ASLIB

DIRECTORY OF INFORMATION SOURCES IN THE UNITED KINGDOM

16th EDITION

Routledge
Taylor & Francis Group

LONDON AND NEW YORK

First published 1928
Sixteenth edition 2010

©Routledge 2010
Albert House, 1–4 Singer Street, London, EC2A 4BQ
(Routledge is an imprint of the Taylor & Francis Group, an **informa** business)

ISBN 978-1-85743-576-4
ISSN 1743–8616

Editor: Sheila Garrard

Proofreaders: Sheila Garrard, Justin Lewis, Etty Payne

Senior Editor, European Directories: Michael Salzman

Editorial Director: Paul Kelly

Typeset in 7pt Palatino

Typeset by AMA DataSet Limited, Preston
Printed and bound in Great Britain by MPG Books, Bodmin, Cornwall

ASLIB

DIRECTORY OF INFORMATION SOURCES IN THE UNITED KINGDOM

FOREWORD

The 16th edition of the ASLIB DIRECTORY OF INFORMATION SOURCES IN THE UNITED KINGDOM offers the reader a wealth of information sources on a potentially limitless range of topics. The pursuers of great learning and of minority hobbies, the great collections, the charitable organisations, the statutory bodies and the defenders of individual rights are there, ready and willing to pass on help, advice, erudition and entertainment.

The information in the directory can be used in a variety of ways. Browsing can, of course, be fun, and an hour might well go by unnoticed as the reader discovers organisations where answers can be obtained to longstanding questions. Where a named institution is sought, the Main Directory offers entries listed alphabetically, by the name of the organisation, while the list of Abbreviations and Acronyms, which follows the Main Directory, can provide a full name for a puzzling acronym.

However, the reader who is seeking a source of information on a specific topic may prefer to turn first to the extensive Subject Index which forms the final section of the book. Organisations are grouped there by subject and, in the case of broad topics, under sub-headings.

As we were preparing to go to press, the UK government announced plans to introduce legislation enabling the abolition or merger of many of the country's quasi-autonomous non-governmental organisations (quangos). These changes, if they are enacted, will be reflected in the next edition of the ASLIB DIRECTORY OF INFORMATION SOURCES IN THE UNITED KINGDOM.

Most of the information that appears in this directory has been provided by the organisations concerned and we are very grateful to those individuals who have given their time to check and update their entry for the new edition.

November 2010

CONTENTS

Main Directory

1 STOP DATA LIMITED

1 Stop Data House, 46 High Street, Ewell, Surrey, KT17 1RW

Tel: 020 8786 9111
Fax: 020 8786 9115
E-mail: info@1stopdata.com

Enquiries:
Enquiries to: Managing Director

Founded:
2001

Formerly called:
Graham and Trotman; Gale Direct (part of the Gale Group) (year of change 2001)

Incorporates the former:
Graham & Whiteside Limited (year of change 2001)

Organisation type and purpose:
Service industry, publishing house.
Business and professional information supplier.

Subject coverage:
Business, professional, academic.

Printed publications:
Trade Associations and Professional Bodies of the UK (15th ed)

Electronic and video publications:
International Associations Database
International Libraries Database
International Major Marketer's Datafile
International Research Centre's Database
Major Companies Database
UK Medical File
UK Companies Database
Ward's Database of US Companies

Publications list:
Available in print

Access to staff:
Contact by letter, by telephone, by fax, by e-mail and via website
Hours: Mon to Fri, 0900 to 1700

100 BLACK MEN OF LONDON

The Bridge, 12–16 Clerkenwell Road, London, EC1M 5PQ

Tel: 0870 121 4100
E-mail: info@100bmol.org.uk

Website:
http://www.100bmol.org.uk

Founded:
2001

Organisation type and purpose:
A non-profit organisation formed by a group of African–Caribbean men who aim to help the youth of their community to achieve their full potential, supported by programmes with an emphasis on mentoring, education, economic development and health and wellbeing.

Links with:
100 Black Men of America Inc.
website: http://www.100blackmen.org

174 TRUST

Duncairn Complex, Duncairn Avenue, Belfast, BT14 6BP, Northern Ireland

Website:
http://www.174trust.org
News, projects.

Founded:
1982

Organisation type and purpose:
Registered charity (charity number: XN62669A/AR)
To effect change in North Belfast by social action and community development so that North Belfast would become a place of co-operation, prosperity and hope.

Subject coverage:
The 174 Trust is a non-denominational Christian organisation that facilitates a variety of essential community projects in North Belfast. Located in the New Lodge community, the Trust offers opportunities and assistance to people of all ages. The 174 Trust is committed to a process of community development based on building relationships with local people, working together to identify and meet local needs.

Electronic and video publications:
174 Trust Profile Document
Director's Report (annually)
Order electronic and video publications from:
Download from website

Publications list:
Available online

Access to staff:
Contact by letter and via website

1745 ASSOCIATION

Ferry Cottage, Corran, Ardgour, Fort William, Inverness-shire, PH33 7AA

Tel: 01855 841306
E-mail: c.aikman@btinternet.com

Website:
http://www.1745association.org.uk

Enquiries:
Enquiries to: Honorary Secretary

Founded:
1946

Organisation type and purpose:
Membership association (membership is by subscription), present number of members: 300, voluntary organisation.

Subject coverage:
History of the whole Jacobite Movement from 1688 to 1788, particularly with reference to Scotland; the Risings of 1715 and 1745 and their aftermath.

Printed publications:
Brochure (on the Association)
Muster Roll of Prince Charles Edward Stuart's Army 1745–46 (1984, Aberdeen University Press, enlarged edition 2001)
Reports of Association's Meetings, etc
The Jacobite (3 times a year)

Access to staff:
Contact by letter and by telephone
Hours: Mon to Fri, 0900 to 1700

2ND AIR DIVISION MEMORIAL LIBRARY (USAAF)

The Forum, Millennium Plain, Norwich, Norfolk, NR2 1AW

Tel: 01603 774747
Fax: 01603 774749
E-mail: 2admemorial.lib@norfolk.gov.uk

Website:
http://www.2ndair.org.uk

Organisation type and purpose:
Library administered by the Board of Governors of the 2nd Air Division Memorial Trust, a UK registered charity, working in consultation with Norfolk County Council Library Authority and the Executive Committee of the 2nd Air Division Association.

Subject coverage:
Books, periodicals and film on all aspects of American history, culture and life, and specialised material about the Second World War in the air and about the special relationship between the peoples of the UK (particularly East Anglia) and the USA. The Library does not hold any official military personnel records.

Museum or gallery collection, archive, or library special collection:
Archive collection deposited with Norfolk Record Office

Library catalogue:
All or part available online

Access to staff:
Contact by letter, by telephone, by fax, by e-mail and in person
Hours: Mon to Sat, 0900 to 1700

Access to building, collection or gallery:
Mon to Sat, 0900 to 1700; closed on bank holidays

3M UNITED KINGDOM PLC

3M House, PO Box 1, Bracknell, Berkshire, RG12 1JU

Tel: 01344 858000
Fax: 01344 858278

Website:
http://www.3M.com
Profiles on subsidiaries, global company and product information, innovations and new products, press releases.

Enquiries:
Enquiries to: Business Intelligence Manager

Founded:
1902

Organisation type and purpose:
Manufacturing industry.

Subject coverage:
Manufacture and marketing of adhesives, adhesive tape, medical products, coated abrasives, reflective products, electrical products, fluorochemicals, reinforced plastics, static eliminators, film cleaners, traffic control, and decorative and recreational products.

Part of:
Minnesota Mining and Manufacturing Company USA

4CHILDREN

City Reach, 5 Greenwich View Place, London, E14 9NN

Tel: Information Helpline: 020 7512 2100
Fax: 020 7512 2010
E-mail: info@4Children.org.uk

Website:
http://www.4Children.org.uk
Campaigns and activities, comprehensive publications catalogue.

Re-launched:
(year of change 2004)

Organisation type and purpose:
A national charity (registered charity number 288285) all about children and families.

Subject coverage:
Works with government, local authorities, children's service providers, and children and parents to ensure joined-up support for all children and young people aged 0–19 in their local community. 4Children is at the forefront of delivery and supporting innovative children's services, ensuring that all children and families get the support they need in their community, from children's centres to extended schools, childcare to play provision, parenting support to support for young people.
Provides information and support to parents through its dedicated Information Helpline and publications. Also works with employers to highlight the many ways that they can help parents to balance work and family responsibilities.
Offers authoritative advice and strategic support to help turn policy into practice working with government departments such as the Treasury, Department for Children, Schools and Families,

continued overleaf

and Department of Health. The organisation has also supported over 100 local authorities to deliver childcare and develop children's and young people's plans, etc.

Library catalogue:
All or part available online

Electronic and video publications:
Comprehensive list of publications available online
Order electronic and video publications from:
4Children by post, tel., fax, or e-mail

Publications list:
Available online

Access to staff:
Contact by letter, by telephone, by fax and by e-mail

AAA-NORCAP

Formal name: Adults Affected by Adoption-NORCAP

112 Church Road, Wheatley, Oxfordshire, OX33 1LU

Tel: 01865 875000
Fax: 01865 875686
E-mail: enquiries@norcap.org

Website:
http: adultsaffectedbyadoption-NORCAP

Enquiries:
Enquiries to: Administrator
Other contacts: Registrar

Founded:
1982

Organisation type and purpose:
Adoption support agency (Ofsted reg. no. 67018), registered charity (charity number 1063428).

Subject coverage:
Advice on searching for those within the adoption triangle. Research service and intermediary service.

Museum or gallery collection, archive, or library special collection:
Microfiche of births, marriages and deaths for England and Wales 1904–1999

Printed publications:
SFFC Action Pack, 'Something that never went away'
Order printed publications from: AAA-NORCAP

Access to staff:
Contact by letter, by telephone, by fax, by e-mail and via website. Appointment necessary.
Hours: Mon to Fri, 0930 to 1300 and 1330 to 1600

Access to building, collection or gallery:
Prior appointment required

Access for disabled people:
Level entry, access to all public areas

ABBEYFIELD SOCIETY

53 Victoria Street, St Albans, Hertfordshire, AL1 3UW

Tel: 01727 857536
Fax: 01727 846168
E-mail: post@abbeyfield.com

Website:
http://www.abbeyfield.com
Details of services and current information on topics relating to older people.

Enquiries:
Enquiries to: Public Relations
Direct tel: 01727 734091
Direct e-mail: j.burder@abbeyfield.com

Founded:
1956

Organisation type and purpose:
To provide housing and innovative services for older people across the UK in 750 sheltered houses and 80 care homes.

Subject coverage:
Legal and financial information for starting and running Abbeyfield societies and houses, including housing for older and frail older people.

Museum or gallery collection, archive, or library special collection:
Books, journal articles, photographs

Trade and statistical information:
The Abbeyfield Profile (latest statistics).

Library catalogue:
All or part available in-house

Printed publications:
What is Abbeyfield? (leaflet)
Any Questions? (leaflet)
Focus (6 times a year)
Manual of Information (free to each Society)
The Abbeyfielder (2 times a year)

Publications list:
Available in print

Access to staff:
Contact by letter, by telephone, by fax, by e-mail and via website. Appointment necessary. All charged.
Hours: Mon to Fri, 0900 to 1700

Access to building, collection or gallery:
No prior appointment required

ABC-CLIO

PO Box 1437, Oxford, OX4 9AZ

Tel: 01844 238448
E-mail: salesinternational@abc-clio.com

Website:
http://www.abc-clio.com/international

Enquiries:
Enquiries to: International Sales Director

Founded:
1955

Formerly called:
Clio Press Limited

Organisation type and purpose:
Publishing house.

Subject coverage:
Own publications of general reference in history (World and US) humanities, language arts, library professional development, and general interest.

Library catalogue:
All or part available online

Printed publications:
America: History and Life, World Bibliographical Series, Reference books

Electronic and video publications:
America: History and Life (CD-ROM and web), World Geography (web), World History FullText (web)

Publications list:
Available online and in print

Access to staff:
Contact by letter, by telephone, by fax, by e-mail and via website
Hours: Mon to Fri, 0900 to 1700

Parent body:
ABC-CLIO Inc
130 Cremona Drive, Suite C, Santa Barbara, CA 93117, USA; tel: +1 805 968 1911; website: http://www.abc-clio.com

ABERDEEN & GRAMPIAN CHAMBER OF COMMERCE

Acronym or abbreviation: AGCC

Greenhole Place, Bridge of Don, Aberdeen, AB23 8EU

Tel: 01224 343900
Fax: 01224 343943
E-mail: info@agcc.co.uk

Website:
http://www.agcc.co.uk
Membership organisation.

Enquiries:
Enquiries to: Policy and Communications Manager
Direct tel: 01224 343913
Direct e-mail: kate.yuill@agcc.co.uk

Founded:
1877

Formerly called:
Aberdeen Chamber of Commerce (year of change 2001)

Organisation type and purpose:
Membership association (membership is by subscription), present number of members: 1300.

Printed publications:
Business eNews (free to members)
Business Bulletin (free to members)
Scottish Chambers of Commerce Directory (free to members, £50 non-members)

Access to staff:
Contact by letter, by telephone, by fax, by e-mail, in person and via website. Appointment necessary.
Hours: Mon to Fri, 0900 to 1700

Access to building, collection or gallery:
Link for directions: http://www.agcc.co.uk/contact-us

ABERDEEN AND NORTH EAST SCOTLAND FAMILY HISTORY SOCIETY

Acronym or abbreviation: ANESFHS

The Family History Research Centre, 158–164 King Street, Aberdeen, AB24 5BD

Tel: 01224 646323
Fax: 01224 639096
E-mail: enquiries@anesfhs.org.uk

Website:
http://www.anesfhs.org.uk
Publications list, society details, membership application form, ancestor chart index, monumental inscriptions index, meetings syllabus, projects.

Enquiries:
Enquiries to: Secretary
Direct e-mail: press.office@anesfhs.org.uk
Other contacts: Press Officer

Founded:
1978

Organisation type and purpose:
Membership association (membership is by subscription), present number of members: 5,000, voluntary organisation, registered charity (charity number SCO 12478).

Subject coverage:
Genealogy relating to the North East of Scotland, census, parish register information for North East parishes, family history.

Museum or gallery collection, archive, or library special collection:
Reference library of books on local and family history
Collection of ancestor charts submitted by members
Historical maps of the area
Parish information
Microfiche of major indexes e.g. IGI, General Register House, Scottish Record Office, BMD for England from 1837
1881 Census (CD-ROM)
Members' research interests
Deryk Cameron Memorial Collection: OPRs and Census (microfilm) for Shetland

Library catalogue:
All or part available in-house

Printed publications:
Journal (quarterly, members)
Membership List
Monumental inscriptions
Census 1851
Aberdeenshire Poll Book 1696
Books on church history and other local subjects

Publications list:
Available online and in print

Access to staff:
Contact by letter, by telephone, by e-mail, in person and via website. Non-members charged.
Hours: Mon to Fri, 1000 to 1600; Sat, 1000 to 1300
Members only Tue to Fri, 1900 to 2200
Special comments: Reference library for members only.

Access for disabled people:
At no. 160 entrance

Member organisation of:
Aberdeen and Grampian Tourist Board
  Exchange House, 26–28 Exchange Street, Aberdeen, AB11 6PH; tel: 01224 288828; fax: 01224 288838; e-mail: aberdeen.information@ visitscotland.com; website: http://www .visitscotland.com
Scottish Association of Family History Societies
  website: http://www.safhs.org.uk

ABERDEEN ANGUS CATTLE SOCIETY

Pedigree House, 6 King's Place, Perth, Tayside, PH2 8AD

Tel: 01738 622477
Fax: 01738 636436
E-mail: info@aberdeen-angus.co.uk

Website:
http://www.aberdeen-angus.com

Enquiries:
Enquiries to: Chief Executive

Founded:
1879

Organisation type and purpose:
Breed Society.

Subject coverage:
Pedigree Aberdeen Angus cattle.

Printed publications:
Aberdeen Angus Herdbook (annually)
Aberdeen Angus Review (annually)

Access to staff:
Contact by telephone, by e-mail and via website
Hours: Mon to Fri, 0900 to 1700

ABERDEEN CITY AND ABERDEENSHIRE ARCHIVES

The Town House, Broad Street, Aberdeen, AB10 1AQ

Tel: 01224 522513; minicom no. 01224 522381
Fax: 01224 638556
E-mail: archives@aberdeencity.gov.uk

Website:
http://www.aberdeencity.gov.uk/archives

Enquiries:
Enquiries to: Duty Archivist

Founded:
1980

Organisation type and purpose:
Local authority archives service for Aberdeen City and Aberdeenshire Councils.

Subject coverage:
Aberdeen City and Aberdeenshire Archives exists to collect and preserve historical records relating to the City of Aberdeen and its locality and to secure significant modern records for future generations.

Information services:
Reference library, photocopying/scanning available, e-mail, telephone & postal enquiries, research service, microfilm reader/printer, internet access, laptop facilities, digital photography allowed.

Museum or gallery collection, archive, or library special collection:
Aberdeen holds the finest and most complete collection of medieval and early modern burgh records in Scotland, with council minutes dating back to 1398. Also available are various Aberdeenshire burgh records, school records, valuation rolls, poor relief records, electoral registers, and many more.

Non-library collection catalogue:
All or part available online and in-house

Library catalogue:
All or part available in-house

Printed publications:
Information Leaflets

Microform publications:
Council Registers 1600 to 1883 (microfilm)
Burgh Sasine Registers (microfilm)
Microfilm of other council records

Access to staff:
Contact by letter, by telephone, by fax, by e-mail, in person and via website. Appointment necessary.
Hours: Old Aberdeen House: Mon to Wed, 0930 to 1300 and 1400 to 1630
The Town House: Wed to Fri, 0930 to 1630
Special comments: Researchers by prior appointment.

Access to building, collection or gallery:
Old Aberdeen House is served by a car park. The Town House is served by fee-paying city centre car parks.
Hours: Old Aberdeen House Archive: Mon to Wed, 0930 to 1300 and 1400 to 1630
The Town House Archive: Wed to Fri, 0930 to 1630
Special comments: A visitor badge will be provided by front desk staff.

Access for disabled people:
Old Aberdeen House has wheelchair access on the ground floor, but no accessible toilet facilities. The Town House may be inaccessible to larger wheelchairs, but alternative arrangements can be made. Accessible toilet facilities are available.
Hours: Access is available during normal opening hours.

Also at:
Aberdeen City and Aberdeenshire Archives – Old Aberdeen House Branch
  Old Aberdeen House, Dunbar Street, Aberdeen, AB24 3UJ; tel: 01224 481775; fax: 01224 495830; e-mail: archives@aberdeencity.gov.uk; website: http://www.aberdeencity.gov.uk/archives

ABERDEEN CITY LIBRARY AND INFORMATION SERVICES

Acronym or abbreviation: ACL

Central Library, Rosemount Viaduct, Aberdeen, AB25 1GW

Tel: 01224 641985
Fax: 01224 636811

Website:
http://www.aberdeencity.gov.uk/libraries

Enquiries:
Enquiries to: Information Librarian
Direct tel: 01224 652502
Direct fax: 01224 641985
Direct e-mail: informationcentre@aberdeencity.gov .uk

Founded:
1887

Formerly called:
Aberdeen Arts & Recreation Division – Library Services

Organisation type and purpose:
Public library.
Business and Technical Dept.

Subject coverage:
Public library service covering all subjects including audio-visual lending service. Scottish history, genealogy and tartans.
Specialist business service provides company product information, technical standards, patents and trademarks, and reference and lending services covering all aspects of business management, science and technology.

Museum or gallery collection, archive, or library special collection:
British and other technical standards
British, European and US Patents
Cosmo Mitchell Collection on dancing
Collection of company and product directories
George Washington Wilson Collection of photographs
Health and safety data on CD-ROM
Oil and gas collection
Statistics and market research
Walker Collection of music
Patents and Trade Marks

Trade and statistical information:
Data on oil and gas explorations including technical standards.
Patent information centre for north of Scotland.
Company and product information relating to UK, Europe, and USA.

Library catalogue:
All or part available online and in-house

Electronic and video publications:
Community Contacts Online

Access to staff:
Contact by letter, by telephone, by fax, by e-mail and in person. Appointment necessary.
Hours: Mon and Wed 0900 to 2000; Tue, Thu, Fri and Sat, 0900 to 1700

ABERDEEN COLLEGE

Gallowgate, Aberdeen, AB25 1BN

Tel: 01224 612000 ext 2138
Fax: 01224 612001
E-mail: gallowlib@abcol.ac.uk

Website:
http://www.abcol.ac.uk/library

Enquiries:
Enquiries to: Librarian
Direct tel: 01224 612138
Direct e-mail: kapp@abcol.ac.uk

Founded:
1992

Formerly called:
Aberdeen College of Commerce, Aberdeen College of Further Education, Aberdeen Technical College (year of change 1992)

Organisation type and purpose:
College of further education.

Subject coverage:
Business and commercial, technical, at further education level.
Art, social sciences, catering.

Library catalogue:
All or part available in-house

Access to staff:
Contact by telephone and by e-mail
Hours: Mon to Thu, 0830 to 2130; Fri, 0830 to 1700; Sat, Sun, 0900 to 1700

Access for disabled people:
Parking provided, ramped entry, toilet facilities

ABERDEEN INTERNATIONAL YOUTH FESTIVAL

Acronym or abbreviation: AIYF

continued overleaf

Custom House, 35 Regent Quay, Aberdeen, AB11 6JR

Tel: 01224 213800
Fax: 01224 213833
E-mail: info@aiyf.org

Website:
http://www.aiyf.org
Full information about the Aberdeen International Youth Festival, its associated summer schools, programme of events, how to buy tickets, etc.

Enquiries:
Enquiries to: Director
Other contacts: General Manager

Founded:
1973

Organisation type and purpose:
Registered charity (charity number SCO 14935), suitable for ages: 12 to 25.
Annual international youth arts festival welcoming youth orchestras, choirs, jazz, dance and theatre groups from around the world to take part in a non-competitive festival. Up to 1,000 young participants up to the age of 25 reside at the University, give public performances and experience different cultures and art forms.

Subject coverage:
Youth orchestras, choirs, jazz and wind bands, all forms of youth dance groups and theatre companies worldwide. Education: ballet summer school plus Scottish traditional music summer school and opera project.

Publications list:
Available online and in print

Access to staff:
Contact by letter, by telephone, by fax, by e-mail and via website
Hours: Mon to Fri, 0900 to 1700

Access to building, collection or gallery:
Hours: Mon to Fri, 0900 to 1700

ABERDEENSHIRE HERITAGE

Formal name: Aberdeenshire Museums Service

Station Road, Mintlaw, Peterhead, Aberdeenshire, AB42 5EE

Tel: 01771 622807
Fax: 01771 623558
E-mail: heritage@aberdeenshire.gov.uk

Website:
http://www.aberdeenshire.gov.uk/ahc.htm
Details of the museums.

Enquiries:
Enquiries to: Curatorial Officer, Documentation and Conservation
Direct e-mail: david.bertie@aberdeenshire.gov.uk
Other contacts: Senior Museums & Heritage Officer

Founded:
1996

Created by the merger of:
North East of Scotland Agricultural Heritage Centre, North East of Scotland Museums Service (NESMS) (year of change 1996)

Organisation type and purpose:
Local government body, museum.

Subject coverage:
Northeast Scotland local history, geology, archaeology, natural history, fishing, shipping and whaling of northeast Scotland, Banff silver, numismatics, details of museums in the north east of Scotland.

Museum or gallery collection, archive, or library special collection:
Large photograph collection relating to the north east of Scotland
Peterhead Port Books
Some fishing boat records on microfilm

Printed publications:
Literary Families (Bertie D M, 50p)

Master and Pupil (Bertie D M, 50p)
Access to staff:
Contact by letter, by telephone, by fax and by e-mail. Appointment necessary.
Hours: Mon to Fri, 0900 to 1630

Access to building, collection or gallery:
Hours: Mon to Fri, 0900 to 1630

Access for disabled people:
Hours: Mon to Fri, 0900 to 1630

Branch museums:
Aberdeenshire Farming Museum
    Aden Country Park, Mintlaw, Peterhead, AB42 5FQ
Arbuthnot Museum
    St Peter Street, Peterhead, AB42 1LA; tel: 01771 622807
Banchory Museum
    Bridge Street, Banchory, Kincardineshire, AB31 5SX; tel: 01771 622807
Banff Museum
    High Street, Banff, Banffshire, AB45 1AE; tel: 01771 622807
Brander Museum
    The Square, Huntly, Aberdeenshire, AB54 8AE; tel: 01771 622807
Carnegie Museum
    The Square, Inverurie, Aberdeenshire, AB51 3SN; tel: 01771 622807
Fordyce Joiner's Workshop Visitor Centre
    Church Street, Fordyce, Banffshire, AB45 2SL; tel: 01771 622807
Maud Railway Museum
    Maud Railway Station, Maud, Aberdeenshire, AB42 5LY; tel: 01771 622807
Sandhaven Meal Mill
    Sandhaven, Fraserburgh, Aberdeenshire, AB43 4EP; tel: 01771 622807
Tolbooth Museum
    The Harbour, Stonehaven, Kincardineshire, AB39 2JU; tel: 01771 622807

Parent body:
Aberdeenshire Council

ABERDEENSHIRE LIBRARY AND INFORMATION SERVICE

Acronym or abbreviation: ALIS

Meldrum Meg Way, Oldmeldrum, Inverurie, Aberdeenshire, AB51 0GN

Tel: 01651 872707
Fax: 01651 872142
E-mail: alis@aberdeenshire.gov.uk

Website:
http://www.aberdeenshire.gov.uk/libraries

Enquiries:
Enquiries to: Principal Libraries Officer

Founded:
1996

Organisation type and purpose:
Public library, school library service, covers the area of Aberdeenshire.

Subject coverage:
Local history, community information, leisure, educational and cultural, open learning through links with colleges.

Information services:
Public enquiry service.

Education services:
Library service to schools.

Museum or gallery collection, archive, or library special collection:
George MacDonald Collection (manuscripts and books)
Strichen Local History Collection (estate papers)

Library catalogue:
All or part available online

Printed publications:
Libraries – Worth Looking Into (information leaflet)

Libraries – Worth Looking Into (guide to services)
Family History Research Guide

Electronic and video publications:
Clubs Directory (online)

Access to staff:
Contact by letter, by telephone, by fax, by e-mail, in person and via website
Hours: Headquarters: Mon to Fri, 0900 to 1700; Sat, 0900 to 1630
Special comments: Opening hours in branches vary.

Constituent part of:
Education, Learning and Leisure Service of Aberdeenshire Council

ABERTAY HISTORICAL SOCIETY

c/o Alder Archaeology, 55 South Methven Street, Perth, PH1 5NX

Tel: 01738 622393
Fax: 01738 631626
E-mail: csmith@alderarchaeology.co.uk

Website:
http://www.abertay.org.uk
Bookshop.

Enquiries:
Enquiries to: Honorary Sales Secretary

Founded:
1947

Organisation type and purpose:
Membership association (membership is by subscription), present number of members: 150, voluntary organisation.

Subject coverage:
History of Dundee, Tayside and Fife.

Library catalogue:
All or part available online and in print

Printed publications:
Dundee's Literary Lives, vols 1 and 2, (Andrew Murray Scott, 2003, £7 each plus p&p)
Victorian Dundee at Worship (Ian McCraw, 2002, £7 plus p&p)
Patrons, Poverty & Profit – Organised Charity in Nineteenth-Century Dundee (Lorraine Walsh, 2000, £3 plus p&p)
The Demands of the People – Dundee Radicalism 1850–1870 (Michael St John, 1997, £2.50 plus p&p)
Making the Vote Count: The Arbroath Women Citizens' Association, 1931–1945 (Sarah F. Browne, 2007, £6.00 plus p&p)
A Noble and Potent Lady: Katherine Campbell, Countess of Crawford (Mary Verschuur, 2006, £7.50 plus p&p)
The Guildry of Dundee (Annette M. Smith, 2005, £7.50 plus p&p)
The Schoolmaster Engineer: Adam Anderson of Perth and St Andrews (Kenneth Cameron, 2006, £7.50 plus p&p)
One Artful and Ambitious Individual: Alexander Riddoch (1745–1822) (Enid Gauldie, 1989, £3.00 plus p&p)
Broughty Castle and the Defence of the Tay (Sir F Mudie, David M Walker & Iain MacIvor, 2010, £7.50 plus p&p)
The 1915 Rent Strikes: an East Coast Perspective (Ann Petrie, 2008, £7.50 plus p&p)
Order printed publications from: The Sales Secretary; e-mail: csmith@suat.co.uk

Publications list:
Available online and in print

Access to staff:
Contact by letter, by telephone, by fax and by e-mail
Hours: Mon to Fri, 0900 to 1700

ABERYSTWYTH LIBRARY

Corporation Street, Aberystwyth, Ceredigion, SY23 2BU

Tel: 01970 633703

Fax: 01970 625059
E-mail: llyfrgell.library@ceredigion.gov.uk

Website:
http://www.ceredigion.gov.uk/libraries

Enquiries:
Enquiries to: Librarian
Direct tel: 01970 633713
Direct e-mail: williamh@ceredigion.gov.uk

Organisation type and purpose:
Public library.

Subject coverage:
Welsh local history (Ceredigion); Welsh language publications; Welsh literature.

Museum or gallery collection, archive, or library special collection:
Local history

Library catalogue:
All or part available online and in-house

Access to staff:
Contact by letter, by telephone, by fax, by e-mail and in person
Hours: Mon to Fri, 0900 to 1700

Access to building, collection or gallery:
No access other than to staff

Also at:
Ceredigion County Council
Bibliographical Department

Branch libraries:
Aberaeron Library
County Hall, Aberaeron, Ceredigion, SA46 0AT; tel: 01545 570382; e-mail: aeronllb@ceredigion.gov.uk
Cardigan Library
Cardigan, Ceredigion, SA43 1JL; tel: 01239 612578; fax: 01239 612285; e-mail: teifillb@ceredigion.gov.uk
Lampeter Library
Market Street, Lampeter, Ceredigion, SA48 7DR; tel: 01570 423606; e-mail: pedrllb@ceredigion.gov.uk
Llandysul Library
Llandysul, Ceredigion, SA44 4QS; tel: 01559 362899; e-mail: tysulllb@ceredigion.gov.uk
New Quay Library
Church Street, New Quay, Ceredigion
Tregaron Library
Secondary School, Tregaron, Ceredigion, SY25 6HG; tel: 01974 298009; e-mail: caronllb@ceredigion.gov.uk

ABERYSTWYTH UNIVERSITY – HUGH OWEN LIBRARY

Penglais, Aberystwyth, Ceredigion, SY23 3DZ

Tel: 01970 622400
Fax: 01970 622404
E-mail: is@aber.ac.uk

Website:
http://voyager.aber.uk
Library OPAC.
http://www.aber.ac.uk/en/is
University information services.

Enquiries:
Enquiries to: Director of Information Services

Founded:
1872

Formerly called:
University College of Wales, Aberystwyth (year of change 1994)

Organisation type and purpose:
University library.

Subject coverage:
Accounting and business studies, economics, applied plant biology, genetics and plant breeding, botany, zoology, physical geography including meteorology, biochemistry, biometry, biology, microbiology, cell and immune biology, physics, mathematics, computer science, business studies, theatre, film and television studies, sports science,

English and American literature, European literature/languages (French, Spanish, Italian, German), classical studies, history, visual art, social sciences, education, agriculture and agricultural botany and biochemistry, agricultural economics, law, Celtic studies, Welsh, Irish, Breton, Gaelic, Cornish and Manx, politics, international politics, library and information studies.

Museum or gallery collection, archive, or library special collection:
18th- and 19th-century Legal Texts (microfiche Inter Documentation Zug)
Archive of British Master Potters
British Official Publications and Statistical Collection
British Sessional Papers 1801–1930 (Readex microprint)
British Society of Rheology Collection
Canadian Official Publications. Selective Depository 1979–
Celtic Collection
David De Lloyd papers (original compositions and material on Welsh folksongs)
Diplomatic documents
Duff Collection of pamphlets on classical studies
Early American Imprints from 1639 to 1800 (Readex Microprint)
English Legal Sources (microfiche Inter Documentation Zug)
Gregynog Press Collection
George Powell Collection
J C Hotten publications. (Victorian publisher 1856–1873)
J O Francis archive (prompt copies, etc. of his plays)
Learning materials for Welsh Language schools
Lily Newton papers on water pollution
Richard Ellis papers (relating to Edward Lhuyd)
Rudler Collection of 19th-century geological pamphlets
T F Roberts MSS (UCW during his Principalship, 1891–1919)
Thomas Webster Letters (19th-century British geologists)
Three Centuries of Drama: English section 1500–1800 (Readex Microprint) UN and League of Nations publications
David Davies Memorial Library (international politics)

Trade and statistical information:
Statistics Collection, official publications, European documentation, Celtic collection.

Non-library collection catalogue:
All or part available online and in-house

Library catalogue:
All or part available online

Printed publications:
Aberystwyth and District: a bibliography of the earth and environmental sciences, 1991
Bible in Welsh and the vernacular, 1988
Bibliographical Handlists
Books printed before 1701 in the Hugh Owen Library (1972, out of print)
Catalog Adnoddau Addysg (Catalogue of Educational Resources in Welsh) 1987
Catalogue of the Scott Blair Collection (British Society of Rheology), 1991
Electronic Information Resources, 1999
Exhibition Catalogues
Glossary of library terms, 1991
Print Collection of the University College of Wales/ Casgliad Printiau Coleg Prifysgol Cymru, 1984
Richard Ellis Papers: handbook and schedule (compiled by Brynley F Roberts, 1983)
The College Library 1872–1976 (T G Lloyd, 1977)
Information Services Guide 2006/2007

Access to staff:
Contact by letter and by telephone. Appointment necessary. Access for members only. Letter of introduction required.
Hours: Term time: Mon to Fri, 0900 to 2200; Sat, 1200 to 1800; Sun, 1200 to 1800
Vacations: Mon to Fri, 0900 to 1730
Special comments: No reference service on weekends.

Access for disabled people:
Hours: Term time: Mon to Fri, 0900 to 2200; Sat, 1200 to 1800; Sun, 1200 to 1800
Vacations: Mon to Fri, 0900 to 1730

Constituent institution of the:
University of Wales

ABERYSTWYTH UNIVERSITY – THOMAS PARRY LIBRARY

Llanbadarn Fawr, Aberystwyth, Ceredigion, SY23 3AS

Tel: 01970 622417
Fax: 01970 621868
E-mail: parrylib@aber.ac.uk

Website:
http://edina.ac.uk/landlifeleisure
Land, Life and Leisure – rural information database
http://www.irs.aber.ac.uk
Institute of Rural Sciences.

Enquiries:
Enquiries to: Site Librarian
Direct e-mail: eet@aber.ac.uk
Other contacts: Rural Studies Librarian for agricultural and rural studies enquiries.

Founded:
1996

Formerly called:
Welsh Institute of Rural Studies Library Aberystwyth; Information and Library Studies Library, University of Wales Aberystwyth (year of change 1991)

Subject coverage:
Librarianship; information science; Welsh librarianship; African librarianship; archives and records management; library buildings; planning; children's literature; physical and historical bibliography; publishing, printing and book trade. Agriculture as practised in the UK (animal production; crop production; farm management; farm mechanisation); forestry; organic husbandry; rural planning; countryside management and conservation; tourism; equine studies.

Museum or gallery collection, archive, or library special collection:
Appleton Collection (Victorian colour printing and publishers binding)
Bibliographical collection (private presses and fine printing)
Children's Collection including Horton Collection of early children's books and ephemera
Library literature (library annual reports and guides)
Press cuttings (librarianship and related subjects)
Simon Collection (Curwen Press and related material)
Welsh Studies Collection
Whittinghams Collection (Chiswick Press)
Agricultural and countryside grant information
Agricultural press notices
Countryside management press notices

Non-library collection catalogue:
All or part available in-house

Library catalogue:
All or part available online

Electronic and video publications:
Land Life and Leisure: farming and countryside index

Access to staff:
Contact by letter, by telephone, by fax and by e-mail. Appointment necessary.
Hours: Term time: Mon to Thu, 0900 to 2100; Fri, 0900 to 1930; Sat, 1200 to 1800
Vacations: Mon to Fri, 0900 to 1730

Access for disabled people:
Ramped entry

Parent body:
University of Wales Aberystwyth
Directorate of Information Services

ABILITYNET

PO Box 94, Warwick, CV34 5WS

Tel: 01926 312847/0800 269545
Fax: 01926 407425
E-mail: enquiries@abilitynet.org.uk

Website:
http://www.abilitynet.org.uk

Enquiries:
Enquiries to: Information Officer

Formerly called:
Foundation for Communication for the Disabled,
The Computability Centre

Organisation type and purpose:
Registered charity (charity number 1067673),
consultancy.
Providing information on making computers
accessible for people with disabilities.

Subject coverage:
Computer access for people with disabilities

Printed publications:
Factsheets

Access to staff:
Contact by letter, by telephone, by fax, by e-mail,
in person and via website
Hours: Mon to Fri, 0900 to 1700

ABINGDON AND WITNEY COLLEGE

Witney Campus, Library and Resource Centre,
Holloway Road, Witney, Oxfordshire, OX28 6NE

Tel: 01993 208010
Fax: 01993 703006

Website:
http://www.oxfe.ac.uk/witney/home.htm
College prospectus, etc.

Enquiries:
Enquiries to: Librarian

Formerly called:
West Oxfordshire College Learning Resources
Centre

Organisation type and purpose:
Suitable for ages: 16+.
College of further education.

Subject coverage:
General further education; stud and stable
husbandry; racing industry.

**Museum or gallery collection, archive, or library
special collection:**
Thoroughbred horse management

Non-library collection catalogue:
All or part available in-house

Library catalogue:
All or part available in-house

Access to staff:
Contact by letter, by telephone, by fax and in
person
Hours: Mon, Tue, Thu, 0830 to 1900; Wed, 0830 to
1700; Fri, 0830 to 1630
Special comments: Non-students, reference only.

Access for disabled people:
Parking provided, ramped entry, toilet facilities

Member organisation of:
COLRIC
Open University Study Centre

ABORTION RIGHTS

18 Ashwin Street, London, E8 3DL

Tel: 020 7923 9792
E-mail: choice@abortionrights.org.uk

Website:
http://www.abortionrights.org.uk

Enquiries:
Enquiries to: Administrator

Founded:
2003

Created by the merger of:
National Abortion Campaign (NAC) and Abortion
Law Reform Association (ALRA)

Organisation type and purpose:
National organisation, membership association
(membership is by subscription), voluntary
organisation.
Campaigning for equal access to safe, free abortion
on request.

Subject coverage:
Abortion in the UK and worldwide; contraception;
new reproductive technology; no counselling.

Printed publications:
Campaign and membership leaflets and factsheets
Abortion: the facts (£2.50 plus p&p)

Access to staff:
Contact by letter, by telephone, by e-mail and via
website. Appointment necessary.
Hours: Varies each week

Links with:
Education for Choice
    The Resource Centre, 356 Holloway Road,
    London, N7 6PA; tel: 020 7700 8190; e-mail: efc@
    efc.org.uk; website: http://www.efc.org.uk
Voice for Choice
    e-mail: vfc@vfc.org.uk; website: http://www.vfc
    .org.uk

ABP – PORT OF IPSWICH

Old Custom House, Key Street, Ipswich, Suffolk,
IP4 1BY

Tel: 01473 231010
Fax: 01473 230914
E-mail: ipswich@abports.co.uk

Website:
http://www.ABPorts.co.uk
Port facilities, etc.

Enquiries:
Enquiries to: Sales Manager
Direct fax: 01473 225364

Founded:
1997

Formerly called:
Port of Ipswich; Ipswich Port Authority (year of
change 1997)

Organisation type and purpose:
Service industry.

Subject coverage:
Port facilities and operation; discharge and loading
of containers, roll-on/roll-off, general cargo, bulk
solid and bulk liquid vessels.

Printed publications:
Development Notes (History of the Port)
Port of Ipswich Handbook (annually)

Parent body:
Associated British Ports (ABP)

ABP MARINE ENVIRONMENTAL RESEARCH

Acronym or abbreviation: ABP Research

Suite B, Waterside House, Town Quay,
Southampton, S014 2AQ

Tel: 023 80711 840
Fax: 023 80711 841
E-mail: enquiries@abpmer.co.uk

Website:
http://www.abpmer.co.uk
ABP Research – capability profile, current news
items, project experience, case studies, recent
reports and publications.

Enquiries:
Enquiries to: Technical Marketing Manager
Other contacts: Library and Information Services

Founded:
1950

Formerly called:
British Transport Docks Board (year of change
1983); ABP Research and Consultancy Limited
(year of change 2002)

Organisation type and purpose:
Consultancy, research organisation.
Specialists in water environment consultancy.

Subject coverage:
Dock and harbour engineering; rivers, estuaries
and coastal research; maritime hydraulics and
structures; hydrographic surveying and dredging
research; port operations and management.

**Museum or gallery collection, archive, or library
special collection:**
Comprehensive library covering all aspects of
    water environment science and hydraulics
    research inclusive of over 400 reports and
    technical guidance notes

Printed publications:
Annual Report, brochures (free)
Technical Reports (for purchase subject to client
    permission)

Electronic and video publications:
Environmental Risk Assessment Package
Estuary Database – UK-wide Directory/
    Information system describing a wide range of
    estuary features, resources etc

Access to staff:
Contact by telephone, by fax, by e-mail and via
website
Hours: Mon to Fri, 0900 to 1700
Special comments: Library searches will be charged
at commercial rates, available on application.

Parent body:
Associated British Ports Holdings plc
    150 Holborn, London, EC1N 2LR; tel: 020 7430
    1177; fax: 020 7430 1384

AC OWNERS' CLUB LIMITED

Acronym or abbreviation: ACOC

Thatch End, Godmanstone, Dorset, DT2 7AQ

Tel: 01300 342058
Fax: 01799 522513
E-mail: rish.morpeth@virgin.net

Website:
http://www.racecar.co.uk/acoc

Enquiries:
Enquiries to: Membership Secretary

Founded:
1949

Organisation type and purpose:
Membership association (membership is by
subscription), present number of members: 700.

Subject coverage:
The AC motor car.

**Museum or gallery collection, archive, or library
special collection:**
The Club Library contains: documents,
    publications, etc., concerning AC cars from the
    early years of the 20th century to date

Library catalogue:
All or part available in-house

Printed publications:
Magazine (monthly, by subscription only)
Registers 1910–2001 (£50)

Access to staff:
Contact by letter, by telephone and by e-mail
Hours: Mon to Sat, 0900 to 2000

ACADEMY OF ANCIENT MUSIC

Acronym or abbreviation: AAM

32 Newnham Road, Cambridge, CB3 9EY

Tel: 01223 301509
Fax: 01223 327377
E-mail: info@aam.co.uk

Website:
http://www.aam.co.uk
History, news, feature articles, concert listings and a complete discography of the orchestra's recordings.

Enquiries:
Enquiries to: Administrator
Direct e-mail: s.fryer@aam.co.uk

Founded:
1973

Organisation type and purpose:
Registered charity (charity number 1085485). Period instrument orchestra.

Subject coverage:
Performance of classical and baroque music.

Electronic and video publications:
Extensive CD discography
Order electronic and video publications from: Record shops

Access to staff:
Contact by e-mail
Hours: Mon to Fri, 0900 to 1800

ACADEMY OF EXECUTIVES AND ADMINISTRATORS

Acronym or abbreviation: AEA

Warwick Corner, 42 Warwick Road, Kenilworth, Warwickshire, CV8 1HE

Tel: 01926 866623
E-mail: info@group-ims.com

Website:
http://www.group-ims.com

Enquiries:
Enquiries to: Administrative Director

Founded:
2002

Organisation type and purpose:
Professional body (membership is by subscription, qualification), range of professional diploma courses available.

Printed publications:
The Academy of Executives and Administrators Journal

Access to staff:
Contact by letter, by telephone, by e-mail and via website

Links with:
Institute of Management Specialists
  at the same address
Institute of Manufacturing and Professional Business and Technical Management
  at the same address
The Academy of Multi-Skills
  at the same address

ACADEMY OF EXPERTS

Acronym or abbreviation: TAE

3 Gray's Inn Square, Gray's Inn, London, WC1R 5AH

Tel: 020 7430 0333
Fax: 020 7430 0666
E-mail: admin@academy-experts.org

Website:
http://www.academy-experts.org

Enquiries:
Enquiries to: Chief Executive

Founded:
1987

Organisation type and purpose:
Professional body (membership is by qualification), consultancy.

Subject coverage:
All matters pertaining to experts, especially in contentious matters. Accreditation of practising experts and qualified dispute resolvers. Matters involving alternative dispute resolution (ADR) including training, accreditation and appointments. Cost-efficient dispute resolution, provision of standards for experts, mediators and others.

Museum or gallery collection, archive, or library special collection:
Directory of Experts
Register of Qualified Dispute Resolvers

Printed publications:
The Model Form of Experts Report (£10)
Resolving Your Disputes by Mediation (£7)
The Expert (£60)
Order printed publications from: Website

Access to staff:
Contact by letter and by e-mail
Hours: Mon to Fri, 0900 to 1700

Access to building, collection or gallery:
Prior appointment required

ACADEMY OF MULTI-SKILLS

Acronym or abbreviation: AMS

Warwick Corner, 42 Warwick Road, Kenilworth, Warwickshire, CV8 1HE

Tel: 01926 866623
E-mail: info@group-ims.com

Website:
http://www.group-ims.com

Enquiries:
Enquiries to: Administrative Director

Founded:
1995

Organisation type and purpose:
International organisation, professional body (membership is by qualification), training organisation, range of professional diploma courses available.
For all groups and types of people who are multi-skilled. The multi-skilled should register with the academy.

Subject coverage:
The principal aim of the Academy is to bring together and help people who have multi-skilled potential, those who wish to lift themselves to higher positions in life by perfecting and securing recognition for their skills. Most people possess more potential than they realise, are already multi-skilled, or have never had their hidden multi-skills recognised. The Academy can help to support and expand their careers.

Printed publications:
Journals from any of the international, professional bodies (£7 per copy to non-members)
Journals issued to members

Access to staff:
Contact by letter, by telephone, by e-mail and via website

Links with:
Professional Business and Technical Management (PBTM) (founded 1983)
  at the same address
The Academy of Executives & Administrators (AEA) (founded 2002)
  at the same address
The Institute of Management Specialists (IMS) (founded 1971)
  at the same address
The Institute of Manufacturing (IManf) (founded 1978)
  at the same address

ACAS

Formal name: Advisory, Conciliation and Arbitration Service

Information Centre, 22nd floor Euston Tower, 286 Euston Road, London, NW1 3JJ

Tel: 020 7210 3911
E-mail: library@acas.org.uk

Website:
http://www.acas.org.uk
Press releases, details of ACAS publications including full text of some publications. Local public enquiry telephone numbers.

Enquiries:
Enquiries to: Senior Information Manager

Founded:
1974

Organisation type and purpose:
Statutory body.

Subject coverage:
Industrial relations, industrial arbitration and conciliation, trade unions, employee involvement, organisational behaviour, employment law, quality of working life, total quality management, stress, personnel management, management of change.

Printed publications:
Advisory booklets
Advisory handbooks
Annual reports
Ask ACAS leaflets
Codes of Practice
Advice Leaflets
Getting It Right – Guides for small firms
Self Help Guides
Research Papers
Order printed publications from: ACAS Publications, PO Box 235, Hayes, Middlesex, UB3 1HF; tel: 0870 242 9090; fax: 020 8867 3225; e-mail: acas@ eclogistics.co.uk

Publications list:
Available online and in print

Access to staff:
Contact via website. Appointment necessary.
Hours: Mon to Fri, 1000 to 1600

Branches:
11 regional centres

ACCOUNTS COMMISSION FOR SCOTLAND

110 George Street, Edinburgh, EH2 4LH

Tel: 0131 625 1605
E-mail: info@audit-scotland.gov.uk

Website:
http://www.audit-scotland.gov.uk
Audit Scotland publications published on behalf of Accounts Commission and Auditor General.
http://www.accounts-commission.gov.uk
Commission's publications.

Enquiries:
Enquiries to: Corporate Service Department; Secretary and Business Manager
Direct tel: 0131 625 1614
Other contacts: Secretary; Audit Scotland Reception

Founded:
1975

Organisation type and purpose:
Statutory body.

Subject coverage:
The performance of Scottish Councils, and police and fire boards. Audit and value for money review in local government in Scotland.

Library catalogue:
All or part available online

Printed publications:
Annual Report and Accounts
A selection of publications relating to local government, most of which are available free of charge from the Accounts Commission (see website)
Order printed publications from: http://www.audit-scotland.gov.uk

continued overleaf

Publications list:
Available online and in print

Access to staff:
Contact by letter, by telephone and by e-mail
Hours: Mon to Fri, 0900 to 1700

ACCRINGTON CENTRAL LIBRARY

St James' Street, Accrington, Lancashire, BB5 1NQ

Tel: 01254 872385
Fax: 01254 301066
E-mail: accrington.library@lancashire.gov.uk

Website:
http://www.lancashire.gov.uk/libraries
Includes library catalogue.

Enquiries:
Enquiries to: Reference Librarian
Direct tel: 01254 306905

Founded:
1908

Formerly called:
Hyndburn Central Library (year of change 1994)

Organisation type and purpose:
Public library.

Subject coverage:
Local history of the Hyndburn District of
Lancashire, and the county of Lancashire; history
of the Accrington Pals (11th Service Battalion, East
Lancashire Regiment) in World War I and
generally; World War I collection (includes war
graves, memorial registers and official histories).

**Museum or gallery collection, archive, or library
special collection:**
Commonwealth War Graves Commission
Registers for World War I
Funder Finder computerised database, for groups
in need, provides an index to trusts who can
supply funding to voluntary organisations

Trade and statistical information:
Small area statistics for Hyndburn district of
Lancashire. Census figures for Lancashire.
General statistics, eg: Annual Abstract of
statistics.

Non-library collection catalogue:
All or part available online

Library catalogue:
All or part available online

Printed publications:
Leaflets (irregular)

Access to staff:
Contact by letter, by telephone, by fax, by e-mail
and in person
Hours: Mon and Tue, 0930 to 1930; Wed, 0930 to
1230; Thu and Fri, 0930 to 1700; Sat, 0930 to 1600

Part of:
Lancashire County Library & Information Service

ACE CREDIT UNION SERVICES

Acronym or abbreviation: NFCU

3rd Floor, 20 Great North Road, Newcastle upon
Tyne, NE2 4PS

Tel: 0191 257 2219
Fax: 0191 259 1884

Enquiries:
Enquiries to: Chairman
Other contacts: National Co-ordinator

Founded:
1964

Formerly called:
National Federation of Credit Unions

Organisation type and purpose:
Advisory body.

Subject coverage:
Information, technical advice and training in the
registering and operating of credit unions for
communities, organisations and employees.

Printed publications:
Newsletter (4 times a year)
Leaflets available on request

Electronic and video publications:
Available on request

Publications list:
Available in print

Access to staff:
Contact by letter, by telephone and by fax.
Appointment necessary.
Hours: Mon to Fri, 0900 to 1700

ACE STUDY TOURS

Babraham, Cambridge, CB2 4AP

Tel: 01223 835055
Fax: 01223 837394
E-mail: ace@study-tours.org

Website:
http://www.study-tours.org

Enquiries:
Enquiries to: Secretary

Founded:
1958

Formerly called:
Association for Cultural Exchange

Organisation type and purpose:
Service industry.
Tour operator for educational study tours and
courses in England, Europe and worldwide.

Subject coverage:
International adult education.

Printed publications:
Annual brochure
Summer Newsletter
Winter/Spring brochure
Bulletins
Newsletter

Access to staff:
Contact by letter, by telephone, by fax and by e-
mail
Hours: Mon to Fri, 0900 to 1700

ACEVO

Formal name: Association of Chief Executives of
Voluntary Organisations

83 Victoria Street, London, SW1H 0HW

Tel: 0845 345 8481
Fax: 0845 345 8482
E-mail: info@acevo.org.uk

Website:
http://www.acevo.org.uk

Enquiries:
Enquiries to: Receptionist/Publications Officer
Direct e-mail: membership@acevo.org.uk
Other contacts: Head of Policy & Communications
for press and policy.

Founded:
1987

Formerly called:
Association of Chief Executives of National
Voluntary Organisations (ACENVO)

Organisation type and purpose:
Professional body, present number of members: c.
1,800, voluntary organisation, training
organisation.
Networking organisation.

Subject coverage:
All matters relating to chief executives of voluntary
organisations, training, education, legal advice,
support, mentoring, twinning, fundraising,
helpline.

Library catalogue:
All or part available online

Printed publications:
Basic Guides to Good Practice
Appraising the Chief Executive: A Guide
Chief Executive Remuneration Survey
Codes of Conduct for Chief Executives and
Trustees
Model Contract for Chief Executives
Model Job Descriptions
Partners in Leadership: a New Style of Governance
and Management for Professionally Managed
Charities
Planning for Partnership: the Relationship between
Chairs and Trustees

Publications list:
Available online and in print

Access to staff:
Contact by letter, by telephone, by fax, by e-mail
and via website
Hours: Mon to Fri, 0900 to 1700

ACPPLD

Formal name: Association of Chartered
Physiotherapists for People with Learning
Disabilities

CIG Liaison Officer, Chartered Society of
Physiotherapy, 14 Bedford Row, London, WC1R
4ED

Tel: 020 7306 6611

Website:
http://www.acppld.org.uk
All about the association, membership, overview
of service provision.

Organisation type and purpose:
Professional body (membership is by subscription),
present number of members: 250.

Subject coverage:
Physiotherapy for people with learning disabilities.

Access to staff:
Contact by letter, by telephone and via website.
Appointment necessary.
Hours: Mon to Fri, 0900 to 1700

Clinical interest group within the:
Chartered Society of Physiotherapy

ACT

Formal name: Association for Children's Palliative
Care

Brunswick Court, Brunswick Square, Bristol, BS2
8PE

Tel: 0117 916 6422
Fax: 0117 916 6430
E-mail: info@act.org.uk

Website:
http://www.act.org.uk

Enquiries:
Enquiries to: Information and Administration
Officer

Founded:
1993

Subject coverage:
ACT (Association for Children's Palliative Care)
aims to provide information on support services
available for families whose children have life-
threatening or terminal conditions, regardless of
the particular disease involved. It is involved in
consultation and contact between service providers
and campaigns to encourage the development of
children's palliative care services.

Information services:
Helpline (tel: 0845 108 2201).

Trade and statistical information:
National information service on support services available for families with a child/children with life-limiting or life-threatening conditions.

Library catalogue:
All or part available online and in-house

Printed publications:
See website

Publications list:
Available online and in print

Access to staff:
Contact by letter, by telephone, by fax, by e-mail and via website. Appointment necessary.
Hours: Access to Families/Health Professionals: Mon to Fri, 0900 to 1700

Access to building, collection or gallery:
Prior appointment required

ACTION AGAINST ALLERGY

Acronym or abbreviation: AAA

PO Box 278, Twickenham, Middlesex, TW1 4QQ

Tel: 020 8892 2711/4949
Fax: 020 8892 4950
E-mail: aaa@actionagainstallergy.freeserve.co.uk

Website:
http://www.actionagainstallergy.co.uk

Enquiries:
Enquiries to: Executive Director

Founded:
1978

Organisation type and purpose:
Registered charity (charity number 276637), patient support organisation.
Provides information about allergic illness and related conditions to patients and professionals in the health care field.

Subject coverage:
Allergies, allergy-related illness.

Information services:
Find-a-Doctor service; wide range of information leaflets concerning allergic illness

Education services:
Occasional workshops for parents and professionals

Museum or gallery collection, archive, or library special collection:
Information leaflets list available on request with sae
Various papers on different aspects of allergic illness

Printed publications:
Allergy Newsletter (3 times a year, £15 per annum UK, US$30, or sterling equivalent, overseas, free to members)
Information packs (£3 each)
Names and addresses of specialists (search fee of £5)
Various leaflets
Order printed publications from: Postal address or online

Publications list:
Available online and in print

Access to staff:
Contact by letter, by telephone, by fax, by e-mail and via website
Hours: Mon to Fri, 0930 to 1700

Access to building, collection or gallery:
No access other than to staff

ACTION ASTHMA

Allen & Hamburys Limited, Department G, Freepost DR83, Ashford, Kent, TN24 0YX

Tel: 020 8990 3011/2430

Subject coverage:
Asthma.

Access to staff:
Contact by letter
Hours: Mon to Fri, 0900 to 1700

Access to building, collection or gallery:
No access other than to staff

Access for disabled people:
Access to all public areas

Other address:
GlaxoSmithKline
Building 10, Stockley Park West, Uxbridge, UB11 1BT

ACTION FOR BLIND PEOPLE

Information & Advice Centre, 14–16 Verney Road, London, SE16 3DZ

Tel: 020 7635 4800; National Freephone Helpline 0800 915 4666
Fax: 020 7635 4900
E-mail: info@actionforblindpeople.org.uk

Website:
http://www.actionforblindpeople.org.uk

Enquiries:
Enquiries to: Information Officer

Founded:
1857

Organisation type and purpose:
Voluntary organisation, registered charity (charity number 205913).
To provide services for visually impaired people.

Subject coverage:
Visual impairment: service provision, general awareness, aids and equipment, accommodation and residential care, leisure and holidays, education, employment and training, welfare rights and grants.

Library catalogue:
All or part available in-house

Printed publications:
Brochures or leaflets on most of the following subject headings: Information and Advice, Accommodation, Holidays, Employment, Leisure, Welfare Rights, Benefit Briefings

Electronic and video publications:
Most publications available on audio tape, or via email

Publications list:
Available online and in print

Access to staff:
Contact by letter, by telephone, by fax, by e-mail and via website. Appointment necessary.
Hours: Mon to Fri, 0900 to 1700

Access for disabled people:
Ramped entry, toilet facilities

ACTION FOR KIDS, CHARITABLE TRUST

Acronym or abbreviation: AFK

Ability House, 15A Tottenham Lane, Hornsey, London, N8 9DJ

Tel: 020 8347 8111; minicom no. 020 8347 3486
Fax: 020 8347 3482
E-mail: info@actionforkids.org

Website:
http://www.actionforkids.org
Remit and service provision of the charity, and news updates.

Enquiries:
Enquiries to: Information Officer

Founded:
1992

Organisation type and purpose:
Registered charity (charity number 1068841).
Provides grants for the provision of mobility aid, provides work experience programmes for disabled young people, assists children and young people suffering physical and mental disability to lead full and independent lives.

Subject coverage:
The relief of physical and mental disability – through independence, created by the provision of mobility aids that are not available on the NHS and by supported-into-work learning programmes, both in-house and via outreach, for disabled young people. Equipment provided for those up to age 21; work-related training for those up to age 26.

Printed publications:
Annual Review
Booklets (free)
Newsletter (3 times a year)

Electronic and video publications:
DVD

Access to staff:
Contact by letter, by telephone, by fax, by e-mail and via website. Appointment necessary.
Hours: Mon to Fri, 0900 to 1730

Access to building, collection or gallery:
Hours: Mon to Fri, 0900 to 1730

Access for disabled people:
Full disabled access and facilities: parking provided, access to all public areas

ACTION FOR ME

Formal name: Action for Myalgic Encephalomyelitis
Acronym or abbreviation: AfME

Third Floor, Canningford House, 38 Victoria Street, Bristol, BS1 6BY

Tel: 0845 123 2314
Fax: 0117 9279552
E-mail: admin@afme.org.uk

Website:
http://www.afme.org.uk
Information on ME and the services provided by Action for ME.

Enquiries:
Enquiries to: Administrator
Direct e-mail: media@afme.org.uk

Founded:
1987

Formerly called:
ME Action

Organisation type and purpose:
National organisation, membership association (membership is by subscription), present number of members: 8,000+, voluntary organisation, registered charity (charity number 1036419).
Over 150 local support groups.
Provides information and support to people with ME and campaigns to government and the medical profession for better understanding and treatment.

Subject coverage:
Information on myalgic encephalomyelitis (ME), chronic fatigue syndrome, and post-viral fatigue syndrome.

Library catalogue:
All or part available in-house and in print

Printed publications:
Contact Action for ME for details.
Order printed publications from: AfME Information Service
PO Box 1302, Wells, Somerset, BA5 1YE

Publications list:
Available in print

Access to staff:
Contact by letter, by telephone, by fax and by e-mail
Hours: Mon to Fri, 0930 to 1700
Special comments: Please telephone initially

continued overleaf

Access to building, collection or gallery:
No access other than to staff

Access for disabled people:
Special comments: Please telephone initially

Also at:
Action for ME
73 Watling Street, London, EC4M 9BL; tel: 020
7329 2299; fax: 020 7329 3600; e-mail: london@
afme.org.uk

ACTION FOR SOUTHERN AFRICA

Acronym or abbreviation: ACTSA

28 Penton Street, London, N1 9SA

Tel: 020 7833 3133
Fax: 020 7837 3001
E-mail: actsa@actsa.org

Website:
http://www.actsa.org

Enquiries:
Enquiries to: Office Manager

Founded:
1994

Formerly called:
Anti-Apartheid Movement

Organisation type and purpose:
Membership association (membership is by
subscription), voluntary organisation.
Lobbying support of Southern Africa,
campaigning for peace, democracy and
development in Southern Africa.

Subject coverage:
Peace, democracy and development in Southern
Africa, South Africa, Lesotho, Swaziland,
Botswana, Namibia, Angola, Zambia, Zimbabwe,
Mozambique, Malawi, Tanzania, Mauritius,
Democratic Republic of Congo, Seychelles.

Printed publications:
ACTSA News (quarterly)

Publications list:
Available online

Access to staff:
Contact by letter, by telephone, by fax, by e-mail
and via website
Hours: Mon to Fri, 0930 to 1730

Access to building, collection or gallery:
Prior appointment required

ACTION ON ELDER ABUSE

Acronym or abbreviation: AEA

PO Box 60001, London, SW16 9BY

Tel: 020 8835 9280
Fax: 020 8696 9328
E-mail: enquiries@elderabuse.org.uk

Website:
http://www.elderabuse.org.uk

Founded:
1993

Organisation type and purpose:
International organisation, membership
association (membership is by subscription),
present number of members: 550, voluntary
organisation, registered charity (charity number
1048397).
To prevent the abuse of older people by raising
awareness, encouraging education and research,
and collecting and disseminating information.

Subject coverage:
The abuse of older people by someone in any
relationship of trust at home or in care settings.

Information services:
Helpline freephone: 080 8808 8141

Non-library collection catalogue:
All or part available in-house

Library catalogue:
All or part available in-house

Printed publications:
Action on Elder Abuse
Briefing Pack
Elder abuse – what is it?

Publications list:
Available online and in print

Access to staff:
Contact by letter, by telephone, by fax, by e-mail
and via website
Hours: Mon to Fri, 0900 to 1700

ACTION ON PRE-ECLAMPSIA

Formal name: Action on Pre-eclampsia
Acronym or abbreviation: APEC

84–88 Pinner Road, Harrow, Middlesex, HA1 4HZ

Tel: 020 8863 3271 (Administration)\ 020 8427 4217
(Helpline) Mon to Fri, 1000 to 1300
Fax: 020 8424 0653
E-mail: info@apec.org.uk

Website:
http://www.apec.org.uk

Enquiries:
Enquiries to: Chief Executive

Founded:
1991

Organisation type and purpose:
Membership association (membership is by
subscription), present number of members: 1000,
voluntary organisation, registered charity (charity
number 1013557).
To prevent or ease suffering from pre-eclampsia by
means of enhanced public awareness, increased
professional knowledge and skill, and the
provision of immediate and continuing support for
affected families.

Subject coverage:
Pre-eclampsia.

Printed publications:
Information pack, available to order
Leaflet, send an sae

Publications list:
Available online

Access to staff:
Contact by letter, by telephone, by fax, by e-mail
and via website. Non-members charged.
Hours: Mon to Fri, 0900 to 1700

ACTION ON SMOKING AND HEALTH

Acronym or abbreviation: ASH

First Floor, 144–145 Shoreditch High Street,
London, E1 6JE

Tel: 020 7739 5902
Fax: 020 7613 0531
E-mail: enquiries@ash.org.uk

Website:
http://www.ash.org.uk

Enquiries:
Enquiries to: Research Manager

Founded:
1971

Organisation type and purpose:
National organisation, voluntary organisation,
registered charity (charity number 262067).

Subject coverage:
Smoking and its effect on health, tobacco industry,
tobacco control activities, statistics on tobacco and
smoking, covering the UK and other countries.

Printed publications:
Reports on Smoking & Health, Tobacco Industry,
Tobacco Advertising, Tobacco Policy, Tobacco &
Economics and Resource Guides

30 referenced Factsheets; 5 'At a glance' fact sheets
Regular reports
Order printed publications from: Online shop on ASH
website

Electronic and video publications:
All published items are on the website

Publications list:
Available online and in print

Access to staff:
Contact by letter, by telephone, by e-mail and via
website
Hours: Mon to Fri, 0900 to 1700
Special comments: No public access to office.

Access to building, collection or gallery:
No access other than to staff

ACTION WITH COMMUNITIES IN RURAL KENT

15 Manor Road, Folkestone, Kent, CT20 2AH

Tel: 01303 850816
Fax: 01303 850244
E-mail: info@ruralkent.org.uk

Website:
http://www.ruralkent.org.uk

Enquiries:
Enquiries to: Director

Founded:
1923

Organisation type and purpose:
Membership association (membership is by
subscription), present number of members: 400,
registered charity (charity number 212796).

Subject coverage:
All rural issues.

Printed publications:
Oast to Coast (magazine)
Rural News (newsletter)

Publications list:
Available in print

Access to staff:
Contact by letter, by telephone, by fax and by e-
mail
Hours: Mon to Fri, 0900 to 1700

Access to building, collection or gallery:
Prior appointment required

ACTIONAID SCHOOLS AND YOUTH

Acronym or abbreviation: AA

Chataway House, Leach Road, Chard, Somerset,
TA20 1FR

Tel: 01460 238000
Fax: 01460 67191
E-mail: deved@actionaid.org.uk

Website:
http://www.actionaid.org
Education resource catalogue.

Enquiries:
Enquiries to: Schools Co-ordinator
Other contacts: Press Officer

Founded:
1972

Formerly called:
ActionAid Education

Organisation type and purpose:
International organisation, registered charity.
Non-governmental organisation. Development
education unit for the charity.

Subject coverage:
Development, geographical and environmental
information for Key Stages 1 to 4 of the National
Curriculum.

Non-library collection catalogue:
All or part available online, in-house and in print

Printed publications:
Education Catalogue

Electronic and video publications:
CD-ROMs of educational resources for Key Stages 1–4

Publications list:
Available online

Access to staff:
Contact by letter, by telephone, by fax, by e-mail, in person and via website. Appointment necessary.
Hours: Mon to Fri, 0900 to 1700

Access for disabled people:
Parking provided, toilet facilities

Parent body:
ActionAid UK
  Hamlyn House, MacDonald Road, Archway, London, N19 5PG

Subsidiary body:
Azione Aiuto
  Via Trincea delle Frasche 2, Milano, I-20136, Italy

ACTORS' BENEVOLENT FUND

6 Adam Street, London, WC2N 6AD

Tel: 020 7836 6378
Fax: 020 7836 8978
E-mail: office@abf.org.uk

Website:
http://www.actorsbenevolentfund.co.uk
Guidelines for applicants, how to become a member, how to make a donation, history of the Fund and online shop.

Enquiries:
Enquiries to: General Secretary
Other contacts: Assistant General Secretary

Founded:
1882

Organisation type and purpose:
Registered charity (charity number 206524), members are all actors (membership is by subscription).
To care for actors and theatrical stage managers unable to work because of poor health, an accident or old age.

Subject coverage:
Provides one-off or long-term financial aid and support and help in claiming benefits.

Printed publications:
History Booklet (Lowrie, P., written to celebrate the Fund's 120th anniversary, £1.50)
Order printed publications from: Website

Access to staff:
Contact by letter, by telephone, by fax and by e-mail

Member organisation of:
Combined Theatrical Charities

ACUMEDIC CENTRE FOR CHINESE MEDICINE

1 Wyle Cop, Shrewsbury, Shropshire, SY1 1UT

Tel: 01743 236100
Fax: 01743 236100

Enquiries:
Enquiries to: Manager

Founded:
1989

Formerly called:
Acumedic Ltd

Organisation type and purpose:
Service industry.

Subject coverage:
Acupuncture and traditional Chinese herbal medicine.

Access to staff:
Contact by telephone
Hours: Mon to Fri, 0900 to 1700

Affiliated to:
Acumedic
  17 Carlisle Road, Colindale, London, NW9 0HD

Parent body:
Acumedic Centre
  101 Camden High Street, London, NW1 7JN; tel: 020 7388 6704; fax: 020 7387 5766; e-mail: infon@ acumedic.com

ADAM SMITH COLLEGE

Library, St Brycedale Avenue, Kirkcaldy, Fife, KY1 1EX

Tel: 01592 223411
Fax: 01592 640225
E-mail: library@adamsmith.ac.uk

Website:
http://www.adamsmithcollege.ac.uk

Enquiries:
Enquiries to: Learner Resources Manager

Created by the merger of:
Fife College of Further and Higher Education, and Glenrothes College (year of change 2005)

Organisation type and purpose:
College of further and higher education.

Subject coverage:
General.

Non-library collection catalogue:
All or part available in-house

Library catalogue:
All or part available online

Access to staff:
Contact by telephone, by e-mail and in person
Hours: Mon to Thu, 0850 to 2100; Fri, 0850 to 1620; Sat, 0900 to 1200

ADAM SMITH LIBRARY

University of Glasgow, 40 Bute Gardens, Glasgow, G12 8RT

Tel: 0141 330 5648
E-mail: adamsmith@lib.gla.ac.uk

Enquiries:
Enquiries to: Adam Smith Librarian
Direct e-mail: k.ross@lib.gla.ac.uk

Founded:
1968

Organisation type and purpose:
University library.
Library of the Faculty of Law, Business & Social Sciences.

Subject coverage:
Anthropology, economics, politics, psychology, sociology, town and regional planning.

Non-library collection catalogue:
All or part available online and in-house

Library catalogue:
All or part available online and in-house

Access to staff:
Contact by letter, by telephone and by e-mail.
Appointment necessary.
Hours: Term time: Mon to Thu, 0900 to 2100; Fri, 0900 to 1700
Vacations: Mon to Fri, 0900 to 1700

Access for disabled people:
Parking provided, ramped entry

ADAMSON PUBLISHING

8 The Moorings, Norwich, NR3 3AX

Tel: 01603 623336
Fax: 01603 624767
E-mail: sales@adamsonbooks.com

Website:
http://www.adamsonbooks.com

Enquiries:
Enquiries to: Managing Director

Founded:
1984

Formerly called:
Adamson Books (year of change 2003)

Organisation type and purpose:
Publishing house.

Subject coverage:
Information for school governors, headteachers and teaching assistants.

Information services:
Clerkwise

Non-library collection catalogue:
All or part available online and in print

Library catalogue:
All or part available online

Printed publications:
The School Governors' Yearbook (annually)
Parent Governors (2006)
Staff Governors (2006)
Community Governors (2006)
Foundation Governors (2006)
Local Authority Governors (2006)
School Self-Evaluation and Inspection (2009)
Being Strategic (2nd edn, 2009)
Monitoring and Evaluation (2009)
Accountability (2nd edn, 2010)
The Green School (2008)
Policies (4th edn, 2010)
Teaching Assistants: The Complete Handbook (2004)
Joined-up Governance (2002)
Start Here (rev. edn 2010)
Performance Management Revisited (2007)
Headteachers and Governing Bodies (2nd edn, 2010)
Order printed publications from: Marston Book Services

Electronic and video publications:
Order electronic and video publications from: Adamson Publishing

Publications list:
Available online

Access to staff:
Contact by letter, by telephone, by fax and by e-mail
Hours: Mon to Fri, 0900 to 1700

Access to building, collection or gallery:
No access other than to staff

ADAS UK LIMITED

Acronym or abbreviation: ADAS

Woodthorne Wergs Road, Wolverhampton, West Midlands, WV6 8TQ

Tel: 01902 754190
Fax: 01902 743602
E-mail: mark.talbot@adas.co.uk

Website:
http://www.globalfarmers.com
E-commerce agricultural trading exchange.
http://www.adas.co.uk
Information about ADAS.
http://www.rbnet.co.uk
RBN (Rural Business network) joint venture between ADAS, CLA and the NFU.

Enquiries:
Enquiries to: Facilities
Direct tel: 01902 693483
Direct fax: 01902 693438
Direct e-mail: mark.talbot@adas.co.uk

Founded:
1997

continued overleaf

Formerly called:
ADAS Executive Agency from 1992 to 1997; MAFF (year of change 1992)

Organisation type and purpose:
Architectural and environmental consultancy.

Subject coverage:
Land-based industries, agricultural and environment-related subjects, food.

Printed publications:
ADAS Research (annually, free)
Insight (4 times a year, free)

Access to staff:
Contact by letter, by telephone, by fax and by e-mail. Appointment necessary. All charged.
Hours: Mon to Fri, 0830 to 1700

Access to building, collection or gallery:
Hours: Mon to Fri, 0830 to 1700 (by invitation only)

Access for disabled people:
Mon to Fri, 0830 to 1700
Hours: Phone before visit

ADDACTION

67–69 Cowcross Street, London, EC1M 6PU

Tel: 020 7251 5860
Fax: 020 7251 5890
E-mail: info@addaction.org.uk

Website:
http://www.addaction.org.uk
Information including: press releases, news clippings, fundraising news and donor forms, information about Addaction, research reports.

Enquiries:
Enquiries to: Administrator
Other contacts: Press Office (for media enquiries)

Founded:
1967

Formerly called:
Association for Prevention of Addiction (APA) (year of change 1997)

Organisation type and purpose:
Registered charity (charity number 1001957).
Addaction provides drug and alcohol treatment services at over 70 projects throughout the country. To solve drug and alcohol problems and to campaign for innovative approaches to solving drug and alcohol problems.

Subject coverage:
Drug and alcohol addiction and misuse.

Non-library collection catalogue:
All or part available online

Printed publications:
Annual Report (£2)
Information booklets: including, Parents' Guide to Drugs

Publications list:
Available online

Access to staff:
Contact by letter, by telephone, by fax and by e-mail
Hours: Mon to Fri, 0900 to 1700

Founder member of:
Alcohol Concern
SCODA

ADFAM

Formal name: National Charity for Families and Friends of Drug Users

25 Corsham Street, London, N1 6DR

Tel: 020 7553 7640
Fax: 020 7253 7991
E-mail: admin@adfam.org.uk

Website:
http://www.adfam.org.uk

Information and resources for families affected by drug/alcohol use and any professionals who work and come into contact with them, including training information, publications and a database of local services across the country.

Enquiries:
Enquiries to: Policy and Communications Coordinator
Direct tel: 020 7553 7640
Direct e-mail: admin@adfam.org.uk

Founded:
1984

Organisation type and purpose:
Voluntary organisation, registered charity (charity number 1067428), training organisation.
A national organisation working with families affected by drugs and alcohol and a leading agency in substance-related family work; provides a range of publications and resources for families about substances and criminal justice and operates an online message board and searchable database of local support groups that helps families hear about and talk to people who understand their situation; runs a range of training programmes on substances and family support; consultancy; direct support services at London prisons for families of prisoners with drug problems.

Subject coverage:
Families and drug use, family dynamics, effects of drug use on the family, training in family support skills, setting up family support groups, drug education for parents, help for families of drug-using prisoners.

Printed publications:
Prison Drugs and You – For the families and friends of prisoners using drugs
Are you worried about your Mum, Dad or Carer using Drugs or Alcohol (for children)
Living with a Drug User – A booklet for parents of drug users
Living with a Drug User – A booklet for partners of drug users
A Guide to Setting Up a Family / Friend Support Group
Families in Focus – England
'Journeys' series for all family members including parents, partners, grandparents, children, siblings
Selection of Criminal Justice Posters

Electronic and video publications:
Putting it into words (website)
Turning it around (£5)
Order electronic and video publications from: http://www.adfam.org.uk

Publications list:
Available online and in print

Access to staff:
Contact by letter, by telephone, by fax and by e-mail
Hours: Mon to Fri, 0900 to 1700
Special comments: Donations welcomed for provision of information.

ADHESIVE TAPE MANUFACTURERS ASSOCIATION

Acronym or abbreviation: ATMA

Sussex House, 8–10 Homesdale Road, Bromley, Kent, BR2 9LZ

Tel: 020 8464 0131
Fax: 020 8464 6018
E-mail: tradeassn@craneandpartners.com

Enquiries:
Enquiries to: Secretary

Organisation type and purpose:
Trade association.

Subject coverage:
Pressure-sensitive tapes, technical aspects and applications of adhesive tapes.

Publications list:
Available in print

Affiliated to:
European association (AFERA)

ADOLESCENT AND CHILDREN'S TRUST

Acronym or abbreviation: TACT

The Courtyard, 303 Hither Green Lane, Hither Green, London SE13 6TJ

Tel: 020 8695 8142
E-mail: enquiries@tactcare.org.uk

Website:
http://www.tactcare.org.uk
The UK's largest fostering and adoption charity.

Founded:
1993

Organisation type and purpose:
Charity prodiving fostering and adoption services across the UK.

Subject coverage:
Adoption and fostering services.

Access to staff:
Contact by telephone and by e-mail
Hours: Mon to Fri, 0900 to 1700

ADOPTION UK

46 The Green, South Bar Street, Banbury, Oxfordshire, OX16 9AB

Tel: 01295 752240
Fax: 01295 752241
E-mail: admin@adoptionuk.org.uk

Website:
http://www.adoptionuk.org
Information about Adoption UK and includes printable membership form.

Enquiries:
Enquiries to: Helpline Adviser

Founded:
1970–71

Formerly called:
Parent to Parent Information on Adoption Services (PPIAS) (year of change 1999)

Organisation type and purpose:
Membership organisation for prospective adopters and adoptive parents, present number of members: over 4,500, registered charity (charity number 326654).
Membership subscription £20–£40 per annum.To provide information, advice, support, and training.

Subject coverage:
Adoption for children (permanent family placement), especially for those who are racially mixed, who have a physical or mental disability or who are older than the usual age for adoption; support and information service for prospective and existing adoptive families.

Museum or gallery collection, archive, or library special collection:
Adoptive families willing to speak to members about any given experience (adoption)

Non-library collection catalogue:
All or part available in-house

Library catalogue:
All or part available in print

Printed publications:
Adoption Today (6 times a year)
Children Who Wait (monthly)
Oh, Brother (£5)
Adoption Law for Adopters (£10)

Electronic and video publications:
Attachment in Adopted and Foster Children (Hughes D, tape)
Annual General Meeting 2001 (Hughes D, tape)

Publications list:
Available online and in print

Access to staff:
Contact by letter, by telephone, by fax, by e-mail, in person and via website. Appointment necessary. Access for members only.
Hours: Mon to Fri, 0900 to 1700 office; Mon to Fri, 1000 to 1600 helpline
Special comments: Helpline Telephone is answered in person during office hours and by answerphone at all other times.

Access for disabled people:
Access to all public areas, toilet facilities

Links with:
all adoption agencies and local authorities in the UK

ADULT RESIDENTIAL COLLEGES ASSOCIATION

Acronym or abbreviation: ARCA

6 Bath Road, Felixstowe, Suffolk, IP11 7JW

Tel: 01394 278161
Fax: 01394 271083
E-mail: arcasec@aol.com

Website:
http://www.arca.uk.net
Information on ARCA colleges and courses

Enquiries:
Enquiries to: Honorary Secretary

Founded:
1983

Organisation type and purpose:
Membership association (membership is by subscription, qualification), present number of members: 30 institutions, voluntary organisation, suitable for ages: adults.
To promote residential short-term liberal adult education for the benefit of the general public.

Subject coverage:
First stop call to member colleges for public enquiries.

Access to staff:
Contact by letter, by telephone, by fax and by e-mail
Hours: Mon to Fri, 0900 to 1700

ADVANTAGE AUSTRIA / THE AUSTRIAN TRADE COMMISSION

Formal name: Austrian Embassy – Commercial Section

45 Princes Gate, Exhibition Road, London, SW7 2QA

Tel: 020 7584 4411
Fax: 020 7584 7946
E-mail: london@advantageaustria.org

Website:
http://www.advantageaustria.org/uk

Enquiries:
Enquiries to: Information Officer

Organisation type and purpose:
Official Austrian Foreign Trade Promotion Organisation and the largest provider of services in the area of Austrian foreign trade.

Subject coverage:
The gateway to Austria for international companies looking for world-class suppliers; for over 60 years, the official representative of Austrian business in Britain, providing Austrian companies with the knowledge, advice and practical support they need to establish trade and investment links with the UK.

Printed publications:
Austria Export Magazine: current facts and figures, company profiles and market insights of many different sectors of the Austrian economy

Order printed publications from: e-mail: london@advantageaustria.org

Electronic and video publications:
Austria Export Magazine: current facts and figures, company profiles and market insights of many different sectors of the Austrian economy
Order electronic and video publications from: e-mail: london@advantageaustria.org

Access to staff:
Contact by e-mail and via website
Hours: Mon to Fri, 0830 to 1700

Access to building, collection or gallery:
Hours: Mon to Fri, 0830 to 1700

ADVERTISING ASSOCIATION

Acronym or abbreviation: AA

7th Floor North, Artillery House, 11–19 Artillery Row, London, SW1P 1RT

Tel: 020 7340 1100
Fax: 020 7222 1504
E-mail: aa@adassoc.org.uk

Website:
http://www.adassoc.org.uk/inform/content.html
Student briefings, links to list, position papers, publications list, press releases, information sheets, reading lists, 'Getting into advertising: a careers guide'.

Founded:
1926

Organisation type and purpose:
The Advertising Association is a federation of trade bodies and organisations representing the advertising and promotional marketing industries, including advertisers, agencies, the media and support services in the UK.

Subject coverage:
Advertising, marketing, public relations, communications, sales promotion, the media.

Library catalogue:
All or part available in-house

Printed publications:
Books
Research monographs and statistical publications
See website for full list

Electronic and video publications:
Getting Into Advertising: Careers Booklet (website)
Student Briefings on advertising (website)

Publications list:
Available online and in print

Access to staff:
Contact by letter, by telephone, by e-mail and via website. Appointment necessary.
Special comments: See AA website for details.

Members:
Cinema Advertising Association (CAA)
Communication Advertising and Marketing Education Foundation (CAM)
Data Publishers Association (DPA)
Direct Marketing Association (UK) Limited (DMA)
Direct Selling Association (DSA)
Incorporated Society of British Advertisers (ISBA)
Institute of Practitioners in Advertising (IPA)
Institute of Sales Promotion (ISP)
Interactive Advertising Bureau (UK) (IAB)
Internet Advertising Association – UK Chapter (IAA UK Chapter)
ITV plc (ITV)
Mail Order Traders' Association (MOTA)
Market Research Society (MRS)
Marketing Communication Consultants Association
Newspaper Publishers Association Limited (NPA)
Newspaper Society (NS)
Outdoor Advertising Association of Great Britain Limited (OAA)
Periodical Publishers Association (PPA)
Point of Purchase Advertising International (POPAI)
Radio Centre

Royal Mail (RM)
Satellite and Cable Broadcasters' Group (SCBG)
Scottish Newspaper Publishers Association (SNPA)

ADVERTISING STANDARDS AUTHORITY

Acronym or abbreviation: ASA

Mid City Place, 71 High Holborn, London, WC1V 6QT

Tel: 020 7492 2222
Fax: 020 7242 3696
E-mail: enquiries@asa.org.uk

Website:
http://www.asa.org.uk
Advertising standards codes plus information about the role and remit of the Authority.

Enquiries:
Enquiries to: Enquiries Team

Founded:
1962

Organisation type and purpose:
Advisory body, professional body, trade association.
Regulates UK advertising.

Subject coverage:
Pre-publication advice on interpretation of the advertising codes available for advertisers, agencies and the media for all non-broadcast ads.

Museum or gallery collection, archive, or library special collection:
Various research and briefing notes

Trade and statistical information:
Data on the number and nature of complaints about advertising.

Printed publications:
Guide to the Advertising Standards Authority
Annual Report
Advertising Codes
Complaints Procedure

Access to staff:
Contact by letter, by telephone, by fax, by e-mail and via website
Hours: Mon to Fri, 0900 to 1730

Access to building, collection or gallery:
No access other than to staff

Access for disabled people:
Ramped entry

Links with:
Committee of Advertising Practice
   Mid City Place, 71 High Holborn, London, WC1V 6QT; tel: 020 7492 2222; fax: 020 7242 3696; e-mail: advice@cap.org.uk; website: http://www.cap.org.uk
European Advertising Standards Alliance
   website: http://www.easa-alliance.org

ADVICE SERVICE CAPABILITY SCOTLAND

11 Ellersly Road, Edinburgh, EH12 6HY

Tel: 0131 313 5510
Fax: 0131 346 1681
E-mail: ascs@capability-scotland.org.uk

Website:
http://www.capability-scotland.org.uk

Enquiries:
Enquiries to: Advice Worker

Founded:
1946

Organisation type and purpose:
A national disability information and advice service, specialising in information on cerebral palsy.

continued overleaf

Subject coverage:
Information on a range of disability issues including cerebral palsy.

Museum or gallery collection, archive, or library special collection:
A small lending library with resources about cerebral palsy and children's books about disability

Library catalogue:
All or part available online

Publications list:
Available online and in print

Access to staff:
Contact by letter, by telephone, by fax, by e-mail and in person
Hours: Mon to Fri, 0900 to 1700

Access for disabled people:
Parking provided, ramped entry, toilet facilities

ADVISORY CENTRE FOR EDUCATION

Acronym or abbreviation: ACE

1c Aberdeen Studios, 22 Highbury Grove, London, N5 2DQ

Tel: 020 7354 8318 (Business line only)
Fax: 020 7354 9069
E-mail: enquiries@ace.dialnet.com

Website:
http://www.ace-ed.org.uk/pdf/publications.pdf
Publications list.
http://www.ace-ed.org.uk/advice.html
Advice pages including downloadable booklets on bullying, SEN, exclusion, school admissions, choosing a school and taking matters further.
http://www.ace-ed.org.uk
Home page.

Enquiries:
Enquiries to: Information Officer
Direct tel: 020 7354 8318

Founded:
1960

Organisation type and purpose:
National organisation (membership is by subscription), voluntary organisation, registered charity (charity number 313142), publishing house.
Advises on parents' rights in education.
Independent national education advice service for parents.

Subject coverage:
Education in the statutory school years 5 to 16, guidance for parents, special education, exclusion from school, education law, governors' duties, choosing a school. Advice available for England and Wales only.

Museum or gallery collection, archive, or library special collection:
Education 5–16 books, pamphlets, cuttings

Non-library collection catalogue:
All or part available in-house

Printed publications:
ACE Bulletin (6 times a year, free to members)
Stop Press (monthly)
A range of books and information leaflets for parents, teachers and governors including:
Governors' briefings (6 titles)
Governors' Handbook (5th ed., 2001)
Home Education Pack
Index to the School Standards and Framework Act (1999)
Outside, Looking In: children's and families' experiences of exclusion (The Children's Society, 2001)
School Governors: a plain guide for people like you (Sallis J, 1999)
Special Educational Handbook – The law on children with special needs (Updated 2002)
The Special Educational Needs and Disability Discrimination Act 2001

Order printed publications from: e-mail: enquiries@ace.dialnet.com

Publications list:
Available online and in print

Access to staff:
Contact by telephone. Appointment necessary.
Hours: Free telephone advice line, Mon to Fri, 1400 to 1700: tel 0808 800 5793
Special comments: Advice is given by telephone only. Internet Web pages also provide downloadable information.

Access to building, collection or gallery:
No access other than to staff

ADVISORY COMMITTEE ON PROTECTION OF THE SEA

Acronym or abbreviation: ACOPS

11 Dartmouth Street, London, SW1H 9BN

Tel: 020 7799 3033
Fax: 020 7799 2933
E-mail: acopsorg@netcomuk.co.uk

Website:
http://www.acops.org

Enquiries:
Enquiries to: Programme Officer

Founded:
1952

Organisation type and purpose:
Advisory body, registered charity.
Non-Governmental Organisation.

Subject coverage:
Protection of the marine environment.

Printed publications:
ACOPS Brochure
Annual Oil Pollution Survey around the coasts of the UK
Newsletters
Reports of Conferences
Yearbook (every 2 years)

Access to staff:
Contact by letter, by telephone, by fax and by e-mail
Hours: Mon to Fri, 0900 to 1700

ADVISORY SERVICE FOR SQUATTERS

Acronym or abbreviation: ASS

Angel Alley, 84B Whitechapel High St, London, E1 7QX

Tel: 020 3216 0099
Fax: 020 3216 0098
E-mail: advice@squat.freeserve.co.uk

Website:
http://www.squatter.org.uk

Enquiries:
Enquiries to: Information Officer

Founded:
1975

Organisation type and purpose:
Advisory body, voluntary organisation.

Subject coverage:
Squatting history, housing struggles, surveys of squatters and their lifestyles (1970), law relating to squatting, practical and legal advice to squatters and homeless persons.

Museum or gallery collection, archive, or library special collection:
Books, photographs, some files on family squatting associations
Documents, relating to squatting in Europe, mainly Holland, France and Germany
Late 1970s bibliography of articles on squatting

Trade and statistical information:
Files on squatting in Europe and the world.

Printed publications:
Squatters Handbook (12th ed., £1.50 plus 50p postage)

Access to staff:
Contact by letter, by telephone, by fax, by e-mail, in person and via website
Hours: Mon to Fri, 1400 to 1800

Links with:
COHRE
Hauikstraat 38 bis, Utrecht, 3514 TR, Netherlands
Droit au Logement
3 bis rue de Vaucouleurs, 75011 Paris, France

ADVOCACY RESOURCE EXCHANGE

Acronym or abbreviation: ARX

Unit 3, 60 Duke Street, Liverpool, L1 5AA

Tel: 0151 734 3047
E-mail: chris@advocacyresource.net

Website:
http://www.leevalley.co.uk/cait
Information on CAIT and citizen advocacy.
http://www.citizenadvocacy.org.uk

Enquiries:
Enquiries to: Information Officer

Founded:
1988

Formerly called:
Citizen Advocacy Information & Training (CAIT); Advocacy Alliance; National Citizen Advocacy (year of change 1994)

Organisation type and purpose:
Voluntary organisation, registered charity (charity number 1035082), training organisation.
CAIT supports the development of local citizen advocacy schemes, through the provision of information, training and networking.
The support of people disadvantaged through age, mental or physical health, or learning difficulties.

Subject coverage:
Citizen advocacy.

Museum or gallery collection, archive, or library special collection:
Collection of policies, publicity material and training programmes used by local citizen advocacy schemes
Small library of books and articles on citizen advocacy

Printed publications:
CAIT Newsletter (quarterly)
CAPE: Standards for Citizen Advocacy Program Evaluation (1979, £11.50)
Citizen Advocacy – A Powerful Partnership (1998, £15.40)
List of Citizen Advocacy and Related Advocacy Groups (£3)
Standing By Me – a collection of stories of citizen advocacy partnerships (1998, £8)

Publications list:
Available online and in print

Access to staff:
Contact by letter, by telephone, by fax and via website. Appointment necessary.
Hours: Mon to Fri, 0900 to 1700

Access to building, collection or gallery:
No prior appointment required

Access for disabled people:
Parking provided, access to all public areas, toilet facilities

Funded by:
London Boroughs Grants Committee

Has:
some 200 schemes in the UK

ADVOCATES FOR ANIMALS

10 Queensferry Street, Edinburgh, EH2 4PG

Tel: 0131 225 6039
Fax: 0131 220 6377
E-mail: info@advocatesforanimals.org

Website:
http://www.onekind.org

Founded:
1912

Formerly called:
Scottish Society for the Prevention of Vivisection
(year of change 1990)

Organisation type and purpose:
A leading animal protection charity inspiring a
movement of people who care about animals.

Subject coverage:
Achieving better animal welfare in the UK and
beyond through positive OneKind public
awareness and political influence campaigns,
animal investigations and education.

**Museum or gallery collection, archive, or library
special collection:**
Photographic archive
Video loan library

Trade and statistical information:
Data on the use and abuse of animals in the United
Kingdom and abroad.

Printed publications:
OneKind magazine (twice yearly)

Access to staff:
Contact by letter, by telephone, by fax, by e-mail
and via website. Appointment necessary.
Hours: Mon to Fri, 0900 to 1700

Links with:
St Andrew Animal Fund
10 Queensferry Street, Edinburgh, EH2 4PG; tel:
0131 225 2116; fax: 0131 220 6377

ADVOCATES LIBRARY

Faculty of Advocates, Parliament House,
Edinburgh, EH1 1RF

Tel: 0131 260 5683
Fax: 0131 260 5663
E-mail: inqdesk@advocates.org.uk

Website:
http://www.advocates.org.uk/library/index.html

Enquiries:
Enquiries to: Reader Services Librarian

Founded:
1689

Organisation type and purpose:
Professional body (membership is by
qualification), present number of members: 460.
The Advocates Library is a private library
servicing members of the Scottish bar.
Legal deposit law materials for Scotland.

Subject coverage:
Law, jurisprudence, Roman law and civil law.

**Museum or gallery collection, archive, or library
special collection:**
Materials from other common law and
Commonwealth jurisdictions, Roman, canon and
civil law
Roman-Dutch collection
Session Papers (printed pleadings)

Non-library collection catalogue:
All or part available online

Library catalogue:
All or part available online

Access to staff:
Contact by letter, by telephone, by fax, by e-mail
and via website. Access for members only.
Hours: Mon to Fri, 0900 to 1700

Special comments: Private library, stock made
available to public via NLS

Access to building, collection or gallery:
Prior appointment required

AEA TECHNOLOGY ENVIRONMENT

Culham, Abingdon, Oxfordshire, OX14 3ED

Tel: 0870 190 1900
Fax: 0870 190 6318
E-mail: enquiry@aeat.co.uk

Website:
http://www.aeat-env.com

Enquiries:
Enquiries to: Information Officer

Founded:
April 1994

Formerly called:
National Environmental Technology Centre;
Environmental Safety Centre, Warren Spring
Laboratory (year of change 1994)

Organisation type and purpose:
Environmental consultancy.

Subject coverage:
Air pollution, marine pollution, industrial effluent,
waste management, recycling, cleaner technology,
contaminated land, biotechnology, project hubs,
future energy solutions, environmental and risk
consultancy, chemical emergency response,
environmental policy and climate change.

Publications list:
Available online and in print

Access to staff:
Contact by letter, by telephone, by fax, by e-mail
and via website
Hours: Mon to Fri, 0900 to 1700

Registered office:
AEA Technology plc
329 Harwell, Didcot, Oxfordshire, OX11 0QJ

AERO INDEX LIMITED

39 Waylands Mead, The Knoll, Beckenham, Kent,
BR3 5XT

Tel: 020 8650 3973

Website:
http://www.aeroindex.com

Enquiries:
Enquiries to: Managing Director
Direct e-mail: jr@aeroindex.freeserve.co.uk

Founded:
1993

Organisation type and purpose:
Publishing house.

Subject coverage:
World aerospace industry.

Printed publications:
Aero Index (3 vols, 2002)

Access to staff:
Contact by fax
Hours: Mon to Fri, 0900 to 1700

AEROPLANE COLLECTION LIMITED

Acronym or abbreviation: TAC

7 Mayfield Avenue, Stretford, Manchester, M32
9HL

Tel: 0161 866 8255
E-mail: aeroplanecol@aol.com

Enquiries:
Enquiries to: Chairman
Direct e-mail: mayfieldsparkes@aol.com

Founded:
1962

Formerly called:
Northern Aircraft Preservation Society

Organisation type and purpose:
Registered charity.
Preservation of aviation-related artefacts.

Subject coverage:
Aircraft and aero engine preservation, historical
aviation research.

**Museum or gallery collection, archive, or library
special collection:**
Very detailed collections of books, pictures,
photographs and some drawings, all relating to
aviation

Access to staff:
Contact by letter, by e-mail and in person
Hours: Mon to Fri, day time

AETHELFLAED

1 Auckland Road, London, SW11 1EW

Tel: 020 7924 5868

Enquiries:
Enquiries to: Honorary Treasurer

Founded:
1999

Organisation type and purpose:
Learned society (membership is by subscription),
present number of members: 23, voluntary
organisation, research organisation.
To encourage research and awareness concerning
Aethelflaed, Lady of the Mercians, daughter of
Alfred The Great.

Subject coverage:
Anglo-Saxon England, Aethelflaed, Lady of the
Mercians, Old English, Alfred The Great.

Printed publications:
Newsletter (members only)
Bibliography (members only)

Access to staff:
Contact by letter
Hours: Mon to Fri, 0900 to 1700

AETHERIUS SOCIETY

Formal name: The Aetherius Society

757 Fulham Road, London, SW6 5UU

Tel: 020 7736 4187; 020 7731 1094
Fax: 020 7731 1067
E-mail: info@aetherius.co.uk

Website:
http://www.aetherius.org

Founded:
1955

Organisation type and purpose:
International organisation, membership
association, voluntary organisation, training
organisation, publishing house.
Religious and educational organisation.
Service to humanity.

Subject coverage:
UFOs, cosmic contacts and life on other planets,
aspects of metaphysics, new age thought, use of
prayer, spiritual healing, self-development, psychic
development, yoga, enlightenment and spiritual
ecology.

Education services:
Workshops and lectures.

Printed publications:
Wide range of literature including:
Contact With a Lord of Karma (£9.99)
Operation Space Power (£9.99)
The Nine Freedoms (£14.99)
Visit to the Logos of Earth (£9.99)
The Twelve Blessings (£12.99)
Contacts with the Gods from Space (£9.99)

continued overleaf

Realise Your Inner Potential (£9.99)
Order printed publications from: Postal address

Electronic and video publications:
Unique CD library of lectures by George King,
  DSc, PhD (individual CDs for sale)
DVDs
Order electronic and video publications from: Postal
address

Publications list:
Available online and in print

Access to staff:
Contact by letter, by telephone, by fax, by e-mail,
in person and via website. Appointment necessary.
Hours: Mon to Fri, 0900 to 2100; weekends, variable
hours

Also at:
The Aetherius Society
  Northern UK Branch, 350 Sheffield Road,
  Birdwell, Barnsley, South Yorkshire, S70 5TU; tel:
  01226 744659
The Inner Potential Centre
  36 Kelvedon Road, London, SW6 5BW; tel: 020
  7736 4187; e-mail: info@innerpotential.org

Branches:
2 branches and 10 groups in UK

AFASIC

1st Floor, 20 Bowling Green Lane, London, EC1R
0BD

Tel: 020 7490 9410 (admin); 0845 355 5577 (helpline)
Fax: 020 7251 2834
E-mail: info@afasic.org.uk

Website:
http://www.afasic.org.uk

Enquiries:
Enquiries to: Information Officer
Other contacts: Helpline Manager (for individual
support for parents seeking help)

Founded:
1968

Formerly called:
Association for All Speech Impaired Children

Organisation type and purpose:
Membership association (membership is by
subscription), voluntary organisation, registered
charity (charity number 1045617).
Afasic is the UK charity representing children and
young adults with speech, language and
communication impairments, working for their
inclusion in society and supporting their parents
and carers.

Subject coverage:
Speech and language difficulties. Speech and
language impairments in children and young
people; special educational facilities; speech and
language therapy; advice to parents; training days.

Printed publications:
Newsletter (3 times a year)
Publications include:
Choosing a School
Glossary Sheets: individual sheets explaining
  terms
Principles for Education Provision
The Proposed Statement
Leaflets on a variety of subjects (free)
Check website or request publications list for
  prices

Publications list:
Available online and in print

Access to staff:
Contact by letter, by telephone, by fax, by e-mail
and via website
Hours: Office: Mon to Thu, 0900 to 1700; Fri, 0900
to 1600
Helpline: Mon to Fri, 1030 to 1430

Access to building, collection or gallery:
Prior appointment required

Also at:
Afasic Cymru
  Titan House, Cardiff Bay Business Centre, Lewis
  Road, Cardiff, CF24 5BS; tel: 029 2046 5854; e-
  mail: jeannette@afasiccymru.org.uk
Afasic Scotland
  1 Prospect 3, Gemini Crescent, Dundee
  Technology Park, Dundee, DD2 1TY; tel: 01382
  561891; fax: 01382 568391; e-mail: admin@
  afasicscotland.org.uk

AFFINITY

PO Box 246, Bridgend, CF31 9FD

Tel: 01656 646152
E-mail: admin@affinity.org.uk

Website:
http://affinity.org.uk/

Enquiries:
Enquiries to: Director

Founded:
1952

Organisation type and purpose:
Membership association, registered charity
(charity number 258924).
Council of Churches; consultancy service.

Subject coverage:
Evangelical Christianity, especially the co-
ordination of churches outside the Ecumenical
Movement.

Printed publications:
Table Talk (3 times a year, £3)
Foundations (theological journal, 2 times a year, £4
  per issue)
Affinity (magazine, 3 times a year, free)
Bulletin (3 times a year, online)

Access to staff:
Contact by letter, by telephone and by e-mail.
Appointment necessary.

AFGHAN ACADEMY IN UK

PO Box 1570, London, W7 3ZJ

Tel: 020 8579 8436\ 07952 578473
Fax: 020 8579 8436

Enquiries:
Enquiries to: Director
Other contacts: Co-ordinator for reports and works
of the other committees within Afghan Academy.

Founded:
1991

Formerly called:
Afghan Link Association (year of change 1991);
Afghanistan, Centre for Research and
Development of Thoughts (year of change 1995);
Afghan Academy (year of change 1997)

Organisation type and purpose:
Membership association (membership is by
subscription), voluntary organisation.
Cultural and welfare.
Afghan Academy provides educational, cultural
and welfare services to the Afghan Community. It
promotes art and artistic activities among Afghans
and works to present Afghan art and culture.

Subject coverage:
Afghanistan; Afghan refugees in UK;
Afghanistan's cultural heritage; Afghan societies in
and outside Afghanistan.

**Museum or gallery collection, archive, or library
special collection:**
Publications in Persian/Pushto languages

Printed publications:
Almost all publications are in Persian/Pushto
  languages

Electronic and video publications:
The selection of videos covers the monthly
  seminars which have been held since 1995

Publications list:
Available online and in print

Access to staff:
Contact by letter, by telephone and by fax.
Appointment necessary.
Hours: 24-hour emergency telephone and fax

Access to building, collection or gallery:
Prior appointment required

AFRICA CENTRE

38 King Street, Covent Garden, London, WC2E 8IT

Tel: 020 7836 1973
Fax: 020 7836 1975

Website:
http://www.africacentre.org.uk

Organisation type and purpose:
The Centre seeks to project a positive face of Africa
in London, providing a focal point for all forms of
cultural and social activities related to Africa
through meetings, talks, visual arts exhibitions,
cinema, literature and the performing arts.

Subject coverage:
Contemporary African culture and creativity.

AFRICAN BIRD CLUB

Acronym or abbreviation: ABC

c/o Birdlife International, Wellbrook Court, Girton
Road, Cambridge, CB3 0NA

E-mail: secretary@africanbirdclub.org

Website:
http://www.africanbirdclub.org
Aims of the club, membership details and club
news, selected articles from previously published
bulletins.

Enquiries:
Enquiries to: Secretary
Direct e-mail: chairman@africanbirdclub.org
Other contacts: Chairman

Founded:
1994

Organisation type and purpose:
Membership association (membership is by
subscription), present number of members: 1,200,
registered charity (charity number 1053920).
To promote African ornithology.

Subject coverage:
African ornithology and all activities related to the
study and conservation of African birds.

Printed publications:
Bulletin of the African Bird Club (journal, 2 times a
  year, £9 per issue)

Access to staff:
Contact by letter, by e-mail and via website
Hours: Mon to Fri, 0900 to 1700

AFRICAN STUDIES ASSOCIATION OF THE UNITED KINGDOM

Acronym or abbreviation: ASAUK

SOAS, University of London, Thornhaugh Street,
Russell Square, London, WC1H 0XG

Tel: 020 7898 4390
Fax: 020 7898 4389
E-mail: asa@soas.ac.uk

Enquiries:
Enquiries to: Honorary Secretary

Founded:
1963

Organisation type and purpose:
Learned society.

Subject coverage:
Symposia and conferences on topics of current
importance in Africa.

Printed publications:
African Affairs (quarterly, membership includes subscription)
African Studies Association Newsletter (quarterly with African Affairs)

Access to staff:
Contact by letter, by telephone and by e-mail
Hours: Mon to Fri, 0900 to 1700

Affiliated to:
Royal African Society
at the same address

AFTAID

Formal name: AFTAID – Aid for the Aged in Distress

Epworth House, 25 City Road, London, EC1Y 1AA

Tel: 0870 803 1950
Fax: 0870 803 2128
E-mail: info@aftaid.org.uk

Website:
http://www.aftaid.org.uk
The charity and its work, case histories, how to apply.

Founded:
1982

Created by the merger of:
Aid for the Aged and Aged in Distress

Formerly called:
Aid for the Aged

Organisation type and purpose:
Registered charity (number 299276), voluntary organisation.
Offers direct financial assistance in the form of grants, often in emergency situations and covering a wide range of issues that are not being addressed elsewhere.
Applications are welcomed from the social services, other charities and caring bodies as well as families and the individuals themselves.

Subject coverage:
A relatively small charitable organisation that is near unique. For instance, help with winter heating comes in many forms, but if old radiators burst and an elderly couple can't pay for replacements, they lose their central heating. There are no official channels to explore for direct action to replace a useless radiator, but there is AFTAID.

Access to staff:
Contact by letter, by telephone, by fax, by e-mail and via website

AGCAS

Formal name: Association of Graduate Careers Advisory Services

AGCAS Administration Office, Millennium House, 30 Junction Road, Sheffield, S11 8XB

Tel: 0114 251 5750
Fax: 0114 251 5751

Website:
http://www.agcas.org.uk
Events, news, resources, jobs, people.

Enquiries:
Enquiries to: Chief Executive
Direct e-mail: margaret.dane@agcas.org.uk

Organisation type and purpose:
A registered charity in England and Wales (number 1078508) and Scotland (number SC038805), the professional association for higher education (HE) careers practitioners, using the expertise and resources of its membership for the collective benefit of its members, HE careers services, their clients and customers, and the sector overall. Has influence with government, employers, professional bodies, the academic community and the guidance community.

Subject coverage:
Graduate careers advice.

Information services:
AGCAS e-mail discussion lists provide instant virtual access to over 2,000 careers professionals, based mostly in the UK but also in the Republic of Ireland and world-wide; members use these lists to participate in general or targeted discussions.

Special visitor services:
Professional conferences and events across the UK.

Education services:
Professional training courses are delivered online and through residential courses.

Printed publications:
Phoenix (quarterly journal, free to members)

Electronic and video publications:
ARENA (monthly newsletter, free to members)

Access to staff:
Contact by letter, by telephone, by fax and by e-mail

AGE CONCERN ENGLAND

Acronym or abbreviation: ACE

Astral House, 1268 London Road, London, SW16 4ER

Tel: 020 8765 7200\ Minicom no. 020 8679 2832 (text phone)
Fax: 020 8765 7211
E-mail: ace@ace.org.uk

Website:
http://www.ageconcern.org.uk
Large website giving information about the organisation, news, fact sheets, reading lists, etc.

Enquiries:
Enquiries to: Library Resources Manager

Formerly called:
National Council on Ageing

Organisation type and purpose:
Registered charity (charity number 261794).
Hub of a network of about 1,400 Age Concern organisations that provide services on a local basis.
National charity that aims to promote the well-being of all older people, and involve them in all aspects of society.

Subject coverage:
All aspects of the welfare of older people including: housing, health and social services, income maintenance, welfare rights, heating, transport and consumer affairs.

Museum or gallery collection, archive, or library special collection:
Library of books, journals and a large amount of grey material

Library catalogue:
All or part available in-house

Printed publications:
Book List
Books and videos on a wide range of subjects
Briefings
Factsheets
Monthly Information Bulletin

Publications list:
Available in print

Access to staff:
Contact by letter, by telephone, by fax, by e-mail and via website. Appointment necessary.
Hours: Mon to Fri, 0930 to 1700
Special comments: Reference only.

Access to building, collection or gallery:
Prior appointment required

Access for disabled people:
Ramped entry, toilet facilities

AGE CONCERN LONDON

Acronym or abbreviation: ACL

21 St. George's Road, London, SE1 6ES

Tel: 020 7820 6770
Fax: 020 7820 1063
E-mail: general@aclondon.org.uk

Website:
http://www.ageconcern.org.uk

Enquiries:
Enquiries to: Communication Officer
Direct e-mail: pwoodward@aclondon.org.uk

Founded:
1966

Formerly called:
Greater London Conference on Old People's Welfare

Organisation type and purpose:
Voluntary organisation, registered charity (charity number 249335), research organisation.
Working across the capital to improve the quality of life for older people and to enhance their status and influence.

Subject coverage:
Referral to local Age Concern organisations in the London boroughs. Details available via website or by calling National Age Concern Information Line 0800 009966. Also available in phone book.

Printed publications:
Directories including:
Age Concern in London Directory
Elders' Health: The Voice of Experience (2000, £4)
Hospital Aftercare Schemes in London (£3)
AGE Factsheets (free, also see http://www.ageconcern.org.uk)
Primary Care Briefings (free – SAE)
Poverty and Ethnic Minority Elders (1996, £4)
Reports (various titles, £5 each)
Getting Transport to Health Services in London (leaflet)
Older People and Housing Benefit Administration in London
A helicopter would be nice – transport to health services for older Londoners (£10)
Order printed publications from: Publications Administrator, Age Concern London
e-mail: vduncan@aclondon.org.uk

Publications list:
Available online and in print

Access to staff:
Contact by letter, by telephone, by fax, by e-mail and via website
Hours: Mon to Fri, 0930 to 1700
Telephone answered: Mon to Fri, 1100 to 1200 and 1500 to 1600
Answerphone at all other times
Special comments: Building not accessible.

Links with:
Age Concern organisations in London

AGE CONCERN SCOTLAND

113 Rose Street, Edinburgh, EH2 3DT

Tel: 0131 220 3345
Fax: 0131 220 2779
E-mail: enquiries@acscot.org.uk

Enquiries:
Enquiries to: Information Officer
Direct tel: 0131 625 9331
Direct e-mail: pamela.stewart@acscot.org.uk

Founded:
1943

Formerly called:
Scottish Old People's Welfare Council (year of change 1974)

Organisation type and purpose:
Membership association (membership is by subscription), present number of members: 512, voluntary organisation, training organisation, consultancy, research organisation.
To promote the interests of older people in Scotland.

continued overleaf

Subject coverage:
Housing; residential accommodation; welfare rights; health; income maintenance; day services; needs of older people and those who work with them or care for them; voluntary services; ageing; statutory services; community care; insurance services.

Library catalogue:
All or part available in-house

Printed publications:
Adage (newsletter, 6 times a year)
Leaflets on money, health, housing, care training and community care
Books for personal use, including:
Better Health in Retirement (Roberts Dr A, 2001)
The Retirement Handbook (New Edition)
Using Your Home as Capital 2000–2001
Your Rights 2000–2001, a guide to money benefits for older people
Carers Handbook Series (12 titles)
Books and training packs for professional use
Policy Books

Electronic and video publications:
Home Maintenance Video for Older Householders (Free, 2000)

Publications list:
Available in print

Access to staff:
Contact by letter, by telephone, by fax and by e-mail. Appointment necessary.
Hours: Mon to Fri, 0900 to 1700

Access to building, collection or gallery:
Prior appointment required
Hours: Mon to Fri, 0900 to 1700

Access for disabled people:
Toilet facilities
Special comments: Chairlift entry

AGE ENDEAVOUR FELLOWSHIP

Registered Office, The Old Well House, 130 Holland Park Avenue, London W11 4VE

Enquiries:
Enquiries to: Chairman

Formerly called:
Employment Fellowship

Organisation type and purpose:
Registered charity.

Subject coverage:
Funding of elderly and respite care.

AGE NI

3 Lower Crescent, Belfast, BT7 1NR

Tel: 028 9024 5729
Fax: 028 9023 5497
E-mail: info@ageni.org

Website:
http://www.ageni.org

Enquiries:
Direct e-mail: info@ageni.org

Formerly called:
Age Concern Northern Ireland and Help the Aged NI (year of change 2009)

Organisation type and purpose:
Voluntary organisation.
To enhance and improve the lives of older people, to create a powerful voice for older people.

Subject coverage:
In Northern Ireland, there are more people over the age of 50 than under the age of 19 and, in the next 20 years, the number of people over 50 will increase by more than 30%. This carries significant consequences for the fabric of the community. It affects planning for the way of life: education systems, health and social care, work life, family life. Policy decisions taken today will influence how current teenagers live in the next 30 years and

beyond. It is important that this message is delivered and acted upon now. NI exists to make people think differently about what it means to get older, because age affects everyone in many different ways.

Information services:
Advice and advocacy.

Printed publications:
Annual Report (free)
Annual Policy Report (free)
Work of Age Concern (free)
Your Rights (annually)
Ageing Well (leaflets)

Access to staff:
Contact by letter, by telephone, by fax, by e-mail and via website
Hours: Mon to Fri, 0900 to 1700
Special comments: Advice and advocacy freephone no. 0808 808 7575; lines open Mon to Fri, 0900 to 1600

AGECARE – THE ROYAL SURGICAL AID SOCIETY

Formal name: Royal Surgical Aid Society

47 Great Russell Street, London, WC1B 3PB

Tel: 020 7637 4577
Fax: 020 7323 6878
E-mail: enquiries@agecare.org.uk

Website:
http://www.agecare.org.uk
General information about the Society and its two homes.

Enquiries:
Enquiries to: Chief Executive

Founded:
1862

Formerly called:
RSAS AgeCare

Organisation type and purpose:
Registered charity (charity number 216613).
Service provider and facilitator.

Subject coverage:
Improvement of the care and well-being of older people, who are physically frail or suffering from dementias, through continuous development of good practice in the Society's own homes, seeking pre-eminence in training, supporting research, promoting awards for excellence and contributing to the exchange of knowledge.

Printed publications:
Annual Report
Information on Homes
Newsletter

Access to staff:
Contact by letter, by fax and by e-mail
Hours: Mon to Fri, 0900 to 1700

Homes for the elderly in:
Crowborough, Droitwich, Sevenoaks and Shepperton

AGRICULTURAL ECONOMICS SOCIETY

Acronym or abbreviation: AES

The Mount Lodge, Church Street, Whitchurch, Hampshire, RG28 7AR

Tel: 01256 892705
Fax: 01256 893090
E-mail: secretariat.aes@googlemail.com

Website:
http://www.aes.ac.uk
Information about the Society, its journal, etc.
Membership application information.

Enquiries:
Enquiries to: Administrator

Founded:
1926

Organisation type and purpose:
Learned society (membership is by subscription), present number of members: c. 900.

Subject coverage:
Agricultural economics.

Printed publications:
EuroChoices (3 times a year)
Journal of Agricultural Economics (3 times a year)

Access to staff:
Contact by letter, by telephone, by fax and by e-mail
Hours: Mon to Fri, 0900 to 1700

AGRICULTURAL ENGINEERS ASSOCIATION

Acronym or abbreviation: AEA

Samuelson House, Paxton Road, Orton Centre, Peterborough, Cambridgeshire, PE2 5LT

Tel: 01733 362925
Fax: 01733 370664
E-mail: ab@aea.uk.com

Website:
http://www.aea.uk.com
Membership details, statistics of industry; industry news; directory of members' products for export.
http://www.ope-groundscare.co.uk
Details of Association, news and statistics.
http://www.aea-farm-machinery.co.uk
Details of Association, news and statistics.

Enquiries:
Enquiries to: Director General

Founded:
1875

Organisation type and purpose:
Trade association. To provide a service to agricultural machinery manufacturers and outdoor power turfcare, landscape, forestry and leisure industries.

Subject coverage:
European and national technical legislation and regulations relating to agriculture and outdoor power vehicles, agricultural tractors, machinery and equipment, including construction and use, health and safety, standards, type approval, vehicle licensing and environmental issues, economics, statistics, technical and legal aspects.

Trade and statistical information:
Data on UK and European markets for agricultural machinery and tractors, economics, statistics, overseas export technical; legal; standards; related to industries (agricultural machinery manufacturers and outdoor power turfcare), landscape, forestry and leisure industries and sole importers.

Printed publications:
OPE Directory and Price Guide (twice a year, £45 hard copy, £30 (CD) annual UK subscription, £35 annual EU and £65 annual rest of world)

Access to staff:
Contact by letter, by telephone, by fax, by e-mail and via website. Non-members charged.
Hours: Mon to Fri, 0900 to 1700
Special comments: Directory of members on web page.

Access for disabled people:
Parking provided, toilet facilities

AGRICULTURAL INDUSTRIES CONFEDERATION

Acronym or abbreviation: AIC

Confederation House, East of England Showground, Peterborough, PE2 6XE

Tel: 01733 385230
Fax: 01733 385270

E-mail: enquiries@agindustries.org.uk

Website:
http://www.agindustries.org.uk/
Fertiliser statistics, publications available, press releases, background briefing to fertilisers.

Enquiries:
Direct e-mail: paul.rooke@agindustries.org.uk

Founded:
2003

Created by the merger of:
the Fertiliser Manufacturers Association (1875) and the UK Agricultural Supply Trade Association (1917)

Organisation type and purpose:
Trade association (membership is by election or invitation), present number of members: 34.
To represent its membership to government and to co-operate with other organisations with shared interests. To promote an understanding of the issues relating to plant nutrients.

Subject coverage:
Fertilisers: production, storage, transport, safety, statistics, use and environmental effects.

Trade and statistical information:
Summary of fertiliser use in the UK, including historical data.

Printed publications:
Nutrients for Plants (free)
Understanding Garden Fertilisers (free)
Mineral Fertiliser Manufacture (free)
Crop Production
Good Earth – The Science of Arable Farming (£5)
Fertiliser Review (annual, free)
Guidance leaflets on best fertiliser practice, quality and advice
Health & Safety Handbook

Publications list:
Available in print

Access to staff:
Contact by letter
Hours: Fri, 0900 to 1600

Access to building, collection or gallery:
No prior appointment required

Links with:
European Fertilizer Manufacturers Association
tel: + 322 675 3550; fax: + 322 675 3961; e-mail: main@efma.be
International Fertilizer Industry Association
tel: 00 33 1 539 30500; fax: 00 33 1 539 30547; e-mail: ifa@fertilizer.org

AHMADIYYA MUSLIM ASSOCIATION (UK)

Acronym or abbreviation: AMA (UK)

The London Mosque, 16 Gressenhall Road, London, SW18 5QL

Tel: 020 8875 4321
Fax: 020 8874 4779

Website:
http://www.al-islam.org

Enquiries:
Enquiries to: National Secretary, Publications
Direct tel: 01438 231311; 07974 202225
Direct fax: 01438 231311
Direct e-mail: arshadahmedi@hotmail.com

Founded:
1889

Formerly called:
Jamaat Ahmadiyya, London Mosque

Organisation type and purpose:
International organisation, present number of members: over 200m. worldwide, registered charity (charity number 299081).
Religious Community.

Subject coverage:
Philosophy and teachings of Islam, correct interpretation of the Holy Qur'an and sayings of the Holy Prophet of Islam, facility in many Western and Eastern European languages.

Museum or gallery collection, archive, or library special collection:
Approximately 1,000 books on Islam and related subjects in English, Arabic and Urdu
Past editions of the Muslim Herald
Translation and Exegesis of the Qur'an in various European and Eastern languages

Printed publications:
Selected sayings of the Holy Prophet – in 90 different languages (50p each)
Translations of the Holy Qur'an – in 50 different languages (between £5 and £10, depending on language)
Review of Religions (monthly, in English)
Many other books on Islam available at cost
Order printed publications from: Secretary, Publications, at the same address; e-mail: ishaatuk@aol.com

Publications list:
Available in print

Access to staff:
Contact by letter, by telephone and by fax.
Appointment necessary.
Hours: Mon to Fri, 1030 to 1930; calls may remain unattended during prayers
Special comments: Library and consulting facility available by prior arrangement.

Access to building, collection or gallery:
No prior appointment required

Constituent bodies:
Lajna Imaullah (UK)
at the same address
Majlis Ansarullah (UK)
at the same address; tel: 020 8687 7845
Majlis Khuddamul Ahmadiyya (UK)
at the same address; tel: 020 8687 7904

AHMED IQBAL ULLAH RACE RELATIONS RESOURCE CENTRE

Ground Floor, Devonshire House, Precinct Centre, Oxford Road, Manchester, M13 9PL

Tel: 0161 275 2920
E-mail: rrarchive@manchester.ac.uk

Website:
http://www.racearchive.org.uk

Founded:
1999

Organisation type and purpose:
Resource centre founded to combat racist ideas about black people.

Subject coverage:
Books, periodical articles, cuttings, video and audio tapes and ephemeral material on key themes of history, politics, culture and identity, women, education and employment, housing, immigration, social services, and criminal justice; also an expanding local history section focused on the history of Manchester's African, Asian and Caribbean communities.

Access to building, collection or gallery:
Hours: Mon to Fri, 0930 to 1630
Special comments: Appointment requested for group visits.

AIIC (UNITED KINGDOM AND IRELAND REGION)

Formal name: International Association of Conference Interpreters (Association Internationale des Interprètes de Conférence)
Acronym or abbreviation: AIIC

12 Vicars Road, London, NW5 4NL

Tel: 020 7284 3112

Fax: 020 7284 0240
E-mail: info@aiic-uk-ireland.com

Website:
http://www.aiic.net
Advice for users of interpretation, for would-be interpreters, for interpreters, for venues, etc.

Enquiries:
Enquiries to: Administrator

Formerly called:
AIIC (British Isles Region) (year of change 1999)

Organisation type and purpose:
International organisation, professional body, service industry, consultancy.
Promotes high standards for conference interpreters.

Subject coverage:
Interpreting, especially conference interpreting, including: training, research, qualifications, requirements, practice.

Museum or gallery collection, archive, or library special collection:
Bibliography of publications
Research in the field of interpreting

Access to staff:
Contact by letter, by telephone, by fax, by e-mail and via website. Appointment necessary.
Hours: Mon to Fri, 0900 to 1700

Parent body:
AIIC
10 Avenue de Sécheron, Geneva, CH-1202, Switzerland; tel: +41 22 908 1540; fax: +41 22 732 4151; e-mail: info@aiic.net

AIM25: ARCHIVES IN LONDON AND THE M25 AREA

C/o Director of Archive Services, King's College London, Strand, London, WC2R 2LS

E-mail: aim25@ulcc.ac.uk

Website:
http://www.aim25.ac.uk

Enquiries:
Enquiries to: Project Dir
Direct tel: 020 7848 2187
Direct e-mail: aim25@ulcc.ac.uk

Organisation type and purpose:
To provide electronic access to collection level descriptions of the archives of over ninety higher education institutions and learned societies within the greater London area.

Subject coverage:
Social sciences, military history, teaching, medicine, overseas development, vocational history, history of higher education, biography, literary history.

Non-library collection catalogue:
All or part available online

Access to staff:
Contact by letter, by telephone, by e-mail and via website

AIR DESPATCH ASSOCIATION

E-mail: via website

Website:
http://www.air-despatch.co.uk
Contacts, online shop, roll of honour, reunions, lost touch service, air despatch units, photographs.

Enquiries:
Enquiries to: Hon. Secretary
Direct e-mail: hmebmp@aol.com
Other contacts: Membership Officer

Organisation type and purpose:
Veterans' association, open to service personnel of all ranks who have been on the strength of an Air Despatch unit of the British Army (membership is by subscription).

continued overleaf

Subject coverage:
Air Despatchers served world-wide on training, operations and famine relief duties.

Printed publications:
The Open Door (newsletter, free to members)

Electronic and video publications:
The Open Door (newsletter)
Order electronic and video publications from:
Download from website

Access to staff:
Contact via website

AIR LEAGUE

Broadway House, Tothill Street, London, SW1H 9NS

Tel: 020 7222 8463
E-mail: via website

Website:
http://www.airleague.co.uk
Mission, activities, news, events, scholarships and bursaries.

Founded:
1909

Organisation type and purpose:
Registered charity, membership association (membership is by subscription).
To generate national understanding of the importance to the UK of aviation and aerospace, and to excite the interest of young people in these areas by helping them to become involved.

Subject coverage:
Helping young people by providing careers and support by way of flying and engineering scholarships and bursaries.

Electronic and video publications:
Newsletter
Order electronic and video publications from:
Download from website

Access to staff:
Contact by letter, by telephone and via website

AIR TRANSPORT USERS COUNCIL

Acronym or abbreviation: AUC

CAA House, 45–59 Kingsway, London, WC2B 6TE

Tel: 020 7240 6061
Fax: 020 7240 7071

Website:
http://www.auc.org.uk

Enquiries:
Enquiries to: Chief Executive

Founded:
1973

Formerly called:
Air Transport Users Committee

Organisation type and purpose:
Independent consumer group, supported by an annual grant from the Civil Aviation Authority.
To represent effectively the requirements of all transport users by means of consultation, advocacy or campaigning, as appropriate.

Subject coverage:
All matters concerning and affecting air transport users.

Printed publications:
Annual Report
Flight Plan (booklet, passenger guide to the planning and use of air travel)

Access to staff:
Contact by letter and by telephone
Hours: Mon to Fri, 0900 to 1700

Access to building, collection or gallery:
No access other than to staff

Member of:
Federation of Air Transport User Representatives in Europe (FATURE)

AIRCRAFT RESEARCH ASSOCIATION LIMITED

Acronym or abbreviation: ARA

Manton Lane, Bedford, MK41 7PF

Tel: 01234 350681
Fax: 01234 328584
E-mail: ara@ara.co.uk

Website:
http://www.ara.co.uk
Publicity material.

Enquiries:
Enquiries to: Librarian
Direct e-mail: krentle@ara.co.uk

Founded:
1954

Organisation type and purpose:
Research organisation.
Association of major companies.

Subject coverage:
Aerodynamics, wind tunnel testing, mathematical modelling, analysis and computing code generation, model design and manufacture.

Library catalogue:
All or part available in-house

Access to staff:
Contact by letter, by telephone, by fax and by e-mail
Hours: Mon to Fri, 0800 to 1600

AIRFIELDS OF BRITAIN CONSERVATION TRUST

Acronym or abbreviation: ABCT

PO Box 26319, Glasgow, G76 6AH

Website:
http://www.abct.org.uk
The Trust and its activities.

Founded:
2006

Organisation type and purpose:
Registered charity (charity number 1112829).
A recently established charity, Airfields of Britain Conservation Trust is designed to acknowledge the enormous and unique contribution airfields have made in numerous spheres since 1909. A memorial is intended to be erected at each known disused airfield site in Britain in order to provide a permanent reminder for future generations. Historical information will be made publicly available and facilities provided to allow new factual details to be collated. Education advice and support will also be offered in practical ways to assist young people who display clear enthusiasm about Britain's airfields or aviation in general for potential future careers in these areas.

Subject coverage:
Establishing memorials and mobilising communities to preserve local airfields.

Electronic and video publications:
Airfield e-mail updates
Order electronic and video publications from: Register via website

Access to staff:
Contact by letter and via website

AIRSHIP ASSOCIATION LIMITED

P.O. Box 715, Folkestone, CT20 9ER, United Kingdom

E-mail: treasurer@airship-association.org

Website:
http://www.airship-association.org

Information about the Airship Association, airships and forthcoming events, e.g., conferences, symposia.

Enquiries:
Enquiries to: The Treasurer

Founded:
1972

Organisation type and purpose:
Professional body.
To promote the use of airships for surveillance, load-carrying, advertising and scientific purposes.

Subject coverage:
Design, construction and operation of all types of modern airships; provision of information about airship designers and manufacturers, aeronautical engineers.

Information services:
e-mail: info@airship-association.org

Printed publications:
Airship Journal (quarterly)
Various airship-related information sheets
Books about modern airship technology

Access to staff:
Contact by letter, by e-mail and via website. Non-members charged.
Hours: Mon to Fri, 0900 to 1700

AL-ANON FAMILY GROUPS UK AND EIRE AND ALATEEN

61 Great Dover Street, London, SE1 4YF

Tel: 020 7403 0888
Fax: 020 7378 9910
E-mail: enquiries@al-anonuk.org.uk

Website:
http://www.al-anonuk.org.uk
Publication list, general information about the organisation, some extracts from the literature.

Enquiries:
Enquiries to: Public Information Secretary
Other contacts: General Secretary

Founded:
1951

Organisation type and purpose:
International organisation, membership association (membership is by qualification), voluntary organisation, registered charity.
Al-Anon is active worldwide and offers understanding and support for families and friends of problem drinkers, whether the alcoholic is still drinking or not. Alateen, a part of Al-Anon, is for young people aged 12 to 17 who have been affected by someone else's drinking, usually that of a parent.

Subject coverage:
Alcoholics, alcoholism, and its effects on family and friends.

Information services:
Confidential helpline

Printed publications:
Prices do change and literature is subject to availability:
Al-Anon Community Resource Book
Al-Anon's Twelve Steps & Twelve Traditions (£7.60)
Alateen – Hope for Children of Alcoholics
Al-Anon Family Groups – Classic Edition (£10.70)
ALATEEN: A Day at a Time (£6.85)
Courage to Change (£12)
From Survival to Recovery: Growing Up in an Alcoholic Home (£12.70)
One Day at a Time in Al-Anon (£6.60, or in large print £10.65)
A wide range of Al-Anon leaflets, pamphlets and posters, including some in Asian languages
A wide range of leaflets and pamphlets from Alateen

Publications list:
Available online and in print

Access to staff:
Contact by letter, by telephone, by fax, by e-mail and via website
Hours: Mon to Fri, 1000 to 1600
Confidential Helpline 020 7403 0888: daily, 1000 to 2200

Constituent bodies:
Almost 1000 self-help groups meet in UK and Eire, and 30,000 worldwide

ALBANY TRUST

239a Balham High Road, London, SW17 7BE

Tel: 020 8767 1827
E-mail: info@albanytrust.org

Website:
http://www.albanytrust.org.uk/

Enquiries:
Enquiries to: Administrator

Founded:
1958

Organisation type and purpose:
Learned society, registered charity (charity number 233564).
Counselling and psychotherapy service.

Subject coverage:
Relationships, personal and sexual counselling.

Access to staff:
Contact by telephone
Hours: Mon to Fri, 0900 to 1700

Incorporates the:
Sexual Law Reform Society

ALBINISM FELLOWSHIP

PO Box 77, Burnley, Lancashire, BB11 5GN

Tel: 01282 771900
E-mail: info@albinism.org.uk

Website:
http://www.albinism.org.uk

Founded:
1979

Formerly called:
Albino Fellowship (year of change 1990)

Organisation type and purpose:
National organisation for UK & Ireland.
Membership association (membership is by subscription), present number of members: 450, voluntary organisation, registered charity (charity number SCO 09443).
Aims to provide information, advice and support to people with albinism, their families and the professionals working with them.

Subject coverage:
Albinism.

Printed publications:
Introductory leaflet (free)
Six-monthly newsletters (members only)
Albinism Lives: Personal and Photographic
  Perspectives on Albinism
Order printed publications from: Via website or fellowship address

Publications list:
Available online

Access to staff:
Contact by letter, by telephone, by e-mail and via website
Hours: Answerphone

ALBION VEHICLE PRESERVATION TRUST

Acronym or abbreviation: AVPT

18 Netherdale Drive, Paisley, Renfrewshire, PA1 3DA

E-mail: albionregister@yahoo.co.uk

Website:
http://www.albion-trust.org.uk

Organisation type and purpose:
Preservation trust (Scottish charity no. SC028791) maintaining a 1950 Albion Valiant heavy coach and a 1967 Viking coach. Keeps a register of more than 1,000 surviving Albion vehicles worldwide.

Subject coverage:
Albion vehicles.

Links with:
Biggar Albion Foundation
  The Albion Club, 9 Edinburgh Road, Biggar, Lanarkshire, ML12 6AX

ALCOHOL CONCERN

64 Leman Street, London, E1 8EU

Tel: 020 7264 0510
Fax: 020 7488 9213
E-mail: contact@alcoholconcern.org.uk

Website:
http://www.alcoholconcern.org.uk
Work of organisation, press releases, factsheets.
http://ourworld.compuserve.com/homepages/
dolomite_publishing
Directory of Alcohol Services.

Enquiries:
Enquiries to: Information Team
Direct e-mail: info@alcoholconcern.org.uk

Founded:
1984

Organisation type and purpose:
Membership association (membership is by subscription), present number of members: 1,000, voluntary organisation, registered charity (charity number 291705).
To raise public awareness of the problems of alcohol abuse; to improve services for problem drinkers and to promote preventive action.
National agency on alcohol misuse. Works to reduce the incidence and costs of alcohol-related harm and to increase the range and quality of services available to people with alcohol-related problems. Provides information and encourages debate on the wide range of public policy issues affected by alcohol, including public health, housing, children and families, crime and licensing. Supports specialist and non-specialist service providers helping to tackle alcohol problems at a local level, whilst also working to influence national alcohol policy.

Subject coverage:
Alcohol use and misuse, treatment, health and social effects, policies.

Information services:
Factsheets, directory of alcohol services, leaflets and extensive library database of journal articles, books, research papers, booklets and leaflets.

Special visitor services:
Office not open to the public.

Printed publications:
Alcohol Concern Straight Talk Magazine
  (quarterly)
Alcohol Education Booklets
Alcohol Services Directory 2007 (price £25 incl. p&p, from http://www.ris.org.uk)
A number of book titles on alcohol-related topics
Leaflets
Order printed publications from: The online bookshop

Publications list:
Available online and in print

Access to staff:
Contact by letter, by telephone, by fax, by e-mail and via website. Appointment necessary.

Access to building, collection or gallery:
Office is not open to the public
Hours: Mon to Fri, 0930 to 1630

ALCOHOL FOCUS SCOTLAND

Acronym or abbreviation: AFS

2nd Floor, 166 Buchanan Street, Glasgow, G1 2LW

Tel: 0141 572 6700
Fax: 0141 333 1606
E-mail: enquiries@alcohol-focus-scotland.org.uk

Website:
http://www.alcohol-focus-scotland.org.uk

Enquiries:
Enquiries to: Chief Executive

Founded:
1973

Formerly called:
Scottish Council on Alcohol (SCA); Scottish Council on Alcoholism (year of change 1985)

Organisation type and purpose:
Voluntary organisation, registered charity (charity number SCO 09538), training organisation.

Subject coverage:
All issues relating to alcohol misuse and abuse, counselling and training.

Museum or gallery collection, archive, or library special collection:
Information service
Collection includes: journals, conference reports and proceedings, educational materials and videos

Printed publications:
Annual Report
UK Alcohol Statistics Book (every two years)
Young People and Alcohol in Scotland (report)
Many publications on alcohol and alcohol related problems.

Publications list:
Available online and in print

Access to staff:
Contact by letter, by telephone, by fax, by e-mail and via website. Appointment necessary.
Hours: Mon to Fri, 0900 to 1700

Local councils:
Alcohol & Drugs Support – South West
  The Sun Project, Unit 4, Kelloholm Business Estate, Greystone Avenue, Sanquhar, DG4 6RB; tel: 01659 67137; fax: 01659 67484; e-mail: mail@sunproject.ssbusiness.co.uk
Alcohol & Drugs Support – South West Scotland
  82 King Street, Castle Douglas, DG7 1AT; tel: 01556 503550; fax: 01556 503550; e-mail: alcohol.info@virgin.net
Alcohol Advisory and Counselling Service
  62 Dee Street, Aberdeen, AB11 6DS; tel: 01224 573887; fax: 01224 213479; e-mail: info@aacs.co.uk
Alcohol Counselling – Inverness
  34A Tomnahurich Street, Inverness, IV3 5DS; tel: 01463 220995; fax: 01463 729292
Alcohol Counselling Service – Ross/Sutherland
  4 Ardross Road, Alness, Ross-Shire, IV17 0PU; tel: 01349 880771; fax: 01349 880771; e-mail: alness@acsras.org
Alcohol Counselling Service Ross/Sutherland
  Estate Office, 1 Duke Street, Golspie, Sutherland, KW10 6RF; tel: 01408 634200; fax: 01408 634200; e-mail: golspie@acsras.org
Ayrshire Council on Alcohol
  3rd Floor, 64 Fort Street, Ayr, KA7 3EH; tel: 01292 281238; fax: 01292 290355
Ayrshire Council on Alcohol
  2 Bridge Lane, Kilmarnock, KA1 1QH; tel: 01563 541155; fax: 01563 573232
Borders Council on Alcohol
  42 High Street, Galashiels, TD1 1RZ; tel: 01896 757657; fax: 01896 757657
Bute Council on Alcohol & Drugs
  26 Bishop Street, Rothesay, PA20 9DG; tel: 01700 505855
Caithness Council on Alcohol
  Rhind House Annexe, West Banks Avenue, Wick, KW1 5LU; tel: 01955 603462; fax: 01955 603462

continued overleaf

Counselling & Support Service for Alcohol &
Drugs
   13 Pitt Terrace, Stirling, FK8 2EZ; tel: 01786
450721; fax: 01786 449671; e-mail: info@
counsellingservices.ssnet.co.uk
Cowal Council on Alcohol
   Ballochyle House, Kirk Street, Dunoon, PA23
7DP; tel: 01369 704406
Cumbernauld & Lancashire Counselling Services
   2nd Floor, Carron House, Town Centre,
Cumbernauld, G67 1ER; tel: 01236 738689; fax:
01236 780538; e-mail: info@ckas.fsnet.co.uk
Dumbarton Area Council on Alcohol
   West Bridgend Lodge, West Bridgend,
Dumbarton, G82 4AD; tel: 01389 731456; fax:
01389 734690; e-mail: email@daca0.fsnet.co.uk
Dumbarton Area Council on Alcohol
   82 Dumbarton Road, Clydebank, G81 1UG; tel:
0141 952 0881; fax: 0141 952 0124; e-mail: email@
daca0fsnet.co.uk
Edinburgh & Lothian Council on Alcohol
   40 Shandwick Place, Edinburgh, EH2 4RT; tel:
0131 225 8888; fax: 0131 220 4090; e-mail:
alcoholcounselling@elca.fsbusiness.co.uk
Fife Alcohol Advisory Service
   17 Tolbooth Street, Kirkcaldy, KY1 1RW; tel:
01592 206200; fax: 01592 206201; e-mail: faas@
fass.org.uk
Glasgow Council on Alcohol
   1st Floor, Bristol & West House, 82 Union Street,
Glasgow, G1 3QS; tel: 0141 226 3883; helpline
4774; fax: 0141 226 3014; e-mail: info.gca@virgin
.net
Inverclyde Counselling Service
   2A Newton Street, Greenock, PA16 8UJ; tel:
01475 786695
Islay Council on Alcohol
   The Claddich Centre, Shore Street, Bowmore, Isle
of Islay, PA43 7JB; tel: 01496 810226
Kintyre Alcohol & Drugs Advisory Service
   Castlehill, Campbeltown, PA28 2AN; tel: 01586
553555; fax: 01586 553555
Lochaber Council on Alcohol
   Caol Shopping Centre, Caol, Fort William,
Inverness-shire, PH33 7DR; tel: 01397 702340;
fax: 01397 702304; e-mail: lca@lochaber84
.freeserve.co.uk
Mid Argyll Council on Alcohol
   PO Box 9559, Lochgilphead, Argyll, PA30 8YE;
tel: 01546 602880; fax: 01546 602880
Monklands Council on Addictions
   81C Hallcraig Street, Airdrie, ML6 6AN; tel:
01236 753263; fax: 01236 767937
Moray Council on Addictions
   252 High Street, Elgin, IV30 1BE; tel: 01343
552211; fax: 01343 547000; e-mail: mca@moray
.gov.uk
Oban Council on Alcohol
   Market Street Centre, Market Street, Oban, PA34
4HR; tel: 01631 566090
Orkney Council on Alcohol
   43 Junction Road, Kirkwall, Orkney, KW15 1AF;
tel: 01856 874738; fax: 01856 873937; e-mail:
oacas@btclick.com
Renfrew Council on Alcohol
   Mirren House, Back Sneddon Street, Paisley, PA3
2AF; tel: 0141 887 0880; fax: 0141 887 8063; e-
mail: rcapaisley@compuserve.com
Ross-shire Council on Alcohol
   66 High Street, Invergordon, IV18 0DH; tel:
01349 852438
Shetland Alcohol Trust, Alcohol Advice Centre
   44 Commercial Street, Lerwick, Shetland, ZE1
0AB; tel: 01595 695363; fax: 01595 692801; e-mail:
aac@care4free.net
Skye & Lochalsh Council on Alcohol
   Highland Council Offices, Dunvegan Road,
Portree, Isle of Skye, IV51 9HD; tel: 01478 612633
Tayside Council on Alcohol
   13 King Street, Dundee, DD1 2JD; tel: 01382
223965; fax: 01382 227142; e-mail: enquiries@tca
.sol.co.uk

ALCOHOLICS ANONYMOUS

Acronym or abbreviation: AA

PO Box 1, 10 Toft Green, York, YO1 7NJ

Tel: 01904 644026
Fax: 01904 629091

Website:
http://www.alcoholics-anonymous.org.uk
General information.

Enquiries:
Enquiries to: General Secretary

Founded:
1935

Organisation type and purpose:
International organisation, voluntary organisation,
registered charity (charity number 226745).

Subject coverage:
Alcoholism, recovery from alcoholism.

Printed publications:
40 plus leaflets on all aspects of AA's work and
   organisation including:
A Newcomer Asks (50p)
Is there an Alcoholic in your life? (50p)
This is AA (80p)
Books include:
Alcoholics Anonymous (£8)
Twelve Steps and Twelve Traditions (£6)

Electronic and video publications:
Message to Young People (video, £10)
One Day at a Time (video, £10)

Publications list:
Available in print

Access to staff:
Contact by letter, by telephone and by fax
Hours: Mon to Thu, 0900 to 1700; Fri, 0900 to 1630

Also at:
Northern Service Office (Scotland)
   tel: 0141 226 2214
Southern Service Office (London)
   tel: 020 7833 0022

ALEXANDER STUDIO

Danceworks, 16 Balderton Street, London, W1K
6TN

Tel: 020 7629 1808

Enquiries:
Enquiries to: Managers

Organisation type and purpose:
Professional body.

Subject coverage:
Stress management, psychophysical health, poise
and grace for performing artists, relief from
muscular aches and pains.

Electronic and video publications:
From Stress to Freedom (1990, video, from STAT
   Books)

All teachers are members of the:
Society of Teachers of the Alexander Technique
(STAT)

ALFA LAVAL LIMITED

Acronym or abbreviation: A-L; Alfa

7 Doman Road, Camberley, Surrey, GU15 3DN

Tel: 01276 63383
Fax: 01276 685035

Website:
http://www.alfalaval.com

Enquiries:
Enquiries to: Public Relations Manager
Direct tel: 01276 413632
Direct fax: 01276 413524
Direct e-mail: peter.rose@alfalaval.com

Founded:
1923

Formerly called:
Alfa-Laval Flow Ltd, Alfa-Laval Separation Ltd,
Alfa-Laval Sharples Ltd, Alfa-Laval Thermal Ltd

Organisation type and purpose:
Manufacturing industry.

Subject coverage:
Heat transfer technology, sanitary pumps, valves
and fittings.

Access to staff:
Contact by letter, by telephone, by fax, by e-mail
and via website
Hours: Mon to Fri, 0900 to 1700

Access for disabled people:
Level entry, toilet facilities

Other addresses:
Alfa Laval Limited
   8H May Brook Road, Sutton Coldfield, West
   Midlands, B76 1AL; tel: 0121 351 3131; fax: 0121
   351 7888
Alfa Laval Limited
   Office 5 – 9th Floor, Salveson Tower, Blaikies
   Quay, Aberdeen, AB11 5PW; tel: 01224 424300;
   fax: 01224 424315

ALFA ROMEO 1900 REGISTER

Mariners, 14 Lower Station Road, Billingshurst,
West Sussex, RH14 9SX

E-mail: ar.01177@yahoo.co.uk

Website:
http://www.ar1900reg.org

Enquiries:
Enquiries to: Factotum

Founded:
1977

Organisation type and purpose:
International organisation, membership
association (membership is by qualification),
present number of members: 500.
Register – The register lists cars rather than
owners, i.e. cars with owners, not owners with
cars.
To record all Alfa Romeo 6C2300, 6C2500 and 1900
still extant and to provide information on these
models.

Subject coverage:
The Register of Alfa Romeo 6C2300, 6C2500 and
1900 also tries to assist on other uncommon post-
war Alfa Romeos, including brochure information.

Printed publications:
Photocopies of handbooks, manuals, parts books
   and brochures

Access to staff:
Contact by letter and by telephone

Also at:
North American Register
   302 Brown Thrush Road, Savannah, Georgia,
   31419, USA

ALFA ROMEO GIULIA 105 REGISTER

144 Sussex Way, Enfield, Cockfosters, Barnet,
Hertfordshire, EN4 0BG

Tel: 020 8351 8565

Enquiries:
Enquiries to: Secretary

Organisation type and purpose:
Membership association.

Subject coverage:
Alfa Romeo Giulia 105 cars.

Access to staff:
Contact by letter, by telephone and by fax.
Appointment necessary.
Hours: Mon to Fri, 0900 to 1700

Parent body:
Alfa Romeo Owners Club

ALL ENGLAND LAWN TENNIS & CROQUET CLUB

Church Road, Wimbledon, London, SW19 5AE

Tel: 020 8944 1066
Fax: 020 8947 3354

Website:
http://www.wimbledon.org

Enquiries:
Enquiries to: Club Secretary
Direct tel: 020 8971 2252
Other contacts: Curator for Wimbledon Lawn Tennis Museum.

Founded:
1868

Organisation type and purpose:
Membership association (membership is by election or invitation), present number of members: 375 plus honorary members. Private tennis club.

Subject coverage:
Lawn tennis and croquet.

Access to staff:
Contact by letter, by telephone and by fax. Appointment necessary.
Hours: Mon to Fri, 0900 to 1700

ALL ENGLAND NETBALL ASSOCIATION LIMITED

Acronym or abbreviation: AENA Ltd

Netball House, 9 Paynes Park, Hitchin, Hertfordshire, SG5 1EH

Tel: 01462 442344
Fax: 01462 442343
E-mail: info@aena.co.uk

Website:
http://www.england-netball.co.uk
Chat pages, structure of AENA, where to play, calendar of events.
Departmental sections: development, umpiring, coaching, England squads.

Enquiries:
Enquiries to: Communications Officer
Direct e-mail: siobhana@aena.co.uk

Founded:
1926

Merged with:
English Schools Netball Association (year of change 1994)

Organisation type and purpose:
National organisation, membership association (membership is by subscription, election or invitation), present number of members: 55,000 individual members.
Governing body of netball in England.

Subject coverage:
International, national, regional, county and club netball; development, performance, disability, coaching, umpiring, awards.

Museum or gallery collection, archive, or library special collection:
Archives and photographs

Printed publications:
Coaching Manual
First Step Netball
High Five
Know the Game
Netball Magazine (quarterly)
Official Netball Rules
Planning a Tournament
Netball Skills
With Netball in Mind
Order printed publications from: The Sports Motive
fax: 01926 888832

Electronic and video publications:
Umpiring and coaching videos (see merchandise catalogue)

Publications list:
Available in print

Access to staff:
Contact by letter, by e-mail and via website
Hours: Mon to Fri, 0900 to 1700

Member of:
International Federation of Netball Associations
tel: 0121 446 4451; fax: 0121 446 5857; e-mail: ifna@btinternet.com

ALL NATIONS CHRISTIAN COLLEGE

Acronym or abbreviation: ANCC

Easneye, Ware, Hertfordshire, SG12 8LX

Tel: 01920 461243
Fax: 01920 462997
E-mail: library@allnations.ac.uk

Website:
http://www.allnations.ac.uk
Information about college facilities, courses and faculty members.

Enquiries:
Enquiries to: Librarian
Direct tel: 01920 443504
Direct e-mail: k.wiseman@allnations.ac.uk

Founded:
1971

Created by the merger of:
All Nations Missionary College, Mount Hermon Missionary Training College, Ridgelands Bible College (year of change 1971)

Formerly called:
All Nations Bible College (year of change 1962)

Organisation type and purpose:
Training institution for Christian mission.

Subject coverage:
Christianity, theology, missiology, anthropology, world religions, intercultural studies.

Information services:
Library and information services.

Special visitor services:
Open to external members – please contact the Librarian for information.

Education services:
Library and information facilities for All Nations Christian College students and staff.

Museum or gallery collection, archive, or library special collection:
Archives of constituent colleges

Non-library collection catalogue:
All or part available in print

Library catalogue:
All or part available online and in-house

Access to staff:
Contact by letter, by telephone, by fax, by e-mail, in person and via website. Appointment necessary. Letter of introduction required. Non-members charged.
Hours: Mon to Fri, 0930 to 1700
Special comments: External library membership restricted to church leaders, mission leaders, and theological students.

Access for disabled people:
Ramped entry, access to all public areas, toilet facilities

ALL WHEEL DRIVE CLUB

Acronym or abbreviation: AWDC

Registered Office: c/o Vallance Lodge & Co, Units 082–086, 555 White Hart Lane, London, N17 7RN

E-mail: secretary@awdc.co.uk

Website:
http://www.awdc.co.uk

General club information. Club magazine information. Rights of Way information.

Enquiries:
Enquiries to: Membership Administrator
Direct tel: 01825 731875

Founded:
1968

Organisation type and purpose:
National organisation, membership association (membership is by subscription), present number of members: 2600, voluntary organisation. Organisation of off-road motorsport events and other activities for 4x4 vehicles.

Subject coverage:
Off-road motor sport, its environmental impact, guidance for landowners, unsurfaced vehicular rights of way, their existence and usage. Recreational use of cross-country motorised vehicles.

Access to staff:
Contact by letter and by e-mail
Hours: Mon to Fri, 0900 to 1700

Affiliated to:
Motor Sports Association

Has:
branches throughout the country

ALLARD OWNERS CLUB

1 Brooklyn Court, Woking, Surrey, GU22 7TQ

Tel: 01483 773428
Fax: 01483 773428

Enquiries:
Enquiries to: Secretary

Founded:
1951

Organisation type and purpose:
Membership association.

Subject coverage:
Allard cars.

Printed publications:
Newsletter (monthly, members only)

Access to staff:
Contact by letter
Hours: Mon to Fri, 0900 to 1700

Access to building, collection or gallery:
No access other than to staff

ALLEGRO CLUB INTERNATIONAL

23 Birchview Close, Yateley, Hampshire, GU46 6DL

Website:
http://www.allegroclubint.org.uk
Membership application and club news.

Enquiries:
Enquiries to: Membership Secretary
Direct e-mail: ian.sc@dial.pipex.com

Founded:
1990

Organisation type and purpose:
Membership association.
Car owners club.

Subject coverage:
Providing parts for Allegro cars, helping those who wish to buy or sell such cars, organising gatherings, pooling information for owners, gathering history of Allegro cars. The club has an archive of Allegro-related material.

Printed publications:
Quartic (magazine, several times a year, members)
List of Allegro parts for sale (members)
Used Allegro listings for sale (members)

Access to staff:
Contact by letter. Access for members only.

continued overleaf

Hours: Mon to Fri, 0900 to 1700

Access to building, collection or gallery:
No access other than to staff

ALLERGY UK

Planwell House, LEFA Business Park, Edgington
Way, Sidcup, DA14 5BH

Tel: 01322 619898
Fax: 01322470330
E-mail: info@allergyuk.org

Website:
http://www.allergyuk.org
http://www.allergyfoundation.com

Enquiries:
Enquiries to: Membership Enquiries
Direct e-mail: raegan@allergyuk.org
Other contacts: Chairman

Founded:
1991

Formerly called:
British Allergy Foundation (BAF) (year of change
2001)

Organisation type and purpose:
A national medical charity providing information
and support to people with allergies, intolerances
and sensitivites (charity number 1003726).
To raise awareness of allergy, provide information
for sufferers and raise funds for research.

Subject coverage:
All allergy-related disorders, including: respiratory
(nose and lungs), dermatological, eye disorders,
food-related problems, venom allergy, drug
allergy, occupational allergic diseases.

**Museum or gallery collection, archive, or library
special collection:**
Data on prevalence of allergic disorders

Printed publications:
We Can Help You leaflets and over 80 factsheets on
how to manage your condition

Publications list:
Available in print

Access to staff:
Contact by letter, by telephone, by fax, by e-mail,
in person and via website. Appointment necessary.
Hours: Mon to Fri, 0900 to 1700
Special comments: Helpline: Mon to Fri.

Affiliated to:
British Society for Allergy and Clinical
Immunology
 tel: 020 8398 9240; fax: 020 8398 2766; e-mail: s
 .duff@co.puserve.com

Has:
Local support groups at various UK locations
(contact via main office)

Member of:
European Federation of Asthma & Allergy
Associations (EFA)

ALLIANCE OF LITERARY SOCIETIES

Acronym or abbreviation: ALS

59 Bryony Road, Selly Oak, Birmingham, B29 4BY

Tel: 0121 475 1805
E-mail: l.j.curry@bham.ac.uk

Website:
http://www.allianceofliterarysocieties.org.uk
Information about member societies with details of
contacts and future events.

Enquiries:
Enquiries to: Membership Secretary
Direct e-mail: johnshorland@aol.com

Founded:
1973

Organisation type and purpose:
Membership association (membership is by
subscription), present number of members: 115,
suitable for ages: 10+.
Uniting literary societies. Provides mutual help
and advice on the running of societies, funding,
etc., and encourages working together to save
threatened places of literary significance.

Subject coverage:
Addresses of member societies; literary enquiries;
literary society, etc.

Printed publications:
ALSo... annual journal (£7 for non-members, £4 for
 members, both inc. p&p)
Newsletter (2 times a year, free to member
 societies)

Access to staff:
Contact by letter, by e-mail and via website

ALPINE CLUB LIBRARY

55 Charlotte Road, London, EC2A 3QF

Tel: 020 7613 0745
Fax: 020 7613 0755
E-mail: library@alpine-club.org.uk

Website:
http://www.alpine-club.org.uk
Description of Alpine Club, calendar of events and
expedition reports, Himalayan Index, a database of
references to the literature of attempts and ascents
of peaks over 6000m in the Himalayas and
adjacent areas.

Enquiries:
Enquiries to: Librarian
Other contacts: Archivist; Photo Librarian

Founded:
1857

Organisation type and purpose:
Membership association (membership is by
subscription), registered charity (charity number
313051).
Mountaineering club.
Caters specifically for those who climb in the Alps
and the Greater Ranges of the world.

Subject coverage:
Historical and current information on
mountaineering and mountain ranges worldwide
including Himalayan database, ski
mountaineering, walking, high altitude medicine
and climbing equipment.

**Museum or gallery collection, archive, or library
special collection:**
Alpine Club Records
The library has one of the most comprehensive
 collections of mountaineering literature in the
 world including journals, early books,
 photographs, manuscripts, newspaper cuttings
 from 1891, diaries and correspondence, guide
 books and reports
Expedition Reports
Records of the former Ladies' Alpine Club

Non-library collection catalogue:
All or part available in print

Library catalogue:
All or part available in-house

Printed publications:
The Alpine Club (corporate author) Alpine Club
 Library Catalogue: Books and Periodicals
 (Volume one, London, Heinemann, 1982)
Alpine Journal: annual record of mountain
 exploration and achievement (free to members)
Guide Books: cover most popular regions of the
 Alps (detailed English language guide books of
 the region)
Newsletter
Year Books of the Ladies' Alpine Club 1910–1975
 (Merz J, index Alpine Club Library, 2000)

Access to staff:
Contact by letter, by telephone, by fax and by e-
mail. Appointment necessary. Non-members
charged.

Hours: Tue, Wed, 1000 to 1700

Access for disabled people:
Special comments: Library on first floor, no lift.

Affiliated to:
British Mountaineering Council
 177–179 Burton Road, Manchester, M20 2BB; tel:
 0870 010 4878; fax: 0161 445 4500; e-mail: info@
 thebmc.co.uk

Parent body:
Alpine Club
 at the same address

ALPINE GARDEN SOCIETY

Acronym or abbreviation: AGS

AGS Centre, Avon Bank, Pershore, Worcestershire,
WR10 3JP

Tel: 01386 554790
Fax: 01386 554801
E-mail: ags@alpinegardensociety.org

Website:
http://www.alpinegardensociety.org
Information on the Society, news, updated
information, show reports, extracts from
publications. Forthcoming events, expeditions, etc.
Members' seed exchange.

Enquiries:
Enquiries to: Director and Secretary to the Society

Founded:
1929

Organisation type and purpose:
International organisation, membership
association (membership is by subscription),
present number of members: 13,850, voluntary
organisation, registered charity (charity number
207478), suitable for ages: all.
Specialist horticultural plant society.
To disseminate knowledge of alpine and rock
garden plants – alpines is a generic term to
encompass small hardy plants, including
perennials, bulbs, ferns, dwarf conifers, etc.

Subject coverage:
Horticultural, with specialist knowledge of the
cultivation of alpines and rock plants, small hardy
plants, including perennials, bulbs, ferns, dwarf
conifers etc. Locations: where to travel in the world
to find alpine specimens. Conservation: the Society
encourages conservation and discourages
indiscriminate collecting.

**Museum or gallery collection, archive, or library
special collection:**
Specialist Library – reference books
Slide Library – hire/loan service

Non-library collection catalogue:
All or part available in-house

Library catalogue:
All or part available in-house

Printed publications:
Bulletin (quarterly)
Encyclopaedia of Alpines
Leaflets
Newsletter (quarterly)
Seed list
Booklist contains over 100 titles covering:
Bulbous plants
Specific Genera
Floras and Guides to Continents and Countries

Electronic and video publications:
The Plant Finder Reference Library 1999/2000 (CD-
ROM)

Publications list:
Available online and in print

Access to staff:
Contact by letter, by telephone, by fax, by e-mail,
in person and via website. Appointment necessary.
Hours: Mon to Thu, 0900 to 1730; Fri, 0900 to 1700

Access for disabled people:
Parking provided, ramped entry, toilet facilities

Has:
60 local groups

Seed Distribution Limited:
Alpine Garden Society
11 Boston Close, Culcheth, Warrington, WA3 4LW

ALUMINIUM FEDERATION

Formal name: Aluminium Federation Limited
Acronym or abbreviation: ALFED

National Metalforming Centre, 47 Birmingham Road, West Bromwich, West Midlands, B70 6PY

Tel: 0121 601 6363
Fax: 0870 183 9714
E-mail: alfed@alfed.org.uk

Website:
http://www.alfed.org.uk

Enquiries:
Enquiries to: Librarian
Direct tel: 0121 601 6746
Other contacts: Technical Executive

Founded:
1963

Formerly called:
Aluminium Development Association

Organisation type and purpose:
Trade association (membership is by subscription), present number of members: 200. Information centre.

Subject coverage:
Technical and commercial information on aluminium and its alloys, extrusion, coating, anodising, rolling.

Museum or gallery collection, archive, or library special collection:
Library with largest collection in the world on aluminium; full range of traditional library services

Non-library collection catalogue:
All or part available online

Library catalogue:
All or part available in-house

Printed publications:
Handbooks and videos
The Properties of Aluminium and its Alloys (10th edn, £35 (UK) incl. p&p)
UK Aluminium Industry Fact Sheets
Technical and promotional brochures on rolled products, extrusions, anodising and finishing and safety

Publications list:
Available online and in print

Access to staff:
Contact by letter, by telephone, by fax, by e-mail and via website
Hours: Mon to Fri, 0900 to 1700
Special comments: Members and bona fide students only.

Member organisations:
Aluminium Alloys Recycling and Melting Association (AARMA)
at the same address
Aluminium Extruders Association (AEA)
at the same address
Aluminium Finishing Association (AFA)
at the same address
Aluminium Primary Producers Association (APPA)
at the same address
Aluminium Rolled Products Manufacturers Association (ARPMA)
at the same address
Aluminium Stockholders Association (ASA)
at the same address; tel: 0121 601 6716; fax: 0121 601 6375
Diecasting Society (DCS)
at the same address
European Aluminium Particulate Association
at the same address

ALUMINIUM PACKAGING RECYCLING ORGANISATION

Acronym or abbreviation: ALUPRO

1 Brockhill Court, Brockhill Lane, Redditch, Worcestershire, B97 6RB

Tel: 01527 597757
Fax: 01527 594140
E-mail: info@alupro.org.uk

Website:
http://www.alupro.org.uk
All information on aluminium can and aluminium foil recycling in the United Kingdom.

Enquiries:
Enquiries to: Communications Director

Founded:
1994

Formerly called:
Aluminium Can Recycling Association (ACRA), Aluminium Foil Recycling Campaign (AFRC) (year of change 1999)

Organisation type and purpose:
Membership association.
Promotes collection of aluminium packaging through all routes: local authority collection and kerbside systems, 'cash for cans' recycling centres.

Subject coverage:
Viable collection opportunities for aluminium, recycling technology, foil in energy from waste plants. Packaging waste legislation.

Printed publications:
Information pack (free)
Education pack (free)

Access to staff:
Contact by letter, by telephone, by fax, by e-mail and via website
Hours: Mon to Fri, 0900 to 1700

ALVIS OWNER CLUB

4 Field Lane, Normanby-By-Spital, Market Rasen, Lincolnshire, LN8 2HB

Tel: 01673 878148
E-mail: gensec@alvisoc.org

Website:
http://www.alvisoc.org

Enquiries:
Enquiries to: General Secretary

Founded:
1951

Organisation type and purpose:
Membership association (membership is by subscription).

Subject coverage:
Technical information, historic information, help and advice on matters concerning the use and restoration of Alvis vehicles.

Printed publications:
Bulletin (monthly)

Access to staff:
Contact by e-mail and via website. Appointment necessary.
Hours: Mon to Fri, 0900 to 1700

ALVIS REGISTER

The Vinery, Wanborough Hill, Wanborough, Guildford, Surrey, GU3 2JR

Tel: 01483 810308
Fax: 01483 810308
E-mail: enquiries@alvisregister.com

Enquiries:
Enquiries to: Registrar
Direct e-mail: joining@alvisregister.com

Founded:
1948

Organisation type and purpose:
Membership association (membership is by subscription), present number of members: 520.

Subject coverage:
Alvis cars.

Access to staff:
Contact by letter and by telephone
Hours: Mon to Fri, 0900 to 1700

ALZHEIMER SCOTLAND

Formal name: Alzheimer Scotland – Action on Dementia

22 Drumsheugh Gardens, Edinburgh, EH3 7RN

Tel: 0131 243 1453
Fax: 0131 243 1450
E-mail: alzheimer@alzscot.org

Website:
http://www.alzscot.org/local/index.html
Information about the organisation, about dementia and caring for people who have dementia, database of services and list of publications.

Enquiries:
Enquiries to: Information Manager
Direct e-mail: mthom@alzscot.org

Founded:
1994

Organisation type and purpose:
Membership association, voluntary organisation, registered charity (charity number SC022315). Provision and promotion of services for people with dementia and their carers. Has a network of branches and services across Scotland; for information contact the National Office.

Subject coverage:
Information relating to statistics on numbers of people in Scotland with dementia. Range of services offered in Scotland. Information on all aspects of dementia and on government policy.

Printed publications:
Annual Report
A variety of policy reports, including:
This is my home: quality of care for people with dementia living in care homes (2005)
Good for You Good for Your Brain: the evidence on risk reduction and dementia (2006)
The Dementia Epidemic – where Scotland is now and the challenge ahead (2007)
Meeting our needs? The level and quality of dementia support services in Scotland (2008)
Let's get personal – personalisation and dementia (2010)
Various booklets and leaflets about coping with dementia, including:
Branches and Services of Alzheimer Scotland (information sheet, 25p standard print, 40p large print)
Dementia: Money and Legal Matters – a guide for carers (2-volume booklet)
We Care About Dementia: about the work of Alzheimer Scotland (leaflet, free)
What is Dementia? (leaflet, 10p)
Newsletter: Dementia in Scotland (4 times a year, £1.50, free to members)

Publications list:
Available online and in print

Access to staff:
Contact by letter, by telephone, by fax, by e-mail and via website. Appointment necessary.
Hours: 24-hour Dementia Helpline 0808 808 3000

Branches:
Alzheimer Scotland, Argyll & Clyde Regional Headquarters
32 Riccartsbar Avenue, Paisley, PA2 6BG; tel: 0141 887 4902; fax: 0141 840 1815; website: http://www.alzscot.org/pages/regions/argyll.htm

27

continued overleaf

Alzheimer Scotland, Ayrshire and Dumfries &
Galloway Regional Office
  1 Gordon Street, Dumfries, DG1 1EG; tel: 01387
  261303; fax: 01387 251899; website: http://www
  .alzscot.org/pages/regions/ayrshiredumf.htm
Alzheimer Scotland, Forth Valley & Lanarkshire
Regional Office
  Lanarkshire Information and Advice Centre, Old
  Town Hall, High Road, Motherwell, ML1 3HU;
  tel: 01698 275300; fax: 01698 251867; website:
  http://www.alzscot.org/pages/regions/forth.htm
Alzheimer Scotland, Glasgow and East
Dunbartonshire Regional Office
  81 Oxford Street, Glasgow, G5 9EP; tel: 0141 418
  3930; fax: 0141 418 3945; website: http://www
  .alzscot.org/pages/regions/glasgow.htm
Alzheimer Scotland, Grampian, Tayside and
Shetland Regional Office
  First Floor, 492 Union Street, Aberdeen, AB10
  1TS; tel: 01224 644077; fax: 01224 644088;
  website: http://www.alzscot.org/pages/regions/
  grampian.htm
Alzheimer Scotland, Highland, Western Isles and
Orkney Regional Office
  3 Gordon Terrace, Inverness, IV2 3HD; tel: 01463
  711707; fax: 01463 711715; website: http://www
  .alzscot.org/pages/regions/highland.htm
Alzheimer Scotland, Lothian, Fife and Borders
Regional Office
  22 Drumsheugh Gardens, Edinburgh, EH3 7RN;
  tel: 0131 243 1453; fax: 0131 243 1450; website:
  http://www.alzscot.org/pages/regions/lothian
  .htm

ALZHEIMER'S RESEARCH TRUST

The Stables, Station Road, Great Shelford,
Cambridge, CB22 5LR one:

Tel: 01223 843899
Fax: 01223 843325
E-mail: enquiries@alzheimers-research.org.uk

Website:
http://www.alzheimers-research.org.uk
The charity and its aims, information about
dementia, research and grants, news and events.

Founded:
1992

Organisation type and purpose:
A registered charity (number 1077089).
A leading research charity for dementia, dedicated
to funding scientific studies to find ways to treat,
cure or prevent Alzheimer's disease, vascular
dementia, Lewy Body disease and fronto-temporal
dementia.

Subject coverage:
Funds vital research and provides free information
on dementia and the progress being made by
research.

Printed publications:
Alzheimer's Facts (booklet)
Order printed publications from: tel: 01223 843899; e-
mail: enquiries@alzheimers-research.org.uk

Electronic and video publications:
e-Newsletter
Order electronic and video publications from: via
website

Publications list:
Available online

Access to staff:
Contact by letter, by telephone, by fax, by e-mail
and via website

ALZHEIMER'S SOCIETY

Acronym or abbreviation: AS

Devon House, 58 St Katharine's Way, London, E1W
1LB

Tel: 020 7423 3500
Fax: 020 7423 3501
E-mail: info@alzheimers.org.uk

Website:
http://www.alzheimers.org.uk
Description of services.

Enquiries:
Enquiries to: Director of Information and Education
Direct e-mail: enquiries@alzheimers.org.uk

Founded:
1979

Formerly called:
Alzheimer's Disease Society (ADS) (year of change
1999)

Organisation type and purpose:
National organisation, membership association
(membership is by subscription), present number
of members: 25,000, voluntary organisation,
registered charity (charity number 296645),
research organisation.
Serves England, Wales and Northern Ireland.
To provide care for people with Alzheimer's
disease and other forms of dementia and research
into the condition.
To provide support for their carers and families.

Subject coverage:
Dementia and dementia care.

**Museum or gallery collection, archive, or library
special collection:**
Dementia Knowledge Centre with over 12,500
  items including books, articles, dvds and videos

Library catalogue:
All or part available in-house

Printed publications:
Annual Report
Fact sheets, booklets
General leaflets (available in 16 languages)
Living with dementia (monthly magazine)

Electronic and video publications:
In their own words (free dvd)

Publications list:
Available online and in print

Access to staff:
Contact by letter, by telephone, by fax, by e-mail,
in person and via website. Appointment necessary.
Non-members charged.
Hours: Mon to Fri, 0900 to 1700

Access to building, collection or gallery:
No access other than to staff
Hours: Mon to Fri, 0900 to 1700

Access for disabled people:
Toilet facilities

AMATEUR BOXING ASSOCIATION OF ENGLAND LIMITED

Acronym or abbreviation: ABA

Crystal Palace, National Sports Centre, London,
SE19 2BB

Tel: 020 8778 0251
Fax: 020 8778 9324

Website:
http://www.amateurboxingassociation.co.uk

Enquiries:
Enquiries to: Secretary
Direct e-mail: hannah.mclafferty@abae.org.uk

Founded:
1993

Formerly called:
Amateur Boxing Association

Organisation type and purpose:
Membership association (membership is by
election or invitation), voluntary organisation,
training organisation.
Governing body of amateur boxing in England.

Subject coverage:
History of boxing, coaching, officials, membership.

**Museum or gallery collection, archive, or library
special collection:**
Literature on the Association

Printed publications:
Boxing News

Access to staff:
Contact by letter. Appointment necessary.
Hours: Mon to Fri, 0900 to 1600

Affiliated to:
European Boxing Association (EABA)
International Amateur Boxing Association (AIBA)

AMATEUR FOOTBALL ALLIANCE

Acronym or abbreviation: AFA

55 Islington Park Street, London, N1 1QB

Tel: 020 7359 3493
Fax: 020 7359 5027
E-mail: a.f.a@dial.pipex.com

Website:
http://www.amateur-fa.org

Enquiries:
Enquiries to: General Secretary

Founded:
1907

Organisation type and purpose:
Membership association (membership is by
election or invitation, subscription, qualification),
present number of members: 320 affiliated clubs,
340 affiliated referees.
Regional governing body for association football.

Subject coverage:
Recreational amateur football.

Printed publications:
Handbook (annually)
AFA Record (magazine, 3 times a year, £4)

Access to staff:
Contact by letter, by telephone, by fax, by e-mail
and via website
Hours: Mon to Fri, 0915 to 1645

Parent body:
The Football Association

AMATEUR SWIMMING ASSOCIATION

Acronym or abbreviation: ASA

Harold Fern House, Derby Square, Loughborough,
Leicestershire, LE11 5AL

Tel: 01509 618700
Fax: 01509 618701
E-mail: customerservices@swimming.org

Enquiries:
Enquiries to: Customer Services Manager

Founded:
1869

Organisation type and purpose:
Governing body of swimming.

Subject coverage:
Swimming; diving; water polo; synchronised
swimming; competitive swimming; examinations
and awards; education and teaching; student
research; swimming for people with a disability;
aquatic exercise.

Printed publications:
ASA Handbook
Books and handbooks on swimming and coaching,
  babies and children, synchronised swimming,
  diving, special needs, masters, survival, aquafit,
  water polo, nutrition
Information brochures
Swimming (monthly)
Order printed publications from: ASA Merchandising
Ltd

Unit 1, Kingfisher Enterprise Park, 50 Arthur Street, Redditch, Worcestershire, B98 8LG, tel: 0800 220292, fax: 01527 514277, e-mail: sales@asa-awards.co.uk

Electronic and video publications:
Videos

Publications list:
Available in print

Access to staff:
Contact by letter, by telephone, by fax and by e-mail
Hours: Mon to Fri, 0900 to 1700

Houses the:
Institute of Swimming Teachers and Coaches

Member of:
Central Council of Physical Recreation
Sports Council

AMATEUR SWIMMING ASSOCIATION, WATER POLO COMMITTEE

Acronym or abbreviation: ASA

177 Urmston Lane, Stretford, Manchester, M32 9EH

Tel: 0161 866 8588
Fax: 0161 865 6041
E-mail: juliemikepolo@supanet.com

Enquiries:
Enquiries to: Committee Administrator

Organisation type and purpose:
Membership association.

Subject coverage:
Water polo.

Access to staff:
Contact by letter, by telephone, by fax and by e-mail
Hours: Sun to Sat, 0900 to 2000

Access to building, collection or gallery:
No access other than to staff

Connections with:
Amateur Swimming Association
Harold Fern House, Derby Square,
Loughborough, LE11 5AL; tel: 01509 618700; fax: 01509 618701

AMBER FOUNDATION

Shurnhold Trading Estate, Melksham, Wiltshire, SN12 8DE

Tel: 01225 792622
Fax: 01225 792629

Website:
http://www.amber-web.org
Full details of the Foundation and its work, including an online Practical Housing Units (PHUs) forum.

Enquiries:
Enquiries to: Chief Executive
Direct tel: 01594 837934 (Chief Exec.); 02380 276531 (PR and Fundraising Director)
Direct fax: 01594 837934
Other contacts: PR and Fundraising Director

Founded:
1995

Organisation type and purpose:
Registered charity (charity number 1051388) for young unemployed people, who are often also homeless.
To help reduce the level of unemployment within the 18–30 age group, working with ex-offenders, ex-drug users, alcoholics, those who have lost their motivation and self-esteem and those who just need a leg up to move forward, by giving them time and space in a residential environment to rebuild their lives and build their self confidence and self esteem so they are motivated to seek employment. Amber works with the individual,

giving them the required confidence and practical skills that they are lacking. Its long-term plan is to expand further and open centres in other areas of the country.

Subject coverage:
Runs three residential centres providing temporary 24-hour care and support, offers accredited training courses, including adult literacy and numeracy, and tenancy and housing-related issues. Broader, transferable skills are developed in personal development and team work and leadership courses that involve personal fitness and a wide range of outdoor activities. The charity's Practical Housing Units are also being used by prisons, housing societies, charities for the homeless and other large and small organisations.

Education services:
PHUs: 10 modules, accredited by AQA; a complete package of staff training and programme supervision, student learning materials/resources, and registration, verification and certification of achieved PHUs.

Printed publications:
Report and Accounts
Newsletter (twice yearly, free)
Order printed publications from: Report and Accounts, e-mail: sue.condie@amberweb.org
Newsletter, tel: 02380 276531; or order via website

Electronic and video publications:
Report and Accounts
Newsletter (twice yearly)
Order electronic and video publications from: available on website

Access to staff:
Contact by letter, by telephone, by fax, by e-mail and via website

Also at:
Ashley Court Residential Centre
Chawleigh, nr Chulmleigh, Devon, EX18 7EX; tel: 01769 581011; fax: 01769 581379
Bythesea Lodge Residential Centre
Bythesea Road, Trowbridge, Wiltshire, BA14 8HR; tel: 01225 759900; fax: 01225 759909
Farm Place Residential Centre
Stane Street, Ockley, Dorking, Surrey, RH5 5NG; tel: 01306 627927; fax: 01306 627426

AMBER VALLEY BOROUGH COUNCIL

Acronym or abbreviation: AVBC

PO Box 15, Town Hall, Market Place, Ripley, Derbyshire, DE5 3XE

Tel: 01773 570222\ Minicom no. 01773 841490
E-mail: enquiry@ambervalley.gov.uk

Website:
http://www.ambervalley.gov.uk
Information about Amber Valley and the services that the council provides.

Enquiries:
Enquiries to: Chief Executive

Organisation type and purpose:
Local government body (membership is by election or invitation), present number of members: 45.

Subject coverage:
Local government issues.

Printed publications:
Amber Valley News (free, early March)

Access to staff:
Contact by letter, by telephone, by fax, by e-mail and in person. Appointment necessary.
Hours: Mon to Fri, 0900 to 1700

Access for disabled people:
Parking provided, toilet facilities

AMBLESS

Shalom House, Lower Celtic Park, Enniskillen, Co Fermanagh, BT74 6HP

Tel: 028 6632 0320
Fax: 028 6632 0320

Enquiries:
Enquiries to: Secretary
Other contacts: Chief Executive

Founded:
1984

Formerly called:
I Am Blessed Ministries (year of change 1990)

Incorporates the former:
DAP, Disasters, Accidents Involving People (year of change 1996)

Organisation type and purpose:
Non-profit-making organisation. Ambless is a national charity with a Christian ethos, that works to alleviate distress, suffering, heartache, grief, loneliness and trauma that accidents can cause. The services provided are confidential and discreet and are available to patients, their families and carers. Ambless relies entirely on the free-will support of the general public. Operates the 24-hour Ambless Accident Supportline (028 6632 0321 – tel, fax, SMS text and voicemail) and Ambless Care Car (tel 07920 793456).

Subject coverage:
Professional counselling, befriending, information and advice and practical support for people who have suffered an accident, and for their families and carers.

Museum or gallery collection, archive, or library special collection:
I am Blessed (newsletter)
Our Companion (newsletter)

Printed publications:
Fundraising Ideas (annually)
Ambless Inspirational Catalogue (quarterly)
Healthy Living Factsheet (annually)
Our Companion (newsletter, 8 times a year)
Info Pack (free)
SOS Helpcards, leaflets, etc.

Access to staff:
Contact by letter, by telephone, by fax and in person. Appointment necessary.
Hours: Mon to Sat, 1000 to 2200

Access for disabled people:
Parking provided

AMBULANCE SERVICE INSTITUTE

Acronym or abbreviation: ASI

2 Appletree Close, Oakley, Basingstoke, Hampshire, RG23 7HL

Fax: 01256 782650
E-mail: ambservinst.uk@virgin.net

Website:
http://www.asi-international.com

Enquiries:
Enquiries to: Honorary Secretary

Founded:
1976

Formerly called:
Institute of Ambulance Officers, Institute of Certified Ambulance Personnel, National Institute of Ambulance Instructors

Organisation type and purpose:
International organisation, professional body, registered charity, training organisation.

Subject coverage:
Ambulance Service organisation, administration and operation; training and qualifying examinations.

Printed publications:
asi International (official publication)

Publications list:
Available online

continued overleaf

Access to staff:
Contact by letter, by fax, by e-mail and via website
Hours: Mon to Fri, 0900 to 1700

AMBULANCE SERVICE NETWORK

The NHS Confederation, 3rd Floor, 29 Bressenden Place, London, SW1E 5DD

Tel: 020 7074 3200
E-mail: liz.kendall@nhsconfed.org

Website:
http://www.nhsconfed.org/ambulance-trusts/index.cfm

Enquiries:
Enquiries to: Information Officer

Founded:
1994

Created by the merger of:
the Ambulance Service Association (ASA) and the NHS Confederation (NHSC)

Formerly called:
Association of Chief Ambulance Officers (ACAO) (year of change 1994)

Organisation type and purpose:
National organisation, trade association (membership is by qualification), present number of members: 39 Corporate members.
Corporate membership for NHS Ambulance Services.

Subject coverage:
NHS Ambulance Services.

Trade and statistical information:
Data on Ambulance personnel, finance and operations.

Printed publications:
The Future of the Ambulance Services in the UK to 2010 (£5)
Operational Arrangements for Civil Emergencies (£25)
Guidance on Chemical Incidents (£25)
Mailing list of UK Ambulance Services (£25)
Order printed publications from: Administrative Assistant, Ambulance Service Association
As main address

Access to staff:
Contact by letter
Hours: Mon to Fri, 0900 to 1730

Access to building, collection or gallery:
Prior appointment required

Access for disabled people:
Parking provided, ramped entry, access to all public areas, toilet facilities

AMERICAN AUTO CLUB UK

Acronym or abbreviation: AAC UK

2 Cumbers Cottage, Sandy Lane, Hanmer, Whitchurch, Shropshire, SY13 3DL

Tel: 01948 830754
Fax: 01948 830754
E-mail: secaacuk@aol.com

Website:
http://www.american-auto-club.co.uk
Membership and events details.

Enquiries:
Enquiries to: Chief Executive Officer
Other contacts: Membership Secretary, President

Founded:
1981

Organisation type and purpose:
International organisation, membership association (membership is by subscription), present number of members: 2600.
To expand interest and ownership of American automobiles in the UK.

Subject coverage:
Technical information on American automobiles, registrations, valuations for insurance purposes, location of parts. Recognised by DVLA for providing vehicle data to obtain year-related registrations. There are 47 area representatives covering the United Kingdom and the United States to locate spares etc.

Museum or gallery collection, archive, or library special collection:
Collection of books relating to production and data of American cars, trucks and motor cycles

Printed publications:
Magazine (monthly, free to members)

Access to staff:
Contact by letter, by telephone, by fax and by e-mail
Hours: Mon to Fri, 0900 to 1700

Access to building, collection or gallery:
No access other than to staff

AMERICAN CHURCH IN LONDON

Acronym or abbreviation: ACL

Whitefield Memorial Church, Tottenham Court Road, London, W1T 4TD

Tel: 020 7580 2791
Fax: 020 7580 5013
E-mail: info@amchurch.co.uk

Website:
http://www.amchurch.co.uk

Enquiries:
Enquiries to: Secretary
Direct e-mail: churchsecretary@amchurch.co.uk
Other contacts: (1) Senior Pastor; (2) Associate Pastor; (3) Church Secretary

Organisation type and purpose:
Church.

Access to staff:
Contact by telephone, by fax, by e-mail and via website
Hours: Mon to Fri, 0900 to 1700

Member organisation of:
The United Reform Church (URC)

AMERICAN EMBASSY

Formal name: Embassy of The United States of America

Information Resource Centre, American Embassy, 24 Grosvenor Square, London, W1A 1AE

Tel: 020 7894 0925 (1000 to 1200); 020 7894 0643
Fax: 020 7629 8288
E-mail: reflond@state.gov

Website:
http://london.usembassy.gov

Enquiries:
Enquiries to: Resource Centre Director
Direct tel: 020 7499 5684

Organisation type and purpose:
National government body.
Embassy unit.
To respond to enquiries about the US from journalists, media researchers, academics, libraries, members of parliament, government departments.

Subject coverage:
United States government, politics, legislation, society, current affairs.

Museum or gallery collection, archive, or library special collection:
Approximately 30 US journal subscriptions in appropriate subject areas (news, current affairs, politics etc)
Approximately 2,000 books
CIS (Congressional Information Service) microfiche collection
Selected US Government reports and documents

Trade and statistical information:
Only basic economic and trade-related statistical data on the US.
Market survey-type information is not held.

Library catalogue:
All or part available in print

Access to staff:
Contact by letter, by telephone, by fax and by e-mail. Appointment necessary.
Hours: Mon to Fri, 0900 to 1700

Access to building, collection or gallery:
Prior appointment essential

Parent body:
Department of State
Washington DC, 20520, United States of America; website: http://www.america.gov; http://www.state.gov

AMERICAN TECHNICAL PUBLISHERS LIMITED

Acronym or abbreviation: ATP

IHS, Willoughby Road, Bracknell, Berkshire, RG12 8FB

Tel: 01344 328039
Fax: 01344 328005 emeastore@ihs.com
E-mail: emeastore@ihs.com

Website:
http://www.ameritech.co.uk/
Search facility for technical book and standards.
http://www.ihsatp.com/

Enquiries:
Enquiries to: Managing Director

Founded:
1980

Organisation type and purpose:
Distributor of standards and technical information.

Subject coverage:
Providers of technical standards and books of USA engineering societies and publishers.

Printed publications:
Engineering Publications Catalogues

Electronic and video publications:
ASTM Standards on CD-ROM

Access to staff:
Contact by letter, by telephone, by fax, by e-mail and via website
Hours: Mon to Fri, 0800 to 1730

AMERICAN UNIVERSITY IN LONDON

97–101 Seven Sisters Road, London, N7 7QP

Tel: 020 7263 2986
Fax: 020 7281 2815
E-mail: aul@ukbusiness.com or info@aul.edu

Website:
http://www.aul.edu

Enquiries:
Enquiries to: Registrar
Direct e-mail: aul@ukbusiness.com or inf@aul.edu

Founded:
1986

Organisation type and purpose:
University department or institute.

Non-library collection catalogue:
All or part available online

Library catalogue:
All or part available in-house

Access to staff:
Contact by letter, by telephone, by fax, by e-mail and in person. Appointment necessary.
Hours: Mon to Fri, 0900 to 1700

Access to building, collection or gallery:
No prior appointment required

AMIIS

Formal name: Advocacy, Mediation and Independent Investigation Service

Astolat, Coniers Way, Guildford, Surrey, GU4 7HL

Tel: 01483 531308
Fax: 01483 301072
E-mail: mediation@amiis.com

Website:
http://www.amiis.com
Description of services.

Enquiries:
Enquiries to: Head of Service
Direct e-mail: david@amiis.com

Organisation type and purpose:
Membership association (membership is by election or invitation), voluntary organisation. Resolving problems/complaints for social service users and carers in Surrey.

Subject coverage:
Social service users and carers.

Access to staff:
Contact by letter, by telephone, by fax, by e-mail and in person
Hours: Mon to Fri, 0900 to 1700

Access for disabled people:
Parking provided
Special comments: Access via separate door and lift. Please telephone to make arrangements.

AMNESTY INTERNATIONAL

Acronym or abbreviation: AI

Peter Benenson House, 1 Easton Street, London, WC1X 0DW

Tel: 020 7413 5500
Fax: 020 7956 1157
E-mail: via website

Website:
http://www.amnesty.org/en/library
Library.
http://www.amnesty.org.uk/news/index.html
Press releases, Amnesty magazine, letter writing activities.
http://www.amnesty.org.uk/amnesty/index.html
Introduction to AIUK.
http://www.amnesty.org.uk/support/index.html
Events and fundraising.
http://www.amnesty.org.uk/action/index.html
Campaigning news.

Enquiries:
Enquiries to: Information Officer
Direct e-mail: press@amnesty.org

Founded:
1961

Organisation type and purpose:
International organisation, membership association (membership is by subscription), voluntary organisation.
Human rights campaigning.
Seeks release of prisoners of conscience; against death penalty, torture, political killings and disappearances; for fair trials for political prisoners.

Subject coverage:
Human rights violations worldwide.

Museum or gallery collection, archive, or library special collection:
Collection of recent AI reports on human rights issues

Library catalogue:
All or part available online

Printed publications:
Amnesty (magazine)
Books and video catalogue
Wire (magazine for international members)
Order printed publications from: Marketing and Supply Team, at postal address

Microform publications:
AI reports available on microfiche

Electronic and video publications:
Videos available for purchase

Publications list:
Available online and in print

Access to staff:
Contact by letter, by telephone, by fax, by e-mail and via website
Hours: Mon to Fri, 1000 to 1800

Access to building, collection or gallery:
No prior appointment required

AMR

PO Box 8715, London, SE23 3ZB

Tel: 020 8699 1887
E-mail: amr.org@btinternet.com

Website:
http://www.amr.org
Introduction to the organisation, aims and objectives, forthcoming events, publications, membership information, etc.

Enquiries:
Enquiries to: Executive Officer

Founded:
1989

Organisation type and purpose:
Membership association (membership is by subscription), present number of members: 75, voluntary organisation, registered charity (charity number 1069744).
Generation, application and dissemination of knowledge. Learned societies in the fields of education, humanities and science and technology.

Subject coverage:
Islam; Islam and education/science and technology/humanities; specific information in the fields of art and Islam, music and Islam; GCSE/AS/A-level Islamic Studies; science courses; networking services; providing referrals, knowledge of British Muslim community.

Information services:
Building engaged Islamic personalities and characters through inter-generational family-based education, training and social interaction within a safe and enjoyable environment.

Printed publications:
AMR News (quarterly)
Annual reports, proceedings
Publications/recordings (available direct and from book order agencies)
Non-registered publications/recordings (only available direct)
Order printed publications from: AMR as above

Electronic and video publications:
Tapes of selected talks

Publications list:
Available online and in print

Access to staff:
Contact by letter, by telephone and by e-mail
Hours: Any day of the week – via answering machine message or e-mail

Access to building, collection or gallery:
No access other than to staff

Affiliated to:
Muslim Council of Britain (MCB)
PO Box 52, Wembley, HA9 0XW; tel: 020 8903 9024

AMSPAR LIMITED

Formal name: Association of Medical Secretaries, Practice Managers, Administrators and Receptionists Limited

Tavistock House North, Tavistock Square, London, WC1H 9LN

Tel: 020 7387 6005
Fax: 020 7388 2648
E-mail: info@amspar.co.uk

Website:
http://www.amspar.com

Enquiries:
Enquiries to: Membership Secretary

Founded:
1964

Organisation type and purpose:
Professional body (membership is by subscription, qualification, election or invitation), present number of members: 4,000, registered charity (charity number 313310), suitable for ages: 16+. National registered awarding body for professional qualifications.

Subject coverage:
Professional qualifications for General Practice Managers, medical secretaries, medical receptionists, delivered via a network of approved centres and colleges throughout the United Kingdom.

Printed publications:
Quarterly Magazine
Careers leaflets
College lists

Access to staff:
Contact by letter, by telephone, by fax and by e-mail. Appointment necessary.
Hours: Mon to Fri, 0900 to 1700

ANAESTHETIC RESEARCH SOCIETY

Acronym or abbreviation: ARS

University Department of Anaesthesia and Intensive Care, Queen's Medical Centre, Nottingham, NG7 2UH

Tel: 0115 823 1002
Fax: 0115 970 0739

Website:
http://www.ars.ac.uk

Enquiries:
Enquiries to: Honorary Secretary
Direct e-mail: jonathan.hardman@nottingham.ac.uk

Founded:
1958

Organisation type and purpose:
Learned society.
Presentation and publication of ongoing research in anaesthesia and related subjects.

Subject coverage:
Anaesthesia; intensive care; acute and chronic pain relief.

Museum or gallery collection, archive, or library special collection:
Abstracts published twice a year in the British Journal of Anaesthesia

Printed publications:
British Journal of Anaesthesia (abstracts only)

Access to staff:
Contact by letter, by fax, by e-mail and via website
Hours: Mon to Fri, 0900 to 1700

ANAPHYLAXIS CAMPAIGN

PO Box 275, Farnborough, Hampshire, GU14 6SX

Tel: 01252 542029 (Helpline); 01252 546100 (Administration)
Fax: 01252 377140
E-mail: info@anaphylaxis.org.uk

Website:
http://www.anaphylaxis.org.uk

Founded:
1994

continued overleaf

ASLIB DIRECTORY of INFORMATION SOURCES

Organisation type and purpose:
Membership association (membership is by subscription), present number of members: 6,800, registered charity (charity number 1085527). Offers support and guidance to those with life-threatening allergies, raises awareness in the food industry, medical profession, etc., promotes research.

Subject coverage:
Anaphylaxis, allergic reactions.

Printed publications:
Cyril the Squirrel (children's book, £5.25)

Electronic and video publications:
Action for Anaphylaxis (information video, £16.50; DVD, £18; both incl p&p)
The New Kid (children's information video, £2 incl p&p)

Access to staff:
Contact by letter, by telephone, by fax, by e-mail and via website
Hours: Mon to Fri, 0900 to 1700
Special comments: Answerphone outside office hours; membership queries to PO Box address.

Also at:
Anaphylaxis Campaign Office
1 Alexandra Road, Farnborough, Hampshire, GU14 6BU; tel: 01252 542029; fax: 01252 377140; e-mail: info@anaphylaxis.org.uk

ANATOMICAL SOCIETY OF GREAT BRITAIN AND IRELAND

Acronym or abbreviation: ASGBI

Department of Anatomy, University College, Cork, Republic of Ireland

Tel: 00 35321 4902115
Fax: 00 35321 4273518
E-mail: anatomy@ucc.ie

Website:
http://www.blackwell-science.com
Information on the society.
http://www.journals.cup.org
Information on the Journal of Anatomy.

Enquiries:
Enquiries to: Honorary Secretary
Other contacts: (1) Membership Secretary (2) Treasurer for (1) membership queries (2) financial queries.

Founded:
1887

Organisation type and purpose:
Learned society.

Subject coverage:
Gross anatomy, anthropology, histology, cell biology, developmental biology, pathological anatomy, biomechanics and related topics.

Museum or gallery collection, archive, or library special collection:
Human embryology database

Printed publications:
Journal of Anatomy (8 times a year, pub. Blackwells)
Order printed publications from: Blackwell Science Limited
Osney Mead, Oxford, OX2 0EL, tel: 01865 206206, fax: 01865 721205

Access to staff:
Contact by letter, by e-mail and via website
Hours: Mon to Fri, 0900 to 1700

ANCIENT AND HONOURABLE GUILD OF TOWN CRIERS

Formal name: The Ancient and Honourable Guild of Town Criers
Acronym or abbreviation: AHGTC

10 Weston Road, Guildford, Surrey, GU2 8AS

Tel: 01483 532796

Fax: 01483 833489
E-mail: secretary@ahgtc.org.uk

Website:
http://www.ahgtc.org.uk
History, how to join, events.

Enquiries:
Enquiries to: Secretary
Other contacts: Membership Secretary (for appointment of new Town Criers, new members)

Founded:
1978

Organisation type and purpose:
International organisation, membership association.

Subject coverage:
Town crying for local authorities and commercial interests, non-political. Town crying competitions, information, history and organisation; charters the World Town Criers Championship, the European Towncriers Championship.

Printed publications:
Newsletter (quarterly, members only)

Access to staff:
Contact by letter, by telephone, by fax, by e-mail and via website
Hours: Mon to Fri, 0900 to 2200

Access to building, collection or gallery:
No access other than to staff

Constituent bodies:
World Town Criers Championships Limited at the same address

ANCIENT MONUMENTS SOCIETY

Acronym or abbreviation: AMS

St Ann's Vestry Hall, 2 Church Entry, London, EC4V 5HB

Tel: 020 7236 3934
E-mail: office@ancientmonumentssociety.org.uk

Website:
http://www.ancientmonumentssociety.org.uk

Enquiries:
Enquiries to: Secretary

Founded:
1924

Organisation type and purpose:
National organisation, learned society (membership is by subscription), present number of members: 2,000, voluntary organisation, registered charity (charity number 209605). Study and conservation of ancient monuments, historic buildings of all ages and fine old craftsmanship.

Subject coverage:
Historic buildings of all ages and types, their dating, conservation and care, new uses; planning law as it relates to them; sources of money for their restoration.

Library catalogue:
All or part available in-house

Printed publications:
Newsletters (three times a year)
Transactions (annually)

Publications list:
Available in print

Access to staff:
Contact by letter, by telephone and by e-mail
Hours: Mon to Fri, 0900 to 1700

Access to building, collection or gallery:
No access other than to staff

Links with:
Friends of Friendless Churches

ANDREA ADAMS TRUST

Acronym or abbreviation: AAT

Hova House, 1 Hova Villas, Hove, East Sussex, BN3 3DH

Tel: 01273 704900
Fax: 01273 704900
E-mail: elaine@andreaadamstrust.org

Website:
http://www.andreaadamstrust.org

Enquiries:
Enquiries to: Office Manager

Founded:
1997

Organisation type and purpose:
Registered charity (charity number 1064539), training organisation, consultancy. National Workplace Bullying Advice Line, training and mediation for business and industry.

Subject coverage:
Workplace bullying.

Trade and statistical information:
Statistical information on workplace bullying and rates of occurrence.

Printed publications:
Bullying at Work (Adams A and Crawford N, 1992, pub Virago)
Factsheet on workplace bullying (£3 with A4 sae)
Guide to Workplace Bullying: The Legal Position
Guide to Workplace Bullying: Summary of latest research

Publications list:
Available in print

Access to staff:
Contact by letter, by telephone, by fax, by e-mail and via website
Hours: Mon to Fri, 0900 to 1700
Special comments: No visitors.

Access to building, collection or gallery:
No access other than to staff

ANGELA THIRKELL SOCIETY

54 Belmont Park, London, SE13 5BN

Tel: 020 8244 9339
E-mail: penny.aldred@ntlworld.com

Website:
http://www.angelathirkellsociety.com

Enquiries:
Enquiries to: Secretary

Founded:
1980

Organisation type and purpose:
Membership association.
Literary society.

Subject coverage:
Life and works of Angela Thirkell and her family.

Printed publications:
Publications for members only

Publications list:
Available in print

Access to staff:
Contact by letter, by telephone and by e-mail
Hours: Mon to Fri, 0900 to 1700

Links with:
Alliance of Literary Societies (ALS)
e-mail: l.j.curry@bham.ac.uk; website: http://www.allianceofliterarysocieties.org.uk

ANGLESEY ANTIQUARIAN SOCIETY AND FIELD CLUB

Acronym or abbreviation: AAS

Llangefni Library, Education and Leisure Department, Isle of Anglesey County Council, Lôn y Felin, Llangefni, Anglesey, LL77 7RT

Tel: 01248 752092
Fax: 01248 750197

E-mail: hanesmon@btinternet.com

Website:
http://www.hanesmon.btinternet.co.uk
Introduction, membership, publications, meetings, excursions, transactions, constitution, committees.

Enquiries:
Enquiries to: Honorary Librarian and Curator
Other contacts: Honorary General Secretary for general information regarding the Society.

Founded:
1911

Organisation type and purpose:
Learned society, registered charity (charity number 507837).

Subject coverage:
Anglesey; its history, antiquities, archaeology, natural science, geology and literature.

Museum or gallery collection, archive, or library special collection:
Collection of printed materials, manuscripts and artefacts pertaining to Anglesey
Lucy Williams, Holyhead Collection
Transactions and Proceedings of various historical and antiquarian societies
William Williams, Pentraeth (1839–1915) Collection

Non-library collection catalogue:
All or part available in-house

Printed publications:
A New Natural History of Anglesey (Jones W E ed, 1990, £7.50 plus p&p)
Index to Transactions 1913–1985 (Jones D comp, 1987, £3 plus p&p)
Newsletter (2 times a year, free to members)
Prehistoric Anglesey (Lynch F, 2nd ed., 1991, £17 plus p&p)
Portraits of an Island (Ramage H, 2nd ed., 2001, £12.95 plus p&p)
Transactions (annually, free to members, some back issues available £6 per volume)
Order printed publications from: Publications Officer, Anglesey Antiquarian Society and Field Club Bryn Eglwys, Llanddyfnan, Llangefni, Anglesey, LL75 8UL, tel: 01248 450310

Publications list:
Available online

Access to staff:
Contact by letter, by telephone and by fax.
Appointment necessary.
Hours: Mon to Fri, 0900 to 1700

Access for disabled people:
Parking provided, level entry, toilet facilities
Special comments: Lift available.

ANGLESEY ARCHIVES SERVICE

Formal name: Gwasanath Archifau Ynys Mon / Anglesey Archives Service

Shire Hall, Glanhwfa Road, Llangefni, Anglesey, LL77 7TW

Tel: 01248 752080
Fax: 01248 751289
E-mail: archifau@anglesey.gov.uk

Website:
http://www.ynysmon.gov.uk
Summary of holdings and purpose of Record Office.

Enquiries:
Enquiries to: Archivist

Founded:
1974

Formerly called:
Llangefni Area Record Office of Gwynedd Archives and Museums Service (year of change 1996)

Organisation type and purpose:
Local government body.
Record Office.

Subject coverage:
Usual holdings of a county record office including parish records, quarter sessions records, poor law unions, local authorities, family and business collections.

Non-library collection catalogue:
All or part available in-house

Access to staff:
Contact by letter, by telephone, by fax, by e-mail and in person
Hours: Mon, Wed, Thu, Fri, 0900 to 1645; Tue, 1400 to 1645 (1400 to 1845 every 2nd and 4th Tue)
Special comments: Member of the County Archives Research Network; tickets issued on day of visit with suitable identification.

Access to building, collection or gallery:
No prior appointment required
Hours: Mon, Wed, Thu, Fri, 0915 to 1645; Tue, 1400 to 1645 (1400 to 1845 every 2nd and 4th Tue)
Special comments: Closed: first full week in Nov; St David's day. No prior appointment required except for microform.

Access for disabled people:
Toilet facilities
Hours: Mon, Wed, Thu, Fri, 0915 to 1645; Tue, 1400 to 1645 (1400 to 1845 every 2nd and 4th Tue)
Special comments: Stairlift, with prior arrangement access to a ground floor room can be arranged.

ANGLIA RUSKIN UNIVERSITY

Acronym or abbreviation: ARU

University Library, Queen's Building, Rivermead Campus, Bishop Hall Lane, Chelmsford, Essex, CM1 1SQ

Tel: 01245 683757
E-mail: firstname.lastname@anglia.ac.uk

Website:
http://www.libweb.anglia.ac.uk
Access to digital library, including library catalogue, library user information pages, Harvard referencing pages.

Enquiries:
Enquiries to: University Librarian

Formerly called:
Cambridge College of Arts & Technology, Essex Institute, Chelmer Institute of Higher Education, Anglia Polytechnic University

Organisation type and purpose:
University library.

Subject coverage:
Law, business, management, telecommunications, languages, built environment, computing, education, nurse education, social welfare, humanities, technology, science, art, design, music, social science, English, women's studies, forensic science, chemistry, communications and media, history, optometry, psychology, politics.

Museum or gallery collection, archive, or library special collection:
French Resistance Archive (Cambridge)

Library catalogue:
All or part available online

Printed publications:
Battling with books: health and safety in the Library
Order printed publications from: Acquisitions, University Library, Queen's Building, Rivermead Campus, Bishop Hall Lane, Chelmsford, Essex, CM1 1SQ

Access to staff:
Contact by letter, by telephone, by e-mail, in person and via website
Hours: Varies between sites, telephone for details or see web page for contact details
Special comments: Appropriate identification should be carried.

Access for disabled people:
Parking provided, level entry, toilet facilities

Also at:
Anglia Ruskin University
University Library, Cambridge Road Campus, East Road, Cambridge, CB1 1PT; tel: 01223 698301

ANGLIA SUPPORT PARTNERSHIP

Acronym or abbreviation: ASP

Kingfisher House, Hinchingbrooke Business Park, Huntingdon, Cambridgeshire, PE29 6FH

Tel: 01480 398708
Fax: 01480 398501
E-mail: asplibrary@asp.nhs.uk

Website:
http://www.nowledge.asp.nhs.uk
Information about the health authority, its partners, local information, demographics, full text Public Health Report and HIMP

Enquiries:
Enquiries to: Head of Knowledge Services
Direct tel: 01480 398622
Direct e-mail: hilary.jackson@cambs-ha.nhs.uk

Founded:
1999

Formerly called:
Cambridge and Huntingdon Health Authority, Cambridge Health Authority, Cambridgeshire Family Health Services Authority, Huntingdon Health Authority, North West Anglia Health Authority, Cambridgeshire Health Authority

Organisation type and purpose:
Shared Services Organisation

Subject coverage:
Health management, evidence-based health care, public health, social care.

Library catalogue:
All or part available online

Access to staff:
Appointment necessary.
Hours: Mon to Fri, 0900 to 1700

Access to building, collection or gallery:
No prior appointment required

Access for disabled people:
Access to all public areas

ANGLICAN SOCIETY FOR THE WELFARE OF ANIMALS

Acronym or abbreviation: ASWA

PO Box 7193, Hound Green, Hook, Hampshire, RG27 8GT

Tel: 01252 843093
Fax: 01252 843093
E-mail: angsocwelanimals@aol.com

Website:
http://www.aswa.org.uk

Enquiries:
Enquiries to: Honorary Secretary

Founded:
1970

Organisation type and purpose:
Membership association, registered charity (charity number 1087270).
An Anglican, Christian animal welfare organisation.

Subject coverage:
Animal welfare, religious, educational, aiming to raise awareness of animal welfare issues amongst clergy and Christians.

Printed publications:
Pamphlets on a variety of animal issues written from a Christian perspective, eg use of animals for experimentation, hunting etc

Publications list:
Available in print

continued overleaf

Access to staff:
Contact by letter, by telephone, by fax, by e-mail and via website. Appointment necessary.
Hours: Mon to Fri, 0900 to 1700

Access to building, collection or gallery:
Prior appointment required

ANGLING TRUST

Eastwood House, 6 Rainbow Street, Leominster, Herefordshire, HR6 8DQ

Tel: 0844 770 0616
Fax: 0115 906 1251
E-mail: admin@anglingtrust.net

Website:
http://www.anglingtrust.net/fl/mapping/map.asp
The trust, membership, find a club, news, competitions, events, club and fisheries information, Fish Legal.

Founded:
2009

Created by the merger of:
six angling and conservation organisations

Organisation type and purpose:
Single governing and representative body for all game, coarse and sea anglers and angling in England, membership association (membership is by subscription).

Subject coverage:
Lobbies government, campaigns on environmental and angling issues and runs national and international competitions; fights pollution, commercial over-fishing at sea, over-abstraction, poaching, unlawful navigation, local bans and a host of other threats to angling.

Access to staff:
Contact by letter, by telephone, by fax and by e-mail

Development arm:
Angling Development Board (ADB)

Legal arm:
Fish Legal
website: http://www.fishlegal.net/landing
.asp?section=158&sectionTitle=Fish+Legal

ANGLO ARGENTINE SOCIETY

Acronym or abbreviation: AAS

2 Belgrave Square, London, SW1X 8PJ

Tel: 020 7235 9505
Fax: 020 7235 9505
E-mail: angloargentinesociety@hotmail.co.uk

Enquiries:
Enquiries to: Secretary

Founded:
1948

Organisation type and purpose:
International organisation, membership association (membership is by subscription), present number of members: 1,100, registered charity (charity number 208002).
To develop relationships between Argentina and the United Kingdom.

Subject coverage:
Anglo-Argentine relations.

Access to staff:
Contact by letter, by telephone, by fax, by e-mail and in person
Hours: Mon, Wed and Thu, 1330 to 1730

ANGLO BRAZILIAN SOCIETY

32 Green Street, London, W1K 7AU

Tel: 020 7493 8493
Fax: 020 7493 8493
E-mail: anglo@braziliansociety.freeserve.co.uk

Enquiries:
Enquiries to: General Secretary

Founded:
1943

Organisation type and purpose:
Membership association (membership is by subscription), registered charity.
To promote close and friendly relations between Brazil and the UK.

Subject coverage:
Brazil: its people, intellectual, artistic and cultural life.

Museum or gallery collection, archive, or library special collection:
Library of Brazilian books

Access to staff:
Contact by letter, by telephone and by e-mail
Hours: Tue, Wed, Thu, 1000 to 1600

Member of:
Hispanic and Luso-Brazilian Council
2 Belgrave Square, London, SW1X 8PJ

ANGLO EUROPEAN COLLEGE OF CHIROPRACTIC

Acronym or abbreviation: AECC

13–15 Parkwood Road, Bournemouth, BH5 2DF

Tel: 01202 436200
E-mail: library@aecc.ac.uk

Website:
http://www.aecc.ac.uk
Course information; college prospectus; clinic and research information.

Enquiries:
Enquiries to: Librarian
Direct tel: 01202 436307
Direct fax: 01202 436308
Direct e-mail: doneill@aecc.ac.uk

Founded:
1965

Organisation type and purpose:
University department or institute.

Subject coverage:
Chiropractic.

Library catalogue:
All or part available in-house

Access to staff:
Contact by letter, by telephone, by fax, by e-mail and via website. Appointment necessary. Non-members charged.
Hours: Mon to Fri, 0900 to 1700

Access to building, collection or gallery:
Prior appointment required

Access for disabled people:
Parking provided, ramped entry, level entry

ANGLO JEWISH ASSOCIATION

Acronym or abbreviation: AJA

Suite 5, 107 Gloucester Place, London, W1U 6BY

Tel: 020 7486 5055
Fax: 020 7486 5155
E-mail: info@anglojewish.org.uk

Website:
http://www.anglojewish.co.uk

Founded:
1871

Organisation type and purpose:
Voluntary organisation, registered charity (charity number 256946), suitable for ages: undergraduates and postgraduate students at university.

Subject coverage:
Jewish affairs, grants and loans for higher education.

Museum or gallery collection, archive, or library special collection:
Archives since 1871 (held at Southampton University)

Access to staff:
Contact by letter, by telephone and by fax
Hours: Mon to Thu, 0900 to 1500

Affiliated to:
Consultative Council of Jewish Organisations (UN)

ANGLO NORSE SOCIETY

25 Belgrave Square, London, SW1X 8QD

Tel: 020 7235 9529

Enquiries:
Enquiries to: Honorary Secretary

Organisation type and purpose:
Membership association (membership is by subscription), present number of members: 500, registered charity (charity number 263933).
A society promoting understanding between Britain and Norway.

Subject coverage:
Encouraging exchanges of an artistic, social, literary and scientific nature. Teaching of Norwegian in UK.

Printed publications:
Textbooks for the teaching of Norwegian
Anglo-Norse Review (2 times a year)
Newsletter (quarterly)

Access to staff:
Contact by letter and by telephone
Hours: Tue and Thu only, 1100 to 1600

ANGLO SCOTTISH FAMILY HISTORY SOCIETY

c/o Manchester & Lancashire FHS, Clayton House, 59 Piccadilly, Manchester, M21 2AQ

Tel: 0161 236 9750
Fax: 0161 237 3812
E-mail: office@mlfhs.org.uk

Website:
http://www.mlfhs.org.uk
Full catalogue and price list – subject index.

Enquiries:
Enquiries to: General Secretary

Founded:
1964

Organisation type and purpose:
Membership association (membership is by subscription), present number of members: c. 4500, registered charity (charity number 515599 (M&LFHS)).
Promotion of family history research.

Subject coverage:
Genealogy.

Museum or gallery collection, archive, or library special collection:
Extensive collection of genealogical material

Non-library collection catalogue:
All or part available in-house

Library catalogue:
All or part available in-house

Printed publications:
Extensive list of indexes and transcripts

Microform publications:
Extensive list of indexes and transcripts

Electronic and video publications:
Specialist indexes and transcripts (CD-ROM)

Publications list:
Available online and in print

Access to staff:
Contact by letter, by telephone, by fax, by e-mail, in person and via website

Hours: Mon, Fri, 1015 to 1300; Tue, Thu, 1015 to 1600

Parent body:
Manchester & Lancashire FHS (M&LFHS)
At the same address

ANGLO THAI SOCIETY

9 Old Hay Close, Dore, Sheffield, South Yorkshire, S17 3GP

Enquiries:
Enquiries to: Secretary

Organisation type and purpose:
Voluntary organisation.

Subject coverage:
Relations between Thailand and Great Britain; history, culture, economy, national institutions and external relations of Thailand.

Access to staff:
Contact by letter
Hours: Mon to Fri, 0900 to 1700

ANGLO TURKISH SOCIETY

43 Montrose Place, London, SW1X 7DU

Tel: 020 7235 8148 or 01420 562506
Fax: 01420 562506

Enquiries:
Enquiries to: General Secretary
Direct tel: 01420 562506

Founded:
1953

Organisation type and purpose:
Membership association (membership is by subscription), voluntary organisation, registered charity (charity number 278727).

Subject coverage:
Cultural and social Anglo-Turkish links.

Access to staff:
Contact by letter
Hours: Mon to Fri, 0900 to 1700

ANGLO-AUSTRIAN MUSIC SOCIETY

Acronym or abbreviation: AAMS

158 Rosendale Road, London, SE21 8LG

Tel: 020 8761 0444
Fax: 020 8766 6151
E-mail: info@aams.org.uk

Website:
http://www.aams.org.uk

Enquiries:
Enquiries to: General Secretary

Founded:
1942

Organisation type and purpose:
Membership association, registered charity (charity number 219021).
Concerts by Austrian artists. The Richard Tauber Prize for singers.

Access to staff:
Contact by letter, by fax and by e-mail
Hours: Mon to Fri, 0900 to 1700

ANGLO-HELLENIC LEAGUE

Acronym or abbreviation: AHL

16–18 Paddington Street, London, W1U 5AS

Tel: 020 7486 9410
Fax: 020 7486 4254
E-mail: anglohellenic.league@virgin.net

Enquiries:
Enquiries to: Administrator

Founded:
1913

Organisation type and purpose:
Membership association (membership is by subscription), present number of members: 710, registered charity (charity number 278892).
To strengthen the ties between Great Britain and Greece, and promote social and cultural relations between the peoples of the two countries.

Subject coverage:
Great Britain and Greece relationships.

Printed publications:
The Anglo-Hellenic Review (ISSN 1351–9107, 2 times a year, £2 each issue, free to members)

Access to staff:
Contact by letter and by telephone
Special comments: Closed during August.

ANGLO-ISRAEL ASSOCIATION

Acronym or abbreviation: AIA

PO Box 47819, London, NW11 7WD

Tel: 020 8458 1284
Fax: 020 8458 3484
E-mail: info@angloisraelassociation.com

Website:
http://www.angloisraelassociation.com

Enquiries:
Enquiries to: Executive Director

Founded:
1949

Organisation type and purpose:
Membership association (membership is by subscription), present number of members: 250, voluntary organisation, registered charity (charity number 313523).
Friendship organisation promoting Anglo-Israeli relations in the UK.

Subject coverage:
Israel and its place in the Middle East, Israeli life, scholarships.

Printed publications:
Annual newsletter
Pamphlets
Publicity material

Publications list:
Available in print

Access to staff:
Contact by letter, by telephone, by fax, by e-mail and via website. Appointment necessary.
Hours: Mon to Thu, 1000 to 1630

Access to building, collection or gallery:
No access other than to staff

Links with:
Israel, Britain and the Commonwealth Association Tel-Aviv, Israel

ANGLO-NORMAN TEXT SOCIETY

Acronym or abbreviation: ANTS

School of Languages, Birkbeck College, Malet Street, London, WC1E 7HX

E-mail: i.short@bbk.ac.uk

Website:
http://www.bbk.ac.uk/ants

Enquiries:
Enquiries to: Honorary Secretary

Founded:
1938

Organisation type and purpose:
Learned society, research organisation, publishing house.

Subject coverage:
Anglo-Norman language and literature; mediaeval French language and literature; publication of texts of historical, legal, linguistic and literary value.

Printed publications:
Annual Texts Series
Occasional Publications Series
Plain Texts Series
Medieval French Textual Studies (Vols 1–4, occasional)

Publications list:
Available online and in print

Access to staff:
Contact by letter, by e-mail and via website

ANGUS ARCHIVES

Hunter Library, Restenneth Priory, Forfar, DD8 2SZ

Tel: 01307 468644
E-mail: angus.archive@angus.gov.uk

Website:
http://www.angus.gov.uk/history/archives
Features on Angus people, places and documents. Resources listed for archives, photographs and books.
Contacts for Angus libraries and museums.

Enquiries:
Enquiries to: Archivist

Founded:
1989

Formerly called:
Angus Local Studies Centre

Organisation type and purpose:
Local government body.

Subject coverage:
Burgh and county history, village history, family history, Angus people, archives of Angus.

Museum or gallery collection, archive, or library special collection:
Over 800 sets of manuscript collections comprising papers belonging to individuals, businesses and societies in Angus, Arbroath, Brechin, Carnoustie, Edzell, Ferryden, Forfar, Kirriemuir, Montrose and Newtyle. These include:
Antiquities of Forfarshire, 19th century
Poems of Betty Stuart, Kinnaird Castle, 1911
Arbroath Ladies Clothing Society, 1840–1927
Papers of William Dorward, mariner in Arbroath, 1803–1871
Royal Naval Lifeboat Institute, Arbroath Branch, 1854–1983
Brechin Dispensary 1823–1870
Papers of Frederick A Ferguson, Town Clerk of Brechin, 1925–1959
Brechin Guildry papers, 1628–c.1900
Caledonian Railway – Carnoustie Station Lavatory charges, 1920–1974
Carnoustie Townswomen's Guild, 1964–1984
Papers concerning Rev Robert Inglis and Inglis Memorial Hall, 1837–1903
Forfar Baptist Church, 1872–1926
Forfar Tract Society, 1858–1940
Correspondence of J M Barrie, Kirriemuir, 1844–1892
Monifieth Scouts minute book, 1950–1969
Montrose Trades Library, 1855–1904
George Fairweather, Funeral Director, Baltic Street, Montrose, 1911–1971
Correspondence of George Paton, merchant in Montrose, 1762–1766
Newtyle Collection of William Murdoch Duncan, 1970s

Non-library collection catalogue:
All or part available online, in-house and in print

Library catalogue:
All or part available online and in-house

Printed publications:
Indexes to a large number of records, collections, and photographs

continued overleaf

Electronic and video publications:
6,000 photographs

Access to staff:
Contact by letter, by telephone, by e-mail, in person and via website. Appointment necessary.
Hours: Mon to Fri, 1000 to 1600

Access to building, collection or gallery:
Hours: Mon to Fri, 1000 to 1600

ANGUS COUNCIL

Cultural Services, Administration Unit, County Buildings, Market Street, Forfar, Tayside, DD8 3WF

Tel: 01307 461460
Fax: 01307 462590
E-mail: cultural@angus.gov.uk

Website:
http://www.angus.gov.uk
Information on council services, events, departments, etc.

Enquiries:
Enquiries to: Senior Cultural Services Manager
Other contacts: Libraries Manager

Founded:
1996

Formerly a part of:
Angus District Council; Tayside Regional Council; Dundee City Council (year of change 1996)

Organisation type and purpose:
Local government body.
Public library, archives, art galleries and exhibition, museum, education resources service, halls and theatre.
The Libraries and Museums Service is a major community facility within Angus whose purpose is to give unbiased access to information.

Subject coverage:
General, Scottish and local history.

Museum or gallery collection, archive, or library special collection:
John C. Ewing, Forfar Library (Scottish Material)
Montrose Library (original Montrose Subscription Library)
R. W. Inglis Free Library, Edzell
On microfiche and available for consultation are the following:
British Standards
Census and Parish Records
Evaluation Volumes
International Genealogical Index
Local Newspapers

Library catalogue:
All or part available online and in-house

Publications list:
Available in print

Access to staff:
Contact by letter, by telephone, by fax, by e-mail and in person
Hours: Mon to Fri, 0900 to 1700

Links with:
Chartered Institute of Library and Information Professionals (CILIP)
Chartered Institute of Library and Information Professionals, Scotland (CILIPS)
Scottish Museums Council
SLIC

ANIMAL CONCERN

PO Box 5178, Dumbarton, Strathclyde, G82 5YJ

Tel: 01389 841639
Fax: 01389 841639
E-mail: animals@jfrobins.force9.co.uk

Website:
http://www.animalconcern.org
News about Animal Concern and its campaigns.

Enquiries:
Enquiries to: Campaigns Consultant
Direct tel: 07721 605521
Direct fax: 08707060327
Direct e-mail: animals@jfrobins.force9.co.uk

Founded:
1876

Formerly called:
Scottish Anti-Vivisection Society (SAVS) (year of change 1988)

Organisation type and purpose:
Membership association (membership is by subscription), present number of members: c. 250, voluntary organisation, suitable for all ages. Pressure group.
The elimination of animal exploitation.

Subject coverage:
All animal rights and welfare issues.

Printed publications:
Animal Concern News (2 or 3 times a year, free)
Annual Report (free)
Range of fact sheets
Range of leaflets
Order printed publications from: Office at above address

Access to staff:
Contact by letter, by telephone, by fax, by e-mail and via website. Appointment necessary.
Hours: 24-hour access

Access to building, collection or gallery:
No access other than to staff

ANIMAL HEALTH TRUST

Acronym or abbreviation: AHT

Lanwades Park, Kentford, Newmarket, Suffolk, CB8 7UU

Tel: 01638 751000
Fax: 01638 750410
E-mail: library@aht.org.uk

Website:
http://www.aht.org.uk

Enquiries:
Enquiries to: Librarian

Founded:
1947

Organisation type and purpose:
Registered charity (charity number 209642), research organisation.
The advancement of veterinary science.

Subject coverage:
Veterinary science includes cancer, skin diseases, eye problems, genetics, haematology, immunology, clinical chemistry, microbiology, mycology, pathology, radiography, surgery and epidemiology.

Non-library collection catalogue:
All or part available in-house

Library catalogue:
All or part available in-house

Printed publications:
Animal Health Trust News (quarterly)
Annual Report

Publications list:
Available online

Access to staff:
Contact by letter, by telephone, by fax and by e-mail. Appointment necessary.
Hours: Mon to Fri, 0900 to 1700

Access to building, collection or gallery:
Prior appointment required

ANIMALS' REFUGE

Formal name: The National Equine (and Smaller Animals) Defence League

Oak Tree Farm, Wetheral Shields, Carlisle, CA4 8JA

Tel: 01228 560082
Fax: 01228 560985
E-mail: heatherm@animalrefuge.co.uk

Website:
http://www.animalrefuge.co.uk
The refuge, rehoming, events.

Enquiries:
Enquiries to: Director

Founded:
1909

Formerly called:
National Equine Defence League

Organisation type and purpose:
Registered charity (number 280700).
An animal refuge and rehoming service. The League works to protect all kinds of animals through its Animals' Refuge near Carlisle.

Subject coverage:
Provides a home to horses, donkeys, sheep, cattle and goats, and provides a temporary haven for dogs, cats and other small pets awaiting new homes through the League's Adoption Programme.

Special visitor services:
School visits, talks, tours, events, dog warden service.

Access to staff:
Contact by letter, by telephone and by e-mail

Access to building, collection or gallery:
Hours: Refuge: Sun to Mon, 0930 to 1600
Kennels: Sun to Mon, 1300 to 1600

ANNE FRANK TRUST UK

Acronym or abbreviation: AFTUK

Star House, 104–108 Grafton Road, London NW5 4BA

Tel: 020 7284 5858
E-mail: info@annefrank.org.uk

Website:
http://www.annefrank.org.uk

Enquiries:
Enquiries to: Executive Director
Other contacts: Administrator

Founded:
1990

Formerly called:
Anne Frank Educational Trust (AFETUK)

Organisation type and purpose:
Membership association (membership is by subscription), registered charity (charity number 1003279), suitable for ages: all.

Subject coverage:
Holocaust education, anti-racism education, citizenship education.

Printed publications:
Dear Anne (magazine for Young Friends of the Anne Frank Educational Trust)
Diary (journal)
Anne Frank: A History for Today
Anne Frank Journal
Beyond the Diary

Electronic and video publications:
Dear Kitty (video)
A Book of Dreams (video)
Eyewitnesses (video)
Anne Frank Remembered (video)

Publications list:
Available online and in print

Access to staff:
Contact by letter, by telephone, by fax and by e-mail
Hours: Mon to Fri, 0900 to 1700

Access to building, collection or gallery:
No access other than to staff
Hours: Mon to Fri, 0930 to 1630

ANNUITY BUREAU, THE

The Tower, 11 York Road, London, SE1 7NX

Tel: 020 7902 2300
Fax: 020 7621 1888
E-mail: web-enquiry@annuity-bureau.co.uk

Website:
http://www.annuity-bureau.co.uk

Enquiries:
Enquiries to: Head of Marketing
Direct tel: 020 7902 2328
Direct fax: 020 7902 0388
Direct e-mail: david@bureauxltd.co.uk

Founded:
1991

Organisation type and purpose:
Service industry.

Subject coverage:
Financial service and advice at retirement.

Printed publications:
Income Drawdown (free)
You and Your Annuity (free)

Publications list:
Available online and in print

Access to staff:
Contact by letter, by telephone, by fax, by e-mail and via website
Hours: Mon to Fri, 0900 to 1700

Access for disabled people:
Parking provided, ramped entry

Northern Region Branch:
Annuity Bureau
Sunhill Laithe, Sunhill, Fleets Lane, Rystone, Skipton, BD23 6NA; tel: 01756 731 900; fax: 01756 730 443

ANTHROPOLOGY LIBRARY

British Museum Department of Ethnography, 6 Burlington Gardens, London, W1S 3EX

Tel: 020 7323 8031
Fax: 020 7323 8013

Website:
http://www.thebritishmuseum.ac.uk
http://lucy.ukc.ac.uk/AIO.html
The Index to the Anthropology Library's journal collection is available through Anthropological Index online, a free internet service.

Enquiries:
Enquiries to: Senior Librarian
Other contacts: Reading Room Supervisor for Reading Room enquiries, appointments, bibliographical information etc.

Formerly called:
British Museum Ethnography Library, Museum of Mankind Library (year of change 2001)

Organisation type and purpose:
National government body, museum.
The Anthropology Library is a major anthropological collection with its origins in the nineteenth century. It incorporates the former library of the Royal Anthropological Institute (RAI).

Subject coverage:
Its scope is worldwide and covers every aspect of anthropology: cultural anthropology, archaeology, some biological anthropology, linguistics, and related fields such as history, sociology and description and travel.
Material culture, ethnography, tribal art and anthropology of indigenous African, American, Asian, Oceanic and some European societies.
Archaeology of the New World.

Museum or gallery collection, archive, or library special collection:
Incorporates former library of the Royal Anthropological Institute
The library includes the Henry Christy and the Sir Eric Thompson collections and a significant Pictorial Collection
The collection contains around 120,000 books and pamphlets and 4000 journal titles (of which 1450 are current)

Library catalogue:
All or part available online

Access to staff:
Contact by letter, by telephone and by fax. Appointment necessary.
Hours: Mon to Fri, 0900 to 1700
Special comments: Visitors by prior appointment except Fellows and Junior Fellows of the RAI. Fellows and Junior Fellows of the RAI can borrow items donated by the RAI.
Other visitors and researchers may have access, by appointment, for reference purposes only.

Departmental library of the:
British Museum
currently housed in the former Museum of Mankind; tel: 020 7323 8031; fax: 020 7323 8013; e-mail: ethnography@thebritishmuseum.ac.uk

ANTHROPOSOPHICAL SOCIETY IN GREAT BRITAIN

Acronym or abbreviation: AS IN GB

Rudolf Steiner House, 35 Park Road, London, NW1 6XT

Tel: 020 7723 4400
Fax: 020 7724 4364

Website:
http://www.anth.org.uk
Anthroposophical Society; Rudolf Steiner Press Catalogue; Steiner Waldorf Education.

Enquiries:
Enquiries to: Librarian
Direct tel: 020 7224 8398
Direct fax: 020 7224 8398
Direct e-mail: rsh-library@anth.org.uk
Other contacts: Executive Secretary

Founded:
1923

Organisation type and purpose:
International organisation, learned society, registered charity (charity number 220480).

Subject coverage:
Anthroposophy (science of the spirit and the spiritual world); every field of art, science, religion, philosophy and social life from that aspect, including education, special needs education, medicine, agriculture and social sciences.

Museum or gallery collection, archive, or library special collection:
Art prints, photographs, archive material, eg: letters, journals
Books and MSS relating to Rudolf Steiner (1861–1925) and his work

Library catalogue:
All or part available in-house

Printed publications:
Catalogues of related publishers
Catalogue of Rudolf Steiner Press Publications
Information leaflets based on aspects of Steiner-based work
New View (magazine)
Rudolf Steiner House Programme (termly)

Electronic and video publications:
Small selection of videos

Access to staff:
Contact by letter, by telephone, by fax, by e-mail and in person
Hours: Office: 1030 to 1800
Bookshop: Mon to Fri, 1030 to 1400 and 1500 to 1800; Sat, 1030 to 1400 and 1500 to 1700

Library: Tue to Thu, 1100 to 1300 and 1400 to 1700 (Tue, 1930 term time); Fri, 1300 to 1800; Sat, 1200 to 1700

Associated with:
Anthroposophical Medical Association
tel: 01299 861561; fax: 01299 861375
Association of Camphill Communities
tel: 01653 694197; fax: 01653 600001; e-mail: info@camphill.org.uk
Bio-Dynamic Agricultural Association
tel: 01453 759501
Committee for Steiner Special Education
Emerson College (Forest Row)
tel: 01342 822238; fax: 01342 826055; e-mail: mail@emerson.org.uk
Peredur Centre for the Arts (Schools) of Eurhythmy and Speech Formation (East Grinstead)
Rudolf Steiner Press
Steiner Waldorf Schools Fellowship
tel: 01342 822115; fax: 01342 826004; e-mail: mail@waldorf.compulink.co.uk
Tobias School of Art (East Grinstead)
tel: 01342 313655; fax: 01342 313655
Triodos Bank (Bristol), and others
tel: 0117 973 9339; fax: 0117 973 9303

ANTI-SLAVERY INTERNATIONAL

Thomas Clarkson House, The Stableyard, Broomgrove Road, London, SW9 9TL

Tel: 020 7501 8920
Fax: 020 7738 4110
E-mail: antislavery@antislavery.org

Website:
http://www.antislavery.org
ASI website, with details of campaigns, news, resources (including the library, publications etc).
http://www.antislavery.org/breakingthesilence
UNESCO's Breaking the Silence free educational portal on the Transatlantic Slave Trade
http://www.recoveredhistories.org
A digital archive of 18th- and 19th-century literature on Transatlantic Enslavement.

Enquiries:
Enquiries to: Librarian
Direct tel: 020 7501 8939
Direct e-mail: j.howarth@antislavery.org

Founded:
1839

Organisation type and purpose:
Registered charity (charity number 1049160), research organisation.

Subject coverage:
Modern forms of slavery, child labour, child prostitution, indigenous peoples, domestic workers, child domestic workers, history of slavery, female genital mutilation, servile marriage, bonded labour, descent-based slavery, migrant labour, forced prostitution, child prostitution, codes of conduct, trafficking of people, Transatlantic Slave Trade, abolition, forced labour and the supply chain.

Museum or gallery collection, archive, or library special collection:
A collection of eighteenth- and nineteenth-century tracts on slavery including Transatlantic Slavery
Binns Collection and supplementary historical and slavery collection (also in microfilm)
Books, documents and research papers on modern forms of slavery
Collection of ILO publications on slavery
Collection of United Nations publications on slavery
Large collection of literature on child labour, bonded labour and trafficking
Slides and photography relevant to exploited labour including Congo atrocities c. 1900

Non-library collection catalogue:
All or part available in-house

Library catalogue:
All or part available in-house

continued overleaf

Printed publications:
Anti-Slavery Reporter (4 times a year, free to
members, subscription £25, annually)
Redefining Prostitution as Sex Work on the
International Agenda
Slavery in Sudan
The Cocoa Industry in West Africa: A history of
exploitation
The Migration-Trafficking Nexus: Combating
trafficking through the protection of migrants'
human rights
Arrested Development: Discrimination and slavery
in the 21st century
Voices of Child Domestic Workers
Forced Labour in North Korean Prison Camps
Women in Ritual Slavery in India
Trafficking for Forced Labour in Europe
Contemporary Forms of Slavery in Argentina,
Bolivia, Brazil, Paraguay, Peru and Uruguay
Order printed publications from: Publications Officer
tel: 020 7501 8922, fax: 020 7738 4110, e-mail: b
.shand@antislavery.org

Microform publications:
Aborigines Protection Society
Anti-Slavery Reporter 1825 to date
Binns Collection and supplementary historical and
slavery collection (microfilm from Academic
Microforms)
Annual Reports 1880–2000 and Publications and
Reports of Anti-Slavery International and
predecessors, 1880–1979 by Adam Matthews

Electronic and video publications:
The Changing Face of Slavery (video and teacher's
pack, £15)
Our News Our Views (video and teacher's pack,
£14)
Hell on Earth: Slavery today

Publications list:
Available online and in print

Access to staff:
Contact by letter, by telephone, by e-mail and via
website. Appointment necessary.
Hours: Mon to Fri, 1000 to 1700

Access to building, collection or gallery:
Hours: Mon to Fri, 1000 to 1700 by appointment

Member of:
End Child Prostitution, Pornography and
Trafficking (ECPAT, Ethical Trading Initiative (ETI)
Grosvenor Gardens House, 35–37 Grosvenor
Gardens, London, SW1W 0BS; tel: 020 7233 9887;
fax: 020 7233 9869; e-mail: info@ecpat.org.uk;
website: http://www.ecpat.org.uk

ANTIGUA AND BARBUDA TOURIST OFFICE

2nd floor, 45 Crawford Place, London, W1H 4LP

Tel: 020 7258 0070
Fax: 020 7258 3826
E-mail: tourisminfo@antigua-barbuda.com

Website:
http://www.antigua-barbuda.com

Enquiries:
Enquiries to: Director of Tourism

Organisation type and purpose:
To promote Antigua and Barbuda's tourist
industry.

Subject coverage:
History of the islands, tourism including:
weddings and honeymoons, water sports,
sightseeing, golf, tennis, maps, sailing, special
events, meetings and incentives, family holidays.

Trade and statistical information:
Tourism statistics.

Printed publications:
General information leaflets

Electronic and video publications:
CD-ROM, videos, available on loan
Slides available on Leonardo databank

Access to staff:
Contact by letter, by telephone, by fax, by e-mail,
in person and via website
Hours: Mon to Fri, 0930 to 1500
Special comments: Contact by telephone is from
0900 to 1700.

Links with:
Ministry of Tourism, Culture and Environment

ANTIQUARIAN BOOKSELLERS ASSOCIATION

Acronym or abbreviation: ABA

Sackville House, 40 Piccadilly, London, W1J 0DR

Tel: 020 7439 3118
Fax: 020 7439 3119
E-mail: admin@aba.org.uk

Website:
http://www.aba.org.uk

Enquiries:
Enquiries to: Administrator

Founded:
1906

Organisation type and purpose:
Trade association.

Printed publications:
List of members, with fields of specialisation

Access to staff:
Contact by letter, by telephone, by fax and by e-
mail
Hours: Mon to Fri, 0930 to 1730

Access to building, collection or gallery:
No access other than to staff

Affiliated to:
International League of Antiquarian Booksellers
website: http://www.ilab.org

ANTIQUARIAN HOROLOGICAL SOCIETY

Acronym or abbreviation: AHS

New House, High Street, Ticehurst, Wadhurst,
East Sussex, TN5 7AL

Tel: 01580 200155
Fax: 01580 201323
E-mail: secretary@ahsoc.demon.co.uk

Website:
http://www.ahsoc.demon.co.uk

Enquiries:
Enquiries to: Administrator

Founded:
1953

Organisation type and purpose:
Learned society, registered charity (charity number
260925).
Practises and promotes the study of antiquarian
horology and allied disciplines in 13 countries.

Subject coverage:
Promotes the study of clocks and watches, and the
history of time measurement in all its forms.

**Museum or gallery collection, archive, or library
special collection:**
Library is housed at the Guildhall Library, London

Printed publications:
Antiquarian Horology (quarterly)
Books on horology including:
Norfolk & Norwich Clocks & Clockmakers (Bird C
and Y, eds)
Suffolk Clocks & Clockmakers (Haggar and Miller)
The Clockmakers of Hertfordshire (Tyler E J)

Publications list:
Available online and in print

Access to staff:
Contact by letter, by telephone, by fax and by e-
mail
Hours: Mon to Fri, 0900 to 1700

ANTIQUE COLLECTORS' CLUB

Acronym or abbreviation: ACC

Sandy Lane, Old Martlesham, Woodbridge,
Suffolk, IP12 4SD

Tel: 01394 389950
Fax: 01394 389999
E-mail: sales@antique-acc.com

Website:
http://www.antique-acc.com

Enquiries:
Enquiries to: Marketing Director
Direct tel: 01394 389966
Direct e-mail: sarah.smye@antique-acc.com

Founded:
1966

Organisation type and purpose:
Publishing house.

Subject coverage:
Art, antiques, architecture, design, fashion,
gardens and gardening.

Printed publications:
Antique Collecting (10 times a year)
Guide to the Antique Shops of Britain (annually)
An extensive range of titles covering:
Jewellery
Textiles
Horology
Glass
Art Reference, etc.

Publications list:
Available online and in print

Access to staff:
Contact by letter, by telephone, by fax, by e-mail
and in person
Hours: Mon to Fri, 0900 to 1730

Also at:
Antique Collectors' Club
5 Church Street, Woodbridge, Suffolk, IP12 1DS;
tel: 01394 385501; fax: 01394 384434

ANTRIM COURT SERVICE

30 Castle Way, Antrim, BT41 4AQ

Tel: 028 94 462661
Fax: 028 94 463301
E-mail: antrimcourthouse@courtsni.gov.uk

Enquiries:
Enquiries to: The Clerk of Petty Sessions

Formerly called:
Northern Ireland Court Service

Organisation type and purpose:
National government body.

Access for disabled people:
Parking provided, access to all public areas, toilet
facilities

ANXIETY UK

Zion CRC, 339 Stretford Road, Hulme,
Manchester, M15 4ZY

Tel: 0844 477 5774
Fax: 0161 226 7727
E-mail: info@anxietyuk.org.uk

Website:
http://www.anxietyuk.org.uk
National anxiety disorders charity.

Enquiries:
Enquiries to: Chief Executive

Founded:
1970

Formerly called:
National Phobics Society

Organisation type and purpose:
Registered charity, voluntary organisation (charity
number 1113403).

Subject coverage:
Anxiety disorders, of which there are over 400 classifications, and specific help for those suffering from anxiety disorders, i.e. phobias, agoraphobia, obsessional and compulsive disorders; depression; help for people with tranquillisers – withdrawal and/or addiction; panic attacks; Body Dysmorphic Disorder; social phobia; Generalised Anxiety Disorder (GAD).

Printed publications:
Bibliographies and self-help papers
Clinical Hypnotherapy
Contacts lists
Fact sheets
Network of Self-help Groups
Person-Centred Counselling
Quarterly magazine: Anxious Times
Cognitive Behavioural Therapy
Complementary Therapies

Publications list:
Available online and in print

Access to staff:
Contact by letter, by telephone, by fax, by e-mail, in person and via website. Appointment necessary. Access for members only. Non-members charged.
Hours: Mon to Fri, 0930 to 2100; message service outside office hours
Special comments: When corresponding by letter, please enclose an sae.

Access for disabled people:
Access to all public areas

APEX TRUST

Formal name: Apex Charitable Trust Limited

7th Floor, 3 London Wall Buildings, London Wall, London EC2M 5PD

Tel: 020 7638 5931
Fax: 020 7638 5977
E-mail: jobcheck@apextrust.com

Website:
http://www.apextrust.com
Full description of the work of the Apex Trust – mission, services, operation, staff profiles, publications, how to make donations.

Enquiries:
Enquiries to: Chief Executive

Founded:
1965

Organisation type and purpose:
National organisation, registered charity (charity number 284736).
The Trust aims to reduce overall crime in society by the appropriate employment of people with a criminal record; by operating 28 projects in prisons and the community giving direct advice to ex-offenders; by raising this issue with employers; and by working with other statutory and voluntary organisations in raising this issue.

Subject coverage:
Employment of ex-offenders; placing techniques; social skills training; careers advice; training in probation and after-care service, social services and prison service; attitudes and policies of professional bodies; unemployment and crime.

Museum or gallery collection, archive, or library special collection:
No library or collections

Printed publications:
Apex Fidelity Bond (free)
People Management (£1 plus 70p per copy p&p)
Releasing the Potential (£2.50 plus 70p per copy p&p)
Straight for Work (£3.50 plus 70p per copy p&p)
Work Matters (£3.50 plus 70p per copy p&p)

Publications list:
Available online and in print

Access to staff:
Contact by letter, by telephone, by fax, by e-mail and via website. Appointment necessary.

Hours: Mon to Fri, 1000 to 1800

Access to building, collection or gallery:
Prior appointment required
Hours: Mon to Fri, 1000 to 1800

APOSTROPHE PROTECTION SOCIETY

Acronym or abbreviation: APS

23 Vauxhall Road, Boston, Lincolnshire, PE21 0JB

Tel: 01205 350056
E-mail: john.richards2@virgin.net

Enquiries:
Enquiries to: Chairman

Founded:
2001

Organisation type and purpose:
Voluntary organisation.
To urge the correct use of the apostrophe and to give advice.

Subject coverage:
Correct use of the apostrophe.

Access to staff:
Contact by letter and by e-mail
Hours: Mon to Fri, 0900 to 1700

APPLIED ARTS SCOTLAND

ECA, School of Design and Applied Arts, Hunter Building, Lauriston Place, Edinburgh, EH3 9DF

Tel: 0131 221 6143
E-mail: office@appliedartsscotland.org.uk

Enquiries:
Enquiries to: Administrator
Other contacts: Convenor for policy matters.

Founded:
1992

Formerly called:
Association for Applied Arts (AAS) (year of change 2000)

Organisation type and purpose:
Membership association (membership is by subscription), present number of members: 300, voluntary organisation, registered charity (charity number SCO 22604).
To promote contemporary applied arts produced in Scotland.

Subject coverage:
Applied Arts Scotland holds a commissioning register of slides and information from around 300 makers in Scotland. They offer a commissioning service to public and private companies, galleries, retail outlets etc.

Printed publications:
The Bulletin (monthly)

Publications list:
Available in print

Access to staff:
Contact by letter, by telephone and by e-mail.
Access for members only. Non-members charged.
Hours: Mon, 0930 to 1730

Access to building, collection or gallery:
No prior appointment required
Special comments: Commissioning register.

ARAB HORSE SOCIETY

Acronym or abbreviation: AHS

Windsor House, The Square, Ramsbury, Marlborough, Wiltshire, SN8 2PE

Tel: 01672 520782
Fax: 01672 520880

Enquiries:
Enquiries to: Honorary Secretary
Direct tel: 01323 811385
Direct fax: 01323 811533

Direct e-mail: jean-mary.crozier@virgin.net

Founded:
1918

Organisation type and purpose:
Membership association (membership is by subscription), present number of members: 3950, registered charity (charity number 213366).
Breeding of Arabian horse and its derivatives, horse shows, amateur flat racing.

Subject coverage:
Stud book and race records for Arab, Anglo-Arab and part bred Arab horses.

Museum or gallery collection, archive, or library special collection:
Library mainly on breed stud books from 1918 when the Society was founded

Trade and statistical information:
World data on Arab horse registration.

Printed publications:
Journal (2 times a year, free to members)
Newsletter (3 times a year, free to members)

Access to staff:
Contact by letter, by telephone, by fax, by e-mail and in person
Hours: Mon to Fri, 0900 to 1700

Access to building, collection or gallery:
No prior appointment required

Affiliated to:
British Horse Society
ECAHO
WAHO

ARAB WORLD DOCUMENTATION UNIT

Acronym or abbreviation: AWDU

IAIS Building, Exeter University, Stocker Road, Exeter, Devon, EX4 4ND

Tel: 01392 264041
Fax: 01392 264035
E-mail: awdu@exeter.ac.uk

Website:
http://www.library.ex.ac.uk/awdu/bombaydiaries.htm
Descriptive listing of the extracts from the Bombay Diaries held at the centre.
http://www.library.ex.ac.uk/awdu
Introduction to the Arab World Documentation Unit and summary of holdings.
http://www.library.ex.ac.uk/awdu/KeyTitlesList.html
Key Titles List: a detailed catalogue of major holdings.
http://lib.exeter.ac.uk
University of Exeter Library online catalogue.

Enquiries:
Enquiries to: AWDU Librarian
Direct tel: 01392 264051
Direct e-mail: j.p.c.auchterlonie@exeter.ac.uk
Other contacts: Library Assistant (AWDU)

Founded:
1979

Formerly called:
Centre for Arab Gulf Studies Documentation Unit (CAGS) (year of change 2001)

Organisation type and purpose:
University library, research organisation.
Reference and research library; documentation unit.
To further the study of the Gulf and Arabian Peninsula region, Arab countries and other Middle East topics.

Subject coverage:
Arab Countries, especially Arabian Peninsula and Gulf region; current documentation (often including back-runs to the mid-20th century) with emphasis on statistical material, economic reports, development plans, etc. from governments and official sources including international

continued overleaf

organisations, commercial sources such as banks, monetary agencies, commerce and industry, and academic and political sources and news media. History of the region, 16th to 20th century, including published, microform and photocopied archives.

Middle East studies: especially economic, political and sociological. Palestine and the Arab–Israeli Conflict.

International petroleum studies.

Museum or gallery collection, archive, or library special collection:
Archives held as photocopies or films:
Bombay Archives 1780–1830 (15,000 pages selected for relevance to the Gulf, Red Sea and Arabian Peninsula region, with typed transcripts and detailed index (this collection is unique, being the only copy in Europe)
Some Portuguese archives of the region 1560–1752
French consular correspondence on Muscat 1783–1810
Relevant selections from the National Archives of USA, National Archives of India, UK Foreign Office and India Office records 1800–1959
Microfiche edition Palestine: the British Mandate
Published books from Archive Editions of the region
A substantial library on Palestine, Israel and the Arab–Israeli conflict, including governmental, international, commercial, academic and political publications, plus unpublished and archival materials and research documentation, e.g. papers on Arrabeh 1850–1950
Press cuttings: classified microfiche collection on the Middle East 1957–82
CAABU collection of press cuttings on the Arab World 1968–2001
BBC Summary of World Broadasts for the Middle East in hard copy or microfiche, 1955–2001
Videos and DVDs of Arab feature films (mainly Egyptian), Iranian feature films and some documentaries on the Middle East
Large collection of modern maps on the Middle East

Trade and statistical information:
Trade information for countries of the region and regional trade (Middle East).
Statistical information, on every aspect of the countries and the Middle East region. Primary countries covered: Bahrain, Iraq, Kuwait, Oman, Saudi Arabia, UAE, Yemen, Iran, Palestine, Israel, (also Lebanon, Jordan, Syria and Egypt).

Non-library collection catalogue:
All or part available online

Library catalogue:
All or part available online

Access to staff:
Contact by letter, by telephone, by fax, by e-mail, in person and via website
Hours: Mon to Fri, 0900 to 1700
Special comments: A prior appointment for visitors is essential.

Access for disabled people:
Parking provided, level entry, toilet facilities

Parent body:
Exeter University Library
Stocker Road, Exeter, EX4 4PT; tel: 01392 264051; fax: 01392 263871; website: http://as.exeter.ac.uk/library

ARBORICULTURAL ASSOCIATION

Acronym or abbreviation: AA

Ampfield House, Winchester Road, Ampfield, Romsey, Hampshire, SO51 9PA

Tel: 01794 368717
Fax: 01794 368978
E-mail: admin@trees.org.uk

Website:
http://www.trees.org.uk

Enquiries:
Enquiries to: Chief Executive

Founded:
1964

Incorporates the former:
Association of British Tree Surgeons and Arborists

Organisation type and purpose:
National organisation, professional body, membership association (membership is by subscription), present number of members: 2000, registered charity.
To advance the science of arboriculture for the public benefit.

Subject coverage:
Production, selection, planning and maintenance of ornamental trees, shrubs and amenity woodlands; tree surveys, inspection, pathology; legal matters.

Non-library collection catalogue:
All or part available online

Printed publications:
Arboricultural Journal (quarterly)
Directories of Registered Consultants and Approved Contractors
Newsletter (4 times a year)
A Guide to Tree Pruning
Tree Survey and Inspection
A Guide to Good Climbing Practice
Twelve Leaflets to be purchased as a set, including:
Trees Suitable for Small Gardens
A Guide to Tree Planting
Trees, Subsidence, and other Structural Damage (A Householder's Guide)
Guide to the Use of MEWPs in Arboriculture
Order printed publications from: Postal address

Publications list:
Available online and in print

Access to staff:
Contact by letter, by telephone, by fax, by e-mail and via website
Hours: Mon to Fri, 0900 to 1700

Access to building, collection or gallery:
No prior appointment required

Access for disabled people:
Parking provided

Has:
8 regional branches

ARC

Formal name: Association for Real Change

ARC House, Marsden Street, Chesterfield, Derbyshire, S40 1JY

Tel: 01246 555043
Fax: 01246 555045
E-mail: contact.us@arcuk.org.uk

Website:
http://www.arcuk.org.uk

Enquiries:
Enquiries to: Chief Executive

Founded:
1976

Formerly called:
Association of Residential Communities

Organisation type and purpose:
Professional body (membership is by subscription), present number of members: 300 organisations, voluntary organisation, registered charity (charity number 285575), training organisation, publishing house.

Subject coverage:
Learning disability (mental handicap), social care, vocational training in health and social care, management, sexual abuse.

Non-library collection catalogue:
All or part available in-house and in print

Publications list:
Available online

Access to staff:
Contact by letter, by telephone, by fax, by e-mail and via website. Appointment necessary.
Hours: Mon to Fri, 0900 to 1700

Access to building, collection or gallery:
No prior appointment required
Hours: Mon to Fri, 0900 to 1700
Special comments: Library, members only.

Also at:
ARC Cymru
Unit 3A, MENTEC, Deiniol Road, Bangor, LL57 2UP; tel: 01248 361990
ARC Northern Ireland
43 Marsden Gardens, Cave Hill, Belfast, BT15 5AL; tel: 028 9022 9020; fax: 028 9020 9300; e-mail: arc.ni@arcuk.org.uk
ARC Scotland
Unit 13, Hardengreen Business Centre, Eskbank, Dalkeith, Midlothian, EH22 3NX; tel: 0131 663 4444; fax: 0131 663 5522; e-mail: arc.scotland@arcuk.org.uk
ARC Training Consortium
ARC House, Marsden Street, Chesterfield, Derbyshire, S40 1JY; tel: 01246 564970; fax: 01246 55504; e-mail: consortium@arcuk.org.uk

ARC ANTENATAL RESULTS & CHOICES

Acronym or abbreviation: ARC

73 Charlotte Street, London, W1P 1LB

Tel: 020 7631 0280
Fax: 020 7631 0280
E-mail: info@arc-uk.org

Website:
http://www.arc.uk.org

Enquiries:
Enquiries to: Director

Founded:
1988

Formerly called:
Support Around Termination for Abnormality (SATFA) (year of change 1998)

Organisation type and purpose:
Membership association, present number of members: 1,400, voluntary organisation, registered charity (charity number 299770).

Subject coverage:
Helping parents through antenatal testing, decision-making, offering continued support to parents whatever decision they make about the future of the pregnancy, training of health care professionals to provide appropriate services.

Printed publications:
Another Pregnancy
Help for Fathers
Help for Grandparents
Talking to Children
Parents' Handbook – Support Around Termination For Abnormality
Parents' Handbook – Continuing a pregnancy after the diagnosis of an abnormality
ARC Information leaflet
ARC News
Supporting Parents' Decisions

Publications list:
Available online and in print

Access to staff:
Contact by letter, by telephone, by fax, by e-mail and in person. Appointment necessary.
Hours: Mon to Fri, 1000 to 1700

ARCHAEOLOGY SCOTLAND

Formal name: Council for Scottish Archaeology
Acronym or abbreviation: CSA

Causewayside House, 160 Causewayside, Edinburgh, EH9 1PR

Tel: 0131 668 4189

Fax: 0131 668 4275
E-mail: info@scottisharchaeology.org.uk

Website:
http://www.scottisharchaeology.org.uk

Enquiries:
Enquiries to: Director
Other contacts: Assistant Director for co-ordinator of Young Archaeologists' Club Scottish network

Founded:
1944

Formerly called:
The Council for British Archaeology Scotland (CBA Scotland)

Organisation type and purpose:
National organisation, membership association (membership is by subscription), present number of members: c. 900, voluntary organisation, registered charity (charity no. SCO 001723), suitable for ages: 8 to 16.
To promote informed opinion concerning the conservation of Scotland's archaeological heritage.

Subject coverage:
Archaeology, including education, careers, excavations, sources of information on sites, cultural resource management and integrated environmental approaches, who to contact in other bodies etc.

Museum or gallery collection, archive, or library special collection:
Inventory of the Scottish Church Heritage – A database of all sites in Scotland and how to access further details

Printed publications:
Discovery & Excavation in Scotland (annually, some out of print)
Scottish Archaeological News (3 times a year)

Publications list:
Available in print

Access to staff:
Contact by letter, by telephone and by fax.
Appointment necessary.
Hours: Mon to Fri, 0900 to 1700

Sister body of the:
Council for British Archaeology

ARCHDEACON SHARP LIBRARY

The College, Durham, DH1 3EH

Tel: 0191 386 2489
Fax: 0191 386 4267 (Durham Chapter Office)
E-mail: library@durhamcathedral.co.uk

Enquiries:
Enquiries to: Assistant Librarian

Organisation type and purpose:
Theological library.
A library of modern theology in English.

Subject coverage:
Theology : 20th century printed theology in English.

Non-library collection catalogue:
All or part available online

Library catalogue:
All or part available online

Access to staff:
Contact by letter, by telephone, by e-mail and in person
Hours: Mon to Fri, 0900 to 1300 and 1400 to 1700
Special comments: Closed for first two weeks of July.

Parent body:
Trustees of Lord Crewe's Charities
c/o Chapter Clerk, Durham Cathedral, The College, Durham, DH1 3EH; tel: 0191 386 4266; fax: 0191 386 4267

ARCHERY GB

Lilleshall National Sports Centre, Near Newport, Shropshire, TF10 9AT

Tel: 01952 677888
Fax: 01952 606019
E-mail: enquiries@archerygb.org

Website:
http://www.archerygb.org

Enquiries:
Enquiries to: Enquiries Officer

Founded:
1861

Formerly called:
Grand National Archery Society (year of change 2008)

Organisation type and purpose:
Membership association (membership is by subscription), present number of members: 30,000.
Governing body for the sport of archery in the United Kingdom.

Subject coverage:
Target archery; field archery; clout and flight shooting; coaching; addresses of UK Clubs and of overseas associations.

Museum or gallery collection, archive, or library special collection:
Archers Register 1864–1915
Colonel Walrond Photographs Collection

Printed publications:
Archery UK (quarterly, free to members)
Does Fitness Count
Principles of Practice and Preparation for Tournaments

Electronic and video publications:
Coaching DVD

Access to staff:
Contact by letter, by telephone, by fax and by e-mail
Hours: Mon to Fri, 0900 to 1700

Member organisation of:
AAS
tel: 01295 721463
British Olympic Association
tel: 020 8871 2677; fax: 020 8871 9104
Central Council of Physical Recreation
tel: 020 7828 3163; fax: 020 7630 8820
English Federation of Disability Sport
tel: 0161 247 5294; fax: 0161 247 6895
Fédération Internationale de Tir à l'Arc (FITA)
tel: + 4121 614 3050; fax: + 4121 614 3055

ARCHIFDY CEREDIGION ARCHIVES

County Offices, Marine Terrace, Aberystwyth, Ceredigion, SY23 2DE

Tel: 01970 633697/8
Fax: 01970 633663 (Attention: Archives)
E-mail: archives@ceredigion.gov.uk

Enquiries:
Enquiries to: Archivist

Founded:
1974

Formerly called:
Dyfed Archives; Cardiganshire Record Office (year of change 1996)

Organisation type and purpose:
Local government body.

Subject coverage:
Historical information, often in manuscript form, concerning the County of Ceredigion, formerly Cardiganshire.

Access to staff:
Contact by letter, by telephone, by fax, by e-mail and in person
Hours: Mon to Fri, 1000 to 1300 and 1400 to 1600

Access for disabled people:
Toilet facilities
Special comments: Disability lift and separate entrance.

ARCHIFDY MEIRIONNYDD ARCHIVES

Ffordd y Bala, Dolgellau, Gwynedd, LL40 2YF

Tel: 01341 424681/424682
Fax: 01341 424683
E-mail: archives.dolgellau@gwynedd.gov.uk

Website:
http://www.gwynedd.gov.uk/Archives

Enquiries:
Enquiries to: Area Archivist

Organisation type and purpose:
Local government body.

Subject coverage:
Local history.

Non-library collection catalogue:
All or part available online and in-house

Library catalogue:
All or part available in-house

Access to staff:
Contact by letter, by telephone, by fax, by e-mail and in person
Hours: Wed closed
Special comments: Closed first full week in November.

ARCHITECTS REGISTRATION BOARD

Acronym or abbreviation: ARB

8 Weymouth Street, London, W1W 5BU

Tel: 020 7580 5861
Fax: 020 7436 5269
E-mail: info@arb.org.uk

Website:
http://www.arb.org.uk

Enquiries:
Enquiries to: Policy Adviser
Direct e-mail: suey@arb.org.uk

Founded:
1997

Formerly called:
Architects Registration Council of the United Kingdom (ARCUK) (year of change 1997)

Organisation type and purpose:
Statutory body.
UK statutory regulator of the architects' profession.

Printed publications:
Register of Architects (for purchase)

Publications list:
Available in print

Access to staff:
Contact by letter, by telephone, by fax and by e-mail
Hours: Mon to Fri, 0900 to 1700

Access for disabled people:
Ramped entry, toilet facilities

ARCHITECTURAL AND SPECIALIST DOOR MANUFACTURERS ASSOCIATION

Acronym or abbreviation: ASDMA

3 Coates Lane, High Wycombe, Buckinghamshire, HP13 5EY

Tel: 01494 447370
E-mail: specialdoors@gmail.com

Website:
http://www.asdma.com

continued overleaf

List of members and free download of publications.

Enquiries:
Enquiries to: General Secretary

Founded:
1989

Organisation type and purpose:
Trade association (membership is by qualification, election or invitation), present number of members: 14 full, 7 associate, 2 sponsoring.
To promote the use of and correct fitting of specialist timber doorsets, through the adoption of quality and BS Standards, and fair conditions of contract.

Subject coverage:
Specialist timber doors, particularly fire, smoke, security and sound-attenuating.

Printed publications:
Members' list – free

Access to staff:
Contact by letter, by telephone and by e-mail
Hours: Mon to Fri, 0900 to 1700

ARCHITECTURAL ASSOCIATION

Acronym or abbreviation: AA

34–36 Bedford Square, London, WC1B 3ES

Tel: 020 7887 4035
Fax: 020 7414 0782
E-mail: hsklar@aaschool.ac.uk

Website:
http://www.aaschool.ac.uk
Main address for the AA; links to pages for the library, photo library and publications.

Enquiries:
Enquiries to: Librarian
Direct tel: 020 7887 4035
Direct e-mail: hsklar@aaschool.ac.uk
Other contacts: Deputy Librarian; Archivist

Founded:
1847

Organisation type and purpose:
Professional body, membership association (membership is by subscription).
School of architecture.

Subject coverage:
Architecture, building, planning, landscape design.

Museum or gallery collection, archive, or library special collection:
AA Archives
Early works on architecture
History of the Association
Material on the Architectural Association from 1847 onwards
Material on the Modern Movement
Rare and early works on architecture

Non-library collection catalogue:
All or part available online

Library catalogue:
All or part available online

Printed publications:
AA Association/School of Architecture:
AA Files
AA School of Architecture Prospectus (annually)
AArchitecture (irregular)
Projects Review (annually)
School of Architecture Projects Review (annually)
Various monograph publications (annually)
AA Library:
Online bibliographies
Guide to the Library
AA Slide Library:
History of the Slide Library
Introduction to the Slide Library
Order printed publications from: Publications, Architectural Association

Publications list:
Available online and in print

Access to staff:
Access for members only. Non-members charged.
Hours: Term time: Mon to Fri, 1000 to 2100; Sat, 1100 to 1700
Vacations: 1000 to 1800
Special comments: Closed August to mid-September.

Constituent bodies:
AA Photo Library

ARCHITECTURAL CLADDING ASSOCIATION

Acronym or abbreviation: ACA

60 Charles Street, Leicester, LE1 1FB

Tel: 0116 253 6161
Fax: 0116 251 4568
E-mail: aca@britishprecast.org

Website:
http://www.britishprecast.org

Enquiries:
Enquiries to: Secretary

Organisation type and purpose:
Trade association.

Subject coverage:
Precast concrete architectural cladding.

Printed publications:
Cast in Concrete: reconstructed stone and precast concrete – a guide for architects (£25)
Code of Practice for the Safe Erection of Precast Concrete Cladding (£25)
Façade (newsletter)

Access to staff:
Contact by letter, by telephone, by fax and by e-mail
Hours: Mon to Fri, 0900 to 1700

Product association of the:
British Precast Concrete Federation

ARCHITECTURAL GLAZING SERVICES

Acronym or abbreviation: AGS

PO Box 2210, London, W1A 1WF

Tel: 0800 028 3708
Fax: 020 7535 5676
E-mail: info@cobaltco.co.uk

Website:
http://www.vanceva.com

Enquiries:
Enquiries to: Information Officer
Direct tel: 020 7535 5678
Direct e-mail: wendy@cobaltco.co.uk

Founded:
October 2001

Incorporated:
Laminated Glass Information Centre (formed in 1990) (LGIC), date of change, October 2001

Organisation type and purpose:
Private venture information centre, sponsored by Solutia SA/NV.
To offer advice to architects, specifiers, trade and industry, media and general public.

Subject coverage:
Safety, security, acoustic, solar-resistant laminated glass, also coloured and patterned laminated glass, laminated glass. Available in automotive and architectural sectors.

Printed publications:
Bulletin
Factsheets on regulations, safety, security etc
Questions and Answers on Laminated Glass

Electronic and video publications:
Variety of information (CD-ROM)

Publications list:
Available in print

Access to staff:
Contact by letter, by telephone, by fax and by e-mail
Hours: Mon to Fri, 0900 to 1700

Access to building, collection or gallery:
No access other than to staff

ARCHITECTURAL HERITAGE FUND

Acronym or abbreviation: AHF

Alhambra House, 27–31 Charing Cross Road, London, WC2H 0AU

Tel: 020 7925 0199
Fax: 020 7930 0295
E-mail: ahf@ahfund.org.uk

Website:
http://www.ahfund.org.uk
Details of services and publications available along with historical objects and activities.

Founded:
1976

Organisation type and purpose:
Registered charity (number 266780).
To promote the conservation of historic buildings in the United Kingdom for beneficial new use by providing advice, information and financial assistance in the form of grants and low-interest working capital loans for projects undertaken by building preservation trusts and other suitable charities. The AHF cannot assist private individuals.

Subject coverage:
The permanent preservation of buildings that are listed, scheduled or in a conservation area and of acknowledged historic merit. Projects must involve a change either in the ownership of a property or its use.

Museum or gallery collection, archive, or library special collection:
Back issues of own publications

Printed publications:
Annual Review (for sale)
How to Rescue a Ruin – by setting up a Buildings Preservation Trust (1997, for sale)

Electronic and video publications:
Standard Governing Documents for a Buildings Preservation Trust

Publications list:
Available in print

Access to staff:
Contact by letter, by telephone, by fax and by e-mail. Appointment necessary.
Hours: Mon to Fri, 0900 to 1700

Access to building, collection or gallery:
Mon to Fri, 0900 to 1700

Links with:
UK Association of Preservation Trusts (APT)
Alhambra House, 27–31 Charing Cross Road, London, WC2H 0AU; tel: 020 7930 1629; fax: 020 7930 0295; e-mail: apt@ahfund.org.uk; website: http://www.ukapt.org.uk

ARCHITECTURAL HERITAGE SOCIETY OF SCOTLAND

Acronym or abbreviation: AHSS

The Glasite Meeting House, 33 Barony Street, Edinburgh, EH3 6NX

Tel: 0131 557 0019
Fax: 0131 557 0049
E-mail: nationaloffice@ahss.org.uk

Website:
http://www.ahss.org.uk

Formerly called:
Scottish Georgian Society

Organisation type and purpose:
Learned society (membership is by subscription), present number of members: 1,100, voluntary organisation, registered charity (charity number SCO 07554) and registered as a company limited by guarantee (SC356726).
The Society exists to promote the study and protection of Scottish architecture.

Subject coverage:
Architectural conservation and history, planning for listed buildings, protection of the built environment, heritage.

Printed publications:
Architectural Heritage (journal, annually, free to members, price varies, c. £20)
Magazine (2 times a year, free to members)

Access to staff:
Contact by letter, by telephone, by fax, by e-mail and via website. Appointment necessary.
Hours: Mon to Fri, 0900 to 1700

ARCHITECTURE AND SURVEYING INSTITUTE

Acronym or abbreviation: ASI

St Mary House, 15 St Mary Street, Chippenham, Wiltshire, SN15 3WD

Tel: 01249 444505
Fax: 01249 443602
E-mail: mail@asi.org.uk

Website:
http://www.asi.org.uk

Enquiries:
Enquiries to: Chief Executive

Founded:
1926

Amalgated with the:
Guild of Incorporated Surveyors (GIS), date of change, October 1999

Formerly called:
Architects and Surveyors Institute (ASI), Construction Surveyors Institute (CSI), Faculty of Architects and Surveyors (FAS)

Organisation type and purpose:
International organisation, professional body (membership is by subscription, qualification), present number of members: 5500, service industry, suitable for ages: all.
To promote and extend the practice, knowledge and study of architecture and surveying.

Subject coverage:
Architecture, surveying, building contracts and associated documentation, careers, examinations.

Printed publications:
ASI Journal (6 times a year, free to members, others on subscription)
Build Safe (An Aid to C.D.M.)
Contract Administration Forms
Contract Documents
European Single Market: Matters Affecting the Construction Industry
Newsletters (ad hoc)
Private Practice Register
Order printed publications from: ASI Services Limited, St Mary House, 15 St Mary Street, Chippenham, Wiltshire, SN15 3JN, tel: 01249 658262, fax: 01249 443602, e-mail: asinst@aol.com

Publications list:
Available in print

Access to staff:
Contact by letter, by telephone, by fax and by e-mail. Appointment necessary.
Hours: Mon to Fri, 0930 to 1600

Member of:
Construction Industry Council
Construction Industry Standing Conference
European Group of Surveyors

Subsidiary body:
ASI Services Limited

ARCHITECTURE FOUNDATION

60 Bastwick Street, London, EC1V 3TN

Tel: 020 7253 3334
Fax: 020 7253 3335
E-mail: mail@architecturefoundation.org.uk

Website:
http://www.architecturefoundation.org.uk

Enquiries:
Enquiries to: Press and PR Co-ordinator
Direct e-mail: claire@architecturefoundation.org.uk

Founded:
1991

Organisation type and purpose:
Membership association (membership is by subscription), present number of members: 150, voluntary organisation, registered charity (charity number 1006361), suitable for ages: all, research organisation.

Access to staff:
Contact by letter, by telephone, by e-mail and via website. Appointment necessary.
Hours: Tue to Sun, 1200 to 1800

Access for disabled people:
Ramped entry, toilet facilities

ARCHITECTURE+DESIGN SCOTLAND

Acronym or abbreviation: A+DS

Bakehouse Close, 146 Canongate, Edinburgh, EH8 8DD

Tel: 0131 556 6699
Fax: 0131 556 6633
E-mail: info@ads.org.uk

Website:
http://www.ads.org.uk/

Founded:
1927

Organisation type and purpose:
To promote good architecture, design and planning in Scotland's built environment.

Subject coverage:
Planning, design of building, urban environment, architecture, all aspects of planning and design of the environment.

Non-library collection catalogue:
All or part available online

Library catalogue:
All or part available online

Access to staff:
Contact by letter, by fax and by e-mail
Hours: Mon to Fri, 0900 to 1700

Access for disabled people:
Level entry, toilet facilities
Special comments: Ground floor only.

Sponsoring department:
Scottish Executive Education Department (SEED)

ARCHIVE OF ART AND DESIGN

Acronym or abbreviation: AAD

Word and Image Department, Victoria and Albert Museum, 23 Blythe Road, London, W14 0QX

Tel: 020 7602 7493
Fax: 020 7602 0980
E-mail: archive@vam.ac.uk

Website:
http://www.vam.ac.uk/resources/archives

Enquiries:
Enquiries to: Archivist

Founded:
1978

Organisation type and purpose:
Museum.

Archive collection of principally 20th-century archives of designers, design associations and companies involved in the design process.

Subject coverage:
British design, design, graphic design, product design, illustration, textiles, fashion, ephemera.

Museum or gallery collection, archive, or library special collection:
Over 250 archives, including:
Krazy Kat Arkive of 20th-century popular culture
Papers of individual designers, craftspeople and artists
Heal & Son Ltd, bedding and furniture manufacturers and retailers
Edward Barnard & Sons Ltd, silversmiths
Art and Crafts Exhibition Society
John French, fashion photographer
Eileen Gray, interior and furniture designer and architect
Ambassador, the British export magazine for textiles and fashion

Non-library collection catalogue:
All or part available online and in-house

Library catalogue:
All or part available online

Printed publications:
Cumulative list of titles of the archive groups collected by the Archive from 1978 to August 1991 (published in Journal of Design History vol. 4, no. 4, 1991 pp. 2558)
Annual returns and updates
Guide to the Archive of Art and Design, Victoria & Albert Museum (2001, £45)
Order printed publications from: Fitzroy Dearborn Publishers, 310 Regent Street, London, W1B 3AX
Publications Department, V & A Museum, South Kensington, SW7 2RL; tel. 020 7942 2000

Publications list:
Available in print

Access to staff:
Contact by letter, by telephone, by fax and by e-mail. Appointment necessary.
Hours: Tue to Fri, 1000 to 1630

Access to building, collection or gallery:
Prior appointment required
Hours: Tue to Fri, 1000 to 1630
Special comments: Reference only.

Constituent part of:
Victoria and Albert Museum's Word and Image Department

Links with:
Artists' Papers Register
website: http://www.apr.ac.uk
National Register of Archives

ARCHIVES AND RECORDS ASSOCIATION

Acronym or abbreviation: ARA

Prioryfield House, 20 Canon Street, Taunton, Somerset, TA1 1SW

Tel: 01823 327030
Fax: 01823 271719
E-mail: ara@archives.org.uk

Website:
http://www.archives.org.uk

Founded:
1947

Created by the merger of:
National Council on Archives, Society of Archivists, and Association of Chief Archivists in Local Government (year of change 2010)

Organisation type and purpose:
Principal professional body for archivists, archive conservators and records managers in the United Kingdom and Ireland.

continued overleaf

To promote the care and preservation of archives and the better administration of archive repositories; to advance the training of its members; and to encourage relevant research and publication.

Subject coverage:
Archives, records management, archives conservation.

Publications list:
Available online and in print

Access to staff:
Contact by letter, by telephone, by fax, by e-mail and via website. Appointment necessary.
Hours: Mon to Fri, 0830 to 1630

Member organisation of:
International Council on Archives

ARCHIVES AND SPECIAL COLLECTIONS, ANDERSONIAN LIBRARY, UNIVERSITY OF STRATHCLYDE

Andersonian Library, Curran Building, 101 St James Road, Glasgow, G4 0NS

Tel: 0141 548 2497
E-mail: archives@strath.ac.uk

Website:
http://www.strath.ac.uk/archives

Enquiries:
Enquiries to: University Archivist

Founded:
1796

Organisation type and purpose:
University department or institute.

Subject coverage:
Official records of the University of Strathclyde and its antecedents, plus deposited collections.

Museum or gallery collection, archive, or library special collection:
Institutional archives of the University of Strathclyde and its antecedent institutions back to 1796
Institutional archives of Jordanhill College and its antecedent institutions back to 1828
Other, deposited, archival collections, such as Patrick Geddes Papers

Non-library collection catalogue:
All or part available online and in-house

Printed publications:
Catalogue of the Papers of Sir Patrick Geddes
Order printed publications from: University Archivist

Access to staff:
Contact by letter, by telephone, by e-mail, in person and via website
Hours: Mon to Fri, 0900 to 1700

Access to building, collection or gallery:
Hours: Mon to Fri, 0900 to 1700

Access for disabled people:
Lift

ARG EUROPE LIMITED

Unit 2, 58a Alexandra Road, Ponders End, Enfield, Middlesex, EN3 7EH

Tel: 020 8804 8008
Fax: 020 8805 7600
E-mail: enquiries@arggroup.org

Website:
http://www.asbestos-removal.co.uk
All aspects of work carried out by the company.

Enquiries:
Enquiries to: Managing Director

Founded:
1984

Formerly called:
Asbestos Removal (Groves) Limited (year of change 1997)

Organisation type and purpose:
Service industry.
Asbestos removal, asbestos surveys.

Subject coverage:
Asbestos in buildings, advice on treatment, removal and identification. Asbestos surveys.

Non-library collection catalogue:
All or part available in-house

Library catalogue:
All or part available in-house

Access to staff:
Contact by letter, by e-mail and via website
Hours: Mon to Fri, 0900 to 1700

Access to building, collection or gallery:
No access other than to staff

ARGYLL & BUTE COUNCIL

Kilmory, Lochgilphead, Argyll, PA31 8RT

Tel: 01546 602127
Fax: 01546 604138

Website:
http://www.argyll-bute.gov.uk

Founded:
1996

Organisation type and purpose:
Local government body.

Subject coverage:
Argyll and Bute Council, services and amenities, corporate services, education, environmental services, finance, housing, legal services, personnel services, planning development and tourism, property and technical services, roads and transportation, social services, council tax and other payments, registration of births, deaths and marriages.

Printed publications:
ABC News: The Newspaper of Argyll and Bute Council

Access to staff:
Contact by letter, by telephone and by fax. Appointment necessary.
Hours: Mon to Fri, 0900 to 1700

ARGYLL & BUTE COUNCIL LIBRARY AND INFORMATION SERVICE

Sandbank Business Park, Highland Avenue, Sandbank, Dunoon, Argyll, PA23 8QZ

Tel: 01369 703214
Fax: 01369 705797
E-mail: libraryhq@argyll-bute.gov.uk

Website:
http://www.argyll-bute.gov.uk
Includes list of own publications.

Enquiries:
Enquiries to: Culture and Libraries Manager
Other contacts: Head of Community Regeneration (for overall responsibility for libraries, museums and arts)

Founded:
1996

Incorporates the former:
Argyll and Bute District Library, Helensburgh and Lomond Area of Dumbarton District Library (year of change 1996)

Organisation type and purpose:
Public library.

Subject coverage:
Local studies for Argyll and Bute.

Museum or gallery collection, archive, or library special collection:
MacGrory Collection (photographs of Campbeltown and Kintyre, 1890 to 1910)
Robertson Collection (local history)

Non-library collection catalogue:
All or part available in-house

Library catalogue:
All or part available online

Printed publications:
Local history publications (various titles, listed online)

Access to staff:
Contact by letter, by telephone, by fax, by e-mail and in person. Appointment necessary.
Hours: Mon to Fri, 0900 to 1700

Access for disabled people:
Hours: Mon to Fri, 0900 to 1700

Parent body:
Argyll and Bute Council
Kilmory, Lochgilphead, Argyll, PA31 8RT; tel: 01546 602127; fax: 01546 604138; website: http://www.argyll-bute.gov.uk

ARGYLL, THE ISLES, LOCH LOMOND, STIRLING & TROSSACHS TOURIST BOARD

Acronym or abbreviation: AILLSTTB

Old Town Jail, St John Street, Stirling, FK8 1EA

Tel: 01786 445222
Fax: 01786 471301

Website:
http://www.scottish-heartlands.org
Information on general area and accommodation providers.

Enquiries:
Enquiries to: Chief Executive

Founded:
1996

Formerly called:
Bute & Cowal Tourist Board, Forth Valley Tourist Board, Loch Lomond, Stirling & Trossachs Tourist Board, West Highlands & Islands of Argyll Tourist Board (year of change 1996)

Organisation type and purpose:
Statutory body, membership association (membership is by subscription).
To promote the area through marketing and visitor services activities at home and abroad.

Subject coverage:
Advice to members on marketing, business planning and development.
Accommodation bookings through local and national schemes, promotion through the Board's publications e.g. accommodation guide.

Museum or gallery collection, archive, or library special collection:
Slide library available for hire

Printed publications:
Accommodation Guide
Holiday and short breaks guide
Visitor guides
What's On Guides

Publications list:
Available in print

Access to staff:
Contact by letter, by telephone, by fax and by e-mail
Hours: Mon to Fri, 0900 to 1700

Access to building, collection or gallery:
No prior appointment required

Tourist Information Centres:
Aberfoyle (April to October)
Main Street, Aberfoyle; tel: 01877 382352

Alva (all year)
  Mill Trail Visitor Centre, West Stirling Street, Alva; tel: 01259 769696
Ardgartan (April to October)
  Glen Croe, Ardgartan; tel: 01301 702432
Balloch (April to October)
  Balloch Road, Balloch; tel: 01389 753533
Bo'ness (April to September)
  Car Park, Seaview Place, Bo'ness; tel: 01506 826626
Bowmore (all year)
  The Square, Isle of Islay, Bowmore; tel: 01496 810254
Callander (March to December and weekends only during January and February)
  Rob Roy & Trossachs Visitor Centre, Ancaster Square, Callander; tel: 01877 330342
Campbeltown (all year)
  MacKinnon House, The Pier, Campbeltown; tel: 01586 552056
Craignure (all year)
  The Pier, Isle of Mull; tel: 01680 812377
Drymen (May to September)
  Drymen Library, The Square, Drymen; tel: 01306 660068
Dumbarton (all year)
  Milton, A82 Northbound; tel: 01389 742306
Dunblane (May to September)
  Stirling Road, Dunblane; tel: 01786 824428
Dunoon (all year)
  7 Alexandra Parade, Dunoon; tel: 01369 703785
Falkirk (all year)
  2–4 Glebe Street, Falkirk; tel: 01324 620244
Helensburgh (April to October)
  Clock Tower, The Pier, Helensburgh; tel: 01436 672642
Inveraray (all year)
  Front Street, Inveraray; tel: 01499 302063
Killin (March to November)
  Breadalbane Folklore Centre, Falls of Dochart, Killin; tel: 01567 820254
Lochgilphead (April to October)
  Lochnell Street, Lochgilphead; tel: 01546 602344
Oban (all year)
  Argyll Square; tel: 01631 563122
Rothesay (all year)
  Isle of Bute, Rothesay; tel: 01700 502151
Stirling (all year)
  Royal Burgh of Stirling, Visitor Centre, Castle Esplanade; tel: 01786 479901
Stirling (all year)
  41 Dumbarton Road, Stirling; tel: 01786 475019
Stirling (April to October)
  M9/M80 Junction 9, Motorway Service Area, Stirling; tel: 01786 814111
Tarbet (Loch Fyne) (April to October)
  Harbour Street, Tarbet (Loch Fyne); tel: 01880 820429
Tarbet (Loch Lomond) (April to October)
  Main Street, Tarbet (Loch Lomond); tel: 01301 702260
Tobermory (April to October)
  The Pier, Isle of Mull, Tobermory; tel: 01688 302182
Tyndrum (April to October)
  Main Street, Tyndrum; tel: 01838 400246

ARIC

Formal name: aric

Department of Environmental and Geographical Sciences, Manchester Metropolitan University, Chester Street, Manchester, M1 5GD

Tel: 0161 247 1593
Fax: 0161 247 6332
E-mail: aric@mmu.ac.uk

Website:
http://www.doc.mmu.ac.uk/aric/
Factsheets, newsletters on air quality issues.

Enquiries:
Enquiries to: Information Officer
Other contacts: All enquiries to the Information Officer

Founded:
1984

Formerly called:
Acid Rain Information Centre (ARIC) (year of change 1991); Atmospheric Research and Information Centre (ARIC) (year of change 1999)

Organisation type and purpose:
Consultancy, research organisation.
Information centre.
To provide world class research and education in atmospheric and sustainability issues to encourage responsible development.

Subject coverage:
Air quality issues, acid rain, greenhouse effect, ozone depletion, transport, waste, sustainability, energy efficiency.

Museum or gallery collection, archive, or library special collection:
Many reference books on acidification, global climate change and urban air quality

Library catalogue:
All or part available in-house

Printed publications:
A wide range of publications on acid rain, air pollution, global change and ozone depletion

Electronic and video publications:
Educational material: Atmosphere, Climate & Environment (by aric for teachers and librarians, CD-ROM, £20 plus VAT)

Publications list:
Available in print

Access to staff:
Contact by letter, by telephone, by fax, by e-mail and via website. Appointment necessary.
Hours: Mon to Fri, 0900 to 1700

Supported by:
Department for Environment, Food and Rural Affairs (DEFRA)

ARMAGH PUBLIC LIBRARY

Abbey Street, Armagh, BT61 7DY

Tel: 028 3752 3142
Fax: 028 3752 4177
E-mail: armroblib@aol.com

Enquiries:
Enquiries to: Assistant Keeper
Other contacts: Administration Officer for access to cataloguing of collection.

Founded:
1771

Organisation type and purpose:
Registered charity, museum, public library, historic building, house or site, research organisation.

Museum or gallery collection, archive, or library special collection:
17th and 18th century books on theology, philosophy, classic and modern literature, voyages and travels, history, medicine, law
Medieval and 17th and 18th century manuscripts
Engravings by Piranesi, Hogarth and Bartolozzi

Library catalogue:
All or part available online

Access to staff:
Contact by letter, by telephone and by e-mail. Appointment necessary.
Hours: Mon to Fri, 1000 to 1300 and 1400 to 1600
Special comments: Other times by prior arrangement.

Access to building, collection or gallery:
No prior appointment required

Access for disabled people:
Ramped entry
Special comments: Chairlift to library.

ARMENIAN GENERAL BENEVOLENT UNION (LONDON)

Acronym or abbreviation: AGBU

25 Cheniston Gardens, London, W8 6TG

E-mail: arline.medazoumian@agbu.org.uk

Website:
http://www.agbu.org.uk

Enquiries:
Enquiries to: Hon. Sec.
Direct e-mail: arline.medazoumian@agbu.org.uk

Founded:
1910

Organisation type and purpose:
To support the educational, cultural and social life of the UK Armenian community and promote Armenian culture and heritage within the UK.

Printed publications:
Hoosharar (4 a year, in English and Armenian)

Access to staff:
Contact by letter and by e-mail

Branch of:
Armenian General Benevolent Union (AGBU)
55 East 59th Street, New York, NY 10022–1112, USA; tel: (212) 319–6383; fax: (212) 319–6507; e-mail: agbuwb@agbu.org; website: http://www.agbu.org

ARMITT MUSEUM AND LIBRARY

Rydal Road, Ambleside, Cumbria, LA22 9BL

Tel: 01539 431212
Fax: 01539 431313
E-mail: info@armitt.com

Website:
http://www.armitt.com

Founded:
1909

Organisation type and purpose:
Art, literature and artefacts relating to the Lake District and its famous inhabitants.

Subject coverage:
Art, archaeology, archives, books, geology, photography and local history of the Lake District.

Museum or gallery collection, archive, or library special collection:
Library of 10,000 items relating to the Lake District
Archives (manuscripts, letters, folk songs, local account books, Poor Law records and deeds)
Newspapers and parish magazines
Beatrix Potter illustrations

Library catalogue:
All or part available in-house

Access to staff:
Contact by letter, by telephone, by e-mail and via website. Appointment necessary.

Access to building, collection or gallery:
Hours: Museum: Mon to Sat, 1000 to 1700 (last admission, 1630)
Library: Mon to Fri, 1000 to 1600

ARMY RECORDS SOCIETY

Acronym or abbreviation: ARS

Heritage House, PO Box 21, Baldock, Hertfordshire, SG7 5SH

Tel: 01462 896688
Fax: 01462 896677
E-mail: ars@hall-mccartney.co.uk

Website:
http://www.armyrecordssociety.org.uk
Membership information, publication information, society news.

Founded:
1985

Organisation type and purpose:
Learned society (membership is by subscription).
National organisation for publishing volumes of historical documents relating to history of the British Army.

continued overleaf

Subject coverage:
British army history (by publications).

Printed publications:
Annual volumes:
The Military Papers of Lieutenant-Colonel Sir Cuthbert Headlam, 1910–1942 (2010)
The First World War Letters of General Lord Horne (2009)
Wolseley and Ashanti (2009)
Montgomery and the Battle of Normandy (2008)
Major-General Oliver Nugent and the Ulster Division, 1915–1918 (2007)
Kitchener and the War in South Africa (2006)
Romaine's Crimean War (2006)
Military Miscellany II (2005)
Allenby in Palestine (2004)
At Wellington's Right Hand. The letters of Lt. Col. Sir Alexander Gordon, 1808–15 (2003)
Rawlinson in India (2003)
The Journal of Corporal Todd (2002)
Sir Hugh Rose and the Central India Campaign 1858 (1999)
Lord Roberts and the War in South Africa 1899–1902 (2000)
The Journal of Corporal William Todd, 1745–1762 (2001)
An Eighteenth Century Secretary at War (1988)
Colonel Samuel Bagshawe and the Army of George II (1990)
John Peebles' American War, 1776–82 (1997)
Letters of a Victorian Army Officer: Edward Wellesley, 1840–1854 (1995)
Lord Chelmsford's Zululand Campaign, 1878–1879 (1994)
Military Miscellany 1 (1996)
Montgomery and the English Army (1991)
Roberts in India, 1876–1893 (1993)
The Army and the Curragh Incident, 1914 (1986)
The British Army and Signals Intelligence in the First World War (1992)
The Napoleonic War Journal of Captain Thomas Brown (1987)
The Maratha War Papers of Arthur Wellesley, 1803 (1998)
The Military Correspondence of Field Marshal Sir William Robertson, Chief of the Imperial General Staff, 1915–1918 (1989)
The Military Correspondence of FM Sir Henry Wilson (1985)
Order printed publications from: Pub Army Records Society, Heritage House, PO Box 21, Baldock, Hertfordshire, SG7 5SHl tel: 01462 896688; fax: 01462 896677; e-mail: ars@hallmccartney.co.uk

Publications list:
Available online and in print

Access to staff:
Contact by letter and via website

Membership Administrators:
Hall McCartney Limited
Heritage House, PO Box 21, Baldock, Hertfordshire, SG7 5SH; tel: 01462 896688; fax: 01462 896677; e-mail: ars@hall-mccartney.co.uk

AROMATHERAPY COUNCIL

Acronym or abbreviation: AOC

PO Box 6522, Desborough, Kettering, Northamptonshire, NN14 2YX

Tel: 0870 7743477
E-mail: info@aromatherapycouncil.co.uk

Website:
http://www.aromatherapycouncil.co.uk

Enquiries:
Enquiries to: Secretary
Direct e-mail: publications@aromatherapycouncil.co.uk

Founded:
1991

Formerly called:
Aromatherapy Organisations Council (AOC); Aromatherapy Consortium (year of change 2006)

Organisation type and purpose:
Regulatory authority.

Subject coverage:
Aromatherapy.

Publications list:
Available online

Access to staff:
Contact by letter, by telephone and by e-mail

Access to building, collection or gallery:
No access other than to staff

AROMATHERAPY TRADE COUNCIL

Acronym or abbreviation: ATC

Fairfield Enterprise Centre, Lincoln Way, Fairfield Industrial Estate, Louth, Lincolnshire. LN11 0LS

Tel: 01507 617761
E-mail: info@a-t-c.org.uk

Website:
http://www.a-t-c.org.uk
Background information to the ATC, list of members, the regulation and responsible marketing of essential oils and aromatherapy products.

Enquiries:
Enquiries to: Administrator

Founded:
1992

Organisation type and purpose:
Trade association for the specialist aromatherapy essential oil trade.

Subject coverage:
The regulation and responsible marketing of essential oils and aromatherapy products.

Trade and statistical information:
Data on responsible marketing of essential oils. Guidelines on the regulation of essential oils and aromatherapy products.

Printed publications:
General information booklet (free on receipt of A5 sae)
Membership list (free as above)
ATC Guidelines on the Regulation, Labelling, Advertising & Promotion of Aromatherapy Products (£100, incl. p&p)

Access to staff:
Contact by letter, by telephone, by fax, by e-mail and via website
Hours: Mon to Fri, 0900 to 1700

ARON VECHT AND ASSOCIATES

95 Corringham Road, London, NW11 7DL

Tel: 020 8316 8429
Fax: 020 8316 8405
E-mail: phosphors@vecht.com

Website:
http://www.aronvechtandassociates.com
http://www.vecht.com

Enquiries:
Enquiries to: Principal
Direct tel: 020 8455 4361
Direct fax: 020 8201 9555
Direct e-mail: phosphor@vecht.com

Founded:
1987

Formerly called:
Phosphor Consultants (year of change 1987)

Organisation type and purpose:
International organisation, consultancy, research organisation.

Subject coverage:
Materials science, semiconductors, phosphors, displays and thin films, as well as ultra-pure chemicals used in the electronics industry,

assessment of new technologies in these areas for investment and marketing. Specific areas of expertise include: chemical vapour deposition of thin films, electro-luminescence, liquid crystals and cathode ray phosphors.

Printed publications:
See website

Electronic and video publications:
Specialist phosphors prepared on request (purchase order)

Publications list:
Available in print

Access to staff:
Contact by letter, by telephone, by fax, by e-mail and via website
Hours: Mon to Fri, 0900 to 2400

ART AND ARCHITECTURE SOCIETY

Acronym or abbreviation: A&A

70 Cowcross Street, London, EC1M 6EJ

Tel: 020 7733 2436
Fax: 020 7733 2436
E-mail: a&a@tsib.demon.co.uk

Website:
http://www.artandarchitecture.co.uk
Full information on events, current activities, artists' network, and links for the A&A Society.

Enquiries:
Enquiries to: Honorary Secretary

Founded:
1982

Organisation type and purpose:
Learned society (membership is by subscription), present number of members: c 400, voluntary organisation.
Furthering artistic collaboration between those creating the built environment.

Subject coverage:
Public art, art works, commissions, policy, environmental art, urban design, artists and craftsmen working on architectural commissions, sculpture parks.

Printed publications:
Brochure (free)
Journal of Art and Architecture (4 times a year, free to members)
Manifesto (£3)
Register of Artists and Craftsmen in Architecture (£10 plus p&p)

Access to staff:
Contact by letter, by telephone, by fax, by e-mail and via website
Hours: Mon to Fri, 0900 to 1700

ART DIRECTORS & TRIP PHOTO LIBRARY

57 Burdon Lane, Cheam, Surrey, SM2 7BY

Tel: 020 8642 3593
Fax: 020 8395 7230
E-mail: images@artdirectors.co.uk

Website:
http://www.artdirectors.co.uk

Enquiries:
Enquiries to: Manager

Organisation type and purpose:
Commercial image library.

Subject coverage:
Photography, usage of colour pictures for printing, brochures, advertising, audiovisuals, etc. Areas covered: worldwide geography, lifestyle, business and economy, nature and ecology, landscapes, holiday travel, religion and backgrounds.

Non-library collection catalogue:
All or part available online

Library catalogue:
All or part available online

Access to staff:
Contact by letter, by telephone, by fax and by e-mail. Appointment necessary.
Hours: Mon to Fri, 0900 to 1800

Member organisation of:
British Association of Picture Libraries and Agencies (BAPLA)

ART FUND

Formal name: National Art Collections Fund
Acronym or abbreviation: NACF

Millais House, 7 Cromwell Place, London, SW7 2JN

Tel: 020 7225 4800
Fax: 020 7225 4848
E-mail: info@artfund.org

Website:
http://www.artfund.org

Enquiries:
Enquiries to: Communications Department
Direct fax: 020 7225 4808/4848

Founded:
1903

Organisation type and purpose:
National organisation, membership association (membership is by subscription), present number of members: 80,000, registered charity (charity number 209174). Art charity giving to museums and galleries across the country for the purchase of works of art. The Art Fund is entirely self-funded, raising the money from membership subscriptions, donations and legacies. It also campaigns on behalf of museums and galleries, particularly on issues such as free admission to national collections and funding for acquisitions.

Subject coverage:
Art current affairs, art history, bequests, grants.

Non-library collection catalogue:
All or part available online

Printed publications:
Art Quarterly (quarterly, members only)
Members' Guide (list of over 500 museums, galleries and historic houses with free entry to the permanent collections for members)
Review (annual, members only)

Access to staff:
Contact by letter, by telephone, by fax, by e-mail and via website
Hours: Mon to Fri, 0930 to 1730

ART LIBRARIES SOCIETY OF THE UK AND IRELAND

Acronym or abbreviation: ARLIS/UK & Ireland

Word and Image Department, Victoria and Albert Museum, South Kensington, London, SW7 2RL

Tel: 020 7942 2317
Fax: 020 7942 2394
E-mail: arlis@vam.ac.uk

Website:
http://www.arlis.org.uk

Enquiries:
Enquiries to: Business Manager

Founded:
1969

Organisation type and purpose:
International organisation, professional body, registered charity (charity number 1048642). Corporate voice of art and design libraries in the UK and Ireland, making their views known to the appropriate professional and educational bodies.

Subject coverage:
Art, architecture and design librarianship.

Printed publications:
Artists' books: A cataloguers' manual (2006)
First Steps in Archives: A Practical Guide (2004)
Trade Literature: Cataloguing and Classification Guidelines (2004)
A Library and Information Plan for the Visual Arts (1993)
Art Libraries Journal vols 1–29, 1976–2004 (prices on application)
Art Libraries Journal and ARLIS News-sheet: Ten Year Indexes, 1976–85 and 1986–95
Art Libraries Journal (quarterly)
Directory of members (annually)
Art Exhibition Documentation in Libraries: cataloguing guidelines (2000)
Guidelines on stock disposal (2000)
News-sheet (6 times a year)

Publications list:
Available online and in print

Access to staff:
Contact by letter, by telephone, by fax, by e-mail, in person and via website. Appointment necessary.
Hours: Mon to Fri, 1000 to 1700

ARTHRITIC ASSOCIATION

One Upperton Gardens, Eastbourne, East Sussex, BN21 2AA

Tel: 01323 416550
Fax: 01323 639793
E-mail: info@arthriticassociation.org.uk

Website:
http://www.arthriticassociation.org.uk
General.

Enquiries:
Direct e-mail: info@arthriticassociation.org.uk

Founded:
1942

Organisation type and purpose:
Membership association (membership is by subscription), present number of members: 4000, registered charity (charity number 292569). To relieve the suffering from arthritis and allied illnesses using complementary techniques.

Subject coverage:
Arthritis and allied illnesses.

Non-library collection catalogue:
All or part available in-house

Printed publications:
Home Treatment Book and Dietary Guidance Chart
The Arthritic Association News (magazine, spring and autumn)
Books by the late Charles de Coti-Marsh
Arthritis – The Conquest
Diet for Arthritis
Prescription for Energy

Electronic and video publications:
Tapes of the Home Treatment for Blind and Partially Sighted

Access to staff:
Contact by letter, by telephone, by fax, by e-mail and via website. Appointment necessary.
Hours: Mon to Fri, 1000 to 1300 and 1400 to 1600

ARTHRITIS CARE

18 Stephenson Way, London, NW1 2HD

Tel: 0808 800 4050 (answerphone helpline)
Fax: 020 7380 6505
E-mail: helpline@arthritiscare.org.uk

Website:
http://www.arthritiscare.org.uk

Enquiries:
Enquiries to: Information Manager
Direct tel: 020 7380 6577
Direct e-mail: info@arthritiscare.org.uk

Founded:
1947

Formerly called:
British Rheumatism Association (year of change 1980)

Organisation type and purpose:
Membership association (membership is by subscription), present number of members: 44,000, voluntary organisation, registered charity (charity number 206563).
National voluntary organisation with over 580 branches.

Subject coverage:
Health and well-being of people with arthritis, exercise, self-management, aids and equipment, and holidays.

Trade and statistical information:
Statistics on impact of arthritis

Library catalogue:
All or part available in-house

Printed publications:
Arthritis News (6 times a year for members)
Booklets and factsheets

Electronic and video publications:
Arthritis News Magazine on tape for people with sight impairments
All booklets are available on audio CD

Publications list:
Available in print

Access to staff:
Contact by letter, by telephone, by fax, by e-mail and via website. Appointment necessary.
Hours: Mon to Fri, 0900 to 1700
Special comments: Helpline hours are 1000 to 1600

Access to building, collection or gallery:
Prior appointment required

Access for disabled people:
Toilet facilities

ARTHRITIS RESEARCH CAMPAIGN EPIDEMIOLOGY UNIT

Acronym or abbreviation: ARC Unit

School of Epidemiology and Health Sciences, Stopford Building, University of Manchester, Oxford Road, Manchester, M13 9PT

Tel: 0161 275 3235
Fax: 0161 275 5043
E-mail: arcstaff@fs1.ser.man.ac.uk

Website:
http://www.arc.org.uk
Official website of the Arthritis Research Campaign, background to the ARC, information about arthritis, publications.
http://www.arc.man.ac.uk
Background to work of unit, staff and publications, courses and job vacancies.

Enquiries:
Enquiries to: Information Officer

Founded:
1954

Formerly called:
Arthritis and Rheumatism Council

Organisation type and purpose:
Registered charity (charity number 207711), university department or institute, research organisation.
Research into the epidemiology of the rheumatic diseases.

Subject coverage:
Epidemiology of rheumatic diseases i.e. incidence and prevalence data on rheumatic diseases.

Museum or gallery collection, archive, or library special collection:
Rheumatic disease journals

Printed publications:
Leaflets, booklets and information sheets for patients
Health Care Needs Assessment

continued overleaf

Medical Student handbook
Reports on Rheumatic Diseases: Series 3 (for
medical professionals)
Order printed publications from: ARC Trading Ltd
Brunel Drive, Northern Road Industrial Estate,
Newark, Nottinghamshire, NG24 2DE

Electronic and video publications:
Teaching Slides (4 sets)
Video : Help is at Hand (£4.95)
Video: Reaching a Balance – Arthritis and the
Family (£4.95)

Publications list:
Available in print

Access to staff:
Contact by letter, by telephone, by fax, by e-mail
and via website. Appointment necessary. Non-
members charged.
Hours: Mon to Fri, 0800 to 1600

Parent body:
Arthritis Research Campaign
Copeman House, St Mary's Court, Chesterfield,
Derbyshire, S41 7TD; tel: 01246 558033; fax:
01246 558007

ARTIFICIAL INTELLIGENCE
APPLICATIONS INSTITUTE

Acronym or abbreviation: AIAI

University of Edinburgh, 80 South Bridge,
Edinburgh, EH1 1HN

Tel: 0131 650 2732
Fax: 0131 650 6513
E-mail: aiai@ed.ac.uk

Website:
http://www.aiai.ed.ac.uk/
Complete description of AIAI and its work.

Enquiries:
Enquiries to: Commercial Director
Other contacts: Training Secretary; Publications
Secretary

Founded:
1984

Organisation type and purpose:
University department or institute, consultancy,
research organisation.
Technology transfer.

Subject coverage:
Artificial intelligence, knowledge-based systems,
modelling, methods, planning, scheduling,
information management, process management,
intelligent workflow.

**Museum or gallery collection, archive, or library
special collection:**
Edinburgh AI Library
Exchange arrangements with international AI
Research centres has led to a collection of over
15,000 AI research papers

Printed publications:
Institute Reports
Newsletter
Project Reports
Technical Reports

Electronic and video publications:
Many technical reports available via ftp

Publications list:
Available online

Access to staff:
Contact by letter, by telephone, by fax, by e-mail
and via website. Appointment necessary.
Hours: Mon to Fri, 0900 to 1700

Parent body:
University of Edinburgh
tel: 0131 650 1000; fax: 0131 650 2147; e-mail:
communications.office@ed.ac.uk

ARTS AND BUSINESS

Acronym or abbreviation: A&B

Nutmeg House, 60 Gainsford Street, Butlers
Wharf, London, SE1 2NY

Tel: 020 7378 8143
Fax: 020 7407 7527
E-mail: head.office@AandB.org.uk

Website:
http://www.aandb.org.uk

Enquiries:
Enquiries to: Information Officer

Founded:
1975

Formed from:
Association for Business Sponsorship of the Arts
(ABSA) (year of change 2000)

Organisation type and purpose:
National organisation, membership association,
service industry, registered charity (charity number
274040), consultancy.
To help business people support the arts and the
arts to inspire business people, because good
business and great art enrich society.

Subject coverage:
Arts sponsorship advice to businesses and arts
organisations, tax advice, evaluation, research,
consultancy, arts funding, the Board Bank, Skills
Bank and mentoring placements. Corporate art
collections and creative and development training.

Trade and statistical information:
Business Investment (of the arts) figures since 1990
Archive surveys.

Library catalogue:
All or part available in-house

Printed publications:
A Creative Education
A&B Literature & Statistics
Art Collecting
Business Investment in the Arts 2002/2003
Creative Connections
Cultural Sponsorship in Europe
Did it Deliver?
Did it Make A Difference?
Did it Work for You?
Funding and Friendship
It Worked for Them
Recreating Communities: Business, the Arts and
Regeneration
The Sponsorship Manual

Publications list:
Available online and in print

Access to staff:
Contact by letter, by telephone, by fax, by e-mail
and via website. Appointment necessary.
Hours: Mon to Fri, 0930 to 1730

Access to building, collection or gallery:
Prior appointment required
Hours: Thu, Fri, 0930 to 1730

Arts & Business Offices and Staff:
Arts & Business Cymru/Wales
16 Museum Place, Cardiff, CF10 3BH; tel: 029
2030 3023; fax: 029 2030 3024; e-mail: cymru@
AandB.org.uk
Arts & Business East
67 Regent Street, Cambridge, CB2 1AB; tel: 01223
321421; fax: 01223 365536; e-mail: east@AandB
.org.uk
Arts & Business East Midlands
Carlton Studios, Lenton Lane, Nottingham, NG7
2NA; tel: 0115 964 5648; fax: 0115 964 5488; e-
mail: nottingham@AandB.org.uk
Arts & Business North West
127–129 Portland Buildings, Portland Street,
Manchester, M1 4PZ; tel: 0161 236 2058; fax:
0161 236 2068; e-mail: north.west@AandB.org.uk
Arts & Business Northern Ireland
53 Malone Road, Belfast, BT9 6RY; tel: 028 9066
4736; fax: 028 9066 4500; e-mail: northern
.ireland@AandB.org.uk
Arts & Business Scotland
6 Randolph Crescent, Edinburgh, EH3 7TH; tel:
0131 220 2499; fax: 0131 220 2296; e-mail:
scotland@AandB.org.uk

Arts & Business South East, Brighton Office
4 Frederick Terrace, Frederick Place, Brighton,
East Sussex, BN1 1AX; tel: 01273 738333; fax:
01273 738666; e-mail: south.east@AandB.org.uk
Arts & Business South East, Eastleigh Office
The Point Dance and Arts Centre, Leigh Road,
Eastleigh, Hampshire, SO50 9DE; tel: 023 8061
9172; fax: 023 8061 9173; e-mail: south.east@
AandB.org.uk
Arts & Business South West
61 Park Street, Bristol, BS1 5NU; tel: 0117 929
0522; fax: 0117 929 1756; e-mail: south.west@
AandB.org.uk
Arts & Business South West, Exeter Office
Civic Centre, Paris Street, Exeter, Devon, EX1 1JJ;
tel: 01392 434272
Arts & Business West Midlands
Suite 16–18, 21 Bennetts Hill, Birmingham, B2
5QP; tel: 0121 248 1200; fax: 0121 248 1202; e-
mail: midlands@AandB.org.uk
Arts & Business Yorkshire
Dean Clough, Halifax, West Yorkshire, HX3 5AX;
tel: 01422 367860; fax: 01422 363254; e-mail:
yorkshire@AandB.org.uk
Cumbria
Arts & Business North West, Community
Foundation, Unit 6B, Lakeland Business Park,
Cockermouth, Cumbria, CA13 0QT; tel: 01900
829376; e-mail: elaine/wise@AandB.org.uk
Highlands and Islands Office
Suites 4/5 – 4th Floor, Ballantyne House, 84
Academy Street, Inverness, IV1 1LU; tel: 01463
720886; fax: 01463 720895; e-mail: inverness@
AandB.org.uk
North Wales Office
1–2 Chapel Street, Llandudno, LL30 2SY; tel:
01492 574003; e-mail: lorraine.hopkins@AandB
.org.uk
North Wales Office
Room 40, The Town Hall, Lloyd Street,
Llandudno, LL30 2UP; tel: 01492 574003; e-mail:
lorraine.hopkins@AandB.org.uk
The Sponsors Club for Arts & Business
Cale Cross House, 156 Pilgrim Street, Newcastle
upon Tyne, NE1 6SU; tel: 0191 222 0945; fax:
0191 230 0689; e-mail: northern@AandB.org.uk

Member of:
Comité Européen pour le Rapprochement de la
Culture (CEREC)
c/ Tuset 8, 1°, 2°, Barcelona, 08006, Spain; tel: 00
34 93 237 2682; fax: 00 34 93 237 22 84; e-mail:
contact@cerec.org

ARTS AND HUMANITIES
RESEARCH COUNCIL

Acronym or abbreviation: AHRC

Polaris House, North Star Avenue, Swindon, SN2
1FL

Tel: 01793 416000
Fax: 01793 416001

Website:
http://www.ahrc.ac.uk

Founded:
1998

Formerly called:
Arts and Humanities Research Board (year of
change 2005)

Organisation type and purpose:
Supports world-class research and postgraduate
study that furthers understanding of human
culture and creativity: from ancient history and
heritage science to modern dance and digital
content.

Access to staff:
Contact by letter, by telephone, by fax, by e-mail
and via website

ARTS AND MINDS

Formal name: Cambridgeshire and Peterborough
Foundation for the Arts and Mental Health

47–51 Norfolk St, Cambridge, CB1 2LD

Tel: 07758 334660
E-mail: info@artsandminds.org.uk

Website:
http://www.artsandminds.org.uk
Description of aims, objectives and projects,
officers, recent events, collaborators.

Enquiries:
Enquiries to: Executive Director
Direct tel: 07545 641810
Direct e-mail: gavin.clayton@artsandminds.org.uk
Other contacts: Admin and Finance Officer

Incorporates the former:
portfolio of the Millennium Arts Project
established under the auspices of the Friends of
Fulbourn Hospital and the Community

Organisation type and purpose:
Registered charity (charity number 273281).
To promote and support access to all forms of the
arts for mental health service users, learning-
disabled people and offenders, many of whom
have mental health issues and some of whom have
learning disabilities.

Subject coverage:
Co-ordinates current arts activities; stimulates
provision where access to participation in the arts
is weak; provides a forum for the discussion of arts
and mental health issues, particularly those
affecting the relationship between the statutory
and voluntary sectors; raises funds for the arts and
mental health activities from statutory and
charitable sources, commercial sponsorship, and
the sale of works of art produced by participants;
commissions providers to offer arts and mental
health activities; trains artists participating in
activities sponsored by the Foundation;
collaborates with other arts and mental health
organizations in Cambridgeshire; disseminates
information about the arts and mental health.

Special visitor services:
Holds an annual Autumn Event seminar.

Access to staff:
Contact by letter, by telephone, by fax and by e-
mail

Links with:
About 20 mental health charities and other
charities and organisations

ARTS COUNCIL ENGLAND, LONDON

2 Pear Tree Court, London, EC1R 0DS

Tel: 020 7608 6100\ Minicom no. 020 7608 4101\
0845 300 6200
Fax: 020 7608 4100
E-mail: firstname.surname@artscouncil.org.uk

Website:
http://www.artscouncil.org.uk/regions

Enquiries:
Enquiries to: Administrator
Other contacts: Publishing Administrator

Organisation type and purpose:
Registered charity (charity number 1036733).
London Arts Board is the arts funding and
development agency for the capital.

Printed publications:
Annual Reports: 1998/99; 1999/00; 2000/01 London:
The Creative City
Artists in Residence – A Teachers' Handbook
(1997, £5 plus £1.50 p&p)
Creative Partnerships
Dance Rehearsal Space Use in London (1996)
Getting On-Line (1997)
A Guide to the London Arts Board
Funding Programmes 1999/00; 2000/01; 2001/02;
2002/03
Musicians Go to School (1998, £10)
Large number of reports and guides including:
Local Authority Arts & Education Directory (1997/
98)

Refugee Directory

Publications list:
Available online and in print

Access to staff:
Contact by letter, by telephone, by fax and by e-
mail
Hours: Mon to Fri, 0900 to 1700
Special comments: Access to staff also by textphone.

ARTS COUNCIL ENGLAND, SOUTH EAST

Sovereign House, Church Street, Brighton, BN1
1RA

Tel: 0845 300 6200
Fax: 0870 242 1257 0845 300 6200
E-mail: enquiries@artscouncil.org.uk

Website:
http://www.artscouncil.org.uk/regions/
The official website of the English Regional Arts
Boards. Grants information, information menu,
staff list, snapshot of region covered, background
to South East Arts.

Enquiries:
Enquiries to: Press Officer
Direct tel: 01273 763053
Direct e-mail: chloe.barker@artscouncil.org.uk

Founded:
1992

Formerly called:
Southern & South East Arts

Organisation type and purpose:
Advisory body, registered charity.
Arts funding body, range of information sheets,
website, annual review, bi-monthly newsletter.
Regional Arts Development.

Subject coverage:
All areas of arts funding for professional artists
and art organisations, arts grants, local authority
contacts, venues and promoters and National
Lottery applications.

**Museum or gallery collection, archive, or library
special collection:**
South East Arts Visual Art and Craft Collection
(catalogue available)

Trade and statistical information:
Arts research data (available to clients only). Local
authority contacts, press contacts.

Printed publications:
Annual Report
Arts Resources leaflet
Festivals! Festivals!: The South East Arts Guide to
Arts Festivals
General Information leaflet
Getting On-line, guide to the Internet
Information Services Menu
Literature supplement
Marketing Guides
Newsletter (once every two months, free) with the
following 2 supplements:
Visual Arts and Crafts supplement
South East Arts Gallery Guide
Various arts strategies

Publications list:
Available in print

Access to staff:
Contact by letter, by telephone, by fax, by e-mail
and via website
Hours: Mon to Thu, 0900 to 1730; Fri, 0900 to 1700

Access to building, collection or gallery:
Prior appointment required
Hours: As above

Access for disabled people:
Ramped entry
Special comments: Third floor, lifts available.

Also at:
Southern & South East Arts
Union House, Eridge Road, Tunbridge Wells,
Kent, TN4 8HF; tel: 01892 507200; fax: 0870
2421259; e-mail: infotw@ssea.co.uk

Parent body:
Arts Council of England
14 Great Peter Street, London, SW1P 3NQ; tel:
020 7333 0100; text phone: 020 7973 6564; fax: 020
7973 6590; e-mail: enquiries@artscouncil.org.uk;
website: http//www.artscouncil.org.uk

ARTS COUNCIL OF ENGLAND

Acronym or abbreviation: ACE

Library, 14 Great Peter Street, London, SW1P 3NQ

Tel: 020 7333 0100\ Minicom no. 020 7973 6564
Fax: 020 7973 6590
E-mail: enquiries@artscouncil.org.uk

Website:
http://www.artscouncil.org.uk
Aims and objectives, information regarding
funding programmes, new initiatives, gateway to
key arts support organisations.

Enquiries:
Enquiries to: Information Officer
Direct tel: 020 7973 6517

Founded:
1945

Formerly called:
Arts Council of Great Britain (year of change 1994)

Organisation type and purpose:
National government body.
Non-Departmental Public Body (NDPB)
Government grant-aided institution, incorporated
under Royal Charter, national body for funding
and development of the arts.
To develop and improve knowledge,
understanding and practice of the arts; increase the
accessibility of the arts; advise and co-operate with
government, local authorities and other bodies.

Subject coverage:
Cultural policy, marketing, management, economy
and financing of the arts, fundraising and
sponsorship.

**Museum or gallery collection, archive, or library
special collection:**
Market research reports on the arts

Trade and statistical information:
Data on the level of central government funding of
the arts.

Printed publications:
Information leaflets available in large print, audio
tape or Braille
Range of bibliographies and fact sheets on cultural
policy
Order printed publications from: Marston Book
Services
PO Box 269, Abingdon, Oxfordshire, OX14 4YN,
tel: 01235 465500, fax: 01235 465555

Publications list:
Available online

Access to staff:
Contact by letter, by telephone, by fax and via
website
Hours: Mon to Fri, 1000 to 1300 and 1400 to 1700
Special comments: Due to limited space, priority is
given to artist and art administrator groups, for
other categories it is a library of last resort.

Access to building, collection or gallery:
Prior appointment required

Regional Arts Boards:
East England Arts Area covered: Bedfordshire,
Cambridgeshire, Essex, Hertfordshire, Norfolk,
Suffolk, Lincolnshire; unitary authority of Luton
Eden House, 48–49 Bateman Street, Cambridge,
CB2 1LR; tel: 01223 454400; fax: 01223 248075

continued overleaf

East Midlands Arts Board Area covered: Derbyshire (excluding High Peak District), Leicestershire, Northamptonshire, Nottinghamshire; unitary authorities of Derby, Leicester, Rutland
   Mountfields House, Epinal Way, Loughborough, Leicestershire, LE11 0QE; tel: 01509 218292; fax: 01509 262214

London Arts Board Area covered: The area of the 32 London Boroughs and the City of London
   Elme House, 133 Long Acre, Covent Garden, London, WC2E 9AF; tel: 020 7240 1313; fax: 020 7240 4580

North West Arts Area covered: Lancashire, Cheshire, Merseyside, Greater Manchester and High Peak Districts of Derbyshire
   Manchester House, 22 Bridge Street, Manchester, M3 3AB; tel: 0161 834 6644; fax: 0161 834 6969

Northern Arts Area covered: Cumbria, Durham, Northumberland; unitary authorities of Darlington, Hartlepool, Middlesbrough, Redcar & Cleveland, Stockton; metropolitan districts of Newcastle, Gateshead, North Tyneside, Sunderland & South Tyneside
   9–10 Osborne Terrace, Jesmond, Newcastle upon Tyne, NE2 1NZ; tel: 0191 281 6334; fax: 0191 281 3276

South East Arts Board Area covered: Kent, Surrey, East and West Sussex, unitary authority of Brighton and Hove
   10 Mount Ephraim, Tunbridge Wells, Kent, TN4 8AS; tel: 01892 515210; fax: 01892 549383

South West Arts Area covered: Cornwall, Devon, Dorset (except districts of Bournemouth, Christchurch & Poole), Gloucestershire and Somerset; unitary authorities of Bristol, Bath and North East Somerset, South Gloucestershire, North Somerset
   Bradninch Place, Gandy Street, Exeter, EX4 3LS; tel: 01392 218188; fax: 01392 413554

Southern Arts Board Area covered: Berkshire, Buckinghamshire. Hampshire, Isle of Wight. Oxfordshire, Wiltshire; unitary authorities of Bournemouth, Milton Keynes, Poole, Southampton, Swindon
   13 St Clement Street, Winchester, Hampshire, SO23 9DQ; tel: 01962 855099; fax: 01962 861186

West Midlands Arts Board Area covered: Hereford & Worcester, Shropshire, Staffordshire, Warwickshire; metropolitan districts of Birmingham, Coventry, Dudley, Sandwell, Solihull, Walsall, Wolverhampton; unitary authority of Stoke-on-Trent
   82 Granville Street, Birmingham, B1 2LH; tel: 0121 631 3121; fax: 0121 643 7239

Yorkshire & Humberside Arts Board Area covered: North Yorks; unitary authorities of York, Hull, East Riding, North Lincs; metropolitan districts of Barnsley, Bradford, Calderdale, Doncaster, Kirklees, Leeds, Rotherham, Sheffield, Wakefield
   21 Bond Street, Dewsbury, West Yorkshire, WF13 1AX; tel: 01924 455555; fax: 01924 466 522

ARTS COUNCIL OF ENGLAND (NORTHERN ARTS)

Central Square, Forth Street, Newcastle upon Tyne, NE1 3PJ

Tel: 0845 300 6200
Fax: 0191 230 1020

Website:
http://www.arts.org.uk/directory/regions/northern

Enquiries:
Enquiries to: Communications Officer
Direct e-mail: kathryn.goodfellow@artscouncil.org.uk

Formerly called:
Northern Arts

Organisation type and purpose:
Local government body, advisory body, professional body (membership is by subscription), registered charity (charity number 517711), training organisation, consultancy, research organisation.

Art funding body.
Regional arts board responsible for almost all national and regional arts funding in the North.

Subject coverage:
Music, drama, performing arts, visual arts, crafts, literature, film, photography, video, community arts, arts funding and organisation, Millennium Fund and lottery.

Museum or gallery collection, archive, or library special collection:
Fundraising library
Slide library (artists index)

Library catalogue:
All or part available in-house and in print

Printed publications:
Annual Report
Northern Review (monthly)

Access to staff:
Contact by letter, by telephone, by fax, by e-mail and via website. Appointment necessary.
Hours: Mon to Fri, 0900 to 1700
Special comments: First floor access only; stairs above, not accessible by lift.

Access to building, collection or gallery:
No prior appointment required

ARTS COUNCIL OF WALES

Acronym or abbreviation: ACW

9 Museum Place, Cardiff, CF10 3NX

Tel: 029 2037 6500\ Minicom no. 029 2039 0027
Fax: 029 2022 1447
E-mail: information@artswales.org.uk

Website:
http://www.artswales.org.uk

Enquiries:
Enquiries to: Information Officer

Founded:
1994

Formerly called:
Welsh Arts Council (year of change 1994)

Organisation type and purpose:
National government body, advisory body, statutory body (membership is by election or invitation), present number of members: 18 members on ACW's Council, 150+ on panels and committees, registered charity (charity number 1034245).
Distributes National Assembly for Wales and National Lottery funds for the arts in Wales.

Subject coverage:
Development of all art forms in Wales, funding for arts activities from National Assembly for Wales and National Lottery sources.

Library catalogue:
All or part available online and in print

Printed publications:
Annual Report and Corporate Plan summary 1999–2002
Artists Notes (newsletter, quarterly, for visual artists)
ArtsFile (bi-monthly newsletter for the arts in Wales)
Crefft (quarterly newsletter for craftspeople)
Building a Creative Society – consultation paper and responses to strategic proposals to develop a practical way forward for the arts in Wales from 1999–2004
Directory of Publishers in Wales
The Arts and Young People in Wales
The Economic Impact of the Arts and Cultural Industries in Wales

Publications list:
Available online and in print

Access to staff:
Contact by letter, by telephone, by fax, by e-mail and via website
Hours: Carmarthen and Colwyn Bay Offices: Mon to Fri, 0900 to 1700

Cardiff Office: Mon to Fri, 0900 to 1730

Other addresses:
Arts Council of Wales
   Cardiff; tel: 029 2037 6500; fax: 029 2022 1447; e-mail: information@ccc-acw.org.uk
Arts Council of Wales
   36 Prince's Drive, Colwyn Bay, LL29 8LA; tel: 01492 533440 Minicom 01492 532288; fax: 01492 533677; e-mail: information@ccc-acw.org.uk
Arts Council of Wales
   6 Gardd Llydaw, Jackson's Lane, Carmarthen, SA31 1QD; tel: 01267 234248; fax: 01267 233084; e-mail: information@ccc-acw.org.uk

ARUN DISTRICT COUNCIL

Arun Civic Centre, Maltravers Road, Littlehampton, West Sussex, BN17 5LF

Tel: 01903 737500\ Minicom no. 01903 732765
Fax: 01903 730442

Website:
http://www.arun.gov.uk
General information about Arun District, including tourism and visitor information, What's New, council information.

Enquiries:
Enquiries to: Public Relations Manager

Founded:
1974

Organisation type and purpose:
Local government body.

Subject coverage:
Tourism, strategy co-ordination, consultation processes, customer care.

Printed publications:
Annual report (free)
Arun's Customer Panel (free)
Civic Guide (free)
Customer Care handbooks for staff (price on application)
Tourism Brochure (free)
Order printed publications from: Head, Strategy Unit at the same address, e-mail: strategy.unit@arun.gov.uk

Access to staff:
Contact by letter, by telephone, by fax and by e-mail. Appointment necessary.
Hours: Mon to Thu, 0845 to 1715; Fri, 0845 to 1645

ASBESTOS CONTROL AND ABATEMENT DIVISION

Acronym or abbreviation: ACAD

Tica House, Allington Way, Yarm Road Business Park, Darlington, Co Durham, D21 4QB

Tel: 01325 466704
Fax: 01325 487691
E-mail: enquiries@tica-acad.co.uk

Website:
http://www.tica-acad.co.uk
Membership information, current news and developments, etc.

Enquiries:
Enquiries to: Operations Manager
Other contacts: ACAD Training Co-ordinator for training enquiries.

Founded:
1994

Formed from:
Insulation and Environmental Training Association (IETA), Insulation and Environmental Training Trust Limited (IETTL)

Organisation type and purpose:
Advisory body, trade association (membership is by subscription), present number of members: 117 members, 39 associate members, service industry, training organisation, consultancy, research organisation.

Subject coverage:
Safe removal of asbestos using latest technology, technical, health and safety advice, training courses. National Vocational Qualifications (NVQs).

Trade and statistical information:
Data on health and safety matters relating to asbestos products, removal and waste handling, for the United Kingdom, Europe and some international information.

Printed publications:
Best Practical Means (series of advice documents)
Practical Information Sheets
Quarterly magazine
Technical publications
Monthly newsletter

Publications list:
Available in print

Access to staff:
Contact by letter, by telephone, by fax, by e-mail, in person and via website. Appointment necessary. Non-members charged.
Hours: Mon to Fri, 0900 to 1700

Access to building, collection or gallery:
Prior appointment required

Access for disabled people:
Parking provided

Parent body:
Thermal Insulation Contractors Association (TICA)

ASCEND

Formal name: Ascend Worldwide

Cardinal Point, Newall Road, Heathrow Airport, Hounslow, Middlesex, TW6 2AS

Tel: 020 8564 6700
Fax: 020 8897 0300
E-mail: info@ascendworldwide.com

Website:
http://www.ascendworldwide.com
Lists of all services available; loss adjusting; consultancy; database; publications, valuations etc.
https://online.ascendworldwide.com//Login/PortalLogin.aspx
Aviation information on fleets, aircraft, prices, news and publications
http://www.ascendv1.com
Aircraft valuations
http://www.ascendspacetrak.com/Home/Login.aspx
Detailed information on insurance losses, launches and satellites

Enquiries:
Direct e-mail: uk@ascendworldwide.com

Founded:
1964

Formerly a part of:
Airclaims Limited (year of change 2006)

Organisation type and purpose:
International organisation, service industry, consultancy, publishing house.
Aviation Loss Adjuster and Information Provider.

Subject coverage:
Commercial aviation, including airline fleets, aircraft, current and future values, accidents, information on communications satellites and launchers (ie commercial astronautics).

Non-library collection catalogue:
All or part available in-house

Library catalogue:
All or part available in-house

Printed publications:
Ascend fast track ™ (bi-monthly)
V1EWPoint (quarterly)
Aviation Pocket Book
Space Intelligence News (monthly)
Space Review (monthly)

Electronic and video publications:
Airline Finance & Traffic (2 times a year, CD-ROM and disc)
Airline Order Backlog (4 times a year, disc)
Fleet Developments (2 times a year, CD-ROM and disc)
Jet Scoresheet (2 times a year, CD-ROM)
Aircraft Programmes (annually, CD-ROM and disc)
Jet Storage Update (monthly)
Major Loss Record (updated every other month, CD-ROM)
Market Intelligence, MI (monthly)
SpaceTrak (database, monthly)
Turbine Airliner Fleet Survey (2 times a year)

Publications list:
Available online and in print

Access to staff:
Contact by letter, by telephone, by fax, by e-mail, in person and via website
Hours: Mon to Fri, 0900 to 1700

Headquarters address:
Ascend Asia
 35/F Central Plaza, 18 Harbour Road, Wanchai, Hong Kong; tel: +852 2813 6366; fax: +652 2813 6357; e-mail: asia@ascendworldwide.com; website: http://www.ascendworldwide.com
Ascend USA
 380 Lexington Avenue, 17th Floor, New York, NY 10168, USA; tel: +1 212 551 1118; fax: +1 212 551 1001; e-mail: usa@ascendworldwide.com; website: http://www.ascendworldwide.com

ASHFIELD DISTRICT COUNCIL

Council Offices, Urban Road, Kirkby-in-Ashfield, Nottinghamshire, NG17 8DA

Tel: 01623 450000
Fax: 01623 457590
E-mail: info@ashfield-dc.gov.uk

Website:
http://www.ashfield-dc.gov.uk

Enquiries:
Enquiries to: Chief Executive

Founded:
1974

Organisation type and purpose:
Local government body.

Subject coverage:
Local government services.

Access for disabled people:
Parking provided, toilet facilities
Special comments: Audio Loop System.

ASHFORD BOROUGH COUNCIL

Acronym or abbreviation: ABC

Civic Centre, Tannery Lane, Ashford, Kent, TN23 1PL

Tel: 01233 637311\ Minicom no. 01233 637311
Fax: 01233 645654
E-mail: media@ashford.gov.uk

Website:
http://www.ashford.gov.uk

Enquiries:
Enquiries to: Chief Executive
Direct e-mail: john.bunnett@ashford.gov.uk
Other contacts: Marketing and Communications Manager for press issues and general publicity.

Organisation type and purpose:
Local government body.

Subject coverage:
Local government services.

Printed publications:
Ashford Borough Guide
Ashford Borough Review
Holiday Guide 2000
Millennium Guide 2000

Electronic and video publications:
Tourism (CD-ROM)

Access to staff:
Contact by letter and by e-mail. Appointment necessary.
Hours: Mon to Fri, 0900 to 1700

ASHFORD LIBRARY

15 Park Mall, Ashford, Kent, TN24 8RY (until Summer 2011)

Tel: 01233 620649
Fax: 01233 646580
E-mail: ashfordlibrary@kent.gov.uk

Website:
http://www.kent.gov.uk/libs
Kent Libraries website with access to online catalogue.

Enquiries:
Enquiries to: Librarian

Organisation type and purpose:
Public library.

Subject coverage:
General, local railways, local studies.

Museum or gallery collection, archive, or library special collection:
Local Railway Collection
Local studies

Library catalogue:
All or part available online

Access to staff:
Contact by letter, by telephone, by fax, by e-mail, in person and via website
Hours: Mon to Wed and Fri, 0900 to 1800; Thu, 0900 to 2000; Sat, 0900 to 1700

Access to building, collection or gallery:
Hours: Mon to Wed and Fri, 0900 to 1800; Thu, 0900 to 2000; Sat, 0900 to 1700

ASIA HOUSE

63 New Cavendish Street, London, W1G 7LP

Tel: 020 7307 5454
Fax: 020 7307 5459
E-mail: enquiries@asiahouse.co.uk

Website:
http://www.asiahouse.org

Founded:
1996

Organisation type and purpose:
A non-profit, non-political organisation serving as a focal point for the development of understanding of business, and of diplomatic and cultural interaction, between Asia and Britain. Runs a programme of events for the public.

Subject coverage:
The organisation's geographical scope extends west–east from Iran to Japan and north–south from the central Asian republics to Indonesia

Access to building, collection or gallery:
Hours: Mon to Fri, 0900 to 1900; Sat (only when there is an exhibition in the gallery), 1000 to 1800

ASIAN ART IN LONDON

Acronym or abbreviation: AAL

32 Dover Street, London, W1S 4NE

Tel: 020 7499 2215
Fax: 020 7499 2216
E-mail: info@asianartinlondon.com

Website:
http://www.asianartinlondon.com
Full list of participating galleries and auction houses, calendar of events.

Enquiries:
Enquiries to: Project Manager

continued overleaf

Founded:
1998

Organisation type and purpose:
Membership association (membership is by subscription), present number of members: 40–50. Annual event.
AAL is an annual event that promotes private dealers, auction houses, societies, academic institutions and museums that deal in and provide Asian Art.

Subject coverage:
Chinese, Japanese, Islamic and Middle Eastern, Indian, South East Asian, Himalayan and Tibetan, Korean art, antique and contemporary art.

Non-library collection catalogue:
All or part available in-house

Printed publications:
AAL Journal 2000
AAL Journal 2001
AAL Guidebook (annually)
AAL Leaflet (annually)

Access to staff:
Contact by letter, by telephone, by fax, by e-mail, in person and via website. Appointment necessary.
Hours: Mon to Fri, 0900 to 1800

Access to building, collection or gallery:
Prior appointment required
Hours: Mon to Fri, 0900 to 1800

ASIAN FAMILY COUNSELLING SERVICE

Acronym or abbreviation: AFCS

Suite 51, The Lodge, Windmill Place, 24 Windmill Lane, Southall, Middlesex, UB2 4NJ

Tel: 020 8571 3933; 020 8813 9714
Fax: 020 8571 3933
E-mail: afcs@btconnect.com

Website:
http://www.asianfamilycounselling.org.uk

Enquiries:
Enquiries to: Administrator

Founded:
1985

Organisation type and purpose:
Voluntary organisation, registered charity (charity number 517595), training organisation, consultancy.

Subject coverage:
Marital and family counselling service.

Access to staff:
Contact by letter, by telephone, by fax and by e-mail. Appointment necessary. All charged.
Hours: Mon to Fri, 1000 to 1600

Access for disabled people:
Wheelchair access not available.

ASIAN STUDIES CENTRE

Acronym or abbreviation: ASC

St Antony's College, Woodstock Road, Oxford, OX2 6JF

Tel: 01865 274559
Fax: 01865 274559
E-mail: asian@sant.ox.ac.uk

Website:
http://www.sant.ox.ac.uk/asian

Enquiries:
Enquiries to: Secretary

Founded:
1982

Formerly called:
Far East Centre (year of change 1982)

Organisation type and purpose:
Research organisation.

A scholarly Centre for Asian Studies within St Antony's College conducting seminars and special talks on Asia; funded by endowment at St Antony's College.

Subject coverage:
History; anthropology; international relations; politics; economics; Asia, with special reference to Japan, Korea, China (including Hong Kong, Taiwan and Tibet), India and Southeast Asia.

Museum or gallery collection, archive, or library special collection:
A collection of c. 4,000 books and periodicals; access restricted to members of St Antony's College
The Asian Studies Collection is held in the St Antony's College Library (books primarily related to international relations in Asia)

Access to staff:
Contact by letter, by telephone, by fax, by e-mail, in person and via website. Appointment necessary.
Hours: Mon, Tue, Thu, Fri, 0930 to 1600

ASIAN WOMEN'S RESOURCE CENTRE

Acronym or abbreviation: AWRC

108 Craven Park, London, NW10 8QE

Tel: 020 8961 6549
Fax: 020 8838 1823
E-mail: asianwomencentre@aol.com

Website:
http://www.asianwomencentre.org.uk

Enquiries:
Enquiries to: Director
Direct tel: 020 8961 5701

Founded:
1980

Organisation type and purpose:
Voluntary organisation, registered charity (charity number 1049058).
Advice centre.

Subject coverage:
Educational and social resources for Asian women living in England.

Printed publications:
Asian Women at Risk of Self-Harm and Suicide
Gender Equality Duty
HIV/Sexual Health Posters (available, free)
Posters about domestic violence

Access to staff:
Contact by letter, by telephone, by fax, by e-mail, in person and via website. Appointment necessary.
Hours: Mon to Fri, 1000 to 1700

Access for disabled people:
Ramped entry

ASKHAM BRYAN COLLEGE

Askham Bryan, York, YO23 3FR

Tel: 01904 772277
Fax: 01904 772288

Website:
http://www.askham-bryan.ac.uk
General college website.

Enquiries:
Enquiries to: Learning Resources Manager
Direct tel: 01904 772234
Direct e-mail: lrc@askham-bryan.ac.uk

Founded:
1948

Organisation type and purpose:
College of further and higher education – land based.

Subject coverage:
Agriculture, agricultural engineering, horticulture, landscape design, arboriculture, greenkeeping, agribusiness, business, management, forestry,

equine management, animal care/management, environmental management and conservation, community education, food production, botany, veterinary sciences, nursing, outdoor education, LLLD, motor sports, construction, land-based technology, land management, gamekeeping; careers information.

Library catalogue:
All or part available in-house

Printed publications:
Farming in Yorkshire (annually)
Order printed publications from: Rural Business Research Unit, Askham Bryan College
tel: 01904 772218; fax: 01904 700129; e-mail: ml@askham-bryan.ac.uk

Access to staff:
Contact by letter, by telephone, by e-mail, in person and via website. Appointment necessary.
Hours: Term Time: Mon to Tue, 0845 to 2030; Wed to Fri, 0845 to 1700; Sun, 1245 to 1730
Vacations: Mon to Fri, 0900 to 1700
Special comments: Non-members of the college may use the library for reference only.

Access for disabled people:
Parking provided, ramped entry, power-assisted front door

Affiliated to:
Harper Adams University College, University College York St John

Also at:
Askham Bryan College
Bedale Centre, Benkhill Drive, Bedale, Yorkshire, DL8 2EA; tel: 01677 422344
Askham Bryan College
Guisborough Centre, Avenue Place, Redcar Road, Guisborough, Cleveland, TS14 6AX; tel: 01287 633870
Askham Bryan College
Harrogate Centre, Great Yorkshire Showground, Harrogate, North Yorkshire, HG2 8BW; tel: 01423 870600
Askham Bryan College
Thirsk Rural Business Centre, Blakey Lane, Thirsk, YO7 3AB; tel: 01845 574928

In collaboration with:
Wakefield College, Yorkshire Coast College, Bradford College

Part of:
DEFRA Farm Management Survey Organisation

ASLIB PROFESSIONAL RECRUITMENT LIMITED

Acronym or abbreviation: APR

Holywell Centre, 1 Phipp Street, London, EC2A 4PS

Tel: 020 7613 3031
Fax: 020 7613 5080
E-mail: recruit@aslib.com

Website:
http://www.aslib.com
Recruitment application form, APR literature and job advertisements.

Enquiries:
Enquiries to: Manager
Other contacts: Recruitment Consultant

Organisation type and purpose:
Library and Information Recruitment Specialists.

Subject coverage:
Recruitment of both temporary and permanent library and information staff for placement in all sectors.

Printed publications:
Brochures
CVs and Interview guidelines

Access to staff:
Contact by letter, by telephone, by fax, by e-mail and via website. Appointment necessary.
Hours: Mon to Fri, 0915 to 1715

Wholly owned subsidiary of:
Aslib

ASLIB, THE ASSOCIATION FOR INFORMATION MANAGEMENT

Howard House, Wagon Lane, Bingley, BD16 1WA

Tel: 01274 785248
Fax: 01274 785200
E-mail: hshukla@aslib.com

Website:
http://www.aslib.com
Home page. Open Learning programme – constructing a thesaurus.
http://www.managinginformation.com
Information update and Copyright Courier.

Enquiries:
Enquiries to: Relationship Manager
Direct e-mail: dheath@aslib.com

Founded:
1924

Organisation type and purpose:
International organisation, membership association (membership is by subscription), members in some 70 countries.
Aslib actively promotes best practice in the management of information resources. It lobbies on all aspects of the management of, and legislation concerning, information at local, national and international levels.

Subject coverage:
Information management, information science, librarianship, applications of information technology, automation of information and library services, online information retrieval, information sources, records management, CD-ROM, thesaurus and database construction, data protection, intellectual property, information governance.

Printed publications:
Aslib corporate members receive discounts on titles published under the Aslib imprint by Emerald and Taylor & Francis
Managing Information (10 times a year)

Publications list:
Available online and in print

Access to staff:
Contact by letter, by telephone, by fax, by e-mail and via website. Appointment necessary. Non-members charged.
Hours: Mon to Fri, 0915 to 1715

Member of:
European Council of Information Associations (ECIA)

ASPARAGUS GROWERS' ASSOCIATION

133 Eastgate, Louth, Lincolnshire, LN11 9QG

Tel: 01507 602427
Fax: 01507 607165
E-mail: crop.association@pvga.co.uk

Website:
http://www.british-asparagus.co.uk

Enquiries:
Enquiries to: Membership Secretary

Founded:
1984

Organisation type and purpose:
National organisation, trade association.

Access to staff:
Contact by letter, by telephone, by fax and by e-mail
Hours: Mon to Fri, 0900 to 1700

ASSIST UK

Formal name: Assist UK Independence

1 Portland Street, 4th Floor, Manchester, M1 3BE

Tel: 0161 2388776
E-mail: general.info@assist-uk.org

Website:
http://www.assist-uk.org

Enquiries:
Enquiries to: Chief Executive
Other contacts: Communications Officer

Founded:
1985

Formerly called:
Disabled Living Centres Council (DLCC) (year of change 2005)

Organisation type and purpose:
A membership organisation leading a network of Disability and Independent Living Centres and services.
The central point for local experience to feed national learning and support local delivery, ensuring that advice and product and service support is available free and impartially at the point of client contact.

Subject coverage:
Creating a Disabled Living Centre, providing contact with Disabled Living Centres, working with other organisations to provide access to their services for disabled living.

Printed publications:
Briefing (monthly, free to members)
Newsletter (quarterly, free to members)
Community equipment services . . . why we should care? (£35 plus £1.35 p&p)
Getting Started (£30 plus p&p)
Disability Equipment Services: What's the Problem? (Winchcombe M, 1997, £5 plus £1 p&p)
Equipped for Change (£5 plus £1 p&p)
Equipped for Life (£5 plus £2.50 p&p)
Who's for an Easier Life? (Winchcombe M, 1996, £5 plus £1 p&p)

Electronic and video publications:
Copy of summary of Community equipment services . . . why we should care? (tape)
Your Disabled Living Centre (video, £10 to buy, £5 to rent for two weeks, both plus £1 p&p)

Publications list:
Available online and in print

Access to staff:
Contact by letter, by telephone, by e-mail and via website. Appointment necessary.
Hours: Mon to Fri, 0900 to 1630

Access to building, collection or gallery:
Prior appointment required

Access for disabled people:
Parking provided, level entry, access to all public areas, toilet facilities

Member organisations:
45 Disabled / Independent Living Centres

ASSOCIATED BRITISH PORTS HOLDINGS PLC

Acronym or abbreviation: ABPH

150 Holborn, London, EC1N 2LR

Tel: 020 7430 1177
Fax: 020 7430 1384
E-mail: pr@abports.co.uk

Website:
http://www.abports.co.uk

Enquiries:
Enquiries to: Corporate Communications Manager
Direct e-mail: mcollins@abports.co.uk

Founded:
1983

Formerly called:
British Transport Docks Board (year of change 1983)

Organisation type and purpose:
Service industry.
Ports, transport and property company.
Ports owner and operator; subsidiaries include property, ferry, transport services, auto-processing terminals, computer and research companies, and dredging division.

Subject coverage:
Transport, the port industry, property development and investment, shipping, auto-processing, research, computing, dredging.

Printed publications:
Annual Report
Fact Book
Ports '99 and 2000 – A Guide to ABP's 23 Ports (fact book, free of charge)
Interim Report
Port Brochures
Ports Magazine

Access to staff:
Contact by letter, by telephone and by fax
Hours: Mon to Fri, 0830 to 1800

ASSOCIATION FOR ARCHERY IN SCHOOLS

Acronym or abbreviation: AAS

Bloxham School, Banbury, Oxfordshire, OX15 4PE

Tel: 01295 721463
Fax: 01295 721463

Website:
http://www.aasinfo.demon.co.uk

Enquiries:
Enquiries to: Secretary
Direct tel: 01295 724338
Direct e-mail: cfe@blockhamschool.com

Founded:
1963

Organisation type and purpose:
Membership association (membership is by subscription), voluntary organisation, suitable for ages: Under 18.
Promotion of Archery in schools and colleges.

Subject coverage:
Archery achievement (a Badge Scheme); formation of archery clubs; equipment; coaching; tournaments.

Printed publications:
Directory (annually, free)
Junior Archery World – JAW
Newsletter (3 times a year, free)

Access to staff:
Contact by letter, by telephone, by fax, by e-mail and via website
Hours: Answerphone/Fax during working day; personal contact late night, 2300 to 0200

Affiliated to:
Fédération Internationale de Tir à l'Arc (FITA)
Grand National Archery Society (GNAS)
National Council for School Sports (NCSS)

ASSOCIATION FOR ASTRONOMY EDUCATION

Formal name: Association for Astronomy Education
Acronym or abbreviation: AAE

Royal Astronomical Society, Burlington House, Piccadilly, London, W1J 0BQ

Website:
http://www.aae.org.uk
General introduction to Association for Astronomy Education.

Enquiries:
Enquiries to: Secretary
Direct e-mail: secretary@aae.org.uk

Founded:
1981

continued overleaf

Organisation type and purpose:
Membership association (membership is by subscription), present number of members: 120, registered charity (charity number 1046041).
To promote astronomy education at all levels and to support teachers through training, information and resources.

Subject coverage:
Astronomy education.

Printed publications:
Earth and Beyond – Resources for primary teachers
Earth and Space – Resources for secondary teachers
Order printed publications from: ASE Publications College Lane, Hatfield, Hertfordshire, AL10 9AA, tel: 01707 283000

Access to staff:
Contact by letter, by e-mail and via website
Hours: Mon to Fri, 0900 to 1700

ASSOCIATION FOR BETTER LIVING AND EDUCATION

Acronym or abbreviation: ABLE

Saint Hill Manor, East Grinstead, West Sussex, RH19 4JY

Tel: 01342 301902
Fax: 01342 327539

Website:
http://www.able.org

Enquiries:
Enquiries to: Executive Director

Founded:
1985

Organisation type and purpose:
Membership association, voluntary organisation, .
To work in the field of eradicating drug abuse, crime, illiteracy and forwarding a non-religious moral code.

Printed publications:
10 Things your friends may not know about DRUGS
Solutions Magazine
The Way to Happiness (booklet)

Access to staff:
Contact by letter, by telephone and by fax
Hours: Mon to Sat, 1000 to 2200

ASSOCIATION FOR CAREERS EDUCATION AND GUIDANCE

Acronym or abbreviation: ACEG

Tel: 01295 720809
Fax: 01295 720809
E-mail: info@aceg.org.uk

Website:
http://www.aceg.org.uk
The society, its aims, services and publications.

Enquiries:
Enquiries to: General Secretary

Founded:
1969

Formerly called:
National Association of Careers Teachers (year of change 1974); National Association of Careers & Guidance Teachers (year of change 2006)

Organisation type and purpose:
Membership association with over 1,600 members, the professional subject association for careers education and guidance (CEG) in schools and colleges in England and Wales. Members are careers practitioners in schools and colleges and those working in Connexions partnerships and local authorities who support these practitioners.

Committed to promoting the highest standards in CEG for all young people through excellence and innovation in careers work; campaigns on appropriate matters.

Subject coverage:
Careers and education guidance in schools and colleges in England and Wales.

Printed publications:
Produces regular journals and newsletters
Other publications include:
Better Practice: A guide to delivering effective career learning 11–19
What Do Careers Co-ordinators Do?
Essential Reading
Other occasional papers

Publications list:
Available online

Access to staff:
Contact by telephone, by fax and by e-mail

ASSOCIATION FOR CERAMIC TRAINING & DEVELOPMENT

Acronym or abbreviation: ACTD

St James House, Webberley Lane, Stoke-on-Trent, Staffordshire, ST3 1RJ

Tel: 01782 597016
Fax: 01782 597015
E-mail: actd@actd.co.uk

Enquiries:
Enquiries to: Director

Founded:
1993

Organisation type and purpose:
National training organisation.

Non-library collection catalogue:
All or part available in-house

Library catalogue:
All or part available in-house

Access to staff:
Contact by letter
Hours: Mon to Fri, 0900 to 1700

ASSOCIATION FOR CLINICAL BIOCHEMISTRY

Acronym or abbreviation: ACB

130–132 Tooley Street, London, SE1 2TU

Tel: 020 7403 8001
Fax: 020 7403 8006
E-mail: enquiries@acb.org.uk

Website:
http://www.acb.org.uk
General information about the Association.
General information for careers in clinical biochemistry.

Enquiries:
Enquiries to: Administrator

Founded:
1953

Organisation type and purpose:
Professional body, trade union, present number of members: 2,200.

Subject coverage:
Clinical biochemistry, chemical pathology, biochemical medicine, clinical chemistry, clinical sciences.

Museum or gallery collection, archive, or library special collection:
Archives of the Association

Non-library collection catalogue:
All or part available in-house

Library catalogue:
All or part available online

Printed publications:
Annals of Clinical Biochemistry (6 times a year, for sale)
News Sheet (monthly, free to members and for sale)
Diabetes & Laboratory Medicine
Neonatology & Laboratory Medicine
A Practical Guide to Accreditation in Laboratory Medicine
Poisoning & Laboratory Medicine
Biochemical Investigations in Laboratory Medicine
Liver Disease and Laboratory Medicine
Cancer and Clinical Biochemistry
Clinical Investigations and Statistics in Laboratory Medicine
Primary Care and Laboratory Medicine
Intensive Care & Clinical Biochemistry
Therapeutic Drug Monitoring & Clinical Biochemistry

Electronic and video publications:
Clinical Cases (CD-ROM, for purchase):
Calcium Cases
Diabetes Cases
Proteins Cases

Publications list:
Available online and in print

Access to staff:
Contact by letter, by fax and by e-mail
Hours: Mon to Fri, 0900 to 1700

Access for disabled people:
Ramped entry, access to all public areas, toilet facilities

Associated, for professional matters, with the:
Association of Clinical Cytogeneticists (ACC)
Association of Clinical Microbiologists (ACM)

Linked, for scientific and educational matters, with the:
International Federation of Clinical Chemistry and Laboratory Medicine (IFCC)

ASSOCIATION FOR COACHING

Acronym or abbreviation: AC

66 Church Road, London, W7 1LB

Tel: 0845 225 5048 or 020 8566 2400
Fax: 0845 225 5049
E-mail: enquiries@associationforcoaching.com

Website:
http://www.associationforcoaching.com
Information on the organisation and its members

Enquiries:
Enquiries to: Chairman
Direct tel: 07884 434547
Direct e-mail: ktulpa@associationforcoaching.com

Founded:
2002

Organisation type and purpose:
National organisation, advisory body, professional body (membership is by qualification, election or invitation).

Subject coverage:
Advancing education and best practice in coaching; executive, business, performance, private.

Access to staff:
Contact by telephone, by fax, by e-mail, in person and via website
Hours: Mon to Fri, 0900 to 1700

ASSOCIATION FOR CONTINENCE ADVICE

Acronym or abbreviation: ACA

c/o Fitwise Management Ltd, Drumcross Hall, Bathgate, EH48 4JJ

Tel: 01506 811077
Fax: 01506 811477
E-mail: aca@fitwise.co.uk

Website:
http://www.fitwise.co.uk

Enquiries:
Enquiries to: Membership Secretary;
Administration Officer
Direct e-mail: katie@fitwise.co.uk

Founded:
1980

Organisation type and purpose:
International organisation, advisory body,
membership association (membership is by
subscription), present number of members: 491,
voluntary organisation, registered charity, training
organisation, consultancy.
Membership organisation for healthcare
professionals working with people with bladder
and bowel dysfunction.

Printed publications:
Quarterly Newsletter

Access to staff:
Contact by letter, by telephone, by fax, by e-mail
and via website
Hours: Mon to Fri, 0900 to 1700

Access to building, collection or gallery:
Hours: Mon to Fri, 0900 to 1700

Access for disabled people:
via delivery area

Branches:
Has 10 regional branches

ASSOCIATION FOR EDUCATION WELFARE MANAGEMENT

Acronym or abbreviation: AEWM

1 The Boundary, Bradford, West Yorkshire, BD8
0BQ

Tel: 01924 305519 (daytime), 01274 542295
(evening)
Fax: 01924 305646

Enquiries:
Enquiries to: General Secretary
Direct e-mail: frances.molloy@ed.lancscc.gov.uk
Other contacts: Assistant Secretary (publicity)

Founded:
1917

Organisation type and purpose:
National organisation, professional body
(membership is by subscription), present number
of members: 150.
Promotes good practice and provides professional
support, responds to government initiatives.

Subject coverage:
Education welfare management.

Access to staff:
Contact by letter and by e-mail
Hours: Mon to Fri, 0900 to 1700

ASSOCIATION FOR GROUP AND INDIVIDUAL PSYCHOTHERAPY

Acronym or abbreviation: AGIP

1 Fairbridge Road, London, N19 3EW

Tel: 020 7272 7013
Fax: 020 7272 6945
E-mail: office@agip.org.uk

Website:
http://www.agip.org.uk

Enquiries:
Enquiries to: Administrator

Founded:
1974

Organisation type and purpose:
Registered charity (charity number 1083030),
training organisation.
Provision of services in psychotherapy.

Subject coverage:
Psychoanalytic psychotherapy, training, clinical
and supervision services.

Special visitor services:
Low-fee psychotherapy clinic.

Education services:
Education and training in psychotherapy.

Services for disabled people:
By arrangement.

Access to staff:
Contact by letter, by telephone, by fax, by e-mail
and via website
Hours: Mon to Fri, 0900 to 1230

Member of:
United Kingdom Council for Psychotherapy

ASSOCIATION FOR HUMANISTIC PSYCHOLOGY IN BRITAIN

Acronym or abbreviation: AHPB

BM Box 3582, London, WC1N 3XX

Tel: 08457 078506
E-mail: admin@ahpb.org.uk

Website:
http://www.ahpb.org.uk
Outline of organisation, index pages of journal,
links to American Association.

Enquiries:
Enquiries to: Administrator

Founded:
1969

Organisation type and purpose:
Professional body, voluntary organisation,
registered charity (charity number 290548).

Subject coverage:
Humanistic psychology; counselling and
psychotherapy; training.

Printed publications:
Newsletter
Self and Society (journal)
Order printed publications from: admin@ahpb.org.uk

Electronic and video publications:
Guide to Humanistic Psychology (online)

Access to staff:
Contact by letter, by telephone, by e-mail and via
website
Hours: 24-hour answering machine.

ASSOCIATION FOR INDUSTRIAL ARCHAEOLOGY

Acronym or abbreviation: AIA

The Wharfage, Coach Road, Coalbrookdale,
Telford, Shropshire, TF8 7DQ

Tel: 01952 432141
Fax: 01952 432237

Enquiries:
Enquiries to: Secretary
Other contacts: Correspondence Secretary

Founded:
1973

Organisation type and purpose:
Advisory body, learned society (membership is by
subscription), voluntary organisation, research
organisation, publishing house.

Subject coverage:
Industrial archaeology; conservation; preservation.

Education services:
Group education facilities, resources for Further or
Higher Education.

Printed publications:
IA News (4 times a year)
Industrial Archaeology Review (2 times a year)
Order printed publications from: Sales Officer

Barn Cottage, Bridge Street, Bridgnorth,
Shropshire, WV15 6AF, tel: 01746 765159

Publications list:
Available in print

Access to staff:
Contact by letter, by telephone and by fax
Hours: Mon to Fri, 0900 to 1700

Access to building, collection or gallery:
No prior appointment required

Also at:
AIA Liaison Officer
School of Archaeological Studies, University of
Leicester, University Road, Leicester, LE1 7RH;
tel: 0116 252 5337; fax: 0116 252 5005; e-mail:
aia@le.ac.uk

Links with:
Ironbridge Gorge Museum Trust
tel: 01952 433522

ASSOCIATION FOR LANGUAGE LEARNING

Acronym or abbreviation: ALL

University of Leicester, University Road, Leicester,
LE1 7RH

Tel: 0116 229 7600
E-mail: info@all-languages.org.uk

Website:
http://www.all-languages.org.uk

Enquiries:
Enquiries to: Director
Other contacts: Advertising, Courses and
Conference Assistant for advertising enquiries.

Founded:
1990

Organisation type and purpose:
Professional body, membership association
(membership is by subscription), present number
of members: 4800, registered charity (charity
number 1001826).
Support for teachers of all modern foreign
languages in all sectors of education.

Subject coverage:
Modern foreign language teaching and learning at
all levels of education from primary to university,
adult education and training, Asian languages,
French, German, Italian, Portuguese, Russian,
Spanish teaching in schools and universities,
teaching materials and sources of auxiliary
teaching materials.

Printed publications:
Language Learning Journal (twice a year)
Francophonie (journal, twice a year)
German Teaching (journal, twice a year)
Rusistika (journal, annually)
Tuttitalia (journal, twice a year)
Vida Hispánica (journal, twice a year)
Language World (newsletter, quarterly)

Publications list:
Available in print

Access to staff:
Contact by letter, by telephone, by fax, by e-mail,
in person and via website
Hours: Mon to Fri, 0900 to 1700

Affiliated to:
Fédération Internationale de Professeurs de
Français (FIPF)
Fédération Internationale de Professeurs de
Langues Vivantes (FIPLV)
IDV
MAPRYAL

ASSOCIATION FOR LATIN LITURGY

Acronym or abbreviation: ALL

47 Western Park Road, Leicester, LE3 6HQ

Tel: 0116 285 6158

continued overleaf

E-mail: enquiries@latin-liturgy.org

Website:
http://www.latin-liturgy.org
Full information on the association and its
publications.

Enquiries:
Enquiries to: Chairman
Direct e-mail: enquiries@latin-liturgy.org

Founded:
1969

Organisation type and purpose:
Learned society, membership association
(membership is by subscription), present number
of members: 300.
Religious (Roman Catholic). Shares aims with the
Latin Liturgy Assoc. (USA), the Vereniging voor
Latijnse Liturgie (Netherlands) and Pro Liturgia
(France). There is a formal Federation of the three
European associations.
To promote understanding of the value of the
Catholic liturgy and its music in Latin, and in a
practical way to encourage its use.

Subject coverage:
The Latin liturgy of the Roman Catholic Church
and its associated music in the past and at the
present day. The teaching of ecclesiastical Latin.
Advice on printed texts connected with the above.

Printed publications:
Adoremus (£1.50)
A New Approach to Latin for the Mass (£12) (CD –
   Orate Fratres – is available for use with this book
   or separately, £12)
A Voice for all Time (£6)
Latin Gregorian Chant Sung Mass Booklets:
Lux et Origo (Mass I, 75p)
Cunctipotens genitor Deus (Mass IV, 75p)
Kyrie magnae (Mass V, 75p)
Cum Jubilo (Mass IX, 75p)
De Angelis (Mass VIII, 75p)
Orbis Factor (Mass XI, 75p)
Advent and Lent (Mass XVII, 75p)
Requiem (75p)
Organ Accompaniment (Mass VIII, £5)
Latin in the Liturgy (1988, available free on
   request)
Newsletter (3 times a year, members)
Orders from outside UK: please add 25%
Order printed publications from: Publications
Manager, 47 Western Park Road, Leicester, LE3
6HQ; e-mail: sales@latin-liturgy.org.uk

Electronic and video publications:
CD: Orate Fratres (Pronunciation and singing of
   Latin at Mass, £12); orders from outside UK:
   please add 25%
Order electronic and video publications from:
Publications Manager, 47 Western Park Road,
Leicester, LE3 6HQ; e-mail: sales@latin-liturgy.org
.uk

Publications list:
Available online and in print

Access to staff:
Contact by letter, by e-mail and via website
Hours: Mon to Fri, 0900 to 1700

ASSOCIATION FOR LEARNING TECHNOLOGY

Acronym or abbreviation: ALT

Gipsy Lane, Headington, Oxford, OX3 0BP

Tel: 01865 484125
Fax: 01865 484165
E-mail: admin@alt.ac.uk

Website:
http://www.alt.ac.uk

Enquiries:
Enquiries to: Director of Development
Other contacts: Administrator for membership
enquiries or conference booking information.

Founded:
1993

Organisation type and purpose:
Learned society (membership is by subscription),
present number of members: 700, registered
charity (charity number 1063519).

Subject coverage:
Innovative teaching and learning in further and
higher education, application of learning
technology, interchange and representation of the
membership.

Printed publications:
ALT-J (journal, 3 times a year)
ALT-N (newsletter, quarterly, subscription
   included in membership fee)
An Introduction to Learning Technology Within
   Tertiary Education in the UK (Handbook)
Enabling Active Learning (Conference abstracts)
Changing Education, Changing Technology
   (Conference abstracts)
Changing Face of Learning Technology (book)
Integrating Technology into the Curriculum
   (Conference abstracts)
Virtual Campus, Real Learning (Conference
   abstracts)

Electronic and video publications:
Media Active 94: Conference Proceedings (CD-
   ROM)
Harnessing Multimedia for Higher Education (CD-
   ROM, £20)

Publications list:
Available in print

Access to staff:
Contact by letter, by telephone, by fax, by e-mail
and via website
Hours: Mon to Fri, 0900 to 1700

Access to building, collection or gallery:
No access other than to staff

ASSOCIATION FOR LOW COUNTRIES STUDIES

Acronym or abbreviation: ALCS

Department of Germanic Studies, University of
Sheffield, Jessop West, 1 Upper Hanover Street,
Sheffield, S3 7RA

Tel: 0114 222 4396
E-mail: alcs@sheffield.ac.uk

Website:
http://alcs.group.shef.ac.uk

Enquiries:
Enquiries to: Administrator

Founded:
1995

Organisation type and purpose:
Learned society (membership is by subscription).
To promote the scholarly study of the language,
culture, history and society of the Low Countries;
to encourage research in Low Countries Studies; to
increase public awareness of the Low Countries,
especially the Dutch Language, and Dutch and
Flemish culture, history and society; to represent
the interests of Low Countries Studies in higher
education at national and international level.

Subject coverage:
Study of language, literature, history, art, politics,
geography and culture of the Low Countries, i.e.
the Netherlands and Belgium (particularly
Flanders).

Printed publications:
Dutch Crossing: A Journal for Low Countries
   Studies (3 times a year; individuals £31 per year)
Order printed publications from: http://
alcs.group.shef.ac.uk/aboutus/subscription.htm

Publications list:
Available online

Links with:
University Council for Modern Languages in
Higher Education (UCML)

ASSOCIATION FOR MANAGEMENT EDUCATION AND DEVELOPMENT

Acronym or abbreviation: AMED

1st Floor, 62 Paul Street, London, EC2A 4NA

Tel: 020 7613 4121
Fax: 01923 859999
E-mail: ahatherill@aol.com

Website:
http://www.amed.org.uk
Articles from journal.
http://www.amed.co.uk
Current events, news, chat rooms, e-newsletters.

Enquiries:
Enquiries to: Membership Secretary
Direct tel: 01923 859999
Direct e-mail: allyson@management.org.uk
Other contacts: Office Manager

Founded:
1978

Organisation type and purpose:
Membership association (membership is by
subscription), present number of members: 1,200.
For the development and propagation of
management, organisational learning and
education.

Subject coverage:
Learning, knowledge management, change
management, board and director development,
organisation developments, management
development, management consultancy.

Library catalogue:
All or part available online

Printed publications:
AMED News (newsletter, monthly)
Conference Proceedings
Organisations and People (journal, quarterly)
Order printed publications from: AMED
The Gardeners Cottage, Shenley Park, Radlett
Lane, Shenley, WD7 9DW

Electronic and video publications:
Conference Proceedings (CD-ROM)

Publications list:
Available in print

Access to staff:
Contact by letter, by telephone, by fax, by e-mail
and via website
Hours: Mon to Fri, 0900 to 1700

ASSOCIATION FOR MEDICAL OSTEOPATHY

8–10 Boston Place, London, NW1 6QH

Tel: 020 7262 5250
Fax: 020 7723 7492

Enquiries:
Enquiries to: Honorary Secretary
Other contacts: Membership Secretary

Founded:
1911

Formerly called:
Association of Medical Osteopaths, British
Osteopathic Association (BOA), London College of
Osteopathic Medicine

Organisation type and purpose:
Professional body (membership is by
qualification), present number of members: 120.
Medically qualified osteopaths trained at the
London College of Osteopathic Medicine.

Subject coverage:
Osteopathic medicine; UK sources of treatment.

Library catalogue:
All or part available in-house

Printed publications:
Directory of Osteopathic Physicians (biennial)
Newsletter (quarterly)

Access to staff:
Contact by letter, by telephone and by fax. Access for members only.
Hours: Mon to Fri, 0930 to 1700

Access to building, collection or gallery:
No access other than to staff

Access for disabled people:
Level entry, toilet facilities

At the same address is the:
Osteopathic Association Clinic
tel: 020 7262 1128; fax: 020 7723 7492

Close links with:
Osteopathic Trusts Limited
tel: 020 7262 5250; fax: 020 7723 7492

ASSOCIATION FOR PALLIATIVE MEDICINE OF GREAT BRITAIN AND IRELAND

Acronym or abbreviation: APM

76 Botley Road, Park Gate, Southampton, SO31 1BA

Tel: 01489 565665
E-mail: sabine.tuck@palliative-medicine.org

Website:
http://www.palliative-medicine.org

Enquiries:
Enquiries to: Administrator

Founded:
1985

Organisation type and purpose:
Professional body, membership association (membership is by subscription, qualification), present number of members: 1,050, registered charity (charity number 1053572).

Subject coverage:
Palliative Medicine

Printed publications:
Clinical governance documents
APM newsletter (for members)
SpR research documents
Manual for trainers in palliative medicine
Palliative medicine curriculum

Access to staff:
Contact by letter, by telephone and by e-mail
Hours: Mon to Fri

ASSOCIATION FOR PASTORAL CARE OF THE MENTALLY ILL

Acronym or abbreviation: APCMH

Cornerstone House, 14 Willis Road, Croydon, Surrey, CR0 2XX

Tel: 020 8665 6718
Fax: 020 8665 1972
E-mail: apcmh@croydononline.org

Enquiries:
Enquiries to: Development Officer

Founded:
1984

Organisation type and purpose:
Voluntary organisation.

Subject coverage:
Mental health especially spirituality and mental health promotion.

Printed publications:
General information leaflet and information on mental health including in minority languages

Access to staff:
Contact by letter, by telephone, by fax and by e-mail
Hours: Mon, Wed, Fri, 0830 to 1530

Access to building, collection or gallery:
No access other than to staff

National Office:
APCMH
c/o Marylebone Park Church, Marylebone Road, London, NW1 5LT; tel: 01483 538936

ASSOCIATION FOR PERIOPERATIVE PRACTICE

Acronym or abbreviation: AFPP

Daisy Ayris House, 6 Grove Park Court, Harrogate, North Yorkshire, HG1 4DP

Tel: 01423 508079
Fax: 01423 531613
E-mail: hq@afpp.org.uk

Website:
http://www.afpp.org.uk
Information about the association, job forum, updated daily, main articles from journal each month, journal index, join membership online and application form, discussion forum, list of national events.

Enquiries:
Enquiries to: Chairman

Founded:
1964

Formerly called:
National Association of Theatre Nurses (year of change 2005)

Organisation type and purpose:
Advisory body, membership association (membership is by subscription), training organisation.

Subject coverage:
Operating theatre nursing (all surgical specialisations); theatre technique; staffing of operating theatres; non-nursing staff in theatres; planning; patient care; anaesthetic room nursing; recovery room nursing; legal implications of patients' safety and accidents; sterilisation.

Museum or gallery collection, archive, or library special collection:
Journals on nursing (national)
Journals on perioperative nursing (national and international)
Books on theatre nursing and related topics

Printed publications:
British Journal of Theatre Nursing (monthly)
Journal of Perioperative Practice (monthly)
Journal of Advanced Perioperative Care (twice a year)
Order printed publications from: AFPP directly or website

Publications list:
Available online and in print

Access to staff:
Contact by letter, by telephone, by fax, by e-mail and via website
Hours: Mon to Fri, 0830 to 1630

ASSOCIATION FOR PHYSICAL EDUCATION

Acronym or abbreviation: AFPE

Building 25, London Road, Reading, Berkshire, RG1 5AQ

Tel: 0118 378 6240
Fax: 0118 378 6242
E-mail: enquiries@afpe.org.uk

Website:
http://www.afpe.org.uk

Enquiries:
Enquiries to: Chief Executive

Founded:
2006

Organisation type and purpose:
Professional body (membership is by subscription), registered charity (charity number 1114673), research organisation.

Subject coverage:
Physical education, continuing professional development, health and fitness education.

Museum or gallery collection, archive, or library special collection:
PEA Archives in the Library, Sheffield University

Printed publications:
PE Matters
Assessment for Learning in Physical Education
Case Law in Physical Education and School Sport
Achieving Excellence
Self-evaluation in Physical Education
Developing the Process
A guide to Self-review in Physical Education

Publications list:
Available in print

Access to staff:
Contact by letter, by telephone, by fax, by e-mail and via website. Appointment necessary.
Hours: Mon to Fri, 0900 to 1700

Access to building, collection or gallery:
Prior appointment required

Access for disabled people:
Parking provided

ASSOCIATION FOR POST NATAL ILLNESS

Acronym or abbreviation: APNI

145 Dawes Road, London, SW6 7EB

Tel: 020 7386 0868
Fax: 020 7386 8885
E-mail: info@apni.org

Website:
http://www.apni.org
Details of Association and leaflets.

Enquiries:
Enquiries to: Information Officer

Founded:
1979

Organisation type and purpose:
Membership association, present number of members: 1,800, voluntary organisation, registered charity (charity number 280510).
Provides information and support to mothers suffering from postnatal depression, information for health professionals, supports research into postnatal illness.

Subject coverage:
The management and treatment of postnatal illness.

Printed publications:
Coping with Postnatal Depression (Marshall F, Shelden Press 1993, £5.99)
Depression after Childbirth (Dalton K, OUP)
Leaflets including:
Puerperal Psychosis (10p per copy, not suitable for general display)
Postnatal Depression (75p each, over 200, 60p each)
The Baby Blues and Postnatal Depression (100 copies £10)
Health Visitors Notes for Guidance (75p per copy, only available to Health Visitors, Midwives and Community Psychiatric Nurses)

Publications list:
Available in print

Access to staff:
Contact by letter, by telephone, by fax, by e-mail and via website
Hours: Mon to Fri, 1000 to 1400

ASSOCIATION FOR PROFESSIONALS IN SERVICES FOR ADOLESCENTS

Acronym or abbreviation: APSA

1 Arun House, River Way, Uckfield, East Sussex, TT22 1SL

Tel: 01825 760 886
Fax: 01825 768 864
E-mail: apsa@bhm.co.uk

Website:
http://www.apsa-web.uk
Information about the Association and its publications.

Enquiries:
Enquiries to: Administrator
Other contacts: Membership Secretary for subscription enquiries.

Founded:
1970

Organisation type and purpose:
Professional body (membership is by subscription), present number of members: 605, registered charity.
To promote the study, understanding, and care of adolescents.

Subject coverage:
Subjects related to disturbed adolescents.

Printed publications:
Journal of Adolescence (6 times a year)
Newsletters (3 times a year, members)
Rapport Journal (4 times a year)

Access to staff:
Contact by letter, by telephone, by fax, by e-mail and via website
Hours: Mon to Fri, 0900 to 1700

ASSOCIATION FOR PROJECT MANAGEMENT

Acronym or abbreviation: APM

150 West Wycombe Road, High Wycombe, Buckinghamshire, HP12 3AE

Tel: 0845 458 1944
Fax: 01494 528937
E-mail: info@apm.org.uk

Website:
http://www.apm.org.uk
Details of the Association.

Enquiries:
Enquiries to: Chief Executive
Other contacts: Head of Professional Development; Head of Membership; Head of Marketing

Founded:
1972

Formerly called:
Association of Project Managers (year of change 1997)

Organisation type and purpose:
National organisation, professional body (membership is by subscription), present number of members: 17,000, registered charity (charity number 290927).
Promotion of the professions of Project Management both in the UK and internationally and the development of the art and science of project management.

Subject coverage:
Project management across all sectors of business and industry.

Printed publications:
International Journal of Project Management (8 times a year by subscription)
Project Magazine (10 times a year, members: free)
Project Risk Analysis and Management Guide 2nd edition
APM Body of Knowledge 5th Edition
Standard Terms for the Appointment of a Project Manager
Starting out in Project Management – A Study Guide for the APM Introductory Certificate in Project Management 2nd edition
Project Management Pathways
APM Competence Framework
APM Yearbook 2006–7 The Business of Projects
APM Yearbook 2005–6 Insights in Project and Programme Management
Earned Value Management – Guideline for the United Kingdom
Contract Strategy for Successful Project Management
Directing Change: A Guide to the Governance of Project Management
Co-Directing Change: Guide to the Governance of Multi-Owned Projects
Models to Improve the Management of Projects
APM Introduction to Programme Management
Order printed publications from: Turpin Distribution: 01767 604951

Electronic and video publications:
APM/BSi product containing BS6079, the APM Body of Knowledge and the APMP Examination Syllabus
APM Project Management Standards
A Guide to Knowledge Management
Order electronic and video publications from: Turpin Distribution: 01767 604951

Access to staff:
Contact by letter, by telephone, by fax and by e-mail
Hours: Mon to Fri, 0900 to 1700

Access to building, collection or gallery:
Hours: Mon to Fri, 0900 to 1700

Access for disabled people:
Parking provided, level entry
Hours: Mon to Fri, 0900 to 1700

Affiliated to:
International Project Management Association (IPMA)
Service Secretariat, PO Box 30, Monmouth, NP5 4YZ; tel: 01594 531007; fax: 01594 531008; e-mail: ipma@btinternet.com; website: http://www.ipma.co.uk

ASSOCIATION FOR PUBLIC SERVICE EXCELLENCE

Acronym or abbreviation: APSE

2nd floor Washbrook House, Lancastrian Office Centre, Talbot Road, Old Trafford, Manchester, M32 0FP

Tel: 0161 772 1810
Fax: 0161 772 1811
E-mail: enquiries@apse.org.uk

Website:
http://www.apse.org.uk
APSE's services.

Enquiries:
Enquiries to: Secretariat
Other contacts: Principal Advisor for publications, press releases, briefing notes

Founded:
1981

Formerly called:
Association of Direct Labour Organisations (ADLO) (year of change 2000)

Organisation type and purpose:
Local government body, advisory body, professional body (membership is by subscription), present number of members: 270, training organisation, consultancy, research organisation.
To consult, develop, promote and advise on best practice in the delivery of public services.

Subject coverage:
Public sector contracting, service delivery issues such as quality, structures, etc, best value, PFI, TUPE, housing stock transfers, best value consultancy, local government benchmarking.

Museum or gallery collection, archive, or library special collection:
Small library and resource unit

Trade and statistical information:
Data on local government direct service provision.

Non-library collection catalogue:
All or part available online

Library catalogue:
All or part available online

Printed publications:
Housing Stock Transfer: The Only Answer?
Internal Service Provision: The Best Value Option?
Report on Hand-Arm Vibration
Structuring towards Best Value
Inspecting Best Value
New Millennium Service Provider
The Involvement of DLOs and DSOs in Local Authority PFI Scheme
Pursuing Excellence in Local Government (Volumes 1 to 3)
Housing Options
The Ingredients for Success
The Future Role of Elected Members
The Composting and Disposal of Green Waste
A Guide to Local Authority Charging and Trading
Construction Skill Shortages in the Public Sector
Environmental Services: At the Heart of Every Community
Delivering the Liveability Agenda
Soft FM
Maximising Local Potential
Towards a Future for Public Employment
The Future of Local Government in Wales
Governance, Neighbourhoods & Service Delivery
Catering within Education: Tackling health in schools
Creating resilient local economies: exploring the economic footprint of public services Insourcing: A guide to bringing local authority services back in house
Think Twice: The role of elected members in commissioning
An elected member guide to performance management
The ensuring Council; Governance, neighbourhoods and service delivery
More bang for the public buck; A guide to using procurement to achieve community benefits
Under one Roof
Order printed publications from: e-mail: enquiries@apse.org.uk

Publications list:
Available online and in print

Access to staff:
Contact by letter, by telephone, by fax, by e-mail and via website. Appointment necessary. Access for members only. Non-members charged.
Hours: Mon to Fri, 0900 to 1700

Access to building, collection or gallery:
No access other than to staff

Access for disabled people:
Access to all public areas

Also at:
Association for Public Service Excellence (Scottish APSE)
Brandon House Business Centre, Unit 18–20, 23–25 Brandon Street, Hamilton, ML3 8DA; tel: 01698 459051; fax: 01698 200316; e-mail: enquiries@apse.org.uk

ASSOCIATION FOR RATIONAL EMOTIVE BEHAVIOUR THERAPY

PO Box 39207, London, SE3 7XH

Tel: 020 8293 4334
Fax: 020 8293 4114
E-mail: rebtadmin@managingstress.com

Website:
http://rebt.bizland.com
Information about the Association, membership details, recognised courses, publications

Enquiries:
Enquiries to: Honorary Secretary
Other contacts: Membership Secretary

Founded:
1993

Formerly called:
Association for Rational Emotive Behaviour
Therapists (year of change 2002)

Organisation type and purpose:
Professional body (membership is by subscription,
qualification), present number of members: 85.
To promote the art and science of rational emotive
behaviour therapy.

Non-library collection catalogue:
All or part available online

Printed publications:
The Rational Emotive Behaviour Therapist Journal

Electronic and video publications:
Online journal

Access to staff:
Contact by letter, by telephone, by e-mail and via
website
Hours: Mon to Fri, 1000 to 1700

ASSOCIATION FOR ROAD TRAFFIC SAFETY AND MANAGEMENT

Acronym or abbreviation: ARTSM

Office 8, Epic House, 128 Fulwell Road,
Teddington, TW11 0RQ

Tel: 020 8977 6952
Fax: 020 8977 8339

Website:
http://www.artsm.org.uk

Enquiries:
Enquiries to: General Secretary
Direct e-mail: philip.crickmay@artsm.org.uk

Founded:
1933

Formerly called:
Association of Road Traffic Sign Makers (ARTSM)
(year of change 1995)

Organisation type and purpose:
Trade association (membership is by subscription,
qualification), present number of members: 41.

Subject coverage:
Transport, road safety, pedestrian safety, road
traffic signs, permanent and portable variable
message signs, portable traffic signals, sign
luminaires, street lighting, street name plates,
traffic cones and lamps, sign erection, sign design-
computer systems, vehicle detection and control.

Printed publications:
Brochure of members and products (free)

Access to staff:
Contact by letter, by telephone, by fax, by e-mail
and via website. Appointment necessary.
Hours: Mon, Tue, Thu, 0900 to 1700

ASSOCIATION FOR SCIENCE EDUCATION

Acronym or abbreviation: ASE

College Lane, Hatfield, Hertfordshire, AL10 9AA

Tel: 01707 283000
Fax: 01707 266532
E-mail: info@ase.org.uk

Website:
http://www.ase.org.uk
Membership information, safety, publications,
Association policies.

Enquiries:
Enquiries to: Chief Executive

Other contacts: Executive Director (Professional and
Curriculum Innovation) – bookselling operations;
Co-ordinator Journals – magazines

Founded:
1901

Organisation type and purpose:
Professional body (membership is by subscription),
present number of members: 15,000, registered
charity (charity number 313123), suitable for ages:
3 to 19, publishing house.
Educational organisation.

Subject coverage:
Primary, secondary and further education science
education, study for its improvement, school safety
issues.

Printed publications:
Education in Science (5 times a year)
Many publications for teachers of science
Primary Science (5 times a year)
Science Teacher Education (3 times a year)
School Science Review (4 times a year)

Electronic and video publications:
Videos

Publications list:
Available online and in print

Access to staff:
Contact by letter, by telephone, by fax, by e-mail
and via website. Appointment necessary.
Hours: Mon to Fri, 0900 to 1700

Links with:
40 International Science Teacher Education
Associations

ASSOCIATION FOR SCOTTISH LITERARY STUDIES

Acronym or abbreviation: ASLS

Department of Scottish Literature, 7 University
Gardens, University of Glasgow, Glasgow, G12
8QH

Tel: 0141 330 5309
Fax: 0141 330 5309
E-mail: office@asls.org.uk

Website:
http://www.asls.org.uk
Articles, teaching materials, information on
publications and conferences, and links to other
sites of interest.

Enquiries:
Enquiries to: Manager

Founded:
1970

Organisation type and purpose:
International organisation, membership
association (membership is by subscription),
present number of members: 600, registered
charity (charity number SC006535), publishing
house.
ASLS is an educational charity promoting the
languages and literature of Scotland, from the
study of classic texts to encouraging contemporary
talent.

Subject coverage:
Languages and literature of Scotland.

Printed publications:
Books and edited editions
ASLS Annual Volumes Series
New Writing Scotland Series
ASLS Occasional Papers Series
Scotnotes (24 titles relating to specific authors or
books)
ScotLit (2 times a year)
Scottish Language (annually)
Scottish Literary Review (2 times a year)

Electronic and video publications:
The International Journal of Scottish Literature at
http://www.ijsl.stir.ac.uk
The Bottle Imp at http://www.thebottleimp.org.uk

Publications list:
Available online and in print

Access to staff:
Contact by letter, by telephone, by fax, by e-mail
and via website
Hours: Mon to Fri, 0900 to 1700

ASSOCIATION FOR SHARED PARENTING

Acronym or abbreviation: A.S.P.

PO Box 2000, Dudley, West Midlands, DY1 1YZ

Tel: 01789 751157
Fax: 01789 751081
E-mail: spring.cott@btopenworld.com

Website:
http://www.sharedparenting.org.uk
http://www.sharedparenting.f9.co.uk/

Enquiries:
Enquiries to: Honorary Secretary
Direct e-mail: owner@sharedparenting.org.uk

Founded:
1993

Formerly called:
Families Need Fathers (West Midlands Branch)
(FNF) (year of change 1993)

Organisation type and purpose:
Membership association (membership is by
subscription), present number of members: 80,
voluntary organisation, registered charity (charity
number 1042874).
To promote the right of children to have sufficient
contact with both parents after separation or
divorce.

Subject coverage:
The Children Act 1989, parental responsibility,
family court procedures, divorce and children,
maintaining contact with children after separation
or divorce, how to manage your solicitor, use of
child contact centre.

Printed publications:
Leaflets and occasional magazine

Access to staff:
Contact by letter and by telephone
Hours: Daily, 0800 to 2200

Other branches in:
Leicestershire
tel: 0116 254 8453

ASSOCIATION FOR SPECIALIST FIRE PROTECTION

Acronym or abbreviation: ASFP

Kingsley House, Ganders Business Park, Kingsley,
Bordon, Hampshire, GU35 9LU

Tel: 01420 471612
Fax: 01420 471611
E-mail: info@asfp.org.uk

Website:
http://www.asfp.org.uk
All the publications produced by ASFP on fire
protection of steelwork, ductwork, fire dampers,
partitions, floors, firestopping, etc. are freely
downloadable from the website.

Enquiries:
Direct e-mail: info@asfp.org.uk

Founded:
1975

Organisation type and purpose:
Trade association, present number of members: 64.
Represents UK manufacturers, distributors,
contractors, consultants, testing houses and others
involved in passive fire protection products and
services. Produces a wide range of relevant
publications.

Subject coverage:
Passive fire protection products and services.

continued overleaf

Information services:
Technical information on passive fire protection is
provided by ASFP Technical Officer.

Library catalogue:
All or part available online

Printed publications:
List of members and services (free)
Fire Stopping & Penetration Seals for the
 Construction Industry (Red Book)
Fire Protection for Structural Steel in Buildings
 (Yellow Book)
Fire Resisting Ductwork (Blue Book), European
 Version
Fire Retardant Coating Systems (Orange Book)
Fire & Smoke Resisting Dampers (Grey Book)
Fire Resisting Non Load-Bearing Partitions (Purple
 Book)
Fire Protection for Timber Floors (Green Book)
Code of practice for sprayed nonreactive coatings
 for FP steelwork
Code of Practice Boards for FP steelwork
CoP spec and onsite use of Intumescent coatings
 for fire protection of structural steelwork
Class O and Class 1

Publications list:
Available online and in print

Access to staff:
Contact by letter, by telephone, by fax, by e-mail
and via website
Hours: Mon to Fri, 0900 to 1700

ASSOCIATION FOR SPINA BIFIDA AND HYDROCEPHALUS

Acronym or abbreviation: ASBAH

ASBAH House, 42 Park Road, Peterborough,
Cambridgeshire, PE1 2UQ

Tel: 01733 555988
Fax: 01733 555985
E-mail: helpline@asbah.org

Website:
http://www.asbah.org
Information on the disabilities (spina bifida/
hydrocephalus), topic sheets.

Enquiries:
Enquiries to: Helpline and Information Service
Direct tel: 0845 450 7755
Direct e-mail: briand@asbah.org

Founded:
1966

Organisation type and purpose:
Voluntary organisation, registered charity (charity
number 249338).
40 affiliated local associations in UK.
Provides information, advice and support to
families/individuals with spina bifida and/or
hydrocephalus.

Subject coverage:
Spina bifida, hydrocephalus, (antenatal testing,
welfare and help as to benefit entitlement,
education, mobility, continence, training and
employment, aids and appliances in relation to
spina bifida or hydrocephalus only).

Printed publications:
Link (journal, bi-monthly, £6.80 annual
 subscription)
Annual Report
Below the Belt (ASBAH, £7)
Benny Bear Books (£2 each)
Hydrocephalus and its implications for teaching
 and learning (£9)
Hydrocephalus and YOU (Holgate, L and
 Batchelor, R, £7.50)
The Statementing Process for Children with Special
 Needs (ASBAH)
Information sheets
Your Child and Hydrocephalus (£9.99)

Publications list:
Available online and in print

Access to staff:
Contact by letter, by telephone, by fax, by e-mail
and via website
Hours: Mon to Fri, 0900 to 1700. Helpline: Mon to
Fri, 1000 to 1600

ASSOCIATION FOR THE CONSERVATION OF ENERGY

Acronym or abbreviation: ACE

Westgate House, Prebend Street, London, N1 8PT

Tel: 020 7359 8000
Fax: 020 7359 0863
E-mail: info@ukace.org

Website:
http://members.aol.com/aceuk/home.htm
Access to briefing notes, general information.

Enquiries:
Enquiries to: Office Manager
Other contacts: Research Director for research
function.

Founded:
1981

Organisation type and purpose:
Membership association (membership is by
subscription, election or invitation), present
number of members: 18, research organisation.
Campaigning organisation.
To increase investment in energy conservation.

Subject coverage:
Energy conservation (policy rather than product
related), greenhouse effect, CO_2 emissions, fuel
poverty.

**Museum or gallery collection, archive, or library
special collection:**
Material on energy conservation policy

Publications list:
Available in print

Access to staff:
Contact by letter, by telephone, by fax, by e-mail
and via website
Hours: Mon to Fri, 0930 to 1730
Special comments: Strictly no personal callers.

Links with:
British Energy Efficiency Federation

ASSOCIATION FOR UNIVERSITY AND COLLEGE COUNSELLING

Acronym or abbreviation: AUCC

British Association for Counselling and
Psychotherapy, 15 St John's Business Park,
Lutterworth, Leicestershire, LE17 4HB

Tel: 01455 883300; minicom no. 01455 0307
Fax: 01455 550243
E-mail: bacp@bacp.co.uk

Website:
http://www.bacp.co.uk
http://www.counselling.co.uk

Enquiries:
Enquiries to: Administrator

Founded:
1971

Formerly called:
Association of Student Counsellors (year of change
1997)

Organisation type and purpose:
Voluntary organisation.
To promote counselling in institutions of post-
compulsory education.

Subject coverage:
Provision of counselling services in post-
compulsory education, practice of student
counselling, careers counselling, training and
professional development of members, advisory

service to members for their institutional
provision, appropriate conditions of service for
counsellors in institutions.

Trade and statistical information:
Statistical survey of institutions (available to
 contributing members only).

Printed publications:
Advisory Service for Institutions (free)
Association for Student Counselling (free)
Directory of Training Courses (via BACP)
Executive Council (free)
Guidelines for the ASC Recognition of Training
 Courses (free)

Publications list:
Available online and in print

Access to staff:
Contact by letter, by telephone, by fax, by e-mail
and via website. Appointment necessary.
Hours: Mon to Fri, 0900 to 1700

Access to building, collection or gallery:
Prior appointment required
Hours: Mon to Fri, 0900 to 1700

Access for disabled people:
Parking provided, ramped entry, toilet facilities

Constituent part of:
British Association for Counselling and
Psychotherapy

ASSOCIATION OF ACCOUNTING TECHNICIANS

Acronym or abbreviation: AAT

154 Clerkenwell Road, London, EC1R 5AD

Tel: 020 7837 8600
Fax: 020 7837 6970
E-mail: info@aat.org.uk

Website:
http://www.aat.org.uk

Enquiries:
Enquiries to: Communications Manager
Direct tel: 020 7415 7670
Direct fax: 020 7415 7699
Direct e-mail: kate.martin@aat.org.uk

Founded:
1980

Organisation type and purpose:
International organisation, professional body
(membership is by subscription, qualification),
present number of members: 105,000, registered
charity (charity number 1050724), suitable for ages:
16+.
The Association of Accounting Technicians is the
only dedicated professional body approved to
award National Vocational Qualifications (NVQs)
and Scottish Vocational Qualifications (SVQs) in
Accounting.
The Association was established in 1980 to provide
a recognised qualification body for Accounting
Technicians.

Subject coverage:
Training as an Accounting Technician – NVQs/
SVQs in Accounting AAT Qualifications.
Membership of the AAT and Continuing
Professional Development.

Printed publications:
The Guide (free)
Approved Assessment Centres (free)
Accounting for Success (free)
Skillcheck leaflet (free)
Student Records (free)
Accounting Portfolio Leaflet (free)

Publications list:
Available online and in print

Access to staff:
Contact by letter, by telephone, by fax, by e-mail,
in person and via website. Appointment necessary.
Hours: Mon to Fri, 0900 to 1700

Access to staff:
Contact by letter, by telephone, by fax, by e-mail
and via website
Hours: Mon to Fri, 0900 to 1700. Helpline: Mon to
Fri, 1000 to 1600

ASSOCIATION OF AMERICAN DANCING

Acronym or abbreviation: AAD

Aspenshaw Hall, Thornsett, High Peak, Derbyshire, SK22 1AU

Tel: 01663 744986
E-mail: email@a-a-d.wanadoo.co.uk

Website:
http://www.the-aad.org.uk

Enquiries:
Enquiries to: Director

Founded:
1936

Organisation type and purpose:
Professional body, membership association (membership is by qualification), training organisation.
Examination and teaching body in dance disciplines.

Subject coverage:
Most dance forms, particularly ballet, mime, tap, acrobatic and modern stage dancing.

Library catalogue:
All or part available in-house

Printed publications:
Many publications on theory, enchainements, ballet, including:
Tap, acrobatic, modern, ballet, mime syllabus
Mime Vocabulary Grades 1, 2 and Preliminary
Mime Vocabulary Elementary, Intermediate, Advanced
Authentic Time Steps and Breaks Theory and Dance
The Theory of Tap Dancing for the Graduate
The Theory of Ballet, Each Grade
Order printed publications from: General Secretary, Association of American Dancing

Electronic and video publications:
CDs available for purchase, members only

Publications list:
Available in print

Access to staff:
Contact by letter, by telephone, by e-mail and via website. Appointment necessary.
Hours: Mon to Fri, 1000 to 1700

Access to building, collection or gallery:
Hours: Mon to Fri, 1000 to 1700

Access for disabled people:
Hours: Mon to Fri, 1000 to 1700

Affiliated to:
Council for Dance Education and Training (UK)
London

ASSOCIATION OF APPLIED BIOLOGISTS

Acronym or abbreviation: AAB

C/o Warwick HRI, Wellesbourne, Warwickshire, CV35 9EF

Tel: 01789 470382
Fax: 01789 470234
E-mail: rebecca@aab.org.uk

Website:
http://www.aab.org.uk
Home page: Details about Association, contents list for Annals of Applied Biology, programmes and booking forms for Association's meetings. Instructions to authors for Annals, publications list.

Enquiries:
Enquiries to: Executive Officer

Founded:
1904

Organisation type and purpose:
International organisation, learned society (membership is by election or invitation), present number of members: 800, registered charity (charity number 275655), training organisation, publishing house.

Subject coverage:
Plant breeding, pathology, physiology, virology, entomology, nematology, host plant resistance to diseases and pests, plant microbial interactions, bio-control, crop physiology, weeds and crop agronomy, post-harvest biology, pesticide application.

Printed publications:
AAB News (newsletter, members, 2 times a year)
Annals of Applied Biology (6 times a year)
Aspects of Applied Biology (papers and contributions from meetings)

Electronic and video publications:
Description of Plant Viruses (CD-ROM)
Molecular Biology Notebook (CD-ROM)

Publications list:
Available online and in print

Access to staff:
Contact by letter, by telephone, by fax and via website. Appointment necessary.
Hours: Mon to Fri, 0900 to 1700

Access to building, collection or gallery:
Prior appointment required

Access for disabled people:
Parking provided, toilet facilities

Affiliated to:
Institute of Biology

ASSOCIATION OF ART & ANTIQUES DEALERS

Formal name: The Association of Art & Antiques Dealers
Acronym or abbreviation: LAPADA

535 Kings Road, London, SW10 0SZ

Tel: 020 7823 3511
Fax: 020 7823 3522
E-mail: lapada@lapada.org

Website:
http://www.lapada.org

Enquiries:
Enquiries to: Chief Executive

Founded:
1974

Formerly called:
London and Provincial Antique Dealers Association (LAPADA)

Organisation type and purpose:
Trade association (membership is by qualification), present number of members: 600.

Subject coverage:
Trade in art and antiques.

Publications list:
Available online and in print

Access to staff:
Contact by letter, by telephone, by fax, by e-mail and via website
Hours: Mon to Fri, 0900 to 1700

Member organisation of:
Confédération Internationale des Négociants en Oeuvres d'Art (CINOA)

ASSOCIATION OF ART HISTORIANS

Acronym or abbreviation: AAH

Cowcross Court, 70 Cowcross Street, London, EC1M 6EJ

Tel: 020 7490 3211
E-mail: admin@aah.org.uk

Website:
http://www.aah.org.uk
Association information and publications.

Enquiries:
Enquiries to: Administrator

Founded:
1974

Organisation type and purpose:
Membership association.

Subject coverage:
Art history, art, design, architecture, photography, film and media, museum studies, conservation, cultural studies.

Printed publications:
Art History (5 times a year)
The Art Book (4 times a year)
Bulletin (3 times a year, free to members)
Order printed publications from: Wiley-Blackwell Publishing

Electronic and video publications:
Available via the publishers' website to members

Publications list:
Available online

Access to staff:
Contact by letter, by telephone, by fax and by e-mail
Hours: Mon to Fri, 0930 to 1730

Links with:
College Art Association (CAA)
USA
Scottish Society of Art Historians (SSAH)

ASSOCIATION OF AUTHORS' AGENTS

Acronym or abbreviation: AAA

President, Anthony Goff, c/o David Higham Associates Ltd, 5–8 Lower John Street, Golden Square, London, W1F 9HA

Tel: 020 7434 5900
E-mail: anthonygoff@davidhigham.co.uk

Website:
http://www.agentsassoc.co.uk
The association, directory of members, code of practice, contacts, FAQs.
http://www.writersservices.com
Listing of UK literary agents.

Organisation type and purpose:
A voluntary body and membership organisation for literary agents.
To provide a forum for member agencies to discuss industry matters, to uphold a code of good practice, and to provide a vehicle for representing the interests of agents and authors.

Subject coverage:
Literary agents and their work. Members have each practiced as literary agents for a period of three years or more, are based in the UK, have a list of clients who are actively engaged in writing, and abide by a code of practice as detailed on the website.

Access to staff:
Contact by letter, by telephone and by e-mail

Also at:
Secretary, James Wills
c/o Watson, Little Ltd, 48–56 Bayham Place, London, NW1 0EU; tel: 020 7388 7529; e-mail: jw@watsonlittle.com

ASSOCIATION OF BAKERY INGREDIENT MANUFACTURERS

Acronym or abbreviation: abim

4a Torphichen Street, Edinburgh, EH3 8JQ

Tel: 0131 229 9415
Fax: 0131 229 9407
E-mail: abim@abim.org.uk

continued overleaf

Website:
http://www.abim.org.uk

Enquiries:
Enquiries to: Executive Secretary

Founded:
1917

Formerly called:
Bakery Allied Traders' Association (BATA) (year of change 1999)

Organisation type and purpose:
Trade association (membership is by subscription). Acts as lobbying organisation for trade sector.

Subject coverage:
Bakery ingredients.

Printed publications:
Code of Good Hygiene Practice (£2.50 plus 75p p&p)
Occupational Allergy Guidelines and Material Safety Data Sheets (£5 plus £1 p&p)

Publications list:
Available online

Access to staff:
Contact by letter, by telephone, by fax, by e-mail and via website. Appointment necessary. Access for members only.
Hours: Mon to Fri, 0900 to 1700

Access to building, collection or gallery:
Prior appointment required

Member of:
FEDIMA
FMBRA
Food and Drink Federation
UKBICC

ASSOCIATION OF BLIND PIANO TUNERS

Acronym or abbreviation: ABPT

31 Wyre Crescent, Lynwood, Darwen, Lancashire, BB3 0JG

Tel: 0844 736 1976
E-mail: abpt@uk-piano.org

Website:
http://www.uk-piano.org
A wealth of information on pianos, tuning, piano history, makers, movers, teachers, accompanists and piano entertainers in the UK.

Enquiries:
Enquiries to: Secretary

Organisation type and purpose:
A registered charity (number 294885).
To serve the professional and particular needs of its members and other blind and partially sighted piano tuners throughout the world; to continue as the leading authority and association for blind or partially sighted piano tuners, insisting that only those professionally trained, examined, and qualified are accepted into membership, ensuring that the public knows that an ABPT member will offer skilled, professional, and reliable service.

Subject coverage:
Pianos and piano tuning.

Education services:
Offers ongoing training to piano tuners who wish to acquire extra levels of ability.

Access to staff:
Contact by letter, by telephone and by e-mail

ASSOCIATION OF BREASTFEEDING MOTHERS

Acronym or abbreviation: ABM

PO Box 207, Bridgwater, Somerset, TA6 7YT

Tel: 08444 122948 (admin); 08444 122949 (helpline)
E-mail: info@abm.me.uk

Website:
http://www.abm.me.uk

Enquiries:
Enquiries to: Administrator

Founded:
1979

Organisation type and purpose:
Membership association (membership is by subscription), registered charity (charity number 280537).
Promotion of breastfeeding and provision of counselling for mothers with breastfeeding problems, training breastfeeding counsellors.

Subject coverage:
Support and information on breastfeeding for mothers and health professionals; counsellor training available.

Information services:
Breastfeeding helpline

Printed publications:
A series of leaflets on breastfeeding
Magazine (to members, 3 times a year)

Publications list:
Available online and in print

Access to staff:
Contact by letter, by telephone, by e-mail and via website
Hours: Daily, 0930 to 2230

ASSOCIATION OF BRITISH & IRISH WILD ANIMAL KEEPERS

Acronym or abbreviation: ABWAK

Twycross Zoo, Burton Road, Atherstone, Warwickshire, CV9 3PX

Tel: 01827 880250
Fax: 01827 880700
E-mail: amy.hulse@twycrosszoo.org

Website:
http://www.abwak.co.uk

Enquiries:
Enquiries to: Honorary Secretary
Direct fax: 01827 881049

Founded:
1974

Organisation type and purpose:
Professional body.

Subject coverage:
Animal husbandry and zoos.

Printed publications:
Careers leaflet
Management Guidelines
Proceedings of Symposia (annually)
RATEL members' journal (quarterly)
Order printed publications from: Publications Officer, Leeds Castle, Maidstone, Kent, ME17 1PL

Publications list:
Available in print

Access to staff:
Contact by letter, by e-mail and via website
Hours: Mon to Fri, 0900 to 1700

ASSOCIATION OF BRITISH CERTIFICATION BODIES LIMITED

Acronym or abbreviation: ABCB

Sandover Centre, 129A Whitehorse Hill, Chislehurst, Kent, BR7 6DQ

Tel: 020 8295 1128
Fax: 020 8467 8095
E-mail: tinman@abcb.org.uk

Website:
http://www.abcb.org.uk/
Members list, SME Workbook for ISO 9000:2000.

Enquiries:
Enquiries to: Chief Executive

Founded:
1984

Organisation type and purpose:
National organisation, trade association (membership is by subscription, qualification), present number of members: 25.
To promote ABCB as the UK's centre of excellence for product, quality management and environmental certification for the benefit of its members.

Trade and statistical information:
List of members.

Printed publications:
Newsletter (periodic, free)

Access to staff:
Contact by letter, by telephone, by fax and by e-mail
Hours: Mon to Fri, 0900 to 1700

ASSOCIATION OF BRITISH CHORAL DIRECTORS

Acronym or abbreviation: abcd

15 Granville Way, Sherborne, Dorset, DT9 4AS

Tel: 01935 389482
Fax: 0870 128 4085
E-mail: rachel.greaves@abcd.org.uk

Website:
http://www.abcd.org.uk

Enquiries:
Enquiries to: General Secretary
Other contacts: Membership Secretary

Founded:
1986

Organisation type and purpose:
A registered charity (number 1085226), membership association (membership is by subscription and is open to individuals and organisations employed or involved in music), current number of members: over 700 individual members and 55 associate and corporate members.
A forum for conductors of choral music in the United Kingdom.
To promote, improve and maintain the education, training and development of choral directors with a view to improving standards in all sectors of choral activity.

Subject coverage:
Choral music and directors of choral music.

Education services:
Regional and national training courses and conventions.

Printed publications:
Mastersinger (journal, 4 a year)

Access to staff:
Contact by letter, by telephone, by fax and by e-mail

ASSOCIATION OF BRITISH CLIMATOLOGISTS

Acronym or abbreviation: ABC

School of Environmental Science, University College Northampton, Park Campus, Boughton Green Road, Northampton, NN2 7AL

Tel: 01604 735500
Fax: 01604 720636
E-mail: chris.holt@northampton.ac.uk

Website:
http://itu.reading.ac.uk/rms/abcgroup.html

Enquiries:
Enquiries to: Honorary Secretary

Founded:
1970

Organisation type and purpose:
Learned society (membership is by subscription).

Subject coverage:
All aspects of climatology, e.g. building climatology, agricultural climatology; climatic change.

Printed publications:
Directory of British Climatologists
Mailings (3 times a year, to members)

Access to staff:
Contact by letter, by fax and by e-mail
Hours: Mon to Fri, 0900 to 1700

Specialist group of the:
Royal Meteorological Society
104 Oxford Road, Reading, Berkshire

ASSOCIATION OF BRITISH CORRESPONDENCE COLLEGES

Acronym or abbreviation: ABCC

PO Box 17926, London, SW19 3WB

Tel: 020 8544 9559
E-mail: info@homestudy.org.uk

Website:
http://www.homestudy.org.uk

Enquiries:
Enquiries to: Secretary

Founded:
1955

Organisation type and purpose:
Trade association (membership is by qualification), present number of members: 22.

Subject coverage:
Distance education; academic, professional, commercial and technical courses.

Access to staff:
Contact by letter, by telephone, by e-mail and via website
Hours: Mon to Fri, 1430 to 1800 (variable)

ASSOCIATION OF BRITISH CYCLING COACHES

Acronym or abbreviation: ABCC

1 Small Drove, Weston, Spalding, Lincolnshire. PE12 6HS

Tel: 01406 370744
Fax: 01406 373150
E-mail: abccadmin@lincscyclecoaching.co.uk

Website:
http://www.abcc.co.uk

Enquiries:
Enquiries to: Administrator

Founded:
before 1970

Formerly called:
British Cycling Coaches Association (BCCA) (year of change c.1990)

Organisation type and purpose:
Membership association (membership is by qualification), present number of members: 702, voluntary organisation, training organisation. To educate, qualify and maintain a register of cycling coaches.

Subject coverage:
Cycling coaching.

Printed publications:
Cycle Coaching (4 times a year, non-ABCC coaches £20)

Electronic and video publications:
Two training presentations for Time Trial Coaching – available individually or as pair.
Order electronic and video publications from: Administrator

Access to staff:
Contact by letter, by telephone, by fax, by e-mail and via website
Hours: Mon to Fri, 0900 to 1700

ASSOCIATION OF BRITISH DISPENSING OPTICIANS

Acronym or abbreviation: ABDO

ABDO College, Godmersham Park, Godmersham, Canterbury, Kent, CT4 7DT

Tel: 01227 738829
Fax: 01227 733900
E-mail: general@abdolondon.org.uk

Website:
http://www.abdo.org.uk

Enquiries:
Enquiries to: Reception
Direct tel: 01227 733905
Other contacts: Head of Distance Learning Department (for education matters)

Founded:
1989

Formerly called:
Association of Dispensing Opticians

Organisation type and purpose:
Professional body (membership is by subscription, qualification), present number of members: 6,400, training organisation.

Subject coverage:
Optics and opticians.

Printed publications:
Books (available for purchase)
Dispensing Optics (journal)
Order printed publications from: ABDO College Bookshop

Publications list:
Available online and in print

Access to staff:
Contact by letter, by telephone, by fax and via website. Appointment necessary. Access for members only.
Hours: Mon to Fri, 0900 to 1700

Access for disabled people:
Parking provided, ramped entry, toilet facilities

ASSOCIATION OF BRITISH HEALTHCARE INDUSTRIES

Acronym or abbreviation: ABHI

111 Westminster Bridge Road, London, SE1 7HR

Tel: 020 7960 4360
Fax: 020 7960 4361
E-mail: enquiries@abhi.org.uk

Website:
http://www.abhi.org.uk

Founded:
1988

Created by the merger of:
British Health Care Export Council (BHEC) and British Health Care Trade and Industry Confederation (BHTIC) (year of change 1988)

Organisation type and purpose:
Trade association (membership is by subscription, qualification), present number of members: 200. To promote medical technology and systems for better health care and to be a facilitator of industry growth and health-care development by supporting the industry.

Subject coverage:
The medical devices industry, technical and regulatory affairs, NHS, overseas trade.

Printed publications:
Annual Report
Focus (journal, quarterly)

Publications list:
Available online

Access to staff:
Contact by letter, by telephone, by fax, by e-mail and via website. Appointment necessary.
Hours: Mon to Fri, 0900 to 1700

Access to building, collection or gallery:
No prior appointment required
Hours: Mon to Fri, 0900 to 1700
Special comments: Members can use the library.

Access for disabled people:
Access to all public areas

ASSOCIATION OF BRITISH INSURERS

Acronym or abbreviation: ABI

51 Gresham Street, London, EC2V 7HQ

Tel: 020 7600 3333
Fax: 020 7696 8999
E-mail: info@abi.org.uk

Website:
http://www.abi.org.uk
Site has three main sections providing information to different audiences:
(a) All site visitors – explanation of ABI's role, ability to view and print a range of consumer information sheets, press releases, details of ABI members, hot links to insurance company sites
(b) Insurance information service (by subscription) – most newsletters, circulars, daily press summary, ability to view and download ABI's statistical publications
(c) Members – all the above plus information confidential to the membership, all newsletters, copies of ABI briefings, representations and submissions.

Enquiries:
Enquiries to: Consumer Support Adviser
Direct tel: 020 7216 7416

Founded:
1985

Formerly called:
British Insurance Association, Fire Offices Committee, Life Offices Association

Organisation type and purpose:
Trade association (membership is by subscription, qualification).

Subject coverage:
UK insurance industry, EC insurance sector, statistics.

Printed publications:
Annual Report (free)
Consumer advice leaflets, information sheets, reports (prices vary)
Order printed publications from: Download from website or ring 020 7216 7617 after consulting website publications list

Publications list:
Available online

Access to staff:
Contact by letter, by telephone, by fax, by e-mail and via website. Access for members only.
Hours: Mon to Fri, 0900 to 1300 and 1400 to 1700

ASSOCIATION OF BRITISH INTRODUCTION AGENCIES

Acronym or abbreviation: ABIA

Suite 109, 315 Chiswick High Rd, Chiswick, London, W4 4HH

Tel: 020 8742 0386

Website:
http://www.abia.org.uk
List of member agencies, code of practice, general information for members of the public.

Enquiries:
Enquiries to: Press Officer
Direct tel: 07530 415 388
Direct e-mail: press@abia.org.uk

Founded:
1981

continued overleaf

Organisation type and purpose:
Trade association, membership association
(membership is by qualification), present number
of members: 30, research organisation.
To monitor, regulate and disseminate information
regarding the industry, enforcing the code of
conduct supported by the Office of Fair Trading.

Subject coverage:
Introduction agencies, including marriage bureaux
and introduction and dating agencies.

Trade and statistical information:
Available upon request.

Printed publications:
Code of Practice (free)
List of current members (free)

Access to staff:
Contact by letter, by fax, by e-mail and via
website
Hours: Telephone between 0930 to 1700
Special comments: No visitors.

ASSOCIATION OF BRITISH INVESTIGATORS

Acronym or abbreviation: ABI

48 Queens Road, Basingstoke, Hampshire, RG21
7RE

Tel: 01256 816390
Fax: 01256 479547
E-mail: info@theabi.org.uk

Website:
http://www.theabi.org.uk
Membership listing, history, information regarding
publications.

Enquiries:
Enquiries to: Company Secretary
Other contacts: President for Administrative Head
of organisation.

Founded:
1913

Organisation type and purpose:
International organisation, trade association
(membership is by qualification), present number
of members: 400.
Association for private investigators.
Representation and training.

Subject coverage:
Any legally obtainable information about
individuals, corporations, associations, trusts etc
worldwide.

Printed publications:
Investigate (4 times a year, members or by
subscription)
Directory of Members (annually, £25)
Process Servers Guide (£30)
Best Practice Guide for Professional Investigators

Access to staff:
Contact by letter, by telephone, by fax and by e-
mail
Hours: Mon to Fri, 0900 to 1700

ASSOCIATION OF BRITISH ORCHESTRAS

Acronym or abbreviation: ABO

20 Rupert Street, London, W1D 6DF

Tel: 020 7287 0333
Fax: 020 7287 0444
E-mail: info@abo.org.uk

Website:
http://www.abo.org.uk
General information about the ABO, its
membership, events and activities.

Enquiries:
Enquiries to: Director
Direct e-mail: mark@abo.org.uk

Founded:
1947

Organisation type and purpose:
The ABO exists to support, develop and advance
the interests and activities of the orchestral
profession in the UK.
The ABO's key activities centre around Advocacy,
Services, Information and Learning and are
delivered through conferences, seminars,
negotiations, training opportunities, education
initiatives and representation.
Full membership is open to professional orchestras
that have been in existence for more than two years
and have given at least 24 performances. Associate,
Corporate and Individual membership is also
available.

Subject coverage:
Professional orchestras in the UK.

Library catalogue:
All or part available online

Printed publications:
ABO Update (monthly newsletter for members
only)
Factsheets
Annual Report
Other reports on specialist subjects

Publications list:
Available online and in print

Access to staff:
Contact by letter, by telephone, by fax, by e-mail
and via website. Appointment necessary.
Hours: Mon to Fri, 0930 to 1730

Access to building, collection or gallery:
Prior appointment required

ASSOCIATION OF BRITISH PEWTER CRAFTSMEN

Acronym or abbreviation: ABPC

Unit 10, Edmund Road Business Centre
135 Edmund Road, Sheffield, S2 4ED

Tel: 0114 252 7550
Fax: 0114 252 7555
E-mail: enquiries@abpcltd.co.uk

Website:
http://www.abpcltd.co.uk

Enquiries:
Enquiries to: Secretary

Organisation type and purpose:
Trade association.

Subject coverage:
Manufacture of articles of pewter.

**Museum or gallery collection, archive, or library
special collection:**
Collections at Pewter Hall, Oat Lane, London

Printed publications:
Pewter Review (3 times a year)

Access to staff:
Contact by letter, by telephone and by fax
Hours: Mon to Fri, 0900 to 1700

ASSOCIATION OF BRITISH PHILATELIC SOCIETIES LIMITED

Acronym or abbreviation: ABPS

c/o Royal Philatelic Society, 41 Devonshire Place,
London, W1G 6JY

E-mail: secretary@abps.org.uk

Website:
http://www.abps.org.uk
Details of ABPS, its function and all UK affiliates
who welcome visitors to their meetings.

Enquiries:
Enquiries to: Secretary
Direct e-mail: secretary@abps.org.uk; chair@abps
.org.uk

Founded:
1994

Formerly called:
British Philatelic Federation (BPF) (year of change
1994)

Organisation type and purpose:
National UK organisation and membership
association (membership is by subscription),
present number of members: 15,000 mainly
through 19 area federations and over 300 local and
specialist stamp, postal history and post card
collecting clubs and societies
Federation of Stamp collectors, societies, etc.

Subject coverage:
Philately generally, stamp collecting, postal history
including postcards.

Printed publications:
ABPS News (quarterly)
Congress Handbook (annually)
ABPS Directory (alternate years)
Speakers' List (alternate years)

Publications list:
Available online and in print

Access to staff:
Contact by letter, by e-mail and via website.
Appointment necessary.
Hours: Mon to Fri, 0900 to 1700

Affiliated to:
Fédération Internationale de Philatélie (FIP)
Federation of European Philatelic Federations
(FEPA)

ASSOCIATION OF BRITISH PICTURE RESTORERS

Formal name: The Association of British Picture
Restorers
Acronym or abbreviation: ABPR

PO BOX 258 , Norwich, NR13 4WY

Tel: 01603 516237
Fax: 0160 351 0985
E-mail: office@bapcr.org.uk

Website:
http://www.bapcr.org.uk/
Future meetings, journals, training, information
about ABPR and conservation enquiries.

Enquiries:
Enquiries to: Secretary

Founded:
1943

Organisation type and purpose:
Professional body.

Subject coverage:
Restoration and conservation of oil paintings;
professional training.

Printed publications:
Conference Preprints
Journal (2 times a year)
Newsletter
Training leaflet

Access to staff:
Contact by letter, by telephone, by fax and by e-
mail
Hours: Mon to Fri, 0930 to 1730

Affiliated to:
IIC
IPC
SSCR

ASSOCIATION OF BRITISH RIDING SCHOOLS

Acronym or abbreviation: ABRS

Queen's Chambers, 38–40 Queen Street, Penzance,
Cornwall, TR18 4BH

Tel: 01736 369440
Fax: 01736 351390
E-mail: office@abrs-info.org

Website:
http://www.abrs-info.org
All exam syllabi, general information from ABRS, membership information.

Enquiries:
Enquiries to: General Secretary

Founded:
1954

Organisation type and purpose:
National organisation, advisory body, professional body (membership is by subscription), voluntary organisation, training organisation.
Professional association for proprietors, managers and staff of riding establishments.

Subject coverage:
Standards of instruction; horsemastership, welfare of horses and ponies in riding establishments, problems of riding establishments.

Printed publications:
101 Riding Exercises (£19.99 inc. p&p)
The Principles of Teaching Riding (£12.99 inc. p&p)
Studies in Equitation (£24.95; or as CD, £12.95)
Drills & Formation Riding (£7.50 inc. p&p)
ABRS Tests Guidelines Book (£7.00 inc. p&p)
ABRS Examination Syllabi (free on receipt of sae)
Order printed publications from: ABRS

Publications list:
Available online and in print

Access to staff:
Contact by letter, by telephone, by fax and by e-mail
Hours: Mon to Fri, 0930 to 1730

Member organisation of:
British Equestrian Federation (BEF)
British Equestrian Trade Association (BETA)
Central Council of Physical Recreation (CCPR)
SEA
SSA

ASSOCIATION OF BRITISH THEATRE TECHNICIANS

Acronym or abbreviation: ABTT

55 Farringdon Road, London, EC1M 3JB

Tel: 020 7242 9200
Fax: 020 7242 9303
E-mail: office@abtt.org.uk

Website:
http://www.abtt.org.uk
Theatre – technical, careers and training.

Enquiries:
Enquiries to: Administrator

Founded:
1961

Organisation type and purpose:
Membership association (membership is by subscription), voluntary organisation, registered charity, training organisation.

Subject coverage:
Technical aspects of theatre; design and planning of theatre buildings; training and careers in the technical theatre.

Library catalogue:
All or part available in-house

Printed publications:
ABTT Codes of Practice (for sale to members and non-members):
Technical Standards for Places of Entertainment (pub Jun 2008, £45 members, £50 non-members)
Modern Rules of Management for Places of Public Entertainment (£20 members, £25 non-members)
Flying (£15 members, £20 non-members)
Fibre Ropes (£10 members, £15 non-members)
Wire Ropes (£10 members, £15 non-members)
A Modern Approach to Emergency Lighting in Theatre (£6 members, £10 non-members)
Firearms and Ammunition: Acquisition, Possession and Use (£6 members, £10 non-members)

Pyrotechnics & Smoke Effects (£6 members, £10 non-members)
Design Guide – Guard Rails (£5 members, £10 non-members)
Guidance Note on Exit Signs (free)
Guidance Note on Water and check list (free)
Plus other publications
Time & Space (Exhibition Catalogue 1999 SBTD, £17.95 members, £18.95 non-members)

Publications list:
Available online and in print

Access to staff:
Contact by letter, by telephone, by fax and by e-mail
Hours: Mon to Fri, 1000 to 1700

Affiliated to and at the same address as:
Society of British Theatre Designers

ASSOCIATION OF BRITISH THEOLOGICAL AND PHILOSOPHICAL LIBRARIES

Acronym or abbreviation: ABTAPL

Website:
http://www.newman.ac.uk/abtapl/index.html
http://www.le.ac.uk/abtapl/
Union list of Periodicals.

Enquiries:
Enquiries to: Honorary Secretary
Other contacts: Chairman

Founded:
1954

Organisation type and purpose:
National organisation, professional body (membership is by subscription), present number of members: 200.

Subject coverage:
Theology, religious studies, philosophy, librarianship.

Printed publications:
Bulletin (3 times a year)
Guide to the Theological Libraries of Great Britain and Ireland
Union List of Theological Periodicals

Access to staff:
Contact by letter, by fax and by e-mail
Hours: Mon to Fri, 0900 to 1700
Special comments: Voluntary organisation, no paid staff.

Links with:
American Theological Libraries Association
Conseil International des Associations des Bibliothèques de Théologie
Library Association

ASSOCIATION OF BRITISH TRAVEL AGENTS

Acronym or abbreviation: ABTA

67–71 Newman Street, London, W1T 3AH

Tel: 020 7637 2444
Fax: 020 7637 0713
E-mail: abta@abta.co.uk

Website:
http://www.abta.com

Enquiries:
Enquiries to: Information Officer
Direct tel: 0901 201 5050 (charged at 50p per min)
Direct fax: 020 7307 1992
Other contacts: Policy and Research Executive for research.

Founded:
1950

Organisation type and purpose:
Trade association.

Subject coverage:
Travel destinations, travel advice, details of ABTA members.

Printed publications:
Annual Report
ABTA Codes of Conduct (£25)
ABTA Magazine (monthly £24)
ABTA Members Handbook (£40)
ABTA Members List (£30)
Order printed publications from: ABTA Magazine, Absolute Publishing
197–199 City Road, London, EC1V 1JN

Electronic and video publications:
ABTA Members Database

Access to staff:
Contact by telephone. All charged.
Hours: Mon to Fri, 0830 to 1800

Access for disabled people:
Ramped entry, toilet facilities

Subsidiary body:
ABTA National Training Board
Waterloo House, 11–17 Chertsey Road, Woking, Surrey; tel: 01483 727321; fax: 01483 756698

ASSOCIATION OF BROADCASTING DOCTORS

Acronym or abbreviation: ABD

PO Box 15, Sindalthorpe House, Ely, Cambridgeshire, CB7 4SG

Tel: 01353 688456 or 688588
Fax: 01353 688451
E-mail: info@abdoctors.com

Website:
http://www.broadcasting-doctor.org
Medical news, members' specialities, aims, medical links.

Enquiries:
Enquiries to: Director
Other contacts: Administrator

Founded:
1988

Organisation type and purpose:
Professional body (membership is by election or invitation), present number of members: 755, voluntary organisation, training organisation, consultancy.
Support for clinicians who also broadcast.

Subject coverage:
Medical broadcasting, all medical specialities. The provision of medical practitioners and specialists as contributors to radio and television, and of producers and journal editors.

Museum or gallery collection, archive, or library special collection:
Library of written and recorded material

Printed publications:
Newsletter (monthly)

Electronic and video publications:
Various audio tapes on medical topics

Access to staff:
Contact by letter, by telephone, by fax, by e-mail and via website
Hours: 0600 to 1900, seven days a week

Administered by:
Soundplan Broadcasting Services Limited at the same address

ASSOCIATION OF BROKERS & YACHT AGENTS

Acronym or abbreviation: ABYA

The Glass Works, Penns Road, Petersfield, Hants, GU32 2EW

Tel: 01730 710425
Fax: 01730 710423
E-mail: info@ybdsa.co.uk

Website:
http://www.abya.co.uk

continued overleaf

Information on the Association, including membership

Enquiries:
Enquiries to: Chief Executive
Direct e-mail: info@ybdsa.co.uk
Other contacts: Tonnage Measurers

Founded:
1912

Organisation type and purpose:
National organisation, professional body (membership is by qualification, election or invitation), present number of members: 150. Training and maintaining of standards, support of yacht brokers.

Subject coverage:
Brokerage of yachts and small craft; training; tonnage measurement as required for registration by the Department of Trade; certification under the MCA Small Commercial Vessel Code; registration and its benefits; codes of practice; forms of contract.

Library catalogue:
All or part available in-house

Printed publications:
Brochures, leaflets and rules
Training Pack Block I (£75)
Sample Report Pack (£10)

Publications list:
Available online and in print

Access to staff:
Contact by letter, by telephone, by fax, by e-mail, in person and via website. Appointment necessary.
Hours: Mon to Fri, 0900 to 1700

Access to building, collection or gallery:
Prior appointment required

Access for disabled people:
Parking provided

Parent body:
Yacht Brokers Designers & Surveyors Association (YBDSA)

Sister bodies:
Professional Charter Association (PCA)
Yacht Designers and Surveyors Association (YDSA)

ASSOCIATION OF BUILDING COMPONENT MANUFACTURERS LIMITED

Acronym or abbreviation: ABCM

Clark House, 3 Brassey Drive, Aylesford, Kent, ME20 7QL

Tel: 01622 715577
Fax: 08700 54 39 15
E-mail: abcm@building-components.org

Website:
http://www.building-components.org

Enquiries:
Enquiries to: Director

Founded:
1965

Organisation type and purpose:
Trade association (membership is by subscription).

Access to staff:
Contact by letter, by telephone, by fax, by e-mail and via website
Hours: Mon to Fri, 0900 to 1700

ASSOCIATION OF BUILDING ENGINEERS

Acronym or abbreviation: ABE

Lutyens House, Billing Brook Road, Weston Favell, Northampton, NN3 8NW

Tel: 01604 404121
Fax: 01604 784220

E-mail: building.engineers@abe.org.uk

Website:
http://www.abe.org.uk

Enquiries:
Enquiries to: Marketing & Events Manager
Direct e-mail: info@abe.org.uk
Other contacts: Editor ABE Journal

Founded:
1925

Formerly called:
Incorporated Association of Architects and Surveyors (IAAS) (year of change 1993)

Incorporates the former:
Institute of Maintenance and Building Management (IMBM) (year of change 2008)

Organisation type and purpose:
Professional body.
To specialise in the technology of building.

Subject coverage:
Building surveying and construction in general, architecture, technology of building, town planning, valuation, estate management.

Education services:
Provision of relevant training courses to those specialising in the technology of building. For details on all courses / to access the prospectus, see: http://www.abe.org.uk.

Printed publications:
Building Engineer (journal, monthly, £40 a year incl. p&p)

Access to staff:
Contact by letter, by telephone, by fax, by e-mail and via website. Appointment necessary. Non-members charged.
Hours: Mon to Fri, 0900 to 1700

Access to building, collection or gallery:
Hours: Mon to Fri, 0900 to 1700

Member organisation of:
Construction Industry Council
Construction Industry Standing Conference
L'Association d'experts européens du bâtiment et de la construction

ASSOCIATION OF BUSINESS RECOVERY PROFESSIONALS

Acronym or abbreviation: R3

8th Floor, 120 Aldersgate Street, London, EC1A 4JQ

Tel: 020 7566 4200
Fax: 020 7566 4224
E-mail: association@r3.org.uk

Website:
http://www.r3.org.uk

Enquiries:
Enquiries to: Chief Executive Officer
Direct tel: 020 7566 4219

Founded:
1990

Organisation type and purpose:
National organisation, professional body, trade association, membership association (membership is by subscription), present number of members: 4,000.
A strong voice for all those who work with underperforming businesses and people in financial difficulty.

Subject coverage:
Business recovery, rescue and renewal, including insolvency.

Printed publications:
The Ostrich's Guide to Business Survival
Understanding Insolvency
Making a Career as an Insolvency Practitioner
Creditors' Guides
Is a Voluntary Arrangement Right For Me?
Order printed publications from: http://www.r3.org.uk

Electronic and video publications:
Business Recovery Training Package

Publications list:
Available online and in print

Access to staff:
Contact by letter, by telephone, by fax and by e-mail
Hours: Mon to Fri, 0900 to 1700

Access to building, collection or gallery:
Prior appointment required

Access for disabled people:
Access to all public areas, toilet facilities

ASSOCIATION OF CATERING EXCELLENCE

Acronym or abbreviation: ACE

Bourne House, Horsell Park, Woking, Surrey, GU21 4LY

Tel: 01483 765111
Fax: 01483 751991
E-mail: admin@acegb.org

Website:
http://www.acegb.rg

Enquiries:
Enquiries to: Administrator

Founded:
1948

Organisation type and purpose:
Professional body (membership is by subscription, qualification), service industry.

Subject coverage:
Contract catering and all subjects allied to staff catering.

Access to staff:
Contact by letter, by telephone, by fax and by e-mail. Non-members charged.
Hours: Mon to Fri, 0900 to 1700

ASSOCIATION OF CEREAL FOOD MANUFACTURERS

Acronym or abbreviation: ACFM

6 Catherine Street, London, WC2B 5JJ

Tel: 020 7836 2460
Fax: 020 7836 0580

Enquiries:
Enquiries to: Executive Secretary

Organisation type and purpose:
Trade association.
Lobbying organisation.

Subject coverage:
Breakfast cereal products and related legislation.

Access to staff:
Appointment necessary. Access for members only.
Hours: Mon to Fri, 0900 to 1700

Affiliated to:
CEEREAL
Rond Point, Schuman 9 bte 11, Brussels, B-1040, Belgium

Umbrella organisation:
Food and Drink Federation
6 Catherine Street, London, WC2B 5JJ

ASSOCIATION OF CERTIFIED FRAUD EXAMINERS (UK)

Acronym or abbreviation: ACFE(UK)

840 Melton Road, Thurmaston, Leicester, LE4 8BN

Tel: 0116 260 6961
Fax: 0116 2604 0141
E-mail: acfe@associationhq.org.uk

Website:
http://www.acfe.org.uk

Enquiries:
Enquiries to: Executive Secretary

Founded:
January 1997

Organisation type and purpose:
Membership association (membership is by subscription, qualification), present number of members: 500.
UK Chapter.

Printed publications:
The Beacon
The White Paper (journal, 6 times a year)
Fraud Examiners Manual

Electronic and video publications:
Self-study video/workbook courses
Fraud Examiners Manual
Occupational Fraud and Abuse

Publications list:
Available online and in print

Access to staff:
Contact by letter, by telephone, by fax and by e-mail. Appointment necessary.
Hours: Mon to Fri, 0900 to 1700

Headquarters:
ACFE
The Gregor Building, 716 West Avenue, Austin, Texas, 78701, USA

ASSOCIATION OF CHARITABLE FOUNDATIONS

Acronym or abbreviation: ACF

Central House, 14 Upper Woburn Place, London, WC1H 0AE

Tel: 020 7255 4499
Fax: 020 7255 4496
E-mail: acf@acf.org.uk

Website:
http://www.acf.org.uk
General information about ACF and about UK trusts and foundations, including guidance on applying for funding, publications.

Enquiries:
Enquiries to: Chief Executive

Founded:
1989

Organisation type and purpose:
Membership association (membership is by subscription), voluntary organisation, registered charity (charity number 1105412).
Membership body for more than 300 charitable grant-making trusts and foundations.

Subject coverage:
Philanthropy, charitable grant-making, relevant aspects of charity and investment law.

Printed publications:
Annual Report
Trust and Foundation News (magazine, 4 times a year, free to members)
Funders' News (monthly bulletin only for members)
Variety of texts on charitable and grant-making issues (see website for details)

Publications list:
Available online

Access to staff:
Contact by letter, by e-mail and via website. Appointment necessary.
Hours: Mon to Fri, 0930 to 1730

ASSOCIATION OF CHARITY OFFICERS

Acronym or abbreviation: ACO

Five Ways, 57–59 Hatfield Road, Potters Bar, Hertfordshire, EN6 1HS

Tel: 01707 651777

Fax: 01707 660477
E-mail: info@aco.uk.net

Enquiries:
Enquiries to: Chief Executive
Other contacts: Administrative Officer; Helpline Co-ordinator (for queries relating to grants from a member charity).

Founded:
1946

Incorporates the former:
Occupational Benevolent Funds Alliance (OBFA)

Organisation type and purpose:
Professional body, membership association (membership is by subscription), present number of members: over 200 charities, registered charity (charity number 1118605).
Association of over 200 charities who give non-contributory relief by means of financial grants and in other ways. ACO itself has no funds for grant aid.
The professional association for benevolent funds and charities helping people in need.

Subject coverage:
Charities; benevolent funds, residential and nursing home care of older people in the voluntary sector; effects of legislation, interest of members. ACO offers training on Access to Benevolence to all those charities and benevolent funds helping people in need. Also gives guidelines and information on best practice.

Museum or gallery collection, archive, or library special collection:
ACO holds details of a large number of grant-making charities which might help individuals in need (not projects)

Trade and statistical information:
Database of member funds.

Printed publications:
Annual Review
Benchmarks – How much do charities pay in grants?
Helping Charities Helping People
Directory of members (for members only)
GP Healthcare for older people in care and sheltered accommodation managed by charities
Individuals in Need – Guidelines for Grantmakers
News-sheet (for members only)
Sheltered Housing for Older People – The Occupational Benevolent Funds Alliance (OBFA) – GP charges
Benevolence in the 21st century (survey)

Access to staff:
Contact by letter, by telephone, by fax and by e-mail. Appointment necessary.
Hours: Mon to Fri, 1000 to 1600

ASSOCIATION OF CHARTERED CERTIFIED ACCOUNTANTS

Acronym or abbreviation: ACCA

29 Lincoln's Inn Fields, London, WC2A 3EE

Tel: 020 7059 5000
Fax: 020 7059 5050
E-mail: info@accaglobal.com

Website:
http://www.accaglobal.com
Students, members, employers, learning providers, general, find an accountant.

Enquiries:
Direct tel: 0044 141 582 2000 (ACCA Connect for admin queries)

Founded:
1904

Created by the merger of:
London Association of Accountants and (Scottish-based) Corporation of Accountants (year of change 1939); Association of Certified and Corporate Accountants (ACCA) and Institution of Certified Public Accountants (year of change 1941)

Formerly called:
London Association of Accountants (year of change 1933); London Association of Certified Accountants (year of change 1939); Association of Certified and Corporate Accountants (ACCA) (year of change 1971); Association of Certified Accountants (year of change 1984); Chartered Association of Certified Accountants (year of change 1996)

Organisation type and purpose:
The global body for professional accountants employed in industry, financial services, the public sector, or in public practice, current number of members: 140,000 members and 404,000 students.

Subject coverage:
Supports members and students throughout their careers, providing services through a network of 83 offices and active centres world-wide.

Museum or gallery collection, archive, or library special collection:
Online technical library

Electronic and video publications:
Accounting Link (e-bulletin for employers)
Accounting and Business (monthly magazine for members)
Student Accountant (magazine for students)
Sector-specific magazines and booklets include: In Practice, In Practice Ireland, Corporate Sector Review, Public Eye, Financial Services Review and Health Service Review
Technical fact sheets address topics such as sustainability reporting, insolvency and internal audit
Order electronic and video publications from:
Download from website

Publications list:
Available online

Access to staff:
Contact by letter, by telephone, by fax and by e-mail

ASSOCIATION OF CHARTERED PHYSIOTHERAPISTS IN INDEPENDENT HEALTHCARE

Acronym or abbreviation: ACPIHC

14 Bedford Row, London, WC1R 4ED

Tel: 020 7306 6666

Enquiries:
Enquiries to: Chair
Direct tel: 020 7908 3742
Direct e-mail: annie.karim@hcahealthcare.co.uk

Formerly called:
Association of Chartered Physiotherapists in Independent Hospitals & Charities (ACPIH)

Organisation type and purpose:
National organisation, advisory body, professional body.
To assist Chartered Physiotherapists working in independent hospitals and give information about physiotherapy within independent hospitals.

Subject coverage:
Physiotherapy in independent hospitals or charities.

Printed publications:
Standards & Guidelines Document

Access to staff:
Contact by letter, by telephone and by e-mail
Hours: Mon to Fri, 0900 to 1700

Group within the:
Chartered Society of Physiotherapy

ASSOCIATION OF CHARTERED PHYSIOTHERAPISTS IN MANAGEMENT

Acronym or abbreviation: ACPM

14 Bedford Row, London, WC1R 4ED

continued overleaf

Tel: 020 7306 6666
Fax: 020 7306 6611

Enquiries:
Enquiries to: Honorary Secretary
Other contacts: Chairman

Founded:
1944

Formerly called:
Association of District and Superintendent
Chartered Physiotherapists (ADSCP)

Organisation type and purpose:
Professional body.

Subject coverage:
Physiotherapy.

Printed publications:
Guidelines for External Assessors (£5)

Access to staff:
Contact by letter, by telephone and by fax
Hours: Mon to Fri, 0900 to 1700

Group within the:
Chartered Society of Physiotherapy

ASSOCIATION OF CHARTERED PHYSIOTHERAPISTS IN OCCUPATIONAL HEALTH AND ERGONOMICS

Acronym or abbreviation: ACPOHE

c/o Chartered Society of Physiotherapy, 14 Bedford
Row, London, WC1R 4ED

Tel: 020 7242 1941

Website:
http://www.acpohe.org.uk

Enquiries:
Enquiries to: Chairman
Direct tel: 01284 748200
Direct e-mail: nicola.hunter@buryphysio.co.uk; jan
.vickery@milligan-and-hill.co.uk
Other contacts: Membership Secretary

Founded:
1948

Formerly called:
Association of Chartered Physiotherapists in
Occupational Health (ACPOH)

Organisation type and purpose:
National organisation, professional body
(membership is by subscription, qualification),
present number of members: 550.
Occupational interest group of the Chartered
Society of Physiotherapy.

Subject coverage:
Occupational health physiotherapy, ergonomics,
education and training, health promotion and
fitness in the workplace, work hardening and
conditioning, functional capacity evaluation, pre-
employment screening, health and safety (risk
assessment and risk management), moving and
handling, workplace design, rehabilitation.

Printed publications:
Guidelines for Practice
Information leaflets (on request)
Newsletter (3 times a year, for members)

Access to staff:
Contact by letter, by telephone, by e-mail and via
website
Hours: Mon to Fri, 0900 to 1700

Constituent part of:
Chartered Society of Physiotherapy
as above

ASSOCIATION OF CHARTERED PHYSIOTHERAPISTS IN RESPIRATORY CARE

Acronym or abbreviation: ACPRC

School of Health and Population Sciences, 52
Pritchatts Road, University of Birmingham,
Edgbaston, Birmingham, B15 2TT

Tel: 0121 415 8606
E-mail: c.r.liles@bham.ac.uk

Organisation type and purpose:
Membership association (membership is by
subscription), present number of members: over
500.

Subject coverage:
Respiratory diseases, cardiorespiratory
physiotherapy, education, research, audit,
management, physiotherapy techniques.

Printed publications:
ACPRC Journal (annually)
Newsletter (4 times a year)
Respiratory Review (annually)

Access to staff:
Contact by letter, by telephone and by fax
Hours: Mon to Fri, 0900 to 1700

Special Interest Group within the:
Chartered Society of Physiotherapy
   tel: 020 7306 6666; fax: 020 7306 6611

ASSOCIATION OF CHARTERED PHYSIOTHERAPISTS IN WOMEN'S HEALTH

Acronym or abbreviation: ACPWH

14 Bedford Row, London, WC1R 4ED

Tel: 020 7306 6666

Website:
http://www.acpwh.org.uk

Enquiries:
Enquiries to: Secretary
Direct e-mail: juliabraytq@hotmail.com
Other contacts: Chairman for when Secretary is
unavailable.

Founded:
1948

Formerly called:
Association of Chartered Physiotherapists in
Obstetrics and Gynaecology (year of change 1993)

Organisation type and purpose:
National organisation, professional body
(membership is by subscription), present number
of members: 700.

Subject coverage:
Physiotherapy in obstetrics and gynaecology;
antenatal education and advice; postnatal
education advice and exercise, female and male
bladder and bowel dysfunction; musculoskeletal
problems relating to pregnancy or gynaecological
in nature, particularly pelvic floor weakness.

Printed publications:
Information leaflets (lists available through the
   Secretary)
Journal (2 times a year)

Publications list:
Available in print

Access to staff:
Contact by letter and by e-mail

Group within the:
Chartered Society of Physiotherapy
   at the same address; tel: 020 7306 6666

ASSOCIATION OF CHARTERED PHYSIOTHERAPISTS INTERESTED IN NEUROLOGY

Acronym or abbreviation: ACPIN

14 Bedford Row, London, WC1R 4ED

Tel: 020 7306 6666
Fax: 020 7306 6611
E-mail: enquiries@csp.org.uk

Website:
http://www.acpin.net

Enquiries:
Enquiries to: Professional Adviser

Organisation type and purpose:
Professional body.

Subject coverage:
Physiotherapy; neurology.

Printed publications:
Synapse (Apr and Nov)
Guidance on manual handling for treatment
Recommendations of Physiotherapy Practice in
   Neurology
Standards of Physiotherapy Practice in Neurology

Access to staff:
Contact by telephone and via website
Hours: Mon to Fri, 0900 to 1700

Group within the:
Chartered Society of Physiotherapy

ASSOCIATION OF CHIEF POLICE OFFICERS OF ENGLAND, WALES AND NORTHERN IRELAND

Acronym or abbreviation: ACPO

1st Floor, 10 Victoria Street, London, SW1H 0NN

Tel: 020 7084 8950
E-mail: info@acpo.pnn.police.uk

Website:
http://www.acpo.police.uk
The association, news, policies.

Organisation type and purpose:
A voluntary association of chief officers
(membership is by subscription) open to police
officers who hold the rank of Chief Constable,
Deputy Chief Constable, or Assistant Chief
Constable, or their equivalents, in the 44 forces of
England, Wales and Northern Ireland, national
police agencies and certain other forces in the UK,
the Isle of Man and the Channel Islands, and
certain senior non-police staff, current number of
members: 349.
ACPO is not a staff association and works on
behalf of the Service, rather than its own members.
Works in the public interest and, in equal and
active partnership with government and the
Association of Police Authorities, leads and co-
ordinates the direction and development of the
police service in England, Wales and Northern
Ireland. In times of national need ACPO – on
behalf of all chief officers – coordinates the
strategic policing response.

Subject coverage:
Police service in England, Wales and Northern
Ireland.

Electronic and video publications:
Press releases
Order electronic and video publications from:
Download from website

Publications list:
Available online

Access to staff:
Contact by letter, by telephone, by e-mail and via
website

Links with:
ACPO Criminal Records Office (ACRO)
   e-mail: http://www.acpo.police.uk/acro
ACPO Vehicle Crime Intelligence Service (AVCIS)
   website: http://www.acpo.police.uk/avcis
National Coordinator Domestic Extremism
(NCDE)
   website: http://www.acpo.police.uk/ncde

ASSOCIATION OF CHRISTIAN COMMUNITIES AND NETWORKS

Acronym or abbreviation: NACCAN

Community House, Eton Road, Newport, Gwent,
NP19 0BL

Tel: 01633 265486
E-mail: moderator@naccan.freeserve.com.uk

Enquiries:
Enquiries to: Moderator

Founded:
1971

Formerly called:
National Association of Christian Communities
and Networks (year of change 1999)

Organisation type and purpose:
International organisation, membership
association (membership is by subscription),
present number of members: 286, voluntary
organisation, registered charity (charity number
283972), training organisation.
Links together Networks, Groups, Communities
and individuals from a wide variety of Christian
traditions committed to living out the implications
of what Christian Community means.

Subject coverage:
Linking, informing, affirming Christian
communities and networks in Britain, particularly
those taking new initiatives in the local scene, with
some contacts overseas also.

Trade and statistical information:
Information provided on communities and
networks in membership.

Printed publications:
Christian Community (newsletter, 4 times a year,
free to members, otherwise donation for p&p)
Directory of Christian Communities and Groups
(£5 including p&p, on request)
Results of research projects

Access to staff:
Contact by letter, by telephone and by e-mail.
Appointment necessary.
Hours: Mon, Thu, 1000 to 1600; Tue, Wed, and Fri,
0900 to 1700. Ansaphone 24 hours

Affiliated to:
CCBI
CYTUN

ASSOCIATION OF CHRISTIAN COUNSELLORS

Acronym or abbreviation: ACC

29 Momus Boulevard, Coventry, Warwickshire,
CV2 5NA

Tel: 0845 124 9569
Fax: 0845 124 9571
E-mail: office@acc-uk.org

Website:
http://www.acc-uk.org
General and specific information, joining,
accreditation, links with ACC Europe, training
organisations.

Enquiries:
Enquiries to: Chief Executive
Direct e-mail: ceo@acc-uk.org

Founded:
1992

Organisation type and purpose:
Professional body, registered charity (charity
number 1018559).

Subject coverage:
Christian counselling, training in Christian
counselling, accreditation for Christian counsellors,
affiliation for Christian Counselling agencies,
referrals for those requiring Christian counselling.

Printed publications:
Information Pack
Personal Counselling Porfolio
Code of Ethics
Training Criteria (for courses)
Accreditation Applications
Accord (magazine, quarterly)

Electronic and video publications:
Accreditation forms

Access to staff:
Contact by letter, by telephone, by fax, by e-mail,
in person and via website
Hours: Mon to Fri, 0900 to 1700

Access to building, collection or gallery:
No prior appointment required

ASSOCIATION OF CIRCUS PROPRIETORS OF GREAT BRITAIN

Acronym or abbreviation: ACP

PO Box 131, Blackburn, Lancashire, BB1 9GJ

Tel: 01254 814789
Fax: 01254 814789
E-mail: malcolmclay@talk21.com

Website:
http://www.circus-uk.co.uk
Details of individual members with links to their
websites giving details of their shows and routes.

Enquiries:
Enquiries to: Secretary
Direct e-mail: malcolm@circus-uk.co.uk

Founded:
1932

Organisation type and purpose:
Advisory body, trade association (membership is
by election or invitation), present number of
members: 14.
To monitor the circus industry in the UK and to
advise on standards of animal welfare, and the
training and keeping of performing animals.

Subject coverage:
Circus training and career opportunities in the
circus; the welfare of performing animals and the
ethics of animal training. Acts as the consultative
body for Government and other authorities on
legislation or other proposals affecting the circus
industry.

Printed publications:
The Association's brochure

Access to staff:
Contact by letter, by telephone, by fax, by e-mail,
in person and via website. Appointment necessary.
Hours: Mon to Fri, 0900 to 1700

Member organisation of:
Variety and Entertainments Council (VAEC)

ASSOCIATION OF CLINICAL PATHOLOGISTS

Acronym or abbreviation: ACP

189 Dyke Road, Hove, East Sussex, BN3 1TL

Tel: 01273 775700
Fax: 01273 773303
E-mail: info@pathologists.org.uk

Website:
http://www.pathologists.org.uk
Membership information, meetings, etc.

Enquiries:
Enquiries to: General Administrator

Founded:
1927

Organisation type and purpose:
International organisation, learned society,
professional body (membership is by election or
invitation), registered charity (charity number
209555).

Subject coverage:
Clinical pathology.

Printed publications:
ACP News (quarterly)
Journal of Clinical Pathology (monthly)
Programme of Postgraduate Education (annually)
Year Book

Access to staff:
Contact by letter, by telephone, by fax, by e-mail
and via website. Appointment necessary. Access
for members only.
Hours: Mon to Fri, 0900 to 1700

ASSOCIATION OF COLLEGES

Acronym or abbreviation: AoC

2–5 Stedham Place, London, WC1A 1HU

Tel: 020 7034 9900
Fax: 020 7034 4650
E-mail: enquiries@aoc.co.uk

Website:
http://www.aoc.co.uk

Enquiries:
Enquiries to: Director of Communications

Founded:
1997

Formerly called:
Association for Colleges (AfC), Colleges'
Employers Forum (CEF) (year of change 1996)

Organisation type and purpose:
Membership association (membership is by
subscription), present number of members: 450,
service industry, suitable for ages: 16+.
Colleges of further education.
Representation of the interests of further education
colleges, sixth form colleges, tertiary and specialist
colleges throughout the UK by lobbying, member
consultations, conferences and seminars and
research.

Subject coverage:
Further education, 16–19 year-olds' education,
sixth form colleges, general further education and
specialist colleges, adult education, lifelong
learning, training.

Museum or gallery collection, archive, or library special collection:
The Association holds a historical library of
information

Library catalogue:
All or part available online

Printed publications:
Regular bulletins are issued to the sector on
matters related to current further education
delivery
Weekly bulletins on all aspects of colleges' activity
are published free
FE Now (magazine, 4 times a year, £25
subscriptions to non-members)

Publications list:
Available online and in print

Access to staff:
Contact by letter, by telephone, by fax, by e-mail
and via website. Appointment necessary.
Hours: Mon to Fri, 0830 to 1700

ASSOCIATION OF COMMONWEALTH ARCHIVISTS AND RECORD MANAGERS

Acronym or abbreviation: ACARM

c/o IRMT, 4th Floor, 7 Hatton Garden, London,
EC1N 8AD

Tel: 020 7831 4101
E-mail: newsletter@acarm.org

Website:
http://www.acarm.org

Enquiries:
Enquiries to: Membership Secretary
Direct fax: 020 7831 6303

Founded:
1984

Organisation type and purpose:
Individual and institutional membership
organisation (membership by subscription).

continued overleaf

ACARM seeks to promote professional development and the sharing of solutions to the problems of managing records and archives (in paper and electronic formats) throughout the Commonwealth.

Printed publications:
Newsletter (3 times a year)

Access to staff:
Contact by letter, by telephone, by e-mail and via website

ASSOCIATION OF COMMONWEALTH UNIVERSITIES

Acronym or abbreviation: ACU

John Foster House, 36 Gordon Square, London, WC1H 0PF

Tel: 020 7380 6700
Fax: 020 7387 2655
E-mail: info@acu.ac.uk

Website:
http://www.acu.ac.uk
Full range of information about the ACU and its services.
http://www.csfp-online.org
http://www.obhe.ac.uk

Enquiries:
Enquiries to: Secretary General

Founded:
1913

Organisation type and purpose:
International organisation, membership association (membership is by subscription), present number of members: 487 universities, registered charity (charity number 314137). Voluntary association of universities which aims to strengthen through international co-operation and understanding its 487 members in 35 Commonwealth countries or regions including the UK.

Subject coverage:
Commonwealth-wide university / higher education information; administers several scholarship and fellowship schemes; advertises academic, administrative and technical job vacancies at HE institutions in the Commonwealth. Hosts Policy and Research Unit. Hosts the Observatory on Borderless Higher Education (OBHE).

Museum or gallery collection, archive, or library special collection:
18,500 volume reference library

Printed publications:
ACU Bulletin; controlled circulation (ACU member universities only) (5 times a year)
International Awards
Commonwealth Universities Yearbook
Community of Universities: An Informal Portrait of the Association of Universities of the British Commonwealth 1913–1963
Mapping borderless higher education: policy, markets and competition: selected reports from the Observatory on Borderless Higher Education (OBHE)
The Commonwealth of Universities: the Story of the ACU 1963–1988
Universities and development: a report on the socioeconomic role of universities in the developing countries of the Commonwealth
Who's Who of Executive Heads: Vice-Chancellors, Presidents, Principals, Rectors

Publications list:
Available online and in print

Access to staff:
Contact by letter, by telephone, by e-mail and via website. Appointment necessary.
Hours: Mon to Fri, 0930 to 1730

Access to building, collection or gallery:
No prior appointment required
Hours: Library: Mon to Fri, 1000 to 1300 and 1400 to 1700

Formal consultative relations with:
UNESCO

Works closely with:
Commonwealth Secretariat

ASSOCIATION OF COMMUNITY HEALTH COUNCILS FOR ENGLAND AND WALES

Acronym or abbreviation: ACHCEW

Tel: 020 7609 8405
Fax: 020 7700 1152
E-mail: mailbox@achcew.org.uk

Website:
http://www.achcew.org.uk

Enquiries:
Enquiries to: Director

Founded:
1977

Organisation type and purpose:
Membership association.
Providing forum, support and research facilities.

Subject coverage:
Community Health Councils: constitution, research and activities, representation of the patient/consumer in primary and institutional health care services, NHS complaints procedures.

Museum or gallery collection, archive, or library special collection:
Library of Reports published by individual Community Health Councils

Printed publications:
Health News Briefings (over 40)
Health Perspectives – topic papers
Patients' Rights Factsheets
Distance Learning Pack – Skills for CHC Chairs
Nationwide Casualty Watch 2001
Why are we waiting? Snapshot surveys of the impact of emergency pressures on patient care (2000)
Directory of Community Health Councils (2000)

Publications list:
Available in print

Access to staff:
Appointment necessary.
Hours: Mon to Fri, 0900 to 1700
Special comments: No disabled access.

ASSOCIATION OF COMMUNITY WORKERS

Acronym or abbreviation: ACW

Stephenson Buildings, Elswick Road, Newcastle upon Tyne, NE4 6SQ

Tel: 0191 272 4341
E-mail: lesleyleach@acw1.fsbusiness.co.uk

Enquiries:
Enquiries to: Information Officer

Founded:
1969

Organisation type and purpose:
Membership association (membership is by subscription), voluntary organisation.

Subject coverage:
Community work, organisation and practice, collective action, policies and activities.

Printed publications:
Community Work Skills Manual
Community Work (monthly newsletter)
Talking Point (monthly discussion paper)

Publications list:
Available in print

ASSOCIATION OF CONSULTANT ARCHITECTS LTD

Acronym or abbreviation: ACA

98 Hayes Road, Bromley, Kent, BR2 9AB

Tel: 020 8325 1402
Fax: 020 8466 9079
E-mail: office@acarchitects.co.uk

Website:
http://www.acarchitects.co.uk

Enquiries:
Enquiries to: Secretary-General

Founded:
1975

Organisation type and purpose:
Membership association (membership is by qualification, subscription), present number of members: 200.
Represents the interests of architects in private practice.

Subject coverage:
Architectural practices and practice.

Trade and statistical information:
Data on specialist services provided by member architectural practices.

Library catalogue:
All or part available online

Printed publications:
ACA Form of Building Agreement (3rd edn 1998, 2003 revision, £14.00)
ACA Form of Subcontract (3rd edn 1998, 2003 revision, £10.00)
GUIDE to ACA Form of Building Agreement (3rd edn 1998, 2003 revision, £12.00)
ACA98 – The Appointment of a Consultant Architect for Small Works (£5.00)
PPC2000 – ACA Standard Form of Contract for Project Partnering (amended 2008, £20.00)
SPC2000 – ACA Standard Form of Specialist Contract for Project Partnering (amended 2008, £20.00)
TPC2005 – ACA Standard Form of Contract for Term Partnering (amended 2008, £20.00)
GUIDE to ACA Project Partnering Contracts PPC2000 and SPC2000 (£20.00)
Introduction to Pricing under PPC2000 (£5.00)
SPC International – ACA Standard Form of Specialised Contract for Project Partnering (£20.00)
PPC International – ACA Standard Form of Contract for Project Partnering (£20.00)
ACA Conciliation Agreement 1998 (£4.00)
ACA Certificate – Agreeing Extended Period for the Consideration of a Planning Application (£12.00)
ACA Architect's Instruction (pad of 100, £14.00)
ACA Interim Certificate (for 2003 revision, pad of 100, £14.00)
ACA Taking-Over Certificate (pad of 50, £10.00)
ACA Final Certificate (pad of 50, £10.00)
ACA SFA/08 – ACA Standard Form of Agreement for the Appointment of an Architect (£20.00)

Publications list:
Available online and in print

Access to staff:
Contact by letter, by telephone, by fax, by e-mail and via website
Hours: Mon to Fri, 0900 to 1730

ASSOCIATION OF CONSULTING ACTUARIES

Acronym or abbreviation: ACA

1 Wardrobe Place, London, EC4V 5AG

Tel: 020 7248 3163
Fax: 020 7236 1889
E-mail: acahelp@aca.org.uk

Enquiries:
Enquiries to: Honorary Secretary

Founded:
1952

Organisation type and purpose:
Trade association (membership is by subscription, qualification), present number of members: 1,000. Association of Fellows of the Institute or Faculty of Actuaries engaged in consulting work.

Subject coverage:
Consultancy in retirement benefits and pension arrangements, sickness and hospital benefit schemes, investment policy, financial planning of funds, operational research and other statistical applications, mergers, life and general insurance, damages and divorce settlements.

Printed publications:
Annual Review
List of Members
Newsletters

Publications list:
Available online and in print

Access to staff:
Contact by letter, by telephone, by fax, by e-mail and via website
Hours: Mon to Fri, 0900 to 1700

Access to building, collection or gallery:
Prior appointment required

ASSOCIATION OF CONSULTING SCIENTISTS LIMITED

Acronym or abbreviation: ACS

PO Box 4040, Thorpe-le-Soken, Clacton-on-Sea, Essex, CO16 0EL

Tel: 01255 862526
Fax: 01255 862526
E-mail: secretary@consultingscientists.co.uk

Website:
http://www.consultingscientists.com
Directory of members and services

Enquiries:
Enquiries to: Secretary
Direct e-mail: sg@sgconsult.co.uk

Founded:
1958

Organisation type and purpose:
Advisory body, professional body (membership is by election or invitation), present number of members: 21, consultancy, research organisation. The Association provides a forum for all member scientists practising as consultants.

Subject coverage:
Consulting activities – expert witnesses, health and safety, microbiological testing, laboratory testing.

Printed publications:
Newsletter (online)

Access to staff:
Contact by letter, by telephone and by fax
Hours: Mon to Fri, 0900 to 1700
Special comments: Part time.

Subsidiary body:
Forensic and Expert Witness Group
Testing Laboratories Group

ASSOCIATION OF CONTACT LENS MANUFACTURERS

Acronym or abbreviation: ACLM

PO Box 735, Devizes, Wiltshire, SN10 3TQ

Tel: 01380 860418
Fax: 01380 860863
E-mail: secgen@aclm.org.uk

Website:
http://www.aclm.org.uk
Contact lens information for consumers and practitioners.

Enquiries:
Enquiries to: Secretary General

Founded:
1962

Organisation type and purpose:
National organisation, trade association (membership is by subscription, election or invitation), present number of members: 25, manufacturing industry.
Members represent over 95% of the UK market.
To promote and increase the wearing of contact lenses.

Subject coverage:
Contact lenses, contact lens care products, contact lens materials.

Non-library collection catalogue:
All or part available online and in print

Printed publications:
ACLM Year Book

Publications list:
Available online

Access to staff:
Contact by letter, by telephone, by fax, by e-mail and via website
Hours: Mon to Fri, 0900 to 1700

ASSOCIATION OF CORPORATE TREASURERS

Acronym or abbreviation: ACT

51 Moorgate, London, EC2R 6BH

Tel: 020 7847 2540
Fax: 020 7374 8744
E-mail: enquiries@treasurers.org

Website:
http://www.treasurers.org

Enquiries:
Enquiries to: Head of Marketing & Communications
Direct tel: 020 7847 2547
Direct e-mail: snewell@treasurers.org
Other contacts: Chief Executive (for enquiries relating to the ACT or treasury profession)

Founded:
1979

Organisation type and purpose:
Professional body (membership is by qualification).

Subject coverage:
Treasury, risk management, corporate finance

Education services:
Provider of treasury qualifications

Library catalogue:
All or part available in-house

Printed publications:
The Treasurer magazine, The International Treasurer's Handbook, The Asia Treasurer's Handbook
Order printed publications from: http://www.global-investor.com

Electronic and video publications:
The Treasurer magazine, The International Treasurer's Handbook (online)

Publications list:
Available online

Access to staff:
Contact by letter, by telephone, by fax and by e-mail
Hours: Mon to Fri, 0900 to 1700

Access to building, collection or gallery:
No prior appointment required

Access for disabled people:
Level entry, access to all public areas, toilet facilities

ASSOCIATION OF COST ENGINEERS

Acronym or abbreviation: ACostE

Administration Office, Lea House, 5 Middlewich Road, Sandbach, Cheshire, CW11 1XL

Tel: 01270 764798
Fax: 01270 766180
E-mail: enquiries@acoste.org.uk; info@acoste.org.uk

Website:
http://www.acoste.org.uk
Resources, online training, qualifications, contacts.

Organisation type and purpose:
A professional association for cost engineers, an international organisation with members from many countries around the world.
Plays a key role in setting standards and in recognition of cost engineers and project control professionals.

Subject coverage:
Prediction, planning and control of the true cost of projects have become key functions in many organisations. ACostE can take a key role in understanding why spending on major projects often significantly exceeds the initial cost estimate. Introduction of good practice and standards in project control is necessary for success.

Library catalogue:
All or part available online

Printed publications:
Project Control Professional (journal, members free, non-members £8.50 current issue, £6.00 back issues)
Cost Engineering Terminology, revised October 2000 (£10.00)
Standard Method of Measurement for Industrial Engineering Projects (£11.50)
Standard Code of Accounts (£20.00)
Guide to Association Indices (£10.00)
Industrial Engineering Projects (members £80.00, non-members £95.00)
Order printed publications from: Journal: website
Books: Merchandise Department, The Association of Cost Engineers, Administration Office, Lea House, 5 Middlewich Road, Sandbach, Cheshire, CW11 1XL; tel: 01270 764798

Electronic and video publications:
Terminology Document
Cost Indices document
Order electronic and video publications from: Download from website

Publications list:
Available online

Access to staff:
Contact by letter, by telephone, by fax and by e-mail
Hours: Mon to Fri, 0900 to 1600
Special comments: Out of these hours there is an answering service.

ASSOCIATION OF CRICKET STATISTICIANS AND HISTORIANS

Acronym or abbreviation: ACS

Archives Department, Glamorgan Cricket, Sophia Gardens, Cardiff, CF11 9XR

Tel: 0115 945 5407
E-mail: office@acscricket.com

Website:
http://acscricket.com

Enquiries:
Enquiries to: Secretary

Founded:
1973

Formerly called:
Association of Cricket Statisticians (year of change 1994)

continued overleaf

Organisation type and purpose:
International organisation, learned society (membership is by subscription), present number of members: 1,300, voluntary organisation, suitable for ages: all, research organisation, publishing house.
To research and publish all aspects of cricket history and statistical record.

Subject coverage:
Cricket and cricketers at all levels throughout the world, both historical and contemporary.

Printed publications:
Journal (quarterly free to members)
ACS International Cricket Year Book
Second Eleven Annual
Books (two or three per annum, free to members) total over 200 including:
County and State Booklets
Famous Cricketers series of 100
First Class Match Scores (16 books by groups of years or single years 1801 to 1910)
Statistical Surveys by year 1862 to 1880

Access to staff:
Contact by letter, by telephone, by fax and in person

Access for disabled people:
Level access, ground floor, direct access to street, wide door

ASSOCIATION OF DENTAL IMPLANTOLOGY

Acronym or abbreviation: ADI

98 South Worple Way, London, SW14 8ND

Tel: 020 8487 5555
Fax: 020 8487 5566
E-mail: via website

Website:
http://www.adi.org.uk
Patients' section, including find a dentist; Professionals' section, including news, events, courses, study clubs, mentor register; members' area.

Founded:
1987

Organisation type and purpose:
A registered charity (number 800238), representative body (but not a governing body) of implant dentistry in the United Kingdom encompassing clinicians, consultants, oral surgeons, technicians, hygienists, nurses and individuals from the healthcare sector.
Membership is by subscription and is open to all who hold an interest in dental implants; has over 1,700 active members drawn from every UK county plus several countries abroad.
Dedicated to providing on-going postgraduate education to the dental profession in order to extend awareness of dental implant treatment as an option for improving patient oral health and to improving the standards of implant dentistry by providing continuing education and encouraging scientific research.

Subject coverage:
A broad-based association of general dentists, oral and maxillofacial surgeons, periodontists, prosthodontists, orthodontists, laboratory technicians, auxiliaries, post-graduate dental students and manufacturer representatives.

Access to staff:
Contact by letter, by telephone, by fax and via website

ASSOCIATION OF DIRECTORS OF SOCIAL SERVICES

Acronym or abbreviation: ADSS

ADSS Office, London Borough of Hammersmith and Fulham, 145 King Street, Hammersmith, London, W6 9XY

Tel: 020 8741 8147
Fax: 020 8753 5739

Website:
http://www.adss.org.uk
ADSS branches, policy statements. ADSS offices, forthcoming events and values statements.

Enquiries:
Enquiries to: Honorary Secretary
Direct e-mail: team@adass.org.uk
Other contacts: Administrator

Organisation type and purpose:
Local government body, professional body.

Subject coverage:
Social services.

Printed publications:
Publications include:
ADSS Handbook (£25)
ADSS Inform (approx quarterly, £20 a year)
Selection of ADSS Guidelines, Policy Statements and Reports (no charge)

Publications list:
Available in print

Access to staff:
Contact by letter, by telephone, by fax and by e-mail
Hours: Mon to Fri, 0900 to 1700

ASSOCIATION OF DISABLED PROFESSIONALS

Acronym or abbreviation: ADP

BCM ADP, London, WC1N 3XX

Tel: 01204 431638
Fax: 01204 431638
E-mail: adp.admin@ntlworld.com

Website:
http://www.adp.org.uk
http://www.disabled-entrepreneurs.net
Website of the Disabled Entrepreneurs' Network.

Enquiries:
Enquiries to: Development Officer

Founded:
1971

Organisation type and purpose:
Voluntary organisation, registered as a charitable company limited by guarantee (company number 6390586; charity number 1121706).

Subject coverage:
Education, training and employment opportunities for disabled people, career prospects. Also provides support to disabled people in self-employment.

Printed publications:
Quarterly (house bulletin, free to members)
Occasional surveys
The Employment of Disabled Teachers (£4.05 including p&p)
Setting up in business? A Resource Guide for disabled people and their advisors (£2.50 including p&p to disabled people; £17.50 to organisations)
What Happens When Nurses Become Disabled? (£5 including p&p)

Access to staff:
Contact by letter, by telephone, by fax, by e-mail and via website
Hours: 24-hour answerphone

Also at:
Association of Disabled Professionals
Beechers Brook, 16 Aintree Drive, Waterlooville, Hampshire, PO7 8NG

ASSOCIATION OF DOMESTIC MANAGEMENT

Acronym or abbreviation: ADM

3 Hagg Bank Cottages, Wylam, Northumberland, NE41 8JT

Tel: 01661 853097
Fax: 01661 853097
E-mail: adm@adom.demon.co.uk

Website:
http://www.adom.demon.co.uk
Summary of publications, magazine, information on conferences. exhibitions and membership.

Enquiries:
Enquiries to: Business Manager

Founded:
1974

Organisation type and purpose:
Professional body.

Subject coverage:
Facilities management.

Printed publications:
Excel (quarterly, magazine)
Standards for Environmental Cleanliness in Hospitals (£25, joint publication with Infection Control Nurses Association)
Minimum Frequencies (publ. Dec 2001, £5)

Publications list:
Available in print

Access to staff:
Contact by letter, by telephone, by fax, by e-mail and via website. Appointment necessary.
Hours: Tue, Thu and Fri, 0830 to 1515

Access to building, collection or gallery:
No access other than to staff

Founder member of:
ADM Conference & Exhibition Ltd
British Cleaning Council

Has links with:
CAMRASO
Hefma
NHS Estates
The Knowledge Centre

ASSOCIATION OF DRAINAGE AUTHORITIES

Acronym or abbreviation: ADA

1st Floor Offices, 1 Claremont Road, Surbiton, Surrey, KT6 4QS

Tel: 0844 209 0089
Fax: 020 8399 9368
E-mail: admin@ada.org.uk

Enquiries:
Enquiries to: Chief Executive

Founded:
1937

Organisation type and purpose:
Advisory body, membership association.

Subject coverage:
Flood risk-management, lowland drainage, water level management.

Printed publications:
ADA Gazette (official journal of the Association, 4 times a year)

Access to staff:
Contact by letter, by telephone and by e-mail
Hours: Mon to Fri, 0900 to 1700

ASSOCIATION OF DRUM MANUFACTURERS

Acronym or abbreviation: ADM

St John's House, 4 London Road, Crowborough, East Sussex, TN6 2TT

Tel: 01892 654414
Fax: 01892 654981
E-mail: enquiries@the-adm.co.uk

Website:
http://www.the-adm.co.uk

Enquiries:
Enquiries to: Secretary

Founded:
1896

Organisation type and purpose:
Trade association, present number of members: 15.

Subject coverage:
Drum manufacturing.

Access to staff:
Contact by letter
Hours: Mon to Fri, 0900 to 1700

ASSOCIATION OF EASTERN MOTOR CLUBS

Acronym or abbreviation: AEMC

9 Dales Court, Dales Road, Ipswich, IP1 4JR

Tel: 01473 463444
Fax: 01473 463444

Website:
http://www.aemc.co.uk
Clubs in association, events and championships, marshals information.

Enquiries:
Enquiries to: Honorary Secretary

Founded:
1950

Organisation type and purpose:
Membership association (membership is by qualification), voluntary organisation.

Subject coverage:
Motor car sports in East Anglia for amateur enthusiasts.

Access to staff:
Contact by letter, by telephone and by fax
Hours: Mon to Fri, 0900 to 1700

Recognised by the:
Motor Sports Association (MSA)
   Riverside Park, Colnbrook, Slough, SL3 0HG; tel: 01753 765000; fax: 01753 682938; website: http://www.msauk.org

ASSOCIATION OF ELECTORAL ADMINISTRATORS

Acronym or abbreviation: AEA

PO Box 201, South Eastern, Liverpool, L16 5HH

Tel: 0151 281 8246
Fax: 0151 281 8246
E-mail: gina.armstrong@aea-elections.co.uk

Website:
http://www.aea-elections.co.uk
General information about the Association, members' area with frequently asked questions, diary, etc.

Enquiries:
Enquiries to: Executive Director (Resources)

Founded:
1987

Organisation type and purpose:
Advisory body, professional body (membership is by subscription), present number of members: 1,000, training organisation, consultancy.
To offer impartial and professional advice on electoral arrangements and the democratic process at central and local government.
Ballot services organisation providing services to the NHS, private organisations and charitable institutions.

Subject coverage:
Elections, electoral processes, electoral registration, training.

Museum or gallery collection, archive, or library special collection:
Basic practice publications
Archival records of Association business

Printed publications:
Quarterly bulletin (free)

Access to staff:
Contact by letter, by telephone, by fax, by e-mail and via website
Hours: Mon to Fri, 0900 to 1700

ASSOCIATION OF ELECTRICITY PRODUCERS

Acronym or abbreviation: AEP

1st Floor, 17 Waterloo Place, London, SW1Y 4AR

Tel: 020 7930 9390
Fax: 020 7930 9391
E-mail: enquiries@aepuk.com

Enquiries:
Enquiries to: Chief Executive
Direct tel: 020 7747 2931
Direct e-mail: rhunter@aepuk.com

Founded:
1987

Organisation type and purpose:
Trade association (membership is by subscription), present number of members: 100, service industry.

Subject coverage:
Electricity generation, competition in electricity production, liberalised electricity markets, renewable energy.

Publications list:
Available in print

Access to staff:
Contact by letter, by telephone, by fax and by e-mail. Appointment necessary.
Hours: Mon to Fri, 0900 to 1700

ASSOCIATION OF EUROPEAN BRAND OWNERS

Acronym or abbreviation: MARQUES

840 Melton Road, Thurmaston, Leicester, LE4 8BN

Tel: 0116 264 0080
Fax: 0116 264 0141
E-mail: info@marques.org

Website:
http://www.marques.org

Enquiries:
Enquiries to: Secretary General

Founded:
1987

Formerly called:
Association of European Trade Mark Proprietors (year of change 1997)

Organisation type and purpose:
International organisation, trade association (membership is by subscription).

Subject coverage:
Brand names, trade mark protection.

Access to staff:
Contact by letter, by telephone, by fax, by e-mail and via website
Hours: Mon to Fri, 0900 to 1700

ASSOCIATION OF EVENT ORGANISERS LIMITED

Acronym or abbreviation: AEO

119 High Street, Berkhamsted, Hertfordshire, HP4 2DJ

Tel: 01442 285810
Fax: 01442 875551
E-mail: info@aeo.org.uk

Website:
http://www.aeo.org.uk

Enquiries:
Enquiries to: Director General

Other contacts: Commercial Manager for administration, membership, exhibition enquiries.

Founded:
1930

Formerly called:
Association of Exhibition Organisers Ltd (year of change 2006)

Organisation type and purpose:
Trade association.

Subject coverage:
Exhibitions and events world-wide, when, where and who; career information for exhibition organisers.

Printed publications:
AEO brochure
Careers Information (free)
Code of Practice (free)
Exhibition Issues
How to Exhibit

Electronic and video publications:
Make a Stand (DVD)
How to Exhibit (e-learning)

Access to staff:
Contact by letter, by telephone, by fax, by e-mail and via website. Appointment necessary.
Hours: Mon to Fri, 0900 to 1700

Member organisation of:
Union des Foires Internationales (UFI)
   35 bis rue Jouffroy d'Abbans 5F, Paris 75017, France

ASSOCIATION OF FLIGHT ATTENDANTS

Acronym or abbreviation: AFA

AFA Council 07, United Airlines Cargo Centre, Shoreham Road East, Heathrow Airport, Hounslow, Middlesex, TW6 3UA

Tel: 020 8276 6723
Fax: 020 8276 6706
E-mail: afalhr@unitedafa.org

Website:
http://www.afalhr.org.uk

Enquiries:
Enquiries to: General Secretary

Organisation type and purpose:
International organisation, trade union (membership is by qualification), present number of members: 800.

Subject coverage:
Airline safety and security, cabin crew issues.

Access to staff:
Contact by letter, by telephone, by fax, by e-mail, in person and via website
Hours: Mon to Fri, 0900 to 1700

Access to building, collection or gallery:
Prior appointment required

Access for disabled people:
Parking provided, access to all public areas, toilet facilities

ASSOCIATION OF FRIENDLY SOCIETIES

Acronym or abbreviation: AFS

Denzell House, Denzell Gardens, Dunham Road, Bowden, Cheshire, WA14 4QE

Tel: 0161 952 5051
Fax: 0161 929 5163
E-mail: info@afs.org.uk

Website:
http://www.afs.org.uk
About the movement, its members, what they do, what the AFS is doing, private site for member societies.

continued overleaf

Enquiries:
Enquiries to: Administrator

Founded:
1995

Formed by the merger of:
Association of Collecting Friendly Societies and other existing organisations of Friendly Societies, National Conference of Friendly Societies

Organisation type and purpose:
Trade association.

Subject coverage:
Matters relating to member societies and the Friendly Society Movement, particularly information on legislation and regulation applying to them, financial services and welfare state reform.

Printed publications:
Newsletter (6 times a year, annual subscription)
Yearbook (for sale)

Access to staff:
Contact by letter, by telephone, by fax and by e-mail. Appointment necessary.
Hours: Mon to Fri, 0900 to 1700

Access to building, collection or gallery:
Prior appointment required

ASSOCIATION OF GENEALOGISTS AND RESEARCHERS IN ARCHIVES

Acronym or abbreviation: AGRA

29 Badgers Close, Horsham, West Sussex, RH12 5RU

E-mail: agra@agra.org.uk

Website:
http://www.agra.org.uk
Details of members, advice on using a professional researcher, events organised by AGRA

Enquiries:
Enquiries to: Secretary

Founded:
1968

Organisation type and purpose:
National organisation, professional body (membership is by subscription, qualification), present number of members: 100, consultancy, research organisation.

Subject coverage:
Family history, family trees, locating missing relatives, translations, surname studies, manorial records, histories of properties, palaeography, census and probate research, baptism and marriage indexes, army and navy records.

Printed publications:
List of Members (annually £2.50 inc. p&p, or 6 International Reply Coupons, available from Post Offices worldwide, to overseas enquirers)
Newsletter (members only)

Access to staff:
Contact by letter, by e-mail and via website
Hours: Mon to Fri, 0900 to 1700

ASSOCIATION OF GEOTECHNICAL AND GEOENVIRONMENTAL SPECIALISTS

Acronym or abbreviation: AGS

Forum Court, 83 Copers Cope Road, Beckenham, Kent, BR3 1NR

Tel: 020 8658 8212
Fax: 020 8663 0949
E-mail: ags@ags.org.uk

Website:
http://www.ags.org.uk

Full information about the AGS, newsletters, members, etc. Also edition III of the AGS Electronic Format for SI data – download (Acrobat) plus discussion forum.

Enquiries:
Enquiries to: Administrator

Founded:
1990

Organisation type and purpose:
Trade association.

Subject coverage:
Geotechnics e.g. foundations (design and construction), site investigation, laboratory testing, geoenvironment testing, remediation, monitoring, geotechnical design, geoenvironmentalism.

Printed publications:
Collateral Warranties (members £15, non-members £20)
Electronic Transfer of Geotechnical Data from Ground Investigation (3rd ed., members £20, non-members £40)
Guide to the Selection of Geotechnical Soil Laboratory Testing (£40 members, £55 non-members)
Guidelines for Combined Geoenvironmental and Geotechnical Investigation (members £28, non-members £45)

Access to staff:
Contact by letter, by telephone, by fax and by e-mail
Hours: Mon to Fri, 0900 to 1700

Members of:
Ground Forum

ASSOCIATION OF GOLF WRITERS

Acronym or abbreviation: AGW

1 Pilgrims Bungalow, Mulberry Hill, Chilham, Kent, CT4 8AH

Tel: 01227 732496
Fax: 01227 732496
E-mail: enquiries@agwgolf.org

Website:
http://www.agwgolf.org

Enquiries:
Enquiries to: Administrator
Other contacts: Honorary Secretary

Founded:
1938

Organisation type and purpose:
Membership association.

Subject coverage:
Golf; sports writing.

Printed publications:
Annual handbook

Access to staff:
Contact by letter, by telephone, by fax and by e-mail
Hours: Mon to Fri, 0900 to 1700

ASSOCIATION OF GRACE BAPTIST CHURCHES (SE)

Acronym or abbreviation: AGBC(SE)

7 Arlington Way, London, EC1R 1XA

Tel: 020 7278 1200
Fax: 020 7278 3598
E-mail: assoc@agbcse.org.uk

Website:
http://www.agbcse.org.uk

Enquiries:
Enquiries to: Association Secretary
Other contacts: Company Secretary for finance and legal.

Founded:
1871

Organisation type and purpose:
Registered charity (charity number 276352). To promote the unity and prosperity of associated churches and devise and employ means for the furtherance of the Gospel in London, Berkshire, Buckinghamshire, Essex, Hampshire, Hertfordshire, Kent, Oxfordshire, Surrey and Sussex.

Access to staff:
Contact by letter, by telephone, by fax and by e-mail
Hours: Mon to Fri, 0900 to 1700

Access to building, collection or gallery:
Prior appointment required

Access for disabled people:
Ramped entry

ASSOCIATION OF GRADUATE RECRUITERS

Acronym or abbreviation: AGR

The Innovation Centre, Warwick Technology Park, Gallows Hill, Warwick, CV34 6UW

Tel: 01926 623236
Fax: 01926 623237
E-mail: info@agr.org.uk

Website:
http://www.agr.org.uk

Enquiries:
Enquiries to: Chief Executive

Founded:
1968

Organisation type and purpose:
Professional body.

Subject coverage:
Graduate recruitment from the employer's viewpoint.

Trade and statistical information:
Graduate vacancies and salaries information.

Printed publications:
Graduate Recruiter (magazine, six times a year, for the graduate recruitment market)

Publications list:
Available online and in print

Access to staff:
Contact by letter, by telephone, by fax, by e-mail and via website
Hours: Mon to Fri, 0900 to 1700

Access for disabled people:
Parking provided, access to all public areas, toilet facilities

ASSOCIATION OF HEAD TEACHERS AND DEPUTES IN SCOTLAND

Acronym or abbreviation: AHDS

PO Box 18532, Inverurie, AB51 0WS

Tel: 0845 260 7560
E-mail: info@ahds.org.uk

Website:
http://www.ahds.org.uk

Enquiries:
Enquiries to: General Secretary

Founded:
1975

Organisation type and purpose:
Trade union

Subject coverage:
Trade Union support for headteachers and deputes from Scotland's nursery, primary and special schools

Access to staff:
Contact by letter, by telephone, by e-mail, in

person and via website. Appointment necessary.
Hours: Mon to Fri, 0900 to 1700

ASSOCIATION OF ILLUSTRATORS

Acronym or abbreviation: AOI

81 Leonard Street, London, EC2A 4QS

Tel: 020 7613 4328
Fax: 020 7613 4417
E-mail: info@a-o-illustrators.demon.co.uk

Website:
http://www.aoisupplement.co.uk
Images Annual online.

Enquiries:
Enquiries to: Membership Secretary

Founded:
1974

Organisation type and purpose:
Trade association (membership is by subscription).

Subject coverage:
Illustration and illustrators; ethics, copyright law, fees and standard practice.

Printed publications:
AOI Booklet: Listing Services (free)
Despatch: (journal, monthly, free, members only)
Images: Yearbook of the Best of British Illustration
Rights: The Illustrator's Guide to a Professional
  Practice (for sale to non-members)
Survive: A Guide to Starting in Illustration

Access to staff:
Contact by telephone, by fax and by e-mail.
Appointment necessary.
Hours: Mon to Fri, 0900 to 1700

Within the:
Joint Ethics Committee for the Visual Arts

ASSOCIATION OF INDEPENDENT COMPUTER SPECIALISTS

Acronym or abbreviation: AICS

Honeyhill, Bismore, Eastcombe, Stroud, Gloucestershire, GL6 7DG

Tel: 0845 123 5399
E-mail: honsec@aics.org.uk

Website:
http://www.aics.org.uk
Full information about the Association, contact information for prospective new members and for those looking to use the services of members.

Enquiries:
Enquiries to: Honorary Secretary

Founded:
1972

Organisation type and purpose:
Trade association for individuals and independent firms whose main business is the supply of computer-related services, including consultancy.

Subject coverage:
Introduction to members offering specific specialist computer-related services.

Printed publications:
Newsletter (quarterly)

Electronic and video publications:
Electronic newsletter to members

Access to staff:
Contact by telephone, by e-mail and via website
Hours: Mon to Fri, 0900 to 1700

Access to building, collection or gallery:
No access other than to staff

ASSOCIATION OF INDEPENDENT LIBRARIES

Acronym or abbreviation: AIL

The Leeds Library, 18 Commercial Street, Leeds, West Yorkshire, LS1 6AL

Tel: 0113 245 3071

Enquiries:
Enquiries to: Honorary Secretary
Direct tel: 01473 253992

Founded:
1989

Organisation type and purpose:
National organisation.
To promote an interest in libraries, reading, literature generally and in the many and varied special collections.

Access to staff:
Contact by letter and by telephone. Appointment necessary.
Hours: Mon to Fri, 0900 to 1700

ASSOCIATION OF INDEPENDENT MUSEUMS

Acronym or abbreviation: AIM

4 Clayhall Road, Gosport, PO12 2BY

Tel: 023 9258 7751
E-mail: aimadmin@aim-museums.co.uk

Website:
http://www.aim-museums.co.uk

Founded:
1977

Organisation type and purpose:
Professional body, trade association (membership is by subscription), present number of members: 800, voluntary organisation.
National museum association for those institutions not directly administered by central or local government.

Subject coverage:
Museum development; management; administration; fundraising; marketing; display; publications, particularly for the independent sector.

Printed publications:
AIM Bulletin (6 times a year for members)
AIM Guidelines on specific topics, generally relating to establishment of specific roles within museums

Access to staff:
Contact by letter, by telephone and by e-mail
Hours: Mon to Fri, 0900 to 1700

ASSOCIATION OF INDEPENDENT PSYCHOTHERAPISTS

Acronym or abbreviation: AIP

PO Box 1194, London, N6 5PW

Tel: 020 7700 1911
E-mail: info@aip.org.uk

Website:
http://www.aip.org.uk

Founded:
1988

Organisation type and purpose:
Professional body (membership is by election or invitation), voluntary organisation, training organisation, consultancy.

Subject coverage:
Psychotherapy.

Information services:
Psychotherapy referral service, e-mail: referrals@aip.org.uk

Education services:
Psychotherapy training; e-mail training@aip.org.uk

Access to staff:
Contact by letter, by telephone and by e-mail
Hours: Mon to Fri, 0900 to 1700

Also at:
Association of Independent Psychotherapists
  8 Victoria Mansions, 135 Holloway Road,
  London, N7 8LZ

ASSOCIATION OF INDEPENDENT TOUR OPERATORS LIMITED

Acronym or abbreviation: AITO

133a St Margaret's Road, Twickenham, Middlesex, TW1 1RG

Tel: 020 8744 9280
Fax: 020 8744 3187
E-mail: info@aito.co.uk

Website:
http://www.aito.co.uk
AITO members.

Enquiries:
Enquiries to: Chairman

Founded:
1976

Organisation type and purpose:
Trade association (membership is by subscription), present number of members: 157.

Subject coverage:
Overseas tour operations.

Printed publications:
Consumer Handbook 2007

Publications list:
Available online and in print

Access to staff:
Contact by letter, by telephone, by fax and by e-mail
Hours: Mon to Thu, 0900 to 1730; Fri, 0900 to 1700

ASSOCIATION OF INTERIOR SPECIALISTS LIMITED

Acronym or abbreviation: AIS

Olton Bridge, 245 Warwick Road, Solihull, West Midlands, B92 7AH

Tel: 0121 707 0077
Fax: 0121 706 1949
E-mail: info@ais-interiors.org.uk

Website:
http://www.ais-interiors.org.uk
General information.

Enquiries:
Enquiries to: Chief Executive

Founded:
1998

Formed by the merger of:
Partitioning & Interiors Association Limited (PIA), Suspended Ceilings and Interiors Association Limited (SCIA) (year of change 1998)

Organisation type and purpose:
A single source serving the interiors fit-out industry, the AIS is a trade association that represents some 466 companies involved in the manufacture, supply and installation of all aspects of interior fit-outs and refurbishments, with particular emphasis on ceilings and partitions. Its members operate in retail and commercial offices, the public sector, banks and building societies, hotels and leisure, airports and hospitals.

Subject coverage:
All aspects of interior fit-out, including industrial and commercial partitioning, operable walls, suspended ceilings, drylining, access flooring. Manufacture, supply and installation.

Printed publications:
AIS – Serving the Interiors Sector (promotional leaflet)
Ceilings Site Guide
Directory of products and services
Fact File Information Sheets on various topics
Health and Safety Handbook

continued overleaf

Interiors Focus (journal, 2 times a year, aimed at
   specifiers of commercial/interior design)
Interiors Insight (4 times a year)
Occasional market research on system partitioning
Partitioning Site Guide
Register of members
Raised Access Flooring Guide
Wallcoverings Guide
Drylining Guide

Access to staff:
Contact by letter, by telephone, by fax, by e-mail
and via website
Hours: Mon to Fri, 0900 to 1700

Access to building, collection or gallery:
No prior appointment required

Members of:
National Specialist Contractors Council (NSCC)
   Construction House, 54–56 Leonard Street,
   London, EC2A 4JX; tel: 020 7608 5090; fax: 020
   7608 5081

ASSOCIATION OF INTERNATIONAL ACCOUNTANTS

Acronym or abbreviation: AIA

AIA Head Office, Staithes 3, The Watermark,
Metro Riverside, Newcastle upon Tyne, NE11 9SN

Tel: 0191 493 0277
E-mail: aia@aiaworldwide.com

Website:
http://www.aiaworldwide.com/
AIA prospectus, press releases, syllabus, reading
lists, structure, membership information,
examinations, events, recruitment.

Enquiries:
Enquiries to: Membership Services
Direct e-mail: membership.services@aiaworldwide
.com

Founded:
1928

Organisation type and purpose:
International organisation, professional body
(membership is by qualification).
Accounting body.
Under the Companies Act 1989 the AIA
Accountancy qualification is a recognised
professional qualification for company auditors in
the United Kingdom.

Subject coverage:
Financial and management accountancy,
investigations, auditing, management consultancy,
taxation.

Printed publications:
International Accountant (available to all
   members) and those wishing to subscribe

Publications list:
Available online

Access to staff:
Contact by letter, by telephone, by fax, by e-mail
and via website
Hours: Mon to Fri, 0900 to 1700

Access to building, collection or gallery:
No access other than to staff

Access for disabled people:
Parking provided

Affiliated to:
Asociación Española de Expertos Contables y
Fiscales
European Accounting Association (EAA)
International Association for Accounting and
Research (IAAER)
International Institute of Accountants (New
Zealand)

Other addresses:
AIA Hong Kong Branch
   Room 1003, 10F Emperor Group Centre, 288
   Hennessy Road, Wanchai, Hong Kong; tel: 00
   852 2845 4982; fax: 00 852 2845 7495; e-mail:
   aiahkbr@netvigator.com

Persatuan Alumni Akauntan – Cawangan
Malaysia
   Suite 20–10, Level 20, Wisma Uoa II, 21 Jalan,
   Pinang, 50450 Kuala Lumpur, Malaysia; tel: 00
   60 3 2166 3020; fax: 00 60 3 2166 4020; e-mail:
   paaicm@tm.net.my

ASSOCIATION OF JEWISH REFUGEES IN GREAT BRITAIN

Acronym or abbreviation: AJR

1 Hampstead Gate, 1A Frognal, London, NW3
6AL

Tel: 020 7431 6161
Fax: 020 7431 8454
E-mail: enquiries@ajr.org.uk

Website:
http://www.ajr.org.uk

Enquiries:
Enquiries to: Administrator
Direct e-mail: susie@ajr.org.uk

Founded:
1941

Organisation type and purpose:
Membership association, present number of
members: 3,500, voluntary organisation, registered
charity (charity number 211239).
Representation and welfare for Jewish refugees
from Nazi persecution, and their families.

Subject coverage:
Matters pertaining to former Jewish refugees from
Nazi persecution in fields of restitution,
compensation, social welfare, old age homes,
accommodation, historical and political matters.

Printed publications:
AJR Journal (monthly, £3 to non-members, free to
   members)

Access to staff:
Contact by letter, by telephone, by fax, by e-mail
and via website
Hours: Mon to Thu, 0930 to 1700; Fri, 0930 to 1330

Access to building, collection or gallery:
No prior appointment required

Access for disabled people:
Toilet facilities

Affiliated to:
AJR Charitable Trust
   at the same address

Also:
Association of Jewish Refugees Day Centre
   15 Cleve Road, London, NW6 3RL; tel: 020 7328
   0208

ASSOCIATION OF KI AIKIDO

Acronym or abbreviation: AKA

17 Langland Gardens, London, NW3 6QE

Tel: 020 7435 1330
E-mail: charlie@harris.u-net.com

Website:
http://www.happyaikido.com
Information about Aikido.

Enquiries:
Direct e-mail: happyaikido@happyaikido.com

Founded:
1987

Organisation type and purpose:
Training organisation.
Training in martial art of Aikido, self-defence and
calmness under pressure in daily life.

Subject coverage:
Martial art of Ki Aikido.

Access to staff:
Contact by telephone and by e-mail. Appointment
necessary.

Hours: Wed, 2000 to 2200; Sat, 1100 to 1330; Sun,
1700 to 1900

Access to building, collection or gallery:
Prior appointment required

Access for disabled people:
Hours: Wed, 2000 to 2200; Sat, 1100 to 1330; Sun,
1700 to 1900

ASSOCIATION OF LANDSCAPE CONTRACTORS OF IRELAND (NORTHERN REGION)

Acronym or abbreviation: ALCI

22 Summerhill Park, Bangor, BT20 5QQ

Tel: 028 9127 2823
Fax: 028 9127 2823
E-mail: secretary@alci.org.uk

Enquiries:
Enquiries to: Secretary

Founded:
1971

Organisation type and purpose:
Trade association.
Representation of the landscape contracting
industry in Ireland.

Subject coverage:
Training needs and educational matter relating to
the landscaping industry, including contract
procedures, standards of quality and
workmanship, and management.

Printed publications:
Who's Who 2001/2002 (brochure with the aims,
   objectives, conditions of membership and list of
   members, available free, direct)

Access to staff:
Contact by letter, by telephone, by fax and by e-
mail. Appointment necessary.
Hours: Mon to Fri, 0900 to 1700

Access to building, collection or gallery:
Prior appointment required

Works closely with:
British Association of Landscape Industries
Institute of Groundsmen

ASSOCIATION OF LASER USERS

Acronym or abbreviation: AILU

100 Ock Street, Abingdon, Oxfordshire, OX14 5DH

Tel: 01235 539595
Fax: 01235 550499
E-mail: admin@ailu.org.uk

Website:
http://www.ailu.org.uk
Directory, technical information on laser
processing, product guide, United Kingdom
statistics.

Enquiries:
Enquiries to: Executive Secretary

Founded:
1995

Organisation type and purpose:
Professional body, membership association
(membership is by subscription), present number
of members: 350, manufacturing industry.
To disseminate information and aid networking.

Subject coverage:
Laser use in industry. Manufacturers and supplies
of laser and laser-related equipment and services.
Laser applications topics, including materials
processing and measurement.

Trade and statistical information:
Centres for UK laser activity.

Printed publications:
Introduction to Laser Materials Processing (£18)
Laser Materials Processing: Challenge and
   Opportunities in Europe (proceedings, 1997, £45)

The Industrial Laser User (magazine, 4 times a
year, members only)

Access to staff:
Contact by letter, by telephone, by fax, by e-mail
and via website
Hours: Mon to Fri, 0900 to 1700

ASSOCIATION OF LAW COSTS DRAFTSMEN

Acronym or abbreviation: ALCD

Church Cottage, Church Lane, Stuston, Diss,
Norfolk, IP21 4AG

Tel: 01379 741404
Fax: 01379 742702
E-mail: enquiries@alcd.org.uk

Website:
http://www.alcd.org.uk
Details of the Association and information on
joining.

Enquiries:
Enquiries to: Administrator

Founded:
1977

Organisation type and purpose:
Professional body (membership is by
qualification), present number of members: 850.
Membership subscription is required.
Law Costs Draftsmen are specialists in the law
who operate by advising upon and applying laws
and directions that relate to the evaluation and
recovery of solicitors' fees.

Printed publications:
ALCD (monthly)

Publications list:
Available in print

Access to staff:
Contact by letter, by telephone, by fax, by e-mail
and via website
Hours: Mon to Fri, 0900 to 1700

ASSOCIATION OF LAW TEACHERS

Acronym or abbreviation: ALT

City Law School, 4 Gray's Inn Place, London,
WC1R 5DX

Tel: 020 7404 5787, ext 368
E-mail: amanda.fancourt.1@city.ac.uk

Enquiries:
Enquiries to: Honorary Secretary

Founded:
1965

Organisation type and purpose:
Professional body (membership is by subscription),
present number of members: 500, research
organisation.

Subject coverage:
Legal education, academic law.

Printed publications:
ALT Bulletin and e-newsletter
The Law Teacher (3 times a year)
Order printed publications from: Nigel Duncan
(Editor The Law Teacher), City Law School, 4
Gray's Inn Place, London, WC1R 5DX

Access to staff:
Contact by letter, by telephone, by fax and by e-
mail
Hours: Mon to Fri, 0900 to 1700

ASSOCIATION OF LEADING VISITOR ATTRACTIONS

Acronym or abbreviation: ALVA

4 Westminster Palace Gardens, Artillery Row,
London, SW1P 1RL

Tel: 020 7222 1728
E-mail: info@alva.org.uk

Website:
http://www.alva.org.uk

Enquiries:
Enquiries to: Information Officer

Founded:
1989

Organisation type and purpose:
Trade association.

Access to staff:
Contact by letter, by telephone, by fax, by e-mail,
in person and via website. Appointment necessary.
Hours: Mon to Fri, 0900 to 1700

Access to building, collection or gallery:
Prior appointment required

ASSOCIATION OF LEARNED AND PROFESSIONAL SOCIETY PUBLISHERS

Acronym or abbreviation: ALPSP

1 Abbey Cottages, The Green, Sutton Courtenay,
Oxfordshire, OX14 4AF

Tel: 01235 847776
Fax: 0870 706 0332
E-mail: ian.russell@alpsp.org

Website:
http://www.alpsp.org

Enquiries:
Enquiries to: Chief Executive

Founded:
1972

Organisation type and purpose:
ALPSP is the international association for the
community of scholarly and professional
publishers and those who work with them.
Membership is open to organizations working in
research-based publishing or a related industry.
ALPSP advocates best practice, carries out research
and other projects, monitors national and
international issues, represents members' interests
to the wider world and provides an extensive
professional development programme. The
Association provides co-operative services such as
the ALPSP Learned Journals Collection and the
ALPSP e-books Collection.

Subject coverage:
Scholarly journal and book publishing; learned
and professional society publishing; not-for-profit
publishing (e.g. learned societies, university
presses, non-governmental organisations etc.).

Printed publications:
Learned Publishing (quarterly, non-members
institutional rate: £185 per year (2010 price), print
plus electronic; full prices on website)
Various research reports, white papers, etc.
Order printed publications from: Ian Hunter, Finance
and Admin Manager, 51 Middletons Road, Yaxley,
Peterborough, Cambridgeshire, PE7 3NU; e-mail:
admin@alpsp.org; tel: 0173 324 7178

Electronic and video publications:
Learned Publishing (quarterly journal)
ALPSP Alert (monthly electronic newsletter)

Publications list:
Available online

Access to staff:
Contact by letter, by telephone, by fax, by e-mail,
in person and via website. Appointment necessary.
Hours: Mon to Fri, 0900 to 1700

Links with:
Copyright Licensing Agency
Publishers Licensing Society
Publishing Skills Group

ASSOCIATION OF LIBERAL DEMOCRAT COUNCILLORS

Acronym or abbreviation: ALDC

Birchcliffe Centre, Birchcliffe, Hebden Bridge, West
Yorkshire, HX7 8DG

Tel: 01422 843785
Fax: 01422 843036
E-mail: info@aldc.org

Website:
http://www.aldc.org

Enquiries:
Enquiries to: Information Officer

Organisation type and purpose:
Membership association (membership is by
subscription).

Access to staff:
Contact by letter, by telephone, by fax, by e-mail
and via website. Access for members only.
Hours: Mon to Fri, 0900 to 1700

ASSOCIATION OF LICENSED MULTIPLE RETAILERS

Acronym or abbreviation: ALMR

9B Walpole Court, Ealing Studios, London, W5
5ED

Tel: 020 8579 2080
Fax: 020 8579 7579
E-mail: info@almr.org.uk

Website:
http://www.almr.org.uk
The association, business news, calendar of events,
hot topics, legislative and regulatory issues,
directory of members, members' area.

Organisation type and purpose:
A network of entrepreneurial retailers and
industry suppliers that champions the smaller
independent companies that own and operate
pubs, bars and restaurants in the UK.

Subject coverage:
Core membership is the smaller independent
company that operates managed pubs and bars at
every level in the market, many of which also have
a bias towards food, entertainment and sports.
They may be either leasehold or freehold or other
ownership basis. The ALMR's title assumes
'multiple' sites, but 2 is an acceptable threshold.

Electronic and video publications:
ALMR Matters
Press releases
Order electronic and video publications from:
Download from website

Publications list:
Available online

Access to staff:
Contact by letter, by telephone, by fax and by e-
mail

ASSOCIATION OF LLOYD'S MEMBERS

Acronym or abbreviation: ALM

100 Fenchurch Street, London, EC3M 5LG

Tel: 0207 488 0033
Fax: 020 7488 7555
E-mail: mail@alm.ltd.uk

Website:
http://www.alm.ltd.uk
Aims, key issues, publications, news, conferences.

Enquiries:
Enquiries to: Consultant
Direct e-mail: edward.vale@alm.ltd.uk; linda
.evans@alm.ltd.uk
Other contacts: Senior Administrator / Membership
Enquiries

continued overleaf

Founded:
c. 1984

Organisation type and purpose:
Represents private capital at Lloyd's insurance market, membership is by subscription.
To represent and advance members' interests whether they participate on an unlimited or a limited liability basis, either alone or in group vehicles.

Subject coverage:
Private underwriters at Lloyd's.

Printed publications:
Publications are free to members:
ALM News (six times a year)
Equitasian (normally two issues each year)
Annual Lloyd's Market Results Summary (May)
Annual Lloyd's Market Results & Prospects (August)
ALM's Annual Tax Briefing (April) including ALM expenses.
Other Special Briefing Papers

Publications list:
Available online

Access to staff:
Contact by letter, by telephone, by fax and by e-mail

ASSOCIATION OF LONDON CHIEF LIBRARIANS

Acronym or abbreviation: ALCL

c/o London Libraries Development Agency, 6 Charing Cross Road, London. WC2H 0HF

Tel: 020 7641 5266
Fax: 020 7641 5266
E-mail: andy.ryan@llda.org.uk

Website:
http://www.llda.org.uk

Enquiries:
Enquiries to: Honorary Secretary
Other contacts: President

Founded:
1965

Organisation type and purpose:
Local government body, professional body, public library.

Subject coverage:
London public libraries.

Access to staff:
Contact by letter, by telephone, by fax and by e-mail
Hours: Mon to Fri, 0900 to 1700

ASSOCIATION OF LONDON GOVERNMENT

Acronym or abbreviation: ALG

59½ Southwark Street, London, NW6 7NE

Tel: 020 7934 9999
Fax: 020 7934 9991
E-mail: info@alg.gov.uk

Website:
http://www.alg.gov.uk

Enquiries:
Enquiries to: Press and Publications Manager

Founded:
2000

Formerly called:
London Borough Grants Committee (LBGC) (year of change 1997); London Boroughs Grants Unit (LBGU) (year of change 2000)

Organisation type and purpose:
Local government body.
Grant-making body, as defined by Section 48 of the Local Government Act 1985.
To distribute grants to voluntary organisations on a London-wide basis.

Subject coverage:
Strategic funding of the voluntary sector in London, grant applications and monitoring processes; funding initiatives; the LBG and London Boroughs Grant Committee; advice and guidance for voluntary organisations; funding sources and other information.

Printed publications:
Information Pack
London Grants News (quarterly)
A variety of other publications

Publications list:
Available in print

Access to staff:
Contact by letter, by telephone, by fax, by e-mail, in person and via website
Hours: Mon to Fri, 0915 to 1715

Access for disabled people:
Parking provided, ramped entry, access to all public areas, toilet facilities

ASSOCIATION OF MANUFACTURERS OF POWER GENERATING SYSTEMS

Acronym or abbreviation: AMPS

Samuelson House, 62 Forder Way, Hampton, Peterborough, PE7 8JB

Tel: 0845 644 8748
Fax: 01733 314767
E-mail: ab@amps.org.uk

Website:
http://www.amps.org.uk

Enquiries:
Enquiries to: Director General

Founded:
1977

Organisation type and purpose:
Trade association (membership is by subscription).
The international promotion of the UK power generation systems industry.

Subject coverage:
Promotion of the interests and sales of the United Kingdom's manufacturers of diesel and gas driven electrical generating systems worldwide. By representation on British, European and International Standards Committees, EUROPGEN and other bodies, to speak with one voice on all issues of technical standards, legislation and commercial policy that affect members' interests. To help members maintain the highest technical standards, quality and customer support.

Trade and statistical information:
Data on worldwide market for diesel and gas turbine electrical power generating systems – volume and value.

Printed publications:
Directory of Members
A Guide to Earthing of Private Generating Sets up to 5MW – single and parallel operation
Technical guidelines to the first 6 parts of the Generating Set Standard ISO 8528

Electronic and video publications:
Directory of AMPS members, activities and products (CD-ROM, free of charge)

Publications list:
Available in print

Access to staff:
Contact by letter, by telephone, by fax and by e-mail
Hours: Mon to Fri, 0830 to 1700

Member of:
British Electrotechnical and Allied Manufacturers' Association (BEAMA)
Electrical Generating System Association, USA (EGSA)
Electricity Supply Association of Australia Limited (ESSA)

European Generating Set Association (EUROPGEN)
Institution of Diesel and Gas Turbine Engineers (IDGTE)

ASSOCIATION OF MBAS

Formal name: Association of Masters in Business Administration

25 Hosier Lane, London, EC1A 9LQ

Tel: 020 7246 2686
Fax: 020 7246 2687
E-mail: info@mbaworld.com

Website:
http://www.mbaworld.com

Enquiries:
Enquiries to: Company Secretary
Direct e-mail: p.north@mbaworld.com
Other contacts: Membership Secretary

Founded:
1967

Formerly called:
Business Graduates Association (BGA) (year of change 1987)

Organisation type and purpose:
Professional body, membership association (membership is by subscription, qualification), present number of members: 9,000, registered charity (charity number 313412), suitable for ages: 24+.
To promote and improve management standards.

Subject coverage:
MBA courses worldwide, accreditation of MBA courses, funding for MBA courses.

Trade and statistical information:
Data on the number of MBA courses available and the numbers of students graduating each year.
Salary and careers data of MBAs.

Printed publications:
Annual address book of members (free to members only)
Annual Report (free)
Official MBA Handbook (annually)
MBAs: Salaries and Careers (biennially)

Access to staff:
Contact by letter, by telephone, by fax, by e-mail, in person and via website. Appointment necessary.
Hours: Mon to Fri, 0900 to 1700

ASSOCIATION OF MEDICAL RESEARCH CHARITIES

Acronym or abbreviation: AMRC

61 Gray's Inn Road, London, WC1X 8TL

Tel: 020 7269 8820
Fax: 020 7269 8821
E-mail: info@amrc.org.uk

Website:
http://www.amrc.org.uk

Enquiries:
Enquiries to: Chief Executive

Founded:
1987

Organisation type and purpose:
Membership association of charities that fund medical research in the UK.
Membership is by application.
Members must use peer review, have a research strategy in place, and sign up to AMRC position statements in order to qualify for membership.
Present number of members: 114.
Registered charity (charity no. 296772), company limited by guarantee (company no. 2107400).
Aims to further medical research in the UK generally; in particular to further effectiveness of those charities in which a principal activity is medical research.

Subject coverage:
Advice and guidance on best practice in medical research. Information on the contribution of charities to UK medical research.

Trade and statistical information:
Data on the funding of medical research charities, including distribution and types of funds.

Electronic and video publications:
Online guide to member charities
Guidance documents on best practice in medical research funding available to download from website

Access to staff:
Contact by letter, by telephone, by fax, by e-mail and via website. Appointment necessary.
Hours: Mon to Fri, 0930 to 1730

Access to building, collection or gallery:
Prior appointment required

Access for disabled people:
Toilet facilities

ASSOCIATION OF MOTOR RACING CIRCUIT OWNERS LTD

Acronym or abbreviation: AMRCO Ltd

BARC, Thruxton Circuit, Andover, Hampshire, SP11 8PN

Tel: 01264 882200
Fax: 01264 882233
E-mail: amrco@barc.net

Website:
http://www.motorsportsuk.co.uk

Enquiries:
Enquiries to: Honorary Secretary

Founded:
1962

Organisation type and purpose:
Trade association, membership association (membership is by subscription, qualification), present number of members: 18.
To represent the interests of UK motor sport circuit owners.

Subject coverage:
Motor sport organisation and race circuit management. Circuits include: Anglesey, Brands Hatch, Cadwell Park, Castle Combe, Croft, Donington Park, Goodwood, Kirkistown, Knockhill, Lydden Hill, Mallory Park, Mondello Park, Oulton Park, Pembrey, Rockingham, Silverstone, Snetterton and Thruxton.

Access to staff:
Contact by letter
Hours: Mon to Fri, 0900 to 1700

ASSOCIATION OF MUSLIM SCHOOLS

Acronym or abbreviation: AMS

512 Berridge Road West, Nottingham, NG7 5JU

Tel: 0115 841 1919
Fax: 0115 841 5806
E-mail: ams@webstar.co.uk

Enquiries:
Enquiries to: Director

Founded:
1992

Organisation type and purpose:
Membership association (membership is by subscription), present number of members: 52 schools, training organisation, consultancy. Members are full-time Muslim schools.
To enhance the development of Muslim schools.

Subject coverage:
Muslim schools, Islamic education, general education, Islam.

Printed publications:
Al Madaris (termly, free)

Access to staff:
Contact by letter, by telephone and by fax
Hours: Mon to Fri, 0900 to 1700

Connections with:
Association of Muslim Schools
PO Box 537, Lenasia, 1820, South Africa

ASSOCIATION OF NATIONAL TOURIST OFFICE REPRESENTATIVES

Acronym or abbreviation: ANTOR

ANTOR Executive Secretary, 39 Pennington Close, Colden Common, Winchester, Hampshire, SO21 1UR

Tel: 0870 241 9084
Fax: 01962 711239
E-mail: esther@antor.com

Website:
http://www.antor.com

Founded:
1952

Organisation type and purpose:
International organisation, professional body (membership is by subscription, election or invitation), present number of members: over 90 National Tourist Office members, voluntary organisation.

Subject coverage:
Tourism in each member country, tourist planning facilities.

Access to staff:
Contact by letter, by telephone, by e-mail and via website. Appointment necessary.
Hours: Telephone has an answering machine

ASSOCIATION OF NATURAL BURIAL GROUNDS

Acronym or abbreviation: ANBG

The Natural Death Centre, In the Hill House, Watley Lane, Twyford, Winchester, SO21 1QX

Tel: 01962 712 690
E-mail: contact@naturaldeath.org.uk

Website:
http://www.naturaldeath.org.uk
Addresses and descriptions of all woodland burial sites; criteria for association members.

Enquiries:
Enquiries to: Manager

Founded:
1994

Organisation type and purpose:
Registered charity.

Subject coverage:
Association for the 240+ green burial grounds (and 50 more at planning stage) where body is buried with a tree planted instead of a headstone; legal, ecological, and other issues pertaining to such a burial method.

Trade and statistical information:
Details of sites run by councils, farmers and wildlife trusts.

Printed publications:
The Natural Death Handbook (4th ed, £15.50 inc. p&p), lists all the woodland burial grounds in the UK, recommended funeral directors, suppliers of cardboard coffins, how to arrange a funeral without a funeral director, green, DIY funerals, etc., plus information on how to set up a woodland burial ground.

Access to staff:
Contact by letter, by telephone, by e-mail and via website
Hours: Mon to Fri, 1100 to 1400

Links with:
Natural Death Centre charity at the same address; website: http://www.naturaldeath.org.uk

ASSOCIATION OF NEWSPAPER AND MAGAZINE WHOLESALERS

Acronym or abbreviation: ANMW

PO Box 40, 4 Acre Road, Reading, Berkshire RG2 0XZ

Tel: 0845 1213210
E-mail: enquiries@anmw.co.uk

Website:
http://www.anmw.co.uk

Enquiries:
Enquiries to: Chairman
Direct e-mail: howard.birch@smithsnews.co.uk

Founded:
1904

Organisation type and purpose:
Trade association.

Subject coverage:
Wholesaling of newspapers and magazines within the United Kingdom.

Access to staff:
Contact by letter, by telephone, by fax and by e-mail
Hours: Mon to Fri, 0900 to 1700

ASSOCIATION OF NOISE CONSULTANTS

Acronym or abbreviation: ANC

The Old Pump House, 1A Stonecross, St Albans, Hertfordshire, AL1 4AA

Tel: 020 8253 4518
E-mail: info@theanc.co.uk

Website:
http://www.association-of-noise-consultants.co.uk

Enquiries:
Enquiries to: Manager

Founded:
1973

Organisation type and purpose:
Professional body, present number of members: 115 corporate members.

Subject coverage:
To help potential clients identify the services of consultancy advice in the fields of noise and vibration.

Non-library collection catalogue:
All or part available online

Printed publications:
Aims and Objectives
Membership Directory
ANC Guidelines – Noise Measurement in Buildings
ANC Guidelines – Measurement and Assessment of Groundborne Noise and Vibration

Publications list:
Available online

Access to staff:
Contact by telephone and by e-mail
Hours: Mon to Fri, 0900 to 1700

Access to building, collection or gallery:
No access other than to staff

ASSOCIATION OF NORTHUMBERLAND LOCAL HISTORY SOCIETIES

Acronym or abbreviation: ANLHS

PO Box 423, Newcastle upon Tyne, NE3 9AZ

E-mail: mail@anlhs.org.uk

continued overleaf

Website:
http://www.anlhs.org.uk

Enquiries:
Enquiries to: Secretary

Founded:
1966

Formerly called:
Northumberland Local History Society (year of change 1979)

Organisation type and purpose:
Membership association (membership is by subscription), present number of members: 130 individual, 53 societies, voluntary organisation, registered charity (charity number 251179). Umbrella organisation supporting affiliated local history societies in Northumberland and Newcastle. Annual research project, lectures and meetings.

Subject coverage:
History of the geographic county of Northumberland (including Tyne and Wear and North Tyneside), excluding family history.

Museum or gallery collection, archive, or library special collection:
At Northumberland Collection Service:
War Memorials Index of Northumberland
Shops and Businesses of Northumberland

Printed publications:
Tyne and Tweed (annually autumn, £4.50 plus p&p)
Order printed publications from: The Secretary

Publications list:
Available online

Access to staff:
Contact by letter, by e-mail and via website

Affiliated to:
British Association for Local History

ASSOCIATION OF NURSES IN SUBSTANCE ABUSE

Acronym or abbreviation: ANSA

37 Star Street, Ware, Hertfordshire, SG12 7AA

Tel: 0870 241 3503
Fax: 0192 0462 730
E-mail: info@ansauk.org

Website:
http://www.ansa.uk.net

Enquiries:
Enquiries to: Chairman

Founded:
1983

Organisation type and purpose:
Membership association (membership is by subscription).
Membership organisation for nurses and other allied professions working in the field of substance misuse or with an interest in this area of work.

Subject coverage:
All aspects of substance misuse, its effects and treatment.

Printed publications:
List on the website

Publications list:
Available in print

Access to staff:
Contact by letter, by telephone, by e-mail and via website

ASSOCIATION OF OPTOMETRISTS

Acronym or abbreviation: AOP

61 Southwark Street, London, SE1 0HL

Tel: 020 7261 9661

Fax: 020 7261 0228
E-mail: postbox@aop.org.uk

Website:
http://www.aop.org.uk
About the Association, our activities and services.

Enquiries:
Enquiries to: Chief Executive

Founded:
1946

Formerly called:
Association of Optical Practitioners (AOP) (year of change 1987)

Organisation type and purpose:
Professional body (membership is by subscription), present number of members: 9000.

Subject coverage:
Optometry, including eye care and protection in industry, DIY, drivers' vision, sports vision, eye care for the elderly, children, road safety.

Printed publications:
Annual Report
General selection of leaflets on aspects of eye care
Insider (members newsletter, quarterly)
Optometry Today (fortnightly)
Order printed publications from: Editor, Optometry Today
Victoria House, 178–180 Fleet Road, Fleet, Hampshire, GU13 8DA, tel: 01252 816266, fax: 01252 816176, e-mail: info@optometry.co.uk

Access to staff:
Contact by letter, by telephone, by fax, by e-mail and via website. Appointment necessary.
Hours: Mon to Fri, 0830 to 1730

Access to building, collection or gallery:
Prior appointment required

Houses the:
Optical Functional Whitley Council
Optometric Fees Review Committee

ASSOCIATION OF PAEDIATRIC CHARTERED PHYSIOTHERAPISTS

Acronym or abbreviation: APCP

42 Cammo Grove, Edinburgh, EH4 8EX

Tel: 0131 339 7555
Fax: 0131 476 3388
E-mail: c.h.shaw@cableinet.co.uk

Enquiries:
Enquiries to: Secretary
Other contacts: Chairman

Founded:
1973

Organisation type and purpose:
Advisory body, professional body.

Subject coverage:
Physiotherapy treatment for children in areas of speciality i.e. respiratory care, neuro-developmental, cerebral palsy, learning disability, dyspraxia, orthopaedic, neonatal care.

Publications list:
Available in print

Access to staff:
Contact by letter, by telephone, by fax and by e-mail
Hours: Mon to Fri, 0900 to 1700

Parent body:
Chartered Society of Physiotherapy
  tel: 020 7306 6666

ASSOCIATION OF PERSONAL INJURY LAWYERS

Acronym or abbreviation: APIL

11 Castle Quay, Nottingham, NG7 1FW

Tel: 0115 958 0585
Fax: 0115 958 0885

E-mail: via website
Website:
http://www.apil.org.uk
Press room, publications, legal information, safety watch, code of conduct, find a personal injury lawyer.

Founded:
1990

Organisation type and purpose:
A not-for-profit organisation that exists to help its 4,700 members fight for the rights of injured people, a trusted organisation in the promotion, encouragement and development of expertise in personal injury law.
To promote full and just compensation for all types of personal injury; to promote and develop expertise in the practice of personal injury law; to promote wider redress for personal injury in the legal system; to campaign for improvements in personal injury law; to promote safety standards and alert the public to hazards; to provide a communication network for its members.

Subject coverage:
Personal injury, personal injury law.

Electronic and video publications:
Accident or Negligence? A Guide on how to avoid preventable injury (booklet)
A guide to your rights to advice and compensation following injury or illness caused by someone else's negligence and how to find legal assistance
Press releases
Order electronic and video publications from:
Download from website

Publications list:
Available online

Access to staff:
Contact by letter, by telephone, by fax and by e-mail

ASSOCIATION OF PHOTOGRAPHERS LIMITED

Acronym or abbreviation: AOP

81 Leonard Street, London, EC2A 4QS

Tel: 020 7739 6669
Fax: 020 7739 8707
E-mail: general@aophoto.co.uk

Website:
http://www.aophoto.co.uk

Enquiries:
Enquiries to: Membership Secretary
Other contacts: Chief Executive

Founded:
1968

Formerly called:
Association of Fashion, Advertising and Editorial Photographers (AFAEP)

Organisation type and purpose:
Trade association (membership is by subscription, election or invitation), present number of members: 1900.
To support and promote the interests of photographers in the areas of fashion, editorial and advertising photography.

Subject coverage:
Copyright, standards and ethics, education.

Museum or gallery collection, archive, or library special collection:
Careers Information
Photographic Reference Books

Printed publications:
Beyond The Lens
Image Magazine (monthly)
The Awards Book (annually)
Order printed publications from: Ventura BHP
The Plant Shop, Lenham Road, Kingswood, Maidstone, Kent, ME17 1LZ, tel: 01622 844417, fax: 01622 844418

Electronic and video publications:
Careers Information for Libraries

Access to staff:
Access for members only.
Hours: Mon to Fri, 0930 to 1800

Access for disabled people:
Level entry

ASSOCIATION OF PHYSICAL & NATURAL THERAPISTS

Acronym or abbreviation: APNT

27 Old Gloucester Street, London, WC1N 3XX

Tel: 07966 181 588
E-mail: apntsource@lineone.net

Website:
http://www.apnt.org.uk
Therapy schools links, news, membership information.

Enquiries:
Enquiries to: General Secretary

Founded:
1986

Organisation type and purpose:
National organisation, membership association (membership is by subscription), training organisation.

Access to staff:
Contact by telephone and by e-mail
Hours: Mon to Fri, 0900 to 1700

Member of:
Aromatherapy Organisations Council
British Complementary Medicine Association

ASSOCIATION OF PIONEER MOTOR CYCLISTS

Acronym or abbreviation: APMC

Heather Bank, May Close, Liphook Road, Headley, Bordon, Hampshire, GU35 8LR

Tel: 01428 712666

Enquiries:
Enquiries to: Honorary Secretary
Direct e-mail: john@barraclough40.freeserve.co.uk
Other contacts: News Editor

Organisation type and purpose:
International organisation, membership association.
All members have held motorcycle driving licences for 50 years for Pioneer Status and 40 years for Companion Member.
For motorcyclists to combine knowledge and meet socially during the year.

Subject coverage:
History of motor cycles and motorcycling.

Museum or gallery collection, archive, or library special collection:
Available only to members on application
Large collection of books, bound volumes of periodicals and other ephemera relating to the history of motor cycles and motorcycling (personal property of the present secretary)

Printed publications:
Newsletter (quarterly)
Rules and Register of Members (revised and updated in alternate years)

Access to staff:
Contact by letter and by telephone. Letter of introduction required.
Hours: Mon to Fri, 0900 to 1700

ASSOCIATION OF PLAY INDUSTRIES

Acronym or abbreviation: API

Federation House, National Agricultural Centre, Stoneleigh Park, Warwickshire, CV8 2RF

Tel: 024 7641 4999
Fax: 024 7641 4990
E-mail: api@api-play.org

Enquiries:
Enquiries to: Association Manager
Direct tel: 024 7641 4999 ext 208

Founded:
1984

Organisation type and purpose:
Trade association (membership is by subscription), present number of members: 60.

Subject coverage:
Manufacturers and suppliers of play equipment and impact-absorbing surfaces.

Printed publications:
Directory of Members
Guide to the Provision of Rubber Impact Absorbing Surfaces
Guide to Installation
Standard Form of Contract

Access to staff:
Contact by letter, by telephone, by fax and by e-mail
Hours: Mon to Fri, 0900 to 1700

Member of:
Federation of European Play Industries (FEPI)

Part of:
The Federation of Sports and Play Associations

Subsidiary body:
Constructors Section
Indoor Play Section
Outdoor Play Section
Surfacing Section

ASSOCIATION OF PLEASURE CRAFT OPERATORS / CANAL BOATBUILDERS ASSOCIATION

Acronym or abbreviation: APCO/CBA

Parkland House, Audley Avenue, Newport, Shropshire, TF10 7BX

Tel: 01952 813572
Fax: 01952 820363
E-mail: info@apco.org.uk

Website:
http://www.britishmarine.co.uk
Lists activities and Group Associations of British Marine Federation.

Enquiries:
Enquiries to: Administrator
Direct e-mail: info@apco.org.uk

Founded:
1954

Organisation type and purpose:
Trade association.
Operation of hireboats, passenger, hotel boats and all business involved in the inland waterways of England & Wales, including boat building and maintenance.

Subject coverage:
Information about boating holidays on the inland waterways of England and Wales and other businesses on the inland waterways. General information about the Association's aims.

Printed publications:
Membership List (annually, free)

Access to staff:
Contact by letter, by telephone and by fax
Hours: Mon to Fri, 0900 to 1600

Group Associations of the:
British Marine Federation (BMF)
tel: 01784 473377; fax: 01784 439678; e-mail: info@britishmarine.co.uk

ASSOCIATION OF PLUMBING AND HEATING CONTRACTORS

Acronym or abbreviation: APHC

Ensign House, Ensign Business Centre, Westwood Way, Coventry, Warwickshire, CV4 8JA

Tel: 024 7647 0626
Fax: 024 7647 0942
E-mail: enquiry@aphc.co.uk

Website:
http://www.licensedplumber.co.uk
Member company details, Association details.

Enquiries:
Enquiries to: National Director
Direct e-mail: members@aphc.co.uk
Other contacts: Commercial Director (for membership, PR, publications, database information, business development and marketing)

Founded:
1925

Formerly called:
National Association of Plumbing and Domestic Engineers; National Association of Plumbing Heating and Mechanical Services Contractors (year of change 1997)

Organisation type and purpose:
Trade association, consultancy.

Subject coverage:
Plumbing, heating, air conditioning, sprinkler systems, building dynamics and building maintenance services.
Training (BPEC certification), modern apprenticeships, training grants to employers, trainee placement (BSI Training Limited).

Museum or gallery collection, archive, or library special collection:
Archive of trade association journals relating to plumbing

Trade and statistical information:
List of member firms including sole traders.

Printed publications:
Bulletin (monthly, for members)
Members' Reference Book

Electronic and video publications:
Members list (disc format, for purchase)

Access to staff:
Contact by letter, by telephone, by fax, by e-mail and via website. Appointment necessary. Non-members charged.
Hours: Mon to Fri, 0900 to 1700

Affiliated to:
British Plumbing Employers Council (BPEC)
British Plumbing Employers Council Certification Limited (BPEC)
Joint Industry Board (JIB)
Union Internationale de la Couverte et Plomberie (UICP)
9 rue la Pérouse, 75784 Paris Cedex 16, France

ASSOCIATION OF POLICY MARKET MAKERS

Acronym or abbreviation: APMM

Holywell Centre, 1 Phipp Street, London, EC2A 4PS

Tel: 020 7739 3949
Fax: 020 7613 2990
E-mail: enquiries@apmm.org

Website:
http://www.apmm.org
Full description of market. Ability to access the market. Links to members' sites.

Enquiries:
Enquiries to: Executive Director

Founded:
1992

continued overleaf

Organisation type and purpose:
Trade association (membership is by subscription), present number of members: 8 companies.
To establish and maintain an orderly market in Traded Endowment Policies (TEPs). To provide objective information. To act as a focus and a voice for the market.

Printed publications:
A Fair Deal for All
The Association of Policy Market Makers

Access to staff:
Contact by letter, by telephone, by fax, by e-mail and via website
Hours: Mon to Fri, 0830 to 1745

ASSOCIATION OF PORT HEALTH AUTHORITIES

Acronym or abbreviation: APHA

3rd Floor, Walbrook Wharf, 78–83 Upper Thames Street, London, EC4R 3TD

Tel: 08707 444505
Fax: 0207 2482114
E-mail: office@porthealth.co.uk

Website:
htp://www.porthealth.co.uk

Enquiries:
Enquiries to: Executive Secretary

Founded:
1899

Organisation type and purpose:
Membership association (membership is by subscription).
Health control of ships, aircraft and imported food control.

Subject coverage:
EU and UK law relating to public health, food control and pollution; environmental health relating to ships, and aircraft, fish and shellfish production.

Museum or gallery collection, archive, or library special collection:
Minutes and Papers from 1898 to date

Printed publications:
Port Health Handbook (published annually)
Airport Catering – Guidance for Inspectors
Order printed publications from: e-mail: office@porthealth.co.uk

Electronic and video publications:
Norovirus on Cruise Ships Guidance
Identification Marking of Fishery Products
Importer Advice Notes
Good Practice Guides
Code of Practice for Infectious Diseases on Aircraft
Order electronic and video publications from: website: http://www.porthealth.co.uk

Publications list:
Available online

Access to staff:
Contact by letter, by telephone, by fax and by e-mail. Appointment necessary.
Hours: Mon to Fri, 0900 to 1700

Access to building, collection or gallery:
By appointment

ASSOCIATION OF PRACTISING ACCOUNTANTS

Acronym or abbreviation: APA

Devonshire House, 60 Goswell Road, London, EC1M 7AD

Tel: 020 7566 4000
Fax: 020 7566 4010

Website:
http://www.apa-uk.co.uk

Enquiries:
Enquiries to: Secretary

Direct tel: 01727 896067
Direct fax: 01727 896026
Direct e-mail: jmellish@kingstonsmith.co.uk

Founded:
1988

Organisation type and purpose:
Membership Association (membership is by election or invitation).

Subject coverage:
Accountancy.

Printed publications:
Becoming a chartered accountant
Order printed publications from: website: http://www.apa-uk.co.uk

Access to staff:
Contact by letter, by e-mail and via website
Hours: Mon to Fri, 0900 to 1700

ASSOCIATION OF PRINTING MACHINERY IMPORTERS

Acronym or abbreviation: APMI

65 Hazlewell Road, London, SW15 6UT

Tel: 020 8780 2966
Fax: 020 8780 2864

Enquiries:
Enquiries to: Secretary

Founded:
1959

Organisation type and purpose:
Trade association (membership is by election or invitation), present number of members: 39.

Subject coverage:
Printing machinery and equipment imported into the United Kingdom.

Printed publications:
For members only

Access to staff:
Contact by letter, by telephone and by fax
Hours: Mon to Fri, 0900 to 1700

ASSOCIATION OF PRIVATE CLIENT INVESTMENT MANAGERS AND STOCKBROKERS

Acronym or abbreviation: APCIMS

1st Floor, 114 Middlesex Street, London, E1 7JH

Tel: 020 7247 7080
Fax: 020 7377 0939
E-mail: info@apcims.co.uk

Website:
http://www.apcims.co.uk
Information about APCIMS members, services they offer and directory of firms across UK and Ireland.

Enquiries:
Enquiries to: Head of Information
Direct e-mail: jasonb@apcims.co.uk

Founded:
1990

Organisation type and purpose:
Trade association.

Subject coverage:
Investment and stockbroking for private individuals.

Printed publications:
Annual Report (information on APCIMS' activities throughout the year, free)
Directory (of over 200 members with an outline of services, annually, free)

Access to staff:
Contact by letter, by telephone, by fax, by e-mail and via website

Hours: Mon to Fri, 0900 to 1730

Access to building, collection or gallery:
No access other than to staff

ASSOCIATION OF PROFESSIONAL LANDSCAPERS

Acronym or abbreviation: APL

19 High Street, Theale, Reading, Berkshire, RG7 5AH

Tel: 0118 9303132
Fax: 0118 9303453
E-mail: apl@the-hta.org.uk

Enquiries:
Enquiries to: Administrator
Other contacts: Publicity Officer for PR & Publicity.

Founded:
1994

Organisation type and purpose:
Trade association (membership is by subscription), present number of members: 114.

Subject coverage:
Landscape gardening.

Access to staff:
Contact by letter, by telephone, by fax, by e-mail and via website

Specialist group within:
Horticultural Trades Association (HTA)
19 High Street, Theale, Reading, Berkshire, RG7 5AH; tel: 01189 303132; fax: 01189 323453; e-mail: info@the-hta.org.uk

ASSOCIATION OF PROFESSIONAL MUSIC THERAPISTS

Acronym or abbreviation: APMT

2nd Floor, 24–27 White Lion Street, London, N1 9PD

Tel: 020 7837 6100
Fax: 020 7837 6142
E-mail: apmtoffice@aol.com

Website:
http://www.apmt.org

Enquiries:
Enquiries to: Administrator

Founded:
1976

Organisation type and purpose:
Professional body (membership is by qualification), present number of members: 600.
To maintain high standards of practice and training. To assist music therapists in development and all matters pertaining to their profession.

Subject coverage:
Music therapy; learning difficulties; mental health disabilities; autism; special needs; career literature.

Printed publications:
British Journal of Music Therapy (2 times a year)
Newsletter (2 times a year)
Music Therapy and Mental Health
Music Therapy for People with Learning Disabilities
Music Therapy Research Register (1993)
Careers and information leaflets
Documents on music therapy in mental health, education and mental handicap

Publications list:
Available online and in print

Access to staff:
Contact by letter, by telephone, by fax and by e-mail
Hours: Mon to Fri, 0930 to 1530

Links with:
British Society for Music Therapy
2nd Floor, 24–27 White Lion Street, London, N1 9PD; tel: 020 7837 6100; fax: 020 7837 6142; e-mail: info@bsmt.org

ASSOCIATION OF PROFESSIONAL RECORDING SERVICES LIMITED

Acronym or abbreviation: APRS

PO Box 22, Totnes, Devon, TQ9 7YZ

Tel: 01803 868600
Fax: 01803 868444
E-mail: info@aprs.co.uk

Website:
http://www.aprs.co.uk
Details about the association, members' services and exhibition.

Enquiries:
Enquiries to: Executive Director
Other contacts: Administration (for Head Office)

Founded:
1947

Formerly called:
Association of Professional Recording Studios

Organisation type and purpose:
International organisation, trade association (membership is by subscription, qualification), present number of members: 200.
Membership is by subscription for individuals and by qualification for companies.
Furthering standards and needs of companies and individuals in audio-related industries.

Subject coverage:
Professional sound recording and related technology.

Printed publications:
APRS Handbook (members)
Sound Recording Practice (5th edn, 2007)
The Master Tape Book (currently out of print, but being updated)
APRS Quarterly Bulletin

Access to staff:
Contact by letter, by telephone, by fax, by e-mail and via website. Appointment necessary.
Hours: Mon to Fri, 0900 to 1700

Links with:
Music Producers Guild (MPG)

ASSOCIATION OF PROFESSIONAL TOURIST GUIDES

Acronym or abbreviation: APTG

128 Theobald's Road, London WC1X 8TN

Tel: 020 7611 2545
E-mail: aptg@aptg.org.uk

Website:
http://www.aptg.org.uk
Details of the association, information about Blue Badge Tourist Guides and some tourism events.

Enquiries:
Enquiries to: Administrator

Founded:
1989

Organisation type and purpose:
Professional body (membership is by qualification), present number of members: 470.
Membership association for Blue Badge Tourist Guides.

Subject coverage:
Tourism issues.

Printed publications:
Register of Members – A listing of London-based Blue Badge Tourist Guides
Tourist Guide's Directory – Opening times and admission prices of historic sites, stately homes, cathedrals, etc. across the UK

Publications list:
Available in print

Access to staff:
Contact by letter, by telephone and by e-mail

Hours: Mon to Fri, 1000 to 1530

Access to building, collection or gallery:
No access other than to staff

ASSOCIATION OF PROFESSIONAL VIDEOMAKERS

Acronym or abbreviation: APV

Ambler House, Helpringham, Lincolnshire, NG34 0RB

Tel: 01529 421717
Fax: 01529 421742
E-mail: jan@videomakers.com

Website:
http://www.apv.org.uk

Enquiries:
Enquiries to: Information Officer

Founded:
1995

Organisation type and purpose:
Membership association (membership is by subscription), present number of members: 500.

Subject coverage:
Video production and associated trades, skills.

Access to staff:
Contact by letter, by telephone, by fax and by e-mail
Hours: Mon to Fri, 0900 to 1700

ASSOCIATION OF PUBLISHING AGENCIES

Acronym or abbreviation: APA

Queens House, 55–56 Lincoln's Inn Fields, London, WC2A 3LJ

Tel: 020 7404 4166
Fax: 020 7404 4167
E-mail: info@apa.co.uk

Website:
http://apa.co.uk

Enquiries:
Enquiries to: Director
Direct tel: 020 7400 7516
Other contacts: Marketing Executive for other principal contact.

Founded:
1993

Organisation type and purpose:
Trade association (membership is by subscription, qualification), present number of members: 32.

Subject coverage:
Customer magazine publishing. Publishing agencies.

Trade and statistical information:
Statistics on the size of the UK contract publishing market. Data on customer magazines published by UK agencies.

Printed publications:
Annual Directory of Publishing Agencies (free)
APA Information Pack (free)
APA Membership Pack (free)

Access to staff:
Contact by letter, by telephone, by fax, by e-mail and via website
Hours: Mon to Fri, 0900 to 1730

Parent body:
Periodical Publishers Association (PPA) at the same address

ASSOCIATION OF RADICAL MIDWIVES

Acronym or abbreviation: ARM

16 Wytham Street, Oxford, OX1 4SU

Tel: 01865 248159

E-mail: sarahmontagu@gmail.com

Website:
http://www.midwifery.org.uk
General information, reprints from journals, links to useful organisations.

Enquiries:
Enquiries to: Secretary

Founded:
1976

Subject coverage:
Midwifery, maternity care, childbirth, breastfeeding, post-natal care.

Printed publications:
Midwifery Matters (journal, quarterly, £30 a year subscription)
What is a Midwife? (leaflet, free for single copies, p&p for bulk supplies)
Choices in Childbirth (leaflet, free for single copies, p&p for bulk supplies)

Publications list:
Available online

Access to staff:
Contact by letter, by telephone and by e-mail
Hours: Mon to Fri, 0900 to 1700

ASSOCIATION OF REFLEXOLOGISTS (UK)

Acronym or abbreviation: AoR

5 Fore Street, Taunton, TA1 1HX

Tel: 0870 5673320
E-mail: info@aor.org.uk

Website:
http://www.aor.org.uk
Reflexology organisations worldwide, information on courses, training standards, career opportunities.

Enquiries:
Enquiries to: Executive Director
Direct tel: 01278 733393
Direct fax: 01278 733665
Direct e-mail: aoreo@reflexology.org
Other contacts: Chairman for policy.

Founded:
1984

Organisation type and purpose:
Professional body, membership association (membership is by qualification).
Awarding Body for Practitioner Qualification in Reflexology.
Accrediting Body for Practitioner Courses in Reflexology.

Subject coverage:
Reflexology, complementary therapies, integrated health.

Trade and statistical information:
Information on courses, reflexology organisations worldwide, training standards, career opportunities.

Printed publications:
Journal (quarterly)
Leaflets on Reflexology
List of Accredited Practitioners Courses in Reflexology (free)
Register of Practitioners (free)
Sales Catalogue

Publications list:
Available in print

Access to staff:
Contact by letter, by telephone, by fax and by e-mail
Hours: Mon to Fri, 0900 to 1700

Member of:
International Council of Reflexologists
Reflexology in Europe Network

continued overleaf

Other departments at:
AoR Administration
  Katepwa House, Ashfield Park Avenue, Ross-on-Wye, Herefordshire, HR9 5AX; tel: 01989 567667; fax: 01989 567676; e-mail: aor@assocmanagement.co.uk
AoR Training and Education
  19 Benson Road, Henfield, West Sussex, BN5 9HY; tel: 01273 492385; fax: 01273 495920; e-mail: aor@reflexology.org

ASSOCIATION OF RELOCATION AGENTS

Acronym or abbreviation: ARA

PO Box 189, Diss, Norfolk, IP22 1PE

Tel: 08700 737475
Fax: 08700 718719
E-mail: info@relocationagents.com

Website:
http://www.relocationagents.com
Details of different services available from relocation companies and a geographic database of member and other relocation companies worldwide.

Enquiries:
Enquiries to: Chief Executive

Founded:
1986

Organisation type and purpose:
Trade association.

Subject coverage:
Relocation services, setting up relocation agencies, relocation industry.

Printed publications:
Directory of Members (annually, free)
Guide to Homesearch: information pack for those considering setting up a relocation agency (annually, £75)
The ARA Guide to the UK (once every two years, £12)

Access to staff:
Contact by letter, by telephone, by fax, by e-mail and via website
Hours: Mon to Fri, 0900 to 1700

ASSOCIATION OF RESEARCHERS IN MEDICINE & SCIENCE

Acronym or abbreviation: ARMS

c/o Henry Wellcome, LINE, Dorothy Hodgkin Building, Whitson Street, University of Bristol, Bristol, BS1 3NY.

Tel: 0117 331 3050
Fax: 0117 331 3049
E-mail: david.jessop@bris.ac.uk

Website:
http://www.hop.man.ac.uk/arms/arms.html
Membership, committee, interests and newsletters, aims, links.

Enquiries:
Enquiries to: Chairman
Direct tel: 07973 675422

Founded:
1978

Organisation type and purpose:
Voluntary organisation, research organisation.

Subject coverage:
Medical and scientific research, contract research, science policy, conditions of employment etc.

Printed publications:
Newsletter (4 times a year)
Surveys of contract research

Access to staff:
Contact by letter, by fax, by e-mail and via website
Hours: Mon to Fri, 0900 to 1700

ASSOCIATION OF RESIDENTIAL LETTING AGENTS

Acronym or abbreviation: ARLA

Arbon House, 6 Tournament Court, Edgehill Drive, Warwick, CV34 6LG

Tel: 01926 496800
Fax: 01926 417788
E-mail: info@arla.co.uk

Website:
http://www.arla.co.uk

Enquiries:
Enquiries to: Administrator

Founded:
1981

Organisation type and purpose:
Trade association (membership is by subscription). National professional and regulatory body for agents specialising in residential letting and management.

Subject coverage:
Private sector residential rental property; law and property; management and administration.

Printed publications:
Members Magazine (every other month)

Access to staff:
Contact by letter, by telephone, by fax and by e-mail
Hours: Mon to Fri, 0900 to 1730

Access to building, collection or gallery:
No access other than to staff

ASSOCIATION OF RESIDENTIAL MANAGING AGENTS LTD

Acronym or abbreviation: ARMA

178 Battersea Park Road, London, SW11 4ND

Tel: 020 7978 2607
Fax: 020 7498 6153
E-mail: info@arma.org.uk

Website:
http://www.arma.org.uk

Enquiries:
Enquiries to: Secretary

Founded:
1991

Organisation type and purpose:
Trade association (membership is by subscription), present number of members: 200+, service industry.
Trade association representing managers of residential leasehold blocks of flats in England and Wales.

Subject coverage:
Matters relating to block management of residential property.

Printed publications:
See publications online

Publications list:
Available online

Access to staff:
Contact by letter, by fax, by e-mail and via website
Hours: Mon to Fri, 0900 to 1700

Access to building, collection or gallery:
No access other than to staff

ASSOCIATION OF SCHOOL AND COLLEGE LEADERS

Acronym or abbreviation: ASCL

130 Regent Road, Leicester, LE1 7PG

Tel: 0116 299 1122
Fax: 0116 299 1123

Website:
http://www.ascl.org.uk

Founded:
1977

Organisation type and purpose:
Professional body, trade union. Represents more than 14,000 senior leaders in secondary schools and colleges.

Subject coverage:
Secondary and further education.

Printed publications:
Magazine, poilcy and guidance papers, books.

Publications list:
Available in print

Access to staff:
Contact by letter, by telephone and by fax
Hours: Mon to Fri, 0900 to 1700

ASSOCIATION OF SCOTTISH COMMUNITY COUNCILS

Acronym or abbreviation: ASCC

28 Bank Street, Brechin, DD9 6AX

Tel: 01356 623330
E-mail: secretary@ascc.org.uk

Website:
http://www.ascc.org.uk
General information

Enquiries:
Enquiries to: Secretary

Founded:
1993

Organisation type and purpose:
Membership association (membership is by subscription), present number of members: 600, voluntary organisation.

Subject coverage:
Scottish Community Councils.

Museum or gallery collection, archive, or library special collection:
Complete database for all Scottish community councils

Printed publications:
Newsletter (quarterly, free, direct)
1999 Survey (£5, direct)

Access to staff:
Contact by letter, by telephone, by fax and by e-mail. Appointment necessary.
Hours: Mon to Fri, 0900 to 1700

ASSOCIATION OF SCOTTISH VISITOR ATTRACTIONS

Acronym or abbreviation: ASVA

Argyll's Lodging, Castle Wynd, Stirling, FK8 1EG

Tel: 01786 475152
Fax: 01786 474288
E-mail: info@asva.co.uk

Website:
http://www.asva.co.uk

Enquiries:
Enquiries to: Administrator
Other contacts: Development Manager

Founded:
1989

Organisation type and purpose:
Trade association (membership is by subscription), present number of members: 400.

Subject coverage:
All aspects of visitor attraction in Scotland, development, operations and marketing.

Publications list:
Available in print

Access to staff:
Contact by letter, by telephone, by fax, by e-mail and via website
Hours: Mon to Fri, 0900 to 1700

ASSOCIATION OF SEA TRAINING ORGANISATIONS

Acronym or abbreviation: ASTO

Unit 10, North Meadow, Royal Clarence Yard, Gosport, Hampshire, PO12 1BP

Tel: 023 9250 3222
Fax: 023 9250 3222
E-mail: office@asto.org.uk

Website:
http://www.asto.org.uk
Exact copy of brochure including links to ASTO members website.

Enquiries:
Enquiries to: Business Manager

Founded:
1971

Organisation type and purpose:
Membership association (membership is by election or invitation), registered charity, training organisation.

Subject coverage:
Sail training for young people and adults, able-bodied or disabled, personal development for young people.

Printed publications:
Publicity material
Sail to Adventure, directory of sail training opportunities (updated every 2 years)

Access to staff:
Contact by letter, by telephone and by fax
Hours: Mon to Fri, 0900 to 1700

Supported by:
Royal Yachting Association

ASSOCIATION OF SHOW AND AGRICULTURAL ORGANISATIONS

Acronym or abbreviation: ASAO

PO Box 4575, Sherborne, Dorset, DT9 4XA

Tel: 07711 205833
Fax: 01749 823169
E-mail: asaosecretary@asao.co.uk

Website:
http://www.asao.co.uk
List of members events.

Enquiries:
Enquiries to: Secretary
Direct e-mail: paul.hooper@bathandwest.co.uk

Founded:
1923

Organisation type and purpose:
National organisation, trade association (membership is by subscription), present number of members: 187, voluntary organisation, registered charity (charity number 1023932).

Subject coverage:
Organisation of agricultural and similar shows.

Publications list:
Available in print

Access to staff:
Appointment necessary.
Hours: Mon to Fri, 0900 to 1700

ASSOCIATION OF SINGER CAR OWNERS

Acronym or abbreviation: ASCO

39 Oakfield, Rickmansworth, Hertfordshire, WD3 8LR

Tel: 01923 778575

Website:
http://www.asco.org.uk
General information about the club, photographs of Singer cars, membership form.

Enquiries:
Enquiries to: General Secretary

Founded:
1976

Organisation type and purpose:
Membership association (membership is by subscription), present number of members: 200.

Subject coverage:
Restoration, technical advice, source materials on all aspects of Singer cars.

Printed publications:
Magazine (once every two months, free to members)

Access to staff:
Contact by letter and by telephone
Hours: Mon to Sun, 1000 to 1900

ASSOCIATION OF SOCIAL ANTHROPOLOGISTS OF THE COMMONWEALTH

Acronym or abbreviation: ASA

50 Fitzroy Street, London, W1T 5BT

E-mail: admin@theasa.org

Website:
http://www.theasa.org

Enquiries:
Enquiries to: Administrator

Organisation type and purpose:
Professional body (membership is referenced).

Subject coverage:
Social anthropology and its various sub-fields.

Printed publications:
ASA Monographs (annually, pub. Berg)
ASA Research Methods (published periodically by Academic Press and Berg)

Electronic and video publications:
Annals (online)
ASAonline
ASAfilm (online)

Publications list:
Available online

Access to staff:
Contact by letter and by e-mail
Hours: Mon to Fri, 0900 to 1700
Special comments: Office is remote so best access is via e-mail.

Links with:
Association of Learned Societies in the Social Sciences

ASSOCIATION OF STAINLESS FASTENER DISTRIBUTORS

Acronym or abbreviation: ASFAD

Ikon Trading Estate, Droitwich Road, Hartlebury, DY10 4EU

E-mail: info@bafd.org

Website:
http://www.bafd.org

Enquiries:
Enquiries to: General Secretary

Founded:
1984

Organisation type and purpose:
Trade association (membership is by qualification, election or invitation).

Subject coverage:
Sources of supply of stainless fasteners and distribution.

Access to staff:
Contact by letter, by telephone, by fax and by e-mail. Access for members only.
Hours: Mon to Fri, 0900 to 1700

Members of:
European Fastener Distributors Association (EFDA)
Germany

Parent body:
British Association of Fastener Distributors (BAFD) at the same address

ASSOCIATION OF SUPERVISORS OF MIDWIVES

Acronym or abbreviation: ASM

West Yorkshire Health Authority, Blenheim House West One, Duncombe Street, Leeds, West Yorkshire, LS14PL

Tel: 0113 295 2094
Fax: 0113 295 2222
E-mail: jean.duerden@westyorks.nhs.uk

Enquiries:
Enquiries to: Honorary Secretary

Founded:
1910

Subject coverage:
Supervision of midwives.

Printed publications:
Journal (annually, members only)

Access to staff:
Contact by letter, by telephone, by fax and by e-mail
Hours: Mon to Fri, 0900 to 1700

ASSOCIATION OF SUPPLIERS TO THE BRITISH CLOTHING INDUSTRY

Acronym or abbreviation: ASBCI

Unit 5, 25 Square Road, Halifax, West Yorkshire, HX1 1QG

Tel: 01422 354666
Fax: 01422 381184
E-mail: info@asbci.co.uk

Website:
http://www.asbci.co.uk
The association, members, technical area, publications, conferences, news.

Founded:
1992

Incorporates the former:
British Interlining Manufacturers Association

Organisation type and purpose:
Represents and provides technical support to members in all the key sectors connected with supplying the British clothing industry; has over 100 members.

Subject coverage:
Fibres, fabrics, linings, interlinings, adhesives, dyers, sewing threads, buttons, zips, trims, sleeve head rolls, shoulder pads, machinery, presses, waistbands, garment processors, clothing consultants, clothing manufacturers, retailers, drycleaners, launderers, domestic detergent manufacturers, chemical suppliers, computer suppliers to the clothing industry, textile testing houses, research organisations, textile universities, and training bodies.

Printed publications:
Range of technical booklets:
Tried & Tested (introduction to colour and laboratory test methods and procedures; members £10 excl. p&p, non-members £15 excl. p&p)

continued overleaf

Caring For Your Clothes (care labelling and aftercare of apparel; members £10 excl. p&p, non-members £15 excl. p&p)
Wrinkle Free (members £5 excl. p&p, non-members £10 excl. p&p)
Make or Break (threads, needles and stitches; members £10 excl. p&p, non-members £15 excl. p&p)
Colour Clues – An introduction to the colouration of textiles and clothing (members £5 excl. p&p, non-members £10 excl. p&p)
ASBCI Interlinings, Books 1–5 (members £10 each, non-members £15 each)
Joining Forces (buttons, zips, poppers, etc.; members £10, non-members £15)
Technical bulletins:
Linings – What to Consider when Selecting a Garment Lining (members £4.50, student members £2.50, non-members £5.00, overseas non-members £7.00, all incl. p&p)
Wet Cleaning (members £4.50, student members £2.50, non-members £5.00, overseas non-members £7.00, all incl. p&p)

Electronic and video publications:
Conference proceedings
Order electronic and video publications from:
Download from website

Publications list:
Available online

Access to staff:
Contact by letter, by telephone, by fax and by e-mail

ASSOCIATION OF SURGEONS OF GREAT BRITAIN AND IRELAND

Acronym or abbreviation: ASGBI

The Royal College of Surgeons, 35–43 Lincoln's Inn Fields, London, WC2A 3PN

Tel: 020 7973 0300
Fax: 020 7430 9235

Website:
http://www.asgbi.org.uk
An association representing general surgery and all its related specialities throughout the United Kingdom and Ireland.

Enquiries:
Enquiries to: Chief Executive
Direct e-mail: admin@asgbi.org.uk

Founded:
1920

Organisation type and purpose:
Professional body, membership association (membership is by subscription, election or invitation), present number of members: 1,100, registered charity (charity number 1068016).
The advancement of the science and art of surgery.

Subject coverage:
General surgery and the specialities thereof: upper and lower GI, vascular, endocrine, transplant, breast, laparascopic surgery.

Access to staff:
Contact by letter, by telephone, by fax, by e-mail, in person and via website
Hours: Mon to Fri, 0900 to 1700

ASSOCIATION OF TANK AND CISTERN MANUFACTURERS

Acronym or abbreviation: ATCM

22 Grange Park, St Arvans, Chepstow, Monmouthshire, NP16 6EA

Tel: 01291 623634
E-mail: imcc@atcmtanks.org.uk

Website:
http://www.atcmtanks.org.uk
For tank and cistern manufacturers who provide quality liquid-storing vessels. The ATCM purpose, its objectives, technical information related to tank products, members list, sizing aids and other downloads, together with links related to industry requirements and standards.

Enquiries:
Enquiries to: Chairman
Other contacts: Secretary

Founded:
1969

Formerly called:
Plastic Tanks and Cisterns Manufacturers Association (year of change 1992)

Organisation type and purpose:
Trade association (membership is by subscription), present number of members: 16, manufacturing industry.
The ATCM is a group of like-minded manufacturers who co-operate and promote with common interest the manufacture of tanks and cistern products conforming to highest possible standards of quality.
Co-operation between members in technical matters, standard production in UK and Europe, and action on behalf of members when making representations to government and regulatory authorities.

Subject coverage:
Manufacture and installation of tanks and cisterns for the storage of water, oil or chemical products.

Information services:
Technical papers posted on the ATCM web site avilable for download.

Non-library collection catalogue:
All or part available online

Library catalogue:
All or part available online

Access to staff:
Contact by letter, by telephone, by e-mail and via website
Hours: Mon to Fri, 0900 to 1700

Member organisation of:
Chartered Institute of Plumbing and Heating Engineering

ASSOCIATION OF TAXATION TECHNICIANS

Acronym or abbreviation: ATT

12 Upper Belgrave Street, London, SW1X 8BB

Tel: 020 7235 2544
Fax: 020 7235 2562
E-mail: info@att.org.uk

Website:
http://www.att.org.uk
Website of the ATT.

Enquiries:
Enquiries to: Head of Education Department

Founded:
1989

Organisation type and purpose:
Professional body, registered charity (charity number 803480), training organisation.

Subject coverage:
Taxation.

Museum or gallery collection, archive, or library special collection:
Tax Library located at King's College, London (members only)

Printed publications:
Annual Report (free on written request)
Essential Accounting for the Tax Technician (£25)
Essential Law for the Tax Adviser (£35 to non-members, £30 to members or students)
List of members (apply for cost)
Tax Adviser (journal, monthly, £64 subscription to non-members)

Access to staff:
Contact by letter, by telephone, by fax, by e-mail and via website

Hours: Mon to Fri, 0900 to 1700

Access to building, collection or gallery:
No access other than to staff

Associated with:
Chartered Institute of Taxation
12 Upper Belgrave Street, London, SW1X 8BB; tel: 020 7235 9381; fax: 020 7235 2562; e-mail: post@ciot.org.uk

ASSOCIATION OF TEACHERS OF MATHEMATICS

Acronym or abbreviation: ATM

Unit 7, Prime Industrial Park, Shaftesbury Street, Derby, DE23 8YB

Tel: 01332 346599
Fax: 01332 204357
E-mail: admin@atm.org.uk

Website:
http://www.atm.org.uk

Enquiries:
Enquiries to: Administrative Officer

Founded:
1952

Organisation type and purpose:
International organisation, membership association (membership is by subscription), present number of members: 3500, registered charity (charity number 293125).
Mathematics Association.

Subject coverage:
Mathematics education at primary, secondary and tertiary levels.

Printed publications:
Software products
Mathematics Teaching incorp Micromath (6 times a year)
E-Newsletter and many other publications

Publications list:
Available online and in print

Access to staff:
Contact by letter, by telephone, by fax and by e-mail
Hours: Mon to Fri, 0900 to 1630

ASSOCIATION OF TECHNICAL LIGHTING AND ACCESS SPECIALISTS

Acronym or abbreviation: ATLAS

4c St Mary's Place, The Lace Market, Nottingham, NG1 1PH

Tel: 0115 955 8818
Fax: 0115 941 2238
E-mail: info@atlas.org.uk

Website:
http://www.atlas-1.org.uk

Enquiries:
Enquiries to: Secretary
Direct e-mail: info@atlas.org.uk

Founded:
1946

Formerly called:
National Federation of Master Steeplejacks and Lightning Conductor Engineers (NFMS&LCE)

Organisation type and purpose:
Trade association.

Subject coverage:
Steeplejacking and lightning conductor engineering.

Member organisation of:
National Specialist Contractors Council

ASSOCIATION OF THE BRITISH PHARMACEUTICAL INDUSTRY

Acronym or abbreviation: ABPI

12 Whitehall, London, SW1A 2DY

Tel: 0870 890 4333
Fax: 020 7747 1400
E-mail: abpi@abpi.org.uk

Website:
http://www.abpi.org.uk
Information about ABPI, press area, publications, education and training, associated links, member services.

Enquiries:
Enquiries to: Information Officer
Direct e-mail: ccoomber@abpi.org.uk
Other contacts: Information Services Executive

Founded:
1929

Organisation type and purpose:
Trade association.
Represents the pharmaceutical industry operating in the UK in a way that assures patients access to the best available medicines, creates a favourable political, economic and regulatory environment, encourages innovative research and development, and affords fair commercial returns.

Subject coverage:
General information on the UK pharmaceutical industry, careers, education and training.

Library catalogue:
All or part available in-house

Printed publications:
Annual Review (free)
Books, briefings and leaflets
Resources for Schools (Key Stage 3 and 4), list of schools and careers materials
Order printed publications from: abpi@edist.co.uk

Publications list:
Available online

Access to staff:
Contact by letter, by telephone, by fax, by e-mail and via website. Access for members only.
Hours: Mon to Fri, 0830 to 1630
Special comments: Priority given to members.

Access to building, collection or gallery:
No access other than to staff
Special comments: Members only.

Also at:
ABPI Cymru Wales
  2 Caspian Point, Pierhead Street, Cardiff Bay, CF10 4DQ; tel: 0870 890 4333; fax: 029 2045 4298; e-mail: wales@abpi.org.uk
ABPI Northern Ireland
  224 Lisburn Road, Belfast, BT9 6GE; tel: 029 2045 4297
ABPI Scotland
  Third Floor East, Crichton House, 4 Crichton's Close, Canongate, Edinburgh, EH8 8DT; tel: 0870 890 4333; fax: 0131 523 0491

Associated with:
Office of Health Economics
  tel: 020 7747 8850; fax: 020 7747 8851; e-mail: ohegeneral@ohe.org; website: http://www.ohe .org

Member organisation of:
European Federation of Pharmaceutical Industry's Associations (EFPIA)
  Brussels; tel: +32 2 6262555; fax: +32 2 6262566
International Federation of Pharmaceutical Manufacturers' Associations (IFPMA)
  Geneva; tel: +41 22 338 32 00; fax: +41 22 338 32 99

ASSOCIATION OF TOWN CENTRE MANAGEMENT

Acronym or abbreviation: ATCM

Queen Anne's Gate, Westminster, London, SW1H 9BT

Tel: 020 7222 0120; 0300 330 0980
E-mail: office@atcm.org

Website:
http://www.atcm.org
The website is designed to provide a wealth of information on town centre management, ranging from a daily news service, information on events and conferences, policy briefs, case studies, background on ATCM, details of award winners and Town Centre Management job vacancies. Some areas are available to all, others to members only – go to Join Us on the menu bar to find out how.

Organisation type and purpose:
Europe's largest membership organisation dedicated to helping town and city centres realise their natural roles both as prosperous locations for business and investment, and as focal points for vibrant, inclusive communities. Members are primarily public private partnerships from across the UK as well as both public and private sector stakeholders.
ATCM works with all those interested in promoting the vitality and viability of town and city centres, in the UK and further afield and has 4 principal areas of work: places, people, partnerships and policy.

Subject coverage:
Has an extensive knowledge bank of good practice initiatives in town and city centres that have made a difference to that centre, and these are accessible to members on line, through publications and through the events programme. Runs training programmes in both personal and technical skills for those engaged in the management of centres and, in partnership with universities and others, offers access to academic and vocational qualifications. Supports partnership creation, development and review through a wide range of programmes that can involve large or small groups and through various publications and works closely with policy makers to ensure that the critical role that town and city centres play in society is never underestimated.

Printed publications:
Business Improvement Districts: A Good Practice Guide from the ATCM (£15)
Retail Markets – Present Status Future Prospects (£15)
Step Change – Summary Report (£10 plus p&p)
Young People and Town Centres (£10)
A Firm Basis (£15)
Developing Structures to Deliver Town Centre Management (£15)
Getting it Right – A Good Practice Guide (£15)
Key Performance Indicators (£15)
Town Centre Managers – Selection, Management, Development (£15)
Car Parks are for People (£15)
Creche Facilities in Town Centres (£15)
Entrepreneurial Management (£15)
Managing Liveability (£15)
Safe and Secure Town Centres (£15)
Managing Urban Spaces in Town Centres (£15)
Business Improvement Districts (£45)
A New Town Centre Managers Survival Kit (£10)

Publications list:
Available online

Access to staff:
Contact by letter, by telephone and by e-mail

ASSOCIATION OF TRANSLATION COMPANIES LIMITED

Acronym or abbreviation: ATC

5th Floor Greener House, 66–68 Haymarket, London, SW1Y 4RF

Tel: 020 7930 2200
Fax: 020 7451 7051
E-mail: info@atc.org.uk

Website:
http://www.atc.org.uk

Enquiries:
Enquiries to: General Secretary

Founded:
1976

Organisation type and purpose:
Professional body, trade association (membership is by subscription, qualification), present number of members: 85.
To provide the use of professionally produced translations by commerce and industry and to regulate translation companies who are members.

Subject coverage:
Information on the sourcing of translation, matching language and specialist subject matter.

Museum or gallery collection, archive, or library special collection:
Libraries, of some members, on unusual subjects, of specialist technical and other glossaries, of translations of foreign technical standards

Trade and statistical information:
The ATC conducts regular surveys of the translation profession, some of the results may be purchased by interested parties.

Printed publications:
ATC Members' Directory (free to those purchasing translations, £25 plus VAT to those selling their services to others).

Access to staff:
Contact by letter, by telephone, by fax, by e-mail and via website. Appointment necessary.
Hours: Mon to Fri, 0900 to 1700

ASSOCIATION OF TUTORS

Acronym or abbreviation: AOT

Sunnycroft, 63 King Edward Road, Northampton, NN1 5LY

Tel: 01604 624171

Website:
http://www.tutor.co.uk

Enquiries:
Enquiries to: Secretary

Founded:
1958

Organisation type and purpose:
Professional body (membership is by election or invitation).

Subject coverage:
All aspects of tutoring.

Access to staff:
Contact by letter
Hours: Mon to Fri, 0900 to 1700

ASSOCIATION OF UNIVERSITY ADMINISTRATORS

Acronym or abbreviation: AUA

AUA National Office, University of Manchester, Oxford Road, Manchester, M13 9PL

Tel: 0161 275 2063
Fax: 0161 275 2036
E-mail: aua@manchester.ac.uk

Website:
http://www.aua.ac.uk
AUA, membership, networks, events, partners and resources, professional development.

Founded:
1961

Created by the merger of:
Association of Polytechnic Administrators (APA) and the Conference of University Administrators (CUA)

Formerly called:
Meeting of University Academic Administrative Staff

continued overleaf

Organisation type and purpose:
Professional association.
To advance and assist in the advancement of education by fostering sound methods of leadership, management and administration in further and higher education by education, training, and other means; to advance and promote the professional development of all who work in professional services roles in higher education and to be an authoritative advocate and champion for the sector. Has over 4,000 members in the UK and world-wide associated with 150 branches based in universities, higher education colleges and HE-related bodies.

Subject coverage:
Professional services roles in higher education.

Education services:
Offers post-graduate certificate and continuing professional development framework.

Printed publications:
perspectives (quarterly international journal)
newslink (quarterly newsletter)
Good Practice Guides
Order printed publications from: Available to members

Electronic and video publications:
aua-news (weekly electronic bulletins)
aua-forum (e-mail list for sharing information and best practice)
Order electronic and video publications from: Available to members

Access to staff:
Contact by letter, by telephone, by fax and by e-mail

ASSOCIATION OF UNIVERSITY CHIEF SECURITY OFFICERS

Acronym or abbreviation: AUCSO

E-mail: aucsec@aim.com

Website:
http://www.aucso.org.uk
AUCSO, membership, regions, services, news, conferences.

Enquiries:
Enquiries to: Secretary

Founded:
1984

Organisation type and purpose:
A forum for security professionals charged with responsibility for the provision and management of security services and personal safety in universities, colleges and institutions of learning within the UK, Ireland and Europe. Currently, 123 universities and HE colleges or institutions are members.
To promote a common purpose in the application of law enforcement policies and security programmes, as it applies to the security and personal safety of staff and students on campus; to exchange experiences and promote partnership working among members, the police service and other agencies to identify trends in crime and disorder and to identify or share solutions; to identify and promote excellence, professionalism and raise standards in security services and to encourage the development of strategic planning and common policies to complement teaching, learning and research; to establish areas of expertise among members, share information and good practices; to consider and debate new and existing legislation, government directives and areas of potential risk, identifying solutions and future needs, and to liaise on these matters with government or other organisations; to identify and encourage the professional training, development and career paths for all members; to promote interest, discussion, consultation, formulation of ideas and policy; to promote the activities of the Association and its members regionally, nationally and internationally.

Subject coverage:
Exchange of knowledge and keeping up to date with crime trends, legislation and other information related to security services. Members can provide advice to each other either by the e-mail list, by arranging visits, or at regional meetings. They are also invited to attend and address the annual conference held at different universities within the UK and Ireland each spring.

Access to staff:
Contact by e-mail

ASSOCIATION OF VETERINARY TEACHERS AND RESEARCH WORKERS

Acronym or abbreviation: AVTRW

Department of Agriculture for Northern Ireland, Veterinary Sciences Division, Stoney Road, Stormont, Belfast, BT4 3SD

Tel: 02890 525606
Fax: 02890 525754
E-mail: john.mcevoy@dardni.gov.uk

Website:
http://www.avtrw.org.uk
Information on the Association and the annual conferences.

Enquiries:
Enquiries to: Honorary Secretary
Other contacts: Affiliated to British Veterinary Association

Founded:
1946

Organisation type and purpose:
International organisation, professional body (membership is by subscription), present number of members: 850.

Subject coverage:
Veterinary teaching and research.

Printed publications:
Proceedings for the 2000 Annual Conference: Research in Veterinary Science, Vol 68, Supp; A, June 2000.
Proceedings for the 2001 Annual Conference: Research in Veterinary Science, Vol 70, Supp; A, April 2001.
Guidelines for the recognition and assessment of pain in animals (1989, ISBN 0 900767 56 1)
Order printed publications from: UFAW
8 Hamilton Close, Potters Bar, Hertfordshire, EN6 3QD

Access to staff:
Contact by letter, by telephone, by fax and by e-mail
Hours: Mon to Fri, 0900 to 1700

Affiliated to:
British Veterinary Association
tel: 020 7636 6541; fax: 020 7436 2970; e-mail: bvahq@bva.co.uk

ASSOCIATION OF WHEELCHAIR CHILDREN

Acronym or abbreviation: AWC

6 Woodman Parade, North Woolwich, London E16 2LL

Tel: 0844 544 1050
Fax: 0844 544 1055
E-mail: headoffice@wheelchairchildren.org.uk

Website:
http://www.wheelchairchildren.org.uk
Comprehensive, up to date list of all training course locations and how to attend courses.
How to help the charity.

Enquiries:
Enquiries to: Fundraising Co-ordinator
Direct tel: 0870 121 0053
Direct fax: 0870 121 0051

Founded:
1990

Organisation type and purpose:
Registered charity (charity number 1057894).
To provide expert training and advice for wheelchair-using children throughout the UK, to help them become more independently mobile, both in the home and out of doors.

Subject coverage:
Information, support and training for children in wheelchairs throughout the UK.

Printed publications:
Annual Report
Get Mobile (leaflet)

Access to staff:
Contact by letter, by telephone, by fax, by e-mail, in person and via website
Hours: Mon to Fri, 0900 to 1700
Special comments: First floor office.

National Headquarters at:
Association of Wheelchair Children
6 Woodman Parade, North Woolwich, London, E16 2LL; tel: 0870 121 0050; fax: 0870 121 0051; e-mail: hq@awc.btinternet.com

ASSOCIATION OF WOMEN BARRISTERS

Acronym or abbreviation: AWB

Administrator, General Council of The Bar, 2–3 Cursitor Street, London, EC4A 1NE

Tel: 020 7242 1289
Fax: 020 7242 1107
E-mail: jbradley@barcouncil.org.uk

Website:
http://www.womenbarristers.co.uk

Enquiries:
Enquiries to: Chairwoman
Other contacts: Administrator for contact details.

Founded:
1991

Organisation type and purpose:
National organisation, membership association (membership is by subscription), present number of members: c. 500.

Subject coverage:
Women barristers.

Printed publications:
Order printed publications from: Administrator

Electronic and video publications:
Newsletters online

Publications list:
Available online

Access to staff:
Contact by letter, by telephone, by e-mail and via website
Hours: Mon to Fri, 0900 to 1700
Special comments: Personal visits not recommended to Administrator's office.

ASSOCIATION OF YOUNG PEOPLE WITH ME

Acronym or abbreviation: AYME

9a Vermont Place, Tongwell, Milton Keynes, MK15 8JA

Tel: 08451 232389
E-mail: info@ayme.org.uk

Website:
http://www.ayme.org.uk

Enquiries:
Enquiries to: Manager

Founded:
1995

Organisation type and purpose:
National organisation, membership association (membership is by qualification), present number of members: 3,500, registered charity (charity number 1082059).

Subject coverage:
Advice and information for young people with ME / CFS aged 0 to 25 years and their families.

Printed publications:
Information Resource Pack

Publications list:
Available online and in print

Access to staff:
Contact by letter, by telephone, by fax, by e-mail, in person and via website
Hours: Mon to Fri, 1000 to 1400

Access to building, collection or gallery:
No prior appointment required
Hours: Mon to Fri, 1000 to 1400

Access for disabled people:
Parking provided, toilet facilities

ASTA BEAB CERTIFICATION SERVICES

Intertek House, Cleeve Road, Leatherhead, Surrey, KT22 7SB

Tel: 01372 370900
Fax: 01372 370999
E-mail: info@beab.co.uk

Website:
http://www.uk.intertek-etlsemko.com/
Currently offers contacts information, services and buyers guide. Future intention is to offer a more comprehensive service for customers, business partners and the general public.

Enquiries:
Enquiries to: Administrative Officer

Founded:
2004

Created by the merger of:
the Association of Short-circuit Testing Authorities (ASTA) and the British Electrotechnical Approvals Board (BEAB)

Organisation type and purpose:
Trade association.

Subject coverage:
Safeguarding and protection of the public by testing and approving electrical appliances and electrotechnical equipment to British Standards.

Printed publications:
Mark of Safety (leaflet)
Update (magazine, quarterly)
BEAB Product and Services Guide
BEAB Brochure Pack

Publications list:
Available online and in print

Access to staff:
Contact by letter, by telephone, by fax, by e-mail and via website. Appointment necessary.
Hours: Mon to Thu, 0900 to 1700; Fri, 0900 to 1630

Constituent part of:
Intertek Testing Services (ITS)

ASTHMA UK

Summit House, 70 Wilson Street, London, EC2A 2DB

Tel: 020 7786 4900
Fax: 020 7256 6075
E-mail: info@asthma.org.uk

Website:
http://www.asthma.org.uk

Enquiries:
Enquiries to: Administrator

Founded:
1990

Organisation type and purpose:
Membership association (membership is by subscription), voluntary organisation, registered charity (charity number 802364).
Provides information, advice and support to people with asthma and their carers; provides funding for research into asthma and related allergies.

Subject coverage:
Asthma, medication, anyone involved, e.g. people with asthma, family, health professionals.

Printed publications:
Annual Report
Asthma Magazine (4 times a year)
General Information on Asthma in adults, babies and children for health professionals and for primary and secondary schools
Order printed publications from: Website

Electronic and video publications:
Managing Your Asthma (video only in Bengali, Gujerati, Hindi, Punjabi, Urdu)

Publications list:
Available online and in print

Access to staff:
Contact by letter
Hours: Helpline only: 0900 to 1900

Access to building, collection or gallery:
No access other than to staff

Also at:
Asthma UK Cymru
   3rd floor, Eastgate House, 35–43 Newport Road, Cardiff, CF24 0AB; tel: 029 2043 5400
Asthma UK Northern Ireland
   Ground floor, Unit 2, College House, City Link Business Park, Durham Street, Belfast, BT12 4HQ; tel: 0800 151 3035
Asthma UK Scotland
   4 Queen Street, Edinburgh, EH2 1JE; tel: 0131 226 2544; fax: 0131 226 2401

ASTON MARTIN OWNERS CLUB LIMITED

Acronym or abbreviation: AMOC

Drayton St Leonard, Wallingford, Oxfordshire, OX10 7BG

Tel: 01865 400400
Fax: 01865 400200
E-mail: hqstaff@amoc.org

Website:
http://www.amoc.org
Details of Club. News of activities. Contacts.

Enquiries:
Enquiries to: Secretary
Direct e-mail: secretary@amoc.org

Founded:
1935

Organisation type and purpose:
International organisation, membership association (membership is by subscription), present number of members: 5,000.
To provide for the needs and interests of owners of Aston Martin cars.

Subject coverage:
Aston Martin history, technical information.

Museum or gallery collection, archive, or library special collection:
Large archive of material relating to Aston Martins including: drawings for pre-war cars; racing history; brochures; etc

Printed publications:
AM Magazine (4 times a year)
AM Register (every 4 years)
News sheet (11 times a year)

Access to staff:
Contact by letter, by telephone, by fax, by e-mail and via website. Appointment necessary. Non-members charged.
Hours: Mon to Fri, 0900 to 1700

Access to building, collection or gallery:
Special comments: Wed afternoon, open to public

ASTON UNIVERSITY, LIBRARY & INFORMATION SERVICES

Library & Information Services, Aston Triangle, Birmingham, B4 7ET

Tel: 0121 204 3000
Fax: 0121 204 4530
E-mail: library@aston.ac.uk

Website:
http://library.aston.ac.uk
Web catalogue
http://www.aston.ac.uk/lis/general.htm
Times of opening
http://www.aston.ac.uk/lis/
Home page containing Annual Report, link to Library catalogue, general information

Enquiries:
Enquiries to: Enquiries
Direct tel: 0121 204 4525

Founded:
1895

Organisation type and purpose:
University Library.

Subject coverage:
Applied psychology, environmental health, ophthalmic optics, sociology and social history, political and economics studies, environmental planning and design, biological sciences, chemistry and chemical engineering, computer studies, electrical and electronic engineering, languages and linguistics, management, mathematics, mechanical engineering, pharmacy and pharmacology, production technology, international business and company information.

Library catalogue:
All or part available online

Printed publications:
Library information leaflets

Access to staff:
Contact by e-mail and via website. Access for members only.
Hours: Term time: service hours; Mon, Tue, Thu, 0900 to 1800; Wed, 1000 to 1800; Fri, 0900 to 1700; Sat, 1000 to 1300; reference hours are longer
Vacations: Mon to Fri; 0900 to 1700
For full details – see website at http://www.aston.ac.uk/lis
Special comments: An access control system is in use, for details see website at http://www.aston.ac.uk/lis
Non-members of the university can use printed resources only.

ASTRA ZENECA UK LIMITED

Brixham Environmental Laboratory, Freshwater Quarry, Brixham, Devon, TQ5 8BA

Tel: 01803 882882
Fax: 01803 882974

Website:
http://www.brixham.astrazeneca.com
Available services and points of contact.

Enquiries:
Enquiries to: Marketing Officer
Direct e-mail: neil.mccrae@astrazeneca.com

Formerly called:
ICI Brixham Laboratory; ICI Group Environmental Laboratory (year of change 1993); Brixham Environmental Laboratory, Zeneca (year of change 2000)

continued overleaf

Organisation type and purpose:
Research organisation.
Company Laboratory of Zeneca Limited providing a service to Zeneca business and external clients.

Subject coverage:
Ecology, effluents, environment and environmental sciences, estuaries, marine sciences, mathematics, oceanography, hydrology, waste treatment, toxicology, environmental assessment, groundwater monitoring.

Museum or gallery collection, archive, or library special collection:
Ray Society publications

Non-library collection catalogue:
All or part available online

Library catalogue:
All or part available in-house

Printed publications:
Cadmium as an environmental pollutant (1980) – Bibliography
Mercury Bibliography (over 1,000 references on mercury as an environmental pollutant, 1975)
Reports on the flora and fauna of estuaries
Summary of the Data on the Toxicity of Various Materials to Aquatic Life (16 titles)

Publications list:
Available online

Access to staff:
Contact by letter, by telephone, by fax, by e-mail and via website. All charged.
Hours: Mon to Fri, 0900 to 1700

ASTROLOGICAL ASSOCIATION, THE

Acronym or abbreviation: AA

BCM 450, London, WC1N 3XX

Tel: 0208 625 0098
E-mail: office@astrologicalassociation.com

Website:
http://www.astrologicalassociation.com
Information about the AA and general astrological information.

Enquiries:
Enquiries to: Media Enquiries
Direct e-mail: media@astrologicalassociation.com

Founded:
1958

Organisation type and purpose:
International organisation, membership association (membership is by subscription), present number of members: 1600, voluntary organisation, suitable for ages: all.
To give out information on astrology. To inform members of current trends and developments. A forum for the exchange of astrological research.

Subject coverage:
Astrology, history of astrology, historical studies, research practice, data collection of natal data on famous and infamous.

Printed publications:
Astrology & Medicine Newsletter (for astrologers who are interested in healing, 3 times a year)
Astrological Journal (6 times a year)
Correlation: journal of research into astrology (biennial)
Culture & Cosmos (looks at the social & historical setting of astrology, 2 times a year)

Electronic and video publications:
Collection of cassette tapes of conference seminars list available direct from the AA office (£7 each, £18 for 3)

Access to staff:
Contact by letter, by telephone, by fax, by e-mail and via website. Non-members charged.
Hours: Mon, Tue, Wed, Fri, 1100 to 1700; closed Thu

ASUCPLUS

Acronym or abbreviation: ASUC

Tournai Hall, Evelyn Woods Road, Aldershot, Hampshire, GU11 2LL

Tel: 01252 357833
Fax: 01252 357831
E-mail: admin@asuc.org.uk

Website:
http://www.asuc.org.uk

Enquiries:
Enquiries to: Secretary

Founded:
1992

Organisation type and purpose:
Trade association, present number of members: 21. Members are specialists in subsidence repair techniques and engineered foundation solutions, including new-build foundations and basement development.

Subject coverage:
Subsidence repair, foundations.

Access to staff:
Contact by letter, by telephone, by fax, by e-mail and via website
Hours: Mon to Fri, 0900 to 1700

ATAXIA UK

Lincoln House, Kennington Business Park, 1–3 Brixton Road, London, SW9 6DE

Tel: 020 7582 1444
Fax: 020 7582 9444

Website:
http://www.ataxia.org.uk

Enquiries:
Enquiries to: Administrator
Direct e-mail: cmcgowan@ataxia.org.uk

Founded:
1964

Formerly called:
Friedreich's Ataxia Group (FAG) (year of change 2001)

Organisation type and purpose:
Registered charity (charity number 102391).
Helpline, limited welfare grants for those who have ataxia, local branches, contacts and meetings. To raise money for research into ataxias and to provide information, advice and support to sufferers and their families, carers, professionals, and the general public.

Subject coverage:
Ataxias, Friedreich's, Cerebellar and other diseases of the nervous system, beginning in childhood or early adulthood, research projects funded by the Group, management and care of sufferers.

Printed publications:
Leaflets for information purposes
The Ataxian (magazine, quarterly)

Electronic and video publications:
2 DVDs available

Publications list:
Available online and in print

Access to staff:
Contact by letter, by telephone, by fax, by e-mail and via website
Hours: Mon to Fri, 0900 to 1700
Special comments: Answerphone available out of office hours.

Branches:
40 local branches throughout the UK

ATHENAEUM LIVERPOOL

Church Alley, Liverpool, L1 3DD

Tel: 0151 709 7770
Fax: 0151 709 0418

E-mail: library@theathenaeum.org.uk

Website:
http://www.theathenaeum.org.uk
Description and brief history of the club and library with three illustrations.

Enquiries:
Enquiries to: Librarian

Founded:
1797

Organisation type and purpose:
Membership association (membership is by subscription, election or invitation), present number of members: 543.

Subject coverage:
General collection: Merseyside, Lancashire and Cheshire, including maps, views, playbills. Genealogy, 19th-century economic pamphlets, 18th-century individual plays, natural history.

Museum or gallery collection, archive, or library special collection:
18th-century plays
Blanco White and South American Collection
Eshelby Collection
Genealogy
Jackson pamphlets
Liverpool playbills
Robert Gladstone pamphlets and 17th-century law
Roscoe Collection
Teignmouth Bibles
Topography
Yorkshire history

Non-library collection catalogue:
All or part available in-house and in print

Library catalogue:
All or part available in-house

Printed publications:
Catalogue of the Library 1864 (£35 post free)
The Athenaeum Liverpool 1797 to 1997 (Carrick N and Ashton E L, 1997, £13.75 post free)
The Athenaeum Liverpool 1928 (McKenna, £2 post free)

Microform publications:
Diary ... of the Brig Henricus 1807–20 (Piper R, 1994, 7 microfiches, £14)

Access to staff:
Contact by letter, by telephone, by fax, by e-mail, in person and via website. Appointment necessary. Letter of introduction required.
Hours: Members: 0900 to 1600; others: Tue to Thu, 1300 to 1600

ATLANTIC SALMON TRUST LIMITED

Acronym or abbreviation: AST

Suite 3/11, King James VI Business Centre, Friarton Road, Perth, PH2 8DG

Tel: 01738 472032
E-mail: director@atlanticsalmontrust.org

Website:
http://www.atlanticsalmontrust.org

Enquiries:
Enquiries to: Deputy Director (England & Wales)
Direct e-mail: ivorllewelyn@atlanticsalmontrust.org

Founded:
1967

Formed from:
Atlantic Salmon Research Trust (ASRT) (year of change 1980)

Organisation type and purpose:
Voluntary organisation.
Conservation and enhancement of stocks of wild Atlantic salmon and sea trout.

Subject coverage:
Wild Atlantic salmon and sea trout management and conservation.

Printed publications:
Atlantic Salmon Facts

Blue Books on salmon and sea trout matters
Posters
Journal (2 times a year)

Publications list:
Available in print

Access to staff:
Contact by letter, by telephone and by fax.
Appointment necessary.
Hours: Mon to Fri, 0930 to 1630

Associated with:
Association Internationale de Défense du Saumon
Atlantique (France)
International Atlantic Salmon Foundation
(Canada)
  tel: 00 1 506 529 4581; fax: 00 1 506 529 4438

ATOMIC WEAPONS ESTABLISHMENT

Acronym or abbreviation: AWE

Aldermaston, Reading, Berkshire, RG7 4PR

Tel: 0118 981 4111
Fax: 0118 981 5320

Website:
http://www.awe.co.uk
Background information on Company, services,
contacts.

Enquiries:
Enquiries to: Librarian
Direct tel: 0118 982 5722
Direct e-mail: library@awe.co.uk

Formerly called:
Atomic Weapons Research Establishment (AWRE)

Organisation type and purpose:
Research organisation.

Subject coverage:
Science, technology and engineering supporting
the Company's programme.

Library catalogue:
All or part available in-house

Access to staff:
Contact by telephone and by e-mail. Appointment
necessary.
Hours: Mon to Fri, 0830 to 1600

Access to building, collection or gallery:
Prior appointment required

Access for disabled people:
Parking provided, ramped entry

ATTEND

The King's Fund, 11–13 Cavendish Square,
London, W1G 0AN

Tel: 0845 4500285
Fax: 0207 307 2571
E-mail: info@attend.org.uk

Website:
http://www.attend.org.uk
Information on members, services and projects.
Includes a members-only section providing
detailed advice and information on running a
successful voluntary organisation.

Enquiries:
Enquiries to: Chief Executive
Other contacts: Communications Officer (for
general external enquiries)

Founded:
1949

Formerly called:
National Association of Hospital and Community
Friends (year of change 2006)

Organisation type and purpose:
National organisation, membership association
(membership is by subscription), present number
of members: 700, voluntary organisation,
registered charity (charity number 5713403).

Subject coverage:
Volunteering in the health sector. Legal, financial
and general advice relating to running Friends'
charities in hospital or the community.

Information services:
Information and advice to members on volunteer-
related issues.

Education services:
Attend Academy provides accredited
qualifications in volunteer management and
courses in volunteer-related issues.

Services for disabled people:
Attend ABI supports people with Acquired Brain
Injury back into work, volunteering or education.

**Museum or gallery collection, archive, or library
special collection:**
Archive information available relating to the
  history of the National Association of Hospital
  and Community Friends

Non-library collection catalogue:
All or part available in-house

Printed publications:
Friends Connect magazine available to members.
Shop Talk magazine available to members.

Publications list:
Available online and in print

Access to staff:
Contact by letter, by telephone, by fax, by e-mail,
in person and via website. Appointment necessary.
Hours: Mon to Fri, 0900 to 1700

Access to building, collection or gallery:
Prior appointment required

Access for disabled people:
Parking provided, ramped entry, access to all
public areas, toilet facilities

Member organisations:
700 independent affiliated health and social care
charities across the UK

AUDAX UNITED KINGDOM

Acronym or abbreviation: AUK

8 Nap View, Awliscombe, Honiton, Devon, EX14
3PL

Tel: 01404 46588 (day)
Fax: 01404 46501
E-mail: ian@audax.uk.net

Website:
http://www.audax.uk.net/cal/
Calendar of Events.
http://www.audax.uk.net/faq.htm
FAQ.
http://www.audax.uk.net
Homepage.

Enquiries:
Enquiries to: Honorary Secretary

Founded:
1976

Organisation type and purpose:
National organisation, membership association
(membership is by subscription), present number
of members: 3,800.
Produces calendars of, validates and keeps records
of long-distance cycle rides registered as Brevets de
Randonneurs.

Subject coverage:
Calendar of Brevets de Randonneurs cycling
events in the UK; links to international events and
cycling-related information.

**Museum or gallery collection, archive, or library
special collection:**
Results of successful Brevets de Randonneurs cycle
  rides in the UK from 1987

Trade and statistical information:
365 events of between 50 and 1,400 km calendared
  in 2001, in the UK, with 14,000 successful riders.

Non-library collection catalogue:
All or part available in-house

Printed publications:
Arrivée (magazine, quarterly, available to members
  only)
Calendar/Handbook (annually, £4)
Order printed publications from: Audax United
Kingdom
10 Huntingdon Drive, The Park, Nottingham, NG7
1BW, e-mail: young@lineone.net

Access to staff:
Contact by letter, by telephone, by fax, by e-mail
and via website
Hours: Mon to Fri, 0900 to 1700

Affiliated with:
The Cyclist Touring Club

Associated with:
Audax Club Parisien

Member of:
Les Randonneurs Mondiaux

AUDIO ENGINEERING SOCIETY LTD

Acronym or abbreviation: AES

PO Box 645, Slough, SL1 8BJ

Tel: 01628 663725
Fax: 0870 762 6137
E-mail: uk@aes.org

Website:
http://www.aes.org

Enquiries:
Enquiries to: Administrator

Founded:
1970

Organisation type and purpose:
International organisation, professional body.

Subject coverage:
Audio engineering.

**Museum or gallery collection, archive, or library
special collection:**
Society's Publications

Printed publications:
AES Standards, Drafts and Information
  Documents
Anthology Series: collected papers of archival
  quality reproduced exactly as they appeared in
  the Journal and other authoritative sources
Conference Proceedings and Collected Papers
Cumulative Indices
Directory of Educational Programs, 1998
Journal Issues
CD-ROM Preprints

Electronic and video publications:
An Afternoon with Jack Mullin (video)

Publications list:
Available online and in print

Access to staff:
Contact by telephone
Hours: Mon to Fri, 0900 to 1700

Access to building, collection or gallery:
No access other than to staff

Affiliated to:
Audio Engineering Society Inc
  60 East 42nd Street, New York, NY, 10165, USA;
  tel: +1 212 661 8528; fax: +1 212 682 0477; e-mail:
  hq@aes.org

AUDIO VISUAL ASSOCIATION

Acronym or abbreviation: AVA

156 High Street, Bushey, Watford, Hertfordshire,
WD23 3HF

Tel: 020 8950 5959
Fax: 020 8950 7560

continued overleaf

Enquiries:
Enquiries to: Chairman

Founded:
1977

Organisation type and purpose:
Membership association.
To represent professionals involved in audiovisual, video and multimedia.

Subject coverage:
Professional audiovisual up to broadcast standard including multimedia.

Access to staff:
Contact by letter and by telephone
Hours: Mon to Fri, 0900 to 1700

Specialist interest group of the:
British Institute of Professional Photography

AUDIT COMMISSION

1st Floor, Millbank Tower, Millbank, London, SW1P 4HQ

Tel: 0844 798 1212
Fax: 0844 798 2945
E-mail: audit-commission@audit-commission.gov
.uk

Website:
http://www.audit-commission.gov.uk

Enquiries:
Enquiries to: Public enquiries team
Direct tel: 0844 798 3131
Direct e-mail: public-enquiries@audit-commission
.gov.uk

Founded:
1982

Organisation type and purpose:
Statutory body.

Subject coverage:
Local government and health service.

Printed publications:
Order printed publications from: Audit Commission, PO Box 3570, Dorcan Three Hundred, Murdock Road, Dorcan, Swindon, SN3 9AR.; tel: 0800 50 20 30; e-mail: ac-orders@audit-commission.gov.uk

Publications list:
Available online

Access to staff:
Contact by letter, by telephone, by fax, by e-mail and via website. Appointment necessary.
Hours: Mon to Fri, 0900 to 1700

AUSTIN 3 LITRE OWNERS' CLUB

78 Croft Street, Ipswich, Suffolk, IP2 8EF

Tel: 01473 684867
E-mail: n.kidby@virgin.net

Enquiries:
Enquiries to: Secretary

Organisation type and purpose:
International organisation, membership association (membership is by subscription), present number of members: 45.
To provide a service to owners of 1967–1971 Austin 3 litre cars, provide bimonthly newsletter and a spares service.

Subject coverage:
All mechanical information on Austin 3 litres, details of part numbers for spares, history of Austin 3 litres.

Museum or gallery collection, archive, or library special collection:
Selected archive material i.e. road tests, period advertisements, magazine articles

Printed publications:
Newsletter (issued to members)
Austin 3 Litre Owners Club Newsletter (6 times a year)

Access to staff:
Contact by letter, by telephone and by fax. Appointment necessary.
Hours: Mon to Fri, 0900 to 2100

AUSTIN A40 FARINA CLUB

2 Ivy Cottages, Fullers Vale, Headley Down, Bordon, Hampshire, GU35 8NR

E-mail: thinton@surrart.ac.uk

Website:
http://www.a40farinaclub.org

Enquiries:
Enquiries to: Events and Publicity Officer
Direct tel: 01628 673472
Direct e-mail: the.minters@btopenworld.com

Founded:
1979

Organisation type and purpose:
Membership association.
Actively pursuing the recognition of the A40 in its true light and seeking to ensure its continuing place in the history of British motor cars.

Subject coverage:
All aspects of the Austin A40 Farina MkI and MkII (1958–1967), including history, information, owners' register, technical advice.

Museum or gallery collection, archive, or library special collection:
Archives, books and magazines on the A40

Printed publications:
Farina News (magazine, quarterly)

Access to staff:
Contact by letter, by e-mail and via website
Hours: Mon to Fri, 1800 to 2200; Sat, Sun, any reasonable time

Other addresses:
Austin A40 Farina Club
    26 Wootton Way, Maidenhead, Berkshire, SL6 4QU; tel: 01628 673472; e-mail: the.minters@ btopenworld.com
Austin A40 Farina Club
    75 Tennal Road, Harbourne, Birmingham, B32 2JB
Events & Publicity Officer
Membership Secretary

AUSTIN BIG SEVEN REGISTER

101 Derby Road, Chellaston, Derby, DE73 5SB

Enquiries:
Enquiries to: Registrar

Founded:
1969

Organisation type and purpose:
Membership association.
Car club for 1937–39 Austin Big Seven.
To register all cars of this marque which have survived and are being restored or used.

Subject coverage:
Technical information, advice and information, spares advice.

Museum or gallery collection, archive, or library special collection:
Books, documents, technical information, relating to 1937–39 Austin Big Sevens

Printed publications:
Hand Books & Technical Journal sheets
Newsletter (2 or 3 times a year)

Access to staff:
Contact by letter and by telephone
Hours: Mon to Sat, 1800 to 2000

Member organisation of:
Austin Seven Clubs Association
Federation of Austin Clubs, Registers and Associations
    e-mail: austinfederation@aol.com
Federation of British Historic Motor Vehicle Clubs

AUSTIN CAMBRIDGE/ WESTMINSTER CAR CLUB

Acronym or abbreviation: ACWCC

26 Railton Jones Close, Stoke Gifford, South Gloucestershire, BS34 8BF

Tel: 0117 9314881
E-mail: acwcc@blueyonder.co.uk

Website:
http://www.acwcc.org

Enquiries:
Enquiries to: Information Officer

Founded:
1980

Organisation type and purpose:
International organisation, membership association (membership is by subscription), present number of members: 120.

Subject coverage:
Austin Cambridge 1954–69, Morris Oxford 1959–71, MG Magnette 1959–68, Riley 1959–69, Wolseley 1959–71, Austin Westminster 1954–68, 3L Austin 1968–71; spares, stockists, advice.

Printed publications:
Newsletter

Access to staff:
Contact by letter, by telephone and by e-mail
Hours: Mon to Fri, 0900 to 2100

AUSTIN MAXI CLUB

Formal name: Austin Maxi Owners Club

27 Queen Street, Bardney, Lincolnshire, LN3 5XF

Tel: 01526 398377
Fax: 01526 398377

Website:
http://www.austinmaxiclub.org

Enquiries:
Enquiries to: Membership Secretary

Founded:
1989

Organisation type and purpose:
Membership association.

Subject coverage:
Austin Maxi, its continuation of use, availability of spares.

Access to staff:
Contact by letter
Hours: Mon to Fri, 0900 to 1700

AUSTRALASIAN PLANT SOCIETY

Acronym or abbreviation: APS

1 Iffin Cottages, Iffin Lane, Canterbury, Kent, CT4 7BE

Tel: 01227 780038
E-mail: secretary@anzplantsoc.org.uk

Website:
http://www.anzplantsoc.org.uk

Enquiries:
Enquiries to: Honorary Secretary

Founded:
1988

Formerly called:
Australian Plant Society (year of change 1992)

Organisation type and purpose:
National organisation (membership is by subscription), present number of members: 150.

Subject coverage:
Details about wild plants of Australia and New Zealand.

Museum or gallery collection, archive, or library special collection:
Colour slides

Books about Antipodean plants

Non-library collection catalogue:
All or part available in-house

Printed publications:
Newsletter (two times a year, to members only)
Seed Germination information (to members only)
Information pack (members only)

Access to staff:
Contact by letter, by telephone and by e-mail
Hours: Daily, 0900 to 1700

AUSTRALIA'S NORTHERN TERRITORY TOURIST COMMISSION

Acronym or abbreviation: NTTC

1st Floor, Beaumont House, Lambton Road, London, SW20 0LW

Tel: 020 8944 2992
Fax: 020 8944 2993

Website:
http://www.ntholidays.com
Holiday and touring information for Australia's Northern Territory.

Enquiries:
Enquiries to: Manager
Direct e-mail: fburrows@tourismnt.australia.com

Organisation type and purpose:
Marketing office for Australia's Northern Territory.

Subject coverage:
Holiday information for Australia's Northern Territory.

Printed publications:
Tour Guides (free)

Electronic and video publications:
Some videos (available on loan for travel agent training)

Access to staff:
Contact by letter, by telephone, by fax and by e-mail
Hours: Mon to Fri, 0900 to 1700
Special comments: Office not open to the general public.

Parent body:
Northern Territory Tourist Commission
PO Box 1155, Darwin, NT 0801, Australia

AUSTRALIAN BUSINESS

Swire House, 59 Buckingham Gate, London, SW1E 6AJ

Tel: 0870 8900720
Fax: 020 7379 0721
E-mail: enquiries@australianbusiness.co.uk

Website:
http://www.australianbusiness.co.uk

Enquiries:
Enquiries to: Director

Organisation type and purpose:
Membership association.

Subject coverage:
Trade between Australia and New Zealand, and the UK.

Access to staff:
Contact by fax and by e-mail. Non-members charged.
Hours: Mon to Fri, 0900 to 1700

AUSTRIAN CULTURAL FORUM

Acronym or abbreviation: ACF

28 Rutland Gate, London, SW7 1PQ

Tel: 020 7225 7300
Fax: 020 7225 0470
E-mail: office@acflondon.org

Website:
http://www.acflondon.org

Enquiries:
Enquiries to: Librarian
Direct e-mail: librarian@acflondon.org

Founded:
1956

Formerly called:
Austrian Cultural Institute (ACI) (year of change 2001)

Organisation type and purpose:
National government body.
Cultural affairs body.

Subject coverage:
Cultural aspects of Austrian life.

Museum or gallery collection, archive, or library special collection:
Austrian studies

Non-library collection catalogue:
All or part available in-house

Library catalogue:
All or part available online

Printed publications:
Leaflets from Foreign Ministry on various subjects
Own small series on Austrian themes, issues

Access to staff:
Contact by letter, by telephone and by e-mail.
Appointment necessary.
Hours: Mon to Thu, 1430 to 1630 (library)

Access to building, collection or gallery:
via Rutland Gate
Hours: Mon to Thu, 1430 to 1630 (library)

Constituent part of:
Austrian Embassy

AUSTRIAN EMBASSY

18 Belgrave Mews West, London, SW1X 8HU

Tel: 020 7235 3731/2/3 and 7344 0290
Fax: 020 7344 0292
E-mail: embassy@austria.org.uk

Website:
http://www.austria.org.uk
General information on Austria, information on consular matters, information for Austrians living in the UK, information on culture, trade and tourism.

Enquiries:
Enquiries to: Information Officer
Other contacts: Consul General for consular matters.

Organisation type and purpose:
Embassy and Consulate.

Subject coverage:
General information on Austria, consular service, assistance to Austrian citizens living in the UK.

Museum or gallery collection, archive, or library special collection:
Information material (booklets, pamphlets etc.) available by letter or fax to the Information Officer

Library catalogue:
All or part available in-house

Electronic and video publications:
Video on Austria (for short term loan, contact the Austrian Cultural Forum)

Access to staff:
Contact by letter, by telephone, by fax, by e-mail, in person and via website. Appointment necessary.
Hours: Consulate: Mon to Fri, 0900 to 1200

Connections with:
Austrian Cultural Forum
28 Rutland Gate, London, SW7 1PQ; tel: 020 7584 8653; fax: 020 7225 0470; e-mail: culture@austria.org.uk

Austrian Trade Commission
45 Princes Gate, Exhibition Road, London, SW7 2QA; tel: 020 7584 4411; fax: 020 7584 2565; e-mail: london@wko.at

Parent body:
Austrian Federal Ministry of Foreign Affairs
Ballhausplatz 2, Wien, A-1014, Austria; tel: + 43 1 53115; website: http://www.bmaa.gv.at

AUTHORS' LICENSING & COLLECTING SOCIETY LIMITED

Acronym or abbreviation: ALCS

Marlborough Court, 14–18 Holborn, London, EC1N 2LE

Tel: 020 7395 0600
Fax: 020 7395 0660
E-mail: alcs@alcs.co.uk

Website:
http://www.alcs.co.uk
Information on ALCS.

Enquiries:
Enquiries to: Communications Manager

Founded:
1977

Organisation type and purpose:
International organisation, membership association, present number of members: 18,000 full members, 35,000 associate members.
British collecting society for all writers. Ensures hard-to-collect revenues due to authors are efficiently collected and speedily distributed.
Campaigns to raise awareness of copyright issues and authors' rights among writers.

Subject coverage:
Database of film, broadcasting and literary information containing information on British writers and film and television works including foreign episode titles, details of daily programming in the United Kingdom and several other European Countries that relate to writers' works. Also a database of books holding details of works photocopied since licensing introduced in 1984.
Information on literary estates and literary agents.

Printed publications:
Information leaflets
Newsletter (members and interested parties only)

Access to staff:
Contact by letter, by telephone, by fax, by e-mail and via website. Appointment necessary.
Hours: Mon to Fri, 0930 to 1750

Affiliations with:
NUJ and other writers' organisations
Society of Authors
Writers Guild of Great Britain

Constituent member of:
Copyright Licensing Agency (CLA)
Educational Recording Agency (ERA)

Lead partner in:
BCC
CISAC
EU Imprimatur Project
European Writers' Congress
IFRRO

AUTISM INDEPENDENT UK

Acronym or abbreviation: SFTAH

199–203 Blandford Avenue, Kettering, Northamptonshire, NN16 9AT

Tel: 01536 523274
Fax: 01536 523274
E-mail: autism@autismuk.com

Website:
http://www.autismuk.com

Enquiries:
Enquiries to: Chief Executive
Direct e-mail: keithlovett@ntlworld.com

continued overleaf

Founded:
1987

Formerly called:
Society for the Autistically Handicapped

Organisation type and purpose:
National organisation, voluntary organisation, registered charity (charity number 803003), training organisation.

Subject coverage:
Specialised information: autism, Asperger's Syndrome, education, care and treatment, training, statementing.

Library catalogue:
All or part available online and in print

Printed publications:
Society leaflets, fact file (Autism) and Holiday Home brochure (free – send SAE)
In-depth Autism, specialised areas and general information

Publications list:
Available online

Access to staff:
Contact by letter, by telephone, by fax, by e-mail, in person and via website. Appointment necessary.
Hours: Every day, 0900 to 1700, answerphone at other times
Special comments: Appointments necessary for reference library.

Access to building, collection or gallery:
Prior appointment required

Access for disabled people:
Special comments: One step

AUTO-CYCLE UNION

Acronym or abbreviation: ACU

ACU House, Wood Street, Rugby, CV21 2YX

Tel: 01788 566400
Fax: 01788 573585
E-mail: admin@acu.org.uk

Website:
http://www.acu.org.uk
Motorcycling disciplines, resources, advice and support, clubs, promoters, associations, membership, insurance, news, events.

Enquiries:
Enquiries to: General Secretary
Direct e-mail: gary@acu.org.uk

Founded:
1903

Formerly called:
Auto-Cycle Club (year of change 1907)

Organisation type and purpose:
The Governing Body for motorcycle sport throughout Britain.
To provide all participants in motorcycle sport with enjoyable, safe and competitive days of sporting action. Has over 630 clubs divided into 20 centres.

Subject coverage:
The sport of motorcycling at all levels.

Electronic and video publications:
Newsletter
Order electronic and video publications from: website

Access to staff:
Contact by letter, by telephone, by fax and by e-mail

Member organisation of:
Fédération Internationale de Motorcyclisme (FIM)

AUTOMATIC DOOR SUPPLIERS ASSOCIATION LIMITED

Acronym or abbreviation: ADSA

411 Limpsfield Road, Warlingham, Surrey, CR6 9HA

Tel: 01883 624961
Fax: 01883 626841
E-mail: admin@adsa.org.uk

Website:
http://www.adsa.org.uk
All about the association, including list of members, objects and rules, BS7036 and test dates

Enquiries:
Enquiries to: Office Manager

Founded:
1985

Organisation type and purpose:
Trade association, consultancy.

Subject coverage:
Supply/installation of automatic doors and the safety aspects of these.

Printed publications:
British Standard – BS 7036 1996: Code of Practice for Provision and Installation of Safety Devices for Automatic Power Operated Pedestrian Door Systems (copies from BSI, Chiswick)

Access to staff:
Contact by letter, by telephone, by fax, by e-mail, in person and via website
Hours: Mon to Fri, 0900 to 1700

AUTOMATIC VENDING ASSOCIATION

Acronym or abbreviation: AVA

1 Villiers Court, 40 Upper Mulgrave Road, Cheam, Surrey, SM2 7AJ

Tel: 020 8661 1112
Fax: 020 8661 2224

Website:
http://www.ava-vending.co.uk
AVA services and members. Refreshment vending. General information. Links to members, technical information.

Enquiries:
Enquiries to: Director
Direct e-mail: janette@ava-vending.co.uk

Founded:
1929

Formerly called:
Automatic Vending Association of Britain (AVAB) (year of change 2000)

Organisation type and purpose:
Trade association.

Subject coverage:
Availability and suitability of automatic vending machines systems for catering or retailing services, UK vending market, explaining refreshment vending.

Trade and statistical information:
Size of the installed vending machine base and the products being sold through it, available as the AVA Census.

Electronic and video publications:
AVA Census (CD-ROM)
Water – Don't let the bugs get you down (DVD)

Publications list:
Available online

Access to staff:
Contact by letter, by telephone, by fax, by e-mail and via website
Hours: Mon to Fri, 0900 to 1700

Access for disabled people:
Parking provided, level entry, toilet facilities

AUTOMOBILE ASSOCIATION

Acronym or abbreviation: AA

AA Press Office, Fanum House, Basing View, Basingstoke, RG21 4EA

Tel: 01256 495969

E-mail: press.office@theaa.com

Website:
http://www.theaa.com

Enquiries:
Enquiries to: Press Officer

Founded:
1905

Organisation type and purpose:
Service industry.

Subject coverage:
Motoring developments (non-commercial): technical, statistical, legislative, environmental and related transport and travel.

Museum or gallery collection, archive, or library special collection:
Archives of the Association from 1905

Access to staff:
Contact by letter, by telephone and by e-mail
Hours: Mon to Fri, 0900 to 1700

AUTOMOTIVE DISTRIBUTION FEDERATION

Acronym or abbreviation: ADF

68 Coleshill Road, Hodge Hill, Birmingham, B36 8AB

Tel: 0121 784 3535
Fax: 0121 784 4411
E-mail: admin@adf.org.uk

Enquiries:
Enquiries to: Secretary

Founded:
1930

Formerly called:
Motor Factors Association (MFA) (year of change 1990)

Organisation type and purpose:
Trade association (membership is by subscription), present number of members: 340 companies. The Automotive Distribution Federation represents the opinions of manufacturers, importers and wholesale distributors (motor factors) of vehicle parts and accessories.

Subject coverage:
Manufacturers, importers and wholesale distributors (motor factors) of vehicle parts and accessories.

Printed publications:
Eyes and Ears (newsletter, 6 times a year, free to members, £15 annual subscription)

Access to staff:
Contact by letter, by telephone, by fax, by e-mail and via website. Appointment necessary.
Hours: Fri, 0900 to 1630

AUTOVIA CAR CLUB

43 Tilbury Road, Tilbury Juxta Clare, Halstead, Essex, CO9 4JJ

Tel: 01787 237676
E-mail: glthomas@gotadsl.co.uk

Enquiries:
Enquiries to: Secretary

Founded:
1990

Organisation type and purpose:
National organisation.

Subject coverage:
Riley Autovia cars.

Access to staff:
Contact by letter and by telephone
Hours: Mon to Fri, 0900 to 1700

AVERT

4 Brighton Road, Horsham, West Sussex, RH13
5BA

Tel: 01403 210202
Fax: 01403 211001
E-mail: info@avert.org

Website:
http://www.avert.org
Wide range of material on HIV/AIDS including
United Kingdom and US AIDS statistics,
educational material, medical and self-help
information. Links to other HIV/AIDS related sites.

Enquiries:
Enquiries to: Information Officer

Founded:
1986

Formerly called:
Aids Education and Research Trust

Organisation type and purpose:
Registered charity (charity number 1074849).
To combat HIV and AIDS world-wide.

Subject coverage:
HIV and AIDS information.

**Museum or gallery collection, archive, or library
special collection:**
Reference library

Trade and statistical information:
Statistics on epidemiology of HIV and AIDS in
  United Kingdom especially.

Printed publications:
All publications are now available for free online,
  including:
HIV and AIDS: Information for Young People
Sex and Sexual Relationships
Teens, STDs and HIV/AIDS
Changing Times: Information about Puberty
STD Booklet
Information about contraception

Publications list:
Available online and in print

Access to staff:
Contact by letter, by telephone, by fax, by e-mail
and via website
Hours: Mon to Fri, 0900 to 1700

Access to building, collection or gallery:
Prior appointment required
Hours: Mon to Fri, 0900 to 1700

Access for disabled people:
Parking provided, ramped entry, level entry, access
to all public areas, toilet facilities

AVIATION ENVIRONMENT
FEDERATION

Acronym or abbreviation: AEF

Broken Wharf House, 2 Broken Wharf, London,
EC4V 3DT

Tel: 020 7248 2223
Fax: 020 7329 8160
E-mail: info@aef.org.uk

Website:
http://www.aef.org.uk
Summary of objectives, membership information,
summary of newsletters/members briefing notes.
http://www.aef.org.uk/publications.htm

Enquiries:
Enquiries to: Information Officer

Founded:
1975

Formerly called:
Airfields Environment Federation (year of change
1993)

Organisation type and purpose:
National organisation, membership association
(membership is by subscription), present number
of members: 110, voluntary organisation,
consultancy, research organisation.
Addresses all the environmental impacts of aircraft
and aerodrome operations.

Subject coverage:
Environmental and amenity effects and impacts of
aviation.

**Museum or gallery collection, archive, or library
special collection:**
Environmental statements
Industry and government reports
Papers, journals
Planning inquiry documents

Trade and statistical information:
World data on the environmental performance of
  the aviation industry.

Printed publications:
Annual Report
Newsletter (6 times a year)
Aviation and its Environmental Effects (Logan M,
  1995, £5 plus 50p p&p)
Aviation, the Environment & Planning Law: An
  AEF Handbook (Bingham A, Johnson T eds,
  1995, £20 plus £1 p&p)
The Development of Surface Access Links to
  Airports: The Environmental Issues (Johnson T,
  1997, £5 plus 50p p&p)
The Environmentalist Viewpoint (Logan M, 1997,
  £5 plus 50p p&p)
Papers, briefings and reports

Publications list:
Available online and in print

Access to staff:
Contact by letter, by telephone, by fax, by e-mail
and via website. Appointment necessary. Non-
members charged.
Hours: Mon to Fri, 0930 to 1630

Access to building, collection or gallery:
Prior appointment required

Co-ordinator of:
Green Skies
  tel: 020 7248 2223; e-mail: info@greenskies.org

Member organisation of:
European Environment Bureau
  Brussels, Belgium

AVON LOCAL HISTORY AND
ARCHAEOLOGY

Acronym or abbreviation: ALHA

5 Parrys Grove, Bristol, BS9 1TT

Tel: 0117 968 4979
Fax: 0117 968 4979
E-mail: wm.evans@btopenworld.com

Website:
http://www.avonlocalhistandarch.co.uk
Activities, and contact details of member groups
and societies

Founded:
1976

Organisation type and purpose:
Umbrella organisation for local groups and
societies.
County local history liaison.
Promotion of local history in the region and a co-
ordinating forum.

Subject coverage:
Local history and archaeology in Avon (Bristol and
Bath) area; especially contacts and club collections.

Printed publications:
Newsletter (quarterly, annual subscription £5 by e-
  mail, £6 on paper), local history booklets (£3.50
  each)
Order printed publications from:
mikeleigh@blueyonder.co.uk

Publications list:
Available in print

Access to staff:
Contact by letter, by telephone, by fax and by e-
mail

Links with:
some 80 affiliated groups and societies

AVON PARK INTERNATIONAL
RACING ASSOCIATION

Acronym or abbreviation: APIRA

The Annex, Half Moon Farm, Rushall, Diss,
Norfolk, IP21 4QD

Tel: 01379 740100
Fax: 01379 740100
E-mail: wendy@apira.org.uk

Website:
http://www.shakespearecountyraceway.com
Race dates, contacts, information on the area, news
updates.

Enquiries:
Enquiries to: General Secretary
Direct fax: 01789 252030
Direct e-mail: wendy@shakespearecountyraceway
.org.uk
Other contacts: Events Information and Race-
Meetings Secretary; Membership Secretary

Founded:
1990

Formerly called:
NDRC-NDRA

Organisation type and purpose:
International organisation, membership
association (membership is by subscription),
present number of members: 350
Motor sports racing organisation for drag racing.

Subject coverage:
Drag car racing covered by the Motorsport
Association and the Auto Cycle Union.

Printed publications:
Newsletters (website)
Order printed publications from: LA Performance
Services
60 Berry Road, Paignton, Devon, TQ3 3QJ, tel:
01803 554308, e-mail: la.racing@virgin.net

Publications list:
Available online

Access to staff:
Contact by letter, by telephone, by fax, by e-mail,
in person and via website. Letter of introduction
required.
Hours: Mon to Fri, 0900 to 1700

Access to building, collection or gallery:
No prior appointment required
Hours: Racing commences 1000 to 1800

Access for disabled people:
Parking provided, level entry, access to all public
areas, toilet facilities
Special comments: Viewing ramp for disabled
wheelchair persons and their carers.

Affiliated to:
Auto Cycle Union
  ACU House, Wood Street, Rugby, Warwickshire,
  CV21 2YX; tel: 01788 566400; fax: 01788 573585;
  website: http://www.acu.org.uk
The Motor Sports Association (MSA)
  Motor Sports House, Riverside Park, Colnbrook,
  Slough, Berkshire, SL3 0HG; tel: 01753 681736;
  fax: 01753 682936; website: http://www.msauk
  .org

Track Owner:
Avon Park International Racing Association
  Airfield House, Long Marston, Stratford Upon
  Avon, Warwickshire, CV37 8LL; tel: 01789
  414119; fax: 01789 262030; website: http://www
  .shakespearecountyraceway.org.uk

AWDURDOD PARC CENEDLAETHOL ERYRI / SNOWDONIA NATIONAL PARK AUTHORITY

Acronym or abbreviation: APCE / SNPA

Swyddfa'r Parc Cenedlaethol, Penrhyndeudraeth, Gwynedd, LL48 6LF

Tel: 01766 770274
Fax: 01766 771211
E-mail: parc@eryri-npa.gov.uk

Website:
http://www.eryri-npa.gov.uk

Founded:
1951

Organisation type and purpose:
Local government body.

Subject coverage:
Farming; woodland management; ecology; planning; visitor services; conservation; demography; education; agriculture.

Printed publications:
Maps, guides, walking routes

Microform publications:
Photographs

Access to staff:
Contact by letter, by telephone, by fax, by e-mail and via website
Hours: Mon to Fri, 0900 to 1700

Access for disabled people:
Parking provided, level entry, toilet facilities

AXIS

Formal name: Axis – the online resource for contemporary art

Studio 17/18, 46 The Calls, Leeds, LS6 4EX

Tel: 0113 2429830
Fax: 0113 2179665
E-mail: info@axisweb.org

Website:
http://www.axisweb.org
A directory of over 2,600 professional UK contemporary artists and curators, information about how to join the directory, interviews, discussions, art news, debates, and a showcase for the artists to watch.

Enquiries:
Enquiries to: Head of Audience Development
Direct e-mail: kara@axisweb.org
Other contacts: Projects Coordinator

Founded:
1991

Formerly called:
Axis – visual arts information service

Organisation type and purpose:
Registered charity (charity number 10022841); online directory of UK contemporary visual artists and curators; contemporary art information service. Axis is a contemporary visual arts service that provides information about professional artists and curators living/working in the UK to a national and international audience.

Subject coverage:
Directory of artists and curators, visual arts information service; featured artists, news and commentary about UK contemporary art.

Trade and statistical information:
Online directory of UK contemporary visual artists and curators.

Non-library collection catalogue:
All or part available online

Access to staff:
Contact by letter, by telephone, by fax, by e-mail, in person and via website. Appointment necessary.
Hours: Mon to Fri, 0900 to 1700

Funded by:
Arts Council England
    website: http://www.artscouncil.org.uk
The Arts Council of Wales
    website: http://www.artswales.org.uk

AXREM

Formal name: Association of Healthcare Technology Providers for Imaging, Radiotherapy and Care

Broadwall House, 21 Broadwall, London, SE1 9PL

Tel: 020 7207 9660
Fax: 020 7642 8096
E-mail: peter.lawson@axrem.org.uk

Website:
http://www.axrem.org.uk/

Enquiries:
Enquiries to: Director

Organisation type and purpose:
Trade association.

Subject coverage:
Commerce and technology of the medical diagnostic imaging and radio-therapy equipment.

AYRSHIRE CATTLE SOCIETY OF GREAT BRITAIN AND IRELAND

17 Barns Street, Ayr, Scotland, KA7 1XB

Tel: 01292 267123
Fax: 01292 611973
E-mail: society@ayrshirescs.org

Website:
http://www.ayrshirescs.org
Details of services and breed.

Enquiries:
Enquiries to: General Manager

Founded:
1877

Organisation type and purpose:
International organisation, advisory body, membership association (membership is by subscription), present number of members: 1,000, registered charity (charity number SC007015). Breed Society.

Subject coverage:
Ayrshire cattle breeding and pedigrees; production records; linear type evaluations; AI use with Ayrshire cattle; livestock pedigree record systems.

Museum or gallery collection, archive, or library special collection:
Books, microfilm and tape journals since 1923
Herd books since 1877

Printed publications:
Herd Directory (2 yearly)
Ayrshire Journal (April and September)

Access to staff:
Contact by letter, by telephone, by fax, by e-mail and via website. Appointment necessary.
Hours: Mon to Fri, 0900 to 1700

Affiliated to:
World Federation of Ayrshire Breed Societies

AIDIS GROUP LTD

Acronym or abbreviation: AIDIS

Salamanca Square, 9 Albert Embankment, London, SE1 7SP

Tel: 0207 091 4500
Fax: 0207 091 4545
E-mail: enquiries@adsgroup.org.uk

Website:
http://www.adsgroup.org.uk
Full information on the AIDIS.

Enquiries:
Enquiries to: Director – Overseas and Exports
Direct tel: 01428 602622

Direct fax: 01428 602628
Direct e-mail: b.salzmann@the-dma.org.uk

Created by the merger of:
Association of Police and Public Security Suppliers (APPSS), the Defence Manufacturers Association (DMA) and the Society of British Aerospace Companies (SBAC).

Organisation type and purpose:
The trade organisation advancing UK aeroSpace, defence and security industries, with Farnborough International Limited as a wholly-owned subsidiary. AIDIS also encompasses the British Aviation Group (BAG).

Museum or gallery collection, archive, or library special collection:
Deso publications
AIDIS publications
Exhibition catalogues
Foreign industry directories
Many Jane's books
Several defence periodicals
Library of Information maintained

Trade and statistical information:
Some data on the UK defence industry and export markets.

Library catalogue:
All or part available in-house

Printed publications:
Draft forms of contract and agency agreement
List of EDMAG members and their products and services
MOD new management strategy
Police and Security Requirements in the 90s – Implications and Opportunities for Industry
Public Sector Purchasing Agencies
Worldwide Directory of Main Defence Contractors

Publications list:
Available in print

Access to staff:
Contact by letter, by telephone, by fax, by e-mail and via website. Appointment necessary.
Hours: Mon to Fri, 0900 to 1730

Access to building, collection or gallery:
No prior appointment required

BACH CHOIR, THE

33 Upham Park Road, London, W4 1PQ

Tel: 020 8742 3661
Fax: 020 8742 3661
E-mail: genman@thebachchoir.org.uk

Website:
http://www.thebachchoir.org.uk
Information about the choir, concerts, booking information, how to join, etc.

Enquiries:
Enquiries to: General Manager
Direct e-mail: pr@thebachchoir.org.uk

Founded:
1876

Organisation type and purpose:
Membership association (membership is by subscription, qualification), present number of members: 250, registered charity (charity number 238287).
Choral Society.

Subject coverage:
The performance of choral music.

Access to staff:
Contact by letter, by telephone, by fax and by e-mail. Appointment necessary. Letter of introduction required.
Hours: Mon to Fri, 0900 to 1700

BACKCARE

16 Elmtree Road, Teddington, Middlesex, TW11 8ST

Tel: 020 8977 5474\Helpline: 0845 130 2704
Fax: 020 8943 5318
E-mail: info@backcare.org.uk

Website:
http://www.backcare.org.uk

Enquiries:
Enquiries to: Communications Manager

Founded:
1968

Formerly called:
Back Pain Association (BPA); National Back Pain
Association (NBPA) (year of change 1999)

Organisation type and purpose:
Advisory body, membership association, voluntary
organisation, registered charity (charity number
256751).
Charity dedicated to educating people on how to
avoid preventable back pain, and supporting those
living with back pain.
Research.

Subject coverage:
Back pain, encouragement of research into causes
and treatment, prevention of damage by proper
use of the body, formation of branches to inform
and aid people with back pain.

Printed publications:
Annual Report
Training, advisory and educational publications
   including:
Advisory posters
Better Backs for Children
Information Packs
Manual Handling: an ergonomic approach
Talkback (magazine, quarterly, free to supporters)
The Handling of Patients (guide for health
   professionals, 4th ed.)

Electronic and video publications:
Fighting Back (video, £15.99)
Catering for Lifters (training video, £24.95)

Publications list:
Available online and in print

Access to staff:
Contact by letter, by telephone, by fax, by e-mail
and via website
Hours: Mon to Fri, 0900 to 1700

BACKPACKERS CLUB

49 Lyndhurst Road, Exmouth, Devon, EX8 3DS

Tel: 01395 265159
E-mail: wjbeed@genie.co.uk

Website:
http://www.catan.demon.co.uk/backpack/
Club information.

Enquiries:
Enquiries to: General Secretary

Founded:
1972

Organisation type and purpose:
National organisation, membership association
(membership is by subscription).
Leisure, camping club.

Subject coverage:
Specialist organisation for lightweight camping,
catering for walkers, cyclists and canoeists
(national/international).

**Museum or gallery collection, archive, or library
special collection:**
Extensive Club Library of camping books and
   walking guides

Library catalogue:
All or part available in-house

Printed publications:
Backpack (magazine, quarterly, members)
Camp Site Directories, Farm and Long Distance
   Paths (members only)

Electronic and video publications:
Camp Site Directories, Farm and Long Distance
   Paths (members only)

Access to staff:
Contact by letter and by telephone
Hours: Mon to Fri, 0900 to 1700 and answerphone

BACTA

Formal name: British Amusement Catering Trades
Association

Bacta House, Regent's Wharf, 6 All Saints Street,
London, N1 9RQ

Tel: 020 7713 7144
Fax: 020 7713 0446
E-mail: info@bacta.org.uk

Enquiries:
Enquiries to: Public Relations Manager
Direct tel: 020 7841 3234

Founded:
1974

Organisation type and purpose:
Trade association.
Represents Britain's pay-to-play leisure machines
industry.

Subject coverage:
Manufacture and operation of coin-operated
leisure machines.

Trade and statistical information:
Data on pay-to-play leisure machines.

Printed publications:
Amusing Britain
Booklet on the industry
Guide to the Gaming Act 1968 (updated
   periodically)
History of BACTA

Access to staff:
Contact by letter, by telephone, by fax and by e-
mail
Hours: Mon to Fri, 0900 to 1700

Access to building, collection or gallery:
No prior appointment required

Links with:
Euromat
National Amusements Council

BACUP NATURAL HISTORY SOCIETY

Acronym or abbreviation: BACUP 'NAT'

24 Yorkshire Street, Bacup, Lancashire, OL13 9AE

Enquiries:
Enquiries to: General Secretary
Direct tel: 01706 873042
Other contacts: Museum Curator, tel: 01706 873961

Founded:
1878

Organisation type and purpose:
Learned society (membership is by subscription),
present number of members: 70, voluntary
organisation, registered charity, museum.

Subject coverage:
Natural history – flora, fauna, fossils, local history
and domestic bygones.

**Museum or gallery collection, archive, or library
special collection:**
Library of over 2,000 books
Copies of Bacup newspapers from 1863
Some 4,000 photographs of old Bacup and its mills,
   houses, farms, churches, public houses etc

Non-library collection catalogue:
All or part available in-house

Library catalogue:
All or part available in-house

Access to staff:
Contact by letter and in person
Hours: Mon to Fri, 0900 to 1700

Has a section:
Bacup Camera Club
   at the same address

BADMINTON ENGLAND

Formal name: Badminton Association of England
Ltd

National Badminton Centre, Bradwell Road,
Loughton Lodge, Milton Keynes,
Buckinghamshire, MK8 9LA

Tel: 01908 268400
Fax: 01908 268412
E-mail: enquiries@badmintonengland.co.uk

Website:
http://www.badmintonengland.co.uk
General information and contacts.

Enquiries:
Other contacts: Press Officer

Founded:
1893

Organisation type and purpose:
Professional body.
Governing body of the sport of badminton in
England.

Subject coverage:
Badminton: rules-regulations, courts, lighting,
playing facilities, shuttles, coaching, events,
championships, players, general information.

**Museum or gallery collection, archive, or library
special collection:**
A number of historic books on badminton

Printed publications:
Badminton (magazine 4 times a year)
BADMINTON England Handbook (annually)
Power & Precision (coaching magazine)
The Diary (annually)
The Laws (annually)

Electronic and video publications:
Videos, DVDs

Publications list:
Available online and in print

Access to staff:
Contact by letter, by telephone, by fax, by e-mail
and in person. Appointment necessary.
Hours: Mon to Thu, 0900 to 1700; Fri, 0900 to 1530

Affiliated to:
British Olympic Association
Central Council of Physical Recreation
Commonwealth Games Council
European Badminton Union
   tel: + 49 2151 503020; fax: + 49 2151 503111; e-
   mail: ebu.gen.sec@t-online.de
International Badminton Federation
   tel: 00603 92837 155; e-mail: info@intbadfed.org
Sport England

BADMINTONSCOTLAND

Formal name: Scottish Badminton Union Ltd

The Cockburn Centre, 40 Bogmoor Place, Glasgow,
G51 4TQ

Tel: 0141 445 1218
Fax: 0141 425 1218
E-mail: enquiries@badmintonscotland.org.uk

Website:
http://www.badmintonscotland.org.uk
All about badminton in Scotland.

Founded:
1911

Organisation type and purpose:
Governing body of the sport of badminton in
Scotland.

Printed publications:
Scottish Badminton (4 times a year, £6 a year)

continued overleaf

Access to staff:
Contact by letter, by telephone, by e-mail and via website
Hours: Mon to Fri, 0900 to 1700

Access to building, collection or gallery:
Prior appointment required

BAE SYSTEMS

Advanced Technology Centre, West Hanningfield Road, Great Baddow, Chelmsford, Essex, CM2 8HN

Tel: 01245 473331
Fax: 01245 242388
E-mail: arthur.jones@baesystems.com

Enquiries:
Enquiries to: Senior Information Officer
Direct tel: 01245 242394
Direct e-mail: baddow.library@baesystems.com

Formerly called:
GEC Marconi Research Centre, Marconi Research Centre

Organisation type and purpose:
Manufacturing industry, research organisation.

Subject coverage:
Electronics, communications, radar, avionics, antennas, microwave research, remote sensing, radio propagation.

Library catalogue:
All or part available in-house

Access to staff:
Contact by letter, by telephone, by fax and by e-mail
Hours: Mon to Fri, 0900 to 1600

Access to building, collection or gallery:
Prior appointment required

BALINT SOCIETY

Tollgate Health Centre, 220 Tollgate Road, London, E6 5JS

Tel: 020 7439 9399
Fax: 020 7473 9388
E-mail: david.watt@gp-f84093.nhs.uk

Website:
http://www.balint.co.uk
Membership, FAQ, programme.

Enquiries:
Enquiries to: Honorary Secretary

Founded:
1969

Organisation type and purpose:
Learned society, professional body, registered charity, training organisation, research organisation.

Subject coverage:
Research and education on the doctor-patient relationship.

Museum or gallery collection, archive, or library special collection:
Balint Archives

Printed publications:
Journal of the Balint Society

Access to staff:
Contact by letter, by telephone, by fax and by e-mail
Hours: Mon to Fri, 0900 to 1700

Links with:
International Balint Federation

BALLIOL COLLEGE LIBRARY

Balliol College, Oxford, OX1 3BJ

Tel: 01865 277709
Fax: 01865 277803
E-mail: library@balliol.ox.ac.uk

Website:
http://www.balliol.ox.ac.uk/library

Enquiries:
Enquiries to: Librarian
Direct tel: 01865 277770

Founded:
1263

Organisation type and purpose:
College of University of Oxford

Subject coverage:
Information relating to collections.

Museum or gallery collection, archive, or library special collection:
Archives
Early printed books
Mediaeval manuscripts
Modern manuscripts
Special collections relating to history of Balliol and to former members

Non-library collection catalogue:
All or part available online, in-house and in print

Library catalogue:
All or part available online and in-house

Printed publications:
Catalogue of Jowett Papers

Microform publications:
Mediaeval manuscripts available from World Microfilms

Access to staff:
Contact by letter, by e-mail and via website.
Appointment necessary.
Hours: Mon to Fri, 0900 to 1700

BALTIC EXCHANGE

38 St Mary Axe, London, EC3A 8BH

Tel: 020 7623 5501
Fax: 020 7369 1622
E-mail: enquiries@baltic exchange.co.uk

Website:
http://www.balticexchange.com
General information on the Baltic Exchange; specific market information for members only.

Enquiries:
Enquiries to: Chief Executive
Other contacts: Development Manager for membership, marketing, press and PR.

Founded:
1900

Organisation type and purpose:
International organisation, professional body, trade association, membership association (membership is by subscription), present number of members: 700 corporate.
Shipping Exchange.
To match bulk ships and bulk cargoes, and to buy and sell bulk vessels.

Subject coverage:
Shipping, including chartering, freight rates, sale and purchase of ships.

Trade and statistical information:
Four daily bulk shipping indices and daily market reports.

Printed publications:
Shipping (magazine, 6 times a year)

Access to staff:
Contact by letter, by telephone, by fax, by e-mail and via website. Appointment necessary.
Hours: Mon to Fri, 0900 to 1700

BANGOR UNIVERSITY – ARCHIVES DEPARTMENT

Bangor, Gwynedd, LL57 2DG, Cymru

Tel: 01248 382966
Fax: 01248 382979
E-mail: e.w.thomas@bangor.ac.uk

Website:
http://www.archiveshub.ac.uk
http://www.bangor.ac.uk/is/library/archives.html

Enquiries:
Enquiries to: Archivist

Founded:
1884

Organisation type and purpose:
University library.
Archives Department within University Library.

Subject coverage:
University of Wales, Bangor; North Wales – history, people, topography; estate and family papers from counties of Anglesey, Caernarfon, Flint, Denbigh and Merioneth. Subject areas include: literary, historical and antiquarian manuscripts; industrial and business enterprises records e.g. mines and quarries; records of religious and educational bodies; records of ownership of land and property; personal and family archives; farming and agricultural records; records of a political nature; genealogical records; records of plantations in Jamaica and the West Indies; hunting records.

Non-library collection catalogue:
All or part available in-house

Library catalogue:
All or part available online

Access to staff:
Contact by letter, by telephone, by fax, by e-mail and in person
Hours: Mon to Fri, 0900 to 1300 and 1400 to 1700

BANGOR UNIVERSITY – LIBRARY AND ARCHIVE SERVICE

Acronym or abbreviation: UWB

College Road, Bangor, Gwynedd, LL57 2DG

Tel: 01248 382981
Fax: 01248 382979
E-mail: library@bangor.ac.uk

Website:
http://www.bangor.ac.uk/library

Enquiries:
Enquiries to: Librarian
Direct tel: 01248 383772
Direct e-mail: g.griffiths@bangor.ac.uk
Other contacts: Library Secretary for departmental secretary.

Formerly called:
Bangor University College of North Wales Library (year of change 1997)

Organisation type and purpose:
University library.

Subject coverage:
Accountancy, banking, finance, administration and social policy, environmental planning, leisure and tourism, communication and media studies; agriculture and forest studies, biological sciences, chemistry; education, ITT – primary and secondary; electronic engineering and computing systems; English and linguistics; health and physical education; health and midwifery, radiography; history, Welsh history, archaeology; mathematics; modern languages (French, German, Spanish, Russian, Italian); music; ocean studies; psychology; sociology, social policy, criminology; theology and religious studies; Welsh and Celtic language, literature and traditions.

Museum or gallery collection, archive, or library special collection:
Archive of Welsh Music
Bangor Cathedral Library (on deposit)
Frank Brangwyn Collection
G S Evans Collection of botanical materials
Local (North Wales) estate records
Welsh material (particularly historical, religious, literary; printed and manuscript)

Non-library collection catalogue:
All or part available in-house

Access to staff:
Contact by letter, by fax, by e-mail and via website. Appointment necessary.
Hours: Hours vary from library to library, please phone or see web pages

Access to building, collection or gallery:
No prior appointment required

Other addresses:
Adeilad Deiniol Library
   University of Wales, Bangor, Adeilad Deiniol, Deiniol Road, Bangor, Gwynedd, LL57 2UX; tel: 01248 382963; fax: 01248 383826; e-mail: library@bangor.ac.uk
Dean Street Library (School of Electronics)
   University of Wales, Bangor, Dean Street, Bangor, Gwynedd, LL57 1UT; tel: 01248 382986; e-mail: library@bangor.ac.uk
Fron Heulog Library (School of Healthcare Sciences)
   University of Wales, Bangor, Ffriddoedd Road, Bangor, Gwynedd, LL57 2EF; tel: 01248 383131; e-mail: library@bangor.ac.uk
Normal Site Library
   University of Wales, Bangor, Ffordd Caergybi, Bangor, Gwynedd, LL57 2PX; tel: 01248 383048; fax: 01248 383976; e-mail: library@bangor.ac.uk
Wolfson Library (School of Ocean Sciences)
   School of Ocean Sciences, University of Wales, Bangor, Askew Street, Menai Bridge, Anglesey, LL59 5EY; tel: 01248 382985; e-mail: library@bangor.ac.uk
Wrexham Maelor Library (School of Healthcare Sciences)
   School of Nursing and Midwifery Studies, Archimedes Centre, Technology Park, Wrexham, Clwyd, LL13 7YP; tel: 01978 316370; fax: 01978 311154; e-mail: library@bangor.ac.uk

BANK OF ENGLAND

Information Centre, Threadneedle Street, London, EC2R 8AH

Tel: 020 7601 4715
Fax: 020 7601 4356
E-mail: informationcentre@bankofengland.co.uk

Website:
http://www.bankofengland.co.uk
General information about the Bank, press releases, publications.

Enquiries:
Enquiries to: Information Centre Manager

Founded:
1694

Organisation type and purpose:
Central bank.

Subject coverage:
UK and overseas banking and financial economics, history of British banking, banking and monetary statistical data, central banking.

Museum or gallery collection, archive, or library special collection:
19th-century government reports on banking and finance
Acts of Parliament from 1693
Collections include United Kingdom 17th- to 19th-century economic tracts
Sets include:
The Course of the Exchange (Castaing, Shergold, Lutyens and Wetenhall) from 1698 to 1898

Library catalogue:
All or part available in-house

Printed publications:
Bank of England Discussion Papers
Bank of England Inflation Report
Bank of England Quarterly Bulletin
Bank of England Annual Report
Financial Stability Review
Bank of England Working Paper Series
Order printed publications from: Publications Group, Bank of England, Threadneedle Street, London, EC2R 8AH; tel: 020 7601 4886

Electronic and video publications:
Some data available on website

Publications list:
Available online

Access to staff:
Appointment necessary.
Hours: Mon to Fri, 0900 to 1730

BANKRUPTCY ASSOCIATION

4 Johnson Close, Abraham Heights, Lancaster, LA1 5EU

Tel: 01539 469474
E-mail: mcqueen314@btinternet.com

Website:
http://www.theba.org.uk

Enquiries:
Enquiries to: Founder

Founded:
1983

Formerly called:
Association of Bankrupts (year of change 1991); Bankruptcy Association of Great Britain and Ireland (year of change 2000)

Organisation type and purpose:
Membership association (membership is by subscription).
To provide advice and support to those who experience bankruptcy and its long-term effects.

Subject coverage:
Insolvency in general, but particularly personal bankruptcy, debt, liquidation and reform of insolvency law.

Printed publications:
Newsletter (quarterly)
Bankruptcy Explained (£14.95)
Boom to Bust: The Great 1990s Slump (£12.95)
How to Settle Debts with Creditors (£9.95)
Saving the Family Home in Bankruptcy (£14.95)
Choosing the Correct Legal Format for Running a Business (£14.95)

Publications list:
Available online and in print

Access to staff:
Contact by letter, by telephone, by e-mail and via website. Appointment necessary. Access for members only.
Special comments: Helpline for general enquiries: Mon to Fri, 1230 to 1700

BAPTIST HISTORICAL SOCIETY

Acronym or abbreviation: BHS

Baptist House, PO Box 44, 129 Broadway, Didcot, Oxfordshire, OX11 8RT

Tel: 01235 517700
Fax: 01235 517715
E-mail: stephen.bhs@dsl.pipex.com

Website:
http://www.baptisthistory.org.uk

Enquiries:
Enquiries to: Honorary Secretary

Founded:
1908

Organisation type and purpose:
Learned society (membership is by subscription), present number of members: 550, registered charity (charity number 271367).
Study and recording of Baptist Church history and theology.

Subject coverage:
Baptist Church history and theology, including original church records and published bibliographies.

Printed publications:
Baptist Quarterly (journal, quarterly)

Publications list:
Available online and in print

Access to staff:
Contact by letter, by e-mail and via website
Hours: Mon to Fri, 0900 to 1700

Also at:
Angus Library
   Regents Park College, Oxford, OX1 2LB; tel: 01865 288120; e-mail: angus.library@regents.ox.ac.uk
Honorary Secretary
   Baptist Historical Society, 60 Strathmore Avenue, Hitchin, Hertfordshire, SG5 1ST; tel: 01462 431816; e-mail: stephen.bhs@dsl.pipex.com

BAPTIST UNION OF SCOTLAND

14 Aytoun Road, Glasgow, G41 5RT

Tel: 0141 423 6169
Fax: 0141 424 1422
E-mail: admin@scottishbaptist.org.uk

Website:
http://www.scottishbaptist.org.uk

Enquiries:
Enquiries to: General Director
Other contacts: Communications Coordinator

Founded:
1869

Organisation type and purpose:
Voluntary organisation, registered charity (charity number SC004960).
Church organisation.

Subject coverage:
Baptist Church life and organisation; current ministerial conditions and persons; denominational budget, policies, programmes and development.

Trade and statistical information:
Statistics of Baptist Churches in Scotland.

Printed publications:
Scottish Baptist Yearbook (directory of members' churches and reports of committees)

Publications list:
Available in print

Access to staff:
Contact by letter, by telephone, by fax and by e-mail. Appointment necessary.
Hours: Variable

Access to building, collection or gallery:
Hours: Mon to Thu, 0900 to 1600; Fri, 0900 to 1500
Special comments: Closed weekends and public holidays

Access for disabled people:
Hours: Mon to Thu, 0900 to 1600; Fri, 0900 to 1500
Special comments: Closed weekends and public holidays

Affiliated to:
Baptist World Alliance
European Baptist Federation
Evangelical Alliance
Fellowship of British Baptists

BAR ASSOCIATION FOR COMMERCE, FINANCE AND INDUSTRY

Acronym or abbreviation: BACFI

PO Box 4352, Edlesborough, Dunstable, Bedfordshire, LU6 9EF

Tel: 01525 222244
E-mail: secretary@bacfi.org

Website:
http://www.bacfi.org

Enquiries:
Enquiries to: Secretary

Founded:
1965

continued overleaf

Created by the merger of:
BACFI and Employed & Non Practising Bar
Association (ENPBA) (year of change 2004)

Organisation type and purpose:
Membership association (membership is by
subscription).

Subject coverage:
Professional interests of barristers working in-
house or outside chambers. It runs training
seminars and provides networking events for
members and represents their views on the Bar
Council and with the Bar Standards Board.

**Museum or gallery collection, archive, or library
special collection:**
Archive of BACFI responses to Bar Council and
Bar Standards Board consultations and
Professional Issues information on http://
www.bacfi.org

Access to staff:
Contact by letter, by telephone, by e-mail and via
website

BARBICAN LIBRARY

Barbican Centre, Silk Street, London, EC2Y 8DS

Tel: 020 7638 0569
Fax: 020 7638 2249
E-mail: barbicanlib@cityoflondon.gov.uk

Website:
http://www.cityoflondon.gov.uk/barbicanlibrary
Description of services, events and activities.
http://www.musicpreserved.org
Music Preserved.

Enquiries:
Enquiries to: Librarian

Founded:
1982

Organisation type and purpose:
Local government body, public library.

Subject coverage:
General lending library collection with strengths in
London history, fine and performing arts,
including art history, painting, sculpture, ceramics,
photography, cinema, film and theatre, music and
finance.

Services for disabled people:
CCTV magnifier, large and trackerball keyboards,
induction loops, Jaws and ZoomText available on
some PCs.

**Museum or gallery collection, archive, or library
special collection:**
Crime fiction collection
Libraries of the Gilbert and Sullivan Society
Music Preserved archive studio of live
performance recordings (audio and video) not
available commercially, includes interviews with
artists
The Society of Technical Analysts

Non-library collection catalogue:
All or part available online and in-house

Library catalogue:
All or part available online and in-house

Access to staff:
Contact by letter, by telephone, by fax, by e-mail
and in person. Appointment necessary.
Hours: Mon and Wed, 0930 to 1730; Tue and Thu,
0930 to 1930; Fri, 0930 to 1400; Sat, 0930 to 1600

Access to building, collection or gallery:
No prior appointment required

Access for disabled people:
Parking provided, level entry, access to all public
areas
Special comments: Stairlift to Music Library.

Branch libraries:
City of London Libraries, Archives and Guildhall
Art Gallery Dept
Guildhall Library, Aldermanbury, London; tel:
020 7382 1852

Parent body:
City of London
tel: 020 7332 1852

BARBOUR ENVIRONMENT, HEALTH & SAFETY

Building B, Kingswood, Kings Ride, Ascot,
Berkshire, SL5 8AJ

Tel: 0845 300 0241
Fax: 01344 884845
E-mail: barbour-marketing@ubm.com

Website:
http://www.barbour-ehs.com
Health, safety and environment information on
legislation and regulations.

Enquiries:
Enquiries to: Marketing Manager
Direct tel: 01344 899240

Founded:
1947

Organisation type and purpose:
Publishing house.
Information providers.

Subject coverage:
A leading UK supplier of specialist information
services to professionals working in the health,
safety and environment sectors. Its services are
used across a variety of commercial and public
organisations in the UK and Ireland and are
designed to help improve decision making,
understanding of complex information areas,
reduction of risks and management of projects.

Information services:
Barbour Environment, Health & Safety Online
Information Service

Non-library collection catalogue:
All or part available online

Library catalogue:
All or part available online and in print

Access to staff:
Contact by letter, by telephone, by fax, by e-mail
and via website
Hours: Mon to Fri, 0900 to 1700

Access to building, collection or gallery:
Hours: Mon to Fri, 0900 to 1700

Access for disabled people:
Accessible
Hours: Mon to Fri, 0900 to 1700

Branch of:
United Business Media Plc
website: http://www.ubm.com

Links with:
Barbour ABI
The Chapter House, Hinderton Hall Estate,
Neston, Cheshire, CH64 7UX; tel: 0151 353 3500;
fax: 0151 353 3501; e-mail: info@barbour-abi
.com; website: http://www.barbour-abi.com

BAREMA

Formal name: Trade Association for Anaesthetic &
Respiratory Equipment

The Stables, Sugworth Lane, Radley, Oxon., OX14
2HX

Tel: 01865 736393
Fax: 01865 736393
E-mail: barema@btinternet.com

Website:
http://barema.org.uk
Separate members' and visitors' sections; list of
members, find a supplier, exhibitions, code of
practice.

Enquiries:
Enquiries to: Secretary

Organisation type and purpose:
Trade association for anaesthetic & respiratory
equipment.
To promote co-operation between registered
companies engaged in the manufacture,
distribution and servicing of anaesthetic and
respiratory equipment and generally to further the
individual and collective interests of these
companies; to encourage and expand the use of
safe and effective products in health care markets;
to create an environment whereby the innovation
of technically advanced products can be
developed; to work in partnership with health care
professionals to influence the regulatory
environment by providing responsible input; to
strive to improve patient safety, through active
participation in the preparation and promotion of
Technical Safety Standards and procedures for
anaesthetic, respiratory and associated devices; to
maintain an ongoing, close relationship with the
medical profession through mutual participation
in matters leading to enhancement of the
knowledge base of all and consequent
improvement of devices, procedures and in patient
health and safety.

Access to staff:
Contact by letter, by telephone, by fax and by e-
mail

BARING FOUNDATION

60 London Wall, London, EC2M 5TQ

Tel: 020 7767 1348
Fax: 020 7767 7121
E-mail: baring.foundation@uk.ing.com

Website:
http://www.baringfoundation.org.uk

Enquiries:
Enquiries to: Administration Officer

Founded:
1969

Organisation type and purpose:
Registered charity (charity number 258583).
Grant-making charity.

Subject coverage:
Three grant programmes: Strengthening the
Voluntary Sector Independence programme; Arts
programme; International Development
programme

Printed publications:
A full list of publications can be found on the
website http://www.baringfoundation.org.uk/
publications.htm or requested by e-mail

Publications list:
Available online and in print

Access to staff:
Contact by letter, by telephone, by fax, by e-mail
and via website
Hours: Mon to Fri, 0900 to 1700

Access for disabled people:
Access to all public areas, toilet facilities

BARKING AND DAGENHAM ADULT & COMMUNITY SERVICES DEPARTMENT

Central Library, Barking, Essex, IG11 8DQ

Tel: 020 8724 8723
Fax: 020 8724 8733
E-mail: reference@lbbd.gov.uk

Website:
http://www.lbbd.gov.uk/4-libraries/lib-menu.html

Enquiries:
Enquiries to: Librarian

Founded:
1888

Organisation type and purpose:
Local government body, public library.

Subject coverage:
Printing, journalism, publishing and newspapers, local history.
Fiction (Joint Fiction Reserve) B-BAI.

Museum or gallery collection, archive, or library special collection:
Fanshawe manuscripts and portraits

Non-library collection catalogue:
All or part available online and in-house

Library catalogue:
All or part available online and in-house

Publications list:
Available online and in print

Access to staff:
Contact by letter, by telephone, by fax, by e-mail, in person and via website. Appointment necessary.
Hours: Barking Library: Mon to Thu, 0900 to 2130; Fri, 0900 to 1900; Sat, 0900 to 1700; Sun, 1000 to 1600

Access to building, collection or gallery:
No prior appointment required

Access for disabled people:
Access to all public areas

Also at:
Local History Collection housed at Local Studies Centre, Valence House Museum
Becontree Avenue, Dagenham, Essex, RM8 3HT; tel: 020 8270 6896
Valence Library
Becontree Avenue, Dagenham, Essex, RM8 3HT; tel: 020 8270 6896

Parent body:
London Borough of Barking and Dagenham

BARNABAS TRUST

Freepost TN2186, Tonbridge, Kent, TN11 9BR

Tel: 01732 366766
Fax: 01732 366767
E-mail: headoffice@barnabas.org.uk

Website:
http://www.barnabas.org.uk

Enquiries:
Enquiries to: Chief Executive

Founded:
1978

Formerly called:
Belgrave Trust (year of change 1978)

Organisation type and purpose:
Registered charity (charity number 276346).

Subject coverage:
Holiday centres for groups of young people including church, secular and school.

Access to staff:
Contact by letter, by telephone, by fax, by e-mail and via website. Appointment necessary.
Hours: Mon to Fri, 0900 to 1700

BARNARDO'S

Tanners Lane, Barkingside, Ilford, Essex, IG6 1QG

Tel: 020 8550 8822
Fax: 020 8551 6870

Website:
http://www.barnardos.co.uk

Enquiries:
Enquiries to: Information Officer
Direct tel: 020 8498 7556
Direct e-mail: barninfo@compuserve.com
Other contacts: Librarian

Founded:
1867

Formerly called:
Dr Barnardo's (year of change 1988)

Organisation type and purpose:
Voluntary organisation, registered charity (charity number 216250).
Child care organisation.
To help the most vulnerable children and young people transform their lives and fulfil their potential.

Subject coverage:
Social welfare policy and practice. Child care, social services with families, neighbourhoods and communities.

Museum or gallery collection, archive, or library special collection:
Archives, dating from 1860s (held by Liverpool University, restricted access)
Films, dating from 1920s
History of Barnardo's
Photographs, dating from 1874 (estimated 500,000)

Printed publications:
Annual Review
Barnardo's Today (twice a year)
Library Bulletin (monthly)
Order printed publications from: Child Care Publications
Barnardo's Trading Estate, Paycocke Road, Basildon, Essex, SS14 3DR, tel: 01268 520224, fax: 01268 284804

Electronic and video publications:
Videos (large number)

Publications list:
Available in print

Access to staff:
Appointment necessary.
Hours: Mon to Fri, 0930 to 1630

Access for disabled people:
Parking provided, level entry, toilet facilities

BARNET AND DISTRICT LOCAL HISTORY SOCIETY

Barnet Museum, 31 Wood Street, Barnet, Hertfordshire, EN5 4BE

Tel: 020 8440 8066

Website:
http://www.barnetmuseum.co.uk

Enquiries:
Enquiries to: Honorary Secretary

Founded:
1927

Organisation type and purpose:
Learned society, voluntary organisation, museum.

Subject coverage:
Local history of Barnet and District, historical and archaeological records.

Museum or gallery collection, archive, or library special collection:
Books, documents, maps, costumes, exhibitions and artefacts relating to history of Barnet

Library catalogue:
All or part available in-house

Printed publications:
Bulletins (list available)
Educational materials
Newsletter (occasional)
A range of titles on local history including:
800 years of Barnet Market (Cobben J L and Willcocks D, 1999, £5)
Barnet and District Local History
Barnet at War (Reboul P and Heathfield J, £7.99 plus £1 p&p)
Historic Barnet, Gelder W
Monumental Inscriptions in Chipping Barnet Church (50p)
Monumental Inscriptions in East Barnet Church (50p)
The Book of Totteridge (Griffiths D, £10 plus 80p p&p)

Publications list:
Available in print

Access to staff:
Contact by letter and in person
Hours: Tue, Wed, Thu, 1430 to 1630; Sat, 1030 to 1230 and 1400 to 1600
Special comments: Donations appreciated

Affiliated to:
Hertfordshire Association for Local History
London and Middlesex Archaeological Society

BARNET LIBRARIES, MUSEUMS AND LOCAL STUDIES

Building 4, North London Business Park, Oakleigh Road South, London, N11 1NP

Tel: 020 8359 7774
E-mail: hendon.library@barnet.gov.uk

Website:
http://www.barnet.gov.uk/libraries
General description of services.
http://www.libraries.barnet.gov.uk
Library catalogue.

Enquiries:
Enquiries to: Reference Librarian, Hendon Library
Direct tel: 020 8359 2628
Direct fax: 020 8359 2885
Direct e-mail: hendon.library@barnet.gov.uk
Other contacts: Information and Heritage Manager for borough-wide reference and information services.

Founded:
1965

Organisation type and purpose:
Local government body, public library.

Subject coverage:
General, local studies.

Museum or gallery collection, archive, or library special collection:
Local history including the
C O Banks Collection on Finchley

Non-library collection catalogue:
All or part available online

Library catalogue:
All or part available in-house

Printed publications:
Various local history and local information publications

Publications list:
Available in print

Access to staff:
Contact by letter, by telephone, by fax, by e-mail and via website. Appointment necessary.
Hours: Mon to Fri, 0900 to 1700

BARNET LOCAL STUDIES & ARCHIVES CENTRE

Formal name: London Borough of Barnet Local Studies and Archives Centre

80 Daws Lane, London, NW7 4SL

Tel: 020 8359 3960
E-mail: library.archives@barnet.gov.uk

Website:
www.barnet.gov.uk/archives
Contact details and location, brief list of holdings, link to useful resources, entry to Barnet Image database.

Enquiries:
Enquiries to: Local Studies Manager
Other contacts: Heritage Officer; Local Studies Assistant

Founded:
1974

Organisation type and purpose:
Local government body.

continued overleaf

Subject coverage:
Local history.

Information services:
Public computers with internet access.

Special visitor services:
Arranged individually.

Education services:
Relevant work undertaken with local primary, secondary and further education establishments.

Services for disabled people:
Disabled access to all public facilities.

Museum or gallery collection, archive, or library special collection:
Local reference collections
Local archive/MSS collections
Photographic and maps collections

Non-library collection catalogue:
All or part available online and in-house

Library catalogue:
All or part available online and in-house

Access to staff:
Contact by letter, by telephone, by e-mail and in person. Appointment necessary.
Hours: Tue, Wed, Fri, 0930 to 1630; Thu, 1300 to 1900; first and third Sat of each month, 0930 to 1630

Access to building, collection or gallery:
Prior appointment required
Special comments: Fully accessible, sited on ground floor.

Access for disabled people:
Low level ramp to entry; all public areas on ground floor and accessible

BARNETT RESEARCH CENTRE AT TOYNBEE HALL

Formal name: Toynbee Hall

28 Commercial Street, London, E1 6LS

Tel: 020 7392 2939
Fax: 020 7377 5964
E-mail: info@toynbeehall.org.uk

Website:
http://www.toynbeehall.org.uk
History of organisation; description of services; details of events; news page; message board.

Enquiries:
Enquiries to: Librarian/Archivist
Direct tel: 020 7392 2939
Direct e-mail: barnettresearchcentre@toynbeehall
.org.uk

Founded:
1884

Organisation type and purpose:
Voluntary organisation.

Museum or gallery collection, archive, or library special collection:
Specialist library on the history of social policy and welfare, archives of Toynbee Hall

Non-library collection catalogue:
All or part available online and in-house

Library catalogue:
All or part available in-house

Printed publications:
Annual Report
Magazine (2 times a year)
The Toynbee Journal (onnline)

Electronic and video publications:
Photographs, oral history collection

Access to staff:
Contact by letter, by telephone, by e-mail, in person and via website. Appointment necessary.
Hours: Tue to Thu, 0930 to 1630

Access to building, collection or gallery:
No appointment required, but we welcome enquiries in advance of visits

BARNSLEY ARCHIVE AND LOCAL STUDIES DEPARTMENT

Central Library, Shambles Street, Barnsley, South Yorkshire, S70 2JF

Tel: 01226 773950
Fax: 01226 773955
E-mail: archives@barnsley.gov.uk

Website:
http://www.barnsley.gov.uk/archives

Enquiries:
Enquiries to: Archives and Local Studies Officer
Other contacts: Local Studies Librarian (for local studies enquiries)

Organisation type and purpose:
Local government body.

Subject coverage:
Relating to Barnsley Metropolitan Borough Council.

Museum or gallery collection, archive, or library special collection:
Census enumeration returns (microfilm or microfiche)
IGI for northern counties of England and Ireland
GRO Index for births, marriages and deaths
Local newspapers (mainly on microfilm)
Local publications such as annual reports and newsletters of organisations, church magazines, council minutes
Parish register copies (printed or microfilm)
Deeds, wills, estate papers
Local photographs and maps

Non-library collection catalogue:
All or part available online, in-house and in print

Library catalogue:
All or part available in-house

Printed publications:
The Family History Handbook (£7.50)
Family History Starter Pack (£5.00)

Publications list:
Available online and in print

Access to staff:
Contact by letter, by telephone, by fax, by e-mail, in person and via website

Access to building, collection or gallery:
Hours: Mon, 0930 to 1300 and 1400 to 1700; Tue, Thu and Fri, 0930 to 1300 and 1400 to 1730; Wed, 0930 to 1300 and 1400 to 1800; Sat, 0930 to 1300

BARNSLEY CHAMBER OF COMMERCE AND INDUSTRY

Acronym or abbreviation: BCCI

Business Innovation Centre, Innovation Way, Wilthorpe, Barnsley, South Yorkshire, S75 1JL

Tel: 01226 217770
Fax: 01226 215729
E-mail: info@barnsleychamber.co.uk

Enquiries:
Enquiries to: Chief Executive

Founded:
1882

Organisation type and purpose:
Membership association (membership is by subscription), present number of members: 800, service industry.
Chamber of Commerce.

Subject coverage:
Policy, representation, export service, debt recovery, general business advice.

Trade and statistical information:
Trade surveys.

Publications list:
Available in print

Access to staff:
Contact by letter, by telephone, by fax, by e-mail and in person

Hours: Mon to Fri, 0900 to 1700

Access for disabled people:
Parking provided, ramped entry, level entry, toilet facilities

BARNSLEY METROPOLITAN BOROUGH COUNCIL

Town Hall, Barnsley, South Yorkshire, S70 2TA

Tel: 01226 770770
Fax: 01226 773099
E-mail: townhall@barnsley.gov.uk

Website:
http://www.barnsley.gov.uk
Pages on economic development, tourism, newsline, events, best value.

Enquiries:
Enquiries to: Chief Executive

Founded:
1974

Organisation type and purpose:
Local government body.

Subject coverage:
Local government services provided to 227,000 citizens covering education, housing, social services, planning, highways, economic development and training.

Printed publications:
Order printed publications from: Public Relations officer
at the same address, tel: 01226 773400, fax: 01226 773399

Access to staff:
Contact by letter, by telephone, by fax, by e-mail, in person and via website
Hours: Mon to Fri, 0900 to 1700

Access for disabled people:
Ramped entry

BARNSLEY METROPOLITAN BOROUGH LIBRARY SERVICES

Central Library, Shambles Street, Barnsley, South Yorkshire, S70 2JF

Tel: 01226 773930
Fax: 01226 773955
E-mail: barnsleylibraryenquiries@barnsley.gov.uk

Website:
http://www.barnsley.gov.uk/libraries

Enquiries:
Enquiries to: Chief Librarian
Direct tel: 01226 773926

Organisation type and purpose:
Public library.

Subject coverage:
General lending and information; multimedia; local studies and archives (historical and other information on the Barnsley Metropolitan District).

Museum or gallery collection, archive, or library special collection:
Barnsley Archive Collection
Barnsley Local History Collection
Dransfield Collection (local history of Penistone)

Library catalogue:
All or part available online

Access to staff:
Contact by letter, by telephone, by fax, by e-mail, in person and via website
Hours: Mon and Wed, 0930 to 1900; Tues, Thurs and Fri, 0930 to 1730; Sat, 0930 to 1600 for Central Library
Special comments: Hours for specific departments vary.

Access for disabled people:
Level entry, access to all public areas, toilet facilities

Parent body:
Barnsley Metropolitan Borough Council

BARWICK-IN-ELMET HISTORICAL SOCIETY

G. Thornton (Chairman), 8 Richmondfield Lane, Barwick-in-Elmet, Leeds, LS15 4EZ

Website:
http://www.barwickinelmethistoricalsociety.com
The society's site is devoted to the publication of the history of the Yorkshire parish of Barwick-in-Elmet.

Enquiries:
Enquiries to: Secretary
Direct tel: 01132 867341
Direct e-mail: gday63@googlemail.com

Founded:
1984

Organisation type and purpose:
Membership assocation, current mems: over 55. To record, research and publish on the history of this Yorkshire parish.

Museum or gallery collection, archive, or library special collection:
The society has a resource centre in Barwick-in-Elmet containing a wide range of documents and photographs, mostly secondary copies.

Non-library collection catalogue:
All or part available in-house

Printed publications:
The Barwicker (quarterly journal)
Books:
Bygone Barwick
Pen Sketches of Barwick-in-Elmet
The Maypole Stayed Up
A Greater Wonder: A History of Methodism in the village
Barwick School: Education in a Yorkshire Village
Map of Barwick-in-Elmet (2000)
Brief History (2000)
Photographs of the Parish of Barwick-in-Elmet in Bygone Days.
Order printed publications from: e-mail: editor
.barwicker@googlemail.com

Publications list:
Available online

Access to staff:
Contact by letter, by telephone, by e-mail and via website

BASEC

Formal name: British Approvals Service for Cables

23 Presley Way, Crownhill, Milton Keynes, Buckinghamshire, MK8 0ES

Tel: 01908 267300
Fax: 01908 267255
E-mail: mail@basec.org.uk

Website:
http://www.basec.org.uk
Cable certification.
http://www.env-basec.org.uk
Environmental certification.

Enquiries:
Enquiries to: Chief Executive

Founded:
1971

Formerly called:
British Approvals Service for Electric Cables (BASEC)

Organisation type and purpose:
Service industry.
Certification Body.

Subject coverage:
ISO 9000 certification, cable, ancillary product, instruments, installation, rod rolling, stockists; quality certification; product certification for

cables; UK cable market certificate holders; new product assessment (cables). Environmental certification to ISO 14001 and/or EMAS. Certification of Health and Safety management systems to OHSAS 18001.

Museum or gallery collection, archive, or library special collection:
Worldwide ISO 9000 cable manufacturers listings

Printed publications:
List of Certificate Holders for Cables (certified product plus ISO 9000)

Access to staff:
Contact by letter, by telephone, by fax, by e-mail and via website
Hours: Mon to Thu, 0900 to 1700; Fri, 0900 to 1300

BASIC SKILLS AGENCY AT NIACE

Acronym or abbreviation: BSA at NIACE

21 DeMontfort Street, Leicester, LE1 7GE

Tel: 0116 204 4200
Fax: 0116 285 4515
E-mail: enquiries@niace.org.uk

Website:
http://archive.basic-skills.co.uk/aboutus

Enquiries:
Enquiries to: Information Officer
Other contacts: Director (Literacy, Language and Numeracy & Workplace)

Founded:
1975

Formerly called:
ALBSU; Basic Skills Agency (year of change 2008)

Organisation type and purpose:
The BSA became an independent charity with government support in 1990. The Agency's work was critical for developing a strategy for literacy, language and numeracy and a range of work in the schools sector. In the light of changing circumstances the BSA's board sought an effective partner to take forward its work with adults and young people. Following competition, NIACE, working with Tribal, was successful in offering a way forward. The BSA's work in Wales will be assimilated into the Welsh Assembly Government in line with Welsh Assembly policy.

Subject coverage:
Basic literacy (including English for speakers of other languages, ESOL), numeracy and related basic skills.

Trade and statistical information:
Data on the scale of need in England and Wales.

Printed publications:
Approximately 250 titles including:
Basic Skills Research
Basic Skills Resources, posters, books, teaching-packs
Magazine (quarterly, free)
Order printed publications from: Basic Skills Agency Prolog-UK, PO Box 5050, Sherwood Park, Annesly, Nottingham, NG15 0DL

Electronic and video publications:
Video and audio cassettes, computer software

Publications list:
Available online and in print

Access to staff:
Contact by letter, by telephone, by fax, by e-mail and via website
Hours: Mon to Fri, 0900 to 1730

Constituent part of:
NIACE
website: http://www.niace.org.uk

Links with:
Basic Skills Cymru
website: http://www.basic-skills-wales.org/bsastrategy/en/home/index.cfm
Tribal
website: http://www.tribalgroup.co.uk

BASILDON DISTRICT COUNCIL

The Basildon Centre, St Martin's Square, Basildon, Essex, SS14 1DL

Tel: 01268 533333
Fax: 01268 294350

Website:
http://www.basildondistrict.com

Enquiries:
Enquiries to: Public Relations Manager
Direct tel: 01268 294157
Direct fax: 01268 294148
Direct e-mail: marketingcommunications@basildon.gov.uk

Organisation type and purpose:
Local government body.

Subject coverage:
Detailed information about Basildon Council services and policies. General information about Basildon. The District Council is responsible for providing a wide range of services in a thriving district of 165,000 people. It is helping lead a significant set of partnerships to regenerate the area, the most important examples being: Community Safety, Thames Gateway, South Essex, and Gardener's Lane South.

Printed publications:
District Diary (council newspaper)
Miscellaneous information leaflets and lists
Press Releases

Access to staff:
Contact by letter, by telephone, by fax and by e-mail
Hours: Mon to Fri, 0900 to 1715

BASINGSTOKE AND DEANE BOROUGH COUNCIL

Civic Offices, London Road, Basingstoke, Hampshire, RG21 4AJ

Tel: 01256 844844
Fax: 01256 844707
E-mail: information@basingstoke.gov.uk

Website:
http://www.basingstoke.gov.uk
General information about the council, tourism and leisure, business information, local services, what's going on?

Enquiries:
Enquiries to: Head of Corporate Communications
Direct tel: 01256 845485
Direct e-mail: m.reid@basingstoke.gov.uk

Founded:
1974

Organisation type and purpose:
Local government body.

Subject coverage:
Local government including: environmental health, leisure, events, housing needs, planning, development, local plans, policy and committees, business development.

Printed publications:
General information leaflets on many subjects

Access to staff:
Contact by letter, by telephone, by fax, by e-mail, in person and via website
Hours: Mon to Thu, 0830 to 1700; Fri, 0830 to 1630

Access for disabled people:
Parking provided, ramped entry, level entry, toilet facilities

BASINGSTOKE COLLEGE OF TECHNOLOGY

Acronym or abbreviation: BCOT

Worting Road, Basingstoke, Hampshire, RG21 8TN

Tel: 01256 354141
Fax: 01256 306444

continued overleaf

E-mail: information@bcot.ac.uk

Website:
http://www.bcot.ac.uk

Enquiries:
Enquiries to: Learning Resources Manager
Direct tel: 01256 306383
Direct e-mail: learning.resources@bcot.ac.uk

Organisation type and purpose:
College of further education.

Subject coverage:
General library to support GCSE, A-levels, NVQs, BTEC, some HND and HNC; engineering; building; business studies.

Library catalogue:
All or part available online

Access to staff:
Contact by letter, by telephone, by fax, by e-mail and in person
Hours: Term time: Mon, 0845 to 1700; Tue to Thu, 0845 to 1900; Fri, 0845 to 1630; Sat closed
Vacations: Mon to Fri, 0845 to 1700; Sat closed
Special comments: Visitors need to make an appointment in advance for security arrangments.

Links with:
University of Portsmouth
   Winston Churchill Avenue, Portsmouth, Hampshire, PO1 2UP
University of Winchester

BASKETMAKERS' ASSOCIATION

64 Lakes Lane, Newport Pagnell, Milton Keynes, MK16 8HR

Tel: 0845 201 1936
E-mail: honsec@basketassoc.org

Website:
http://www.basketassoc.org
General information, membership details, sales and course details.

Founded:
1975

Organisation type and purpose:
Membership association (membership is by subscription), present number of members: 1,000–1,200.
To promote the craft of basketmaking and chair seating.

Subject coverage:
All forms of basketry; willow work, cane work, rush work, coil work; hedgerow basketry; chair seating; straw work; growth and preparation of materials; history, tools, books and equipment, courses list nationwide (send large sae to publications sales).

Printed publications:
Newsletter (quarterly, members only)
Basketwork Through the Ages (Bobart H H, reprinted by the Basketmakers Association)
An Introduction to the Art of Basketmaking (Okey T, 1911, classic reprinted by the BA)
The Basketmakers List, Wage Rates and Specifications at 1956 (reprinted by the BA)
Order printed publications from: Sales, Basketmakers Association
216 Walton Road, East Molesey, Surrey, KT8 0HR

Electronic and video publications:
How To Make Round Baskets (video)
How to Make Oval Willow Baskets with Cross Handles (video)
Lowestoft Trawl (documentary video)
Devon Maund (documentary video)
Willow Class (documentary video)
George Chambers making a Porthleven Lobster Pot (video)
Colin Manthorpe making a Quarter Aran Herring Basket (video)

Access to staff:
Contact by letter, by telephone, by fax and by e-mail
Hours: Mon to Fri, 0900 to 1700

BAT CONSERVATION TRUST

Acronym or abbreviation: BCT

15 Cloisters House, 8 Battersea Park Road, London, SW8 4BG

Tel: 0845 1300 228
Fax: 020 7627 2628
E-mail: enquiries@bats.org.uk

Website:
http://www.bats.org.uk
Information about bats and the Bat Conservation Trust.

Enquiries:
Enquiries to: Chief Executive

Founded:
1991

Organisation type and purpose:
National organisation, membership association (membership is by subscription), present number of members: 4,000, voluntary organisation, registered charity (charity number 1012361), training organisation, consultancy, research organisation.
BCT is the UK organisation solely devoted to the conservation of bats and their habitats through: conservation projects, research, supporting and educating people who find bats in their property, and encouraging appreciation of these animals.

Subject coverage:
Biology and conservation of bats.

Library catalogue:
All or part available in-house

Printed publications:
Bat News (newsletter, quarterly, free to BCT members)
Bats (leaflet, free with sae)

Publications list:
Available in print

Access to staff:
Contact by letter, by telephone, by fax, by e-mail and via website
Hours: Mon to Fri, 0900 to 1700

Umbrella group for:
over 90 voluntary bat groups in the UK

BATH AND NORTH EAST SOMERSET COUNCIL

Formal name: Bath and North East Somerset
Acronym or abbreviation: B&NES

Riverside, Temple Street, Keynsham, Somerset, BS31 1CA

Tel: 01225 477000
E-mail: communications_marketing@bathnes.gov.uk

Website:
http://www.bathnes.gov.uk
General Council information on Bath and North East Somerset Council and surrounding areas.

Enquiries:
Enquiries to: Information and Publications Officer
Direct tel: 01225 477413
Direct fax: 01225 477499
Other contacts: Communications & Marketing Manager

Founded:
1996

Formed from:
Avon County Council, Bath City Council, Wansdyke District Council (year of change 1996)

Organisation type and purpose:
Local government body.
Local authority.
To provide local services.

Subject coverage:
Education, environmental health, economic development, housing, libraries, planning, roads, social services and many others.

Printed publications:
Annual Reports (free)
Bath and Beyond (free)
Council News (free)
Your Guide to Council Services (free)
Performance Plan
Order printed publications from: Information and Publicity Officer, Bath and North East Somerset Council
Guildhall, High Street, Bath, Somerset, BA1 5AW, e-mail: juliet_williams@bathnes.gov.uk

Access to staff:
Contact by letter, by telephone, by fax, by e-mail and in person. Appointment necessary.
Hours: Mon to Thu, 0830 to 1700; Fri, 0830 to 1630

Access for disabled people:
Parking provided

Other addresses:
Guildhall
   High Street, Bath, BA1 5AW; tel: 01225 477000
The Hollies
   Midsomer, Wotton, BA3 2OP

BATH AND NORTH EAST SOMERSET RECORD OFFICE

Guildhall, High Street, Bath, BA1 5AW

Tel: 01225 477421
Fax: 01225 477439
E-mail: archives@bathnes.gov.uk

Website:
http://www.batharchives.co.uk
Introductory information, family history, house history and principal collections, leaflets and link to on-line catalogue.

Enquiries:
Enquiries to: Archivist

Formerly called:
Bath City Record Office (year of change 1996)

Organisation type and purpose:
Local government body.
Record office.

Subject coverage:
History of Bath and district.

Museum or gallery collection, archive, or library special collection:
Official records of the City of Bath from the 12th century
Records of local businesses, families and organisations
Collections of photographs, maps and plans

Non-library collection catalogue:
All or part available online and in-house

Access to staff:
Contact by letter, by telephone, by fax, by e-mail and in person
Hours: Tue to Thu, 0900 to 1300 and 1400 to 1700; Fri, 0900 to 1300 and 1400 to 1630

Access for disabled people:
By prior arrangement

BATH PRESERVATION TRUST

Acronym or abbreviation: BPT

No 1 Royal Crescent, Bath, BA1 2LR

Tel: 01225 338727
Fax: 01225 481850
E-mail: admin@bptrust.demon.co.uk

Website:
http://www.bath-preservation-trust.org.uk

Enquiries:
Enquiries to: Administrator
Other contacts: Director

Founded:
1934

Organisation type and purpose:
Membership association (membership is by subscription), present number of members: 1070, registered charity (charity number 203048). Buildings preservation trust.

Subject coverage:
The trust exists to preserve the historic character and amenities of Bath.

Printed publications:
Annual Report
Newsletter (annual)

Access to staff:
Contact by letter
Hours: Mon to Fri, 0900 to 1700

Access to building, collection or gallery:
Prior appointment required

BATH ROYAL LITERARY AND SCIENTIFIC INSTITUTION

16–18 Queen Square, Bath, Somerset, BA1 2HN

Tel: 01225 312084
Fax: 01225 442460
E-mail: admin@brlsi.org

Website:
http://www.brlsi.org

Enquiries:
Enquiries to: Administrator

Founded:
1824

Organisation type and purpose:
Membership organisation (membership by donation/subscription).
Research institution, museum and library.

Subject coverage:
Literature, geology, natural history, archaeology, fine art, photography, social history and local history of Bath.

Museum or gallery collection, archive, or library special collection:
Library:
Rev. Leonard Jenyns Collection (science and natural history)
Christopher Edmund Broome Collection (botany, especially the lower plants, fungi and algae)
Parliamentary Collection
Libraries of the Bath Natural History and Antiquarian Field Club and the Bath District of the Somerset Archaeological and Natural History Society
Geology:
Moore Collection (32 Plesiosaurs and Ichthyosaurs)
William Lonsdale Collection (rocks and fossils)
Natural history:
Jenyns Herbarium of British Plants (3,000 specimens)
Broome Herbarium (6,600 British and European specimens)
Shell Collection (17,000 specimens)
Other collections for archaeology, social history, fine art, photography and archives

Non-library collection catalogue:
All or part available online and in-house

Access to staff:
Contact by letter, by telephone, by fax, by e-mail and via website

BATH SPA UNIVERSITY

Library, Newton Park, Bath, BA2 9BN

Tel: 01225 875490
Fax: 01225 875493

Website:
http://www.bathspa.ac.uk/srvices/library/

Enquiries:
Enquiries to: Head of Library and Information Services

Created by the merger of:
Bath College of Education (Home Economics), Newton Park College and Bath Academy of Art

Organisation type and purpose:
The university is an accredited institution for the award of its own degrees up to taught Masters level.

Subject coverage:
Education (primary and secondary), English, history, study of religions, environmental biology, geography, creative arts, fine art, ceramics, graphic design, social sciences, psychology, food management, music, visual culture, health studies, business studies, dance.

Library catalogue:
All or part available online

Access to staff:
Contact by letter and by telephone. Appointment necessary. Non-members charged.
Hours: Mon to Fri, 0900 to 1700

Access for disabled people:
Level entry via ramp, lifts

Library is part of the:
UK Libraries Plus

BATHROOM MANUFACTURERS ASSOCIATION

Acronym or abbreviation: BMA

Federation House, Station Road, Stoke-on-Trent, Staffordshire, ST4 2RT

Tel: 01782 747123
Fax: 01782 747161
E-mail: info@bathroom-association.org.uk

Website:
http://www.bathroom-association.org.uk

Enquiries:
Enquiries to: CEO

Formerly called:
Council of British Ceramic Sanitaryware Manufacturers (CBCSM) (year of change 1987); British Bathroom Council (BBC) (year of change 1999); Bathroom Association (BA) (year of change 2001)

Organisation type and purpose:
Trade association.

Subject coverage:
Information on bathroom products sold in the UK, including sanitaryware, baths, taps and showers, and bathroom refurbishment.

Museum or gallery collection, archive, or library special collection:
Factsheets on bathroom refurbishment

Printed publications:
Factsheets (notes on bathroom design and suppliers of equipment, sae 43p)

Access to staff:
Contact by letter, by fax, by e-mail and via website
Hours: Mon to Fri, 0900 to 1700

BATTERSEA DOGS & CATS HOME

4 Battersea Park Road, London, SW8 4AA

Tel: 020 7622 3626
Fax: 020 7622 6451
E-mail: info@battersea.org.uk

Website:
http://www.battersea.org.uk
Features include online rehoming application form, reporting of a lost dog or cat to the Lost Dogs & Cats Line, downloadable Battersea leaflets and a selection of current canine and feline residents.

Founded:
1860

Formerly called:
The Temporary Home for Lost & Starving Dogs; The Dogs Home Battersea; Battersea Dogs Home (year of change 2005)

Organisation type and purpose:
Registered charity (charity number 206394).
Animal rescue and rehoming.

Subject coverage:
Practical problems, help to owners of lost dogs and cats, rehoming of animals, advice on pet ownership and behavioural problems.

Printed publications:
Annual Report
Lots of leaflets for new dog and cat owners and advice for people thinking about taking on a dog or cat (also downloadable from the website)
Paws Magazine (in-house supporter publication) and Fantail (for supporters under the age of 16 years)

Publications list:
Available in print

Access to staff:
Contact by letter, by telephone, by fax, by e-mail, in person and via website. Appointment necessary. All charged.
Hours: Office hours

Access to building, collection or gallery:
at postal address
Hours: 24 hours, for stray dogs and cats only

Also at:
Battersea Dogs & Cats Home
Crowhurst Lane, Ash, Kent; tel: 01474 874994
Battersea Dogs & Cats Home
Priest Hill, Old Windsor, Berkshire, SL4 2JN; tel: 01784 432989

Member organisation of:
Association of Dogs and Cats Homes

BATTERY VEHICLE SOCIETY

Acronym or abbreviation: BVS

Sorgwm, Cwmdu, Powys, NP8 1RT

Tel: 01874 730320
E-mail: battery@zetnet.co.uk

Website:
http://www.bvs.org.uk
Current Society activities and other relevant activities.

Enquiries:
Enquiries to: Enquiries Officer
Other contacts: Secretary

Founded:
1973

Organisation type and purpose:
Learned society (membership is by subscription), present number of members: 350, voluntary organisation, research organisation.

Subject coverage:
Battery, hybrid and solar electric traction: technical, commercial, recreational and historic aspects.

Museum or gallery collection, archive, or library special collection:
Books, periodicals, brochures, drawings, diagrams, photographs

Trade and statistical information:
Data on the availability of battery-electric cars and light commercials, and parts thereof.

Printed publications:
Battery Car Conversions & Supplement
Battery Road Vehicles: Brief History
Battery Vehicle Review (6 times a year)
Serendipity (Competition Car)

Access to staff:
Contact by letter, by telephone and by e-mail
Hours: Mon to Fri, 0800 to 2200

Affiliated to:
Royal Automobile Club
Transport Trust

BBC CYMRU WALES

Acronym or abbreviation: BBC

Research & Archives, Ty Oldfield – MO28, Llandaff, Cardiff, CF5 2YQ

Tel: 029 2032 3309
Fax: 029 2032 2798
E-mail: edith.hughes@bbc.co.uk

Website:
http://www.bbc.wales.com
General information on all departments.

Enquiries:
Enquiries to: Manager Research & Archives

Founded:
1928

Organisation type and purpose:
National broadcaster.

Subject coverage:
TV film and videotape, radio productions, film transfer servcice (fee payable).

Museum or gallery collection, archive, or library special collection:
Film and TV archive
News cuttings
Radio Times – 1928 to present
Sound archive
Stills collection

Electronic and video publications:
Hanes BBC Wales / BBC Wales: A History (bilingual, CD-ROM)

Access to staff:
Contact by letter, by telephone, by fax and by e-mail. Appointment necessary.
Hours: Mon to Fri, 0930 to 1730

BBC HAYMARKET EXHIBITIONS LIMITED

2–14 Shortlands, London, W6 8DJ

Tel: 020 8267 8300
Fax: 020 8267 8350

Website:
http://www.haymarketgroup.com

Enquiries:
Enquiries to: Operations Director

Organisation type and purpose:
Exhibition organisers.

Subject coverage:
Organisation of consumer exhibitions.

Access to staff:
Contact by letter
Hours: Mon to Fri, 0930 to 1730

Connections with:
Haymarket Exhibitions Limited
At the same address

BBC INFORMATION AND ARCHIVE

Formal name: British Broadcasting Corporation
Acronym or abbreviation: BBC I&A

BC3 D4 Broadcast Centre, Media Village, 201 Wood Lane, London, W12 7TP

Tel: 020 8008 2288
Fax: 020 8936 9002
E-mail: research.gateway@bbc.co.uk

Website:
http://www.bbc.co.uk/archive

Founded:
1932

Organisation type and purpose:
Media.
National broadcaster.

Access to staff:
Contact by telephone, by fax and by e-mail. All charged.
Hours: Mon to Fri, 0930 to 1730

BBC MONITORING

Acronym or abbreviation: BBC

Caversham Park, Reading, Berkshire, RG4 8TZ

Tel: 0118 948 6289
Fax: 0118 946 3823
E-mail: marketing@mon.bbc.co.uk

Website:
http://www.monitor.bbc.co.uk

Enquiries:
Enquiries to: Business Development and Customer Relations

Founded:
1939

Organisation type and purpose:
International organisation, publishing house.
Foreign Affairs news service compiled from international news media monitoring.

Subject coverage:
Continually updated political and economic news from more than 140 countries. Coverage includes government policy, international relations, security issues, globalisation, energy, trade, investment and human rights.

Printed publications:
All former printed publications are now only available on electronic formats

Microform publications:
Microfiche and microfilm of the SWB publications can be purchased from UMI (USA) and Information Publications International Limited (UK)

Electronic and video publications:
Subscribers can choose from a variety of 'push' and 'pull' formats:
Global Newsline – daily news, available on different regions of the world, sent by email
International Reports – news service tailored to individual needs, sent by email
BBC Monitoring Online – searchable internet news database with email alerts, archive and reference materials
Additional specialist reports are available for Central Asia and the international broadcast industry

Publications list:
Available online

Access to staff:
Contact by letter, by telephone, by fax, by e-mail and via website. All charged.
Hours: Open 24 hours; main office 0900 to 1730

Access to building, collection or gallery:
No access other than to staff

Links with:
BBC World Service, BBC

BBC SCOTLAND

40 Pacific Quay, Glasgow, G51 1DA

Tel: 0141 422 6000
E-mail: enquiries.scot@bbc.co.uk

Website:
http://www.bbc.co.uk/scotland/

Enquiries:
Enquiries to: Organiser, Library Services

Organisation type and purpose:
National government body.
Broadcasting organisation.

Subject coverage:
Information relevant to BBC Scotland broadcast output, Scotland and related topics form the basis of all collections.

Museum or gallery collection, archive, or library special collection:
BBC Scotland radio broadcasts from 1949 onwards (tape and disc)
BBC Scotland TV broadcasts from 1952 onwards (film and tape)
Scottish press cuttings from 1968 onwards (microform)

Access to staff:
Contact by letter and by fax. All charged.
Hours: Mon to Fri, 0900 to 1700

Access to building, collection or gallery:
No access other than to staff

Access for disabled people:
Parking provided, level entry, toilet facilities
Special comments: Access to most areas

Also at the same address::
BBC Radio Scotland, BBC Alba, Radio nan Gaidheal

BBC WRITTEN ARCHIVES CENTRE

Formal name: British Broadcasting Corporation
Acronym or abbreviation: BBC

Peppard Road, Caversham Park, Reading, Berkshire, RG4 8TZ

Tel: 0118 948 6281
Fax: 0118 946 1145
E-mail: heritage@bbc.co.uk

Website:
http://www.bbc.co.uk/historyofthebbc/contacts/wac.shtml
History of the BBC and information about the archives.
http://www.bbc.co.uk/aboutthebbc
General information and contacts for all aspects of the BBC's work and programmes.

Founded:
1922

Organisation type and purpose:
International organisation.
Broadcasting organisation.

Subject coverage:
Correspondence, minutes of meetings, news bulletins, scripts, press cuttings and other detailed information relating to the whole of the BBC's output, regional and national, at home and overseas; papers relating to the history and development of the BBC, including technical development, from 1922, constitute a major source for 20th-century social and political history, biography, music, drama and the arts in the 20th century, as well as broadcasting itself.

Museum or gallery collection, archive, or library special collection:
Collection of press cuttings on all aspects of broadcasting (1922–mid 1960s)
Complete sets of Radio Times from 1923
The Listener and all BBC Schools publications

Non-library collection catalogue:
All or part available in-house

Library catalogue:
All or part available in-house

Printed publications:
Order printed publications from: BBC Worldwide Ltd, Media Centre, 201 Wood Lane, London, W12 7TQ; tel: 020 8433 2000

Access to staff:
Contact by letter, by telephone, by fax, by e-mail and via website. Appointment necessary.
Hours: Mon to Fri, 0930 to 1730
Special comments: No loans.

Access to building, collection or gallery:
Prior appointment required
Hours: Wed to Fri, 0945 to 1700

Access for disabled people:
Parking provided, access to all public areas, toilet facilities

BBC YOUNG MUSICIAN OF THE YEAR

Room 3223, White City, 201 Wood Lane, London, W12 7TS

Tel: 020 8752 4212
Fax: 020 8752 4050
E-mail: young.musician@bbc.co.uk

Website:
http://www.bbc.co.uk/youngmusician

Enquiries:
Enquiries to: Artistic Administrator

Founded:
1978

Organisation type and purpose:
National organisation.
Music competition.

Subject coverage:
Competition for young classical musicians.

Access to staff:
Contact by letter, by telephone, by fax, by e-mail and via website
Hours: Mon to Fri, 0900 to 1700

BEAFORD ARTS

Greenwarren House, Beaford, Winkleigh, Devon, EX19 8DU

Tel: 01805 603201
Fax: 01805 603202
E-mail: lyn@beaford-arts.co.uk

Website:
http://www.beaford-arts.co.uk

Enquiries:
Enquiries to: Director
Direct tel: 01805 603734

Founded:
1972

Formerly called:
Beaford Archive, Beaford Photographic Archive

Organisation type and purpose:
Registered charity (charity number 279784).
Photographic Archive.

Subject coverage:
Old North Devon from 1850 to present day, including all aspects of life from domestic to industrial and from childhood to old age; images of farming, transport, leisure, costume, trades and crafts, landscapes and streetscapes.

Museum or gallery collection, archive, or library special collection:
The Old Archive of 9,000 negatives and prints of images taken from the 1850s until World War II and after
The New Archive, the lifetime's study of North Devon by James Ravilious, 8,300 negatives and prints
Contemporary collection currently 4,000 negatives and prints

Printed publications:
Publicity Leaflet (free, 3 times a year)

Access to staff:
Contact by letter, by telephone, by fax and by e-mail. Appointment necessary.
Hours: Mon to Fri, 0900 to 1800

Access to building, collection or gallery:
Prior appointment required
Hours: Telephone for information on access to library and archive.

Access for disabled people:
Toilet facilities
Special comments: Wheelchair access to archive

BEAT

Formal name: Eating Disorders Association

1st Floor, Wensum House, 103 Prince of Wales Road, Norwich, Norfolk, NR1 1DW

Tel: 0300 123 3355
Fax: 01603 664915
E-mail: info@b-eat.co.uk

Website:
http://www.b-eat.co.uk

Enquiries:
Enquiries to: Information Officer
Direct e-mail: media@b-eat.co.uk

Founded:
1989

Incorporates the former:
Anorexic Aid, Anorexic Family Aid, Eating Disorders Association

Organisation type and purpose:
Membership association (membership is by subscription), present number of members: 3,200, registered charity (charity number 801343). Help and support in respect of eating disorders for anyone affected (sufferers, carers, friends, etc.).

Subject coverage:
Eating disorders including anorexia nervosa, bulimia and obesity; offers help, understanding and support to people with an eating disorder and to their family and friends through helplines and online services, and provides education, training and research.

Printed publications:
European Eating Disorders Review (members £25, non-members £45, every 3 months)
Upbeat (free to members, every 3 months)

Publications list:
Available online

Access to staff:
Contact by telephone, by fax, by e-mail and via website
Hours: Administration only: 0900 to 1700
Special comments: Youth Helpline: Mon to Fri, 1630 to 2030; tel. 0845 634 7650
Adult Helpline: Mon to Fri, 1030 to 2030; tel. 0845 634 1414.

BEATSON INSTITUTE FOR CANCER RESEARCH

Garscube Estate, Switchback Road, Bearsden, Glasgow, G61 1BD

Tel: 0141 330 3953
Fax: 0141 942 6521
E-mail: library@beatson.gla.ac.uk

Website:
http://www.beatson.gla.ac.uk

Enquiries:
Enquiries to: Scientific Administrator
Direct tel: 0141 330 8722

Founded:
1912

Formerly called:
CRC Beatson Laboratories; Beatson Institute for Cancer Research (year of change 1967)

Organisation type and purpose:
Research organisation.

Subject coverage:
Molecular biology, cell biology, molecular pathology, cancer research, proteomics, pharmacology, medical oncology, radiation oncology.

Museum or gallery collection, archive, or library special collection:
Historical collection relating to Sir George Beatson and the founding of the Royal Glasgow Cancer Hospital

Non-library collection catalogue:
All or part available in-house

Library catalogue:
All or part available in-house

Printed publications:
Cancer Research UK Beatson Institute for Cancer Research Scientific Report (annual, contains a list of papers by staff)

Publications list:
Available in print

Access to staff:
Contact by letter, by telephone, by fax and by e-mail. Appointment necessary.

Access to building, collection or gallery:
Prior appointment required

Access for disabled people:
Parking provided, level entry, toilet facilities

Links with:
University of Glasgow

BEAULIEU ARCHIVES

John Montagu Building, Beaulieu, Brockenhurst, Hampshire, SO42 7ZN

Tel: 01590 612345
Fax: 01590 612624
E-mail: info@beaulieu.co.uk

Website:
http://www.beaulieu.co.uk

Enquiries:
Enquiries to: Archivist

Founded:
1952

Organisation type and purpose:
Museum.
Montagu family & Beaulieu estate private archives.
Private estate and leisure destination.

Subject coverage:
Family of Lords Montagu of Beaulieu, Beaulieu Estate and Parish, Buckler's Hard 18th-century shipbuilding village, Beaulieu Abbey. Ditton Park Estate, Slough, Buckinghamshire.

Museum or gallery collection, archive, or library special collection:
Beaulieu History
Archive of the Montagu family

Non-library collection catalogue:
All or part available in-house

Printed publications:
Wheels Within Wheels: An Unconventional Life (Lord Montagu of Beaulieu)
An Album of Old Beaulieu & Buckler's Hard (Susan Tomkins)
Beaulieu: The Finishing School for Secret Agents (Cyril Cunningham)
Buckler's Hard guidebook
Buckler's Hard: a rural shipbuilding centre (A J Holland)
John Montagu of Beaulieu (Paul Tritton)
Palace House & Beaulieu Abbey (guidebook)
The Beaulieu Record (H E R Widnell)
all prices from Shops Manager
Order printed publications from: Shops Manager, Beaulieu Enterprises Limited
John Montagu Building, Beaulieu, Brockenhurst, Hampshire, SO42 7ZN, tel: 01590 614639, fax: 01590 612624, e-mail: info@beaulieu.co.uk

Access to staff:
Contact by letter, by telephone, by fax, by e-mail and via website. Appointment necessary.
Hours: Mon to Fri, 1000 to 1500

Access for disabled people:
Parking provided, ramped entry, toilet facilities
Special comments: Access to Archives by ramped entry and lift.

BEAUMONT SPECIALIST FABRICATIONS LIMITED

Woodlands Road, Mere, Wiltshire, BA12 6BT

Tel: 01747 860481
Fax: 01747 861076

continued overleaf

E-mail: sales@beaumont-chimneys.co.uk

Website:
http://www.beaumont-chimneys.co.uk

Enquiries:
Enquiries to: Director

Founded:
2001

Formerly called:
Beaumont Chimneys (year of change 1949); F E
Beaumont Limited (year of change 2001)

Organisation type and purpose:
Manufacturing industry.
Design, manufacturing, installation, inspection and
maintenance of steel chimneys and associated
items.

Subject coverage:
Steel chimneys, flue liners, flue ducting,
aerodynamic stabiliser vanes, counterbalance
dampers.

Printed publications:
General sales literature

Access to staff:
Contact by letter, by telephone and by fax
Hours: Mon to Thu, 0845 to 1700; Fri, 0845 to 1600

BEAVERBROOK FOUNDATION

11 Old Queen Street, London, SW1H 9JA

Tel: 020 7222 7474
Fax: 020 7222 2198

Website:
http://www.beaverbrookfoundation.org

Enquiries:
Enquiries to: Secretary

Organisation type and purpose:
Registered charity.

Access to staff:
Contact by letter
Hours: Mon to Fri, 0900 to 1700

BEDFORD CENTRAL LIBRARY

Harpur Street, Bedford, MK40 1PG

Tel: 01234 718178 Main number; 01234 718168
Reference Library
Fax: 01234 342163
E-mail: via website

Website:
http://www.bedford.gov.uk
Click on Libraries for Bedfordshire Libraries
Virtual Library.

Enquiries:
Enquiries to: The Library Manager
Direct e-mail: bedfordshirelibraries@bedford.gov.uk
.

Organisation type and purpose:
Local government body, public library.

Subject coverage:
Local community information, business
information, local studies, family history, John
Bunyan.

**Museum or gallery collection, archive, or library
special collection:**
Bedford Old Library
Bedfordshire Local Studies Library
Fowler Collection
Frank Mott Harrison Collection (John Bunyan)
George Offor Collection
General Registrar's Index to Births, Marriages and
   Deaths, including the overseas index (microfiche)
Mark Rutherford Collection 1837–2002

Non-library collection catalogue:
All or part available online

Library catalogue:
All or part available online

Access to staff:
Contact by letter, by telephone, by fax, by e-mail,
in person and via website
Hours: Mon, Tue, Wed, Fri, 0900 to 1800; Thu, 0900
to 1300; Sat, 0900 to 1700

Access for disabled people:
Lift, wide doors, toilet facilities

Parent body:
Bedford Borough Council

BEDFORD COLLEGE

Cauldwell Street, Bedford, MK42 9AH

Tel: 01234 291000; Learning Resources Centre:
01234 291320
Fax: 01234 342674

Website:
http://www.bedford.ac.uk
College website.

Enquiries:
Enquiries to: Library and Resource Centre Manager
Direct tel: 01234 291321
Direct e-mail: hcjones@bedford.ac.uk

Founded:
1993

Created by the merger of:
Shuttleworth College (formerly part of Writtle
College) and Bedford College (year of change
2009)

Organisation type and purpose:
Suitable for ages: 14+.

Subject coverage:
Engineering (mechanical, electrical, electronic,
motor vehicle, aeronautical engineering),
construction, business studies, art and design,
English as a foreign language, leisure, sport,
tourism, catering, computing, performing arts,
health, social and child care, hair, beauty and
holistic therapies, agriculture, animal care, equine
studies, horticulture, land management.

**Museum or gallery collection, archive, or library
special collection:**
Learning and Skills Council information and
   reports

Non-library collection catalogue:
All or part available in-house

Library catalogue:
All or part available online

Access to staff:
Contact by letter, by telephone, by e-mail and via
website. Appointment necessary.
Hours: Term time: Mon to Thu, 0830 to 1830; Fri,
0830 to 1630
Vacations: Mon to Fri, 1000 to 1600
Special comments: Closed on some Fridays in
vacation until mid-August. Please ring for details.

Access for disabled people:
Access to all public areas, toilet facilities, parking
provided, ramped entry

BEDFORDSHIRE AND LUTON
ARCHIVES AND RECORDS
SERVICE

Acronym or abbreviation: BLARS

Riverside Building, Borough Hall, Cauldwell
Street, Bedford, MK42 9AP

Tel: 01234 228833/4; 01234 228777
Fax: 01234 228854
E-mail: archive@bedford.gov.uk

Website:
http://www.bedford.gov.uk/archive
Typical local authority archive holdings: records of
churches, businesses, estates, institutions and
individuals. Local map and picture collection. Also
incls contact details; advice on holdings; history of
local Bedfordshire places; 'community pages'.

Enquiries:
Enquiries to: Archivist
Other contacts: Ops Manager (Customer Services &
Outreach)

Founded:
1913

Formerly called:
Bedfordshire Record Office (year of change 1997)

Please select:

Organisation type and purpose:
Local government body; archive repository.
The Service collects and preserves a
comprehensive and evolving archive illustrating
all aspects of Bedfordshire life and history,
including contemporary records of archival value;
facilitates public and community access to the
records; and promotes their use for business,
education, cultural and recreational purposes.

Subject coverage:
Bedfordshire history – all aspects; documents
recording or illustrating: the topography,
ownership, occupations and use of land in
Bedfordshire; human activity in Bedfordshire, e.g.
the social, economic, religious, cultural, political,
administrative life and history of the county's
inhabitants, communities, organisations and
government at all levels.

Information services:
Advice on holdings is free; there is a charge for
research.

Education services:
Limited: small groups can be catered for on site;
talks offered to local societies.

Services for disabled people:
See website for advice. Hearing loop and
adjustable chairs on site

**Museum or gallery collection, archive, or library
special collection:**
Unique archive material from a variety of sources.
Major holdings include quarter sessions archives,
county council, district and parish council
archives, Bedford estate papers, Lucas (Wrest
Park) collection, Whitbread Family papers,
Bedford archdeaconry records, ecclesiastical
parish records, Pym Family papers and estate
archives, and records from Orlebar estate,
Methodist Church, Beds and Herts Regiment,
Poor Law unions and London Brick Company

Non-library collection catalogue:
All or part available online

Library catalogue:
All or part available online

Printed publications:
Many titles, including:
Guides to Holdings – specific subject areas (e.g.
   family history, property history, educational
   sources, women's and ethnic minority sources;
   irregular)
Newsletter (quarterly)
Bedfordshire 1851 Census Index (several vols,
   those out of print available on microfiche)
Series of free service leaflets, including: Summary
   List of Archive Holdings, Guide for Visitors,
   Service Charter, Enquiries and Research Services
Bedfordshire Parish Register series (all places up to
   1812)
Order printed publications from: Archive

Microform publications:
Bedfordshire Parish Register Series (vols 144)
Order microform publications from:
archive@bedford.gov.uk

Electronic and video publications:
n/a

Publications list:
Available online

Access to staff:
Contact by letter, by telephone, by fax, by e-mail,
in person and via website
Hours: Mon 0900 to 1900; Tue, Wed and Fri, 0900 to
1700

Closed Thu and weekends

Access to building, collection or gallery:
same as opening hours
Hours: As access to staff

Access for disabled people:
Access to all public areas
Hours: As standard opening hours
Special comments: Access possible, please contact
the service in advance. Guidance on website.

Parent body:
Bedford Borough Council
Borough Hall, Bedford, MK42 9AP; tel: 01234
267422; fax: 01234 221606; e-mail: centralp@
bedford.gov.uk; website: http://www.bedford
.gov.uk

BEDFORDSHIRE FAMILY HISTORY SOCIETY

PO Box 214, Bedford, MK42 9RX

E-mail: bfhs@bfhs.org.uk

Website:
http://www.bfhs.org.uk

Enquiries:
Enquiries to: Honorary Secretary

Founded:
1977

Organisation type and purpose:
Membership association (membership is by
subscription), present number of members: 1,000,
registered charity (charity number 281677).
To bring together those interested in family history,
genealogy and heraldry, primarily in Bedfordshire.

Printed publications:
Bedfordshire Parish Registers Series (as the
microfiche, in hard copy from Bedfordshire and
Luton Archives and Records Service)
Bedfordshire Parish Registers Series
Bedfordshire Strays Index Vols 1 and 2
Poor Law Papers 1622–1834
Index to 1851 Census of Bedfordshire
Bedfordshire Churches in the Nineteenth Century
(4 vols)
Bedfordshire Wills 1531–1539

Microform publications:
Bedfordshire Parish Registers Series (microfiche,
over 120 parishes, i.e. all the pre-1812 parish
registers)
Bedfordshire Parish Registers Series (microfiche)
Monumental Inscriptions for 86 parishes

Electronic and video publications:
Luton General Cemetery (Rothesay Road)
Registers 1854–2003
Bedfordshire Parish Registers Index (PRIME, CD)

Publications list:
Available in print

Access to staff:
Contact by letter, by e-mail and via website
Hours: Mon to Fri, 0900 to 1700

BEDFORDSHIRE HISTORICAL RECORD SOCIETY

Acronym or abbreviation: BHRS

48 St Augustine's Road, Bedford, MK40 2ND

Tel: 01234 309548
E-mail: rsmart@ntlworld.com

Website:
http://www.bedfordshirehrs.org.uk
Publications list.

Enquiries:
Enquiries to: Honorary Secretary

Founded:
1913

Organisation type and purpose:
Learned society (membership is by subscription),
present number of members: 300, registered
charity (charity number 1098629).
Record publishing society (historical source
materials for Bedfordshire).
Publication of materials for the history of
Bedfordshire.

Subject coverage:
Bedfordshire local history, archival sources.

**Museum or gallery collection, archive, or library
special collection:**
The Fowler Library (owned by BHRS but housed
by the University of Northampton)

Non-library collection catalogue:
All or part available online and in print

Printed publications:
Historical source materials, edited records,
monographs, diaries and documents

Microform publications:
Some titles available on microfiche (Chadwyck-
Healey)

Publications list:
Available online and in print

Access to staff:
Contact by letter, by telephone, by e-mail and via
website
Hours: Mon to Fri, 0900 to 1700

BEES FOR DEVELOPMENT

Acronym or abbreviation: BfD

Troy, Monmouth, NP25 4AB

Tel: 01600 713648
Fax: 01600 716167
E-mail: info@beesfordevelopment.org

Website:
http://www.beesfordevelopment.org

Enquiries:
Enquiries to: Director

Founded:
1993

Organisation type and purpose:
International organisation, training organisation,
consultancy.

Subject coverage:
Beekeeping in developing countries.

Library catalogue:
All or part available in-house

Access to staff:
Contact by letter, by telephone, by fax, by e-mail
and via website. Appointment necessary.
Hours: Mon to Fri, 0900 to 1700
Special comments: Strictly by prior appointment.

Access to building, collection or gallery:
Prior appointment required

BELARUS EMBASSY

Formal name: The Embassy of the Republic of
Belarus

6 Kensington Court, London, W8 5DL

Tel: 020 7937 3288
Fax: 020 7361 0005
E-mail: uk@belembassy.org

Website:
http://www.uk.belembassy.org

Enquiries:
Enquiries to: Ambassador

Organisation type and purpose:
National government body.
Embassy.

Subject coverage:
Belarus and Belarusian governmental matters,
economy and trade.

Trade and statistical information:
Belarusian market.

Access to staff:
Contact by letter, by telephone, by fax and by e-
mail
Hours: Mon to Fri, 0900 to 1800

Access to building, collection or gallery:
No access other than to staff

BELFAST AND LISBURN WOMEN'S AID

Support & Resource Centre, 30 Adelaide Park,
Belfast, BT9 6FY

Tel: 028 9066 6049; 24-hour helpline: 0800 9171 414
E-mail: admin@belfastwomensaid.org.uk

Website:
http://www.belfastwomensaid.org.uk
Women's Aid and its aims and work, domestic
violence, youth pages, contact information.

Organisation type and purpose:
Registered charity.
Provides confidential support, information and
emergency accommodation for women and
children affected by domestic violence.
To provide temporary refuge for women and their
children suffering mental, physical or sexual abuse
within the home; to offer support and advice to
any woman who asks for it, whether or not she is
living in a refuge, and to offer supportive aftercare
to women leaving the refuge; to encourage the
woman to take control of her own future, whether
this involves returning home or beginning an
independent life; to recognise and care for the
needs of the children involved; to educate and
inform the public, the media, the courts and
statutory and voluntary agencies, always mindful
of the fact that abused women are a direct result of
the general position of women in our society.

Subject coverage:
Women's Aid's 3 refuges – in Belfast and in
Lisburn, its outreach work, personal development
training, awareness-raising for statutory and
voluntary agencies, young people's projects, and
inter-agency work.

Education services:
Awareness-raising training for statutory and
voluntary agencies. Links with schools and youth
clubs throughout Belfast and Lisburn to promote
healthy and non-abusive relationships.

Printed publications:
Leaflets and other publications
Annual report
Order printed publications from: Above address

Electronic and video publications:
Leaflets and other publications
Annual report
Order electronic and video publications from:
Download from website

Access to staff:
Contact by letter, by telephone, by e-mail and in
person

Access to building, collection or gallery:
Hours: 0900 to 1730

BELFAST CARERS' CENTRE

Suites 2–5 Second Floor, Merrion Business Centre,
58 Howard Street, Belfast, BT1 6PJ

Tel: 028 9043 4700
Fax: 028 9024 9999
E-mail: info@carerscentre.org

Website:
http://www.carerscentre.org

Enquiries:
Enquiries to: Manager
Direct e-mail: r.devlin@carerscentre.org

Founded:
2002

continued overleaf

Formerly called:
Princess Royal Trust Limited

Organisation type and purpose:
Registered charity.

Subject coverage:
Information and support for carers.

Museum or gallery collection, archive, or library special collection:
Range of information material pertinent to carers.

Publications list:
Available online and in print

Access to staff:
Contact by letter, by telephone, by fax, by e-mail and via website. Appointment necessary.
Hours: Mon to Fri, 0900 to 1700

Access to building, collection or gallery:
No prior appointment required
Hours: Mon to Fri, 0900 to 1700

BELFAST CITY COUNCIL

Development Department, The Cecil Ward Building, 8–10 Linenhall Street, Belfast, BT2 8BP

Tel: 028 9032 0202\ Minicom no. 028 9027 0405
Fax: 028 9027 0325

Website:
http://www.development.belfastcity.gov.uk
Arts, projects, markets, planning and development, tourism, events, industrial, economic development, estates, gasworks site, procurement.

Enquiries:
Enquiries to: Director
Direct e-mail: shawa@belfastcity.co.uk
Other contacts: Head of Capital Works, Tourism Manager, Events Manager, Culture and Arts Manager,

Organisation type and purpose:
Local government body.

Subject coverage:
Economic development, arts, tourism development and events in Belfast.

Printed publications:
Arts Strategy and Arts Directory
Relocation Brochure
Strategy for economic development
Tourism guides for Belfast

Access to staff:
Contact by letter, by telephone, by fax and by e-mail. Appointment necessary.
Hours: Mon to Fri, 0900 to 1700

Access to building, collection or gallery:
Prior appointment required

Connections with:
Belfast First Stop Business Shop (First Stop Shop)
  tel: 028 9027 8399
Belfast Visitor & Convention Bureau (BVCB)
  tel: 028 9023 9026
Investment Belfast Limited (IBL)
  tel: 028 9031 136

BELFAST INSTITUTE OF FURTHER AND HIGHER EDUCATION

Acronym or abbreviation: BIFHE

Gerald Moag Campus, Millfield, Belfast, BT1 1HS

E-mail: information-servicesbelfastinstitute.ac.uk

Website:
http://www.belfastinstitute.ac.uk
All relevant information about courses and services is either available now or will be shortly.

Enquiries:
Enquiries to: Information Officer
Direct e-mail: information_services@belfastinstitute.ac.uk
Other contacts: Director

Founded:
1991

Formerly called:
College of Business Studies, College of Technology, Rupert Stanley College

Subject coverage:
Education and training at all levels in all subjects except mining, agriculture and marine technology.

Printed publications:
Adult Education News (twice a year, free)
Annual Report (free)
General Prospectus (annually, free)
Higher Education Prospectus (annually, free)

Access to staff:
Contact by letter, by telephone, by fax, by e-mail and in person
Hours: Mon to Thu, 0900 to 1700; Fri, 0900 to 1600

BELFAST PUBLIC LIBRARIES

Royal Avenue, Belfast, BT1 1EA

Tel: 028 9050 9150
Fax: 028 9033 2819
E-mail: info@libraries.belfast-elb.gov.uk

Enquiries:
Enquiries to: Chief Librarian
Direct e-mail: outreach.belb@librariesni.org.uk

Founded:
1888

Formerly called:
Belfast City Libraries

Organisation type and purpose:
Local government body, public library.

Subject coverage:
Departmentalised as follows:
General Reference Library; social sciences, philosophy, religion, history, arts, literature, science, medicine, law
Local History Library; local studies and Irish material
Music Library; music, records, cassettes, CDs, scores
Business Library; business information
Electronic Information Services; internet access, CD-ROM, on-line searching, software application, e-mail.

Museum or gallery collection, archive, or library special collection:
Belfast Theatre Posters
Early Belfast printed books
F J Bigger Collection
Grainger, Moore, Riddell and Horner Collections
Irish and Belfast Newspapers from 1761
Irish folksong and music records
Irish history, archaeology and antiquarian material
J S Crone Collection
UN Depository Library

Printed publications:
Reading lists on specific topics

Access to staff:
Contact by letter, by telephone, by fax, by e-mail and in person
Hours: Mon, Thu, 0900 to 2000; Tue, Wed, Fri, 0900 to 1730; Sat, 0900 to 1300

Access for disabled people:
Level entry, access to all public areas, toilet facilities

BELGIAN EMBASSY

103 Eaton Square, London, SW1W 9AB

Tel: 020 7470 3700
Fax: 020 7259 6213
E-mail: info@belgium-embassy.co.uk

Website:
http://belgium.fgov.be
Guide to the Federal Administration, decisions of the Federal Council of Ministers, information from the Federal Information Service, all about Belgium, hyperlinks to other sites, an address for all questions.

http://www.belgium.fgov.be
Belgium on the Internet (Federal information service).
http://www.belgium-embassy.co.uk
Belgian Events (in-house publication), general information.

Enquiries:
Enquiries to: Information Officer

Organisation type and purpose:
Diplomatic mission.

Subject coverage:
General (politics, media, monarchy, etc), culture, economics, working and living in Belgium, visas and passports.

Printed publications:
Bulletin of Belgian Events in Great Britain (6 times a year)

Heads or is associated with the:
Anglo-Belgian Club
  60 Knightsbridge, London, SW1X 7LF; tel: 020 7235 2121; fax: 020 7243 9470
Belgian Consulates
Belgian Tourist Office Brussels-Ardennes
  217 Marsh Wall, London, E14 9FJ; tel: 020 7531 0390; fax: 020 7531 0393; e-mail: info@belgium-tourism.net
Belgo-Luxembourg Chamber of Commerce
  Riverside House, 27–29 Vauxhall Grove, London, SW8 1SY; tel: 020 7820 7839; fax: 020 7793 1628
Tourism Flanders-Brussels
  31 Pepper Street, London, E14 9RW; tel: 020 7867 0311; fax: 020 7458 0045; e-mail: info@flanders-tourism.org

BELIZE HIGH COMMISSION

Third Floor, 45 Crawford Place, London, W1H 4LP

Tel: 020 7723 3603
Fax: 020 7723 9637
E-mail: bzhc-lon@btconnect.com

Website:
http://www.belizehighcommission.com

Enquiries:
Enquiries to: High Commissioner
Other contacts: The First Secretary for Consular and Administrative Affairs

Organisation type and purpose:
National government body.
Diplomatic mission of the government of Belize.

Subject coverage:
Belize: economics, tourism, politics, investment, trade, social structure, citizenship and visas.

Printed publications:
Free information packs on Belize (on request)
Application forms (visa, passports)

Access to staff:
Contact by letter, by telephone, by fax and by e-mail. Appointment necessary.
Hours: Mon to Fri, 1000 to 1800

Access to building, collection or gallery:
Prior appointment required
Hours: Consular Hours: Mon to Wed, 1030 to 1400

BELL COLLEGE TECHNICAL INFORMATION SERVICE

Acronym or abbreviation: BECTIS

Bell College of Technology, Almada Street, Hamilton, South Lanarkshire, ML3 0JB

Tel: 01698 285658
Fax: 01698 286856
E-mail: bectis@bell.ac.uk

Website:
http://www.bell.ac.uk

Enquiries:
Enquiries to: Information Officer

Organisation type and purpose:
Commercial information service.
To make the resources of Bell College Library available to the industrial community.

Subject coverage:
Industrial, commercial and public authorities information, technical and managerial subjects, British Standards.

Printed publications:
BECTIS Bulletin (10 times a year)

Access to staff:
Contact by letter, by telephone, by fax, by e-mail and in person
Hours: Mon to Fri, 0830 to 1630

Access to building, collection or gallery:
No access other than to staff
Hours: Term time: Mon to Thu, 0830 to 2100; Fri, 0830 to 1630; Sat 0900 to 1300

BENESH INSTITUTE

36 Battersea Square, London, SW11 3RA

Tel: 020 7326 8031
Fax: 020 7924 3129
E-mail: beneshinstitute@rad.org.uk

Website:
http://www.benesh.org

Enquiries:
Enquiries to: Director

Founded:
1962

Formerly called:
Institute of Choreology

Organisation type and purpose:
Professional body (membership is by subscription), registered charity (charity number 312826), suitable for ages: 16+.
Education and research institute in movement notation.

Subject coverage:
Benesh Movement Notation, anthropology, choreography, computer research, dance techniques, dance repertoire, ethnic dance, physiotherapy.

Museum or gallery collection, archive, or library special collection:
Choreographic scores in Benesh Movement Notation

Library catalogue:
All or part available online

Printed publications:
A range of publications relating to Benesh Movement Notation, including:
Movement Study and Benesh Movement Notation
Benesh Movement Notation Elementary Solo Syllabus
Order printed publications from: http://www.radenterprises.co.uk

Electronic and video publications:
Benesh Notation Editor computer software
Order electronic and video publications from: http://www.radenterprises.co.uk

Publications list:
Available online

Access to staff:
Contact by letter, by telephone, by fax and by e-mail. Appointment necessary. Non-members charged.
Hours: Mon to Thu, 1000 to 1800; Fri, 1000 to 1730

Access to building, collection or gallery:
Prior appointment required
Hours: Mon to Thu, 1000 to 1800; Fri, 1000 to 1730

Access for disabled people:
Ramped entry, toilet facilities
Special comments: Wheelchair access to first two floors.

Links with:
The Royal Academy of Dance
at the same address; tel: 020 7326 8000; fax: 020 7924 3129; e-mail: info@rad.org.uk; website: http://www.rad.org.uk

BERKELEY ENTHUSIASTS CLUB

41 Gorsewood Road, St Johns, Woking, Surrey, GU21 1UZ

Tel: 01483 475330

Enquiries:
Enquiries to: Secretary

Founded:
1963

Organisation type and purpose:
Membership association (membership is by subscription), present number of members: 300, voluntary organisation.

Subject coverage:
Preservation of all types of 3- and 4-wheeled Berkeley sports cars, sources of cars, parts, technical advice.

Printed publications:
Newsletter (monthly, members)

Access to staff:
Contact by letter
Hours: Mon to Fri, 0900 to 1700

BERKSHIRE ARCHAEOLOGICAL SOCIETY

Acronym or abbreviation: BAS

43 Laburnham Road, Maidenhead, Berkshire, SL6 4DE

Tel: 01628 631225

Enquiries:
Enquiries to: Honorary Secretary

Founded:
1871

Organisation type and purpose:
Learned society.

Subject coverage:
Berkshire archaeology and history.

Museum or gallery collection, archive, or library special collection:
Library of rare books on Berkshire
Pre-1998 archaeological periodicals from UK mostly, some from elsewhere, for sale from October 1998, please apply for catalogue

Printed publications:
Berkshire Archaeological Journal

Access to staff:
Contact by letter
Hours: Mon to Fri, 0900 to 1700
Special comments: International reply coupon requested if outside UK.

Member of:
Council for British Archaeology

Practical Arm:
Berkshire Field Research Group

BERKSHIRE LOCAL HISTORY ASSOCIATION

Acronym or abbreviation: BLHA

The Bailiwick, Tag Lane, Hare Hatch, Twyford, Reading, Berkshire, RG10 9ST

Tel: 0118 940 2376
E-mail: peter@bailiwick1.co.uk

Enquiries:
Enquiries to: Chairman
Other contacts: Newsletter Editor

Founded:
1976

Organisation type and purpose:
Membership association (membership is by subscription), present number of members: 40 corporate bodies, 80 individuals, voluntary organisation.
Acts to liaise with and disseminate information about the activities of its members interested in local and family history, and archaeology.

Subject coverage:
Various aspects of the history of Berkshire, its towns, parishes, people, landscape, etc depending on research and interests of members.

Printed publications:
Berkshire Old and New (annually for sale to non-members, free to members)
Newsletter (3 times a year, free to members)

Access to staff:
Contact by letter, by telephone and by e-mail
Hours: Mon to Fri, 0900 to 1700

Affiliated to:
British Association of Local History

Members include:
Berkshire Archaeological Society
tel: 01628 631225
Berkshire Family History Society
tel: 0118 984 3995
Berkshire Industrial Archaeology Group
tel: 0118 978 5234
Berkshire Library Service
Berkshire Record Office
tel: 0118 901 5132; fax: 0118 901 5131; e-mail: arch@reading.gov.uk
many local history and historical societies in the county

Other addresses:
Berkshire Local History Association
18 Foster Road, Abingdon, Oxfordshire, OX14 1YN

BERKSHIRE RECORD OFFICE

9 Coley Avenue, Reading, Berkshire, RG1 6AF

Tel: 0118 937 5132
Fax: 0118 937 5131
E-mail: arch@reading.gov.uk

Website:
http://www.berkshirerecordoffice.org.uk

Enquiries:
Enquiries to: County Archivist

Founded:
1948

Organisation type and purpose:
Local government body.

Subject coverage:
Family and local history relating to Berkshire (including area now in Oxfordshire).

Museum or gallery collection, archive, or library special collection:
Business archives, charity archives, church archives, estate and family archives, local government archives, hospital archives, court archives

Non-library collection catalogue:
All or part available online and in-house

Electronic and video publications:
See: http://www.berkshirenclosure.org.uk

Access to staff:
Contact by letter, by telephone, by fax, by e-mail and in person. Appointment necessary.
Hours: Mon, closed; Tue and Wed, 0900 to 1700; Thu, 0900 to 2100; Fri, 0900 to 1630
Special comments: Closed for two weeks' stocktaking, usually last week in November and first week in December.

Access for disabled people:
Parking provided, level entry, access to all public areas, toilet facilities

Parent body:
Bracknell Forest Council

continued overleaf

Reading Borough Council
Royal Borough of Windsor and Maidenhead
Slough Borough Council
West Berkshire Council
Wokingham Borough Council

BERKSHIRE, BUCKINGHAMSHIRE AND OXFORDSHIRE WILDLIFE TRUST

Acronym or abbreviation: BBOWT

The Lodge, 1 Armstrong Road, Littlemore, Oxford, OX4 4XT

Tel: 01865 775476
Fax: 01865 711301
E-mail: info@bbowt.org.uk

Website:
http://www.bbowt.org.uk

Enquiries:
Enquiries to: Information Officer
Direct e-mail: wildinfo@bbowt.org.uk

Founded:
1961

Formerly called:
Berkshire, Buckinghamshire and Oxfordshire Naturalists' Trust (BBONT) (year of change 1999)

Organisation type and purpose:
Voluntary organisation, registered charity (charity number 204330).
Environmental, conservation, wildlife organisation.

Subject coverage:
All aspects of wildlife in Berkshire, Buckinghamshire and Oxfordshire.

Museum or gallery collection, archive, or library special collection:
Guides to nature reserves in these three counties

Printed publications:
Where to go for wildlife in Berkshire, Buckinghamshire and Oxfordshire (available free on joining)

Access to staff:
Contact by letter, by telephone, by fax, by e-mail and via website. Appointment necessary.
Hours: Mon to Fri, 0900 to 1700

Parent body:
Wildlife Trusts
   UK Office, The Kiln, Waterside, Mather Road, Newark, Notts, NG24 1NT; tel: 0870 036 7711; fax: 0870 036 0101; e-mail: enquiry@ wildlifetrusts.org

BERLIOZ SOCIETY

450b Lea Bridge Road, Leyton, E10 7DY

Tel: 020 8539 9122
E-mail: sqing@btinternet.com

Website:
http://www.theberliozsociety.org.uk

Enquiries:
Enquiries to: Honorary Secretary

Founded:
1952

Organisation type and purpose:
Membership association (membership is by subscription), present number of members: 240.

Subject coverage:
Music of Berlioz, life of Berlioz, performances of Berlioz' work, Berlioz' writing.

Non-library collection catalogue:
All or part available in-house

Library catalogue:
All or part available in-house

Printed publications:
Bibliography (by Michael Wright)

The Society Bulletin (approximately 3 times a year, £10 a year, free to members)
Order printed publications from: Bulletin, Berlioz Society, 450b Lea Bridge Road, London, E10 7DY

Access to staff:
Contact by letter, by telephone, by e-mail and via website

Access to building, collection or gallery:
No access other than to staff

BERMUDA TOURISM

26 York Street, London, W1U 6PZ

Tel: 0207 096 4246
Fax: 0207 096 0509
E-mail: ukeurope@bermudatourism.com

Enquiries:
Enquiries to: Manager
Other contacts: Sales Administration Co-ordinator

Founded:
1985

Formerly called:
Bermuda Tourism BCB Limited

Organisation type and purpose:
National Tourist Office.

Subject coverage:
Bermuda, tourism and travel.

Printed publications:
Tourist literature and brochures on Bermuda updated annually

Access to staff:
Contact by e-mail
Hours: Mon to Fri, 0900 to 1700

Access to building, collection or gallery:
No access other than to staff

BERTRAND RUSSELL PEACE FOUNDATION LIMITED

Acronym or abbreviation: BRPF

Russell House, Bulwell Lane, Nottingham, NG6 0BT

Tel: 0115 978 4504
Fax: 0115 942 0433
E-mail: elfeuro@compuserve.com

Website:
http://www.russfound.org
Bertrand Russell Peace Foundation was launched in 1963, and was established to carry forward Russell's work for peace, human rights and social justice. Over forty years later, it continues to do so.
http://www.spokesmanbooks.com
Spokesman is the publishing imprint of the Bertrand Russell Peace Foundation. It publishes in many areas including politics, peace and disarmament, history, drama and philosophy.

Enquiries:
Enquiries to: Secretary
Direct tel: 0115 970 8318
Direct e-mail: julia@brpf.demon.co.uk

Founded:
1963

Organisation type and purpose:
International organisation (membership is by election or invitation), research organisation, publishing house.
To investigate the causes of international and social conflict and to work for peace and disarmament.

Subject coverage:
International relations, politics, economics, civil liberties.

Printed publications:
The Spokesman Journal
Spokesman Books
Order printed publications from: http:// www.spokesmanbooks.com

Publications list:
Available online and in print

Access to staff:
Contact by letter, by telephone, by fax, by e-mail and via website
Hours: Mon to Fri, 0900 to 1700

Access to building, collection or gallery:
Prior appointment required

BERWICK-UPON-TWEED RECORD OFFICE

Council Offices, Wallace Green, Berwick-upon-Tweed, Northumberland, TD15 1ED

Tel: 01289 301865
Fax: 01289 330540
E-mail: berwickarchives@woodhorn.org.uk

Website:
http://www.northumberland.gov.uk/collections
Contains information about the office and sources kept.

Enquiries:
Enquiries to: Archivist

Founded:
1980

Organisation type and purpose:
Local government body.
Record office.

Subject coverage:
Local and family history of North Northumberland including Berwick-upon-Tweed.

Museum or gallery collection, archive, or library special collection:
Berwick Borough Archives, 16th to 20th centuries
Berwick Salmon Fisheries company records
Ford and Etal Estate records
IGI (England, Scotland and Ireland, microfiche)
North Northumberland census returns, 1841 to 1901 (microfilm)
North Northumberland parish registers (microfilm)
GRO Birth, Marriage and Death Indexes, 1837 to 1955 (microfiche)

Non-library collection catalogue:
All or part available in-house

Printed publications:
Berwick-on-Tweed Illustrated, 1894–1994 (£5, inc. p&p)

Microform publications:
Printed list of microfiche publications (transcripts of parish registers and census) available on receipt of sae

Publications list:
Available online and in print

Access to staff:
Contact by letter, by telephone, by fax, by e-mail and in person
Hours: Only Wed, Thu, 0930 to 1300 and 1400 to 1700

Access for disabled people:
Level entry, toilet facilities

Parent body:
Woodhorn Trust
   Woodhorn, QEII Country Park, Ashington, Northumberland, NE63 9YF; tel: 01670 528080; website: htttp://www.experiencewoodhorn.com

BEVIN BOYS ASSOCIATION

Acronym or abbreviation: BBA

23 Great Cranford Street, Poundbury, Dorchester, Dorset, DT1 3SQ

Tel: 01305 261269

Enquiries:
Enquiries to: Archivist / Public Relations
Other contacts: Vice President / National Chairman

Founded:
1989

Organisation type and purpose:
Voluntary organisation.
To encourage comradeship, and organise reunions and events throughout the UK for all ex-Bevin Boys who worked in the coal mines to serve their National Service in lieu of service in the Forces during WWII. Bevin Boys were so named after Ernest Bevin the wartime Minister of Labour and National Service.

Printed publications:
Newsletter (members only)

Access to staff:
Contact by letter and by telephone
Hours: Mon to Fri, 0900 to 1700

BEXLEY LIBRARY SERVICE

Central Library, Townley Road, Bexleyheath, Kent, DA6 7HJ

Tel: 020 8303 7777 ext. 3450
Fax: 020 8304 7058
E-mail: centrallibrary@bexley.gov.uk

Website:
http://www.bexley.gov.uk

Enquiries:
Enquiries to: Library Manager

Organisation type and purpose:
Local government body, public library.

Subject coverage:
General.

Museum or gallery collection, archive, or library special collection:
Government publications

Non-library collection catalogue:
All or part available online

Library catalogue:
All or part available online

Access to staff:
Contact by letter, by telephone, by fax, by e-mail and in person
Hours: Mon, Tue, Wed, Fri, 0930 to 1730; Thu 0930 to 2000; Sat, 0930 to 1700; Sun 1000 to 1400

Branch of:
South East Area Libraries Information Co-operative (SEAL)

BEXLEY LOCAL STUDIES AND ARCHIVE CENTRE

Central Library, Townley Road, Bexleyheath, Kent, DA6 7HJ

Tel: 020 8303 7777 ext. 7470
Fax: 020 8304 7058
E-mail: archives@bexley.gov.uk

Website:
http://www.bexley.gov.uk/localstudies/index.html

Enquiries:
Enquiries to: Local Studies Manager
Other contacts: Archivist (for archive collection enquiries)

Founded:
1972

Formerly called:
Bexley Local Studies Society

Organisation type and purpose:
Public library, Diocesan Record Office for Rochester and Southwark, Local Authority Record Office for Bexley

Subject coverage:
Historical information for area now covered by London Borough of Bexley.

Non-library collection catalogue:
All or part available online and in-house

Library catalogue:
All or part available online and in-house

Printed publications:
Publications on the history of Bexley, Sidcup, Crayford, Erith

Microform publications:
Local parish registers, census, GRO indexes and newspapers (for reference only)

Electronic and video publications:
Image database for the local area (online)

Publications list:
Available online

Access to staff:
Contact by letter, by telephone, by fax, by e-mail, in person and via website
Hours: Mon to Fri, 0930 to 1730; Thu, 0930 to 2000; Sat, 0930 to 1700

Access for disabled people:
Access to all public areas, toilet facilities

Parent body:
London Borough of Bexley
Civic Offices, Bexleyheath, Kent; tel: 020 8303 7777; website: http://www.bexley.gov.uk

BFI NATIONAL ARCHIVE

Formal name: British Film Institute

Curatorial Unit, 21 Stephen Street, London, W1T 1LN

Tel: 020 7255 1444
Fax: 020 7580 7503
E-mail: information.unit@bfi.org.uk

Website:
http://www.bfi.org.uk/national archive
http://www.bfi.org.uk
General information on the bfi Collections.

Founded:
1935

Organisation type and purpose:
National government body.
Cultural organisation.

Subject coverage:
Art and history of the cinema and of television, the documentary record of the 20th century. Films, video and TV programmes produced, shown, distributed or transmitted in the UK; preservation and restoration; cataloguing of film and TV material.

Museum or gallery collection, archive, or library special collection:
The Archive holds approximately 450,000 titles dating from 1895 to the present day
The Collection comprises features and short films, animation, documentaries, newsreels, television programmes, amateur films and videos

Non-library collection catalogue:
All or part available online and in-house

Printed publications:
See bfi website

Access to staff:
Contact by letter, by telephone, by fax, by e-mail and in person
Hours: Mon to Fri, 1000 to 1730

Access to building, collection or gallery:
Appointment required

BFI – Imax Cinema:

1 Charlie Chaplin Walk, South Bank, Waterloo, London, SE1 8XR; tel: 020 7902 1234

Founder member of:
International Federation of Film Archives

BFMS

Formal name: British False Memory Society
Acronym or abbreviation: BFMS

Bradford on Avon, Wiltshire, BA15 1NF

Tel: 01225 868682
Fax: 01225 862251
E-mail: bfms@bfms.org.uk

Website:
http://www.bfms.org.uk

Enquiries:
Enquiries to: Administrator

Founded:
1993

Formerly called:
ACAP, British False Memory Society

Organisation type and purpose:
Registered charity (charity number 1040683). Formed in 1993 to raise awareness of dangers of 'recovered memory therapy', which has given rise to an epidemic of decades-delayed, uncorroborated allegations against parents of childhood sexual abuse. Comprehensive archive on damage to patients and families as a result of false allegations influenced by therapy and associated beliefs; legal implications of 'recovered memory' and unreliable allegations in the criminal and civil courts, with case histories and contacts.

Subject coverage:
False memory/recovered memory including legal implications.

Museum or gallery collection, archive, or library special collection:
Books, videos, audio cassettes, academic papers and newspaper, journal and magazine cuttings

Non-library collection catalogue:
All or part available in-house

Library catalogue:
All or part available in-house

Printed publications:
Fractured Families (book)
List of academic articles (by request)
Brochure
Newsletters
Booklet

Electronic and video publications:
Various videos related to false memories

Access to staff:
Contact by letter, by telephone, by fax, by e-mail and via website. Appointment necessary. Access for members only.
Hours: Mon to Fri, 0915 to 1700
Special comments: Lift serves the first two flights of stairs, but not the third flight of stairs.

Access to building, collection or gallery:
Hours: Mon to Fri, 0915 to 1700

Access for disabled people:
Ramped entry
Special comments: Lift to 1st floor only.

BFWG CHARITABLE FOUNDATION

Formal name: FfWG

20 Fern Road, Storrington, Pulborough, West Sussex, RH20 4LW

Tel: 01903 746723
Fax: 01903 746723
E-mail: valconsidine@toucansurf.com

Website:
http://www.ffwg.org.uk

Enquiries:
Enquiries to: Company Secretary
Direct e-mail: jean.c@blueyonder.co.uk (re grants)
Other contacts: Grants Administrator (for details relating to grant applications)

Founded:
1925

Formerly called:
Crosby Hall (year of change 1993)

Organisation type and purpose:
Registered charity (charity number 312903).

continued overleaf

Grant awarding charity.
Grants to help women graduates with their living expenses while registered for study or research at an approved institution of higher education in Great Britain.

Access to staff:
Contact by letter, by telephone, by fax, by e-mail, in person and via website. Appointment necessary.
Hours: Mon to Fri, 0900 to 1645

Member organisation of:
International Federation of University Women (IFUW)
8 rue de l'Ancien Port, 1201, Geneva, Switzerland; tel: +41 22 731 1280; fax: +41 22 738 0440; e-mail: ifuw@ifuw.org
University Women of Europe (UWE)

Parent body:
British Federation of Women Graduates (BFWG)
4 Mandeville Courtyard, 142 Battersea Park Road, London, SW11 4NB; tel: 020 7498 8037; fax: 020 7498 8037; e-mail: bfwg@bfwg.demon.co.uk

BG GROUP PLC

Information Centre, 100 Thames Valley Park Drive, Reading, Berkshire, RG6 1PT

Tel: 0118 929 2496
Fax: 0118 929 2482
E-mail: padraig.cronin@bg-group.com

Enquiries:
Enquiries to: Commercial Intelligence Manager
Other contacts: Information Analyst

Formerly called:
British Gas (year of change 1997); BG plc (year of change 1999)

Organisation type and purpose:
International organisation, industrial commercial company.
Gas exploration and production, overseas gas-related ventures.

Subject coverage:
Oil/gas exploration and production, LNG, power generation, gas transmission and distribution.

Library catalogue:
All or part available in-house

Access to staff:
Contact by letter, by telephone and by fax
Hours: Mon to Fri, 0900 to 1700

Access to building, collection or gallery:
Prior appointment required

Access for disabled people:
Parking provided, access to all public areas

BHF GROUP

225 Bristol Road, Edgbaston, Birmingham, B5 7UB

Tel: 0121 446 6688
Fax: 0121 446 5215
E-mail: info@bhfgroup.co.uk

Website:
http://www.bhfgroup.co.uk

Enquiries:
Enquiries to: Information Officer

Founded:
1899

Organisation type and purpose:
Trade association.
Trade Federation.
Represents more than 4,000 primary retail outlets in hardware, ironmongery, DIY, building supplies and agricultural machinery.

Subject coverage:
Finance clearing house, merchandising company, insurance, inter-firm comparison, computer systems, information service, training, shop design, direct mail.

Printed publications:
Grey List (monthly)
Hardware Today (monthly)
Home Décor & Furnishings (bi-monthly)
CHA Times (bi-monthly)
BAGMA Bulletin (bi-monthly)
Garden Machinery Price Guide (monthly)
Members Handbook (Annual)

Access to staff:
Contact by letter and by e-mail. Access for members only.
Hours: Mon to Fri, 0900 to 1700

Links with:
British Retail Consortium
DTI De-Regulation Task Force
Eurocommerce Limited
International Hardware Association
Rainy Day Trust

BHR GROUP LIMITED

The Fluid Engineering Centre, Cranfield, Bedfordshire, MK43 0AJ

Tel: 01234 750422
Fax: 01234 750074
E-mail: contactus@bhrgroup.com

Website:
http://www.bhrgroup.com

Enquiries:
Enquiries to: Manager – Information Service
Direct tel: 01234 756530
Direct e-mail: nguy@bhrgroup.co.uk

Founded:
1947

Organisation type and purpose:
Consultancy, research organisation.
Independent technology organisation.

Subject coverage:
Fluid dynamics and process engineering, more specifically: pumps and other fluid machines, fluid power, tribology, abrasive waterjet and plain water jet cutting and cleaning technology, fluid sealing and containment integrity, multiphase flow, pipeline technology; flow in pipes, cavitation, flow measurement and control, hydraulic transport of solid materials in pipelines, open channel flow, civil engineering, hydraulic structures (dams, spillways, flood defences, cooling systems, etc.), fluid effects on structures, industrial aerodynamics, biotechnology; process technology, process intensification, fluid control, valves, oil and gas production improvement, oil and gas transport, water and waste water treatment, water supply modelling software systems, knowledge-based software tools for water resource allocation planning, biodiesel production; knowhow for reduction of emissions, computational fluid dynamics (CFD), pipeline pigging and pipe protection, mixing – batch and inline, filtration and separation.

Non-library collection catalogue:
All or part available online and in-house

Library catalogue:
All or part available in-house

Publications list:
Available online

Access to staff:
Contact by letter, by telephone, by fax, by e-mail, in person and via website
Hours: Mon to Fri, 0900 to 1700
Special comments: Charges, either by subscription or one-off, for certain services; details on request.

Access to building, collection or gallery:
By arrangement

BIAB ONLINE – BRITISH AND IRISH ARCHAEOLOGICAL BIBLIOGRAPHY

Acronym or abbreviation: biab online

c/o The British Academy, 10 Carlton Terrace, London, SW1Y 5AH

Tel: 020 7969 5223 or 5444
Fax: 020 7969 5300 (shared)
E-mail: info@biab.ac.uk

Website:
http://www.biab.ac.uk
biab online exists to support research work of all kinds and includes almost 200,000 publication references from over three centuries of scholarship; coverage extends across all aspects of archaeology and the historic environment, and every chronological period, with a geographical focus on Britain and Ireland. Over 2,000 new references are added each year, including: online and hard-copy sources; local, regional, national and international publications; books, articles, conference proceedings and grey literature. Additional data and functionality following the 2010 relaunch include: over 55,000 grey literature references from England's Archaeological Investigations Project (AIP); user accounts – allowing users to save and refine their searches, and download results (subject to terms and conditions).

Access to the biab online service is free to all.

Enquiries:
Enquiries to: Chief Bibliographer & Editor

Founded:
1968

Formerly called:
British Archaeological Abstracts (year of change 1991); British Archaeological Bibliography (year of change 1997)

Organisation type and purpose:
Research organisation.
biab online is a service provided by the Council for British Archaeology (CBA) with the support of funding from English Heritage, Society of Antiquaries of London, Cadw, the Heritage Council of the Republic of Ireland, RCAHMW, RCAHMS, Historic Scotland, Society of Antiquaries of Scotland, Archaeology Scotland, and the Northern Ireland Environment Agency. It provides the abstracts and indexing service for British and Irish Archaeology and is now available online at http://www.biab.ac.uk.
To compile and publish a comprehensive bibliography for the archaeology of Great Britain and Ireland.

Subject coverage:
Archaeology of Great Britain and Republic of Ireland; publications relating to the archaeology of Great Britain and Ireland.

Museum or gallery collection, archive, or library special collection:
Electronic data on archaeology bibliography from 1695 to 1980, citations only; 1967 to present, citations and abstracts

Electronic and video publications:
Online database and web pages

Access to staff:
Contact by letter, by telephone, by fax and by e-mail. Appointment necessary.
Hours: Mon to Fri, 1000 to 1730
Special comments: Staff are part-time – e-mailing ahead is recommended

Links with:
Council for British Archaeology (CBA)
St Mary's House, 66 Bootham, York, YO30 7BZ; tel: 01904 671 417; fax: 01904 671 384; website: http://www.britarch.ac.uk

BIBIC

Formal name: British Institute for Brain Injured Children

Knowle Hall, Bridgwater, Somerset, TA7 8PJ

Tel: 01278 684060
Fax: 01278 685573
E-mail: info@bibic.org.uk

Website:
http://www.bibic.org.uk

Enquiries:
Enquiries to: Marketing Co-ordinator
Other contacts: Family Services Director

Founded:
1972

Organisation type and purpose:
National organisation, voluntary organisation, registered charity (charity number 1057635). Caters for children from the age of 6 months to 18 years. BIBIC exists to maximise the potential of children with conditions affecting their social, sensory communication, motor and learning abilities.

Subject coverage:
BIBIC's home-based therapy helps rehabilitate children variously diagnosed as having autism, autistic tendencies, brain damage, brain injury, cerebral palsy, developmental delay, Downs syndrome, dyslexia, epilepsy, hydrocephalus, learning difficulties, learning disability, microcephalus, dyspraxia, attention deficit hyperactivity disorders (ADHD). It draws not only on sensory-motor techniques but also incorporates aspects derived from speech therapy, physiotherapy and occupational therapy in a medically overseen environment. Bursary funding for children from disadvantaged backgrounds is available.

Printed publications:
Milestones (newsletter, 2 times a year, free)

Electronic and video publications:
CD and DVD

Access to staff:
Contact by letter, by telephone, by fax, by e-mail and via website. Appointment necessary.
Hours: Mon to Fri, 0900 to 1700

Access for disabled people:
Parking provided, ramped entry, toilet facilities, lift, stair lift.
Special comments: Access to most public areas

BIBLE SOCIETY

Formal name: British & Foreign Bible Society
Acronym or abbreviation: BFBS

Contact Centre, Stonehill Green, Westlea, Swindon, Wiltshire, SN5 7DG

Tel: 01793 418100
Fax: 01793 418118
E-mail: contactus@biblesociety.org.uk

Website:
http://www.biblesociety.org.uk

Enquiries:
Enquiries to: Contact Centre
Direct tel: 01793 418222

Founded:
1804

Organisation type and purpose:
Registered charity (charity number 232759). Helping church people to own, use, value and share the Bible.

Subject coverage:
Bible translation and distribution of the scriptures throughout the world, printing history, linguistics, church growth, mission, bible commentaries, social and religious trends, research reports relating to these.

Museum or gallery collection, archive, or library special collection:
Catalogue of manuscripts
Historical catalogue of printed Bibles with sectional revisions for African, English, Indian and Chinese scriptures
Scriptures Library and Archive (28,000 volumes in more than 2,000 languages) now housed in Cambridge University Library, access via Contact Centre, Swindon

Printed publications:
Bibles
Bible Translations – update and background
Word in Action (3 times a year, free)
Bible in TransMission (3 times a year, free to clergy)
Resources relating to projects
Order printed publications from: website: http://www.bibleresources.org.uk

Electronic and video publications:
Complete Bible on microchip in pocket computer
New Testament on diskette
Cassettes
Videos

Publications list:
Available online

Access to staff:
Contact by letter, by fax and by e-mail.
Appointment necessary.
Hours: Mon to Fri, 0900 to 1700

Access for disabled people:
Parking provided, ramped entry, access to all public areas, toilet facilities

Founder member of:
United Bible Society – a fellowship of national bible societies around the world (UBS)

BIBLE TEXT PUBLICITY MISSION

PO Box 2677, Romford, RM7 8XF

Tel: 01708 733293
E-mail: billturner:tiscali.co.uk

Website:
http://www.btpm.org.uk
Mission statement, details of poster sites, meanings of posters.

Organisation type and purpose:
A Christian Mission committed to proclaiming the contents of the Bible on posters in public places.

Subject coverage:
Posters in railway stations and tube stations.

Information services:
Tel. for discussion of any issues arising from the posters, or for help and guidance.

Access to staff:
Contact by letter, by telephone and by e-mail

Member organisation of:
Evangelical Alliance

BIBLIOGRAPHICAL SOCIETY

Formal name: The Bibliographical Society

C/o Institute of English Studies, Room 306, Senate House, Malet Street, London, WC1E 7HU

E-mail: secretary@bibsoc.org.uk

Website:
http://www.bibsoc.org.uk

Enquiries:
Enquiries to: Hon. Sec.

Founded:
1892

Organisation type and purpose:
Learned society.
Membership organisation (membership by subscription)
To promote and encourage study and research in the fields of: historical, analytical, descriptive and textual bibliography, and the history of printing, publishing, bookselling, bookbinding and collecting.
To hold meetings at which papers are read and discussed. To print and publish a journal and books concerned with bibliography.
To maintain a bibliographical library.
To support bibliographical research by awarding grants and bursaries.

Museum or gallery collection, archive, or library special collection:
Society's library is housed at Stationers' Hall. Members wishing to borrow books should apply to the Hon. Librarian: Robin Myers, Stationers' Company, Stationers' Hall, London EC4M 7DD.
The catalogue for the library is now available electronically, via the catalogue of the School of Advanced Study at the University of London (go to http://catalogue.ulrls.lon.ac.uk/ and select Bibliographical Society from the options).

Library catalogue:
All or part available online

Publications list:
Available online

Access to staff:
Contact by letter and by e-mail

BIBRA TOXICOLOGY ADVICE & CONSULTING LTD

Westmead House, 123 Westmead Road, Sutton, Surrey, SM1 4JH

Tel: 020 8722 4701
Fax: 020 8722 4706
E-mail: info@bibratoxadvice.co.uk

Website:
http://www.bibra-information.co.uk/
General information on services.

Enquiries:
Enquiries to: Information Officer
Other contacts: Sales Manager

Founded:
1960

Created by the merger of:
BIBRA Information Services Ltd and Toxicology Advice & Consulting Ltd (year of change 2007)

Formerly called:
TNO BIBRA International Limited

Organisation type and purpose:
Consultancy, research organisation.
Independent research and advice on the health effects of chemicals.

Subject coverage:
Chemical toxicology and ecotoxicology and safety in use, including industrial chemicals, food additives, food contaminants such as packaging migrants, pesticides, feed additives and other agricultural chemicals, cosmetics and toiletry components, dry excipients, surgical products, tobacco additives and air and water pollutants, international legislation on the foregoing subjects, need for and design of toxicological tests on specific materials.

Museum or gallery collection, archive, or library special collection:
Unique collection of over 400,000 specially selected up-to-date research papers, reports, expert comment, and legislative material relating to the health effects of chemicals

Printed publications:
Toxicology and Regulatory News (monthly; formerly TNO BIBRA Bulletin)
Food and Chemical Toxicology
Toxicity Profiles
Toxicology In Vitro

Access to staff:
Contact by letter, by telephone, by fax and by e-mail
Hours: Mon to Fri, 0900 to 1715

Parent body:
TNO Nutrition and Food Research Institute Utrechtseweg 48, PO Box 360, Zeist, Netherlands; tel: +31 3 694 4754; fax: +31 3 695 7928; e-mail: infodesk@tno.nl

BICYCLE ASSOCIATION OF GREAT BRITAIN LIMITED

Acronym or abbreviation: BA

Starley House, Eaton Road, Coventry, Warwickshire, CV1 2FH

Tel: 024 7655 3838
Fax: 024 7622 8366
E-mail: office@ba-gb.com

Enquiries:
Enquiries to: Secretary

Organisation type and purpose:
Trade association.

Subject coverage:
British bicycle industry, manufacture, statistics, imports, accessories.

Trade and statistical information:
UK market for bicycles.

Printed publications:
Order printed publications from: Secretary

Publications list:
Available in print

Access to staff:
Contact by letter and by telephone
Hours: Mon to Fri, 0900 to 1700

Access to building, collection or gallery:
No access other than to staff

BIGGAR ALBION FOUNDATION

The Albion Archive, 9 Edinburgh Road, Biggar, Lanarkshire, ML12 6AX

Tel: 01899 221497
E-mail: info@albionarch.co.uk

Website:
http://www.albion-trust.org.uk

Enquiries:
Enquiries to: Secretary

Founded:
1999

Organisation type and purpose:
Foundation responsible for the Albion Club (membership is open to all those interested in Albion vehicles), the Albion Archive, the Biggar Rally and the Albion museum.

Subject coverage:
Albion vehicles (1899–1976).

Information services:
Identification of Albion lorries/vehicles for DVLA.

Special visitor services:
Archive.

Museum or gallery collection, archive, or library special collection:
Albion archive of material relating to Albion commercial vehicles

Printed publications:
Albion Magazine (quarterly)

Links with:
Albion Vehicle Preservation Trust
    18 Netherdale Drive, Paisley, Renfrewshire, PA1 3DA

BILLINGS NATURAL FAMILY PLANNING CENTRE

Acronym or abbreviation: The BOM Trust

The Basement, 58b Vauxhall Grove, London, SW8 1TB

Tel: 020 7793 0026
Fax: 020 7793 0026

Enquiries:
Enquiries to: Director General
Other contacts: Secretary for book and literature orders.

Founded:
1987

Formerly called:
Billings Family Life Centre, Billings Natural Family Planning Centre

Organisation type and purpose:
International organisation, national organisation, professional body (membership is by qualification, election or invitation), voluntary organisation, registered charity (charity number 10077245), suitable for ages: 12 to 22, training organisation, consultancy.

Subject coverage:
Literature, teaching and teacher training in the Billings Ovulation Method providing a means of natural family planning for the achievement or avoidance of pregnancy. Teacher training and education courses in human sexuality which, while addressing all aspects of the human person including fertility, teach chastity.

Access to staff:
Contact by letter, by telephone and by fax. Appointment necessary.
Hours: Mon, Tue, Wed, Fri, 1000 to 1800
Special comments: Evening and weekend appointments.
Charges made to all users (with exceptions). May close during state school holidays.

Access to building, collection or gallery:
Prior appointment required
Hours: Mon to Fri, 1000 to 1700; plus some evenings and Sats
Special comments: Closed on some evenings, some weekends and some school holidays.

Affiliated with the:
World Organisation of Ovulation Method Billings (WOOMB)

Other addresses:
Billings NFP Centre (Hours: Tue and Thu, 0930 to 1230)
    Margaret House, 132 Huntley Street, Aberdeen, AB10 1SU; tel: 01224 643300; e-mail: mariesandison@hotmail.com

Parent body:
Billings Family Life Centre (WOOMB)
    27 Alexandra Parade, North Fitzroy, 3068, Australia; tel: + 61 3 948 1722 / 1 800 336 860; fax: + 61 3 9482 4208; e-mail: billings@ozemail.com .au; website: http://www.woomb.org

BINGO ASSOCIATION, THE

Lexham House, 75 High Street North, Dunstable, Bedfordshire, LU6 1JF

Tel: 01582 860921
Fax: 01582 860925
E-mail: info@bingo-association.co.uk

Website:
http://www.bingo-association.co.uk
Industry news; press releases.

Enquiries:
Enquiries to: Chief Executive
Other contacts: Administration Manager for centre of activity.

Founded:
1985

Formerly called:
Bingo Association of Great Britain (year of change 1998)

Organisation type and purpose:
Trade association (membership is by qualification, election or invitation, present number of members: 125.

Subject coverage:
Licensed bingo in Great Britain; Gaming Act 1968 and the law appertaining to licensed bingo, where, how and when you can play; history of bingo.

Printed publications:
Industry Factsheet
Code of Practice

Management Guide (£10 per copy plus postage)

Access to staff:
Contact by letter, by telephone, by fax, by e-mail, in person and via website. Appointment necessary.
Hours: Mon to Fri, 0900 to 1700

BIO INDUSTRY ASSOCIATION SCOTLAND

Acronym or abbreviation: BIA Scotland

Centre House, Midlothian Innovation Centre, Pentlandfield, Roslin, Midlothian, EH25 9RE

Tel: 0131 440 6161
Fax: 0131 440 2871

Website:
http://www.bioindustry.org

Enquiries:
Enquiries to: Director
Direct e-mail: sjohnstone@bioindustry.org

Founded:
2001

Formerly called:
Scottish Biomedical Association (SbA) (year of change 2001)

Organisation type and purpose:
Trade association.

Subject coverage:
All aspects associated with the promotion of the healthcare industry, biomedical and biotechnology sectors in Scotland.

Printed publications:
Annual Review
Membership directory (members only)
Membership Information
Order printed publications from: Bio Industry Association
14/15 Belgrave Square, London, SW1X 8PS, tel: 020 7565 7192, fax: 020 7565 7191, e-mail: rgrant@ bioindustry.org

Electronic and video publications:
BIS-Database of biotech industry in the UK – contains details of companies, products (CD-ROM)

Publications list:
Available in print

Access to staff:
Contact by letter, by telephone, by fax and by e-mail. Appointment necessary.
Hours: Mon to Fri, 0900 to 1700

Parent body:
BIA
    14–15 Belgrave Square, London, SW1X 8PS; tel: 020 7565 7190; fax: 020 7565 7191

BIOCHEMICAL SOCIETY

Third Floor, Eagle House, 16 Procter Street, London, WC1V 6NX

Tel: 020 7280 4100
Fax: 020 7280 4170
E-mail: genadmin@biochemistry.org

Website:
http://www.biochemistry.org
http://www.portlandpress.com

Enquiries:
Enquiries to: Membership Secretary
Direct e-mail: membership@biochemistry.org

Founded:
1911

Organisation type and purpose:
National organisation, learned society (membership is by election or invitation), present number of members: 7200, registered charity (charity number 253894), publishing house.

Subject coverage:
Biochemistry, biotechnology, biomolecular sciences, molecular biology, genetics, cell biology.

Museum or gallery collection, archive, or library special collection:
Contact Archivist at: genadmin@biochemistry.org

Printed publications:
Biotechnology and Applied Biochemistry (6 times a year)
Biochemical Journal (fortnightly)
Biochemical Society Transactions (quarterly)
Essays in Biochemistry (2 times a year)
Graduate Employment Survey (annually)
Symposia (annually)
The Biochemist (6 times a year)
Biology of the Cell (12 times a year)
Order printed publications from: Portland Press Commerce Way, Colchester, CO2 8HP, tel: 01206 796351, fax: 01206 799331, e-mail: sales@portland -services.com

Publications list:
Available online and in print

Access to staff:
Contact by letter, by telephone, by fax, by e-mail and via website
Hours: Mon to Fri, 0900 to 1700

Links with:
Portland Press
  tel: 020 7580 5530; fax: 020 7323 1136; e-mail: editorial@portlandpress.com

Members of:
Association of Learned and Professional Society Publishers
Federation of European Biochemical Societies
International Union of Biochemistry and Molecular Biology

Other address:
Biochemical Society
  Commerce Way, Colchester, CO2 8HP; tel: 01206 796351; fax: 01206 799331; e-mail: membership@ biochemistry.org

BIOINDUSTRY ASSOCIATION

Acronym or abbreviation: BIA

14–15 Belgrave Square, London, SW1X 8PS

Tel: 020 7565 7190
Fax: 020 7565 7191
E-mail: admin@bioindustry.org

Website:
http://www.bioindustry.org
About BIA, its members, benefits of bioscience, news, events, publications, careers.

Organisation type and purpose:
The trade association for innovative enterprises in the UK's bioscience sector.
To promote the human health benefits of new bioscience technologies, encouraging the commercial success of the bioscience industry by focusing on emerging enterprise and the related interests of companies with whom such enterprise trades.
Supports member interests by lobbying government and parliament in the UK and Brussels, providing high quality information and business services, and attracting investment from both private and government sources.

Subject coverage:
The Association defines bioscience companies as those that are developing products or services that are derived from the study of living systems, or use living systems in their research, development and/ or manufacturing activities. Such companies will typically be working in the fields of human or animal healthcare, including: diagnostics; therapeutics; vaccines and nutrition; environmental protection or remediation; or will be companies providing technical or commercial services to such companies.

Electronic and video publications:
Annual Review
NewsCAST (weekly e-mail news bulletin)
Regulatory Briefing (quarterly newsletter on regulatory issues)

An extensive list of reports, surveys and examinations of the bioscience sector in the UK
Order electronic and video publications from:
Download from website

Publications list:
Available online

Access to staff:
Contact by letter, by telephone, by fax and by e-mail

BIOMEDICAL RESEARCH EDUCATION TRUST

Acronym or abbreviation: BRET

25 Shaftesbury Avenue, London, W1D 7EG

Tel: 020 7287 2595
Fax: 020 7287 2595
E-mail: t.g@bret.org.uk

Website:
http://www.bret.org.uk
Information otherwise found in leaflets, information about obtaining speakers.

Enquiries:
Enquiries to: Director
Direct e-mail: ted@tgriffiths.net

Founded:
1988

Organisation type and purpose:
Service industry, registered charity (charity number 292366), training organisation.
Information for schools and other interested groups about why animals are used for medical research.

Subject coverage:
Animal welfare, information for schools, biomedical research.

Printed publications:
Information About Animal Research (leaflet, free)
Schools Resources Guide (leaflet, free)
Why Is Animal Research Necessary? (leaflet, free)

Electronic and video publications:
Animals and Human Kidney (video, free to schools on request)
Choices (video, free to schools on request)
Inside the Animal House (video available for viewing only with a speaker)
The Use of Animals in Medical Research (video, free to schools on request)
What About People? (video, free to schools on request)

Access to staff:
Contact by letter, by telephone, by fax, by e-mail and via website
Hours: Mon to Fri, 0900 to 1700

Parent body:
Research Defence Society

BIOSS INTERNATIONAL

Acronym or abbreviation: BIOSS

Box 3, Brunel Science Park, Kingston Lane, Uxbridge, Middlesex, UB8 3PQ

Tel: 01895 270072
Fax: 01895 254760
E-mail: info@biosseurope.com

Website:
http://www.bioss.com
EDAC, a website that provides organisation and individual development procedures on-line, based on the analysis by trained practitioners from three instruments known as MCPA, an executive development instrument, Launchpad, a psychometric instrument, a modified version of CPA (Career Path Appreciation).

Enquiries:
Enquiries to: Secretary General
Other contacts: Secretary & Registrar (Finance and Legal)

Founded:
1968

Formerly called:
Bioss International Ltd; Brunel Institute of Organisation and Social Studies (year of change 2001)

Organisation type and purpose:
International organisation, advisory body, membership association (membership is by qualification, election or invitation), present number of members: over 200, registered charity (charity number 1016381).

Subject coverage:
Social policy, social organisation, social relationships, social institutions, social stratification and mobility, individual behaviour and capacity, education, church and the community, youth in society.
Career path appreciation, mapping and appraisal.
The use and management of strategic information and the management of change and Organisation Mapping.

Printed publications:
Conference papers, books, working papers
A list of locally produced papers is held at the address

Access to staff:
Contact by letter, by telephone, by fax, by e-mail and via website. Appointment necessary.
Hours: Mon to Fri, 0900 to 1700

Other officers worldwide:
BIOSS International
  Information at same address

BIOTECHNOLOGY AND BIOLOGICAL SCIENCES RESEARCH COUNCIL

Acronym or abbreviation: BBSRC

Polaris House, North Star Avenue, Swindon, Wiltshire, SN2 1UH

Tel: 01793 413200
Fax: 01793 413382
E-mail: external.relations@bbsrc.ac.uk

Website:
http://www.bbsrc.ac.uk
Information on the organisation, funding, research committees, studentships, fellowships and special initiatives. Oasis database of recent BBSRC-funded research.

Formerly called:
AFRC, Science and Engineering Research Council (year of change 1994)

Organisation type and purpose:
Research organisation.

Subject coverage:
Agriculture, food, biotechnology, pharmaceutical, chemical and healthcare industries.

Printed publications:
Annual Report
BBSRC Business Strategic Plan

Electronic and video publications:
Oasis database of recent BBSRC-funded research

Access to staff:
Contact by e-mail. Appointment necessary.
Hours: Mon to Fri, 0900 to 1700

BIRDLIFE INTERNATIONAL

Wellbrook Court, Girton Road, Cambridge, CB3 0NA

Tel: 01223 277318
Fax: 01223 277200
E-mail: birdlife@birdlife.org

Website:
http://www.birdlife.org

continued overleaf

Information about the organisation. How to contact Partners. Publications. Information on important bird areas and globally threatened bird species.

Enquiries:
Enquiries to: Communications Manager
Direct tel: 01223 279813
Direct e-mail: martin.fowlie@birdlife.org.uk
Other contacts: Information Scientist & Librarian

Founded:
1922

Formerly called:
International Council for Bird Preservation (year of change 1993)

Organisation type and purpose:
International organisation (membership is by subscription), registered charity (charity number 1042125), research organisation.
Carries out field projects, research and advocacy relating to threatened bird species and their habitats.

Subject coverage:
Status of bird species throughout the world especially all endangered species; conservation problems and priorities concerning threatened bird species and their habitats.

Museum or gallery collection, archive, or library special collection:
Library and reprint collection relating to threatened birds

Trade and statistical information:
World data on threatened bird species.

Library catalogue:
All or part available in-house

Printed publications:
Books:
Bird Conservation series (12 titles)
Birds in Europe
Important Bird Areas
Red Data Books (3 titles)
Threatened Birds of the World
Periodical publications:
Annual Report
BirdLife International Africa (newsletter, 2 times a year)
BirdLife International Asia (newsletter, quarterly)
World Birdwatch (magazine, quarterly, annual subscription £25)
Order printed publications from: For books only: NHBS Limited, 2–3 Wills Road, Totnes, Devon, tel: 01803 865913, fax: 01803 865280, e-mail: sales@nhbs.co.uk
For Threatened Birds of the World: Lynx Edicions, Passeig de Gràcia, Barcelona, 12 E-08007, Spain, tel: +34 93 301 07 77, fax: +34 93 302 1475, e-mail: lynx@hbw.com

Access to staff:
Contact by letter, by telephone, by fax, by e-mail and via website
Hours: Mon to Fri, 0900 to 1700

Access to building, collection or gallery:
By prior appointment only
Hours: Mon to Fri, 0900 to 1700

Access for disabled people:
Toilet facilities

Partnership of:
National conservation organisations worldwide, present in more than 100 countries or territories

BIRKBECK COLLEGE LIBRARY

Library, Malet Street, London, WC1E 7HX

Tel: 020 7631 6064
Fax: 020 7631 6066
E-mail: library-help@bbk.ac.uk

Website:
http://www.bbk.ac.uk/lib
Library services.

Enquiries:
Enquiries to: Librarian

Direct tel: 020 7631 6250
Direct e-mail: p.payne@bbk.ac.uk

Founded:
1823

Organisation type and purpose:
University library.

Subject coverage:
Applied linguistics, economics, English, film studies, French, geography, German, history, history of art, philosophy, politics, psychology, occupational psychology, sociology, Spanish, chemistry, botany, zoology, statistics, computer science, crystallography, geology, law, management and business studies.

Library catalogue:
All or part available online

Printed publications:
Leaflets on Library services – all on website

Access to staff:
Contact by letter, by telephone, by fax, by e-mail and via website. Non-members charged.
Hours: Term time: Mon to Fri, 1000 to 2215; Sat, 1000 to 1745; Sun, 1000 to 1745
Vacations: times vary, check website

Access to building, collection or gallery:
Hours: Term time: Mon to Sun, 0830 to 2345
Vacations: times vary, check website

Parent body:
University of London

BIRMINGHAM AND DISTRICT BUTCHERS ASSOCIATION

Acronym or abbreviation: BBA

30 Manor House, Moat Lane, Birmingham, B5 5BD

Tel: 0121 622 4900

Enquiries:
Enquiries to: Secretary

Founded:
1878

Organisation type and purpose:
Trade association.

Subject coverage:
All aspects relating to the running of a retail butcher's shop, including current legislation and consumer opinion on a daily basis.

Access to staff:
Contact by letter and by telephone
Hours: Mon to Fri, 0900 to 1300, with 24-hour answering service

BIRMINGHAM AND MIDLAND INSTITUTE

Acronym or abbreviation: BMI

9 Margaret Street, Birmingham, B3 3BS

Tel: 0121 236 3591
Fax: 0121 212 4577
E-mail: admin@bmi.org.uk

Website:
http://www.bmi.org.uk

Enquiries:
Enquiries to: Administrator

Founded:
1854

Incorporates the former:
Birmingham Library (founded 1779) (year of change 1955)

Organisation type and purpose:
Learned society (membership is by subscription), present number of members: 300, registered charity (charity number 522852).
Founded by Act of Parliament in 1854 for the Diffusion and Advancement of Science, Literature and Art amongst all Classes of Persons resident in Birmingham and the Midland Counties.

Subject coverage:
Science, literature and art.

Museum or gallery collection, archive, or library special collection:
18th-century volumes
19th- and 20th-century volumes on history, literature, natural history, science, travel, biography, autobiography, poetry
Late 19th- and early 20th-century fiction
Classical music books, records, CDs

Non-library collection catalogue:
All or part available in-house

Library catalogue:
All or part available in-house and in print

Printed publications:
BMI Insight (annual magazine, free to members)

Access to staff:
Contact by letter, by telephone, by fax, by e-mail and in person. Appointment necessary. Non-members charged.
Hours: Mon to Fri, 0900 to 1800

Access to building, collection or gallery:
Prior appointment required
Hours: Library: Mon to Fri, 1000 to 1800
Special comments: Members only. Charge for non-members research. Reference only for non-members.

Access for disabled people:
Ramped entry
Hours: As above

BIRMINGHAM ARCHIVES AND HERITAGE

Birmingham Central Library, Chamberlain Square, Birmingham, B3 3HQ

Tel: 0121 303 4549
Fax: 0121 464 1176
E-mail: archives.heritage@birmingham.gov.uk

Website:
http://www.birmingham.gov.uk/archivesandheritage
Part guide to records held.

Organisation type and purpose:
Local government body; public library; archives; records office. To collect, preserve and make available for research archival collections, printed reference material, maps and family history sources relating to the City of Birmingham, 12th to 21st centuries.

Subject coverage:
Sources for local and family history in the Birmingham area.

Museum or gallery collection, archive, or library special collection:
Original archive materials, including local authority records, church records, business records, estate and family records, public records (e.g. courts, hospitals, coroners), maps and photographs, and printed reference books.

Non-library collection catalogue:
All or part available online and in-house

Library catalogue:
All or part available online and in-house

Access to staff:
Contact by letter, by telephone, by fax, by e-mail, in person and via website
Hours: Open-access research area for published and printed material, microfiche and microfilm collections, Mon to Fri, 0900 to 2000 (except bank holidays); Sat, 0900 to 1700. Archives searchroom area for original documents, archive collections, photographs, rare and fragile material, Tue, Wed, Fri and Sat, 1000 to 1700; Thu, 1000 to 2000
Special comments: Official proof of identity is required for viewing archive material, photographs and any other material served in the archives searchroom area

BIRMINGHAM ASSOCIATION OF YOUTH CLUBS

Acronym or abbreviation: BAYC

Hilda Simister House, 581 Pershore Road, Selly Park, Birmingham, B29 7EL

Tel: 0845 241 0923
Fax: 0845 241 0924
E-mail: info@bayc.org

Enquiries:
Enquiries to: Chief Executive
Other contacts: Principal Development Officer for affiliations and support services.

Founded:
1898

Organisation type and purpose:
Membership association, voluntary organisation, registered charity (charity number 1090789). Youth Club Association.
Servicing agency for mixed youth groups in Birmingham and the Black Country.

Subject coverage:
Good practice in youth work; networks and contacts; volunteering opportunities for young people; project design and development; curriculum development; specialist work with young women and young men; accreditator of young people's voluntary activity, capacity building for youth groups.

Museum or gallery collection, archive, or library special collection:
Resources on work with girls and young women, boys and young men, youth work policy and practice, residential centres and projects, action research with young people, involving disabled young people as volunteers

Trade and statistical information:
Profile of youth groups in Birmingham and surrounding areas.

Printed publications:
Annual Report
Newsletter (monthly)
Promotional material for specific projects
Publications available through national body, UK Youth

Access to staff:
Contact by letter, by telephone, by fax and by e-mail. Appointment necessary.
Hours: Mon to Fri, 0915 to 1800

Access for disabled people:
Parking provided, ramped entry

Affiliated to:
UK Youth
2nd Floor, Kirby House, 20–24 Kirby Street, London, EC1N 8TS; tel: 020 7242 4045; fax: 020 7242 4125; e-mail: info@ukyouth.org

BIRMINGHAM AUTOMOTIVE SAFETY CENTRE

Acronym or abbreviation: BASC

School of Engineering (Mechanical and Manufacturing Engineering), University of Birmingham, Edgbaston, Birmingham, B15 2TT

Tel: 0121 414 5156
Fax: 0121 414 4180

Website:
http://barc.bham.ac.uk

Enquiries:
Enquiries to: Manager
Direct tel: 0121 414 7384
Direct e-mail: a.m.hassan@bham.ac.uk

Founded:
1970

Formerly called:
Accident Research Centre; Accident Research Unit (year of change 1999)

Organisation type and purpose:
University department or institute, training organisation, consultancy, research organisation.

Subject coverage:
Injuries and vehicle design, accident causation, transport, safety, product liability.

Access to staff:
Contact by letter, by telephone, by fax, by e-mail and via website. Appointment necessary.
Hours: Mon to Fri, 0900 to 1700

BIRMINGHAM BIBLIOGRAPHICAL SOCIETY

c/o Information Services, The University of Birmingham, Edgbaston, Birmingham, B15 2TT

Tel: 0121 414 3132

Enquiries:
Enquiries to: Honorary Secretary
Direct e-mail: j.hinks@bham.ac.uk

Organisation type and purpose:
Learned society.

Subject coverage:
Bibliographical and allied subjects, printing, booktrade etc; West Midlands Bibliography; local history of the book trade. On-going research project on the West Midlands book trade.

Printed publications:
West Midlands Book Trade Project; Working papers 1–7 covering the period to 1839, published 1975–1987

Access to staff:
Contact by e-mail
Hours: Mon to Fri, 0900 to 1700

BIRMINGHAM BOTANICAL GARDENS AND GLASSHOUSES

Acronym or abbreviation: BBHS

Westbourne Road, Edgbaston, Birmingham, B15 3TR

Tel: 0121 454 1860
Fax: 0121 454 7835
E-mail: admin@birminghambotanicalgardens.org.uk

Website:
http://www.birminghambotanicalgardens.org.uk

Enquiries:
Enquiries to: Chief Executive
Other contacts: Plant Collections Manager (for scientific and educational enquiries)

Founded:
1832

Also known as:
Birmingham Botanical and Horticultural Society Limited

Organisation type and purpose:
Membership association (membership is by subscription), present number of members: 5,000, registered charity (charity number 528981), suitable for all ages.
The Company, which is limited by guarantee, is an educational charity the aims of which are: to further public education in botany, horticulture and zoology, and provide facilities for research; to maintain and operate the Birmingham Botanical Gardens and Glasshouses for the above purpose, and for the recreation of the public.

Subject coverage:
Horticulture, history of Birmingham Botanical Gardens.

Museum or gallery collection, archive, or library special collection:
7,000 plants

Non-library collection catalogue:
All or part available in-house and in print

Library catalogue:
All or part available in-house and in print

Printed publications:
Annual report and accounts (online)
Information sheets (10p to £1.50)
Newsletters
Souvenir Guide (£2)

Electronic and video publications:
Guides (audio, braille and large print, free of charge)

Publications list:
Available online

Access to staff:
Contact by letter, by telephone, by fax, by e-mail and via website. Appointment necessary.
Hours: Mon to Fri, 0900 to 1700 (variable according to season)

Access for disabled people:
Parking provided, ramped entry, access to all public areas, toilet facilities

BIRMINGHAM BOYS AND GIRLS UNION

Acronym or abbreviation: BBGU

Woodlands Camp, Bournevale, Walsall, West Midlands, WS9 0SH

Tel: 0121 353 7329
Fax: 0121 353 7329

Enquiries:
Enquiries to: Warden

Founded:
1906

Organisation type and purpose:
Registered charity (charity number 522487), suitable for ages: 7+.
Residential outdoor activity centre giving priority to disadvantaged and handicapped groups.

Subject coverage:
Outdoor education; animal sanctuary; environmental.

Printed publications:
Brochures
Newsletter

Access to staff:
Contact by letter, by telephone and in person. Appointment necessary.
Hours: Mon to Fri, 0900 to 1700

Access for disabled people:
Parking provided, ramped entry, toilet facilities

BIRMINGHAM BURNS CENTRE

Selly Oak Hospital, Raddlebarn Road, Birmingham, B29 6JD

Tel: 0121 627 1627
Fax: 0121 627 8782

Enquiries:
Enquiries to: Clinical Lead in Burns
Direct tel: 0121 627 8784
Direct e-mail: remopapini@doctors.org.uk
Other contacts: Burns & Plastic Surgery Co-ordinator for clinical service lead in burns.

Founded:
1944

Formed from:
Birmingham Accident Hospital, date of change, October 1995

Formerly called:
West Midlands Regional Burns Unit (year of change 1993)

Organisation type and purpose:
Hospital.
Hospital department specialising in care of burn victims.

continued overleaf

Subject coverage:
Care of burns, epidemiology, pathology, acute care, aftercare and rehabilitation, aspects of clinical use of cultured skin and skin substitutes.

Access to staff:
Contact by letter, by telephone, by fax and by e-mail. Appointment necessary.
Hours: 24 hours

Access for disabled people:
Toilet facilities

Part of:
National Health Service

BIRMINGHAM CHAMBER OF COMMERCE AND INDUSTRY

Acronym or abbreviation: BCI

75 Harborne Road, Edgbaston, Birmingham, B15 3DH

Tel: 0121 454 6171\ Minicom no. 0845 606 2666
Fax: 0121 455 8670
E-mail: info@birminghamchamber.org.uk

Website:
http://www.bci.org.uk

Enquiries:
Enquiries to: Information Officer

Founded:
1813

Organisation type and purpose:
Trade association, membership association (membership is by subscription).

Subject coverage:
Business information, export documentation, export advice and trade missions, business management and policy.

Museum or gallery collection, archive, or library special collection:
Business directories and databases
British Standards

Printed publications:
Newspaper/Bulletin (monthly)
Surveys, reports and handbooks
Members Directory (annually)

Access to staff:
Contact by letter, by telephone, by fax, by e-mail, in person and via website. Non-members charged.
Hours: Mon to Fri, 0900 to 1700

Access for disabled people:
Parking provided, ramped entry, access to all public areas, toilet facilities

Member of:
Association of British Chambers of Commerce

Partner in:
Birmingham Economic Development Partnership
Business Link Birmingham

BIRMINGHAM CHINESE SOCIETY

11 Allcock Street, Birmingham, B9 4DY

Tel: 0121 773 0099 / 0870 2030100
Fax: 0121 733 3636
E-mail: ichu@jobs4brum.org.uk

Website:
http://website.lineone.net/~b.chinese.s

Enquiries:
Enquiries to: Manager

Founded:
1988

Organisation type and purpose:
Voluntary organisation, registered charity (charity number 1049035), training organisation.
Umbrella organisation.

Subject coverage:
Information and advice centre, employment, business; training, ESOL, IT, Chinese input, basic food hygiene course, intermediate food hygiene

course, first aid, home maintenance course; health, mental health, men and women; business offering advice to local Chinese businesses; translation and interpreting service, Cantonese, Mandarin, Haka, Vietnamese to English.

Access to staff:
Contact by letter, by telephone, by fax, by e-mail, in person and via website. Appointment necessary.
Hours: Mon to Fri, 1000 to 1700

BIRMINGHAM CITY UNIVERSITY

Kenrick Library, Perry Barr, Birmingham, B42 2SU

Tel: 0121 331 5000 (main switchboard)
Fax: 0121 356 2875

Website:
http://library.bcu.ac.uk

Enquiries:
Enquiries to: Director of Library and Learning Resources
Direct tel: 0121 331 6300
Direct e-mail: judith.andrews@bcu.ac.uk

Organisation type and purpose:
University library.

Subject coverage:
Construction technology, quantity surveying, computer studies, architecture, economics, management, communications studies, English, nursing, midwifery and community health, law, sociology, social work, accounting, finance, speech therapy, town planning, landscape architecture, housing, government, banking, fine art, art education, fashion and textiles, foundation and community studies, jewellery, silversmithing and horology, three-dimensional design, visual communication, education, music, psychology, media, electrical engineering, mechanical engineering, acting, drama.

Museum or gallery collection, archive, or library special collection:
Birmingham Flute Society Library
Royal College of Organists Library
Early Printed Music Collection (pre- c.1850)
Material samples from late 19th century to mid-20th century
Piranesi engravings (15 vols)

Library catalogue:
All or part available online

Publications list:
Available online and in print

Access to staff:
Contact by letter, by telephone, by fax, by e-mail, in person and via website. Appointment necessary.
Hours: Mon to Fri, 0900 to 1700

Access to building, collection or gallery:
No prior appointment required. Kenrick Library has controlled access and identification is required.

BIRMINGHAM CIVIL JUSTICE CENTRE

Formal name: Ministry of Justice, Midlands Region Judicial and Court Library Service

The Library, The Priory Courts, 33 Bull Street, Birmingham, B4 6DW

Tel: 0121 681 3446
Fax: 0121 681 3444
E-mail: mike.troon@justice.gsi.gov.uk; joanne.jarvie@justice.gsi.gov.uk

Organisation type and purpose:
National government body, Ministry of Justice (MoJ) Regional Library Service.
To provide a legal information service for judiciary and MoJ staff throughout the Midlands Region (including all court libraries).

Subject coverage:
Law reports, public general acts and measures, statutory instruments, legal books and periodicals.

Library catalogue:
All or part available in-house

Access to staff:
Appointment necessary.
Hours: Mon to Fri, 0830 to 1530
Special comments: The Priory Courts Library is primarily for the use of the judiciary and staff of the Ministry of Justice in the Midlands Region.

Access to building, collection or gallery:
Prior appointment required

BIRMINGHAM EARLY MUSIC FESTIVAL LTD

Acronym or abbreviation: BEMF

PO Box 15747, Birmingham, B132 9FY

Tel: 07 745 887 326
Fax: 0121 427 1511
E-mail: info@bemf.net

Website:
http://www.bemf.net
Information about the organisation, including details of this year's festival and online ticket purchase.

Enquiries:
Enquiries to: Administrator

Founded:
1992

Organisation type and purpose:
Registered charity (charity number 1039399).
Runs annual festival of early music.

Subject coverage:
Early music.

Access to staff:
Contact by letter, by telephone, by e-mail and via website
Hours: Mon to Fri, 0900 to 1700

Access to building, collection or gallery:
No access other than to staff

BIRMINGHAM ECONOMIC STRATEGY

Development Strategy, PO Box 14439, Birmingham, B2 2JE

Tel: 0121 303 3719
Fax: 0121 303 3076
E-mail: beic.enquiry.line@birmingham.gov.uk

Website:
http://www.birminghameconomy.org.uk

Enquiries:
Enquiries to: Information Service
Other contacts: Business Centre Manager (for major projects, strategies, analysis)

Founded:
1994

Organisation type and purpose:
Local government body, research organisation.
Source of information and analysis on the operation of the Birmingham economy and labour market.

Subject coverage:
The Birmingham economy and labour market.

Museum or gallery collection, archive, or library special collection:
Wide variety of reports and information on the Birmingham economy

Trade and statistical information:
Data on the Birmingham economy, economic forecasts, volume of investment, employment (occupation, sector), unemployment, impact & evaluation studies.

Access to staff:
Contact by letter, by telephone, by fax, by e-mail and via website. Appointment necessary.
Hours: Mon to Fri, 0900 to 1700
Special comments: Charges made for some services.

Access for disabled people:
Level entry, access to all public areas

Affiliated to:
Birmingham Economic Development Partnership Limited

Parent body:
Birmingham City Council

BIRMINGHAM FOCUS ON BLINDNESS

Acronym or abbreviation: Birmingham Focus

48–62 Woodville Road, Harborne, Birmingham, B17 9AT

Tel: 0121 478 5200; 0121 478 5222 (helpline)
Fax: 0121 478 5280
E-mail: info@birminghamfocus.org.uk

Website:
http://www.birminghamfocus.org.uk

Enquiries:
Enquiries to: Chief Executive
Direct tel: 0121 478 5201
Direct e-mail: rob@birminghamfocus.org.uk
Other contacts: Marketing Manager

Founded:
1846

Formerly a part of:
Birmingham Royal Institution for the Blind (BRIB) (year of change 1997)

Formerly called:
BRIB – Working with Blind People (year of change 1998)

Organisation type and purpose:
Registered charity (charity number 1065745). Welfare organisation.

Subject coverage:
Welfare of blind and partially sighted people in Birmingham, training and development, low vision assessment, rehabilitation and aids, blindness with multiple disabilities.

Printed publications:
In Focus News (quarterly; large print, audio, Braille)
Focal Bulletin
Leaflets on Services and Volunteers, Legacies, etc.

Electronic and video publications:
All publications available in large print, audio, Braille or e-mail

Access to staff:
Contact by letter, by telephone, by fax, by e-mail, in person and via website. Appointment necessary.
Hours: Mon to Fri, 0900 to 1700

Member organisation of:
National Association of Local Societies for Visually Impaired (NALSVI)
Queen Alexandra College

BIRMINGHAM LAW SOCIETY

8 Temple Street, Birmingham, B2 5BT

Tel: 0121 633 6901
Fax: 0121 633 3507
E-mail: info@birminghamlawsociety.co.uk

Website:
http://www.birminghamlawsociety.co.uk

Founded:
1818

Organisation type and purpose:
Professional body (membership is by subscription).

Subject coverage:
Law.

Library catalogue:
All or part available in-house

Access to staff:
Contact by letter, by telephone, by fax and by e-mail. Appointment necessary. Access for members only.
Hours: Mon to Fri, 0900 to 1700

Access to building, collection or gallery:
Prior appointment required

BIRMINGHAM LIBRARIES

Acronym or abbreviation: BLS

Central Library, Chamberlain Square, Birmingham, B3 3HQ

Tel: 0121 303 4511\ Minicom no. 0121 235 4511
Fax: 0121 233 4458
E-mail: centrallibrary@birmingham.gov.uk

Website:
http://www.birmingham.gov.uk/libraries

Enquiries:
Enquiries to: Librarian
Direct tel: 0121 303 4220
Direct e-mail: centrallibrary@birmingham.gov.uk
Other contacts: Information Officer for fee-based business information service.

Founded:
1866

Formerly called:
Birmingham Public Libraries (BPL); Birmingham Library Services (BLS) (year of change 2001)

Organisation type and purpose:
Public library.

Subject coverage:
Local studies and history; Birmingham information, history, geography, maps, genealogy, photographs; science, technology management, environment, engineering, motor manuals, information technology, building, manufacturing, general and production management; social sciences, politics, economics, law, education (including open learning, school governor information), community information, health information, philosophy, religion, transport; arts, languages and literature; fine and performing arts, music, scores, sets of vocal scores, sound recordings; business information, telephone and trade directories, company information, annual reports, statistics, market research reports, marketing, company histories; archives.

Museum or gallery collection, archive, or library special collection:
Archives (of Birmingham)
Baskerville Collection
Boulton and Watt and Priestley collections
British Standards
Early and fine printing
Francis Bedford Collection of photographs
Francis Frith Collection of photographs
Kings Norton and Sheldon Parochial libraries
Local history of Birmingham and surrounding counties
Marston Rudland Collection of engraved portraits
Milton, Johnson, Cervantes, War poetry collections
National organ archive
Official publications
Parker Collection of early children's books and games
Patents (British, European, US and PCT)
Railway collection
Shakespeare
Stone Collection of Victorian and Edwardian photographs
Trade union collection
UN depository library

Non-library collection catalogue:
All or part available in-house

Library catalogue:
All or part available online

Printed publications:
Literature and art bibliographies
Local history publications
Statistics and market research

Building the City – a series of fourteen books to date, tracing the history of different areas of the city, each title is illustrated with over 200 photographs mainly drawn from the Birmingham Central Library Archives, £9.99 each volume:
Acocks Green
Northfield
Moseley, Balsall Heath and Highgate
Yardley
Old Harbourne
Kings Heath
Kings Norton
Edgbaston
Erdington
Handsworth, Hockley and Handsworth Wood
Sutton Coldfield
Sutton Coldfield the Second Selection
Hall Green
Aston and Perry Barr
The Heart of the City – a series of books
Birmingham Transport
Birmingham Pubs
Contrasts in a Victorian City
Birmingham Between The Wars
Central Birmingham 1870–1920
Central Birmingham 1920–1970
Other series include Sounds of the City, Shaping the City, Capturing the City, The Man from the City, Life and Death in the City, news from the City
Order printed publications from: Room Bookings and Sales, Birmingham Library Services
tel: 0121 303 2868

Electronic and video publications:
Birmingham – A Journey Through Time (1932–1945, £12.99, video)
Birmingham – A Journey Through Time Part 2 (1946–1969, £12.99, video)
Sutton Coldfield – A Journey Through Time (£12.99, video)

Publications list:
Available in print

Access to staff:
Contact by letter, by telephone, by fax, by e-mail, in person and via website
Hours: Mon, Tue, Thu, Fri, 0900 to 2000; Sat, 0900 to 1700
Special comments: Archives section has restricted opening hours, closing at 1700 each day and all day Wednesday.

Houses the:
Diocesan Record Office
Information Direct

Member of:
UK Patents Information Network

Parent body:
Birmingham City Council

BIRMINGHAM LOCAL MEDICAL COMMITTEE

36 Harborne Road, Edgbaston, Birmingham, B15 3AF

Tel: 0121 454 5008
Fax: 0121 455 0758

Enquiries:
Enquiries to: Executive Secretary / Business manager
Other contacts: Doctors

Founded:
1911

Organisation type and purpose:
Professional body.

Subject coverage:
Advice on range of medical and medico/legal matters to GPs.

Access to staff:
Contact by letter and by fax
Hours: Mon to Fri, 1030 to 1530

continued overleaf

Access to building, collection or gallery:
Appointment required

Access for disabled people:
Parking provided, ramped entry

BIRMINGHAM ROYAL BALLET

Acronym or abbreviation: BRB

Thorp Street, Birmingham, B5 4AU

Tel: 0121 245 3500
Fax: 0121 245 3571
E-mail: info@brb.org.uk

Website:
http://www.brb.org.uk
General information on the company, its dancers and productions.

Enquiries:
Enquiries to: Communications Director
Direct e-mail: keithlongmore@brb.org.uk

Founded:
1990

Formed from:
Sadler's Wells Royal Ballet (SWRB) (year of change 1989)

Organisation type and purpose:
Ballet company.

Subject coverage:
Information concerning Birmingham Royal Ballet and its history.

Museum or gallery collection, archive, or library special collection:
Cast lists, photographs, programmes

Trade and statistical information:
Casting, performance dates.

Non-library collection catalogue:
All or part available in-house

Library catalogue:
All or part available in-house

Electronic and video publications:
Some videos of performances available

Access to staff:
Contact by letter and by e-mail
Hours: Mon to Fri, 0900 to 1700

Access to building, collection or gallery:
Prior appointment required
Hours: Mon to Fri, 0930 to 1730

Access for disabled people:
Level entry

BIRMINGHAM SCHOOL OF ACTING

Acronym or abbreviation: BSA

Level 0 – Millennium Point, Curzon Street, Birmingham, B4 7XG

Tel: 0121 331 7220
Fax: 0121 331 7221

Website:
http://www.bsa.bcu.ac.uk

Enquiries:
Enquiries to: Director
Direct tel: 0121 331 7224
Direct e-mail: stephen.simms@bcu.ac.uk
Other contacts: Registrar, Admissions Manager, Marketing Manager

Founded:
1936

Formerly called:
Birmingham School of Speech and Drama; Birmingham School of Speech Training & Dramatic Art Ltd

Organisation type and purpose:
Birmingham School of Acting is a small specialist institution offering full-time higher education courses at undergraduate and postgraduate level and part-time and summer school courses for adults, young people and children. Birmingham School of Acting is a faculty of Birmingham City University and its acting courses are accredited by the National Council for Drama Training (NCDT).

Subject coverage:
Acting technique, extending natural talent for the professional theatre, dance, fencing and stage fighting, stage management, radio technique, voice production and speech training, relaxation and stress management.

Museum or gallery collection, archive, or library special collection:
Drama and play collection

Library catalogue:
All or part available in-house

Printed publications:
Prospectus (also at: http://www.bsa.bcu.ac.uk/ Contact/BSA%20Prospectus%202008%20- %2009.pdf)

Electronic and video publications:
CD-ROM

Publications list:
Available in print

Access to staff:
Contact by letter, by telephone, by fax, by e-mail and via website. Appointment necessary.
Hours: Mon to Fri, 0900 to 1700

Access for disabled people:
All levels entry, toilet facilities

BISCUIT, CAKE, CHOCOLATE & CONFECTIONERY ASSOCIATION

Acronym or abbreviation: BCCCA

6 Catherine Street, London, WC2B 5JJ

Tel: 020 7420 7200
Fax: 020 7420 7201
E-mail: office@bccca.org.uk

Website:
http://www.bccca.org.uk

Enquiries:
Enquiries to: Director

Founded:
1901

Organisation type and purpose:
Trade association.

Subject coverage:
Cocoa, chocolate, confectionery products, cakes and biscuits.

Trade and statistical information:
Data on the sales of biscuits, cakes, chocolate and confectionery for the home market and for export.

Printed publications:
Annual Review

Electronic and video publications:
Microbiology & Hygiene Factsheets (CD-ROM, £10)

Member of:
CAOBISCO, the corresponding EC professional organisation
Food and Drink Federation

BISHOP AUCKLAND COLLEGE LIBRARY

Woodhouse Lane, Bishop Auckland, Co Durham, DL14 6JZ

Tel: 01388 443000
Fax: 01388 609294
E-mail: enquiries@bacoll.ac.uk

Website:
http://www.bishopaucklandcollege.ac.uk
Courses available.

Enquiries:
Enquiries to: Learning Resources Manager
Direct tel: extn 2264

Formerly called:
Bishop Auckland College Student Resource Centre (year of change 1998)

Organisation type and purpose:
Suitable for ages: 16+.
College library.

Subject coverage:
Engineering, construction, business studies, creative and community subjects, hairdressing, crafts, caring, art and design, information technology, leisure and tourism.

Non-library collection catalogue:
All or part available in-house

Library catalogue:
All or part available in-house

Access to staff:
Contact by letter, by telephone, by fax and by e-mail
Hours: Term time: Mon to Thu, 0900 to 1930; Fri, 0900 to 1600
Vacations: Mon to Thu, 0900 to 1630; Fri, 0900 to 1600

Access for disabled people:
Parking provided, ramped entry, level entry, access to all public areas, toilet facilities
Special comments: Library is on first floor.

BISHOPSGATE INSTITUTE

230 Bishopsgate, London, EC2M 4QH

Tel: 020 7392 9270
Fax: 020 7392 9275
E-mail: library@bishopsgate.org.uk

Website:
http://www.bishopsgate.org.uk/library

Enquiries:
Enquiries to: Library Manager
Other contacts: Deputy Library Manager

Founded:
1894

Organisation type and purpose:
Independent free public library.

Subject coverage:
London history and topography, labour and trade union history, economic and political history, co-operation and the co-operative movement in London and the South East, secularism, humanism, republicanism, pacifism, anarchism.

Museum or gallery collection, archive, or library special collection:
London Collection (50,000 volumes); Howell Collection (7,000 volumes); Labour History (10,000 volumes); Holyoake Collection (1,000 items); Bradlaugh Papers (3,000 items); London Cooperative Society Collection (20,000 items); archives of: Raphael Samuel; Bernie Grant; Republic; British Humanist Association; Rationalist Association; Stop the War Coalition.

Non-library collection catalogue:
All or part available online and in-house

Library catalogue:
All or part available online and in-house

Printed publications:
James Ince (Umbrellas): two centuries of an East London family business

Access to staff:
Contact by letter, by telephone, by e-mail and in person
Hours: Mon, Tue, Thu and Fri, 1000 to 1730; Wed, 1000 to 2000

Special comments: Library closes at 1400 on the 1st Fri of each month.

Access to building, collection or gallery:
No prior appointment required

BISHOPTHORPE LOCAL HISTORY GROUP

39 Acaster Lane, Bishopthorpe, York, YO23 2SA

Tel: 01904 704584
E-mail: historygroup@bishopthorpe.net

Website:
http://www.bishopthorpe.net/mt/history

Enquiries:
Enquiries to: Chairman

Founded:
1998

Organisation type and purpose:
Membership association (membership is by subscription), present number of members: 11, voluntary organisation.

Subject coverage:
Local and family history relating to the parish of Bishopthorpe.

Museum or gallery collection, archive, or library special collection:
Bishopthorpe photographs, ephemera and administration records of local groups.

Non-library collection catalogue:
All or part available in-house

Printed publications:
Bishopthorpe: Reaping the Past, 1800–1900 (£4.95 plus p&p, out of print)
Bishopthorpe Remembered (£2.95 plus 75p p&p, out of print)
Bishopthorpe History Trail (Free)

Access to staff:
Contact by letter, by telephone and by e-mail
Hours: Mon to Fri, 0900 to 1700

BITTER OWNERS CLUB

Treasurer and Membership Secretary, 6 Swanston Field, Whitchurch on Thames, RG8 7HP UK

Tel: 01189 845214
E-mail: info@bitter-owners-club.com

Website:
http://www.bitter-owners-club.com/

Enquiries:
Enquiries to: Secretary

Founded:
1988

Organisation type and purpose:
Membership association (membership is by subscription), present number of members: 55, service industry.
Classic car club.
To promote and encourage Bitter owners and prospective buyers of the cars.

Subject coverage:
Bitter cars.

Museum or gallery collection, archive, or library special collection:
Collection of over 5000 pictures of Bitter cars
Collection of archive press articles and road tests

Trade and statistical information:
Values and numbers of Bitter cars.

Non-library collection catalogue:
All or part available in-house

Printed publications:
Club magazine (6 times a year, included in £34 membership fee)
Bitter the Cars (Griffith P B, A4 100pp, £12.95 plus £2 p&p)

Access to staff:
Contact by letter, by telephone, by fax and by e-mail. Appointment necessary.
Hours: Mon to Sun, 0900 to 2100

Member of:
Classic Car Association

BITUMEN WATERPROOFING ASSOCIATION (UK) LTD

Acronym or abbreviation: BWA

19 Regina Crescent, Ravenshead, Nottingham, NG15 9AE

Tel: 01623 430574
Fax: 01623 798098
E-mail: info@bwa-europe.com

Website:
http://www.bwa-europe.com
Membership, meetings, general activities, congress.

Enquiries:
Enquiries to: Chief Executive

Founded:
1968

Organisation type and purpose:
International organisation, trade association (membership is by subscription, qualification, election or invitation), manufacturing industry, service industry.

Subject coverage:
Technical investigations, market survey projects, PR role.

Printed publications:
Past Congress Book of Proceedings (£39)

Access to staff:
Contact by letter, by telephone, by fax, by e-mail, in person and via website
Hours: Mon to Fri, 0900 to 1700

UK registered office:
Bitumen Waterproofing Association (UK) Ltd
Newstead House, Pelham Road, Nottingham, NG5 1AP; tel: 0115 960 8412; fax: 0115 969 1878

BLABY DISTRICT COUNCIL

Council Offices, Desford Road, Narborough, Leicestershire, LE9 5EP

Tel: 0116 275 0555\ Minicom no. 0116 284 9786
Fax: 0116 275 0368

Website:
http://www.blaby.gov.uk
Publications and leaflets, and ordering.

Enquiries:
Enquiries to: Public Relations Manager
Direct tel: 0116 272 7556
Direct e-mail: djm@blaby.gov.uk

Organisation type and purpose:
Local government body.

Subject coverage:
Local government services.

Printed publications:
A range of publications and leaflets available from the Council Offices covering services and leisure activities

Publications list:
Available online

Access to staff:
Contact by letter, by telephone, by fax, by e-mail, in person and via website
Hours: Mon to Thu, 0845 to 1715; Fri, 0845 to 1645

Access for disabled people:
Parking provided, level entry, access to all public areas, toilet facilities
Special comments: Access to all public areas.

BLACK COUNTRY CHAMBER OF COMMERCE

Formal name: Black Country Chamber & Business Link
Acronym or abbreviation: BCCBL

Dudley Court South, Waterfront East, Level Street, Brierley Hill, West Midlands, DY5 1XW

Tel: 0845 113 1234
Fax: 01384 360560

Website:
http://www.bccbl.com

Enquiries:
Enquiries to: Information Officer
Direct e-mail: gemmabutler@blackcountrychamber.co.uk

Founded:
2001

Organisation type and purpose:
Membership association (membership is by subscription), present number of members: 2500, service industry.

Subject coverage:
Business information and services for business.

Non-library collection catalogue:
All or part available online

Library catalogue:
All or part available online and in-house

Access to staff:
Contact by letter, by telephone, by fax, by e-mail, in person and via website. Non-members charged.
Hours: Mon to Thu, 0830 to 1730; Fri, 0830 to 1700
Special comments: SME business within the Black Country and members of the Black Country Chamber of Commerce.

Access for disabled people:
Access to all public areas, toilet facilities

BLACK COUNTRY INVESTMENT

The Deckhouse, Waterfront West, Dudley Road, Brierley Hill, DY5 1LW

Tel: 0845 815 1515
E-mail: enquiries@bci-uk.com

Website:
http://www.bci-uk.com
Black Country property location facility, general information concerning the Black Country.

Enquiries:
Enquiries to: Enquiry Officer
Direct e-mail: jane_mcgreen@blackcountryconsortium.co.uk

Founded:
2001

Formerly called:
Business Link Sandwell (year of change 2001)

Organisation type and purpose:
Local government body.

Subject coverage:
Property location information within the Black Country, general information concerning the Black Country.

Printed publications:
Black Country Investment Property Finder
Black Country Investment Services Brochure
Newsletter (quarterly)

Access to staff:
Contact by letter, by telephone, by fax, by e-mail and via website
Hours: Mon to Fri, 0900 to 1700

BLACK COUNTRY SOCIETY

Acronym or abbreviation: BCS

PO Box 71, Kingswinford, West Midlands, DY6 9YN

continued overleaf

E-mail: editor@blackcountrysociety.co.uk

Website:
http://www.blackcountrysociety.co.uk

Enquiries:
Enquiries to: Editor
Other contacts: Membership Secretary (for subscriptions)

Founded:
1967

Organisation type and purpose:
Learned society (membership is by subscription), present number of members: 2,000, voluntary organisation.
To foster interest in the Black Country area of the West Midlands past, present and future.

Subject coverage:
Local history, industrial archaeology, geography and culture; the past, present and future of the Black Country region; family and social history in the Black Country

Museum or gallery collection, archive, or library special collection:
Photographic collection (now deposited in the Black Country Living Museum)

Printed publications:
Black Countryman (quarterly, £2.75)
Booklets on local topics including:
Black Country Humour
Black Country Stories
William Fowler's Kingswinford
The Gospels in Black Country Dialect
The Black Country as seen through Antique Maps – a survey from 1579 (Richardson E, £5.95)
Bostin' Fittle
Order printed publications from: Publications, BCS PO Box 71, Kingswinford, West Midlands, DY6 9YN, tel: 01384 295606

Electronic and video publications:
CD-ROM containing first 10 volumes (40 issues) of The Blackcountryman magazine

Publications list:
Available online and in print

Access to staff:
Contact by letter, by telephone, by e-mail and via website
Hours: Mon to Fri, 0900 to 1700

Access to building, collection or gallery:
No access other than to staff

Also at:
Advertising/Distribution/Publications
32 Lawnswood Avenue, Wordsley, Stourbridge, West Midlands, DY8 5LP; tel: 01384 295606

Constituent bodies:
Four subsidiary groups, all with same contact details as BCS

BLACK WELSH MOUNTAIN SHEEP BREEDERS ASSOCIATION

Touch Stone, 3 Quarry Cottages, Bourton on the Hill, Moreton-in-Marsh, Gloucestershire, GL56 9AJ

Tel: 01386 701538
Fax: 01386 701383

Enquiries:
Enquiries to: Secretary

Founded:
1920

Organisation type and purpose:
Membership association (membership is by subscription), present number of members: 250, registered charity.
Sheep breeders association.

Access to staff:
Contact by letter, by telephone and by fax
Hours: Mon to Fri, 0900 to 1700

BLACKBURN COLLEGE LIBRARY

Feilden Street, Blackburn, Lancashire, BB2 1LH

Tel: 01254 292120
Fax: 01254 682700

Website:
http://catalogue.blackburn.ac.uk

Enquiries:
Enquiries to: Learning Resources Manager

Organisation type and purpose:
College of Further Education.

Subject coverage:
Wide subject coverage for FE and HE in FE curriculum.

Library catalogue:
All or part available online

Printed publications:
Library guide
Study skills and projects and assignments guides
Available for library users only

Access to staff:
Contact by letter, by telephone and in person. Appointment necessary. Non-members charged.
Hours: Term time: Mon to Thu, 0845 to 2000; Fri, 0845 to 1500; Sat, 0900 to 1230
Vacations: Mon to Fri, 0900 to 1630
Special comments: Associate membership is available (annual subscription) to members of the public; occasional users may prefer single admission fee for each visit.

Access for disabled people:
Access to all public areas

Associate college of:
Lancaster University

BLACKBURN WITH DARWEN BOROUGH COUNCIL

Town Hall, Blackburn, Lancashire, BB1 7DY

Tel: 01254 585585
Fax: 01254 680870

Website:
http://www.council.blackburnworld.com

Enquiries:
Enquiries to: Public Relations Manager

Organisation type and purpose:
Local government body.

BLACKFRIARS LIBRARY

64 St Giles, Oxford, OX1 3LY

Tel: 01865 278400
Fax: 01865 278403

Website:
http://www.bfriars.ox.ac.uk

Enquiries:
Enquiries to: Librarian
Direct e-mail: librarian@blackfriars.ox.ac.uk

Organisation type and purpose:
Library.

Subject coverage:
Philosophy, theology and scripture (particularly in relation to the Roman Catholic tradition and the medieval contribution of Dominican authors such as St Thomas Aquinas); life, work and history of the Dominican Order.

Museum or gallery collection, archive, or library special collection:
1 papyrus, 5 MSS, some cuneiform tablets, 26 incunabula and some 350 books printed before 1700, including many Dominican authors
Autograph letters of George Tyrrell SJ
Private press items, including many from St Dominic's Press
Works from the Library of André Raffalovich

Library catalogue:
All or part available online

Access to staff:
Contact by letter, by telephone, by e-mail, in person and via website. Access for members only. Letter of introduction required.
Hours: Mon to Fri, 0900 to 1700

Access to building, collection or gallery:
Prior appointment required

A permanent private hall of:
University of Oxford

In collaboration with other libraries of the:
English Dominicans

Serves a priory and *studium generale* of the:
English Province of the Friars of the Order of Preachers (Dominicans)

BLACKHEATH SCIENTIFIC SOCIETY

Mycenae House Community Centre, Mycenae Road, London, SE3 7SE

E-mail: richardjbuchanan@aol.com

Website:
http://www.bss.btik.com

Enquiries:
Other contacts: Honorary Secretary: 79 Ashridge Crescent, Shooters Hill, London, SE18 3EA

Founded:
1857

Organisation type and purpose:
Learned society (membership is by subscription, election or invitation), voluntary organisation.
Airing of information on developments in science and technology to qualified and non-qualified public; members.

Subject coverage:
Current scientific and technological developments. Coverage is wide and does include occasionally an historical lecture.

Printed publications:
Minutes of meetings and agendas

Access to staff:
Contact by letter, by telephone and by e-mail. Appointment necessary.
Hours: Mon to Fri, 0900 to 2200

BLACKPOOL AND THE FYLDE COLLEGE

Ashfield Road, Bispham, Blackpool, Lancashire, FY2 0HB

Tel: 01253 352352
Fax: 01253 356127
E-mail: lrc@blackpool.ac.uk

Website:
http://www.blackpool.ac.uk

Enquiries:
Enquiries to: Learning Resources
Direct tel: 01253 352352
Direct e-mail: lrc@blackpool.ac.uk

Founded:
1934

Organisation type and purpose:
Education for ages 16+.

Library catalogue:
All or part available online

Access to staff:
Contact by letter, by telephone, by fax and by e-mail. Appointment necessary.
Hours: Mon to Fri, 0900 to 1700

BLACKPOOL CENTRAL LIBRARY

Queen Street, Blackpool, Lancashire, FY1 1PX

Tel: 01253 478080

Fax: 01253 478082
E-mail: central.library@blackpool.gov.uk

Website:
http://www.blackpool.gov.uk
General council services and information.

Organisation type and purpose:
Local government body, public library.

Subject coverage:
General, local history of Blackpool and Fylde area.

Library catalogue:
All or part available online

Access to staff:
Contact by letter, by telephone, by fax, by e-mail and in person
Hours: Closed – undergoing refurbishment and remodelling until Sept 2011
Special comments: Local history items are for use in the library only.

Access for disabled people:
Access to all public areas

BLACKWELL PUBLISHING LIMITED

9600 Garsington Road, Oxford, OX4 2DQ

Tel: 01865 776868
Fax: 01865 714591

Website:
http://www.blackwell-science.com
Catalogue of books and journals.
http://www.blackwellpublishers.co.uk
Catalogue of books and journals.
http://www.blackwellpublishing.com
Merger site
http://www.blackwell-synergy.com
Journals online.

Enquiries:
Enquiries to: Marketing Co-ordinator

Founded:
1939

Formerly called:
Blackwell Scientific Publications Limited (BSPL) (year of change 1995); Blackwell Publishers Limited (BPL), Blackwell Science Limited (BSL) (year of change 2001)

Organisation type and purpose:
Publishing house.

Subject coverage:
Books and journals in medicine, humanities, life and social sciences, as listed in catalogues.

Printed publications:
Catalogues and journal lists

Electronic and video publications:
Roists Essential Immunology (CD-ROM)
Rook's Textbook of Dermatology (CD-ROM)
Synergy (journals online)

Publications list:
Available online and in print

Access to staff:
Contact by letter and by telephone
Hours: Mon to Fri, 0900 to 1700

Other addresses:
Blackwell Publishing Asia
54 University Street, Carlton South 3053, Victoria, Australia; tel: 00 61 3 9374 0300; fax: 00 61 3 9347 5001
Blackwell Publishing Limited
108 Cowley Road, Oxford, OX4 1JF
Blackwell Publishing Limited
10 rue Casimir Delavigne, 75006 Paris, France; tel: +33 1 53 10 33 10; fax: +33 1 53 10 33 15; e-mail: aboydsquires@compuserve.com
Blackwell Publishing, Inc
Commerce Place, 350 Main Street, Malden, MA 02148–5018, USA; tel: 00 1 781 388 8250; fax: 00 1 781 388 8255

Blackwell Wissenschaft-Verlag
Kurfürstendamm 57, Charlottenburg, Berlin, D-10707, Germany; tel: +49 30/32 79 06 -0; fax: +49 30/32 79 06 -10; e-mail: verlag@blackwis.de

Sister company:
B H Blackwell Limited

BLACKWELL UK LIMITED

Acronym or abbreviation: Blackwell's

Beaver House, Hythe Bridge Street, Oxford, OX1 2ET

Tel: 01865 792792
Fax: 01865 200285
E-mail: sales@blackwell.co.uk

Website:
http://www.blackwell.com
Databases of books, series and CD-ROMs.

Enquiries:
Enquiries to: International Sales Manager
Direct fax: 01865 200285

Founded:
1879

Also known as:
Blackwell's, Blackwell's Book Services

Organisation type and purpose:
International organisation, service industry.
Booksellers.
Academic Library Suppliers

Subject coverage:
Academic books, CD-ROM, music, microform, cataloguing and bibliographic services, eBook services.

Non-library collection catalogue:
All or part available online

Printed publications:
Advance information on books not yet published
Subject bibliographies
Trade catalogues

Electronic and video publications:
EBooks
Collection Manager (Web-based library Collection Development/Acquisitions service)

Publications list:
Available online

Access to staff:
Contact by letter, by telephone, by fax, by e-mail and via website. Appointment necessary.
Hours: Mon to Fri, 0900 to 1700

BLAENAU GWENT COUNTY BOROUGH COUNCIL

Municipal Offices, Civic Centre, Ebbw Vale, Gwent, NP23 6XB

Tel: 01495 350555
Fax: 01495 301255

Website:
http://www.blaenau-gwent.gov.uk

Enquiries:
Enquiries to: Public Relations Officer
Direct tel: 01495 355112
Direct fax: 01495 355093

Organisation type and purpose:
Local government body.
Unitary authority.

Subject coverage:
Local government services.

Printed publications:
Valley's Voice (magazine)
Official guide and street atlas
A-Z guide to services

Access to staff:
Contact by letter, by telephone and by fax
Hours: Mon to Fri, 0900 to 1700

BLAENAU GWENT COUNTY BOROUGH LIBRARIES

c/o Ebbw Vale Library, 21 Bethcar Street, Ebbw Vale, Gwent, NP23 6HH

Tel: 01495 303069
Fax: 01495 350547

Enquiries:
Enquiries to: Principal Librarian
Direct tel: 01495 355950
Direct fax: 01495 355900
Direct e-mail: sue.white@blaenau-gwent.gov.uk

Organisation type and purpose:
Local government body, public library.

Subject coverage:
General subjects, local studies and self-help, European information, adult basic information.

Museum or gallery collection, archive, or library special collection:
Main information collections housed at Ebbw Vale Library
European information housed at Ebbw Vale Library
Main local history collections housed at Tredegar Library
National Assembly Information housed at Ebbw Vale Library

Non-library collection catalogue:
All or part available online and in-house

Library catalogue:
All or part available online and in-house

Printed publications:
History of Ebbw Vale

Publications list:
Available in print

Access to staff:
Contact by letter, by telephone, by fax, by e-mail and in person. Appointment necessary.
Hours: Mon to Fri, 0900 to 1700; Sat 0900 to 1300

Library HQ:
Blaenau Gwent County Borough Council Leisure Services, Anvil Court, Church Street, Abertillery, NP13 1DB; tel: 01495 355950; fax: 01495 355900; e-mail: sue.white@blaenau-gwent.gov.uk

BLATCHINGTON COURT TRUST

Acronym or abbreviation: BCT

Ridgeland House, 165 Dyke Road, Hove, East Sussex, BN3 1TL

Tel: 01273 727222
Fax: 01273 722244
E-mail: blatchington.court@virgin.net

Website:
http://www.blatchington-court.co.uk

Enquiries:
Enquiries to: Client Services Manager

Founded:
1993

Organisation type and purpose:
Voluntary organisation, registered charity (charity number 306350), suitable for ages: 0 to 30. Primarily grant giving charity to promote education and employment and provide grants for young visually impaired people for computers and sensory equipment. Also help with Family Support and Advocacy.

Subject coverage:
Services and facilities for visually impaired young people, mainly in Sussex; help includes: family support service, advocacy service, IT training, education and employment.

Printed publications:
Information Packs about the specific work of BCT (free of charge)

continued overleaf

Access to staff:
Contact by letter, by telephone, by fax, by e-mail, in person and via website
Hours: Mon to Fri, 0900 to 1700

Access to building, collection or gallery:
No prior appointment required

Access for disabled people:
Parking provided, ramped entry

BLC LEATHER TECHNOLOGY CENTRE

Acronym or abbreviation: BLC

Leather Trade House, Kings Park Road, Moulton Park, Northampton, NN3 6JD

Tel: 01604 679999
Fax: 01604 679998
E-mail: info@blcleathertech.com

Website:
http://www.blcleathertech.com
Services, training, member directory, consultancy.

Enquiries:
Enquiries to: Information Officer

Founded:
1920

Formerly called:
British Leather Confederation

Organisation type and purpose:
International organisation, trade association, training organisation, consultancy, research organisation.

Subject coverage:
Manufacture and use of leather; raw hides and skins; fellmongering; treatment and disposal of industrial wastes; chemistry and testing of leather; tanning; physical and mechanical testing of leather; leather dyes and surface coatings: safety in the leather industry; cleaner processing in the leather industry.

Printed publications:
BLC Journal (monthly, confidential to members)
Farming and Abattoir Practices Leading to Impaired Leather Quality
Guide to Fellmongering
Leather Clothing; its manufacture and maintenance
Leather Descriptions and Definitions
Leather under the Microscope
Member/Product Directory

Electronic and video publications:
Leather Online CD-ROM (available to members only)

Access to staff:
Contact by letter, by telephone, by fax, by e-mail and via website
Hours: Mon to Fri, 0900 to 1700

Incorporates the:
British Leather Confederation

BLENHEIM PROJECT

321 Portobello Road, London, W10 5SY

Tel: 020 8960 5599
Fax: 020 8960 0508
E-mail: blenpro@dircon.co.uk

Website:
http://www.theblenheimproject.org

Enquiries:
Enquiries to: Administrator

Founded:
1966

Organisation type and purpose:
Voluntary organisation, registered charity (charity number 1015237).
Drugs counselling.

Subject coverage:
Counselling for drug users, their friends and family, use and effects, alternative therapies, detox teas.

Printed publications:
Changing Gear (£1.20 plus p&p)
Drugs – Check This Out (£1.20 plus p&p)
How to Help (£1.20 plus p&p)
How to Stop (£1.20 plus p&p)
What's the Crack – Professional – Information on how to help crack and cocaine users (£5)
What's the Crack – User's Guide – Information for crack and cocaine users (£1.50)

Publications list:
Available in print

Access to staff:
Contact by letter, by telephone, by fax, by e-mail, in person and via website
Hours: Mon to Fri, 1000 to 1700; Drop in: Mon to Fri, 1300 to 1600; Tue, 1800 to 2100

BLOOD PRESSURE ASSOCIATION

60 Cranmer Terrace, London, SW17 0QS

Tel: 020 8772 4994 (head office); 0845 241 0989. (information line)

Website:
http://www.bpassoc.org.uk
Symptoms, causes, medicines and lifestyle, support services, resources for health professionals, A–Z of blood pressure, online shop.

Founded:
2000

Organisation type and purpose:
Registered charity in England and Wales (charity number 1058944), membership organisation (membership is by subscription).
Dedicated to lowering the nation's blood pressure to prevent disability and death from stroke and heart disease.
To help people take control of, or prevent, high blood pressure.

Subject coverage:
The vision is that everyone will know their blood pressure numbers, in the same way that they know their height or weight, and take steps to keep them healthy both now and in the future.

Information services:
Booklets, magazine, e-newsletters, website, information line and other activities.

Special visitor services:
UK's biggest blood pressure testing event, Know your Numbers! Week.

Printed publications:
Magazine (free to members)

Electronic and video publications:
e-Newsletter
Order electronic and video publications from: via website

Publications list:
Available online

Access to staff:
Contact by letter and by telephone
Hours: Information line: Mon to Fri, 1100 to 1500

BLOOMSBURY HEALTHCARE LIBRARY

Ground Floor, Bonham Carter House, 52 Gower Street, London, WC1E 6EB

Tel: 020 7436 1414
Fax: 020 7436 5111

Website:
http://www.chllib.demon.co.uk
Library services, NVQ's, external sources, services to region.

Enquiries:
Enquiries to: Librarian

Founded:
1997

Organisation type and purpose:
NHS Library.
Library services for all healthcare staff in associated organisations.

Subject coverage:
Nursing, midwifery, health visiting, sociology, psychology, education, management, physiotherapy, occupational therapy, dietetics, clinical governance, NHS policy, radiography, librarianship.

Non-library collection catalogue:
All or part available online

Library catalogue:
All or part available online

Printed publications:
Current Awareness Bulletin (monthly)

Access to staff:
Contact by letter, by telephone and by fax.
Appointment necessary. Non-members charged.
Hours: Mon to Fri, 0900 to 1700

Access to building, collection or gallery:
No prior appointment required

BLUEFACED LEICESTER SHEEP BREEDERS ASSOCIATION

Acronym or abbreviation: BFLSBA

The Secretary, Riverside View, Warwick Road, Carlisle CA1 2BS

Tel: 01228 598022
Fax: 01228 598021
E-mail: info@blueleicester.co.uk

Website:
http://www.blueleicester.co.uk

Founded:
1962

Organisation type and purpose:
National government body, membership association (membership is by subscription).
Sheep breeders' association.
Sheep registration.

Subject coverage:
Bluefaced Leicester sheep.

Access to staff:
Contact by letter, by telephone, by fax, by e-mail and via website
Hours: Mon to Fri, 0900 to 1500

Access to building, collection or gallery:
Prior appointment required

BMS WORLD MISSION

PO Box 49, Baptist House, 129 Broadway, Didcot, Oxfordshire, OX11 8XA

Tel: 01235 517700
Fax: 01235 517601
E-mail: mail@bmsworldmission.org

Website:
http://www.bmsworldmission.org
Information about mission personnel, prayer requests, ways to support BMS, resources and five channels for user groups: ministers, BMS reps in churches, those seeking mission opportunities, 24:7 Partners and campaigners.

Enquiries:
Enquiries to: General Director

Founded:
1792

Formerly called:
Baptist Missionary Society (BMS)

Organisation type and purpose:
Voluntary organisation, registered as a charity in England and Wales (number 233782) and in Scotland (number SC037767).

BMS World Mission is a Christian mission organisation aiming to share life in all its fullness with the world's peoples by: enabling them to know Christ; alleviating suffering and injustice; improving the quality of life with people as the primary agent of change – motivating, training, sending and resourcing them. Has missions in 4 continents.

Subject coverage:
Christian missions worldwide involving church planting and evangelism; development initiatives; disaster relief; educational programmes; health programmes; and other specialised activities.

Museum or gallery collection, archive, or library special collection:
Archives of the 19th century relating to the establishment of missions and some rare books at Regents Park College, Oxford

Printed publications:
engage magazine
Mission Catalyst (for ministers)
The Equipment (for BMS Reps)
FACE (resource for all-age church events)
Prayer Guide
Order printed publications from: Resources, tel: 01235 517617; e-mail: resources@bmsworldmission.org

Publications list:
Available online

Access to staff:
Contact by letter, by telephone, by fax, by e-mail and via website. Appointment necessary.
Hours: Mon to Fri, 0900 to 1700

BMT GROUP LTD

Goodrich House, 1 Waldegrave Road, Teddington, Middlesex, TW11 8LZ

Tel: 020 8943 5544
Fax: 020 8943 5347
E-mail: dgriffiths@bmtmail.com

Website:
http://www.bmt.org
http://www.marinescienceandtechnology.com
http://www.marinetechnologyabstracts.com
The Marine Technology Abstracts database contains bibliographic information providing a reference and description for over 90,000 technical articles, reports, books, conference and transaction papers and other material on all aspects of maritime technology.

Enquiries:
Enquiries to: Librarian
Direct tel: 020 8614 4277

Founded:
1985

Organisation type and purpose:
Consultancy, research organisation.

Subject coverage:
Fluid mechanics, naval architecture, ocean engineering, industrial aerodynamics as related to the commercial shipping, maritime defence, ports and harbours, and offshore oil and gas industries.

Museum or gallery collection, archive, or library special collection:
Report material of former National Maritime Institute
Report material of former ship, aero and maritime science divisions of the National Physical Laboratory
Transactions of Royal Institution of Naval Architects, Society of Naval Architects and Marine Engineers, North-east Coast Institution of Engineers and Shipbuilders, Institution of Engineers and Shipbuilders in Scotland

Library catalogue:
All or part available in-house

Printed publications:
40 Years of Progress: A History of the Wallsend Research Station 1945–1985 (£25)

BMT Abstracts: 1946 to date (monthly, £220 per year)
BMT Focus (3–4 times a year, free)
Codes of Practice (£50)
Engineering Economics and Ship Design (£30, students £15)
NMI Technical Reports (from £40 each)
Research reports and technical memoranda (from £40)
Shipbuilding Industry and Steelwork Manufacturing Standards
Ship Design Manuals (£1,000 each)
Ships in the Making: a history of ship model testing at Teddington and Feltham 1910–1994 (D. Bailey, Lloyd's of London Press, 1995, £45)

Electronic and video publications:
Marine Technology Abstracts (online)

Publications list:
Available in print

Access to staff:
Contact by letter, by telephone, by fax, by e-mail and via website. All charged.
Hours: Mon to Thu, 0830 to 1700; Fri, 0830 to 1630

Access to building, collection or gallery:
No prior appointment required

Also at:
BMT Group Ltd
Northumbria House, Davy Bank, Wallsend, Tyne and Wear, NE28 6UY; tel: 0191 263 6899; fax: 0191 263 8754; e-mail: gsmith@bmtmail.com

BMT GROUP LTD – WALLSEND

Acronym or abbreviation: BMT

Northumbria House, Oceana Business Park, Wallsend, Tyne and Wear, NE28 6UZ

Tel: 0191 262 5242
Fax: 0191 263 8754
E-mail: gilliansmith@bmtmail.com

Website:
http://www.bmt.org
http://www.marinescienceandtechnology.com
News and events listings for the maritime professional.
http://www.marinetechnologyabstracts.com
The Marine Technology Abstracts database contains bibliographic information providing a reference and description for over 90,000 technical articles, reports, books, conference and transaction papers and other material on all aspects of maritime technology, dating back as far as 1940 and drawn from all major marine engineering publications, published worldwide in at least 10 languages.

Enquiries:
Enquiries to: Librarian

Founded:
1985

Organisation type and purpose:
Consultancy, research organisation.

Subject coverage:
Maritime and civil engineering research, naval architecture, fluid mechanics, ocean engineering, marine engineering, wind engineering, offshore technology, industrial aerodynamics, marine traffic operations, port and harbour design operations and related subjects.

Museum or gallery collection, archive, or library special collection:
Stock/Holdings: 1,000 books and 10,000 reports on related subjects
Reports and Technical Memoranda of British Ship Research Association (BSRA)
Special Collections:
Transactions of Royal Institution of Naval Architects
Transactions of Society of Naval Architects & Marine Engineers
Transactions of North East Coast Institution of Engineers and Shipbuilders

Transactions of Engineers and Shipbuilders in Scotland
Reports and Technical Memoranda of British Ship Research Association (BSRA)
Transactions of Engineers and Shipbuilders in Scotland
Transactions of North East Coast Institution of Engineers and Shipbuilders
Transactions of Royal Institution of Naval Architects
Transactions of Society of Naval Architects & Marine Engineers

Library catalogue:
All or part available in-house

Printed publications:
BMT Abstracts (monthly, £220 p.a.)
BMT Focus (quarterly)
Code of Procedure for Marine Instrumentation and Control Equipment
Engineering Economics and Ship Design
Recommended Practice for the Protection and Painting of Ships
Ship Design Manual: Hydrodynamics (5 volumes, £1,000)
Ship Design Manual: Marine Structures (7 volumes, £1,000)
Ship Design Manual: Noise (£1,000)
Technical Reports (list available)

Electronic and video publications:
Marine Technology Abstracts (online, jointly with Institute of Marine Engineers)
Order electronic and video publications from: website: http://www.marinetechnologyabstracts.com

Publications list:
Available in print

Access to staff:
Contact by letter, by telephone, by fax and by e-mail. All charged.
Hours: Mon to Thu, 0830 to 1700; Fri, 0830 to 1630

Access to building, collection or gallery:
Prior appointment required

Constituent part of:
BMT Group Ltd
Goodrich House, 1 Waldegrave Road, Teddington, Middlesex, TW11 8LZ; tel: 020 8943 5544; fax: 020 8943 5347; e-mail: dgriffiths@ bmtmail.com

BMT MARINE & OFFSHORE SURVEYS LTD.

Acronym or abbreviation: SA

4th Floor, Holland House, 1–4 Bury Street, London, EC3A 5AW

Tel: 0207 648 9650
Fax: 0207 929 5564
E-mail: enquiries@bmtmarinerisk.com

Website:
http://www.wreckage.org
Publications including International Directory.

Enquiries:
Enquiries to: Director, Business Development
Direct tel: 020 7648 9652
Other contacts: Chief Executive; Managing Director

Founded:
1856

Organisation type and purpose:
International organisation, professional body, membership association (membership is by election or invitation), service industry, consultancy.
Marine survey and risk management.
From offices around the world, the SA's surveyors, marine engineers and master mariners are on call; being involved in loss prevention and pre-risk assessment, they travel constantly to ships that are in trouble.

Subject coverage:
Marine surveying and consultancy, insurance loss prevention, marine damage assessment, marine casualty investigation.

continued overleaf

Printed publications:
Salvage Lines (newsletter, quarterly)

Access to staff:
Contact by letter, by telephone, by fax, by e-mail and via website
Hours: Mon to Fri, 0900 to 1730

Has:
offices worldwide

Parent body:
British Maritime Technology Limited (BMT)
Goodrich House, 1 Waldegrave Road, Teddington, TW11 8LZ; tel: 020 8943 5544; fax: 020 8943 5347; e-mail: enquiries@bmtmail.com

BOARD OF DEPUTIES OF BRITISH JEWS

Acronym or abbreviation: BoD

6 Bloomsbury Square, London, WC1A 2LP

Tel: 020 7543 5400
Fax: 020 7543 0010
E-mail: info@bod.org.uk

Website:
http://www.bod.org.uk

Enquiries:
Enquiries to: Researcher
Direct e-mail: jci@bod.org.uk

Founded:
1760

Organisation type and purpose:
Membership association (membership is by election or invitation), voluntary organisation, registered charity.
Lay representative body for Jewish community in the UK.

Subject coverage:
Information about Judaism and about the British Jewish community.

Museum or gallery collection, archive, or library special collection:
Jewish Way of Life Exhibition

Printed publications:
Order printed publications from: As above

Publications list:
Available online

Access to staff:
Contact by letter, by telephone, by fax, by e-mail and via website
Hours: Mon to Fri, 0930 to 1730
Closed for public and Jewish holidays, early closing on Fridays and evenings of Jewish holidays

Access to building, collection or gallery:
Prior appointment required

BOARD OF GRADUATE STUDIES

Formal name: University of Cambridge Board of Graduate Studies
Acronym or abbreviation: BGS

University of Cambridge, 4 Mill Lane, Cambridge, CB2 1RZ

Tel: 01223 760606
Fax: 01223 338723
E-mail: admissions@gradstudies.cam.ac.uk

Website:
http://www.admin.cam.ac.uk/univ/gsprospectus
Prospectus and orders
http://www.admin.cam.ac.uk/offices/gradstud

Enquiries:
Enquiries to: Admissions Office

Founded:
1284

Organisation type and purpose:
University department or institute.
University graduate admissions.

Subject coverage:
All academic subjects studied at the university: arts, humanities, social sciences, physical sciences, biological sciences, engineering, management, technology.

Printed publications:
Prospectus (online)

Access to staff:
Contact by letter, by telephone, by fax and by e-mail
Hours: Mon to Fri, 1000 to 1600

Access to building, collection or gallery:
Mon to Fri, 1000 to 1600

Access for disabled people:
Mon to Fri, 1000 to 1600

Parent body:
University of Cambridge
Cambridge; website: http://www.cam.ac.uk

BOARDING SCHOOLS' ASSOCIATION

Acronym or abbreviation: BSA

Grosvenor Gardens House, 35–37 Grosvenor Gardens, London, SW1W 0BS

Tel: 020 7798 1580
Fax: 020 7798 1581
E-mail: bsa@boarding.org.uk

Website:
http://www.boarding.org.uk

Enquiries:
Enquiries to: National Director
Direct e-mail: office@boarding.org.uk

Founded:
1965

Organisation type and purpose:
National professional society of schools with boarding facilities.

Subject coverage:
Boarding school education in both independent and maintained sectors, with specialist areas in: training, publication, information, National Boarding Standards.

Printed publications:
Magazine (2 times a year)
For full list of publications see website

Publications list:
Available online and in print

Access to staff:
Contact by letter, by telephone, by fax, by e-mail, in person and via website. Appointment necessary. Access for members only. Non-members charged.
Hours: Mon to Fri, 0900 to 1700

Links with:
GSA
HMC
IAPS
ISA
ISC
SHMIS
State Boarding Schools' Association (SBSA)

BOBATH CENTRE FOR CHILDREN WITH CEREBRAL PALSY

Bradbury House, 250 East End Road, London, N2 8AU

Tel: 020 8444 3355
Fax: 020 8444 3399
E-mail: info@bobathlondon.co.uk

Website:
http://www.bobathlondon.co.uk

Enquiries:
Enquiries to: Director for Referrals
Other contacts: (1) Course Organiser (2) Appointments Organiser for (1) training (2) treatment information.

Founded:
1957

Formerly called:
Western Cerebral Palsy Centre

Organisation type and purpose:
Registered charity (charity number 229663), treatment organisation, training organisation, research organisation.
Treatment of children with cerebral palsy and related conditions; training of therapists; research.
Treatment of adults with neurological disability.

Subject coverage:
Cerebral palsy, brain damage, treatment of these conditions.

Printed publications:
A Neurodevelopmental Treatment of Cerebral Palsy
The Bobath Concept Evolution and Application
The Motor Disorders of Infantile Hemiplegia and their Treatment
The Neuro-Developmental Treatment (Bobath K & B)
The Prevention of Mental Retardation in Patients with Cerebral Palsy
Treatment Principals and Planning in Cerebral Palsy

Electronic and video publications:
Teaming with Success (video, £49.95, £20 a month to hire)
The Bobath Approach to the Treatment of Children with Cerebral Palsy (video, £50 to buy, £20 a month to hire)

Publications list:
Available online and in print

Access to staff:
Contact by letter, by telephone, by fax, by e-mail and via website. Appointment necessary.
Hours: Mon to Fri, 0900 to 1700

Access for disabled people:
Parking provided, level entry, access to all public areas, toilet facilities

Connections with:
Bobath Children's Therapy Centre Wales
19 Park Road, Whitchurch, Cardiff, CF4 7BP; tel: 029 2052 2600; fax: 029 2052 1477
Bobath Scotland
Golden Jubilee National Hospital, Beardmore Street, Clydebank, G81 4HX; tel: 0141 435 3270; fax: 0141 435 3279
British Association of Bobath Trained Therapists

BODLEIAN JAPANESE LIBRARY

Acronym or abbreviation: BJL

27 Winchester Road, Oxford, OX2 6NA

Tel: 01865 284506
Fax: 01865 284500
E-mail: japanese@bodleian.ox.ac.uk

Website:
http://www.bodleian.ox.ac.uk/bjl
http://solo.bodleian.ox.ac.uk/
SOLO: Search Oxford Libraries Online.

Enquiries:
Enquiries to: Bodleian Japanese Librarian
Direct e-mail: japanese@bodleian.ox.ac.uk

Founded:
1993

Created by the merger of:
The Japanese collections of the Bodleian Library and the former Nissan Institute Library (year of change 1993)

Organisation type and purpose:
University library.

Subject coverage:
Japanese studies.

Library catalogue:
All or part available online

Access to staff:
Contact by letter, by telephone, by fax, by e-mail, in person and via website. Non-members charged.

Access to building, collection or gallery:
Hours: Term time: Mon to Fri, 0915 to 1900; Sat, 1000 to 1300
Vacations: Mon to Fri, 0915 to 1700
Special comments: Must be accredited readers of the Bodleian Library.

Access for disabled people:
Ramped entry, toilet facilities

Parent body:
Bodleian Library
Broad Street, Oxford, OX1 3BG; tel: 01865 277000; fax: 01865 277182; website: http://www.bodleian.ox.ac.uk

BODLEIAN LAW LIBRARY

St Cross Building, Manor Road, Oxford, OX1 3UR

Tel: 01865 271462
Fax: 01865 271475
E-mail: law.library@bodleian.ox.ac.uk

Website:
http://www.bodleian.ox.ac.uk/law

Enquiries:
Enquiries to: Law Librarian
Other contacts: Academic Services Librarian for services offered by the library, ILL, copies of materials.

Founded:
c.1602

Organisation type and purpose:
University library.

Subject coverage:
Law; criminology; legal bibliography.

Museum or gallery collection, archive, or library special collection:
Law from the jurisdiction of the British Isles, most Commonwealth countries, USA, most European countries; public international law; European Documentation Centre

Non-library collection catalogue:
All or part available online

Library catalogue:
All or part available online

Access to staff:
Contact by letter, by telephone, by fax, by e-mail and via website. Appointment necessary.
Hours: Mon to Fri, 0900 to 1700

Access for disabled people:
Ramped entry, toilet facilities, lift
Special comments: Lift

Constituent part of:
Bodleian Libraries
Broad Street, Oxford, OX1 3BG; website: http://www.bodleian.ox.ac.uk

BODLEIAN LIBRARY

Broad Street, Oxford, OX1 3BG

Tel: 01865 277000
Fax: 01865 277182
E-mail: enquiries@bodley.ox.ac.uk

Website:
http://www.lib.ox.ac.uk/olis/
OLIS Oxford University Library Information Service.
http://www.ouls.ox.ac.uk/bodley
Bodleian library information.

Enquiries:
Enquiries to: Librarian
Other contacts: Director of University Library Services and Bodley's Librarian

Founded:
1598

Organisation type and purpose:
University library.
University and copyright library, of the University of Oxford.

Subject coverage:
Comprehensive range of a university and copyright library dating from 1602; strong coverage in Orientalia, Hebraica, medieval MSS, incunabula, English 16th- and 17th-century literature and history, modern political papers, music (manuscripts and printed); maps.

Museum or gallery collection, archive, or library special collection:
Clarendon State Papers
Douce, Francis (1757–1834) Collection (MSS and early printed works)
Gough, Richard (1735–1809) Collection (British topography)
Harding Collection (music, scores and libretti)
John Johnson Collection of Printed Ephemera
Locke, John (1632–1704) Papers and library
Malone Collection of Shakespearean and British drama
Opie, Peter Mason (1918–1982) Collection (children's literature)
Rawlinson, Richard (1690–1755) Collection
Rawlinson, Thomas (1681–1725) Collection
Selden, John (1584–1654) Collection
UN and EC documents

Non-library collection catalogue:
All or part available online and in print

Library catalogue:
All or part available online and in print

Printed publications:
Catalogues, Union Lists, Histories, Picture books
Order printed publications from: Marketing and Publishing Division, Bodleian Library
Broad Street, Oxford, OX1 3BG, tel: 01865 277091, fax: 01865 277218, e-mail: sales@bodley.ox.ac.uk

Microform publications:
Colour transparencies and film strips

Electronic and video publications:
Pre-1920 catalogue on CD-ROM (OUP)
A tour of the Bodleian Library (The Library, 1998, 25 minute video, PAL/NTEC)

Publications list:
Available online and in print

Access to staff:
Contact by letter, by telephone, by fax and by e-mail. Non-members charged.
Hours: Mon to Fri, 0900 to 1900 or 2200
Special comments: Admission Form (available on web) required. No access below undergraduate level; access to undergraduates of other universities only during vacations.

Central Bodleian site:
Admissions Office (for enquiries about becoming a reader at the library)
tel: 01865 277180; fax: 01865 277105; e-mail: admissions@bodley.ox.ac.uk
Bodleian Japanese Library at the Nissan Institute (for Japanese collections)
27 Winchester Road, Oxford, OX2 6NA; tel: 01865 284506; fax: 01865 284500; e-mail: japanese@bodley.ox.ac.uk
Bodleian Law Library (for law, excluding ecclesiastical law)
Manor Road, Oxford, OX1 3UR; tel: 01865 271463; fax: 01865 271475; e-mail: law.library@bodley.ox.ac.uk
Department of Oriental Books and Manuscripts (books and manuscripts in Oriental languages, except Japanese and the languages of the Indian subcontinent)
tel: 01865 277034; fax: 01865 277029; e-mail: oriental@bodley.ox.ac.uk
Department of Special Collections & Western Manuscripts (manuscripts, rare and early printed books, modern political papers in Western languages)
tel: 01865 277158; fax: 01865 277182; e-mail: western.manuscrpts@bodley.ox.ac.uk

Eastern Art Library
Pusey Lane, Oxford, OX1 2LE; tel: 01865 278202; fax: 01865 278190; e-mail: eastern.art.library@bodley.ox.ac.uk
European Documentation Centre (receives all European Union publications)
Bodleian Library, Manor Road, Oxford, OX1 3UR; tel: 01865 271463; fax: 01865 271475; e-mail: edc@bodley.ox.ac.uk
Hooke Library (for science)
South Parks Road, Oxford, OX1 3UB; tel: 01865 272812; fax: 01865 272821; e-mail: hooke@bodley.ox.ac.uk
Imaging Services (all photocopy and photographic enquiries)
tel: 01865 277061; fax: 01865 287127; e-mail: repro@bodley.ox.ac.uk
Indian Institute Library (for books and mânuscripts from the Indian subcontinent)
Bodleian Library, Broad Street, Oxford, OX1 3BG; tel: 01865 277081; fax: 01865 277182; e-mail: indian.institute@bodley.ox.ac.uk
Institute for Chinese Studies Library
Walton Street, Oxford, OX1 2HG; tel: 01865 280430; fax: 01865 280431; e-mail: chinese.studies.library@bodley.ox.ac.uk
John Johnson Collection (printed ephemera)
tel: 01865 277047; fax: 01865 277182; e-mail: jjcoll@bodley.ox.ac.uk
Map Room (for maps and geography-related resources)
tel: 01865 277013; fax: 01865 277139; e-mail: maps@bodley.ox.ac.uk
Marketing & Publishing Division (library publications and merchandise, publication of material from the library)
tel: 01865 277091; fax: 01865 277218; e-mail: sales@bodley.ox.ac.uk
Modern Papers (modern political papers)
tel: 01865 277046; fax: 01865 277182; e-mail: modern.papers@bodley.ox.ac.uk
Music Room (for music resources)
tel: 01865 277063; fax: 01865 277182; e-mail: music@bodley.ox.ac.uk
Oriental Institute Library
Pusey Lane, Oxford, OX1 2LE; tel: 01865 278202; fax: 01865 278190; e-mail: library@orinst.ox.ac.uk
Philosophy Library (admission restricted to University members)
10 Merton Street, Oxford, OX1 4JJ; tel: 01865 276927; fax: 01865 276932; e-mail: philosophy.library@bodley.ox.ac.uk
Preservation & Conservation Department (preservation and conservation of the collections)
tel: 01865 277086; fax: 01865 277182; e-mail: prescons@bodley.ox.ac.uk
Radcliffe Science Library (for science, covering the physical and life sciences)
Parks Road, Oxford, OX1 3QP; tel: 01865 272800; fax: 01865 272821; e-mail: rsl.enquiries@bodley.ox.ac.uk
Reader Services Department (reader services relating to printed books and journals in Western languages)
tel: 01865 277162; fax: 01865 287112; e-mail: reader.services@bodley.ox.ac.uk
Rhodes House Library (for African and Commonwealth history and politics)
South Parks Road, Oxford, OX1 3RG; tel: 01865 270908; fax: 01865 270912; e-mail: rhodes.house.library@bodley.ox.ac.uk
Systems Section (Bodleian's database network and www pages)
tel: 01865 277074; fax: 01865 277182; e-mail: systems@bodley.ox.ac.uk
Technical Services Department (status of items on order, receipt of legal deposit material, reporting errors in the Oxford union catalogue, OLIS)
tel: 01865 277017; fax: 01865 277036; e-mail: technical.services@bodley.ox.ac.uk
Vere Harmsworth Library (for American history and politics)
South Parks Road, Oxford, OX1 3TG; tel: 01865 282700; fax: 01865 282709; e-mail: vhl@bodley.ox.ac.uk

Parent body:
University of Oxford
tel: 01865 270000; fax: 01865 270708

BODLEIAN LIBRARY OF COMMONWEALTH AND AFRICAN STUDIES AT RHODES HOUSE

South Parks Road, Oxford, OX1 3RG

Tel: 01865 270908
Fax: 01865 270912
E-mail: rhodes.house.library@bodleian.ox.ac.uk

Website:
http://www.bodleian.ox.ac.uk/rhodes
Library website.

Enquiries:
Enquiries to: Subject Consultant or Archivist

Founded:
1929

Formerly called:
Rhodes House Library

Organisation type and purpose:
University library.

Subject coverage:
History of the Commonwealth (excluding the Indian sub-continent) and Africa south of the Sahara.

Museum or gallery collection, archive, or library special collection:
C J Rhodes Papers
Colonial Records (collection of papers of colonial servants)
Papers of the Anti-Apartheid Movement
Papers of the Anti-Slavery Society
Papers of the United Society for the Propagation of the Gospel
Scicluna Collection (Malta)
Sir Roy Welensky Papers

Library catalogue:
All or part available online

Printed publications:
African medical history: a guide to personal papers in Rhodes House Library, Oxford
Manuscript collections in Rhodes House Library: accessions 1978 to 1994
Papers of Sir Roy Welensky, 1907–1991 in Rhodes House Library: a catalogue

Microform publications:
Manuscript catalogues available from the Bodleian Library

Publications list:
Available in print

Access to staff:
Contact by letter, by telephone, by e-mail and in person. Letter of introduction required. Non-members charged.
Hours: Term time: Mon to Fri, 0900 to 1900; Sat, 0900 to 1300
Vacations: Mon to Fri, 0900 to 1700

Access for disabled people:
Access difficult due to steps at building entrance and within building. Please contact staff in advance for material to be moved to an accessible reading room.

Constituent part of:
Bodleian Library
University of Oxford

BOLSOVER DISTRICT COUNCIL

Acronym or abbreviation: BDC

Sherwood Lodge, Bolsover, Derbyshire, S44 6NF

Tel: 01246 242424; minicom no. 01246 242450
Fax: 01246 242423
E-mail: enquiries@bolsover.gov.uk

Website:
http://www.bolsover.gov.uk

Enquiries:
Enquiries to: Communications Officer
Direct tel: 01246 242323
Direct e-mail: scott.chambers@bolsover.gov.uk

Founded:
1974

Organisation type and purpose:
Local government body.

Printed publications:
Intouch Newspaper (free, direct)
Days Out (pocket guide, free, direct)
Various tourism publications (free, direct)
Customer Information Booklets
Various Council publications (housing, planning, leisure, tourism, environmental health)
Order printed publications from: Contact Centres, Bolsover District Council, Sherwood Lodge, Bolsover, Derbyshire S44 6NF

Electronic and video publications:
Intouch Newspaper (online)

Publications list:
Available online and in print

Access to staff:
Contact by letter, by telephone, by fax, by e-mail, in person and via website
Hours: Mon to Fri, 0900 to 1700

Access for disabled people:
Parking provided, ramped entry, toilet facilities

BOLTON LIBRARIES

Central Library, Civic Centre, Le Mans Crescent, Bolton, Lancashire, BL1 1SE

Tel: 01204 333173
Fax: 01204 332225
E-mail: josie.butterworth@bolton.gov.uk

Website:
http://www.bolton.gov.uk/libraries
Includes access for library members to online information resources.

Enquiries:
Enquiries to: Team Librarian
Direct tel: 01204 332853
Direct e-mail: central.library@bolton.gov.uk

Founded:
1853

Organisation type and purpose:
Local government body, public library.

Subject coverage:
General, science and technology, textiles, local studies, business information, childcare information, career information, health and social care information.

Information services:
In-depth information service, tourist information service, Bolton NHS library, social care library

Museum or gallery collection, archive, or library special collection:
Textiles collection, special periodicals collection, rare books collection, Lancashire collection, British Standards, childcare information, careers

Trade and statistical information:
Mainly official British statistics, EU statistics, UN statistics.

Library catalogue:
All or part available online

Access to staff:
Contact by letter, by telephone, by fax, by e-mail and in person
Hours: Mon, Tue and Thu, 0900 to 1930; Wed and Fri, 0900 to 1730; Sat, 0900 to 1700

Access to building, collection or gallery:
Hours: Mon, Tue and Thu, 0815 to 1930; Wed and Fri, 0815 to 1730; Sat, 0900 to 1700

Access for disabled people:
Ramped entry, toilet facilities
Hours: Mon, Tue and Thu, 0815 to 1930; Wed and Fri, 0815 to 1730; Sat, 0900 to 1700

BOLTON METROPOLITAN BOROUGH COUNCIL

Acronym or abbreviation: Bolton Council

Town Hall, Bolton, Greater Manchester, BL1 1RU

Tel: 01204 333333
Fax: 01204 392808
E-mail: bolton@bolton.gov.uk

Website:
http://www.bolton.gov.uk

Organisation type and purpose:
Local government body.

Subject coverage:
Local government services.

BOND OWNERS' CLUB

Acronym or abbreviation: BOC

42 Beaufort Avenue, Hodge Hill, Birmingham, B34 6AE

Tel: 0121 784 4626
Fax: 0121 784 4626

Website:
http://www.bondownersclub.co.uk
Details of the club, Bond cars and includes membership form.

Enquiries:
Enquiries to: General Secretary

Founded:
1951

Organisation type and purpose:
International organisation, membership association.

Subject coverage:
Information on Bond cars and the Bond Owners' Club, spares availability and technical advice.

Museum or gallery collection, archive, or library special collection:
Production records and original archive material

Printed publications:
Bond Related Information, Handbooks and Parts Lists

Access to staff:
Contact by letter, by telephone and by fax.
Appointment necessary.
Hours: Evenings and weekends

BOOK AID INTERNATIONAL

39–41 Coldharbour Lane, London, SE5 9NR

Tel: 020 7733 3577
Fax: 020 7978 8006
E-mail: info@bookaid.org

Website:
http://www.bookaid.org
Information about the organisation and its work, copies of newsletter, interchange and details of how people can support organisation's work.

Enquiries:
Enquiries to: Administrator

Founded:
1954

Organisation type and purpose:
Registered charity (charity number 313869). Working in partnership with organisations in developing countries to support their work in literacy, education, training and publishing.

Subject coverage:
Education, book provision and publishing in developing countries, especially Africa.

Printed publications:
Annual Review and Three Year Plan
Newsletter (irregular)
Posters and pamphlets

Access to staff:
Contact by letter, by telephone, by fax, by e-mail and via website. Appointment necessary.
Hours: Mon to Fri, 0900 to 1700

BOOK PRODUCTION CONSULTANTS LTD

Acronym or abbreviation: BPC

25–27 High Street, Chesterton, Cambridge, CB4 1ND

Tel: 01223 352790
Fax: 01223 460718
E-mail: bpc@bpccam.co.uk

Website:
http://www.bpccam.co.uk

Enquiries:
Enquiries to: Marketing Manager
Direct e-mail: jl@bpccam.co.uk

Founded:
1973

Organisation type and purpose:
Service industry, publishing house.
Complete one-stop publishing service, from conception to distribution, for books, magazines, institutional journals, guides, catalogues, brochures, newsletters, catalogues and company histories.

Subject coverage:
Service publishing including: guides and magazines, corporate manuals and brochures, books and journals, all subjects covered.

Publications list:
Available in print

Access to staff:
Contact by letter, by telephone, by fax and by e-mail
Hours: Mon to Fri, 0900 to 1730

Constituent bodies:
Granta Editions

BOOK TRUST

Formal name: Book Trust

Book House, 45 East Hill, London, SW18 2QZ

Tel: 020 8516 2977
Fax: 020 8516 2978
E-mail: query@booktrust.org.uk

Website:
http://www.booktrust.org.uk

Organisation type and purpose:
To provide reviews, information and advice giving readers the widest possible access to books.

Subject coverage:
Books, publishing, reading, literary prizes

Access to staff:
Contact by letter, by telephone, by fax, by e-mail and via website

BOOKPLATE SOCIETY

Yarkhill, Upper Bucklebury, Reading, Berkshire, RG7 6QH

E-mail: publications@bookplatesociety.org

Website:
http://www.bookplategb.org
Membership details, list of publications.

Enquiries:
Enquiries to: Honorary Secretary

Founded:
1972

Organisation type and purpose:
International organisation, membership association (membership is by subscription), present number of members: 250, registered charity (charity number 295678), publishing house.
Voluntary association of bookplate collectors, artists and bibliophiles.
To promote the collection and study of bookplates.

Subject coverage:
History of bookplates, bookplate artists, bookplate literature.

Museum or gallery collection, archive, or library special collection:
Society Archive

Printed publications:
Newsletter (twice a year)
The Bookplate Journal
Books about bookplates (usually biennually) including:
The Bookplates of Edward Gordon Craig (Blatchley, J, 1997)
Bookplates by Robert Osmond (Lee, B N, 1998)
The Bookplates of Edmund Hort New (Lee, B N, 1999/2000)
Scottish Bookplates (Lee, B N and Campbell, I, 2006)
Bookplates in the Trophy Style (Latcham, P, 2006)
Some Bookplates of Heralds (Lee, B N, 2003)
Order printed publications from: The Bookplate Society
Address as above

Publications list:
Available online

Access to staff:
Contact by letter and by e-mail
Hours: Weekends and evenings

Affiliated to:
Fédération Internationale des Sociétés d'Amateurs d'Ex-Libris (FISAE)

BOOKS EXPRESS

PO Box 10, Saffron Walden, Essex, CB11 4EW

Tel: 01799 513726
Fax: 01799 513248
E-mail: info@books-express.co.uk

Website:
http://www.books-express.co.uk
Ordering information, lists of specialist publications.

Enquiries:
Enquiries to: Senior Partner
Direct e-mail: duncan@books-express.co.uk
Other contacts: Bibliographic Services Manager (for website enquiries, bibliographic enquiries)

Founded:
1983

Organisation type and purpose:
Service industry.
Specialist bookseller and information service.
North American and European academic publishers.

Subject coverage:
Official publications, government documents and electronic information from Commonwealth of Australia (AGPS), Federal Government of Canada (CCG-P), Federal Government of USA (USGPO), Queensland Department of Primary Industry, and Library Cataloguing Materials from United States Library of Congress.

Museum or gallery collection, archive, or library special collection:
Comprehensive database of official publications for sale from Australia, Canada, USA and Queensland
US and European academic publications

Printed publications:
Over 60,000 titles and journals including:
USA government books, documents and grey literature
Canadian government books, documents and grey literature
Australian government books, documents and grey literature
Queensland Department of Primary Industries
US Code of Federal Regulations
English-French French-English bilingual glossaries and vocabularies in over 60 subjects

Access to staff:
Contact by letter, by telephone, by fax, by e-mail and via website. Appointment necessary.
Hours: Mon to Fri, 1000 to 1800

BOOKSELLERS ASSOCIATION OF THE UK & IRELAND LIMITED

Acronym or abbreviation: BA

272 Vauxhall Bridge Road, London, SW1V 1BA

Tel: 020 7802 0802
Fax: 020 7802 0803
E-mail: mail@booksellers.org.uk

Website:
http://www.booksellers.org.uk

Enquiries:
Enquiries to: Chief Executive

Founded:
1895

Organisation type and purpose:
Trade association, present number of members: 4,400 mostly retail outlets.
Representing and promoting retail booksellers nationwide.

Subject coverage:
Book trade regulations, market conditions, legislation, shopfitting, distribution, national book tokens, careers, etc.

Printed publications:
The Complete Guide to Starting and Running a Bookshop (£28.00)
Bookselling Essentials (magazine)
Directory of BA Members (annually, £34)
Directory of UK and Irish Book Publishers
Labels of special interest to booksellers and publishers

Publications list:
Available in print

Wholly-owned companies:
batch.co.uk
   e-mail: mail@batch.co.uk
Book Tokens Limited
   e-mail: mail@booktokens.co.uk

BORDER HERITAGE

Loophill, Canonbie, Dumfries & Galloway, DG14 0XF

Tel: 01387 371780
Fax: 01387 381243

Website:
http://www.borderheritage.com
Family history on video.

Enquiries:
Enquiries to: Managing Director
Direct e-mail: amillar@scotborders.gov.uk

Founded:
1997

Organisation type and purpose:
Local history society.

Subject coverage:
Scottish/English border history, films, books.

Museum or gallery collection, archive, or library special collection:
Extensive video tape collection on Border family history
Books

Non-library collection catalogue:
All or part available online

continued overleaf

Printed publications:
Various publications (available direct or via website)
Various products (available direct or via website)

Publications list:
Available online

Access to staff:
Contact by letter, by telephone, by fax and by e-mail
Hours: Mon to Fri, 0900 to 1700

Access to building, collection or gallery:
Prior appointment required

BORDER UNION AGRICULTURAL SOCIETY

Showground Office, Springwood Park, Kelso, Borders, TD5 8LS

Tel: 01573 224188
Fax: 01573 226778
E-mail: bordunion@aol.com

Enquiries:
Enquiries to: Secretary

Founded:
1813

Organisation type and purpose:
Voluntary organisation, publishing house.
Agricultural Society.
Organisation and promotion of agricultural, rural and canine activities.

Subject coverage:
Shows and exhibitions, agricultural, canine and general, rural life. Access to rural historical records for the locality. Information on present day rural activities.

Museum or gallery collection, archive, or library special collection:
Society records dating from 1813

Printed publications:
Border Union Show: Catalogue (annually in July, charge)
Border Union Show: Prize Schedule (annually in April, free)
Championship Dog Show: Schedule and Catalogue (annually, Schedule February, free, Catalogue June, charge)
Kelso Ram Sales: Catalogue (annually in September, charge)

Access to staff:
Contact by letter, by telephone and by fax
Hours: Mon to Fri, 0900 to 1700

Member of:
Association of Show and Agricultural Organisations

BORGWARD DRIVERS' CLUB

158 Willow Avenue, Edgbaston, Birmingham, B17 8HG

Tel: 0121 429 7169
E-mail: borgwardclub@btinternet.com

Website:
http://www.borgward.co.uk
History of company and description of cars plus pictures.

Enquiries:
Enquiries to: Secretary

Founded:
1980

Organisation type and purpose:
Membership association (membership is by subscription), present number of members: 70, voluntary organisation.
To further the promotion of Borgward, Lloyd, Goliath, and Hansa cars in the United Kingdom.

Subject coverage:
Borgward cars, Lloyd cars, Goliath cars, Hansa cars and spares for same.

Printed publications:
Newsletters (6 times a year)

Access to staff:
Contact by letter, by telephone, by e-mail and via website
Hours: Sun to Sat, 0900 to 2000

BORTHWICK INSTITUTE FOR ARCHIVES

University of York, Heslington, York, YO1 5DD

Tel: 01904 321160
E-mail: bihr500@york.ac.uk

Website:
http://www.york.ac.uk/inst/bihr
Summary details of holdings, publications and access, list of publications.

Enquiries:
Enquiries to: Keeper of Archives

Founded:
1953

Organisation type and purpose:
University department or institute.
Historical research institute and archives.

Subject coverage:
Ecclesiastical, social, economic, local and political history, medical history, architectural history and the history of Southern Africa.

Museum or gallery collection, archive, or library special collection:
Archives of the Archbishopric of York c. 1200 to present day
Archives of the Centre for Southern African Studies
Archives of the Earls of Halifax
Atkinson-Brierley architectural archive
York Health Trust Archives
The Institute houses c. 500,000 wills and inventories 1320–1858, for Yorkshire

Non-library collection catalogue:
All or part available online, in-house and in print

Printed publications:
Borthwick Papers (many relate to the history of York, twice a year)
Borthwick Texts and Studies including:
The Jewish Communities of Medieval England (R.B. Dobson, Helen Birkett, 2010)
The York sede vacante register, 1423–1426 (Joan Kirby, 2009)
Foundations of Medieval Scholarship: records in honour of David Crook (Sean Cunningham & Paul Brand, 2008)
The Foundations of the History of the Abbeys and Byland and Jervaulx (Janet Burton, 2007)
Order printed publications from: Borthwick Institute, University of York, Heslington, York, YO10 5DD

Publications list:
Available online and in print

Access to staff:
Contact by letter, by telephone, by fax, by e-mail, in person and via website
Hours: Mon to Fri, 0915 to 1645

Access for disabled people:
Lift available to building and within building, height-adjustable desks available

Constituent part of:
University of York

BOSS FEDERATION

Formal name: British Office Supplies and Services Federation

Farringdon Point, 29–35 Farringdon Road, London, EC1M 3JF

Tel: 0845 450 1565
Fax: 020 7915 8414
E-mail: info@bossfederation.co.uk

Website:
http://www.bossfederation.com
Membership benefits and services, industry standards, support services, regional committees.

Founded:
1905

Formerly called:
Stationers Proprietary Articles Trade Association

Organisation type and purpose:
A non-profit making organisation, the trade association that serves the UK office supplies and services industry.
Provides a range of initiatives, cost-saving benefits and services to enhance the business performance of its members, and plays a strategic role in the support, promotion and protection of the office products industry.

Subject coverage:
Represents all businesses, from the smallest retailer to the largest manufacturer, along the distribution chain in the office products industry, covering stationery, office machines and supplies, office furniture, office systems and related product areas.

Access to staff:
Contact by letter, by telephone, by fax and by e-mail

Branches:
Has 8 regional committees throughout the UK

Federation includes:
Rubber Stamp Manufacturers Guild (RSMG)
Writing Instruments Associaton (WIA)

BOTANICAL SOCIETY OF SCOTLAND

Acronym or abbreviation: BSS

c/o Royal Botanic Garden Edinburgh, 20a Inverleith Row, Edinburgh, EH3 5LR

Tel: 0131 552 7171
Fax: 0131 248 2901

Website:
http://www.botsocscot.org.uk

Enquiries:
Enquiries to: General Secretary

Founded:
1836

Organisation type and purpose:
Learned society (membership is by subscription, election or invitation), voluntary organisation, recognised Scottish charity, no. 016283).
Incorporates the Cryptogamic Society of Scotland.

Subject coverage:
Plant science; Scottish flora: plant identification, ecological studies and botanical conservation.

Museum or gallery collection, archive, or library special collection:
Library is incorporated within that of the Royal Botanic Garden Edinburgh

Printed publications:
Plant Ecology and Diversity: previously Botanical Journal of Scotland (twice a year)
BSS News (twice a year)
Checklists of the Flowering Plants and Ferns of East Lothian, West Lothian and Midlothian
Flora of Sutherland (J. Anthony)
A Map of the Flora of Mainland Inverness-shire (in collaboration with the Botanical Society of the British Isles)
Plant Life of South West Asia
Plant Life of Edinburgh and the Lothians (2002)

Access to staff:
Contact by letter

BOTANICAL SOCIETY OF THE BRITISH ISLES

Acronym or abbreviation: BSBI

Department of Botany, Natural History Museum, Cromwell Road, London, SW7 5BD

Tel: 020 7492 5002 (answerphone only)
E-mail: dpearman4@aol.com

Website:
http://www.bsbi.org.uk
General information about the Society.

Enquiries:
Enquiries to: Honorary General Secretary (for specific plant enquiries)
Other contacts: Honorary Assistant Secretary (for all general enquiries)

Founded:
1836

Organisation type and purpose:
Learned society (membership is by subscription), present number of members: 2,800 approx, voluntary organisation, research organisation, publishing house.
The study and conservation of the British and Irish vascular plant and charophyte flora, its form and distribution. Research into the taxonomy, ecology, biogeography of the flora, maintenance of a botanical recording network and collaboration with other statutory and voluntary bodies.

Subject coverage:
British flowering plants and ferns, identification of wild plants, local floras.

Museum or gallery collection, archive, or library special collection:
Database at University of Leicester, c/o Dr R J Gornall, University Road, Leicester, LE1 7RH

Printed publications:
Large number of publications including:
BSBI News (3 times per annum, to members only)
Conference Reports
Handbooks on Identification, etc., including:
Dandelions of Great Britain and Ireland (235 species, £17.50)
Plant Crib 1998 (£18.75)
Roses of Great Britain and Ireland (£12.50)
Willows and Poplars of Great Britain and Ireland (£12.50)
Watsonia: Journal and Proceedings of the Botanical Society of the British Isles (2 parts annually)
Order printed publications from: Botanical Society of the British Isles Publications, c/o Summerfield Books, 3 Phoenix Park, Skelton, Penrith, Cumbria, CA11 95DE; tel: 01768 484909; fax: 01768 484910; e-mail: info@summerfieldbooks.com

Publications list:
Available in print

Access to staff:
Contact by letter, by telephone and by e-mail
Hours: Mon to Fri, 0900 to 1700
Special comments: Answerphone provides a letter reply only.

BOTANIX LIMITED

Hop Pocket Lane, Paddock Wood, Tonbridge, Kent, TN12 6DQ

Tel: 01892 833415
Fax: 01892 836905
E-mail: sales@botanix.co.uk

Website:
http://www.botanix.co.uk
Pure hop aromas, hop-based antifoams, hop-based bittering products, hops and hop pellets

Enquiries:
Enquiries to: Sales Director

Founded:
1987

Organisation type and purpose:
International organisation, manufacturing industry.

Subject coverage:
Production and sales of hop-based products for the brewing industry; marketing of English hops and hop products.

Access to staff:
Contact by letter, by telephone, by e-mail and via website. Appointment necessary.
Hours: Mon to Fri, 0900 to 1730

Member organisation of:
Institute of Brewing and Distilling

BOUNDARY COMMISSION FOR SCOTLAND

Thistle House, 91 Haymarket Terrace, Edinburgh, EH12 5HD

Tel: 0131 538 7510
Fax: 0131 538 7511
E-mail: secretariat@scottishboundaries.gov.uk

Website:
http://www.bcomm-scotland.gov.uk
Information on boundaries of constituencies in Scotland for Scottish and Westminster parliaments, and on the periodic reviews of those boundaries.

Enquiries:
Enquiries to: Secretary

Founded:
1945

Organisation type and purpose:
Statutory body, advisory non-departmental public body, constituted under the Parliamentary Constituencies Act 1986, reporting to the Scotland Office.

Subject coverage:
Parliamentary boundaries.

Printed publications:
Periodical and Interim Reports
Order printed publications from: The Stationery Office

Electronic and video publications:
Reports available from website as PDF files

Publications list:
Available online

Access to staff:
Contact by letter, by telephone, by fax, by e-mail and via website
Hours: Mon to Fri, 0900 to 1700

BOURNEMOUTH AND POOLE COLLEGE

North Road, Parkstone, Poole, Dorset, BH14 0LS

Tel: 01202 747600
Fax: 01202 205477
E-mail: enquiries@thecollege.co.uk

Website:
http://www.thecollege.co.uk

Enquiries:
Enquiries to: Librarian
Direct tel: 01202 205631

Subject coverage:
FE courses (GCSE, A-level, AS-level, AVCE, GMVQ, NVQ) in the following subjects: construction, engineering, social care, child care, theatre and performing arts, hairdressing, floristry, beauty therapy, catering, tourism, hotel operations, business studies, computing, media studies, management, teacher training, art and design, science, languages, social sciences, law.
HE courses (BSC and BEng Foundation, HND, HNC) in the following subjects: conservation sciences, computing, electronics, design engineering, business, business information technology, computer-aided design, geography and coastal conservation, popular music, tourism and leisure management, mechanical and production engineering, building studies.

Museum or gallery collection, archive, or library special collection:
249 journals
6000 audio visual items (videos, tapes)
70,776 books to support courses listed

Library catalogue:
All or part available in-house

Access to staff:
Contact by letter and by e-mail
Hours: Mon to Thu, 0900 to 1900; Fri, 0900 to 1700

Access for disabled people:
Parking provided, ramped entry, access to all public areas, toilet facilities

BOURNEMOUTH UNIVERSITY

Library and Learning Centre, Talbot Campus, Fern Barrow, Poole, Dorset, BH12 5BB

Tel: 01202 524111
Fax: 01202 513293

Website:
http://www.bournemouth.ac.uk/library
Information about all library services

Enquiries:
Enquiries to: University Librarian
Direct tel: 01202 965044
Direct fax: 01202 965475
Direct e-mail: jascott@bmth.ac.uk
Other contacts: Deputy University Librarian

Founded:
1979

Organisation type and purpose:
University library.

Subject coverage:
Computing, IT, electronics and information systems, psychology, communications and sociology, economics and industry, finance, taxation and accountancy, law, management, marketing, retailing, advertising and public relations, health and community studies, social policy, nursing and midwifery, biological and environmental sciences, design, production and manufacture, food hospitality, tourism, recreation and leisure, media studies, archaeology and heritage conservation.

Museum or gallery collection, archive, or library special collection:
Wedlake and Greening: Archaeology
Ernst and Young: Taxation and Revenue Law
BBC Radio 4 Analysis Programme
Broadcasting Audience Research
Independent Local Radio Programme Sharing Digitization Project Archive
Segrue Journalism Collection
TV Times Project
Printed and electronic sources covering history of broadcasting, public relations and advertising; product design, interior design and engineering

Trade and statistical information:
Collection of government and EC official statistics.
A range of unofficial statistics.
Business information.
Company data.
Market Research.

Printed publications:
Bournemouth University Occasional Papers on Library and Information Services (BUOPOLIS)
British Nursing Index
Conference Proceedings
Order printed publications from: Academic Services, Bournemouth University
tel: 01202 965725, fax: 01202 965475, e-mail: gfowler@bournemouth.ac.uk

Electronic and video publications:
British Nursing Index online and on CD-ROM

Access to staff:
Contact by letter, by e-mail and via website. Appointment necessary.
Hours: Term time: Mon to Thu, 0900 to 2100; Fri, 0915 to 1715; Sat, 1200 to 1800; Sun 1200 to 1700

continued overleaf

Members:
Southern Universities Purchasing Consortium
(SUPC)

BOVIS LEND LEASE LIMITED (EUROPE)

Acronym or abbreviation: BLLE

142 Northolt Road, Harrow, Middlesex, HA2 0EE

Tel: 020 8271 8000
Fax: 020 8271 8188

Website:
http://www.bovislendlease.com
Information on Bovis Lend Lease worldwide.

Enquiries:
Enquiries to: Librarian
Direct tel: 020 8271 8124 (Information Centre)
Direct e-mail: caroline.massey@eu.bovislendlease
.com

Founded:
1885

Organisation type and purpose:
Service industry.
Construction company.
Project and construction management,
consultancy, creative solutions.

Subject coverage:
Building construction.

Library catalogue:
All or part available in-house

Access to staff:
Contact by letter, by e-mail and via website.
Appointment necessary.
Hours: Mon to Fri, 0900 to 1700

Access to building, collection or gallery:
No access other than to staff

Parent body:
Lend Lease Limited

Regional offices in:
Birmingham, Bristol, Edinburgh, Glasgow,
Manchester, Dublin, Belfast

BOWLS ENGLAND

Acronym or abbreviation: BE

Lyndhurst Road, Worthing, West Sussex, BN11
2AZ

Tel: 01903 820222
Fax: 01903 820444
E-mail: enquiries@bowlsengland.com

Website:
http://www.bowlsengland.com

Enquiries:
Enquiries to: Chief Executive

Founded:
1903

Organisation type and purpose:
National organisation, professional body, present
number of members: 132,000.
National governing body of the game.

Subject coverage:
The game of bowls.

Access to staff:
Contact by letter, by telephone and by fax.
Appointment necessary.
Hours: Mon to Fri, 0900 to 1700

Access for disabled people:
Parking provided, level entry

Also at:
Bowls England
   Victoria Park, Archery Road, Royal Leamington
   Spa, Warwickshire, CV31 3PT; tel: 01926 430686;
   fax: 01926 332024

BOX CULVERT ASSOCIATION

Acronym or abbreviation: BoxCA

60 Charles Street, Leicester, LE1 1FB

Tel: 0116 253 6161
Fax: 0116 251 4568
E-mail: boxca@britishprecast.org

Website:
http://www.boxculverts.org.uk

Enquiries:
Enquiries to: Secretary

Organisation type and purpose:
Trade association.

Subject coverage:
Precast concrete box culverts.

Printed publications:
Brochure (free)
Site Use Guide (free)
Specification (1991, £3)

Access to staff:
Contact by letter, by telephone, by fax and by e-mail
Hours: Mon to Fri, 0900 to 1700

Product association of the:
British Precast Concrete Federation

BOYS' BRIGADE

Acronym or abbreviation: BB

Felden Lodge, Felden Lane, Hemel Hempstead,
Hertfordshire, HP3 0BL

Tel: 01442 231681
Fax: 01442 235391
E-mail: felden@boys-brigade.org.uk

Website:
http://www.boys-brigade.org.uk
History, events, guestbook.

Enquiries:
Enquiries to: Chief Executive

Founded:
1883

Organisation type and purpose:
Voluntary organisation.
Youth organisation.

Subject coverage:
Church-based youth work with boys and young
men in nearly 3,000 churches of most
denominations.

Museum or gallery collection, archive, or library special collection:
Archives relating to the founding (in 1883) and
   subsequent history of the Brigade

Printed publications:
Annual Report
BB Gazette (6 times a year)
Order printed publications from: The Supplies
Manager, The Boys' Brigade
Alington Road, Eynesbury, St Neots,
Cambridgeshire, PE19 2RD, tel: 01480 470515, fax:
01480 470516, e-mail: bus-cent@boys-brigade.org
.uk

Access to staff:
Contact by letter, by fax and by e-mail
Hours: Mon to Fri, 0900 to 1700

BP VIDEO LIBRARY

52–54 Southwark Street, London, SE1 1UN

Tel: 020 7357 7521
Fax: 020 7357 9953
E-mail: bpvl@bp.com

Website:
http://www.bpvideolibrary.com

Enquiries:
Enquiries to: Librarian

Organisation type and purpose:
Suitable for ages: all.
Distribution library.

Subject coverage:
Oil industry, refining, exploration, energy,
environment, motoring, power and engineering.

Museum or gallery collection, archive, or library special collection:
Video programmes covering wide area of the oil
   industry

Library catalogue:
All or part available in print

Electronic and video publications:
Videos

Publications list:
Available in print

Access to staff:
Contact by letter, by telephone, by fax and by e-mail
Hours: Mon to Fri, 0900 to 1700

BPA CONSULTING LIMITED

Atlas House, Spring Court, Station Road, Dorking,
Surrey, RH4 1EB

Tel: 01306 875500
Fax: 01306 888179
E-mail: bpa@bpaconsulting.com

Enquiries:
Enquiries to: Director

Founded:
1971

Organisation type and purpose:
Consultancy.

Subject coverage:
Strategic consultants to the electronics industry,
specialising in inter-connection and packaging.

Publications list:
Available online and in print

Access to staff:
Contact by letter, by telephone, by fax and by e-mail
Hours: Mon to Fri, 0900 to 1730

BRACE

Formal name: Bristol Research into Alzheimer's and
Care of the Elderly

Frenchay Hospital, Frenchay, Bristol, BS16 1LE

Tel: 0117 340 4831
Fax: 0117 340 4831
E-mail: admin@alzheimers-brace.org

Website:
http://www.alzheimers-brace.org
Current research projects funded, brief statistical
information and FAQs on dementia and
Alzheimer's disease.

Founded:
1987

Organisation type and purpose:
Registered charity (charity number 297965).
One of only a few charities that exists specifically
to finance dementia research.
Aims to help support a continuing programme of
research into conditions of the elderly, particularly
Alzheimer's Disease, and also to raise awareness of
the disease and its effects, not only on the sufferer
but also on family life. Supports research projects
undertaken in universities and hospitals in the
South West of the UK, particularly in Bristol, which
is a centre of excellence for neuroscience research.

Subject coverage:
High quality, peer-reviewed research projects in
different aspects of dementia research. The projects
range from the development of more accurate
methods of diagnosis and evaluating treatments to

examining a person's genetic make-up to see why some people suffer from dementia when others live into old age without developing the condition.

Information services:
Provides speakers for external events and group meetings.

Electronic and video publications:
Newsletter
Order electronic and video publications from: Website

Access to staff:
Contact by letter, by telephone, by fax, by e-mail and via website

BRACKENHURST LIBRARY

The Nottingham Trent University, Brackenhurst, Nottingham Road, Southwell, Nottinghamshire, NG25 0QF

Tel: 01636 817000 (switchboard); 01636 817049 (library)
Fax: 01636 815404

Enquiries:
Enquiries to: Information Specialist
Direct e-mail: heather.parsonage@ntu.ac.uk

Organisation type and purpose:
University library, suitable for ages: 16+.

Subject coverage:
Agriculture, food science, horticulture and floristry, equine studies and horse management, land management, small animal care.

Access to staff:
Contact by telephone
Hours: Term time: Mon to Thu, 0830 to 2100; Fri, 0830 to 1730

Department of:
Nottingham Trent University

BRACKNELL AND WOKINGHAM COLLEGE

Church Road, Bracknell, Berkshire, RG12 1DJ

Tel: 01344 460200
Fax: 01344 420360
E-mail: study@bracknell.ac.uk

Website:
http://www.bracknell.ac.uk
General and course information.

Enquiries:
Enquiries to: Learning Resources Centre Manager
Direct tel: ext 239/240
Direct e-mail: marketing@bracknell.ac.uk

Founded:
1962

Organisation type and purpose:
Suitable for ages: 16+.

Subject coverage:
General education up to and including A Level; AVCE and BTEC National Diploma; art, design and media studies; business and leisure; marketing, personnel and accountancy; computing and IT; engineering; health and social care; EFL; modern languages; access; teacher training, including PGCE.

Library catalogue:
All or part available in-house

Access to staff:
Contact by letter, by telephone, by e-mail, in person and via website
Hours: Mon to Thu, 0900 to 1930; Fri, 0900 to 1500
Special comments: Limited opening in College vacation.

Access for disabled people:
Parking provided, ramped entry, access to all public areas, toilet facilities

Other addresses:
Bracknell & Wokingham College
  Montague House, Broad Street, Wokingham, Berkshire, RG11 1AU; tel: 0118 902 9150; fax: 0118 902 9160
Bracknell & Wokingham College
  Wick Hill Centre, Wick Hill, Sandy Lane, Bracknell, RG12 2JG; tel: 01344 390400 ext 421 or 422; fax: 01344 390490
Bracknell & Wokingham College
  Woodley Hill House, Eastcourt Avenue, Earley, Reading, RG6 1HH; tel: 0118 926 1621; fax: 0118 966 0321

BRACKNELL FOREST BOROUGH COUNCIL

Easthamstead House, Town Square, Bracknell, Berkshire, RG12 1AQ

Tel: 01344 424642\ Minicom no. 01344 352045
Fax: 01344 352810
E-mail: 106005.521@compuserve.com

Website:
http://www.bracknell-forest.gov.uk

Enquiries:
Enquiries to: Public Relations Manager
Other contacts: Borough Administrator

Organisation type and purpose:
Local government body.

Subject coverage:
Leisure, environmental health, housing services, planning, development and control, council tax, refuse collection, street lighting, landscape maintenance, drains, sewer clearance and cesspools, services for residents of the borough of Bracknell Forest.

Trade and statistical information:
Data on the local population of Bracknell, amenities, services and employment.

Printed publications:
Annual Report
Bracknell 'The Making of Our New Town' (book)
Community plan
Guide to the Borough of Bracknell Forest

Electronic and video publications:
Live, work and play, the Bracknell Forest way (video)
What's Important to You? (video)

Access to staff:
Contact by letter, by telephone and by fax
Hours: Mon to Fri, 0900 to 1700

BRACKNELL FOREST COUNCIL LIBRARY AND INFORMATION SERVICE

Bracknell Central Library, Town Square, Bracknell, Berkshire, RG12 1BH

Tel: 01344 423149
Fax: 01344 411392
E-mail: bracknell.library@bracknell-forest.gov.uk

Website:
http://www.bracknell-forest.gov.uk/libraries

Organisation type and purpose:
Local government body, public library.

Museum or gallery collection, archive, or library special collection:
Photographic collection of the development of Bracknell town, and local studies collection.

Library catalogue:
All or part available online

Access to staff:
Contact by letter, by telephone, by fax, by e-mail and in person
Hours: Mon, 0930 to 1700; Tue, Thu, Fri, 0930 to 1900; Sat, 0930 to 1600
Closed Wed and Sun

Access to building, collection or gallery:
Special comments: No lift access at Bracknell Library.

Access for disabled people:
Ramp and automatic doors

BRACKNELL FOREST HERITAGE

Environment & Leisure, Time Square, Market Street, Bracknell, RG12 1JD

Tel: 01344 351754
E-mail: heritage@bracknell-forest.gov.uk

Website:
http://www.bracknell-forest.gov.uk/leis-heritage

Enquiries:
Enquiries to: Heritage Officer

Organisation type and purpose:
Heritage strategy arm of Bracknell Forest Borough Council.

Subject coverage:
The heritage strategy covers a broad range of heritage concerns and interests across the borough.

Access to staff:
Contact by letter, by telephone and by e-mail

BRADFORD CATHEDRAL

Formal name: Cathedral Church of St Peter, Bradford

Cathedral Office, Stott Hill, Bradford, West Yorkshire, BD1 4EH

Tel: 01274 777720
Fax: 01274 777730
E-mail: info@bradfordcathedral.org

Website:
http://www.bradfordcathedral.org
Information about the Cathedral including music and times of services.

Enquiries:
Enquiries to: Cathedral Secretary

Founded:
7th century

Organisation type and purpose:
Place of worship, historic listed building, concert and exhibition venue, education resource – visits programme, Bradford heritage.

Subject coverage:
Christian worship and faith; local history; William Morris Glass.

Education services:
For school and group visits contact the Education Officer

Access to staff:
Contact by letter, by telephone, by fax, by e-mail, in person and via website
Hours: Mon to Fri, 0900 to 1700; Sun, services only
Special comments: Groups by prior appointment.

Access to building, collection or gallery:
Hours: Mon to Fri, 0900 to 1630; Sat, 0900 to 1600 (phone ahead for confirmation)

Access for disabled people:
Access for most areas, parking provided, level entry, toilet facilities

Constituent part of:
Diocese of Bradford
  Kadugli House, Elmsley Street, Steeton, Keighley, BD20 6SE; tel: 01535 650555; fax: 01535 650550; e-mail: office@kadugli.org.uk; website: http://www.bradford.anglican.org

BRADFORD CHAMBER OF COMMERCE & INDUSTRY

Acronym or abbreviation: CMS

Devere House, Vicar Lane, Little Germany, Bradford, West Yorkshire, BD1 5AH

continued overleaf

Tel: 01274 772777
Fax: 01274 771081
E-mail: information@bradfordchamber.co.uk

Website:
http://www.bradfordchamber.co.uk

Enquiries:
Enquiries to: Chief Executive
Other contacts: Enterprise and Marketing Manager

Organisation type and purpose:
Trade association (membership is by subscription),
present number of members: 1100.
Chamber of Commerce.
Provision of business services to members.

Subject coverage:
All business information, international trade
documentation, business representation, training
services.

Printed publications:
Contact (annually)
Construction Review (annually)
Directory of members (annually)
Export/Import Guide (annually)

Access to staff:
Access for members only. Non-members charged.
Hours: Mon to Fri, 0900 to 1700

BRADFORD LIBRARIES, ARCHIVES AND INFORMATION

Central Library, Princes Way, Bradford, West
Yorkshire, BD1 1NN

Tel: 01274 433600
Fax: 01274 395108
E-mail: public.libraries@bradford.gov.uk

Website:
http://www.bradford.gov.uk

Enquiries:
Enquiries to: Head of Service: Libraries Archives &
Information

Founded:
1872

Organisation type and purpose:
Local government body, public library.

Subject coverage:
Business information; local studies including oral
history; photography; Indic languages especially
Urdu; multicultural material, particularly
children's material.

**Museum or gallery collection, archive, or library
special collection:**
Arthur Blackburn Monumental Inscriptions
  Collection
Bradford Heritage Recording Unit (local oral
  history)
Dickons Collection (mainly Bradford history)
Federer Collection (Yorkshire books and
  pamphlets)
Lees Botanical Collection (19th century flora)
Snowdon Collection (political and social history of
  the late 19th and early 20th centuries)

Library catalogue:
All or part available online

Printed publications:
Key Companies in Bradford (directory of 1300
  companies in Bradford, for purchase)
DIVA database of community and voluntary
  organisations in the Bradford district

Electronic and video publications:
Key Companies in Bradford (directory of 1300
  companies in Bradford, CD-ROM, for purchase)

Publications list:
Available in print

Access to staff:
Contact by letter, by telephone, by fax, by e-mail
and in person

Access for disabled people:
Access to all public areas, toilet facilities

Houses the library of:
Bradford Antiquarian Society

BRADFORD MECHANICS' INSTITUTE LIBRARY

76 Kirkgate, Bradford, West Yorkshire, BD1 1SZ

Tel: 01274 722857
E-mail: bmi-library@tiscali.co.uk

Enquiries:
Enquiries to: Administrator

Founded:
1832

Organisation type and purpose:
Registered charity (charity number 509231).
Independent subscription library.

Subject coverage:
Lending library; local history collection, history of
Bradford and environs, history of the Institute.

Printed publications:
Newsletter (quarterly, members only)

Access to staff:
Contact by letter and by telephone. Access for
members only.

Access to building, collection or gallery:
Hours: Mon to Fri, 0900 to 1630; Sat, 0900 to 1200
Special comments: Library open to members only by
subscription.

Member organisation of:
Association of Independent Libraries

BRADFORD SCHOOL OF MANAGEMENT

Heaton Mount, Keighley Road, Bradford, West
Yorkshire, BD9 4JU

Tel: 01274 234485
Fax: 01274 234444
E-mail: edp.ubmc@bradford.ac.uk

Website:
http://www.brad.ac.uk
All brochures, full course details.
http://www.brad.ac.uk/acad/management

Enquiries:
Enquiries to: Director
Direct tel: 01274 234466
Other contacts: Programme Administrators

Founded:
1962

Organisation type and purpose:
University department or institute.
Creation and delivery of executive education and
development programmes.

Subject coverage:
Management development; marketing; finance and
accounting; human resource management;
strategic management; negotiation skills; effective
manager programmes; company programmes.

**Museum or gallery collection, archive, or library
special collection:**
Business Library

Printed publications:
Open courses brochure (annually, free)

Publications list:
Available online and in print

Access to staff:
Contact by letter, by telephone, by fax, by e-mail
and in person
Hours: Mon to Fri, 0900 to 1700

Access to building, collection or gallery:
No prior appointment required
Hours: Mon, Tue, Thu, Fri, 0900 to 1700; Wed, 0900
to 2100; Sat, 0900 to 1200

Access for disabled people:
Parking provided, level entry, toilet facilities

Parent body:
University of Bradford
  tel: 01274 232323

BRADFORD UNIVERSITY SCHOOL OF MANAGEMENT LIBRARY

Emm Lane, Bradford, West Yorkshire, BD9 4JL

Tel: 01274 234402
Fax: 01274 234398
E-mail: j.finder@bradford.ac.uk

Website:
http://www.brad.ac.uk/lss/library
Library services, catalogue, subject guides.

Enquiries:
Enquiries to: Librarian

Founded:
1962

Organisation type and purpose:
University library, consultancy.

Subject coverage:
All aspects of management.

**Museum or gallery collection, archive, or library
special collection:**
Research publications, projects and theses on a
  wide variety of management topics
Library with business information services

Library catalogue:
All or part available online

Access to staff:
Contact by letter, by telephone, by fax, by e-mail
and in person. Non-members charged.
Hours: Mon to Fri, 0900 to 1700

Access to building, collection or gallery:
No prior appointment required
Hours: Term Time: Mon, Tue, Thu, Fri, 0845 to
1730; Wed, 0845 to 2000; Sat, 1000 to 1400
Vacation: Mon to Fri, 0845 to 1730

Parent body:
University of Bradford Library
  Richmond Road, Bradford, West Yorkshire, BD7
  1DP; tel: 01274 233400; fax: 01274 233398; e-mail:
  j.j.horton@bradford.ac.uk (university librarian)

BRAIN AND SPINE FOUNDATION

3.36 Canterbury Court, Kennington Park, 1–3
Brixton Road, London, SW9 6DE

Tel: 020 7793 5900
Fax: 020 7793 5939
E-mail: info@brainandspine.org.uk

Website:
http://www.brainandspine.org.uk
General information about the services provided.

Enquiries:
Enquiries to: Administrator

Founded:
1992

Organisation type and purpose:
Registered charity (charity number 1098528).
To improve the prevention, treatment and care of
disorders of the brain and spine, funds medical
research and develops an education programme to
increase the knowledge and understanding of
neurological disorders for the profession and
general public.

Subject coverage:
Disorders of the brain and spine.

Information services:
tel: 0808 808 1000

Printed publications:
Leaflets and information booklets for patients and
  carers covering a wide range of neurological
  disorders (free to patients and carers, for
  purchase by all others, various prices)

Electronic and video publications:
Disability and Rehabilitation (training video for medical students, free to medical students, available for purchase to all others)

Publications list:
Available online and in print

Access to staff:
Contact by letter, by telephone, by fax, by e-mail and via website. Appointment necessary.
Hours: Mon to Fri, 0900 to 1700

Member organisation of:
Association of Medical Research Charities (AMRC)
National Council for Voluntary Organisations (NCVO)
Neurological Alliance
Spinal Injuries Forum

BRAIN RESEARCH TRUST

Acronym or abbreviation: BRT

15 Southampton Place, London, WC1A 2AJ

Tel: 020 7404 9982
Fax: 020 7404 9983
E-mail: info@brt.org.uk

Website:
http://www.brt.org.uk

Enquiries:
Enquiries to: Chief Executive

Founded:
1971

Organisation type and purpose:
Registered charity (charity number 263064). Promotes and supports neurological research at UCL, Institute of Neurology, Queen Square, London.

Subject coverage:
World class neurological research.

Printed publications:
Annual Report
Newsletter

Publications list:
Available online

Access to staff:
Contact by letter, by telephone, by fax and by e-mail. Appointment necessary.
Hours: Mon to Fri, 0900 to 1700

BRAINTREE DISTRICT COUNCIL

Causeway House, Braintree, Essex, CM7 9HB

Tel: 01376 552525\ Minicom no. 01376 557766
Fax: 01376 552626

Website:
http://www.braintree.gov.uk
Elections, local services, local information.

Enquiries:
Enquiries to: Public Relations Manager
Direct tel: 01376 557752

Founded:
1974

Organisation type and purpose:
Local government body.

Publications list:
Available online

Access to staff:
Contact by letter and by telephone. Appointment necessary.
Hours: Mon to Fri, 0900 to 1700

Access for disabled people:
Parking provided, ramped entry, access to all public areas, toilet facilities

BRAINWAVES NI

Tel: 028 9335 3995

E-mail: brainwavesni@hotmail.com

Website:
http://www.brainwaves-ni.org
The charity and its aims, useful links, contact details.

Enquiries:
Enquiries to: Secretary

Founded:
1994

Organisation type and purpose:
Registered charity (charity number XO 1519/94) dedicated to providing support and information to those people affected by brain tumour. Free membership is open to all.

Subject coverage:
Provides information and signposts to appropriate and accurate quality materials, raises awareness of the needs of those just recently diagnosed or living with a brain tumour, and the needs of their families and carers, organises and runs social activities for members, provides financial support, where appropriate, makes donations towards research.

Information services:
Hosts a number of information and networking meetings – see website.

Electronic and video publications:
Newsletter
Leaflet
Order electronic and video publications from:
Download from website

Publications list:
Available online

Access to staff:
Contact by telephone and by e-mail
Hours: Answerphone available if phone is not answered

BRAM STOKER SOCIETY

Acronym or abbreviation: B S Society

c/o 43 Castle Court, Killiney Hill Road, Killiney, Co. Dublin, Ireland

E-mail: gothicalbert@eircom.net

Website:
http://www.bibliomania.com
http://www.vampyreempire.com

Enquiries:
Enquiries to: Registrar & Journal Editor

Founded:
1980

Organisation type and purpose:
Learned society (membership is by subscription), present number of members: 120.
The promotion of the serious study and appreciation of Bram Stoker, his works, and influence in the areas of fiction, cinema, theatre and music, as well as his importance in the Gothic Horror literary genre.

Subject coverage:
The Vampire in fiction, Count Dracula, Bram Stoker, the Gothic Horror genre in film and literature and the Irish Supernatural tradition in folklore and literature.

Museum or gallery collection, archive, or library special collection:
An archive of 5,000 books, MSS and documents relating to Bram Stoker held at The Chairperson's address

Printed publications:
Newsletter (quarterly, to members by subscription)
Journal of scholarly articles (annually, to members by subsription)
Order printed publications from: Editor (Dr Albert Power), The B S Society Journal
43 Castle Court, Killiney Hill Road, Killiney, County Dublin, Ireland

Publications list:
Available in print

Access to staff:
Contact by letter, by e-mail and in person. Appointment necessary. Access for members only. Non-members charged.
Hours: Mon to Fri, 0900 to 1700

Access to building, collection or gallery:
Prior appointment required
Special comments: Prior appointment by application to Chairperson in advance, to consult archives held at his private house.
The Annual Summer School held in Dublin, 1st weekend of July.

Affiliated to:
The Bram Stoker Club
  Trinity College, Dublin
The Bram Stoker Memorial Association of New York

Chairperson's address:
The B S Society
  1 Lakelands Close, Stillergan, County Dublin, Ireland; tel: 00 35 31 288 1970; fax: 00 35 31 288 1970

Close links with:
Dracula Society of London

BRANCH LINE SOCIETY

Acronym or abbreviation: BLS

73 Norfolk Park Avenue, Sheffield, S2 2RB

Tel: 0114 275 2303
Fax: 0114 275 2303

Website:
http://www.branchline.org.uk
Details of society activities plus news archive.

Enquiries:
Enquiries to: General Secretary
Other contacts: Sales Officer (for sales and membership recruitment enquiries only)

Founded:
1955

Organisation type and purpose:
Membership association (membership is by subscription), present number of members: 900, voluntary organisation.

Subject coverage:
Minor and branch railway lines, primarily in the British Isles but also in the rest of Europe and other parts of the world.

Printed publications:
Branch Line News (twice monthly, members only)
List of occasional publications available from the Society
Order printed publications from: Sales Officer, Branch Line Society, 37 Osberton Place, Sheffield, S11 8XL; tel: 0114 263 1094; fax: 0114 263 1094; e-mail: bls .sales@tesco.net

Access to staff:
Contact by letter, by telephone and by fax. Appointment necessary.
Hours: Mon to Sun, 0900 to 2200

BRASS BAND HERITAGE TRUST

Acronym or abbreviation: BBHT

1 Clumber Close, Poynton, Cheshire, SK12 1PG

E-mail: pehindmarsh@btinternet.com

Enquiries:
Enquiries to: Director
Direct tel: 01625 873820

Founded:
1996

Organisation type and purpose:
Registered charity (charity number 1037552).

continued overleaf

To promote, present activities and foster the future of the Brass Band movement in the UK. The Trust is an active commissioner of new repertoire for brass bands.

Subject coverage:
Commissioning new works for brass band for national and regional events; supporting the activities of young composers and youth brass bands nationwide.

Access to staff:
Contact by letter, by telephone and by e-mail
Hours: Mon to Fri, 0900 to 1700

BREAKTHROUGH DEAF/HEARING INTEGRATION

Acronym or abbreviation: Breakthrough

Alan Geale House, The Close, Westhill Campus, Bristol Road, Birmingham, B29 6LN

Tel: 0121 415 2289 (voice and text)
Fax: 0121 415 2323
E-mail: info@breakthrough-dhi.org.uk

Website:
http://www.breakthrough-dhi.org.uk

Enquiries:
Enquiries to: Information Officer

Founded:
1971

Organisation type and purpose:
National organisation, voluntary organisation, registered charity (charity number 261951), training organisation.
Self help group.
Development of innovative work with deaf and hearing people through contact, information and training.

Subject coverage:
Integration between deaf and hearing adults through contact, information and training.

Museum or gallery collection, archive, or library special collection:
Information service on all aspects of deafness

Printed publications:
An OBE Investiture at Buckingham Palace (Michael Jackson, booklet, £2.50)
Have You Heard? (information booklet, £4)
Hear my Silence (Jacqui Parkes, selected poems, £4)
Laminated Fingerspelling Mats (A3 £3, A4 £2.50)
Summary of Services, Information and Publications on Deafness in the United Kingdom (booklet, £4)

Access to staff:
Contact by letter and via website
Hours: Mon to Fri, 0900 to 1700

Access for disabled people:
Parking provided, toilet facilities

Regional centres at:
Breakthrough (London) Ealing & Hammersmith & Fulham
  2 Erconwald Street, East Acton, London, W12 0BS; tel: 020 8749 4111 (voice/fax); 020 8749 8186 (text); 020 8749 7854 (video); e-mail: london .ealing@breakthrough-dhi.org.uk and london .hammersmith
Breakthrough (London) Ealing & Hammersmith & Fulham
  The Hall, Peyton Place, Greenwich, London, SE10 8RS; tel: 020 8853 5661; 020 8858 7689 (text); 020 8858 2954 (video); fax: 020 8853 5661; e-mail: london.greenwich@breakthrough-dhi.org.uk
Breakthrough (London) Harrow
  2nd Floor, Premier House, 1 Canning Road, Wealdstone, HA7 7TS; tel: 020 8424 0983 (voice/fax); 020 8424 4626 (text); 020 8861 4625 (video); e-mail: london.harrow@breakthrough-dhi.org.uk

Breakthrough (London) Tower Hamlets
  Trinity Centre, Key Close, London, E1 4HG; tel: 010 7790 8478 (voice/fax); 020 7791 0105 (text); 020 7790 7453 (video); e-mail: london.tower .hamlets@breakthrough-dhi.org.uk
Breakthrough (North)
  John Haswell House, 8/9 Gladstone Terrace, Gateshead, Tyne and Wear, NE8 4DY; tel: 0191 478 7920 (voice/fax) 0191 478 6363 (text) 0191 478 4369 (video phone); e-mail: north@breakthrough -dhi.org.uk
Breakthrough (Southern Counties)
  Farnborough Centre, 67 Albert Road, Farnborough, Hampshire, GU14 6SL, Text 01252 372978 (video); tel: 01252 510051; 522765; fax: 01252 524642; e-mail: southern.counties@ breakthrough-dhi.org.uk
Breakthrough (Southern Counties)
  Aldershot Centre, Princess Gardens, 2A High Street, Aldershot, Hants, GU11 1BJ; tel: 01252 313882 (voice/text) 01242 310041 (video); fax: 01252 337546; e-mail: southern.counties@ breakthrough-dhi.org.uk
Breakthrough (West Midlands)
  1 College Walk, Bristol Road, Selly Oak, Birmingham, B29 6LE; tel: voice/fax 415 5900, Minicom 0121 472 5488
Breakthrough London Services Team
  The Hall, Peyton Place, London, SE10 8RS; tel: 020 8269 0307 (voice/fax); 020 8269 0287 (text); 020 8269 0242 (video); e-mail: london.services@ breakthrough-dhi.org.uk

BREAST CANCER CARE – GLASGOW

Acronym or abbreviation: BCC

2nd Floor, 40 St Enoch Square, Glasgow, G1 4DH

Tel: 0141 221 2244
Fax: 0141 221 9499
E-mail: sco@breastcancercare.org.uk

Website:
http://www.breastcancercare.org.uk

Enquiries:
Enquiries to: Head of National Development
Direct e-mail: press@breastcancercare.org.uk
Other contacts: National Manager responsible for all services provided in Scotland.

Founded:
1973

Organisation type and purpose:
National organisation, voluntary organisation, registered charity (charity number 1017658).

Subject coverage:
Breast cancer in women and men, information, help and support.

Library catalogue:
All or part available online and in print

Printed publications:
Breast Cancer and Breast Care (£6)
A range of leaflets and booklets on subjects related to breast cancer (free)
Order printed publications from: Publications Department, Breast Cancer Care
Kiln House, 210 New Kings Road, London, SW6 4NZ, tel: 0808 800 6000 or 0141 221 2244, fax: 020 7384 3387, e-mail: bcc@breastcancercare.org.uk

Electronic and video publications:
Treating Breast Cancer (audio tape)

Publications list:
Available online and in print

Access to staff:
Contact by letter, by telephone, by fax, by e-mail and via website. Appointment necessary.
Hours: Mon to Fri, 0900 to 1700

Access for disabled people:
Level entry, toilet facilities

BREAST CANCER CARE – LONDON

Acronym or abbreviation: BCC

Kiln House, 210 New Kings Road, London, SW6 4NZ

Tel: 020 7384 2984\ Minicom no. 020 7731 6395
Fax: 020 7384 3387
E-mail: info@breastcancercare.org.uk

Website:
http://www.breastcancercare.org.uk
Full range of patient information, ordering publications, making donations, discussion forums, ask the nurse email service, news, fundraising, press, recruitment.

Enquiries:
Enquiries to: Administrator

Founded:
1973

Organisation type and purpose:
National organisation, membership association, present number of members: 400, voluntary organisation, registered charity (charity number 1017658).
To provide information and support to those affected by breast cancer.

Subject coverage:
Breast cancer; treatments, general information, prostheses, after-care, support groups.

Printed publications:
Newsletter (quarterly)
Several booklets and 30 factsheets dealing with breast cancer, its treatment and support for sufferers (free but charge for bulk order postage), all publications are available in large print on request

Electronic and video publications:
Treating Breast Cancer (tape)
Diagnosing and Treating Breast Cancer (URDU) (tape)

Publications list:
Available online and in print

Access to staff:
Contact by letter, by telephone, by fax, by e-mail and via website
Hours: Helpline: Mon to Fri, 1000 to 1700; Sat, 1000 to 1400

Access to building, collection or gallery:
Prior appointment required

Access for disabled people:
Parking provided, ramped entry, toilet facilities
Special comments: Parking must be requested prior to visit.

Also at Northern Office:
Breast Cancer Care
  Volsenc House, 14–18 West Bar Green, Sheffield, S1 2DA; tel: 0114 276 0296; fax: 0114 276 0293

Also at Scotland Office:
Breast Cancer Care
  46 Gordon Street, Glasgow, G1 3PU; tel: 0141 221 2244; fax: 0141 221 9499

Subsidiary body:
Lavender Trust Charity

BRECON BEACONS NATIONAL PARK AUTHORITY

Acronym or abbreviation: BBNPA

Plas y Ffynnon, Cambrian Way, Brecon, Powys, LD3 7HP

Tel: 01874 624437
Fax: 01874 622574
E-mail: enquiries@breconbeacons.org

Enquiries:
Enquiries to: Public Relations Officer
Other contacts: Chief Executive for statutory and legal matters.

Founded:
1957

Organisation type and purpose:
Local government body, advisory body, statutory body, present number of members: 24, public library, research organisation, publishing house. National park authority, two thirds of the authority members are appointed by the constituent unitary authorities; one third are appointed by the Welsh Assembly.
To protect and conserve wildlife, landscape and cultural heritage; to promote opportunities for quiet enjoyment of the countryside; a local planning authority.

Subject coverage:
Landscape conservation and countryside recreation within the Brecon Beacons National Park. Ecology/archaeology/planning, local area knowledge.

Printed publications:
Park Update Newsletter
Welcome Guide
Tourism Newsletter
Unitary Development Plan
State of the Park report
Leaflets, books and maps for walkers, cavers, cyclists, horseriders, and tourism employees.

Publications list:
Available in print

Access to staff:
Contact by letter, by telephone, by fax, by e-mail and in person. Appointment necessary.
Hours: Mon to Fri, 0900 to 1700

BRECON BEACONS NATIONAL PARK VISITOR CENTRE

Libanus, Brecon, Powys, LD3 8ER

Tel: 01874 623366
Fax: 01874 624515
E-mail: visitor.centre@breconbeacons.org

Website:
http://www.breconbeacons.org
Events, education, location map.

Enquiries:
Enquiries to: Information Officer

Founded:
1957

Organisation type and purpose:
Local government body, service industry, suitable for ages: all.
To provide an information and education service relating to the Brecon Beacons National Park.

Subject coverage:
Activities within the Brecon Beacons National Park, specialised publications on offer, education resources.

Library catalogue:
All or part available in-house

Printed publications:
Various leaflets and small books on walks and sites of interest within the Brecon Beacons National Park under the headings: Maps, Recreational, Cultural, Historical, Nature Guides.

Publications list:
Available in print

Access to staff:
Contact by letter, by telephone, by fax, by e-mail, in person and via website
Hours: Sun to Sat, 0930 to 1700

Access to building, collection or gallery:
No prior appointment required
Hours: Sun to Sat, 0930 to 1700

Access for disabled people:
Parking provided, ramped entry, access to all public areas, toilet facilities
Special comments: Hearing loop/induction installed.

Other addresses:
Brecon Beacons National Park Authority
Plas y Ffynnon, Cambrian Way, Brecon, Powys, LD3 7HP; tel: 01874 624437

BRENT ARCHIVES

Willesden Green Library Centre, 95 High Road, Willesden, London NW10 2SF

Tel: 020 8937 3541
Fax: 020 8937 3601
E-mail: archives@brent.gov.uk

Website:
http://www.brent.gov.uk/archives
Online catalogue of archive and museum collections and database of digitised images and photographs.

Enquiries:
Enquiries to: Borough Archivist
Direct tel: 020 8937 3677

Founded:
1976/7

Organisation type and purpose:
Local government body.
Archive.

Subject coverage:
Government and local history of London Borough of Brent and predecessors (Willesden, Wembley, etc).

Education services:
Schools sessions and lectures, talks and sessions for adult learners.

Non-library collection catalogue:
All or part available online and in-house

Library catalogue:
All or part available online

Printed publications:
List available on website.
Order printed publications from: Brent Archives, Willesden Green Library Centre, 95 High Road, Willesden, London NW10 2SF

Publications list:
Available online and in print

Access to staff:
Contact by letter, by telephone, by fax, by e-mail, in person and via website
Hours: Tue and Wed, 0900 to 1700; Thu, 1300 to 2000; Sat, 0900 to 1700

Access for disabled people:
Fully accessible

Links with:
Brent Museum
Willesden Green Library Centre, 95 High Road, Willesden, London, NW10 2SF; tel: 020 937 3600

BREWER'S COMPANY

Brewer's Hall, Aldermanbury Square, London, EC2V 7HR

Tel: 020 7600 1801
Fax: 020 7776 8939
E-mail: clerksecretary@brewershall.co.uk

Website:
http://www.brewershall.co.uk

Enquiries:
Enquiries to: The Clerk

Founded:
1437

Organisation type and purpose:
Membership association (membership is by election or invitation).
City of London Livery Company.

Access to staff:
Contact by letter, by telephone, by fax and by e-mail

BREWERY HISTORY SOCIETY

10 Ringstead Court, Ringstead Road, Sutton, Surrey, SM1 4SH

Tel: 020 8642 7189

Enquiries:
Enquiries to: Archivist

Founded:
1971

Organisation type and purpose:
Membership association (membership is by subscription), present number of members: 700, voluntary organisation, research organisation, publishing house.

Subject coverage:
History of the British brewery industry.

Museum or gallery collection, archive, or library special collection:
Histories of brewing industry, yearbooks, directories, periodicals

Non-library collection catalogue:
All or part available in-house

Library catalogue:
All or part available in-house

Printed publications:
Brewery History Journal (quarterly)
Wide variety of books including:
Beers and Brewing
Brewery Histories, by region
Brewery Transport
Bottles
Historical Research
Hops and Maltings
Inns and Pubs
Inn Signs
Order printed publications from: Paul Travis
Long High Top, Heptonstall, Hebden Bridge, West Yorkshire, HX7 7PF

Publications list:
Available in print

Access to staff:
Contact by letter, by telephone and in person.
Appointment necessary.
Hours: Mon to Fri, 0900 to 1700

BREWING, FOOD & BEVERAGE INDUSTRY SUPPLIERS ASSOCIATION

Acronym or abbreviation: BfBi

3 Brewery Road, Wolverhampton, West Midlands, WV1 4JT

Tel: 01902 422303
Fax: 01902 795744
E-mail: info@bfbi.org.uk

Website:
http://www.bfbi.org.uk

Enquiries:
Enquiries to: Chief Executive

Founded:
1907

Organisation type and purpose:
Trade association (membership is by subscription), present number of members: 430.

Printed publications:
Annual Directory of Members and classified listings (pub June, £95, direct)

Publications list:
Available in print

Access to staff:
Contact by letter, by telephone, by fax and by e-mail
Hours: Mon to Fri, 0900 to 1700

BRIDGEMAN ART LIBRARY LIMITED

17–19 Garway Road, London, W2 4PH

Tel: 020 7727 4065
Fax: 020 7792 8509
E-mail: info@bridgeman.co.uk

Website:
http://www.bridgeman.co.uk
A searchable archive of thousands of images from the collection.

Enquiries:
Enquiries to: Marketing Manager

Founded:
1972

Organisation type and purpose:
Service industry.
Commercial company; formerly Cooper-Bridgeman Library; fine art photographic library/agency; agency agreements with photographic libraries outside the UK.
Fine art photo archive (commercial).

Subject coverage:
Large format colour transparencies of paintings, sculpture, prints, manuscripts, the decorative arts, antiques and antiquities.

Museum or gallery collection, archive, or library special collection:
Over 150,000 large format colour transparencies growing by more than 500 new pictures each week, of the works from more than 1000 museums, galleries and private collections, including contemporary artists

Library catalogue:
All or part available online and in print

Printed publications:
Catalogues of complete collections

Electronic and video publications:
Catalogue (online, free registration)

Publications list:
Available online and in print

Access to staff:
Contact by telephone, by fax, by e-mail and via website. Appointment necessary.
Hours: Mon to Fri, 0930 to 1730

Access to building, collection or gallery:
Prior appointment required

Members of:
British Association of Picture Libraries & Agencies (BAPLA)
Vine Hill, London, EC1

Other address:
Bridgeman Art Library International
65 East 93rd Street, New York, NY 10128, USA; tel: 00 1 212 828 1238; fax: 00 1 212 828 1255; e-mail: info@bridgemanart.com
Bridgeman Giraudon
36 rue des Bourdonnais, 75001 Paris, France; tel: + 33 1 55 80 79 10; fax: + 33 1 55 80 79 11; e-mail: paris@bridgeman.fr

BRIDGEND COUNTY BOROUGH COUNCIL

Civic Offices, Angel Street, Bridgend, Mid Glamorgan, CF31 1LX

Tel: 01656 643643
Fax: 01656 646966

Website:
http://www.bridgend.gov.uk
Tourism and general information.

Enquiries:
Enquiries to: Public Relations Manager
Direct tel: 01656 643210/17
Direct fax: 01656 643215

Founded:
April 1996

Organisation type and purpose:
Local government body.

Subject coverage:
Economic and business database, traffic surveys, transport infrastructure, trading standards, public protection, planning, local plan, mineral extraction, design and print, information technology, demographic information.

Access to staff:
Contact by letter, by telephone, by fax and by e-mail
Hours: Mon to Thu, 0830 to 1700; Fri, 0830 to 1630

Access for disabled people:
Ramped entry, toilet facilities

BRIDGEND LIBRARY AND INFORMATION SERVICE

Coed Parc, Park Street, Bridgend, Mid Glamorgan, CF31 4BA

Tel: 01656 754800
Fax: 01656 645719
E-mail: blis@bridgend.gov.uk

Website:
http://www.bridgend.gov.uk/libraries

Enquiries:
Enquiries to: Librarian

Founded:
1996

Organisation type and purpose:
Public library.

Subject coverage:
Local history (Mid Glamorgan), family history (Glamorgan area).

Museum or gallery collection, archive, or library special collection:
Local studies (Mid Glamorgan and areas surrounding Bridgend County Borough)

Non-library collection catalogue:
All or part available online

Library catalogue:
All or part available online

Access to staff:
Contact by letter, by telephone, by fax, by e-mail and in person
Hours: Mon to Fri, 0830 to 1900; Sat, 0830 to 1700

Access for disabled people:
Parking provided, ramped entry

BRIDGNORTH & DISTRICT HISTORICAL SOCIETY

Barn Cottage, Bridge Street, Bridgnorth, Shropshire, WV15 6AF

Tel: 01746 765159

Enquiries:
Enquiries to: Treasurer and Publicity

Organisation type and purpose:
Membership association (membership is by subscription), present number of members: 120, voluntary organisation, registered charity.

Subject coverage:
History of Bridgnorth and district.

BRIDGNORTH DISTRICT COUNCIL

Westgate, Bridgnorth, Shropshire, WV16 5AA

Tel: 01746 765131
Fax: 01746 764414

Website:
http://www.bridgnorth.gov.uk

Enquiries:
Enquiries to: Public Relations Manager
Direct tel: 01746 713111

Direct e-mail: lscreen@bridgnorth-dc.gov.uk

Founded:
1974

Organisation type and purpose:
Local government body.

Access to staff:
Contact by letter, by telephone, by fax, by e-mail and in person
Hours: Mon to Fri, 0900 to 1700

Access for disabled people:
Ramped entry

BRIDLEDOWN CHILDREN'S FARM AND WILDLIFE CENTRE

Bridledown, West Hougham, Dover, Kent, CT13 7AG

Tel: 01304 201382
Fax: 01304 204757
E-mail: bridledown.dover@virgin.net

Enquiries:
Enquiries to: Information Officer

Founded:
1968

Organisation type and purpose:
Suitable for ages: Key Stages 1 and 2.
Stray dogs' kennels and children's activity farm.
Finding homes for stray dogs.

Subject coverage:
Teaching the importance of wildlife, farming in the community and hands-on fun for the family.

Access to staff:
Contact by letter, by telephone, by fax, by e-mail, in person and via website
Hours: Daily, 1000 to 1700

Access for disabled people:
Access to all public areas

BRIGHTON AND HOVE CITY LIBRARIES

Jubilee Library, Jubilee Street, Brighton, BN1 1GE

Tel: 01273 296969; 01273 290800
Fax: 01273 296976
E-mail: libraries@brighton-hove.gov.uk

Website:
http://www.citylibraries.info

Enquiries:
Enquiries to: Library Manager

Founded:
1869

Organisation type and purpose:
Local government body, public library.

Subject coverage:
Local studies, fine arts, early printed books, business and European studies.

Museum or gallery collection, archive, or library special collection:
Bloomfield Collection (rare books)
Cobden Collection (2,500 items from Richard Cobden's library)
Elliot Collection (3,000 Greek and Hebrew texts)
Lewes Collection (3,000 European language books in fine arts)
Long Collection (3,000 classical texts)
Matthews Collection (3,500 oriental (Middle East) books)
Wolseley Collection (late 19th-century British military history and horticulture and topography of Sussex, including Field Marshal Wolseley's letters)

Library catalogue:
All or part available online

Access to staff:
Contact by letter, by telephone, by fax, by e-mail and in person

Access to building, collection or gallery:
Hours: Mon and Tue, 1000 to 1900; Wed, Fri and Sat, 1000 to 1700; Thu, 1000 to 2000; Sun, 1100 to 1600
Special comments: Some special collections materials and rare books require membership of rare books scheme. Baby changing area available.

Access for disabled people:
Jubilee Library is fully accessible and has adult change facilities; guide dogs are welcome

BRINSBURY CAMPUS

Formal name: Chichester College

North Heath, Pulborough, West Sussex, RH20 1DL

Tel: 01243 786321
Fax: 01243 539481
E-mail: info@chichester.ac.uk

Website:
http://www.chichester.ac.uk
General.

Enquiries:
Enquiries to: Information Officer

Formerly called:
Brinsbury College (year of change 2002)

Organisation type and purpose:
Suitable for ages: 16+, training organisation.

Subject coverage:
Land-based training.

Library catalogue:
All or part available online

Printed publications:
Course Directory
Information leaflets
Section leaflets

Access to staff:
Contact by letter, by telephone, by fax, by e-mail and in person
Hours: Mon to Fri, 0900 to 1700

Access for disabled people:
Parking provided, ramped entry, toilet facilities, lifts

Headquarters address:
Chichester College
  Westgate Fields, Chichester, West Sussex PO19 1SB; tel: 01243 786321; fax: 01243 539481; e-mail: info@chichester.ac.uk; website: http://www .chichester.ac.uk

BRISTOL AND GLOUCESTERSHIRE ARCHAEOLOGICAL SOCIETY

Acronym or abbreviation: BGAS

Stonehatch, Oakridge Lynch, Stroud, Gloucestershire, GL6 7NR

Tel: 01285 760460
E-mail: john@loosleyj.freeserve.co.uk

Website:
http://www.bgas.org.uk

Enquiries:
Enquiries to: General Secretary
Other contacts: Chairman (for special correspondence); Editor

Founded:
1876

Organisation type and purpose:
Learned society (membership is by subscription), present number of members: 900, voluntary organisation, registered charity (charity number 202014), suitable for ages: 18+, publishing house. Promotes the study of the history and antiquities of Bristol and Gloucestershire, including South Gloucestershire; encourages their conservation and publishes records, reports and papers.

Subject coverage:
History, archaeology and antiquities of Gloucestershire including South Gloucestershire and Bristol.

Museum or gallery collection, archive, or library special collection:
Archaeological Library: Bristol, Gloucestershire and neighbouring counties

Non-library collection catalogue:
All or part available online

Library catalogue:
All or part available online

Printed publications:
Newsletter (twice a year)
Monographs (occasional)
Transactions (annually)
Record Series (vols of edited texts) including:
Historic Churches and Church Life in Bristol (ed. J. Bettey)
Archives and Local History in Bristol and Gloucestershire (ed. J. Bettey)
Bigland's Historical Monumental and Genealogical Collections Relative to the County of Gloucester (four parts, ed. B. Firth, each part £30)
Cheltenham Probate Records 1660–1740 (ed. A. J. H. Sale, £30)
Original Acta of St Peter's Abbey, Gloucester, c.1122–1263 (ed. R. B. Patterson, £30)
The Cartulary of St Augustine's Abbey, Bristol (ed. D. Walker, £30)
Register of Llanthony Priory, 1457–65, 1501–25 (ed. J. Rhodes, £30)
Transportees from Gloucestershire to Australia 1783–1842 (ed. I. Wyatt, £20)
A Calendar of the Registers of Apprentices of the City of Gloucester 1595–1700 (ed. J. Barlow, £30)
Abstracts of Feet of Fines for Gloucestershire, 1199–1299 (ed. C. R. Elrington, £30)
Catalogue of Medieval Muniments at Berkeley Castle (ed. B. Wells-Furby, two vols, £30 each)
Notes on the Diocese of Gloucester by Chancellor Richard Parsons c.1700 (ed. J. Fendley, £30)
Abstracts of Feet of Fines for Gloucestershire, 1200–1359 (ed. C. R. Elrington, £30)
Gloucester Cathedral Chapter Act Book 1616–1687 (ed. S. Eward, £30)
Order printed publications from: Stockholder, Bristol and Gloucestershire Archaeological Society, 17 Estcourt Road, Gloucester, GL1 3LU; tel. 01452 528930

Publications list:
Available online and in print

Access to staff:
Contact by letter, by telephone, by e-mail and via website

Links with:
Committee for Archaeology in Gloucestershire (CAG)
  at same address

BRISTOL AND WESTERN ENGINEERING MANUFACTURERS ASSOCIATION LIMITED

Acronym or abbreviation: BEMA

Engineers House, The Promenade, Clifton Down, Bristol, BS8 3NB

Tel: 0117 906 4830
Fax: 0117 906 4827
E-mail: enquiries@bema.co.uk

Enquiries:
Enquiries to: Director

Founded:
1936

Organisation type and purpose:
Trade association.
Engineering Companies in South West and South Wales.

Subject coverage:
Personnel matters including employment law, wage rates, technical and business matters affecting small engineering companies, health and safety legislation and training courses.

Trade and statistical information:
Sources of engineering products and services in the South West and South Wales.

Printed publications:
Engineering Handbook (quarterly)
Bulletin (quarterly)

Access to staff:
Contact by letter and by fax
Hours: Mon to Fri, 0900 to 1700

Affiliated to:
Engineering Industries Association

Member of:
CBI

BRISTOL CENTRAL LIBRARY

Central Library, College Green, Bristol, BS1 5TL

Tel: 0117 903 7200
Fax: 0117 922 1081
E-mail: bristol_library_service@bristol-city.gov.uk

Website:
http://www.bristol-city.gov.uk/librarycatalogue

Enquiries:
Enquiries to: Reference enquiries
Direct tel: 0117 903 7202
Direct e-mail: refandinfo@bristol-city.gov.uk

Founded:
1613

Organisation type and purpose:
Local government body, public library.
Central lending, music, reference and business libraries.

Subject coverage:
Bristol local history; slave trade; modern literature; caving and potholing; doctrinal theology; genealogy; British Standards and British Patents; non-performing arts, both fine and applied.

Museum or gallery collection, archive, or library special collection:
Private Press books; Early Printed books (Bristol)
Stuckey Lean Collection (folklore and proverbs) (Bristol)
Thomas Chatterton Collection (Bristol)

Non-library collection catalogue:
All or part available online

Library catalogue:
All or part available online

Access to staff:
Contact by letter, by telephone, by fax, by e-mail and in person. Appointment necessary.
Hours: Mon, Tue and Thu, 0930 to 1930; Wed 1000 to 1700, Fri and Sat, 0930 to 1700; Sun, 1300 to 1700

Access for disabled people:
Ramped entry, toilet facilities

Parent body:
Bristol City Council
  Culture and Leisure Services

BRISTOL CITY COUNCIL

The Council House, College Green, Bristol, BS1 5TR

Tel: 0117 922 2000
Fax: 0117 922 2024
E-mail: simon_caplan@bristol-city.gov.uk

Website:
http://www.bristol-city.gov.uk

Enquiries:
Enquiries to: Head of Corporate Communications
Direct tel: 0117 922 2650
Direct fax: 0117 922 4330

continued overleaf

Organisation type and purpose:
Local government body.

Subject coverage:
Full range of local authority information.

Access to staff:
Contact by letter, by telephone, by fax, by e-mail, in person and via website. Appointment necessary.
Hours: Mon to Fri, 0900 to 1700

BRISTOL RECORD OFFICE

B Bond Warehouse, Smeaton Road, Bristol, BS1 6XN

Tel: 0117 922 4224
Fax: 0117 922 4236
E-mail: bro@bristol.gov.uk

Website:
http://www.bristol.gov.uk/recordoffice

Enquiries:
Enquiries to: Archivist

Organisation type and purpose:
Local government body.

Subject coverage:
Historical archives relating to the city of Bristol from the 12th century to the present day.

Non-library collection catalogue:
All or part available online and in-house

Library catalogue:
All or part available online and in-house

Printed publications:
Handlists and Aids to Research
Introductory leaflet
Registers and Bishop's Transcripts of births, baptisms, marriages and burials in Bristol Record Office, includes Anglican and Nonconformist registers
Index to Bristol's wills 1793–1858
Bristol: The Home Front, records in Bristol Record Office relating to World War II
The Poor Law in Bristol: a handlist of records
Information leaflets, books and pamphlets including:
Bristol Record Office: what we do and how to use us
Family History at Bristol Record Office
Sources for Ships, Seaman and Emigrants
Sources for the History of Buildings
Records relating to Slavery
Maps: Bristol Parish Boundaries c.1900; Ancient parishes of Bristol; South Gloucestershire and North Somerset Parishes, 1830; Mathews' New and Correct plan of the City and suburbs of Bristol, 1794
Antiquaries of Gloucestershire and Bristol (Gray I, 1981)
Bristol Apprentice Books 1566–1593
Bristol Cathedral: history and architecture (ed. J. Rogan, 2000)
Historic Churches and Church Life in Bristol
Views of Bristol Churches (43 city churches, 6 country churches and 10 nonconformist churches)
Bristol Record Society Publications
Historical Association (Bristol Branch) Publications

Electronic and video publications:
Bristol: Bristol's VE Day: a City celebrates (DVD)
Bristol Historical Sources (CD)
Wills index 1791–1858 (online)
List of parish register holdings (online)

Publications list:
Available in print

Access to staff:
Contact by letter, by telephone, by fax, by e-mail and in person
Hours: Tue to Fri, 0930 to 1630; first two Thu of month, 0930 to 1900; first two Sat of month, 1000 to 1600

Access for disabled people:
Parking provided, ramped entry, access to all public areas, toilet facilities

BRISTOL SOCIETY, THE

Leigh Court, Abbots Leigh, Bristol, BS8 3RA

Tel: 0117 915 2335
Fax: 01275 374423

Enquiries:
Enquiries to: Membership Secretary
Direct e-mail: sally.allen@bcci.westec.co.uk
Other contacts: Chairman

Founded:
1992

Organisation type and purpose:
Learned society (membership is by subscription), present number of members: 300.
Lecture society.

Access to staff:
Contact by letter and by telephone
Hours: Mon to Fri, 0900 to 1700

Other addresses:
The Bristol Society
Somerset House, 18 Canynge Road, Clifton, Bristol, BS8 3JX; tel: 0117 923 9234; fax: 0117 923 9237

BRISTOL-MYERS SQUIBB PHARMACEUTICALS LIMITED

141–149 Staines Road, Hounslow, Middlesex, TW3 3JA

Tel: 020 8572 7422
Fax: 020 8754 3789

Website:
http://www.b-ms.co.uk/

Enquiries:
Enquiries to: Librarian
Direct tel: 020 8754 3610
Direct fax: 020 8572 7370

Organisation type and purpose:
Manufacturing industry.

Subject coverage:
Pharmaceutical industry, cardiovascular disease, oncology.

Library catalogue:
All or part available in-house

Access to staff:
Contact by letter
Hours: Mon to Fri, 0900 to 1700

Access to building, collection or gallery:
No access other than to staff

BRITAIN-AUSTRALIA SOCIETY

c/o Swire House, 59 Buckingham Gate, London, SW1E 6AJ

Tel: 020 7630 1075
Fax: 020 7828 2260

Website:
http://www.britain-australia.org.uk

Enquiries:
Enquiries to: National Director
Direct e-mail: natdir@britain-australia.org.uk

Founded:
1971

Organisation type and purpose:
Membership association (membership is by subscription).
Society for development of strong Anglo-Australian relations.

Subject coverage:
All aspects of life in Australia.

Printed publications:
BritOz Magazine (3 times a year, members only)

Access to staff:
Contact by letter, by telephone, by fax, by e-mail and via website. Appointment necessary.
Hours: Mon to Fri, 1000 to 1630

BRITAIN-RUSSIA CENTRE

Acronym or abbreviation: BRC

11 Belgrave Road, London, SW1V 1RB

Tel: 020 7931 6455
Fax: 020 7233 9736
E-mail: mail@bewc.org

Website:
http://www.bewc.org

Enquiries:
Enquiries to: Information Officer

Founded:
1959

Organisation type and purpose:
Membership association.
To promote understanding and contacts between UK and countries of former USSR, excluding Baltic States.

Subject coverage:
General information on Russia and other republics of former USSR; arts and humanities, literature, history, geography and travel, politics and society.

Library catalogue:
All or part available in-house

Access to staff:
Contact by letter and via website. Appointment necessary.
Special comments: The Centre is not a public body.

Also known as:
British East-West Centre (BEWC)
at the same address; tel: 020 7823 1990

BRITISH & INTERNATIONAL FEDERATION OF FESTIVALS FOR MUSIC, DANCE AND SPEECH

Festivals House, 198 Park Lane, Macclesfield, Cheshire, SK11 6UD

Tel: 0870 774 4290
Fax: 0870 774 4292
E-mail: liz@federationoffestivals.org.uk

Website:
http://www.festivals.demon.co.uk

Enquiries:
Enquiries to: Chief Executive
Direct tel: 01625 611578

Founded:
1921

Organisation type and purpose:
Membership association (membership is by qualification), voluntary organisation, registered charity (charity number 213125), training organisation.
Consists of festival organisers, adjudicators, accompanists and private members.

Subject coverage:
Amateur festivals, all aspects of the performing arts, particularly music, speech, drama and dance, adjudication in all these disciplines.

Printed publications:
Newsletter (3/4 per annum, free, for members only)
Year Book (annually, for sale)

Access to staff:
Contact by letter, by telephone, by fax and by e-mail
Hours: Mon to Fri, 0930 to 1730

Headquarters of the:
Amateur Competitive Festival Movement

BRITISH ABRASIVES FEDERATION

Acronym or abbreviation: BAF

Toad Hall, Hinton Road, Horst, Berkshire, RG10 0BS

Tel: 08456 121380

Fax: 08456 121380
E-mail: info@thebaf.org.uk

Website:
http://www.the-british-abrasives-federation.org
.uk
The BAF, its organisation, objectives, membership,
technical pages and access to the FEPA site.

Enquiries:
Enquiries to: Secretary General

Organisation type and purpose:
Trade association.

Subject coverage:
Use, care and protection of grinding wheels and
other abrasive products; British and European
safety standards.

Printed publications:
Abrasive Grain Booklets
Diamond and Superabrasive Wheel and Grain
  Booklets
FEPA Safety Code for the use, care and protection
  of Abrasive Wheels (£9.50)

Access to staff:
Contact by letter, by telephone, by fax, by e-mail
and via website
Hours: Mon to Fri, 0900 to 1700

Affiliated to:
Fédération Européenne des Fabricants de Produits
Abrasifs (FEPA)
  Secretariat, 20 avenue Reille, 75014 Paris, France;
  tel: 00 331 4581 2590; fax: 00 331 4581 6294; e-
  mail: fepa@compuserve.com

Product groups:
Abrasive Grain
Bonded Abrasives
Coated Abrasives
Superabrasives

BRITISH ACADEMY

Formal name: British Academy: The National
Academy for the Humanities and Social Sciences

10 Carlton House Terrace, London, SW1Y 5AH

Tel: 020 7969 5200
Fax: 020 7969 5300
E-mail: secretary@britac.ac.uk

Website:
http://www.britac.ac.uk
Information about the British Academy as a
learned society; its funding programmes for
humanities and social sciences.

Enquiries:
Enquiries to: Secretary
Direct fax: 020 7969 5414

Founded:
1902

Organisation type and purpose:
National organisation, learned society
(membership is by election or invitation), present
number of members: 851 ordinary, 307
corresponding, 18 hon fellows, registered charity
(charity number 233176).
Directory of all UK Learned Bodies in the social
sciences and humanities.
Promotes advanced research in humanities and
social sciences.

Subject coverage:
Humanities and social sciences.

Printed publications:
Lectures and Symposia
Research Series
Policy Documents

Publications list:
Available online and in print

Access to staff:
Contact by letter, by fax and by e-mail
Hours: Mon to Fri, 0930 to 1730

Access to building, collection or gallery:
No access other than to staff

Access for disabled people:
Access to all public areas

BRITISH ACADEMY OF COMPOSERS, SONGWRITERS AND AUTHORS

Acronym or abbreviation: BASCA

British Music House, 26 Berners Street, London,
W1T 3LR

Tel: 020 7636 2929
Fax: 020 7636 2212
E-mail: info@basca.org.uk

Website:
http://www.basca.org.uk
News, events, links page, register of members.

Enquiries:
Enquiries to: Information Officer

Founded:
1999

Organisation type and purpose:
Professional body, trade association.

Subject coverage:
Advice on publishing contracts in classical music,
recommended commissioning fees, copyright
advice, music hire fees, competitions.
Music, songwriting; music industry; copyright;
authors' royalties from broadcast and public
performances; music publishing; creative
workshops.

Printed publications:
The Works (quarterly, members on subscription)

Access to staff:
Contact by letter, by telephone, by fax and by e-
mail. Appointment necessary.
Hours: Mon to Fri, 1000 to 1700

BRITISH ACADEMY OF DRAMATIC COMBAT

Acronym or abbreviation: BADC

3 Castle View, Helmsley, North Yorkshire, YO62
5AU

Tel: 01439 770546
E-mail: info@badc.co.uk

Website:
http://www.badc.co.uk

Enquiries:
Enquiries to: Secretary

Organisation type and purpose:
Professional body.

Subject coverage:
Stage and screen combats of all kinds; weapons for
use in the theatre; safety in stage fighting; history
of armed combat, training in stage and screen
combat.

Library catalogue:
All or part available in-house

Access to staff:
Contact by letter, by telephone, by e-mail and via
website
Hours: Any reasonable time

BRITISH ACADEMY OF FILM AND TELEVISION ARTS

Acronym or abbreviation: BAFTA

195 Piccadilly, London, W1J 9LN

Tel: 020 7734 0022
Fax: 020 7734 1792

Website:
http://www.bafta.org

Enquiries:
Enquiries to: Public Relations Manager
Direct fax: 020 7734 1009
Other contacts: Membership Officer

Founded:
1947

Organisation type and purpose:
Professional body (membership is by subscription,
qualification, election or invitation), registered
charity (charity number 216726).

Access to staff:
Contact by letter and by fax. Appointment
necessary.
Hours: Mon to Fri, 0900 to 1700

Access to building, collection or gallery:
Prior appointment required

Access for disabled people:
Level entry

Also at:
BAFTA Cymru
  Chapter Arts Centre, Market Road, Canton,
  Cardiff, CF5 1QE; tel: 029 2022 3898; fax: 029
  2066 4189
BAFTA East Coast
  31 West 56th Street, New York, NY 10019, USA;
  tel: 00 1 212 254 2681; fax: 00 1 212 258 2653
BAFTA LA
  930 South Robertson Boulevard, Los Angeles,
  California, CA 90035–1626, USA; tel: 00 1 310
  652 4121; fax: 00 1 310 854 6002
BAFTA North
  International Media Centre, Adelphi House, The
  Crescent, Salford, Manchester, M3 3EN; tel: 0161
  831 9733; fax: 0161 831 9733
BAFTA Scotland
  74 Victoria Crescent Road, Glasgow, G12 9JN;
  tel: 0141 357 4317; fax: 0141 337 1432

BRITISH ACADEMY OF MANAGEMENT

Acronym or abbreviation: BAM

Ground Floor, 137 Euston Road, London, NW1
2AA

Tel: 0207 383 7770
Fax: 0207 383 0377
E-mail: bam@bam.ac.uk

Website:
http://www.bam.ac.uk
News, membership, publications, training and
events, conference.

Founded:
1986

Organisation type and purpose:
Professional association representing the
community of management academics.

Subject coverage:
Management studies.

Electronic and video publications:
British Journal of Management (quarterly, free to
  members)
Newsletter

Access to staff:
Contact by letter, by telephone, by fax and by e-
mail

BRITISH ACCREDITATION COUNCIL

Formal name: British Accreditation Council for
Independent Further and Higher Education
Acronym or abbreviation: BAC

44 Bedford Row, London, WC1R 4LL

Tel: 020 7447 2584
Fax: 020 7447 2585
E-mail: info@the-bac.org

Website:
http://www.the-bac.org

continued overleaf

Enquiries:
Enquiries to: Chief Executive
Other contacts: Head of Administration

Founded:
1984

Organisation type and purpose:
Registered charity (charity number 326652).
Inspection and accreditation of privately funded
institutions of further and higher education.

Printed publications:
Leaflet about BAC (free)
Accreditation Handbooks (free)
Review (free)

Publications list:
Available online

Access to staff:
Contact by letter, by telephone, by fax, by e-mail
and via website
Hours: Mon to Fri, 0830 to 1630

Access for disabled people:
Lift
Hours: Mon to Fri, 0830 to 1630

BRITISH ACTIVITY HOLIDAY ASSOCIATION

Acronym or abbreviation: BAHA

The Hollies, Oak Bank Lane, Hoole Village,
Chester, CH2 4ER

Tel: 01244 301342
E-mail: info@baha.org.uk

Website:
http://www.baha.org.uk
Information about members and required
standards.

Enquiries:
Enquiries to: Secretary

Founded:
1986

Organisation type and purpose:
Trade association (membership is by qualification),
present number of members: 31, service industry,
suitable for ages: all.

Subject coverage:
Activities offered by members; recommended
standards of safety in activity holidays; legislation
covering activity holidays.

Printed publications:
Guide to members (free)
Members' manual (for members only)

Access to staff:
Contact by letter, by telephone, by fax and by e-mail
Hours: Mon to Thu, 0930 to 1230

Access to building, collection or gallery:
No access other than to staff

BRITISH ACUPUNCTURE COUNCIL

Acronym or abbreviation: BAcC

63 Jeddo Road, London, W12 9HQ

Tel: 020 8735 0400
Fax: 020 8735 0404
E-mail: info@acupuncture.org.uk

Website:
http://www.acupuncture.org.uk
Training, research, membership, how to find a
practitioner, health and safety; general
acupuncture information.

Enquiries:
Enquiries to: Administrator

Founded:
1995

Organisation type and purpose:
Advisory body, professional body, membership
association (membership is by subscription,
qualification), present number of members: 3,000.
Research organisation.
Governing body of the acupuncture profession
working to maintain common standards of
education, ethics, discipline and codes of practice
to ensure the health and safety of the public at all
times. It is committed to promoting research and
enhancing the role that traditional acupuncture can
play in the health of the nation.

Subject coverage:
Acupuncture, ethics, practice, research, training
and educational developments.

Printed publications:
Code of Ethics
Code of Safe Practice
Guide to Safe Practice
Health Committee Procedures
Code of Professional Conduct
European Journal of Oriental Medicine (EJOM)
Information leaflet
Reading List
Register of Practitioner Members (annually, £7)
Training List
Disciplinary Procedures
Standards of acupuncture
(all codes relate to members only)

Electronic and video publications:
BAcC Powerpoint presentation (for members only)

Access to staff:
Contact by letter, by telephone, by fax, by e-mail
and via website. Appointment necessary.
Hours: Mon to Fri, 0930 to 1730
Special comments: Office not open to the public.

BRITISH ADHESIVE AND SEALANTS ASSOCIATION

Acronym or abbreviation: BASA

5 Alderson Road, Worksop, Nottinghamshire, S80
1UZ

Tel: 01909 480888
Fax: 01909 473834
E-mail: secretary@basaonline.org

Website:
http://www.basaonline.org

Enquiries:
Enquiries to: Secretary

Organisation type and purpose:
Trade association.

Subject coverage:
Information on the manufacturers and suppliers of
adhesives and sealants.

Printed publications:
Members Handbook (annually)
Adhesives and Sealants, A Resource Pack for
Schools (free)
Information on other publications available at
website: http://www.basaonline.org

Access to staff:
Contact by letter
Hours: Mon to Fri, 0900 to 1700

BRITISH AEROSOL MANUFACTURERS' ASSOCIATION

Acronym or abbreviation: BAMA

Kings Buildings, Smith Square, London, SW1P 3JJ

Tel: 020 7828 5111
Fax: 020 7834 8436
E-mail: enquiries@bama.co.uk

Website:
http://www.bama.co.uk

Enquiries:
Enquiries to: Director
Direct e-mail: enquiries@bama.co.uk
Other contacts: PR Manager (for press, statistics)

Founded:
1961

Organisation type and purpose:
Trade association.

Subject coverage:
Aerosols.

Trade and statistical information:
Data on UK production of aerosols.

Printed publications:
The BAMA Standard for Consumer Safety and
Good Manufacturing Practice
BAMA Annual Report
BAMA Test Methods
Guides to Safety

Access to staff:
Contact by letter, by telephone, by fax and by e-mail
Hours: Mon to Fri, 0900 to 1700

Access to building, collection or gallery:
Prior appointment required

Affiliated to:
European Aerosol Federation
Brussels

BRITISH AGENTS REGISTER

Acronym or abbreviation: BAR

24 Mount Parade, Harrogate, North Yorkshire,
HG1 1BP

Tel: 01423 560608
Fax: 01423 561204
E-mail: info@agentsregister.com

Website:
http://www.agentsregister.com

Enquiries:
Enquiries to: Director
Other contacts: Membership Secretary

Founded:
1963

Organisation type and purpose:
Membership association (membership is by
subscription), service industry.

Subject coverage:
Commercial sales agents and their advantages in
developing sales plus payable services to assist
manufacturers in finding sales agents and a
monthly publication detailing agencies, available
by annual subscription.

Printed publications:
Handbook for the Manufacturers Agents (£10)
Operating an Agency Sales Force (£45)
The EC Guide to Agency Agreements and
Contracts (£25)

Access to staff:
Contact by letter, by telephone, by fax, by e-mail
and via website
Hours: Mon to Fri, 0900 to 1700

Access to building, collection or gallery:
Prior appointment required

BRITISH AGRICULTURAL & GARDEN MACHINERY ASSOCIATION

Acronym or abbreviation: BAGMA

Entrance B, Level 1, Salamander Quay West, Park
Lane, Harefield, Middlesex, UB9 6NZ

Tel: 0870 205 2834
Fax: 0870 205 2835
E-mail: info@bagma.com

Website:
http://www.bagma.com

Enquiries:
Enquiries to: Information Officer
Direct e-mail: information@bhfgroup.co.uk
Other contacts: Director General

Founded:
1917

Organisation type and purpose:
Trade association (membership is by subscription, qualification), service industry, training organisation.

Subject coverage:
Agricultural and garden machinery dealer industry.

Printed publications:
Garden Machinery Price Guide
Market Guide to Used Farm Tractors and
    Machinery
Technical Specification
Order printed publications from: Indices Publications Ltd
14–16 Church Street, Rickmansworth, Hertfordshire, WD31 1RQ, tel: 01923 711434, fax: 01923 896063

Access to staff:
Contact by letter, by telephone, by fax and by e-mail. Appointment necessary.
Hours: Mon to Fri, 0900 to 1700

BRITISH AGRICULTURAL HISTORY SOCIETY

Acronym or abbreviation: BAHS

University of Exeter, Department of History, Amory Building, Rennes Drive, Exeter, Devon, EX4 4RJ

Tel: 01392 263284
Fax: 01392 263305
E-mail: bahs@exeter.ac.uk

Website:
http://www.bahs.org.uk

Enquiries:
Enquiries to: Membership Secretary
Other contacts: Editorial, tel no: 0118 931 8662

Founded:
1952

Organisation type and purpose:
Learned society (membership is by subscription), present number of members: 970.
To further the study of rural and agricultural history.

Subject coverage:
British agricultural history and rural economics.

Printed publications:
Agricultural History Review (1 volume per
    annum, in two parts)

Access to staff:
Contact by letter, by e-mail and via website
Hours: Mon to Fri, 0900 to 1700

BRITISH AIKIDO BOARD

6 Halkingcroft, Langley, Slough, Berkshire, SL3 7AT

Tel: 01753 577878
Fax: 01753 577331

Enquiries:
Enquiries to: General Secretary

Founded:
1975

Organisation type and purpose:
National government body, membership association (membership is by subscription), voluntary organisation, training organisation.
Governing body for Aikido in UK.

Subject coverage:
Aikido.

Access to staff:
Contact by letter and by telephone
Hours: Mon to Fri, 0900 to 1700
Special comments: Enclose an sae for reply to letter.

BRITISH AMATEUR RUGBY LEAGUE ASSOCIATION

Acronym or abbreviation: BARLA

West Yorkshire House, 4 New North Parade, Huddersfield, West Yorkshire, HD1 5JP

Tel: 01484 544131
Fax: 01484 519985
E-mail: info@barla.org.uk

Website:
http://www.barla.org.uk
Everything related to Rugby League

Enquiries:
Enquiries to: Membership Secretary
Direct e-mail: msd@barla.org.uk

Founded:
1973

Organisation type and purpose:
Membership association (membership is by subscription), present number of members: 42 leagues.
Controlling body of the sport.

Subject coverage:
Rugby League.

Printed publications:
The Bulletin (journal, bi-monthly, free to clubs,
    £1.50 per issue to others, £6 a year)

Publications list:
Available online and in print

Access to staff:
Contact by letter, by telephone, by fax, by e-mail and in person
Hours: Mon to Fri, 0900 to 1700

Access to building, collection or gallery:
No prior appointment required

Access for disabled people:
Parking provided

Links with:
Rugby League Coach Education Programme (RLCEP)

BRITISH AMBULANCE SOCIETY

21 Victoria Road, Horley, Surrey, RH6 9BN

Tel: 01293 776636 (answerphone)
Fax: 01293 776636
E-mail: basochq@aol.com

Website:
http://www.britambsoc.org.uk

Enquiries:
Enquiries to: General Secretary

Founded:
1974

Organisation type and purpose:
International organisation, advisory body, membership association (membership is by subscription), present number of members: 300, voluntary organisation, museum, research organisation.
To encourage the research of the British Ambulance Service and its vehicles. To provide an educational medium for all ambulance-related subjects. To create a museum appertaining to the history of the British ambulance service.

Subject coverage:
Ambulances, the ambulance service, history and operation (past, present and future).

Museum or gallery collection, archive, or library special collection:
Vehicles and uniforms
Reference library of model and badge collection
Journals, documents, pictures, photographs,
    publications, statistical information, videos

Printed publications:
Ambulance Scene (newsletter, 5 times a year)
Ambulance World (journal, formerly Bells &
    Beacons International, quarterly)

Access to staff:
Contact by letter, by telephone, by fax and by e-mail. Appointment necessary. Non-members charged.
Hours: After 2000 for phone contact or 24-hour answerphone
Special comments: Access by prior appointment.

Access to building, collection or gallery:
No prior appointment required

Links with:
Council Vehicle Society / Fleet Data Register
Fire Service Preservation Group
Professional Car Society (USA)
St John Ambulance Brigade

Membership Secretary:
British Ambulance Society
    Falklands, 251 Kings Drive, Eastbourne, East
    Sussex, BN21 2UR; tel: 01323 508233

Public Relations Officer:
British Ambulance Society
    25 West Rise, Tonbridge, Kent, TN9 2PG; tel:
    01732 508525; e-mail: chrisbatten@virgin.net

BRITISH AMERICAN BUSINESS INC

Acronym or abbreviation: BABi

75 Brook Street, London, W1K 4AD

Tel: 020 7467 7400
Fax: 020 7493 2394
E-mail: ukinfo@babinc.org

Website:
http://www.babinc.org

Enquiries:
Enquiries to: Director – Commercial
Direct e-mail: cwells@babinc.org
Other contacts: Director – Membership

Founded:
2000

Organisation type and purpose:
International organisation, membership association (membership is by subscription), present number of members: 630 corporate, 2400 individuals, service industry, suitable for ages: 20 to 60.
Leading transatlantic business organisation dedicated to helping its member companies build and expand their international business.
As a not-for-profit organisation, BABi's mission is to provide practical business benefits for its member companies.

Subject coverage:
Focuses closely on US and UK company information and trading relationships. Through BABi's collection of databases, it is possible to trace and highlight the ownership of company affiliates and subsidiaries worldwide, including information on US subsidiaries in the UK and UK subsidiaries in the US.

Trade and statistical information:
US company data.

Printed publications:
Network New York London (quarterly, available to
    members and selected journalists, organisations
    etc)
British American Business – publication giving
    information and advice to companies looking to
    expand into or open offices in the UK (handbook,
    annually)
Membership Directory – lists all member
    companies (annually, members only)
UK and USA (magazine)
Order printed publications from: Publications Manager, BABi

Publications list:
Available online and in print

Access to staff:
Contact by letter, by telephone, by fax, by e-mail and via website. Appointment necessary. Non-members charged.

continued overleaf

Hours: Mon to Fri, 0900 to 1700

Affiliated to:
British-American Business Inc
20th Floor, 52 Vanderbilt Avenue, New York, NY, 1022, USA; tel: + 1 212 661 4060; fax: + 1 212 661 4074; e-mail: info@babinc.org

BRITISH AMERICAN TOBACCO

Acronym or abbreviation: BAT

Regent's Park Road, Southampton, SO15 8TL

Tel: 023 8079 3603
Fax: 023 8079 3800
E-mail: val_rice@britamtob.com

Website:
http://www.bat.com
Company information, tobacco history.

Enquiries:
Enquiries to: Information Manager

Founded:
1956

Organisation type and purpose:
Manufacturing industry.

Subject coverage:
Tobacco growing, cigarette manufacture, tobacco history.

Library catalogue:
All or part available in-house

Access to staff:
Contact by letter, by fax and by e-mail
Hours: Mon to Fri, 0900 to 1700

Parent body:
British American Tobacco (Investments) Limited
tel: 020 7845 1000; fax: 020 7845 0555

BRITISH AND FOREIGN SCHOOL SOCIETY ARCHIVES

Acronym or abbreviation: BFSS Archives

BFSS Archives, c/o Brunel University Archives, Brunel University, Kingston Lane, Uxbridge, Middlesex UB8 3PH

Tel: 01895 265390; 01784 436111
E-mail: bfss.archive@brunel.ac.uk

Website:
http://www.bfss.org.uk
http://www.brunel.ac.uk/about/administration/archivesandrecords

Enquiries:
Enquiries to: Archivist

Founded:
1808

Organisation type and purpose:
Registered charity (charity number 314286).

Subject coverage:
The Archives document the history of 19th- and 20th-century elementary education and teacher training.

Museum or gallery collection, archive, or library special collection:
Surviving records of the BFSS from the beginning of the 19th century including minute books 1808–1834, correspondence of the Secretaries of the Society 1814–1897, overseas correspondence, annual reports
Letters of Joseph Lancaster 1810–1812
Records of the Society's teacher training colleges, mainly 1830–1976, including Borough Road College, Saffron Walden College, Stockwell College and some from Darlington College
Student registers and other official records of student progress
Lists of British Schools and some original records including pamphlets, annual reports and Newcastle Commision returns
The Educational Record 1848–1929
Student magazines

Student photos from 19th century
Prints and photographs, paintings and engravings, architects' plans
Books and pamphlets on education dating from the 19th century, including works by Lancaster, Bell, Pestalozzi and Froebel.

Non-library collection catalogue:
All or part available online

Access to staff:
Contact by letter, by telephone, by e-mail, in person and via website. Appointment necessary. Non-members charged.
Hours: Reading room open by appointment only, Mon to Wed, 0930 to 1500

Access to building, collection or gallery:
The Archives Reading Room is not on the Uxbridge campus. Contact the archivist for address and directions
Hours: Reading room open by appointment only, Mon to Wed, 0930 to 1500

Access for disabled people:
Ground floor reading room, disabled toilet
Hours: As above

Administered by:
Brunel University Archives
Brunel University Archives, Brunel University, Kingston Lane, Uxbridge, Middlesex UB8 3PH; tel: 01895 265390; 01784 436111; e-mail: bfss .archive@brunel.ac.uk; website: http://www .brunel.ac.uk/about/administration/ archivesandrecords

BRITISH AND IRISH ASSOCIATION OF LAW LIBRARIANS

Acronym or abbreviation: BIALL

Lincoln's Inn Library, London, WC2A 3TN

Tel: 020 7242 4371
Fax: 020 7404 1864
E-mail: susanfrost@compuserve.com

Website:
http://www.biall.org.uk

Enquiries:
Enquiries to: Administrator

Founded:
1969

Organisation type and purpose:
Professional body.
To provide better administration and exploitation of law libraries and legal information units; unite and co-ordinate the interests, opinions and activities of legal information professionals into a single influential voice.

Subject coverage:
Law librarianship, exchange of information and improvement of service, history of law and the courts, legal bibliography. Salary information in legal information sector.

Trade and statistical information:
Salary survey.

Printed publications:
Bibliography of Commonwealth Law Reports
Directory of Law Libraries (5th ed.)
History of the British and Irish Association of Law Librarians 1969–1999 (Blake, M)
Manual of Law Librarianship (Moys E ed., 2nd ed.)
Newsletter (4 times a year)
Legal Information Management (4 times a year)
Sources of Biographical Information on Past Lawyers (Holborn, G)
Order printed publications from: BIALL
Administrator, BIALL
26 Myton Crescent, Warwick, CV34 6QA, tel: 01926 491717, fax: 01926 491717, e-mail: susanfrost@ compuserve.com

Access to staff:
Contact by letter, by telephone, by fax, by e-mail and via website

Hours: Administrator available Mon to Fri, 0900 to 1200, or answerphone available

Administrator's Office:
British and Irish Association of Law Librarians (BIALL)
26 Myton Crescent, Warwick, CV34 6QA; tel: 01926 491717; fax: 01926 491717; e-mail: susanfrost@compuserve.com

Cooperation with:
other national law librarianship associations such as CALL and AALL

BRITISH AND IRISH ORTHOPTIC SOCIETY

Acronym or abbreviation: BIOS

4th Floor, 14 Bedford Row, London, WC1R 4ED

Tel: 0207 306 1135
Fax: 0207 242 8452
E-mail: bios@orthoptics.org.uk

Website:
http://www.orthoptics.org.uk

Enquiries:
Enquiries to: Executive Officer

Founded:
1937

Organisation type and purpose:
Professional body, trade union, present number of members: 1,400.

Subject coverage:
Orthoptics, binocular vision, amblyopia.

Museum or gallery collection, archive, or library special collection:
National archive of orthoptics

Printed publications:
British and Irish Orthoptic Journal (annually)
Order printed publications from: email: membership@ orthoptics.org.uk

Electronic and video publications:
Newsletter (monthly, for members)

Publications list:
Available online and in print

Access to staff:
Contact by e-mail
Hours: Mon to Fri, 0900 to 1700

Access to building, collection or gallery:
Prior appointment required

Access for disabled people:
Special comments: By appointment.

BRITISH ANTARCTIC SURVEY

Acronym or abbreviation: BAS

High Cross, Madingley Road, Cambridge, CB3 0ET

Tel: 01223 221400
Fax: 01223 362616
E-mail: information@bas.ac.uk

Website:
http://www.antarctica.ac.uk

Enquiries:
Enquiries to: Information Officer

Organisation type and purpose:
International organisation, national government body, research organisation.

Subject coverage:
Antarctic research as follows: atmospheric sciences: upper air and surface meteorology (including ozone observations), geomagnetism, aurora and airglow, ionosphere and whistlers; earth sciences: glaciology and physical oceanography, marine and land geophysics (including seismology), geology (including economic geology), topographical survey, hydrography and hydrographic surveys,

quaternary studies; life sciences: taxonomy, biogeography, bioclimatology, marine biology, freshwater biology, pedology, terrestrial ecology, physiology (including human physiology); also: polar equipment and travel techniques, including the operation of ships, aircraft and vehicles.

Museum or gallery collection, archive, or library special collection:
BAS Archive Collection – Expeditions from 1943
BAS Herbaria – Code: AAS (Antarctic and Sub-Antarctic plants)
Geology Rock Collection
Sea ice records, and field data and maps for all scientific work carried out

Library catalogue:
All or part available in-house

Printed publications:
Antarctic Science (journal from 1989, quarterly, pub CUP)
BAS Annual Report
British Antarctic Survey Bulletin (collections of shorter papers, ceased publication 1988)
British Antarctic Survey Scientific Reports (monographs, ceased publication 1991)
Leaflets, booklets, posters and postcards

Electronic and video publications:
CD-ROM for polar bibliographies

Access to staff:
Contact by letter, by fax, by e-mail and via website
Hours: Mon to Fri, 0900 to 1700

Access to building, collection or gallery:
Prior appointment required
Special comments: Access to library by prior appointment only.

Access for disabled people:
Parking provided, level entry, toilet facilities

Funded institute of the:
Natural Environment Research Council (NERC) Polaris House, North Star Avenue, Swindon, SN2 1EU; tel: 01793 411500; fax: 01793 411501

BRITISH ANTIQUE DEALERS' ASSOCIATION

Acronym or abbreviation: BADA

20 Rutland Gate, London, SW7 1BD

Tel: 020 7589 4128
Fax: 020 7581 9083
E-mail: info@bada.org

Website:
http://www.bada.org

Enquiries:
Enquiries to: Secretary-General

Founded:
1918

Organisation type and purpose:
Trade association (membership is by election or invitation), present number of members: 400.

Subject coverage:
Buying, selling, valuation and care of antiques.

Printed publications:
Handbook (annual)
Consumer information sheets, including:
Buying Antiques with Confidence
Care of Antiques
Careers in Antiques
Information on Shippers
List of members
Newsletter (for members)

Publications list:
Available in print

Access to staff:
Contact by letter, by telephone, by fax, by e-mail, in person and via website
Hours: Mon to Fri, 0930 to 1700

Links with:
Confédération des Négociants en Oeuvres d'Art

BRITISH ANTIQUE FURNITURE RESTORERS ASSOCIATION LTD

Acronym or abbreviation: BAFRA

Head Office, The Old Rectory, Warmwell, Dorchester, Dorset, DT2 8HQ

Tel: 01305 854822
Fax: 01305 854822
E-mail: headoffice@bafra.org.uk

Website:
http://www.bafra.org.uk

Enquiries:
Enquiries to: Executive Secretary
Other contacts: Chief Executive Officer

Founded:
1979

Organisation type and purpose:
International organisation, national organisation, advisory body, professional body, trade association (membership is by subscription, qualification), present number of members: 102 in all categories, suitable for ages: 18 to 60, publishing house. Although a trade association, BAFRA is also a professional body in the conservation and restoration field.
To provide the public and private heritage sector and antique trade with a network of highly skilled and accredited conservators/restorers across Britain.

Subject coverage:
Furniture conservation and restoration, furniture history, training in furniture conservation and restoration.

Information services:
Unlimited, in the areas of furniture, clocks, barometers, mechanical music, textile conservation.

Education services:
BAFRA-designed training in all aspects of furniture conservation and restoration.

Printed publications:
BAFRA Directory of Members
BAFRA (Journal, 2 times a year)
Order printed publications from: BAFRA Head Office

Publications list:
Available in print

Access to staff:
Contact by letter, by telephone, by fax, by e-mail and via website. Appointment necessary.
Hours: Mon to Fri, 0900 to 1700

BRITISH APPAREL & TEXTILE CONFEDERATION

Acronym or abbreviation: BATC

5 Portland Place, London, W1B 1PW

Tel: 020 7636 7788
Fax: 020 7636 7515
E-mail: batc@dial.pipex.com

Website:
http://www.batc.co.uk

Enquiries:
Enquiries to: Director General

Organisation type and purpose:
Trade association.

Subject coverage:
Apparel and textile industry.

Access to staff:
Contact by letter, by fax and by e-mail
Hours: Mon to Fri, 0900 to 1700

Access to building, collection or gallery:
Prior appointment required

Member of:
European Clothing and Textile Association (EURATEX)

BRITISH APPROVALS FOR FIRE EQUIPMENT

Acronym or abbreviation: BAFE

Neville House, 55 Eden Street, Kingston Upon Thames, Surrey, KT1 1BW

Tel: 020 8541 1950
Fax: 020 8547 1564
E-mail: info@bafe.org.uk

Enquiries:
Enquiries to: General Secretary
Direct e-mail: info@bafe.org.uk
Other contacts: BAFE Scheme Administrator

Founded:
1984

Organisation type and purpose:
The organisation writes and adopts schemes of third party accreditation for the fire protection industry.

Subject coverage:
Active fire protection equipment, services.

Printed publications:
BAFE brochure/supplement (free)
List of approved manufacturers/suppliers (free)

Access to staff:
Contact by letter, by telephone and by fax
Hours: Mon to Fri, 0900 to 1700

BRITISH ARACHNOLOGICAL SOCIETY

Acronym or abbreviation: BAS

31 Duxford Close, Redditch, Worcestershire, B97 5BY

E-mail: secretary@britishspiders.org.uk

Website:
http://www.britishspiders.org.uk
Information about the Society and its publications.

Enquiries:
Enquiries to: Honorary Secretary

Organisation type and purpose:
Learned society (membership is by subscription), present number of members: 700, registered charity (charity number 260346).

Subject coverage:
Arachnida (spiders, harvestmen, pseudoscorpions).

Museum or gallery collection, archive, or library special collection:
Library of books, papers and microfiche available to members

Printed publications:
Bulletin of the British Arachnological Society (3 times a year)
How to Begin the Study of Spiders (booklet)
Newsletter (3 times a year)
Society Handbook
Specialist Books
Order printed publications from: Francis Farr-Cox, 1 Winchester Road, Burnham on Sea, Somerset, TA8 1HY; e-mail: sales@britishspiders.org.uk

Access to staff:
Contact by letter, by e-mail and via website
Hours: Mon to Fri, 0900 to 1700

Links with:
American Arachnological Society
Centre de Documentation Arachnologique

BRITISH ARCHITECTURAL LIBRARY

Acronym or abbreviation: BAL

Royal Institute of British Architects, 66 Portland Place, London, W1B 1AD

Tel: 020 7580 5533
Fax: 020 7631 1802
E-mail: info@inst.riba.org

continued overleaf

Website:
http://www.architecture.com
Information regarding library holdings, on-line catalogue.

Enquiries:
Enquiries to: Director
Other contacts: Archivist; Curator of Drawings

Founded:
1834

Organisation type and purpose:
Professional body.
Library of a professional organisation; the title given above was designated in 1975; includes the Sir Banister Fletcher Library.

Subject coverage:
Architecture; architectural history; building; construction; planning; landscape architecture; conservation; design; applied and decorative arts; interior design; topography.

Museum or gallery collection, archive, or library special collection:
Biography Files (over 15,000 vertical files on architects and others)
Books Collection (some 135,000 volumes)
Collection on the Modern Movement
Drawings and Archives Collection (some 500,000 drawings, predominantly British from the 15th century onwards, at the RIBA Study Rooms in the Victoria and Albert Museum)
Early Imprints Collection (some 4,000 books on architecture, printed before 1841)
Handley-Read Collection on Victorian decorative arts
Manuscripts Collection (important papers of architects, architectural historians, practices, firms and societies, 17th century to present, at the RIBA Study Rooms in the Victoria and Albert Museum)
Periodicals Collection (700 current titles and 1,400 that have ceased publication)
Photographs Collection (some 1.5m. images including postcards and slides)

Non-library collection catalogue:
All or part available online and in print

Library catalogue:
All or part available online and in-house

Printed publications:
Architectural Keywords
Architectural Publications Index (quarterly)
Architecture Database
British Architectural Library Guides
RIBA Drawings Collection Catalogue (20 volumes)
RIBA List of Recommended Books (annually)
Order printed publications from: Directory of British Architects 1834–1914 (2001)

Microform publications:
Microfiche and microfilm of catalogues, drawings, manuscripts, rare books and early journals

Electronic and video publications:
Architecture database on Dialog (file 179)
Architectural publications index, on disc (APId) available on CD-ROM

Publications list:
Available online

Access to staff:
Contact by letter, by telephone, by fax, by e-mail, in person and via website
Hours: Tue, Wed, Fri, 1000 to 1700; Sat, 1000 to 1330; Mon, Thu, closed
Special comments: Appointment necessary for access to Photographs Collection.

Access for disabled people:
Ramped entry, level entry

BRITISH ART MEDAL SOCIETY

Acronym or abbreviation: BAMS

c/o Department of Coins and Medals, British Museum, London, WC1B 3DG

Tel: 020 7323 8568

Fax: 020 7323 8171
E-mail: jlarkin@thebritishmuseum.ac.uk

Website:
http://www.bams.org.uk
Activities of the Society and medals issued by it.

Enquiries:
Enquiries to: Secretary

Founded:
1982

Organisation type and purpose:
Learned society, voluntary organisation, registered charity (charity number 288869).
To encourage, develop and support the practice and study of medallic art.

Subject coverage:
Medals and coins; commissioning of medals; sculpture; history of art; contemporary art.

Printed publications:
The Medal (twice a year)
Contemporary art medals: the BAMS student medal project (annual, £2)
The Pingo family and medal making in 18th-century Britain (Eimer, C. £19.95)
Designs on Posterity: drawings for medals (Jones, M. £35)
Christian Wermuth: a German medallist of the Baroque age (Wohlfahrt, C. £95)
Modern Hungarian medals (£3)
British art medals 1982–2002 (Attwood, P. £10)
The British Columbia medals of John Lobban (£8.50)
Order printed publications from: Galata Print Ltd, The Old White Lion, Market Street, Llanfyllin, Powys, SY22 5BX; fax: 01691 648765

Publications list:
Available in print

Access to staff:
Contact by letter, by telephone, by fax and by e-mail. Appointment necessary.
Hours: Mon to Fri, 1000 to 1700

BRITISH ARTS FESTIVALS ASSOCIATION

Acronym or abbreviation: BAFA

2nd Floor, 28 Charing Cross Road, London, WC2H 0DB

Tel: 020 7240 4532
Fax: 020 7247 5010
E-mail: info@artsfestivals.co.uk

Website:
http://www.artsfestivals.co.uk
Map, calendar and A-Z directory for over 100 arts festivals in the UK with direct links to their websites and links to European festival networks.

Enquiries:
Enquiries to: Co-ordinator

Founded:
1970

Organisation type and purpose:
Membership association (membership is by subscription), present number of members: 110, voluntary organisation, registered charity (charity number 1010867).
BAFA is the meeting point of arts festivals in the UK, and is a point of information for member festivals.
Promotes and co-ordinates information in more than 100 arts festivals.

Subject coverage:
Arts festivals, dates, and programmes etc.

Printed publications:
Free annual arts festivals calendar published each winter for succeeding year
Festivals Mean Business (research report, 2001, £30 inc. p&p)

Publications list:
Available in print

Access to staff:
Contact by letter, by telephone, by fax, by e-mail and via website
Hours: Mon to Fri, 0900 to 1700

Access to building, collection or gallery:
No access other than to staff

Affiliated to:
European Festivals Association (EFA)
Chateau di Coppet, Case Postale 26, Coppet, CH 1296, Switzerland; tel: 00 41 22 776 8673; fax: 00 41 22 776 4275; e-mail: geneva@euro-festival.net; website: http://www.euro-festival.net

BRITISH ASSOCIATION FOR AMERICAN STUDIES

Acronym or abbreviation: BAAS

School of English and American Studies, University of Leicester, University Road, Leicester, LE2 7RH

Tel: 0116 223 1068
Fax: 0116 252 2065
E-mail: catherine.morley@baas.ac.uk

Website:
http://www.baas.ac.uk

Enquiries:
Enquiries to: Secretary
Other contacts: Chair

Founded:
1955

Organisation type and purpose:
Learned society, professional body.
To promote, support and encourage the study of the USA in the United Kingdom.

Subject coverage:
History, literature, politics, sociology, geography, film, culture of the USA.

Printed publications:
Journal of American Studies (3 times a year)
BAAS American Studies paperbacks series
Newsletter (twice a year)
Pamphlets in American Studies (no longer published, backlist in print)
Ryburn/BAAS Reprint Library
US Studies Online (BAAS Postgraduate Journal)

Microform publications:
BRRAM series (British Records Relating to America)

Publications list:
Available in print

Access to staff:
Contact by letter, by telephone, by fax and by e-mail
Hours: Variable hours

Links with:
American Studies Association (US)
Canadian Association for American Studies
European Association for American Studies
International American Studies Association
Irish Association for American Studies
United Kingdom Council for Area Studies

BRITISH ASSOCIATION FOR APPLIED LINGUISTICS

Acronym or abbreviation: BAAL

c/o Dovetail Management Consultancy, London, SE15 3WB

Tel: 020 7639 0090
Fax: 020 7635 6014
E-mail: admin@baal.org.uk

Website:
http://www.baal.org.uk

Enquiries:
Enquiries to: Administrator

Founded:
1967

Organisation type and purpose:
Learned society, membership association
(membership is by subscription), present number
of members: 750 individual, 9 associate
(publishers), 20 university departments and
libraries.
To promote the study of language in use, to foster
interdisciplinary collaboration and to provide a
common forum for those engaged in the theoretical
study of language and those interested in its
practical use.

Subject coverage:
Applied linguistics.

Printed publications:
The following publications are available to
members only:
Membership list
Newsletter (3 times a year)
Proceedings of Annual Meeting (pub. John
Benjamin Publishing Company)

Access to staff:
Contact by letter, by fax and by e-mail
Hours: Thu, 0900 to 1700 (call to confirm)

Links with:
Association Internationale de Linguistique
Appliquée (AILA)

BRITISH ASSOCIATION FOR CANADIAN STUDIES

Acronym or abbreviation: BACS

31 Tavistock Square, London, WC1H 9HA

Tel: 020 7862 8687
Fax: 020 7117 1875
E-mail: jodie.robson@canadian-studies.net

Website:
http://www.canadian-studies.net
About BACS: conferences and other events; British
Journal of Canadian Studies and BACS Newsletter;
Access Canada.

Enquiries:
Enquiries to: Administrator

Founded:
1975

Organisation type and purpose:
Learned society.

Subject coverage:
General information on Canadian studies in
Britain, on Canadian academics visiting the UK,
travel grants to scholars, specialist groups on
Canada/UK architecture, business and economic
studies, Canada in schools, history, social policy,
library and resources, Aboriginal studies.

Printed publications:
BACS Newsletter (two issues per annum, winter
and summer)
British Journal for Canadian Studies (two issues
per annum)
Occasional workshop and bibliographical
publications
Order printed publications from: BACS

Access to staff:
Contact by letter, by telephone, by e-mail and via
website. Appointment necessary.
Hours: Mon to Fri, 0900 to 1700

Member organisation of:
International Council for Canadian Studies
250 City Centre Avenue, Suite 303, Ottawa,
Ontario, K1R 6K7, Canada; website: http://www
.iccs-ciec.ca

BRITISH ASSOCIATION FOR CANCER RESEARCH

Acronym or abbreviation: BACR

c/o Leeds Institute of Molecular Medicine, Clinical
Sciences Building, St James's University Hospital,
Beckett Street, Leeds, LS9 7TF

Tel: 0113 206 5611

Fax: 0113 242 9886
E-mail: bacr@leeds.ac.uk

Website:
http://www.bacr.org.uk

Enquiries:
Enquiries to: BACR Administrative Secretary

Founded:
1960

Organisation type and purpose:
National organisation, learned society
(membership is by election or invitation), present
number of members: 1,100, representing all aspects
of clinical and experimental research.
Registered charity (charity number 289297).
Organises scientific meetings/workshops on cancer
research within the United Kingdom, and provides
a platform for presentation of original clinical and
experimental research. Funds exchanges between
laboratories to encourage knowledge transfer and
engender collaboration both nationally and
internationally; provides opportunities for senior
investigators to undergo further training to enable
them to keep abreast of new investigative/research
methods, and for junior investigators and research
students to present their work at other meetings/
conferences.

Subject coverage:
Cancer research.

Printed publications:
Newsletter (annual)

Access to staff:
Contact by letter, by telephone, by fax, by e-mail
and via website
Hours: Mon to Fri, 0900 to 1700

Links with:
European Association for Cancer Research
Institute of Biology

BRITISH ASSOCIATION FOR CEMETERIES IN SOUTH ASIA

Acronym or abbreviation: BACSA

135 Burntwood Lane, London, SW17 0AJ

E-mail: rosieljai@clara.co.uk

Website:
http://members.ozemail.com.au/~clday/bacsa.htm
http://www.bacsa.org.uk

Enquiries:
Enquiries to: Honorary Secretary

Founded:
1976

Organisation type and purpose:
Membership association (membership is by
subscription), present number of members: over
1800, registered charity (charity number 273422),
research organisation, publishing house.

Subject coverage:
Information on cemeteries in South Asia
(excluding war graves).

**Museum or gallery collection, archive, or library
special collection:**
An archive maintained in the British Library –
Oriental and India Office Collections

Printed publications:
Chowdikar (journal, twice a year, members)
Over 30 books and booklets on Records,
Monumental Inscriptions and Biographical
Details published by BACSA (prices vary, 50p
p&p per item)
Series of paperback books about the lives of
Europeans in South Asia: written by BACSA
members (prices vary, £1 p&p per item)
including:
Canals and Campaigns: An Engineer Officer on
India, 1877 (Moncrieff, Maj-Gen Sir George,
1987)
India Served and Observed (Archer W and M,
1994)

Memoirs of an Adventurous Dane in India: 1904–
1947 (Hansen A P, 1999)
The Calcutta of Begum Johnson (Edwards-Stuart I,
1990)
Statues of the Raj (Steggles M, 2000)
A Railway Family in India (Stevenage P, 2001)
Who Was Dr Jackson: Two Calcutta Families
(Benett, 2002)
Willingly to War (Norris, 2004)

Publications list:
Available in print

Access to staff:
Contact by letter, by e-mail and via website
Hours: Mon to Fri, 0900 to 2000

BRITISH ASSOCIATION FOR CHEMICAL SPECIALITIES

Acronym or abbreviation: BACS

Simpson House, Windsor Court, Clarence Drive,
Harrogate, HG1 2PE

Tel: 01423 700249
Fax: 01423 520297
E-mail: enquiries@bacsnet.org

Website:
http://www.bacsnet.org
General data about the Associates and programme
of events.

Enquiries:
Enquiries to: Secretariat

Founded:
1977

Organisation type and purpose:
Trade association (membership is by subscription),
present number of members: 155.

Subject coverage:
The British Association for Chemical Specialities
(BACS) is the trade association representing
manufacturers and formulators of speciality
chemicals and intermediates. Major classes of
performance and effect chemicals covered by
BACS include maintenance products for consumer
and industrial use, disinfectants and industrial
biocides, including water treatment chemicals and
services, speciality surfactants and personal care
and cosmetic ingredients.

Printed publications:
Proceedings of Chemical Symposia for current and
previous years
BACS Code of Practice on the Control of
Legionellae
BACS Guide to the Choice of Disinfectants
BACS Review of Worldwide Disinfectant Test
Methods
BACS Annual Review
Understanding Germs, Hygiene and Health

Publications list:
Available online

Access to staff:
Contact by letter, by telephone, by fax and by e-
mail. Appointment necessary.
Hours: Mon to Fri, 0900 to 1700

BRITISH ASSOCIATION FOR COMMUNITY CHILD HEALTH

Acronym or abbreviation: BACCH

5–11 Theobalds Road, London, WC1X 8SH

Tel: 020 7092 6084
Fax: 020 7092 6194
E-mail: bacch@rcpch.ac.uk

Website:
http://www.bacch.org.uk

Enquiries:
Enquiries to: Administrator

Subject coverage:
Community paediatrics, child development.

continued overleaf

Printed publications:
Standards for Child Development Services (free)
Directory of Child Development Centres (£6)
Child Health Rights: a Practitioners Guide (£5)

Publications list:
Available online

Access to staff:
Contact by letter, by telephone, by fax, by e-mail, in person and via website
Hours: Mon to Fri, 0900 to 1700

Groups in the organisation:
British Academy for Childhood Disability (BACD)
    at the same address
Child – Public Health Interest Group (C-PHIG)
    at the same address
Child Protection Interest Group (CPIG)
    at the same address

BRITISH ASSOCIATION FOR COUNSELLING & PSYCHOTHERAPY

Acronym or abbreviation: BACP

15 St John's Business Park, Lutterworth, LE17 4HB

Tel: 01455 883300; minicom no. 01455 550307
E-mail: enquiries@bacp.co.uk

Website:
http://www.counselling.co.uk
Membership details, accreditation criteria, Code of Ethics, publications, services available.
http://www.bacp.co.uk/

Enquiries:
Enquiries to: Information Officer
Other contacts: Membership Services Manager (for membership); Accreditation Manager (for accreditation)

Founded:
1977

Organisation type and purpose:
National organisation, learned society, professional body (membership is by subscription), present number of members: 15,000 individuals, 800+ organisations, registered charity (charity number 298361).
Counselling help in local areas of England, Wales, Scotland and Northern Ireland; agencies and individuals, available on the website or on receipt of an SAE.

Subject coverage:
Counselling, psychotherapy, training, personal development, stress management, employee assistance programmes, post-trauma.

Printed publications:
Variety of books and pamphlets on counselling
    and psychotherapy, research, special interests
    and careers and training, including:
Good Practice Guidance for Counsellors in Schools
    (£9 members, £11 non-members)
Counselling Journal (monthly)
Divisional journals or newsletters (7)
Handbook of Counselling (2nd ed., 1997, £17.99
    members, £18.99 non-members)
List of counsellors and counselling organisations in
    your area (on receipt of an A5 sae or on website)
Research Study I False Memory Syndrome (£3
    members, £3.50 non-members)
Research Study II Child Sexual Abuse (£3
    members, £3.50 non-members)
Training and Careers in Counselling (pamphlet, on
    receipt of an A5 sae)
List of publications and audio-visual aids, on
    request

Electronic and video publications:
Finding a Therapist (UK) (available only online)

Publications list:
Available online and in print

Access to staff:
Contact by letter, by fax and by e-mail
Hours: Mon to Fri, 0845 to 1700

Divisions of BAC:
Association for Pastoral Care and Counselling (APCC)
Association for Student Counselling (ASC)
Association of Independent Practitioners (AIP)
BACP Healthcare
BACP Workplace
Counselling Children & Young People (CCYP)

Member of:
Standing Conference for the Advancement of Counselling

BRITISH ASSOCIATION FOR CRYSTAL GROWTH

Acronym or abbreviation: BACG

BAE Systems Infra-red Limited, PO Box 217, Millbrook Industrial Estate, Southampton, SO15 0EG

Tel: 023 8070 2300
Fax: 023 8031 6777
E-mail: pete.capper@baesystems.com

Website:
http://bacg.newi.ac.uk

Enquiries:
Enquiries to: Honorary Secretary

Founded:
1969

Organisation type and purpose:
International organisation, national organisation, membership association (membership is by qualification), present number of members: 400, registered charity (charity number 261780), suitable for ages: 21+.
Interdisciplinary in nature and representing crystal growth in industry, research laboratories and higher education in the UK.
To encourage scientific and technological communication on crystal growth including all types of inorganic and organic crystals.

Subject coverage:
Crystal growth of inorganic and organic crystalline materials including metals, ceramics, polymers and electronic-device materials.

Printed publications:
Newsletter (2 times a year, free to members)

Access to staff:
Contact by letter, by telephone, by fax and by e-mail
Hours: Mon to Fri, 0900 to 1700

Affiliated to:
International Organisation for Crystal Growth (IOCG)

BRITISH ASSOCIATION FOR IMMEDIATE CARE

Acronym or abbreviation: BASICS

Turret House, Turret Lane, Ipswich, Suffolk, IP4 1DL

Tel: 01473 218407
Fax: 01473 280585
E-mail: admin@basics.org.uk

Website:
http://www.basics.org.uk

Enquiries:
Enquiries to: Chief Executive

Founded:
1977

Organisation type and purpose:
Membership association (membership is by subscription), present number of members: 1,400, registered charity (charity number 276054), training organisation.

Subject coverage:
Emergency medical care.

Printed publications:
Newsletter (3 times a year)
Other publications on immediate medical care

Access to staff:
Contact by letter, by telephone, by fax, by e-mail and via website
Hours: Mon to Thu, 0830 to 1700; Fri, 0830 to 1630

BRITISH ASSOCIATION FOR INFORMATION AND LIBRARY EDUCATION AND RESEARCH

Acronym or abbreviation: BAILER

c/o Dr Vesna Brujic-Okretic, Head of Department of Information Science, School of Informatics, City University London, Northampton Square, London, EC1V 0HB

Tel: 020 7040 8551
E-mail: v.brujic-okretic@city.ac.uk

Website:
http://www.bailer.org.uk
Contains details of all BAILER members as well as links to departmental websites and documents of relevance to BAILER members.

Enquiries:
Enquiries to: Chairman

Founded:
1992

Organisation type and purpose:
Professional body, university department or institute.
Comprising teaching and research staff of information and library schools and departments in the UK and Ireland. Acts as a national forum for matters relating to information and library education and research and aims to reflect and focus the evolution of the field of information and library studies through the development and encouragement of its members.

Subject coverage:
Education and research in library and information studies, including theory and practice in digital information management and dissemination.

Printed publications:
Directory of Courses in Information and Library
    Studies in the UK

Access to staff:
Contact by e-mail
Hours: Mon to Fri, 0900 to 1700

BRITISH ASSOCIATION FOR LOCAL HISTORY

Acronym or abbreviation: BALH

PO Box 6549, Somersal Herbert, Ashbourne, DE6 5WH

Tel: 01283 585947
E-mail: info@balh.co.uk

Website:
http://www.balh.co.uk
Details of BALH and abstracts of recent articles in The Local Historian available.

Enquiries:
Enquiries to: Secretary General
Direct e-mail: mail@balh.co.uk

Founded:
1982

Organisation type and purpose:
Membership association (membership is by subscription), present number of members: 2500, voluntary organisation, registered charity (charity number 285467), publishing house.

Subject coverage:
Local history, family history, genealogy, industrial archaeology, vernacular architecture, archive services, library services, museum services.

Printed publications:
Annual Report

Publications include:
The Local Historian (journal, quarterly)
Concise Index to the Local Historian Volumes 1–27
From Chantry to OXFAM – A short history of
charities and charity legislation (Alvey N, 1996)
Local History News (magazine, quarterly)
How Much is that Worth? (Munby L, 1996)
Local History Catalogue
Newspapers and Local History (Murphy M, 1991)
Reading Tudor and Stuart Handwriting (Munby L,
1988)
The Late Victorian Town (Grace F, 1991)
Writing Local History: A Practical Guide (Dymond
D, 2000)

Publications list:
Available online and in print

Access to staff:
Contact by letter and by fax
Hours: Mon to Fri, 0900 to 1700

BRITISH ASSOCIATION FOR PAEDIATRIC NEPHROLOGY

Acronym or abbreviation: BAPN

Renal Unit, Royal Hospital for Sick Children,
Yorkhill, Glasgow, G3 8SJ

Tel: 0141 201 0122
Fax: 0141 201 0859

Website:
http://bapn.uwcm.ac.uk

Enquiries:
Enquiries to: Speciality Coordinator

Organisation type and purpose:
Professional body.

Subject coverage:
All aspects of kidney disease in children, including
the treatment of renal failure; research.

Printed publications:
Paediatric Nephrology in the nineties (1995)
Reports, 1974 and 1979, on the siting of units for
the care of children with chronic renal failure in
the United Kingdom
The Provision of Services in the UK for Children
and Adolescents with Renal Disease (1995)

Access to staff:
Contact by letter
Hours: Mon to Fri, 0900 to 1700

Close links with:
Renal Association
Royal College of Paediatrics and Child Health

BRITISH ASSOCIATION FOR PERFORMING ARTS MEDICINE

Acronym or abbreviation: BAPAM

4th Floor, Totara Park House, 34–36 Gray's Inn
Road, London, WC1X 8HR

Tel: 020 7404 5888
Fax: 020 7404 3222
E-mail: admin@bapam.org.uk

Website:
http://www.bapam.org.uk
Basic information about BAPAM.

Enquiries:
Enquiries to: Chief Executive
Other contacts: (1) Administrator; (2) Clinic
Manager; for (1) Membership; (2) Volunteering,
helpline, clinic.

Founded:
1984

Organisation type and purpose:
National organisation, membership association,
registered charity (charity number 10823295),
training organisation, research organisation.
To provide medical assessment and diagnosis for
performers with performance-related injury and/or
illness.

Subject coverage:
Medical and psychological problems of performing
artists.

**Museum or gallery collection, archive, or library
special collection:**
Small specialist library

Trade and statistical information:
Data on specific medical problems of performers.

Printed publications:
Journal (2 times a year)
Newsletter (quarterly)
Journal, Newsletter and Membership (£35 a year)

Access to staff:
Contact by letter, by telephone and by e-mail.
Appointment necessary.
Hours: Tues to Fri, 0900 to 1830; Mon, 0900 to 1500

Access to building, collection or gallery:
Prior appointment required

Access for disabled people:
Lift and level floors

Subsidiary body:
Association of Medical Advisors to British
Orchestras

BRITISH ASSOCIATION FOR PERINATAL MEDICINE

Acronym or abbreviation: BAPM

50 Hallam Street, London, W1W 6DE

Tel: 020 7307 5627
Fax: 020 7307 5601
E-mail: bapm@rcpch.ac.uk

Website:
http://www.bapm-london.org
All information on the Association including
publications

Enquiries:
Enquiries to: Administrator
Direct e-mail: bryan.gill@leedsth.nhs.uk

Founded:
1976

Organisation type and purpose:
Professional body.

Subject coverage:
All aspects of perinatal medicine.

Printed publications:
Various documents available for purchase and for
free download from the website including:
Guidelines Relating to the Birth of Extremely
Immature Babies (March 2000)
National Census of Availability of Neonatal
Intensive Care (September 2000)
Standards for Hospitals Providing Neonatal
Intensive and High Dependency Care (2nd ed
December 2001)
Training Needs of Professionals Responsible for
Resuscitation of Babies at Birth (October 1998)

Publications list:
Available online

Access to staff:
Contact by letter, by telephone, by fax and by e-
mail
Hours: Mon to Fri, 0900 to 1700

BRITISH ASSOCIATION FOR PRINT AND COMMUNICATION

Acronym or abbreviation: BAPC

Catalyst House, 720 Centennial Road, Centennial
Park, Elstree, Herts, WD6 3SY

Tel: 020 8736 5862
Fax: 020 8224 9090
E-mail: info@bapc.co.uk

Website:
http://www.bapc.co.uk

Enquiries:
Enquiries to: Executive Director
Other contacts: Chairman for public relations

Founded:
1978

Organisation type and purpose:
National organisation, trade association
(membership is by subscription, qualification).

Subject coverage:
Trade association within the print sector, providing
its members with a wide range of facilities and
benefits to help printers survive and succeed,
including free legal advice, marketing support,
technical assistance, product assessment, seminars,
conferences, magazines and newsletters, tailored
insurance and credit-check scheme, health, safety
and employment hotline, arbitration, mentoring
and distance-learning schemes.

Access to staff:
Contact by letter, by telephone, by e-mail and via
website
Hours: Mon to Fri, 0900 to 1700

Access to building, collection or gallery:
Prior appointment required

BRITISH ASSOCIATION FOR PSYCHOLOGICAL TYPE

Acronym or abbreviation: BAPT

17 Royal Crescent, Cheltenham, Gloucestershire,
GL50 3DA

Tel: 01242 282990
Fax: 01242 282990
E-mail: office@bapt.org.uk

Website:
http://www.bapt.org.uk

Enquiries:
Enquiries to: General Secretary

Founded:
1989

Organisation type and purpose:
Professional body (membership is by subscription),
present number of members: 200, voluntary
organisation, registered charity (charity number
1045772), consultancy.

Subject coverage:
Advice on Psychological Type including
workshops and register of practitioners.

Information services:
Library of Psychological Type

Library catalogue:
All or part available in-house and in print

Publications list:
Available online

Access to staff:
Contact by letter, by telephone and by e-mail
Hours: Mon to Fri, 0900 to 1700

Access to building, collection or gallery:
No access other than to staff

BRITISH ASSOCIATION FOR PSYCHOPHARMACOLOGY

Acronym or abbreviation: BAP

36 Cambridge Place, Hills Road, Cambridge, CB2
1NS

Tel: 01223 358395
Fax: 01223 321268
E-mail: susan@bap.org.uk

Website:
http://www.bap.org.uk

Enquiries:
Enquiries to: Administrator
Direct tel: 01223 358428

Founded:
1974

continued overleaf

Organisation type and purpose:
International organisation, learned society (membership is by subscription), present number of members: 1050, registered charity (charity number 277825).

Subject coverage:
Psychopharmacology: behavioural pharmacology, neurochemical pharmacology, psychopharmacological treatment in psychiatry.

Printed publications:
Journal of Psychopharmacology (8 times a year, free to members, on subscription to others)
Newsletters (for members)

Access to staff:
Contact by letter, by fax, by e-mail and via website
Hours: Mon to Fri, 0900 to 1700

BRITISH ASSOCIATION FOR SEXUAL AND RELATIONSHIP THERAPY

Acronym or abbreviation: BASRT

PO Box 13686, London, SW20 9ZH

Tel: 020 8543 2707
Fax: 020 8543 2707
E-mail: info@basrt.org.uk

Website:
http://www.basrt.org.uk

Enquiries:
Enquiries to: Administrator

Founded:
1976

Organisation type and purpose:
National organisation, membership association (membership is by subscription, qualification), present number of members: 760, voluntary organisation, registered charity (charity number 1101961).
Professional body for clinicians and therapists who treat sexual and relationship problems.
To further education of professionals working in field of sexual and relationship therapy, to set and maintain ethical standards, to promote research and raise public awareness of sexual and relationship therapy.

Subject coverage:
A professional body for clinicians and therapists who treat sexual and relationship problems.

Printed publications:
Sexual and Relationship Therapy (journal, quarterly)
List of qualified practitioners
Order printed publications from: Taylor & Francis plc, Rankine Road, Basingstoke, RG24 8PR; tel: 020 7017 6318; e-mail: info@tandf.co.uk

Publications list:
Available in print

Access to staff:
Contact by letter, by telephone, by fax, by e-mail and via website
Hours: Mon to Fri, 0900 to 1430

BRITISH ASSOCIATION FOR SHOOTING AND CONSERVATION

Marford Mill, Chester Road, Rossett, Wrexham, Clwyd, LL12 0HL

Tel: 01244 573000
Fax: 01244 573001
E-mail: enq@basc.org.uk

Website:
http://www.basc.org.uk
About shooting and British Association for Shooting and Conservation.

Enquiries:
Enquiries to: Head of Media and Communications
Direct tel: 01244 573032
Direct fax: 01244 573040

Other contacts: Press Officer

Founded:
1908

Organisation type and purpose:
Membership association (membership is by subscription), present number of members: 120,000.
Cross-party lobbying organisation, representing United Kingdom shooting sports.

Subject coverage:
Firearms, political lobbying, public relations, land management, education and training, ecology, quarry species management, research.

Trade and statistical information:
Data on shooting sports, quarry species, firearms ownership, access issues, and shooting and conservation.

Printed publications:
Codes of Practice
Factsheets
Guides
Handbook of Shooting
Magazine (quarterly)
Specialist newsletters

Publications list:
Available in print

Access to staff:
Contact by letter, by telephone, by fax, by e-mail and via website
Hours: Mon to Fri, 0900 to 1700

Other addresses:
BASC Northern Ireland
    Courtyard Cottage, Galgorm Castle, Ballymena, Co Antrim, BT42 1HL
BASC Scotland
    Trochry, Dunkeld, Tayside, PH8 0DY; tel: 01350 723226; fax: 01350 723227; e-mail: scotland@basc.org.uk

BRITISH ASSOCIATION FOR THE STUDY AND PREVENTION OF CHILD ABUSE AND NEGLECT

Acronym or abbreviation: BASPCAN

17 Priory Street, York, YO1 6ET

Tel: 01904 613605
Fax: 01904 642239
E-mail: baspcan@baspcan.org.uk

Website:
http://www.baspcan.org.uk

Founded:
1979

Organisation type and purpose:
Professional body (membership is by subscription), present number of members: 1,800, registered charity (charity number 279119).
Networking.
Multi-disciplinary networking association for professionals working in the field of child protection. Membership applications invited.

Subject coverage:
Child abuse.

Printed publications:
Child Abuse Review (newsletter, quarterly, free to members)
Journal (6 times a year, free to members)

Access to staff:
Contact by letter, by telephone, by e-mail and via website
Hours: Mon to Fri, 0900 to 1700

BRITISH ASSOCIATION OF ADVISERS AND LECTURERS IN PHYSICAL EDUCATION

Acronym or abbreviation: BAALPE

Sports Development Centre, Loughborough University, Loughborough, Leicestershire, LE11 3TU

Tel: 01509 228378
Fax: 01509 228378
E-mail: baalpe@lboro.ac.uk

Website:
http://www.baalpe.org

Enquiries:
Enquiries to: General Secretary
Direct tel: 01746 769487
Direct fax: 01746 769487
Other contacts: 1) Finance and Membership Officer; 2) Continuing Professional Development (CPD) Manager for (1) Finance and membership issues (2) CPD/training.

Founded:
1921

Organisation type and purpose:
National organisation, professional body, trade union (membership is by qualification, election or invitation), present number of members: 450.
The development and maintenance of high standards in all areas and all phases of physical education in schools.

Subject coverage:
Teaching and coaching of physical activities; equipment and apparatus; training of teachers in primary and secondary schools; health of young people; safety in physical activities; consultancy on safe practice providing expert witnesses for court cases related to physical education/leisure; recreation, leisure, health, safety related to physical education and recreation; curriculum and management issues in physical education; initial teacher's training and CPD for PE.

Museum or gallery collection, archive, or library special collection:
Bulletin copies since 1920s (foundation time)

Non-library collection catalogue:
All or part available online

Printed publications:
Bulletin of physical education (quarterly)
Order printed publications from: Dudley LEA (BAALPE Publications)
Saltwells EDC, Bowling Green Road, Dudley, West Midlands, tel: 01384 813706/7, fax: 01384 813801

Electronic and video publications:
Videos

Publications list:
Available online and in print

Access to staff:
Contact by letter, by telephone, by fax, by e-mail and via website
Hours: Permanent 24-hour answerphone on 01509 228378.

Affiliated to:
Central Council of Physical Recreation
Fédération Internationale Éducation Physique

BRITISH ASSOCIATION OF ART THERAPISTS

Acronym or abbreviation: BAAT

5 Tavistock Place, London, WC1H 9SN

Tel: 020 7383 3774
Fax: 020 7431 2450
E-mail: baat@ukgateway.net

Website:
http://www.baat.co.uk

Enquiries:
Enquiries to: Honorary Secretary

Founded:
1964

Organisation type and purpose:
Professional body, voluntary organisation.

Subject coverage:
Art therapy and art education in special schools; training in art therapy; research in art therapy; professional standards; conditions of work; art therapy in all areas of child, adult and elderly care; mental health; learning disabilities; physical and neurological problems; dementia; autism etc.

Printed publications:
BAAT Register of Art Therapists (price £5)
Code of Ethics and Principles of Professional Practice (price £2.50)
Inscape (journal of BAAT twice a year, Individual subscription £11; Institutional subscription £21)

Access to staff:
Contact by letter, by telephone, by fax, by e-mail and via website
Hours: Mon to Fri, 0900 to 1700

Access to building, collection or gallery:
No access other than to staff

BRITISH ASSOCIATION OF AUDIOLOGICAL PHYSICIANS

Acronym or abbreviation: BAAP

c/o Department of Neuro-otology, The National Hospital for Neurology and Neurosurgery, Queen Square, London, WC1N 3BG

Tel: 020 7837 3611 ext 3386
Fax: 029 7829 8775
E-mail: honsec.baap@virgin.net

Website:
http://www.baap.org.uk
Information regarding the hospital speciality of audiological medicine. Names of contacts and some physicians. Curriculum for trainees; constitution, policy document.

Enquiries:
Enquiries to: Honorary Secretary

Founded:
1976

Organisation type and purpose:
National organisation, professional body (membership is by subscription, qualification, election or invitation), present number of members: 90.

Subject coverage:
Audiological medicine; audiology; hearing aids; auditory rehabilitation; hearing loss; balance disorders; neuro-otology; auditory electrophysiology. Vestibular medicine; vestibular rehabilitation; noise-induced hearing loss; cochlear implants; universal newborn screening for hearing loss; auto-immune inner ear disease.

Printed publications:
Career's Focus Article: BMJ
Careers leaflet
Policy document
Guidelines for referral
Promotional poster

Publications list:
Available online

Access to staff:
Contact by letter, by telephone, by fax, by e-mail and via website
Hours: Mon to Fri, 0900 to 1700

Connections with:
National Council for Professionals in Audiology (NCPA)
c/o Ellen Godden BSA, Brighton Road, Reading

BRITISH ASSOCIATION OF AVIATION CONSULTANTS

Acronym or abbreviation: BAAC

Queen Anne's Gate Buildings, London, SW1H 9HP

Tel: 0207 630 5358
Fax: 0207 828 0667
E-mail: committee@baac.org.uk

Website:
http://www.baac.org.uk

Enquiries:
Enquiries to: Chairman
Direct e-mail: peter.mw@jacobs-consultancy.com
Other contacts: Honorary Secretary for administration.

Founded:
1972

Organisation type and purpose:
Professional body (membership is by qualification), present number of members: 80.
Aviation consultancy.

Subject coverage:
Aviation worldwide.

Printed publications:
Register of Members (annual)

Publications list:
Available online and in print

Access to staff:
Contact by e-mail
Hours: Mon to Fri, 0900 to 1700

BRITISH ASSOCIATION OF COLLIERY MANAGEMENT, TECHNICAL, ENERGY AND ADMINISTRATIVE MANAGEMENT

Acronym or abbreviation: BACM-TEAM

17 South Parade, Doncaster, South Yorkshire, DN1 2DR

Tel: 01302 815551
Fax: 01302 815552
E-mail: enquiries@bacmteam.org.uk

Website:
http://www.bacmteam.org.uk

Enquiries:
Enquiries to: General Secretary
Other contacts: Office Manager

Founded:
1947

Organisation type and purpose:
Trade union (membership is by subscription), present number of members: 4300.

Subject coverage:
Mining, European energy, employment law.

Printed publications:
BACMTEAM Focus (quarterly newsletter to members)

Access to staff:
Contact by letter, by telephone and by e-mail
Hours: Mon to Fri, 0830 to 1700

Access to building, collection or gallery:
No prior appointment required

Affiliated to:
TUC

Member of:
ECSC
FICME
MIF

BRITISH ASSOCIATION OF CONFERENCE DESTINATIONS

Acronym or abbreviation: BACD

6th Floor, Charles House, 148–149 Great Charles Street, Birmingham, B3 3HT

Tel: 0121 212 1400
Fax: 0121 212 3131
E-mail: info@bacd.org.uk

Website:
http://www.bacd.org.uk

Enquiries:
Enquiries to: Executive Director

Other contacts: Marketing Executive for library and information services.

Founded:
1969

Organisation type and purpose:
Trade association.
Association of local authorities, convention bureaux and tourist boards.
To promote the British Isles as a conference destination.

Subject coverage:
Conference and exhibition facilities in British Isles, information/research on the conference industry, consultancy advice on conference infrastructure developments.

Museum or gallery collection, archive, or library special collection:
Library of reports and publications

Trade and statistical information:
Data on the value, size, and trends etc, in the conference and business tourism sectors.

Printed publications:
Surveys and papers including:
BACD Library Index
British Conference Destinations Directory (2002 ed., £15 plus £1.50 p&p)
Conferences: A 21st Century Industry (1998, Longmans)

Electronic and video publications:
Conference organiser database information available for purchase on disk

Access to staff:
Contact by letter, by telephone, by fax and by e-mail. Appointment necessary.
Hours: Mon to Fri, 0900 to 1700

Member of:
The Council for Travel and Tourism
LGM House, Mill Green Road, Haywards Heath, West Sussex, RH16 1XQ; tel: 01444 452277; fax: 01444 452244

BRITISH ASSOCIATION OF DENTAL NURSES

Acronym or abbreviation: BADN

11 Pharos Street, Fleetwood, Lancashire, FY7 6BG

Tel: 01253 778631
Fax: 01253 773266
E-mail: admin@badn.org.uk

Website:
http://www.badn.org.uk

Enquiries:
Enquiries to: Executive Secretary
Direct tel: 01253 778800
Direct e-mail: xs@badn.org.uk

Founded:
1940

Organisation type and purpose:
Professional body, trade union (membership is by subscription).

Subject coverage:
Education, training, employment, salaries and conditions of employment, advice seminars, annual conference, local group network, national groups for DNs in specific areas of dentistry.

Museum or gallery collection, archive, or library special collection:
Library available to members

Printed publications:
British Dental Nurses Journal (quarterly, UK £35, overseas £40)

Publications list:
Available in print

Access to staff:
Contact by letter, by telephone, by fax, by e-mail and via website
Hours: Mon to Fri, 0900 to 1700

BRITISH ASSOCIATION OF DERMATOLOGISTS

Acronym or abbreviation: BAD

4 Fitzroy Square, London, W1T 5HQ

Tel: 020 7383 0266
Fax: 020 7388 5263
E-mail: admin@bad.org.uk

Website:
http://www.skinhealth.co.uk
Information on skin disease and dermatology in the UK.

Enquiries:
Enquiries to: Executive Officer

Founded:
1920

Organisation type and purpose:
Learned society, professional body (membership is by qualification, election or invitation), present number of members: 800.
A body of international specialists of dermatology formed to promote and represent the best interests of dermatologists and patients affected by diseases of the skin. Its objects are: to promote for public benefit greater knowledge and understanding of diseases of the skin, and improve the teaching of dermatology at all levels by organising and sponsoring scientific meetings, conferences and seminars; to stimulate and promote appropriate medical and scientific research; to collect, evaluate and disseminate data and information on all matters relating to the well-being of patients.

Subject coverage:
Dermatology.

Museum or gallery collection, archive, or library special collection:
A small specialised library of historically significant books in relation to dermatology, which can only be viewed privately since it is a private collection controlled from the Association's offices
Willan Library

Printed publications:
British Journal of Dermatology

Access to staff:
Contact by letter
Hours: Mon to Fri, 0900 to 1700

BRITISH ASSOCIATION OF DRAMATHERAPISTS

Acronym or abbreviation: BADth

Waverley, Battledown Approach, Cheltenham, Gloucestershire, GL52 6RE

Tel: 01242 235515
E-mail: enquiries@badth.org.uk

Website:
http://www.badth.org.uk

Enquiries:
Enquiries to: Administrator

Founded:
1977

Organisation type and purpose:
Professional body (membership is by qualification, election or invitation), present number of members: 650, voluntary organisation, training organisation, research organisation, publishing house.

Information services:
Information about dramatherapy and dramatherapy training.

Printed publications:
The Dramatherapy Journal (3 times per year)
The Prompt Newsletter (quarterly)
Order printed publications from: e-mail: enquiries@badth.org.uk

Publications list:
Available in print

Access to staff:
Contact by letter, by telephone, by e-mail and via website
Hours: Mon to Fri, variable hours

BRITISH ASSOCIATION OF FASTENER DISTRIBUTORS

Formal name: British Association of Fastener Distributors Limited
Acronym or abbreviation: BAFD

136 Hagley Road, Edgbaston, Birmingham, B16 9PN

Tel: 0121 454 4141
E-mail: info@bafd.org

Website:
http://www.bafd.org

Enquiries:
Enquiries to: General Secretary

Founded:
1945

Organisation type and purpose:
National organisation, trade association (membership by subscription), present number of members: 60.

Subject coverage:
Distribution of fasteners and construction fixings.

Access to staff:
Contact by e-mail
Hours: Mon to Fri, 0900 to 1700

Affiliated to:
European Fastener Distributors Association (EFDA)
  Germany

BRITISH ASSOCIATION OF FRIENDS OF MUSEUMS

Acronym or abbreviation: BAFM

c/o Deborah Woodland MSc, BAfM Hon. Secretary, The Shrubbery, 14 Church Street, Whitchurch, Hampshire, RG28 7AB

Tel: 0870 224 8904
E-mail: secretary@bafm.org.uk

Website:
http://www.bafm.org.uk

Enquiries:
Enquiries to: Honorary Secretary
Other contacts: Administrator

Organisation type and purpose:
National organisation, membership association, voluntary organisation, registered charity (charity number 270253), museum, art gallery, historic building, house or site, consultancy.
To inform, encourage and support all those, whether in groups or as individuals, who wish to work in and for museums in a voluntary capacity.

Subject coverage:
Museums, the organisation and management of friends, groups, supporters and volunteers in museums of all kinds. Setting up a group, good practice, model constitution, contacts worldwide.

Printed publications:
The Handbook for Heritage Volunteer Managers and Administrators (£5)
Handbook for Friends – How to set up and Run a Group of Friends for your Local Museum, Art Gallery, Theatre, Historic House, Garden or Archaeological Site (£6.80)
Insurance for Friends of Museums (£2)
Newsletter (3 times a year, free to members)
Information Sheets (14, free to members)

Publications list:
Available online and in print

Access to staff:
Contact by letter, by telephone, by fax, by e-mail and via website. Appointment necessary.
Hours: Mon to Fri, 0900 to 1700

Links with:
Association of Independent Museums
Museum Association
World Federation of Friends of Museums
  Paris, France

BRITISH ASSOCIATION OF GREEN CROP DRIERS LIMITED

Acronym or abbreviation: BAGCD

March Hares, Montagu Road, Canwick, Lincoln, LN4 2RW

Tel: 01522 523322
Fax: 01522 568539
E-mail: info@bagcd.org

Website:
http://www.bagcd.org

Enquiries:
Enquiries to: Secretary

Founded:
1963

Organisation type and purpose:
National organisation, trade association (membership is by election or invitation), present number of members: 30, manufacturing industry.

Subject coverage:
All production, political and nutritional aspects of drying grass and lucerne for animal feed.

Access to staff:
Contact by letter, by telephone, by fax and by e-mail
Hours: Mon to Fri, 0900 to 1700

Access to building, collection or gallery:
No access other than to staff

Links with:
European Dehydrators Association – Commission Intersyndicale des Deshydrateurs Européens (CIDE)
  tel: +33 2 33 85 12 38; fax: +33 2 33 85 12 38; e-mail: ericguillemot@aol.com

BRITISH ASSOCIATION OF LANDSCAPE INDUSTRIES

Acronym or abbreviation: BALI

Landscape House, NAC, Stoneleigh Park, Warwickshire, CV8 2LG

Tel: 024 7669 0333
Fax: 024 7669 0077
E-mail: contact@bali.org.uk

Website:
http://www.bali.co.uk

Enquiries:
Enquiries to: Chief Executive

Founded:
1972

Organisation type and purpose:
Trade association (membership is by subscription, qualification, present number of members: 645, training organisation.
Industry training organisation for landscaping.
BALI is the national body representing Landscape Contractors in the UK.

Subject coverage:
Environmental landscaping, all landscape work and supplies, all facets of landscaping.

Printed publications:
BALI Who's Who Membership Directory is available to potential clients, architects and designers on request
Model tender documents

Access to staff:
Contact by letter and by telephone
Hours: Mon to Fri, 0900 to 1700

Founder member of:
Confederation of British Industry (CBI)

Industry Lead Body for Amenity Horticulture
(ILBAH)
Joint Council for Landscape Industries (JCLI)
National Specialist Contractors Council (NSCC)

BRITISH ASSOCIATION OF LIBERTARIAN FEMINISTS

25 Chapter Chambers, Esterbrook Street, London,
SW1P 4NN

Tel: 020 7821 5502
Fax: 020 7834 2031
E-mail: admin@libertarian.co.uk

Website:
http://www.libertarian.co.uk

Enquiries:
Enquiries to: Director
Direct e-mail: chris@rand.demon.co.uk

Publications list:
Available online

BRITISH ASSOCIATION OF MOUNTAIN GUIDES

Acronym or abbreviation: BMG

Siabod Cottage, Capel Curig, Conwy, LL24 0ES

Tel: 01690 720386
Fax: 01690 720248
E-mail: guiding@bmg.org.uk

Website:
http://www.bmg.org.uk

Enquiries:
Enquiries to: Honorary Secretary
Direct tel: 07878 303229
Other contacts: President (for discipline, conduct)

Founded:
1975

Organisation type and purpose:
Professional body (membership is by
qualification), present number of members: 183,
service industry.

Subject coverage:
Guides for climbing and mountaineering, climbing
instruction, advice and consultancy on
mountaineering affairs.

Electronic and video publications:
News from the Mountains (3 times a year, in-
house, members only)

Access to staff:
Contact by letter, by telephone, by fax and by e-
mail
Hours: Mon to Fri, 0900 to 1700

Links with:
Union Internationale des Associations de Guides
de Montagne (The International Federation of
Mountain Guide Associations)
Armin Oehrli, Sekretar IVBV/UIAGM,
Badweidli, 3780 Gstaad, Switzerland; tel: +41
(0)33 744 54 77; fax: +41 (0)33 744 54 77; website:
http://www.ivbv.info

BRITISH ASSOCIATION OF NUMISMATIC SOCIETIES

Acronym or abbreviation: BANS

The Manchester Museum, The University of
Manchester, Oxford Road, Manchester M13 9PL

Tel: 0161 275 2643
E-mail: phyllis.stoddart@manchester.ac.uk

Website:
http://www.coinclubs.freeserve.co.uk
Lists member societies, publications and
conferences.

Enquiries:
Enquiries to: Honorary Secretary

Founded:
1953

Organisation type and purpose:
National organisation, membership association
(membership is by subscription), present number
of members: 60.
A coordinating body for liaison and research
among local numismatics societies.

Subject coverage:
Numismatics.

**Museum or gallery collection, archive, or library
special collection:**
Collections of slides of coins for lecturing purposes
(for loan to affiliated societies)

Printed publications:
Doris Stockwell Memorial Papers

Electronic and video publications:
Videotaped lectures

Publications list:
Available in print

Access to staff:
Contact by letter, by telephone and by e-mail
Hours: Mon to Fri, 0900 to 1700

BRITISH ASSOCIATION OF PAPER HISTORIANS

Acronym or abbreviation: BAPH

c/o Ian Hendry, 27 North End, Longhoughton,
Alnwick, NE66 3JG

Tel: 01665 577988
E-mail: ifhendry@btinternet.com

Website:
http://www.baph.org.uk

Enquiries:
Enquiries to: Membership Secretary

Founded:
1989

Organisation type and purpose:
Membership association (membership is by
subscription).

Subject coverage:
Paper making history, paper mill sites, raw
materials, communities; paper watermarks, users
and conservation.

Printed publications:
BAPH (quarterly)
BAPH News
Conference Papers

Publications list:
Available online

Access to staff:
Contact by letter, by e-mail and via website
Hours: Mon to Fri, 0900 to 1700

BRITISH ASSOCIATION OF PHARMACEUTICAL WHOLESALERS

Acronym or abbreviation: BAPW

90 Long Acre, London, WC2E 9RA

Tel: 020 7031 0590
Fax: 020 7031 0591
E-mail: mail@bapw.net

Website:
http://www.bapw.net/

Enquiries:
Enquiries to: Executive Director

Founded:
1967

Organisation type and purpose:
Trade association (membership is by subscription).

Subject coverage:
Pharmaceuticals.

Printed publications:
Members Directory

Access to staff:
Contact by letter, by telephone, by fax and by e-
mail. Appointment necessary.
Hours: Mon to Thu, 0900 to 1700; Fri, 0900 to 1600

Affiliated to:
Groupement International de la Répartition
Pharmaceutique Européenne (GIRP)
International Federation of Pharmaceutical
Wholesalers (IFPW)

BRITISH ASSOCIATION OF PICTURE LIBRARIES AND AGENCIES

Acronym or abbreviation: BAPLA

59 Tranquil Vale, Blackheath, London, SE3 0BS

Tel: 020 8297 1198
Fax: 020 8852 7211
E-mail: enquiries@bapla.org.uk

Website:
http://www.bapla.org.uk
Search accredited libraries and agencies by name
or subject. Details of vacancies in the industry, the
work of BAPLA and its publications.

Enquiries:
Enquiries to: Administrator

Founded:
1975

Organisation type and purpose:
National organisation, advisory body, trade
association (membership is by subscription),
present number of members: 400.
Free referral service to picture researchers to assist
them in locating the best source of photographic
imagery.
To develop and maintain a professional framework
for the industry.

Subject coverage:
Picture libraries.

**Museum or gallery collection, archive, or library
special collection:**
Members' specialist collections

Trade and statistical information:
1999 UK Picture Library Industry Survey. Data on
UK Picture Industry.
2000 European Picture Library Industry Survey.
Pricing Trends Survey 2001.

Non-library collection catalogue:
All or part available online

Publications list:
Available online

Access to staff:
Contact by letter, by telephone, by fax, by e-mail
and via website. Appointment necessary.
Hours: Mon to Fri, 0930 to 1800

Access to building, collection or gallery:
By appointment only

Member organisation of:
British Copyright Council
British Photographers Liaison Committee (BPLC)
9–10 Domingo Street, London, EC1Y 0TA
CEPIC
Picture Agency Council of America
Picture Industry Council

BRITISH ASSOCIATION OF PSYCHOTHERAPISTS

Acronym or abbreviation: BAP

37 Mapesbury Road, London, NW2 4HJ

Tel: 020 8438 2414
Fax: 020 8452 0310
E-mail: library@bap-psychotherapy.org

Website:
http://www.bap-psychotherapy.org

continued overleaf

Enquiries:
Enquiries to: Librarian

Founded:
1951

Organisation type and purpose:
National organisation, professional body, membership association (membership is by qualification, election or invitation), present number of members: 500, registered charity (charity number 281720), training organisation.

Subject coverage:
Analytic psychotherapy (child, adolescent and adult), registration of psychotherapists, training in adult and child psychotherapy (Jungian and Freudian), clinical assessment and referral service.

Museum or gallery collection, archive, or library special collection:
Books and journals on psychotherapy

Library catalogue:
All or part available online

Printed publications:
Journal
Details of short courses
General information booklet
List of qualified practitioners
Monographs of papers from public conferences
Pamphlets on the Clinical Service and Reduced Fee
  Scheme
Training Prospectus – Child and Adult
Order printed publications from: Administrator

Publications list:
Available in print

Access to staff:
Contact by letter, by telephone, by fax, by e-mail and via website. Appointment necessary.
Hours: Mon to Fri, 0930 to 1700

Access for disabled people:
Parking provided, toilet facilities
Special comments: No lift to the 1st floor.

Constituent bodies:
British Psychoanalytic Council
  Suite 7, 19–23 Wedmore Street, London, N19
  4RU; tel: 020 7561 9240; fax: 020 7561 9005; e-
  mail: mail@psychoanalytic-council.org; website:
  http://www.psychoanalytic-council.org

BRITISH ASSOCIATION OF REMOVERS

Acronym or abbreviation: BAR

Tangent House, 62 Exchange Road, Watford, Herts, WD18 0TG

Tel: 01923 699480
Fax: 01923 699481
E-mail: info@bar.co.uk

Website:
http://www.bar.co.uk
The British Association of Removers is the largest and most established trade association for the professional removals and storage industry in the UK.

Enquiries:
Enquiries to: General Secretary
Direct e-mail: james.falkner@bar.co.uk
Other contacts: Executive Assistant

Founded:
1900

Organisation type and purpose:
Trade association.

Subject coverage:
Removal, storage, shipping etc, of household goods and effects and commercial, office furniture and effects.

Printed publications:
Removals and Storage (monthly)

Access to staff:
Contact by letter, by telephone, by fax, by e-mail and via website

Hours: Mon to Fri, 0900 to 1700

Affiliated to:
Fédération des Entreprises de Déménagement du Marché Commun (FEDEMAC)
Fédération Internationale des Déménageurs Internationaux (FIDI)

Associated with:
Freight Transport Association
Road Haulage Association

BRITISH ASSOCIATION OF SETTLEMENTS AND SOCIAL ACTION CENTRES

Acronym or abbreviation: bassac

33 Corsham Street, London, N1 6DR

Tel: 0845 241 0375
Fax: 0845 241 0376
E-mail: info@bassac.org.uk

Website:
http://www.bassac.org.uk

Enquiries:
Enquiries to: Administrator

Founded:
c. 1919–20

Organisation type and purpose:
National organisation, membership association (membership is by subscription), present number of members: 100, voluntary organisation, registered charity (charity number 1028784). Network of 70 independent organisations.

Subject coverage:
Social welfare, community development, member settlements and social action centres, inner-city projects, urban regeneration, community work, funding (members only).

Library catalogue:
All or part available in-house

Printed publications:
see website

Publications list:
Available online

Access to staff:
Contact by letter, by telephone, by fax, by e-mail and via website. Appointment necessary.
Hours: Mon to Fri, 0930 to 1730
Special comments: Primarily, information provided to members.

Access for disabled people:
Level entry, access to all public areas, toilet facilities; lift

Member organisation of:
International Federation of Settlements (IFS)
  Canada; tel: +1 416 469 5711; e-mail: ifs.agnes@
  woodgreen.org

BRITISH ASSOCIATION OF SKI PATROLLERS (BASP UK LTD)

Acronym or abbreviation: BASP

20 Lorn Drive, Glencoe, Ballachulish, Argyll, PH49 4HR

Tel: 01855 811443
E-mail: firstaid@basp.org.uk

Website:
http://www.basp.org.uk
Ski patrol. First aid training, membership, international ski patrol, newsletters.

Enquiries:
Enquiries to: Administrator

Founded:
1987

Organisation type and purpose:
Professional body (membership is by subscription), present number of members: 120, education, suitable for ages: 18+, training organisation.

Training and grading of ski patrollers, first aid training.

Subject coverage:
Ski patrolling, first aid training, specialist advanced mountain medicine.

Printed publications:
BASP Outdoor First Aid and Safety Manual (ISBN 09528435 52)

Publications list:
Available in print

Access to staff:
Contact by letter, by telephone, by e-mail and via website
Hours: Mon to Fri, 0900 to 1700

BRITISH ASSOCIATION OF SNOWSPORTS INSTRUCTORS

Acronym or abbreviation: BASI

Morlich House, 17 The Square, Grantown-on-Spey, Morayshire, PH26 3HG

Tel: 01479 861717
Fax: 01479 873657
E-mail: basi@basi.org.uk

Website:
http://www.basi.org.uk

Enquiries:
Enquiries to: Chief Executive
Direct e-mail: fergus@basi.org.uk

Founded:
1963

Formerly called:
British Association of Ski Instructors BASI (year of change 2005)

Organisation type and purpose:
Membership association (membership is by subscription, qualification), present number of members: 5,700, training organisation.

Subject coverage:
Training and grading of snowsport instructors; skiing and ski teaching; snowboard teaching.

Printed publications:
Alpine Manual: features more than 200
  photographs and diagrams and reference
  material for professionals (£25 plus £5 p&p)
BASI News (quarterly, members)
Information Pack
Snowboard Handbook (£10)
Telemark handbook (£10)

Electronic and video publications:
Various technical skiing videos
Boarding Skool 1 – beginners s/b (video, £19.95
  plus p&p)
Central Theme Video: designed to complement
  manual (£10 plus £2 p&p)
Boarding Skool 2 – advanced s/b (video, £19.95
  plus p&p)
CD-ROM Manual (£30 plus £1 p&p)
Ski Skool – beginners ski video (£14.95)
Ski Skool again – advanced ski video (£19.95)
Order electronic and video publications from:
roz@basi.org.uk

Publications list:
Available online and in print

Access to staff:
Contact by letter, by telephone, by fax, by e-mail, in person and via website. Appointment necessary. Letter of introduction required.
Hours: Mon to Fri, 0900 to 1700

Access to building, collection or gallery:
Through reception
Hours: Mon to Fri, 0900 to 1700

Access for disabled people:
Parking provided, ramped entry
Hours: as above
Special comments: Ground floor access only.

Affiliated to:
Snowsports GB

BRITISH ASSOCIATION OF SOCIAL WORKERS

Acronym or abbreviation: BASW

16 Kent Street, Birmingham, B5 6RD

Tel: 0121 622 3911
Fax: 0121 622 4860
E-mail: reception@basw.co.uk

Website:
http://www.basw.co.uk

Founded:
1970

Organisation type and purpose:
Professional body.

Subject coverage:
Social work and social welfare in all field and residential settings (public, charitable and private agencies and independent practice), including child care, child abuse, mental health, learning disabilities, old age, physical handicap, personal and family problems, adult and juvenile offenders, community work, poverty, social services management, education and training in social services, social services employment.

Museum or gallery collection, archive, or library special collection:
Archives of the founding associations

Printed publications:
BASW Publications (books and pamphlets)
British Journal of Social Work (8 times a year)
Practice (4 times a year)
Professional Social Work (monthly)
Venture Press Books
Practitioner Guides Series (Expanding Horizons Series)

Publications list:
Available in print

Access to staff:
Contact by letter, by telephone, by fax and by e-mail

Affiliated to:
International Federation of Social Workers

BRITISH ASSOCIATION OF SPORTS AND EXERCISE SCIENCES

Acronym or abbreviation: BASES

Chelsea close, off Amberley road, Armley, Leeds, LS12 4HP

Tel: 0113 289 1020
Fax: 0113 231 9606 and 0113 289 1020
E-mail: jbairstow@bases.org.uk

Website:
http://www.bases.org.uk

Enquiries:
Enquiries to: Executive Officer
Direct e-mail: cpalmer@bases.org.uk
Other contacts: Office Manager for general information and membership.

Founded:
1983

Organisation type and purpose:
Learned society, professional body, membership association (membership is by subscription, qualification), present number of members: 2855.

Subject coverage:
Sport and exercise sciences; psychology, physiology, biomechanics, nutrition, elite sport, health promotion, exercise and associated careers.

Printed publications:
Annual Report (free)
BASES Newsletter (4 times a year)
Accreditation Sheets
Advice List/Career Information
Biomechanical Analysis of Movement in Sport and Exercises (£20)
Members Handbook
Physiological Testing Guidelines (£30)

Access to staff:
Contact by letter, by telephone, by fax, by e-mail and via website
Hours: Mon to Fri, 0830 to 1645

Access to building, collection or gallery:
No prior appointment required
Hours: Mon to Fri, 0900 to 1700

Access for disabled people:
Parking provided, ramped entry, toilet facilities

Affiliated to:
European Federation of Sports Psychology
International Society of Biomechanics

BRITISH ASSOCIATION OF SURGICAL ONCOLOGY

Acronym or abbreviation: BASO~ACS

at the Royal College of Surgeons, 35–43 Lincoln's Inn Fields, London, WC2A 3PE

Tel: 020 7405 5612
Fax: 020 7404 6574

Website:
http://www.baso.org.uk

Enquiries:
Enquiries to: Honorary Secretary

Founded:
1972

Organisation type and purpose:
Learned society (membership is by subscription), present number of members: 650, registered charity (charity number 269736).

Subject coverage:
Cancer surgery; oncology.

Library catalogue:
All or part available online

Printed publications:
European Journal of Surgical Oncology

Access to staff:
Contact by letter
Hours: Mon to Fri, 0900 to 1700

BRITISH ASSOCIATION OF TEACHERS OF DANCING

Acronym or abbreviation: BATD

23 Marywood Square, Glasgow, G41 2BP

Tel: 0141 423 4029
Fax: 0141 423 0677
E-mail: enquiries@batd.co.uk

Website:
http://www.batd.co.uk

Enquiries:
Enquiries to: General Secretary

Founded:
1892

Organisation type and purpose:
International organisation, professional body (membership is by qualification, election or invitation), present number of members: 3000, suitable for ages: 16+.
Registered Friendly Society, no. 11SA(S).
To promote the art of dancing and aid members in times of distress.

Subject coverage:
All dancing activities.

Printed publications:
Printed syllabus and books available for sale to qualified dance teachers

Access to staff:
Contact by letter, by telephone, by fax, by e-mail, in person and via website
Hours: Mon to Fri, 0900 to 1700

Affiliated to:
Central Council of Physical Recreation

Representation on:
British Council of Ballroom Dancing
Scottish Official Board of Highland Dancing
Stage Dance Council International

BRITISH ASSOCIATION OF TEACHERS OF THE DEAF

Acronym or abbreviation: BATOD

175 Dashwood Avenue, High Wycombe, Buckinghamshire, HP12 3DB

Tel: 01494 464190
Fax: 01494 464190
E-mail: secretary@batod.org.uk

Website:
http://www.batod.org.uk
Whole range of Association's interests plus formal submissions to government bodies.

Enquiries:
Enquiries to: Secretary
Other contacts: Magazine Editor and Publications Editor for matters related to magazine and publications.

Founded:
1977

Organisation type and purpose:
National organisation, professional body (membership is by subscription), present number of members: 1650, voluntary organisation, suitable for ages: all, training organisation, consultancy, research organisation, publishing house.

Subject coverage:
National curriculum (hearing impaired), communication, teacher of deaf training, examination special arrangements, special education (hearing impaired), educational audiology, educational legislation.

Museum or gallery collection, archive, or library special collection:
Archived history at University of Birmingham

Printed publications:
BATOD journal (4 times a year, free to members)
BATOD magazine (5 times a year, free to members)
Information leaflets and guidelines

Publications list:
Available online and in print

Access to staff:
Contact by letter, by telephone, by fax, by e-mail and via website. Appointment necessary.
Hours: Answerphone 24-hours

Affiliated to:
European Federation of Associations of Teachers of the Deaf (FEAPDA)
C/o 175 Dashwood Avenue, High Wycombe, Buckinghamshire, HP12 3DB; tel: 01494 464190; fax: 01494 464190; e-mail: president@feapda.org; website: http://www.feapda.org

BRITISH ASSOCIATION OF UROLOGICAL SURGEONS

Acronym or abbreviation: BAUS

Royal College of Surgeons of England, 35–43 Lincoln's Inn Fields, London, WC2A 3PE

Tel: 020 7869 6950
Fax: 020 7404 5048
E-mail: admin@baus.org.uk

Enquiries:
Enquiries to: Chief Executive

Founded:
1945

Organisation type and purpose:
Professional body.

Subject coverage:
Urology; urological surgery.

continued overleaf

Access to staff:
Contact by letter, by fax and by e-mail
Hours: Mon to Fri, 0900 to 1700

BRITISH AUTOMOBILE RACING CLUB LIMITED

Acronym or abbreviation: BARC

Thruxton Circuit, Andover, Hampshire, SP11 8PN

Tel: 01264 882200
Fax: 01264 882233
E-mail: info@barc.net

Website:
http://www.barc.net

Enquiries:
Enquiries to: Chief Executive

Founded:
1912

Organisation type and purpose:
Membership association.
Motor Sport organisation.

Subject coverage:
Motor racing, motor racing and motor racing safety.

Museum or gallery collection, archive, or library special collection:
Early photographs, motoring books, minutes, Brooklands programmes, etc.

Printed publications:
Race Meeting Programmes
Startline magazine (6 times a year, for members)
Programme of Events booklet (yearly)

Access to staff:
Contact by letter, by telephone, by fax, by e-mail, in person and via website
Hours: Mon to Fri, 0900 to 1700
Special comments: By appointment for research.

Access for disabled people:
Parking provided, toilet facilities

Affiliated to:
Royal Automobile Club Motor Sports Association
tel: 01753 681736; fax: 01753 682938

BRITISH AVIATION PRESERVATION COUNCIL

Acronym or abbreviation: BAPC

c/o Museum of Science and Industry, Liverpool Road, Castlefield, Manchester, M3 4JP

Tel: 0161 832 2244
Fax: 0161 834 5135
E-mail: n.forder@msim.org.uk

Enquiries:
Enquiries to: Chairman

Founded:
1967

Organisation type and purpose:
International organisation, advisory body, membership association (membership is by subscription), present number of members: 162.
Co-ordinating body.
To link national, local authority, independent and service museums with private collections, voluntary groups and other organisations in the advancement of the preservation of Britain's aviation heritage.

Subject coverage:
Preservation, restoration and exhibition of historic aviation, archives and associated records.

Printed publications:
All publications are free to members, non-members will be charged postage and packing at cost
Logbook: BAPC Members' Manual
National Aviation Heritage Register
Register of Historic Aero Engines (internal draft document)
Stopping the Rot (seminar papers)

Wants, Disposals and Sales listings: distributed quarterly
Order printed publications from: British Aviation Preservation Council
1 Calfe Fen Close, Soham, Ely, CB7 5GD

Access to staff:
Contact by letter, by telephone, by fax and by e-mail
Hours: Mon to Fri, 0900 to 1700

Affiliated to:
Association of British Transport Museums
European Aviation Representation Council
Transport Trust

There are some:
6 observers, 3 honorary members, 139 member organisations and 12 affiliated member organisations

BRITISH BALLET ORGANIZATION

Acronym or abbreviation: BBO

39 Lonsdale Road, Barnes, London, SW13 9JP

Tel: 020 8748 1241
Fax: 020 8748 1301
E-mail: info@bbo.org.uk

Website:
http://www.bbo.org.uk

Enquiries:
Enquiries to: Director

Founded:
1930

Organisation type and purpose:
Membership association, registered charity (charity number 277177), suitable for ages: all.
Examining body for ballet, tap, jazz and modern dancing at all ages. Teaching qualifications in ballet and tap dancing. Teacher training programme.

Subject coverage:
Examinations in ballet, tap, jazz and modern dancing, in the UK, Australia, New Zealand, Spain, Cyprus, Jordan and Kuwait. Dance and teacher training and examinations.

Museum or gallery collection, archive, or library special collection:
Archives of the British Ballet Organization
Archives of the Espinosa Family (founders)

Printed publications:
Bulletin (2 times a year)
Magazine (once a year)
Syllabus: Ballet and tap dancing (primary to advanced)
Syllabus: Modern (primary to intermediate)
Syllabus: Jazz (primary to elementary)
Order printed publications from: BBO Dance Supplies Limited
39 Lonsdale Road, Barnes, London, SW13 9JP, tel: 020 8748 1241, fax: 020 8748 1301, e-mail: info@bbo .org.uk

Electronic and video publications:
Ballet: Primary to advanced (tape)
Grade 1 to 5 (CD)
Jazz: Primary to Grade 7 (tape)

Access to staff:
Contact by letter, by fax and by e-mail
Hours: Mon to Fri, 0900 to 1700
Special comments: Open to anyone wishing to join and study the British Ballet Organization method.

Access for disabled people:
Parking provided

Registered with:
The Council for Dance Education and Training (CDET(UK))

BRITISH BANDSMAN

66–78 Denington Road, Wellingborough, Northamptonshire, NN8 2QH

Tel: 01933 445442

E-mail: info@britishbandsman.com

Website:
http://www.britishbandsman.com

Enquiries:
Enquiries to: Information Officer
Other contacts: Managing Editor

Founded:
1887

Organisation type and purpose:
Publishing house.

Subject coverage:
Brass bands.

Printed publications:
By subscription and newsagent

Access to staff:
Contact by letter
Hours: Mon to Fri, 0900 to 1630

Parent body:
Kapitol Media and Events Limited
64 London End, Beaconsfield, Buckinghamshire, HP18 9QH; tel: 01494 674411; fax: 01494 670932; e-mail: info@britishbandsman.com

BRITISH BANKERS' ASSOCIATION

Acronym or abbreviation: BBA

Pinners Hall, 105–108 Old Broad Street, London, EC2N 1EX

Tel: 020 7216 8800
Fax: 020 7216 8905
E-mail: info@bba.org.uk

Website:
http://www.bba.org.uk
General banking information sheets, British Bankers' Association information, publications list.

Founded:
1919

Organisation type and purpose:
Trade association.

Subject coverage:
Banks and banking; specific information for member banks; some limited information for general public.

Trade and statistical information:
Monthly statistical information of bank lending (available on website).

Printed publications:
Abstract of Banking Statistics (annually, May)

Publications list:
Available online and in print

Access to staff:
Contact by letter
Hours: Mon to Fri, 0900 to 1700

Access to building, collection or gallery:
By appointment only

Member of:
European Banking Federation

BRITISH BANKING HISTORY SOCIETY

Acronym or abbreviation: BBHS

71 Mile Lane, Cheylesmore, Coventry, West Midlands, CV3 5GB

Tel: 024 7650 3245
E-mail: info@cheque-collectors.co.uk

Website:
http://www.banking-history.co.uk
General information.

Enquiries:
Enquiries to: Honorary Secretary

Founded:
1980

Organisation type and purpose:
Membership association (membership is by subscription).

Subject coverage:
The collection of cheques and research into banking history.

Printed publications:
Counterfoil (journal, quarterly, available by subscription only to members of the society)

Access to staff:
Contact by letter, by telephone and by e-mail
Hours: Mon to Fri, 0900 to 1700

BRITISH BASKETBALL ASSOCIATION

Acronym or abbreviation: BBA

Linen Hall, Suite 446, 162–168 Regent Street, London, W1B 5TE

Tel: 020 7993 6864
E-mail: info@bbauk.com

Website:
http://www.bbauk.com

Founded:
2007

Organisation type and purpose:
Formed by a consortium of business, sports, marketing and basketball professionals primarily to create a commercially viable professional basketball league in the United Kingdom.

BRITISH BATTERY MANUFACTURERS ASSOCIATION

Acronym or abbreviation: BBMA

3 London Wall Buildings, London Wall, London, EC2M 5SY

Tel: 020 7826 2690
Fax: 020 7826 2601
E-mail: info@bbma.co.uk

Website:
http://www.bbma.co.uk

Enquiries:
Enquiries to: Secretary
Other contacts: Executive

Founded:
1986

Organisation type and purpose:
Trade association.

Subject coverage:
Standards, safety, statistics, UK and European legislation, environmental interest, disposal and recycling of portable batteries, both primary (non-rechargeable) and secondary (rechargeable).

Printed publications:
Battery Compartment Guidelines
Battery Ingestion Guidelines
Battery Safety Guidelines
Powering Everyday Life: An introduction to the BBMA
Environmental Initiatives by the Battery Industry

Publications list:
Available online and in print

Access to staff:
Contact by letter, by telephone, by fax and by e-mail
Hours: Mon to Fri, 0900 to 1700

Member of:
European Portable Battery Association

BRITISH BAVARIAN WARMBLOOD ASSOCIATION

Acronym or abbreviation: BBWA

Sittyton, Straloch, Newmachar, Aberdeen, AB21 0RP

Tel: 01651 882226
Fax: 01651 882313
E-mail: bbwa@bbwa.co.uk

Website:
http://www.bbwa.co.uk
Information on the various aspects of the Association.

Enquiries:
Enquiries to: Secretary

Founded:
1987

Organisation type and purpose:
Membership association (membership is by subscription), present number of members: 80.

Subject coverage:
Bavarian Warmblood horses, breeding, registration, grading and performance testing.

Access to staff:
Contact by telephone
Hours: Mon to Fri, 0900 to 1700

Parent body:
Landesverband Bayerischer Pferdezuechter eV Landshamer Str. 11, 81929 Munich, Germany; tel: + 49 89 926967; fax: + 49 89 907405

BRITISH BEEKEEPERS ASSOCIATION

Acronym or abbreviation: BBKA

National Agricultural Centre, Stoneleigh Park, Warwickshire, CV8 2LG

Tel: 024 7669 6679
Fax: 024 7669 0682
E-mail: bbka@britishbeekeepers.com

Website:
http://www.britishbeekeepers.com

Enquiries:
Enquiries to: General Secretary

Founded:
1874

Organisation type and purpose:
Membership association (membership is by subscription), present number of members: 12,521, registered charity (charity number 212025). To further the craft of beekeeping.

Subject coverage:
Bees and beekeeping; examinations in beekeeping.

Museum or gallery collection, archive, or library special collection:
AVA library of slides, tapes etc
Library of numerous collections

Printed publications:
Honey Recipe leaflets (50p)
Advisory leaflets on many aspects of beekeeping (50p)
Leaflets of bee management (50p)
BBKA News (for members)
Bee Craft (monthly by subscription)
First Steps in Beekeeping
Honeybee Swarms – What to Do?
Bees in the Curriculum – Schools pack (£15 inc. p&p in United Kingdom; £30 inc. p&p overseas)

Microform publications:
Honeybee Anatomy, 8 coloured transparency plates in folder complete with index (£4)

Publications list:
Available in print

Access to staff:
Contact by letter, by telephone, by fax and by e-mail. Appointment necessary.
Hours: Mon to Fri, 0930 to 1230 and 1300 to 1430

BRITISH BEER & PUB ASSOCIATION

Market Towers, 1 Nine Elms Lane, London, SW8 9NQ

Tel: 020 7627 9191
Fax: 020 7627 9123
E-mail: enquiries@beerandpub.com

Website:
http://www.beerandpub.com
Career information.

Enquiries:
Enquiries to: Secretary

Founded:
1904

Organisation type and purpose:
Trade association.

Subject coverage:
Beer, brewing, the brewing industry, public houses, licensing system.

Museum or gallery collection, archive, or library special collection:
Trade periodicals and annuals back to 1880

Printed publications:
Statistical Handbook (annually)

Publications list:
Available in print

Access to staff:
Contact by letter
Hours: Mon to Fri, 0900 to 1700

Access for disabled people:
Level entry

Member of:
Confederation of British Industry

BRITISH BERRICHON DU CHER SHEEP SOCIETY LIMITED

Acronym or abbreviation: BdC

The Lodge, Sutton Bassett, Market Harborough, Leicestershire, LE16 8HL

Tel: 01858 462427
Fax: 01858 462427

Enquiries:
Enquiries to: Secretary

Founded:
1986

Organisation type and purpose:
Membership association (membership is by subscription).
Breed Society.

Subject coverage:
British Berrichon Du Cher sheep breed.

Printed publications:
Promotional leaflets available free

Access to staff:
Contact by letter, by telephone and by fax
Hours: Mon to Fri, 0900 to 1700

BRITISH BIOMAGNETIC ASSOCIATION

Acronym or abbreviation: BBA

31 St Marychurch Road, Torquay, Devon, TQ1 3JF

Tel: 01803 293346
Fax: 01803 293346
E-mail: secretary@britishbiomagneticassoc.fsnet.co.uk

Enquiries:
Enquiries to: Secretary
Other contacts: Course Administrator

Founded:
1976

Organisation type and purpose:
Professional body (membership is by qualification), present number of members: 250, training organisation, research organisation.
Postgraduate Training.

continued overleaf

Subject coverage:
Magnetic effects on acupuncture points, acupuncture at postgraduate level, radionic practice.

Access to staff:
Contact by letter, by telephone, by fax and by e-mail
Hours: Not Wed or Fri afternoon

BRITISH BIRD COUNCIL

Acronym or abbreviation: BBC

1st Floor Offices, 1159 Bristol Road South, Northfield, Birmingham, B31 2SL

Tel: 0121 476 5999

Website:
http://www.britishbirdcouncil.com

Enquiries:
Enquiries to: Administrator
Direct tel: 01902 700319
Direct fax: 01902 701140
Direct e-mail: rogercaton@birdexpert.fsnet.co.uk

Founded:
1970

Organisation type and purpose:
Non-governmental organisation.
Department for the Environment, Food & Rural Affairs approved supplier of rings for birds.

Subject coverage:
Rings to identify British birds.

Access to staff:
Contact by letter
Hours: Mon to Fri, 0900 to 1700

Access to building, collection or gallery:
No access other than to staff

Affiliated society:
Cleveland British Bird Club
Eastern Federation of British Bird Fanciers
Lancashire British Bird & Hybrid Club
London & Home Counties British Bird & Mule Club
National British Bird & Mule Club
North Derbyshire British Bird & Mule Club
Sandwell British Bird & Hybrid Club
Scottish British Bird & Mule Club
Severn Counties Foreign & British Bird Society
South Coast British Bird & Hybrid Club
Staffordshire British Bird & Mule Club
Welsh British Bird & Mule Club
Yorkshire British Bird & Hybrid Club

Affiliated to:
National Council for Aviculture

BRITISH BIRDWATCHING FAIR

Acronym or abbreviation: Birdfair

Fishponds Cottage, Hambleton Road, Oakham, Rutland, LE15 8AB

Tel: 01572 771079
Fax: 01572 756611
E-mail: info@birdfair.org.uk

Website:
http://www.birdfair.org.uk

Enquiries:
Enquiries to: Administrator

Founded:
1989

Organisation type and purpose:
Voluntary organisation.
Conservancy organisation.
Three-day event at Egleton Nature Reserve, Rutland Water, the purpose of which is a celebration of birdwatching and a way of raising funds for international bird conservation.

Subject coverage:
Birdwatching and conservation.

Trade and statistical information:
Approximately 300 exhibitions and 23,000 visitors.

Access to staff:
Contact by letter, by telephone, by fax and by e-mail
Hours: Mon to Fri, 0900 to 1700
Special comments: Preferred access order: e-mail, letter, fax, telephone.

Access for disabled people:
Parking provided, toilet facilities

Links with:
Leicestershire & Rutland Wildlife Trust
tel: 0116 2720444; fax: 0116 2720404; e-mail: info@lrwt.org.uk; website: http://www.lrwt.org.uk
Royal Society for the Protection of Birds
tel: 01767 680551; website: http://www.rspb.org.uk

BRITISH BLIND AND SHUTTER ASSOCIATION

Acronym or abbreviation: BBSA

42 Heath Street, Tamworth, Staffordshire, B79 7JH

Tel: 01827 52337
Fax: 01827 310827
E-mail: info@bbsa.org.uk

Website:
http://www.bbsa.org.uk
Members' details, technical product information.

Enquiries:
Enquiries to: Secretary

Founded:
1919

Organisation type and purpose:
National organisation, advisory body, trade association (membership is by subscription), present number of members: 390.
Represents manufacturers and suppliers.

Subject coverage:
Internal and external blinds, awnings and security grilles and shutters.

Printed publications:
Blinds and Shutters Buyers Guide 2006/7
Blinds and Shutters (quarterly)
Openings (trade journal)

Access to staff:
Contact by letter, by telephone, by fax and by e-mail
Hours: Mon to Thu, 0900 to 1700; Fri, 0900 to 1630

BRITISH BLIND SPORT

Acronym or abbreviation: BBS

4–6 Victoria Terrace, Leamington Spa, Warwickshire, CV31 3AB

Tel: 01926 424247
Fax: 01926 427775
E-mail: info@britishblindsport.org.uk

Website:
http://www.britishblindsport.org.uk

Enquiries:
Enquiries to: Admin. Manager

Founded:
1975

Organisation type and purpose:
Membership association, voluntary organisation, registered charity (charity number 271500).
Providing sport and recreation for blind and partially sighted people.

Subject coverage:
General information about sports for the blind and partially sighted, specialist sports, classification of sight categories.

Printed publications:
Newsletter (4 times a year)

Electronic and video publications:
Tape copy of newsletter

Access to staff:
Contact by letter and by e-mail
Hours: Mon to Thu, 0900 to 1700; Fri, 0900 to 1630

Affiliated to:
International Blind Sport Association

BRITISH BOARD OF AGRÉMENT

Acronym or abbreviation: BBA

Bucknalls Lane, Garston, Watford, Hertfordshire, WD25 9BA

Tel: 01923 665300
Fax: 01923 665301
E-mail: mail@bba.star.co.uk

Website:
http://www.bbacerts.co.uk
Information on the BBA. Listings of approved products and installers. Test services information.

Enquiries:
Enquiries to: Information Officer
Direct e-mail: athomas@bba.star.co.uk
Other contacts: Sales and Communications Director

Founded:
1966

Organisation type and purpose:
Approvals body for the construction industry.

Subject coverage:
Testing and approval of building and civil engineering products (successful assessments are published as Agrément Certificates, which contain essential technical data for designers and users).

Museum or gallery collection, archive, or library special collection:
3,500 agrément certificates dating from 1966

Non-library collection catalogue:
All or part available online

Library catalogue:
All or part available online

Printed publications:
Directory of Approved Installers
Index of Certificates (quarterly, with monthly updates)
Methods of Assessment and Testing
Supplement to the Approved Documents supporting the Building Regulations

Microform publications:
All publications available on microfiche

Electronic and video publications:
Agrément Certificates

Publications list:
Available in print

Access to staff:
Contact by letter, by fax, by e-mail and via website
Hours: Mon to Fri, 0900 to 1730

Access to building, collection or gallery:
Mon to Fri
Hours: Mon to Fri, 0900 to 1730

Member organisation of:
European Organisation for Technical Approvals (EOTA)
tel: +32 2 502 6900; fax: +32 2 502 3814; e-mail: info@eota.be
European Union of Agrément (UEATC)
tel: 01923 665412; fax: 01923 665301; e-mail: jblaisdale@bba.star.co.uk

BRITISH BOTTLERS' INSTITUTE

Acronym or abbreviation: BBI

c/o Binsted Group, Attwood House, Mansfield Park, Four Marks, Hampshire, GU34 5PZ

Tel: 01420 568901
Fax: 01420 565994

E-mail: bbi@binstedgroup.com

Website:
http://www.bbi.org.uk

Enquiries:
Enquiries to: President
Direct e-mail: secretary@bbi.org.uk

Founded:
1953

Organisation type and purpose:
Trade association (membership is by election or invitation), present number of members: 135.

Subject coverage:
Bottling, canning and packaging of beverages, including beers, mineral waters, soft drinks, fruit juices, ciders, wines, spirits.

Access to staff:
Contact by letter, by telephone, by fax and by e-mail
Hours: Mon to Fri, 0900 to 1700

BRITISH BRICK SOCIETY

Acronym or abbreviation: BBS

Brick Development Association, 26 Store Street, London, WC1E 7BT

Tel: 020 7323 7030
Fax: 020 7580 3795
E-mail: michael@mhammett.freeserve.co.uk

Website:
http://www.britishbricksoc.free-online.co.uk

Enquiries:
Enquiries to: Honorary Secretary
Direct tel: 01494 520599

Founded:
1972

Organisation type and purpose:
Learned society (membership is by subscription), present number of members: c.300.
To promote the study and recording of all aspects of the archaeology and history of bricks, brickmaking and brickwork.

Subject coverage:
Historical aspects of brickmaking in the United Kingdom and of brickwork structures.

Printed publications:
INFORMATION (newsletter, c.20pp, members, 3 times a year)
All book issues kept in print and Index available

Access to staff:
Contact by letter, by telephone, by fax and by e-mail
Hours: Mon to Fri, 0900 to 1700

Also at:
Honorary Secretary
 9 Bailey Close, High Wycombe,
 Buckinghamshire, HP13 6QA; tel: 01494 520299;
 e-mail: michael@mhammett.freeserve.co.uk

Links with:
British Archaeological Association, Brick Section

BRITISH BRYOLOGICAL SOCIETY

Acronym or abbreviation: BBS

6 Church View, Wootton, Northampton, NN4 7LJ

Website:
http://www.britishbryologicalsociety.org.uk
Meetings, referees and recording, Tropical Bryology Group, membership enquiries.

Enquiries:
Enquiries to: General Secretary

Founded:
1896

Organisation type and purpose:
Learned society (membership is by subscription), present number of members: 600, registered charity (charity number 228851).

To promote a wide interest in bryology.

Subject coverage:
Study and conservation of mosses and liverworts (bryophytes) worldwide.

Museum or gallery collection, archive, or library special collection:
Bryological library
Herbarium of approximately 30,000 dried specimens of bryophytes

Printed publications:
Census Catalogue of British Bryophytes
Field Bryology – the Bulletin of the British Bryological Society (3 times a year)
Journal of Bryology (4 times a year)
Occasional publications: BBS Special Volumes
Mosses and Liverworts of Britain and Ireland: a Field Guide

Access to staff:
Contact by letter
Hours: Mon to Fri, 0900 to 1700

BRITISH BUDDHIST ASSOCIATION

Acronym or abbreviation: BBA

11 Biddulph Road, London, W9 1JA

Tel: 020 7286 5575
Fax: 020 7289 5545

Enquiries:
Enquiries to: Director

Founded:
1974

Organisation type and purpose:
Voluntary organisation.
Specialists in teaching and practice of early Buddhism. The BBA is non-sectarian and seeks to express devotion in ways suitable to Western practitioners.

Subject coverage:
Educational, religious and meditation aspects of the Buddha's teaching. The Association promotes educational, religious and meditation aspects of the Buddha's teaching at evening and weekend sessions both in London and at country retreats, to augment private study and practice.

Access to staff:
Contact by letter and by fax
Hours: Mon to Fri, 0900 to 1700

Access to building, collection or gallery:
Prior appointment required

BRITISH BULGARIAN CHAMBER OF COMMERCE

Acronym or abbreviation: BBCC

PO Box 123, Bromley, Kent, BR1 4ZX

Tel: 020 8464 5007
E-mail: info@bbcc.bg

Website:
http://www.bbcc.bg

Enquiries:
Enquiries to: Executive Director

Founded:
1993

Organisation type and purpose:
International organisation, membership association (membership is by subscription).

Subject coverage:
Promotion of business between the United Kingdom and Bulgaria.

Electronic and video publications:
BBCC Weekly Newsletter (e-mail)

Access to staff:
Contact by e-mail

Hours: Mon to Fri, 0900 to 1700

Access to building, collection or gallery:
No access other than to staff

BRITISH BURN ASSOCIATION

Acronym or abbreviation: BBA

35–43 Lincloln's Inn Fields, London, WC2A 3PE

Tel: 020 7869 6923
Fax: 020 7869 6929
E-mail: info@britishburnassociation.org

Website:
http://www.britishburnassociation.co.uk

Enquiries:
Enquiries to: Honorary Secretary

Founded:
1967

Organisation type and purpose:
Professional body (membership is by subscription, qualification), registered charity (charity number 260167).
Disseminate knowledge and research into the care of, recovery from and prevention of burns.

Subject coverage:
Burn prevention; burn treatment, care and rehabilitation.

Printed publications:
Burncare (newsletter)

Access to staff:
Contact by letter, by telephone, by fax and by e-mail
Hours: Mon to Fri, 0900 to 1700

Affiliated to:
International Society for Burn Injuries

BRITISH BUSINESS AWARDS ASSOCIATION

The Stables, Highfield Park, Creaton, Northampton, NN6 8NT

Tel: 01604 505480

Enquiries:
Enquiries to: Information Officer

BRITISH BUTTON SOCIETY

Acronym or abbreviation: BBS

E-mail: british.button.society@care4free.net

Website:
http://www.britishbuttonsociety.org

Enquiries:
Enquiries to: Secretary
Other contacts: Membership Secretary for information regarding membership.

Founded:
1976

Organisation type and purpose:
Membership association (membership is by subscription), present number of members: 350 (approx).
Members, collect and research the background to old, interesting buttons; uniform and dress.

Subject coverage:
History of button manufacturers, collection and research into all types of buttons i.e. modern/antique dress, military/service uniform, all types of civilian uniform, livery. Not present day manufacturers or sources of supply.

Printed publications:
Button Lines (quarterly, to paid-up members only)

Access to staff:
Contact by letter
Hours: Mon to Fri, 0900 to 1700

continued overleaf

Membership Secretary:
British Button Society
  Jersey Cottage, Parklands Road, Patchway,
  Bower Ashton, Bristol, BS3 2JR

BRITISH CABLES ASSOCIATION

Acronym or abbreviation: BCA

37a Walton Road, East Molesey, Surrey, KT8 0DH

Tel: 020 8941 4079
Fax: 020 8783 0104

Enquiries:
Enquiries to: Secretary General
Direct e-mail: peter.smeeth@btconnect.com

Organisation type and purpose:
Trade association.

Subject coverage:
Insulated cables.

Access to staff:
Contact by e-mail
Hours: Mon to Fri, 0900 to 1700

Access to building, collection or gallery:
No access other than to staff

BRITISH CACTUS AND SUCCULENT SOCIETY

Acronym or abbreviation: BCSS

49 Chestnut Glen, Hornchurch, Essex, RM12 4HL

Tel: 01708 447778
Fax: 01444 454061
E-mail: bcss@bcss.org.uk

Website:
http://www.bcss.org.uk
Worldwide information on events related to cacti
and succulents; branch programmes and events;
nurseries.

Enquiries:
Enquiries to: Membership Secretary
Direct tel: 01455 614410
Direct e-mail: membership@bcss.org.uk
Other contacts: Secretary (for general enquiries);
Publicity Officer

Founded:
1983

Organisation type and purpose:
Learned society (membership is by subscription),
present number of members: 3,500, registered
charity (charity number 290786).
To educate the general public on all aspects of the
subject.

Subject coverage:
All aspects concerned with the growing,
propagation and conservation of succulent plants.

Printed publications:
Journal (quarterly, members only)
Publications available for purchase
Order printed publications from: Publications
Manager, BCSS, Brenfield, Bolney Road, Ansty,
West Sussex, RH17 5AW, tel: 01444 459151, fax:
01444 454061, e-mail: bcss@bcss.org.uk

Publications list:
Available online

Access to staff:
Contact by letter, by telephone, by fax, by e-mail
and via website
Hours: Mon to Fri, 0900 to 1700

Access to building, collection or gallery:
No prior appointment required
Special comments: Members only for reference
library, no borrowing.

Also at:
Membership Secretary, British Cactus and
Succulent Society
  6 Castlemaine Drive, Hincley, Leicester, LE10
  1RY; tel: 01455 614410; e-mail: membership@bcss
  .or.uk; website: http://www.bcss.org.uk

BRITISH CALCIUM CARBONATES FEDERATION

Acronym or abbreviation: BCCF

c/o Omya UK Ltd, Omya House, Stephensons Way,
Wyvern Business Park, Chaddesden, Derby, DE21
6LY

Tel: 01332 887435
Fax: 01332 887043
E-mail: mike.nocivelli@omya.com

Website:
http://www.calcium-carbonate.org.uk

Enquiries:
Enquiries to: Secretary

Founded:
1943

Organisation type and purpose:
Trade association.

Subject coverage:
Calcium carbonates (chalk whiting), production
and uses.

Printed publications:
List of members

Access to staff:
Contact by letter, by telephone, by fax and by e-
mail
Hours: Mon to Fri, 0900 to 1700

BRITISH CANOE UNION

Acronym or abbreviation: BCU

John Dudderidge House, Adbolton Lane, West
Bridgford, Nottingham, NG2 5AS

Tel: 0115 982 1100
Fax: 0115 982 1797

Website:
http://www.bcu.org.uk
General information on the sport and recreation of
canoeing and kayaking.

Enquiries:
Enquiries to: Chief Executive
Other contacts: PA to Chief Executive

Organisation type and purpose:
Membership association (membership is by
subscription), present number of members: 23,000.
Governing body for the sport and recreation of
canoeing and kayaking.

Subject coverage:
All aspects of canoeing.

**Museum or gallery collection, archive, or library
special collection:**
Archival films

Printed publications:
Booklets on canoeing
Canoe Focus
Coaching Handbook

Access to staff:
Contact by letter and by e-mail
Hours: Mon to Fri, 0900 to 1700

Access to building, collection or gallery:
No prior appointment required

Affiliated to:
British Olympic Association
  tel: 020 8871 2677; fax: 020 8871 9104
Central Council of Physical Recreation
  tel: 020 7828 3163; fax: 020 7630 8820
Commonwealth Games Federation for England
  tel: 020 7388 6643; fax: 020 7388 6744
European Canoe Association
International Canoe Federation

BRITISH CARTOGRAPHIC SOCIETY

Acronym or abbreviation: BCS

c/o Royal Geographical Society, 1 Kensington Gore,
London, SW7 2AR

Tel: 0115 9328684
Fax: 0115 9328684
E-mail: admin@cartography.org.uk

Website:
http://www.cartography.org.uk
News, membership, job vacancies, directories
(corporate members, freelance cartographers,
students), publications.

Enquiries:
Enquiries to: Administrator

Founded:
1963

Organisation type and purpose:
Learned society (membership is by subscription),
present number of members: 700, registered
charity (charity number 240034).
To promote the art and science of map-making.

Subject coverage:
Cartography, history of cartography, map libraries
curatorship, GIS, technical developments and
automation in cartography, design, technology,
education and careers in cartography.

**Museum or gallery collection, archive, or library
special collection:**
Library housed at the National Library of Scotland
Exchange and subscription journals
Map design awards entries
Reference works

Printed publications:
Working in The Map industry (2007) – brief guide
  for young people seeking a career in the map
  world; the full version (Careers in Cartography)
  may be viewed on the Society's website
The Cartographic Journal (4 times a year, free to
  members and on subscription to non-members)
Maplines (Society newsletter for members, 3 times
  a year)
Directory of UK Map Collections (1995, £10
  members, £15 non-members). An updated
  version may be viewed on the Society's website
Index to the Cartographic Journal 1964–1996 (£10
  members, £15 non-members)
Military Publisher's Designations: a list of
  publishers' designations appearing on military
  maps past and present (£1.20)
Qualifications: a collection of papers, discussions
  and proposals from the 1991 meeting of RICS on
  qualifications in Mapping and Surveying
  (Lawrence, P., ed., £5.50)
Recording our Changing Landscape (1994, £9)
Order printed publications from: The Cartographic
Journal from Maney Publishing, tel: 0113 243 2800;
website: http://www.maney.co.uk
All other publications from the Administration
address

Publications list:
Available in print

Access to staff:
Contact by letter, by telephone, by fax, by e-mail
and via website
Hours: Mon to Fri, 0900 to 1700; answerphone
when absent

Also at:
British Cartographic Society (Administration)
  15 The Crescent, Stanley Common, Ilkeston,
  Derby, DE7 6GL; tel: 0115 9328684; fax: 0115
  9328684

BRITISH CARTON ASSOCIATION

Farringdon Point, 29–35 Farringdon Road,
London, EC1M 3JF

Tel: 020 7915 8300
Fax: 020 7405 7785

Website:
http://bpif.org.uk
General information about BPIF, current press
releases.

Enquiries:
Enquiries to: Manager
Direct e-mail: chris.selby@bpif.org.uk

Founded:
1933

Organisation type and purpose:
Trade association.
To represent manufacturers of printed folding cartons.

Subject coverage:
Cartons, folding cartons, carton board, employment affairs, technical, legal, training advice, statistics, health and safety, environment.

Trade and statistical information:
Printing industry statistics, consumption and production of cartons.

Printed publications:
ECMA Folding Carton Dictionary (five languages)
European Carton Manufacturers Association Code
Glossary of folding carton terms
Handbook of Carton Board and Carton Test Procedures

Publications list:
Available in print

Access to staff:
Contact by letter and by e-mail
Hours: Mon to Fri, 0900 to 1700

Affiliated to:
British Printing Industries Federation
tel: 020 7915 8300; fax: 020 7405 7784

BRITISH CARTOON ARCHIVE

Acronym or abbreviation: BCA

Templeman Library, University of Kent, Canterbury, Kent, CT2 7NU

Tel: 01227 823127
Fax: 01227 823127
E-mail: j.m.newton@kent.ac.uk

Website:
http://www.cartoons.ac.uk
Online catalogue with 140,000 images of British political and social-comment cartoons, plus cartoonists' biographies and supporting material. Users can register to create their own groups of cartoons, for research or teaching purposes.

Founded:
1973

Formerly called:
Centre for the Study of Cartoons and Caricature

Organisation type and purpose:
Created as a research centre and picture library with the objectives of conserving and cataloguing cartoons; encouraging research into all aspects and periods of cartooning; planning and promoting exhibitions of cartoon originals; and servicing teaching in a variety of disciplines.

Subject coverage:
Cartoons.

Museum or gallery collection, archive, or library special collection:
Archive of 150,000 pieces of original cartoon artwork, plus 90,000 cuttings, with 140,000 cartoons available for viewing online in the database.
Library of more than 5,000 books, periodicals, cuttings, slides, videos and cassettes about cartoons, caricature and humour.

Non-library collection catalogue:
All or part available online

Library catalogue:
All or part available online

Publications list:
Available online

Access to staff:
Contact by letter, by telephone, by fax, by e-mail, in person and via website. Appointment necessary.
Hours: Mon to Fri, 0900 to 1700

Access to building, collection or gallery:
Varies during University terms and holidays

BRITISH CATTLE VETERINARY ASSOCIATION

Acronym or abbreviation: BCVA

The Green, Frampton on Severn, Gloucester, GL2 7EP

Tel: 01452 740816
Fax: 01452 741117
E-mail: office@cattlevet.co.uk

Website:
http://www.bcva.org.uk

Enquiries:
Enquiries to: Secretariat

Organisation type and purpose:
Learned society.

Subject coverage:
Veterinary science related to cattle and cattle production.

Printed publications:
Abstracts
Meetings Papers

Access to staff:
Contact by letter, by telephone, by fax, by e-mail and via website
Hours: Mon to Fri, 0900 to 1700

Affiliated to:
British Veterinary Association

BRITISH CAVE RESEARCH ASSOCIATION

Acronym or abbreviation: BCRA

The Old Methodist Chapel, Great Hucklow, Buxton, Derbyshire, SK17 8RG

Tel: 01298 873800
E-mail: enquiries@bcra.org.uk

Website:
http://www.bcra.org.uk
Full description of BCRA services, meetings, publications. Contents list of Caves and Caving, Cave and Karst Science.

Enquiries:
Enquiries to: Secretary

Founded:
1973

Organisation type and purpose:
National organisation, membership association (membership is by subscription), present number of members: 1000, registered charity (charity number 267828), research organisation, publishing house.
The national organisation for the study of sciences associated with caving, caves and karst.

Subject coverage:
Speleology (British and foreign), biospeleology, hydrology, cave chemistry, physics and geophysics, cave archaeology and palaeontology, cave survey and photography, regional studies (NW Yorkshire, Derbyshire, Mendip, South Wales and Devon limestone regions); geology, geomorphology, erosion of limestones, cave rescue and medicine, ropes, ladders, lights.

Museum or gallery collection, archive, or library special collection:
National Caving Library, including old and rare works, British and foreign publications virtually a complete collection of published material on speleology

Non-library collection catalogue:
All or part available in-house

Printed publications:
Caves and Caving (quarterly, formerly BCRA Bulletin up to 1978)
Cave and Karst Science (quarterly to vol.12, 1986 then 3 times a year)
Cave Studies, series of occasional booklets

Current Titles in Speleology CTS/BBS/SA (annually up to 1993, now incorporated within the Bulletin Bibliographique Spéléologique/Speleological Abstracts)
Several books, full list on request
Order printed publications from: Publications Sales Officer, BCRA
Village Farm, Great Thirkleby, Thirsk, YO7 2AT, tel: 01845 501424

Electronic and video publications:
CTS/BBS/SA (CD-ROMS)

Access to staff:
Contact by letter, by telephone and by e-mail
Hours: Usually 0900 to 2100 but not guaranteed

Access to building, collection or gallery:
Prior appointment required for access to library
Hours: Mon to Fri, 0900 to 1700
Special comments: Contact: BCRA, Holt House, Holt Lane, Lea, Matlock, Derbyshire, DE4 5GQ, tel: 01629 534775, email: librarian@bcra.org.uk

Associated with the:
British Caving Association

BRITISH CAVING ASSOCIATION

Acronym or abbreviation: BCA

The Old Methodist Chapel, Great Hucklow, Buxton, Derbyshire, SK17 8RG

E-mail: secretary@british-caving.org.uk

Website:
http://www.british-caving.org.uk
Information on organisation, members training, conservation, access.

Enquiries:
Enquiries to: Publications and Information Officer
Direct e-mail: publications@british-caving.org.uk
Other contacts: Training coordinator for leadership qualification queries.

Founded:
1969

Organisation type and purpose:
Advisory body, statutory body, membership association (membership is by subscription), present number of members: 5000, voluntary organisation, training organisation.
Governing body of the sport of caving in the UK.

Subject coverage:
Caving training and equipment, cave conservation and access, research and science, rescue, registry data, diving; mine history, overseas caving expeditions, caving in general, caving clubs.

Trade and statistical information:
Statistics on caving accidents.

Printed publications:
Cave Conservation Handbook
Cave Conservation Policy
Equipment, library and film lists
Instructor and Leadership Qualifications in caving
Legal Aspects of Access Underground (£1)
National Caving Code
Protect our Caves
Radon Underground
So You Want to Go Caving
Speleoscene (newsletter, 6 times a year)
Weil's Disease Leaflet

Electronic and video publications:
Lost Caves of Britain (video, £10)

Publications list:
Available online and in print

Access to staff:
Contact by letter, by telephone, by e-mail, in person and via website
Hours: 24 hours every day
Special comments: Voluntary organisation, officers have other occupations.

Affiliated to:
European Speleological Federation
International Speleological Union

continued overleaf

Umbrella organisation of the:
5 Regional Caving Councils
British Cave Rescue Organisation
British Cave Research Association
National Association on Mining History
Organisations
William Pengelly Cave Studies Trust

BRITISH CERAMIC CONFEDERATION

Acronym or abbreviation: BCC

Federation House, Station Road, Stoke-on-Trent, Staffordshire, ST4 2SA

Tel: 01782 744631
Fax: 01782 744102
E-mail: bcc@ceramfed.co.uk

Website:
http://www.ceramfed.co.uk

Enquiries:
Enquiries to: Chief Executive

Organisation type and purpose:
Trade association.
Representative body for UK ceramics manufacturing industry.

Subject coverage:
Ceramics manufacturing industry.

Printed publications:
Careers Brochure
List of Member Companies

Access to staff:
Contact by letter, by fax and by e-mail
Hours: Mon to Fri, 0900 to 1700
Special comments: No personal callers. Information available to members only.

Links with:
Cerame Unie

BRITISH CERAMIC PLANT AND MACHINERY MANUFACTURERS ASSOCIATION

Acronym or abbreviation: BCPMMA

Founded:
1962

Organisation type and purpose:
Trade association (membership is by subscription), present number of members: 75, manufacturing industry, publishing house.
Exhibition Organisers.

Subject coverage:
Plant, machinery and raw materials and/or turn-key projects for the manufacture of the complete range of ceramic products, including building bricks, sewer pipes, roofing/wall/floor tiles, tableware, sanitary ware, art pottery, porcelain insulators, refractories etc.

Printed publications:
Global Ceramic Review (quarterly)

Access to staff:
Contact by letter, by telephone, by fax, by e-mail, in person and via website. Appointment necessary. Access for members only. Non-members charged.
Hours: Mon to Fri, 0900 to 1700

Affiliated to:
British Ceramic Confederation

BRITISH CHAMBERS OF COMMERCE

Acronym or abbreviation: BCC

4 Westwood House, Westwood Business Park, Coventry, Warwickshire, CV4 8HS

Tel: 024 7669 4484
Fax: 024 7669 5844
E-mail: info@britishchambers.org.uk

Website:
http://www.britishchambers.org.uk

Enquiries:
Enquiries to: Managing Director
Direct e-mail: s.turvey@britishchambers.org.uk

Organisation type and purpose:
Membership association.
Chamber of commerce.

Subject coverage:
Export advice and guidance, international trade advice, links to local and overseas chambers of commerce.

Trade and statistical information:
European economics.
UK economics and business statistics.

Printed publications:
British Chambers of Commerce Quarterly
  Economic Survey
European Economic Survey
Other specific policy reports
Small Firms Survey
Order printed publications from: 65 Petty France, St James's Park, London, SW1H 9EU

Publications list:
Available online and in print

Access to staff:
Contact by letter, by telephone, by fax, by e-mail and via website. Appointment necessary.
Hours: Mon to Fri, 0845 to 1645 (Coventry Office), 0900 to 1700 (London Office)

Parent body:
The British Chambers of Commerce
  65 Petty France, St James Park, London, SW1H 9EU; tel: 020 7654 5800; fax: 020 7654 5819; e-mail: info@britishchambers.org.uk

BRITISH CHEMICAL ENGINEERING CONTRACTORS ASSOCIATION

Acronym or abbreviation: BCECA

1–4 Regent Street, London, SW1Y 4NR

Tel: 020 7839 6514
Fax: 020 7930 3466
E-mail: ian.corbidge@bceca.org.uk

Website:
http://www.bceca.org.uk

Enquiries:
Enquiries to: Director

Founded:
1966

Organisation type and purpose:
Trade association (membership is by subscription, qualification, election or invitation), present number of members: 20.

Subject coverage:
Process plant contracting and the activities of member companies, their qualifications and experience.

Trade and statistical information:
Industry statistics, member companies order, intake and exports.

Printed publications:
Target – Careers Information and Graduate
  Employers

Access to staff:
Contact by letter, by telephone and by e-mail
Hours: Mon to Thu, 1000 to 1600

BRITISH CHINESE ARTISTS' ASSOCIATION

Acronym or abbreviation: BCAA

Tel: 020 7813 0086
Fax: 020 7482 5292

Enquiries:
Enquiries to: Information Officer

Other contacts: Arts & Education for education work.

Founded:
1991

Organisation type and purpose:
Voluntary organisation, registered charity (charity number 1059823), suitable for ages: 5+, training organisation, consultancy, research organisation. To raise the profile of Chinese arts and artists through education for the public benefit through the promotion of the full spectrum of arts practised by artists of Chinese origins in Britain.

Subject coverage:
Database of Chinese artists in London and UK, in performing arts, visual arts, design, music and film. Education projects, research, general advice to public, media sector.

Access to staff:
Contact by letter, by telephone, by fax and by e-mail. Appointment necessary.
Hours: Mon to Fri, 0900 to 1700

BRITISH CHIROPODY AND PODIATRY ASSOCIATION

Acronym or abbreviation: BChA

The New Hall, Bath Road, Maidenhead, Berkshire, SL6 4LA

Tel: 01628 632449
Fax: 01628 674483
E-mail: smae_institute@compuserve.com

Enquiries:
Enquiries to: Membership Secretary

Founded:
1959

Organisation type and purpose:
Professional body (membership is by qualification, election or invitation), present number of members: over 10,000, service industry, training organisation, consultancy, research organisation, publishing house.

Subject coverage:
Chiropody, chiropodists, podiatry, all matters pertaining to feet and footware care.

Printed publications:
Fact sheets on: verruca and calluses, diabetes and footsore, flat foot, bunions, general advice on footcare
Magazine (on subscription)

Publications list:
Available in print

Access to staff:
Contact by letter, by telephone, by fax, by e-mail and via website
Hours: Mon to Fri, 0900 to 1700

Access to building, collection or gallery:
No prior appointment required

Affiliated to:
School of Surgical Chiropody

BRITISH CHIROPRACTIC ASSOCIATION

Acronym or abbreviation: BCA

59 Castle Street, Reading, Berkshire, RG1 7SN

Tel: 0118 950 5950
Fax: 0118 958 8946
E-mail: enquiries@chiropractic-uk.co.uk

Website:
http://www.chiropractic-uk.co.uk
Information on chiropractic research data; membership of BCA.

Enquiries:
Enquiries to: Press Officer
Direct e-mail: jdoyle@publicasity.co.uk

Founded:
1925

Organisation type and purpose:
Advisory body, statutory body, professional body (membership is by subscription), present number of members: 816, voluntary organisation.

Subject coverage:
Chiropractic within the UK.

Museum or gallery collection, archive, or library special collection:
Library of resource material
Photographs and slides of chiropractors, their work and related topics

Printed publications:
Annual Report
Register of all BCA members
Variety of leaflets (available on request)

Access to staff:
Contact by letter, by telephone, by fax, by e-mail and via website. Appointment necessary. Access for members only.
Hours: Mon to Fri, 0900 to 1700

Access to building, collection or gallery:
No access other than to staff

BRITISH CHRISTMAS TREE GROWERS ASSOCIATION

Acronym or abbreviation: BCTGA

13 Wolrige Road, Edinburgh, EH16 6HX

Tel: 0131 664 1100
Fax: 0131 664 2669
E-mail: rogermhay@btinternet.com

Website:
http://www.bctga.co.uk

Enquiries:
Enquiries to: General Secretary

Founded:
1979

Organisation type and purpose:
National organisation, trade association (membership is by subscription), present number of members: 380.
Promotion of real Christmas trees.

Subject coverage:
Growing, cultivating and marketing real Christmas trees.

Printed publications:
Newsletter
Care of Tree leaflets
History of Christmas Trees

Access to staff:
Contact by letter, by telephone, by fax and by e-mail. Appointment necessary.
Hours: Mon to Fri, 0900 to 1700

BRITISH CLEANING COUNCIL LIMITED

Acronym or abbreviation: BCC Ltd

PO Box 1328, Kidderminster, Worcestershire, DY11 5ZJ

Tel: 01562 851129
Fax: 01562 851129

Enquiries:
Enquiries to: General Secretary/Treasurer
Direct e-mail: info@britishcleaningcouncil.org
Other contacts: Press Office, tel no: 01942 612616 for public relations

Founded:
1982

Organisation type and purpose:
Trade association (membership is by election or invitation), research organisation.
Co-ordinating body for UK cleaning industry.

Subject coverage:
All matters relating to cleaning and hygiene, including cleaning of buildings, internally and externally, and cleaning of outside areas.

Publications list:
Available in print

Access to staff:
Contact by letter, by telephone, by fax and by e-mail. Appointment necessary. Non-members charged.
Hours: Mon to Fri, 0900 to 1700

Member organisations:
18 member organisations

BRITISH CLOTHING INDUSTRY ASSOCIATION LIMITED

Acronym or abbreviation: BCIA

5 Portland Place, London, W1B 1PW

Tel: 020 7636 7788
Fax: 020 7636 7515
E-mail: bcia@dial.pipex.com

Enquiries:
Enquiries to: Director

Organisation type and purpose:
Trade association.

Subject coverage:
Clothing industry.

Printed publications:
News sheets (for members)
UK Fashion Exhibition Calendar

BRITISH COFFEE ASSOCIATION

Acronym or abbreviation: BCA

Federation House, 6 Catherine Street, London, WC2B 5JJ

Tel: 020 7836 2460
Fax: 020 7836 0580

Enquiries:
Enquiries to: Executive Secretary

Organisation type and purpose:
Trade association.

Subject coverage:
Coffee.

Access to staff:
Access for members only.
Hours: Mon to Fri, 0900 to 1700

Member of:
Food and Drink Federation

BRITISH COLOSTOMY ASSOCIATION

Acronym or abbreviation: BCA

15 Station Road, Reading, Berkshire, RG1 1LG

Tel: 0118 939 1537
Fax: 0118 956 9095
E-mail: sue@bcass.org.uk

Website:
http://www.bcass.org.uk

Enquiries:
Enquiries to: Secretary

Founded:
1967

Organisation type and purpose:
Membership association, voluntary organisation, registered charity (charity number 298299).
25 area organisers, to help people who have, or are about to have, a colostomy.

Subject coverage:
Help and advice to anyone who has, or is about to have, a colostomy.

Printed publications:
Literature available from Head Office or from 25 area organisers (free of charge)

Publications list:
Available in print

Access to staff:
Contact by letter, by telephone, by fax, by e-mail and via website. Appointment necessary.
Hours: Mon to Thu, 0900 to 1700; Fri, 0900 to 1500

Access to building, collection or gallery:
Prior appointment required

Connections with:
Macmillan Cancer Relief (MCR)
tel: 020 7840 7840; fax: 020 7840 7841; website: http://www.macmillan.org.uk

BRITISH COMPLEMENTARY MEDICINE ASSOCIATION

Acronym or abbreviation: BCMA

PO Box 5122, Bournemouth, BH8 0WG

Tel: 0845 345 5977
E-mail: office@bcma.co.uk

Website:
http://www.bcma.co.uk
General information.

Enquiries:
Enquiries to: Administrator

Founded:
1992

Organisation type and purpose:
National organisation, professional body, membership association (membership is by subscription, qualification), present number of members: 86 organisations, voluntary organisation.

Subject coverage:
Complementary therapies and therapists.

Printed publications:
Code of Conduct
Complaint Investigation and Disciplinary Procedure
Membership list
Helping you to be Better Informed about Comp. Therapies (leaflet, free)
Protecting Patients, Promoting Professionalism (leaflet, free)

Access to staff:
Contact by letter, by telephone, by e-mail and via website
Hours: Mon, Tue, Thu and Fri, 1000 to 1700

Access to building, collection or gallery:
No access other than to staff

BRITISH COMPRESSED AIR SOCIETY

Acronym or abbreviation: BCAS

33–Devonshire Street, London, W1G 6PY

Tel: 020 7935 2464
Fax: 020 7935 3077
E-mail: society@britishcompressedair.co.uk

Website:
http://www.britishcompressedair.co.uk

Enquiries:
Enquiries to: Executive Director

Organisation type and purpose:
Trade association.
Technical body for the compressed air industry.

Subject coverage:
Compressed air, gas and vacuum equipment and use; European and British legislation affecting the industry.

Printed publications:
Installation guide
Tools guide – pneumatic
Condensate publication booklet
Pipe joined guide
Publications on services, legislation, regulations, tools, terminology, symbols, product liability

Publications list:
Available in print

continued overleaf

Access to staff:
Contact by letter, by telephone, by fax and by e-mail. Appointment necessary.
Hours: Mon to Fri, 0900 to 1700

BRITISH COMPRESSED GASES ASSOCIATION

Acronym or abbreviation: BCGA

1 Gleneagles House, Vernongate, Derby, DE1 1UP

Tel: 01332 225120
Fax: 01332 225101
E-mail: enquiries@bcga.co.uk

Website:
http://www.bcga.co.uk

Enquiries:
Enquiries to: Secretary

Founded:
1971

Organisation type and purpose:
National organisation, trade association. Representation of about 35 companies who manufacture or distribute gases, or manufacture cylinders to contain them or equipment to use them. It does not represent the interests of the compressed air or natural gas industries.

Subject coverage:
Compressed and liquefied industrial, medical and food gases e.g. oxygen, nitrogen, carbon dioxide, acetylene, chlorine etc; cylinders, regulators, valves etc; safety in handling, transport and use.

Printed publications:
Codes of Practice
Guidance notes
Technical Reports
A Method for Estimating the Offsite Risks from
  Bulk Storage of Liquefied Oxygen
Avoidance and Detection of Internal Corrosion of
  Gas Cylinders
Carriage of Gas Cylinders by Road in Cars and
  Vans – Guidance for Drivers at Work: 1996
  (leaflet)
The Safe Handling of Gas Cylinders at Waste
  Facilities (leaflet)
The Safe Use of CO2 and CO2/N2 Cylinders in the
  Beverage Dispense Industry
The Safe Use of Non-Refillable Gas Containers
  (Cylinders)

Publications list:
Available online

Access to staff:
Contact by e-mail
Hours: Mon to Fri, 0900 to 1700

Affiliated to:
European Industrial Gases Association (EIGA)

BRITISH COMPUTER ASSOCIATION OF THE BLIND

Acronym or abbreviation: BCAB

c/o RNIB, 58–72 John Bright Street, Birmingham, B1 1BN

Tel: 0845 430 8627
E-mail: secretary@bcab.org.uk

Website:
http://www.bcab.org.uk
General information; membership and contact details.

Enquiries:
Enquiries to: Administrator

Founded:
1969

Organisation type and purpose:
National government body, professional body, membership association (membership is by subscription, qualification), present number of members: 250, voluntary organisation, registered charity (charity number SCO232324), suitable for ages: all, training organisation.
A society pursuing all matters of interest to blind people in the computer field.

Subject coverage:
Training, advice on computer access devices for the visually impaired, support groups.

Printed publications:
Newsletter (quarterly)

Electronic and video publications:
Membership CD (3 times a year)

Access to staff:
Contact by letter, by telephone, by fax and by e-mail
Hours: Mon to Fri, 0900 to 1700

Access to building, collection or gallery:
No access other than to staff

BRITISH COMPUTER SOCIETY

Acronym or abbreviation: BCS

1st Floor, Block D, North Star House, North Star Avenue, Swindon, SN2 1FA

Tel: 01793 417417
Fax: 01793 417444
E-mail: bcshq@bcs.org.uk

Website:
http://www.bcs.org.uk

Enquiries:
Enquiries to: Public Relations Manager
Direct tel: 01793 417433
Direct e-mail: aduckworth@hq-bcs.org.uk

Founded:
1957

Organisation type and purpose:
Professional body.

Subject coverage:
Computers and their applications, commercial data processing, programming and programming languages, information technology, safety-critical and business-critical systems, computers for the disabled and computer misuse (including hacking and viruses).

Museum or gallery collection, archive, or library special collection:
The Society's Library is online

Library catalogue:
All or part available online

Printed publications:
Computer Bulletin (6 times a year)
Distributed Systems Engineering Journal
  (quarterly, jointly with the IEE and the IoP)
Formal Methods in Computing (quarterly, pub.
  jointly with Springer-Verlag)
HCI Journal (4 times a year, pub. jointly with
  Butterworth)
High Integrity Systems (4 times a year, pub. jointly
  with Oxford University Press)
Information Technology and Nursing (pub. BCS
  Nursing Specialist Group)
Software Engineering Journal (10 times a year, pub.
  jointly with OUP)
The Computer Journal (6 times a year)

Publications list:
Available in print

Access to staff:
Contact by letter, by telephone, by fax and by e-mail
Hours: Mon to Fri, 0915 to 1715

Associated with:
numerous similar Information Technology Societies

Member of:
Council of European Professional Information Societies

UK member of:
IFIP

BRITISH CONSTRUCTIONAL STEELWORK ASSOCIATION LIMITED

Acronym or abbreviation: BCSA

Head Office, 4 Whitehall Court, Westminster, London, SW1A 2ES

Tel: 020 7839 8566
Fax: 020 7976 1634
E-mail: postroom@steelconstruction.org

Website:
http://www.steelconstruction.org

Enquiries:
Enquiries to: Director General
Direct fax: 020 7839 4729
Direct e-mail: derek.tordoff@steelconstruction.org

Founded:
1906

Organisation type and purpose:
Trade association.

Subject coverage:
Constructional steelwork.

Publications list:
Available online and in print

Access to staff:
Contact by letter, by telephone, by fax and by e-mail
Hours: Mon to Fri, 0900 to 1700

BRITISH CONTRACT FURNISHING ASSOCIATION

Acronym or abbreviation: BCFA

Project House, 25 West Wycombe Road, High Wycombe, Buckinghamshire, HP11 2LQ

Tel: 01494 896790
Fax: 01494 896779
E-mail: enquiries@bcfa.org.uk

Website:
http://www.bcfa.org.uk
Members' benefits, list of members.

Enquiries:
Enquiries to: Chief Executive

Founded:
1970

Organisation type and purpose:
Trade association.

Subject coverage:
British manufacture or supply of goods and services for the contract furnishing sector.

Printed publications:
BCFA Members' Directory
Order printed publications from: BCFA

Access to staff:
Contact by telephone, by fax, by e-mail and via website
Hours: Mon to Fri, 0900 to 1700

Access for disabled people:
Ramped entry

BRITISH COPYRIGHT COUNCIL

Acronym or abbreviation: BCC

29–33 Berners Street, London, W1T 3AB

Tel: 01986 788122
E-mail: info@britishcopyright.org

Website:
http://www.britishcopyright.org

Enquiries:
Enquiries to: Secretary

Organisation type and purpose:
Membership association (membership is by subscription), present number of members: 31. Liaison committee.

Discussion forum for the Council's member associations on matters of common concern relating to copyright in literary, musical, dramatic and artistic works.

Subject coverage:
Copyright and rights in performances in the UK.

Access to staff:
Contact by letter and by e-mail

BRITISH CORRESPONDENCE CHESS ASSOCIATION

Acronym or abbreviation: BCCA

61 Swanswell Road, Solihull, West Midlands, B92 7ET

Tel: 0121 707 3850
E-mail: s.grayland@sky.com

Website:
http://www.bcca.info
Current activities and tournaments taking place within the association

Enquiries:
Enquiries to: General Secretary

Founded:
1906

Organisation type and purpose:
Membership association (membership is by subscription), present number of members: 250, voluntary organisation.

Subject coverage:
Postal chess, e-mail chess and chess in general.

Printed publications:
Correspondence Chess (quarterly)

Access to staff:
Contact by letter, by telephone, by e-mail and via website
Hours: Mon to Fri, 0900 to 1700

Links with:
British Federation for Correspondence Chess
    tel: 01206 542753

BRITISH COUNCIL – INFORMATION CENTRE

Acronym or abbreviation: BC

Bridgewater House, 58 Whitworth Street, Manchester, M1 6BB

Tel: 0161 957 7755\ Minicom no. 0161 957 7188
Fax: 0161 957 7762
E-mail: general.enquiries@britishcouncil.org

Website:
http://www.britishcouncil.org
The work of the British Council in general.

Founded:
1934

Organisation type and purpose:
International organisation, service industry, registered charity (charity number 209131). Non-government organisation.
Promoting art, cultural, and educational co-operation between Britain and other countries.

Subject coverage:
British education system, English language teaching and learning, higher education courses, English literature, visual arts, science and technology education, overseas development, work of the British Council overseas, environment, government, law and social development.

Museum or gallery collection, archive, or library special collection:
The unit holds small collections of leaflets, prospectuses, reports, etc. in its fields of interest, but it has no major holdings of books or runs of periodicals

Printed publications:
Address book of British Council offices overseas

Information sheets on studying and living in Britain
British Council Annual Report
English language courses and schools in UK (brochure)

Access to staff:
Contact by letter, by telephone, by fax, by e-mail and via website
Hours: Mon to Fri, 1000 to 1645

Access to building, collection or gallery:
No access other than to staff
Hours: Mon to Fri, 1000 to 1700

Funded by:
Foreign and Commonwealth Office

BRITISH COUNCIL – VISUAL ARTS DEPARTMENT

10 Spring Gardens, London, SW1A 2BN

Tel: 020 7389 3050
Fax: 020 7389 3101
E-mail: visual.arts@britishcouncil.org

Website:
http://www.britishcouncil.org/arts

Enquiries:
Enquiries to: Resources Officer
Other contacts: Research Officer for bibliographic enquiries.

Founded:
1934

Organisation type and purpose:
International organisation, national organisation, registered charity (charity number 209131).
To develop and enlarge overseas knowledge and appreciation of British achievements in the fields of contemporary visual art.

Subject coverage:
Painting, sculpture, printmaking, design, photography, crafts, architecture, video, installation, performance.

Museum or gallery collection, archive, or library special collection:
Art collection specialising in British Art, especially post-1945

Non-library collection catalogue:
All or part available online, in-house and in print

Library catalogue:
All or part available online and in-house

Printed publications:
Distributed by Cornerhouse, Manchester
Order printed publications from: Cornerhouse Publications
70 Oxford Street, Manchester, M1 5NH, tel: 0161 200 1503, fax: 0161 200 1504, e-mail: publications@cornerhouse.org

Publications list:
Available online

Access to staff:
Appointment necessary.
Hours: Mon to Fri, 1000 to 1700
Special comments: Library: by appointment only. Art Collection: online only.

Access to building, collection or gallery:
By appointment only
Hours: Mon to Fri, 1000 to 1700

BRITISH COUNCIL EDUCATION AND TRAINING GROUP

10 Spring Gardens, London, SW1A 2BN

Tel: 0161 957 7755
Fax: 0161 957 7762
E-mail: general.enquiries@britishcouncil.org

Website:
http://www.educationuk.org
Advice and information on studying in the UK.
http://www.globalgateway.org

Advice and information on international school linking, including an interactive database where schools can register and look for partners.
http://www.britishcouncil.org/learning
Information on the British Council's range of services in the area of education and training.

Enquiries:
Enquiries to: Information Officer
Other contacts: Director

Organisation type and purpose:
International organisation, registered charity (charity number 209131).
The British Council Education and Training Group promotes and enhances quality education and training in the UK and world-wide by strengthening education, training and youth co-operation between the UK and other countries; increasing international recognition of the range and quality of learning opportunities, including English language teaching, provided by the UK; supporting education and training reform; sharing creativity, innovation and best practice between the UK and other countries; delivering a range of quality programmes in international education, training, youth and sport.

Subject coverage:
For international students: information and advice on studying in the UK and on British courses, qualifications and examinations.
For the UK education and training field: information and advice on working internationally, setting up educational partnerships, international professional development and exchange opportunities, the promotion of UK education and training overseas.

Access to staff:
Contact by letter, by telephone, by fax, by e-mail and via website
Hours: Mon to Fri, 1000 to 1645

Also at:
Belfast Office
    Norwich Union Building, 7 Fountain Street, Belfast, BT1 5EG; tel: 028 9024 8220; fax: 028 9023 7592
Cardiff Office
    1 Kingsway, Cardiff, CF10 3AQ; tel: 029 2092 4300; fax: 029 2092 4301
Edinburgh Office
    3rd Floor, The Tun, 4 Jackson's Entry, Holyrood Road, Edinburgh, EH8 8PJ; tel: 0131 524 5700; fax: 0131 524 5701
Manchester Office
    Bridgewater House, 58 Whitworth Street, Manchester, M1 6BB; tel: 0161 957 7755; fax: 0161 957 7762

Parent body:
British Council
    10 Spring Gardens, London, SW1A 2BN

BRITISH COUNCIL FOR OFFICES

Acronym or abbreviation: BCO

78–79 Leadenhall Street, London, EC3A 3DH

Tel: 020 7283 0125
Fax: 020 7626 1553
E-mail: mail@bco.org.uk

Website:
http://www.bco.org.uk

Enquiries:
Enquiries to: Chief Executive
Other contacts: Assistant Secretary

Founded:
1990

Organisation type and purpose:
Membership association (membership is by subscription), present number of members: 1,553.
The British Council for Offices' mission is to research, develop and communicate best practice in all aspects of the office sector. It delivers this by providing a forum for the discussion and debate of relevant issues.

continued overleaf

Printed publications:
Best Practice in the Specification for Offices
Good Practice in the Selection of Construction
  Materials
Management Guidance – Security
International Benchmarking
Annual Review
Members' Handbook (available to members only)
Order printed publications from: website: http://
www.bco.org.uk/research

Publications list:
Available online

Access to staff:
Contact by letter, by telephone, by fax, by e-mail
and via website. Appointment necessary.
Hours: Mon to Fri, 0930 to 1730

BRITISH COUNCIL FOR PREVENTION OF BLINDNESS

Acronym or abbreviation: BCPB

4 Bloomsbury Square, London, WC1A 2RP

Tel: 020 7404 7114
E-mail: info@bcpb.org

Website:
http://www.bcpb.org
About BCBP, funding research, new treatments,
fellowships and research grants.

Founded:
1976

Organisation type and purpose:
Registered charity (number 270941).
Funds both UK-based and overseas research into
the causes of blindness throughout the world,
together with specific community-based disease
prevention projects in developing countries. Also
funds the training of eyecare professionals from
developing countries through Fellowship
programmes.

Subject coverage:
Prevention of blindness.

Access to staff:
Contact by letter, by telephone and by e-mail

BRITISH COUNCIL OF CHINESE MARTIAL ARTS

c/o 110 Frensham Drive, Nuneaton, Warwickshire,
CV10 9QL

Tel: 024 7639 4642
E-mail: info@bccma.com

Website:
http://www.bccma.com

Enquiries:
Enquiries to: Secretary General

Organisation type and purpose:
Membership association (membership is by
subscription, qualification).
Governing body of the sport.

Subject coverage:
Traditional Chinese martial arts, freestyle martial
arts, Tai Chi and Chi Gung and Chinese boxing
(Sanshou).

Access to staff:
Contact by letter, by telephone, by e-mail and via
website
Hours: Mon to Fri, 1000 to 1600

Affiliated to:
European Wu Shu Federation
International Wu Shu Federation

Member of:
Sports Council

BRITISH COUNCIL OF DISABLED PEOPLE

Acronym or abbreviation: BCODP

Suites 1–2, Litchurch Plaza, Litchurch Lane, Derby,
DE24 8AA

Tel: 01332 295551\ Minicom no. 01332 295581
Fax: 01332 295580
E-mail: bcodp@bcodp.org.uk

Website:
http://www.bcodp.org.uk

Enquiries:
Enquiries to: Chief Executive

Founded:
1981

Organisation type and purpose:
Registered charity.

Subject coverage:
Campaigning and lobbying, representing the
interests of disabled people at national level and
above; supporting new and existing organisations
run by and for disabled people to represent their
interests.

Printed publications:
Making Your Own Choices
Cashing in on Independence
From Local to National
Demolishing Special Needs
Everything You Need to Know About Getting &
  Using Direct Payments
The Way Forward – a BCODP Resource Pack
Users' Ability to Manage Direct Payments
Notes on the Disability Discrimination Act as at
  April 2000

Publications list:
Available in print

Access to staff:
Contact by letter, by telephone, by fax and by e-
mail
Hours: Mon to Fri, 0900 to 1700

Access for disabled people:
Parking provided, ramped entry, access to all
public areas, toilet facilities

BRITISH COUNCIL OF SHOPPING CENTRES

Acronym or abbreviation: BCSC

1 Queen Anne's Gate, Westminster, London, SW1H
9BT

Tel: 020 7222 1122
Fax: 020 7222 4440
E-mail: info@bcsc.org.uk

Website:
http://www.bcsc.org.uk

Enquiries:
Enquiries to: Head of Secretariat
Other contacts: Events Manager for BCSC Events.

Founded:
1984

Organisation type and purpose:
Membership association.
To provide a forum for all those involved in the
development and management of shopping
centres.

Subject coverage:
Matters relating to shopping centres.

Publications list:
Available in print

Access to staff:
Contact by letter, by telephone and by e-mail
Hours: Mon to Fri, 0900 to 1730

Access to building, collection or gallery:
No access other than to staff

BRITISH CROWN GREEN BOWLING ASSOCIATION

Acronym or abbreviation: BCGBA

94 Fishers Lane, Pensby, Wirral, Merseyside, CH61
8SB

Tel: 0151 648 5740
Fax: 0151 648 0733
E-mail: jac21up@aol.com

Website:
http://www.bowls.org

Enquiries:
Enquiries to: Chief Executive
Other contacts: Financial Officer

Founded:
1907

Organisation type and purpose:
Membership association.
Governing body of crown green bowls.

Subject coverage:
Crown green bowls; coaching; manufacture and
maintenance of crown greens.

Printed publications:
Handbook (annually, £1.75)

Access to staff:
Contact by letter, by telephone and by fax
Hours: Mon to Fri, 0900 to 1700

BRITISH CUTLERY AND SILVERWARE ASSOCIATION

Acronym or abbreviation: BCSA

Unit 10 Edmund Road Business Centre, Sheffield,
S2 4ED

Tel: 0114 252 7850
Fax: 0114 252 7855
E-mail: enquiries@secas.co.uk

Website:
http://www.secas.co.uk
Under construction.

Enquiries:
Enquiries to: Chief Executive

Organisation type and purpose:
Trade association.

Subject coverage:
Trade marks, patterns, care of cutlery and
silverware, sources of supply.

Printed publications:
Buyers Guide
History of the Industry

BRITISH CYCLING FEDERATION

Acronym or abbreviation: BCF

National Cycling Centre, Stuart Street, Manchester,
M11 4DQ

Tel: 0161 274 2000
Fax: 0161 274 2001
E-mail: info@britishcycling.org.uk

Website:
http://new.britishcycling.org.uk

Enquiries:
Enquiries to: Company Secretary
Direct tel: 0161 274 2038

Founded:
1959

Organisation type and purpose:
Membership association (membership is by
subscription), present number of members: 32,000.
Promotional and governing body for the sport and
pastime of cycling.

Subject coverage:
All forms of cycling, including cycle racing,
coaching, touring, leisure cycling.

Printed publications:
BCF Quarterly Handbook 2002 (£10 annually)

Access to staff:
Contact by letter, by telephone, by fax, by e-mail,
in person and via website. Non-members charged.

Hours: Mon to Thu, 0845 to 1700; Fri, 0845 to 1545

Access for disabled people:
Access to all public areas

BRITISH DANCE COUNCIL

Acronym or abbreviation: BDC

Terpsichore House, 240 Merton Road, South Wimbledon, London, SW19 1EQ

Tel: 020 8545 0085
Fax: 020 8545 0225
E-mail: secretary@british-dance-council.org

Website:
http://www.british-dance-council.org
Information about the BDC

Enquiries:
Enquiries to: Manager

Founded:
1929

Organisation type and purpose:
Membership association.
Official Board of Ballroom Dancing.
Promotion and regulation of ballroom dancing, dance sport and social dancing in Great Britain.

Subject coverage:
Ballroom dancing.

Printed publications:
Ballroom Dancing as a Career
Ballroom Dancing in Great Britain
Researching into Dance
Leaflets, include:
Charts, scripts and books
Let's Dance – fun, health, sports, making friends

Publications list:
Available in print

Access to staff:
Contact by letter, by telephone, by fax, by e-mail and via website. Appointment necessary.
Hours: Mon to Fri, 1000 to 1600

Corporate member:
Allied Dancing Association
   71 Haileybury Road, Woolton, Liverpool, L25 8SN; tel: 0151 428 1312
British Association of Teachers of Dancing
   23 Marywood Square, Glasgow, G41 2BP; tel: 0141 423 4029
Imperial Society of Teachers of Dancing
   Imperial House, 22/26 Paul Street, London, EC2A 4QE; tel: 020 7377 1577; fax: 020 7247 8979
International Dance Teachers Association
   International House, 76 Bennett Road, Brighton, BN2 5JL; tel: 01273 685652/3; fax: 01273 674388; e-mail: idta@fastnet.co.uk
National Association of Teachers of Dancing
   44–47 The Broadway, Thatcham, Berkshire, RG19 3HP; tel: 01635 868888; fax: 01635 872301
National Resource Centre of Dance
   University of Surrey, Guildford, Surrey, GU2 5HX; tel: 01483 259316
Northern Counties Dance Teachers' Association
   67 Elizabeth Drive, Palmersville, Newcastle upon Tyne, NE12 9QP; tel: 0191 268 1830
Scottish Dance Teachers' Alliance
   339 North Woodside Road, Glasgow, G20 6ND; tel: 0141 339 8944
United Kingdom Alliance
   Centenary House, 30/40 Station Road, Blackpool, FY4 1EU; tel: 01253 408828; fax: 01253 408066

Member of:
World Dance and Dance Sport Council
   at the same address; tel: 020 8545 0223; fax: 020 8544 9825

BRITISH DARTS ORGANISATION

Acronym or abbreviation: BDO

2 Pages Lane, Muswell Hill, London, N10 1PS

Tel: 020 8883 5544
Fax: 020 8883 0109

E-mail: britishdarts.org@btconnect.com
Website:
http://www.bdodarts.com

Enquiries:
Enquiries to: Director

Founded:
1973

Organisation type and purpose:
Membership association (membership is by subscription), voluntary organisation.
Incorporates 66 member county darts organisations in England, Scotland and Wales; plus associations with over 60 countries worldwide.
Promoters of darts.

Subject coverage:
Promotion and organisation of the sport of darts at all levels, i.e. local darts league, Inter County Championships and International and World Championships; rules and regulations governing the sport of darts (updated annually). Promoters of the BBC televised Lakeside World Professional Darts Championships and Winmau World Masters annually.

Printed publications:
Annual Yearbook and Darts Diary (published 1 September)
Current Playing Rules for the Sport of Darts

Access to staff:
Contact by letter
Hours: Mon to Fri, 0900 to 1700

Member of:
Central Council of Physical Recreation
World Darts Federation (WDF)

BRITISH DEAF ASSOCIATION

Acronym or abbreviation: BDA

10th Floor, Coventry Point, Market Way, Coventry, CV1 1EA

Tel: 02476 550936 (voice), 02476 550393 (text), 84 12 97 143 (videophone)
Fax: 02476 221541
E-mail: bda@bda.org.uk

Website:
http://www.bda.org.uk

Founded:
1890

Organisation type and purpose:
Membership association, voluntary organisation, registered charity.
Membership-led charity campaigning on behalf of nearly 70,000 deaf people in Britain.
To advance and protect the interests of the Deaf Community, to increase deaf people's access to the facilities and lifestyles of hearing people, and to ensure a greater awareness of their rights and responsibilities as members of society.

Subject coverage:
Profound deafness; British sign language; deaf community, culture and heritage.

Printed publications:
Publication list available on website
British Deaf News (monthly)
Information Directory
Information pack

Publications list:
Available online

Access to staff:
Contact by letter, by telephone, by fax, by e-mail, in person and via website
Hours: Mon to Fri, 0900 to 1700
Textphone also available during evening hours.
Special comments: Voice and textphone also available for access.

Access for disabled people:
Level entry, toilet facilities

Has regional offices in:
Belfast, Cardiff, Glasgow and Preston

Representative organisation of UK on the:
European Union of the Deaf
World Federation of the Deaf (affiliated to the United Nations)

BRITISH DEAF HISTORY SOCIETY

Acronym or abbreviation: BDHS

11–13 Wilson Patten Road, Warrington, Cheshire, WA1 1PG

Tel: 01925 632463
E-mail: info.bdhs@btconnect.com

Website:
http://www.bdhs.org.uk

Organisation type and purpose:
Membership organisation focusing on history related to deafness.

Subject coverage:
History related to deafness.

BRITISH DEAF SPORTS COUNCIL

Acronym or abbreviation: BDSC

Bridge Street, Otley, West Yorkshire, LS21 1B

Tel: 01943 850214 / Minicom: 01943 850081
Fax: 01943 850828
E-mail: enquiries@britishdeafsportscouncil.org.uk

Website:
http://www.britishdeafsportscouncil.org.uk/

Enquiries:
Enquiries to: Administrator

Founded:
1930

Organisation type and purpose:
Membership association (membership is by subscription), registered charity (charity number 1014541).

Subject coverage:
Sports for hearing impaired people.

Access to staff:
Contact by letter, by telephone and by fax
Hours: Mon to Thu, 0930 to 1330 and 1430 to 1730; Fri, 0930 to 1330 and 1430 to 1700
Special comments: Stamped addressed envelope preferred.

BRITISH DEER FARMERS ASSOCIATION

Acronym or abbreviation: BDFA

Old Stoddah, Penruddock, Penrith, Cumbria, CA11 0RY

Tel: 01768 483810
Fax: 01768 483809
E-mail: bdfa@old-stoddah.demon.co.uk

Website:
http://www.deer.org.uk

Enquiries:
Enquiries to: Secretary

Organisation type and purpose:
National organisation, trade association (membership is by subscription).
National association representing deer farmers and venison processors.

Subject coverage:
Deer farming; farmed venison.

Printed publications:
Deer Farming (journal, quarterly by subscription direct from BDFA)

Access to staff:
Contact by e-mail and via website
Hours: Mon to Fri, 0900 to 1700

BRITISH DENTAL ASSOCIATION

Acronym or abbreviation: BDA

64 Wimpole Street, London, W1G 8YS

Tel: 020 7563 4545
Fax: 020 7935 6492
E-mail: r.farbey@bda.org

Website:
http://www.bda.org

Enquiries:
Enquiries to: Librarian
Other contacts: Head of Library Services

Founded:
1880

Organisation type and purpose:
National organisation, professional body
(membership is by subscription).

Subject coverage:
Dentistry and the dental profession.

Museum or gallery collection, archive, or library special collection:
Rare historical dental texts
DVD and video collection

Printed publications:
British Dental Journal (2 times a month)
Occasional publications
BDA News

Access to staff:
Contact by letter. Appointment necessary. Letter of introduction required.
Hours: Mon to Fri, 0900 to 1800

Access to building, collection or gallery:
Prior appointment required for non-members, except to museum
Hours: Mon to Fri, 0900 to 1800

BRITISH DENTAL HEALTH FOUNDATION

Acronym or abbreviation: BDHF

Smile House, 2 East Union Street, Rugby, Warwickshire, CV22 6AJ

Tel: 0870 770 4000
Fax: 0870 770 4010
E-mail: feedback@dentalhealth.org.uk

Website:
http://www.dentalhealth.org.uk
Dental health advice, press releases, on-line shopping.
http://www.dentalhelpline.org
Public enquiry service, individual response to personal enquiries on dental issues.

Enquiries:
Enquiries to: Public Relations Department
Direct tel: 0870 770 4014
Direct e-mail: pr@dentalhealth.org.uk

Founded:
1971

Organisation type and purpose:
International organisation (membership is by subscription, election or invitation), present number of members: 1400, voluntary organisation, registered charity (charity number 263198).
To promote dental health to the public.

Subject coverage:
Free, impartial and independent advice on dental health for the public and the media.

Library catalogue:
All or part available online and in print

Printed publications:
Annual Report
Foundation Focus (members newsletter)
Word of Mouth Yearbook (for health professionals)
Patient information leaflets (for the general public)

Electronic and video publications:
Do I Have to Go to the Dentist? (audio book)
Happy & Gappy (audio tape)
Just Five Minutes a Day (video)

Everything you always wanted to know about mouth cancer, but were afraid to ask (CD-ROM)
Other titles cover tooth whitening, implants and bad breath (CD-ROM)

Publications list:
Available online and in print

Access to staff:
Contact by letter, by telephone, by fax and by e-mail
Hours: Mon to Fri, 0900 to 1700

BRITISH DISABLED WATER SKI ASSOCIATION

Acronym or abbreviation: BDWSA

The Tony Edge National Centre, Heron Lake, Hythe End, Wraysbury, Middlesex, TW19 6HW

Tel: 01784 483664
Fax: 01784 482747
E-mail: southern@bdwsa.org

Website:
http://www.bdwsa.org

Enquiries:
Enquiries to: Honorary Secretary
Other contacts: Chairman

Founded:
1979

Organisation type and purpose:
Membership association (membership is by subscription), present number of members: 200, registered charity (charity number 1063678).
Teaching disabled people to water ski.

Subject coverage:
Tuition and equipment for disabled water skiers.

Printed publications:
Brochures

Publications list:
Available in print

Access to staff:
Contact by letter, by telephone, by fax, by e-mail, in person and via website
Hours: Mon to Fri, 0900 to 1700

Access for disabled people:
Parking provided, level entry, access to all public areas, toilet facilities

Parent body:
British Water Ski Federation
390 City Road, London, EC1V 2QA; tel: 020 7833 2856

BRITISH DRAGON BOAT RACING ASSOCIATION

Acronym or abbreviation: BDA

13 The Prebend, Northend, Southam, Warwickshire, CV47 2TR

Tel: 01295 770734
Fax: 01295 770734
E-mail: dacogswell@aol.com

Website:
http://www.dragonboat.com

Enquiries:
Enquiries to: Company Secretary and Treasurer

Founded:
1987

Organisation type and purpose:
National government body, membership association (membership is by subscription), present number of members: 867, voluntary organisation.
Governing body of the sport.

Subject coverage:
The BDA in general, dragon boat racing, boats, sponsoring of dragon boat racing, dragon boat purchase and specification, dragon boat events.

Printed publications:
BDA Handbook
BDA Magazine
Calendar of events
Various leaflets on specific subjects

Access to staff:
Contact by letter, by telephone, by fax, by e-mail and via website
Hours: Mon to Fri, 0900 to 2100

Access to building, collection or gallery:
Prior appointment required

Parent body:
International Dragon Boat Federation
HKTA , 35th Floor, Jardine House, Central, Hong Kong

Subsidiary body:
Dragon Boats UK

BRITISH DRILLING ASSOCIATION LIMITED

Acronym or abbreviation: BDA

Wayside, 55 London End, Upper Boddington, Daventry, Northamptonshire, NN11 6DP

Tel: 01327 264622
Fax: 01327 264623
E-mail: info@britishdrillingassociation.co.uk

Website:
http://www.britishdrillingassociation.co.uk

Enquiries:
Enquiries to: Executive Secretary

Founded:
1975

Organisation type and purpose:
Professional body, trade association.

Subject coverage:
Ground drilling, including ground investigation, ground improvement, water well drilling, mining and quarrying, mineral exploration and some aspects of tunnelling.

Printed publications:
Newsletter (6 times a year)

Access to staff:
Contact by letter, by telephone, by fax, by e-mail and via website
Hours: Mon to Fri, 0900 to 1700

BRITISH DRIVING SOCIETY

Acronym or abbreviation: BDS

83 New Road, Helmingham, Stowmarket, Suffolk, IP14 6EA

Tel: 01473 892001
Fax: 01473 892005
E-mail: email@britishdrivingsociety.co.uk

Website:
http://www.britishdrivingsociety.co.uk
Various

Enquiries:
Enquiries to: Executive Secretary

Founded:
1957

Organisation type and purpose:
Membership association (membership is by subscription), present number of members: 6000, voluntary organisation.
To encourage and assist those interested in the driving of horses and ponies.

Subject coverage:
Driving of horses and ponies.

Printed publications:
Annual book of driving shows/trials/competitions (for members)
Annual journal (for members)
Book List
Newsletter (quarterly, for members)

Publications list:
Available online and in print

Access to staff:
Contact by letter, by telephone, by fax, by e-mail and via website
Hours: Mon to Fri, 0900 to 1700

Affiliated to:
Joint National Horse Education and Training Council

BRITISH DYSLEXIA ASSOCIATION

Acronym or abbreviation: BDA

Unit 8, Bracknell Beeches, Old Bracknell Lane, Bracknell, RG12 7BW

Tel: 0845 251 9002 (helpline); 0845 251 9003 (office)
Fax: 0845 215 9005
E-mail: helpline@bdadyslexia.org.uk

Website:
http://www.bdadyslexia.org.uk

Founded:
1960

Organisation type and purpose:
Membership association, voluntary organisation, registered charity (charity number 289243), training organisation.
Co-ordinates 120 independent local associations.

Subject coverage:
Dyslexia; education and training for the young, adults and professionals in education, health and employment, medical and psychological information. The charity offers advice, information and help to dyslexic people, their families and the professionals who support them, and works to raise awareness and understanding and to effect change.

Printed publications:
Achieving Dyslexia-Friendly Schools (available as a download)
Code of Practice for Employers
Conference proceedings (every 2 or 3 years)
Dyslexia – An International Journal of Research and Practice
Dyslexia Contact (magazine, 3 times a year)
Dyslexia Handbook

Publications list:
Available online and in print

Access to staff:
Contact by letter, by telephone, by fax, by e-mail and via website
Hours: Mon to Fri, 1000 to 1600; Wed, 1700 to 1900

Member organisations:
local dyslexia associations and corporate members

BRITISH EARTH SHELTERING ASSOCIATION

Acronym or abbreviation: BESA

15 Maes-y-Fron Terrace, Abercrave, Swansea Valley, SA9 1XE

Tel: 01639 730006
E-mail: caerllan@compuserve.com, undergroundwoods@hotmail.co.uk

Enquiries:
Enquiries to: Honorary Secretary

Founded:
1981

Organisation type and purpose:
Membership association.

Subject coverage:
Design and construction of earth sheltering structures, energy efficiency and architecture.

Printed publications:
Newsletter (3–4 times a year, £2 non-members, free to members)

Access to staff:
Contact by letter, by telephone, by fax, by e-mail and via website. Appointment necessary.
Hours: Mon to Fri, 0900 to 1700

BRITISH ECOLOGICAL SOCIETY

Acronym or abbreviation: BES

Charles Darwin House, 12 Roger Street, London, WC1N 2JU

Tel: 020 7685 2500
Fax: 020 7685 2501
E-mail: info@britishecologicalsociety.org

Website:
http://www.BritishEcologicalSociety.org
Details of the society's activities.

Enquiries:
Enquiries to: Executive Director

Founded:
1913

Organisation type and purpose:
Learned society.
To promote the science of ecology through research, and to use the findings of such research to educate the public and influence policy decisions that involve ecological matters.

Subject coverage:
Ecology, as a branch of natural science.

Printed publications:
Ecological Issues Booklets (1 or 2 each year)
Journal of Animal Ecology (6 times a year)
Journal of Applied Ecology (6 times a year)
Journal of Ecology (6 times a year)
Functional Ecology (6 times a year)
Symposium volumes

Electronic and video publications:
Methods in Ecology and Evolution (1–2 times a year)

Publications list:
Available in print

Access to staff:
Contact by letter, by telephone, by fax and by e-mail

BRITISH EDITORIAL SOCIETY OF BONE AND JOINT SURGERY

Acronym or abbreviation: BESBJS

22 Buckingham Street, London, WC2N 6ET

Tel: 020 7782 0010
Fax: 020 7782 0995
E-mail: info@jbjs.org.uk

Website:
http://www.jbjs.org.uk
Information about all publications and content hosted online.

Enquiries:
Enquiries to: Managing Director
Other contacts: Circulations Manager (for ordering subscriptions)

Founded:
1948

Organisation type and purpose:
Registered charity (charity number 209299), publishing house.
The advancement and improvement of education in orthopaedic surgery and allied branches of surgery.

Subject coverage:
Bone and joint surgery.

Museum or gallery collection, archive, or library special collection:
Watson-Jones Library Bequest

Non-library collection catalogue:
All or part available online

Library catalogue:
All or part available in-house

Printed publications:
Journal of Bone and Joint Surgery, British Volume
The History of the ABC Club of Travelling Fellows

Microform publications:
Journal of Bone and Joint Surgery, British Volume

Electronic and video publications:
Journal of Bone and Joint Surgery, British Volume

Publications list:
Available online and in print

Access to staff:
Contact by letter, by telephone, by fax, by e-mail and via website. Appointment necessary.
Hours: Mon to Fri, 0900 to 1700

Access to building, collection or gallery:
Prior appointment required

BRITISH EDUCATIONAL SUPPLIERS ASSOCIATION LIMITED

Acronym or abbreviation: BESA

20 Beaufort Court, Admirals Way, London, E14 9XL

Tel: 020 7537 4997
Fax: 020 7537 4846
E-mail: besa@besa.org.uk

Website:
http://www.besa.org.uk

Enquiries:
Enquiries to: Information Manager / Research Assistant

Founded:
1933

Organisation type and purpose:
Trade association.

Subject coverage:
Educational equipment and materials, home and export.

Printed publications:
Annual Report
BESA Book – UK Education and Training: The directory of products and suppliers (annual, free on request)
Memorandum and Articles of Association
Promotional literature (all free on request):
ETEMA Brochure
ESPA Brochure
eIC Factfile
UK Show Brochures
BETT
The Education Show
Education Show London
Special Needs London
Specialist Schools Trust National Conference Exhibition
BESA International Conference
ICT in UK State Schools
ICT in UK State Schools
ICT in UK Schools
English Schools Budgets
Early Years Resourcing report
Resources in English Schools – Full Report
Resources in English Schools – Summary Report
Resources in English Schools – Full Report
Resources in English Schools – Summary report
Single-issue reports on a variety of subjects, such as the Licensing Survey Report commissioned by ESPA
A variety of BESA commissioned foreign market reports

Electronic and video publications:
BESA CD Rom (available to overseas enquirers / potential trade partners) BESA Members directory (online) UK Education and Training: The directory of products and Suppliers
UK Show Brochures – BETT
The Education Show

continued overleaf

Access to staff:
Contact by letter, by telephone, by fax, by e-mail and via website
Hours: Mon to Fri, 0900 to 1700

Special interest group the:
British Educational Distributors and Contractors Group
British Educational Furniture Manufacturers Group
Educational Software Publishers Association

BRITISH ELASTIC ROPE SPORTS ASSOCIATION

Acronym or abbreviation: BERSA

33a Canal Street, Oxford, OX2 6BQ

Tel: 01865 311179
Fax: 01865 426007
E-mail: info@bersa.org

Website:
http://www.bersa.org

Enquiries:
Enquiries to: Chairman

Founded:
1989

Organisation type and purpose:
Professional body.
National governing body for the safety and regulation of bungee jumping and other sports involving elastic ropes.

Subject coverage:
General and specialist information on current clubs and their locations, history of the sport and of the Association, recognised equipment and its safe use. Training of operatives within clubs, insurance and accident investigation, inspection of sites, risk assessment and product development to BERSA Certification Mark standard.

Printed publications:
The BERSA Code of Safe Practice (£42)

Access to staff:
Contact by letter, by telephone, by fax and by e-mail. Appointment necessary.
Hours: Mon to Fri, 0900 to 1700
Special comments: Charges made for some services.

BRITISH ELECTROTECHNICAL COMMITTEE

Acronym or abbreviation: BEC

389 Chiswick High Road, London, W4 4AJ

Tel: 020 8996 7458
Fax: 020 8996 7460
E-mail: mike.graham@bsi-global.com

Website:
http://www.bsi-global.com

Enquiries:
Enquiries to: Secretary

Founded:
1908

Organisation type and purpose:
Advisory body.
Represents the UK in European and international electrotechnical bodies.

Subject coverage:
International and European electrotechnical standardisation and its relationship with British Standards.

Museum or gallery collection, archive, or library special collection:
Full Collection of British, European and
  international standards

Library catalogue:
All or part available in-house

Printed publications:
Order printed publications from: Customer Services, BSI

at the same address

Microform publications:
Order microform publications from: Technical Indexes Ltd, Willoughby Road, Bracknell, Berkshire, RG12 4DW

Publications list:
Available online and in print

Access to staff:
Contact by letter, by telephone, by fax and by e-mail
Hours: Mon to Fri, 0900 to 1700

Access to building, collection or gallery:
Prior appointment required

Access for disabled people:
Parking provided, ramped entry, level entry, access to all public areas, toilet facilities

Links with:
BSI
  at the same address

BRITISH ENERGY

Barnett Way, Barnwood, Gloucester, GL4 3RS

Tel: 01452 652769
Fax: 01452 654163

Website:
http://www.british-energy.co.uk
General information about the company including details of power stations. Graduate positions also noted.

Enquiries:
Enquiries to: Corporate Librarian

Organisation type and purpose:
Electricity generator.

Subject coverage:
Nuclear engineering, electrical engineering, heat transfer, physics and mechanical engineering, health and safety, management.

Access to staff:
Appointment necessary.
Hours: Mon to Thu, 0900 to 1700; Fri, 0900 to 1600

BRITISH ENERGY

Acronym or abbreviation: BE

Corporate Library, British Energy, Barnett Way, Barnwood, Gloucester, GL4 3RS

Tel: 01452 652222
Fax: 01452 654163

Website:
http://www.british-energy.com

Enquiries:
Enquiries to: Library and Information Officer
Direct tel: 01452 652769; 01452 653660
Direct e-mail: bwd.library@british-energy.com

Founded:
1996

Please select:

Organisation type and purpose:
Service industry.
Electricity generator.

Subject coverage:
Power generation; nuclear technology; electricity supply industry.

Library catalogue:
All or part available in-house

Access to staff:
Contact by telephone and by e-mail. Appointment necessary.
Hours: Mon to Fri, 0900 to 1600

Access to building, collection or gallery:
Prior appointment required

Constituent part of:
EDF Energy

BRITISH ENGINEERS' CUTTING TOOLS ASSOCIATION

Acronym or abbreviation: BECTA

c/o Institute of Spring Technology, Henry Street, Sheffield, S3 7EQ

Tel: 0114 278 9143
E-mail: nstamp@mta.org.uk

Enquiries:
Enquiries to: Secretary

Organisation type and purpose:
Trade association.

Subject coverage:
Cutting tools manufactured from high-speed steel.

Access to staff:
Contact by letter, by telephone, by fax and by e-mail
Hours: Mon to Fri, 0900 to 1700

Affiliated to:
Federation of British Engineers' Tool Manufacturers

BRITISH EQUESTRIAN FEDERATION

Acronym or abbreviation: BEF

National Agricultural Centre, Stoneleigh, Kenilworth, Warwickshire, CV8 2RH

Tel: 024 7669 8871
Fax: 024 7669 6484
E-mail: info@bef.co.uk

Website:
http://www.bef.co.uk
General information on the work of the BEF, international competitions in the UK and articles of equestrian interest.

Enquiries:
Enquiries to: Chief Executive

Organisation type and purpose:
International organisation, national government body, advisory body, membership association (membership is by election or invitation). Represents the sport on the National Olympic Committee of the British Olympic Association.

Subject coverage:
BEF provides knowledge regarding international equestrian matters concerning competition, rules and regulations. Member disciplines provide specialist discipline knowledge.

Access to staff:
Contact by letter, by telephone, by fax, by e-mail and via website. Appointment necessary.
Hours: Mon to Fri, 0900 to 1700

Access to building, collection or gallery:
Prior appointment required

Access for disabled people:
Level entry

Member disciplines:
Association of British Riding Schools (ABRS)
  tel: 01736 369440; fax: 01736 351390; e-mail: office@abrs.org
British Dressage Limited
  tel: 024 7669 8843; e-mail: name.surname@ britishdressage.co.uk
British Equestrian Trade Association (BETA)
  tel: 01937 587062; fax: 01937 582728; e-mail: clairewilliams@beta-uk.org
British Equestrian Vaulting Limited
  tel: 0976 421789; fax: 01203 463027; e-mail: julievaulting@hotmail.com
British Eventing
  tel: 024 7669 8856; e-mail: name.surname@ britisheventing.com
British Horse Driving Trials Association
  tel: 01347 878789; e-mail: bhdta@dial.pipex.com
British Horse Society
  tel: 01926 707700; fax: 01926 707800
British Reining Horse Association (BRHA)
  tel: 01342 892203; fax: 01342 893441

British Show Jumping Association
 tel: 024 7669 8800; e-mail: nameinitial@bsja.co.uk
Endurance GB
 tel: 024 7669 8863
Pony Club
 tel: 024 7669 8300; fax: 024 7669 6386; e-mail:
 name@pcuk.org
Scottish Equestrian Association (SEA)
 tel: 01475 540687; fax: 01475 540348; e-mail:
 patsypup@aol.com

BRITISH EQUESTRIAN TRADE ASSOCIATION

Acronym or abbreviation: BETA

East Wing, Stockeld Park, Wetherby, West
Yorkshire, LS22 4AW

Tel: 01937 587062
Fax: 01937 582728
E-mail: info@beta-uk.org

Enquiries:
Enquiries to: Secretary
Direct e-mail: tinar@beta-int.com

Founded:
1977

Organisation type and purpose:
Trade association.

Subject coverage:
Equestrian business and trade, including saddlery,
pharmaceutical products, breeding, feedstuffs,
transport, stalling, exporting, importing and other
related matters.

Information services:
BETA International Trade Fair

Printed publications:
British Equestrian Directory and Trade Supplement
Equestrian Trade News (monthly)
Newsletter

Access to staff:
Contact by letter, by telephone, by fax and by e-
mail
Hours: Mon to Fri, 0900 to 1700

Links with:
EMC Limited, publishers

Subsidiary body:
BETA Trade Fairs

BRITISH ESSENCE MANUFACTURERS ASSOCIATION

Acronym or abbreviation: BEMA

PO Box 172, Cranleigh, GU6 8WU, England

Tel: 01483 275411
E-mail: secretariat@bemaorg.org

Website:
http://www.bemaorg.org

Enquiries:
Enquiries to: Secretary

Founded:
1917

Organisation type and purpose:
Trade association.

Subject coverage:
Food and drink flavourings, UK, EEC and global
legislation.

Access to staff:
Contact by letter and by e-mail
Hours: Mon to Fri, 0900 to 1700

Links with:
British Fragrance Association
Food and Drink Federation

BRITISH EXPERTISE

10 Grosvenor Gardens, London, SW1W 0DH

Tel: 020 7824 1920

Fax: 020 7824 1929
E-mail: mail@britishexpertise.org

Website:
http://www.britishexpertise.org

Enquiries:
Enquiries to: Chief Executive

Founded:
1965

Formerly called:
BCCB (British Consultants & Construction Bureau)
(year of change 2006)

Organisation type and purpose:
Trade association.
Bureau of multi-disciplined consultants. Primary
information source on business prospects
worldwide.
Promotion of British Consultancy of all disciplines
worldwide.

Subject coverage:
Overseas projects and British consultancy expertise
in all disciplines and specialisations; engineers,
architects, planners, management and economics,
surveyors, agriculture, mining, healthcare,
education and training, environment, tourism,
security, legal, banking, catering, energy,
transportation, leisure, IT, maritime, water
engineering, fire, telecommunications, corrosion,
acoustics, chemical, contractors and construction.

Trade and statistical information:
Knowledge of all countries and multilateral
 funding agencies.

Access to staff:
Contact by letter, by telephone, by fax, by e-mail
and via website. Appointment necessary.
Hours: Mon to Thu, 0900 to 1715; Fri, 0900 to 1700

BRITISH EXPORTERS ASSOCIATION

Acronym or abbreviation: BExA

Broadway House, Tothill Street, Westminster,
London, SW1H 9NQ

Tel: 020 7222 5419
Fax: 020 7799 2468
E-mail: hughbailey@bexa.co.uk

Website:
http://www.bexa.co.uk

Enquiries:
Enquiries to: Director

Founded:
1940

Organisation type and purpose:
Trade association.
Lobby organisation.

Subject coverage:
Exporting.

BRITISH FALCONERS' CLUB

Acronym or abbreviation: BFC

Westfield, Meeting Hill, Worstead, North
Walsham, Norfolk, NR28 9LS

Tel: 01692 404057
Fax: 01692 404057
E-mail: admin@britishfalconersclub.co.uk

Website:
http://www.britishfalconersclub.co.uk

Enquiries:
Enquiries to: Director
Other contacts: Public Relations Officer (for
publicity and press releases)

Founded:
1927

Organisation type and purpose:
Membership association (membership is by
 subscription), present number of members: 1,266.

Subject coverage:
Promotion of falconry in the British Isles and
promotion of captive breeding for birds of prey.

**Museum or gallery collection, archive, or library
special collection:**
The Alexander Library, Oxford University
 Zoological Department Library
The A. K. Bell Library, Perth

Printed publications:
Journal (annually, free to members)
Newsletter (2 times a year, free to members)

Access to staff:
Contact by letter, by telephone, by fax, by e-mail
and via website
Hours: Mon and Tue, 0900 to 1500; Wed and Thu,
0900 to 1300

Access to building, collection or gallery:
No access other than to staff

Branches:
12 regional clubs in the United Kingdom, and
overseas members

Member organisation of:
Countryside Alliance
Federation of Field Sports Associations of the EEC
(FACE)
International Association of Falconry and
Conservation of Birds of Prey (IAF)
Standing Conference on Countryside Sports
(SCCS)

BRITISH FASHION COUNCIL

Acronym or abbreviation: BFC

5 Portland Place, London, W1B 1PW

Tel: 020 7636 7788
Fax: 020 7636 7515

Website:
http://www.britishfashioncouncil.com
http://www.londonfashionweek.co.uk

Enquiries:
Enquiries to: Administrator

Organisation type and purpose:
Trade association.

Subject coverage:
Fashion; fashion exhibitions and London Fashion
Week.

Printed publications:
UK Fashion Exhibition Calendar

BRITISH FEDERATION OF BRASS BANDS

Acronym or abbreviation: BFBB

Unit 12, Maple Estate, Stocks Lane, Barnsley, South
Yorkshire, S75 2BL

Tel: 01226 771015
Fax: 01226 732630
E-mail: natoffice@bfbb.co.uk

Website:
http://www.bfbb.co.uk
General information and contact points of the
Federation.

Enquiries:
Enquiries to: Secretary

Founded:
1968

Organisation type and purpose:
Membership association (membership is by
subscription), present number of members: 310,
registered charity (charity number BFBB 1065181;
BBHT 1037552).
National umbrella body.
Working for all brass bands in the UK.

Subject coverage:
Amateur brass band movement in the UK.

continued overleaf

Museum or gallery collection, archive, or library special collection:
Brass Band Music Library

Non-library collection catalogue:
All or part available in-house

Library catalogue:
All or part available in-house

Access to staff:
Contact by letter, by telephone, by fax, by e-mail, in person and via website
Hours: Mon to Fri, 0900 to 1700

Also at:
British Federation of Brass Bands (BFBB)
122 Main Street, Bingley, BD16 2HL; tel: 01274 511280; fax: 01274 511281

BRITISH FEDERATION OF WOMEN GRADUATES

Acronym or abbreviation: BFWG

4 Mandeville Courtyard, 142 Battersea Park Road, London, SW11 4NB

Tel: 020 7498 8037
E-mail: office@bfwg.org.uk

Website:
http://www.bfwg.org.uk
Scholarships, local, national, regional, international meetings and events.

Enquiries:
Other contacts: President/Vice-Presidents

Founded:
1907

Organisation type and purpose:
International organisation, membership association (membership is by subscription), present number of members: over 800 in England and Wales; 180,000 Worldwide, voluntary organisation, registered charity (charity number 273043).
BFWG is a non-profit, international non-governmental organisation working locally, nationally and globally to improve the status of women and girls, to promote lifelong education, and to enable graduate women to use their expertise to effect change.

Subject coverage:
National pre-doctoral research scholarships for women entering their final year towards a PhD degree, lobbying of government, EU, UN; educational exchange plus international fellowships for members of IFUW.

Museum or gallery collection, archive, or library special collection:
Archives held in The Women's Library, Old Castle Street, London, E1 7NT

Printed publications:
BFWG News (4 times a year, free to members); also available on line to members

Access to staff:
Contact by letter, by telephone, by e-mail and via website. Appointment necessary.
Hours: Varied – by arrangement

Access to building, collection or gallery:
Prior appointment required

Other branches:
Approximately 20 Associations in England and Wales

Other offices in:
79 Countries

Parent body:
International Federation of University Women
10 Rue de Lac, Geneva, CH-1207; tel: 00 41 22 731 2380; fax: 00 41 22 738 0440; e-mail: ifuw@ifuw.org; website: http://www.ifuw.org

Subsidiary:
British Federation of Women Graduates Charitable Foundation (BFWG (CF))
Contact details as per BFWG above

BRITISH FENCING

1 Baron's Gate, 33–35 Rothschild Rd, London, W4 5HT

Tel: 020 8742 3032
Fax: 020 8742 3033
E-mail: headoffice@britishfencing.com

Website:
http://www.britishfencing.com
About fencing, governance, academy, international, clubs, membership, events.

Organisation type and purpose:
National governing body for the Olympic sport of fencing in the British Isles (excluding the Republic of Ireland).
To promote and develop the sport of fencing in the British Isles (excluding the Republic of Ireland).

Subject coverage:
The sport of fencing.

Electronic and video publications:
To The Point (Newsletter, monthly)
The Sword (magazine)

Publications list:
Available online

Access to staff:
Contact by letter, by telephone, by fax and by e-mail
Hours: Mon to Thu, 0930 to 1700; Fri, 0930 to 1600
Special comments: Telephone contact.

Links with:
England Fencing
at the same address
Guernsey Union d'Escrime
Jersey Fencing
Northern Ireland Fencing
Scottish Fencing
Welsh Fencing

BRITISH FILM INSTITUTE – NATIONAL LIBRARY

Acronym or abbreviation: BFI

21 Stephen Street, London, W1T 1LN

Tel: 020 7255 1444
E-mail: library@bfi.org.uk

Website:
http://www.bfi.org.uk/library

Enquiries:
Enquiries to: Information Officer
Direct fax: 020 7436 0165
Other contacts: Curator of Special Collections (for access to special collections)

Founded:
1933

Organisation type and purpose:
National organisation, registered charity.
Grant-aided education/cultural body.
To enable everyone to experience, enjoy and discover more about the world of film and television.

Subject coverage:
All aspects of world cinema; UK broadcast television, with some restrictions.

Museum or gallery collection, archive, or library special collection:
Rare and old books on cinema and pre-cinema
The following are accessed via the library:
Collections, over 200, donated by organisations associated with film and TV
Newspaper cuttings (over 1.5m. dating back to 1930s)
Includes the former ITC (Independent Television Commission) Library collection
Periodicals collection (believed to be largest of its kind in the world)
Published and unpublished scripts (over 20,000)

Trade and statistical information:
Film production statistics, television viewing figures.

Non-library collection catalogue:
All or part available online and in-house

Library catalogue:
All or part available online and in-house

Printed publications:
See website for details
Order printed publications from: Some items from BFI only

Microform publications:
Cinema Pressbooks 1920–40
Film Weekly
Picturegoer
Order microform publications from: Cinema Pressbooks 1920–40 and Picturegoer via Proquest Chadwyck-Healey

Electronic and video publications:
Film Index International
Order electronic and video publications from: Via Proquest Chadwyck-Healey

Publications list:
Available online and in print

Access to staff:
Contact by letter, by telephone, by fax, by e-mail, in person and via website. Non-members charged.

Access to building, collection or gallery:
No prior appointment required
Hours: Reading room: Mon and Fri, 1030 to 1730; Tue and Thu, 1030 to 2000; Wed, 1300 to 2000; closed Sat and Sun
Information line: Mon to Fri, 1000 to 1200 and 1500 to 1700
Special collections by appointment.
Special comments: Special collections: users required to be annual-pass holders. Charges made to some users.
Visitors travelling from some distance recommended to reserve place.

Access for disabled people:
Level entry, toilet facilities

Constituent bodies:
Collections and Information: National Film and Television Archive

BRITISH FIRE ADVISORY SERVICES LIMITED

3 Otterbourne Place, Willington, Maidstone, Kent, ME15 8JL

Tel: 01622 755365
Fax: 01622 755365
E-mail: bfas@zoom.co.uk

Enquiries:
Enquiries to: Director
Other contacts: Senior Consultant

Founded:
2000

Organisation type and purpose:
Consultancy.
A non-political organisation not funded by public money.

Subject coverage:
Fire risk assessment; advice on all fire safety-related legislation; fire fighting procedures; means of escape from fire for disabled persons.

Access to staff:
Contact by letter, by telephone, by fax and by e-mail. Appointment necessary. All charged.
Hours: Mon to Fri, 0900 to 1700

BRITISH FLUE AND CHIMNEY MANUFACTURERS' ASSOCIATION

Acronym or abbreviation: BFCMA

2 Waltham Court, Milley Lane, Hare Hatch, Reading, Berkshire, RG10 9TH

Tel: 0118 940 3416
Fax: 0118 940 6258
E-mail: info@feta.co.uk

Website:
http://www.feta.co.uk

Enquiries:
Enquiries to: Commercial Manager

Founded:
1977

Organisation type and purpose:
Trade association.

Subject coverage:
Natural draught flues and chimneys for all fuels.

Printed publications:
Guide to Choosing and Using Flues and Chimneys
  for Domestic Solid Fuel and Woodburning
  Appliances (2007)
Guide to Flues and Chimneys for Gas Appliances
  (2007)

Publications list:
Available online

Access to staff:
Contact by letter, by telephone, by fax and by e-mail
Hours: Mon to Thu, 0830 to 1630; Fri, 0830 to 1600

Links with:
Federation of Environmental Trade Associations
  at the same address

BRITISH FLUID POWER ASSOCIATION

Acronym or abbreviation: BFPA

Cheriton House, Cromwell Park, Chipping Norton,
Oxfordshire, OX7 5SR

Tel: 01608 647900
Fax: 01608 647919
E-mail: enquiries@bfpa.co.uk

Website:
http://www.bfpa.co.uk
Trade association profile, members' products
guide, publications, news, training information.

Enquiries:
Enquiries to: Director

Founded:
1959

Organisation type and purpose:
Trade association.
Trade association for manufacturers and
distributors of hydraulic and pneumatic
equipment.

Subject coverage:
Hydraulic and pneumatic equipment.

Trade and statistical information:
General production and trade statistics UK and
  Europe (specific data available to members only),
  technical information, product sourcing,
  exhibitions.

Printed publications:
Annual Membership Directory & Year Book
Guides, guidelines, data sheets, codes of practice,
  etc. (over 40 titles)

Publications list:
Available online and in print

Access to staff:
Contact by letter, by telephone, by fax, by e-mail
and via website
Hours: Mon to Thu, 0900 to 1700; Fri, 0900 to 15.20

Access for disabled people:
Parking provided

Sister association:
British Fluid Power Distributors Association
  at the same address

BRITISH FLUORIDATION SOCIETY

Acronym or abbreviation: BFS

Ward 4, Booth Hall Children's Hospital,
Charlestown Road, Manchester, M9 7AA

Tel: 0161 918 5223
E-mail: bfs@bfsweb.org

Website:
http://www.bfsweb.org/
History of fluoridation, BFS publications.

Enquiries:
Enquiries to: Information Officer
Direct e-mail: bfs@bfsweb.org
Other contacts: Administrator, tel no: 01565 872445,
fax: 01565 873936

Founded:
1969

Organisation type and purpose:
Learned society (membership is by subscription),
research organisation.

Subject coverage:
Fluoridation of public water supplies; safety,
benefits, effectiveness; fluoride supplements.

Printed publications:
Booklets on legal cases and scientific cases
Fluoridation – Safety First
Fluoride – The Dental Benefits
How Fluoridation Works
News and Information Bulletin
Society Briefings
Reading List

Electronic and video publications:
Five six-minute videos on fluoridation and dental
  decay

Publications list:
Available in print

Access to staff:
Contact by letter, by telephone, by fax, by e-mail
and via website
Hours: Mon to Fri, 0900 to 1700

BRITISH FLUTE SOCIETY

Acronym or abbreviation: BFS

The Nook, How Mill, Brampton, Cumbria, CA8
9JY

Tel: 01228 670306
E-mail: membership@bfs.org.uk

Enquiries:
Enquiries to: Membership Secretary

Organisation type and purpose:
Membership association.
To promote the flute and flute playing, provide an
opportunity for enthusiasts to contact each other.

Subject coverage:
Flutes and flute making, music, instruments,
history, players, events worldwide.

Printed publications:
Pan (journal, quarterly)

Access to staff:
Contact by letter, by telephone and by e-mail
Hours: Mon to Fri, 0900 to 1700

BRITISH FOOTWEAR ASSOCIATION

Acronym or abbreviation: BFA

3 Burystead Place, Wellingborough,
Northamptonshire, NN8 1AH

Tel: 01933 229005
Fax: 01933 225009
E-mail: info@britfoot.com

Website:
http://www.britfoot.com
Industry summary, consumer information, details
of member firms.

Founded:
1890

Organisation type and purpose:
National organisation, trade association
(membership is by subscription), present number
of members: 100, manufacturing industry, service
industry.

Subject coverage:
Footwear manufacture: labour relations, working
conditions, environmental and safety legislation,
export information and labelling.

Access to staff:
Contact by letter, by telephone, by fax, by e-mail
and via website. Non-members charged.
Hours: Mon to Fri, 0900 to 1700

Access to building, collection or gallery:
Prior appointment required

BRITISH FRANCHISE ASSOCIATION

Acronym or abbreviation: BFA

Thames View, Newtown Road, Henley-on-
Thames, Oxfordshire, RG9 1HG

Tel: 01491 578050
Fax: 01491 573517

Website:
http://www.british-franchise.org.uk
Comprehensive information on franchising and
publication ordering service.

Enquiries:
Enquiries to: Director General
Direct e-mail: mailroom@thebfa.org

Founded:
1977

Organisation type and purpose:
Advisory body, trade association (membership is
by subscription), present number of members: 280,
training organisation, research organisation,
publishing house.
To develop and continuously improve the
standards of good practice in franchising.

Subject coverage:
Franchising: an introduction to franchising to
individuals looking to invest in a franchise
opportunity.
Guidance to businesses on how to franchise their
business.

Trade and statistical information:
Annual survey and statistics on the extent and
  performance of franchising in the UK.

Printed publications:
The Franchisee Guide (to purchase, direct from the
  BFA)
The Franchisor Guide (to purchase, direct from the
  BFA)

Electronic and video publications:
Your Introduction to Franchising (video, £9.95 or
  free with Franchisee or Franchisor Guide, direct)

Publications list:
Available online

Access to staff:
Contact by letter, by telephone, by fax, by e-mail
and via website
Hours: Mon to Fri, 0900 to 1700

BRITISH FRIENDS OF RAMBAM MEDICAL CENTRE

Formal name: The British Friends of Rambam
Medical Center
Acronym or abbreviation: BFRMC

The Director, 10 North Crescent, London, N3 3LL

Tel: 020 8371 1500
Fax: 020 8271 1501
E-mail: alexanderpasse@dsl.pipex.com

Enquiries:
Enquiries to: Director

continued overleaf

Founded:
1993

Organisation type and purpose:
Registered charity (charity number 1028061).
The purchase of medical equipment for all
departments of the Rambam Medical Centre.

Access to staff:
Contact by letter
Hours: Mon to Fri, 0900 to 1700

BRITISH FRIESLAND SHEEP SOCIETY

Weir Park Farm, Christow, Exeter, Devon, EX6 7PB

Tel: 01647 252549
E-mail: 1nf0@baber.co.uk

Website:
http://www.baber.co.uk

Founded:
1980

Subject coverage:
British Friesland sheep.

BRITISH FUCHSIA SOCIETY

Acronym or abbreviation: BFS

PO Box 178, Evesham, Worcestershire, WR11 3WY

Tel: 01386 45158
E-mail: editor@thebfs.org.uk

Website:
http://www.thebfs.org.uk
Society details and news, pictures of fuchsias,
cultural information.

Enquiries:
Enquiries to: Honorary Secretary

Founded:
1938

Organisation type and purpose:
Membership association (membership is by
subscription), present number of members: 3,500,
registered charity (charity number 1038334).
To encourage, improve and research the cultivation
of fuchsias and their various cultivars.

Subject coverage:
All matters related to the culture of fuchsias,
availability of specific cultivars (limited to those
grown in the UK).

Printed publications:
Fuchsia Annual (free to members, limited quantity
    may be available to non-members)
Bulletins (2 times a year, free to members, limited
    quantity may be available to non-members)

Access to staff:
Contact by letter, by telephone and via website
Hours: Mon to Fri, 0900 to 1700

Affiliated to the:
Royal Horticultural Society

Has:
300 affiliated local societies

BRITISH FURNITURE MANUFACTURERS FEDERATION

Members:
High Wycombe Furniture Manufacturers Society
London and South Eastern Furniture
Manufacturers Association
Midlands and North West Furniture
Manufacturers Association
Northern Furniture Manufacturers Association
Scottish Furniture Manufacturers Association
West of England & South Wales Furniture
Manufacturers Association

BRITISH GEAR ASSOCIATION

Acronym or abbreviation: BGA

Suite 43, Imex Business Park, Shobnall Road,
Burton-on-Trent, Staffordshire, DE14 2AU

Tel: 01283 515521
Fax: 01283 515841
E-mail: admin@bga.org.uk

Website:
http://www.bga.org.uk

Enquiries:
Enquiries to: Office Manager
Other contacts: Technical Executive for technical
enquiries.

Organisation type and purpose:
Trade association, membership association
(membership is by subscription).
Association for the Mechanical Power
Transmission Industry.

Subject coverage:
Technical, research, education, training and
economic aspects related to the mechanical power
transmissions industry.

**Museum or gallery collection, archive, or library
special collection:**
Congress papers on mechanical power
    transmission subjects

Trade and statistical information:
Statistical Profile of the Power Transmission
    Industry, members: 1 CD copy free of charge, UK
    non-members: £250 for hard copy, £120 + VAT for
    CD, outside UK: please ask for quote.

Printed publications:
Buyers Guide & Members Handbook
Gear Technology Manual
Gear Technology Teaching Pack
Technical Publications

Publications list:
Available online and in print

Access to staff:
Contact by letter, by telephone, by fax, by e-mail
and via website
Hours: Mon to Fri, 0900 to 1700

Member of:
European Committee of Associations of
Manufacturers of Gears and Transmission Parts
    tel: + 49 69 66 03 1526; fax: + 49 69 66 03 1459

BRITISH GEOLOGICAL SURVEY

Acronym or abbreviation: BGS

Natural History Museum, Cromwell Road,
London, SW7 5BD

Tel: 020 7589 4090
Fax: 020 7584 8270
E-mail: bgslondon@bgs.ac.uk

Website:
http://www.bgs.ac.uk
BGS publications.
http://www.geologyshop.com

Enquiries:
Enquiries to: Manager

Founded:
1845

Organisation type and purpose:
Research organisation.
Scientific research (earth sciences).

Subject coverage:
Geological sciences, earth sciences, geology and
associated subjects, economic resources,
environmental geology, hydrogeology,
geochemistry, regional geology (UK and overseas),
geophysics, palaeontology, engineering geology,
minerals, remote sensing, seismology, volcanology,
petrology, biostratigraphy, petroleum geology,
fluid processes, marine geology, coastal geology,
geological maps, natural hazards.

**Museum or gallery collection, archive, or library
special collection:**
1:10,000 / 1:10,560 National Grid and County Series
    Geological maps of the British Isles and other
    scale geological maps
Indexes to field notebooks and BGS archives
Manuscript graphic indexes to BGS maps
All BGS publications including:
BGS Memoirs, open file, technical and research
    reports

Trade and statistical information:
World mineral statistics.
UK Minerals Year-book.

Library catalogue:
All or part available online

Printed publications:
Catalogue of Geological Maps and Books
Sale collection of BGS and some non-BGS
    publications, including maps
Guide to the London BGS Information Office
New Releases list
Various leaflets on the Services of the Survey
Printed publications list of the most popular items

Publications list:
Available online and in print

Access to staff:
Contact by letter, by telephone, by fax, by e-mail,
in person and via website
Hours: Mon to Fri; tel., 0900 to 1700; visitors, 1000
to 1700

Access for disabled people:
Toilet facilities
Special comments: Lift available to office level.

BRITISH GEOLOGICAL SURVEY – MARINE OPERATIONS AND ENGINEERING

Formal name: British Geological Survey
Acronym or abbreviation: BGS

2A Nivensknowe Road, Loanhead, Midlothian,
EH20 9AU

Tel: 0131 448 2700
Fax: 0131 448 2545
E-mail: enquiries@bgs.ac.uk

Website:
http://www.bgs.ac.uk/science/marine_operations/
home.html
Description of all facilities available from BGS with
further specific information on help index.

Enquiries:
Enquiries to: Information Officer
Direct tel: 0131 667 1000 (Murchison House); 01159
363 100 (Keyworth)
Direct fax: 0131 668 4140 (Murchison House); 01159
363 200 (Keyworth)
Other contacts: Head of Marine Operations and
Engineering

Founded:
1835

Organisation type and purpose:
National government body, professional body,
research organisation.
National onshore and offshore data archive for
geology and geoscience.
Geological survey, geophysical survey and
monitoring (geomagnetism and earthquakes).

Subject coverage:
Geological, geophysical, geotechnical field data
maps, reports, computer databased archive files
and maps, seismic hazards. Geomagnetic
observations and predictions. Offshore geophysical
and geological surveys. Specialised offshore
sampling and coring equipment. Coastal and
environmental monitoring and data collection.

Trade and statistical information:
Documentation relating to mineral statistics,
    earthquake statistics and similar data.

Non-library collection catalogue:
All or part available in-house

Library catalogue:
All or part available in-house

Printed publications:
Publications available from bookshops at the offices in London, Keyworth and Edinburgh, HMSO and some outdoor sports/hillwalking/climbing shops
Annual Reports
Geological and geophysical reports
Maps and surveying documents
Order printed publications from: Information Officer, British Geological Survey, Murchison House, West Main Road, Edinburgh, EH9 3LA; tel: 0131 667 1000; fax: 0131 668 2683
Information Officer, British Geological Survey, Keyworth, Nottingham, NG12 5GG; tel: 0115 936 3100; fax: 0115 936 3200

Microform publications:
Contact BGS Keyworth and Murchison House

Electronic and video publications:
Contact BGS or see website

Publications list:
Available online and in print

Access to staff:
Contact by letter, by fax, by e-mail and via website. Appointment necessary. All charged.
Hours: Mon to Thu, 0900 to 1700; Fri, 0900 to 1630
Special comments: There may be data exchange arrangements.
Access times may vary. Please check with staff concerned.

Access for disabled people:
Parking provided
Special comments: Access varies dependent on building.

Constituent part of:
The Natural Environment Research Council (NERC)
Polaris House, North Star Avenue, Swindon, Wiltshire, SN2 1EU; tel: 01793 411500; fax: 01793 411501

Main Office:
British Geological Survey
Platt Lane, Nicker Hill, Keyworth, Nottingham, NG12 5GG; tel: 01159 363 100; fax: 01159 363 200; e-mail: enquiries@bgs.ac.uk; website: http://www.bgs.ac.uk

North UK Office:
British Geological Survey
Murchison House, West Main Road, Edinburgh, EH19 3LA; tel: 0131 667 1000; fax: 0131 668 4140; e-mail: enquiries@bgs.ac.uk; website: http://www.bgs.ac.uk

BRITISH GEOLOGICAL SURVEY – RESEARCH KNOWLEDGE SERVICES

Acronym or abbreviation: BGS

Kingsley Dunham Centre, Keyworth, Nottinghamshire, NG12 5GG

Tel: 0115 936 3205
Fax: 0115 936 3015
E-mail: libuser@bgs.ac.uk

Website:
http://www.bgs.ac.uk
Access to the high-level data index and to online public access catalogue (OPAC).
http://nora.nerc.ac.uk
NERC Open Research Archive.

Enquiries:
Enquiries to: Head of Research Knowledge Services

Founded:
1835

Organisation type and purpose:
National government body, consultancy, research organisation, publishing house.
The mission of the BGS is to: advance geoscientific knowledge of the United Kingdom landmass and its adjacent continental shelf; provide

comprehensive, objective and up-to-date geoscientific information, advice and services; enhance the United Kingdom science base.

Subject coverage:
Earth sciences and related subjects.

Museum or gallery collection, archive, or library special collection:
500,000 volumes
14,000 serials incl world-wide
BGS archives
National collection of field survey records (NGRC)
BGS and British Association for the Advancement of Science geological photographs (80,000)
World-wide collections of geological maps and related texts (200,000)

Trade and statistical information:
Minerals statistics.

Non-library collection catalogue:
All or part available online and in-house

Library catalogue:
All or part available online

Printed publications:
BGS Catalogue of geological maps, books, and data
Earthwise (House magazine)
Earthworks (House magazine)
Order printed publications from: Sales Desk, British Geological Survey

Electronic and video publications:
For BGS publications in OPAC see: http://geolib.bgs.ac.uk (GEOLIB)
Order electronic and video publications from: Sales at http://www.bgs.ac.uk/contacts/sales.html

Publications list:
Available online and in print

Access to staff:
Contact by letter, by telephone, by fax, by e-mail, in person and via website
Hours: Mon to Thu, 0900 to 1700; Fri, 0900 to 1630

Access to building, collection or gallery:
Prior appointment required
Hours: Mon to Thu, 0900 to 1700; Fri, 0900 to 1630
Special comments: Library available for reference only.

Access for disabled people:
Parking provided, ramped entry, level entry, toilet facilities

Also at:
British Geological Survey
Maclean Building, Crowmarsh Gifford, Wallingford, Oxfordshire, OX10 8BB; tel: 01491 838800; fax: 01491 692345; website: http://www.bgs.ac.uk/contacts/sites/wallingford/wahome.html
British Geological Survey
Columbus House, Greenmeadow Springs, Tongwynlais, Cardiff, CF15 7NE; tel: 029 2052 1962; fax: 029 2052 1963; website: http://www.bgs.ac.uk/contacts/sites/cardiff/home.html
British Geological Survey
Hydrogeological Enquiries and National Wells Records Archive; tel: 01491 692299; fax: 01491 692345; e-mail: hydro@bgs.ac.uk
British Geological Survey
Murchison House, West Mains Road, Edinburgh, EH9 3LA; tel: 0131 667 1000; fax: 0131 668 2683; e-mail: enquiry@bgs.ac.uk; website: http://www.bgs.ac.uk/contacts/sites/edinburgh/mhhome.html
British Geological Survey
London Information Office, Natural History Museum Earth Galleries, Exhibition Road, South Kensington, London, SW7 2DE; tel: 020 7589 4090; fax: 020 7584 8270; e-mail: bgslondon@bgs.ac.uk; website: http://www.bgs.ac.uk/contacts/sites/london/liohome.html
Geological Survey of Northern Ireland
Colby House, Stranmills Court, Belfast, BT9 5BF; tel: 028 9038 8462; fax: 028 9038 8461
National Geological Records Centre (North)
tel: 0131 650 0307; fax: 0131 667 2785; e-mail: ngrcn@bgs.ac.uk

National Geological Records Centre (South)
tel: 0115 936 3109; fax: 0115 936 3276; e-mail: ngis@bgs.ac.uk

Parent body:
Natural Environment Research Council
Polaris House, North Star Avenue, Swindon, SN2 1EU; tel: 01793 411500; fax: 01793 411501; website: http://www.nerc.ac.uk

BRITISH GEOTECHNICAL ASSOCIATION

Acronym or abbreviation: BGA

Institution of Civil Engineers, 1 Great George Street, London, SW1P 3AA

Tel: 020 7665 2233
Fax: 020 7799 1325
E-mail: bga@icc.org.uk

Website:
http://www.ice.org.uk
Meetings of the British Geotechnical Society.

Enquiries:
Enquiries to: Administrator

Organisation type and purpose:
Learned society.

Subject coverage:
Soil mechanics; foundation engineering; rock and ice mechanics; geotechnical engineering; details of conferences and proceedings in the field.

Printed publications:
Geotechnique (quarterly)

Access to staff:
Contact by letter
Hours: Mon to Fri, 0900 to 1700

Affiliated to:
Institution of Civil Engineers

Member of:
International Society for Rock Mechanics
International Society for Soil Mechanics and Ground Engineering

BRITISH GERIATRICS SOCIETY

Acronym or abbreviation: BGS

Marjory Warren House, 31 St John's Square, London, EC1M 4DN

Tel: 020 7608 1369
Fax: 020 7608 1041
E-mail: general.information@bgs.org.uk

Website:
http://www.bgs.org.uk

Enquiries:
Enquiries to: Administrator

Founded:
1947

Organisation type and purpose:
Advisory body, professional body (membership is by qualification), voluntary organisation, registered charity (charity number 268762).
Voluntary association of physicians and scientists concerned with improving standards of treatment, and encouraging research in the illnesses of elderly people.

Subject coverage:
Promotion of high standards of health and treatment for the elderly, the teaching of geriatric medicine, the training of medical and paramedical staff, and research into age-related disease.

Printed publications:
Compendium of Guidelines, Policy Statements and Statements of Good Practice
Fact sheets on a range of practical issues (keeping warm, eating well, etc)
Publications for Carers, NHS Decision Makers and Researchers

Publications list:
Available online and in print

continued overleaf

Access to staff:
Contact by letter, by telephone, by fax, by e-mail and via website
Hours: Mon to Fri, 0900 to 1700
Special comments: The society does not deal specifically with the public, but aims its activities at doctors with an interest in elderly care.

BRITISH GLASS MANUFACTURERS CONFEDERATION

Acronym or abbreviation: BGMC

Northumberland Road, Sheffield, South Yorkshire, S10 2UA

Tel: 0114 268 6201
Fax: 0114 268 1073
E-mail: info@britglass.co.uk

Website:
http://www.britglass.co.uk

Enquiries:
Enquiries to: Librarian
Direct e-mail: t.green@britglass.co.uk
Other contacts: Recycling Officer

Founded:
1959

Organisation type and purpose:
Advisory body, trade association (membership is by subscription, qualification), present number of members: 144, training organisation, consultancy, research organisation.

Subject coverage:
Glass, recycling, statistics, education, economics, legislation, safety, specifications, HSE, training and consultancy, environmental services.

Trade and statistical information:
Production and recycling statistics.

Library catalogue:
All or part available in-house

Printed publications:
Digest of Information and Patent Review (quarterly, on subscription)
Making Glass
Teachers' Notes on Recycling
Technical Manuals
TEC Publications
Wall Charts

Electronic and video publications:
Video on bottle banks
First Glass Packaging
Ollie Recycles (CD-ROM)

Publications list:
Available in print

Access to staff:
Contact by letter, by telephone and by e-mail.
Appointment necessary. Non-members charged.
Hours: Mon to Fri, 0900 to 1700

Access to building, collection or gallery:
Prior appointment required
Hours: Mon to Fri, 0900 to 1700

Access for disabled people:
Parking provided, toilet facilities

Member of:
(ETSU)
British Standards Institution
European Domestic Glassware Organisation
European Glass Manufacturers
Scientific Glassware Association

BRITISH GLIDING ASSOCIATION

Acronym or abbreviation: BGA

Kimberley House, 47 Vaughan Way, Leicester, LE1 4SE

Tel: 0116 253 1051
Fax: 0116 251 5939

Website:
http://www.gliding.co.uk

Enquiries:
Enquiries to: Secretary
Direct e-mail: keith@gliding.co.uk

Founded:
1929

Organisation type and purpose:
Membership association (membership is by election or invitation), present number of members: 9500, voluntary organisation.
Governing body for the sport.

Subject coverage:
Gliding.

Printed publications:
Sailplane and Gliding (6 times a year)

Access to staff:
Contact by letter, by telephone, by fax, by e-mail and in person
Hours: Mon to Fri, 0900 to 1700

Affiliated to:
Fédération Aéronautique Internationale
Royal Aero Club of the United Kingdom

BRITISH GLOVE ASSOCIATION

Acronym or abbreviation: BGA

Sussex House, 8–10 Homesdale Road, Bromley, Kent, BR2 9LZ

Tel: 020 8464 0131
Fax: 020 8464 6018
E-mail: tradeassn@craneandpartners.com

Website:
http://www.gloveassociation.org

Enquiries:
Enquiries to: Secretary

Organisation type and purpose:
Trade association.

Subject coverage:
Glove production, glove types (dress, sports, industrial and protective).

Museum or gallery collection, archive, or library special collection:
The Worshipful Company of Glovers is responsible for two glove collections, both at the Museum of Costume, Bath
The Duplicate Royal Coronation Gloves Collection
The Spence Collection

Sponsors the:
Worshipful Company of Glovers

BRITISH GOAT SOCIETY

Acronym or abbreviation: BGS

34–36 Fore Street, Bovey Tracey, Newton Abbot, Devon, TQ13 9AD

Tel: 01626 833168
Fax: 01626 834536
E-mail: secretary@allgoats.com

Website:
http://www.allgoats.com

Enquiries:
Enquiries to: Secretary

Founded:
1879

Organisation type and purpose:
Voluntary organisation.
Registration body, over 90 local and regional societies are affiliated.

Subject coverage:
Goat husbandry and management; registration of stock.

Printed publications:
Books on husbandry, etc

Leaflets or pamphlets on goatkeeping, feeding, goats' milk, etc
Monthly Journal
Year Book and Herd Book

Publications list:
Available in print

Access to staff:
Contact by letter, by telephone and by e-mail
Hours: Mon to Fri, 0900 to 1700

BRITISH GRASSLAND SOCIETY

Acronym or abbreviation: BGS

Unit 32c, Stoneleigh Deer Park, Stareton, Kenilworth, Warwickshire, CV8 2LY

Tel: 02476 696 600
E-mail: office@britishgrassland.com

Website:
http://www.britishgrassland.com

Enquiries:
Enquiries to: Administrator

Founded:
1945

Organisation type and purpose:
Learned society, present number of members: 800, registered charity (charity number 261800).
BGS is a forum for those with an active interest in the science and practice of temperate grassland production and utilisation.

Subject coverage:
The advancement of methods of production and utilisation of grass and forage crops for the promotion of agriculture and the public benefit; the advancement of education and research in grass and forage crop production and utilisation, and the publication of the results of such research.

Publications list:
Available in print

Access to staff:
Contact by letter, by fax and via website
Hours: Mon to Fri, 0900 to 1700

BRITISH GREYHOUND RACING BOARD LIMITED

Acronym or abbreviation: BGRB

32 Old Burlington Street, London, W1S 3AT

Tel: 020 7292 9900
Fax: 020 7292 9909

Enquiries:
Enquiries to: Chief Executive

Founded:
1976

Organisation type and purpose:
Advisory body, statutory body, trade association.

Subject coverage:
Greyhound racing.

Trade and statistical information:
Information and statistics on greyhound racing.

Access to staff:
Contact by letter and by telephone
Hours: Mon to Fri, 0930 to 1700

BRITISH GUILD OF TRAVEL WRITERS

Acronym or abbreviation: BGTW

51B Askew Crescent, London, W12 9DN

Tel: 020 8749 1128
Fax: 020 8181 6663
E-mail: secretariat@bgtw.org

Website:
http://www.bgtw.org

About the Guild, current committee, membership criteria, code of conduct, Guild awards, sale of yearbook.

Enquiries:
Enquiries to: Administrator

Founded:
1960

Organisation type and purpose:
Membership association (membership is by election or invitation), present number of members: 250.
Professional travel writers, authors, broadcasters and photographers.

Subject coverage:
Travel, tourism, journalism, photography, radio, television, video.

Printed publications:
Yearbook (£108 to purchase via website)

Publications list:
Available in print

Access to staff:
Contact by letter, by telephone, by fax and by e-mail
Hours: Mon to Fri, 0900 to 1700

BRITISH GYMNASTICS

Acronym or abbreviation: BG

Ford Hall, Lilleshall National Sports Centre, Newport, Shropshire, TF10 9NB

Tel: 01952 822300
Fax: 01952 820326
E-mail: information@british-gymnastics.org

Website:
http://www.baga.co.uk

Enquiries:
Enquiries to: Public Relations Manager
Direct fax: 01952 822338
Direct e-mail: vera.a@british-gymnastics.org
Other contacts: Chief Executive for policy of the association.

Founded:
1888

Organisation type and purpose:
Membership association (membership is by subscription), present number of members: 100,000, training organisation.
National governing body of the sport.

Subject coverage:
Gymnastics, women's and men's; rhythmic gymnastics, trampolining, sports acrobatics, general gymnastics, gymnastics for people with disabilities, sports aerobics, competitions, courses, membership, technical information, awards and publications, events, promotion and publicity, judging.

Museum or gallery collection, archive, or library special collection:
Large library

Non-library collection catalogue:
All or part available in-house

Printed publications:
Books, guides, training and teaching materials
Calendar of Events
Gymnast (magazine, 6 times a year, subscription agents, telephone: 01580 200657)
Gym News (6 times a year)
Wall charts
Order printed publications from: World Wide Subscription Ltd, Unit 4, Gibbs Reed Farm, Pashley Road, Ticehurst, Wadhurst, East Sussex, TN5 7HE, tel: 01580 200657

Electronic and video publications:
Videos

Publications list:
Available in print

Access to staff:
Contact by letter, by telephone, by fax, by e-mail, in person and via website. Appointment necessary.
Hours: Mon to Thu, 0900 to 1700; Fri, 0900 to 1630

Access to building, collection or gallery:
Prior appointment required
Hours: Mon to Thu, 0900 to 1700; Fri, 0900 to 1630
Special comments: Library at Lilleshall HQ may be visited on request, for information and research.

Access for disabled people:
Parking provided

Constituent part:
British Trampoline Federation (BTF)

European governing body is:
UEG
   Switzerland; tel: +41 21 613 7332; fax: +41 21 613 7331; e-mail: info@ueg.org

World governing body is:
FIG
   Switzerland; tel: +41 32 494 6410; fax: +41 32 494 6419; e-mail: fig.gymnastics@worldsport.org

BRITISH HALLMARKING COUNCIL

No 1 Colmore Square, Birmingham, B4 6AA

Tel: 0870 763 2000
Fax: 0870 763 1814
E-mail: david.gwyther@martineau-uk.com

Website:
http://www.britishhallmarkingcouncil.gov.uk/

Enquiries:
Enquiries to: Secretary

Founded:
1973

Organisation type and purpose:
Statutory body.
Created by the Hallmarking Act of 1973; supervisory body for the activities of the Independent Assay Offices.

Subject coverage:
Hallmarking in the United Kingdom.

Printed publications:
Annual Report

Access to staff:
Contact by letter
Hours: Mon to Fri, 0900 to 1700

BRITISH HANG GLIDING AND PARAGLIDING ASSOCIATION

Acronym or abbreviation: BHPA

8 Merus Court, Meridian Business Park, Leicester, LE19 1RJ

E-mail: office@bhpa.co.uk

Website:
http://www.bhpa.co.uk
Skywings magazine.

Enquiries:
Enquiries to: Office Manager

Founded:
1992

Organisation type and purpose:
Membership association.
Governing body of the sport.

Subject coverage:
Hang gliding and paragliding; availability, training, licensing of instructors, safety regulations, national competitions, development of new techniques and equipment, courses, conventions.

Printed publications:
Directory of Clubs
Leaflets, posters, handbooks and textbooks
Safety Standards Manuals and Codes of Practice
Skywings Magazine (monthly)

Access to staff:
Contact by letter, by telephone, by fax, by e-mail and via website
Hours: Mon to Fri, 0900 to 1700

Affiliated to:
Fédération Aéronautique Internationale

Constituent bodies:
British Association of Parascending Clubs
British Hang Gliding Association

Representation on:
Royal Aero Club of the United Kingdom

BRITISH HARDMETAL ASSOCIATION

Acronym or abbreviation: BHA

c/o Institute of Spring Technology, Henry Street, Sheffield, S3 7EQ

Tel: 0114 278 9143

Enquiries:
Enquiries to: Secretary

Organisation type and purpose:
Trade association.

Subject coverage:
Hardmetal and associated products.

Access to staff:
Contact by letter, by telephone, by fax and by e-mail
Hours: Mon to Fri, 0900 to 1700

Affiliated to:
Federation of British Engineers' Tool Manufacturers

BRITISH HEALTH CARE ASSOCIATION

Acronym or abbreviation: BHCA

PO Box 6752, Elgin, IV30 9BN

Tel: 01343 544841
E-mail: info@bhca.org.uk

Website:
http://www.bhca.org.uk
Full details of BHCA, together with a list of member organisations.

Enquiries:
Enquiries to: National Secretary
Other contacts: President

Founded:
1947

Organisation type and purpose:
Trade association (membership is by subscription).
To promote and advance the interest of member organisations; to lobby, consult and negotiate on their behalf and undertake and arrange for the arbitration of disputes. To determine and administer an ethical code of conduct for the resolution of disputes.

Subject coverage:
Health care cash plan insurance.

Museum or gallery collection, archive, or library special collection:
History of the Association

Library catalogue:
All or part available online and in print

Access to staff:
Contact by letter, by telephone, by e-mail and via website
Special comments: Office operates irregular part-time hours only.

Member organisations:
BHSF Limited (BHSF Ltd)
   Gamgee House, 2 Darnley Road, Birmingham, B16 8TE; tel: 0121 454 3601; e-mail: enquiries@bhsf.co.uk; website: http://www.bhsf.co.uk

continued overleaf

Bolton and District Hospital Saturday Council
Regent House, Folds Point, Folds Road, Bolton, BL1 2RZ; tel: 01204 522775; e-mail: info@hospital-saturday.org.uk; website: http://www.hospital-saturday.org.uk

Engage Mutual Assurance
Hornbeam Park Avenue, Harrogate, HG2 8XE; tel: 0800 169 4321; e-mail: mail@engagemutual.com; website: http://www.engagemutual.com

Gwent Hospitals Contributory Fund
13 Cardiff Road, Newport, NP20 2EH; tel: 01633 266152; e-mail: admin@ghcf.co.uk; website: http://www.ghcf.co.uk

HSF health plan
24 Upper Ground, London, SE1 9PD; tel: 020 7928 6662; e-mail: marketing@hsf.eu.com; website: http://www.hsf.eu.com

Medicash
Merchants Court, 2–12 Lord Street, Liverpool, L2 1TS; tel: 0800 011 2222; e-mail: info@medicash.org; website: http://www.medicash.org

National Friendly
4–5 Worcester Road, Clifton, Bristol, BS8 3JL; tel: 0800 195 9246; e-mail: enquiries@nationalfriendly.co.uk; website: http://www.nationalfriendly.co.uk

Paycare
George Street, Wolverhampton, WV2 4DX; tel: 01902 371000; e-mail: enquiries@paycare.org; website: http://www.paycare.org

Simplyhealth
Hambleden House, Waterloo Court, Andover, SP10 1LQ; tel: 0800 980 7890; e-mail: customerservices@simplyhealth.co.uk; website: http://www.simplyhealth.co.uk

Sovereign Health Care
Royal Standard House, 26 Manningham Lane, Bradford, West Yorkshire, BD1 3DN; tel: 01274 841130; e-mail: cs@sovereignhealthcare.co.uk; website: http://www.sovereignhealthcare.co.uk

Westfield Health
Westfield House, 87 Division Street, Sheffield S1 1HT; tel: 0845 602 1629; e-mail: enquiries@westfieldhealth.com; website: http://www.westfieldhealth.com

WHA Healthcare
60 Newport Road, Cardiff, CF2 1YG; tel: 029 2048 5461; e-mail: mail@whahealthcare.co.uk; website: http://www.whahealthcare.co.uk

WHCA
Worcester House, 9 St Mary's Street, Worcester, WR1 1HA; tel: 01905 729090; e-mail: orchard@whcaorchard.com; website: http://www.whcaorchard.com

BRITISH HEALTHCARE TRADES ASSOCIATION

Acronym or abbreviation: BHTA

1 Webbs Court, Buckhurst Avenue, Sevenoaks, Kent, TN13 1LZ

Tel: 01732 458868
Fax: 01732 459225
E-mail: bhta@bhta.com

Website:
http://www.bhta.com
List of members.

Enquiries:
Enquiries to: Director

Founded:
1917

Organisation type and purpose:
Trade association (membership is by subscription), present number of members: 320.

Subject coverage:
BHTA's aim is to be seen as the body that effectively represents the sector of the British health care industry that serves those with special physical needs.

Trade and statistical information:
Membership lists available for general circulation. All other information available to members only.

Printed publications:
Exporters List (free)
General membership list (free)
Surgical Instrument Directory (free)
Wheelchair Distributors Membership List (free)

Publications list:
Available in print

Access to staff:
Contact by letter, by telephone, by fax, by e-mail and via website
Hours: Mon to Fri, 0900 to 1700

Access to building, collection or gallery:
No access other than to staff

BRITISH HEART FOUNDATION

Acronym or abbreviation: BHF

14 Fitzhardinge Street, London, W1H 6DH

Tel: 020 7935 0185
Fax: 020 7486 5820

Website:
http://www.bhf.org.uk

Enquiries:
Enquiries to: Director of Communications
Direct tel: 020 7487 7183
Direct fax: 020 7224 5082
Other contacts: Editor

Founded:
1961

Organisation type and purpose:
Registered charity (charity number 225971), research organisation.
Medical research charity working in the field of cardiovascular disease. Producers of a statistical database.
Funds vital research, rehabilitation programmes, life-saving cardiac equipment and educational initiatives, BHF nurses and co-ordinates heart support groups. Encourages people to learn emergency life support skills.

Subject coverage:
Research into the causes, diagnosis, treatment and prevention of heart disease, public education and information, information to the medical profession, rehabilitation, heart support groups, emergency life support skills training.

Trade and statistical information:
Coronary heart disease statistics.

Printed publications:
Annual Medical and Research Reports (free to members of the medical profession)
Annual Review, Report and Accounts
Heart Information Series (constantly updated and available)
Leaflets, newsletters and booklets for children and adults (some available in Welsh and Asian versions, free)
Cardiopulmonary resuscitation (CPR)
Diet information
Exercise information
Heart information series

Electronic and video publications:
Educational videos, including those for patients, available for a donation of approximately £5

Publications list:
Available online and in print

Access to staff:
Contact by letter and by telephone. Appointment necessary.
Hours: Mon to Fri, 0900 to 1700

Has:
9 regional offices

Member of:
International Society and Federation of Cardiologists

Regional Offices:
Region 1
4–6 Bridge Street, Tadcaster, North Yorkshire, LS24 9AL; tel: 01937 835421

Region 10
6 Terrace Walk, Bath, BA1 1LN; tel: 01225 463616
Region 2
2 Kiln House Yard, Baldock Street, Royston, Hertfordshire, SG8 5AY; tel: 01763 242414
Region 3
4 Shore Place, Edinburgh, EH6 6UU; tel: 0131 555 5891
Region 5
Oak House B, Ransom Wood Business Park, Southwell Road West, Mansfield, Nottinghamshire, NG21 0HJ; tel: 01623 624558
Region 6
21 Cathedral Road, Cardiff, CF11 9HA; tel: 029 2038 2368
Region 7
7 Queen Avenue, Dale Street, Liverpool, L2 4TZ; tel: 0151 236 6988
Region 8
239A High Street, Erdington, Birmingham, B23 6SS; tel: 0121 382 3168
Region 9
33 High Street, Ticehurst, Wadhurst, East Sussex, TN5 7AS; tel: 01580 200443

BRITISH HEDGEHOG PRESERVATION SOCIETY

Acronym or abbreviation: BHPS

Hedgehog House, Dhustone, Ludlow, Shropshire, SY8 3PL

Tel: 01584 890801
Fax: 01584 891313
E-mail: info@britishhedgehogs.org.uk

Website:
http://www.britishhedgehogs.org.uk

Enquiries:
Enquiries to: Chief Executive

Founded:
1982

Organisation type and purpose:
National organisation, membership association (membership is by subscription), present number of members: 11,000, registered charity (charity number 326885).
National organisation with some foreign members. To heighten awareness of needs of hedgehogs.

Subject coverage:
Hedgehog care.

Printed publications:
Background to the BHPS
Education packs
Leaflets (12 titles)
Newsletter (2 times a year, for members)
Project packs
Treating Sick Hedgehogs (intended for Veterinary Surgeons)

Access to staff:
Contact by letter, by telephone, by e-mail and via website
Hours: Mon to Fri, 0900 to 1700

BRITISH HELICOPTER ADVISORY BOARD LIMITED

Acronym or abbreviation: BHAB

Graham Suite, West Entrance, Fairoaks Airport, Chobham, Woking, Surrey, GU24 8HX

Tel: 01276 856100
Fax: 01276 856126

Website:
http://www.bhab.demon.co.uk

Enquiries:
Enquiries to: Chief Executive
Other contacts: Executive Assistant for information regarding membership or helicopter charter, services.

Founded:
1969

Organisation type and purpose:
Trade association (membership is by subscription).
To promote and advise on civil helicopter
operations.

Subject coverage:
All aspects of helicopter operations.

Printed publications:
Code of Flight Conduct for Helicopter Pilots
Information Handbook (annually)
Pilot Training Leaflet
The Civil Helicopter in the Community

BRITISH HERBAL MEDICINE ASSOCIATION

Acronym or abbreviation: BHMA

PO Box 583, Exeter, EX1 9GX

Tel: 0845 680 1134
Fax: 0845 680 1136
E-mail: secretary@bhma.info

Website:
http://www.bhma.info

Enquiries:
Enquiries to: Secretary

Founded:
1964

Organisation type and purpose:
Trade association.
BHMA provides an advisory service to
government and is involved in scientific research
and legislation.

Subject coverage:
Herbs and herbal medicine; herbal products;
Medicines Act (1968); advertising regulations on
herbs, suppliers etc.; training facilities for herbal
practitioners; research.

Printed publications:
British Herbal Compendium (1992 and 2005)
British Herbal Pharmacopoeia (1983, 1990, 1996)
A Guide to Traditional Herbal Medicines
Code of Advertising
Occasional Papers

Access to staff:
Contact by letter, by telephone, by fax and by e-
mail
Hours: Mon to Fri, 1000 to 1600

BRITISH HERNIA CENTRE

87 Watford Way, Hendon Central, London, NW4
4RS

Tel: 020 8201 7000
E-mail: experts@hernia.org

Website:
http://www.hernia.org
Comprehensive information, including
explanations on hernia in plain English.
Award winning website.

Enquiries:
Enquiries to: Chief Executive

Founded:
1990

Organisation type and purpose:
Specialist hospital.
The largest tension-free specialist hernia centre in
the world.

Subject coverage:
All aspects of hernias, treatment and cure.

Library catalogue:
All or part available online

Printed publications:
Explanatory booklets on all types of Hernia
Various academic publications

Publications list:
Available online

Access to staff:
Contact by letter, by telephone, by fax, by e-mail
and via website. Appointment necessary.
Hours: Mon to Fri, 0900 to 1700
Special comments: Telephone lines open 24 hours.

Links with:
BHC – Grosvenor Hospitals Group Limited

BRITISH HERPETOLOGICAL SOCIETY

Acronym or abbreviation: BHS

Zoological Society of London, Regent's Park,
London, NW1 4RY

Tel: 01674 671676
E-mail: secretary@thebhs.org

Website:
http://www.thebhs.org

Enquiries:
Enquiries to: Secretary

Founded:
1947

Organisation type and purpose:
Learned society (membership is by subscription),
present number of members: 600, voluntary
organisation, registered charity.
Study of herpetology.

Subject coverage:
Herpetology, study and protection of amphibians
and reptiles, particularly British and European;
captive breeding of species in vivaria as a
conservation tool.

**Museum or gallery collection, archive, or library
special collection:**
Scientific journals from various countries
Corkhill Collection of books and bound papers

Printed publications:
Bulletin (4 times a year)
Herpetological Journal (4 times a year)
NatterJack newsletter (12 times a year)
The Care and Breeding of Captive Reptiles
The Reptiles and Amphibians of Dorset

Access to staff:
Contact by letter, by telephone and by e-mail
Hours: Mon to Fri, 1730 to 1930

Constituent bodies:
Conservation committee, research committee,
captive breeding committee, education committee,
including a young members' group (Young
Herpetologists Club)

BRITISH HOLIDAY AND HOME PARKS ASSOCIATION

Acronym or abbreviation: BH & HPA Ltd

6 Pullman Court, Great Western Road, Gloucester,
GL1 3ND

Tel: 01452 526911
Fax: 01452 508508

Enquiries:
Enquiries to: Director General

Founded:
1950

Organisation type and purpose:
Trade association.

Subject coverage:
The interests of owners and managers of holiday
and residential parks nationwide.

Printed publications:
BH & HPA Journal
BH & HPA Members' Handbook (free for
qualifying individuals)

Access to staff:
Contact by letter
Hours: Mon to Fri, 0900 to 1700

BRITISH HOLISTIC MEDICAL ASSOCIATION

Acronym or abbreviation: BHMA

PO Box 371 Bridgwater Somerset, TA6 9BG

Tel: 01278 722000
E-mail: admin@bhma.org

Website:
http://www.bhma.org

Enquiries:
Enquiries to: Chairman

Founded:
1983

Organisation type and purpose:
Membership association (membership is by
subscription), present number of members: 650,
voluntary organisation, registered charity (charity
number 289459), training organisation, research
organisation, publishing house.
BHMA is an organisation of professionals and
members of the public who care about the future of
healthcare and want to adopt a more holistic
approach in their own life and work.
The BHMA is furthering the development of
holistic healthcare through bringing together the
many people who can contribute to a system for
the 21st century by holding conferences,
workshops, seminars and by facilitating a network
of regional groups.

Subject coverage:
Holistic medical practice; complementary
therapies, their application in and outside
orthodox medical practice; training.

Printed publications:
Journal of Holistic Healthcare (quarterly)

Electronic and video publications:
Self help CDs: Coping with Stress, The Breath of
Life, Getting to Sleep, Introducing Meditation,
Imagery for Relaxation, Coping with Persistent
Pain

Access to staff:
Contact by letter, by telephone, by e-mail and via
website
Hours: Mon to Fri, 1000 to 1600
Answerphone checked regularly
Special comments: If contacting by letter please
enclose an sae.

Access to building, collection or gallery:
Prior Appointment Required

BRITISH HOMEOPATHIC ASSOCIATION

Acronym or abbreviation: BHA

Hahnemann House, 29 Park Street West, Luton,
LU1 3BE

Tel: 0870 444 3950
Fax: 0870 444 3960
E-mail: info@trusthomeopathy.org

Website:
http://www.trusthomeopathy.org

Enquiries:
Enquiries to: Chief Executive

Founded:
1902

Organisation type and purpose:
Membership association, registered charity
(charity number 235900).
To promote homeopathy and raise funds for
research and education.

Subject coverage:
Homeopathy practised by statutorily registered
healthcare professionals – doctors, dentists, nurses,
vets, pharmacists, podiatrists, midwives,
osteopaths

Information services:
Information on medical homeopathy.

continued overleaf

Printed publications:
Health & Homeopathy (4 times a year, free to members, subscription £25)
Order printed publications from: British Homeopathic Association

Access to staff:
Contact by letter, by telephone, by e-mail and via website. Appointment necessary.
Hours: Mon to Fri, 0900 to 1700

Access to building, collection or gallery:
Prior appointment required

Access for disabled people:
Hours: Mon to Fri, 0900 to 1700

BRITISH HOROLOGICAL FEDERATION

Acronym or abbreviation: BHF

Upton Hall, Upton, Newark, Nottinghamshire, NG23 5TE

Tel: 01636 813795
Fax: 01636 812258
E-mail: clocks@bhi.co.uk

Website:
http://www.bhi.co.uk/bhfhome.htm

Enquiries:
Enquiries to: Secretary General

Founded:
1932

Organisation type and purpose:
Trade association.

Subject coverage:
Clocks and watches, manufacturers and suppliers, horological technology (including standards), horological trade fairs, European directives for the horological industry.

Printed publications:
Horological Journal (monthly, members only)

Access to staff:
Contact by fax
Hours: Mon to Fri, 0900 to 1700

Member of:
European Committee for the Industry

Other address:
British Horological Federation
  tel: 01636 706965; fax: 01636 706965; e-mail: gevansbhf@aol.com

Sister organisation at the same address the:
British Horological Institute

BRITISH HOROLOGICAL INSTITUTE

Acronym or abbreviation: BHI

Upton Hall, Upton, Newark, Nottinghamshire, NG23 5TE

Tel: 01636 813795
Fax: 01636 812258
E-mail: clocks@bhi.co.uk

Website:
http://www.bhi.co.uk

Enquiries:
Enquiries to: General Manager
Other contacts: Education Team for education related services and facilities.

Founded:
1858

Organisation type and purpose:
Professional body, membership association (membership is by subscription), present number of members: 3500, museum, historic building, house or site, training organisation.
To protect and further the science and art of horology.

Subject coverage:
Horology.

Museum or gallery collection, archive, or library special collection:
Library and museum

Printed publications:
Horological Journal

Access to staff:
Contact by letter, by telephone, by fax, by e-mail and via website. Appointment necessary. Letter of introduction required. Non-members charged.
Hours: Mon to Fri, 0900 to 1700

Access to building, collection or gallery:
Prior arrangement necessary
Hours: By appointment for members only. Group visits for non-mems by prior arrangement

Access for disabled people:
Parking provided, level entry, toilet facilities
Special comments: Access to ground floor only.

BRITISH HORSE SOCIETY

Acronym or abbreviation: BHS

Abbey Park, Stareton, Kenilworth, Warwickshire CV8 2XZ

Tel: 01926 707700 / 0844 848 1666
Fax: 01926 707800
E-mail: enquiry@bhs.org.uk

Website:
http://www.bhs.org.uk
Information on the BHS and its work in fulfilling people's passion for horses.
http://www.britishhorse.com
The BHS Bookshop online.

Enquiries:
Enquiries to: Director of Membership, Marketing and Communications
Direct tel: 01926 707738
Direct fax: 01926 707746
Other contacts: Chief Executive

Founded:
1947

Created by the merger of:
Institute of the Horse and Pony Club and the National Horse Association of Great Britain

Organisation type and purpose:
Membership association (membership is by subscription), registered charity (charity number 210504 and SC038516).
Represents all equine interests and has the following objectives: to promote and advance the education, training and safety of the public in all matters relating to the horse; to promote the use, breeding, well-being, safety, environment, health and management of the horse for the public benefit; to promote community participation in healthy recreation involving the horse; to promote and facilitate the prevention of cruelty, neglect or harm to horses and to promote the relief, safety, sanctuary, rescue and welfare of horses in need of care, attention and assistance; to promote and secure the provision, protection and preservation of rights of way and of access for ridden and driven horses over public roads, highways, footpaths, bridleways, carriageways, public paths and other land.

Subject coverage:
Equine welfare, equestrian safety, access and riding rights of way, qualifications, training and careers, riding schools, horse and pony breeds, riding clubs, competitions.

Museum or gallery collection, archive, or library special collection:
Library deposited with Warwickshire College, Moreton Morrell

Trade and statistical information:
Data on statistics relating to equestrian activities.

Printed publications:
A large range of books on all the subjects above including:
British Horse (magazine, six times a year)
Riding and Road Safety Manual

Where to Ride, Train & Stable your Horse (inc. register of Instructors)
Year Book
Order printed publications from: website: http://www.britishhorse.com

Electronic and video publications:
Tapes for teaching
Videos of events, training and entertainment

Access to staff:
Contact by letter, by telephone, by fax, by e-mail and in person
Hours: Mon to Thu, 0835 to 1700; Fri, 0835 to 1500

Access for disabled people:
Ramped entry, level entry, toilet facilities

Affiliated to:
The British Equestrian Federation (BEF)
  National Agriculture Centre, Stoneleigh Park, Kenilworth, Warwickshire, CV8 2RH; tel: 01203 698871; fax: 01203 696484

Affiliates:
British Riding Clubs
  The British Horse Society, Abbey Park, Stareton, Kenilworth, Warwickshire CV8 2XZ; tel: 01926 707700; fax: 01926 707764

Represented by the BEF in matters concerned with the:
Fédération Equestre Internationale (FEI)

BRITISH HORSEBALL ASSOCIATION

Acronym or abbreviation: BHA

67 Clifford Road, New Barnet, Barnet, Hertfordshire, EN5 5NZ

Tel: 020 8441 1799
Fax: 020 8441 1060

Website:
http://www.horseball.org.uk

Enquiries:
Enquiries to: Chairman
Direct e-mail: jim@horseball.org.uk

Founded:
1991

Organisation type and purpose:
Membership association.
National governing body.
To control and develop the game of horseball.

Subject coverage:
The game of horseball.

Printed publications:
Newsletter (free to members)
Rule Book for Horseball

Publications list:
Available online and in print

Access to staff:
Contact by letter, by telephone, by fax, by e-mail and via website. Appointment necessary.
Hours: Mon to Fri, 0900 to 1700

BRITISH HOSPITALITY ASSOCIATION

Acronym or abbreviation: BHA

Queen's House, 55–56 Lincoln's Inn Fields, London, WC2A 3BH

Tel: 020 7404 7744
Fax: 020 7404 7799
E-mail: bha@bha.org.uk

Website:
http://www.bha-online.org.uk
FAQs, information research bank, key personnel, mission statement.

Enquiries:
Enquiries to: Information Officer
Direct e-mail: bill@bha.org.uk

Founded:
1910

Organisation type and purpose:
Trade association (membership is by subscription).

Subject coverage:
Hotels, restaurants, industrial catering, motorway catering, employment in the hotel and catering industry (legislation and conditions), computer software for hotels etc, licensing law, food hygiene.

Trade and statistical information:
Contract catering survey.
Starting a small hotel or restaurant business.

Printed publications:
British Hospitality Trends and Statistics
Contract Catering Survey
Hospitality Matters (magazine, 6 times a year)
Starting a Small Hotel or Restaurant Business
Statutory Notices and Stationery
Systematic Assessment of the Food Environment (SAFE)
Order printed publications from: Office Manager

Publications list:
Available in print

Access to staff:
Contact by letter, by telephone, by fax, by e-mail and via website. Access for members only.
Hours: Mon to Fri, 0900 to 1700

Access to building, collection or gallery:
No prior appointment required

Member of:
European Federation of Contract Catering Organisations (FERCO)
  Brussels
European Hotel, Restaurant and Catering Association (HOTREL)
  Brussels
International Hotel and Restaurants Association (IHRA)
  Paris

Other addresses:
British Hospitality Association
  c/o Dundas & Wilson, Saltire Court, Edinburgh, EH1 2EN; tel: 0131 200 7484; fax: 0131 228 8888; e-mail: john.a.loudon@dundas.wilson.com

BRITISH HUMANIST ASSOCIATION

Acronym or abbreviation: BHA

1 Gower Street, London, WC1E 6HD

Tel: 020 7079 3580
Fax: 020 7079 3588
E-mail: info@humanism.org.uk

Website:
http://www.humanism.org.uk
Introductory information to main beliefs and areas of work.

Enquiries:
Enquiries to: Reception
Other contacts: Assistant to the Chief Executive

Founded:
1896

Organisation type and purpose:
Learned society, membership association (membership is by subscription), present number of members: 4,000, service industry, registered charity (charity number 285987), suitable for ages: all.

Subject coverage:
Humanism, moral education, ethics, law as it relates to religious privilege, reform of religious education and collective worship, non-religious funerals, weddings and baby namings.

Museum or gallery collection, archive, or library special collection:
Archive, books, international journals

Printed publications:
BHA News (six times a year)

Books on naming ceremonies, weddings and funerals and other topics, including:
Humanism
Humanist Anthology
Problems with Arguments for the Existence of God

Electronic and video publications:
The Great Detective Story (video)

Publications list:
Available online and in print

Access to staff:
Contact by letter, by telephone, by fax, by e-mail and via website. Appointment necessary.
Hours: Mon to Fri, 0900 to 1700

Affiliated to:
Religious Education Council

Has:
50 regional and local groups, parliamentary group; branch details are available from Head Office

Member organisation of:
European Humanist Federation
International Humanist and Ethical Union

BRITISH HUMANITARIAN AID

11 Devon Road, Canterbury, Kent, CT1 1RP

Tel: 01227 453434
Fax: 01227 787728
E-mail: office@britishhumanitarianaid.co.uk

Enquiries:
Enquiries to: Director
Direct tel: 07774 100 273 (mobile)

Founded:
1992

Organisation type and purpose:
Voluntary organisation, registered charity (charity number 1031547).
Aid to the needy abroad, mainly children, presently Ukraine.

Subject coverage:
Convoying of humanitarian aid to those in need, Ukraine, supplying aid. Ukraine – centre for adults and children in need, helping 4 orphanages in Ukraine for physically and mentally handicapped children.

Printed publications:
Newsletter (3 times a year)

Access to staff:
Contact by letter, by telephone, by fax, by e-mail and via website
Hours: Mon to Fri, 0900 to 1700

BRITISH HYPNOTHERAPY ASSOCIATION

Acronym or abbreviation: BHA

67 Upper Berkeley Street, London, W1H 7QX

Tel: 020 7723 4443
E-mail: therapy@the-wordsmith.co.uk

Website:
http://www.british-hypnotherapy-association.org

Enquiries:
Enquiries to: Secretary

Founded:
1958

Organisation type and purpose:
International organisation, national organisation, advisory body, learned society, professional body (membership is by qualification), present number of members: 348, training organisation, consultancy, research organisation.
The organisation of practitioners who have had at least four years of relevant training and who comply with professional standards of competence and ethics in psychotherapy involving hypnotherapy.

To maintain a register of competent qualified practitioners and raise standards in the treatment of nervous problems.

Subject coverage:
Hypnotherapy; hypno-analysis; psychotherapy; psychodynamics; nervous problems; emotional problems; birth; parenthood; human relationships; phobias; compulsions, lack of confidence; fears; learning difficulties; parent problems; migraine; psoriasis; psychosexual problems; anxiety etc.

Printed publications:
Amongst many are:
British Medical Hypnotists and the General Medical Council
Choosing a Hypnotherapist
How to Assess Therapy Organisations
Hypnosis in Psychotherapy
The Hypnotherapy Handbook

Publications list:
Available in print

Access to staff:
Contact by letter and by telephone. Appointment necessary.
Hours: Mon to Fri, 0900 to 1700

BRITISH IMAGING AND PHOTOGRAPHIC ASSOCIATION

Acronym or abbreviation: BIPA

Ambassador House, Brigstock Road, Thornton Heath, Surrey, CR7 7JG

Tel: 020 8665 5395
Fax: 020 8665 6447
E-mail: bipa@admin.co.uk

Website:
http://www.bipa.org

Enquiries:
Enquiries to: Chief Executive

Founded:
1918

Organisation type and purpose:
Trade association.

Subject coverage:
Photographic and imaging products.

Access to staff:
Contact by letter, by fax and by e-mail
Hours: Mon to Fri, 0900 to 1700

BRITISH IN VITRO DIAGNOSTIC ASSOCIATION

Acronym or abbreviation: BIVDA

1 Queen Anne's Gate, London, SW1H 9BT

Tel: 020 7957 4633
Fax: 020 7957 4644
E-mail: enquiries@bivda.co.uk

Website:
http://www.bivda.co.uk

Enquiries:
Enquiries to: Director-General

Founded:
1992

Organisation type and purpose:
Trade association (membership is by subscription), present number of members: 120 companies.

Subject coverage:
In vitro diagnostics; laboratory medicine.

Access to staff:
Contact by letter, by telephone, by fax, by e-mail and via website
Hours: Mon to Fri, 0900 to 1700

BRITISH INDUSTRIAL FURNACE CONSTRUCTORS ASSOCIATION

Acronym or abbreviation: BIFCA

continued overleaf

National Metalforming Centre, 47 Birmingham Road West Bromwich B70 6PY

Tel: 0121 601 6350
Fax: 0121 601 6387
E-mail: enquiry@bifca.org.uk

Website:
http://www.bifca.org.uk
List of members, products and services, exhibitions and conferences, members area, recruitment area, useful links.

Enquiries:
Enquiries to: Secretary

Organisation type and purpose:
Trade association.

Subject coverage:
Design and manufacture of furnaces, refurbishment, ancillary equipment and control systems.

Access to staff:
Contact by letter, by telephone, by fax, by e-mail and via website. Appointment necessary.
Hours: Mon to Fri, 0900 to 1700

Access to building, collection or gallery:
Prior appointment required

Federated member of the:
Metcom Organisation (Mechanical and Metal Trades Confederation) (METCOM)
tel: 0141 332 0826; fax: 0141 332 5788; website: http://www.metcon.org.uk

Founder member of:
European Committee of Furnace and Heating Equipment Associations (CECOF)
Frankfurt, Germany; tel: + 49 69 66031413; fax: + 49 69 66031692; e-mail: cecof@vdma.org

BRITISH INDUSTRIAL TRUCK ASSOCIATION

Acronym or abbreviation: BITA

5–7 High Street, Sunninghill, Berkshire, SL5 9NQ

Tel: 01344 623800
Fax: 01344 291197
E-mail: info@bita.org.uk

Enquiries:
Enquiries to: Secretary General
Other contacts: Technical Officer for technical matters.

Founded:
1942

Organisation type and purpose:
Trade association, present number of members: 130.
Represents UK manufacturers of industrial trucks, UK suppliers to the industry and importers of trucks, components and accessories.

Subject coverage:
Industrial trucks (lift trucks), operator safety, code books and guidance notes for the industry.

Printed publications:
Publications on operational safety and training

Publications list:
Available online and in print

Access to staff:
Contact by letter, by telephone, by fax and by e-mail
Hours: Mon to Thu, 0900 to 1700; Fri, 0900 to 1630

Member of:
British Materials Handling Federation
tel: 0121 200 2100; fax: 0121 200 1306

BRITISH INFECTION SOCIETY

Acronym or abbreviation: BIS

Department of Infection and Tropical Medicine, Leicester Royal Infirmary, Infirmary Square, Leicester, LE1 5WW

Tel: 0116 258 6952
Fax: 0116 258 5067
E-mail: martin.wiselka@uhl-tr.nhs.uk

Website:
http://www.britishinfectionsociety.org

Enquiries:
Enquiries to: Honorary Secretary

Founded:
1997

Organisation type and purpose:
Learned society.

Subject coverage:
Infection and communicable diseases and within that general context, public health, microbiology, zoonoses.

Printed publications:
Journal of Infection (12 times a year, free to society members, otherwise on subscription, pub. W B Saunders Company)

Access to staff:
Contact by letter, by fax and by e-mail
Hours: Mon to Fri, 0900 to 1700

BRITISH INSTITUTE AT ANKARA

Acronym or abbreviation: BIAA

10 Carlton House Terrace, London, SW1Y 5AH

Tel: 020 7969 5204
Fax: 020 7969 5401
E-mail: biaa@britac.ac.uk

Website:
http://www.biaa.ac.uk

Enquiries:
Enquiries to: Administrator

Founded:
1948

Organisation type and purpose:
Learned society, registered charity (charity number 313940), research organisation, publishing house. The British Institute at Ankara (BIAA) supports, promotes and publishes British research focused on Turkey and the Black Sea littoral in all academic disciplines within the arts, humanities and social sciences, whilst maintaining a centre of excellence in Ankara focused on the archaeology and related subjects of Turkey.

Subject coverage:
British research focused on Turkey and the Black Sea littoral in all academic disciplines within the arts, humanities and social sciences.

Museum or gallery collection, archive, or library special collection:
Library (52,000 vols), maps, inscription squeezes, pottery, botanical and bone collections, field work archives, photographs and slides

Non-library collection catalogue:
All or part available online and in-house

Library catalogue:
All or part available online and in-house

Printed publications:
BIAA Monographs :
A Catalogue of Glass Vessels in Afyon Museum (C. S. Lightfoot, 1989)
Anatolian Iron Ages 2 (ed. A. Çilingiroglu and D. French, 1991)
Anatolian Iron Ages 3 (ed. A. Çilingiroglu and D. French, 1994)
Anatolian Iron Ages 5 (ed. A. Çilingiroglu and G. Darbyshire, 2005)
An Epigraphical Survey in the Kibyra-Olbasa Region Conducted by A. S. Hall: Regional Epigraphic Catalogues of Asia Minor III (N. P. Milner, 1998)
At Empires' Edge. Project Paphlagonia Regional Survey in North-Central Turkey (Matthews, R., Glatz, C. (eds) 2009)
Canhasan Sites 1, Canhasan I: Stratigraphy and Structures (D. French, 1998)
Canhasan Sites 2, Canhasan I: The Pottery (D. French, 2005)
Greek and Latin Inscriptions in the Konya Archaeological Museum (B. H. McLean, 2002)
Greek, Roman and Byzantine Coins in the Museum at Amasya (Ancient Amaseia), Turkey (S. Ireland, 2000)
Inhabiting Çatalhöyük: Reports from the 1995–99 Seasons (ed. I. Hodder, 2005)
On the Surface: Çatalhöyük 1993–1995 (ed. I. Hodder, 1997)
Recent Turkish Coin Hoards and Numismatic Studies (ed. C. S. Lightfoot, 1991)
Roman Bath Buildings in Lycia (A. Farrington, 1995)
Roman Roads and Milestones of Asia Minor 2: An Interim Catalogue of Milestones (D. French, 1988)
Studies in the Ancient Coinage of Turkey (ed. R. Ashton, 1996)
Studies in the History and Topography of Lycia and Pisidia. In Memoriam A. S. Hall (ed. D. French, 1994)
Survey of Medieval Castles of Anatolia I: Kutahya (C. Foss, 1985)
Survey of Medieval Castles of Anatolia II: Nicodma (C. Foss, 1996)
The Asvan Sites 3 (A. G. Sagona, 1994)
The Black Sea: Past, Present and Future (Erkut and Mitchell, 2007)
The Eastern Frontier of the Roman Empire (ed. D. French and C. S. Lightfoot, 1989)
The Greek and Latin Inscriptions in the Burdur Archaeological Museum (Horsley, 2007)
The Madra River Delta: Regional Studies on the Aegean Coast of Turkey (Lambrianides and Spencer, 2007)
The Ottoman House; Papers of the Amasya Symposium 24–27 September 1996 (ed. S. Ireland and W. Bechhoefer, 1998)
Tille Hôyük I, The Medieval Period (J. Moore, 1993)
Tille Hôyük IV, The Late Bronze Age and the Iron Age Transition (G. D. Summers, 1993)
Tille Hoyuk 3.1. the Iron Age: Introduction, Stratification and Architecture (S. Blaylock, 2010)
Towards Reflexive Method in Archaeology: The Example at Çatalhöyük (ed. I. Hodder, 2000)
BIAA Occasional Publications:
A Classical Map of Asia Minor (W. M. Calder and G. E. Bean, 1958)
Beycesultan Vol. I, Vol. II, Vol. III.1, Vol. III.2
The Sultantepe Tablets Vol. I (O. R. Gurney and J. J. Finkelstein, 1957)
The Sultantepe Tablets Vol. II (O. R. Gurney and P. Hullin, 1964)
BIAA Annual Publications:
Anatolian Studies, Vols 1 (1951) to 59 (2009; prices vary)
The Indexes to Anatolian Studies Vols 1–10, 11–20, 21–30, 31–40
Anatolian Archaeology, Vols 1 (1995) to 15 (2009)
Special Anniversary Volume: Fifty Years' Work by the British Institute of Archaeology at Ankara (ed. R. Matthews, 1997)
Order printed publications from: Oxbow Books, Park End Place, Oxford, OX1 1HN; tel: 01865 241249; website: http://www.oxbowbooks.com

Publications list:
Available online and in print

Access to staff:
Contact by letter, by telephone, by fax, by e-mail, in person and via website. Appointment necessary.
Hours: Mon to Fri, 0900 to 1700

Also at:
British Institute at Ankara
Tahran Caddesi 24, 06700 Kavaklidere, Ankara, Turkey; tel: +90 312 427 5487; fax: +90 312 428 0159

Parent body:
British Academy
10 Carlton House Terrace, London, SW1Y 5AH

BRITISH INSTITUTE FOR ALLERGY AND ENVIRONMENTAL THERAPY

Acronym or abbreviation: BIAET

Ffynnonwen, Llangwyryfon, Aberystwyth, Ceredigion, SY23 4EY

Tel: 01974 241376
Fax: 01974 241795
E-mail: allergy@onetel.com

Website:
http://www.allergy.org.uk
Information about allergies and the Institute's diploma: The Identification and Treatment of Allergic Disorders.

Enquiries:
Enquiries to: Principal

Founded:
1987

Organisation type and purpose:
Professional body.

Subject coverage:
Allergies; clinical ecology.

Education services:
Diploma:The Identification and Treatment of Allergic Disorders (DipAET).

Access to staff:
Contact by letter, by telephone and by fax
Hours: Mon to Fri, 0900 to 1500

BRITISH INSTITUTE FOR LEARNING & DEVELOPMENT

Acronym or abbreviation: BILD

Trym Lodge, 1 Henbury Road, Westbury on Trym, Bristol, BS9 3HQ

Tel: 0117 959 6517
Fax: 0117 959 6518
E-mail: info@thebild.org

Website:
http://www.thebild.org/
On-line database of members' products, services and courses.

Enquiries:
Enquiries to: Marketing and Development Manager
Other contacts: General Manager

Founded:
1990

Formerly called:
the British Learning Association (formed by merger in 2003 of the British Association for Open Learning and The Forum for Technology in Training) (year of change 2007)

Organisation type and purpose:
International organisation, national organisation, trade association, membership association (membership is by subscription), present number of members: 300, registered charity (charity number 328229).
To build a dynamic community, with global reach, committed to inculcating excellence and best practice in learning.

Subject coverage:
Open, flexible and distance learning and e-learning. All aspects associated with this area.

Printed publications:
Guide to the BAOL Quality Mark-UK (£26.25, UK inc. p £28.83, Europe inc. p&p)
Ensuring Quality in open learning (£41.45, UK inc. p £42.25, Europe inc. p&p)
Open Learning Today (journal, 4 times a year, £55 per annum, £65 per annum overseas)

Access to staff:
Contact by letter, by telephone, by fax, by e-mail and via website. Appointment necessary.
Hours: Mon to Fri, 0900 to 1700

BRITISH INSTITUTE IN EASTERN AFRICA

Acronym or abbreviation: BIEA

10 Carlton House Terrace, London, SW1Y 5AH

Tel: 020 7969 5201
Fax: 020 7969 5401
E-mail: biea@britac.ac.uk

Website:
http://www.biea.ac.uk

Enquiries:
Enquiries to: Secretary

Founded:
1960

Organisation type and purpose:
Learned society (membership is by subscription), registered charity (charity number 1061622).

Subject coverage:
Research into the history, archaeology and related subjects of eastern Africa.

Printed publications:
Azania (journal, free to members)
Journal of East African Studies (journal, free to members)
Order printed publications from: Membership enquires via website: http://www.biea.ac.uk
Sponsored publications can be ordered through Oxbow Books, 10 Hythe Bridge St, Oxford, OX1 1EW, tel: 01865 241249, fax: 01865 794449

Access to staff:
Contact by letter, by telephone, by fax, by e-mail and via website
Hours: Thu and Fri, 0900 to 1700

Also at:
British Institute in Eastern Africa
PO Box 30710, Nairobi, Kenya; tel: 00 254 2 43721; fax: 00 254 2 43365; e-mail: office@biea.ac.uk

BRITISH INSTITUTE OF AGRICULTURAL CONSULTANTS

Acronym or abbreviation: BIAC

The Estate Office, Torry Hill, Milstead, Sittingbourne, Kent, ME9 0SP

Tel: 01795 830100
Fax: 01795 830243
E-mail: info@biac.co.uk

Website:
http://www.biac.co.uk

Enquiries:
Enquiries to: Chief Executive
Direct e-mail: anthony.hyde@farmline.com

Founded:
1957

Organisation type and purpose:
Professional body.

Subject coverage:
Agriculture, horticulture, forestry, silviculture, arboriculture, crop production, livestock production, mechanisation, land drainage and reclamation, landscape planning, chemicals and fertilisers, plant pathology, farm and estate management, farm buildings, pollution, soils, management, finance, planning appeals, agricultural education and law, fish farming, photography, snail farming, deer farming, historic houses and gardens, leisure and amenity, environment and conservation, arbitration.

Printed publications:
Curricula Vitae of Overseas Consultants
Curricula Vitae of Business Management Consultants
List of members and their specialist services

Electronic and video publications:
Membership List
Overseas Consultants List

Access to staff:
Contact by letter, by telephone, by fax, by e-mail and via website
Hours: Mon to Fri, 0900 to 1700

BRITISH INSTITUTE OF CLEANING SCIENCE

Acronym or abbreviation: BICSc

9 Premier Court, Boarden Close, Moulton Park, Northampton, NN3 6LF

Tel: 01604 678710
Fax: 01604 645988
E-mail: info@bics.org.uk

Website:
http://www.bics.org.uk

Enquiries:
Enquiries to: Executive Director
Direct tel: 01604 678715
Direct e-mail: stan@bics.org.uk
Other contacts: Business Development Manager

Founded:
1961

Organisation type and purpose:
Membership association (membership is by qualification), present number of members: 5,000, service industry, suitable for ages: 18+.
Education and training body for the cleaning industry.

Subject coverage:
Education, training and general information regarding the cleaning industry, cleaning of buildings, internally and externally; cleaning of outside areas; education and training.

Printed publications:
Cleaning Industry Handbook (pub. Market Place Publishing for the Institute, annually, free to members)
Newsletter (quarterly, members only)
BICSc supplies a number of educational products connected with the Cleaning Operator Proficiency Certificate (COPC), Food Premises Cleaning Certificate (FPCC), Healthcare Professional Cleaning Certificate (HPCC), Cleaning Supervisors Skills Certficate (CSSC) and the Car Valeting Certificate (CVC). Also specialist manuals. Some items are restricted to members.

Electronic and video publications:
2 training DVDs

Publications list:
Available online and in print

Access to staff:
Contact by letter, by telephone, by fax, by e-mail and via website. Appointment necessary.
Hours: Mon to Fri, 0830 to 1700

Links with:
British Cleaning Council

BRITISH INSTITUTE OF FACILITIES MANAGEMENT

Acronym or abbreviation: BIFM

Number One Building, The Causeway, Bishop's Stortford, Hertfordshire, CM23 2ER

Tel: 0845 058 1356
Fax: 01279 712 669
E-mail: admin@bifm.org.uk

Website:
http://www.bifm.org.uk
General information, publications for members only.

Enquiries:
Enquiries to: Membership Team
Direct tel: 0845 058 1356
Direct fax: 01279 712 669
Direct e-mail: membership@bifm.org.uk

Access to staff:
Contact by letter, by telephone, by fax, by e-mail and via website
Hours: Mon to Fri, 0900 to 1700

continued overleaf

Founded:
1993

Organisation type and purpose:
Professional body (membership is by subscription, election or invitation), present number of members: 12,500.
To promote awareness of facilities management and provide support, education, training and information to members.

Subject coverage:
All aspects of facilities management, including space planning, lighting, business continuity planning, measurement protocol.

Trade and statistical information:
Survey of members' responsibilities.
Research Directory.

Printed publications:
FM World
Best practice guides on: Procuring and Running Catering Contracts, Selecting FM Software, Procuring and Running Cleaning Contracts, Inclusive Access and the DDA, FM Procurement, Security Management, Procuring and Running Guarding Contracts, Implementing a Sustainability Policy, Project Financial Appraisal, Refurbishing Office Interiors, Managing Fire Safety, Commercial Removals (£10 to non-members)

Electronic and video publications:
BIFM Weekly News

Publications list:
Available online and in print

Access to staff:
Contact by letter, by telephone, by fax, by e-mail and via website. Appointment necessary.
Hours: Mon to Fri, 0900 to 1715

BRITISH INSTITUTE OF GRAPHOLOGISTS

Acronym or abbreviation: BIG

PO Box 3060, Gerrards Cross, Buckinghamshire, SL9 9XP

Tel: 01753 891 241

Website:
http://www.britishgraphology.org
Example analysis on monthly basis, history, background, free lesson on monthly basis, mailing list, information pack available, services offered, details of library, lectures and membership.

Enquiries:
Enquiries to: General Secretary

Founded:
1983

Organisation type and purpose:
Learned society.
To promote understanding and recognition of graphology.

Subject coverage:
Graphology consultancy in: vocational guidance; information and professional training; personnel selection etc.

Printed publications:
Books and monographs
The Graphologist (quarterly)

Access to staff:
Contact by letter, by telephone and by e-mail
Hours: Mon to Fri, 0900 to 1700

Also at:
Association of Disabled Professionals
Netley Lodge, 134 Old Woking Road, Woking, Surrey, GU22 8NY

Subsidiary body:
Graphology Research & Education Trust (GRET)
55 Whitton Avenue East, Greenford, Middlesex, UB6 0BQ; tel: 020 8902 4183

BRITISH INSTITUTE OF HOMEOPATHY

Acronym or abbreviation: BIH

Endeavour House, 80 High Street, Egham, Surrey, TW20 9HE

Tel: 01784 473800
Fax: 01784 473801
E-mail: britinsthom@compuserve.com

Website:
http://www.britinsthom.com
All course information.

Enquiries:
Enquiries to: Managing Director

Founded:
1986

Organisation type and purpose:
International organisation, training organisation.

Subject coverage:
Homoeopathic medicine, homoeopathic pharmacy, herbal medicine, anatomy, physiology, pathology, nature of disease. Bach flower therapy, nutrition, differential diagnosis, aromatherapy.

Printed publications:
International Newsletter (3 times a year)

Electronic and video publications:
Audio and videotapes and CD-ROM which form an integral part of the courses

Access to staff:
Contact by letter, by telephone, by fax, by e-mail and in person. Appointment necessary.
Hours: Mon to Fri, 0900 to 1700

Access to building, collection or gallery:
No prior appointment required

Parent body:
The British Institute of Homeopathy Limited
tel: 01784 440467; fax: 01784 449887; e-mail: britinsthom@compuserve.com

BRITISH INSTITUTE OF HUMAN RIGHTS

Acronym or abbreviation: BIHR

School of Law, King's College London, 3rd Floor, 26–29 Drury Lane, London, WC2B 5RL

Tel: 020 7848 1818
Fax: 020 7848 1814
E-mail: admin@bihr.org

Website:
http://www.bihr.org

Enquiries:
Enquiries to: Administrator

Founded:
1970

Organisation type and purpose:
Registered charity (charity number 1101575).
Conducting research, organising lectures, conferences, etc. in the human rights field.

Subject coverage:
Human rights with particular application to education; European Convention on Human Rights.

Printed publications:
Aspects of incorporation of the European Convention on Human Rights into Domestic Law
The Best Interests of the Child: International Co-operation on Child Abduction
Human Rights for the New Millennium
Human Rights Protection

Access to staff:
Contact by letter and by e-mail
Hours: Mon to Fri, 0930 to 1730

Close links with:
King's College, London

Connections with:
Council of Europe
Other human rights organisations through the Human Rights Network

BRITISH INSTITUTE OF INDUSTRIAL THERAPY

Acronym or abbreviation: BIIT

243 Shelley Road, Wellingborough, Northamptonshire, NN8 3EN

Tel: 01933 675327
Fax: 01933 675327

Enquiries:
Enquiries to: Administrator

Founded:
1981

Organisation type and purpose:
Professional body (membership is by subscription), present number of members: 110, voluntary organisation, registered charity (charity number 283951), consultancy.
National charitable organisation with members from both statutory and voluntary sector units.

Subject coverage:
Rehabilitation through work therapy and associated social education and training for the relief and rehabilitation of the mentally disabled. Advancement of science and practice of industrial therapy. Educational courses for those working in the field of industrial therapy. Consultancy service on work rehabilitation for members.

Printed publications:
Specialised information leaflets (members only)

Access to staff:
Appointment necessary.
Hours: Mon to Fri, 0900 to 1700
Special comments: Answerphone if not available.

Chairman:
British Institute of Industrial Therapy
Lewin Cottage, Jeremy's Lane, Bolney, Haywards Heath, West Sussex, RH17 5QE; tel: 01444 881054

BRITISH INSTITUTE OF INNKEEPING

Acronym or abbreviation: BII

Wessex House, 80 Park Street, Camberley, Surrey, GU15 3PT

Tel: 01276 684449
Fax: 01276 23045
E-mail: info@bii.org

Website:
http://www.bii.org
Information on all BII products and services.
http://www.barzone.co.uk
Careers information for the sector.

Enquiries:
Enquiries to: Reception
Direct fax: 01276 682214
Direct e-mail: reception@bii.org

Founded:
1981

Organisation type and purpose:
Professional body (membership is by qualification, election or invitation), present number of members: 16,000, registered charity (charity number 283945), training organisation.
BII is the professional body for the licensed retail sector. BII's aim is to provide skills, information and qualifications to help members run more successful businesses. BIIAB is a wholly-owned subsidiary awarding qualifications for licensed hospitality.

Subject coverage:
Qualifications for those entering or already in the licensed retail sector (pubs) and off licences.
Information on careers in licensed retailing.

Trade and statistical information:
Data relating to careers in the licensed retail sector (pubs).

Printed publications:
biiBusiness (business magazine, 10 times a year, members and on subscription)
Handbooks for specific qualifications

Publications list:
Available online

Access to staff:
Contact by letter, by telephone, by fax, by e-mail, in person and via website
Hours: Mon to Fri, 0900 to 1700

Links with:
BIIAB – qualifications for licensed hospitality
tel: 01276 684449; fax: 01276 23045; e-mail: info@bii.org

BRITISH INSTITUTE OF INTERIOR DESIGN

Acronym or abbreviation: BIID

Units 109–111 The Chambers, Chelsea Harbour, London, SW10 0XF

Tel: 0207 349 0800
Fax: 0207 349 0500
E-mail: info@biid.org.uk

Website:
http://www.biid.org.uk
Appointing a designer, find designers, find suppliers, CPD, events, careers, publications.

Founded:
2002

Created by the merger of:
Interior Decorators & Designers Association (originally set up in 1966) and International Interior Design Association (UK Chapter) (year of change 2002)

Formerly called:
The British Interior Design Association (BIDA) (year of change 2009)

Organisation type and purpose:
Professional organisation for interior designers in the UK, its growing national and international membership represents both the commercial and residential sectors, from heritage to cutting edge. Committed to encouraging and supporting creativity and competence in the field of interior design through facilitating best practice, practical professional support, development opportunities and education.

Subject coverage:
Interior design.

Printed publications:
Order printed publications from: http://www.ribabookshops.com

Publications list:
Available online

Access to staff:
Contact by letter, by telephone, by fax and by e-mail

Member organisation of:
Construction Industry Council

Represented on the board of:
International Federation of Interior Architects and Designers

BRITISH INSTITUTE OF INTERNATIONAL AND COMPARATIVE LAW

Acronym or abbreviation: BIICL

Charles Clore House, 17 Russell Square, London, WC1B 5JP

Tel: 020 7862 5151
Fax: 020 7862 5152
E-mail: info@biicl.org

Website:
http://www.biicl.org
Details of services offered by the Institute.

Enquiries:
Enquiries to: Director

Founded:
1952

Organisation type and purpose:
International organisation, consultancy, research organisation.
Commonwealth Legal Advisory Service.

Subject coverage:
Public international law; EC law; human rights law; private international law; comparative law; Commonwealth law.

Printed publications:
Bulletin of Legal Developments (fortnightly)
International and Comparative Law Quarterly (ICLQ)
Newsletter (quarterly)
Various monographs, please contact to order catalogue

Publications list:
Available online and in print

Access to staff:
Contact by letter, by telephone, by fax and by e-mail
Hours: Mon to Fri, 0930 to 1730

BRITISH INSTITUTE OF LEARNING DISABILITIES

Acronym or abbreviation: BILD

Campion House, Green Street, Kidderminster, Worcestershire, DY10 1JL

Tel: 01562 723010
Fax: 01562 723029
E-mail: enquiries@bild.org.uk

Website:
http://www.bild.org.uk

Enquiries:
Enquiries to: Information Administrator
Direct tel: 01562 723014
Direct e-mail: k.brackley@bild.org.uk

Founded:
1972

Organisation type and purpose:
Professional body (membership is by subscription), registered charity (charity number 1019663), training organisation, consultancy, research organisation, publishing house.
Receives financial support from the Department of Health.
Aims to improve the quality of life of people with learning disabilities, through advancing education, research and practice and by promoting better ways of working with and for children and adults with learning difficulties.

Subject coverage:
Learning disability and multi-handicap, medical, nursing, social, educational and environmental needs.

Library catalogue:
All or part available in-house

Printed publications:
A selection of books and journals relating to all aspects of disability; research, good practice, everyday living and study materials, including:
British Journal of Learning Disabilities (quarterly)
Current Awareness Service (monthly)
Good Autism Practice (2 times a year)
Journal of Applied Research in Intellectual Disabilities (quarterly)
Learning Disability Bulletin (quarterly)
The SLD Experience (3 times a year)
A Place at the Table? (Simons K)
Crossing Boundries (Edited by Brighman L, Atkinson D, et al, 2000)

Forgotten Lives: Exploring the History of Learning Disability (Edited by Atkinson D, Jackson M, Walmsley J)
Pathways to Citizen Advocacy (Brooke J, 16 training units)
Shared Ownership for People with Learning Difficulties (Dixon T, 2001)
Order printed publications from: BookSource, 32 Finlas Street, Cowlair's Estate, Glasgow, G22 5DU; tel: 08702 402182; fax: 0141 557 0189

Publications list:
Available online and in print

Access to staff:
Contact by letter, by telephone, by fax, by e-mail and via website. Appointment necessary.
Hours: Mon to Thu, 0900 to 1300 and 1400 to 1700; Fri, 0900 to 1300 and 1400 to 1630

Access to building, collection or gallery:
Prior appointment required

Access for disabled people:
Parking provided, level entry, access to all public areas, toilet facilities

BRITISH INSTITUTE OF MUSCULOSKELETAL MEDICINE

Acronym or abbreviation: BIMM

34 The Avenue, Watford, Hertfordshire, WD17 4AH

Tel: 01923 220999
Fax: 01923 249037

Website:
http://www.bimm.org.uk

Enquiries:
Enquiries to: Honorary Secretary
Direct e-mail: deena@bimm.org.uk
Other contacts: Secretary for non-medical enquiries.

Founded:
1992

Organisation type and purpose:
Professional body (membership is by subscription), present number of members: 340, registered charity, training organisation, research organisation.
Dissemination of knowledge to medical profession of musculoskeletal medicine.

Subject coverage:
Musculoskeletal medicine, including manual/manipulative medicine, all aspects of mechanical disorders of the spine and peripheral joints, and sports injuries. This specifically includes soft tissue disorders/injuries of muscles, ligaments, tendons and fascia.

Printed publications:
Patient Information Leaflets
Journal of Orthopaedic Medicine (4 times a year)
Membership list of Practitioners
Newsletter (4 times a year)

Access to staff:
Contact by letter, by telephone, by fax and by e-mail
Hours: Mon to Fri, 0900 to 1700

Access to building, collection or gallery:
No access other than to staff

Affiliated to:
British League Against Rheumatism (BLAR)
Fédération Internationale de Médecine Manuelle (FIMM)

BRITISH INSTITUTE OF NON-DESTRUCTIVE TESTING

Acronym or abbreviation: BINDT

Newton Building, St George's Avenue, Northampton, NN2 6JB

Tel: 01604 893811
Fax: 01604 893861
E-mail: info@bindt.org

continued overleaf

Website:
http://www.bindt.org
Membership data, details of publications, events, certification.

Enquiries:
Enquiries to: Secretary

Founded:
1954

Organisation type and purpose:
Learned society.
To promote the science and practice of non-destructive testing and all other associated materials testing disciplines.

Subject coverage:
Non-destructive testing, condition and health monitoring and all other materials and quality testing disciplines. Various specialist groups for NDT application e.g. aerospace, service inspection, condition monitoring and diagnostic technology group.

Library catalogue:
All or part available in-house

Printed publications:
Insight (journal, monthly, with quarterly European issues)
NDT News (monthly)
NDT Yearbook (annually)
A wide range of technical titles on related subjects including:
Basic Metallurgy for Non-Destructive Testing (ed Taylor J L)
Mathematics and Formulae in NDT (Halmshaw R)
Infrared Thermography Handbooks
Vibration Monitoring & Analysis Handbook
Order printed publications from: website: http://www.bindt.org

Electronic and video publications:
DVD: The Unseen World of NDT
Order electronic and video publications from: tel: 01604 893811

Publications list:
Available online

Access to staff:
Contact by letter, by telephone, by fax, by e-mail and via website

A nominated body of the:
Engineering Council

Member organisation of:
European Federation for Non-Destructive Testing
International Committee for Non-Destructive Testing

BRITISH INSTITUTE OF OCCUPATIONAL HYGIENISTS

Acronym or abbreviation: BIOH

5–6 Melbourne Business Court, Millennium Way, Pride Park, Derby, DE24 8LZ

Tel: 01332 298101
Fax: 01332 298099
E-mail: admin@bohs.org

Website:
http://www.bioh.org

Enquiries:
Enquiries to: Media Enquiries
Direct tel: 01332 250701
Direct e-mail: anthea@bohs.org

Founded:
1997

Organisation type and purpose:
Professional body (membership is by subscription, qualification), registered charity (charity number 1066537).

Subject coverage:
Occupational hygiene.

Access to staff:
Contact by letter, by telephone, by fax and by e-mail

Hours: Mon to Fri, 0830 to 1630

Access to building, collection or gallery:
No access other than to staff

BRITISH INSTITUTE OF ORGAN STUDIES

Acronym or abbreviation: BIOS

Ashcroft, 10 Ridgegate Close, Reigate, Surrey, RH2 0HT

Tel: 01737 241355
E-mail: hughesmelvin@hotmail.com

Website:
http://www.bios.org.uk
Current officers, National Pipe Organ Register with search facilities, British Organ Archive Handlist.
Directory of British Organ-builders.

Enquiries:
Enquiries to: Secretary
Direct e-mail: c.kearl@blueyonder.co.uk
Other contacts: Hon. Archivist; Membership Secretary

Founded:
1976

Organisation type and purpose:
Learned society (membership is by subscription), present number of members: c. 650, voluntary organisation, registered charity (charity number 283936), suitable for ages: 11–80.

Subject coverage:
Conservation, history and restoration of historic British pipe organs; information on repertoire and performance practice.

Museum or gallery collection, archive, or library special collection:
British Organ Archive (largest single collection of original records, order books, designs, working drawings, etc. of organ builders from 1820); housed in Birmingham Central Library

Non-library collection catalogue:
All or part available online

Printed publications:
BIOS Journal (annually)
BIOS Reporter (quarterly)
Directory of British Organ-builders
Guidance Leaflets:
Sound Advice – The Care of your Pipe Organ
Grants – Funding for work on historic instruments
Order printed publications from: Positif Press, British Institute of Organ Studies, 130 Southfield Road, Oxford, OX4 1PA, tel: 01865 243220; fax: 01865 243272; e-mail: john.f.brennan@btinternet.com

Publications list:
Available online

Access to staff:
Contact by letter, by fax, by e-mail and via website. Appointment necessary. Letter of introduction required.
Hours: Mon to Fri, 0900 to 1700
Special comments: Visitors to British Organ Archive require a letter of introduction and should arrange a prior appointment with Birmingham Central Library (City Archives), where the Archive is held.

Access to building, collection or gallery:
Prior appointment required
Hours: Mon, Tue, Fri, Sat, 0900 to 1700; Thu, 0900 to 2000

Constituent bodies:
British Organ Archive (BOA)
National Pipe Organ Register (NPOR)

BRITISH INSTITUTE OF PROFESSIONAL PHOTOGRAPHY

Acronym or abbreviation: BIPP

1 Prebandal Court, Oxford Road, Aylesbury, Buckinghamshire, HP19 8EY

Tel: 01296 718530
Fax: 01296 336367
E-mail: info@bipp.com

Website:
http://www.bipp.com

Enquiries:
Enquiries to: Project Manager
Direct e-mail: marketing@bipp.com

Founded:
1901

Organisation type and purpose:
Professional body.

Subject coverage:
Imaging.

Printed publications:
The Photographer (bi-monthly, £30 for annual UK subscription)

Access to staff:
Contact by letter, by telephone, by fax and by e-mail
Hours: Mon to Fri, 0900 to 1700

BRITISH INSTITUTE OF RADIOLOGY

Acronym or abbreviation: BIR

36 Portland Place, London, W1B 1AT

Tel: 020 7307 1405
Fax: 020 7307 1414
E-mail: infocentre@bir.org.uk

Website:
http://www.bir.org.uk
British Institute of Radiology home page and sample journal pages, library and archives pages.

Enquiries:
Enquiries to: General Secretary
Direct tel: 020 7307 1406
Other contacts: Information Centre Manager

Founded:
1897

Organisation type and purpose:
Professional body, registered charity (charity number GB 233 7553 63).

Subject coverage:
Radiology, radiography, diagnostic imaging, ultrasound, radiation protection, radiation physics, radiotherapy and oncology, computed tomography, radiobiology, nuclear medicine, NMR, MRI (magnetic resonance imaging), history of radiology.

Museum or gallery collection, archive, or library special collection:
Hugh Davies Bequest
KC Clark Slide Collection of 3,500 glass slides

Library catalogue:
All or part available online

Printed publications:
Annual Report
British Journal of Radiology (monthly with a Congress supplement)
Imaging
Dentomaxillofacial Radiology
Special Reports

Publications list:
Available online and in print

Access to staff:
Contact by letter, by telephone, by fax and by e-mail. Appointment necessary. All charged.
Hours: Mon, Wed and Fri, 0900 to 1700; Tue and Thu, 1000 to 1800

BRITISH INSURANCE BROKERS' ASSOCIATION

Acronym or abbreviation: BIBA

8th Floor, John Stow House, 18 Bevis Marks, London, EC3A 7JB

Tel: 0870 950 1790
Fax: 020 7626 9676
E-mail: enquiries@biba.org.uk

Website:
http://www.biba.org.uk
Details of local insurance brokers for consumers.

Enquiries:
Enquiries to: Chief Executive

Founded:
1978

Organisation type and purpose:
Trade association.
Representing insurance brokers and independent intermediaries for the sale of general insurance.

Subject coverage:
The sale of general insurance products through an insurance broker or independent intermediary.

Printed publications:
The Broker (quarterly)

Access to staff:
Contact by letter, by telephone, by fax, by e-mail and via website
Hours: Mon to Fri, 0900 to 1700

BRITISH INSURANCE LAW ASSOCIATION

Acronym or abbreviation: BILA

London Metropolitan University, 84 Moorgate, London, EC2M 6SQ

Tel: 020 7320 1490
Fax: 020 7320 1497
E-mail: bila@lgu.ac.uk

Website:
http://www.bila.org.uk

Enquiries:
Enquiries to: Administrator

Founded:
1964

Organisation type and purpose:
Learned society.
Education and exchange of ideas.

Subject coverage:
Law affecting any branch of insurance.

Printed publications:
Bulletin (3 times per annum)
Technical papers, including government and law reforms

Access to staff:
Contact by letter, by fax, by e-mail and via website
Hours: Mon to Fri, 0900 to 1700

Affiliated to:
International Insurance Law Association (AIDA)

BRITISH INTERIOR TEXTILES ASSOCIATION

Acronym or abbreviation: BITA

5 Portland Place, London, W1B 1PW

Tel: 020 7636 7788
Fax: 020 7636 7515
E-mail: bita@dial.pipex.com

Website:
http://www.interiortextiles.co.uk

Enquiries:
Enquiries to: Secretary

Founded:
1917

Organisation type and purpose:
Trade association.

Subject coverage:
Furnishing textiles industry, manufacture and distribution. UK and EC legislation affecting the industry.

Printed publications:
Directory of Products and Services
Newsletter

Electronic and video publications:
CD-ROM of members and services

Publications list:
Available in print

Access to staff:
Contact by letter, by fax, by e-mail and via website. Appointment necessary.
Hours: Mon to Fri, 0900 to 1730

Access to building, collection or gallery:
Prior appointment required

BRITISH INTERNATIONAL FREIGHT ASSOCIATION

Acronym or abbreviation: BIFA

Redfern House, Browells Lane, Feltham, Middlesex, TW13 7EP

Tel: 020 8844 2266
Fax: 020 8890 5546
E-mail: bifa@bifa.org

Website:
http://www.bifa.org
Background information to BIFA, its organisation, aims, structure, news, members, associate organisations, trading conditions, etc, as well as detailed information on the range of training services available.

Enquiries:
Direct e-mail: information@bifa.org

Founded:
1944

Organisation type and purpose:
Trade association.
To represent the international freight services industry.

Subject coverage:
Practical help and advice on any aspect of running a freight forwarding business or any industry-related issues that may affect member companies.

Publications list:
Available online and in print

Access to staff:
Contact by letter, by telephone, by fax and by e-mail. Access for members only. Non-members charged.
Hours: Mon to Fri, 0900 to 1700

Incorporates:
Institute of Freight Professionals

BRITISH INTERNATIONAL STUDIES ASSOCIATION

Acronym or abbreviation: BISA

16 Ridge Croft, Stone, Staffordshire, ST15 8PN

Tel: 01785 818788
Fax: 01785 818788
E-mail: pkellybisa@compuserve.com

Website:
http://www.bisa.ac.uk

Enquiries:
Enquiries to: Administrator

Founded:
1975

Organisation type and purpose:
Membership association (membership is by subscription), present number of members: c. 1000, registered charity.
To promote the study of International Relations and related subjects through teaching, research and the facilitation of contact between scholars.

Subject coverage:
International studies, IR theory, strategy, IPE, environment, UN and International organisations.

Printed publications:
Review of International Studies (Academic Journal and BISA Newsletter available free to members, review available for purchase)

Publications list:
Available in print

Access to staff:
Contact by letter, by e-mail and via website
Hours: Mon to Fri, 0900 to 1700

BRITISH INTERPLANETARY SOCIETY

Acronym or abbreviation: BIS

27–29 South Lambeth Road, London, SW8 1SZ

Tel: 020 7735 3160
Fax: 020 7820 1504
E-mail: mail@bis-spaceflight.com

Website:
http://www.bis-spaceflight.com

Enquiries:
Enquiries to: Executive Secretary

Founded:
1933

Organisation type and purpose:
Learned society, registered charity (charity number 250556).
Promotion of studies in space research, technology and applications.

Subject coverage:
Space research and technology, space applications and astronomy.

Museum or gallery collection, archive, or library special collection:
Specialised library contains about 8000 books and reports (members only)

Printed publications:
Journal of the British Interplanetary Society (6 times a year)
Spaceflight (monthly)
Space Chronicle (2 times a year)

Electronic and video publications:
Space videos

Access to staff:
Contact by letter, by telephone, by fax, by e-mail and via website
Hours: Mon to Fri, 0930 to 1700

Founder member of:
International Astronautical Federation

BRITISH INVESTMENT CASTING TRADE ASSOCIATION

Acronym or abbreviation: BICTA

National Metalforming Centre, 47 Birmingham Road, West Bromwich, West Midlands, B70 6PX

Tel: 0121 601 6390
Fax: 0121 601 6391
E-mail: admin@cmfed.co.uk

Enquiries:
Enquiries to: Manager

Founded:
1958

Organisation type and purpose:
Trade association.

Subject coverage:
All aspects of the foundry process known as investment (or lost wax) casting – technology of process, markets for investment castings, equipment and consumables used in process, related (foundry) subjects.

Museum or gallery collection, archive, or library special collection:
Books on investment casting

continued overleaf

Copies of proceedings of: BICTA Conferences, EICF (European Investment Casters' Federation) Conferences, World Investment Casting Conference, US Investment Casting Institute Conferences
Miscellaneous technical papers

Trade and statistical information:
Data on output of investment castings.

Printed publications:
Abstracts (members only)
Bicta Bulletin (3 times a year, magazine issued to members and others interested in investment casting)

Publications list:
Available online and in print

Access to staff:
Contact by letter, by telephone, by fax and by e-mail. Appointment necessary. Non-members charged.
Hours: Mon to Thu, 0900 to 1700; Fri, 0900 to 1530

BRITISH IRIS SOCIETY

Acronym or abbreviation: BIS

Aulden Farm, Aulden, Leominster, Herefordshire, HR6 0JT

Tel: 01568 720129
E-mail: jill@auldenfarm.co.uk

Website:
http://www.britishirissociety.org.uk

Enquiries:
Enquiries to: Honorary Secretary

Founded:
1922

Organisation type and purpose:
Voluntary organisation, registered charity (charity number 261896), research organisation.

Subject coverage:
Irises and iridaceae: origins, breeding, cultivation, taxonomy, history.

Museum or gallery collection, archive, or library special collection:
The Genus Iris: original paintings by W R Dykes
Miscellaneous printed material not available in public libraries
Slide library
Paintings by Paul Furse
Paintings by Caparne

Printed publications:
Alphabetical Table and Cultivation Guide to the Species of the Genus Iris and other titles
Cultivation of Irises (2 parts)
First Steps in Iris Growing
Irises for the Water Garden
Year Books (1929 to date)
Introducing Iris
List of Iris Suppliers
Order printed publications from: Postal address; or e-mail: jill@auldenfarm.co.uk

Access to staff:
Contact by letter, by telephone and by e-mail
Hours: Mon to Fri, 0900 to 1700

Affiliated to:
Iris societies around the world
Royal Horticultural Society

Also at:
Enrolment Secretary, Mrs J. Christison
Mill House, Woodlands Lane, Chichester, West Sussex, PO19 5PA; tel: 01243 781887; e-mail: jillchar@btinternet.com
Membership Secretary, British Iris Society
15 Parkwood Drive, Rawtenstall, Lancashire, BB4 6RP; tel: 01706 212840; e-mail: ehf.bis@btinternet.com

Member organisation of:
National Plant Societies Federation

BRITISH JEWELLERS' ASSOCIATION

Acronym or abbreviation: BJA

10 Vyse Street, Birmingham, B18 6LT

Tel: 0121 237 1110
Fax: 0121 237 1113
E-mail: info@bja.org.uk

Website:
http://www.bja.org.uk

Enquiries:
Enquiries to: Senior Co-ordinator

Organisation type and purpose:
Membership association (membership is by subscription).

Subject coverage:
Jewellery manufacturing and silversmithing, designers, jewellery tools, members who supply these services.

Printed publications:
Retail Jeweller & British Jeweller (magazine)
The British Jeweller Yearbook
Jewellery in Britain
Order printed publications from: British Jewellers' Association
338 Goswell Road, London, EC1V 7QP

Access to staff:
Contact by letter, by telephone, by fax, by e-mail and via website
Hours: Mon to Fri, 0900 to 1700

BRITISH JEWELLERY GIFTWARE AND FINISHING FEDERATION

Acronym or abbreviation: BJGF

Federation House, 10 Vyse Street, Birmingham, B18 6LT

Tel: 0121 236 2657
Fax: 0121 236 3921

Website:
http://www.bjgf.org.uk
The federation and its services to members.

Founded:
1887

Formerly called:
Birmingham Jewellers & Silversmiths Association (BJSA) (year of change 1946); British Joint Association of Goldsmiths, Silversmiths, Horlogical and Kindred Trades (BJA) (year of change 1970); British Jewellery & Giftware Federation (year of change 2004)

Incorporates the former:
Fancy Goods Association (changed name to Giftware Association in 1966) (year of change 1948)

Organisation type and purpose:
Represents the interests of 2,500 member companies operating in the jewellery, gift and home, leathergoods and surface engineering industries, employing between them 46,000 people.
To provide professional central services to the six trade associations operating within it.

Access to staff:
Contact by letter, by telephone and by fax

Federated associations:
British Jewellers' Association (BJA)
British Travelgoods and Accessories Association (BTAA)
Giftware Association (GA)
Jewellery Distributors' Association (JDA)
Surface Engineering Association (SEA)

BRITISH JIGSAW PUZZLE LIBRARY

Acronym or abbreviation: BJPL

Clarendon, Parsonage Road, Herne Bay, Kent, CT6 5TA

Tel: 01227 742222
E-mail: jigsawman@britishjigsawpuzzlelibrary.co.uk

Website:
http://www.britishjigsawpuzzlelibrary.co.uk
Subscription information, brief history, types of jigsaw puzzles, contact information.

Enquiries:
Enquiries to: Secretary

Founded:
1933

Organisation type and purpose:
Membership association (membership is by subscription).
Library of wooden jigsaw puzzles.
Leisure and therapy.

Subject coverage:
Jigsaw puzzles (subscription loan service).
Lending library of wooden jigsaw puzzles.
Puzzles exchanged by post.
Stock contains jigsaws with large pieces suitable for stroke victims and people with disabilities.

Trade and statistical information:
Collection of over 3,500 high quality craftsman-cut wooden puzzles.

Printed publications:
History of The Jigsaw Puzzle Library (£4)

Access to staff:
Contact by letter, by telephone, by e-mail and via website. Appointment necessary.
Hours: Mon to Fri, 0900 to 1700

Access to building, collection or gallery:
No access other than to staff

BRITISH JUDO COUNCIL

Acronym or abbreviation: BJC

1A Horn Lane, Acton, London, W3 9NJ

Tel: 020 8992 9454
Fax: 020 8993 3526

Enquiries:
Enquiries to: General Secretary

Organisation type and purpose:
Voluntary organisation.

Subject coverage:
Judo.

Access to staff:
Contact by letter and by telephone. Appointment necessary.
Hours: Mon to Fri, 0900 to 1500

BRITISH KENPO KARATE UNION

Acronym or abbreviation: BKKU

16 York Road, Exeter, Devon, EX4 6BA

Tel: 07778 921623
E-mail: info@bkku.com

Website:
http://www.bkku.com

Enquiries:
Enquiries to: Secretary

Founded:
1981

Organisation type and purpose:
Membership association (membership is by subscription), present number of members: 100, service industry, training organisation.

Subject coverage:
Kenpo karate.

Access to staff:
Contact by e-mail
Hours: Mon to Fri, 0900 to 1700

BRITISH KIDNEY PATIENT ASSOCIATION

Acronym or abbreviation: BKPA

Bordon, Hampshire, GU35 9JZ

Tel: 01420 472021/2
Fax: 01420 475831

Enquiries:
Enquiries to: Chief Executive

Organisation type and purpose:
National Charity.
To help kidney patients and their families.

Subject coverage:
Renal dialysis and transplantation, material and physical needs of patients and their relatives, lobbying for more facilities.

Printed publications:
Questions & Answers on Series: Kidney Transplantation, Donation, Failure, CAPD, Nephrotic Syndrome in Children, Polycystic Disease, Alport's Syndrome, Renal Diabetes, Haemolytic Uraemic Syndrome
Silver Lining Appeal (annually)
The Home Dialysis Patient
Timbo: A Struggle for Survival by Mrs E D Ward
The Kidney Question – education pack (free of charge, £5.30 p&p)
Work of the BKPA

Electronic and video publications:
Videos

Publications list:
Available in print

Access to staff:
Contact by letter, by telephone and by fax.
Appointment necessary.
Hours: Mon to Fri, 0900 to 1700

BRITISH KORFBALL ASSOCIATION

Acronym or abbreviation: BKA

Registrations Officer, 50 Mayfair Avenue, Worcester Park, Surrey, KT4 7SL

Tel: 020 8337 6729
E-mail: registrations@korfball.co.uk

Website:
http://www.korfball.co.uk
Links to IKF and other national body sites including UK.
Rules of the sport, contact person for clubs and areas, noticeboard, national league fixtures and results.

Enquiries:
Enquiries to: General Secretary
Direct e-mail: secretary@korfball.co.uk
Other contacts: Development Officer

Founded:
1946

Organisation type and purpose:
Voluntary organisation.
Governing body for the sport.

Subject coverage:
Rules of Korfball, lists of clubs, coaches and referees, coaching and refereeing courses.

Printed publications:
Handbook of Clubs
Korfball Magazine

Access to staff:
Contact by letter and by e-mail
Hours: Answerphone, if unavailable during office hours; personal contact by phone, normally in the evenings

Affiliated to:
International Korfball Federation
PO Box 85394, 3508 AJ Utrecht, The Netherlands; tel: + 31 30 6566354; fax: + 31 30 6570468; e-mail: office@ihf.org; website: http://www.ihf.org

General Secretary:
British Korfball Association
PO Box 179, Maidstone, Kent, ME14 1LU; e-mail: secretary@korfball.co.uk

BRITISH LIBRARY – ASIA, PACIFIC AND AFRICA COLLECTIONS

Acronym or abbreviation: APAC

96 Euston Road, London, NW1 2DB

Tel: 020 7412 7873
Fax: 020 7412 7641
E-mail: apac-enquiries@bl.uk

Website:
http://www.bl.uk/collections/asiapacificafrica.html

Enquiries:
Enquiries to: Reference Services

Founded:
1753

Organisation type and purpose:
Non-departmental public body.

Subject coverage:
Languages, literature, religion, art, social and political life of the various regions of Asia and North Africa, both historical and contemporary; principal linguistic and geographical sections are: Hebrew (with Coptic, Syriac, Ethiopian, etc), Islamic (Arabic, Turkish, Iranian, etc.), South Asian, South-East Asian, Far Eastern.
Official British records relating to the Indian sub-continent from 1600 to 1947, humanities and social sciences relating to the sub-continent, activities of the British in the sub-continent and in other areas of Asia where the East India Company was active, material in Indian vernacular languages, Indian studies in the broadest sense.

Education services:
Free monthly training sessions for first-time users of the family history sources.

Museum or gallery collection, archive, or library special collection:
Drawings and prints, including miniatures (over 29,000 items)
Each language section contains rare and specialised collections of manuscripts and printed books
East India Company material, including collections on factories or early trading stations, and the Company's maritime activities
Government of India Publications (70,200 vols)
Manuscripts in European languages (over 100 major collections)
Manuscripts in Oriental languages (over 27,000 items)
Maps: topographical, subject (railways, canals, irrigation, etc.)
Oriental language newspapers and official publications
Photographs, including some 187,000 photographs of scenes in India, pre-1947 and 2,300 negative plates of Indian inscriptions and antiquities
Records of the Crown Representative and of the Residents in the Indian Princely States

Non-library collection catalogue:
All or part available online, in-house and in print

Library catalogue:
All or part available online, in-house and in print

Printed publications:
Annual Report
Detailed catalogues of the collections
Guide to the Department of Oriental Manuscripts and Printed Books (1977)
Guide to the India Office Library
Guide to the India Office Records (1982)
List of catalogues is available from the Department
Newsletter

Publications list:
Available in print

Access to staff:
Contact by letter, by telephone, by fax, by e-mail and in person
Hours: Mon, 1000 to 1700; Tue to Sat, 0930 to 1700

Access for disabled people:
Ramped entry, access to all public areas, toilet facilities
Special comments: Parking spaces for disabled people are in Midland Road.

Constituent part of:
British Library

BRITISH LIBRARY – BUSINESS AND INTELLECTUAL PROPERTY CENTRE

96 Euston Road, London, NW1 2DB

Tel: 020 7412 7454 (enquiries and holdings information)
Fax: 020 7412 7453
E-mail: bipc@bl.uk

Website:
http://www.bl.uk/bipc

Organisation type and purpose:
Information service.

Subject coverage:
Business and intellectual property information on patents, designs, trademarks, copyright, markets, companies, and products covering all sectors in the United Kingdom and overseas.

Museum or gallery collection, archive, or library special collection:
Various electronic databases, patent specifications, market research reports, trade directories, trade journals and trade literature collection

Trade and statistical information:
Range of national and international trade statistics.

Non-library collection catalogue:
All or part available online and in-house

Library catalogue:
All or part available online

Access to staff:
Contact by letter, by telephone, by fax, by e-mail, in person and via website

Access to building, collection or gallery:
Hours: Mon, 1000 to 2000; Tue to Thu, 0930 to 2000; Fri to Sat, 0930 to 1700
Special comments: No access to first-time users after 1700.

Access for disabled people:
Ramped entry, toilet facilities
Special comments: Parking spaces for disabled people are in Midland Road.

BRITISH LIBRARY – CARTOGRAPHIC AND TOPOGRAPHIC MATERIALS

Acronym or abbreviation: BL

96 Euston Road, London, NW1 2DB

Tel: 020 7412 7702
Fax: 020 7412 7780
E-mail: maps@bl.uk

Website:
http://www.bl.uk

Enquiries:
Enquiries to: Head of Cartographic and Topographic Materials
Direct tel: 020 7412 7701
Direct e-mail: peter.barber@bl.uk

Organisation type and purpose:
Non-departmental public body.

Subject coverage:
Cartographic materials (atlases, maps, globes), cartobibliography, celestial atlases and maps, history of cartography, remotely sensed imagery,

continued overleaf

topographical views and panoramas, gazeteers, geographical information systems, digital mapping.

Museum or gallery collection, archive, or library special collection:
Crace Collection (maps of London)
King George III Topographical and Maritime Collections
Ministry of Defence mapping archive
Ordnance Survey manuscript drawings
Ordnance Survey publications, including large-scale plans (the United Kingdom's definitive collection)
Royal United Services Institution map collection

Non-library collection catalogue:
All or part available online, in-house and in print

Library catalogue:
All or part available online, in-house and in print

Printed publications:
County Atlases of the British Isles Vol III – the period 1764–1789 (D. Hodson, 1997, £35)
Images and Icons of the New World – Essays on American Cartography (K. S. Cook, 1996, £17.50)
Lie of the Land: The Secret Life of Maps (A. Carlucci and P. Barber, 2001, £9.95)
Mappa Mundi: The Hereford World Map (P. D. A. Harvey, 1996, £17.95 or £10.95 paper)
Mapping Time and Space: How Medieval Mapmakers Viewed Their World (E. Edson, 1997, £19.95 paper)
Maps as Prints in the Italian Renaissance (D. Woodward, 1996, £16)
The Charting of the Oceans – Ten Centuries of Maritime Maps (P. Whitfield, 1996, £20)
The Dictionary of Land Surveyors and Local Mapmakers of Great Britain and Ireland 1530–1850 (S. Bendall, 1997, £75)
The Image of the World – 20 Centuries of World Maps (P. Whitfield, 1997, £12.95)
The Mapping of the Heavens (P. Whitfield, 1997, £12.95)
Magnificent Maps: Power, Propaganda and Art (P. Barber, T. Harper, 2010, £17.95)
Order printed publications from: Turpin Distribution Ltd, Blackhorse Road, Letchworth, Hertfordshire, SG6 1HN; tel. 01462 672555; fax 01462 480497; e-mail turpin@turpinltd.com

Publications list:
Available online and in print

Access to staff:
Contact by letter, by telephone, by fax, by e-mail, in person and via website. Appointment necessary.
Hours: Mon, 1000 to 1700; Tue to Sat, 0930 to 1700

Access for disabled people:
Ramped entry, toilet facilities
Special comments: Parking spaces for disabled people are in Midland Road.

BRITISH LIBRARY – DEPARTMENT OF MANUSCRIPTS

Formal name: British Library Department of Western Manuscripts
Acronym or abbreviation: BL MSS

96 Euston Road, London, NW1 2DB

Tel: 020 7412 7513
Fax: 020 7412 7745
E-mail: mss@bl.uk

Website:
http://www.bl.uk/collections/manuscripts.html
Information on the manuscripts reading room and collections.

Enquiries:
Enquiries to: Reading Room Manager
Other contacts: Manuscripts Librarian (for subject enquiries)

Founded:
1753

Organisation type and purpose:
Non-departmental public body.

Subject coverage:
Primarily material written by hand in Western languages, covering virtually all aspects of history, literature and culture, including maps dating from the classical period to the present day and early (pre-1500) music.

Museum or gallery collection, archive, or library special collection:
Additional MSS
Arundel MSS
Ashley MSS
Burney MSS
Collections of Charters, Rolls, Seals, Papyri and Ostraca
Cotton MSS
Egerton MSS
Hargrave MSS
Harley MSS
King's MSS
Lansdowne MSS
Lord Chamberlain's Plays
Modern Playscripts
Photocopies of exported manuscripts
Royal MSS
Sloane MSS
Stowe MSS
Yates Thompson MSS
Zweig MSS
Facsimile collection

Non-library collection catalogue:
All or part available online and in print

Printed publications:
Guide to the Catalogues and Indexes of the Department of Manuscripts (M. A. E. Nickson, 3rd edn, London 1998)
Index of Manuscripts in the British Library (10 vols, Chadwyck-Healey, 1984–86 and supplements)
Manuscripts Collections
Using the Manuscripts Reading Room
Other collection guides

Access to staff:
Contact by letter, by telephone, by fax, by e-mail and via website
Hours: Mon, 1000 to 1700; Tue to Sat, 0930 to 1700

Access for disabled people:
Ramped entry, access to all public areas, toilet facilities
Special comments: Parking spaces for disabled people are in Midland Road.

BRITISH LIBRARY – DIALTECH

96 Euston Road, London, NW1 2DB

Tel: 020 7412 7951 or 7946
Fax: 020 7412 7947
E-mail: dialtech@bl.uk

Website:
http://www.gemcatcher.com
Gives a description of the GEM service provided by EINS, details of costs, training courses available etc. Also gives access to the GEM databases if the GEM customer has a password.
http://www.bl.uk/
Services provided by Dialtech.

Enquiries:
Enquiries to: Manager
Direct e-mail: roy.kitley@bl.uk

Organisation type and purpose:
To provide the UK national centre for EINS (European Information Network Services) which gives access to the GEM online information service in science, technology and business information. Support is also given to customers in Australia, New Zealand, Ireland, Canada and the USA.

Subject coverage:
Bibliographic and factual databases in science, technology and business information.

Printed publications:
Newsletter (irregular, free)

Access to staff:
Contact by letter, by telephone, by fax, by e-mail and via website. Appointment necessary. All charged.
Hours: Mon to Fri, 0930 to 1700

Access for disabled people:
Ramped entry, toilet facilities
Special comments: Parking spaces for disabled people are in Midland Road.

Represents the:
European Information Network Services (EINS)

BRITISH LIBRARY – DOCUMENT SUPPLY

Acronym or abbreviation: BLDS

Boston Spa, Wetherby, West Yorkshire, LS23 7BQ

Tel: 01937 546060
Fax: 01937 546333
E-mail: dsc-customer-services@bl.uk

Website:
http://www.bl.uk/catalogue
Free access to Integrated Catalogue. Includes online document ordering link for both registered and non-registered customers.
http://www.bl.uk/docsupply
Web pages dedicated to British Library Document Supply service.
http://www.bl.uk/inside
A fully integrated searching and ordering service based on the British Library's Document Supply collection.
http://www.bl.uk
General British Library site.

Enquiries:
Enquiries to: Customer Services
Direct tel: 01937 546060
Direct fax: 01937 546333
Direct e-mail: dsc-customer-services@bl.uk

Founded:
1962

Organisation type and purpose:
National Library Service.
To provide a document supply and loan service to researchers in every field of enquiry anywhere in the world. A small Reading Room also operates on-site (open Mon to Fri, 0930 to 1600: tel: 01937 546070).

Subject coverage:
Science, technology, law, finance, industry, medicine, humanities, social sciences and all allied subjects.

Museum or gallery collection, archive, or library special collection:
Over 250,000 journal series in total (50,000 current subscriptions)
Over 3 million books
All British official publications since 1962
All EC official publications since 1973
Conference Proceedings (over 370,000)
Local authority material (28,000)
Music (over 129,000 scores)
Reports (over 4,300,000, mainly US and in microform)
Russian science and technology monographs (over 220,000)
Theses and Dissertations (over 580,000 UK, US, and some European)
Translations (over 570,000)
Microform research collections – includes one of the largest medieval manuscript collections in Europe
Access to all United Kingdom and international patents

Non-library collection catalogue:
All or part available online and in print

Printed publications:
British Library publications can be purchased online from http://www.bl.uk/bookshop
Order printed publications from: Turpin Distribution Services Ltd

Blackhorse Road, Letchworth, Hertfordshire, SG6
1HN, tel: 01462 488900, fax: 01462 480947, e-mail:
turpin@rsc.org

Electronic and video publications:
British National Bibliography

Publications list:
Available in print

Access to staff:
Contact by letter, by telephone, by fax, by e-mail,
in person and via website
Hours: Customer Services open: Mon to Fri, 0830 to
1700 (except for English public holidays)
Document supply staff work 'around the clock'
from Mon at 0800 to Sat at 0200 (except for English
public holidays)
Special comments: Charges made for document
supply and interlibrary loan. Orders must be sent
online or by email.

Access for disabled people:
For visitors to the Boston Spa site, parking
provided, ramped entry, toilet facilities

Affiliated to:
National Bibliographic Service
  Boston Spa; tel: 01937 546585; fax: 01937 546586;
  e-mail: nbs-info@bl.uk

Parent body:
British Library
  tel: 020 7412 7111; fax: 020 7412 7168; e-mail:
  press-and-pr@bl.uk

BRITISH LIBRARY – ECCLES CENTRE FOR AMERICAN STUDIES

96 Euston Road, London, NW1 2DB

Tel: 020 7412 7551
Fax: 020 7412 7792
E-mail: eccles-centre@bl.uk

Website:
http://www.bl.uk/ecclescentre

Enquiries:
Enquiries to: Director

Founded:
1991

Organisation type and purpose:
Information agency.
To support the study and understanding of North
America in the United Kingdom through the
resources of the British Library.

Subject coverage:
North American collections in the British Library,
North American educational activities in the
United Kingdom, general information on the USA
and Canada.

Publications list:
Available online

Access to staff:
Contact by letter, by telephone, by fax, by e-mail,
in person and via website. Appointment necessary.
Hours: Mon to Fri, 0900 to 1700
Special comments: Please telephone for opening
times.

Access to building, collection or gallery:
No prior appointment required

Parent body:
The British Library
  96 Euston Road, London, NW1 2DB; tel: 020
  7412 7000

BRITISH LIBRARY – ENVIRONMENTAL INFORMATION SERVICE

Acronym or abbreviation: EIS

96 Euston Road, London, NW1 2DB

Tel: 020 7412 7477
Fax: 020 7412 7954

E-mail: eis@bl.uk

Website:
http://www.bl.uk/environment
Environmental Information Service at the British
Library: lists of environmental organisations by
topic and A–Z, all hypertext linked, and resources
on the Internet.

Enquiries:
Enquiries to: Information Officer
Other contacts: Head of Science and Technology
Information Services

Founded:
1989

Organisation type and purpose:
Consultancy, research organisation.
Information service.

Subject coverage:
Scientific and technological aspects of
environmental information.

**Museum or gallery collection, archive, or library
special collection:**
Access to all British Library collections including
environmental newsletters and corporate
environmental reports

Printed publications:
Amongst many are:
How to Find Information – Environment (1998)

Publications list:
Available in print

Access to staff:
Contact by letter, by telephone, by fax and by e-
mail
Hours: Mon to Fri, 0930 to 1700
Special comments: Reader Pass needed.
Charges made for on-line searches and detailed
enquiries.

Access for disabled people:
Ramped entry, toilet facilities
Special comments: Parking spaces for disabled
people are in Midland Road.

Part of:
British Library (same address)

BRITISH LIBRARY – HEALTH CARE INFORMATION SERVICE

Acronym or abbreviation: HCIS

96 Euston Road, London, NW1 2DB

Tel: 020 7412 7489
Fax: 020 7412 7954
E-mail: hcis@bl.uk

Website:
http://www.bl.uk/health
British Library website, Healthcare information
page.
http://www.bl.uk/services/publications/onlineshop
.html
Publications list.

Enquiries:
Enquiries to: Information Officer
Direct fax: 020 7412 7947
Direct e-mail: fiona.mclean@bl.uk
Other contacts: Head of HCIS

Founded:
1995

Organisation type and purpose:
Non-departmental public body.

Subject coverage:
Biomedicine and healthcare, medical information,
consumer health information, complementary
medicine, allied healthcare, occupational therapy,
physiotherapy, palliative care, rehabilitation,
nursing, health informatics.

**Museum or gallery collection, archive, or library
special collection:**
UK Publications (and selected overseas) including
patents and historical material, as well as a wide
range of relevant books, journals, grey literature
and databases

Trade and statistical information:
Health Care Statistics for the United Kingdom.

Non-library collection catalogue:
All or part available in-house

Library catalogue:
All or part available online

Printed publications:
AMED Thesaurus
Complementary Medicine Index (monthly, also in
  electronic format)
Employment Health: Psychosocial Stress in the
  Workplace (Grimshaw J, 1999)
Directory of Organisations in Allied and
  Complementary Health Care (Madge D, 2000)
Guide to Libraries and Information Sources in
  Medicine and Health Care (Dale P, 3rd ed., 2001)
List of Journals Indexed for AMED
Health Care Updates – 29 titles including
  Alcoholism, Asthma, Depression, Drug
  Dependence, Eating Disorders, Obesity,
  Parkinson's Disease, Epilepsy, Health Care in
  Britain, Dementia, Schizophrenia, Smoking and
  Women's Health (monthly, also in electronic
  format)
Occupational Therapy Index (monthly, also in
  electronic format)
Palliative Care Index (monthly, also in electronic
  format)
Physiotherapy Index (monthly, also in electronic
  format)
Podiatry Index (quarterly, also in electronic format)
Rehabilitation Index (monthly, also in electronic
  format)
How to Find Information series (brief guides):
Social Sciences (Grimshaw J, 2000)
Health Care (Madge D, 2001)
Complementary and Alternative Health Care
  (Madge D, 2001)
Genetically Modified Foods (Lee, 2000)
Order printed publications from: Health Care
Information Service (North)
Boston Spa, Wetherby, West Yorkshire, LS23 7BQ,
tel: 01937 546361, fax: 01937 546458, e-mail: anita
.jackson@bl.uk

Electronic and video publications:
Allied and Alternative Medicine Database (AMED)
(CD-ROM)

Publications list:
Available online and in print

Access to staff:
Contact by letter, by telephone, by fax, by e-mail
and via website. Appointment necessary.
Hours: Mon to Fri, 1000 to 1700
Special comments: Voicemail out of hours.

Access for disabled people:
Ramped entry, toilet facilities
Special comments: Parking spaces for disabled
people are in Midland Road.

Other address:
Health Care Information Service (North) and
Reading Room (North)
The British Library
  Boston Spa, Wetherby, West Yorkshire, LS23
  7BQ; tel: 01937 546364; fax: 01937 546458

Parent body:
British Library

BRITISH LIBRARY – LIBRARIANSHIP AND INFORMATION SCIENCES SERVICE

Acronym or abbreviation: LIS

96 Euston Road, London, NW1 2DB

Tel: 020 7412 7676

continued overleaf

Fax: 020 7412 7691
E-mail: lis@bl.uk

Website:
http://www.bl.uk
Description of services and collections; recent accessions lists including journal holdings; links to useful sites and services.
http://catalogue.bl.uk
British Library integrated catalogue.

Enquiries:
Enquiries to: Reference Specialist

Organisation type and purpose:
National library.

Subject coverage:
All aspects of librarianship and information science.

Museum or gallery collection, archive, or library special collection:
Collections include British material acquired by legal deposit and selected non-British material on librarianship, information science and related subjects

Non-library collection catalogue:
All or part available online

Library catalogue:
All or part available online

Printed publications:
Leaflet and reader guide

Access to staff:
Contact by letter, by telephone, by fax, by e-mail and in person
Hours: Mon, 1000 to 2000; Tue, Wed, Thu, 0930 to 2000; Fri, Sat, 0930 to 1700
Special comments: A Readers Pass is required for entry to the Reading Rooms, see details on website.

Access for disabled people:
Accessible to the disabled

BRITISH LIBRARY – METADATA SERVICES

Boston Spa, Wetherby, West Yorkshire, LS23 7BQ

Tel: 01937 546548
Fax: 01937 546586
E-mail: bd-info@bl.uk

Website:
http://www.bl.uk
British Library website (collections, catalogues and services), including the British Library Integrated Catalogue (online).

Founded:
2002

Formerly called:
National Bibliographic Service; Bibliographic Development (year of change 2010)

Organisation type and purpose:
National government body, public library.
To develop metadata standards with reference to their application in British Library bibliographic products and services, and in a variety of EC and other projects.

Subject coverage:
The development of bibliographic standards at national and international levels; the British National Bibliography; support for metadata products and services; projects in support of the UK library and information community.

Museum or gallery collection, archive, or library special collection:
Metadata Services does not have its own collections but makes available the MARC records of the British National Bibliography and the British Library collections

Printed publications:
British National Bibliography (BNB): lists by subject all forthcoming and new books and serials published in the UK and Ireland with full author and title indexes (options include weekly list, cumulations, annual vol.). Also available in .pdf format.
Serials in the British Library (SBL): lists all serials acquired through legal deposit together with titles purchased by the London Reading Rooms (three printed issues and an annual cumulative vol.)
Current Serials Received (CSR): over 60,000 current serial titles received by the British Library and available for document supply (annual vol.)
Index of Conference Proceedings (ICP): newly acquired by the British Library and available for document supply (annual vol.)
The UKMARC Exchange Record Format (1997) (also available online)
The UKMARC Manual: a cataloguer's guide to the bibliographic format (4th ed., 1996, with updates 1997–2002) (also available online)
Order printed publications from: Available from: Extenza-Turpin, Stratton Business Park, Pegasus Drive, Biggleswade, Bedfordshire, SG18 8QB; tel: 01767 604955; fax: 01767 601640; e-mail: turpin@ extenza-turpin.com

Electronic and video publications:
Exchange data services:
BNB MARC Weekly File
British Library holdings (Humanities & Social Sciences, Science Technology and Business)
British Library Document Supply Centre Monographs / Conferences / Serials files
Library of Congress weekly 'Books All' file (distribution in the UK and Europe)
Order electronic and video publications from: The British Library, Bibliographic Data Licensing, Boston Spa, Wetherby, West Yorkshire, LS23 7BQ; tel: 01937 546797; fax: 01937 546586; e-mail: data -licensing@bl.uk

Publications list:
Available in print

Access to staff:
Contact by letter, by telephone, by fax and by e-mail. Appointment necessary.
Hours: Mon to Fri, 0900 to 1700

BRITISH LIBRARY – MUSIC COLLECTIONS

96 Euston Road, London, NW1 2DB

Tel: 020 7412 7772
Fax: 020 7412 7751
E-mail: music-collections@bl.uk

Website:
http://www.bl.uk/collections/music/music.html
http://www.bl.uk/reshelp/findhelprestype/music

Enquiries:
Enquiries to: Head of Music Collections
Direct tel: 020 7412 7529

Founded:
1973

Organisation type and purpose:
Non-departmental public body.

Subject coverage:
All aspects of printed and manuscript music, including music history, music printing, bibliography of music, availability of music, music copyright, popular music, etc. NB for recorded music, see British Library Sound Archive.

Information services:
Music Reference Service.

Museum or gallery collection, archive, or library special collection:
Hirsch Collection
Royal Music Library
Royal Philharmonic Society Archive

Non-library collection catalogue:
All or part available in-house

Library catalogue:
All or part available online and in print

Printed publications:
Catalogue of Printed Music in the British Library to 1980 (62 vols, 1980–87)
Stefan Zweig Collection: catalogue of the music manuscripts (1999)

Electronic and video publications:
CPM PLUS (2nd ed., CD-ROM catalogue of printed music in the British Library to 1996)

Publications list:
Available in print

Access to staff:
Contact by letter, by telephone, by fax, by e-mail and via website. Appointment necessary.
Hours: Mon, 1000 to 2000; Tue, Wed, Thu, 0930 to 2000; Fri, Sat, 0930 to 1700
Special comments: Reader's Pass required to use reading rooms.

Access for disabled people:
Ramped entry, access to all public areas, toilet facilities
Special comments: 3 parking bays in Ossulton Street.

BRITISH LIBRARY – NATIONAL PRESERVATION OFFICE

Acronym or abbreviation: NPO

96 Euston Road, London, NW1 2DB

Tel: 020 7412 7612
Fax: 020 7412 7796
E-mail: npo@bl.uk

Website:
http://www.bl.uk/npo/
Basic information via the British Library's home pages; lists of publications, etc.
http://www.bl.uk/services/npo/npo.html

Enquiries:
Enquiries to: Information Officer
Other contacts: Director

Founded:
1984

Organisation type and purpose:
Research organisation.
Independent national advisory body.
Independent national focus for debate and information on preservation, conservation and security in libraries and archives.

Subject coverage:
Preservation, conservation, disaster control, security, surrogacy.

Printed publications:
see website for details, http://www.bl.uk/services/ npo/publications.html

Access to staff:
Contact by letter, by telephone, by fax, by e-mail and via website
Hours: Mon to Fri, 0900 to 1700
Special comments: Visitors by prior appointment only (no casual callers).

Funded by:
British Library
Cambridge University Library
The Bodleian Library, Oxford University
The National Archives
The National Library of Scotland
The National Library of Wales
Trinity College Library, Dublin

Policies guided by the:
National Preservation Office Board

BRITISH LIBRARY – NEWSPAPERS

Colindale Avenue, London, NW9 5HE

Tel: 020 7412 7353
Fax: 020 7412 7379
E-mail: newspaper@bl.uk

Website:
http://www.bl.uk/collections/newspapers.html

Organisation type and purpose:
The national archive collections in the United Kingdom of British and overseas newspapers; the only large, integrated national newspaper service in the world, combining facilities for the collection, preservation, and use of newspapers all on one site.
Our collections, which also include popular magazines and periodicals, are made available in hard copy, in microform, and on CD-ROM in the Newspaper Reading Rooms in Colindale, north west London. Subject to restrictions, facilities are available for the photocopying, microfilming, and photographic and film reproduction of items from the collections in our care.

Museum or gallery collection, archive, or library special collection:
British Library Newspapers Web Catalogue
The British Library Online Newspaper Archive (Pilot version only)
British and Irish Newspapers
Overseas Newspapers
Periodicals and Comics
Visual Arts collections
Microform Series
Chatham House Press Cuttings
Special collections:
British and Irish Cinema and Film Periodicals
British Comics Collection
British Football Programmes
British Military History Collections 1801–1945
The Burney Collection of Newspapers
Current Foreign (Non-British Isles) Newspapers
The Dutch Underground Press 1940–1945
Early American Newpapers
Early English Newspapers
Early Indian Newspapers
The Francis Place Collection (British Politics and Economics)
General Strike Newspapers 1926
German-language Newspapers and Journals Published in London since 1810
Modern Music Periodicals: Pop and Jazz
Northern Ireland Political Literature: Periodicals 1966–1989
The Thomason Tracts (English Newsbooks, 1640–61)
Tuskegee Institute News Clippings File (African-Americans 1899–1966)
Victorian Illustrated Newspapers and Journals

Printed publications:
Newsletter

Electronic and video publications:
Abstracts and Indexes to Newspapers and Journals
Full-Text, Word-Searchable Newspapers and Journals
Chronological and Subject Guides based on News and Newspapers
Other databases

Access to staff:
Hours: Mon to Fri, 0900 to 1700

BRITISH LIBRARY – PHILATELIC COLLECTIONS

96 Euston Road, London, NW1 2DB

Tel: 020 7412 7635
Fax: 020 7412 7780
E-mail: philatelic@bl.uk

Website:
http://www.bl.uk/collections/philatelic

Founded:
1973

Organisation type and purpose:
Non-departmental public body.

Subject coverage:
Philately, postal history, philatelic literature, history of philately.

Museum or gallery collection, archive, or library special collection:
Over 50 main collections, including:

Board of Inland Revenue Stamping Department Archive
Crown Agents Philatelic and Security Printing Archive
Fletcher Collection
Foreign and Commonwealth Office Collection
Harrison Collection
Tapling Collection (perhaps the most important and unique)

Non-library collection catalogue:
All or part available in-house

Printed publications:
Newsletter
Catalogue of the Crawford Library of Philatelic Literature at the British Library (Sir E. Bacon, £90)
Stamps (R. F. Schoolley-West, 1987, £6.95)
The Care and Preservation of Philatelic Materials (T. J. Collings and R. F. Schoolley-West, £12.95)
The British Library Treasures in Focus – Stamps (David Beech, 2009, £3.99)

Access to staff:
Contact by letter, by telephone, by fax and by e-mail. Appointment necessary.
Hours: Mon to Fri, 0900 to 1700

Access to building, collection or gallery:
Prior appointment required
Hours: Mon to Fri, 1000 to 1600
Special comments: Reader's pass required

Access for disabled people:
Ramped entry, toilet facilities

BRITISH LIBRARY – READER REGISTRATION OFFICE

96 Euston Road, London, NW1 2DB

Tel: 020 7412 7676
Fax: 020 7412 7794
E-mail: reader-registration@bl.uk

Website:
http://www.bl.uk
Admissions information.

Founded:
1973

Organisation type and purpose:
Non-departmental public body.

Subject coverage:
Applications for a Reader's Pass and information about access to the Library.

Printed publications:
Application for a Reader's Pass

Access to staff:
Contact by letter, by telephone, by fax, by e-mail and in person
Hours: Mon, 1000 to 1800; Tue, Wed, Thu, 0930 to 1800; Fri, Sat, 0930 to 1630

Access for disabled people:
Ramped entry, toilet facilities
Special comments: Parking spaces for disabled people are in Midland Road and Ossulton Street

BRITISH LIBRARY – READING ROOMS AT ST PANCRAS

96 Euston Road, London, NW1 2DB

Tel: 020 7412 7676
Fax: 020 7412 7609
E-mail: reader-services-enquiries@bl.uk

Website:
http://www.bl.uk

Organisation type and purpose:
Non-departmental public body.

Access to staff:
Contact by letter, by telephone, by fax, by e-mail, in person and via website
Hours: Mon to Fri, 0900 to 1700
Special comments: Reader's Pass required, apply to the Reader Admissions Office.

Direct lines:
General enquiries; reader services and advance reservations
tel: 020 7412 7676; fax: 020 7412 7789; e-mail: reader-services-enquiries@bl.uk
Humanities 1 and 2; includes the Library and Information Sciences Service and the Recorded Sound Information Service
tel: 020 7412 7440 (Humanities and LISS), 020 7412 7676 (RSIS)
Manuscripts
tel: 020 7412 7513
Maps
tel: 020 7412 7702
Oriental and India Office
tel: 020 7412 7873
Rare Books and Music; includes the Music Service and the Listening and Viewing Service
tel: 020 7412 7772 (Early Printed Collections), 020 7412 7673 (Music Service)
Reader Admissions Office; information about access to the Library
tel: 020 7412 7677; fax: 020 7412 7794
Readers' Advisor; information about assistance for users with disabilities
tel: 020 7412 7666; fax: 020 7412 7557; e-mail: lydia.butler@bl.uk
Science, Technology & Innovation Information Services; British and EPO patents
tel: 020 7412 7919
Science, Technology & Innovation Information Services; Business
tel: 020 7412 7454/7977
Science, Technology & Innovation Information Services; Foreign patents
tel: 020 7412 7902
Science, Technology & Innovation Information Services; Science and Technology
tel: 020 7412 7288/7494/7496
Science, Technology & Innovation Information Services; Social Sciences
tel: 020 7412 7536

BRITISH LIBRARY – RESEARCH SERVICE

96 Euston Road, London, NW1 2DB

Tel: 020 7412 7903
Fax: 020 7412 7930
E-mail: patents-information@bl.uk

Website:
http://www.bl.uk/reshelp/experthelp/researchservice
Explains about the priced research services offered by the British Library.

Enquiries:
Enquiries to: Information Expert

Founded:
1973

Organisation type and purpose:
Information service.

Subject coverage:
Patent, market research, company, scientific and newspaper information.

Museum or gallery collection, archive, or library special collection:
The Business & IP Centre has a very extensive collection of business and patent material

Library catalogue:
All or part available online

Printed publications:
History of Science and Technology:
British Patents of Invention, 1617–1977: A Guide for Researchers
The Indefatigable Mr Woodcroft: The Legacy of Invention
Inventing the 19th Century: The Great Age of Victorian Inventions
Inventing the 20th Century: 100 Inventions that Shaped the World
James Watt and the Patent System
Michael Hill on Science, Invention and Information

continued overleaf

New and Improved: Inventors and Inventions that Have Changed the Modern World

Rooms near Chancery Lane: The Patent Office under the Commissioners, 1852–1883

Patents:

How to Find Information: Patents on the Internet

International Guide to Official Industrial Property Publications (3rd edn)

Introduction to Patents Information (4th edn, 2002)

Trade Marks: An Introductory Guide and Bibliography (2nd edn)

Order printed publications from: Turpin Distribution Services, Blackhorse Road, Letchworth, Hertfordshire, SG6 1HN; tel. 01462 672555; fax 01462 480947; e-mail turpin@turpinltd.com

Publications list:
Available online and in print

Access to staff:
Contact by letter, by telephone, by fax, by e-mail, in person and via website

Access to building, collection or gallery:
Hours: Mon to Fri, 1000 to 1300 and 1400 to 1700
Special comments: Reader Pass required by visitors. Ring for details of admission procedure.

Access for disabled people:
Ramped entry, toilet facilities

BRITISH LIBRARY – SOCIAL SCIENCES AND OFFICIAL PUBLICATIONS REFERENCE SERVICE

96 Euston Road, London, NW1 2DB

Tel: 020 7412 7676
Fax: 020 7412 7761
E-mail: social-sciences@bl.uk

Website:
http://catalogue.bl.uk
The British Library integrated catalogue.
http://www.bl.uk/socialsciences
Description of collections and services, including collection guides and finding aids.

Enquiries:
Enquiries to: Social Sciences Reference Service

Founded:
1753

Organisation type and purpose:
Non-departmental public body.

Subject coverage:
Government, national and local; politics and administration; sociology; economics; education and training policy and administration; transport and the environment; social care, health and welfare services; social security; theory of management; housing and homelessness; law.

Museum or gallery collection, archive, or library special collection:
Legal deposit collection of British official publications

Electoral registers for whole of United Kingdom from 1947 and extensive earlier collection

Depository for United Nations publications, some UN agencies, World Bank, International Labour Organization, European Union, OECD and World Health Organization

Worldwide collections of publications of governments and inter-governmental organisations, including microfiche of US Federal GPO publications (both depository and non-depository) from 1982 (extensive earlier collection in hard copy) and full-text electronic resources including Congressional Serial Set Online, Congressional Hearings Digital Collection 1823–1979, Congressional Record, Declassified Documents Reference System and Digital National Security Archive

Reading room open access collections include:
National Statistics Collection

Social Sciences collection of recent English-language books and serials

UK Parliamentary materials and legislation

Note: The British Library has one of the largest collections of social science publications worldwide, accessible through the Social Sciences Reading Room, but this is not organised as a discrete collection

Trade and statistical information:
The National Statistics Collection based in SS&OP (focus on social and demographic statistics for the UK).

Library catalogue:
All or part available online

Electronic and video publications:
Welfare Reform on the Web: free current awareness service, available at the website, http://www.bl.uk/welfarereform/index.html

Access to staff:
Contact by letter, by telephone, by fax, by e-mail and in person
Hours: Telephone enquiries: Mon to Fri, 0930 to 1700

Access to building, collection or gallery:
No access other than to reading rooms
Hours: Reading Room: Mon, 1000 to 2000; Tue, Wed, Thu, 0930 to 2000; Fri, Sat, 0930 to 1700
Special comments: Readers Pass required.

Access for disabled people:
Ramped entry, access to all public areas, toilet facilities

Constituent part of:
British Library, Operations and Services

BRITISH LIBRARY SOUND ARCHIVE

96 Euston Road, London, NW1 2DB

Tel: 020 7412 7676
Fax: 020 7412 7441
E-mail: sound-archive@bl.uk

Website:
http://www.bl.uk/soundarchive
Information on collections and services; fellowships; the current issue of Playback newsletter.
http://cadensa.bl.uk
Catalogue of the British Library Sound Archive.
http://sounds.bl.uk
Online sounds (44,500 selected recordings of music, spoken word, and natural environments)

Enquiries:
Enquiries to: Head of the Sound Archive
Direct tel: 020 7412 7424
Direct fax: 020 7412 7422
Direct e-mail: richard.ranft@bl.uk

Founded:
1955

Formerly called:
British Institute of Recorded Sound (year of change 1983)

Organisation type and purpose:
Registered charity (charity number 292096). Non-departmental public body.

Subject coverage:
All aspects of recorded sound, in particular music, including classical music, world and traditional music, popular music and jazz; spoken word, including poetry and drama, oral history, language and dialect; wildlife sounds including birds, mammals, insects, reptiles, amphibians and fish; sound effects; also the United Kingdom music business, broadcasting and the technology of recording.

Information services:
Sound Archive Information Service, e-mail: sound-archive@bl.uk

Special visitor services:
Listening & Viewing Service, website: http://www.bl.uk/reshelp/inrrooms/stp/sound/listening.html

Museum or gallery collection, archive, or library special collection:
Classical Music Collection
Drama and Literature Collection
Library of printed reference sources
Music video
National Deposit Collection of published phonograms
Oral History Collection
Popular Music Collection
Radio recordings
Record catalogues, national and international
Wildlife Sounds
World and Traditional Music Collection
Broadcast TV and radio news

Trade and statistical information:
Data on the United Kingdom record industry.

Non-library collection catalogue:
All or part available online

Library catalogue:
All or part available online

Printed publications:
Numerous CD publications, see website

Publications list:
Available online

Access to staff:
Contact by letter, by telephone, by fax, by e-mail and in person
Hours: Mon, 1000 to 2000; Tue, Wed and Thu, 0930 to 2000; Fri and Sat, 0930 to 1700
Special comments: Listening and viewing service by appointment.

Access to building, collection or gallery:
Special comments: Reader's Pass required.

Access for disabled people:
Ramped entry, access to all public areas, toilet facilities
Special comments: Parking spaces for disabled people are in Midland Road.

Parent body:
British Library
96 Euston Road; website: htpp://www.bl.uk

BRITISH LIMBLESS EX-SERVICE MEN'S ASSOCIATION

Acronym or abbreviation: BLESMA

Frankland Moore House, 185–187 High Road, Chadwell Heath, Romford, Essex, RM6 6NA

Tel: 020 8590 1124
Fax: 020 8599 2932
E-mail: headquarters@blesma.org

Website:
http://www.blesma.org
BLESMA supports all those ex-Service men and women who have lost limbs, the use of their limbs, or one or both eyes. From the outbreak of World War II and all conflicts since, up to and including the present conflict in Afghanistan, many Members of BLESMA went to War young and whole, but came home disabled for life. The Association offers them the fellowship of shared experience and the welfare support they need and has fought for their interests over many years.
While the Association does not wish to receive new Members, owing to the current conflict in Afghanistan and, as service life takes its inevitable toll, it is unavoidable that it will do so. It is here to assist them in their recovery and rehabilitation from their injuries. It receives no government grants and relies wholly on the generosity of the public.

Enquiries:
Enquiries to: General Secretary
Other contacts: National Welfare Officer (for all welfare matters)

Founded:
1932

Organisation type and purpose:
National organisation, membership association
(membership is by subscription), present number
of members: 5,000 including widows, voluntary
organisation, registered charity (charity number:
England – 1084189; Scotland – SCO10315).
National charity dealing specifically with
amputation and rehabilitation. Operates
residential and nursing homes. Grant-making
organisation providing advice on pensions and
allowances.

Subject coverage:
Amputation and rehabilitation, general welfare,
prosthetics and orthotics, pension advice and
casework, financial grants, research and
development, residential homes, counselling.

Printed publications:
Better Health for the Amputee, 1987
BLESMAG – House Journal (3 times a year)
Driving After Amputation (2001)
Newsletter (2 times a year, members)
Out on a Limb, 1982
The Amputee Guide 1997

Electronic and video publications:
Welfare video

Publications list:
Available in print

Access to staff:
Contact by letter, by telephone, by fax, by e-mail
and via website
Hours: Mon to Fri, 0900 to 1700

Access for disabled people:
Parking provided, ramped entry, toilet facilities

Also at:
The Ancaster BLESMA Home, Crieff
  Alligan Road, Crieff, Perthshire, PH7 3JU; tel:
  01764 652480; fax: 01764 652550; e-mail: crieff@
  blesma.org
The Elizabeth Frankland Moore Home
  539 Lytham Road, Blackpool, Lancashire, FY4
  1RA; tel: 01253 343313; fax: 01253 408994; e-
  mail: blackpool@blesma.org

Headquarters address:
International Society of Prosthetics and Orthotics
(ISPO)

Links with:
Royal Association for Disability and Rehabilitation
(RADAR)
World Veterans Federation (WVF)

BRITISH LIME ASSOCIATION

Acronym or abbreviation: BLA

156 Buckingham Palace Road, London, SW1W 9TR

Tel: 020 7730 8194
Fax: 020 7730 4355

Website:
http://www.bla.org
http://www.britishlime.org
http://www.qpa.org

Enquiries:
Enquiries to: Public Relations Manager
Direct e-mail: clements@qpa.org
Other contacts: Lime Product Officer

Organisation type and purpose:
Trade association.

Subject coverage:
Lime, limestone, chalk dolomite, health and safety,
environmental matters.

Trade and statistical information:
Data on industry statistics.

Printed publications:
Lime Posters for schools
Lime Stabilisation Manual

Publications list:
Available in print

Access to staff:
Contact by letter, by telephone, by fax, by e-mail
and via website
Hours: Mon to Fri, 0900 to 1700

Parent body:
Quarry Products Association (QPA)
  tel: 020 7730 8194; fax: 020 7730 4355; e-mail:
  info@qpa.org

BRITISH LIVER TRUST

2 Southampton Road, Ringwood, Hampshire,
BH24 1HY

Tel: 01425 481320
Fax: 01425 481335
E-mail: info@britishlivertrust.org.uk

Website:
http://www.britishlivertrust.org.uk

Founded:
1988

Organisation type and purpose:
National organisation, registered charity (charity
number 298858), suitable for: adults, research
organisation.
Education on liver disease. The charity produces
information on all aspects of liver disease and
funds research.

Subject coverage:
Information on liver disease.

Information services:
Liver disease information helpline: 0800 652 7330

Printed publications:
Bulletin (newsletter, twice a year)
Publications on liver disease (order form and price
  list available from the British Liver Trust)
Order printed publications from: e-mail:
publications@britishlivertrust.org.uk

Publications list:
Available online and in print

Access to staff:
Contact by letter, by telephone, by fax, by e-mail
and via website
Hours: Mon to Fri, 0900 to 1700

Access to building, collection or gallery:
No access other than to staff

BRITISH LLAMA AND ALPACA ASSOCIATION

Acronym or abbreviation: BLAA

Banks Way House, Effingham Common,
Leatherhead, Surrey, KT24 5JB

Tel: 01372 458350
Fax: 01372 451131

Website:
http://www.llama.co.uk
Information on all four species of camelid and
camels, breeding, breeders list, events, conference,
links, etc.
http://www.alpaca.co.uk
Information on all four species of camelid and
camels, breeders list, events, conference, links, etc.

Enquiries:
Enquiries to: Honorary Secretary

Founded:
1987

Organisation type and purpose:
Membership association (membership is by
subscription), present number of members: 432,
registered charity (charity number 802688).
Owners and breeders association.
To promote good husbandry and the establishment
of sound breeding programmes to improve and
increase British stock; to guide and foster the
growing interest in camelids.

Subject coverage:
Welfare guidelines, trekking, sheep guarding, pets,
information from conference proceedings, social
days, showing and judging camelids, contacts to
visit, camelid fibre.

Printed publications:
Books available mainly imports from USA, but
  stocks usually held:
Along Came A Llama (Ruck R J, £7.95)
Caring for Llamas (Hoffman C, £17)
GALA: The Guanaco, Alpaca and Llama
  Advertiser (constantly updated, free initially
  then £1 per update)
Llama and Alpaca Neonatal Care (Smith B and
  Timms R, £20.95)
Medicine and Surgery of South American
  Camelids, Llama, Alpaca, Vicuna, Guanacos
  (Fowler M E, £75)
The Veterinary Clinics of North America: Llama
  Medicine (ed La Rue Johnson, £35)

Publications list:
Available in print

Access to staff:
Contact by letter, by telephone and by fax
Hours: Mon to Fri, 0900 to 1700

Access to building, collection or gallery:
No access other than to staff

BRITISH LUGGAGE AND LEATHERGOODS ASSOCIATION

Acronym or abbreviation: BLLA

Federation House, 10 Vyse Street, Birmingham,
B18 6LT

Tel: 0121 237 1107
Fax: 0121 236 3921
E-mail: enquries@blla.org.uk

Website:
http://www.blla.org.uk
Product search available, members area,
consumers area, retailer and product/brand search.

Enquiries:
Enquiries to: Chief Executive
Direct e-mail: diana.fiveash@blla.org.uk

Founded:
1918

Organisation type and purpose:
Trade association (membership is by subscription,
election or invitation), present number of
members: 102.
National trade body for those manufacturing and
supplying luggage, travel goods, briefcases,
handbags, small leathergoods and accessories.

Subject coverage:
Luggage, travel goods, briefcases, handbags, small
leathergoods and accessories.

Printed publications:
Buyer's Guide (£20)
BLLANews (newsletter, free)
Fashion Extras

Publications list:
Available online

Access to staff:
Contact by letter, by telephone, by fax, by e-mail
and via website. Appointment necessary.
Hours: Mon to Thu, 0930 to 1630; Fri, 0900 to 1600

Access to building, collection or gallery:
Prior appointment required

Access for disabled people:
Parking provided, access to all public areas, toilet
facilities

Parent body:
British Jewellery and Giftware Federation Limited
  Federation House, 10 Vyse Street, Birmingham,
  B18 6LT; tel: 0121 236 2657; fax: 0121 236 3921

BRITISH LUNG FOUNDATION

73–75 Goswell Road, London EC1V 7ER

Tel: 020 7831 5831
Fax: 020 7831 5832

Website:
http://www.lunguk.org/

Enquiries:
Enquiries to: Press Officer
Direct tel: 020 7688 5564
Direct e-mail: casey.purkiss@blf-uk.org

Founded:
1984

Organisation type and purpose:
Registered charity (charity number 326730).
Raising funds for, and promoting research into,
diseases of the lung.

Subject coverage:
Diseases of the chest and lungs, their prevalence,
treatment, social and economic effects and research
into these diseases; maintaining healthy lungs;
effects of atmospheric pollution and occupational
respiratory disease.

Printed publications:
Annual Report with research reports (free)
Breathe Easy Club (free)
Leaflets on specific lung disorders (free)
Press releases on research work in lung disease

Publications list:
Available online and in print

Access to staff:
Contact by letter, by telephone, by fax and by e-mail
Hours: Mon to Fri, 0900 to 1700

Member of:
Association of Medical Research Charities
Long-Term Medical Conditions Alliance

Regional Offices:
British Lung Foundation
  The Nuffield House, Queen Elizabeth Hospital,
  Birmingham, B15 2TH; tel: 0121 627 2260; fax:
  0121 697 8323
British Lung Foundation
  Orchard Street Business Centre, 3 Charles Place,
  Bristol, BS8 4QW; tel: 0117 925 5810; fax: 0117
  925 5809; e-mail: susan@blfsw.fsnet.co.uk
British Lung Foundation
  Sir G B Hunter Memorial Hospital, The Green,
  Wallsend, Tyne & Wear, NE28 7PB; tel: 0191 263
  0276; fax: 0191 262 2660
British Lung Foundation (North West)
  Moroney House, Cardiothoracic Centre, Thomas
  Drive, Liverpool, L14 3LB; tel: 0151 228 4723;
  fax: 0151 228 4723
British Lung Foundation Scotland
  The Beacon, 176 St Vincent Street, Glasgow, G2
  5SG; tel: 0141 249 6810; e-mail: redballoon@
  blfscotland.org.uk

BRITISH LYMPHOLOGY SOCIETY

Acronym or abbreviation: BLS

PO Box 196, Shoreham, Sevenoaks, TN13 9BF

Tel: 01959 525524
Fax: 01959 525524
E-mail: admin@blsac.demon.co.uk

Website:
http://www.lymphoedema.org/bls

Enquiries:
Enquiries to: Administrator

Founded:
1985

Organisation type and purpose:
Professional body (membership is by subscription),
present number of members: 600, registered
charity (charity number 1042561).

Subject coverage:
Lymphoedema.

Printed publications:
Introduction Leaflet (p&p only)
Screening Tools
Equipment Catalogue
Directory of Lymphoedema Treatment Centres
  (2000–2001)
Guidelines for the use of Manual Lymphatic
  Drainage and Self-Administered Massage in
  Lymphoedema

Publications list:
Available online and in print

Access to staff:
Contact by letter, by telephone, by fax, by e-mail
and via website
Hours: Tue to Thu, 0900 to 1700

Access to building, collection or gallery:
Prior appointment required

BRITISH MARINE FEDERATION

Marine House, Thorpe Lea Road, Egham, Surrey,
TW20 8BF

Tel: 01784 473377
Fax: 01784 439678
E-mail: info@britishmarine.co.uk

Website:
http://www.britishmarine.co.uk
A resource for members of the BMF, boaters and
those needing to know more about the industry
and the Federation.

Enquiries:
Direct tel: 01784 223663
Direct e-mail: membership@britishmarine.co.uk

Founded:
1913

Formerly called:
Boat, Yacht and Allied Trades Association (year of
change 1947); Ship and Boat Builders National
Federation (year of change 1986); British Marine
Industries Federation (year of change since 1986)

Organisation type and purpose:
Trade association for the leisure and small
commercial marine industry, including leisure
boats – seagoing and inland, small commercial
workboats, superyachts, hire fleets, and all the
equipment and services needed for those craft.
Members come from over 4,300 businesses in the
UK leisure, superyacht and small commercial
marine markets.

Subject coverage:
Promotes the marine industry, provides showcases
for its products in the UK and overseas, liaises with
governments, authorities and agencies, conducts
research on UK and international marine markets,
provides technical, regulatory and manufacturing
information and advice, provides strategy, advice
and practical assistance on environmental issues,
assists with training and recruitment, advises and
represents on legal and financial matters.

Trade and statistical information:
Numerous statistics and market research projects
  to provide members with valuable information
  on the marine industry and to enable BMF to
  highlight the size and importance of the industry
  to government and the media.

Printed publications:
A number of books, magazines, reports,
  informational guides (see website)

Electronic and video publications:
A number of books, magazines, reports,
  informational guides and cd-roms (see website)
Order electronic and video publications from: Many
available to download from website.

Publications list:
Available online

Access to staff:
Contact by letter, by telephone, by fax and by e-mail

Constituent bodies:
12 Region and 18 Group Associations

BRITISH MARINE INDUSTRIES FEDERATION SCOTLAND

Acronym or abbreviation: BMIF Scotland

Westgate, Toward, Dunoon, Argyll, PA23 7UA

Tel: 01369 870251
Fax: 01369 870251
E-mail: bmif-s@clydemarinepress.co.uk

Website:
http://www.bmif.co.uk

Enquiries:
Enquiries to: Administrator

Founded:
1921

Organisation type and purpose:
Trade association (membership is by election or
invitation), present number of members: 55,
training organisation.
Representing members of the Scottish Marine
industry.

Subject coverage:
Yacht and boat building in Scotland, chandlery
manufacture, wholesale and retail, marina
operations, marine electronics, yacht chartering
and other related marine operations in Scotland.

Access to staff:
Contact by letter, by telephone, by fax and by e-mail
Hours: Mon to Fri, 0900 to 1700

Member of:
British Marine Industries Federation
  Meadlake Place, Thorpe Lea Road, Egham,
  Surrey, TW20 8HE

BRITISH MARITIME LAW ASSOCIATION

Acronym or abbreviation: BMLA

Andrew Taylor, Reed Smith LLP, The Broadgate
Tower, 20 Primrose Street, London, EC2A 2RS

Tel: 020 3116 3000
Fax: 020 3116 3999
E-mail: adtaylor@reedsmith.com

Website:
http://www.bmla.org.uk
Purposes, constitution, executive committee,
general membership, document archive, contacts.

Enquiries:
Enquiries to: Secretary and Treasurer

Founded:
1908

Organisation type and purpose:
Professional association, acts as an adviser to UK
government bodies responsible for maritime
legislation or regulation and co-operates with its
international parent body, the CMI, in research and
drafting of international instruments for the
harmonisation of maritime and mercantile law.
Membership consists of representatives from the
following groups: shipowners, shippers,
merchants, manufactures, insurers, insurance
brokers, tug owners, shipbuilders, port and
harbour authorities, bankers, classifications
societies or other societies or bodies interested in
the objects of the Association. The Association also
has a number of individual members who may be
employees of corporate or institute members or
barristers or others without a corporate identity.
To promote the study and the advancement of
British maritime and mercantile law; to promote
and consider with foreign and other maritime law
associations proposals for the unification of
maritime and mercantile law in the practice of
different nations; to afford opportunities for
members to discuss matters of national and
international maritime law; to collect and circulate

amongst its members information regarding maritime and mercantile law and to establish a collection of publications and documents of interest to members.

Subject coverage:
Maritime and mercantile law.

Access to staff:
Contact by letter, by telephone, by fax and by e-mail

Member organisation of:
Comité Maritime International

BRITISH MATCHBOX LABEL AND BOOKLET SOCIETY

Acronym or abbreviation: BML&BS

122 High Street, Melbourn, Cambridgeshire, SG8 6AL

Tel: 01763 260399
E-mail: secretary@phillumeny.com

Website:
http://www.phillumeny.com

Enquiries:
Enquiries to: Secretary

Founded:
1945

Organisation type and purpose:
Membership association (membership is by subscription), present number of members: 450.

Subject coverage:
Matchbox labels and bookmatch collecting, hardware, advertising and other material pertaining to the hobby of collecting these items.

Printed publications:
Books and catalogues by collectors
Magazine (6 times a year)
Membership list (to members only)
Order printed publications from: Bookshop Manager, BML&BS, e-mail: webmaster@phillumeny.com

Access to staff:
Contact by letter, by telephone, by e-mail and via website
Hours: Mon to Fri, 0900 to 1700

BRITISH MATERIALS HANDLING FEDERATION

Acronym or abbreviation: BMHF

National Metalforming Centre, 47 Birmingham Road, West Bromwich, B70 6PY

Tel: 0121 601 6350
Fax: 0121 601 6387
E-mail: enquiry@bmhf.org.uk

Website:
http://www.bmhf.org.uk
Overview of BMHF, details of member associations, products/services, useful links, recruitment facility.

Enquiries:
Enquiries to: General Secretary

Organisation type and purpose:
Trade association.
The UK's voice in Europe on materials handling matters.

Subject coverage:
Heavy lifting and handling equipment, continuous handling equipment, industrial trucks, mobile cranes, lifts, escalators, passenger conveyors, series lifting equipment, storage equipment and methods, powered access vehicles.

Printed publications:
English language versions of FEM's technical publications

Access to staff:
Contact by letter, by telephone, by fax and by e-mail
Hours: Mon to Fri, 0900 to 1700

BRITISH MEASUREMENT AND TESTING ASSOCIATION

Acronym or abbreviation: BMTA

East Malling Enterprise Centre, New Road, East Malling, Kent, ME19 6BJ

Tel: 01732 897452
Fax: 01732 897453
E-mail: kgb@bmta.co.uk

Website:
http://www.bmta.co.uk
Membership list, member company information, meeting notices and reports, etc.

Enquiries:
Enquiries to: Executive Secretary
Other contacts: Assistant Secretary

Founded:
1990

Organisation type and purpose:
Membership association (membership is by subscription), present number of members: 90.
An Association for organisations concerned with measurement or testing.

Subject coverage:
Testing and calibration; European issues relating to testing and product conformity.

Printed publications:
Newsletter
Directory of European Testing and Analytical Laboratories
Measurement Good Practice Guide No 36, Estimating Uncertainties in Testing

Access to staff:
Contact by telephone, by fax, by e-mail and via website
Hours: Mon to Fri, 0900 to 1700

UK member of:
EUROLAB

BRITISH MEDICAL ACUPUNCTURE SOCIETY

Acronym or abbreviation: BMAS

BMAS House, 3 Winnington Court, Northwich, Cheshire, CW8 1AQ

Tel: 01606 786782
Fax: 01606 786783
E-mail: admin@medical-acupuncture.org.uk

Website:
http://www.medical-acupuncture.co.uk

Enquiries:
Enquiries to: Support Manager to Medical Director
Direct e-mail: bmaslondon@aol.com

Founded:
1980

Organisation type and purpose:
National organisation, professional body (membership is by subscription, election or invitation), registered charity (charity number 1057942).

Subject coverage:
Medical acupuncture; medically qualified practitioners who practise acupuncture; education, promotion, professional support.

Printed publications:
Acupuncture in Medicine (quarterly)
Newsletter (2 times a year)
Patient information leaflet

Electronic and video publications:
Electronic journal available

Publications list:
Available online

Access to staff:
Contact by letter, by telephone, by fax, by e-mail and via website
Hours: Mon to Fri, 0900 to 1700 (Head Office); Mon to Fri, 1000 to 1800 (London office)

Access to building, collection or gallery:
No access other than to staff

Also at:
Medical Director
BMAS, The Royal London Homoeopathic Hospital, 60 Great Ormond Street, London, WC1N 3HR; tel: 020 7713 9437; fax: 020 7713 6286; e-mail: bmaslondon@aol.com; website: http://www.medical-acupuncture.co.uk

Links with:
International Council for Medical Acupuncture and Related Techniques (ICMART)
Rue de l'Amazone 62, 1050 Brussels, Belgium

BRITISH MEDICAL ASSOCIATION

Acronym or abbreviation: BMA

BMA House, Tavistock Square, London, WC1H 9JP

Tel: 020 7383 6625
Fax: 020 7388 2544
E-mail: bma.library@bma.org.uk

Website:
http://www.bma.org

Enquiries:
Enquiries to: Librarian

Organisation type and purpose:
Professional body, trade union.

Subject coverage:
Current clinical information, medical ethics, computers and medicine.

Museum or gallery collection, archive, or library special collection:
Hastings, Sir Charles (1794–1866) Collection (c. 400 volumes pre-1866 which belonged to the founder of the Association)

Access to staff:
Contact by letter. Appointment necessary. Access for members only. Letter of introduction required. Non-members charged.
Hours: Mon to Fri, 0900 to 1700

BRITISH MEDICAL ASSOCIATION SCOTLAND

Acronym or abbreviation: BMA

14 Queen Street, Edinburgh, EH2 1LL

Tel: 0131 247 3000
Fax: 0131 247 3001
E-mail: bmascotland@bma.org.uk

Website:
http://www.bma.org.uk
http://www.bma.org.uk/scotland

Enquiries:
Enquiries to: Scottish Secretary

Founded:
1832

Organisation type and purpose:
National organisation, professional body, trade union (membership is by subscription).
Represents the interests of and provides services for 140,044 members in UK, including 19,000 medical students and 3,000 overseas members.

Access to staff:
Contact by letter, by telephone, by fax and by e-mail. Access for members only.
Hours: Mon to Fri, 0900 to 1700

Access to building, collection or gallery:
Prior appointment required

Access for disabled people:
Parking provided, disabled lift, toilet facilities

Headquarters address:
BMA
BMA House, Tavistock Square, London, WC1H 9JP; tel: 020 7387 4499

BRITISH MEDICAL ULTRASOUND SOCIETY

Acronym or abbreviation: BMUS

36 Portland Place, London, W1B 1LS

Tel: 020 7636 3714
Fax: 020 7323 2175
E-mail: secretariat@bmus.org

Website:
http://www.bmus.org

Enquiries:
Enquiries to: Chief Executive Officer

Founded:
1984

Organisation type and purpose:
Learned society, present number of members: 2,200.
The advancement of science and technology in medical ultrasound; maintenance of the highest standards in these fields; to advance and encourage education and research in these areas.

Subject coverage:
Diagnostic medical ultrasound.

Printed publications:
BMUS Journal (quarterly)

Access to staff:
Contact by letter, by telephone, by fax, by e-mail and via website
Hours: Mon to Fri, 0900 to 1700

Links with:
European Federation of Ultrasound in Medicine & Biology (EFSUMB)
36 Portland Place, London, W1B 1LS; fax: 020 7099 7140; e-mail: 020 7436 7934; website: http://www.efsumb.org

BRITISH MENSA LIMITED

Acronym or abbreviation: MENSA

St John's House, St John's Square, Wolverhampton, West Midlands, WV2 4AH

Tel: 01902 772771
Fax: 01902 392500
E-mail: enquiries@mensa.org.uk

Website:
http://www.mensa.org.uk
How to join, puzzles, general information.

Enquiries:
Enquiries to: Financial Controller
Direct e-mail: info@mensa.org.uk
Other contacts: PA to GM

Founded:
1946

Organisation type and purpose:
Learned society, membership association (membership is by qualification), present number of members: 27,000.
Society for people with high IQ.
Association for people of high intelligence (IQ scope above 98th percentile).

Subject coverage:
Measurement of intelligence, gifted children, puzzles.

Printed publications:
Home Test
Invigilated Test
Books via bookshops

Access to staff:
Contact by letter, by telephone, by fax and by e-mail
Hours: Mon to Fri, 0830 to 1630

BRITISH MENSWEAR GUILD

Acronym or abbreviation: BMG

5 Portland Place, London, W1B 1PW

Tel: 020 7580 8783

Fax: 020 7436 8833
E-mail: director@british-menswear-guild.co.uk

Website:
http://www.british-menswear-guild.co.uk
Information about members, listing of relevant trade shows and special events, information on joining the BMG.

Enquiries:
Enquiries to: Director

Founded:
1959

Organisation type and purpose:
Trade association.

Subject coverage:
Manufacturing of top quality men's clothing and accessories, clothing trade exhibitions in the United Kingdom and Europe.

Trade and statistical information:
Available from the Department of Trade and Industry.

Printed publications:
List of member companies (free)
Press releases with information about the Guild and its member companies (free)
Year book (annually, free)

Access to staff:
Contact by letter, by telephone, by fax and by e-mail
Hours: Mon to Fri, 0900 to 1700

BRITISH METALS RECYCLING ASSOCIATION

Acronym or abbreviation: BMRA

16 High Street, Brampton, Huntingdon, Cambridgeshire, PE28 4TU

Tel: 01480 455249
Fax: 01480 453680
E-mail: admin@recyclemetals.org

Website:
http://www.britmetrec.org.uk
Educational literature, membership list, annual report, benefits, code of practice, history.

Enquiries:
Enquiries to: Director General

Founded:
1919

Organisation type and purpose:
Trade association.

Subject coverage:
Ferrous and non-ferrous scrap metal recycling.

Access to staff:
Contact by letter, by telephone, by fax, by e-mail and via website
Hours: Mon to Fri, 0900 to 1700

Access to building, collection or gallery:
No access other than to staff

BRITISH MICROCIRCULATION SOCIETY

Acronym or abbreviation: BMS

c/o Prof Giovanni E. Mann, Cardiovascular Division, King's College London, 150 Stamford Street, London, SE1 9NH

Tel: 020 7848 4306
Fax: 020 7848 4500
E-mail: giovanni.mann@kcl.ac.uk

Website:
http://www.microcirculation.org.uk
Full information about the Society and full updates.

Enquiries:
Enquiries to: President

Founded:
1963

Organisation type and purpose:
Learned society, present number of members: 225.
Promotion of all aspects of research into microvascular function.

Subject coverage:
Microcirculation, blood flow in small vessels, capillary function, endothelial function, tissue fluid balance, vessel growth, vasculature in disease, nitric oxide, inflammation, oedema.

Museum or gallery collection, archive, or library special collection:
Annual proceedings

Printed publications:
Constitution, Rules and List of Members (containing a summary of members' research interests, every 2 years)
Scientific abstracts (annually)
Journal of Vascular Research

Access to staff:
Contact by fax and by e-mail
Hours: Mon to Fri, 0900 to 1700

Affiliated to:
European Society for Microcirculation

BRITISH MICROLIGHT AIRCRAFT ASSOCIATION

Acronym or abbreviation: BMAA

Bullring, Deddington, Banbury, Oxfordshire, OX15 0TT

Tel: 01869 338888
Fax: 01869 337116
E-mail: general@bmaa.org

Website:
http://www.bmaa.org

Enquiries:
Enquiries to: Chief Executive

Founded:
1978

Organisation type and purpose:
National organisation, membership association (membership is by subscription), present number of members: 4,000, service industry.
Promotion of affordable aviation in microlight aircraft.

Subject coverage:
Information on every aspect of microlight flying.

Access to staff:
Contact by letter, by telephone, by fax, by e-mail and via website
Hours: Mon to Fri, 0900 to 1700

Authorised company of:
Civil Aviation Authority (CAA)

Links with:
Fédération Aéronautique Internationale (FAI)
Royal Aero Club of Great Britain

BRITISH MILKSHEEP SOCIETY

Acronym or abbreviation: BMS

The Row, Roweltown, Carlisle, Cumbria, CA6 6LX

Tel: 01697 748217
E-mail: parsonstherow@freenetname.co.uk

Enquiries:
Enquiries to: Secretary

Founded:
1982

Organisation type and purpose:
Membership association (membership is by subscription, qualification), present number of members: 131, voluntary organisation.
To promote the British Milksheep, advertise the breed, assist members with exports, collate pedigree breeding data, organise meetings for members.

Subject coverage:
Information on the British Milksheep, on milking sheep and pedigree data of British Milksheep.

Affiliation to:
National Sheep Association (NSA)
  Sheep Centre, Malvern, Worcestershire

BRITISH MINIGOLF ASSOCIATION

Acronym or abbreviation: BMGA

E-mail: via website for (general enquiries); membership@minigolf.org.uk (fo

Website:
http://www.minigolf.org.uk
Statutes, rules of minigolf, where to play, events, news, membership.

Enquiries:
Enquiries to: Chairman
Direct e-mail: chairman@minigolf.org.uk

Organisation type and purpose:
A non-profit making organisation, a membership association (membership is by subscription).
The UK's governing body for minigolf sport, including crazy golf and adventure golf.
To promote and increase the profile of minigolf in the UK, to represent the interests of its members at both national and international level, with regards to the authorities, other sport associations, the media and the public, to bring together those who enjoy playing minigolf, including adventure golf and crazy golf, to encourage the playing of minigolf as a competitive sport, to organise national tournaments, including a British Open and British Championship, to encourage the development of new, skill-based, minigolf courses in the UK.

Subject coverage:
Minigolf of all types.

Electronic and video publications:
Newsletter
Order electronic and video publications from:
Download from website

Publications list:
Available online

Access to staff:
Contact by e-mail and via website

Member organisation of:
European Minigolf Federation
World Minigolf Federation

BRITISH MODEL FLYING ASSOCIATION

Acronym or abbreviation: BMFA

Chacksfield House, 31 St Andrews Road, Leicester, LE2 8RE

Tel: 0116 244 0028
Fax: 0116 244 0645
E-mail: admin@bmfa.org

Website:
http://www.bmfa.org
News, clubs, calendar of events, resources, what's new?

Enquiries:
Enquiries to: Chief Executive

Founded:
1922

Organisation type and purpose:
Membership association (membership is by subscription, election or invitation), present number of members: 28,000, voluntary organisation.
National governing body for model flying.

Subject coverage:
Model flying legislation, model aircraft building and flying, flying site retention, national and international model flying competitions.

Printed publications:
Acquisition and Retention of Flying Sites – Book
BMFA/BHPA Code for Shared Use of Sites
BMFA: Why Join (annually)
BMFA: Members Handbook (annually)
BMFA News (6 times a year)
BMFA: Your voice
Leaflets on wide range of model flying topics

Access to staff:
Contact by letter, by telephone, by fax, by e-mail, in person and via website
Hours: Mon to Fri, 0900 to 1700

Links with:
Fédération Aéronautique Internationale (FAI)
General Aviation Awareness Council (GAAC)
Royal Aero Club of the United Kingdom (RAeC)

BRITISH MODEL SOLDIER SOCIETY

Acronym or abbreviation: BMSS

12 Savay Lane, Denham, Buckinghamshire, UB9 5NH

Tel: 01895 832757
E-mail: model.soldiers@btinternet.com

Website:
http://www.model.soldiers.btinternet.co.uk
Description of the society; details of branches, meetings and shows; advice on modelling and painting; photos of model soldiers; how to join the society.

Enquiries:
Enquiries to: Honorary Secretary

Founded:
1935

Organisation type and purpose:
International organisation, voluntary organisation.
To promote research and scholarship of military history, weaponry, uniforms, etc. through the media of military models.

Subject coverage:
Collecting, making and painting model soldiers, military vehicles and weapons, military uniforms and operations of all periods, campaigns of all military bodies of all nationalities and periods.

Museum or gallery collection, archive, or library special collection:
The Society's National Collection of all types of figures of a military nature

Printed publications:
Bulletin (quarterly, free to members)
Bulletin Extra (quarterly, free to members)
Handbook sheets (when published, free to members)

Access to staff:
Contact by letter, by telephone and by e-mail.
Access for members only.
Hours: Mon to Fri, 0900 to 1700

BRITISH MUSEUM

Acronym or abbreviation: BM

Great Russell Street, London, WC1B 3DG

Tel: 020 7323 8000
Fax: 020 7323 8616
E-mail: information@thebritishmuseum.ac.uk

Website:
http://www.thebritishmuseum.ac.uk
General information about galleries, opening times, access for disabled visitors.
http://www.britishmuseum.co.uk
British Museum Company (retail and mail order).

Enquiries:
Enquiries to: Information Officer
Direct tel: 020 7323 8299
Other contacts: Visitor Information Manager

Founded:
1753

Organisation type and purpose:
Museum.
National museum.

Subject coverage:
The history, culture and ethnography of much of the world from prehistoric times to the present day.
The collections are displayed in the following departments:
Greek and Roman Department
Ancient Near East Department
Oriental Department
Japanese Department
Prehistory and Early Europe Department
Medieval and Modern Europe Department
Coins and Medals Department
Egyptian Department
Ethnography Department
Prints and Drawings Department.

Information services:
Helpline available, tel: 020 7323 8299.

Special visitor services:
Guided tours, tape recorded guides, materials and/ or activities for children.

Education services:
Group education facilities, resources for Key Stages 1 and 2, 3 and 4.

Services for disabled people:
For the visually impaired; for the hearing impaired.

Museum or gallery collection, archive, or library special collection:
Records of the buildings, staff and administration, 1753 to the present day, are in the Central Archives
The departments hold manuscript records relating to the history of the collections
These include the papers of Charles Townley relating to his collection of classical antiquities, 1760–1805

Non-library collection catalogue:
All or part available online and in-house

Printed publications:
Books, children's books, scholarly titles
Full list of publications is available from the British Museum Company Limited, The British Museum Press
Order printed publications from: British Museum Company Ltd, 46 Bloomsbury Street, London, WC1B 3QQ; tel: 020 7323 1234; fax: 020 7436 7315; e-mail: sales.products@bmcompany.co.uk

Publications list:
Available in print

Access to staff:
Contact by letter, by telephone, by fax, by e-mail, in person and via website
Hours: Mon to Sun, 0900 to 1730

Access for disabled people:
Parking provided, ramped entry, level entry, access to all public areas, toilet facilities
Special comments: Pre-booking required for parking.

BRITISH MUSIC HALL SOCIETY

Acronym or abbreviation: BMHS

82 Fernlea Road, London, SW12 9RW

Tel: 020 8673 2175

Enquiries:
Enquiries to: Honorary Secretary

Founded:
1963

Organisation type and purpose:
Learned society (membership is by subscription), present number of members: 950, consultancy, research organisation.
Study group.
To preserve the history of British Music Hall and Variety, and recall the artists who created it.

continued overleaf

Subject coverage:
The British music halls and variety theatre from 1800 to present day.

Museum or gallery collection, archive, or library special collection:
Removed from Passmore Edwards Museum, now in storage awaiting a new venue, information from the Historian/Archivist

Printed publications:
The Call Boy (quarterly, for members only)

Access to staff:
Contact by letter and by telephone. Non-members charged.
Hours: Mon to Fri, 1830 to 2230

Access to building, collection or gallery:
No prior appointment required
Special comments: Contact Historian/Archivist, 76 Royal Close, Chichester, West Sussex, PO19 2FL, enclose sae, tel 01243 783322.

BRITISH MUSIC SOCIETY

Acronym or abbreviation: BMS

7 Tudor Gardens, Upminster, Essex, RM14 3DE

Tel: 01708 224795
E-mail: sct.bms1943@amserve.com

Website:
http://www.britishmusicsociety.co.uk
Membership and catalogue.

Enquiries:
Enquiries to: Honorary Treasurer

Founded:
1978

Organisation type and purpose:
Membership association (membership is by subscription), present number of members: 600, voluntary organisation, registered charity (charity number 1043838).
To promote an interest in the music of lesser-known British composers of serious music, especially between 1850 and 1975 and where they do not have their own society or trust.

Subject coverage:
Promotion of British composers from about 1800 to the present day, especially between 1850 and 1975.

Printed publications:
Publications include:
Aspects of British Song (£6)
British Composer Profiles (£6.25)
British Music (journal, annual, 31 volumes, £5 per volume)
British Opera in Retrospect (£6)
Monographs (occasional series, £5)
Newsletter (quarterly, free to members)
British Choral Music (£8.95)
Goodnight to Flamboro (Baines W, £10.99)
Parrotcisms: the autobiography of Professor Ian Parrott (£8.99)

Electronic and video publications:
British choral and instrumental music (cassette tapes and CDs)

Publications list:
Available online and in print

Access to staff:
Contact by letter, by telephone and by e-mail. Appointment necessary.
Hours: Mon to Fri, 0900 to 1700

BRITISH MYCOLOGICAL SOCIETY

Acronym or abbreviation: BMS

Joseph Banks Building, Royal Botanic Gardens, Kew, Richmond-upon-Thames, Surrey, TW9 3AB

Tel: 020 8332 5720
Fax: 020 8332 5720
E-mail: info@britmycolsoc.org.uk

Website:
http://www.britmycolsoc.org.uk

Information about society and its activities, links to other scientific sites.

Enquiries:
Enquiries to: General Secretary
Direct tel: 0151 231 2203
Direct fax: 0151 207 4726
Direct e-mail: g.p.sharples@livjm.ac.uk
Other contacts: Membership Secretary for membership application.

Founded:
1896

Organisation type and purpose:
Learned society, registered charity (charity number 276503).
To promote mycology in all its aspects by publications, meetings and such other means as the society deems appropriate.

Subject coverage:
Mycology, biodiversity, biotechnology, conservation, ecology, genetics, fungal pathogens of plants and animals, systematics.

Museum or gallery collection, archive, or library special collection:
Books

Printed publications:
Field Mycology (quarterly)
Guides and Keys (variable)
Mycologist (quarterly)
Mycological Research (monthly)
Symposium Volumes (annually)
Order printed publications from: Books, The Librarian and Archivist
British Mycological Society, c/o Herbarium, Royal Botanic Gardens, Kew, Richmond, Surrey, TA9 3AE, tel: 020 8332 5720, e-mail: v.barkham@rbgkew.org.uk

Publications list:
Available in print

Access to staff:
Contact by letter, by fax and by e-mail
Hours: Mon to Fri, 0900 to 1700

Book collection housed with:
Librarian and Archivist
British Mycological Society, c/o Herbarium, Royal Botanic Gardens, Kew, Richmond-upon-Thames, Surrey, TW9 3AE; tel: 020 8332 5720; e-mail: v.barkham@rbgkew.org.uk

BRITISH NATIONAL CARNATION SOCIETY

Acronym or abbreviation: BNCS

Linfield, Duncote, Towcester, Northamptonshire, NN12 8AH

Tel: 01327 351594
E-mail: betty@induncote.freeserve.co.uk

Enquiries:
Enquiries to: Membership Secretary

Founded:
1948

Organisation type and purpose:
National organisation, membership association (membership is by subscription), present number of members: c 400, voluntary organisation.

Subject coverage:
Carnations and pinks (Dianthus family); culture and hybridisation; exhibitions and competitions.

Printed publications:
The following publications are available for purchase:
How to Grow Border Carnations
How to Grow Perpetual Flowering Carnations
How to Grow Pinks
Newsletter (two times a year)
Rules for judging, standards and classifications
The Carnation Yearbook

Access to staff:
Contact by e-mail
Hours: Evenings

Affiliated to:
Royal Horticultural Society

BRITISH NATIONAL LYMPHOMA INVESTIGATION

Acronym or abbreviation: BNLI

UCL & CRC Cancer Trials Centre, 222 Euston Road, London, NW1 2DA

Tel: 020 7679 8060
Fax: 020 7679 6061
E-mail: bnli@ctc.ucl.ac.uk

Website:
http://www.bnli.ucl.ac.uk/
Trial information, staff information, links to other sites.

Enquiries:
Enquiries to: Senior Data Manager

Founded:
1970

Organisation type and purpose:
Professional body, registered charity (charity number 263424).

Subject coverage:
Lymphoma investigation.

Publications list:
Available in print

Access to staff:
Contact by letter and by e-mail
Hours: Mon to Fri, 0900 to 1700

BRITISH NATIONAL TEMPERANCE LEAGUE

Acronym or abbreviation: BNTL

30 Keswick Road, Worksop, Nottinghamshire, S81 7PT

Tel: 01909 477882
E-mail: bntl@btconnect.com

Website:
http://www.bntl.org

Enquiries:
Enquiries to: Chief Executive Officer

Founded:
1834

Organisation type and purpose:
Voluntary organisation, registered charity (charity number 224555), suitable for ages: 5–18.
Promoting drug-free lifestyles; providing education and resources on the subject.

Subject coverage:
Alcohol and drug education, history of temperance organisations (general), training.

Museum or gallery collection, archive, or library special collection:
Livesey Library held at the University of Central Lancashire in Preston: temperance history and 19th-century social reform, includes items bequeathed by William E. Moss

Printed publications:
Annual Report
Drugs and their Dangers (Key Stage 1)
Alcohol and Your Body (Key Stage 2)
Basic Drug Awareness (Key Stage 2)

Electronic and video publications:
Basic Drug Awareness Resource Box (suitable for ages: 14+)
Basic Alcohol Awareness Resource Box (suitable for ages: 14+)

Access to staff:
Contact by letter, by telephone, by e-mail and in person
Hours: Mon to Thu, 0900 to 1700

BRITISH NATURALISTS' ASSOCIATION

Acronym or abbreviation: BNA

PO Box 5682, Corby, Northamptonshire, NN17 2ZW

Tel: 0844 892 1817
E-mail: secretary@bna-naturalists.org

Website:
http://www.bna-naturalists.org
General natural history; branch details.

Enquiries:
Enquiries to: General Secretary

Founded:
1905

Organisation type and purpose:
Membership association (membership is by subscription), registered charity (charity number 296551).
One of the oldest natural history societies in the UK.
Educational charity.

Subject coverage:
Natural history in general.

Museum or gallery collection, archive, or library special collection:
Books, records and documents

Printed publications:
British Naturalist (4 times a year)
Country-Side magazine (2 times a year)
How to Begin the Study series (5 titles)
Spiders, Amphibians, Slugs and Snails, Natural History, Mosses and Liverworts

Access to staff:
Contact by letter, by telephone and by e-mail
Hours: Mon to Fri, 1830 to 2200

Has:
12 branches
24 affiliated societies

BRITISH NON-FERROUS METALS FEDERATION

Acronym or abbreviation: BNFMF

5 Grovelands Business Centre, Boundary Way, Hemel Hempstead, HP2 7TE

Tel: 01442 275705
Fax: 01442 275716
E-mail: bnfmf@copperuk.org.uk

Founded:
1945

Organisation type and purpose:
Trade association.

Subject coverage:
Trade association for producers in the UK of copper and copper alloy semi-fabricated products: strip, tube, wire, rod, bar and profiles, for electrical and other engineering purposes.

Access to staff:
Contact by letter, by fax and by e-mail
Hours: Mon to Fri, 0900 to 1700

Administered by:
Copper Development Association
5 Grovelands Business Centre, Boundary Way, Hemel Hempstead, HP2 7TE; tel: 01442 275705; fax: 01442 275716; website: http://www.copperinfo.co.uk

BRITISH NUCLEAR ENERGY SOCIETY

Acronym or abbreviation: BNES

Institution of Civil Engineers, 1–7 Great George Street, London, SW1P 3AA

Tel: 020 7665 2241
Fax: 020 7799 1325
E-mail: ianandrews@ice.org.uk

Website:
http://www.bnes.org.uk
Details of BNES, Nuclear Energy journal, events.

Enquiries:
Enquiries to: Secretary

Founded:
1962

Organisation type and purpose:
Learned society, professional body (membership is by subscription), present number of members: 1100, registered charity (charity number 261687).

Subject coverage:
Nuclear energy for power generation; fuel; safety.

Printed publications:
Conference Proceedings
Nuclear Energy (6 times a year)
Order printed publications from: Stk Publishing Ltd 6 Yarde Hill Orchard, Sidmouth, Devon, EX10 9J2

Access to staff:
Contact by letter, by telephone, by fax and by e-mail
Hours: Mon to Fri, 0900 to 1700

Affiliated to:
European Nuclear Society
tel: + 41 31 382 6111; fax: + 41 31 382 6845
Institution of Civil Engineers
tel: 020 7222 7722; fax: 020 7222 7500

Constituent bodies:
Institute of Energy
tel: 020 7580 7124; fax: 020 7580 4420
Institute of Marine Engineers
tel: 020 7382 2600; fax: 020 7382 2670; e-mail: imare@imare.org.uk
Institute of Materials
tel: 020 7839 4071; fax: 020 7839 1702
Institute of Measurement and Control
tel: 020 7387 4989; fax: 020 7388 8431
Institute of Physics
tel: 020 7470 4800; fax: 020 7470 4848
Institution of Chemical Engineers
tel: 01788 578214; fax: 01788 560833
Institution of Civil Engineers
tel: 020 7222 7722; fax: 020 7222 7500
Institution of Electrical Engineers
tel: 020 7240 1871
Institution of Incorporated Engineers
Institution of Mechanical Engineers
tel: 020 7222 7899; fax: 020 7222 4557
Institution of Nuclear Engineers
tel: 020 8698 1500; fax: 020 8695 6409
Royal Society of Chemistry
tel: 020 7437 8658; fax: 020 7437 8883

BRITISH NUCLEAR FUELS PLC

Magnox Generation, Berkeley Centre, Berkeley, Gloucestershire, GL13 9PB

Tel: 01453 810451
Fax: 01453 812529

Enquiries:
Enquiries to: Information Officer
Direct tel: 01453 812562
Direct fax: 01453 813914

Founded:
1996

Organisation type and purpose:
Electricity generator.

Subject coverage:
Nuclear engineering, electrical engineering, physics, mechanical engineering, health and safety, robotics.

Access to staff:
Contact by telephone and by fax
Hours: Mon to Fri, 0900 to 1700

BRITISH NUCLEAR MEDICINE SOCIETY

Acronym or abbreviation: BNMS

Regent House, 291 Kirkdale, London, SE26 4QD

Tel: 020 8676 7864
Fax: 020 8676 8417
E-mail: office@bnms.org.uk

Website:
http://www.bnms.org.uk

Enquiries:
Enquiries to: Administrator

Founded:
1969

Organisation type and purpose:
Learned society.
Affiliated to the European Nuclear Medicine Society and to the World Federation of Nuclear Medicine; the British Association for Radiopharmacy is an affiliate society.

Subject coverage:
Nuclear medicine; clinical uses of unsealed radioactive isotopes and radiopharmaceuticals.

Printed publications:
Nuclear Medicine Communications

Electronic and video publications:
Myocardial Perfusion (CD-ROM)

BRITISH NUMBER PLATE MANUFACTURERS ASSOCIATION

Acronym or abbreviation: BNMA

PO Box 23, South Shore, Blackpool, Lancs FY4 3DA

Tel: 01253 345287
Fax: 01253 344595

Website:
http://www.bnma.org/

Enquiries:
Enquiries to: Press Officer

Organisation type and purpose:
Trade association.

Subject coverage:
Road vehicle number plates.

Access to staff:
Contact by letter, by fax and by e-mail
Hours: Mon to Fri, 0900 to 1700

BRITISH NUMISMATIC SOCIETY

Acronym or abbreviation: BNS

c/o Warburg Institute, Woburn Square, London, WC1H 0AB

Tel: 01223 332915
E-mail: secretary@britnumsoc.org

Website:
http://www.britnumsoc.org

Enquiries:
Enquiries to: Honorary Secretary

Founded:
1903

Organisation type and purpose:
Learned society.

Subject coverage:
British numismatics: coins, currency, medals and tokens of Great Britain and Ireland, Empire and Commonwealth; numismatics more generally, especially the literature; history of minting techniques.

Museum or gallery collection, archive, or library special collection:
Library

Printed publications:
British Numismatic Journal (annually, free to members)
British Numismatic Society Special Publications (occasional)

Affiliated to:
British Association of Numismatic Societies

BRITISH NUMISMATIC TRADE ASSOCIATION

Acronym or abbreviation: BNTA

PO Box 2, Rye, East Sussex, TN31 7WE

Tel: 01797 229988
Fax: 01797 229988
E-mail: bnta@lineone.net

Website:
http://www.bnta.net

Enquiries:
Enquiries to: General Secretary

Founded:
1973

Organisation type and purpose:
Trade association.

Subject coverage:
The purchase and sale of numismatic items including coins, medals and decorations.

Printed publications:
Membership Directory (dealers who specialise in purchase and sale of numismatic items, annually, free)

Publications list:
Available in print

Access to staff:
Contact by letter, by telephone, by fax and by e-mail
Hours: Mon to Fri, 0900 to 1700

BRITISH NURSING ASSOCIATION

Acronym or abbreviation: BNA

258 Capability Green, Luton, Bedfordshire, LU1 3LU

Tel: 0845 452 3311
Fax: 0845 452 3312
E-mail: info@bna.co.uk

Website:
http://www.bna.co.uk

Founded:
1949

Organisation type and purpose:
Professional body, service industry.
Provision of nurses and carers to support people in their own homes, hospitals, NHS Trusts, social services departments, prisons and industry.

Subject coverage:
Nursing, staffing, occupational health, first aid courses, social services, nursing homes, family health services authorities, insurance companies, GP practices, prisons, individual clients in their own homes.

Printed publications:
BNA branch address list
Brochures about services available

Access to staff:
Contact by letter, by telephone, by e-mail, in person and via website
Hours: Mon to Fri, 0900 to 1700
Special comments: 24 hour emergency on-call at local BNA branches.

Has:
over 160 branches nationwide

Holding Group:
Nestor Healthcare Group
The Colonnades, Beaconsfield Close, Hatfield, Hertfordshire; tel: 01707 255635; fax: 01707 255633

Member of:
REC
UKHCA

Other companies in the group include:
Abigail Care
At Home Care
Forensic Medical Services
Grosvenor Nursing Agency

Home Nursing Agency
Kensington and Knightsbridge Nurses Bureau
Mayfair Specialist Nurses
Medic International
Medico Nursing
Nestor Medical Duty Services
Nestor Primecare
Nightingales
United Kingdom Underwriting Services
Worldwide Healthcare Exchange

BRITISH NUTRITION FOUNDATION

Acronym or abbreviation: BNF

High Holborn House, 52–54 High Holborn, London, WC1V 6RQ

Tel: 020 7404 6504
Fax: 020 7404 6747
E-mail: postbox@nutrition.org.uk

Website:
http://www.nutrition.org.uk
Nutrition information. Information on resources, press contacts and events.

Founded:
1967

Organisation type and purpose:
National organisation, registered charity (charity number 251681), suitable for ages: 5 to 18, consultancy, publishing house.
Independent scientific charity.
Provides scientifically based information on nutrition and related health matters, also provides health education resources for Primary and Secondary schools.

Subject coverage:
Nutrition and related health matters, science of nutrition and its application, food and diet, diet-related health problems, nutrition education, food labelling, food safety.

Printed publications:
BNF Briefing Papers
BNF Nutrition Bulletin and Conference Proceedings
BNF Nutrition Facts
Diet and Heart Disease: A round table of factors (2nd ed., 1996, £29.99)
Food – A Fact of Life (educational materials for 11 to 16 year olds, prices vary)
McCance and Widdowson – A Scientific Partnership of 60 years (book, 1993, £10)
Task Force Reports – comprehensive and authoritative reviews of a particular area of nutrition science (7 titles)

Electronic and video publications:
Teaching Food Safety (primary)
Interactive Food Facts (secondary)

Publications list:
Available online and in print

Access to staff:
Contact by letter, by fax, by e-mail and via website
Hours: Mon to Fri, 0900 to 1700
Special comments: Stamped addressed envelope is useful for information.

BRITISH OAT AND BARLEY MILLERS ASSOCIATION

Acronym or abbreviation: BOBMA

4A Torphichen Street, Edinburgh, EH3 8JQ

Tel: 0131 229 9415
Fax: 0131 229 9407

Enquiries:
Enquiries to: Executive Secretary
Direct e-mail: tom.hollis@fdf.org.uk

Organisation type and purpose:
Trade association.
Acts as a lobbying organisation for trade sector.

Subject coverage:
Supply of oats and barley.

Access to staff:
Contact by telephone and by e-mail. Appointment necessary. Access for members only.
Hours: Mon to Fri, 0900 to 1700

Affiliated to the European organisation:
CEEREAL
Rond-Point Schuman 9, bte 11, Brussels, B-1040, Belgium; tel: 00 3 22 230 4354; fax: 00 3 22 230 9493

Umbrella organisation:
Food and Drink Federation (FDF)
6 Catherine Street, London, WC2B 5JJ; tel: 020 7836 2460; fax: 020 7836 0580; e-mail: fdf@fdf.org.uk

BRITISH OCCUPATIONAL HYGIENE SOCIETY

Acronym or abbreviation: BOHS

5–6 Melbourne Business Court, Millennium Way, Pride Park, Derby, DE24 8LZ

Tel: 01332 298101
Fax: 01332 298099
E-mail: admin@bohs.org

Website:
http://www.bohs.org

Enquiries:
Enquiries to: Press Officer
Direct e-mail: anthea@bohs.org

Founded:
1953

Organisation type and purpose:
Learned society, registered charity (charity number 801417).

Subject coverage:
Occupational hygiene; recognition, evaluation and control of the workplace; physical and chemical factors affecting the health or well-being of workers or the community, emphasis on health hazards at work and indoor air quality.

Printed publications:
Annals of Occupational Hygiene (pub. OUP)
Newsletter (joint publication with the British Institute of Occupational Hygienists)

Access to staff:
Access for members only.
Hours: Mon to Thu, 0830 to 1630; Fri, 0830 to 1600

Access to building, collection or gallery:
No access other than to staff

BRITISH OLYMPIC ASSOCIATION

Acronym or abbreviation: BOA

60 Charlotte Street, London, W1T 2NU

Tel: 020 7842 5700
E-mail: boa@boa.org.uk

Website:
http://www.olympics.org.uk
Role of the BOA, London 2012, Olympic fact sheets, summer games, winter games, youth games, Team GB, education.

Founded:
1905

Organisation type and purpose:
BOA is the national Olympic committee for the United Kingdom, with sole responsibility for raising funds for Team GB. Working with the Olympic governing bodies, it selects Team GB from the best sportsmen and women who will go on to compete in the 26 summer and 7 winter Olympic sports. BOA is the strong, independent voice for British Olympic Sport.
BOA's role is to prepare and lead the nation's finest athletes at the Olympic Games and it has the responsibility for developing the Olympic Movement throughout the UK. In addition, it

delivers extensive support services to Britain's Olympic athletes and their national governing bodies throughout each Olympic cycle to assist them in their preparations for, and performances at the Games.

Subject coverage:
Preparation of Team GB for the Olympic Games.

Access to staff:
Contact by letter, by telephone and by e-mail

Member organisations:
The 33 national governing bodies of each Olympic sport, both summer and winter

BRITISH ORCHID COUNCIL

Acronym or abbreviation: BOC

Hall Farm House, Shelton, Newark on Trent, NG23 5JG

Tel: 01949 850713
E-mail: bocsecretary@tiscali.co.uk

Website:
http://www.british-orchid-council.info
Details of the organisation.

Enquiries:
Enquiries to: Secretary

Founded:
1971

Organisation type and purpose:
Membership association (membership is by subscription), registered charity (charity number 1002945).

Subject coverage:
Orchids: their study, cultivation, breeding and conservation.

Museum or gallery collection, archive, or library special collection:
Slide (35mm) Library

Library catalogue:
All or part available in-house

Printed publications:
Grower's and Buyer's Guide (annually)

Access to staff:
Contact by letter, by telephone and by e-mail
Hours: Sun to Sat, 0800 to 2100

BRITISH ORGAN DONOR SOCIETY

Acronym or abbreviation: BODY

Balsham, Cambridge, CB1 6DL

Tel: 01223 893636
Fax: 01223 893636 (telephone first)
E-mail: body@argonet.co.uk

Website:
http://www.argonet.co.uk/body

Enquiries:
Enquiries to: Administrator

Founded:
1984

Organisation type and purpose:
Voluntary organisation, registered charity (charity number 294925).

Subject coverage:
Aspects of transplantation and organ donation other than specific medical details; help available to donor recipient and waiting recipient families, especially where there are emotional problems; information to nurses and researchers about the emotional side of organ donation.

Printed publications:
Information Pack (free upon request)
Newsletter (2 times a year)
The Gift of Life (3 vols, £4.95 each)
Whole Body Donation and Society

Electronic and video publications:
The Race for Life (video, £17.50 incl. p&p)

Access to staff:
Contact by letter, by telephone, by fax, by e-mail and via website
Hours: Mon to Fri, 0900 to 1700
Special comments: 24 hour answerphone, no office access or personal answers.

Member organisation of:
Council of TIME (transplants in mind)

BRITISH ORIENTEERING FEDERATION

Acronym or abbreviation: BOF

Riversdale, Dale Road North, Darley Dale, Matlock, Derbyshire, DE4 2HX

Tel: 01629 734042
Fax: 01629 733769
E-mail: mail@bof.cix.co.uk

Website:
http://www.britishorienteering.org.uk/index.html

Enquiries:
Enquiries to: Secretary General
Other contacts: (1) Director of Coaching (2) Marketing and Membership Manager

Founded:
1967

Organisation type and purpose:
Governing body of the sport.

Subject coverage:
Orienteering, maps, forests and adventure; competitive events, specialised coaching awards, teachers' and leaders' certificates, NVQ qualifications.

Publications list:
Available in print

Access to staff:
Contact by letter, by telephone, by fax and in person
Hours: Mon to Fri, 0900 to 1700

Affiliated to:
International Orienteering Federation (IOF)
   Radio Katu 20, FI-00093 SLU, Finland

BRITISH ORNITHOLOGISTS' UNION

Acronym or abbreviation: BOU

The Natural History Museum, Akeman Street, Tring, Hertfordshire, HP23 6AP

Tel: 01442 890080
Fax: 020 7942 6150
E-mail: bou@bou.org.uk

Website:
http://www.bou.org.uk
Information on the organisation, publications, conferences and meetings, etc.

Enquiries:
Enquiries to: Administrator
Direct tel: 01733 390392
Direct fax: 01733 390408
Direct e-mail: stevedudley@bou.org.uk

Founded:
1858

Organisation type and purpose:
International organisation, learned society, registered charity (charity number 249877).

Subject coverage:
Ornithology.

Printed publications:
A Dictionary of Birds
Checklist Series (19 in series)
Status of Birds in Britain and Ireland 1971
The Ibis (quarterly)

Electronic and video publications:
Ibis (online)

Publications list:
Available online and in print

Access to staff:
Contact by letter, by telephone, by fax and by e-mail
Hours: Mon to Fri, 0900 to 1700

Member of:
Biological Council

BRITISH OVERSEAS TRADE BOARD

Acronym or abbreviation: BOTB

China and Hong Kong Branch:
China
   tel: 020 7215 5252 or 4827
Hong Kong
   tel: 020 7215 4829

Exports to North America Branch:
consumer goods
   tel: 020 7215 4595 or 4593
industrial goods
   tel: 020 7215 4608 or 4606

Latin America, Caribbean and Australasia Branch:
Australia, Papua New Guinea
   tel: 020 7215 5319/21
Caribbean
   tel: 020 7215 5297
Latin America
   tel: 020 7215 5059
New Zealand, the Pacific Islands
   tel: 020 7215 4760

Market branches:
East Europe Branch
   tel: 020 7215 5258
Exports to Europe Branch
   tel: 020 7215 5336

Middle East Branch:
Arabian Gulf
   tel: 020 7215 5096
Egypt
   tel: 020 7215 4947
North Africa
   tel: 020 7215 5358
other Middle East countries
   tel: 020 7215 5501

South Asia and Far East Branch:
Burma, Indonesia
   tel: 020 7215 4738
India, Sri Lanka
   tel: 020 7215 4825
Indo-China, North Korea
   tel: 020 7215 4736
Japan
   tel: 020 7215 4804
Pakistan, Bangladesh, Nepal
   tel: 020 7215 4821/4
Singapore, Malaysia, Brunei
   tel: 020 7215 5143
South Korea
   tel: 020 7215 4808
Thailand, the Philippines
   tel: 020 7215 5253

Sub-Saharan Africa Branch:
Sub-Saharan Africa
   tel: 020 7215 4969/70

BRITISH PARACHUTE ASSOCIATION

Acronym or abbreviation: BPA

5 Wharf Way, Glen Parva, Leicester, LE2 9TF

Tel: 0116 278 5271
Fax: 0116 247 7662
E-mail: skydive@bpa.org.uk

Website:
http://www.bpa.org.uk
Operations manual governing the sport

continued overleaf

http://www.skydivemag.com
Subscription and advertising information

Enquiries:
Enquiries to: Membership Services

Founded:
1962

Organisation type and purpose:
Membership association.
Governing body for Sport Parachuting in the
United Kingdom.
Parachuting in the UK.

Subject coverage:
Sport parachuting, technical information, safety
information, diary of events, skydiving and people
in the sport.

Printed publications:
Skydive – magazine (6 times a year, members and
by subscription)

Electronic and video publications:
UK Sport Parachuting (Skydiving) Operations
Manual, governing the conduct of the sport in
the United Kingdom (available online).

Publications list:
Available online

Access to staff:
Contact by letter, by telephone, by fax, by e-mail,
in person and via website
Hours: Mon to Fri, 0900 to 1700

Links with:
Fédération Aéronautique Internationale, through
the Royal Aero Club of the United Kingdom

BRITISH PEST CONTROL ASSOCIATION

Acronym or abbreviation: BPCA

1 Gleneagles House, Vernon Gate, Derby, DE1 1UP

Tel: 0870 609 2687
Fax: 01332 295904

Website:
http://www.BPCA.org.uk
Post code searchable database to find members,
training course and exams, open discussion forum,
members-only section.

Enquiries:
Enquiries to: Public Relations Manager
Direct tel: 01332 225114
Direct e-mail: sofi@bpca.org.uk

Founded:
1942

Organisation type and purpose:
National organisation, trade association
(membership is by qualification), present number
of members: 420, training organisation.

Subject coverage:
Public hygiene, pest control.

Printed publications:
Newsletter
Professional Pest Controller (magazine)

Publications list:
Available online

Access to staff:
Contact by letter, by telephone, by fax, by e-mail
and via website
Hours: Mon to Thu, 0830 to 1700; Fri, 0830 to 1600

Access to building, collection or gallery:
No access other than to staff

Access for disabled people:
Parking provided, ramped entry, level entry, access
to all public areas, toilet facilities

BRITISH PHARMACOLOGICAL SOCIETY

Acronym or abbreviation: BPS

16 Angel Gate, City Road, London, EC1V 2PT

Tel: 020 7417 0171
Fax: 020 7417 0114
E-mail: info@bps.ac.uk

Website:
http://www.bps.ac.uk
Information about BPS and pharmacology.

Founded:
1931

Organisation type and purpose:
Learned society (membership is by qualification,
election or invitation), present number of
members: 2,700, registered charity (charity number
1030623).
To promote and advance pharmacology (including
without limitation clinical pharmacology).

Subject coverage:
Pharmacology, drug use.

Printed publications:
British Journal of Clinical Pharmacology (monthly)
British Journal of Pharmacology (twice a month)
Careers in Pharmacology

Access to staff:
Contact by letter, by telephone, by fax and by e-mail
Hours: Mon to Fri, 0900 to 1700
Special comments: Press enquiries only – no general
information service.

Access to building, collection or gallery:
No access other than to staff

BRITISH PHOTOGRAPHIC & IMAGING ASSOCIATION

Acronym or abbreviation: BPIA

Ambassador House, Brigstock Road, Thornton
Heath, Surrey, CR7 7JG

Tel: 020 8665 6181
Fax: 020 8665 6447
E-mail: bpia@admin.co.uk

Website:
http://www.bpia.co.uk
List of members and products with hot links to
their sites and description of Association activities.

Enquiries:
Enquiries to: Secretary General

Founded:
1952

Organisation type and purpose:
Trade association.

Subject coverage:
Imported photographic and imaging products and
accessories.

Access to staff:
Contact by e-mail
Hours: Mon to Fri, 0900 to 1700

BRITISH PIG ASSOCIATION

Acronym or abbreviation: BPA

Trumpington Mews, 40B High Street,
Trumpington, Cambridge, CB2 2LS

Tel: 01223 845100
Fax: 01223 846235
E-mail: bpa@britishpigs.org

Website:
http://www.britishpigs.org.uk

Enquiries:
Enquiries to: Chief Executive

Founded:
1884

Organisation type and purpose:
Trade association.
Representative body for the UK pig industry and
pedigree recording society.

Subject coverage:
Pig industry matters; non-technical aspects of pig
breeding and production in the UK; UK pedigree
pig breeds.

**Museum or gallery collection, archive, or library
special collection:**
Herd Books for Pedigree Pig Breeds from 1884

Printed publications:
Pig Industry (magazine, monthly)
Publicity and membership leaflets

Access to staff:
Appointment necessary.
Hours: Mon to Fri, 0900 to 1700

BRITISH PLASTICS FEDERATION

Acronym or abbreviation: BPF

6 Bath Place, Rivington Street, London, EC2A 3JE

Tel: 020 7457 5000
Fax: 020 7457 5045
E-mail: reception@bpf.co.uk

Website:
http://www.bpf.co.uk/bpf/books_online/
bpf_publications/

Enquiries:
Direct e-mail: mcairns@bpf.co.uk

Founded:
1933

Organisation type and purpose:
National organisation, trade association
(membership is by subscription), present number
of members: 400 companies.
To promote and safeguard the UK plastics
industry.

Subject coverage:
Plastics industry, commercial and technical;
economic trends and statistics, biological safety,
environmental information, fire hazards and
prevention, industrial health and safety, plastics in
building, processing and moulding, reinforced
plastics, thermoplastics, thermosets.

**Museum or gallery collection, archive, or library
special collection:**
Many and varied publications, photographs,
illustrations related to the plastics industry

Non-library collection catalogue:
All or part available online

Library catalogue:
All or part available online

Printed publications:
Factsheets
Many publications on market information,
material and processing, health and safety,
windows, doors and conservatories
Product Information for the Plastics Industry

Publications list:
Available online and in print

Access to staff:
Contact by letter, by telephone, by fax, by e-mail
and via website
Hours: Mon to Fri, 0900 to 1700

Access for disabled people:
Parking provided, ramped entry, access to all
public areas, toilet facilities

Affiliated associations:
Association of Flexible Calendared uPVC Sheet
Manufacturers
British Laminated Fabricators Association Limited
British Rigid Urethane Foam Manufacturers
Association
Flexible Packaging Association
Gauge and Toolmakers Association
Northern Ireland Polymers Association
Packaging and Industrial Films Association
Plastics Consultancy Network
Polymer Machinery Manufacturers and
Distributors Association
Scottish Plastics and Rubber Association

Member of:
European Plastics Converters Association

BRITISH POLAROGRAPHIC RESEARCH INSTITUTE

Acronym or abbreviation: BPRI

6 Beechvale, Hillview Road, Woking, Surrey, GU22 7NS

Enquiries:
Enquiries to: Director of Research

Founded:
1955

Organisation type and purpose:
Advisory body, research organisation.

Subject coverage:
Polarographic operational research (theory and methodology); polarographic mathematical, physical and chemophysical depolarisational processes and phenomena; polarophilosophy, polarology, polaronomy, polarometry, polaroscopy, polarography, polarological sciences; polaroengineering sciences, radiopolarography, communication-radiopolarography, medical communication-radiopolarography, deaf-mute communication radiopolarography, stroke-communication radiopolarography. Cardiopolarographic therapy, cardiac-immobility polarography, cancer diagnostic polarography, psychoanalytical polarography, psychomotivation polarography. Space-communication radiopolarography, fog-prevention gas-phase polarography, fog and (CO) jet-stream-dispersal polarography, cot death (CO) poisoning (prevention) polarography, learning disabilities, (communication), photon-polarography, and very many other applications and uses of polarography.

Printed publications:
Reprints of Research Papers, following Journal publication

Access to staff:
Contact by letter
Hours: Mon to Fri, 0900 to 1700

Links with:
Institute of Pure Polarology Research
National Institute of Applied Polarology Research
Polarographic Society
UK Polaromatics R E – National Centres for Polarological and Polarographic Operational Research

Parent body:
British Polarological Research Society (BPRS)
6 Beechvale, Hillview Road, Woking, Surrey, GU22 7NS

BRITISH POLIO FELLOWSHIP

Acronym or abbreviation: BPF

Ground Floor Unit A, Eagle Office Centre, The Runway, South Ruislip, Middlesex, HA4 6SE

Tel: 0800 018 0586
Fax: 020 8842 0555
E-mail: info@britishpolio.org.uk

Website:
http://www.britishpolio.org.uk

Enquiries:
Enquiries to: Chief Executive
Other contacts: Information and Benefits Manager (for support and information)

Founded:
1939

Organisation type and purpose:
Registered charity (charity number 1108335, England; SC038863, Scotland).

Subject coverage:
Support for people who have had polio and their carers, information available on the late effects of polio, often referred to as post-polio syndrome.

Information services:
Information in relation to post-polio syndrome, benefits.

Printed publications:
The Bulletin (6 times a year, free to members)
Information on the late effects of polio

Electronic and video publications:
Living with the Late Effects of Polio (video, £8 inc. p&p)

Publications list:
Available online and in print

Access to staff:
Contact by letter, by telephone, by fax, by e-mail and in person. Appointment necessary.
Hours: Mon to Thu, 0900 to 1700; Fri, 0900 to 1600

Access for disabled people:
Parking provided, level entry, access to all public areas, toilet facilities

BRITISH PORTS ASSOCIATION

Acronym or abbreviation: BPA

Africa House, 64–78 Kingsway, London, WC2B 6AH

Tel: 020 7242 1200
Fax: 020 7430 7474
E-mail: info@britishports.org.uk

Website:
http://www.britishports.org.uk

Enquiries:
Enquiries to: Director
Direct e-mail: monica.williams@britishports.org.uk
Other contacts: Association Secretary

Founded:
1993

Organisation type and purpose:
Trade association.

Subject coverage:
Port industry and policy.

Access to staff:
Contact by letter, by telephone, by fax, by e-mail and via website. Appointment necessary.
Hours: Mon to Fri, 0900 to 1700

Affiliated to:
European Seaports Organisation (ESPO)
International Association of Ports and Harbours (IAPH)

BRITISH POSTAL MUSEUM AND ARCHIVE

Acronym or abbreviation: BPMA

Freeling House, Phoenix Place, London, WC1X 0DL

Tel: 020 7239 2570
Fax: 020 7239 2576
E-mail: info@postalheritage.org.uk

Website:
http://www.postalheritage.org.uk

Enquiries:
Enquiries to: Archive Assistant
Other contacts: Head of Archive/Collections Manager (for offers of donation of records/objects); Philatelic Curator (for appointments for access to philatelic collections)

Founded:
1896

Formerly called:
Post Office Heritage (year of change 2001)

Incorporates the former:
National Postal Museum; Post Office Archives (year of change 1998); Consignia Heritage Services (year of change 2004)

Organisation type and purpose:
Archive and museum service.

Subject coverage:
All aspects of British postal history.

Museum or gallery collection, archive, or library special collection:
An archive of historical records of Royal Mail Group plc, from 1636 to the present day, including working files, staff records, reports and visual records such as maps, posters, artwork and photographs.
Stamps of Great Britain from the Penny Black onwards, and their artwork, and British postal markings from 1661.
Museum collection: letter boxes, vehicles, uniforms, postal equipment, paintings, signs, etc.

Non-library collection catalogue:
All or part available online and in-house

Printed publications:
Postal Reform and the Penny Black: A New Appreciation (D. Muir, 1990)
Moving the Mail: By Road (J. Stray, 2006)
Range of information sheets and leaflets on various aspects of postal history (available free of charge)

Publications list:
Available online

Access to staff:
Contact by letter, by telephone, by fax, by e-mail and in person
Hours: Mon, Tue, Wed, Fri, 1000 to 1700; Thu, 1000 to 1900; Sat, see website
Special comments: Philatelic collections available by appointment only. Cannot undertake research on behalf of members of the public, although will provide access to the records.

Access for disabled people:
Level entry, access to all public areas, toilet facilities

BRITISH POSTMARK SOCIETY

Acronym or abbreviation: BPS

12 Dunavon Park, Strathaven, Lanarkshire, ML10 6LP

Tel: 01357 522430
E-mail: johlen@stracml10.freeserve.co.uk

Website:
http://www.britishpostmarksociety.org.uk

Enquiries:
Enquiries to: General Secretary

Founded:
1958

Organisation type and purpose:
Membership association (membership is by subscription), present number of members: 237, voluntary organisation; registered charity (charity number 1102748).

Subject coverage:
British postmarks, postal history, postal mechanisation markings.

Museum or gallery collection, archive, or library special collection:
Cuttings and reprints (10 titles by W G Stitt-Dibden and 29 titles by J A Mackay)
Cuttings collected under subject headings, available for loan to members; information provided to non-members by the Librarian Postmark Library

Library catalogue:
All or part available online and in-house

Printed publications:
Bulletin (4 times a year, £13 UK, £18 overseas)
Special Event Postmarks of the United Kingdom (3 volumes, price for 3 volumes £21.50 plus £3 p&p)
Special Event Postmarks of the United Kingdom, volume 4 1994–2003, Finch A and Peachey Cm 2004 (£9.50 plus £2 p&p)
Twenty Years of First Day Postmarks (£3.50 plus 75p p&p)

continued overleaf

Skeleton Postmarks of England and Wales, 3rd edn, Awcock P and Frost L (£18.50 plus £2.50 p&p)
Order printed publications from: Publications, British Postmark Society, 19 Moorland Road, Hemel Hempstead, Hertfordshire, HP1 1NH

Publications list:
Available online and in print

Access to staff:
Contact by letter, by telephone, by e-mail and via website
Hours: Mon to Fri, 0900 to 1700

BRITISH POTATO TRADE ASSOCIATION

Acronym or abbreviation: BPTA

12 Buckstone Hill, Edinburgh, EH10 6TH

Tel: 0131 623 0183
Fax: 0131 623 5295
E-mail: charlie.greenslade@bpta.org.uk

Website:
http://www.bpta.org.uk

Enquiries:
Enquiries to: Secretary

Founded:
1940

Created by the merger of:
National Association of Seed Potato Merchants (NASPM) and Scottish Potato Trade Association (SPTA) (year of change 2006)

Organisation type and purpose:
Trade association (membership is by subscription, election or invitation), present number of members: 110.

Subject coverage:
All matters pertaining to seed potato merchanting.

Access to staff:
Contact by letter, by telephone, by fax, by e-mail and in person
Hours: Mon to Thu, 1400 to 1800

BRITISH POULTRY COUNCIL

Acronym or abbreviation: BPC

Europoint House, 5 Lavington Street, London, SE1 0NZ

Tel: 020 7202 4760
Fax: 020 7928 6366
E-mail: bpc@poultry.uk.com

Website:
http://www.poultry.uk.com

Enquiries:
Enquiries to: Chief Executive

Founded:
2001

Incorporates the former:
BCA (Co-operative & Export) Limited; British Chicken Association; British Goose Producers Association; British Poultry Breeders and Hatcheries Association; British Turkey Federation; Duck Producers Association; Hen Packers Association; Poultry Industry Conference

Organisation type and purpose:
Trade association (membership is by election or invitation).

Subject coverage:
Poultry meat industry.

Access to staff:
Contact by letter, by telephone and by e-mail. Appointment necessary.
Hours: Mon to Fri, 0900 to 1700

BRITISH PRECAST CONCRETE FEDERATION

Acronym or abbreviation: BPCF

60 Charles Street, Leicester, LE1 1FB

Tel: 0116 253 6161
Fax: 0116 251 4568
E-mail: info@britishprecast.org

Website:
http://www.britishprecast.org

Enquiries:
Enquiries to: Secretary

Organisation type and purpose:
Trade association.

Subject coverage:
Precast concrete.

Publications list:
Available online

Access to staff:
Contact by letter, by telephone, by fax, by e-mail and via website
Hours: Mon to Fri, 0900 to 1700

Access to building, collection or gallery:
No access other than to staff

Members:
Concrete Lighting Column Association
Concrete Lintel Association

BRITISH PREGNANCY ADVISORY SERVICE

Acronym or abbreviation: bpas

20 Timothy's Bridge Road, Stratford Enterprise Park, Stratford upon Avon, CV37 9BF

Tel: 0845 730 4030
Fax: 0845 365 5051
E-mail: info@bpas.org

Website:
http://www.bpas.org
Full details of bpas services.

Founded:
1968

Organisation type and purpose:
National organisation, advisory body and registered charity (charity number 289145). bpas is the UK's leading provider of abortion care.

Subject coverage:
Pregnancy testing; pre- and post-abortion counselling; abortion assessment, treatment and aftercare; vasectomy; female sterilisation; vasectomy reversal; contraception; unplanned pregnancy and online STI testing and treatment.

Printed publications:
Information leaflets: general; abortion; other services and other resources
Order printed publications from: e-mail: marketing@bpas.org

Publications list:
Available online and in print

Access to staff:
Contact by letter, by telephone, by fax, by e-mail and via website
Hours: Mon to Fri, 0800 to 2100; Sat, 0830 to 1800; Sun, 0930 to 1430

Branches:
Branches nation-wide
   tel: 0845 730 4030

BRITISH PRINTING INDUSTRIES FEDERATION

Acronym or abbreviation: BPIF

Farringdon Point, 29–35 Farringdon Road, London, EC1M 3JF

Tel: 0870 240 4085
Fax: 020 7405 7784

E-mail: info@bpif.org.uk

Website:
http://www.britishprint.com
Careers, information about the industry, members services, training and news.

Enquiries:
Enquiries to: Director of Corporate Affairs
Direct tel: 020 7915 8378
Direct fax: 020 7915 8395
Direct e-mail: andrew.brown@bpif.org.uk

Founded:
1901

Organisation type and purpose:
National organisation, advisory body, trade association, present number of members: 2500, training organisation, consultancy.

The British Printing Industries Federation is the leading trade association and business support organisation for the UK printing industry. The BPIF runs a strong regional network of advisors and business centres to support printing companies in the UK, offering a 'one-stop shop' for skills solutions, and delivering expert assistance across the full range of business activities from sales and marketing to environmental and risk management, from training to insurance and pensions.

As a leading trade association the BPIF also works closely with government and international institutions. Regularly consulted by government and other national and international trade associations, the BPIF is in a strong position to lobby and influence public policy on behalf of the industry both in the UK, in Europe and other parts of the globe.

Subject coverage:
British printing industry and paper; employment affairs, education and training, industrial relations, technical, consultancy, environment, health and safety, waste management.

Trade and statistical information:
Surveys for the UK printing industry.

Printed publications:
Action (newsletter, fortnightly)
Company staff salaries (Salary Survey), UK
Directions – Survey of Trends in the Printing Industry (quarterly)
Manpower Survey Report (annually)
Print & Profitability Survey
Printing for Profit Report (annually)
Salary Survey Report (annually)
Wages Survey (Manpower Survey)
Order printed publications from: Information Officer

Publications list:
Available in print

Access to staff:
Contact by letter, by telephone, by fax, by e-mail and via website. Appointment necessary. Non-members charged.
Hours: Mon to Fri, 0900 to 1700

Access to building, collection or gallery:
No access other than to staff
Hours: Mon to Fri, 0930 to 1630

Access for disabled people:
Parking provided, ramped entry, access to all public areas, toilet facilities

Affiliated to:
Intergraf

Regional business centres:
BPIF Eastern (Bedfordshire, Buckinghamshire, Cambridgeshire, Essex (East and North), Hertfordshire, Norfolk and Suffolk)
   7 Kings Court, Willie Snaith Road, Newmarket, Suffolk, CB8 7SG; tel: 01638 565180; fax: 01638 665235; e-mail: east@bpif.org.uk

BPIF Midland (Derbyshire (except High Peak and Chesterfield areas), Leicestershire, Lincolnshire, Northamptonshire, Nottinghamshire, Shropshire, Staffordshire, Warwickshire, West Midlands and Worcestershire)
  Unit 2 Villiers Court, Meridien Business Park, Birmingham Road, Coventry, West Mids, CV5 9RN; tel: 01676 526030; fax: 01676 526033; e-mail: mid@bpif.org.uk
BPIF North Eastern (Cleveland, Derbyshire (Chesterfield area), Durham, Humberside, Northumberland, Tyne and Wear, North Yorkshire, South Yorkshire and West Yorkshire)
  142 Thornes Lane, Wakefield, West Yorkshire, WF2 7XG; tel: 01924 203330; fax: 01924 290092; e-mail: ne@bpif.org.uk
BPIF North Western (Cheshire, Cumbria, Derbyshire (High Peak district), Lancashire, Greater Manchester, Merseyside, Isle of Man, Clwyd, Gwynedd and Northern Ireland)
  8th Floor, Trafford House, Chester Road, Stretford, Manchester, M32 0RS; tel: 0161 886 8400; fax: 0161 877 4455; e-mail: nw@bpif.org.uk
BPIF South Eastern (Berkshire, Hampshire, Kent, Greater London, Surrey, Sussex and the Isle of Wight)
  Farringdon Point, 29–35 Farringdon Road, London, EC1M 3JF; tel: 020 7915 8400; fax: 020 7404 7304; e-mail: se@bpif.org.uk
BPIF South Western (Avon, Cornwall, Devon, Dorset, Gloucestershire, Herefordshire, Oxfordshire, Somerset, Wiltshire, Dyfed, Mid Glamorgan, South Glamorgan, West Glamorgan, Gwent and Powys)
  Lindsey House, Oaklands Business Park, Bristol, BS37 5NA; tel: 01454 333 331; fax: 01454 333 331; e-mail: sw@bpif.org.uk

Subsidiary of BPIF, access through BPIF Head Office:
Book Production Section
British Binders and Finishers Association (BBFA)
British Carton Association (BCA)
British Engraved Stationery Association (BESA)
British Roll Label Association (BRLA)
Business Documents Section
Digital Interest Group
Direct Marketing Special Products Section
Heidelberg Users Group
Inplant Printers
Magazine & Media Section
Promotional Finishers Association (PFA)
Young Managing Printers (YMP)

BRITISH PROMOTIONAL MERCHANDISE ASSOCIATION

Formal name: British Promotional Merchandise Association Limited
Acronym or abbreviation: BPMA

Arena House, 66–68 Pentonville Road, London, N1 9HS

Tel: 020 7689 5555
Fax: 020 7837 5326
E-mail: enquiries@bpma.co.uk

Website:
http://www.bpma.co.uk

Enquiries:
Enquiries to: Secretary

Founded:
1965

Organisation type and purpose:
Trade association, present number of members: 800. Members are manufacturers and suppliers of products and services to the sales promotion industry.

Printed publications:
BPMA Yearbook (trade journal for the sales promotion industry)
Promotion News (trade journal, 12 times a year)

Access to staff:
Contact by letter, by telephone, by fax, by e-mail and via website
Hours: Mon to Fri, 0900 to 1700

BRITISH PROPERTY FEDERATION

Acronym or abbreviation: BPF

5th Floor, St Albans House, 57–59 Haymarket, London, SW1Y 4QX

Tel: 020 7828 0111
Fax: 020 7834 3442
E-mail: info@bpf.org.uk

Website:
http://www.bpf.org.uk

Enquiries:
Enquiries to: Operations Manager
Direct tel: 020 7802 0100
Direct e-mail: mhoyte@bpf.org.uk

Founded:
1974

Organisation type and purpose:
Trade association, present number of members: 450.

Subject coverage:
Property taxation (direct and indirect) accounting standards, private rented sector, planning and environment, property legislation, landlord/tenant relationship, impact of development on archaeology.

Printed publications:
BPF Short-Term Commercial Lease
BPF Research Report: Business Parking Standards: The effects of PPG13 (2001, free to members, £15 non-members)
BPF/IPD Annual Lease Review 2001
Form of Agreement for Collateral Warranty Co Wa/F (3rd ed)
Good Practice in the Selection of Construction Materials

Publications list:
Available in print

Access to staff:
Contact by letter, by telephone, by fax and by e-mail. Appointment necessary.
Hours: Mon to Fri, 0930 to 1700

Access to building, collection or gallery:
24-hour access

Access for disabled people:
Access to all public areas

Subsidiary company:
BPF Commercial Ltd
  at the same address

BRITISH PSYCHIC AND OCCULT SOCIETY

Acronym or abbreviation: BPOS

PO Box 1112, London, N10 3XE

Tel: 020 8442 1233
Fax: 020 8442 1233

Website:
http://www.dfarrant.co.uk
Brief description of BPOS.

Enquiries:
Enquiries to: General Secretary

Founded:
1967

Organisation type and purpose:
Learned society, present number of members: 374, research organisation.
Psychic research and investigation, including ghosts, poltergeists, unexplained apparitions and other phenomena, unsolved mysteries etc.

Subject coverage:
Psychic research in general, i.e. unexplained phenomena, psychic disturbances, mysterious or unexplained events relating to 'ghosts', 'vampires' etc.

Printed publications:
Dark Journey: True Cases of Ghostly Phenomena from the Files of the BPOS
Vampyre Syndrome: The Truth Behind the Highgate Vampire Legend (publ BPOS)
Shadows in the Night: Distant Dreams and Lost Reality (publ BPOS)
Beyond the Highgate Vampire (1997, publ BPOS)
Dark Secrets (2001, publ BPOS)
Man, myth and Manchester, Ser. 1–8 (2001–2004, publ BPOS)
Order printed publications from: BPOS Publications

Electronic and video publications:
In Search of the Highgate Vampire (video 45 mins, £9.99 plus £1.50 p&p)
The British Psychic and Occult Society (Electronic Press Kit, CD-ROM, £4.99 plus 50p p&p)

Access to staff:
Contact by letter and by fax
Hours: Mon to Fri, 0900 to 1700

Access to building, collection or gallery:
No access other than to staff

BRITISH PSYCHOANALYTIC COUNCIL

Formal name: The British Psychoanalytic Council
Acronym or abbreviation: BPC

West Hill House, 6 Swains Lane, London, N6 6QS

Tel: 020 7267 3626
Fax: 020 7267 4772
E-mail: mail@psychoanalytic-council.org

Website:
http://www.psychoanalytic-council.org
Information on training, finding a therapist, registration of psychotherapists, member institutions, issues relating to psychoanalysis and psychodynamic psychotherapy.

Enquiries:
Enquiries to: Honorary Secretary
Other contacts: Chief Executive Officer; Head of Services

Founded:
1993

Formerly called:
British Confederation of Psychotherapists (year of change 2005)

Organisation type and purpose:
Professional body, voluntary organisation.
To publish a register of appropriately qualified psychotherapists.

Subject coverage:
Register lists psychoanalysts, Jungian analysts, psychoanalytic psychotherapists and child psychotherapists.

Printed publications:
Register, includes brief description of psychotherapy and how to find a therapist; lists referral services and reduced-fee schemes offered by member societies

Access to staff:
Contact by letter, by telephone, by fax, by e-mail and via website
Hours: Mon to Fri, 0930 to 1730

Members:
British Association of Psychotherapists
  37 Mapesbury Road, London, NW2 4HJ; tel: 020 8452 9823; fax: 020 8452 5182; e-mail: admin@ bap-psychotherapy.org; website: http://www .bap-psychotherapy.org
British Psychoanalytical Society and the Institute of Psychoanalysis
  112A Shirland Road, London, W9; tel: 020 7563 5000; fax: 020 7563 5001; website: http://www .psychoanalysis.org.uk
Lincoln Clinic and Centre for Psychotherapy
  23 Abbeville Mews, 88 Clapham Park Road, London, SW4 7BX; tel: 020 7978 1545; fax: 020 7720 4721; e-mail: info@lincoln-psychotherapy .org.uk

continued overleaf

London Centre of Psychotherapy
32 Leighton Road, London, NW5 2QE; tel: 020 7482 2002; fax: 020 7482 4222; e-mail: info@lcp-psychotherapy.org.uk; website: http://www.lcp-psychotherapy.org.uk

North of England Association of Psychoanalytic Psychotherapists
Claremont House, off Framlington Place, Newcastle upon Tyne, NE2 4AA; tel: 0191 282 4547; fax: 0191 282 4542

Northern Ireland Association for the Study of Psycho-Analysis
32 Upper Malone Park, Upper Malone Road, Belfast, BT9 6PP; tel: 028 9047 3254

Scottish Association of Psychoanalytical Psychotherapists
172 Leith Walk, Edinburgh, EH6 5EA; tel: 0131 454 3240; fax: 0131 454 3241

Scottish Institute of Human Relations
172 Leith Walk, Edinburgh, EH6 5EA; tel: 0131 226 9610; fax: 0131 454 3241; e-mail: info@sihr.org.uk; website: http://www.sihr.org.uk

Severnside Institute for Psychotherapy
11 Orchard Street, Bristol, BS1 5EH; tel: 0117 923 2354; fax: 0117 923 2354; e-mail: sipsychotherapy@blueyonder.co.uk

Society of Analytical Psychology
1 Daleham Gardens, London, NW3 5BY; tel: 020 7435 7696; fax: 020 7731 1495; e-mail: office.sap@btconnect.com; website: http://www.jungian-analysis.org

Tavistock Clinic and Tavistock Society of Psychotherapists
120 Belsize Lane, London, NW3 5BA; tel: 020 7435 7111; fax: 020 7447 3709; e-mail: info@tavi-port.org; website: http://www.tavi-port.org

Partner organisation:
Association of Psychoanalytic Psychotherapists in the National Health Service
5 Windsor Road, London, N3 3SN; tel: 020 8349 9873; fax: 020 8343 3197; e-mail: joycepiper@compuserve.com

BRITISH PSYCHOLOGICAL SOCIETY

Acronym or abbreviation: BPS

St Andrews House, 48 Princess Road East, Leicester, LE1 7DR

Tel: 0116 254 9568
Fax: 0116 247 0787
E-mail: mail@bps.org.uk

Website:
http://www.bps.org.uk
Information pages being developed.

Enquiries:
Enquiries to: Help Desk

Founded:
1901

Organisation type and purpose:
Learned society, professional body.
Empowered to maintain Register of Chartered Psychologists; 20 specialist divisions or sections.

Subject coverage:
Psychology, specialist groups in educational, medical, clinical, criminological and legal, mathematical, statistical and computing, social, developmental, cognitive, consciousness and experimental psychology, counselling psychology, occupational psychotherapy, history and philosophy of psychology, neuropsychology, teaching of psychology, psychology of women, transpersonal psychology.

Museum or gallery collection, archive, or library special collection:
Archives

Printed publications:
British Journal of Clinical Psychology (quarterly)
British Journal of Developmental Psychology (quarterly)
British Journal of Educational Psychology (3 times a year)

British Journal of Mathematical and Statistical Psychology (2 times a year)
British Journal of Medical Psychology (quarterly)
British Journal of Psychology (quarterly)
British Journal of Social Psychology (quarterly)
Directory of Chartered Psychologists (annually)
Information sheets (list available from the Society)
Journal of Occupational and Organisational Psychology (quarterly)
Register of Chartered Psychologists (annually)
Selection and Development Review (6 times a year)
The Psychologist: incorporating the Bulletin of the British Psychological Society (monthly)

Access to staff:
Contact by telephone, by e-mail and via website
Hours: Mon to Fri, 0900 to 1700

Affiliated to:
European Federation of Professional Psychological Associations
International Union of Psychological Science

BRITISH PTERIDOLOGICAL SOCIETY

Acronym or abbreviation: BPS

Department of Botany, Natural History Museum, Cromwell Road, South Kensington, London, SW7 5BD

Tel: 020 8850 3218
Fax: 020 8850 3218
E-mail: secretary@ebps.org.uk

Website:
http://www.ebps.org.uk
Information about the Society and about ferns generally.

Enquiries:
Enquiries to: Honorary Secretary
Direct e-mail: horticulturalinformation@ebps.org.uk
Other contacts: Horticultural Information Officer for horticultural information.

Founded:
1891

Organisation type and purpose:
International organisation, learned society (membership is by subscription), present number of members: 760, voluntary organisation.
Membership comprises amateur and professional pteridologists.
To promote the growing, study and conservation of ferns and fern allies, both of wild species and cultivated varieties and to encourage interest in their taxonomy, distribution and ecology.

Subject coverage:
Ferns and fern allies: their morphology, ecology, distribution, taxonomy, conservation. All aspects of fern growing.

Printed publications:
BPS Bulletin (annually, free to members)
Fern Gazette (twice a year, free to members)
Occasional Pamphlets, for sale
Pteridologist (annually, free to members)
Special Publication Series produced at irregular intervals, for sale

Access to staff:
Contact by letter, by telephone, by fax and by e-mail
Hours: Mon to Fri, 0900 to 1700

Affiliated to:
National Council for the Conservation of Plants and Gardens
National Plant Societies Federation
Plantlife
Royal Horticultural Society

BRITISH PUMP MANUFACTURERS ASSOCIATION

Acronym or abbreviation: BPMA

National Metalforming Centre, 47 Birmingham Road, West Bromwich, B70 6PY

Tel: 0121 601 6350
Fax: 0121 601 6387
E-mail: enquiry@bpma.org.uk

Website:
http://www.bpma.org.uk
LIst of Members. Pump Search facility. Events.

Enquiries:
Enquiries to: Administration
Direct e-mail: admin@bpma.org.uk
Other contacts: Technical Director

Founded:
1941

Organisation type and purpose:
Trade association, present number of members: 80.

Subject coverage:
Manufacture and marketing of pumps.

Education services:
Training in pump technology.

Printed publications:
Buyers Guide
Order printed publications from: http://www.bpma.org.uk or admin@bpma.org.uk

Publications list:
Available online and in print

Access to staff:
Contact by telephone, by fax, by e-mail and via website
Hours: Mon to Fri, 0900 to 1700

Affiliated to:
European Committee of Pump Manufacturers (EUROPUMP)

Parent body:
Mechanical and Metal Trades Confederation (METCOM)

BRITISH PUPPET AND MODEL THEATRE GUILD

Acronym or abbreviation: BPMTG

65 Kingsley Avenue, West Ealing, London, W13 0EH

Tel: 020 8997 8236
E-mail: peter@peterpuppet.co.uk

Website:
http://www.puppetguild.org.uk
Up-to-date listing of puppetry events in the UK & world-wide, news, views and discussion of puppetry matters.

Enquiries:
Enquiries to: Honorary Chairman
Direct tel: 07931 550365

Founded:
1924

Organisation type and purpose:
Membership association (membership is by subscription), voluntary organisation.
To promote and encourage the art of puppetry in all its forms.

Subject coverage:
Puppetry, model theatre, workshops, technical assistance, festivals, exhibitions.

Museum or gallery collection, archive, or library special collection:
Archive, books on puppetry and collection of puppets including the Lanchester Marionettes, stored in Bridgnorth, Shropshire; viewing by appointment

Non-library collection catalogue:
All or part available online

Printed publications:
Newsletter (bi-monthly)
Puppet Master (magazine, annual)

Access to staff:
Contact by letter and by telephone. Non-members charged.

Hours: Any reasonable time

Access to building, collection or gallery:
Prior appointment required

BRITISH RACING SPORTS CAR CLUB

Acronym or abbreviation: BRSCC

Westway House, Castle Combe, Chippenham, Wiltshire, SN14 7EY

Tel: 01249 782417
Fax: 01249 782392

Website:
http://www.castlecombecircuit.co.uk

Enquiries:
Enquiries to: Vice President
Direct e-mail: jo@brscc.co.uk

Founded:
1946

Organisation type and purpose:
Membership association (membership is by subscription), present number of members: 4500.

Access to staff:
Contact by letter, by telephone, by fax, by e-mail and via website
Hours: Mon to Fri, 0900 to 1700

BRITISH RECORDS ASSOCIATION

Acronym or abbreviation: BRA

c/o Finsbury Library, 245 St John Street, London, EC1V 4NB

Tel: 020 7833 0428
Fax: 020 7833 0416
E-mail: britrecassoc@hotmail.com

Website:
http://www.britishrecordsassociation.org.uk

Enquiries:
Enquiries to: Honorary Secretary
Direct tel: 020 7834 6242
Direct fax: 020 7828 8317
Direct e-mail: karen.stapley@girlguiding.org.uk
Other contacts: Chairman, Vice-Chair, Chair – Records Preservation Section; Administrative Officer

Founded:
1932

Organisation type and purpose:
National organisation, membership association (membership is by subscription), present number of members: 800, registered charity (charity number 227464). Council includes representatives of the British Academy, the Library Association, the National Archives, the Society of Archivists, etc.
Preservation and promotion of archival material as an historical source.

Subject coverage:
Archive management, archive services, use of documentary sources (in general), information management, preservation, conservation, care; deposit and use of historical records, manuscripts and archives, advice to record owners and keepers, friends of record offices, publication of records and archive user guides.

Printed publications:
Archives (journal, 2 times a year)
Sources for the History of London 1939–45: a Guide and Bibliography (Creaton H)
Guidelines series on records preservation
Irish History from 1700. A Guide to the Sources in the Public Record Office (Prochaska A)
Materials for the Local and Regional Study of Schooling, 1700–1900 (Stephens WB and Unwin RW)
Newsletter (2 times a year)
Sources for the History of English Nonconformity 1660–1830 (Mullet M)
Indexing for Editors (Hunnisett RF, out of print)

Records of the Established Church in England, excluding Parochial Records (Owen DM)
Manorial Records (Harvey PDA)
Documenting the History of Houses (Alcock NW)
Seals (New E)
Order printed publications from: BRA

Publications list:
Available online and in print

Access to staff:
Contact by letter, by telephone, by fax and by e-mail. Appointment necessary.
Hours: Mon, Tue, Thu, 0900 to 1700
Special comments: Please telephone for an appointment.

Constituent bodies:
Records Preservation Section

Links with:
Scottish Records Association

BRITISH RED CROSS SOCIETY

Acronym or abbreviation: British Red Cross

UK Office, 44 Moorfields, London, EC2Y 9AL

Tel: 0844 871 1111
Fax: 020 7562 2000
E-mail: information@redcross.org.uk

Website:
http://www.redcross.org.uk

Enquiries:
Enquiries to: Information Officer
Direct tel: 0844 412 2804

Founded:
1870

Organisation type and purpose:
Voluntary organisation, registered charity (England and Wales charity number 220949; Scotland charity number SC037738).

Subject coverage:
Improvement of health, prevention of disease, first aid, nursing, welfare, training, community services, family reunions, transport, medical equipment loans, fundraising, voluntary work.

Museum or gallery collection, archive, or library special collection:
Collection of international humanitarian law documents and Red Cross policies, practices and procedures

Printed publications:
Lifeline: update of work (quarterly)

Publications list:
Available online and in print

Access to staff:
Contact by letter, by telephone, by fax, by e-mail and via website. Appointment necessary.
Hours: Mon to Fri, 0930 to 1730

Access to building, collection or gallery:
Prior appointment required
Hours: Mon to Fri, 0900 to 1700

Access for disabled people:
Ramped entry, access to all public areas, toilet facilities

Also at:
British Red Cross Museum and Archives same address; tel: 020 7201 5153; e-mail: enquiry@redcross.org.uk; website: http://www.redcross.org.uk/museumandarchives

Links with:
International Committee of the Red Cross
International Federation of Red Cross and Red Crescent Societies

BRITISH REED GROWER'S ASSOCIATION

Acronym or abbreviation: BRGA

c/o Brown & Co, The Atrium, St George's Street,, Norwich, Norfolk, NR3 1AB

Tel: 01603 629871
Fax: 01603 616199
E-mail: ian.lonsdale@brown-co.com

Website:
http://www.brga.org.uk
Online general information on the BRGA, copies of Buying and Selling Reed and Norfolk Reed Roofing Today information leaflets, 2009 update of The Reed pamphlet, as well as general updates on reed.

Enquiries:
Enquiries to: Secretary

Founded:
1965

Organisation type and purpose:
Trade association (membership is by subscription), present number of members: 38, suitable for ages: all.
Promotion of reed and sedge growing; co-ordination of supply to thatchers, monitoring supply and demand; promotion of research into improved production, maintaining close links with the thatching trade, environmental groups, government agencies and local authorities; lobbying over important relevant issues.

Subject coverage:
Reed bed management and creation, marketing reed and sedge.

Trade and statistical information:
Guideline information on cost of reed and sedge.

Printed publications:
Buying and Selling Reed (free)
New Wetland Harvests – New Life for the Broads Fens (free)
Norfolk Reed, Roofing Today (free)
Reedbed Management for Bitterns (free)
2009 update of The Reed (free)
Reedbed Management for Commercial and Wildlife Interests (Hawke C J and José P V, published in conjunction with RSPB £14.95)

Publications list:
Available in print

Access to staff:
Contact by letter, by telephone, by fax, by e-mail and via website. Non-members charged.
Hours: Mon to Fri, 0900 to 1700

BRITISH REFLEXOLOGY ASSOCIATION

Acronym or abbreviation: BRA

Monks Orchard, Whitbourne, Worcester, WR6 5RB

Tel: 01886 821207
Fax: 01886 822017
E-mail: bra@britreflex.co.uk

Website:
http://www.britreflex.co.uk

Enquiries:
Enquiries to: Chairman

Founded:
1985

Organisation type and purpose:
Membership association, training organisation.

Subject coverage:
Reflexology and reflexology training.

Printed publications:
Footprints (magazine, quarterly, £10 per year)
Reflexology: A Way to Better Health (Nicola Hall, £10.99 plus p&p)
Reflexology for Women (Nicola Hall, £9.99 plus p&p)
Register of Reflexologists (£3 plus 50p p&p)

Electronic and video publications:
Reflexology: A Way to Better Health – The Practical Technique (DVD, £15.99 plus p&p)
Reflexology: A Way to Better Health – The Practical Technique (video, £14.99 plus p&p)

continued overleaf

Publications list:
Available online and in print

Access to staff:
Contact by letter, by telephone, by fax, by e-mail and via website. Appointment necessary.
Hours: Mon to Thu, 0900 to 1600

Official teaching body:
The Bayly School of Reflexology
Monks Orchard, Whitbourne, Worcestershire, WR6 5RB; tel: 01886 821207; fax: 01886 822017; e-mail: bayly@britreflex.co.uk; website: http://www.britreflex.co.uk

BRITISH REFRACTORIES & INDUSTRIAL CERAMICS ASSOCIATION

Acronym or abbreviation: BRICA

Federation House, Station Road, Stoke-on-Trent, Staffordshire, ST4 2SA

Tel: 01782 744631
Fax: 01782 744102
E-mail: ragb@ceramfed.co.uk

Website:
http://www.ceramfed.co.uk

Enquiries:
Enquiries to: Secretary
Direct e-mail: andrewm@ceramfed.co.uk

Organisation type and purpose:
Trade association.

Subject coverage:
Refractory and ceramics materials industry, commercial and industrial relations within it.

Printed publications:
Refractories Industry of Great Britain (1991)

Access to staff:
Contact by letter, by telephone, by fax and by e-mail
Hours: Mon to Fri, 0900 to 1700

Member of:
British Ceramic Confederation
at the same address

BRITISH RETAIL CONSORTIUM

Acronym or abbreviation: BRC

Second Floor, 21 Dartmouth Street, London, SW1H 9BP

Tel: 020 7854 8900
Fax: 020 7854 8901
E-mail: info@brc.org.uk

Website:
http://www.brc.org.uk

Enquiries:
Enquiries to: Marketing and Business Information Director
Direct e-mail: krishan.rama@brc.org.uk

Founded:
1992

Organisation type and purpose:
Trade association.

Subject coverage:
Retailing, consumer affairs.

Trade and statistical information:
Retailing.

Publications list:
Available online

Access to staff:
Contact by letter, by fax, by e-mail and via website
Hours: Mon to Fri, 0900 to 1700

Branch office:
Scottish Retail Consortium
PO Box 13737, Gullane, EH31 2WX; tel: 07830 152423; e-mail: src@brc.org.uk

BRITISH RETINITIS PIGMENTOSA SOCIETY

Formal name: RP Fighting Blindness
Acronym or abbreviation: BRPS

PO Box 350, Buckingham, MK18 1GZ

Tel: 01280 821334
E-mail: info@brps.org.uk

Website:
http://www.brps.org.uk
http://www.fightingblindness.org.uk

Enquiries:
Enquiries to: Chief Executive Officer

Founded:
1975

Organisation type and purpose:
Membership association (membership is by subscription), present number of members: 3,000, charity, research organisation.
Run by volunteers, it aims to raise funds for scientific research to provide treatments leading to a cure for RP.
Provides welfare support and guidance service to members and their families.

Subject coverage:
Retinitis pigmentosa (RP), medical advice, progress of research, aids to sufferers.

Printed publications:
Quarterly Newsletter (available in large print and Braille)

Electronic and video publications:
Monthly e-bulletin
Quarterly Newsletter (available on tape, by e-mail or computer diskette)

Publications list:
Available in print

Access to staff:
Contact by letter, by telephone, by fax and by e-mail

BRITISH RIGID URETHANE FOAM MANUFACTURERS' ASSOCIATION LIMITED

Acronym or abbreviation: BRUFMA

12a High Street East, Glossop, Derbyshire, SK13 8DA

Tel: 01457 855884
Fax: 01457 855884
E-mail: brufma@brufma.co.uk

Website:
http://www.brufma.co.uk

Enquiries:
Enquiries to: Chief Executive
Direct e-mail: mel.price@brufma.co.uk

Founded:
1967

Organisation type and purpose:
Trade association.

Subject coverage:
BRUFMA is a trade association that was incorporated in 1978 to represent the manufacturers of the wide range of PIR/PUR insulation products produced in the UK. Its membership comprises the major companies in the industry, both manufacturers of finished insulation products and suppliers of the various raw materials.

Publications list:
Available online

Access to staff:
Contact by e-mail and via website. Appointment necessary.
Hours: Mon to Fri, 0915 to 1700

Affiliated to:
Construction Products Association

BRITISH ROSE GROWERS ASSOCIATION

Acronym or abbreviation: BRGA

c/o Horticultural Trades Association, 19 High Street, Theale, Reading, Berkshire, RG7 5AH

Tel: 0118 930 3132
Fax: 0118 930 4989
E-mail: info@the-hta.org.uk

Enquiries:
Enquiries to: Administrator
Direct e-mail: info@the-hta.org.uk

Founded:
1976

Organisation type and purpose:
Trade association (membership is by election or invitation), present number of members: 70.

Printed publications:
Find That Rose (2006/07, £3.00, inc. p&p, available from Editor)
Order printed publications from: The Editor, British Rose Growers Association
303 Mile End Road, Colchester, CO4 5EA

Access to staff:
Contact by letter, by telephone and by fax
Hours: Mon to Fri, 0900 to 1700

BRITISH ROWING

The Priory, 6 Lower Mall, Hammersmith, London, W6 9DJ

Tel: 020 8237 6700
Fax: 020 8237 6749
E-mail: info@britishrowing.org

Website:
http:www.britishrowing.org

Founded:
1882

Formerly called:
Amateur Rowing Association (year of change 2009)

Organisation type and purpose:
Membership association, voluntary organisation, publishing house, training organisation.
Governing body of the sport in England.

Subject coverage:
All aspects of rowing: learning, training, coaching, rules, organisation, clubs, competitions, international and Olympic representation.

Museum or gallery collection, archive, or library special collection:
British Rowing Almanack & Year Book (from 1869)
Reference library of historic and contemporary books associated with rowing

Library catalogue:
All or part available in-house

Printed publications:
British Rowing Almanack (annually in April, members £23 plus £2 p&p)
Rowing & Regatta (magazine, 9 a year, free to members)
Whole Sport Plan (free to every club)

Access to staff:
Contact by letter, by telephone, by fax and in person
Hours: Mon to Fri, 0900 to 1700
Special comments: Library by prior appointment.

Also at:
International Office, British Rowing
tel: 020 8237 6767; fax: 020 8563 2265; e-mail: info@gbrowingteam.org.uk
Satellite Office, British Rowing
Bedford Satellite Office, Unit 3, Greensbury Farm, Thurleigh Road, Bolnhurst, Beds, MK44 2ET; fax: 01234 378899; e-mail: 01234 37886

Members:
British Olympic Association
tel: 020 8871 2677; fax: 020 8871 9104

Central Council of Physical Recreation
tel: 020 7854 8500; fax: 020 7854 8501
Commonwealth Games Federation
tel: 020 7388 6643
Fédération Internationale des Sociétés d'Aviron
tel: +41 21 617 8373; fax: +41 21 617 8375; e-mail: info@fisa.org

BRITISH SAFETY COUNCIL

Acronym or abbreviation: BSC

70 Chancellors Road, London, W6 9RS

Tel: 020 8741 1231
Fax: 020 8741 4555
E-mail: mail@britsafe.org

Website:
http://www.britsafe.org
Information on the Council, its services and products.

Founded:
1957

Organisation type and purpose:
Advisory body, professional body (membership is by subscription), present number of members: 10,000, registered charity, training organisation. To promote health, safety and environmental best practice for the increase of productivity and the benefit of society.

Subject coverage:
Occupational health, safety and environmental issues, training, risk management, audits, award schemes, advisory and assessment schemes, and related publications.

Printed publications:
Health and Safety at Work Act Newsletter
Safety Management (magazine, 11 times a year, free to members or £60 annual UK Subscription)
British Safety Council Guides and posters (monthly, free to members)

Access to staff:
Contact by letter, by telephone, by fax, by e-mail and via website. Appointment necessary.
Hours: Mon to Fri, 0900 to 1700

Access for disabled people:
Level entry, access to all public areas, toilet facilities

BRITISH SAFETY INDUSTRY FEDERATION

Acronym or abbreviation: BSIF

93 Bowen Court, St Asaph Business Park, Glascoed Road, St Asaph, Denbighshire, LL17 0JE

Tel: 01745 585600
Fax: 01745 585800
E-mail: b.s.i.f@virgin.net

Enquiries:
Enquiries to: Secretary General

Founded:
1994

Organisation type and purpose:
Trade association (membership is by qualification), present number of members: 180, service industry. Single voice for UK safety industry.

Subject coverage:
Lead association for the PPE directive, access to supply chain for safety products, access to information on safety industry.

Access to staff:
Contact by letter, by telephone and by fax. Non-members charged.
Hours: Mon to Fri, 0900 to 1600

Access to building, collection or gallery:
No access other than to staff

Access for disabled people:
Parking provided, ramped entry, toilet facilities

BRITISH SCHOOL OF OSTEOPATHY

Acronym or abbreviation: BSO

275 Borough High Street, London, SE1 1JE

Tel: 020 7407 0222
Fax: 020 7089 5300
E-mail: admin@bso.ac.uk

Website:
http://www.bso.ac.uk
Information on the BSc Hons course in osteopathy and about the clinic.

Enquiries:
Enquiries to: Librarian
Direct tel: 020 7089 5324
Direct e-mail: willp@bso.ac.uk

Founded:
1917

Organisation type and purpose:
Registered charity (charity number 312873). Private institution of higher education.

Subject coverage:
Medicine, complementary medicine, osteopathy.

Museum or gallery collection, archive, or library special collection:
J. M. Littlejohn collection of osteopathic books
Special collection of osteopathic books and periodicals

Library catalogue:
All or part available online

Printed publications:
Bibliography on palpation
How to do research
Spinal Outcomes
Study methods

Access to staff:
Contact by letter, by telephone, by fax, by e-mail and in person. Non-members charged.
Hours: Mon to Fri, 0900 to 1700

Access for disabled people:
Parking provided, ramped entry, access to all public areas, toilet facilities

Links with:
University of Bedfordshire
Park Square, Luton, Bedfordshire, LU1 3JU; tel: 01234 793006; website: http://www.beds.ac.uk

BRITISH SCHOOL OF SHIATSU-DO

Acronym or abbreviation: BSS-Do

Unit 3, Thane Works, Thane Villas, London, N7 7NU

Tel: 020 7700 3355
Fax: 020 7700 3355
E-mail: london@shiatsu-do.co.uk

Website:
http://www.shiatsu-do.co.uk

Enquiries:
Enquiries to: Registrar
Direct tel: 020 7700 3355

Founded:
1983

Organisation type and purpose:
Training organisation.

Subject coverage:
Shiatsu-Do, Shiatsu.

Printed publications:
British School of Shiatsu-Do handbook (£6.99)

Electronic and video publications:
BSS-Do video (£14.99)

Access to staff:
Contact by letter, by telephone, by fax, by e-mail and in person
Hours: Mon to Fri, 1100 to 1300 and 1400 to 1800

Access to building, collection or gallery:
No prior appointment required
Hours: Mon to Fri, 0900 to 1900

Access for disabled people:
Parking provided
Special comments: No wheelchair access

BRITISH SCHOOL OF YOGA

Acronym or abbreviation: BSY GROUP

Stanhope Square, Holsworthy, Devon, EX22 6DF

Tel: 0800 731 9271
E-mail: info@bsygroup.co.uk

Website:
http://www.bsygroup.co.uk

Enquiries:
Enquiries to: Information Officer

Founded:
1946

Organisation type and purpose:
Learned society (membership is by qualification), training organisation.

Subject coverage:
Complementary therapies, stress management, counselling, alternative therapies, self improvement, beauty therapies, yoga, new age, fitness training.

Publications list:
Available online and in print

Access to staff:
Contact by letter, by telephone, by fax, by e-mail and via website. Appointment necessary.
Hours: Mon to Fri, 0900 to 1800

BRITISH SCHOOLBOY MOTORCYCLE ASSOCIATION

20 Glenpark Crescent, Kingscourt, Stroud, Gloucestershire, GL5 5DT

Tel: 01453 766516
Fax: 01453 764877

Enquiries:
Enquiries to: Information Officer

Founded:
1969

Organisation type and purpose:
Membership association.

Subject coverage:
Motorcycling for those of school age.

Access to staff:
Contact by letter
Hours: Mon to Fri, 0900 to 1700

BRITISH SCHOOLS CYCLING ASSOCIATION

Acronym or abbreviation: BSCA

21 Bedhampton Road, North End, Portsmouth, Hampshire, PO2 7JX

Tel: 023 9264 2226
Fax: 023 9266 0187
E-mail: susanknight@bsca.fsnet.co.uk

Website:
http://www.bsca.org.uk

Enquiries:
Enquiries to: General Secretary

Founded:
1967

Organisation type and purpose:
Membership association (membership is by subscription).
School sports governing body.

Access to staff:
Contact by letter, by telephone and by fax

continued overleaf

Hours: Answerphone in operation

Connections with:
National Council for Schools' Sport

BRITISH SCHOOLS EXPLORING SOCIETY

Acronym or abbreviation: BSES Expeditions

Royal Geographical Society, 1 Kensington Gore, London, SW7 2AR

Tel: 020 7591 3141
Fax: 020 7591 3140
E-mail: info@bses.org.uk

Website:
http://www.bses.org.uk

Enquiries:
Enquiries to: Executive Director

Founded:
1932

Organisation type and purpose:
Learned society (membership is by qualification), registered charity (charity number 802196), suitable for ages: 16 to 24, training organisation. The British Schools Exploring Society is a pioneering youth development charity undertaking scientific research expeditions. For over 75 years its aim has been to recruit, train and develop the leaders and scientists of the future who are able to inspire others.

Subject coverage:
Expeditions to areas such as Svalbard, Greenland, northern Norway, Peruvian Amazon, Ladakh and South Georgia. Other destinations include Canada, Kenya, Botswana, Zimbabwe, Australia, Papua New Guinea, Iceland and Namibia. Field work in associated sciences eg glaciology, geology, botany, survey, art and photography. All associated expedition planning and logistics, including budgets.

Museum or gallery collection, archive, or library special collection:
Library (private) of exploration books
Slides of past expeditions
Video collection made from 8mm/16mm film etc, of BSES expeditions, mainly Arctic areas, since 1932

Printed publications:
Annual Report (details of expeditions run by Society since 1932)
Expedition Reports (annually)
The Explorer Newsletter (2 times a year)
Scientific Reports from expeditions

Electronic and video publications:
Videos of expeditions since 1932 to present day

Access to staff:
Contact by letter, by telephone, by fax, by e-mail and in person. Appointment necessary.
Hours: Mon to Fri, 0930 to 1730

Links with:
Royal Geographical Society
at the same address

BRITISH SCHOOLS GYMNASTIC ASSOCIATION

Acronym or abbreviation: BSGA

Orchard House, 15 North Common Road, Uxbridge, Middlesex, UB8 1PD

Tel: 01895 233377
Fax: 01895 814031
E-mail: crhamilton@lineone.net

Enquiries:
Enquiries to: General Secretary

Organisation type and purpose:
National organisation, voluntary organisation.
National schools sports organisation – voluntarily staffed.

Subject coverage:
Coaching of gymnastics for boys and girls; organisation of national gymnastic competitions.

Printed publications:
Annual Handbook

Affiliated to:
British Amateur Gymnastics Association

BRITISH SCIENCE ASSOCIATION

Wellcome Wolfson Building, 165 Queen's Gate, London, SW7 5HD

Tel: 0870 770 7101
Fax: 0870 770 7102
E-mail: via website

Website:
http://www.britishscienceassociation.org/web
What's on, regions and branches, press office, contacts, publications.

Enquiries:
Enquiries to: Chief Executive

Founded:
1831

Formerly called:
British Association for the Advancement of Science (BA) (year of change 2009)

Organisation type and purpose:
A registered charity (charity number 212479 in England and Wales and SCO39236 in Scotland) that exists to advance the public understanding, accessibility and accountability of the sciences and engineering in the UK.

Subject coverage:
Organises major initiatives across the UK, including the annual British Science Festival, National Science and Engineering Week, programmes of regional and local events, and an extensive programme for young people in schools and colleges.

Education services:
Extensive programme for young people in schools and colleges.

Electronic and video publications:
Reports on topics as diverse as mental health and the effect of climate change on business
Evidence to Select Committees and advice to the OSI
Reports from conferences, working lunches and events
Order electronic and video publications from:
Download from website

Publications list:
Available online

Access to staff:
Contact by letter, by telephone, by fax and by e-mail

BRITISH SCIENCE FICTION ASSOCIATION LIMITED

Acronym or abbreviation: BSFA

8 West Avenue Road, London, E17 9SE

E-mail: bsfachair@gmail.com

Website:
http://www.bsfa.co.uk
BSFA website.
http://www.mjckeh.demon.co.uk/
BSFA magazine index.

Enquiries:
Enquiries to: Administrator

Founded:
1958

Organisation type and purpose:
Voluntary organisation.
Amateur association and company limited by guarantee dedicated to the enjoyment and promotion of science fiction.

Subject coverage:
Science fiction in general; publication sources; writers' forum; book reviews.

Museum or gallery collection, archive, or library special collection:
BSFA Library (based at Science Fiction Foundation, Liverpool University)

Printed publications:
Focus (2 times a year, for writers)
Matrix (news magazine, 6 times a year)
Vector (critical journal, 6 times a year)
A Very British Genre (a critical history of UK Science Fiction, Chapbook, free to members, non-members £5)
Omegatropic – Collection of fiction and non-fiction (Baxter S, £8 paperback, £20 hardback)

Publications list:
Available online

Access to staff:
Contact by letter, by e-mail and via website
Hours: Mon to Fri, 0900 to 1700

BRITISH SECURITY INDUSTRY ASSOCIATION LIMITED

Acronym or abbreviation: BSIA

Kirkham House, John Comyn Drive, Worcester, WR3 7NS

Tel: 0845 389 3889
Fax: 0845 389 0761
E-mail: info@bsia.co.uk

Website:
http://www.bsia.co.uk
Members' list, news, articles, events, information.

Enquiries:
Enquiries to: Press contacts
Direct e-mail: a.beesley@bsia.co.uk

Founded:
1967

Organisation type and purpose:
Trade association (membership is by subscription). To promote and encourage high standards of ethics, equipment and service throughout the industry.

Subject coverage:
All aspects of security, including guard and patrol services, security equipment manufacture and installation, physical and electronic security, access control, closed circuit television, locks and safes.

Trade and statistical information:
UK security industry market size by sector.

Printed publications:
Codes of practice
Information pack (free)
Security Direct
Spectrum (newsletter, 2 times a year, free)

Publications list:
Available online and in print

Access to staff:
Contact by letter, by telephone, by e-mail and via website
Hours: Mon to Fri, 0900 to 1715

BRITISH SHOOTING SPORTS COUNCIL

Acronym or abbreviation: BSSC

PO Box 53608, London, SE24 9YN

Tel: 020 7095 8181
Fax: 020 7095 8181
E-mail: djpbssc@btconnect.com

Website:
http://www.bssc.org.uk

Enquiries:
Enquiries to: Secretary

Founded:
1956

Organisation type and purpose:
Advisory body.
To promote and safeguard the lawful use of firearms and air weapons for sporting and recreational purposes in the United Kingdom amongst all sections of the community, to co-ordinate and present the views of member associations and other bodies.

Subject coverage:
The lawful manufacture and use of firearms, air weapons and ammunition in the United Kingdom, for sporting and recreational purposes. National policy for the use of firearms and air weapons.

Museum or gallery collection, archive, or library special collection:
Archive of Council

Printed publications:
Annual Report
Order printed publications from: BSSC, PO Box 53608, London, SE24 9YN

Electronic and video publications:
Annual Report and miscellaneous publications on website

Access to staff:
Contact by letter, by telephone and by e-mail
Hours: Mon to Fri, 0900 to 1700

Access to building, collection or gallery:
No access other than to staff

Links with:
Home Office Consultee on Shooting Issues
   tel: 020 7273 2623; fax: 020 7273 4284
World Forum of Shooting Sports Associations (WFSA)
   tel: +39 06 592 5971; fax: +39 06 322 0016

Member organisations:
Association of Professional Clay Target Shooting Grounds
   tel: 01295 678141; fax: 01295 670100
British Association for Shooting and Conservation
   tel: 024 4457 3000; fax: 024 4457 3001
Clay Pigeon Shooting Association
   tel: 01483 485400; fax: 01483 485410
Countryside Alliance
   tel: 020 7582 5432; fax: 020 7793 8484
Gun Trade Association
   tel: 01684 291865; fax: 01684 291864
Muzzle Loaders Association
   tel: 01734 590080; fax: 01734 590080
National Rifle Association
   tel: 01483 797777; fax: 01483 797285
National Small Bore Rifle Association
   tel: 01483 485500; fax: 01483 476392
Sportsman Association
   tel: 01772 863900; fax: 01772 866373
United Kingdom Practical Shooting Association
   tel: 01702 342501; fax: 01702 431775

BRITISH SHOW JUMPING ASSOCIATION

Acronym or abbreviation: BSJA

British Equestrian Centre, National Agricultural Centre, Stoneleigh Park, Kenilworth, Warwickshire, CV8 2LR

Tel: 024 7669 8800
Fax: 024 7669 6685
E-mail: bsja@bsja.co.uk

Website:
http://www.bsja.co.uk

Enquiries:
Enquiries to: Chief Executive

Founded:
1925

Organisation type and purpose:
Membership association.
National governing body.

Subject coverage:
National and international show jumping.

Printed publications:
Directory (monthly)

Rules Year Book (annually)
Show Jumper (magazine, quarterly)

Access to staff:
Contact by letter, by telephone, by fax and by e-mail
Hours: Mon to Fri, 0900 to 1700

BRITISH SIGN & GRAPHICS ASSOCIATION

Acronym or abbreviation: BSGA

5 Orton Enterprise Centre, Bakewell Road, Orton Southgate, Peterborough, Cambridgeshire, PE2 6XU

Tel: 01733 230033
Fax: 01733 230993
E-mail: info@bsga.co.uk

Website:
http://www.bsga.co.uk

Enquiries:
Enquiries to: Director

Founded:
1978

Organisation type and purpose:
Trade association.

Subject coverage:
Illuminated and non-illuminated signs.

Trade and statistical information:
Data on UK and European sign manufacturing markets.

Printed publications:
BSGA News (quarterly)
Sign Directions Magazine (bi-monthly)

Publications list:
Available in print

Access to staff:
Contact by letter, by telephone, by fax, by e-mail and via website. Appointment necessary.
Hours: Mon to Thu, 0900 to 1700; Fri 0900 to 1600

Affiliated to:
European Federation of Illuminated Signs and the Outdoor Advertising Council

BRITISH SIKH FEDERATION

Acronym or abbreviation: BSF

PO Box 242, Wolverhampton, West Midlands, WV4 5DH

Tel: 01242 226517
Fax: 01242 226517
E-mail: british_sikh_fed@btopenworld.com

Website:
http://www.british-sikh-federation.org

Enquiries:
Enquiries to: General Secretary
Direct tel: 07221 507055

Founded:
1984

Organisation type and purpose:
Voluntary organisation.
Tackles UK political and religious issues of a serious nature for the British Sikh community.

Subject coverage:
Politics, religion, legal and business issues as they relate to the Sikh community, contacts for other Sikh organisations, interests of 600,000 British Sikhs.

Access to staff:
Contact by letter and by e-mail. Access for members only.
Hours: Mon to Fri, 0900 to 1700

BRITISH SIMMENTAL CATTLE SOCIETY

National Agricultural Centre, Stoneleigh Park, Kenilworth, Warwickshire, CV8 2LG

Tel: 024 7669 6513
Fax: 024 7669 6724
E-mail: information@britishsimmental.co.uk

Website:
http://www.britishsimmental.co.uk

Enquiries:
Enquiries to: General Secretary

Founded:
1970

Organisation type and purpose:
Membership association (membership is by subscription), registered charity (charity number 985570).
Registration and promotion of Simmentals.

Subject coverage:
Breeds of beef cattle.

Printed publications:
Annual Review (free to members)

Access to staff:
Contact by letter, by telephone and by fax.
Appointment necessary.
Hours: Mon to Fri, 0900 to 1700

BRITISH SMALL ANIMAL VETERINARY ASSOCIATION

Acronym or abbreviation: BSAVA

Woodrow House, 1 Telford Way, Waterwells Business Park, Quedgeley, Gloucestershire, GL2 4AB

Tel: 01452 726700
Fax: 01452 726701
E-mail: adminoff@bsava.com

Website:
http://www.bsava.com

Enquiries:
Enquiries to: Administration Officer

Founded:
1957

Organisation type and purpose:
Membership association (membership is by subscription, qualification), present number of members: 5700, registered charity (charity number 1024811).
To foster and promote high scientific and educational standards of small animal medicine and surgery in practice, teaching and research.

Subject coverage:
Health, welfare and diseases of small animals, birds and fish; veterinary science and medicine.

Printed publications:
An Introduction to Veterinary Anatomy and Physiology
Flea Allergic Skin Disease in Cats (£1 plus p&p)
Journal of Small Animal Practice (monthly)
Manual of Anaesthesia in Small Animal Practice
Manual of Canine Behaviour (£30.50 plus p&p)
Manual of Companion Animal Nutrition and Feeding (£60 plus p&p)
Manual of Exotic Pets
Manual of Feline Behaviour (£17 plus p&p)
Manual of Ornamental Fish
Manual of Psittacine Birds
Manual of Reptiles
Manual of Small Animal Neurology (2nd ed., 1995)
Practical Veterinary Nursing (3rd ed.)

Electronic and video publications:
BSAVA Congress Lectures 1995–2001 are available on CD-ROM

Parent body:
British Veterinary Association

BRITISH SNORING AND SLEEP APNOEA ASSOCIATION LIMITED

Acronym or abbreviation: BSSAA

1 Duncroft Close, Reigate, Surrey, RH2 9DE

Tel: 01737 245638
Fax: 01737 248744
E-mail: helpline@britishsnoring.co.uk

Website:
http://www.britishsnoring.co.uk

Enquiries:
Enquiries to: Helpline staff
Other contacts: Information Officer, Help Line Manager

Founded:
1991

Organisation type and purpose:
International organisation, national organisation, membership association, voluntary organisation.

Subject coverage:
Snoring and sleep apnoea and related topics, including surgery, treatment and prevention.

Printed publications:
Information leaflets available (A4 sae plus £2.50 donation cheque)
Sound Asleep (quarterly, £10 a year)
Library articles (£1.50 each)
Back issues of Sound Asleep (£5 each)

Access to staff:
Contact by letter, by telephone, by fax, by e-mail and via website
Hours: Mon to Fri, 0900 to 1700

BRITISH SOCIETY FOR ALLERGY AND CLINICAL IMMUNOLOGY

Acronym or abbreviation: BSACI

BSACI Secretariat, 66 Weston Park, Thames Ditton, Surrey, KT7 0HL

Tel: 020 8398 9240
Fax: 020 8398 2766
E-mail: susanmduff@cs.com

Website:
http://www.bsaci.soton.ac.uk/bsaci/
Membership information.

Enquiries:
Enquiries to: Administrator
Other contacts: President, Secretary, Newsletter Editor

Founded:
1948

Organisation type and purpose:
Learned society (membership is by qualification), present number of members: 580, registered charity.
The recognition of allergy and clinical immunology as a specialised branch of medicine; to advance and encourage study of the subject.

Subject coverage:
Allergy, clinical immunology.

Printed publications:
Clinical and Experimental Allergy (journal, monthly)

Access to staff:
Contact by letter, by telephone, by fax and by e-mail
Hours: Mon to Fri, 0900 to 1700

Affiliated to:
EAACI
IAACI

BRITISH SOCIETY FOR CELL BIOLOGY

Acronym or abbreviation: BSCB

School of Biosciences, Faculty of Medical Sciences, University of Newcastle, Newcastle upon Tyne, NE2 4HH

Tel: 0191 222 5264
Fax: 0191 222 6706
E-mail: michael.whitaker@ncl.ac.uk

Website:
http://www.bscb.org
News, information about scientific meetings, contact details, educational content.

Enquiries:
Enquiries to: Secretary

Founded:
1965

Organisation type and purpose:
Learned society.

Subject coverage:
Research in the general field of cell and molecular biology and cytology, applications of cell biology in the commercial and biomedical fields.

Printed publications:
BSCB Handbook of Members

Access to staff:
Contact by letter, by telephone, by fax and by e-mail. Appointment necessary.
Hours: Mon to Fri, 0900 to 1700

Constituent society of the:
European Cell Biology Organization

BRITISH SOCIETY FOR CLINICAL CYTOLOGY

Acronym or abbreviation: BSCC

PO Box 352, Uxbridge, Middlesex, UB10 9AU

Tel: 01895 274020
Fax: 01895 274080
E-mail: mail@bscc.uk.net

Website:
http://www.clinicalcytology.co.uk

Enquiries:
Enquiries to: Secretariat
Direct e-mail: mail@bscc.uk.net

Organisation type and purpose:
Learned society.

Subject coverage:
Clinical cytology; diagnostic cytopathology; education and training for medical and non-medical personnel.

Printed publications:
Newsletter (3 times a year)

Access to staff:
Contact by letter, by telephone, by fax and by e-mail
Hours: Mon, Wed, Thu, 0900 to 1700

Access to building, collection or gallery:
No access other than to staff

Affiliated to:
International Academy of Cytology

Has:
9 affiliated regional cytology societies

Member of:
European Federation of Cytology Societies

BRITISH SOCIETY FOR DENTAL RESEARCH

Acronym or abbreviation: BSDR

Restorative Dentistry, The Dental School, Framlington Place, Newcastle upon Tyne, NE2 4BW

Tel: 0191 222 7823
Fax: 0191 222 8191
E-mail: a.w.g.walls@ncl.ac.uk

Website:
http://www.bsdr.org.uk

Details of meetings, registration, constitutions, management committee members, BSDR Research Groups – Contacts, newsletter, BSDR competitions.

Enquiries:
Enquiries to: Honorary Secretary

Founded:
1952

Organisation type and purpose:
International organisation, learned society, registered charity, research organisation.

Subject coverage:
Dental public health, forensic dentistry, oral and dental sciences, dental materials, implant research, restorative dentistry, oral medicine, oral microbiology and immunology, oral pathology, oral surgery, mineralised tissues, oral anatomy and histology, oral biochemistry and physiology.

Printed publications:
Journal of Dental Research (monthly, from IADR Headquarters 1619 Duke Street, Alexandria, VA, USA)
Newsletter (annually)

Access to staff:
Contact by letter, by telephone, by fax, by e-mail and via website
Hours: Mon to Fri, 0900 to 1700

Affiliated to:
International Association for Dental Research 1619 Duke Street, Alexandria, VA, USA

BRITISH SOCIETY FOR DEVELOPMENTAL BIOLOGY

Acronym or abbreviation: BSDB

Department of Developmental Neurobiology, UMDS, Guy's Hospital, London, SE1 9RT

Tel: 020 7955 4798
Fax: 020 7955 4886
E-mail: bsdb@kcl.ac.uk

Website:
http://www.ana.ed.ac.uk/BSDB

Enquiries:
Enquiries to: Secretary
Direct tel: 020 7848 6547
Direct fax: 020 7848 6550
Direct e-mail: ivor.mason@kcl.ac.uk

Founded:
1964

Organisation type and purpose:
Learned society.

Subject coverage:
Developmental biology.

Printed publications:
Newsletter

Access to staff:
Contact by letter
Hours: Mon to Fri, 0900 to 1700

Affiliated to:
United Kingdom Life Sciences Council

BRITISH SOCIETY FOR GEOMORPHOLOGY

Acronym or abbreviation: BSG

Royal Geographical Society (with IBG), 1 Kensington Gore, London, SW7 2AR

E-mail: bsg@rgs.org

Website:
http://www.geomorphology.org.uk

Enquiries:
Enquiries to: Honorary Secretary
Other contacts: Administrator

Founded:
1960

Organisation type and purpose:
Learned society.

Subject coverage:
Geomorphology: landforms, earth surface processes, sedimentology, earth materials, hydrology, Quaternary stratigraphy, Quaternary studies; fluvial, coastal, glacial, periglacial, tropical and arid environment processes and landforms; land deposits.

Printed publications:
BGRG Technical Bulletins (30 titles, Hardisty, University of Hull)
Earth Surface Processes and Landforms (journal, 13 times a year, John Wiley)
Symposium Series (John Wiley)
Order printed publications from: John Wiley & Sons, 43 Leinster Gardens, London, W2 3AN

Access to staff:
Contact by letter and by e-mail
Hours: Mon to Fri, 0900 to 1700

Links with:
Royal Geographical Society (with IBG)

BRITISH SOCIETY FOR HAEMATOLOGY

Acronym or abbreviation: BSH

100 White Lion Street, London, N1 9PF

Tel: 020 7713 0990
Fax: 020 7837 1931
E-mail: info@b-s-h.org.uk

Website:
http://www.b-s-h.org.uk

Enquiries:
Enquiries to: Administrator

Founded:
1962

Organisation type and purpose:
Learned society, registered charity (charity number 1005735).

Subject coverage:
General haematology, including diagnosis and treatment of blood diseases, leukaemia, haemophilia and other bleeding diseases, lymphomas. Equipment used in haematological laboratories, quality control and standards in haematological laboratories, blood transfusion and blood products (preparation and clinical use).

Printed publications:
Newsletters
Publicity material

Access to staff:
Contact by letter, by telephone, by fax, by e-mail and via website
Hours: Flexible

BRITISH SOCIETY FOR IMMUNOLOGY

Acronym or abbreviation: BSI

Vintage House, 37 Albert Embankment, London, SE1 7TL

Tel: 020 3031 9800
Fax: 020 7582 2882
E-mail: bsi@immunology.org

Website:
http://www.immunology.org
Society activities, publications, meetings, conferences and events, immunology-related jobs.

Founded:
1956

Organisation type and purpose:
Learned society (membership is by subscription, qualification, election or invitation), present number of members: 4,000, registered charity (charity number 1043255).

Subject coverage:
Immunology; biochemical immunology, materno-foetal immunology, comparative and veterinary immunology, mucosal immunology, neuroimmunology, histocompatibility and immunogenetics, clinical immunology.

Printed publications:
Clinical & Experimental Immunology (monthly)
Immunology (monthly)
Immunology News (6 times a year)

Electronic and video publications:
Immunology online
Clinical & Experimental Immunology online

Publications list:
Available in print

Access to staff:
Contact by letter, by telephone, by fax, by e-mail and via website. Appointment necessary.
Hours: Mon to Fri, 0900 to 1700

Member organisation of:
European Federation of Immunological Societies
International Union of Immunological Societies
Society of Biology

BRITISH SOCIETY FOR MEDICAL AND DENTAL HYPNOSIS

Acronym or abbreviation: BSMDH (MET&S)

(Metropolitan and South), Flat 23, Broadfield Heights, Broadfield Avenue, Edgware, Middlesex, HA8 8PF

Tel: 020 8905 4342
Fax: 020 8958 8069

Enquiries:
Enquiries to: Referral Secretary

Founded:
1960

Organisation type and purpose:
Learned society.

Subject coverage:
Use of hypnosis in dentistry and medicine. Training of doctors, dentists and clinical psychologists. Referral service for members of public, medical and dental practitioners.

Access to staff:
Contact by letter and by telephone
Hours: Mon to Fri, 0900 to 1700
Special comments: Telephone for referral requests.

Links with:
European Society for Hypnosis
International Society of Hypnosis

BRITISH SOCIETY FOR MERCURY FREE DENTISTRY

Acronym or abbreviation: BSMFD

225 Old Brompton Road, London, SW5 0EA

Tel: 020 7373 3655
Fax: 020 7736 2480

Enquiries:
Enquiries to: President

Organisation type and purpose:
Advisory body, professional body, registered charity.

Subject coverage:
Mercury poisoning from dental amalgam filling.

Access to staff:
Contact by letter and by telephone. All charged.
Hours: Mon to Fri, 0900 to 1700

BRITISH SOCIETY FOR MUSIC THERAPY

Acronym or abbreviation: BSMT

2nd Floor, 24–27 White Lion Street, London, N1 9PD

Tel: 020 7837 6100
Fax: 020 7837 6142
E-mail: info@bsmt.org

Website:
http://www.bsmt.org
Information on music therapy, training and publications.

Enquiries:
Enquiries to: Administrator
Other contacts: Chairperson

Founded:
1958

Organisation type and purpose:
International organisation, learned society (membership is by subscription), present number of members: 850, registered charity (charity number 260837). BSMT and APMT will be forming a new organisation together under a new name in the winter of 2010.
To promote the use and development of music therapy.

Subject coverage:
Use and development of music therapy.

Non-library collection catalogue:
All or part available online, in-house and in print

Library catalogue:
All or part available online, in-house and in print

Printed publications:
BSMT bulletin (2 times a year, members)
BSMT information booklet
BSMT booklist
Index of articles in the British Journal of Music Therapy
British Journal of Music Therapy (2 times a year, members)
Conference paper – Changes; exploring clinical, professional and global perspectives BSMT/APMT Conference – February 2004 (conference paper, £12 plus £2 p&p)
Conference paper – Community, Relationship and Spirit: Continuing the dialogue and debate BSMT/APMT Conference February 2004 (conference paper, £12 plus £2 p&p)
BSMT also sells a large number of books on music therapy

Electronic and video publications:
Music for Life (CD, £11.70)
Music Therapy at the Child Development Centre, Cambridge (video, £16 plus £2 p&p)
Timothy – Music therapy with a little boy who has Asperger Syndrome (video, £16 plus £2 p&p)
Training as a Music Therapist, the MA in Music Therapy at APU (video, £16 plus £2 p&p)
Music Therapy for Children on the Autistic Spectrum (video, £16 plus £2 p&p)
Joshua and Barry – Music therapy with a partially-sighted little boy with cerebral palsy (video, £16 plus £2 p&p)
Sounds and Meaning – Group Music Therapy with People with Profound Learning Difficulties and their Carers (video, £19 plus £2 p&p)
Ice Calm – Background Patterns for Improvisation (CD, £9 plus £2 p&p)
Music Therapy with Children (CD-Rom, £15.95 plus £2 p&p)

Publications list:
Available online and in print

Access to staff:
Contact by letter, by telephone, by fax and by e-mail. Appointment necessary.
Hours: Mon to Thu, 0930 to 1530

Access to building, collection or gallery:
No access other than to staff

Links with:
Association of Professional Music Therapists
2nd Floor, 24–27 White Lion Street, London, N1 9PD; tel: 020 7837 6100; fax: 020 7837 6142; e-mail: apmtoffice@aol.com; website: http://www.apmt.org

BRITISH SOCIETY FOR PARASITOLOGY

Acronym or abbreviation: BSP

24 The Paddock, Hitchin, SG4 9EF

Tel: 01462 624081; 01462 451618
Fax: 01462 648693
E-mail: hedgepigs@aol.com

Website:
http://www.bsp.uk.net
Information on BSP and benefits of membership;
details of meetings and registration; secure
members-only area

Enquiries:
Enquiries to: Honorary General Secretary
Direct e-mail: info@bsp.uk.net; at info@bsp.uk.net
(Secretariat)
Other contacts: Secretariat

Founded:
1962

Organisation type and purpose:
International organisation, national organisation,
learned society (membership is by subscription),
present number of members: 1000, registered
charity (charity number 206847), suitable for ages:
18 plus.

Subject coverage:
All aspects of parasitology including human,
animal, fish and plant diseases caused by parasites;
study of parasites including physiology,
biochemistry, immunology, ecology, pathology.

Printed publications:
Autumn Symposium Proceedings (annually,
Cambridge University Press)
Newsletter (for members, quarterly)

Access to staff:
Contact by letter, by telephone, by fax, by e-mail
and via website
Hours: Mon to Fri, 0900 to 1700

BRITISH SOCIETY FOR RESTORATIVE DENTISTRY

Acronym or abbreviation: BSRD

Department of Restorative Dentistry, The Royal
London Hospital, Whitechapel, London, E1 1BB

Enquiries:
Enquiries to: Honorary Secretary

Organisation type and purpose:
Learned society.

Subject coverage:
General or specialised information on restorative
dentistry, the conservation of teeth and the
improvement of their appearance (the Society does
not recommend by name individual dentists able
to carry out this work).

Printed publications:
European Journal of Prosthodontics and
Restorative Dentistry (quarterly)
Members Newsletter

Access to staff:
Contact by letter
Hours: Mon to Fri, 0900 to 1700

BRITISH SOCIETY FOR RHEUMATOLOGY

Acronym or abbreviation: BSR

Bride House, 18–20 Bride Lane, London, EC4Y 8EE

Tel: 020 7842 0900
Fax: 020 7842 0901
E-mail: bsr@rheumatology.org.uk

Website:
http://www.rheumatology.org.uk

Enquiries:
Enquiries to: Chief Executive

Founded:
1984

Organisation type and purpose:
Learned society, registered charity.

Subject coverage:
Rheumatology, education for medical staff,
research conferences, information for providers/
purchasers of rheumatology services, also runs
British Health Professionals in Rheumatology
(BHPR) and Arthritis and Musculoskeletal Alliance
(ARMA).

**Museum or gallery collection, archive, or library
special collection:**
The Heberden Library – based at the Royal College
of Physicians

Trade and statistical information:
Can provide access to epidemiological information
eg number of people with osteoarthritis in UK.

Printed publications:
Annual Report
Rheumatology (journal, monthly, free to members,
on subscription to others)
BSR Newsletter (3 times a year)
Handbook (annually, members only)
Information for Purchasers of Rheumatology
Services

Access to staff:
Contact by letter
Hours: Mon to Fri, 0830 to 1730

Access to building, collection or gallery:
Prior appointment required

Access for disabled people:
Parking provided

Member of:
Arthritis & Musculoskeletal Alliance (ARMA)
at the same address
European League Against Rheumatism (EULAR)

BRITISH SOCIETY FOR STRAIN MEASUREMENT

Acronym or abbreviation: BSSM

71 Hillview Drive, Clarkston, Glasgow, G76 7JJ

Tel: 0141 577 6297
Fax: 0141 577 6281
E-mail: bssmsec@moragmac.clara.net

Enquiries:
Enquiries to: Honorary Secretary

Founded:
1964

Organisation type and purpose:
Learned society.

Subject coverage:
Strain measurement by strain gauges, brittle
lacquers, photoelasticity extensometers, strain
transducers and other optical methods;
experimental stress analysis and other
experimental engineering evaluation, theoretical
analysis, engineering measurements by
transducers; data logging and data handling.

Printed publications:
Strain (quarterly)

Access to staff:
Contact by letter, by telephone, by fax and by e-
mail
Hours: Mon to Fri, 0900 to 1700

BRITISH SOCIETY FOR THE HISTORY OF PHARMACY

Acronym or abbreviation: BSHP

840 Melton Road, Thurmaston, Leicester, LE4 8BN

Tel: 0116 264 0083
Fax: 0116 264 0141
E-mail: bshp@associationhq.org.uk

Website:
http://www.bshp.org

Enquiries:
Enquiries to: Secretary

Founded:
1967

Organisation type and purpose:
Learned society.

Subject coverage:
History of pharmacy in Britain, pharmaceutical
antiques.

Printed publications:
Pharmaceutical Historian (4 times a year)
Transactions (occasional)

Access to staff:
Contact by letter and by e-mail
Hours: Mon to Fri, 0900 to 1700

Affiliated to:
Royal Pharmaceutical Society of Great Britain

BRITISH SOCIETY FOR THE HISTORY OF SCIENCE

Acronym or abbreviation: BSHS

PO Box 3401, Norwich, Norfolk, NR7 7JF

Tel: 01603 516236
E-mail: office@bshs.org.uk

Website:
http://www.bshs.org.uk
History of science information and activities.

Enquiries:
Enquiries to: Executive Secretary

Founded:
1947

Organisation type and purpose:
International organisation, learned society
(membership is by subscription), present number
of members: 700, registered charity (charity
number 258854).
To promote and further the study of the history
and philosophy of science.

Subject coverage:
History and philosophy of science.

Non-library collection catalogue:
All or part available online

Printed publications:
British Journal for the History of Science (4 times a
year, free to members, £134 a year to non-
members)
List of Theses in History of Science in British
Universities and Polytechnics (online)
Monograph Series (12 current titles)
Newsletter (3 times a year, free to members, £10 a
year to non-members)
Viewpoint
Order printed publications from: British Journal for
the History of Science, Cambridge University
Press, FREEPOST, The Edinburgh Building,
Shaftesbury Road, Cambridge, CB2 1BR

Electronic and video publications:
British Journal for the History of Science (Online by
arrangement with Cambridge University Press)
Wheeler Library online project (in preparation)

Publications list:
Available online and in print

Access to staff:
Contact by letter, by telephone, by fax, by e-mail
and via website. Appointment necessary.
Hours: Mon to Fri, 0900 to 1700

Links with:
Association for Science Education
History of Science Society (USA)
e-mail: info@hssonline.org; website: http://www
.hssonline.org

BRITISH SOCIETY FOR THE STUDY OF PROSTHETIC DENTISTRY

Acronym or abbreviation: BSSPD

Division of Restorative Dentistry, University Dental School and Hospital, Wilton, Cork, Republic of Ireland

Tel: 00 353 21 490 1186
Fax: 00353 21 490 1193
E-mail: finbarralen@hotmail.com

Website:
http://www.derweb.ac.uk/bsspd

Enquiries:
Enquiries to: Honorary Secretary

Organisation type and purpose:
Learned society.

Subject coverage:
Prosthetic dentistry.

Access to staff:
Contact by letter, by fax and by e-mail
Hours: Mon to Fri, 0900 to 1700

Affiliated to:
European Prosthodontic Association

Conference organiser:
British Society for the Study of Prosthetic Dentistry Birmingham Dental School, St Chad's Queensway, Birmingham; e-mail: c.w.barclay@bham.ac.uk

BRITISH SOCIETY OF AESTHETICS

Acronym or abbreviation: BSA

c/o Kathleen Stock, Dept. of Philosophy, University of Sussex, Falmer, Brighton, BN1 9QN

E-mail: kathleen@british-aesthetics.org

Website:
http://www.british-aesthetics.org

Enquiries:
Enquiries to: Honorary Secretary

Founded:
1965

Organisation type and purpose:
International organisation, learned society (membership is by subscription).

Subject coverage:
Aesthetics, philosophy of the arts and criticism, theory of beauty.

Printed publications:
British Journal of Aesthetics
BSA Newsletter

Access to staff:
Contact by letter, by e-mail and via website
Hours: Mon to Fri, 0900 to 1700

Member of:
British Philosophical Association
International Association of Aesthetics

Organisers of the:
Collaborative European Conferences

BRITISH SOCIETY OF ANIMAL SCIENCE

Acronym or abbreviation: BSAS

PO Box 3, Penicuik, Midlothian, EH26 0RZ

Tel: 0131 445 4508
Fax: 0131 535 3120
E-mail: bsas@ed.sac.ac.uk

Website:
http://www.bsas.org.uk

Enquiries:
Enquiries to: Secretary
Direct tel: 01848 331437
Direct fax: 01848 331437

Other contacts: Finance Officer for membership and financial matters.

Founded:
1943

Organisation type and purpose:
National organisation, learned society (membership is by subscription), present number of members: 1100, service industry, registered charity, suitable for ages: 18+.
Educational society.

Subject coverage:
Animal science in most areas and species, research, welfare, nutrition, breeding/genetics.

Printed publications:
Animal Science (6 times a year)
Occasional Publications (proceedings of conferences or meetings, 1 or 2 times a year) including:
Animal Choices
Animal Production in Developing Countries
Hill and Upland Livestock Production
Safety & Quality of Food from Animals
Metabolic Stress in Dairy Cows
Milk Composition
Fertility in the High Producing Dairy Cow
Animal Welfare – Who Writes The Rules
Challenge of Genetic Change in Animal Production

Electronic and video publications:
Various CD-ROMs to purchase, direct
Annual Meeting Proceedings (CD-ROM)
Animal Science – BSAS Journal (CD-ROM)

Publications list:
Available in print

Access to staff:
Contact by letter, by telephone, by fax and by e-mail
Hours: Mon to Fri, 0900 to 1700

Member of:
Biological Society
European Association for Animal Production (EAAP)
Via A Torlonia 15/A, Rome, I-00161, Italy

BRITISH SOCIETY OF AUDIOLOGY

Acronym or abbreviation: BSA

80 Brighton Road, Reading, Berkshire, RG6 1PS

Tel: 0118 966 0622
Fax: 0118 935 1915
E-mail: bsa@thebsa.org.uk

Website:
http://www.thebsa.org.uk
Information about the society.

Enquiries:
Enquiries to: Administrator

Founded:
1966

Organisation type and purpose:
National organisation, professional body (membership is by subscription), present number of members: 1400, registered charity (charity number 261060).
Umbrella organisation in audiology services.

Subject coverage:
Audiology; otology; hearing; hearing loss; clinical audiological practice.

Museum or gallery collection, archive, or library special collection:
Hearing aid museum (now at Thackray Museum, Leeds)

Library catalogue:
All or part available in-house

Printed publications:
International Journal of Audiology (12 times a year, pub. Informa)
BSA News (3 times a year)

Careers in Audiology
Educational pamphlets and booklets
Procedures in Audiology

Access to staff:
Contact by letter, by telephone, by fax and by e-mail
Hours: Mon to Fri, 0900 to 1400

Access to building, collection or gallery:
No access other than to staff

BRITISH SOCIETY OF CLINICAL AND ACADEMIC HYPNOSIS

Acronym or abbreviation: BSCAH

Inspiration House, Redbrook Grove, Sheffield, S20 6RR

Tel: 0844 884 3116
Fax: 0844 884 3116
E-mail: bscah@btinternet.com

Website:
http://www.bscah.com
Information about hypnosis, list of approved practitioners, professional training and events, links to resources.

Enquiries:
Enquiries to: Secretary

Founded:
1952

Created by the merger of:
British Society of Medical and Dental Hypnosis (BSMDH) and British Society of Experimental and Clinical Hypnosis (BSECH – founded 1977) (year of change 2007)

Formerly called:
British Society of Dental Hypnosis (year of change 1955); Dental and Medical Society for the Study of Hypnosis (year of change 1968); British Society of Medical and Dental Hypnosis (BSMDH) (year of change 2007)

Organisation type and purpose:
A non-profit making registered charity (charity number 1012806), a national organisation of health care practitioners and academics.
To promote the safe and responsible use of hypnosis in medicine, dentistry, and psychology, and to educate both professional colleagues and the public about hypnosis and its uses; to promote and maintain the highest professional standards in the practice of hypnosis for clinical or experimental purposes and in the dissemination of information concerning hypnosis; to advance the science of hypnosis and promote the evidence-base for clinical hypnosis as a therapeutic tool, by using research to guide interventions and clinical practice to guide research.

Subject coverage:
Clinical hypnosis. Believes that the safe use of clinical hypnosis as a therapeutic tool is best in the hands of practitioners who are qualified to treat patients without hypnosis. Encourages the conduct of research and audit of practices of the subject of clinical hypnosis and the publication of the useful results of that research.

Access to staff:
Contact by letter, by telephone, by fax and by e-mail

Constituent part of:
European Society of Hypnosis
International Society of Hypnosis

BRITISH SOCIETY OF DOWSERS

Acronym or abbreviation: BSD

4–5 Cygnet Centre, Worcester Road, Hanley Swan, Worcs, WR8 0EA

Tel: 01684 576969
Fax: 01684 311388
E-mail: info@britishdowsers.org

continued overleaf

Website:
http://www.britishdowsers.org
Full details of the society and its activities.

Enquiries:
Enquiries to: Director

Founded:
1933

Organisation type and purpose:
International organisation, learned society
(membership is by subscription), present number
of members: 1,600, registered charity (charity
number 295911), training organisation.

Subject coverage:
Dowsing (water divining) for geophysical,
medical, agricultural and other purposes;
radiesthesia; professional operators.

**Museum or gallery collection, archive, or library
special collection:**
Library of books on dowsing, radiesthesia and
allied subjects

Non-library collection catalogue:
All or part available online

Printed publications:
Dowsing Today (3 times a year, to members only)

Electronic and video publications:
Swings and Roundabouts Electronic Newsletter

Access to staff:
Contact by letter, by telephone, by fax, by e-mail,
in person and via website. Appointment necessary.
Hours: Mon to Fri, 0900 to 1300 and 1400 to 1700

Access to building, collection or gallery:
Mon to Fri, 1030 to 1500

BRITISH SOCIETY OF
GASTROENTEROLOGY

Acronym or abbreviation: BSG

3 St Andrews Place, Regent's Park, London, NW1
4LB

Tel: 020 7935 3150
Fax: 020 7487 3734
E-mail: enquiries@bsg.org.uk

Website:
http://www.bsg.org.uk
Information on membership. Working Party
Reports and Guidelines all produced in-house.

Enquiries:
Enquiries to: Chief Executive

Founded:
1937

Organisation type and purpose:
Learned society, professional body (membership is
by qualification), registered charity (charity
number 258713), research organisation.

Subject coverage:
Clinical and scientific aspects of the structure and
function of the gastrointestinal system and its
appendages; liver disease; gastrointestinal
endoscopy.

Printed publications:
GUT (monthly, free to members)

Electronic and video publications:
Various clinical guidelines available (website)

Publications list:
Available online

Access to staff:
Contact by letter, by telephone, by fax, by e-mail
and via website
Hours: Mon to Fri, 0900 to 1700

BRITISH SOCIETY OF
GERONTOLOGY

Acronym or abbreviation: BSG

PO Box 607, 8 Queenswood Grove, York, YO24
4PP

E-mail: britishgerontology@yahoo.co.uk

Website:
http://www.britishgerontology.org

Enquiries:
Enquiries to: Administrator

Founded:
1971

Organisation type and purpose:
Learned society (membership is by subscription),
present number of members: 650, registered
charity (charity number 264385).

Subject coverage:
Quality of life in old age. Implications of ageing
societies and populations. Social care of older
people.

Printed publications:
Ageing and Society (6 times a year, Cambridge
University Press)
Ageing in Society: An introduction to social
gerontology (1993, Sage Publications)
Directory of Members' Research (2002, BSG)
Generations Review (quarterly, free to members,
BSG)

Publications list:
Available in print

Access to staff:
Contact by letter and by e-mail
Hours: Mon to Fri, 0900 to 1700

Member organisation of:
Academy of Learned Societies for the Social
Sciences (ALSISS)
  tel: 020 7468 2296; fax: 020 7468 2296; e-mail:
  andy.cawdell@the-academy.org.uk
International Association of Gerontology –
European Region
  tel: + 34 91 807 0874; fax: + 34 91 807 5637
International Association of Gerontology (IAG)
  tel: + 61 8 8201 7552; fax: + 61 8 8201 7551; e-mail:
  cas@flinders.edu.au

BRITISH SOCIETY OF HEARING
AID AUDIOLOGISTS

Formal name: British Society of Hearing Aid
Audiologists Limited
Acronym or abbreviation: BSHAA

9 Lukins Drive, Great Dunmow, Essex, CM6 1XQ

Tel: 01371 876623
Fax: 01371 876623
E-mail: secretary@bshaa.com

Website:
http://www.bshaa.com
General information on hearing difficulty,
directory of Hearing Aid Dispensers.

Enquiries:
Enquiries to: Executive Secretary

Founded:
1954

Organisation type and purpose:
Professional body, trade association, membership
association (membership is by subscription),
present number of members: 650.

Subject coverage:
Hearing aid audiology; education and research in
acoustics relating to hearing aids.

Printed publications:
Newsletter (quarterly)

Access to staff:
Contact by letter and by telephone
Hours: Mon to Sun, 0900 to 1700

**Approved education body for the examinations
of the:**
Hearing Aid Council

BRITISH SOCIETY OF
HYPNOTHERAPISTS

Acronym or abbreviation: BSH

37 Orbain Road, Fulham, London, SW6 7JZ

Tel: 020 7385 1166
Fax: 020 7385 1166
E-mail: syhyp@onetel.net

Website:
http://www.bsh1950.fsnet.co.uk

Enquiries:
Enquiries to: Secretary

Founded:
1950

Organisation type and purpose:
Professional body.

Subject coverage:
Clinical and educational applications of
hypnotherapy; information on training courses,
training standards and qualifications;
hypnotherapy for patients suffering from
functional nervous problems and unwanted habits
such as smoking; phobias, depression and
insomnia; stammering, asthma etc (psychosomatic
conditions); hypnotherapy as complementary to
orthodox medicine.

Access to staff:
Contact by letter, by telephone, by fax and by e-
mail
Hours: Mon to Fri, 0900 to 1700

Access to building, collection or gallery:
No access other than to staff

BRITISH SOCIETY OF MAGAZINE
EDITORS

Acronym or abbreviation: BSME

Administrator, c/o Gill Branston & Associates, 137
Hale Lane, Edgware, Middlesex, HA8 9QP

Tel: 020 8906 4664
E-mail: via website

Website:
http://www.bsme.com
List of members, news, events, BSME awards,
BSME network, BSME TV.

Enquiries:
Direct fax: 020 8959 2137
Direct e-mail: info@gillbranston.com

Organisation type and purpose:
A membership association (membership is by
subscription), the only society exclusively for
magazine editors in the UK. Full membership is
open to serving editors, website editors, editors-in-
chief and editorial directors of recognised
consumer, business or customer magazines
published in the UK; members include the editors
of magazines and websites as diverse as Prima,
Glamour, YOU Magazine, Supply Management,
Elle, Take a Break, Handbag.com and Waitrose
Food Illustrated.
To represent the needs and views of all magazine
editors, and enhance their status, acting as a voice
for the industry.

Subject coverage:
Editing magazines.

Access to staff:
Contact by letter, by telephone, by fax, by e-mail
and via website

BRITISH SOCIETY OF MASTER
GLASS PAINTERS

Acronym or abbreviation: BSMGP

5 Tivoli Place, Ilkley, West Yorkshire, LS29 8SU

E-mail: bsmgp@cix.co.uk

Website:
http://www.bsmgp.org.uk
Events, courses, portfolios of work.

Enquiries:
Enquiries to: Honorary Secretary

Founded:
1921

Organisation type and purpose:
Learned society, voluntary organisation.
To promote and elevate the art and craft of glass painting and staining and the conservation and appreciation of historic stained glass.

Subject coverage:
Glass painting, use of decorative glass in churches and secular buildings, conservation and restoration services by accredited craftsmen.

Printed publications:
Directory of members' work
Newsletter (quarterly)
The Journal of Stained Glass

Access to staff:
Contact by letter, by e-mail and via website
Hours: Mon to Fri, 0900 to 1700
Special comments: Please enclose sae for reply.

BRITISH SOCIETY OF NEURORADIOLOGISTS

Acronym or abbreviation: BSNR

Department of Radiology, Hull Royal Infirmary, Anlaby Road, Hull, East Yorkshire

Tel: 01482 674083
Fax: 01482 320137
E-mail: rjvbartlett50@hotmail.com

Enquiries:
Enquiries to: Honorary Secretary

Founded:
1970

Organisation type and purpose:
Learned society.

Subject coverage:
Neuroradiology: training, post availability and career prospects.

Printed publications:
Effective Neuroradiology

Access to staff:
Contact by letter, by telephone, by fax and by e-mail
Hours: Mon to Fri, 0900 to 1700

Recognised by the:
Royal College of Radiologists

BRITISH SOCIETY OF PERIODONTOLOGY

Acronym or abbreviation: BSP

BSP Administrative Manager, P O Box 334, Leeds, LS19 9FJ

Tel: 0844 335 1915
Fax: 0844 335 1915

Website:
http://www.bsperio.org.uk

Enquiries:
Enquiries to: Administrator

Founded:
1949

Organisation type and purpose:
Learned society, registered charity (charity number 265815).

Subject coverage:
Dentistry, periodontology, periodontics, periodontal diseases, dental hygiene.

Printed publications:
Newsletter
Policy document on periodontology in general dental practice (revised Mar 2001)

Access to staff:
Contact by letter, by telephone, by fax, by e-mail and via website
Hours: Mon to Fri, 0900 to 1700

BRITISH SOCIETY OF PLANT BREEDERS LIMITED

Acronym or abbreviation: BSPB

Woolpack Chambers, Market Street, Ely, Cambridgeshire, CB7 4ND

Tel: 01353 653200
Fax: 01353 661156
E-mail: enquiries@bspb.co.uk

Website:
http://www.bspb.co.uk
Introduction to plant breeding and the work and role of the BSPB.

Enquiries:
Enquiries to: Chief Executive
Other contacts: Technical Liaison Manager

Organisation type and purpose:
Membership association (membership is by subscription, qualification).
To liaise with official bodies and other organisations on technical and legislative matters concerning plant breeding, issue licences and to collect and redistribute royalties.

Subject coverage:
Plant breeding, technical and legislative matters.

Printed publications:
Leaflets (free)

Access to staff:
Contact by letter, by telephone, by fax and by e-mail
Hours: Mon to Fri, 0900 to 1700

Access to building, collection or gallery:
Prior appointment required

BRITISH SOCIETY OF SOIL SCIENCE

Acronym or abbreviation: BSSS

c/o Macaulay Land Use Research Institute, Craigiebuckler, Aberdeen, AB9 2QJ

Tel: 01224 318611
Fax: 01224 208065
E-mail: j.gauld@mluri.sari.ac.uk

Enquiries:
Enquiries to: Administrator

Organisation type and purpose:
Learned society (membership is by subscription), voluntary organisation.

Subject coverage:
Soil science, soil management, environmental management, education, agriculture, agricultural management.

Printed publications:
European Journal of Soil Science (quarterly)
Intermittent publications in relation to soil science in school curriculum and careers
Soil Use and Management (quarterly)

Access to staff:
Contact by telephone, by fax and by e-mail
Hours: Mon to Fri, 0900 to 1700

BRITISH SOCIOLOGICAL ASSOCIATION

Acronym or abbreviation: BSA

Bailey Suite, Palatine House, Belmont Business Park, Belmont, Durham, DH1 1TW

Tel: 0191 383 0839
Fax: 0191 383 0782
E-mail: enquiries@britsoc.org.uk

Website:
http://www.britsoc.co.uk

Enquiries:
Enquiries to: Enquiries
Other contacts: Membership Development Officer (for member enquiries); Events Officer (for events); Publications Officer (for publications)

Founded:
1951

Organisation type and purpose:
The BSA is the professional association for sociology in Britain, representing the intellectual interests of members. Membership is open to anyone who is engaged in, has influenced, or is interested in contributing to the promotion of sociology. Members include individuals in research, teaching and learning, as well as practitioners in many fields. Present number of members: 2,250. Registered charity (charity number 1080235).

Subject coverage:
Sociology.

Information services:
Website/IT Officer

Printed publications:
Newsletter (members only)
Sociology (journal, for purchase through SAGE Publications or free with membership)
Work, Employment and Society (journal, subscriptions through SAGE Publications or free with membership)
Cultural Sociology (journal, subscriptions through SAGE Publications)
Order printed publications from: website: http://www.britsoc.co.uk/publications/pubsjournals.htm

Electronic and video publications:
The World of Sociology (DVD)

Access to staff:
Contact by letter, by telephone, by fax, by e-mail and via website
Hours: Mon to Fri, 0900 to 1700

Access to building, collection or gallery:
Prior appointment required
Hours: Mon to Fri, 0900 to 1700

Access for disabled people:
Parking provided

BRITISH SOFT DRINKS ASSOCIATION LIMITED

Acronym or abbreviation: BSDA

20–22 Stukeley Street, London, WC2B 5LR

Tel: 020 7430 0356
Fax: 020 7831 6014
E-mail: bsda@britishsoftdrinks.com

Website:
http://www.britishsoftdrinks.com

Enquiries:
Enquiries to: Media Director
Other contacts: Administration (for publications)

Founded:
1987

Organisation type and purpose:
Trade association.

Subject coverage:
UK soft drinks, fruit juices, bottled water industries.

Publications list:
Available online and in print

Access to staff:
Contact by letter, by telephone, by fax, by e-mail and via website. Appointment necessary. Non-members charged.
Hours: Mon to Fri, 0900 to 1700

Member organisation of:
AIJN
EFBW

continued overleaf

UNESDA

Subsections are:
Bottled Waters Group
Fruit Juice Committee

BRITISH SOFTBALL FEDERATION

Acronym or abbreviation: BSF

c/o Baseball Softball UK, Ariel House, 74A
Charlotte Street, London W1T 4QJ

Tel: 07729 854193
E-mail: carmel.keswick@britishsoftball.org

Website:
http://www.baseballsoftballuk.com
Comprehensive information on softball in the UK.

Enquiries:
Enquiries to: Executive Secretary

Founded:
1984

Organisation type and purpose:
Membership association.
Governing body of the sport.

Subject coverage:
Playing and coaching of softball, umpiring, team locations, national teams.

Printed publications:
Softball Starter Pack
Schools/Youth Starter Pack
Idiot's Guide to Softball
Softball Scoring Guide
How to Run a Tournament
Basic Skills Coaching Manual

Publications list:
Available online and in print

Access to staff:
Contact by letter, by e-mail and via website
Hours: Mon to Fri, 0900 to 1700

Affiliated to:
European Softball Federation
International Softball Federation

BRITISH SPORTING ART TRUST

Acronym or abbreviation: BSAT

99 High Street, Newmarket, Suffolk, CB8 8JL

Tel: 01638 664429
E-mail: bsatrust@btconnect.com

Website:
http://www.bsat.co.uk

Founded:
1977

Organisation type and purpose:
An independent registered charity (no. 274156)
with membership by subscription.

Subject coverage:
Sporting art.

Museum or gallery collection, archive, or library special collection:
Representative collection of British sporting paintings
Library of books, transparencies, catalogues, magazines and archive material

Printed publications:
A Bibliography of British Sporting Artists

BRITISH STAMMERING ASSOCIATION

Acronym or abbreviation: BSA

15 Old Ford Road, London, E2 9PJ

Tel: 020 8983 1003; helpline: 0845 603 2001
Fax: 020 8983 3591
E-mail: mail@stammering.org

Website:
http://www.stammering.org
Information about BSA and about stammering.

Enquiries:
Enquiries to: Helpline

Organisation type and purpose:
National organisation, membership association
(membership is by subscription), present number
of members: 1,200, voluntary organisation,
registered charity (charity number 278170).
To help stammerers help themselves and promote
wider understanding of condition.

Subject coverage:
Stammering, speech therapy, medical/health, self-help.

Museum or gallery collection, archive, or library special collection:
Postal library
Regional directories of speech therapy provision
Research information database

Library catalogue:
All or part available online

Printed publications:
Books for professionals, teachers, parents and pupils
Newsletter (quarterly)
Selection of leaflets providing information about stammering for all age ranges

Electronic and video publications:
Audio tape, Slow Prolonged Speech (£4.95)

Publications list:
Available online and in print

Access to staff:
Contact by letter, by telephone, by fax, by e-mail
and via website. Appointment necessary.
Hours: Mon to Fri, 0900 to 1700

Member organisation of:
European League of Stuttering Associations
(ELSA)

BRITISH STANDARDS SOCIETY

Acronym or abbreviation: BSS

389 Chiswick High Road, London, W4 4AL

Tel: 020 8996 7081
Fax: 020 8996 7091
E-mail: bss@bsi-global.com

Website:
http://www.bsi.global.com/

Enquiries:
Enquiries to: Secretary
Direct tel: 01923 252361
Direct fax: 01923 252361
Direct e-mail: pam.hall@bsi-global.com

Founded:
1960

Organisation type and purpose:
Professional body (membership is by subscription),
present number of members: 500.
Voluntary association of individuals concerned
with the application of standards; established and
administered by BSI.

Subject coverage:
Application of standards in design, manufacturing,
services, quality assurance, information technology
and in-service support; special interest groups on
building, electronics and management systems,
health and environment, consumer products and
services, information technology.

Museum or gallery collection, archive, or library special collection:
Library of papers on various aspects of
standardisation available to members only

Printed publications:
Members' Handbook (annually)
Newsletter (quarterly)

PD 3542: 1998 Standards and Quality
Management: an integrated approach (BSI, £50,
members of BSI and BSS £25)
PD 6614: 1999 Obsolescence Management: guide to
the subscription of components in electronic
equipment (BSI, £50, members of BSI and BSS
£25)
PD 6615: 1998 Guide to setting up a parts database
(BSI, £36, members of BSI & BSS £15)
PD 6667: 2000 Obsolescence Management:
suppliers guide to the substitution of
components in electronic equipment (BSI, £36,
members of BSS & BSI £18)
Programme of meetings (annually)
Order printed publications from: Customer Services,
BSI
389 Chiswick High Road, London, W4 4AL, tel:
020 8996 9001, fax: 020 8996 7001, website: http://
www.bsi-global.com

Access to staff:
Contact by letter, by telephone, by fax and by e-mail
Hours: Mon to Fri, 0900 to 1700

Parent body:
British Standards Institution
tel: 020 8996 9000; fax: 020 8996 7001; website:
http://www.bsi-global.com

UK member of:
International Federation of Standards Users
(IFAN)
tel: +41 22 749 0331; fax: +41 22 749 0155; e-mail:
ifan@iso.ch

BRITISH STARCH INDUSTRY ASSOCIATION

Acronym or abbreviation: BSIA

Federation House, 6 Catherine Street, London,
WC2B 5JJ

Tel: 020 7836 2460
Fax: 020 7836 0580

Enquiries:
Enquiries to: Executive Secretary
Direct e-mail: tom.hollis@fdf.org.uk

Organisation type and purpose:
Trade association.

Subject coverage:
Maize refining and wheat refining, production of
starch, glucose and other derived products.

Access to staff:
Contact by letter, by fax and by e-mail
Hours: Mon to Fri, 0930 to 1730

BRITISH SUB-AQUA CLUB

Acronym or abbreviation: BSAC

Telford's Quay, South Pier Road, Ellesmere Port,
Cheshire, CH65 4FL

Tel: 0151 350 6200
E-mail: info@bsac.com

Website:
http://www.bsac.com
BSAC, learn to dive, snorkelling, membership,
clubs, dive tips, courses, diving information.

Founded:
1953

Organisation type and purpose:
The UK national governing body for underwater
activities.
Works in conjunction with the Health & Safety
Executive, the Marine Coastguard Association, the
RNLI, HM Treasury's Receiver of Wrecks, DEFRA
and other diving agencies to ensure the continued
development, safety and enjoyment of scuba
diving for all; also works in partnership with a
wide range of conservation and environmental
organisations to help safeguard the UK's precious
waters and marine life for divers – both now and
for future generations – to enjoy.

Subject coverage:
Run by divers, for divers, BSAC provides all the training and support needed to get the best out of this exciting sport.

Electronic and video publications:
Council meeting and AGM minutes
Annual report
Order electronic and video publications from:
Download from website

Publications list:
Available online

Access to staff:
Contact by letter, by telephone and by e-mail

BRITISH SUNDIAL SOCIETY

Acronym or abbreviation: BSS

c/o The Royal Astronomical Society, Burlington House, Piccailly, London,W1J0BQ

Tel: 01663 762415
E-mail: graham@sheardhall.co.uk

Website:
http://www.sundialsoc.org.uk
Types of dials, books in print, equation of time, national sundial societies, information about the British Sundial Society.

Enquiries:
Enquiries to: Secretary

Founded:
1989

Organisation type and purpose:
Learned society (membership is by subscription), present number of members: 500, voluntary organisation, registered charity (charity no. 1032530).
A society for those interested in gnomonics and sundials generally.

Subject coverage:
Constructing sundials, makers of sundials, sundial bibliography, history of sundials, location of sundials (British), restoration of sundials, gnomonics, speakers' panel.

Museum or gallery collection, archive, or library special collection:
Photographs of most existing British sundials
Detailed records of over 6,000 existing sundials in the British Isles
Books on sundials
Quarterly all-colour Bulletin with learned articles and descriptions and mathematics of sundials

Trade and statistical information:
List of dial makers in the UK who are members of the society.

Non-library collection catalogue:
All or part available in print

Printed publications:
Make a Sundial (book for schools, 70pp)
Sundial Books in English from 1900 (A4 sheet)
Sundial Makers (D/S A4 sheet)
Sundial Register (locations, details, 210pp)
Sundial Glossary (terminology, equations, 84pp)
Biographical Index of British Sundial Makers from the Seventh Century to 1920 (117pp)
Several other monographs (list available)
Order printed publications from: British Sundial Society

Microform publications:
Sets of Slides for lectures:
Basic Theory
Early History
Early British Dials

Electronic and video publications:
Looking at Sundials (education video available for purchase direct)
Sundial Calculations

Publications list:
Available online

Access to staff:
Contact by letter, by telephone, by e-mail and via website. Appointment necessary.
Hours: Mon to Fri, 0900 to 1700

Links with:
European sundial societies
North American Sundial Society
Public Monuments and Sculpture Association

BRITISH SURFING ASSOCIATION

Acronym or abbreviation: BSA

c/o The International Surfing Centre, Fistral Beach, Newquay, Cornwall, TR7 1HY

Tel: 01637 876474
Fax: 01637 878608
E-mail: info@britsurf.co.uk

Website:
http://www.nationalsurfingcentre.com
http://www.gbsurf.org
http://www.britsurf.co.uk

Enquiries:
Enquiries to: National Director
Other contacts: Assistant to National Director

Founded:
1966

Organisation type and purpose:
Membership association.
Governing body of the sport.

Subject coverage:
Surfing; courses for beginners, teachers and coaches.

Trade and statistical information:
Information on surfing related business available.

Printed publications:
BSA Guide to Surfing in Britain (£3.95)
General fact sheets on surfing
Newsletters

Access to staff:
Contact by letter, by telephone, by fax and by e-mail
Hours: Mon to Fri, 0900 to 1700

Access to building, collection or gallery:
No prior appointment required

Affiliated to:
Central Council of Physical Recreation
International Surfing Association

BRITISH SUZUKI INSTITUTE

Acronym or abbreviation: BSI

Kensington Charity Centre, 4th Floor, Charles House, 375 Kensington High Street, London W14 8QH

Tel: 020 7471 6780
Fax: 020 7471 6778
E-mail: info@britishsuzuki.com

Website:
http://www.britishsuzuki.org.uk/

Enquiries:
Enquiries to: General Secretary

Founded:
1978

Organisation type and purpose:
Membership association (membership is by subscription), present number of members: c. 1600, registered charity (charity number 278005), training organisation.
To further education by Suzuki method.

Subject coverage:
Information about the Suzuki approach to instrumental teaching, provision of training courses in music and general education. The emphasis is on teaching very young children with parental involvement.

Museum or gallery collection, archive, or library special collection:
A small library on Suzuki method includes musical tapes and CDs

Printed publications:
Ability Development (journal, 3 times a year)
Annual Report
Music, books
Suzuki method pamphlets and information

Electronic and video publications:
Tapes and CDs relating to Suzuki method

Publications list:
Available in print

Access to staff:
Contact by letter, by telephone, by fax and by e-mail. Appointment necessary.
Hours: Mon to Fri, 0930 to 1630
Special comments: 24 hour answerphone.

Affiliated to:
European Suzuki Association
at the same address
International Suzuki Association
3–10–3 Fukhshi, Matsumoto, Nagawo, 390, Japan

BRITISH TARANTULA SOCIETY

Acronym or abbreviation: BTS

81 Phillimore Place, Radlett, Hertfordshire, WD7 8NJ

Tel: 01923 856071

Website:
http://www.bts.ndirect.co.uk
Details of Society and its services, articles and photographs.

Enquiries:
Enquiries to: Honorary Secretary
Direct e-mail: angehale@thebts.co.uk

Founded:
1984

Organisation type and purpose:
Membership association (membership is by subscription), present number of members: over 700, voluntary organisation, suitable for ages: all, research organisation.
Membership is predominantly UK but is also worldwide.

Subject coverage:
Keeping, conservation, captive breeding and management of tropical arachnids (tarantulas and scorpions).

Museum or gallery collection, archive, or library special collection:
Reference library

Library catalogue:
All or part available online

Printed publications:
Journal (quarterly, members only)
Publicity material

Access to staff:
Contact by letter and by telephone. Non-members charged.
Hours: 24-hour answerphone

BRITISH TAXPAYERS ASSOCIATION LIMITED

Acronym or abbreviation: British Taxpayers

Barclays House, 51 Bishopric, Horsham, West Sussex, RH12 1BS

Tel: 01403 271919
Fax: 01403 271912
E-mail: enquiries@britishtaxpayers.com

Website:
http://www.britishtaxpayers.com

Enquiries:
Enquiries to: Managing Director

continued overleaf

Direct fax: 01403 271912

Founded:
1919

Organisation type and purpose:
Consultancy.

Subject coverage:
Income, capital gains and inheritance tax, overseas income and trusts, expatriate taxation, national insurance contributions, tax return preparation, personal financial planning, remuneration planning, employee benefits, revenue investigations, incentive schemes.

Museum or gallery collection, archive, or library special collection:
Research library on all UK taxation matters

Trade and statistical information:
Full data on UK personal taxation.

Printed publications:
Publications available online via http://www.britishtaxpayers.com

Publications list:
Available online

Access to staff:
Contact by letter, by telephone, by fax, by e-mail and in person
Hours: Mon to Fri, 0900 to 1700

Affiliated to:
British Taxpayers Financial Planning
  tel: 020 7456 0450; fax: 020 7247 0411; e-mail: mail@british-taxpayers.com
The Taxpayers' Society
  tel: 01403 271919; fax: 01403 271912; e-mail: tps@british-taxpayers.com

Also at:
British Taxpayers
  78 Park Street, Horsham, West Sussex, RH12 1BS; tel: 01403 271919; fax: 01403 271912; e-mail: mail@british-taxpayers.co.uk

BRITISH TECHNION SOCIETY

62 Grosvenor Street, London, W1K 3JF

Tel: 020 7495 6824
Fax: 020 7355 1525
E-mail: bts62@apl.com

Website:
http://www.britishtechnionsociety.org
Full history of BTS.

Enquiries:
Enquiries to: Executive Director

Founded:
1951

Organisation type and purpose:
Registered charity (charity number 206922).
To raise funds for Technion, Haifa, Israel.

Subject coverage:
Promotion of Technion, fund-raising for Technion.

Printed publications:
Newsletter and other printed material (no charge)

Access to staff:
Contact by letter, by telephone, by fax and in person
Hours: Mon to Fri, 0900 to 1700

Parent body:
Technion
  Israel Institute of Technology, Haifa, 32000, Israel

BRITISH TENPIN BOWLING ASSOCIATION

Acronym or abbreviation: BTBA

114 Balfour Road, Ilford, Essex, IG1 4JD

Tel: 0208 478 1745
Fax: 0208 514 3665
E-mail: admin@btba.org.uk

Website:
http://www.btba.org.uk

Founded:
1961

Organisation type and purpose:
Governing body of the tenpin bowling sport in Britain.
Provides official rules; recognises bowling achievements in sanctioned play; provides tournament competition; and provides services to sanctioned leagues.

Subject coverage:
Tenpin bowling in Britain at all levels.

Access to staff:
Contact by letter, by telephone, by fax and by e-mail

BRITISH TEXTILE MACHINERY ASSOCIATION

Acronym or abbreviation: BTMA

Mount Pleasant, Glazebrook Lane, Glazebrook, Warrington, WA3 5BN

Tel: 0161 775 5740
Fax: 0161 775 5485
E-mail: btma@btma.org.uk

Website:
http://www.btma.org.uk

Enquiries:
Enquiries to: Director

Founded:
1940

Organisation type and purpose:
Trade association (membership is by subscription), present number of members: 50, manufacturing industry.
To promote the British textile machinery industry world-wide.

Subject coverage:
Textile machinery for natural and synthetic products.

Printed publications:
Directory of Members and Products (annually, free)

Access to staff:
Contact by letter, by telephone, by fax, by e-mail and via website. Appointment necessary.
Hours: Mon to Fri, 0700 to 1600

BRITISH THYROID FOUNDATION

Acronym or abbreviation: BTF

2nd Floor, 3 Devonshire Place, Harrogate, HG1 4AA

Tel: 01423 709707

Website:
http://www.btf-thyroid.org

Enquiries:
Enquiries to: Membership Secretary

Founded:
1991

Organisation type and purpose:
Voluntary organisation, registered charity.
To support sufferers of thyroid disorders.

Subject coverage:
Thyroid disorders.

Printed publications:
General introductory leaflet: contains membership information (free)
Newsletter: includes telephone numbers of local support groups (quarterly, members)
Pamphlets on thyroid disorders (members)

Access to staff:
Contact by letter and by telephone
Hours: Mon to Fri, 1000 to 1400

BRITISH TINNITUS ASSOCIATION

Acronym or abbreviation: BTA

Acorn Business Park, Woodseats Close, Sheffield S8 0TB

Tel: 0114 250 9933 \ Minicom 0114 258 5694
Fax: 0114 258 2279
E-mail: info@tinnitus.org.uk

Website:
http://www.tinnitus.org.uk/

Enquiries:
Enquiries to: Operations Manager
Direct tel: 0114 273 0122
Other contacts: Membership Secretary

Founded:
1992

Organisation type and purpose:
Membership association (membership is by subscription), present number of members: 10,000, voluntary organisation, registered charity (charity number 1011145).
The sole national voluntary organisation for people with tinnitus, close links with tinnitus associations in other countries, self-help groups.
To raise an increasing awareness of the condition, support new research, promote better medical services and provide support for sufferers.

Subject coverage:
Tinnitus; help or treatments available; information on research in progress.

Printed publications:
Information leaflets
Medical Leaflets (6, free for sae)
Quiet (journal, quarterly; £10 a year)

Electronic and video publications:
New World relaxation tapes
Video cassette for hire

Publications list:
Available in print

Access to staff:
Contact by letter, by telephone, by fax and by e-mail
Hours: Mon to Fri, 0930 to 1630 (plus 24hr answerphone)

BRITISH TOY & HOBBY ASSOCIATION LIMITED

Acronym or abbreviation: BTHA

80 Camberwell Road, London, SE5 0EG

Tel: 020 7701 7271
Fax: 020 7708 2437
E-mail: admin@btha.co.uk

Website:
http://www.btha.co.uk

Enquiries:
Enquiries to: Director General

Founded:
1944

Organisation type and purpose:
Trade association.

Subject coverage:
Toys and hobbies, toy industry, UK toy exports and imports, toy safety, advertising of toys and responsible manufacturing.

Printed publications:
Advertising Toys to Children in the UK and Europe (£4.50)
BTHA Sourcebook
British Toys and Hobbies Briefing
Directory of Members (annually)
Games (£4.50)
Hundred popular toys and games for blind and partially sighted children (1996, free)
Intergenerational Play (£4.50)
Play Value (£4.50)
Television Advertising and Children (£25)
Toys and Play in Child Development (£4.50)

War Toys (£4.50)

Access to staff:
Contact by letter, by telephone, by fax and by e-mail
Hours: Jun to Sep, Mon to Thu, 0830 to 1700; Fri, 0830 to 1630

Houses the:
British Toy Council
British Toy Fairs (International) Limited
website: http://www.toyfair.co.uk

Member of:
International Council of Toy Industries
website: http://www.toy-icti.org
Toy Industries of Europe
website: http://www.tietoy.org

BRITISH TOY COUNCIL LIMITED

80 Camberwell Road, London, SE5 0EG

Tel: 020 7701 7271
Fax: 020 7708 2437
E-mail: admin@btha.co.uk

Enquiries:
Enquiries to: Secretary

Founded:
1967

Organisation type and purpose:
Trade association.

Subject coverage:
Standards of design, development, quality and safety of toys; preparation and implementation of these standards UK and international.

Museum or gallery collection, archive, or library special collection:
Some international toy safety standards

Access to staff:
Contact by letter
Hours: Mon to Fri, 0900 to 1700

Subsidiary of:
British Toy and Hobby Association
website: http://www.btha.co.uk

BRITISH TOYMAKERS GUILD

Acronym or abbreviation: BTG

PO Box 4498, Bradford-on-Avon, BA15 5BB

Tel: 01225 442440
E-mail: info@toymakersguild.co.uk

Website:
http://www.toymakersguild.co.uk
Guild representing traditional toys and toymakers.

Enquiries:
Enquiries to: Manager

Founded:
1956

Organisation type and purpose:
International organisation, trade association (membership is by subscription, qualification), present number of members: 200.

Subject coverage:
Toys.

Trade and statistical information:
Data on the traditional toy sector.

Printed publications:
A Closer Look at the Traditional Toy Sector
A Guide to Self Certification
Marketing Traditional Toys
Yearly Catalogue

Access to staff:
Contact by letter, by telephone, by e-mail and via website. Appointment necessary.
Hours: Mon to Fri, 0900 to 1700

BRITISH TROLLEYBUS SOCIETY

Acronym or abbreviation: BTS

2 Josephine Court, Southcote Road, Reading, Berkshire, RG30 2DG

Tel: 0118 958 3974

Enquiries:
Enquiries to: Honorary Secretary

Founded:
1961

Organisation type and purpose:
Membership association (membership is by subscription), present number of members: 320, voluntary organisation, registered charity (charity number 1033666).

Subject coverage:
History and development of British trolleybus systems in particular, and foreign systems in general; history and development of bus operation in the Thames Valley area, development of public transport in West Yorkshire area.

Printed publications:
Bus Fare (monthly)
Trolleybus (monthly)
Wheels (monthly)

Access to staff:
Contact by letter and by telephone
Hours: Mon to Fri, 0900 to 1700

Associated with:
Sandtoft Transport Centre

There are groups in:
Bradford and Reading

BRITISH TROUT ASSOCIATION

Acronym or abbreviation: BTA

British Trout Association, The Rural Centre, West Mains, Ingliston, EH28 8NZ

Tel: 0131 472 4080
Fax: 0131 472 4083
E-mail: mail@britishtrout.co.uk

Website:
http://www.britishtrout.co.uk
Information on organisation, list of members and their addresses.

Enquiries:
Enquiries to: Honorary Secretary

Organisation type and purpose:
National organisation, trade association (membership is by subscription).
Information for members only.

Access to staff:
Contact by e-mail
Hours: Mon to Fri, 0900 to 1700

BRITISH TRUST FOR CONSERVATION VOLUNTEERS SCOTLAND

Acronym or abbreviation: BTCV Scotland

Balallan House, 24 Allan Park, Stirling, FK8 2QG

Tel: 01786 479697
Fax: 01786 465359
E-mail: scotland@btcv.org.uk

Website:
http://www.btcv.org.uk/scotland

Enquiries:
Enquiries to: Administrator

Founded:
1984

Organisation type and purpose:
National organisation, membership association (membership is by subscription), present number of members: 5,000, voluntary organisation, registered charity (charity number 261009), training organisation.
Environmental organisation.

To involve people in improving the quality of Scotland's environment through practical conservation.

Subject coverage:
Information provided on all aspects of practical conservation and community regeneration work.

Printed publications:
Annual Review
Environmental Skills books
Conserver Magazine
CLAN Bulletin Magazine

Electronic and video publications:
Green Gym (video)

Access to staff:
Contact by letter, by telephone, by fax, by e-mail, in person and via website
Hours: Mon to Fri, 0900 to 1700

Access to building, collection or gallery:
No prior appointment required

Access for disabled people:
Parking provided, toilet facilities

Also at:
Edinburgh, Glasgow, Falkirk, Aberdeen, Inverness, Fife

Constituent bodies:
285 affiliated local conservation groups, collectively known as Community Local Action Network (CLAN)

Constituent part of:
British Trust for Conservation Volunteers (BTCV)

Links with:
Action Recycle
27 Winchester Avenue, Denny, FK6 6QE; tel: 01324 826826; fax: 01324 882533; e-mail: action-recycle@btcv.org.uk

BRITISH TRUST FOR ORNITHOLOGY

Acronym or abbreviation: BTO

The Nunnery, Thetford, Norfolk, IP24 2PU

Tel: 01842 750050
Fax: 01842 750030
E-mail: applications@bto.org

Website:
http://www.bto.org

Enquiries:
Enquiries to: Senior Development Officer
Direct e-mail: sam.bailey@bto.org

Founded:
1933

Organisation type and purpose:
Membership association (membership is by subscription), present number of members: 12,500, registered charity (charity number 216652 England & Wales, SC039193 Scotland), research organisation.

Subject coverage:
British and migratory birds, their habitats and population levels, breeding season, mortality, migration, using information gathered by members. Understanding, appreciation and conservation of birds.

Museum or gallery collection, archive, or library special collection:
Largest data collection on British birds in the UK
Second largest ornithological library of books and journals in the UK
Breeding Bird Survey (data from 1994 onwards)
Common Birds Census (data from 1962 to 2000)
Ornithological Sites Register (data from 1960s onwards)
Waterway Bird Survey (data 1974 onwards)
Wetland Bird Survey (data from 1993 onwards)
Nest Record Scheme (data from 1930s onwards)
National Ringing Scheme (data from 1909 onwards)

continued overleaf

Non-library collection catalogue:
All or part available online, in-house and in print

Library catalogue:
All or part available in-house

Printed publications:
Contact BTO for price details:
Bird Study (3 times a year)
BTO News (6 times a year)
Bird Table (4 times a year)
Occasional technical guides, books
Research reports
Ringing and Migration (2 times a year)
The New Atlas of Breeding Birds in Britain and
Ireland: 1988–1991

Publications list:
Available online and in print

Access to staff:
Contact by letter, by telephone, by fax and by e-mail
Hours: Mon to Fri, 0900 to 1700

Access to building, collection or gallery:
Prior appointment required
Special comments: Members only, preferably by prior appointment

Access for disabled people:
Parking provided, level entry, toilet facilities

Also at:
British Trust for Ornithology (Scottish Office) (BTO Scotland)
School of Biological & Environmental Sciences, Cottrell Building, University of Stirling, Stirling, FK9 4LA.; tel: 01786 466560; fax: 01786 466561

BRITISH TUNNELLING SOCIETY

Acronym or abbreviation: BTS

Institution of Civil Engineers, 1 Great George Street, London, SW1P 3AA

Tel: 020 7665 2229
Fax: 020 7799 1325
E-mail: bts@ice.org.uk

Website:
http://www.ice.org.uk
http://www.britishtunnelling.org.uk
Meetings of the British Tunnelling Society listed.

Founded:
1971

Organisation type and purpose:
Learned society.

Subject coverage:
All aspects of tunnel design, construction and maintenance.

Museum or gallery collection, archive, or library special collection:
Library tunnelling section of the ICE library

Printed publications:
Tunnels and Tunnelling (10 times a year, free to members)

Access to staff:
Contact by letter, by telephone and via website
Hours: Mon to Fri, 0900 to 1700
Special comments: Access to library/archives of Institution of Civil Engineers on payment of a fee.

Affiliated to:
Institution of Civil Engineers

National section of the:
International Tunnelling Association

BRITISH TURNED PARTS MANUFACTURERS ASSOCIATION

Acronym or abbreviation: BTMA

PTC, Snitterfield Lane, Norton Lindsey, Warwick, CV35 8JQ

Tel: 01789 730877
Fax: 01789 730899
E-mail: iangold@btma.org

Website:
http://www.btma.org

Enquiries:
Enquiries to: Director

Organisation type and purpose:
Trade association.

Subject coverage:
Precison-turned parts and machined components.

Education services:
CNC setter training courses for members

Non-library collection catalogue:
All or part available online and in print

Printed publications:
Buyer's Guide
Order printed publications from: Postal address

Access to staff:
Contact by letter, by telephone, by fax, by e-mail and via website

Access to building, collection or gallery:
Special comments: No access

BRITISH UNIDENTIFIED FLYING OBJECT RESEARCH ASSOCIATION

Acronym or abbreviation: BUFORA

41 Castlebar Road, Ealing, London, W5 2DJ

Tel: 020 8997 3496
E-mail: enquiries@bufora.org.uk

Website:
http://www.bufora.org.uk

Founded:
1962

Organisation type and purpose:
Non-membership Association conducting objective/scientific based investigative research into the UFO phenomenon.

Subject coverage:
Field investigations, research, investigator training, support in all areas pertaining to UFOs and related paranormal phenomena

Printed publications:
Website with free access to all material therein, unless otherwise stated.

Access to staff:
Contact by letter, by telephone, by e-mail and via website
Hours: Access via e-mail 24 hours
Special comments: Telephone evenings after 1830 and weekends

BRITISH UNION CONFERENCE OF SEVENTH-DAY ADVENTISTS

Acronym or abbreviation: BUC

Stanborough Park, Garston, Watford, Hertfordshire, WD25 9JZ

Tel: 01923 672251
Fax: 01923 893212
E-mail: info@adventist.org.uk

Website:
http://www.adventist.org.uk
General information about the Seventh-day Adventist Church, links to other sites and to other Christian sites.

Enquiries:
Enquiries to: Communications Director
Direct e-mail: vhulbert@adventist.org.uk

Organisation type and purpose:
Registered charity (charity number 209780). British Isles Headquarters of the Seventh-day Adventist Church.

Subject coverage:
Seventh-day Adventist beliefs and history, health and temperance.

Museum or gallery collection, archive, or library special collection:
Rare collections relating to Church history are housed at the denominational college, Newbold College, Binfield, nr Bracknell, Berkshire, RG42 4AN

Printed publications:
Encounter Youth Magazine, Messenger, Life.info Focus Magazine

Electronic and video publications:
Satellite Television Channel – The Hope Channel – on Hotbird, http://www.hopetv.org.uk

Access to staff:
Contact by letter, by telephone, by fax, by e-mail and via website
Hours: Mon to Thu, 0900 to 1700; Fri, 0900 to 1200

Access to building, collection or gallery:
Hours: Mon to Thu, 0900 to 1700; Fri, 0900 to 1200

Access for disabled people:
Disabled access available

Also at the same address:
Seventh-day Adventist Association Limited
website: http://www.adventist.org.uk

Parent body:
General Conference of Seventh-day Adventists
12501 Old Columbia Pike, Silver Spring, MD 20904–6600, USA

Subsidiary body:
Adventist Development and Relief Agency (ADRA-uk)
at the same address; tel: 01923 681723; website: http://adra.org.uk

BRITISH UNION FOR THE ABOLITION OF VIVISECTION

Acronym or abbreviation: BUAV

16a Crane Grove, Islington, London, N7 8NN

Tel: 020 7700 4888
Fax: 020 7700 0252
E-mail: info@buav.org

Website:
http://www.buav.org

Enquiries:
Other contacts: Media Manager for media enquiries

Founded:
1898

Organisation type and purpose:
The BUAV works to create a world where nobody wants to or believes in the need to experiment on animals. It campaigns peacefully to end animal testing. Through undercover investigations, political lobbying, the promotion of cruelty-free products, legal and scientific expertise and media activities, it works to make the world a better place for animals.

Subject coverage:
Animal protection, campaigning, Cruelty Free, laboratory animals and the campaign against vivisection.

Museum or gallery collection, archive, or library special collection:
BUAV archive material (1898 to present day) held at Brynmor Jones Library, University of Hull, available to bona fide researchers by appointment

Library catalogue:
All or part available in-house

Printed publications:
Annual Report
BUAV Update, supporter newsletter
Fact sheets on campaign issues

Access to staff:
Contact by letter, by telephone, by fax, by e-mail and via website. Appointment necessary. Letter of introduction required.
Hours: Mon to Fri, 0900 to 1700

Access to building, collection or gallery:
Hours: Mon to Fri, 0900 to 1700

Access for disabled people:
via lift
Hours: Mon to Fri, 0900 to 1700

Affiliated to:
European Coalition to End Animal Experiments at the same address

BRITISH UNION OF SOCIAL WORK EMPLOYEES

Acronym or abbreviation: BUSWE

BUSWE House, 208 Middleton Road, Manchester, M8 4NA

Tel: 0161 720 7727
Fax: 0161 795 4524
E-mail: buswe@buswe.fsnet.co.uk

Enquiries:
Enquiries to: General Secretary

Founded:
1976

Organisation type and purpose:
Trade union, present number of members: 3,500.

Subject coverage:
UK social work structure and services, industrial relations.
Development of a broad knowledge base; education of the public and others as to the purpose and impact of social care practices and procedures; creation of the optimal circumstances for the employment of social care practitioners; participation in the setting and evolution of professional standards of social care; support of initiatives that promote the expansion of opportunities within which individuals can expand their development potential; re-establishment of education and training of social care employees in order that the demands of evolving standards and practices can be met.

Access to staff:
Contact by letter, by telephone and by e-mail. Appointment necessary.
Hours: Mon to Fri, 0900 to 1700

Access to building, collection or gallery:
Prior appointment required
Hours: Mon to Fri, 0900 to 1700

Access for disabled people:
Parking provided

BRITISH UNIVERSITIES FILM & VIDEO COUNCIL

Acronym or abbreviation: BUFVC

77 Wells Street, London, W1T 3QJ

Tel: 020 7393 1500
Fax: 020 7393 1555
E-mail: ask@bufvc.ac.uk

Website:
http://www.bufvc.ac.uk
Annual information on BUFVC membership, services and publications. HERMES, RGO, BUND, MIGr and TRILT databases.

Enquiries:
Enquiries to: Head of Information
Direct tel: 020 7393 1508
Direct e-mail: luke@bufvc.ac.uk
Other contacts: Library and Database Manager for general information. Also newsreels@bufvc.ac.uk and rgo@bufvc.ac.uk

Founded:
1948

Merged with:
Learning on Screen (year of change 2004)

Organisation type and purpose:
Registered charity (no. 313582), research organisation, publishing house.

Reference Library founded 1972; instrumental in founding the Consortium for Drama and Media in Higher Education, providing the secretariat since 1974; assumed responsibility for administration of Slade Film History Register, 1975; took over production of HELPIS catalogue from Council for Educational Technology, 1976; Audio-Visual Reference Centre opened, 1978; took over distribution of the films of the Interuniversity History Film Consortium, 1981, launched British Universities Newsreel Project 1995; launched British Universities Newsreel (Scripts) Project 1999; launched Researcher's Guide Online and Moving Image Gateway (2001); launched Television & Radio Index for Learning and Teaching (2002).

Subject coverage:
Audio-visual media, including computer-based multi-media, materials and techniques for degree-level teaching and research, resource lists on the history of science and invention, Shakespeare, post-war British history, physics and astronomy, teaching, guides to film, and newsreel collections.

Museum or gallery collection, archive, or library special collection:
BKSTS book library
Issue sheets for all British newsreels and cinemagazines, as well as details of unissued material, held in the Slade Film History Register
Newsreel commentary scripts, dope sheets and other original documents from Reuters Television
Records of the Scientific Film Association
Subject index to television documentary programmes broadcast by BBC and ITV from 1987 to 2001

Printed publications:
Annual Report
As You Like It: Audio Visual Shakespeare (3rd ed.)
Buying and Clearing Rights: Print, Broadcast and Multimedia
Film and Television Collections in Europe: The MAP-TV Guide
Filming History: BUFVC Handbook (3rd ed.)
Researchers' Guide to British Film and Television Collections (6th ed. 2001)
Researchers' Guide to British Newsreels vol. I, (1983); vol. II, (1988); vol. III, (1993)
Viewfinder (4 times per annum)

Microform publications:
British Newsreels Issue Sheets 1913–1970 on Microfiche

Electronic and video publications:
The BUFVC Newsreel Project (CD-ROM)
Origins of the Cold War (CD-ROM)

Publications list:
Available in print

Access to staff:
Contact by letter, by telephone, by fax and by e-mail. Appointment necessary. Non-members charged.
Hours: Mon to Fri, 0930 to 1730
Special comments: Information service open for enquiries 1200 to 1730.

Supported by:
the Joint Information Systems Committee (JISC)

BRITISH UNIVERSITIES SPORTS ASSOCIATION

Acronym or abbreviation: BUSA

8 Union Street, London, SE1 1SZ

Tel: 020 7357 8555
Fax: 020 7403 1218
E-mail: office@busa.org.uk

Website:
http://www.busaresults.org.uk
Results of sports matches and league information. Contact information and sponsor information.

Enquiries:
Enquiries to: Public Relations Manager

Organisation type and purpose:
National government body, membership association (membership is by qualification, present number of members: 147, registered charity (charity number 223324).

Subject coverage:
Governing body for University Sport in the UK. Organises tournaments in 42 sports for 147 member institutions.

BRITISH URBAN REGENERATION ASSOCIATION

Acronym or abbreviation: BURA

63–66 Hatton Garden, London, EC1N 8LE

Tel: 020 7539 4030
Fax: 020 7404 9614
E-mail: info@bura.org.uk

Website:
http://www.bura.org.uk

Enquiries:
Enquiries to: Business Development Director

Founded:
1990

Organisation type and purpose:
Trade association (membership is by subscription, election or invitation), present number of members: 550, voluntary organisation. Promoting an integrated approach to improving the quality of life in urban areas, taking fully into account the interdependence of the social, economic and environmental issues involved.

Subject coverage:
Urban regeneration; contaminated land; sustainable development; annual awards: BURA Award for Best Practice in Urban Regeneration; The Secretary of State for the Environment, Transport and the Regions' Award for Partnership in Regeneration; Best Practice in Community Regeneration Awards; Best Practice in Promoting Sport in the Community Awards.

Printed publications:
Urban Regeneration Handbook
Research Papers
Newsletter (quarterly)
Conference Reports

Access to staff:
Contact by letter, by telephone, by fax and by e-mail. Appointment necessary.
Hours: Mon to Fri, 0930 to 1730

Standing committees and working groups include:
Contaminated Land Working Group
Urban Policy Group

Works in partnership with:
Association of Town Centre Management
Civic Trust
Local Government Association
Royal Town Planning Institute
Town and Country Planning Association
Urban Villages Forum

BRITISH URUGUAYAN SOCIETY

Shreelane, 222 Brooklands Road, Weybridge, Surrey, KT13 0RJ

Tel: 01932 847455
Fax: 01932 847455

Enquiries:
Enquiries to: Secretary

Founded:
1945

Organisation type and purpose:
Membership association (membership is by subscription), present number of members: 270, registered charity (charity number 275362). Educational charity promoting knowledge of Uruguay in Britain and of Britain in Uruguay.

continued overleaf

Subject coverage:
History, geography and culture of Uruguay; educational contacts for students; some limited information on business, trade and travel, not specialists but have contacts and are willing to help wherever possible.

Museum or gallery collection, archive, or library special collection:
The Society's library is on permanent loan to the Library of the Hispanic and Luso-Brazilian Council at 2 Belgrave Square, London, SW1, where it is open to the public weekdays, 0930 to 1730

Printed publications:
El Hornero (journal, 2 times a year, in English with some Spanish articles, free to members, otherwise £2 per copy)
History of the British Uruguayan Society 1945–1995 (1997) (£5 inc. p&p)
Tales of Uruguay (anthology of members' reminiscences, 1988, £5 inc. p&p)
History of the Uruguayan Short Story (Adams J, in preparation)

Access to staff:
Contact by letter and by telephone
Hours: Mon to Fri, 0900 to 1700

Affiliated to:
Hispanic and Luso-Brazilian Council
tel: 020 7235 2303; fax: 020 7235 3587

BRITISH VALVE & ACTUATOR ASSOCIATION

Acronym or abbreviation: BVAMA

9 Manor Park, Banbury, OX16 3TB

Tel: 01295 221270
Fax: 01295 268965
E-mail: enquiry@bvaa.org.uk

Website:
http://www.bvaa.org.uk
Members information, product locator, members only information.

Enquiries:
Enquiries to: Director

Founded:
1939

Organisation type and purpose:
Trade association.

Subject coverage:
Industrial valves for the control of fluids.

Printed publications:
Valve Users Manual
Valves and Actuators from Britain (sale item only, 7th ed.)

Publications list:
Available online and in print

Access to staff:
Contact by letter, by telephone, by fax and by e-mail
Hours: Mon to Fri, 0900 to 1700

Access to building, collection or gallery:
Prior appointment required

BRITISH VENDEEN SHEEP SOCIETY

Formal name: British Vendeen Sheep Society Ltd
Acronym or abbreviation: BVSS

Darkes House, Conderton, Tewkesbury, Gloucestershire, GL20 7PP

Tel: 01386 725229
E-mail: info@vendeen.co.uk

Website:
http://www.vendeen.co.uk
Subscribing, flocks, sheep for sale.

Enquiries:
Enquiries to: Secretary

Founded:
1985

Organisation type and purpose:
National organisation, membership association (membership is by subscription), present number of members: 40, registered charity.
To promote and improve the breed of British Vendeen sheep.

Subject coverage:
Breeding of and breeding from British Vendeen sheep.

Printed publications:
Flock Book

Access to staff:
Contact by letter, by telephone, by fax, by e-mail and in person. Appointment necessary.
Hours: Any reasonable time

BRITISH VETERINARY ASSOCIATION

Acronym or abbreviation: BVA

7 Mansfield Street, London, W1G 9NQ

Tel: 020 7636 6541
E-mail: bvahq@bva.co.uk

Website:
http://www.bva.co.uk
General information on BVA services including annual congress.

Enquiries:
Enquiries to: Head of Media
Direct e-mail: press@bva.co.uk

Founded:
1882

Organisation type and purpose:
Professional body (membership is by subscription, election or invitation), present number of members: 10,000.
Houses the BVA Animal Welfare Foundation.
There are 2 branches (Scottish and Welsh), 30 territorial divisions and 20 specialist divisions within the Association.
The national representative body for the British veterinary profession.

Subject coverage:
Veterinary science, including animal health and welfare and public health.

Printed publications:
Handbooks, guidelines, etc
In Practice (monthly)
Journal of the Association of Veterinary Students (quarterly)
Veterinary Record (weekly)
Off The Record (monthly)
Publication list available for purchase
Order printed publications from: Ten Alps Subscriber Services, Coach House, Turners Drive, Thatcham, Berkshire RG19 4QB
6 Bourne Enterprise Centre, Wrotham Road, Borough Green, Wrotham, Kent, TN15 8DG, tel: 01732 884023, fax: 01732 884034

Publications list:
Available online and in print

Access to staff:
Contact by letter, by telephone, by e-mail and via website. Access for members only.
Hours: Mon to Fri, 0930 to 1700

Member organisation of:
Commonwealth Veterinary Association
Federation of Veterinarians in Europe
Inter-Professional Group
Parliamentary and Scientific Committee
Pet Advisory Committee
Pet Health Council
World Veterinary Association

Specialist divisions at the same address:
Association for Veterinary Teaching and Research Work
Association of Government Vets
Association of Veterinarians in Industry
Association of Veterinary Students
British Cattle Veterinary Association
British Equine Veterinary Association
British Laboratory Animals Veterinary Association
British Small Animal Veterinary Association
British Veterinary Hospitals Association
British Veterinary Poultry Association
British Veterinary Zoological Society
Fish Veterinary Society
Goat Veterinary Society
Pig Veterinary Society
Royal Army Veterinary Corps Division
Sheep Veterinary Society
Society for the Study of Animal Breeding
Society of Greyhound Veterinarians
Society of Practising Veterinary Surgeons
Veterinary Deer Society
Veterinary Public Health Association

BRITISH VETERINARY NURSING ASSOCIATION

Acronym or abbreviation: BVNA

82 Greenway Business Centre, Harlow Business Park, Harlow, Essex, CM19 5QE

Tel: 01279 408644
Fax: 01279 408645
E-mail: bvna@bvna.co.uk

Website:
http://www.bvna.org.uk
Careers, CPD and congresses, online shop, news, helplines and support.

Founded:
1965

Organisation type and purpose:
The only national representative body for veterinary nurses.
To promote animal health and welfare through the ongoing development of professional excellence in veterinary nursing.

Subject coverage:
Veterinary nursing.

Information services:
BVNA Members Helpline

Printed publications:
VNJ (monthly journal, free to members)

Electronic and video publications:
Position statements
Order electronic and video publications from:
Download from website

Access to staff:
Contact by letter, by telephone, by fax and by e-mail
Hours: Mon to Thu, 0900 to 1700; Fri, 0900 to 1600

BRITISH VIDEO ASSOCIATION

Acronym or abbreviation: BVA

167 Great Portland Street, London, W1W 5PE

Tel: 020 7436 0041
Fax: 020 7436 0043
E-mail: general@bva.org.uk

Website:
http://www.bva.org.uk

Enquiries:
Enquiries to: Director General

Founded:
1980

Organisation type and purpose:
Trade association.
Represent the interests of UK video rights owners.

Subject coverage:
Trends in market of video rental and retail sales.

Trade and statistical information:
Quarterly statistical press release.

Printed publications:
British Video Association Yearbook

Access to staff:
Contact by letter, by telephone, by fax, by e-mail and via website. Appointment necessary.
Hours: Mon to Fri, 0930 to 1730

Affiliated to:
British Screen Advisory Council
tel: 020 7287 1111
International Video Federation
tel: 00 322 503 4063

BRITISH VOICE ASSOCIATION

Acronym or abbreviation: BVA

330 Grays Inn Road, London, WC1X 8EE

Tel: 020 7713 0064
Fax: 020 7915 1388
E-mail: administrator@britishvoiceassociation.org .uk

Website:
http://www.britishvoiceassociation.org.uk

Enquiries:
Enquiries to: Administrator

Founded:
1991

Organisation type and purpose:
Professional body, registered charity.
An umbrella group for all professionals involved with the care of the human voice – from laryngologists and speech and language therapists to voice and singing teachers.

Subject coverage:
Multidisciplinary voice; otolaryngology; speech and language therapy; teachers of singing; singers; voice trainers, students of all of the above.

Printed publications:
List of voice clinics in the UK
Newsletter (3 times a year and published in print and web form)
Logopedics Phoniatrics Vocology (journal, 2 issues – previously 4, but issues 1 & 2, and 3 & 4, are now sent out together)
List of members (members only)

Electronic and video publications:
Newsletter (online, 3 times a year)

Publications list:
Available online and in print

Access to staff:
Contact by letter, by telephone, by fax, by e-mail and via website
Hours: Mon to Fri, 0900 to 1700

Access for disabled people:
Parking provided, ramped entry, toilet facilities
Special comments: Please check for parking availability.

BRITISH WATCH AND CLOCKMAKERS GUILD

Acronym or abbreviation: BWCMG

PO Box 2368, Romford, Essex, RM1 2YZ

Tel: 01708 750616
E-mail: sec@bwcmg.org

Website:
http://www.bwcmg.org

Enquiries:
Enquiries to: Honorary Secretary

Founded:
1907

Organisation type and purpose:
Trade association (membership is by election or invitation).
Trade organisation to protect the interests of those engaged in the watch, clock and general horological industry.

Subject coverage:
Horological and allied crafts.

Printed publications:
Members newsletter (3 times a year) and annual yearbook

Access to staff:
Contact by letter, by telephone and by e-mail
Hours: Mon to Fri, 1300 to 1800

BRITISH WATER

1 Queen Anne's Gate, London, SW1H 9BT

Tel: 020 7957 4554
Fax: 020 7957 4565
E-mail: info@britishwater.co.uk

Website:
http://www.britishwater.co.uk

Enquiries:
Enquiries to: Chief Executive
Other contacts: (1) International Director (2) Technical Director (3) UK Director for (1) inward/ outward trade missions (2) standards/regulations/ technology (3) industrial/municipal/domestic (POU) equipment.

Founded:
1993

Organisation type and purpose:
Trade association (membership is by subscription). The British water and waste water industry worldwide.

Subject coverage:
Plant for the treatment of water for potable or industrial use; disinfection of swimming pools; plant for the treatment of domestic and municipal sewage and liquid industrial waste, and for industrial and waterworks sludges; domestic water softeners etc; statistics. With some 200 members, it promotes the involvement of all sectors in water-related projects, working closely with government and government departments at home and overseas; it organises outward and inward missions, seminars, exhibitions and other platforms to promote the technical, financial and administrative expertise of the British water sector. The organisation operates technical committees concerned with all aspects of the industry's activities and collaborates with British and European agencies in the development of standards.

Non-library collection catalogue:
All or part available online and in-house

Library catalogue:
All or part available online

Printed publications:
Annual Report
Codes of Practice for Swimming Pool Ozone Plant and Water Softeners
Guidance documents
Membership list including products, services and buyers' guide
Standards

Publications list:
Available online

Access to staff:
Contact by letter, by telephone, by fax, by e-mail and via website. Appointment necessary.
Hours: Mon to Fri, 0900 to 1700

Access to building, collection or gallery:
Prior appointment required

Links with:
Aqua Europa
Geelseweg 56, B-2250, Olen, Belgium
METCOM
Savoy Tower, Glasgow, G2 3BZ; tel: 0141 332 5788; fax: 0141 332 0826

BRITISH WATER SKI & WAKEBOARD

Unit 3 The Forum, Hanworth Lane, Chertsey, Surrey, KT16 9JX

Tel: 01932 560007
Fax: 01932 570028
E-mail: via website

Website:
http://www.britishwaterski.org.uk
Waterskiing, ski clubs, ski schools, safety and welfare, instructor courses, events, news, contacts.

Founded:
1951

Formerly called:
British Water Ski; British Water Ski Federation (BWSF) (year of change 1999)

Organisation type and purpose:
The national governing body for water skiing in Great Britain, a non-profit making organisation.

Subject coverage:
Responsible for the development of the sport; co-ordination of national and international competition; selection of national teams; training and registration of coaches and officials; increasing the opportunities for participation in water skiing for all residents, including the disabled; actively encourages newcomers to the sport, promotes good practice and safety and works to enhance and improve standards of coaching and driving; has highly active competition programmes in all divisions of the sport.

Access to staff:
Contact by letter, by telephone, by fax and via website

Affiliated to:
International Water Ski & Wakeboard Federation (IWWF)

Member organisation of:
Boating Alliance
Central Council for Physical Recreation (CCPR)
European Boating Association
Parliamentary Waterways Group
ROSPA

BRITISH WEIGHT LIFTERS ASSOCIATION LIMITED

Acronym or abbreviation: BWLA

Lilleshall National Sports Centre, near Newport, Shropshire, TF10 9AT

Tel: 01952 604201
Fax: 01952 604265
E-mail: steve.cannon@uklifting.demon.co.uk

Website:
http://www.bwla.netcalm.co.uk
General information.

Enquiries:
Enquiries to: Chief Executive Officer

Organisation type and purpose:
Membership association (membership is by subscription), present number of members: 4,000, voluntary organisation.
Sports governing body.

Subject coverage:
Weightlifting, powerlifting, weight training and fitness training with weights.

Printed publications:
The BWLA Safe Weight Training Manual
The BWLA Handbook
The British Weight Lifter (magazine)
Training books

Publications list:
Available in print

Access to staff:
Contact by letter, by telephone and by fax
Hours: Mon to Fri, 0900 to 1700

Affiliated to:
European Powerlifting Federation
European Weightlifting Federation
International Powerlifting Federation
International Weightlifting Federation

continued overleaf

Links with:
British Olympic Committee
Central Council of Physical Recreation
Commonwealth Games Council

Welsh Divisional Association:
British Amateur Weight Lifters Association
  Pennant Blaenau, Ammanford, Dyfed, SA18 3BZ

BRITISH WEIGHTS AND MEASURES ASSOCIATION

Acronym or abbreviation: BWMA

PO Box 590, London, WC1 X0U

Tel: 020 8922 0089 (24-hour answer machine)

Website:
http://www.bwmaonline.com
http://www.footrule.org

Enquiries:
Enquiries to: Director
Other contacts: Press Officer, tel no: 01568 708820, fax 01568 708765

Founded:
c1868

Organisation type and purpose:
Membership association.
To oppose compulsory metrication and to explain the good reasons for using traditional weights and measures.

Subject coverage:
The advantages of British weights and measures and the disadvantages of metrication.

Printed publications:
The Yardstick (quarterly, £10 a year)
The Footrule (newsletter, free to members)

Access to staff:
Contact by letter, by telephone and by fax
Hours: Mon to Fri, 0900 to 1700

Access to building, collection or gallery:
Prior appointment required

Access for disabled people:
Level entry, toilet facilities

BRITISH WHEEL OF YOGA, THE

25 Jermyn Street, Sleaford, Lincolnshire, NG34 7RU

Tel: 01529 306851
Fax: 01529 303233
E-mail: office@bwt.org.uk

Website:
http://www.bwy.org.uk

Enquiries:
Enquiries to: Central Office Manager
Direct tel: 01529 303881
Direct e-mail: office@bwy.org.uk

Founded:
1965

Organisation type and purpose:
National organisation, membership association (membership is by subscription), present number of members: 8400, registered charity (charity number 264993), training organisation.
The governing body for yoga in Great Britain, non-political, non-sectarian.
To encourage and help all persons to a greater knowledge and understanding of all aspects of Yoga and its practice by the provision of study, education and training, to maintain and improve the standard of teaching.

Subject coverage:
Yoga: philosophy involving meditation and physical discipline; training of yoga teachers; yoga for therapy and for the elderly and less able.

Printed publications:
Quarterly Regional Newsletter
Spectrum: quarterly magazine (for members)
Order printed publications from: BWY Services

e-mail: office@bwy.org.uk

Electronic and video publications:
British Wheel of Yoga (video/DVD)

Access to staff:
Contact by letter, by telephone, by fax, by e-mail and via website
Hours: Mon to Fri, 0900 to 1700

Affiliated to:
European Union of National Federations of Yoga

Member of:
Central Council of Physical Recreation

BRITISH WHEELCHAIR SPORTS FOUNDATION

Acronym or abbreviation: BWSF

Guttmann Road, Stoke Mandeville, Aylesbury, Buckinghamshire, HP21 9PP

Tel: 01296 395995
Fax: 01296 424171
E-mail: infos@bwsf.org.uk

Website:
http://www.bwsf.org.uk

Enquiries:
Enquiries to: Chief Executive
Other contacts: Head of Public Relations

Founded:
1952

Organisation type and purpose:
National organisation, membership association (membership is by subscription, election or invitation), present number of members: 1500, voluntary organisation, registered charity (charity number 265498).
National body for wheelchair sport – sport for disabled people.

Subject coverage:
Wheelchair sports; archery, athletics, basketball, bowls, fencing, rugby, shooting, snooker, swimming, table tennis, tennis, weightlifting, wintersports – sledge hockey and handcycling.

Printed publications:
Handbook (annually, free)
Newsletter (quarterly, free to members)

Access to staff:
Contact by letter, by telephone, by e-mail and via website. Appointment necessary.
Hours: Mon to Fri, 0900 to 1700

Access to building, collection or gallery:
Prior appointment required

Access for disabled people:
Access to all public areas

Affiliated to:
British Paralympic Association
  tel: 020 8681 9655

Member of:
International Paralympic Committee
International Stoke Mandeville Wheelchair Sports Federation
  tel: 01296 436179
Royal Association for Disability and Rehabilitation
  tel: 020 7250 3222

BRITISH WILDLIFE PUBLISHING LTD

The Old Dairy, Milton on Stour, Gillingham, Dorset, SP8 5PX

Tel: 01747 835511
Fax: 01747 835522
E-mail: enquiries@britishwildlife.com

Website:
http://www.britishwildlife.com
Details of BW magazine.

Enquiries:
Enquiries to: Information Officer

Founded:
1989

Organisation type and purpose:
Publishing house.

Subject coverage:
Natural history, environment, conservation.

Printed publications:
British Wildlife (magazine, 6 times a year, for purchase)
Conservation Land Management (magazine, 4 times a year, for purchase)
Order printed publications from: British Wildlife Publishing, The Old Dairy, Milton on Stour, Gillingham, Dorset, SP8 5PX; tel: 01747 835511

Access to staff:
Contact by letter and by fax
Hours: Mon to Fri, 0900 to 1700

BRITISH WILDLIFE RESCUE CENTRE

Acronym or abbreviation: BWRC

Amerton Working Farm, Amerton, Stafford, ST18 0LA

Tel: 01889 271308
E-mail: ahardy@thebwrc.co.uk

Website:
http://www.britishwildliferescure.co.uk

Enquiries:
Enquiries to: Owner

Founded:
1991

Organisation type and purpose:
Voluntary organisation, suitable for ages: all.

Subject coverage:
Rescue and rehabilitation of British wildlife, animal hospital, centre open to the public, school parties welcome, visits to schools, national curriculum subjects covered.

Printed publications:
Newsletter (quarterly, free on receipt of sae)

Access to staff:
Contact by letter, by telephone and in person
Hours: Summer: Sun to Sat, 1000 to 1800
Winter: Sun to Sat, 1000 to 1700
Special comments: Closed Christmas Day, New Year's Day

Access for disabled people:
Hours: Summer: Sun to Sat, 1000 to 1800
Winter: Sun to Sat, 1000 to 1700

Member and working links with:
Royal Society for the Prevention of Cruelty to Animals (RSPCA)

Member of:
British Wildlife Rehabilitation Council
  website: http://www.bwrc.co.uk

Postal address only:
British Wildlife Rescue Centre
  35 Marston Road, Stafford, ST16 3BT; tel: 01785 247486; e-mail: ahardy@thebwrc.org.uk; website: http://www.thebwrc.co.uk

BRITISH WIRELESS FOR THE BLIND FUND

Acronym or abbreviation: BWBF

10 Albion Place, Maidstone, Kent, ME14 5DZ

Tel: 01622 754757
Fax: 01622 751727
E-mail: info@blind.org.uk

Website:
http://www.blind.org.uk
Information and details of products and services provided by the charity.

Founded:
1929

Organisation type and purpose:
Registered charity (charity number 211849).
To provide the comfort of radio listening to the
registered blind in need.

Subject coverage:
Free permanent loan of radio, radio/cassette
players, CD/radio/cassette and internet radio for
registered blind people and partially sighted
people.

Services for disabled people:
Provision of radios and associated equipment to
registered blind and registered partially sighted
people resident in the United Kingdom, over the
age of 8 and in need. Sets can be sold to those who
do not qualify through the trading arm of the
charity.

Printed publications:
Annual Report and Accounts
Deed of Covenant (brochures)
Make a Will (brochures)
Talkabout (newsletter)
Info Leaflets

Access to staff:
Contact by letter, by telephone, by fax, by e-mail
and via website. Appointment necessary.
Hours: Mon to Fri, 0900 to 1700

Access for disabled people:
Full disabled access

BRITISH WOMEN PILOTS' ASSOCIATION

Acronym or abbreviation: BWPA

Brooklands Museum, Brooklands Road,
Weybridge, Surrey, KT13 0QN

E-mail: info@bwpa.co.uk

Website:
http://www.bwpa.co.uk

Enquiries:
Enquiries to: Chairman
Direct e-mail: info@bwpa.co.uk

Founded:
1955

Organisation type and purpose:
Membership association (membership is by
subscription).

Subject coverage:
Women in aviation, careers in aviation.

Information services:
Careers, recreational pilot training.

Education services:
Talks to schools.

Printed publications:
Quarterly newsletter
Newsletter (members only)

Access to staff:
Contact by letter, by e-mail and via website
Hours: Mon to Fri, 0900 to 1700

BRITISH WOODWORKING FEDERATION

Acronym or abbreviation: BWF

Royal London House, 22–25 Finsbury Square,
London, EC2A 1DX

Tel: 0844 209 2610
E-mail: via website

Website:
http://www.bwf.org.uk
BWF and its member services; code of conduct;
total support services; schemes for windows, fire
doors and stairs; training, including in health and
safety, management, site work, and timber and
sustainability; careers; news and events;
publications.

Enquiries:
Enquiries to: Chief Executive

Other contacts: Membership Director; Technical
Manager

Organisation type and purpose:
Membership organisation (membership is by
subscription), trade association.
Represents leading manufacturers, distributors
and installers of a variety of joinery and
woodworking products and ensures that they
comply with the highest technical and regulatory
standards.

Subject coverage:
Joinery and woodworking.

Electronic and video publications:
A wide range of publications to support members
and the joinery industry, including:
BWF Employee Handbook
Machine Safety Cards
Model Company Policies
Contractual and Employment Guidance
Technical Advice
Order electronic and video publications from: Most
publications can be downloaded free by members;
further copies can be ordered direct

Publications list:
Available online

Access to staff:
Contact by letter, by telephone and via website

Access to building, collection or gallery:
Entrance via north-east corner of Finsbury Sq.

Member organisation of:
Construction Confederation
Construction Products Association
TRADA
Trade Association Forum

BRITISH YOUTH COUNCIL

Acronym or abbreviation: BYC

Downstream Building, The Mezzanine 2, 1 London
Bridge, SE1 9BG

Tel: 0845 458 1489
Fax: 0845 458 1847
E-mail: mail@byc.org.uk

Website:
http://www.byc.org.uk
What BYC does; outline of activities; list of
publications.

Enquiries:
Enquiries to: Policy and Press Officer
Direct tel: 0845 458 1489
Direct e-mail: helen.deakin@byc.org.uk

Founded:
1948

Organisation type and purpose:
Membership association (membership is by
subscription), present number of members: 130
member organisations, voluntary organisation,
registered charity (charity number 305973).
The British Youth Council is the independent voice
of young people in the UK.
Representing the views of young people to
government and decision-makers at national and
international levels.

Subject coverage:
Interests and views of young people, advocacy for
the increased participation of young people in
society.

Printed publications:
Publications include:
BYC News – Quarterly Newsletter
A Young Person's Guide to Lobbying
Listening to the Unheard: The National Youth
Consultation for the European Youth Policy
(2000)
Peer Education – The British Youth Council's
Manual
State of the Young Nation – A Report by the British
Youth Council (1998)
Youth Index – an information and analysis service
with 2 publications:

Youth Agenda (monthly)
Youth Update (monthly)
Order printed publications from: Policy and Research
Officer, British Youth Council
at the same address, tel: 020 7422 8644, e-mail:
louise.king@byc.org.uk

Publications list:
Available in print

Access to staff:
Contact by letter, by telephone, by e-mail and via
website. Appointment necessary.
Hours: Mon to Fri, 0930 to 1800

Access to building, collection or gallery:
Prior appointment required

Access for disabled people:
Ramped entry

BRITISH-GERMAN ASSOCIATION

Acronym or abbreviation: BGA

34 Belgrave Square, London, SW1X 8QB

Tel: 020 7235 1922
Fax: 020 7235 1902
E-mail: bgalondon@compuserve.com

Enquiries:
Enquiries to: Honorary Treasurer
Direct tel: 020 7244 7663
Direct fax: 020 7373 3415

Founded:
1951

Organisation type and purpose:
Membership association (membership is by
subscription), present number of members: 1,000,
registered charity (charity number 206062).
Promotion of Anglo-German relations on an
educational and cultural basis.

Subject coverage:
All aspects of German affairs and British-German
cultural and educational relations.

Printed publications:
British-German Review (quarterly, for members)
Diary of Activities (for members)
Order printed publications from: Editor-in-Chief,
British-German Review
April House, Balcombe, Sussex, RH17 6LF, tel:
01444 811237, fax: 01444 811237

Access to staff:
Contact by letter, by telephone and by fax
Hours: Mon to Fri, 1100 to 1600

Connected with:
Deutsch Englische Gesellschaft (DEG)
Jaegerstrasse 54/5, 10112 Berlin, Germany; tel:
030 203 983

BRITISH-ISRAEL-WORLD FEDERATION

Acronym or abbreviation: BIWF

121 Low Etherley, Bishop Auckland, DL14 0HA

Tel: 01388 834395
Fax: 01388 835957
E-mail: admin@britishisrael.co.uk

Website:
http://www.britishisrael.co.uk
Publications catalogue, basis outline of belief/
research, membership details.

Enquiries:
Enquiries to: Administrator

Founded:
1919

Organisation type and purpose:
International organisation, national organisation
(membership is by subscription), present number
of members: 300, registered charity (charity
number 208079), research organisation, publishing
house.

continued overleaf

Christian heritage research into Anglo-Saxon-Celtic peoples as the modern-day descendants of the ancient Hebrew race and nation of Israel which spread to the west from the Assyrian and Babylonian Captivities.

Subject coverage:
Migrations of Israel in Europe; scriptural evidence, bible prophecy, early Christian Church, 1st century in Britain, charts of royal descent, heraldry showing British links with Israel, current events.

Museum or gallery collection, archive, or library special collection:
Books in library, not open to public

Printed publications:
The following are published by The Covenant Publishing Company Limited
The Origin and Early History of Christianity in Britain
Eating for Life
Celt, Druid and Culdee
The Hidden Treasure of the Parables
Royal House of Britain an Enduring Dynasty
Order printed publications from: The Covenant Publishing Company Limited
at the same address

Publications list:
Available online and in print

Access to staff:
Contact by letter, by telephone, by fax, by e-mail and via website. Appointment necessary.
Hours: Mon to Fri, 0900 to 1700

Access to building, collection or gallery:
Prior appointment required
Hours: Access for publications by prior appointment

Access for disabled people:
Parking provided, toilet facilities
Special comments: Level entry at rear from parking area.

Associated with similar:
Christian Israel Organisations in: Australia, Canada, Holland, New Zealand, South Africa and USA

BRITISH-ITALIAN SOCIETY

The Offices of Venice in Peril Fund, Hurlingham Studios (Unit 4), Ranelagh Gardens, London, SW6 3PA

Tel: 020 8150 9167
E-mail: jj@british-italian.org

Website:
http://www.british-italian.org

Enquiries:
Enquiries to: General Secretary

Founded:
1941

Organisation type and purpose:
Learned society, membership association (membership is by subscription), present number of members: 500, registered charity (charity number 253386).
To increase understanding of Italy in this country and to promote friendship between Great Britain and Italy.

Subject coverage:
General information on Italy.
No employment contacts.

Printed publications:
Rivista (quarterly, for members or by subscription)

Access to staff:
Contact by letter, by telephone, by fax and by e-mail
Hours: 3 days per week variable

Access to building, collection or gallery:
Prior appointment required

BRITISH-KAZAKH SOCIETY

Formal name: British-Kazakh Society

105 Salisbury Road, London, NW6 6RG

Tel: 020 7596 5176
Fax: 020 7596 5115
E-mail: info@bksoc.org.uk

Website:
http://www.bksoc.org.uk

Founded:
2002

Organisation type and purpose:
Individual and corporate membership organisation (membership by subscription)
To promote relations between the UK and Kazakhstan.

Access to staff:
Contact by letter, by telephone, by fax, by e-mail and via website

BRITISH–SERBIAN BENEVOLENT TRUST

Acronym or abbreviation: B-SBT

Glebelands, Star Lane, Rockland St Mary, Norwich, NR14 7BX

Tel: 01508 480262
Fax: 01508 480262
E-mail: orns@lineone.net

Enquiries:
Enquiries to: Chairman

Founded:
1917

Organisation type and purpose:
National organisation, registered charity (charity number 254179).
Charitable trust.

Subject coverage:
The relief of children resident in Serbia who are in conditions of need, hardship or distress.

Access to staff:
Contact by letter, by telephone, by fax and by e-mail. Appointment necessary.
Hours: Mon to Fri, 0900 to 1700

BRITTEN-PEARS LIBRARY

Formal name: Britten-Pears Foundation

The Red House, Golf Lane, Aldeburgh, Suffolk, IP15 5PZ

Tel: 01728 451700
Fax: 01728 453076
E-mail: enquiries@britten-pears.org

Website:
http://www.britten-pears.org
General information; access; collections; catalogue; exhibitions; publications; bibliography.

Enquiries:
Enquiries to: Director of Collections and Heritage
Other contacts: Archivist; Curator; Librarian; Promotions Manager

Founded:
1980

Organisation type and purpose:
Registered charity (charity number 295595), research organisation, publishing house.
Private research library.

Subject coverage:
Benjamin Britten's life, career and music, Peter Pears's life and career, English song (books and music), Gustav Holst's music, English Opera Group/English Music Theatre, Aldeburgh Festival, music in general.

Museum or gallery collection, archive, or library special collection:
Benjamin Britten's manuscripts (some on permanent loan from the British Library)
Britten's collection of printed music
Britten's personal papers (including correspondence and diaries)
Printers' copies, proofs and early editions of Britten's works
Peter Pears's collection of printed music
Pears's personal papers (including correspondence)
Extensive collection of sound recordings and video cassettes (chiefly relating to Britten and Pears)
English Opera Group/English Music Theatre Archive
Aldeburgh Festival Archive
Archive of press cuttings and programmes (chiefly relating to Britten and Pears)
Photographic archives (chiefly relating to Britten and Pears)
Manuscripts of works by other composers, including Bax, Bedford, L Berkeley, M Berkeley, Bridge, Crosse, Maxwell Davies, C A Gibbs, Greene, Harvey, Henze, G Holst, I Holst, Knussen, Lehmann, Lutoslawski, Maconchy, C Matthews, D Matthews, Maw, Moeran, Nash, Oldham, Quilter, Rainier, Saxton, Seiber, Shostakovich, Stanford, Tippett, Turnage, Weir, Wellesz, Williamson
Literary manuscripts, including those of W H Auden, Ronald Duncan, E M Forster, Thomas Hardy, Wilfred Owen, Myfanwy Piper, William Plomer, Edith Sitwell
English Song (from 16th century to present day)
Julian Herbage material relating to Thomas Arne
Holst Library, a lending library for use of students attending the Britten-Pears School for Advanced Musical Studies

Non-library collection catalogue:
All or part available online

Library catalogue:
All or part available online

Printed publications:
Benjamin Britten: A Catalogue of the Published Works
Britten and the Far East: Asian Influences in the Music of Benjamin Britten
The Making of Peter Grimes: A Facsimile of Benjamin Britten's Composition Draft
On Mahler and Britten: Essays in Honour of Donald Mitchell on His Seventieth Birthday
The Travel Diaries of Peter Pears
Britten's Gloriana: Essays and Sources
A Britten Source Book
Music of Forty Festivals: A list of works performed at the Aldeburgh Festivals from 1948 to 1987
Transcripts of the Prince of Hesse Memorial Lectures 1990 to 2000
Imogen Holst: a life in music
Benjamin Britten: New perspectives on his life and work

Publications list:
Available online and in print

Access to staff:
Contact by letter, by telephone, by fax, by e-mail and via website. Appointment necessary.
Hours: Mon to Fri, 1000 to 1300 and 1415 to 1715; closed on bank holidays

Access to building, collection or gallery:
Prior appointment required

Access for disabled people:
Level entry, toilet facilities

Administers the:
Holst Library

BRITTEN-PEARS YOUNG ARTIST PROGRAMME

Acronym or abbreviation: BPP

Snape Maltings Concert Hall, Snape, Saxmundham, Suffolk, IP17 1SP

Tel: 01728 688671
Fax: 01728 688171
E-mail: britten-pears@aldeburgh.co.uk

Website:
http://www.aldeburgh.co.uk

Information about the Britten-Pears Young Artist Programme, including courses for 2005 and an on-line application form.

Enquiries:
Enquiries to: Assistant
Other contacts: Administrator for orchestral enquiries.

Founded:
1972

Organisation type and purpose:
Music school.
The Britten-Pears Programme offers a unique opportunity for young professionals and advanced students to study intensively with some of the world's most respected musicians.

Access to staff:
Contact by letter, by telephone, by fax, by e-mail and via website
Hours: Mon to Fri, 0930 to 1730

Parent body:
Aldeburgh Productions
   Snape Maltings Concert Hall, Snape, Saxmundham, Suffolk, IP17 1SP; tel: 01708 687100; fax: 01728 687120; e-mail: info@ aldeburgh.co.uk

BRITTLE BONE SOCIETY

Acronym or abbreviation: BBS

Grant-Paterson House, 30 Guthrie Street, Dundee, DD1 5BS

Tel: 01382 204446 Freephone 08000 282459
Fax: 01382 206771

Enquiries:
Enquiries to: Chief Executive
Direct e-mail: annette@brittlebone.org

Founded:
1968

Organisation type and purpose:
Registered charity (Scottish registered charity SCO10951).
Promoting research and providing information and support for people and their relatives.

Subject coverage:
The society seeks to promote research into the causes, inheritance and treatment of osteogenesis imperfecta, characterised by excessive fragility of the bones. It also provides advice, encouragement and practical help for patients and their relatives facing the difficulties of living with brittle bones, practical aspects of living with brittle bones, education, wheelchairs and other equipment.

Publications list:
Available in print

Access to staff:
Contact by letter, by telephone and by e-mail.
Appointment necessary.
Hours: Mon to Fri, 0900 to 1630

Access to building, collection or gallery:
Hours: Mon to Fri, 0900 to 1630

Charity Shop:
BBS Shop
   112 City Road, Dundee; tel: 01382 667603

BROADCASTING GROUP OF THE SOCIETY OF AUTHORS

Acronym or abbreviation: SoA

84 Drayton Gardens, London, SW10 9SB

Tel: 020 7373 6642
Fax: 020 7373 5768
E-mail: info@societyofauthors.org

Organisation type and purpose:
Trade union.

Subject coverage:
Writing for radio and television.

Access to staff:
Contact by letter and by e-mail
Hours: 0930 to 1730

BROADCASTING, ENTERTAINMENT, CINEMATOGRAPH AND THEATRE UNION

Acronym or abbreviation: BECTU

373–377 Clapham Road, London, SW9 9BT

Tel: 020 7346 0900
Fax: 020 7346 0901
E-mail: info@bectu.org.uk

Website:
http://www.bectu.org.uk

Enquiries:
Enquiries to: Administrator

Founded:
1991

Incorporates the former:
ABS, ACTT, BETA, FAA, NATTKE (year of change 1991)

Organisation type and purpose:
Trade union, present number of members: 26,000.

Subject coverage:
The interests of workers in broadcasting, film, theatre and related areas of the arts and media.

Museum or gallery collection, archive, or library special collection:
Documents of the Unions dating back to 1890 (uncatalogued)

Printed publications:
Stage, Screen and Radio (journal, 8 times a year)

Access to staff:
Contact by letter, by telephone, by e-mail and via website. Access for members only.
Hours: Mon to Fri, 0900 to 1700

Access for disabled people:
Wheelchair lift, toilet facilities, induction loop

Affiliated to:
Trades Union Congress

Affiliated via Federation of Entertainment Unions to:
Irish Congress of Trade Unions
Labour Party
Uni-Media Entertainment International
Wales Trades Union Congress

Member organisations:
Scottish Trades Union Congress

BROADLAND DISTRICT COUNCIL

Thorpe Lodge, 1 Yarmouth Road, Thorpe St Andrew, Norwich, Norfolk, NR7 0DU

Tel: 01603 431133
Fax: 01603 300087
E-mail: reception@broadland.gov.uk

Website:
http://www.broadland.gov.uk
Services for local people, tourism and business development information.

Enquiries:
Enquiries to: Communications Manager
Direct tel: 01603 430523
Direct fax: 01603 430614
Direct e-mail: angi.doy@broadland.gov.uk

Founded:
1974

Organisation type and purpose:
Local government body.

Subject coverage:
Broadland District Council area, services and amenities.

Education services:
Broadland Council Training Services

Printed publications:
Training Prospectus & Business Directory
Broadland News (4 times a year)
Property Register
Order printed publications from: e-mail: news@ broadland.gov.uk

Electronic and video publications:
Order electronic and video publications from: website: http://www.broadland.gov.uk

Access to staff:
Contact by letter, by telephone, by fax, by e-mail and via website. Appointment necessary.
Hours: Mon to Fri, 0900 to 1700

Access to building, collection or gallery:
Hours: Mon to Fri, 0900 to 1700

Access for disabled people:
Parking provided, ramped entry

BROADS AUTHORITY, THE

18 Colegate, Norwich, Norfolk, NR3 1BQ

Tel: 01603 610734
Fax: 01603 765710
E-mail: broads@broads-authority.gov.uk

Website:
http://www.broads-authority.gov.uk
General and Press.

Enquiries:
Enquiries to: Information Officer

Founded:
1989

Organisation type and purpose:
Local government body.
Equivalent to national park.

Subject coverage:
The Broads: conservation (including planning), recreation, navigation.

Printed publications:
Broads Authority Research Series
Broads Design and Management Information
Project Design Series (prices vary)
Research Series (prices vary)
The Broads Plan 2004 (£5, inc. p&p)
Various general titles including:
Broads Fact pack: two books covering all aspects of
   the Broads life and landscape (£2.99)
Broad Walks: maps and guides to eight walks in
   the Bure Valley (£2.50)
Hathor, goddess of love and joy: the story of a
   Norfolk pleasure wherry (£2)

Publications list:
Available online and in print

Access to staff:
Contact by letter, by telephone, by fax and by e-mail. Appointment necessary.
Hours: Mon to Fri, 0900 to 1700

BROADS SOCIETY

Solar Via, Happisburgh, Norwich, Norfolk, NR12 0QU

Tel: 01692 651321
E-mail: broads_society.admin@bigfoot.com

Website:
http://www.broads-society.org.uk
Description of Broads environment, ecology, recreation, navigation and role of Society in preservation and enhancement.

Enquiries:
Enquiries to: Administrator
Other contacts: Chairman

Founded:
1956

continued overleaf

Organisation type and purpose:
Membership association (membership is by subscription), present number of members: 1,700, voluntary organisation, registered charity (charity number 1078434).
Voluntary body dedicated to securing a sustainable future for The Broads as a unique and protected landscape in which leisure, tourism and the local economy can thrive in harmony with the natural environment.

Subject coverage:
Wetland conservation, navigation on inland waters.

Museum or gallery collection, archive, or library special collection:
Collection of all back issues of quarterly magazine

Printed publications:
The Harnser (magazine, quarterly, ISSN 1368–5554, free to members, back issues available free from Administrator)

Access to staff:
Contact by letter, by telephone, by e-mail and via website
Hours: Any reasonable time; 24-hour answering service

Also at:
Broads Society Editor
Grebe Cottage, New Road, Catfield, Great Yarmouth, NR29 5BQ; tel: 01692 584179; e-mail: harnser2006@yahoo.co.uk

BROMLEY COLLEGE OF FURTHER AND HIGHER EDUCATION

Acronym or abbreviation: BCFHE

Rookery Lane, Bromley, Kent, BR2 8HE

Tel: 020 8295 7000
Fax: 020 8295 7099
E-mail: library@bromley.ac.uk

Website:
http://www.bromley.ac.uk
Qualifications offered; international information; information request form; College news; course list and course details.

Enquiries:
Enquiries to: Librarian
Direct tel: 020 8295 7024
Direct e-mail: judym@bromley.ac.uk

Founded:
1959

Organisation type and purpose:
Suitable for ages: all.
Library of a college of further and higher education.

Subject coverage:
Life science, engineering (electrical, mechanical and motor vehicle), social work, business, finance, law, IT, software engineering, hairdressing and beauty therapy, leisure, travel and tourism, counselling, teaching and training, media, built environment, sport.

Library catalogue:
All or part available online and in-house

Access to staff:
Contact by telephone, by e-mail and via website.
Appointment necessary.
Hours: Mon to Fri, 0900 to 1700

Access for disabled people:
Parking provided, ramped entry, toilet facilities

Also at:
Old Town Hall Site
Tweedy Road, Bromley, BR2 8HE; tel: 020 8295 7091

BROMLEY HOUSE LIBRARY

Acronym or abbreviation: BHL

Bromley House, Angel Row, Nottingham, NG1 6HL

Tel: 0115 947 3134
E-mail: enquiries@bromleyhouse.org

Website:
http://www.bromleyhouse.org

Enquiries:
Enquiries to: Librarian

Founded:
1816

Organisation type and purpose:
Membership association (membership is by subscription), present number of members: 1,000, registered charity (charity number 1074752).
Private library for research purposes.

Subject coverage:
Victorian fiction, history, local history, biography, travel, theology.

Printed publications:
Bromley House 1752–1991 (ed Coope R and Corbett J, £6, pbk)

Access to staff:
Contact by letter, by telephone and by e-mail.
Appointment necessary. Access for members only.
Letter of introduction required.
Hours: Mon to Fri, 0930 to 1700

Access for disabled people:
No disabled access
Special comments: Situated on first floor and above.

BROMLEY PUBLIC LIBRARIES

Central Library, High Street, Bromley, Kent, BR1 1EX

Tel: 020 8460 9955
Fax: 020 8466 7860
E-mail: informationservices@bromley.gov.uk

Website:
http://www.bromley.gov.uk/libraries

Enquiries:
Enquiries to: Principal Library Service Manager

Organisation type and purpose:
Local government body, public library.

Subject coverage:
General; geography, travel and history of all countries, excluding Europe, history and studies of the London Borough of Bromley.

Museum or gallery collection, archive, or library special collection:
Crystal Palace collection
H. G. Wells collection
Harlow bequest (Orpington and Kent)
Walter de la Mare collection

Library catalogue:
All or part available online

Printed publications:
Bibliographies
Catalogue of the H. G. Wells collection
Various local history publications
Order printed publications from: Local Studies Librarian, Central Library, High Street, Bromley, BR1 1EX; tel. 020 8461 7170; fax 020 8466 7860; e-mail localstudies.library@bromley.gov.uk

Access to staff:
Contact by letter, by telephone, by e-mail and in person
Hours: Central Library: Mon, Wed, Fri, 0930 to 1800; Tue, Thu, 0930 to 2000; Sat, 0930 to 1700
Branch Libraries: open at 0930, but are all closed one day a week (Burnt Ash three days, Hayes three days), so telephone first

Branch libraries:
Anerley Library
Anerley Town Hall, Anerley Road, Anerley, SE20 8BD; tel: 020 8778 7457
Beckenham Library
Beckenham Road, Beckenham, BR3 4PE; tel: 020 8650 7292

Biggin Hill Library
Church Road, Biggin Hill, TN16 3LB; tel: 01959 574468
Burnt Ash Library
Burnt Ash Lane, Bromley, BR1 5AF; tel: 020 8460 3405
Chislehurst Library
Red Hill, Chislehurst, BR7 6DA; tel: 020 8467 1318
Hayes Library
Hayes Street, Hayes, BR2 7LH; tel: 020 8462 2445
Mottingham Library
31 Mottingham Road, Mottingham, SE9 4QZ; tel: 020 8857 5406
Orpington Library
The Priory, Church Hill, Orpington, BR6 0HH; tel: 01689 831551
Penge Library
186 Maple Road, Penge, SE20 8HT; tel: 020 8778 8772
Petts Wood Library
Frankswood Road, Petts Wood, BR5 1BP; tel: 01689 821607
Shortlands Library
110 Shortlands Road, Bromley, BR2 0JP; tel: 020 8460 9692
Southborough Library
Southborough Lane, Bromley, BR2 8HP; tel: 020 8467 0355
St Paul's Cray Library
Mickleham Road, St Paul's Cray, Kent, BR5 2RW; tel: 020 8300 5454
West Wickham Library
Glebe Way, West Wickham, BR4 0SH; tel: 020 8777 4139

Parent body:
The London Borough of Bromley

BROMYARD AND DISTRICT LOCAL HISTORY SOCIETY

5 Sherford Street, Bromyard, Herefordshire, HR7 4DL

Tel: 01885 488755
E-mail: bromyard.history@virgin.net

Website:
http://www.bromyardhistorysociety.org.uk

Founded:
1966

Organisation type and purpose:
A registered charity (no. 1051572), with a local history centre run by volunteers.

Subject coverage:
History of Bromyard and the surrounding area.

Museum or gallery collection, archive, or library special collection:
Archive of documents, books, maps, newspapers and photographs

Printed publications:
Newsletter

Publications list:
Available online

Access to building, collection or gallery:
Hours: Thu and Fri, 1000 to 1300 and 1400 to 1630; Sat, 1000 to 1230

BRONTË SOCIETY

The Brontë Parsonage Museum, Church Street, Haworth, Keighley, West Yorkshire, BD22 8DR

Tel: 01535 642323
Fax: 01535 647131
E-mail: bronte@bronte.org.uk

Website:
http://www.bronte.info
Information about the Brontë Parsonage Museum and the Brontë Society.

Enquiries:
Enquiries to: Library and Information Officer
Direct tel: 01535 640199

Direct e-mail: sarah.laycock@bronte.org.uk
Other contacts: Director, Brontë Parsonage Museum
for all matters concerning the museum.

Founded:
1893

Organisation type and purpose:
Learned society (membership is by subscription),
present number of members: 1,750, voluntary
organisation, registered charity (charity number
529952), suitable for ages: all.
Entrusted with the ownership and care of the
Brontë Parsonage Museum.
To stimulate interest in the writing and the history
of the Brontë Family and to promote
understanding of their contemporary significance
as an integral part of the intellectual, cultural and
historical heritage of world literature.

Subject coverage:
The writings of the Brontës and those associated
with them; interpretations of their lives and works,
subsequent biographies, monographs and
scholarly criticism.

**Museum or gallery collection, archive, or library
special collection:**
Books, manuscripts, drawings, furnishings and
artefacts owned by the Brontës
Bonnell Collection: archive of manuscripts,
drawings, first editions, Brontës' own books
Brontë Society General Collection: archive of
manuscripts, letters, drawings, first editions,
Brontës' own books, furniture, personal
memorabilia
Grolier Collection of manuscripts
Seton Gordon Collection of manuscripts

Non-library collection catalogue:
All or part available in-house

Printed publications:
The Art of The Brontës (catalogue)
Journal of the Brontë Studies (journal, 3 times a
year, by subscription, reduced rate for members)
The Brontë Parsonage Museum (Guide to the
house, with Brontë chronology)
The Brontë Society Gazette (newsletter, free to
members)

Access to staff:
Contact by letter, by telephone, by fax, by e-mail
and via website. Appointment necessary.
Hours: Mon to Fri, 1000 to 1630
Special comments: Visitors to the research library by
prior appointment. Academic reference required in
advance for access to primary sources.

Links with:
Irish Brontë Society

Member organisation of:
Alliance of Literary Societies (ALS)
Association of Independent Museums (AIM)
Yorkshire and Humberside Museums Council
(YMHC)

BROOKLANDS SOCIETY LIMITED

Rudgelands, 4 Blackstone Hill, Redhill, Surrey,
RH1 6BE

Tel: 01737 217221
Fax: 01737 764401
E-mail: reynolds@rudgelands.prestel.co.uk

Website:
http://www.brooklands.org.uk

Enquiries:
Enquiries to: Assistant Secretary

Founded:
1967

Organisation type and purpose:
International organisation, learned society,
membership association (membership is by
subscription), present number of members: 1350,
voluntary organisation.

Subject coverage:
Brookland motor course and airfield, history and
preservation of relics.

**Museum or gallery collection, archive, or library
special collection:**
Large archive of films, photographs and artefacts
related to the Brooklands motor course and the
personalities involved for the period 1907–1987

Printed publications:
The following are available free or for purchase
direct:
Occasional Historic Publications
Quarterly Gazette
Quarterly Newsletter

Publications list:
Available online and in print

Access to staff:
Contact by letter, by telephone, by fax, by e-mail
and via website. Appointment necessary.

Access to building, collection or gallery:
Prior appointment required

Affiliated to:
Brooklands Museum Trust
Brooklands Museum, Brooklands Road,
Weybridge, Surrey, KT13 0QN

Website management:
Brooklands Society Limited
Hartland, Copse Corner, 38 Coxheath Road,
Church Crookham, Hampshire, GU13 0QC; tel:
01252 408877; fax: 01252 408878; e-mail:
brooklands@hartland.co.uk

BROOM'S BARN RESEARCH STATION

Higham, Bury St Edmunds, Suffolk, IP28 6NP

Tel: 01284 812200
Fax: 01284 811191

Website:
http://www.broomsbarn.ac.uk
Advisory information for UK sugar beet growers
and advisers, areas of research, job vacancies.

Enquiries:
Enquiries to: Information Officer
Direct tel: 01284 812230
Direct e-mail: mike.may@bbsrc.ac.uk

Organisation type and purpose:
Research organisation.
Agricultural research station for English sugar beet
crop.

Subject coverage:
Sugar beet crop rotation: seed quality, fertiliser
practice, irrigation, crop agronomy; sugar beet
crop protection: seedling pests and diseases, beet
cyst nematode, virus yellows and vector aphids,
leaf diseases, rhizomania, weed control.

Library catalogue:
All or part available in-house

Printed publications:
Growers Guide (every 4 to 5 years)
Reprints of Scientific Papers (free)
Station Guide (free)

Access to staff:
Contact by letter, by telephone, by fax and by e-
mail
Hours: Mon to Thu, 0830 to 1700; Fri, 0830 to 1630

Funded by:
Biotechnology and Biological Sciences Research
Council

BROUGH SUPERIOR CLUB

Flint Cottage, St Pauls Walden, Hitchin,
Hertfordshire, SG4 8DN

Tel: 01438 871714

Enquiries:
Enquiries to: Secretary

Organisation type and purpose:
Voluntary organisation.

Subject coverage:
Preservation and use of W.E. Brough and Brough
Superior Motorcycles, and any knowledge relating
to these.

BROUGHAM HALL CHARITABLE TRUST

Acronym or abbreviation: BHCT

Brougham Hall, Brougham, Penrith, Cumbria,
CA10 2DE

Tel: 01768 868184
Fax: 01768 862306
E-mail: juliachurchill@sky.com

Website:
http://www.broughamhall.co.uk

Enquiries:
Enquiries to: Administrator

Founded:
1986

Organisation type and purpose:
Registered charity (charity number 517943),
museum, historic building, house or site, suitable
for ages: school leavers and undergraduates;
training organisation, consultancy, research
organisation, publishing house.

Subject coverage:
Vernacular crafts, architecture, stone masonry,
political history.

**Museum or gallery collection, archive, or library
special collection:**
A collection of books, documents, manuscripts,
pictures, photographs and other materials

Library catalogue:
All or part available in-house

Printed publications:
A History of Brougham Hall and Highhead Castle
(Philimore, 1992, £30)
Windsor of the North (Ross, 1999, £9)
Order printed publications from: Brougham Hall,
Brougham, Penrith, Cumbria, CA10 2DE

Publications list:
Available in print

Access to staff:
Contact by letter
Hours: Mon to Fri, 0900 to 1700
Special comments: Prior appointment preferred.

Access to building, collection or gallery:
No prior appointment required
Hours: Mon to Fri, 0900 to 1700

Access for disabled people:
Parking provided, ramped entry, level entry, toilet
facilities
Special comments: Access to most areas, including
cafe.

BROXBOURNE BOROUGH COUNCIL

Borough Offices, Bishops' College, Churchgate,
Cheshunt, Hertfordshire, EN8 9XQ

Tel: 01992 785555\ Minicom no. 01992 785581
Fax: 01992 785578
E-mail: enquiry@broxbourne.gov.uk

Website:
http://www.broxbourne.gov.uk

Enquiries:
Enquiries to: Senior Communications Officer

Founded:
1974

Organisation type and purpose:
Local government body.

continued overleaf

Subject coverage:
Local information, tourism, recycling, refuse, environment, leisure facilities, social housing, building control, planning and development, council tax.

Access to staff:
Contact by letter, by telephone, by fax, by e-mail and via website
Hours: Mon, Wed, Thu, 0800 to 1800; Tue, 0800 to 1930; Fri, 0800 to 1730; Sat, 0900 to 1300

Access for disabled people:
Parking provided, level entry, access to all public areas, toilet facilities

Also at:
Broxbourne Borough Council
Unit 5, Broxbourne Business Centre, New River Estate, Cheshunt, Waltham Cross, Hertfordshire, EN8 0NP; tel: 01992 642240; fax: 01992 642216; e-mail: broxserv@broxbourne.gov.uk

BRUNEL INSTITUTE FOR BIOENGINEERING

Acronym or abbreviation: BIB

Information Unit, Brunel University, Uxbridge, Middlesex, UB8 3PH

Tel: 01895 266926
Fax: 01895 274608
E-mail: dawn.brandl@brunel.ac.uk

Website:
http://www.brunel.ac.uk

Enquiries:
Enquiries to: Information Officer

Founded:
1983

Organisation type and purpose:
University department or institute.
Commercial institute attached to Brunel University.

Subject coverage:
Mainly countercurrent chromatography and centrifugal partition chromatography, but will compile bibliographies on any relevant subject

Printed publications:
Bibliography of counter-current chromatography 1964–2004 (£50)

Access to staff:
Contact by letter, by telephone, by fax, by e-mail and in person. Appointment necessary. Non-members charged.
Hours: Fri, 0730 to 1500

Access for disabled people:
Toilet facilities

BRUNEL UNIVERSITY

Library, Uxbridge, Middlesex, UB8 3PH

Tel: 01895 266154
Fax: 01895 203263
E-mail: library@brunel.ac.uk

Website:
http://www.brunel.ac.uk/life/study/library

Enquiries:
Direct tel: 01896 266154

Founded:
1965

Organisation type and purpose:
University library.

Subject coverage:
Biology, computer science, economics, electrical engineering, government, human sciences, law, mathematics, health sciences, arts and media, education, design, management, government, social work, sports science, occupational therapy, physiotherapy, sports medicine, sports science, education, social work, arts and humanities.

Museum or gallery collection, archive, or library special collection:
Collection of Working Class autobiographies
Channel Tunnel Library and Archive (Runnymede Campus)
Clinker and Garnett Railway Collection (Runnymede Campus)
I K Brunel photographs (please direct enquiries to Library Office)
Maria Grey Archives (Runnymede Campus)
Murray Collection (Victorian children's books) (Runnymede Campus)
Salmon Collection (books and pamphlets on Joseph Lancaster in the British and Foreign School Society Archives) (Runnymede Campus)

Library catalogue:
All or part available online

Access to staff:
Contact by letter, by telephone and by e-mail. Appointment necessary.
Hours: Hours may vary during weekends, vacations and semesters

Access for disabled people:
Access to all public areas, toilet facilities

BSA FRONT-WHEEL DRIVE CLUB

Acronym or abbreviation: BSAFWDC

93 Barkby Road, Syston, Leicestershire, LE7 2AH

Tel: 0116 260 9663

Website:
http://www.bsafwdc.co.uk

Enquiries:
Enquiries to: Information Officer

Founded:
1959

Organisation type and purpose:
To preserve the BSA front-wheel drive car and to maintain its position in the history of motor-engineering.

Subject coverage:
BSA front-wheel drive 3- and 4-wheel cars produced from 1929 to 1939. Also caters for RWD cars.

Printed publications:
Front Wheels (bulletin, monthly, members)

BSA OWNERS' CLUB

Formal name: Birmingham Small Arms Owners' Club

PO Box 27, Crewe, Cheshire, CW1 6GE

E-mail: bsaoc@bsaoc.demon.co.uk

Website:
http://www.bsaoc.demon.co.uk
General information on club and news of forthcoming events. Links to like-minded URLs.

Enquiries:
Enquiries to: National Secretary

Founded:
1958

Organisation type and purpose:
Membership association (membership is by subscription), present number of members: 4000. Support for owners of BSA Motorcycles worldwide in terms of technical help and opportunity to get together with other motorcyclists.

Subject coverage:
Information and technical advice on motorcycles produced by the Birmingham Small Arms Co. This includes original factory machine dispatch books, an archive of technical and publicity material. The club also offers social events for BSA owners through regional branch meetings and national and international rallies. International branches also exist.

Library catalogue:
All or part available in-house

Printed publications:
The Star (magazine, monthly, members)
Occasional handbook for members

Access to staff:
Contact by letter, by e-mail and via website. Non-members charged.
Hours: Mon to Fri, 0900 to 1700

BSEM

Formal name: British Society for Ecological Medicine

c/o New Medicine Group, PO Box 3AP, London, W1A 3AP

Tel: 020 7100 7090
E-mail: info@ecomed.org.uk

Website:
http://www.ecomed.org.uk

Enquiries:
Enquiries to: Administrator

Founded:
1993

Organisation type and purpose:
Membership association (membership is by subscription), present number of members: 160, registered charity (charity number 326372).

Subject coverage:
Nutritional and environmental medicine.

Publications list:
Available in print

Access to staff:
Contact by letter, by telephone and by e-mail
Hours: Mon, Tue and Thu, 0900 to 1700

BSI

Formal name: British Standards Institution

389 Chiswick High Road, London, W4 4AL

Tel: 020 8996 7004, Library
Fax: 020 8996 7005
E-mail: library@bsi-global.com

Website:
http://www.bsi-global.com
Information on BSI's products and services. On-line catalogue of BSI publications. British Standards on-line (subscription service).

Enquiries:
Enquiries to: Librarian
Direct tel: 020 8996 7041
Direct e-mail: mary.yates@bsi-global.com

Founded:
1901

Organisation type and purpose:
Professional body (membership is by subscription), present number of members: 20,000.
National Standards body.

Subject coverage:
British, international and overseas standards and technical requirements covering most subject areas, certification schemes, European Community legislation, environmental issues.

Museum or gallery collection, archive, or library special collection:
BSI current and obsolete standards
Books on quality and environmental management
International and overseas national standards and related specifications (Library)

Printed publications:
British Standards
Business Standards (monthly)
BSI Root Thesaurus
BSI Standards Catalogue (annually, with supplement monthly, cumulative)
BSI Update (monthly)

Microform publications:
British Standards on microform, available from
Technical Indexes

Electronic and video publications:
Electronic catalogue (monthly)
British Standards are available online via web site
on a subscription basis
PERINORM, CD-ROM (updated monthly)
Various electronic books of standards

Publications list:
Available online and in print

Access to staff:
Contact by letter, by telephone, by fax, by e-mail,
in person and via website. Non-members charged.
Hours: Mon to Fri, 0900 to 1700
Special comments: Free to members and students.

Access for disabled people:
Parking provided, access to all public areas, toilet
facilities

Controls:
BSI Product Services, Hemel Hempstead

Member of:
European Committee for Electrotechnical
Standardization (CENELEC)
European Committee for Standardization (CEN)
International Electrotechnical Commission (IEC)
International Organization for Standardization
(ISO)

BSI PRODUCT SERVICES

Formal name: British Standards Institution Product
Services
Acronym or abbreviation: BSI

Kitemark House, Maylands Avenue, Hemel
Hempstead Industrial Estate, Hemel Hempstead,
Hertfordshire, HP2 4SQ

Tel: 08450 765600
Fax: 01442 278630
E-mail: product.services@bsigroup.com

Website:
http://www.bsigroup.com
Corporate website of BSI
http://www.kitemark.com
Dedicated web portal for Kitemark (UK symbol of
quality and trust)

Enquiries:
Enquiries to: Customer Service

Founded:
1901

Organisation type and purpose:
Service industry.
Product testing and certification services.

Subject coverage:
Product testing information in the following areas:
construction, engineering, fire, personal protective
equipment, electrical and electronic, lighting,
environmental, healthcare, services, automotive
services, combustion equipment, building and
construction products, engineering and scientific
products, transport and recreation, electronics,
communications systems, electrical machines,
lighting, cables, Canadian Standards Association,
electromagnetic compatibility, electrical and
mechanical calibration. Support for product
development, product certification, voluntary
(Kitemark schemes) and mandatory (CE marking).

**Museum or gallery collection, archive, or library
special collection:**
National and International Standards
National Standards Body Library based at HQ
Chiswick

Library catalogue:
All or part available online and in print

Printed publications:
Annual BSI Buyers Guide (listing all certified and
registered products and licensees; free)
Catalogue of THE documents (2 a year, free)

Order printed publications from: BSI Customer
Services
389 Chiswick High Road, London, W4 4AL, tel:
020 8996 9001

Access to staff:
Contact by letter, by telephone, by fax, by e-mail
and via website. Appointment necessary.
Hours: Mon to Fri, 0900 to 1700

Access for disabled people:
Parking provided, ramped entry

Parent body:
British Standards Institution
389 Chiswick High Road, London, W4 4AL; tel:
020 8996 9000; website: http://www.bsigroup
.com

BSI-DISC

389 Chiswick High Road, London, W4 4AL

Tel: 020 8996 9000
Fax: 020 8996 7448
E-mail: disc.enquiries@bsi-global.com

Website:
http://www.brainstorm.co.uk/reg/DISC
Basic information on a variety of activities,
products and services.

Enquiries:
Enquiries to: Membership Secretary
Direct tel: 020 8996 7180

Founded:
1990

Organisation type and purpose:
International organisation, membership
association (membership is by subscription),
present number of members: 5000, training
organisation, publishing house.
The standards development and publishing service
for the information and communications
technology sector.

Subject coverage:
Information management systems, data protection,
document scanning and storage, IT service
management, risk assessment, disaster recovery,
training and workshops, records management,
telecommunications.

Printed publications:
Publications and standards (for purchase, price on
application)

Electronic and video publications:
Data Protection (interactive CD-ROM)
TickIT Guide v5.0 (interactive CD-ROM)

Publications list:
Available online and in print

Access to staff:
Contact by letter, by telephone, by fax, by e-mail
and via website
Hours: Mon to Fri, 0900 to 1700

Access to building, collection or gallery:
Prior appointment required

Access for disabled people:
Parking provided, level entry, access to all public
areas, toilet facilities

Parent body:
British Standards Institution

BSRIA

Old Bracknell Lane West, Bracknell, Berkshire,
RG12 7AH

Tel: 01344 465600
Fax: 01344 465626
E-mail: bsria@bsria.co.uk

Website:
http://www.bsria.co.uk
Full information covering all BSRIA activities;
building services engineering books on bookshop
page.

Enquiries:
Enquiries to: Information and Knowledge Manager
Direct tel: 01344 465522
Direct e-mail: information@bsria.co.uk

Founded:
1955

Formerly called:
Heating and Ventilating Research Association
(year of change 1959); Building Services Research
and Information Association (year of change 1975)

Organisation type and purpose:
Membership association (membership is by
subscription), present number of members: 650,
consultancy, research organisation.
An independent research testing and information
organisation offering laboratory facilities, site
investigations and consultancy for building
services.

Subject coverage:
Heating; ventilation and air conditioning; building
and energy management; technical information;
equipment consultancy and testing; water quality
and legionella; research; marketing research;
management consultancy.

Information services:
Building services and construction online, physical
and phone enquiry services for BSRIA members.

Trade and statistical information:
Market research facilities for building service
industry.

Library catalogue:
All or part available online, in-house and in print

Printed publications:
Visit: http://www.bsria.co.uk/bookshop for details
of over 300 building services and construction
guides
Order printed publications from: BSRIA Bookshop
Address as before

Publications list:
Available online and in print

Access to staff:
Contact by letter, by telephone, by fax, by e-mail
and via website. Appointment necessary. Non-
members charged.
Hours: Mon to Fri, 0830 to 1700

Access to building, collection or gallery:
Prior appointment required
Hours: Mon to Fri, 0830 to 1700
Special comments: Members only.

Access for disabled people:
Parking provided, level entry, access to all public
areas

BSS

Formal name: Broadcasting Support Services

Head Office, Suite C International House, 7 High
Street, Ealing, London, W5 5DB

Tel: 020 8799 9000
Fax: 020 8799 9099
E-mail: marketing@bss.org

Website:
http://www.bss.org
Information about bss.

Enquiries:
Enquiries to: Business Development Executive
Direct tel: 0845 600 1317
Direct fax: 020 8799 9099
Direct e-mail: marketing@bss.org

Founded:
1975

Organisation type and purpose:
National organisation, registered charity (charity
number 282264), consultancy.
BSS provides tailored communications solutions to
broadcasters, charities and organisations, through
the provision of helplines, and distribution
services. BSS also processes credit card and online
donations.

continued overleaf

Subject coverage:
Charity providing communications solutions through: helplines provision, donation processing for appeals, design, print and distribution services.

Printed publications:
BSS leaflet (available on request)

Electronic and video publications:
Presentation of BSS services

Access to staff:
Contact by telephone, by fax, by e-mail and via website
Hours: Mon to Fri, 0930 to 1730

Access to building, collection or gallery:
Prior appointment required

Access for disabled people:
Parking provided

Offices in:
Leicester, Manchester and London

BT ARCHIVES

Formal name: British Telecommunications plc Archives

Third Floor, Holborn Telephone Exchange, 268–270 High Holborn, London, WC1V 7EE

Tel: 020 7440 4220
Fax: 020 7242 1967
E-mail: archives@bt.com

Website:
http://www.bt.com/archives
Information on BT Archives, facilities, and the history of the BT Group.
http://www.connected-earth.com
The innovative telecommunications heritage partnership initiative founded by BT.
http://www.bt.com/archivesonline
Online catalogue of BT Archives' unique collection of documents, photographs, film, advertising material and artefacts.
http://www.bt.com/archives-telefocus
BT Archives image gallery – facility to search, browse and purchase historic photographs and advertisements.

Enquiries:
Enquiries to: Customer Services Leader
Other contacts: Archivist, BT Connected Earth Curator

Founded:
1846

Organisation type and purpose:
BT Archives is the corporate memory of the world's oldest communications company; prior to 1984 records are public records, which BT Archives looks after on behalf of the nation.

Subject coverage:
The unique and nationally significant archive charts the development of communications in the UK and across the world, from the birth of the electric telegraph in the 1830s to the explosion of the internet and the rise of competition.
The collection illustrates the leading role that the UK, BT and its predecessors played in the progress of communications technology and its influence on society.

Museum or gallery collection, archive, or library special collection:
Archives of British Telecommunication plc and its predecessors, including private telegraph and telephone companies, Post Office Telecommunications and BT (public corporation)
Major collections include:
Private telegraph and telephone companies, 1830s–1910s
Post Office Telecommunications, 1870 (nationalisation) to 1981
Records of BT plc, 1984 to date
Historical phone books, 1880 to date
Photographic records, 19th century to date
Film and audio, 1930 to date

Reference library of printed sources including journals, periodicals, technical and historical works, 1769 to date

Non-library collection catalogue:
All or part available online and in-house

Library catalogue:
All or part available online and in-house

Printed publications:
Events in Telecommunications History (free and online)
Order printed publications from: http://www.bt.com/history

Access to staff:
Contact by letter, by telephone, by fax, by e-mail, in person and via website. Appointment necessary.
Hours: Mon to Fri, 0900 to 1700; research appointments Tue and Thu, 1000 to 1600

Access to building, collection or gallery:
By appointment
Hours: Tue and Thu, 1000 to 1600

BT GROUP

Antares Building, Room 1/3, Martlesham Heath, Ipswich, Suffolk, IP5 3RE

E-mail: library@bt.com

Website:
http://www.bt.com

Enquiries:
Enquiries to: Library and information services manager

Organisation type and purpose:
Research organisation.

Subject coverage:
Telecommunications, electronics, computing, internet, information technology, business, management, learning and development.

Library catalogue:
All or part available in-house

Access to staff:
Contact by e-mail
Hours: Mon to Fri, 0900 to 1700

Access to building, collection or gallery:
No access other than to staff

BTCV – BARN COUNTRYSIDE CENTRE

Formal name: British Trust for Conservation Volunteers

Philips Park, Whitefield, Manchester, M45 7QJ

Tel: 0161 796 6404
Fax: 0161 796 8846

Website:
http://www.btcv.org
All aspects of the charity locally and nationally.

Enquiries:
Enquiries to: Manager

Founded:
1959

Organisation type and purpose:
Membership association (membership is by subscription), voluntary organisation, registered charity.

Access to staff:
Contact by letter, by telephone and by fax
Hours: Mon to Fri, 0900 to 1700

Access for disabled people:
Parking provided, ramped entry, access to all public areas, toilet facilities

BTCV – WALLINGFORD

Formal name: British Trust for Conservation Volunteers
Acronym or abbreviation: BTCV

36 St Mary's Street, Wallingford, Oxfordshire, OX10 0EU

Tel: 01491 821600
Fax: 01491 839646
E-mail: information@btcv.org.uk

Website:
http://www.btcv.org

Enquiries:
Enquiries to: Information Officer
Direct e-mail: e.hudson@btcv.org.uk
Other contacts: PR Manager for media contacts.

Founded:
1959

Organisation type and purpose:
Membership association (membership is by subscription), present number of members: 5000, voluntary organisation, registered charity (charity number 261009), training organisation.
BTCV is the UK's leading practical conservation charity supporting people from all sectors of the community in positive action to improve our environment.
BTCV's purpose is to ensure that the potential of voluntary action for the environment is fully realised.

Subject coverage:
Volunteering, particularly in relation to conservation and the environment. Practical conservation operations in woodlands, waterways, wetlands, footpaths and sand dunes, hedging, dry stone walling and fencing. Environmental skills training, e.g. hedge-laying, dry stone walling. Community groups – support network for groups involved in conservation. BTCV is the UK's leading conservation charity supporting over 84,000 volunteers each year in action to improve their local environment. Information on conservation working holidays both in Britain and abroad.

Museum or gallery collection, archive, or library special collection:
Slide-photo library

Printed publications:
BTCV Conservation Holidays
Practical handbooks and educational material
The Conserver (quarterly, free to members)
A range of titles on conservation and related subjects including:
Drystone Walling (Brooks A, 1999)
Fencing (Agate E)
Footpaths (Agate E)
Trees and Aftercare (ed Kiser B)
Waterways and Wetlands (Agate E)
Woodlands (Brooks A)
Order printed publications from: BTCV Enterprises, The Conservation Centre, Balby Road, Doncaster, South Yorkshire, DN4 0RH, tel: 01302 572200, fax: 01308 310167

Publications list:
Available in print

Access to staff:
Contact by letter, by telephone, by fax, by e-mail and via website
Hours: Mon to Fri, 0900 to 1700

Has:
130 offices throughout the UK

BTTG

Formal name: British Textile Technology Group

Wira House, West Park Ring Road, Leeds, West Yorkshire, LS16 6QL

Tel: 0113 259 1999
Fax: 0113 278 0306
E-mail: info@bttg.co.uk

Website:
http://www.bttg.co.uk
Services available from BTTG.

Enquiries:
Enquiries to: Customer Services
Direct tel: 0161 445 8141

Direct fax: 0161 434 9957
Other contacts: Pat Widdowson

Founded:
1988

Organisation type and purpose:
International organisation, membership association (membership is by subscription), present number of members: 120, training organisation, consultancy, research organisation. Specialised centre of excellence in textile-related testing, investigation and evaluation.
UKAS accredited textile testing laboratory. Research and technical services for the textile and related industries.

Subject coverage:
Textiles of all types (sourcing, processing, use, performance), carpets, cleaning science, biotechnology, polymers, testing of textiles and many other products including toys, flammability research, forensic science, water, effluent, energy, noise, safety etc.
Technical textiles, personal protective equipment, fire testers, chemical and biochemical sciences, laundry products, textile ecology (Oeko-Tex), microscopy, toys, spinning and non-wovens, certification, training etc.

Museum or gallery collection, archive, or library special collection:
Research results

Printed publications:
Books on textile topics (15 titles for purchase)
BTTG Independent (news magazine, 4 times a year, free subscription)
Services promotional literature (free)

Access to staff:
Contact by letter, by telephone, by fax, by e-mail and via website
Hours: Mon to Fri, 0900 to 1700

Other addresses:
BTTG (British Textile Technology Group)
Shirley House, Wilmslow Road, Didsbury, Manchester, M20 2RB; tel: 0161 445 8141; fax: 0161 434 4957; e-mail: info@bttg.co.uk
BTTG Fire Technology Services
Unit 4B, Stag Industrial Estate, Atlantic Street, Broadheath, Altrincham, Cheshire, WA14 5DW; tel: 0161 929 8056; fax: 0161 929 8070; e-mail: pmeaton@bttg.co.uk
BTTG Spinning and Non-Wovens
Unit B6, Newton Business Park, Talbot Road, Hyde, SK14 4UQ; tel: 0161 368 2630; fax: 0161 368 1305; e-mail: info@bttg.co.uk

BUCKINGHAMSHIRE ARCHAEOLOGICAL SOCIETY

Formal name: Buckinghamshire Archaeological and Architectural Society
Acronym or abbreviation: BAS

County Museum, Church Street, Aylesbury, Buckinghamshire, HP20 2QP

Tel: 01296 387341
E-mail: bucksas@buckscc.gov.uk

Website:
http://www.bucksas.org.uk

Enquiries:
Enquiries to: Honorary Librarian/Archivist

Founded:
1847

Organisation type and purpose:
Learned society (membership is by subscription), present number of members: 569 plus 16 affiliated societies.

Subject coverage:
History and archaeology of Buckinghamshire in all aspects.

Non-library collection catalogue:
All or part available in-house and in print

Library catalogue:
All or part available in-house and in print

Printed publications:
Newsletter (2 times a year)
Records of Buckinghamshire (annually, since 1857)
Buckinghamshire in the 1760s and 1820s: The County Maps of Jefferys & Bryant (2001, £15 plus £3 p&p)
Historic Views of Buckinghamshire (2004)
Milton Keynes Monograph Series: (various prices plus £3 p&p)
Illustrated History of Early Buckinghamshire (2010, £15.99 plus £2.50 p&p)
Watermills of Buckinghamshire (2007, £12.99 plus £2.50 p&p)

Publications list:
Available in print

Access to staff:
Contact by letter, by telephone, by e-mail and in person. Appointment necessary. Non-members charged.
Hours: Members only: Mon to Sat, 1000 to 1700; Sun, 1400 to 1700
Non-members: Wed, 1000 to 1600

Access for disabled people:
Parking provided, ramped entry to building, level entry to library

BUCKINGHAMSHIRE CHILTERNS UNIVERSITY COLLEGE

Queen Alexandra Road, High Wycombe, Buckinghamshire, HP11 2JZ

Tel: 01494 522141
Fax: 01494 524392
E-mail: advice@bcuc.ac.uk

Website:
http://www.bcuc.ac.uk

Enquiries:
Enquiries to: Marketing Officer
Direct fax: 01494 471585

Organisation type and purpose:
College of higher education; formerly High Wycombe College of Technology and Art and Newland Park College of Education; connection with Missenden Abbey Management Centre.

Subject coverage:
Art and design, arts and social sciences, built environment, business and management, computing, engineering and technology, furniture, health studies, leisure and tourism.

Printed publications:
College Prospectus, updated annually, distributed freely

Publications list:
Available in print

Access to staff:
Contact by letter
Hours: Mon to Fri, 0900 to 1700

Access to building, collection or gallery:
Prior appointment required

Access for disabled people:
Parking provided, ramped entry

BUCKINGHAMSHIRE FAMILY HISTORY SOCIETY

PO Box 403, Aylesbury, Buckinghamshire, HP21 7GU

Subject coverage:
Buckinghamshire family history.

Access to staff:
Contact by letter
Hours: Mon to Fri, 0900 to 1700

BUCKINGHAMSHIRE LIBRARY SERVICE

The Gallery Suite, County Hall, Walton Street, Aylesbury, Buckinghamshire, HP20 1UU

Tel: 0845 230 3232
E-mail: library@buckscc.gov.uk

Website:
http://www.buckscc.gov.uk/bcc/content/index .jsp?contentid=-342380260

Enquiries:
Enquiries to: Head of Culture and Learning

Organisation type and purpose:
Local government body, public library.

Subject coverage:
General, Buckinghamshire, business information, careers and courses information.

Information services:
Libraries Information Service (see below).

Museum or gallery collection, archive, or library special collection:
Buckinghamshire Collection (at the Centre for Buckinghamshire Studies, Aylesbury)
Early Children's Book Collection (at Chesham), County Museum (Aylesbury)

Library catalogue:
All or part available online

Access to staff:
Contact by letter, by telephone, by fax, by e-mail, in person and via website
Hours: Mon to Fri, 0900 to 1700
Special comments: Access hours to libraries vary.

Branch libraries:
Aylesbury Study Centre
County Hall, Walton Street, Aylesbury, Buckinghamshire, HP20 1UU; tel: 0845 2303132
Centre for Buckinghamshire Studies
County Hall, Walton Street, Aylesbury, Buckinghamshire, HP20 1UU; tel: 01296 382250; fax: 01296 382771
Chesham Study Centre
Chesham Library, Elgiva Lane, Chesham, Buckinghamshire, HP5 2JD; tel: 0845 2303132
High Wycombe Study Centre
High Wycombe Library, 5 Eden Place, High Wycombe, Buckinghamshire, HP11 2DH; tel: 0845 2303132

Member organisation of:
Buckinghamshire Culture and Learning Department
European Public Information Centre Network (EPIC)
County Hall, Walton Street, Aylesbury, Buckinghamshire, HP20 1UU; tel: 01296 383252; fax: 01296 382405; e-mail: lib-info@buckscc.gov .uk
Libraries Information Service
County Hall, Walton Street, Aylesbury, Buckinghamshire, HP20 1UU; tel: 0845 230 3132; fax: 01296 382405; e-mail: lib-info@buckscc.gov .uk; website: http://www.bucks.gov.uk

BUCKINGHAMSHIRE RECORD SOCIETY

Centre for Buckinghamshire Studies, County Hall, Aylesbury, Buckinghamshire, HP20 1UU

Tel: 01296 383013
Fax: 01296 382771
E-mail: archives@buckscc.gov.uk

Website:
http://www.bucksinfo.net/brs

Enquiries:
Enquiries to: Honorary Secretary

Founded:
1947

Formerly called:
Buckinghamshire Archaeological Society (Records Branch)

Organisation type and purpose:
Learned society (membership is by subscription), voluntary organisation, registered charity (charity number 262004).

continued overleaf

To publish volumes based on original records illustrative of the history of Buckinghamshire; to concern itself with the collection, preservation and listing of public and private records relating to the county, including, if necessary, the raising of separate funds for this purpose.

Subject coverage:
Local history of Buckinghamshire.

Printed publications:
Vols include:
Vol. 19 The Courts of the Archdeaconry of Buckingham 1483–1525 (edited with an introduction, E. M. Elvey, 1975)
Vol. 23 The Autobiography of Joseph Mayett of Quainton 1783–1839 (edited with an introduction, A. Kussmaul, 1986)
Vol. 26 Descriptions of Lord Cobham's Gardens at Stowe 1700–1750 (edited by G. B. Clarke)
Vol. 28 Buckinghamshire Dissent and Parish Life 1669–1712 (edited by J. Broad, 1993)
Vol. 31 Recollections of Nineteenth Century Buckinghamshire (edited by I. Toplis, G. Clarke, I. Beckett and H. Hanley, 1998)
Vol. 32 An Index to Buckinghamshire Probate Records, 1420–1660 (edited by J. Hunt, R. Bettridge and A. Toplis, with introduction by H. Hanley, 2001)
Vol. 33 The Household Book (1510–51) of Sir Edward Don (edited by R. A. Griffiths, 2004)
Vol. 34 The Buckinghamshire Eyre of 1286 (edited by L. Boatwright, 2006)
Order printed publications from: The Society

Electronic and video publications:
Vols 1–22 in digital format.
Vol. 8 The Subsidy Roll for Buckinghamshire 1524 (edited by A. B. Chibnall and A. V. Woodman, 1950, with index by G. M. de Fraine)
Vol. 17 The Certificate of Musters for Buckinghamshire 1522 (edited by A. B. Chibnall, 1973)
Vol. 22 The Buckinghamshire Posse Comitatus 1798 (edited by I. F. W. Beckett, 1985)
Order electronic and video publications from: The Society

Publications list:
Available online and in print

Access to staff:
Contact by letter, by telephone, by fax and by e-mail. Appointment necessary.
Hours: Tue to Fri, 0900 to 1715

Access for disabled people:
Ramped entry, access to all public areas, toilet facilities

BUDDHIST SOCIETY

58 Ecclestone Square, London, SW1V 1PH

Tel: 020 7834 5858
Fax: 020 7976 5238
E-mail: info@thebuddhistsociety.org

Website:
http://www.the buddhistsociety.org
Library catalogue.

Enquiries:
Enquiries to: Librarian (for enquiries related to the literature of Buddhism)
Direct e-mail: library@thebuddhistsociety.org

Founded:
1924

Organisation type and purpose:
Membership association (membership is by subscription), present number of members: 2,000.
Religious society.

Subject coverage:
All aspects of Buddhism.

Library catalogue:
All or part available online and in-house

Printed publications:
Leaflets on Buddhism and the Society's activities
Middle Way (quarterly, free to members)

Electronic and video publications:
CD recordings, mostly of lectures given at the Society

Publications list:
Available online and in print

Access to staff:
Contact by letter, by telephone, by fax, by e-mail and in person
Hours: Mon to Fri, 1400 to 1800; Sat, 1400 to 1700

Links with:
European Buddhist Union
World Federation of Buddhists

BUGATTI OWNERS' CLUB LIMITED

Prescott Hill, Gotherington, Cheltenham, Gloucestershire, GL52 9RD

Tel: 01242 673136
Fax: 01242 677001
E-mail: club@bugatti.co.uk

Website:
http://www.prescott-hillclimb.com
http://www.prescott-hillclimb-school.uk

Enquiries:
Enquiries to: Secretary

Founded:
1929

Organisation type and purpose:
Membership association (membership is by subscription).

Subject coverage:
Speed Hill Climb meetings, Speed Hill Climb driver school, Bugatti information.

Access to staff:
Contact by letter, by telephone, by fax and by e-mail
Hours: Mon to Fri, 0900 to 1700

Access for disabled people:
Parking provided, toilet facilities

BUILDERS CONFERENCE

Crest House, 19 Lewis Road, Sutton, Surrey, SM1 4BR

Tel: 020 8770 0111
Fax: 020 8770 7736
E-mail: info@buildersconf.co.uk

Website:
http://www.buildersconference.co.uk

Enquiries:
Enquiries to: General Manager

Founded:
1935

Organisation type and purpose:
Trade association, registered charity (charity number 281742), research organisation.

Subject coverage:
Building.

Trade and statistical information:
A comprehensive tender reporting and market information service in the UK market.

Access to staff:
Contact by letter, by telephone, by fax and by e-mail. Appointment necessary.
Hours: Mon to Thu, 0830 to 1700; Fri 0830 to 1630

BUILDING COST INFORMATION SERVICE

Acronym or abbreviation: BCIS

Royal Institution of Chartered Surveyors, Parliament Square, London, SW1P 3AD

Tel: 020 7695 1500
Fax: 020 7695 1501

E-mail: bcis@bcis.co.uk;

Website:
http://www.bcis.co.uk
Information about BCIS publications and services.

Enquiries:
Enquiries to: Executive Director
Direct tel: 020 7695 1502

Founded:
1961

Organisation type and purpose:
Membership association, consultancy, research organisation.
Voluntary association for the exchange of information; open to all those willing to exchange information.
To provide information on the construction and property markets.

Subject coverage:
Construction industry information; statistical and econometric studies, facilities management information, building cost information, building economic forecasting, analysis of prices; property occupancy and costs; building maintenance management and costs; facilities management; life cycle costs.

Trade and statistical information:
Statistics on price and cost trends in UK construction.
Statistics on the level of prices for UK building construction.
Data on occupancy costs.
Data on expenditure on maintenance of buildings in the UK.

Printed publications:
BCIS Bulletin Service
Building Maintenance Price Book
Guide to Dayworks
Quarterly Review of Building Prices
Standard Form of Cost Analysis
Studies on building maintenance (c. 100 titles)

Electronic and video publications:
BCIS online data service

Access to staff:
Contact by letter, by telephone, by fax, by e-mail and via website. Access for members only. All charged.
Hours: Mon to Fri, 0900 to 1700

Constituent part of:
Royal Institution of Chartered Surveyors

BUILDING RESEARCH ESTABLISHMENT LIMITED

Acronym or abbreviation: BRE

Bucknalls Lane, Garston, Watford, Hertfordshire, WD25 9XX

Tel: 01923 664000
Fax: 01923 664010
E-mail: enquiries@bre.co.uk

Website:
http://www.bre.co.uk
Home page.
http://www.brebookshop.com
On-line book shop.
http://www.bre.co.uk/askbre
On-line advice service.

Enquiries:
Enquiries to: Administrator

Founded:
1921

Organisation type and purpose:
Consultancy, research organisation.

Subject coverage:
Building materials, building services, construction industry, structural design, fire science, timber construction, radioactive waste disposal, indoor environment (sick building syndrome), energy conservation, contaminated land.

Fire statistics; self-heating, ignition and growth of fire; structural aspects of fire in buildings; detection, extinction and suppression of fire; heat and smoke detectors; explosion hazards; combustion products, smoke, toxicity; smoke control and ventilation; human behaviour, escape and risk; combustion theory and modelling; sprinklers and extinguishing agents; special fire hazards in industries and materials.

Library catalogue:
All or part available in-house

Printed publications:
Publications list available on-line
Order printed publications from: BRE Press, distributed by IHS, Willoughby Road, Bracknell, Berkshire, RG12 8FB, tel: 01344 328038, e-mail: brepress@ihsatp.com, website http://www.brebookshop.com

Publications list:
Available online and in print

Access to staff:
Contact by letter, by telephone, by fax, by e-mail and via website. All charged.
Hours: Mon to Fri, 0900 to 1700
Special comments: Not normally open to visitors.

Access to building, collection or gallery:
No access other than to staff
Special comments: Collections not open to the public

Access for disabled people:
Access to all public areas, toilet facilities

Member of:
Construction Industry Information Group (CIIG)
  26 Store Street, London, WC1E 7BT
European Network of Building Research Institutions (ENBRI)
International Council for Research and Innovation in Building and Construction (CIB)
International Network for Fire Information and Reference Exchange (INFIRE)

Other addresses:
Scottish Laboratory
  Kelvin Road, East Kilbride, Glasgow, G75 0RZ; tel: 01355 233001

BUILDING SOCIETIES ASSOCIATION

Acronym or abbreviation: BSA

6th Floor, York House, 23 Kingsway, London, WC2B 6UJ

Tel: 020 7520 5900
Fax: 020 7240 5290
E-mail: simon.rex@bsa.org.uk

Website:
http://www.bsa.org.uk

Enquiries:
Enquiries to: Information Services Manager

Organisation type and purpose:
Trade association.

Subject coverage:
Building society industry, housing finance, the mortgage market, savings markets, related financial services.

Library catalogue:
All or part available in-house

Publications list:
Available online

Access to staff:
Contact by letter, by telephone, by fax, by e-mail and via website. Appointment necessary.
Hours: Mon to Fri, 0900 to 1700

Access to building, collection or gallery:
Appointment required
Hours: Mon to Fri, 0900 to 1700

BURDEN NEUROLOGICAL INSTITUTE

Acronym or abbreviation: BNI

Frenchay Park Road, Bristol, BS16 1JB

Tel: 0117 918 6720
E-mail: burdeninstitute@hotmail.com

Enquiries:
Enquiries to: Director
Direct e-mail: n.j.scolding@bris.ac.uk

Founded:
1939

Organisation type and purpose:
University department or institute, research organisation.

Subject coverage:
Research in neurological diseases and stem-cell therapies.

Museum or gallery collection, archive, or library special collection:
Research journals in the fields of neurology, neurophysiology, neuropsychology, psychiatry, psychophysiology

Access to staff:
Contact by letter, by telephone and by e-mail
Hours: Mon to Fri, 0900 to 1700

Access to building, collection or gallery:
Prior appointment required

Access for disabled people:
Level entry, access to all public areas, toilet facilities

Associated institute of the:
University of Bristol

BUREAU OF ANALYSED SAMPLES LIMITED

Acronym or abbreviation: BAS

Newham Hall, Newby, Middlesbrough, Cleveland, TS8 9EA

Tel: 01642 300500
Fax: 01642 315209
E-mail: enquiries@basrid.co.uk

Website:
http://www.basrid.co.uk

Enquiries:
Enquiries to: Managing Director

Founded:
1935

Organisation type and purpose:
Manufacturing industry.

Subject coverage:
Certified reference materials (CRM), sources of supply.

Non-library collection catalogue:
All or part available online, in-house and in print

Library catalogue:
All or part available online, in-house and in print

Printed publications:
Catalogue of Certified Reference Materials produced by BAS and other leading CRM producers

Publications list:
Available online and in print

Access to staff:
Contact by letter, by telephone, by fax, by e-mail and via website
Hours: Mon to Thu, 0900 to 1700; Fri, 0900 to 1630

BUREAU VAN DIJK ELECTRONIC PUBLISHING LIMITED

Northburgh House, 10 Northburgh Street, London, EC1V 0PP

Tel: 020 7549 5000

Fax: 020 7549 5010
E-mail: uk@bvdep.com

Website:
http://www.bankscope.bvdep.com
Detailed information for over 23,000 banks worldwide.
http://www.cameo.bvdep.com
UK Electoral Roll on the internet.
http://www.mintforbusiness.com
Companies, news, industry research and directors in a single business information database
http://www.fame.bvdep.com
Detailed information for 3m UK and Irish companies.
http://www.bvdep.com
Information on the Bureau's products and services.
http://www.amadeus.bvdep.com
Detailed information for over 8m European companies.

Enquiries:
Enquiries to: Marketing Manager

Founded:
1970

Organisation type and purpose:
Publishing house.
Provider of business information solutions on disk and via the Internet.

Subject coverage:
Company information for the UK, Europe and worldwide.
Detailed information on banks worldwide.
Detailed information on insurance companies worldwide.
UK electoral roll on the internet.

Access to staff:
Contact by letter, by telephone, by fax, by e-mail and via website
Hours: Mon to Fri, 0830 to 1830

BURNLEY BOROUGH COUNCIL

Town Hall, Manchester Road, Burnley, Lancashire, BB11 1JA

Tel: 01282 425011
Fax: 01282 438772

Enquiries:
Enquiries to: Public Relations Manager
Direct tel: 01282 477180
Direct fax: 01282 424764
Direct e-mail: srichardson@burnley.gov.uk

Organisation type and purpose:
Local government body.

Subject coverage:
Local government services.

BURTON COLLEGE LIBRARY

Lichfield Street, Burton-on-Trent, Staffordshire, DE14 3RL

Tel: 01283 494431
Fax: 01283 494800
E-mail: library@burton-college.ac.uk

Enquiries:
Enquiries to: Librarian

Subject coverage:
Electrical, electronic, mechanical and automobile engineering, plastics and rubber technology, mathematics and pure sciences, construction, business and management studies, computer science, nursery nursing, catering, art, drama and design.

Library catalogue:
All or part available online

Affiliated to:
College Librarians in Staffordshire (COLLIS)
Forum for Information Resources in Staffordshire (FIRST)
LA/CoFHE (West Midlands Circle)

BURTON HOSPITALS NHS FOUNDATION TRUST LIBRARY & INFORMATION SERVICE

Queen's Hospital, Belvedere Road, Burton-on-Trent, Staffordshire, DE13 0RB

Tel: 01283 511511 extn 2104
Fax: 01283 593174
E-mail: library.bur@burtonh-tr.wmids.nhs.uk

Enquiries:
Enquiries to: Library Services Manager

Founded:
1973

Organisation type and purpose:
NHS Medical Library.

Subject coverage:
Medicine, general aspects and specialities, including nursing.

Library catalogue:
All or part available online and in-house

Access to staff:
Contact by letter, by telephone, by fax, by e-mail and in person. Appointment necessary. Non-members charged.
Hours: Mon to Fri, 0900 to 1630

BURTON UPON TRENT FAMILY AND LOCAL HISTORY CENTRE

Acronym or abbreviation: F&LHC

Burton upon Trent Public Library, Riverside, High Street, Burton upon Trent, Staffordshire, DE14 1AH

Tel: 01283 239556
Fax: 01283 239571
E-mail: burton.library@staffordshire.gov.uk

Website:
http://www.staffordshire.gov.uk/libraries
Burton Library opening hours and location.
http://www.staffordshire.gov.uk/leisure/archives/burtoncentre
Contact information and list of available resources.

Enquiries:
Enquiries to: Team Leader: ICT, Information and Local Studies

Founded:
1977

Organisation type and purpose:
Public library.

Subject coverage:
Civic, educational, Burton Workhouse, and church (including some nonconformist) records, etc.; copies of census from 1841–1901 inclusive; pre- and post-WWII local newspapers; and a range of material relating to Burton and the surrounding areas in East Staffordshire and South Derbyshire.

Information services:
Free computer and internet access for all. Free access to online subscriptions such as Ancestry.com and a range of Oxford Reference titles such as the Dictionary of National Biography, Grove Art, Grove Music, and Oxford English Dictionary.

Special visitor services:
Cafe facilities are available during library opening hours, serving hot and cold drinks and snacks.

Education services:
Guided tours can be arranged for groups or classes.

Services for disabled people:
The F&LHC is located on the ground floor. A large-print keyboard and trackerball mouse are available on request. A reader-magnifier is located on the first floor (accessible by a passenger lift).

Non-library collection catalogue:
All or part available online and in-house

Library catalogue:
All or part available online

Access to staff:
Contact by letter, by telephone, by fax, by e-mail and in person
Hours: Mon, Wed and Fri, 0830 to 1800; Tue, 1000 to 1800; Thu, 0830 to 2000; Sat, 0830 to 1630

Access to building, collection or gallery:
Hours: Mon, Wed and Fri, 0830 to 1800; Tue, 1000 to 1800; Thu, 0830 to 2000; Sat, 0830 to 1630

Access for disabled people:
Limited parking available at the front of the building, ramped entry, access to all public areas, toilet facilities

BURY ARCHIVE SERVICE

Moss Street, Bury, BL9 0DR

Tel: 0161 253 6782
Fax: 0161 253 5878
E-mail: archives@bury.gov.uk

Website:
http://www.bury.gov.uk
http://archives.bury.gov.uk
Online catalogue.

Enquiries:
Enquiries to: Archivist

Founded:
1986

Organisation type and purpose:
Public Archive Service.

Subject coverage:
Local history, geography, government of Bury and district, other local information.

Museum or gallery collection, archive, or library special collection:
The archives of local authorities in the Bury area, 1675 to present
Deposited archives of various local organisations (business, trade union, church, voluntary, sports, etc.) and individuals, mostly c. 1780 to present

Non-library collection catalogue:
All or part available online, in-house and in print

Printed publications:
Newsletter (quarterly)
Routes Guide to Family History

Access to staff:
Contact by letter, by telephone, by fax, by e-mail and in person. Appointment necessary.
Hours: Tue, Wed, 1300 to 1600; Thu, Fri, 1000 to 1600; Sat, 2nd of the month, 1000 to 1600
Special comments: Appointment recommended but not always essential.

Access to building, collection or gallery:
Hours: Tue to Fri, 1000 to 1700; Sat, 1000 to 1630

Access for disabled people:
Ramp and lift access, bathrooms

Location:
Bury Council, Environment and Development Services
Knowsley Place, Bury

BURY COLLEGE

Learning Resources Centre, Bury College, Market Street, Bury, Lancashire, BL9 0BD

Tel: 0161 280 8280

Website:
http://www.burycollege.ac.uk

Enquiries:
Enquiries to: Resource Librarian
Direct tel: 0161 280 8214/59
Direct e-mail: louise.binns@burycollege.ac.uk
Other contacts: Learning Resources Manager

Organisation type and purpose:
Further education college, suitable for ages: 16+.

Subject coverage:
Paper-making, health studies, catering, computing, business studies, hairdressing.

Library catalogue:
All or part available online and in-house

Access to staff:
Contact by letter, by telephone, by fax and by e-mail. Appointment necessary.
Hours: Mon to Fri, 0900 to 1700

Access to building, collection or gallery:
No prior appointment required

Access for disabled people:
Access to all public areas

BURY COUNCIL LIBRARIES

Reference and Information Services, Bury Library, Manchester Road, Bury, BL9 0DG

Tel: 0161 253 5871
Fax: 0161 253 5857
E-mail: information@bury.gov.uk

Website:
http://www.bury.gov.uk/libraries
Libraries pages include community contacts database, guide to web, branch libraries, archives, library catalogue, magazines, online library services.

Enquiries:
Enquiries to: Reference and Information Services Librarian

Founded:
1901

Organisation type and purpose:
Local government body, public library.

Subject coverage:
General, business, local history and genealogical information, careers, social science.

Information services:
Online library services.

Services for disabled people:
Visual impairment unit, hearing impairment unit, housebound library service.

Non-library collection catalogue:
All or part available online

Library catalogue:
All or part available online

Printed publications:
Bury Community Contacts Lists (20p each)
Routes: Guide to sources for family historians (£5)
Order printed publications from: Reference Information Services, Bury Library

Electronic and video publications:
Bury Community Contacts
Order electronic and video publications from: Website

Publications list:
Available online and in print

Access to staff:
Contact by letter, by telephone, by fax, by e-mail, in person and via website

Access to building, collection or gallery:
Hours: Mon, Tue, Thu, Fri, 0930 to 1730; Wed, 0930 to 1930; Sat, 0930 to 1630

Access for disabled people:
Disabled access available
Hours: As above

Branch libraries:
16 branch libraries throughout Bury Metroplitan Borough Council

BUS USERS UK

PO Box 2950, Stoke on Trent, ST4 9EW

Tel: 01782 442855
Fax: 01782 442856
E-mail: enquiries@bususer.org

Website:
http://www.bususers.org

Details of work of Bus Users UK and membership application, good practice guide, guide to making a complaint about bus services.

Enquiries:
Enquiries to: Chairman

Founded:
1985

Formerly called:
National Federation of Bus Users (year of change c. 2004)

Organisation type and purpose:
National organisation, membership association, voluntary organisation.

Subject coverage:
An independent group, formed to give bus passengers a voice. Has the ear of all the major bus companies and a lot of the smaller ones too, of their trade organisation and of the Government and local authorities.

Printed publications:
BUS USER (newsletter, 4 times a year, for members)
Good Practice Guide (free)

Access to staff:
Contact by letter, by telephone, by fax and by e-mail
Hours: Mon to Fri, 0900 to 1300

Access to building, collection or gallery:
No access other than to staff

BUSINESS AND PROFESSIONAL WOMEN UK LIMITED

Acronym or abbreviation: BPW UK Ltd

74 Fairfield Rise, Billericay, Essex, CM12 9NU

Tel: 01277 623867
E-mail: hq@bpwuk.co.uk

Website:
http://www.bpwuk.co.uk

Founded:
1938

Organisation type and purpose:
Membership association (membership is by subscription), present number of members: 500, voluntary organisation.
Lobbying and networking organisation.

Subject coverage:
The interests of all working women, equality, women in the workplace and public life, support for them personally or in their work, networking system.

Printed publications:
Annual Review
BPW News (quarterly, free to members, subscription)
Bi-monthly bulletin

Access to staff:
Contact by letter, by telephone, by e-mail and via website

Links with:
International Federation of Business and Professional Women
   tel: +1 631 422 7849; fax: +1 631 792 1192; e-mail: presidents.office@bpw-international.org

Member organisations:
There are 26 clubs in the United Kingdom

BUSINESS AND TRADE STATISTICS LIMITED

Acronym or abbreviation: BTS

Lancaster House, More Lane, Esher, Surrey, KT10 8AP

Tel: 01372 463121
Fax: 01372 469847
E-mail: info@worldtradestats.com

Website:
http://www.worldtradestats.com

Enquiries:
Enquiries to: Managing Director

Founded:
1986

Organisation type and purpose:
Service industry.

Subject coverage:
External trade statistics for the UK, all the European Community countries and Switzerland, Norway, USA, Canada, Mexico, Japan, Hong Kong, South Korea, Taiwan, Singapore, Australia, New Zealand.

Museum or gallery collection, archive, or library special collection:
Historical data back to 1979

Trade and statistical information:
Statistical databases.
Production Statistics (PRODCOM) for UK.
UK consumption statistics for beer, wine, spirits, tobacco, hydrocarbons and expenditure in betting and gambling.

Printed publications:
Printed reports

Electronic and video publications:
Online, CD-ROM and floppy disks provision

Publications list:
Available in print

Access to staff:
Contact by letter, by telephone, by fax and by e-mail. Appointment necessary.
Hours: Mon to Fri, 0900 to 1700

BUSINESS ARCHIVES COUNCIL OF SCOTLAND

Acronym or abbreviation: BACS

c/o University of Glasgow Archive Services, 77 Dumbarton Road, Glasgow, G11 6PW

Tel: 0141 330 4159
Fax: 0141 330 4158

Website:
http://www.gla.ac.uk/archives/bacs

Enquiries:
Enquiries to: Surveying Officer
Direct e-mail: k.king@archives.gla.ac.uk

Founded:
1960

Organisation type and purpose:
National organisation, membership association (membership is by subscription), registered charity (charity number SCO 02565).

Subject coverage:
Scottish business history, locating records of Scottish business history, preserving, appraising and listing.

Printed publications:
Scottish Business and Industrial History (journal)
Order printed publications from: Editor, Scottish Business and Industrial History, c/o Business Archives Council of Scotland; e-mail: bacs@ archives.gla.ac.uk

Electronic and video publications:
Publications online, including detailed index to the journal Scottish Business and Industrial History

Publications list:
Available online

Access to staff:
Contact by letter, by telephone, by fax, by e-mail, in person and via website. Appointment necessary.
Hours: Mon to Fri, 0900 to 1700

Access to building, collection or gallery:
No access other than to staff

BUSINESS CONTINUITY INSTITUTE

Acronym or abbreviation: BCI

10 Southview Park, Marsack Street, Caversham, RG4 5AF

Tel: 0118 947 8215
E-mail: email bci@thebci.org

Website:
http://www.thebci.org
BCI, regional forums, standards, training, conference, workshops, jobs, online bookstore.

Founded:
1994

Organisation type and purpose:
Membership association, professional organisation for business continuity management, number of members: 5,000 in 90 countries.
To enable individual members to obtain guidance and support from fellow business continuity practitioners; to promote the highest standards of professional competence and commercial ethics in the provision and maintenance of business continuity planning and services.

Subject coverage:
The art and science of business continuity management world-wide.

Printed publications:
Business continuity and disaster recovery books, software tools and templates, videos and research reports
Order printed publications from: Online bookstore.

Electronic and video publications:
ENewsletters (for members)
BCI Workshop Reports (members may download free from: http://www.bcipartnership.com/ publications.html, non-members £95 per copy)
Continuity Magazine (members may download free from: http://www.bcipartnership.com/ publications.html)

Publications list:
Available online

Access to staff:
Contact by letter, by telephone and by e-mail

Links with:
Risk Management Institution of Australasia (RMIA)

Member organisation of:
Risk Federation

BUSINESS IN THE COMMUNITY

Acronym or abbreviation: BITC

137 Shepherdess Walk, London, N1 7RQ

Tel: 0870 600 2482
Fax: 020 7253 1877

Website:
http://www.bitc.org.uk

Enquiries:
Enquiries to: Executive Secretary
Other contacts: Information Officer for publications

Founded:
1982

Organisation type and purpose:
Membership association (membership is by subscription, election or invitation), present number of members: 650 companies, voluntary organisation, registered charity (charity number 297716).
BITC's mission is to inspire businesses to increase the quality and extent of their contribution to social and economic regeneration by making corporate social responsibility an essential part of business excellence.

Subject coverage:
Development of companies' positive impact on society through specialised campaigns.

continued overleaf

Printed publications:
Information pack (free)
Specialist publications available upon request

Publications list:
Available in print

Access to staff:
Contact by telephone
Hours: Mon to Fri, 0900 to 1700

Offices at:
Business in the Community, East Midlands
3rd Floor, 30–34 Hounds Gate, Nottingham,
NG1 7AB; tel: 0115 911 6666; fax: 0115 911 6667
Business in the Community, East of England
PO Box 93, 58 High Street, Newmarket, CB8
8ZN; tel: 01638 663272; fax: 01638 666841
Business in the Community, North East
Design Works, William Street, Felling, Tyne &
Wear, NE10 0JP; tel: 0191 469 5333; fax: 0191 469
5353
Business in the Community, North West
Suite 17, St James Court, Wilderspool Causeway,
Warrington, WA4 6RS; tel: 01925 230317; fax:
01925 652644
Business in the Community, Northern Ireland
c/o TK-ECC Limited, 770 Upper Newtownards
Road, Dundonald, Belfast, BT16 1UL; tel: 028
9041 0410; fax: 028 9041 9030
Business in the Community, South East
137 Shepherdess Walk, London, N1 7RQ; tel:
0870 600 2482; fax: 020 7253 1877
Business in the Community, South West
165 Whiteladies Road, Bristol, BS8 2RN; tel: 0117
923 8750; fax: 0117 923 8270
Business in the Community, Wales
Fourth Floor, Empire House, Mount Stuart
Square, Cardiff, CF10 5FN; tel: 029 2048 3348;
fax: 029 2046 1513
Business in the Community, West Midlands
c/o Cadbury Limited, 83 Bournville Lane,
Birmingham, B30 2HP; tel: 0121 451 2227; fax:
0121 451 2782
Business in the Community, Yorkshire &
Humberside
Progress House, 99 Bradford Road, Pudsey,
Leeds, LS28 6AT; tel: 0113 236 1888; fax: 0113 236
0555

Sister organisation:
Scottish Business in the Community
PO Box 408, Bankhead Avenue, Edinburgh, E11
4EX; tel: 0131 442 2020; fax: 0131 442 3555

BUSINESS INSTITUTE

University of Ulster at Jordanstown, Shore Road,
Newtownabbey, Co. Antrim, BT37 0QB

Tel: 028 9036 6417
Fax: 028 9036 6831
E-mail: j.mccoy@ulster.ac.uk

Website:
http://www.business.ulster.ac.uk/businst
Description and breakdown of all activities.

Enquiries:
Enquiries to: Director

Founded:
1984

Organisation type and purpose:
University department or institute, training
organisation, consultancy, research organisation.
Provider of management development,
management education and research.

Subject coverage:
Training and education in all areas of business,
small business research, personal and
organisational development.

Printed publications:
Course brochures available on request

Access to staff:
Contact by letter, by telephone, by fax, by e-mail
and via website

Hours: Mon to Fri, 0900 to 1700

Access to building, collection or gallery:
No prior appointment required

BUSINESS LINK EAST MIDLANDS

Innovation House, Riverside Park, Raynesway,
Derby, DE21 7BF

Tel: 0845 058 6644
E-mail: info@businesslinkem.co.uk

Website:
http://www.businesslink.gov.uk/eastmidlands

Branches:
Derbyshire Area Office – Pride Park
Business Link East Midlands, Commerce House,
2 Victoria Way, Pride Park, DE24 8AN; tel: 01332
614150
Leicestershire Area Office
Business Link East Midlands, Unit 5, Merus
Court, Meridian Business Park, Leicester , LE19
1RJ; tel: 0116 240 5200; website: http://www
.embltd.co.uk
Lincolnshire & Rutland Area Office
Business Link East Midlands, Commerce House,
Outer Circle Road, Lincoln, LN2 4HY; tel: 01522
523333
Northamptonshire Area Office
Business Link East Midlands, Opus House,
Moulton Road, Northampton, NN3 6JA; tel:
01604 782443
Nottinghamshire Area Office
Business Link East Midlands, Nottingham
Commerce House, 8 Experian Way, NG2
Business Park, Nottingham, NG2 1EP; tel: 0115
850 0000

BUSINESS LINK IN LONDON

Link House, 1st and 2nd Floor, 292–308 Southbury
Road, Enfield, EN1 1TS

Tel: 0845 6000 787
E-mail: info@bllondon.co.uk

Website:
http://www.businesslink.gov.uk/london

Enquiries:
Enquiries to: Information Officer

Organisation type and purpose:
National government body, local government
body, consultancy.
Training business support services for SMEs in
South London (boroughs of Bexley, Greenwich,
Lewisham, Sutton, Bromley and Croydon).

Subject coverage:
Business advisory service for SMEs in London.

Trade and statistical information:
Access to a wide range of trade and statistical
information pertinent to London SMEs.

Printed publications:
A range of booklets, pamphlets, fact sheets etc,
pertinent to London SMEs

Electronic and video publications:
A range of CD-ROM and online services available
directly and via partner organisations

Access to staff:
Contact by letter, by telephone, by fax and by e-
mail
Hours: Mon to Fri, 0900 to 1730

Access to building, collection or gallery:
Prior appointment required

BUSINESS LINK IN THE EAST OF ENGLAND

Zenith Court, 4 Bishops Square Business Park,
Hatfield, Hertfordshire, AL10 9NE

Tel: 08457 171615
E-mail: questions@businesslinkeast.org.uk

Website:
http://www.businesslink.gov.uk/east

Branches:
Business Link Office in Bedford
Priory Business Park, Stannard Way, Bedford,
MK44 3RZ; tel: 08457 171615
Business Link Office in Cambridge
St Johns Innovation Centre, Cowley Road,
Cambridge, CB4 0WS; tel: 08457 171615
Business Link Office in Chatteris
South Fens Business Centre, Fenton Way,
Chatteris, Cambridgeshire, PE16 6TT; tel: 08457
171615
Business Link Office in Colchester
Suites 3 & 5 The Centre, The Crescent, Colchester
Business Park, Colchester, Essex, CO4 9QQ; tel:
08457 171615
Business Link Office in Harlow
Unit FF27, Harlow Enterprise Hub, Kao
Hockham Building, Edinburgh Way, Harlow,
Essex, CM20 2NQ; tel: 08457 171615
Business Link Office in Hatfield
4 Bishops Square, Hatfield Business Park,
Hatfield, Hertfordshire, AL10 9NE; tel: 08457
171615
Business Link Office in Ipswich
Felaw Maltings, South Kiln, 42 Felaw Street,
Ipswich, Suffolk, IP2 8SQ; tel: 08457 171615
Business Link Office in King's Lynn
St Ann's House, St Ann's Street, King's Lynn,
Norfolk, PE30 1LT; tel: 08457 171615
Business Link Office in Luton
Business Competitiveness Centre, Kimpton
Road, Luton, Bedfordshire, LU2 0SX; tel: 08457
171615
Business Link Office in Norwich
Henderson Business Centre, Ivy Road, Norwich,
Norfolk, NR5 8BF; tel: 08457 171615
Business Link Office in Peterborough
Export House, Minerva Business Park, Lynch
Wood, Peterborough, PE2 6FT; tel: 08457 171615
Business Link Office in Southend
University of Essex, Southend Campus, Elmer
Approach, Southend on Sea, Essex, SS1 1LW; tel:
08457 171615

BUSINESS LINK IN THE NORTH EAST

Acronym or abbreviation: BLTV

Spectrum 6, Spectrum Business Park, Seaham,
Durham, SR7 7TT

Tel: 0845 600 9006
E-mail: enquiries@businesslinknortheast.co.uk

Website:
http://www.teesbusinesslink.co.uk

Enquiries:
Enquiries to: Customer Liaison Officer
Other contacts: Information Researcher for
Information Research Service.

Founded:
1995

Formerly called:
Business Link Teesside (year of change 1998);
Business Link Tees Valley (year of change 2007)

Organisation type and purpose:
Service industry.
Business support organisation, a partnership of
local public and private business support
organisations throughout Tees Valley.
To provide a single point of access to the business
support network for all Tees Valley businesses.

Subject coverage:
All business-related topics including business
information on companies, markets, products,
finance, legislation. Business Information Research
Service offered on chargeable basis, plus mailing
lists, company financial reports, financial
assistance searches.

Museum or gallery collection, archive, or library special collection:
Local business information including literature on business support services
Business information directories, CD-ROM and online services, including Kompass, Corporate Profound, Equifax, Experian, Grantfinder

Trade and statistical information:
Access to online services, including Corporate Profound for market research. International Trade team access DTI services.

Library catalogue:
All or part available in-house

Printed publications:
Promotional literature only

Access to staff:
Contact by letter, by telephone, by fax, by e-mail, in person and via website
Hours: Mon to Thu, 0830 to 1700; Fri, 0830 to 1630
Special comments: Charges made for some services.

Branches:
Business Link Office at Gateshead Civic Centre
  Regent Street, Gateshead, NE8 1PQ
Business Link Office at Gateshead Gear House
  Gear House, Saltmeadows Road, Gateshead, NE8 3AH
Business Link Office at Gateshead Greenfield Business Centre
  Mulgrave Terrace, Gateshead, NE8 1PQ
Business Link Office at Gateshead PNE Design Works
  William Street, Felling, Gateshead, NE10 0JP
Business Link Office at Sunderland Business & Innovation Centre
  Wearfield, Enterprise Park East, Sunderland, SR5 2TA
Business Link Office at Sunderland NECC
  NECC Premises, Havelock Buildings, High Street West, Sunderland, SR1 1DW
Business Link Office in Alnwick
  Alnwick Advice Centre, 50–52 Bondgate Within, Alnwick, Northumberland, NE66 1JD
Business Link Office in Ashington
  Wansbeck Advice Centre, Hirst Arcade, Woodhorn Road, Ashington, Northumberland, NE63 9AS
Business Link Office in Barnard Castle
  Enterprise Agency for Wear Valley & Teesside, Enterprise House, Harmire Enterprise Park, Barnard Castle, Durham, DL12 8XT
Business Link Office in Berwick-upon-Tweed
  Berwick Advice Centre, 45 Castlegate, Berwick-upon-Tweed, Northumberland, TD15 1LF
Business Link Office in Bishop Auckland
  Enterprise Agency for Wear Valley & Teesside, Innovation House, 26 Longfield Road, South Church Enterprise Park, Bishop Auckland, Durham, DL14 6XB
Business Link Office in Blyth
  Blyth Advice Centre, 8 Bridge Street, Blyth, NE24 1BL
Business Link Office in Byker
  Enterprise Support Centre East, 135–137 Shields Road, Byker, Newcastle-upon-Tyne, NE6 1DN
Business Link Office in Consett
  DIDA, Steel House, Ponds Court Business Park, Genesis Way, Consett, Durham, DH8 5XP
Business Link Office in Darlington
  Darlington Imperial Centre, Grange Road, Darlington, DL1 5NQ
Business Link Office in Durham
  Pity Me Office, Abbey Business Centre, Abbey Road, Pity Me, Durham, DH1 5JZ
Business Link Office in Hartlepool
  Brougham Enterprise Centre, Brougham Terrace, Hartlepool, TS24 8EY
Business Link Office in Hebburn
  21 Station Road, Hebburn, Tyne and Wear, NE31 1NX
Business Link Office in Hexham
  Tynedale Advice Centre, 3 Cattle Market, Hexham, Northumberland, NE46 1NJ
Business Link Office in Jarrow
  5–7 Grange Road, Jarrow, Tyne and Wear, NE32 3JY

Business Link Office in Middlesbrough
  Middlesbrough Council, Civic Centre, Middlesbrough
Business Link Office in Morpeth
  Morpeth Advice Centre, 35 Newgate Street, Morpeth, NE61 1AT
Business Link Office in Newcastle-upon-Tyne
  1 Portman House, Portland Road, Newcastle-upon-Tyne, NE2 1AQ
Business Link Office in Newton Aycliffe
  Evans Business Incubation Centre – Evans Easy Space Ltd, Durham South Way, Aycliffe Industrial Estate, Newton Aycliffe, DL5 6XP
Business Link Office in North Shields
  North Tyneside Business Centre, Howard House, 54A Saville Street, North Shields, Tyne and Wear, NE30 1NT
Business Link Office in Redcar
  Redcar Station Business Centre, Station Road, Redcar, TS10 1RD
Business Link Office in South Shields
  25–27 Market Place, South Shields, Tyne and Wear, NE33 1JF
Business Link Office in Stockton-on-Tees
  Stockton Borough Council – Stockton Business Centre, 70–74 Brunswick Street, Stockton-on-Tees, TS18 1DW

BUSINESS LINK IN THE SOUTH EAST

Elizabeth House, Duke Street, Woking, Surrey, GU21 5AS

Tel: 0845 600 9006
E-mail: info@businesslinksoutheast.co.uk

Website:
http://www.businesslink.gov.uk/southeast

Branches:
Business Link Office in Hampshire and the Isle of Wight
  1st Floor, Regus Business Centre, Solent Business Park, Whiteley, Fareham, Hampshire, PO15 7FH; tel: 0845 600 9006; e-mail: info@businesslinksoutheast.co.uk
Business Link Office in Kent
  26 Kings Hill Avenue, West Malling, Kent, ME19 4AE; tel: 0845 699 9006; e-mail: info@businesslinksoutheast.co.uk
Business Link Office in Milton Keynes, Oxfordshire and Buckinghamshire
  Midshires House, Midshires Business Park, Smeaton Close, Aylesbury, Buckinghamshire, HP19 8HL; tel: 0845 600 9006; e-mail: info@businesslinksoutheast.co.uk
Business Link Office in Surrey
  2nd Floor, Elizabeth House, Duke Street, Woking, Surrey, GU21 5AS; tel: 0845 600 9006; e-mail: info@businesslinksoutheast.co.uk
Business Link Office in Sussex
  Greenacre Court, Station Road, Burgess Hill, West Sussex, RH15 9DS; tel: 0845 600 9006; e-mail: info@businesslinksoutheast.co.uk

BUSINESS LINK IN THE SOUTH WEST

Great Western Business Centre, Emlyn Square, Swindon, Wiltshire SN1 5BP

Tel: 0845 600 9966
E-mail: info@businesslinksw.co.uk

Website:
http://www.businesslink.gov.uk/southwest/

Enquiries:
Enquiries to: Information Manager
Other contacts: Information Officer

Founded:
2007

Created by the merger of:
Business Link Devon and Cornwall and Business Link Somerset (1997)

Organisation type and purpose:
Service industry.

Access point for those in Somerset wishing to start, run or develop a business.

Subject coverage:
Company information, market information, legal and technical information, financial information, business information.

Access to staff:
Contact by letter, by telephone, by fax and by e-mail
Hours: Mon to Fri, 0830 to 1700

Access to building, collection or gallery:
Prior appointment required
Hours: Mon to Fri, 0900 to 1700

Access for disabled people:
Yes
Hours: Mon to Fri, 0900 to 1700

Branches:
Business Link Office in Bodmin
  Bodmin Business Centre, Harleigh Road, Bodmin, Cornwall, PL31 1AH; tel: 0845 600 9966; e-mail: enquiries@blpeninsula.co.uk
Business Link Office in Dorset
  Arena Business Centre, Holyrood Close, Poole, Dorset, BH17 7FJ; tel: 0845 600 9966; e-mail: enquiry@businesslinksw.co.uk
Business Link Office in Exeter
  Unit 3, 4 Cranmere Court, Lustleigh Close, Matford Business Park, Exeter, EX2 8PW; tel: 0845 600 9966; e-mail: enquiries@blpeninsula.co.uk
Business Link Office in Gloucestershire
  Chargrove House, Shurdington, Cheltenham, GL51 4GA; tel: 0845 600 9966; e-mail: enquiry@businesslinksw.co.uk
Business Link Office in Plymouth
  Tamar Science Park, 5 Research Way, Derriford, Plymouth, PL6 8BT; tel: 0845 600 9966; e-mail: enquiries@blpeninsula.co.uk
Business Link Office in Somerset
  Ground Floor, Agriculture House, Blackbrook Park Avenue, Blackbrook Business Park, Taunton, TA1 2FU; tel: 0845 600 9966; e-mail: enquiries@blpeninsula.co.uk
Business Link Office in the West of England
  Leigh Court Business Centre, Abbots Leigh, Bristol, BS8 3RA; tel: 0845 600 9966; e-mail: enquiry@businesslinksw.co.uk
Business Link Office in Wiltshire
  Great Western Business Centre, Emlyn Square, Swindon, SN1 5BP; tel: 0845 600 9966; e-mail: enquiry@businesslinksw.co.uk

BUSINESS LINK NORTHWEST

Brian Johnson Way, Preston, Lancashire, PR2 5PE

Tel: 0845 006 6888
E-mail: info@businesslinknw.co.uk

Website:
http://www.businesslink.gov.uk/northwest
About the organisation, what's new, services, press releases, case studies, contacts and how to find it, how-to guides, interactive tools, events directory, business support directory, press releases.

Enquiries:
Enquiries to: Business Adviser
Direct e-mail: info@businesslinknw.co.uk

Founded:
2007

Incorporates the former:
Business Link for Cumbria (year of change 2007)

Organisation type and purpose:
Free-to-use, independent business support and information service funded by the Northwest Regional Development Agency.

Subject coverage:
Provides access to independent business advisers who can work directly with businesses to identify their needs and access relevant solutions. This includes advisers with specialisms, including: finance, innovation, resource efficiency and skills and training. It also includes advisers with expertise in a wide range of industry sectors.

continued overleaf

Non-library collection catalogue:
All or part available online and in-house

Library catalogue:
All or part available online

Access to staff:
Contact by letter, by telephone, by fax, by e-mail and via website. Appointment necessary.
Hours: Enquiry line: Mon to Fri, 0800 to 2000; Sat, Sun, 0800 to 1400

Access for disabled people:
Parking provided, ramped entry, access to all public areas

Funded by:
Northwest Regional Development Agency

BUSINESS LINK WEST MIDLANDS

Advantage House, 19 Ridgeway, Quinton Business Park, Quinton, Birmingham, West Midlands, B32 1AL

Tel: 0845 113 1234
E-mail: info@businesslinkwm.co.uk

Website:
http://www.businesslinkwm.co.uk/
Guide to services

Enquiries:
Enquiries to: Business Support Team
Other contacts: Marketing Manager

Founded:
1995

Formerly called:
Business Link Staffordshire (year of change 2007)

Organisation type and purpose:
Service industry.

Subject coverage:
General business advice, grants, legislation, mailing lists, published market research.

Access to staff:
Contact by letter, by telephone, by fax, by e-mail, in person and via website
Hours: Mon to Fri, 0830 to 1730

Access to building, collection or gallery:
Prior appointment required

Access for disabled people:
Parking provided, level entry, toilet facilities

Other office:
Business Link Staffordshire
Cannock

BUSINESS LINK YORKSHIRE

1 Capitol Court, Capitol Business Park, Dodworth, Barnsley, S75 3TZ

Tel: 0845 6 048 048
E-mail: info@businesslinkyorkshire.co.uk

Website:
http://www.businesslink.gov.uk/yorkshire/

Enquiries:
Enquiries to: Managing Director
Other contacts: Information Adviser for all enquiries.

Founded:
1998

Formerly called:
Business Link (Boothferry) Limited, Business Link (Grimsby and Cleethorpe) Limited, Business Link (Hull and East Riding) Limited, Business Link (North Lincolnshire) Limited (year of change 1998); Business Link (Humberside) Limited (year of change 2001); Business Link Humber (year of change 2008)

Organisation type and purpose:
Local government body, research organisation. Business information service, market intelligence and research.

To help SMEs increase their competitiveness by access to market information and business advisory services.

Subject coverage:
Business information, credit ratings, mailing lists, market research UK and international.

Access to staff:
Contact by letter, by telephone, by fax, by e-mail, in person and via website
Hours: Mon to Fri, 0800 to 1700
Special comments: Businesses in the Humberside area (North Lincolnshire, North East Lincolnshire, Hull, East Riding of Yorkshire).

Other offices:
Business Link Humber
  10–14 Hainton Square, Grimsby, DN32 9BB; tel: 01472 312121; fax: 01472 312131
Business Link Humber
  Kingsway Centre, Kingsway, Scunthorpe, DN17 1AL; tel: 01724 867190
Business Link Humber
  Bridlington Business Centre, Bessingby Industrial Estate, Bridlington, YO16 4SF; tel: 01262 401399; fax: 01262 401633; e-mail: info@blhumber.co.uk
Business Link Humber
  East Riding Small Business Centre, Annie Reed Road, Beverley, HU17 0LF; tel: 01482 880460; fax: 01482 880442
Business Link Humber
  Berkeley House, Doncaster Road, Scunthorpe, DN15 7DQ; tel: 01724 270444; fax: 01724 276773
Business Link Humber
  The Old Goole Shipyard, Swinefleet Road, Goole; tel: 01405 722630
Business Link Humber (HABAC)
  Samman House, Bowlalley Lane, Hull, HU3 1XR; tel: 01482 607100; fax: 01482 607102

Parent body:
A4E Consult

Part of:
Business Link Network

BUSINESS SERVICES ASSOCIATION

Acronym or abbreviation: BSA

Warnford Court, 29 Throgmorton Street, London, EC2N 2AT

Tel: 020 7786 6300
Fax: 020 7786 6309
E-mail: holly.edwards@bsa-org.com

Website:
http://www.bsa-org.com

Enquiries:
Enquiries to: Director General
Direct tel: 020 7786 6301
Direct e-mail: norman.rose@bsa-org.com

Founded:
1993

Organisation type and purpose:
Trade association (membership is by subscription), present number of members: 19, service industry. Leading representative of major companies in the business services industry. BSA is secretary of the Parliamentary All Party Group for Business Services and represents the views of the industry to government.
Has close links with UK and EU government monitoring policies and legislation. It develops policy papers on issues of employment and social policy including Best Value in local government contracting, public sector pensions and National Minimum Wage.

Subject coverage:
Support services, public sector market testing, employment legislation, government tendering, EU markets, PFI, local government contracting, pensions, training.

Trade and statistical information:
Data on private companies competing for public sector markets.

Printed publications:
Briefing brochure on the BSA
Newsletter (quarterly)

Access to staff:
Contact by letter, by telephone, by fax and by e-mail
Hours: Mon to Fri, 0900 to 1700

Access to building, collection or gallery:
No access other than to staff

BUSINESS SOFTWARE ALLIANCE

Acronym or abbreviation: BSA

79 Knightsbridge, London, SW1X 7RB

Tel: 020 7245 0304
Fax: 020 7245 0310

Website:
http://www.bsa.org

Enquiries:
Enquiries to: Communications Manager

Founded:
1988

Organisation type and purpose:
International organisation, trade association. Alliance of Microsoft, Novell/WordPerfect, Adobe, Autodesk, Bentley Systems, Apple, Borland, CNC/Mastercam, Macromedia, Symantec and Unigraphics Solutions.

Subject coverage:
Software piracy, its occurrence and prevention, software management.

Trade and statistical information:
Statistics on software piracy and what this has cost in jobs and taxes in Europe.

Electronic and video publications:
Audit Disk (for purchase)

Access to staff:
Contact by letter, by telephone and by fax
Hours: Mon to Fri, 0900 to 1700

Access to building, collection or gallery:
No access other than to staff

Headquarters of the:
BSA
  1180 18th Street NW, Suite 700, Washington, DC, 20036, USA; tel: + 1 202 872 5500; fax: + 1 202 872 5501

BUSINESS WEST

Formal name: Bristol Chamber of Commerce and Initiative (trading as Business West)

Leigh Court Business Centre, Abbots Leigh, Bristol, BS8 3RA

Tel: 01275 373373
Fax: 01275 370706
E-mail: info@businesswest.co.uk

Website:
http://www.businesswest.co.uk

Enquiries:
Enquiries to: Information Services Manager

Founded:
1826

Organisation type and purpose:
Membership association (membership is by subscription), present number of members: 2400, service industry.
Business Link.

Subject coverage:
Industrial, commercial and financial affairs in Bristol and region: overseas trade, travel and marketing; overseas trade documentation; transport and shipping procedures; general

business information; export credit insurance; EU legislation and public sector tenders information; credit referencing.

Museum or gallery collection, archive, or library special collection:
Company Information and Market Information, UK and worldwide
EC legislation: Official journal (L, C and S series)
Electronic Database Information
Standard reference material for business information

Trade and statistical information:
UK and European statistics.
CSO data.
Tradstats.

Printed publications:
Directory of Members

Access to staff:
Contact by telephone, by fax and by e-mail. Non-members charged.
Hours: Mon to Fri, 0900 to 1700

Affiliated to:
Bristol Euro Info Centre (EIC)
at the same address

BUSINESS-COMMUNITY CONNECTIONS, CRAIGMILLAR AND SOUTH EDINBURGH

Castlebrae Community High School, 2a Greendykes Road, Edinburgh, EH16 4DP

Tel: 0131 652 0367
Fax: 0131 661 9811
E-mail: janet@ednet.co.uk

Website:
http://www.craigmillarinfo.co.uk

Enquiries:
Enquiries to: Manager

Founded:
1991

Formerly called:
Friends of Craigmillar (year of change 2000)

Organisation type and purpose:
Registered charity.
To act as a link between the business and community sector to generate jobs for local people and to create innovative working links.

Subject coverage:
Links between community groups and the private sector.

Printed publications:
Newsletter (quarterly, free)

Microform publications:
Slides

Access to staff:
Contact by letter, by telephone and by fax
Hours: Mon to Fri, 0900 to 1700

Access to building, collection or gallery:
Prior appointment required

Access for disabled people:
Parking provided, level entry

BUTTERFLY CONSERVATION

Acronym or abbreviation: BC

Manor Yard, East Lulworth, Wareham, Dorset, BH20 5QP

Tel: 0870 7744 309
Fax: 0870 7706 150
E-mail: info@butterfly-conservation.org

Website:
http://www.butterfly-conservation.org

Enquiries:
Enquiries to: Publicity Officer
Direct e-mail: cmallinson@butterfly-conservation .org

Founded:
1968

Formerly called:
British Butterfly Conservation Society Limited (BBCS)

Organisation type and purpose:
Membership association (membership is by subscription), present number of members: 11,500, registered charity (charity number 254937), the UK charity taking action to save butterflies, moths and their habitats.
Conservation society.

Subject coverage:
Butterfly and moth conservation, species information, habitat information, research, monitoring, nature reserves.

Printed publications:
Butterfly Magazine (3 times a year, free to members)
Species Action Plans for each of 22 threatened species (£5 each inc. p&p)
Booklets, occasional papers
Saving Butterflies – a practical guide to the conservation of butterflies (ed Dunbar D, £5 soft, £7 hard inc. p&p)

Publications list:
Available in print

Access to staff:
Contact by letter, by telephone, by fax and by e-mail
Hours: Mon to Fri, 0900 to 1700

Associated with:
Butterfly Recording Scheme
English Nature
JCCBI
Wildlife Link

Has:
32 branches

BUTTERFLY HOUSE

Formal name: Seaforde Gardens and Tropical Butterfly House

Seaforde Demense, Seaforde, Downpatrick, Co Down, BT30 8PG

Tel: 028 4481 1225
Fax: 028 4481 1370
E-mail: plants@seafordegardens.com

Enquiries:
Enquiries to: Owner

Founded:
1988

Subject coverage:
Gardens, maze and tropical butterfly house

Access to staff:
Contact by letter, by fax and by e-mail

Access to building, collection or gallery:
Hours: Easter to end September: Mon to Sat, 1000 to 1700; Sun, 1300 to 1800

Access for disabled people:
Parking provided, access to all public areas, toilet facilities

BUTTERWORTH-HEINEMANN

Linacre House, Jordan Hill, Oxford, OX2 8DP

Tel: 01865 310366
Fax: 01865 314519
E-mail: bhmarketing@repp.co.uk

Website:
http://www.bh.com
Comprehensive details of all available and forthcoming titles.

Enquiries:
Enquiries to: Administrator
Direct tel: 01865 314492
Direct e-mail: maggie.harte@repp.co.uk

Founded:
1990

Formerly called:
Butterworth Scientific Limited, Heinemann Professional Publishing

Organisation type and purpose:
Publishing house.
Books and electronic products. An Imprint of Elsevier Science.

Subject coverage:
Software development; information systems; strategy formulation and implementation, architecture, networking, data communications, programming, IS/IT management, personal computing, internet, business, open learning fields for tertiary and professional qualification.

Printed publications:
Numerous titles under the following headings:
IS/IT Management
Networking and Data Communications
Personal Computing
Software Development/Programming
Systems/Intervals/Architecture
Order printed publications from: Customer Services Department, Reed Publishers, Oxford
PO Box 382, Halley Court, Jordan Hill, Oxford, OX2 8RU, tel: 01865 888110, fax: 01865 314029, e-mail: bhuk.orders@repp.co.uk

Publications list:
Available online and in print

Access to staff:
Contact by letter, by fax, by e-mail and via website
Hours: Mon to Fri, 0900 to 1700

Parent body:
Elsevier Science

BUTTONHOOK SOCIETY

2 Romney Place, Maidstone, Kent, ME15 6LE

Tel: 01622 752949
Fax: 01622 752949
E-mail: buttonhooksociety@tiscali.co.uk

Website:
http://www.thebuttonhooksociety.com

Enquiries:
Enquiries to: Chairman

Founded:
1979

Organisation type and purpose:
International organisation, learned society (membership is by subscription), research organisation.
Archives of over 70,000 buttonhooks.
Research into origins and social history associated with buttonhooks.

Subject coverage:
Buttonhooks, their origins, history, social context, materials and construction, costume, sources of information and areas of further research.

Information services:
Speakers list available

Museum or gallery collection, archive, or library special collection:
Computerised archival material on known buttonhooks in collections, sorted by type and material

Non-library collection catalogue:
All or part available in-house

Printed publications:
Antique buttonhooks (Bettersley B)
Buttonhooks and Shoehorns (Sue Brandon, pub. Shire Books)
Buttonhooks (Booker J)
Collecting Buttonhooks (Compton C)
Compendium of Buttonhooks
Glovehook in Colour (Moorehead P G)
Newsletter (6 times a year, for members)
The Boutonneur

continued overleaf

Buttonhooks to Trade, to Treasure (Bettersley B)
Specialities & Novelties in Shoe Store Supplies
 (1920 US Catalogue reprint)

Publications list:
Available in print

Access to staff:
Contact by letter, by telephone, by e-mail and via
website
Hours: Mon to Fri, 0900 to 1700

Associated with:
Button Society
Costume Society

Other addresses:
Overseas coordinator for American members
 Box 287, White Marsh, Maryland, 21162–0287,
 USA

BYRON SOCIETY

Byron House, 6 Gertrude Street, London, SW10
0JN

Tel: 020 7352 5112

Enquiries:
Enquiries to: Honorary Director

Founded:
1972

Organisation type and purpose:
Learned society.

Subject coverage:
Lord Byron's life and works, and those of his
contemporaries (1788–1824).

Printed publications:
The Byron Journal (annually, £5 per copy)

Access to staff:
Contact by letter
Hours: Mon to Fri, 0900 to 1700

Includes the:
International Byron Society; maintains contact with
many literary societies

CAB INTERNATIONAL

Formal name: Centre for Agriculture and
Biosciences International
Acronym or abbreviation: CABI

Wallingford, Oxfordshire, OX10 8DE

Tel: 01491 832111
Fax: 01491 833508
E-mail: cabi@cabi.org

Website:
http://www.cabi.org/
Full range of products and services, together with
information on our scientific institutes, developing
country initiatives and training programmes.

Enquiries:
Enquiries to: Director General

Founded:
1929

Formerly called:
Imperial Agricultural Bureaux (year of change
1948); Commonwealth Agricultural Bureaux (year
of change 1985)

Incorporates:
Bureau of Hygiene and Tropical Diseases (year of
change 1993)

Organisation type and purpose:
International organisation, membership
association (membership is by election or
invitation), present number of members: 41
countries, training organisation, consultancy,
research organisation.
Intergovernmental organisation, granted
international status under the International
Organisations Act of 1985.
Provides information, scientific and development
services in the applied life sciences.

Subject coverage:
Agriculture, forestry and forest products, field
crops, grasslands, horticulture, crop protection,
plant and animal breeding, veterinary science,
water pollution and quality, leisure, recreation and
tourism. Rural sociology and development. Public
health, communicable diseases, tropical diseases,
community health and medicine, environmental
science, soils, land and water management,
biotechnology, biodiversity, biosystematics,
integrated pest management, biological control,
human and animal nutrition, human and animal
parasitology, AIDS.

Printed publications:
Abstract journals (over 50 current titles)
Primary journals
Review journals
Annotated bibliographies (over 3,000 titles)
Annual Report
Directories
Distribution maps of pests
Identification keys
Newsletters
Review articles
Reference textbooks
Training manuals etc
Order printed publications from: Publishing Division,
CAB International
Wallingford, Oxfordshire, OX10 8DE

Microform publications:
Contact marketing department

Electronic and video publications:
CABCD (CAB ABSTRACTS database) series in CD
 format
Electronic multimedia compendium on CD-ROM
 eg Crop Protection Compendium
Many abstract products on CD-ROM and diskette
CD-ROM Topics in International Health (resource
 collection for researchers, professionals and
 students, more titles available in 1999)

Publications list:
Available in print

Access to staff:
Contact by letter, by fax, by e-mail and via
website
Hours: Mon to Fri, 0900 to 1700

Access for disabled people:
Parking provided, level entry

Member countries:
Australia, Bahamas, Bangladesh, Belize, Botswana,
Brunei Darussalam, Canada, People's Republic of
China, Chile, Colombia, Cyprus, Fiji, Gambia,
Ghana, Guyana, Hungary, India, Indonesia,
Jamaica, Kenya, Malawi, Malaysia, Mauritius,
Myanmar, New Zealand, Nigeria, Pakistan, Papua
New Guinea, Philippines, Sierra Leone, Solomon
Islands, South Africa, Sri Lanka, Tanzania,
Trinidad & Tobago, Uganda, United Kingdom, UK
Dependent Territories, Vietnam, Zambia,
Zimbabwe

Other addresses:
CAB International
 Headquarters, CABI Publishing, Wallingford,
 Oxfordshire, OX10 8DE; tel: 01491 832111; fax:
 01491 829292; e-mail: publishing@cabi.org
CAB International Africa Regional Centre
 ICRAF Complex, PO Box 633, Village Market,
 Nairobi, Kenya; tel: + 254 2 524462; fax: + 254 2
 522150; e-mail: arc@cabi.org
CAB International Caribbean Regional Centre
 Gordon Street, Curepe, Trinidad & Tobago, West
 Indies; tel: + 1 868 645 7628; fax: + 1 868 663 2859;
 e-mail: crc@cabi.org
CAB International North America
 CABI Publishing, 10 East 40th Street, Suite 3203,
 New York, NY 10016, USA; tel: +1 212 481 7018
 and +1 800 528 4841; fax: +1 212 686 7993; e-mail:
 cabi-nao@cabi.org
CAB International South-East Asia Regional
Centre
 MARDI, PO Box 210, 43409 UPM Serdang,
 Malaysia; tel: +60 3 894 32921; fax: +60 3 894
 36400; e-mail: searc@cabi.org

CABI Bioscience Switzerland Centre
 1 Rue des Grillons, CH-2800 Delémont,
 Switzerland; tel: + 41 32 421 4870; fax: + 41 32 421
 4871; e-mail: swiss.centre@cabi-bioscience.ch
CABI Bioscience UK Centre
 Bakeham Lane, Egham, Surrey, TW20 9TY; tel:
 0178 470111; fax: 01491 829100; e-mail:
 bioscience.egham@cabi.org
CABI Bioscience UK Centre
 Silwood Park, Buckhurst Road, Ascot, Berkshire,
 SL5 7TA; tel: 01491 829129; fax: 01212 686 7993

Registered with the:
United Nations

CABRINI CHILDREN'S SOCIETY

49 Russell Hill Road, Purley, Surrey, CR8 2XB

Tel: 020 8668 2181
Fax: 020 8763 2274
E-mail: info@cabrini.org.uk

Website:
http://www.cabrini.org.uk
Information on the work of the society and how
people can support the organisation.

Enquiries:
Enquiries to: Executive Director

Founded:
1887

Formerly called:
Catholic Children's Society (Arundel & Brighton,
Portsmouth and Southwark (year of change 2009)

Organisation type and purpose:
The Catholic Children's Society is a regional social
care agency. It works primarily in disadvantaged
communities helping to improve the emotional
wellbeing and outcomes for children, young
people and families. It supports people from a
diverse range of backgrounds, cultures and faiths.
It places children's needs at the centre of
everything it does.

Subject coverage:
Adoption, post-adoption care, fostering, schools
counselling, community projects and catechetical
programmes and residential care for people with
learning difficulties.

Access to staff:
Contact by letter, by telephone, by fax and by e-
mail
Hours: Mon to Fri, 0930 to 1730

Access to building, collection or gallery:
Hours: Mon to Fri, 0930 to 1730

Also at:
Hove Adoption, Catholic Children's Society
Adoption
 Linkline House, 65 Church Road, Hove, BN3
 2BD; tel: 01273 821234; e-mail: hoveadoption@
 cabrini.org
Purley Adoption, Catholic Children's Society
Adoption
 49 Russell Hill Road, Purley, CR8 2XB; tel: 020
 8668 2181; e-mail: info@cabrini.org.uk
Reading Adoption, Catholic Children's Society
Adoption
 50 Mount Pleasant, Reading, RG1 2TD; tel: 0118
 987 5121; e-mail: reading@cabrini.org
Winchester Adoption, Catholic Children's Society
Adoption
 7 Bridge Street, Winchester, SO23 0HN; tel:
 01962 842024; e-mail: adoption,winchester@
 cabrini.org
Winchester Fostering, Catholic Children's Society
Fostering
 7a Bridge Street, Winchester, SO23 0HN; tel:
 01962 842024; e-mail: fostering.winchester@
 cabrini.org

Cabrini Residential Care:
Cabrini
 3a Healy Drive, Orpington, Kent, BR6 9LB; tel:
 01689 891401; e-mail: cabrini@cabrini.org

Catechetical Programmes:
Fountains Centre
24 Knebworth Road, Bexhill on Sea, TN39 4JJ;
tel: 01424 730536; e-mail: fountainscentre@
cabrini.org

Dartford Community Project:
Hubert House, Dartford
Mallard Close, Knights Manor Estate, Dartford,
DA1 5HU; tel: 01322 224500; e-mail:
huberthouse@cabrini.org

Peckham Community Project:
Bird in Bush, Peckham
616 Old Kent Road, Peckham, London, SE15 1JB;
tel: 020 7639 3030; e-mail: birdinbush@cabrini
.org

Schools Counselling:
Schools Counselling
49 Russell Hill Road, Purley, CR8 2XB; tel: 020
8668 2181; e-mail: info@cabrini.org

Vauxhall Community Project:
St Anne's, Vauxhall
42–46 Harleyford Road, Vauxhall, London, SE11
5AY; tel: 020 7735 7049; e-mail: vauxhall@cabrini
.org

CAERNARFON AREA RECORD OFFICE

County Offices, Shirehall Street, Caernarfon,
Gwynedd, LL55 1SH

Tel: 01286 679088
Fax: 01286 679637
E-mail: annrhydderch@gwynedd.gov.uk

Website:
http://www.llgc.org.uk/cac/cac0053.htm
Basic information, telephone numbers, classes of
records, services to public.
http://www.gwynedd.gov.uk/archives

Enquiries:
Enquiries to: Archivist

Founded:
1947

Organisation type and purpose:
Local government body.

Subject coverage:
Local government archives, parish material,
estates, industrial (predominantly slate), maritime
records.

Non-library collection catalogue:
All or part available online

Printed publications:
Several publications of Gwynedd historical interest
Maritime Wales (journal, annually)

Publications list:
Available online

Access to staff:
Contact by letter, by telephone, by fax, by e-mail
and in person
Hours: Mon, closed; Tue, Thu, Fri, 0930 to 1230 and
1330 to 1700; Wed, 0930 to 1230 and 1330 to 1900
Special comments: CARN Reader's ticket required.

Access for disabled people:
Level entry, access to all public areas, toilet
facilities

CAERNARVONSHIRE HISTORICAL SOCIETY

County Offices, Caernarfon, Gwynedd, LL55 1SH

Tel: 01286 679088
Fax: 01286 679637

Enquiries:
Enquiries to: Honorary Secretary

Founded:
1939

Organisation type and purpose:
Learned society, voluntary organisation, registered
charity.
Historical Society.

Subject coverage:
Local history in the former county of Caernarvon
(now Gwynedd).

Printed publications:
Transactions (annually)

Access to staff:
Contact by letter, by telephone and by fax
Hours: Mon to Fri, 0900 to 1700

Member of:
Federation of Local History Societies in
Caernarvonshire

CAERPHILLY COUNTY BOROUGH COUNCIL

Nelson Road, Tredomen, Ystrad Mynach, Mid
Glamorgan, CF82 7WF

Tel: 01443 815588 or 01495 226622
Fax: 01443 863029

Website:
http://www.caerphilly.gov.uk
Information on the area: tourism, business
opportunities, training. Information on the
Council; news and views.

Enquiries:
Enquiries to: Communications Manager
Direct tel: 01443 864262
Direct fax: 01443 864246
Direct e-mail: rosemarymathews@caerphilly.gov.uk

Founded:
1996

Formerly called:
Gwent County Council, Islwyn Borough Council,
Mid Glamorgan County Council, Rhymney Valley
District Council

Organisation type and purpose:
Local government body.

Subject coverage:
Socio-economic data about the county borough.

Printed publications:
Caerphilly County Borough Ward Profiles based
on census of population conducted every 10
years
Caerphilly Street Atlas
Caerphilly Insight: A Profile of Caerphilly County
Borough

Access to staff:
Contact by letter
Hours: Mon to Thu, 0830 to 1700; Fri, 0830 to 1630

CAIRNGORM REINDEER CENTRE, THE

Glenmore Forest Park, Visitors Centre, Aviemore,
Inverness-shire, PH22 1QU

Tel: 01479 861228
Fax: 01479 861228
E-mail: reindeerinfo@btinternet.com

Enquiries:
Enquiries to: Director

Founded:
1952

Organisation type and purpose:
Promotion and research of reindeer.

Subject coverage:
Reindeer breeding and general husbandry, training
to harness, import/export of reindeer to and from
the UK.

Printed publications:
Rangifer Tarandus, Reindeer (small booklet)
Velvet Antlers, Velvet Noses (Smith T, pub.
Hodder and Stoughton)

Publications list:
Available in print

Access to staff:
Contact by letter, by fax and by e-mail
Hours: Mon to Fri, 0900 to 1700

CAITHNESS ARCHIVE CENTRE

Acronym or abbreviation: CAC

Wick Library, Sinclair Terrace, Wick, Caithness,
KW1 5AB

Tel: 01955 606432
Fax: 01955 603000
E-mail: north.highlandarchive@highland.gov.uk

Website:
http://www.highland.gov.uk/educ/publicservices/
archivedetails/northarchive.htm

Enquiries:
Enquiries to: Caithness Archivist

Founded:
1995

Formerly called:
North Highland Archive (year of change 2009)

Organisation type and purpose:
Local government body.
Local archive and record office.

Subject coverage:
Maritime history, poor relief, council
administration, police activity, education, planning
(building development). Less significant: WWII,
archaeology, trade, estates and agriculture,
nursing, church activity.

**Museum or gallery collection, archive, or library
special collection:**
Local and family history sources including census/
OPR microfilms, maps, valuations rolls, school
records, council and parochial board records,
and private collections of major local significance
such as Wick Harbour Trust
A number of smaller private collections come from
local businesses or major landowning
professional families

Non-library collection catalogue:
All or part available online and in-house

Library catalogue:
All or part available in-house

Printed publications:
Beyond the Registers: family history from archives
and ephemera (£1.50)
Guide to the Highland Council Archive (£7)
Guide to printed sources at the North Highland
Archive (£2.50)
Leaflet, newsletter and numerous information
sheets (free)

Access to staff:
Contact by letter, by telephone, by fax, by e-mail
and in person
Hours: Mon, Thu, Fri, 1000 to 1300 and 1400 to
1730; Tue, 1000 to 1300 and 1400 to 2000; Wed,
1000 to 1300
Special comments: May be advisable to book in the
summer months to ensure access to microfilm
readers.

Access to building, collection or gallery:
No access other than to staff

Access for disabled people:
On request

Parent body:
Highland Council Archive, Inverness

CALDERDALE COLLEGE

Learning Resources Centre, Francis Street, Halifax,
West Yorkshire, HX1 3UZ

Tel: 01422 399312
Fax: 01422 399320
E-mail: info@calderdale.ac.uk

continued overleaf

Website:
http://www.calderdale.ac.uk
Details of college departments, courses and
facilities.

Enquiries:
Enquiries to: Head of Learning Resources

Formerly called:
Percival Whitley College of Further Education
Library and Resources

Organisation type and purpose:
Further educational college

Subject coverage:
All subjects covered by the further education
curriculum; building construction; information
technology; health and safety; further and adult
education; chemistry; physics; biology;
mathematics; computing; commercial art; business;
strongest subjects are business and social care,
graphic and fine arts, photography, service
industries, health and caring.

Library catalogue:
All or part available online

Access to staff:
Contact by letter, by telephone, by fax and by e-
mail. Appointment necessary. Letter of
introduction required.
Hours: Mon to Thu, 0845 to 2000; Fri, 0915 to 1600;
Sat, 1000 to 1300 (term only).
Special comments: Restricted hours during college
vacations.

Access for disabled people:
Level entry, access to all public areas, toilet
facilities

Member organisation of:
Leeds Metropolitan University Regional University
Network
  website: http://www.leedsmet.ac.uk/regional/
  new
Welcome!
  website: http://welcome.hud.ac.uk

CALDERDALE FAMILY HISTORY SOCIETY

Acronym or abbreviation: CFHS

22 Well Grove, Hove Edge, Brighouse, West
Yorkshire, HD6 2LT

Tel: 01484 714311
E-mail: mail@cfhsweb.co.uk

Website:
http://www.cfhsweb.co.uk
Full information concerning the Society, its
publications and how to become a member.

Enquiries:
Enquiries to: Chairman

Founded:
1985

Organisation type and purpose:
Membership association (membership is by
subscription).
The Society exists to encourage interest in, and
assist in, matters relating to genealogy and family
history, and to record and preserve genealogical
material for future generations.

Subject coverage:
Genealogy, family history, particularly with
relation to Halifax (West Yorkshire) and
surrounding areas.

**Museum or gallery collection, archive, or library
special collection:**
Calderdale War Dead, other local summary
information

Non-library collection catalogue:
All or part available in print

Library catalogue:
All or part available in-house

Printed publications:
Halifax St. John's Parish Church Baptisms 1813–
  1838, Marriages 1754–1837 and Burials 1813–
  1937
Elland St. Mary's Parish Church Baptisms 1559–
  1850, Marriages 1559–1837 and Burials 1559–
  1843
1851 Census – All areas within the Halifax
  Registration District
Monumental Inscriptions
Order printed publications from: Publications Officer,
Calderdale Family History Society, 22 Well Grove,
Hove Edge, Brighouse, HD6 2LT; tel: 01484 714311;
e-mail: publications@cfhsweb.co.uk

Microform publications:
Halifax Parish Church Baptisms 1813–1838,
  Marriages 1754–1837 and Burials 1813–1937
Elland St. Mary's Parish Church Baptisms 1559–
  1850, Marriages 1559–1837 and Burials 1559–
  1843
1851 Census Hebden Bridge
1841 and 1851 Census Todmorden

Electronic and video publications:
CDs: Halifax Census (1881); St Mary Elland Births,
  Deaths and Marriages (1558–1837); St John
  Halifax Births, Deaths and Marriages (1812–
  1837); Censuses (1801–1831)

Publications list:
Available in print

Access to staff:
Contact by letter, by telephone and by e-mail
Hours: Sun to Sat, 1000 to 2100; Research Room,
Brighouse Library, Tue, 1330 to 1630 and Thu, 1000
to 1300

CALDERDALE LIBRARIES

Central Library, Northgate, Halifax, West
Yorkshire, HX1 1UN

Tel: 01422 392630
Fax: 01422 392615
E-mail: libraries@calderdale.gov.uk

Website:
http://www.calderdale.gov.uk

Enquiries:
Enquiries to: Information Services Team Leader
Direct tel: 01422 392631
Direct fax: 01422 349458
Direct e-mail: reference.library@calderdale.gov.uk

Founded:
1882

Formerly called:
Halifax Central Library, Halifax Public Libraries

Organisation type and purpose:
Local government body, public library, suitable for
all ages.

Subject coverage:
General; Calderdale local history.

Services for disabled people:
Access to all units, including assistive technology
for full access to IT services

**Museum or gallery collection, archive, or library
special collection:**
Edwards Bindings (Halifax late 18th and early 19th
  centuries)
Horsfall Turner Local History Collection
  (Calderdale)
Milner Collection (publications of William Milner
  dating 1834–1913)
Phyllis Bentley Collection (MS books and work
  books)
Some incunabula

Library catalogue:
All or part available online and in-house

Access to staff:
Contact by letter, by telephone, by fax, by e-mail
and in person
Hours: Mon, Tue, Thu and Fri, 0930 to 1900; Sat,
0930 to 1700

Access for disabled people:
Access to all public areas

Branch libraries:
21 local branches, 2 mobile libraries

Parent body:
Calderdale Metropolitan Borough Council
  Town Hall, Crossley Street, Halifax, HX1 1UJ;
  tel: 01422 357257; fax: 01422 393102

CALEDONIAN RAILWAY ASSOCIATION

Acronym or abbreviation: CRA

63 Andrew Drive, Clydebank, Dunbartonshire,
G81 1BU

E-mail: dwhind@ukonline.co.uk

Website:
http://www.crassoc.org.uk
The association – membership, officers & contacts,
notice board; resources – archive, photographs,
The True Line journal, bibliography, other
resources; Caledonian Railway – map of system,
heritage; services – publications, reprints, staff/
family history, modelling; events – exhibitions,
meetings.

Enquiries:
Enquiries to: Secretary

Founded:
1983

Organisation type and purpose:
Voluntary organisation, research organisation.

Subject coverage:
Research and study of former Caledonian Railway
Company, including locomotive drawings, coach
and wagon drawings, signal box track diagrams,
industrial relations, architecture, publicity
material, shipping services, tickets and history.

**Museum or gallery collection, archive, or library
special collection:**
At University of Glasgow Business Archive, 13
  Thurso Street, Glasgow, G11 6PE; website: http://
  www.gla.ac.uk/archives; e-mail:
  enquiries@gla.ac.uk; tel: 0141 330 5515

Printed publications:
Locomotive drawings, carriage drawings, wagon
  drawings
Signal box track diagrams
Reprints of public and working timetables, etc.
The True Line (journal, quarterly)
Order printed publications from: Sales Officer,
Caledonian Railway Association, 73 Victoria Park
Drive North, Glasgow, G14 9PS

Publications list:
Available online

Access to staff:
Contact by letter, by telephone and by e-mail

CALOUSTE GULBENKIAN FOUNDATION

98 Portland Place, London, W1B 1ET

Tel: 020 7636 5313
Fax: 020 7908 7580
E-mail: info@gulbenkian.org.uk

Website:
http://www.gulbenkian.org.uk
Information on how to apply for grants,
Foundation priorities for grants and recent
publications

Enquiries:
Enquiries to: Information Officer

Founded:
1956

Organisation type and purpose:
Charitable foundation.

Subject coverage:
Arts, education, social welfare, Anglo-Portuguese cultural relations.

Printed publications:
Advice to applicants (free)
Annual report (free)
Reports include:
Art not Chance: Nine artists' diaries
Centres for Curiosity and Imagination
Children and Violence
Creating Chances: Arts interventions in Pupil Referral Units and Learning Support Units
Experience and Experiment: The UK Branch of the Calouste Gulbenkian Foundation 1956–2006
Fit to Dance? The Report of the National Inquiry into Dancers' Health and Injury
Hospice Without Walls
Joining In: An Investigation into Participatory Music
Let's Act Locally – The Growth of Local Exchange Trading Systems
Mediation in Action
Passport: A framework for personal and social development
Public Interest: New models for delivering public services?
Rethinking Families
Science, not Art: Ten scientists' diaries
Serious Play: An evaluation of arts activities in Pupil Referral Units and Learning Support Units
Social Enterprise in Anytown
Strange and Charmed: Science and the contemporary visual arts
Taking Children Seriously: A Proposal for a Children's Rights Commissioner (New edition)
The Arts in Schools: – principles, practice and provision
The Turning World: Stories from the London International Festival of Theatre
Tomorrow's Parents: Developing Parenthood Education in Schools
UK Review of Effective Government Structures for Children 2001
Understanding the Stranger: Building Bridges Commmunity Handbook
Why Restorative Justice? Repairing the harm caused by crime
Wild Reckoning: An anthology provoked by Rachel Carson's 'Silent Spring'
Wise Before the Event – coping with crises in school
Plus others – see Publications List (free)
Order printed publications from: Central Books Ltd, 99 Wallis Road, London E9 5LN, tel: 0845 458 9911, fax: 0845 458 9912; e-mail: orders@centralbooks.com website: www.centralbooks.co.uk

Publications list:
Available online and in print

Access to staff:
Contact by letter, by telephone, by fax and by e-mail
Hours: Mon to Fri, 0930 to 1730
Special comments: Telephone messages taken all day.

Parent body:
Calouste Culbenkian Foundation
Avenida de Berna 45A, Lisbon, 1067–001, Portugal; tel: 00 35121 782 3000; fax: 00 35121 782 3021; e-mail: info@gulbenkian.pt; website: www.gulbenkian.pt

CAMANACHD ASSOCIATION

Alton House, 4 Ballifeary Road, Inverness, IV3 5PJ

Tel: 01463 715931
E-mail: admin@shinty.com

Website:
http://www.shinty.com
Fixtures, leagues, contacts, news, etc.

Enquiries:
Enquiries to: Executive Officer
Direct e-mail: executive@camanachd.co.uk

Founded:
1893

Organisation type and purpose:
Membership association (membership is by subscription).
National governing body of the game.
To foster and develop the game of Shinty.

Subject coverage:
The game of Shinty.

Access to staff:
Contact by fax
Hours: Mon to Fri, 0900 to 1700

CAMBERWELL COLLEGE OF ARTS

Peckham Road, London, SE5 8UF

Tel: 020 7514 6302
Fax: 020 7514 6310
E-mail: info@camberwell.arts.ac.uk

Website:
http://www.camberwell.arts.ac.uk

Enquiries:
Enquiries to: Information Assistant
Direct tel: 020 7514 6302
Direct e-mail: info@camberwell.arts.ac.uk

Founded:
1898

Formerly called:
Camberwell College of Arts and Crafts

Organisation type and purpose:
College of higher and further education.

Subject coverage:
Fine art (drawing, painting, photography and sculpture); ceramics; textiles; graphic design; illustration; 3D Design, printing; print making; typographic design; bookbinding; silversmithing and metalwork; conservation of prints, drawings, textiles and artefacts; book illustration; photography and film.

Museum or gallery collection, archive, or library special collection:
Books and ephemera by and about Walter Crane
Books on poster art
Thorold Dickinson Cinema Collection

Non-library collection catalogue:
All or part available online

Library catalogue:
All or part available online

Access to staff:
Contact by letter, by telephone and by e-mail.
Appointment necessary. Access for members only.
Hours: Mon, Fri, 1000 to 1700; Tue, Thu, 1000 to 2000; Wed, 1000 to 1930

Parent body:
University of the Arts London
272 High Holborn, London; tel: 0207 514 6130; e-mail: info@arts.ac.uk; website: htp://www.arts.ac.uk

CAMBRIDGE ASSESSMENT

Syndicate Buildings, 1 Hills Road, Cambridge, CB1 2EU

Tel: 01223 553311
Fax: 01223 460278

Enquiries:
Enquiries to: Chief Executive

Founded:
1858

Formerly called:
University of Cambridge Local Examinations Syndicate

Organisation type and purpose:
Examining body.
UK Examinations offered through OCR (which is part of Cambridge Assessment) include GCSE, GCE at A/AS, and vocational qualifications

Subject coverage:
Specifications and question papers in all subjects for which papers are set, numerous examinations and assessment services.

Printed publications:
Occasional Publications on specification or research matters
Past Papers – generally previous 3 years available
Regulations and specifications (annually)

Subsidiary body:
Oxford Cambridge and RSA Examinations (OCR)
1 Hills Road, Cambridge; tel: 01223 552552; fax: 01223 552553

CAMBRIDGE BIBLIOGRAPHICAL SOCIETY

University Library, West Road, Cambridge, CB3 9DR

Tel: 01223 333123
Fax: 01223 333160
E-mail: nas1000@cam.ac.uk

Website:
http://www.lib.cam.ac.uk/cambibsoc

Enquiries:
Enquiries to: Secretary
Other contacts: Treasurer (for subscription enquiries)

Founded:
1949

Organisation type and purpose:
Learned society.

Subject coverage:
Bibliography (historical), rare books, manuscripts, book collecting.

Printed publications:
Transactions Vol II, part 1 (1954) to Vol XII, part 1 (2000) (1954–1999, £8 each part), Vol XII, part 2 (2001–) (2000 onwards, £12 each part)
Monographs (occasional) including:
A Hand-List of English Provincial Newspapers, 1700–1760 (G. A. Cranfield, reprint with two supplements, £4.50)
A Hand-List of Irish Newspapers, 1685–1750 (R. L. Munter, £4.50)
English Embossed Bindings 1825–1850 (£8.50)
The Caxton Master and his Patrons (£8.50)
Sir Frederick Madden at Cambridge (£7)
A catalogue of books belonging to Dr Jonathan Swift (£9)
Andrew Perne Quarter-centenary studies (£7)
Garrett Godfrey's accounts (£8)
The Recovery of the Past in Elizabethan England (£8)
Thomas Gascoigne, Libraries and Scholarship (£12)
Cambridge Act and Tripos Verses (£18)
Order printed publications from: The Secretary (address as above)

Publications list:
Available in print

Access to staff:
Contact by letter, by telephone and by e-mail
Hours: Mon to Fri, 0930 to 1245 and 1400 to 1730

CAMBRIDGE CRYSTALLOGRAPHIC DATA CENTRE

Acronym or abbreviation: CCDC

12 Union Road, Cambridge, CB2 1EZ

Tel: 01223 336408
Fax: 01223 336033
E-mail: admin@ccdc.cam.ac.uk

Website:
http://www.ccdc.cam.ac.uk
Overview of the Cambridge Structural Database System, organisation of CCDC, contact information.

continued overleaf

Enquiries:
Enquiries to: Executive Director

Founded:
1987

Organisation type and purpose:
Registered charity (charity number 800579).
Research organisation.
Independent non-profit institution.

Subject coverage:
Chemical structure and substructure searching,
crystal structures of organic, organometallic
compounds.

Museum or gallery collection, archive, or library special collection:
Reprint collection
Structural data on CD-ROM

Access to staff:
Contact by e-mail and via website
Hours: Mon to Fri, 0900 to 1700
Special comments: Academic and industrial
scientists.

Access to building, collection or gallery:
No access other than to staff

Access for disabled people:
Level entry

Links with:
International Union of Crystallography
University of Cambridge

CAMBRIDGE PHILOSOPHICAL SOCIETY

Bene't Street, Cambridge, CB2 3PY

Tel: 01223 334743
E-mail: philosoc@hermes.cam.ac.uk

Website:
http://www.cambridgephilosophicalsociety.org

Enquiries:
Enquiries to: Executive Secretary

Founded:
1819

Organisation type and purpose:
Learned society.
To promote scientific enquiry.

Subject coverage:
Science, biology and mathematics.

Printed publications:
Biological Reviews (1 volume, 4 issues a year, £118
per volume, 2002)
Mathematical Proceedings (2 volumes, 3 issues
each a year, £326 per volume, 2002)

Microform publications:
Transactions (available on microfilm, £77)

Access to staff:
Contact by letter and by e-mail. Appointment
necessary.
Hours: Mon to Fri, 0900 to 1630

CAMBRIDGE REFRIGERATION TECHNOLOGY

Acronym or abbreviation: CRT

140 Newmarket Road, Cambridge, CB5 8HE

Tel: 01223 365101
Fax: 01223 461522
E-mail: dgoddard@crtech.demon.co.uk

Website:
http://www.crtech.co.uk
Newsletters, refrigerant information, commodity
information, CRT services.

Enquiries:
Enquiries to: Information Officer
Direct tel: 01223 461352

Founded:
1965

Organisation type and purpose:
Research organisation.
Research association; connection with IIR (Paris),
RIB, Institute of Refrigeration.

Subject coverage:
Transportation of perishable cargoes; specialist
knowledge on all storage and stowage techniques
of fruits and vegetables; transport, both road
vehicles and sea freight – reefers and containers;
refrigeration equipment; refrigerants; CFCs; food
legislation.

Museum or gallery collection, archive, or library special collection:
Early books and ship drawings from 1850s of
refrigeration equipment and refrigerated ships

Trade and statistical information:
Data on UNEP and all environmental
organisations, especially connected with use of
solvents, refrigerants, and foams.

Non-library collection catalogue:
All or part available online

Printed publications:
Evaluation of Refrigerant R502 Alternative for use
in Air Cooled Refrigeration Equipment
Instrumentation for Transport Equipment
Pressure Drops through Loaded Containers
Refrigerated Transport for the Grocery Industry
Transport of Perishable Foodstuffs 3 vols.

Publications list:
Available in print

Access to staff:
Contact by letter, by telephone, by fax, by e-mail
and via website. Appointment necessary. Non-
members charged.
Hours: Mon to Fri, 0900 to 1700

Access to building, collection or gallery:
Prior appointment required

Access for disabled people:
Parking provided

CAMBRIDGE UNION SOCIETY

Acronym or abbreviation: CUS

Keynes Library, Bridge Street, Cambridge, CB2
1UB

Tel: 01223 568439
Fax: 01223 566444
E-mail: eak12@cus.cam.ac.uk

Enquiries:
Enquiries to: Assistant Librarian

Founded:
1815

Organisation type and purpose:
Membership association (membership is by
subscription), registered charity, historic building,
house or site.
To provide services for members, including
debates, bar, meeting rooms and library.

Subject coverage:
Strong subjects: music, biography, fiction, travel,
leisure interests.
General subjects: history, geography; English,
French, German and Italian literature; art,
architecture, politics, sociology, anthropology,
theology, philosophy.

Museum or gallery collection, archive, or library special collection:
Erskine Allon Music Library
Fairfax Rhodes Collection (mainly art and
literature)
Extensive collection of biographies and memoirs

Non-library collection catalogue:
All or part available online

Library catalogue:
All or part available in-house

Access to staff:
Contact by letter, by telephone, by e-mail and in
person. Appointment necessary. Access for
members only. Letter of introduction required.
Hours: Term time: Mon to Fri, 1300 to 1800
Special comments: Open to non-members by prior
appointment only.

Access to building, collection or gallery:
Prior appointment required

CAMBRIDGE UNIVERSITY LIBRARY

West Road, Cambridge, CB3 9DR

Tel: 01223 333000
Fax: 01223 333160
E-mail: library@lib.cam.ac.uk

Website:
http://www.lib.cam.ac.uk

Founded:
1400

Organisation type and purpose:
University library.
Legal Deposit Library.

Subject coverage:
Extensive and general.

Museum or gallery collection, archive, or library special collection:
Acton Library
Adversaria
Almanacks
Armorial bindings
Bible Society Library and Archives
Book sales (English sales catalogues)
Bookplates and book stamps
Bradshaw Collection (Irish books)
Cambridge Collection
Chapbooks
Darwin Library and papers
Early English printed books
Ely Diocesan and Chapter Records
Gerhardie Collection
Hunter-McAlpine Collection (history of
psychiatry)
Incunabula
Jardine-Matheson Archives
Keynes Collection (Sir Geoffrey Keynes' personal
library)
Madden Collection of Ballads
Madden Collection of Maps
Music
Norton Collection (early European printing 1501–
1520)
Official Publications
Peterborough Cathedral Library
Portraits
Royal Commonwealth Society's Library
Royal Greenwich Observatory Archives
Taylor-Schechter Genizah Collection
University Archives
Vickers Archives
Wade Collection (Chinese books)
War Collection 1914–1919

Non-library collection catalogue:
All or part available online, in-house and in print

Printed publications:
Cambridge University Libraries Directory
Exhibition catalogues
General books
Genizah series
Specialised catalogues
Order printed publications from: Library Offices,
Cambridge University Library; tel: 01223 333048; e-
mail: admin@lib.cam.ac.uk

Publications list:
Available online and in print

Access to building, collection or gallery:
Prior appointment required
Hours: Mon to Fri, 0900 to 1915; Sat, 0900 to 1700
Easter Full Term: Mon to Fri, 0900 to 2200

Special comments: Closed between Christmas and New Year, Bank Holidays, Sept 16 to 23. A prior appointment is advised to obtain reader's ticket.

Access for disabled people:
Parking provided, ramped entry, toilet facilities
Special comments: Recommended to contact Library before first visit.

Also at the same address:
Cambridge Bibliographical Society
University Archives
   tel: 01223 333147/8

Organisationally, it includes the:
Betty & Gordon Moore Library
   Centre for Mathematical Sciences, Wilberforce
   Road, Cambridge, CB3 0WD; tel: 01223 765670;
   fax: 01223 765678; e-mail: moore-library@lib.cam
   .ac.uk
Cambridge University Medical Library
   Clinical School Building, Box 111,
   Addenbrooke's Hospital, Hills Road, Cambridge,
   CB2 2SP; tel: 01223 336750; fax: 01223 331918; e-
   mail: library@medschl.cam.ac.uk
Central Science Library
   Bene't Street, Cambridge, CB2 3PY; tel: 01223
   334742; fax: 01223 334748; e-mail: lib-csl
   -inquiries@lists.cam.ac.uk
Squire Law Library
   10 West Road, Cambridge, CB3 9DZ; tel: 01223
   330077; fax: 01223 330048; e-mail: dfw1003@cam
   .ac.uk

CAMBRIDGE UNIVERSITY PRESS

Acronym or abbreviation: CUP

The Edinburgh Building, Shaftesbury Road, Cambridge, CB2 8RU

Tel: 01223 312393
Fax: 01223 325959
E-mail: information@cambridge.org

Website:
http://www.cambridge.org

Enquiries:
Enquiries to: Sales Manager

Founded:
1534

Organisation type and purpose:
University department or institute, publishing house.

Subject coverage:
The Press publishes in all main academic and educational subject areas, including English Language Teaching, Schoolbooks, Humanities, Social Sciences, STM and Reference books, Bibles and prayer books, educational software and CD-ROMs.

Printed publications:
About 1500 titles a year
230 learned journals
Online catalogue; also subject lists and lists of
   journals

Publications list:
Available online and in print

Access to staff:
Contact by letter, by telephone, by fax, by e-mail and via website
Hours: Mon to Fri, 0900 to 1700

CAMBRIDGESHIRE ARCHIVES

Box RES 1009, Shire Hall, Castle Hill, Cambridge, CB3 0AP

Tel: 01223 699399
Fax: 01223 718823
E-mail: cambs.archives.cambridge@cambridgeshire
.gov.uk

Website:
http://www.cambridgeshire.gov.uk/leisure/
archives

Enquiries:
Enquiries to: Senior Archivist Public Services
Other contacts: Archives and Local Studies Manager (for matters of general policy, broad issues); Principal Archivist (for collections-related matters)

Founded:
1930

Formerly called:
Cambridgeshire Record Office (alias County Record Office Cambridge) (year of change 2008)

Organisation type and purpose:
Local government body.
Record office.

Subject coverage:
Historical matters of all kinds relating to the area of the former county of Cambridgeshire and the Isle of Ely; matters relating to the County Council of Cambridgeshire since 1974.

Museum or gallery collection, archive, or library special collection:
Cambridge Borough, 13th to 20th centuries
Land drainage authorities including the former
   Bedford Level Corporation 1663–1920

Non-library collection catalogue:
All or part available online and in-house

Library catalogue:
All or part available in-house

Printed publications:
A Century of Cambridgeshire Parish Councils
   (Batcheler K C, 1994, £4.95)
Archaeology of Cambridgeshire 1. South-West
   Cambridgeshire (Taylor A, 1997, £9.95)
Archaeology of Cambridgeshire 2. South-East
   Cambridgeshire and the Fen Edge (Taylor A,
   1998, £11.95)
Changing Landscapes: The Ancient Fenland (Coles
   J and Hall D, 1998, £4.95)
Guide to Education Records in the County Record
   Office Cambridge (Black A, 1972, £1)
Reproduction posters, prints and maps
Order printed publications from: See website

Microform publications:
Microform of parish register transcripts (about 80
   sets)
Order microform publications from: Cambridgeshire
Family History Society; website: http://
www.cfhs.org.uk

Publications list:
Available in print

Access to staff:
Contact by letter, by telephone, by e-mail and in person
Hours: Tue, Wed, Thu, 0900 to 1245 and 1345 to 1715; Fri, 0900 to 1245 and 1345 to 1615; Tue, 1715 to 2100 by appointment only

Branches:
Huntingdonshire Archives
   Huntingdon; tel: 01480 375842

Constituent part of:
Cambridgeshire Archives and Local Studies
(CALS)

Parent body:
Cambridgeshire County Council
   tel: 01223 717111

CAMBRIDGESHIRE CHAMBERS OF COMMERCE

Vision Park, Histon, Cambridge, CB24 9ZR

Tel: 01223 237414
Fax: 01223 237405
E-mail: enquiries@cambscci.co.uk

Enquiries:
Enquiries to: Chief Executive

Founded:
1917

Formerly called:
Cambridge and District Chamber of Commerce and Industry

Organisation type and purpose:
Membership association (membership is by subscription), present number of members: 1,100. Chamber of Commerce.

Subject coverage:
International trade services, relevant information and back-up services.

Museum or gallery collection, archive, or library special collection:
UK, Local and International Trade Library

Trade and statistical information:
On-line access to trade statistics.

Printed publications:
Cambridge Directory of Industry and Commerce
   (annually)
Cambridge Chamber Newsletter (12 times a year)
Export Newsletter (monthly)

Access to staff:
Contact by letter, by telephone, by fax, by e-mail and in person
Hours: Mon to Fri, 0900 to 1700

Access to building, collection or gallery:
No access other than to staff
Hours: Mon to Fri, 0900 to 1700

Member of:
Association of British Chambers of Commerce

CAMBRIDGESHIRE RECORDS SOCIETY

Cambridgeshire Archives, Box RES1009, Shire Hall, Castle Hill, Cambridge, CB3 0AP

Tel: 01223 716858; 01223 699399
Fax: 01223 718823
E-mail: cambs.archives@cambridgeshire.gov.uk

Website:
http://www.cambsrecordsociety.co.uk/index.php

Enquiries:
Enquiries to: Secretary

Founded:
1972

Formerly called:
Cambridge Antiquarian Records Society (year of change 1987)

Organisation type and purpose:
A not-for-profit record publishing society of around 120 individual and institutional members publishing texts of documentary sources and reproductions of maps, etc., relating to Cambridgeshire and adjoining areas.

Subject coverage:
History of Cambridgeshire, documentary sources.

Printed publications:
Edited texts and documents including:
A Cambridgeshire Lieutenancy Letter Book 1595–
   1605 (ed. E. J. Bourgeois)
Romilly's Cambridge Diary 1842–47 and 1848–64
   (ed. M. E. Bury and J. D. Pickles)
Edmund Pettis's Survey of St Ives 1728 (ed. M.
   Carter)
Churchwardens' Book of Bassingbourn 1496–
   c.1540 (ed. D. Dymond)
Cartulary of the Hospital of St John Cambridge
   (ed. M. G. Underwood)
Order printed publications from: from the Society

Publications list:
Available online and in print

Access to staff:
Contact by letter, by telephone, by fax and by e-mail

Links with:
Cambridge Antiquarian Society (CAS)
   Haddon Library, Faculty of Archaeology and
   Anthropology, Pembroke Street, Cambridge, CB2
   3RA

CAMDEN LOCAL STUDIES AND ARCHIVES CENTRE

Holborn Library, 32–38 Theobalds Road, London, WC1X 8PA

Tel: 020 7974 6342
Fax: 020 7974 6284
E-mail: localstudies@camden.gov.uk

Website:
http://www.camden.gov.uk/localstudies

Enquiries:
Enquiries to: Senior Officer: Local Studies and Archives

Organisation type and purpose:
Local government body, public library.
Archives service.

Subject coverage:
Local studies, local history of Camden including Hampstead, Holborn and St Pancras, archives, conservation.

Museum or gallery collection, archive, or library special collection:
Local books and printed materials
Local newspapers
Ephemera
Local directories
Electoral registers
Illustrations
Maps
Census returns for Camden Area 1841–1901 (microfilm)
Archives of the London Borough of Camden and its predecessor bodies
Deposited archives including Highgate Cemetery registers (microfilm)
Special collections including:
Bellmoor Collection (compiled by Hampstead historian Thomas J. Barratt)
Eleanor Farjeon Collection
Heal Collection (compiled by local historian Sir Ambrose Heal on St Pancras to 1913)
Kate Greenaway Collection (available by special application only)

Non-library collection catalogue:
All or part available in-house

Printed publications:
A large number of books about the history of the area and particular places, including:
Beating the Bounds of Camden: A long distance walk (M. J. Holmes, ISBN 0 901389 79 X)
Camden Celebrates Cinema 100 – A guide to film locations in Camden (ISBN 0 901 389 86 2)
Camden Town 1791–1991: a pictorial record (V. Hart, R. Knight, L. Marshall, ISBN 0 901389 70 6)
The Cinemas of Camden (M. Aston, ISBN 0 901389 88 9)
Hampstead and Highgate Directory 1885/1886 (ISBN 0901389 48X)
A History of Camden: Hampstead, Holborn and St Pancras (J. Richardson, ISBN 0 948667 58 3)
Memories of Holborn (ed. M. Waugh, ISBN 0 901389 53 6)
Somers Town: A record of change (M. J. Holmes, ISBN 0 901389 50 1)
Twelve Views of Camden: A portfolio of prints (ISBN 0 901389 09 9)
Wartime Camden (ed. V. Hart and L. Marshall, ISBN 0 901389 40 4)
Camden Past and Present: A guide to the Camden Local Studies and Archives Centre (M. Aston, M. J. Holmes, R. G. Knight, ISBN 0 901389 99 4)
Studying Camden: A students' guide to Camden Local Studies and Archives Centre (M. Aston, ISBN 1 900846128)
King's Cross: A tour in time (M. Aston and L. Marshall, ISBN 1900846187)
Little Italy: The story of London's Italian quarter (T. Allen, ISBN 9781900846219)

Publications list:
Available online and in print

Access to staff:
Contact by letter, by telephone, by fax, by e-mail, in person and via website

Hours: Mon, Tue, Thu, Fri, 1000 to 1900; Sat, 1000 to 1700; Wed and Sun closed.
Special comments: Appointments needed for some archives held in outstore.

Parent body:
London Borough of Camden
Culture and Environment Directorate

CAMPAIGN AGAINST ARMS TRADE

Acronym or abbreviation: CAAT

11 Goodwin Street, London, N4 3HQ

Tel: 020 7281 0297
Fax: 020 7281 4369
E-mail: enquiries@caat.org.uk

Website:
http://www.caat.org.uk

Enquiries:
Enquiries to: Research Co-ordinator

Founded:
1974

Organisation type and purpose:
Voluntary organisation.

Subject coverage:
UK arms exports.

Publications list:
Available in print

Access to staff:
Appointment necessary.
Hours: Mon to Fri, 1030 to 1730

CAMPAIGN FOR AN INDEPENDENT BRITAIN

Acronym or abbreviation: CIB

81 Ashmole Street, London, SW8 1NF

Tel: 020 8340 0314
Fax: 020 7582 7021
E-mail: info@cibhq.co.uk

Website:
http://www.cibhq.co.uk

Enquiries:
Enquiries to: Honorary Secretary
Direct tel: 020 8348 3784
Direct fax: 020 8347 8246
Other contacts: Chairman

Founded:
1976

Formerly called:
Safeguard Britain Campaign (year of change 1983); British Anti-Common Market Campaign (year of change 1989)

Organisation type and purpose:
Membership association (membership is by subscription), present number of members: 3000.
To recoup self-government from the European Union.

Subject coverage:
European Community and its impact on the United Kingdom.

Printed publications:
A price not worth paying: the economic cost of EMU (Burkitt B et al, £4.50)
The Common Fisheries Policy – End or Mend? (Mitchell A, £2.50)
There IS an Alternative: Britain and its relationship with the EU (Burkitt B, et al, £4.50 inc. p&p)

Publications list:
Available in print

Access to staff:
Contact by letter, by telephone and by fax
Hours: Mon to Fri, 0900 to 1700

CAMPAIGN FOR FREEDOM OF INFORMATION

Acronym or abbreviation: CFoI

Suite 102, 16 Baldwins Gardens, London, EC1N 7RJ

Tel: 020 7831 7477
Fax: 020 7831 7461
E-mail: admin@cfoi.demon.co.uk

Website:
http://www.cfoi.org.uk

Founded:
1984

Organisation type and purpose:
Not-for-profit organisation working to improve public access to official information and ensure that the Freedom of Information Act is implemented effectively.

Subject coverage:
Freedom of information. Data protection/access to personal files.

Printed publications:
Various publications available free via website or to purchase in paper form

Publications list:
Available online and in print

Access to staff:
Contact by letter, by telephone, by fax and by e-mail
Hours: Mon to Fri, 1000 to 1600

Access to building, collection or gallery:
Prior appointment required

CAMPAIGN FOR HOMOSEXUAL EQUALITY

Acronym or abbreviation: CHE

PO Box 342, London, WC1X 0DU

Tel: 07702 326151
Fax: 020 8743 6252
E-mail: secretary@c-h-e.fsnet.co.uk

Enquiries:
Enquiries to: Secretary

Founded:
1969

Organisation type and purpose:
Membership association (membership is by subscription), present number of members: 200, voluntary organisation.
Pressure group.
To promote acceptance of homosexuality.

Subject coverage:
Discrimination against homosexuals and bisexuals.

Printed publications:
Annual Report
Newsletter
Variety of leaflets on the subject (free)

Electronic and video publications:
Audio Cassette: Coming Out (£6)

Publications list:
Available in print

Access to staff:
Contact by letter and by telephone
Hours: Mon to Fri, 0900 to 1700

CAMPAIGN FOR NATIONAL PARKS

Acronym or abbreviation: CNP

6–7 Barnard Mews, London, SW11 1QU

Tel: 020 7924 4077
Fax: 020 7924 5761
E-mail: info@cnp.org.uk

Website:
http://www.cnp.org.uk

General information.

Enquiries:
Enquiries to: Chief Executive

Founded:
1936

Organisation type and purpose:
Voluntary organisation, registered charity (charity number 295336).

Subject coverage:
National Parks of England and Wales; conservation and protection.

Printed publications:
Various – list on receipt of sae

Publications list:
Available online and in print

Access to staff:
Contact by letter, by telephone, by e-mail and via website. Appointment necessary. Non-members charged.
Hours: Mon to Fri, 0900 to 1700

Access to building, collection or gallery:
Prior appointment required

Member organisations:
over 40 organisations

CAMPAIGN FOR PRESS AND BROADCASTING FREEDOM

Acronym or abbreviation: CPBF

2nd Floor, Vi & Garner Smith House, 23, Orford Road, Walthamstow, London, E17 9NL

Tel: 020 8521 5932
E-mail: freepress@cpbf.org.uk

Website:
http://www.cpbf.org.uk
All about the Campaign for Press and Broadcasting Freedom.

Enquiries:
Enquiries to: National Organiser

Founded:
1979

Organisation type and purpose:
Membership association, voluntary organisation, research organisation.
Campaign for diversity and democracy in the media.

Subject coverage:
Media ownership, right of reply, new media technologies, democracy and diversity in the media.

Museum or gallery collection, archive, or library special collection:
Books and videos on media issues

Printed publications:
Free Press (6 times a year, £1 per copy)
Shafted: The Media, the Miners' Strike and the Aftermath, edited by Granville Williams £12.50 inc. p&p)
Order printed publications from: CPBF

Access to staff:
Contact by letter, by telephone, by e-mail, in person and via website. Appointment necessary.
Hours: Mon to Fri, 1000 to 1800

Access to building, collection or gallery:
Prior appointment required

Access for disabled people:
Level entry

CAMPAIGN FOR REAL ALE LIMITED

Acronym or abbreviation: CAMRA

230 Hatfield Road, St Albans, Hertfordshire, AL1 4LW

Tel: 01727 867201

Fax: 01727 867670
E-mail: camra@camra.org.uk

Website:
http://www.camra.org.uk

Enquiries:
Enquiries to: Research and Information Manager
Direct tel: 01727 798449
Direct e-mail: iain.loe@camra.org.uk

Founded:
1971

Organisation type and purpose:
National organisation, membership association (membership is by subscription), present number of members: 118,000, voluntary organisation, publishing house.
Consumer organisation.
To act as the champion of the consumer in relation to the UK drinks industry.

Subject coverage:
Brewing industry, traditional beer and public houses, consumer protection, foreign breweries and beer.

Services for disabled people:
Tapes of members' newspaper available.

Museum or gallery collection, archive, or library special collection:
Issues of What's Brewing – the newspaper of the campaign – back to the early 70s
Good Beer Guides back to 1st edition 1974

Trade and statistical information:
Some statistics on the UK Brewing Industry.

Printed publications:
Beer, Bed & Breakfast
Brew Your own Real Ale at Home
Good Beer Guides (annually, 1974–2002)
Good Beer Guide to Belgium & Holland
Good Beer Guide to Prague & the Czech Republic
Good Beer Guide to Munich & Bavaria
The Best Pubs (series of local guides)
What's Brewing (monthly, available to members)
Good Bottled Beer Guide
Dictionary of Beer
London Pub Guide
CAMRA's Good Cider Guide
Good Beer Guide to Germany

Access to staff:
Contact by letter, by telephone, by fax, by e-mail and via website. Appointment necessary.
Hours: Mon to Fri, 0900 to 1700

Access to building, collection or gallery:
Prior appointment required
Hours: Mon to Fri, 0900 to 1700

Access for disabled people:
Parking provided

Links with:
European Beer Consumer Union (EBCU)
230 Hatfield Road, St Albans, Hertfordshire, AL1 4LW; tel: 01727 867201; fax: 01727 867670; e-mail: ebcu@camra.org.uk

CAMPAIGN FOR STATE EDUCATION

Acronym or abbreviation: CASE

98 Erlanger Road, London, SE14 5TH

Tel: 07932 149942
E-mail: case@casenet.org.uk

Website:
http://www.casenet.org.uk

Enquiries:
Enquiries to: Contact

Founded:
1963

Formerly called:
Campaign for the Advancement of State Education

Organisation type and purpose:
Membership association (membership is by subscription), voluntary organisation.
Education campaign group.

Subject coverage:
State education, funding, class size, contacts, government policy, comprehensive education.

Printed publications:
Parents and Schools (5 times a year, £20 year's subscription, £15 members)

Publications list:
Available online and in print

Access to staff:
Contact by letter, by telephone, by fax and by e-mail

Access to building, collection or gallery:
No access other than to staff

CAMPAIGN FOR THE PROTECTION OF RURAL WALES

Acronym or abbreviation: CPRW

Ty Gwyn, 31 High Street, Welshpool, Powys, SY21 7YD

Tel: 01938 552525 or 556212
Fax: 01938 552741
E-mail: deb@cprwmail.org.uk

Website:
http://www.cprw.org.uk
General information.

Enquiries:
Enquiries to: Liaison Officer

Founded:
1928

Formerly called:
Council for the Protection of Rural Wales

Organisation type and purpose:
Voluntary organisation, registered charity (charity number 239899).
Protection of Wales countryside and coasts from inappropriate development.

Subject coverage:
Active protection of the Welsh countryside and its villages; planning; amenities; legislation.

Museum or gallery collection, archive, or library special collection:
Library of environmental publications

Printed publications:
Rural Wales (magazine, 3 times a year, free to members, others on request)

Access to staff:
Contact by e-mail and via website. Appointment necessary.
Hours: Mon to Fri, 0900 to 1700

CAMPAIGN TO PROTECT RURAL ENGLAND – DORSET BRANCH

Acronym or abbreviation: CPRE Dorset

The Little Keep, Bridport Road, Dorchester, Dorset, DT1 1SQ

Tel: 01305 265808
E-mail: info@dorset-cpre.org.uk

Website:
http://www.dorset-cpre.org.uk
Information on local campaigns (Litter, Green Belt, Wind Farms, etc.), group contacts, membership, news items and reference information.

Enquiries:
Enquiries to: Director

Founded:
1926

Organisation type and purpose:
Membership association (membership is by subscription), voluntary organisation, registered charity (charity number 211974).

continued overleaf

To improve, protect and preserve for the benefit of the public, the countryside and the country towns and villages of the county of Dorset.

Subject coverage:
Planning procedures appropriate to county structure plan, minerals and waste local plans, district and borough local plans and planning applications within the county; issues relevant to the protection of the countryside; litter and transport issues.

Printed publications:
Dorset Review (2 times a year)

Access to staff:
Contact by letter, by telephone, by e-mail and via website. Appointment necessary.
Hours: Tue, 0900 to 1600; and most Thu, 0900 to 1500
Special comments: 24-hour answerphone and fax.

National office:
Campaign to Protect Rural England (CPRE)
128 Southwark Street, London, SE1 0SW; tel: 020 7981 2800; fax: 020 7981 2899; e-mail: info@cpre.org.uk

CAMPAIGN TO PROTECT RURAL ENGLAND – OXFORDSHIRE BRANCH

Acronym or abbreviation: CPRE Oxfordshire

Punches Barn, Waterperry Road, Holton, Oxfordshire, OX33 1PP

Tel: 01865 874780
E-mail: campaign@cpreoxon.org.uk

Website:
http://www.cpreoxon.org.uk
Campaign news and advice on protecting the countryside.

Enquiries:
Enquiries to: Campaign Manager
Direct e-mail: campaign@cpreoxon.org.uk

Founded:
1931

Organisation type and purpose:
Membership association (membership is by subscription).
A company limited by guarantee, registered in England, no. 04443278.
Registered charity (charity no. 1093081).
Branch of the national charity.

Subject coverage:
Protection of the local countryside, planning applications, transport, development, conservation issues relating to rural environment, hedgerows, dry stone walls.

Printed publications:
The Oxford Green Belt Way (£5 plus £1 p&p)
Order printed publications from: Order directly from the office. Please send cheques payable to CPRE Oxfordshire.

Access to staff:
Contact by letter, by telephone, by e-mail and via website. Appointment necessary.
Hours: Mon, Tue, Thu and Fri, 1000 to 1300
Special comments: Officer is only part-time.

CAMPAIGN TO PROTECT RURAL ENGLAND – SHROPSHIRE BRANCH

Acronym or abbreviation: CPRE

Bear Steps Office, St Alkmond's Square, Shrewsbury, Shropshire, SY1 1UH

Tel: 01743 356511
Fax: 01743 344994
E-mail: cpre@civic.plus.net

Enquiries:
Enquiries to: Secretary

Founded:
1926

Organisation type and purpose:
Membership association (membership is by subscription), present number of members: 550, voluntary organisation, registered charity (charity number 218782), suitable for ages: all.
The care and improvement of the whole of the countryside.

Subject coverage:
Environmental conservation.

Access to staff:
Contact by letter, by telephone, by fax and by e-mail
Hours: Mon to Fri, 1000 to 1600
Special comments: Shrewsbury office open on Monday and Thursday only. National office is open Monday to Friday inclusive.

National Office at:
Campaign to Protect Rural England
128 Southwark Street, London, SE1 0SW; tel: 020 7981 2800; fax: 020 7981 2899

CAMPBELL HOOPER

35 Old Queen Street, London, SW1H 9JD

Tel: 020 7222 9070
Fax: 020 7222 5591
E-mail: danieleilon@campbellhooper.com

Website:
http://www.campbellhooper.com
Information relating to the firm.

Enquiries:
Enquiries to: Partner
Direct tel: 020 7654 5115
Direct fax: 020 7654 5226

Founded:
1760

Organisation type and purpose:
Solicitors.
Legal advice, transactional work and litigation.

Subject coverage:
Computer software copyright issues, intellectual property advice and litigation, employment, commercial property, company law and commercial law, private client and trust issues.

Printed publications:
Order printed publications from: Marketing Administrator, Campbell Hooper
35 Old Queen Street, London, SW1H 9JD, tel: 020 7222 9070, fax: 020 7222 5591, e-mail: marketing@campbellhooper.com

Publications list:
Available online

Access to staff:
Contact by letter, by telephone, by fax, by e-mail and via website. Appointment necessary.
Hours: Mon to Fri, 0900 to 1800

CAMPDEN BRI

Chipping Campden, Gloucestershire, GL55 6LD

Tel: 01386 842000
Fax: 01386 842100
E-mail: information@campden.co.uk

Website:
http://www.campden.co.uk

Enquiries:
Enquiries to: Information Officer
Direct tel: 01386 842045
Direct e-mail: info@campden.co.uk

Founded:
1919

Created by the merger of:
Campden & Chorleywood Food Research Association and Brewing Research International (year of change 2008)

Formerly called:
Campden Food and Drink Research Association (year of change 1995); Campden & Chorleywood Food Research Association (year of change 2008)

Organisation type and purpose:
Consultancy, research organisation.

Subject coverage:
Food science and technology associated with the preservation (canning, aseptic, chill, modified atmosphere packaging, freezing, dehydration) of foods, microbiology, chemistry, biochemistry and sensory quality evaluation of processed foods, suitability of raw materials for processing.

Museum or gallery collection, archive, or library special collection:
Old books on milling and baking equipment and products

Publications list:
Available online

Access to staff:
Contact by letter, by telephone, by fax, by e-mail and via website. Non-members charged.
Hours: Mon to Fri, 0900 to 1700

CAMPING AND CARAVANNING CLUB

Greenfield House, Westwood Way, Coventry, Warwickshire, CV4 8JH

Tel: 0845 130 7631
Fax: 024 7669 4886

Website:
http://www.campingandcaravanningclub.co.uk
Information about the Club's services and sites.

Enquiries:
Enquiries to: Public Relations Manager
Direct tel: 024 7647 5204
Direct e-mail: jon.dale@thefriendlyclub.co.uk
Other contacts: Public Relations Executive

Founded:
1901

Formerly called:
Camping Club of Great Britain and Ireland

Organisation type and purpose:
Membership association.
Owning and running over 100 campsites on behalf of members, although most sites are also open to non-members.

Subject coverage:
Technical assistance to members with tents, caravans, trailer tents, motor caravans. General assistance on camping law and information to official bodies, media, trade, etc.

Museum or gallery collection, archive, or library special collection:
Historical archives relative to the club and camping in general

Printed publications:
Camping and Caravanning (magazine, monthly)
Carefree International Travel Service Brochure (annually)
Club Handbook (free to all members)
Member Services Directory (annually)
Your Big Sites Book (every 2 years)
Your Place in the Country (annually)

Access to staff:
Contact by letter and by e-mail
Hours: Mon to Fri, 0845 to 1645

Access for disabled people:
Parking provided, lift
Special comments: Access to all floors

CANADA WOOD UK

PO Box 1, Farnborough, Hampshire, GU14 6WE

Tel: 01252 522545
Fax: 01252 522546
E-mail: office@canadawooduk.org

Website:
http://www.canadawooduk.org

Enquiries:
Enquiries to: UK Consultant

Incorporates the former:
CertiWood, Coastal Forest Products Association
(CFPA), Council of Forest Industries (COFI), Forest
Products Association of Canada (FPAC), Quebec
Wood Export Bureau (QWEB), Western Red Cedar
Export Association (WRCEA).

Organisation type and purpose:
Advisory body (membership is by subscription,
qualification), manufacturing industry.
Industry association representing, in the United
Kingdom, Canadian timber and plywood
manufacturers through various agencies and
associations.
Providing technical information and advice on
member-company products to architects,
engineers, specifiers and the construction and
wood-utilising industries generally.

Subject coverage:
Technical advisory service for application and use
of wood and plywood in construction.

Information services:
RIBA-accredited CPD presentations, technical
literature and free advice over the phone.

Education services:
RIBA-accredited CPD presentations on Canadian
wood, timber buildings and green design.

Trade and statistical information:
Worldwide exports of Canadian timber and
plywood.

Printed publications:
Technical literature on Canadian timber species,
plywood, structural grading (free of charge)

Access to staff:
Contact by letter, by telephone, by fax and by e-
mail. Appointment necessary.
Hours: Mon to Fri, 0900 to 1700

Also at:
Maritime Lumber Bureau
PO Box 459, Amherst, Nova Scotia, B4H 4A1,
Canada; tel: +1 902 667 3889; fax: +1 902 667 0401

CANADA-UNITED KINGDOM CHAMBER OF COMMERCE

38 Grosvenor Street, London, W1K 4DP

Tel: 020 7258 6576 or 020 7258 6578
Fax: 020 7258 6594
E-mail: info@canada-uk.org

Website:
http://www.canada-uk.org
About the Chamber, its services and resource links.

Enquiries:
Enquiries to: Manager
Direct tel: 020 7258 6576

Founded:
1921

Organisation type and purpose:
Membership association (membership is by
subscription), present number of members: 330.

Subject coverage:
Enquiries about trade and investment between
Canada and the United Kingdom in both
directions.

Printed publications:
Link Newsletter (faxed/e-mailed monthly)

Access to staff:
Contact by letter, by telephone, by fax, by e-mail
and via website. Appointment necessary. Non-
members charged.
Hours: Mon to Fri, 0900 to 1700

CANCER PREVENTION RESEARCH TRUST

231 Roehampton Lane, London, SW15 4LB

Tel: 020 8785 7786
Fax: 020 8785 6466
E-mail: cprt@talk21.com

Website:
http://www.cancerpreventionresearch.org.uk

Enquiries:
Enquiries to: Director

Founded:
1973

Organisation type and purpose:
International organisation, national organisation,
voluntary organisation, registered charity (charity
number 265985), research organisation.

Subject coverage:
Cancer prevention, cancer research.

Printed publications:
Cancer Prevention and Health News (newsletter,
monthly, free with sae)

Access to staff:
Contact by letter, by telephone, by fax, by e-mail,
in person and via website
Hours: Mon to Fri, 0900 to 1700

Access to building, collection or gallery:
No prior appointment required

Access for disabled people:
Toilet facilities

CANNING HOUSE LIBRARY

Formal name: Hispanic and Luso-Brazilian Council
Acronym or abbreviation: HLBC

Hispanic and Luso-Brazilian Council, Canning
House, 2 Belgrave Square, London, SW1X 8PJ

Tel: 020 7235 2303
Fax: 020 7838 9258
E-mail: library@canninghouse.org

Website:
http://www.canninghouse.org

Enquiries:
Enquiries to: Library and Information Services
Manager
Direct tel: ext. 208
Direct e-mail: library@canninghouse.org

Founded:
1943

Organisation type and purpose:
Registered charity, cultural lending and reference
library (65,000 vols).
Promotes relations between the UK and Latin
America, Spain and Portugal.

Subject coverage:
Most subjects relating to Latin America, the
Caribbean, Portugal and its former colonies, and
Spain, including history, archaeology, politics,
economics, sociology, anthropology, religion,
geography, natural history, travel, literature,
language, art, music, cinema, food and drink.

**Museum or gallery collection, archive, or library
special collection:**
R. B. Cunninghame Graham Collection
W. H. Hudson Collection
George Canning Collection
Rare books (travel accounts, history, literature and
language, religion, anthropology, natural history,
etc.)
Feature films from Latin America, Spain and
Portugal, on DVD and video

Non-library collection catalogue:
All or part available online and in-house

Library catalogue:
All or part available online

Printed publications:
British Bulletin of Publications on Latin America,
the Caribbean, Portugal and Spain (twice a year)

Cultural Centre Newsletter (electronic, bi-monthly)
Information leaflets
Printed catalogue (to 1973, subject and author)
Order printed publications from: Worldwide
Subscription Services, e-mail: enquiries@
worldwidesubscriptions.com

Publications list:
Available online

Access to staff:
Contact by letter, by telephone, by fax, by e-mail,
in person and via website
Hours: Mon to Fri, 1400 to 1800

Links with:
ACLAIIR, REDIAL, SALALM

CANTERBURY CATHEDRAL ARCHIVES

Acronym or abbreviation: CCA

The Precincts, Canterbury, Kent, CT1 2EH

Tel: 01227 865330; minicom no. 01622 605249
Fax: 01227 865222
E-mail: archives@canterbury-cathedral.org

Website:
http://www.canterbury-cathedral.org/archives
.html
Main archives site.

Enquiries:
Enquiries to: Archivist / Manager
Other contacts: Canon Librarian

Founded:
597

Organisation type and purpose:
Local government body.
Cathedral archives.

Subject coverage:
Archives relating to Canterbury, especially the
Cathedral, City, Diocese and Archdeaconry
parishes.

**Museum or gallery collection, archive, or library
special collection:**
Archives of Christ Church, dating from the 8th
century, including charters, financial records and
manorial records
Archives of the post-Reformation Dean and
Chapter, to the present day, including
photographs and architectural drawings
Records of the City of Canterbury, dating from the
12th century
Records of the Diocese of Canterbury
Parish records for Church of England parishes in
the Archdeaconry of Canterbury
Records of individuals, families, businesses and
organisations in the district of Canterbury
Collections of artefacts

Non-library collection catalogue:
All or part available online and in-house

Microform publications:
Stock of microfilm of deposits, especially
genealogical sources (available for purchase)

Publications list:
Available online and in print

Access to staff:
Contact by letter, by telephone, by fax, by e-mail,
in person and via website. Appointment necessary.
Hours: Mon to Thu, 0900 to 1700; 1st and 3rd Sat,
0900 to 1300

Access for disabled people:
Parking provided, subject to availability
Special comments: Lift to search room; hearing loop.

Parent body:
Dean and Chapter of Canterbury
Cathedral House, The Precincts, Canterbury, CT1
2EH; tel: 01227 762862; fax: 01227 865222
Kent County Council
Sessions House, County Hall, Maidstone, Kent,
ME14 1XQ; tel: 08458 247247; fax: 01622 697186

CANTERBURY CATHEDRAL LIBRARY

Acronym or abbreviation: CCL

The Precincts, Canterbury, Kent, CT1 2EH

Tel: 01227 865287
Fax: 01227 865222
E-mail: library@canterbury-cathedral.org

Website:
http://www.canterbury-cathedral.org
Summary of collections, opening hours, history of the library.
http://opac.ukc.ac.uk
Catalogue.

Enquiries:
Enquiries to: Librarian
Direct tel: 01227 865288
Direct e-mail: librarian@canterbury-cathedral.org
Other contacts: Canon Librarian

Founded:
597

Organisation type and purpose:
Registered charity.
Cathedral library.

Subject coverage:
Church history, Kentish history, bibliography, anti-slavery literature, early natural science books, printed historical sources, Oxford Movement, Roman Catholic controversy.

Museum or gallery collection, archive, or library special collection:
50,000 books in total: 30,000 pre-19th-century books and pamphlets held on computer database
Anti-slave trade tracts (19th century)
Herbals and other natural history books
Howley-Harrison Library (12,800 books bequeathed by Benjamin Harrison, Archdeacon of Maidstone, 1887)
Local history and cathedral history collection
Mendham Collection on Roman Catholic Controversy
Parish collections for Elham and Preston-next-Wingham

Library catalogue:
All or part available online and in print

Printed publications:
The Slave Trade: bibliography of the collection (revised edn 2001, £12)
In Foreign Parts: books and pamphlets on the World Beyond Western Europe printed before 1900 (2000, £12)
The Oxford Movement: 19th-century books and pamphlets in the Cathedral Library (1999, £10)
Catalogue of Canterbury Cathedral Library's pre-1801 books (1998)
Catalogue of the Mendham Collection (1994)
Order printed publications from: e-mail: canterburysources@canterbury-cathedral.org
Adam Matthews Publications, Marlborough, Wiltshire (for the Cathedral pre-1801 catalogue)

Access to staff:
Contact by letter, by telephone, by e-mail and via website. Appointment necessary.
Hours: Mon to Thu, 0900 to 1700; 1st and 3rd Sat, 0900 to 1300

Access for disabled people:
Parking provided
Special comments: Lift to first floor where library is situated.

Affiliated to the:
University of Kent at Canterbury
tel: 01227 764000

Parent body:
Dean and Chapter of Canterbury Cathedral
The Precincts, Canterbury, CT1 2EH; tel: 01227 762862

CANTERBURY CHRIST CHURCH UNIVERSITY – LIBRARY

North Holmes Road, Canterbury, Kent, CT1 1QU

Tel: 01227 767700
Fax: 01227 470442

Website:
http://www.canterbury.ac.uk/library

Enquiries:
Enquiries to: Director of Library Services
Direct tel: 01227 782352

Founded:
1962

Organisation type and purpose:
University library.

Subject coverage:
Applied social sciences, art, business and management studies, education, English and language studies, geography, history, IT, law and criminal justice studies, media, music, nursing and allied health professions, religious studies, social work, and sports science.

Museum or gallery collection, archive, or library special collection:
Elizabeth Gaskell Collection

Library catalogue:
All or part available online

Access to staff:
Contact by letter, by telephone, by e-mail, in person and via website. Non-members charged.
Hours: Mon to Fri, 0900 to 1700

Access to building, collection or gallery:
Hours: Main library: Mon to Fri, 0730 to 2100; Sat, Sun, 0900 to 1700

Access for disabled people:
Building is fully accessible

Also at:
Broadstairs Learning Centre
Northwood Road, Broadstairs, CT10 2WA; tel: 01843 609103; website: http://www.canterbury.ac.uk/library
Salomons Campus
David Salomons Estate, Broomhill Road, Southborough, Tunbridge Wells, TN3 0TG; tel: 01895 507516; website: http://www.canterbury.ac.uk/library

CANTERBURY CITY COUNCIL

Military Road, Canterbury, Kent, CT1 1YW

Tel: 01227 862000
Fax: 01227 862020
E-mail: firstname.familyname@canterbury.gov.uk

Website:
http://www.canterbury.co.uk

Enquiries:
Enquiries to: Chief Executive

Founded:
1974

Organisation type and purpose:
Local government body.

Subject coverage:
Local government.

Access to staff:
Contact by letter, by telephone, by fax, by e-mail, in person and via website. Appointment necessary.
Hours: Mon to Fri, 0900 to 1700

CAPEL

Formal name: Capel: The Chapels Heritage Society

5 Cuffnell Close, Liddell Park, Llandudno, Conwy, LL30 1UX

Tel: 01492 860449
E-mail: obadiah1@btinternet.com

Website:
http://www.capeli.org.uk
General information about the society and list of forthcoming events in English and Welsh.

Enquiries:
Enquiries to: Honorary Secretary
Other contacts: Treasurer for subscription/membership

Organisation type and purpose:
Membership association (membership is by subscription), present number of members: 300, voluntary organisation, registered charity (charity number 518411).
Presentation of the nonconformist heritage of Wales.

Subject coverage:
Nonconformist history, chapels in Wales.

Printed publications:
Newsletter (twice a year)

Publications list:
Available online and in print

Access to staff:
Contact by letter and by e-mail
Hours: Mon to Fri, 0900 to 1700

CAPEL MANOR COLLEGE

Bullsmore Lane, Enfield, Middlesex, EN1 4RQ

Tel: 08456 122122
Fax: 01992 717544
E-mail: enquiries@capel.ac.uk

Website:
http://www.capel.ac.uk/

Enquiries:
Enquiries to: Student Registrar

Formerly called:
Capel Manor Horticultural and Environmental Centre

Organisation type and purpose:
Further education college.
Specialist horticultural college and gardens open to the public.

Subject coverage:
Horticulture, garden design, arboriculture, countryside management, floristry, balloon artistry.

Library catalogue:
All or part available in-house

Access to staff:
Contact by letter, by telephone and by e-mail.
Appointment necessary.
Hours: Mon to Fri, 0900 to 1700

Access for disabled people:
Parking provided, level entry, access to all public areas, toilet facilities

Also at:
Capel Manor College at Castle Green
Gale Street, Dagenham, RM9 4UN; tel: 020 8724 1528
Capel Manor College at Crystal Palace
Crystal Palace Park, Ledrington Road, SE19 2BS; tel: 020 8778 5572
Capel Manor College at Gunnersbury Park
Popes Lane, Gunnersbury Park, Acton, W3 8LQ; tel: 020 8993 6266; fax: 020 8993 6266
Capel Manor College at Regent's Park
The Store Yard, Inner Circle, Regent's Park, NW1 4NR; tel: 020 7486 7930

CAPRI CLUB (INTERNATIONAL)

Acronym or abbreviation: CCI

Capri Club HQ, Badgers Hill, Sheriffs Lench, Evesham, Worcestershire, WR11 4SN

Tel: 01386 860860
Fax: 01386 861455
E-mail: capriclub@btclick.com

Website:
http://www.capriclub.co.uk/

Enquiries:
Enquiries to: Membership Secretary

Founded:
1983

Formerly called:
Capri 70 Owners Club, Capri Owners Club

Organisation type and purpose:
Membership association (membership is by subscription), present number of members: 8000.

Subject coverage:
Ford Capris 1969 to 1987.

Printed publications:
Catalogue (annually to members)
Club Magazine (monthly to members)
Mk3 Biography Book (£12.95 plus postage)

Electronic and video publications:
Capri – Documentary (video, £14.95 plus postage)
Convention '97 (video, £14.95, plus postage)
Summer Camp '97 (video, £14.95, plus postage)
Summer Camp '98 (video, £14.95 plus postage)
Summer Camp '99 (video, £14.95 plus postage)
Summer Camp '00 (video, £14.95 plus postage)
Summer Camp '01 (video, £14.95 plus postage)

Access to staff:
Contact by letter, by telephone, by fax, by e-mail and in person
Hours: Mon to Fri, 0900 to 1700

CARADON DISTRICT COUNCIL

Luxstowe House, Liskeard, Cornwall, PL14 3DZ

Tel: 01579 341000\ Minicom no. 01579 341010
Fax: 01579 341001
E-mail: postroom@caradon.gov.uk

Website:
http://www.caradon.gov.uk
Gives information about Caradon District Council and about the area.

Enquiries:
Enquiries to: Chief Executive
Direct tel: 01579 341022
Direct fax: 01579 341002
Other contacts: Corporate Communications Officer for public relations and media enquiries.

Founded:
1974

Organisation type and purpose:
Local government body.

Access to staff:
Contact by letter, by telephone, by fax, by e-mail and in person. Appointment necessary.
Hours: Mon to Fri, 0830 to 1700

Access for disabled people:
Parking provided, ramped entry, toilet facilities

CARDIFF LIBRARIES

Cardiff Central Library, The Hayes, Cardiff, CF10 1FL

Tel: 029 2038 2116
Fax: 029 2078 0989
E-mail: centrallibrary@cardiff.gov.uk

Website:
http://www.cardiff.gov.uk/libraries
Service point profiles, opening hours, catalogue, online resources, events, fines and charges, bilingual Facebook pages.

Enquiries:
Enquiries to: Central Library Manager
Direct e-mail: nrichards@cardiff.gov.uk
Other contacts: Adult Non-Fiction; Children's Librarian; Community Languages Librarian; Information Librarian; Leisure Librarian; Local Studies Librarian; Music Librarian; Stock Manager; Welsh Librarian

Founded:
1882

Formerly called:
South Glamorgan County Libraries (year of change 1996)

Organisation type and purpose:
Local government body, public library.

Subject coverage:
Adult Non-Fiction department: business, law, education, history, art, language and literature, military studies, social sciences, religion and philosophy, transport, life sciences, geography, science and technology, travel, gardening, food and drink.
Music department: books, scores, CDs, DVDs, performance area and baby grand piano.
Information department: business and commercial directories for UK and worldwide, telephone directories for UK, Eire, Jersey and Guernsey, British Standards online, statistical information, European Union information, census statistics, maps and atlases, community information, National Assembly for Wales linked libraries collection, trade journals.
Cardiff Capital Collection: local studies and geneaology, census returns.
The Wales Collection: material in Welsh and English relating to Wales.
Leisure Library includes: fiction, talking books, DVDs, biographies, newsroom.
Children's Library Service.
Community Languages Department: 14 community languages.

Museum or gallery collection, archive, or library special collection:
Manuscripts, fine bindings, private press books, early printed books, limited editions
Cardiff Local Collection including photographs, maps and newspapers

Non-library collection catalogue:
All or part available in-house

Library catalogue:
All or part available online

Access to staff:
Contact by letter, by telephone, by fax, by e-mail, in person and via website
Hours: Mon, Tue, Wed, Fri, 0900 to 1800; Thu, 0900 to 1900; Sat, 0900 to 1730; Sun, 1100 to 1500 ground floor only

Access for disabled people:
Level entry, access to all public areas, toilet facilities, lifts to all floors.

Parent body:
Cardiff County Council
Housing and Neighbourhood Renewal

CARDIFF NATURALISTS SOCIETY

The Library, National Museum Wales, Cathays Park, Cardiff, CF10 3NP

Tel: 029 2057 3202
Fax: 029 2057 3216
E-mail: library@museumwales.ac.uk

Enquiries:
Enquiries to: Librarian

Founded:
1867

Organisation type and purpose:
Learned society.

Subject coverage:
Natural history of the Glamorgan area; zoology; ornithology; botany; entomology.

Museum or gallery collection, archive, or library special collection:
Library, mainly periodicals via exchange agreements
Morrey Salmon Ornithology Archive

Library catalogue:
All or part available in-house

Printed publications:
Newsletter (quarterly)

Access to staff:
Contact by letter, by telephone and by fax. Appointment necessary.
Hours: Tue to Fri, 1000 to 1700

Access for disabled people:
Parking provided, ramped entry, toilet facilities
Special comments: Lift.

CARDIFF UNIVERSITY – INFORMATION SERVICES

PO Box 430, Cardiff, CF24 0DE

Tel: 029 2087 9362
Fax: 029 2037 1921
E-mail: library@cardiff.ac.uk

Website:
http://www.cardiff.ac.uk/insrv

Enquiries:
Enquiries to: University Librarian and Senior Assistant Director, Information Services
Direct e-mail: petersjm@cardiff.ac.uk

Founded:
1883

Formerly called:
University of Wales, Cardiff, Library

Organisation type and purpose:
University library.
Information service.

Subject coverage:
Humanities, religious studies, education, music, social sciences, law, Welsh language, literature, history and culture, archaeology, language, literature and history of other Celtic countries, engineering, biosciences, optometry, pharmacy, physics, chemistry, earth sciences, architecture, business studies, town planning, computer studies, journalism, mathematics, medicine, nursing and health care.

Museum or gallery collection, archive, or library special collection:
British Government, EC and UN publications
Carmarthen Presbyterian College Library
Architecture rare books collection
Companies information (business studies)
Pre-1800 and fine or rare post-1800 books, including some manuscripts (those of the poets Edward Thomas and Anne Griffiths in particular)
Salisbury Library (Welsh and Celtic material)
Tennyson Collection
Welsh Hymnology collection
Welsh Ballads collection
History of Medicine
China Studies
Cochrane Archive
Centre for the History of Evaluation in Healthcare (CHEHC)
Osman Collection (photojournalism)
Cudlipp Collection (journalism)
Richard Stott Daily Mirror papers (journalism)
Tom Harrison Mass Observation Collection
Mackworth Collection (Music)
Aylward Collection (Music)
UN Deposit Collection
Former Cardiff City Library collection of 15C–19C books

Non-library collection catalogue:
All or part available online

Library catalogue:
All or part available online

Publications list:
Available online

Access to staff:
Contact by letter, by telephone, by e-mail and in person
Hours: 0900 to 1700

Access to building, collection or gallery:
No prior appointment required

Access for disabled people:
Parking provided, ramped entry, level entry, toilet facilities

continued overleaf

Special comments: Cardiff University Information Services are distributed across the campus. All areas are accessible but by different means – some areas ramped or level entry.

CARDIFF UNIVERSITY – RESEARCH AND COMMERCIAL DIVISION

Acronym or abbreviation: CU

7th Floor, 30–36 Newport Road, Cardiff, CF24 0DE

Tel: 029 2087 5834
Fax: 029 2087 4189
E-mail: whittinghamj@cf.ac.uk

Website:
http://www.cardiff.ac.uk/racdv

Enquiries:
Enquiries to: Research Information Officer

Formerly called:
Cardiff University, Research and Consultancy Division, Cardiff University

Organisation type and purpose:
University Division, consultancy, research policy, research support, research funding, University expertise, technology transfer, IP, business development, commercial support.

Subject coverage:
Architecture, semiconductors, engineering, pharmacy, computing, geology, marine research, magnetics technology, aerospace, chemistry, motors, astronomy, insect biology, systems dynamics, EDI, Cardiff University Innovation Network, planning, optometry, medicine, dentistry, nursing, health care, social sciences, history, archaeology, religion, politics, music, Welsh, journalism, English, philosophy, business, physics, biosciences, languages, psychology, law.

Library catalogue:
All or part available online

Printed publications:
Annual Reports
University Prospectuses

Access to staff:
Contact by e-mail and via website
Hours: Mon to Fri, 0800 to 1600

CARDIFF UNIVERSITY – SIR HERBERT DUTHIE LIBRARY

Acronym or abbreviation: CU

Heath Park, Cardiff, CF14 4XN

Tel: 029 2074 2874
Fax: 029 2074 3651
E-mail: duthieliby@cf.ac.uk

Website:
http://cardiff.ac.uk/insrv/libraries
University Library homepage.

Enquiries:
Enquiries to: Director of Library Services
Direct e-mail: library@cf.ac.uk

Founded:
1931

Formerly called:
Welsh National School of Medicine Library; University of Wales College of Medicine (year of change 2004)

Incorporates the former:
Combined Training Institute, Institute of Healthcare Studies, South East Wales Institute of Nursing and Midwifery

Organisation type and purpose:
University library.
NHS library.

Subject coverage:
Medicine; dentistry; nursing (including relevant sociology and social sciences); basic medical sciences; professions allied to medicine; library and information sciences (especially academic medical and life sciences).

Museum or gallery collection, archive, or library special collection:
Health and Safety
Historical collection (medicine and some dentistry)

Non-library collection catalogue:
All or part available online and in-house

Library catalogue:
All or part available online

Printed publications:
AWHILES Handbook
Periodicals lists

Access to staff:
Contact by letter, by telephone, by fax and by e-mail. Appointment necessary.
Hours: Duthie Library: Sep to Jun: Mon to Fri, 0900 to 2100; Sat, 0900 to 1700; Jul and Aug: Mon to Fri, 0900 to 1900; Sat, 0900 to 1230
Special comments: Full library service provided to NHS employees in South Glamorgan; extension services to NHS employees throughout Wales; fee for some services for external users. Certain services to staff and students of Welsh HE institutions.

Access for disabled people:
Parking provided, level entry, access to all public areas
Special comments: Located within hospital building.

Branch libraries:
Cardiff University
Library, School of Nursing Studies, Grounds of St Cadoc's Hospital, Caerleon, Newport, NP6 1XR; tel: 01633 430919; fax: 01633 430717; e-mail: caerleonliby@cf.ac.uk
Cardiff University
Library, School of Nursing & Healthcare Studies, Ty Dewi Sant Building, Heath Park, Cardiff, CF4 4XN; tel: 029 2068 7713; fax: 029 2068 7715; e-mail: healthcliby@cardiff.ac.uk
Cardiff University
Sir Herbert Duthie Medical Library, Heath Park, Cardiff, CF14 4XN; tel: 029 2074 2875; fax: 029 2074 3651; e-mail: duthieliby@cf.ac.uk
Cardiff University
Brian Cooke Dental Library, Heath Park, Cardiff, CF4 4XY; tel: 029 2074 2523; fax: 029 2074 3651; e-mail: dentliby@cf.ac.uk
University of Wales College of Medicine
Cancer Research Wales Library, Velindre Hospital, Whitchurch, Cardiff, CF4 7XL; tel: 029 2031 6291; fax: 029 2031 6927; e-mail: crwlibrary@wales.nhs.uk
University of Wales College of Medicine
Archie Cochrane Library, University Hospital Llandough, Penarth, CF64 2XX; tel: 029 2071 1711, extn 5497; e-mail: cochraneliby@cf.ac.uk

Member organisation of:
All-Wales Health Information and Libraries Extension Service (AWHILES)
NHS Regional Librarians Group
Standing Conference of National University Libraries
University Medical School Librarians Group
Welsh Higher Education Libraries' Forum (WHELF)

CARE FOR THE WILD INTERNATIONAL

Acronym or abbreviation: CWI

The Granary, Tickfold Farm, Marches Road, Kingsfold, Horsham, West Sussex, RH12 3SE

Tel: 01306 627900
Fax: 01306 627901
E-mail: info@careforthewild.com

Website:
http://www.careforthewild.com

Details of latest appeals and information on animal-fostering programmes; gift catalogue.

Enquiries:
Enquiries to: Reception & Administration
Other contacts: Cashier & Administration

Founded:
1984

Organisation type and purpose:
Registered charity (charity number 288802). To alleviate suffering and the exploitation of wildlife around the world.

Subject coverage:
A charity dedicated to the conservation and welfare of wildlife around the world. Working with partners, to protect wildlife and its habitat, rescue and rehabilitate displaced wild animals, and act as a global voice for wildlife protection through campaigns, research and education.

Information services:
Information on wildlife issues and the charity's work.

Printed publications:
Care for the Wild News (twice a year)
Order printed publications from: tel: 01306 627900; or e-mail: info@careforthewild.com

Publications list:
Available in print

Access to staff:
Contact by letter, by telephone, by fax, by e-mail, in person and via website. Appointment necessary.
Hours: Mon to Fri, 0900 to 1700

Also at:
Care for the Wild Kenya
PO Box 34334, Nairobi, Kenya; tel: + 254 2 21977/8; fax: + 254 2 219717

CARE PROGRAMME APPROACH ASSOCIATION

Walton Hospital, Whitecoats Lane, Chesterfield, Derbyshire, S40 3HW

Tel: 01246 515975
Fax: 01246 515976
E-mail: cpa.association@derbysmhservices.nhs.uk

Enquiries:
Enquiries to: Administrator
Direct fax: 01246 515974
Other contacts: Secretary

Founded:
April 1996

Subject coverage:
Application of CPA in mental health, CPAA standards and criteria.

Printed publications:
The Approach (quarterly)
CPA Handbook (2004)

Access to staff:
Contact by letter, by telephone, by fax and by e-mail
Hours: Mon to Fri, 0900 to 1700

Access to building, collection or gallery:
No access other than to staff, prior appointment required

Access for disabled people:
Parking provided, toilet facilities

Regional Representatives addresses:
obtainable from CPAA

CAREERS GROUP, UNIVERSITY OF LONDON

Stewart House, 32 Russell Square, London, WC1B 5DN

Tel: 020 7863 6014
Fax: 020 7863 6003
E-mail: careers@careers.lon.ac.uk

Website:
http://www.careers.lon.ac.uk

Enquiries:
Enquiries to: Information & Research Specialist

Organisation type and purpose:
University department or institute.
Careers service.

Subject coverage:
Careers advice, recruitment information,
occupational information.

Printed publications:
How to write a CV
How to complete an application form
How to change your career
How to analyse and promote your skills for work
How to succeed at interviews
Graduate entry into medicine
Getting into international development
Recruitment agencies

Access to staff:
Contact by letter, by telephone, by fax, by e-mail
and via website. Non-members charged.
Hours: Mon to Thu, 0930 to 1700; Fri, 1100 to 1700

CARERS UK

20 Great Dover Street, London, SE1 4LX

Tel: 020 7378 4999; 0808 808 7777 (carers' line)
Fax: 020 7378 9787
E-mail: info@carersuk.org

Website:
http://www.carersuk.org

Enquiries:
Enquiries to: Chief Executive
Other contacts: Information Officer (for professional
enquiries); Advice Officer / Carers' line (for carers)

Founded:
1988

Formerly called:
Carers National Association (year of change 2001)

Organisation type and purpose:
National organisation, voluntary organisation,
registered charity (charity number 246329).
Campaigning organisation.
To give information and advice to carers and
professionals, develop support groups, campaign
at all levels of national and local government, and
with service providers, on behalf of carers.

Subject coverage:
Information on any subject of concern or interest to
carers, e.g. benefits, community care, residential
care, practical caring, money worries, emotional
support, housing, holdings, council tax, etc.

Trade and statistical information:
Data on the numbers of carers in the United
Kingdom.

Printed publications:
Leaflets
Information booklets
Caring (magazine)

Publications list:
Available online and in print

Access to staff:
Contact by letter, by telephone, by fax, by e-mail
and via website
Hours: Mon to Fri, 0900 to 1700
Carers' line: Wed, Thu, 1000 to 1200 and 1400 to
1600

Branches:
Carers Northern Ireland
58 Howard Street, Belfast, BT1 6PJ; tel: 028 9043
9843; fax: 028 9032 9299; e-mail: info@carersni.co
.uk; website: http://www.carersni.org
Carers Scotland
The Cottage, 21 Pearce Street, Glasgow, G51 3UT;
tel: 0141 445 3070; fax: 0141 445 3096; e-mail:
info@carerscotland.org; website: http://www
.carerscotland.org

Carers Wales
River House, Ynys Bridge Court, Gwaelod-y-
Garth, Cardiff, CF15 9SS; tel: 029 2081 1370; fax:
029 2081 1575; e-mail: info@carerswales.org;
website: http://www.carerswales.org

CARITAS – SOCIAL ACTION

Acronym or abbreviation: CCWC

39 Eccleston Square, London, SW1V 1BX

Tel: 020 7901 4875
E-mail: caritas@cbcew.org.uk

Website:
http://www.caritas-socialaction.org.uk

Enquiries:
Enquiries to: Director

Founded:
2002

Formerly called:
Catholic Child Welfare Council

Organisation type and purpose:
Membership association, present number of
members: 22 corporate members, voluntary
organisation, registered charity (charity number
1101431).
Umbrella organisation for Roman Catholic
agencies concerned with the care and welfare of
children and families.

Subject coverage:
Services to children and families provided by
Catholic Children's Societies and other Catholic
social care agencies. Adoption and fostering of
children, post-adoption support work, birth
records counselling, family support projects,
support of children through Catholic schools and
parishes, child migration.

Printed publications:
Directory of Catholic Diocesan Children's Societies
and other Caring Services (every 2–3 years,
current edn 2000, £1.50)
Other occasional publications

Access to staff:
Contact by letter, by telephone and by e-mail.
Appointment necessary.
Hours: Mon to Fri, 1000 to 1700
Special comments: Office is not always staffed.

Member organisations:
Catholic Childrens Societies
Diocesan care agencies
Some religious congregations

CARLISLE CITY COUNCIL

Civic Centre, Carlisle, Cumbria, CA3 8QG

Tel: 01228 817000
Fax: 01228 817013
E-mail: customerservices@carlisle.gov.uk

Website:
http://www.carlisle.gov.uk

Organisation type and purpose:
Local government body.

Subject coverage:
Policy and performance, property, community
services, building and mechanised services, leisure
and amenity services and housing, environmental
services.

Access to staff:
Contact by letter, by telephone, by fax and by e-
mail
Hours: Mon to Thu, 0900 to 1700; Fri, 0900 to 1600

CARLISLE COLLEGE LEARNING RESOURCE CENTRE

Acronym or abbreviation: Carlisle College LRC

Victoria Place, Carlisle, Cumbria, CA1 1HS

Tel: 01228 822760

Fax: 01228 822710
E-mail: lrc@carlisle.ac.uk

Website:
http://www.carlisle.ac.uk

Enquiries:
Enquiries to: LRC Officer

Formerly called:
Carlisle Technical College

Organisation type and purpose:
College of further and higher education.

Library catalogue:
All or part available online

Access to staff:
Contact by letter, by telephone and by e-mail.
Appointment necessary.
Hours: Term time: Mon, Wed, 0830 to 1700; Tue,
Thu, 0830 to 1900; Fri, 0830 to 1600
Special comments: For reference only.

CARLISLE PUBLIC LIBRARY

11 Globe Lane, Carlisle, Cumbria, CA3 8NX

Tel: 01228 227310
Fax: 01228 607333
E-mail: carlisle.library@cumbriacc.gov.uk

Website:
http://www.cumbria.gov.uk/libraries

Enquiries:
Enquiries to: Area Library Manager

Organisation type and purpose:
Local government body, public library.

Subject coverage:
General.

Library catalogue:
All or part available online

Access to staff:
Contact by letter, by telephone, by fax, by e-mail
and in person
Hours: Mon, Wed and Fri, 0930 to 1730; Tue and
Thu, 0930 to 1900; Sat 0930 to 1600; Sun 1200 to
1600

Parent body:
Cumbria Library Services

CARMARTHENSHIRE ARCHIVE SERVICE

Parc Myrddin, Richmond Terrace, Carmarthen,
SA31 1DS

Tel: 01267 228232
Fax: 01267 228237
E-mail: archives@carmarthenshire.gov.uk

Enquiries:
Enquiries to: Archivist

Founded:
1959

Formerly called:
Dyfed Archives Services (year of change 1996)

Organisation type and purpose:
Local government body.

Subject coverage:
Aspects of the history of Carmarthenshire, church
and chapel records 16th–20th century, estate
records 13th–20th century, business records 18th–
20th century, local government records 16th–20th
century, maps of the county 18th–20th century.

**Museum or gallery collection, archive, or library
special collection:**
Cawdor Collection containing the Golden Grove
Book, an 18th-century collection of pedigrees
relating to the whole of Wales
Records of local historical interest, including parish
registers

Printed publications:
Carmarthen Book of Ordinances 1569–1606 (£3.95,
incl p&p £5)

continued overleaf

Leaflets and booklets
Summaries of the holdings of the Offices
Topic lists

Publications list:
Available in print

Access to staff:
Contact by letter, by telephone, by fax, by e-mail
and in person. Appointment necessary.
Hours: Mon, closed; Tue, 0930 to 1930 (1700 to 1930
by appointment only); Wed to Fri, 0930 to 1700
Special comments: For reservations at other times,
phone for appointment

Links with:
Carmarthen Reference Library
   St Peter's Street, Carmarthen; tel: 01267 224822
Carmarthenshire Museums Service
   Abergwili, Carmarthen; tel: 01267 231691

CARMARTHENSHIRE COLLEGE (COLEG SIR GAR)

Graig Campus, Sandy Road, Llanelli,
Carmarthenshire, SA15 4DN

Tel: 01554 748000
Fax: 01554 756088
E-mail: admissions@colegsirgar.ac.uk

Website:
http://www.colsirgar.ac.uk
Course details and college information.

Enquiries:
Enquiries to: Marketing Officer
Direct tel: 01554 748112
Direct e-mail: debbie.williams@colegsirgar.ac.uk

Founded:
1984

Formerly called:
Llanelli Technical College

Organisation type and purpose:
Suitable for ages: 16+.
Higher and further education establishment.

Subject coverage:
Access and general education; business,
management, and office technology, catering,
hairdressing and beauty therapy, computing and
applied science, creative and performing arts,
engineering and construction, foundation and
community education, health, social and child
care, sport, leisure, tourism and land-based
studies.

Printed publications:
Prospectus (free)
Faculty leaflets (free)
Course leaflets (free)

Access to staff:
Contact by letter, by telephone, by fax, by e-mail,
in person and via website. All charged.
Hours: Mon to Thu, 0845 to 2100; Fri, 0845 to 1630

Access for disabled people:
Parking provided, toilet facilities

Has:
5 sites (11,000 students, 500 staff)

Parent body:
Funding Council for Wales
   Lambourne House, Cardiff Business Park,
   Llanishen, Cardiff, CF4 5GL

Subsidiary body:
CCTA Enterprises Ltd

CARMARTHENSHIRE COUNTY LIBRARIES

Carmarthen Library, St. Peter's Street, Carmarthen,
SA31 1LN

Tel: 01267 224824
Fax: 01267 223189
E-mail: library@carmarthenshire.gov.uk

Enquiries:
Enquiries to: Regional Library Manager

Founded:
1996

Formerly called:
Dyfed County Library, Llanelli Borough Library
(year of change 1996)

Organisation type and purpose:
Local government body, public library.

Subject coverage:
General, local history and other matters relating to
the county of Carmarthenshire, history of Wales,
Welsh languages and literature.

**Museum or gallery collection, archive, or library
special collection:**
Carmarthenshire Antiquarian Society Collection
Video collection on physical and mental disabilities

Library catalogue:
All or part available online and in-house

Printed publications:
Booklets and exhibition catalogues and other
   publications, including:
Facsimile copies of classic local history studies
   previously out of print
A History of Gorslas 1804–2007(£12)
Llanarthney Past and Present (Jones T & D £12)
Capeli Llanelli / Llanelli Chapels (Huw Edwards
   2009 £25/£15)
Order printed publications from: Carmarthen Library

Publications list:
Available online and in print

Access to staff:
Contact by letter, by telephone, by fax, by e-mail
and in person
Hours: Mon to Wed and Fri, 0900 to 1900; Thu and
Sat, 0900 to 1700

Access to building, collection or gallery:
No prior appointment required

Access for disabled people:
Ramped entry

CARNEGIE LEADERS IN LEARNING PARTNERSHIP

Churchwood, Headingley Campus, Leeds
Metropolitan University, Leeds, LS6 3QS

Tel: 0113 812 6138
Fax: 0113 275 5927
E-mail: info@carnegieleaders.org.uk

Website:
http://www.carnegieleaders.org.uk

Please select:
Carnegie Leaders in Learning Partnership is a
partnership between CCDU Ltd and Leeds
Metropolitan University.

Organisation type and purpose:
Carnegie Leaders in Learning Partnership exists to
enable individuals, teams and organisations to
achieve their potential.

Subject coverage:
Consultancy – working collaboratively with clients
to understand requirements and design and
deliver solutions. Examples of solutions delivered
include: competency development, coaching,
impact evaluation, quality improvement,
leadership development and assessment and
moderation.

Printed publications:
Getting it Right Series of practical guides:
Succesful Presentations
Facilitation: getting the most out of working with
   groups
Mentoring in Organisations
Mentoring in Medicine

Publications list:
Available online and in print

Access to staff:
Contact by letter, by telephone, by fax, by e-mail
and via website
Hours: Mon to Fri, 0900 to 1700

CARNEGIE UNITED KINGDOM TRUST

Comely Park House, New Row, Dunfermline, Fife,
KY12 7EJ

Tel: 01383 721445
Fax: 01383 620682
E-mail: raji@carnegieuk.org

Website:
http://www.carnegieuktrust.org.uk
Publications and general information.

Enquiries:
Enquiries to: Chief Executive
Other contacts: Communications Director

Founded:
1913

Organisation type and purpose:
Registered charity (charity number SCO 12799).

**Museum or gallery collection, archive, or library
special collection:**
Archives (held in National Archives of Scotland)

Printed publications:
Annual Report, obtainable in all main public and
   reference libraries, ISBN prefix 0900259
Policy Guidelines, available free from Trust office
   on receipt of an sae

Publications list:
Available online and in print

Access to staff:
Contact by letter, by telephone and by e-mail
Hours: Mon to Fri, 0900 to 1700

CARNIVOROUS PLANT SOCIETY

Acronym or abbreviation: CPS

1 Orchard Close, Ringwood, Hampshire, BH24
1LP

Enquiries:
Enquiries to: Chairman
Other contacts: Membership Secretary for
membership enquiries.

Founded:
1978

Organisation type and purpose:
Membership association (membership is by
subscription), present number of members: 600,
voluntary organisation, registered charity (charity
number 281423).
To bring together all those interested in
carnivorous plants whether beginners or experts.
To increase people's knowledge both in
horticulture and in the wild, including
conservation.

Subject coverage:
Botany and horticulture of carnivorous plants; seed
bank; conservation of carnivorous plants in their
habitats.

Printed publications:
Guide to Carnivorous Plants
Journal (annual)
Newsletters (4 times a year)

Access to staff:
Contact by letter
Hours: Mon to Fri, 0900 to 1700

Affiliated to:
Royal Horticultural Society

Membership Secretary:
Carnivorous Plant Society
   100 Lambley Lane, Burton Joyce, Nottingham,
   NG14 5BL

CARPENTERS' COMPANY

Carpenters' Hall, Throgmorton Avenue, London,
EC2N 2JJ

Tel: 020 7588 7001
Fax: 020 7638 6286
E-mail: info@carpentersco.com

Website:
http://www.thecarpenterscompany.co.uk
Building Crafts College, Rustington Convalescent
Home, Wyatts Almshouses, Carpenters Craft
Competititon.

Enquiries:
Enquiries to: The Clerk

Founded:
1271

Organisation type and purpose:
Professional body (membership is by election or
invitation), present number of members: 150.
City of London Livery Company that supports the
construction industry, craft of carpentry and
charitable giving.

Access to staff:
Contact by letter
Hours: Mon to Fri, 0900 to 1700

CARPET FOUNDATION, THE

MCF Complex, 60 New Road, Kidderminster,
Worcestershire, DY10 1AQ

Tel: 01562 755568
Fax: 01562 565405
E-mail: info@carpetfoundation.com

Website:
http://www.carpetfoundation.com

Enquiries:
Enquiries to: Commercial Director

Founded:
1999

Organisation type and purpose:
Membership association (membership is by
subscription), present number of members: 12.
To promote the image of carpets and to improve
knowledge about them to this end.

Subject coverage:
Pile carpets (especially wool carpets), carpet tiles
and most other wall-to-wall textile floor coverings
– but NOT oriental or machine washable rugs.

Printed publications:
CarpetCare
Carpet Foundation Brochure

Access to staff:
Contact by letter, by telephone, by fax, by e-mail
and via website
Hours: Mon to Fri, 0900 to 1700

CARSHALTON COLLEGE

Nightingale Road, Carshalton, Surrey, SM5 2EJ

Tel: 020 8544 4444
Fax: 020 8544 4440
E-mail: cs@carshalton.ac.uk

Website:
http://www.carshalton.ac.uk
General introduction to the college; information on
courses.

Enquiries:
Enquiries to: Systems Librarian
Direct tel: 020 8544 4344
Other contacts: e-Learning Librarian

Subject coverage:
Art and design, media, multimedia, music
technology, business studies, secretarial and
administration, accounting, early years, health and
social care, residential care, dental care,
construction, electrical installation, motor vehicle
engineering, hairdressing, beauty therapy,
hospitality and catering, information technology,
software engineering, sports science, uniformed
services, ESOL, pre-entry and entry level
vocational studies, and teacher training. Level 4
courses in management, accounting, care, early
years, teaching and learning support, and teacher
training.

Library catalogue:
All or part available in-house

Printed publications:
Course leaflets
Prospectus

Access to staff:
Contact by letter, by telephone, by fax, by e-mail
and in person. Appointment necessary.
Hours: Mon to Fri, 0900 to 1700

Access to building, collection or gallery:
Prior appointment required

Access for disabled people:
Parking provided, level entry, lifts to all floors,
toilet facilities

CAST METALS FEDERATION

Acronym or abbreviation: CMF

National Metalforming Centre, 47 Birmingham
Road, West Bromwich, West Midlands, B70 6PY

Tel: 0121 601 6390
Fax: 0121 601 6391

Website:
http://www.castmetalsfederation.com
Casting enquiries, supplier enquiries, technical
enquiries, casting processes, members section.

Enquiries:
Enquiries to: Chief Executive

Founded:
2001

Formed from:
British Foundry Association (BFA), British
Investment Casting Trade Association (BICTA),
British Metal Castings Association (BMCA) (year
of change 2001)

Organisation type and purpose:
National organisation, trade association
(membership is by subscription).
The single trade body for the UK cast metals sector.

Subject coverage:
Promotion of Best Of British castings, influencing
and forming legislation, guidance and information
on environmental, health, safety, statistics,
markets, costs, prices, contracts, best practice,
benchmarking.

Printed publications:
CMF Newsletter

Access to staff:
Appointment necessary.
Hours: Mon to Fri, 0900 to 1700

CASTINGS TECHNOLOGY INTERNATIONAL

Advanced Manufacturing Park, Brunel Way,
Rotherham, S60 5WG

Tel: 0114 254 1144
Fax: 0114 254 1155
E-mail: info@castingstechnology.com

Website:
http://www.castingstechnology.com
Services provided by the organisation, Cti.

Enquiries:
Enquiries to: Information Officer

Founded:
1996

Formerly called:
British Cast Iron Research Association and the
Castings Development Centre (year of change
2001)

Organisation type and purpose:
International organisation, membership
association (membership is by subscription),
present number of members: 300, research
organisation.

Subject coverage:
Cast metals technology includes environmental
and working conditions, melting and molten metal
treatment, moulding and coremaking, process and

quality control, NDE guaranteed quality,
automation and advanced manufacturing
technology (AMT), new cast materials, new
applications for castings, casting design and choice
of materials ferrous and non-ferrous, operating
economics, design and production control, and
costing.

**Museum or gallery collection, archive, or library
special collection:**
National and International Standards
The Cti Library is devoted solely to the technology
of metal castings production

Non-library collection catalogue:
All or part available in-house

Library catalogue:
All or part available in-house

Publications list:
Available online and in print

Access to staff:
Contact by letter, by telephone, by fax and by e-
mail. Access for members only.
Hours: Mon to Fri, 0800 to 1600

CASTLE BROMWICH HALL GARDENS TRUST

Acronym or abbreviation: CBHGT

Chester Road, Castle Bromwich, Birmingham, B36
9BT

Tel: 0121 749 4100
Fax: 0121 749 4100
E-mail: enq@cbhgt.swinternet.co.uk

Website:
http://www.cbhgt.swinternet.co.uk
Admission/opening hours, special events, friends'
organisation, photographs and history.

Enquiries:
Enquiries to: Secretary

Founded:
1985

Organisation type and purpose:
Registered charity (charity number 516855),
historic building, house or site.
Historic gardens and maze.
Restoration of walled gardens to their 18th-century
glory.

Subject coverage:
Historical and horticultural. The Hall and Gardens
were built in 1599 by Sir Edward Devereux who
was MP for Tamworth. In 1657 the estate was
purchased by Sir John Bridgeman I and later
extended by his son Sir John Bridgeman II to its
present boundaries. The gardens are of some 10
acres and include a 19th-century holly maze.

Information services:
Lectures by special arrangement.

Special visitor services:
Guided tours.

Library catalogue:
All or part available in-house

Printed publications:
Brochure

Access to staff:
Contact by letter and by telephone
Hours: Mon to Fri, 0900 to 1700

Access for disabled people:
Level entry, access to all public areas, toilet
facilities

CASTLE COMBE CIRCUIT LIMITED

Castle Combe, Chippenham, Wiltshire, SN14 7EY

Tel: 01249 782417
Fax: 01249 782392
E-mail: sales@castlecombecircuit.co.uk

continued overleaf

Website:
http://www.castlecombecircuit.co.uk
Full programme of events, availability of courses/content/etc, services provided

Enquiries:
Enquiries to: Managing Director

Founded:
1950

Organisation type and purpose:
Service industry.
Racing circuit.

Subject coverage:
All usages of the circuit, racing and other, motorsports, learning to race.

Printed publications:
Annual fixtures and courses (free)
Race school brochures (free)

Access to staff:
Contact by letter, by telephone, by fax, by e-mail, in person and via website
Hours: Mon to Fri, 0900 to 1700; Sat, 0900 to 1600

Subsidiary body:
Castle Combe Exhibitions Limited
  tel: 01249 782417; fax: 01249 782392; e-mail: sales@castlecombecircuit.co.uk
Castle Combe Racing School
  tel: 01249 782929; fax: 01249 782392; e-mail: sales@castlecombecircuit.co.uk

CASTOR MANUFACTURERS ASSOCIATION

Acronym or abbreviation: CMA

1 Perch Close, Marlow, Buckinghamshire, SL7 2BQ

Tel: 01628 475648
Fax: 01628 475648

Enquiries:
Enquiries to: General Secretary

Founded:
1963

Organisation type and purpose:
Trade association.

Subject coverage:
Furniture, hospital and industrial castors.

Printed publications:
CMA Brochure detailing aims and objectives of the association and a list of members with products classified into industry types

Access to staff:
Contact by letter, by telephone and by fax
Hours: Mon to Fri, 0900 to 1700

Member of:
British Materials Handling Federation
BSI
FIRA

CASUALTIES UNION

Acronym or abbreviation: CU

Casualties Union Headquarters, PO Box 1942, London, E17 6YU

Tel: 08700 780590
Fax: 08700 780590
E-mail: hq.cu@casualtiesunion.org.uk

Website:
http://www.casualtiesunion.org.uk

Enquiries:
Enquiries to: Headquarters Administrator
Other contacts: Honorary Treasurer (for financial matters)

Founded:
1942

Organisation type and purpose:
Membership association (membership is by subscription or invitation), present number of members: 450, voluntary organisation, registered charity (charity number 234672), suitable for ages: 8+.
To advance for the public benefit education and training in first aid, the treatment of illness, nursing, rescue, accident prevention, care in the community and similar activities, particularly through casualty simulation.

Subject coverage:
Casualty simulation, training and provision of skilled acting casualties, demonstrations and emergency exercises for training first aid, rescue, ambulance and hospital personnel.

Museum or gallery collection, archive, or library special collection:
Some archives are stored at the Wellcome Trust, London.

Printed publications:
Casualty Simulation (quarterly, free to members including associates)
More Ways Than One of Fighting a War (E. Claxton, £3)
The Struggle for Peace – the history of CU's founding and early development (E. Claxton, £3 each or the pair for £5)
Order printed publications from: e-mail: hq.cu@casualtiesunion.org.uk

Access to staff:
Contact by letter, by telephone, by fax and by e-mail
Hours: Mon to Fri, 1100 to 2100

CATERHAM AND DISTRICT LOCAL HISTORY CENTRE

Caterham Valley Library, Stafford Road, Caterham, Surrey, CR3 6JG

Tel: 08456 009009
Fax: 01883 330872
E-mail: libraries@surreycc.gov.uk

Website:
http://www.surreycc.gov.uk/caterhamlocalhistory

Organisation type and purpose:
A partnership between Surrey Libraries, Surrey History Centre, the Bourne Society, East Surrey Museum and East Surrey Family History Society.

Subject coverage:
Local and family history of the parishes of Caterham, Chaldon, Chelsham, Farleigh, Godstone, Tatsfield, Titsey, Warlingham, Whyteleafe and Woldingham.

Access to building, collection or gallery:
Hours: 1st Tue of the month, 1400 to 1600; 2nd and 4th Sat of the month, 1000 to 1200

CATERING EQUIPMENT DISTRIBUTORS ASSOCIATION OF GREAT BRITAIN

Acronym or abbreviation: CEDA

PO Box 683, Inkberrow, Worcestershire, WR7 4WQ

Tel: 01386 793911
E-mail: peterkay@ceda.co.uk

Website:
http://www.ceda.co.uk

Enquiries:
Enquiries to: Managing Director

Founded:
1972

Organisation type and purpose:
Trade association, membership association (membership is by subscription).
The official organisation of the catering equipment dealer and supply industry.

Subject coverage:
Provision, installation, service and design of commercial kitchens, catering equipment and kitchen utensils.

Printed publications:
Membership List (free of charge)
Newsletter (free of charge)
Association Information (free of charge)

Publications list:
Available online

Access to staff:
Contact by letter, by telephone, by e-mail and via website. Appointment necessary.
Hours: Mon to Fri, 0900 to 1700

CATES

Formal name: Campaign Against the Trade of Endangered Species

23 Clifton Road, Henlow, Bedfordshire, SG16 6BL

Enquiries:
Enquiries to: Secretary
Other contacts: Director

Founded:
1985

Formerly called:
North Herts FOE Endangered Species Campaign (year of change 1985)

Organisation type and purpose:
Advisory body (membership is by subscription), present number of members: 200, voluntary organisation, research organisation.

Subject coverage:
Environmental subjects including: tropical rainforests, endangered species campaign, tree planting/woodland management, introduction/reintroduction (ie plant or animal species), behavioural and genetic extinction, pesticides and architecture.

Museum or gallery collection, archive, or library special collection:
Earth Matters Magazines (Friends of the Earth)
TRAFFIC Bulletins

Non-library collection catalogue:
All or part available in-house

Printed publications:
CATES membership and all publications £7, or:
Behavioural and Genetic Extinction (free, sae)
Campaign sheets
Housing Policy/Development (£1.50)
Information material
Pesticide Infractions/HSE's Response portfolio (£1.50)
Reintroduction/Introduction (free, sae)
Tree Planting/Woodland Management (£3)

Publications list:
Available in print

Access to staff:
Contact by letter
Hours: Mon to Fri, 0900 to 1700

CATHEDRAL ORGANISTS' ASSOCIATION

Acronym or abbreviation: COA

Royal School of Church Music, 19 The Close, Salisbury, SP1 2EB

Tel: 01722 424840
Fax: 01722 424849
E-mail: coa@rscm.com

Enquiries:
Enquiries to: Secretary

Founded:
1946

Organisation type and purpose:
Professional body.

To provide opportunities for all cathedral organists to meet at 2 conferences per year and for the exchange of useful information.

Subject coverage:
Cathedral music today, education of choristers and the choir school situation today.

Access to staff:
Contact by letter, by telephone, by fax and by e-mail. Access for members only.
Hours: Mon to Fri, 0900 to 1700

CATHEDRALS AND CHURCH BUILDINGS LIBRARY

Formal name: Cathedrals and Church Buildings Division of the Archbishops' Council of the Church of England

Church House, Great Smith Street, London, SW1P 3AZ

Tel: 020 7898 1884
Fax: 020 7898 1881
E-mail: vaughan.whibley@c-of-e.org.uk

Website:
http://www.churchcare.co.uk
Advice on care of church buildings.
http://www.cofe.anglican.org/about/librariesandarchives
Libraries and archives of the Church of England.

Enquiries:
Enquiries to: Honorary Librarian

Founded:
1921

Organisation type and purpose:
The Library supports the work of the Church Buildings Council (CBC) and the Cathedrals Fabric Commission for England (CFCE). The CBC advises churches and dioceses on matters relating to architecture and ecclesiastical planning regulations; it also dispenses grants, for conservation of furnishings of historical or artistic significance in Church of England churches, on behalf of charitable organisations. The CFCE oversees the Church's own system of planning controls for cathedrals and provides guidance and advice on such issues.

Subject coverage:
Ecclesiastical art and architecture, with special reference to the cathedral and church buildings and furnishings of the Church of England; conservation of works of art in Church of England churches, general and specific information on a wide range of topics relating to churches and their contents including ecclesiology; liturgy; heraldry; ecclesiastical history; symbolism; hagiography.

Museum or gallery collection, archive, or library special collection:
Library of c.13,000 books and over 100 periodical titles on ecclesiastical art and architecture; liturgy; ecclesiology; National Association of Decorative and Fine Arts Society (NADFAS) church recorders reports; National Survey of English Churches, with documentary and photographic material, postcards and guide books relating to about 18,000 churches

Library catalogue:
All or part available in print

Access to staff:
Contact by letter, by telephone, by fax, by e-mail and in person. Appointment necessary.
Hours: Tue, Wed, 1030 to 1600

Constituent part of:
Cathedrals Fabric Commission for England
Church House, Great Smith Street, London SW1P 3AZ; tel: 020 7898 1884; fax: 020 7898 1881; e-mail: vaughan.whibley@c-of-e.org.uk
Church Buildings Council

Parent body:
Archbishops' Council of the Church of England

CATHEDRALS FABRIC COMMISSION FOR ENGLAND

Acronym or abbreviation: CFCE

Church House, Great Smith Street, London, SW1P 3NZ

Tel: 020 7898 1866
Fax: 020 7898 1881
E-mail: enquiries@cfce.c-of-e.org.uk

Enquiries:
Enquiries to: Secretary

Founded:
1991

Formerly called:
Cathedrals Advisory Committee (CAC) (year of change 1991)

Organisation type and purpose:
Advisory and research body.
Statutory church body.

Subject coverage:
Care of cathedrals in England.

Library catalogue:
All or part available in-house

Access to staff:
Contact by letter
Hours: Mon to Fri, 0930 to 1630
Special comments: By appointment only.

Access to building, collection or gallery:
Prior appointment required

Access for disabled people:
Ramped entry, access to all public areas

Parent body:
Archbishops' Council of the Church of England

CATHOLIC AGENCY FOR OVERSEAS DEVELOPMENT

Acronym or abbreviation: CAFOD

Romero Close, Stockwell Road, London, SW9 9TY

Tel: 020 7733 7900
Fax: 020 7274 9630
E-mail: hqcafod@cafod.org.uk

Website:
http://www.cafod.org.uk
Information about CAFOD, its publications, campaigns, contact, library and information centre.

Enquiries:
Enquiries to: Information Services Manager
Direct tel: 020 7326 5600

Founded:
1962

Organisation type and purpose:
Voluntary organisation, registered charity (charity number 285776).
Specialised library.
Development and relief NGO working in the third world.

Subject coverage:
Computing, development economics, debt, trade, environment, land, information technology, theology, women, children in Africa, Asia, the Pacific, Latin America, the Caribbean and Eastern Europe.

Trade and statistical information:
A number of UN and World Bank statistical reports.

Library catalogue:
All or part available in-house

Printed publications:
An extensive selection of educational material relevant to Third World environmental, economic, justice and religious issues
CAFOD Bulletin
CAFOD Reports
Fruits of the Earth
Food and Land

Order printed publications from: e-mail: afarragh@cafod.org.uk

Electronic and video publications:
Videos on all aspects of the work

Publications list:
Available in print

Access to staff:
Contact by letter, by telephone, by fax, by e-mail and via website. Appointment necessary.
Hours: Mon to Fri, 1030 to 1630

Access to building, collection or gallery:
No access other than to staff

Regional Offices:
CAFOD East
Chigwell Convent, 803 Chigwell Road, Woodford Green, Essex, IG8 8AX; tel: 020 8502 9722
CAFOD East Midlands
61 Staton Road, Rearsby, Leicestershire, LE7 4YY; tel: 01664 424346
CAFOD Leeds and Hallam
St William of York, Eccleshall Road, Sheffield, S11 8TL; tel: 0114 268 7817
CAFOD Liverpool
St Joseph's, Upholland, Lancashire, WN8 0PZ; tel: 01695 633284
CAFOD North East
Ushaw College, Durham, DH7 9BJ; tel: 0191 373 5001
CAFOD North West
St Walburge, Weston Street, Preston, Lancashire, PR2 2QE; tel: 01772 733310
CAFOD South
St John's Seminary, Wonersh, Surrey, GU5 0QX; tel: 01483 898866
CAFOD South West
The Mount, Taunton, Somerset, TA1 3NR; tel: 01823 338903
CAFOD Southwark
Hubert House, Mallard Close, Temple Hill, Dartford, Kent, DA1 5HU; tel: 01322 294924; fax: 01322 279223; e-mail: southwark@cafod.org.uk
CAFOD Wales
St Mary's Parish Centre, Union Street, Carmarthen, Dyfed, SA31 3DE; tel: 01267 221549
CAFOD West Midlands
23 Glebe Street, Walsall, West Midlands, WS1 3NX; tel: 01922 722944
CAFOD Westminster
The Benedictine Centre for Spirituality, 29 Bramley Road, Cockfosters, London, N14 4HE; tel: 020 8449 6970

CATHOLIC BISHOPS' CONFERENCE OF ENGLAND AND WALES

Department for International Affairs, 39 Eccleston Square, London, SW1V 1BX

Tel: 020 7901 4861
Fax: 020 7901 4821

Enquiries:
Enquiries to: Secretary

Founded:
1968

Formerly called:
Commission for International Justice and Peace

Organisation type and purpose:
Advisory body, professional body, registered charity.
Promotion of international justice and peace including development. The Department is an advisory body for the Catholic Bishops of England and Wales, and has four analytical groups dealing with: international justice and peace, European affairs, refugees and migrants, environmental issues.

Subject coverage:
Catholic teaching on international affairs, development, and justice and peace issues.

continued overleaf

Access to staff:
Contact by letter
Hours: Mon to Fri, 0900 to 1700

Subsidiary body:
National Liaison Committee of Diocesan Justice and Peace Groups

CATHOLIC CENTRAL LIBRARY

Lancing Street, London, NW1 1ND

Tel: 020 7383 4333
Fax: 020 7388 6675
E-mail: librarian@catholic-library.org.uk

Website:
http://www.catholic-library.org.uk
Membership details, periodical holdings, latest new book list, mission register holdings (baptism, marriage etc).

Enquiries:
Enquiries to: Librarian
Other contacts: Director

Organisation type and purpose:
Registered charity (charity number 1064460/0). A theological library.

Subject coverage:
Catholic Church in England and in countries of the world, Roman Catholic current affairs, theology, ecumenism, scripture, ecclesiastical history, comparative religion and Christian sociology.

Museum or gallery collection, archive, or library special collection:
19th-century Roman Catholic pamphlets, tracts and directories
Ecumenism
Papal documents and magisterial statements
Post-Reformation English Catholic history
Vatican Council II

Printed publications:
List of additions to the library (3 times a year)

Access to staff:
Contact by letter, by telephone, by fax, by e-mail, in person and via website
Hours: Mon, Tue, Thu, Fri, 1030 to 1700; Wed, 1030 to 1900

Access for disabled people:
Level entry, access to all public areas, toilet facilities

CATHOLIC EDUCATION SERVICE

Formal name: Catholic Education Service for England and Wales
Acronym or abbreviation: CESEW

39 Eccleston Square, London, SW1V 1BX

Tel: 020 7901 1900
Fax: 020 7901 1939
E-mail: general@cesew.org.uk

Website:
http://www.cesew.org.uk

Enquiries:
Enquiries to: Office Manager

Founded:
1847

Formerly called:
Catholic Poor Schools Committee

Organisation type and purpose:
Promoting and supporting Catholic education in England and Wales.

Subject coverage:
Catholic education.

Printed publications:
http://www.cesew.org.uk
Order printed publications from:
general@cesew.orguk

Publications list:
Available online and in print

Access to staff:
Contact by letter, by telephone, by fax, by e-mail and via website. Appointment necessary.
Hours: Mon to Fri, 0900 to 1700

The education agency of the:
Bishops' Conference of England and Wales

CATHOLIC INSTITUTE FOR INTERNATIONAL RELATIONS

Acronym or abbreviation: CIIR

Unit 3 Canonbury Yard, 190a New North Road, London, N1 7BJ

Tel: 020 7288 8600
Fax: 020 7359 0017
E-mail: info@ciir.org

Website:
http://www.ciir.org
Information on all aspects of CIIR's work.

Enquiries:
Enquiries to: Information Officer
Other contacts: Advocacy Officer for issue/region based information request.

Organisation type and purpose:
Membership association (membership is by subscription), registered charity (charity number 294329).
CIIR works for justice, development and the eradication of poverty through a combination of technical assistance and advocacy for political change.

Subject coverage:
Social, economic, cultural and political analysis and expertise in geographic regions: Dominican Republic, El Salvador, Nicaragua, Honduras, Ecuador, Peru, Namibia, Zimbabwe, Somalia, Yemen, East Timor.

Printed publications:
Burma's Excluded Majority: Women, dictatorship and the democracy movement (briefing, O'Shannassy T)
Contagion and Cure: Tackling the crisis in global finance (comment series, Woodward D)
Education for the Future: Environment and sustainable development in Peru (ed Chauvin L O)
Families in the War on Drugs: Peasant families, alternative development and the war on drugs in Bolivia (Blickman T)
Reaping the Whirlwind: Economic reform and food security in Zimbabwe (Chisvo M, Jimat Consultants)
Storm Warnings: Hurricanes Georges and Mitch and the lessons for development (Mowforth M)
Thinking Strategically about Politics and Poverty (Moore M and Putzel J)
Trade and Food Security: An assessment of the Uruguay Round Agreement on Agriculture (discussion paper, Murphy S)

Publications list:
Available in print

Access to staff:
Contact by e-mail and via website. Appointment necessary.
Hours: Mon to Fri, 0930 to 1730

Access to building, collection or gallery:
Prior appointment required

Other addresses:
International Cooperation for Development (ICD)
At the same address

CATHOLIC RECORD SOCIETY

Acronym or abbreviation: CRS

12 Melbourne Place, Wolsingham, Co. Durham, DL13 3EH

Tel: 01388 527747

Website:
http://www.catholicrecordsociety.org

Enquiries:
Enquiries to: Honorary Secretary

Founded:
1905

Organisation type and purpose:
Learned society, present number of members: 600.

Subject coverage:
Catholic history of England and Wales from the Reformation (not genealogical).

Non-library collection catalogue:
All or part available online

Printed publications:
Annual Report
Newsletter (annually)
Recusant History (2 times a year)
Volume of Records or a Monograph (approx. every 2 years)

Access to staff:
Contact by letter and by telephone
Hours: Mon to Fri, 0900 to 1700

CATHOLIC YOUTH SERVICES

Acronym or abbreviation: CYS

39 Eccleston Square, London, SW1V 1BX

Tel: 020 7901 4870
Fax: 020 7901 4873
E-mail: cys@btinternet.com

Enquiries:
Enquiries to: Director

Organisation type and purpose:
Statutory body, voluntary organisation, registered charity.
Training agency.

Subject coverage:
Youth, youth service, youth work.

Printed publications:
CYS News (quarterly)
Catholic Curriculum Youth Work Document (£3)
Ecumenical Pack (£2)
Guidelines to Good Practice (£3.95)
Induction Pack for Youth Workers (£3.95)
National Youth Sunday Pack (£2)

Access to staff:
Contact by letter, by telephone and by fax. Appointment necessary.
Hours: Mon to Fri, 0900 to 1700

Also at:
Assistant Director
Newman College, Genners Lane, Bartley Green, Birmingham, B32 3NT; tel: 0121 411 1033; fax: 0121 475 0012

Member of:
British Youth Council
Council of Churches for Britain and Ireland (Youth Unit)
National Council for Voluntary Youth Services

Sponsored by:
Roman Catholic Bishops' Conference

CBD RESEARCH LIMITED

Chancery House, 15 Wickham Road, Beckenham, Kent, BR3 5JS

Tel: 020 8650 7745
Fax: 020 8650 0768
E-mail: cbd@cbdresearch.com

Website:
http://www.cbdresearch.com

Enquiries:
Enquiries to: Company Secretary

Founded:
1961

Organisation type and purpose:
Publishing house.

Subject coverage:
Sources of business information; directories and guides to associations, societies and institutions of all kinds in Great Britain and Europe.

Library catalogue:
All or part available in-house and in print

Printed publications:
Amongst many are:
American Companies: A Guide to Sources of Information
Asian and Australian Companies: a Guide to Sources of Information
Centres, Bureaux and Research Institutes
Councils, Committees and Boards including Government Agencies and Authorities
Current British Directories
Current European Directories
Directory of British Associations and Associations in Ireland
Directory of European Industrial and Trade Associations
Directory of European Professional and Learned Societies
European Companies: A Guide to Sources of Information
Pan-European Associations
Statistics-Europe: Sources for social, economic and market research

Electronic and video publications:
Directory of British Associations and Associations in Ireland (19th edn, 2009, CD-ROM)
Mailing lists of associations to the client's specifications, in print or mailing-label format.

Publications list:
Available online and in print

Access to staff:
Contact by letter, by telephone, by fax, by e-mail, in person and via website. Appointment necessary.
Hours: Mon to Fri, 0800 to 1700

Member organisation of:
Data Publishers Association (DPA)
Independent Publishers Guild (IPG)

CCUSA

Formal name: Camp Counsellors USA

1st Floor North, Devon House, 171–177 Great Portland Street, London, W1W5PQ

Tel: 020 7637 0779
Fax: 0207 580 6209
E-mail: info@ccusa.co.uk

Website:
http://www.ccusa.com
Information and application forms

Enquiries:
Enquiries to: Marketing Manager
Direct e-mail: jamiem@ccusa.co.uk

Founded:
1986

Formerly called:
Camp Counsellors USA (CCUSA) (year of change 2001)

Organisation type and purpose:
International organisation.
Student work & travel specialists.
Recruitment for summer work placements in the USA and gap years to Australia or New Zealand, work experience in Brazil or Russian summer camps.

Subject coverage:
Work experience placements and travel.

Printed publications:
Brochure (free, on request)

Access to staff:
Contact by letter, by telephone, by fax, by e-mail, in person and via website
Hours: Mon to Fri, 0900 to 1700

Also at the same address:
Work Experience USA (WEUSA)

CEEBIS

Formal name: Central and East European Business Information Service

Glasgow University Library, Hillhead Street, Glasgow, G12 8QE

Tel: 0141 330 6735
Fax: 0141 330 4952
E-mail: t.konn@lib.gla.ac.uk

Enquiries:
Enquiries to: Information Officer

Founded:
1990

Formerly called:
Soviet and East European Business Information Service

Organisation type and purpose:
University library, consultancy.

Subject coverage:
Economic, social and political background for all countries of Eastern Europe and the former Soviet Union, general and specialised business information services.

Museum or gallery collection, archive, or library special collection:
50 current newspaper titles
75,000 monographs
600 journals
Back runs of newspapers held on microfilm

Trade and statistical information:
Statistics, company data, legislation.

Access to staff:
Appointment necessary. All charged.
Hours: Mon to Fri, 0900 to 1700

CELTIC MEDIA FESTIVAL

249 West George Street, Glasgow, G2 4QE

Tel: 0141 302 1737
Fax: 0141 302 1738
E-mail: info@celticmediafestival.co.uk

Website:
http://www.celticmediafestival.co.uk

Enquiries:
Enquiries to: Festival Producer

Founded:
1980

Formerly called:
Celtic Film and Television Festival; Celtic Film and Television Association

Organisation type and purpose:
International organisation, trade association (membership is by subscription, election or invitation), registered charity (charity number SC 028708).
Celebrates and showcases the best of film and broadcasting from the Celtic countries and regions of Scotland, Ireland, Wales, Cornwall and Brittany. The festival is a unique platform for debate and international co-production development.

Access to staff:
Contact by letter, by telephone and by e-mail
Hours: Mon to Fri, 0930 to 1730

CEMENT ADMIXTURES ASSOCIATION

Acronym or abbreviation: CAA

38a Tilehouse Green Lane, Knowle, West Midlands, B93 9EY

Tel: 01564 776362
Fax: 01564 776362
E-mail: info@admixtures.org.uk

Website:
http://www.admixtures.org.uk
Comprehensive range of information, technical and environmental sheets for free download.

Enquiries:
Enquiries to: Secretary

Organisation type and purpose:
Trade Association.

Subject coverage:
Admixtures for concrete, mortar, grout and sprayed concrete; curing compounds for concrete.

Printed publications:
Admixture Information Sheets
Admixture Technical Sheets
Admixture Environmental Sheets

Member organisation of:
European Federation of Concrete Admixtures Associations (EFCA)
Cobblers Cottage, Chester Road, Daresbury, Warrington, Cheshire, WA4 4AJ; tel: 01925 740581; fax: 01925 740581; e-mail: roland .harbron@talktalk.net; website: http://www.efca .info

CENTER FOR AUTISM & RELATED DISORDERS

Acronym or abbreviation: CARD

Acorn House, 13 Moorfield Road, Orpington, Kent, BR6 0HG

Tel: 01689 837373
Fax: 01689 896656
E-mail: carduk@kentseuk.freeserve.co.uk

Website:
http://www.cardhq.com

Enquiries:
Enquiries to: Clinic Supervisor

Founded:
1998

Organisation type and purpose:
National organisation, suitable for ages: 2–8.
Special Needs Education.

Subject coverage:
Design and implementation of home-based teaching programmes for children with autism and related disorders based on the Lovaas technique.

Printed publications:
Brochures (on application)

Access to staff:
Contact by letter, by telephone and by e-mail
Hours: Mon to Fri, 0900 to 1700

Access to building, collection or gallery:
Prior appointment required

Headquarters:
Center for Autism & Related Disorders
2330 Ventura Boulevard, Woodland Hills, California, CA 91364, USA; tel: +1 818 223 0123

CENTRAL ARBITRATION COMMITTEE

Acronym or abbreviation: CAC

Euston Tower, 22nd Floor, 286 Euston Road, London, NW1 3JJ

Tel: 020 7904 2300
Fax: 020 7904 2301
E-mail: enquiries@cac.gov.uk

Website:
http://www.cac.gov.uk
Press releases, information about organisation, latest applications, decisions and hearings, annual report, guidance.

Founded:
1976

Organisation type and purpose:
National government body, permanent independent arbitration body.
To promote fair and efficient arrangements in the work place, by resolving collective disputes (in England, Scotland and Wales), either by voluntary agreement or, if necessary, through adjudication.

continued overleaf

Subject coverage:
Disclosure of information (Trade Union and Labour Relations (Consolidation) Act 1992: Section 183); voluntary arbitration (1992 Act: Section 212); industrial relations; statutory recognition (Employment Relations Act 1999). Considers applications and complaints under the Information and Consultation of Employees Regulations 2004 and performs a similar role in relation to European Works Councils, European Companies, European Co-operative Societies and Cross-Border Mergers.

Museum or gallery collection, archive, or library special collection:
Copies of past awards as issued by the Industrial Court, Industrial Arbitration Board and Central Arbitration Committee, from 1919
Applications and decisions on all cases
Guidelines to Statutory Recognition Procedures

Printed publications:
CAC Annual Report (free)
CAC information leaflet (free)
Statutory Guidelines to Recognition (free)
Information and Consultation Guidance (free)

Publications list:
Available online

Access to staff:
Contact by letter, by telephone, by fax, by e-mail and via website
Hours: Mon to Fri

Access to building, collection or gallery:
Prior appointment required

Access for disabled people:
Access to all public areas, toilet facilities

CENTRAL BEDFORDSHIRE LIBRARIES

Operations Unit, Dunstable Library, Vernon Place, Dunstable, LU5 4HA

Tel: 0300 300 8060
Fax: 01582 471290
E-mail: dunstable.library@centralbedfordshire.gov.uk

Website:
http://www.galaxy.bedfordshire.gov.uk/cgi-bin/vlib.sh
Bedfordshire's Virtual Library.

Enquiries:
Enquiries to: Libraries Manager
Other contacts: Service Development Manager, Adult, Community & Information

Organisation type and purpose:
Local government body. Public library service offering access to information, books, spoken word, DVDs and CDs for all ages and interests.

Subject coverage:
Local information on Bedfordshire and its history, agriculture; local government information; life and works of John Bunyan; medieval English history; aeronautics; automobile engineering.

Education services:
Homework centres and a virtual homework centre.

Non-library collection catalogue:
All or part available online and in-house

Library catalogue:
All or part available online

Printed publications:
Asian Bedford and European Bedfordshire
Order printed publications from: Download free from the Virtual Library

Microform publications:
Catalogue of holdings

Access to staff:
Contact by letter, by telephone, by fax, by e-mail, in person and via website
Hours: Mon to Sat

CENTRAL COUNCIL FOR BRITISH NATURISM

Acronym or abbreviation: CCBN or British Naturism

30–32 Wycliffe Road, Northampton, NN1 5JF

Tel: 01604 620361
Fax: 01604 230176
E-mail: headoffice@british-naturism.org.uk

Website:
http://www.british-naturism.org.uk

Enquiries:
Enquiries to: Secretary General
Other contacts: Public Relations Office, 07799 677732, Archivist 01223 840947

Founded:
1964

Organisation type and purpose:
National organisation, membership association (membership is by subscription), present number of members: 20,000, voluntary organisation. National organisation of clubs and individuals.

Subject coverage:
History of, and present facilities for, naturism and naturist sunbathing throughout the world.

Museum or gallery collection, archive, or library special collection:
Archives of CCBN and its predecessors
Magazines and books concerning naturism throughout the world

Printed publications:
British Naturism (quarterly)
Members Handbook (approximately every other year)

Publications list:
Available online and in print

Access to staff:
Contact by letter, by telephone, by fax, by e-mail and via website
Hours: Mon to Fri, 0900 to 1630

Affiliated to:
International Naturist Federation

CENTRAL COUNCIL OF CHURCH BELL RINGERS

Acronym or abbreviation: CCCBR

E-mail: secretary@cccbr.org.uk

Website:
http://www.cccbr.org.uk
Information about the Council, its committees, publications and affiliated societies, and Doves' Guide to the Church Bells of Britain and Ringing Peals of the World.

Enquiries:
Enquiries to: Honorary Secretary
Direct e-mail: honlibrarian@cccbr.org.uk
Other contacts: Honorary Librarian

Founded:
1891

Organisation type and purpose:
Advisory body, membership association (membership is by election or invitation), present number of members: 230, voluntary organisation, registered charity (charity number 270036).
To promote and foster the ringing of church bells for Christian worship and on other occasions, to represent ringers to national bodies, etc., to advise on all matters concerned with bells and bellringing.

Subject coverage:
Bells and their fittings (both historical and engineering aspects); technical aspects of change ringing; history of change ringing; assistance with disposal of bells from redundant churches; advice on fund-raising for bells and their maintenance.

Museum or gallery collection, archive, or library special collection:
Unique collection of books and manuscripts on bells, bellfounders, bell-ringers and bell-ringing in the English tradition, covering the British Isles and overseas

Non-library collection catalogue:
All or part available online, in-house and in print

Printed publications:
The Ringing World (weekly journal);
Central Council Publications:
Towers and Bells Handbook
Change Ringing History (3 volumes)
Publications on various aspects of bell ringing under the following general headings:
Technical – learning
Technical – teaching
Recruiting
Maintenance, restoration, etc.
History
Method collections, etc.
Order printed publications from: The Ringing World, 35A High Street, Andover, Hampshire, SP10 1LJ; tel: 01264 366620; e-mail: subs@ringingworld.co.uk; website: http://www.ringingworld.co.uk
Central Council Publications, e-mail: pubs@cccbr.org.uk; website: http://www.cccbr.org.uk/pubs

Electronic and video publications:
Also available from Central Council Publications:
Bell Handling – A Tutor's Companion (video)
Listening to Ringing (two cassettes or CDs)

Publications list:
Available online

CENTRAL GURDWARA LONDON

Formal name: The Central Gurdwara (Khalsa Jatha) London

62 Queensdale Road, London, W11 4SQ

Tel: 020 7603 2789
Fax: 0207 480 7636
E-mail: ksg@khalsa.com

Website:
http://www.centralgurdwara.org.uk

Enquiries:
Enquiries to: General Secretary
Direct tel: 020 7481 8176

Founded:
1908

Formerly called:
Central Gurdwara (British Isles Khalsa Jatha) London

Organisation type and purpose:
Membership association (membership is by subscription), present number of members: 1,000, registered charity (charity number 258324), public library, suitable for all ages.
Sunday school.
Religious congregations; education; births, marriages, death rites; library; music.

Subject coverage:
Sikhism

Non-library collection catalogue:
All or part available in-house

Library catalogue:
All or part available in-house

Printed publications:
Newsletter (monthly)

Access to staff:
Contact by letter, by telephone, by fax, by e-mail and in person
Hours: Access to the Executive Committee by phone, or Sunday evening on the premises. Wed and Fri, 1900 to 2030

Access to building, collection or gallery:
No access other than to staff
Hours: Daily, 0500 to 2030

CENTRAL LIBRARY, DERBY

The Wardwick, Derby, DE1 1HS

Tel: 01332 641702
Fax: 01332 369570
E-mail: central.library@derby.gov.uk

Enquiries:
Direct e-mail: askusaquestion@derby.gov.uk

Founded:
1879

Organisation type and purpose:
Local government body, public library.

Museum or gallery collection, archive, or library special collection:
An extensive manuscript collection, files of newspapers, Derbyshire census (both on microfilm), photographs, engravings, maps and family records
Local studies collection incorporates the Devonshire and Bemrose family libraries
The collection of printed books and pamphlets includes works published in 17th, 18th, 19th and 20th centuries. This is housed at the Local Studies Library, 25B Irongate, Derby, DE1 3GL

Library catalogue:
All or part available online and in-house

Access to staff:
Contact by letter, by telephone, by fax, by e-mail, in person and via website

Access for disabled people:
Ramped entry, access to all public areas, toilet facilities

Part of:
Derby City Libraries
  website: http://www.derby.gov.uk/libraries

CENTRAL SCHOOL OF BALLET

Acronym or abbreviation: CSB

10 Herbal Hill, Clerkenwell Road, London, EC1R 5EG

Tel: 020 7837 6332
Fax: 020 7833 5571
E-mail: info@csbschool.co.uk

Website:
http://www.centralschoolofballet.co.uk

Enquiries:
Enquiries to: Assistant Administrator
Other contacts: Senior School Administrator (for admission process)

Founded:
1982

Organisation type and purpose:
Registered charity (charity number 285398), dance training organisation.
Affiliate Member of the Conservatoire for Dance & Drama.

Access to staff:
Contact by letter, by telephone, by fax, by e-mail, in person and via website
Hours: Mon, Wed, Fri, Sat, 0900 to 1830; Tue, Thu, 0900 to 2100

Access to building, collection or gallery:
Prior appointment required

Graduate touring company:
Ballet Central
  at the same address; e-mail: info@csbschool.co.uk; website: http://www.balletcentral.co.uk

CENTRAL SCHOOL OF SPEECH AND DRAMA

Acronym or abbreviation: CSSD, Central

Embassy Theatre, 64 Eton Avenue, London, NW3 3HY

Tel: 020 7559 3942
Fax: 020 7722 4132
E-mail: library@cssd.ac.uk

Website:
http://www.cssd.ac.uk/pages/library.htmll
Library pages.

Enquiries:
Enquiries to: Head of Library Services
Other contacts: Library, Media, Computer Services Managers (for library, media, computer enquiries)

Founded:
1906

Organisation type and purpose:
University library, HE College library.
Higher education.

Subject coverage:
Theatre, drama, art and design, drama education.

Museum or gallery collection, archive, or library special collection:
Library of c. 32,000 vols

Library catalogue:
All or part available online

Electronic and video publications:
DVD and video collections

Access to staff:
Contact by telephone. Appointment necessary.
Non-members charged.
Hours: Telephone for hours as times vary for term time and holidays

Access to building, collection or gallery:
Prior appointment required
Hours: Hours vary, see website for details
Special comments: Charges for borrowing and copying.

Access for disabled people:
Toilet facilities
Special comments: Access via side-entrance, phone beforehand.

CENTRAL SCIENCE LABORATORY

Acronym or abbreviation: CSL

Sand Hutton, York, North Yorkshire, YO41 1LZ

Tel: 01904 462000
Fax: 01904 462111
E-mail: science@csl.gov.uk

Website:
http://www.csl.gov.uk

Enquiries:
Enquiries to: Information Centre Manager
Direct tel: 01904 462272

Founded:
1992

Organisation type and purpose:
National government body, research organisation.

Subject coverage:
Plant pathology (bacteriology, plant health and disease assessment, disease control, mycology, virology), agricultural entomology (general entomology, vertebrate pest assessment, biology and control, fumigation, insect systematics), crop protection, biochemistry, chemistry (biological efficiency, analytical methods for pest formulations and residues in crops, safety to users), toxicology and industrial hygiene related to pesticides.
Biology and control of invertebrate pests of stored products, moulds on stored products, mycotoxins.
Food safety, food quality, food authenticity, pesticide residues in food and water. Microbiology.
Alternative crops, GMOs. Conservation, environmental protection and environmental effects of pesticides, ecotoxicology. Mammal and bird ecology, invasive species, avian risks to aviation ('birdstrike'), animal health and welfare,

zoonoses. Risk assessment, epidemiology, modelling and bioinformatics relevant to the above areas.

Museum or gallery collection, archive, or library special collection:
Cowan collection on Bees and Beekeeping – a collection containing works from the 17th century to date
Original drawings of invertebrate pest species
Photographic images of pest species and plant diseases

Trade and statistical information:
Annual Pesticide Usage Survey Reports.

Printed publications:
Annual Pesticide Usage Survey Reports
Annual Report and Accounts (priced, TSO)
Insect Identification Cards (priced, available directly)
Photographs (priced, available directly)
Research papers
Science Review (priced, TSO)

Publications list:
Available online

Access to staff:
Contact by letter, by telephone and by e-mail.
Appointment necessary.
Hours: Mon to Thu, 0900 to 1700, Fri 0900 to 1630
Special comments: Some charges may be made.

Access to building, collection or gallery:
Appointment necessary

Constituent part of:
Department for Environment, Food and Rural Affairs (DEFRA)

CENTRAL SCOTLAND FAMILY HISTORY SOCIETY

Acronym or abbreviation: CSFHS

11 Springbank Gardens, Dunblane, Perthshire, FK15 9JX

Website:
http://www.csfhs.org.uk

Enquiries:
Enquiries to: Honorary Secretary

Founded:
1990

Organisation type and purpose:
Membership association (membership is by subscription).

Subject coverage:
Family history of the area.

Printed publications:
Stirling Burgess Lists
Various 1851 Census Indexes

Publications list:
Available online

CENTRAL ST MARTINS COLLEGE OF ART AND DESIGN

Acronym or abbreviation: CSM

Southampton Row, London, WC1B 4AP

Tel: 020 7514 7000
Fax: 020 7514 7033

Website:
http://www.csm.arts.ac.uk
College website including pages on the Museum and Study Collection (this collection holds the college archives and other special collections).
http://www.arts.ac.uk/library
Library website, including catalogue.

Enquiries:
Enquiries to: Learning Resources Manager
Direct tel: 020 7514 7029
Direct e-mail: s.gilmour@csm.arts.ac.uk

continued overleaf

Other contacts: Assistant Learning Resources Manager (for requests for access by potential external users)

Founded:
1896

Incorporates the former:
ILEA Art Schools; Central School of Art and Design, St Martins School of Art (year of change 1989); Drama Centre London (year of change 2000); Byam Shaw School of Art (year of change 2003)

Organisation type and purpose:
University department or institute, suitable for ages: 18+.
College of Higher Education.

Subject coverage:
Fine arts, graphic design, product and industrial design, fashion design, textile design, jewellery design, ceramic design, photography, animation, film and video, theatre design and scenography, performing arts

Museum or gallery collection, archive, or library special collection:
Materials and Products Collection
Fashion files

Non-library collection catalogue:
All or part available online

Library catalogue:
All or part available online

Printed publications:
Guide to the Special Collections and Archives within the Libraries of the University of the Arts London

Publications list:
Available online

Access to staff:
Contact by letter, by telephone, by fax, by e-mail and via website. Appointment necessary.
Hours: Mon to Fri, 0900 to 1700

Also at:
Central St Martins College of Art and Design
109 Charing Cross Road, London, WC2H 0DU; tel: 020 7514 7190; fax: 020 7514 7189

Parent body:
University of the Arts London
272 High Holborn, London, WC1; tel: 020 7514 6000; e-mail: p.christie@arts.ac.uk

CENTRAL SUSSEX COLLEGE

Learning Resource Centre (LRC), Crawley Campus, College Road, Crawley, West Sussex, RH10 1NR

Tel: 01293 442281
Fax: 01293 442399
E-mail: lrc@centralsussex.ac.uk

Enquiries:
Enquiries to: LRC Manager
Other contacts: Deputy LRC Manager

Founded:
2005

Created by the merger of:
Crawley College and Haywards Heath Sixth Form College (year of change 2005)

Organisation type and purpose:
Further education, higher education.

Subject coverage:
Business and finance, beauty therapy, catering, computing and IT, engineering, construction, hairdressing, health and social care, languages, management, education, the arts, social sciences, travel and tourism.

Library catalogue:
All or part available in-house

Access to staff:
Contact by letter, by telephone and by e-mail. Appointment necessary.

Hours: Mon to Fri, 1000 to 1600

Access for disabled people:
Access to most areas

CENTRE FOR ACCESSIBLE ENVIRONMENTS

Acronym or abbreviation: CAE

70 South Lambeth Road, Vauxhall, London, SW8 1RL

Tel: 020 7840 0125
Fax: 020 7840 5811
E-mail: info@cae.org.uk

Website:
http://www.cae.org.uk

Enquiries:
Enquiries to: Information Officer
Other contacts: Technical Officer for help on design or access audit requests.

Founded:
1970

Formerly called:
Centre on Environment for the Handicapped

Organisation type and purpose:
Registered charity (charity number 1050820).

Subject coverage:
Information and advice on the design of the built environment for disabled and older people.

Museum or gallery collection, archive, or library special collection:
Specialist library on the environment and disability

Library catalogue:
All or part available in-house

Printed publications:
Access by Design (journal, 4 times a year)

Electronic and video publications:
Designing for Accessibility (available via our website and access audits and in alternative formats)
Keeping up with the Past (38-minute video on making access improvements to historic buildings)

Publications list:
Available in print

Access to staff:
Contact by letter, by telephone, by fax, by e-mail and via website. Appointment necessary.
Hours: Mon to Fri, 0900 to 1700

CENTRE FOR AGRICULTURAL STRATEGY

Acronym or abbreviation: CAS

The University of Reading, PO Box 237, Earley Gate, Reading, Berkshire, RG6 6AR

Tel: 0118 931 8150
Fax: 0118 935 3423
E-mail: casagri@reading.ac.uk

Website:
http://www.rdg.ac.uk/AgriStrat
Staff, aims of the centre, publications, forthcoming conferences.

Enquiries:
Enquiries to: Director

Founded:
1980

Organisation type and purpose:
University department or institute, research organisation.

Subject coverage:
Agriculture, including food, horticulture, forestry, agroforestry, fish production; environment; long-term planning and forecasting for the agricultural industries, worldwide.

Printed publications:
Papers, contributed by outside authors
Reports, prepared by the Centre staff
Order printed publications from: Publications Department, Centre for Agricultural Strategy at the same address, tel: 0118 931 8152, fax: 0118 935 3423, e-mail: t.m.hicks@rdg.ac.uk

Publications list:
Available in print

Access to staff:
Contact by letter, by telephone, by fax, by e-mail, in person and via website
Hours: Mon to Fri, 0900 to 1700

Established by the:
Nuffield Foundation as an independent, non-profit distributory organisation

Part of:
University of Reading within the Faculty of Agriculture and Food

CENTRE FOR ALTERNATIVE TECHNOLOGY

Acronym or abbreviation: CAT

Machynlleth, Powys, SY20 9AZ

Tel: 01654 705989
E-mail: info@cat.org.uk

Website:
http://www.cat.org.uk
Information about services provided by CAT, description of visitors centre, online mail order catalogue, details of courses, education, training, consultancy and publications.

Enquiries:
Enquiries to: Free Information Service

Founded:
1975

Organisation type and purpose:
International organisation, national organisation, membership association (membership is by subscription), registered charity (charity number 265239), suitable for ages: all, training organisation, consultancy, research organisation, publishing house.
Visitor Centre.
Display and research in sustainable, environmental, alternative technology and energy conservation issues.

Subject coverage:
Small-scale renewable energy, wind, water and solar energy, energy efficiency, environmentally sound buildings, organic gardening, alternative sewage systems, reed beds, compost toilets, green tourism, environmental visitor centres, green building technology, education.

Printed publications:
Clean Slate (journal, quarterly)
Do-It-Yourself Plans
Educational material (10 titles)
Periodic publication of information sheets on all aspects of alternative technology
Resource lists
Books
Order printed publications from: CAT Mail Order, at the same address; tel: 01654 705959 or 0845 330 4592; fax: 01654 705999; e-mail: mail.order@cat.org.uk

Publications list:
Available online and in print

Access to staff:
Contact by letter, by telephone, by e-mail, in person and via website
Hours: Mon to Fri, 0930 to 1730
Also Sat, Sun for visitors to the centre
Special comments: In person access may be restricted – please phone for details.

Access to building, collection or gallery:
No prior appointment required
Hours: Mon to Sun, 1000 to 1730

Special comments: Entrance fee.

Access for disabled people:
Parking provided, level entry, access to most public areas, toilet facilities

CENTRE FOR APPLIED RESEARCH IN EDUCATION

Acronym or abbreviation: CARE

School of Education and Professional Development, University of East Anglia, Norwich, Norfolk, NR4 7TJ

Tel: 01603 456161
Fax: 01603 451412
E-mail: c.stephens@uea.ac.uk

Website:
http://www.uea.ac.uk/care/
CARE Web has information on research projects/initiatives, personnel and publications. Details of research degree programmes.

Enquiries:
Enquiries to: Director's Secretary
Direct tel: 01603 592638

Founded:
1970

Organisation type and purpose:
University department or institute, consultancy, research organisation.
University policy and curriculum research centre with degree teaching function; a constituent of the School of Education while maintaining its own identity.

Subject coverage:
Curriculum research, evaluation, development, dissemination, particularly in relation to centralised innovation projects; policy research and evaluation; information technology in education; computer-based education; bilingual education; in-service teacher education, particularly school-focused with an action research element; naturalistic methods of inquiry; problems and effects of teaching about race relations; library access and independent study for sixth-form students; performing arts evaluation; police training; AIDS/HIV education; research on youth; funding and contracting of social research, higher education research, disaffected pupils and curriculums; research/evaluation of nurse, midwife and GP education.

Museum or gallery collection, archive, or library special collection:
Archive of major research and curriculum development projects

Printed publications:
CARE publications on methodology
Monographs (24 titles published commercially)
Prospectus
Research and Evaluation Reports (40 titles)

Publications list:
Available in print

Access to staff:
Contact by e-mail
Hours: Mon to Fri, 0900 to 1700

CENTRE FOR ARMENIAN INFORMATION AND ADVICE

Hayashen, 105A Mill Hill Road, London, W3 8J

Tel: 020 8992 4621
Fax: 020 8993 8953
E-mail: info@caia.org.uk

Website:
http://www.caia.org.uk

Founded:
1986

Organisation type and purpose:
To enhance the quality of life for disadvantaged members of the Armenian community in London, specifically those in poverty and isolation, through the provision of welfare, educational and cultural services.
To promote understanding of the Armenian heritage, history and culture among the Armenian community and the wider public.
Registered charity (charity number 1088534)

Printed publications:
Armenian Voice (4 times a year, in English and Armenian)

Access to staff:
Contact by letter, by telephone, by fax, by e-mail and via website. Appointment necessary.
Hours: Mon to Fri, 0900 to 1600 (phone for appointment)

CENTRE FOR BUCKINGHAMSHIRE STUDIES

County Hall, Aylesbury, Buckinghamshire, HP20 1UU

Tel: 01296 382587 (Archives); 01296 382250 (Local Studies)
Fax: 01296 382771
E-mail: archives@buckscc.gov.uk; localstudies@buckscc.gov.uk

Website:
http://www.buckscc.gov.uk/archives
Introductory information, family history information, conservation leaflet, internet links, list of newspapers, house history information.
http://www.buckscc.gov.uk (click on P in A-Z index, then Photographs of Buckinghamshire)
Database for images of over 20,000 photographs.
http://www.nationalarchives.gov.uk/a2a
Many of the Centre's archive catalogues are available online on the Access to Archives website.
http://www.buckscc.gov.uk/libraries
Much Local Studies Library stock is in the main Library catalogue.

Enquiries:
Enquiries to: Archivist

Founded:
1938

Formerly called:
Buckinghamshire Record Office (year of change 1997); Buckinghamshire Records and Local Studies Service (year of change 2002)

Organisation type and purpose:
Local government body.

Subject coverage:
Local authority records, including Buckinghamshire Quarter Sessions (from1678) and County Council (from 1889), Church of England parish records, also records of non-conformist churches, records of Archdeaconry of Buckinghamshire (including wills 1483–1858) etc., family and estate records, business records.

Museum or gallery collection, archive, or library special collection:
Microfiche copies of National Probate Index, 1858–1943
Microfiche copies of General Register Office index to births, deaths and marriages, 1837–2004
Microfilm copies of most of the Buckinghamshire Parish Registers held in the archives are available in the Local Studies Library

Non-library collection catalogue:
All or part available online

Library catalogue:
All or part available online and in-house

Printed publications:
Newsletter (4 times a year)
The Buckinghamshire Sheriffs (992–1992) (Hanley H. A., 1992)
Leaflets:
Your County Archives
Genealogical Sources

Local History Sources
Public House History Sources
How to Care for Your Family Archives

Publications list:
Available online and in print

Access to staff:
Contact by letter, by telephone, by fax, by e-mail, in person and via website
Hours: Tue, Wed and Fri, 0900 to 1730; Thu 0900 to 2000; Sat, 0900 to 1600.
(Archive Searchroom closes Tue to Fri, 1715; Sat, 1545)
Special comments: CARN Readers Ticket required for archive searchroom; can be issued on presentation of proof of identity, name, address, signature.
A reservation is strongly advised for a microfilm/microfiche reader in the Local Studies Library and for a seat in the archive searchroom.

Access for disabled people:
Ramped entry, toilet facilities
Special comments: Access to all public areas.

Parent body:
Culture and Learning Service of Buckinghamshire County Council

CENTRE FOR BUSINESS AND PUBLIC SECTOR ETHICS

Acronym or abbreviation: CBPSE

Suite 131, 23 King Street, Cambridge, CB1 1AH

Tel: 01954 710086
Fax: 01954 710103
E-mail: info@ethicscentre.org

Website:
http://www.ethicscentre.org
http://www.ethicspress.com

Enquiries:
Enquiries to: Director

Founded:
1988

Organisation type and purpose:
International organisation, registered charity (charity number 1045986), training organisation, consultancy, research institute, publishing house.

Subject coverage:
Business ethics, corporate governance, government and political ethics, corporate and social responsibility, ethical systems, ethical audit, public administration and policy, environmental ethics, sustainable development, anti-corruption.

Non-library collection catalogue:
All or part available online and in print

Library catalogue:
All or part available online and in print

Printed publications:
See http://www.ethicspress.com
Business Ethics
Environmental Ethics
Espionage and Secrecy
Government Ethics
The British Philosophy of Administration
Ethics and Anti-corruption

Publications list:
Available online and in print

Access to staff:
Contact by letter, by telephone, by fax, by e-mail and via website. Appointment necessary.
Hours: Mon to Fri, 0900 to 1700

Access to building, collection or gallery:
No access other than to staff

Also at:
Centre for Business and Public Sector Ethics
St Andrew's Castle, St Andrew's Street South, Bury St Edmunds, IP33 3PH; tel: 01954 710086; fax: 01954 710103; e-mail: info@ethicscentre.org

CENTRE FOR CELL & TISSUE RESEARCH

Acronym or abbreviation: CCTR

Department of Biology, University of York, PO Box 373, York, YO10 5YW

Tel: 01904 432936
Fax: 01904 432936
E-mail: cmj4@york.ac.uk

Enquiries:
Enquiries to: Marketing Coordinator
Other contacts: Director

Founded:
1981

Organisation type and purpose:
University department or institute.
Commercial Unit.
The development and use of equipment.

Subject coverage:
Low temperature preparation techniques for electron microscopy, rapid freezing, cryo-sem, cryo ultra-microtomy freeze fracture for transmission electron microscopy, freeze-etching, low temperature embedding.

Access to staff:
Contact by letter, by telephone, by fax and by e-mail
Hours: Mon to Fri, 0900 to 1700

CENTRE FOR CLASSICAL HOMOEOPATHY

Homoeopathy Clinic, 2a Meal Market, Hexham, Northumberland, NE46

Tel: 01434 322084
E-mail: francishannon@hotmail.com

Website:
http://www.hompath.club24.co.uk
Introduction to Principal and information about service and email address.
http://www.yell.co.uk/sites/homeopathy
Addresses and telephone numbers of clinics.

Enquiries:
Enquiries to: Director

Founded:
1979

Formerly called:
Hannon Clinic of Natural Medicine

Organisation type and purpose:
Service industry, consultancy. To treat sick people by means of homoeopathic medicine. Specialising in chronic diseases such as arthritis, asthma, eczema and psoriasis.

Subject coverage:
Treatment of chronic diseases by means of homoeopathic medicine.

Printed publications:
Brief Introduction to Homeopathy (leaflet)
Guide to Self-help with Homeopathy (leaflet)

Access to staff:
Contact by letter, by telephone, by e-mail and via website. Appointment necessary.
Hours: Mon to Fri, 0900 to 1700

Also at:
Homoeopathy Clinic
Lindisfarne, 71 Westgate Road, Newcastle Upon Tyne
Homoeopathy Clinic
1 Red Gables, Chatsworth Road, Carlisle, CA1

CENTRE FOR COACHING

156 Westcombe Hill, London, SE3 7DH

Tel: 0845 680 2065
E-mail: admin@centreforcoaching.com

Website:
http://www.centreforcoaching.com

Details of accredited training courses, services, consultancy and products.

Enquiries:
Enquiries to: Director

Founded:
2001

Organisation type and purpose:
Training organisation, consultancy, research organisation.

Subject coverage:
Coaching, life coaching, performance coaching, business coaching, executive coaching, stress management coaching, health coaching, psychological coaching, cognitive coaching, training.

Non-library collection catalogue:
All or part available online

Printed publications:
Life Coaching: A Cognitive Behavioural Approach
Handbook of Coaching Psychology
Dealing with People Problems at Work
Conquer Your Stress
Creating a Balance: Managing Stress

Electronic and video publications:
Articles available online

Publications list:
Available online

Access to staff:
Contact by letter, by telephone and by e-mail.
Appointment necessary.
Hours: Mon to Fri, 1000 to 1700

Links with:
Centre for Stress Management
156 Westcombe Hill, London, SE3 7DH

Member organisation of:
Association for Coaching

CENTRE FOR COMBUSTION AND ENERGY STUDIES

University of Leeds, Leeds, West Yorkshire, LS2 9JT

Tel: 0113 343 2498
Fax: 0113 244 0572

Website:
http://www.mech-eng.leeds.ac.uk/cces/ce.html

Enquiries:
Enquiries to: Deputy Director
Direct tel: 0113 343 2108
Direct fax: 0113 242 4611
Direct e-mail: comb-energy@mech-eng.leeds.ac.uk

Organisation type and purpose:
University department or institute, consultancy, research organisation.
Consortium of University Departments of Chemistry, Fuel and Energy Engineering and Mechanical Engineering.

Subject coverage:
Combustion; fundamentals and applications in engines, furnaces, power generation; flames; control and diagnostics; heat transfer; pollution emission control; energy; analysis, conservation, cogeneration; alternative sources; fuels; analysis, reserves, conversion technologies; fire and explosion hazards.

Printed publications:
Research Project Summaries
Short Course Information (2 times a year)
Specialist MSC Course brochures

Access to staff:
Contact by letter, by telephone and by e-mail
Hours: Mon to Fri, 0900 to 1700

Access for disabled people:
Access to all public areas

CENTRE FOR COMPLEMENTARY AND INTEGRATED MEDICINE

56 Bedford Place, Southampton, SO15 2DT

Tel: 023 8033 4752
Fax: 023 8023 1835
E-mail: info@complemed.co.uk

Website:
http://www.complemed.co.uk
Services the centre provides.

Enquiries:
Enquiries to: Manager

Founded:
1982

Organisation type and purpose:
Service industry, training organisation, research organisation.
Medical Practice.
To provide services, planning and research within complementary medicine.

Subject coverage:
A multi-disciplinary, medically based clinical practice within the field of complementary medicine encompassing training and research in homoeopathy, osteopathy, acupuncture, environmental medicine, clinical ecology (food and chemical sensitivity).

Printed publications:
Books of interest to doctors and therapists including:
Modern Chinese Acupuncture (a review, Lewith G and N, £12.99)
Books of interest to the lay public including:
Allergy and intolerance (Lewith G et al, £8.99)

Publications list:
Available in print

Access to staff:
Contact by letter, by telephone, by fax and via website
Hours: Mon to Thu, 0900 to 1300

Also at:
21 Harcourt House, 19 Cavendish Square, London W1G 0PL; tel: 020 7935 7848

CENTRE FOR COMPOSITE MATERIALS

Imperial College of Science, Technology and Medicine, Prince Consort Road, London, SW7 2BY

Tel: 020 7594 5084
Fax: 020 7594 5083
E-mail: composites@ic.ac.uk

Website:
http://www.cm.ic.ac.uk
General.

Enquiries:
Enquiries to: Director

Founded:
1983

Organisation type and purpose:
University department or institute.
MSc in composite materials, research degrees, contract research and testing for industry.

Subject coverage:
Testing, characterisation, design, mathematical modelling of fibre-reinforced plastics, metals and ceramics.

Printed publications:
Annual Report
Newsletter (2 times a year)
Post-experience courses (annually)
Postgraduate research brochure (annually)

Access to staff:
Contact by letter, by telephone, by fax and by e-mail. Appointment necessary.
Hours: Mon to Fri, 0900 to 1700

CENTRE FOR CONSERVATION STUDIES

Department of Archaeology, University of York, The Kings Manor, York, YO1 7EP

Tel: 01904 433997
Fax: 01904 433902
E-mail: pab11@york.ac.uk

Website:
http://www.york.ac.uk/depts/arch
Information on the department, research, staff, CPD courses.

Enquiries:
Enquiries to: Postgraduate Administrator

Created by the merger of:
Institute of Advanced Architectural Studies (IAAS), Institute of Advanced Architectural Studies Centre for the Conservation of Parks and Gardens (year of change 1997)

Organisation type and purpose:
University department or institute, suitable for ages: 18+.
Award of MA and DPhil degrees. Short courses open to the public.

Subject coverage:
Architectural conservation, cultural heritage management, landscape studies.

Museum or gallery collection, archive, or library special collection:
Library housed at the Kings Manor Library, University of York

Library catalogue:
All or part available online

Publications list:
Available in print

Access to staff:
Contact by letter, by telephone, by fax, by e-mail, in person and via website. Appointment necessary.
Hours: Mon to Fri, 0900 to 1700

Access to building, collection or gallery:
No access other than to staff
Hours: Mon to Fri, 0900 to 1700
Special comments: Borrowing restricted to university members and subscribers, but access is free.

CENTRE FOR CONTEMPORARY ART AND THE NATURAL WORLD

Acronym or abbreviation: CCANW

Haldon Forest Park, Exeter, Devon, EX6 7XR

Tel: 01392 832277
E-mail: info@ccanw.co.uk

Website:
http://www.ccanw.co.uk

Founded:
2001

Organisation type and purpose:
A registered limited company (no. 4141506) and registered charity (no. 1092019), seeking to increase access to the arts by breaking down physical, psychological and intellectual barriers, while working with different communities, embracing cultural diversity and social inclusion.

Subject coverage:
Man's artistic relationship with the natural world.

CENTRE FOR CONTEMPORARY ARTS

Acronym or abbreviation: CCA

350 Sauchiehall Street, Glasgow, G2 3JD

Tel: 0141 332 7521
Fax: 0141 332 3226
E-mail: gen@cca-glasgow.com

Website:
http://www.cca-glasgow.com

Enquiries:
Enquiries to: Head of Administration & Resources

Founded:
1993

Organisation type and purpose:
Voluntary organisation, registered charity, art gallery.
Arts centre.
To support artists in making possible the creation of original works, increasing the accessibility and strengthening the understanding of contemporary arts through a range of activities including talks, tours, writers' events, classes and workshops.

Subject coverage:
Contemporary visual and performing arts especially in Scotland.

Printed publications:
Catalogues for CCA commissioned or joint commissioned exhibitions 1993–1998

Publications list:
Available in print

Access to staff:
Contact by telephone and by e-mail
Hours: Mon to Fri, 0900 to 1700

Access for disabled people:
Access to all public areas

CENTRE FOR CONTEMPORARY BRITISH HISTORY

Acronym or abbreviation: CCBH

K.6.52, King's College London, Strand, London, WC2R 2LS

Tel: 020 7836 5454 ext. 7045
E-mail: virginia.preston@kcl.ac.uk

Website:
http://www.ccbh.ac.uk

Founded:
1986

Formerly called:
Institute of Contemporary British History

Organisation type and purpose:
University department or institute, age range: higher, research organisation, publishing house.

Subject coverage:
British history since 1945, oral history, information about research and scholars in these fields both in the UK and overseas, Conservative Party in the 20th century, Labour Party in the 20th century, current affairs (political), political economy.

Printed publications:
Edited volumes and monographs
Modern History Review (quarterly)
13 Witness Seminar transcriptions published in hard copy and online, including:
Britain and Europe
Development of Concord
1967 Abortion Act
Rhodesian UDI

Publications list:
Available in print

Access to staff:
Contact by letter, by telephone, by fax, by e-mail and via website. Appointment necessary.

CENTRE FOR COUPLE RELATIONSHIPS

Acronym or abbreviation: TCCR

Tavistock Centre, 120 Belsize Lane, London, NW3 5BA

Tel: 020 8938 2353
Fax: 020 7435 1080
E-mail: tccr@tccr.org.uk

Website:
http://www.tccr.org.uk

Enquiries:
Enquiries to: Information Officer
Other contacts: Director

Founded:
1948

Organisation type and purpose:
Voluntary organisation, registered charity (charity number 211058), training organisation, consultancy, research organisation.
Psychotherapy Organisation working nationally and internationally; learned institute concerned with the couple relationship.

Subject coverage:
Training, consultancy and research organisation offering psychotherapy to couples, teaching, training and consultancy to other practitioners working with couples, research. Areas of particular interest: couple psychotherapy, divorce, infertility, unemployment, family transitions, divorce court welfare, mediation, inter-agency collaboration.

Printed publications:
Annual Report
In Brief (newsletter, annually)
Training Prospectus (annually)
In House publications include:
Brief Casework with a Marital Problem (Guthrie L and Mattinson J, 1975, £4.50, ISBN: 901882–03–8)
Marital Interaction and Some Illnesses in Children (Mainprice J, 1977, £4.50, ISBN: 901882–09–7)
The Reflection Process in Casework Supervision (Mattison J, 2nd ed 1991)
Marriage and Mental Handicap (Mattison J, 1975, £9.50, ISBN: 90188212–7)
Mate and Stalemate: Working with Marital Problems in a Social Services Department (Mattinson J and Sinclair I, 1981, £9.50 ISBN 0–901882–16-X)
Shared Fantasy in Marital Problems (Bannister K and Pincus L, 1975, £4.50)
Staff Supervision in a Turbulent Environment (Hughes L and Pengelly P, 2nd ed. 1991 £14.95)
Order printed publications from: Karnac (Books) Ltd 58 Gloucester Road, London, SW7 4DQ, tel: 020 7584 3303, fax: 020 7823 7743

Electronic and video publications:
Teaching videos

Publications list:
Available online and in print

Access to staff:
Contact by letter, by telephone, by fax, by e-mail and via website. Appointment necessary.
Hours: Mon to Fri, 0900 to 1700

Member of:
International Union of Family Organisations
United Kingdom Council for Psychotherapy

Parent body:
Tavistock Institute of Medical Psychology

CENTRE FOR CRIME AND JUSTICE STUDIES

Acronym or abbreviation: CCJS

King's College London, Strand, WC2R 2LS

Tel: 020 7848 1688
Fax: 020 7848 1689
E-mail: info@crimeandjustice.org.uk

Website:
http://www.kcl.ac.uk/ccjs
http://www.crimeinfo.org
http://www.kcl.ac.uk/istd

Enquiries:
Enquiries to: Director
Other contacts: Research and Development Officer

Founded:
1931

Formerly called:
Institute for the Study and Treatment of Delinquency (ISTD)

continued overleaf

Organisation type and purpose:
Membership association (membership is by subscription), present number of members: 926, voluntary organisation, registered charity (charity number 251588), research organisation.
To promote the exchange of knowledge, experience and understanding of criminal justice matters among interested individuals and to provide an independent, objective and non-campaigning forum for debate.

Subject coverage:
Criminology, criminal justice, delinquency.

Museum or gallery collection, archive, or library special collection:
The E T Jensen Library (over 2000 volumes on Criminology) now in the King's College Library

Printed publications:
Annual Report
British Journal of Criminology (quarterly, pub. OUP)
Conference Reports (for sale)
Criminal Justice Matters (newsletter, quarterly)
Occasional papers (for sale)

Publications list:
Available online and in print

Access to staff:
Contact by letter, by telephone, by fax, by e-mail and via website
Hours: Mon to Fri, 0900 to 1700

CENTRE FOR CRIMINOLOGY

Formal name: The Centre for Criminology
Acronym or abbreviation: CCR

Manor Road Building, Manor Road, Oxford, OX1 3UQ

Tel: 01865 274444/8
Fax: 01865 281924
E-mail: ccr@crim.ox.ac.uk

Website:
http://www.crim.ox.ac.uk
Information about CCR, its research activities, staff, visiting academics and graduate programmes.
http://www.lib.ox.ac.uk/olis
University of Oxford's online union library catalogue.

Enquiries:
Enquiries to: Administrator

Founded:
1996

Formerly called:
Penal Research Unit (year of change 1973); The Centre for Criminological Research and Probation Studies Unit (year of change 2004)

Organisation type and purpose:
University department or institute, research organisation.
Research centre. Provider of graduate programmes at Master's and DPhil level

Subject coverage:
Policing and security; sentencing and punishment; public opinion, politics and crime control; victims; extra-legal governance and organized crime, and crime, rehabilitation and desistance.

Printed publications:
Meeting Expectations. The Application of Restorative Justice to the Police Complaints Process (Hill R, Cooper K, Young R and Hoyle C, 2003, Occasional Paper No.21, £14.50)
Introducing Restorative Justice to the Police Complaints System: Close Encounters of the Rare Kind (Hill R, Cooper K, Hoyle C and Young R, 2003, Occasional Paper No.20, £10)
The Changing Face of Crime and Criminal Policy in Europe (Hood R and Courakis N E (eds), 1999, Occasional Paper No.19, £14.50)
Bullying in Prisons (O'Donnell I and Edgar K, 1998, Occasional Paper No.18, £15.50)

The Changing Face of Crime and Criminal Policy in Europe (Hood R and Courakis N E eds, 1999, £10)
Victims with Learning Disabilities: Negotiating the Criminal Justice System (Sanders A et al, 1997, Occasional Paper No.17, £14.50)
Paroling with New Criteria: Evaluating the Impact and Effects of Changes in the Parole System: Phase Two (Hood R and Shute S, 1995, Occasional Paper No.16, £10.50)
Armed Robbery: A Study in London (Morrison S and O'Donnell I, 1994, Occasional Paper No.15, £5)
Reported and Unreported Racial Incidents in Prisons (Burnett R and Farrell G, 1994, Occasional Paper No.14, £12.50)
Parole in Transition: Evaluating the Impact and Effects of Changes in the Parole System: Phase One, Establishing the Base-Line (Hood R and Shute S, 1994, Occasional Paper No.13, £10)
Probation Partnerships. A Study of Roles, Relationships and Meanings (Gibbs A, 1998, Occasional Paper Nr.7, £12.50)
New Politics, New Probation? Proceedings of the Probation Studies Unit Second Colloquium (Faulkner D and Gibbs A (eds), 1998, Occasional Paper No.6, £15.50)
Increasing the Employability of Offenders. An enquiry into Probation Service Effectiveness (Bridges A, 1998, Occasional Paper No.5, £10)
Straight Thinking on Probation (STOP): The Mid Glamorgan Experiment (Raynor P and Vanstone M, 1997, Occasional Paper No.4, £12.50)
The Probation Service: Responding to Change. Proceedings of the Probation Studies Unit First Colloquium (Burnett R (ed), 1997, Occasional Paper No.3, £15.50)
Victim-Offender Mediation: Limitations and Potential (Robinson G, 1996, Occasional Paper No.2, £10)
A System for Evaluating Probation Practice. Report of a method devised and piloted by the Oxford Probation Studies Unit and Warwickshire Probation Service (Roberts C, Burnett R, Kirby A and Hamill H, 1996, Occasional Paper No.1, £12.50)

Access to staff:
Contact by letter, by telephone, by fax, by e-mail and via website. Appointment necessary.
Hours: Mon to Fri, 0915 to 1700

Access to building, collection or gallery:
Please arrange appointment in advance
Hours: Mon to Fri, 0900 to 1700
Special comments: University card required.

Access for disabled people:
Please arrange appointment in advance
Hours: Mon to Fri, 0900 to 1700
Special comments: University card required.

CENTRE FOR DEAF EDUCATION

Acronym or abbreviation: CfDE

City Lit, Keeley Street, Covent Garden, London, WC2B 4BA

Tel: 020 7492 2725; minicom 020 7492 2746
Fax: 020 7492 2745
E-mail: deafedu@citylit.ac.uk

Website:
http://www.citylit.ac.uk

Enquiries:
Enquiries to: Head of Centre
Other contacts: Centre Administrator and Centre Co-ordinators

Formerly called:
Central London AEI Centre for the Deaf; Deaf Education and Learning Support (year of change 2010)

Please select:

Organisation type and purpose:
Professional body, suitable for ages: 18+, training organisation.
Academic institution, formerly under the Inner London Education Authority.

Subject coverage:
Training, courses and support for deaf people and for those wishing to work with deaf people. Provides support for deaf students in over 30 further education and higher education colleges.

Library catalogue:
All or part available in-house

Printed publications:
Prospectus
Course leaflets
Start to Sign books
Books on wordprocessing, writing CVs

Publications list:
Available online

Access to staff:
Contact by letter, by telephone, by fax and by e-mail. Appointment necessary.
Hours: Mon to Fri, 0900 to 1700

Access to building, collection or gallery:
No prior appointment required

Access for disabled people:
Street-level entry, toilet facilities

CENTRE FOR DEFENCE AND INTERNATIONAL SECURITY STUDIES

Acronym or abbreviation: CDISS

Cartmel College, University of Lancaster, Bailrigg, Lancaster, LA1 4YL

Tel: 01524 594254
Fax: 01524 594258
E-mail: cdiss@lancaster.ac.uk

Website:
http://www.cdiss.org
CDISS Research Programme, 450 pages on Ballistic Missile Defence, details of all CDISS publications.

Enquiries:
Enquiries to: Executive Secretary
Direct e-mail: p.elliott@lancaster.ac.uk
Other contacts: Director

Founded:
1990

Formed by the merger of:
Centre for Defence and Security Analysis (CDSA), Centre for the Study of Arms Control and International Security (CSACIS) (year of change 1990)

Organisation type and purpose:
Membership association (membership is by election or invitation), present number of members: 54, university department or institute, research organisation.

Subject coverage:
Ballistic missile defence; defence management; civil-military relations; military technology; maritime and naval policy.

Museum or gallery collection, archive, or library special collection:
150+ Defence Journal Titles 1983–1999 as Abstracts and indexed in The Lancaster Index

Non-library collection catalogue:
All or part available online and in print

Library catalogue:
All or part available in-house

Printed publications:
Bailrigg Debating Points
Bailrigg Memoranda
Bailrigg Papers including:
Future Conditional: War & Conflict after Next (ed Edmonds M, 2002, £15)
Bailrigg Studies including:
Landmarks in Defense Literature (Edmunds M and Gray B, 2001 £9.95)
100 Years of the Trade. RN Submarines: Past, Present & Future (ed Edmonds M, 2001, £25)
Defense & Security Analysis

Electronic and video publications:
Lancaster Index (CD-ROM for purchase with the
  search programme (Windows format))

Publications list:
Available in print

Access to staff:
Contact by letter, by telephone, by fax, by e-mail
and via website
Hours: Mon to Fri, 0900 to 1700

Access to building, collection or gallery:
No access other than to staff
Hours: University Library: 0900 to 2100 term time
Special comments: Permission required.

Connections with:
ANEPE
  Santiago, Chile
CERSA Toulouse University
CISSM Maryland University
Defence Research Centre
  Tokyo, Japan
SIIA
  Johannesburg, South Africa

CENTRE FOR DEVELOPMENT STUDIES

Acronym or abbreviation: CDS

University of Wales, Swansea, Singleton Park,
Swansea, West Glamorgan, SA2 8PP

Tel: 01792 295332
Fax: 01792 295682
E-mail: h.lewis@swansea.ac.uk

Website:
http://www.swan.ac.uk/cds/index.htm
http://www.swan.ac.uk/cds/devres/index.htm
For publications.

Enquiries:
Enquiries to: Admissions Secretary

Founded:
1976

Organisation type and purpose:
International organisation, university department
or institute, training organisation, consultancy,
research organisation, publishing house.

Subject coverage:
Development planning, in particular social
development; monitoring, evaluation and impact
assessment; development policy; regional
development; rights-based approaches;
development management; environmental
planning; population and development;
participatory development; health planning; sexual
and reproductive health; crime and justice systems;
children's rights; governance; poverty reduction;
sustainable livelihoods; corporate social
responsibility.

Printed publications:
CDS Prospectus
Papers in International Development
Resources in Social Development Practice
Research Issues in Natural Resource Management

Publications list:
Available online and in print

Access to staff:
Contact by letter, by telephone, by fax, by e-mail,
in person and via website. Appointment necessary.
Hours: Mon to Fri, 0900 to 1700

Links with:
Resource Centre for Department for International
Development, in the fields of social development,
health and population

CENTRE FOR ECOLOGY AND HYDROLOGY

Acronym or abbreviation: CEH

Maclean Building, Crowmarsh Gifford,
Wallingford, Oxfordshire, OX10 8BB

Tel: 01491 838800
Fax: 01491 692424
E-mail: wllibrary@ceh.ac.uk

Website:
http://www.ceh.ac.uk
CEH homepage.
http://cehlib.ceh.ac.uk/olibcgi
On-line library catalogue.
http://www.ceh.ac.uk/library/index.html
CEH Library Service homepage.

Enquiries:
Enquiries to: Librarian

Founded:
1962

Formerly called:
Institute of Hydrology (IH) (year of change 2000)

Organisation type and purpose:
Research organisation.

Subject coverage:
Hydrology, ecology, biodiversity, biogeochemistry,
environmental science.

**Museum or gallery collection, archive, or library
special collection:**
Hurst Collection (Nile hydrology)
Rofe Collection (water legislation)

Library catalogue:
All or part available online

Printed publications:
One-off special publications, e.g. Flood Estimation
  Handbook
Further information available at the CEH website

Publications list:
Available online

Access to staff:
Appointment necessary.
Hours: Mon to Fri, 0900 to 1700

Houses the editorial office of the:
International Association of Hydrological Sciences

Parent body:
Natural Environment Research Council (NERC)

CENTRE FOR ECOLOGY AND HYDROLOGY – EDINBURGH RESEARCH STATION

Acronym or abbreviation: CEH

Bush Estate, Penicuik, Midlothian, EH26 0QB

Tel: 0131 445 4343
Fax: 0131 445 3943
E-mail: bulib@ceh.ac.uk

Website:
http://www.ceh.ac.uk
Comprehensive information on the work of the
Institute and its research stations, publications
lists.

Enquiries:
Enquiries to: Librarian
Direct tel: 0131 445 8509

Founded:
2000

Created by the merger of:
Institute of Freshwater Ecology (IFE), Institute of
Hydrology (IH), Institute of Terrestrial Ecology
(ITE), Institute of Virology and Environmental
Microbiology (IVEM) (year of change 2000)

Formerly a part of:
Nature Conservancy Council (year of change 1973)

Organisation type and purpose:
Research organisation.

Subject coverage:
Factors determining the structure, composition
and processes of terrestrial ecological systems and
the abundance and performance of individual
species and organisms, scientific bases for
predicting and modelling future environmental

trends, human impact, land use, conservation and
the protection and management of the
environment.

Library catalogue:
All or part available online

Printed publications:
Annual Report
Provisional atlases of the flora and fauna of Britain
  and Ireland
Research publications series (pub HMSO)
Symposium series (pub HMSO)
Order printed publications from: Publications Section,
CEH Wallingford, OX10 8BB

Access to staff:
Contact by letter, by telephone, by fax, by e-mail
and via website. Appointment necessary.
Hours: Mon to Fri, 0900 to 1700
Special comments: Researchers only.

Also at:
Bangor Research Unit
  Environment Centre for Wales, Deiniol Road,
  Bangor, Gwynedd, LL57 2UW; tel: 01248 374500
CEH Lancaster
  Lancaster Envionment Centre, Library Avenue,
  Bailrigg, LA1 4AP; tel: 01524 595906; fax: 01539
  534705
Centre for Ecology and Hydrology
  Maclean Building, Crowmarsh Gifford,
  Wallingford, Oxfordshire, OX10 8BB; tel: 01491
  838800

Parent body:
Natural Environment Research Council

CENTRE FOR ECOLOGY AND HYDROLOGY – MONKS WOOD

Acronym or abbreviation: CEH

Abbots Ripton, Huntingdon, Cambridgeshire,
PE28 2LS

Tel: 01487 772400
Fax: 01487 773467

Website:
http://www.ceh.ac.uk/html/unicorn.htm
Library catalogue

Enquiries:
Enquiries to: Librarian
Direct tel: 0131 445 8512
Direct fax: 0131 445 4343
Direct e-mail: sjpr@ceh.ac.uk

Founded:
2000

Formed from:
Institute of Freshwater Ecology (IFE), Institute of
Hydrology (IH), Institute of Terrestrial Ecology
(ITE), Institute of Virology and Environmental
Microbiology (IVEM) (year of change 2000)

Organisation type and purpose:
Research organisation.
One of the Centres and Surveys of the Natural
Environment Research Council. UK body for
research, survey and monitoring in terrestrial and
freshwater environments.

Subject coverage:
Environmental science, aquatic ecology, terrestrial
ecology, hydrology, microbiology, environmental
chemistry, hydrobiology.

**Museum or gallery collection, archive, or library
special collection:**
Various collections of original (unpublished) data

Library catalogue:
All or part available online

Publications list:
Available online

Access to staff:
Contact by letter, by telephone, by fax and by e-
mail. Appointment necessary.
Hours: Mon to Fri, 0900 to 1700

Access to building, collection or gallery:
Prior appointment required

continued overleaf

Special comments: Any bona fide researcher with a scientific not-for-profit research need which cannot easily be met through their own organisation's resources may use the libraries at the discretion of the Site Director

Access for disabled people:
Parking provided

Other addresses:
CEH Bangor
Orton Building, Bangor, Deiniol Road, Bangor, Gwynedd, LL57 2UP; tel: 01248 370045; fax: 01248 3553656; e-mail: bae@ceh.ac.uk
CEH Dorset
Winfrith Technology Centre, Dorchester, Dorset, DT2 8ZD; tel: 01305 213500; fax: 01305 213600
CEH Edinburgh
Bush Estate, Penicuik, Midlothian, EH26 0QB; tel: 0131 445 4343; fax: 0131 445 3943
CEH Lancaster
Lancaster Environment Centre, Library Avenue, Bailrigg, Lancaster, LA1 4AP; tel: 01524 595 800; fax: 01524 61536; e-mail: lanacaster@ceh.ac.uk
CEH Oxford
Mansfield Road, Oxford, OX1 3SR; tel: 01865 281630; fax: 01865 281696; e-mail: oxford -enquiries@ceh.ac.uk
CEH Wallingford
Maclean Building, Crowmarsh Gifford, Wallingford, Oxfordshire, OX10 8BB; tel: 01491 838800; fax: 01491 692424
CEU Banchory
Hill of Brathens, Banchory, Aberdeenshire, AB31 4BW; tel: 01330 826303; fax: 01330 823303

Parent body:
Natural Environment Research Council (NERC)
Polaris House, North Star Avenue, Swindon, SN2 1EY; tel: 01793 411500; fax: 01793 411501

CENTRE FOR ECONOMIC PERFORMANCE

Acronym or abbreviation: CEP

London School of Economics, Houghton Street, London, WC2A 2AE

Tel: 020 7955 7048
Fax: 020 7955 7595
E-mail: cep_info@lse.ac.uk

Website:
http://cep.lse.ac.uk
http://cep.lse.ac.uk/papers/
Publications list.

Enquiries:
Enquiries to: Administrator

Founded:
1990

Organisation type and purpose:
University department or institute, research organisation.
Researching the factors affecting the economic performance of nations and firms.

Subject coverage:
Economic aspects of the labour market, including employment, unemployment, inflation and income distribution; economics of education and human capital, economic growth, corporate performance, industrial relations, skills and job satisfaction, globalisation, internet economy, productivity and innovation, and wellbeing.

Library catalogue:
All or part available online

Publications list:
Available online and in print

Access to staff:
Contact by e-mail and via website
Hours: Mon to Fri, 0900 to 1700

Access to building, collection or gallery:
No access other than to staff

Access for disabled people:
Access to all public areas

Parent body:
London School of Economics (LSE)
Houghton Street, London, WC2A 2AE

CENTRE FOR ECONOMIC POLICY RESEARCH

Acronym or abbreviation: CEPR

90–98 Goswell Road, London, EC1V 7RR

Tel: 020 7878 2900
Fax: 020 7878 2999
E-mail: cepr@cepr.org

Website:
http://www.cepr.org

Enquiries:
Enquiries to: External Relations Manager

Founded:
1983

Organisation type and purpose:
Registered charity, research organisation.

Subject coverage:
Economic policy.

Printed publications:
Books
CEPR Bulletin (4 times a year)
CEPR Discussion Papers
Economic Policy (journal, 2 times a year)
European Economic Perspectives (newsletter, 6 times a year)
Order printed publications from: tel: 020 7878 2903, e-mail: orders@cepr.org

Publications list:
Available online and in print

Access to staff:
Contact by e-mail
Hours: Mon to Fri, 0900 to 1700

Links with:
Centre for Economic Policy Research International Foundation (US)

CENTRE FOR EFFECTIVE DISPUTE RESOLUTION

Acronym or abbreviation: CEDR

70 Fleet Street, London, EC4Y 1EU

Tel: 020 7536 6000
Fax: 020 7536 6001
E-mail: info@cedr.co.uk

Website:
http://www.cedr.co.uk

Enquiries:
Enquiries to: Administration Manager, Corporate Resources

Founded:
1990

Organisation type and purpose:
International organisation, advisory body, membership association (membership is by subscription), present number of members: 450, registered charity (charity number 106369), training organisation, consultancy, research organisation.
Experts in mediation and other forms of effective dispute resolution for commercial disputes.
CEDR is an independent organisation supported by industry and professional advisers and founded to promote and encourage more effective commercial resolution of disputes.

Subject coverage:
Alternative dispute resolution (ADR) information services and training, negotiating training, mediation and alternative dispute resolution techniques, mediation training for lawyers, UK and worldwide, commercial alternative dispute resolution services, extensive mediation and conflict resolution training.

Printed publications:
Booklets and research reports (annually)
Newsletter (quarterly)
International Mediation: the art of business diplomacy
Commercial Dispute Resolution – An ADR Practice Guide
Court Referred ADR – a guide for the judiciary
ADR for Corporate Counsel and Executives

Electronic and video publications:
CEDR ADR video

Publications list:
Available online and in print

Access to staff:
Contact by letter, by telephone, by fax, by e-mail, in person and via website. Appointment necessary.
Hours: Mon to Fri, 0900 to 1800

CENTRE FOR ENERGY, PETROLEUM AND MINERAL LAW AND POLICY

Acronym or abbreviation: CEPMLP

CEPMLP Information Service, Carnegie Building, Geddes Quadrangle, University of Dundee, Dundee, DD1 4HN

Tel: 01382 384302
Fax: 01382 385854
E-mail: r.m.carstairs@dundee.ac.uk

Website:
http://www.cepmlp.org

Enquiries:
Enquiries to: Information Services Manager
Direct e-mail: r.m.carstairs@dundee.ac.uk

Formerly called:
Centre for Petroleum and Mineral Law and Policy (CPMLP) (year of change 1997)

Organisation type and purpose:
University library, training organisation, consultancy, research organisation, publishing house.

Subject coverage:
Oil and gas law, policy and economics; mineral law, policy and economics; natural resources law, policy and economics; environmental law and policy.

Education services:
Access given to external research scholars, but by prior arrangement only.

Museum or gallery collection, archive, or library special collection:
Petroleum, mining and environmental laws, worldwide
Contracts and agreements collection

Library catalogue:
All or part available online and in-house

Printed publications:
Books
Conference Proceedings
Professional Papers Series
Seminar Papers Series

Electronic and video publications:
DVD available
Order electronic and video publications from: Online store

Publications list:
Available online and in print

Access to staff:
Contact by letter, by telephone, by fax, by e-mail, in person and via website. Appointment necessary. Non-members charged.
Hours: Mon to Fri, 0930 to 1230 and 1400 to 1700

CENTRE FOR ENGLISH LANGUAGE TEACHING

Acronym or abbreviation: CELT

Airthrey Castle, University of Stirling, Stirling, FK9 4LA

Tel: 01786 467934
Fax: 01786 466131
E-mail: celt@stir.ac.uk

Website:
http://www.celt.stir.ac.uk/
CELT course information.

Enquiries:
Enquiries to: Associate Director
Other contacts: Director

Founded:
1981

Organisation type and purpose:
University department or institute.
Provides English language courses for non-native speakers of English.

Subject coverage:
Courses in English as a foreign language lasting from 4 weeks to 3 years for anyone over the age of 17; courses in the teaching of English as a foreign language.

Printed publications:
Full publicity material on all courses prepared each November and available throughout the year to enquirers

Access to staff:
Contact by letter, by telephone, by fax, by e-mail and via website
Hours: Mon to Fri, 0900 to 1700

CENTRE FOR ENVIRONMENT, FISHERIES AND AQUACULTURE SCIENCE, THE

Acronym or abbreviation: Cefas

Lowestoft Laboratory, Lowestoft, Suffolk, NR33 0HT

Tel: 01502 562244
Fax: 01502 524525
E-mail: lowlibrary@cefas.co.uk

Website:
http://www.cefas.co.uk

Enquiries:
Enquiries to: Librarian

Organisation type and purpose:
National government body.
Main Cefas laboratory.

Subject coverage:
Fisheries, fishing and aquatic environmental research; marine biology; oceanography; aquaculture; marine pollution; fish diseases; marine radiobiology.

Printed publications:
Annual Report
Shellfish News
Trout News
Order printed publications from: tel: 01502 524380, fax: 01502 542525, e-mail: lowlibrary@cefas.co.uk

Publications list:
Available online and in print

Access to staff:
Contact by letter, by telephone, by fax and by e-mail. Appointment necessary.
Hours: Mon to Thu, 0900 to 1700; Fri, 0900 to 1600

Access to building, collection or gallery:
No access other than to staff

Access for disabled people:
Parking provided, ramped entry, toilet facilities

Also at:
Cefas Weymouth Laboratory
  Barrack Road, The Nothe, Weymouth, Dorset, DT4 8UB; tel: 01305 206600; e-mail: weylibrary@cefas.co.uk

Constituent part of:
Department for Environment, Food and Rural Affairs (DEFRA)

CENTRE FOR ENVIRONMENTAL DATA AND RECORDING

Acronym or abbreviation: CEDaR

National Museums Northern Ireland, 153 Bangor Road, Cultra, Holywood, County Down, Northern Ireland

Tel: 028 9039 5256
E-mail: damian.mcferran@nmni.com

Website:
http://www.nmni.com/cedar

Enquiries:
Enquiries to: Records Centre Manager

Organisation type and purpose:
National government body, museum, university department or institute, research organisation.
Funded by Northern Ireland Environment Agency (NIEA) and funding in-kind from NMNI.

Subject coverage:
Natural history, flora and fauna, and geology of Northern Ireland and its coastal waters.

Museum or gallery collection, archive, or library special collection:
Databases of the location, date, vice-county, recorder, species and grid reference
Over 200,000 local natural history records
Over 1m. species and site records

Non-library collection catalogue:
All or part available in-house

Library catalogue:
All or part available in-house

Access to staff:
Contact by letter, by telephone, by fax, by e-mail and via website. Appointment necessary.
Hours: Mon to Fri, 0900 to 1700

Access to building, collection or gallery:
Prior appointment required

CENTRE FOR ENVIRONMENTAL INITIATIVES

Acronym or abbreviation: The CEI

Old School House, Mill Lane, Carshalton, Surrey, SM5 2JY

Tel: 020 8770 6611
Fax: 020 8647 0719
E-mail: info@ecolocal.org.uk

Website:
http://www.thecei.org.uk
Newsletters, reports and community projects.

Enquiries:
Enquiries to: Director

Founded:
1987

Formerly called:
Centre for Environmental Information (year of change 1993)

Organisation type and purpose:
Voluntary organisation, registered charity (charity number 800377), suitable for ages: all, training organisation, consultancy, research organisation.
Local agenda 21, sustainable development, community involvement in sustainability.
The CEI's aim's to achieve and sustain strong, vibrant communities within a healthy environment.

Subject coverage:
Local agenda 21, sustainable development, community involvement and participation in sustainable development, community consultation techniques.

Printed publications:
Available for purchase directly

Publications list:
Available in print

Access to staff:
Contact by letter. Appointment necessary.

Hours: Mon to Fri, 1000 to 1630
Special comments: Building accessible to the disabled, but there are no disabled toilets.

Access to building, collection or gallery:
Prior appointment required
Hours: Mon to Fri, 1000 to 1630

CENTRE FOR ENVIRONMENTALLY RESPONSIBLE TOURISM

PO Box 14, Benfleet, Essex, SS7 3LW

Tel: 01268 752827
Fax: 0870 139 2802
E-mail: cert.desk@virgin.net

Enquiries:
Enquiries to: Chief Executive

Founded:
1994

Organisation type and purpose:
International organisation (membership is by subscription), voluntary organisation.

Access to staff:
Contact by e-mail
Hours: Mon to Fri, 0900 to 1700

Access to building, collection or gallery:
No access other than to staff

CENTRE FOR EPIDEMIOLOGY AND HEALTH SERVICES RESEARCH

Formal name: Centre for Epidemiological Research CER
Acronym or abbreviation: CEHSR

Brunel University, School of Health Sciences and Social Care, Mary Seacole Building (Room 301B), Uxbridge, Middlesex, UB8 3PH

Tel: 01895 268818
Fax: 01895 269853

Website:
http://www.brunel.ac.uk/research/centres/cehsr

Enquiries:
Enquiries to: Centre Director
Direct tel: 01895 268759
Direct e-mail: alex.farrow@brunel.ac.uk
Other contacts: Senior Investigator

Founded:
1992

Formerly called:
Centre for Evaluation Research (CER) (year of change 1992)

Organisation type and purpose:
Professional body (membership is by subscription), university department or institute, consultancy, research organisation.
To undertake evaluative research in the field of healthcare and welfare.

Subject coverage:
Evaluation research investigating the quality and effectiveness of health and welfare (including education and training) services; includes methods and techniques of evaluation and quality assurance.

Printed publications:
Welfare or Welfare State (Marsland D, hardback, £45; paperback, £14.99)
Regular publications on research methods, social policy and evaluation studies

Publications list:
Available in print

Access to staff:
Contact by letter, by telephone and by e-mail.
Appointment necessary.
Hours: Mon to Fri, 0900 to 1700

Parent body:
Brunel University

CENTRE FOR EUROPEAN REFORM

Acronym or abbreviation: CER

14 Great College Street, Westminster, London, SW1P 3RX

Tel: 020 7233 1199
Fax: 020 7233 1117
E-mail: info@cer.org.uk

Website:
http://www.cer.org.uk

Organisation type and purpose:
Think tank. Discussion forum. Conducts research and seminars.

Subject coverage:
Political, economic and social challenges facing Europe. Pro-European but not uncritical.

Printed publications:
Longer publications, in a wide range of research topics, are available for purchase in hard copy format:
Reports
Working papers
Essays

Electronic and video publications:
All publications, in a wide range of research topics, are available for downloading from the website free of charge as PDF files

Publications list:
Available online

CENTRE FOR FACILITIES CONSULTANCY LIMITED

PO Box 7490, Chelmsford, CM2 8YW

Tel: 0870 607 0201
Fax: 01245 403 262
E-mail: centre@globalnet.co.uk

Website:
http://www.facilities-centre.com

Enquiries:
Enquiries to: Chairman
Other contacts: Office Manager for absence of the Chairman.

Founded:
1992

Organisation type and purpose:
Service industry, training organisation, consultancy.
Facilities management consulting and training.

Subject coverage:
All aspects of facilities management consultancy including strategic reviews, accommodation strategy, outsourcing, cost savings, business continuity, performance measurement, health and safety, skills training, specifications, impartial advice and information on facilities management in UK and overseas. Training in non-clinical aspects of NHS Trusts, eg: violence, aggression, quality aspects.

Printed publications:
UK FM Overview (newsletter)

Access to staff:
Contact by letter, by telephone, by fax, by e-mail and via website. Appointment necessary.
Hours: Mon to Fri, 0900 to 1700

Access for disabled people:
Access to all public areas

CENTRE FOR GLOBAL ENERGY STUDIES

Acronym or abbreviation: CGES

17 Knightsbridge, London, SW1X 7LY

Tel: 020 7235 4334
Fax: 020 7235 4338
E-mail: marketing@cges.co.uk

Website:
http://www.cges.co.uk

Enquiries:
Enquiries to: Marketing Manager
Direct tel: 020 7309 3610
Direct e-mail: jenni.wilson@cges.co.uk

Founded:
1990

Organisation type and purpose:
International organisation, research institute (oil and gas).

Subject coverage:
Oil market subscription reports, studies, special reports, events and oil market consulting.

Trade and statistical information:
Oil and gas/energy.

Printed publications:
Global Oil Report (6 times a year, annual subscription £1500)
Monthly Oil Report (market analysis and comment, monthly, annual subscription £500)
Special Reports on specific areas of oil and gas
Order printed publications from: website: http://www.cges.co.uk, e-mail: marketing @cges.co.uk

Publications list:
Available online and in print

Access to staff:
Contact by letter, by telephone, by fax, by e-mail and via website
Hours: Mon to Fri, 0930 to 1730

CENTRE FOR HEALTH ECONOMICS

Acronym or abbreviation: CHE

University of York, Heslington, York, YO10 5DD

Tel: 01904 433707
Fax: 01904 433644
E-mail: jmg1@york.ac.uk

Website:
http://www.york.ac.uk/inst/che/welcome.html
Descriptions of organisations and staff, projects, publications.

Enquiries:
Enquiries to: Information Service Manager
Direct e-mail: cheweb@york.ac.uk
Other contacts: Director for research opportunities.

Founded:
1983

Organisation type and purpose:
University department or institute, training organisation, research organisation.
Centre for research and training in the factors affecting the demand for and supply of health, and the consequences for the provision of care.

Subject coverage:
Health economics, health technology assessment, community care, economics of addiction, health services manpower, quality of life.

Museum or gallery collection, archive, or library special collection:
Health economics working papers

Library catalogue:
All or part available in-house

Printed publications:
Discussion Papers (over 100)
Occasional Papers
Technical Papers
Order printed publications from: Publications Office, Centre for Health Economics
at same address, tel: 01904 433648, fax: 01904 433644, e-mail: chepub@york.ac.uk

Publications list:
Available online and in print

Access to staff:
Contact by letter, by telephone, by fax, by e-mail and via website. Appointment necessary.

Hours: Mon to Fri, 0900 to 1700
Special comments: Closed 23 Dec to 2 Jan.

Connections with:
NHS Centre for Reviews and Dissemination (CRD)
tel: 01904 433707; fax: 01904 433661; e-mail: revdis@york.ac.uk

Parent body:
University of York
tel: 01904 430000; fax: 01904 433433

Part of:
Institute for Research into the Social Sciences (IRISS)
tel: 01904 433523; fax: 01904 433524

CENTRE FOR HEALTH INFORMATICS

Acronym or abbreviation: CHI

City University London, Northampton Square, London, EC1V 0HB

Tel: 020 7040 8367
Fax: 020 7040 8364
E-mail: a.v.roudsari@city.ac.uk

Website:
http://www.city.ac.uk/chi

Enquiries:
Enquiries to: Director

Founded:
1983

Formerly called:
Centre for Measurement and Information in Medicine (year of change 2005)

Organisation type and purpose:
University department or institute, research organisation.

Subject coverage:
e-health and telecare, high-dependency medicine and public health; decision support systems (including computer-aided learning); integrated policy modelling for ICT-enhanced public healthcare; healthcare technologies, with emphasis upon methodologies for assessment and evaluation.

Museum or gallery collection, archive, or library special collection:
Annual Reports

Printed publications:
Annual Report
Occasional Technical Reports

Access to staff:
Contact by letter, by telephone, by fax, by e-mail and via website. Appointment necessary.
Hours: Mon to Fri, 0900 to 1700; other times by arrangement

Constituent part of:
Cass Business School of City University London

Links with:
School of Engineering and Mathematical Sciences of City University London
School of Informatics of City University London

CENTRE FOR HUMAN GENETICS

Children's Hospital, Western Bank, Sheffield, South Yorkshire, S10 2TH

Tel: 0114 271 7000
Fax: 0114 273 7467
E-mail: o.quarrell@sheffield.ac.uk

Enquiries:
Enquiries to: Director
Other contacts: Head of Department

Organisation type and purpose:
Professional body.

Subject coverage:
Genetics, medical genetics, cytogenetics.

Access to staff:
Contact by letter
Hours: Mon to Fri, 0900 to 1700

Links with:
Sheffield Children's Hospital

CENTRE FOR INDEPENDENT TRANSPORT RESEARCH IN LONDON

Acronym or abbreviation: CILT

Room 208, The Colourworks, 2 Abbot Street, London, E8 3DP

Tel: 020 7275 9900\ Minicom no. 020 7275 9123
Fax: 020 7254 6777

Website:
http://www.cilt.dial.pipex.com/
Descriptions of work; archive of papers and articles generated by that work; selected articles from the magazine; links to other useful web sites.

Enquiries:
Enquiries to: Researchers

Founded:
1983

Formerly called:
The Campaign to Improve London's Transport (CILT) (year of change 1988)

Organisation type and purpose:
Membership association (membership is by subscription), present number of members: 30, voluntary organisation, registered charity (charity number 1001580), consultancy, research organisation, publishing house.
Research and resource unit.
To explore ways of making public transport more accessible, efficient and safe for all those who want to use it.

Subject coverage:
Transport, environment, transport planning, operational issues, women's transport needs, disability access, related issues.

Museum or gallery collection, archive, or library special collection:
Books, documents, reports, own publications, transport journals

Printed publications:
Variety of publications including:
Accessible Transport in East London (S Bell & D Hardle, 1998, £30, £10 for community groups)
Can the Boroughs Keep London Moving? (1992, £3)
The Complete 'Green Transport Plan' for Local Authorities (D Hurdle, 1998, £15)
Green Commuter Plans – London Boroughs' Progress (£10)
Lewisham Community Transport Study (A Peck et al, 1993, £13)
Motorcycling – Time to Apply the Brakes (£10)
Red Routes into Green Routes (G Smith, 1993)
Traffic and Transport: a guide to understanding and influencing the transport system (UK £10.50 inc. p&p, overseas £34 inc. p&p)
Stage or Terminus: a review of 50 years of London's public transport (K Fuller, 1985, £1)
Street Trams for London (C Wood, 1994, £12.50)
Transition (journal, replaces CILT Journal, quarterly, UK £18 a year, overseas £23, free to affiliates)

Electronic and video publications:
Transition (available on tape, on request)

Publications list:
Available online and in print

Access to staff:
Contact by letter, by telephone, by fax, by e-mail and via website. Appointment necessary.
Hours: Mon to Fri, by arrangement

Access to building, collection or gallery:
Prior appointment required

Access for disabled people:
Ramped entry, access to all public areas, toilet facilities
Special comments: Lift to second floor. Heavy gates and doors, but staff will come down to assist if requested. Very poor pavements in the surroundings.

CENTRE FOR INFORMATION QUALITY MANAGEMENT

Acronym or abbreviation: CIQM

Penbryn, Bronant, Aberystwyth, Ceredigion, SY23 4TJ

Tel: 01974 251302
E-mail: lisqual@cix.co.uk

Website:
http://www.i-a-l.co.uk/index.htm

Enquiries:
Enquiries to: Managing Director

Founded:
1993

Organisation type and purpose:
Professional body, training organisation, consultancy, research organisation.
CIQM represents the professional interests of the information community with respect to the quality, evaluation and selection of informational resources and databases.

Subject coverage:
CIQM acts as a clearing house for database and internet resource quality issues, and as a research and consulting organisation for all matters concerning the provision of good quality electronic information. Has worked to establish a methodology for database resource and internet resource quality assurance: database labelling.

Publications list:
Available online and in print

Access to staff:
Contact by letter, by telephone, by e-mail and via website. Appointment necessary.
Hours: Mon to Fri, 0900 to 1700

Access to building, collection or gallery:
Prior appointment required

Access for disabled people:
Parking provided

Affiliated to:
CILIP
  7 Ridgmount Street, London
UKeiG: UK electronic information Group
  Piglet Cottage, Redmire, Leyburn, North Yorkshire, DL8 4EH; tel: 01969 625751

Parent body:
Information Automation Limited (IAL)
  at the same address; tel: 01974 251302

CENTRE FOR INSTITUTIONAL STUDIES

Acronym or abbreviation: CIS

Duncan House, Stratford High Street, London, E15 2JB

Tel: 020 8223 3333 \ Minicom 020 8223 2853

Website:
http://www.uel.ac.uk

Enquiries:
Enquiries to: Press Officer
Direct tel: 020 8223 8194
Direct e-mail: h.esselink@uel.ac.uk

Founded:
1970

Organisation type and purpose:
University department or institute, research organisation.

Subject coverage:
Public policy and institutions, education policy, administration, local government, the voluntary sector, volunteering, urban regeneration, management of voluntary organisations, youth justice, community safety, social enterprise, community action, philosophy of Karl Popper.

Museum or gallery collection, archive, or library special collection:
Reference library

Printed publications:
CIS Commentaries on public policy issues (occasional)
Working papers (occasional)

Publications list:
Available in print

Access to staff:
Contact by letter, by telephone, by fax and by e-mail
Hours: Mon to Fri, 0900 to 1700

Access for disabled people:
Ramped entry, toilet facilities

CENTRE FOR INTER-CULTURAL DEVELOPMENT

Formal name: Diversity Works Ltd
Acronym or abbreviation: CI-CD

Diversity Works Ltd, 27 Langland Gardens, London, NW3 6QE

Tel: 020 7431 1712
E-mail: johntwitchin@diversityworks.co.uk

Website:
http://www.diversityworks.co.uk
Cultural competence and cross-cultural communication: research and training services, global and domestic, are set out via CI-CD home page.

Enquiries:
Enquiries to: Director
Other contacts: Co-Director

Founded:
1993

Organisation type and purpose:
Consultancy, research, training provision for (a) international business (b) domestic public services (c) university courses and international students.

Subject coverage:
Managing diversity; awareness and skills of cross-cultural communication; training DVD production; equal opportunities policy implementation; anti-discrimination law; recruiting, performance measuring and appraisal, customer care across cultures, diversity policy development.

Information services:
DVD resources for training in diversity and in cross-cultural communication available on request

Special visitor services:
Visitors welcome to examine DVD training resources and library of 5,000 books and articles.

Education services:
Visiting lectures in cross-cultural communication for MBA courses, and linguistics courses at postgraduate levels

Museum or gallery collection, archive, or library special collection:
Library of training resources: research papers, books and DVD/video packages

Non-library collection catalogue:
All or part available online

Library catalogue:
All or part available in-house

Printed publications:
Appraisal Interviewing across Cultures (training manual)
Attitudes to Islam (training manual)
Counselling and Advice across Cultures (training manual)

continued overleaf

Crosstalk (training manual)
Equal Opps at Work Race (training manual)
Evidence Unseen (training manual)
Information sheets (free)
Recruitment Interviewing Across Cultures
(training manual)
Multicultural Education, Staff Development in
Multicultural Practice (book)
The Black and White Media Book (£10.95)
What Makes You Say That? – Cultural Diversity at
Work (training manual)
Order printed publications from: Diversity Works
Ltd.

Electronic and video publications:
22 DVD training documentaries on cultural
diversity; catalogue available
Order electronic and video publications from: Diversity
Works Ltd.

Publications list:
Available online

Access to staff:
Contact by letter, by telephone, by fax, by e-mail,
in person and via website. Appointment necessary.
Hours: Mon to Fri, 1030 to 1700

Access to building, collection or gallery:
Hours: 1030 to 1700

Associates in:
Australia, Malaysia, Hong Kong, USA, Finland,
South Africa

CENTRE FOR INTERFIRM COMPARISON

Acronym or abbreviation: CIFC

32 St Thomas Street, Winchester, Hampshire, SO23
9HJ

Tel: 01962 844144
Fax: 01962 843180
E-mail: enquiries@cifc.co.uk

Website:
http://www.cifc.co.uk

Enquiries:
Enquiries to: Managing Director

Founded:
1959

Organisation type and purpose:
Consultancy, research organisation.
To organise benchmarking projects and properly
conducted interfirm comparisons between firms or
organisations in the same industry or trade, as a
service to them.

Subject coverage:
Benchmarking studies, interfirm comparison,
management ratios, financial information systems,
industry surveys, industry statistics.

Access to staff:
Contact by letter, by telephone, by fax, by e-mail
and via website. Appointment necessary.
Hours: Mon to Fri, 0900 to 1700

CENTRE FOR JAPANESE AND EAST ASIAN STUDIES

Acronym or abbreviation: CJEAS

PO Box 427, Pinner, Middlesex, HA5 3FX

Tel: 020 8429 2839
Fax: 0208 429 9236
E-mail: ruth.taplin@btinternet.com

Website:
http://www.jie.org.uk
Access to the Journal of Interdisciplinary
Economics.

Enquiries:
Enquiries to: Director
Direct tel: 0208–429–2839
Direct fax: 0208–429–9236
Direct e-mail: ruth.taplin@btinternet.com

Founded:
1989

Organisation type and purpose:
Briefings, research, translation of Japanese,
Chinese, Korean from English and into English,
interpreters

Subject coverage:
East and South-East Asia. Specialised translations
and interpretations of the languages of the region,
bespoke marketing strategies, research, cultural
training such as company briefings. Content
analysis of medical and pharmaceutical clinical
trials, and legal reports. Japanese, Chinese and
Korean Intellectual Property Law consultancy.

Printed publications:
The Journal of Interdisciplinary Economics (editor,
Dr Ruth Taplin)
Order printed publications from: Routledge, 2 Park
Square, Milton Park, Abingdon, Oxford, OX14
4RN (for other publications by Dr Taplin in Asian
Studies, Economics and Law)

Publications list:
Available online and in print

Access to staff:
Contact by letter, by telephone, by fax, by e-mail
and in person. Appointment necessary.
Hours: Mon to Fri, 0900 to 1700

CENTRE FOR LAW AND SOCIETY

Formal name: Criminology & Law
Acronym or abbreviation: CLS

Faculty of Law, University of Edinburgh, Old
College, South Bridge, Edinburgh, EH8 9YL

Tel: 0131 650 2025
Fax: 0131 650 2005
E-mail: elizabeth.goodwin-andersson@ed.ac.uk

Enquiries:
Enquiries to: Director

Formerly called:
Centre for Criminology and the Social and
Philosophical Study of Law

Organisation type and purpose:
University department or institute.

Subject coverage:
Official data on crime, crime surveys, policy
analysis on crime and punishment, policy advice
on crime and punishment, comparative knowledge
on criminal justice policy, legal theory.

Access to staff:
Contact by letter, by telephone, by fax and by e-
mail
Hours: Mon to Fri, 0900 to 1700

Access for disabled people:
Ramped entry, toilet facilities
Special comments: Lifts.

CENTRE FOR LEBANESE STUDIES

Acronym or abbreviation: CLS

c/o 14a Airlie Gardens, London, W8 7AL

Tel: 020 7221 3809
E-mail: info@lebanesestudies.com

Website:
http://lebanesestudies.com

Enquiries:
Enquiries to: Director
Direct e-mail: shehadi@herald.ox.ac.uk

Founded:
1984

Organisation type and purpose:
Learned society (membership is by subscription),
registered charity (charity number 298375),
research organisation, publishing house.

Subject coverage:
The Centre initiates and publishes research papers
and books on relevant historical, economic,
political, sociological and cultural issues affecting
Lebanon.

Printed publications:
A Vision of the Middle East: An Intellectual
Biography of Albert Hourani (Al-Sudairi A)
CLS Bulletins report on various conferences and
seminars (3 vols)
Index to the Archives of the Centre for Lebanese
Studies (Shultz K)
Papers on Lebanon – 17 analytical essays dealing
with historical, political and economic issues
Prospects for Lebanon – 9 analytical essays dealing
with policy aspects of relevant and current issues
The Breakdown of the State in Lebanon 1967 to
1976 (El Khazen F)
The Politics of Interventionism in Ottoman
Lebanon, 1830 to 1861 (Farah C)
Titles of more recent publications available on
request

Publications list:
Available in print

Access to staff:
Contact by letter, by telephone, by fax, by e-mail
and via website. Appointment necessary.
Hours: Mon to Fri, 1030 to 1730

Access to building, collection or gallery:
Prior appointment required

Access for disabled people:
Ramped entry, access to all public areas, toilet
facilities

CENTRE FOR LOCAL ECONOMIC STRATEGIES

Acronym or abbreviation: CLES

Express Networks, 1 George Leigh Street,
Manchester, M4 5DL

Tel: 0161 236 7036
Fax: 0161 236 1891
E-mail: info@cles.org.uk

Website:
http://www.cles.org.uk

Enquiries:
Enquiries to: Information Officer

Founded:
1986

Organisation type and purpose:
Membership association, registered charity
(charity number 1089503).

Subject coverage:
Regeneration, economic development, local
government, employment and labour markets,
sector studies, urban and regional economics,
community initiatives, European issues, European
legislation and links.

**Museum or gallery collection, archive, or library
special collection:**
Large collection of local government publications,
published, semi-published, grey literature,
committee reports etc

Library catalogue:
All or part available in-house

Publications list:
Available online

Access to staff:
Contact by letter, by telephone, by fax and by e-
mail. Appointment necessary. Non-members
charged.
Hours: Mon to Fri, 0900 to 1700

Subsidiary body:
CLES European Research Network (CERN)

CENTRE FOR MANAGEMENT CREATIVITY

Acronym or abbreviation: CMC

High Trenhouse, Malham Moor, Settle, North Yorkshire, BD24 9PR

Tel: 01729 830322
Fax: 01729 830519
E-mail: helen@centreformanagementcreativity.com

Website:
http://www.centreformanagementcreativity.com

Enquiries:
Enquiries to: Business Development Manager

Founded:
1985

Organisation type and purpose:
Service industry, training organisation, consultancy. Managing change.

Subject coverage:
Strategic thinking, team development, culture change, management techniques, personal development.

Printed publications:
Newsletters (members only)
MagNotes for structuring thoughts

Electronic and video publications:
Visual Concept software

Access to staff:
Contact by letter, by telephone, by fax, by e-mail and via website. Appointment necessary.
Hours: Mon to Fri, 0900 to 1700

Access for disabled people:
Parking provided, ramped entry, toilet facilities

CENTRE FOR MANX STUDIES

Formal name: School of Archaeology, Classics and Egyptology, University of Liverpool
Acronym or abbreviation: CMS

The Stables, University Centre, Old Castletown Road, Douglas, Isle of Man, IM2 1QB

Tel: 01624 695777
Fax: 01624 695783
E-mail: cms@liv.ac.uk

Website:
http://www.liv.ac.uk/manxstudies

Enquiries:
Enquiries to: Secretary
Other contacts: Administrator

Founded:
1992

Organisation type and purpose:
Centre for the academic study of anything Manx; undergraduate and postgraduate research organisation.

Subject coverage:
Research related to the Isle of Man, particularly earth sciences, archaeology, architecture, history, music, language and social studies.

Education services:
BA in History and Heritage Management (with IOM Dept Education); MA in Manx Studies; MPhil; PhD.

Museum or gallery collection, archive, or library special collection:
Collection of reference-only books on Manx topics

Non-library collection catalogue:
All or part available online

Library catalogue:
All or part available online

Printed publications:
For list of publications see website: http://www.liv.ac.uk/manxstudies
Order printed publications from: Secretary

Publications list:
Available online and in print

Access to staff:
Contact by letter, by telephone, by fax, by e-mail, in person and via website
Hours: Mon to Fri, 0900 to 1700

Access to building, collection or gallery:
No prior appointment required
Hours: Mon to Fri, 0900 to 1700

Links with:
Isle of Man Department of Education
St George's Court, Upper Church Street, Douglas, Isle of Man, IM1 2SG

Parent body:
School of Archaeology, Classics and Egyptology, University of Liverpool
PO Box 147, Liverpool, L69 3BX; tel: 0151 794 2000; fax: 0151 708 6502; website: http://www.liv.ac.uk

CENTRE FOR MARINE TECHNOLOGY

University of Salford, 43 The Crescent, Salford, Manchester, M5 4WT

Tel: 0161 295 5081
Fax: 0161 295 5380
E-mail: r.hughes@salford.ac.uk

Enquiries:
Enquiries to: Director

Organisation type and purpose:
University department or institute.

Subject coverage:
Offshore processing of oil and gas; enhanced oil recovery; simulation of oil and gas production; underwater life support systems.

Access to staff:
Contact by letter, by telephone, by fax and by e-mail
Hours: Mon to Fri, 0900 to 1700

Associated with:
Marinetech North West

CENTRE FOR MASS COMMUNICATION RESEARCH

Acronym or abbreviation: CMCR

University of Leicester, 104 Regent Road, Leicester, LE1 7LT

Tel: 0116 252 5293
Fax: 0116 252 5276
E-mail: cmcr@le.ac.uk

Website:
http://www.le.ac.uk/cmcr/
General departmental website and useful links.
http://www.le.ac.uk/cmcr/dl
Information on the MA in Mass Communications (by Distance Learning).

Enquiries:
Enquiries to: General Office Manager/PA to Head of Department
Direct e-mail: hlh7@leicester.ac.uk

Founded:
1966

Organisation type and purpose:
University department or institute, suitable for ages: 18+, research organisation.

Subject coverage:
Mass media, sociological research on mass media and communications, media and health, science communications, media and environment, media and politics, popular music industry, film, globalisation, culture, national identity, television and food.

Museum or gallery collection, archive, or library special collection:
Current and pre-current year British national newspapers, limited access available

Trade and statistical information:
Data on use of media in health education, structure of the media industries, viewing, listening, reading behaviour.

Access to staff:
Contact by telephone and by e-mail. Appointment necessary.
Hours: Mon to Fri, 0900 to 1700

Access to building, collection or gallery:
Prior appointment required

CENTRE FOR MEDICAL EDUCATION

Acronym or abbreviation: CME

Tay Park House, 484 Perth Road, Dundee, DD2 1LR

Tel: 01382 631968
Fax: 01382 645748
E-mail: p.a.wilkie@dundee.ac.uk

Website:
http://www.dundee.ac.uk/meded/

Enquiries:
Enquiries to: Director
Direct tel: 01382 631973
Direct e-mail: r.m.harden@dundee.ac.uk
Other contacts: AMEE Administrator for membership of Association for Medical Education in Europe.

Organisation type and purpose:
University department or institute.

Subject coverage:
Medical education: curriculum design, development and assessment; teaching and learning methods, evaluation management and administration, technology-based learning in medicine and health sciences, distance learning, vocational training and continuing medical and nursing education; diploma and masters of medical education; diploma in advanced nursing studies, degree in nursing studies, masters in palliative care.

Museum or gallery collection, archive, or library special collection:
Extensive collection of books and journals on medical and general education

Library catalogue:
All or part available in-house

Printed publications:
Distance learning programmes on a variety of topics in medicine and health care
Newsletter (free)

Publications list:
Available in print

Access to staff:
Contact by letter, by telephone, by fax, by e-mail and via website. Appointment necessary.
Hours: Mon to Fri, 0900 to 1700

Access for disabled people:
Parking provided, ramped entry

CENTRE FOR MEDIEVAL STUDIES

Acronym or abbreviation: CMS

King's Manor, York, YO1 7EP

Tel: 01904 433910
Fax: 01904 433918
E-mail: gmg501@york.ac.uk

Website:
http://www.york.ac.uk/inst/cms
Information on centre and courses offered.

Enquiries:
Enquiries to: Administrator

Founded:
1968

Organisation type and purpose:
University department or institute.

continued overleaf

Subject coverage:
Medieval studies.

Library catalogue:
All or part available in print

Access to staff:
Contact via website

CENTRE FOR MULTIMODAL THERAPY

156 Westcombe Hill, Blackheath, London, SE3 7DH

Tel: 0845 680 2065
E-mail: admin@managingstress.com

Website:
http://www.centreforcoaching.com
http://www.managingstress.com
Books, articles, course details, details about staff.

Enquiries:
Enquiries to: Director
Other contacts: Co-ordinator

Founded:
1990

Organisation type and purpose:
Training organisation, consultancy, research organisation, publishing house.

Subject coverage:
Multimodal therapy, stress management, stress counselling, training for counsellors, psychologists and therapists.

Electronic and video publications:
Audio tapes for relaxation and hypnosis
Some articles are freely available to download from the website

Publications list:
Available online

Access to staff:
Contact by letter, by telephone, by e-mail and via website. Appointment necessary.
Hours: Mon to Fri, 1000 to 1700

Parent body:
Centre for Stress Management

CENTRE FOR ORGANISATIONAL MANAGEMENT

Zenith House, Craigholm, Shooters Hill, London, SE18 3RR

Tel: 020 8319 1449
E-mail: almeric.powerone@btinternet.com

Website:
Under review

Enquiries:
Enquiries to: Director & Founder
Direct tel: 07523 528 895; 020 8319 1449

Founded:
1985

Formerly called:
Centre for Performance Improvement (year of change 1990)

Organisation type and purpose:
Organisational leadership coaching and transference consultancy practice.
To transfer understanding and skills that will directly transmit into an organisation's overall performance. To support the development of understanding and skills enabling the development of the collective use of both human resources and technical assets to reinforce an organisation's overall performance.

Subject coverage:
The development and application of skills in the following areas: Organisational Leadership, Organisational Design and Development, Organisational and Personal Decision-making, Motivational Skills Transference, Creating and Developing Focused Effective Teams and Work-Groups, Influencing and Negotiating, Conflict

Resolution, Organisational Communication, Systems Design, Development, and Management, Contract Management, Simultaneous Problem-solving; many other problems that naturally present themselves in any continuous performance improvement programme.

Access to staff:
Contact by letter, by telephone, by e-mail and in person. Appointment necessary.
Hours: Mon to Fri, 0900 to 1700

Access for disabled people:
Parking provided, ramped entry

CENTRE FOR PERSONAL AND PROFESSIONAL DEVELOPMENT

The Brewery, High Street, Twyford, Winchester, Hampshire, SO21 2RG

Tel: 01962 715838
Fax: 01962 711419
E-mail: ann@cppd.co.uk

Enquiries:
Enquiries to: Managing Director
Other contacts: Administrator

Founded:
1994

Organisation type and purpose:
Training organisation, consultancy.
Counselling services.
To provide counselling, training and consultancy services to both individuals and organisations, personal and professional development.

Subject coverage:
Counselling, psychotherapy, family and marital therapy, hypnotherapy, personal and professional development, training.

Access to staff:
Contact by letter, by telephone and by e-mail. Appointment necessary.
Hours: Mon to Fri, 0900 to 1700

Access to building, collection or gallery:
Prior appointment required

Access for disabled people:
Parking provided

CENTRE FOR POLICY ON AGEING

Acronym or abbreviation: CPA

25–31 Ironmonger Row, London, EC1V 3QP

Tel: 020 7553 6500
Fax: 020 7553 6501
E-mail: ageinfo@cpa.org.uk

Website:
http://www.cpa.org.uk
AGEINFO – bibliographic database updated monthly, NDAR – National database of ageing research, SAP – Single Assessment Process national resource.

Enquiries:
Enquiries to: Director
Other contacts: Librarian

Founded:
1947

Organisation type and purpose:
Registered charity (charity number 207163). Independent policy and information unit promoting and formulating effective policies to improve services etc for older people.

Subject coverage:
Social aspects of gerontology in Britain and, to a lesser extent, Europe, USA, etc; includes health care, housing, adult education/leisure, employment, retirement, social policy etc for older people.

Museum or gallery collection, archive, or library special collection:
Reference library (by appointment only)

International collection on gerontology, over 500 core journals and 49,000 monographs, reports, statistical sources, legislation, etc

Library catalogue:
All or part available online and in-house

Printed publications:
Many books and reports including:
Ageing and Society (5 times a year)
Directory of Services for Elderly People
European Directory of Old Age
New Literature on Old Age (6 times a year)
Old Age: a register of social research 1985–1990 (biennial)
Order printed publications from: Central Books, 99 Wallis Road, London, E9 5LN, tel: 020 8986 5488, fax: 020 8533 5821, e-mail: peter@centralbooks.com

Electronic and video publications:
AGEINFO (CD-ROM with quarterly updates, Internet with monthly updates, comprises three databases: 50,000 plus bibliographic items; 4,500 national and international organisations; calendar of events)

Publications list:
Available online and in print

Access to staff:
Contact by letter, by telephone, by fax and by e-mail. Appointment necessary.
Hours: Mon, 1400 to 1700; Tue to Fri, 1000 to 1700

Access to building, collection or gallery:
Prior appointment required

Established by:
Nuffield Foundation

CENTRE FOR RADIOGRAPHIC AND MEDICAL STUDIES

Cranfield University, Shrivenham, Swindon, Wiltshire, SN6 8LA

Tel: 01793 785756
Fax: 01793 785744
E-mail: j.laxon@rmcs.cranfield.ac.uk

Enquiries:
Enquiries to: Director
Direct tel: 01793 785227
Direct e-mail: berridge@rcms.cranfield.ac.uk
Other contacts: Undergraduate Admissions Officer (for undergraduate admissions through UCAS)

Founded:
1992

Formerly called:
Oxford Centre for Radiographic Studies (year of change 1997)

Incorporates the former:
Joint Services School of Radiography, Northampton School of Radiography, Oxford Regional School of Radiography

Organisation type and purpose:
University department or institute.

Subject coverage:
Radiography, radiobiology, radiation physics, radiation dosimetry, medical ultrasound, veterinary radiography and ultrasound, dental radiography, radiation protection, imaging, oncology, forensic radiography, radiation effects on materials.

Printed publications:
Course literature and undergraduate and post-graduate prospectus (free on request)

Publications list:
Available in print

Access to staff:
Contact by letter, by telephone, by fax and by e-mail
Hours: Mon to Fri, 0900 to 1700

Access for disabled people:
Parking provided, ramped entry, access to all public areas, toilet facilities

CENTRE FOR RATIONAL EMOTIVE BEHAVIOUR THERAPY

Broadway House, 3 High Street, Bromley, Kent, BR1 1LF

Tel: 020 8228 1185

Website:
http://www.managingstress.com
Course details, books, articles.

Enquiries:
Enquiries to: Director
Direct e-mail: jason.jones@bsmhft.nhs.uk
Other contacts: Co-ordinator

Founded:
1990

Formerly called:
Centre for Rational Emotive Therapy

Organisation type and purpose:
Training organisation, consultancy, research organisation, publishing house. Counselling and training centre.

Subject coverage:
Rational emotive behaviour therapy, counselling, coaching and training.

Printed publications:
Rational Interviews (£6.95 plus 75p p&p)
Think Rationally (£1.95 inc. p&p)

Electronic and video publications:
Audio tapes for relaxation and self hypnosis

Publications list:
Available online

Access to staff:
Contact by letter, by telephone, by e-mail and via website. Appointment necessary.
Hours: Mon to Fri, 1000 to 1700

Affiliated to:
Centre for Coaching
Centre for Multimodel Therapy
Centre for Problem Focused Training and Therapy
Centre for Stress Management

CENTRE FOR RESEARCH IN ETHNIC RELATIONS

Acronym or abbreviation: CRER

University of Warwick, Coventry, Warwickshire, CV4 7AL

Tel: 024 7652 3605
Fax: 024 7652 4324
E-mail: crer@warwick.ac.uk

Website:
http://www.warwick.ac.uk/CRER
Searchable citations of reports and pamphlets including ethnic minority health from medical literature. Information about CRER research and postgraduate teaching. Publications ordering information.

Enquiries:
Enquiries to: Librarian
Direct tel: 024 7652 2972
Other contacts: Publications Manager for publications.

Organisation type and purpose:
University department or institute, research organisation.

Subject coverage:
All aspects of British, and increasingly of European, race and ethnic relations: employment, health, housing, education, politics, social services, etc; migrant workers in Europe; refugees; community studies.

Museum or gallery collection, archive, or library special collection:
Large indexed press clippings collection; videos and ephemera collection
Over 200 periodicals and newspapers
Over 8000 pamphlets and reports

Resources Centre maintained and staffed part-time, reinforcing the university library's collection of material on race and ethnic relations

Trade and statistical information:
National Ethnic Minority Data Archive (statistical, survey and census data, primarily for Britain).

Library catalogue:
All or part available online

Printed publications:
British Pakistanis – Demographic, Social and Economic Position (Muhammad Anwar, £10)
National Ethnic Minority Archive: 1991 Census Statistical Papers
Making Monitoring Work (Jones A, £20)
Research Papers, Bibliographies and Monographs in Ethnic Relations
Order printed publications from: Publications Manager, Centre for Research in Ethnic Relations tel: 024 7652 3607, fax: 024 7652 4324, e-mail: bains@warwick.ac.uk

Publications list:
Available online and in print

Access to staff:
Contact by letter, by telephone, by fax and by e-mail
Hours: Mon to Fri, 0900 to 1600

Access for disabled people:
Ramped entry, toilet facilities

Parent body:
University of Warwick
tel: 024 7652 3523

CENTRE FOR REVIEWS AND DISSEMINATION

Acronym or abbreviation: CRD

University of York, Heslington, York, YO10 5DD

Tel: 01904 321040
Fax: 01904 321041
E-mail: crd-info@york.ac.uk

Website:
http://www.york.ac.uk/inst/crd
Searchable databases: NHS Economic Evaluation Database; Database of Abstracts of Reviews of Effects; Health Technology Assessment Database.

Full text of CRD reports

Enquiries:
Enquiries to: Information Service Manager

Founded:
1994

Organisation type and purpose:
Part of the National Institue of Health Research and an academic department of the University of York.
To provide information to the NHS on the effects of treatments and the delivery and organisation of care.

Subject coverage:
Systematic reviews of the effects of health care interventions. Cost-effectiveness information.

Library catalogue:
All or part available in-house

Printed publications:
CRD Reports
Also available full text on website
Order printed publications from: Publications Officer, Centre for Reviews and Dissemination, at same address, tel: 01904 321441; fax: 01904 321035

Electronic and video publications:
Database of Abstracts of Reviews of Effects
NHS Economic Evaluation Database
Health Technology Assessment Database

Publications list:
Available online

Access to staff:
Contact by e-mail

Parent body:
University of York
York, YO10 5DD; tel: 01904 430000; fax: 01904 433433

CENTRE FOR SOCIAL ANTHROPOLOGY AND COMPUTING

Acronym or abbreviation: CSAC

University of Kent, Canterbury, Kent, CT2 7NS

Tel: 01227 764000
Fax: 01227 827289
E-mail: csa-c@lucy.ukc.ac.uk

Website:
http://www.lucy.ukc.ac.uk/
http://www.csac.anthropology.ac.uk/
http://www.era.anthropology.ac.uk/
http://www.lucy.ukc.ac.uk/online_pubs.html
Summary of online publications.
http://www.lucy.ukc.ac.uk/AIO.html
Anthropological Index Online – online bibliography.
http://www.aio.anthropology.org.uk/
Registration for updates to AIO.

Enquiries:
Enquiries to: Director
Direct e-mail: m.d.fischer@ukc.ac.uk
Other contacts: Deputy Director

Organisation type and purpose:
University department or institute.

Subject coverage:
Anthropology, anthropological computing, teaching and learning materials.

Printed publications:
CSAC Monographs (prices on request from CSAC Office)
South-East Asian Studies Occasional Paper Series
Order printed publications from: CSAC Office
Eliot College, University of Kent, Canterbury, CT2 7NS

Electronic and video publications:
Experience Rich Anthropology (CD-ROM and via website)
Era Sampler (CD-ROM)

Publications list:
Available online and in print

Access to staff:
Contact by letter, by e-mail and via website
Hours: Mon to Fri, 0900 to 1700

Affiliated to:
Department of Anthropology
University of Kent, Canterbury, CT2 7NS; tel: 01227 764000

CENTRE FOR SOCIO-LEGAL STUDIES

Acronym or abbreviation: CSLS

University of Oxford, Manor Road Building, Manor Road, Oxford, OX1 3UQ

Tel: 01865 284220
Fax: 01865 284221
E-mail: admin@csls.ox.ac.uk

Website:
http://www.cslc.ox.ac.uk
History of centre; events; research staff and profiles; areas of research; student programme; visitors programme; directions; library information.

Enquiries:
Enquiries to: Administrator

Founded:
1972

Organisation type and purpose:
University department or institute, research organisation.

continued overleaf

Subject coverage:
Role and function of law in societies, law and the media, human rights, social history, procedures for adjudication and dispute settlement, law and psychology, law and economics, families and the law especially divorce, compensation for illness and injury, medicine and law, regulation of health and safety at work, regulation of public and private sector, regulation of business practice.

Museum or gallery collection, archive, or library special collection:
Small specialised socio-legal library, open for outside use by appointment

Printed publications:
Annual Reports (including details of current research projects)
Bibliographies in socio-legal studies
Oxford Socio-Legal Studies series (pub. OUP)
Research Reviews of subject areas (e.g. law and economics)
Working papers and conference papers

Publications list:
Available in print

Access to staff:
Contact by letter, by fax, by e-mail and via website. Appointment necessary.
Hours: Mon to Fri, 0900 to 1700

CENTRE FOR SPEECH TECHNOLOGY RESEARCH

Acronym or abbreviation: CSTR

University of Edinburgh, 2 Buccleuch Place, Edinburgh, EH8 9LW

Tel: 0131 650 2804
Fax: 0131 650 4587
E-mail: evelcen@cogsci.ed.ac.uk

Website:
http://www.cstr.ed.ac.uk/
Home page.

Enquiries:
Enquiries to: Secretary

Founded:
1984

Organisation type and purpose:
University department or institute, research organisation.

Subject coverage:
Phonetics, dialogue engineering, speech synthesis, speech signal processing and coding, hidden markov modelling, neural networks, transputer DSP and PC prototyping, speaker verification, expert software.

Printed publications:
Annual published papers volume
Annual Report

Access to staff:
Contact by letter, by telephone, by fax and by e-mail
Hours: Mon to Fri, 0900 to 1700

Links with:
research organisations throughout Europe

Member of:
European Network in Language and Speech (ELSNET)

CENTRE FOR STRESS MANAGEMENT

Acronym or abbreviation: CFSM

156 Westcombe Hill, Blackheath, London, SE3 7DH

Tel: 0845 680 2065
E-mail: admin@managingstress.com

Website:
http://www.managingstress.com
Information about the centre including courses and staff. Also articles about stress, stress management and relaxation methods.

Enquiries:
Enquiries to: Director
Other contacts: Co-ordinator

Founded:
1987

Organisation type and purpose:
Training organisation, consultancy, research organisation, publishing house.

Subject coverage:
Stress management, stress counselling, stress audits, positive approaches to managing pressure and stress, assertion and communication skills, self-esteem and self-acceptance, challenging irrational beliefs and public beliefs.

Printed publications:
General Information and Training Programme
How to Deal with Stress (Sunday Times) £9.99
How to Deal with Stress ISBN 10: 0–7494–4866–0

Electronic and video publications:
Audio tapes – relaxation, hypnosis

Publications list:
Available in print

Access to staff:
Contact by letter, by telephone, by e-mail and via website. Appointment necessary.
Hours: Mon to Fri, 1000 to 1700

Affiliated to:
Centre for Multimodal Therapy
    tel: 020 8318 4448
Centre for Problem Focused Training and Therapy
Centre for Rational Emotive Behaviour Therapy
Institute for Complementary Medicine
UK Centre for Cognitive Behaviour Therapy,
Centre for Coaching, International Academy for Professional Development, Centres of Expertise

Also at:
Centre for Stress Management
    Porthleven, Cornwall

CENTRE FOR STUDIES ON INCLUSIVE EDUCATION LIMITED

Acronym or abbreviation: CSIE

New Redland, Frenchay Campus, Coldharbour Lane, Bristol, BS16 1QU

Tel: 0117 328 4007
Fax: 0117 328 4005
E-mail: admin@csie.org.uk

Website:
http://www. csie.org.uk

Enquiries:
Enquiries to: Director

Founded:
1982

Formerly called:
Centre for Studies on Integration in Education (CSIE) (year of change 1994)

Organisation type and purpose:
Voluntary organisation, registered charity (charity number 327805), suitable for ages: 0 to 19.
The Centre is committed to working towards an end to segregated education and developing inclusive education, with support, for all in the mainstream.
The Centre publishes the Index for Inclusion, which helps break down barriers to learning and participation. The Index facilitates inclusive school development by investigating the culture, policy and practice of a school.

Subject coverage:
Inclusion of all children with disabilities or difficulties in learning into society during school years from nurseries to colleges; parental involvement in assessment and placement; the 1996 and 2001 Education Acts; LEA policy and practice on inclusion.

Printed publications:
A wide range of leaflets, publications and free material on Inclusive Education is available
Booklets, survey reports, factsheets including:
Human Rights and School Change – The Newham Story
Inclusive Education – The Right to Belong to the Mainstream
Index for Inclusion: developing learning and participation in schools
Index for Inclusion – developing learning participation and play in early years and childcare
Learning supporters and inclusion
Developing a Single Equality Policy (2010)

Publications list:
Available online and in print

Access to staff:
Contact by letter, by telephone, by fax and via website. Appointment necessary.
Hours: Mon to Fri, 0900 to 1700

Access to building, collection or gallery:
Prior appointment required

Access for disabled people:
Parking provided, ramped entry, access to all public areas, toilet facilities

Links with:
Alliance for Inclusive Education (ALLFIE)
Council for Exceptional Children (ERIC)
    1920 Association Drive, Reston, Virginia, 20191–1589, USA
Parents for Inclusion

CENTRE FOR SUSTAINABLE ENERGY

Acronym or abbreviation: CSE

3 St Peter's Court, Bedminster Parade, Bristol, BS3 4AQ

Tel: 0117 934 1400
Fax: 0117 934 1410
E-mail: info@cse.org.uk

Website:
http://www.cse.org.uk
The Centre for Sustainable Energy helps people and organisations from the public, private and voluntary sectors meet the twin challenges of rising energy costs and climate change.

Enquiries:
Enquiries to: Office Administrator
Direct tel: 0117 9341408

Founded:
1979

Formerly called:
Urban Centre for Appropriate Energy (UCAT)

Organisation type and purpose:
National government body.
Established to stimulate the development of new and renewable energy sources wherever they have the prospect of being economically attractive and environmentally acceptable, in order to contribute to diverse, secure and sustainable energy supplies, reduction in the emission of pollutants, and encouragement of internationally competitive industries.

Subject coverage:
Biosciences, commercialisation, energy from waste, solar energy, wave and tidal energy, wind energy.

Printed publications:
The programme has produced over 1,700 publications in the last ten years including brochures, technology status reports, case studies, factsheets, newsletters, project summaries and contractor reports; with the exception of contractor reports these are sent to enquirers free of charge and do not need to be returned; a loan service operates for contractor reports
Order printed publications from: e-mail: kirsty.mitchell@cse.org.uk

Publications list:
Available online

Access to staff:
Contact by letter, by telephone, by fax, by e-mail and via website. Appointment necessary.
Hours: Mon to Fri, 0900 to 1730

Links with:
Centre for Alternative Energy
Machynlleth, Powys, Wales, SY20 9AZ; tel: 01654 702782; website: http://www.cat.org.uk

CENTRE FOR THE ECONOMICS AND MANAGEMENT OF AQUATIC RESOURCES

Acronym or abbreviation: CEMARE

University of Portsmouth, Boathouse No. 6, College Road, HM Naval Base, Portsmouth, PO1 3LJ

Tel: 023 9284 4082
Fax: 023 9284 4614
E-mail: christopher.martin@port.ac.uk

Website:
http://www.port.ac.uk/cemare
Home page; reading room; research; consultancy; training; publications.

Enquiries:
Enquiries to: Librarian

Founded:
1970

Formerly called:
Centre for Marine Resource Economics, Marine Resources Research Unit

Organisation type and purpose:
University department or institute, consultancy, research organisation.

Subject coverage:
Fisheries economics, agricultural economics, environmental economics, coastal zone management, aquaculture, recreational fisheries.

Museum or gallery collection, archive, or library special collection:
2,000 books, 10,000 reports, 5,000 reprints, 165 serial titles (60 current)
Large collection of FAO Fisheries publications on hard copy and microfiche

Non-library collection catalogue:
All or part available online and in-house

Printed publications:
CEMARE Miscellaneous Papers (irregular)
CatchUp Alumni Newsletter (irregular)
CEMARE Reports (irregular)
CEMARE Research Papers (irregular)

Publications list:
Available online and in print

Access to staff:
Contact by e-mail and via website. Appointment necessary.
Hours: Mon to Fri, 1000 to 1700

Member of:
BIASLIC
EURASLIC
IAALD
IAMSLIC

CENTRE FOR THE HISTORY OF TECHNOLOGY, SCIENCE AND SOCIETY

University of Bath, Claverton Down, Bath, BA2 7AY

Tel: 01225 311508
E-mail: hssraab@bath.ac.uk

Enquiries:
Enquiries to: Honorary Director

Founded:
1964

Organisation type and purpose:
University department or institute, research organisation.
The National Cataloguing Unit for the Archives of Contemporary Scientists is now in the University Library.

Subject coverage:
History of technology in all periods and all forms, technology and society, history of engineering, especially in Britain, engineering biography, Victorian engineering, history of stationary steam power, industrial archaeology, national heritage and conservation.

Museum or gallery collection, archive, or library special collection:
Watkins collection (photographs and documentation of stationary steam engines), now with the National Buildings Record, English Heritage, Swindon

Printed publications:
Papers in scientific journals
Research reports
Works on industrial archaeology, the steam engine, engineering biographies, especially I K Brunel, gunpowder history etc. (12 titles, independently published)

Access to staff:
Contact by letter and by e-mail
Hours: Mon to Fri, 0900 to 1700

CENTRE FOR THE STUDY OF FINANCIAL INNOVATION

Acronym or abbreviation: CSFI

5 Derby Street, London, W1J 7AB

Tel: 020 7493 0173
Fax: 020 7493 0190
E-mail: info@csfi.org.uk

Website:
http://www.csfi.org.uk
Information about the centre, future events and past events. Minutes of past meetings, publications and how to purchase. Information about sponsors.

Enquiries:
Enquiries to: Director
Direct e-mail: andrew@csfi.org.uk
Other contacts: Director of Studies (for research, themes); Sponsorship Manager (for membership)

Founded:
1993

Organisation type and purpose:
Membership association (membership is by subscription), present number of members: c. 70, registered charity (charity number 1017352), research organisation.

Subject coverage:
Banking, regulation, risk, e-finance, SMEs, development finance, Europe, insurance, technology.

Printed publications:
Reports (10 to 12 per annum, for purchase)

Electronic and video publications:
Pdfs available for purchase

Publications list:
Available online and in print

Access to staff:
Contact by letter, by fax and by e-mail
Hours: Mon to Fri, 0900 to 1700

Access to building, collection or gallery:
Prior appointment required

CENTRE FOR THE STUDY OF GLOBALISATION AND REGIONALISATION

Acronym or abbreviation: CSGR

Department of Economics, University of Warwick, Coventry, Warwickshire, CV4 7AL

Tel: 024 7657 2533
Fax: 024 7657 2548
E-mail: csgr@warwick.ac.uk

Website:
http://www.warwick.ac.uk/fac/soc/CSGR
http://www.csgr.org

Enquiries:
Enquiries to: Research Fellow

Organisation type and purpose:
University department or institute, research organisation.

Subject coverage:
Globalisation, regionalisation, trade, finance

CENTRE FOR THE STUDY OF INTERRELIGIOUS RELATIONS

Acronym or abbreviation: CSIR

University of Birmingham, Elmfield House, Bristol Road, Birmingham, B29 6LQ

Tel: 0121 415 8373
Fax: 0121 415 8376
E-mail: d.r.thomas.1@bham.ac.uk

Website:
http://www.bham.ac.uk/theology

Enquiries:
Enquiries to: Administrative Secretary
Direct e-mail: h.ingram@bham.ac.uk

Founded:
2007

Formerly called:
Centre for the Study of Islam and Christian-Muslim Relations (year of change 2007)

Organisation type and purpose:
University department, research organisation

Subject coverage:
Interreligious relations; Christian-Muslim relations; philosophy of religion; religion in South Asia.

Museum or gallery collection, archive, or library special collection:
Mingana Collection of Islamic Arabic, Christian Arabic and Syriac Manuscripts

Library catalogue:
All or part available online

Printed publications:
Islam and Christian-Muslim Relations (journal)
Newsletter
Order printed publications from:
h.ingram@bham.ac.uk

Electronic and video publications:
Islam and Christian-Muslim Relations (journal)
Order electronic and video publications from: Taylor & Francis

Publications list:
Available online and in print

Access to staff:
Contact by letter, by telephone, by fax, by e-mail, in person and via website. Appointment necessary.
Hours: Mon to Fri, 0900 to 1700

Access to building, collection or gallery:
Doors security locked; wall phone to secretaries available
Hours: 0900 to 1700

Access for disabled people:
Parking provided, toilet facilities

CENTRE FOR THE STUDY OF PUBLIC POLICY

Acronym or abbreviation: CSPP

Edward Wright Building, University of Aberdeen, Aberdeen, AB24 3QY

E-mail: cspp@abdn.ac.uk

continued overleaf

Website:
http://www.abdn.ac.uk/cspp
http://www.russiavotes.org

Enquiries:
Enquiries to: Director
Direct e-mail: cspp@abdn.ac.uk

Founded:
1976

Organisation type and purpose:
University department or institute, research organisation.
Concerned with the problems of public policy, especially post-Communist societies and new democracies in the European Union. Specialised databases of public opinion, surveys of 20 countries.

Subject coverage:
Public policy generally; the growth of government; public finance and political economy; elections, transformation of post-Communist societies; social capital.

Museum or gallery collection, archive, or library special collection:
A variety of machine-readable survey data sets

Non-library collection catalogue:
All or part available online and in print

Printed publications:
CSPP Monograph series: Studies in Public Policy (about 16 times a year)
Journal of Public Policy (pub. CUP)

Electronic and video publications:
Massive survey database on 20 countries

Publications list:
Available online and in print

Access to staff:
Contact by letter, by e-mail and via website. Appointment necessary.
Hours: Mon to Fri, 0900 to 1700

Headquarters address:
research institutes in Eastern and Western Europe and the United States

CENTRE FOR TRADITIONAL CHINESE MEDICINE

78 Haverstock Hill, London, NW3 2BE

Tel: 020 7284 2898
Fax: 020 7485 8875
E-mail: centcm@netcomuk.co.uk

Enquiries:
Enquiries to: Director

Founded:
1992

Organisation type and purpose:
Professional body, consultancy.

Subject coverage:
Chinese herbal medicine, acupuncture and Chinese massage.

Museum or gallery collection, archive, or library special collection:
Chinese herbal samples
Chinese medical books

Access to staff:
Contact by letter, by telephone, by fax and by e-mail
Hours: Mon to Fri, 0930 to 1730

CENTRE OF AFRICAN STUDIES LIBRARY

University of Cambridge, Mond Building, Free School Lane, Cambridge, CB2 3RF

Tel: 01223 334398
Fax: 01223 769325
E-mail: afrlib@hermes.cam.ac.uk

Website:
http://www.african.cam.ac.uk/library.htm
http://www.african.cam.ac.uk
Website for Centre of African studies, of which library is part

Enquiries:
Enquiries to: Librarian
Direct e-mail: meg23@cam.ac.uk
Other contacts: Assistant Librarian

Founded:
1965

Organisation type and purpose:
University department or institute (library).

Subject coverage:
Africa (mainly sub-Saharan): its history, geography, literature, economics and politics and its social, developmental, cultural and artistic affairs.

Library catalogue:
All or part available online

Publications list:
Available in print

Access to staff:
Contact by letter, by telephone, by fax, by e-mail, in person and via website. Appointment necessary.
Hours: Mon to Fri, 0900 to 1730
Special comments: The library hours may be shortened during the summer vacation, so please check before visiting.

Access to building, collection or gallery:
Hours: Mon to Fri, 0900 to 1730
Special comments: After hours and at weekend, authorised card entry only (no access to library).

Access for disabled people:
By side door; intercom to request door opening
Hours: Mon to Fri, 0900 to 1730

Links with:
UK Libraries and Archives Group on Africa (SCOLMA)

Parent body:
University of Cambridge

CENTRE OF CANADIAN STUDIES

University of Edinburgh, 15A George Square, Edinburgh, EH8 9LD

Tel: 0131 650 4129
Fax: 0131 650 6535
E-mail: centreofcanadianstudies@ed.ac.uk

Website:
http://www.cst.ed.ac.uk

Enquiries:
Enquiries to: Administrator
Other contacts: Director

Organisation type and purpose:
University department or institute.

Subject coverage:
Canada.

Publications list:
Available online

Access to staff:
Contact by letter, by telephone, by fax, by e-mail, in person and via website. Appointment necessary.
Hours: Mon to Thu, 0900 to 1700; Fri, 0900 to 1230

Access to building, collection or gallery:
No access other than to staff

CENTRE OF MEDICAL LAW AND ETHICS

Acronym or abbreviation: CMLE

King's College London, Strand, London, WC2R 2LS

Tel: 020 7848 2382
Fax: 020 7848 2575
E-mail: cmle.enq@kcl.ac.uk

Website:
http://www.kcl.ac.uk/cmle

Enquiries:
Enquiries to: Administrator
Other contacts: Director

Founded:
1978

Organisation type and purpose:
University department or institute.

Subject coverage:
Medical ethics, medical and healthcare law.

Museum or gallery collection, archive, or library special collection:
Specialist collection of medical, law and ethics books and periodicals held by King's College Library, Chancery Lane, London WC2

Printed publications:
Advance Directives and AIDS (£5)
Dispatches (newsletter, 3 issues per academic year, £12.50)
Manual for Research Ethics Committees (updated annually)
Occasional Papers Series (frequency and price varies; OPS1 £12, OPS2 £8, OPS3 £13)

Publications list:
Available in print

Access to staff:
Contact by letter, by telephone, by fax and by e-mail. Appointment necessary.
Hours: Mon to Fri, 0930 to 1300, 1400 to 1730

Part of:
School of Law
King's College London, London

CENTRE OF SOUTH ASIAN STUDIES

Laundress Lane, Cambridge, CB2 1SD

Tel: 01223 338094
Fax: 01223 767094
E-mail: webmaster@s-asian.cam.ac.uk

Website:
http://www.s-asian.cam.ac.uk
Library guide, list of microfilms held of South Asian newspapers, list of collections in archive, list of memoirs in archive, list of microforms held of government archives, handlist of archive, databases of film and photographic collections.

Enquiries:
Enquiries to: Librarian

Founded:
1964

Organisation type and purpose:
University library, university department or institute, research organisation.

Subject coverage:
South Asia (India, Sri Lanka, Pakistan, Bangladesh, Nepal) and Southeast Asia (Burma, Thailand, Laos, Cambodia, Vietnam, Malaysia, Singapore, Indonesia, Philippines); social sciences, history (17th century onwards), geography, agriculture, economics, development, etc.

Museum or gallery collection, archive, or library special collection:
7,500 microforms on South and Southeast Asia
30,000 monographs on South and Southeast Asia
Cambridge South Asian Archive of the personal papers relating to the British period in India
Indian Newspapers on microfilm from the 19th century onwards
50 hours of cinefilm now on DVD

Non-library collection catalogue:
All or part available online and in print

Library catalogue:
All or part available online

Printed publications:
Archive Guides and Handlists

Cambridge South Asian Archive (pub. Chadwyck-Healey; 5 volumes, continuing)
Cambridge South Asian Studies (pub. Cambridge University Press; some 60 titles)
Central Government of India publications held by libraries in London, Oxford and Cambridge
Centre's Annual Reports
Government of Ceylon publications held by libraries in London, Oxford and Cambridge
Government of Pakistan publications held by libraries in London, Oxford and Cambridge
Library Quarterly Accessions Lists
Serial publications of the Indian Government held by libraries in London, Oxford and Cambridge
Union Catalogues

Access to staff:
Contact by letter and via website. Appointment necessary. Letter of introduction required.
Hours: Mon to Fri, 0930 to 1730
Special comments: Closed Christmas and Easter.

Constituent part of:
University of Cambridge

CENTRE OF WEST AFRICAN STUDIES

Acronym or abbreviation: CWAS

University of Birmingham, Edgbaston, Birmingham, B15 2TT

Tel: 0121 414 5128
Fax: 0121 414 3228
E-mail: cwas@bham.ac.uk

Website:
http://www.bham.ac.uk/WestAfricanStudies

Enquiries:
Enquiries to: Director
Direct tel: 0121 414 5125
Direct e-mail: tmccaskie@aol.com
Other contacts: Secretary, CWAS for routine requests for information, publications.

Founded:
1963

Organisation type and purpose:
Museum, university department or institute, suitable for ages: 18+, research organisation.

Subject coverage:
History (social, Islamic, South African), geography, political science, Yoruba language, literature (African and Caribbean), popular culture, sociology – all related to West Africa and, in some cases, Eastern or Southern Africa. Specialisms in Benin, Ghana, Mali, Nigeria, Senegambia and Sierra Leone, African development studies, African cultural anthropology.

Museum or gallery collection, archive, or library special collection:
Cadbury Papers
CMS archives
Danford Collection of African Art and Artefacts
Early West African newspapers
Extensive holdings of books on Africa
John Figueroa Papers
Joseph Chamberlain Papers
R E Bradbury Papers (Benin)
William Bascom Collection (Yoruba)

Printed publications:
Birmingham University African Studies series nos 1–5 (for purchase, direct)
Sierra Leone Studies (volume produced 1987 and 1990, for purchase, direct)

Publications list:
Available online

Access to staff:
Contact by letter, by e-mail and via website. Appointment necessary.
Hours: Mon to Fri, 0930 to 1700

Access to building, collection or gallery:
Prior appointment required

CENTREPOINT

Neil House, 7 Whitechapel Road, London, E1 1DU

Tel: 020 7426 5300

Website:
http://www.centrepoint.org.uk

Enquiries:
Enquiries to: Information Officer
Direct e-mail: john.raynham@centrepoint.org

Organisation type and purpose:
Voluntary organisation, registered charity.

Subject coverage:
Housing and support to homeless 16–25 year olds, research with young people at risk.

Publications list:
Available online and in print

Access to staff:
Contact by letter and by telephone
Hours: Mon to Fri, 0900 to 1700

Access to building, collection or gallery:
No prior appointment required

CEP ASSOCIATES

1st Floor NYMCA, North View, Ashington, Northumberland, NE63 9XQ

Tel: 01670 521805
Fax: 01670 521805
E-mail: patdreyer@cepassociates.fsnet.co.uk

Website:
http://www.cepassociates@fsnet.co.uk
Course information; company information; application forms.

Enquiries:
Enquiries to: Information Officer

Founded:
1991

Formerly called:
Community Education Project

Organisation type and purpose:
Suitable for ages: 18+, training organisation, consultancy.

Subject coverage:
Community education.

Access to staff:
Contact by letter, by telephone, by fax, by e-mail, in person and via website. Appointment necessary.
Hours: Mon to Fri, 0900 to 1700

Access for disabled people:
Ramped entry

CERAM RESEARCH LTD

Queens Road, Penkhull, Stoke-on-Trent, Staffordshire, ST4 7LQ

Tel: 01782 764444
Fax: 01782 412331
E-mail: enquiries@ceram.com

Website:
http://www.ceram.com
Services available.

Enquiries:
Enquiries to: Information Manager
Direct tel: 01782 764241
Direct e-mail: ann.pace@ceram.com

Founded:
1948

Organisation type and purpose:
Membership association (membership is by subscription), present number of members: 300, research organisation.
Research and technology organisation for ceramics and materials industries.

Subject coverage:
Production and service behaviour of ceramic materials and pottery (tableware, tiles, sanitary ware, electrical porcelain); refractories; technical ceramics for engineering and electrical applications; clay and calcium silicate-based building products (bricks, sewer pipes) and their behaviour in structures; evaluation of properties, and physical and chemical testing methods.

Museum or gallery collection, archive, or library special collection:
Graves Library (on bricks and building)
Mellor Memorial Library

Trade and statistical information:
Statistical information on ceramics industry (worldwide).
Material information on ceramics industry (worldwide).

Non-library collection catalogue:
All or part available in-house

Library catalogue:
All or part available in-house

Printed publications:
Progress (two a year, members only)

Electronic and video publications:
World Ceramics (database internet subscription – Cambridge Scientific Abstracts)

Publications list:
Available online and in print

Access to staff:
Contact by letter, by telephone, by fax, by e-mail, in person and via website. Appointment necessary. Access for members only. Letter of introduction required. Non-members charged.
Hours: Mon to Thu, 0845 to 1715; Fri, 0845 to 1645

CEREDIGION ARCHIVES

County Office, Marine Terrace, Aberystwyth, Ceredigion, SY23 2DE

Tel: 01970 633697
Fax: 01970 633663
E-mail: archives@ceredigion.gov.uk

Website:
http://www.archifdy-ceredigion.org.uk

Enquiries:
Enquiries to: Archivist

Founded:
1974

Formerly called:
Dyfed Archives, Cardiganshire Area Office (year of change 1996)

Organisation type and purpose:
Local government body.
Local government county record office.

Non-library collection catalogue:
All or part available online and in-house

Access to staff:
Contact by letter, by telephone, by fax, by e-mail, in person and via website
Hours: Mon, 1400 to 1900; Tue to Fri, 1400 to 1630

Access to building, collection or gallery:
No prior appointment required

Access for disabled people:
Toilet facilities
Special comments: Disability lift

Parnet body:
Ceredigion County Council

CEREDIGION COUNTY COUNCIL

Neuadd Cyngor Ceredigion, Penmorfa, Aberaeron, Ceredigion, SA46 0PA

Tel: 01545 570881
Fax: 01545 572009
E-mail: info@ceredigion.gov.uk

continued overleaf

Website:
http://www.ceredigion.cix.co.uk/cyngor/
General, tourism, economic development.

Enquiries:
Enquiries to: Public Relations Manager
Direct tel: 01545 572002

Founded:
1996

Formerly called:
Cardiganshire County Council, Dyfed County
Council; Cyngor Dosbarth Ceredigion (year of
change 1996)

Organisation type and purpose:
Local government body.

Access to staff:
Contact by letter, by telephone, by fax, by e-mail,
in person and via website
Hours: Mon to Fri, 0900 to 1700

CERTIFICATION OFFICE FOR TRADE UNIONS AND EMPLOYERS' ASSOCIATIONS

22nd Floor, Euston Tower, 286 Euston Road,
London, NW1 3JJ

Tel: 020 7210 3734
Fax: 020 7210 3612
E-mail: info@certoffice.org

Website:
http://www.certoffice.org

Enquiries:
Enquiries to: Manager
Direct tel: 020 7210 3719

Founded:
1976

Organisation type and purpose:
National government body.
Independent statutory body.
To ensure trade unions and employers' associations
comply with the relevant legislation.

Subject coverage:
Information on financial returns of trade unions
and employers' associations, mergers between
trade unions and employers' associations, trade
union independence, elections for trade union
officers and members of executive, trade union
political fund rules.

**Museum or gallery collection, archive, or library
special collection:**
Certification Officers' annual reports from 1976
Trade union and employers' associations annual
returns, rules and constitutions from 1976
Trade union and employers' associations merger
documents from 1976

Printed publications:
Annual Report
A guide to political fund review ballots (2000 free)
Financial irregularities in trade unions and
employers associations. The approach of the
Certification Officer in exercising his powers of
investigation (2000)
Guidance for trade unions and employers'
associations wishing to establish a political fund
(1994 free)
Guidance for trade unions wishing to apply for a
certificate of independence (2000 free)
Making a complaint to the Certification Officer
against a trade union (1999 free)
Mergers: a guide to the statutory requirements for
transfers of engagements and amalgamation of
employers' associations (2000 free)
Mergers: a guide to the statutory requirements for
transfers of engagements and amalgamations of
trade unions (2000 free)

Publications list:
Available in print

Access to staff:
Contact by letter, by telephone and by e-mail
Hours: Mon to Fri, 0900 to 1700

Access to building, collection or gallery:
No prior appointment required
Hours: Mon to Fri 0930 to 1630

Access for disabled people:
Toilet facilities

CHAMBER BUSINESS

The Business Competitiveness Centre, Kimpton
Road, Luton, Bedfordshire, LU2 0LB

Tel: 01582 522448
Fax: 01582 522450

Enquiries:
Enquiries to: Information Officer
Direct e-mail: info@chamber-business.com

Founded:
2001

Formerly called:
Bedfordshire & Luton Chamber of Commerce,
Business Link Bedfordshire (year of change 2001)

Organisation type and purpose:
Membership association (membership is by
subscription), present number of members: 1400,
service industry, training organisation,
consultancy, research organisation.

Subject coverage:
Business, companies, grants, funding,
employment, exporting, HR, credit.

Access to staff:
Contact by e-mail
Hours: Mon to Fri, 0900 to 1700

Access for disabled people:
Parking provided, ramped entry, access to all
public areas, toilet facilities

CHAMBER OF COMMERCE HEREFORDSHIRE AND WORCESTERSHIRE

Head Office, Severn House, Prescott Drive,
Warndon Business Park, Worcester, WR4 9NE

Tel: 0845 641 1641
Fax: 0845 641 4641
E-mail: enquiries@hwchamber.co.uk

Website:
http://www.hwchamber.co.uk

Enquiries:
Enquiries to: Information Services & Quality
Executive

Founded:
1993

Formerly called:
HAWTEC Hereford & Worcester (year of change
1996/97); Business Link Herefordshire and
Worcestershire (year of change 1998/99)

Organisation type and purpose:
National organisation, advisory body, professional
body, membership association (membership is by
subscription), present number of members: 1,400.
Business support services, business advice and
information, membership services.

Subject coverage:
Information on Herefordshire and Worcestershire.

Information services:
Business Reference Library for Chamber Members;
On-line Resource Centre.

**Museum or gallery collection, archive, or library
special collection:**
Business Reference library

Library catalogue:
All or part available online

Printed publications:
Business Direction (6 times a year)
Chamber Quarterly Economic Survey (quarterly
survey of members' views on the economy, etc.)

Economic Assessment (annual report in
conjunction with Worcestershire County
Council)

Access to staff:
Contact by letter, by telephone, by fax, by e-mail,
in person and via website. Appointment necessary.
Access for members only. Non-members charged.
Hours: Mon to Fri, 0830 to 1730

Access for disabled people:
Parking provided, ramped entry, level entry, access
to all public areas, toilet facilities

Affiliated to:
British Chamber of Commerce Accredited
Chamber (BCC)

Also at:
Chamber of Commerce Herefordshire and
Worcestershire
Crossway House, Holmer Road, Hereford, HR4
9SS; tel: 0845 641 1641; e-mail: enquiries@
hwchamber.co.uk

CHAMBER OF COMMERCE TRAINING COMPANY LIMITED

Enterprise House, Castle Street, Worcester, WR1
3EN

Tel: 01905 744450
Fax: 01905 744451

Enquiries:
Enquiries to: Chief Executive
Direct e-mail: jennyj@hwchamber.co.uk
Other contacts: Administrator

Founded:
1982

Organisation type and purpose:
Training organisation.

Subject coverage:
Offers broad range of training services from IT
internet training through to MIG and TIG welding
training.

Printed publications:
Products, services brochures, on request

Access to staff:
Contact by letter, by telephone, by fax and by e-
mail
Hours: Mon to Fri, 0830 to 1730

Access for disabled people:
Parking provided, ramped entry, level entry, access
to all public areas, toilet facilities

CHANGING FACES

The Squire Centre, 33/37 University Street,
London, WC1E 6JN

Tel: 0845 4500 275
Fax: 0845 4500 276
E-mail: info@changingfaces.org.uk

Website:
http://changingfaces.org.uk

Enquiries:
Enquiries to: National Infomation and Advice
Worker

Founded:
1992

Organisation type and purpose:
Registered charity (charity number 1011222).
To provide information, advice and counselling to
children, adults (and families) affected by
disfigurement. Also provides training and
resources to health and social care professionals,
schools and employers.

Subject coverage:
Facial disfigurement.

Information services:
Online counselling via young people's website:
http://www.iface.org.uk.

Library catalogue:
All or part available in-house

Printed publications:
Reading list available to purchase
Up to three books available free to clients, at a charge to all others
Handling other people's reactions
Managing the effects of burns
When a medical skin condition affects the way you look
When facial paralysis affects the way you look
Talking to health professionals about disfigurement
Also a selection of other guides and booklets for adults, children and professionals
Order printed publications from: Full details on website; available from same address

Electronic and video publications:
Video on managing day-to-day challenges of living with disfigurement (available at cost)

Publications list:
Available online and in print

Access to staff:
Contact by letter, by telephone, by fax, by e-mail, in person and via website. Appointment necessary.
Hours: Mon to Fri, 0900 to 1700

Access for disabled people:
Full access

CHANNEL CROSSING ASSOCIATION, THE

Acronym or abbreviation: CCA

Bolden's Wood, Fiddling Lane, Stowting, Ashford, Kent, TN25 6AP

Tel: 01303 812011
Fax: 01303 812011
E-mail: channelcrossings@aol.com

Website:
http://www.channelcrossingassociation.com

Enquiries:
Enquiries to: Information Officer

Founded:
2001

Organisation type and purpose:
International organisation, membership association (membership is by subscription). To act as a body competent to organise and/or control selected sporting activities which take place in the Channel (eg Channel swims and crossings undertaken by unorthodox craft) and to liaise with the British and French Coastguards and Maritime Authorities, to maintain a register of professional pilots with experience of providing escort and pilotage for these activities.

Subject coverage:
Professional escort and pilotage across Strait of Dover and effective liaison with coastguard agencies of UK and France.

Printed publications:
Information/Registration Pack (available for purchase, direct)

Access to staff:
Contact by telephone, by e-mail and via website
Hours: Mon to Fri, 0900 to 1700

Access to building, collection or gallery:
No access other than to staff

Wholly-owned subsidiary of:
Channel Crossings Association Limited at the same address

CHANNEL SWIMMING ASSOCIATION LIMITED

Acronym or abbreviation: CSA

Bolden's Wood, Fiddling Lane, Stowting, Ashford, Kent, TN25 6AP

Tel: 01303 814788

Fax: 01303 813835
E-mail: swimsecretary@aol.com

Website:
http://www.channelswimmingassociation.com

Enquiries:
Enquiries to: General Secretary

Founded:
1927

Organisation type and purpose:
Voluntary organisation.

Subject coverage:
All information on Channel swimming since 1875, assistance for channel swimmers, observation and ratification of swims.

Museum or gallery collection, archive, or library special collection:
Photographs and press cuttings from 1875

Printed publications:
Handbook
Information Pack
Captain Webb and 100 Years of Channel Swimming

Access to staff:
Contact by telephone and by e-mail
Hours: Mon to Fri, 0900 to 1700

CHANNEL VIEW PUBLICATIONS LTD

Acronym or abbreviation: CVP

St Nicholas House, 31–34 High Street, Bristol, BS1 2AW

Tel: 0117 315 8562
Fax: 0117 315 8563
E-mail: info@multilingual-matters.com

Website:
http://www.multilingual-matters.com

Enquiries:
Enquiries to: Managing Director

Founded:
1980

Formerly called:
Multilingual Matters Limited (year of change 2008)

Organisation type and purpose:
Publishing house.

Subject coverage:
Languages, linguistics, translations, education, bilingualism, travel and tourism.

Printed publications:
Order printed publications from: http://www.channelviewpublications.com

Publications list:
Available online and in print

Access to staff:
Contact by letter, by telephone, by fax, by e-mail and via website
Hours: Mon to Fri, 0900 to 1700

CHANTRAINE SCHOOL OF DANCE

25A Menelik Road, London, NW2 3RJ

Tel: 020 7435 4247 and 07956 308031
Fax: 020 7435 4247
E-mail: patricia.woodall@yahoo.com

Website:
htttp://www.chantrainedance.co.uk

Enquiries:
Enquiries to: Director
Direct e-mail: info@chantrainedance.co.uk

Founded:
1978

Organisation type and purpose:
International organisation.
Dance school.

The School teaches the Chantraine Dance of Expression, created in France since 1958 by Alain and Françoise Chantraine, for the harmony and development of the person. Open to all ages – children from 4, to adults without age limit – and all levels – beginners to professional dancers; it aims to broaden and deepen the scope of dance as an expressive art linked with life, and to promote well-being and joy. It offers regular classes, short courses, choreographic ensemble and professional training.

Subject coverage:
The Chantraine Dance of Expression has three dimensions – artistic, pedagogic and human. They cover an extensive choreographic repertoire and a teaching method with five main aspects – rhythm, interiority, technique, creativity and choreography. The approach takes in the main styles – contemporary, classical, jazz and dances of other cultures – while going beyond style alone, as well as relationships with the other arts and the natural world.

Printed publications:
'La Danse de la Vie' (F Chantraine, 1998, Cerf, £7.00; in French)
'Poems/Poèmes' by Alain Chantraine, in French with translations by P.Woodall (£3.50, from Chantraine School).
Leaflets describing the Chantraine approach to dance and listing the classes available (revised annually, free)

Access to staff:
Contact by letter, by telephone, by fax, by e-mail, in person and via website. Appointment necessary.
Hours: Daily, 0830 to 2100

Also at:
High Wycombe Chantraine Centre
13 Queens Road, High Wycombe, Buckinghamshire, HP13 6AQ; tel: 01494 447741; e-mail: jgreenstreet@live.co.uk; website: http://www.chantrainedance.co.uk
Wanstead Chantraine Centre
27 Blake Hall Crescent, London, E11 3RH; tel: 020 8989 8604; e-mail: kategreen@yahoo.co.uk; website: http://www.chantrainedance.co.uk

Parent body:
Ecole de Danse Chantraine
12 avenue Ste-Foy, 92200 Neuilly sur Seine, France; tel: + 33 1 46 24 01 89; fax: + 33 1 46 24 64 11; e-mail: centredeneuilly@dansechantraine.com; website: http://www.dansechantraine.com

CHAPELS SOCIETY

c/o 47 Salisbury Drive, Midway, Swadlincote, DE11 7LD

Tel: 01283 558169
E-mail: chapelssociety@gmail.com

Website:
http://www.britarch.ac.uk/chapelsoc/index.html

Enquiries:
Enquiries to: Honorary Secretary

Founded:
1988

Organisation type and purpose:
Seeks to promote knowledge of the architectural and historical importance of places of worship outside the established Church, primarily the buildings of Christian bodies (Protestant, Roman Catholic, and Orthodox) but also those of other faiths.
The Chapels Society is a learned society administered by volunteers and is a registered charity in England (number 1014207). Membership of the Chapels Society is by annual subscription.

Subject coverage:
Nonconformist places of worship in England and comparable buildings throughout UK.

Printed publications:
A series of occasional publications and a newsletter (three times a year)

continued overleaf

Order printed publications from: Honorary Editor, Chapels Society, c/o 31 Melrose Avenue, Reading, RG6 7BN

Publications list:
Available online

Access to staff:
Contact by letter, by e-mail and via website
Special comments: Contact by e-mail.

Links with:
Capel (Welsh Chapels Heritage Society)
    website: http://www.capeli.org.uk/index.php
Historic Chapels Trust
    website: http://www.hct.org.uk/
The Association of Denominational Historical Societies & Cognate Libraries
    website: http://www.adhscl.org.uk/

CHARITIES AID FOUNDATION

Acronym or abbreviation: CAF

Kings Hill, West Malling, Kent, ME19 4TA

Tel: 01732 520000
Fax: 01732 520001
E-mail: enquiries@cafonline.org

Website:
http://www.cafonline.org/research
Latest research on the Voluntary Sector.
http://www.cafonline.org/info
Practical informtion on CAF and the Sector.
http://www.cafonline.org
Dynamic interactive guide to the services and activities of CAF worldwide. Other sites include information resources for the non-profit sector and facilities for online giving to charity.

Enquiries:
Enquiries to: Information Officer
Direct tel: 01732 520081/2/3
Other contacts: Press Officer for PR enquiries.

Founded:
1924

Organisation type and purpose:
International organisation, registered charity (charity number 268369), consultancy, research organisation.
CAF provides a range of services to charities and their supporters worldwide.
Exists to increase the flow of funds to the voluntary sector. Advises on how to give tax-effectively and provide charities with banking, investment and administration services.

Subject coverage:
Tax-effective giving, resources in the voluntary sector, loans for charities, international giving, administration and investment services for charities. Information on the charitable sector, lists of specific areas of charities, advice and support for charities seeking to use the Internet.

Trade and statistical information:
Income and expenditure of top 500 charities.
Size and scope of UK voluntary sector.
Levels of individual giving.
Corporate giving in the UK.
Local Authority and central government support for the voluntary sector.
Grant-making Trusts in the UK.

Printed publications:
A Lot of Give – trends in charitable giving for the 21st century (£14.99 plus p&p)
Coming Full Circle – the role of charitable funds in London's health (Pharaoh C and Mocroft I, £10 plus p&p)
Dimensions 2000 Series:
Income From Government Sources (£10 plus p&p)
An Update on CAF's Top 500 Fundraising Charities (£6 inc. p&p)
Patterns of Independent Grant-Making in the UK (£25 plus p&p)
Healthy Relationships (1998, £12 plus p&p)
Benchmarking Charity Costs (1998, £10 plus p&p)

Publications list:
Available in print

Access to staff:
Contact by letter, by telephone, by fax, by e-mail and via website. Appointment necessary.
Hours: Mon to Fri, 0900 to 1700

Access for disabled people:
Parking provided, level entry, access to all public areas, toilet facilities

Offices also at:
Charities Aid Foundation
    114–118 Southampton Row, London, WC1B
    5AA; tel: 020 7400 2300; fax: 020 7831 0134; e-mail: enquiries@cafonline.org

Overseas offices:
CAF America
    King Street Station, 1800 Diagonal Road, Suite 150, Alexandria, Virginia 22314–2840, USA; tel: 00 1 703 549 8931; fax: 00 1 703 549 8934; e-mail: info@cafamerica.org
CAF Brussels
    Rue Dejonckerstraat 46, Brussels, B-1060, Belgium; tel: 00 32 2 544 0050; fax: 00 32 2 544 0880; e-mail: cafbrussels@cafonline.org
CAF Bulgaria
    65 Vitosha Blvd, 2nd Floor, Sofia, 100, Bulgaria; tel: 00 359 2 981 1901; fax: 00 359 2 981 1901; e-mail: bcaf@cafonline.org
CAF India
    25 Navjeevan Vihar, Ground Floor, New Delhi, 110017, India; tel: 00 91 11 652 2206; fax: 00 91 11 618 6646; e-mail: cafindia@cafonline.org
CAF Russia (based in Moscow)
    14/6 Ulitsa Sadovnicheskaya 57, Moscow, 113035, Russia; tel: 00 7 095 792 5929; fax: 00 7 095 792 5929; e-mail: cafrussia@cafonline.org
CAF Southern Africa
    41 de Korte Street, Braamfontein 2017, Gauteng, South Africa; tel: 00 27 11 339 1136; fax: 00 27 11 339 1152; e-mail: cafsouthafrica@cafonline.org
CAF West Africa
    F-146/5 Second Soula Street, North Labone Estates, PO Box 05–2956, OSU, Accra, Ghana; tel: 00 233 21 771 953; fax: 00 233 21 7011 260; e-mail: cafwestafrica@cafonline.org

CHARITIES EVALUATION SERVICES

Acronym or abbreviation: CES

4 Coldbath Square, London, EC1R 5HL

Tel: 020 7713 5722
Fax: 020 7713 5692
E-mail: enquiries@ces-vol.org.uk

Website:
http://www.ces-vol.org.uk

Enquiries:
Enquiries to: Information Officer

Organisation type and purpose:
Registered charity (charity number 803602), training organisation.

Access to staff:
Contact by letter, by telephone, by fax, by e-mail and via website. Appointment necessary.
Hours: Mon to Fri, 0900 to 1730

Access for disabled people:
Parking provided, level entry, toilet facilities

CHARITY COMMISSION FOR ENGLAND AND WALES

Charity Commission Direct, PO Box 1227, Liverpool, L69 3UG

Tel: 0845 300 0218
Fax: 0151 703 1555
E-mail: enquiries@charitycommission.gsi.gov.uk

Website:
http://www.charitycommission.gov.uk

Enquiries:
Direct e-mail: pressenquiries@charitycommission .gsi.gov.uk

Organisation type and purpose:
Central government body; includes the Central Register of Charities.

Subject coverage:
General advice to charity trustees, information on the Commission to members of the public, effective use of charitable monies, charity law, history, administration and management.

Museum or gallery collection, archive, or library special collection:
19th-century reports of the former Commissioners for Inquiring concerning Charities
Unreported vols concerning charities (mid-19th century to 1947)

Library catalogue:
All or part available in-house

Printed publications:
Annual Report
Guidance leaflets on charity administration
Order printed publications from: The Stationery Office

Publications list:
Available online

Access to staff:
Contact by letter, by telephone, by fax, by e-mail, in person and via website. Appointment necessary.
Hours: Mon to Fri, 0900 to 1700
Special comments: Central Register of Charities open 1000 to 1600 by appointment only.

Access to building, collection or gallery:
Prior appointment required
Hours: 1000 to 1600

Access for disabled people:
Level entry, access to all public areas, toilet facilities

CHARLES WILLIAMS SOCIETY

Flat 8, 65 Cadogan Gardens, London, SW3 2RA

Tel: 020 7581 9917
E-mail: brian.horne2@btinternet.com

Website:
http://www.charleswilliamssociety.org.uk

Enquiries:
Enquiries to: Librarian

Founded:
1976

Organisation type and purpose:
Learned society.
To promote interest in, and provide opportunities for, study of Charles Williams' writings.

Subject coverage:
Life and works of Charles Walter Stansby Williams, author, theologian and poet, 1886–1945.

Museum or gallery collection, archive, or library special collection:
Members' lending and reference libraries are located at CMRS, St Michael's Hall, Shoe Lane, Oxford, OX1 2DP

Printed publications:
Quarterly (newsletter for members, 4 a year)
Occasional publications

Access to staff:
Contact by letter, by telephone, by e-mail and via website
Hours: Mon to Fri, 0900 to 1700

CHARLOTTE M. YONGE FELLOWSHIP

Acronym or abbreviation: CMYF

8 Anchorage Terrace, Durham, DH1 3DL

Tel: 0191 384 7857
E-mail: c.e.schultze@durham.ac.uk

Website:
http://www.cmyf.org.uk

Enquiries:
Enquiries to: Membership Secretary

Founded:
1995

Organisation type and purpose:
Membership association (membership is by subscription), present number of members: 160. Literary society for all those interested in the work of Victorian novelist, Charlotte M. Yonge.

Subject coverage:
The works, life and milieu of Victorian novelist, Charlotte M. Yonge (1823–1901).

Museum or gallery collection, archive, or library special collection:
Collection of books by and relating to Charlotte M. Yonge, accessible to members, located in Oxford, United Kingdom

Printed publications:
Review (twice a year, to members; individual issues available for purchase by non-members)
Journal (approx. biennial, to members; also available for purchase by non-members)
Books (essay vol. on Yonge, 2007)
Reprinted works by Yonge (one in 2009, others forthcoming)
Order printed publications from: Details on website

Publications list:
Available online

Access to staff:
Contact by letter, by e-mail and via website
Hours: Mon to Fri, 0900 to 1700

Access to building, collection or gallery:
No access other than to staff

CHARTERED INSTITUTE FOR SECURITIES & INVESTMENT

Acronym or abbreviation: CISI

8 Eastcheap, London, EC3M 1AE

Tel: 020 7645 0600
Fax: 020 7645 0601

Website:
http://www.secinst.co.uk
Qualifications, membership, CPD and events, education, careers, ethics.

Enquiries:
Enquiries to: Client Services
Direct tel: 020 7645 0680
Direct e-mail: clientservices@cisi.org

Founded:
1992

Royal Charter granted:
(year of change 2009)

Organisation type and purpose:
A registered charity, a professional body for those who work in the securities and investment industry in the UK and in a growing number of major financial centres round the world. Has more than 40,000 members in 89 countries.
To promote, for the public benefit, the advancement and dissemination of knowledge in the field of securities and investments; to develop high ethical standards for practitioners in securities and investments and to promote such standards in the UK and overseas; to act as an authoritative body for the purpose of consultation and research in matters of education or public interest concerning investment in securities.

Subject coverage:
Securities and investments industry.

Electronic and video publications:
Annual Report and Accounts
A wide range of brochures and fact sheets on the following topics: qualifications, membership, events, international, careers
Press releases
Examination workbooks (available to purchase via the website)

Order electronic and video publications from:
Download from website; for multiple hard copies, contact Client Services, tel: 0207 645 0600; e-mail: clientservices@cisi.org

Publications list:
Available online

Access to staff:
Contact by letter, by telephone, by fax and by e-mail

Also at:
CISI Northern Ireland
CISI Scotland

Branches:
10 network branches in England and Wales, 3 offshore branches

CHARTERED INSTITUTE OF ARBITRATORS

Acronym or abbreviation: CIArb

International Centre for Arbitration and Mediation, 12 Bloomsbury Square, London, WC1A 2LP

Tel: 020 7421 7444
Fax: 020 7404 4023
E-mail: info@ciarb.org

Website:
http://www.ciarb.org
Information about the Institute, dispute resolution and details about education and training, membership and resources for practitioners.

Enquiries:
Enquiries to: Member Services Assistant
Direct tel: 020 7421 7439
Direct e-mail: kmurray@ciarb.org
Other contacts: The Legal Counsel (for legal enquiries)

Founded:
1915

Organisation type and purpose:
The Institute is globally recognised as the professional home for all dispute resolvers and is a resource centre for those who benefit from cost-effective, private dispute resolution; number of members: 11,000 worldwide; the CIArb is a global authority on dispute resolution. CIArb membership offers individuals from a variety of sectors internationally recognised standards of excellence. The Institute also provides dispute resolution services for public sector, consumer and commercial markets, providing bespoke solutions for the efficient settlement of disputes.

Subject coverage:
Commercial arbitration, mediation, adjudication, dispute resolution, aspects of law, arbitration clauses, appointment of arbitrators, arbitration acts, international arbitration, international conventions on arbitration, enforcement of arbitration awards, training of arbitrators, duties of expert witnesses and advocacy, alternative dispute resolution procedures.

Museum or gallery collection, archive, or library special collection:
Volumes on arbitration procedure and practice throughout the world
Legal texts covering dispute resolution

Library catalogue:
All or part available online and in-house

Printed publications:
Arbitration Journal, Institute Newsletter (quarterly, arbitration rules)

Access to staff:
Contact by letter, by telephone, by fax, by e-mail and via website. Appointment necessary.
Hours: Mon to Fri, 0830 to 1730

Access to building, collection or gallery:
Library available to members
Hours: Mon to Fri, 0830 to 1730

Access for disabled people:
Toilet facilities, lifts

Branches:
30 branches world-wide

CHARTERED INSTITUTE OF ARCHITECTURAL TECHNOLOGISTS

Acronym or abbreviation: CIAT

397 City Road, Islington, London, EC1V 1NH

Tel: 020 7278 2206
Fax: 020 7837 3194
E-mail: info@ciat.org.uk

Website:
http://www.ciat.org.uk

Enquiries:
Enquiries to: Communications Director
Other contacts: Assistant Communications Director

Founded:
1965

Formerly called:
Society of Architectural & Associated Technicians (year of change 1986); British Institute of Architectural Technicians (year of change 1994); British Institute of Architectural Technologists (year of change 2005)

Organisation type and purpose:
Professional body (membership is by subscription), present number of members: 9,500. International qualifying body for Chartered Architectural Technologists and Professional Architectural Technicians.

Subject coverage:
Careers advice, practice and technical advice, education guidance, recognition of the CIAT qualifications, continuing professional development, consultative panel for construction documents, architecture and construction awards.

Printed publications:
Architectural Technology (journal, 6 times a year)
Becoming a Member (free)
Careers Handbook (free)
Code of Conduct (free)

Publications list:
Available in print

Access to staff:
Contact by letter, by telephone, by fax, by e-mail, in person and via website
Hours: Mon to Fri, 0900 to 1700

Access to building, collection or gallery:
Prior appointment required

Member organisation of:
Construction Industry Council

CHARTERED INSTITUTE OF BANKERS IN SCOTLAND

Acronym or abbreviation: CIOBS

38B Drumsheugh Gardens, Edinburgh, EH3 7SW

Tel: 0131 473 7777
Fax: 0131 473 7788
E-mail: info@ciobs.org.uk

Website:
http://www.ciobs.org.uk
General information on the Institute, full details of the educational programmes.

Enquiries:
Enquiries to: Chief Executive
Other contacts: Director of Education (for information on qualifications and courses; Business Development Manager (for marketing and development issues)

Founded:
1875

continued overleaf

Formerly called:
Institute of Bankers in Scotland (year of change 1991)

Organisation type and purpose:
Professional body (membership is by subscription, qualification, election or invitation), present number of members: 11,500, registered charity (charity number SCO 13927).

Subject coverage:
Banking and finance, administration and management.

Museum or gallery collection, archive, or library special collection:
Scottish Bank Notes from 1727 to the present

Printed publications:
Handbooks on Scottish banking practice
Workbooks relating to the financial services sector
Scottish Banker (6 times a year)

Publications list:
Available in print

Access to staff:
Contact by letter, by telephone, by fax, by e-mail and via website. Appointment necessary.
Hours: Mon to Fri, 0900 to 1700

CHARTERED INSTITUTE OF BUILDING

Acronym or abbreviation: CIOB

Englemere, Kings Ride, Ascot, Berkshire, SL5 7TB

Tel: 01344 630700
Fax: 01344 630777
E-mail: reception@ciob.org.uk

Website:
http://www.constructors.org
Membership access for library database, membership database.
http://www.ciob.org.uk
Public access for the CIOB and its services plus members-only area.

Enquiries:
Enquiries to: LIS Manager
Direct fax: 01344 630764
Direct e-mail: lis@ciob.org.uk

Founded:
1834

Organisation type and purpose:
International organisation, professional body (membership is by qualification), present number of members: 38,000 individuals, 320 firms, registered charity (charity number 280795), suitable for ages: 18+, research organisation, publishing house.

Subject coverage:
Processes of management in construction: eg; law; contracts; human resources; costs; planning and programming; education and training.

Museum or gallery collection, archive, or library special collection:
Photographic collection on Construction Management Processes (small)
Building Law Reports
Conference Proceedings, 1970 to date
Construction Law Reports

Library catalogue:
All or part available online

Printed publications:
Construction History (annually)
Construction Information Quarterly (4 times a year)
Construction Manager (formerly Chartered Builder, 10 times a year)
Order printed publications from: Construction Books Direct, Englemere Limited
The White House, Englemere, Kings Ride, Ascot, SC5 7JR, tel: 01344 630810

Publications list:
Available online

Access to staff:
Contact by letter, by telephone, by fax, by e-mail and via website. Appointment necessary. Access for members only. Non-members charged.
Hours: Mon to Fri, 0830 to 1700 (phone)

Access to building, collection or gallery:
Appointment required
Hours: Mon to Fri, 0930 to 1630
Special comments: Members only.

Access for disabled people:
Parking provided, ramped entry, access to all public areas, toilet facilities

Affiliated to:
CIRIA
  tel: 020 7222 8891
Conseil International du Bâtiment (CIB)
Construction Industry Computing Association
  tel: 01223 236336; e-mail: postmaster@cica.org.uk

CHARTERED INSTITUTE OF ENVIRONMENTAL HEALTH

Acronym or abbreviation: CIEH

Chadwick Court, 15 Hatfields, London, SE1 8DJ

Tel: 020 7928 6006
Fax: 020 7827 5862
E-mail: info@cieh.org

Website:
http://www.cieh.org
Information about the Chartered Institute, including press releases and policy statements.

Enquiries:
Enquiries to: Information Officer
Direct tel: 020 7827 5821
Direct fax: 020 7827 6322

Founded:
1883

Formerly called:
Association of Public Sanitary Inspectors (year of change 1891); Sanitary Inspectors Association (year of change 1957); Association of Public Health Inspectors (year of change 1975); Environmental Health Officers Association (year of change 1981); Institution of Environmental Health Officers (year of change 1994)

Organisation type and purpose:
Professional body (membership is by qualification), registered charity (charity number 290350).
Registration board and examining body for Environmental Health Officers.

Subject coverage:
Environmental health, housing, pollution control, food safety, health and safety at work, and noise.

Museum or gallery collection, archive, or library special collection:
Complete set of the CIEH journal: Environmental Health Practitioner 1895 to 2009

Library catalogue:
All or part available in-house

Printed publications:
Environmental Health News (fortnightly)
Journal of Environmental Health Research (twice a year)
Reports and guidance on environmental protection, food hygiene, general environmental health, health and safety, housing, and pest control

Publications list:
Available online

Access to staff:
Contact by letter, by telephone, by fax, by e-mail and via website. Appointment necessary.
Hours: Mon to Fri, 0900 to 1700

Access to building, collection or gallery:
Library access for CIEH members and researchers, by appointment
Hours: Library: Mon to Fri, 0900 to 1700

CHARTERED INSTITUTE OF HOUSING

Acronym or abbreviation: CIH

Octavia House, Westwood Way, Coventry, Warwickshire, CV4 8JP

Tel: 024 7685 1700
Fax: 024 7669 5110

Website:
http://www.cih.org
Some information on policy, training and publications.

Enquiries:
Enquiries to: Information Officer
Other contacts: Good Practice Manager

Formerly called:
Institute of Housing

Merged with:
Institute of Rent Officers and Rental Valuers, date of change, February 1999

Organisation type and purpose:
Professional body (membership is by subscription), present number of members: over 17,000, registered charity (charity number 244067/R), training organisation, research organisation.

Subject coverage:
Housing (social and private rented sector), housing finance, CCT, homelessness, housing management and good practice.

Museum or gallery collection, archive, or library special collection:
15,000 books and reports and about 35 journal titles held in library

Trade and statistical information:
Housing statistics, stock sizes, tenure type.

Printed publications:
Briefing papers on current topics of housing interest
Housing (magazine, monthly)
Inside Housing (magazine, weekly)
Yearbook
Many good practice books, guides and manuals including:
Manual on Housing Benefit and Valuation
Order printed publications from: Publications Officer
tel: 02476 851700

Electronic and video publications:
Housing Management Standards Manual: Hypertext edition

Publications list:
Available online and in print

Access to staff:
Contact by letter, by telephone and by e-mail. Access for members only.
Hours: Mon to Fri, 0900 to 1700
Special comments: Members only.

Access to building, collection or gallery:
No prior appointment required

Other addresses:
CIH London
  9 White Lion Street, Islington, London, N1 9XJ; tel: 020 7837 4280; fax: 020 7278 2705
CIH Scotland
  6 Palmerston Place, Edinburgh, EH12 5AA; tel: 0131 225 4544; fax: 0131 225 4566
CIH Wales
  4 Purbeck House, Lambourne Crescent, Cardiff Business Park, Llanishen, Cardiff, CF4 5GJ; tel: 029 2076 5760; fax: 029 2076 5761

CHARTERED INSTITUTE OF JOURNALISTS

Acronym or abbreviation: CIOJ

2 Dock Offices, Surrey Quays Road, London, SE16 2XU

Tel: 020 7252 1187
Fax: 020 7232 2302
E-mail: memberservices@cioj.co.uk

Website:
http://www.ioj.co.uk

Enquiries:
Enquiries to: General Secretary
Other contacts: Treasurer (for all financial matters)

Founded:
1884

Formerly called:
Institute of Journalists (IOJ) (year of change 1978)

Organisation type and purpose:
International organisation, professional body, trade union (membership is by subscription, election or invitation), present number of members: 1,150.

Subject coverage:
Journalism, broadcasting.

Museum or gallery collection, archive, or library special collection:
Newspaper and journalistic library

Printed publications:
CIOJ Journal (quarterly, free to members)
Directory of Chartered Institute of Freelance Journalists
CIOJ Update (newsletter)

Access to staff:
Contact by letter, by telephone, by fax, by e-mail and via website. Appointment necessary.
Hours: Mon to Fri, 0900 to 1700

Access to building, collection or gallery:
No prior appointment required

Links with:
British Copyright Council
Campaign for Freedom of Information
Independent Unions Training Council
Journalists' Copyright Fund
Media Society
National Council for the Training of Journalists

CHARTERED INSTITUTE OF LIBRARY AND INFORMATION PROFESSIONALS

Acronym or abbreviation: CILIP

7 Ridgmount Street, London, WC1E 7AE

Tel: 020 7255 0500; 020 7255 0505 (minicom, textphone)
Fax: 020 7255 0501
E-mail: info@cilip.org.uk

Website:
http://www.cilip.org.uk

Enquiries:
Enquiries to: Information and Advice Team
Direct tel: 020 7255 0620
Other contacts: Chief Executive

Founded:
1877

Formerly called:
The Institute of Information Scientists (IIS), The Library Association (LA) (year of change 2002)

Organisation type and purpose:
CILIP is the leading professional body for librarians, information specialists and knowledge managers. CILIP forms a community of around 36,000 people engaged in library and information work, of whom approximately 18,000 are CILIP members and about 15,000 are regular customers of CILIP Enterprises.

Subject coverage:
Librarianship, libraries, information science and services, education for the profession, salaries and conditions, qualifications and professional development, service provision guidelines and standards, databases, copyright, legislation, local authorities, recruitment agency.

Library catalogue:
All or part available in-house

Printed publications:
Library and Information Gazette

Directories and published works from Facet Publishing
Library and Information Update
Chartered Institute of Library and Information Professionals' Yearbook

Publications list:
Available in print

Access to staff:
Contact by letter, by telephone, by fax and by e-mail. Appointment necessary.
Hours: Mon to Fri, 0900 to 1700
Special comments: Tel. enquiries taken 1000 to 1600.

CHARTERED INSTITUTE OF LIBRARY AND INFORMATION PROFESSIONALS IN SCOTLAND

Acronym or abbreviation: CILIPS

1st Floor Building C, Brandon Gate, Leechlee Road, Hamilton, ML3 6AU

Tel: 01698 458888
Fax: 01698 283170
E-mail: cilips@slainte.org.uk

Website:
http://www.slainte.org.uk

Enquiries:
Enquiries to: Director
Direct e-mail: e.fulton@slainte.org.uk

Founded:
1908

Created by the merger of:
The Scottish Library Association and the Institute of Information Scientists (IIS) (year of change 2002)

Organisation type and purpose:
Professional body, registered charity (charity number 313014).

Subject coverage:
Librarianship and library resources in Scotland.

Printed publications:
IS News

Electronic and video publications:
Information Scotland

Access to staff:
Contact by letter, by telephone and by e-mail

Access to building, collection or gallery:
Appointment only
Hours: 0900 to 1700

Affiliated to:
CILIP
   website: http://www.cilip.org.uk

CHARTERED INSTITUTE OF LINGUISTS

Acronym or abbreviation: IoL

Saxon House, 48 Southwark Street, London, SE1 1UN

Tel: 020 7940 3100
Fax: 020 7940 3101
E-mail: info@iol.org.uk

Website:
http://www.iol.org.uk
Membership, examinations, assessments, employment possibilities, the Linguist, Members' Discussion Forum, Find-a-Linguist service, Chartered Linguist site.

Enquiries:
Enquiries to: Director of Communications
Direct tel: 020 7940 3135
Direct fax: 020 7940 3121
Direct e-mail: cetty.zambrano@iol.org.uk
Other contacts: (1) Central Registration Department (2) Registrar for (1) examination queries (2) membership eligibility.

Founded:
1910

Organisation type and purpose:
International organisation, professional body (membership is by qualification), present number of members: 6,500.
To promote the interests of professional linguists and maintain standards within the language world.

Subject coverage:
Language learning; courses; methods; availability and training of translators and interpreters; qualifications; language grammar books and dictionaries; employment of translators; examinations in languages; careers with languages; language in general; public service interpreters; language assessments.

Museum or gallery collection, archive, or library special collection:
Journals and magazines relating to languages or linguistics received from appropriate organisations overseas
Monolingual minor language works
Technical and/or specialised multilingual dictionaries

Trade and statistical information:
Survey of freelance notes for translators and interpreters.

Library catalogue:
All or part available in-house

Printed publications:
Publications for language and translator's qualifications available
1998 Freelance Rates Survey (full report, £15 plus p&p)
Information sheets for translators
The Linguist (6 times a year)
Translator's Information Pack (members free, non-members £5 plus p&p)
Order printed publications from: Membership Department

Publications list:
Available online and in print

Access to staff:
Contact by letter, by telephone, by fax, by e-mail and via website
Hours: Mon to Fri, 0900 to 1700

Access to building, collection or gallery:
By appointment with a contact
Hours: Mon to Fri, 0900 to 1700

Access for disabled people:
Wheelchair access not available due to the heritage condition and age of the building, disabled persons can be assisted by staff at the main entrance

CHARTERED INSTITUTE OF LOGISTICS AND TRANSPORT (UK)

Acronym or abbreviation: CILT (UK)

Logistics and Transport Centre, Earlstrees Court, Earlstrees Road, Corby, Northamptonshire, NN17 4AX

Tel: 01536 740100
Fax: 01536 740101
E-mail: enquiry@ciltuk.org.uk

Website:
http://www.ciltuk.org.uk
Services, products and activities.

Enquiries:
Enquiries to: Chief Executive
Other contacts: Director Corporate Communications

Founded:
1999

Organisation type and purpose:
Professional body (membership is by qualification), present number of members: 23,000, registered charity (charity number 1004963).

continued overleaf

Subject coverage:
Information technology, logistics, warehousing, transport, materials management, materials handling, inventory systems, stock control, storage, distribution, road, rail, air and sea transport, transport planning, transport operations, transport infrastructure provision.

Library catalogue:
All or part available online and in-house

Printed publications:
Logistics and Transport Focus (10 times a year, free to members)

Publications list:
Available in print

Access to staff:
Contact by letter, by telephone, by fax, by e-mail and via website. Appointment necessary.
Hours: Mon to Fri, 0900 to 1700

Access to building, collection or gallery:
No access other than to staff and members
Hours: Mon to Fri, 0900 to 1700
Special comments: Charge to non-members.

CHARTERED INSTITUTE OF LOSS ADJUSTERS

Acronym or abbreviation: CILA

Warwick House, 65/66 Queen Street, London EC4R 1EB

Tel: 020 7337 9960
Fax: 020 7929 3082
E-mail: info@cila.co.uk

Website:
http://www.cila.co.uk

Enquiries:
Enquiries to: Executive Director

Founded:
1941

Organisation type and purpose:
Professional body (membership is by qualification), present number of members: Approx 2600.

Subject coverage:
Insurance, loss adjusting, property, liability.

Printed publications:
Publication list available direct

Publications list:
Available in print

Access to staff:
Contact by letter
Hours: Mon to Fri, 0900 to 1700

CHARTERED INSTITUTE OF MARKETING

Acronym or abbreviation: CIM

Moor Hall, Cookham, Maidenhead, Berkshire, SL6 9QH

Tel: 01628 427500
Fax: 01628 427499
E-mail: info@cim.co.uk

Website:
http://www.cim.co.uk
Outline of CIM services and events.

Enquiries:
Enquiries to: Information Services Manager
Direct tel: 01628 427333
Direct fax: 01628 427349
Direct e-mail: library@cim.co.uk
Other contacts: Head of Marketing Communications

Founded:
1911

Organisation type and purpose:
Professional body.

Subject coverage:
Consumer and industrial products and services, retail, wholesale and distribution sectors, marketing planning, implementation and control techniques, marketing communications, marketing support services, human resources.

Museum or gallery collection, archive, or library special collection:
6,000 books held on marketing and management specifically, relevant marketing journals, market research reports, miscellaneous other reports
Members also have access to online journals from their desktops

Trade and statistical information:
Market research reports and government statistics.

Non-library collection catalogue:
All or part available in-house

Library catalogue:
All or part available online and in-house

Printed publications:
Books, marketing and sales texts (joint ventures and own publications)
The marketer (magazine, 10 times a year)
Twice-yearly papers published on topics such as segmentation, marketing law, communications, sponsorship and technology
Order printed publications from: CIM Direct, at the same address: tel: 01628 427427; fax: 01628 427439; e-mail: cimdirect@cim.co.uk

Publications list:
Available online and in print

Access to staff:
Contact by letter, by telephone, by fax, by e-mail, in person and via website. Appointment necessary. Non-members charged.
Hours: Mon to Fri, 0900 to 1700 for telephone and e-mail enquiries
Wed to Fri, 0900 to 1700 for personal visits
Special comments: Charges may be made to non-members for usage, prior appointment required. Some services free to members.

Also at:
The Chartered Institute of Marketing (Scotland)
3rd Floor, 100 Wellington Street, Glasgow, G2 6DH; tel: 0141 221 7700; fax: 0141 221 7766
The Chartered Institute of Marketing Ireland
13 Harbour Court, Heron Road, Belfast, BT3 9HB; tel: 028 9045 1005; fax: 028 9046 9004

Member organisation of:
European Marketing Council (EMC)
tel: +32 2 7421780; fax: +32 2 7421785; e-mail: infodesk@emc.be

CHARTERED INSTITUTE OF PATENT ATTORNEYS

Acronym or abbreviation: CIPA

95 Chancery Lane, London, WC2A 1DT

Tel: 020 7405 9450
Fax: 020 7430 0471
E-mail: mail@cipa.org.uk

Website:
http://www.cipa.org.uk
General basic information on patents, trademarks, designs and copyright, careers information, lists of firms of patent attorneys (also known as patent agents), general news, links to other relevant sites.

Enquiries:
Enquiries to: Institute Manager

Founded:
1882

Formerly called:
The Chartered Institute of Patent Agents (year of change 2006)

Organisation type and purpose:
Professional body.

Subject coverage:
Patents, designs, trademarks, copyright.

Printed publications:
CIPA – Journal of the CIPA (£100 a year)
Directory of Firms of Patent Agents (free, and online)
Information Pack for Inventors (free, and online)
Membership list (£25)
Register of Patent Agents (annually, £25, free online)

Access to staff:
Contact by letter, by telephone, by fax, by e-mail and via website
Hours: Mon to Fri, 0900 to 1730

CHARTERED INSTITUTE OF PERSONNEL AND DEVELOPMENT

Acronym or abbreviation: CIPD

151 The Broadway, London, SW19 1JQ

Tel: 020 8612 6200
Fax: 020 8612 6232
E-mail: cipd@cipd.co.uk

Website:
http://www.cipd.co.uk
2,000 pages on CIPD services and access for members to the LIS webcat.

Enquiries:
Enquiries to: Head of Library and Information Services
Direct tel: 020 8612 6210
Direct fax: 020 8612 6232
Direct e-mail: lis@cipd.co.uk

Founded:
2000

Organisation type and purpose:
Professional body, registered charity (charity number 1079797), training organisation, research organisation.

Subject coverage:
Personnel management, industrial relations, employment law, training.

Museum or gallery collection, archive, or library special collection:
Comprehensive collection of publications for the European Centre for the Development of Vocational Training (CEDEFOP)

Printed publications:
People Management (journal, fortnightly)
Wide range of publications on personnel development and general management for managers and students

Electronic and video publications:
Available on website:
Careers information
Case Studies
Quick Facts
Reports
Surveys

Publications list:
Available in print

Access to staff:
Contact by letter, by telephone, by fax, by e-mail, in person and via website. Non-members charged.
Hours: Mon to Fri, 0900 to 1730
Special comments: Primarily for members only.

UK contact for:
European Centre for the Development of Vocational Training (CEDEFOP)
International Federation of Training and Development Organisations (IFTDO)

CHARTERED INSTITUTE OF PUBLIC FINANCE AND ACCOUNTANCY

Acronym or abbreviation: CIPFA Scotland

22 Logie Mill, Edinburgh, EH7 4HG

Tel: 0131 551 2100
Fax: 0131 551 2223

E-mail: scotland@cipfa.org.uk

Website:
http://www.cipfascotland.org.uk

Founded:
1885

Organisation type and purpose:
Professional body (membership is by qualification), present number of members: 13,000, registered charity (charity number 231060).

Subject coverage:
Financial management in the public services, especially as regards Scotland.
Accountancy and finance training and qualifications.

Trade and statistical information:
Information published on the expenditure and income of all Scottish local authorities; two annual publications of statistics (Rating Review).

Printed publications:
Publications and newsletters regarding financial management in the public services in Scotland.
Scottish News (quarterly)

Publications list:
Available in print

Access to staff:
Contact by letter, by telephone, by fax, by e-mail and via website
Hours: Mon to Fri, 0900 to 1700
Special comments: Not a public office.

Headquarters address:
CIPFA
3 Robert Street, London, WC2N 6BH; tel: 020 7543 5600; fax: 020 7543 5700; e-mail: info@cipfa.org.uk

CHARTERED INSTITUTE OF PUBLIC RELATIONS

Acronym or abbreviation: CIPR

32 St James's Square, London, SW1Y 4JR

Tel: 020 7766 3333
Fax: 020 7766 3344
E-mail: info@cipr.co.uk

Website:
http://www.cipr.co.uk

Founded:
1948

Organisation type and purpose:
Professional body, present number of members: 9,000.

Subject coverage:
Public relations practice in central and local government, industry and commerce, consultancies and voluntary organisations.

Printed publications:
Annual Report (free)
Profile (magazine, members)
The CIPR Planning, Research and Evaluation Toolkit (£35 members, £85 non-members, plus £1 p&p)
Other publications include:
The PR in Practice series
Order printed publications from: website: http://www.cipr.co.uk/publications

Publications list:
Available in print

Access to staff:
Contact by letter, by telephone, by fax, by e-mail and via website. Appointment necessary.
Hours: Mon to Fri, 0900 to 1800

Member organisation of:
European Confederation of Public Relations (CERP)
Global Alliance

CHARTERED INSTITUTE OF TAXATION

Acronym or abbreviation: CIOT

12 Upper Belgrave Street, London, SW1X 8BB

Tel: 020 7235 9381
Fax: 020 7235 2562

Website:
http://www.tax.org.uk
Information on taxation and the Institute.

Enquiries:
Enquiries to: Head of Education Department
Direct e-mail: rbaxter@ciot.org.uk

Founded:
1930

Formerly called:
Institute of Taxation (year of change 1994)

Organisation type and purpose:
Professional body, registered charity (charity number 1037771), training organisation.

Subject coverage:
UK taxation, information on examinations in taxation and careers in the profession.

Museum or gallery collection, archive, or library special collection:
Tax Library at King's College London (members only)

Printed publications:
Annual Report (free)
Essential Law for the Tax Adviser
Essential Accounting for the Tax Technician
Directory of Chartered Tax Advisers
Tax Adviser (journal, monthly, free to members, subscription for non-members)

Access to staff:
Contact by letter, by telephone, by fax, by e-mail and via website
Hours: Mon to Fri, 0900 to 1700

Access to building, collection or gallery:
No access other than to staff

Sister body to:
Association of Taxation Technicians
at the same address; tel: 020 7235 2544; fax: 020 7235 4571; e-mail: info@att.org.uk

UK Representative Body on the:
Confédération Fiscale Européenne

CHARTERED INSTITUTION OF BUILDING SERVICES ENGINEERS

Acronym or abbreviation: CIBSE

222 Balham High Road, London, SW12 9BS

Tel: 020 8675 5211
Fax: 020 8675 5449

Website:
http://www.cibse.org

Enquiries:
Enquiries to: Information Officer

Founded:
1977

Formerly called:
Illuminating Engineering Society (IES), Institution of Heating and Ventilating Engineers (IHVE) (year of change 1977); Chartered Institution of Building Services (CIBS) (year of change 1982)

Organisation type and purpose:
Professional body, registered charity (charity number 278104).
Provides the Secretariat of the National Illumination Committee of Great Britain.

Subject coverage:
All engineering services within buildings: design, installation, commissioning, maintenance, acoustics, air conditioning, communications, controls, electrical services, energy management,

fire protection, heating, internal transportation, lighting, maintenance, public health, refrigeration, safety, security, ventilating, facilities management.

Printed publications:
Building Services (technical journal, monthly)
Building Services Engineering Research and Technology (technical journal, quarterly)
Lighting Research and Technology (technical journal, quarterly)
Lighting Register (annual)
Minimising the risk of Legionnaires' disease (2000)
Register of Building Services Consultants (annually and online)
A comprehensive range of information on building services including: guides, reference books, technical memoranda, commissioning and building energy codes, application manuals and research publications

Electronic and video publications:
Register of Building Services Consultants (online, annually)
CIBSE Guide C: Reference data (2001) (CD-ROM)
CIBSE Guide J: Weather, solar and illuminance data (CD-ROM)

Publications list:
Available online and in print

Access to staff:
Contact by letter, by telephone, by fax and by e-mail
Hours: Mon to Fri, 0900 to 1700

CHARTERED INSTITUTION OF WASTES MANAGEMENT

Acronym or abbreviation: CIWM

9 Saxon Court, St Peter's Gardens, Northampton, NN1 1SX

Tel: 01604 620426
Fax: 01604 621339
E-mail: technical@ciwm.co.uk

Website:
http://www.ciwm.co.uk

Enquiries:
Enquiries to: Technical Officer

Founded:
1898

Formerly called:
Institute of Public Cleansing (IPC), Institute of Solid Wastes Management (ISWM), Institute of Wastes Management (IWM)

Organisation type and purpose:
National organisation, professional body, registered charity, training organisation, research organisation.

Subject coverage:
Refuse collection; refuse disposal; street cleaning; litter abatement and control; resource recovery; incineration of waste and heat utilisation; analysis of wastes, best practice and technical articles and publications on waste and resource management, biological treatment, strategy, healthcare waste.

Museum or gallery collection, archive, or library special collection:
Comprehensive technical library on all aspects of wastes management

Library catalogue:
All or part available online

Printed publications:
Briefing Notes and Technical Publications (irregular)
Scientific & Technical Review (quarterly)
CIWM (monthly)

Electronic and video publications:
CD-ROM access in library
Videos on environmental and waste management issues (for hire)

Publications list:
Available online and in print

continued overleaf

Access to staff:
Contact by letter, by telephone, by fax, by e-mail and via website. Appointment necessary.
Hours: Mon to Fri, 0900 to 1630

Access to building, collection or gallery:
Prior appointment required
Hours: Mon to Fri, 0900 to 1700

Access for disabled people:
Toilet facilities

Member organisation of:
International Solid Waste Association (ISWA)
Overgarden Oven Vandet 48E, 1415 Copenhagen, Denmark; tel: +45 32 96 15 88; fax: +45 32 96 15 84; e-mail: iswa@inet.vni2.dk

CHARTERED INSTITUTION OF WATER AND ENVIRONMENTAL MANAGEMENT

Acronym or abbreviation: CIWEM

15 John Street, London, WC1N 2EB

Tel: 020 7831 3110
Fax: 020 7405 4967
E-mail: admin@ciwem.org

Website:
http://www.ciwem.org

Enquiries:
Enquiries to: Executive Director

Founded:
1895

Created by the merger of:
Institute of Water Pollution Control, Institution of Public Health Engineers, Institution of Water Engineers and Scientists (year of change 1987)

Formerly called:
Institution of Water and Environmental Management (year of change 1995)

Organisation type and purpose:
Professional body (membership is by qualification), present number of members: 11,500, registered charity (charity number 1043409).

Subject coverage:
Water treatment, water pollution control, treatment and disposal of sewage and trade waste, sewers and sewerage waste disposal, environmental issues.

Printed publications:
Global Environment (annually)
Water and Environment Journal (4 times a year)
Journal of Flood Risk Management (4 times a year, online only)
WEM magazine (10 times a year)
Proceedings of Conferences and Symposia
Information Booklet on CIWEM
Manuals (on waste water treatment, river engineering, etc.)
A large selection of publications on environmental issues

Access to staff:
Contact by letter, by telephone, by fax, by e-mail and via website. Appointment necessary.
Hours: Wed, 1000 to 1600

Access to building, collection or gallery:
Prior appointment required

Access for disabled people:
Hours: Mon to Fri, 0900 to 1700

Founder member of:
Society of Environment

Nominated body of:
Engineering Council
Science Council

CHARTERED INSURANCE INSTITUTE

Acronym or abbreviation: CII

20 Aldermanbury, London, EC2V 7HY

Tel: 020 7417 4416/5
Fax: 020 7417 0110
E-mail: knowledge@cii.co.uk

Website:
http://www.cii.co.uk
http://www.cii.co.uk/knowledge
CII Knowledge Services

Founded:
1934

Organisation type and purpose:
Professional body for those working in the insurance and financial services industry, with 92,000 members.

Subject coverage:
Insurance, United Kingdom and overseas, risk, financial services and related subjects.

Trade and statistical information:
Overseas insurance markets, UK insurance market.

Non-library collection catalogue:
All or part available online

Library catalogue:
All or part available online

Printed publications:
Research reports
Textbooks
The Journal (6 times a year)
Financial Solutions (6 times a year)
Order printed publications from: 31 Hillcrest Road, London, E18 2JB, tel: 020 8989 8464, fax: 020 8530 3052, e-mail: customer.serv@cii.co.uk

Electronic and video publications:
Online market and technical information on the CII Knowledge Services website (mostly members only)

Access to staff:
Contact by letter, by telephone, by fax, by e-mail, in person and via website. Non-members charged.
Hours: Mon to Fri, 0900 to 1700

Access for disabled people:
Ramped entry, access to all public areas, toilet facilities

Branches:
Insurance Institute of London and 60 others

Constituent bodies:
Personal Finance Society
same address; tel: 020 8989 8464
Society of Mortgage Professionals
same address; tel: 020 8989 8464

CHARTERED MANAGEMENT INSTITUTE

Acronym or abbreviation: CMI

Management House, Cottingham Road, Corby, Northamptonshire, NN17 1TT

Tel: 01536 204222
Fax: 01536 201651
E-mail: mic.enquiries@managers.org.uk

Website:
http://www.managers.org.uk
Information on the Institute, its services and membership; links to other useful sites.
http://www.managers.org.uk/bookshop
Publications catalogue.

Enquiries:
Enquiries to: Head of Information Services
Direct tel: 01536 207423
Direct fax: 01536 401013
Direct e-mail: bob.norton@managers.org.uk

Founded:
1992

Organisation type and purpose:
Professional body, membership association (membership is by subscription, qualification, election or invitation), present number of members: 74,000, registered charity (charity number 1091035), research organisation.

Subject coverage:
Techniques, skills, theories and practices of management.

Non-library collection catalogue:
All or part available online

Printed publications:
Annual Report
Business in a Week (series)
Checklists
Professional Manager (6 times a year)
Reading lists, fact sheets
The Management Thinkers

Electronic and video publications:
Checkpoint (checklists and thinkers, CD-ROM)

Publications list:
Available online

Access to staff:
Contact by letter, by telephone, by fax, by e-mail, in person and via website
Hours: Mon to Fri, 0900 to 1700
Special comments: Non-members may use the library for reference free of charge. Use of other services will incur a charge.

Access for disabled people:
Parking, level entry, access to all areas, toilet facilities
Special comments: Ramped fire exits

Administrative Office:
Chartered Management Institute
3rd Floor, 2 Savoy Court, London, WC2R 0EZ; tel: 020 7497 0580; fax: 020 7497 0463; e-mail: secretariat@managers.org.uk

CHARTERED PHYSIOTHERAPISTS IN MENTAL HEALTHCARE

Acronym or abbreviation: CPMH

14 Bedford Row, London, WC1R 4ED

Tel: 020 7306 6666
E-mail: enquiries@csp.org.uk

Website:
http://www.csp.org.uk

Enquiries:
Enquiries to: General Secretary

Formerly called:
Association of Chartered Physiotherapists in Psychiatry (ACPP) (year of change 1994)

Organisation type and purpose:
International organisation, advisory body, professional body (membership is by subscription, qualification, election or invitation), present number of members: 150, training organisation.

Subject coverage:
Physiotherapy, psychiatry, mental healthcare.

Access to staff:
Contact by letter, by telephone and by fax
Hours: Mon to Fri, 0900 to 1700

Group within the:
Chartered Society of Physiotherapy

CHARTERED QUALITY INSTITUTE

Acronym or abbreviation: CQI

12 Grosvenor Crescent, London, SW1X 7EE

Tel: 020 7245 6722
Fax: 020 7245 6788
E-mail: info@thecqi.org

Website:
http://www.thecqi.org

Formerly called:
Institute of Quality Assurance (year of change 2007)

Organisation type and purpose:
Professional body.

Subject coverage:
All aspects of quality assurance and quality management.

Printed publications:
Quality World Monthly Magazine
Order printed publications from: via website

Publications list:
Available in print

Access to staff:
Contact by letter, by telephone, by fax, by e-mail and via website. Appointment necessary.
Hours: Mon to Thu, 0900 to 1700; Fri, 0900 to 1600

Access to building, collection or gallery:
Prior appointment required

Constituent part of:
International Register of Certificated Auditors
tel: 020 7245 6833; fax: 020 7245 6755; e-mail: irca@irca.org; website: http://www.irca.org

CHARTERED SOCIETY OF DESIGNERS

Acronym or abbreviation: CSD

1 Cedar Court, Royal Oak Yard, Bermondsey Street, London, SE1 3GA

Tel: 020 7357 8088
Fax: 020 7407 9878
E-mail: info@csd.org.uk

Website:
http://www.csd.org.uk

Enquiries:
Enquiries to: Director

Founded:
1930

Formerly called:
Society of Industrial Artists & Designers (year of change 1977)

Organisation type and purpose:
Professional body (membership is by subscription, qualification, election or invitation). Registered charity (no. 279393).

Subject coverage:
Industrial, product and engineering design, fashion and textile design, interior and exhibition design, graphic design and illustration, professional practice in all the foregoing, design copyright and registration, intellectual property law.

Printed publications:
A Guide to Business Practice: Graphic, Textile, Product and Interior
Chartered Designers Newsletter (6 times a year, free to members)
Introductory Pack
Protecting Your Designs
The Professional Practice of Design

Electronic and video publications:
Electronic forms

Access to staff:
Contact by letter, by fax and by e-mail
Hours: Mon to Fri, 0930 to 1730

Member of:
Bureau of European Designers Association (BEDA)

CHARTERED SOCIETY OF PHYSIOTHERAPY

Acronym or abbreviation: CSP

14 Bedford Row, London, WC1R 4ED

Tel: 020 7306 6666
Fax: 020 7306 6611

E-mail: enquiries@csp.org.uk

Website:
http://www.csp.org.uk
Information on the society and its role. Resources include information papers, online library catalogue, careers information and Physiotherapy Frontline magazine. CSP Members can access the full text of the Physiotherapy Journal.

Enquiries:
Enquiries to: Chief Executive

Founded:
1894

Organisation type and purpose:
Professional body, educational body, trade union (membership is by subscription, qualification), present number of members: 47,000 with 50 groups, research organisation.

Subject coverage:
Physical rehabilitation and therapy, treatment techniques, conditions such as back pain, physiotherapy.

Services for disabled people:
Facilities in the Learning Resource Centre for literature searching, reading documents and accessing the Internet are available for blind, visually impaired, dyslexic and disabled members. These include a scanner and speech synthesis system (Cicero), a magnifier/screen reader (Zoomtext 8.0) and a screen reader (JAWS for windows 8.0). A CCTV is also available.

Museum or gallery collection, archive, or library special collection:
CSP Learning Resource Centre holding 180 English language journals; Society's Journals from 1916; foreign language journals; CSP specific interest group literature; books; documents; theses and dissertations

Non-library collection catalogue:
All or part available in-house

Library catalogue:
All or part available in-house

Printed publications:
Annual Report
Factsheets and Guidelines, mainly for members
Frontline (magazine, 2 a month)
Information papers
Physiotherapy (journal, quarterly)
Standards of Physiotherapy Practice

Electronic and video publications:
Electronic Library on website

Publications list:
Available online and in print

Access to staff:
Contact by letter, by telephone, by fax, by e-mail and via website. Appointment necessary.
Hours: Mon to Fri, 0900 to 1700

Connections with:
Universities for validation of courses

Groups at the same address:
Acupuncture Association of Chartered Physiotherapists
    website: http://www.aacp.uk.com
Aquatic Therapy Association of Chartered Physiotherapists
Association of Chartered Physiotherapists for People with Learning Disabilities
    website: http://www.acppld.org.uk
Association of Chartered Physiotherapists in Animal Therapy
    website: http://www.acpat.org.uk
Association of Chartered Physiotherapists in Cystic Fibrosis
Association of Chartered Physiotherapists in Electrotherapy
Association of Chartered Physiotherapists in Energy Medicine
    website: http://www.energymedphysio.org.uk
Association of Chartered Physiotherapists in Independent Hospitals and Charities

Association of Chartered Physiotherapists in Management
    website: http://www.physiomanagers.org.uk
Association of Chartered Physiotherapists in Occupational Health and Ergonomics
    website: http://www.acpohe.org.uk
Association of Chartered Physiotherapists in Oncology and Palliative Care
    website: http://www.acpopc.org.uk
Association of Chartered Physiotherapists in Orthopaedic Medicine and Injection Therapy
    website: http://www.acpom.org.uk
Association of Chartered Physiotherapists in Reflex Therapy
Association of Chartered Physiotherapists in Respiratory Care
    website: http://www.acprc.org
Association of Chartered Physiotherapists in Sports Medicine
    website: http://www.acpsm.org
Association of Chartered Physiotherapists in the Community
Association of Chartered Physiotherapists in Therapeutic Riding
Association of Chartered Physiotherapists in Vestibular Rehabilitation
Association of Chartered Physiotherapists in Women's Health
    website: http://www.acpwh.org.uk
Association of Chartered Physiotherapists interested in Cardiac Rehabilitation
Association of Chartered Physiotherapists interested in Massage
Association of Chartered Physiotherapists interested in Neurology
    website: http://www.acpin.net
Association of Chartered Physiotherapists working with Older People
    website: http://www.agile-uk.org
Association of Orthopaedic Chartered Physiotherapists
    website: http:// www.aocp.co.uk
Association of Paediatric Chartered Physiotherapists
British Association of Bobath Trained Therapists
    website: http://www.bobath.org.uk/babtt/index.html
British Association of Chartered Physiotherapists in Amputee Rehabilitation
    website: http://www.bacpar.org.uk
British Association of Hand Therapists Ltd
    website: http://www.hand-therapy.co.uk
Chartered Physiotherapists in International Health and Development
Chartered Physiotherapists in Mental Healthcare (CPMH)
    website: http://www.cpmh.org.uk
Chartered Physiotherapists Promoting Continence
    website: http://www.cppc.org.uk
Chartered Physiotherapists working as Extended Scope Practitioners
Craniosacral Therapy Association of Chartered Physiotherapists
    website: http://www.craniosacral.co.uk
Manipulation Association of Chartered Physiotherapists
    website: http://www.macp-online.co.uk
McKenzie Institute Mechanical Diagnosis and Therapy Practitioners
    website: http://www.mckenzieinstitute.co.uk
Medico Legal Association of Chartered Physiotherapists
    website: http://www.mlacp.org.uk
Physio First
    website: http://www.physiofirst.org.uk
Physiotherapy Pain Association for Chartered Physiotherapists
    website: http://www.ppaonline.co.uk
Physiotherapy Research Society
    website: http://www.prs-uk.org/
Rheumatic Care Association of Chartered Physiotherapists
    website: http://www.rheumatology.org.uk

Umbrella group:
Manipulation Association of Chartered Physiotherapists
    website: http://www.macpweb.org

CHARTERED SURVEYORS TRAINING TRUST

Acronym or abbreviation: CSTT

16th Floor Tower Building, 11 York Road, Waterloo, London SE1 7NX

Tel: 020 7871 0454
E-mail: info@cstt.org.uk

Website:
http://www.cstt.org.uk

Enquiries:
Enquiries to: Chief Executive

Organisation type and purpose:
Registered charity (charity number 327456), training organisation.
Training for the professions of the built environment.

Access to staff:
Contact by letter, by telephone and by e-mail
Hours: Mon to Fri, 0900 to 1700

CHARTERED SURVEYORS' COMPANY

75 Meadway Drive, Horsell, Woking, Surrey, GU21 4TF

Tel: 01483 727113
E-mail: wccsurveyors@btinternet.com

Website:
http://www.surveyorslivery.org.uk

Enquiries:
Enquiries to: The Clerk
Direct tel: 01483 727113
Direct e-mail: wccsurveyors@btinternet.com

Founded:
1977

Organisation type and purpose:
Membership association (membership is by election or invitation).
City of London Livery Company.

Access to staff:
Contact by letter, by telephone, by e-mail and via website

CHATHAM DOCKYARD HISTORICAL SOCIETY

Acronym or abbreviation: CDHS

The Museum of The Royal Dockyard, The Historic Dockyard, Chatham, Kent, ME4 4TZ

Tel: 01634 832028

Website:
http://www.cdhs.org.uk

Enquiries:
Enquiries to: Honorary Secretary
Direct tel: 01634 718546
Direct e-mail: john_lambert@talk21.com

Founded:
1980

Organisation type and purpose:
Learned society, registered charity (charity number 287263), museum, historic building, house or site, suitable for ages: 8+, research organisation.
To spread the knowledge of the dockyard and promote the museum.

Subject coverage:
History of the Navy and its men, ships, etc. Workers and trades in the dockyard.

Information services:
Catalogue in preparation.

Special visitor services:
Guided tours, materials and/or activities for children.

Services for disabled people:
Displays and/or information at wheelchair height.

Museum or gallery collection, archive, or library special collection:
Extensive reference library
Reserve Collection of artefacts in addition to those on show

Printed publications:
Research papers Nos 1 to 26 (available direct):
No. 1 The Royal Marines in Chatham (40p)
No. 2 Convicts in the Dockyard (40p)
No. 3 Chatham Built Submarines (40p)
No. 4 Naval Cannon (40p)
No. 5 Bugler Timmins (15p)
No. 6 HMS Chatham (40p)

Access to staff:
Contact by letter, by telephone, by e-mail, in person and via website
Hours: Mon to Fri, 1030 to 1700
Special comments: via historic dockyard.

Access to building, collection or gallery:
No prior appointment required
Hours: Apr to end Oct: Daily, 1030 to 1700
Nov, Feb, Mar: Wed, Sat, Sun, 1030 to 1700
Special comments: Closed to the public Dec and Jan.

Access for disabled people:
Parking provided, level entry, toilet facilities

CHELMSFORD BOROUGH COUNCIL

Civic Centre, Duke Street, Chelmsford, Essex, CM1 1JE

Tel: 01245 606606
Fax: 01245 606747
E-mail: mailbox@chelmsfordbc.gov.uk

Website:
http://www.chelmsford bc.gov.uk
General information.

Enquiries:
Enquiries to: Chief Executive
Other contacts: Head of Publicity and Marketing

Organisation type and purpose:
Local government body.

Subject coverage:
All local authority services.

Museum or gallery collection, archive, or library special collection:
Chelmsford Museum
Essex Regiment Museum

Printed publications:
Economic development information
Tourism and Information leaflets (free)

Access to staff:
Contact by letter and by telephone. Appointment necessary.
Hours: Mon to Thu, 0845 to 1645; Fri, 0845 to 1615
Special comments: Closed until 1000 last Wed of month for staff training.

CHELMSFORD CATHEDRAL LIBRARY

The Cathedral Centre, New Street, Chelmsford, Essex, CM1 1TY

Tel: 01245 294489
Fax: 01245 294499
E-mail: office@chelmsfordcathedral.org.uk

Website:
http://www.chelmsfordcathedral.org.uk

Enquiries:
Enquiries to: Librarian
Other contacts: Canon Theologian

Organisation type and purpose:
Voluntary organisation, suitable for ages: adults.
Theological lending library.
Early collections reference only, together with those Cathedral Archives that are not in the County Record Office.

Subject coverage:
19th- and early 20th-century theology; contemporary works in biblical, liturgical, missionary, ecumenical and behavioural, inter-faith studies; Essex church history.

Museum or gallery collection, archive, or library special collection:
Appointment required to view the collections marked *:
Ante-Nicene Fathers, 10 vols
*Historic Collection
*Essex Church History
*Knightbridge Library (mainly Puritan theology and patristics: 571 vols of 16th and 17th centuries)
Nicene; Past Nicene Fathers, 2 series, 28 vols

Non-library collection catalogue:
All or part available in-house

Library catalogue:
All or part available in-house

Access to staff:
Contact by letter, by telephone, by fax, by e-mail, in person and via website
Hours: Mon to Fri, 0900 to 1600
Special comments: Appointment required for certain collections.

Access to building, collection or gallery:
No prior appointment required
Hours: Mon to Fri, 0900 to 1600
Special comments: Prior appointment is required for Historic and Essex Collections.

Access for disabled people:
Level entry, toilet facilities

Constituent part of:
Chelmsford Cathedral
Cathedral Centre, New Street, Chelmsford, CM1 1TY; tel: 01245 294489; fax: 01245 294499; e-mail: office@chelmsfordcathedral.org.uk; website: http://www.chelmsfordcathedral.org.uk

Member organisation of:
Cathedral Libraries and Archives Associations

CHELSEA PHYSIC GARDEN

66 Royal Hospital Road, London, SW3 4HS

Tel: 020 7352 5646
Fax: 020 7376 3910
E-mail: enquiries@chelseaphysicgarden.co.uk

Website:
http://www.cpgarden.demon.co.uk
Visual promotion of work and activities of the Garden.

Enquiries:
Enquiries to: Curator
Direct tel: 020 7352 5646 ext .3

Founded:
1673

Organisation type and purpose:
Registered charity (charity number 286513), research organisation.
Botanic garden.
Research and education in botany, horticulture especially medicinal plants.

Subject coverage:
Medicinal plants and herbalism, history of plant introductions, history of the Chelsea Physic Garden and its curators.

Services for disabled people:
One wheelchair available to reserve.

Museum or gallery collection, archive, or library special collection:
Library ex Society of Apothecaries
Thomas Moore Clematis Herbarium
Photographic archive of the Chelsea Physic Garden

Non-library collection catalogue:
All or part available in-house

Library catalogue:
All or part available in-house

Printed publications:
Guide Books
Research Publications relating to previous
 Curators
Seed List (annually)
Work of Garden

Publications list:
Available in print

Access to staff:
Appointment necessary.
Hours: Mon to Fri, 0900 to 1700

Access to building, collection or gallery:
Hours: Public openings: April to October, Wed,
Thu, Fri, 1200 to 1700, Sun and Bank Holidays,
1200 to 1800. Members: all year Mon to Fri, 0930 to
1700 (or dusk if earlier); April to October, Sun, 1200
to 1800.

Access for disabled people:
Through 66 Royal Hospital Road

CHELTENHAM LIBRARY

Clarence Street, Cheltenham, Gloucestershire,
GL50 3JT

Tel: 01242 532686/7
Fax: 01242 532684
E-mail: cheltenham.library@gloucestershire.gov.uk

Website:
http://www.gloucestershire.gov.uk
All Gloucestershire libraries, details of Cheltenham
special collections.

Enquiries:
Enquiries to: Librarian
Direct tel: 0845 230 5421
Direct e-mail: ask@gloucestershire.gov.uk

Founded:
1897

Organisation type and purpose:
Local government body, public library.

Subject coverage:
General reference, local studies – Cheltenham and
environs, art.

**Museum or gallery collection, archive, or library
special collection:**
Art collection – 6,000 items covering fine and
 applied arts

Library catalogue:
All or part available online

Access to staff:
Contact by letter, by telephone, by fax, by e-mail
and in person
Hours: Mon, Wed, Fri, 0900 to 1900; Tue, Thu, 0900
to 1730; Sat, 0900 to 1600

Access for disabled people:
Ramped entry

Member organisation of:
ARLIS

Parent body:
Gloucestershire County Council, Libraries &
Information

CHEMICAL INDUSTRIES
ASSOCIATION

Acronym or abbreviation: CIA

Kings Buildings, Smith Square, London, SW1P 3JJ

Tel: 020 7834 3399
Fax: 020 7834 4469
E-mail: enquiries@cia.org.uk

Website:
http://www.chemistry-industry.org.uk
Overview of the chemical industry and its
products.
http://www.sourcerer.co.uk
Sourcerer, a directory of products and services.
News about chemicals.
http://www.cia.org.uk

Overview of the association, its activities and the
industry it serves.

Enquiries:
Enquiries to: General Secretary
Other contacts: Head of Media Relations for press
enquiries.

Founded:
1965

Organisation type and purpose:
National organisation, advisory body, trade
association, membership association (membership
is by subscription), present number of members:
200, manufacturing industry, training organisation,
publishing house.
Employers' Federation.

Subject coverage:
Chemical and allied industries economic aspects,
e.g. production, investment, employees and
employment, safety, law, trade, tariffs, statistics;
not information on individual companies, technical
information limited to the extent of staff expertise.
Comprehensive product information on Sourcerer
(See Internet home pages), health, safety, and
environment.

Printed publications:
Publications dealing with: safety, health and
 environment, public affairs, community
 relations, business development, science and
 technology, employment, schools liaison etc
Directory of Chemical Products and Buyers Guide
 (annually)
Directory of Chemical Services (annually)
Responsible Care
Guidance manuals, codes of practice, statistics, etc
Order printed publications from: Publications Orders
at the same address, fax: 020 7834 4469, e-mail:
publications@cia.org.uk

Electronic and video publications:
Audio and video programmes:
Chemicals with Care
Policy Against Pollution
PSGO – Product Stewardship reference and guide
 (CD-ROM)

Publications list:
Available in print

Access to staff:
Contact by letter, by telephone, by fax, by e-mail
and via website. Appointment necessary. Access
for members only.
Hours: Mon to Fri, 0900 to 1700
Special comments: No library facilities available.
CIA and Sourcerer online 24 hours a day.

Access to building, collection or gallery:
Prior appointment required

Affiliated associations:
Association of the British Pharmaceutical Industry
(ABPI)
 tel: 020 7930 3477; fax: 020 7747 1411
British Aerosol Manufacturers Association
(BAMA)
 tel: 020 7828 5111; fax: 020 7834 8436; e-mail:
 bama@compuserve.com
British Agrochemicals Association (BAA)
 tel: 01733 349225; fax: 01733 562523; e-mail:
 reception@brit-agro.prestel.co.uk
British Association for Chemical Specialities
(BACS)
 tel: 01524 849606; fax: 01524 849194
British Chemical Distributors & Traders
Association (BCDTA)
 tel: 020 8686 4545; fax: 020 8686 7768
Fertiliser Manufacturers Association (FMA)
 tel: 01733 331303; fax: 01733 332909
National Sulphuric Acid Association (NSAA)
 tel: 01244 322200; fax: 01224 345155
Picon Ltd
 tel: 01372 824513; fax: 01372 824628
Soap and Detergent Industry Association (SDIA)
 tel: 01444 450884; fax: 01444 450951
Solvents Industry Association (SIA)
 tel: 01206 252268; fax: 01206 252268

Member of:
Confederation of British Industry (CBI)
 tel: 020 7395 8247; fax: 020 7240 1578
European Chemical Industry Council (CEFIC)
 Brussels, Belgium; tel: 00 32 2 676 7211; fax: 00 32
 2 676 7300; e-mail: mde@cefic.be

CHERWELL DISTRICT COUNCIL

Bodicote House, Bodicote, Banbury, Oxfordshire,
OX15 4AA

Tel: 01295 252535; minicom no. 01295 221572
Fax: 01295 270028
E-mail: janet.ferris@cherwell.dc.gov.uk

Website:
http://www.cherwell.gov.uk

Enquiries:
Enquiries to: Communications Manager
Direct tel: 01295 221577

Organisation type and purpose:
Local government body.

Subject coverage:
Local government services.

Access to staff:
Contact by letter, by telephone, by fax, by e-mail
and via website. Appointment necessary.
Hours: Mon to Thu, 0840 to 1715; Fri, 0840 to 1620

CHESHIRE ARCHIVES AND
LOCAL STUDIES SERVICE

Cheshire Record Office, Duke Street, Chester,
Cheshire, CH1 1RL

Tel: 01244 972574
Fax: 01244 973812
E-mail: recordoffice@cheshire.gov.uk

Website:
http://www.cheshire.gov.uk/recordoffice
General information and index of Cheshire wills
1492–1940; publications; online catalogue; tithe
maps online; family history pages.

Enquiries:
Enquiries to: County Archivist

Founded:
1949

Created by the merger of:
Cheshire County Record Office and Chester City
Record Office (year of change 2000)

Formerly called:
Cheshire County Record Office (year of change
2000); Cheshire and Chester Archives and Local
Studies (year of change 2009)

Organisation type and purpose:
Local government body.

Subject coverage:
History of ancient county of Cheshire,
development of Cheshire and its communities.

**Museum or gallery collection, archive, or library
special collection:**
Antiquarian Collections
Archives of local authorities, courts, the diocese,
 parishes, nonconformist churches, private estates
 and businesses
Central Local Studies Collection includes books,
 journals, maps, pamphlets, etc.

Non-library collection catalogue:
All or part available online, in-house and in print

Library catalogue:
All or part available online

Printed publications:
Census Indexes of Cheshire 1851, 1881, 1891
Township Packs, selected material from the
 standard printed sources
Cheshire in the Civil War – a learning resource
 pack with contemporary documents intended for
 school use (£7.50)
Cheshire Parish Registers – A summary guide (B.
 Langston, 2002)

continued overleaf

The Ancient Parishes, Townships and Chapelries of Cheshire (booklet and map, F. I. Dunn, £4.50 plus 45p p&p)
Various local history publications

Microform publications:
Directories for Cheshire and Lancashire (some 15, 1789–1924)

Publications list:
Available online and in print

Access to staff:
Contact by letter, by telephone, by fax, by e-mail, in person and via website
Hours: Mon, 1300 to 1700; Tue to Fri, 0900 to 1700; 3rd Sat in month, 0900 to 1600

Access to building, collection or gallery:
Special comments: CARN Readers' Ticket required, booking recommended.

Access for disabled people:
Ramped entry, level entry, access to all public areas, toilet facilities, parking available

Parent body:
Cheshire West and Chester Council

CHESHIRE COMMUNITY ACTION

Acronym or abbreviation: CCA

96 Lower Bridge Street, Chester, Cheshire, CH1 1RU

Tel: 01244 323602
Fax: 01244 401036
E-mail: enquiries@cheshireaction.org.uk

Website:
http://www.cheshireaction.org.uk

Enquiries:
Enquiries to: Chief Executive
Direct e-mail: alison.roylance@cheshireaction.org.uk
Other contacts: Assistant Chief Executive

Founded:
1930

Formerly called:
Cheshire Community Council (year of change 2008)

Organisation type and purpose:
Advisory body, membership association (membership is by subscription), voluntary organisation, registered charity (charity number 1074676).
To promote the quality of life in Cheshire communities, especially rural communities.

Subject coverage:
Management and funding of charities and voluntary bodies, community development and voluntary action, rural community services.

Information services:
Community development, grants, funding.

Museum or gallery collection, archive, or library special collection:
Data on rural communities and services in Cheshire
Directories of funding sources
Grantfinder national computer database on funding sources

Printed publications:
Village Halls Newsletter (sample free)
Cheshire Community Action Newsletter (quarterly, by subscription)
Rural Briefings (send an sae)
Annual Report
Order printed publications from: Website, or see contact details

Electronic and video publications:
Order electronic and video publications from: Website

Publications list:
Available online

Access to staff:
Contact by letter, by telephone, by fax, by e-mail, in person and via website. Appointment necessary.
Hours: Mon to Thu, 0900 to 1630; Fri, 0900 to 1600

Access to building, collection or gallery:
Hours: Mon to Fri, 0900 to 1700
Special comments: Parking can be a problem.

Access for disabled people:
No disabled access
Special comments: Stairs; no lifts or ramps.

Also at:
Satellite office
Unit 20, Blakemere Craft Centre, Chester Road, Sandiway, Cheshire, CW8 2EB

Parent body:
ACRE (Action with Communities in Rural England)
Somerford Court, Somerford Road, Cirencester, Gloucestershire, GL7 1TW

CHESHIRE EAST LIBRARIES

Macclesfield Library, Jordangate, Macclesfield, Cheshire, SK10 1EE

Tel: 01625 374000
Fax: 01625 612818
E-mail: macclesfield.infopoint@cheshireeast.gov.uk

Website:
http://www.cheshireeast.gov.uk/libraries

Formerly called:
Cheshire Libraries and Archives

Organisation type and purpose:
Local government body, public library.

Subject coverage:
Full range of general reference and information from local to international, e.g. community, business, travel, law, leisure.

Museum or gallery collection, archive, or library special collection:
Collection of books written by, and with paintings or drawings by, Charles F. Tunnicliffe, bird artist
Extensive local history collection including works on the silk industry of Macclesfield

Library catalogue:
All or part available online

Access to staff:
Contact by letter, by telephone, by fax, by e-mail, in person and via website
Hours: Mon, Tue, Thu, 0900 to 1900; Wed, Fri, 0900 to 1700; Sat, 0900 to 1300

Access for disabled people:
Level entry, access to all public areas, toilet facilities

Headquarters address:
Cheshire East Council
Westfields, Middlewich Road, Sandbach, Cheshire

CHESHIRE MUSEUMS SERVICE

162 London Road, Northwich, Cheshire, CW9 8AB

Tel: 01606 271640
Fax: 01606 350420
E-mail: cheshiremuseums@cheshire.gov.uk

Website:
http://www.saltmuseum.org.uk

Enquiries:
Enquiries to: Heritage and Museums Officer

Founded:
1974

Organisation type and purpose:
Local government body, museum.

Subject coverage:
Archaeology and field monuments, excavations at Northwich and Middlewich, museology, curatorship, history of the salt industry.

Museum or gallery collection, archive, or library special collection:
Main collections relate to the industrial and social history of Mid-Cheshire with particular emphasis on salt. Material held ranges from industrial equipment, packaging, domestic items and art, to photographs, also archaeological excavation archives for Cheshire, excluding Chester district

Non-library collection catalogue:
All or part available in-house

Publications list:
Available online and in print

Access to staff:
Contact by letter, by telephone and by e-mail
Hours: Mon to Fri, 0900 to 1700

Access for disabled people:
Parking provided, ramped entry, toilet facilities lift access to first floor

Administers:
Salt Museum
Stretton Watermill

CHEST HEART & STROKE SCOTLAND

Acronym or abbreviation: CHSS

65 North Castle Street, Edinburgh, EH2 3LT

Tel: 0131 225 6963
Fax: 0131 220 6313
E-mail: admin@chss.org.uk

Website:
http://www.chss.org.uk

Enquiries:
Enquiries to: Finance Director

Founded:
1959

Formerly called:
Chest Heart and Stroke Association (year of change 1991)

Organisation type and purpose:
Registered charity (charity number SC 018761).

Subject coverage:
Medical welfare.

Information services:
Advice Line, tel: 0845 077 6000

Printed publications:
Order printed publications from: Website, e-mail or telephone

Publications list:
Available online and in print

Access to staff:
Hours: Mon to Fri, 0900 to 1630

Access to building, collection or gallery:
No access other than to staff

Regional Offices:
Glasgow
tel: 0141 633 1666
Inverness
tel: 01463 713433

CHESTER COMMUNITY HISTORY & HERITAGE

Formal name: Chester Community History & Heritage
Acronym or abbreviation: CHH

St Michael's Church, Bridge Street Row East, Chester, Cheshire, CH1 1NW

Tel: 01244 402110
Fax: 01244 312243
E-mail: chh@cheshirewestandchester.gov.uk

Website:
http://www.chester.gov.uk/heritage/history/home.html
Chester history and heritage

http://www.chester.gov.uk/heritage/history/family
-history.html
Internet tutorials for family history enthusiasts.
1901 Census vouchers for sale
http://www.chesterimagebank.com
Image Bank online

Enquiries:
Enquiries to: Community Heritage Officer

Founded:
2000

Formerly called:
Chester Archives, Chester City Record Office (year
of change 2000)

Organisation type and purpose:
Local government body, suitable for ages: all.

Subject coverage:
Family history, local history, community history,
conservation archaeology.

Information services:
Library available for reference (for conditions see
Access); Guided tours for parties – walks and talks.

Special visitor services:
Materials and/or activities for children.

Education services:
Group education facilities, resources for Key
Stages 1 and 2.

**Museum or gallery collection, archive, or library
special collection:**
General Register Office Index 1837–1969
Census for Chester District 1841–1901
1881 census for UK
Electoral registers for Chester, IGI for Cheshire,
Lancashire, Shropshire, Staffordshire, Derbyshire
and Wales
Parish registers for Chester
Local newspapers, maps
Chester photographic survey team, street by street
ongoing record since 1950s with some early
photographs
Local history library
Archaeological library

Printed publications:
Books, pamphlets and leaflets on Chester and
surrounding district including:
Our House
History of the Rows
Tudor Chester
Millennium Trail of Chester
History of Chester (Ormerod G)

Electronic and video publications:
Chester Revealed (CD-ROM)

Access to staff:
Contact by letter, by telephone, by fax, by e-mail
and in person
Hours: Mon to Thu, 1000 to 1600

Access to building, collection or gallery:
Hours: Mon to Thu, 1000 to 1600

CHESTER-LE-STREET AND CITY OF DURHAM ENTERPRISE AGENCY

Acronym or abbreviation: CDC Enterprise Agency

7 Millennium Place, Durham City, DH1 1WA

Tel: 0191 384 5407
Fax: 0191 386 3934
E-mail: enquiries@cdcbp.org.uk

Website:
http://www.cdcbp.org.uk

Enquiries:
Enquiries to: Chief Executive

Founded:
1986

Organisation type and purpose:
Voluntary organisation, consultancy, training
organisation.
Business advice, information and training.

Subject coverage:
Business information.

Printed publications:
Available free

Access to staff:
Contact by letter, by telephone, by fax, by e-mail,
in person and via website. Appointment necessary.
Hours: Mon to Fri, 0900 to 1700

Access for disabled people:
Ramped entry, full disabled access

Also at:
Chester-le-Street and City of Durham Enterprise
Agency
Mile House, Newcastle Road, Chester-le-Street,
Co Durham, DH3 3RA; tel: 0191 389 2648; fax:
0191 387 1684; e-mail: enquiries@cdcbp.org.uk

Links with:
Chester-le-Street District Council
tel: 0191 387 1919
Durham City Council
tel: 0191 386 6111

CHESTERFIELD BOROUGH COUNCIL

Acronym or abbreviation: CBC

Town Hall, Chesterfield, Derbyshire, S40 1LP

Tel: 01246 345345
Fax: 01246 345252
E-mail: info@chesterfieldbc.gov.uk

Website:
http://www.chesterfieldbc.gov.uk
Details of Chesterfield Council services, economic
development, tourism.

Enquiries:
Enquiries to: Public Relations Manager

Organisation type and purpose:
Local government body.

Subject coverage:
Local government services and amenities.

Printed publications:
A-Z of Council Services
Chesterfield Tourist Guide
Community Housing News (twice a year)
Our Town (newspaper, 4 times a year, free)

Access to staff:
Contact by letter, by e-mail and via website
Hours: Mon to Fri, 0900 to 1700

CHESTERFIELD LIBRARY

New Beetwell Street, Chesterfield, Derbyshire, S40
1QN

Tel: 01629 533400
Fax: 01246 209304
E-mail: chesterfield.library@derbyshire.gov.uk;
asklibrary@derbyshire.gov

Website:
http://www.derbyshire.gov.uk/leisure/libraries
Not all local studies materials included, otherwise
comprehensive.

Enquiries:
Enquiries to: Senior Librarian
Direct tel: 01629 533444

Organisation type and purpose:
Local government body, public library.

Subject coverage:
Marketing information, disabled services, music
and drama.

Information services:
Library Information Service, tel: 01629 533444

**Museum or gallery collection, archive, or library
special collection:**
Asa Lees collection (dogs, especially s.c. fox
terriers): a collection of printed items (including
Kennel Gazette 1880–1973 and Stud Book 1859–
1973) and manuscript correspondence, pedigrees
and show reports
Stephenson Collection (railway history)

Non-library collection catalogue:
All or part available online

Library catalogue:
All or part available online

Access for disabled people:
Level entry, access to all public areas, toilet
facilities

CHESTERTON LTD

10 Gillingham Street, London, SW1V 1HJ

Tel: 020 3040 8240

Website:
http://www.chesterton.co.uk
Details of range of services offered by Chesterton,
commercial properties in United Kingdom, job
vacancies.

Enquiries:
Enquiries to: Senior Information Officer

Organisation type and purpose:
Service industry, consultancy.
Commercial Company.
Property agents and consultants.

Subject coverage:
Property, including offices, retail, industrial,
residential, leisure, investment, UK, Europe, USA,
Japan, South East Asia, companies.

Library catalogue:
All or part available in-house

Printed publications:
Commercial Property Bulletin (available on a
monthly basis by email)
Licensed Leisure Bulletin (available on a quarterly
basis by email)
Retailer News Property Bulletin (available on a
quarterly basis by email)
Banking & Finance Property Bulletin (available on
a quarterly basis by email)
Various Property related research reports – details
on application

Publications list:
Available online

Access to staff:
Contact by letter, by telephone, by fax and by e-
mail
Hours: Mon to Fri, 0900 to 1730

Access to building, collection or gallery:
No prior appointment required

Other addresses:
Chesterton Ltd
Head Office, 54 Brook Street, London, W1A 2BU;
tel: 020 7499 0404; fax: 020 7629 7804

CHESTERTON SOCIETY, THE

11 Lawrence Leys, Bloxham, Near Banbury,
Oxfordshire, OX15 4NU

Tel: 01295 720869\ 07766 711984 (Mobile)
Fax: 01295 720869
E-mail: roberthughes11@talktalk.net@onetel.com

Enquiries:
Enquiries to: Honorary Secretary

Founded:
1964

Organisation type and purpose:
International organisation, national organisation,
learned society (membership is by subscription),
present number of members: 1500, voluntary
organisation.

continued overleaf

To inform and educate members on the writing of G K Chesterton.

Subject coverage:
Words and writings of G K Chesterton.

Non-library collection catalogue:
All or part available in-house and in print

Library catalogue:
All or part available in-house and in print

Printed publications:
The G K Chesterton Quarterly (for purchase)
Order printed publications from: Secretary, Chesterton Society
As main address

Publications list:
Available in print

Access to staff:
Contact by letter, by telephone, by fax, by e-mail and in person
Hours: Any reasonable time

CHETHAM'S LIBRARY

Long Millgate, Manchester, M3 1SB

Tel: 0161 834 7961
Fax: 0161 839 5797
E-mail: librarian@chethams.org.uk

Website:
http://www.chethams.org.uk
Archival finding aids.

Enquiries:
Enquiries to: Librarian
Other contacts: Archivist (for archival enquiries); Senior Librarian (for systems)

Founded:
1653

Organisation type and purpose:
Registered charity (charity number DG/526702C-1/E), museum, historic building, house or site.
Free public library, founded in 1653, for research and consultation.

Subject coverage:
History and topography of the North-West of England, rare books.

Museum or gallery collection, archive, or library special collection:
Archival Collections re Manchester
Halliwell-Phillipps Collection of broadsides
History of Lancashire and Cheshire
Incunabula
John Byrom's Collection

Non-library collection catalogue:
All or part available online

Library catalogue:
All or part available online

Printed publications:
A Catalogue of Proclamations, Broadsides, Ballads, and Poems, presented to the Chetham Library by James O. Halliwell (Phillipps) (London, privately printed, 1851)
A Catalogue of the Collection of Tracts for and against Popery (published in or about the reign of James II) in the Manchester Library founded by Humphrey Chetham (Thomas Jones ed., Manchester, 1859–65, 2 vols, Chetham Society, Original Series, 48 and 64)
A Catalogue of the Library of John Byrom (Compiled by B. B. B. R. Wheatley, privately printed, 1848)
A selection from the list of historical manuscripts in the Chetham Library (compiled in 1930 by G. H. Tupling, in Bulletin of the Institute of Historical Research, vol. X (1932–33), pp. 69–72)
Bibliothecae Chethamensis Catalogus (Manchester, 1701–1883, 6 vols)
Catalogue of the John Radcliffe Collection (compiled by C. T. E. Phillips, Manchester, 1937)

Access to staff:
Contact by letter, by telephone, by fax and by e-mail. Appointment necessary.

Hours: Mon to Fri, 0930 to 1630

Access for disabled people:
Parking provided, ramped entry

CHEVIOT SHEEP SOCIETY

Holm Cottage, Langholm, Dumfries & Galloway, DG13 0JP

Tel: 013873 80222

Website:
http://www.cheviotsheep.org

Enquiries:
Enquiries to: General Secretary

Organisation type and purpose:
Membership association (membership is by subscription), present number of members: 114, registered charity.
To promote and encourage the breeding of Cheviot sheep.

Subject coverage:
South country Cheviot sheep; record of ram pedigrees.

Printed publications:
British Sheep Book (8th ed., pub. National Sheep Association)
Flock Book (annually, includes list of members, for members only)
Information booklets and pamphlets

Member of:
National Sheep Association
The Sheep Centre, Malvern, Worcestershire

CHICHESTER CHAMBER OF COMMERCE & INDUSTRY

Acronym or abbreviation: CCCI

3 Chapel Street, Chichester, West Sussex, PO19 1BU

Tel: 01243 531765
Fax: 01243 531765
E-mail: office@chichestercci.org.uk

Website:
http://www.chichesteri.org.uk

Enquiries:
Enquiries to: Membership Secretary

Founded:
1970

Organisation type and purpose:
Advisory body, membership association (membership is by subscription), voluntary organisation.

Subject coverage:
Local business information.

Printed publications:
Chichester Business News
Chichester Chamber Business Directory

Access to staff:
Contact by letter, by telephone, by fax and by e-mail. Appointment necessary.
Hours: Mon to Fri, 0900 to 1700

CHICHESTER DISTRICT COUNCIL

East Pallant House, 1 East Pallant, Chichester, West Sussex, PO19 1TY

Tel: 01243 785166
Fax: 01243 776766
E-mail: helpline@chichester.gov.uk

Website:
http://www.chichester.gov.uk

Enquiries:
Enquiries to: Information Services Officer
Direct tel: 01243 534679

Founded:
1974

Organisation type and purpose:
Local government body.

Subject coverage:
Archaeology in Chichester district, tourist information, local government information, business information, housing needs, environmental health, waste management, recycling, development control and building control, council tax, business and economic development.

Trade and statistical information:
Local business information (including statistics), local tourism information (including statistics), crime audit information (including statistics).

Printed publications:
Initiatives – the magazine of Chichester District Council
Archaeological Report
Community Safety Strategy
Chichester District Community Plan
Business Directory
Tourism Leaflet/Guide
Order printed publications from: Information Services Officer, Chichester District Council
tel: 01234 534679

Electronic and video publications:
Initiatives (tape, free, for the partially sighted)

Access to staff:
Contact by letter, by telephone, by fax and by e-mail
Hours: Mon to Thu, 0845 to 1710; Fri, 0845 to 1700

Access for disabled people:
Parking provided, ramped entry, level entry, toilet facilities

Other area offices:
Midhurst Area Office
North Street, Midhurst, West Sussex, GU29 9DW; tel: 01730 812251
Petworth Area Office
The Old Bakery, Golden Square, Petworth, West Sussex, GU28 0AP; tel: 01798 342241

CHILD ACCIDENT PREVENTION TRUST

Acronym or abbreviation: CAPT

Canterbury Court 1.09, 1–3 Brixton Road, London, SW9 6DE

Tel: 020 7608 3828
Fax: 020 7608 3674
E-mail: safe@capt.org.uk

Website:
http://www.capt.org.uk

Founded:
1981

Organisation type and purpose:
Advisory body, voluntary organisation, registered charity (charity number 1053549), consultancy, research organisation.
Researches childhood accidents, examines modes of prevention, promotes the importance of a child's safe environment, spreads information about nature and prevention of accidents to children and young people.

Subject coverage:
Prevention of children's accidents, child development, child's environment, road accidents, home accidents, leisure accidents, injury types (burns, scalds, poisonings, falls, suffocations, etc.), accident prevention (United Kingdom, international), product safety, accident prevention and health services, safety education, accident compensation and post-accident disability.

Publications list:
Available in print

Access to staff:
Contact by letter, by telephone, by fax, by e-mail and via website. Appointment necessary.
Hours: Mon to Fri, 0930 to 1700

CHILD BEREAVEMENT CHARITY

Acronym or abbreviation: CBC

Aston House, High Street, West Wycombe, Buckinghamshire, HP14 3AG

Tel: 01494 446648 (information and support)
Fax: 01494 440057
E-mail: enquiries@childbereavement.org.uk

Website:
http://www.childbereavement.org.uk

Enquiries:
Enquiries to: Chief Executive

Founded:
1994

Formerly called:
Child Bereavement Trust (year of change 2007)

Organisation type and purpose:
Supporting families, educating professionals.

Subject coverage:
Provides support to families and professionals when a child dies or when a child is bereaved of someone important in their lives. Services offered include a support and information line, interactive website with a Families and Professionals Forum, resources and Professionals Training Programme.

Information services:
Support and information for bereaved families and the professionals who care for them.

Education services:
Educating professionals and offering bereavement training in schools.

Museum or gallery collection, archive, or library special collection:
Resources include DVDs, CD-ROMs, books, leaflets, research

Printed publications:
Resources
Order printed publications from: website: http://www.childbereavement.org.uk

Publications list:
Available online and in print

Access to staff:
Contact by letter, by telephone, by fax, by e-mail and via website. Appointment necessary.
Hours: Mon to Fri, 0900 to 1700

Access to building, collection or gallery:
No access other than to staff

Access for disabled people:
Parking provided

CHILD DEATH HELPLINE

Acronym or abbreviation: CDH

York House, 37 Queen Square, London, WC1N 3BH

Tel: 0800 282986; 0808 800 6019 (Helpline)
Fax: 020 7813 8516
E-mail: contact@childdeathhelpline.org

Website:
http://www.childdeathhelpline.org.uk

Enquiries:
Enquiries to: Head of Department
Direct tel: 020 7813 8551
Other contacts: Administrator

Founded:
1995

Organisation type and purpose:
Voluntary organisation.
A national freephone service for all those affected by the death of a child of any age, from pre-birth to adult, under any circumstances, however recently or long ago.

Subject coverage:
Support for those bereaved by the death of a child whether recent or many years ago.

Printed publications:
Information Pack

Publications list:
Available online and in print

Access to staff:
Contact by letter, by telephone, by fax and by e-mail
Hours: Mon to Fri, 0900 to 1700
Special comments: Helpline open: Mon, Thu and Fri, 1000 to 1300 and 1900 to 2200; Tue and Wed, 1000 to 1600 and 1900 to 2200

Also at:
Child Death Helpline Department
  Great Ormond Street Hospital NHS Trust, London, WC1N 3JH; tel: 020 7813 8551; fax: 020 7813 8516
The Alder Centre
  Alder Hey Children's Hospital, Eaton Road, Liverpool, L12 2AP; tel: 0151 252 5391; fax: 0151 252 5513

CHILD GROWTH FOUNDATION

Acronym or abbreviation: CGF

2 Mayfield Avenue, Chiswick, London, W4 1PW

Tel: 020 8994 7625 or 8995 0257
Fax: 020 8995 9075
E-mail: cgflondon@aol.com

Website:
http://www.heightmatters.org.uk
General information on growth, assessing appropriateness.
http://www.tss.org.uk
Turner Syndrome, assessing appropriateness.

Enquiries:
Enquiries to: Administrator

Founded:
1977

Organisation type and purpose:
Membership association (membership is by subscription), present number of members: 1100, registered charity (charity number 274325).
Parent support and to promote public and professional awareness of growth and growth related problems.

Subject coverage:
All aspects of growth disorders and related problems, including Silver Russell Syndrome; Soto's Syndrome; Turner's Syndrome; growth hormone deficiency and insufficiency, multiple pituitary hormone deficiency, achondroplasia and bone dysplasias, premature sexual maturation, intrauterine growth retardation.

Printed publications:
Baby Check (a checklist to determine whether babies up to six months old need medical attention)
Leaflets for all growth disorders
Newsletter (2 times a year, members, annual membership UK £15, overseas £22.50)

Publications list:
Available in print

Access to staff:
Contact by letter, by telephone and by fax
Hours: Mon to Fri, 0900 to 1600

CHILD POVERTY ACTION GROUP

Acronym or abbreviation: CPAG

94 White Lion Street, London, N1 9PF

Tel: 020 7837 7979
Fax: 020 7837 6414
E-mail: staff@cpag.co.uk

Website:
http://www.cpag.org.uk

Enquiries:
Enquiries to: Information Officer

Founded:
1965

Organisation type and purpose:
Membership association (membership is by subscription), voluntary organisation, registered charity (charity number 294841), training organisation, research organisation, publishing house.
Promotes action for relief of poverty among families with children.

Subject coverage:
Poverty in the United Kingdom; social policy and administration; welfare rights and benefits; social security; children; social security law, appeals and reviews.

Museum or gallery collection, archive, or library special collection:
CPAG Library

Library catalogue:
All or part available in-house

Printed publications:
Child Support Handbook (annual)
Benefits for Students Handbook
Poverty Journal
Housing Benefit and Council Tax Legislation
Welfare Rights Bulletin (6 times a year)
Paying for Care Handbook
Welfare Benefits and Tax Credits Handbook (annual)
Order printed publications from: CPAG

Electronic and video publications:
Welfare Benefits and Tax Credits Handbook (online)

Publications list:
Available online and in print

Access to staff:
Contact by letter, by telephone, by fax and by e-mail. Appointment necessary.
Hours: Mon to Fri, 0900 to 1700

Access to building, collection or gallery:
Prior appointment required
Hours: Mon to Fri, 0900 to 1700

Access for disabled people:
Parking provided, ramped entry, access to all public areas, toilet facilities
Hours: Mon to Fri, 0900 to 1700

Also at:
Child Poverty Action Group in Scotland
  Unit 9, Ladywell, 94 Duke St, Glasgow, G4 0UW; tel: 0141 552 3303; fax: 0141 552 4404; e-mail: staff@cpagscotland.org.uk

Links with:
Citizens' Rights Office
  Department for Welfare Benefits and Tax Credits, at the same address

CHILD PSYCHOTHERAPY TRUST

Acronym or abbreviation: CPT

Star House, 104–108 Grafton Road, Kentish Town, London, NW5 4BD

Tel: 020 7284 1355
Fax: 020 7284 2755
E-mail: cpt@globalnet.co.uk

Website:
http://www.childpsychotherapytrust.org.uk

Enquiries:
Enquiries to: Administrator

Founded:
1987

Organisation type and purpose:
Voluntary organisation, registered charity (charity number 327361).
Provide information on children's behaviour and emotional development, promote understanding of psychoanalytic work, promote the training of

continued overleaf

child psychotherapists, and increase the access of children in need of help to child psychotherapy provision.

Subject coverage:
Concerned with providing information about child psychotherapy within the National Health Service. Child and adolescent mental health, emotional and behavioural problems, and supporting psychotherapists through providing training awards.

Library catalogue:
All or part available in-house

Printed publications:
The Child Psychotherapy Review (newsletter, subscription)
Putting child psychotherapy on the map (booklet)
Won't they just grow out of it? (factsheet)
Attending to difficult behaviour (leaflet)
Crying and sleeping (leaflet)
Divorce and separation (leaflet)
Separations in early years (leaflet)
Sibling rivalry (leaflet)
Tempers and tears (leaflet)
Your new baby, your family and you (leaflet)
Key Stages in Your Child's Emotional Development (booklet)

Electronic and video publications:
Won't they just grow out of it? (video)

Publications list:
Available in print

Access to staff:
Contact by letter, by telephone, by fax and by e-mail
Hours: Mon to Fri, 0900 to 1700

CHILDLINE

2nd Floor, Royal Mail Building, Studd Street, London, N1 0QW

Tel: 020 7239 1000 (Admin only)
Fax: 020 7239 1001 (Admin only)
E-mail: info@childline.org.uk (Admin only)

Website:
http://www.childline.org.uk

Enquiries:
Enquiries to: Executive Director
Other contacts: Information Officer

Founded:
1986

Organisation type and purpose:
Voluntary organisation, registered charity (charity number 1003758).
To provide help and support to children and young people in trouble or danger. It also brings to public attention issues affecting children's welfare and rights.

Subject coverage:
ChildLine is the free, national helpline for children and young people in danger and distress. It provides a confidential phone counselling service for any child with any problem 24 hours a day, every day. It listens, comforts and protects. Trained counsellors provide support and advice, and refer children in danger to appropriate helping agencies. ChildLine also raises public awareness of issues affecting children's welfare and rights.

Printed publications:
A selection of literature related to trauma in young people, including:
Beyond the Limit – Children who live with parental alcohol misuse (Houston A, Kork S, Macleod M)
No Home and Alone – Runaway and homeless young people calling ChildLine (Keep G)
Saving Young Lives – Calls to ChildLine about Suicide (McConville B)

Publications list:
Available online and in print

CHILDLINK ADOPTION SOCIETY

10 Lion Yard, Tremadoc Road, Clapham, London, SW4 7NQ

Tel: 020 7501 1700
Fax: 020 7498 1791
E-mail: enquiries@adoptchildlink.org.uk

Website:
http://www.adoptchildlink.org.uk

Enquiries:
Enquiries to: Administrator

Founded:
1913

Formerly called:
Church Adoption Society (year of change 1990)

Organisation type and purpose:
Voluntary organisation, registered charity (charity number 211419).
Adoption.

Subject coverage:
Adoption; counselling for children, parents and adopters; relevant childcare.

Printed publications:
Brochure
Newsletter

Access to staff:
Contact by letter, by telephone, by fax, by e-mail and via website
Hours: Mon to Fri, 0930 to 1700

Access to building, collection or gallery:
No access other than to staff

CHILDREN 1ST

Formal name: Royal Scottish Society for Prevention of Cruelty to Children
Acronym or abbreviation: RSSPCC

83 Whitehouse Loan, Edinburgh, EH9 1AT

Tel: 0131 446 2300
Fax: 0131 446 2339
E-mail: info@children1st.org.uk

Website:
http://www.children1st.org.uk

Enquiries:
Enquiries to: Chief Executive

Founded:
1884

Organisation type and purpose:
Voluntary organisation (charity number SCO 16092).

Subject coverage:
Child protection, child abuse and neglect, parent support.

Printed publications:
Factsheets (also available online)
Order printed publications from: website: http://www.children1st.org.uk/shop

Publications list:
Available online

Access to staff:
Contact by letter, by telephone, by fax, by e-mail, in person and via website. Appointment necessary.
Hours: Mon to Fri, 0900 to 1700

Links with:
NSPCC
tel: 020 7825 2500

CHILDREN IN SCOTLAND

Princes House, 5 Shandwick Place, Edinburgh, EH2 4RG

Tel: 0131 228 8484
Fax: 0131 228 8585
E-mail: info@childreninscotland.org.uk

Website:
http://www.childreninscotland.org.uk/children

Enquiries:
Enquiries to: Communications Manager

Formerly called:
Scottish Child and Family Alliance

Organisation type and purpose:
Membership association (membership is by subscription), present number of members: 406, voluntary organisation, registered charity (charity number SCO 03527).
National co-ordinating agency of over 300 members who work with children and families throughout Scotland.

Subject coverage:
Information relevant to children and families in Scotland, e.g. education, welfare, health, services, special needs, early years and rural development.

Printed publications:
Publications catalogue available on application

Publications list:
Available online and in print

Access to staff:
Contact by letter, by telephone, by fax, by e-mail and via website. Appointment necessary.
Hours: Mon to Fri, 0900 to 1700

Affiliated to:
Children in Wales
National Children's Bureau

CHILDREN LAW UK

44 Queen Anne Street, London, W1G 8HG

Tel: 020 7224 3566
Fax: 020 7224 3577
E-mail: info@childrenlawuk.org.uk

Enquiries:
Enquiries to: Secretary

Founded:
1974

Formerly called:
British Juvenile and Family Courts Society (BJFCS) (year of change 2001)

Organisation type and purpose:
Registered charity (charity number 265966).
Working for children and families in legal proceedings throughout the UK.
Aims to inform and educate professionals, to commission research and disseminate findings and to enrich national policy development in order to foster a judicial process that works in the interests of children, young people, families and the wider community.

Subject coverage:
Forum for information and debate on national and international policy and practice; best European practice and research; authoritative and independent contribution to youth and family court policy across the UK.

Access to staff:
Contact by letter, by telephone, by fax and by e-mail
Hours: Mon to Fri, 0900 to 1700

Affiliated to:
The International Association of Juvenile and Family Court Magistrates

CHILDREN WITH AIDS CHARITY

Acronym or abbreviation: CWAC

Calvert House, 5 Calvert Avenue, London E2 7JP

Tel: 020 7033 8620
Fax: 020 7739 3902
E-mail: info@cwac.org

Website:
http://www.cwac.org
Services, news and events website.

Enquiries:
Enquiries to: CEO

Other contacts: Services Co-ordinator; Education & Outreach Manager; Executive Fundraiser

Founded:
1992

Organisation type and purpose:
Membership association (membership registration), present number of members: 160 voluntary and statutory organisations, registered charity (charity number 1027816), suitable for ages: under 18.
Leaflets, DVDs and resources available re paediatric HIV in the UK.

Subject coverage:
Medicine, HIV/Aids.

Non-library collection catalogue:
All or part available in-house

Library catalogue:
All or part available in-house

Printed publications:
Booklet on Disclosure
Talking with Children about Illness and HIV (£5.00)
Voices of Young People (£3.50)
Me My Health & My Medicines (£8.50)
Your Body your Blood Worksheets
Order printed publications from: e-mail: info@cwac .org

Electronic and video publications:
Problem video (for 7 to 10 year olds, HIV transmission and hygiene)
The Cloakroom video (for all teenagers on keeping secrets)
HIV: Risky Business (for 12–15 year olds, on HIV transmission)

Access to staff:
Contact by letter, by telephone, by e-mail and via website. Appointment necessary.
Hours: Mon to Fri, 1000 to 1630

Access to building, collection or gallery:
No access other than to staff

CHILDREN WITH LEUKAEMIA

Formal name: Children with Cancer UK

51 Great Ormond Street, London, WC1N 3JQ

Tel: 020 7404 0808
Fax: 020 7404 3666
E-mail: info@leukaemia.org

Website:
http://www.leukaemia.org

Enquiries:
Enquiries to: Media Enquiries
Direct e-mail: tina@tinapriceconsultants.com

Founded:
1989

Formerly called:
Foundation for Children with Leukaemia;
Children with Leukaemia UK; Paul O'Gorman
Foundation for Children with Leukaemia

Organisation type and purpose:
Voluntary organisation, registered charity (charity number 1035538).

Subject coverage:
Childhood leukaemia; other childhood cancers.

Access to staff:
Contact by letter, by telephone and by fax
Hours: Mon to Fri, 0900 to 1700

CHILDREN'S CLINIC AT DOLPHIN HOUSE

Formal name: Dolphin House Children's Clinic

14 New Road, Brighton, East Sussex, BN1 1UF

Tel: 01273 324790
Fax: 01273 729491
E-mail: info@thechildrensclinic.org.uk

Enquiries:
Enquiries to: Practice Manager

Founded:
1983

Formerly called:
Foundation for Traditional Medicine

Organisation type and purpose:
Registered charity (charity number 288174), suitable for ages: 0 to 18.
Registered charity that focuses on providing a comprehensive range of complementary therapies to babies, children and young people, regardless of family means, mainly focusing on familes and children who are socially and economically excluded.

Subject coverage:
Complementary therapies for children: treating children with acupuncture, homoeopathy, paediatric/cranial osteopathy, creative art therapy, nutritional advice, herbal medicine, reflexology, healing.

Access to staff:
Contact by letter, by telephone, by fax and in person
Hours: Mon to Sat, 0900 to 1730

CHILDREN'S LEGAL CENTRE

Acronym or abbreviation: CLC

The University of Essex, Wivenhoe Park, Colchester, Essex, CO4 3SQ

Tel: 01206 877910 (administration)
Fax: 01206 877963
E-mail: clc@essex.ac.uk

Website:
http://www.childrenslegalcentre.com; http://www .lawstuff.org.uk

Enquiries:
Enquiries to: Child Law Advice Line Freephone
Direct tel: 0808 802 0008

Founded:
1981

Organisation type and purpose:
Advisory body, registered charity (charity number 281222).
Independent national charity concerned with law and policy affecting children and young people.
To give free and confidential advice for children, young people and their advisers, on any aspect of children's legal rights; to lobby for changes in the law.

Subject coverage:
Law and policy affecting children and young people in England and Wales, welfare and rights of children and young people.

Printed publications:
Legal guides and information sheets
Reports and handbooks
At What Age Can I...? (£6.50)
At The Police Station (£4.95)
Working with Young People (£24.95)
You and the Police: fact cards for young people (£4.50 per 10)

Access to staff:
Contact by letter, by telephone, by fax, by e-mail and via website
Hours: Mon to Fri, 0900 to 1700

CHILDREN'S LIVER DISEASE FOUNDATION

Acronym or abbreviation: CLDF

36 Great Charles Street, Birmingham, B3 3JY

Tel: 0121 212 3839
Fax: 0121 212 4300
E-mail: info@childliverdisease.org

Website:
http://www/childliverdisease.org

Enquiries:
Enquiries to: Chief Executive

Founded:
1980

Organisation type and purpose:
Registered charity (charity number 1067331).
To raise awareness of paediatric liver disease, to give support both to children with liver disease and to their families, to promote research and to provide new facilities and trained staff.

Subject coverage:
Children's liver diseases.

Printed publications:
Leaflets
Annual Report

Access to staff:
Contact by letter, by telephone, by fax, by e-mail, in person and via website. Appointment necessary.
Hours: Mon to Fri, 0900 to 1700

CHILDREN'S SOCIETY, THE

Formal name: Church of England Children's Society
Acronym or abbreviation: TCS

Edward Rudolf House, Margery Street, London, WC1X 0JL

Tel: 020 7841 4400
E-mail: information@the-childrens-society.org.uk

Website:
http://www.the-childrens-society.org.uk

Founded:
1881

Organisation type and purpose:
Voluntary organisation, registered charity (charity number 221124).

Subject coverage:
Child care; neighbourhood and community work with the Church; advocacy; independent living; runaways; conciliation; fundraising; voluntary organisations.

Museum or gallery collection, archive, or library special collection:
Archive material documenting the development of the Society since it was founded in 1881
Collection of 10,000 photographic images depicting child welfare mainly at the turn of the century

Printed publications:
The Children's Society produces a range of titles covering the following subjects:
Adoption, Fostering and Care
Child Abuse and Prostitution
Children in Communities
Disability
Faltering Growth
PSE and Citizenship Resources
Poverty and Homelessness
School Exclusion and Reintegration
Young Runaways
Youth Justice
Divorce and Children (Smith R)
Hitting and Hurting – Living in a Violent Family (Pickering F)
On Small Shoulders – Learning from the Experiences of Former Young Carers (Frank J, Tatum C and Tucker S)
Order printed publications from: Publishing Department, The Children's Society
tel: 020 7837 4415, e-mail: publishing@the -childrens-society.org.uk

Publications list:
Available in print

Access to staff:
Contact by letter, by telephone, by e-mail and via website
Hours: Mon to Fri, 0930 to 1700
Special comments: Enquiries from the general public by telephone, letter or email only. No visitors.

Access to building, collection or gallery:
No access other than to staff

CHILLED FOOD ASSOCIATION

Acronym or abbreviation: CFA

PO Box 6434, Kettering, NN15 5XT

Tel: 01536 514365
E-mail: cfa@chilledfood.org

Website:
http://www.chilledfood.org
CFA and membership benefits, library of
information (members only).

Enquiries:
Enquiries to: Secretary-General

Founded:
1989

Organisation type and purpose:
Trade association (membership is by qualification),
present number of members: 21, manufacturing
industry.

Subject coverage:
Food safety, food hygiene, HACCP, technology,
chilled food manufacture.

Library catalogue:
All or part available online, in-house and in print

Printed publications:
Shelf life of ready to eat foods in relation to L
  monocytogenes – Guidance for food business
  operators
Best Practice Guidelines for the Production of
  Chilled Foods
Food Safety and Hygiene Training in Multicultural
  Environments
Guidance on the practical implementation of the
  EU Microbiological Criteria Regulations
Microbiological Testing and Interpretation
  Guidelines
Handwash posters
Water Quality Management: Guidelines for the
  Chilled Food Industry
High Risk Areas Best Practice Guidelines
Pesticides Due Diligence
Packaging Hygiene Guidelines
Hygiene Design Guidelines
Microbiological Guidance for Growers
Veterinary Residues Management Guidance
Order printed publications from: http://
www.chilledfood.org/shop

Publications list:
Available online and in print

Access to staff:
Contact by letter, by telephone, by e-mail and via
website. Appointment necessary. Access for
members only.
Hours: Mon to Fri, 0900 to 1700
Special comments: Detailed information available to
members only.

Access to building, collection or gallery:
No access other than to staff

Links with:
European Chilled Food Federation
  website: http://www.ecff.net

CHILTERN SOCIETY

The White Hill Centre, White Hill, Chesham,
Buckinghamshire, HP5 1AG

Tel: 01494 771250
Fax: 01494 793745
E-mail: office@chilternsociety.org.uk

Website:
http://www.chilternsociety.org.uk
Information about the Society.

Enquiries:
Enquiries to: Office Manager

Founded:
1965

Organisation type and purpose:
Membership association (membership is by
subscription), present number of members: 7250,
voluntary organisation, registered charity (charity
number 1085163).
Local amenity society.

Subject coverage:
Conservation in the Chilterns, trees and
woodlands, rivers and wetlands, rights of way,
waymarking, historic works and buildings,
planning, mineral resources and water supplies
etc.

Library catalogue:
All or part available online, in-house and in print

Printed publications:
Chiltern News (quarterly, free to members)
The Chiltern Way & Chiltern Way Extensions
Circular Walks in Buckinghamshire
Chiltern Walks in Herts, Beds & Bucks
Chiltern Walks in Oxon and West Bucks
Treasures of the Chilterns and many more.
Over 40 books, on walks and cycle routes
  throughout the region
26 Chiltern Society Footpath Maps
Order printed publications from: Chiltern Society
office

Electronic and video publications:
Caring for the Chilterns, describing the work of the
  Society (video)
The Chiltern Hills – Land of flint & beech (12.99)
St Albans – A city to inspire (video, £12.99)

Publications list:
Available online and in print

Access to staff:
Contact by letter, by telephone, by fax, by e-mail
and via website. Appointment necessary.
Hours: Mon to Fri, 0900 to 1700

Affiliated to:
Civic Trust
CPRE

Founders of:
Chiltern Open Air Museum
The Chiltern Woodland Project Limited

CHINA SOCIETY

16 Bridge Street, Christchurch, Dorset, BH23 1EB

Tel: 01202 482717

Enquiries:
Enquiries to: Chairman

Founded:
1906

Organisation type and purpose:
Learned society.

Subject coverage:
Generalised information only on Chinese art,
history and current affairs.

Printed publications:
Booklets

Access to staff:
Contact by letter and by telephone
Hours: Mon to Fri, 0900 to 2000

CHINA-BRITAIN BUSINESS COUNCIL

Acronym or abbreviation: CBBC

1 Warwick Row, London, SW1E 5ER

Tel: 020 7802 2000
Fax: 020 7802 2029

Website:
http://www.cbbc.org

Enquiries:
Enquiries to: Information Centre Manager
Direct tel: 020 7802 2014
Direct fax: 020 7802 2029
Direct e-mail: leo.liu@cbbc.org

Founded:
1998

Organisation type and purpose:
National government body, advisory body.

Subject coverage:
People's Republic of China: business and trade,
economy.

**Museum or gallery collection, archive, or library
special collection:**
Business guides, reference books, China statistical
  year books

Trade and statistical information:
UK-China trade statistics.

Library catalogue:
All or part available in-house

Printed publications:
China-Britain Business Review (monthly, £150
  annually)

Access to staff:
Contact by letter, by telephone, by fax, by e-mail
and via website. Appointment necessary.
Hours: Mon to Fri, 0900 to 1700

Access to building, collection or gallery:
Prior appointment required
Hours: Mon to Fri, 0900 to 1700

CHINESE INFORMATION AND ADVICE CENTRE

Acronym or abbreviation: CIAC

1st Floor, 53 New Oxford Street, London, WC1A
1BL

Tel: 020 7692 3471
Fax: 020 7692 3476
E-mail: ciac@ciac.co.uk

Enquiries:
Enquiries to: Information Officer
Direct tel: 020 7692 3473
Direct e-mail: cheng@ciac.co.uk
Other contacts: Tel: 020 7692 3474

Founded:
1983

Organisation type and purpose:
National government body, advisory body,
voluntary organisation, registered charity, training
organisation.
Advice agency for Chinese community,
specialising in immigration, asylum, matrimonial,
employment law to Chinese Community ONLY.
Also undertakes specific project work and
undertakes cases re: domestic violence issues;
matrimonial law; only sees women users.

Subject coverage:
Immigration, matrimonial, employment law
advice only; only sees women users re matrimonial
advice.

Non-library collection catalogue:
All or part available in-house

Library catalogue:
All or part available in-house

Printed publications:
Fact sheet on immigration and asylum law in
  Chinese
Annual Report (available free, directly from CIAC)
Service Directory of all Chinese community centres
  in London (available at a cost from CIAC)

Access to staff:
Contact by letter, by telephone, by fax and by e-
mail. Appointment necessary.
Hours: Mon to Fri, 0930 to 1800
Special comments: Not accessible to wheelchairs.

CHIPPENDALE SOCIETY

Temple Newsam House, Leeds, West Yorkshire,
LS15 0AE

Tel: 0113 264 7321

Fax: 0113 260 2285

Enquiries:
Enquiries to: Honorary Curator

Founded:
1965

Organisation type and purpose:
Learned society (membership is by subscription), registered charity.

Subject coverage:
Life and work of Thomas Chippendale Senior and Junior, furniture, wood carving.

Museum or gallery collection, archive, or library special collection:
Furniture, manuscripts, designs

Printed publications:
Newsletter (3 times a year, members)

Access to staff:
Contact by letter
Hours: Mon to Fri, 0900 to 1700

CHIROPRACTIC PATIENTS' ASSOCIATION

Acronym or abbreviation: CPA

8 Centre One, Lysander Way, Old Sarum Park, Salisbury, Wiltshire, SP4 6BU

Tel: 01722 415027
Fax: 01722 415028
E-mail: c.p.a@dial.pipex.com

Website:
http://www.chiropatients.org.uk

Enquiries:
Enquiries to: Chairman
Other contacts: Membership Secretary

Founded:
1966

Formerly called:
British Pro Chiropractic Association; Chiropractic Advancement Association (CAA) (year of change 1996)

Organisation type and purpose:
National organisation, membership association (membership is by subscription), voluntary organisation, registered charity (charity number 328135), suitable for all ages.
Voluntary association of chiropractic patients that aims to ensure patient welfare, provide a patient helpline, make chiropractic treatment more easily accessible via the NHS, and fund chiropractic research and education.

Subject coverage:
All aspects that relate patients to the provision of chiropractic treatment in the United Kingdom.

Printed publications:
Back Chat (magazine, free to members)
Information leaflet/Q & As (free)

Access to staff:
Contact by letter, by telephone, by fax, by e-mail and via website
Hours: Mon to Fri, 0900 to 1700

Access to building, collection or gallery:
No access other than to staff

CHOIR SCHOOLS ASSOCIATION

Acronym or abbreviation: CSA

The Minster School, Deangate, York, YO1 7JA

Tel: 01904 624900
Fax: 01904 557232

Enquiries:
Enquiries to: Administrator

Organisation type and purpose:
Professional body, registered charity (charity number 326868).

To supply information about choir schools. The Bursary Trust provides financial help to families in need of assistance.

Subject coverage:
Choir schools, information about entry, location, bursaries.

Printed publications:
Choir Schools Today (journal, annually)
Could My Child be a Chorister
List of members

Access to staff:
Contact by letter and by telephone
Hours: Mon to Fri, 0900 to 1700
Special comments: Office is open on Monday and Wednesday only during term-time.

At the same address is the:
CSA Bursary Trust

CHRIS MCALLISTER LIMITED

Formal name: Chris McAllister Associates

2 Riverside Walk, Annan, Dumfries and Galloway, DG12 6BE

Tel: 01461 205866
Fax: 01461 205838
E-mail: chris@chrismca.com

Website:
http://www.chrismca.com
How to make NVQs easy; CD-ROM portfolio (with or without interactive content); NVQs and SVQs in management, learning and development, etc. Useful information on e-portfolios and free downloadable resources.

Enquiries:
Enquiries to: Principal Consultant
Direct tel: 07802 251713

Founded:
1985

Organisation type and purpose:
Training organisation, consultancy.

Subject coverage:
Trainer training, management training, assessor and verifier training, open learning, customer service training, advice and guidance training, team leadership training.

Special visitor services:
Delivers NVQs and SVQs anywhere in the United Kingdom (and abroad, usually by telephone).

Education services:
NVQs/SVQs in Management, Learning and Development, etc., including Assessor and Verifier training.

Services for disabled people:
Telephone tutoring (as required).

Non-library collection catalogue:
All or part available online

Library catalogue:
All or part available online

Electronic and video publications:
Workbooks online as PDFs: A1.pdf and V1.pdf
Order electronic and video publications from: http://www.chrismca.com

Publications list:
Available online

Access to staff:
Contact by letter, by telephone, by fax, by e-mail, in person and via website. Appointment necessary.
Hours: Mon to Fri, 0900 to 1700

Access to building, collection or gallery:
Only by appointment
Hours: Mon to Fri, 0900 to 1700

Access for disabled people:
No disabled access

Links with:
Chartered Institute of Personnel and Development (CIPD)
  tel: 020 8971 9000

Institute for Leadership and Management (ILM)
  tel: 01593 251346

CHRIST CHURCH LIBRARY

Christ Church, Oxford, OX1 1DP

Tel: 01865 276169
E-mail: library@chch.ox.ac.uk

Website:
http://www.chch.ox.ac.uk/library
General information on the library.

Enquiries:
Enquiries to: Librarian

Founded:
1546

Organisation type and purpose:
College library.

Subject coverage:
Manuscript and printed music of the 16th and 17th centuries; theology, particularly the Vulgate; theatre.

Museum or gallery collection, archive, or library special collection:
Brady Collection of theatrical prints and plays
Manuscript and printed music of 16th and 17th centuries
Medieval and Renaissance manuscripts, especially Greek
Printed books and pamphlets of 17th and 18th centuries

Non-library collection catalogue:
All or part available online, in-house and in print

Microform publications:
Microfilms of music manuscript, printed music and other manuscripts
Order microform publications from: See website
http://www.chch.ox.ac.uk/library

Access to staff:
Contact by letter and by e-mail. Appointment necessary. Letter of introduction required.
Hours: Mon to Fri, 0900 to 1700

Constituent part of:
University of Oxford

CHRIST'S COLLEGE LIBRARY

St Andrew Street, Cambridge, CB2 3BU

Tel: 01223 334950
E-mail: library@christs.cam.ac.uk

Website:
http://www.christs.cam.ac.uk/info/library
Library guide, admissions information, guide to the college.

Enquiries:
Enquiries to: College Librarian

Founded:
1505

Organisation type and purpose:
University library.

Subject coverage:
General academic subjects.

Museum or gallery collection, archive, or library special collection:
C. Lesingham Smith Collection of early scientific books
Collection of editions of the works of John Milton
Robertson Smith Oriental Collection
Stephen Gazelee Coptic Collection
W. H. D. Rouse Indian Collection
Wratislaw Slavonic Collection
David Stanbury Darwin Collection
Donald Dickson C. P. Snow Collection

Non-library collection catalogue:
All or part available in-house

Library catalogue:
All or part available online and in-house

continued overleaf

Access to staff:
Contact by letter, by telephone and by e-mail.
Appointment necessary. Access for members only.
Letter of introduction required.
Hours: Mon to Fri, 0900 to 1700

Access for disabled people:
Parking provided, ramped entry, access to all
public areas

CHRISTCHURCH BOROUGH COUNCIL

Civic Offices, Bridge Street, Christchurch, Dorset,
BH23 1AZ

Tel: 01202 495000
Fax: 01202 482200
E-mail: post@christchurch.gov.uk

Website:
http://www.dorsetforyou.com
Council information and services, tourism,
community business and transport.
http://www.christchurchtourism.info
Tourism.

Enquiries:
Enquiries to: Chief Executive
Direct tel: 01202 495126
Direct fax: 01202 482060
Direct e-mail: m.turvey@christchurch.gov.uk

Organisation type and purpose:
Local government body.

Access to staff:
Contact by letter, by telephone, by fax, by e-mail,
in person and via website. Appointment necessary.
Hours: Mon to Thu, 0845 to 1715; Fri, 0845 to 1645

Access for disabled people:
Parking provided, ramped entry, toilet facilities,
hearing loop, interpreting (by appointment)

CHRISTIAN AID

PO Box 100, London SE1 7RT

Tel: 020 7620 4444
E-mail: info@christian-aid.org

Website:
http://www.christian-aid.org.uk

Founded:
1945

Organisation type and purpose:
International organisation, registered charity
(charity number 1105851).
International development aid agency committed
to working with all people to combat poverty.

Subject coverage:
Combatting poverty. Information on 700 partners
in 60 countries that it works with. Campaign work
on cancellation of 3rd World debt and Trade for
Life. Emergency work around the world.

Printed publications:
Resources Catalogue for Schools

Electronic and video publications:
Tapes, disks and videos available direct through
  Christian Aid and through publishing house

Publications list:
Available online and in print

Access to staff:
Contact by letter, by telephone, by fax, by e-mail,
in person and via website
Hours: Mon to Fri, 0930 to 1615

Access for disabled people:
Level entry, access to all public areas, toilet
facilities
Special comments: Lift available.

Also at:
Christian Aid
  35 Lower Marsh, London, SE1 7RL; tel: 020 7620
  4444

Parent body:
The British Council of Churches

CHRISTIAN AID SCOTLAND

The Pentagon Centre, 36 Washington Street,
Glasgow, G3 8AZ

Tel: 0141 221 7475
Fax: 0141 241 6145
E-mail: glasgow@christian-aid.org

Website:
http://www.christianaidscotland.org

Enquiries:
Enquiries to: Head of Christian Aid Scotland

Founded:
1955

Organisation type and purpose:
International organisation, registered charity
(Scottish Charity number SC039150).

Access to staff:
Contact by letter, by telephone, by fax, by e-mail
and in person. Appointment necessary.
Hours: Mon to Fri, 0900 to 1600

Also at:
Christian Aid
  41 George IV Bridge, Edinburgh, EH1 1EL; tel:
  0131 240 1254
Christian Aid
  28 Glasgow Road, Perth, PH2 0NX; tel: 01738
  643982

CHRISTIAN AID, INFORMATION RESOURCES CENTRE

PO Box 100, London, SE1 7RT

Tel: 020 7523 2414
Fax: 020 7620 0719
E-mail: irc@christian-aid.org

Website:
http://www.christian-aid.org

Enquiries:
Enquiries to: Senior Information Officer

Organisation type and purpose:
Voluntary organisation, registered charity.
An official agency of the British and Irish Churches
working with local organisations in 60 countries,
strengthening their efforts to eradicate poverty and
increase self-reliance; also provides grants to
refugees and disaster victims.

Subject coverage:
Needs of the world's poor; poverty issues;
development education; emergencies, refugees and
interchurch aid.

Library catalogue:
All or part available in-house

Printed publications:
Order printed publications from: Supporter Relations
Department

Access to staff:
Contact by letter, by telephone, by e-mail, in
person and via website. Appointment necessary.
Hours: Mon to Fri, 1000 to 1700

CHRISTIAN ALLIANCE HOUSING SERVICES LIMITED

2 Exton Street, London, SE1 8UE

Tel: 020 7593 0470
Fax: 020 7593 0478
E-mail: mail@caha.org.uk

Website:
http://www.caha.org.uk

Enquiries:
Enquiries to: Director

Organisation type and purpose:
Membership association (membership is by
election or invitation), registered charity.

Subject coverage:
Residential accommodation and information.

Access to staff:
Contact by letter and by telephone
Hours: Mon to Fri, 0900 to 1700

CHRISTIAN ASSOCIATION OF BUSINESS EXECUTIVES

Acronym or abbreviation: CABE

24 Greencoat Place, London, SW1P 1BE

Tel: 020 7798 6040
Fax: 020 7798 6044

Enquiries:
Enquiries to: Director

Founded:
1943

Organisation type and purpose:
Membership association, registered charity.

Access to staff:
Contact by letter
Hours: Mon to Fri, 1000 to 1700

CHRISTIAN BUSINESSMEN'S COMMITTEE (BROMLEY)

Acronym or abbreviation: CBMC

Fair Winds, Goatsfield Road, Tatsfield, Westerham,
Kent, TN16 2 BU

Tel: 01959 577745
E-mail: roy@lifesroadmap.co.uk

Website:
http://www.cbmcbromley.org.uk
Sharing the claims of Jesus Christ with
businessmen.

Enquiries:
Enquiries to: Secretary

Founded:
1967

Organisation type and purpose:
International organisation, membership
association (membership is by election or
invitation).
Religious – Christian Gospel.
A Christian organisation witnessing to
businessmen sharing Christ with businessmen and
professional men in the market place.

Access to staff:
Contact by letter, by telephone, by fax and by e-
mail
Hours: Mon to Fri, 0900 to 1700

CHRISTIAN COMMUNITY

22 Baylie Street, Stourbridge, DY8 1AZ

Tel: 01384 377190
E-mail: info@thechristiancommunity.co.uk

Website:
http://www.thechristiancommunity.co.uk
Communities, 7 sacraments.

Founded:
1922

Organisation type and purpose:
Movement for religious renewal.

Subject coverage:
Ordained priests, both men and women, work
together with the members of the congregations to
create free sacramental communities for
celebrating The Act of Consecration of Man and
the other sacraments.

Printed publications:
Order printed publications from: Floris Books, see
website: http://www.florisbooks.co.uk

Electronic and video publications:
Newsletter
Perspectives (quarterly journal)

Access to staff:
Contact by letter, by telephone and by e-mail

Christian Community sites in:
North America, Australia and New Zealand,
Germany and France

Christian Community training centres in:
Chicago, USA, and Hamburg and Stuttgart,
Germany

CHRISTIAN COPYRIGHT LICENSING (EUROPE) LTD

Acronym or abbreviation: CCL

PO Box 1339, Eastbourne, East Sussex, BN21 1AD

Tel: 01323 417711
Fax: 01323 417722
E-mail: info@ccli.co.uk

Website:
http://www.ccli.com
Information on international copyright licensing
and copyright education.

Enquiries:
Enquiries to: Church/School Representative

Founded:
1991

Organisation type and purpose:
International organisation.
Copyright licensing.

Subject coverage:
Hymn and worship song copyright, non-
commercial licences for reproducing and
photocopying text or audio/visual recordings of
hymns and worship songs by churches, schools
and Christian organisations.

Printed publications:
Copyright education brochure including licence
   application form

Access to staff:
Contact by letter, by telephone, by fax, by e-mail
and via website
Hours: Mon to Fri, 0830 to 1630

Parent body:
Christian Copyright Licensing International
   17201, NE Sacramento Street, Portland, OR
   97230, USA

CHRISTIAN EDUCATION

1020 Bristol Road, Selly Oak, Birmingham, B29 6LB

Tel: 0121 472 4242
Fax: 0121 472 7575
E-mail: enquiries@christianeducation.org.uk

Website:
http://www.christianeducation.org.uk
Resource list, courses, online catalogue,
downloads.

Enquiries:
Enquiries to: Director

Founded:
2001

Formerly called:
National Sunday School Union (NSSU), SCM in
Schools (SCM) (year of change 1965); Christian
Education Movement (CEM), National Christian
Education Council (NCEC) (year of change 2001)

Organisation type and purpose:
National organisation, membership association
(membership is by subscription), registered charity
(charity number 1086990), suitable for ages: lifelong, training organisation, consultancy, research
organisation, publishing house.

Subject coverage:
Religious education for all ages; ecumenism.

Printed publications:
Books, guides and leaflets supporting teachers of
   5–16 year olds
Resource (termly periodical)
RE Today (termly periodical)
BJRE (termly periodical)

Electronic and video publications:
Videos for RE in secondary schools and others

Publications list:
Available in print

Access to staff:
Contact by letter, by telephone, by fax and via
website
Hours: Mon to Fri, 0900 to 1700

Other addresses:
RE Today Services
   1020 Bristol Road, Selly Oak, Birmingham, B29
   6LB; tel: 0121 472 4242; fax: 0121 472 7575

Subsidiary body:
Professional Council for Religious Education
(PCfRE)
   tel: 0191 213 5227; fax: 0191 213 5227; e-mail:
   rachel@retoday.org.uk

CHRISTIAN ENQUIRY AGENCY

Acronym or abbreviation: CEA

27 Tavistock Square, London, WC1H 9HH

Tel: 020 8144 7177
E-mail: enquiry@christianity.org.uk

Website:
http://www.christianity.org.uk
Information about the Christian faith, links to other
sites, opportunity to request literature, prayer or
help for a journey of faith.

Enquiries:
Enquiries to: Administrator

Founded:
1988

Organisation type and purpose:
Registered charity (charity number 297393).
To provide information about the Christian faith.

Subject coverage:
Christian faith.

Printed publications:
Christian Enquiry Agency News

Access to staff:
Contact by letter, by telephone, by e-mail and via
website
Hours: Mon to Fri, 0800 to 1600
Special comments: Hours are variable, but voicemail
and answerphone operate.

Works in association with:
all major churches in Britain and Ireland, and
many Christian organisations.

CHRISTIAN POLICE ASSOCIATION

Acronym or abbreviation: CPA

Bedford Heights, Manton Lane, Bedford, MK41
7PH

Tel: 01234 272 865
E-mail: info@cpauk.net

Website:
http://www.cpauk.net

Enquiries:
Enquiries to: Executive Director

Organisation type and purpose:
Membership association (membership is by
election or invitation), present number of
members: 2,000, registered charity (charity number
220482).

Access to staff:
Contact by letter, by telephone, by fax and by e-
mail
Hours: Mon to Fri, 0900 to 1700

CHRISTIAN SCIENCE COMMITTEES ON PUBLICATION

10 Tideway Yard, 125 Mortlake High Street,
London, SW14 8SN

Tel: 020 8150 0245
Fax: 020 8487 1566
E-mail: londoncs@csps.com

Website:
http://christianscience.co.uk

Enquiries:
Enquiries to: District Manager

Organisation type and purpose:
Registered charity (charity number 230940).
To provide information on Christian Science and
Church of Christ, Scientist.

Subject coverage:
Christian Science, the writings of Mary Baker
Eddy, the Bible and general information on The
Church of Christ Scientist.

Information services:
Information about Christian Science, Mary Baker
Eddy, and Church of Christ, Scientist.

CHRISTIANS ABROAD

Acronym or abbreviation: Cab

The Bon Marche Centre, 241–251 Ferndale Road,
London, SW9 8BJ

Tel: 08707 707990
Fax: 08707 707991
E-mail: director@cabroad.org.uk

Website:
http://www.cabroad.org.uk
http://www.wse.org.uk

Enquiries:
Enquiries to: Information Officer

Founded:
1972

Organisation type and purpose:
Voluntary organisation, registered charity (charity
number 265867).
To offer opportunities for individuals with
Christian commitment to work for development
overseas through Christians Abroad, and
debriefing sessions for review and reflection for
those returning from overseas service.
To provide a consultancy for overseas recruitment
and personnel management to agencies placing
persons overseas in mission, and development on
all matters deriving from the organisation's
experience in the international movement of
personnel. As World Service Enquiry, providing
information and advice about volunteering or
working in the developing world.

Subject coverage:
Work in aid, development and mission overseas;
recruitment and personnel management in mission
work overseas.

Printed publications:
Guide to Volunteering and Working for
   Development; Opportunities Abroad; The
   Survival Guide – A travellers e-book guide.

Publications list:
Available online and in print

Access to staff:
Contact by telephone, by e-mail and via website
Hours: Mon to Fri, 0900 to 1700

Access to building, collection or gallery:
No access other than to staff

CHRISTIE CHARITY

Formal name: The Christie NHS Foundation Trust

Appeals Office, Wilmslow Road, Withington, Manchester, M20 4BX

Tel: 0161 446 3988
Fax: 0161 446 3991
E-mail: via website

Website:
http://www.christies.org
The charity, its work, its fund raising.

Founded:
1901

Organisation type and purpose:
Registered charity (charity number 1049751).
Raises money to fund projects at The Christie hospital that are outside the scope of the NHS, such as a new radiopharmacy, communications skills training for nursing staff, a new state-of-the-art surgical robot, groundbreaking cancer research and the wig service.

Printed publications:
Successes (magazine)
Order printed publications from: Website

Electronic and video publications:
E-newsletter
Press release archive
Order electronic and video publications from: Website

Access to staff:
Contact by letter, by telephone, by fax and via website

CHRISTIE HOSPITAL & PATERSON INSTITUTE FOR CANCER RESEARCH

Medical Library, Wilmslow Road, Withington, Manchester, M20 4BX

Tel: 0161 446 3000
Fax: 0161 446 3454
E-mail: sglover@picr.man.ac.uk

Website:
http://www.christie.nhs.uk

Enquiries:
Enquiries to: Librarian
Direct tel: 0161 446 3456

Founded:
1932

Organisation type and purpose:
Research organisation.
Medical library.
Cancer.

Subject coverage:
Oncology; radiotherapy; treatment and research.

Library catalogue:
All or part available in-house

Access to staff:
Contact by telephone and by e-mail
Hours: Mon to Wed, 0900 to 1900; Thu, 0800 to 1730; Fri, 0800 to 1700; Sat, 0900 to 1300
Special comments: NHS or academic staff only.

CHURCH MISSION SOCIETY

Acronym or abbreviation: CMS

Watlington Road, Oxford, OX4 6BZ

Tel: 01865 787552
Fax: 01865 776375
E-mail: margaret.acton@cms-uk.org

Website:
http://www.cms-uk.org

Enquiries:
Enquiries to: Records Manager

Founded:
1799

Formerly called:
Church Missionary Society

Organisation type and purpose:
Registered charity (charity number 220297).
Anglican Missionary Society.

Subject coverage:
Mission work and local church growth, particularly in Asia and Africa.

Museum or gallery collection, archive, or library special collection:
Extensive archive collection located at Birmingham University Library. Contact Special Collections, Main Library, University of Birmingham, Edgbaston, Birmingham, B15 2TT

Library catalogue:
All or part available online

Printed publications:
Catalogues for all sections of the archive collection available (various prices)
CMS Newsletter (6 times a year)
Yes (5 times a year)

Access to staff:
Appointment necessary.
Hours: Mon to Fri, 0900 to 1700

CHURCH MONUMENTS SOCIETY

Acronym or abbreviation: CMS

The Membership Secretary, 55 Bowden Park Road, Crownhill, Plymouth, PL6 5NG

E-mail: churchmonuments@aol.com

Website:
http://www.churchmonumentssociety.org

Enquiries:
Enquiries to: Honorary Secretary
Other contacts: Honorary Publicity Officer

Founded:
1979

Organisation type and purpose:
Learned society, registered charity (charity number 279597).
To promote, for the public benefit, the study, care and conservation of funerary monuments of all countries and all periods.

Subject coverage:
Art, architecture, history, costume, heraldry, lettering, geology, genealogy, iconography, epigraphy.

Printed publications:
Church Monuments (journal, annually)
Newsletter (twice a year)
Order printed publications from: Honorary Membership Secretary, Church Monuments Society, 55 Bowden Park Road, Crownhill, Plymouth, PL6 5NG; tel. 01752 773634

Access to staff:
Contact by letter, by telephone, by fax, by e-mail and via website

CHURCH OF ENGLAND BOARD OF EDUCATION

Acronym or abbreviation: BOE

Church House, Great Smith Street, London, SW1P 3AZ

Tel: 020 7898 1500
Fax: 020 7898 1520
E-mail: janina.ainsworth@c-of-e.org.uk

Website:
http://www.cofe.anglican.org/about/education
Overview, specific links to each area of the Board's work in education.
http://www.churchschools.co.uk
Subscription service for teachers, head teachers and governors of all Church schools; resources, up-to-date information on Church school issues.
http://www.natsoc.org.uk

Collective workshop, RE centre resources, information about church schools, National Society publications.

Formerly called:
General Synod Board of Education

Organisation type and purpose:
Advisory body, voluntary organisation, suitable for ages: all.
To promote the Church's interest in education.

Subject coverage:
Church of England schools, church colleges, chaplains in colleges and universities, adult work in the Church, children's work (including Sunday schools), religious education, history of church colleges of education, training/adult education, youth work/youth council.

Publications list:
Available in print

Access to staff:
Contact by letter, by telephone, by fax, by e-mail and via website
Hours: Mon to Fri, 0900 to 1700

Constituent bodies:
Lifelong Learning Team
tel: 020 7898 1505; fax: 020 7898 1520; e-mail: gabriella.disalvo@c-of-e.org.uk
Schools Strategy Team
tel: 020 7898 1491; fax: 020 7898 1520; e-mail: veronica.elks@c-of-e.org.uk
Training & Development Team
tel: 020 7898 1512; fax: 020 7898 0520; e-mail: julia.eden@c-of-e.org.uk

Links with:
National Society (CofE) for Promoting Religious Education
tel: 020 7898 1518; fax: 020 7898 1493; e-mail: peter.churchill@c-of-e.org.uk

Parent body:
Archbishops' Council of the Church of England
tel: 020 7898 1000

CHURCH OF ENGLAND RECORD CENTRE

Acronym or abbreviation: CERC

15 Galleywall Road, South Bermondsey, London, SE16 3PB

Tel: 020 7898 1030
Fax: 020 7898 1043
E-mail: archivist@c-of-e.org.uk

Website:
http://www.cofe.anglican.org/

Enquiries:
Enquiries to: Operations Manager

Founded:
1990

Formerly called:
Church Commissioners' Archives, General Synod Archives, National Society Archives (year of change 1990)

Organisation type and purpose:
Church Administration.

Subject coverage:
Church of England; administration, buildings, education, finance, history, legislation, liturgy, ministry, mission, social responsibility.

Museum or gallery collection, archive, or library special collection:
Church Commissioners' Archives
General Synod Archives
National Society Archives

Non-library collection catalogue:
All or part available in print

Library catalogue:
All or part available online

Printed publications:
Sources for Anglican Clergy, 16th to 20th centuries

Keep or Bin – The Care of your Parish Records

Electronic and video publications:
Keep or Bin – The Care of your Parish Records
Save or Delete – Care of Diocesan Records

Access to staff:
Contact by letter, by telephone, by fax and by e-mail. Appointment necessary.
Hours: Mon to Fri, 0900 to 1700
Special comments: Reading room at Lambeth Palace Library

Access to building, collection or gallery:
Prior appointment required for reading room at Lambeth Palace Library

Access for disabled people:
Parking provided, toilet facilities

CHURCH OF JESUS CHRIST OF LATTER-DAY SAINTS

Church Offices, 751 Warwick Road, Solihull, West Midlands, B91 3DQ

Tel: 0121 712 1200

Website:
http://www.familysearch.org
Personal Ancestral File download facility.
http://www.lds.org/newsroom
Information for journalists.
http://www.mormon.org
For those wanting to know more about the Church and its teachings.
http://www.lds.org
Basic information on the Church, its history and beliefs.

Founded:
1830

Also known as:
Mormons (nickname)

Organisation type and purpose:
International organisation, membership association (membership is by qualification), present number of members: 180,000 UK and Ireland, 11,000,000 worldwide, registered charity (charity number 242451).
Church, religious organisation.

Subject coverage:
Theology, especially early Christian church, revelation; certain fields of health, especially cancer; self-sufficiency; family relationships; genealogy, especially the use of computer held genealogical records, such as the IGI (International Genealogical Index).

Printed publications:
Church News (weekly newspaper, on subscription)
Ensign (monthly magazine on subscription)
The New Era (magazine for youth, monthly, on subscription)
The Friend (magazine for children up to 12 years, monthly, on subscription)
Order printed publications from: Latter-Day Saints Distribution
399 Garrett Green Lane, Birmingham, B33 0UH, tel: 0121 785 2200

Electronic and video publications:
British Vital Records Index (CD-ROM, £13.50)
Family History Source Guide (CD-ROM, £10)
Personal Ancestral File (computer software for genealogical management, v3.0, floppy disk only 3.5 or 5.25 ins MS-DOS, £11.80)
Personal Ancestral File (computer software for genealogical management, v4.0, CD-ROM, for Windows £3.80 or free download from website)
Pedigree Resource File (CD-ROM, set of five, £19)
Order electronic and video publications from: Latter-Day Saints Distribution
399 Garrett Green Lane, Birmingham, B33 0UH, tel: 0121 785 2200

Access to staff:
Contact by letter, by telephone, by fax, by e-mail and via website. Appointment necessary.

Hours: Mon to Fri, 0900 to 1700

Access for disabled people:
Access to all public areas, toilet facilities

CHURCH OF SCOTLAND

121 George Street, Edinburgh, EH2 4YN

Tel: 0131 225 5722
Fax: 0131 220 3133
E-mail: fmacdonald@cofscotland.org.uk

Website:
http://www.churchofscotland.org.uk

Enquiries:
Enquiries to: Principal Clerk

Founded:
500 AD

Organisation type and purpose:
National church.

Subject coverage:
Church of Scotland.

Printed publications:
Life and Work (monthly)

Access to staff:
Contact by letter
Hours: Mon to Fri, 0900 to 1700

CHURCH UNION

Formal name: The Church Union
Acronym or abbreviation: CU

(may change; currently at) Faith House, 7 Tufton Street, Westminster, London, SW1P 3QN

Tel: 020 7222 6952
E-mail: secretary@churchunion.co.uk

Website:
http://www.churchunion.co.uk

Enquiries:
Enquiries to: The Secretary
Direct tel: 020 7388 3588
Other contacts: Chairman, tel: 01371 830132; Publication, tel: 01684 575893; Treasurer, tel: 01709 546441; Membership, tel: 020 7222 6952

Founded:
1859

Formerly called:
Tufton Books; Church Literature Association (publication arm of CU) (year of change 1997)

Organisation type and purpose:
Membership association (membership is by subscription), present number of members: 2000, registered charity (charity number 243535), publishing house.

Subject coverage:
The Catholic Movement within the Church of England, founded at the time of the Oxford Movement, to promote catholic faith and order, it continues this work today by providing support and encouragement to those lay people and priests who wish to see catholic faith, order, morals and spirituality maintained and upheld, and who wish to promote catholic unity. The Union is a publisher of books and tracts and has part-time staff who can advise on matters liturgical, legal and musical.

Museum or gallery collection, archive, or library special collection:
Lord Halifax's personal Library: history of the English Church Union and Anglo-Catholic congresses

Printed publications:
Church Observer (quarterly)
Modern works on liturgy and theological matters
Following published by Canterbury Press Norwich:
Order for the Eucharist (Hunwicke J, ISBN 0–85191–097–1, £6.99)

Order of Mass:
Order One: ISBN 0–8591–089–0 (per pack of 50, £22.50)
Order One: ISBN 0–8591–109–9 (per pack of 10, £4.50)
Order One: ISBN 0–8591–069–8 (singles, 50p)
Traditional: ISBN 0–8591–008–2 (per pack of 50, £22.50)
Traditional: ISBN 0–8591–174–9 (per pack of 10, £4.50)
Traditional: ISBN 0–8591–098-X (singles, 50p)
Following published by Tufton Books and CLA:
Another Look at St John's Gospel (Clutterbuck I, ISBN 0–85191–240–0, £5.95)
Baptism of Children, Order of Service (single copy/copies, ISBN 0–85191–240–0, 50p)
Baptism of Children, Order of Service (pack(s) of 10, ISBN 0–85191–241–9, £4.50)
Baptism of Children, Order of Service (pack(s) of 50, ISBN 0–85191–236–2, £22.50)
Celebration With the Sick and Dying (Pinchin T, ISBN 0–85191–270–2, £1.95)
CREDO (course book, Urwin L, ISBN 0–85191–310–5, £16.50 (out of print), book and video pack, £32.50 inc. VAT)
Parish Cards
What We Do In Church and Why (Straszak E)
Word of God for the People of God (Chadd L, ISBN 0–85191–160–9, £3.50)
Youthful Spirit (Ward P and Urwin L, ISBN 0–85191–233–8, £6.99)
Order printed publications from: Canterbury Press, St Mary's Works, St Mary Plain, Norwich, NR3 3BH, tel: 01603 612914

Electronic and video publications:
CREDO (video, Urwin L, ISBN 0–85191–310–5, £19 inc VAT)
Order electronic and video publications from: Canterbury Press

Publications list:
Available in print

Access to staff:
Contact by letter, by telephone and by e-mail. Appointment necessary.
Hours: Mon to Fri, 0900 to 1700
Special comments: Via tel only

Access to building, collection or gallery:
Prior appointment required

Also trades as:
Tufton Books

CHURCHES RACIAL JUSTICE NETWORK

Acronym or abbreviation: CRJN

39 Eccleston Square, London SW1V 1BX

Tel: 020 7901 4890
Fax: 020 7901 4894
E-mail: info@ctbi.org.uk

Website:
http://www.ctbi.org.uk

Enquiries:
Enquiries to: RJN Desk

Founded:
1992

Organisation type and purpose:
National organisation, voluntary organisation, registered charity (charity number 259688).
Church organisation.

Subject coverage:
Racial justice and community relations in Britain.

Library catalogue:
All or part available online

Printed publications:
Racial Justice Sunday Pack (2nd Sunday September)

Publications list:
Available online and in print

continued overleaf

Access to staff:
Contact by letter, by telephone, by fax, by e-mail and via website. Appointment necessary.
Hours: Mon to Fri, 0930 to 1700

Access for disabled people:
Level entry

Affiliated to:
All community race relations bodies

CHURCHES TOGETHER IN BRITAIN AND IRELAND

Acronym or abbreviation: CTBI

39 Eccleston Square, London SW1V 1BX

Tel: 020 7901 4890
Fax: 020 79014894
E-mail: info@ctbi.org.uk

Website:
http://www.ctbi.org.uk

Enquiries:
Enquiries to: General Secretary

Founded:
1947

Formerly called:
British Council of Churches (year of change 1990)

Organisation type and purpose:
National organisation, membership association (membership is by subscription, qualification), present number of members: 37 member churches, registered charity (charity number 1113299). Fellowship of Churches in the United Kingdom and the Republic of Ireland; member churches – Protestant, Anglican, Orthodox, Roman Catholic, Pentecostal, Salvation Army, Quaker, Ecumenical.

Subject coverage:
Ecumenical co-operation: Christianity; relations with other churches and other faiths; Christian perspectives on public affairs, international affairs, race relations, mission and evangelisation, women's issues, inter-faith relations.

Printed publications:
Ecumenical studies
Reports on current issues
World Council of Churches Publications
Order printed publications from: CTBI Publications, Church House Bookshop, Great Smith Street, London, SW1P 3BN

Publications list:
Available online and in print

Access to staff:
Contact by letter, by telephone, by fax, by e-mail and via website. Appointment necessary.
Hours: Mon to Fri, 0900 to 1700

Access to building, collection or gallery:
Prior appointment required

Access for disabled people:
Level entry, access to all public areas, toilet facilities

Affiliated to:
Conference of European Churches
World Council of Churches

Links with:
Churches Together in England, Scotland, Wales
Irish Council of Churches

CHURCHES' CONSERVATION TRUST, THE

1 West Smithfield, London EC1A 9EE

Tel: 020 7213 0660
Fax: 020 7213 0678
E-mail: central@tcct.org.uk

Website:
http://www.visitchurches.org.uk
Details of all 325 churches – opening arrangements, location, short architectural description.

Enquiries:
Enquiries to: Public Relations Manager

Founded:
1969

Formerly called:
Redundant Churches Fund (year of change 1994)

Organisation type and purpose:
Statutory body, registered charity (charity number 258612).
The care and conservation of redundant churches in England.

Subject coverage:
Conservation of churches, redundant churches.

Printed publications:
County lists (free)
Guidebooks and postcards for churches under the care of The Churches Conservation Trust (available from the churches or direct)

Publications list:
Available online and in print

Access to staff:
Contact by letter, by telephone and by fax
Hours: Mon to Fri, 0900 to 1700

Access to building, collection or gallery:
No prior appointment required

CHURCHILL ARCHIVES CENTRE

Churchill College, Cambridge, CB3 0DS

Tel: 01223 336087
Fax: 01223 336135
E-mail: archives@chu.cam.ac.uk

Website:
http://www.chu.cam.ac.uk/archives
Visitor information, holdings guide.

Enquiries:
Enquiries to: Director of the Archives

Founded:
1973

Organisation type and purpose:
University department or institute.
College library and archive.

Subject coverage:
Churchill Family; diplomacy, foreign policy and international relations, 1900 to date; political life and government policy, 1900 to date; military and naval history, 1900 to date; history of science and technology, 1900 to date.

Museum or gallery collection, archive, or library special collection:
Papers of Sir Winston Churchill, together with papers of about 570 other individuals and institutions

Non-library collection catalogue:
All or part available online and in-house

Library catalogue:
All or part available in-house

Access to staff:
Contact by letter, by telephone, by fax, by e-mail and via website. Appointment necessary.
Hours: Mon to Fri, 0900 to 1700

Access to building, collection or gallery:
Prior appointment required, ID required

Access for disabled people:
Parking provided, ramped entry, toilet facilities, lift to reading rooms

CIBA SPECIALTY CHEMICALS PLC

Hawkhead Road, Paisley, Renfrewshire, PA2 7BG

Tel: 0141 887 1144
Fax: 0141 840 2283

Enquiries:
Enquiries to: Information Manager
Direct tel: 0141 887 1144 ext 5287
Direct e-mail: ailsa.morrison@cibasc.com

Other contacts: Library Assistant for general.

Formerly called:
Ciba-Geigy Pigments (year of change 1997)

Organisation type and purpose:
Manufacturing industry.

Subject coverage:
Organic pigments, colour chemistry.

Library catalogue:
All or part available in-house

Access to staff:
Contact by letter, by telephone and by e-mail.
Appointment necessary.
Hours: Mon to Fri, 0900 to 1700

Access to building, collection or gallery:
Prior appointment required

CILT, THE NATIONAL CENTRE FOR LANGUAGES

Acronym or abbreviation: CiLT

20 Bedfordbury, London, WC2N 4LB

Tel: 020 7379 5110
Fax: 020 7379 5082
E-mail: library@cilt.org.uk

Website:
http://www.nacell.org.uk
Information about language learning for under 11 year olds in the UK.
http://www.blis.org.uk
Databases of language and cultural expertise services in the field of business and employment.
http://www.cilt.org.uk
Information about the activities of CILT, CILT Cymru, the Comenius Centres, the Regional Language Networks. Links to CILT Cymru, Scottish CILT, Northern Ireland CILT, BLIS and NACELL websites.

Enquiries:
Enquiries to: Librarian

Founded:
1966

Organisation type and purpose:
Registered charity (charity number 313938).
Supported by Central Government grants.

Subject coverage:
Promotion of a greater national capability in languages, including languages for employment, and to support the work of all those concerned with language teaching and learning from primary to graduate level. Research into teaching methods and learning resources in French, German, Italian, Russian, Spanish, and many other languages; English as a second language in Britain; community languages; examinations.

Museum or gallery collection, archive, or library special collection:
Books and periodicals
Teaching materials, textbooks, visual aids, software, video and audio recordings

Trade and statistical information:
Education statistics and labour market data at http://www.cilt.org.uk/statistics

Non-library collection catalogue:
All or part available online

Library catalogue:
All or part available online

Printed publications:
Methodology texts, language promotion resources, project and conference documents, downloadable free resources
Catalogue of publications (annual, over 100 titles listed)
Courses, training & events for teachers of MFL and language professionals (annotated list – 3 times a year)
Information sheets (free, see website)
Business of Language (bulletin)
Community Languages (bulletin)

Curriculum guides for community languages (5 titles forthcoming)
Early Language Learning Bulletin (3 times a year)
European Languages Portfolio (2 titles)
Higher (research and higher education bulletin – 3 times a year)
InfoTech series (5 titles)
Language Teaching (the international abstracting journal for language teachers and applied linguists, quarterly, jointly with the British Council, pub. CUP)
Languages 2006 (yearbook)
Links (language teacher training bulletin – 2 times a year)
MFL (secondary language teachers' bulletin – 3 times a year)
Netword (bulletin for further and adult education – 2 times a year)
Advanced Pathfinder series (6 titles)
Pathfinder series (also New and Classic Pathfinders – 18 titles)
Reflections on practice series (6) on professional development
Regional Language Audits (free, see website)
Resource files (5 titles)
Young Pathfinder series (13 titles for primary languages)
Order printed publications from: Central Books Ltd, 99 Wallis Road, London, E9 5LN, tel: 0845 458 9910 (mail order/enquiries) 0845 458 9911 (trade orders), fax: 0845 458 9912, e-mail: mo@centralbooks.com

Electronic and video publications:
Early Language Learning DVD
Hocus & Lotus (video, CD and other materials for teaching young children)

Publications list:
Available online and in print

Access to staff:
Contact by letter, by telephone, by fax, by e-mail and in person
Hours: Mon to Fri, 1030 to 1700
Extended opening hours during school terms: Wed, 1030 to 2000; Sat, 1000 to 1300

Affiliated to:
A network of Comenius Centres in England
CILT Cymru
    tel: 029 2048 0137; fax: 029 2048 0145; e-mail: bethan.enticott@ciltcymru.org.uk; website: http://www.ciltcymru.org.uk
Northern Ireland CILT
    tel: 028 9097 5955; fax: 028 9032 6571; e-mail: nicilt@qub.ac.uk; website: http://www.qub.ac.uk/edu/nicilt
Scottish CILT
    tel: 01786 466290; fax: 01786 466291; e-mail: scilt@stir.ac.uk; website: http://www.scilt.stir.ac.uk/

CIMA

Formal name: Chartered Institute of Management Accountants

26 Chapter Street, London, SW1P 4NP

Tel: 020 7663 5441
Fax: 020 7663 5442

Website:
http://www.cimaglobal.com
Detailed information about the Institute, including examinations; list of members in practice; useful articles; bulletin boards for queries. Publications, courses, knowledge bank.
http://www.cimaglobal.com/main/resources/knowledge

Enquiries:
Enquiries to: Information Manager (TAS)
Direct tel: 020 8849 2259
Direct fax: 020 8849 2464
Direct e-mail: tas@cimaglobal.com

Founded:
1919

Formerly called:
Institute of Cost and Management Accountants

Organisation type and purpose:
Professional body (membership is by qualification).

Subject coverage:
Cost, financial and management accountancy; finance and financial management.

Museum or gallery collection, archive, or library special collection:
Archive of own publications from 1934
Historical collection of books relating to cost and management accounting

Library catalogue:
All or part available in-house

Printed publications:
List of Members (annually)
Management Accounting Research (in association with Academic Press)
Financial Management (11 times a year, from Journal Department)
Order printed publications from: Publishing Sales Department
tel: 020 8849 2270, fax: 020 8849 2465, e-mail: publishing-sales@cimaglobal.com

Electronic and video publications:
List of Members (annually, CD-ROM)

Publications list:
Available online

Access to staff:
Contact by letter, by telephone, by fax, by e-mail, in person and via website. Access for members only.
Hours: Mon to Fri, 1000 to 1600
Special comments: Members and bona fide researchers only.

Access to building, collection or gallery:
Prior appointment required

CIMTECH LIMITED

University of Hertfordshire, Innovation Centre, College Lane, Hatfield, Herts, AL10 9AB

Tel: 01707 281060
Fax: 01707 281061
E-mail: c.cimtech@herts.ac.uk

Website:
http://www.cimtech.co.uk

Enquiries:
Enquiries to: Office Manager

Founded:
1967

Formerly called:
HERTIS Information and Research, National Centre for Information Management and Technology (CIMTECH)

Organisation type and purpose:
Membership association (membership is by subscription), service industry, training organisation, consultancy, publishing house.

Subject coverage:
Image processing, electronic content, document and records management, microfilm, optical disks, CD-ROM, electronic publishing, document imaging, recognition technology, workflow management, business process re-engineering, data and document capture.

Printed publications:
Publications include the following:
Managing Information and Documents (available foc and online)

Electronic and video publications:
Information Management and Technology (online, 10 a year, subscription £80.00 per year)

Publications list:
Available online

Access to staff:
Contact by letter, by telephone, by fax, by e-mail and via website. Appointment necessary. All charged.

Hours: Mon to Thu, 0900 to 1700; Fri, 0900 to 1600

Parent body:
University of Hertfordshire

CINE GUILDS OF GREAT BRITAIN

Acronym or abbreviation: CGGB

72 Pembroke Road, London, W8 6NX

Tel: 020 7602 8319
Fax: 020 7602 8319
E-mail: cineguildsgb@btinternet.com

Enquiries:
Enquiries to: Secretary

Founded:
1990

Organisation type and purpose:
To promote the British film industry.

Subject coverage:
The British film industry.

Access to staff:
Contact by letter and by e-mail
Hours: Mon to Fri, 0900 to 1700

Access to building, collection or gallery:
No access other than to staff

CINEMA ADVERTISING ASSOCIATION LIMITED

Acronym or abbreviation: CAA

12 Golden Square, London, W1F 9JE

Tel: 020 7534 6363
Fax: 020 7534 6227

Enquiries:
Enquiries to: Secretary
Direct e-mail: sam.newsom@carltonscreen.com

Organisation type and purpose:
Trade association.

Subject coverage:
Cinema advertising medium (UK), standards of advertising practice, research.

Museum or gallery collection, archive, or library special collection:
Advertising Film Archives

Printed publications:
CAVIAR (annual research study; Cinema and Video Industry Audience Research)
Cinema Coverage and Frequency Guide (annually, free)

Access to staff:
Contact by telephone and by e-mail
Hours: Mon to Fri, 0900 to 1700

Access to building, collection or gallery:
No access other than to staff

Access for disabled people:
Access to all public areas, toilet facilities

Member of:
Advertising Association

CINEMA THEATRE ASSOCIATION

Acronym or abbreviation: CTA

59 Harrowdene Gardens, Teddington, Middlesex, TW11 0DJ

Tel: 020 8977 2608
E-mail: atunger@blueyonder.co.uk

Website:
http://www.cta-uk.org.
General information on the association's activities, including the archive and publications.

Enquiries:
Enquiries to: Honorary Secretary

continued overleaf

Other contacts: Chairman (for cinemas threatened by planning proposals); Public Relations Officer (for press releases and enquiries); Archivist (for archive)

Founded:
1967

Organisation type and purpose:
Advisory body, membership association (membership is by subscription), present number of members: 1,400, voluntary organisation, research organisation.
To promote interest in Britain's cinema-building legacy, to visit and research cinema buildings, to monitor threatened cinemas of architectural importance and campaign for their protection, to maintain an archive.
The Association arranges visits to cinemas and theatres in the UK and abroad. The CTA is often consulted by local planning authorities on planning applications.

Subject coverage:
Cinema buildings, history, architecture, ownership, lighting, projection, stage facilities, programmes, publicity, etc. (primarily in the United Kingdom).

Museum or gallery collection, archive, or library special collection:
Archive of photographs and related material
George Coles (cinema architect) photograph collection, plans and drawings
John Squires colour slide collection of cinemas
Kine Year Books (incomplete run)
Opening programmes of cinemas, photo collection, plans and drawings, and related material

Printed publications:
CTA Bulletin (6 times a year, members only)
Picture House (magazine, annually)
Over 30 books on the History of Cinemas in Britain including:
Cheshire Cinemas
Cinemas in Britain (Gray R)
Clyde Coast Picture Palaces
Halifax & Surrounding Area
Ribbon of Dreams, Cardiff
The Essoldo Circuit

Publications list:
Available online and in print

Access to staff:
Contact by letter, by telephone and by e-mail.
Non-members charged.
Special comments: Collections available for reference by appointment.

Access to building, collection or gallery:
Prior appointment required

CINTO

Formal name: Cleaning Industry National Training Organisation

3 Moulton Court, Anglia Way, Moulton Park, Northampton, NN3 6JA

Tel: 01604 645731
Fax: 01604 645988
E-mail: info@cleaningnto.org

Website:
http://www.cleaningnto.org
About the NTO, qualifications, advanced foundation modern apprenticeships, national standards.

Enquiries:
Enquiries to: Executive Director

Founded:
1997

Formerly called:
Cleaning and Support Services Industry Training Organisation (CSSITO); Cleaning Industry Lead Body (year of change 1997); Cleaning and Support Services National Training Organisation (CSSNTO) (year of change 2000)

Organisation type and purpose:
Training organisation.

Subject coverage:
Education and training for the cleaning and support services industry, both private and public sectors, National Standards, National Vocational Qualifications (NVQs), Scottish Vocational Qualifications (SVQs), modern apprenticeships, labour market information, skills needs, qualification structures, how to start a cleaning business.

Trade and statistical information:
Labour market information.

Printed publications:
Advanced Modern Apprenticeship Framework
National Standards for Cleaning
Foundation Modern Apprenticeship
Vocational Qualifications Information

Publications list:
Available online and in print

Access to staff:
Contact by letter, by telephone, by fax, by e-mail and via website. Appointment necessary.
Hours: Mon to Fri, 0830 to 1600

Links with:
DfES
QCA
SQA

CIRIA

Formal name: Construction Industry Research and Information Association

Classic House, 174–180 Old Street, London, EC1V 9BP

Tel: 020 7549 3300
Fax: 020 7253 0523
E-mail: enquiries@ciria.org

Website:
http://www.ciria.org.uk
Introduction to the Association, outline of research and information themes, details of participation routes and services. Recent publications and forthcoming events.

Enquiries:
Enquiries to: Customer Services

Founded:
1960

Organisation type and purpose:
Advisory body, professional body, membership association (membership is by subscription), research organisation, publishing house.
Providing best practice guidance for construction and the environment.

Subject coverage:
Building; structural design; construction management; materials; ground engineering; site operations; contaminated land; water engineering and environmental management; structural engineering; health and safety; quality management; information technology.

Library catalogue:
All or part available online and in print

Printed publications:
Annual Report
Reports
CIRIA News (quarterly)
A range of over 400 publications under the headings of:
Building Construction and Technology
Construction Management
Environment Management
Ground Engineering
Water Engineering

Publications list:
Available online and in print

Access to staff:
Contact by letter, by telephone, by fax, by e-mail, in person and via website
Hours: Mon to Fri, 0900 to 1700

CISION UK

Cision House, 16–22 Baltic Street West, London, EC1Y 0UL

Tel: 020 7251 7220
Fax: 020 7689 1164
E-mail: info.uk@cision.com

Website:
http://uk.cision.com/

Enquiries:
Enquiries to: Information Officer

Founded:
1852

Formerly called:
Romeike Limited

Organisation type and purpose:
Media monitoring and press clipping agency.
Media monitoring and analysis.

Subject coverage:
Press clippings; media analysis; online summaries.

Access to staff:
Contact by letter, by telephone, by fax, by e-mail and in person
Hours: Mon to Fri, 0900 to 1700

Member of:
Association of Media Evaluation Companies (AMEC)
Fédération Internationale des Bureaux d'Extraits de Presse (FIBEP)
International Association of Broadcast Monitors (IABM)
Public Relations Consultants Association (PRCA)

CITB-CONSTRUCTIONSKILLS

Acronym or abbreviation: CITB

Head Office, Bircham Newton, King's Lynn, Norfolk, PE31 6RH

Tel: 01485 577577
Fax: 01485 577684

Website:
http://www.citb.co.uk
Careers, training and publications.

Enquiries:
Enquiries to: Resource Centre
Direct tel: 01485 577682
Direct e-mail: information.centre@citb.co.uk

Founded:
1964

Organisation type and purpose:
Statutory body, registered charity (charity number 264289), training organisation.
Statutory body.
An integral part of the construction industry concerned with craft, technicians, safety, supervisory, management training and manpower.

Subject coverage:
Building; civil engineering and related management; training; health and safety in the industry.

Printed publications:
A large number of publications on:
Craft and Operative Training
Health and Safety
National and Scottish Vocational Qualifications
Prevocational Education and Equal Opportunities
Technical, Supervisory and Management Training
Order printed publications from: CITB Publications Department
tel: 01485 577800, fax: 01485 577758

Electronic and video publications:
Computer-based training packages
Videos, particularly on safety

Access to staff:
Appointment necessary.
Hours: Mon to Fri, 0900 to 1700

CITIZENS ADVICE CYMRU

Acronym or abbreviation: CAC

Quebec House, 5–19 Cowbridge Road East,
Cardiff, CF11 9AB

Tel: 029 2037 6750
Fax: 029 2034 1541

Website:
http://www.adviceguide.org.uk

Enquiries:
Enquiries to: Office Manager

Organisation type and purpose:
Registered charity.
Advice and information service.
CAC provides central administrative support for
Citizens Advice Bureaux.

Subject coverage:
Information on services provided by, and levels of
use of, the Citizens Advice Bureaux in the South
Wales area.

Trade and statistical information:
Number and type of enquiries received and
financial grant aid achieved.

Access to staff:
Contact by letter, by telephone and by fax
Hours: Mon to Fri, 0900 to 1700

Parent body:
National Association of Citizens Advice Bureaux
Myddelton House, 115–123 Pentonville Road,
London, N1 9LZ

CITIZENS ADVICE SCOTLAND

Formal name: Scottish Association of Citizens
Advice Bureaux – Citizens Advice Scotland
Acronym or abbreviation: CAS

Spectrum House, 2 Powderhall Road, Edinburgh,
EH7 4GB

Tel: 0131 550 1000
Fax: 0131 550 1001
E-mail: info@cas.org.uk

Website:
http://www.cas.org.uk

Enquiries:
Enquiries to: Press Officer
Other contacts: Chief Executive

Founded:
1975

Organisation type and purpose:
Membership association, voluntary organisation,
registered charity (Scottish charity number
SC016637).
Policy-making body and provider of services to
Citizens Advice Bureaux in Scotland.

Subject coverage:
Citizens Advice Bureau services in Scotland and
advice centres generally; all aspects of welfare law,
Commissioners' decisions, social security,
employment, housing, consumer affairs, money
advice, Scots Law; expertise in training, volunteer
development and advice service development.

**Museum or gallery collection, archive, or library
special collection:**
Library of information related to Welfare Law

Non-library collection catalogue:
All or part available online

Library catalogue:
All or part available in-house

Printed publications:
Annual Report
Range of free information leaflets including:
CAB Information System
Getting Divorced
Neighbour Problems
Social Policy Evidence Reports

Microform publications:
CAB Information System (to members)

Electronic and video publications:
CAB Information System (CD-ROM)

Publications list:
Available online and in print

Access to staff:
Contact by letter and by telephone
Hours: Mon to Fri, 0900 to 1700

CITIZENS' BAND RADIO GOOD PUBLICITY GROUP

Acronym or abbreviation: CB Radio Good Publicity
Group

Hillview, Mid-Holmwood Lane, Dorking, RH5
4HD

Tel: 01306 881137
E-mail: cbrgpg@muddymail.com

Enquiries:
Enquiries to: Manager

Founded:
1997

Incorporates the former:
Communication Eleven, County Hunters DX
Group

Organisation type and purpose:
Advisory body, voluntary organisation.
Increase public awareness of the positive sides to
citizens band radio (CB Radio). Practical help and
advice on installation and use of CB radio
equipment in vehicles, homes and business
premises.

Subject coverage:
Citizens' band radio, advice on which radios are
legal and which are illegal, help with keeping a CB
station within legal limits; specific installation
advice regarding CB in off-road vehicles, especially
Land Rovers and farm machines; information on
specialist products available; microphone wiring
database to stop mic compatibility problems; CB
radio advice for potential new users, who may be
curious as to what CB radio could do for them or
their business.

Printed publications:
4WD CB Guide (for off-road drivers, free)
Caravan CB Guide (for caravan enthusiasts, free)
CB Catalogue (free)
Farm CB Guide (for farmers, free)

Access to staff:
Contact by letter, by telephone and by e-mail.
Appointment necessary.
Hours: Mon to Fri, 0900 to 1700

Also at:
Citizens' Band Radio Good Publicity Group
PO Box 198, Reigate, Surrey, RH2 0FX

CITROËN CAR CLUB

Acronym or abbreviation: CCC

PO Box 348, Bromley, Kent, BR2 8QT

Tel: 07000 248 258
Fax: 07000 248 258
E-mail: member@citroencarclub.net

Website:
http://www.citroencarclub.org.uk
The club and its cars, membership application
form.

Enquiries:
Enquiries to: Membership Administration

Founded:
1949

Organisation type and purpose:
Membership association (membership is by
subscription), present number of members: 3000,
voluntary organisation.

Subject coverage:
Citroën cars, past and present.

**Museum or gallery collection, archive, or library
special collection:**
Comprehensive library of all back issues of
Citroënian and most English language
publications and books on Citroën

Printed publications:
Club magazine (monthly, available on
subscription)

Access to staff:
Contact by letter, by telephone, by fax, by e-mail
and via website
Hours: 1000 to 1900 only
Special comments: Club membership list enquiries
are not normally available, but all enquiries will be
considered on merit.

CITY & GUILDS LAND BASED SERVICES

Building 500, Abbey Park, Stareton, Warwickshire,
CV8 2LG

Tel: 024 7685 7300
Fax: 024 7669 6128
E-mail: information@cityandguilds.com

Website:
http://www.nptc.org.uk

Enquiries:
Enquiries to: Customer Support

Founded:
1970

Organisation type and purpose:
City & Guilds Land Based Services is an awarding
body for the land-based industries. It seeks to
promote competence and professionalism in the
workforce of land-based and related industries by
the encouragement of continous learning and the
recognition of skill. To this end, it oversees a range
of qualifications, including Certificates of
Competence, NVQs, SVQs, work-based
qualifications, Certificates, Extended Certificates,
Diplomas, Subsidiary and Extended Diplomas.

Subject coverage:
Agriculture, horticulture, forestry and timber,
floristry, animal care, equine, countryside and
environment, land-based machinery.

Printed publications:
Fliers and posters covering all the qualifications

Access to staff:
Contact by letter, by telephone, by fax, by e-mail
and via website. Appointment necessary.
Hours: Mon to Fri, 0830 to 1700

CITY AND COUNTY OF SWANSEA LIBRARY & INFORMATION SERVICE

Library HQ, Civic Centre, Oystermouth Road,
Swansea, SA1 3SN

Tel: 01792 636430
Fax: 01792 636235
E-mail: swansea.libraries@swansea.gov.uk

Website:
http://www.swansea.gov.uk/libraries
http://www.libraries.swansea.gov.uk

Enquiries:
Enquiries to: Librarian
Direct tel: 01792 636464
Direct fax: 01792 636235
Direct e-mail: libraryline@swansea.gov.uk

Founded:
1996

Organisation type and purpose:
Local government body, public library.

Subject coverage:
Welsh language material, culture and history of
Wales, history of Swansea, Dylan Thomas.

continued overleaf

Information services:
Library Line, a dedicated enquiry service to help
with any issues about Swansea Libraries, and local
studies and general information enquiries, is
available: Mon to Fri, 0830 to 1800; Sat, 1000 to
1600.

**Museum or gallery collection, archive, or library
special collection:**
Local studies collections focussing on the history,
culture and people of Swansea, but also in
relation to Wales in general; antiquarian
collection of books and periodicals covering
Wales and the Celtic nations.

Non-library collection catalogue:
All or part available online and in-house

Library catalogue:
All or part available online and in-house

Electronic and video publications:
Index to The Cambrian Newspaper (South Wales)
1804–1880s, with miscellaneous later entries
from The Cambrian and other local newspapers
(mainly relating to births, marriages and deaths)
to c.1914

Access to staff:
Contact by letter, by telephone, by fax, by e-mail,
in person and via website. Appointment necessary.
Hours: Central Library open Tue to Fri, 0830 to
2000; Sat and Sun, 1000 to 1600
Local Studies Librarian available by appointment

Parent body:
City and County of Swansea
  Civic Centre, Oystermouth Road, Swansea, SA1
  3SN; tel: 01792 636000

CITY AND ISLINGTON COLLEGE

The Marlborough Building, 383 Holloway Road,
London, N7 0RN

Tel: 020 7700 9333
Fax: 020 7700 4268

Website:
http://www.candi.ac.uk

Enquiries:
Enquiries to: Director of Students
Direct tel: 020 7700 9214
Other contacts: Head of Learning Resources

Formed by the amalgamation of:
City and East London College, Islington 6th Form
Centre and Adult Education Service, North
London College

Organisation type and purpose:
Suitable for ages: 16+.
Further education college.

Subject coverage:
Applied optics, engineering technology, access
courses, GNVQ and A levels, business studies,
health and leisure, ESOL, wide range of adult
education courses, health and community care,
wide range of IT resources, media, visual and
performing arts.

Library catalogue:
All or part available online

Publications list:
Available online and in print

Access to staff:
Contact by letter, by telephone, by fax and by e-
mail
Hours: Mon to Thu, 0900 to 2000; Fri, 0900 to 1700;
Sat, 1100 to 1600 at Camden, Springhouse and
Willen

Access to building, collection or gallery:
No access other than to staff

CITY BUSINESS LIBRARY

Acronym or abbreviation: CBL

Aldermanbury, London, EC2V 7HH

Tel: 020 7332 1812 (enquiries)

E-mail: cbl@cityoflondon.gov.uk

Website:
http://www.cityoflondon.gov.uk/cbl

Enquiries:
Enquiries to: Business Librarian
Direct e-mail: goretti.considine@cityoflondon.gov
.uk

Founded:
1970

Organisation type and purpose:
Free public reference library, open to all; current
worldwide business information; free business
training events.

Subject coverage:
Company data (including facility to create free B2B
mailing lists), market research, country economies,
import/export, management, finance, marketing.

Services for disabled people:
Induction loop; Jaws and ZoomText software for
those with visual impairment.

**Museum or gallery collection, archive, or library
special collection:**
Worldwide trade directories
Worldwide company data – financials and profiles
Worldwide market research

Trade and statistical information:
Worldwide financial statistics.

Library catalogue:
All or part available online

Printed publications:
City Business Library Information sheets to help
visitors use the Library's resources

Publications list:
Available online and in print

Access to staff:
Contact by letter, by telephone, by e-mail, in
person and via website
Hours: Mon to Sat, 0930 to 1700

Access for disabled people:
Internal lift for Library entry, access to all public
areas, toilet facilities

Constituent part of:
City of London library service

CITY COLLEGE BRIGHTON AND HOVE

Acronym or abbreviation: CCBH

Pelham Tower, Pelham Street, Brighton, East
Sussex, BN1 4FA

Tel: 01273 667733
Fax: 01273 667748
E-mail: lrc@ccb.ac.uk

Website:
http://www.ccb.ac.uk
LRC catalogue and other online resources.

Enquiries:
Enquiries to: LRC Manager

Formerly called:
Brighton College of Technology (BCT) (year of
change 2001)

Organisation type and purpose:
College of further education library.

Subject coverage:
Art and design, business, child care and education,
construction, digital media and photography,
ESOL, electrical, electronic, mechanical and motor
vehicle engineering, general humanities,
hairdressing and beauty therapy, hospitality and
catering, media and journalism, music and
performing arts, science, travel and tourism.

Library catalogue:
All or part available online

Access to staff:
Contact by letter, by telephone and by e-mail.
Appointment necessary.

Hours: Term time: Mon to Thu, 0900 to 2000; Fri,
0900 to 1700; vacation: 0900 to 1700 (variable)

Access to building, collection or gallery:
Special comments: Visitors who wish to use the LRC
should come during less busy times (after 1600)
and report to the Enquiry Desk on arrival.

CITY LITERARY INSTITUTE

Acronym or abbreviation: City Lit

Keeley Street, London, WC2B 4BA

Tel: 020 7492 2600
E-mail: infoline@citylit.ac.uk

Website:
http://www.citylit.ac.uk

Enquiries:
Enquiries to: Head of Learning Centre
Direct tel: 020 7492 2666
Direct fax: lc-enquiries@citylit.ac.uk

Organisation type and purpose:
Adult education institute.

Subject coverage:
Education of deaf and partially hearing adults,
speech therapy for stammerers and hearing
impaired people.

**Museum or gallery collection, archive, or library
special collection:**
Sign language videos, CD-ROMs and books, deaf
culture and deaf awareness, aural rehabilitation,
speech therapy

Non-library collection catalogue:
All or part available online

Library catalogue:
All or part available online

Access to staff:
Contact by telephone
Hours: Term Time: Mon, 1200 to 2000; Tue to Fri,
1030 to 2000; Sat, 1200 to 1600

Access to building, collection or gallery:
No prior appointment required
Hours: Mon, 1200 to 2000; Tue to Fri, 1030 to 2000;
Sat, 1200 to 1600

CITY OF BRADFORD METROPOLITAN DISTRICT COUNCIL

City Hall, Bradford, West Yorkshire, BD1 1HY

Tel: 01274 432111
Fax: 01274 432065

Website:
http://www.bradford.gov.uk

Organisation type and purpose:
Local government body.

Subject coverage:
Local government services.

CITY OF LONDON SOLICITORS' COMPANY

Acronym or abbreviation: CLSC

4 College Hill, London, EC4R 2RB

Tel: 020 7329 2173
Fax: 020 7329 2190
E-mail: mail@citysolicitors.org.uk

Website:
http://www.citysolicitors.org.uk

Enquiries:
Enquiries to: The Clerk

Founded:
1908

Organisation type and purpose:
Membership association (membership is by
election or invitation).
City of London Livery Company.

Access to staff:
Contact by letter, by telephone, by fax, by e-mail and via website

CITY OF SALFORD

Civic Centre, Chorley Road, Swinton, Salford, Greater Manchester, M27 5FJ

Tel: 0161 794 4711
Fax: 0161 794 6595

Website:
http://www.salford.gov.uk

Enquiries:
Enquiries to: Public Relations Manager
Direct tel: 0161 793 3157
Direct fax: 0161 793 3234
Direct e-mail: margaret.hynes@salford.gov.uk
Other contacts: Chief Executive for formal complaints.

Organisation type and purpose:
Local government body.

Subject coverage:
Business of a local authority – metropolitan authority – Greater Manchester. Arts and leisure, libraries, museums, education, social services, housing, planning issues, environmental issues.

Printed publications:
Civic Guide On Salford People (magazine)

Access to staff:
Contact by letter, by telephone, by fax, by e-mail, in person and via website
Hours: Mon to Fri, 0830 to 1630

Access for disabled people:
Parking provided, ramped entry, access to all public areas, toilet facilities

Includes:
Rushmoor Local History Gallery at the same address

CITY OF SUNDERLAND

Civic Centre, Sunderland, Tyne and Wear, SR2 7DN

Tel: 0191 553 1000

Website:
http://www.sunderland.gov.uk

Enquiries:
Enquiries to: Chief Executive

Organisation type and purpose:
Local government body.

Subject coverage:
Local government services.

Access to staff:
Contact by letter, by telephone, by fax and by e-mail. Appointment necessary.
Hours: Mon to Fri, 0900 to 1700

CITY OF WESTMINSTER ARCHIVES CENTRE

Acronym or abbreviation: COWAC

10 St Ann's Street, London, SW1P 2DE

Tel: 020 7641 5180\ Minicom no. 020 7641 4879
Fax: 020 7641 5179
E-mail: archives@westminster.gov.uk

Website:
http://www.westminster.gov.uk/archives
General information, location, opening hours, publications for sale, talks and events, what we do.

Enquiries:
Enquiries to: Librarian
Other contacts: City Archivist, Manager for the Business Unit Manager.

Organisation type and purpose:
Local government body, public library. Archive.

Subject coverage:
Local studies, conservation, local history, archives, Westminster history, Marylebone history, Paddington history.

Museum or gallery collection, archive, or library special collection:
A M Broadley Collections (Annals of the Haymarket, and Some Social, Political and Literary Landmarks of Bath and Piccadilly)
Artisans', Labourers' & General Dwellings Company Limited (annual reports and accounts 1880–1956)
Francis Edwards Limited (booksellers catalogues 1938–1982)
Manuscript notes on local subjects including an 82-volume scrapbook, Inns, Taverns, Alehouses, Coffee Houses, etc. in and around London, compiled by D Foster c. 1900
Marylebone Gardens (over 50 songs of the 18th century sung in the gardens, some by William Defesch and James Hook)
The Ashbridge Collection (books, maps, prints, watercolours and drawings relating to St Marylebone)
The parliamentary representation of Westminster from the 13th century to the present day
The Preston Blake Collection: books by and about William Blake, papers, letters, periodicals, catalogues, transparencies.
Theatre Collection (some 28,000 theatre programmes, and playbills, news cuttings, portraits, financial records, correspondence)
St Marylebone Housing Association
Whiteley's (catalogues for general goods, wines, cigars, provisions etc, staff magazine 1885–1958)
Books and pamphlets; rare books; newspapers and periodicals; official local government records; prints and photographs; census; parish registers; wills, from 1460 onwards; maps and plans; directories and electoral registers; business records

Non-library collection catalogue:
All or part available online and in-house

Library catalogue:
All or part available online

Printed publications:
Guides to sources of information particularly genealogical material
Maps from 1755 onwards
Books on the history, architecture and development of the area including:
Regent's Park – A study of the development of the area from 1086 to the present day (Saunders A, £4.50 plus p&p)
St John's Wood and Maida Vale Past (Tames R, £14.95 plus p&p)
Growth of St Marylebone and Paddington (Whitehead J, 3rd ed., 2001, £12.95 plus p&p)
Westminster History Review (annual, vol 1 1997, £3.99 plus p&p)
Guide to Sources for Family History held by Westminster Archives (Cory E, 1997, £3 plus p&p)
Tracing the History of Your House (Kenney A, 1996, £3.50 plus p&p)
Local interest publications include:
Blitz over Westminster (includes City of Westminster Civil Defence Bomb Incident Photographs 1940–44, Harrison R, 1990, £3.50 plus p&p)
Covent Garden Past (Richardson J, 1995, £14.95 plus p&p)
Diary of William Tayler, footman 1837 (Wise D ed, 1998, £7.50 plus p&p)
Order printed publications from: Publications Officer, City of Westminster Archives Centre
Address as main

Microform publications:
Gillow Archive
Local Newspapers (some fifty covering various periods)
Twentieth century Post Office London directories
Name index to St Martin-in-the-Fields Poor Law Settlements Part 1, 1750 to 1775 (7 microfiches, £5 plus p&p)

St Marylebone Census Name Index for 1821 and 1831 (£5 each plus p&p)
Order microform publications from: St Marylebone Census Name Index for 1821 and 1831, published by The Family History Shop, Norwich

Publications list:
Available online and in print

Access to staff:
Contact by letter, by telephone, by fax, by e-mail, in person and via website
Hours: Mon, Closed, Fri, Sat, 1000 to 1700; Tue to Thu, 1000 to 1900

Access to building, collection or gallery:
No prior appointment required

Access for disabled people:
Ramped entry, access to all public areas, toilet facilities
Special comments: Parking provided by prior arrangement.

CITY OF YORK & DISTRICT FAMILY HISTORY SOCIETY

The Raylor Centre, James Street, Lawrence Street, York, YO10 3DW

Tel: 01904 412204
E-mail: secretary@yorkfamilyhistory.org.uk

Website:
http://www.yorkfamilyhistory.org.uk/

Enquiries:
Enquiries to: Secretary

Founded:
1975

Organisation type and purpose:
Membership association (membership is by subscription), registered charity.

Subject coverage:
Family history.

Printed publications:
For purchase, direct only

Microform publications:
Microfiche, for purchase, direct only

Electronic and video publications:
CD-ROM, for purchase direct only

Publications list:
Available online and in print

Access to staff:
Contact by letter, by e-mail and via website

CITY OF YORK LIBRARIES

Museum Street, York, YO1 7DS

Tel: 01904 655631
Fax: 01904 611025
E-mail: reference.library@york.gov.uk

Website:
http://www.york.gov.uk
City of York Council information.
http://www.york.gov.uk/libraries

Enquiries:
Enquiries to: Head of Library Service
Direct tel: 01904 553316
Other contacts: Information Services Librarian tel: 01904 552824 reference.library@york.gov.uk.

Founded:
1891

Organisation type and purpose:
Local government body, public library.

Subject coverage:
General, York and Yorkshire.

Museum or gallery collection, archive, or library special collection:
Rowland Collection of oboe music
Sir John Marriott Memorial Library on modern European history from the French Revolution

continued overleaf

Non-library collection catalogue:
All or part available in-house

Library catalogue:
All or part available online

Access to staff:
Contact by letter, by telephone, by fax, by e-mail and in person
Hours: Lending library: Mon, Tue, Fri, 0930 to 2000; Wed, Thu, 0930 to 1730; Sat, 0930 to 1600
Reference library: Mon, Tue, Wed, Fri, 0900 to 2000; Thu, 0900 to 1730; Sat, 0900 to 1600

Access to building, collection or gallery:
No prior appointment required

Access for disabled people:
Lift, ramped entry, access to all public areas, toilet facilities
Hours: as above

Has:
15 libraries and 1 mobile library covering the City of York Council area

Parent body:
City of York Council
tel: 01904 613161

CITY UNIVERSITY LONDON – DEPARTMENT OF COMPUTING

Northampton Square, London, EC1V 0HB

Tel: 020 7040 8432
Fax: 020 7040 8587

Website:
http://www.soi.city.ac.uk/doc/
Full departmental profile and details.

Enquiries:
Enquiries to: Administrator

Formerly called:
Department of Business Computing, Department of Computer Science

Organisation type and purpose:
University department or institute.

Subject coverage:
Undergraduate courses in computer science, computer science with distributed systems or AI, software engineering, business computing and information systems. Postgraduate courses in business systems analysis and design and object oriented software systems.

Publications list:
Available online

Access to staff:
Contact by letter and by e-mail. Appointment necessary.
Hours: Mon to Fri, 0900 to 1700

Access to building, collection or gallery:
Prior appointment required

Access for disabled people:
Ramped entry, access to all public areas, toilet facilities

CITY UNIVERSITY LONDON – DEPARTMENT OF LANGUAGE AND COMMUNICATION SCIENCE

Northampton Square, London, EC1V 0HB

Tel: 020 7040 8281
Fax: 020 7040 8577
E-mail: lcsadmin@city.ac.uk

Website:
http://www.city.ac.uk/lcs

Enquiries:
Enquiries to: Programme Officer

Organisation type and purpose:
University department or institute.

Subject coverage:
Disorders of speech, training of speech therapists, research into disorders of speech, alternative and augmentative aids to human communication.

Museum or gallery collection, archive, or library special collection:
MSc and MPhil/PhD theses in field of disorders of human communication

Access to staff:
Contact by telephone and by e-mail
Hours: Mon to Fri, 0900 to 1700

CITY UNIVERSITY LONDON – LIBRARY

Northampton Square, London, EC1V 0HB

Tel: 020 7040 8191
Fax: 020 7040 8194
E-mail: library@city.ac.uk

Website:
http://www.city.ac.uk/library

Enquiries:
Enquiries to: Director of Information Services and Libraries
Direct tel: 020 7040 8162

Founded:
1894

Organisation type and purpose:
University library.

Subject coverage:
Cultural policy and management; banking; business; finance; language and communication science; computer science; engineering; information science; journalism; law; management; mathematics; music; optometry; property valuation; social science; nursing; midwifery.

Museum or gallery collection, archive, or library special collection:
Erna Auerbach Collection (art history)
Kipling Society Collection
Rosencweig Collection (Jewish music), now transferred to the School of Oriental and African Studies
Walter Fincham Collection (optics)

Library catalogue:
All or part available online

Printed publications:
Library information leaflets

Access to staff:
Contact by e-mail
Hours: Mon to Fri, 0900 to 1700

Access for disabled people:
Ramped entry, toilet facilities

CIVIC TRUST

17 Carlton House Terrace, London, SW1Y 5AW

Tel: 020 7930 0914
Fax: 020 7321 0180
E-mail: pride@civictrust.org.uk

Website:
http://www.civictrust.org.uk
Home page, information and publications.

Enquiries:
Enquiries to: Librarian

Founded:
1957

Organisation type and purpose:
National organisation, membership association (membership is by subscription), present number of members: 3000 members, 60 corporate members, voluntary organisation, registered charity (charity number 1068759).
Working in partnership to improve the built environment for the benefit of the community.

Subject coverage:
Urban environment, architecture, planning, transport, conservation, regeneration, community involvement, civic societies.

Printed publications:
Civic Focus – News from the Civic Trust (available on subscription)
2001 Civic Trust Awards Report
A New Framework for Freight Transport (1995)
Brownfield Housing – 12 Years On (1999)
Effective Partnerships for Voluntary and Community Groups (1999)
Effective Partnerships for Managers and Board Managers
Investing in the High Street (1999)
Small Town Vitality: The Impact of New Housing (2000)
Sustainable Renewal of Suburban Areas (1999)

Publications list:
Available online and in print

2nd Office:
Civic Trust Northern Office
6th Floor, The View, Gostins Building, 32–36 Hannover Street, Liverpool, L1 4LN; tel: 0151 709 1969; fax: 0151 709 2022; e-mail: northernoffice@civictrust.org.uk

Partner organisations:
Civic Trust for Wales
3rd Floor, Empire House, Mount Stuart Square, Cardiff, CF10 5FN; tel: 01222 484606; website: http://www.civictrustwales.org
North East Civic Trust
Blackfriars, Monk Street, Newcastle upon Tyne, NE1 4XN
Scottish Civic Trust
42 Miller Street, Glasgow, G2 1DT; tel: 0141 221 1466

CIVIL AID

Formal name: National Voluntary Civil Aid Services
Acronym or abbreviation: NVCAS

c/o Crinoids, 106 Church Road, Teddington, Middlesex, TW11 8EY

Tel: 020 8977 2806
Fax: 020 8943 5556

Enquiries:
Enquiries to: President
Other contacts: General Secretary, tel no: 020 8942 9126

Founded:
1968

Emerged for reasons of political expediency:
Civil Defence Corps (year of change 1968)

Organisation type and purpose:
National organisation, membership association (membership is by subscription), present number of members: 300, voluntary organisation, registered charity (charity number 266349), suitable for ages: 16+, training organisation.
An autonomous, self-funded organisation which emerged in 1968 when the Civil Defence Corps was stood down for reasons of political expediency. Duke of Edinburgh's Award training organisation.
To train its members and the public in disaster mitigation and relief, and to provide aid for any peace-time disaster.

Subject coverage:
First aid, fire prevention and control, emergency feeding, rescue techniques, communications, rest centres, information centres.

Printed publications:
Newsletter

Access to staff:
Contact by letter, by telephone and by fax
Hours: Mon to Fri, 0900 to 1700

Links with:
The Institute of Civil Defence and Disaster Studies
The National Council for Civil Protection

Registered Office:
Civil Aid
  Phoenix House, Greenlands Avenue, Kingsway,
  Derby

CIVIL AVIATION AUTHORITY

Acronym or abbreviation: CAA

Library and Information Centre, Civil Aviation
Authority Safety Regulation Group, Aviation
House, South Area, Gatwick Airport, West Sussex,
RH6 0YR

Tel: 01293 573725
Fax: 01293 573181
E-mail: infoservices@caa.co.uk ·

Website:
http://www.caa.co.uk

Enquiries:
Enquiries to: Manager
Direct tel: 01293 573966
Direct e-mail: vagn.pedersen@caa.co.uk
Other contacts: Librarian for information enquiries

Founded:
1972

Carries out the functions of the former:
Air Registration Board, Air Transport Licensing
Board

Incorporates the former:
Safety Regulation Group Library

Organisation type and purpose:
Statutory body, public authority, aviation
regulatory body.

Subject coverage:
Civil aviation, electronics including air traffic
control, aircraft, flightcrew, airports,
telecommunications, radar, etc.

**Museum or gallery collection, archive, or library
special collection:**
Historical aviation collection

Trade and statistical information:
UK airlines and airports statistics.

Library catalogue:
All or part available in-house

Publications list:
Available in print

Access to staff:
Contact by letter, by telephone, by fax, by e-mail
and in person
Hours: Mon to Fri, 0930 to 1630; 1st Wed of each
month, 1000 to 1630
Special comments: Reference use only to visitors.

Access to building, collection or gallery:
No prior appointment required

Access for disabled people:
Parking provided, level entry, access to all public
areas

CIVIL ENGINEERING CONTRACTORS ASSOCIATION

Acronym or abbreviation: CECA

1 Birdcage Walk, London, SW1H 9JJ

Tel: 020 7340 0450
Fax: 020 7222 7514
E-mail: enquiries@ceca.co.uk

Website:
http://www.ceca.co.uk

Enquiries:
Direct e-mail: lauraellis@ceca.co.uk

Founded:
1996

Organisation type and purpose:
Trade association.

Subject coverage:
Construction, including training and careers, legal
affairs, industrial relations, safety, economics,
statistics.

Printed publications:
Economic Reports
Contracts and associated publications
Guides, technical reports and manuals
Newsline (monthly)
Press Abstracts

Access to staff:
Contact by letter, by telephone, by fax, by e-mail
and via website
Hours: Mon to Fri, 0900 to 1730

Member of:
Construction Confederation

CIVIL SERVICE APPEAL BOARD

Acronym or abbreviation: CSAB

22 Whitehall, London, SW1A 2WH

Tel: 020 7276 3832
Fax: 020 7276 3836
E-mail: csab@cabinet-office.x.gsi.gov.uk

Website:
http://www.cabinet-office.gov.uk/civilservice/
1999/appealboard/csab.htm
CSAB Annual Reports, 1997/98 and 1998/99.
http://www.civilserviceappealboard.gov.uk

Enquiries:
Enquiries to: Secretary
Direct e-mail: keith.wright@cabinet-office.x.gsi.gov
.uk

Founded:
1971

Organisation type and purpose:
Advisory body.
An advisory non-departmental public body that
hears appeals from civil servants against: dismissal
and early retirement; part- or non-payment of the
amount of compensation paid to civil servants
dismissed on inefficiency grounds; refusal to allow
participation in political activities or forfeiture of
superannuation benefits.

Printed publications:
Civil Service Appeal Board Annual Report
  (annually, free)

Access to staff:
Contact by letter, by telephone, by fax and by e-
mail
Hours: 0900 to 1700

CIVITAS: THE INSTITUTE FOR THE STUDY OF CIVIL SOCIETY

The Mezzanine, Elizabeth House, 39 York Road,
London, SE1 7NQ

Tel: 020 7401 5470
Fax: 020 7401 5471
E-mail: robert.whelan@civitas.org.uk

Website:
http://www.civitas.org.uk

Enquiries:
Enquiries to: Deputy Director

Formerly called:
Health & Welfare Unit of the Institute of Economic
Affairs (year of change 2000)

Organisation type and purpose:
Registered charity (charity number 1085494),
research organisation, publishing house.

Subject coverage:
Health, education, welfare, criminal justice, the
family.

Publications list:
Available online and in print

Access to staff:
Contact by letter, by telephone, by fax, by e-mail
and via website
Hours: Mon to Fri, 0900 to 1700

CLACKMANNANSHIRE COUNCIL

Greenfield, Alloa, Clackmannanshire, FK10 2AD

Tel: 01259 450000
Fax: 01259 452010
E-mail: info@clacksweb.org.uk

Website:
http://www.clacksweb.org.uk

Enquiries:
Enquiries to: Communications and Marketing
Manager
Direct tel: 01259 452023
Direct fax: 01259 452117
Direct e-mail: rfry@clacks.gov.uk
Other contacts: Chief Executive

Founded:
1996

Formerly called:
Central Regional Council, Clackmannan District
Council

Organisation type and purpose:
Local government body.

Subject coverage:
Scottish local government; Clackmannanshire as
an inward investment area.
Schools, nurseries, adult and community
education, trading standards, environmental
health, roads maintenance, property maintenance
and design, social work, housing, licensing, council
tax.

Printed publications:
Corporate Performance Report (free)
Business Directory (for purchase)
Business Information Leaflets (free)
Clackmannanshire Area Guide (free)
Community Safety Plane (free)
Economic Development Strategy (free)
Clackmannanshire Community Plan (free)
Building Clackmannanshire: Economic
  Development Framework (free)
Order printed publications from: http://
www.clacksweb.org.uk

Publications list:
Available in print

Access to staff:
Contact by letter, by telephone, by fax, by e-mail
and via website
Hours: Mon to Fri, 0900 to 1700

Access for disabled people:
Parking provided, level entry, toilet facilities

CLACKMANNANSHIRE LIBRARIES

Acronym or abbreviation: CL

Alloa Library, 26–28 Drysdale Street, Alloa,
Clackmannanshire, FK10 1JL

Tel: 01259 722262
Fax: 01259 219469
E-mail: libraries@clacks.gov.uk

Website:
http://www.clacksweb.org.uk/culture/
libraryservice

Enquiries:
Enquiries to: Information Librarian and Archivist
Other contacts: Special Services Co-ordinator; Team
Leader of Public Services

Founded:
1996

continued overleaf

Formerly called:
Clackmannan District Libraries (year of change 1996); Central Region Archives Department; Central Region Schools Library Service (year of change 1997)

Organisation type and purpose:
Local government body, museum, public library. Archive service.

Subject coverage:
General, local studies, archives, schools material.

Museum or gallery collection, archive, or library special collection:
Walter Murray Local Studies Collection; Clackmannanshire Archives

Non-library collection catalogue:
All or part available in-house

Library catalogue:
All or part available online

Printed publications:
A range of books on local history and society including:
Books on Alloa and Clackmannanshire
Local Railways (2 vols)
Poems of the Maestro (3 vols) and of the Wanderer (3 vols)
Statistical Accounts of six areas of Clackmannanshire
Order printed publications from: Special Services Co-ordinator, at the same address

Publications list:
Available online and in print

Access to staff:
Contact by letter, by telephone, by fax, by e-mail and in person

Access to building, collection or gallery:
No prior appointment required
Hours: Alloa Library: Mon, Wed, Thu, Fri, 0930 to 1900; Tue, 0930 to 1630; Sat, 0900 to 1600
Other libraries vary, all close for lunch, telephone first
Special comments: Orders for items from Archive Store (Mon to Fri only) to be lodged no later than 1700 for delivery same day.

Access for disabled people:
Level entry

Branch libraries:
Alva Community Access Point
   153 West Stirling Street, Alva; tel: 01259 760652; fax: 01259 760364
Clackmannan Community Access Point
   Main Street, Clackmannan; tel: 01259 721579; fax: 01259 212493
Dollar Community Access Point
   Dollar Civic Centre, Park Place, Dollar; tel: 01259 743253; fax: 01259 743328
Menstrie Community Access Point
   Dumyat Leisure Centre, Main Street East, Menstrie; tel: 01259 769439; fax: 01259 762941
Sauchie Community Access Point
   42–48 Main Street, Sauchie; tel: 01259 721679; fax: 01259 218750
Tillicoultry Branch Library
   99 High Street, Tillicoultry; tel: 01259 751685
Tullibody Branch Library
   Leisure Centre, Abercromby Place, Tullibody; tel: 01259 218725

Parent body:
Clackmannanshire Council
   tel: 01259 450000; fax: 01259 452230

CLAN RANALD TRUST FOR SCOTLAND

Unit 35 New Street, Warsely Car Park, Edinburgh, EH8 8DW

Tel: 0131 558 9191

Website:
http://www.clanranald.org
History, images, costume.

Enquiries:
Enquiries to: Chief Executive
Direct e-mail: info@clanranald.org
Other contacts: Administrator

Founded:
1996

Organisation type and purpose:
Membership association (membership is by election or invitation), present number of members: 50 (charity number SCO 24881), suitable for ages: 14+.
Promotes Scottish Medieval History through education and entertainment. Constructing large motte and baille fortress in the Carronn Valley near Stirling for tourism and education.

Subject coverage:
Film, TV, combat team, period room dressing, entertainment, gala days and open events, pipers and drummers, actors, special events, walk-ons, experienced extras for film.

Library catalogue:
All or part available online

Printed publications:
Direct for free, unless commercial

Electronic and video publications:
Showcase video
Music CD-ROM

Publications list:
Available online

Access to staff:
Contact by letter, by telephone, by e-mail and via website. Appointment necessary.
Hours: Mon to Fri, 1200 to 1800

Access for disabled people:
Parking provided, level entry

Links with:
Kirkpatrick McAndrew Clan Trust
McFarlane Clan Trust
Wallace Clan Trust

CLAN TARTAN CENTRE

Formal name: Edinburgh Woollen Mills
Acronym or abbreviation: EWM

James Pringle Weavers at Leith Mills, Leith Mills, 70–74 Bangor Road, Leith, Edinburgh, EH6 5JU

Tel: 0131 553 5161
Fax: 0131 553 4415

Website:
http://www.foreverscotland.com

Enquiries:
Enquiries to: Public Relations Manager
Other contacts: Manager

Subject coverage:
Clan history, research and retail tartan and accessories, gifts, crystal, cashmere, woollens, ladies and gents fashion, designer labels, shoes, whisky shop, golf company and Scottish foods.

Printed publications:
Leaflets available on request for Corporate Business, Tourist and Local

Access to staff:
Contact by letter, by telephone, by fax and by e-mail. Appointment necessary.
Hours: Mon to Sat, 0900 to 1700; Sun, 1000 to 1700

Access for disabled people:
Parking provided, level entry

Head Office:
Edinburgh Woollen Mill
   Waverley Mill, Langholm, Dumfriesshire, DG13 2BR; tel: 01387 380611

CLARINET HERITAGE SOCIETY

Acronym or abbreviation: CHS

47 Hambalt Road, London, SW4 9EQ

Tel: 020 8675 3877

Enquiries:
Enquiries to: Honorary Secretary

Founded:
1980

Organisation type and purpose:
International organisation, advisory body, learned society, professional body (membership is by subscription), training organisation, consultancy, research organisation, publishing house.
To promote new and rare music and general awareness for the clarinet, research, recording, study and performance.

Subject coverage:
Discovery, publication and sound recordings of rare, unknown music for the clarinet; history; performance and teaching; inventions and innovations.

Education services:
Clarinet lessons from beginner to professional coaching by internationally acclaimed teacher and performer.

Museum or gallery collection, archive, or library special collection:
Book manuscript
Musical instruments and tools of a noted master clarinettist
Various limited music for clarinet

Printed publications:
Clarinet tutor and method
Music by Heinrich Baermann
Personal memoirs of the music business from a professional clarinettist
Recording: The Art of Clarinet and Piano (Stephen Bennett, clarinet, Joyce Riddell, piano, for sale)
Sheet music: August Henrik Winding, 3 Fantasy Pieces for Clarinet and Piano (for sale)

Electronic and video publications:
Cassette and CD music audio

Access to staff:
Contact by letter, by telephone, by e-mail and via website. Appointment necessary. Non-members charged.
Hours: Mon to Fri, 0900 to 1700

Access to building, collection or gallery:
Prior appointment required

CLASSIC KAWASAKI CLUB

Acronym or abbreviation: CKC

PO Box 528, Kings Langley, Herts WD5 5AF

Tel: 020 8737 9755
Fax: 0115 913 4223
E-mail: classkawa@aol.com

Website:
http://kawaportal.org
Reference, photographs, adverts, message board.

Enquiries:
Enquiries to: Membership Secretary
Direct tel: 07779094462
Direct e-mail: downpipe3@ntlworld.com

Founded:
1980

Formerly called:
Kawasaki Triples Club (year of change 1996)

Organisation type and purpose:
International organisation, membership association (membership is by subscription), present number of members: 1100, museum.

Subject coverage:
Historical reference for Kawasaki motorcycles.

Museum or gallery collection, archive, or library special collection:
Technical, historical and reference data held on computer and hard copy

Printed publications:
Magazine (6 times a year, members)

Electronic and video publications:
Reference Guides (CD-ROM)

Access to staff:
Contact by letter, by telephone, by fax, by e-mail and via website. Appointment necessary.
Hours: Mon to Fri, 0900 to 1700

Access to building, collection or gallery:
No prior appointment required
Special comments: Museum visits by appointment only.

Has connections with:
Various worldwide clubs

CLASSIC SALOON CAR CLUB (GB)

Acronym or abbreviation: CSCC

15 Biddenham Turn, Garston, Hertfordshire, WD2 6PU

Tel: 01923 893518

Website:
http://www.csccgb.co.uk
Clubs rules and technical regulations with details of present car racing activities and records of same since 1975.

Enquiries:
Enquiries to: Registrar
Direct e-mail: robslater@csccgb.co.uk

Founded:
1975

Organisation type and purpose:
Membership association (membership is by subscription).

Subject coverage:
Recreating the great touring car racing of the past in the spirit of the period but to the standards of modern motorsport, showing, racing and enjoying historic racing touring cars.

Access to staff:
Contact by letter, by e-mail and via website
Hours: Mon to Fri, 0900 to 1700

Affiliated club:
British Automobile Racing Club
  Thruxton Circuit, Andover, Hants, SP11 8PN; tel: 01264 772696

Registered with Sport Governing Body:
The Motorsports Association
  Motorsports House, Riverside Park, Colnbrook, Berks, SL3 0HG; tel: 01753 765000; fax: 01753 682938

CLASSICAL ASSOCIATION

Acronym or abbreviation: CA

Senate House, Malet Street, London, WC1E 7HU

Tel: 020 7862 8706
Fax: 020 7862 8729
E-mail: office@classicalassociation.org

Website:
http://www.classicalassociation.org
General information about the Association.

Enquiries:
Enquiries to: Secretary

Founded:
1904

Organisation type and purpose:
Membership association (membership is by subscription), present number of members: 4,000, registered charity.

Subject coverage:
Classical studies generally.

Printed publications:
CA News (included in the subscription)
Classical Quarterly
Classical Review
Greece and Rome
Presidential Address (included in subscription)

Order printed publications from: The Secretary, Classical Association, at the same address

Access to staff:
Contact by letter, by telephone, by fax and by e-mail
Hours: Mon to Thu, 0900 to 1700

Affiliated to:
International Federation for Classical Studies (FIEC)

CLEANING AND HYGIENE SUPPLIERS ASSOCIATION

Acronym or abbreviation: CHSA

PO Box 770, Marlow, Buckinghamshire, SL7 2SH

Tel: 01628 478273
Fax: 01628 478286
E-mail: secretary@chsa.co.uk

Website:
http://www.chsa.co.uk

Enquiries:
Enquiries to: General Secretary

Founded:
1969

Organisation type and purpose:
Trade association (membership is by subscription), present number of members: 200.

Subject coverage:
Supply chain issues.

Access to staff:
Contact by letter, by telephone, by fax, by e-mail and via website
Hours: Mon to Fri, 0900 to 1700

Access to building, collection or gallery:
No access other than to staff

CLEANING AND SUPPORT SERVICES ASSOCIATION

Acronym or abbreviation: CSSA

Warnford Court, 29 Throgmorton Street, London, EC2N 2AT

Tel: 020 7920 9632
Fax: 020 7256 9360
E-mail: alarge@cleaningassoc.org

Website:
http://www.cleaningassoc.org
News and information.

Enquiries:
Enquiries to: Director General

Founded:
1967

Organisation type and purpose:
Trade association.

Subject coverage:
Site support services, industry; especially, cleaning, hygiene, building maintenance.

Trade and statistical information:
Trade information.

Printed publications:
Membership Directory
Trade Brochures

Publications list:
Available online and in print

Access to staff:
Contact by letter, by telephone, by fax, by e-mail and via website
Hours: Mon to Fri, 0800 to 1630

Links with:
AssetSkills
European Federation of Cleaning Industries (EFCI)
Trade Association Forum (TAF)
World Federation of Building Service Contractors (WFBSC)

CLEAPSS

The Gardiner Building, Brunel Science Park, Kingston Lane, Uxbridge, Middlesex, UB8 3PQ

Tel: 01895 251496
Fax: 01895 814372
E-mail: science@cleapss.org.uk

Website:
http://www.cleapss.org.uk
Information about the services offered; lists of current publications; dates and content of forthcoming courses; membership information; news items.

Enquiries:
Enquiries to: Director

Founded:
1963

Formerly called:
CLEAPSE (year of change 1988)

Organisation type and purpose:
Local government body, advisory body, membership association (membership is by subscription), present number of members: all state-funded, local authority schools in all 182 local authorities in England, Wales and Northern Ireland and off-shore islands (not Scotland), 2,000 associate members, training organisation, consultancy.
Information service.
To offer guidance on practical science and technology in schools and colleges, including health and safety, facilities, resources, laboratories, technicians, etc.

Subject coverage:
Primary and secondary school and college practical science and design & technology, facilities, resources and health and safety.

Library catalogue:
All or part available online

Printed publications:
Mostly free, but only available to members
Order printed publications from: Members can access via security password on website

Publications list:
Available online

Access to staff:
Contact by letter, by telephone, by fax, by e-mail and via website. Access for members only. Non-members charged.
Hours: Mon to Fri, 0900 to 1700

CLECKHEATON LIBRARY

Cultural Services, Kirklees Metropolitan Council, Whitcliffe Road, Cleckheaton, West Yorkshire, BD19 3DX

Tel: 01274 335170
Fax: 01274 335171
E-mail: cleckheaton.library@kirklees.gov.uk

Website:
http://www.kirklees.gov.uk/libraries
Library address etc, photographs, facilities, opening hours, services.

Enquiries:
Enquiries to: Librarian

Organisation type and purpose:
Public library.

Museum or gallery collection, archive, or library special collection:
Spen Valley Historical Society Collection

Non-library collection catalogue:
All or part available in-house

Library catalogue:
All or part available in-house

Access to staff:
Contact by letter, by telephone, by fax, by e-mail and in person

continued overleaf

Hours: Mon, 0900 to 2000; Tue and Thu, 0900 to 1930; Wed, 0900 to 1300; Fri, 0900 to 1700; Sat, 0900 to 1600

Access for disabled people:
Parking provided, ramped entry, toilet facilities, wheelchair lift

CLEFT LIP AND PALATE ASSOCIATION

Acronym or abbreviation: CLAPA

First Floor, Green Man Tower, 332b Goswell Road, London, EC1V 7LQ

Tel: 020 7833 4883
Fax: 020 7833 5999
E-mail: info@clapa.com

Website:
http://www.clapa.com
What is cleft lip and palate, news and articles, publications, how to make contact with CLAPA, what is the cleft lip and palate association.

Enquiries:
Enquiries to: Chief Executive
Other contacts: Community Fundraiser (for volunteers wanting to get involved in CLAPA)

Founded:
1979

Organisation type and purpose:
Registered charity (England and Wales charity number 1108160, Scotland SC041034).
To offer support to families affected by cleft lip and/or palate.

Subject coverage:
Cleft lip and/or palate.

Information services:
Information via website, email, letter and phone enquiries.

Printed publications:
Antenatal Diagnosis of Cleft Lip and Palate
CLAPA News and Annual Report
Cleft Lip & Palate: A Guide for Sonographers
Help for Parents
Help with Feeding
How does your Palate Work?
Pharyngoplasty
Treatment of Cleft Lip and Palate – a parent's guide

Publications list:
Available online and in print

Access to staff:
Contact by letter, by telephone, by fax, by e-mail and via website
Hours: Mon to Fri, 0900 to 1700

CLEVELAND COLLEGE OF ART AND DESIGN LIBRARY

Acronym or abbreviation: CCAD

Green Lane, Linthorpe, Middlesbrough, Cleveland, TS5 7RJ

Tel: 01642 288000
Fax: 01642 288828

Website:
http://www.ccad.ac.uk
Course information, admission policy.

Enquiries:
Enquiries to: Learning Resource Manager
Direct tel: 01642 298732
Direct e-mail: ann.kenyon@ccad.ac.uk

Organisation type and purpose:
College of further and higher education.

Subject coverage:
Fine and applied arts and crafts, art history, design history, history of architecture, interior design and layout, jewellery, ceramics, textiles, graphics, printmaking, painting, sculpture, photography and fashion.

Library catalogue:
All or part available online

Printed publications:
Library Handbook (annually)

Access to staff:
Contact by letter, by telephone and by e-mail. Appointment necessary.
Hours: Mon, Tue, 0900 to 1900; Thu, 0900 to 1700; Fri, 0900 to 1630
Special comments: Limited access during vacation periods.

Access for disabled people:
Ramped entry

CLEVELAND COLLEGE OF ART AND DESIGN LIBRARY – HARTLEPOOL ANNEXE

Acronym or abbreviation: CCAD

Church Square, Hartlepool, Cleveland, TS24 7EX

Tel: 01429 422000
Fax: 01429 422122

Enquiries:
Enquiries to: Librarian
Other contacts: Learning Resource Manager

Organisation type and purpose:
HE students, full and part time

Subject coverage:
Fine and applied arts and crafts, art history, design history, history of architecture, interior design and layout, jewellery, ceramics, textiles, printmaking and photography.

Library catalogue:
All or part available online

Printed publications:
Library Handbook (annually)
List of periodicals, acquisitions, videos and DVDs

Access to staff:
Contact by letter and by telephone. Appointment necessary.
Hours: Mon to Fri, 0900 to 1700

Access to building, collection or gallery:
Hours: 0900 to 1700

Access for disabled people:
Fully accessible

Parent body:
Cleveland College of Art and Design
Green Lane, Linthorpe, Middlesbrough, TS5 7RJ; tel: 01642 288000; fax: 01642 288828; website: http://www.ccad.ac.uk

CLEVELAND, NORTH YORKS & SOUTH DURHAM FHS

1 Oxgang Close, Redcar, Cleveland, TS10 4ND

Tel: 01642 486615
Fax: 01642 486615
E-mail: pjoiner@lineone.net

Website:
http://www.wesite.lineone.net/~pjoiner/cfhs/cfhs.html

Enquiries:
Enquiries to: General Secretary

Founded:
1980

Organisation type and purpose:
International organisation, membership association (membership is by subscription), number of members: 2,000, voluntary organisation, research organisation.

Subject coverage:
Family history.

Printed publications:
Journal
Monumental Inscriptions (over 250 churches and cemeteries)

Parish Register transcriptions
Thirsk and Helmsley areas
Various historical publications
1851 Census Indexes for North Yorkshire and South Durham (over 125 vols)
Workhouse Census Index (18 indices)
1881 Census Index (3 booklets)

Microform publications:
Guisborough Area (HO 107 2375), 3 fiche, covers about 50 parishes or sub-districts including Danby
Parish registers, Monumental Inscriptions and Returns of Papists
Pickering Area (HO 107 2373), 3 fiche, covers Pickering and about 20 neighbouring districts
1851 Census Index for Northern Yorkshire & Southern Durham (in microfiche)
1851 Census Indexes Guisborough, Helmsley, Pickering and Thirsk Areas
1881 Census Index (in microfiche)
1881 Census Indexes South Durham
1891 Census Indexes North Riding, Yorkshire, South Durham
Order microform publications from: as for printed publications

Publications Manager, Cleveland, North Yorkshire & South Durham FHS
106 The Avenue, Nunthorpe, Middlesbrough, Cleveland, TS7 0AH

Publications list:
Available in print

Access to staff:
Contact by letter, by fax and by e-mail
Hours: Mon to Fri, 0900 to 1700

CLIFFORD CHANCE

200 Aldersgate Street, London, EC1A 4JJ

Tel: 020 7600 1000
Fax: 020 7600 5555

Website:
http://www.cliffordchance.com
Includes list of publications.

Enquiries:
Enquiries to: Head of Information Sourcing

Founded:
1987

Formerly called:
Clifford Turner Coward Chance (year of change 1987)

Organisation type and purpose:
Service industry.
Law Firm.

Subject coverage:
Commercial aspects of UK, European and international law, publications for clients and professional contacts.

Non-library collection catalogue:
All or part available in-house

Library catalogue:
All or part available in-house

Printed publications:
Aspects of EC law and procedures
Newsletters on a range of subjects; several on European matters
Setting up business in (series)
Technical publications on banking, commercial, company, employment, environment, funds, insolvency, intellectual property, media, computer & communications, pensions & employee benefits, property, securities, shipping and tax law etc
Order printed publications from: Clifford Chance Publications
c/o Jevons Brown, 19 Bedford Row, London, WC1R 4EB, tel: 020 7404 2917, fax: 020 7600 5555

Publications list:
Available online and in print

Access to staff:
Access for members only.
Hours: Mon to Fri, 0900 to 1730
Special comments: Publications for clients and professional contacts.

Has:
offices worldwide

CLIMB

Formal name: Children Living with Inherited Metabolic Diseases

Climb Building, 176 Nantwich Road, Crewe, CW2 6BG

Tel: 0800 652 3181 (free phone); 0845 241 2172; 0845 241 2173
Fax: 0845 241 2174
E-mail: info.svcs@climb.org.uk

Website:
http://www.climb.org.uk
The charity, its services, supported diseases, research, news, events, online shop.

Enquiries:
Enquiries to: Information Research Officer
Other contacts: Membership Services

Organisation type and purpose:
A registered charity (number 1089588). The National Information Centre for Metabolic Diseases. A national organisation working on behalf of children, young people and families affected by metabolic disease and providing a resource for children, adults, families and professionals.
To maintain and advance its position as the primary provider of Metabolic Disease-specific information and support to children, young people, adults, families and professionals in the United Kingdom and to provide information and support to families world-wide; to fund educational and primary research programmes; and to investigate treatments and medical services.

Subject coverage:
Funding research and facilitating medical treatment, providing information, advice and support for families and professionals, supporting families through grants to help meet equipment and other costs, educating professionals and others about this group of diseases.

Information services:
Up-to-date, sourced information covering over 730 metabolic conditions, each supported disorder having an information pack containing information for professionals and families. For disease-specific information and support, e-mail: fam.svcs@climb.org.uk (for family services); cya.svcs@climb.org.uk (for children and young people's services); ir.svcs@climb.org.uk (for information research). Additional information and support available in relation to the health system, benefits, welfare rights, medicine, empowerment, personal issues, education and jobs, links with other specialists and families, care, social services, accessing education or special needs support, attaining services available locally, diagnosis, sharing information with family members, and advice on genetic counselling and issues around genetic testing.

Printed publications:
Members magazine (3 a year)

Electronic and video publications:
Newsletter
Information leaflets
Order electronic and video publications from:
Download from website

Publications list:
Available online

Access to staff:
Contact by letter, by telephone, by fax and by e-mail
Hours: Mon to Fri, 1000 to 1600

CLOTHWORKERS' COMPANY, THE

Formal name: Worshipful Company of Clothworkers of the City of London

Clothworkers' Hall, Dunster Court, Mincing Lane, London, EC3R 7AH

Tel: 020 7623 7041
Fax: 020 7397 0107
E-mail: enquiries@clothworkers.co.uk

Website:
http://www.clothworkers.co.uk

Founded:
1528

Organisation type and purpose:
Membership association (membership is by election or invitation).
City of London Livery Company.

Museum or gallery collection, archive, or library special collection:
Archive
Plate Collection

Non-library collection catalogue:
All or part available in-house

Library catalogue:
All or part available in-house

Publications list:
Available online

Access to staff:
Contact by letter, by telephone, by fax, by e-mail, in person and via website. Appointment necessary. Letter of introduction required.

Access to building, collection or gallery:
No public access

Access for disabled people:
Wheelchair access, lift access

CLUB FOR ACTS AND ACTORS

Acronym or abbreviation: CAA

20 Bedford Street, London, WC2E 9HP

Tel: 020 7836 3172
Fax: 020 7836 3172
E-mail: office@thecaa.org

Enquiries:
Enquiries to: Secretary
Other contacts: Chairman (for initiations); Treasurer (for financial matters)

Founded:
1897

Formerly called:
Concert Artistes' Association (CAA) (year of change early 1990s)

Organisation type and purpose:
Membership association (membership is by subscription, election or invitation), present number of members: 1,010 plus a few Honorary Members, registered charity (charity number 211012).

Museum or gallery collection, archive, or library special collection:
Archive Material: old members list, photographs, concert programmes, posters, etc.

Printed publications:
But – What Do You Do in the Winter: 100 years of the CAA from 1987 to 1997 (L. Parker, £9 incl. p&p, available direct)

Access to staff:
Contact by letter, by telephone, by fax and by e-mail. Appointment necessary.
Hours: Mon to Fri, 0930 to 1700

Access to building, collection or gallery:
Special comments: Entry door, stairs to first floor office.

CLUB GTI

PO Box 6506, Sutton in Ashfield, Nottinghamshire, NG17 1NG

Tel: 07891 963823
E-mail: info@clubgti.com

Website:
http://www.clubgti.com
Information on the vehicles, events, contact details.

Enquiries:
Enquiries to: Chairman
Direct e-mail: secretary@clubgti.com

Organisation type and purpose:
International organisation, national organisation, membership association (membership is by subscription), present number of members: 3600.

Subject coverage:
Club GTI is a non-profit making organisation for enthusiasts of the Volkswagen GTI and associated models within the Volkswagen group of companies. The club is independent of the manufacturer, importer or dealer network.

Printed publications:
Publications available through membership

Access to staff:
Contact by letter, by telephone, by e-mail and via website
Hours: Mon to Fri, 0900 to 1700

CLUB LOTUS

58 Malthouse Court, Dereham, Norfolk , NR20 4UA

Tel: 01362 694459 or 691144
Fax: 01362 695522
E-mail: jane@clublotus.co.uk

Website:
http://www.club-lotus.co.uk/

Enquiries:
Enquiries to: Membership Secretary
Direct e-mail: annemarie@clublotus.co.uk

Founded:
1956

Organisation type and purpose:
International organisation, membership association (membership is by subscription), present number of members: 10,000.
Lotus enthusiasts.

Subject coverage:
Lotus cars, technical information and all aspects.

Museum or gallery collection, archive, or library special collection:
Complete book list of current titles

Access to staff:
Contact by letter, by telephone, by fax and by e-mail. Appointment necessary.
Hours: Fri, 0900 to 1500

CLUB MARCOS INTERNATIONAL

Acronym or abbreviation: CMI

26 Blackberry Close, Chippenham, Wiltshire, SN14 6RG

Tel: 01249 464795
E-mail: info@clubmarcos.net

Website:
http://www.clubmarcos.org.uk

Enquiries:
Enquiries to: Membership Secretary

Founded:
1986

Organisation type and purpose:
Membership association (membership is by subscription).

Subject coverage:
The Marcos marque.

continued overleaf

Access to staff:
Contact by letter, by telephone, by e-mail and via
website
Hours: Evenings and weekends; 24-hour
answerphone

CLUB TRIUMPH

42 Greenlands Road, Staines, Middlesex, TW18
4LR

Tel: 01784 465351
Fax: 01784 465351
E-mail: enquiries@club.triumph.org.uk

Website:
http://www.club.triumph.org.uk
Club information.

Enquiries:
Enquiries to: Secretary

Founded:
1954

Organisation type and purpose:
Membership association (membership is by
subscription), present number of members: 1500,
voluntary organisation.
Classic car club.

Subject coverage:
Technical and other advice on Triumph cars.

Library catalogue:
All or part available in-house

Printed publications:
Directory (members only)
Newsletter (members only)
Library List (members only)
Magazine (members only)

Access to staff:
Contact by letter, by telephone, by fax, by e-mail
and via website
Hours: Mon to Fri, 0900 to 1700

Public Relations Officer:
Club Triumph
   1 Bure Homage Gardens, Mudeford,
   Christchurch, Dorset, BH23 4DR; tel: 01425
   278320; e-mail: charles.collin@ntlworld.com

CLUB TRIUMPH (EASTERN)

39 Maltings Road, Great Baddow, Chelmsford,
Essex, CM2 8HQ

E-mail: enquiries@clubtriumph.org

Website:
http://clubtriumph.org
Club history, contact information, updates and
reports on club activities, events calendar, links,
guestbook.

Enquiries:
Enquiries to: Publicity Officer
Direct e-mail: enquiries@clubtriumph.org

Founded:
1960

Formerly called:
Triumph Sports Owners Association

Incorporates the former:
Club Triumph Limited

Organisation type and purpose:
Membership association (membership is by
subscription), voluntary organisation.
To bring together like-minded enthusiasts of the
Triumph Marque and to provide technical back-
up. To promote enjoyment of the Triumph marque
of motor car in a social environment.

Subject coverage:
The Triumph motor car: the technology, enjoyment
and use of all models.

**Museum or gallery collection, archive, or library
special collection:**
Triumph motor car history

Triumph-related technical information (hard copy
only)

Printed publications:
Club Magazine (6 times a year, free to subscribers,
   back issues available for purchase, £1 each plus
   p&p)

Access to staff:
Contact by letter, by e-mail and via website.
Appointment necessary.

Affiliated to:
RACMSA

CLUBS FOR YOUNG PEOPLE

Acronym or abbreviation: CYP

371 Kennington Lane, London, SE11 5QY

Tel: 020 7793 0787
Fax: 020 7820 9815
E-mail: office@clubsforyoungpeople.org.uk

Website:
http://www.clubsforyoungpeople.org.uk/
http://www.nacyp.org.uk

Enquiries:
Enquiries to: National Director
Other contacts: Director of Fundraising Officer for
communications.

Founded:
1925

Formerly called:
National Association of Boys' Clubs (NABC) (year
of change 2005)

Organisation type and purpose:
Membership association, present number of
members: 400,000, voluntary organisation,
registered charity (charity number 306065),
suitable for ages: 11 to 25, training organisation.
To offer young people the knowledge,
understanding and help they need which will
utilise their full potential as they prepare for life in
society and their responsibilities as adults.

Subject coverage:
Youth leadership training; sports; creative
activities; adventure opportunities, development
training, youth clubs.

Printed publications:
Club Connection (magazine, quarterly, produced
   by NACYP, distributed to its 2500 clubs, free)
Realising Young People's Potential – Corporate
   Brochure
Leaders Guide – A tool for youth workers,
   managers and volunteers (£11.25 inc. p&p)
Working with Young People – A guide to
   protecting leaders and young people (£28.80 inc.
   p&p)

Access to staff:
Contact by letter, by fax, by e-mail and via
website
Hours: Mon to Fri, 0900 to 1700

Affiliated to:
British Youth Council
National Council for Voluntary Youth Services
National Youth Agency

Has:
3000 youth clubs affiliated

CLYDEBANK LOCAL HISTORY
SOCIETY

14 Birch Road, Parkhall, Clydebank, Strathclyde,
G81 3NZ

Tel: 0141 562 3212
E-mail: s_david.carson@ntlworld.com

Enquiries:
Enquiries to: Chairman
Direct tel: 01389 383043

Founded:
1977

Organisation type and purpose:
Voluntary organisation.

Subject coverage:
Local history of Clydebank and district.

Printed publications:
Journal (annually)

Electronic and video publications:
Video (55 minutes)

Access to staff:
Contact by letter, by telephone and by e-mail
Hours: Mon to Fri, 0900 to 1700

Access for disabled people:
Access via ramp at side entrance in Hall Street

Links with:
Scottish Civic Trust

CMR INTERNATIONAL LIMITED

Formal name: Centre for Medicines Research
International

Novellus Court, 61 South Street, Epsom, Surrey,
KT18 7PX

Tel: 01372 846100
Fax: 01372 846101
E-mail: information@cmr.org

Website:
http://www.cmr.org
Description of the work of CMR International, list
of publications.

Enquiries:
Enquiries to: Information Assistant

Founded:
1981

Formerly called:
Centre for Medicines Research (CMR)

Organisation type and purpose:
Membership association (membership is by
subscription), present number of members: 55,
consultancy, research organisation.
To collect data and conduct research into the
development of medicines.

Subject coverage:
Innovation of new chemical entities, safety
evaluation of medicines, international medicines
regulations, research and development in the
pharmaceutical industry and benchmarking.

**Museum or gallery collection, archive, or library
special collection:**
Small collection of c. 400 books on the drug
   development process

Trade and statistical information:
International pharmaceutical research and
   development expenditure. New chemical entities
   reaching the world market. Development times
   for new medicines. Regulatory review times in
   major markets.

Printed publications:
Annual lectures
Newsletter
An extensive list of books and reports relating to
   the pharmaceutical industry dealing with R&D
   Expenditure, Safety Evaluation, Regulations,
   Socio-economics
CMR International Lecture Series
Papers in professional journals

Publications list:
Available in print

Access to staff:
Contact by letter, by e-mail and via website
Hours: Mon to Fri, 0900 to 1700

CO-OPERATIVE AND SOCIAL
ENTERPRISE DEVELOPMENT
AGENCY LTD

Acronym or abbreviation: CASE-DA

94 New Walk, Leicester, LE1 7EA

Tel: 0116 222 5010
Fax: 0116 222 5495
E-mail: enquiries@case-da.co.uk

Website:
http://www.case-da.co.uk

Enquiries:
Enquiries to: Information Officer

Organisation type and purpose:
Voluntary organisation.
Advice, training and support to people who want to set up Social Enterprise.

Subject coverage:
Industrial and service co-operatives; how to set up and run co-operatives and social enterprises; their projects, markets, available skills and finance, legal and taxation problems, education, training, publicity.

Printed publications:
Brochure

Access to staff:
Contact by letter, by telephone, by fax, in person and via website
Hours: Mon to Fri, 0900 to 1700

CO-OPERATIVE COLLEGE

Holyoake House, Hanover Street, Manchester, M60 0AS

Tel: 0161 246 2902
Fax: 0161 246 2946
E-mail: archive@co-op.ac.uk

Website:
http://www.archive.coop

Enquiries:
Enquiries to: Head of Archive and Learning Resources
Direct tel: 0161 246 2925
Direct e-mail: gillian@co-op.ac.uk

Founded:
1911

Formerly called:
Co-operative College, J J Worley Memorial Library; Co-operative Union Library (year of change 2000)

Organisation type and purpose:
Registered charity, suitable for ages: adults, consultancy, research organisation.

Subject coverage:
Co-operation, co-operative history and co-operative society history and histories, nationally and internationally; co-operative film archive, co-operative archive, international economic development centre for alternative industrial and technological systems archive, co-operative oral history archive.

Museum or gallery collection, archive, or library special collection:
CAITS Archive
Co-operation and Owenism history collection (c. 2,000 items)
Co-operative Society History
J J Worley Memorial Library
Midlands Co-operative Society Archive
Robert Owen Collection (3,000 items)
George Jacob Holyoake Collection (4,000 items)
National Co-operative Film Archive
Co-operative Oral History Archive
Edward Owen Greening Collection
Co-operative Women's Guild
Rochdale Equitable Pioneers Society Collection
Co-operative Party Collection
Co-operative Press Collection
Co-operative Group South East, South Midlands and Northern Region Collection
Co-operative Youth Movements

Non-library collection catalogue:
All or part available online

Library catalogue:
All or part available online

Printed publications:
Holdings lists for special collections

Publications list:
Available in print

Access to staff:
Contact by letter, by telephone, by fax, by e-mail and via website. Appointment necessary.
Hours: Mon to Fri, 1000 to 1700

Access to building, collection or gallery:
By appointment
Hours: Mon to Fri, 1000 to 1700

Access for disabled people:
By appointment
Hours: Mon to Fri, 1000 to 1700

COBALT DEVELOPMENT INSTITUTE

Acronym or abbreviation: CDI

167 High Street, Guildford, Surrey, GU1 3AJ

Tel: 01483 578877
Fax: 01483 573873
E-mail: info@thecdi.com

Website:
http://www.thecdi.com

Enquiries:
Enquiries to: General Manager
Other contacts: Administration Manager

Founded:
1982

Formerly called:
Centre d'Information du Cobalt (CIC) (year of change 1970)

Organisation type and purpose:
Trade association (membership is by subscription). Representing the world's main cobalt producers and users; purpose is to promote cobalt and provide information on it to any interested party.

Subject coverage:
All aspects of cobalt – sources, statistics, uses, properties, extraction, environmental aspects.

Non-library collection catalogue:
All or part available in-house

Library catalogue:
All or part available in-house

Printed publications:
Cobalt Monograph Series: Superalloys, Chemicals, Catalysts, Environment, Electronics (for purchase)
Cobalt News (quarterly, free)
Cobalt Facts

Publications list:
Available online and in print

Access to staff:
Contact by letter, by telephone, by fax, by e-mail and via website. Appointment necessary.
Hours: Mon to Fri, 0900 to 1700

COCKBURN ASSOCIATION

Formal name: Cockburn Association (The Edinburgh Civic Trust)

Trunk's Close, 55 High Street, Edinburgh, EH1 1SR

Tel: 0131 557 8686
Fax: 0131 337 9387

Website:
http://www.cockburnassociation.org.uk

Founded:
1875

Organisation type and purpose:
A registered Scottish charity.

Subject coverage:
Conservation and enhancement of Edinburgh's landscape and historic and architectural heritage.

CODRINGTON LIBRARY

All Souls College, High Street, Oxford, OX1 4AL

Tel: 01865 279379
Fax: 01865 279299
E-mail: codrington.library@all-souls.ox.ac.uk

Website:
http://www.all-souls.ox.ac.uk/library

Enquiries:
Enquiries to: Librarian in Charge
Direct tel: 01865 279318

Organisation type and purpose:
College Library.

Subject coverage:
Law, history, strategic studies.

Museum or gallery collection, archive, or library special collection:
400 manuscripts including the Luttrell-Wynne Papers
British and continental early-printed books
18th-century English newspapers
Material relating to the letters of Junius
Neo-Latin and inscriptional literature

Library catalogue:
All or part available online

Access to staff:
Contact by letter and by e-mail. Appointment necessary. Letter of introduction required.
Hours: Term time: Mon to Fri, 0930 to 1830
Vacations: Mon to Fri, 0930 to 1630

COELIAC UK

3rd floor, Apollo Centre, Desborough Road, PO Box 220, High Wycombe, Buckinghamshire, HP11 2HY

Tel: 01494 437278
Fax: 01494 474349
E-mail: info@coeliac.co.uk

Enquiries:
Enquiries to: Chief Executive
Direct tel: Helpline: 0845 305 2060

Founded:
1968

Formerly called:
Coeliac Society of the United Kingdom, The Coeliac Society (year of change 2001)

Organisation type and purpose:
Registered charity (charity number 1048167 in England and Wales and SC039804 in Scotland). To support the health, welfare and rights of coeliacs, those with Dermatitis Herpetiformis (DH). Supports other medically diagnosed patients whose health and quality of life can be improved by following the dietary regime beneficial to coeliacs. To provide easily accessible written, verbal and electronic advice, information and resources to these individuals and groups. To educate the public and those in appropriate sectors of health, government, commerce and industry on the conditions and the issues. To promote and commission research into the causes, alleviation, treatment, care and cure of the coeliac and DH conditions.

Subject coverage:
General management of a gluten-free diet for those medically diagnosed as having the coeliac condition or dermatitis herpetiformis.

Printed publications:
Coeliac Handbook
Crossed Grain Magazine (2 times a year)
List of Gluten Free Manufactured Products (annually, members)
A selection of free leaflets on health and eating information
Publications for purchase include:
Gluten Free Diet booklet (£1 plus p&p)
World Travel Guide (£10 plus p&p)

Electronic and video publications:
Leaflets available to download (online)

continued overleaf

Access to staff:
Contact by letter, by telephone, by fax and by e-mail
Hours: Mon to Fri, 0900 to 1700
Helpline: Mon, Tue, Thu, Fri, 1000 to 1600; Wed, 1100 to 1600

COFFEE TRADE FEDERATION

Acronym or abbreviation: CTF

63A Union Street, London, SE1 1SG

Tel: 020 7403 3088
Fax: 020 7403 7730

Website:
http://www.coffeetradefederation.co.uk

Enquiries:
Enquiries to: Secretary
Direct e-mail: coffeetradefed@compuserve.com

Organisation type and purpose:
Trade association.

Subject coverage:
Coffee trade.

Printed publications:
Arbitration Rules
Brochure
Standard Contracts

Publications list:
Available online

Access to staff:
Contact by letter, by telephone, by fax and by e-mail
Hours: Mon to Fri, 1000 to 1600

COIL WINDING INTERNATIONAL MAGAZINE

Formal name: Coil Winding International & Electrical Insulation Magazine

PO Box 936, Alder Hills, Poole, Dorset, BH12 3HB

Tel: 01202 743906
Fax: 01202 736018
E-mail: coilwind@bournemouth-net.co.uk

Website:
http://www.coilwinding.co.uk

Enquiries:
Enquiries to: Editor

Founded:
1976

Organisation type and purpose:
Publishing house.

Subject coverage:
Electric motors; transformers; electromagnetic materials and components.

Printed publications:
Coil Winding International (magazine, 3 times a year)

Access to staff:
Contact by fax and by e-mail
Hours: Mon to Fri, 0900 to 1700

Access to building, collection or gallery:
Prior appointment required

COKE OVEN MANAGERS' ASSOCIATION

Acronym or abbreviation: COMA

Universal Contractors Limited, Strata Industrial Estate, Rotherham Road, Dinnington, Sheffield, South Yorkshire, S25 3RF

Tel: 01909 518778
Fax: 01909 518838

Website:
http://coke-oven-managers.org

Enquiries:
Enquiries to: Honorary Secretary

Direct e-mail: steve.holmes@corusgroup.com

Founded:
1917

Organisation type and purpose:
Professional body.

Subject coverage:
Coke ovens, coking, carbonisation.

Museum or gallery collection, archive, or library special collection:
Complete set of COMA Yearbooks

Printed publications:
Coke Oven Managers' Association Bulletin (2 times a year)
Coke Oven Managers' Association Year Book (annually)

COLCHESTER BOROUGH COUNCIL

PO Box 884, Town Hall, Colchester, Essex, CO1 1FR

Tel: 01206 282222
Fax: 01206 282288

Website:
http://www.colchester.gov.uk

Enquiries:
Enquiries to: Chief Executive

Organisation type and purpose:
Local government body.

Access to staff:
Contact by letter, by telephone, by fax and in person
Hours: Mon to Fri, 0900 to 1700

COLCHESTER INSTITUTE LIBRARY

Sheepen Road, Colchester, Essex, CO3 3LL

Tel: 01206 712642
Fax: 01206 711712
E-mail: library.helpdesk@colchester.ac.uk

Website:
http://library.colchester.ac.uk

Enquiries:
Enquiries to: Head of Learning Resources and Student Services
Direct tel: 01206 712280
Direct e-mail: cilla.summers@colchester.ac.uk

Organisation type and purpose:
Suitable for ages: 16+.
College of further and higher education.

Subject coverage:
Music, art and design, catering and hospitality studies, health studies, business studies, leisure and recreation, construction, automobile and general engineering, humanities, social sciences, science, education.

Museum or gallery collection, archive, or library special collection:
Music scores, including wind band scores

Library catalogue:
All or part available online

Access to staff:
Contact by letter, by telephone, by fax, by e-mail, in person and via website. Non-members charged.
Hours: Mon to Fri, 0900 to 1700

Links with:
Essex University

COLD ROLLED SECTIONS ASSOCIATION

Acronym or abbreviation: CRSA

National Metalforming Centre, 47 Birmingham Road, Birmingham, B70 6PY

Tel: 0121 601 6350
Fax: 0121 601 6373
E-mail: crsa@crsauk.com

Website:
http://www.crsauk.com

Enquiries:
Enquiries to: Secretary

Organisation type and purpose:
Trade association.

Subject coverage:
Cold roll-formed steel sections.

Printed publications:
Safe Working of Cold Roll Forming Lines
Cold Roll Forming: How it can benefit your business – A Designer's Guide

Access to staff:
Contact by telephone and by e-mail
Hours: Mon to Fri, 0900 to 1700

Connections with:
Confederation of British Metalforming (CBM) National Metalforming Centre, 47 Birmingham Road, Birmingham, B70 6PY; tel: 0121 601 6350; fax: 0121 601 6373; e-mail: info@britishmetalforming.com; website: http://www.britishmetalforming.com

COLEG LLANDRILLO LIBRARY RESOURCE CENTRE

Formal name: Library Learning Technology Service

Llandudno Road, Rhos-on-Sea, Colwyn Bay, Conwy, LL28 4HZ

Tel: 01492 546666
Fax: 01492 543052
E-mail: info@llandrillo.ac.uk

Website:
http://www.llandrillo.ac.uk

Enquiries:
Enquiries to: Library Resource Manager
Direct tel: 01492 542342
Direct fax: 01492 548267
Direct e-mail: library1@llandrillo.ac.uk

Organisation type and purpose:
Library resource centre for a college of further education, higher education and work-based learning.

Subject coverage:
A Level, GCSE and International Baccalaureate; business and management, further education, computer studies, special needs, hospitality management, leisure and tourism, health care and counselling, engineering, construction, motor vehicle technology, languages, art, office technology and secretarial studies.

Non-library collection catalogue:
All or part available online

Library catalogue:
All or part available online

Printed publications:
Library fact sheets (annually)

Access to staff:
Contact by letter, by telephone, by fax, by e-mail and via website. Appointment necessary. Non-members charged.
Hours: Term time: Mon, 0830 to 1600; Tue to Thu, 0830 to 2000; Fri, 0930 to 1630; Sat, 1000 to 1500
Vacations: Mon to Thu, 0830 to 1700; Fri 0830 to 1630

Branches:
Abergele Community College
Denbigh Community College
Rhyl Community College

COLLECTIONS TRUST

Downstream Building, CAN Mezzanine, 1 London Bridge, London, SE1 9BG

Tel: 020 7022 1889

E-mail: office@collectionstrust.org.uk

Website:
http://www.collectionstrust.org.uk

Enquiries:
Enquiries to: Marketing Officer

Incorporates the former:
MDA (year of change 2008)

Organisation type and purpose:
Professional body, registered charity (charity number 273984).

Subject coverage:
Professional collections management and related information technology and legal issues.

Printed publications:
Publications include:
Documentation: a practical guide
SPECTRUM
Order printed publications from: website: http://www.collectionstrust.org.uk/books

Publications list:
Available online and in print

Access to staff:
Contact by letter, by telephone, by fax, by e-mail and via website. Appointment necessary.
Hours: Mon to Fri, 0900 to 1700

Access to building, collection or gallery:
No prior appointment required

COLLEGE OF ARMS

Formal name: Corporation of the Kings, Heralds and Pursuivants of Arms; also known as Heralds' College.

Queen Victoria Street, London, EC4V 4BT

Tel: 020 7248 2762
Fax: 020 7248 6448
E-mail: enquiries@college-of-arms.gov.uk

Website:
http://www.college-of-arms.gov.uk

Enquiries:
Enquiries to: Officer in Waiting
Other contacts: Archivist for study of books or manuscripts.

Founded:
1484

Organisation type and purpose:
Advisory body, professional body (membership is by election or invitation), present number of members: 11, historic building, house or site, consultancy, research organisation.
Repository of the official registers of armorial bearings and genealogies of England, Wales, Northern Ireland and Commonwealth families.
Heraldry and genealogy.

Subject coverage:
Heraldry, grants of arms, genealogy, ceremonial, precedence, changes of name.

Museum or gallery collection, archive, or library special collection:
Some of the Arundel MSS
Unique manuscript collections of heraldic and genealogical material

Non-library collection catalogue:
All or part available in-house and in print

Library catalogue:
All or part available in-house

Printed publications:
Louise Campbell and Francis Steer, A Catalogue of Manuscripts in the College of Arms: Collections vol. 1 (1988)

Access to staff:
Contact by letter, by telephone, by fax, by e-mail, in person and via website
Hours: Mon to Fri, 1000 to 1600
Special comments: Groups of visitors by appointment with Officer in Waiting.

Access to building, collection or gallery:
Prior appointment required
Hours: Mon to Fri, 1000 to 1600
Special comments: Contact Archivist, telephone 020 7236 1627

COLLEGE OF CRANIO-SACRAL THERAPY

Acronym or abbreviation: CCST

9 St Georges Mews, Primrose Hill, London, NW1 8XE

Tel: 020 7586 0148 or 7483 0120
Fax: 020 7586 9550
E-mail: info@ccst.co.uk

Website:
http://www.ccst.co.uk

Enquiries:
Enquiries to: Administrator

Founded:
1986

Organisation type and purpose:
Training organisation, research organisation. Clinic.

Subject coverage:
Cranio-sacral therapy, general health and wellbeing, physical and psychological; birth trauma, baby and child health, learning difficulties, meningitis, resolution of obscure and intractable conditions.

Printed publications:
Articles (free)
Course brochure (free)
Information leaflets (free)

Access to staff:
Contact by letter, by telephone, by fax and by e-mail
Hours: Mon to Fri, 0900 to 1800

Access to building, collection or gallery:
No prior appointment required

Also at:
Primrose Hill Natural Health Centre
9 St George's Mews, London, NW1 8XE; tel: 020 7586 0148; fax: 020 7586 9550

COLLEGE OF EMERGENCY MEDICINE

Acronym or abbreviation: CEM

Churchill House, 35 Red Lion Square, London, WC1R 4SG

Tel: 020 7404 1999
Fax: 020 7067 1267
E-mail: cem@collemergencymed.ac.uk

Website:
http://www.collemergencymed.ac.uk

Organisation type and purpose:
Became a College by Royal Charter 2008. Seeks to advance education and research in emergency medicine. Sets standards for training. Administers examinations in emergency medicine for the award of fellowship and membership of the College. Recommends trainees for CCT in Emergency Medicine. Present number of fellows and members: 2,900. Registered charity (charity number 1122689).

Subject coverage:
Emergency medicine.

Access to staff:
Contact by letter, by telephone, by e-mail and via website
Hours: 0900 to 1700

COLLEGE OF ESTATE MANAGEMENT

Acronym or abbreviation: CEM

Whiteknights, Reading, Berkshire, RG6 6AW

Tel: 0800 019 9697
Fax: 0118 921 4620
E-mail: courses@cem.ac.uk

Website:
http://www.cem.ac.uk

Enquiries:
Enquiries to: Admission Officer
Direct e-mail: prospectuses@cem.ac.uk

Founded:
1919

Organisation type and purpose:
Registered charity (charity number 313223), suitable for ages: 18+, research organisation.

Subject coverage:
Undergraduate, professional and postgraduate courses for the property professions, construction industry and those associated. Course subjects include estate management, arbitration, shopping centre management, property investment, building conservation, construction and real estate, project management, construction, surveying, facilities management, valuation.

Printed publications:
All Write! Effective Writing for Professional People (Bailey A, 2000)
Introduction to Civil Engineering Construction (Holmes R, 1995)
Research reports

Electronic and video publications:
No

Publications list:
Available online and in print

Access to staff:
Contact by letter, by telephone, by fax, by e-mail and via website. Appointment necessary.
Hours: Mon to Fri, 0830 to 1730

Access to building, collection or gallery:
No prior appointment required

COLLEGE OF HEALTH CARE CHAPLAINS

Acronym or abbreviation: CHCC

Unite Health Sector, 128 Theobald's Road, London, WC1X 8TN

Tel: 020 3371 2004
Fax: 0870 731 5043
E-mail: william.sharpe@unitetheunion.org

Website:
http://www.healthcarechaplains.org
Home page details of CHCC.

Enquiries:
Enquiries to: Registrar

Founded:
1993

Organisation type and purpose:
Trade union (membership is by subscription), present number of members: 1,000, training organisation, research organisation, Allied Health Care Chaplains.

Subject coverage:
Pastoral care, ethics in health care, inter-faith relationships in health care.

Library catalogue:
All or part available online and in-house

Printed publications:
Journal (3 times a year, free to members, available to purchase to non-members)
Newsletter (4 times a year, available to members)
Occasional papers

Publications list:
Available online and in print

Access to staff:
Contact by letter, by telephone, by fax, by e-mail and via website

continued overleaf

Hours: Mon to Fri, 0900 to 1700

Autonomous section of:
Unite the Union
    website: http://www.unitetheunion.org

COLLEGE OF INTEGRATED CHINESE MEDICINE

Acronym or abbreviation: CICM

19 Castle Street, Reading, Berkshire, RG1 7SB

Tel: 0118 950 8880
Fax: 0118 950 8890
E-mail: info@cicm.org.uk

Website:
http://www.cicm.org.uk
The college offers a BSc. (Hons) in Chinese Acupuncture in collaboration with Kingston University. It also offers a continuing professional development course for Chinese medicine practitioners and a course in health topics for the wider public. It has a teaching and regular clinic for acupuncture, tuina and Chinese herbal medicine.

Enquiries:
Enquiries to: Reception

Founded:
1992

Organisation type and purpose:
Training organisation.

Subject coverage:
Training in acupuncture, tuina and Chinese herbal medicine.

Library catalogue:
All or part available online, in-house and in print

Access to staff:
Contact by letter, by fax, by e-mail and in person. Appointment necessary. Letter of introduction required.
Hours: Mon to Fri, 0900 to 1800

Access to building, collection or gallery:
Hours: Every Day except over Christmas and Easter, 0900 to 1800

Access for disabled people:
None to library, but provision would be made for access to requested books or journals

Member organisations:
British Acupuncture Acreditation Board
    63 Jeddo Road, London, W12 9HQ; tel: 020 8735 0466; website: http://www.baab.co.uk

COLLEGE OF MASONS

42 Magdalen Road, Wandsworth, London, SW18 3NP

Tel: 020 8874 8363
Fax: 020 8871 1342

Enquiries:
Enquiries to: Honorary Secretary

Founded:
1893

Organisation type and purpose:
Membership association.

Subject coverage:
Masonry and all worked materials: building, decoration, carving, lettering, sculpture, restoration, cleaning, fixings, memorials and monuments, granite, marble, slate and stone.

Access to staff:
Contact by letter, by telephone and by fax
Hours: Mon to Fri, 0900 to 1700

COLLEGE OF NORTH EAST LONDON

Acronym or abbreviation: CONEL

High Road, Tottenham, London, N15 4RU

Tel: 020 8802 3014
Fax: 020 8442 3091
E-mail: jdunster@staff.conel.ac.uk

Website:
http://www.conel.ac.uk

Enquiries:
Enquiries to: Learning Resources Team Leader
Direct tel: 020 8442 3877

Founded:
1990

Formerly called:
Haringey College, Tottenham College of Technology

Organisation type and purpose:
College of further education.

Subject coverage:
Subjects Basic Skills to A levels: accountancy; business studies; building and engineering; health care; art; design; media; hairdressing; beauty therapy; floristry; information technology; environmental health; housing; public administration; electronics; general education; sports and recreation.

Library catalogue:
All or part available in-house

Access to staff:
Contact by telephone, by e-mail and via website
Hours: Mon to Thu, 0900 to 2000; Fri 0900 to 1630; Sat, 1000 to 1600

Access to building, collection or gallery:
Prior appointment required

Access for disabled people:
Ramped entry, toilet facilities

COLLEGE OF NORTH WEST LONDON

Acronym or abbreviation: CNWL

Dudden Hill Lane, Willesden, London, NW10 2XD

Tel: 020 8208 5000
Fax: 020 8451 2718
E-mail: cic@cnwl.ac.uk

Website:
http://www.cnwl.ac.uk

Enquiries:
Enquiries to: Head of Learning Resources
Direct tel: 020 8208 5145

Organisation type and purpose:
Further education.

Subject coverage:
Fashion; catering; creative and media studies; building services, plumbing, electrical and electronics engineering; construction; refrigeration; business studies; auto engineering; access provision; ESOL, EFL, modern foreign languages, interpreting, IELTS.

Museum or gallery collection, archive, or library special collection:
Technical index – for construction

Trade and statistical information:
Available from website.

Library catalogue:
All or part available online

Access to staff:
Contact by letter, by telephone and by e-mail
Hours: Mon to Fri, 0900 to 1700

Also at:
College of North West London
    Wembley Park, North End Road, Middlesex, HA9 0AD
College of North West London
    Willesden Centre, Denzil Road, London, NW2 7BZ; tel: 020 8208 5050; fax: 020 8451 2718

COLLEGE OF OCCUPATIONAL THERAPISTS

106–114 Borough High Street, London, SE1 1LB

Tel: 020 7450 2316
Fax: 020 7450 2364

Enquiries:
Enquiries to: Librarian
Direct e-mail: library@cot.co.uk

Organisation type and purpose:
Professional body (membership is by subscription), present number of members: c. 29,000, registered charity.

Subject coverage:
All aspects of occupational therapy in a variety of formats.

Museum or gallery collection, archive, or library special collection:
Archives
Code of Practice documents (for reference only)
Conferences file
Government and legal publications
National collection of occupational therapy literature
Organisations file
Practice records and references

Printed publications:
Current Awareness Bulletin
Professional Practice briefings
Occupational therapy-related publications
Order printed publications from: Sales department

Publications list:
Available online and in print

Access to staff:
Contact by letter, by telephone, by fax, by e-mail, in person and via website. Access for members only. Non-members charged.
Hours: Mon to Fri, 0900 to 1700

Access for disabled people:
Level entry, toilet facilities

Parent body:
British Association of Occupational Therapists

COLLEGE OF OPTOMETRISTS

Library, The College of Optometrists, 42 Craven Street, London, WC2 5NG

Tel: 020 7839 6000
Fax: 020 7839 6800
E-mail: library@college-optometrists.org

Website:
http://www.college-optometrists.org

Enquiries:
Enquiries to: Librarian

Founded:
1901

Organisation type and purpose:
Learned society, professional body (membership is by qualification).

Subject coverage:
Anatomy and physiology of the eye, physiology and psychology of vision, vision defects and their correction, spectacles and contact lenses, geometric and visual optics, optometry and its history.

Museum or gallery collection, archive, or library special collection:
Early books on vision

Library catalogue:
All or part available online

Access to staff:
Contact by letter, by telephone, by fax, by e-mail, in person and via website. Appointment necessary. Non-members charged.
Hours: Mon to Fri, 0900 to 1300 and 1400 to 1700

Administered by:
College of Optometrists

COLLEGE OF PIPING

16–24 Otago Street, Glasgow, G12 8JH

Tel: 0141 334 3587
Fax: 0141 587 6068
E-mail: info@piping.scot.net

Website:
http://www.college-of-piping.co.uk/index.html

Enquiries:
Enquiries to: Chairman
Other contacts: Principal for day to day responsibility.

Founded:
1944

Organisation type and purpose:
Voluntary organisation, museum.

Subject coverage:
Highland bagpipe and its music.

Printed publications:
Piping Times (monthly)
Tutors for piping and Piobaireachd

Access to staff:
Contact by letter, by telephone, by fax, by e-mail and in person
Hours: Mon to Fri, 0900 to 1700

Access for disabled people:
Parking provided

COLLEGE OF PSYCHIC STUDIES

Acronym or abbreviation: CPS

16 Queensberry Place, London, SW7 2EB

Tel: 020 7589 3292
Fax: 020 7589 2824
E-mail: admin@collegeofpsychicstudies.co.uk

Website:
http://www.psychic-studies.org.uk
Programme, publications, services, history, membership.

Enquiries:
Enquiries to: Administrator
Direct tel: 020 7838 4401
Other contacts: Librarian for books and research.

Founded:
1884

Formerly called:
London Spiritualist Alliance (year of change 1955); College of Psychic Science (year of change 1970)

Organisation type and purpose:
Membership association (membership is by subscription), present number of members: 2190, registered charity (charity number 212728), suitable for ages: 18+, training organisation, research organisation.
Educational charity, advice and resource centre.

Subject coverage:
Psychic research, parapsychology, occult, healing, meditation, New Age, psychic development, spiritual philosophy.

Museum or gallery collection, archive, or library special collection:
Small specialist collection of books, manuscripts, photographs and artefacts relating to psychic research and the college's history. No public access. Research by prior arrangement with the Librarian

Printed publications:
Light (journal, annually)
Programme booklet (3 times a year)
Mediumship Made Simple (Northage I, £7.99)
Journey Beyond (Northage I, £3.50)

Electronic and video publications:
Soulwork – Home Study Pack (workbook and double CD)
Psychic Development CD (Jan 2002)
Meditation CD (Jan 2002)

Publications list:
Available in print

Access to staff:
Contact by letter, by telephone, by fax, by e-mail and via website. Appointment necessary.
Hours: Mon to Fri, 1030 to 1900; Sat, 0915 to 1415
Special comments: Library for members only, no direct access to archives unless by special appointment with the Librarian.

COLLEGE OF TEACHERS

3rd Floor, 33 John Street, London, WC1N 2AT

Tel: 020 7404 2008
Fax: 020 7404 2008
E-mail: gen@cot4.freeserve.co.uk

Enquiries:
Enquiries to: Chief Executive

Founded:
1849

Formerly called:
College of Preceptors

Organisation type and purpose:
Professional body.
To make public the concerns of the teaching profession and to support the profession through its publications and qualifications.

Subject coverage:
Professional development of teachers, education, especially teacher education.

Printed publications:
Aldrich: School and Society in Victorian Britain
Course Book on methods of teaching
Education Today (termly)
Newsletter

Publications list:
Available in print

Access to staff:
Appointment necessary.
Hours: Mon to Fri, 0930 to 1700

COLLEGE OF TRADITIONAL ACUPUNCTURE

Acronym or abbreviation: CTA

Haseley Manor, Hatton, Warwickshire, CV35 7LU

Tel: 01926 484158
Fax: 01926 485444
E-mail: jeanette.harper@cta-uk.net

Website:
http://www.acupuncture-coll.ac.uk
Information about: Five-element acupuncture; the college and courses offered and college events.

Enquiries:
Enquiries to: Administrator

Founded:
1960s

Formerly called:
Oriental Medical College Ltd t/a The College of Traditional Acupuncture UK (year of change 1994)

Organisation type and purpose:
Registered charity (charity number 1039702), suitable for ages: 20+.
Private college offering 3-year part-time licentiate in acupuncture for qualification as professional practitioners. Programme is fully accredited by the British Acupuncture Accreditation Board and validated as BA(Hons) by Oxford Brookes University.

Subject coverage:
Acupuncture, complementary medicine.

Access to staff:
Contact by letter, by telephone, by fax and by e-mail

Hours: Mon to Fri, 0900 to 1700

Access for disabled people:
Parking provided, ramped entry, access to all public areas, toilet facilities

COLOMBIAN EMBASSY

3 Hans Crescent, Knightsbridge, London, SW1X 0LN

Tel: 020 7589 9177
Fax: 020 7581 1829
E-mail: mail@colombianembassy.co.uk

Website:
http://www.colombiaemb.co.uk

Enquiries:
Enquiries to: Ambassador

Organisation type and purpose:
National government body.
Embassy.

Subject coverage:
Colombia, general information and economic statistics.

Printed publications:
Publications for schools

Also at:
Colombian Consulate General
3rd Floor, 15–19 Great Titchfield Street, London, W1P 7FB; tel: 020 7637 9893; fax: 020 7637 5604; e-mail: consulco@consulco.demon.co.uk

Links with:
Proexport (Trade Office)
9 Berkeley Street, London, W1X 5AD; tel: 020 7491 3535; fax: 020 7491 4295; e-mail: cici@ proexport-london.co.uk

COMBAT STRESS

Formal name: Ex-Services Mental Welfare Society

Tyrwhitt House, Oaklawn Road, Leatherhead, Surrey, KT22 0BX

Tel: 01372 841600
Fax: 01372 841601
E-mail: contactus@combatstress.org.uk

Website:
http://www.combatstress.com
Treatment centres, welfare offices – their role in the society, fundraising including calendar of events, details for those wishing to donate.

Enquiries:
Enquiries to: Director Fundraising & Communications
Direct tel: 01372 841615
Direct e-mail: robert.marsh@combatstress.org.uk; faye.waters@combatstress.org.uk

Founded:
1919

Organisation type and purpose:
Registered charity (charity number 206002).
Supports three treatment centres and 15 welfare officers in the UK and Republic of Ireland. The Ex-Services Mental Welfare Society, also known as Combat Stress, is the only charity to specialise in helping those of all ranks of the Armed Forces and Merchant Navy who suffer from psychological disorders caused through or exacerbated by service.

Printed publications:
Annual Report
Combat Stress Newsletter (twice a year)

Microform publications:
Film of the Society's work

Access to staff:
Contact by letter, by telephone, by fax, by e-mail and via website. Appointment necessary.
Hours: Mon to Fri, 0730 to 1600

continued overleaf

Branches:
Combat Stress Regional Offices
Hollybush House, Hollybush by Ayr, Ayrshire, KA6 7EA; tel: 01292 561315; fax: 01292 561351; e-mail: bill.middleton@combatstress.org.uk; website: http://www.combatstress.org.uk
Combat Stress Welfare Support Team North
Audley Court, Audley Avenue, Newport, Shropshire, TF10 7BP; tel: 01952 822712; fax: 01952 811751; e-mail: mike.burrows@combatstress.org.uk; website: http://www.combatstress.org.uk

COMHAIRLE NAN EILEAN SIAR

Acronym or abbreviation: CNES

Council Offices, Sandwick Road, Stornoway, Isle of Lewis, HS1 2BW

Tel: 01851 703773
Fax: 01851 705349

Website:
http://www.w-isles.gov.uk

Enquiries:
Enquiries to: Chief Executive
Direct tel: 01851 709500
Direct fax: 01851 706022
Direct e-mail: m.burr@cne-siar.gov.uk
Other contacts: Communications Officer

Founded:
1975

Formerly called:
Western Isles Council (WIC) (year of change 1998)

Organisation type and purpose:
Local government body.

Subject coverage:
All areas of community service.

Museum or gallery collection, archive, or library special collection:
Library (open to the public)

Access to staff:
Contact by letter, by telephone, by fax, by e-mail and in person
Hours: Mon to Fri, 0900 to 1700

Access for disabled people:
Parking provided, ramped entry, level entry, access to all public areas, toilet facilities

Affiliated to:
Conference of Peripheral Maritime Regions

Council Offices:
Comhairle Nan Eilean Siar
Castlebay, Isle of Barra; tel: 01871 810431; fax: 01871 810254
Comhairle Nan Eilean Siar
Tarbert, Isle of Harris; tel: 01859 502367; fax: 01859 502283
Comhairle Nan Eilean Siar
Balivanich, Benbecula; tel: 01870 602425; fax: 01870 602332

COMIC BOOK POSTAL AUCTIONS LIMITED

Acronym or abbreviation: COMPAL

PO Box 58386, London, NW1W 9RE

Tel: 020 7424 0007
Fax: 020 7424 0008
E-mail: comicbook@compalcomics.com

Website:
http://www.compalcomics.com

Enquiries:
Enquiries to: Managing Director

Founded:
1992

Organisation type and purpose:
Publishing house.
Comic book auctions by post.

Subject coverage:
Comics.

Non-library collection catalogue:
All or part available online

Library catalogue:
All or part available online

Access to staff:
Contact by letter, by telephone, by fax and via website
Hours: Mon to Fri, 0900 to 1700

COMIC RELIEF EDUCATION DISTRIBUTION

Education House, Drywall Estate, Castle Road, Sittingbourne, Kent, ME10 3RL

Tel: 01795 437988
Fax: 01795 474871
E-mail: info@edist.co.uk

Enquiries:
Enquiries to: Information Officer

Organisation type and purpose:
Registered charity (charity number 326568).

Access to staff:
Contact by letter, by telephone, by fax and by e-mail
Hours: Mon to Fri, 0900 to 1700

Access to building, collection or gallery:
No access other than to staff

Head Office:
Comic Relief
5th Floor, 89 Albert Embankment, London, SE1 7TP

COMMEMORATIVE COLLECTORS SOCIETY

Lumless House, Gainsborough Road, Winthorpe, Newark, Nottinghamshire, NG24 2NR

Tel: 01636 671377
E-mail: commemorativecollectorssociety@hotmail.com

Website:
http://www.commemorativecollecting.co.uk

Enquiries:
Enquiries to: Honorary Secretary

Founded:
1972

Organisation type and purpose:
International organisation, membership association (membership is by subscription), present number of members: 3649, voluntary organisation, research organisation.
International society of private collectors of all types of popular commemorabilia.
To represent the interests of members, research and record/maintain archive of commemorative items and commemorative collections.

Subject coverage:
Popular/mass-produced commemorative items of any kind, in any material or medium, identification of items/events/manufacturer (if known) and historical background.

Museum or gallery collection, archive, or library special collection:
Archive of information on 12,731 different items, worldwide events, 1660–2006
Commemorative Museum Trust Collection of over 5762 pieces from 1761–2006
Library of related material
Photographic Library of over 10,822 black and white photographs of popular commemorative items in any medium from 1660 to the present day. These include foreign commemoratives covering 71 countries to date

Trade and statistical information:
Market size and value for commemorative items.

Printed publications:
Members Journal
Members Newsletter
Special Reviews for major events i.e. Royal Jubilees, coronations etc

Access to staff:
Contact by letter, by telephone, by e-mail and in person. Appointment necessary.
Hours: Mon to Sun, 0900 to 1700

Access to building, collection or gallery:
Prior appointment required
Hours: 0930 to 1700

Access for disabled people:
Level entry
Hours: 0930 to 1700

COMMITTEE OF SCOTTISH CLEARING BANKERS

Acronym or abbreviation: CSCB

Drumsheugh House, 38b Drumsheugh Gardens, Edinburgh, EH3 7SW

Tel: 0131 473 7770
Fax: 0131 473 7799
E-mail: info@scotbanks.co.uk

Enquiries:
Enquiries to: Operations Co-ordinator

Organisation type and purpose:
Trade association, present number of members: 4.

Subject coverage:
Most aspects of Scottish banking.

Trade and statistical information:
Aggregate statistics of Scottish clearing banks.

Access to staff:
Contact by letter, by telephone, by fax and by e-mail
Hours: Mon to Fri, 0900 to 1700

COMMITTEE ON THE ADMINISTRATION OF JUSTICE

Acronym or abbreviation: CAJ

2nd Floor, Sturgen Building, 9–15 Queen Street, Belfast, BT1 6EA

Tel: 028 9031 6000
Fax: 028 9031 4583
E-mail: info@caj.org.uk

Website:
http://www.caj.org.uk

Enquiries:
Enquiries to: Office Manager

Founded:
1981

Organisation type and purpose:
Membership association, voluntary organisation, research organisation.
Civil liberties group.

Subject coverage:
Civil liberties and human rights in Northern Ireland.

Museum or gallery collection, archive, or library special collection:
Information from newspaper cuttings, legislation, conference reports, government publications, etc. on a variety of subjects including administration of the courts, bill of rights, right to silence, miscarriages of justice, police and policing, equality and criminal justice

Printed publications:
A large number of publications including conference papers, submissions and responses. Many publications are available to buy online.

Publications list:
Available online and in print

Access to staff:
Contact by letter, by telephone, by fax and by e-mail. Appointment necessary.
Hours: Mon to Fri, 0900 to 1700

Links with:
International Federation of Human Rights
17 passage de la Main d'Or, 75011 Paris, France

COMMONWEAL COLLECTION

J B Priestley Library, University of Bradford, Richmond Road, Bradford, West Yorkshire, BD7 1DP

Tel: 01274 233404
Fax: 01274 233398
E-mail: commonweal@bradford.ac.uk

Website:
http://www.bradford.ac.uk/library/services/commonweal/index.php
Information about the collection, including how to become a member, and access to an online catalogue.

Enquiries:
Enquiries to: Secretary to the Trustees
Other contacts: Special Collections Librarian (archives)

Founded:
1958

Organisation type and purpose:
Voluntary organisation, registered charity (charity number 1053157), public library.
To provide a resource for all issues relating to non-violence and non-violent social change.
Mission Statement: The Commonweal Collection is an independent specialist library devoted to issues around non-violent social change, working to promote justice and peace. Commonweal aims to provide literature.

Subject coverage:
Theory and practice of non-violence; non-violence and peace research; Gandhi and other pacifists and political radicals; peace education; critique of war; disarmament; nuclear power and weaponry; alternative society; spirituality; ecological issues; human rights; gender issues.

Museum or gallery collection, archive, or library special collection:
Over 11,000 books and pamphlets available for loan, over 230 current alternative journals available for reference
Archival material documenting non-violent campaigns and the peace movement in Britain, including:
Collection of printed materials on Gandhi
Peace News Archives
Papers from the International Seminar on Training in Nonviolent Action
Papers from the London Office of the United Farm Workers, USA
Papers of Hugh Brock (Editor of Peace News, 1955–1964)

Library catalogue:
All or part available online

Printed publications:
Annual Report
Gandhi: A Bibliography, a complete list of the 450 books and journals held in the Commonweal Collection by and about Mohandas K Gandhi (1995, 50pp, £5 inc. p&p)
Guide to the Collections
The Commonweal Collection: a short history (Barlow S, 1996)
Travels of an International Voluntary Service Worker (Huggett D, 1996)
Bibliographies:
Citizenship and the National Curriculum
Circle Time Resources
Religious Education
Conflict Resolution and Bullying (for teachers)

Electronic and video publications:
List of videos available, may be borrowed

Access to staff:
Contact by letter, by telephone and in person
Hours: Term time: Mon to Thu, 0800 to 2400; Fri, 0800 to 2100; Sat, Sun, 0845 to 2100
Vacations: Mon to Fri, 0845 to 2100; Sat, Sun, 0845 to 1800

Access for disabled people:
Level entry, access to all public areas, toilet facilities, lifts

Parent body:
Commonweal Trust

COMMONWEALTH ASSOCIATION OF SURVEYING AND LAND ECONOMY

Acronym or abbreviation: CASLE

University of the West of England, Faculty of Built Environment, Frenchay Campus, Coldharbour Lane, Bristol, BS16 1QY

Tel: 0117 328 3036
Fax: 0117 328 3036
E-mail: susan.spedding@uwe.ac.uk

Website:
http://www.casle.org
http://www.casle.conferences.co.uk

Enquiries:
Enquiries to: Administrator

Founded:
1969

Organisation type and purpose:
Membership association.

Subject coverage:
Education and training in surveying and land management subjects throughout the Commonwealth.

Printed publications:
Introduction to Facilities Management
Building Maintenance
CASLE Newsletter
Project Manuals on surveying topics
Survey Review Ltd – Land Surveyors Journal (quarterly)
Order printed publications from: Survey Review, CASLE
Room 2Q20A, Faculty of the Built Environment, University of the West of England, Bristol, BS16 1QY, tel: As main numbers

Access to staff:
Contact by letter, by telephone, by fax and by e-mail. Appointment necessary.
Hours: Mon to Fri, 0900 to 1700

COMMONWEALTH BROADCASTING ASSOCIATION

Acronym or abbreviation: CBA

17 Fleet Street, London, EC4Y 1AA

Tel: 020 7853 5550
Fax: 020 7583 5549
E-mail: cba@cba.org.uk

Website:
http://www.cba.org.uk

Enquiries:
Enquiries to: Secretary General

Founded:
1945

Organisation type and purpose:
International organisation, professional body, membership association (membership is by election or invitation), present number of members: 100, training organisation, consultancy, research organisation.

To support quality broadcasting throughout the Commonwealth.

Subject coverage:
Broadcasting in Commonwealth countries.

Printed publications:
Commonwealth Broadcaster
Commonwealth Broadcasting Directory
Order printed publications from: Postal address or email: cba@cba.org.uk

Electronic and video publications:
Commonwealth Photographic Awards (CD, available to member organisations)
Commonwealth Short Stories (CD, annually, available to member organisations)

Publications list:
Available online

Access to staff:
Contact by letter, by telephone, by fax, by e-mail and via website
Hours: Mon to Fri, 0930 to 1730

Access to building, collection or gallery:
No access other than to staff and visitors

COMMONWEALTH FORCES HISTORY TRUST

37 Davis Road, Acton, London, W3 7SE

Tel: 020 8749 1045

Enquiries:
Enquiries to: Secretary

Founded:
1988

Organisation type and purpose:
Registered charity.

Subject coverage:
All the different units of the Defence Forces of the British Commonwealth and Empire outside the United Kingdom, from 1066 to 1946, including the American Loyalists and the Indians who fought as Allies of the King in the American Revolution and/or the War of 1812.

Museum or gallery collection, archive, or library special collection:
Books and Journals
Indices
Letters
Photographs
Tape recordings

Access to staff:
Contact by letter and by telephone. Appointment necessary.
Hours: Mon to Fri, 0900 to 1600

COMMONWEALTH FORESTRY ASSOCIATION

Acronym or abbreviation: CFA

The Crib, Dinchope, Craven Arms, Shropshire, SY7 9JJ

Tel: 01588 672868
Fax: 0870 0116645
E-mail: cfa@cfa-international.org

Website:
http://www.cfa-international.org

Enquiries:
Enquiries to: Membership Manager
Direct e-mail: jenny@cfa-international.org

Founded:
1921

Organisation type and purpose:
Professional body.

Subject coverage:
Forestry, forest products, related environmental subjects.

Museum or gallery collection, archive, or library special collection:
Commonwealth Forestry Conference Proceedings
Commonwealth Forestry Review

Printed publications:
Commonwealth Forestry Handbook (periodic)

continued overleaf

International Forestry Review (quarterly)
The World's Forests – Rio plus 5: international
initiatives towards sustainable management
The World's Forests – Rio plus 8

Access to staff:
Contact by letter, by telephone, by fax, by e-mail
and via website
Hours: Mon to Fri, 0900 to 1700

Member organisation of:
Commonwealth Professional Associations
Commonwealth Trust

COMMONWEALTH HUMAN ECOLOGY COUNCIL

Acronym or abbreviation: CHEC

Church House, Newton Road, London, W2 5LS

Tel: 020 7792 5934
Fax: 020 7792 5948
E-mail: chec@btopenworld.com

Website:
http://www.checinternational.org

Enquiries:
Enquiries to: Chief Executive
Other contacts: Chairman, Governing Board

Founded:
1969

Formerly called:
Committee on Nutrition in the Commonwealth

Organisation type and purpose:
Promotion of a human ecological approach to
sustainable development, international
organisation, professional body, present number of
members: 92 individuals and 3 corporate,
voluntary organisation, registered charity (charity
number 272018), research organisation.
Joint government and non-government
composition.

Subject coverage:
Human ecology, Commonwealth, human
settlements, poverty programmes, health
education, sustainable fisheries.

Non-library collection catalogue:
All or part available in-house

Library catalogue:
All or part available in-house

Printed publications:
Bibliographies, books and papers to purchase
CHEC Journal (free to members)
CHEC Points (free to all)
Conference Proceedings
Order printed publications from: from CHEC

Publications list:
Available in print

Access to staff:
Contact by letter, by telephone, by fax and by e-
mail. Appointment necessary.
Hours: Mon to Thu, 1030 to 1700

Access to building, collection or gallery:
By Appointment

Access for disabled people:
No access

Links with:
Commission on Sustainable Development
Economic and Social Council for Asia and the
Pacific (ESCAP)
IUCN Education Commission
UN Centre for Human Settlements
UN ECOSOC
UN Environment Programme (UNEP)
UNESCO Education
World Health Organisation (WHO)

COMMONWEALTH JEWISH COUNCIL

Acronym or abbreviation: CJC

BCM Box 6871, London, WC1N 3XX

Tel: 020 7222 2120
Fax: 020 7222 1781
E-mail: info@cjc.org.uk

Website:
http://www.cjc.org.uk
Members, projects, contacts with the
Commonwealth, about CJC, etc.

Enquiries:
Enquiries to: Administrator

Founded:
1982

Organisation type and purpose:
Registered charity (charity number 287564).
Commonwealth Jewish Trust.
CJC is the political arm of the organisation that
provides the Commonwealth link between
countries, high commissioners and ambassadors.

Subject coverage:
Commonwealth, Jewish communities, Judaism.

Printed publications:
Newsletter (2 times a year)

Access to staff:
Contact by letter, by telephone, by fax and by e-
mail
Hours: Mon to Fri, 0915 to 1745

Access to building, collection or gallery:
No access other than to staff

COMMONWEALTH LOCAL GOVERNMENT FORUM

Acronym or abbreviation: CLGF

16A Northumberland Avenue, London, WC2N
5AP

Tel: 020 7389 1490
Fax: 020 7389 1499
E-mail: linfo@clgf.org.uk

Website:
http://www.clgf.org.uk

Founded:
1995

Organisation type and purpose:
International organisation, local government body,
membership association, present number of
members: 160.

Subject coverage:
Local government in Commonwealth countries.

Special visitor services:
Only for CLGF members.

**Museum or gallery collection, archive, or library
special collection:**
Documentation on local government in
Commonwealth countries

Non-library collection catalogue:
All or part available in-house and in print

Library catalogue:
All or part available online

Printed publications:
Annual Report (annually)
Bulletin (quarterly)
Reports on aspects of local government in
Commonwealth Countries (available free to
members)
Commonwealth Local Government Handbook

Electronic and video publications:
CLGF E-news

Publications list:
Available online and in print

Access to staff:
Contact by letter, by fax and by e-mail
Hours: Mon to Fri, 0900 to 1700

Access to building, collection or gallery:
Prior appointment required

COMMONWEALTH PARLIAMENTARY ASSOCIATION

Acronym or abbreviation: CPA

Suite 700, Westminster House, 7 Millbank, London,
SW1P 3JA

Tel: 020 7799 1460
Fax: 020 7222 6073
E-mail: hq.sec@cpahq.org

Website:
http://www.cpahq.org
Aims of the organisation, publications,
subscriptions, conference information, newsletters
and latest news.

Enquiries:
Enquiries to: Secretary General

Founded:
1911

Organisation type and purpose:
International organisation, professional body
(membership is by qualification), present number
of members: 14,000, registered charity, training
organisation, research organisation, publishing
house.
To promote knowledge and education about the
constitutional, legislative, economic, social and
cultural systems within a parliamentary
democratic framework, with particular reference to
countries of the Commonwealth.

Subject coverage:
Parliaments of the Commonwealth (membership,
practice and procedures etc), constitutions,
standing orders, names of Commonwealth MPs,
elections.

**Museum or gallery collection, archive, or library
special collection:**
Books on parliamentary practice and procedure,
the Commonwealth, Commonwealth
constitutions and standing orders
PA publications, including specialist monographs

Printed publications:
The Parliamentarian (quarterly journal, annual
subscription: UK £28; worldwide £36 air mail,
£30 surface)

Electronic and video publications:
The Commonwealth Way (video, £10)
The Parliamentarian (on microfilm, from
University Microfilms International, 300 North
Zeeb Road, Ann Arbor, Michigan, USA)

Publications list:
Available online

Access to staff:
Contact by letter, by telephone, by fax, by e-mail
and via website. Appointment necessary. Non-
members charged.
Hours: Fri, 0900 to 1600

Access to building, collection or gallery:
Prior appointment required

Access for disabled people:
Ramped entry

Has:
branches in more than 165 national, state,
provincial and territorial parliaments in the
Commonwealth

COMMONWEALTH PHARMACEUTICAL ASSOCIATION

Acronym or abbreviation: CPA

1 Lambeth High Street, London, SE1 7JN

Tel: 020 7572 2364
Fax: 020 7572 2508

Website:
http://www.rpsgb.org.uk/international.html
Background and objectives of CPA.

Enquiries:
Enquiries to: Administrator

Founded:
1970

Organisation type and purpose:
Membership association (membership is by subscription), present number of members: 600. An association of professional pharmaceutical bodies and personal members from 39 Commonwealth countries.
To establish, develop and maintain the highest possible professional standards of pharmacy throughout the Commonwealth in order to achieve better health outcomes within communities.

Subject coverage:
Pharmacy.

Access to staff:
Contact by telephone, by fax and by e-mail.
Appointment necessary.
Hours: Mon to Fri, 0900 to 1700

Access for disabled people:
Ramped entry, toilet facilities

COMMONWEALTH SCIENCE COUNCIL

Formal name: Commonwealth Science Council
Acronym or abbreviation: CSC

Marlborough House, Pall Mall, London, SW1Y 5HX

Tel: 020 7747 6220/6219
Fax: 020 7839 6174
E-mail: science@commonwealth.int

Website:
http://www.commonwealthknowledge.net

Enquiries:
Enquiries to: Information Officer
Direct tel: 020 7747 6219
Direct e-mail: t.ruredzo@commonwealth.int

Organisation type and purpose:
International organisation.
The CSC is an innovative, creative and proactive organisation that seeks to leverage the science and technology capability in the public and industry domain within the Commonwealth through networking of both knowledge and finance, using modern information technologies to facilitate the application of S&T by member countries for sustainable economic, environmental, social and cultural development.

Subject coverage:
Science and technology.

Printed publications:
Commonwealth Scientist (newsletter, quarterly)
Knowledge Networking for Development: Science and Technology for the Millennium
Paths to Prosperity – Science and technology in the Commonwealth 1999/2000
Biodiversity in Small States
Biodiversity Management Procedures Guide
Information Pack
Order printed publications from: The Publications Unit
tel: 020 7747 6342, fax: 020 7839 9081

Access to staff:
Contact by e-mail
Hours: Mon to Fri, 0900 to 1700

Access to building, collection or gallery:
Prior appointment required
Hours: Mon to Fri, 0930 to 1730

Access for disabled people:
Level entry, toilet facilities

COMMONWEALTH SECRETARIAT

Marlborough House, Pall Mall, London, SW1Y 5HX

Tel: 020 7747 6164
Fax: 020 7747 6168
E-mail: library@commonwealth.int

Website:
http://www.thecommonwealth.org
Publications, information on the Commonwealth.

Enquiries:
Enquiries to: Head of Library and Archives
Other contacts: Archivist and Records Management Officer

Founded:
1965

Organisation type and purpose:
International organisation.

Subject coverage:
Commonwealth, development, trade, agriculture, statistics, economics, technology, industry, politics, education, women and development, youth, health and science.

Museum or gallery collection, archive, or library special collection:
Collection of Commonwealth Secretariat Publications
Commonwealth Secretariat Archive, released after 30 years

Library catalogue:
All or part available in-house

Printed publications:
Publications catalogue available online
Order printed publications from: Publications Manager, Communications and Public Affairs Division, Commonwealth Secretariat; tel. 020 7747 6342; fax 020 7839 9081

Publications list:
Available online and in print

Access to staff:
Contact by letter, by telephone, by e-mail and in person. Appointment necessary.
Hours: Mon to Fri, 0915 to 1700

Access for disabled people:
Access to all public areas, toilet facilities
Special comments: Lift from ground floor.

COMMONWEALTH WAR GRAVES COMMISSION

Acronym or abbreviation: CWGC

2 Marlow Road, Maidenhead, Berkshire, SL6 7DX

Tel: 01628 634221
Fax: 01628 771208
E-mail: general.enq@cwgc.org

Website:
http://www.cwgc.org
The Debt of Honour Register, information on the task of the Commission, the world-wide commitment, country membership, commissioners, areas and agencies, publications, services and comments.

Enquiries:
Enquiries to: Enquiries Section
Direct tel: 01628 507200
Direct e-mail: casualty.enq@cwgc.org

Founded:
1917

Formerly called:
Imperial War Graves Commission (year of change 1964)

Organisation type and purpose:
An international organisation, the Commonwealth War Graves Commission was established by Royal Charter of 21 May 1919, the provisions of which were amended and extended by a Supplemental Charter of 8 June 1964.
Its duties are to mark and maintain the graves of the members of the forces of the Commonwealth who died in the two world wars, to build and maintain memorials to the dead whose graves are unknown, and to keep records and registers.

Subject coverage:
The Commission's work is guided by four fundamental principals:

1) that each of the dead should be commemorated individually by name either on the headstone on the grave or by an inscription on a memorial;
2) that the headstones and memorials should be permanent;
3) that the headstones should be uniform;
4) that there should be no distinction made on account of military or civil rank, race or creed.

Information services:
media@cwgc.org

Education services:
education@cwgc.org

Non-library collection catalogue:
All or part available in-house

Library catalogue:
All or part available in-house

Printed publications:
Annual Report
Cemetery and memorial registers: the dead of the two world wars
Information sheets and booklets pertaining to the Commission's work
Education information sheets and booklets
Michelin Road Atlas: Cemeteries & Memorials in Belgium & Northern France – a compact road atlas with maps in Michelin's 1:200,000 series, overprinted to show the locations of each Commonwealth cemetery and memorial in Belgium and Northern France
Remembered – published to mark the Commission's 90th anniversary in 2007; features images by award-winning photographer Brian Harris, previously unreleased photographs from the Commission's own archives and a new history of the CWGC
Remembering Fromelles – an in-depth look at the first war cemetery built by the CWGC in 50 years; dedicated on 19 July 2010
The Unending Vigil – a history of the CWGC by Philip Longworth
Recipients of the Victoria & George Cross – a 96-page book that details the 374 recipients of the Victoria Cross and George Cross whose graves and memorials are in the Commission's care.
Order printed publications from: website: http://www.cwgc.org

Electronic and video publications:
A Debt of Honour – this DVD seeks to illustrate how the war cemeteries and memorials came to be established in some 150 countries throughout the world and how, through its work, the Commission records and honours those who died. Commentary by Michael Palin. This DVD also includes two short remembrance presentations – One Boy and Some Go Early, aimed at Upper Primary and Secondary school students
The Glory Days: Football in times of war
Order electronic and video publications from: website: http://www.cwgc.org

Publications list:
Available online and in print

Access to staff:
Contact by letter, by telephone, by fax, by e-mail and via website. Appointment necessary.
Hours: Mon to Thu, 0830 to 1700; Fri, 0830 to 1630

Access to building, collection or gallery:
Prior appointment required

Access for disabled people:
Level entry, toilet facilities

Branches:
Outer Area Office (not Europe or the Mediterranean)
  2 Marlow Road, Maidenhead, Berkshire, SL6 7DX; tel: 01628 634221; fax: 01628 771643; e-mail: outer.area@cwgc.org
United Kingdom Area Office
  Jenton Road, Sydenham, Leamington Spa, Warwickshire, CV31 1XS; tel: 01926 330137; fax: 01926 456595; e-mail: ukaoffice@cwgc.org

COMMONWEALTH YOUTH EXCHANGE COUNCIL

Acronym or abbreviation: CYEC

7 Lion Yard, Tremadoc Road, London, SW4 7NQ

Tel: 020 7498 6151
Fax: 020 7720 5403
E-mail: mail@cyec.org.uk

Website:
http://www.cyec.org.uk

Enquiries:
Enquiries to: Chief Executive
Other contacts: Grants and Administration Officer for Youth Exchange Information Enquiries

Founded:
1970

Organisation type and purpose:
Voluntary organisation, registered charity (charity number 1086375).
National voluntary youth organisation.
Education – informal (young people's social and personal education via youth work) via international youth exchange projects.
Not able to help individuals interested in an international experience or overseas applicants.

Subject coverage:
Group youth exchanges between Britain and other Commonwealth countries for young people aged 16–25 years.

Printed publications:
Journeys Inward Journey Outward (personal record achievement for youth exchange groups)
Contact (Handbook)
Leaflets and Guidelines (free)
Crossing Frontiers (workbook for youth exchange groups)
Commonwealth (4 poster set)

Publications list:
Available in print

Access to staff:
Contact by letter, by telephone, by fax and by e-mail. Appointment necessary.
Hours: Mon to Fri, 1100 to 1800
Special comments: Send stamped addressed envelope.

Access to building, collection or gallery:
Hours: Mon to Fri, 1000 to 1700

Branch Office:
CYEC Scotland
Development Officer, 30 Wyvis Crescent, Conon Bridge, Dingwall, Highland, IV7 8BZ; tel: 01349 861110; fax: 01349 861110; e-mail: cyecscotland@btinternet.com

COMMUNICATIONS POLICY PROGRAMME

Acronym or abbreviation: CPJRU

City University, Northampton Square, London, EC1V 0HB

Tel: 020 7040 8908
Fax: 020 7040 8558
E-mail: socscipg@city.ac.uk

Website:
http://www.city.ac.uk/human/sociology
http://www.staff.city.ac.uk/p.iosifidis

Enquiries:
Enquiries to: Director
Direct e-mail: p.iosifidis@city.ac.uk

Founded:
1984

Formerly called:
Communications Policy and Journalism Research Unit, Communications Policy Centre

Organisation type and purpose:
University department or institute.

Subject coverage:
Communications Policy; New Media Technologies; Information Society.

Access to staff:
Contact by letter, by telephone, by fax and by e-mail
Hours: Mon to Fri, 0900 to 1700

COMMUNIST PARTY OF BRITAIN

Acronym or abbreviation: CPB

BCM Box 928, London WC1N 3XX

Tel: 020 7254 8444
E-mail: office@cpgb.org.uk

Website:
http://www.cpgb.org.uk

Enquiries:
Enquiries to: Organiser

Founded:
1998

Formerly called:
Communist Party of Great Britain (CPGB) (year of change 1991)

Organisation type and purpose:
National organisation (membership is by subscription), present number of members: 1350.
Political party.

Printed publications:
Pamphlets:
British Road to Socialism New 7th Edition 2001 (£2.50 inc. p&p)
Case for Trade Unions (£2.50 inc. p&p)
Women & Class (Davis M, 1999, £2.50 inc. p&p)
What We Stand For, introduction to the CPB (2001, £1.50 inc. p&p)
Stop the War – Terror and the New World Order (2001, £1.50 inc. p&p)
Books:
Fashioning a New World (Davis M, 2001, £8 inc. p&p)
The Communist Party of Great Britain – An historical analysis to 1941 (Murray A, £5 inc. p&p)
Communist Review (journal, quarterly, £2 inc. p&p)
The African Resource Wars of the 21st Century (Dreapir L, £1.50 inc. p&p)
The National Question (Greaves C D, 2002, £1.20 inc. p&p)
Challenge – Journal of the Young Communist League (quarterly, £1.30 inc. p&p)

Publications list:
Available in print

Access to staff:
Contact by letter, by telephone, by fax and by e-mail
Hours: Mon to Fri, 0900 to 1700

Access for disabled people:
Parking provided, access to all public areas

COMMUNITIES AND LOCAL GOVERNMENT AND DEPARTMENT FOR TRANSPORT

Acronym or abbreviation: CLG/DfT

Information Centre, Eland House, Bressenden Place, London, SW1E 5DU

Tel: 0303 444 1111

Website:
http://www.dft.gov.uk
Department for Transport web site.
http://www.communities.gov.uk
Communities and Local Government web site.

Founded:
2002

Organisation type and purpose:
National government body.

Subject coverage:
Provides an internal service to policy divisions of Communities and Local Government and Department for Transport. Subject areas cover devolution and the regions, housing, homelessness, urban policy, planning, local and regional government, neighbourhood renewal, social exclusion, rent assessment panels and fire services. For DfT: railways and aviation, transport strategy, roads, local transport, maritime transport.

Non-library collection catalogue:
All or part available in-house

Library catalogue:
All or part available in-house

Printed publications:
Order printed publications from: CLG and DfT Publications, Cambertown Ltd, Cambertown House, Goldthorpe Industrial Estate, Goldthorpe, Rotherham, S63 9BL; tel: 0300 123 1124

Publications list:
Available online

Access to staff:
Contact by letter, by telephone, by e-mail and via website. Appointment necessary.
Hours: Mon to Fri, 0900 to 1700

COMMUNITIES SCOTLAND

Thistle House, 91 Haymarket Terrace, Edinburgh, EH12 5HE

Tel: 0131 313 0044
Fax: 0131 313 2680

Website:
http://www.communitiesscotland.gov.uk
Complete picture of Scottish Homes and its activities, including same day publication of news releases, latest publications, etc.

Enquiries:
Enquiries to: Librarian
Direct tel: 0131 479 5016
Direct e-mail: johnstoner@communitiesscotland.gov.uk

Founded:
2001

Formerly called:
Housing Corporation in Scotland, Scottish Special Housing Association; Scottish Homes (year of change 1989–2001)

Organisation type and purpose:
National government body.
The national housing agency for Scotland.

Subject coverage:
Wide-ranging information on all aspects of housing in Scotland, including joint funding arrangements, establishment and funding of housing associations and housing co-operatives; approval of landlords; urban renewal; housing management; modernisation and rehabilitation techniques; private developers; rural housing.

Library catalogue:
All or part available in-house

Printed publications:
Annual Report
Dozens of Newsletters on specific subjects
Home News
Research Reports
Strategic Plan

Access to staff:
Contact by letter, by telephone and by e-mail.
Appointment necessary.
Hours: Mon to Thu, 0830 to 1700; Fri, 0830 to 1630

Access to building, collection or gallery:
Prior appointment required

Access for disabled people:
Ramped entry, toilet facilities

COMMUNITY ACTION NORTHUMBERLAND

Acronym or abbreviation: CAN

Tower Buildings, 9 Oldgate, Morpeth, Northumberland, NE61 1PY

Tel: 01670 517178
Fax: 01670 511400
E-mail: info@ca-north.org.uk

Website:
http://www.ca-north.org.uk

Enquiries:
Enquiries to: Director
Direct e-mail: davidfrancis@ca-north.org.uk

Founded:
1951

Formerly called:
Northumberland Rural Community Council; (year of change 1974); Community Council of Northumberland (year of change 2007)

Organisation type and purpose:
Voluntary organisation, registered charity (charity number 224798). Community development and voluntary sector support.

Subject coverage:
Voluntary organisations, community initiatives and parish councils in Northumberland. Information needed by these groups e.g. grant aid, law, project development, working together, further sources of help.

Printed publications:
Northumberland Community News (6 times a year, free)
Various guides, directories and research reports

Access to staff:
Contact by letter, by telephone, by fax, by e-mail and in person. Appointment necessary.
Hours: Mon to Thu, 0900 to 1700; Fri, 0900 to 1630

Affiliated to:
ACRE; NAVCA
Voluntary Organisations Network North East

COMMUNITY AND DISTRICT NURSING ASSOCIATION

Acronym or abbreviation: CDNA

32–38 Uxbridge Road, Ealing, London, W5 2BS

Tel: 020 8280 5342
Fax: 020 8280 5341
E-mail: info@cdnaonline.org

Website:
http://www.cdna.tvu.ac.uk

Enquiries:
Enquiries to: Chairman
Other contacts: Professional Officer for information on professional and clinical issues.

Founded:
1971

Organisation type and purpose:
Professional body, trade union (membership is by subscription), present number of members: 5500.

Access to staff:
Contact by letter, by telephone, by fax, by e-mail and via website
Hours: Mon to Fri, 0900 to 1700

COMMUNITY AND YOUTH WORKERS' UNION, THE

Acronym or abbreviation: CYWU

302 The Argent Centre, 60 Frederick Street, Birmingham, B31 3HS

Tel: 0121 233 3344
Fax: 0121 344 3345
E-mail: kerry@cywu.org.uk

Website:
http://www.cywu.org.uk

Enquiries:
Enquiries to: Administrator
Direct e-mail: kerry.jenkins@unitetheunion.org

Founded:
1938

Organisation type and purpose:
Trade union (membership is by subscription), present number of members: 4500.

Subject coverage:
Community and youth work.

Printed publications:
Rapport (tabloid journal, fortnightly)
Youth Work and Community Work into the twenty-first Century
Planning for a Sufficient Youth Service
The Struggle for Statutory Youth Service Provision
Employment Practice and Policies in Youth and Community Work (£16.95, available from Russell House Publishing)
Health and Safety in Youth and Community Work – A Resource Manual
Managing Aggression and Violence – A Model for Youth and Community Centres of legal compliance, safe working practices and good personal safety habits for staff (1996, £19.50 available from Pepar Publications)
Order printed publications from: CYWU

Pepar Publications
The Gatehouse, 112 Park Hill Road, Harborne, Birmingham, B17 0HD
Russell House Publishing Limited
4 St George's House, Uplyme Road Business Park, Lyme Regis, DT7 3LS

Publications list:
Available in print

Access to staff:
Contact by e-mail
Hours: Mon to Fri, 0900 to 1700

Affiliated to:
GFTU
TUC

COMMUNITY COMPOSTING NETWORK

Acronym or abbreviation: CCN

67 Alexandra Road, Sheffield, South Yorkshire, S2 3EE

Tel: 0114 258 0483
Fax: 0114 258 0483
E-mail: info@communitycompost.org

Website:
http://www.communitycompost.org

Enquiries:
Enquiries to: Co-ordinator

Founded:
1995

Organisation type and purpose:
National organisation, membership association (membership is by subscription), present number of members: 200, voluntary organisation.
Provides advice and support to existing and 'would be' community composting projects across the UK.

Printed publications:
The Growing Heap (newsletter, 4 times a year, free to members)
Community Composting Guide (£15 members, £55, non members, incl. p&p)

Access to staff:
Contact by letter, by telephone, by fax, by e-mail and via website. Appointment necessary.
Hours: Mon to Fri, 0900 to 1700

COMMUNITY COUNCIL FOR BERKSHIRE

Acronym or abbreviation: CCB

27 Eldon Square, Reading, Berkshire, RG1 4DP

Tel: 0118 961 2000
Fax: 0118 961 2600
E-mail: admin@ccberks.co.uk

Website:
http://www.ccberks.org.uk

Enquiries:
Enquiries to: PA to Chief Executive

Founded:
1973

Organisation type and purpose:
Voluntary organisation, registered charity (charity number 1056367).
To enable all people, communities and organisations to work better by working together.

Subject coverage:
Information on voluntary sector support in Berkshire, rural communities, funding advice, community buildings information and advice service, village shops, rural disadvantage, community developments, community training, training on how to connect with hard-to-reach groups, etc.

Printed publications:
Amongst many are:
Community (newsletter, free to members)
Making the Links Best Practice Guide
East Berkshire Community Transport Travel Guide

Access to staff:
Contact by letter, by telephone, by fax and by e-mail. Appointment necessary.
Hours: Mon to Fri, 0900 to 1700

Access to building, collection or gallery:
Prior appointment required

COMMUNITY COUNCIL OF DEVON

Acronym or abbreviation: CCD

School Huts, County Hall, Topsham Road, Exeter, Devon, EX2 4QB

Tel: 01392 383443
Fax: 01392 382062
E-mail: info@devonrcc.org.uk

Website:
http://www.devonrcc.org.uk
General information, reports, corporate plan, directions, links.

Enquiries:
Enquiries to: Chief Executive
Other contacts: (1) Parish Councils Officer (2) Playing Fields Officer for (1) information on Parish Councils (2) information and advice on playing fields.

Founded:
1961

Organisation type and purpose:
Voluntary organisation, registered charity (charity number 1074047).
Rural community council.

Subject coverage:
Village halls in Devon, Parish Council contacts in Devon, Charities Information Bureau, Devon Playing Fields Association, information on sources of funding, community development, parish appraisals, children's play in Devon.

Printed publications:
Annual Report
Village Green (newsletter, quarterly)

Access to staff:
Contact by letter, by telephone, by e-mail and in person
Hours: Mon to Fri, 0900 to 1700

COMMUNITY COUNCIL OF SHROPSHIRE

Acronym or abbreviation: CCS

continued overleaf

1 College Hill, Shrewsbury, Shropshire, SY1 1LT

Tel: 01743 360641
Fax: 01743 233335
E-mail: ccs@collegehill.org.uk

Website:
http://www.collegehill.org.uk
Detailed information about the Council's services;
latest issue of the quarterly newsletter 'Buzz'.

Enquiries:
Enquiries to: Director

Founded:
1961

Organisation type and purpose:
Registered charity (charity number 218783),
training organisation.

Subject coverage:
Advice for voluntary organisations, especially in
rural areas, rural transport, rural housing,
promotion of volunteering, funding, training,
charities, parish councils.

Printed publications:
Annual Report
Information sheets on all aspects of village life,
from 'Public Entertainment Licences' to 'Coping
with VAT on Fuel and Power' (£1 per copy inc.
p&p)

Publications list:
Available in print

Access to staff:
Contact by letter, by telephone, by fax, by e-mail
and in person
Hours: Mon to Fri, 0900 to 1700

Member of:
Federation of Rural Community Councils
William House, Skipton Road, Skelton, York,
YO3 6XW

COMMUNITY DEVELOPMENT FOUNDATION

Acronym or abbreviation: CDF

Unit 5, Angel Gate, 320–326 City Road, London,
EC1V 2PT

Tel: 020 7833 1772
Fax: 020 7837 6584
E-mail: admin@cdf.org.uk

Website:
http://www.cdf.org.uk

Enquiries:
Enquiries to: Information and Marketing Officer
Direct e-mail: tessa.norton@cdf.org.uk

Founded:
1968

Formerly called:
Community Projects Foundation

Organisation type and purpose:
National government body, voluntary
organisation, registered charity (charity number
306130), consultancy, research organisation.
Promotion of community development.

Subject coverage:
Community development, community work, social
policy, environment and planning, housing, health,
education, social welfare, local government,
economic development, employment and
unemployment, voluntary sector; youth work,
ethnic and racial issues, poverty, regeneration,
social inclusion and capacity building.

Non-library collection catalogue:
All or part available in-house

Library catalogue:
All or part available in-house

Printed publications:
Community Currents: the Community
Development Information Digest (6 times a year,
£20.90 a year)

Community Groups Handbook (Pearse M and
Smith J, 1990)

Electronic and video publications:
CommunityWISE (CD-ROM)

Publications list:
Available online and in print

Access to staff:
Contact by letter, by telephone, by fax, by e-mail
and via website. Appointment necessary.
Hours: Mon to Fri, 0900 to 1700

Access to building, collection or gallery:
Prior appointment required

Access for disabled people:
Special comments: No wheelchair access.

Supported by:
central and local government

COMMUNITY FIRST

Wyndhams, St Joseph's Place, Devizes, Wiltshire,
SN10 1DD

Tel: 01380 722475
Fax: 01380 728476
E-mail: reception@communityfirst.org.uk

Enquiries:
Enquiries to: Director

Founded:
1965

Organisation type and purpose:
Membership association (membership is by
subscription), voluntary organisation, registered
charity (charity number 288117).
Working in partnership with communities and
funders to encourage and support social, economic
and environmental initiatives in Wiltshire and
Swindon.

Subject coverage:
Rural community development, village halls,
sports clubs, children's play, parish and town
councils, funding and support for voluntary
groups, rural projects and services, rural housing,
community transport, rural policy, rural economic
development.

Printed publications:
Leaflets and other publications including:
Annual Report
Newsletter

Publications list:
Available in print

Access to staff:
Contact by letter, by telephone and by e-mail.
Appointment necessary.
Hours: Mon to Thu, 0900 to 1700; Fri, 0900 to 1600

Access for disabled people:
Parking provided, ramped entry, toilet facilities

Member of:
ACRE Network of Rural Community Councils

COMMUNITY FIRST IN HEREFORDSHIRE AND WORCESTERSHIRE

141 Church Street, Malvern, Worcestershire, WR14
2AN

Tel: 01684 573334
Fax: 01684 573367
E-mail: info@comfirst.org.uk

Website:
http://www.comfirst.org.uk
Information about the organisation's work.

Enquiries:
Enquiries to: Chief Executive Officer

Founded:
1975

Formerly called:
Rural Community Council; Community Council of
Hereford and Worcester (year of change 2001)

Organisation type and purpose:
Voluntary organisation, registered charity (charity
number 703072).
Sub-regional development agency working with
communities and voluntary organisations in
Herefordshire and Worcestershire.
Mission – To build better communities.

Subject coverage:
Rural transport initiatives, learning and skills in
the voluntary sector, information and training for
voluntary sector, community resource centres,
village halls in Herefordshire and Worcestershire;
ICT support for voluntary sector, business advice,
social enterprise support.

Printed publications:
Newsline (every other month, free to members)

Publications list:
Available in print

Access to staff:
Contact by letter, by telephone, by fax, by e-mail
and via website. Appointment necessary.
Hours: Mon to Fri, 0900 to 1700

Access to building, collection or gallery:
Prior appointment required

Access for disabled people:
Parking provided, ramped entry, toilet facilities

Other offices:
Community First – Hereford Office
41a Bridge Street, Hereford; tel: 01432 267820

COMMUNITY FOUNDATION FOR NORTHERN IRELAND

Acronym or abbreviation: NIVT

City Link, Albert House, Belfast, BT12 4HQ

Tel: 028 9024 5927
Fax: 028 9032 9839
E-mail: info@communityfoundation.org

Enquiries:
Enquiries to: Director

Founded:
1979

Organisation type and purpose:
Registered charity (charity number XN45242).

Access to staff:
Contact by letter
Hours: Mon to Fri, 0900 to 1700

COMMUNITY FOUNDATION NETWORK

Arena House, 66–68 Pentonville Road, London, N1
9HS

Tel: 020 7713 9326
Fax: 020 7713 9327
E-mail: network@communityfoundations.org.uk

Website:
http://www.communityfoundations.org.uk

Enquiries:
Enquiries to: Director

Founded:
1991

Formerly called:
Association of Community Trusts and Foundations
(ACTAF) (year of change 1999)

Organisation type and purpose:
Membership association (membership is by
subscription), present number of members: 68,
voluntary organisation, registered charity (charity
number 1004630).
Membership is restricted to active community
foundations, although any interested body may
subscribe as an associate.

Promotion, support and development of
community foundations throughout the UK.

Subject coverage:
Community foundation development and
management.

Trade and statistical information:
Fund development and grant-making in
community foundations in UK. Advice on the
development of community foundations.

Library catalogue:
All or part available in-house

Printed publications:
A number of free information sheets
Occasional reports – most recent is The Price of
Giving, Diana Leat, 2002, £10
Newsletter (3 issues a year, annual subscription
£25)

Publications list:
Available online and in print

Access to staff:
Contact by letter, by telephone, by fax, by e-mail
and via website. Appointment necessary.
Hours: Mon to Fri, 0900 to 1700

COMMUNITY LINCS

The Old Mart, Church Lane, Sleaford, Lincolnshire,
NG34 7DF

Tel: 01529 302466
Fax: 01529 414267
E-mail: office@communitylincs.com

Website:
http://www.communitylincs.com
General information, services, etc.

Enquiries:
Enquiries to: Chief Executive's PA
Direct e-mail: teresa.palmer@communitylincs.com

Founded:
1927

Organisation type and purpose:
Voluntary organisation, registered charity (charity
number 1046569). Rural Community
Development.

Subject coverage:
Rural development in Lincolnshire.

Printed publications:
Annual Report (£1)
Grants for rural projects available from CCL (free)
Rural Links (magazine, 2 a year)

Publications list:
Available in print

Access to staff:
Contact by letter, by telephone, by fax and by e-
mail. Appointment necessary.
Hours: Mon to Fri, 0900 to 1700

Access for disabled people:
Ramped entry, access to all public areas, toilet
facilities

Affiliated to:
Federation of Rural Community Councils

Connections with:
Lincolnshire Association of Local Councils
Lincolnshire Playing Fields Association

COMMUNITY MATTERS

12–20 Baron Street, Islington, London, N1 9LL

Tel: 020 7837 7887
Fax: 020 7278 9253

Enquiries:
Enquiries to: Chief Executive
Other contacts: Performance Improvement &
Information Manager

Founded:
1945

Formerly called:
National Federation of Community Organisations
(NFCO)

Organisation type and purpose:
Membership association (membership is by
subscription), present number of members: 1500
member organisations, voluntary organisation,
registered charity (charity number 1002383),
training organisation, consultancy, research
organisation, publishing house.
To support and help develop local community
groups and associations and make sure their
interests are represented locally and nationally.

Subject coverage:
Good management of charities and community
organisations; managing community activities;
managing social contractual relations; managing
community premises, legislation affecting charities
and voluntary organisations managing buildings.

Printed publications:
Annual Report and accounts
Community (magazine, quarterly, £10 a year)
Community Start Up: How to start a community
group and keep it going (£9.95)
How to Manage Your Money, if you have any
Information Sheets (65 titles; single copies free to
some members)
Law Monitoring Group Bulletin (quarterly, £10 a
year)
Managing Your Community Building
Occupying Community Premises
Organising for a Better Community

Electronic and video publications:
Model Constitution for a Community Association
(book and disc)
Occupying Community Premises (book, Dawson J,
and disc)

Publications list:
Available in print

Access to staff:
Contact by letter, by telephone, by fax and by e-
mail. Appointment necessary. Non-members
charged.
Hours: Mon to Fri, 0900 to 1700

Affiliated to:
Community Sector Coalition
International Federation of Settlements
National Council for Voluntary Organisations

COMMUNITY MEDIA ASSOCIATION

Acronym or abbreviation: CMA

15 Paternoster Row, Sheffield, South Yorkshire, S1
2BX

Tel: 0114 279 5219
Fax: 0114 279 8976
E-mail: admin@commedia.org.uk

Website:
http://www.commedia.org.uk
Airflash (articles from), information sheets,
publication list, membership application form,
policy papers, project descriptions, fundraising
contacts.

Enquiries:
Enquiries to: Financial/Office Manager

Founded:
1983

Formerly called:
Community Radio Association (CRA) (year of
change 1997)

Organisation type and purpose:
National organisation, membership association
(membership is by subscription), present number
of members: 600, voluntary organisation, training
organisation, consultancy.
The CMA's primary purpose is to support the
development of local media projects for
community-based, creative and cultural
expression, community development, information

and entertainment. Media forms include
community radio, community TV, cable
broadcasting and multimedia on the internet.

Subject coverage:
Community Radio – general information on start
up, training, fundraising, consultancy, licence
application. Community media including TV, cable
and internet broadcasting.

**Museum or gallery collection, archive, or library
special collection:**
Airflash – Complete Set
Broadcast – Hard Copies Only
The Radio Magazine – Hard Copies Only

Non-library collection catalogue:
All or part available in-house and in print

Printed publications:
Airflash (magazine, quarterly)
CMA basic information pack which includes
publications list

Publications list:
Available online and in print

Access to staff:
Contact by letter, by telephone, by fax, by e-mail
and via website. Appointment necessary.
Hours: Mon to Fri, 0930 to 1730

Access to building, collection or gallery:
Prior appointment required
Hours: Mon to Fri, 0930 to 1730

Access for disabled people:
Access to all public areas, toilet facilities

Member organisation of:
World Association of Community Radio
Broadcasters (AMARC)
705 Bourget, bureau 100, Montreal, Quebec, H2C
2M6, Canada; tel: + 1 514 982 0351; fax: + 1 514
849 7129; website: http://www.amarc.org

COMMUNITY MUSIC WALES

Acronym or abbreviation: CMW

2 Leckwith Place, Canton, Cardiff, CF11 6QA

Tel: 029 2038 7620
Fax: 029 2023 3022
E-mail: admin@communitymusicwales.org.uk

Website:
http://www.communitymusicwales.org.uk

Enquiries:
Enquiries to: Administrator
Direct e-mail: gethin.evans@communitymusicwales
.org.uk

Founded:
1990

Organisation type and purpose:
Voluntary organisation, registered charity (charity
number 1009867), training organisation.
Concerned with developing music projects,
targeting groups of people who, through reasons
of disability or disadvantage, have little chance of
taking part in mainstream music activities.

Subject coverage:
Use of music technology in working with people
with disabilities, training for community
practitioners, role of music in working with young
people at risk.

**Museum or gallery collection, archive, or library
special collection:**
Small library of reference books

Access to staff:
Contact by letter, by telephone and by fax.
Appointment necessary.
Hours: Mon to Fri, 0900 to 1700

Access for disabled people:
Level entry, toilet facilities

COMMUNITY PRACTITIONERS AND HEALTH VISITING ASSOCIATION

Acronym or abbreviation: Unite/CPHVA

128 Theobald's Road, London, WC1X 8TN

Tel: 020 7611 2500
E-mail: infocphva@unitetheunion.org

Website:
http://www.unitetheunion.org/cphva
http://www.cphvabookshop.com
Publications online.

Founded:
1896

Organisation type and purpose:
National organisation, trade union, membership association (membership is by subscription). The CPHVA is an autonomous body of Unite. It gives information on professional issues and labour relations to members.

Subject coverage:
Health visiting, child care and development, community care of elderly and handicapped, health promotion, accident prevention, community nursing, clinical effectiveness, practice nursing, school nursing, mental health.

Information services:
Archives of the Association, available from The Wellcome Institute, 183 Euston Road, London, NW1 2BE.

Non-library collection catalogue:
All or part available online and in-house

Library catalogue:
All or part available online and in-house

Printed publications:
Annual Report
Community Practitioner (formerly Health Visitor, journal, monthly)
Action for Health
Action for School Health
Domestic Violence
Health Visitors, Working for Older People
Legal and Professional Issues in Child Protection
Men's Health
Postnatal Depression
Poverty and Public Health
Protecting the Child
Order printed publications from: McMillan Scott, Garrard House, 2–6 Homesdale Road, Bromley, Kent, BR2 2WL; tel. 020 8249 4454; fax 020 8289 7955

Publications list:
Available online and in print

Access to staff:
Contact by letter, by telephone, by fax, by e-mail, in person and via website. Access for members only.

Access to building, collection or gallery:
Special comments: Library and information service for members only.

Constituent part of:
Unite – The Union
128 Theobald's Road, London, WC1X 8TN; tel: 020 7611 2500; fax: 020 7611 2555; website: http://www.unitetheunion.org

COMMUNITY SELF BUILD AGENCY

Acronym or abbreviation: CSBA

Swale Foyer, Bridge Road, Sheerness, Kent, ME12 1RH

Tel: 01795 663 073
Fax: 01795 581 804
E-mail: info@communityselfbuildagency.org.uk

Website:
http://www.communityselfbuildagency.org.uk

Enquiries:
Enquiries to: Director

Direct e-mail: j.gillespie@communityselfbuildagency.org.uk

Founded:
1989

Organisation type and purpose:
National organisation.
To promote and advise on the development of community self build housing projects for those in housing need.

Subject coverage:
Community Self Build, where a group of local people in housing need come together to build homes for themselves.

Printed publications:
Basic publications available free
Other publications for sale direct

Publications list:
Available in print

Access to staff:
Contact by letter, by telephone and by e-mail. Appointment necessary.
Hours: Mon to Fri, 0930 to 1730

COMMUNITY SERVICE VOLUNTEERS

Acronym or abbreviation: CSV

237 Pentonville Road, London, N1 9NJ

Tel: 020 7278 6601
Fax: 020 7833 0149
E-mail: information@csv.org.uk

Website:
http://www.csv.org.uk

Founded:
1962

Organisation type and purpose:
National organisation, voluntary organisation, registered charity (charity number 291222).

Subject coverage:
Volunteering and employment and media training. Volunteering for young people, older people, employees and students. Mentoring and befriending, work with young offenders, social action broadcasting, citizenship in schools, the environment, Millennium Awards, Millennium Volunteers, advice and expertise in volunteer management. Make a Difference Day – the largest single day of volunteering – is co-ordinated by CSV.

Printed publications:
Annual Review
Information leaflets and pamphlets
CSV Reports On (series on volunteering issues)

Publications list:
Available online and in print

Access to staff:
Contact by letter, by telephone, by fax, by e-mail and via website
Hours: Mon to Fri, 0900 to 1730

Access for disabled people:
Level entry, toilet facilities

COMMUNITY TRANSPORT ASSOCIATION

Acronym or abbreviation: CTA

Highbank, Halton Street, Hyde, Cheshire, SK14 2NY

Tel: 0161 351 1475
Fax: 0161 351 7221
E-mail: info@ctauk.org

Website:
http://www.ctauk.org
Information on Community Transport Association Services, events and publications.

Enquiries:
Enquiries to: Advice Service
Direct tel: 0845 130 6195
Direct e-mail: advice@ctauk.org

Founded:
1978

Organisation type and purpose:
National organisation, advisory body, trade association (membership is by subscription), present number of members: 1,500, voluntary organisation, registered charity (charity no. 1002222), training organisation, consultancy. Representation and support services for non-profit transport sector.

Subject coverage:
All aspects of non-profit transport operations; service planning and development; accessibility and technical equipment; community development; employment and volunteering issues.

Information services:
Advice and information for operators of not-for-profit transport.

Museum or gallery collection, archive, or library special collection:
Historical records of CTA
Photograph library

Printed publications:
CTA journal, other advice leaflets and publications available through the website

Publications list:
Available online

Access to staff:
Contact by letter, by telephone, by fax and by e-mail
Hours: Mon to Fri, 0900 to 1700

COMPANIES HOUSE

Crown Way, Cardiff, CF14 3UZ

Tel: 030 3123 4500
Fax: 029 2038 0900
E-mail: enquiries@companieshouse.gov.uk

Website:
http://www.companieshouse.gov.uk
General Companies House information, products and services, press notices, complete set of guidance notes.

Enquiries:
Enquiries to: Cardiff Contact Centre
Direct e-mail: press@companieshouse.gov.uk

Founded:
1844

Organisation type and purpose:
National government body. To incorporate limited companies and to maintain a register of information on them for public information.

Subject coverage:
Information on limited companies entered in the register.

Printed publications:
Companies House Annual Report
Guide to Incorporation of Companies
Guide to Public Search
Guide to Registering Foreign Companies
Guide to Sensitive Words
Guide to Winding up
The Register: Customer newsletter
Enforcement Concordat (What You Can Expect from Companies House) and How to Complain and Who to Contact
Guide for Company Directors and Secretaries

Electronic and video publications:
Companies House Direct: Remote access online system
'Its the Company you Keep': Video aimed at explaining the need for compliance under the Companies Act
Directory of current names (CD-ROM)

Directory of change of name and dissolved companies (CD-ROM)

Access to staff:
Contact by letter, by telephone, by fax, by e-mail, in person and via website. All charged.
Hours: Mon to Fri, 0900 to 1700

Also at:
Companies House
London Search Room, 21 Bloomsbury Street, London, WC1B 3XD; tel: 0870 33 33 636; fax: 029 2038 0900

Executive Agency of:
Department for Business, Enterprise and Regulatory Reform

COMPANIES HOUSE SCOTLAND

37 Castle Terrace, Edinburgh, EH1 2EB

Tel: 0870 3333636
Fax: 0131 535 5820

Website:
http://www.companieshouse.gov.uk
About Companies House, notes for guidance, products and services. Press notices. At Head Office in Cardiff.

Enquiries:
Enquiries to: Registrar
Direct tel: 0131 535 5855
Direct fax: 0131 535 5879
Direct e-mail: jhenderson@companieshouse.gov.uk

Founded:
1856

Formerly called:
Companies Registration Office (year of change 1988)

Organisation type and purpose:
National government body, statutory body.
Executive agency within the Department of Trade and Industry.
To incorporate and dissolve limited companies, to examine and file documents relating to the Companies Act, to make this information available to the public.

Subject coverage:
Information on Scottish limited companies from statutory documents filed by the company directors, including financial information, details of directors, capital changes and members.

Printed publications:
A series of guidance notes (approx 20)

Microform publications:
Microfiche copies of Company records (£6.50 or £9.50 by post)

Electronic and video publications:
CH-Direct (online service)
CH-Monitor
CD-ROM
Magnetic tapes

Publications list:
Available in print

Access to staff:
Contact by letter, by telephone, by fax, by e-mail and via website. Appointment necessary.
Hours: Mon to Fri, 0900 to 1700
Special comments: Closed on Public and Bank Holidays.

Head Office:
Companies House
Crown Way, Cardiff, CF4 3UZ; tel: 0870 3333636; fax: 029 2038 0900

Other branches at:
Companies House
25 Queen Street, Leeds, LS 2TW; tel: 0113 233 8338; fax: 0113 2338335
Companies House
75 Mosley Street, Manchester, M2 2HR; tel: 0161 236 7500; fax: 0161 237 5258

Companies House
Central Library, Chamberlain Square, Birmingham, B3 3HQ; tel: 0121 233 9047; fax: 0121 233 9052
Companies House
7 West George Street, Glasgow, G2 1BQ; tel: 0141 221 5513; fax: 0141 221 3244

COMPANY OF DESIGNERS

232 Kempshott Lane, Basingstoke, Hampshire, RG22 5LR

Tel: 01256 472757
E-mail: mike-preedy@company-of-designers.co.uk

Enquiries:
Enquiries to: Managing Director

Founded:
1995

Organisation type and purpose:
Service industry, consultancy, publishing house.
Design consultancy.
Design for print: books, annual reports and accounts, brochures, leaflets, promotional literature

Access to staff:
Contact by letter, by telephone and by e-mail
Hours: Mon to Fri, 0900 to 1700

Access to building, collection or gallery:
Prior appointment required

COMPANY OF SECURITY PROFESSIONALS

Formal name: Worshipful Company of Security Professionals

Willowcroft, Old Forest Road, Winnersh, Wokingham, Berkshire, RG41 1HY

Tel: 01189 794675
Fax: 01189 794675
E-mail: clerk@wcosp.org

Website:
http://www.professionalsecurity.co.uk/company

Enquiries:
Enquiries to: Clerk
Direct e-mail: john@troon.wanadoo.co.uk

Organisation type and purpose:
To promote, support and encourage standards of excellence, integrity and honourable practice in conducting the profession of security practitioners and to aid societies and other organisations connected to the security profession.

Access to staff:
Contact by letter, by telephone and by e-mail

COMPANY OF WATERMEN AND LIGHTERMEN OF THE RIVER THAMES

Acronym or abbreviation: Company of Watermen

Watermen's Hall, 16 St Mary Hill, London, EC3R 8EF

Tel: 020 7283 2373
Fax: 020 7283 0477
E-mail: admin@watermenshall.org

Website:
http://www.watermenshall.org

Enquiries:
Enquiries to: Clerk

Founded:
1555

Organisation type and purpose:
Statutory body, membership association (membership is by election or invitation), present number of members: 400, voluntary organisation, training organisation.

A working guild promoting the work of watermen and lightermen on the River Thames, training apprentices and having charitable interests.

Subject coverage:
Watermen and Lightermen of the River Thames.

Library catalogue:
All or part available in-house

Printed publications:
History of the Company (4 vols, £75)
The Life and Charities of Thomas Mann (£5.50)
Thomas Doggetts Pictur'd Book (£7)
The History of the Company Vol 5 (forthcoming, £25)
Order printed publications from: Watermen's Hall

Publications list:
Available online and in print

Access to staff:
Contact by letter, by telephone, by fax, by e-mail, in person and via website. Appointment necessary.
Non-members charged.
Hours: Mon to Fri, 0900 to 1700

Access to building, collection or gallery:
By appointment
Hours: Mon to Fri, 0900 to 1700

Access for disabled people:
Accessible, lift to all floors
Special comments: Disabled access entrance at 16 St Mary-at-Hill

COMPASSIONATE FRIENDS, THE

Acronym or abbreviation: TCF

53 North Street, Bedminster, Bristol, BS3 1EN

Tel: 0845 120 3785
Fax: 0845 120 3786
E-mail: info@tcf.org.uk

Website:
http://www.tcf.org.uk

Enquiries:
Enquiries to: Helpline Worker

Founded:
1969

Organisation type and purpose:
National organisation, registered charity (charity number 1082335).
Offers support and friendship to bereaved parents and their families after the death of a child or children.

Subject coverage:
Support and friendship for bereaved parents and their families by those with a similar experience, including loss through suicide and murder.

Printed publications:
Newsletter (quarterly, available through membership scheme)
SIBBS (Support in Bereavement for Brothers and Sisters) (quarterly, newsletter)
Leaflets covering many aspects of bereavement including:
A father's grief
Grieving couples
When your adult child dies
When your child has been murdered
When your grandchild dies

Electronic and video publications:
Bereavement Services (video)

Publications list:
Available online and in print

Access to staff:
Contact by letter, by telephone, by fax, by e-mail and via website
Hours: Mon to Fri, 0900 to 1700

Subsidiary body:
Support in Bereavement for Brothers and Sisters (SIBBS)
at the same address

COMPETITION COMMISSION

Acronym or abbreviation: CC

Victoria House, Southampton Row, London, WC1B 4AD

Tel: 020 7271 0100
Fax: 020 7271 0367
E-mail: info@cc.gsi.gov.uk

Website:
http://www.competition-commission.org.uk

Enquiries:
Enquiries to: Information Centre Manager

Formerly called:
Monopolies and Mergers Commission (MMC) (year of change 1999)

Organisation type and purpose:
Statutory body.

Subject coverage:
Monopolies; mergers; industrial economics; competition policy.

Printed publications:
Information pack on the Commission

Publications list:
Available online and in print

Constituent part of:
Department for Business, Enterprise and Regulatory Reform (BERR)

COMPLEMENTARY THERAPISTS ASSOCIATION

PO Box 6955, Towcester, NN12 6WZ

Tel: 0845 202 2941
Fax: 0844 779 8898
E-mail: info@complementary.assoc.org.uk

Website:
http://www.complementary.assoc.org.uk

Enquiries:
Enquiries to: Administrator

Founded:
2003

Created by the merger of:
The International Therapists Examination Council (ITEC) and the Guild of Complementary Practitioners (GCP, which had previously merged with the Holistic Association of Reflexologists)

Organisation type and purpose:
National organisation, professional body (membership is by subscription, qualification). Member of the Parliamentary Group for Alternative & Complementary Medicine.
To maintain a national and international register of professional members, available to the general public and to other professionals.
To establish standards of professional training and qualification appropriate to the various disciplines.

Subject coverage:
Complementary medicine including aromatherapy, massage, reflexology, sports therapy, nutrition, Shiatsu, homoeopathy and Reiki.

Printed publications:
The Essential Guide to Hand and Foot Reflexology
The Theory and Practice
The Ancient Answers to Modern Ailments
Healing Points (quarterly magazine)
Reflexology: A Step-by-Step Guide
The Complete Book of Massage
Reflexology and the Intestinal Link, Chart
Reflexology and the Intestinal Link

Microform publications:
Lecture pack – Reflexology (Overhead transparencies)

Electronic and video publications:
The Timeless Art of Self Healing, video

Access to staff:
Contact by letter, by telephone, by fax, by e-mail and via website
Hours: Mon to Fri, 0900 to 1700

Affiliated to:
British School of Reflexology

Member of:
British Complementary Medicine Association

COMPLIANCE INSTITUTE

107 Barkby Road, Leicester LE4 9LG

Tel: 0116 246 1316
Fax: 0116 274 2239
E-mail: hlacey.compinst@nsconnect.co.uk

Website:
http://www.complianceinstitute.co.uk/
General information

Enquiries:
Enquiries to: Secretary

Founded:
1990

Formerly called:
UK Association of Compliance Officers (year of change 1997)

Organisation type and purpose:
Professional body (membership is by subscription).

Subject coverage:
Regulation – guide and assistance to Compliance staff.

Printed publications:
The Gazette (for purchase)

Access to staff:
Contact by letter
Hours: Mon to Fri, 0900 to 1700

COMPOSITES PROCESSING ASSOCIATION LIMITED

Acronym or abbreviation: CPA

Sarum Lodge, St Anne's Court, Talygarn, Pontyclun, Mid Glamorgan, CF72 9HH

Tel: 01443 228867
Fax: 01443 239083
E-mail: info@composites-proc-assoc.co.uk

Website:
http://www.composites-proc-assoc.co.uk
Full directory of products and services in UK composites industry. Service and product finder. Details of all member companies. Details of National and International Standards relating to composites. Links.

Enquiries:
Enquiries to: Association Secretary

Founded:
1989

Organisation type and purpose:
Trade association, consultancy.

Subject coverage:
Raw materials, manufacturing processes, applications, research and development activity, technical exchange, international activity as related to reinforced plastic composites.

Trade and statistical information:
National and international composites industry, market statistics, market sectors, data on composite shipments worldwide.

Access to staff:
Contact by letter, by telephone, by fax, by e-mail and via website. Appointment necessary.
Hours: Mon to Fri, 0900 to 1700

Member of:
American Composites Manufacturers Association Composites Fabricators Association, 1655 North Fort Myer Drive, Suite 510, Arlington, VA22209, USA; tel: + 1 703 525 0511; fax: + 1 703 525 0743; e-mail: info@acmanet.org; website: http://www.acmanet.org

COMPUTER USERS' FORUM

Acronym or abbreviation: CUF

1 Stuart Road, Thornton Heath, Surrey, CR7 8RA

Tel: 07831 196693
E-mail: postmaster@cr78ra1uk.cix.co.uk

Enquiries:
Enquiries to: Secretary

Founded:
1980

Organisation type and purpose:
Advisory body, professional body, membership association (membership is by subscription, election or invitation), present number of members: over 5,000, training organisation, consultancy, research organisation.

Subject coverage:
Expertise and knowledge in the use of computers.

Access to staff:
Contact by letter and by e-mail. All charged.
Hours: Mon to Fri, 0900 to 1700

Access to building, collection or gallery:
No access other than to staff

COMPUTING SUPPLIERS FEDERATION

Acronym or abbreviation: CSF

26–27 Brookside Business Park, Colde Meece, Stone, Staffordshire, ST15 0TZ

Tel: 01785 769090
Fax: 01785 769082
E-mail: info@csf.org.uk

Website:
http://www.csf.org.uk
Free downloads, organisational information, members-only area, case study database.

Enquiries:
Enquiries to: Managing Director

Founded:
1985

Formerly called:
Computer Graphics Suppliers Association (CGSA) (year of change 1995); Association of Visual Communicators (AVC) (year of change 1997)

Organisation type and purpose:
Trade association (membership is by subscription, qualification, election or invitation), present number of members: 200.
The CSF is a not-for-profit trade association representing specialist sectors of the IT industry.

Subject coverage:
Information management, imaging and workflow. CAD, CAM, PDM, EDM and other engineering applications, platforms and IT peripherals (including monitors, printers, workstations and storage equipment). Electronic presentations equipment (including projectors, video communications and conferencing systems).

Non-library collection catalogue:
All or part available online and in print

Printed publications:
eEngineering – Collaborating to Survive
Engineering Data across the Enterprise
Implementing Design Technology
Information Management – The Business Case
Innovation – the third dimension – using design technology to grow your business
Justifying Investing in Design Technology
Monitors Matter

New Display Technologies – making the right choice
Video Communications in the Workplace

Publications list:
Available online

Access to staff:
Contact via website
Hours: Mon to Fri, 0900 to 1700

Access for disabled people:
Parking provided, level entry, access to all public areas

CONCHOLOGICAL SOCIETY OF GREAT BRITAIN AND IRELAND

Acronym or abbreviation: CSGBI

1 Court Farm, Hillfarrance, Taunton, Somerset, TA4 1AN

Tel: 01823 461482
E-mail: c_m_gillard@compuserve.com

Website:
http://www.conchsoc.org
Publications, meetings, recording schemes, conservation, how to join, contacts, members' interests, links, news.

Enquiries:
Enquiries to: General Secretary

Founded:
1876

Organisation type and purpose:
Learned society (membership is by subscription), present number of members: 420, registered charity (charity number 208205), suitable for ages: all.
To promote the study of the Mollusca in all its aspects.

Subject coverage:
Distribution of molluscs, marine and non-marine in the United Kingdom, conservation of molluscan species and their habitats, environmental impact assessment, in general all aspects of conchology world-wide, marine, non-marine and fossil.

Museum or gallery collection, archive, or library special collection:
Distribution records
Non-marine held at NHM
Marine computerised database

Trade and statistical information:
Holds national records of non-marine and marine biogeographical distribution.

Non-library collection catalogue:
All or part available in-house and in print

Printed publications:
Atlas of the Non-Marine Mollusca of the British Isles
Conchologists Newsletter (4 a year, back numbers available)
Concordance to the Field Card for British Marine Mollusca
Journal of Conchology (2 times a year, some back numbers available)
List of Members (occasional and annual amendments)
Programme of Events (annually)
Special publications (irregular)
Packs of reprints from the Journal grouped by subject
Sea Area Atlas of the Marine Mollusca of Britain & Ireland (Seaward D R)
Order printed publications from: CSGBI, Hilliers Freith, Henley on Thames, Oxon, RG9 6PJ

Publications list:
Available in print

Access to staff:
Contact by letter, by telephone, by e-mail and via website
Hours: After 1700 weekdays and weekends
Special comments: Please note that all officers of the Society are volunteers.

Affiliated to:
Council for Nature

CONCORD MEDIA

The Rosehill Centre, 22 Hines Road, Ipswich, Suffolk, IP3 9BG

Tel: 01473 726012
Fax: 01473 274531
E-mail: sales@concordmedia.org.uk

Website:
http://www.concordmedia.org.uk
DVDs on social work, child care, race relations, the arts, crime & justice, mental health, etc.

Enquiries:
Enquiries to: Office Manager

Founded:
1965

Formerly called:
Concord Film Council (year of change 1984); Concord Video & Film Council (year of change 2006)

Organisation type and purpose:
Registered charity, public library.
Video and film library.

Subject coverage:
Social sciences, arts, development education, peace, counselling, medical and mental health.

Library catalogue:
All or part available online

Printed publications:
Catalogues

Electronic and video publications:
DVDs

Publications list:
Available online and in print

Access to staff:
Contact by letter, by telephone, by fax and by e-mail
Hours: Mon, Tue, Thu, Fri, 0900 to 1700; closed Wed

Access for disabled people:
Parking provided, level entry, toilet facilities

CONCRETE ADVISORY SERVICE

Acronym or abbreviation: CAS

Riverside House, 4 Meadows Business Park, Station Approach, Blackwater, Camberley, Surrey, GU17 9AB

Tel: 01276 607140
Fax: 01276 607141
E-mail: consoc@concrete.org.uk

Website:
http://www.concrete.org.uk

Organisation type and purpose:
National organisation, advisory body, membership association (membership is by subscription), consultancy.
Specialist consultancy in concrete and cementitious materials and applications.

Subject coverage:
Concrete and cementitious materials, design, construction, application, trouble-shooting.

Non-library collection catalogue:
All or part available online

Printed publications:
Purchase through http://www.concretebookshop.com

Publications list:
Available online and in print

Access to staff:
Contact by letter and by telephone. Access for members only. All charged.
Hours: Mon to Fri, 0900 to 1730

Parent body:
Concrete Society
At the same address

CONCRETE PIPE ASSOCIATION

Acronym or abbreviation: CPA

Tournai Hall, Evelyn Woods Road, Aldershot Hampshire GU11 2LL

Tel: 01252 357834
Fax: 01252 357831
E-mail: lauren.fairley@corrosionprevention.org.uk

Website:
http://www.corrosionprevention.org.uk

Enquiries:
Enquiries to: Director

Founded:
1932

Organisation type and purpose:
Trade association.

Subject coverage:
Manufacture and use of precast concrete pipe products for drainage systems; foul and surface water drainage systems.

Printed publications:
Information Sheets
Technical Bulletins

Electronic and video publications:
Videos

Publications list:
Available in print

Access to staff:
Contact by letter, by telephone and by fax
Hours: Mon to Fri, 0900 to 1700
Special comments: Library for members only. Information freely available to enquirers.

Affiliated to:
British Precast Concrete Federation
International Bureau of Concrete Manufacturers
International Concrete Pipe Commission

CONCRETE REPAIR ASSOCIATION

Acronym or abbreviation: CRA

Tournai Hall, Evelyn Woods Road, Aldershot, Hampshire GU11 2LL

Tel: 01252 357835
Fax: 01252 357831
E-mail: admin@cra.org.uk

Website:
http://www.concreterepair.org.uk

Enquiries:
Enquiries to: Secretary
Direct e-mail: publications@cra.org.uk

Founded:
1989

Organisation type and purpose:
Trade association, present number of members: 32. Represents contractors, manufacturers and consultants involved in the concrete repair industry.

Printed publications:
Directory of Members
Application of Measurement of Protective Coatings
Standard Method of Measurement for Concrete Repair
The Route to a Successful Concrete Repair

Publications list:
Available in print

Access to staff:
Contact by letter, by telephone, by fax, by e-mail and via website
Hours: Mon to Fri, 0900 to 1700

CONCRETE SOCIETY

Riverside House, 4 Meadows Business Park,
Station Approach, Blackwater, Camberley, Surrey,
GU17 9AB

Tel: 01276 607140
Fax: 01276 607141
E-mail: infoservices@concrete.org.uk

Website:
http://www.concrete.org.uk
http://www.concretebookshop.com

Founded:
1966

Organisation type and purpose:
Learned society.

Subject coverage:
Concrete in the construction industry.

Information services:
contact: Manager, Information Services

Education services:
contact: Head, Training & Education

Museum or gallery collection, archive, or library special collection:
Library, archives and photographic collection
    established by the former Cement & Concrete
    Association in 1937

Library catalogue:
All or part available online, in-house and in print

Printed publications:
Concrete (journal, monthly)
Data sheets
Proceedings of symposia
Technical reports and papers
Order printed publications from: e-mail: enquiries@
concretebookshop.com

Publications list:
Available online and in print

Access to staff:
Contact by letter, by telephone, by fax, by e-mail,
in person and via website. Appointment necessary.
Non-members charged.
Hours: Mon to Fri, 0900 to 1700

Access to building, collection or gallery:
Hours: Mon to Fri, 0900 to 1700

Administers:
Glassfibre Reinforced Concrete Society
    tel: 01276 607140; fax: 01276 607141; e-mail:
    grc_advisor@concrete.org.uk

Links with:
Institute of Concrete Technology
    tel: 01276 607140; e-mail: k.calverley@concrete
    .org.uk

CONCRETE TILE MANUFACTURERS' ASSOCIATION

Acronym or abbreviation: CTMA

60 Charles Street, Leicester, LE1 1FB

Tel: 0116 253 6161
Fax: 0116 251 4568
E-mail: info@britishprecast.org

Website:
http://www.britishprecast.org

Enquiries:
Enquiries to: Secretary

Organisation type and purpose:
Trade association.

Subject coverage:
Precast concrete roof tiles.

Publications list:
Available online

Access to staff:
Contact by letter, by telephone, by fax and by e-
mail
Hours: Mon to Fri, 0900 to 1700

Links with:
British Precast Concrete Federation

CONFED

Formal name: Confederation of Education Service
Managers

The Humanities Building, University of
Manchester, Oxford Road, Manchester, M13 9PL

Tel: 0161 275 8810
Fax: 0161 275 8811
E-mail: confedoffice@confed.org.uk

Website:
http://www.confed.org.uk
Outline of CONFED activities.

Enquiries:
Enquiries to: General Secretary
Other contacts: Administrator, President

Founded:
1972

Formed by the merger of:
Association of Chief Education Officers (ACEO),
Society of Chief Inspectors and Advisers (SCIA),
Society of Education Officers (SEO) (year of
change 2002)

Organisation type and purpose:
Professional body (membership is by subscription,
qualification), present number of members: 900.

Subject coverage:
Administration and management of the education
service in local authorities in England and Wales.

Publications list:
Available in print

Access to staff:
Contact by letter, by telephone, by fax and by e-
mail
Hours: Mon to Thu, 0900 to 1700; Fri, 0900 to 1300

CONFEDERATION OF AERIAL INDUSTRIES LIMITED

Acronym or abbreviation: CAI

Fulton House Business Centre, Fulton Road,
Wembley Park, Middlesex, HA9 0TF

Tel: 020 8902 8998
Fax: 020 8903 8719
E-mail: office@cai.org.uk

Website:
http://www.cai.org.uk

Enquiries:
Enquiries to: Secretary
Direct e-mail: suzanne@cai.org.uk

Founded:
1978

Organisation type and purpose:
Trade association.

Subject coverage:
Aerials, satellite dishes, cables and allied
equipment, manufacture, supply, installation.

Trade and statistical information:
Training for the industry.

Printed publications:
Codes of Practice for domestic aerials, door entry
    systems, satellite dishes and MATV/SMATV
    systems
Feedback
Members Directory
Year Planner

Access to staff:
Contact by letter, by telephone, by fax and by e-
mail
Hours: Mon to Fri, 0900 to 1700

CONFEDERATION OF AFRICAN PROFESSIONALS (CAP) UK

Acronym or abbreviation: CAP UK

BBI Business Centre, 53 Peckham Park Road,
Peckham, London SE15 6TU

E-mail: capuk@bbinitiative.com

Enquiries:
Enquiries to: Chairman/President
Direct e-mail: sunny@sunnylambe.com

Founded:
1998

Organisation type and purpose:
International organisation, national organisation,
professional body, membership association
(membership is by subscription, qualification,
election or invitation), present number of
members: 200, voluntary organisation, suitable for
ages: all, consultancy, research organisation.
To provide a voice and networking opportunity for
professionals of African origin.

Access to staff:
Contact by letter, by telephone, by fax and by e-
mail. Appointment necessary. Letter of
introduction required.
Hours: Mon to Fri, 0900 to 1700

Access to building, collection or gallery:
Prior appointment required

Access for disabled people:
Parking provided, level entry, access to all public
areas, toilet facilities

CONFEDERATION OF BRITISH INDUSTRY

Acronym or abbreviation: CBI

Centre Point, 103 New Oxford Street, London,
WC1A 1DU

Tel: 020 7379 7400
Fax: 020 7240 0988 or 1578

Website:
http://www.cbi.org.uk
Policy information, press office, events,
publications, membership information.

Enquiries:
Enquiries to: Information Officer
Direct tel: 020 7395 8247
Direct e-mail: press.office@cbi.org.uk

Founded:
1965

Organisation type and purpose:
Membership association (membership is by
subscription), manufacturing industry, service
industry.
Representative organisation for member
companies, employers organisations and trade
associations.

Subject coverage:
Public policy (international, national and regional),
economic situation and trends, taxation, human
resources, industrial relations, conditions of
employment, education and training,
manufacturing, research and development,
overseas affairs, commercial and company law,
industrial property law, industrial effluent, energy
and water resources, innovation, information
society.

Trade and statistical information:
See publications.

Library catalogue:
All or part available in-house

Printed publications:
Business Voice (monthly)
Distributive Trades Survey (monthly)
Economic & Business Outlook (quarterly)
Financial Services Survey (quarterly)
Industrial Trends Survey (monthly)
Various monographs

Order printed publications from: CBI Publications, tel: 020 7395 8071

Access to staff:
Contact by letter, by telephone, by fax and by e-mail. Appointment necessary.
Hours: Mon to Fri, 0930 to 1730

CONFEDERATION OF BRITISH WOOL TEXTILES LIMITED

Acronym or abbreviation: CBWT

Textile House, Red Doles Lane, Huddersfield, HD2 1YF

Tel: 01484 346500
Fax: 01484 346501
E-mail: info@cbwt.co.uk

Website:
http://www.cbwt.co.uk

Enquiries:
Enquiries to: Administation
Direct e-mail: slawka@cbwt.co.uk

Founded:
1979

Organisation type and purpose:
Trade association (membership is by subscription), present number of members: 180.
Promotion and protection of interests of the British wool textiles industry, provision of services to member companies.

Subject coverage:
UK wool textile industry; international trade practice and technical specifications relating to the raw materials and end products.

Trade and statistical information:
Data on the British wool textile industry.

Access to staff:
Contact by fax, by e-mail and via website
Hours: Mon to Fri, 0900 to 1700

Member of:
British Apparel and Textile Confederation (BATC)
   tel: 020 7636 7788; fax: 020 7636 7515; e-mail: batc@dial.pipex.com
INTERLAINE (EEC)
   tel: + 32 2 513 06 20; fax: + 32 2 514 06 65
International Wool Textile Organization (IWTO)
   tel: + 32 2 513 06 20; fax: + 32 2 514 06 65; e-mail: info@iwto.org

CONFEDERATION OF FOREST INDUSTRIES (UK) LTD

Acronym or abbreviation: ConFor

5 Dublin Street Lane South, Edinburgh, EH1 3PX

Tel: 0131 524 8080
Fax: 0131 538 7222
E-mail: mail@confor.org.uk

Website:
http://www.confor.org.uk

Enquiries:
Enquiries to: Chief Executive

Founded:
1983

Formed from:
merged with Forestry and Timber Association (FTA), 2006; Association of Professional Foresters (APF), Timber Growers Association (TGA) (year of change 2002)

Formerly called:
Timber Growers United Kingdom Limited (year of change 1994)

Organisation type and purpose:
Trade association (membership is by subscription), present number of members: 2500.

Subject coverage:
Forestry and woodland ownership. Timber production.

Printed publications:
9 Regional Newsletters (quarterly, members only)
Timber Grower Magazine (quarterly)

Access to staff:
Contact by letter, by telephone, by fax, by e-mail and via website. Non-members charged.
Hours: Mon to Fri, 0900 to 1700

Access to building, collection or gallery:
Prior appointment required

CONFEDERATION OF INDIAN ORGANISATIONS (UK)

Acronym or abbreviation: CIO

5 Westminster Bridge Road, London, SE1 7XW

Tel: 020 7928 9889
Fax: 020 7620 4025
E-mail: headoffice@cio.org.uk

Website:
http://www.cio.org.uk

Enquiries:
Enquiries to: Chief Executive
Other contacts: Information Officer

Founded:
1975

Organisation type and purpose:
National organisation, membership association (membership is by subscription), present number of members: 150, voluntary organisation, registered charity (charity number 1075501), training organisation, research organisation.
A national South Asian umbrella organisation.
Representation of the needs of South Asian community and voluntary organisations.

Subject coverage:
Information about South Asians in the UK including statistics, organisations, health issues, information resources in ethnic languages, issue-based participatory research, social policy, service provision, development of innovative'models of good practice, promotion of anti-racist practices.

Library catalogue:
All or part available in-house

Printed publications:
A Cry for Change (Information Pack, Amanda Webb-Johnson, 1991, £7.50)
CIO's South Asian Mental Health Conference Report (£3.50)
Directory of Mental Health Services for South Asian Communities, 1998 (£5)
Directory of South Asian Voluntary Groups in the United Kingdom (to be published 1999)
Illness or Distress? Alternative Models of Mental Health (£3.50 plus p&p)
Mental Health Assessment and Asian Men (2001)

Publications list:
Available in print

Access to staff:
Contact by letter, by telephone and by fax.
Appointment necessary.
Hours: Mon to Fri, 0900 to 1700

Other addresses:
CIO Leicester Office
   5th Floor, Epic House, Lower Hill Street, Leicester, LE1 3SH; tel: 0116 225 9299; fax: 0116 225 9298

CONFEDERATION OF PAPER INDUSTRIES

Acronym or abbreviation: CPI

1 Rivenhall Road, Swindon, Wiltshire, SN5 7BD

Tel: 01793 889600
Fax: 01793 878700
E-mail: cpi@paper.org.uk

Website:
http://www.corrugated.org.uk
The CPI, news, information, current issues.

Founded:
1974

Organisation type and purpose:
Represents the paper chain from the recovery of used paper through papermaking and conversion to distribution.
To be recognised by the UK government, and the community at large, as the authoritative and effective voice of the UK paper-related industry, defending its interests and promoting its achievements and potential.

Subject coverage:
Supporting members by identifying, analysing, and resolving issues; informing government, the media and the public; presenting the industry's views in a coherent, consistent and targeted manner.

Information services:
Information section on website, including glossary of terms, recycling, papermaking process.

Education services:
School information packs for either primary/junior or secondary pupils.

Trade and statistical information:
Reference guide of industry statistics, 1989–2009.

Electronic and video publications:
Annual Review
Press releases
Fact sheets
Technical bulletins
Order electronic and video publications from:
Download from website

Publications list:
Available online

Access to staff:
Contact by letter, by telephone, by fax and by e-mail. Appointment necessary.
Hours: Mon to Fri, 0900 to 1700

Access to building, collection or gallery:
No access other than to staff

Access for disabled people:
Parking provided, toilet facilities

Constituent bodies:
Association of Makers of Packaging Papers
Association of Makers of Printing and Writing Papers
Association of Makers of Soft Tissue Papers
Corrugated Case Materials Association

Member organisation of:
Confederation of European Paper Industries
   Brussels, Belgium

CONFEDERATION OF PASSENGER TRANSPORT UK

Acronym or abbreviation: CPT

Drury House, 34–43 Russell Street, London, WC2B 5HA

Tel: 020 7240 3131
Fax: 020 7240 6565
E-mail: admin@cpt-uk.org

Website:
http://www.cpt-uk.org/

Enquiries:
Enquiries to: Public Affairs Officer
Direct e-mail: chrisnice@cpt-uk.org
Other contacts: Assistant Director Public Affairs for media and press enquiries.

Formerly called:
Bus and Coach Council

Organisation type and purpose:
Trade association.

Subject coverage:
Public road passenger transport, bus and coach industry, fixed track operators, technical and operations, legal matters, statistics, informed comment.

continued overleaf

Printed publications:
Newsline (newsletter for members, fortnightly)

Publications list:
Available in print

Access to staff:
Contact by letter, by telephone, by fax, by e-mail and via website. Appointment necessary.
Hours: Mon to Fri, 0900 to 1700

Subsidiary of:
Confederation of British Road Passenger Transport Transfed

CONFEDERATION OF ROOFING CONTRACTORS LIMITED

Formal name: CRC

72 Church Road, Brightlingsea, Colchester, Essex, CO7 0JF

Tel: 01206 306600
Fax: 01206 306200
E-mail: enquiries@corc.co.uk

Website:
http://www.corc.co.uk
List of members, benefits of membership, map of country.

Enquiries:
Enquiries to: Membership Co-ordinator
Direct e-mail: mike@corc.co.uk

Founded:
1985

Organisation type and purpose:
Trade association (membership is by subscription), present number of members: 580.
To protect the general public from unscrupulous roofing contractors.

Subject coverage:
All aspects of the roofing industry.

Library catalogue:
All or part available in-house

Printed publications:
Roofing Trades Journal – the biggest circulation roofing magazine in Europe

Publications list:
Available in print

Access to staff:
Contact by letter, by telephone, by fax, by e-mail and via website
Hours: Mon to Fri, 0900 to 1300 and 1400 to 1700

Access to building, collection or gallery:
Prior appointment required

Access for disabled people:
Parking provided, level entry, access to all public areas, toilet facilities

CONFEDERATION OF SHIPBUILDING AND ENGINEERING UNIONS

Acronym or abbreviation: CSEU

140–142 Walworth Road, Walworth, London, SE17 1JW

Tel: 020 7703 2215
Fax: 020 7252 7397

Enquiries:
Enquiries to: General Secretary
Direct e-mail: smehta@hwfisher.co.uk

Founded:
1936

Formed from:
Federation of Engineering & Shipbuilding Trades (FESTUK) (year of change 1936)

Organisation type and purpose:
Trade union (membership is by subscription), present number of members: 1,093,001.

Subject coverage:
Co-ordination and policy of shipbuilding and engineering unions throughout the UK.

Access to staff:
Contact by letter, by telephone and by fax
Hours: Mon to Fri, 0900 to 1700

CONFERENCE INTERPRETERS GROUP

Acronym or abbreviation: CIG

10 Barley Mow Passage, Chiswick, London, W4 4PH

Tel: 020 8995 0801
Fax: 020 8742 1066
E-mail: info@cig-interpreters.com

Website:
http://www.cig-interpreters.com

Enquiries:
Enquiries to: Executive Secretary

Founded:
1979

Organisation type and purpose:
Service industry.
Cooperative grouping; membership restricted to members of AIIC (Association Internationale des Interprètes de Conférence).

Subject coverage:
Interpretation, simultaneous and consecutive.

Access to staff:
Contact by letter, by telephone and by fax
Hours: Mon to Fri, 0900 to 1700

CONGREGATIONAL LIBRARY

c/o 14 Gordon Square, London, WC1H 0AR

Tel: 020 7387 3727

Enquiries:
Enquiries to: Librarian

Founded:
1831

Organisation type and purpose:
Registered charity (charity number 260601), public library.
Managed by Dr Williams's Library.

Subject coverage:
English religious dissent. Congregationalism.

Library catalogue:
All or part available in-house

Printed publications:
Congregational Lecture (occasional)

Publications list:
Available in print

Access to staff:
Contact by letter, by telephone and in person. Appointment necessary.
Hours: Mon, Wed, Fri, 1000 to 1700; Tue, Thu, 1000 to 1830

Parent body:
Congregational Memorial Hall Trust (1978) Limited
   c/o Dr Williams's Library, 14 Gordon Square, London, WC1H 0AR

CONNECT

30 St George's Road, Wimbledon, London, SW19 4BD

Tel: 020 8971 6000
Fax: 020 8971 6002
E-mail: union@connect.uk.org

Website:
http://www.connect.org.uk
http://www.connectuk.org

Services to members and updates of what is happening on negotiations and other industry news.

Enquiries:
Enquiries to: Researcher
Direct tel: 020 8971 6025
Direct fax: 020 8971 6026
Direct e-mail: research@connect.uk.org
Other contacts: Assistant Secretary for overseas publications.

Formerly called:
Society of Telecom Executives (year of change 2000)

Organisation type and purpose:
Trade union (membership is by subscription), present number of members: 18,500, service industry.
Members are managers and professionals in the Communications and IT industry.

Printed publications:
Various members newsletters
The Review (magazine, monthly, members)

Access to staff:
Contact by letter, by telephone and by e-mail. Access for members only. Non-members charged.
Hours: Mon to Fri, 0900 to 1715

Access to building, collection or gallery:
No access other than to staff

Access for disabled people:
Parking provided, ramped entry, access to all public areas, toilet facilities

Field offices at:
CONNECT
   22a Caroline Street, St Paul's Square, Birmingham, B3 1VE; tel: 0121 236 0596 or 2637; fax: 0121 233 2616

CONSERVATION FOUNDATION

1 Kensington Gore, London, SW7 2AR

Tel: 020 7591 3111
Fax: 020 7591 3110
E-mail: info@conservationfoundation.co.uk

Website:
http://www.conservationfoundation.co.uk

Enquiries:
Enquiries to: Executive Director

Founded:
1982

Organisation type and purpose:
International organisation, registered charity (charity number 284656).

Subject coverage:
Initiation and management of environmental projects.

Printed publications:
Parish Pump Newsletter
Annual Report
Healthier Profits, Business Success and the Green Factor
Media information pack (monthly)
What? On Earth

Access to staff:
Contact by letter, by telephone, by fax and by e-mail
Hours: Mon to Fri, 0930 to 1730

CONSTANCE HOWARD RESOURCE AND RESEARCH CENTRE IN TEXTILES

Goldsmiths, University of London, Deptford Town Hall Building, New Cross Road, London, SE14 6AF

Tel: 020 7717 2210
E-mail: connitex@gold.ac.uk

Website:
http://www.goldsmiths.ac.uk/constance-howard

Organisation type and purpose:
An independent centre supported by Goldsmiths (University of London), the Arts Council, the Arts and Humanities Research Council and other bodies.

Subject coverage:
History of textiles since the 1940s.

Museum or gallery collection, archive, or library special collection:
Textile reference library, including many books from Eastern Europe

CONSTRUCTION EMPLOYERS FEDERATION

Acronym or abbreviation: CEF

143 Malone Road, Belfast, BT9 6SU

Tel: 028 9087 7143
Fax: 028 9087 7155
E-mail: mail@cefni.co.uk

Website:
http://www.cefni.co.uk
http://www.constructionfocus.co.uk

Enquiries:
Enquiries to: Deputy Secretary
Direct e-mail: nlucas@cefni.co.uk
Other contacts: Information Officer

Founded:
1945

Formerly called:
Federation of Building and Civil Engineering (FBCE)

Organisation type and purpose:
Advisory body, trade association (membership is by subscription), service industry, voluntary organisation.

Subject coverage:
Construction output data, expenditure, contract problems.

Trade and statistical information:
State of Trade Survey.

Non-library collection catalogue:
All or part available online

Printed publications:
All current forms of building contract

Publications list:
Available in print

Access to staff:
Contact by letter. Access for members only. Letter of introduction required.
Hours: Mon to Fri, 0900 to 1700

CONSTRUCTION EQUIPMENT ASSOCIATION

Acronym or abbreviation: CEA

Ambassador House, Brigstock Road, Thornton Heath, Surrey, CR7 7JG

Tel: 020 8665 5727
Fax: 020 8665 6447
E-mail: cea@admin.co.uk

Website:
http://www.coneq.org.uk

Enquiries:
Enquiries to: Information Officer

Founded:
1942

Formerly called:
Federation of Manufacturers of Construction Equipment and Cranes (FMCEC) (year of change 2000)

Organisation type and purpose:
Trade association (membership is by subscription), present number of members: 100.

The UK trade association serving construction equipment manufacturers, their component and accessory suppliers and service providers.

Subject coverage:
Subjects relating to UK-based manufacturers of construction equipment, relevant components and accessories in the UK.

Electronic and video publications:
Business Tracker (CD-ROM)

Access to staff:
Contact by letter, by telephone, by fax, by e-mail and via website
Hours: Mon to Fri, 0900 to 1700

Member of:
Committee for European Construction Equipment (CECE)
Fédération Européenne de la Manutention (FEM)

CONSTRUCTION FIXINGS ASSOCIATION

Acronym or abbreviation: CFA

Light Trades House, 3 Melbourne Avenue, Sheffield, South Yorkshire, S10 2QJ

Tel: 0114 266 3084
Fax: 0114 267 0910
E-mail: light.trades@virgin.net

Enquiries:
Enquiries to: Secretary

Organisation type and purpose:
Trade association.

Subject coverage:
Construction fixings.

Access to staff:
Contact by letter, by telephone, by fax and by e-mail
Hours: Mon to Fri, 0900 to 1700

Affiliated to:
Federation of British Hand Tool Manufacturers

CONSTRUCTION HEALTH AND SAFETY GROUP

Acronym or abbreviation: CHSG

John Ryder Training Centre, St Ann's Road, Chertsey, Surrey, KT16 9EH

Tel: 01932 561871 or 563121
Fax: 01932 560193
E-mail: info@chsg.co.uk

Website:
http://www.chsg.co.uk

Enquiries:
Enquiries to: Manager
Direct e-mail: gm@chsg.co.uk

Founded:
1953

Organisation type and purpose:
Membership association (membership is by subscription), present number of members: 430, registered charity, training organisation.

Subject coverage:
Construction safety training courses.

Access to staff:
Contact by letter, by telephone, by fax, by e-mail and via website
Hours: Mon to Fri, 0900 to 1700

CONSTRUCTION HISTORY SOCIETY

Acronym or abbreviation: CHS

c/o Library and Information Services Manager, The Chartered Institute of Building, Englemere, Kings Ride, Ascot, Berkshire, SL5 7TB

Tel: 01344 630741

Fax: 01344 630764
E-mail: secretary@constructionhistory.co.uk

Website:
http://www.constructionhistory.co.uk

Enquiries:
Enquiries to: Secretary

Founded:
1982

Formerly called:
Construction History Group (year of change 1985)

Organisation type and purpose:
Learned society (membership is by subscription), present number of members: 300, registered charity.

Subject coverage:
Construction history, construction techniques and materials, company histories, etc.

Printed publications:
CHS Newsletter (2–3 per year, free to members)
Construction History (annual journal, free to members; on sale to others)
The Place of Technology in Architectural History (2001, seminar papers, jtly with Society of Architectural Historians)
Proceedings of the Second International Congress on Construction History (2006, 4 vols, including index – out of print)
Order printed publications from: Society, as above, or via website

Publications list:
Available online

Access to staff:
Contact by letter, by e-mail and via website
Hours: Mon to Fri, 0900 to 1700

Links with:
Building and Construction Industry Interest Group
Society for the History of Technology
Panel for Historical Engineering Works
Institution of Civil Engineers

CONSTRUCTION INDUSTRY COMPUTING ASSOCIATION

Acronym or abbreviation: CICA

National Computing Centre, Oxford House, Oxford Road, Manchester, M1 7ED

Tel: 0161 242 2121
E-mail: michael.dean@ncc.co.uk

Website:
http://www.cica.org.uk

Enquiries:
Enquiries to: Managing Director

Founded:
1973

Organisation type and purpose:
Membership association (membership is by subscription), consultancy, research organisation. To provide impartial information and advice on the use of computers in the construction industry.

Subject coverage:
All areas of construction, including CAD, communications, management, engineering software, building services, quantity surveying; computing services, expert systems, IT strategy and standards.

Museum or gallery collection, archive, or library special collection:
Directory of software for the construction industry

Trade and statistical information:
Data on use of computers in the UK and European Construction Industry.
Data on sales of CAD systems to construction.

Printed publications:
Arup CAD Good Practice Guide
Document Management for Construction
Qualifying the Benefits of IT
The CAD Rating Guide

continued overleaf

Publications list:
Available online and in print

Access to staff:
Contact by letter, by telephone, by e-mail and via website
Hours: Mon to Fri, 0900 to 1700

Commercial branch for consultancy and training:
CICA Services Ltd

CONSTRUCTION INDUSTRY COUNCIL

Acronym or abbreviation: CIC

26 Store Street, London, WC1E 7BT

Tel: 020 7399 7400
Fax: 020 7399 7425
E-mail: cic@cic.org.uk

Website:
http://www.cic.org.uk
General information.

Founded:
1988

Organisation type and purpose:
The Construction Industry Council (CIC) is the representative forum for the professional bodies, research organisations and specialist business associations in the construction industry.

Non-library collection catalogue:
All or part available in print

Printed publications:
E-mail: hsmith@cic.org.uk to obtain copy of list
Order printed publications from: CIC
26 Store Street, London, WC1E 7BT, tel: 020 7399 7400, fax: 020 7399 7425, e-mail: cic@cic.org.uk

Publications list:
Available online and in print

Access to staff:
Contact by letter, by telephone, by fax, by e-mail and via website. Appointment necessary.
Hours: Mon to Fri, 0900 to 1700

Access for disabled people:
lift, toilet facilities

Other address:
Construction Industry Council
26 Store Street, London, WC1E 7BT; tel: 020 7399 7400; fax: 020 7399 7425; e-mail: mail@cic.org.uk

CONSTRUCTION PLANT-HIRE ASSOCIATION

Acronym or abbreviation: CPA

52 Rochester Row, London, SW1P 1JU

Tel: 020 7630 6868
Fax: 020 7630 6765
E-mail: enquiries@cpa.uk.net

Website:
http://www.c-p-a.co.uk
Members services, background of CPA.

Enquiries:
Enquiries to: Director

Founded:
1941

Organisation type and purpose:
Trade association.

Subject coverage:
Construction plant-hire, health and safety, training, statistics and legal aspects.

Printed publications:
Bulletin (10 times a year, members only)
Contract forms, guidance notes and safety notes

Electronic and video publications:
List of members on disc (£100)
M Condition (CD-ROM)

Publications list:
Available in print

Access to staff:
Contact by letter, by telephone and by fax
Hours: Mon to Fri, 0930 to 1700

CONSTRUCTION PRODUCTS ASSOCIATION

Acronym or abbreviation: CPA

The Building Centre, 26 Store Street, London, WC1E 7BT

Tel: 020 7323 3770
Fax: 020 7323 0307
E-mail: enquiries@constructionproducts.org.uk

Website:
http://www.constructionproducts.org.uk
Briefings, press releases/news, meetings and events, hyperlinks to members and other useful sites, industry overview and publications.

Enquiries:
Enquiries to: Director
Other contacts: Communications and External Affairs Director

Founded:
2000

Formed from the merger of:
Association of Construction Product Supplies (ACPS), Building Materials Export Group (BMEG), National Council of Building Material Producers (NCBMP)

Organisation type and purpose:
National organisation, trade association (membership is by subscription), present number of members: 60.
To demonstrate the importance of a growing and profitable construction products sector to the UK economy.

Subject coverage:
Building materials, components and fittings, industry in general; non-specialist information on availability and sources of materials; forecasts of construction industry output; statistics.

Museum or gallery collection, archive, or library special collection:
Economic, technical, wide-ranging other information on construction industry structure and organisation

Printed publications:
Construction Industry forecasts (quarterly)
Annual Report
Construction Market Trends (monthly)
Construction Product Trade Survey (4 times a year)
Weekly Notes (every Friday, members only)

Publications list:
Available online and in print

Access to staff:
Contact by letter, by telephone, by fax, by e-mail and via website. Appointment necessary. Non-members charged.
Hours: Mon to Fri, 0900 to 1700

Member organisation of:
Confederation of British Industry (CBI)
tel: 020 7379 8001
Council of European Producers of Materials for Construction

CONSUMER CREDIT ASSOCIATION

Acronym or abbreviation: CCA

Queens House, Queens Road, Chester, Cheshire, CH1 3BQ

Tel: 01244 312044
Fax: 01244 318035
E-mail: cca@ccauk.org

Website:
http://www.ccauk.org

Enquiries:
Enquiries to: Director

Direct tel: 01244 505907
Direct fax: 01244 322528
Direct e-mail: cca@ccauk.org

Founded:
1978

Created by the merger of:
National Personal Finance Association (NPFA) and Retail Credit Federation (RCF) (year of change 1978)

Organisation type and purpose:
Trade association.
Represents over 500 companies operating in the home credit market.

Subject coverage:
Consumer credit, home credit.

Printed publications:
CCA News (quarterly)

Access to staff:
Contact by letter, by telephone, by fax and by e-mail
Hours: Mon to Fri, 0900 to 1700

CONSUMER FOCUS

4th Floor, Artillery House, Artillery Row, London, SW1P 1RT

Tel: 0207 799 7900
Fax: 0207 799 7901
E-mail: contact@consumerfocus.org.uk

Website:
http://www.consumerfocus.org.uk

Enquiries:
Enquiries to: Communications Assistant

Founded:
2008

Created by the merger of:
energywatch, Postwatch and National Consumer Council (NCC) (year of change 2008)

Organisation type and purpose:
NDPB (Non-departmental public body).

Subject coverage:
Consumer Focus is the independent champion for consumers in the UK, giving a strong voice to consumers on the issues that matter to them and working to secure a fair deal on their behalf. It works with consumers and a range of organisations to tackle the problems customers face and to achieve creative solutions that make a difference to peoples' lives.
It has legislative powers, including the right to investigate any complaint if it is of wider interest; the right to open up information from providers; and the ability to make an official super-complaint about failing services.
It is not a complaints-handling body or a statutory regulator. Consumer complaints or advice requests should be directed to Consumer Direct or Citizens Advice Bureau.

Publications list:
Available online

Access to staff:
Contact by letter, by telephone, by fax and by e-mail
Hours: Mon to Fri, 0900 to 1700

Also at:
Consumer Focus Post (Northern Ireland)
Elizabeth House, 116 Holywood Road, Belfast, BT4 1NY; tel: 028 9067 4833; website: http://www.consumerfocus.org.uk/northern-ireland
Consumer Focus Scotland
Royal Exchange House, 100 Queen Street, Glasgow, G1 3DN; tel: 0141 226 5261; fax: 0141 221 0731; website: http://www.consumerfocus.org.uk/scotland
Consumer Focus Wales
3rd Floor, Capital Tower, Greyfriars Road, Cardiff, CF10 3AG; tel: 02920 787100; fax: 02920 787101; website: http://www.consumerfocus.org.uk/wales

CONSUMER FOCUS SCOTLAND

Royal Exchange House, 100 Queen Street, Glasgow, G1 3DN

Tel: 0141 226 5261; minicom no. 0141 226 8459
Fax: 0141 221 9695
E-mail: mail@consumerfocus-scotland.org.uk

Website:
http://www.consumerfocus.org.uk/scotland

Founded:
2008

Created by the merger of:
Scottish Consumer Council (founded 1975), energywatch, Postwatch (year of change 2008)

Organisation type and purpose:
National government body.
Set up by the government to promote the interests of Scottish consumers, particularly those experiencing disadvantage in society.

Subject coverage:
Consumer issues, including access to information, advice, debt, education, food, health, housing, legal matters, local authorities, rural problems, social security, transport, social services, environmental affairs, food and diet, disability issues.

Printed publications:
Annual Report
Code on Openness
Reports, policy papers and consumer information leaflets on various issues

Publications list:
Available online and in print

Access to staff:
Contact by letter, by telephone, by fax, by e-mail and via website. Appointment necessary.
Hours: Mon to Fri, 0900 to 1700

Part of:
National Consumer Council
20 Grosvenor Gardens, London, SW1W 0DH; tel: 020 7730 3469; fax: 020 7730 0191

CONSUMERS' ASSOCIATION

Acronym or abbreviation: CA

Head Office, 2 Marylebone Road, London, NW1 4DF

Tel: 020 7770 7400
Fax: 01992 827485
E-mail: editor@which.net or support@which.net

Website:
http://www.which.net

Enquiries:
Enquiries to: Customer Services Officer
Direct tel: 01992 589031 ext 4504

Founded:
1957

Organisation type and purpose:
Membership association (membership is by subscription), registered charity, research organisation, publishing house.
The company is Which Limited.

Subject coverage:
Consumer affairs, product testing, consumer law, standards.

Museum or gallery collection, archive, or library special collection:
Local Consumer Group magazines and Overseas Consumer magazines on microfiche

Non-library collection catalogue:
All or part available online and in print

Printed publications:
Numerous Which Guides and Books including:
Daily Consumer News
Drug and Therapeutics Bulletin
Gardening Which? (magazine, quarterly)
Good Food Guide (annually)
Good Hotel Guide

Good Pub Guide
Holiday Which? (magazine, quarterly)
Which? (magazine, monthly)
Which? Way to Health (magazine, 6 times a year)

Electronic and video publications:
Which? Online

Publications list:
Available in print

Access to staff:
Contact by letter, by telephone, by fax, by e-mail and via website
Hours: Which queries Mon to Fri, 0830 to 2000; Sat, 0900 to 1300
Which online Mon to Fri, 0830 to 2100; Sat 0900 to 1500

Connections with:
BEUC
IOCU

Links with:
Research Institute for Consumer Affairs

Other addresses:
Membership Queries
Consumers' Association, Castlemead, Gascoyne Way, Hertford, SG1 1LH

CONTACT A FAMILY

209–211 City Road, London, EC1V 1JN

Tel: 020 7608 8700\ Minicom no. 020 7608 8702
Fax: 020 7608 8701
E-mail: info@cafamily.org.uk

Website:
http://www.cafamily.org.uk
CaF directory containing more than 400 entries giving information on more than 1,200 conditions affecting children. Each entry is accompanied by medical information and details of support groups.

Enquiries:
Enquiries to: Information Officer

Founded:
1979

Organisation type and purpose:
Voluntary organisation, registered charity.
Support for families who care for children with disabilities and special needs.

Subject coverage:
Children with special needs, parent carers, parents' support groups, rare conditions affecting children.

Information services:
Helpline, tel: 0808 808 3555 (Mon to Fri); textphone, tel: 0808 808 3556.

Non-library collection catalogue:
All or part available in-house

Library catalogue:
All or part available in-house

Printed publications:
Connected (magazine, quarterly)
CaF Directory of Specific Conditions & Rare Syndromes in Children with their Family Support Networks
CaF Annual Review
CaF Group Action Pack
A range of factsheets and leaflets for groups, individuals and professionals

Electronic and video publications:
Podcasts available online at http:// www.cafamily.org.uk/news/podcasts.html
Videos available online at http:// www.youtube.com/cafamily

Publications list:
Available online and in print

Access to staff:
Contact by letter, by telephone, by fax, by e-mail and via website
Hours: Mon to Fri, 0900 to 1700

Access to building, collection or gallery:
Prior appointment required

Hours: Mon to Fri, 0900 to 1700

Access for disabled people:
Ramped entry, toilet facilities

CONTACT THE ELDERLY

15 Henrietta Street, Covent Garden, London, WC2E 8QG

Tel: 020 7240 0630
Fax: 020 7379 5781
E-mail: info@contact-the-elderly.org.uk

Website:
http://www.contact-the-elderly.org.uk

Enquiries:
Enquiries to: Friendship Line Officer

Founded:
1965

Formerly called:
CONTACT

Organisation type and purpose:
Voluntary organisation, registered charity (charity number 244681 in England and Wales and SC039377 in Scotland).

Subject coverage:
Contact the Elderly provides monthly Sunday afternoon tea parties for people over 75, who live alone with little or no contact with family and friends. Members are picked up by volunteer drivers and spend afternoons full of fun and laughter at a volunteer host's home: a real lifeline.

Printed publications:
Annual Report and leaflet
Contact the Elderly News

Electronic and video publications:
Videos

Access to staff:
Contact by letter, by telephone, by fax, by e-mail and via website
Hours: Mon to Fri, 0900 to 1700

CONTEMPORARY APPLIED ARTS

2 Percy Street, London, W1P 9FA

Tel: 020 7436 2344
Fax: 020 7436 2446

Website:
http://www.caa.org.uk
Current exhibitions.

Enquiries:
Enquiries to: Press and Promotions Officer

Founded:
1948

Formerly called:
British Crafts Centre (year of change 1989)

Organisation type and purpose:
Membership association (membership is by qualification), present number of members: 250 approx, registered charity.
Gallery.

Subject coverage:
Ceramics, glass, jewellery, furniture, textiles, wood, metalwork.

Printed publications:
Exhibition leaflets (approx 7 times a year)

Access to staff:
Contact by letter and by telephone
Hours: Mon to Sat, 1030 to 1730
Special comments: Closed Bank Holidays and from Christmas to early Jan.

Member of:
Federation of British Crafts Societies (FBCS)

CONTEMPORARY ART SOCIETY

Acronym or abbreviation: CAS

continued overleaf

11–15 Emerald Street, London, WC1N 3QL

Tel: 020 7831 1243
Fax: 020 7831 1214
E-mail: info@contemporaryartsociety.org

Website:
http://www.contemporaryartsociety.org
About the Society, its work with public collections,
becoming a member, forthcoming events, art
consultancy services, news, centenary programme,
annual fundraiser, limited editions.

Founded:
1910

Organisation type and purpose:
The Contemporary Art Society exists to support
and develop public collections of contemporary art
in the UK.

Subject coverage:
Promotion of the understanding, enjoyment and
collecting of contemporary art; acquisition of
works of contemporary art for gifts to public
museums and galleries; an extensive knowledge of
British contemporary art.

**Museum or gallery collection, archive, or library
special collection:**
Extensive data on contemporary artists
Information is held on all CAS purchases since
1910
Office used as a gallery space, rotating exhibitions

Access to staff:
Contact by letter, by telephone, by fax and by e-
mail. Appointment necessary.
Hours: Mon to Fri, 0930 to 1730

CONTEMPORARY GLASS SOCIETY

Acronym or abbreviation: CGS

c/o Broadfield House Glass Museum, Compton
Drive, Kingswinford, West Midlands, DY6 9NS

Tel: 01379 741120
Fax: 01379 741120
E-mail: admin@cgs.org.uk

Website:
http://www.cgs.org.uk

Enquiries:
Enquiries to: Administrator

Founded:
1997

Formerly called:
British Artists in Glass (year of change 1997)

Organisation type and purpose:
International organisation, learned society,
professional body, membership association
(membership is by subscription), present number
of members: 600, manufacturing industry,
voluntary organisation, consultancy.

Subject coverage:
Studio glass-making, exhibitions, individuals
specialising in particular areas of glass-making,
collectors, supporters.

Library catalogue:
All or part available online and in print

Printed publications:
Journal (annually)
Newsletter (quarterly)

Access to staff:
Contact by letter and by e-mail
Hours: Mon to Fri, 0900 to 1700

CONTINYOU

Unit C1, Grovelands Court, Grovelands Est.,
Longford Road, Exhall, Coventry, Warwickshire,
CV7 9NE

Tel: 024 7658 8440
Fax: 024 7658 8441
E-mail: info.coventry@continyou.org.uk

Website:
http://www.continyou.org.uk
Information about ContinYou's work, projects,
consultancy, training, publications.
http://www.continyou.org.uk/publications
Publications list.

Enquiries:
Enquiries to: Publications Co-ordinator
Direct tel: 024 7658 8465

Founded:
2003

Organisation type and purpose:
Voluntary organisation, registered charity (charity
number 1097596).

Subject coverage:
Community-based learning, parental involvement
in education, extended schools, out-of-school-
hours learning, lifelong learning, family learning,
economic and community regeneration, health
improvement, promoting healthy communities.

Printed publications:
Focus (Wales publication)
Bulletin (Supplementary Schools)
Order printed publications from: Publications, Sales,
ContinYou, at the same address; tel: 024 7658 8470;
fax: 024 7658 8441; e-mail: publications.sales@
continyou.org.uk

Publications list:
Available online and in print

Access to staff:
Contact by letter, by telephone, by fax, by e-mail
and via website. Appointment necessary.
Hours: Mon to Thu, 0900 to 1700; Fri 0900 to 1630

CONTRACT FLOORING ASSOCIATION

Acronym or abbreviation: CFA

4C Saint Mary's Place, The Lace Market,
Nottingham, NG1 1PH

Tel: 0115 941 1126
Fax: 0115 941 2238
E-mail: info@cfa.org.uk

Website:
http://www.cfa.org.uk

Founded:
1974

Organisation type and purpose:
Trade association.

Subject coverage:
All types of floorcoverings, incl. carpet, timber,
resilient.

Printed publications:
Contract Flooring Journal
Guide to Contract Flooring
Members Handbook

Publications list:
Available in print

Access to staff:
Contact by letter, by telephone, by fax, by e-mail
and via website
Hours: Mon to Fri, 0900 to 1700

Member organisation of:
National Specialist Contractors Council (NSCC)

CONTROL SYSTEMS CENTRE

Acronym or abbreviation: CSC

UMIST, Department of Electrical Engineering &
Electronics, PO Box 88, Manchester, M60 1QD

Tel: 0161 200 4665
Fax: 0161 200 4647
E-mail: neil@csc.umist.ac.uk

Website:
http://www.csc.umist.ac.uk

Enquiries:
Enquiries to: Head of Centre

Founded:
1966

Organisation type and purpose:
University department or institute, consultancy.
University unit within the Department of Electrical
and Electronic Engineering.
Interdisciplinary research in control and systems
engineering.

Subject coverage:
Control and information technology, multivariable
control system design, computer-aided design,
self-tuning regulators, 2-D system theory, robust
control, fault detection, symbolic programming,
nonlinear systems, optimisation.

Printed publications:
Control System Centre Reports
Control System Centre Book Series: a set of texts on
important developments in control theory and
engineering includes:
Analysis of Piecewise Linear Dynamical Systems
(Pettit N, 1995)
Application of Neural Networks to Adaptive
Control of Nonlinear Systems (Ng G W, 1997)
Change Detection and Input Design in Dynamical
Systems (Kerestecioglu F, 1993)
Pole Assignment for Uncertain Systems (Soylemez
T, 1999)
Possibility Theory with Applications to Data
Analysis (Woklenhauer O, 1998)
Self Tuning Control for Two-Dimensional
Processes (Heath W, 1994)
Symbolic Methods in Control System Analysis and
Design (Munro N, 1999)
Order printed publications from: IEE, RSP and J Wiley

Publications list:
Available in print

Access to staff:
Contact by letter, by telephone, by fax and by e-
mail
Hours: Mon to Fri, 0900 to 1700

CONVENTION OF SCOTTISH LOCAL AUTHORITIES

Acronym or abbreviation: COSLA

Rosebery House, 9 Haymarket Terrace, Edinburgh,
EH12 5XZ

Tel: 0131 474 9200
Fax: 0131 474 9292
E-mail: carol@cosla.gov.uk

Website:
http://www.cosla.gov.uk
Background to COSLA, meeting dates and
agendas, publications list, news releases,
conference facilities.

Enquiries:
Enquiries to: Head of Media and Communications
Direct tel: 0131 474 9205
Direct e-mail: davidk@cosla.gov.uk

Founded:
1975

Organisation type and purpose:
Local government body.

Subject coverage:
Scottish local government, people, boards, and
public bodies.

Printed publications:
The Directory of Scottish Local Government
Order printed publications from: COSLA Connections

Publications list:
Available online and in print

Access to staff:
Contact by letter, by telephone, by fax, by e-mail
and via website
Hours: Mon to Fri, 0900 to 1700

Access to building, collection or gallery:
Main Reception

Hours: Mon to Fri, 0900 to 1700

Also at:
COSLA
Brussels Office, The House of Cities, Municipalities & Regions, Square de Meeus 1 , B-1000 Brussels, Belgium; tel: +32 (0)2 213 8120; fax: +32 (0)2 213 8129; e-mail: cosla@pophost .eunet.be
COSLA
Glasgow Office, Suite 203, 69 Buchanan Street, Glasgow, G1 3HL; tel: 0141 314 3700; fax: 0141 314 3836

CONWY COUNTY BOROUGH COUNCIL

Acronym or abbreviation: CCBC

Bodlondeb, Conwy, LL32 8DU

Tel: 01492 574000
Fax: 01492 592114
E-mail: information@conwy.gov.uk

Website:
http://www.conwy.gov.uk

Enquiries:
Enquiries to: Chief Executive
Direct fax: 01492 576003
Other contacts: Corporate Information and Complaints Manager

Founded:
1996

Created by the merger of:
Colwyn Borough Council and Aberconwy Borough Council (year of change 1996)

Organisation type and purpose:
Local government body.

Subject coverage:
Information on services provided by the Authority for those who live in, work in or visit Conwy County Borough.

Information services:
Corporate Information and Complaints Service, Library and Information Services, Corporate Research and Information Unit, Marketing and Communications Unit, Tourist Information Services

Education services:
Education Services

Services for disabled people:
Physical Disability and Sensory Impairment Service

Trade and statistical information:
Local census information available, business directory, community information directory

Library catalogue:
All or part available online

Printed publications:
Numerous
Order printed publications from: Corporate Information and Complaints Service, Publications Circulation, Reception and Information Desk, Civic Offices, Colwyn Bay, LL29 8AR

Access to staff:
Contact by letter, by telephone, by fax, by e-mail, in person and via website
Hours: Mon to Thu, 0845 to 1715; Fri, 0845 to 1645

Access to building, collection or gallery:
Access is different for each council building, contact for further details

Access for disabled people:
Access is different for each council building, contact for further details

CONWY LIBRARY SERVICE

Formal name: Conwy County Borough Council – Community Development Service – Culture and Information
Acronym or abbreviation: CLIS

The Old Board School, Lloyd Street, Llandudno, LL30 2YG

Tel: 01492 576139
Fax: 01492 577550
E-mail: library@conwy.gov.uk

Website:
http://www.conwy.gov.uk/library
Conwy Library and Information website.
http://www.conwy.gov.uk/llyfrgell
Welsh version of Library and Information website.
http://www.conwy.gov.uk
Conwy County Borough Council website.
http://prism.talis.com/conwy
Online catalogue for North West Wales.

Enquiries:
Enquiries to: Section Head: Culture and Information
Direct e-mail: rhian.williams@conwy.gov.uk

Founded:
1996

Formerly a part of:
Gwynedd and Clwyd Library Services (year of change 1996)

Organisation type and purpose:
Local government body, statutory body, public library.
Information and archives service.

Subject coverage:
Local government information; Welsh history; Welsh language and literature; Welsh reference material, local information.

Museum or gallery collection, archive, or library special collection:
Alice in Wonderland Books Collection at Llandudno library
Archive access points (held at Llandudno and Colwyn Bay libraries)

Trade and statistical information:
Statistical information, e.g. population, social data, etc.

Non-library collection catalogue:
All or part available online

Library catalogue:
All or part available online

Access to staff:
Contact by letter, by telephone, by fax, by e-mail and via website
Hours: Mon to Fri, 0900 to 1700
Special comments: Headquarters visitors by prior appointment only.

Access to building, collection or gallery:
Hours: Opening times vary; contact for further details

Access for disabled people:
Special comments: Headquarters on first floor, with no lift.

Branch libraries:
Abergele Library
Market Street, Abergele, LL22 7BP; tel: 01492 577505; fax: 01745 823376; e-mail: llyfr.lib .abergele@conwy.gov.uk; website: http://www .conwy.gov.uk/library/abergele
Cerrigydrudion Library
King Street, Cerrigydrudion, Corwen, LL21 9UB; tel: 01490 420501; e-mail: llyfr.lib.cerrig@conwy .gov.uk; website: http://www.conwy.gov.uk/ library/cerrigydrudion
Colwyn Bay Library
Woodland Road West, Colwyn Bay, LL29 7DH; tel: 01492 577510; fax: 01492 534474; e-mail: llyfr .lib.baecolwynbay@conwy.gov.uk; website: http: .//www.conwy.gov.uk/library/colwynbay
Conwy Library
Civic Hall, Castle Street, Conwy, LL32 6AY; tel: 01492 596242; fax: 01492 582359; e-mail: llyfr.lib .conwy@conwy.gov.uk; website: http://www .conwy.gov.uk/library/conwy

Deganwy Library
Station Road, Deganwy, Conwy, LL31 9EX; tel: 01492 584705; e-mail: llyfr.lib.deganwy@conwy .gov.uk; website: http://www.conwy.gov.uk/ library/deganwy
Kinmel Bay Library
Community Centre, Kendal Road, Kinmel Bay, LL18 5BT; tel: 01745 353499; e-mail: llyfr.lib .kinmel@conwy.gov.uk; website: http://www .conwy.gov.uk/library/kinmelbay
Llandudno Junction Library
Maes Derw, Llandudno Junction, LL31 9AL; tel: 01492 582266; e-mail: llyfr.lib.cyffordd@conwy .gov.uk; website: http://www.conwy.gov.uk/ library/llandudnojunction
Llandudno Library
Victoria Centre, Mostyn Street, Llandudno, LL30 2RS; tel: 01492 574010; 01492 574020; fax: 01492 876826; e-mail: llyfr.lib.llandudno@conwy.gov .uk; website: http://www.conwy.gov.uk/library/ llandudno
Llanfairfechan Library
Village Road, Llanfairfechan, LL33 0AA; tel: 01248 681014; e-mail: llyfr.lib.llanfairfechan@ conwy.gov.uk; website: http://www.conwy.gov .uk/library/llanfairfechan
Llangernyw Library
Ysgol Bro Cernyw, Llangernyw, Abergele, LL22 8PF; tel: 01745 860413; e-mail: llyfr.lib .llangernyw@conwy.gov.uk; website: http:// www.conwy.gov.uk/library/llangernyw
Llanrwst Library
Plas yn Dre, Station Road, Llanrwst, LL26 0DF; tel: 01492 577545; e-mail: llyfr.lib.llanrwst@ conwy.gov.uk; website: http://www.conwy.gov .uk/library/llanrwst
Penmaenmawr Library
Bangor Road, Penmaenmawr, LL34 6DA; tel: 01492 623619; e-mail: llyfr.lib.penmaenmawr@ conwy.gov.uk; website: http://www.conwy.gov .uk/library/penmaenmawr
Penrhyn Bay Library
Llandudno Road, Penrhyn Bay, Llandudno, LL30 3HN; tel: 01492 548873; e-mail: llyfr.lib .penrhyn@conwy.gov.uk; website: http://www .conwy.gov.uk/library/penrhynbay

Constituent part of:
Conwy County Borough Council
Bodlondeb, Conwy, North Wales, LL32 8DU; tel: 01492 574000; e-mail: information@conwy.gov .uk; website: http://www.conwy.gov.uk

COPELAND BOROUGH COUNCIL

The Copeland Centre, Catherine Street, Whitehaven, Cumbria, CA28 7SJ

Tel: 0845 095 2100
Fax: 0845 095 2140

Website:
http://www.copelandbc.gov.uk

Enquiries:
Enquiries to: General Manager
Direct tel: 01946 598320
Direct fax: 01946 598303
Direct e-mail: jstanforth@copelandbc.gov.uk

Organisation type and purpose:
Local government body.

Subject coverage:
Corporate services, education, environmental services, finance, housing, legal services, personnel services, planning development and tourism, property and technical services, roads and transportation, social services, council tax and other payments, registration of births, deaths and marriages.

Access to staff:
Contact by letter, by telephone, by fax, by e-mail and via website
Hours: Mon to Fri, 0900 to 1700

COPPER DEVELOPMENT ASSOCIATION

Acronym or abbreviation: CDA

5 Grovelands Business Centre, Boundary Way, Hemel Hempstead, HP2 7TE

Tel: 01442 275705
Fax: 01442 275716
E-mail: mail@copperdev.co.uk

Website:
http://www.copperinfo.co.uk
http://www.cda.org.uk
CDA publications.

Enquiries:
Enquiries to: Information Manager

Founded:
1933

Organisation type and purpose:
Advisory body, service industry, research organisation.
Non-trading organisation, sponsored by copper producers and fabricators.

Subject coverage:
Copper, its alloys and compounds, non-ferrous metals, market development and technical data.

Printed publications:
Information Sheets
Technical Notes

Electronic and video publications:
Datadiscs (8 discs for PC)
Megabytes on Copper (56 publications and 8 datadiscs on CD-ROM, £20)
Videos (8, purchase or hire)

Publications list:
Available online

Access to staff:
Contact by letter, by telephone, by fax and in person. Appointment necessary.
Hours: Mon to Fri, 0930 to 1700

COPYRIGHT LICENSING AGENCY

Acronym or abbreviation: CLA

Saffron House, 6–10 Kirby Street, London, EC1N 8TS

Fax: 020 7400 3100
E-mail: cla@cla.co.uk

Website:
http://www.cla.co.uk
Background information on copyright. Interactive questionnaire 'Do you need a photocopying licence?' Publication-specific photocopy and coursepack fees. On-line clearance for registered users.

Enquiries:
Enquiries to: PR Manager
Other contacts: Marketing Manager

Founded:
1982

Organisation type and purpose:
Service industry.
To license photocopying and scanning of extracts and clippings from copyright books, journals and magazines.

Subject coverage:
Copyright licensing, copyright, electronic copying, internet issues.

Trade and statistical information:
Photocopy fees for specific publications.

Printed publications:
Clarion (twice a year, free newsletter)
Annual Report
Various leaflets

Access to staff:
Contact by letter, by telephone and by e-mail
Hours: Mon to Fri, 0900 to 1700
Special comments: Internet online 24 hrs.

Affiliated to:
Association of Learned and Professional Society Publishers
International Federation of Reproduction Rights Organisations
Publishers Association
Publishers Licensing Society (PLS)
    37–41 Gower Street, London, WC1E 6HH; tel: 020 7299 7730; fax: 020 7299 7780; e-mail: pls@pls .org.uk
Society of Authors
Writers' Guild of Great Britain

Parent body:
Authors' Licensing and Collecting Society (ALCS)
    Marlborough Court, 14–18 Holborn, London, EC1N 2LE; tel: 020 7395 0600; fax: 020 7395 0660; e-mail: alcs@alcs.co.uk

CORBY BOROUGH COUNCIL

Deene House, New Post Office Square, Corby, Northamptonshire, NN17 1GD

Tel: 01536 402551
Fax: 01536 464640

Website:
http://www.corby.gov.uk

Enquiries:
Enquiries to: Public Relations Manager

Founded:
1993

Formerly called:
Corby District Council

Organisation type and purpose:
Local government body.

Subject coverage:
Corby Borough, services and amenities.

Access to staff:
Contact by letter, by telephone, by fax and by e-mail. Appointment necessary.
Hours: Mon to Fri, 0900 to 1700

CORD

Formal name: Christian Outreach – Relief and Development

1 New Street, Leamington Spa, Warwickshire, CV1 1HP

Tel: 01926 315301
Fax: 01926 885786
E-mail: info@cord.org.uk

Enquiries:
Enquiries to: Director

Founded:
1967

Formerly called:
Christian Outreach Project Vietnam Orphans (year of change 1999)

Organisation type and purpose:
International organisation, registered charity (charity number 1070684).
An international Christian-based relief and development organisation.

Printed publications:
Compassion in Action (newsletter 6 times a year, free of charge)

Access to staff:
Contact by letter and by e-mail
Hours: Mon to Fri, 0900 to 1700

CORE

3 St Andrew's Place, Regent's Park, London, NW1 4LB

Tel: 020 7486 0341
Fax: 020 7224 2012
E-mail: info@corecharity.org.uk

Website:
http://www.corecharity.org.uk
Patient information, Core activities, details of research awards, newsletter

Enquiries:
Enquiries to: Public Affairs Coordinator
Direct tel: 020 7034 4972

Founded:
1971

Formerly called:
Digestive Disorders Foundation (year of change 2004)

Organisation type and purpose:
Registered charity (charity number 1137029), research organisation.
Core supports research into all aspects of digestive disease.

Subject coverage:
Gastroenterology, including the physiology and pathology of the digestive system; research into causes, prevention and treatment of digestive disorders.

Printed publications:
Annual Report and Accounts, Newsletter (3 annually)
Information leaflets on common digestive disorders including: ulcers, heartburn, irritable bowel syndrome, diverticular disease, coeliac disease, indigestion, constipation, diarrhoea, gallstones, etc. (free plus p&p)
Order printed publications from: Leaflets available from: Core, 3 St Andrews Place, London, NW1 4LB

Publications list:
Available in print

Access to staff:
Contact by letter, by telephone, by fax, by e-mail and via website
Hours: Mon to Fri, 0900 to 1700
Special comments: Please send sae if requiring information.

Close association with:
British Liver Trust
Children's Liver Disease Foundation
Coeliac Society
Crohn's in Childhood Research Appeal
IA – The Ileostomy and Internal Pouch Support Group
IBS Network
National Association for Colitis and Crohn's Disease

CORK INDUSTRY FEDERATION

Acronym or abbreviation: CIF

13 Felton Lea, Sidcup, Kent, DA14 6BA

Tel: 020 8302 4801
Fax: 020 8302 4801

Website:
http://www.cork-products.co.uk
Addresses and products of all members and cork information.

Enquiries:
Enquiries to: Honorary Secretary
Other contacts: Chairman

Founded:
1969

Organisation type and purpose:
Trade association (membership is by subscription).

Subject coverage:
All aspects of cork, for domestic, decorative, industrial and architectural uses, and for use in the wine and spirit trades; advice can be given on roof drainage and insulation, material selection and design.

Museum or gallery collection, archive, or library special collection:
Details of cork products

Access to staff:
Contact by letter, by telephone and by fax

Hours: Mon to Fri, 0900 to 1700

Member organisation of:
European Cork Industry Federation

CORNWALL CENTRE (KRESENN KERNOW)

Alma Place, Redruth, Cornwall, TR15 2AT

Tel: 01209 216760
Fax: 01209 210283
E-mail: cornishstudies.library@cornwall.gov.uk

Website:
http://www.cornwall.gov.uk/cornwallcentre
Library content, including newspapers list, photographic database, timeline of Cornish history.

Enquiries:
Enquiries to: Librarian

Founded:
1974

Organisation type and purpose:
Local government body, public library.
Local studies library and visitor centre.

Subject coverage:
Cornwall

Museum or gallery collection, archive, or library special collection:
Ashley Rowe Collection (general Cornish)
Hambly and Rowe Collection (general Cornish)
A. K. Hamilton Jenkin Collection (Cornish mining)
Cornish Newspapers (around 50 titles, microfilm)
Photographs (over 150,000)
Cornish Census returns
Maps
Parish Register transcriptions
Books and pamphlets about Cornwall

Library catalogue:
All or part available online

Printed publications:
Leaflets (free)
Directories
Newspapers
Parish Register transcripts

Electronic and video publications:
Photographic reproductions (to order)

Access to staff:
Contact by letter, by telephone, by fax, by e-mail and in person
Hours: Mon to Fri, 1000 to 1700; Sat, 1000 to 1600
Special comments: Prior appointment is advisable to view microforms.

Access for disabled people:
Level entry, access to all public areas, toilet facilities

Parent body:
Cornwall Council
Cornwall Library Service, Unit 17, Threemilestone Industrial Estate, Truro, Cornwall, TR4 9LD; tel: 0300 123 4111; fax: 01872 223509; e-mail: libraries@cornwall.gov.uk; website: http://www.cornwall.gov.uk

CORNWALL COLLEGE GROUP

Acronym or abbreviation: CCLS

Learning Services, Cornwall College St Austell, Tregonissey Road, St Austell, Cornwall, PL25 4DJ

Tel: 01726 226401
E-mail: peter.sampson@cornwall.ac.uk

Website:
http://www.cornwall.ac.uk
General information about the College, including courses and services.

Organisation type and purpose:
Further and higher education.

Subject coverage:
General.

Library catalogue:
All or part available online and in-house

Printed publications:
General guides

Access to staff:
Access for members only. Non-members charged.
Hours: Mon to Fri, 0900 to 1630 (minimum)

Also at:
Cornwall College Camborne
Trevenson Road, Redruth, TR15 3RD; tel: 01209 616242
Cornwall College Newquay
Centre for Applied Zoology, Wildflower Lane, Trenance Gardens, Newquay, TR7 2LZ; tel: 01637 857930
Cornwall College Saltash
Church Road, Saltash, PL12 4AE; tel: 01752 850215
Duchy College Rosewarne
Rosewarne, Cambourne, TR14 0AB; tel: 01209 722134
Duchy College Stoke Climsland
Stoke Climsland, Callington, PL17 8PB; tel: 01579 372213
Falmouth Marine School
Killigrew Street, Falmouth, TR11 3QS; tel: 01326 310319; fax: 01326 310331

CORNWALL FAMILY HISTORY SOCIETY

Acronym or abbreviation: CFHS

5 Victoria Square, Truro, Cornwall, TR1 2RS

Tel: 01872 264044
E-mail: secretary@cornwallfhs.com

Website:
http://www.cornwallfhs.com

Enquiries:
Enquiries to: Administrator

Founded:
1976

Organisation type and purpose:
International organisation, membership association (membership is by subscription), present number of members: 5100, voluntary organisation, registered charity (charity number 288686), research organisation.
To promote interest in family history research into Cornish families.

Subject coverage:
All records concerning the tracing of Cornish family histories.

Museum or gallery collection, archive, or library special collection:
Books, documents, indexes, photographs of Cornish families
Much held on computer database
1837–1992 GRO index (microfiche)
1841–1901 Censuses (microfiche)

Printed publications:
Society Journal
A very large number of publications providing: monumental inscriptions, Pre-Civil Registration marriage index, Phillimore marriage index, 1813–37 parish burial index, 1841 census index, 1851 census index, 1861 census index, 1871 census index, 1891 census index; the publications list provides details of which parishes are covered

Microform publications:
Directory of members' interests (microfiche, members only)

Publications list:
Available online and in print

Access to staff:
Contact by letter, by telephone, by e-mail, in person and via website. Non-members charged.
Hours: Mon, 1000 to 1600; Wed to Sat, 1100 to 1500; Tue, closed

CORNWALL LIBRARY SERVICE

Unit 17, Threemilestone Industrial Estate, Truro, Cornwall, TR4 9LD

Tel: 01872 324316
Fax: 01872 223509
E-mail: library@cornwall.gov.uk

Website:
http://www.cornwall.gov.uk

Organisation type and purpose:
Local government body, public library.

Subject coverage:
General; metalliferous mining in Cornwall; county local studies (at Redruth); performing arts (at St Austell); art (at Penzance); maritime studies (at Falmouth); law and business (at Truro).

Museum or gallery collection, archive, or library special collection:
Ashley Rowe Collection (local studies)
Cornish Methodist Historical Association (on deposit)
Hambley Rowe Collection (local studies)
Hamilton Jenkin Collection (local studies)
Rosewarne Collection (local studies)

Non-library collection catalogue:
All or part available online

Library catalogue:
All or part available online

Printed publications:
Subject Index

Parent body:
Cornwall County Council

CORNWALL REFERENCE AND INFORMATION LIBRARY

Union Place, Truro, Cornwall, TR1 1EP

Tel: 01872 272702; Freephone 0800 032 2345
Fax: 01872 223772
E-mail: reference.library@cornwall.gov.uk

Website:
http://www.cornwall.gov.uk/library

Enquiries:
Enquiries to: Librarian

Founded:
1896

Formerly called:
Cornwall County Reference and Information Library

Organisation type and purpose:
Public reference library, Cornwall Centre for Europe Direct

Subject coverage:
Law and business, European information, general reference.

Trade and statistical information:
General statistics.

Non-library collection catalogue:
All or part available online

Library catalogue:
All or part available online

Electronic and video publications:
Community information for Cornwall (available online)

Access to staff:
Contact by letter, by telephone, by fax, by e-mail, in person and via website
Hours: Mon, Tue, Thu and Fri, 0900 to 1800; Wed, 0930 to 1800; Sat, 0900 to 1600

Access for disabled people:
Parking provided, level entry, access to all public areas

Parent body:
Chief Executive's Department
New County Hall, Truro, Cornwall, TR1 3EW; tel: 01872 322000; fax: 01872 323818

CORONA WORLDWIDE

Acronym or abbreviation: CWW

Southbank House, Black Prince Road, London, SE1
7SJ

Tel: 020 7793 4020
Fax: 020 7793 4020
E-mail: corona@coronaworldwide.org

Website:
http://www.corona_worldwide.org
http://www.coronaworldwide.org

Enquiries:
Enquiries to: Administrative Secretary

Founded:
1950

Formerly called:
Women's Corona Society (year of change 2006)

Organisation type and purpose:
International organisation, voluntary organisation,
registered charity (charity number 204802),
suitable for ages: adults.
Notes for newcomers to over 100 countries
worldwide.
To support people going to work and live in other
countries by giving them information about living
conditions there, to welcome people coming to live
in Britain; aim is to promote friendship and
understanding around the world.

Subject coverage:
Living and working in foreign countries.

Printed publications:
Forty Years of Service (the history of the society)
Magazine (yearly, sent to members, available on
request)
Notes for newcomers to various countries (price on
application)

Access to staff:
Contact by letter, by telephone, by fax and by e-
mail
Hours: Tue, Thu, 0900 to 1700

Access to building, collection or gallery:
Hours: 0900 to 1700
Special comments: Security pass at reception.

CORONERS' SOCIETY OF ENGLAND AND WALES

HM Coroner's Court, The Cotton Exchange, Old
Hall Street, Liverpool, L3 9UF

Tel: 0151 233 4708
Fax: 0151 233 4710
E-mail: andre.rebello@liverpool.gov.uk

Website:
http://www.coroner.org.uk

Enquiries:
Enquiries to: Honorary Secretary

Founded:
1846

Organisation type and purpose:
Professional body (membership is by election or
invitation), present number of members: 400.
Membership restricted to coroners, deputies and
assistant deputies, and retired coroners.

Subject coverage:
Law and practice concerning coroners.

**Museum or gallery collection, archive, or library
special collection:**
Minutes and reports 1846–

Access to staff:
Contact by letter and by e-mail
Hours: Mon to Fri, 0900 to 1700

CORPORATION OF INSURANCE, FINANCIAL AND MORTGAGE ADVISERS

Acronym or abbreviation: CIFMA

174 High Street, Guildford, Surrey, GU1 3HW

Tel: 01483 539121
Fax: 01483 301847

Enquiries:
Enquiries to: General Secretary

Founded:
1968

Formerly called:
Corporation of Mortgage Brokers (year of change
1972)

Organisation type and purpose:
Professional body, membership association
(membership is by subscription, qualification),
present number of members: c. 700.
To raise the professional standards in mortgage
broking and the associated life assurance industry
and general insurance industry.

Subject coverage:
Mortgage broking, life insurance and general
insurance.

Printed publications:
Newsletter (free to members)

Access to staff:
Contact by letter, by telephone and by fax
Hours: Mon to Fri, 0900 to 1700

CORPORATION OF LONDON RECORDS OFFICE

Acronym or abbreviation: CLRO

c/o London Metropolitan Archives, 40
Northampton Road, London, EC1R 0HB

Tel: 020 7332 3820
Fax: 020 7833 9136
E-mail: ask.lma@cityoflondon.gov.uk

Website:
http://www.cityoflondon.gov.uk/archives/lma

Enquiries:
Enquiries to: Enquiries Team

Founded:
1876

Formerly called:
City of London Record(s) Office, Guildhall
Record(s) Office

Organisation type and purpose:
Local government body.
Record office.
Custody of the official archives of the Corporation
of the City of London.

Subject coverage:
Archives of national as well as civic interest,
reflecting the interests and activities of the
Corporation, from the 11th to the 20th centuries.

**Museum or gallery collection, archive, or library
special collection:**
Administrative records, such as: Proceedings of the
Courts of Aldermen and Common Council, 15th
century onwards
Financial records
Judicial records, from the civic courts and the
Sessions of Gaol Delivery and Peace, 13th
century onwards
Medieval compilations of City law and custom
Records of admission to the Freedom of the City
Records of the City of London Police
Rentals and deeds relating to property, some of
which lay outside the City
Royal Charters 1067 onwards

Non-library collection catalogue:
All or part available online, in-house and in print

Printed publications:
A variety of histories and calendars of records are
available for purchase; also some free
publications available:
An Introductory Guide to the Corporation of
London Records Office (out of print)
Calendar of Coroners Rolls of the City of London
1300–78 (£15)
Calendar of Early Mayor's Court Rolls 1298–1307
(out of print)
Calendar of Plea and Memoranda Rolls 1323–64,
1364–81, 1381–1412, 1413–37 (all out of print),
1437–57, 1458–82 (£15 each)
Calendar of Wills proved and enrolled in the Court
of Husting, London 1258–1688
Greater London History Sources: Vol. 1 City of
London (available from Guildhall Library, £14.95
hardback, £9.95 paperback)
Information sheets (free publications)
Southwark and the City (out of print)
The Fire Court, Calendar to the Decrees of the
Court of Judicature on disputes as to rebuilding
after the Great Fire: Vol. 1 1667–68, Vol. 2 1667–
68 (£10 each)

Microform publications:
Remembrancia c.1579–1664/65 (pub. World
Microfilms)
The Husting Rolls of Deeds and Wills, 1252–1485
(pub. Chadwyck-Healey, later International
Imaging)
The Making of Modern London: Repertories, 1495–
1692 (pub. Research Publications International)
The Whitechapel Murders Papers (pub. World
Microfilms)

Publications list:
Available online and in print

Access to staff:
Contact by letter, by telephone, by fax, by e-mail,
in person and via website

Access to building, collection or gallery:
Hours: Mon, Wed and Fri, 0930 to 1645; Tue and
Thu, 0930 to 1930; Sat, contact for details
Special comments: Appointments required to view
rare books.

Access for disabled people:
Toilet facilities

CORPORATION OF TRINITY HOUSE

Trinity House, Tower Hill, London, EC3N 4DH

Tel: 020 7481 6900
Fax: 020 7480 7662
E-mail: enquiries@thls.org

Website:
http://www.trinityhouse.co.uk
Information on the history and current operations
of Trinity House including profiles of all 72
lighthouses and latest news, notices to mariners.

Enquiries:
Direct e-mail: paul.howe@thls.org
Other contacts: Media and Communication Officer

Founded:
1514

Organisation type and purpose:
Statutory body, registered charity.
General lighthouse authority for England, Wales
and Channel Islands, a deep sea pilotage authority
and marine charitable organisation.

Subject coverage:
History and current operations of Trinity House.
Aids to navigation – lighthouses, light vessels,
buoyage and radio navigation.

**Museum or gallery collection, archive, or library
special collection:**
Corporations archives dating from 1660 held by
Guildhall Library
Library – mainly nautical books

Printed publications:
Information pack on history and modern day
activities of the Corporation (free)
Trinity House Calendar (for purchase)
Horizon (2 times a year, free)
Order printed publications from: Publications Office
at the same address, tel: 020 7481 6900

Access to staff:
Contact by letter, by telephone, by fax, by e-mail

and via website. Appointment necessary.
Hours: Mon to Fri, 0900 to 1700

CORPS OF COMMISSIONAIRES MANAGEMENT LIMITED

Acronym or abbreviation: The Corps

85 Cowcross Street, London, EC1M 6PF

Tel: 020 7566 0500
Fax: 020 7566 0522
E-mail: info@the-corps.co.uk

Website:
http://www.the-corps.co.uk

Enquiries:
Enquiries to: Executive Director
Other contacts: Sales and Marketing Director

Founded:
1859

Organisation type and purpose:
National organisation, present number of members: 3000, service industry.
Providers of security and facilities support services.
To help (former) members of HM's Uniformed Services find employment (worldwide).

Subject coverage:
Availability of employment using former military/police skills.
Security – manned guarding, receptionists, patrols and key-holding, training.
Recruitment agency, international projects and consultancy.
Facilities support: mailrooms, file management, building administration and management, receptionists.

Museum or gallery collection, archive, or library special collection:
Uncatalogued collection, archive stored photographs of corps members (informal), may or may not be identifiable

Library catalogue:
All or part available in-house

Printed publications:
Directory of Services
L'Esprit (in-house staff magazine, free to staff, clients)
Our Sergeant (history of the Corps of Commissionaires, p.o.a.)

Electronic and video publications:
Corporate Video

Access to staff:
Contact by letter, by telephone and by fax.
Appointment necessary.
Hours: Mon to Fri, 0900 to 1700

Affiliations with:
Similar associations with the same name exist in Commonwealth countries – Canada and Australia

Branches at:
Corps of Commissionaires Management Limited
In 16 major UK towns, See local Yellow Pages; website: http://www.the-corps.co.uk

CORROSION PREVENTION ASSOCIATION

Acronym or abbreviation: CPA

Kingsley House, Ganders Business Park, Kingsley, Bordon, Hampshire, GU35 9LU

Tel: 01420 471614
Fax: 01420 471611
E-mail: admin@corrosion prevention.org.uk

Website:
http://www.corrosionprevention.org.uk
Technical advice and guidance notes produced by the CPA are freely available to download.

Enquiries:
Enquiries to: Secretary

Founded:
1991

Formerly called:
Society for the Cathodic Protection of Re-Inforced Concrete (SCPRC) (year of change 1998)

Organisation type and purpose:
Construction industry association representing consultants, contractors and manufacturers working in the field of corrosion prevention for concrete and masonry-encased steel.

Subject coverage:
The CPA acts as the leading authority and source of information on the subject of cathodic protection and other corrosion techniques and encourages research to ensure better understanding of the preservation of reinforced concrete structures and masonry-clad steel-framed buildings

Library catalogue:
All or part available online

Printed publications:
Brochure and Directory of Members (free)
Cathodic Protection of Reinforced Concrete – Status Report
Reinforced Concrete: History, Properties & Durability (monograph)
Technical Guidance Notes:
No 1: Reinforced Concrete: History, Properties and Durability
No 2: An Introduction to Electrochemical Rehabilitation Techniques
No 3: Cathodic protection of steel in concrete – the international perspective
No 4: Monitoring and maintenance of cathodic protection systems
No 5: Corrosion mechanisms – an introduction to aqueous corrosion
No 6: The principles and practice of galvanic cathodic protection for reinforced concrete structures
No 7: Cathodic protection of early steel framed buildings
No 8: Cathodic protection of steel in concrete – frequently asked questions
No 9: Electrochemical Realkalisation of Steel Reinforced Concrete – A State of the Art Report
No 10: Stray Current
No 11: Impressed Current Anodes for the Cathodic Protection of Atmospherically Exposed Concrete
No 12: Budget Cost and Anode Performance Information for Impressed Current Cathodic Protection of Reinforced Concrete Highway Bridges

Publications list:
Available online and in print

Access to staff:
Contact by letter, by telephone, by fax, by e-mail and via website
Hours: Mon to Fri, 0900 to 1700

CORUS RESEARCH, DEVELOPMENT & TECHNOLOGY

Swinden Technology Centre, Library & Information Services, Moorgate, Rotherham, South Yorkshire, S60 3AR

Tel: 01709 820166
Fax: 01709 825464
E-mail: stc.library@corusgroup.com

Enquiries:
Enquiries to: Information Officer
Direct tel: 01709 825335
Direct e-mail: mike.nott@corusgroup.com

Formerly called:
British Steel plc (year of change 1999)

Organisation type and purpose:
Research organisation.

Subject coverage:
Iron and steel product applications, carbon, alloy and stainless steels, physical metallurgy, environmental sciences, welding, machinability, advanced machining, steel specifications, iron and steel roll technology, iron and steel plant.

Museum or gallery collection, archive, or library special collection:
Steel specifications and standards

Access to building, collection or gallery:
Prior appointment required

Access for disabled people:
Ramped entry

Other services:
Corus Construction Centre
Piling Advisory Service
  PO Box 1, Frodingham House, Scunthorpe, South Humberside, DN16 1BP; tel: 01724 404040
Plates Technical Advisory Centre
  PO Box 30, Motherwell, ML1 1AA; tel: 01698 266233
Stainless Steel Advisory Centre, not now part of British Steel, now Avesta
Strip Products Advisory Service
  PO Box 10, Newport, Gwent; tel: 01633 290011
Technical Hotline
  PO Box 1, Brigg Road, Scunthorpe, DN16 1BP; tel: 01724 405060
Tubes and Open Sections Structural Advisory Service
  PO Box 101, Weldon Road, Corby, Northamptonshire, NN17 1UA; tel: 01536 402121

COSMETIC, TOILETRY AND PERFUMERY ASSOCIATION LIMITED

Acronym or abbreviation: CTPA

Josaron House, 5–7 John Princes Street, London, W1G 0JN

Tel: 020 7491 8891
Fax: 020 7493 8061

Website:
http://www.ctpa.org.uk
General information about legislative controls for cosmetics, overview of CTPA and the cosmetic market. Useful contact points.

Enquiries:
Enquiries to: Company Secretary
Direct e-mail: info@ctpa.org.uk

Founded:
1945

Organisation type and purpose:
Trade association.

Subject coverage:
Cosmetic, toiletry and perfumery industry, legislation, technical information (no market information).

Information services:
Consumer website: http://www.thefactsabout.co.uk

Education services:
Online resource for schools: http://www.catie.org.uk

Electronic and video publications:
The Cost of Microbes (video)

Publications list:
Available online

Access to staff:
Access for members only.
Hours: Mon to Fri, 0900 to 1700

Member organisation of:
European Association of Cosmetic Industries (COLIPA)
  Brussels

COSTUME AND TEXTILE STUDY CENTRE, CARROW HOUSE

301 King Street, Norwich, Norfolk, NR1 2TS

Tel: 01603 223870; text phone 0844 800 8011
E-mail: museums@norfolk.gov.uk

Website:
http://www.museums.norfolk.gov.uk

Organisation type and purpose:
Study centre, with specialist facilities for students and enthusiasts.

Subject coverage:
Period costume, textiles and related material.

COSTUME SOCIETY OF SCOTLAND

Acronym or abbreviation: CSS

16 Muirpark, Eskbank, Dalkeith

Tel: 0131 663 0967
E-mail: tandd@muirpark.plus.com

Website:
http://www.costumesocietyofscotland.org
Images of some clothes, information about programme, membership and events.

Enquiries:
Enquiries to: Secretary
Other contacts: Chairman

Founded:
1965

Organisation type and purpose:
Membership association (membership is by subscription), present number of members: 90, suitable for ages: all, meet on a monthly basis for relevant talks.
To promote interest in all matters relating to costume, design and textiles.

Subject coverage:
Mourning jewellery, Scottish costume, including fisherfolks' dress, textiles and embellishment, historical and contemporary.

Museum or gallery collection, archive, or library special collection:
A small collection of donated clothes from different eras is used for study, illustrating talks and exhibition purposes and may be borrowed for a fee.
Small library of books available to members

Library catalogue:
All or part available in-house

Printed publications:
Costume Society of Scotland Bulletin (A5 b/w plates, annually, £3 inc. p&p, free to members)
Mourning Jewellery – a Collector's Account (Margaret Hunter, A4, 22pp plus 3pp colour plates, £3 inc. p&p)
Order printed publications from: Treasurer, Costume Society of Scotland, 28 Cameron Park, Newington, Edinburgh, EH16 5LA

Access to staff:
Contact by letter, by e-mail and via website
Hours: Mon to Fri, 0900 to 1700

COTSWOLD DISTRICT COUNCIL

Acronym or abbreviation: CDC

Council Offices, Trinity Road, Cirencester, Gloucestershire, GL7 1PX

Tel: 01285 623000
Fax: 01285 623900

Website:
http://www.cotswold.gov.uk

Enquiries:
Enquiries to: Information Officer
Direct tel: 01285 623132
Direct e-mail: claire.mcgine@cotswold.gov.uk

Founded:
1974

Organisation type and purpose:
Local government body.

Subject coverage:
Local government, economic development, tourism, planning, housing, enabling, environmental health; conservation, landscape; arts, leisure, museums; benefits, elections, waste collection, recycling, landcharges.

Printed publications:
Cotswold News (2 times a year, free)

Access to staff:
Contact by letter, by telephone, by fax, by e-mail, in person and via website. Appointment necessary.
Hours: Mon to Fri, 0900 to 1700

Access to building, collection or gallery:
Prior appointment required

Access for disabled people:
Parking provided, ramped entry, level entry

Branch Office:
Cotswold District Council
   Moreton in Marsh, Gloucestershire; tel: 01608 650881; fax: 01608 651542

COTTAGE AND RURAL ENTERPRISES LIMITED

Acronym or abbreviation: CARE

CARE Central Office, 9 Weir Road, Kibworth, Leicestershire, LE8 0LQ

Tel: 0116 279 3225
Fax: 0116 279 6384
E-mail: jp@care-ltd.co.uk

Website:
http://www.care-ltd.co.uk
Services offered by CARE.

Enquiries:
Enquiries to: Chief Executive

Founded:
1966

Organisation type and purpose:
Voluntary organisation, registered charity (charity number 250058).
CARE is a national charity that responds creatively and innovatively to the changing needs of people with learning disabilities.

Subject coverage:
Care of adults with a learning disability in communities where they live and work.

Printed publications:
All About CARE
Principles and Policies (booklet)

Access to staff:
Contact by letter, by telephone, by fax, by e-mail and via website
Hours: Mon to Fri, 0900 to 1700

COUGAR CLUB OF AMERICA

Acronym or abbreviation: CCOA

International Office, 19A Lorne Road. Oxton. Birkenhead. CH43 2JW

Tel: 0151 652 3984
E-mail: international@cougarclub.org

Website:
http://www.cougarclub.org

Enquiries:
Enquiries to: International Manager

Founded:
1980

Organisation type and purpose:
International organisation, membership association (membership is by subscription), present number of members: 1,000.

Subject coverage:
Information regarding 1967 to present, Mercury Cougars, i.e. options, identifications, parts availability, parts suppliers. All this information is free to members.

Printed publications:
At The Sign of the Cat (newsletter, quarterly, free to members)

Access to staff:
Contact by letter and by e-mail
Hours: Mon to Sat, 1000 to 1900

Parent body:
Cougar Club of America
   e-mail: membership@cougarclub.org

COUNCIL FOR ADVANCEMENT AND SUPPORT OF EDUCATION (EUROPE)

Acronym or abbreviation: CASE

Entrance A, Tavistock House North, Tavistock Square, London, WC1H 9HX

Tel: 020 7387 4404
Fax: 020 7387 4408
E-mail: info@eurocase.org.uk

Website:
http://www.case.org
Full information about the organisation and its activities and services.

Enquiries:
Enquiries to: Executive Director
Direct e-mail: jmotion@eurocase.org.uk

Founded:
1994

Organisation type and purpose:
International organisation, registered charity (charity number 1042724), training organisation, consultancy, research organisation, publishing house.
Dissemination of Best Practice in the advancement of education.

Subject coverage:
Educational external relations, in particular alumni relations, communications, fund raising, marketing, philanthropy, public relations, student recruitment.

Printed publications:
A large range of publications on the subject of the Council
CASE CURRENTS (10 times a year, for members)
CASE Directory of Advancement Professionals in Education

Electronic and video publications:
Audio and video cassettes on aspects of institutional advancement

Publications list:
Available in print

Access to staff:
Contact by letter, by telephone, by fax and by e-mail. Access for members only. Non-members charged.
Hours: Mon to Fri, 0900 to 1700

Connections with:
CASE
   Suite 400, 11 Dupont Circle, Washington, DC, 20036–1261, USA

COUNCIL FOR ALUMINIUM IN BUILDING

Acronym or abbreviation: CAB

Bank House, Bond's Mill, Stonehouse, Gloucestershire, GL10 3RF

Tel: 01453 828851
Fax: 01453 828861
E-mail: enquiries@c-a-b.org.uk

Website:
http://www.c-a-b.org.uk

Enquiries:
Enquiries to: Chief Executive
Direct tel: 01453 828856

Founded:
1995

Incorporates the former:
Aluminium Window Association (AWA),
Architectural Aluminium Association (AAA),
Patent Glazing Contractors' Association (PGCA)
(year of change 1995)

Organisation type and purpose:
Trade association.

Subject coverage:
Aluminium in building, patent glazing, curtain
wall, aluminium windows, doors, cladding and
roofing in aluminium, aluminium powder
coatings, anodising, hardware, systems suppliers.

Printed publications:
Curtain Walling and Large Composite Windows,
notes for guidance
Guide to Specification of Windows and Doors
Guide to the Specification of Patent Glazing
Products and Services Guide
Specifying Window Performance BSI/DIN
Comparison
Thermal Assessment Guide to Windows and
Curtain Wall Structures

Publications list:
Available online

Access to staff:
Contact by letter, by telephone, by fax and by e-
mail
Hours: Mon to Fri, 0900 to 1700

Member organisation of:
Centre for Window and Cladding Technology
(CWCT)
Construction Products Association

COUNCIL FOR AWARDS IN CHILDREN'S CARE AND EDUCATION

Acronym or abbreviation: CACHE

8 Chequer Street, St Albans, Hertfordshire, AL1
3XZ

Tel: 01727 847636
Fax: 01727 867609
E-mail: info@cache.org.uk

Website:
http://www.cache.org.uk

Enquiries:
Enquiries to: Chief Executive
Other contacts: Information and Publications
Officer, Marketing Officer

Founded:
1994

Formed by the merger of:
Council for Early Years Awards (CEYA), National
Nursery Examination Board (NNEB), date of
change, April 1994; National Association for
Maternal and Child Welfare (NAMCW) (year of
change 2000)

Organisation type and purpose:
Registered charity (charity number 1036232).
Awarding body.
Offers courses and NVQ assessment in childcare,
education and playwork.

Subject coverage:
Vocational training in child care, education and
playwork; NVQs; early years workers, A&V units
for assessors and verifiers.

**Museum or gallery collection, archive, or library
special collection:**
Archive material regarding the history of the
NNEB and CEYA, and the development of their
awards and courses in child care and education
Pass lists of candidates who have successfully
completed course and awards

Trade and statistical information:
Numbers of candidates registered as training with
the Council.
Post-qualifying employment and progression.
Equal opportunities monitoring.
Number of study centres approved to run Council
awards and which particular courses they offer.
Number of candidates registered for NVQ
assessment.
Number of NVQ Assessment Centres approved by
CACHE to offer NVQ assessment and the
awards they offer.

Printed publications:
Publications on child care, education and
playwork, including titles for NVQs and other
awards

Electronic and video publications:
Current candidate handbooks may be downloaded
from the website for planning purposes

Publications list:
Available online and in print

Access to staff:
Contact by letter, by telephone, by fax, by e-mail
and via website. Appointment necessary.
Hours: Mon to Fri, 0900 to 1700

COUNCIL FOR BRITISH ARCHAEOLOGY

Acronym or abbreviation: CBA

St Mary's House, 66 Bootham, York YO30 7BZ

Tel: 01904 671417
Fax: 01904 671384
E-mail: info@britarch.ac.uk

Website:
http://www.britarch.ac.uk
Electronic information service for British
archaeology, including text from British
Archaeology magazine, news, events, online
databases and bibliography.

Enquiries:
Enquiries to: Office Administrator

Founded:
1944

Organisation type and purpose:
Membership association (membership is by
subscription), present number of members: 10,000
individuals and institutions, registered charity
(charity number 1760254), research organisation,
publishing house.
To promote the study of Britain's historic
environment, provide a forum for archaeological
opinion and improve public knowledge and
enjoyment of the past through participation,
discovery and advocacy.

Subject coverage:
Information on all aspects of Britain's historic
environment (organisation, research in progress,
conservation, legislation, management); specialises
in countryside and urban archaeology, archaeology
of buildings, archaeological science, nautical
archaeology, archaeology in education, calendar of
events and excavations, annual Festival of British
Archaeology and presenting archaeology to young
people.

Printed publications:
A wide variety of publications available for
purchase including:
British Archaeology (6 times a year)
Young Archaeology (4 times a year)
Research Reports, including excavation and
conference reports as well as research syntheses
Practical Handbook Series: a series of short,
practical guides for both professional and
independent archaeologists, historians,
architects, and anyone interested in the past
Research Bulletin surveys

Electronic and video publications:
British and Irish Archaeological Bibliography

Publications list:
Available online and in print

Access to staff:
Contact by letter, by telephone, by fax, by e-mail,
in person and via website. Appointment necessary.
Hours: Mon to Fri, 0900 to 1700

Subsidiary body for 8 to 16 year olds:
Young Archaeologists' Club (YAC)

COUNCIL FOR DANCE EDUCATION AND TRAINING (UK)

Acronym or abbreviation: CDET

Old Brewer's Yard, 17–19 Neal Street, Covent
Garden, London, WC2H 9UY

Tel: 020 7240 5703
Fax: 020 7240 2547
E-mail: info@cdet.org.uk

Website:
http://www.cdet.org.uk
Information on dance education and training.

Enquiries:
Enquiries to: Administrator

Founded:
1979

Organisation type and purpose:
Professional body, registered charity (charity
number 277729).
Professional and representative body for dance
education and training matters.

Subject coverage:
Vocational dance training, including accredited
courses, sources of funding and grants, careers
advice.

**Museum or gallery collection, archive, or library
special collection:**
The first comprehensive source of information in
dance training

Printed publications:
The UK Handbook of Accredited Courses in Dance
and Musical Theatre
Dance Information Sheets
Code of Professional Conduct and Practice for
Teachers of Dance

Access to staff:
Contact by letter, by fax and by e-mail
Hours: Mon to Fri, 0930 to 1700
Special comments: Appointment necessary.

Member organisation of:
CDET
Conference of Professional Dance Schools

COUNCIL FOR MOSQUES

Formal name: Bradford Council for Mosques

6 Claremont, Bradford, West Yorkshire, BD7 1BQ

Tel: 01274 732479

Enquiries:
Enquiries to: Press Officer
Direct e-mail: i.ahmed@pacalis.co.uk

Founded:
1985

Organisation type and purpose:
Voluntary organisation.

Access to staff:
Contact by letter, by telephone, by e-mail and in
person. Appointment necessary.
Hours: Mon to Fri, 0930 to 1900

Access for disabled people:
Ramped entry, toilet facilities

COUNCIL FOR REGISTERED GAS INSTALLERS, THE

Acronym or abbreviation: CORGI

continued overleaf

1 Elmwood, Chineham Park, Crockford Lane, Basingstoke, Hampshire, RG24 8WG

Tel: 01256 372200 or 372300
Fax: 01256 708144
E-mail: enquiries@corgi-gas.co.uk

Website:
http://www.corgi-gas.com
Gas safety information, information about CORGI and its role as National Watchdog for gas safety.

Enquiries:
Enquiries to: Press Officer
Direct tel: 01256 372254
Direct e-mail: publications@corgi-gas.co.uk
Other contacts: Public Relations Manager

Founded:
1991

Formerly called:
Confederation of Registered Gas Installers (CORGI) (year of change 1991)

Organisation type and purpose:
Statutory body, present number of members: 45,000 registered installers.
National watchdog for gas safety. Registration Body.
Inspection of registered businesses, customer complaints regarding gas safety, gas safety publicity, development of nationally accredited certification scheme for individual gas fitting operatives.

Subject coverage:
The national watchdog for gas safety , providing gas safety advice for consumers, technical advice for registered installers, details of registered installers to the public.

Printed publications:
Annual Report (free)
Gas Installer Manual Domestic Series (available to purchase)
The Gas Installer Magazine (10 times a year, free to registered installers)
Order printed publications from: CORGI
Station Approach, Blackwater, Camberley, Surrey, GU17 9PD

Publications list:
Available online and in print

Access to staff:
Contact by letter, by telephone, by fax and by e-mail
Hours: Mon to Thu, 0900 to 1730; Fri, 0900 to 1700

Access for disabled people:
Parking provided, ramped entry, access to all public areas, toilet facilities

COUNCIL FOR THE ADVANCEMENT OF ARAB-BRITISH UNDERSTANDING

Acronym or abbreviation: CAABU

21 Collingham Road, London, SW5 0NU

Tel: 020 7373 8414
Fax: 020 7835 2088
E-mail: caabu@caabu.org

Enquiries:
Enquiries to: Information Officer

Founded:
1967

Organisation type and purpose:
International organisation, membership association (membership is by subscription), present number of members: 900, research organisation.
Lobby, education, non-governmental. To promote understanding between peoples of Arab countries and Britain.

Subject coverage:
The Arab World, Palestine, Iraq.

Museum or gallery collection, archive, or library special collection:
Comprehensive information about all Arab countries

Trade and statistical information:
Newspaper clippings on the Middle East, information service, speakers for schools.

Printed publications:
Regular briefing papers produced on topical issues
Schools information pack (£8 including p&p)

Publications list:
Available online and in print

Access to staff:
Contact by letter, by telephone, by fax and by e-mail. Appointment necessary.
Hours: Mon to Thu, 0930 to 1730; Fri, 0930 to 1630

Access to building, collection or gallery:
Prior appointment required
Hours: Mon to Fri, 0930 to 1730

Chairs the:
European Co-ordinating Committee of Non-governmental Organisations (ECCP) on the question of Palestine

COUNCIL FOR THE HOMELESS (NI)

Acronym or abbreviation: CHNI

4 floor, Andras House, 60 Great Victoria St, Belfast BT2 2BB

Tel: 028 9024 6440
Fax: 028 9024 1266
E-mail: info@chni.org.uk

Website:
http://www.chni.org.uk

Enquiries:
Enquiries to: Information Officer

Founded:
1983

Formerly called:
Northern Ireland Council for Single Homeless

Organisation type and purpose:
Voluntary organisation, registered charity (charity number XO544/83), training organisation.

Subject coverage:
Homelessness, housing benefits, children, finance, health, poverty, legislation, Northern Ireland Housing Executive, organisations and organisational development, individuals' rights, special needs, temporary accommodation, types of housing, women, young people.

Museum or gallery collection, archive, or library special collection:
Housing and Homelessness Journals
Social policy journals
Video library

Access to staff:
Contact by letter, by telephone, by fax, by e-mail and in person
Hours: Mon to Fri, 0900 to 1700

Member organisation of:
European Federation of National Organisations Working with the Homeless (FEANTSA)
Rue Defacqz 1, 1050 Brussels, Belgium; tel: +32 2 538 6669; fax: +32 2 539 4174

COUNCIL FOR VOLUNTARY SERVICE – SOUTH LAKELAND

Acronym or abbreviation: SLCVS

Stricklandgate House, 92 Stricklandgate, Kendal, Cumbria, LA9 4PU

Tel: 01539 742627
Fax: 01539 742628
E-mail: info@slcvs.org

Enquiries:
Enquiries to: Information Officer

Organisation type and purpose:
Advisory body, membership association (membership is by election or invitation), voluntary organisation, registered charity (charity number 503635), training organisation.
Concerning voluntary organisations in South Lakeland.

Subject coverage:
Advice on voluntary organisations in South Lakeland. Advice on fundraising, recruitment, training and management of voluntary organisations. Advice on charity law. Liaison with health and social care providers.

Museum or gallery collection, archive, or library special collection:
Includes the Roger Wilson Library – all on computerised database

Printed publications:
Newsletter (monthly, to affiliated organisations)

Access to staff:
Contact by letter, by telephone, by fax, by e-mail and in person. Appointment necessary.
Hours: Mon to Fri, 0930 to 1630
Special comments: Wheelchair access to all areas.

COUNCIL FOR WORLD MISSION

Acronym or abbreviation: CWM

32–34 Great Peter Street, London, SW1P 2DB

Tel: 020 7222 4214
Fax: 020 7233 1747
E-mail: council@cwmission.org

Website:
http://www.cwmission.org

Enquiries:
Enquiries to: Communications Officer
Direct tel: 020 7227 2505
Direct fax: 020 7222 3510
Direct e-mail: kenwyn.pierce@cwmission.org

Founded:
1795

Formerly called:
London Missionary Society (year of change 1977)

Organisation type and purpose:
International organisation, registered charity.
Ecumenical organisation.
World mission (Reformed Churches and United Churches).

Subject coverage:
Christian world mission.

Museum or gallery collection, archive, or library special collection:
Archives of the former London Missionary Society

Printed publications:
Inside Out (magazine)

Publications list:
Available in print

Access to staff:
Contact by letter, by fax, by e-mail and via website. Appointment necessary.
Hours: Mon to Fri, 0900 to 1700

COUNCIL OF DISABLED PEOPLE

Formal name: Council of Disabled People – Warwickshire and Coventry
Acronym or abbreviation: CDP

Independent Options, Hillmorton Road, Rugby, Warwickshire, CV22 5AB

Tel: 01926 413334
Fax: 01926 413334

Enquiries:
Enquiries to: Director

Organisation type and purpose:
Membership association (membership is by subscription), present number of members: 150, registered charity (charity number 1028144).

Meeting the needs of disabled people.

Subject coverage:
Benefit information, resource teams.

Publications list:
Available in print

Access to staff:
Contact by letter
Hours: Mon to Fri, 0900 to 1700

Access to building, collection or gallery:
Prior appointment required

Access for disabled people:
Parking provided, level entry, access to all public areas, toilet facilities

Other addresses:
The Council of Disabled People – Warwickshire and Coventry
  Fordsfield Centre, Bury Road, Leamington Spa, CV31 3HW

COUNCIL OF MORTGAGE LENDERS

Acronym or abbreviation: CML

North West Wing, Bush House, Aldwych, London, WC2B 4PJ

Tel: 0845 373 6771
Fax: 0845 373 6778

Website:
http://www.cml.org.uk

Enquiries:
Enquiries to: Information Officer
Direct e-mail: tamsin.askew@cml.org.uk

Founded:
1989

Organisation type and purpose:
Trade association.

Subject coverage:
Mortgage lending; housing market; financial services.

Printed publications:
Research Reports (occasional)

Electronic and video publications:
All publications available electronically
CML News and Views (fortnightly, electronic only)
Housing Finance (occasional, electronic only)

Publications list:
Available online and in print

Access to staff:
Contact by letter, by fax, by e-mail and via website
Hours: Mon to Fri, 0900 to 1630

Access to building, collection or gallery:
No access other than to staff

COUNCIL OF NATIONAL GOLF UNIONS

Acronym or abbreviation: CONGU

1 Peerswood Court, Little Neston, Neston, CH64 0US

Tel: 0151 336 3936
E-mail: secretary@congu.com

Website:
http://www.congu.com

Enquiries:
Enquiries to: Secretary

Founded:
1924

Formerly called:
British Golf Unions Joint Advisory Committee (year of change 1960)

Organisation type and purpose:
Membership association.

Subject coverage:
Golf handicaps.

Access to staff:
Contact by letter, by telephone and by e-mail
Hours: Mon to Fri, 0900 to 1700

Links with:
English Golf Union
Golfing Union of Ireland
Royal and Ancient Golf Club of St. Andrews
Scottish Golf Union
Welsh Golfing Union

COUNCIL OF SIKH GURDWARAS IN BIRMINGHAM

Acronym or abbreviation: CSGB

627 Stratford Road, Sparkhill, Birmingham, B11 4LS

Tel: 0121 773 0399
Fax: 0121 773 0699

Enquiries:
Enquiries to: General Secretary
Direct e-mail: csgb@sikh-council.demon.co.uk

Founded:
1989

Organisation type and purpose:
Membership association (membership is by election or invitation), present number of members: 13 organisations, voluntary organisation.
Consultancy on Sikh issues.
To serve and provide a collective voice for Birmingham Sikh community.

Access to staff:
Contact by letter, by telephone, by fax and by e-mail. Appointment necessary.
Hours: Mon to Fri, 1000 to 1800
Special comments: No alcohol, drugs, tobacco.

COUNCIL ON INTERNATIONAL EDUCATIONAL EXCHANGE

Acronym or abbreviation: CIEE

52 Poland Street, London, W1F 7AB

Tel: 020 7478 2020
Fax: 020 7734 7322
E-mail: info@ciee.org

Website:
http://www.councilexchanges.org.uk
Information regarding programmes, electronic publication of Update, a bi-monthly journal produced by CIEE in New York regarding international education activities. Special features include jobsearch database for finding summer jobs/internships in the USA.

Enquiries:
Enquiries to: Regional Director
Direct e-mail: jccooper@fie.org.uk
Other contacts: Programme Co-ordinator for specific programme enquiries.

Founded:
1947

Formerly called:
Council Exchanges (year of change 1999)

Organisation type and purpose:
International organisation, registered charity (charity number 293969).
To arrange international educational exchanges.

Subject coverage:
Work abroad and study abroad opportunities for students and recent graduates: work abroad in USA, Canada, Australia, China and Japan; studies abroad in the USA, France, Spain, Italy and Germany.

Printed publications:
Annual Report
General Brochure

Work Abroad and Study Abroad Programme, information, brochures, application forms

Access to staff:
Contact by letter, by telephone, by fax, by e-mail and via website. Appointment necessary.
Hours: Mon to Fri, 0930 to 1730

Founder member of the:
Year Out Group

Offices in many cities worldwide including:
New York, Paris, Tokyo, Rome, Berlin and Madrid

COUNSEL AND CARE

Formal name: Counsel and Care for the Elderly

Twyman House, 16 Bonny Street, London, NW1 9PG

Tel: 020 7241 8555
Fax: 020 7267 6877
E-mail: advice@counselandcare.org.uk

Website:
http://www.counselandcare.org.uk
Information on Advice Service, training and research projects. Factsheets to download and publications list.

Enquiries:
Enquiries to: Advicework Department
Direct tel: 0845 300 7585

Founded:
1954

Formerly called:
Elderly Invalids Fund

Organisation type and purpose:
National organisation, membership association (membership is by subscription), voluntary organisation, registered charity (charity number 203429).
To provide practical help and advice to people over 60, their families and carers.

Subject coverage:
Advice for older people on welfare benefits, community care, hospital discharge, going into care and help at home. One-off grants for older people.

Printed publications:
Guides and Factsheets (39 titles, updated annually, free to individuals, but charge to organisations for full set, sae requested)
Not Only Bingo
New Appetite for Life
Your care home – is it up to standard?

Publications list:
Available online and in print

Access to staff:
Contact by letter, by telephone, by fax, by e-mail and via website. Appointment necessary.
Hours: Mon, Tue, Thu, Fri, 1000 to 1600; Wed, 1000 to 1300

Access for disabled people:
Level entry, toilet facilities

COUNTERFEITING INTELLIGENCE BUREAU

Formal name: The International Chamber of Commerce – Commercial Crime Services (CCS)
Acronym or abbreviation: CIB

Cinnabar Wharf, 26 Wapping High Street, London, E1W 1NG

Tel: 020 7423 6960
Fax: 020 7423 6961
E-mail: ccs@icc-ccs.org

Website:
http://www.icc-ccs.org/cib/overview.php

Enquiries:
Enquiries to: Director

Founded:
1985

continued overleaf

Organisation type and purpose:
International organisation, membership association (membership is by subscription), consultancy, research organisation.

Subject coverage:
Intellectual property rights, trademarks, counterfeiting, infringements, proactive monitoring, reactive intelligence and investigations, anti-counterfeiting technology assistance.

Museum or gallery collection, archive, or library special collection:
Special reports on counterfeiting

Printed publications:
Commercial Crime International (monthly)
Confidential Bulletin (monthly to members only)
Annual Piracy Report (£15 plus p&p)
Countering Counterfeiting (guide, £50 plus p&p)
Special Reports including:
Industrial Property Protection in East Asia
China Trade – The Risk Factor

Access to staff:
Contact by letter, by telephone, by fax, by e-mail and via website. Appointment necessary.
Hours: Mon to Fri, 0900 to 1700

Access for disabled people:
Ramped entry

Specialised division of:
International Chamber of Commerce

COUNTRY LAND & BUSINESS ASSOCIATION

Acronym or abbreviation: CLA

16 Belgrave Square, London, SW1X 8PQ

Tel: 020 7235 0511
Fax: 020 7235 0528

Website:
http://www.cla.org.uk
Background information and material on Country Landowners Association policies. Contact details for head office and regional offices.

Enquiries:
Enquiries to: Public Relations Manager
Direct e-mail: richardb@cla.org.uk
Other contacts: Finance and Administration Secretary

Founded:
1907

Formerly called:
Country Landowners Association (CLA) (year of change 2000)

Organisation type and purpose:
Membership association (membership is by subscription).
Owners of rural land in England and Wales. 43 branches in England and Wales.

Subject coverage:
Legal, tax and economic aspects of rural landowning; land use, conservation, water and minerals interests.

Printed publications:
Advisory Handbooks (36 titles to date, on sale)
Country Landowner (monthly, for members)
Model forms for agreements and tenancy

Publications list:
Available in print

Access to staff:
Contact by letter. Access for members only.
Hours: Mon to Fri, 0900 to 1700

Connections with:
CBI
Confederation of European Agriculture
European Landowners Organisation
FACE
FWAG
Rural
Rural Voice

Standing Conference on Countryside Sports

Regional Office:
CLA, North West Region
  Dalton Hall, Stable Yard, Burton, Carnforth, Lancashire, LA6 1NJ; tel: 01524 782209; fax: 01524 782248

COUNTRYSIDE AGENCY

John Dower House, Crescent Place, Cheltenham, Gloucestershire, GL50 3RA

Tel: 01242 521381
Fax: 01242 584270

Website:
http://www.countryside.gov.uk
About the Countryside Agency and its work. Publications list.

Enquiries:
Enquiries to: Librarian

Founded:
1999

Formed by the merger of:
Countryside Commission; Rural Development Commission (RDC); Rural Industries Bureau (RIB); National Parks Commission (NPC); Council for Small Industries in Rural Areas (CoSIRA); Development Commission of CoSIRA

Formerly called:
Development Commission (DC)

Organisation type and purpose:
Statutory body.
The 1968 Countryside Act widened its remit to become the Countryside Commission as part of the Department of the Environment; the 1981 Wildlife and Countryside Act gave the Countryside Commission independent status as an independent grant-in-aid corporate body. The Environmental Protection Act 1990 removed the Commission's responsibilities for Wales. From 1st April 1991 these were incorporated in the newly formed Countryside Council for Wales and the Countryside Commission became responsible for England only. In April 1999, the Countryside Commission merged with the Rural Development Commission to become the Countryside Agency responsible for advising government and taking action on issues relating to the social, economic and environmental well-being of the English countryside.
To conserve and enhance England's countryside; to spread social and economic opportunity for people who live there; to help everyone, wherever they live and whatever their background, to enjoy the countryside and share in this priceless asset.
The Countryside Agency works to achieve the aims by: influencing those whose decisions affect the countryside through their expertise and research and by spreading good practice; implementing specific work programmes reflecting priorities set by Parliament, the Government and the Agency Board.

Subject coverage:
Bulk of stock is from the Countryside Commission Library and covers: conservation and enhancement of landscape beauty; provision and improvement of facilities for countryside recreation, access and rights of way, particularly national trails; planning and management of the countryside, specifically national parks, areas of outstanding natural beauty, heritage coasts. Subject coverage is being broadened to include the rural economy and rural communities.

Library catalogue:
All or part available in-house

Printed publications:
A large selection of books, leaflets, posters, reports, research documents and educational material with a reference to all aspects of the countryside, including:
Countryside Focus – Countryside Agency's Newspaper (6 times a year, free)

Eat the view: Promoting sustainable, local produce (2000, free)
Great ways to go – good practice in rural transport (2001, free)
Labour market detachment in rural England (1999)
National Trail Guides, official guide books
Not seen, not heard? Social exclusion in rural areas (2000, free)
Out in the country: where you can go and what you can do (2000 revised, free)
Rural services and social housing 1999–2000 (2001)
Towards tomorrow's countryside: A strategy for the Countryside Agency (2001, free)
Understanding the countryside: The state of the countryside 2001 (national report, free)
Order printed publications from: Countryside Agency Postal Sales (Ref: CA2)
PO Box 124, Walgrave, Northampton, NN6 0TL, tel: 01604 781848, fax: 01604 781714

Electronic and video publications:
The Character of England (CD-ROM)

Publications list:
Available online and in print

Access to staff:
Contact by letter and by telephone
Hours: Mon to Fri, 0900 to 1700
Special comments: The library closes at 1630 on Fridays.

Access to building, collection or gallery:
No access other than to staff
Special comments: Currently in temporary accommodation with no access for visitors.

Affiliated to:
Council of Europe
Federation of Nature and National Parks of Europe
International Union for the Conservation of Nature and Natural Resources (IUCNNR)

Funded by:
Department for Environment, Food and Rural Affairs

Other addresses:
Also some national functions
  Dacre House, 19 Dacre Street, London, SW1H 0DH; tel: 020 7340 2900; fax: 020 7340 2911
East Midlands
  18 Market Place, Bingham, Nottingham, NG13 8AP; tel: 01949 876200; fax: 01949 876222
East of England
  Ortona House, 110 Hills Road, Cambridge, CB2 1LQ; tel: 01223 354462; fax: 01223 313850
North East
  Cross House, Westgate Road, Newcastle upon Tyne, NE1 4XX; tel: 0191 269 1600; fax: 0191 269 1601
North West
  Haweswater Road, Penrith, CA11 7EH; tel: 01768 865752; fax: 01768 890414
North West
  7th Floor, Bridgewater House, Whitworth Street, Manchester, M1 6LT; tel: 0161 237 1061; fax: 0161 237 1062
South East & London
  Sterling House, 7 Ashford Road, Maidstone, ME14 5BJ; tel: 01622 765222; fax: 01622 662102
South West
  2nd Floor, 11–15 Dix's Field, Exeter, EX1 1QA; tel: 01392 477150; fax: 01392 477151
South West
  Bridge House, Sion Place, Clifton Down, Bristol, BS8 4AS; tel: 0117 973 9966; fax: 0117 923 8086
West Midlands
  Strickland House, The Lawns, Park Street, Wellington, Telford, TF1 3BX; tel: 01952 247161; fax: 01952 248700
West Midlands and Doorstep Greens National Project Team
  1st Floor, Vincent House, Tindal Bridge, 92–93 Edward Street, Birmingham, B1 2RA; tel: 0121 233 9399; fax: 0121 233 9286
Yorkshire & The Humber
  4th Floor, Victoria Wharf, No 4 The Embankment, Sovereign Street, Leeds, LS1 4BA; tel: 0113 246 9222; fax: 0113 246 0353

COUNTRYSIDE ALLIANCE

367 Kennington Road, London, SE11 4PT

Tel: 020 7840 9200
Fax: 020 7793 8484
E-mail: info@countryside-alliance.org

Website:
http://www.countryside-alliance.org
Wide variety of information relating to countryside issues.

Enquiries:
Enquiries to: Information Officer
Other contacts: Membership for membership queries.

Founded:
1930

Formed from:
British Field Sports Society (BFSS), Countryside Movement; Countryside Business Group (year of change 1997)

Organisation type and purpose:
Advisory body, membership association (membership is by subscription), present number of members: 85,000, suitable for ages: 10 to 18.
To champion the countryside, country sports and the rural way of life.

Subject coverage:
Rural issues – rural livelihood, businesses, lifestyles and country sports. Land management, access to the countryside and conservation.

Trade and statistical information:
Economic facts relating to country sports and countryside in general.

Printed publications:
Country Sports (magazine, quarterly)

Access to staff:
Contact by letter, by telephone, by fax, by e-mail and via website
Hours: Mon to Fri, 0900 to 1700

Regional Offices:
Countryside Alliance

COUNTRYSIDE COUNCIL FOR WALES

Acronym or abbreviation: CCW

Maes y Ffynnon, Penrhosgarnedd, Bangor, Gwynedd, LL57 2DW

Tel: 01248 385500
Fax: 01248 355782
E-mail: enquiries@ccw.gov.uk

Website:
http://www.ccw.gov.uk

Enquiries:
Enquiries to: Librarian
Other contacts: Public Relations Officer for press.

Formerly called:
Countryside Commission Wales, Nature Conservancy Council (year of change 1991)

Organisation type and purpose:
National government body.
Statutory body funded by a grant from the Welsh Assembly Government.
The Countryside Council for Wales is the government's statutory adviser on wildlife, countryside and maritime conservation matters in Wales.

Subject coverage:
Wildlife, countryside and maritime conservation matters, conservation of plants, mammals, reptiles and amphibians, promotes protection of landscape, opportunities for recreation, planning and management of the countryside.

Printed publications:
Annual Report
National Nature Reserve leaflets
Policy documents

Publications on protected areas in Wales, designated areas, special projects, species projects and habitats series (all bilingual and free of charge)

Publications list:
Available online and in print

Access to staff:
Contact by letter, by telephone, by fax, by e-mail and via website. Appointment necessary.
Hours: Mon to Fri, 0900 to 1700

Access for disabled people:
Parking provided, ramped entry, toilet facilities

Branches:
North Area Office, Countryside Council for Wales
Llys y Bont, Ffordd y Parc, Parc Menai, Bangor, Gwynedd, LL57 4BN; tel: 01248 672500; fax: 01248 679259; e-mail: s.williams@ccw.gov.uk
South and East Area Office, Countryside Council for Wales
Unit 7, Castleton Court, Fortran Road, St Mellons, Cardiff, CF3 0LT; tel: 02920 772400; fax: 02920 772412; e-mail: s.annmorgan@ccw.gov.uk
West Area Office, Countryside Council for Wales
Plas Gogerddan, Aberystwyth, Ceredigion, SY23 3EE; tel: 01970 821100; fax: 01970 828314; e-mail: i.frost@ccw.gov.uk

COUNTRYWIDE HOLIDAYS

Acronym or abbreviation: COUNTRYWIDE

Miry Lane, Wigan, Lancashire, WN3 4AG

Tel: 01942 823456
Fax: 01942 242518
E-mail: countrywidewalking@shearingsholidays.co.uk

Website:
http://www.countrywidewalking.com
Brochure reproduced.

Enquiries:
Enquiries to: Manager
Direct tel: 01942 823529
Direct fax: 01942 825034
Other contacts: (1) Marketing Manager (2) Product Manager for (1) advertising and promotion (2) new products and contracting.

Founded:
1893

Formerly called:
CHA (year of change 1992)

Organisation type and purpose:
Membership association (membership is by subscription).
Holiday company and guest house accommodation provider.

Subject coverage:
Countrywide Holidays specialises in walking and special interest holidays, including bridge, dancing, painting, photography and countryside appreciation. Holidays are offered throughout the UK to individuals, special arrangements are available for groups.

Museum or gallery collection, archive, or library special collection:
Guest House collection brochure
Historical information
Holiday brochures
Newsletters
Transparencies available for loan to journalists for promotion purposes

Printed publications:
Seasonal holiday brochures
Transparencies available for loan to journalists for promotion purposes

Access to staff:
Contact by letter, by telephone, by fax, by e-mail and via website
Hours: Mon to Sat, 0900 to 1700

COUNTY OF HEREFORDSHIRE DISTRICT COUNCIL

Acronym or abbreviation: Herefordshire Council

Brockington, 35 Hafod Road, Hereford, HR1 1SH

Tel: 01432 260000
Fax: 01432 260384

Website:
http://www.herefordshire.gov.uk

Enquiries:
Enquiries to: Chief Executive
Direct tel: 01432 260044
Direct fax: 01432 340189

Founded:
1998

Organisation type and purpose:
Local government body.

Subject coverage:
Local government services.

Access to staff:
Contact by letter, by telephone and by fax
Hours: Mon to Fri, 0900 to 1700

Access to building, collection or gallery:
No access other than to staff

COURT BARN MUSEUM

Formal name: The Guild of Handicraft Trust
Acronym or abbreviation: Court Barn

Church Street, Chipping Campden, Gloucestershire, GL55 6JE

Tel: 01386 841951
E-mail: admin@courtbarn.org.uk

Website:
http://www.courtbarn.org.uk

Enquiries:
Enquiries to: Administrator
Other contacts: Curator

Founded:
1990

Organisation type and purpose:
Registered charity (charity number 1007696), museum, suitable for ages: 5+.
Collections of material relating to art, craft and design in Chipping Campden and the North Cotswolds.
To preserve, promote and encourage an understanding of the work of artists, craftsmen and women, and designers of Chipping Campden and the North Cotswolds.

Subject coverage:
Information and material relating to C R Ashbee's Guild of Handicraft in Chipping Campden 1902–1919, a permanent exhibition of the work of: CR Ashbee in silverwork, jewellery and printed books; Katharine Adams, bookbinder; FL Griggs, illustrator and etcher; Paul Woodroffe, illustrator and stained-glass artist; Alex Miller, carver and sculptor; Gordon Russell, furniture designer; the Winchcombe Pottery; the Hart workshop, silversmiths; and Robert Welch, silversmith and industrial designer.

Special visitor services:
The exhibition at Court Barn accommodates about 20 people; groups of 15 or more should book with the Administrator.

Education services:
Children are welcome; family packs and drawing materials provided. There is a space for classes, workshops, temporary exhibitions and work with schools.

Museum or gallery collection, archive, or library special collection:
The gallery houses the Trust's collections, including the working archive of Robert Welch

Non-library collection catalogue:
All or part available in-house

continued overleaf

Printed publications:
A range of publications on sale at the museum or by post (plus p&p):
A Fertile Field: Stuart Robinson (£2.00)
Alec Miller: J Wilgress (£5.00)
Anthology of the Arts & Crafts Movement: Mary Greenstead (£19.99)
AE Lemmon (1889–1963) Artist & Craftsman: Roy Albutt (£12.95)
Arts & Crafts Gardens: Gertrude Jekyll & Lawrence Weaver (£25.00)
Arts & Crafts Movement: Blakesley (£39.95)
Arts & Crafts Movement: Cumming & Kaplan (£8.95)
Arts & Crafts Movement in the Cotswolds: Mary Greensted (£7.95)
At the Sign of the Rainbow: Betty Miles (£12.50)
Campden 1914–18: Paul R Hughes (£20.00)
A Child in Arcadia. The Chipping Campden boyhood of H T Osborn 1902–07 (£5)
Child in Jerusalem: Felicity Ashbee
Contemporary Crafts: Imogen Racz (£17.99)
Cotswold Arts & Crafts Architecture: Catherine Gordon (£20.00)
CR Ashbee Architect, Designer, Romantic Socialist: Alan Crawford (£25.00)
FL Griggs – The Architect of Dreams: Jerrold Northrop Moore (£39.95)
Frederick Griggs, RA & Chipping Campden: Geoffrey Powell (£1.50)
Fishleys of Fremington: John Edgeler (£25.00)
Good Citizen's Furniture: Annette Carruthers & Mary Greensted (£26.50)
Gordon Russell Vision & Reality: Gordon Russell Museum (£5.00)
Gordon Russell – Designer of Furniture: Jeremy Myerson (£15.00)
Green Fuse, The: The Jerrold Northrop Moore (£35.00)
Inseparable Siblings: Elizabeth Oakley (£12.95)
Janet Ashbee – Love, Marriage and the Arts & Crafts Movement: Felicity Ashbee (£37.50)
Micahel Cardew & Stoneware: John Edgeler (£25.00)
Stained Glass Windows of AJ Davies: Roy Abutt (£16.95)
The Crafts in Britan in the 20th Century: Tanya Harrod (£55.00)
Winchcombe Pottery – The Cardew/Finch Tradition: Ron Wheeler (£17.50)
When So Little Meant So Much: Elizabeth Argent (£7.50)
Harts of Chipping Campden: Richard Russell (£17.50)
Walking the Block: Jane Weir (£16.99)
Robert Welch Designs for Old Hall Tableware: Michael Bennett (£11.95)
Hand Machine: Robert Welch (£15.00)
Nine Lives: Alan Crawford (£3.50)
The Buildings of England – Gloucestershire 1 – The Cotswolds: David Verey & Alan Brookes (£29.95)
The Buildings of England – Gloucestershire 2 – The Vale & the Forest of Dean: David Verey & Alan Brookes (£29.95)

Publications list:
Available in print

Access to staff:
Contact by letter, by telephone and by e-mail. Appointment necessary.
Hours: Any reasonable time during museum opening hours

Access to building, collection or gallery:
Hours: Museum, Apr to Sep: Tue to Sat, 1030 to 1730; Sun, 1130 to 1730
Oct to Mar: Tue to Sat, 1100 to 1600; Sun, 1130 to 1600
Special comments: Mon, closed (except bank holidays); 24 Dec to 1 Jan inclusive, closed.

Access for disabled people:
Special comments: Wheelchair access except in the archive. Staff wil bring archive material to disabled visitors.

COURT OF THE LORD LYON KING OF ARMS

HM New Register House, Edinburgh, EH1 3YT

Tel: 0131 556 7255
Fax: 0131 557 2148

Website:
http://www.lyon-court.com

Enquiries:
Enquiries to: Lyon Clerk

Organisation type and purpose:
Court of Law.
Court of heraldic jurisdiction.

Subject coverage:
The granting and control of heraldry in Scotland.

Museum or gallery collection, archive, or library special collection:
Heraldic, genealogical and associated library (non-lending library, not public)

Non-library collection catalogue:
All or part available in-house

Library catalogue:
All or part available in-house

Access to staff:
Contact by letter, by fax and via website. Appointment necessary.
Hours: Mon to Fri, 1000 to 1230 and 1400 to 1600

COURTAULD INSTITUTE OF ART, BOOK LIBRARY

Somerset House, Strand, London, WC2R 0RN

Tel: 020 7848 2701
Fax: 020 7848 2887
E-mail: booklib@courtauld.ac.uk

Website:
http://www.courtauld.ac.uk

Founded:
1933

Organisation type and purpose:
University department or institute.
Library.

Subject coverage:
Fine arts (painting, sculpture, architecture) in the Western tradition from classical antiquity to the present.

Museum or gallery collection, archive, or library special collection:
Extensive photographic collections administered separately from the Book Library

Non-library collection catalogue:
All or part available online

Library catalogue:
All or part available online and in-house

Access to staff:
Contact by letter, by telephone, by fax, by e-mail and via website. Appointment necessary.
Hours: Term time: 0930 to 2100 (last admission before 1900)
Vacations: 1030 to 1730
Special comments: A last-resort reference library.

Constituent part of:
University of London

COVENT GARDEN MARKET AUTHORITY

Acronym or abbreviation: CGMA

Covent House, New Covent Garden Market, London, SW8 5NX

Tel: 020 7720 2211
Fax: 020 7622 5307
E-mail: info@cgma.gov.uk

Website:
http://www.cgma.gov.uk

Enquiries:
Enquiries to: Information Officer

Founded:
1961

Organisation type and purpose:
Statutory body.
Wholesale market operator.

Subject coverage:
Wholesaling of horticultural produce; operation of the market with over 300 market tenants including wholesalers, catering distributors, importers, hauliers and trade and official bodies.

Trade and statistical information:
Annual turnover figures for traders on New Covent Garden Market.

Printed publications:
Annual Report
Information leaflets
New Covent Garden Market (guide)
Newsletter (quarterly)

Access to staff:
Contact by telephone
Hours: Mon to Fri, 0900 to 1700

Links with:
Department for Environment, Food and Rural Affairs

COVENTRY & WARWICKSHIRE CHAMBER OF COMMERCE

Oak Tree Court, Binley Business Park, Harry Weston Road, Coventry, Warwickshire, CV3 2UN

Tel: 024 7665 4321
Fax: 024 7645 0242
E-mail: info@cw-chamber.co.uk

Website:
http://www.cw-chamber.co.uk

Enquiries:
Enquiries to: Information Officer

Founded:
2001

Formerly called:
Business Link Coventry & Warwickshire; Coventry & Warwickshire Chamber of Commerce Training & Enterprise (year of change 2001)

Organisation type and purpose:
National government body, membership association (membership is by subscription), present number of members: 1800.
Chamber of Commerce.

Subject coverage:
Market research, export, design and innovation, information technology, manufacturing, personal business advisors, finance, start-up advice, training advice.

Museum or gallery collection, archive, or library special collection:
Reference Directories

Trade and statistical information:
Local economic assessments.

Publications list:
Available online

Access to staff:
Contact by letter, by telephone, by fax, by e-mail, in person and via website
Hours: Mon to Fri, 0900 to 1700

Access for disabled people:
Parking provided, ramped entry, access to all public areas, toilet facilities

Other addresses:
Coventry & Warwickshire Chamber of Commerce Progress House, Avenue Farm, Birmingham Road, Stratford Upon Avon, CV37 0HR

COVENTRY CITY ARCHIVES

Formal name: Coventry History Centre

Herbert Art Gallery & Museum, Jordan Well, Coventry, CV1 5QP

Tel: 024 7683 4060
Fax: 024 7683 4060

Enquiries:
Enquiries to: Archivist/Librarian

Founded:
1937

Formerly called:
Coventry Record Office (CRO) (year of change 1995); Coventry Archives (year of change 2008)

Organisation type and purpose:
Local government body, local government archives service.

Subject coverage:
Family history, local history of Coventry including destruction in World War II and post-war reconstruction. Local authority records, Coventry Borough Archives 1182–1881, records of non-conformist churches.

Information services:
Combined Archive and Local History Centre. Resources for local and family history.

Museum or gallery collection, archive, or library special collection:
Archive collections of organisations and individuals who are or have been active in Coventry from the 12th to the 20th centuries
Freemans and Apprentice Records from Coventry 1714 onwards
Cancelled vehicle registration cards to the early 1960s
Local public records, including quarter sessions, magistrates court, coroner's court and hospital records
Large collection of architect plans, building plans and byelaws for all areas of Coventry, 1900 onwards
Collection of oral history tapes (with transcripts) covering most aspects of Coventry's recent history, especially the motor cars and allied trades
Microfilms of Church of England and Roman Catholic registers for Coventry and environs and local cemetery records
Detailed 1851 map of Coventry prepared for the local Board of Health
Plans for reconstruction of Coventry after World War II
Medieval records of the city 12th century onwards, including minutes of the Court Leet 1421 and records of Coventry's trading companies, Guilds
Records of the Blitz and post-war reconstruction of the city
Deposited and donated collections also include local and district trade union records, business records, notably Rootes (and constituent companies, e.g. Singer Motors), Armstrong-Siddley, Armstrong Whitworth, Daimler and Clarke Cluley, records of non-conformist churches, clubs, societies, schools and other local organisations
A large majority of the Coventry City Archives catalogues are computerised on the CALM database, direct customer access on site is available and also at other heritage facilities in the city
Card indexes for Coventry Freemen (women included from 1930s), microfiche indexes of apprenticeship enrolments 1781–1841, microfiche index of building plans and byelaws, card indexes for architects plans (all of these are gradually being transferred to computer catalogue)

Non-library collection catalogue:
All or part available online and in-house

Library catalogue:
All or part available in-house

Printed publications:
Coventry at School
Coventry Celebrates 650 years of Civic Pride (1345–1995)

People to Coventry (migration and settlement from early times)
The Coventry Martyrs
Brief Guide to Records (28 leaflets)
Subject and period guides to archive holdings
Criminals, Courts and Conflict in 14th Century Coventry (A. Gooder, ed. T. Johns)

Publications list:
Available in print

Access to staff:
Contact by letter, by telephone, by fax, by e-mail and in person
Hours: Mon to Fri, 0930 to 1645
Special comments: Identification required to obtain County Archive Research Network (CARN) reader ticket.

Access to building, collection or gallery:
No prior appointment required
Special comments: Preparing to move to new premises.

Access for disabled people:
Lift, access to all public areas, toilet facilities
Special comments: Minimal parking provided.

Links with:
Coventry Arts and Heritage
Herbert Art Gallery and Museum, Jordan Well, Coventry; tel: 02476 832386; fax: 02476 220171; e-mail: info@theherbert.org; website: http://www.theherbert.org

COVENTRY FAMILY HISTORY SOCIETY

Acronym or abbreviation: COVFHS

12 Knoll Drive, Styvechale, Coventry, CV3 5BT

Tel: 024 7669 3904
E-mail: enquiries@covfhs.org

Website:
http://www.covfhs.org

Enquiries:
Enquiries to: General Secretary

Founded:
1994

Organisation type and purpose:
Membership association (membership is by subscription), present number of members: 450, voluntary organisation, registered charity (charity number 1070160).
To promote genealogy, family history and local history studies of Coventry and surrounding parishes and villages.

Subject coverage:
Tracing ancestry, genealogy of local areas.

Printed publications:
Wide variety of books and leaflets, including:
Around Leamington Spa in Old Photographs (£7.95 plus 70p p&p)
Civic Heraldry of Warwickshire (£3 plus 30p p&p)
Coventry at School (£1 plus 30p p&p)
Coventry Through the Ages (£3 plus 30p p&p)
Finding out about Lady Godiva (50p plus 30p p&p)
Moments in Time (special edition, £3.50 plus 30p p&p)
Past in Warwick (£2.50 plus 30p p&p)
Plain and Fancy: ribbon weaving (50p plus 30p p&p)
Watchmaking in Coventry: History Trail (30p plus 30p p&p)
Coventry Family History Society's Publications include:
Beginner's Guide to Family History (3rd edn, £1 plus 30p p&p)
Coventry Family History Quarterly Journals (back issues £1, plus 34p p&p)
Foleshill Workhouse Punishment Book 1864–1900 (£1.50 plus 30p p&p)
Hawkesbury School 1860–1968 (£5 plus 55p p&p)
Order printed publications from: Bookshop Manager, Coventry Family History Society, 88 Howes Lane, Coventry, West Midlands, CV3 6PJ

Microform publications:
Coventry Apprentice Enrolment Registers 1781–1841 (5 vols, £2, explanatory leaflet free with first volume)
Death Registers of the Coventry Workhouse (booklet and 2 fiche, £3)
Census Index for Coventry

Publications list:
Available online and in print

Access to staff:
Contact by letter, by telephone, by e-mail and via website. Appointment necessary. Non-members charged.
Hours: Mon to Fri, 0900 to 1700

Links with:
Federation of Family History Societies

COVENTRY LIBRARIES AND INFORMATION SERVICES

Central Library, Smithford Way, Coventry, Warwickshire, CV1 1FY

Tel: 024 7683 2314; 024 7683 2395 (minicom)
Fax: 024 7683 2440
E-mail: central.library@coventry.gov.uk

Website:
http://www.coventry.gov.uk/libraries

Enquiries:
Enquiries to: Libraries & Information Services Manager
Direct fax: 024 7683 2470

Organisation type and purpose:
Public library.

Subject coverage:
General, industrial relations and trade union affairs, current and historical; Coventry local studies collection; automobile engineering; history of automobiles (local studies, auto engineering, auto history now at Herbert Art Gallery and Museum)

Museum or gallery collection, archive, or library special collection:
Angela Brazil Collection (at Herbert Art Gallery and Museum)
Bartleet Collection on development of the bicycle (at Herbert Art Gallery and Museum)
Workshop Manuals Collection (at Herbert Art Gallery and Museum)
George Eliot Collection (at Herbert Art Gallery and Museum)
Tom Mann Centre for Trade Union and Labour Studies
Waring Brown Collection of newscuttings on engineering (at Herbert Art Gallery and Museum)

Library catalogue:
All or part available online and in-house

Printed publications:
Pamphlets, etc. on local history
Pictures of Coventry

Electronic and video publications:
OPIN (Older People's Information Network – website)
TALIS computer terminals

Publications list:
Available online and in print

Access to staff:
Contact by letter, by telephone, by fax, by e-mail and in person. Appointment necessary.
Hours: Mon to Fri, 0900 to 2000; Sat, 0900 to 1630; Sun, 1200 to 1600

Access to building, collection or gallery:
No access to non-public areas other than with staff permission

Access for disabled people:
Access to all public areas, lifts, toilet facilities

COVENTRY UNIVERSITY – LANCHESTER LIBRARY

Gosford Street, Coventry, Warwickshire, CV1 5DD

Tel: 024 7688 7541
Fax: 024 7688 7525

Website:
http://wwwm.coventry.ac.uk/cu/library
Detailed information on Coventry University
library services.

Enquiries:
Enquiries to: University Librarian

Formerly called:
Lanchester Library of Lanchester Polytechnic

Incorporates the former:
Art & Design Library (year of change 2000)

Organisation type and purpose:
University library.

Subject coverage:
Biology, building construction, business studies,
chemistry, civil engineering, communication
studies, computer science, control engineering and
systems, economics, electrical engineering,
geography and topography, health sciences,
industrial design, life sciences, linguistics,
materials science, mathematics, mechanical
engineering, microbiology, motor vehicle
engineering, operational research, physics,
physiotherapy, politics, production engineering,
social science, social work, statistics, town and
country planning, performing arts, nursing and
midwifery.
Art in general, art history, design, films and
cinema, graphic art and design, photography,
television, communication studies, computer
graphics and industrial design.

**Museum or gallery collection, archive, or library
special collection:**
Lanchester Collection (manuscripts and archives of
  Dr F W Lanchester, pioneer motor car designer
  and engineer, and early theory of flight)

Non-library collection catalogue:
All or part available online

Library catalogue:
All or part available online

Access to staff:
Contact by letter, by telephone, by fax, in person
and via website
Hours: Termtime: Mon to Thu, 0845 to 1900; Fri,
0900 to 1715; Sat, Sun, 1300 to 1700
Vacations: Mon to Fri, 0900 to 1700

Access for disabled people:
Level entry, access to all public areas, toilet
facilities, parking

CPRE

Formal name: Council for the Protection of Rural
England

128 Southwark Street, London, SE1 0SW

Tel: 020 7981 2800
Fax: 020 7981 2899
E-mail: info@cpre.org.uk

Website:
http://www.cpre.org.uk
Information on organisation and publications,
press releases, job opportunities, resources, etc.

Enquiries:
Enquiries to: Librarian
Direct e-mail: publications@cpre.org.uk
Other contacts: Library & Information Unit for
CPRE history and archive information requests.

Founded:
1926

Formerly called:
Council for the Preservation of Rural England
(year of change 1969)

Organisation type and purpose:
Membership association (membership is by
subscription), present number of members: 49,000,
registered charity (charity number 242809),
research organisation.
Independent environment group.
Lobbying locally, Parliament, Whitehall and the EC
for countryside protection.

Subject coverage:
Improvement, protection and management of the
rural scenery and amenities of the countryside and
its towns and villages, in particular, planning,
green belts, development control, access to the
countryside, transport policies, motorways, heavy
lorries, mineral extraction, farmed landscape, land
drainage, water resources, tourism/recreation and
impact on the countryside, forestry and
woodlands, hedgerows, environmental
assessment, energy policies, rural development,
housing and urban regeneration.

**Museum or gallery collection, archive, or library
special collection:**
CPRE documents and archives

Non-library collection catalogue:
All or part available in-house

Library catalogue:
All or part available in-house

Printed publications:
Annual Report
CPRE Voice (4 times a year)
Leaflets (free, send A4 sae)
Campaigners' Guides
Publications under the headings: campaigners'
  guides & briefings, land use change, rural
  development, planning, regional planning,
  sustainable development, housing & urban
  development, roads & transport, agriculture,
  heritage & leisure, trees & forestry, landscape
  features, water & waste, minerals, energy

Publications list:
Available in print

Access to staff:
Contact by letter, by telephone, by fax and by e-
mail. Appointment necessary.
Hours: Mon to Fri, 0930 to 1730
Special comments: Access only to bona fide
researchers on the work of CPRE.

Access to building, collection or gallery:
Prior appointment required

Has:
43 branches and district committees
  in every English county. Contact numbers
  available, from National office

CPRE HERTFORDSHIRE

Acronym or abbreviation: CPRE Herts.

31A Church Street, Welwyn Garden City,
Hertfordshire, AL6 9LW

Tel: 01438 717587
Fax: 01438 714984
E-mail: office@cpreherts.org.uk

Website:
http://www.cpreherts.org.uk

Enquiries:
Enquiries to: Executive Secretary

Founded:
1936

Formerly called:
The Hertfordshire Conservation Society (HCS)
(year of change 1997)

Organisation type and purpose:
Membership association, present number of
members: 1,350 in Hertfordshire, 60,000 nationally,
voluntary organisation, registered charity (charity
number 211299).
Protection of the countryside.

Subject coverage:
Promotes beauty, tranquillity and diversity of rural
Hertfordshire by encouraging the sustainable use
of land and other natural resources in town and
country. Operates through the planning system,
screening planning applications countywide and
raising the alarm where the countryside is
threatened. Influences planning policy through the
local plan process. Offers advice and support to
individuals and local groups embarking on
planning campaigns. Lobbies for sustainable
transport polices and safer country lanes.
Organises the Hertfordshire Village of the Year
competition.

Printed publications:
CPRE Hertfordshire Publications:
Newsletter (3 times a year)
Annual Report

Access to staff:
Contact by letter, by telephone, by fax, by e-mail
and via website
Hours: Mon to Thu, 0930 to 1700

Parent body:
Campaign to Protect Rural England (CPRE)
  128 Southwark Street, London, SE1 0SW; tel: 020
  7981 2800; fax: 020 7981 2899; e-mail: info@cpre
  .org.uk; website: http://www.cpre.org.uk

CPRE LANCASHIRE

Formal name: Campaign to Protect Rural England
Lancashire Branch

Hazelwell's House, Station Road, Bamber Bridge,
Preston, PR5 6TT

Tel: 01772 627510
E-mail: ruralengland@btconnect.com

Enquiries:
Enquiries to: Administration Officer

Founded:
1933

Organisation type and purpose:
Membership association (membership is by
subscription), voluntary organisation, registered
charity (charity number 1107376).
To protect the countryside and the country towns
and villages of Lancashire and parts of Greater
Manchester and Merseyside.

Subject coverage:
Rural land use, planning policy and development
control, material from a wide range of sources.

**Museum or gallery collection, archive, or library
special collection:**
Library set of CPRE publications (campaigners'
  guides, authoritative reports and free leaflets);
  stock can be obtained

Printed publications:
Countrywise (newsletter, quarterly, issued to
  branch members, free on request)
Occasional issue of leaflets (e.g. explaining Tree
  Preservation Orders)

Publications list:
Available online

Access to staff:
Contact by letter, by telephone, by e-mail and in
person. Appointment necessary.
Hours: Mon, Tue and Thu, 0930 to 1230
Special comments: No information service, only
access to the collection and files.

Constituent part of:
CPRE
  Warwick House, 128 Southwark St, London, SE1
  0SW; tel: 020 7981 2800; e-mail: info@cpre.org
  .uk; website: http://www.cpre.org.uk

CRAFTS COUNCIL

44A Pentonville Road, Islington, London, N1 9BY

Tel: 020 7278 7700
Fax: 020 7837 6891

Website:
http://www.craftscouncil.org.uk

Enquiries:
Enquiries to: Research and Information Assistants
Direct tel: 020 7806 2501
Direct e-mail: reference@craftscouncil.org.uk
Other contacts: Research and Information Officer

Founded:
1971

Formerly called:
Crafts Advisory Committee (year of change 1979)

Organisation type and purpose:
National organisation, registered charity (charity number 280956). National development agency for contemporary craft.

Subject coverage:
Contemporary British craft: retail outlets, suppliers of materials, exhibitions, funding sources, business practice, guilds and societies, techniques.

Information services:
Enquiry service by telephone, email and post.

Museum or gallery collection, archive, or library special collection:
Crafts Council Collection, the national collection of works by leading contemporary crafts people, available for loan to public institutions
Online image library of more than 30,000 images of contemporary work

Non-library collection catalogue:
All or part available in-house

Library catalogue:
All or part available in-house

Printed publications:
Books, catalogues, posters, postcards, information lists, exhibition catalogues, factsheets on crafts, lists of courses, careers information, opportunities overseas
Crafts Magazine (6 times a year)

Access to staff:
Contact by letter, by telephone, by e-mail, in person and via website. Appointment necessary.
Hours: Research Library: Wed, Thu, 1000 to 1700
Special comments: By appointment only.

Access to building, collection or gallery:
Reception open to the public, Research Library available by appointment
Hours: Reception: Mon to Fri, 1000 to 1700;
Research Library: Wed, Thu, 1000 to 1700

Access for disabled people:
There is disabled access
Hours: Mon to Fri, 1000 to 1700

Funded by:
Arts Council England
14 Great Peter Street, London, SW1P 3NQ;
website: http://www.artscouncil.org.uk

CRAFTS STUDY CENTRE

University of the Creative Arts, Falkner Road, Farnham, Surrey, GU9 7DS

Tel: 01252 891450
Fax: 01252 891451
E-mail: craftscentre@ucreative.ac.uk

Website:
http://www.csc.ucreative.ac.uk

Enquiries:
Enquiries to: Information & Administration Officer

Founded:
1977

Organisation type and purpose:
A registered charity (261109) functioning as a specialist museum and a research centre of the University for the Creative Arts.

Subject coverage:
Modern calligraphy, furniture and crafts in ceramics, textiles and wood.

Education services:
Research visits welcome by appointment; please telephone 01252 891450

Museum or gallery collection, archive, or library special collection:
Supporting material includes makers' diaries, working notes and photographs dating from the 1920s

Access to staff:
Contact by letter, by telephone, by fax, by e-mail, in person and via website
Hours: Tue to Fri, 1000 to 1700; Sat, 1000 to 1600

Access to building, collection or gallery:
Hours: Tue to Fri, 1000 to 1700; Sat, 1000 to 1600

Access for disabled people:
The Centre is accessible to wheelchair users, induction loop at reception

CRANFIELD PRECISION

Formal name: Cranfield Precision, Divison of Unova UK Limited
Acronym or abbreviation: CP

Woburn House, 3 Adams Close, Kempston, Bedfordshire, MK42 7JE

Tel: 01234 312820
Fax: 01535 367121
E-mail: cpsales@landis-lund.co.uk

Website:
http://www.cranfieldprecision.com
Company profile; products; services; email contacts.

Enquiries:
Enquiries to: Marketing Department

Founded:
1968

Formerly called:
Cranfield Unit for Precision Engineering (CUPE) (year of change 1987)

Organisation type and purpose:
Manufacturing industry, university department or institute, consultancy, research organisation.
OEM design, manufacture and application in machine tools.

Subject coverage:
Precision engineering, including metrology, machine design, servo system design and development, measuring systems (linear and angular), control systems. Applications in semiconductor processing and computer peripheral manufacturing, as well as in automotive, advanced optics, optoelectronics and other ultra-precision manufacturing industries.

Access to staff:
Contact by telephone and by e-mail
Hours: Mon to Fri, 0830 to 1700

Parent body:
Landis Lund, Division of Unova UK Limited
tel: 01535 633211

CRANFIELD UNIVERSITY

Acronym or abbreviation: CU
Cranfield, Bedfordshire, MK43 0AL

Tel: 01234 750111
Fax: 01234 752391
E-mail: hazel.woodward@cranfield.ac.uk

Website:
http://www.cranfieldlibrary.cranfield.ac.uk
Library and Information Service at Cranfield Campus
http://diglib.shrivenham.cranfield.ac.uk
Defence College of Management and Technology
http://www.cranfield.ac.uk
University home page

Enquiries:
Enquiries to: University Librarian
Direct tel: 01234 754446

Organisation type and purpose:
University library.

Subject coverage:
Aerospace engineering; electronics; mechanical engineering; advanced materials; advanced manufacturing techniques, defence science and technology, agricultural engineering; food production; land use; management, water and waste technology, biotechnology, health science, logistics, natural resources.

Museum or gallery collection, archive, or library special collection:
Aeronautical history
Aerospace Technology Reports (NASA, AGARD, AIAA, ARC)
History of ballooning (Kings Norton Library)
British Balloon Library; Kings Norton Collection.

Library catalogue:
All or part available online

Includes the:
Defence College of Management and Technology. Shrivenham

CREATIVESHEFFIELD

Acronym or abbreviation: SF4I

1st Floor, The Fountain Precinct, Balm Green, Sheffield,S1 2JA

Tel: 0114 223 2345
Fax: 0114 223 2346
E-mail: info@creativesheffield.co.uk

Website:
http://www.creativesheffield.co.uk
Information on Sheffield for potential investors, and services provided by Creativesheffield.

Enquiries:
Enquiries to: Director – Operations

Founded:
2007

Formerly called:
Sheffield First for Investment; Sheffield One

Organisation type and purpose:
Local government body.
Provides a single point of contact for inward investment, relocation and business development enquiries, marketing Sheffield and visitor attractions.

Subject coverage:
Industrial and commercial property, sources of financial assistance, the development climate, local partner organisations, statistical information on Sheffield, local labour market and economy.

Information services:
All information on Sheffield as a place to live, work and visit.

Trade and statistical information:
Database of available industrial and commercial property.
General information and statistics on Sheffield.

Printed publications:
Promotional brochures and other material from a variety of local organisations and estate agents

Access to staff:
Contact by letter, by telephone, by fax, by e-mail and via website. Appointment necessary.
Hours: Mon to Fri, 0830 to 1715

Links with:
Yorkshire Forward

Parent body:
Sheffield City Council

CREDIT PROTECTION ASSOCIATION

CPA House, 350 King Street, London, W6 0RX

Tel: 020 8846 0000; freephone: 0800 634 0187
Fax: 020 8741 7459

continued overleaf

E-mail: via website

Website:
http://www.cpa.co.uk

Founded:
1914

Organisation type and purpose:
Membership association providing credit management services to members.

Subject coverage:
Innovative IT connects client-members to essential financial data, enabling instant decision making relating to the granting of credit. Client-members can also instantaneously refer their overdue accounts, which usually results in full settlement days later.

Access to staff:
Contact by letter, by telephone, by fax and via website

Branches:
in or near Falkirk, Bolton, Harrogate, Birmingham, Newmarket and Bristol

CREMATION SOCIETY OF GREAT BRITAIN

Acronym or abbreviation: CSGB

Brecon House, 1st Floor, 16–16a Albion Place, Maidstone, Kent, ME14 5DZ

Tel: 01622 688292/3
Fax: 01622 686698
E-mail: info@cremation.org.uk

Website:
http://www.cremation.org.uk

Enquiries:
Enquiries to: Secretary

Founded:
1874

Organisation type and purpose:
Advisory body, membership association, registered charity.

Subject coverage:
Cremation and its religious, legal, technical, architectural and statistical aspects; crematorium administration.

Museum or gallery collection, archive, or library special collection:
Society's records since 1874. From 1999 these have been transferred to University of Durham Library (Special Collections)

Printed publications:
Directory of Crematoria
Directory of Pet Crematoria
History of Modern Cremation in Great Britain from 1874
May Catholics Choose Cremation?
Pharos International (quarterly)
Provision for Cremation Facilities pack
What You Should Know about Cremation
What is Respectful Disposal?

Access to staff:
Contact by letter, by telephone, by fax and by e-mail
Hours: Mon to Fri, 0900 to 1700

Founder member of the:
International Cremation Federation
tel: +31 70 3518836; fax: +31 70 3518827; e-mail: keizer@facultatieve.com; website: http://www.int-crem-fed.org

CRIME CONCERN TRUST

Beaver House, 147–150 Victoria Road, Swindon, Wiltshire, SN1 3UY

Tel: 01793 863500
Fax: 01793 514654

Website:
http://www.crimeconcern.org.uk

http://www.safer-community.net

Enquiries:
Direct e-mail: john.skillicorn-aston@catch-22.org.uk

Founded:
1988

Organisation type and purpose:
Registered charity (charity number 800735). Working with local and national partners to reduce crime and create safer communities.

Subject coverage:
Crime prevention, burglary reduction, domestic violence, racial harassment, youth crime, car crime, neighbourhood safety, drug misuse prevention, and personal safety.

Library catalogue:
All or part available online

Printed publications:
A Second Chance (1997)

Publications list:
Available online and in print

Access to staff:
Contact by letter, by telephone, by fax, by e-mail and via website
Hours: Mon to Fri, 0900 to 1715

CRIMESTOPPERS TRUST

Acronym or abbreviation: Crimestoppers

Apollo House, 66a London Road, Morden, Surrey, SM4 5BE

Tel: 020 8254 3200
Fax: 020 8254 3201
E-mail: cst@crimestoppers-uk.org

Website:
http://www.crimestoppers-uk.org
Crimestoppers Trust website with detailed information on the charity and its activities. Users can go to the website to e-mail information about crimes.

Enquiries:
Enquiries to: Director
Other contacts: Head of Marketing & Fundraising for any marketing or fundraising enquiries.

Founded:
1986

Formed from:
Community Action Trust (year of change 1995)

Organisation type and purpose:
Registered charity (charity number 1108687). To create an alliance to fight crime.

Subject coverage:
Crimestoppers Trust publicises the Crimestoppers Scheme and supports specific crime-fighting initiatives. To date Crimestoppers have received 320,000 anonymous phone calls leading to 30,000 arrests and the recovery of property valued at £44 million. With other offences taken into consideration, it is estimated that information given to Crimestoppers has helped to clear up almost 100,000 crimes.

Trade and statistical information:
The only UK charity dedicated to solving crimes.

Printed publications:
Publicity material is available for purchase on request

Publications list:
Available online and in print

Access to staff:
Contact by letter, by telephone, by fax, by e-mail and via website. Appointment necessary. Letter of introduction required.
Hours: Mon to Fri, 0900 to 1700

Access to building, collection or gallery:
No access other than to staff, prior appointment required

CRIMINAL BAR ASSOCIATION

Acronym or abbreviation: CBA

2–3 Cursitor Street, London, EC4A 1NE

Tel: 020 7242 1289
Fax: 020 7242 1107
E-mail: videoconference@dial.pipex.com

Website:
http://www.criminalbar.com

Enquiries:
Enquiries to: Administrator

Founded:
1969

Organisation type and purpose:
Professional body (membership is by qualification), present number of members: 2700.

Subject coverage:
Criminal procedure and practice, policy of the specialist organisation for members of the Criminal Bar, criminal justice system.

Printed publications:
CBA Newsletter

Access to staff:
Contact by letter, by fax and by e-mail
Hours: Mon to Fri, 0900 to 1700

Links with:
General Council of The Bar
3 Bedford Row, London, WC1R 4DB; tel: 020 7240 0082; fax: 020 7831 9217

CRIMINAL INJURIES COMPENSATION AUTHORITY

Tay House, 300 Bath Street, Glasgow, G2 4LN 0800 358 3601 0141 331 2287

Tel: 0800 358 3601
Fax: 0141 331 2287

Website:
http://www.cica.gov.uk

Enquiries:
Enquiries to: Media Enquiries
Direct e-mail: philip.gibson@cica.gsi.gov.uk

Formerly called:
Criminal Injuries Compensation Board

Organisation type and purpose:
National government body.
Government board.

Subject coverage:
Scheme for compensating victims of crimes of violence and persons injured while arresting an offender, or preventing an offence, or giving help to a policeman engaged in those things. Application may also be made by the widow, widower, or a close relative and dependant of a person who received fatal injuries in such circumstances, or who received injuries but died from some other cause. Traffic offences are usually excluded.

Printed publications:
Annual Report (HMSO)
Information leaflets
Text of the Scheme

CRISIS

Formal name: Crisis UK trading as Crisis

66 Commercial Street, London, E1 6LT

Tel: 0870 011 3335
Fax: 0870 011 3336
E-mail: enquiries@crisis.org.uk

Website:
http://www.crisis.org.uk
Information on the work of Crisis.

Enquiries:
Enquiries to: Marketing Executive

Founded:
1967

Formerly called:
Crisis at Christmas

Organisation type and purpose:
National organisation, voluntary organisation, registered charity (charity number 1082947). Crisis is a national charity for homeless people.

Subject coverage:
Homelessness, housing, volunteering, fundraising.

Museum or gallery collection, archive, or library special collection:
Photograph library
Reports on homelessness issues

Trade and statistical information:
Statistics on homelessness and housing.

Printed publications:
A Future Foretold – New approaches to meeting the long-term needs of single homeless people
Falling Out (£6.95)
Homeless on Sea (£5)
Healthy Hostels – A Guide to Promoting Health and Well-Being Among homeless People (2001, £7.50 plus p&p)
Homeless Truths (Crane M, 1997, £8)
Homelessness and Loneliness – The Want of Conviviality (2001, £4.50 plus p&p)
In From the Cold (£4)
Leaving Homelessness Behind – New solutions for a new age
Lest We Forget – Ex-servicemen and Homelessness (2000, £7.50 plus p&p)
Prevention is Better than Cure
The Move in Experience (£6.95)
Trouble at Home – Family Conflict, Young People and Homelessness (2001, £7.50 plus p&p)
Sick to Death of Homelessness (£6.95)
Still Dying for a Home (Grenier P, 1996, £8)
Unsafe Streets – Street Homelessness and Crime
Walk on By – Begging, Street Drinking and the Giving Age (2000, £7.50 plus p&p)
Waste Not, Want Not (Cottee P, and Webster J, 1997, £3)

Publications list:
Available online and in print

Access to staff:
Contact by letter, by telephone, by fax, by e-mail and via website
Hours: Mon to Fri, 0930 to 1730; Sat, Sun, closed

Access to building, collection or gallery:
No access other than to staff

CROFTERS COMMISSION

Great Glen House, Leachkin Road, Inverness

Tel: 01463 663450
Fax: 01463 711820
E-mail: info@crofterscommission.org.uk

Website:
http://www.crofterscommission.org.uk

Enquiries:
Enquiries to: Communications Officer
Direct tel: 01463 663424
Direct e-mail: betty.mackenzie@crofterscommission.org.uk

Founded:
1955

Organisation type and purpose:
National government body, advisory body, statutory body.
Non-departmental government body.

Subject coverage:
Crofting regulation
Croft house grants

Non-library collection catalogue:
All or part available online

Printed publications:
Publications available free of charge

Publications list:
Available online and in print

Access to staff:
Contact by letter, by telephone, by fax, by e-mail, in person and via website. Appointment necessary.
Hours: Mon to Thu, 0830 to 1700; Fri, 0830 to 1630

Access for disabled people:
Fully accessible, toilet facilities

CROHN'S IN CHILDHOOD RESEARCH ASSOCIATION

Acronym or abbreviation: CICRA

Parkgate House, 356 West Barnes Lane, Motspur Park, Surrey, KT3 6NB

Tel: 020 8949 6209
Fax: 020 8942 2044
E-mail: support@cicra.org

Website:
http://www.cicra.org

Enquiries:
Enquiries to: Charity Co-ordinator

Founded:
1978

Organisation type and purpose:
Membership association, present number of members: 1,500, registered charity (charity number England and Wales 278212, Scotland SC040700). Free membership offered to all interested parties, including medical professionals.

Subject coverage:
Telephone advice and support for individuals and families of children suffering from Crohn's Disease and Ulcerative Colitis (inflammatory bowel disease). Literature on all aspects of inflammatory bowel disease, especially as it affects children and young people. Membership (free of charge) to all relevant individuals and families, and the medical profession. Annual meeting/open day attended by senior medical professionals.

Printed publications:
Crohn's Disease: Ulcerative Colitis
Children with Crohn's and Colitis – A parent's guide
Children with Crohn's and Colitis – A teacher's guide
Children with Crohn's and Colitis – What do the doctors mean (A–Z of terms)
Children with Crohn's and Colitis – General information
Series of fact sheets on aspects of IBD, particularly as it affects children
Newsletter (quarterly, members)
All the above are free of charge

Publications list:
Available in print

Access to staff:
Contact by letter, by telephone, by fax, by e-mail and via website. Appointment necessary.
Hours: Mon to Fri, 0930 to 1730

Access to building, collection or gallery:
Prior appointment required

Access for disabled people:
Parking provided

CRONER CCH GROUP LIMITED

145 London Road, Kingston Upon Thames, Surrey, KT2 6SR

Tel: 020 8547 3333
Fax: 020 8547 2638
E-mail: info@croner.cch.co.uk

Website:
http://www.croner.cch.co.uk
News stories, articles, questions and answers, in-depth reports and tools.

Enquiries:
Enquiries to: Customer Services Manager

Organisation type and purpose:
Publishing house.
Publishers of business information solutions.

Subject coverage:
Human resources; consumer, business and specialist industry law; exporting, importing, health and safety, transport; freight and haulage, VAT and finance, IT, education, charities, care homes, catering, health service management, environmental management and the control of hazardous substances.

Printed publications:
Loose-leaf, online, software, training, seminar and consultancy products and services

Publications list:
Available in print

Access to staff:
Contact by letter, by telephone, by fax, by e-mail and via website
Hours: Mon to Fri, 0830 to 1730

Part of:
Wolters Kluwer Group

CROP PROTECTION ASSOCIATION (UK) LIMITED

Acronym or abbreviation: CPA

4 Lincoln Court, Lincoln Road, Peterborough, Cambridgeshire, PE1 2RP

Tel: 01733 349225
Fax: 01733 562523
E-mail: info@cropprotection.org.uk

Enquiries:
Enquiries to: Director General

Formerly called:
British Agrochemicals Association Limited (BAA)

Organisation type and purpose:
International organisation, trade association. Represents companies who manufacture and formulate pesticides, and distributors.

Subject coverage:
Agrochemicals, pesticides.

Printed publications:
AGCHEM (quarterly magazine)
CPA Annual Review and Handbook
Educational materials
Pesticides in Perspective (set of 9 leaflets)

Publications list:
Available in print

Access to staff:
Appointment necessary.
Hours: Mon to Fri, 0900 to 1700

Member of:
Crop Life
European Crop Protection Association (ECPA)

CROQUET ASSOCIATION

Acronym or abbreviation: CA

c/o The Cheltenham Croquet Club, Old Bath Road, Cheltenham, GL53 7DF

Tel: 01242 242318
E-mail: caoffice@croquet.org.uk

Website:
http://www.croquet.org.uk

Enquiries:
Enquiries to: Manager

Founded:
1897

Organisation type and purpose:
Membership association (membership is by subscription), present number of individual members: 1,700, member clubs; 168, voluntary organisation.
Governing body of the game.

continued overleaf

Organises tournaments and coaching for players of all abilities.

Subject coverage:
Croquet, handicap ratings, laws of croquet, history.

Printed publications:
Croquet (J. Solomon, £9 inc p&p)
Croquet Coaching Manual (£11.50 inc p&p)
Croquet Gazette (members only, 6 times a year)
Croquet Management (Gaunt and Wheeler £11.50 inc p&p)
Croquet – The Skills of the Game (B. Lamb, £10 inc p&p)
Know the Game (£6.20 inc p&p)
Plus One on Time (D. Gaunt, £10 inc p&p)
Laws of Association Croquet (£4.00 inc p&p)
Laws of Golf Croquet (£2.50 inc p&p)
Basic Laws (£2 inc p&p)
Guide of Golf Croquet (£5 inc p&p)
Order printed publications from: Croquet Association Shop

Publications list:
Available in print

Access to staff:
Contact by letter, by telephone, by e-mail and via website. Appointment necessary.
Hours: Mon to Thu, 0900 to 1600; Fri, 0900 to 1300

CROSS & COCKADE INTERNATIONAL

Acronym or abbreviation: CCI

Hamilton House, Church Street, Wadenhoe, Peterborough, PE8 5ST

Tel: 01832 720522
Fax: 07092 172286
E-mail: chairman@crossandcockade.com

Website:
http://www.crossandcockade.com
Information on the Society, shop, forum, sample articles and news.

Enquiries:
Enquiries to: Membership Secretary
Direct tel: 01237 474703
Direct e-mail: membership.secretary@crossandcockade.com
Other contacts: Managing Editor for journal material

Founded:
1969

Also known as:
First World War Aviation Historical Society

Formerly called:
Cross and Cockade Great Britain 1969

Incorporates the former:
Essex Chapter Cross and Cockade

Organisation type and purpose:
International organisation, learned society (membership is by subscription), present number of members: 1,400, voluntary organisation, consultancy, research organisation, publishing house.
To enable those with a common interest in any aspect of World War I aviation to share those interests, and to meet fellow enthusiasts.

Subject coverage:
Factual information about all aspects of the 1914–1918 war in the air.

Museum or gallery collection, archive, or library special collection:
Photographs and some original documents
Reference books

Printed publications:
Journal (quarterly, free to members, back numbers available, prices vary)
Seminar Papers 1995, 1997
Monographs on Nieuport and FE2 aircraft
Order printed publications from: Sales Manager, Cross and Cockade, 6 Cowper Road, Southgate, London, N14 5RP

Electronic and video publications:
Gazetteer of Northern France
Index of Journal Contents

Publications list:
Available in print

Access to staff:
Contact by letter, by telephone, by e-mail and via website. Appointment necessary. Non-members charged.
Hours: Mon to Fri, 0900 to 1700

Also at:
Advertising Manager, Cross & Cockade International
6 Cowper Road, Southgate, London, N14 5RP; tel: 020 8361 8482; e-mail: advertising.manager@crossandcockade.com
Membership Secretary, Cross & Cockade International
11 Francis Drive, Westward Ho!, EX39 1XE; tel: 01237 474703; e-mail: membership.secretary@crossandcockade.com

CROSSLEY REGISTER

Willow Cottage, Lexham Road, Great Dunham, King's Lynn, Norfolk, PE32 2LS

Tel: 01328 701240
E-mail: malcolmhatfield@globalnet.co.uk

Website:
http://www.crossley-motors.org.uk

Enquiries:
Enquiries to: General Secretary
Direct e-mail: anthonycourtney@tiscali.co.uk
Other contacts: Editor

Founded:
1985

Organisation type and purpose:
Membership association (membership is by subscription), voluntary organisation.

Subject coverage:
The Crossley motor car.

Museum or gallery collection, archive, or library special collection:
Archive material on Crossley Motors Limited
Records from the company of Crossley Motors Limited

Printed publications:
Newsletter (3 times a year)

Access to staff:
Contact by letter, by telephone, by fax and by e-mail
Hours: Mon to Fri, 0900 to 1700

Access to building, collection or gallery:
Prior appointment required

Access for disabled people:
Parking provided

CROSSWORD CLUB

Coombe Farm, Awbridge, Romsey, Hampshire, SO51 0HN

Tel: 01794 524346
Fax: 01794 514988
E-mail: bh@thecrosswordclub.co.uk

Website:
http://www.thecrosswordclub.co.uk
Mainly online brochure offering information about club, including stop-press items, especially about latest puzzles published in Crossword and solutions of earlier puzzles.

Enquiries:
Enquiries to: Editor

Founded:
1978

Organisation type and purpose:
Membership association.

Subject coverage:
All aspects of crosswords, especially difficult examples involving gimmicks; composition; history, etc.

Museum or gallery collection, archive, or library special collection:
Collections of crossword and general dictionaries
Library of books of and about crosswords

Printed publications:
Crossword (monthly, free to members)
Guide to Playfair (£1.25)
Handbook (occasional, free to members)

Access to staff:
Contact by letter, by telephone, by fax and by e-mail. Appointment necessary.
Hours: Generally 1600 to 2000; other times on spec; 24-hour answerphone

CROWN PROSECUTION SERVICE

Acronym or abbreviation: CPS

50 Ludgate Hill, London, EC4M 7EX

Tel: 020 7273 8000
Fax: 020 7796 8651

Website:
http://www.cps.gov.uk
General information.

Enquiries:
Enquiries to: Information Officer
Direct tel: 020 7796 8023
Direct fax: 020 7796 8030
Direct e-mail: cps.pressoffice@cps.gsi.gov.uk

Founded:
1986

Organisation type and purpose:
National government body.

Subject coverage:
Criminal law.

Library catalogue:
All or part available in-house

Printed publications:
Domestic Violence Policy
Domestic Violence Guidance
Prosecutions Leaflet
Introduction to CPS Leaflet
The People Leaflet
The Code for Crown Prosecutors
Witness in Court
Complaints to the CPS
CPS Area Map (Colour)
Order printed publications from: Communications Branch, CPS

Publications list:
Available online

Access to staff:
Contact by letter, by fax and by e-mail
Hours: Mon to Fri, 0900 to 1700

Access to building, collection or gallery:
No access other than to staff

Access for disabled people:
Ramped entry, level entry, access to all public areas, toilet facilities
Special comments: Parking provided in The Courtyard, 1st left turn in Old Bailey.

CROWTHER CENTRE FOR MISSION EDUCATION

Watlington Road, Oxford, OX4 6BZ

Tel: 01865 787400
Fax: 01865 776375
E-mail: info@cms-uk.org

Website:
http://www.cms-uk.org
Online catalogue.

Enquiries:
Enquiries to: Librarian

Direct tel: 01865 787552
Direct e-mail: ken.osborne@cms-uk.org

Founded:
1987

Please select:
Partnership House Mission Studies Library

Organisation type and purpose:
Registered charity (charity number 1131655).
Provides library service to the Anglican missionary
societies. The Partnership House Mission Studies
Library was formed in 1987 from the post-1945
library collections of CMS and the USPG, to which
has been added the library of the South American
Missionary Society. All interested in Christian
Mission are welcome to use the library.

Subject coverage:
Missiology; world-wide Christian church,
especially history; growth and work of
Anglicanism; the ecumenical movement; other
faiths; spirituality; social concerns of the church
(e.g. race, poverty, human rights); area studies.

**Museum or gallery collection, archive, or library
special collection:**
CMS Max Warren collection (comprises the books
from the former Church Missionary Society
Library that were published prior to 1946, plus
copies of all CMS publications)

Non-library collection catalogue:
All or part available online

Library catalogue:
All or part available online and in-house

Printed publications:
Bulletin (including JIST, journals in short –
abstracting service and New Books List)

Access to staff:
Contact by letter, by telephone, by fax, by e-mail,
in person and via website
Hours: Mon to Fri, 0930 to 1700
Special comments: Reference services free of charge.
Loan of books (other than to missions staff) by
annual subscription.

CROYDON COLLEGE LIBRARY

College Road, Fairfield, Croydon, Surrey, CR9 1DX

Tel: 020 8760 5843
E-mail: library@croydon.ac.uk

Website:
http://www.croydon.ac.uk/ipoint
Library services and catalogue access to
eResources, Subject Guides.

Enquiries:
Enquiries to: Librarian

Organisation type and purpose:
Suitable for ages: 16+. College of further education/
higher education.

Subject coverage:
Art and design, theatre, management, nursing,
health studies, child care, social work, law,
construction, business studies, education, travel
and tourism, sport.

Library catalogue:
All or part available online

Access to staff:
Access for members only.
Hours: Main Campus: term time, Mon to Thu, 0830
to 2030; Fri, 0830 to 1700; Sat, 1000 to 1500;
vacations, Mon to Fri, 0930 to 1630; occasionally
closed.
Davidson Campus: term time, Mon to Fri, 0900 to
1700; vacations, closed
Special comments: Library for the use of Croydon
College staff and students only.

Access for disabled people:
Ramped entry, access to all public areas, toilet
facilities

CROYDON LIBRARIES

Central Library, Katharine Street, Croydon, Surrey,
CR9 1ET

Tel: 020 8726 6900
Fax: 020 8253 1004
E-mail: aileen.cahill@croydon.gov.uk

Website:
http://www.croydon.gov.uk/libraries
Covers all general information about the services,
activities and events. Reference and information
specialist areas include: business, law, information,
technology, tourism, community, local and family
history.

Enquiries:
Enquiries to: Assistant Director, Libraries
Direct tel: 020 8253 1001

Founded:
1888

Formerly called:
Croydon Public Library

Organisation type and purpose:
Local government body, public library.

Subject coverage:
General collection, strong in the following areas:
computers, business information, European
information, law, visual arts, Croydon local history.

Information services:
Online access to encyclopedias, dictionaries,
newspaper archives and business sources.

Services for disabled people:
Zoomtext on public PCs, Kurzweil reader, CCTV
enlarger.

**Museum or gallery collection, archive, or library
special collection:**
Archives
Croydon Local Studies Library
IGI complete
1881 Census Index, Surrey only
Riesco Collection of Chinese Ceramics

Library catalogue:
All or part available online

Printed publications:
SWLULOP (edited by Anna Raghunanan)

Access to staff:
Contact by letter, by telephone, by fax, by e-mail,
in person and via website
Hours: Main Library: Mon, 0900 to 1900; Tue, Wed
and Fri, 0900 to 1800; Thu, 0930 to 1800; Sat, 0900
to 1700; Sun, 1400 to 1700

Access to building, collection or gallery:
No access other than to staff
Hours: Main Library: Mon, 0900 to 1900; Tue, Wed
and Fri, 0900 to 1800; Thu, 0930 to 1800; Sat, 0900
to 1700; Sun, 1400 to 1700

Access for disabled people:
Ramped entry, access to all public areas, toilet
facilities, lifts to all floors

CROYDON LOCAL STUDIES
LIBRARY AND ARCHIVES
SERVICE

Central Library, Katharine Street, Croydon, Surrey,
CR9 1ET

Tel: 020 8726 6900 etn 61112
Fax: 020 8253 1012
E-mail: localstudies@croydon.gov.uk

Website:
http://www.croydon.gov.uk/researchcroydon

Enquiries:
Enquiries to: Senior Borough Archivist
Other contacts: Local Studies Librarian

Organisation type and purpose:
Public library.

Subject coverage:
Local history of the Borough of Croydon and the
surrounding area. By virtue of the range of the
collections, local and family history of many parts
of England.

Information services:
Free internet access for family and local history,
including Ancestry library edition.

**Museum or gallery collection, archive, or library
special collection:**
IGI (microfiche)
1841–1901 Census
Books
Maps
Photographs
Newspapers and local periodicals
Large collection of volumes of English local history
    societies, records and transcriptions
Harleian Society volumes
Street directories
Electoral rolls
Telephone directories
Parish registers
GRO indexes of births, marriages and deaths,
    1837–1897
Rate books (advance notice may be required)
Records of Croydon Council and predecessor
    bodies, Croydon schools, Croydon Board of
    Guardians and Workhouse, other local
    organisations and individuals (advance notice
    may be required for some or all of these)

Library catalogue:
All or part available online and in-house

Access to staff:
Contact by letter, by telephone, by fax, by e-mail,
in person and via website
Hours: Mon, 1030 to 1900; Tue, Wed, Fri, 1030 to
1700; 1st and 3rd Sat in month, 1030 to 1700

Access to building, collection or gallery:
No prior appointment required; situated off Level
3
Hours: Mon, 1030 to 1900; Tue, Wed, Fri, 1030 to
1700; 1st and 3rd Sat in month, 1030 to 1700

Access for disabled people:
Ramped entry, access to all public areas, toilet
facilities
Hours: As above

CROYDON NATURAL HISTORY
AND SCIENTIFIC SOCIETY
LIMITED

Acronym or abbreviation: CNHSS

96A Brighton Road, South Croydon, Surrey, CR2
6AD

Tel: 020 8688 3593

Website:
http://www.croydononline.org/hs/cnhss/index.asp

Enquiries:
Enquiries to: Librarian
Other contacts: Membership Secretary for
membership

Founded:
1870

Formed from:
Croydon Microscopical & Natural History Club
(1877–1901), Croydon Microscopical Club (1870–
1877)

Organisation type and purpose:
Learned society (membership is by subscription),
present number of members: 360, voluntary
organisation, registered charity (charity number
260739).
Research and education concerned with the
geology, natural history, archaeology, local history,
etc. of Croydon and adjoining parts of east Surrey
and west Kent.

continued overleaf

Subject coverage:
Archaeology, botany, entomology, geography, geology, industrial archaeology and history, local history, ornithology, zoology, all pertaining to the Croydon area and some parts of NE Surrey, NW Kent and adjoining London Boroughs; particularly strong in natural history, geology and industrial history, and archaeology of the extractive and transport industries.

Museum or gallery collection, archive, or library special collection:
C C Fagg Collection (early land-use surveying, regional survey, etc.)
Strong holdings relating to economic, geological, civil engineering, water supply, etc.
W H Bennett Collection (geological and palaeontological books and journals)

Non-library collection catalogue:
All or part available in-house

Library catalogue:
All or part available in-house

Printed publications:
Accounts of excavations
Croydon Between the Wars (2nd ed, 1993, £4.75 plus p&p)
Croydon in the 1940s and 1950s (1994, £5.25 plus p&p)
Croydon: the Story of a Hundred Years (1870–1970)
Edwardian Croydon Illustrated (2nd ed, 1990, £4.25 plus p&p)
Illustrated local history books
Victorian Croydon Illustrated (2nd ed, 1987, £3.25 plus p&p)
Various publications on the history and natural history of the area

Publications list:
Available in print

Access to staff:
Contact by letter and by telephone. Appointment necessary.
Hours: Any reasonable time

Access to building, collection or gallery:
Prior appointment required
Hours: Any mutually convenient time
Special comments: By arrangement with the librarian.

CRUISING ASSOCIATION

Acronym or abbreviation: CA

1 Northey Street, Limehouse Basin, London, E14 8BT

Tel: 020 7537 2828
Fax: 020 7537 2266
E-mail: office@cruising.org.uk

Website:
http://www.cruising.org.uk

Enquiries:
Enquiries to: Information Officer

Founded:
1908

Organisation type and purpose:
Voluntary organisation.

Subject coverage:
Cruising under sail or power, pilotage, accounts of cruises historical and modern, navigation, seamanship and boat maintenance. Extensive maritime chart collection.

Information services:
Extensive library and information centre of yachting information, available to members of the association.

Museum or gallery collection, archive, or library special collection:
Nautical books (said to be the largest collection in private ownership in Europe)

Non-library collection catalogue:
All or part available online

Library catalogue:
All or part available online

Printed publications:
Cruising Almanac
CRUISING, quarterly magazine of the Cruising Association

Access to staff:
Contact by letter, by telephone, by e-mail, in person and via website. Appointment necessary. Access for members only.
Hours: Mon to Fri, 0930 to 1730

Access for disabled people:
Ramped entry, access to all public areas, toilet facilities

Affiliated to:
Royal Yachting Association

CRUSE BEREAVEMENT CARE

PO Box 800, Richmond, TW9 1RG

Tel: 020 8939 9530
Fax: 020 8940 1671
E-mail: info@cruse.org.uk

Website:
http://www.cruse.org.uk

Founded:
1959

Formerly called:
National Organisation for the Widowed and their Children

Organisation type and purpose:
National organisation, registered charity (charity number 208278).
To provide bereavement support, counselling and advice to anyone who is bereaved by death. This help also includes support groups, a monthly newsletter and a wide variety of leaflets and publications. Includes specialist support and website for children and young people.

Subject coverage:
Welfare of bereaved people; counselling, social support and courses for counsellors.

Printed publications:
A wide range of leaflets and publications – for a mail order catalogue please e-mail
Annual Report
Bereavement Care Journal (for bereavement care workers and professionals)
Books
Leaflets and fact sheets (about 40 titles)
Packs (for educational purposes)

Publications list:
Available online and in print

Access to staff:
Contact by letter, by telephone, by fax, by e-mail and via website
Hours: Mon to Fri, 0930 to 1700

Access to building, collection or gallery:
No access other than to staff

Branches:
Local Cruse branches throughout England, Wales and Northern Ireland and a National Helpline

CRY-SIS HELP LINE

Acronym or abbreviation: CRY-SIS

BM CRY-SIS, London, WC1N 3XX

Tel: 08451 228669
E-mail: info@cry-sis.org.uk

Website:
http://www.cry-sis.org.uk

Enquiries:
Enquiries to: Administrator

Founded:
1981

Formerly called:
The Cry-sis Support Group (year of change 1986); Serene (year of change 1997)

Organisation type and purpose:
National organisation, voluntary organisation, registered charity (charity number 295470). Self-help and support group for families with excessively crying, sleepless and demanding babies.

Subject coverage:
Self-help and support for parents of excessively crying, sleepless and demanding babies.

Printed publications:
See publications list, available by postal application (sae please)
Order printed publications from: BM CRY-SIS, London, WC1N 3XX

Electronic and video publications:
Self-help information sheets available online at http://www.cry-sis.org.uk in easily downloadable form

Publications list:
Available online and in print

Access to staff:
Contact by letter, by telephone, by e-mail and via website
Hours: Mon to Sun, 0900 to 2200
Special comments: Telephone access and postal enquiries only (sae please).

CUED SPEECH ASSOCIATION UK

9 Jawbone Hill, Dartmouth, Devon, TQ6 9RW

Tel: 01803 832784
Fax: 01803 835311
E-mail: info@cuedspeech.co.uk

Website:
http://www.cuedspeech.co.uk

Enquiries:
Enquiries to: Executive Director

Founded:
1975

Formerly called:
National Centre for Cued Speech (NCCS) (year of change 2000)

Organisation type and purpose:
National organisation, membership association (membership is by subscription, election or invitation), present number of members: 75, registered charity (charity number 279523), training organisation.
To provide information and training in cued speech throughout the UK.

Subject coverage:
Cued speech is a simple sound-based system comprising 8 handshapes used in 4 positions near the mouth, in conjunction with the lip patterns of normal speech, to make all the sounds of spoken language fully comprehensible to deaf and hearing-impaired people.

Printed publications:
Newsletter (4 times a year)
The Cued Speech Resource Book for Parents of Deaf Children (£15 plus p&p)
Cued Speech booklet (free)
Cued Speech information sheets and leaflets (free)

Access to staff:
Contact by letter, by telephone, by fax and by e-mail. Appointment necessary.
Hours: Mon to Fri, 0900 to 1700

Access to building, collection or gallery:
No access other than to staff

CULHAM CENTRE FOR FUSION ENERGY (INCORPORATING EFDA-JET)

Formal name: United Kingdom Atomic Energy Authority

Acronym or abbreviation: CCFE

Culham Centre for Fusion Energy, Culham Science Centre, Abingdon, Oxfordshire, OX14 3DB

Tel: 01235 466647
Fax: 01235 466706
E-mail: chris.warrick@ccfe.ac.uk

Website:
http://www.jet.efda.org
Details about the pan-European JET fusion experiment – hosted at the Culham site.
http://www.fusion.org.uk
Descriptive information of the UK's domestic fusion programme and CCFE's role as the host of JET.

Enquiries:
Enquiries to: Communications Manager.

Founded:
1965

Organisation type and purpose:
Research organisation, which is part of a Europe- and world-wide effort to realise nuclear fusion as a viable source of carbon-free, abundant electricity in the future. JET is funded by the EU fusion research organisations under the European Fusion Development Agreement (EFDA) and operated on behalf of the research organisations by CCFE.

Subject coverage:
Research into realising nuclear fusion electricity production in the future.

Information services:
Information on the science and engineering challenges of nuclear fusion research.

Special visitor services:
Open evenings throughout the year – see website: http://www.ccfe.ac.uk.

Education services:
School visits accommodated – see website: http://www.ccfe.ac.uk.

Museum or gallery collection, archive, or library special collection:
Annual reports, annual progress reports and detailed scientific reports in the various fields of relevance to fusion research in the site library

Library catalogue:
All or part available online, in-house and in print

Printed publications:
Brochures:
1. Fusion – A Clean Future
2. JET – A European Success Story
Order printed publications from: 1. Communications Dept, CCFE, Culham Science Centre, Abingdon, Oxon, OX14 3DB or via website: http://www.ccfe.ac.uk
2. Public Information Officer, EFDA-JET Close Support Unit, Culham Science Centre, Abingdon, Oxon, OX14 3DB or via website: http://www.jet.efda.org

Electronic and video publications:
See website: http://www.ccfe.ac.uk

Publications list:
Available online and in print

Access to staff:
Contact by letter, by telephone, by fax and by e-mail. Appointment necessary.

Access to building, collection or gallery:
Prior appointment required for all visitors. For open evenings or group visits of any kind, registration is required
Hours: As required for the visit

Access for disabled people:
Parking provided, ramped entry to buildings; most parts of tour routes are disabled-accessible
Hours: As required for the visit

CULT INFORMATION CENTRE

Acronym or abbreviation: CIC

BCM CULTS, London, WC1N 3XX

Tel: 0845 4500 868

Website:
http://www.cultinformation.org.uk
General information on cults and advice for families with a loved one in a cult. Information about books on the topic, especially 'Cults: A Practical Guide' published by Cult Information Centre.

Enquiries:
Enquiries to: General Secretary

Founded:
1987

Organisation type and purpose:
National organisation, voluntary organisation, registered charity (charity number 1012914), suitable for ages: all, training organisation, consultancy, research organisation.
Information and advice to families, ex-members, the media and researchers on cults. Gives lectures on the dangers of cults to a wide variety of audiences.

Subject coverage:
Cults.

Education services:
The cult information centre gives lectures/talks on the topic of cults to schools, professional groups, clubs, religious institutions, UK companies and community groups.

Museum or gallery collection, archive, or library special collection:
Archive of books and publicity material published relating to cults
Newscuttings
Relevant articles

Printed publications:
Cults: A Practical Guide (£4.99 inc. p&p)
Moonwebs (Freed J, £2.99 inc. p&p)
The Children of God (Davis D, £11 inc. p&p)

Electronic and video publications:
Cults (video)

Publications list:
Available online and in print

Access to staff:
Contact by letter and by telephone
Hours: Mon to Fri, 0900 to 1700

Access to building, collection or gallery:
No access other than to staff

CUMBERLAND AND WESTMORLAND ANTIQUARIAN AND ARCHAEOLOGICAL SOCIETY

Acronym or abbreviation: CWAAS

Brantbeck, Wind Hall Road, Bowness-on-Windermere, LA23 3HX

Tel: 01539 445276
E-mail: info@cwaas.org.uk

Website:
http://www.cwaas.org.uk
Officers, publications, activities, contents of Transactions.
http://www.cumbriacad.ac.uk

Enquiries:
Enquiries to: Honorary Secretary
Other contacts: Publications, tel no: 01228 544120; Library, tel no: 01228 400300

Founded:
1866

Organisation type and purpose:
Learned society (membership is by subscription), present number of members: 850, registered charity (charity number 227786).

Subject coverage:
Archaeology and all aspects of history and customs of Cumberland and Westmorland, including genealogy, heraldry, parish registers, industrial archaeology, historic buildings etc.

Museum or gallery collection, archive, or library special collection:
Books and artefacts are held at Carlisle Museum, Tullie House, Castle Street, Carlisle, access by application to Librarian.
Library is now c/o Cumbria College of Art and Design, Brampton Road, Carlisle, Cumbria
Society's archives are held at Cumbria Record Office, The Castle, Carlisle

Non-library collection catalogue:
All or part available in-house

Library catalogue:
All or part available in-house

Printed publications:
Newsletter (3 times a year)
Medieval Carlisle (Henry Summerson 1993)
Transactions (annually, members)
Parish Registers, some available back to 1927
Other volumes include:
The Building of Hadrian's Wall
The Stained Glass in the Churches of the Anglican Diocese of Carlisle
Prehistoric Habitation Sites on the Limestone Uplands of Eastern Cumbria
Additional new volumes:
The Cumbria Parishes from Bishop Gartrall's 'Notitia' 1714–1725 (1998)
The Lanercost Cartulary (1997)
The Accounts of Sir Daniel Fleming of Rydal Hall 1688–1701 (2001)
Thomas Denton: a Perambulation of Cumberland 1687–88 (2003)
The Websters of Kendal: a North-Western Architectural Dynasty (2004)
Order printed publications from: Publications Officer, Cumberland and Westmorland Antiquarian and Archaeological Society
10 Peter Street, Carlisle, Cumbria, CA3 8QP, tel: 01228 544120

Publications list:
Available in print

Access to staff:
Contact by letter, by e-mail and via website
Hours: Mon to Fri, 0900 to 1700

Access to building, collection or gallery:
No prior appointment required
Special comments: New arrangement are under discussion.

Affiliated to:
Council of British Archaeology (CBA)

Library is now at:
Cumbrian Institute of the Arts
Brampton Road, Carlisle, Cumbria, CA3 9AY; tel: 01228 400300; fax: 01228 514491; website: http://www.cumbriacad.ac.uk

CUMBRIA ARCHIVE SERVICE – BARROW-IN-FURNESS

Cumbria Record Office & Local Studies Library, 140 Duke Street, Barrow in Furness, Cumbria, LA14 1XW

Tel: 01229 407377; minicom no. 01228 606336
Fax: 01229 894364
E-mail: barrow.record.office@cumbriacc.gov.uk

Website:
http://www.cumbria.gov.uk/archives
The general Cumbria Archive Service site.
http://www.cumbria.gov.uk/archives/pubs.asp
For the publications page.
http://www.a2a.pro.gov.uk/default.asp
The Access to Archives website, which includes a limited but growing number of record office catalogues.

Enquiries:
Enquiries to: Area Archivist

Founded:
1975

continued overleaf

Formerly called:
Central Library (Local Studies), Ramsden Square, Barrow, Cumbria Record Office (Barrow) (year of change 1998)

Organisation type and purpose:
Local government body.
Record office.

Subject coverage:
General local history of Barrow-in-Furness and South West Cumbria, genealogy, iron-mining and production, the Furness Railway, naval armaments production and design by Vickers Ltd, Barrow, urban growth and architecture.
Printed sources on Cumbria, chiefly the Furness area, including books, newspapers, journals; also transactions of local academic societies.

Special visitor services:
Has operated a combined searchroom since Oct 1998, jointly controlled by Cumbria Archive Service and Cumbria Library Service.

Museum or gallery collection, archive, or library special collection:
Manorial records for various Furness Manors, 16th to 20th centuries
Microfilm of minute books of Furness Railway 1844–1923 and station staff registers, late 19th century
Records of the Furness Estate of the Duke of Buccleuch, c. 1820–1960
Ships armament drawings (mainly gun mountings) from Vickers Ltd, Barrow, 20th century
Early 19th century handbills, etc. from J Soulby, Ulverston and other local printers

Non-library collection catalogue:
All or part available online and in-house

Library catalogue:
All or part available online

Printed publications:
Information Sheets on: local sources for Family History, Church Registers, House History, Development of Barrow-in-Furness, Industries, Ships and Shipbuilding, Directories and Maps (first issued 1987–89), Manorial Records, Poor Relief (first issued 1989–1990, revised periodically)
The Ellen Rose Fieldhouse Collection: a catalogue of sources covering the history and dialect of the Kirkby-in-Furness area (1992)
See entry for the Carlisle office for publications available at all four offices

Microform publications:
A microfilm edition of Barrow-in-Furness Labour Party Records has been produced by Microform Academic Publishers
Order microform publications from: Microform Academic Publishers, East Ardsley, Wakefield, WF3 2AT

Publications list:
Available in print

Access to staff:
Contact by letter, by telephone, by fax, by e-mail and in person
Hours: Usual opening hours: Mon to Fri, 0930 to 1300 and 1400 to 1700
Offers a full archive and local studies service on the 1st Sat of every month, 1000 to 1300 and 1400 to 1600
Closed the first Mon of every month following the 1st Sat
Local studies and searchroom sources only: Wed, 1700 to 1900

Access for disabled people:
Ramped entry, access to all public areas, toilet facilities

Constituent part of:
Cumbria (County Council) Archive Service

Links with:
Record Offices in Carlisle, Whitehaven and Kendal

CUMBRIA ARCHIVE SERVICE – CARLISLE

Formal name: Cumbria Archive Centre, Carlisle
Acronym or abbreviation: CACC

Cumbria Archive Centre, Lady Gillford's House, Petteril Bank Road, Carlisle, CA1 3AJ

Tel: 01228 227285 or 227284; minicom no. 01228 226336
Fax: 01228 607270 (office hours only)
E-mail: carlisle.record.office@cumbriacc.gov.uk

Website:
http://www.cumbria.gov.uk/archives

Enquiries:
Enquiries to: Assistant County Archivist
Direct tel: 01228 227283
Other contacts: Senior Archivist, Carlisle

Founded:
1962

Incorporates the former:
Joint Archives Committee for the Counties of Cumberland and Westmorland, and The City of Carlisle (year of change 1974)

Organisation type and purpose:
Local government body.
Record office.

Subject coverage:
History of Cumberland, Carlisle and Cumbria, history of property, mining and transport, etc., genealogy.

Museum or gallery collection, archive, or library special collection:
Archive of Catherine Marshall, suffragist and pacifist
Archive of Sir Esme Howard, diplomat

Non-library collection catalogue:
All or part available online and in-house

Printed publications:
A number of publications are available at all four of the Cumbrian Record Offices, including:
Church of England Parishes in Cumbria 1829 (1998)
Cumbrian Ancestors. Notes for Genealogical Searchers (3rd edn, 1998)
Map of Carlisle, 1745
Various subject guides available on Lonsdale estate, railways, tithes, the World Wars

Microform publications:
Original microfilm can be ordered or copies from existing film

Publications list:
Available online and in print

Access to staff:
Contact by letter, by telephone, by fax, by e-mail, in person and via website
Hours: Mon to Fri, 0900 to 1700
Special comments: CARN readers' ticket system.

Access to building, collection or gallery:
There is visitor car parking

Access for disabled people:
Parking provided, ramped entry, toilet facilities; lifts; platform lift

CUMBRIA ARCHIVE SERVICE – KENDAL

Cumbria Record Office, County Offices, Kendal, Cumbria, LA9 4RQ

Tel: 01539 773540; minicom no. 01228 606336
Fax: 01539 773538
E-mail: kendal.record.office@cumbriacc.gov.uk

Website:
http://www.cumbria.gov.uk/archives
Cumbria Archive Service website.

Enquiries:
Enquiries to: Archivist

Founded:
1962

Formerly called:
Westmorland Record Office (year of change 1974)

Organisation type and purpose:
Local government body.
Record office.

Subject coverage:
Records of: the historic county of Westmorland, the Cartmel area formerly in Lancashire north of the sands, Sedbergh, Garsdale and Dent area, formerly in West Riding of Yorkshire.

Museum or gallery collection, archive, or library special collection:
Records of Lady Anne Clifford of Appleby Castle (1590–1676)
Records of Sir Daniel Fleming MP of Rydal Hall (1633–1701)
Records of Thomas H Mawson (1861–1933), landscape architect of Lancaster

Non-library collection catalogue:
All or part available online and in-house

Printed publications:
Selection of books including:
Cumbrian Ancestors, notes for genealogical searchers (1998, £6.99)
The Ellen Rose Fieldhouse Collection Catalogue
Selection of maps, guides and posters including:
Church of England Parishes in Cumbria (map, 1829)
Henry Hoggarth's Plan of Kendal, 1853
John Todd's Plan of Kendal, 1787
John Wood's Plan of Kendal, 1833
Vital Statistics. The Westmorland Census of 1787 (ed Ashcroft L, £9.50 plus p&p)
See entry for the Carlisle office for publications available at all four offices

Publications list:
Available in print

Access to staff:
Contact by letter, by fax, by e-mail and in person
Hours: Mon to Fri, 0900 to 1700
Special comments: Readers' ticket required.

Access for disabled people:
Parking provided, level entry, access to all public areas, toilet facilities

Parent body:
Cumbria (County Council) Archive Service
The Castle, Carlisle

CUMBRIA CHAMBER OF COMMERCE AND INDUSTRY

The Enterprise Centre, James Street, Carlisle, Cumbria, CA2 5DA

Tel: 01228 534120
Fax: 01228 515602
E-mail: info@cumbriachamber.co.uk

Enquiries:
Enquiries to: Chief Executive
Direct e-mail: info@cumbriachamber.co.uk

Founded:
May 2001

Organisation type and purpose:
Membership association (membership is by subscription).

Printed publications:
Journal (two times a year)

Access to staff:
Contact by letter
Hours: Mon to Fri, 0900 to 1700

Has:
41 county groups

CUMBRIA COLLEGE OF ART AND DESIGN LIBRARY

Acronym or abbreviation: CCAD

Brampton Road, Carlisle, Cumbria, CA3 9AY

Tel: 01228 400312
Fax: 01228 514491

Website:
http://www.libraryopac.cumbriacad.ac.uk

Enquiries:
Enquiries to: Librarian
Direct e-mail: cdaniel@cumbriacad.ac.uk

Subject coverage:
Ceramics, textiles, painting, sculpture, printmaking, photography, graphic design, media studies, fashion, product design, heritage management, performing arts, archaeology, history, local history, writing.

Non-library collection catalogue:
All or part available online

Library catalogue:
All or part available online

Access to staff:
Contact by letter, by telephone and by fax. Appointment necessary.
Hours: Mon to Thu, 0845 to 2000; Fri, 0845 to 1600; Sat, 0900 to 1300

Access for disabled people:
Parking provided

Member of:
HCLRG
Northern Regional Library System and ARLIS

CUMBRIA ENVIRONMENTAL AND GEOLOGICAL SERVICES

Acronym or abbreviation: CEGS

Watch Hill, Aspatria, Wigton, Cumbria, CA7 3SB

Tel: 016973 22565
Fax: 016973 21375
E-mail: dred.cegs@bigfoot.com

Enquiries:
Enquiries to: Proprietor

Founded:
1992

Organisation type and purpose:
Consultancy.

Subject coverage:
Contaminated ground investigations (including mine gas monitoring and mine shaft investigations) and reports; knowledge of geology in relation to mine design, geomorphology, mapping and evaluation of mineral reserves; geotechnical site investigations and reports; geological appraisals, investigations, mapping and report writing; environmental surveys (including wildlife – amphibian handling licences held); environmental forestry and habitat management; extensive knowledge of the farming year and farming practices in UK; footpath surveys and countryside management practical skills.

Access to staff:
Contact by letter, by telephone and by e-mail
Hours: Mon to Fri, 0830 to 1900

Access to building, collection or gallery:
Hours: Mon to Fri, 0830 to 1900; other times by appointment

CUMBRIA RECORD OFFICE AND LOCAL STUDIES LIBRARY

Scotch Street, Whitehaven, Cumbria, CA28 7NL

Tel: 01946 506420
Fax: 01946 852919
E-mail: whitehaven.record.office@cumbriacc.gov.uk

Website:
http://www.cumbria.gov.uk/archives/whrec.asp
Guidance on finding the office, details of holdings and information relating to the educational use of the archive service and tracing a Cumbrian family history.
http://www.a2a.org.uk

Online catalogue for part of the collection (see also below).
http://www.cumbria.gov.uk/archives/Online_catalogues/default.asp
Online catalogue provides details of many of the holdings at the four offices in Barrow, Carlisle, Kendal and Whitehaven.

Founded:
1996

Organisation type and purpose:
Local government body.

Subject coverage:
History of West Cumbria and Whitehaven.

Museum or gallery collection, archive, or library special collection:
Whitehaven Local Studies Library (formerly in the Daniel Hay Library, Whitehaven)

Non-library collection catalogue:
All or part available online and in-house

Library catalogue:
All or part available online and in-house

Printed publications:
A variety of publications to inform or entertain, relating to aspects of Cumbrian history and its archives.
Order printed publications from: http://www.cumbria.gov.uk/archives/onlineshop

Publications list:
Available online

Access to staff:
Contact by letter, by telephone, by fax, by e-mail and in person

Access to building, collection or gallery:
Mon, Tue, Thu and Fri, 0930 to 1230 and 1330 to 1700; Wed, 0930 to 1230 and 1330 to 1900; alternate Sat, 0900 to 1300
Special comments: CARN readers' ticket required.

Access for disabled people:
Ramped entry, access to all public areas, toilet facilities

Constituent part of:
Cumbria Archive Service

CUMBRIA TOURISM

Windermere Road, Staveley, Cumbria, LA8 9PL

Tel: 01539 822222
Fax: 01539 825079
E-mail: info@cumbriatourism.org

Website:
http://www.golakes.co.uk

Enquiries:
Enquiries to: Chief Executive

Founded:
1974

Organisation type and purpose:
Membership association (membership is by subscription).

Subject coverage:
Tourism in Cumbria and the Lake District.

Publications list:
Available in print

Access to staff:
Contact by letter, by telephone, by fax and by e-mail
Hours: Mon to Fri, 0900 to 1700

Links with:
local authorities and commercial members
Visit Britain

CURATIVE HYPNOTHERAPY REGISTER

Acronym or abbreviation: CHR

584 Derby Road, Nottingham, NG7 2GZ

Tel: 0115 970 1233
E-mail: info@curativehypnotherapyregister.co.uk

Website:
http://www.curativehypnotherapyregister.co.uk
About hypnosis, hypnotherapy, curative hypnotherapy; information for patients; problems that can be treated; requirements/duty of members; further information sites.

Enquiries:
Enquiries to: The Directors

Founded:
1985

Organisation type and purpose:
International organisation, advisory body, professional body (membership is by subscription, qualification, election or invitation).
To enhance the understanding of hypnotherapy, to provide advice/information on the subject of hypnosis/hypnotherapy; maintains a register of qualified practitioners nationwide.

Subject coverage:
Improving standards of hypnotherapy, list of qualified practitioners nationwide, information about hypnotherapy.

Printed publications:
Register of Qualified Therapists (free of charge)

Publications list:
Available online

Access to staff:
Contact by e-mail and via website
Hours: Mon to Fri, 0900 to 1700

CUTLERY AND ALLIED TRADES RESEARCH ASSOCIATION

Acronym or abbreviation: CATRA

Henry Street, Sheffield, South Yorkshire, S3 7EQ

Tel: 0114 276 9736
Fax: 0114 272 2151
E-mail: info@catra.org

Website:
http://www.catra.org
General information about services, products and helpful advice.

Enquiries:
Enquiries to: Director of Research

Founded:
1952

Organisation type and purpose:
Consultancy, research organisation.

Subject coverage:
Corrosion, grinding, heat treatment, metal finishing, electroplating, metallography, polishes and polishing, stainless steel, silver plate, automation, robotics, quality control, quality testing, cutlery, machine knives, knives, scissors, tools, sharpening, cookware, kitchen gadgets, surgical instruments, hand tools and garden tools.

Printed publications:
Annual Report
Leaflets on the care of cutlery (for sale)
Newsletters
Technical reports (for sale)

Access to staff:
Contact by letter, by telephone, by fax, by e-mail and via website. Appointment necessary. All charged.
Hours: Mon to Fri, 0900 to 1700

Access to building, collection or gallery:
Prior appointment required

Member of:
BSI

CYCLING TIME TRIALS

Acronym or abbreviation: CTT

continued overleaf

77 Arlington Drive, Pennington, Leigh, Lancashire, WN7 3QP

Tel: 01942 603976
Fax: 01942 262326
E-mail: phil.heaton@cyclingtimetrials.org.uk

Website:
http://cyclingtimetrials.org.uk
Information about the organisation and the sport, contact details of clubs, results and records.

Enquiries:
Enquiries to: National Secretary (Corporate & Administration)

Founded:
1937

Formerly called:
Road Time Trials Council (year of change 2002)

Organisation type and purpose:
National organisation, membership association (membership is by subscription), present number of members: 1,064 clubs, voluntary organisation. National governing body for cycling road time trials.

Subject coverage:
Cycle road time trials.

Printed publications:
Annual Handbook (with list of some 2,000 events, £8)
Rules, Regulations, Records, Past Champions, etc.

Electronic and video publications:
Championship DVDs (£6)
Entry forms (disc, £2.50)

Publications list:
Available online and in print

Access to staff:
Contact by letter, by telephone, by fax, by e-mail and via website. Appointment necessary.
Hours: Mon to Fri, 0900 to 1700

Access to building, collection or gallery:
No access other than to staff

Access for disabled people:
Parking provided, ramped entry, access to all public areas, toilet facilities
Hours: Mon to Fri, 0900 to 1700

Links with:
Central Council for Physical Recreation
14–16 Caxton St, London, SW1H 0QT; tel: 020 7976 3900

CYCLISTS' TOURING CLUB

Acronym or abbreviation: CTC

Parklands, Railton, Road, Guildford, Surrey, GU2 9JX

Tel: 0870 873 0060
Fax: 0870 873 0064
E-mail: cycling@ctc.org.uk

Website:
http://www.ctc.org.uk

Enquiries:
Enquiries to: Public Relations Manager
Other contacts: Director

Founded:
1878

Organisation type and purpose:
Membership association.
Promotes cycling for leisure, travel and transport.

Subject coverage:
All aspects of cycling; recreational and utility cycling; technical; legal aid; cycle insurance; mail order; campaigning; information for local/central government; rights and safety of all cyclists; touring; third party insurance; publications; all ages and abilities of cyclists helped.

Museum or gallery collection, archive, or library special collection:
Cycle Archive (CTC est. 1878)

Printed publications:
Route sheets
CTC Cycle Digest (quarterly)
CTC Event Guide
Cycle Away!
CTC Handbook (annually)
Cycle Touring & Campaigning (6 times a year)
Information booklets and sheets
Tours Guide
Various research reports
CTC Cyclists Welcome

Affiliated to:
Alliance Internationale de Tourisme (AIT)
BCF
European Cycling Federation (ECF)
RTTC

CYFA

Formal name: Church Youth Fellowships Association

CPAS, Athena Drive, Tachbrook Park, Warwick, CV34 6NG

Tel: 01926 458458
Fax: 01926 458459
E-mail: thehub@cpas.org.uk

Website:
http://www.cpas.org.uk
Details of events and products.

Enquiries:
Enquiries to: Head
Direct tel: 01926 458438

Founded:
1930

Organisation type and purpose:
To equip, encourage, and enable churches in youth ministry and discipleship.

Subject coverage:
Christian teaching and training for older teenagers, training of adults for youth leadership.

Printed publications:
A range of titles under the following headings:
Youth and Children's Resources
Youth Leadership skills
Worship
Evangelism
Small Groups
Strategy and Leadership
Order printed publications from: 24-hour sales orderline
tel: 01926 458400

Electronic and video publications:
Web-based teaching and resource materials for leaders and youth groups

Publications list:
Available online and in print

Access to staff:
Contact by letter, by telephone, by fax, by e-mail and via website. Appointment necessary.
Hours: Mon to Fri, 0900 to 1700

Affiliated to:
Church Pastoral Aid Society (CPAS)
at the same address

CYNGOR GWYNEDD COUNCIL

Stryd y Jêl, Shirehall Street, Caernarfon, Gwynedd, LL55 1SH

Tel: 01286 672255
Fax: 01286 673993
E-mail: enquiries@gwynedd.gov.uk

Website:
http://www.gwynedd.gov.uk
Council services; bus timetables; library services; tourism brochures; Gwynedd facts and figures.

Enquiries:
Enquiries to: Communications Manager
Direct tel: 01286 679310
Direct fax: 01286 679488

Direct e-mail: siongwilliams@gwynedd.gov.uk

Founded:
1996
Gwynedd County Council (year of change 1996)

Organisation type and purpose:
Local government body.

Subject coverage:
Local government services.

Library catalogue:
All or part available online

Access to staff:
Contact by letter, by telephone, by fax, by e-mail, in person and via website. Appointment necessary.
Hours: Mon to Fri, 0900 to 1700

Other addresses:
Arfon Area Office
Penrallt, Caernarfon, Gwynedd, LL55 1BN; tel: 01286 673113; fax: 01286 672635
Dwyfor Area Office
Ffordd y Cob, Pwllheli, Gwynedd, LL53 5AA; tel: 01758 613131; fax: 01758 613265
Meirionnydd Area Office
Cae Penarlag, Dolgellau, Gwynedd, LL40 1HL; tel: 01341 422341; fax: 01341 423984

CYSTIC FIBROSIS TRUST

11 London Road, Bromley, Kent, BR1 1BY

Tel: 020 8464 7211
Fax: 020 8313 0472
E-mail: enquiries@cftrust.org.uk

Website:
http://www.cftrust.org.uk

Enquiries:
Enquiries to: Chief Executive

Founded:
1964

Formerly called:
Cystic Fibrosis Research Trust

Organisation type and purpose:
Registered charity (charity number 1079049), research organisation.
Affiliated to the International Cystic Fibrosis (Mucoviscidosis) Association and the European Working Group for Cystic Fibrosis.

Subject coverage:
Research into the condition, and advice in coping with cystic fibrosis.

Museum or gallery collection, archive, or library special collection:
Library of books and documents relating to cystic fibrosis

Printed publications:
Publications include:
Annual Review
Booklets/Fact sheets
CF News
Cystic Fibrosis: the facts (£9.95, OUP 1995)
List of Research Projects

Electronic and video publications:
Audio Tapes: advice and information (available also in Urdu and Gujerati)
Videos on Treatment and living with CF (purchase or loan)

Publications list:
Available in print

Access to staff:
Contact by letter, by telephone, by fax, by e-mail and via website. Appointment necessary.
Hours: Mon to Fri, 0900 to 1700

Affiliated to:
European Working Group for Cystic Fibrosis
International Cystic Fibrosis (Mucoviscidosis) Association

Has:
local self-help groups

CYSTITIS AND OVERACTIVE BLADDER FOUNDATION

Acronym or abbreviation: COB Foundation

Kings Court, 17 School Road, Hall Green, Birmingham, B28 8JG

Tel: 0121 702 0820
E-mail: info@cobfoundation.org

Website:
http://www.cobfoundation.org
Full range of information.

Enquiries:
Enquiries to: Development Manager and Charity Administrator

Founded:
1994

Organisation type and purpose:
Membership association (membership is by subscription), registered charity (charity number 1047714).
Support for those with a specific medical condition.

Subject coverage:
Interstitial cystitis, treatments, therapies, medical research data.

Printed publications:
Interstitial Cystitis Survival Guide
Newsletter
Series of Information Leaflets

Electronic and video publications:
Understanding and coping with Interstitial Cystitis (video)
Understanding Interstitial Cystitis (video)

Publications list:
Available in print

Access to staff:
Contact by letter, by telephone, by e-mail and via website
Hours: Mon to Fri, 0900 to 1400

Access for disabled people:
Special comments: Steep narrow stairs.

CZECH AND SLOVAK TOURIST CENTRE

Acronym or abbreviation: CTC

16 Frognal Parade, Finchley Road, London, NW3 5HG

Tel: 020 7794 3264
Fax: 020 7794 3265
E-mail: reservations@cztc.co.uk

Website:
http://www.czech-wedding.co.uk
http://www.czechtravel.co.uk
http://www.czech-slovak-tourist.co.uk

Enquiries:
Enquiries to: Director

Founded:
1994

Formerly called:
Czech Tourist Centre

Organisation type and purpose:
National Slovak Tourist Board/Tour Operator.

Printed publications:
Photograph negatives (free hire, deposit required)

Electronic and video publications:
Videos and CD-ROMs (free hire, deposit required)

Access to staff:
Contact by letter, by telephone, by fax, by e-mail and in person
Hours: Mon to Fri, 1000 to 1800

CZECH CENTRE

13 Harley Street, London, W1G 9QG

Tel: 020 7307 5180
Fax: 020 7323 3709
E-mail: info@czechcentre.org.uk

Website:
http://www.czechcentres.cz/london

Enquiries:
Enquiries to: Administration and Marketing
Direct e-mail: storchova@czechcentre.org.uk

Founded:
1993

Organisation type and purpose:
International organisation.
Information centre of the Czech Republic.

Subject coverage:
Cultural information, activities, tourism, local and foreign investment, exhibitions, trade.

Access to staff:
Contact by letter, by telephone, by fax, by e-mail and via website
Hours: Tue, 1000 to 1900; Wed to Fri, 1000 to 1800

D H LAWRENCE SOCIETY

1 Church Street, Swepstone, Leics, LE67 2SA

Tel: 01530 270367

Enquiries:
Enquiries to: Joint Secretary
Direct tel: 0115 950 3008

Founded:
1974

Organisation type and purpose:
Learned society (membership is by subscription), present number of members: 200.
Study of life and works of D H Lawrence.

Subject coverage:
Life and works of D H Lawrence.

Printed publications:
D H Lawrence Society Journal (annually)
D H Lawrence Society Newsletter (2 times a year)

Access to staff:
Contact by letter and by telephone
Hours: Mon to Fri, 0900 to 1700

DAFFODIL SOCIETY

105 Bramcote Road, Nottingham, NG9 3GZ

Tel: 0115 925 5498
E-mail: rogerbb@lineone.net

Website:
http://www.the daffodil society .com

Enquiries:
Enquiries to: Secretary
Other contacts: Membership Secretary (tel. 01264 790745)

Founded:
1898

Organisation type and purpose:
Membership association (membership is by subscription), societies and individual members, voluntary organisation, registered charity (charity number 1055817).
To encourage the cultivation of the genus Narcissus.

Subject coverage:
Daffodils (genus Narcissus): breeding of new cultivars; control of pest and disease; general cultivation and exhibition.

Printed publications:
Annual Journal (February, for members)
Newsletter (July, for members)
Show Handbook (for sale)
Order printed publications from: Merchandising Manager, The Daffodil Society, 8 Foxdalls, Birch Green, Hertford, SG14 2LS, e-mail: baxterdaffs@ hotmail.com

Access to staff:
Contact by letter, by telephone, by e-mail and via website

DAIRY COUNCIL

Henrietta House, 17–18 Henrietta Street, Covent Garden, London, WC2E 8QH

Tel: 020 7395 4030
Fax: 020 7240 9679
E-mail: info@dairycouncil.org.uk

Website:
http://www.milk.co.uk
Types and composition of milk, range of dairy products, nutritional composition, history of dairying, modern methods of production, processing and manufacture.

Enquiries:
Enquiries to: Communications Manager
Direct e-mail: amanda.ball@dairyco.org.uk

Founded:
1920

Formerly called:
The National Dairy Council (year of change 2001)

Organisation type and purpose:
Trade association.
Promotional organisation for the whole dairy industry in Britain.

Subject coverage:
Dairy industry, milk, dairy products, nutrition, careers in the dairy industry, market data.

Museum or gallery collection, archive, or library special collection:
Foreign Dairy Industry journals
Historical exhibits
Photographic library
United Kingdom and European Community Dairy Facts and Figures

Trade and statistical information:
Consumption data and market research on the liquid milk market, top line data for other dairy products.

Library catalogue:
All or part available in-house

Printed publications:
Press releases
Catalogue of education material (booklets, factsheets, charts and posters, for Key Stage 1 to 4)
Catalogue of nutrition and health material
Consumer leaflets
Dairy Education (termly)
Dairy Mirror (quarterly)
Material for schools and teachers
UK and EC Dairy Facts and Figures
Nutrition and health education material (booklets free of charge)

Electronic and video publications:
The Dairy Channel (video, Key Stage 2, £5)
Discover Milk (CD-ROM, Key Stage 3, 4, GNVQ, £7.50)
Milk IT! (PC, Key Stage 2, £15)
Milk on the Move (video, Key Stage 1 and 2, £10)
The Meal Ticket (video, purchase not hire, £10)

Access to staff:
Contact by letter and by fax. Appointment necessary.
Hours: Mon to Fri, 0900 to 1700

Links to:
The Dairy Industry Federation (for processors)
The Milk Development Council (for farmers)

Other addresses:
Dairy Council for Northern Ireland
456 Antrim Road, Belfast, BT15 5GB; tel: 028 9077 0113

DAIRY UK

93 Baker Street, London, W1U 6QQ

continued overleaf

Tel: 020 7486 7244
Fax: 020 7487 4734
E-mail: info@dairyuk.org

Website:
http://www.dairyuk.org/

Enquiries:
Enquiries to: Secretary
Direct tel: 020 7467 2648
Direct e-mail: sbates@dairyuk.org

Created by the merger of:
Dairy Industry Federation (DIF) and the National Dairymen's Association (NDA)

Formerly called:
Dairy Trade Federation (DTF) (year of change 1993)

Organisation type and purpose:
Trade association.
Represents the interests of United Kingdom dairy companies.

Subject coverage:
Milk and milk products.

Printed publications:
Annual Review (available for purchase)

Access to staff:
Contact by letter, by telephone, by fax and by e-mail
Hours: Mon to Fri, 0900 to 1700

Access for disabled people:
Level entry

Member of:
European Dairy Association
The Dairy Council
United Kingdom Dairy Association

DAIRY UK (NORTHERN IRELAND)

8 Ranfurly Avenue, Bangor, County Down, BT20 3SN

Tel: 028 9147 1300
Fax: 028 9147 1300
E-mail: parcher@dairyuk.org

Enquiries:
Enquiries to: Northern Ireland Director

Founded:
1995

Organisation type and purpose:
Trade association (membership is by subscription), present number of members: 9.

Subject coverage:
Dairy processing industry in Northern Ireland.

Access to staff:
Contact by letter and by e-mail
Hours: Mon to Fri, 0900 to 1700

Access to building, collection or gallery:
Prior appointment required

Access for disabled people:
Parking provided, level entry, access to all public areas, toilet facilities

DAIWA ANGLO-JAPANESE FOUNDATION

Acronym or abbreviation: DAJF

Daiwa Foundation Japan House, 13–14 Cornwall Terrace, London, NW1 4QP

Tel: 020 7486 4348
Fax: 020 7486 2914
E-mail: office@ajf.org.uk

Website:
http://www.dajf.org.uk

Enquiries:
Enquiries to: Receptionist
Direct fax: 020 7486 3049

Founded:
1988

Organisation type and purpose:
Registered charity (charity number 299955).
To support links between the UK and Japan by awarding Daiwa Scholarhips, grant-making, and a year-round programme of events.

Subject coverage:
Japan, Japanese culture and the Japanese people.

Museum or gallery collection, archive, or library special collection:
Library (open to the public)

Access to staff:
Contact by letter, by telephone, by fax, by e-mail and in person. Appointment necessary.
Hours: Mon to Fri, 0930 to 1730
Special comments: Non-commercial enquiries only.

Links with:
Daiwa Anglo-Japanese Foundation
810 TBR Building, 2–10–2 Nagata-cho, Chiyoda-Ku, Tokyo, 100–0614, Japan; tel: 00 813 5501 2980; fax: 00 813 5501 2983; e-mail: dajftkyo@qa2.50-net.ne.jp

DARTINGTON COLLEGE OF ARTS

Dartington Hall Estate, Totnes, Devon, TQ9 6EJ

Tel: 01803 862224
Fax: 01803 861666
E-mail: library@dartington.ac.uk

Website:
http://www.dartington.ac.uk
Prospectus, news.

Enquiries:
Enquiries to: Librarian
Direct tel: 01803 861651

Founded:
1961

Organisation type and purpose:
Higher education in the performing arts.

Subject coverage:
Music, theatre, visual arts, arts management, writing for performance.

Library catalogue:
All or part available online

Access to staff:
Contact by letter, by telephone, by fax, by e-mail, in person and via website. Non-members charged.
Hours: Mon to Fri, 0900 to 2100; Sat, Sun, 1330 to 1730

Access to building, collection or gallery:
No prior appointment required
Hours: Mon to Fri, 0900 to 2100; Sat, Sun, 1330 to 1730

Access for disabled people:
Level entry, toilet facilities

DARTMOOR NATIONAL PARK AUTHORITY

Acronym or abbreviation: DNP/DNPA

Parke, Bovey Tracey, Devon, TQ13 9JQ

Tel: 01626 832093
Fax: 01626 834684
E-mail: hq@dartmoor-npa.gov.uk

Website:
http://www.dartmoor-npa.gov.uk
Copy of Dartmoor Visitor and other information, links to others.

Enquiries:
Enquiries to: Chief Executive
Other contacts: Directors

Founded:
1951

Organisation type and purpose:
Local government body.
National Park Authority.

Subject coverage:
Moorland and woodland management, upland archaeology, recreation management, development control, urban and rural enhancement, listed building protection, farm conservation, species conservation, community support, information and interpretation, design techniques.

Museum or gallery collection, archive, or library special collection:
Books, photographs and slides pertaining to Dartmoor only
Taylor Collection, photographs
Parminter Collection, photographs
Minter Collection (copy archaeological excavations)
French Collection (assorted papers, photographs and artefacts)

Trade and statistical information:
Corporate Plan.

Library catalogue:
All or part available in-house

Printed publications:
A large range of books, leaflets, study pack, factsheets, maps and posters on the moor and the subjects listed
Dartmoor Visitor (newspaper, 2 per year)

Microform publications:
Planning applications, (microfilm, viewing by appointment, no sales)

Electronic and video publications:
CD: Moor Memories – Collection 1: Rabbits, whortleberries and railways. Collection 2: Lovely days. Collection 3: Blacksticks and blizzards.
Virtually Dartmoor website: A Virtual Tour of Higher Uppacott. The Moor Memories project also has an archive of over 100 oral history recordings

Publications list:
Available online and in print

Access to staff:
Contact by letter, by telephone, by fax, by e-mail, in person and via website. Appointment necessary.
Hours: Mon to Thu, 0900 to 1700; Fri, 0900 to 1630

Access to building, collection or gallery:
Prior appointment required

Access for disabled people:
Parking provided, ramped entry, toilet facilities
Special comments: Disabled access to ground floor only.

Also at:
High Moorland Visitor Centre (HMVC)
Princetown, Devon; tel: 01822 890414; e-mail: hmvc@dartmoor-npa.fsbusiness.co.uk

Parent body:
Association of National Park Authorities (ANPA)

DARTMOOR PRESERVATION ASSOCIATION

Acronym or abbreviation: DPA

Duchy Hotel, Tavistock Road, Princetown, Yelverton, Devon, PL20 6QF

Tel: 01822 890646
E-mail: info@dartmoorpreservation.com

Website:
http://www.dartmoorpreservation.com
Independent voice of Dartmoor.

Enquiries:
Enquiries to: Chief Executive

Founded:
1883

Organisation type and purpose:
Membership association (membership is by subscription), present number of members: 2,400, voluntary organisation, registered charity (charity number 215665).
Conservation and amenity interests; campaigning to conserve the special qualities of Dartmoor.

Subject coverage:
All information relevant to Dartmoor.

Printed publications:
Newsletter (free to members)

Access to staff:
Contact by letter, by telephone, by e-mail and via website. Appointment necessary.
Hours: Tue and Thu, 0930 to 1430

DARTMOUTH TOURIST INFORMATION CENTRE

The Engine House, Mayors Avenue, Dartmouth, Devon, TQ6 9YY

Tel: 01803 834224
Fax: 01803 835631
E-mail: holidays@discoverdartmouth.com

Website:
http://www.discoverdartmouth.com

Enquiries:
Enquiries to: Manager

Founded:
1993

Organisation type and purpose:
Advisory body, museum, suitable for ages: 8+.

Subject coverage:
Features the Newcomen Atmospheric Engine, a preserved working steam atmospheric engine which was re-erected here in Thomas Newcomen's home town in 1963 to mark the 300th anniversary of his birth. In 1993 it was combined with a new tourist information centre.

Printed publications:
Discover Dartmouth

Access to staff:
Contact by letter, by telephone, by e-mail, in person and via website
Hours: Mon to Fri, 0930 to 1600

Access to building, collection or gallery:
No prior appointment required
Hours: Apr to Oct: Mon to Sat, 0930 to 1700; Sun, 1000 to 1400
Nov to Mar: Mon to Sat, 0930 to 1600

Access for disabled people:
Level entry, access to all public areas

DATA AND ARCHIVAL DAMAGE CONTROL CENTRE

Acronym or abbreviation: DADCC

4 Bridge Wharf, 156 Caledonian Road, London, N1 9UU

Tel: 020 7837 8215
E-mail: dadcc@netcomuk.co.uk

Website:
http://www.dadcc.com
On-site incident management after fire, flood or bombs to help clients in the decision-making process. Fire-, flood- and bomb-damaged books and documents salavaged. Coaching and mentoring for libraries and museums before and during an incident.

Enquiries:
Enquiries to: Managing Director
Direct tel: 07973 295155

Founded:
1986

Organisation type and purpose:
Training organisation, consultancy; forensic disaster management.

Subject coverage:
Salvage and restoration of books and documents damaged by fires, floods and terrorist activities; disaster planning, health and safety equipment that should be worn when entering disaster sites, training on pre-disaster planning and post-disaster recovery operations; educational literature.

Education services:
Training, talks and papers.

Museum or gallery collection, archive, or library special collection:
Slide reference library in UK disaster case studies

Printed publications:
DADCC brochure online

Getting it Right (free)

Access to staff:
Contact by letter, by telephone, by e-mail, in person and via website. Appointment necessary.
Hours: Mon to Fri, 0900 to 1700

Access to building, collection or gallery:
No access other than to staff

Access for disabled people:
Toilet facilities

DATA PUBLISHERS ASSOCIATION

Acronym or abbreviation: DPA

Queens House, 28 Kingsway, London, WC2B 6JR

Tel: 020 7405 0836
Fax: 020 7404 4167
E-mail: info@dpa.org.uk

Website:
http://www.dpa.org.uk

Enquiries:
Enquiries to: Marketing Co-ordinator
Direct e-mail: sarah.gooch@dpa.org.uk
Other contacts: Executive Director

Founded:
1970

Organisation type and purpose:
Trade association (membership is by subscription), present number of members: 80.
Not a directory publisher or distributor.

Subject coverage:
Directories, directory and data publishing.

Trade and statistical information:
Advertising statistics, business, salaries and benefits for directory publishing.

Printed publications:
Descriptive booklet and List of Members
Newsletter

Publications list:
Available in print

Access to staff:
Contact by letter, by telephone, by fax and by e-mail
Hours: Mon to Fri, 0900 to 1700

Access to building, collection or gallery:
No access other than to staff

Links with:
Advertising Association
Advertising Standards Board of Finance
Confederation of Information Communication Industries
Digital Content Forum
European Association of Directory and Database Publishers
Periodical Publishers Association
Publishing Skills Group

DATSUN OWNERS CLUB

40 Humber Way, Donnington, Telford, Shropshire, TF2 8LJ

Tel: 01342 321000

Website:
http://www.datsunworld.com

Enquiries:
Enquiries to: Archivist
Direct e-mail: datsunownersclub@hotmail.com

Founded:
1993

Organisation type and purpose:
International organisation, membership association (membership is by subscription), present number of members: 300, voluntary organisation.
Preservation of Datsun cars, help with obtaining parts, bringing together owners of this marque.

Subject coverage:
History of Datsuns, technical information, whereabouts of parts or cars.

Museum or gallery collection, archive, or library special collection:
Newspaper and magazine articles
Owners' manuals
Photographs
Spare parts available for Datsun cars
Workshop manuals

Trade and statistical information:
Production numbers of Datsun cars, numbers of examples surviving.

Printed publications:
Datsun Owners Club Newsletter (4 times a year, members, annual subscription £12)

Access to staff:
Contact by letter, by telephone, by e-mail and via website. Appointment necessary.
Hours: Mon to Fri, 1000 to 1900

Archivist:
Datsun Owners Club
7 School Road, Fritton, Norwich, Norfolk, NR15 2QN; tel: 01508 499620; e-mail: nigelg@tinyonline.co.uk

DAVID LEWIS CENTRE FOR EPILEPSY

Acronym or abbreviation: DLC

Mill Lane, Warford, Alderley Edge, Cheshire, SK9 7UD

Tel: 01565 640000
Fax: 01565 640100
E-mail: enquiries@davidlewis.org.uk

Website:
http://www.davidlewis.org.uk

Enquiries:
Enquiries to: Chief Executive

Founded:
1904

Organisation type and purpose:
Registered charity (charity number 1000392).
The David Lewis Centre provides a unique range of services for adults and children with complicated epilepsy. Services include The David Lewis School, The David Lewis College, Children's Epilepsy Outreach Assessments, Adult Social Care Provision, Residential Behaviour Service, Adult Assessment Unit and Residential High Dependency Unit.

Subject coverage:
Epilepsy and associated disabilities, in adults and children, including behaviour problems, understanding, treatment care, stabilisation, rehabilitation, research of adults and children. Adults and children – severe epilepsy and associated problems, assessment, treatment, residential care, education, training and rehabilitation service for children and young people with acquired brain injuries.

Access to staff:
Contact by letter, by telephone, by fax and by e-mail. Appointment necessary.
Hours: Mon to Fri, 0900 to 1700

Access to building, collection or gallery:
Prior appointment required

Access for disabled people:
Ramped entry, toilet facilities

DAVID WILLIAMS PICTURE LIBRARY

Allt-na-Craobh, Old Shore Road, Connel, Argyll, PA37 1PT

Tel: 01631 710586
Fax: 01631 710586

Enquiries:
Enquiries to: Proprietor
Direct e-mail: enquiries@bapla.org.uk

Founded:
1989

Organisation type and purpose:
Commercial picture library.

Subject coverage:
Colour photographic transparencies of Scotland, Iceland, Spain and a number of other countries, photographs of landscapes, landforms, buildings, towns and sites of historical interest.

Museum or gallery collection, archive, or library special collection:
Colour photographic transparencies of Scotland, Iceland, Spain and a number of other countries

Access to staff:
Contact by letter, by telephone, by fax and by e-mail. Appointment necessary.
Hours: ordinary business hours, also evenings and weekends

Member of:
British Association of Picture Libraries and Agencies

DAWSON BOOKS LIMITED

Foxhills House, Rushden, Northamptonshire, NN10 6DB

Tel: 01933 417500
Fax: 01933 417501

Website:
http://www.dawsonbooks.co.uk
Electronic library news.

Enquiries:
Enquiries to: Marketing Manager
Direct e-mail: marketing@dawsonbooks.co.uk

Founded:
1809

Organisation type and purpose:
International organisation, service industry, supplier of books.

Subject coverage:
A market leader in the use of information technology to expedite the book-buying process, providing a total acquisitions package for professional librarians worldwide. Provides the industry with web interfaces, shelf-ready book supply and delivery of eContent through dawsonera.

Printed publications:
Dawson Books brochure of services

Electronic and video publications:
See: http://dawsonenter.com; http://www.enterProfile.com

Access to staff:
Contact by letter, by telephone, by fax and by e-mail
Hours: Mon to Thu, 0845 to 1645, Fri 0845 to 1600

Access to building, collection or gallery:
Prior appointment required

Access for disabled people:
Parking provided, level entry, access to all public areas, toilet facilities

Constituent part of:
Dawson Holdings plc

DAYCARE TRUST

2nd Floor, Novas Contemporary Urban Centre, 73–81 Southwark Bridge Road, London, SE1 0NQ

Tel: 020 7940 7510
Fax: 020 7940 7515
E-mail: info@daycaretrust.org.uk

Website:
http://www.daycaretrust.org.uk
http://www.payingforchildcare.org.uk

Enquiries:
Enquiries to: Information Officer

Founded:
1986

Formerly called:
National Childcare Campaign

Organisation type and purpose:
Voluntary organisation, registered charity (charity number 327279).

Subject coverage:
Childcare, policy and practice; family-friendly employment practices; sources of information on childcare and children's services, consultancy and training.

Trade and statistical information:
Data on childcare in the UK.

Printed publications:
Childwise
Briefing Papers
Policy Papers
Order printed publications from: e-mail: publications@daycaretrust.org.uk

Publications list:
Available online and in print

Access to staff:
Contact by letter, by telephone, by fax, by e-mail and via website. Appointment necessary.
Hours: Mon to Fri, 0900 to 1700

Access for disabled people:
Toilet facilities, lift

DE MONTFORT UNIVERSITY

The Gateway, Leicester, LE1 9BH

Tel: 0116 255 1551
Fax: 0116 255 0307

Website:
http://www.library.dmu.ac.uk

Enquiries:
Enquiries to: Librarian
Direct tel: 0116 257 7165
Direct fax: 0116 257 7046

Organisation type and purpose:
University library.

Subject coverage:
Chemistry, physics, electronics, mechanical engineering, architecture, building, fashion, textiles, graphic art and design, information technology, law, public administration, economics, education, performing arts, speech and speech therapy, sport and physical education, business, health, nursing, midwifery, humanities.

Museum or gallery collection, archive, or library special collection:
HATRA Collection (former Hosiery and Allied Trades Research Association)
Hockliffe Collection of early children's books (Polhill Site)

Library catalogue:
All or part available online

Access to staff:
Contact by letter and by telephone
Hours: Varies between campuses – please consult website for full details.

Access for disabled people:
Parking provided, ramped entry, access to all public areas, toilet facilities

Special comments: Facilities may vary slightly from campus to campus.

Includes the:
Kimberlin Library
City Campus; tel: 0116 255 1551 ext 2677
Polhill Campus Library (Bedford)
tel: 01234 793077

Site libraries:
De Montfort University
Polhill Campus, Polhill Avenue, Bedford, MK41 9EA; tel: 01234 793077; fax: 01234 217738
De Montfort University
Charles Frears Campus, 266 London Road, Leicester, LE2 1RQ; tel: 0116 270 0661; fax: 0116 270 9722
De Montfort University
Kimberlin Library, The Gateway, Leicester, LE1 9BH; tel: 0116 257 7042; fax: 0116 257 7170

DE TOMASO DRIVERS CLUB

Flint Barn, Malthouse Lane, Ashington, West Sussex, RH20 3BU

Tel: 01903 893870
Fax: 01903 893870

Enquiries:
Enquiries to: Secretary

Founded:
1982

Organisation type and purpose:
Membership association.

Subject coverage:
De Tomaso cars.

Museum or gallery collection, archive, or library special collection:
De Tomaso Books
Club Magazines

DEAFAX

No 1 Earley Gate, University of Reading, Whiteknights Road, PO Box 236, Reading, Berkshire, RG6 6AT

Tel: 0118 935 3685
Fax: 0118 935 3686
E-mail: info@deafax.org

Website:
http://www.deafax.org
General information about the organisation's work, regularly updated.

Enquiries:
Enquiries to: Chief Executive
Direct e-mail: helen@deafax.org
Other contacts: Administrator (for general enquiries)

Founded:
1985

Organisation type and purpose:
International organisation, voluntary organisation, registered charity (new charity number 1095398), suitable for ages: all, training organisation, research organisation.
To deliver ICT and English literacy training and provide other support services for deaf children and adults in the UK and internationally.

Subject coverage:
Deaf issues: communications technology, training, literacy, education, support services.

Printed publications:
Information on all aspects of our work is available

Electronic and video publications:
CD-ROM to teach deaf children English literacy skills (available for purchase direct)

Access to staff:
Contact by letter, by telephone, by fax and by e-mail
Hours: Mon to Fri, 0900 to 1700

Access for disabled people:
Parking provided, ramped entry, access to all public areas, toilet facilities
Special comments: Wheelchair accessible.

DEAFBLIND SCOTLAND

21 Alexandra Avenue, Lenzie, Glasgow, G66 5BG

Tel: 0141 777 6111\ Minicom no. 0141 777 6111
Fax: 0141 775 3311
E-mail: info@deafblindscotland.org.uk

Website:
http://www.deafblindscotland.org.uk
History of Deafblind Scotland, services provided, guide/communicator services, news and events.

Enquiries:
Enquiries to: Information Officer
Other contacts: Chief Executive

Founded:
1928

Organisation type and purpose:
Registered charity (charity number 802976).
To serve deafblind people and reduce their isolation through clubs, outings, holidays and provision of information; provide trained guide/communicator service where funding available, training in communication and guiding skills, awareness-raising.

Subject coverage:
Deafblind awareness, communication and guiding skills with deafblind people.

Museum or gallery collection, archive, or library special collection:
Small resource centre of books, articles, reports and publications

Printed publications:
Rainbow (magazine, quarterly)
Snippets (newspaper, fortnightly)
Also available in tape, Braille, Moon and large print formats

Electronic and video publications:
Into Touch: basic communication with deafblind people (video)
Rainbow and Snippets on tape

Access to staff:
Contact by letter, by telephone, by fax, by e-mail and via website
Hours: Mon to Fri, 0900 to 1700
Special comments: 24-hour Helpline.

DEAFBLIND UK

Acronym or abbreviation: DBUK

The National Centre for Deafblindness, John and Lucille van Geest Place, Cygnet Road, Hampton, Peterborough, PE7 8FD

Tel: 01733 358100; Free Helpline 0800 132320; Minicom 01733 358100
Fax: 01733 358356
E-mail: info@deafblind.org.uk

Website:
http://www.deafblind.org.uk

Enquiries:
Enquiries to: Information Officer
Direct e-mail: enquiries@deafblind.org.uk
Other contacts: Chief Executive

Founded:
1928

Formerly called:
National Deaf-Blind Helpers League; National Deafblind League (year of change 1996)

Organisation type and purpose:
Voluntary organisation, registered charity.
To enable those people with a dual sensory impairment to live full and active lives despite their disability. To raise awareness of deafblindness

in the caring professions and amongst the wider public, to ensure sufferers' needs are met in care planning.

Subject coverage:
Activities include visiting/assessing deafblind individuals. Participation in national development/lobbying groups. Contributing to individual community care plans. Information and advice on dual sensory loss. Counselling. Training. Social activities for deafblind people, rehabilitation services, holiday flat, independent living accommodation. Linking deafblind people through magazines and newspapers in touch-based media. Free helpline accessible to deafblind people, their carers and professionals working with deafblind people.

Information services:
Information for people who have a combined sight and hearing loss, and for their families and friends.

Services for disabled people:
Volunteer befriending; interpreters; communicator guides; free helpline; case worker; formatted publications and letters; deafblind clubs; campaigning and raising awareness.

Museum or gallery collection, archive, or library special collection:
Heritage exhibition at the National Centre for Deafblindness explaining the history of combined sight and hearing loss.

Printed publications:
Information leaflets
Open Hand (quarterly, available in print, large print, Braille, Moon, cassette, CD, e-mail)
Order printed publications from: 01733 358100

Access to staff:
Contact by letter, by telephone, by fax, by e-mail and via website. Appointment necessary.
Hours: Mon to Thu, 0830 to 1700; Fri, 0830 to 1600
Free Helpline available daily, 0900 to 2130

Access for disabled people:
Level entry, toilet facilities, handrails, wheelchair and assistance dog friendly, Braille, Moon, Large Print and Audio room markings, tactile map of building.

Also at:
Deafblind UK Training and Rehabilitation Centre
18 Rainbow Court, Paston Ridings, Peterborough, Cambridgeshire, PE4 7UP; tel: 01733 325353; fax: 01733 323101

DEAFNESS RESEARCH UK

330–332 Gray's Inn Road, London, WC1X 8EE

Tel: 020 7833 1733\ Minicom no. 020 7915 1412 (text phone)
Fax: 020 7278 0404
E-mail: contact@deafnessresearch.org.uk

Website:
http://www.deafnessresearch.org.uk

Enquiries:
Enquiries to: Office Manager
Other contacts: Information Officer

Founded:
1985

Formerly called:
Defeating Deafness (year of change 2005)

Organisation type and purpose:
Voluntary organisation, registered charity.
Aims to encourage and finance research into the prevention, diagnosis, treatment and cure of hearing difficulties. It also aims to educate people about hearing problems and their treatments, offering information and advice based upon the most up-to-date evidence available.

Subject coverage:
Cochlear implants, glue ear, hearing aids, tinnitus, hyperacusis, hair cell research, genetics of hearing loss, auditory processing disorder, otosclerosis, Meniere's Disease, cholesteatoma

Printed publications:
Fact sheet on the following topics (please enclose an sae):
Cochlear Implants
Genetics and Deafness
Hair Cell Research
Glue Ear – Facts for Parents
Hyperacusis
Tinnitus
Getting a Hearing Aid on the NHS
Auditory Processing Disorder
Cholesteatoma
Trouble with your ears
In-flight ear health

Publications list:
Available in print

Access to staff:
Contact by letter, by telephone, by fax, by e-mail and via website
Hours: Office hours: Mon to Fri, 0930 to 1730
Helpline: Mon to Fri, 0900 to 1700

Parent body:
The Hearing Research Trust

DEBRA

Debra House, 13 Wellington Business Park, Dukes Ride, Crowthorne, Berkshire, RG45 6LS

Tel: 01344 771961
Fax: 01344 762661
E-mail: debra@debra.org.uk

Website:
http://www.debra.org.uk
All aspects of epidermolysis bullosa.
http://www.debra-international.org

Enquiries:
Enquiries to: Director of Nursing and Social Care
Direct e-mail: claire.mather@debra.org.uk
Other contacts: PR and Press Officer; CEO; Director of Fundraising; Director of Research

Founded:
1978

Formerly called:
Dystrophic Epidermolysis Bullosa Research Association

Organisation type and purpose:
Registered charity (charity number 1084958).
Funds nursing and welfare teams. Commissions research into EB (Epidermolysis Bullosa).

Subject coverage:
Epidermolysis bullosa, all types; education, self-help, care and management, counselling and research.

Library catalogue:
All or part available online

Printed publications:
Coping with Epidermolysis Bullosa
Diagnosis and Treatment (available only for professional use)
Dowling MEARA EB Simplex
Epidermolysis Bullosa: A Guide for Parents, Schools & Playgroups
Epidermolysis Bullosa: An Outline for Professionals
Epidermolysis Bullosa: Teachers' Supplement for Schools & Playgroups
Information Sheets (includes Financial Benefits, Education – Your Rights, Employment Services)
Genetics in EB
Junctional EB – Care and Management (available only for professional nursing staff)
Nutrition for Babies with EB
Play and Development in EB Children
Play and Developmental Needs of a Child with Epidermolysis Bullosa
Pregnancy and Childbirth in EB

Electronic and video publications:
Promotional video (free)

Publications list:
Available online and in print

continued overleaf

Access to staff:
Contact by letter, by telephone, by fax, by e-mail, in person and via website
Hours: Mon to Fri, 0900 to 1700

Access for disabled people:
Access to all public areas, toilet facilities

DEBRETT'S PEERAGE LIMITED

Formal name: Debrett's Limited

18–20 Hill Rise, Richmond, Surrey, TW10 6UA

Tel: 020 8939 2250
Fax: 020 8939 2251
E-mail: people@debretts.co.uk

Website:
http://www.debretts.co.uk
Company, books and diaries, People of Today, recommendations, guide to the season, royal connections.

Enquiries:
Enquiries to: Finance and Operations Manager

Founded:
1769

Organisation type and purpose:
Publishing house.

Subject coverage:
Biographical information – general, peerage, baronetage. Etiquette and manners.

Printed publications:
Debrett's Correct Form
Debrett's Etiquette for Girls
Debrett's Manners for Men
Debrett's Guide to Entertaining
Debrett's Peerage & Baronetage (every 5 years, latest edn 2008)
Debrett's People of Today (annually, December, £120)

Electronic and video publications:
Debrett's People of Today (online, subscription)
Debrett's People of Today (CD-ROM, annually, December)

Access to staff:
Contact by letter, by e-mail and via website
Hours: Mon to Fri, 0900 to 1700
Special comments: By appointment only.

DECORATIVE ARTS SOCIETY

Formal name: The Decorative Arts Society 1850 to the Present
Acronym or abbreviation: DAS

PO Box 136, Woodbridge, Suffolk, IP12 1TG

Website:
http://www.decorativeartssociety.org.uk/

Enquiries:
Enquiries to: Honorary Secretary
Direct e-mail: links@thedecorativeartssociety.org.uk
Other contacts: Membership Secretary for membership applications, subscription rates etc.

Founded:
1975

Organisation type and purpose:
Learned society (membership is by subscription), present number of members: 650, registered charity (charity number 271838).
To encourage the study and appreciation of the Decorative Arts in Britain, Europe and America from 1850 to the present.

Subject coverage:
Decorative arts, 1850 to the present.

Printed publications:
Journal (annual, contains publications list)
Back issues of DAS Journals available for purchase through the Honorary Secretary or from Richard Dennis Publications
Index of Journals Nos 1 to 20 (pub Nov 1997)
Order printed publications from: Richard Dennis Publications, The Old Chapel

Middle Street, Shepton Beauchamp, Ilminster, Somerset, TA19 0LE

Publications list:
Available in print

Access to staff:
Contact by letter
Hours: Mon to Fri, 0900 to 1700

Membership applications:
The Decorative Arts Society
PO Box 136, Woodbridge, Suffolk, IP12 1TG

DEESIDE COLLEGE

Kelsterton Road, Connah's Quay, Deeside, Flintshire, CH5 4BR

Tel: 01244 831531
Fax: 01244 814305
E-mail: enquiries@deeside.ac.uk

Website:
http://www.deeside.ac.uk

Enquiries:
Enquiries to: Manager
Direct tel: 01244 834516
Direct fax: 01244 834526
Direct e-mail: forresl@deeside.ac.uk

Founded:
1993

Organisation type and purpose:
College of Further Education.

Subject coverage:
All subjects including computer studies, management and business studies.

Access to staff:
Contact by letter, by telephone, by fax, by e-mail and via website
Hours: Term time: Mon to Thu, 0830 to 1925; Fri, 0830 to 1625
Vacations: Mon to Thu, 0830 to 1625; Fri, 0830 to 1555

Access for disabled people:
Level entry, access to all public areas

DEFENCE ACADEMY, COLLEGE OF MANAGEMENT AND TECHNOLOGY

Acronym or abbreviation: DA-CMT

Cranfield University, Shrivenham, Swindon, Wiltshire, SN6 8LA

Tel: 01793 785743
Fax: 01793 785555
E-mail: library.barrington@cranfield.ac.uk

Website:
http://www.cranfield.ac.uk
Cranfield University website.
http://diglib.shrivenham.cranfield.ac.uk
Digital library.

Enquiries:
Enquiries to: Head of Library Services
Direct tel: 01793 785481

Organisation type and purpose:
University library.

Subject coverage:
Military science, military technology, computing science, mathematics, ballistics, operational research, statistics, defence procurement, management, political science, social science, international affairs, chemistry, materials science, metallurgy, engineering design, mechanical engineering, aeronautical engineering, military vehicles, thermal power, control and guidance, information technology, electromagnets, electronic engineering, physics, electro-optics, electrical engineering, telecommunications, electronic warfare, command and control, guided weapons, explosives and ammunition, weapons systems, surveillance and target acquisition, military management, defence administration, military

affairs, disaster management, security and resilience, forensic science, forensic archaeology, anthropology.

Museum or gallery collection, archive, or library special collection:
Reports collection of about 50,000 items, reflects the specialised nature of some of the campus courses

Library catalogue:
All or part available online

Electronic and video publications:
Digital Archive
eDefence News (daily)
Inside Knowledge

Access to staff:
Contact by telephone and via website.
Appointment necessary.
Hours: Mon to Fri, 0800 to 1900; Sat, 1000 to 1500

Access for disabled people:
Parking provided, level entry

Constituent bodies:
Defence Academy

DEFENCE MEDICAL LIBRARY

Acronym or abbreviation: RDMC

Fort Blockhouse, Horton Block, Gosport, Hampshire, PO12 2AB

Tel: 023 9276 5751
Fax: 023 9276 5747
E-mail: library@milmed.demon.co.uk

Enquiries:
Enquiries to: College Librarian
Direct tel: 023 9276 5899
Other contacts: Head, Defence Library Services, tel no: 023 9276 5400

Founded:
1997

Organisation type and purpose:
National government body, training organisation, research organisation.
Medical College.
Central medical library for the Ministry of Defence; library for Royal Defence Medical College; linked with the Ministry of Defence medical libraries.

Subject coverage:
Military medicine, general medicine and allied health, primary care, nursing.

Museum or gallery collection, archive, or library special collection:
Royal Army Medical Corps historical collection (housed at Wellcome Institute)

Library catalogue:
All or part available in-house

Printed publications:
Journal of the Royal Army Medical Corps (quarterly)

Access to staff:
Contact by letter, by telephone, by fax and by e-mail. Access for members only.
Hours: Mon to Thu, 0800 to 1630; Fri, 0800 to 1530
Special comments: Services to Defence medical staff and Ministry of Defence staff; to others by written appointment only.

Access to building, collection or gallery:
Prior appointment required

Library for:
MOD Medical Services
Royal Defence Medical College

Links with:
Ministry of Defence Medical Libraries

DELIUS SOCIETY

21 Woodlands Drive, Brooklands, sale, M33 3PQ

Tel: 0161 282 3654
E-mail: secretary@thedeliussociety.org.uk

Enquiries:
Enquiries to: Honorary Secretary

Founded:
1962

Organisation type and purpose:
Membership association.
Society for all who appreciate Delius' music.

Subject coverage:
Life and works of the composer Frederick Delius.

Printed publications:
Delius Society Journal and Newsletter (members)

Access to staff:
Contact by letter
Hours: Mon to Fri, 0900 to 1700

Independent from, but works closely with, the:
Delius Trust

DELPHINIUM SOCIETY

Acronym or abbreviation: DS

2 The Grove, Ickenham, Uxbridge, Middlesex,
UB10 8QH

Tel: 01895 464694
Fax: 01895 235365
E-mail: roger.beauchamp@btinternet.com

Website:
http://www.delphinium-society.co.uk

Enquiries:
Enquiries to: Promotions and Publicity Secretary

Founded:
1928

Organisation type and purpose:
International organisation, membership
association (membership is by subscription),
present number of members: 1,000.
For the study, dissemination and collection of all
information concerning the genus Delphinium and
the closely related genus Consolida. Also to study
the relationship of the genus to other members of
the family Ranunculaceae.

Subject coverage:
All aspects of the genus Delphinium and related-
genus Consolida. Scientific interest in Aconitum.

Information services:
from Promotions and Publicity Secretary

Printed publications:
Yearbook (publ in Apr/May, members only)
Bulletin (publ in Oct, annually, members only)
The Delphinium Garden
Other publications are undergoing revision

Publications list:
Available in print

Access to staff:
Contact by letter, by telephone, by fax, by e-mail
and via website

DELTA

Formal name: Deaf Education through Listening
and Talking

The Con Powell Centre, Alfa House, Molesey
Road, Walton-on-Thames, Surrey, KT12 3PD

Tel: 0845 108 1437; 01932 243018
E-mail: enquiries@deafeducation.org.uk

Website:
http://www.deafeducation.org.uk

Founded:
1988

Organisation type and purpose:
Voluntary organisation, registered charity (charity
number 1115603).
To guide parents and teachers in helping deaf
children to develop normal spoken language and
to live independently within the hearing society,
the practice and philosophy of the natural aural
approach to the education of deaf children.

Subject coverage:
Deaf young people, the development of
independence and communication, the attainment
levels achieved by severely and profoundly deaf
young people.

Printed publications:
Factsheets and booklets for families of deaf
children and for lay people interested in the
natural aural approach to the education of deaf
children (available on request, some free)
Chat (newsletter, twice a year)
Understanding the Natural Aural Approach:
Approaches to Communication (W. Lynas)
Parents' Guide for the Natural Aural Approach,
Vols 1 and 2 (£10 per set)

Electronic and video publications:
Sound Futures
Chattering (e-mail newsletter)
Order electronic and video publications from: e-mail:
enquiries@deafeducation.org.uk

Publications list:
Available online and in print

Access to staff:
Contact by letter, by telephone, by fax, by e-mail
and via website. Appointment necessary.
Hours: Mon to Fri, 0900 to 1700

Access to building, collection or gallery:
No access other than to staff

DELTA BIOTECHNOLOGY LIMITED

Castle Court, Castle Boulevard, Nottingham, NG7
1FD

Tel: 0115 955 3355
Fax: 0115 955 1299

Enquiries:
Enquiries to: Information Manager
Direct e-mail: alison.mitson@aventis.com

Organisation type and purpose:
Research organisation.

Subject coverage:
Recombinant technology.

Access to staff:
Contact by letter, by fax and by e-mail
Hours: Mon to Fri, 0900 to 1700

Parent body:
Aventis Behring

DENBIGHSHIRE COUNTY COUNCIL

Council Offices, Wynnstay Road, Ruthin,
Denbighshire, LL15 1YN

Tel: 01824 706000
Fax: 01824 705026

Website:
http://www.denbighshire.gov.uk
General – councillors' details, news releases,
services, what's on.

Enquiries:
Enquiries to: Public Relations Manager
Direct tel: 01824 706222
Direct fax: 01824 707446
Direct e-mail: sue.appleton@denbighshire.gov.uk

Founded:
1996

Formed from:
Clwyd County Council, Glyndwr District Council,
Rhuddlan Borough Council (year of change 1996)

Organisation type and purpose:
Local government body.

Subject coverage:
Education, social services, housing and
environment, planning, economic development,
highways, transport.

Access to staff:
Contact by telephone
Hours: Mon to Fri, 0900 to 1700

DENBIGHSHIRE HERITAGE SERVICE

46 Clwyd Street, Ruthin, Denbighshire, LL15 1HP

Tel: 01824 708281
Fax: 01824 708258
E-mail: heritage@denbighshire.gov.uk

Website:
http://www.denbighshire.gov.uk

Enquiries:
Enquiries to: Curator
Direct tel: 01824 708223
Direct e-mail: curatorialmanager@denbighshire.gov
.uk

Organisation type and purpose:
Local government body.
Administrative body for the libraries, museums,
art galleries and historical sites that are under the
care of Denbighshire County Council.

Subject coverage:
The conservation of Denbighshire heritage. Ruthin
Gaol, Plas Newydd, Rhyl Museum and Nantclwyd
y Dre.

Information services:
Information on DCC museum collections.

Special visitor services:
Site audio guides; multimedia presentations.

Education services:
For all ages, but focusing on KS2 history.

Access to staff:
Contact by letter, by telephone, by fax, by e-mail
and via website. Appointment necessary.

Parent body:
Denbighshire County Council
tel: 01824 706000

DENBIGHSHIRE HISTORICAL SOCIETY

Formal name: Cymdeithas Hanes Sir Ddinbych /
Denbighshire Historical Society

1 Green Park, Erddig, Wrexham, LL13 7YE.

Tel: 01978 353 363

Website:
http://www.glyndwr.ac.uk/dhs

Enquiries:
Enquiries to: Chairman

Founded:
1950

Organisation type and purpose:
Learned society (membership is by subscription),
present number of members: 350, registered
charity (charity number 519210).

Subject coverage:
General, social, personal and industrial history of
the former county of Denbighshire, defined by the
boundaries prior to 1974 re-organisation.

Printed publications:
Transactions (annually, £10 to non-members)
Order printed publications from: The Treasurer,
Ysgubor Isa, Llanfair D.C., Ruthin, LL15 2UN

Access to staff:
Contact by letter and by telephone
Hours: Mon to Fri, 0900 to 1700

DENBIGHSHIRE RECORD OFFICE

46 Clwyd Street, Ruthin, Denbighshire, LL15 1HP

Tel: 01824 708250
Fax: 01824 708222
E-mail: archives@denbighshire.gov.uk

continued overleaf

Website:
http://www.denbighshire.gov.uk/archives

Enquiries:
Enquiries to: Archivist

Founded:
1972

Formerly called:
Clwyd Record Office (year of change 1996)

Organisation type and purpose:
Local government body.
Archive.
County record office holding material relating to the pre-1974 county of Denbigh and the present area.

Subject coverage:
Local history: former county of Clwyd, and the historic and present county of Denbighshire.

Museum or gallery collection, archive, or library special collection:
Collections relating to historic county of Denbighshire, including quarter sessions; county council; district councils; parish (microfilm); schools; family and estates; census (microfilm); newspapers (microfilm and original)

Non-library collection catalogue:
All or part available online and in-house

Publications list:
Available online and in print

Access to staff:
Contact by letter, by telephone, by fax, by e-mail, in person and via website
Hours: Tue to Fri, 0930 to 1630
Special comments: Reader's ticket, prior appointment for microfilm users.

Access for disabled people:
Parking provided, ramped entry, access to most public areas, toilet facilities

DENTAL LABORATORIES ASSOCIATION LIMITED

Acronym or abbreviation: DLA

44–46 Wollaton Road, Beeston, Nottingham, NG9 2NR

Tel: 0115 925 4888
Fax: 0115 925 4800
E-mail: info@dla.org.uk

Website:
http://www.DLA.ORG.UK

Enquiries:
Enquiries to: Chief Executive

Founded:
1961

Organisation type and purpose:
Trade association.

Subject coverage:
Dental technology; commercial dental laboratories; Department of Health current guidelines and regulations within mechanical dentistry.

Printed publications:
Annual Report
Dental Laboratory (magazine, monthly)
Yearbook
Year Planner

Access to staff:
Contact by letter and by e-mail. Appointment necessary. Non-members charged.
Hours: Mon to Fri, 0900 to 1700

Links with:
Federation of European Dental Laboratory Owners (FEPPD)

DENTAL PRACTITIONERS' ASSOCIATION

Acronym or abbreviation: DPA

61 Harley Street, London, W1G 8QU

Tel: 020 7636 1072
Fax: 020 7636 1086
E-mail: info@uk-dentistry.org

Website:
http://www.UK-Dentistry.org/

Enquiries:
Enquiries to: Chief Executive

Founded:
1954

Organisation type and purpose:
Professional body (membership is by subscription), number of members: 1,200 practices, 3,000 members.
Founded in 1954 by General Dental Practitioners for GDPs. Exclusively promotes the interests of dentists in general practice, providing support, advice and representation at all levels.

Subject coverage:
Dentistry, statistics, dental politics, dento-legal matters, business briefing, management consultancy.

Non-library collection catalogue:
All or part available online and in-house

Printed publications:
General Dental Practitioner (6 times a year)

Publications list:
Available online

Access to staff:
Contact by letter, by telephone, by fax, by e-mail and via website. Appointment necessary. Access for members only.
Hours: Mon to Fri, 1000 to 1600

Access for disabled people:
No

DENTISTS' MEDIA GROUP

Acronym or abbreviation: DMG

PO Box 15, Sindalthorpe House, Ely, Cambridgeshire, CB7 4SG

Tel: 01353 688456
Fax: 01353 688451

Enquiries:
Enquiries to: Administrator
Direct e-mail: peter@dentalconfidence.com

Founded:
1996

Organisation type and purpose:
National organisation, membership association (membership is by election or invitation), present number of members: 170, voluntary organisation, training organisation, consultancy.
To encourage, and to enhance the quality of, broadcasting and writing by dentists on radio and television, local radio in particular and in the press and magazines.

Subject coverage:
The Dentists' Media Group is a source of spokespeople on all aspects of oral health.

Access to staff:
Contact by letter, by telephone, by fax and by e-mail
Hours: Mon to Fri, 0900 to 1700

Access to building, collection or gallery:
Prior appointment required

Access for disabled people:
Ramped entry

Affiliated to and at the same address as:
Association of Broadcasting Doctors (ABD)

DEPARTMENT FOR BUSINESS INNOVATION AND SKILLS

Acronym or abbreviation: BIS

1 Victoria Street, London, SW1H 0ET

Tel: 020 7215 5000; minicom no. 020 7215 6740
E-mail: enquiries@bis.gsi.gov.uk

Website:
http://www.bis.gov.uk

Enquiries:
Enquiries to: Librarian
Direct tel: 0207 215 5006
Direct e-mail: infosource@bis.gsi.gov.uk

Founded:
2009

Created by the merger of:
Department for Business Enterprise and Regulatory Reform, and Department for Innovation, Universities and Skills (year of change 2009)

Formerly called:
Department of Trade and Industry (year of change 2007)

Organisation type and purpose:
National government body.
Government library.

Subject coverage:
Trade policy, export promotion, corporate and consumer affairs, employment relations, innovation and technology, small firms, regional development and inward investment.

Museum or gallery collection, archive, or library special collection:
Archive of publications from the DTI, Department of Energy, Board of Trade, etc.

Library catalogue:
All or part available in-house

Printed publications:
Order printed publications from: BIS Publications Orderline, ADMAIL 528, London, SW1W 8YT; tel. 0845 015 0010; or via website: http://www.bis.gov.uk/publications

Publications list:
Available online

Access to staff:
Contact by letter and by telephone. Appointment necessary.
Hours: Mon to Fri, 0900 to 1700

DEPARTMENT FOR CULTURE, MEDIA AND SPORT

Acronym or abbreviation: DCMS

Library, Room L21, 2–4 Cockspur Street, London, SW1Y 5DH

Tel: 020 7211 6041
Fax: 020 7211 6032

Website:
http://www.lottery.culture.gov.uk
Lottery awards database.
http://www.culture.gov.uk
General information about DCMS.

Enquiries:
Enquiries to: Libraries services to DCMS staff

Founded:
1992

Formerly called:
Department of National Heritage (year of change 1997)

Organisation type and purpose:
National government body.

Subject coverage:
The arts, sport, the National Lottery, libraries, museums and galleries, broadcasting, gambling, film, press freedom and regulation, the built heritage, tourism, the creative industries, cultural property and the Government Art Collection.

Museum or gallery collection, archive, or library special collection:
On the subjects listed

Library catalogue:
All or part available online and in-house

Printed publications:
See DCMS website http://www.culture.gov.uk/
reference_library

Publications list:
Available online

Access to staff:
Contact by letter, by telephone, by fax, by e-mail
and via website. Appointment necessary.
Hours: Mon to Fri, 0900 to 1730

Access for disabled people:
Access to all public areas

DEPARTMENT FOR EDUCATION LIBRARY

Acronym or abbreviation: DfE

Sanctuary Buildings, Great Smith Street, London,
SW1P 3BT

Tel: 0870 000 2288

Website:
http://www.education.gov.uk
http://publications.dcsf.gov.uk

Organisation type and purpose:
National government body.

Subject coverage:
Education policy, children and families policy.

Library catalogue:
All or part available in-house

Access to building, collection or gallery:
Special comments: Library is not open to the public,
please use the public enquiries contact for the
Department.

DEPARTMENT FOR ENVIRONMENT, FOOD AND RURAL AFFAIRS – LIBRARY

Acronym or abbreviation: Defra

Lower Ground Floor, Ergon House, c/o 17 Smith
Square, London, SW1P 3JR

Tel: 020 7238 6575
Fax: 020 7238 6609
E-mail: defra.library@defra.gsi.gov.uk

Website:
http://www.defra.gov.uk

Enquiries:
Enquiries to: Librarian
Direct tel: 020 7238 3327
Direct e-mail: kevin.jackson@defra.gsi.gov.uk

Founded:
2001

Formerly called:
Ministry of Agriculture, Fisheries & Food (MAFF)
(year of change 2001)

Organisation type and purpose:
National government body.
Government departmental library.

Subject coverage:
Agriculture, fisheries, food, particularly temperate
agriculture, environment, nature conservation,
sustainable environment, biodiversity, climate
change adaptation.

Information services:
Helpdesk, tel: 08459 335577

Library catalogue:
All or part available in-house

Printed publications:
Order printed publications from: Defra Library at
above address

Publications list:
Available online

Access to staff:
Contact by e-mail and via website. Appointment
necessary.
Hours: Mon to Fri, 0900 to 1700

Access to building, collection or gallery:
Prior appointment required

Access for disabled people:
Toilet facilities

Also at:
Department for Environment, Food and Rural
Affairs (DEFRA)
   Nobel House, 17 Smith Square, London, SW1P
3JR

DEPARTMENT FOR INTERNATIONAL DEVELOPMENT

Acronym or abbreviation: DFID

Abercrombie House, Eaglesham Road, East
Kilbride, Glasgow, G75 8EA

Tel: 01355 843880
Fax: 01355 843632
E-mail: library@dfid.gov.uk

Website:
http://www.dfid.gov.uk

Enquiries:
Enquiries to: Librarian
Direct tel: 020 7023 0574
Direct fax: 020 7023 0523
Direct e-mail: s-skelton@dfid.gov.uk

Formerly called:
Overseas Development Administration (ODA)
(year of change 1997)

Organisation type and purpose:
National government body.
Central government library.

Subject coverage:
Social and economic development of developing
countries; development aid and policy (especially
for the Third World, but now also for Eastern
Europe).

Access to staff:
Contact by letter, by telephone, by fax, by e-mail
and via website. Appointment necessary.
Hours: Mon to Fri, 0900 to 1700

Access to building, collection or gallery:
Prior appointment required

London Office:
Department for International Development
   1 Palace Street, London, SW1E 5HE; tel: 020 7023
0000; fax: 020 7023 0019

DEPARTMENT FOR WORK AND PENSIONS

Acronym or abbreviation: DWP

Information and Library Services, Room 114,
Adelphi, 111 John Adam Street, London, WC2N
6NT

Tel: 020 7712 2500
Fax: 020 7962 8491
E-mail: library.services@dwp.gsi.gov.uk

Website:
http://www.dwp.gov.uk
Press releases, publications, profiles of ministers,
links to DWP agency pages.

Founded:
2001

Organisation type and purpose:
National government body.
Government departmental library.

Subject coverage:
Social security, social welfare (including National
Insurance, industrial injuries, supplementary
benefits, state and occupational pensions, family

benefits); social policy, poverty, taxation,
distribution of income, public administration,
management; unemployment, employment.

Trade and statistical information:
UK government statistics and world-wide statistics
on social security and social welfare.

Library catalogue:
All or part available in-house

Printed publications:
Journals

Access to staff:
Contact by letter, by telephone, by fax and by e-
mail. Appointment necessary.
Hours: Mon to Fri, 0900 to 1700
Special comments: Library of last resort – if there is
no other service for the information.

Access for disabled people:
Access to all public areas, toilet facilities

DEPARTMENT OF AGRICULTURE AND RURAL DEVELOPMENT LIBRARY

Acronym or abbreviation: DARD

Room 615, Dundonald House, Upper
Newtownards Road, Belfast, BT4 3SB

Tel: 028 9052 4401
Fax: 028 9052 5546
E-mail: library@dardni.gov.uk

Website:
http://www.dardni.gov.uk
Structure of department courses, open
government, agricultural information.

Enquiries:
Enquiries to: Librarian

Organisation type and purpose:
Government department.

Subject coverage:
Agriculture, fisheries, forestry and afforestation,
horticulture, rural development, public
administration.

Library catalogue:
All or part available online

Printed publications:
Accessions lists (regularly)

Access to staff:
Access for members only.
Hours: Mon to Fri, 0900 to 1700

DEPARTMENT OF COMPLEMENTARY THERAPIES

School of Integrated Health, University of
Westminster, 115 New Cavendish Street, London,
W1W 6UW

Tel: 020 7911 5000
Fax: 020 7911 5028
E-mail: course-enquiries@westminster.ac.uk

Website:
http://www.westminster.ac.uk/sih

Founded:
1983

Created by the merger of:
Centre for Community Care and Primary Health,
and London School of Acupuncture and
Traditional Chinese Medicine (year of change
1997)

Organisation type and purpose:
Advisory body, university department or institute,
training organisation, consultancy, research
organisation.

Subject coverage:
Homoeopathy, nutritional therapy, medical
herbalism, remedial massage, professional entry
education in traditional Chinese Medicine,
acupuncture and other complementary therapies,

continued overleaf

development of research base of traditional Chinese acupuncture in the United Kingdom and other complementary therapies.

Library catalogue:
All or part available online and in-house

Printed publications:
Prospectus (by post or electronically)
Order printed publications from: Course Enquiries: course-enquiries@westminster.ac.uk, tel. 020 7911 5000

Access to staff:
Contact by letter, by telephone, by fax, by e-mail and via website
Hours: Mon to Fri, 0900 to 1700

Access to building, collection or gallery:
Prior appointment required
Hours: Mon to Fri, 0900 to 1700

Access for disabled people:
Ramped entry, toilet facilities

DEPARTMENT OF GEOGRAPHY, UNIVERSITY OF CAMBRIDGE

Acronym or abbreviation: Air Photo Library

University of Cambridge, Downing Site, Cambridge, CB2 3EN

E-mail: library@uflm.cam.ac.uk

Website:
http://www.uflm.cam.ac.uk

Founded:
1945

Organisation type and purpose:
University library.

Subject coverage:
Indexed collection of 500,000 vertical and oblique aerial photographs of United Kingdom and Ireland from 1945 onwards. Smaller collection of air photographs of France, the Netherlands and Denmark taken from 1966 to 1974. Emphasis on areas of ecological, historical and archaeological interest.

Non-library collection catalogue:
All or part available online and in-house

Library catalogue:
All or part available in-house

Access to staff:
Hours: Access is not available at this time

Access to building, collection or gallery:
Appointment required

DEPARTMENT OF HEALTH

1W28, Quarry House, Quarry Hill, Leeds, LS2 7UE

Tel: 0113 2545080
Fax: 0113 2545084
E-mail: library.enquiries@dh.gsi.gov.uk

Website:
http://www.dh.gov.uk

Enquiries:
Enquiries to: Customer Services Librarian (Leeds)

Founded:
1834

Organisation type and purpose:
National government body.
Government Department Library Service provided to all staff within the Department of Health.

Subject coverage:
Public health, health services, health services policy and management, social care policy and management, hospital buildings.

Museum or gallery collection, archive, or library special collection:
250,000 monographs
565 printed periodicals
Various databases and some e-journals

Library catalogue:
All or part available online and in-house

Printed publications:
Order printed publications from: DH Publications Order Line, PO Box 777, London, SE1 6XH,; fax: 0870 1555 455; e-mail: dh@prolog.uk.com

Electronic and video publications:
DoH Thesaurus of health and social care terms
DH-Data Thesaurus (available via the DH website)
DH-Data (from DIALOG)
HMIC (from Ovid/Silver Platter)

Access to staff:
Contact by letter. Appointment necessary.
Hours: Mon to Fri, 0900 to 1700

Access to building, collection or gallery:
No access other than to staff
Special comments: Not open to the public. Written requests for access should be addressed to the Customer Services Librarian

Also at:
Chief Librarian, Department of Health Library 1W22, Quarry House, Quarry Hill, Leeds LS2 7UE; tel: 0113 2546742; fax: 0113 2545084; e-mail: library.enquiries@dh.gsi.gov.uk; website: http://www.dh.gov.uk

DEPARTMENT OF HEALTH – LIBRARY INFORMATION SERVICES

Skipton House, 80 London Road, London, SE1 6LH

Tel: 020 7972 2000
Fax: 020 7972 1609

Website:
http://www.doh.gov.uk
General information about the Department of Health.

Enquiries:
Enquiries to: Librarian
Direct tel: 020 7972 6541
Direct fax: 020 7972 5976

Organisation type and purpose:
National government body.
Government department library.

Subject coverage:
Health and social care services, management of the National Health Service, hospitals, public health, environmental health, services for older people and those with disabilities and learning difficulties.

Museum or gallery collection, archive, or library special collection:
Collection of early Poor Law pamphlets
Government Medical Inspectors Local Reports on Public Health, 1869–1907
Local Reports to the General Board of Health, 1848–1857

Library catalogue:
All or part available in-house

Printed publications:
DH-DATA Thesaurus of Health and Social Care Terms
Order printed publications from: DH publications Orderline, PO Box 777, London, SE1 6XH; tel: 08701 555455; fax: 01623 724524; e-mail: dh@prolog.uk.com

Microform publications:
Departmental documents, available from Chadwyck-Healey

Electronic and video publications:
DH-DATA (available through Datastar)
HMIC CD-ROM (available from Ovid)

Access to staff:
Appointment necessary.
Hours: Mon to Fri, 0900 to 1700

Access to building, collection or gallery:
Prior appointment required

DEPARTMENT OF MATERIALS: LOUGHBOROUGH UNIVERSITY

Loughborough University, Loughborough, Leicestershire, LE11 3TU

Tel: 01509 223331
Fax: 01509 223949
E-mail: materials@lboro.ac.uk

Website:
http://www.lboro.ac.uk/materials
Departmental overview, programmes, research groups, academic staff listing, staff room and telephone numbers, ISST, short courses and conferences, opportunities.

Enquiries:
Enquiries to: Development Officer
Direct tel: 01509 228592
Direct e-mail: m.e.white@lboro.ac.uk

Founded:
1967

Formerly called:
Institute of Polymer Technology and Materials Engineering – IPTME (year of change 2008)

Organisation type and purpose:
University department or institute.
Postgraduate education, research and consultancy. Loughborough Materials Characterisation Centre.

Subject coverage:
Polymers; metals; ceramics; materials characterisation centre with advanced thermal method units; Institute of Surface Science and Technology; electron microscope unit; X-ray unit.

Printed publications:
MSc Programmes leaflets
Research brochure
Short course list
Undergraduate programmes brochure

Publications list:
Available in print

Access to staff:
Contact by letter, by telephone, by fax, by e-mail and via website
Hours: Mon to Fri, 0900 to 1700

Links with:
Institute of Surface Science and Technology (ISST) Address as IPTME; tel: 01509 223387; fax: 01509 234225; e-mail: lmcc@lboro.ac.uk

DEPARTMENT OF REGIONAL DEVELOPMENT

Acronym or abbreviation: DRD

Library, Room G-40, Clarence Court, 10–18 Adelaide Street, Belfast, BT2 8GB

Tel: 028 9054 1046
Fax: 028 9054 1081
E-mail: library@drdni.gov.uk

Enquiries:
Enquiries to: Librarian

Formerly called:
Department of the Environment for Northern Ireland (DOE) (year of change 2000)

Organisation type and purpose:
National government body.
There is a Core Department and two Next Steps agencies.

Subject coverage:
Planning, roads, road safety, environmental protection and conservation, local government, urban regeneration and disposal and management of the department's land and property holdings, transport, fire services, pollution, historic monuments, archaeology, water and sewerage services, building construction, public records.

Non-library collection catalogue:
All or part available online and in-house

Library catalogue:
All or part available online and in-house

Access to staff:
Access for members only.
Hours: Mon to Fri, 0900 to 1700
Special comments: Loans and personal access to civil servants only. Brief subject enquiries by letter or telephone from non-civil servants will be dealt with where possible.

Access to building, collection or gallery:
No prior appointment required

Next Steps agencies:
Roads Service
website: http://www.roadsni.gov.uk
Water Service
website: http://www.waterni.gov.uk

DEPAUL UK

1st Floor, 291–299 Borough High Street, London, SE1 1JG

Tel: 020 7939 1220
Fax: 020 7939 1221
E-mail: depaul@depauluk.org

Website:
http://www.depauluk.org

Enquiries:
Enquiries to: Administrator

Founded:
1989

Organisation type and purpose:
Voluntary organisation, registered charity (charity number 802384).

Subject coverage:
Depaul Trust helps young people across the UK who are homeless, vulnerable and disadvantaged, working in the very heart of local communities. It protects young people who become homeless by finding them a place to call their home. Each year it provides over 100,000 bed nights and it is open every day and night.
It prevents young people from becoming homeless by rebuilding family relationships and offering through-the-gate support to young offenders.
It provides young people with the chance to fulfil their potential in the community through education, volunteering, training and jobs.
Since Depaul Trust started in 1989, it has made a difference to over 40,000 young people.

Publications list:
Available online

Access to staff:
Contact by letter, by telephone, by fax, by e-mail and via website
Hours: Mon to Fri, 0900 to 1730

DEPRESSION ALLIANCE

35 Westminster Bridge Road, London, SE1 7JB

Tel: 020 7633 0557
Fax: 020 7633 0559
E-mail: information@depressionalliance.org

Website:
http://www.depressionalliance.org
Information on depression.

Enquiries:
Enquiries to: Office and Communications Co-ordinator

Founded:
1974

Formerly called:
Depressives Associated (year of change 1995); National Depression Campaign (year of change 2000)

Organisation type and purpose:
Membership association (membership is by subscription), present number of members: 3000, voluntary organisation, registered charity (charity number 278532).
To provide support and understanding, information, education, self-help.

Subject coverage:
Depression.

Printed publications:
Free for individuals, charges for organisations and bulk orders
Leaflets on Depression, Self Help, Student Stress Pack, etc
A Single Step (magazine, quarterly)
Order printed publications from: Office Manager, Depression Alliance
As above

Electronic and video publications:
Video: Understanding Depression

Publications list:
Available online and in print

Access to staff:
Contact by letter, by telephone, by fax, by e-mail and via website
Hours: Mon to Fri, 1000 to 1700

Access to building, collection or gallery:
Prior appointment required

Other addresses:
Depression Alliance Cymru
11 Plas Melin, Westbourne Road, Whitchurch, Cardiff, CF4 2BT; tel: 029 2069 2891; fax: 029 2052 7774
Depression Alliance Scotland
3 Grosvenor Gardens, Edinburgh, EH12 5JU; tel: 0131 467 3050; fax: 0131 467 7701

DEPRESSION–UK

Acronym or abbreviation: D–UK

Self Help Nottingham, Ormiston House, 32–36 Pelham Street, Nottingham, NG1 2EG

E-mail: info@depressionuk.org.uk

Website:
http://www.depressionuk.org.uk

Enquiries:
Enquiries to: Honorary Secretary
Direct tel: 0870 774 4320

Founded:
1973

Formerly called:
Depressives Anonymous (year of change 1973)

Please select:
Fellowship of Depressives Anonymous (year of change 2007)

Organisation type and purpose:
Membership association (membership is by subscription), present number of members: 700, voluntary organisation, registered charity (charity number 294482).
Encouragement and support for those with depression and those concerned for them.

Subject coverage:
Depression.

Printed publications:
Newsletter (six times a year, £2 to non-members)
Book List, Leaflets (free), Information Sheet (free)
Order printed publications from: Postal address

Electronic and video publications:
Audio Tape List (free)

Publications list:
Available in print

Access to staff:
Contact by letter, by telephone and by e-mail
Hours: Mon to Fri, 0900 to 1700

DERBY CITY COUNCIL

Council House, Corporation Street, Derby, DE1 2FS

Tel: 01332 293111\ Minicom no. 01332 256666
Fax: 01322 255500
E-mail: via website

Website:
http://www.derby.gov.uk

Enquiries:
Enquiries to: Chief Executive

Organisation type and purpose:
Local government body.

Subject coverage:
All local authority services.

Access to staff:
Contact by letter, by telephone, by fax, by e-mail and in person
Hours: Mon to Thu, 0830 to 1700; Fri, 0830 to 1630

DERBY CITY LIBRARIES

Derby Local Studies Library, 25B Irongate, Derby, DE1 3GL

Tel: 01332 255393
E-mail: localstudies.library@derby.gov.uk

Website:
http://www.derby.gov.uk/libraries/about/local_studies.htm
Guide to library.

Enquiries:
Enquiries to: Librarian

Founded:
1879

Organisation type and purpose:
Public library.
Local studies library providing research facilities.

Subject coverage:
Local studies materials of all types relating to Derby and Derbyshire.

Education services:
Informal family history and local history courses.

Museum or gallery collection, archive, or library special collection:
Printed materials, over 40,000 items including histories of Derby and Derbyshire, street and trade directories, poll books and registers of electors for Derby
Periodicals and newspapers dating from 1732
Maps from 1577
Illustrations and engravings including over 8,500 photographs dating from 1860s to present day
Broadsheets mostly 19th-century items depicting events
Family History including Census returns on microfilm for the whole of Derbyshire 1841 to 1901
IGI (microfiche) for UK
Special collections including family papers, deeds, manuscripts, business records, etc.

Non-library collection catalogue:
All or part available in-house

Library catalogue:
All or part available online and in-house

Printed publications:
General guide to collections (free)

Electronic and video publications:
Parish registers listing
Guide to family history resources

Access to staff:
Contact by letter, by telephone, by e-mail, in person and via website
Hours: Mon, 0900 to 1900; Thu, Fri, 0930 to 1230; Sat, 0930 to 1600
Special comments: Opening hours subject to change; please check website or phone for current opening.

Access to building, collection or gallery:
Hours: As above

Access for disabled people:
Ramped entry
Special comments: Please ring to book a parking space.

continued overleaf

Parent body:
Derby City Council
Derby City Libraries, Regeneration &
Community, Heritage Gate, Friary Street, Derby,
DE1 1QX; tel: 01332 715549; fax: 01332 716607

DERBYSHIRE AND NOTTINGHAMSHIRE CHAMBER OF COMMERCE

Acronym or abbreviation: DNCC

Canal Wharf, Chesterfield, Derbyshire, S41 7NA

Tel: 0845 601 1038
Fax: 01246 233228
E-mail: information@dncc.co.uk

Website:
http://www.dncc.co.uk

Enquiries:
Enquiries to: Information & Research Officer

Founded:
1899

Formerly called:
Derbyshire Chamber and Business Link;
Nottinghamshire Chamber of Commerce and
Industry (year of change 2006 and 2007)

Organisation type and purpose:
Membership association.
Chamber of Commerce.

Subject coverage:
Training, business information, business support,
with emphasis on Derbyshire and
Nottinghamshire. Export advice.

Information services:
Telephone and e-mail enquiry service for business

Printed publications:
InBusiness (monthly magazine, free to members).
Members' Briefing (monthly information bulletin,
free to members)
Directory of Members (annually, free to members)

Electronic and video publications:
Customised databases available for purchase

Access to staff:
Contact by letter, by telephone, by fax, by e-mail
and via website
Hours: Mon to Fri, 0900 to 1700
Special comments: Charges made for incurred costs
and research time.

Member of:
Association of British Chambers of Commerce

DERBYSHIRE COUNTY COUNCIL

Cultural and Community Services Department,
County Hall, Matlock, Derbyshire, DE4 3AG

Tel: 01629 580000
Fax: 01629 585363
E-mail: derbyshire.libraries@derbyshire.gov.uk

Website:
http://www.derbyshire.gov.uk
Full catalogue.
http://www.peaklandheritage.org.uk
http://picturethepast.org.uk

Enquiries:
Enquiries to: Strategic Director of Cultural and
Community Services
Other contacts: Assistant Director (for information
on resources and publications)

Organisation type and purpose:
Local government body, museum, art gallery,
public library.
County and Diocesan Record Office.

Subject coverage:
Derbyshire local studies; local government
information; family history; lead mining.

**Museum or gallery collection, archive, or library
special collection:**
British Cave Research Association Library (at HQ)

George Stephenson Collection of early railway
history (at Chesterfield)

Non-library collection catalogue:
All or part available online and in-house

Library catalogue:
All or part available online

Printed publications:
Various publications on local history, including:
Buxton, a People's History (M. Langham, £6.99)
South Derbyshire and its People: a history (O. Hull,
£10.99)
A Victorian Farmer's Diary (W. Hodkin, £6.95)
Kinder Scout, portrait of a mountain (£12.99)
Boiler Suits, Bofors and Bullets (J. Edgar, £5.99)
Trains and Trails (J. Edgar, £4.99)
Melbourne 1820–1875, a diary (J. J. Briggs, £10.99)
Free but not Easy, Autobiography of Bas Barker of
Chesterfield and his work with the Labour and
Trade Union Movements (B. Barker and L.
Straker, 50p)
Eleven Years Hard, or Ten Paces to the Privy: the
life of a police sergeant's wife in Ilkeston and
Sandiacre 1939–1950 (W. Broughton, £1)
Props, Points and Pig Iron: Life in Renishaw (J.
Edgar, £5.00)
Derbyshire Detail and Character – a celebration of
Derbyshire's towns and villages in pictures (B.
Joyce, G. Michell and M. Williams, £12.99)
Facsimile Trade Directories: Bulmer's Chesterfield
and North East Derbyshire

Electronic and video publications:
See website covering the history of the Peak
District and containing a database of books and
articles held in the library: http://
www.peaklandheritage.org.uk
Picture the Past: a web-based resource containing
historic images from the collections of libraries in
Derby, Derbyshire, Nottingham and
Nottinghamshire: http://
www.picturethepast.org.uk

Publications list:
Available online and in print

Access to staff:
Contact by letter, by telephone, by fax, by e-mail,
in person and via website
Hours: Mon to Fri, 0900 to 1700

Links with:
County local studies library at Matlock
Derbyshire County Council
Main public library at Chesterfield

DERBYSHIRE FAMILY HISTORY SOCIETY

Acronym or abbreviation: DFHS

Bridge Chapel House, St Mary's Bridge, Sowter
Road, Derby, DE1 3AT

Tel: 01332 363876

Website:
http://www.dfhs.org.uk

Enquiries:
Enquiries to: Honorary Secretary

Founded:
1976

Organisation type and purpose:
Membership association (membership is by
subscription), present number of members: 2000,
registered charity (charity number 517162).
Family history research.

Subject coverage:
Family history in Derbyshire.

Services for disabled people:
Quarterly journal on tape for the partially sighted.

Library catalogue:
All or part available in-house and in print

Printed publications:
Journal (4 times a year)
1851 Census Books

Order printed publications from: Booksales Officer,
Derbyshire Family History Society
17 Penrhyn Avenue, Littleover, Derby, DE23 6LB

Microform publications:
Memorial Inscriptions (microfiche)
Melbourne Name Index (microfiche)
1851 Census (microfiche)
1891 Census Index Fiche (microfiche)
How to trace your family tree in Derbyshire
(video)
IGI
Cemetery Records
Order microform publications from: Booksales Officer

Electronic and video publications:
Journal (4 times a year, on tape for blind and
partially sighted members)
1891 Census (work in progress to index the census
in a computer database)
Memorial Inscriptions (work in progress to record
these in a computer database)
Census Indexes 1851 and 1891 (CD-ROM)
Census Index 1861 (disketter)

Publications list:
Available online and in print

Access to staff:
Contact by letter and via website
Hours: Tue, Thu, Sat, 1000 to 1600
Special comments: Telephone 01332 363876 during
these hours only.

Access to building, collection or gallery:
Hours: Tue, Thu, Sat, 1000 to 1600

Access for disabled people:
Special comments: Grade 2 listed building; please
telephone to make arrangements before visiting.

Affiliated to:
Federation of Family History Societies

DERBYSHIRE GRITSTONE SHEEP BREEDERS SOCIETY

The Secretary, 5 Bridge Close, Waterfoot,
Rossendale, Lancashire, BB4 9SN

Tel: 07766 448854
E-mail: info@pmcoppack.com

Website:
http://www.derbyshiregritstone.org.uk

Enquiries:
Enquiries to: Honorary Secretary

Founded:
1906

Organisation type and purpose:
Membership association (membership is by
subscription), registered charity (charity number
265539).
Support for members and to maintain/develop
standard of Derbyshire Gritstone sheep.

Printed publications:
1991 brochure

Access to staff:
Contact by letter
Hours: Mon to Fri, 0900 to 1700

DERBYSHIRE RECORD OFFICE

County Hall, Matlock, Derbyshire, DE4 3AG

Tel: 01629 539202
Fax: 01629 57611
E-mail: record.office@derbyshire.gov.uk

Website:
http://www.derbyshire.gov.uk/recordoffice

Enquiries:
Enquiries to: County and Diocesan Archivist
Direct tel: 01629 539201
Direct e-mail: margaretosullivan@derbyshire.gov
.uk

Organisation type and purpose:
Local government body.

County Record Office.

Subject coverage:
Archives of the County of Derbyshire, the City of Derby and the Diocese of Derby; public records of Derbyshire origin; business, industrial, diocesan, parish, family and estate, manorial, hospital, school, voluntary society and other records from Derby and Derbyshire

Non-library collection catalogue:
All or part available online, in-house and in print

Printed publications:
Derbyshire Record Office Guide (available online)
Annual list of archive accessions (available online and in hard copy, free on request)
Parish Register Guide (dates of original parish registers and surrogate copies of registers of baptisms, banns, marriages and burials available for consultation in the Record Office, with brief administrative history of each parish/township, an introduction to parish registers and a parish map; available online)
Archives First (a series of over 30 short beginners' guides to original sources for aspects of Derbyshire's history; available in hard copy only, price on application)
Information for New Users (available online and in hard copy, free on request)
Index to Estate and Family Archives (available online)
Guides including Railway Records, Military Records for Family Historians (available in hard copy only, price on application)
Outline map of Derbyshire parishes (available in hard copy only, price on application)
Order printed publications from: Derbyshire Record Office

Electronic and video publications:
Ordnance Survey 2nd edn 25in-to-1-mile maps of Derbyshire c.1900 (on CD-ROM, £25 plus postage)
George M. Woodward: collection of 18th–19th-century caricatures (on CD-ROM, price on application)
Order electronic and video publications from: Derbyshire Record Office

Publications list:
Available online and in print

Access to staff:
Contact by letter, by telephone, by fax, by e-mail and in person. Appointment necessary.

Access to building, collection or gallery:
Hours: Mon to Fri, 0930 to 1645, one Sat per month, 1000 to 1600
Special comments: Reader registration required, with proof of identity and address

Parent body:
Derbyshire County Council
    Cultural and Community Services Department, Libraries and Heritage Division

DERBYSHIRE WILDLIFE TRUST

Acronym or abbreviation: DWT

East Mill, Bridgefoot, Belper, Derbyshire, DE56 1XH

Tel: 01773 881188
Fax: 01773 821826
E-mail: enquiries@derbyshirewt.co.uk

Website:
http://www.derbyshirewildlifetrust.org.uk
Details on the work of the trust, events, membership, reserves and how people can get involved.

Enquiries:
Enquiries to: Administration Assistant

Founded:
1962

Organisation type and purpose:
Voluntary organisation, registered charity (charity number 222212).

Printed publications:
Wild Derbyshire

Publications list:
Available in print

Access to staff:
Contact by letter, by telephone, by fax, by e-mail and via website
Hours: Mon to Thu, 0900 to 1700; Fri, 0900 to 1630

Access to building, collection or gallery:
No prior appointment required

Also at:
Countryside Centre, Derbyshire Wildlife Trust
    The Whistlestop Countryside Centre, Matlock Bath Railway Station, Matlock Bath, Derbyshire, DE4 3PT; tel: 01629 580958

DERMATITIS AND ALLIED DISEASES RESEARCH TRUST

Acronym or abbreviation: DERMATRUST

40 Queen Anne Street, London, W1G 9EL

Tel: 01604 781903
Fax: 01604 781514

Enquiries:
Enquiries to: Chairman

Founded:
1996

Organisation type and purpose:
Registered charity (charity number 1016315).
To support the care of patients with skin diseases and to fund research into their causes and develop new treatments.

Subject coverage:
Dermatological diseases, dermatology research.

Access to staff:
Contact by letter and by fax
Hours: Mon to Fri, 0900 to 1700

DESIGN AND ARTISTS COPYRIGHT SOCIETY

Acronym or abbreviation: DACS

33 Great Sutton Street, London, EC1V 0DX

Tel: 020 7336 8811
Fax: 020 7336 8822
E-mail: info@dacs.org.uk

Enquiries:
Enquiries to: Membership Secretary

Founded:
1983

Organisation type and purpose:
International organisation, membership association (membership is by subscription).
DACS is the copyright and collecting society for visual arts in the UK; acting as exclusive licensee on behalf of its national members and as agent for foreign artists and estates. It also actively campaigns to create a fairer working environment for visual creators through collective administration and lobbying on behalf of all artists at both national and international levels on rights-related issues.

Printed publications:
Annual Report
Slide Collection Licensing Scheme Pack

Publications list:
Available online and in print

Access to staff:
Contact by letter, by fax and by e-mail.
Appointment necessary.
Hours: Mon to Fri, 0900 to 1800
Special comments: DACS can only act on behalf of its members, but offers general copyright information to all.

Access to building, collection or gallery:
No prior appointment required

DESIGN AND TECHNOLOGY ASSOCIATION

Acronym or abbreviation: DATA

16 Wellesbourne House, Walton Road, Wellesbourne, Warwickshire, CV35 9JB

Tel: 01789 470007
Fax: 01789 841955
E-mail: data@data.org.uk

Website:
http://www.data.org.uk
Membership, publications, conferences, training.

Enquiries:
Enquiries to: Chief Executive

Founded:
1989

Incorporates:
National Association for Teachers of Home Economics (NATNE), date of change, 1 April 2000

Organisation type and purpose:
Professional body (membership is by subscription), number of members: 4,350, registered charity (charity number 1062270), suitable for ages: preschool to post 18, training organisation, consultancy, research organisation.
Educational organisation of teachers and academic institutions.
To support, develop and enhance design and technology in all sectors of education and society.

Subject coverage:
Design and technology education.
Home economics; nutrition; childcare and development; food and textiles; technology.

Museum or gallery collection, archive, or library special collection:
Books and Resources
All issues of the ATDS journal Housecraft from 1928 to 1982 and NATHE journal MODUS, 1928 to present held at Hamilton House
Computerised database
Domestic science archives held at University of Warwick
Design and Technology Library

Printed publications:
Variety of educational books and resources, including:
Assessment Handbook
Teaching CAD/CAM
DATA Guidance Materials Key Stages 1, 2 and 3
DATA NEWS (newsletter, termly, free to members)
Designing (termly magazine for primary and secondary education)
Modus (8 times a year and 2 educational inserts; 1 issue a year is a Resources Guide)
Primary Coordinators' File
Primary Planning into Practice
Risk Assessment in Secondary School Design and Technology Teaching Environments 2001

Electronic and video publications:
Electronics (educational videos)
CAD/CAM in Practice (CD)

Publications list:
Available in print

Access to staff:
Contact by letter, by telephone, by fax, by e-mail, in person and via website
Hours: Mon to Fri, 0900 to 1700
Special comments: Library access available for members only.

Constituent member of:
Confederation of Design and Technology Associations
Council of Subject Teachers Associations

DESIGN HISTORY SOCIETY

Acronym or abbreviation: DHS

28 New High Street, Oxford, OX3 7AQ

Tel: 01264 353058
E-mail: webadmin@designhistorysociety.org

continued overleaf

Website:
http://www.designhistorysociety.org
Society membership; full range of initiatives including those aimed at students; support of events; access to electronic discussion list.

Enquiries:
Enquiries to: Secretary

Founded:
1977

Organisation type and purpose:
Learned society (membership is by subscription), registered charity (charity number 327326), research organisation.

Subject coverage:
History of architecture and design, including design of fashion and textiles; graphic design; product design; cultural studies.

Printed publications:
Journal of Design History (quarterly)
Newsletter (quarterly)

Access to staff:
Contact by letter, by telephone, by e-mail and via website
Hours: Mon to Fri, 0900 to 1700

DESIGNER BOOKBINDERS

6 Queen Square, London, WC1N 3AR

Tel: 01453 759063
E-mail: secretary@designerbookbinders.org.uk

Website:
http://www.designerbookbinders.org.uk

Enquiries:
Enquiries to: Secretary

Founded:
1951

Formerly called:
Guild of Contemporary Bookbinders; Hampstead Guild of Scribes and Bookbinders (year of change 1955)

Organisation type and purpose:
Membership association, present number of members: 600, voluntary organisation, registered charity (charity number 282018).
Maintenance and improvement of standards of design and craft in hand bookbinding by means of exhibitions, teaching and publications.

Subject coverage:
Art of the hand-bound book, design, craftsmanship, repair and restoration.

Printed publications:
Newsletter (quarterly, for members only)
The New Bookbinder (annually, from 1981; superseded the Designer Bookbinders Review, 1973–1979)
Modern British Bookbinding (exhibition catalogue, 1985, £10)
Leighton House Exhibition (1987, £10)
DB5 (catalogue, 1987, £5)
Fine Words, Fine Books (catalogue, 1991, £10)
DB4 (illustrated directory, 1983, £5)
North American Exhibition Catalogue (2000–2001)
Order printed publications from: Designer Bookbinders Publications Limited
8 Bryn Coetmor, Bethesda, Bangor, Gwynnedd, LL57 3NL, tel: 01248 602591, fax: 01248 602591, e-mail: publications@designerbookbinders.org.uk

Publications list:
Available in print

Access to staff:
Contact by letter, by telephone, by e-mail and via website
Hours: Mon to Fri, 1800 to 2100 (answerphone 0900 to 1800)

Member of:
Federation of British Crafts Societies (FBCS)

DEUX CHEVAUX CLUB OF GREAT BRITAIN

Acronym or abbreviation: 2CVGB

PO Box 602, Crick, Northampton, NN6 7UW

E-mail: secretary@2cvgb.com

Website:
http://www.2cvgb.co.uk

Enquiries:
Enquiries to: Secretary

Founded:
1978

Organisation type and purpose:
International organisation, membership association (membership is by subscription), number of members: 3,000.

Subject coverage:
Information and parts for all Citroën A-series vehicles.

Museum or gallery collection, archive, or library special collection:
Archive on A-series vehicles

Printed publications:
2CVGB News (monthly, £2.50)

Access to staff:
Contact by letter, by e-mail and via website
Hours: Mon to Fri, 0800 to 2200

DEVELOPMENT EDUCATION ASSOCIATION

Acronym or abbreviation: DEA

1st Floor, River House, 143–145 Farringdon Road, London EC1R 3AB

Tel: 020 7812 1282
Fax: 020 7812 1272
E-mail: dea@dea.org.uk

Website:
http://www.dea.org.uk
Main DEA website
http://www.globaldimension.org.uk
Free database of resources for school teachers interested in teaching about global issues. Managed by the DEA on behalf of DFID.

Enquiries:
Enquiries to: Communications Team

Founded:
1993

Organisation type and purpose:
Membership association (membership is by subscription), present number of members: 300, voluntary organisation, registered charity (charity number 291696), suitable for ages: all.
To promote and strengthen the development education movement in UK; to raise public awareness of global and development issues.

Subject coverage:
Provides information on availability of development education resources for researchers, youth and community workers; information and support base to development education practitioners, global perspectives in formal education (schools, higher and further education), youth work, adult and community education.

Museum or gallery collection, archive, or library special collection:
Small resource centre for internal use

Trade and statistical information:
Contact and resource information on development education sector in UK.

Printed publications:
See http://www.dea.org.uk/dea/publications.html for full list of publications.
Development Education Journal (3 times a year, free to members or subscribe through Trentham Books, http://www.trentham-books.co.uk)
Development Education News – newsletter free to members produced 10 times a year.

Order printed publications from: Contact the DEA

Publications list:
Available online and in print

Access to staff:
Contact by letter, by telephone, by fax, by e-mail and via website. Appointment necessary.
Hours: Mon to Fri, 1000 to 1700

DEVON AND EXETER INSTITUTION LIBRARY

7 Cathedral Close, Exeter, Devon, EX1 1EZ

Tel: 01392 251017

Website:
http://www.lib.ex.ac.uk/search
Exeter University Library catalogue search facility.
http://www.ex.ac.uk/library/devonex.html
Description of the library.

Enquiries:
Enquiries to: Librarian in Charge
Direct e-mail: j.p.gardner@exeter.ac.uk

Founded:
1813

Organisation type and purpose:
Membership association, registered charity.
Independent subscription library.

Subject coverage:
History of Exeter, Devon, Cornwall, Somerset, Dorset, 19th-century periodicals, biography, history and topography.

Museum or gallery collection, archive, or library special collection:
18th- and 19th-century local newspapers
Early 19th-century pamphlets, including medical history and locally published
South West Collection
Topographical prints and early maps

Library catalogue:
All or part available online

Printed publications:
The Devon & Exeter Institution 1813–1988 (Longridge RW, 1988, £2)

Access to staff:
Contact by letter, by telephone and by e-mail.
Appointment necessary. Access for members only.
Hours: Mon to Fri, 0900 to 1700

Affiliated to:
University of Exeter

Houses the:
Devon & Cornwall Record Society
Devon Archaeological Society (as Library)
Devon Gardens Trust
Devon History Society

DEVON ARCHAEOLOGICAL SOCIETY

Acronym or abbreviation: DAS

c/o Royal Albert Memorial Museum, Queen Street, Exeter, Devon, EX4 3RX

E-mail: dashonsec@btinternet.com

Website:
http://devonarchaeologicalsociety.org.uk

Enquiries:
Enquiries to: Honorary Secretary
Direct e-mail: dasonline.wanadoo.co.uk

Organisation type and purpose:
Learned society, registered charity.

Subject coverage:
Archaeology of Devon, historic buildings.

Library catalogue:
All or part available online and in-house

Printed publications:
Devon Archaeology (occasional)
Field Guides to Archaeological Sites in Devon
Proceedings (annually)

Newsletter (for members, quarterly)

Publications list:
Available online and in print

Access to staff:
Contact by letter and by e-mail

DEVON ART SOCIETY

27 Barchington Avenue, Torquay, TQ2 8LB

Tel: 01803 310600
E-mail: lynn@drake55.fsnet.co.uk

Enquiries:
Enquiries to: Honorary Secretary
Other contacts: Chairman

Founded:
1912

Organisation type and purpose:
Membership association (membership is by qualification), present number of members: 144.

Subject coverage:
Society for professional and non-professional artists in the Torbay area. Exhibitions held twice yearly. Members meet regularly for workshops and demonstrations. Membership by selection.

Access to staff:
Contact by letter and by telephone
Hours: Mon to Fri, 0900 to 1700

DEVON CATTLE BREEDERS' SOCIETY

Acronym or abbreviation: DCBS

Wisteria Cottage, Iddesleigh, Winkeigh, Devon, EX19 8BG

Tel: 01837 810845
E-mail: lane@dcbs.fsbusiness.co.uk

Enquiries:
Enquiries to: Secretary

Founded:
1884

Formerly called:
Devon Cattle Society (year of change 2000)

Organisation type and purpose:
Membership association (membership is by subscription, qualification, election or invitation), present number of members: c. 330, registered charity (charity number 248836).
Cattle breed society.
To maintain and further the breeding of the Devon breed of cattle.

Subject coverage:
The Herd books of the society which are published on an annual basis are available for reference in the reference sections of the Devon County Library Service at Barnstaple and Exeter.

Printed publications:
Davy's Devon Herd Book (annual herd book £15)
Trade Brochure (descriptive, free of charge)

Access to staff:
Contact by letter, by telephone, by fax, by e-mail and via website. Appointment necessary.
Hours: Mon to Fri, 0900 to 1700

DEVON COUNTY FOOTBALL ASSOCIATION LIMITED

County Headquarters, Coach Road, Newton Abbot, Devon, TQ12 1EJ

Tel: 01626 332077
Fax: 01626 336814
E-mail: hq@devonfa.f9.co.uk

Enquiries:
Enquiries to: General Secretary

Subject coverage:
Association football in Devon.

DEVON LIBRARIES

Great Moor House, Bittern Road, Sowton, Exeter, EX2 7NL

Tel: 01392 384315
Fax: 01392 384316
E-mail: devlibs@devon.gov.uk

Website:
http://www.devon.gov.uk/libraries

Enquiries:
Enquiries to: Head of Libraries

Organisation type and purpose:
Local government body, public library.

Subject coverage:
General.

Museum or gallery collection, archive, or library special collection:
Early children's books collection; Railway Studies collection; Westcountry Studies Library; Pocknell collection of shorthand books; Napoleonic material

Non-library collection catalogue:
All or part available online

Library catalogue:
All or part available online

Printed publications:
Printable factsheets about services and resources on website

Access to staff:
Contact by letter, by telephone, by fax, by e-mail and via website
Hours: Mon to Fri, 0900 to 1700

DEVON LIBRARY SERVICES – NORTH DEVON LIBRARY AND RECORD OFFICE

Tuly Street, Barnstaple, Devon, EX31 1EL

Tel: 01271 388596
Fax: 01271 388599
E-mail: geoff.king@devon.gov.uk

Website:
http://www.devon.gov.uk/library

Enquiries:
Enquiries to: Manager

Formerly called:
Barnstaple Central Library (year of change 1988)

Organisation type and purpose:
Local government body, public library.

Subject coverage:
General, local and family history of North Devon, business, commercial and technical information.

Museum or gallery collection, archive, or library special collection:
Community information database

Non-library collection catalogue:
All or part available online

Library catalogue:
All or part available online

Printed publications:
Leaflets and pamphlets are available on application to the Library

Access to staff:
Contact by letter, by telephone, by fax, by e-mail and in person. Appointment necessary.
Hours: Mon, 0930 to 1900; Tue, Fri, 0900 to 1900; Wed, 0930 to 1300; Thu, 0930 to 1700; Sat, 0930 to 1600

Access for disabled people:
Level entry, access to all public areas, toilet facilities

Accommodates the:
Devon Schools Library Service
tel: 01271 388623
North Devon Athenaeum
tel: 01271 388607

North Devon Branch of the Devon Record Office
tel: 01271 388608

Parent body:
Devon County Council, Library Services

DEVON LIBRARY SERVICES – RAILWAY STUDIES LIBRARY

Formal name: Railway Studies Collection
Acronym or abbreviation: RSC

Newton Abbot Library, Market Street, Newton Abbot, Devon, TQ12 2RJ

Tel: 01626 206422
E-mail: railway.library@devon.gov.uk

Website:
http://www.devon.gov.uk/library/catalogue

Enquiries:
Enquiries to: Librarian
Direct e-mail: moira.andrews@devon.gov.uk

Organisation type and purpose:
Local government body, public library.

Subject coverage:
All aspects of railways in United Kingdom.

Museum or gallery collection, archive, or library special collection:
Back and current issues of a very large range of railway journals and magazines, including many now discontinued, also those relating to railway modelling

Library catalogue:
All or part available online

Printed publications:
Introductory Leaflet (free)
List of Periodical Holdings (free)

Electronic and video publications:
Photographs, postcards, some ephemera

Publications list:
Available online and in print

Access to staff:
Contact by letter, by telephone, by e-mail and in person
Hours: Wed, 1000 to 1300 and 1400 to 1700; Thu, 1000 to 1300; Sat, 1000 to 1300 and 1400 to 1600
Special comments: Staffed by the Friends of the Railway Studies Collection on Saturdays.

Access for disabled people:
Toilet facilities, lift

Administered by:
Devon Library Services

DEVON RECORD OFFICE

Acronym or abbreviation: DRO

Great Moor House, Bittern Road, Sowton Industrial Estate, Exeter, EX2 7NL

Tel: 01392 384253
Fax: 01392 384256
E-mail: devrec@devon.gov.uk

Website:
http://www.devon.gov.uk/record_office.htm
General information; opening times, newsletters, etc.

Enquiries:
Enquiries to: County Archivist

Founded:
1952

Organisation type and purpose:
Local government body.
Archive office.

Subject coverage:
Mainly local political, administrative, ecclesiastical, maritime, social and economic history, including the history of towns, parishes, local institutions, farms and estates, families, houses, crime and punishment, and transport.

continued overleaf

Museum or gallery collection, archive, or library special collection:
City of Exeter records, and the County and City of Exeter quarter sessions
Devon quarter sessions records
Ecclesiastical records of the Diocese of Exeter
Exeter Cathedral Archives in the Cloister Library
Records of the ancient Borough of Barnstaple, in the North Devon Record Office

Non-library collection catalogue:
All or part available online

Printed publications:
Historical Notes on Devon Schools (Bovett R, 1989, £5.00)
Map of Devon parishes (40p)
Newsletter No 1 (May 1988) and later issues published in May and November each year (free on receipt of sae)
Ship's Crew lists: a handlist of records in the Devon Record office (1987, £4.75)
Stopping the Rot: Archive Preservation Good Practice (£3.50)
Please ask for an estimate of the cost of postage and packing before sending remittance

Access to staff:
Contact by letter, by telephone, by fax, by e-mail, in person and via website
Hours: Mon to Fri, 1000 to 1800; some Sats, 0930 to 1230
Special comments: Charges for some postal enquiries.

Constituent bodies:
North Devon Record Office
North Devon Library and Record Office, Tuly Street, Barnstaple, Devon, EX31 1EL; tel: 01271 388607; fax: 01271 388608; e-mail: ndevrec@devon.gov.uk

Links with:
Plymouth and West Devon Record Office

Parent body:
Devon County Council
County Hall, Topsham Road, Exeter; tel: 01392 382000

DEVON WILDLIFE TRUST

Acronym or abbreviation: DWT

Cricklepit Mill, Commercial Road, Exeter, Devon, EX2 4AB

Tel: 01392 279244
Fax: 01392 433221
E-mail: contactus@devonwildlifetrust.org

Website:
http://www.devonwildlifetrust.org
Outlines DWT's work conserving wild areas for the future, including its 40 nature reserves.

Enquiries:
Enquiries to: Chief Executive

Founded:
1962

Formerly called:
Devon Trust for Nature Conservation

Organisation type and purpose:
Registered charity (charity number 213224). Conservation organisation.

Subject coverage:
Wildlife conservation in Devon.

Museum or gallery collection, archive, or library special collection:
Biological Data

Printed publications:
Wild Devon (supporters' magazine, 3 times a year)

Electronic and video publications:
4 wildlife e-newsletter
Order electronic and video publications from: e-mail: contactus@devonwildlifetrust.org

Publications list:
Available online

Access to staff:
Contact by letter, by telephone, by fax and by e-mail
Hours: Mon to Fri, 0900 to 1700

Access to building, collection or gallery:
Hours: Mon to Fri, 0900 to 1700

Access for disabled people:
Hours: Mon to Fri, 0900 to 1700

Links with:
Royal Society for Nature Conservation
The Kiln, Waterside, Mather Lane, Newark, NG24 1WT; tel: 01636 677711; fax: 01636 670001

DEWSBURY COLLEGE

Halifax Road, Dewsbury, West Yorkshire, WF13 2AS

Tel: 01924 465916 ext 286
Fax: 01924 457047

Website:
http://www.dewsbury.ac.uk

Enquiries:
Enquiries to: Learning Resources Manager
Direct tel: 01924 465916 ext 240
Direct e-mail: abismillah@dewsbury.ac.uk
Other contacts: Art and Design Specialist

Formed from:
Wheelwright 6th Form Centre

Formerly called:
DABTAC (year of change 1993)

Subject coverage:
Fashion, graphics, design, media studies, surface pattern design, photography, general subjects in humanities and social studies up to A level, business studies up to HND level.

Library catalogue:
All or part available in-house

Access to staff:
Contact by letter and by e-mail
Hours: Mon to Thurs, 0850 to 2000 Fri 1000 to 1600

Access for disabled people:
Level entry, toilet facilities

Associate college of:
Huddersfield University

DIABETES UK

10 Parkway, London, NW1 7AA

Tel: 020 7424 1000
Fax: 020 7424 1001
E-mail: info@diabetes.org.uk

Website:
http://www.diabetes.org.uk

Enquiries:
Enquiries to: Assistant Media Relations Officer

Founded:
1934

Formerly called:
British Diabetic Association (BDA) (year of change 2000)

Organisation type and purpose:
Advisory body, membership association (membership is by subscription), voluntary organisation, registered charity (charity number 215199), research organisation.
Helping people with diabetes and supporting diabetes research.

Subject coverage:
Diabetes and all aspects of living with diabetes.

Printed publications:
Diabetes Update (newsletter for health professionals 2 times a year)
Diabetic Medicine (journal for the medical profession 10 times a year)
Leaflets and information sheets for people living with diabetes: diet, pregnancy, exercise, travel, children and other matters
Books, reports, publicity literature covering all diabetes related subjects for healthcare professionals and those living with diabetes
Order printed publications from: Distribution Department, British Diabetic Association
PO Box 1, Portishead, Bristol, BS20 8DJ, tel: 0800 585088

Electronic and video publications:
Videos and cassettes

Publications list:
Available in print

Access to staff:
Contact by letter, by telephone, by fax, by e-mail, in person and via website
Hours: Mon to Fri, 0900 to 1700

Has:
450 branches in the UK

Regional Offices:
North West
65 Bewsey Street, Warrington, WA2 7JG; tel: 01925 653281; fax: 01925 653288
Northern & Yorkshire
Birch House, 80 East Mount, Darlington, DL1 1LE; tel: 01325 488606; fax: 01325 488816
Northern Ireland
John Gibson House, 257 Lisbon Road, Belfast, BT9 7EN; tel: 028 9066 6646; fax: 028 9066 6333
Scotland
Unit 3, 4th Floor, 34 West George Street, Glasgow, G2 1AD; tel: 0141 332 2700; fax: 0141 332 4880
Wales
The Board Room, Plas Gwynt, Sophia Close, 30 Cathedral Road, Cardiff, CF1 9TD; tel: 029 2066 8276; fax: 029 2066 8329
West Midlands
1 Eldon Court, Eldon Street, Walsall, West Midlands, WS1 2JP; tel: 01922 614500; fax: 01922 646789

DIAL UK

Formal name: Disablement Information and Advice Line

Birch View, St Catherine's, Tickhill Road, Doncaster, West Yorkshire, DN4 8QN

Tel: 01302 310123; minicom no. 01302 310123
Fax: 01302 310404
E-mail: dialuk@scope.org.uk

Website:
http://www.dialuk.org.uk

Enquiries:
Enquiries to: Head of DIAL UK
Other contacts: Information Officer

Founded:
1981

Now part of Scope's Information and Advice Services:
(year of change 2008)

Organisation type and purpose:
National organisation, advisory body, registered charity (charity number 208231).
The national organisation for the DIAL network of approx 90 disability advice centres run by and for people with disabilities.
Promotes the interests and usage of disability advice centres controlled by disabled people and provides information and support servies to DIAL groups and other disability information providers.
DIAL groups give free, independent advice on all aspects of disability over the telephone, at drop-in centres and in some cases through a home visit.

Subject coverage:
Help for people with disabilities. Information and advice on social, medical or economic problems of all mental, physical and sensory disablements.

Access to staff:
Contact by letter, by telephone and by e-mail

Hours: Mon to Fri, 1000 to 1600

Access for disabled people:
Fully accessible, toilet facilities

DIALOG CORPORATION, THE

Oxford Office, 2 Des Roches Square, Witney, Oxford, OX28 4BE

Tel: 01993 899300
Fax: 01993 899333
E-mail: ondisc@dialog.com

Website:
http://www.dialog.com

Enquiries:
Enquiries to: Manager
Direct e-mail: mike_sullivan@dialog.com
Other contacts: Marketing Executive

Founded:
1972

Formerly called:
DIALOG, DIALOG Europe; KR OnDisc (year of change 1997)

Organisation type and purpose:
International organisation, publishing house.
Providing access to online databases and publishing CD-ROMs and DVD-ROMS.

Subject coverage:
Databases on CD-ROM in science, technology, chemistry, medicine, health, biomedicine, engineering, materials, social sciences, business, law, government, economics, education, humanities, current events, newspapers and journals, indexes to book reviews, companies, and people and associations. Also web browser access to above databases (Intranet/extranet solutions).

Electronic and video publications:
About 80 CD-ROM databases including:
Aerospace Database
ASM Handbook
Business & Industry
Chemical Business News Base
Compendex Plus
EIU Business Intelligence
Encyclopedia of Physical Science and Technology
Environmental Management
Kirk Othmer Encyclopedia
Medline
Metadex
Petroleum Abstracts
Standard & Poor's Corporation
Thomas Register

Access to staff:
Contact by letter, by telephone, by fax, by e-mail and via website
Hours: Mon to Fri, 0900 to 1730

Parent body:
The Dialog Corporation

DIECASTING SOCIETY

Acronym or abbreviation: DCS

The National Metalforming Centre, 47 Birmingham Road, West Bromwich B70 6PY

Tel: 0121 601 6365
Fax: 0870 138 9714
E-mail: dcs@alfed.org.uk

Website:
http://www.dcsoc.org.uk
A chaitable organisation representing the diecasting industry in the UK.

Enquiries:
Enquiries to: Secretary

Founded:
1967

Organisation type and purpose:
Professional body.

Subject coverage:
Diecasting.

Access to staff:
Contact by letter, by telephone, by fax and by e-mail. Appointment necessary.
Hours: Mon to Fri, 0900 to 1700

Administered by:
The Aluminium Federation

DIGNITY IN DYING

181 Oxford Street, London, W1D 2JT

Tel: 020 7479 7730
E-mail: info@dignityindying.org.uk

Website:
http://www.dignityindying.org.uk
Up-to-date news, background information and articles on end-of-life issues. Information on campaign.

Enquiries:
Direct e-mail: jo.cartwright@dignityindying.org.uk

Founded:
1935

Formerly called:
EXIT (year of change 1982)

Organisation type and purpose:
Voluntary organisation.
Promoting living wills, campaigning to change the law so that a competent incurably ill adult who is suffering unbearably can choose medical assistance to die.

Subject coverage:
Voluntary euthanasia, advance directives, living wills, patients' rights, physician-assisted suicide, refusal of medical treatment.

Museum or gallery collection, archive, or library special collection:
Newsletters of World Federation Members
Press cuttings and articles
Extensive collection of books and journal articles

Printed publications:
Information pack
Information leaflets on voluntary euthanasia
Living Wills and Physician Assisted Suicide
VES newsletter (3 times a year)
Living Wills

Access to staff:
Contact by letter, by telephone, by fax, by e-mail and via website
Hours: Mon to Fri, 1000 to 1600
Special comments: Visitors strictly by prior appointment.

Access to building, collection or gallery:
No prior appointment required
Hours: Mon to Fri, 1000 to 1600

Affiliated to:
World Federation of Right to Die Societies

DIRECT MAIL INFORMATION SERVICE

Acronym or abbreviation: DMIS

5 Carlisle Street, London, W1D 3JX

Tel: 020 7494 0483
Fax: 020 7494 0455
E-mail: info@dmis.co.uk

Website:
http://www.dmis.co.uk
Extracts from research reports, statistics, press releases, report ordering facility.

Founded:
1991

Organisation type and purpose:
Consultancy, research organisation.
Run by HBH on behalf of the Royal Mail to provide information to assist the direct mail and marketing industry.

Subject coverage:
Direct mail statistics and research reports.

Museum or gallery collection, archive, or library special collection:
Direct mail research by DMIS and DMSB from 1982 onwards

Printed publications:
The DMIS publishes extracts from some of its reports on the direct mail industry (available free of charge)

Publications list:
Available in print

Access to staff:
Contact by letter, by telephone, by fax, by e-mail and via website
Hours: Mon to Fri, 0900 to 1700

Parent body:
HBH Partnership Limited
at the same address; tel: 020 7494 0482

DIRECT SELLING ASSOCIATION LIMITED

Acronym or abbreviation: DSA

29 Floral Street, London, WC2E 9DP

Tel: 020 7497 1234
Fax: 020 7497 3144
E-mail: info@globalnet.co.uk

Website:
http://www.dsa.org.uk

Enquiries:
Enquiries to: Director

Founded:
1965

Organisation type and purpose:
Trade association (membership is by subscription, election or invitation).
To promote high trading standards in the direct selling of consumer goods.

Subject coverage:
General industry data on direct selling of consumer goods, industry codes of practice, direct selling legislation, details of member companies.

Trade and statistical information:
Annual statistical survey of direct selling of consumer goods in UK, includes DSA members and non-members.

Printed publications:
Direct Selling
Advice leaflet, Shopping at Home (free)
Code of Business Conduct (free)
Code of Practice (free)
List of Members (free)
The Direct Selling of Consumer Goods in UK (annual survey, £20)

Access to staff:
Contact by letter, by fax, by e-mail and via website. Appointment necessary.
Hours: Mon to Fri, 0930 to 1700

Affiliated to:
Federation of European Direct Selling Associations (FEDSA)
Avenue de Tervueren 14, 1040 Brussels, Belgium; tel: + 32 2 7361014; fax: + 32 2 7363497
World Federation of Direct Selling Associations (WFDSA)
Washington, DC, USA; tel: + 1 202 293 5760; fax: + 1 202 463 4569

DIRECTORS GUILD OF GREAT BRITAIN

Acronym or abbreviation: DGGB

4 Windmill Street, London, W1T 2HZ

Tel: 020 7580 9131
Fax: 020 7580 9132
E-mail: info@dggb.org

Website:
http://www.dggb.co.uk
General information and publications list.

continued overleaf

http://www.directorstraining.org.uk
Training information.

Enquiries:
Enquiries to: Chief Executive
Direct e-mail: malcolm@dggb.co.uk

Founded:
1985

Organisation type and purpose:
Trade union (membership is by subscription), number of members: 1,250.

Subject coverage:
Directors' rates, contract advice, guidance to the profession, information on contacting directors and/or other relevant organisations, organising events, masterclasses and conferences. Training website and information.

Non-library collection catalogue:
All or part available online

Printed publications:
Code of Practice for Drama and Radio
Code of Practice for TV Drama, Documentary, Film
Direct Magazine (quarterly)
Directory of Members (every 2 years)
Rate Cards for Recorded and Live Media

Electronic and video publications:
Spotlight CD-ROM (directory of members)

Access to staff:
Contact by letter, by telephone, by fax, by e-mail and via website. Appointment necessary.
Hours: 1000 to 1800

Access for disabled people:
Level entry

Member of:
Federation of European Film Directors (FERA)
   Avenue Everard 59, 1190 Brussels, Belgium
Informal European Theatre Meeting (IETM)
International Association of Audiovisual Writers and Directors (AIDAA)

DISABILITY ALLIANCE

Universal House, 88–94 Wentworth Street, London, E1 7SA

Tel: 020 7247 8776
Fax: 020 7247 8765
E-mail: office@disabilityalliance.org

Website:
http://www.disabilityalliance.org
Factsheets, policy, case law, membership, publications sales, links.

Enquiries:
Enquiries to: Membership and Office Administrator

Founded:
1974

Organisation type and purpose:
National organisation, present number of members: 230 paid member organisations, registered charity (charity number 1063115). Disability Alliance is committed to breaking the link between poverty and disability by providing information about social security benefits to disabled people, their carers and advisers through publications.

Subject coverage:
Social Security benefits and related services for disabled people.

Printed publications:
Including:
Disability Rights Handbook (annually)
ESA Guide
DLA/AA – A guide to making a claim
Updates service (six e-mails per year)
Briefings, factsheets and responses on a range of subjects (available free to download from website)
Order printed publications from: website; e-mail: zuzana@disabilityalliance.org

Electronic and video publications:
Disability Rights Handbook (CD-ROM)

Publications list:
Available online and in print

Access to staff:
Contact by letter, by telephone, by fax, by e-mail and via website
Hours: Mon to Fri, 1000 to 1600
Special comments: Access for the purchase of publications only.

Access to building, collection or gallery:
Prior appointment required
Special comments: Library is only available to Disability Alliance member organisations.

Access for disabled people:
Level entry, toilet facilities

Connections with Disability Benefits Consortium; Coalition on Charging:
230 Alliance Member Organisations

DISABILITY ARTS CYMRU

Sbectrwm, Bwlch Road, Fairwater, Cardiff, CF5 3EF

Tel: 029 2055 1040
Fax: 029 2055 1036
E-mail: post@dacymru.com

Website:
http://www.dacymru.com
All about the charity and its work; publications; showcase of artists' work.

Enquiries:
Enquiries to: Director

Organisation type and purpose:
Registered charity (charity number 514083), membership association (membership is free to the disabled and the unwaged).
Committed to working with individuals and organisations to celebrate the diversity of disabled and deaf people's arts and culture, and develop equality across all art forms.

Subject coverage:
Creates opportunities for disabled and deaf people to develop their skills in the arts, raises the profile of arts by disabled and deaf people, works in partnership with other organisations on arts-related projects, advises on issues related to disability and the arts, provides a consultancy service around policy development and offers arts-specific disability equality training.

Information services:
Information and advice service, free of charge, to arts organisations on a wide range of issues relating to disability and the arts and to individuals on a wide range of issues, including marketing work, making funding applications and skills development.

Printed publications:
What's On (free to members, 2 a month)

Electronic and video publications:
What's On (free to members, 2 a month)
Information sheets:
Essential Tips for Disabled Dancers
Essential Tips for Disabled Actors
Essential Tips for Disabled Writers
Photographing your work
Information sheets taken from Equal Spaces: Best practice guidance for arts providers on disability issues, a document produced by The Arts Council of Wales
Order electronic and video publications from:
Download from website

Publications list:
Available online

Access to staff:
Contact by letter, by telephone, by fax and by e-mail
Special comments: In some circumstances it may be possible to arrange for someone from Disability Arts Cymru to visit an organisation, or for a visit to

be made to the office in Cardiff. Please contact the Disability Arts Cymru office to make an appointment.

Funded by:
Arts Council of Wales

DISABILITY INFORMATION SERVICES

Acronym or abbreviation: DISS

Oaklawn Road, Leatherhead, Surrey KT22 0BT

Tel: 01372 841396

Website:
DISS's services, DissBASE details and development, DISS network contact details for further information, links to disability information providers and others.

Enquiries:
Enquiries to: Manager
Direct e-mail: hue.schoenemann@diss.org.uk

Founded:
1989

Formerly called:
Disability Information Service Surrey (DISS) (year of change 2001)

Organisation type and purpose:
Voluntary organisation, registered charity (charity number 251051).
Information service.

Subject coverage:
Anything connected with disabilities, e.g. equipment, care, employment, holidays, education, social security benefits, self-help groups, recreation, transport and access.

Museum or gallery collection, archive, or library special collection:
Journal articles, leaflets, statistical materials, directories, equipment guides

Printed publications:
Directory of Further Education Opportunities (£25)
DISS Clasification Scheme (£60/£100)
Directory of Supported Employment Opportunities (£25)
DISS introductory leaflet
Disability Information Resources leaflet
DissBASE introductory leaflet
Surrey Disability News (6 times a year)

Electronic and video publications:
DissBASE: over 6,000 records on a national database, plus 3,000 in Surrey; records relate to organisations providing services to disabled people (available for purchase)

Access to staff:
Contact by letter, by telephone, by fax, by e-mail, in person and via website. Appointment necessary.
Hours: Mon to Fri, 1000 to 1300 and 1400 to 1600
Special comments: Also textphone and typetalk.

Access for disabled people:
Parking provided, level entry, access to all public areas, toilet facilities

Parent body:
Queen Elizabeth's Foundation for Disabled People
   Leatherhead Court, Leatherhead, Surrey, KT22
   0BN; tel: 01372 841100; fax: 01372 844072;
   website: http://www.qefd.org

Subsidiary body:
DISS network

DISABILITY PREGNANCY AND PARENTHOOD INTERNATIONAL

Acronym or abbreviation: DPPI

The National Centre for Disabled Parents, Unit F9, 89–93 Fonthill Road, London, N4 3JH

Tel: 0800 018 4730; minicom no. 0800 018 9949
Fax: 020 7263 6399
E-mail: info@dppi.org.uk

Website:
http://www.dppi.org.uk

Enquiries:
Enquiries to: Administrator
Direct tel: 020 7263 3088
Direct e-mail: office@dppi.org.uk

Founded:
1993

Organisation type and purpose:
International organisation, voluntary organisation, registered charity (charity number 1070303).
To produce a quarterly journal on issues related to pregnancy, parenting and disabled people; to provide an information service to disabled parents, professionals and others.

Subject coverage:
Information databases related to all aspects of pregnancy and parenting for disabled people, including: condition-specific information, equipment, adaptations, specialist deaf parenting project, parents' rights, advocacy, local support groups.

Library catalogue:
All or part available in-house

Printed publications:
DPPI Journal (quarterly)
Extensive range of in-house publications on all aspects of disabled parenting
Order printed publications from: tel. 0800 018 4730 or via the website

Electronic and video publications:
DPPI Journal and Information Sheets (audio tape, available on request)
Extensive range of electronic publications on all aspects of disabled parenting
DVD on pregnancy and childbirth for deaf parents
Order electronic and video publications from: tel. 0800 018 4730 or online

Publications list:
Available online and in print

Access to staff:
Contact by letter, by telephone, by fax, by e-mail and via website. Appointment necessary.
Hours: Mon to Thu, 1000 to 1600

Access for disabled people:
Access to all public areas, toilet facilities

DISABILITY SPORT ENGLAND

Acronym or abbreviation: DSE

Disability Sport Events, Belle Vue Centre, Pink Bank Lane, Manchester, M12 5GL

Tel: 0161 953 2499
Fax: 0161 953 2420
E-mail: info@dse.org.uk

Website:
http://www.disabilitysport.org.uk

Enquiries:
Enquiries to: Marketing and Communications Manager
Direct e-mail: sarah@dse.org.uk
Other contacts: tel no: 01325 369554 for information re the BT/DSE swimming programme.

Founded:
1961

Formerly called:
British Sports Association for the Disabled (BSAD)

Organisation type and purpose:
Membership association (membership is by subscription), present number of members: 80,000, voluntary organisation, registered charity (charity number 297035).
Provision, development and coordination of sport for the inclusion of people with disabilities.

Subject coverage:
Sport and recreation for people with disabilities.

Printed publications:
Calendar of Event Guidelines

Information Pack wth membership
Profile Manual with Rules and Procedures

Access to staff:
Contact by letter, by telephone, by fax and by e-mail
Hours: Mon to Fri, 1000 to 1600

Access for disabled people:
Access to all public areas

Links with:
regional branches and associations

Other address:
Disability Sport England (Water Sports)
Darlington, DL1 5QU; tel: 01325 369554

DISABILITY SPORT ENGLAND – DARLINGTON

Acronym or abbreviation: DSE

The Dolphin Centre, The Horse Centre, Darlington, Co Durham, DL1 5QU

Tel: 01325 369554

Enquiries:
Enquiries to: Coordinator for swimming events
Direct e-mail: patbennett@darlingtondse.freeserve.co.uk

Founded:
1961

Organisation type and purpose:
Membership association (membership is by subscription), present number of members: 80,000, voluntary organisation, registered charity (charity number 297035).

Subject coverage:
Water sports, information re the BT/DSE swimming programme.

Access to staff:
Contact by letter, by telephone and by e-mail
Hours: Mon to Fri, 0900 to 1700

Access for disabled people:
Access to all public areas, toilet facilities

Other address:
Disability Sport England
London, N17 0DA; tel: 020 8801 4466; fax: 020 8801 6644; e-mail: info@dse.org.uk

DISABILITY SPORT ENGLAND – WEST MIDLANDS REGION

Wyndley Lane, Sutton Coldfield, West Midlands, B73 6ES

Tel: 0121 354 5369
Fax: 0121 355 5702

Enquiries:
Enquiries to: Administrator

Formerly called:
BSAD

Organisation type and purpose:
Voluntary organisation, registered charity (charity number 297035).

Subject coverage:
Advice on sports opportunities for disabled people.

Printed publications:
Information packs

Access to staff:
Contact by letter and by telephone
Hours: 24-hour answerphone

Other addresses:
Disability Sport England
Darlington, DL1 5QU; tel: 01325 369554

Parent body:
Disability Sport England
Unit 4G, 784–788 High Road, Tottenham, London, N17 0DA; tel: 020 8801 4466; fax: 020 8801 6644

DISABLED DRIVERS INSURANCE BUREAU

Formal name: Chartwell Insurance

292 Hale Lane, Edgware, Middlesex, HA8 8NP

Tel: 020 8958 0901 / 0900
Fax: 020 8958 3220
E-mail: info@chartwellinsurance.co.uk

Website:
http://www.chartwellinsurance.co.uk
Motor insurance for drivers with disabilities.

Enquiries:
Enquiries to: Partner
Direct tel: 020 8958 0919
Other contacts: Manager

Founded:
1965

Formed from:
Chartwell Insurance

Organisation type and purpose:
Service industry.
Insurance intermediary.

Subject coverage:
Motor car insurance for the disabled driver, adapted vehicles i.e. vans, powerchairs, travel and household, breakdown cover.

Printed publications:
Brochure

Access to staff:
Contact by letter, by telephone, by fax and in person
Hours: Mon to Fri, 0900 to 1730

Access to building, collection or gallery:
Mon to Fri, 0900 to 1730

Access for disabled people:
Parking provided, ramped entry, access to all public areas, toilet facilities

Affiliated to:
Chartwell Insurance
at the same address; tel: 020 8958 0900 or 0845 260 7051; fax: 020 8958 3220; e-mail: info@chartwellinsurance.co.uk; website: http://www.chartwellinsurance.co.uk

DISABLED LIVING FOUNDATION

Acronym or abbreviation: DLF

380–384 Harrow Road, London, W9 2HU

Tel: 020 7289 6111\ Minicom no. 0870 603 9176
Fax: 020 7266 2922
E-mail: info@dlf.org.uk

Website:
http://www.dlf.org.uk
Introduction to the work of Disabled Living Foundation with some generalised information. All factsheets for downloading. Information and advice. Discussion base, subscriber service on-line.

Enquiries:
Enquiries to: Information Officer
Other contacts: Director

Founded:
1970

Organisation type and purpose:
Advisory body, voluntary organisation, registered charity (charity number 290069), training organisation, publishing house.
Working for freedom, empowerment and choice for disabled people and others who use equipment or technology to enhance their independence.

Subject coverage:
The DLF works for freedom, empowerment and choice for disabled people and others who use equipment or technology to enhance their independence. It runs a helpline and letter enquiry service offering information and advice about disability equipment, and the London Disability Living Centre with over 600 items for people to try. It produces a wide range of publications on

continued overleaf

choosing and using equipment and offers a specialist subscriber service and training for healthcare professionals and organisations.

Printed publications:
Hamilton index, 24 Sections of detailed product information
Fact sheets on choosing and using equipment
Other general publications on travel, gardening, kitchen design and clothing including:
Flying High
A Garden for You
All Dressed up
A Kitchen for You
Order printed publications from: Marketing and Publication Department, Disabled Living Foundation
at same address

Electronic and video publications:
DLF data CD-ROM – listing over 14,000 product records, 2000 suppliers and 1000 relevant contacts

Publications list:
Available online and in print

Access to staff:
Contact by letter, by telephone, by fax, by e-mail and in person. Appointment necessary.
Hours: Office: Mon to Fri, 0900 to 1700; helpline, Mon to Fri, 1000 to 1600

Access to building, collection or gallery:
Prior appointment required
Hours: Equipment Centre: Mon to Fri, 1000 to 1600

Access for disabled people:
Level entry, toilet facilities

Has:
40 centres in the UK

DISABLED MOTORISTS FEDERATION

Acronym or abbreviation: DMF

c/o Chester-le-Street and District CVS Volunteer Centre, Clarence Terrace, Chester-le-Street, Co Durham, DH3 3DQ

Tel: 0191 416 3172
Fax: 0191 416 3172
E-mail: jkillick2214@yahoo.co.uk

Website:
http://www.healthworks.co.uk/daccess/D-Access/D-Access_Factsheets/dmfgendef.html
http://www.dmfed.org.uk

Enquiries:
Enquiries to: Honorary Secretary
Other contacts: Vice-President

Founded:
1973

Organisation type and purpose:
National organisation, membership association (membership is by subscription, qualification), voluntary organisation, registered charity (charity number 1012874).
Qualification for membership is registered disabled or carer.
To provide information to disabled people and their carers on matters of travel whether by road, rail or air, including advice on suitable hotel accommodation; to act for and on behalf of disabled motorist clubs.

Subject coverage:
Motoring and mobility for the disabled; setting up a local base or club for disabled drivers; vehicle choice; overseas and UK travel; wheelchairs; home adaptations; lifts and hoists; camping and caravanning; route-planning service and route maps.

Information services:
Free information on travel by road, rail, air or sea to all disabled people and their carers.

Printed publications:
The Way Ahead (quarterly, free to members, £5 a year to others)
UK Mainland River Crossings (concessions at tunnels, bridges and ferries, free for sae)
Order printed publications from: from the Honorary Secretary, by letter or e-mail, or see website

Access to staff:
Contact by telephone, by fax and by e-mail. Appointment necessary.
Hours: Mon to Fri, 0900 to 1700

Also at:
Honorary Secretary
  145 Knoulberry Road, Black Fell, Washington, Tyne & Wear, NE37 1JN; tel: 0191 416 3172; fax: 0191 416 3172; e-mail: jkillick2214@yahoo.co.uk

Constituent bodies:
10 member clubs for disabled drivers throughout Britain
  website: http://www.dmfed.org.uk

DISABLED PHOTOGRAPHERS' SOCIETY

Acronym or abbreviation: DPS

PO Box 85, Longfield, Kent, DA3 9BA

E-mail: enquiries@disabledphotographers.co.uk

Website:
http://www.disabledphotographers.co.uk
General information and examples of members' work.

Founded:
1968

Organisation type and purpose:
Membership association (membership is by subscription), present number of members: 500 individuals, 55 groups, voluntary organisation, registered charity (charity number 262866). Encourages disabled people to take an active interest in photography as a therapeutic and creative pursuit primarily by collecting surplus photographic equipment and redistributing it to disabled users who are members of the society.

Subject coverage:
Adaptation of photographic equipment for specific handicaps; advice on equipment and techniques; assistance in adopting photography as a therapeutic/leisure pursuit for disabled and handicapped persons of all ages.

Printed publications:
Annual Exhibition
Fact Sheets
Information Sheets
Newsletter (quarterly, members)

Access to staff:
Contact by letter and by e-mail

DISCRIMINATION LAW ASSOCIATION

PO Box 7722, Newbury, RG20 5WD

Tel: 0845 478 6375
E-mail: info@discriminationlaw.org.uk

Website:
http://www.discriminationlaw.org.uk
Membership, meetings and conferences, submissions and other publications, news.

Enquiries:
Enquiries to: Administrator

Founded:
1995

Organisation type and purpose:
A non-profit network that brings together a broad range of discrimination law practitioners, policy experts, academics and concerned individuals, all united around a commitment to improving equality law, practice, education and advice for those who face discrimination; has 350 members.

Subject coverage:
Activities include submitting responses to government consultations, sharing experiences and expertise through practitioner group meetings, disseminating information and knowledge via the Briefings journal, e-mail updates, conferences and seminars.

Electronic and video publications:
Briefings (journal for lawyers and non-lawyers, 3 a year, free to members)
E-News (monthly news and information service for members)
DLA submissions
Challenging Racism: Using the Human Rights Act
Full list of books published is available only to members
Order electronic and video publications from: website

Publications list:
Available online

Access to staff:
Contact by letter, by telephone, by fax and by e-mail
Hours: Office functions part-time and therefore may not be able to respond to communications immediately
Special comments: Not an advice service; cannot provide advice to the public.

DISFIGUREMENT GUIDANCE CENTRE/LASERFAIR

Acronym or abbreviation: DGC

PO Box 7, Cupar, Fife, KY15 4PF

Tel: 01337 870 281
Fax: 01337 870310

Website:
http://www.dgc.org.uk

Enquiries:
Enquiries to: Director
Other contacts: Publications Officer, tel no: 0133 787 0281, fax: 0133 787 0310

Founded:
1969

Organisation type and purpose:
Voluntary organisation, registered charity, research organisation, publishing house.
UK corporate voice and centre for the disfigured, specialist resource Skin Laser Services and information.

Subject coverage:
All aspects of disfigurement, including treatment developments, especially medical lasers, insurance, compensation advice, research, family problems; skin problems.

Non-library collection catalogue:
All or part available online and in print

Printed publications:
Publications list (please send sae)
Cosmetic-Aid: Skin Camouflage Handbook (free to GPs on request with 50p stamp, £5 to others)
Disfigurement Newsletter (free on receipt of A4 sae)
Skinlaser Directory (annually, free to GPs on receipt of 50p A5 sae, £5 to all others)
Full range of Companion Books on a wide range of topics including: Acne, Social Skills, Birthmarks, Lasers etc

Publications list:
Available in print

Access to staff:
Contact by letter, by telephone and by fax.
Appointment necessary.
Hours: Mon to Fri, 0900 to 1700
Special comments: Please send sae for information.

DIVINE INFORMATION SERVICES

PO Box 2530, Windsor, Berkshire, SL4 1WS

E-mail: informationservices@divine.com

Website:
http://www.divineinformationservices.co.uk
Main site, pdf documents on case studies and products and contact information.

Enquiries:
Enquiries to: UK Marketing Manager

Formerly called:
RoweCom (year of change 2001)

Organisation type and purpose:
International organisation, service industry.
To provide librarians and information specialists with a complete information solution in acting not only as a subscription agent for both print and electronic information resources but also in providing librarians and information specialists with content and information management, content classification, search and taxonomy.

Museum or gallery collection, archive, or library special collection:
Northern Light – Single Point
Print and Electronic Subscription Services

Electronic and video publications:
Content Management
Information Quest
kcentral
klibrary
kstore
New! Single Point
Virtual Library

Access to staff:
Contact by telephone, by fax and by e-mail
Hours: Mon to Fri, 0900 to 1730

Other offices:
Has 19 other offices throughout the world

DOCUMENT OPTIONS LTD

Priestley Way, Crawley, West Sussex, RH10 9NT

Tel: 01293 426677
Fax: 01293 403453
E-mail: sales@document-options.co.uk

Website:
http://www.document-options.co.uk
http://www.document-options.net
Demonstration of web document hosting.

Enquiries:
Enquiries to: Director

Founded:
1970

Organisation type and purpose:
Service industry.
Microfilming and scanning bureau.

Subject coverage:
Reprographic procedures, raster to vector conversion, conversion of microfilm/microfiche to digital data.

Access to staff:
Contact by telephone
Hours: Mon to Fri, 0900 to 1700

DOLMETSCH FOUNDATION INCORPORATED

27 Gilmour Gardens, Alton, Hampshire, GU34 2NR

Tel: 01420 541892

Website:
http://www.dolmetsch.com

Enquiries:
Enquiries to: Secretary

Organisation type and purpose:
Learned society.

Subject coverage:
Early music and instruments, c. 1000 to c. 1750.

Museum or gallery collection, archive, or library special collection:
File from 1929 of the annual journal, The Consort

Access to staff:
Contact by letter
Hours: Mon to Fri, 0900 to 1700

Other addresses:
Dolmetsch Foundation Incorporated
Jesses, Grayswood Road, Haslemere, Surrey, GU27 2BS

DOLMETSCH HISTORICAL DANCE SOCIETY

Acronym or abbreviation: DHDS

17 Well Lane, Stock, Ingatestone, Essex, CM4 9LT

Tel: 01277 840473
Fax: 01277 840473
E-mail: secretary@dhds.org.uk

Website:
http://www.dhds.org.uk
Publications order form; membership details; report on Summer School. Past and future events and conferences. Links to similar sites; photographs. Ability to download articles.

Enquiries:
Enquiries to: Honorary Secretary

Founded:
1970

Organisation type and purpose:
National organisation, membership association, present number of members: 120, registered charity (charity number 270896), research organisation.
To promote the practice of and research into social dance in Europe from the 15th to the 19th century.

Subject coverage:
Information on dances, dancers and dancing masters of the past; information on source material and secondary sources, including society publications; information on teachers and dance classes available; information on performing groups.

Printed publications:
Books and CDs and tapes of dances (from the 15th century onwards) produced annually for Summer School
Conference Proceedings (biennially)
Historical Dance (journal, occasionally)
Dance for Tudors and Stuarts – A resource pack for teachers (book and tape for Key Stage 2, Understanding Victorian Society through Dance)
Order printed publications from: Secretary, Dolmetsch Historical Dance Society, 17 Well Lane, Stock, ingatestone, Essex, CM4 9LT

Electronic and video publications:
Tapes and CDs of dance music
Understanding Victorian Society through Dance (CD)

Publications list:
Available online and in print

Access to staff:
Contact by letter, by telephone, by fax and by e-mail
Hours: No fixed hours.

DOMESTIC APPLIANCE SERVICE ASSOCIATION

Acronym or abbreviation: DASA

2nd Floor, 145–157 St John Street, London, EC1V 4PY

Tel: 0870 224 0343
Fax: 0870 224 0358
E-mail: dasa@dasa.org.uk

Website:
http://www.dasa.org.uk

Enquiries:
Enquiries to: Administrator
Direct e-mail: admin@dasa.org.uk

Founded:
1978

Organisation type and purpose:
Trade association (membership is by qualification), present number of members: 180, service industry.
To promote quality service, efficiency and courtesy in the servicing of domestic appliances.

Subject coverage:
Promotion of good service, efficiency and courtesy to all members of the public, investigation of complaints against member firms, quality management, insurance, training.

Printed publications:
Code of Practice
Quality Criteria
Orbit Newsletter (for members)
Overview of Domestic Appliance Servicing Qualifications
Quality Assessment System

Access to staff:
Contact by letter, by telephone, by fax and by e-mail. Appointment necessary.
Hours: Mon to Fri, 0900 to 1700

Access to building, collection or gallery:
Appointment required

Member organisation of:
British Quality Foundation
tel: 020 7654 5000; fax: 020 7654 5001; e-mail: mail@quality-foundation.co.uk
Electrical and Electronics Servicing Training Council (EESTC)
tel: 020 7836 3357; fax: 020 7497 9006; e-mail: ccrouch@eeb.iie.org.uk

DOMESTIC FOWL TRUST

Station Road, Honeybourne, Evesham, Worcestershire, WR11 5QG

Tel: 01386 833083
Fax: 01386 833364
E-mail: dft@honeybourne.demon.co.uk

Website:
http://www.domesticfowltrust.co.uk

Enquiries:
Enquiries to: Director

Founded:
1975

Organisation type and purpose:
Professional body, consultancy, research organisation.

Subject coverage:
Poultry breeding, old breeds of hens, ducks, geese, turkeys; housing and management of outdoor poultry, poultry health.

Printed publications:
Mail Order Catalogue (free of charge)
Wide range of domestic poultry keeping books (available for purchase)

Access to staff:
Contact by letter, by telephone, by fax, by e-mail and in person
Hours: Mon to Sun, 1030 to 1700

Access to building, collection or gallery:
No access other than to staff
Hours: Mon to Fri, 1030 to 1700

Access for disabled people:
Parking provided, ramped entry, toilet facilities

DOMINICA HIGH COMMISSION

Formal name: High Commission for the Commonwealth of Dominica

1 Collingham Gardens, London, SW5 0HW

Tel: 020 7370 5194

continued overleaf

Fax: 020 7373 8743
E-mail: info@dominicahighcommission.co.uk

Website:
http://www.dominicahighcommission.co.uk

Enquiries:
Enquiries to: Secretary

Organisation type and purpose:
National government body.

Subject coverage:
Dominica, tourism, trade, consular, general information.

Access to staff:
Contact by letter, by fax and by e-mail.
Appointment necessary.
Hours: Mon to Fri, 0930 to 1730

DOMINICAN REPUBLIC TOURIST BOARD

18–21 Hand Court, London, WC1V 6JF

Tel: 020 7242 7778
Fax: 020 7405 4202
E-mail: uk@godominicanrepublic.com

Website:
http://www.godominicanrepublic.com

Enquiries:
Enquiries to: Executive Director

Founded:
1996

Organisation type and purpose:
International organisation, national government body.
Promotion of tourism.

Information services:
Dominican Republic visitor information.

Printed publications:
Brochures, magazines, etc.
Order printed publications from: e-mail: uk@godominicanrepublic.com

Electronic and video publications:
Order electronic and video publications from: e-mail: uk@godominicanrepublic.com

Publications list:
Available online and in print

Access to staff:
Contact by letter, by telephone, by fax, by e-mail, in person and via website
Hours: Mon to Fri, 1000 to 1700

Access to building, collection or gallery:
Hours: Mon to Fri, 1000 to 1700

Access for disabled people:
Level entry, access to public areas, no toilet facilities

DONCASTER AND DISTRICT FAMILY HISTORY SOCIETY

Acronym or abbreviation: DDFHS

8 Tenter Lane, Warmsworth, Doncaster, South Yorkshire, DN4 9PT

Tel: 01302 854809
E-mail: honsecretary@doncasterfhs.co.uk

Website:
http://www.doncasterfhs.co.uk
Publications, membership form, downloads, about the society

Enquiries:
Enquiries to: Honorary Secretary

Founded:
1980

Formerly called:
Doncaster Family History Society (year of change 1990)

Organisation type and purpose:
Membership association (membership is by subscription), voluntary organisation, registered charity (charity number 516226).

Subject coverage:
Genealogy, family history.

Museum or gallery collection, archive, or library special collection:
Archives (held at the Doncaster MBC Archives Service)

Printed publications:
Publications on various topics (for sale)
The Doncaster Ancestor (4 times a year)
Order printed publications from: Doncaster and District Family History Society
Mr K Wishart, 11 Hawthorn Terrace, New Earswick, York, YO32 4BL

Microform publications:
Microfiche of various topics (for sale)
Order microform publications from: Doncaster and District Family History Society
Mr K Wishart, 11 Hawthorn Terrace, New Earswick, York, YO32 4BL

Electronic and video publications:
Various Topics (CD-ROM, for sale)
Order electronic and video publications from:
Doncaster and District Family History Society
Mr K Wishart, 11 Hawthorn Terrace, New Earswick, York, YO32 4BL

Publications list:
Available online and in print

Access to staff:
Contact by letter, by e-mail and via website. Non-members charged.
Hours: Mon to Fri, 0900 to 1700
Special comments: Not after 2100

Access to building, collection or gallery:
Prior appointment required
Special comments: Contact Secretary.

Access for disabled people:
Disabled visitors are advised to contact the Palgrave research room (tel: 01302 311930) or the Secretary prior to their visit
Special comments: Contact Secretary.

DONCASTER ARCHIVES

Formal name: Doncaster Metropolitan Borough Council: Library and Information Services, Doncaster Archives

King Edward Road, Balby, Doncaster, South Yorkshire, DN4 0NA

Tel: 01302 859811
E-mail: doncaster.archives@doncaster.gov.uk

Website:
http://www.doncaster.gov.uk/doncasterarchives

Enquiries:
Enquiries to: Principal Archivist

Founded:
1973

Formerly called:
Doncaster Archives Department

Organisation type and purpose:
Local government body.
Doncaster Archives collects, preserves and gives public access to the documentary heritage of Doncaster Metropolitan Borough from 1194 to the present.

Subject coverage:
The full range of records usually to be found in a local record office, including local government archives, local public records, Church of England parish records, nonconformist church records, family and landed estate records, business archives, political party archives, trade union archives, voluntary society archives, local maps and plans.

Museum or gallery collection, archive, or library special collection:
Includes:
Parish Registers of 36 ancient parishes, transcribed with surname index up to 1837 and many to later dates

Non-library collection catalogue:
All or part available online and in-house

Library catalogue:
All or part available in-house

Printed publications:
Doncaster: A Borough and its Charters (G. H. Martin et al, 1994, £2.50)
Guide to Doncaster Archives (2006, £5, or £7.50 by post)
Leaflets on the department (free)
Order printed publications from: Doncaster Archives, King Edward Road, Balby, Doncaster, South Yorkshire, DN4 0NA

Access to staff:
Contact by letter, by telephone, by e-mail and in person. Appointment necessary.
Hours: Mon to Fri, 0900 to 1245 and 1400 to 1645

Access to building, collection or gallery:
Special comments: Reader's ticket required

DONCASTER COLLEGE

The Hub Learning Resource Centre, Doncaster, South Yorkshire, DN1 2RF

Tel: 01302 553553
Fax: 01302 553559

Website:
http://www.don.ac.uk
Introduction, finding information on the internet, Autodesk Training Centre course registration.

Enquiries:
Enquiries to: Site Librarian at The Hub
Direct tel: 01302 553745
Direct e-mail: infocentre@don.ac.uk
Other contacts: Head of Learning Resources (responsible for all site Learning Resource Centres)

Created by the merger of:
4 Doncaster Colleges of Technology, Art and Design and Education

Organisation type and purpose:
College of further education.

Subject coverage:
Business studies, environmental sciences, engineering (construction, mechanical, production, electrical, mining and mineral), catering, hairdressing and beauty, nursing, modern languages, computing, education and related fields, art and design, sociology, geography and history, travel and tourism, animal care, floristry.

Library catalogue:
All or part available online

Access to staff:
Contact by letter. Appointment necessary. Non-members charged.
Hours: Term time: Mon to Thu, 0845 to 2000; Fri, 0845 to 1700
Vacations: Mon to Fri, 0900 to 1230 and 1330 to 1645

Also at:
Doncaster College
The University Centre LRC, High Melton, Doncaster, South Yorkshire, DN5 7SZ

DONCASTER LIBRARY AND INFORMATION SERVICES

Doncaster Central Library, Waterdale, Doncaster, South Yorkshire, DN1 3JE

Tel: 01302 734305
Fax: 01302 369749
E-mail: reference.library@doncaster.gov.uk

Website:
http://www.doncaster.gov.uk

Enquiries:
Enquiries to: Reference Manager
Direct tel: 01302 734320

Founded:
1869

Organisation type and purpose:
Local government body, public library.

Subject coverage:
General, local studies, railways, horse racing.

Information services:
Reference and information service.

Education services:
Classes held in Library premises.

Services for disabled people:
Reading Aids Unit – serving the visually impaired.

Museum or gallery collection, archive, or library special collection:
Archives: official, ecclesiastical, family and private records held at King Edward Road, Balby, Doncaster, DN4 0NA; tel: 01302 859811
Local Studies Library – 1984–85 Miners' Strike Collection
Local Studies Library – Family Album Project
Local Studies Library – Doncaster Community Archive (CD ROM)
British Standards (online)
Britannica Online
Oxford Online

Trade and statistical information:
Mint UK online.

Library catalogue:
All or part available online

Printed publications:
Local Societies and Organisations
List of Rooms for Hire
List of Places of Worship
List of Speakers and Demonstrators
List of Translators
The Local Studies Library (guide to services)
Order printed publications from: Reference Department

Access to staff:
Contact by letter, by telephone, by fax, by e-mail, in person and via website
Hours: Mon to Thu, 0900 to 1800; Fri, 1000 to 1800; Sat, 0900 to 1700

Access for disabled people:
Access to all public areas, toilet facilities

Member organisation of:
Doncaster Chamber of Commerce
European Public Information Centre
SINTO
South Yorkshire Joint Archives Service
Yorkshire and Humberside Association of Library Services

DONKEY BREED SOCIETY

Acronym or abbreviation: DBS

The Hermitage, Pootings, Edenbridge, Kent, TN8 6SD

Tel: 01732 864414
Fax: 01732 864414
E-mail: societysecretary@donkeybreedsociaty.co.uk

Website:
http://www.donkeybreedingsociety.co.uk

Enquiries:
Enquiries to: Secretary

Founded:
1967

Organisation type and purpose:
Membership association, registered charity (charity number 292268).
To work for the welfare of all donkeys.

Subject coverage:
The care, management and breeding of donkeys, also their welfare, education and general activities such as trekking, showing, driving and light draught work.

Museum or gallery collection, archive, or library special collection:
Library of limited donkey related books (for hire by members)
Stud Book

Printed publications:
Annual Magazine (available by membership subscription and for sale)
Information leaflets (available free to members or for a donation to non-members)
Newsletters (available by membership subscription)

Access to staff:
Contact by letter, by telephone and by fax
Hours: Mon to Fri, 0900 to 1700

DONKEY SANCTUARY

Sidmouth, Devon, EX10 0NU

Tel: 01395 578222
Fax: 01395 579266
E-mail: enquiries@thedonkeysanctuary.com

Website:
http://www.thedonkeysanctuary.org.uk
Information on charities, Adopt a Donkey.

Founded:
1969

Incorporates the:
International Donkey Protection Trust

Organisation type and purpose:
International organisation, registered charity (charity number 264818).

Subject coverage:
Provision of high quality, professional advice, training and support on donkey welfare worldwide.

Printed publications:
The Professional Handbook of the Donkey
Newsletters, reference sheets and many other books and posters

Electronic and video publications:
Basic Donkey Health Care
An Introduction to Donkey Footcare
The Donkey Sanctuary... 40 years on

Publications list:
Available in print

Access to staff:
Contact by letter, by telephone, by fax, by e-mail, in person and via website. Appointment necessary.
Hours: Mon to Fri, 0830 to 1630

Access for disabled people:
Parking provided, level entry, toilet facilities

Connections at the same address with:
The Elisabeth Svendsen Trust for Children and Donkeys
tel: 01395 578222; fax: 01395 579266; e-mail: info@elisabethsvendsentrust.org

DOROTHY L SAYERS SOCIETY

Rose Cottage, Malthouse Lane, Hurstpierpoint, West Sussex, BN6 9JY

Tel: 01273 833444
Fax: 01273 835988
E-mail: jasmine@sayers.org.uk

Website:
http://www.sayers.org.uk

Enquiries:
Enquiries to: Chairman
Other contacts: info@sayers.org.uk

Founded:
1976

Formerly called:
Dorothy L Sayers Historical and Literary Society

Organisation type and purpose:
Membership association (membership is by subscription), present number of members: 500, registered charity (charity number 272120), suitable for ages: all.

Subject coverage:
Life, biographical details and works of Dorothy L Sayers and the subjects in which she was involved such as: Christian theology and apologetics, campanology, genealogy, Dante, drama (secular and religious), literary and theological criticism, broadcasting, the Wimsey family, Sherlock Holmes, detective fiction, the Detection Club, Wimsey chronology, poetry, painting and stage sets, locations and social references in DLS fiction.

Museum or gallery collection, archive, or library special collection:
Archives include writings by DLS (articles, poetry, speeches, letters (personal and press), reviews and introductions and pamphlets); other writings on DLS and her subjects, commentaries and essays, press cuttings, certificates, memorabilia, reviews of her plays and biographies. Most of these items can be copied for members only; copies of much of the work are available at Witham County Library

Printed publications:
Archives List
Bulletin (6 times a year)
Chronology of Lord Peter Wimsey (1983)
DLS, Mystery Maker (J Brabazon, 1981)
DLS, Player of the Game (J Brabazon, 1981)
Does She Cheat? (J Morris, 1983)
Encounters with Lord Peter (Dean C ed. 1991)
Genealogy of DLS (G Lee)
Letters of Dorothy L Sayers (Reynolds B ed. 1997, 1998, 2000)
Poetry of Dorothy L Sayers (Horne R ed. 1996)
Proceedings of Annual Seminars from 1976
Sidelights on Sayers (56 volumes, 1981 to 2008)
Studies in Sayers (Dean C ed., 1993)
Theology of DLS (P de Voil, 1983)
Tour Guides (Oxford, London, Cambridge, the Fens, Galloway) (1983)
Les origines du roman policier (Sayers, 2003)
The Wimsey Family (Scott-Giles & Sayers, 2007)
The Christ of the Creeds (Sayers, 2008)
Order printed publications from: Dorothy L Sayers Society

Access to staff:
Contact by letter, by telephone, by fax, by e-mail and via website. Appointment necessary.
Hours: Mon to Fri, 0900 to 1700

DORSET DOWN SHEEP BREEDERS' ASSOCIATION

Acronym or abbreviation: DDSBA

Havett Farm, Dobwalls, Liskeard, Cornwall, PL14 6HB

Tel: 01579 320273
E-mail: secretary@dorsetdownsheep.org.uk

Website:
http://www.dorsetdownsheep.org.uk

Enquiries:
Enquiries to: Breed Secretary

Founded:
1906

Organisation type and purpose:
National organisation, membership association (membership is by subscription), present number of members: 80, registered charity (charity number 84799).
Promotion of the breed of Dorset Down sheep.

Subject coverage:
Breeding and whereabouts of Dorset Down sheep, and administration of the association since 1906.

continued overleaf

Museum or gallery collection, archive, or library special collection:
Flock Books, 1906 to present day

Printed publications:
Annual Flock Book (available for purchase after Jan each year)

Publications list:
Available in print

Access to staff:
Contact by letter, by telephone and by e-mail

DORSET LIBRARY SERVICE

Headquarters, Colliton Park, Dorchester, Dorset, DT1 1XJ

Tel: 01305 225000
Fax: 01305 224344
E-mail: dorsetlibraries@dorsetcc.gov.uk

Website:
http://www.dorsetforyou.com/libraries

Enquiries:
Enquiries to: Head of Cultural Services

Organisation type and purpose:
Local government body, public library.

Subject coverage:
General lending and reference and information services; also specialist information on all aspects of the County of Dorset.

Museum or gallery collection, archive, or library special collection:
Collections on T E Lawrence and Percy Westerman (Wareham Library)
Collections on Thomas Hardy, the Powys family and William Barnes, John Fowles, Sir Frederick Treves, Sylvia Townsend Warner (Dorchester Library)
Drama and Playsets Collection
Local Studies Collections (Dorset History Centre; Dorchester Library; Weymouth Library; Christchurch Library; Bridport Library)

Non-library collection catalogue:
All or part available online

Library catalogue:
All or part available online

Publications list:
Available in print

Access to staff:
Contact by letter, by telephone, by fax, by e-mail, in person and via website
Hours: Hours vary dependent on service point

Access to building, collection or gallery:
No access other than to staff

Parent body:
Dorset County Council

DORSET NATURAL HISTORY AND ARCHAEOLOGICAL SOCIETY

Dorset County Museum, High West Street, Dorchester, Dorset, DT1 1XA

Tel: 01305 262735
Fax: 01305 257180

Website:
http://www.dorsetcountymuseum.org

Enquiries:
Enquiries to: Director

Founded:
1846

Organisation type and purpose:
Learned society, museum.
Private library.

Subject coverage:
Dorset: local history, natural history, archaeology, social history, fine arts, geology, literature.

Museum or gallery collection, archive, or library special collection:
Dorset Archaeological Archive
Lock and Mann Hardy Collection
Mansel-Pleydell Herbarium
Photographic Collection
Sanders Hardy Collection
Sylvia Townsend Warner (author 1893–1985), manuscripts, notebooks, diaries, letters and publications
Thomas Hardy Memorial Collection
William Barnes (Dorset poet, 1801–1886) manuscripts, notebooks, letters, diaries, scrapbooks and publications

Non-library collection catalogue:
All or part available in-house

Printed publications:
Proceedings (annually)
Various publications about the geology, archaeological investigations and natural history of Dorset

Publications list:
Available in print

Access to staff:
Appointment necessary.
Hours: Mon to Fri, 1000 to 1700

DORSET RECORD OFFICE

Bridport Road, Dorchester, Dorset, DT1 1RP

Tel: 01305 250550\ Minicom no. 01305 267933 (at County Hall)
Fax: 01305 257184
E-mail: archives@dorset-cc.gov.uk

Website:
http://www.dorset-cc.gov.uk/archives

Enquiries:
Enquiries to: County Archivist

Founded:
1955

Organisation type and purpose:
Local government body.
Archives and record office.
The preservation of archives of Dorset and making them accessible, providing an archives service on behalf of Dorset County Council, Bournemouth Borough Council and the Borough of Poole.

Subject coverage:
Standard range of public and private archives including local government, parishes, estates, businesses, families, suitable for history, local history, family history and much else.

Museum or gallery collection, archive, or library special collection:
Standard local record office archives, documents, manuscripts, photographs, sound film
Parish registers, probate records, census records, General Register Office index (microfilm and microfiche)

Non-library collection catalogue:
All or part available in-house

Printed publications:
Free information leaflets: regulations, charter of service, location, research services, copying services, meeting room facilities, Friends of Dorset's Archives and Dorset Parish Records Preservation Project
A map of the parishes of Dorset c. 1900 (40p plus p&p)
Building Accounts of Mapperton Rectory (ed Machin R, £4 plus p&p)
Guide to the Location of the Parish Registers of Dorset (£2 plus p&p)
Guide to the Location of the Nonconformist & Roman Catholic Registers (£1.50 plus p&p)
Guide to the Transcripts held in the County Record Office (£1 plus p&p)
Farming in Dorset: Diary of James Warne, 1758; Letters of George Boswell, 1787–1805 (ed James J F & Bettey J H, £10.75 plus p&p)

List of diaries and memoirs in the Dorset Record Office (50p plus p&p)
List of documents in the Record Office relating to precautions in the county against the threat of French invasion 1797–1814 (10p plus p&p)
Puddletown: House Street and Family (ed Sinclair Williams C L, £5.75 plus p&p)
Railway Records in the Dorset Records Office (£6.95 plus p&p)
The Case Book of Sir Frances Ashley, JP Recorder of Dorchester 1614–1635 (ed Bettey J H, £6.50 plus p&p)
The Love Poems & Letters of William Barnes and Julia Miles (ed Lindgren C, £4 plus p&p)
Touching Witchcrafte and Sorcerye (ed Davies G J, £4 plus p&p)
Who's Afear'd of Family History – A guide to services in DRO (£6.95 plus p&p)
William Whiteway of Dorchester: His Diary 1618 to 1635 (£9.75 plus p&p)

Microform publications:
Microfilm available; photocopies and microfilm printout copies are charged for

Publications list:
Available in print

Access to staff:
Contact by letter, by telephone, by fax, by e-mail and via website. Appointment necessary.
Hours: Mon, Tue, Thu, Fri, 0900 to 1700; Wed, 1000 to 1700; Sat, 0930 to 1230
Special comments: Proof of identity required.

Access for disabled people:
Level entry, toilet facilities

Other addresses:
Dorset Record Office
Archives Management Unit, County Hall, Dorchester, Dorset, DT1 1XJ; tel: 01305 225191; fax: 01305 225175

Parent bodies:
Borough of Poole
Bournemouth Borough Council
Dorset County Council

DOUGLAS PUBLIC LIBRARY

Formal name: Henry Bloom Noble Library

10/12 Victoria Street, Douglas, Isle of Man, IM1 2LH

Tel: 01624 696461
Fax: 01624 696400
E-mail: jmacartney@douglas.gov.im

Website:
http://www.douglas.gov.im

Enquiries:
Enquiries to: Librarian

Founded:
1886

Organisation type and purpose:
Local government body, public library.

Subject coverage:
Isle of Man: historical, social, political, economic and other aspects.

Museum or gallery collection, archive, or library special collection:
Manx Collection

Non-library collection catalogue:
All or part available in-house

Library catalogue:
All or part available online and in-house

Access to staff:
Contact by letter, by telephone, by fax, by e-mail, in person and via website
Hours: Mon to Sat, 0915 to 1730

Access to building, collection or gallery:
Hours: Mon, Tue, Thu, Fri and Sat, 0915 to 1730; Wed, 1000 to 1730

Access for disabled people:
Fully compliant with DOA requirements

DOVE MARINE LABORATORY

Cullercoats, North Shields, Tyne and Wear, NE30 4PZ

Tel: 0191 222 3053
Fax: 0191 252 1054
E-mail: jill.cowans@ncl.ac.uk

Website:
http://www.ncl.ac.uk/marine

Enquiries:
Enquiries to: Secretary
Direct e-mail: c.a.weiss@ncl.ac.uk
Other contacts: Deputy Director

Founded:
1908

Organisation type and purpose:
Research organisation.

Subject coverage:
Marine biology; oceanography; fisheries.

Special visitor services:
Laboratory and meeting room hire.

Education services:
School pupil science classes; UG- and CPO-level training.

Library catalogue:
All or part available in-house

Printed publications:
Reports (marine fauna of the Cullercoats district) (for sale)

Access to staff:
Contact by letter, by telephone, by fax and by e-mail
Hours: Mon to Fri, 0900 to 1700

Access to building, collection or gallery:
By appointment
Hours: Mon to Fri, 0900 to 1700

Access for disabled people:
Access to ground floor only

Part of:
School of Marine Science and Technology
tel: 0191 222 6661; fax: 0191 222 7891

DOVER HARBOUR BOARD

Harbour House, Dover, Kent, CT17 9BU

Tel: 01304 240400
Fax: 01304 240465

Website:
http://www.doverport.co.uk
Ferries: cars, coach, freight. Shipping: cruises, marina, cargo. Commercial: advertising, property.

Enquiries:
Enquiries to: Public Relations Officer
Direct tel: 01304 240400 ext 4801
Direct fax: 01304 241274
Direct e-mail: val.crimmin@doverport.co.uk

Founded:
1606

Also known as:
Port of Dover

Organisation type and purpose:
Statutory body.
Statutory board.

Subject coverage:
Port administration, particularly cross-channel passenger trade and roll-on roll-off traffic, cruise terminal, marina operation and fresh produce cargo facilities.

Printed publications:
All information is free of charge
Annual Report
Port Handbook
Service Brochures
Statistical Digests
Marina Guide

Access to staff:
Contact by letter, by telephone, by fax and via website
Hours: Mon to Fri, 0800 to 1800

DOWN'S HEART GROUP

Acronym or abbreviation: DHG

PO Box 4260, Dunstable, Bedfordshire, LU6 2ZT

Tel: 0844 288 4800
Fax: 0844 288 4808
E-mail: info@dhg.org.uk

Website:
http://www.dhg.org.uk
Online version of information pack plus more recent material, newsletters, conferences, etc.

Enquiries:
Enquiries to: Information Officer
Direct e-mail: sarah@dhg.org.uk
Other contacts: Director

Founded:
1989

Organisation type and purpose:
UK national charity.

Subject coverage:
Heart defects with Down's Syndrome; pre-natal screening for heart defects with Down's Syndrome; bereavement; support for families.

Information services:
information and support offered via phone, e-mail, website, newsletters and conferences.

Special visitor services:
One-to-one visits at hospitals, if possible.

Services for disabled people:
Provides information, research, support for people with Down's Syndrome and heart problems.

Museum or gallery collection, archive, or library special collection:
Archive information at National Office and Information Office

Non-library collection catalogue:
All or part available in-house

Library catalogue:
All or part available online and in print

Printed publications:
Information Pack (£5, free to families)
Newsletter (free to members)
Order printed publications from: National Office

Electronic and video publications:
Heart Problems in Children with Down's Syndrome (video, loaned free to families, £5 to purchase)
I'm Gonna Go For It – following a young man through heart surgery
Order electronic and video publications from: National Office

Publications list:
Available online

Access to staff:
Contact by letter, by telephone, by fax, by e-mail and via website
Hours: 24-hour in emergency; contact or answerphone always available

Access to building, collection or gallery:
Prior appointment required

Member organisation of:
Children's Heart Federation

DOWN'S SYNDROME ASSOCIATION

Acronym or abbreviation: DSA

Langdon Down Centre, 2a Langdon Park, Teddington, TW11 9PS

Tel: 0845 230 0372
Fax: 0845 230 0373

E-mail: info@downs-syndrome.org.uk

Website:
http://www.downs-syndrome.org.uk
Information about Down's Syndrome and the Association; list of publications.

Enquiries:
Enquiries to: Information Officer

Founded:
1971

Organisation type and purpose:
National organisation, membership association (membership is by subscription), present number of members: 12,000, voluntary organisation, registered charity (charity number 1061474).

Subject coverage:
Down's Syndrome: medical, educational and psychological issues, counselling new parents, and general aspects.

Printed publications:
Newsletter (3 times a year)
Literature List – publications of the Association and others under the following headings: play and early learning, speech and language, education, behaviour, benefits, services and legal matters, health, medical and nutrition, leisure, relations and sexuality, bereavement, counselling

Electronic and video publications:
Education: Preparation for life (video)
Play and Say (video)
Down 2 Earth

Publications list:
Available in print

Access to staff:
Contact by letter, by telephone, by fax, by e-mail and via website. Appointment necessary.
Hours: Mon to Fri, 0900 to 1700

DOWN'S SYNDROME SCOTLAND

158–160 Balgreen Road, Edinburgh, EH11 3AU

Tel: 0131 313 4225
Fax: 0131 313 4285
E-mail: info@dsscotland.org.uk

Website:
http://www.dsscotland.org.uk

Founded:
1982

Formerly called:
Scottish Down's Syndrome Association (SDSA) (year of change 2001)

Organisation type and purpose:
Membership association (membership is by subscription), present number of members: 1500+, voluntary organisation, registered charity (charity number SC011012).

Subject coverage:
Down's Syndrome.

Information services:
Telephone, e-mail helplines, website resources, ebulletins and archive.

Education services:
Provides training to parents and professionals on all aspects connected with Down's syndrome.

Services for disabled people:
Making Your Way Through Life Project provides training for adults with Down's syndrome.

Museum or gallery collection, archive, or library special collection:
Resource centre of books and DVDs available for loan

Non-library collection catalogue:
All or part available online, in-house and in print

Library catalogue:
All or part available online

Printed publications:
Annual Review

continued overleaf

Bi-annual Newsletter
A variety of booklets for parents and professionals.
A range of easy-to-read booklets for people with
learning disabilities
Fact sheets

Publications list:
Available online and in print

Access to staff:
Contact by letter, by telephone, by fax, by e-mail,
in person and via website. Appointment necessary.
Hours: Mon to Fri, 0900 to 1700

Access for disabled people:
Level entry, access to all public areas, toilet
facilities

Branches:
in Ayrshire, Central, Grampian, Lothian, Tayside,
West of Scotland

**Sister organisation for England, Wales and
Northern Ireland:**
Down's Syndrome Association
Langdon Down Centre, 2A Langdon Park,
Teddington, Middlesex, TW11 9PS; tel: 0845 230
0372; fax: 0845 230 0373; e-mail: info@downs
-syndrome.org.uk; website: http://www.downs
-syndrome.org.uk

DOZENAL SOCIETY OF GREAT BRITAIN

Acronym or abbreviation: DSGB

32 Lansdowne Crescent, Carlisle, Cumbria, CA3
9EW

Tel: 01228 596834
E-mail: dsgb@dozenalsociety.org.uk

Website:
http://www.dozenalsociety.org.uk

Enquiries:
Enquiries to: Secretary

Founded:
1958

Formerly called:
Duodecimal Society of Great Britain (year of
change 1978)

Organisation type and purpose:
International organisation, learned society
(membership is by subscription), present number
of members: 60, research organisation.
Metrological and numbering systems past, present
and future. Informed consideration of attempts to
impose decimal-metric methods on areas for which
they are not appropriate.
To replace base ten with base twelve.
Technical and social metrologies have differing
requirements and purposes. The first postulates
abstract concepts which need not relate to
anything but one another, to be operated on by
multi-figured calculations. Social use requires
human-sized units that are designated by small
numbers and are in the simple proportions
commonly required and instinctively employed
when making comparisons of size, weight, value,
etc, such as have been evolved down the ages for
our convenience and understanding.

Subject coverage:
Measurement systems and methods of numeration
and arithmetic, past, present and future; principles,
practical imperatives and efficiency in applied
metrology and computation; historical, scientific
and social metrology; derivation, relationships and
purposes of basic units; application of twelve-
based arithmetic; informed criticism of decimal-
metric methods.

**Museum or gallery collection, archive, or library
special collection:**
Books, papers and references on numeration,
calculation and metrology
Duodecimal Bulletins of the Dozenal Society of
America since 1945
Journals of the DSGB from 1960 to date
Media cuttings over present decimalisation era

Wide bibliography of references

Non-library collection catalogue:
All or part available in-house

Library catalogue:
All or part available in-house

Printed publications:
Dozenal Journal (occasional, free to members)
Duodecimal Bulletin of the DSA
Gravity and Mass TGM, A coherent dozenal
metrology based on time

Publications list:
Available in print

Access to staff:
Contact by letter, by telephone, by e-mail and via
website. Appointment necessary.
Hours: Mon to Sun, 0900 to 2100

Links with:
British Weights and Measures Association
11 Greensleeves Avenue, Broadstone, Dorset,
BH18 8BJ; tel: 020 8922 0089; fax:
bwma@email.com; website: http://www.footrule
.org
Dozenal Society of America (DSA)
472 Village Oaks Lane, Babylon Village, NY
11702–3123, USA; tel: +1 631 669 0273; fax:
contact@dozenal.org; website: http://www
.dozenal.org

DR WILLIAMS'S LIBRARY

14 Gordon Square, London, WC1H 0AR

Tel: 020 7387 3727
E-mail: enquiries@dwlib.co.uk

Website:
http://www.dwlib.co.uk

Founded:
1729

Organisation type and purpose:
Registered charity (charity number 214926), public
library.

Subject coverage:
Theology, ecclesiastical history (particularly early
nonconformist history), philosophy, humanities in
general.

**Museum or gallery collection, archive, or library
special collection:**
Henry Crabb Robinson, diaries and
correspondence
New College, London, Collection
Norman Baynes Byzantine Library
George Henry Lewes Library
Philip Doddridge Correspondence
Richard Baxter Correspondence
Roger Morrice Collection

Non-library collection catalogue:
All or part available in-house and in print

Library catalogue:
All or part available in-house and in print

Printed publications:
Friends of Dr Williams's Library Annual Lectures,
1947–

Publications list:
Available online

Access to staff:
Contact by letter, by telephone and by e-mail.
Appointment necessary.
Hours: Mon, Wed, Fri, 1000 to 1700; Tue, Thu, 1000
to 1830

Parent body:
Dr Williams's Trust
14 Gordon Square, London, WC1H 0AR

DRAKE MUSIC

Rich Mix, 35–47 Bethnal Green Road, London, E1
6LA

Tel: 020 7739 5444

Fax: 020 7729 8942
E-mail: info@drakemusicproject.org

Website:
http://www.drakemusicproject.org
Information about Drake Music and its activities;
contact details.

Organisation type and purpose:
Registered charity (charity number 1034374).
Removes disabling barriers to music through
innovative approaches to teaching, learning and
making music. Focuses on nurturing musical and
creative ability through exploring music and
technology in imaginative ways. Enables access to
music making and connects disabled and non-
disabled musicians locally, nationally and
internationally.

Subject coverage:
The team works in areas surrounding London,
Bristol and Manchester, offering training in
disability equality for music, an introduction to
music technology and disability, accessible singing
and Soundbeam. It provides consultancy services
to universities, colleges, PGCE course providers,
venues, music studios and others who wish to
ensure their music facilities and resources are fully
accessible to disabled people. It works in
partnership with schools, universities, arts
organisations, local authorities, music services,
software developers as well as individual artists,
composers, musicians and music technologists to
deliver creative learning for schools, playschemes,
young people and adults.

Electronic and video publications:
Newsletter
Order electronic and video publications from:
Download from website

Access to staff:
Contact by letter, by telephone, by fax, by e-mail
and via website

Also at:
Drake Music North West
Zion Arts Centre, 335 Stretford Road, Hulme,
Manchester, M15 5ZA; tel: 0161 232 6079; e-mail:
gemmanash@drakemusicproject.org
Drake Music South West
C/o Claremont School, Henleaze Park, Westbury-
On-Trym, Bristol, BS9 4LR; tel: 0117 353 3614;
fax: 0117 942 6942 (please add: FAO Drake
Music); e-mail: annamacgregor@
drakemusicproject.org

DRAMA ASSOCIATION OF WALES

Acronym or abbreviation: DAW

The Old Library, Singleton Road, Splott, Cardiff,
CF24 2ET

Tel: 029 2045 2200
Fax: 029 2045 2277
E-mail: teresa@dramawales.org.uk

Website:
http://www.dramawales.org.uk

Enquiries:
Enquiries to: PR & Member Services Officer
Direct e-mail: teresa@dramawales.org.uk
Other contacts: Director; Administrator; North
Wales Development & Welsh Language Officer;
General Assistant

Founded:
1934

Organisation type and purpose:
National organisation, advisory body, membership
association (membership is by subscription),
present number of members: 460, voluntary
organisation, registered charity (charity number
502186), public library, training organisation,
publishing house.

Subject coverage:
Information on all aspects of amateur theatre,
including funding, training, supplies of costumes,
etc., festivals, lottery funding, international
activities and contacts.

Museum or gallery collection, archive, or library special collection:
Largest playscript lending library in the world
Part reference collection of former British Theatre Association (BTA)
Playsets of the former British Theatre Association (BTA) and Inner London Education Authority
Part collection BBC Research Library
Playsets collection of Kensington and Chelsea Libraries

Non-library collection catalogue:
All or part available online

Printed publications:
Dawn (newsletter, quarterly)
Catalogue of one-act and full-length scripts
Order printed publications from: Drama Association of Wales, The Old Library, Singleton Road, Splott, Cardiff, CF24 2ET

Publications list:
Available online and in print

Access to staff:
Contact by letter, by telephone, by fax, by e-mail, in person and via website
Hours: Mon, 1400 to 1630; Tue to Fri, 0900 to 1630

Links with:
CCAT
International Amateur Theatre Association (IATA)
National Association of Youth Theatres (NAYT)
Theatre Information Group (TIG)
Wales Association of the Performing Arts (WAPA)

DRAPERS' COMPANY

Formal name: Worshipful Company of Drapers

Drapers' Hall, Throgmorton Avenue, London, EC2N 2DQ

Tel: 020 7588 5001
Fax: 020 7628 1988
E-mail: mail@thedrapers.co.uk

Website:
http://www.thedrapers.co.uk

Organisation type and purpose:
Membership association (membership is by election or invitation).
City of London Livery Company.
To administer charitable trusts relating to relief of need, education and almshouses, to provide banqueting and catering services, and to foster its heritage and traditions of good fellowship.

Access to staff:
Contact by letter, by telephone, by fax, by e-mail and via website

DRAUGHT PROOFING ADVISORY ASSOCIATION LIMITED

Acronym or abbreviation: DPAA

PO Box 12, Haslemere, Surrey, GU27 3AH

Tel: 01428 654011
Fax: 01428 651401
E-mail: dpaaassociation@aol.com

Website:
http://www.dpaa-association.org.uk

Enquiries:
Enquiries to: Director

Founded:
1985

Organisation type and purpose:
Trade association (membership is by qualification).

Subject coverage:
Draught proofing.

Trade and statistical information:
Statistics on UK market for draught proofing.

Printed publications:
Advisory literature
Register of Members

Access to staff:
Contact by letter, by telephone, by fax, by e-mail and via website
Hours: Mon to Fri, 0900 to 1700

DRIVER AND VEHICLE AGENCY

Acronym or abbreviation: DVA

County Hall, Castlerock Road, Coleraine, BT51 3HS

Tel: 0845 601 4094; textphone 028 7034 1351
Fax: 028 7034 1422

Website:
http://www.dvani.gov.uk

Organisation type and purpose:
Executive Agency within the Department of the Environment (Northern Ireland Government).

Constituent bodies:
Driver and Vehicle and Licensing Northern Ireland (DVLNI)
County Hall, Castlerock Road, Coleraine, BT51 3TA; tel: 0845 402 4000; e-mail: dvlni@doeni.gov.uk; website: http://www.dvlni.gov.uk
Driver and Vehicle Testing Agency (DVTA)
County Hall, Castlerock Road, Coleraine, BT51 3HS; tel: 0845 601 4094; fax: 028 7034 1422; e-mail: dvta@doeni.gov.uk; website: http://www.dvtani.gov.uk

DRIVING INSTRUCTORS ASSOCIATION

Acronym or abbreviation: DIA

Safety House, Beddington Farm Road, Croydon, Surrey, CR0 4XZ

Tel: 020 8665 5151
Fax: 020 8665 5565
E-mail: dia@driving.org

Website:
http://www.driving.org

Enquiries:
Enquiries to: General Manager

Founded:
1978

Organisation type and purpose:
Trade association (membership is by subscription), present number of members: 10,000.

Subject coverage:
Nation-wide, looking after the interests of driving instructors and road safety educationalists.
Providing information, producing magazines and manuals, resource material towards raising standards of driver education, professional qualifications including Diploma in Driving Instruction and degree courses – BSc and BA (Driver Education) Masters and Doctorates. Mail order supplies and requisites – everything for driving schools and driving instructors.

Printed publications:
Driving Instructor Magazine (alternate months)
Driving Magazine (6 times a year)
Newsletter
Resource Material for Diploma in Driving Instruction (Dip.DI) Examinations

Access to staff:
Contact by letter, by telephone, by fax, by e-mail and in person
Hours: Mon to Fri, 0900 to 1700

Links with:
International Association of Driver Education (IVV)
tel: 020 8665 5151; fax: 020 8665 5565; e-mail: ivv@driving.org

DRIVING STANDARDS AGENCY

Acronym or abbreviation: DSA

Stanley House, 56 Talbot Street, Nottingham, NG1 5GU

Tel: 0115 901 2500
Fax: 0115 901 2940
E-mail: pressoffice@dsa.gsi.gov.uk

Website:
http://www.dsa.gov.uk

Enquiries:
Enquiries to: Customer Service Manager
Direct tel: 0115 901 2515/6
Direct fax: 0115 901 2510
Direct e-mail: customerservices@dsa.gov.uk

Founded:
1990

Organisation type and purpose:
National government body.
Government Executive Agency.
To promote road safety in Great Britain through the advancement of driving standards and by testing drivers, riders and driving instructors fairly and efficiently.

Subject coverage:
Driving standards, testing drivers, riders and driving instructors.

Trade and statistical information:
Data on pass and fail characteristics of the theory and practical driving tests.

Printed publications:
For publications see website www.dsa.gov.uk
Order printed publications from: Publications Unit, Driving Standards Agency
Paul Waller Avenue, Harrowden Lane, Cardington, Bedfordshire, MK14 3ST, tel: 01234 742297, fax: 01234 742581, e-mail: publications@dsa.gsi.gov.uk

Electronic and video publications:
For non-book media see website www.dsa.gov.uk

Publications list:
Available in print

Access to staff:
Contact by letter, by telephone, by fax, by e-mail and via website
Hours: Mon to Fri, 0800 to 1800

Access to building, collection or gallery:
Yes
Hours: Mon to Fri, 0800 to 1800

Access for disabled people:
Yes

Executive Agency of:
Department for Transport (DfT)

DRUGSCOPE

Prince Consort House, Suite 204, Second Floor, 109–111 Farringdon Road, London, EC1R 3BW

Tel: 020 7520 7550
Fax: 020 7520 7555
E-mail: info@drugscope.org.uk

Website:
http://www.drugscope.org.uk

Enquiries:
Enquiries to: Information Officer

Founded:
2000

Created by the merger of:
Institute for the Study of Drug Dependence (ISDD), Standing Conference on Drug Abuse (SCODA) (year of change 2000)

Organisation type and purpose:
Membership association (membership is by subscription), present number of members: 850, voluntary organisation, registered charity (charity number 255030), research organisation.
Centre of expertise on drugs.

continued overleaf

To inform policy development and reduce drug-related risk by providing quality drug information, promoting effective responses to drug taking, advising on policy-making and encouraging debate.

Subject coverage:
Drug misuse; besides illegal drugs, also covers over-the-counter medicines, alcohol, presription drugs, benzodiazepines, etc. Specialist advice on local drug services and best practice information on drug treatment and care, prevention and education.

Library catalogue:
All or part available online and in-house

Printed publications:
Publications aimed at young people, drug workers, teachers and other professionals, and various publications for those providing, purchasing, or commissioning drug services or working with drug users including:
Drug Problems: Where to Get Help
Drug Notes
Substance Misuse and Pregnancy
Druglink Guide to Drugs
What Drugs Look Like (poster)
Drugs Misuse (wallchart)

Electronic and video publications:
Drug encyclopedia (CD-ROM)

Publications list:
Available online and in print

Access to staff:
Contact by letter, by telephone, by fax, by e-mail and via website. Appointment necessary. All charged.
Hours: Mon to Fri, 0900 to 1700

Access to building, collection or gallery:
By appointment

Links with:
European Monitoring Centre for Drugs and Drug Addiction (EMCDDA)
United Nations Drug Control Programme (UNDCP)

Member organisation of:
European Association of Libraries and Information Services on Alcohol and Other Drugs (ELISAD)

DRY STONE WALLING ASSOCIATION OF GREAT BRITAIN

Acronym or abbreviation: DSWA

Lane Farm, Crooklands, Milnthorpe, Cumbria, LA7 7NH

Tel: 01539 567953
E-mail: information@dswa.org.uk

Website:
http://www.dswa.org.uk

Enquiries:
Enquiries to: Secretary

Founded:
1968

Organisation type and purpose:
Membership association (membership is by subscription), voluntary organisation, registered charity (charity number 289678), training organisation.
To further all aspects of the craft of dry stone walling.

Subject coverage:
All aspects of the craft of dry stone walling, craft training – formal and informal, skills assessment and certification scheme.

Museum or gallery collection, archive, or library special collection:
Small collection of printed material on the craft

Printed publications:
Register of Certificated Wallers and Dykers (free with sae)

Annual Report
Building and Repairing Dry Stone Walls (Tufnell R, £1.70))
Dry Stone Walling Techniques & Traditions (£9.75)
Dry Stone Walling (Rainsford Hannay F, £5.40)
Technical publications, specification leaflets and books including:
Waller and Dyker (newsletter, 3 times a year, for members)

Electronic and video publications:
Dry Stone Country (video, £15.99 plus £1.01 p&p)
How to Build & Repair Dry Stone Walls (video, £15 plus £1.50 p&p)
DVDs also available for above

Publications list:
Available online and in print

Access to staff:
Contact by letter, by e-mail and via website
Hours: Mon to Fri, 0900 to 1700

Branches:
19 branches throughout the United Kingdom (all honorary/volunteers)

Works closely with:
Conservation Bodies
Government Agencies

DSTL KNOWLEDGE AND INFORMATION SERVICES

Formal name: Defence Science and Technology Laboratory
Acronym or abbreviation: Dstl

Dstl Porton Down, Salisbury, Wiltshire, SP4 0JQ

Tel: 01980 613971
Fax: 01980 613328
E-mail: kisenquiries@dstl.gov.uk

Website:
http://www.dstl.gov.uk
KIS has own pages within Dstl site.

Founded:
2001

Organisation type and purpose:
National government body, research organisation.

Subject coverage:
Operational analysis, military policy, naval systems, general business and management, special operations, radar, electronic warfare, explosives, weapon technologies including pyrotechnics and obscurants research, countermeasures, detection, ordnance, forensics, electronic warfare, electronic detection technologies, operational research, military history, general military- and defence-related topics, biological sciences, chemistry, materials science, historical analysis incl. history of battles, WW1 and WW2, aeronautics and space, military aviation, psychology, physiology, mathematics, statistics, biological sciences, computing and other technology areas at undergraduate / postgraduate level including signal processing, radar, lasers, acoustics and management.

Museum or gallery collection, archive, or library special collection:
KIS has over 700,000 Scientific and Technical reports, which are not publicly available, comprising:
The output from UK government-funded defence R&D and Intelligence programmes since World War ll
Scientific, technical and intelligence reports from non-UK government defence R&D programmes over the same period
13,000 books and access to over 1,000 electronic journals

Non-library collection catalogue:
All or part available in-house

Library catalogue:
All or part available in-house

Printed publications:
Defence Reports Abstracts (monthly bulletin of reports added to stock)
DRIC Spec 1000 (standard for defence R&D reports)
Defence Technology Alerts (monthly SDI service)
Defence Newsletters

Electronic and video publications:
Defence Reports (CD-ROM)

Access to staff:
Contact by letter, by telephone, by fax, by e-mail and via website. Appointment necessary. All charged.
Hours: Mon to Thurs, 0900 to 1700, Fri 0900 to 1630

Access to building, collection or gallery:
Prior appointment required

Agency of:
Ministry of Defence (MOD)

DSTL KNOWLEDGE SERVICES – INFORMATION CENTRE

Formal name: Defence Science and Technology Laboratory
Acronym or abbreviation: Dstl

Porton Down, Salisbury, Wiltshire, SP4 0JQ

Tel: 01980 613000
Fax: 01980 613970
E-mail: knowledge-services@dstl.gov.uk

Website:
http://www.dstl.gov.uk
Website of Dstl. Knowledge Services has pages within site.

Enquiries:
Enquiries to: Team Leader
Direct tel: 01980 6134663
Direct e-mail: damey@dstl.gov.uk
Other contacts: Librarian

Formerly called:
Chemical and Biological Defence Establishment (CBDE), Chemical Defence Establishment (CDE), DERA, PLSD

Organisation type and purpose:
National government body, research organisation.

Subject coverage:
Chemical, physical and meteorological problems of defence against chemical agents; design and development of protective equipment, respirators and clothing; filters and filtration; physiological effects, toxicology and biochemistry of poisonous substances and the development of therapeutic and prophylactic procedures.

Library catalogue:
All or part available in-house

Access to staff:
Contact by letter, by telephone, by fax, by e-mail and via website. Appointment necessary.
Hours: Mon to Thu, 0900 to 1700; Fri, 0900 to 1630

Access to building, collection or gallery:
Prior appointment required

Agency of:
Ministry of Defence (MOD)

Head Office:
Dstl
Room G067 Building A2, Dstl Farnborough, Ively Road, Farnborough, GU14 0LX; tel: 01252 455838; fax: 01252 455959; e-mail: cdstewart@dstl.gov.uk
Head of Knowledge Services

DUDLEY ARCHIVES AND LOCAL HISTORY SERVICE

Acronym or abbreviation: DALHS

Mount Pleasant Street, Coseley, West Midlands, WV14 9JR

Tel: 01384 812770
E-mail: archives.centre@dudley.gov.uk

Website:
http://www.dudley.gov.uk/archives
Information relating to the services via Dudley Council's web pages; being expanded and upgraded, particularly for family history.

Enquiries:
Enquiries to: Archivist

Founded:
1947

Relocated from:
Dudley Library (year of change 1992)

Organisation type and purpose:
Local government body.

Subject coverage:
History of Dudley and the Black Country, in particular the area of the present Metropolitan Borough of Dudley.

Museum or gallery collection, archive, or library special collection:
Printed material re: Dudley and the Black Country and Archives – for details see entry in British Archives (Foster and Sheppard, 3rd edn)
The Dudley Estate Archive (the Earls of Dudley) 12th to 20th century

Non-library collection catalogue:
All or part available online and in-house

Library catalogue:
All or part available online and in-house

Printed publications:
Publication details online via website
Handlists of material, particularly for family historians
Publications relating to the history of the area – lists available

Microform publications:
Local newspapers, parish regsiters, census returns
IGI (microfiche)
GRO Indexes 1837–1960

Electronic and video publications:
Videos, DVDs, CDs, LPs, cassettes

Access to staff:
Contact by letter, by telephone, by e-mail, in person and via website
Hours: Mon: closed; Tue, Wed, Fri: 0900 to 1700; Thu: 0930 to 1900; 1st and 3rd Sat in month: 0930 to 1230
Closed for last full week of every month; see website for details
Special comments: CARN readers' tickets issued with two proofs of identity with name, address and signature; appointments advisable, particularly for microform material; appointments for Saturdays.

Access for disabled people:
Ramped entry, access to all public areas, toilet facilities
Special comments: On-site parking on level.

Parent body:
Dudley Metropolitan Borough Council

DUDLEY COLLEGE

The Broadway, Dudley, West Midlands, DY1 4AS

Tel: 01384 363000
Fax: 01384 363311

Website:
http://www.dudleycol.ac.uk

Enquiries:
Enquiries to: Library Co-ordinator
Direct tel: 01384 363353
Direct e-mail: library@dudleycol.ac.uk

Organisation type and purpose:
College of further and higher education.

Subject coverage:
Management; secretarial and office practice; work study; production control; construction; structural engineering; welding; brickwork; carpentry; joinery; electrical engineering; electronic

engineering; microcomputer technology; hairdressing; beauty therapy; mechanical engineering; production engineering; motor vehicle work, local history, science, humanities.

Non-library collection catalogue:
All or part available in-house

Library catalogue:
All or part available in-house

Access to staff:
Contact by letter, by telephone and by e-mail. Appointment necessary.
Hours: Term time: Mon to Thu, 0900 to 2000; Fri, 0900 to 1630
Vacations: Mon to Thu, 0900 to 1700; Fri, 0900 to 1630
Special comments: Reference facilities for non-students £5 per annum; borrowing facilities for non-students £25 per annum.

Access for disabled people:
Parking provided, level entry, toilet facilities, lift access from disabled parking to ground floor library

Subsidiary body:
International Glass Centre
tel: 01384 363067

DUDLEY PUBLIC LIBRARIES

Dudley Library, St James's Road, Dudley, West Midlands, DY1 1HR

Tel: 01384 815568 (library office)
Fax: 01384 815543
E-mail: dudley.library@dudley.gov.uk

Website:
http://www.dudley.gov.uk/libraries

Founded:
1909

Organisation type and purpose:
Local government body, public library.

Subject coverage:
Dudley and Black Country local studies.

Library catalogue:
All or part available online and in-house

Access to staff:
Contact by letter, by telephone, by fax, by e-mail, in person and via website
Hours: Mon, Wed, Thu, Fri, 0900 to 1900; Tue, 0930 to 1900;Sun, 1000 to 1400

Access for disabled people:
Disabled entrance, public lift

Branch libraries:
Brierley Hill
Coseley
Cradley
Gornal
Halesowen
Kingswinford
Long Lane
Lye
Netherton
Sedgley
Stourbridge
Wordsley

DUGDALE SOCIETY

Shakespeare Centre, Stratford-upon-Avon, Warwickshire, CV37 6QW

Tel: 01789 204016
E-mail: dugdale-society@hotmail.co.uk

Website:
http://www.shakespeare.org.uk/dugdale
Details of membership and publications list.

Enquiries:
Enquiries to: Secretary

Founded:
1920

Organisation type and purpose:
Learned society, membership association (membership is by subscription), present number of members: 350, registered charity (charity number 1051033).

Subject coverage:
Warwickshire: historical records, local history and topography.

Printed publications:
Leaflet detailing the publications of the Society
Occasional Papers based on Warwickshire records
Volumes of Records of Warwickshire

Publications list:
Available online and in print

Access to staff:
Contact by letter and by e-mail
Hours: Mon to Fri, 1000 to 1700

DUKE OF EDINBURGH'S AWARD, THE

Acronym or abbreviation: the Award

Gulliver House, Madeira Walk, Windsor, Berkshire, SL4 1EU

Tel: 01753 727400
Fax: 01753 810666
E-mail: info@theaward.org

Website:
http://www.theaward.org

Enquiries:
Enquiries to: Director
Other contacts: Communications Officer

Founded:
1956

Organisation type and purpose:
Registered charity (charity number 1072490). Voluntary programme of activities and service to others, leading to Awards which are open to all between the ages of 14 and 25; the Award Head Office is advised by national co-ordinating bodies concerned with individual activities.

Subject coverage:
Over 300 different activities from bee-keeping to ballet, first aid to farming, etc; the specialist advice and expertise of the assisting organisations is relied upon by the Award Office, especially in the field of expeditioning.

Printed publications:
Annual Report
Award Handbook
Award Journal (magazine, 3 times a year)
Expedition Guide

Access to staff:
Contact by letter, by telephone, by fax and by e-mail
Hours: Mon to Fri, 0900 to 1700

DUMFRIES AND GALLOWAY ARCHIVE CENTRE

33 Burns Street, Dumfries, DG1 2PS

Tel: 01387 269254
Fax: 01387 264126
E-mail: libs&i@dumgal.gov.uk

Website:
http://www.dumgal.gov.uk/lia

Enquiries:
Enquiries to: Resources Development
Other contacts: Research Officer tel no: 01387 253820 for genealogical research.

Founded:
1987

Organisation type and purpose:
Local government body. Record office.
Preservation of, and research using, local archives.

continued overleaf

Subject coverage:
Local and family history, civic, religious, economic and social history, architecture and genealogical studies.

Museum or gallery collection, archive, or library special collection:
Dumfries Burgh archives
Local Authority archives
Papers of local businesses, societies and families
Sanquhar Burgh archives
Stewart of Shambellie family papers
Walter Newall architectural drawings

Non-library collection catalogue:
All or part available online, in-house and in print

Printed publications:
The following publications are available for purchase:
Ancestor hunting in Dumfries Archive Centre
Court Records
Valuation, Taxation and Voting Records
Monumental Inscriptions
Census 1851 Parish Indexes
Various information sheets, source lists etc
Church records
Health records
Military records
Poor and Welfare records

Publications list:
Available in print

Access to staff:
Contact by letter, by telephone, by fax, by e-mail and in person. Appointment necessary.
Hours: Tue, Wed, Fri, 1100 to 1300 and 1400 to 1700; Thu, 1800 to 2100

Links with:
Ewart Library
Catherine Street, Dumfries, DG1 1JB; tel: 01387 253820; fax: 01387 260294; e-mail: alastairj@ dumgal.gov.uk

Parent body:
Libraries, Information and Archives Service, Dumfries and Galloway Council
tel: 01387 253820; fax: 01387 260294; e-mail: alastairj@dumgal.gov.uk

DUMFRIES AND GALLOWAY COLLEGE

Acronym or abbreviation: DAGCOL

Bankend Road, Dumfries, DG1 4FD

Tel: 01387 734000
Fax: 01387 734040
E-mail: info@dumgal.ac.uk

Website:
http://www.dumgal.ac.uk

Enquiries:
Enquiries to: Marketing Manager
Direct tel: 01387 734090
Direct e-mail: norriss@dumgal.ac.uk

Formerly called:
Dumfries and Galloway College of Technology

Organisation type and purpose:
Suitable for ages: 16+.
College of further and higher education.

Subject coverage:
Mechanical, electrical, electronic and motor vehicle engineering, construction and allied industries, safety, business studies, information technology, accounting, office management, art and design, computing, media/communications, hairdressing, catering, tourism, social care, education, sport.

Library catalogue:
All or part available in-house

Access to staff:
Contact by letter, by telephone, by e-mail and via website. Non-members charged.
Hours: Mon to Thu, 0830 to 1700; Fri, 0845 to 1630

Access for disabled people:
Parking provided, ramped entry, toilet facilities

Also at:
Stranraer Campus
Lewis Street, Stranraer; tel: 01776 706633; website: http://www.dumgal.ac.uk

DUMFRIES AND GALLOWAY COUNCIL

Council Offices, English Street, Dumfries, DG1 2DD

Tel: 01387 260000
Fax: 01387 260034

Website:
http://www.dumgal.gov.uk

Enquiries:
Enquiries to: Communications Manager
Direct tel: 01387 260330
Direct fax: 01387 260334
Direct e-mail: susanbl@dumgal.gov.uk

Founded:
1996

Formerly called:
Annandale and Eskdale District Council, Dumfries and Galloway Regional Council, Nithsdale District Council, Stewartry District Council, Wigtown District Council (year of change 1996)

Organisation type and purpose:
Local government body.

Subject coverage:
All information covering Dumfries and Galloway.

Printed publications:
Annual report
Children's services plan
Community care plan
Corporate plan
Local plans
Structure plan

Access to staff:
Contact by letter, by telephone, by fax, by e-mail, in person and via website
Hours: Mon to Fri, 0900 to 1700

Access for disabled people:
Ramped entry, access to all public areas

DUMFRIES AND GALLOWAY FAMILY HISTORY SOCIETY

Acronym or abbreviation: D&GFHS

Family History Centre, 9 Glasgow Street, Dumfries, DG2 9AF

Tel: 01387 248093
E-mail: publications@dgfhs.org.uk

Website:
http://www.safhs.org.uk
All Family History Societies in the Scottish Association of Family History Societies.
http://www.dgfhs.org.uk
History and current details about the Society including membership details, publications list and order form.
http://homepages.rootsweb.com/~scottish/

Enquiries:
Enquiries to: Honorary Secretary

Founded:
1987

Organisation type and purpose:
Learned society (membership is by subscription), present number of members: 1700, voluntary organisation, registered charity (charity number SC 020596), research organisation, publishing house.
Family history research.

Subject coverage:
Genealogy, family history, local history, especially pertaining to Dumfriesshire, Kircudbrightshire and Wigtownshire.

Museum or gallery collection, archive, or library special collection:
Wigtown Free Press newspaper indexes 1850–1920 and all these newspapers on fiche
Bank of family trees
Books, documents, manuscripts
Dumfries newspapers' indexes 1777–1930
OPRs, IGI and 1841–1901 Census records (film)

Printed publications:
Newsletter (members)
Dumfries and Galloway: some sources for local and family history
Irregular Marriages – Annan, Dumfriesshire 1797– 1854
Irregular Marriages – Portpatrick, Wigtownshire 1759–1826
Census 1851 surname index
Census 1841 surname index
Glenluce Old and New Luce Kirkyards Memorial Transcriptions
Portpatrick Kirkyard Memorial Transcriptions
A Scots Agricultural Glossary: Adam Gray
Stranraer Mls Vol 1 (Bridge, Thistle & Dalrymple St & Ivy Place Burial Grounds)
Stranraer Mls Vol 2 (Sheuchan Cemetry Section 1- Original)
Stranraer Mls Vol 3 (Sheuchan Cemetry Extension & War Memorial)
Stoneykirk & Kirkmadrine Mls
Parish of Balmaclellan – 1792 Census
Looking back on Dalbeattie Granite Industry
Clock and Watchmakers of SW Scotland 1576–1900
1841 Census Record indexed by surname for Wigtownshire, Kirkcudbrightshire and Dumfriesshire
Many publications on local history

Electronic and video publications:
Digital Tours of Dumfries & Galloway (Millennium edition)(CD-ROM, 560 Mb)(6000 images created by Sandy Pittendreigh for D&GFHS)

Publications list:
Available online and in print

Access to staff:
Contact by letter, by telephone, by e-mail, in person and via website. Non-members charged.
Hours: Tue to Fri; Apr to Oct, 1000 to 1600; Nov to Mar 1100 to 1500; Sat, 1000 to 1300

Access to building, collection or gallery:
No prior appointment required

Access for disabled people:
Level entry

DUMFRIES AND GALLOWAY LIBRARIES, INFORMATION AND ARCHIVES

Ewart Library, Catherine Street, Dumfries, DG1 1JB

Tel: 01387 253820
Fax: 01387 260294
E-mail: libs&i@dumgal.gov.uk

Website:
http://www.dumgal.gov.uk/lia
Homepage of the main library website

Enquiries:
Enquiries to: Cultural Services, Libraries Information & Archives Manager
Other contacts: Reference Librarian

Founded:
1903

Formerly called:
Dumfries and Galloway Libraries (year of change 1995)

Organisation type and purpose:
Local government body, public library.

Subject coverage:
General, local studies of Dumfries and Galloway region; civic, religious, genealogy, architecture, economic and social history; Lockerbie Air Disaster at Ewart.

Museum or gallery collection, archive, or library special collection:
Burns Club Collection (at Archive Centre)
Local Authority Archives
Local Studies Collection
Lockerbie Air Disaster Archive
Lord Glendyne Collection
R C Reid Manuscripts (at Ewart)

Non-library collection catalogue:
All or part available online and in-house

Library catalogue:
All or part available online and in-house

Printed publications:
A Historic Walk Through Lockerbie (£2.95)
Dumfries and Galloway Through the Lens series: books old photographs of local scenes (30 books, £2.50 each)
Pigot and Slater: Dumfries and Galloway 19th Century Trade Directories (£12.50)
Robert Burns: Reflections of an Age (£7.99)
Sang 0 the Nith: poetic journey through Burns' Country as seen through the eyes of three generations of Dumfries poets (compiled by Clark J, £25)
With Both Feet off the Ground: Contemporary poetry and prose from Dumfries and Galloway (£4.95)
Posters and maps
Order printed publications from: http://www.dumgal.gov.uk/lia

Publications list:
Available online and in print

Access to staff:
Contact by letter, by telephone, by fax, by e-mail, in person and via website
Hours: Ewart: Mon, to Wed, Fri, 0900 to 1930; Thu, Sat, 0900 to 1700

Access for disabled people:
Parking provided, ramped entry, access to all public areas, toilet facilities

Branches at:
Annan Library
Charles Street, Annan, DG12 5AG; tel: 01461 202809; fax: 01461 20280901461 202809
Castle Douglas Library
King Street, Castle Douglas, DG7 1AE; tel: 01556 502643; fax: 01556 502643
Dalbeattie Library
High Street, Dalbeattie Library, DG5 4AD; tel: 01556 610898; fax: 01556 610898
Dalry Library
Dalry, Castle Douglas, DG7 3UP; tel: 01644 430234; fax: 01644 430234
Dumfries and Galloway Archives
Archive Centre, 33 Burns Street, Dumfries, DG1 2PS; tel: 01387 269254; fax: 01387 264126
Eastriggs Library
Eastriggs Community School, Eastriggs, Annan, DG12 6PZ; tel: 01461 40844; fax: 01461 40844
Gatehouse Library
63 High Street, Gatehouse of Fleet, DG7 2HS; tel: 01557 814646; fax: 01557 814646
Georgetown Library
Gillbrae Road, Dumfries, DG1 4EJ; tel: 01387 256059; fax: 01387 256059
Gretna Library
Richard Greenhow Centre, Central Avenue, Gretna, DG16 5AQ; tel: 01461 338000; fax: 01461 338000
Kirkconnel Library
Greystone Avenue, Kelloholm, DG4 6RA; tel: 01659 67191; fax: 01659 67191
Kirkcudbright Library
Sheriff Court House, Kirkcudbright, DG6 4JW; tel: 01557 331240; fax: 01557 331240
Langholm Library
Charles Street Old, Langholm, DG13 0AA; tel: 01387 380040; fax: 01387 380040
Lochmaben Library
High Street, Lochmaben, Lockerbie, DG11 1NQ; tel: 01387 811865; fax: 01387 811865
Lochside Library
Lochside Road, Dumfries, DG2 0LW; tel: 01387 268751; fax: 01387 268751
Lochthorn Library
Lochthorn, Dumfries, DG1 1UF; tel: 01387 265780; fax: 01387 266424
Lockerbie Library
31–33 High Street, Lockerbie, DG11 2JL; tel: 01576 203380; fax: 01576 203380
Moffat Library
Town Hall, High Street, Moffat, DG10 9HF; tel: 01683 220952; fax: 01683 220952
Newton Stewart Library
Church Street, Newton Stewart, DG8 6ER; tel: 01671 403450; fax: 01671 403450
Port William Library
Church Street, Port William, Newton Stewart, DG8 9QL; tel: 01988 700406; fax: 01988 700406
Sanquhar Library
106 High Street, Sanquhar, DG4 6DZ; tel: 01659 50626; fax: 01659 50626
Stranraer Library
North Strand Street, Stranraer, DG9 7LD; tel: 01776 707400; fax: 01776 703565
Thornhill Library
Townhead Street, Thornhill, DG3 5NW; tel: 01848 330654; fax: 01848 330654
Whithorn Library
St John Street, Whithorn, DG8 8PF; tel: 01988 500406; fax: 01988 500406
Wigtown Library
Wigtown County Buildings, Wigtown, DG8 9JH; tel: 01988 403329; fax: 01988 403329

DUNDEE AND TAYSIDE CHAMBER OF COMMERCE AND INDUSTRY

Chamber of Commerce Buildings, Panmure Street, Dundee, DD1 1ED

Tel: 01382 228545
Fax: 01382 228441
E-mail: admin@dundeechamber.co.uk

Website:
http://www.dundeechamber.co.uk
Membership and service information; publications; news and legislation briefings; electronic business park.

Enquiries:
Enquiries to: Communications Manager
Direct e-mail: juliechristie@dundeechamber.co.uk

Organisation type and purpose:
Advisory body, trade association (membership is by subscription).
To represent the business interests of companies in Tayside.

Subject coverage:
Business services.

Printed publications:
Business Directory, directory and buyers guide (250pp, annually, c. 1800, £7.50)
The Business (16pp, newspaper, 6 times a year, c. 6000 free to subscribers)

Publications list:
Available online and in print

Access to staff:
Contact by letter, by telephone, by fax, by e-mail, in person and via website
Hours: Mon to Fri, 0900 to 1700

Access to building, collection or gallery:
No prior appointment required

Access for disabled people:
Access to all public areas

DUNDEE CITY ARCHIVES

Formal name: Archive Centre of Dundee City Council

21 City Square, Dundee, DD1 3BY

Tel: 01382 434494
Fax: 01382 434666
E-mail: archives@dundeecity.gov.uk

Website:
http://www.dundeecity.gov.uk/archive
Brief list of holdings.
http://www.fdca.org.uk
Resources produced by volunteers.

Enquiries:
Enquiries to: City Archivist

Founded:
1191

Formerly called:
Burgh of Dundee (year of change 1894); City of Dundee District Council (year of change 1996)

Please select:
County of City of Dundee (Dundee Corporation) (year of change 1975)

Organisation type and purpose:
Local government body.

Subject coverage:
Local history from the formation of the Burgh of Dundee in 1191, shipbuilding, Port of Dundee, Customs and Excise, Presbytery records.

Non-library collection catalogue:
All or part available in-house

Printed publications:
Robert Fleming [1845–1892] and the Dundee Merchants (George A. Stout, 1999, £4.95)
Wesleyan Register of Baptisms, Dundee 1785–1898 (Grace Mann and J. G. L. Wright, 2000, £4.95)
The Kirks of Dundee Presbytery 1558–1999 (Ian McCraw, 2000, £9.99)
Dundee Motor Registrations TS1–TS1000 (J. G. L. Wright (ed.), 2003, £4.95)
Caledon Ships (David Middleton, 2008, £9.99)
Order printed publications from: Honorary Sales Secretary, Friends of Dundee City Archive (at same address)

Access to staff:
Contact by letter, by telephone, by fax and by e-mail. Appointment necessary.
Hours: Mon to Fri, 0915 to 1300 and 1400 to 1645

Access to building, collection or gallery:
Report to City Square Reception, 18 City Square
Hours: Mon to Fri, 0915 to 1300 and 1400 to 1645; for local holidays check council website A–Z
Special comments: Visitors will be escorted to City Archives from 18 City Square.

Access for disabled people:
No lift available to Archives; special arrangements can be made to consult records elsewhere for those with difficulty walking

Links with:
Friends of Dundee City Archives
c/o Dundee City Archives; website: http://www.fdca.org.uk

DUNDEE CITY COUNCIL – ARTS & HERITAGE

The McManus: Dundee's Art Gallery & Museum, Albert Square, Meadowside, Dundee, DD1 1DA

Tel: 01382 307200
Fax: 01382 307207
E-mail: themcmanus@dundeecity.gov.uk

Website:
http://www.themcmanus-dundee.gov.uk
http://www.dundeecity.gov.uk

Enquiries:
Enquiries to: Arts & Heritage Manager
Direct tel: 01382 307210
Direct e-mail: john.stewart-young@dundeecity.gov.uk

Founded:
1867

Formerly called:
Dundee Art Galleries & Museums (year of change 1994); Arts & Heritage Dept (year of change 2002); Leisure & Arts Dept (year of change 2006); Leisure & Communities Dept (year of change 2008)

continued overleaf

Organisation type and purpose:
Local government body, museum, art gallery.
Heritage facilities.

Subject coverage:
Tayside and North Fife region: archaeology,
including sites research, history, natural sciences
and environmental studies; museum education
services; fine and applied art; Egyptology;
astronomy; numismatics; field archaeology.

**Museum or gallery collection, archive, or library
special collection:**
Recognised collections of fine and decorative art
and whaling

Non-library collection catalogue:
All or part available online

Printed publications:
Ale and A'thing: the Grocer and Licensed Trade in
Dundee
Art Catalogue
Fishing for the Whale
Local history books
Studies in Archaeology

Access to staff:
Contact by letter, by telephone, by fax, by e-mail,
in person and via website
Hours: Mon to Fri, 0900 to 1700

Access to building, collection or gallery:
Hours: Mon to Sat 1000 to 1700; Sun 1230 to 1600

Access for disabled people:
Level access to both entrances to the building; full
wheelchair access to all public areas and a lift to all
floors; room thresholds have lighting to assist
visitors with partial sight; larger text sizes and
colour coding on displays; guide dogs, hearing
dogs and other recognised assistance dogs are
admitted; accessible toilets incorporating adult
changing are available in the main toilet suite

Branch museums:
Broughty Castle Museum
　Castle Approach, Broughty Ferry, Dundee, DD5
　2TF; tel: 01382 436916; fax: 01382 436951; e-mail:
　broughty@dundeecity.gov.uk; website: http://
　www.dundeecity.gov.uk/broughtycastle
Mills Observatory
　Glamis Road, Balgay Park, Dundee, DD2 2UB;
　tel: 01382 435967; fax: 01382 435962; e-mail: mills
　.observatory@dundeecity.gov.uk; website: http://
　www.dundeecity.gov.uk/mills

DUNDEE CITY COUNCIL LIBRARIES

Leisure and Communites Department, Central
Library, The Wellgate, Dundee, DD1 1DB

Tel: 01382 431500
Fax: 01382 431558
E-mail: central.library@dundeecity.gov.uk

Website:
http://www.dundeecity.gov.uk/library
http://opac.dundeecity.gov.uk/cgi-bin/spydus.exe/
MSGTRN/OPAC/HOME
Library catalogue.
http://www.wighton.com
Wighton database of Scottish national music.
http://www.dundeecity.gov.uk/photodb
Photopolis – database of old Dundee photographs.

Enquiries:
Enquiries to: Head of Libraries, Information &
Cultural Services
Direct tel: 01382 307462
Direct fax: 01382 307487
Direct e-mail: moira.methven@dundeecity.gov.uk
Other contacts: Manager, Central Library

Founded:
1869

Organisation type and purpose:
Local government body, public library.

Subject coverage:
General, business information, ethnic minority
languages, local history, genealogy, art, music,
architecture, patents, Scottish literature, open
learning materials, Scottish Parliament, European
information and early Scottish music.

**Museum or gallery collection, archive, or library
special collection:**
Antiquarian Collection
British Standards
Cynicus Collection (early 20th century cartoons)
Dundee Photographic Survey 1916
Dundee Photographic Survey 1991
Lamb Collection (local history ephemera including
　posters, news cuttings, pamphlets, etc.)
Ower Collection (architecture)
Sir James Ivory Collection (early mathematical and
　scientific works)
Sturrock Collection (fine printing and binding;
　private press books)
Whaling Logbooks
Wighton Collection (1,200 volumes of early music
　of UK, particularly Scottish; some unique items)
William McGonagall Collection
Wilson Collection (turn-of-the-century
　photographs, mainly of Dundee)

Trade and statistical information:
The Central Library has a collection of government
and inter-governmental publications.

Non-library collection catalogue:
All or part available online

Library catalogue:
All or part available online

Electronic and video publications:
Directory of Organisations

Access to staff:
Contact by letter, by telephone, by fax, by e-mail,
in person and via website
Hours: Central Library: Mon, Tue, Thu, Fri, 0900 to
2000; Wed, 1000 to 2000; Sat, 0930 to 1700
Opening times of neighbourhood libraries vary

Access for disabled people:
Parking provided, ramped entry, level entry, access
to all public areas, toilet facilities

Branch libraries:
Ardler Complex
　Turnberry Avenue, Dundee, DD3 3TP; tel: 01382
　432863; fax: 01382 432862; e-mail: ardler.library@
　dundeecity.gov.uk
Arthurstone Community Library
　Arthurstone Terrace, Dundee, DD4 6RT; tel:
　01382 438881; fax: 01382 438886; e-mail:
　arthurstone.library@dundeecity.gov.uk
Blackness Community Library
　225 Perth Road, Dundee, DD2 1EJ; tel: 01382
　435936; fax: 01382 435942; e-mail: blackness
　.library@dundeecity.gov.uk
Broughty Ferry Community Library
　Queen Street, Broughty Ferry, Dundee, DD5
　2HN; tel: 01382 436919; fax: 01382 436913; e-
　mail: broughty.library@dundeecity.gov.uk
Charleston Community Centre and Library
　60 Craigowan Road, Dundee, DD2 4NL; tel:
　01382 436639; fax: 01382 436640; e-mail:
　charleston.library@dundeecity.gov.uk
Coldside Community Library
　150 Strathmartine Road, Dundee, DD3 7SE; tel:
　01382 432849; fax: 01382 432850; e-mail: coldside
　.library@dundeecity.gov.uk
Douglas Community and Library Centre
　Balmoral Avenue, Dundee, DD4 8SD; tel: 01382
　436944; fax: 01382 436922; e-mail: douglas
　.library@dundeecity.gov.uk
Fintry Community Library
　Findcastle Street, Dundee, DD4 9EW; tel: 01382
　432560; fax: 01382 432559; e-mail: fintry.library@
　dundeecity.gov.uk
Hub Community Centre and Library
　Pitkerro Road, Dundee, DD4 8ES; tel: 01382
　438648; fax: 01382 438627; e-mail: hub.library@
　dundeecity.gov.uk

Kirkton Community Centre and Library
　Derwent Avenue, Dundee, DD3 0BW; tel: 01382
　432851; fax: 01382 436321; e-mail: kirkton
　.library@dundeecity.gov.uk
Lochee Community Library
　High Street, Lochee, Dundee, DD2 3AU; tel:
　01382 431835; fax: 01382 431837; e-mail: lochee
　.library@dundeecity.gov.uk
Menzieshill Community Centre and Library
　Orleans Place, Dundee, DD2 4BH; tel: 01382
　432945; fax: 01382 432968; e-mail: menzieshill
　.library@dundeecity.gov.uk
Whitfield Library and Learning Centre
　Whitfield Drive, Dundee, DD4 0DX; tel: 01382
　432561; fax: 01382 432562; e-mail: whitfield
　.library@dundeecity.gov.uk

Parent body:
Dundee City Council
　City Chambers, Dundee, DD1 3BY; tel: 01382
　434000; fax: 01382 434666; e-mail: helpline@
　dundeecity.gov.uk

DUNDEE HERITAGE TRUST

Verdant Works, West Henderson's Wynd, Dundee,
DD1 5BT

Tel: 01382 226659
Fax: 01382 225891
E-mail: info@dundeeheritage.co.uk

Website:
http://www.rrrdiscovery.com
Content of the museum exhibitions, opening hours
and prices, etc., education services, special events,
historical information.

Enquiries:
Enquiries to: Museums Officer

Founded:
1985

Organisation type and purpose:
Registered charity (charity number SC 002268).
Museum.

Subject coverage:
Dundee's industrial history, specifically textiles
(linen and jute). Textile engineering and mill
architecture. RRS Discovery, polar exploration,
Captain Scott and ship restoration and
conservation.

**Museum or gallery collection, archive, or library
special collection:**
Archives (not business archives), photographs and
　objects relating to Dundee textile industries,
　especially linen and jute
Archival photographs and objects relating to RRS
　Discovery and 1901–04 British National
　Antarctic Expedition under Captain Scott

Printed publications:
The Story of the Discovery (£2.50 plus p&p)
Verdant Works – The Story of Dundee and Jute
　(£2.50 plus p&p)
Order printed publications from: Shop Manager,
Dundee Industrial Heritage Ltd
Discovery Point, Discovery Quay, Dundee, DD1
4XA, tel: 01382 309060, fax: 01382 225891, e-mail:
info@dundeeheritage.co.uk

Access to staff:
Contact by letter, by telephone, by fax and by e-
mail. Appointment necessary.
Hours: Mon to Fri, 0900 to 1700

Access to building, collection or gallery:
No access other than to staff
Hours: Verdant Works: April to October, Mon and
Sat 1000 to 1800, Sun 1100 to 1800; November to
March, Wed and Sat 1030 to 1630, Sun 1100 to
1630. Closed Mon and Tue from November to
March. Closed 25 and 26 December and 1 and 2
January. Last admission is 1 hour prior to closing

Also at:
Discovery Point
　Discovery Quay, Dundee, DD1 5BT; tel: 01382
　309060; fax: 01382 225891; e-mail: info@
　dundeeheritage.co.uk

DUNFERMLINE CARNEGIE LIBRARY

Formal name: Fife Council Libraries & Museums

Dunfermline Carnegie Library, Abbot Street, Dunfermline, Fife, KY12 7NL

Tel: 01383 312600
Fax: 01383 312608
E-mail: dunfermline.library@fife.gov.uk

Enquiries:
Enquiries to: Librarian
Direct tel: 01383 312602
Direct e-mail: libraries.museums@fife.gov.uk

Founded:
1883

Formerly called:
Dunfermline District Libraries; Fife Council Libraries (year of change 2008)

Organisation type and purpose:
Local government body, public library.

Subject coverage:
General, local history.

Museum or gallery collection, archive, or library special collection:
Andrew Carnegie Collection
George Reid Collection (medieval manuscripts and early printed books)
Local History Collection of books, maps, photographs, slides
Murison Burns Collection (works of Robert Burns, contains no manuscripts)

Non-library collection catalogue:
All or part available online and in-house

Library catalogue:
All or part available online and in-house

Printed publications:
Local History Publications
Murison Burns Catalogue
Various minor local interest pamphlets (e.g. Witchcraft in Dunfermline)

Electronic and video publications:
Audiobooks

Publications list:
Available in print

Access to staff:
Contact by letter and by e-mail

Access for disabled people:
Parking provided, level entry, access to all public areas, toilet facilities

Parent body:
Fife Council, Housing & Communitites
Fife House, North Street, Glenrothes; website: http://www.fife.gov.uk

DURHAM CATHEDRAL LIBRARY

The College, Durham, DH1 3EH

Tel: 0191 386 2489
Fax: 0191 386 4267 (Chapter Office)
E-mail: library@durhamcathedral.co.uk

Website:
http://www.durhamcathedral.co.uk/library

Enquiries:
Enquiries to: Librarian

Founded:
995

Organisation type and purpose:
Cathedral library.

Subject coverage:
Durham Cathedral; manuscripts and early printed books; Durham local history; pre-1800 sacred and secular music; monasticism; Saxon and medieval monastic manuscripts.

Museum or gallery collection, archive, or library special collection:
Antiquarian mss collections: Allan, Hunter, Longstaffe, Randall, Raine, Sharp
Churchmen's papers: Henson, I.T. Ramsey, J.B. Lightfoot
Music MS part books for organ and choir
Collection of over 12,000 17th- and 18th-century printed theses, mainly from German Universities
Falle Collection of 17th- and 18th-century printed music
Pre-Conquest and medieval books of the monastic house of Durham (manuscripts, c. 300 vols)

Non-library collection catalogue:
All or part available online, in-house and in print

Library catalogue:
All or part available online, in-house and in print

Printed publications:
Guide for readers leaflet

Microform publications:
Microfilms of all medieval manuscripts and of much manuscript and printed early music available

Access to staff:
Contact by letter, by telephone, by e-mail, in person and via website. Appointment necessary. Letter of introduction required.
Hours: Mon to Fri, 0900 to 1300 and 1400 to 1700
Special comments: Closed for first two weeks of July; letter of introduction sometimes required.

Parent body:
Durham Cathedral
The College, Durham, DH1 3EH; tel: 0191 386 4266; fax: 0191 386 4267; e-mail: enquiries@ durhamcathedral.co.uk; website: http://www .durhamcathedral.co.uk

DURHAM COUNTY LOCAL HISTORY SOCIETY

Acronym or abbreviation: DCLHS

St Mary's Grove, Tudhoe, Spennymoor, DL16 6LR

Tel: 01388 816209
E-mail: johnbanham@tiscali.co.uk

Website:
http://www.durhamweb.org.uk/dclhs

Enquiries:
Enquiries to: Secretary

Founded:
1963

Organisation type and purpose:
Learned society, publishing house.

Subject coverage:
Durham, local history, mainly 15th century to present day.

Printed publications:
Journal (twice a year)
Newsletter (quarterly)
Occasional papers (irregular)

Publications list:
Available online

Access to staff:
Contact by letter and by e-mail
Hours: Mon to Fri, 0900 to 1700

DURHAM COUNTY RECORD OFFICE

Acronym or abbreviation: DCRO

County Hall, Durham, DH1 5UL

Tel: 0191 383 3253
Fax: 0191 383 3474
E-mail: record.office@durham.gov.uk

Website:
http://www.durhamrecordoffice.org.uk

Database of all catalogues, information concerning services provided, detailed lists of parish records and indexes, educational resources.

Enquiries:
Enquiries to: County Archivist
Direct tel: 0191 383 4211

Founded:
1961

Organisation type and purpose:
Local government body.
Record office.

Subject coverage:
Archives and records of the County of Durham.

Museum or gallery collection, archive, or library special collection:
Archives and records of the County of Durham
All catalogues of these records are held in a database

Non-library collection catalogue:
All or part available online

Printed publications:
Durham Family History Gazetteer (1996)
Durham Places in the Mid-Nineteenth Century (1996)
Map of parish and chapelry boundaries c. 1800 (1983)
Streatlam and Gibside: The Bowes and Strathmore Families in County Durham (1984)
The Londonderry Papers: Catalogue of documents (1996)
Cemeteries in County Durham
Image of the Soldier
Durham Collieries
Reprints of various historic maps of County
Handlists, subject guides and user guides

Publications list:
Available online and in print

Access to staff:
Contact by letter, by telephone, by fax, by e-mail, in person and via website. Appointment necessary.
Hours: Mon, Tue, Thu, 0845 to 1645; Wed, 0845 to 2000
Special comments: Fri, Sat, Sun and bank holidays closed.

Access to building, collection or gallery:
Prior appointment required

Access for disabled people:
Parking provided, ramped entry, access to all public areas, toilet facilities

DURHAM HISTORICAL ENTERPRISES

3 Briardene, Margery Lane, Durham, DH1 4QU

Tel: 0191 386 1500
E-mail: dhent@dhent.fsnet.co.uk

Website:
http://www.dhent.fsnet.co.uk

Enquiries:
Enquiries to: Proprietor

Founded:
1991

Organisation type and purpose:
Consultancy, research organisation, publishing house.

Subject coverage:
Durham local history, Durham family histories.

Printed publications:
Durham City 1851 Census

Access to staff:
Contact by letter, by telephone and by e-mail
Hours: Mon to Fri, 0900 to 1700

DURHAM LEARNING RESOURCES

Acronym or abbreviation: DLR

continued overleaf

Libraries, Learning and Culture, Adult and Community Services, Sevenhills, Unit 1, Greenhills Industrial Estate, Spennymoor, Co Durham, DL16 6JB

Tel: 0191 370 6220
Fax: 01388 817099
E-mail: dlr@durham.gov.uk

Website:
http://www.durham.gov.uk/dlr

Enquiries:
Enquiries to: Manager
Direct e-mail: patricia.brown@durham.gov.uk

Founded:
1991

Organisation type and purpose:
Local government body, public library.
To support reading and learning in schools by providing: a multimedia loans service to schools in support of the National Curriculum; advice and courses on schools resource centres and learning using books and other resources; books for sale to schools.

Subject coverage:
Information and advice in school resource centre management; information and training on study and library skills; knowledge of loans of museum objects, books, art and other media in support of the National Curriculum; sales of books to schools.

Non-library collection catalogue:
All or part available online

Access to staff:
Contact by letter, by telephone, by fax, by e-mail, in person and via website. Appointment necessary.
Hours: Mon to Thu, 0830 to 1700; Fri, 0830 to 1630

Access for disabled people:
Parking provided

DURHAM UNIVERSITY

Formal name: University of Durham

Mountjoy Research Centre, Stockton Road, Durham, DH1 3UR

Tel: 0191 334 4649
Fax: 0191 334 4634

Enquiries:
Enquiries to: Busienss Relations Manager
Direct e-mail: jonathon.lee@durham.ac.uk

Founded:
1832

Organisation type and purpose:
University department or institute, consultancy, research organisation.

Subject coverage:
All academic departments, particularly, mathematics / statistics; chemistry; physics; geological sciences; computing; business development; economics and finance; engineering; manufacturing, environment. Particular expertise includes photonics, nanotechnology, materials, nuclear magnetic resonance, electronics.

Library catalogue:
All or part available online

DURHAM WILDLIFE TRUST

Bowlees Visitor Centre, Bowlees, Middleton in Teesdale, Co Durham, DL12 0XE

Tel: 01833 622292
Fax: 01833 622292
E-mail: durhamwt@cix.co.uk

Website:
http://www.wildlifetrust.org.uk/durham

Enquiries:
Enquiries to: Manager
Other contacts: Education Officer (tel: 0191 548 0152)

Founded:
1975

Formerly called:
Durham County Conservation Trust

Organisation type and purpose:
National organisation, membership association (membership is by subscription), service industry, voluntary organisation, registered charity (charity number 501038), suitable for ages: all.
Visitor Centre.
To highlight the natural history of Teesdale.

Subject coverage:
Wildlife and conservation in Teesdale and tourist information leaflets.

Museum or gallery collection, archive, or library special collection:
The Fitzhugh Library, previously held here, is now housed at Witham Hall in Barnard Castle

Printed publications:
The Natural History of Upper Teesdale
Durham Wildlife Trust Reserves Guide
Magical Meadows

Publications list:
Available online and in print

Access to staff:
Contact by letter, by telephone, by fax, by e-mail, in person and via website
Hours: 1 Apr to 31 Oct: daily, 1030 to 1730
Special comments: Other times by prior appointment.

Access to building, collection or gallery:
By prior appointment
Hours: Daily, 1030 to 1700

Access for disabled people:
Parking provided, ramped entry, level entry, access to all public areas
Hours: As above
Special comments: Toilet facilities in main car park.

For membership details:
Rainton Meadows Site
  tel: 0191 584 3112; fax: 0191 584 3934; e-mail: durhamwt@cix.compulink.co.uk

Head Office and Visitor Centre:
Durham Wildlife Trust
  Rainton Meadows, Chilton Moor, Houghton-le-Spring, Tyne & Wear, DH4 6PU; tel: 0191 584 3112; fax: 0191 584 3934; e-mail: durhamwt@cix .compulink.co.uk

Visitor Centre at:
Low Barns
  Witton-le-Wear, Bishop Auckland, Co Durham, DL14 0AG; tel: 01388 488728; fax: 01388 488529

DVORAK SOCIETY

Formal name: The Dvorak Society for Czech and Slovak Music

The Secretary, 13 Church Lane, Knutton, Newcastle-under-Lyme, Staffordshire, ST5 6DU

Tel: 01782 631274
E-mail: secretary@dvorak-society.org

Website:
http://www.dvorak-society.org

Enquiries:
Enquiries to: Membership Secretary
Direct tel: 01904 642407
Direct e-mail: membership@dvorak-society.org

Founded:
1974

Formerly called:
Dvorák Society of Great Britain (year of change 1986)

Organisation type and purpose:
Learned society (membership is by subscription, election or invitation), present number of members: 582, registered charity (charity number 267336), suitable for all ages.
The promotion of Czech and Slovak music.

Subject coverage:
History of Czech and Slovak music composers and musicians; contemporary Czech and Slovak music. Concert promotion, record reviews and regular listings of available recordings of Czech and Slovak music.

Museum or gallery collection, archive, or library special collection:
All collections are held c/o The Dvorak Society Library, Cardiff School of Music, Corbett Road, Cardiff, CF10 3ED
John Clapham Collection
Recorded Music Library
Tausky Collection
Melville-Mason Collection
Belohlavek Collection
Dvorak Society Archive

Non-library collection catalogue:
All or part available in-house

Library catalogue:
All or part available in-house

Printed publications:
Czech Music (journal, 2 times a year)
Newsletter (quarterly, members)
Yearbook and Directory
Occasional series of specialist publications

Access to staff:
Contact by letter, by telephone, by e-mail and via website
Hours: Mon to Fri, 0900 to 1700

Access to building, collection or gallery:
No access other than to staff
Special comments: Members only.

Links with:
British Czech and Slovak Association

DYLAN THOMAS SOCIETY OF GREAT BRITAIN, THE

Fernhill, 124 Chapel Street, Mumbles, Swansea, West Glamorgan, SA3 4NH

Tel: 01792 363875

Enquiries:
Enquiries to: Chair

Founded:
1977

Organisation type and purpose:
Learned society (membership is by subscription).

Subject coverage:
Life and works of Dylan Thomas.

Non-library collection catalogue:
All or part available in-house

Printed publications:
Dylan Thomas Remembered
The World I Breathe (talks and lectures to the Society)
The World Winding Home (essays)
I Sang in My Chains (essays and poems commemorating the 50th anniversary of Dylan's death, 2003)

Electronic and video publications:
Dylan Thomas Remembered (audio cassette)
Win Rees as Florence Thomas (Dylan's mother) (video)

DYNIX USERS GROUP

Acronym or abbreviation: DUG

Thompson Library, Staffordshire University, College Rd, Stoke on Trent, ST4 2XS

Tel: 01782 294755
Fax: 01782 295799
E-mail: i.haydock@staffs.ac.uk

Website:
http://www.dynixusers.org.uk

Enquiries:
Enquiries to: Honorary Secretary

Founded:
1995

Incorporates the former:
Horizon Users Group (year of change 2004)

Organisation type and purpose:
Membership association.

Subject coverage:
SirsiDynix Horizon and Dynix Classic library management system.

Access to staff:
Contact by letter, by telephone, by fax and by e-mail
Hours: Mon to Fri, 0900 to 1700

DYSLEXIA ACTION

Park House, Wick Road, Egham, Surrey, TW20 0HH

Tel: 01784 222300
Fax: 01784 222333
E-mail: info@dyslexiaaction.org.uk

Website:
http://www.dyslexiaaction.org.uk
Publications list

Enquiries:
Enquiries to: Information Officer

Founded:
1972

Organisation type and purpose:
Professional body, registered charity (charity number 268502).

Subject coverage:
Dyslexia: assessment of difficulties, teaching children and adults, teacher training, advisory service.

Non-library collection catalogue:
All or part available online

Printed publications:
As We See It (newsletter, information on dyslexia)
Leaflets and booklets including:
General Information
Developing Literacy for Study and Work (Bramley W, £38.50)
Developing Spoken Language Skills (Borwick C and Townend J, £35)
Understanding Dyslexia: a teacher's perspective (Townend J, £1.95)
Units of Sound (Bramley W)
Order printed publications from: DI Trading Limited at the same address

Publications list:
Available online and in print

Access to staff:
Contact by letter, by telephone, by e-mail and via website. Appointment necessary.
Hours: Mon to Fri, 0900 to 1700

Parent body:
Dyslexia Trust

DYSLEXIA INFORMATION CENTRE

Acronym or abbreviation: DIC

Hampton Grange, 21 Hampton Lane, Solihull, West Midlands, B91 2QJ

Tel: 0121 705 4547

Website:
http://www.dyslexiabooks.biz

Enquiries:
Enquiries to: Director
Direct e-mail: petercongdon@blueyonder.co.uk

Founded:
1978

Organisation type and purpose:
Suitable for ages: all, consultancy, publishing house.

The primary purpose of the Centre is to disseminate advice and information on the subject of specific learning difficulties/dyslexia.

Subject coverage:
Gifted children, dyslexic children and adults, left-handed children and adults.

Education services:
Assessment of children and adults suffering from dyslexia, dyspraxia, ADHD, Asperger Syndrome.

Printed publications:
Books, leaflets, teaching guides and workbooks for both children and professionals
Order printed publications from: GCIC, 21 Hampton Lane, Solihull, B91 2QJ

Publications list:
Available online and in print

Access to staff:
Contact by letter, by telephone, by e-mail, in person and via website. Appointment necessary.
Hours: Mon to Fri, 0900 to 1700

Connections with:
Gifted Children's Information Centre at the main address

DYSLEXIA SCOTLAND

Acronym or abbreviation: DS

Stirling Business Centre, Wellgreen, Stirling, FK8 2DZ

Tel: 01786 446650
Fax: 01786 471235
E-mail: info@dyslexiascotland.org.uk

Website:
http://www.dyslexiascotland.org.uk

Enquiries:
Enquiries to: Administrator
Direct e-mail: sharon@dyslexiascotland.org.uk

Founded:
1981

Organisation type and purpose:
National organisation, voluntary organisation, registered charity (charity number SCO 00951).

Subject coverage:
All aspects of dyslexia and its related difficulties.

Printed publications:
Information packs, made up to individual requirements
Leaflets
A wide range of titles on all aspects of dyslexia, education and the family, etc.

Publications list:
Available in print

Access to staff:
Contact by letter, by telephone, by fax and by e-mail. Appointment necessary.
Hours: Helpline: Mon to Fri, 1000 to 1600

Branches:
a wide number of locations throughout Scotland

DYSTONIA SOCIETY

2nd Floor, 89 Albert Embankment, London, SE1 7TP

Tel: 0845 458 6211
Fax: 0845 458 6311
E-mail: info@dystonia.org.uk

Website:
http://www.dystonia.org.uk

Enquiries:
Enquiries to: Helpline
Direct tel: 0845 458 6322

Founded:
1983

Organisation type and purpose:
Membership association (membership is by subscription), present number of members: 3,627, registered charity (charity number 1062595). The Dystonia Society exists to support people who are affected by any form of the neurological movement disorder known as dystonia, and their families and carers, through the promotion of awareness, research and support and information.

Subject coverage:
Neurological disorders known as the dystonias; methods of treatment and care; research to find a cure.

Information services:
Helpline, support and information for those affected by dystonia.

Services for disabled people:
Helpline, support and information for those affected by dystonia.

Printed publications:
Local groups newsletters (3/4 times a year, free to members)
National Newsletter (4 times a year, free to members)
Dystonia Explained
Cervical Dystonia
Blepharospasm
Botulinum Toxin Treatment
Oromandibular Dystonia
Laryngeal Dystonia
Writers Cramp
Myoclonus
Paroxysmal Dystonia
Deep Brain Stimulation
Hemifacial Spasm
Dystonia: Self-Help Techniques
Dystonia – Your Questions Answered
Information pack (free to enquirers)
Various factsheets such as access to benefits, driving and dystonia etc

Electronic and video publications:
See current publications list

Publications list:
Available online and in print

Access to staff:
Contact by letter, by telephone, by fax, by e-mail, in person and via website. Appointment necessary.
Hours: Mon to Fri, 0900 to 1700; Answerphone operates at other times
Access to Helpline: Mon to Fri, 1000 to 1600

Access to building, collection or gallery:
Via main reception, 24 hours

Links with:
Dystonia Medical Research Foundation, USA tel: +1 312 755 0198; website: http://www.dystonia-foundation.org
Parkinson's Disease Society tel: 020 7931 8080; fax: 020 7233 5373

E F BENSON SOCIETY

The Old Coach House, High Street, Rye, East Sussex, TN31 7JF

Tel: 01797 223114
E-mail: oakleyites@yahoo.co.uk

Website:
http://www.efbensonsociety.org
To promote interest in E. F. Benson and the Benson family by lectures, publications, exhibitions, walks and via the Society's annual journal, the Dodo. The Society also sells out-of-print E. F. Benson books.

Enquiries:
Enquiries to: Secretary

Founded:
1985

Organisation type and purpose:
Literary society.

Subject coverage:
E. F. Benson and the Benson Family.

continued overleaf

Education services:
Talks and exhibitions can be arranged.

Printed publications:
Publications available for purchase, see website
Order printed publications from: The Secretary

Publications list:
Available online and in print

Access to staff:
Contact by letter, by telephone, by e-mail and via website. Appointment necessary. Access for members only.
Hours: Sun to Sat, 0900 to 1700

E2V TECHNOLOGIES (UK) LTD

Waterhouse Lane, Chelmsford, Essex, CM1 2QU

Tel: 01245 493493 ext. 3320
Fax: 01245 45341
E-mail: doug.spencer@e2v.com

Website:
http://www.e2v.com
Basic company information, product information.

Enquiries:
Enquiries to: Information Specialist

Founded:
1946

Formerly called:
English Electric Valve Co Ltd (year of change 1999); Marconi Applied Technologies (year of change 2002)

Organisation type and purpose:
Manufacturing industry.

Subject coverage:
Microwave technology, CCD & CMOS sensors, magnetrons, thyratrons, spark gaps, modulators and power supplies.

Museum or gallery collection, archive, or library special collection:
Company library

Non-library collection catalogue:
All or part available in-house

Library catalogue:
All or part available in-house

Access to staff:
Contact by telephone and by e-mail. Appointment necessary.
Hours: Mon to Fri, 0800 to 1600

Access to building, collection or gallery:
Prior appointment required

Access for disabled people:
Parking provided, ramped entry

EALING LIBRARY AND INFORMATION SERVICE

Ealing Central Library, 103 Ealing Broadway Centre, London, W5 5JY

Tel: 020 8567 3656
Fax: 020 8840 2351
E-mail: libuser@ealing.gov.uk

Website:
http://www.ealing.gov.uk/leisure/libraries

Enquiries:
Enquiries to: Manager

Founded:
1965

Organisation type and purpose:
Local government body, public library.

Museum or gallery collection, archive, or library special collection:
Selborne Society Library (Gilbert White's work)

Non-library collection catalogue:
All or part available in-house

Printed publications:
Various publications on the local history of the London Borough of Ealing

Access for disabled people:
Level entry, access to all public areas

Branch libraries:
Acton, Southall, Greenford and West Ealing and seven Community Libraries

EALING, HAMMERSMITH AND WEST LONDON COLLEGE

Acronym or abbreviation: EHWLC

Hammersmith Campus, Learning Centre, Gliddon Road, London, W14 9BL

Tel: 0207 565 1339
E-mail: library@wlc.ac.uk

Website:
http://www.wlc.ac.uk

Enquiries:
Enquiries to: Learning Centre Manager

Organisation type and purpose:
College of further education.

Subject coverage:
Art & design, beauty & holistic therapies, business, construction, engineering, ESOL, hairdressing, health, care & early years, hospitality & catering, information technology, media, performing arts, public services, science, sport, travel, leisure & tourism.

Library catalogue:
All or part available online

Access to staff:
Contact by letter, by telephone and by e-mail
Hours: Mon to Thu, 0800 to 2030; Fri, 0800 to 1800; Sat, 1000 to 1600

Also at:
Acton Campus
 Gunnersbury Lane, Acton, London, W3 8UX; tel: 020 8231 6344
Ealing Campus
 The Green, Ealing, W5 5EW; tel: 020 8231 6037
Southall Campus
 Beaconsfield Road, Southall, Middlesex, UB1 1DP; tel: 020 8231 6142

EAR INSTITUTE & RNID LIBRARIES

Acronym or abbreviation: ILO

Royal National Throat Nose and Ear Hospital, 330 Gray's Inn Road, London, WC1X 8EE

Tel: 020 7915 1445
E-mail: rnidlib@ucl.ac.uk

Website:
http://www.ucl.ac.uk/library/rnidlib.shtml

Enquiries:
Enquiries to: Librarian

Founded:
1946

Organisation type and purpose:
University library. The UCL Ear Institute and RNID Libraries are a collaborative venture between UCL, RNID and the NHS. The libraries are based at the Royal National Throat Nose & Ear Hospital (RNTNEH) and together constitute the largest specialist collection for audiology, deaf studies, and ear, nose and throat (ENT) or otorhinolaryngolgic (ORL) medicine in Europe. As well as providing services to staff and students at UCL, RNID, and the Royal Free Hampstead NHS Trust, the libraries are open to the public and provide reference and enquiry services to anybody conducting research connected with ENT medicine, hearing, or deafness.

Subject coverage:
Otorhinolaryngology, audiology, medical research, facial plastic surgery; deafness & Deaf history.

Museum or gallery collection, archive, or library special collection:
Historical works on otorhinolaryngology, Deaf history & related topics

Library catalogue:
All or part available online

Printed publications:
Annual Report in Postgraduate Prospectus of University College and Middlesex School of Medicine

Access to staff:
Contact by letter, by telephone, by fax, by e-mail, in person and via website. Appointment necessary.
Hours: Mon, Tue, 0900 to 1900; Wed to Fri, 0900 to 1730

Access for disabled people:
Arrange in advance
Special comments: No wheelchair access.

Constituent part of:
Royal Free and University College Medical School
University College London Library Services

EARLY EDUCATION

Formal name: British Association for Early Childhood Education

136 Cavell Street, London, E1 2JA

Tel: 020 7539 5400
Fax: 020 7539 5409
E-mail: office@early-education.org.uk

Website:
http://www.early-education.org.uk
Publications.

Enquiries:
Enquiries to: Chief Executive

Founded:
1923

Formerly called:
Nursery Schools Association (year of change 1974)

Organisation type and purpose:
Membership association (membership is by subscription), present number of members: 7,000, voluntary organisation, registered charity (charity number 313082), suitable for ages: 0 to 8. Promotes the right of all children to an education of the highest quality. Provides a multi-disciplinary network of support for all concerned with the education and care of young children.

Subject coverage:
Information regarding the care and early childhood education of children of up to 8 years.

Museum or gallery collection, archive, or library special collection:
Books concerning early childhood education

Library catalogue:
All or part available in-house

Printed publications:
Order printed publications from: Website

Publications list:
Available online and in print

Access to staff:
Contact by letter, by telephone, by fax and by e-mail. Appointment necessary.
Hours: Mon to Fri, 0900 to 1700

Access to building, collection or gallery:
Prior appointment required
Hours: Mon to Fri, 0900 to 1700

Access for disabled people:
Access to all public areas, toilet facilities
Special comments: Four steps to entrance and no ramp to front door.

Member organisation of:
National Children's Bureau
National Council for Voluntary Organisations
Women's National Commission
World Organization for Early Childhood Education

EARLY ENGLISH TEXT SOCIETY

Acronym or abbreviation: EETS

Lady Margaret Hall, Oxford, OX2 6QA

Website:
http://www.eets.org.uk
General.
http://www.boydell.co.uk/eets.htm
Publications list updated monthly.

Enquiries:
Enquiries to: Executive Secretary
Direct e-mail: vincent.gillespie@ell.ox.ac.uk

Founded:
1864

Organisation type and purpose:
Learned society (membership is by subscription),
present number of members: 1,034.

Subject coverage:
Publications of English texts earlier than 1558;
medieval studies, especially the history of English
language and literature, medieval theology and
sociology, medieval history.

Printed publications:
About 400 texts with at least one new one each
year
Order printed publications from: Oxford University
Press, Saxon Way West, Corby, Northamptonshire,
NN18 9ES (for publications from 2006)
Boydell & Brewer, PO Box 9, Woodbridge, Suffolk,
IP12 3DF (for publications up to 2006)

Publications list:
Available online and in print

Access to staff:
Contact by letter and by e-mail
Hours: Mon to Fri, 0900 to 1700

EARLY MUSIC NETWORK

Acronym or abbreviation: EMN

31 Abdale Road, London, W12 7ER

Founded:
1972

Formerly called:
Early Music Centre (EMC) (year of change 1996)

EARLY YEARS – THE ORGANISATION FOR YOUNG CHILDREN

6C Wildflower Way, Belfast, BT12 6TA

Tel: 028 9066 2825
Fax: 028 9038 1270
E-mail: info@early-years.org

Website:
http://www.early-years.org

Enquiries:
Enquiries to: Information Officer
Direct tel: 028 9038 7935

Founded:
1965

Organisation type and purpose:
Membership association (membership is by
subscription), present number of members: c. 900,
voluntary organisation, registered charity, suitable
for ages: up to 12, training organisation.

Subject coverage:
Information about early childhood, care and
education.

Library catalogue:
All or part available online

Printed publications:
Publications for purchase, direct

Publications list:
Available online and in print

Access to staff:
Contact by telephone, by e-mail, in person and via
website
Hours: Mon to Fri, 0900 to 1700

Access for disabled people:
Parking provided, level entry, access to all public
areas, toilet facilities

EARTH SCIENCE TEACHERS' ASSOCIATION

Acronym or abbreviation: ESTA

E-mail: contact@esta-uk.net

Website:
http://www.esta-uk.net

Enquiries:
Enquiries to: Chairman

Founded:
1967

Organisation type and purpose:
Membership association (membership is by
subscription), present number of members: 700,
voluntary organisation, registered charity (charity
number 1005331).
To encourage and support the teaching of earth
sciences at all levels, whether as a single subject or
as part of science or geography courses.

Subject coverage:
Geology, education, earth science.

Printed publications:
Science of the Earth Packs (Key Stage 3 and Key
Stage 4)
Teaching Earth Sciences (journal, twice a year)
Newsletter (twice a year)

Access to staff:
Contact by e-mail and via website

Constituent bodies:
8 Committees

EAST ASIAN HISTORY OF SCIENCE LIBRARY

8 Sylvester Road, Cambridge, CB3 9AF

Tel: 01223 311545
Fax: 01223 362703
E-mail: jm10019@cam.ac.uk

Website:
http://www.nri.org.uk/library.html
Introduction to the Library and how to access the
catalogue.

Enquiries:
Enquiries to: Librarian

Founded:
1976

Organisation type and purpose:
Registered charity.
Private research institute and library.

Subject coverage:
History of traditional Chinese science, technology
and medicine.

**Museum or gallery collection, archive, or library
special collection:**
Based on personal collection of Dr Joseph
Needham

Non-library collection catalogue:
All or part available online and in-house

Library catalogue:
All or part available online

Printed publications:
Science and Civilization in China (J. Needham et
al, Cambridge, Cambridge University Press)

Access to staff:
Contact by letter, by telephone, by fax, by e-mail
and via website. Appointment necessary.

Hours: Mon to Fri, 0900 to 1700

Access for disabled people:
Parking provided, level entry, access to all public
areas, toilet facilities

EAST AYRSHIRE COUNCIL

Council Headquarters, London Road, Kilmarnock,
Ayrshire, KA3 7BU

Tel: 01563 576000
Fax: 01563 576500
E-mail: the.council@east-ayrshire.gov.uk

Website:
http://www.east-ayrshire.gov.uk

Enquiries:
Enquiries to: Head of Public Relations and
Marketing
Direct tel: 01563 576135
Direct fax: 01563 576068

Founded:
1996

Formerly called:
Cumnock and Doon Valley District Council,
Kilmarnock and Loudoun District Council

Formerly part of:
Strathclyde Regional Council

Organisation type and purpose:
Local government body.
Public relations and marketing.

Subject coverage:
Services and amenities; corporate services,
education, environmental services, finance,
housing, legal services, personnel services,
planning development and tourism, property and
technical services, roads and transportation, social
services, council tax and other payments,
registration of births, deaths and marriages.

Access to staff:
Contact by letter, by telephone, by fax, by e-mail
and via website
Hours: Mon to Thu, 0900 to 1700; Fri, 0900 to 1600

EAST AYRSHIRE LIBRARY, REGISTRATION AND INFORMATION SERVICES

Acronym or abbreviation: EALRIS

Headquarters (North), Dick Institute, 14 Elmbank
Avenue, Kilmarnock, Ayrshire, KA1 3BU

Tel: 01563 554300
Fax: 01563 554311
E-mail: libraries@east-ayrshire.gov.uk

Website:
http://www.east-ayrshire.gov.uk/thelibrary
Online catalogue.

Enquiries:
Enquiries to: Library, Registration and Information
Services Manager
Direct e-mail: gerald.cairns@east-ayrshire.gov.uk

Founded:
1901

Created by the merger of:
Cumnock and Doon Valley District Libraries,
Kilmarnock and Loudoun District Libraries (year
of change 1996)

Formerly called:
East Ayrshire Library and Information Services
(EALIS)

Organisation type and purpose:
Local government body, public library.

Subject coverage:
General, Robert Burns, Ayrshire history and place
names, genealogy, archaeological and historical
sites, remains and monuments in South-West
Scotland.

Services for disabled people:
ICT training in JAWS software.

continued overleaf

Museum or gallery collection, archive, or library special collection:
Braidwood Collection of incunabula and early printed books
Hutton Collection of early printed Bibles
Papers of the Boyd Family, the Earls of Kilmarnock
Robert Burns Collection

Library catalogue:
All or part available online and in-house

Printed publications:
A range of publications on local history and places:
Greetings from Kilmarnock (F. Beattie)
Pictorial History of Newmilns (J. Mair)
Old Catrine and Sorn (R. Wilson)
The Cumnock Pottery (G. Quail)
The Ayrshire Book of Burns Lore (A. M. Boyle)

Publications list:
Available online and in print

Access to staff:
Contact by letter, by telephone, by fax, by e-mail, in person and via website

Access to building, collection or gallery:
Hours: Mon, Tue, Thu and Fri, 0900 to 2000; Wed, 1000 to 1700; Sat, 0900 to 1700;
other libraries vary, telephone for times

Access for disabled people:
Parking provided, ramped entry, access to all public areas, toilet facilities

Also at:
Council Offices
Library Headquarters (South), Lugar, Cumnock, KA18 3JQ; tel: 01563 555459; e-mail: libraries@east-ayrshire.gov.uk

Branch libraries:
Auchinleck
Community Centre, Well Road, Auchinleck, KA18 2LA; tel: 01209 422829; e-mail: libraries@east-ayrshire.gov.uk
Bellfield
79 Whatriggs Road, Kilmarnock, KA1 3RB; tel: 01563 534266; e-mail: libraries@east-ayrshire.gov.uk
Catrine
A. M. Brown Institute, Catrine, KA5 6RT; tel: 01290 551717; e-mail: libraries@east-ayrshire.gov.uk
Crosshouse
Crosshouse Area Centre, Annandale Gardens, Crosshouse, KA2 0LE; tel: 01563 503290; e-mail: libraries@east-ayrshire.gov.uk
Cumnock
25–27 Ayr Road, Cumnock, KA18 1EB; tel: 01290 422804; e-mail: libraries@east-ayrshire.gov.uk
Dalmellington
Townhead, Dalmellington, KA6 7QZ; tel: 01292 550159; e-mail: libraries@east-ayrshire.gov.uk
Dalrymple
Barbieston Road, Dalrymple, KA6 6DZ; tel: 01292 560511; e-mail: libraries@east-ayrshire.gov.uk
Darvel
Town Hall, West Main Street, Dravel, KA17 0AQ; tel: 01560 322754; e-mail: libraries@east-ayrshire.gov.uk
Drongan
Mill O'Shield Road, Drongan, KA6 7AY; tel: 01292 591718; e-mail: libraries@east-ayrshire.gov.uk
Galston
Henrietta Street, Galston, KA4 8HQ; tel: 01563 821994; e-mail: libraries@east-ayrshire.gov.uk
Hurlford
Blair Road, Hurlford, KA1 5BN; tel: 01563 539899; e-mail: libraries@east-ayrshire.gov.uk
Kilmaurs
Irvine Road, Kilmaurs, KA3 2RJ; tel: 01563 539895; e-mail: libraries@east-ayrshire.gov.uk
Mauchline
2 The Cross, Mauchline, KA5 5DA; tel: 01290 550824; e-mail: libraries@east-ayrshire.gov.uk
Muirkirk
Burns Avenue, Muirkirk, KA18 3RQ; tel: 01290 661505; e-mail: libraries@east-ayrshire.gov.uk

New Cumnock
Community Centre, The Castle, New Cumnock, KA18 4AH; tel: 01290 338710; e-mail: libraries@east-ayrshire.gov.uk
Newmilns
Craigview Road, Newmilns, KA16 9DQ; tel: 01560 322890; e-mail: libraries@east-ayrshire.gov.uk
Ochiltree
Main Street, Ochiltree, KA18 2PE; tel: 01290 700425; e-mail: libraries@east-ayrshire.gov.uk
Patna
Doonside Avenue, Patna, KA6 7LX; tel: 01292 531538; e-mail: libraries@east-ayrshire.gov.uk
Stewarton
Stewarton Area Centre, Avenue Street, Stewarton, KA3 5AP; tel: 01563 553670; e-mail: libraries@east-ayrshire.gov.uk

Constituent bodies:
Burns Monument Centre
Kay Park; tel: 01563 553655; e-mail: libraries@east-ayrshire.gov.uk; website: http://www.burnsmonumentcentre.co.uk

Parent body:
East Ayrshire Council (EAC)
Council HQ, London Road, Kilmarnock, KA1 5BU; tel: 01563 576000; fax: 01563 576500; website: http://www.east-ayrshire.gov.uk

EAST CAMBRIDGESHIRE DISTRICT COUNCIL

Acronym or abbreviation: ECDC

The Grange, Nutholt Lane, Ely, Cambridgeshire, CB7 4PL

Tel: 01353 665555
Fax: 01353 665240
E-mail: info@eastcambs.gov.uk

Website:
http://www.eastcambs.gov.uk

Enquiries:
Enquiries to: Chief Executive
Other contacts: Press and PR Officer for corporate communication.

Founded:
1974

Organisation type and purpose:
Local government body.

Subject coverage:
Many subjects relating to East Cambridgeshire district, including Ely, Soham and Littleport. Information about projects both economic and community based, new initiatives and all aspects of tourism.

Non-library collection catalogue:
All or part available online

Printed publications:
ECDC (district newsletter, 2 times a year, free)

Access to staff:
Contact by letter, by telephone, by fax and by e-mail. Appointment necessary.
Hours: Mon to Thu, 0845 to 1700; Fri, 0845 to 1630

Access for disabled people:
Level entry, toilet facilities

EAST DORSET DISTRICT COUNCIL

Acronym or abbreviation: EDDC

Council Offices, Furzehill, Wimborne, Dorset, BH21 4HN

Tel: 01202 886201
Fax: 01202 841390

Website:
http://www.eastdorset.gov.uk/tourism
Tourism in East Dorset.
http://www.eastdorset.gov.uk
All services.

Enquiries:
Enquiries to: Public Relations Manager
Direct tel: ext 2289
Direct e-mail: chief.exec@eastdorset.gov.uk

Organisation type and purpose:
Local government body.

Subject coverage:
Local Government, elections and elected members, electoral roll, environmental health, planning, Council Tax and Housing Benefit, recycling and refuse collection, tourism, local plan and grants.

Access for disabled people:
Parking provided, ramped entry, toilet facilities

EAST DUNBARTONSHIRE LEISURE & CULTURAL SERVICES

Library Headquarters, William Patrick Library, 2–4 West High Street, Kirkintilloch, Glasgow, G66 1AD

Tel: 0141 777 3143
Fax: 0141 777 3140
E-mail: libraries@eastdunbarton.gov.uk

Website:
http://www.eastdunbarton.gov.uk

Enquiries:
Enquiries to: Leisure & Cultural Services Manager
Direct e-mail: mark.grant@eastdunbarton.gov.uk

Founded:
1996

Created by the merger of:
Bearsden and Milngavie District Libraries, Strathkelvin District Libraries (year of change 1996)

Organisation type and purpose:
Local government body; public library service.

Subject coverage:
Local history of Dunbartonshire, Stirlingshire, Lanarkshire and Glasgow; community and government information; leisure, educational and cultural; learning and outreach.

Museum or gallery collection, archive, or library special collection:
Archives of East Dunbartonshire Council and its predecessor authorities, including the former Burghs of Kirkintilloch, Milngavie, Bearsden and Bishopbriggs, the parishes of Baldernock, Cadder, Campsie, Kirkintilloch and New Kilpatrick, and Strathkelvin District Council and Bearsden and Milngavie District Council; also, deposited collections of businesses, organisations and individuals within East Dunbartonshire, including J. F. McEwan Transport History Collection, Lion Foundry Co. Ltd., J. & J. Hay Boatbuilders and Glasgow Garden Suburb Tenants Ltd.

Non-library collection catalogue:
All or part available online

Library catalogue:
All or part available online

Printed publications:
Local publications list (33 titles)
If you belonged (short story, Donald, Jason)
Campsie flowers: a collection of poetry by local authors

Microform publications:
Old Aisle burial register

Publications list:
Available online and in print

Access to staff:
Contact by letter, by telephone, by fax, by e-mail, in person and via website
Hours: Mon to Fri, 0900 to 1700

Access to building, collection or gallery:
No prior appointment required
Hours: Bishopbriggs, Brookwood, Milngavie, William Patrick Libraries: Mon to Thu, 1000 to 2000; Fri and Sat, 1000 to 1700

Lennoxtown, Lenzie, Milton of Campsie, Westerton Libraries: Mon and Thu, 1300 to 2000; Tue, Wed and Fri, 1000 to 1700

Access for disabled people:
Parking provided, ramped entry, level entry, access to all public areas, toilet facilities

Branch libraries:
Bishopbriggs Library
170 Kirkintilloch Road, Bishopbriggs, G64 2LX; tel: 0141 772 4513; fax: 0141 762 5363
Brookwood Library, Bearsden
166 Drymen Road, Bearsden, G61 3RJ; tel: 0141 777 3021; fax: 0141 777 3022
Lennoxtown Library
31 Main Street, Lennoxtown, G65 7HA; tel: 01360 311436; fax: 01360 311436
Lenzie Library
13 Alexandra Avenue, Lenzie, G66 5BG; tel: 0141 776 3021
Milngavie Library
Milngavie Community Education Centre, Allander Road, Milngavie, G62 8PN; tel: 0141 956 2776; fax: 0141 956 2776
Milton of Campsie Library
School Lane, Milton of Campsie, G66 8DL; tel: 01360 311925
Westerton Library
82 Maxwell Avenue, Westerton, Bearsden, G61 1NZ; tel: 0141 943 0780; fax: 0141 943 0780
William Patrick Library
2–4 West High Street, Kirkintilloch, G66 1AD; tel: 0141 777 3141; fax: 0141 777 3140

EAST DURHAM COLLEGE

Acronym or abbreviation: EDC

Houghall Centre, Durham, DH1 3SG

Tel: 0191 375 4710; 0191 375 4756
Fax: 0191 3860419
E-mail: enquiry@edhcc.ac.uk

Website:
http://www.eastdurham.ac.uk

Enquiries:
Enquiries to: Learning Resources Manager
Direct e-mail: jill.forbes@eastdurham.ac.uk

Founded:
1999

Created by the merger of:
Durham College of Agriculture and Horticulture, East Durham Community College (year of change 1999)

Formerly called:
Houghall College

Organisation type and purpose:
Vocational, further and higher education.

Subject coverage:
Agriculture, horticulture, equestrianism, arboriculture, environmental management, small animal care.

Library catalogue:
All or part available in-house

Access to staff:
Contact by letter, by telephone, by fax and by e-mail
Hours: Mon to Thu, 0900 to 2000; Fri, 0900 to 1600

Access to building, collection or gallery:
No access other than to staff

Access for disabled people:
Parking provided, ramped entry, toilet facilities

EAST ENGLAND ARTS

Eden House, 48–49 Bateman Street, Cambridge, CB2 1LR

Tel: 01223 454400\ Minicom no. 01223 306893
Fax: 0870 242 1271
E-mail: info@eearts.co.uk

Website:
http://www.eastenglandarts.co.uk
http://www.axisartists.org.uk

Enquiries:
Enquiries to: Helpdesk

Formed with:
Arts Council of England and the other Regional Arts Boards (year of change 2002)

Formerly called:
Eastern Arts Board

Organisation type and purpose:
Service industry, registered charity (charity number 1036733).
On 1st April 2002, East England Arts joined with the Arts Council of England and the other regional arts boards to form a single development organisation for the arts.
East England Arts is the government arts and culture development agency for the East of England.

Subject coverage:
Arts funding including National Lottery, design, dance, mime and new circus, theatre and puppetry, literature, music, new media, visual arts, regeneration, audience development.

Printed publications:
Annual Report
Eye (newsletter, 6 times a year)
Public Art Galleries & Studio Spaces List
Private Art Galleries List
Regional Press List
Venues List

Publications list:
Available in print

Access to staff:
Contact by letter, by telephone, by fax, by e-mail and via website
Hours: Mon to Fri, 0900 to 1700

Access to building, collection or gallery:
Prior appointment required
Hours: Mon to Fri, 0900 to 1700

Access for disabled people:
Parking provided, ramped entry, access to all public areas, toilet facilities. Lift/elevator access.

EAST HAMPSHIRE DISTRICT COUNCIL

Acronym or abbreviation: EHDC

Penns Place, Petersfield, Hampshire, GU31 4EX

Tel: 01730 266551; 01730 234103 (minicom)
Fax: 01730 267760
E-mail: info@easthants.gov.uk

Website:
http://www.easthants.gov.uk

Enquiries:
Enquiries to: Chief Executive

Founded:
1974

Organisation type and purpose:
Local government body.

Subject coverage:
East Hampshire demographic and environmental information, council service information: planning, council tax, housing, refuse collection and recycling, benefits, tourism and leisure, grants for community groups, animal welfare, countryside, environmental health, business information and advice, and local democracy.

Printed publications:
Partners Magazine

Publications list:
Available online and in print

Access to staff:
Contact by letter, by telephone, by fax, by e-mail, in person and via website
Hours: Mon to Fri, 0900 to 1700

Access to building, collection or gallery:
No prior appointment required

Access for disabled people:
Parking provided, ramped entry

EAST HERTFORDSHIRE DISTRICT COUNCIL

Acronym or abbreviation: EHDC

Wallfields, Pegs Lane, Hertford, SG13 8EQ

Tel: 01279 655261\ Minicom no. 01279 658512
Fax: 01992 552280
E-mail: ce@ehdc.gov.uk

Website:
http://www.eastherts.gov.uk
Council services and news.

Enquiries:
Enquiries to: Public Relations Manager
Direct tel: 01279 655261 ext 449
Direct fax: 01992 505710
Other contacts: Chief Executive for complaints.

Founded:
1974

Organisation type and purpose:
Local government body.

Subject coverage:
Local government services.

Access to staff:
Contact by letter, by telephone, by fax and by e-mail. Appointment necessary.
Hours: Mon to Fri, 0830 to 1700

Other addresses:
Council Offices
The Causeway, Bishop's Stortford, Hertfordshire, CM23 2EN; tel: 01279 655261; e-mail: ce@ehdc.gov.uk

EAST HERTS ARCHAEOLOGICAL SOCIETY

Acronym or abbreviation: EHAS

11 St Leonard's Close, Bengeo, Hertford, Hertfordshire, SG14 3LL

Tel: 01992 423433
E-mail: ehasoc@googlemail.com

Website:
http://www.ehas.org.uk

Enquiries:
Enquiries to: Honorary Secretary

Founded:
1898

Organisation type and purpose:
Learned society (membership is by subscription), present number of members: 86, registered charity (charity number 257254).

Subject coverage:
Archaeological, architectural information, local history in Eastern Hertfordshire.

Library catalogue:
All or part available in-house

Printed publications:
Annual Newsletter
A Century of Archaeology in East Herts
Hertfordshire Archaeology and History (published jointly with the St Albans Archaeological Society)

Access to staff:
Contact by letter, by telephone, by e-mail and via website
Hours: Mon to Fri, 0900 to 1700
Special comments: Membership: adult £10, family £12 a year.

Access to building, collection or gallery:
No prior appointment required

Member of:
Council for British Archaeology

continued overleaf

Hertfordshire Archaeological Council
Hertfordshire Archaeological Trust

EAST KENT ARCHIVES CENTRE

Acronym or abbreviation: EKAC

Enterprise Zone, Honeywood Road, Whitfield,
Dover, Kent, CT16 3EH

Tel: 01304 829306
Fax: 01304 820783
E-mail: eastkentarchives@kent.gov.uk

Website:
http://www.kent.gov.uk/archives

Enquiries:
Enquiries to: Manager

Founded:
2000

Formerly called:
South East Area Office, Folkestone Library (year of
change 1999); Thanet Branch Archives, Ramsgate
Library (year of change 1999)

Organisation type and purpose:
Local government body.
Archive service.

Subject coverage:
Archives relating to Thanet, Dover and Shepway
District Council areas, except Church of England
and civil registration records.

**Museum or gallery collection, archive, or library
special collection:**
Local government, hospital, family and estate and
nonconformist records
Business, schools, shipping registers

Non-library collection catalogue:
All or part available online and in-house

Access to staff:
Contact by letter, by telephone, by e-mail and in
person. Appointment necessary.
Hours: Tue, Wed, Thu, 0900 to 1700

Access for disabled people:
Free parking provided, ramped entry, access to all
public areas including toilet facilities

Also at:
Centre for Kentish Studies (CKS)
  Sessions House, County Hall, Maidstone, ME14
  1XQ; tel: 01622 694363; e-mail: archives@kent
  .gov.uk

Links with:
Kent County Council

EAST LANCASHIRE CHAMBER OF INDUSTRY AND COMMERCE

Red Rose Court, Clayton Business Park, Clayton-
le-Moors, Accrington, Lancashire, BB5 5JR

Tel: 01254 356400
Fax: 01254 388900
E-mail: info@chamberelancs.co.uk

Website:
http://www.chamberelancs.co.uk
http://www.chamberinternet.co.uk

Enquiries:
Enquiries to: Chief Executive

Formerly called:
Blackburn Chamber of Commerce and Industry

Organisation type and purpose:
Membership association.
Chamber of Commerce.

Subject coverage:
Export and import information; general business
advice; business expansion; sources of finance and
grants.

Printed publications:
Business View (6 times a year)
Newsletter (6 times a year)

EAST LOTHIAN ANTIQUARIAN AND FIELD NATURALISTS SOCIETY

Acronym or abbreviation: ELFNSoc

Inchgarth, East Links, Dunbar, East Lothian, EH42
1LT

Tel: 01368 863335
E-mail: s.bunyan@yahoo.co.uk

Website:
http://eastlothianantiquarians.org.uk/site

Enquiries:
Enquiries to: President
Other contacts: The Editor, for publications and
transactions.

Founded:
1924

Organisation type and purpose:
Learned society (membership is by subscription),
present number of members: c. 200, voluntary
organisation. Stimulates and develops knowledge
and awareness of the history and natural history of
East Lothian.

Subject coverage:
East Lothian antiquities, local architecture, history
and natural history, flora and fauna.

**Museum or gallery collection, archive, or library
special collection:**
Local history books
Pictures of local interest (in the care of East Lothian
  Council Library and Museums Service)
Society's Transactions

Printed publications:
Dunbar Parish Church (Donaldson and Bunyan,
  supplement)
Society Transactions
Order printed publications from: S. A. Bunyan

Publications list:
Available in print

Access to staff:
Contact by letter, by telephone and by e-mail
Hours: Mon to Fri, 0900 to 1700
Special comments: Telephone calls may only get
through to an answerphone.

EAST LOTHIAN COUNCIL

John Muir House, Haddington, East Lothian, EH41
3HA

Tel: 01620 827827
Fax: 01620 827888

Website:
http://www.eastlothian.gov.uk

Enquiries:
Enquiries to: Corporate Communications Manager
Direct tel: 01620 827655
Direct fax: 01620 827442

Founded:
1996

Formerly called:
East Lothian District Council, Lothian Regional
Council

Organisation type and purpose:
Local government body.

Subject coverage:
All matters relating to local government; law and
administration, policy and performance, property,
personnel, finance, information technology,
community services, building design direct,
mechanised services, leisure and amenity services,
libraries, education, social services and housing,
environmental services.

Printed publications:
East Lothian Guide
Public Performance Report
A-Z of Council Services

Access to staff:
Contact by letter, by telephone, by fax and by e-
mail
Hours: Mon to Thu, 0900 to 1700; Fri, 0900 to 1600

Access for disabled people:
Parking provided, level entry, toilet facilities

EAST LOTHIAN COUNCIL LIBRARY SERVICE

Library and Museum Headquarters, Dunbar Road,
Haddington, East Lothian, EH41 3PJ

Tel: 01620 828200
Fax: 01620 828201
E-mail: jstevenson@eastlothian.gov.uk

Website:
http://www.eastlothian.gov.uk

Enquiries:
Enquiries to: Librarian
Direct tel: 01620 823307
Direct e-mail: localhistory@eastlothian.gov.uk
Other contacts: Senior Librarian: Local History &
Promotions

Founded:
1996

Organisation type and purpose:
Local government body, public library.

Subject coverage:
General; local history and genealogy for the
County of East Lothian, previously
Haddingtonshire and Inveresk (Musselburgh).

Services for disabled people:
Wi-Fi provided whether building is open or closed.
Staff will assist downstairs with information or
books that are portable. Assistance will be given
with genealogy enquiries, which can also be
handled by e-mail, or post. Please contact 01620
823307 for details.

**Museum or gallery collection, archive, or library
special collection:**
Library of the East Lothian Antiquarian and Field
  Naturalists Society, Latto Collection on
  Musselburgh, Gordon photograph collection
Local history collection (at the Local History
  Centre, Haddington Library, Newtonport,
  Haddington)

Non-library collection catalogue:
All or part available online

Library catalogue:
All or part available online

Printed publications:
Guides to services
Order printed publications from: East Lothian,
Library & Museum HQ, Dunbar Road,
Haddington, EH41 3PJ; e-mail: jstevenson@
eastlothian.gov.uk

Publications list:
Available online

Access to staff:
Contact by letter, by telephone, by e-mail, in
person and via website
Hours: Mon to Fri, 0930 to 1700

Access for disabled people:
Public parking nearby, level entry, access to public
areas, toilet facilities, except Local History Centre
Special comments: Disabled access is not currently
available at the Local History Centre, but special
arrangements will be made where possible. A new
building is in progress, expected to open Nov.
2011, which will provide full disabled access and
toilet facilities. Please check website for details.

EAST MALLING RESEARCH

Acronym or abbreviation: EMR

New Road, East Malling, Kent, ME19 6BJ

Tel: 01732 843833
Fax: 01732 849067

E-mail: enquiries@emr.ac.uk

Website:
http://www.eastmallingresearch.com

Enquiries:
Enquiries to: Information Officer

Founded:
1913

Organisation type and purpose:
Independent company, professional body, registered charity (charity number 211581), research organisation.
Research on fruit and other perennial crops including hardy nursery stock, farm woodland and hops.

Subject coverage:
Horticulture, particularly temperate fruit culture, forestry, woody ornamentals, hops, related plant science, particularly plant physiology, plant pathology, entomology, biochemistry, IPDM, postharvest storage and quality of horticultural crops.

Museum or gallery collection, archive, or library special collection:
Cherry gene database
European apple inventory
Historical books on fruit breeding and horticulture
Index of graft transmittable diseases

Non-library collection catalogue:
All or part available in-house

Library catalogue:
All or part available in-house

Access to staff:
Contact by telephone and by e-mail. Appointment necessary.
Hours: Mon to Fri, 0900 to 1700

Access to building, collection or gallery:
Prior appointment required
Special comments: Open to members of the East Malling Research Association.

EAST MIDLANDS MUSEUMS SERVICE

Acronym or abbreviation: EMMS

Centre for Museum and Heritage Management, Nottingham Trent University, Clifton Lane, Nottingham, NG11 8NS

Tel: 0115 848 3562
E-mail: emms@emms.org.uk

Website:
http://www.emms.org.uk
News, networks, resources, museum listings for the East Midlands museum community.

Enquiries:
Enquiries to: Executive Director
Direct tel: 0115 848 3572
Other contacts: Administrator

Founded:
1981

Organisation type and purpose:
Regional museum network (membership is by subscription), present number of members: 112 (local authorities, independent museums, universities, national bodies and individuals), registered charity (charity number 1009683). Offers support, communication, networking, training, consultancy. Aims to enhance and improve standards in care and public use of museum collections in the East Midlands.

Subject coverage:
Museum management, organisation and practice, museum collections in the East Midlands, collections care, training and advice, Regional Emergencies and Disaster Support Service (prevention, preparedness, reaction and recovery).

Information services:
Advice and information relating to museums in the East Midlands

Regional Emergency and Disaster Support (REDS) Service.

Printed publications:
Annual Report
EmmS News (members only)

Electronic and video publications:
Emergency Manual for Historic Buildings and Collections (interactive CD-ROM, £29.50)

Publications list:
Available online

Access to staff:
Contact by letter, by telephone, by fax, by e-mail, in person and via website. Appointment necessary. Non-members charged.
Hours: Variable

Access to building, collection or gallery:
By appointment
Hours: University opening hours

Access for disabled people:
No restrictions

EAST MIDLANDS ORAL HISTORY ARCHIVE

Acronym or abbreviation: EMOHA

Centre for Urban History, University of Leicester, LE1 7RH

Tel: 0116 252 5065
Fax: 0116 252 5769
E-mail: emoha@le.ac.uk

Website:
http://www.le.ac.uk/emoha

Organisation type and purpose:
A partnership between the University of Leicester's Centre for Urban History, Leicestershire County Council and Leicester City Museums and Library Services.

Subject coverage:
Oral history of the East Midlands (Leicestershire and Rutland).

Museum or gallery collection, archive, or library special collection:
Among the Archive's resources are the collections of the former Leicester Oral History Archive, the Mantle Archive from northwest Leicestershire, the Community History archive of Leicester City Libraries and the sound archive of BBC Radio Leicester

Access to building, collection or gallery:
The Archive is housed on the University of Leicester's satellite campus, at 1 Salisbury Road, Leicester, LE1 7QR

EAST NORTHAMPTONSHIRE COUNCIL

East Northamptonshire House, Cedar Drive, Thrapston, Kettering, Northamptonshire, NN14 4LZ

Tel: 01832 742000
Fax: 01832 734839

Website:
http://www.east-northamptonshire.gov.uk
Local government services, economic development, tourism.

Founded:
1974

Organisation type and purpose:
Local government body.

Subject coverage:
Local government services, economic development, tourism.

Access to staff:
Contact by letter and by telephone
Hours: Mon to Fri, 0900 to 1700

Other office at:
Rushden Centre (One Stop Shop)
  Newton Road, Rushden, Northamptonshire, NN10 0PT; tel: 01933 412000; fax: 01933 410564

EAST OF ENGLAND TOURISM

Formal name: East of England Tourist Board
Acronym or abbreviation: EET

Dettingen House, Dettingen Way, Bury St Edmunds, Suffolk, IP33 3TU

Tel: 01284 727470
Fax: 01284 706657
E-mail: info@eet.org.uk

Website:
http://www.visiteadtofengland.com
http://www.eet.org.uk

Founded:
1972

Formerly called:
East Anglia Tourist Board (year of change 1996); East of England Tourist Board (year of change 2007)

Organisation type and purpose:
Promotion of sustainable tourism throughout the East of England.

Subject coverage:
Tourism in Bedfordshire, Cambridgeshire, Essex, Hertfordshire, Norfolk and Suffolk. Information on research.

Access to staff:
Contact by letter, by telephone, by fax, by e-mail and via website
Hours: Mon to Fri, 0900 to 1700
Special comments: Closed Bank Holidays.

Access to building, collection or gallery:
No public access

EAST OF LONDON FAMILY HISTORY SOCIETY

Acronym or abbreviation: EoLFHS

23 Louvaine Avenue, Wickford, Essex, SS12 0DP

E-mail: society.secretary@eolfhs.org.uk

Website:
http://www.eolfhs.org.uk

Enquiries:
Enquiries to: General Secretary
Direct e-mail: society.secretary@eolfhs.org.uk

Founded:
1978

Organisation type and purpose:
Membership association (membership is by subscription), present number of members: over 3000, suitable for ages: all.
Family history society.

Subject coverage:
Family history and genealogy.

Library catalogue:
All or part available online

Printed publications:
Available from online bookstall or by post
Order printed publications from: East of London Family History Society, Bookstall Manager, 68 Stanfield Road, Dagenham, RM10 8JT

Publications list:
Available online

Access to staff:
Contact by letter, by e-mail and via website
Hours: Mon to Fri, 0900 to 1700
Special comments: Advice only provided, no research undertaken.

Member organisation of:
The Federation of Family History Societies

EAST RENFREWSHIRE COUNCIL

Council Headquarters, Eastwood Park, Giffnock, East Renfrewshire, G42 6UG

Tel: 0141 577 3000
Fax: 0141 620 0884

Enquiries:
Enquiries to: Public Relations Manager
Direct tel: 0141 577 3851
Direct fax: 0141 577 3852
Direct e-mail: RelationsP@eastrenfrewshire.gov.uk

Founded:
1996

Organisation type and purpose:
Local government body.

Subject coverage:
Local government; services and amenities; corporate services, education, environmental services, finance, housing, legal services, personnel services, planning development and tourism, property and technical services, roads and transportation, social services, council tax and other payments, registration of births, death and marriages.

Printed publications:
How to get in touch with the Council

Access to staff:
Contact by letter, by telephone, by fax and by e-mail. Appointment necessary.
Hours: Mon to Fri, 0900 to 1700

EAST RIDING ARCHIVES AND LOCAL STUDIES SERVICE

Acronym or abbreviation: Treasure House

County Hall, Beverley, East Yorkshire, HU17 9BA

Tel: 01482 392790
Fax: 01482 392791
E-mail: archives.service@eastriding.gov.uk

Website:
http://www.eastriding.gov.uk

Created by the merger of:
East Riding Archives Service and Beverley Local Studies Library (year of change 2007)

Organisation type and purpose:
Archive and local studies library.

Subject coverage:
East Riding of Yorkshire local history, topography and culture.

Special visitor services:
Meeting rooms available for hire.

Museum or gallery collection, archive, or library special collection:
Archive with collections of public, local government, church, family and estate and other local records
Local studies library with local studies books, pamphlets and journals, newspapers and directories

Non-library collection catalogue:
All or part available online and in-house

Library catalogue:
All or part available online and in-house

Printed publications:
Guides to records, leaflets on tracing family history, house history and using the East Riding Register of Deeds
Hand Lists

Access to staff:
Contact by letter, by telephone, by fax, by e-mail and in person

Access to building, collection or gallery:
Hours: Mon, Wed, Fri, 0930 to 1700; Tue, Thu, 0930 to 2000; Sat, 0900 to 1600

Access for disabled people:
Disabled access and lift access to all public parts of building

Also at:
East Riding Archives and Local Studies Service Treasure House, Champney Road, Beverley, HU17 9BE

Parent body:
East Riding of Yorkshire Council

EAST RIDING OF YORKSHIRE COUNCIL

Acronym or abbreviation: ERYC

County Hall, Cross Street, Beverley, East Yorkshire, HU17 9BA

Tel: 01482 887700

Website:
http://www.eastriding.gov.uk

Enquiries:
Enquiries to: Chief Executive
Direct tel: 01482 884832

Founded:
1996

Organisation type and purpose:
Local government body.

Subject coverage:
All local government services.

Museum or gallery collection, archive, or library special collection:
Archives of documents collected by Humberside County Council and former East Riding County Council and former East Riding Registry of Deeds held by the East Riding of Yorkshire Council Archives and Records Service

Access to staff:
Contact by letter, by telephone and by fax. Appointment necessary.
Hours: Mon to Fri, 0900 to 1700

EAST STAFFORDSHIRE BOROUGH COUNCIL

Town Hall, Burton-on-Trent, Staffordshire, DE14 2EB

Tel: 01283 508000
Fax: 01283 35412
E-mail: reception@eaststaffsbc.gov.uk

Website:
http://www.eaststaffsbc.gov.uk

Enquiries:
Enquiries to: Public Relations Manager

Organisation type and purpose:
Local government body.

Access to staff:
Contact by letter, by telephone, by fax, by e-mail and via website
Hours: Mon to Fri, 0800 to 1700

Access for disabled people:
Parking provided, level entry, toilet facilities

Other addresses:
East Staffordshire Borough Council Midland Grain Warehouse, Derby Street, Burton on Trent, Staffordshire, DE14 2JJ; tel: 01283 508628; fax: 01283 508388

EAST SURREY BADGER PROTECTION SOCIETY

Acronym or abbreviation: ESBPS

PO Box 911, Warlingham, Surrey, CR6 9AF

Tel: 01883 622455
Fax: 01883 349699
E-mail: esbps@stata.com.net

Website:
http://badger-groups.org.uk/east-surrey

Enquiries:
Enquiries to: Honorary Secretary

Founded:
1979

Formerly called:
Surrey Badger Protection Society (year of change 1997)

Organisation type and purpose:
Registered charity (charity number 800270).

Subject coverage:
Badgers.

Printed publications:
Information leaflets (free)

Access to staff:
Contact by letter and by telephone
Hours: Mon to Fri, 0900 to 1700
Special comments: Also available in evenings and at weekends.

Affiliated to the:
National Federation of Badger Groups
2B Inworth Street, London, SW11 3EP

EAST SURREY FAMILY HISTORY SOCIETY

119 Keevil Drive, London, SW19 6TF

Tel: 01737 554071
E-mail: secretary@eastsurreyfhs.co.uk

Website:
http://scorpio.gold.ac.uk/genuki/sry/esfhs
List of publications, details of society and membership form.

Enquiries:
Enquiries to: Honorary Secretary

Founded:
1977

Organisation type and purpose:
International organisation, membership association (membership is by subscription), present number of members: 2000, registered charity (charity number 286659), suitable for ages: all, research organisation.

Subject coverage:
Family history (genealogy) data relating to East Surrey which includes parts of South London previously in Surrey.

Printed publications:
Introductory booklet (sent to members when they join)
Quarterly Journal (sent to members)
Census indexes for 1851, 1871 and 1891
Monumental inscriptions
Parish Registers
Record publications, Poor Law, Apprenticeships, Settlements etc
Order printed publications from: Census Indexes and Other Publications, East Surrey Family History Society
4 Constance Road, Croydon, Surrey, CR0 2RS

Microform publications:
Directory of Members' Interests – 1995

Publications list:
Available online and in print

Access to staff:
Contact by letter and by e-mail
Hours: Mon to Fri, 0900 to 1700

EAST SUSSEX LIBRARY AND INFORMATION SERVICE

County Hall, Lewes, East Sussex, BN7 1UE

Tel: 01273 481870
Fax: 01273 481716
E-mail: anita.cundall@eastsussex.gov.uk

Website:
http://www.eastsussex.gov.uk/libraries

Founded:
1974

Organisation type and purpose:
Local government body, public library.

Library catalogue:
All or part available online and in-house

Access to staff:
Contact by letter, by telephone, by fax, by e-mail, in person and via website
Hours: Mon to Fri, 0900 to 1700

Group Headquarters at:
Hastings, Eastbourne, Lewes, Bexhill and Uckfield

EAST SUSSEX RECORD OFFICE

Acronym or abbreviation: ESRO

The Maltings, Castle Precincts, Lewes, East Sussex, BN7 1YT

Tel: 01273 482349
Fax: 01273 482341
E-mail: archives@eastsussex.gov.uk

Website:
http://www.eastsussex.gov.uk/useourarchives
Information leaflets, short guide to holdings.
http://www.nationalarchives.gov.uk/archon
Details of all archive repositories in England.
http://www.nationalarchives.gov.uk/a2a
Copies of lists of over 90% of holdings.

Founded:
1949

Organisation type and purpose:
Local government body.
To preserve the documentary heritage of East Sussex, and of the Brighton and Hove Council area, and to make its resources available to the public for research. To act as a Diocesan Record Office for Chichester (East Sussex Parish records).

Subject coverage:
Most aspects of the history and historical geography of East Sussex (including Brighton and Hove), its communities, people, public authorities and organisations, c. 1100 to date.

Museum or gallery collection, archive, or library special collection:
Archives of the usual local authority holdings
Deposited collections, including:
Battle Abbey Archives
Danny Archives
Frewen Archives
Hickstead Place Archives
Sheffield Park Archives concerning John Baker Holroyd, 1st Earl of Sheffield, politician and authority on commercial and agricultural topics, late 18th century
Sussex Archaeological Society records, including papers of the Gage family (American material) and the Fuller family of Rosehill (West Indian material)

Non-library collection catalogue:
All or part available online and in-house

Printed publications:
Annual Report (contains a list of accessions during the year)
Handlist of registers of Births, Baptisms, Marriages, Deaths and Burials (online)
Catalogues of individual archives

Microform publications:
Available for consultation in the Record office (copies of entries provided for a fee)

Publications list:
Available in print

Access to staff:
Contact by letter, by telephone, by fax, by e-mail, in person and via website
Hours: Mon, Tue and Thu, 0845 to 1645; Wed, 0930 to 1645; Fri, 0845 to 1615; Sat 2nd and 4th in the month (booking required), 0900 to 1300 and 1400 to 1645
Special comments: Although it is not compulsory to book in advance, it is strongly reccomended.

Access for disabled people:
Parking provided, ramped entry
Special comments: The public search room is on the first floor and is only accessible via two flights of stairs; there are no disabled toilet facilities on site. Only one parking space, but it is bookable.

EAST YORKSHIRE FAMILY HISTORY SOCIETY

Acronym or abbreviation: EYFHS

Carnegie Heritage Centre, 342 Anlaby Road, Kingston upon Hull, HU3 6JA

Tel: 01482 561216
E-mail: secretary@eyfhs.org.uk

Website:
http://www.eyfhs.org.uk
Family and local history resource.
http://www.eyreg.co.uk
History of roll of the East Yorkshire Regiment.
http://www.heroesofhull.co.uk
Kingston upon Hull's casualties of (any) war, military and civillian.

Enquiries:
Enquiries to: Secretary

Founded:
1977

Organisation type and purpose:
Membership association (membership is by subscription), present number of members: 1,700, registered charity (charity number 519743).
Extensive local and family history library.
Publisher of over 500 family/local history titles.

Subject coverage:
Family history in East Yorkshire.

Information services:
Extensive library and publications catalogue. Local archives 'look-up' service.

Special visitor services:
Free family history help desks across the whole East Riding and every Monday afternoon at the Carnegie.

Education services:
Various family and local history courses at the Carnegie all year round.

Services for disabled people:
Full access to the Carnegie Heritage Centre (ambulant toilets only).

Non-library collection catalogue:
All or part available online, in-house and in print

Library catalogue:
All or part available online, in-house and in print

Printed publications:
Monumental Inscriptions
Parish Register Transcripts
Miscellaneous local and family history publications
1851 Census of the EYFHS area (24 booklets)
1861 Census (on CD-ROM)
A3-size maps
Order printed publications from: The Publications Officers, East Yorkshire Family History Society, 5 Curlew Close, Molescroft, Beverley, East Yorkshire, HU17 7QN

Microform publications:
Births, Marriages and Deaths from Scarborough Newspapers
1891 Census Scarborough Registration District
Order microform publications from: The Publications Officers, East Yorkshire Family History Society, 5 Curlew Close, Molescroft, Beverley, East Yorkshire, HU17 7QN

Electronic and video publications:
1891 Census Scarborough Registration District (disc)
Births, Marriages and Deaths for the Beverley Guardian Newspapers (disc)

Order electronic and video publications from: The Publications Officers, East Yorkshire Family History Society, 5 Curlew Close, Molescroft, Beverley, East Yorkshire, HU17 7QN

Publications list:
Available online and in print

Access to staff:
Contact by letter, by telephone, by e-mail, in person and via website
Hours: Mon to Fri, 0900 to 1700

Access to building, collection or gallery:
Open to the general public
Hours: Mon, 1330 to 1530; Tue and Thu, 1000 to 1600
Special comments: For details of other times and events please contact the Carnegie.

Access for disabled people:
Full disabled access
Hours: No restrictions – as per public timetable
Special comments: No disabled toilet.

Branches:
EYFHS Beverley
e-mail: beverley@eyfhs.org.uk; website: http://www.eyfhs.org.uk
EYFHS Bridlington
e-mail: bridlington@eyfhs.org.uk; website: http://www.eyfhs.org.uk
Scarborough
e-mail: scarborough@eyfhs.org.uk; website: http://www.eyfhs.org.uk

EASTERN AFRICA ASSOCIATION

Acronym or abbreviation: EAA

2 Vincent Street, London, SW1P 4LD

Tel: 020 7828 5511
Fax: 020 7828 5251
E-mail: jcsmall@eaa-lon.co.uk

Website:
http://www.eaa-lon.co.uk

Enquiries:
Enquiries to: Asst Company Secretary

Founded:
1964

Formerly called:
East Africa Association (year of change 1995)

Organisation type and purpose:
Trade association (membership is by subscription), present number of members: 340
To support and promote investment in Eastern Africa.

Subject coverage:
Trade and investment matters in Kenya, Uganda, Tanzania, Ethiopia, Eritrea, Seychelles and Rwanda.

Printed publications:
Newsletter (to members only)

Access to staff:
Contact by letter, by telephone, by fax, by e-mail and via website. Appointment necessary. Access for members only.
Hours: Mon to Fri, 0930 to 1730

Administered by:
The Eastern Africa Association
  PO Box 41272, 5th Floor, Room 512, Jubilee Place, Mama Ngina Street/General Kago Street, Nairobi, Kenya 00100; tel: +254 20 340341; fax: +254 20 214898; e-mail: info@eaa.co.ke; website: http://www.eea-lon.co.uk
The Eastern Africa Association
  Dar-es-Salaam, Tanzania; tel: +255 22 2617124; fax: +255 22 2617145; e-mail: dcrobertsontz@gmail.com
The Eastern Africa Association
  Kampala, Uganda; tel: +256 752 757025; e-mail: aaslund@infocom.co.ug
The Eastern Africa Association
  Kigali, Rwanda; tel: +250 575075; +250 0830 8276; e-mail: steve.caley@finabank.co.rw

continued overleaf

The Eastern Africa Association
  Addis Ababa, Ethiopia; tel: +251 11 662 3372;
  +251 91 125 0745; e-mail: demissie.demissie@
  gmail.com

EASTLEIGH BOROUGH COUNCIL

Civic Offices, Leigh Road, Eastleigh, Hampshire,
SO50 9YN

Tel: 023 8068 8000
Fax: 023 8064 3952

Website:
http://www.eastleigh.gov.uk

Enquiries:
Enquiries to: Chief Executive
Other contacts: Public Relations Officer

Organisation type and purpose:
Local government body.

Subject coverage:
Local government services.

Access to staff:
Contact by letter, by telephone, by fax, by e-mail
and in person. Appointment necessary.
Hours: Mon to Thu, 0830 to 1700; Fri, 0830 to 1630

Access to building, collection or gallery:
No prior appointment required

Access for disabled people:
Parking provided, ramped entry, access to all
public areas, toilet facilities

ECCTIS LIMITED

Acronym or abbreviation: ECCTIS

Oriel House, Oriel Road, Cheltenham,
Gloucestershire, GL50 1XP

Tel: 0871 330 7303
Fax: 01242 258600
E-mail: info@ecctis.co.uk

Website:
http://www.ecctis.co.uk
Course discover online database.

Enquiries:
Enquiries to: Head of Policy and Communications
Direct tel: 01242 258616
Direct e-mail: communications@ecctis.co.uk

Founded:
1990

Carries out the functions of the former:
ECCTIS Ltd (trading as UK NARIC) operates the
NARIC service for the UK under contract from the
Department of Business Innovation and Skills.
As the national agency responsible for providing
information, advice and data on qualifications
from overseas, it offers services to those bringing
individuals into the UK to work or study. (year of
change 1997); ECCTIS Ltd is also the UK National
Europass Centre (UK NEC) for the UK.
UK NEC is the national agency responsible for
promoting Europass within the UK to individuals,
awarding bodies, employers, education
institutions and other stakeholders. The agency is
jointly funded by the European Commission and
the UK Department of Business, Innovation and
Skills (BIS) and sits within a network of 31 other
Europass Centres within the EU / EEA.
Europass helps individuals highlight their abilities
in an effective way. It can help to remove barriers
to working, studying or training in Europe. It is
free and enables people to present their
competencies, skills and qualifications in a clear
way. This European-wide initiative consists of five
documents that help potential employers,
educational establishments and training providers
understand which subjects have been studied,
what training has been completed or how much
experience has been gained working. (year of
change 2005)

Organisation type and purpose:
International organisation (membership is by
subscription), training organisation, consultancy,
research organisation, publishing house.

Subject coverage:
All award-bearing courses, from non-advanced to
postgraduate level, in further and higher education
throughout the UK, in colleges and universities,
including standard entry requirements, course
content and institutional data; non-standard entry
opportunities (i.e. credit transfer).

Printed publications:
Newsletter (3 times a year, free)

Publications list:
Available in print

Access to staff:
Contact by e-mail
Hours: Mon to Fri, 0830 to 1730

Parent body:
Hobsons Ltd

ECHO LANGUAGE SCHOOL

Acronym or abbreviation: ECHO

23 Rutland Gardens, Hove, East Sussex, BN3 5PD

Tel: 01273 202802
Fax: 01273 746464
E-mail: info@echolanguageschool.co.uk

Website:
http://www.echolanguageschool.co.uk
Details of courses; English courses for teenagers.

Enquiries:
Enquiries to: Information Officer
Other contacts: Director of Studies

Founded:
1989

Organisation type and purpose:
Service industry, suitable for ages: 12+.
Residential language school, home tuition.

Subject coverage:
English residential language courses.

Printed publications:
Brochures

Access to staff:
Contact by letter, by telephone, by fax, by e-mail,
in person and via website
Hours: Daily, 0800 to 2000

Access to building, collection or gallery:
No prior appointment required

ECONOMIC AND SOCIAL RESEARCH COUNCIL

Acronym or abbreviation: ESRC

Polaris House, North Star Avenue, Swindon, SN2
1UJ

Tel: 01793 413000
Fax: 01793 413001

Website:
http://www.esrcsocietytoday.ac.uk
ESRC and its research.

Founded:
1965

Formerly called:
Social Science Research Council (year of change
1983)

Organisation type and purpose:
An independent organisation, established by Royal
Charter.
Funds research and training in social and economic
issues.

Subject coverage:
Provides high-quality research on issues of
importance to business, the public sector and
government, and is committed to training world-

class social scientists; nearly two-thirds of the
budget is allocated to research and just under one-
third to postgraduate training.

Printed publications:
Britain in 2010 (magazine, £4.95, available at WH
  Smith and other outlets)
A range of research publications (see website)
Society Now (magazine, 3 a year, available via
  website)
Order printed publications from: ESRC Publications,
Tangent Communications, PO Box 757,
Cheltenham, GL52 2YZ; tel: 01242 283100 Mon to
Fri, 0900 to 1730; fax: 01242 283131; e-mail: esrc@
tangentuk.com

Electronic and video publications:
eNews (6 a year)
Articles
Press briefings
Order electronic and video publications from: website

Publications list:
Available online

Access to staff:
Contact by letter, by telephone and by fax

Funded by:
Department for Business, Innovation and Skills

ECONOMIC HISTORY SOCIETY

University of Glasgow, Department of Economic
and Social History, Lilybank House, Bute Gardens,
Glasgow, G12 8RT

Tel: 0141 330 4662
Fax: 0141 330 4889
E-mail: ehsocsec@arts.gla.ac.uk

Website:
http://www.ehs.org.uk

Enquiries:
Enquiries to: Honorary Secretary

Founded:
1926

Organisation type and purpose:
Learned society, registered charity (charity number
228494; SCO38304).
To promote the study of economic history and to
establish closer relations between students and
teachers of economic and social history.

Subject coverage:
Economic and social history.

Non-library collection catalogue:
All or part available online and in print

Printed publications:
Economic History Review (quarterly)
Refresh (no longer available, except for back issues
  online)
Living Economic and Social History (essays to
  mark the 75th anniversary of the Economic
  History Society)
Order printed publications from: e-mail: ehsocsec@
arts.gla.ac.uk

Publications list:
Available online and in print

Access to staff:
Contact by letter, by telephone, by fax, by e-mail
and via website
Hours: Mon to Fri, 0900 to 1700

ECONOMIC RESEARCH COUNCIL

Acronym or abbreviation: ERC

7 St James's Square, London, SW17 4JU

Tel: 020 7439 0271

Website:
http://www.ercouncil.org

Enquiries:
Enquiries to: Honorary Secretary

Founded:
1943

Organisation type and purpose:
Membership association, registered charity.
To promote education in economics, particularly monetary practice.

Subject coverage:
Education in the science of economics, particularly monetary policy; inflation, taxation, use of resources etc.

Non-library collection catalogue:
All or part available online

Printed publications:
Britain and Overseas (quarterly)

Access to staff:
Contact by letter
Hours: Mon to Fri, 0900 to 1700

ECONOMIC RESEARCH INSTITUTE OF NORTHERN IRELAND LTD

Acronym or abbreviation: ERINI

Pearl Assurance House, 1–3 Donegall Square East, Belfast, BT1 5HB

Tel: 028 9023 2125 or 028 261 8000
Fax: 028 9033 1250/3054

Website:
http://www.niec.org.uk
Information about Council, Council Members, Staff, publications, events and future research. New ERINI website being developed.

Enquiries:
Enquiries to: Director
Direct e-mail: e.moore@erini.ac.uk
Other contacts: Administrator

Founded:
2004

Organisation type and purpose:
Economic research and policy development body.

Subject coverage:
Economics.

Printed publications:
Occasional Papers Series
Publicly Funded R&D and Economic Development in Northern Ireland (December 1999, free)
Plus a wide variety of papers, reports and monographs (all charged) including:
Tough Choices: Setting Health and Social Care Priorities in Northern Ireland (April 2000)
Annual Report 2000–2001 (November 2001)
The Knowledge Driven Economy: Indicators for Northern Ireland (April 2001)
Order printed publications from: The Administration Group, Economic Research Institute of Northern Ireland Ltd
tel: 028 90 232125, fax: 028 90 331250, e-mail: info@niec.org.uk

Publications list:
Available online and in print

Access to staff:
Contact by letter, by telephone, by fax, by e-mail, in person and via website. Appointment necessary.
Hours: Mon to Fri, 0900 to 1700

Also at:
Economic Research Institute of Northern Ireland Ltd
22–24 Mount Charles, Belfast, BT7 6NN

ECONOMIST INTELLIGENCE UNIT LIMITED

Acronym or abbreviation: EIU

26 Red Lion Square, London, WC1R 4HQ

Tel: 020 7576 8000
E-mail: london@eiu.com

Website:
http://www.eiu.com
http://store.eiu.com

Enquiries:
Enquiries to: Client Relations Department
Direct tel: 020 7576 8181
Direct fax: 020 7572 8476
Direct e-mail: london@eiu.com

Organisation type and purpose:
To provide country, industry and management analysis.
To assess and forecast the political, economic and business climates of 201 countries.
To produce intelligence on key industries.

Subject coverage:
Country specific reports – economic and political studies; forecasts; country credit risk; commodities; industry studies – consumer markets, energy, rubber, travel and tourism, automotive, financial services, food, beverages and tobacco, healthcare and pharmaceuticals.

Trade and statistical information:
International business and economic information.

Publications list:
Available online and in print

Incorporates:
Business International Limited

Other offices:
Hong Kong
60F Central Plaza, 18 Harbour Road, Wanchai, Hong Kong; tel: +852 2802 7288
New York
The Economist Building, 111 West 57th Street, New York, NY 10019, USA; tel: +1 212 698 9745

Parent body:
Economist Group

EDEXCEL

One90 High Holborn, London, WC1V 7BH

Tel: 0870 240 9800
E-mail: enquiries@edexcel.org.uk

Website:
http://www.edexcel.org.uk
The Edexcel website or Edexcel On-line Services & Resources allows customers to have access to Edexcel's key information, resources and services 24 hours a day, 7 days a week.

Enquiries:
Enquiries to: Corporate Information Resource Centre Manager
Direct e-mail: sarah.whybrow@pearson.com
Other contacts: Customer Response Centre (CRC) for information and guidance on the full range of Edexcel programmes of study and qualifications.

Founded:
1983

Organisation type and purpose:
Body concerned with academic and vocational qualifications in secondary and tertiary education.

Subject coverage:
The CIRC provides a 'first step' information service for all users of Edexcel qualifications. Guidance, contents, procedures and availability can be given on a wide range of qualifications, both academic and vocational, from Entry Level right through to Professional Development Awards.

Non-library collection catalogue:
All or part available in-house and in print

Library catalogue:
All or part available in-house

Printed publications:
A large number of course-related publications and supporting material for all Edexcel's qualifications including syllabuses, specifications, guidance, past examination papers, teacher support material and student support material
Order printed publications from: Edexcel Publications Adamsway, Mansfield, Nottinghamshire, NG18 4FN, tel: 01623 467467, fax: 01623 450481, e-mail: publications@linneydirect.com

Publications list:
Available in print

Access to staff:
Contact by letter, by telephone, by fax, by e-mail and via website
Hours: Mon to Fri, 0900 to 1700

EDGE HILL COLLEGE OF HIGHER EDUCATION

St Helens Road, Ormskirk, Lancashire, L39 4QP

Tel: 01695 584284
Fax: 01695 579997

Website:
http://www.ehche.ac.uk/ims
Information and media services homepage.

Enquiries:
Enquiries to: Manager
Direct e-mail: pressoffice@edgehill.ac.uk

Formerly called:
Edge Hill College of Further Education, Edge Hill University College

Organisation type and purpose:
University library, university department or institute.
College awards are validated by Lancaster University.

Subject coverage:
Afro-Asian studies, social science, community and race relations, drama, religious studies, English language and literature, biology, science, French, geography (human and physical), British and world history, mathematics, information technology, politics, European literature and culture, organisation and management, teacher education and educational studies, urban development, women's studies, sport studies and health.

Museum or gallery collection, archive, or library special collection:
Education Resource collection
Local history collection

Non-library collection catalogue:
All or part available online

Access to staff:
Contact by letter, by telephone, by e-mail and via website
Hours: Term time: Mon to Fri, 0845 to 2100; Sat, Sun, 1300 to 1700

Affiliated to:
University of Lancaster

EDINBURGH ASSAY OFFICE

Acronym or abbreviation: EAO

Goldsmiths' Hall, 24 Broughton Street, Edinburgh, EH1 3RH

Tel: 0131 556 1144
Fax: 0131 556 1177
E-mail: admin@assay-office.co.uk

Website:
http://www.assayofficescotland.co.uk

Enquiries:
Enquiries to: Assay Master

Organisation type and purpose:
Statutory body.
Established in accordance with the requirements of the Hallmarking Act 1973.

Subject coverage:
Assaying and hallmarking over the past 500 years of gold, silver and platinum.

Museum or gallery collection, archive, or library special collection:
Records of wares hallmarked at Edinburgh since 1799 to present day

Printed publications:
Hallmarks (booklet of the Assay Offices of GB)

continued overleaf

Access to staff:
Contact by letter, by fax, by e-mail and in person
Hours: Mon to Fri, 0800 to 1600

Controlled by the:
Incorporation of Goldsmiths of the City of
Edinburgh

EDINBURGH BIBLIOGRAPHICAL SOCIETY

c/o National Library of Scotland, George IV Bridge,
Edinburgh, EH1 1EW

Tel: 0131 623 3894
E-mail: h.vincent@rarebooks.nls

Website:
http://mcs.qmuc.ac.uk/EBS

Enquiries:
Enquiries to: Secretary

Founded:
1890

Organisation type and purpose:
Learned society.

Subject coverage:
Bibliography (especially Scottish).

Printed publications:
Occasional publications (generally available, price
and frequency variable)
Journal (annually, members only)
Order printed publications from: website: http://
mcs.qmuc.ac.uk/EBS/Publications.htm

Publications list:
Available online and in print

Access to staff:
Contact by letter, by telephone and by e-mail

EDINBURGH CENTRE FOR TROPICAL FORESTS

Acronym or abbreviation: ECTF

Pentlands Science Park, Bush Loan, Penicuik,
Midlothian, EH26 0PH

Tel: 0131 440 0400
Fax: 0131 440 4141
E-mail: mail@ectf-ed.org.uk

Website:
http://www.nmw.ac.uk/ectf/
Objectives of ECTF as a whole and each of its
constituent members. Consultant database.

Enquiries:
Enquiries to: Administrator

Founded:
1991

Organisation type and purpose:
Training organisation, consultancy, research
organisation.
Coordinates the expertise of the members of ECTF
for potential clients.

Subject coverage:
Tropical forestry, land management and
sustainable development of natural resources.

Printed publications:
Rooting Cuttings of Tropical Trees (manual,
Longman K A, £12.50)

Electronic and video publications:
Multiplying Tropical Trees (video, for sale)

Access to staff:
Contact by letter, by e-mail and via website
Hours: Mon to Fri, 0900 to 1700

Member organisations:
Centre for Ecology and Hydrology
Bush Estate, Penicuik, Midlothian, EH26 0QB
Forestry Commission
231 Corstorphine Road, Edinburgh, EH12 7AT
LTS International Limited
Pentlands Science Park, Bush Loan, Penicuik,
Midlothian, EH26 0PH

Royal Botanic Garden
20A Inverleith Row, Edinburgh, EH3 5LR
University of Edinburgh
Darwin Building, Mayfield Road, Edinburgh,
EH9 3JU

EDINBURGH CITY LIBRARIES AND INFORMATION SERVICE

George IV Bridge, Edinburgh, EH1 1EG

Tel: 0131 242 8000
Fax: 0131 242 8009
E-mail: eclis@edinburgh.gov.uk

Website:
http://www.edinburgh.gov.uk/libraries

Enquiries:
Enquiries to: Head of Library and Information
Services

Organisation type and purpose:
Local government body, public library.

Subject coverage:
Architecture, art, design and photography,
business, community information, Edinburgh past
and present, English literature, genealogy,
government information, courses and careers,
consumer information, music, dance (particularly
Scottish), geography, science and technology,
travel, painting, Scotland, Sir Walter Scott and R L
Stevenson, Scottish Parliament.

**Museum or gallery collection, archive, or library
special collection:**
Architectural Copy Books
British Standards (CD-ROM)
Children's Illustrated Books
Cowan Bequest (music)
Dance of Death Collection
Donald Scottish Dance Collection
Early Photography of Edinburgh and Scotland
Early Scottish Printed Music
Edinburgh Printing before 1700
Genealogy Records – Microform
General Register Office Index to Births Deaths and
Marriages 1837–1997 (microfiche)
Henry Dyer Collection of Japanese Prints
Highland Life Collection of Photographs
Individual Family Histories
James Skene Watercolours
Krishnamurti Collection
Robert Louis Stevenson Collection
Marr Collection (music/handbills)
Scottish Artists' Sketchbooks
Scottish Parliament Offficial Publications
Sir Walter Scott Collection

Trade and statistical information:
Business directories UK, government information,
yearbooks and statistics.

Non-library collection catalogue:
All or part available online

Library catalogue:
All or part available online

Printed publications:
Bibliographies, booklets, calendars, postcards (list
available)
Handouts; leaflets on individual service points
Notes for Exhibitors in the Fine Art Library
Welcome wallets and welcome leaflets

Electronic and video publications:
Borrow a box (Multiple CD sets)
CD-ROMs in the Central Library
CD-ROMs in the Fine Art Department

Branch libraries:
Access Services
343 Oxgangs Road North, Edinburgh, EHB 9NE;
tel: 0131 529 5683
Balerno
1 Main Street, Edinburgh, EH14 7EQ; tel: 0131
529 5500; fax: 0131 529 5502; e-mail: balerno
.library@edinburgh.gov.uk

Balgreen
173 Balgreen Road, Edinburgh, EH11 3AT; tel:
0131 529 5585; fax: 0131 529 5583; e-mail:
balgreen.library@edinburgh.gov.uk
Blackhall
56 Hillhouse Road, Edinburgh, EH4 5EG; tel:
0131 529 5595; fax: 0131 336 5419; e-mail:
blackhall.library@edinburgh.gov.uk
Colinton
14 Thorburn Road, Edinburgh, EH13 0BQ; tel:
0131 529 5603; fax: 0131 529 5607; e-mail:
colinton.library@edinburgh.gov.uk
Corstorphine
12 Kirk Loan, Edinburgh, EH12 7HD; tel: 0131
529 5506; fax: 0131 529 5508; e-mail: costorphine
.library@edinburg.gov.uk
Craigmillar
7 Niddrie Marischal Gardens, Edinburgh, EH16
4LX; tel: 0131 529 5597; fax: 0131 529 5601; e-
mail: craigmillar.library@edinburgh.gov.uk
Currie
210 Lanark Road West, Edinburgh, EH14 5NN;
tel: 0131 529 5609; fax: 0131 529 5613; e-mail:
currie.library@edinburgh.gov.uk
Fountainbridge
137 Dundee Street, Edinburgh, EH11 1BG; tel:
0131 529 5616; fax: 0131 529 5621; website:
fountainbridge.library'edinburgh.gov.uk
Gilmerton
64 Gilmerton Dykes Street, Edinburgh, EH17
8PL; tel: 0131 529 5628; fax: 0131 529 5627; e-
mail: gilmerton.library@edinburgh.gov.uk
Granton
Wardieburn Terrace, Edinburgh, EH5 2DA; tel:
0131 529 5630; fax: 0131 529 5634; e-mail:
granton.library@edinburgh.gov.uk
Kirkliston
Station Road, Kirkliston, Edinburgh, EH29 9BE;
tel: 0131 529 5510; fax: 0131 529 5514; e-mail:
kirkliston.library@edinburgh.gov.uk
Leith
28–30 Ferry Road, Edinburgh, EH6 4AE; tel:
0131 529 5517; fax: 0131 554 2720; e-mail: leith
.library@edinburgh.gov.uk
McDonald Road
2 McDonald Road, Edinburgh, EH7 4LU; tel:
0131 529 5636 (also Ethnic Services tel: 0131 529
5644); fax: 0131 529 5646; e-mail: mcdonaldrd
.library@edinburgh.gov.uk
Moredun
92 Moredun Park Road, Edinburgh, EH17 7HL;
tel: 0131 529 5652; fax: 0131 447 5651; e-mail:
moredun.library@edinburgh.gov.uk
Morningside
184 Morningside Road, Edinburgh, EH10 4PU;
tel: 0131 529 5654; fax: 0131 447 4685; e-mail:
morningside.library@edinburgh.gov.uk
Muirhouse
15 Pennywell Court, Edinburgh, EH4 4TZ; tel:
0131 529 5528; fax: 0131 529 5532; e-mail:
muirhouse.library@edinburgh.gov.uk
Newington
17–21 Fountainhall Road, Edinburgh, EH9 2LN;
tel: 0131 529 5536; fax: 0131 667 5491; e-mail:
newington.library@edinburgh.gov.uk
Oxgangs
343 Oxgangs Road North, Edinburgh, EH13
9NE; tel: 0131 529 5549; fax: 0131 529 5554; e-
mail: oxgangs.library@edinburgh.gov.uk
Piershill
30 Piersfield Terrace, Edinburgh, EH8 7BQ; tel:
0131 529 5685; fax: 0131 529 5685; e-mail:
piershill.library@edinburgh.gov.uk
Portobello
14 Rosefield Terrace, Edinburgh, EH15 1AU; tel:
0131 529 5558; fax: 0131 669 2344; e-mail:
portobello.library@edinburgh.gov.uk
Ratho
6 School Wynd, Ratho, Newbridge, Edinburgh,
EH28 8TT; tel: 0131 333 5297; fax: 0131 333 5297;
e-mail: ratho.library@edinburgh.gov.uk
Sighthill
6 Sighthill Wynd, Edinburgh, EH11 4BL; tel:
0131 529 5569; fax: 0131 539 5572; e-mail:
sighthill.library@edinburgh.gov.uk

South Queensferry
9 Shore Road, Edinburgh, EH30 9RD; tel: 0131 529 5576; fax: 0131 529 5578; e-mail: southqueensferry.library@edinburgh.gov.uk
Stockbridge
Hamilton Place, Edinburgh, EH3 5BA; tel: 0131 529 5665; fax: 0131 529 5681; e-mail: stockbridge.library@edinburgh.gov.uk
Wester Hailes
1 West Side Plaza, Edinburgh, EH14 2ET; tel: 0131 529 5667; fax: 0131 529 5671; e-mail: westerhailes.library@edinburgh.gov.uk

Mobile Libraries:
c/o Access Services

Resource Centre (for people with disabilities):
Central Library
George IV Bridge, Edinburgh, EH1 1EG; tel: 0131 242 8136

EDINBURGH COLLEGE OF ART LIBRARY SERVICE

Acronym or abbreviation: ECA

Lauriston Place, Edinburgh, EH3 9DF

Tel: 0131 221 6180
Fax: 0131 221 6293
E-mail: library@eca.ac.uk

Website:
http://www.lib.eca.ac.uk
Access to library catalogue.

Enquiries:
Enquiries to: Reader Services Librarian
Other contacts: Technical Services Librarian

Founded:
1907

Organisation type and purpose:
University library, suitable for ages: adult, research organisation; SFC Small Specialist Institution status.

Subject coverage:
Architecture; landscape architecture; painting and drawing; sculpture; applied arts (jewellery and silversmithing, glass and architectural glass); applied design (furniture and interior and product design, fashion, textiles); visual communications (graphics, photography, animation, film and TV, illustration); urban design; architectural conservation; Islamic architecture, and urbanism.

Library catalogue:
All or part available online

Access to staff:
Contact by letter, by telephone, by e-mail and in person
Hours: Term time: Mon to Thu, 0915 to 2000; Fri, 1000 to 1700; vacations: Mon to Thu, 0915 to 1600; Fri, 1000 to 1600

Access to building, collection or gallery:
Hours: Term time: Mon to Thu, 0915 to 2000; Fri, 0900 to 1700; vacations: Mon to Thu, 0915 to 1600; Fri, 0900 to 1600

EDINBURGH COLLEGE OF PARAPSYCHOLOGY

Acronym or abbreviation: ECP

2 Melville Street, Edinburgh, EH3 7NS

Tel: 0131 220 1433
Fax: 0131 220 1433

Website:
http://www.parapsychology.org.uk

Enquiries:
Enquiries to: Secretary

Founded:
1932

Formerly called:
Edinburgh Psychic College and Library (year of change 1973)

Organisation type and purpose:
Membership association (membership is by subscription), present number of members: 300, voluntary organisation, registered charity (charity number SC 000571), suitable for ages: 18+.
To help the bereaved understand that life continues after physical death, to assist enquirers in this area plus provision of education, in a non-religious context. To promote all aspects of non-religious spiritualism.

Subject coverage:
Parapsychology, mediumship, psychism, survival after death, physical phenomena, spiritualism, spiritual healing, clairvoyance, counselling.

Museum or gallery collection, archive, or library special collection:
Library of 2000 books (catalogue on computer)

Library catalogue:
All or part available in-house

Printed publications:
The Candlestick (newsletter, 3 times a year, free, direct)

Access to staff:
Contact by letter, by telephone, by fax, by e-mail and in person
Hours: Mon to Fri, 1000 to 1600

EDINBURGH DISTRICT ENGINEERING TRAINING ASSOCIATION LIMITED

Acronym or abbreviation: EDETA Ltd

Fleming House, Kinnaird Park, Edinburgh, EH15 3RD

Tel: 0131 454 4840
Fax: 0131 454 4841
E-mail: administration@edeta.org.uk

Website:
http://www.edeta.org.uk
About EDETA, training services, course descriptions and dates, links to useful sites.

Enquiries:
Enquiries to: Manager

Founded:
1970

Organisation type and purpose:
National organisation, advisory body, learned society (membership is by election or invitation), service industry, registered charity, suitable for ages: 18+, training organisation.

Subject coverage:
VQ training in engineering, administration, IT, customer care, health and safety training.

Publications list:
Available online and in print

Access to staff:
Contact by letter, by telephone, by fax, by e-mail, in person and via website. Appointment necessary.
Hours: Mon to Fri, 0900 to 1700

Access for disabled people:
Parking provided, level entry, access to all public areas, toilet facilities

EDINBURGH FESTIVAL FRINGE

180 High Street, Edinburgh, EH1 1QS

Tel: 0131 226 0026\ Minicom no. 0131 220 5594
Fax: 0131 226 0016
E-mail: admin@edfringe.com

Website:
http://www.edfringe.com
Details on how to participate. Annual performance programme, background and history of organisation and public reviews of events.

Enquiries:
Enquiries to: Administrator

Founded:
1947

Organisation type and purpose:
Registered charity.
Arts festival.
Promotion of the performing and visual arts in Edinburgh.

Subject coverage:
Edinburgh Festival Fringe; performance, production, marketing and technical information. Advice and support year-round.

Printed publications:
Annual Performance Programme (postage)
FringeSafe: Technical Handbook (£5)
How to do a Show on the Fringe (£5)
How to Sell a Show on the Fringe (£5)

Access to staff:
Contact by letter, by telephone, by fax and by e-mail. Appointment necessary.
Hours: Mon to Fri, 1000 to 1800

EDINBURGH FILM FOCUS

Acronym or abbreviation: EFF

20 Forth Street, Edinburgh, EH1 3LH

Tel: 0131 622 7337
Fax: 0131 622 7338
E-mail: info@edinfilm.com

Website:
http://www.edinfilm.com
Locations brochure, production guide – directory of facilities, personnel, searchable locations library.

Enquiries:
Enquiries to: Film Commissioner
Other contacts: Location Liaison

Founded:
1989

Formerly called:
Edinburgh and Lothian Screen Industries Office (ELSIO) (year of change 1997)

Organisation type and purpose:
Advisory body, service industry. Local government-funded, independent, film commission. A first point of contact for information and help on filming in Edinburgh, the Lothians and Scottish Borders.

Printed publications:
Location brochure

Access to staff:
Contact by letter, by telephone, by fax, by e-mail and via website. Appointment necessary.
Hours: Mon to Fri, 0900 to 1700

Access to building, collection or gallery:
By appointment
Hours: Mon to Fri, 0930 to 1700

EDINBURGH INTERNATIONAL FESTIVAL

The Hub, Castlehill, Edinburgh, EH1 2NE

Tel: 0131 473 2000; minicom no./Textphone: 0131 473 2098
Fax: 0131 473 2003
E-mail: info@eif.co.uk

Website:
http://www.eif.co.uk
Background and information on Edinburgh International Festival. Full programme listings and booking details.

Enquiries:
Enquiries to: Marketing Manager
Direct tel: 0131 473 2020
Direct fax: 0131 473 2002
Direct e-mail: marketing@eif.co.uk

Founded:
1947

continued overleaf

Organisation type and purpose:
Registered charity (charity number SC 004694).
For promotion of annual arts festival.
Three-week festival presenting over 200
performances of the world's best music, opera,
theatre and dance.

Subject coverage:
Performances in music, opera, dance, theatre.

Printed publications:
Edinburgh International Festival Programme
 (annually)
Newsletter (twice annually)
Annual Review

Access to staff:
Contact by letter, by telephone, by fax, by e-mail
and via website. Appointment necessary.
Hours: Mon to Fri, 0930 to 1730

Access to building, collection or gallery:
No prior appointment required
Hours: Mon to Sun, 0930 to 1700
Special comments: Restricted access when functions
are on.

Access for disabled people:
Level entry, access to all public areas, toilet
facilities

EDINBURGH INTERNATIONAL JAZZ & BLUES FESTIVAL

Formal name: Edinburgh International Jazz and
Blues Festival

29 St Stephen Street, Edinburgh, EH3 5AN

Tel: 0131 225 2202
Fax: 0131 225 3321
E-mail: mikehart@edinburghjazzfestblues.com

Enquiries:
Enquiries to: Director

Founded:
1979

Organisation type and purpose:
Registered charity (charity number SCO12211).
Running an annual jazz and blues festival.

Printed publications:
Annual programme (free)

Access to staff:
Contact by letter, by telephone, by fax and by e-
mail
Hours: Mon to Fri, 0900 to 1700

EDINBURGH INTERNATIONAL SCIENCE FESTIVAL

Acronym or abbreviation: EISF

4 Gayfield Place Lane, Edinburgh, EH1 3NZ

Tel: 0131 558 7666
Fax: 0131 557 9177
E-mail: eisf@scifest.co.uk

Website:
http://www.sciencefestival.co.uk
Background information on the Science Festival
and full programme information.

Enquiries:
Enquiries to: Marketing Manager
Other contacts: Festival Manager

Founded:
1988

Organisation type and purpose:
Registered charity, events suitable for all ages, plus
an extensive schools touring programme.
To reveal science and the excitement of discovery
to the widest possible audience.

Subject coverage:
Public understanding of science. Science
communication. Science shows, workshops and
hands-on events.

Non-library collection catalogue:
All or part available online

Printed publications:
Information brochure
Science Festival Programme (annually, free)
Generation Science Schools Touring Programme
 (annually, free)

Access to staff:
Contact by letter, by telephone, by fax and by e-
mail. Appointment necessary.
Hours: Mon to Fri, 0930 to 1730

Also known as:
The Science Festival

EDINBURGH MATHEMATICAL SOCIETY

Acronym or abbreviation: EMS

School of Mathematics, Edinburgh University, The
King's Buildings, Mayfield Road, Edinburgh, EH9
3JZ

Tel: 0131 650 5040
Fax: 0131 650 6553
E-mail: edmathsoc@ed.ac.uk

Website:
http://www.maths.ed.ac.uk/~ems

Enquiries:
Enquiries to: Honorary Secretary

Founded:
1883

Organisation type and purpose:
Learned society.
Promotion and extension of the mathematical
sciences, pure and applied, particularly in
Scotland.

Subject coverage:
Pure and applied mathematics.

Printed publications:
Proceedings of the Edinburgh Mathematical
 Society (annual vol. in 3 parts)

EDINBURGH NAPIER UNIVERSITY MELROSE CAMPUS LIBRARY

Education Centre, Borders General Hospital,
Melrose, Roxburghshire, TD6 9BD

Tel: 01896 827620; minicom no. 01896 661630
Fax: 01896 823869

Enquiries:
Enquiries to: Librarian
Direct e-mail: moira.mitchell@borders.scot.nhs.uk

Founded:
1974

Organisation type and purpose:
University library also serving NHS.
NHS Library.

Subject coverage:
Nursing, primary care, medicine, psychiatry,
public health, psychology, complementary
therapies, social work, child care, NHS
management.

Non-library collection catalogue:
All or part available online

Library catalogue:
All or part available online

Access to staff:
Contact by letter, by telephone, by fax, by e-mail
and in person. Non-members charged.
Hours: Mon to Thu, 0900 to 2100; Fri, 0900 to 1700

Access to building, collection or gallery:
No prior appointment required

Access for disabled people:
Level entry, toilet facilities

Also at:
Edinburgh Napier University Learning
Information Services (NULIS)
 Craiglockhart Campus, Edinburgh, EH14 1DJ

Links with:
NHS Borders
 Newstead, Melrose

EDINBURGH NAPIER UNIVERSITY LEARNING INFORMATION SERVICES

Craiglockhart Campus, Edinburgh, EH14 1DJ

Tel: 0131 455 4269
Fax: 0131 455 4276

Website:
http://www.napier.ac.uk/napierlife/campuslife/
Libraries/Pages/Libraries.aspx
http://www.napier.ac.uk

Enquiries:
Enquiries to: Director of Learning Information
Services
Direct tel: 0131 455 4270
Direct fax: 0131 455 4242
Direct e-mail: c.pinder@napier.ac.uk

Organisation type and purpose:
University library.

Subject coverage:
Accounting, economics and statistics; arts and
creative industries; computing; engineering and
the built environment; health and social sciences;
life sciences; management and law; marketing,
tourism and languages; nursing, midwifery and
social care.

**Museum or gallery collection, archive, or library
special collection:**
Edward Clark Collection on printing and book
 production
War Poets' collection, material relating to Wilfred
 Owen, Siegfried Sassoon and war poetry
 generally.

Non-library collection catalogue:
All or part available online

Library catalogue:
All or part available online

Printed publications:
General guides to services and collections
Guides to finding information
Subject guides

Access to staff:
Contact by letter, by telephone and by e-mail.
Non-members charged.
Hours: Term time: Mon to Thu, 0845 to 2100; Sat
and Sun, 1000 to 1600

EDINBURGH ROYAL CHORAL UNION

Acronym or abbreviation: ERCU

Craigroyston, Broadgate, Gullane, EH31 2DH

Tel: 01620 843299
E-mail: jane.kirk@ed.ac.uk

Website:
http://www.ercu.org.uk

Enquiries:
Enquiries to: President
Other contacts: Librarian for hire of choral music.

Founded:
1858

Organisation type and purpose:
Membership association (membership is by
qualification), present number of members: 120,
voluntary organisation, registered charity (charity
number SC012050).
Self-governing amateur society whose objects are
the study, practice and performance of music, one
of Scotland's largest independent amateur choirs,
promoting at least three concerts in a season, with
professional orchestras and conductors.

Subject coverage:
Choral music.

Museum or gallery collection, archive, or library special collection:
Large library of choral music available for hire

Library catalogue:
All or part available online

Printed publications:
History of the Edinburgh Royal Choral Union, 1858–1983 (booklet)
Library catalogue

Publications list:
Available online

Access to staff:
Contact by letter, by telephone, by fax, by e-mail and via website
Hours: Mon to Fri, 0900 to 1700

Member of:
National Federation of Music Societies (NFMS) 7–15 Rosebery Avenue, London, EC1R 4SP; tel: 020 7841 0110; fax: 020 7841 0115; e-mail: nfms@nfms.org.uk

EDINBURGH SIR WALTER SCOTT CLUB

Acronym or abbreviation: ESWSC

9, Burnbank Grove, Straiton, Loanhead, Midlothian, EH20 9NX

Tel: 0131 448 1976
E-mail: hontreas@walterscottclub.org.uk

Website:
http://www.walterscottclub.org.uk
The Edinburgh Sir Walter Scott Club.

Enquiries:
Enquiries to: Hon. Secretary
Direct tel: 0131 228 2430
Direct e-mail: honsec@walterscottclub.org.uk

Founded:
1894

Organisation type and purpose:
Learned society (membership is by subscription), present number of members: 250.

Subject coverage:
Life and works of Sir Walter Scott.

Museum or gallery collection, archive, or library special collection:
A few books of Scott minutes of club and council meetings
Tapes of annual dinner speeches

Printed publications:
Annual Bulletin
Occasional leaflets, with forthcoming programme of events

Access to staff:
Contact by e-mail and via website. Appointment necessary.

Links with:
University of Edinburgh, Department of Literature

EDUCATION LAW ASSOCIATION

Acronym or abbreviation: ELAS

37 Grimston Avenue, Folkestone, Kent, CT20 2QD

Tel: 01303 211570
Fax: 01303 211570
E-mail: secretary@educationlawassociation.org.uk

Enquiries:
Enquiries to: Executive Secretary

Founded:
1992

Organisation type and purpose:
Professional body (membership is by subscription), present number of members: 325, registered charity (charity number 1053614), suitable for ages: all, training organisation.

Subject coverage:
Education law.

Access to staff:
Contact by letter, by telephone, by fax and by e-mail
Hours: Mon to Fri, 0900 to 1700
Special comments: No visitors, part-time staff.

EDUCATIONAL AND TELEVISION FILMS LIMITED

Acronym or abbreviation: ETV

247a Upper Street, Highbury Corner, London, N1 1RU

Tel: 020 7226 2298
Fax: 020 7226 8016
E-mail: zoe@etvltd.demon.co.uk

Website:
http://www.etvltd.demon.co.uk
Details of aspects of the collection, fully searchable database online soon.

Enquiries:
Enquiries to: Librarian

Founded:
1950

Organisation type and purpose:
Film library.

Subject coverage:
Footage of and from the history of the British Labour Movement and a wide variety of documentary and technical subjects from the former socialist countries and from the former Soviet Union, former Eastern Bloc countries, Afghanistan, China, Chile, Cuba, Korea and Vietnam, as well as a complete collection from the Spanish Civil War from the Republican side.

Museum or gallery collection, archive, or library special collection:
British Labour History films
Spanish Civil War films
A wide spectrum of international films that have a political relevance to todays news stories

Non-library collection catalogue:
All or part available in-house

Library catalogue:
All or part available in-house

Printed publications:
Catalogues available covering all aspects of the collection

Publications list:
Available in print

Access to staff:
Contact by letter, by telephone, by fax, by e-mail and via website
Hours: Mon to Fri, 0930 to 1730

Access to building, collection or gallery:
Prior appointment required
Hours: Mon to Fri, 0930 to 1730

EDUCATIONAL DISTRIBUTION SERVICE

Education House, Drywall Estate, Castle Road, Murston, Sittingbourne, Kent, ME10 3RL

Tel: 01795 427614
Fax: 01795 437988
E-mail: info@edist.co.uk

Enquiries:
Enquiries to: Managing Director

Founded:
1971

Organisation type and purpose:
International organisation, suitable for ages: all. Library and distribution service for film and video, and all resources and other goods as contracted.

Museum or gallery collection, archive, or library special collection:
GPO classic films

Printed publications:
Educational resources

Publications list:
Available in print

Access to staff:
Contact by letter, by telephone, by fax and by e-mail. Appointment necessary.
Hours: Mon to Fri, 0900 to 1700

Access to building, collection or gallery:
Prior appointment required

EDUCATIONAL GRANTS ADVISORY SERVICE

Acronym or abbreviation: EGAS

501–505 Kingsland Road, London, E8 4AU

Tel: 020 7254 6251 (Tue, Wed and Thu 1400 to 1600 only)
Fax: 020 7249 5443
E-mail: egas.enquiry@family-action.org.uk

Website:
http://www.family-action.org.uk
Information about parent organisation (Family Action) and details of services provided by EGAS.

Enquiries:
Enquiries to: Educational and Grants Manager

Founded:
1962

Parent body formerly called:
Family Welfare Association (year of change 2008)

Organisation type and purpose:
Information and grant giving service. A service provided by Family Action, registered charity number 264713.

Subject coverage:
Post-16 education in England, specialising in charitable funding.

Information services:
Guide to Student Funding, Educational Grants Search

Access to staff:
Contact by letter and by telephone
Hours: Mon to Fri, 0900 to 1700
Special comments: Telephone service only available on Tue, Wed and Thu, from 1400 to 1600

Parent body:
Family Action
501–505 Kingsland Road, London E8 4AU; tel: 020 7254 6251; fax: 020 7249 5443; e-mail: info@family-action.org.uk; website: http://www.family-action.org.uk

EDUCATIONAL INSTITUTE OF SCOTLAND

Acronym or abbreviation: EIS

46 Moray Place, Edinburgh, EH3 6BH

Tel: 0131 225 6244
Fax: 0131 220 3151
E-mail: enquiries@eis.org.uk

Website:
http://www.eis.org.uk

Enquiries:
Enquiries to: General Secretary

Organisation type and purpose:
Trade union (membership is by subscription), present number of members: 58,000.
All sectors of Scottish education.

Subject coverage:
Education and teachers in all sectors (Scotland).

Printed publications:
Scottish Educational Journal

Access to staff:
Contact by letter, by fax and by e-mail
Hours: Mon to Fri, 0900 to 1700

continued overleaf

Affiliated to:
Trades Union Congress

EDUSERV

Royal Mead, Railway Place, Bath, BA1 1SR

Tel: 01225 474300
Fax: 01225 474301
E-mail: contact@eduserv.org.uk

Website:
http://www.eduserv.org.uk
Eduserv's technology services developed for
education and the public sector.

Founded:
1988

Organisation type and purpose:
Non-profit IT services group, dedicated to
developing and delivering technology services for
education and the public sector through services,
including access and identity management;
institution connections to online resources such as
Athens and OpenAthens; licence negotiation and
management; offers on software and data licences
to the education community; web development
and hosting and consultancy. Eduserv also
undertakes forward-thinking research and
innovation that leads to a greater understanding of
technology and shared services, which it provides
to the academic community.

Subject coverage:
Access to protected online resources, web
development and hosting and licence negotiation
for software and data licences.

Access to staff:
Contact by letter, by telephone, by fax, by e-mail
and via website. Appointment necessary.
Hours: Mon to Fri, 0800 to 1800

EEF – THE MANUFACTURERS' ORGANISATION

Acronym or abbreviation: EEF

Broadway House, Tothill Street, Westminster,
London, SW1H 9NQ

Tel: 020 7222 7777
Fax: 020 7222 2782
E-mail: enquiries@eef.org.uk

Website:
http://www.eef.org.uk
About the EEF.

Enquiries:
Enquiries to: Information Services Manager
Direct tel: 020 7654 1574
Direct e-mail: crochester@eef-fed.org.uk

Founded:
1896

Organisation type and purpose:
Trade association.
Employers' Organisation.

Subject coverage:
Representation of the engineering industry's
employer interests, employee relations, personnel
management, education and skills, environmental
issues, health and safety, economics. (Information
derived from surveys of members is not generally
available.)

Non-library collection catalogue:
All or part available in-house

Library catalogue:
All or part available in-house

Printed publications:
Engineering Outlook (4 times a year, £180)
Management and Professional Engineers' Pay
   Survey (annually, £400)

Publications list:
Available in print

Access to staff:
Contact by letter, by telephone, by fax, by e-mail
and via website. Access for members only.
Hours: Mon to Fri, 0900 to 1530

Affiliated to:
Engineering Construction Industry Association
Federation of Engineering Design Companies
Fifteen autonomous organisations, fourteen
regional associations

Links with:
Engineering Council
SEMTA

Member of:
Council of European Employers of the Metal,
Engineering and Technology-Based Industries

EEF YORKSHIRE AND HUMBERSIDE

Acronym or abbreviation: EEF

Fieldhead, Thorner, Leeds, West Yorkshire, LS14
3DN

Tel: 0113 289 2671
Fax: 0113 289 3170
E-mail: team@eef-yandh.org.uk

Website:
http://www.eef.org.uk

Enquiries:
Enquiries to: Director
Direct tel: 0113 289 2863

Founded:
1890

Formerly called:
Engineering and Ship Building Employers
Association (Yorkshire and Humberside)

Organisation type and purpose:
Membership association.
Employers trade association.
Supports engineering and manufacturing
companies.

Subject coverage:
All matters relating to the employment of people.

Printed publications:
A variety of maintained documents are available
   for purchase, including:
Annual Review of the Federation (free to members)
EEF Directory
EEF Employment Guide (updated 3 times a year)
Health and Safety Newsline (newsletter, 4 times a
   year, free to members)
Practical Risk Assessment – guidance for SMEs
Register of Environmental Regulations
Training and Development Guide

Publications list:
Available in print

Access to staff:
Contact by letter and by fax. Appointment
necessary. Non-members charged.
Hours: Mon to Fri, 0900 to 1700

Affiliated to:
EEF
   Tothill Street, London, SW1H 9NQ

EEMA

Formal name: European Electronic Messaging
Association

Alexander House, High Street, Inkberrow,
Worcester, WR7 4DT

Tel: 01386 793028
Fax: 01386 793268
E-mail: info@eema.org

Website:
http://www.eema.org

Enquiries:
Enquiries to: Membership Director
Direct e-mail: jim.dickson@eema.org

Founded:
1987

Organisation type and purpose:
International organisation, trade association.

Subject coverage:
All aspects of electronic business including
security, directory, e-commerce, XML, unified
messaging, legal issues surrounding secure digital
identity and trusted third party products and
services, change management, e-Government and
public sector, CA's and regulation authorities.

Non-library collection catalogue:
All or part available online

Printed publications:
Publications include:
Role Based Access Control
e-Business Glossary
E-mail Best Practice Document
The 16 Steps to Effective E-mail and The Nine No's
   of E-mail
Acceptable Computer Usage Policy
Confidentiality Issues
Practical Policies for Virus Protection
The ECAF Model
LDAP Moving Forward
Internet Personal Naming Standard

Publications list:
Available online and in print

Access to staff:
Contact by letter, by telephone, by fax and by e-
mail
Hours: Mon to Fri, 0900 to 1700

Access to building, collection or gallery:
Prior appointment required

EFFECTIVE TECHNOLOGY MARKETING LIMITED

Acronym or abbreviation: ETM

PO Box 171, Grimsby, Lincolnshire, DN35 0TP

Tel: 01472 816660
Fax: 01472 816660

Website:
http://www.dataresources.co.uk
Publications and conferences.

Enquiries:
Enquiries to: Managing Director

Founded:
1987

Organisation type and purpose:
Publishing house.
Publishers distributor.

Subject coverage:
Business information, Central and Eastern Europe
and the CIS, Russia.

Printed publications:
Business Information Searcher (£95)
Directory of Information & Research Specialists
   2002 (1st ed., £65)
EBRD Directory Business Information Sources on
   Central and Eastern Europe and the CIS (£125)

Publications list:
Available in print

Access to staff:
Contact by letter, by telephone, by fax and by e-
mail
Hours: Mon to Fri, 0900 to 1700

EFNARC

Formal name: European Federation for Specialist
Construction Chemicals and Concrete Systems

EFNARC Secretary, Cobblers Cottage, Chester
Road, Daresbury, Warrington, WA4 4AJ

Tel: 01925 740581
Fax: 01925 740581
E-mail: secretary@efnarc.org

Website:
http://www.efnarc.org

Founded:
1998

Formerly called:
European Federation of Producers and Applicators of Specialist Products for Structures

Organisation type and purpose:
Trade association, present number of members: 15. Represents major European manufacturers involved in specialised construction and concrete systems.

Subject coverage:
Specialised construction and concrete systems.

Non-library collection catalogue:
All or part available online

Printed publications:
European Specification for Sprayed Concrete (English and German editions)
Guidelines for the use of specialist products for Mechanised Tunnelling (TBM)
Specification for Synthetic Resin and Polymer-modified Cementitious Floorings for Industrial Use
Specification and Guidelines for Self-Compacting Concrete
Guidelines for testing fire protection systems for tunnels
Guidelines for Viscosity Modifying Admixtures for Concrete
Specification and Guidelines on Thin Spray-on Liners for Mining and Tunnelling

Publications list:
Available online and in print

Access to staff:
Contact by letter, by telephone, by fax, by e-mail and via website
Hours: Mon to Fri, 0900 to 1700

EGG CRAFTERS GUILD OF GREAT BRITAIN

The Studio, 7 Hylton Terrace, North Shields, Tyne and Wear, NE29 0EE

Tel: 0191 258 3648
E-mail: joanccutts@oal.com

Website:
http://www.geocities.com/eggcraftersguild
http://www.freewebs.com/eggcraftersguild

Enquiries:
Enquiries to: Life President/Founder

Founded:
1979

Organisation type and purpose:
International organisation, membership association (membership is by subscription, election or invitation), present number of members: 800 world-wide, voluntary organisation. Craft organisation.
Members meet at various venues to exhibit and enter competitions; many members sell their eggs, some give Guild talks to organisations.

Subject coverage:
Egg craft (painting and other art work on eggshell); exhibitions; teaching; cutting designs with electric drill. Many eggs are created in the Style of Fabergé, and all are made from real eggs.

Printed publications:
Books
Newsletter (quarterly to members only)

Access to staff:
Contact by letter, by fax and by e-mail.
Appointment necessary.
Hours: Mon to Fri, 0900 to 1600

EGYPT EXPLORATION SOCIETY

Acronym or abbreviation: EES

3 Doughty Mews, London, WC1N 2PG

Tel: 020 7242 1880
Fax: 020 7404 6118
E-mail: contact@ees.ac.uk

Website:
http://www.ees.ac.uk
About the Society and its work, history, photo galleries, library archives, fieldwork, publications, news, payment facilities.

Enquiries:
Enquiries to: Administrator
Direct tel: 020 7242 2268
Other contacts: Deputy Director

Founded:
1882

Formerly called:
The Egypt Exploration Fund (EEF) (year of change 1915)

Organisation type and purpose:
International organisation, learned society (membership is by subscription), present number of members: 3,200, registered charity (charity number 212384), research organisation.

Subject coverage:
Ancient Egypt; archaeology and history of Egypt to AD1900.

Information services:
Library, archives, online resources.

Education services:
Publications, events.

Museum or gallery collection, archive, or library special collection:
Library of Egyptology, archive of photographs, correspondence and other documents relating to the Society and its work.
Archive

Non-library collection catalogue:
All or part available online

Library catalogue:
All or part available online

Printed publications:
Publications prices do not include p&p:
Egyptian Archaeology (2 times a year)
Arabic Documents from the Ottoman Period from Qasr Ibrim (Hinds M et al, 1986, £48)
Archaeological Memoirs (intermittent)
Egyptian Archaeology, The Bulletin of the Egypt Exploration Society (2 times a year, cover price £3)
Excavation Memoirs (intermittent)
Graeco-Roman Memoirs (intermittent)
Meroitic Inscriptions, Part II (Griffith F LI, 1912, £20)
Semna-Kumma I, The Temple of Kumma; and The Temple of Semna (Caminos R A, 1998, two-volume set, £90)
Texts from Excavations (intermittent)
The Anubieion at Saqqara I, The Settlement and the Temple Precinct (Jeffeys D G et al, 1988, £72)
The Inscriptions of Sinai, Part II (Gardiner A H et al, 1955, £40)
The Journal of Egyptian Archaeology (annually, £40, members £34)
The Mephite Tomb of Horemheb, Commander-in-Chief of Tutankhamun, II A Catalogue of the finds (Schneider H D, 1996, £80)
The Tomb of Tia and Tia. A Royal Monument of the Ramesside Period In The Memphite Necropolis (Martin G T, 1997, £96)
The Oxyrhynchus Papyri, Part LXVI (Gonis M et al, 1999, £70)
The Scrolls of Bishop Timotheos (Plumley J M, 1975, £15)
Who Was Who in Egyptology, A Biographical Index from 1700 to Present Day (Bierbrier M L, 1995, £40)
Order printed publications from: The EES, 3 Doughty Mews, London, WC1N 2PG; e-mail: @ees.ac.uk; tel: 020 7242 2266; fax: 020 7404 6118; website: http://www.ees.ac.uk

Publications list:
Available online and in print

Access to staff:
Contact by letter, by telephone, by fax, by e-mail, in person and via website. Appointment necessary. Non-members charged.
Hours: Tue to Fri, 1030 to 1630

Access to building, collection or gallery:
No prior appointment required

Links with:
Foundation for Science and Technology

EGYPTIAN STATE TOURIST OFFICE

Egyptian House, 170 Piccadilly, London, W1V 9DD

Tel: 020 7493 5283
Fax: 020 7408 0295
E-mail: egypt@freenetname.co.uk

Website:
http://www.interoz.com/Egypt
The official Ministry of Tourism website.

Enquiries:
Enquiries to: Director
Direct tel: 020 7495 6489
Other contacts: Deputy Manager

Formerly called:
Egyptian Tourist Authority (UK)

Organisation type and purpose:
National government body.
Promotion of tourism to Egypt.

Subject coverage:
Tourism, travel and transport, schedules and prices in Egypt; visa forms and information; Nile cruises; places of interest; tourist villages, destinations in Egypt. Conference and meeting facilities.

Museum or gallery collection, archive, or library special collection:
A collection of slides of Egypt
Promotional videos on the country
Posters

Printed publications:
Brochures, pictures and maps, Cairo, Luxor, Aswan, Sinai, Alexandria, Red Sea, Oasis
Press releases, statistics

Electronic and video publications:
Videos on different places

Access to staff:
Contact by letter, by telephone, by fax and by e-mail
Hours: Mon to Fri, 0930 to 1630

Links with:
Egyptian Embassy and the Egyptian Consulate
tel: 020 7235 9777; fax: 020 7235 5684

Parent body:
Ministry of Tourism in Egypt
tel: + 202 685 3576/9658; fax: + 202 685 4363/4788

EIL CULTURAL AND EDUCATIONAL TRAVEL

Acronym or abbreviation: EIL UK

287 Worcester Road, Malvern, Worcestershire, WR14 1AB

Tel: 01684 562577
Fax: 01684 562212
E-mail: info@eiluk.org

Website:
http://www.eiluk.org
General information.

Founded:
1936

Formerly called:
(BAEIL)

continued overleaf

Organisation type and purpose:
International organisation, membership
association, registered charity (charity number
1070440), suitable for ages: 16+.
Non-profit making organisation. Recognised by
the Economic and Social Council of the UN
(ECOSOC) as category II non-governmental
organisation.
Cultural and educational exchange.

Subject coverage:
Understanding between countries of the world,
cross-cultural education.

Access to staff:
Contact by letter, by telephone, by fax, by e-mail
and via website
Hours: Mon to Fri, 0900 to 1700

Affiliated to:
UNESCO, category B

ELDERLY ACCOMMODATION COUNSEL

Acronym or abbreviation: EAC

3rd Floor, 89 Albert Embankment, London, SE1
7TP

Tel: 020 7820 1343
Fax: 020 7820 3970
E-mail: enquiries@eac.org.uk

Website:
http://www.housingcare.org
Access to National Database of housing and care
homes

Founded:
1985

Organisation type and purpose:
Registered charity (charity number 292552).
A national charity offering advice and information
about all forms of accommodation and care for
older people.

Subject coverage:
Accommodation options for older people. Elderly
Accommodation Counsel (EAC) is a national
charity, maintaining nation-wide databases of
accommodation specifically for older people –
sheltered, retirement housing to buy and to rent,
extra care schemes and close care housing
(sheltered accommodation where there is a care
home on site), and care homes, both for personal
care and for nursing. The free, independent advice
line offers guidance, advice and detailed
information to help older people choose and fund
the support or accommodation options most suited
to their needs and wishes.

Printed publications:
Accommodation options for older people (booklet)
Regional Guides on housing or on housing and
care homes
Housing Options for Older People (HOOP) Toolkit
HOOP questionnaire

Access to staff:
Contact by letter, by telephone, by fax, by e-mail
and via website
Hours: Mon to Fri, 0900 to 1700

Access to building, collection or gallery:
No access other than to staff

ELECTORAL REFORM INTERNATIONAL SERVICES

6 Chancel Street, Blackfriars, London, SE1 0UU

Tel: 020 7620 3794
Fax: 020 7928 4366
E-mail: erisuk@eris.org.uk

Website:
http://www.eris.org.uk

Organisation type and purpose:
To provide support to emerging democracies for
the further consolidation of democracy and good
governance around the world, with a particular
emphasis of the conduct of credible and
transparent elections

Access to staff:
Contact by letter, by telephone, by fax, by e-mail
and via website

ELECTORAL REFORM SOCIETY LIMITED

Acronym or abbreviation: ERS

6 Chancel Street, Blackfriars, London, SE1 0UU

Tel: 020 7928 1622
Fax: 020 7401 7789

Website:
http://www.electoral-reform.org.uk

Enquiries:
Enquiries to: Chief Executive
Direct e-mail: ers@electoral-reform.org.uk

Founded:
1884

Formerly called:
Proportional Representation Society (year of
change 1969)

Organisation type and purpose:
Learned society, membership association
(membership is by subscription), present number
of members: 2,000, voluntary organisation.
Campaigning organisation.
To campaign for the introduction of proportional
representation by the single transferable vote
method for all elections.

Subject coverage:
All aspects of elections, including electoral law and
practice; voting systems, especially proportional
representation; election monitoring; election
campaigns; balloting in professional, trade union
and other common interest organisations, etc.

**Museum or gallery collection, archive, or library
special collection:**
The Lakeman Library (formerly the Arthur
McDougall Library) houses a collection of works
and papers on political science, elections, election
observations, voting systems, electoral reform,
especially proportional representation in the
United Kingdom and elsewhere. The Library is
maintained by the McDougall Trust

Trade and statistical information:
Statistical information relating to elections in the
UK and elsewhere.

Library catalogue:
All or part available in-house

Printed publications:
Annual Report (members)
Ballot Box (newsletter, members)
Publications include:
Ballot Secrecy (A4 58pp, £10 plus p&p)
What is STV? (leaflet, 50p plus p&p)

Publications list:
Available online and in print

Access to staff:
Contact by letter, by telephone, by fax and by e-
mail. Appointment necessary.
Hours: Mon to Fri, 0930 to 1730
Special comments: Letter of introduction preferred.
Charges may be made to users.

Access to building, collection or gallery:
No prior appointment required
Hours: Mon to Fri, 0930 to 1730

Access for disabled people:
Toilet facilities

Associated charity:
The McDougall Trust
tel: 020 7620 1080; fax: 020 7928 1528; e-mail:
admin@mcdougall.org.uk

Consultative status with:
Economic and Social Council of the United Nations

**Enquiries concerning the conduct of ballots and
surveys only:**
Electoral Reform (Services) Ltd
The Elections Centre, 33 Clarendon Road,
Hornsey, London, N8 0NW; tel: 020 8365 8909;
fax: 020 8365 8587

ELECTRIC RAILWAY SOCIETY

Acronym or abbreviation: ERS

17 Catherine Drive, Sutton Coldfield, West
Midlands, B73 6AX

Tel: 0121 354 8332
E-mail: iwfrew@tiscali.co.uk

Website:
http://www.electric-rly-society.org.uk

Enquiries:
Enquiries to: Honorary Secretary

Founded:
1946

Organisation type and purpose:
Learned society (membership is by subscription).

Subject coverage:
History and development of electric railway and
light railway services and equipment in the British
Isles. Development of rail services around major
cities worldwide. Development of high speed
intercity passenger services worldwide.

**Museum or gallery collection, archive, or library
special collection:**
Some material available for educational purposes
Collection of colour slides depicting tramways,
electric railways, in the United Kingdom
Collection of colour slides depicting coastal ferries
and pleasure steamers in British waters

Printed publications:
The Electric Railway (6 times a year, subscription
£16)
Order printed publications from: Hon. Secretary

Access to staff:
Contact by letter and by e-mail
Hours: Mon to Fri, 0900 to 2200

Access to building, collection or gallery:
No access other than to staff

Affiliated to:
Asociación Uruguaya Amigos del Riel
Cas Correos 857, Montevideo, Uruguay
Railway Society of Southern Africa
PO Box 12375, Jacobs, SA 4026

ELECTRICAL CONTRACTORS' ASSOCIATION

Acronym or abbreviation: ECA

ESCA House, 34 Palace Court, London, W2 4HY

Tel: 020 7313 4800
Fax: 020 7221 7344
E-mail: electricalcontractors@eca.co.uk

Website:
http://www.eca.co.uk
Background, organisation and structure.

Enquiries:
Enquiries to: Head of Marketing
Other contacts: Departmental Heads

Founded:
1901

Organisation type and purpose:
Trade association.

Subject coverage:
Electrical installation work; engineering and
contracting.

Printed publications:
ECA Desk Diary
ECA Registered Electrical Contractors (annually)

Electrical Contractor (monthly)
Information Manual

Access to staff:
Contact by letter, by fax and by e-mail
Hours: Mon to Fri, 0900 to 1700

ELECTRICAL INSTALLATION EQUIPMENT MANUFACTURERS' ASSOCIATION LIMITED

Acronym or abbreviation: EIEMA

Westminster Tower, 3 Albert Embankment, London, SE1 7SL

Tel: 020 7793 3013
Fax: 020 7735 4158
E-mail: cac@beama.org.uk

Website:
http://www.eiema.org.uk

Enquiries:
Enquiries to: Director
Direct tel: 020 7793 3009
Direct e-mail: dd@eiema.demon.co.uk

Organisation type and purpose:
Trade association.

Subject coverage:
Electrical accessories; fuses; switch and fuse gear; miniature, earth leakage and moulded case circuit-breakers; distribution switchboards (cubicle and non-cubicle types); cablejoints and terminators.

Trade and statistical information:
Statistical information is strictly for members only.

Printed publications:
Guide to Busbar Trunking Systems
Guide to Fuse Link Application
Guide to 'IP' Codes for enclosures
Guide to Residual Current Devices
Guide to Switch and Fusegear Devices
Guide to the Forms of Separation
Guide to Type Tested Assemblies and Partially
  Type Tested Assemblies
Member and Product Guide (annually)

Access to staff:
Contact by letter, by telephone, by fax and by e-mail
Hours: Mon to Thu, 0900 to 1700; Fri, 0900 to 1545

Affiliated to:
British Electrotechnical and Allied Manufacturers Association (BEAMA)

ELECTROPHYSIOLOGICAL TECHNOLOGISTS ASSOCIATION

Acronym or abbreviation: EPTA

Department of Clinical Neurophysiology, Great Ormond St Hospital, Great Ormond Street, London, WC1N 3JH

E-mail: eptasec@hotmail.com

Website:
http://www.epta.50megs.com

Enquiries:
Enquiries to: Honorary Secretary

Founded:
1949

Organisation type and purpose:
National organisation, professional body (membership is by
subscription), present number of members: over 600.

Subject coverage:
Electrophysiology especially neurophysiology.

Printed publications:
Quarterly journal (annual subscription)

Access to staff:
Contact by letter and by e-mail
Hours: Mon to Fri, 0900 to 1700

Links with:
International Organisation of Societies for Electophysiology (OSET)
  tel: 01785 258672

ELGAR SOCIETY

The Hon Secretary, 12 Monkhams Drive, Woodford Green, IG8 0LQ

Tel: 020 8504 0292
E-mail: hon.sec@elgar.org

Website:
http://www.elgar.org
Real Audio, extracts, biographical details, merchandise details, branches, networking, multimedia, etc.
http://www.cornucopia.org.uk
Summary catalogue.

Enquiries:
Enquiries to: Honorary Secretary

Founded:
1951

Created by the merger of:
Friends of Elgar's Birthplace

Organisation type and purpose:
International organisation, learned society (membership is by subscription), present number of members: 1,500 UK & world, registered charity (charity number 298062).
Trading Company formed in 2000.
To supply books, CDs, scores and other merchandise.

Subject coverage:
Sir Edward Elgar, his life and music; study, appreciation and performance of his works.
Publicity for concerts, talks and lectures via website.

Museum or gallery collection, archive, or library special collection:
Scores of all Compositions
Memorabilia
Research biographies, etc.

Printed publications:
Elgar Society Journal (3 times a year)
Elgar Society News (3 times a year)
Order printed publications from: Elgar Editions, c/o 20 High Street, Rickmansworth, Hertfordshire, WD3 1ER; or via the website

Electronic and video publications:
Elgar Choral Songs
Elgar's Interpreters on Record
King Olaf
The Black Knight
The Dream of Gerontius
The Elgar Edition
The Elgar Piano
Various CDs of choral/orchestral and piano music

Publications list:
Available online and in print

Access to staff:
Contact by letter, by telephone, by e-mail and via website
Hours: Any reasonable time

Branches:
Bristol (Great Western Branch)
  tel: 01434 776503
Edinburgh (Scottish Branch)
  tel: 01383 727491
London Branch
  tel: 01707 876079
Manchester (North West Branch)
  tel: 0161 998 4404
Southampton (Southern Branch)
  tel: 023 9281 6488
Worcester (West Midlands Branch)
  tel: 01453 882091

ELIZABETH FINN CARE

Acronym or abbreviation: EFC

1 Derry Street, London, W8 5HY

Tel: 020 7396 6700
Fax: 020 7396 6739
E-mail: info@elizabethfinn.org.uk

Website:
http://www.elizabethfinncare.org.uk
www.turn2us.org.uk
turn2us is a new charity offering a groundbreaking online service to help the millions of people in need in the UK. For the first time, people can access information on all benefits and grants available to them from both statutory and voluntary organisations, at no cost, through turn2us. In many cases, applications for support can be made directly from the website and we'll keep people informed by e-mail or by sending a text to their mobile phone.

Enquiries:
Enquiries to: Director of Casework
Direct e-mail: enquiries.casework@elizabethfinn.org .uk

Founded:
1897

Formerly called:
Distressed Gentlefolks Aid Association (DGAA); Homelife DGAA (year of change 1994); Elizabeth Finn Trust (year of change 2005)

Organisation type and purpose:
Voluntary organisation, registered charity (charity number 207812).
Elizabeth Finn Care is the UK's largest independent direct grant-giver dedicated specifically to helping those in poverty. As such, EFC provides support and care for people, including their immediate families, of British or Irish nationality, regardless of religious denomination, political opinion, age or place of residence.

Subject coverage:
High quality care in 12 residential and nursing homes and 10 almshouses cottages; financial support and assistance to people of all ages who live in their own homes or those requiring financial assistance toward care in other homes. The financial support we can provide includes regular allowances and one-off grants to cover specific items, such as wheelchairs, or for household repair and maintenance.

Access to staff:
Contact by letter, by telephone and by fax
Hours: Mon to Fri, 0900 to 1700
Special comments: No personal callers.

ELMBRIDGE BOROUGH COUNCIL

Acronym or abbreviation: EBC

Civic Centre, High Street, Esher, Surrey, KT10 9SD

Tel: 01372 474474\ Minicom no. 01372 474219
Fax: 01372 474972
E-mail: civiccentre@elmbridge.gov.uk

Website:
http://www.elmbridge.gov.uk

Enquiries:
Enquiries to: Communications and Consultation Officer
Direct tel: 01372 474391
Direct fax: 01372 474931
Direct e-mail: lballinger@elmbridge.gov.uk

Founded:
1974

Organisation type and purpose:
Local government body.

Subject coverage:
All aspects of Elmbridge Borough and Elmbridge Borough Council; services, amenities, housing and planning.

Printed publications:
A-Z of Local Services
Elmbridge Review (twice a year)

continued overleaf

Numerous leaflets and booklets available from the housing, planning and finance directorates

Access to staff:
Contact by letter, by telephone, by fax, by e-mail and via website. Appointment necessary.
Hours: Mon to Fri, 0845 to 1700

Access for disabled people:
Level entry, toilet facilities

Parent body:
Surrey County Council
tel: 020 8541 8800

ELSEVIER SCIENCE BIBLIOGRAPHIC DATABASES

Customer Service Department, Linacre House, Jordan Hill, Oxford, OX2 8DP

Tel: 01865 474010
Fax: 01865 474011
E-mail: directenquiries@elsevier.com

Website:
http://www.elsevier.com/
Publications catalogue.

Enquiries:
Enquiries to: Press Officer
Direct e-mail: pressoffice@elsevier.com
Other contacts: Product Manager for telephone queries, email: a.munns@elsevier.co.uk.

Founded:
1960

Organisation type and purpose:
Publishing house.

Subject coverage:
Geology, development studies, human geography, physical geography, textiles, fluids, civil engineering, process engineering, ecology, physical geography, oceanography, geomechanics.

Museum or gallery collection, archive, or library special collection:
Back issues and indexes for 1966 until present

Printed publications:
The annual cumulative index is included in the last issue of each journal:
Ecological Abstracts, ISSN 0305–196X (1838 euro)
Fluid Abstracts: Civil Engineering, ISSN 0962–7170 (1286 euro)
Fluid Abstracts: Process Engineering, ISSN 0962–7162 (monthly, 1286 euro)
Geographical Abstracts: Human Geography, ISSN 0953–9611 (monthly, 1371 euro)
Geographical Abstracts: Physical Geography, ISSN 0954–0504 (monthly, 1800 euro)
Geological Abstracts, ISSN 0954–0512 (12 monthly, 1813 euro)
Geomechanics Abstracts, ISSN1365–1617 (6 times a year, 531 euro)
International Development Abstracts, ISSN 0262–0855 (6 times a year, 847 euro)
World Textile Abstracts, ISSN 0043–9118 (12 monthly, 1276 euro)
Order printed publications from: Elsevier Science, Regional Sales Office
Customer Support Department, PO Box 211, Amsterdam, NL-1000 AE, The Netherlands, tel: 00 31 20 485 3757, fax: 00 31 20 485 3432, e-mail: nlinfo-f@elsevier.nl

Electronic and video publications:
FLUIDEX (on Dialog Silver Platter and EINS)
GEOBASE (on Dialog Silver Platter, OCLC and EINS)
World Textiles (on Silver Platter, STN, Fiz-Technik and EINS)

Publications list:
Available in print

Access to staff:
Contact by letter, by telephone, by fax, by e-mail and via website
Hours: Mon to Fri, 0900 to 1700

Other addresses:
Elsevier Science Bibliographic Databases
 Molenwerf 1, 1014 AE Amsterdam, The Netherlands; tel: 00 31 20 485 3507; fax: 00 31 20 485 3222

Parent body:
Elsevier Science Limited
 The Boulevard, Langford Lane, Kidlington, Oxford, OX5 1GB; tel: 01865 843000; fax: 01865 843010

ELVA OWNERS CLUB

Acronym or abbreviation: EOC

c/o Elva Racing Components Ltd, Unit 3, Gaugemaster Way, Ford Road, Ford, Arundel, BN18 0RX

Tel: 01903 882911
Fax: 01903 882911
E-mail: roger.dunbar@elva.com; elvacars@gmail.com

Website:
http://www.elva.com
Official Elva website.
http://www.elvacourier.com
Official Elva Courier website
http://www.elva-ale.com
Official website for the range of Elva ales.

Enquiries:
Enquiries to: Honorary Secretary
Direct tel: 07976 234470
Direct e-mail: roger@elva.com

Founded:
1979

Organisation type and purpose:
Membership association (membership is by election or invitation), present number of members: 400.
Support for owners and enthusiasts of Elva cars.

Subject coverage:
Information about Elva racing and sports racing cars.

Information services:
A focal point for information relating to ELVA Cars.

Access to staff:
Contact by letter, by telephone, by e-mail and via website. Appointment necessary.
Hours: Mon to Fri, 0900 to 1700

EMBASSY OF DENMARK

55 Sloane Street, London, SW1X 9SR

Tel: 020 7333 0200
Fax: 020 7333 0270
E-mail: lonamb@um.dk

Website:
http://www.dk-export.com

Enquiries:
Enquiries to: Information Officer

Organisation type and purpose:
National government body.

Subject coverage:
Denmark and Danish governmental matters; Danish commerce.

Printed publications:
Focus Denmark
Directory of Danish Subsidiaries of Danish Companies in the UK (priced)

EMBASSY OF FINLAND

38 Chesham Place, London, SW1X 8HW

Tel: 020 7838 6200
Fax: 020 7235 3680
E-mail: sanomat.lon@formin.fi

Website:
http://www.finemb.org.uk

Enquiries:
Enquiries to: Information Officer

Organisation type and purpose:
Embassy.

Access to staff:
Contact by letter, by telephone and via website
Hours: Mon to Fri, 0830 to 1230 and 1330 to 1630
Special comments: Passport and Visa Department Open: Mon to Fri, 0900 to 1200 only; telephone enquiries: Mon to Fri, 1400 to 1600.

EMBASSY OF HONDURAS

115 Gloucester Place, London, W1U 6JT

Tel: 020 7486 4880
Fax: 020 7486 4550
E-mail: hondurasuk@lineone.net

Enquiries:
Enquiries to: Information Officer

Organisation type and purpose:
National embassy.

Subject coverage:
Honduras Republic; Central America.

Access to staff:
Contact by letter, by telephone and by e-mail
Hours: 1000 to 1700

EMBASSY OF ICELAND

2A Hans Street, London, SW1X 0JE

Tel: 020 7259 3999
Fax: 020 7245 9649
E-mail: icemb.london@utn.stjr.is

Website:
http://www.statice.is
Statistical information. Homepage of Statistics of Iceland.
http://www.icetourist.is
Tourism in Iceland. Home page of the Tourist Board of Iceland.
http://www.iceland.org/uk
Embassy homepage.
http://www.iceland.is
Iceland Information Gateway.

Enquiries:
Enquiries to: Information Officer

Organisation type and purpose:
International organisation.

Subject coverage:
Icelandic government matters, Icelandic trade.

Access to staff:
Contact by letter, by fax and by e-mail
Hours: Mon to Fri, 0930 to 1600

EMBASSY OF MONGOLIA

7 Kensington Court, London, W8 5DL

Tel: 020 7937 5238
Fax: 020 7937 1117
E-mail: office@embassyofmongolia.co.uk

Website:
http://www.embassyofmongolia.co.uk

Enquiries:
Enquiries to: Information Officer

Founded:
1969

Organisation type and purpose:
National government body.

Subject coverage:
General information about Mongolia.

Trade and statistical information:
Statistics and information about Mongolian economy.

Printed publications:
Newspaper
Press Releases

Access to staff:
Contact by letter, by telephone, by fax, by e-mail
and in person. Appointment necessary.
Hours: Mon to Fri, 0900 to 1700

EMBASSY OF PERU

52 Sloane Street, London, SW1X 9SP

Tel: 020 7235 1917
Fax: 020 7235 4463
E-mail: postmaster@peruembassy-uk.com

Website:
http://www.peruembassy-uk.com
Peru general information: history, geography and
politics, news, trade and investment, tourism,
cultural and educational information,
programmed activities in the UK and Peru.

Enquiries:
Enquiries to: Economic Advisor (for trade and
investment opportunities, for economic
information)

Organisation type and purpose:
National government body.
Diplomatic representation of Peru in the UK and
Ireland.

Subject coverage:
Peruvian information.

Information services:
Trade and investment opportunities, tourism and
cultural information and advice.

Education services:
Information and advice.

Trade and statistical information:
UK trade with Peru; Peruvian exports and imports;
British investment in Peru; foreign investment in
Peru; economic indicators for Peru; general
statistical information.

Non-library collection catalogue:
All or part available in-house

Library catalogue:
All or part available in-house

Printed publications:
Opportunities (British Peruvian Chamber of
Commerce publication)
Peru Exporta
Alpaca del Peru
Exportar (bilingual publication)
Tourism guides and brochures
Order printed publications from: e-mail: postmaster@
peruembassy-uk.com

Publications list:
Available in print

Access to staff:
Contact by letter, by telephone, by fax, by e-mail,
in person and via website. Appointment necessary.
Hours: Mon to Fri, 0900 to 1700

Access to building, collection or gallery:
Hours: Mon to Fri, 0900 to 1700

Links with:
Consulate General of Peru
52 Sloane Street, London, SW1X 9SP
Naval Attaché Office
5 Falstaff House, 24 Barldolph Road, Richmond,
London, TW9 2LH

EMBASSY OF RWANDA

Acronym or abbreviation: AMBARWA

Uganda House, 58–59 Trafalgar Square, London,
WC2N 5DS

Tel: 020 7930 2570
Fax: 020 7930 2572
E-mail: ambarwanda@compuserve.com

Website:
http://www.ambarwanda.org.uk

Enquiries:
Enquiries to: Administrator
Other contacts: First Secretary for detailed
enquiries.

Founded:
1995

Organisation type and purpose:
National government body.
Embassy or Diplomatic Mission.
Consular and diplomatic relations.

Subject coverage:
Any information regarding Rwanda.

Trade and statistical information:
Trade or statistical information regarding Rwanda.

Access to staff:
Contact by letter, by telephone, by fax and by e-
mail. Appointment necessary.
Hours: Mon to Fri, 0930 to 1300 and 1400 to 1730

Access for disabled people:
Level entry

EMBASSY OF SWEDEN

Press and Information, 11 Montagu Place, London,
W1H 2AL

Tel: 020 7917 6400
Fax: 020 7724 4174
E-mail: ambassaden.london@foreign.ministry.se

Website:
http://www.swedenabroad.com/london

Enquiries:
Enquiries to: Information Officer

Organisation type and purpose:
Embassy.

Subject coverage:
General information on Sweden.

Access to staff:
Hours: Mon to Fri, 0900 to 1230 and 1400 to 1600

EMBASSY OF THE FEDERAL REPUBLIC OF GERMANY

23 Belgrave Square, London, SW1X 8PZ

Tel: 020 7824 1300
Fax: 020 7824 1470
E-mail: info@london.diplo.de

Website:
http://www.london.diplo.de
Services provided by the embassy, and by the
information centre including life, science, economy
and culture in Germany.
http://www.auswaertiges-amt.de
Information of all kinds about Germany.

Enquiries:
Enquiries to: Information Centre

Organisation type and purpose:
Government diplomatic representation.

Subject coverage:
Life, science, economy and culture in Germany.

EMBASSY OF THE REPUBLIC OF BULGARIA

186–188 Queens Gate, London, SW7 5HL

Tel: 020 7584 9433
Fax: 020 7584 4948
E-mail: bgembasy@globalnet.co.uk

Website:
http://www.bulgarianembassy.org.uk

Enquiries:
Enquiries to: Secretary
Other contacts: Trade Counsellor for trade
information.

Founded:
1920

Organisation type and purpose:
National government body.
Embassy.
Diplomatic.

Access to staff:
Contact by letter and by fax. Appointment
necessary.
Hours: Mon to Fri, 0900 to 1700

EMBASSY OF THE REPUBLIC OF CROATIA

21 Conway Street, London, W1T 6BN

Tel: 020 7387 2022/1640
Fax: 020 7387 0310

Enquiries:
Enquiries to: Information Officer

Organisation type and purpose:
National government body.
Diplomatic mission.

Subject coverage:
Information regarding the Republic of Croatia, the
Croatian language, economic data, culture, etc.

Access to staff:
Contact by letter, by telephone, by fax and by e-
mail. Appointment necessary.
Hours: Mon to Fri, 0900 to 1700
Consular Department: Mon to Thu, 1100 to 1400

EMBASSY OF THE REPUBLIC OF LITHUANIA

84 Gloucester Place, London, W1U 6AU

Tel: 020 7486 6401/6402; Consular section 020 7486
6404
Fax: 020 7486 6403
E-mail: lralon@globalnet.co.uk

Website:
http://www.users.globalnet.co.uk/~lralon

Enquiries:
Enquiries to: Head of Chancery
Other contacts: Private Secretary to the Ambassador

Organisation type and purpose:
National government body.

Subject coverage:
Lithuania.

Access to staff:
Contact by letter, by telephone, by fax and by e-
mail. Appointment necessary.
Hours: Consular Section: Mon to Fri, 1000 to 1300

EMBASSY OF THE REPUBLIC OF SLOVENIA

10 Little College Street, London, SW1P 3SH

Tel: 020 7222 5400
Fax: 020 7222 5722
E-mail: vlo@mzz-dkp.gov.si

Website:
http://www.embassy-slovenia.org.uk
Information regarding Slovenia.

Enquiries:
Enquiries to: Information Officer

Founded:
1991

Organisation type and purpose:
National government body.

Subject coverage:
Slovenia and Slovene governmental matters,
Slovene commerce, visa information.

Access to staff:
Contact by letter, by telephone, by fax, by e-mail
and via website. Appointment necessary.
Hours: Mon to Fri, 0900 to 1700
Visas: Mon to Fri, 1000 to 1200

continued overleaf

Access to building, collection or gallery:
Prior appointment required

Other address:
Embassy of the Republic of Slovenia
  Consular Section, 10 Cowley Street, London,
  SW1P

EMBASSY OF THE SLOVAK REPUBLIC

Acronym or abbreviation: Slovak Embassy

25 Kensington Palace Gardens, London, W8 4QY

Tel: 020 7313 6470
Fax: 020 7313 6481
E-mail: mail@slovakembassy.co.uk

Website:
http://www.slovakembassy.co.uk
General information, visa information, links.

Enquiries:
Enquiries to: Information Officer

Founded:
1993

Organisation type and purpose:
National government body.
Embassy.

Subject coverage:
General information on the Slovak Republic and
tourist information.

Trade and statistical information:
General economy and trade information and
  statistics obtainable from the commercial attaché,
  telephone, 020 7727 3099; fax, 020 7727 3667 or
  via website.

Non-library collection catalogue:
All or part available in-house

Library catalogue:
All or part available in-house

Publications list:
Available online

Access to staff:
Contact by letter, by telephone, by fax and by e-
mail. Appointment necessary.
Hours: General: Mon to Thu, 0900 to 1645; Fri, 0900
to 1530
Visa Department: Mon, Wed, 0900 to 1600;
Tue,Thu, Fri, 0900 to 1200

Access to building, collection or gallery:
Prior appointment required
Hours: Open to Public: Mon to Thu, 0900 to 1645;
Fri, 0900 to 1530
Special comments: Visa Information: tel no 020 7313
6470.

EMBASSY OF THE SYRIAN ARAB REPUBLIC

8 Belgrave Square, London, SW1X 8PH

Tel: 020 7245 9012
Fax: 020 7235 4621

Enquiries:
Enquiries to: Information Officer

Organisation type and purpose:
Diplomatic Mission.

EMBASSY OF THE UNION OF MYANMAR

19a Charles Street, London, W1J 5DX

Tel: 020 7499 4340 Option 1 Consular Section; 09001
600 306 Visa Information
Fax: 020 7493 7399
E-mail: memblondon@aol.com

Website:
http://www.myanmar.com

Enquiries:
Enquiries to: Information Officer – Consular Office

Direct tel: 020 7499 4340

Formerly called:
Embassy of the Union of Burma

Organisation type and purpose:
Diplomatic relations and consular services.

Subject coverage:
Consular, travel, investing opportunities, trade.

Printed publications:
Myanmar Visitors' Guide

Electronic and video publications:
CD-ROM on Information available for purchase
  from the Embassy

Access to staff:
Contact by letter, by telephone and by fax.
Appointment necessary.
Hours: Mon to Fri, 0930 to 1630
Visa Section: Mon to Fri, 1000 to 1300

Access to building, collection or gallery:
Hours: Mon to Fri, 0930 to 1630
Special comments: Via Charles Street

EMBASSY OF THE UNITED ARAB EMIRATES

30 Princes Gate, London, SW7 1PT

Tel: 020 7581 1281
Fax: 020 7581 9616
E-mail: information@uaeebassyuk.net

Website:
http://www.uaeebassyuk.net

Enquiries:
Enquiries to: Information and Resources
Direct e-mail: commerce@uaeembassyuk.net

Organisation type and purpose:
National government body.
Embassy.

Subject coverage:
United Arab Emirates.

EMBROIDERERS' GUILD

Apartment 41, Hampton Court Palace, Kingston
Upon Thames, Surrey, KT8 9AU

Tel: 020 8943 1229
Fax: 020 8977 9882
E-mail: administrator@embroiderersguild.com

Website:
http://www.embroiderersguild.com
Details of Young Embroiderers' Guild website;
STITCH with the Embroiderers' Guild; World of
Embroidery.

Enquiries:
Enquiries to: CEO
Direct e-mail: ceo@embroidersguild.com
Other contacts: Head of Heritage

Founded:
1906

Organisation type and purpose:
Membership association (membership is by
subscription), present number of members: 14,000,
registered charity (charity number 234239),
museum, suitable for ages: 5+, publishing house.
To promote the craft of embroidery for all.

Subject coverage:
Historical and contemporary embroidery –
workshops, library, bookshop and educational
resources. Branches nationwide and Young
Embroiderers available for children.

**Museum or gallery collection, archive, or library
special collection:**
Collection of 11,000 pieces of historical and
  contemporary embroidery from the 17th century
  onwards, under the care of a professional
  Curator; exhibitions from the collection travel to
  museums throughout the UK
Specialised library (by appointment)

Printed publications:
Books and booklets on all aspects of the art,
  techniques and history of embroidery and
  related techniques
Contact (newsletter, 3 times a year)
Stitch with the Embroiderers' Guild (6 times a
  year)
The Machine Embroidery Workbook
Embroidery Magazine (6 times a year)
The Workbook
Textile Ideas for Young Embroiderers (3 times a
  year)
Order printed publications from: Magazine Secretary,
Embroiderers' Guild, PO Box 42B, East Molesey,
Surrey, KT8 9BB; tel: 020 8943 1229 extn 28; fax: 020
8977 9882; e-mail: jjardine@embroiderersguild.com

Publications list:
Available online and in print

Access to staff:
Contact by letter, by telephone, by fax, by e-mail
and via website. Appointment necessary.
Hours: Mon to Fri, 1000 to 1630
Special comments: Day pass required on arrival at
Hampton Court Palace.

Access to building, collection or gallery:
No prior appointment required
Hours: Mon to Fri, 1030 to 1630

EMERSON COLLEGE

Formal name: Emerson College Trust Ltd

Forest Row, East Sussex, RH18 5JX

Tel: 01342 822238
Fax: 01342 826055
E-mail: mail@emerson.org.uk

Website:
http://www.emerson.org.uk
Home page; information on the college and all the
courses.

Enquiries:
Enquiries to: Information Officer

Founded:
1962

Organisation type and purpose:
International organisation, registered charity
(charity number 312101), suitable for ages: 18+ no
upper limit, training organisation.
Emerson College is an international centre for
adult education, training and research based on the
work of Rudolph Steiner.

Subject coverage:
Steiner and Waldorf teacher training,
anthroposophy and Rudolf Steiner.
Bio-dynamic, organic agriculture training.

Printed publications:
Course brochures (free)
Prospectus (free)

Access to staff:
Contact by letter, by telephone, by fax, by e-mail
and via website. Appointment necessary.
Hours: Mon to Fri, 0830 to 1645; Reception is closed
1245 to 1400

Access to building, collection or gallery:
Prior appointment required
Special comments: Library is only open to current
full-time students.

Access for disabled people:
Parking provided, ramped entry

Accredited by the:
British Accreditation Council (BAC)
  Westminster Central Hall, Storey's Gate, London,
  SW1H 9NH; tel: 020 7233 3468; fax: 020 7233
  3470; e-mail: info@the-bac.org

EMI MUSIC SOUND FOUNDATION

27 Wrights Lane, London, W8 5SW

Tel: 020 7795 7000

Fax: 020 7795 7296
E-mail: enquiries@emimusicsoundfoundation.com

Website:
http://www.emimusicsoundfoundation.com

Enquiries:
Enquiries to: Chief Executive

Founded:
1997

Organisation type and purpose:
Registered charity (charity number 1104027).

Subject coverage:
Improvement of people's access to music education.

Printed publications:
Annual Review

Publications list:
Available in print

Access to staff:
Contact by letter, by telephone, by fax, by e-mail and via website
Hours: Mon to Fri, 0900 to 1730

EMIE AT NFER

NFER, The Mere, Upton Park, Slough, Berkshire, SL1 2DQ

Tel: 01753 574123
Fax: 01753 531458
E-mail: emie@nfer.ac.uk

Website:
http://www.nfer.ac.uk/emie
Includes: all EMIE publications, access to emiedirect database, links to full text of local authority documents, links to all local authority education services and other relevant sites.

Enquiries:
Enquiries to: Head of Service
Direct tel: 01753 523156
Other contacts: EMIE Information Officers

Founded:
1981

Organisation type and purpose:
Local government body, research organisation. To provide information service and exchange on education management policy and practice for local authority staff working in or with the education service. Part of the National Foundation for Educational Research which is dedicated to providing information on education and children's service policy and practice issues for those working in or with UK local authorities.

Subject coverage:
Information services on educational management policy and practice provided principally to local authority staff and members in England, Wales, Scotland and Northern Ireland. Not curriculum but other matters pertaining to the operation of education and children's services in the UK.

Museum or gallery collection, archive, or library special collection:
Certain categories of documentation only accessible by local authority personnel. Extensive collection of policy level documentation contributed by education and children's services authorities in England, Wales, Scotland and Northern Ireland

Trade and statistical information:
Surveys conducted on various aspects of education and children's service provision.

Printed publications:
All publications free to Local Education Authorities
Abstracts Bulletins – Synopsis and Document Digests
Regular newsletters, abstracts, bulletins, surveys and commentaries on current issues in education and children's services

Publications list:
Available online and in print

Access to staff:
Contact by letter, by telephone, by fax, by e-mail and via website. Appointment necessary.
Hours: Mon to Fri, 0915 to 1715
Special comments: Queries dealt with if resources permit but full range of services limited to local authorities and subscribers to the service

Funded by:
Education and Library Boards in Northern Ireland
Local Authorities in England, Wales, Scotland and Northern Ireland
National Foundation for Educational Research (NFER)

Housed with the:
National Foundation for Educational Research with whose researchers, and library and information services, EMIE co-operates closely

EMMS INTERNATIONAL

Acronym or abbreviation: EMMS

7 Washington Lane, Edinburgh, EH11 2HA

Tel: 0131 313 3828
Fax: 0131 313 4662
E-mail: info@emms.org

Website:
http://www.emms.org

Enquiries:
Enquiries to: Chief Executive

Founded:
1841

Formerly called:
Edinburgh Medical Missionary Society

Incorporates the former:
Emmanuel Healthcare

Organisation type and purpose:
Registered charity (charity number SC032327, company number 224402).
Medical missionary society.

Subject coverage:
History of medical missions; the Nazareth Hospital; placement of medical students for elective periods; medical missions.

Museum or gallery collection, archive, or library special collection:
Records of the Society since its foundation in 1841

Printed publications:
Annual Report
Healing Hand (3 times a year)
Prayer Focus (3 times a year)

Access to staff:
Contact by letter, by telephone, by fax and by e-mail
Hours: Mon to Fri, 0900 to 1700

Links with:
Church of Central Africa Presbyterian
  Malawi
Dr Stephen Alfred
  India
Emmanuel Hospital Association
  India
International Nepal Fellowship

EMPICS

Formal name: EMPICS, A PA Group Photos Company

Pavilion House, 16 Castle Boulevard, Nottingham, NG7 1FC

Tel: 0115 844 7447
Fax: 0115 844 7448
E-mail: info@empics.com

Website:
http://www.empics.com

Enquiries:
Enquiries to: Sales and Marketing Director

Founded:
1867

Organisation type and purpose:
National organisation, service industry.
Picture library.

Subject coverage:
News, sport, and entertainment pictures, past and present.

Museum or gallery collection, archive, or library special collection:
PA
Empire Sport
AP
Emoics Entertainment

Non-library collection catalogue:
All or part available online

Library catalogue:
All or part available online

Electronic and video publications:
Pictures can be sent by ISDN, e-mail and by CD-ROM + FTP or downloads from website

Access to staff:
Contact by telephone, by e-mail and via website
Hours: Mon to Fri, 0900 to 1700

Access to building, collection or gallery:
Prior appointment required
Hours: Mon to Fri, 0930 to 1800

Access for disabled people:
Access to all public areas, toilet facilities

EMPLOYMENT OPPORTUNITIES FOR PEOPLE WITH DISABILITIES

Acronym or abbreviation: Employment Opportunities

Crystal Gate, 3rd Floor, 28–30 Worship Street, London, EC2A 2AH

Tel: 020 7448 5420

Website:
http://www.opportunities.org.uk
Information on Opportunities and the services provided.

Enquiries:
Enquiries to: Administrator
Direct e-mail: samantha.jobber@shaw-trust.org.uk

Founded:
1980

Formerly called:
Opportunities for the Disabled

Organisation type and purpose:
National organisation, registered charity (charity number 280112).
Helps people with disabilities find employment via a network of regional centres around the country.

Subject coverage:
Disability in relation to employment.

Printed publications:
Annual Report and Accounts (May)
Information Leaflets (2)
Seetheability Booklet

Publications list:
Available online and in print

Access to staff:
Contact by letter, by telephone, by fax, by e-mail and via website. Appointment necessary.
Hours: Mon to Fri, 0900 to 1700

Regional Centres:
Bath
  tel: 01225 461005 and minicom; fax: 01225 461158; e-mail: eopps.diropsbath@connectfree.co.uk
Bristol and West
  Bristol; tel: 0117 925 5751 and minicom; fax: 0117 925 5751; e-mail: eopps.bristol@connectfee.co.uk

continued overleaf

East Midlands
   Leicester; tel: 0116 280 7450; minicom 7451; fax:
   0116 280 7449; e-mail: eopps.leicester@
   connectfree.co.uk
Greater London
   London; tel: 020 7580 7545 and minicom; fax: 020
   7255 3115; e-mail: eopps.grtlondon@connectfree
   .co.uk
Greater Manchester
   Manchester; tel: 0161 431 8889 and minicom; fax:
   0161 431 8889; e-mail: eopps.manchester@
   connectfree.co.uk
Merseyside and Deeside
   Wirral; tel: 0151 645 2346 and minicom; fax: 0151
   645 2346; e-mail: eopps.mersey@connectfree.co
   .uk
Newcastle and North East
   Newcastle upon Tyne; tel: 0191 232 1994 and
   minicom; fax: 0191 233 0945; e-mail: eopps
   .newcastle@connectfree.co.uk
Scotland
   Glasgow; tel: 0141 429 8429 and minicom; fax:
   0141 429 4023; e-mail: eopps.glasgow@
   connectfree.co.uk
South East Wales
   Cardiff; tel: 029 2039 4363 and minicom; fax: 029
   2039 8886; e-mail: eopps.cardiff@connectfree.co
   .uk
South Essex
   Essex; tel: 01227 201984 and minicom; fax: 01227
   202355; e-mail: eopps.brentwood@connectfree.co
   .uk
South Hampshire
   Southampton; tel: 02380 228010 and minicom;
   fax: 01329 233911; e-mail: eopps.fareham@
   connectfree.co.uk
South Yorkshire & North Midlands
   Sheffield; tel: 0114 279 5362; fax: 0114 279 7303
   and minicom; e-mail: eopps.sheffield@
   connectfree.co.uk
Surrey and East Sussex
   West Sussex; tel: 01403 262021; minicom 262031;
   fax: 01403 262021; e-mail: eopps.horsham@
   connectfree.co.uk
West Midlands
   Birmingham; tel: 0121 331 4121 and minicom;
   fax: 0121 344 4470; e-mail: eopps.birmingham@
   connectfree.co.uk

EMPLOYMENT RIGHTS ADVICE SERVICE

Acronym or abbreviation: ERAS

Low Pay Unit, 10 Dukes Road, London, WC1H
9AD

Tel: 020 7387 2911
Fax: 020 7387 2250
E-mail: enquiries@lowpayunit.org.uk

Website:
http://www.lowpayunit.org.uk

Enquiries:
Enquiries to: Director
Direct e-mail: bharti.patel@lowpayunit.org.uk
Other contacts: On-line Officer for web site.

Founded:
1974

Organisation type and purpose:
Voluntary organisation, research organisation.
Advice and campaigning body on issues related to
low pay and in-work poverty, campaigning for
better protection for the low paid.

Subject coverage:
Employment legislation and advice, information
on better employment practice.

Trade and statistical information:
Labour market data and earnings.
Poverty statistics.

Printed publications:
For purchase or free to subscribers

Publications list:
Available online and in print

Access to staff:
Contact by letter, by telephone, by fax, by e-mail
and via website
Hours: Mon to Fri, 0930 to 1730
Special comments: No disabled access.

EMPLOYMENT TRIBUNALS SERVICE

Acronym or abbreviation: ETS

The Secretary to the Tribunals, ETS/FSU, First
Floor, 100 Southgate Street, Bury St Edmunds, IP33
2AQ

Tel: 0845 795 9775; Minicom 0845 757 3722
E-mail: buryet@ets.gsi.gov.uk

Website:
http://www.employmenttribunals.gov.uk
Various tribunal information and booklets.

Enquiries:
Enquiries to: Senior Secretariat Officer

Formerly called:
Central Office of the Industrial Tribunals (COIT)

Organisation type and purpose:
National government body.

Subject coverage:
Procedures for Employment Tribunals, statistics
etc.

**Museum or gallery collection, archive, or library
special collection:**
Public registers of applications and tribunal
   decisions held in Bury St Edmunds and Glasgow
   for England and Wales and Scotland respectively

Non-library collection catalogue:
All or part available in-house

Printed publications:
ITL Booklets
Leaflets on employment law
Order printed publications from: DTI Orderline
tel: 0870 1502 500, fax: 0870 1502 333

Electronic and video publications:
Audio Tapes
Braille

Publications list:
Available online

Access to staff:
Contact by letter, by telephone and by fax
Hours: Mon to Fri, 0900 to 1700

Access to building, collection or gallery:
No prior appointment required
Hours: Mon to Fri, 0900 to 1700

Access for disabled people:
Ramped entry

ENABLE SCOTLAND

2nd Floor, 146 Argyle Street, Glasgow, G2 8BL

Tel: 0141 226 4541
Fax: 0141 204 4398
E-mail: enable@enable.org.uk

Website:
http://www.enable.org.uk

Enquiries:
Enquiries to: Information Service
Direct e-mail: info@enable.org.uk
Other contacts: Chief Executive

Founded:
1954

Formerly called:
Scottish Society for the Mentally Handicapped
(year of change 1993)

Organisation type and purpose:
Voluntary organisation, registered charity (charity
number SC 09024).

Subject coverage:
Rights, services, employment, advocacy,
education, community care relating to people with
learning disabilities and their families.

Information services:
A telephone and e-mail enquiry service, a lending
library.

Services for disabled people:
ENABLE Scotland supports people with learning
disabilities and their families in Scotland; provides
accessible, easy-to-read information on many
topics.

**Museum or gallery collection, archive, or library
special collection:**
Small library

Non-library collection catalogue:
All or part available online

Library catalogue:
All or part available online and in-house

Printed publications:
Factsheets and occasional booklets (irregular)
Newslink – ENABLE's newsletter (twice-yearly
   magazine)
Far beyond our Dreams – ENABLE's history
   brochure (2004, free)
Order printed publications from: Information Service

Electronic and video publications:
Newslink (newsletter, twice-yearly, on audio cd)
Various video clips on website

Publications list:
Available online and in print

Access to staff:
Contact by letter, by telephone, by fax, by e-mail
and via website. Appointment necessary.
Hours: Enquiry line: Mon to Fri, 1300 to 1600

Access to building, collection or gallery:
Prior appointment required
Hours: Appointments to use the library may be
made Mon to Fri, 0900 to 1600

Access for disabled people:
Steps into building, lift, level access thereafter,
toilet facilities
Special comments: Steps into building, lift, level
access thereafter.

Member organisation of:
Inclusion Europe

ENDANGERED DOGS DEFENCE AND RESCUE LIMITED

Acronym or abbreviation: EDDR Ltd

PO Box 1544, London, W7 2ZB

Tel: 0844 856 3303
E-mail: info@endangereddogs.com

Website:
http://www.endangereddogs.com
Advice on canine legislation, campaign and
welfare information, current canine issues.

Enquiries:
Enquiries to: Secretary
Direct e-mail: office@endangereddogs.com

Founded:
1999

Formerly called:
Endangered Dogs Defence and Rescue (year of
change 1999)

Organisation type and purpose:
Advisory body, voluntary organisation.
Advice and guidance concerning canine legislation
and welfare.

Subject coverage:
Canine legislation and legal actions, canine rescue/
re-homing, dogs with special needs, promoting
responsible dog ownership, telephone helplines.

Printed publications:
Newsletter (quarterly)

Access to staff:
Contact by letter, by telephone, by e-mail and via website
Hours: All hours

ENERGY INFORMATION CENTRE

Acronym or abbreviation: EIC

Rosemary House, Lanwades Business Park, Newmarket, Suffolk, CB8 7PW

Tel: 01638 751400
Fax: 01638 751801
E-mail: info@eic.co.uk

Enquiries:
Enquiries to: Membership Manager

Founded:
1975

Organisation type and purpose:
Membership association (membership is by subscription), present number of members: 650 corporate members, training organisation, consultancy, research organisation, publishing house.

Subject coverage:
Utilities market information, advice and support, covering electricity, gas, oil and water.

Trade and statistical information:
Data on the production and use of utility services; electricity, gas, oil and water.

Printed publications:
Utility Purchaser's Handbook
Centre News (6 times a year)

Access to staff:
Access for members only.
Hours: Mon to Fri, 0900 to 1730

Access to building, collection or gallery:
Prior appointment required

Access for disabled people:
Toilet facilities

Parent Company:
Metal Bulletin plc
   Park House, Park Terrace, Worcester Park, Surrey, KT4 7HY

ENERGY INSTITUTE

Acronym or abbreviation: EI

61 New Cavendish Street, London, W1G 7AR

Tel: 020 7467 7100
Fax: 020 7255 1472
E-mail: info@energyinst.org

Website:
http://www.energyinst.org
Information about the EI and its publications and events, answers to frequently asked questions on the petroleum and other energy industries, careers and educational information, library information and catalogues and EI statistical services.

Enquiries:
Enquiries to: Library and Information Service Manager
Direct tel: 020 7467 7111
Direct e-mail: ccosgrove@energyinst.org
Other contacts: Information Officer

Founded:
2003

Created by the merger of:
Institute of Petroleum (founded 1913), Institute of Energy (founded 1927) (year of change 2003)

Organisation type and purpose:
Membership association (membership is by subscription), present number of members: 12,000 individuals and 400 corporate, registered charity (charity number 1097899).

Subject coverage:
All forms of energy including renewables, wind, wave, electricity, nuclear, oil and gas. Especially strong on petroleum technology, petroleum geology, exploration, production, refining, transportation, physical and chemical properties of hydrocarbons, methods of analysis, petroleum products and petrochemicals, statistics, business.

Information services:
Quick queries; extended desk research; online searching; statistics service.

Special visitor services:
Access to on-line databases.

Education services:
Training courses.

Museum or gallery collection, archive, or library special collection:
Books dating from the mid-19th century to present day
Periodicals relating to petroleum and other energy industries dating from 1890s

Trade and statistical information:
UK petrol retailing market statistics.
UK refining statistics.
Worldwide petroleum industry statistics.

Non-library collection catalogue:
All or part available online and in-house

Library catalogue:
All or part available online and in-house

Printed publications:
Conference Proceedings
Petroleum Review (monthly)
Energy World (11 issues a year)
Standards and Codes of Safe Practice
Technical papers
Educational publications, including:
Teachers' packs
Career information
Order printed publications from: Portland Customer Services, tel: 01206 796351; e-mail: sales@portland -services.com

Electronic and video publications:
IP Standard Methods for Analysis and Testing of Petroleum and Related Products and British Standards 2000 Parts, (CD-ROM) (annual publication)
Order electronic and video publications from: EI Publications available for purchase electronically, see website: http://www.energyinst.org

Publications list:
Available online and in print

Access to staff:
Contact by letter, by telephone, by fax, by e-mail, in person and via website. Non-members charged.
Hours: Mon to Fri, 0915 to 1700
Special comments: Letter of introduction is required from students.

Access for disabled people:
Special comments: Steps from pavement to front door.

Administers:
Information for Energy Group – IFEG
   at the same address; tel: 020 7467 7115; fax: 020 7255 1472; e-mail: ifeg@energyinst.org; website: http://www.energyinst.org
UKWEC – UK Member Committee of the World Energy Council
   at the same address; tel: 020 7467 7111; fax: 020 7255 1472; e-mail: ukwec@energyinst.org; website: http://www.worldenergy.org/uk

ENFIELD & DISTRICT VETERAN VEHICLE TRUST

Acronym or abbreviation: EDVVT

Whitewebbs Museum, Whitewebbs Road, Enfield, Middlesex, EN2 9HW

Tel: 020 8367 1898
Fax: 020 8363 1904
E-mail: museum@whitewebbs.fsnet.co.uk

Enquiries:
Enquiries to: Information Officer

Founded:
1979

Formerly called:
Enfield and District Veteran Vehicle Society

Organisation type and purpose:
Museum.

Subject coverage:
Vintage and classic cars, motor cycles and commercial vehicles.

Access to staff:
Contact by letter, by telephone, by fax and by e-mail. Appointment necessary.
Hours: Tue, 1200 to 1600
Special comments: Otherwise access by arrangement.

Access for disabled people:
Parking provided, ramped entry, toilet facilities

ENFIELD LIBRAIRES

First Stop Information, Central Library, Cecil Road, Enfield Town, EN2 6TW

Tel: 020 8379 8341
Fax: 020 8379 8401

Website:
http://www.enfield.gov.uk/
Information on Council services and Enfield as a location. Information on local libraries.

Organisation type and purpose:
Local government body, public library.

Subject coverage:
General; local history including material in the museum at Forty Hall; European fiction; lingustics.

Museum or gallery collection, archive, or library special collection:
European Fiction Collection
Linguistics (under the London and SE Region Scheme)
Local History Collection
Sound recordings of J S Bach, jazz artists BAJ to BH and Folk Music (Argentina, Bolivia, Chile, Paraguay, Uruguay) (under the Greater London Audio Specialising Scheme)

Access to staff:
Contact by letter, by telephone, by fax and by e-mail
Hours: Mon to Fri, 0900 to 1700
Special comments: No appointment necessary for general libraries. Appointments are required for local history collections and other special collections.

ENFIELD LOCAL HISTORY UNIT

Formal name: Enfield Local Studies Library & Archives

Thomas Hardy House, 39 London Road, Enfield, EN2 6DS

Tel: 020 8379 2724
E-mail: local.history@enfield.gov.uk

Website:
http://80.169.147.100/museum

Enquiries:
Enquiries to: Librarian

Founded:
1975

Organisation type and purpose:
Archive.

Subject coverage:
Local history material for Local Borough of Enfield area.

Non-library collection catalogue:
All or part available in-house

continued overleaf

Library catalogue:
All or part available in-house

Access to staff:
Contact by letter, by telephone, by e-mail and in person. Appointment necessary.
Hours: Mon, Tue, Thu, Fri, 0930 to 1630

Access to building, collection or gallery:
Hours: as above

Access for disabled people:
Lift

ENGINEERING AND PHYSICAL SCIENCES RESEARCH COUNCIL

Acronym or abbreviation: EPSRC

Polaris House, North Star Avenue, Swindon, Wiltshire, SN2 1ET

Tel: 01793 444000
E-mail: infoline@epsrc.ac.uk

Website:
http://www.epsrc.ac.uk
All matters about EPSRC.

Enquiries:
Enquiries to: Head of Communications & Stakeholder Engagement
Direct tel: 01793 444502
Direct e-mail: david.reid@epsrc.ac.uk

Founded:
1965

Formerly called:
Science Research Council (SRC) (year of change 1981); Science and Engineering Research Council (SERC) (year of change 1994)

Organisation type and purpose:
EPSRC is a non-departmental public body funded by the UK government through the Department for Business Innovation and Skills. It employs around 300 staff in Swindon.

Subject coverage:
The main UK government agency for funding research and training in engineering and the physical sciences, investing more than £850m. a year. Supports research into engineering, mathematics, physics, chemistry, materials science, information and communications technologies.

Printed publications:
EPSRC Annual Report
Pioneer
Connect
College Newsletter

Publications list:
Available online

Access to staff:
Contact by letter, by telephone, by e-mail and via website
Hours: Mon to Fri, 0900 to 1700

ENGINEERING COUNCIL

246 High Holborn, London, WC1V 7EX

Tel: 020 3206 0500
Fax: 020 3206 0501
E-mail: staff@engc.org.uk

Website:
http://www.engc.org.uk
Press releases.

Enquiries:
Enquiries to: Marketing and Communications Director
Direct e-mail: sbrough@engc.org.uk

Founded:
1983

Formerly called:
Engineering Council UK (year of change 2009)

Organisation type and purpose:
Regulatory authority for professional engineers and engineering technicians in the UK. Operates through 35 engineering institutions, which it licenses to assess individuals for inclusion on the ECUK register of Chartered Engineers, Incorporated Engineers and Engineering Technicians, titles that are protected by Royal Charter.

Subject coverage:
The engineering profession, education and training of Chartered Engineers, Incorporated Engineers and Engineering Technicians, continuing professional development.

Printed publications:
Annual Report
UK-SPEC (United Kingdom Standard for Professional Engineering Competence)
Register News (e-bulletin), leaflets on registration.

Publications list:
Available online and in print

Access to staff:
Contact by letter, by telephone, by fax, by e-mail and via website
Hours: Mon to Fri, 0900 to 1700

Access to building, collection or gallery:
Prior appointment required

Nominated institutions:
Association of Cost Engineers
British Computer Society
British Institute of Non-Destructive Testing
Chartered Institution of Building Services Engineers
Chartered Institution of Water and Environmental Management
Energy Institute
IEE
Institute of Acoustics
Institute of Cast Metals Engineers
Institute of Healthcare Engineering & Estate Management
Institute of Highway Incorporated Engineers
Institute of Marine Engineering, Science and Technology
Institute of Materials, Minerals and Mining
Institute of Measurement and Control
Institute of Physics
Institute of Physics & Engineering in Medicine
Institute of Plumbing & Heating Engineers
Institution of Agricultural Engineers
Institution of Chemical Engineers
Institution of Civil Engineers
Institution of Electrical Engineers
Institution of Engineering Designers
Institution of Fire Engineers
Institution of Gas Engineers and Managers
Institution of Highways & Transportation
Institution of Incorporated Engineers
Institution of Lighting Engineers
Institution of Mechanical Engineers
Institution of Nuclear Engineers
Institution of Plant Engineers
Institution of Railway Signal Engineers
Institution of Structural Engineers
Institution of Water Officers
Royal Aeronautical Society
Royal Institution of Naval Architects
Society of Environmental Engineers
Society of Operations Engineers
Welding Institute

ENGINEERING EDUCATION SCHEME IN ENGLAND

Acronym or abbreviation: EES

Weltech Centre, Ridgeway, Welwyn Garden City, Hertfordshire, AL7 2AA

Tel: 01707 393323
Fax: 01707 393133
E-mail: enquiries@eeswgc.demon.co.uk

Website:
http://www.engineering-education.org.uk

Enquiries:
Enquiries to: Director
Direct e-mail: a.ritchie@eeswgc.demon.co.uk

Founded:
1984

Organisation type and purpose:
Registered charity (charity number 1002459), suitable for ages: year 12 students.
To encourage year 12 students into engineering.

Subject coverage:
Engineering education scheme for schools.

Printed publications:
Information File

Access to staff:
Contact by letter, by telephone and by e-mail
Hours: Mon to Fri, 0900 to 1700

Administered by:
Engineering Development Trust

Part of:
Royal Academy of Engineering's Best Programme

ENGINEERING EQUIPMENT AND MATERIALS USERS' ASSOCIATION

Acronym or abbreviation: EEMUA

10–12 Lovat Lane, London, EC3R 8DN

Tel: 020 7621 0011
Fax: 020 7621 0022
E-mail: info@eemua.org

Website:
http://www.eemua.org
http://www.eemua.co.uk/pub-folder/index.htm

Enquiries:
Enquiries to: Executive Director

Founded:
1950

Organisation type and purpose:
Industry Association.
Members are purchasers, specificiers and users of engineering products and services in the chemical process industries, power generation and utilities sectors.
Aims to reduce costs and improve safety and operational effectiveness by sharing experiences and expertise, and by promotion of engineering users' interests.

Subject coverage:
Storage tanks, mechanical, electrical, instrumentation and control engineering, inspection and maintenance, quality assurance and control, health and safety at work.

Library catalogue:
All or part available online

Printed publications:
Technical handbooks

Publications list:
Available online

Access to staff:
Contact by letter, by telephone, by fax, by e-mail and via website. Appointment necessary. Access for members only.
Hours: Mon to Fri, 0900 to 1700

Administers:
Secretariat for the European Committee of User Inspectorates (ECUI)

ENGINEERING INDUSTRIES ASSOCIATION

Acronym or abbreviation: EIA

62 Bayswater Road, London, W2 3PS

Tel: 020 7298 6455
Fax: 020 7298 6456
E-mail: head.office@eia.co.uk

Website:
http://www.eia.uk

Enquiries:
Enquiries to: Director
Other contacts: Administrator (for general enquiries)

Founded:
1940

Organisation type and purpose:
Trade association.

Subject coverage:
Engineering industry; legislation, particularly health and safety and employment law; export practice; overseas missions and exhibitions.

Printed publications:
Buyers Guide and Classified Directory
Database of all members (members only)
History of the Association
Newsletter (6 times a year, members only)

Access to staff:
Contact by letter, by telephone, by fax, by e-mail and via website. Appointment necessary.
Hours: Mon to Fri, 0900 to 1700

Constituent bodies:
five regional groups

Member organisation of:
Bristol and Western Engineering Manufacturers Association (BEMA)
  tel: 0117 906 4830; fax: 0117 906 4827; e-mail: enquiries@bema.co.uk

ENGINEERING INTEGRITY SOCIETY

Acronym or abbreviation: EIS

5 Wentworth Avenue, Sheffield, South Yorkshire, S11 9QX

Tel: 0114 262 1155
Fax: 0114 262 1120
E-mail: cpinder@e-i-s.org.uk

Website:
http://www.e-i-s.org.uk
Information about the Society including conferences and seminars.

Enquiries:
Enquiries to: Secretariat Administrator

Founded:
1985

Organisation type and purpose:
Membership association (membership is by subscription), registered charity (charity number 327121).
Arrangement of courses and conferences to advance the education of persons working in the field of engineering by providing a forum for the interchange of ideas and information on engineering integrity.

Subject coverage:
Durability and fatigue; simulation; test and measurement, noise, vibration and harshness; these are the three Groups which make up the society.

Printed publications:
Engineering Integrity (journal, 2 times a year)

Access to staff:
Contact by letter, by telephone, by fax, by e-mail and via website
Hours: Mon to Fri, 0900 to 1700

ENGINEERING TRAINING COUNCIL FOR NORTHERN IRELAND

Acronym or abbreviation: ETC (NI)

Interpoint, 20–24 York Street, Belfast, BT15 1AQ

Tel: 028 9032 9878
Fax: 028 9031 0301

E-mail: info@etcni.org.uk

Website:
http://www.etcni.org.uk

Enquiries:
Enquiries to: Chief Executive

Founded:
1990

Organisation type and purpose:
Training organisation.

Subject coverage:
Industrial training, employment, qualifications, education and technical issues associated with careers and development of engineers in manufacturing industries.

Access to staff:
Contact by letter, by telephone, by e-mail and via website
Hours: Mon to Fri, 0900 to 1700

ENGINEERINGUK

Weston House, 2nd Floor, 246 High Holborn, London, WC1V 7EX

Tel: 020 3206 0400
Fax: 020 3206 0401
E-mail: info@engineeringuk.com

Website:
http://www.engineeringuk.com

Enquiries:
Enquiries to: Communications Director
Direct e-mail: belgood@engineeringuk.com

Founded:
2002

Formerly called:
Engineering and Technology Board (ETB) (year of change 2002)

Organisation type and purpose:
An independent, not-for-profit organisation.
To promote the vital contribution that engineers, and engineering and technology, make to society; to inspire people at all levels to pursue careers in engineering and technology; to improve the perception of engineers, engineering and technology and to improve the supply of engineers.
Works with partners across business and industry, education and skills, the professional engineering institutions, the Engineering Council and the wider science and engineering communities.

Subject coverage:
The engineering profession, education and training, qualifications of engineers and technicians, careers advice, salary surveys, continuing education and training, career breaks for women, Young Engineers for Britain and the Environment Award for Engineers, Women Into Science and Engineers (WISE) campaign, schools and industry liaison, engineering and technology.

Printed publications:
Annual reports
Newsletter
Surveys, policy statements and discussion documents

Access to staff:
Contact by letter, by telephone, by fax, by e-mail and via website
Hours: Mon to Fri, 0900 to 1700

ENGLAND AND WALES CRICKET BOARD

Acronym or abbreviation: ECB

Lord's Cricket Ground, St John's Wood Road, London, NW8 8QZ

Tel: 020 7432 1200
Fax: 020 7289 5619
E-mail: feedback@ecb.co.uk

Website:
http://lords.org
http://www.ecb.co.uk

Enquiries:
Enquiries to: Administration Manager

Founded:
1997

Formed from:
Cricket Council, National Cricket Association (NCA), Test and County Cricket Board (TCCB) (year of change 1997)

Organisation type and purpose:
Governing body for cricket at all levels in England and Wales.

Subject coverage:
Cricket: coaching, pitches (turf and non-turf), grant aid, competitions, laws of the game, insurance.

Museum or gallery collection, archive, or library special collection:
MCC Cricket Memorial Gallery (information from the Curator, MCC, Lords Cricket Ground)

Printed publications:
Constitution and Rules

Electronic and video publications:
Videos

Access to staff:
Contact by letter, by telephone, by fax and by e-mail. Appointment necessary.
Hours: Mon to Fri, 0900 to 1700

Composed of:
Marylebone Cricket Club
National Cricket Association
Test and County Cricket Board

Member of:
Sports Council

ENGLAND AND WALES CRICKET BOARD ASSOCIATION OF CRICKET OFFICIALS

Acronym or abbreviation: ECB ACO

The England and Wales Cricket Board, Lord's Cricket Ground, London, NW8 8QZ

Tel: 020 7432 1231
E-mail: ecbaco@ecb.co.uk

Website:
http://www.ecb.co.uk/ecbaco
Association and related cricket law, umpire and scorer details.

Enquiries:
Enquiries to: Membership Services Team
Direct tel: 020 7432 1240

Founded:
1953

Created by the merger of:
the Association of Cricket Umpires and Scorers and the ECB Officials Association (year of change 2008)

Formerly called:
Association of Cricket Umpires & Scorers (ACUS) (year of change 1993)

Organisation type and purpose:
International organisation, membership association (membership is by subscription, qualification), present number of members: 9,500, voluntary organisation, training organisation. Examination organisation.
To improve the standard of umpiring and scoring by training, examination and example, and by any other means.

Subject coverage:
The interpretation and application of the laws of cricket.

Printed publications:
A flick through the covers

continued overleaf

Electronic and video publications:
Training videos and slides (purchase through agency)

Access to staff:
Contact by letter, by telephone, by e-mail and via website
Hours: Mon to Fri, 0900 to 1700

ENGLAND SQUASH

Ground Floor, Bell Vue Athletics Centre, Pink Bank Lane, Manchester, M12 5GL

Tel: 0161 231 4499
Fax: 0161 231 4231
E-mail: englandsquash@squash.uk.com

Website:
http://www.englandsquash.com

Enquiries:
Enquiries to: Chair
Other contacts: Administration Manager

Founded:
1930

Formerly called:
Squash Rackets Association (SRA) (year of change 2001)

Organisation type and purpose:
Membership association.
Governing body of squash in England.

Subject coverage:
Coach training and qualification, referee training and qualification, technical and court specification, tournament organisation, grass roots development both player and participation, membership, club and individual.

Trade and statistical information:
Some statistics held for playing numbers in UK.

Printed publications:
Squash and Fitness – The Magazine

Publications list:
Available online and in print

Access to staff:
Contact by letter and by e-mail
Hours: Mon to Fri, 0900 to 1700

Access to building, collection or gallery:
No prior appointment required

Access for disabled people:
Parking provided, level entry, toilet facilities

ENGLISH ASSOCIATION

Acronym or abbreviation: EA

University of Leicester, University Road, Leicester, LE1 7RH

Tel: 0116 252 3982
Fax: 0116 252 2301
E-mail: engassoc@le.ac.uk

Website:
http://www.le.ac.uk/engassoc
Conferences, current contents of publications; student website; current issues and debates; publications.

Enquiries:
Enquiries to: Chief Executive

Founded:
1906

Organisation type and purpose:
International organisation, learned society, professional body (membership is by subscription), present number of members: 1,500, registered charity (charity number 1124890), publishing house.

Subject coverage:
English language and literature; standards of English writing and speech; educational matters relating to the teaching of English.

Museum or gallery collection, archive, or library special collection:
Own publications back to 1906

Printed publications:
Bookmarks, series of books to encourage over 16s to read more widely
English (journal, literary criticism, essays, reviews, original poetry, 3 times a year)
English 4–11 (formerly Primary English, 3 times a year, published jointly with UKLA)
Essays & Studies (annually)
The English Association Newsletter (3 times a year)
The Use of English (journal, 3 times a year)
The Year's Work in Critical and Cultural Theory
The Year's Work in English Studies (annual bibliography)

Publications list:
Available online and in print

Access to staff:
Contact by letter, by telephone, by fax, by e-mail and via website
Hours: Mon to Fri, 0900 to 1700

ENGLISH BASKETBALL ASSOCIATION

Acronym or abbreviation: EBBA

c/o English Institute of Sport, Coleridge Road, Sheffield, S9 5DA

Tel: 0870 77 44 225
Fax: 0870 77 44 226
E-mail: enquiries@ebbaonline.net

Website:
http://www.englandbasketball.co.uk
General information on England Basketball, fixtures, tables, etc.

Enquiries:
Enquiries to: Chief Executive
Other contacts: General Manager

Organisation type and purpose:
Membership association (membership is by subscription), present number of members: 900 clubs; 20,000 individuals.
Governing body of sport.

Subject coverage:
Sport of basketball, coaching, officiating, playing indoor and outdoor basketball.

Printed publications:
Annual Report
A Guide to English Basketball (£4)
Attacking a Zone Defence (£5.50)
Boom Boom Boom – The Rhythm of English Basketball (£12)
Basketball Development Manual
Coaching Basketball (£5.50)
Drills Book – One (£5.50)
Drills Book – Two (£5.50)
Manual for Table Officials (£4.50)
National Competitions Handbook (£7)
Newsletter
Nike Basketball Curriculum Guide (£20)
Official Basketball Rules
Referees Manual (£7.50)
Women in Basketball (£3)

Electronic and video publications:
Basketball Skills Video (£10)

Publications list:
Available in print

Access to staff:
Contact by letter, by telephone, by fax and by e-mail. Appointment necessary.
Hours: Mon to Fri, 0900 to 1700

Affiliated to:
British Olympic Association
Central Council of Physical Recreation
International Basketball Association

ENGLISH BOWLING FEDERATION

Acronym or abbreviation: EBF

The Secretary, 14 Field Close, Worksop, Nottinghamshire, S81 0PF

Tel: 01909 474346
Fax: 01909 474346
E-mail: j.heppel@btinternet.com

Website:
http://www.fedbowls.co.uk

Enquiries:
Enquiries to: Publicity Officer
Direct e-mail: d.nash1@tiscli.co.uk

Founded:
1926

Organisation type and purpose:
National governing body, membership association, present number of members: 13 county bowling associations.
National governing body of the sport.

Subject coverage:
Flat green bowls.

Printed publications:
Laws of the Game
Year Book

Access to staff:
Contact by letter, by telephone and by fax
Hours: Mon to Fri, 0900 to 1700

ENGLISH BRIDGE UNION LIMITED

Acronym or abbreviation: EBU

Broadfields, Bicester Road, Aylesbury, Buckinghamshire, HP19 8AZ

Tel: 01296 317200
Fax: 01296 317220
E-mail: postmaster@ebu.co.uk

Website:
http://www.ebu.co.uk

Enquiries:
Enquiries to: General Manager
Other contacts: Bridge for All helpline for students/teachers wishing to join Bridge for All education programme.

Founded:
1940

Organisation type and purpose:
Membership association (membership is by subscription), present number of members: 30,000.
National governing body for the card game of Duplicate Bridge.

Subject coverage:
Duplicate bridge in England, membership, Master Points, bridge supplies, competition entry, laws and ethics, educating and teaching, Bridge for All, overseas information.

Museum or gallery collection, archive, or library special collection:
Some archive material – books, trophies

Printed publications:
County Newsletter (to County associations)
Bridge for All – Really Easy books
English Bridge (6 times a year, free to members)
Club Newsletter (to affiliated clubs)

Electronic and video publications:
Blue Chip Bridge (CD-ROM)

Access to staff:
Contact by letter, by telephone, by fax, by e-mail, in person and via website
Hours: Mon to Fri, 0830 to 1715

Access for disabled people:
Parking provided, ramped entry, toilet facilities

Member of:
European Bridge League
World Bridge Federation

ENGLISH CHESS FEDERATION

Acronym or abbreviation: ECF

The Watch Oak, Chain Lane, Battle, East Sussex, TN33 0YD

Tel: 01424 775222
Fax: 01424 775904
E-mail: office@englishchess.org.uk

Website:
http://www.bcf.org.uk

Enquiries:
Enquiries to: Manager
Direct e-mail: cynthia@englishchess.org.uk

Founded:
1904

Formerly called:
British Chess Federation (year of change 2005)

Organisation type and purpose:
To control, direct and promote the playing of chess in England, to institute and maintain British Chess Championships, to promote national and international chess tournaments in England,

Museum or gallery collection, archive, or library special collection:
National Chess Library of 8,000 vols (housed at University Centre Hastings)

Library catalogue:
All or part available online

Printed publications:
Chess Moves (bimonthly membership magazine)

Publications list:
Available online

Access to staff:
Contact by letter, by telephone, by fax and by e-mail
Hours: Mon to Fri, 1000 to 1530 (by telephone only)

Access to building, collection or gallery:
Hours: Daily, 0900 to 1730

Access for disabled people:
Hours: Daily, 0900 to 1730

Affiliated to:
World Chess Federation (FIDE)

ENGLISH CIVIL WAR SOCIETY LIMITED

Acronym or abbreviation: ECWS

70 Hailgate, Howden, East Yorkshire, DN14 7ST

Tel: 01430 430695
Fax: 01405 430695
E-mail: press@english-civil-war-society.org

Website:
http://www.english-civil-war-society.org

Enquiries:
Enquiries to: Public Relations Manager

Founded:
1981

Formed from:
King's Army, Roundhead Association

Organisation type and purpose:
Membership association (membership is by subscription), present number of members: 2000, voluntary organisation.
Re-enactment Society specialising in period 1638–1651.

Subject coverage:
Historical re-enactment, English Civil War 1638–1651, film, television and media contacts and expertise, educational interpretation of history, living history, museum activity.

Printed publications:
Friends of the English Civil War Society (newsletter, quarterly, £5 a year)
Information leaflets (individual copies free with sae)
Soldiers' Handbook (50p)

Strife in the Kingdom; information pack on the English Civil War (£1.20)

Publications list:
Available in print

Access to staff:
Contact by letter, by telephone, by fax, by e-mail and via website
Hours: Evenings preferred

ENGLISH COLLECTIVE OF PROSTITUTES

Crossroads Women's Centre, PO Box 287, London, NW6 5QU

Tel: 020 7482 2496\ Minicom no. 020 7482 2496
Fax: 020 7209 4761
E-mail: crossroadswomenscentre@compuserve.com

Website:
http://www.prostitutescollective.net

Enquiries:
Enquiries to: Information Officer

Organisation type and purpose:
Voluntary organisation.
Pressure group.
To establish workers' rights in the sex industry, to be recognised as workers with legal, economic and civil rights. To campaign for the abolition of the prostitution laws, for the right to protection from violence, to health care, to form or join unions and for financial alternatives to prostitution.
To oppose illegal and racist enforcement of the law, and state run prostitution including toleration zones.

Subject coverage:
Prostitution laws, police legality and racism, child custody, taxes, health including HIV and AIDS, benefits.

Printed publications:
Network News
Prostitutes – Our Life
Prostitute Women and AIDS: Resisting the Virus of Repression
Some Mother's Daughter – The hidden movement of prostitute women against violence
The Hooker and the Beak

Access to staff:
Contact by letter, by telephone, by fax, by e-mail, in person and via website. Appointment necessary.
Hours: Tue and Wed, 1200 to 1600; Thu, 1700 to 1900
Telephone lines: Mon to Wed, Fri, 1000 to 1600; Thu, 1000 to 1600, 1700 to 1900

Access for disabled people:
Access to all public areas, toilet facilities

Initiated:
Legal Action for Women (LAW)
e-mail: law@crossroadswomen.net; website: http://www.allwomencount.net

Member of:
International Prostitutes Collective
website: http://www.prostitutescollectives.net
International Wages for Housework Campaign
Wages for Housework Campaign

ENGLISH CROSS-COUNTRY ASSOCIATION

Acronym or abbreviation: ECCA

22 Denham Drive, Berg Estate, Basingstoke, Hampshire, RG22 6LR

Tel: 01256 328401

Enquiries:
Enquiries to: Honorary Secretary

Founded:
1992

Organisation type and purpose:
Membership association, voluntary organisation.

National governing body, controlling body of the sport in England.
Organises and develops cross-country running.

Subject coverage:
Cross-country running.

Printed publications:
Handbook

Access to staff:
Contact by letter, by telephone and by fax
Hours: Mon to Fri, 0900 to 1700

Affiliated to:
United Kingdom Athletics

Member of:
Amateur Athletics Association of England

ENGLISH CURLING ASSOCIATION

Acronym or abbreviation: ECA

14 Donnelly Drive, Bedford, MK14 9TV

Tel: 01234 315174 (home); 01223 372752 (business)
E-mail: jmbroons@ntlworld.com

Website:
http://www.englishcurling.org.uk

Enquiries:
Enquiries to: Secretary

Founded:
1971

Organisation type and purpose:
Membership association, present number of members: 150, suitable for ages: 13+, training organisation.
National governing body of the sport.

Subject coverage:
Sport of curling in general from beginners to world championships.

Access to staff:
Contact by letter, by telephone, by fax, by e-mail and in person. Appointment necessary.
Hours: Mon to Fri, 0900 to 1700

ENGLISH FOLK DANCE AND SONG SOCIETY

Formal name: Vaughan Williams Memorial Library
Acronym or abbreviation: EFDSS

Vaughan Williams Memorial Library, Cecil Sharp House, 2 Regent's Park Road, London, NW1 7AY

Tel: 020 7485 2206
Fax: 020 7284 0534
E-mail: library@efdss.org

Website:
http://www.efdss.org
Multi-media.

Enquiries:
Enquiries to: Library Director
Direct e-mail: library@efdss.org

Founded:
1932

Organisation type and purpose:
Learned society (membership is by subscription), present number of members: 5,000, registered charity.
To document and promote folk arts in England.

Subject coverage:
Folk music including song, dance and drama, customs involving dance and song, singing games, social history, folk tales, oral history, dialects, mainly British material but much information on other English-speaking countries, notably the USA.

Museum or gallery collection, archive, or library special collection:
BBC Archive of folk music recordings
Broadwood Collection (manuscripts, and folk song books on loan)

continued overleaf

Butterworth Collection (manuscripts, dance and song)
Carpenter Collection (manuscripts and tapes from wax cylinders, folk song and drama)
Cecil Sharp Collection (books and manuscripts on folk song and dance)
Collection of 18th-century dancing masters
Gardiner Collection (folk song)
Gilchrist Collection (folk music)
Melusine Wood (historical dance)
Percy Grainger Collection of phonograph recordings from wax cylinders (on tape)
Vaughan Williams manuscripts in the British Library (microfilm)

Library catalogue:
All or part available online and in-house

Printed publications:
Catalogue
Folk Music Journal
English Dance and Song
Library leaflets and bibliographies on aspects of folk music

Electronic and video publications:
Cds, DVDs
Order electronic and video publications from: website: http://folkshop.efdss.org

Publications list:
Available online

Access to staff:
Contact by letter, by telephone, by fax, by e-mail, in person and via website. Access for members only. Non-members charged.
Hours: Tue to Fri, 0930 to 1730; 1st and 3rd Sat each month, 1000 to 1600

Access to building, collection or gallery:
Hours: Tue to Fri, 0930 to 1730; 1st and 3rd Sat each month, 1000 to 1600
Special comments: Sound/audio visual collections closed daily, 1200 to 1400.

Access for disabled people:
To library reading room level only
Hours: Tue to Fri, 0930 to 1730; 1st and 3rd Sat each month, 1000 to 1600
Special comments: To library level, to which materials will be retrieved by staff for disabled users.

ENGLISH GARDENING SCHOOL

At The Chelsea Physic Gardens, 66 Royal Hospital Road, London, SW3 4HS

Tel: 020 7352 4347
Fax: 020 7376 3936
E-mail: egs@dircon.co.uk

Website:
http://www.englishgardeningschool.co.uk
Details of all courses and events, plus online secure booking.

Enquiries:
Enquiries to: Principal

Founded:
1984

Organisation type and purpose:
Suitable for ages: 18+, training organisation, consultancy.

Subject coverage:
Teaching a wide range of amateur and professional gardening courses; horticultural/garden design consultancy; resource for garden designers.

Publications list:
Available in print

Access to staff:
Contact by letter, by telephone, by fax, by e-mail and via website. Appointment necessary.
Hours: Mon to Fri, 0900 to 1700

ENGLISH GOLF UNION

Acronym or abbreviation: EGU

The National Golf Centre, Broadway, Woodhall Spa, Lincolnshire, LN10 9PU

Tel: 01526 354500
Fax: 01526 354020
E-mail: info@englishgolfunion.org

Website:
http://www.englishgolfunion.org

Enquiries:
Enquiries to: Chief Executive

Founded:
1924

Organisation type and purpose:
National government body.
Governing body for the amateur game of men's golf in England.

Subject coverage:
Amateur golf in England, handicapping, standard scratch scores of golf courses.

Non-library collection catalogue:
All or part available online and in-house

Library catalogue:
All or part available in-house

Printed publications:
English Golf (magazine, 6 times a year)
Golfing Year (annually)
Order printed publications from: e-mail: nhayward@englishgolfunion.org

Publications list:
Available in print

Access to staff:
Contact by letter, by fax and by e-mail
Hours: Mon to Fri, 0900 to 1700

Access to building, collection or gallery:
Prior appointment required

Access for disabled people:
Parking provided, ramped entry, toilet facilities

ENGLISH HERITAGE

Acronym or abbreviation: HBMC or EH

Fortress House, 23 Savile Row, London, W1S 2ET

Tel: 0870 333 1181 Customer Services
Fax: 01793 414926

Website:
http://www.open.gov.uk/heritage/ehehome.htm
General information.
http://www.english-heritage.org.uk
General information.

Enquiries:
Enquiries to: Customer Services Department
Other contacts: Nine Regional Education Officers at the appropriate English Heritage Regional offices

Founded:
1984

Formerly called:
Historic Buildings and Monuments Commission for England, Ministry of Works (MOW); Department of the Environment (DOE) (year of change 1983)

Organisation type and purpose:
National government body, advisory body, statutory body, membership association (membership is by subscription).
Heritage conservation.

Subject coverage:
The governments' official adviser on all matters concerning the conversation of the historic environment and the major source of public funding for rescue archaeology, conservation areas, and repairs to historic buildings and ancient monuments.

Museum or gallery collection, archive, or library special collection:
Historical Research Library (mainly architectural)
Listed historic buildings

Historic Plans Collection over 200,000 plans of buildings
Mayson Beeton Collection (London social history)
Lists of scheduled monuments
Photographic library
Register of historic parks and gardens

Non-library collection catalogue:
All or part available in print

Library catalogue:
All or part available in print

Printed publications:
Annual Report and Accounts
Approximately 50 leaflets covering all aspects of the English Heritage
Conservation Bulletin (3 times a year, free)
Archaeological Reports Series
Exploring England's Heritage Series (HMSO)
Guides to sites
Conservation Publications (various free leaflets and priced books)
Many illustrated books on all aspects of the resources under the care of English Heritage including archaeology, architecture, conservation and general publishing titles:
An Atlas of Rural Settlement in England (Roberts B and Wrathmell S, 2000)
Food and Cooking Series (various titles)
Gatekeeper Series (various titles)
Ration Book Recipes (Corbishley G, 1990)
Region and Place (Roberts B and Wrathmell S, 2002)
Stonehenge: Mysteries of the Stones and Landscape (Souden D, 1997)
The Albert Memorial – The Prince Consort National Memorial, its contexts and its conservation (Brooks C ed, 2000)
The Batsford English Heritage Series (various titles)
Order printed publications from: Customer Services, English Heritage
PO Box 569, Swindon, SN2 2YP, tel: 0870 333 1181

Electronic and video publications:
Videos and tapes

Publications list:
Available online and in print

Access to staff:
Contact by letter, by telephone, by fax and in person. Appointment necessary.
Hours: Mon to Fri, 0900 to 1730

Other address:
English Heritage
Customer Services Department, PO Box 569, Swindon, Wiltshire, SN2 5YP

Other office:
National Monuments Record Centre
Kemble Drive, Swindon, Wiltshire, SN2 2GZ; tel: 01793 414600; e-mail: nmrinfo@english-heritage.org.uk

Parent body:
Department for Culture, Media and Sport
2–4 Cockspur Street, London, SW1Y 5DH

Regional Offices:
English Heritage (East Midlands Region)
44 Derngate, Northampton, NN1 1UH; tel: 01604 735400; fax: 01604 735401
English Heritage (East of England Region)
Brooklands, 24 Brooklands Avenue, Cambridge, CB2 2BU; tel: 01223 582700; fax: 01223 582701
English Heritage (London Region)
23 Savile Row, London, W1S 2ET; tel: 020 7973 3000; fax: 020 7973 3000
English Heritage (North East Region)
Bessie Surtees House, 41–44 Sandhill, Newcastle upon Tyne, NE1 3JF; tel: 0191 261 1585
English Heritage (North West Region)
Canada House, 3 Chepstow Street, Manchester, M1 5FW; tel: 0161 242 1400
English Heritage (South East Region)
Eastgate Court, 195–205 High Street, Guildford, Surrey, GU1 3EH; tel: 01483 252000; fax: 01483 252001
English Heritage (South West Region)
29 Queen Square, Bristol, BS1 4ND; tel: 0117 975 0700

English Heritage (West Midlands Region)
112 Colemore Row, Birmingham, B3 3AG; tel: 0121 625 6820

English Heritage (Yorkshire Region)
37 Tanner Row, York, YO1 6WP; tel: 01904 601901

ENGLISH HERITAGE – EDUCATION

1 Waterhouse Square, 138–142 Holborn, London EC1N 2ST

Tel: 020 79733000
E-mail: education@english-heritage.org.uk

Website:
http://www.english-heritage.org.uk/education
Full details of free entry for learning groups, great value Discovery Visits and free learning resources.

Enquiries:
Enquiries to: Director of Education
Direct e-mail: sandra.stancliffe@english-heritage.org.uk

Founded:
1984

Formerly called:
Historic Buildings and Monuments Commission for England (year of change 1984)

Organisation type and purpose:
National government body, advisory body, statutory body, membership association (membership is by subscription), suitable for ages: 5 to 18 (formal and informal).
To provide an advisory and support service for primary and secondary schools in the teaching of history and the use of the historic environment.

Subject coverage:
The historic environment of Britain, its preservation and use. Archaeology, architecture, ancient monuments, conservation and listed buildings.

Printed publications:
Visit the website for online resources. Free 'Learners go free' leaflets and four regional guides (including maps and booking forms) are available for learning groups; e-mail education@english-heritage.org.uk for these, to subscribe to the education enewsletter and to request the bi-annual Heritage Learning magazine – full of topical teaching ideas.
Order printed publications from: English Heritage, c/o Gillards, Trident Works, Temple Cloud, Bristol, BS39 5AZ; tel: 01761 452966; fax: 01761 453408

Publications list:
Available online and in print

Access to staff:
Contact by letter, by telephone, by fax and by e-mail
Hours: Mon to Fri, 0900 to 1700
Special comments: Access for visitors with disabilities should be checked with the regional office before booking a visit.

Also at:
English Heritage
Customer Services Department, National Monuments Record Centre, Kemble Drive, Swindon, Wiltshire, SN2 2GZ; tel: 01793 414926

Branches:
English Heritage
Education Officer, East of England Region; tel: 01223 582715
English Heritage
Education Officer, North of England, 37 Tanner Row, York, YO1 6WP; tel: 01904 601917
English Heritage
Education Officer, West Midlands Region; tel: 0121 625 6864
English Heritage
Education Officer, East Midlands Region, 44 Derngate, Northampton, NN1 1UH; tel: 01604 735440

English Heritage
Education Officer, London Region; tel: 020 7499 5676
English Heritage
Education Officer, South West Region, 29–30 Queen Square, Bristol, BS1 4ND; tel: 0117 975 0720
English Heritage
Education Officer, South East Region, Eastgate Court, 195–205 High Street, Guildford, GU1 3EH; tel: 01483 252013

ENGLISH HERITAGE – NATIONAL MONUMENTS RECORD

Acronym or abbreviation: NMR

Kemble Drive, Swindon, Wiltshire, SN2 2GZ

Tel: 01793 414600
Fax: 01793 414606
E-mail: nmrinfo@english-heritage.org.uk

Website:
http://www.english-heritage.org.uk/nmr
Information and news about the work of the National Monuments Record (NMR), the public archive of English Heritage. Enquiry forms for remote searches of the NMR archives are incorporated within the English Heritage website.
http://www.imagesof england.org.uk
Contemporary photographs of England's listed buildings taken at the turn of the 21st century.
http://www.pastscape.org.uk
England's archaeological, architectural and maritime heritage – nearly 400,000 records held in the national historic environment database.
http://www.english-heritager.org.uk/viewfinder
Historic photographs of England from the 1850s to the present day.
http://www.englishheritagearchives.org.uk
Descriptions of over 1m. images and records of England's buildings and historic sites.

Enquiries:
Enquiries to: Enquiry and Research Services
Other contacts: Customer Services Section

Founded:
1908

Formerly called:
Historic Buildings and Monuments Commission for England (HBMCE) (year of change 1984)

Incorporates the former:
National Archaeological Record, National Buildings Record, National Library of Air Photography; Royal Commission on the Historical Monuments of England (RCHME) (year of change 1999)

Organisation type and purpose:
National government body.
Public archive of English Heritage.

Subject coverage:
Architecture, archaeology, aerial photographs and maritime sites. The archive is of use to anyone interested in the historic built environment, local historians, researchers, archaeologists, architectural historians and environmental consultants.

Museum or gallery collection, archive, or library special collection:
Archive comprises over 10m. photographs, drawings and reports and an extensive book library specialising in architecture, archaeology and the historic environment
Aerial photograph collection includes complete RAF post-war coverage of England, early photographs of sites such as Stonehenge and more recent Ordnance Survey and English Heritage photography
Architectural archive includes interior and exterior photographs of buildings from the early days of photography to the present day. The National Buildings Record collection and photographs taken by Bedford Lemere, Eric De Mare, John Gay and many others are held in the NMR

Archaeological collections include earthwork surveys, aerial photograph interpretations and photographs of historic excavations

Trade and statistical information:
Data on archaeological sites, Scheduled Ancient Monuments and Listed Buildings.

Non-library collection catalogue:
All or part available in-house

Library catalogue:
All or part available in-house

Printed publications:
Many and varied, including:
Work
Seaside Resorts
The Birmingham Jewellery Quarter
Hillforts
Order printed publications from: http://www.english-heritageshop.org.uk

Publications list:
Available online

Access to staff:
Contact by letter, by telephone, by fax, by e-mail, in person and via website
Hours: Tue to Fri, 0930 to 1700
Special comments: Closed over Christmas and New Year (please contact for details)

Access to building, collection or gallery:
Hours: Tue to Fri, 0930 to 1700
Special comments: Limited visitor parking.

Funded by:
Department of Culture, Media and Sport

Links with:
county councils and local planning departments

Parent body:
English Heritage
1 Waterhouse Square, 138–142 Holborn, London, EC1N 2ST

ENGLISH HERITAGE (EAST MIDLANDS REGION)

44 Derngate, Northampton, NN1 1UH

Tel: 01604 735400
Fax: 01604 735401

Website:
http://www.english-heritage.org.uk

Enquiries:
Enquiries to: Marketing Executive

Organisation type and purpose:
National organisation, advisory body, membership association (membership is by subscription), suitable for ages: all.
Independent but government-sponsored body. English Heritage site administration and information service, including dates, times of opening and special events.

Subject coverage:
English Heritage East Midlands Region, administers and cares for properties and sites in Derbyshire, Northamptonshire, Rutland, Lincolnshire and Leicestershire; the conservation and preservation of the historic environment.

Access to staff:
Contact by letter, by telephone and by fax
Hours: Mon to Fri, 0900 to 1700

Heritage sites:
Ashby-de-la-Zouch Castle
South Street, Ashby-de-la-Zouch, Leicestershire, LE6 5PR; tel: 01530 413343
Bolsover Castle
Castle Street, Bolsover, Chesterfield, Derbyshire, S44 6PR; tel: 01246 822844; fax: 01246 241569
Gainsborough Old Hall
Parnell Street, Gainsborough, Lincolnshire, DN21 2NB; tel: 01427 612669; fax: 01427 612779
Hardwick Old Hall
Doe Lea, Chesterfield, Derbyshire, S44 5QJ; tel: 01246 850431

continued overleaf

Kirby Hall
Deene, Corby, Northamptonshire, NN17 3EN;
tel: 01536 203230
Kirby Muxloe Castle
Oakcroft Avenue, Kirby Muxloe, Leicestershire,
LE9 9MD; tel: 01162 386886
Lyddington Bede House
Blue Coat Lane, Uppingham, Rutland, LE15 9LZ;
tel: 01572 822438
Medieval Bishops' Palace
Minster Yard, Lincoln, LN2 1PU; tel: 01522
527468
Peveril Castle
Market Place, Castleton, Derbyshire, S33 8WQ;
tel: 01422 620613
Rushton Triangular Lodge
Rushton, Kettering, Northamptonshire, NN14
1RP; tel: 01536 710761
Sibsey Trader Windmill
Sibsey, Boston, Lincolnshire, PE22 0SY; tel: 01205
460647
Wingfield Manor
Garner Lane, South Wingfield, Alfreton,
Derbyshire, DE5 7NH; tel: 01773 832060

ENGLISH HERITAGE (EAST OF ENGLAND REGION)

Brooklands, 24 Brooklands Avenue, Cambridge,
CB2 2BU

Tel: 01223 582700
Fax: 01223 582701

Website:
http://www.english-heritage.org.uk

Enquiries:
Enquiries to: Regional Marketing Executive – East
of England

Organisation type and purpose:
National organisation, suitable for ages: all.
Independent but government-sponsored body.
English Heritage site information service,
including dates, times of opening and special
events.

Subject coverage:
The conservation and preservation of the historic
environment of Eastern England.

Access to staff:
Contact by letter, by telephone, by fax and by e-
mail
Hours: Mon to Fri, 0900 to 1700

Heritage sites:
Audley End House & Gardens
Saffron Walden, Essex, CB11 4JF; tel: 01799
522399
Berney Arms Windmill
8 Manor Road, Southtown, Norfolk, NR31 0QA;
tel: 01493 85700
Castle Acre Priory and Castle
Stocks Green, Castle Acre, Kings Lynn, Norfolk,
PE32 2XD; tel: 01760 755394
Castle Rising Castle
King's Lynn, Norfolk; tel: 01553 631330
Denny Abbey & The Farmland Museum
Near Waterbeach, Cambridge; tel: 01223 860489
Framlingham Castle
Framlingham, Suffolk, IP8 9BT; tel: 01728 724189
Great Yarmouth Row Houses
South Quay, Great Yarmouth, Norfolk, IP13 2RQ;
tel: 01493 857900
Grime's Graves
Lynford, Thetford, Norfolk, IP26 5DE; tel: 01842
810656
Hill Hall
Epping, Essex; tel: 01223 582700
Landguard Fort
Felixstowe, Suffolk; tel: 01473 218245
Longthorpe Tower
Thorpe Road, Longthorpe, Cambridgeshire, PE1
1HA; tel: 01760 755394
Orford Castle
Orford, Woodbridge, Suffolk; tel: 01394 450472
Saxtead Green Post Mill
The Mill House, Saxtead Green, Suffolk, IP13
9QQ; tel: 01728 685789

Tilbury Fort
No 2 Office Block, The Fort, Tilbury, Essex, RM18
7NR; tel: 01375 858489
West Park Gardens
Silsoe, Luton, Bedfordshire, MK45 4HS; tel:
01525 860152 (weekends only)

ENGLISH HERITAGE (LONDON REGION)

23 Savile Row, London, W1X 1AB

Tel: 020 7973 3000
Fax: 020 7937 3001

Website:
http://www.english-heritage.org.uk

Enquiries:
Enquiries to: Marketing Officer

Organisation type and purpose:
National organisation, membership association,
suitable for ages: all.
Independent but government-sponsored body.
English Heritage sites administration and
information service, including dates, times of
opening and special events.

Subject coverage:
Conservation and preservation of the historic
environment. English Heritage London Region,
administers and cares for its properties and sites in
the London area.

Education services:
Group education facilities.

Access to staff:
Contact by letter and by telephone. Appointment
necessary.
Hours: Mon to Fri, 0900 to 1700

Heritage sites:
Chapter House
East Cloisters, Westminster Abbey, London,
SW1P 3PE; tel: 020 7222 5897; fax: 020 7222 0960
Chiswick House
Burlington Lane, London, W4 2RP; tel: 020 8995
0508; fax: 020 8742 3104
Downe House
Luxted Road, Downe, Biggin Hill, Kent, BR6 7JT;
tel: 01689 859119; fax: 01689 862755
Eltham Palace
Court Yard, Eltham, London, SE9 5QE; tel: 020
8294 2548; fax: 0208 8294 2621
Jewel Tower
Abingdon Street, Westminster, London, SW1P
3JY; tel: 020 7222 2219; fax: 020 7222 2219
Kenwood House
The Iveagh Bequest, Kenwood, Hampstead
Lane, London, NW3 7JR; tel: 020 8348 1286; fax:
020 8793 3891
Marble Hill House
Richmond Road, Twickenham, Middlesex, TW1
2NL; tel: 0208 892 5115; fax: 020 8607 9976
The Wernher Collection at Ranger's House
Chesterfield Walk, Blackheath, London, SE10
8QX; tel: 020 8853 0035; fax: 020 8853 0090
Wellington Arch
Hyde Park Corner, London, W1J 7JZ; tel: 020
7930 2726; fax: 020 7925 1019

ENGLISH HERITAGE (NORTH EAST REGION)

Bessie Surtees House, 41–44 Sandhill, Newcastle
upon Tyne, NE1 3JF

Tel: 0191 269 1200

Website:
http://www.english-heritage.org.uk

Enquiries:
Enquiries to: Marketing Manager

Organisation type and purpose:
National organisation, advisory body, membership
association (membership is by subscription),
suitable for ages: all. Independent but government-
sponsored body.

English Heritage site administration and
information service, including dates, times of
opening and special events.

Subject coverage:
English Heritage North East Region administers
and cares for properties and sites in
Northumberland, Tyne and Wear, County Durham
and Teesside; the conservation and preservation of
the historic environment.

Access to staff:
Contact by letter and by telephone. Appointment
necessary.
Hours: Mon to Fri, 0900 to 1700

Heritage sites:
Aydon Castle
Corbridge, Northumberland, NE45 5PJ
Barnard Castle
Castle House, Barnard Castle, County Durham,
DL12 9AT
Belsay Hall, Castle and Gardens
Belsay, Ponteland, Northumberland, NE20 0DX
Berwick Barracks
The Parade, Berwick upon Tweed,
Northumberland, TD15 1DF
Brinkburn Priory
Long Framlington, Morpeth, Northumberland,
NE65 8AR
Chesters Roman Fort and Museum
Chollerford, Humshaugh, Hexham,
Northumberland, NE46 4EP
Dunstanburgh Castle
14 Queen Street, Alnwick, Northumberland,
NE66 1RD
Etal Castle
Etal Village, Berwick upon Tweed,
Northumberland, TD12 4TN
Finchale Priory
Brasside, Newton Hall, County Durham, DH1
5SH
Hadrian's Wall Museums
Hadrian's Wall Tourism Partnership
Housesteads Roman Fort
Haydon Bridge, Hexham, Northumberland,
NE46 6NN
Lindisfarne Priory
Holy Island, Berwick upon Tweed,
Northumberland, TD15 2RX
Norham Castle
Berwick upon Tweed, Northumberland, TD15
2JY
Prudhoe Castle
Prudhoe, Northumberland, NE42 6NA
Tynemouth Castle and Priory
North Shields, Tyne and Wear, NE30 4BZ
Warkworth Castle and Hermitage
Morpeth, Northumberland, NE66 0UJ

ENGLISH HERITAGE (NORTH WEST REGION)

Canada House, 3 Chepstow Street, Manchester, M1
5FW

Tel: 0161 242 1400
Fax: 0161 242 1401
E-mail: northwest@english-heritage.org.uk

Website:
http://www.english-heritage.org.uk

Organisation type and purpose:
National organisation, advisory body, membership
association (membership is by subscription),
suitable for ages: all.
Independent but government-sponsored body.
English Heritage site administration and
information service, including dates, times of
opening and special events.

Subject coverage:
English Heritage North West Region advises local
planning authoorities on proposals for highly
graded listed buildings, and major new
development in historic areas, and allocates
financial support to the historic environment of the
North West.

Publications list:
Available online

Access to staff:
Contact by letter and by telephone. Appointment necessary.
Hours: Mon to Fri, 0900 to 1700

Heritage sites:
Ambleside Roman Fort
    Ambleside, Cumbria
Beeston Castle
    Beeston, Tarporley, Cheshire, CW6 9TX
Brough Castle
    Brough, Kirby Stephen, Cumbria
Brougham Castle
    Brougham, Penrith, Cumbria, CA10 2AA
Carlisle Castle
    Carlisle, Cumbria, CA3 8UR
Furness Abbey
    Barrow-in-Furness, Cumbria, LA13 0TJ
Hadrian's Wall Museums
    The Roman Site, Corbridge, Northumberland, NE45 5NT
Lanercost Priory
    Lanercost, Brampton, Cumbria, CA8 2HQ
Stott Park Bobbin Mill
    Low Stott Park, Ulverston, Cumbria, LA12 8AX

ENGLISH HERITAGE (SOUTH EAST REGION)

Eastgate Court, 195–205 High Street, Guildford, Surrey, GU1 3EH

Tel: 01483 252000
Fax: 01483 252001
E-mail: southeast@english-heritage.org.uk

Website:
http://www.english-heritage.org.uk/southeast

Enquiries:
Enquiries to: Marketing Assistant

Organisation type and purpose:
National organisation, advisory body, suitable for ages: all.
Independent but government-sponsored body. English Heritage site administration and information service, including dates, times of opening and special events.

Subject coverage:
English Heritage South East Region administers and cares for properties and sites in Kent, Surrey, Sussex, Hampshire and the Isle of Wight; conservation and preservation of the historic environment.

Access to staff:
Contact by letter, by telephone and by fax
Hours: Mon to Fri, 0900 to 1700

Heritage sites:
Abingdon County Hall
    Oxfordshire, 0X14 3HG; tel: 01235 523703
Appuldurcombe House
    Wroxall, Ventnor, Isle of Wight, PO38 3EW; tel: 01983 852484; fax: 01983 840188
Battle Abbey and Battlefield
    High Street, Battle, East Sussex, TN33 0AD; tel: 01424 773792
Bayham Old Abbey
    Bayham, Lamberhurst, Kent, TN8 8DE; tel: 01892 890381
Bishop's Waltham Palace
    Bishop's Waltham, Hampshire, SO32 1DH
Calshot Castle
    Hampshire, SO4 1BR; tel: 02380 892023
Camber Castle
    tel: 01797 223862
Carisbrooke Castle and Museum
    Carisbrooke, Newport, Isle of Wight, PO30 6JY; tel: 01983 522107; e-mail: carismus@lineone.net
Deal Castle
    Victoria Road, Deal, Kent, CT14 7BA; tel: 01304 372762
Dover Castle
    The Keep, Dover, Kent, CT16 1HU; tel: 01304 211067

Down House
    Luxted Road, Downe, Biggin Hill, Kent, BR6 7JT; tel: 01689 859119
Dymchurch Martello Tower
    High Street, Dymchurch, Kent, CT16 1HU
Farnham Castle Keep
    Castle Hill, Farnham, Surrey, GU6 0AG
Fort Brockhurst
    Gunners Way, Elson, Hampshire, PO12 4DS; tel: 02392 378291
Hurst Castle
    Hampshire, SO14 0TP; tel: 01590 642344
Lullingstone Roman Villa
    Lullingstone Lane, Eynsford, Kent, DA4 0JA; tel: 01322 863467
Medieval Merchant's House
    58 French Street, Southhampton, SO23 8NB; tel: 02380 221503
Osborne House
    York Avenue, East Cowes, Isle of Wight, PO32 6JY; tel: 01983 200022; fax: 01983 281380
Pevensey Castle
    Pevensey, East Sussex, BN24 5LE; tel: 01323 762604
Portchester Castle
    Portchester, Hampshire, PO16 9QW; tel: 023 923 78291
Richborough Roman Fort
    Sandwich, Kent, CT13 9JW
Rochester Castle
    Boley Hill, Rochester, Kent, ME1 1SW; tel: 01634 402276
St Augustine's Abbey and Museum
    Longport, Canterbury, Kent, CT1 1TF; tel: 01227 767345; fax: 01227 767345
Temple Manor
    Strood, Rochester, Kent; tel: 01634 827980
Upnor Castle
    Wainscott, Rochester, Kent; tel: 01634 718742
Walmer Castle & Gardens
    Kingsdown Road, Deal, Kent, CT14 7LJ; tel: 01304 364288; fax: 01304 364826
Wolvesey Castle (Old Bishop's Palace)
    College Street, Winchester, SO23 8NB
Yarmouth Castle
    Quay Street, Yarmouth, Isle of Wight, PO41 0PB; tel: 01983 760678

ENGLISH HERITAGE (SOUTH WEST REGION)

Formal name: Historic Monuments & Building Commission for England
Acronym or abbreviation: HMBCE

29 Queen Square, Bristol, BS1 4ND

Tel: 0117 975 0700
Fax: 0117 975 0701
E-mail: southwest@english-heritage.org.uk

Website:
http://www.english-heritage.org.uk/southwest

Founded:
1984

Organisation type and purpose:
National organisation, advisory body, membership association (membership is by subscription), suitable for ages: all, publishing house.
English Heritage South West Region administers and cares for properties and sites in Bristol, Cornwall, Devon, Dorset, Gloucestershire, Isles of Scilly, Somerset, and Wiltshire.

Subject coverage:
The conservation and preservation of the historic environment.

Access to staff:
Contact by letter, by telephone, by fax, by e-mail and in person. Appointment necessary.
Hours: Mon to Fri, 0900 to 1700

Heritage Site:
Berry Pomeroy Castle
    Totnes, Devon, TQ9 6NJ; tel: 01803 866618; e-mail: customers@english-heritage.org.uk; website: http://www.english-heritage.org.uk/berrypomeroy

Chysauster Ancient Village
    Newmill, Penzance, Cornwall, TR20 8XA; tel: 07831 757934; e-mail: customers@english -heritage.org.uk; website: http://www.english -heritage.org.uk/chysauster
Cleeve Abbey
    Washford, Watchet, Somerset, TA23 0PS; tel: 01984 640377; e-mail: customers@english -heritage.org.uk; website: http://www.english -heritage.org.uk/cleeve
Dartmouth Castle
    Castle Road, Dartmouth, Devon, TQ6 0JN; tel: 01803 833588; e-mail: customers@english -heritage.org.uk; website: http://www.english -heritage.org.uk/dartmouth
Farleigh Hungerford Castle
    Farleigh Hungerford, Bath, Somerset, BA3 6RS; tel: 01225 754026; e-mail: customers@english -heritage.org.uk; website: http://www.english -heritage.org.uk/farleighhungerford
Hailes Abbey
    Winchcombe, Cheltenham, Gloucester, GL54 5PB; tel: 01242 602398; e-mail: customers@ english-heritage.org.uk; website: http://www .english-heritage.org.uk/hailes
Launceston Castle
    Castle Lodge, Launceston, Cornwall, PL15 7DR; tel: 01566 772365; e-mail: customers@english -heritage.org.uk; website: http://www.english -heritage.org.uk/launceston
Muchelney Abbey
    Muchelney, Langport, Somerset, TA10 0DQ; tel: 01458 250664; e-mail: customers@english -heritage.org.uk; website: http://www.english -heritage.org.uk/muchelney
Okehampton Castle
    Castle Lodge, Okehampton, Devon, EX20 1JB; tel: 01837 52844; e-mail: customers@english -heritage.org.uk; website: http://www.english -heritage.org.uk/okehampton
Old Sarum
    Castle Road, Salisbury, Wiltshire, SP1 3SD; tel: 01722 335398; e-mail: customers@english -heritage.org.uk; website: http://www.english -heritage.org.uk/oldsarum
Old Wardour Castle
    Tisbury, Salisbury, Wiltshire, SP3 6RR; tel: 01747 870347; e-mail: customers@english-heritage.org .uk; website: http://www.english-heritage.org .uk/oldwardour
Pendennis Castle
    Falmouth, Cornwall, TR11 4LP; tel: 01326 316594; e-mail: customers@english-heritage.org .uk; website: http://www.english-heritage.org .uk/pendennis
Portland Castle
    Castleton, Portland, Dorset, DT5 1AZ; tel: 01305 820539; e-mail: customers@english-heritage.org .uk; website: http://www.english-heritage.org .uk/portland
Restormel Castle
    Lostwithiel, Cornwall, PL22 0BD; tel: 01208 872687; e-mail: customers@english-heritage.org .uk; website: http://www.english-heritage.org .uk/restormel
Sherborne Old Castle
    Castleton, Sherborne, Dorset, DT9 3SA; tel: 01935 812730; e-mail: customers@english -heritage.org.uk; website: http://www.english -heritage.org.uk/sherborne
St Mawes Castle
    St Mawes, Cornwall, TR2 3AA; tel: 01326 270526; e-mail: customers@english-heritage.org.uk; website: http://www.english-heritage.org.uk/ stmawes
Stonehenge
    Stone Circle, Wiltshire, SP4 7DE; tel: 01980 624715 (Information line); e-mail: customers@ english-heritage.org.uk; website: http://www .english-heritage.org.uk/stonehenge
Tintagel Castle
    Tintagel, Cornwall, DL34 0AA; tel: 01840 770328; e-mail: customers@english-heritage.org.uk; website: http://www.english-heritage.org.uk/ tintagel

continued overleaf

Totnes Castle
  Castle Street, Totnes, Devon, TQ9 5NU; tel:
  01803 864406; e-mail: customers@english
  -heritage.org.uk; website: http://www.english
  -heritage.org.uk/totnes

ENGLISH HERITAGE (WEST MIDLANDS REGION)

The Axis, 10 Holliday Street, Birmingham, B1 1TG

Tel: 0121 625 6820

Website:
http://www.english-heritage.org.uk

Organisation type and purpose:
National organisation, advisory body.
Independent but government-sponsored body.
English Heritage West Midlands Region
administers and cares for properties and sites in
Herefordshire, Shropshire, Staffordshire,
Warwickshire, West Midlands and Worcestershire.

Subject coverage:
The conservation and preservation of the historic
environment.
English Heritage site administration and
information service, including dates, times of
opening and special events.

Access to staff:
Contact by letter, by telephone and in person
Hours: Mon to Fri, 0900 to 1700

Heritage Site:
Boscobel House and the Royal Oak
  Brewood, Bishops Wood, Staffordshire, ST19
  9AR
Buildwas Abbey
  Ironbridge, Telford, TF8 7BW
Goodrich Castle
  Goodrich, Ross on Wye, Worcestershire, HR9
  6HY
Halesowen Abbey
Haughmond Abbey
  Upton Magna, Uffington, Shropshire, SY4 4RW
Kenilworth Castle
  Kenilworth, Warwickshire, CV8 1NE
Stokesay Castle
  Craven Arms, Shropshire, SY7 9AH
Wall Roman Site (Letocetum)
  Watling Street, Lichfield, Staffordshire, WS14
  0AW
Wenlock Priory
  Much Wenlock, Shropshire, TF13 6HS
Witley Court
  Great Witley, Worcestershire, WR6 6JT
Wroxeter Roman City
  Wroxeter, Shropshire, SY5 6PH

ENGLISH HERITAGE (YORKSHIRE REGION)

37 Tanner Row, York, YO1 6WP

Tel: 01904 601901

Website:
http://www.english-heritage.org.uk

Organisation type and purpose:
National organisation, advisory body.
Independent but government-sponsored body.
English Heritage Yorkshire Region administers
and cares for properties and sites in East Riding of
Yorkshire, North East Lincolnshire, North
Lincolnshire, North Yorkshire, South Yorkshire
and West Yorkshire.

Subject coverage:
The conservation and preservation of the historic
environment.
English Heritage site administration and
information service, including dates, times of
opening and special events.

Access to staff:
Contact by letter, by telephone and in person
Hours: Mon to Fri, 0900 to 1700

Heritage Site:
Aldborough Roman Site
  Main Street, Boroughbridge, Yorkshire, YO5 9EF
Brodsworth Hall and Gardens
  Brodsworth, Doncaster, South Yorkshire
Byland Abbey
  Coxwold, North Yorkshire, YO6 4BD
Clifford's Tower
  Clifford Street, York, YO11 1HY
Conisbrough Castle
Helmsley Castle
  Helmsley, North Yorkshire, YO6 5AB
Kirkham Priory
  Whitwell-on-the-Hill, North Yorkshire, YO6 7JS
Middleham Castle
  Middleham, Leyburn, North Yorkshire, DL8
  4QG
Mount Grace Priory
  Saddle Bridge, Northallerton, North Yorkshire,
  DL6 3JG
Pickering Castle
  Pickering, North Yorkshire, YO18 7AX
Richmond Castle
  Richmond, North Yorkshire, DL10 4QW
Rievaulx Abbey
  Rievaulx, Helmsley, North Yorkshire, DL10 5LB
Roche Abbey
  Maltby, Rotherham, South Yorkshire, S66 8NW
Scarborough Castle
  Castle Road, Scarborough, North Yorkshire,
  YO11 1HY
Whitby Abbey
  Whitby, North Yorkshire, YO22 4JT

ENGLISH HOCKEY

Acronym or abbreviation: EHA

The Stadium, Silbury Boulevard, Milton Keynes,
Buckinghamshire, MK9 1HA

Tel: 01908 544644
Fax: 01908 241106
E-mail: info@englandhockey.org

Website:
http://www.hockeyonline.co.uk
Official site of English Hockey, including latest
news, results, tables and links to hockey clubs in
England.

Enquiries:
Enquiries to: Marketing Director

Founded:
1886

Formerly called:
Hockey Association (HA) from 1886 to 1997; All
England Womens Hockey Association (AEWHA)
from 1895 to 1997; Mixed Hockey Association
(MHA), National Hockey Foundation (NHF) (year
of change 1997)

Organisation type and purpose:
Membership association (membership is by
subscription), present number of members: 70,000,
suitable for ages: 5 to 65.
Governing body of hockey in England.

Subject coverage:
Hockey in England, its history, past, present and
future development, English hockey in European
and world arenas; league and competition
management, coaching, umpiring and teaching,
technical information, sponsorship and
partnership, international teams, advice on all
aspects of hockey including clubs.

**Museum or gallery collection, archive, or library
special collection:**
Minute books and cash account books from the
  formation of the Association in 1896
Pictorial history
Trophies, gifts, and artefacts presented by guest
  and host nations

Trade and statistical information:
Data on the market profile and on the number of
  participants in hockey, at club level split into
  regions and counties.

Printed publications:
Clothing
Coaching Packs
Handbook of English Hockey
Leaflets and posters
Rules of Hockey

Microform publications:
Coaching videos

Access to staff:
Contact by letter, by telephone, by fax, by e-mail
and via website. Appointment necessary.
Hours: Mon to Fri, 0900 to 1700

Affiliated to:
European Hockey Federation (EHF)
International Hockey Federation (FIH)

Constituent member of:
Great Britain Olympic Hockey Board

ENGLISH INDEPENDENCE PARTY

Acronym or abbreviation: EIP

27 Old Gloucester Street, London, WC1N 3XX

Tel: 020 7278 5221
E-mail: eip_enquiries@yahoo.com

Website:
www.englishindependenceparty.com
Manifesto, bibliography

Enquiries:
Enquiries to: Chairman

Founded:
1991

Formerly called:
English National Party (ENP)

Organisation type and purpose:
National organisation, membership association
(membership is by subscription), voluntary
organisation.
Political party.

Subject coverage:
English nationalism, knowledge about the English
people, UK devolution, UK politics, English
politics, nationalism, English history, culture and
language.

**Museum or gallery collection, archive, or library
special collection:**
Books related to English nationalism, etc.

Printed publications:
Manifesto
Leaflet
Progress Letters

Access to staff:
Contact by letter and by telephone. Appointment
necessary.
Hours: Mon to Fri, 1100 to 2200

Access to building, collection or gallery:
No access other than to staff

ENGLISH INDOOR BOWLING ASSOCIATION LTD

Acronym or abbreviation: EIBA

David Cornwell House, Bowling Green, Leicester
Road, Melton Mowbray, Leicestershire, LE13 0FA

Tel: 01664 481900
Fax: 01664 482888
E-mail: enquiries@eiba.co.uk

Website:
http://www.eiba.co.uk
Full information on the sport, including all
national competitions and how to find a local club.

Enquiries:
Enquiries to: Chief Operating Executive

Founded:
1971

Organisation type and purpose:
National organisation, membership association (membership is by subscription), present number of members: 327 clubs.
National governing body, level-green, indoor bowling.

Subject coverage:
Development of facilities for indoor bowling for men and women, details of events and programme, player profiles.

Printed publications:
EIBA Year Book

Electronic and video publications:
Affiliated clubs' addresses

Access to staff:
Contact by letter, by telephone, by fax, by e-mail, in person and via website. Appointment necessary.
Hours: Mon to Fri, 0900 to 1700

Access to building, collection or gallery:
By appointment

Affiliated to:
British Isles Indoor Bowls Council
World Indoor Bowls Council

ENGLISH LACROSSE ASSOCIATION

Acronym or abbreviation: ELA

Belle Vue Athletics Centre, Pink Bank Lane, Manchester, M12 5GL

Tel: 0161 227 3626
Fax: 0161 227 3625
E-mail: info@englishlacrosse.co.uk

Website:
http://www.englishlacrosse.co.uk
The ELA and its constitution, working policies and guides, lacrosse, its history and rules of the game, members, clubs, fixtures, results and statistics, national squads, news.

Founded:
1996

Created by the merger of:
All England Women's Lacrosse Association and English Lacrosse Union

Organisation type and purpose:
National governing body for lacrosse in England, membership association (membership is by subscription).
To control, promote and develop lacrosse throughout the country, and in the long term lo make lacrosse one of the major team sports in England by substantially increasing participation for all.

Subject coverage:
Lacrosse at all levels.

Education services:
Education programme develops, administers, organises and implements courses and resources for lacrosse coaches, officials, teachers and volunteers.

Printed publications:
Lacrosse talk (national magazine)

Access to staff:
Contact by letter, by telephone, by fax, by e-mail and via website

ENGLISH NATIONAL BALLET

Markova House, 39 Jay Mews, London, SW7 2ES

Tel: 020 7581 1245
Fax: 020 7225 0827
E-mail: info@ballet.org.uk

Website:
http://www.ballet.org.uk
Includes information on ballets, dancers, current news, history of the Company, etc.

Enquiries:
Enquiries to: Assistant to Managing Director
Other contacts: Marketing Manager for general source of information about performances and other activities.

Founded:
1950

Formed from:
Festival Ballet, London Festival Ballet

Organisation type and purpose:
Membership association (membership is by subscription), registered charity (charity number 214005).
English National Ballet is a performing arts organisation. Individuals and companies can provide support and receive services/benefits by joining the Association of English National Ballet or the Council of English National Ballet or by becoming a corporate member/sponsor of the Company.

Subject coverage:
Ballet.

Museum or gallery collection, archive, or library special collection:
English National Ballet Archive includes photographs, designs, set models, music scores, press clippings and books

Printed publications:
In the Wings (magazine, free to associates with membership, minimum £8 a year)

Access to staff:
Contact by letter, by telephone, by fax and by e-mail
Hours: Mon to Fri, 1000 to 1800

Access to building, collection or gallery:
Prior appointment required
Special comments: English National Ballet Archive is available to those undertaking serious study.

ENGLISH NATIONAL OPERA

Acronym or abbreviation: ENO

Lilian Baylis House, 165 Broadhurst Gardens, London, NW6 3AX

Tel: 020 7624 7711
E-mail: ccolvin@eno.org

Website:
http://www.eno.org

Enquiries:
Enquiries to: Archivist

Founded:
1931

Formerly called:
Sadler's Wells Opera (year of change 1974)

Organisation type and purpose:
Registered charity (charity number 257210), historic building, house or site.
Opera production in English.
Encouragement of understanding and appreciation of the dramatic art by providing, presenting, producing, organising, managing, and conducting performances of classical and educational plays, opera, ballet, films and concerts.

Subject coverage:
History and performance of opera at Sadler's Wells Theatre until 1968 and The Coliseum from 1968.

Museum or gallery collection, archive, or library special collection:
Original documents relating to the history and performance of Sadler's Wells Opera and English National Opera

Non-library collection catalogue:
All or part available online and in-house

Access to staff:
Contact by letter, by telephone and by e-mail. Appointment necessary.

Hours: Archives: by appointment

Access for disabled people:
Toilet facilities

ENGLISH PÉTANQUE ASSOCIATION

Acronym or abbreviation: EPA

41 Warwick Road, Southam, Warwickshire, CV47 0HW

Tel: 01926 815982
E-mail: mike.pegg@fipjp.com

Website:
http://www.englishpetanque.org.uk

Enquiries:
Enquiries to: National President

Founded:
1974

Organisation type and purpose:
Membership association.
Governing body of the sport.

Subject coverage:
Pétanque: starting a club, facilities, equipment, coaching, umpiring, competition organisation, leagues.

Printed publications:
EPA Competition Organisers Manual
Pétanque/Boules Explained
Directory of Officers and Clubs
Pétanque: A Comprehensive and Structured Coaching Course
The Official Rules of the Game of Pétanque
Pétanque – The Game of Boules

Publications list:
Available in print

Access to staff:
Contact by e-mail. Appointment necessary.
Hours: Mon to Fri, 0900 to 1700

Member organisation of:
CCPR
Fédération Internationale de Pétanque et Jeu Provençal
Sports Council

ENGLISH PEWTER COMPANY

1 Blackmore Street, Sheffield, South Yorkshire, S4 7TZ

Tel: 0114 272 3920
Fax: 0114 276 1416
E-mail: asharp@englishpewter.co.uk

Website:
http://www.englishpewter.co.uk

Enquiries:
Enquiries to: Managing Director
Direct e-mail: sales@englishpewter.co.uk

Founded:
1977

Organisation type and purpose:
Manufacturing industry.

Subject coverage:
Pewterware.

Non-library collection catalogue:
All or part available online

Library catalogue:
All or part available online

Publications list:
Available online

Access to staff:
Contact by letter, by telephone, by fax and by e-mail. Appointment necessary.
Hours: Mon to Fri, 0900 to 1700

Access to building, collection or gallery:
Prior appointment required

continued overleaf

Also at:
English Pewter Company
  1 Blackmoor Street, Sheffield, S4 7TZ; e-mail:
  sales@englishpewter.co.uk

ENGLISH PLACE-NAME SOCIETY

Acronym or abbreviation: EPNS

Department of English Studies, University of
Nottingham, Nottingham, NG7 2RD

Tel: 0115 951 5919
Fax: 0115 951 5924

Website:
http://www.nottingham.ac.uk/english/research/
EPNS/index.html
Information provided (our purpose, publications,
membership details, personnel)

Enquiries:
Enquiries to: Administrator

Founded:
1923

Organisation type and purpose:
Learned society (membership is by subscription),
registered charity (charity number 257891),
research organisation, publishing house.

Subject coverage:
Etymologies of English place-names, surveyed on a
county basis.

**Museum or gallery collection, archive, or library
special collection:**
English and Scandinavian onomastics
Library including the Olof von Feilitzen bequest

Library catalogue:
All or part available in-house

Printed publications:
Place-Names in Skaldic Verse
The Place-Names of West Thorney
Vocabulary of English Place-Names
Wirral and its Viking Heritage
Journal of the English Place-Name Society (issued
  free to members)
A Dictionary of Lincolnshire Place-Names
Annual county volume on the place-names of that
  county (each county takes several volumes to
  cover it); counties include:
Bedfordshire, Berkshire, Buckinghamshire,
  Cambridgeshire and the Isle of Ely, Cheshire,
  Cornwall, Cumberland, Derbyshire, Devon,
  Dorset, East Riding of Yorkshire and York, Essex,
  Gloucestershire, Hertfordshire,
  Huntingdonshire, Leicestershire, Lincolnshire,
  Middlesex apart from the City of London,
  Norfolk, North Riding of Yorkshire,
  Northamptonshire, Nottinghamshire,
  Oxfordshire, Rutland, Shropshire, Staffordshire,
  Surrey, Sussex, Warwickshire, West Riding of
  Yorkshire, Westmoreland, Wiltshire,
  Worcestershire

Publications list:
Available online and in print

Access to staff:
Contact by letter, by telephone and by fax.
Appointment necessary. Non-members charged.
Hours: Mon to Fri, 0900 to 1700

Affiliated to:
AHRB
Institute for Navneforskning
  University of Copenhagen
Ortnamnssällskapets
  University of Uppsala
Sydsvenska Ortnamnssällskapets
  University of Lund

Supported by:
British Academy

ENGLISH PLAYING CARD
SOCIETY

Acronym or abbreviation: EPCS

Little Paddock, Charlton Mackrell, Somerton,
Somerset, TA11 7BG

Tel: 01458 223812
E-mail: secretary@epcs.org

Website:
http://www.wopc.co.uk/epcs

Enquiries:
Enquiries to: Secretary

Founded:
1984

Organisation type and purpose:
Membership association (membership is by
subscription), present number of members: 120.

Subject coverage:
All aspects of the manufacture and designs of
English playing cards/card games and related
subjects, including ephemera.

Printed publications:
Newsletter (3 times a year)

Access to staff:
Contact by telephone and by e-mail. Appointment
necessary.
Hours: Mon to Fri, 0900 to 1700

ENGLISH RACKETBALL
ASSOCIATION

50 Tredegar Road, Wilmington, Dartford, Kent,
DA2 7AZ

Tel: 01322 272200
Fax: 01322 289295
E-mail: idw@kentsra.co.uk

Website:
http://www.kentracketball.co.uk

Enquiries:
Enquiries to: Secretary

Founded:
1984

Created by the merger of:
British Racketball Association (BRA) and Squash
Rackets Association (SRA) (year of change 1998)

Organisation type and purpose:
Voluntary organisation.
Governing body of the sport.

Subject coverage:
Rules of racketball, coaching, tournaments,
promoting racketball within Local Authority
leisure centres and private squash clubs.

Access to staff:
Contact by letter, by telephone and by fax
Hours: Mon to Fri, 0900 to 1700

ENGLISH SCHOOLS' ATHLETIC
ASSOCIATION

Acronym or abbreviation: ESAA

26 Newborough Green, New Malden, Surrey, KT3
5HS

Tel: 020 8949 1506
Fax: 020 8942 0943

Enquiries:
Enquiries to: Honorary Secretary

Founded:
1925

Organisation type and purpose:
Voluntary organisation.

Subject coverage:
Schools' athletics.

Printed publications:
Awards Scheme Brochure (annually, free)
History of English Schools AA 1925 to 1995 (£8.50
  inc. p&p)
Handbook (annually, £3 inc. p&p)

Access to staff:
Contact by letter, by telephone and by fax

Hours: Mon to Fri, 0900 to 1700

Affiliated to:
Amateur Athletic Association of England
Central Council of Physical Recreation
National Council for School Sports
UK Athletics

ENGLISH SCHOOLS' FOOTBALL
ASSOCIATION

Acronym or abbreviation: ESFA

4 Parker Court, Staffordshire Technology Park,
Stafford, ST18 0WP

Tel: 01785 785970
Fax: 01785 256246
E-mail: office@esfa.co.uk

Website:
http://www.esfa.co.uk/esfa
Competition draws and results.

Enquiries:
Enquiries to: Chief Executive

Founded:
1904

Organisation type and purpose:
Membership association, registered charity
(charity number 306003).

Subject coverage:
Organisation of extra-curricular football for
schools in England, regulations for schoolboy or
girl footballers, competition rules.

Printed publications:
Annual Handbook (£7 plus p&p)
Annual Report
The ESFA Guide to the Teaching of Soccer in
  Schools (£2.95 inc. p&p)
Kicks (3 times a year, free)
Other publications available from the Football
  Association

Publications list:
Available in print

Access to staff:
Contact by letter, by telephone, by fax and by e-
mail. Appointment necessary.
Hours: Mon to Fri, 0900 to 1700

Affiliated to:
Football Association
  tel: 020 7745 4545

Has:
500 member associations

ENGLISH SHORT MAT BOWLING
ASSOCIATION

Acronym or abbreviation: ESMBA

Wytheford Hall, Shawbury, Shrewsbury,
Shopshire, SY4 4JJ

Tel: 01952 770218
Fax: 01952 770567

Website:
http://www.shortmatbowlsesmba.com

Enquiries:
Enquiries to: General Secretary
Other contacts: Umpires Director; Competition
Secretary; Membership Secretary

Founded:
1984

Organisation type and purpose:
Membership association (membership is by
subscription), present number of members: c.
27,000, voluntary organisation.
National governing body of the game in England,
sports association.

Subject coverage:
The game of short mat bowls.

Printed publications:
Rule Book (£2)

Electronic and video publications:
Video (£10)

Access to staff:
Contact by letter
Hours: Daily, 0900 to 1700

ENGLISH SPEAKING BOARD (INTERNATIONAL) LIMITED

Acronym or abbreviation: ESB

26a Princes Street, Southport, Merseyside, PR8 1EQ

Tel: 01704 501730
Fax: 01704 539637
E-mail: admin@esbuk.org

Website:
http://www.esbuk.org
Full range of syllabus available plus contact information for interested organisations.

Enquiries:
Enquiries to: Chief Administration Officer

Founded:
1953

Organisation type and purpose:
International organisation, advisory body, professional body, voluntary organisation, registered charity (charity number 272565), suitable for ages: 5+, training organisation. Examining body.

Subject coverage:
Oral education, communication, speech, English language, English teaching.

Printed publications:
Creative Oral Assessment (Burniston, 1982)
English Speaking Board: an introduction (leaflet)
Forty Years of Achievement: ESB 1953–1993
Speaking English (formerly Spoken English, 2 times a year)

Publications list:
Available in print

Access to staff:
Contact by letter, by telephone, by fax, by e-mail and via website
Hours: Mon to Fri, 0900 to 1700

Access for disabled people:
Parking provided

Affiliated to:
Australia Speech Communication Association
ESB New South Wales
New Zealand Speech Board

ENGLISH SPEAKING UNION OF THE COMMONWEALTH

Acronym or abbreviation: ESU

Page Memorial Library, Dartmouth House, 37 Charles Street, London, W1J 5ED

Tel: 020 7529 1550
Fax: 020 7495 6108
E-mail: esu@esu.org

Website:
http://www.esu.org

Enquiries:
Enquiries to: Librarian
Direct e-mail: library@esu.org

Founded:
1948

Organisation type and purpose:
International organisation, membership association (membership is by subscription), present number of members: 6104, registered charity (charity number 273136).
Promotion of international understanding; scholarships, exchange programmes, cultural events.

Subject coverage:
History, literature and culture of the United States.

Museum or gallery collection, archive, or library special collection:
ESU Archive (photographs, letters, documents)
Adlai Stevenson Memorial Collection
Main collection c. 12,000 books of US interest (history, literature, arts, social sciences)
Winifred Nerney Collection: publishers and literary figures

Access to staff:
Contact by letter, by telephone, by fax and by e-mail. Appointment necessary.
Hours: Mon to Fri, 1000 to 1700

Affiliated to:
The English Speaking Union of the United States
144 East 39th Street, New York, NY 10016, USA; tel: +1 212 818 1200; fax: +1 212 867 4177; e-mail: info@esuus.org; website: http://www.esuus.org

ENGLISH STRING ORCHESTRA LIMITED/ENGLISH SYMPHONY ORCHESTRA

Formal name: English Symphony Orchestra
Acronym or abbreviation: ESO

The Old Hop Store, Three Counties Showground, Malvern, Worcestershire, WR13 6SP

Tel: 01684 560696
Fax: 01684 560656
E-mail: info@eso.co.uk

Enquiries:
Enquiries to: Head of Finance and Administration
Direct e-mail: alison@eso.co.uk
Other contacts: Administrator

Founded:
1980

Organisation type and purpose:
Registered charity (charity number 293345).
Orchestra.

Subject coverage:
Orchestral performance and touring, music, orchestration, programme notes.
3 Youth Orchestras for grades 1–8, regular courses, bespoke concerts/programmes, indoor and outdoor. Box office services for customer events.

Electronic and video publications:
Recordings on CD and cassette by Nimbus (discography is available)

Publications list:
Available in print

Access to staff:
Contact by letter, by telephone, by fax, by e-mail and via website
Hours: Mon to Fri, 1000 to 1700

ENGLISH TABLE TENNIS ASSOCIATION

Acronym or abbreviation: ETTA

Queensbury House, Havelock Road, Hastings, East Sussex, TN34 1HF

Tel: 01424 722525
Fax: 01424 422103
E-mail: admin@etta.co.uk; vanda.jones@etta.co.uk (events)

Website:
http://www.etta.co.uk

Enquiries:
Enquiries to: National Communications Officer
Direct e-mail: richard.pettit@etta.co.uk

Founded:
1901

Formerly called:
Ping Pong Association (PPA) (year of change 1901); Table Tennis Association (year of change 1903); United Table Tennis and Ping Pong Association (UTTPPA) (year of change 1904); Table Tennis Association (TTA) (year of change 1922);

English Table Tennis Association (ETTA) (year of change 1927); English Table Tennis Association Limited (year of change 2001)

Organisation type and purpose:
Governing body of the sport.

Subject coverage:
Table tennis: competition and administration; historical, technical and developmental aspects of table tennis.

Printed publications:
Official Handbook
Table Tennis News (8 times a year)

Access to staff:
Contact by letter, by telephone, by fax and by e-mail. Appointment necessary.
Hours: Mon to Fri, 0900 to 1700

Links with:
European Table Tennis Union (ETTU)
25 rue des Capucins, 1313, Luxembourg; tel: +352 223030; +352 223031; fax: +352 223060; e-mail: ettu@pt.lu
International Table Tennis Federation (ITTF)
Avenue Mon-Repos 30, Lausanne, 1005, Switzerland; tel: + 41 21 340 7090; fax: + 41 21 340 7099; e-mail: ittf@ittf.com

ENGLISH TOURING OPERA

Acronym or abbreviation: ETO

52–54 Rosebery Avenue, London, EC1R 4RP

Tel: 0207 833 2555
Fax: 0207 713 8686
E-mail: admin@englishtouringopera.org.uk

Website:
http://www.englishtouringopera.org.uk
Company background, friends, repertoire, educational work, tour venues and dates.

Enquiries:
Enquiries to: Chief Executive
Other contacts: Marketing Manager, Education Manager, Head of Development & Marketing – Fundraising

Founded:
1979

Formerly called:
Opera 80 Limited (year of change 1979–1992)

Organisation type and purpose:
Service industry, registered charity.
To take opera throughout England to venues that otherwise would receive little or no professional opera and in so doing to provide opportunities for singers in the early stages of their careers.

Subject coverage:
Opera, touring opera, opera in education and for special needs.

Access to staff:
Contact by letter, by telephone, by fax and by e-mail
Hours: Mon to Fri, 1000 to 1800

ENGLISH VOLLEYBALL ASSOCIATION

Acronym or abbreviation: EVA

27 South Road, West Bridgford, Nottinghamshire, NG2 7AG

Tel: 01509 631699
Fax: 01509 631699

Enquiries:
Enquiries to: Chief Executive
Other contacts: Director

Founded:
1972

Organisation type and purpose:
Membership association (membership is by subscription), present number of members: 23,000, voluntary organisation.

continued overleaf

Subject coverage:
Volleyball; coaching; refereeing; competitions (domestic and international); equipment recommendations, rules, qualifications, awards, beach volleyball, mini volleyball.

Printed publications:
Volleyball International Rules (£5.31)

Electronic and video publications:
Introducing Volleyball (video, £18)
Volleyball – A Movement Education (video, £18)

Publications list:
Available online and in print

Access to staff:
Contact by letter, by telephone, by fax, by e-mail and via website. Appointment necessary.
Hours: Mon to Fri, 0930 to 1630

Affiliated to:
European Volleyball Confederation
International Volleyball Federation

ENGLISH WOMEN'S GOLF ASSOCIATION

Acronym or abbreviation: EWGA

11 Highfield Road, Edgbaston, Birmingham, B15 3EB

Tel: 0121 456 2088
Fax: 0121 452 5978
E-mail: office@englishwomensgolf.org

Website:
http://www.englishwomensgolf.org
Information about all championships, recent news, player profiles, information for juniors, details of grants available.

Enquiries:
Enquiries to: Chief Executive

Founded:
1952

Organisation type and purpose:
Membership association (membership is by subscription), present number of members: 135,000, voluntary organisation.
National governing body of the game, training organisation for juniors.
Administers ladies golf in England.

Subject coverage:
Ladies golf, entry to golf clubs, queries on handicaps and rules of golf, championship organisation.

Museum or gallery collection, archive, or library special collection:
Yearbook
Histories and Centenary Books from County Associations and Golf Clubs

Printed publications:
Yearbook (£5)

Access to staff:
Contact by letter, by telephone, by e-mail and via website. Appointment necessary.
Hours: Mon to Fri, 0830 to 1730

Affiliated to:
Ladies Golf Union
The Scores, St Andrews, Fife, KY16 9AT

ENGLISH-SPEAKING UNION SCOTLAND

Acronym or abbreviation: ESU Scotland

23 Atholl Crescent, Edinburgh, EH3 8HQ

Tel: 0131 229 1528
Fax: 0131 229 1533
E-mail: secretary@esuscotland.org.uk

Website:
http://www.esuscotland.org.uk

Enquiries:
Enquiries to: Secretary

Founded:
1918

Organisation type and purpose:
International organisation, membership association (Scottish charity number 000653). World-wide educational charity, represented in over 50 countries. Members contribute to a wide range of international and cultural events; the promotion of the awareness of current affairs; the use of the English language to create a more harmonious world. Runs international scholarships and exchanges, organises conferences and cultural events, and teaches English as a foreign language. The main providers of training and competitions in speech and debate for Scottish schools, also providing training in public speaking and presentation skills for adults.

Subject coverage:
Public speaking and debating, English language, culture, current affairs.

Education services:
Training for schools in speech and debate. Training for adults in public speaking and presentation skills. Teaching English as a foreign language. Resources for school debate online. Cultural events and public debates. Scholarships.

Museum or gallery collection, archive, or library special collection:
American Studies Library, over 1,200 vols of North American interest, covering literature, criticism, history, politics and society

Non-library collection catalogue:
All or part available online

Library catalogue:
All or part available online

Printed publications:
Newsletter (monthly, free)

Access to staff:
Contact by letter, by telephone, by fax, by e-mail and via website. Appointment necessary.
Hours: Mon to Fri, 0900 to 1700

Links with:
English-Speaking Union of the Commonwealth Dartmouth House, 37 Charles Street, London, W1J 5ED; tel: 020 7529 1550; fax: 020 7495 6108; e-mail: esu@esu.org; website: http://www.esu .org

ENT UK

Formal name: Trading as: British Academic Conference in Otolaryngology (BACO) and British Association of Otorhinolaryngology – Head and Neck Surgery (BAO-HNS)

The Royal College of Surgeons, 35–43 Lincoln's Inn Fields, London, WC2A 3PE

Tel: 020 7404 8373
Fax: 020 7404 4200
E-mail: entuk@entuk.org

Website:
http://www.entuk.org

Enquiries:
Enquiries to: Administration Manager
Direct tel: 020 7611 1731
Direct fax: 020 7404 4200
Other contacts: Honorary Secretary

Founded:
2008

Created by the merger of:
British Association of Otorhinolaryngologists – Head and Neck Surgeons and the British Academic Conference in Otolaryngology (year of change 2008)

Organisation type and purpose:
Professional body (membership is by subscription, election or invitation), present number of members: 1,353, registered charity (charity number 1125524).

The Association aims to promote the highest quality and standards of medical and surgical practice of the Specialty for the benefit of patients and to encourage its future advancement through education, research and audit.

Subject coverage:
Laryngology, otology, rhinology, head and neck surgery.

Publications list:
Available in print

Access to staff:
Contact by letter, by telephone, by fax, by e-mail and via website. Appointment necessary.
Hours: Mon to Fri, 0930 to 1730
Special comments: For doctors only.

ENTERPRISE EUROPE NETWORK

E-mail: info@eiscltd.eu

Website:
http://www.enterprise-europe-network.ec.europa .eu/network_en.htm
Click on the United Kingdom in the map of Europe, or on 'the united Kingdom' in the list of countries beneath the map, to call up a list of Local Partner Organisations that have been established in the UK

Founded:
2008

Organisation type and purpose:
An initiative of the European Commission to establish a network of contact points, in the Member States of the European Union and in a number of non-EU countries, offering information and advice to companies (particularly small and medium-sized enterprises) on EU matters.

ENTERPRISE EUROPE YORKSHIRE

Bradford Design Exchange, 34 Peckover Street, Bradford, West Yorkshire, BD1 5BD

Tel: 01274 434262
Fax: 01274 432136
E-mail: info@ee-yorkshire.com

Website:
http://www.ee-yorkshire.com
News, events, business co-operation opportunities from Europe.

Enquiries:
Enquiries to: Manager

Founded:
1990

Incorporates the former:
West Yorkshire European Information Centre (WYEIC) (year of change 2008)

Organisation type and purpose:
Member of Enterprise Europe Network.
Provision of information and advice to business on EU legislation, innovation and technology transfer, and trading in Europe.

Subject coverage:
EU legislation and policies, European business information, innovation, technical standards, research and development, and the environment.

Information services:
Enquiry service, tenders information service, alerting service, European partner search service.

Museum or gallery collection, archive, or library special collection:
EC official journal prior to 1989 on microfiche
Collection of EC official documentation held

Electronic and video publications:
News from Europe
Order electronic and video publications from: via website

Access to staff:
Contact by letter, by telephone, by fax, by e-mail, in person and via website. Appointment necessary.

Hours: Mon to Fri, 0900 to 1700

Parent body:
Bradford City Council
  Department of Regeneration

ENTRUST CARE

Clifton House, 3 St Paul's Road, Foleshill, Coventry, Warwickshire, CV6 5DE

Tel: 024 7666 5450
Fax: 024 7666 5450
E-mail: admin@entrustcare.co.uk

Website:
http://www.entrustcare.co.uk

Enquiries:
Enquiries to: General Manager

Founded:
1969
Association for Brain-Damaged Children and Young Adults (year of change 2005)

Organisation type and purpose:
Membership association (membership is by subscription), present number of members: 70, voluntary organisation, registered charity (charity number 500452).
Localised.
Respite and residential care in the Coventry area only.

Subject coverage:
Self-help group providing respite care to children and residential care to adults with learning and physical disabilities.

Printed publications:
Information Leaflet
Newsletter (2 times a year)

Access to staff:
Contact by letter, by telephone, by fax and by e-mail. Appointment necessary. Access for members only. All charged.
Hours: Mon to Fri, 0900 to 1500

Access for disabled people:
Parking provided, ramped entry

Links with:
CVS Coventry

ENVIRONMENT AGENCY – BRISTOL

Rio House, Waterside Drive, Aztec West, Almondsbury, Bristol, BS32 4UD

Tel: 01454 624400
Fax: 01454 624409
E-mail: enquiries@environment-agency.gov.uk

Website:
http://www.environment-agency.gov.uk
Contact information, state of the environment report, press releases, newsletter, Board meetings agendas & summaries, guidance notes, bathing water quality data, river habitat data, river flow data, Annual Report, environmental strategy, Corporate Plan, some consultation papers.
http://www.environment-agency.gov.uk/fish
Instant dealing of full, junior, eight-day and one-day fishing licences

Enquiries:
Enquiries to: Information & Marketing Manager
Direct tel: 0117 914 2856
Direct fax: 0117 914 2760

Founded:
1 April 1996

Formed from:
County Council Waste Regulatory Functions; London Waste Regulation Authority (year of change 1996)

Formerly called:
Her Majesty's Inspectorate of Pollution (HMIP), National Rivers Authority (NRA)

Organisation type and purpose:
National government body.
Non departmental public body.
Environmental regulation.

Subject coverage:
Water quality, water resources, conservation, water recreation, navigation, waste management, pollution control, sustainable development, environmental policy, environmental legislation, fisheries.

Museum or gallery collection, archive, or library special collection:
Principal Public Registers are:
Integrated Pollution Control (IPC) Register (industrial processes; applications, authorisations, variations, appeals, restrictions, monitoring records, enforcement and prohibition notices, revocations, convictions and appeals)
Register of Industrial Works (the 'Air Register'; industrial processes with the potential to cause air pollution)
Radioactive Substances (RAS) Register (use, accumulation and disposal of radioactive materials; applications, registrations, authorisations, variations, cancellations, enforcement and prohibition notices, convictions and appeals)
Water Quality & Pollution Control Register (discharge consent applications, decisions and appeals, changes of holder, revocations, water quality objectives, monitoring records including bathing waters, maps of freshwater limits, maps of 'controlled' coastal waters)
Water Abstraction and Impounding Register (licence applications, decisions and appeals, successions, revocations)
Maps of Waterworks (location of resource mains, water mains, discharge pipes and underground works)
Maps of Main Rivers (for each area covered by the Agency's Regional Flood Defence Committees)
Waste Management Licence Register (relating to the recovery or disposal of waste; applications, working plans, inspection reports, monitoring information, modifications, revocations, suspensions, appeals, surrenders, convictions, exemptions to licences)
Carriers and Brokers of Controlled Waste Register (applications to carry waste)
Other Registers:
Works Discharge Register (information on owners or occupiers of premises which abut watercourses who have requested to be registered in order to receive notification of discharges caused by the Agency)
Genetically Modified Organisms Register, held on behalf of the Department of the Environment, Food and Rural Affairs (releases of genetically modified organisms)
Chemical Release Inventory (releases from processes regulated under Integrated Pollution Control)
Special Waste Notifications (consignment notes: disposal and location records – non-commercially confidential, summaries of Special Waste – when prepared by the disposal authority)

Trade and statistical information:
Public Registers in a combination of paper and computer files, details of water quality, consents to discharge to water, water and effluent sample data.

Non-library collection catalogue:
All or part available in-house

Library catalogue:
All or part available in-house

Printed publications:
Publications include:
Annual Report
Corporate Plan (annually)
Bathing Water Quality in England and Wales
Fisheries Technical Reports
Groundwater Vulnerability Map
Otters and River Habitat Management
Weather Radar and Flood Warning Services
Research and Development Outputs
Angling Guides
Order printed publications from: Free publications, Environment Agency
Rio House, Waterside Drive, Aztec West, Almondsbury, Bristol, BS12 4UD
Priced publications, The Stationery Office
PO Box 276, London, SW8 5DT
R&D Reports, Foundation for Water Research
Allen House, The Listons, Liston Road, Marlow, Buckinghamshire, SL7 1FD
Regional publications, Environment Agency Regional Offices

Publications list:
Available in print

Access to staff:
Contact by letter, by telephone, by fax, by e-mail and via website. Appointment necessary.
Hours: Mon to Fri, 0900 to 1700

Access to building, collection or gallery:
Prior appointment required
Hours: Mon to Fri, 0900 to 1700

Access for disabled people:
Parking provided, ramped entry, toilet facilities

Libraries and Information Service:
Agency Libraries are open to the public for reference purposes, by appointment during working hours. They hold publications of the former National Rivers Authority and Her Majesty's Inspector of Pollution
Environment Agency Anglian
  Kingfisher House, Goldhay Way, Orton Goldhay, Peterborough, Cambridgeshire, PE2 5ZR; tel: 01733 371811; fax: 01733 464397
Environment Agency Head Office
  Rio House, Waterside Drive, Aztec West, Almondsbury, Bristol, BS32 4UD; tel: 01454 624400; fax: 01454 624004
Environment Agency North East Region
  Tyneside House, Skinnerburn Road, Newcastle Business Park, Newcastle upon Tyne, NE4 7AR; tel: 0191 203 4000; fax: 0191 203 4004
Environment Agency North West
  Richard Fairclough House, Knutsford Road, Warrington, WA4 1HG; tel: 01925 653999; fax: 01925 639670
Environment Agency South West Region
  Manley House, Kestrel Way, Exeter, EX2 7LQ; tel: 01392 444000; fax: 01392 444238
Environment Agency Southern Region
  Guildbourne House, Chatsworth Road, Worthing, West Sussex, BN11 1LD; tel: 01903 832000; fax: 01903 821832
Environment Agency Thames
  Kings Meadow House, Kings Meadow Road, Reading, RG1 8DQ; tel: 0118 953 5000; fax: 0118 950 0388
Environment Agency Welsh
  Rivers House/Plas-yr-Afon, St Mellons Business Park, Fortran Road, Cardiff, CF3 0LT; tel: 029 2077 0088; fax: 029 2036 1437

Sponsoring department:
Department of the Environment, Transport and the Regions

ENVIRONMENT AGENCY – TEWKESBURY

Area Office, Riversmeet House, Newtown Industrial Estate, Northway Lane, Tewkesbury, Gloucestershire, GL20 8JG

Tel: 01684 850951
Fax: 01684 293599

Website:
http://www.environment-agency.gov.uk

Enquiries:
Enquiries to: Customer Contact Team

Founded:
1996

Formerly called:
Her Majesty's Inspectorate of Pollution, National Rivers Authority, Waste Regulation Authorities

continued overleaf

Organisation type and purpose:
National government body, professional body.
To protect and improve the environment and
contribute towards sustainable development
through the integrated management of air, land
and water. We have specific responsibilities for
water resources, pollution prevention and control,
flood defence, fisheries, conservation, recreation
and navigation throughout England and Wales.

**Museum or gallery collection, archive, or library
special collection:**
Public Register Information

Printed publications:
Available free from the Agency or for purchase
from HMSO

Electronic and video publications:
CD-ROM and Videos, available free or for
purchase

Access to staff:
Contact by letter, by telephone and by fax
Hours: Mon to Fri, 0900 to 1700

Links with:
DEFRA
The Welsh Office

Main sponsor in the Government is:
The Department for Environment, Food & Rural
Affairs (DEFRA)

Sub-Area Office:
Environment Agency
Brooke House, Spartan Close, Tachbrook Park
Industrial Estate, Leamington Spa,
Warwickshire, CV34 6RR; tel: 01926 889474; fax:
01926 887657

ENVIRONMENTAL AWARENESS
TRUST

Acronym or abbreviation: EAT

23 High Street, Wheathampstead, Hertfordshire,
AL4 8BB

Tel: 01582 834580
Fax: 01582 834547

Enquiries:
Enquiries to: Executive Director

Founded:
1990

Organisation type and purpose:
Registered charity (charity number 100042).
Prime purpose is the development of a National
Exploratorium of the Global Environment open to
members of the public of all ages.

Subject coverage:
Global environment.

Access to staff:
Contact by letter, by telephone and by fax
Hours: Mon to Fri, 0900 to 1700

ENVIRONMENTAL
COMMUNICATORS'
ORGANIZATION

Acronym or abbreviation: ECO Journalists

8 Hooks Cross, Watton-at-Stone, Hertford, SG14
3RY

Tel: 01920 830527
Fax: 01920 830538
E-mail: alanmassam@btinternet.com

Enquiries:
Enquiries to: Chairman
Direct tel: 01920 830527
Other contacts: Press spokesman for press releases.

Founded:
1972

Organisation type and purpose:
Membership association (membership is by
election or invitation).
Pressure group.

To bring a green interpretation of significant events
to the attention of professional journalists and
broadcasters.

Subject coverage:
Information on environmental topics provided for
journalists.

Printed publications:
Countryside (bi-monthly price £1.95)
Newsletter (Occasional, 6 times a year)

Access to staff:
Contact by letter, by fax and by e-mail
Hours: Mon to Fri, 0900 to 1700

Affiliated to:
Foundation for Ethnobiology
tel: 01992 893632; e-mail: conradgorinsky@
hotmail.com

ENVIRONMENTAL HEALTH
REGISTRATION BOARD

Acronym or abbreviation: EHRB

Chartered Institute of Environmental Health,
Chadwick Court, 15 Hatfields, London, SE1 8DJ

Tel: 020 7928 6006
E-mail: g.telfer@cieh.org

Website:
http://www.ehrb.co.uk

Enquiries:
Enquiries to: Principal Education Officer
Direct tel: 020 7827 5929

Formerly called:
Public Health Inspectors Registration Board
(PHIEB)
Environmental Health Officers Registration Board
(year of change 2003)

Organisation type and purpose:
Publicly listed company.

Subject coverage:
Registration of student and qualified
environmental health officers. Development and
accreditation of courses for other environmental
professional staff.

Information services:
Provides information on how to become an
environmental health officer, lists accredited
environmental health degree courses in the UK
and accredited courses for technician qualifications
such as Higher Certificate in Food Premises
Inspection.

Access to staff:
Contact by letter, by telephone, by e-mail and via
website
Hours: Mon to Fri, 0900 to 1700

Administered by:
Chartered Institute of Environmental Health
Chadwick Court, 15 Hatfields, London, SE1 8DJ;
tel: 020 7928 6006

ENVIRONMENTAL INDUSTRIES
COMMISSION LIMITED, THE

Acronym or abbreviation: EIC

45 Weymouth Street, London, W1G 8ND

Tel: 020 7935 1675
Fax: 020 7486 3455
E-mail: info@eic-uk.co.uk

Website:
http://www.eic-uk.co.uk
Information on current EIC activities.

Enquiries:
Enquiries to: Director

Founded:
1995

Formed from:
Association of Environmental Consultancies (AEC)

Organisation type and purpose:
National organisation, trade association
(membership is by subscription), present number
of members: 210.

Subject coverage:
Contact with members. Information about EIC
members and in which fields they specialise.
Information about membership for potential
members.

Printed publications:
Handbook of EIC's Environmental Consultancies
Group Members (free)

Publications list:
Available in print

Access to staff:
Contact by telephone
Hours: Mon to Fri, 0930 to 1800

ENVIRONMENTAL
INVESTIGATION AGENCY

Acronym or abbreviation: EIA

62–63 Upper Street, London, N1 0NY

Tel: 020 7354 7960
Fax: 020 7354 7961
E-mail: ukinfo@eia-international.org

Website:
http://www.eia-international.org

Enquiries:
Enquiries to: Administrator

Founded:
1984

Organisation type and purpose:
Voluntary organisation, registered charity.
Independent wildlife and environmental
campaigning organisation.

Subject coverage:
Research, investigations and monitoring of illegal
trade in endangered animal species and
environmentally damaging commodities.
Provision of documented information on such
activities to governmental authorities and the
media to generate improved enforcement
measures.

Printed publications:
Various publications including:
Chilling Facts About a Burning Abuse – CFC
Smuggling in the European Union (£5)
Corporate Power, Corruption & Destruction of the
World's Forests (£5)
The Global War Against Small Cetaceans (£5)
The Political Wilderness – India's Tiger Crisis (£5)
The Politics of Extinction – The Orangutang Crisis/
The Destruction of Indonesia's Forests (£5)

Microform publications:
Film and Photographs (for sale)

Access to staff:
Contact by letter, by telephone, by fax and by e-
mail
Hours: Mon to Fri, 0930 to 1800

ENVIRONMENTAL LAW
FOUNDATION

Acronym or abbreviation: ELF

Suite 309, 16 Baldwins Gardens, London, EC1N
7RJ

Tel: 020 7404 1030
Fax: 020 7404 1032
E-mail: info@elflaw.org

Website:
http://www.elflaw.org

Enquiries:
Enquiries to: Administrator
Direct e-mail: membership@elflaw.org
Other contacts: Director

Founded:
1992

Organisation type and purpose:
Advisory body, present number of members: 450, voluntary organisation, registered charity, research organisation.
Provides advice and assistance, refers communities to lawyers and experts to resolve environmental problems.

Subject coverage:
Environmental law; how the law can be used to resolve environmental problems, access to justice.

Museum or gallery collection, archive, or library special collection:
Case information (not available to the public)

Trade and statistical information:
Data on communities taking legal action to protect and improve the environment of the UK.

Printed publications:
Reports:
Annual Reports
ELFline (regular publication)
Environmental Risk: The Responsibilities of the Law and Science
Human Rights and the Environment
Environmental Briefings
Leaflets:
Green Issues

Publications list:
Available in print

Access to staff:
Contact by letter, by telephone, by fax and by e-mail
Hours: Mon to Fri, 1030 to 1630
Special comments: Information provided in response to specific requests only.

ENVIRONMENTAL NETWORK LIMITED

Acronym or abbreviation: ENL

The Hillocks, Tarland, Aboyne, Aberdeenshire, AB34 4TJ

Tel: 01339 881446
Fax: 01339 881618
E-mail: mail@env-net.com

Website:
http://www.env-net.com

Enquiries:
Enquiries to: Managing Director

Founded:
1993

Organisation type and purpose:
Multi-disciplinary European network organisation for R&D in environmental management and sustainable development.

Subject coverage:
Environmental assessment, planning and management, sustainable development, rural resource management and development; software development.

Access to staff:
Contact by letter, by telephone, by fax, by e-mail and via website. Appointment necessary.
Hours: Britain: Mon to Fri, 0900 to 1700 GMT
Germany: Mon to Fri, 0900 to 1700 GMT+1

Also at:
Umweltnetzwerk Deutschland
Oberilfingerstrasse 3, 72160 Horb, Germany; tel: +49 1577 6826343

ENVIRONMENTAL PROTECTION UK

44 Grand Parade, Brighton, East Sussex, BN2 9QA

Tel: 01273 878770
Fax: 01273 606626
E-mail: info@environmental-protection.org.uk

Website:
http://www.environmental-protection.org.uk

Enquiries:
Enquiries to: Administration Officer
Direct tel: 01273 878775

Founded:
1899

Formerly called:
National Society for Clean Air and Environmental Protection

Organisation type and purpose:
National organisation, membership association (membership is by subscription), present number of members: 1775, registered charity (charity number 221026).
The Society is a non-governmental, non-political organisation, bringing together pollution expertise from industry, local and central government and technical, academic and institutional bodies.
Seeks to inform debate and influence changes in policy and practice in the areas of air quality, climate change, noise and land quality.

Subject coverage:
Air quality, noise, contaminated land; policy and legislation.

Museum or gallery collection, archive, or library special collection:
Archive Collection on Air Pollution and Environment

Non-library collection catalogue:
All or part available in-house

Library catalogue:
All or part available in-house

Printed publications:
Books, information leaflets, factsheets, reports and schools resources
Pollution Control Handbook
Teaching Resources
Order printed publications from:
shop@environmental-protection.org.uk

Publications list:
Available online and in print

Access to staff:
Contact by letter, by telephone, by fax, by e-mail and via website. Appointment necessary.
Hours: Mon to Fri, 0900 to 1700

Access to building, collection or gallery:
Prior appointment required

ENVIRONMENTAL SERVICES ASSOCIATION

Acronym or abbreviation: ESA

154 Buckingham Palace Road, London, SW1W 9TR

Tel: 020 7824 8882
Fax: 020 7824 8753
E-mail: info@esauk.org

Website:
http://www.esauk.org
Searchable database of membership, details of publications and press statements, ESA events and industry legislation.
http://www.epolitix.com/forum/esa

Enquiries:
Enquiries to: Chief Executive
Other contacts: Deputy Chief Executive/Members' Services

Founded:
1969

Formerly called:
National Association of Waste Disposal Contractors (NAWDC) (year of change 1996)

Incorporates the former:
Energy from Waste Association (EWA) (year of change 2001)

Organisation type and purpose:
Trade association.

ESA is the UK's sectoral trade association for waste and secondary resource management, an industry accounting for 0.5% GDP.

Subject coverage:
Information on integrated solutions to waste across the full spectrum of biological, mechanical and thermal treatment processing options, to achieve sustainable waste management.

Museum or gallery collection, archive, or library special collection:
Library containing printed products

Non-library collection catalogue:
All or part available in-house

Library catalogue:
All or part available in-house

Printed publications:
ESA Directory (A listing of waste facilities in the UK)
Resource Management & Recovery Magazine
ESA Membership Directory
Annual Statement
Weekly Policy Bulletin

Electronic and video publications:
Virtual Tour of an Energy from Waste Plant (CD-ROM)
Energy, Waste and the Environment (video)

Publications list:
Available online and in print

Access to staff:
Contact by letter, by telephone, by fax, by e-mail, in person and via website. Appointment necessary. Access for members only. All charged.
Hours: Mon to Fri, 0900 to 1700

Access to building, collection or gallery:
Prior appointment required

Access for disabled people:
Ramped entry

Member of:
European Waste Management Association (FEAD)
Avenue des Gaulois 19, Brussels, B-1040, Belgium; tel: 00 32 2 732 3213; fax: 00 32 2 734 9592; e-mail: wg@fead.be
WAMITAB
3 The Lakes, Peterbridge House, Northampton, NN4 7HE; tel: 01604 231950; fax: 01604 232457; e-mail: info.admin@wamitab.org.uk

Other addresses:
Northern Ireland Environmental Services Association (NIESA)
PO Box 21, Belfast, BT1 4WD; tel: 0870 241 3298; e-mail: niesa@esauk.org
Scottish Environmental Services Association (SESA)
48 Edinburgh Road, Coatbridge, Lanarkshire, ML5 4UG; tel: 01236 437480; e-mail: sesa@esauk.org
Welsh Environmental Services Association (WESA)
PO Box 4061, Cardiff, CF14 3YY; tel: 020 7591 3205; e-mail: wesa@esauk.org

ENVIRONMENTAL TRANSPORT ASSOCIATION

Acronym or abbreviation: ETA

ETA Services Limited, 10 Church Street, Weybridge, Surrey, KT13 8RS

Tel: 01932 828882
Fax: 01932 829015
E-mail: eta@eta.co.uk

Website:
http://www.eta.co.uk
Details campaigns, services, factsheets.

Enquiries:
Enquiries to: Public Relations Co-ordinator

Founded:
1990

447

continued overleaf

Organisation type and purpose:
National organisation, membership association (membership is by subscription), present number of members: 20,000, service industry.
Breakdown recovery and other insurance issues.
Motoring breakdown organisation campaigning for greener transport.

Subject coverage:
Specialist information on transport and environment issues.

Printed publications:
The following publications are for both ETA members and non-members
Going Green (ETA members magazine, £5)
Car Buyer's Guide 2001 (£5)
Car Buyer's Guide 2002 (£5)
CFD Good Practice Guide (£5)
Community Tourism Guide (£9.99)
Cutting Your Car Use (£4.95)
Real Costs of Motoring (£3.50)
The Cyclists' Sourcebook (£20)

Publications list:
Available online and in print

Access to staff:
Contact by letter, by telephone, by fax, by e-mail and via website
Hours: Mon to Fri, 0800 to 1800

Access to building, collection or gallery:
Prior appointment required

Access for disabled people:
Parking provided

Affiliated to:
European Federation for Transport and Environment (T&E)
Boulevard de Waterloo 34, 1000 Brussels, Belgium; tel: 00 322 502 9909; fax: 00 322 502 9908
Transport 2000 (T2000)
The Impact Centre, 12 Hoxton Street, London, N1 6NG; tel: 020 7613 0743; fax: 020 7615 5280

ENVIROWISE

Harwell International Business Centre, Harwell, Didcot, Oxfordshire, OX11 0QJ

Tel: 0800 585794
Fax: 0870 190 6713
E-mail: helpline@envirowise.gov.uk

Website:
http://www.envirowise.gov.uk

Enquiries:
Enquiries to: Helpline Advisor

Founded:
1994

Organisation type and purpose:
Government funded advice and information service for business.

Subject coverage:
Waste minimisation, cleaner technology, environment: all subjects including legislation, for all industry and service sectors.

Printed publications:
All free to UK organisations under the following headings including guides and case studies:
Best Practice tailored to various engineering/ manufactoring industries
Information about the Programme
Reducing Water Waste
Reducing Packaging Waste
Resource Efficiency Clubs
Reducing Solvent Use
Cleaner Technology
Information to Help Business Support
Organisations Help Businesses in the:
Printing, Foundry, Engineering, Glass, Plastics, Paper & Board, Textiles, Metal Finishing, Chemicals, Ceramics and Food and Drink Industries

Electronic and video publications:
Resource Efficiency and Waste Minimisation (guides and software)

Publications list:
Available online and in print

Access to staff:
Contact by letter, by telephone, by fax, by e-mail and via website
Hours: Mon to Fri, 0900 to 1700
Special comments: UK only except for Web access.

Access for disabled people:
Access to all public areas, toilet facilities

EPHEMERA SOCIETY

PO Box 112, Northwood, Middlesex, HA6 2WT

Tel: 01923 829079
Fax: 01923 825207

Website:
http://www.ephemera-society.org.uk
Membership information and list of fairs.

Enquiries:
Enquiries to: Secretary

Founded:
1975

Organisation type and purpose:
Membership association.

Subject coverage:
Preservation, study and presentation of printed and handwritten ephemera, identification, dating and conservation, valuation and disposal of collections of ephemera.

Museum or gallery collection, archive, or library special collection:
Centre collection based on Rickards Collection
Centre for Ephemera Studies Collection based on Rickards Collection at University of Reading

Printed publications:
The Ephemerist (quarterly, journal index and first 100 issues available to purchase)

Access to staff:
Contact by letter, by telephone and by fax
Hours: Mon to Fri, 0900 to 1700

Associated with:
Foundation for Ephemera Studies

Associated with offshoot ephemera societies in:
America, Australia, Canada and Austria

Contact Centre for Ephemera Studies is the:
University of Reading

EPILEPSY ACTION

New Anstey House, Gateway Drive, Yeadon, Leeds, West Yorkshire, LS19 7XY

Tel: 0113 210 8800
Fax: 0113 391 0300
E-mail: epilepsy@epilepsy.org.uk

Website:
http://www.epilepsy.org.uk
Information on all aspects of epilepsy, children's pages, news pages, medical pages, merchandise pages.

Enquiries:
Direct tel: 0808 800 5050
Direct fax: 0808 800 5555
Direct e-mail: helpline@epilepsy.org.uk

Founded:
1950

Organisation type and purpose:
Voluntary organisation.
Provides information and support to people with epilepsy, their families and any professionals involved.

Subject coverage:
Epilepsy Action represents the interests of people with epilepsy. Services include a national information service, an epilepsy helpline, consultation to professionals, staging of conferences, etc. The Association assists in the formation of local groups, funds social research and promotes a greater awareness of epilepsy among lay and professional people.

Information services:
Advice and information in a variety of languages for people with epilepsy, their families and carers.

Education services:
Advice and information for education professionals on working with children and young people with epilepsy.

Printed publications:
Books, leaflets, pamphlets
Epilepsy Today (bimonthly)
Epilepsy Professional (quarterly)

Electronic and video publications:
Videos and DVDs available for hire from the library

Publications list:
Available online and in print

Access to staff:
Contact by letter, by telephone, by fax, by e-mail and via website
Hours: Mon to Thu, 0900 to 1630; Fri, 0900 to 1600

Affiliated to:
International Bureau for Epilepsy
International League Against Epilepsy

Also at:
International Bureau for Epilepsy
PO Box 21, 2100, AA Heemstede, Netherlands

EPILEPSY CONNECTIONS

100 Wellington Street, Glasgow, G2 6DH

Tel: 0141 248 4125
Fax: 0141 248 5887
E-mail: info@epilepsyconections.org.uk

Website:
http://www.epilepsyconnections.org.uk
Services, news and events.

Founded:
2000

Organisation type and purpose:
A registered Scottish charity (number SC030677) that provides information and support to people with epilepsy, their families, friends and those with whom they live and work.
Runs a variety of projects within the Greater Glasgow & Clyde and Forth Valley Health Board areas.

Subject coverage:
Epilepsy.

Special visitor services:
Counselling appointments in the Glasgow office are available to adults affected by epilepsy, and to their family and carers.

Education services:
Training and Education Programmes for anyone with a personal or professional interest in epilepsy.

Electronic and video publications:
Newsletter (quarterly)
Guidance and advice leaflets on a wide range of issues to do with living with epilepsy
Disability Living Allowance infomation pack
Safety infomation pack
Concessionary travel information
Order electronic and video publications from:
Download from website

Publications list:
Available online

Access to staff:
Contact by letter, by telephone, by fax and by e-mail
Hours: Counselling appointments: Mon afternoons

EPILEPSY RESEARCH UK

Acronym or abbreviation: ERUK

PO Box 3004, London, W4 1XT

Tel: 020 8995 4781
Fax: 020 8995 4781
E-mail: info@eruk.org.uk

Website:
http://www.epilepsyresearch.org.uk
Information about epilepsy

Enquiries:
Enquiries to: Research and Information Executive
Other contacts: Information Executive (for research enquiries)

Founded:
2007

Created by the merger of:
The Epilepsy Research Foundation and the Fund for Epilepsy (year of change 2007)

Formerly called:
British Epilepsy Research Foundation (year of change 2003)

Organisation type and purpose:
Voluntary organisation, registered charity (charity number 1100394), research organisation.
Promotes and supports basic and clinical scientific research into epilepsy throughout the United Kingdom. Independent research is supported, carried out by the best available research team.

Subject coverage:
Epilepsy.

Museum or gallery collection, archive, or library special collection:
Information available relating to epilepsy research

Printed publications:
Grant Awards
Annual Report and Accounts
General leaflets
Focus (newsletter)

Access to staff:
Contact by letter, by telephone, by fax, by e-mail and via website. Appointment necessary.
Hours: Mon to Fri, 0900 to 1700

Access to building, collection or gallery:
Prior appointment required

Member organisation of:
Association of Medical Research Charities (AMRC)
Joint Epilepsy Council (JEC)

EPILEPSY SCOTLAND

48 Govan Road, Glasgow, G51 1JL

Tel: 0808 800 2200
Fax: 0141 419 1709
E-mail: enquiries@epilepsyscotland.org.uk

Website:
http://www.epilepsyscotland.org.uk
General information on Epilepsy Scotland plus literature to download.

Enquiries:
Enquiries to: Helpline

Founded:
1954

Organisation type and purpose:
National organisation, membership association (membership is by subscription), present number of members: 500, voluntary organisation, registered charity (charity number SCO 00067), training organisation, consultancy.
Campaigning, lobbying and policy organisation.
Helpline and information service.
Training.

Support Services in Edinburgh and Glasgow

Subject coverage:
Social aspects of epilepsy and associated disabilities, epilepsy in relation to employment, driving, the law, the family, etc., understanding of epilepsy, support systems, professional training, community care, research and policy comment.

Printed publications:
Many publications, professional guidelines, reports and factsheets, see website for more details
Order printed publications from: e-mail: enquiries@epilepsyscotland.org.uk; tel: 0808 800 2200

Electronic and video publications:
See website for details

Publications list:
Available online and in print

Access to staff:
Contact by letter, by telephone, by fax, by e-mail, in person and via website. Appointment necessary.
Hours: Mon to Fri, 0900 to 1700

Access to building, collection or gallery:
Prior appointment required

Access for disabled people:
Parking provided, ramped entry, toilet facilities

Affiliated to:
International Bureau for Epilepsy
Joint Epilepsy Council of UK and Ireland

EPPING FOREST DISTRICT COUNCIL

Acronym or abbreviation: EFDC

Civic Offices, High Street, Epping, Essex, CM16 4BZ

Tel: 01992 564000
Fax: 01992 578018

Website:
http://www.eppingforestdc.gov.uk

Enquiries:
Enquiries to: Information Officer
Direct e-mail: contactus@eppingforestdc.gov.uk
Other contacts: Public Relations Manager

Founded:
1974

Organisation type and purpose:
Local government body.

Subject coverage:
All areas relating to local council matters. Most areas relating to the district.

Museum or gallery collection, archive, or library special collection:
EFDC Museum, Sun Street, EN9 1OZ

Access to staff:
Contact by letter, by telephone, by fax and by e-mail
Hours: Mon to Fri, 0900 to 1700

Access to building, collection or gallery:
Hours: Mon to Fri, 0900 to 1700

Access for disabled people:
Accessible for disabled

EPPING FOREST FIELD CENTRE

Acronym or abbreviation: FSC

Pauls Nursery Road, High Beech, Loughton, Essex, IG10 4AF

Tel: 020 8502 8500
Fax: 020 8502 8502
E-mail: enquiries.ef@field-studies-council.org

Founded:
1970

Formerly called:
Epping Forest Conservation Centre (year of change 1992)

Organisation type and purpose:
Membership association (membership is by qualification), registered charity.
Environmental education.

Subject coverage:
Environmental field work for schools at all levels, environmental and natural history courses for adults, out-of-school activities and environmental birthday parties.

Education services:
Environmental field work for schools at all levels.
Environmental and natural history courses for adults.

Printed publications:
Promotional Literature
FSC Courses Brochure (annually, from head office)
Order printed publications from: FSC Publications, Preston Montford, Montford Bridge, Shrewsbury, Shropshire, SY4 1HW; tel. 01743 852140; fax 01743 852101; e-mail publications@field-studies-council.org

Publications list:
Available in print

Access to staff:
Contact by letter, by telephone, by fax and by e-mail. Appointment necessary.
Hours: Mon to Fri, 0900 to 1700
Special comments: Centre must be booked for teaching, lectures, use of library, etc.

Access to building, collection or gallery:
Prior appointment required

Access for disabled people:
Parking provided

Constituent part of:
Field Studies Council
tel: 01743 852100; fax: 01743 852101

EQUALITY & HUMAN RIGHTS COMMISSION

Acronym or abbreviation: EHRC

2nd Floor, Arndale House, Arndale Centre, Manchester, M4 3AQ

Tel: 0161 829 8100
Fax: 0161 829 8110
E-mail: info@equalityhumanrights.com; library@equalityhumanrights.com

Website:
http://www.equalityhumanrights.com
The Commission has a statutory remit to promote and monitor human rights; and to protect, enforce and promote equality across the seven 'protected' grounds – age, disability, gender, race, religion and belief, sexual orientation and gender reassignment.

Enquiries:
Enquiries to: Library & Information Services Manager
Direct tel: 0161 829 8308
Direct e-mail: david.sparrow@equalityhumanrights.com

Founded:
2007

Organisation type and purpose:
National organisation, statutory body.
The elimination of unlawful sex and marriage discrimination, to promote equality of opportunity between men and women and to keep the Sex Discrimination (1975) and Equal Pay (1970) Acts under review.

Subject coverage:
Equal opportunity and sex discrimination (including law, education, employment, equal pay, etc.).

Information services:
Workplace library.

continued overleaf

Trade and statistical information:
Statistical information on women and men available on website, via publications list, or by application to the Research, Statistics and Information Unit.

Library catalogue:
All or part available in-house

Printed publications:
A large number of free guides on equal pay and sex equality (free, directly from EOC)

Publications list:
Available online and in print

Access to staff:
Contact by letter, by telephone, by fax, by e-mail and via website. Appointment necessary.
Hours: Mon to Fri, 0900 to 1700
Special comments: Access by arrangement only.

Access for disabled people:
Fully accessible.

Also at:
Equal Opportunities Commission
Windsor House, Windsor Lane, Cardiff, CF10 3GE; tel: 029 2034 3552; fax: 029 2064 1709; e-mail: wales@eoc.org.uk
Equal Opportunities Commission
St Stephens House, 279 Bath Street, Glasgow, G2 4JL; tel: 0141 248 5833; fax: 0141 248 5834; e-mail: scotland@eoc.org.uk

EQUALITY COMMISSION FOR NORTHERN IRELAND

Acronym or abbreviation: ECNI

Equality House, 79 Shaftesbury Square, Belfast, BT2 7DP

Tel: 028 9089 0890
Fax: 028 9024 8687; textphone 028 9050 0589
E-mail: information@equalityni.org

Website:
http://www.equalityni.org

Enquiries:
Enquiries to: Information Officer

Founded:
1999

Created by the merger of:
Commission for Racial Equality for Northern Ireland, Equal Opportunities Commission for Northern Ireland, Fair Employment Commission for Northern Ireland, Northern Ireland Disability Council (year of change 1999)

Organisation type and purpose:
Statutory body.

Subject coverage:
Equality of opportunity in employment, education, goods, facilities and services; issues related to women in society.

Museum or gallery collection, archive, or library special collection:
Women in employment and in society generally, women's education, discrimination law, race issues

Library catalogue:
All or part available in-house

Printed publications:
All single copies of printed publications are available free of charge:
Annual Report
Booklets and leaflets on equal opportunities, with regard to: sex, race, disability, fair employment, sexual orientation
Research reports on employment and education

Publications list:
Available online and in print

Access to staff:
Contact by letter, by telephone, by fax, by e-mail, in person and via website. Appointment necessary.
Hours: Mon to Fri, 0900 to 1700

Access to building, collection or gallery:
Special comments: Library is reference only.

Access for disabled people:
Parking provided, level entry, access to all public areas, toilet facilities

EQUITY

Guild House, Upper St Martin's Lane, London, WC2H 9EG

Tel: 020 7379 6000
Fax: 020 7379 7001
E-mail: info@equity.org.uk

Website:
http://www.equity.org.uk

Enquiries:
Enquiries to: General Secretary
Direct fax: 020 7379 6074

Founded:
1930

Organisation type and purpose:
Trade union (membership by subscription).
To represent artists from across the entire spectrum of arts and entertainment, to negotiate minimum terms and conditions of employment throughout the entire world of entertainment and to endeavour to ensure these take account of social and economic changes, to lobby government and other bodies on issues of paramount importance to the membership.

Printed publications:
Equity Magazine

Access to staff:
Contact by letter, by telephone, by fax, by e-mail and via website. Access for members only.
Hours: Mon to Fri, 0930 to 1730

Access to building, collection or gallery:
Hours: Mon to Fri, 0930 to 1730

Access for disabled people:
Hours: Mon to Fri, 0930 to 1730

Affitialted to:
Trades Union Congress (TUC)

ERC GROUP LTD

Acronym or abbreviation: ERC

3 Kings Court, Newmarket, Suffolk, CB8 7SG

Tel: 01638 667733
Fax: 01638 667744
E-mail: marketing@erc-world.com

Website:
http://www.erc-world.com

Enquiries:
Enquiries to: Director

Founded:
1961

Organisation type and purpose:
International organisation, service industry, consultancy, research organisation.

Subject coverage:
Food, drinks, tobacco, ophthalmics, OTC pharmaceuticals, cosmetics and toiletries, personal care, home goods. Geographical research specialisation extends to Eastern and Western Europe, Pacific Rim, Latin America, China, the USA, Middle East, India, South Africa, plus other global markets.

Printed publications:
Over 150 market research reports on the subjects listed, some by country, others by manufacturer, or product within the category

Electronic and video publications:
Disc, CD-ROM

Publications list:
Available online

Access to staff:
Contact by letter, by telephone, by fax, by e-mail and via website. Appointment necessary.
Hours: Mon to Fri, 0930 to 1730

Access for disabled people:
Level entry

EREWASH BOROUGH COUNCIL

Town Hall, Ilkeston, Derbyshire, DE7 5RP

Tel: 0115 907 2244\ Minicom no. 0115 949 9478
Fax: 0115 907 1121
E-mail: enquiries@erewash.gov.uk

Website:
http://www.erewash.gov.uk

Enquiries:
Enquiries to: Public Relations Manager
Direct tel: 0115 9071159

Organisation type and purpose:
Local government body.

Subject coverage:
Local government services.

Access to staff:
Contact by letter
Hours: Mon to Thu, 0830 to 1700; Fri, 0830 to 1630

Access for disabled people:
Ramped entry, access to all public areas, toilet facilities

ERGONOMICS INFORMATION ANALYSIS CENTRE

Acronym or abbreviation: EIAC

Electronic, Electrical and Computer Engineering, University of Birmingham, Edgbaston, Birmingham, B15 2TT

Tel: 0121 414 4239
Fax: 0121 414 3476
E-mail: ergo-abs@bham.ac.uk

Website:
http://www.eee.bham.ac.uk/eiac

Enquiries:
Enquiries to: Manager

Founded:
1968

Organisation type and purpose:
University department or institute.

Subject coverage:
Ergonomics, human factors, human-computer interaction.

Electronic and video publications:
Ergonomics Abstracts (online)
Order electronic and video publications from: Taylor and Francis Ltd, 4 Park Square, Milton Park, Abingdon, Oxfordshire; tel. 020 7017 6000; fax 020 7017 6336; e-mail richard.steele@tandf.co.uk

Access to staff:
Contact by letter, by telephone, by fax and by e-mail. Appointment necessary. All charged.
Hours: Mon to Fri, 0800 to 1600

Access for disabled people:
Parking provided, ramped entry, access to all public areas, toilet facilities

ERGONOMICS SOCIETY

Acronym or abbreviation: ES

Devonshire House, Devonshire Square, Loughborough, Leicestershire, LE11 3DW

Tel: 01509 234904
Fax: 01509 235666
E-mail: ergsoc@ergonomics.org.uk

Website:
http://www.ergonomics.org.uk

3

General information on: the society, ergonomics, society members.
http://www.ergonomics4schools.com
Information and advice for students of ergonomics in schools.

Enquiries:
Enquiries to: Honorary Secretary
Other contacts: Business Manager

Founded:
1949

Organisation type and purpose:
Professional body.

Subject coverage:
Ergonomics and human factors, work design, environmental sciences, equipment design, human and computer interaction.

Printed publications:
Applied Ergonomics (quarterly, pub Elsevier)
Behaviour and Information Technology (pub Taylor & Francis)
Ergonomics (monthly, pub Taylor & Francis)
Register of Ergonomics Consultants
Register of Professional Ergonomists
Work & Stress (quarterly, pub Taylor & Francis)

Electronic and video publications:
Register of Ergonomics Consultants
Register of Professional Ergonomists

Access to staff:
Contact by letter, by telephone, by fax and by e-mail
Hours: Mon to Fri, 0900 to 1630

Affiliated to:
International Ergonomics Association

ERIC (EDUCATION AND RESOURCES FOR IMPROVING CHILDHOOD CONTINENCE)

Acronym or abbreviation: ERIC

36 Old School House, Britannia Road, Kingswood, Bristol, BS15 8DB

Tel: Helpline: 0845 370 8008
Fax: 0117 960 0401
E-mail: info@eric.org.uk

Website:
http://www.eric.org.uk
Information, leaflets and resources to download and message boards for children, parents and health professionals on potty training, bedwetting, daytime wetting, constipation and soiling.
http://www.ericshop.org.uk
Resources to help manage childhood wetting and soiling – including bedding protection, bedwetting alarms, absorbent and washable underwear, literature and much more.

Enquiries:
Enquiries to: Training and Media enquiries
Direct tel: 0117 301 2102

Founded:
1988

Organisation type and purpose:
Registered Charity (number 1002424), national child health charity.
Support and information on potty training, childhood bedwetting, daytime wetting, constipation and soiling.

Subject coverage:
Potty training, bedwetting (nocturnal enuresis), daytime wetting, soiling and constipation in children and young people.

Information services:
ERIC Helpline.

Education services:
ERIC Training.

Printed publications:
ERIC has a range of leaflets available to download free from website: http://www.eric.org.uk, or these can be purchased in bulk.

Visit http://www.ericshop.org.uk to view ERIC's range of books and literature for children, parents and health professionals.

A free catalogue is available on request – call 0117 301 2100 to receive a copy
Order printed publications from: website: http://www.ericshop.org.uk

Publications list:
Available online and in print

Access to staff:
Contact by letter, by telephone, by fax, by e-mail and via website
Hours: Helpline, Mon to Fri, 1000 to 1600

Member organisation of:
THA

ESCP-EAP EUROPEAN SCHOOL OF MANAGEMENT

Formal name: Ecole Supérieure de Commerce de Paris – Ecole des Affaires de Paris
Acronym or abbreviation: ESCP-EAP

Parsifal College, 527 Finchley Road, Hampstead, London, NW3 7BG

Tel: 020 7443 8800
Fax: 020 7443 8845
E-mail: kstokes@escp-eap.net

Website:
http://www.escp-eap.net
Information about educational facilities and history of ESCP-EAP centres in London, Paris, Berlin, Madrid and Turin.

Enquiries:
Enquiries to: Business Librarian
Direct tel: 020 7443 8875

Founded:
1973

Formed by the merger of:
Ecole des Affaires de Paris (EAP) and Ecole Supérieure de Commerce de Paris (ESCP) (year of change 1999)

Organisation type and purpose:
Registered charity (charity number 293027), suitable for ages: c. 18–30.

Subject coverage:
Management.

Library catalogue:
All or part available in-house

Access to staff:
Contact by letter, by telephone, by fax, by e-mail and via website
Hours: Mon to Fri, 0900 to 1700
ESCP-EAP European School of Management Heubnerweg 6, 14059 Berlin, Germany
ESCP-EAP European School of Management Corso Stati Uniti 38, 10128 Turin, Italy
Other addresses:
ESCP-EAP European School of Management Arroyofresno 1, 28035 Madrid, Spain

Parent body:
ESCP-EAP
79 avenue de la République, 75543 Paris Cedex 11, France

ESDU

133 Houndsditch, London, EC3A 7BX

Tel: 020 3159 3300
Fax: 020 3159 3299
E-mail: esdu@ihs.com

Website:
http://www.esdu.com
Full product and company information (on public site). Product delivery via same web address for subscribers with user name/password.

Enquiries:
Enquiries to: Sales Office Supervisor

Other contacts: Technical Director; Director of Finance

Founded:
1940

Formerly called:
Engineering Sciences Data Unit; Royal Aeronautical Society (RAeS) (year of change 1970)

Organisation type and purpose:
International organisation, service industry, research organisation, publishing house.
Profit-making company, but utilising large number of committees where (250+) members give time voluntarily.
Suppliers of validated engineering data and software.

Subject coverage:
Acoustic fatigue; aerodynamics; composites; dynamics; fatigue (endurance data and fracture mechanics); fluid mechanics, internal flow; heat transfer; metallic materials data; mechanisms; noise; aircraft performance; physical data (in chemical and mechanical engineering); stress and strength; structures; transonic aerodynamics; tribology; wind engineering; computer software.

Printed publications:
ESDU Catalogue of Validated Engineering Methods and Software

Electronic and video publications:
ESDU Subject Index (CD-ROM)
Supporting computer programs and computerised data and design procedures

Publications list:
Available online

Access to staff:
Contact by letter, by telephone, by fax, by e-mail and via website. Appointment necessary.
Hours: Mon to Fri, 0900 to 1700

Access to building, collection or gallery:
No access other than to staff

Access for disabled people:
Level entry

Work is endorsed by the:
Institution of Chemical Engineers
Institution of Mechanical Engineers
Royal Aeronautical Society

ESI LTD

Formal name: Endat Standard Indexes Ltd
Acronym or abbreviation: ESI

Ochil House, Springkerse Business Park, Stirling, FK7 7XE

Tel: 01786 407000
Fax: 01786 407003
E-mail: info@esi.info

Website:
http://www.esi.info
Company profile, electronic versions of printed directories.

Enquiries:
Enquiries to: Managing Director

Founded:
1989

Formerly called:
Environmental Data Research Limited (EDR), Landscape Promotions (year of change 1999)

Organisation type and purpose:
Research organisation, publishing house.

Subject coverage:
Landscape, civil engineering, horticulture, architectural landscape, products, users, local authorities, consulting engineers, facilities managers, engineers, process engineering, regulatory authorities, environmental management, water utilities, manufacturing industry, interior design.

continued overleaf

Trade and statistical information:
Product information for designers and specifiers involved with process engineering and environmental management. Produce information for specifiers, buyers and estimators in the design and construction industry in both private and public sectors.

Printed publications:
Available in print and online:
ESI External Works (landscape design, civil engineering)
ESI Building Products (architectural design, construction)
ESI Interior Design (interior furnishings, fittings and finishes)
ESI PENTEC (engineering, manufacturing and environmental management)

Publications list:
Available online

Access to staff:
Contact by letter, by fax, by e-mail and via website
Hours: Mon to Fri, 0900 to 1700

ESPERANTO – ASOCIO DE BRITIO

Formal name: Esperanto Association of Britain
Acronym or abbreviation: EAB

Esperanto House, Station Road, Barlaston, Stoke-on-Trent, Staffordshire, ST12 9DE

Tel: 01782 372141
E-mail: eab@esperanto-gb.org

Website:
http://www.esperanto-gb.org

Enquiries:
Enquiries to: Office Manager
Direct tel: 0845 230 1887
Other contacts: Honorary Librarian

Founded:
1976

Formerly called:
British Esperanto Association (BEA) (year of change 1976)

Organisation type and purpose:
National organisation, membership association (membership is by subscription), present number of members: 700, voluntary organisation, registered charity (charity number 272676), suitable for all ages.
Esperanto library, book sales, courses, etc.
For the promotion of the international language, Esperanto.

Subject coverage:
Esperanto, international language movements in general, and related subjects.

Museum or gallery collection, archive, or library special collection:
Rare publications dating from 1887

Non-library collection catalogue:
All or part available in-house

Library catalogue:
All or part available in-house

Printed publications:
Large number of both fiction and non-fiction publications
La Brita Esperantisto (twice a year, in Esperanto)
EAB Update (quarterly)

Electronic and video publications:
Cassettes, videos, discs and CDs

Publications list:
Available in print

Access to staff:
Contact by letter, by telephone, by fax, by e-mail and via website. Appointment necessary.
Hours: Mon to Fri, 0900 to 1700, telephone transfer in operation when the office is not manned

Access to building, collection or gallery:
Prior appointment required

Access for disabled people:
Parking provided, level entry, access to all public areas

Links with:
Esperanto Teachers Association
1 Regent Avenue, Skipton, Yorkshire, BD23 1AZ; tel: 01756 799912
Regional federations in the United Kingdom
World Esperanto Organisation
Rotterdam, The Netherlands; tel: + 31 10 436 1044; fax: + 31 10 436 1751; e-mail: uea@inter.nl.net

ESSENTIA GROUP, THE

Lower Ground, Skypark, 72 Finnieston Square, Glasgow, G3 8ET

Tel: 0141 568 4000
Fax: 0141 568 4001
E-mail: info@essentiagroup.com

Enquiries:
Enquiries to: Managing Director
Other contacts: Accounts Manager, Information Officer

Founded:
1979

Formerly called:
Network Scotland (year of change 2000)

Organisation type and purpose:
Advisory body, registered charity (charity number SCO 02866).
Tax File Ref: CR44419/1.

Subject coverage:
Telephone counselling and information services on predominantly health-related topics.

Access to staff:
Contact by letter, by telephone and by e-mail
Hours: Mon to Fri, 0900 to 1700 (office)

Access to building, collection or gallery:
No access other than to staff

Access for disabled people:
Access to all public areas

Connections with:
NHS Helpline
tel: 0800 22 44 88
Sexwise
tel: 0800 28 29 30
Smokeline
tel: 0800 84 84 84

ESSEX ARCHAEOLOGICAL AND HISTORICAL CONGRESS

Acronym or abbreviation: Essex Congress

c/o Cllr Norman Jacobs, Honorary Secretary, 101 Farmleigh Ave, Clacton-on-Sea, Essex, CO15 4UL

Fax: 01621 890868
E-mail: essexahc@aol.com

Founded:
1964

Organisation type and purpose:
Membership association (membership is by subscription), registered charity (charity number 27604).

Subject coverage:
Archaeology, local history and conservation of geographical county of Essex.

Printed publications:
Essex Journal (2 times a year)

Connections with:
British Association for Local History
Council for British Archaeology
Rural Community

ESSEX COUNTY COUNCIL LIBRARIES

County Hall, Market Road, Chelmsford, Essex CM1 1LQ

Tel: 0845 603 7628
E-mail: answers.direct@essex.gov.uk

Website:
http://www.essex.gov.uk/libraries
General information on Essex Libraries and links to other specialised online services.

Founded:
1926

Organisation type and purpose:
Local government body, public library.

Subject coverage:
General library service with 73 service points and 12 mobile libraries.

Museum or gallery collection, archive, or library special collection:
Performing Arts Service
Business Information Service
Castle Collection example 18th century subscription library (Colchester)
Jazz archive (Loughton)
Victorian Studies Centre (Saffron Walden)

Non-library collection catalogue:
All or part available online

Library catalogue:
All or part available online

Access to staff:
Contact by letter, by telephone, by e-mail, in person and via website
Hours: Mon to Fri, 0830 to 1900; Sat 0830 to 1700; Sun 1000 to 1630

Access for disabled people:
Access to all public areas

Parent body:
Essex County Council

ESSEX COUNTY COUNCIL LIBRARIES – BASILDON LIBRARY

St Martin's Square, Basildon, Essex, SS14 1EE

Tel: 01268 288533
Fax: 01268 286326
E-mail: basildon.library@essex.gov.uk

Website:
http://askchris.essexcc.gov.uk
Book reviews/recommendations.
http://www.essexcc.gov.uk/libraries
General information on Essex Libraries.

Enquiries:
Enquiries to: Customer Service Supervisor – Basildon
Direct tel: 0845 438438

Organisation type and purpose:
Local government body, public library.
Basildon

Subject coverage:
General.

Information services:
0845 438438

Access to staff:
Contact by letter, by telephone, by fax, by e-mail, in person and via website
Hours: Mon, Fri, 0900 to 1800; Tue, 0900 to 1900; Wed, 0900 to 1800; Thu, 1000 to 1800; Sat, 0900 to 1700; Sun, 1300 to 1600

Access for disabled people:
Level entry, access to all public areas.

ESSEX COUNTY COUNCIL LIBRARIES – BRAINTREE LIBRARY

Fairfield Road, Braintree, Essex, CM7 3YL

Tel: 01376 320752
Fax: 01376 553316
E-mail: braintree.library@essex.gov.uk

Enquiries:
Enquiries to: Group Manager

Organisation type and purpose:
Local government body, public library.

Subject coverage:
General.

Access to staff:
Contact by letter, by telephone, by fax, by e-mail
and in person
Hours: Mon to Fri, 0900 to 1900; Sat, 0900 to 1700;
Sun, 1300 to 1600

ESSEX COUNTY COUNCIL LIBRARIES – CHELMSFORD CENTRAL LIBRARY

PO Box 882, Market Road, Chelmsford, Essex,
CM1 1LH

Tel: 01245 492758
Fax: 01245 436503
E-mail: chelmsford.library@essex.gov.uk

Website:
http://www.essex.gov.uk/libraries
General information on Essex Libraries, online
catalogue and free access to ebooks and eaudio
books.
http://askchris.essex.gov.uk
Book reviews and recommendations.

Enquiries:
Enquiries to: Group Manager – Chelmsford

Organisation type and purpose:
Local government body, public library.
District library for Chelmsford.

Subject coverage:
General, local history and studies, particularly of
Chelmsford from c.1903, business, Learndirect
Centre, statistics, Europe.

Library catalogue:
All or part available online

Access to staff:
Contact by letter, by telephone, by fax, by e-mail,
in person and via website
Hours: Mon to Fri, 0830 to 1900; Sat, 0830 to 1730;
Sun, 1230 to 1630

Access for disabled people:
Ramped entry, access to all public areas, toilet
facilities
Special comments: Induction loop to counter and
enquiry desks, minicom (textphone), automatic
doors.

ESSEX COUNTY COUNCIL LIBRARIES – COLCHESTER CENTRAL LIBRARY

Trinity Square, Colchester, Essex, CO1 1JB

Tel: 01206 245900
Fax: 01206 254901
E-mail: colchester.library@essex.gov.uk

Website:
http://www.essex.gov.uk/libraries
Full information on Essex Libraries, with useful
links.

Organisation type and purpose:
Local government body, public library.

Subject coverage:
General, local & family history.

Services for disabled people:
Home library service, hearing loop, additional
services for visually impaired & learning-disabled
customers.

**Museum or gallery collection, archive, or library
special collection:**
Castle Library (18th-century subscription library)

Essex Local Studies Collection

Library catalogue:
All or part available online and in-house

Access to staff:
Contact by letter, by telephone, by fax, by e-mail,
in person and via website
Hours: Mon to Fri, 0830 to 1930; Sat, 0830 to 1700;
Sun, 1230 to 1630

Access for disabled people:
Level entry, access to all public areas, toilet
facilities
Special comments: Escalator to 1st floor; lift
available.

Branch libraries:
Greenstead Library
  Hawthorne Avenue, Colchester, Essex, CO4 3QE;
  tel: 01206 862758; fax: 01206 798754; e-mail:
  greenstead.library@essex.gov.uk
Prettygate Library
  Prettygate Road, Colchester, Essex, CO3 4EQ;
  tel: 01206 563700; fax: 01206 571283; e-mail:
  prettygatelibrary@essexcc.gov.uk
Stanway Library
  10 Villa Road, Stanway, Colchester, Essex, CO3
  0RH; tel: 01206 545022; e-mail: stanway.library@
  essexcc.gov.uk

Headquarters address:
Essex County Council Libraries
  Goldlay Gardens, Chelmsford, Essex, CM2 0EW;
  tel: 01245 284981

Mobile libraries:
Three mobile libraries serving surrounding area.

ESSEX COUNTY COUNCIL LIBRARIES – HARLOW LIBRARY

The High, Harlow, Essex, CM20 1HA

Tel: 01279 413772
Fax: 01279 424612
E-mail: harlow.library@essexcc.gov.uk

Website:
http://www.essexcc.gov.uk/libraries
General information on Essex Libraries.
http://www.askchris.essexcc.gov.uk
Book reviews/recommendations.

Enquiries:
Enquiries to: District Manager – Harlow/Epping

Organisation type and purpose:
Local government body, public library.
District Library – Harlow/Epping Forest District.

Subject coverage:
Essex County Council Libraries Language and
Literature Librarian is based at Harlow Library,
responsible for County collection of language
books, audio and video courses, non-English
fiction and literature stock.

**Museum or gallery collection, archive, or library
special collection:**
International Genealogical Index (IGI UK) on
  microfiche
LASER joint fiction reserve (authors S-SS)

Access to staff:
Contact by letter, by telephone, by fax and in
person
Hours: Mon, Tue, Thu, Fri, 0900 to 1900; Wed, 1000
to 1900; Sat, 0900 to 1700; Sun, 1300 to 1600

Access for disabled people:
Level entry, access to all public areas
Special comments: Induction loop at counter and
enquiry desk.

Parent body:
Essex County Council Libraries

ESSEX COUNTY COUNCIL LIBRARIES – SAFFRON WALDEN LIBRARY

2 King Street, Saffron Walden, Essex, CB10 1ES

Tel: 01799 523178
Fax: 01799 513642
E-mail: saffronwalden.library@essex.gov.uk

Website:
http://www.essex.gov.uk

Enquiries:
Enquiries to: Librarian

Organisation type and purpose:
Local government body, public library.
Houses a Victorian studies centre based on the old
Town Library Collection.

Subject coverage:
Victorian studies with special emphasis on art,
literature and natural history, local studies relating
to Saffron Walden and its environs.

**Museum or gallery collection, archive, or library
special collection:**
Herts and Essex Observer (1939–2004, microfilm)
Saffron Walden Observer (1994–2004)
Saffron Walden Weekly News (1881–2004,
  microfilm)
Local census returns 1841, 1851, 1861, 1871, 1881,
  1891 and 1901 (microfilm)
The Library of Saffron Walden Literary and
  Scientific Institute
Victorian Studies collection

Non-library collection catalogue:
All or part available online and in-house

Library catalogue:
All or part available online

Access to staff:
Contact by letter, by telephone, by fax, by e-mail
and in person
Hours: Mon to Fri, 0900 to 1900; Sat, 0900 to 1700;
Sun, 1300 to 1600

Access for disabled people:
Level entry, access to all public areas, toilet
facilities

ESSEX RECORD OFFICE – CHELMSFORD

Acronym or abbreviation: ERO

Wharf Road, Chelmsford, Essex, CM2 6YT

Tel: 01245 244644
Fax: 01245 244655
E-mail: ero.enquiry@essex.gov.uk

Website:
http://www.essex.gov.uk/ero
http://www.essex.gov.uk/heritage
Description of services offered, outline of archive
holdings, publications and exhibitions, online
catalogue SEAX, events calendar.

Enquiries:
Enquiries to: Archive Service Manager

Founded:
1938

Incorporates the former:
Essex Record Office – Colchester (year of change
2007)

Organisation type and purpose:
Local government body.
Record office.

Subject coverage:
Topography and history of Essex, genealogy.

Special visitor services:
Conference facilities.

Education services:
Heritage Education Officer.

**Museum or gallery collection, archive, or library
special collection:**
Extensive collections of local government, parish,
  estate and family, business and other archives
  relating to the county of Essex; library of Essex
  local history books, journals and newspapers;
  Essex Sound and Video Archive

continued overleaf

Non-library collection catalogue:
All or part available online, in-house and in print

Library catalogue:
All or part available in-house

Printed publications:
Over 70 publications in print, including:
Colchester, 1815–1914 (A. J. F. Brown)
Elizabethan Life (F. G. Emmison, 5 vols)
Essex Illustrated – a county, its people and its past
Essex Quarter Sessions Order Book, 1652–1661 (ed. D. H. Allen)
Examples of English Handwriting, 1150–1750 (H. Grieve)
Foulness (J. R. Smith)
Genealogist's Guide to Essex Sources
John Horace Round (W. R. Powell)
Picture booklets (Medieval Essex, Elizabethan Essex, etc., list available)
Prosperity and Poverty – Rural Essex, 1700–1815 (A. F. J. Brown)
Reproductions of maps
Seax series of Teaching Portfolios (list available)
The Sleeper and the Shadows (H. Grieve, 2 vols)
List of new archival accessions (annual)
Order printed publications from: Address above

Microform publications:
Microfilm and microfiche of a wide variety of records can be made to order
Order microform publications from: Address above

Electronic and video publications:
Digital images of a wide variety of records can be made to order
Order electronic and video publications from: Address above

Publications list:
Available online and in print

Access to staff:
Contact by letter, by telephone, by fax, by e-mail, in person and via website
Hours: Mon, 0900 to 2030; Tue to Thu, 0900 to 1700; Fri and Sat, 0900 to 1600

Access to building, collection or gallery:
Public entrance is situated on river side of building, not on Wharf Road side
Hours: From 0830

Access for disabled people:
Parking provided, level entry, access to all public areas, toilet facilities
Hours: From 0830

Links with:
Saffron Walden Archive Access Point
Saffron Walden Library, 2 King Street, Saffron Walden, CB10 1ES; tel: 01799 523178; e-mail: ero.saffronwalden@essex.gov.uk

ESSEX SOCIETY FOR ARCHAEOLOGY AND HISTORY

Hollytrees Museum, High Street, Colchester, Essex, CO1 1UG

Enquiries:
Enquiries to: Secretary
Direct tel: 01277 363106

Founded:
1852

Formerly called:
Essex Archaeological Society

Organisation type and purpose:
Learned society.

Subject coverage:
Essex archaeology and history.

Museum or gallery collection, archive, or library special collection:
Library is now housed at the University of Essex
17th and 18th century books (history and religion)
Archaeological journals
Brass rubbing collection (A H Brown)
Definitive collection of rubbings of Essex brasses (Christy, Porteous and Smith)
Essex Parish histories and county biography

Essex prints and photographs
Transcripts of Essex Parish Registers

Non-library collection catalogue:
All or part available in print

Library catalogue:
All or part available in print

Printed publications:
Catalogues of non-book library materials (in preparation)
Essex Archaeological News (quarterly newsletter)
Essex Archaeology and History (annual transactions)
Order printed publications from: Secretary

Access to staff:
Contact by letter. Appointment necessary.
Hours: Mon to Fri, 0900 to 1700

Affiliated to:
Council for British Archaeology
Essex Historical and Archaeological Congress

ESSO PETROLEUM COMPANY LIMITED

Esso Refinery, Fawley, Southampton, SO45 1TX

Tel: 023 8089 2511
Fax: 023 8089 6712

Enquiries:
Enquiries to: IMS Administrator
Direct tel: 023 8089 6113
Direct fax: 023 8089 6334
Direct e-mail: rob.gostt@exxonmobil.com

Organisation type and purpose:
Manufacturing industry.

Subject coverage:
Chemical engineering; combustion; corrosion; petroleum and petroleum products; oil refining; oil transport and storage; plant maintenance; pollution.

Museum or gallery collection, archive, or library special collection:
British and American industrial standards

Access to staff:
Contact by telephone, by fax and by e-mail
Hours: Mon to Fri, 0830 to 1630

Constituent part of:
ExxonMobil Corporation, USA

ESTONIAN EMBASSY

Formal name: Embassy of the Republic of Estonia

16 Hyde Park Gate, London, SW7 5DG

Tel: 020 7589 3428
Fax: 020 7589 3430
E-mail: embassy.london@estonia.gov.uk

Website:
http://www.estonia.gov.uk

Enquiries:
Enquiries to: Secretary

Formerly called:
Estonian Information Bureau (year of change 1992)

Organisation type and purpose:
National government body.
Diplomatic Mission/Embassy.

Subject coverage:
All information on Estonia: travel, economical, political, cultural, etc.

Access to staff:
Contact by letter, by telephone, by fax, by e-mail and via website
Hours: The Consular Section (for Visas): Mon, Fri, 1000 to 1300; Tue, Thu, 1300 to 1600

Access to building, collection or gallery:
Prior appointment required

ETHICAL INVESTMENT RESEARCH SERVICE

Acronym or abbreviation: EIRIS

80–84 Bondway, London, SW8 1SF

Tel: 020 7840 5700
Fax: 020 7735 5323
E-mail: ethics@eiris.org

Website:
http://www.eiris.org

Enquiries:
Enquiries to: Partnerships and Development Manager

Founded:
1983

Organisation type and purpose:
Registered charity (charity number 1020068), consultancy, research organisation.
Provides research on the ethical aspects of corporate activities for ethical investors. Provides (non-financial) information on ethical or socially responsible investment.

Subject coverage:
Helping investors match their investments with their ethical (incl. environmental) principles.
Providing (non-financial) information on ethical or socially responsible investment.

Trade and statistical information:
Collated information on retail ethical funds.

Printed publications:
Does Ethical Investment Pay (download from web)
The Ethical Investor (newsletter, 4 times a year, and supplement, 2 times a year, annual subscription £15, or available online)
The following supplements are available free:
Guide to ethical banking
Guide to ethical share ownership
Guide on charities and ethical investment
Order printed publications from: EIRIS Orderline tel: 0845 606 0324

Electronic and video publications:
All EIRIS's supplements and newsletters can be downloaded free from www.eiris.org
Ethical Portfolio Manager (software for institutional investors)

Publications list:
Available online and in print

Access to staff:
Contact by letter, by telephone, by fax, by e-mail and via website
Hours: Mon to Fri, 0900 to 1700
Special comments: Charges for some services made to all users. Some information available free via website.

Member of:
Global Partners for Corporate Responsibility Research
UK Social Investment Forum

ETON COLLEGE LIBRARY

Eton College, Windsor, Berkshire, SL4 6DB

Tel: 01753 671221
Fax: 01753 801507
E-mail: collections@etoncollege.org.uk

Founded:
1440

Organisation type and purpose:
Registered charity.
A rare book and manuscript library, maintained by collegiate body (Provost and Fellows). A research library.

Museum or gallery collection, archive, or library special collection:
16th-century continental books
17th- and 18th-century English pamphlets (to c.1730)
Armenian printed books (16th–19th centuries)
Bibliography

Classical school books (15th–19th centuries)
Drawings and engravings after the antique
(Topham Collection)
Drawings of Rome and its environs
English literature 19th and 20th centuries (Hardy,
Browning, Swinburne, Anne Thackeray Ritchie,
Edward Gordon Craig, Susan Hill, Moelwyn
Merchant, Anthony Powell, Etonian authors)
Fine bindings
Incunabula
Local history collections (Eton and Windsor)
Photographic collection
Pre-Restoration English drama
Private presses
Topographical prints and drawings (mostly local)
Western and oriental manuscripts

Non-library collection catalogue:
All or part available in-house

Library catalogue:
All or part available in-house and in print

Access to staff:
Contact by letter, by telephone, by fax, by e-mail
and via website. Appointment necessary.
Hours: Mon to Fri, 0930 to 1300 and 1400 to 1700

ETON FIVES ASSOCIATION

Acronym or abbreviation: EFA

3 Bourchier Close, Sevenoaks, Kent, TN13 1PD

Tel: 01732 458775
E-mail: efa@etonfives.co.uk

Website:
http://www.etonfives.co.uk
About Eton Fives, association information, courts,
historical and other articles, merchandise and
equipment, league and tournament results, clubs
and schools, picture gallery, contacts.

Enquiries:
Enquiries to: Secretary

Founded:
c. 1928

Organisation type and purpose:
National organisation, membership association
(membership is by subscription, election or
invitation), present number of members: 700 plus
50 friends.
Controlling body of the game.
To promote the playing of Eton Fives; to review
and publish the rules and laws of the game.

Subject coverage:
Eton Fives court specifications; lighting; equipment
(gloves and balls); laws of the game; court location;
court availability; archives.

**Museum or gallery collection, archive, or library
special collection:**
Archives: include books, documents, manuscripts,
pictures, photographs and other material

Library catalogue:
All or part available online

Printed publications:
Annual Handbook
Coaching and Playing Manual

Access to staff:
Contact by letter, by telephone, by e-mail and via
website
Hours: Sun to Sat, 0800 to 2200

EUROMONITOR INTERNATIONAL

60–61 Britton Street, London, EC1M 5UX

Tel: 020 7251 8024
Fax: 020 7608 3149
E-mail: info@euromonitor.com

Website:
http://www.euromonitor.com
Complete listing of market research reports,
reference products and consultancy, searchable by
industry, country or product.

Enquiries:
Enquiries to: Marketing Manager

Founded:
1972

Organisation type and purpose:
Professional body, consultancy, research
organisation, publishing house.

Subject coverage:
International marketing information and analysis,
food, drinks, tobacco, tourism, household cleaning,
healthcare, cosmetics and toiletries, household
goods, domestic electrical appliances, consumer
electronics, leisure, automotives, catering,
financial, consumer lifestyles, retailing, Europe,
Eastern Europe, North and South America,
Australasia, Japan and China, South East Asia.

**Museum or gallery collection, archive, or library
special collection:**
Large in-house international library which
includes directories, national statistics (Europe),
trade and marketing press (Europe), company
reports (international) and key data and surveys
on consumer goods markets around the world

Trade and statistical information:
Data on overall and specific consumer markets to
include key trends and developments, market
size, sources of supply, market sectors, usership
and purchasing patterns, prices and margins,
brands and manufacturers, advertising,
promotions and new products, retail
distribution, future outlook.

Library catalogue:
All or part available in print

Printed publications:
World Directory of Business Information Libraries

Electronic and video publications:
World Consumer Markets (internet)
World Consumer Lifestyles: Data (internet)
Market Research Monitor (internet)
World Marketing Data and Statistics (internet)
World Marketing Forecasts (internet)

Publications list:
Available online and in print

Access to staff:
Contact by letter, by telephone, by fax, by e-mail
and via website
Hours: Mon to Fri, 0930 to 1730

EUROPEAN ASSOCIATION FOR
BRAZING AND SOLDERING

Acronym or abbreviation: EABS

5 Kent Drive, Congleton, Cheshire, CW12 1SD

Tel: 01260 271703
Fax: 01260 276729
E-mail: eabs@btconnect.com

Website:
http://www.brazingandsoldering.org
Aims and objectives, training courses available,
newsletter, technical articles, response form for
technical advice, detail and booking forms for
technical training seminars.

Enquiries:
Enquiries to: Secretariat

Founded:
1970

Formerly called:
British Association for Brazing and Soldering
(BABS) (year of change 2000)

Organisation type and purpose:
Training organisation.
To provide a consultancy service and technical
information in the promotion of brazing and
soldering technology.

Subject coverage:
Brazing (low and high temperature), soldering,
diffusion bonding, adhesives, ceramics, metals,
process equipment, consumables, standards.

Printed publications:
EABS Newsletter (2 or 3 times a year)

Access to staff:
Contact by letter, by telephone, by fax, by e-mail
and via website. Non-members charged.
Hours: Mon to Fri, 0830 to 1630

EUROPEAN ASSOCIATION FOR
PASSIVE FIRE PROTECTION

Acronym or abbreviation: EAPFP

Tournai Hall, Evelyn Woods Road, Aldershot,
Hampshire, GU11 2LL

Tel: 01252 357836
Fax: 01252 357831
E-mail: admin@eapfp.com

Website:
http://www.eapfp.com

Enquiries:
Enquiries to: Secretary

Founded:
1988

Formerly called:
European Association for Specialist Fire Protection
(EASFP)

Organisation type and purpose:
Trade association, present number of members: 7.
Corporate voice for European manufacturers and
contractors involved in passive fire protection to
steelwork, timber and other specialist applications.

Subject coverage:
Fire protection to steelwork, timber and other
specialist fire protection applications including
penetration seals and ductwork.

Printed publications:
Conference papers
EAPFP Folder (members' details and other
information, free)

Publications list:
Available online and in print

Access to staff:
Contact by letter, by telephone, by fax, by e-mail
and via website
Hours: Mon to Fri, 0900 to 1700

EUROPEAN ASSOCIATION OF
SCIENCE EDITORS

Acronym or abbreviation: EASE

PO Box 6159, Reading, RG19 9DE

Tel: 0118 970 0322
Fax: 0118 970 0322
E-mail: secretary@ease.org.uk

Website:
http://www.ease.org.uk
Information about EASE and application form for
potential members and subscribers to the journal,
Editor's Bookshelf, recent copies of EASE's
quarterly journal, list of conferences and meetings,
job advertisements, courses offered by members,
links to useful sites, how to join EASE web forum,
how to join EASE, payment facility for
subscriptions and handbooks, Members' Area,

Enquiries:
Enquiries to: Secretary or Membership Secretary
Direct e-mail: secretary@ease.org.uk; membership@
ease.org.uk

Founded:
1982

Created by the merger of:
European Association of Earth Science Editors
(Editerra), European Life Sciences Editors'
Association (ELSE) (year of change 1982)

Organisation type and purpose:
International organisation, professional body.

Subject coverage:
Editing and copy-editing in the sciences.

continued overleaf

Printed publications:
European Science Editing (journal for members and subscribers, quarterly, £65 to non-members)
Science Editors' Handbook (included in membership fee: new chapters issued from time to time, after editorial approval; available to non-members £35 plus p&p – see website: http://www.ease.org.uk for details and price)
Order printed publications from: e-mail: membership@ease.org.uk; website: http://www.ease.org.uk

Access to staff:
Contact by letter, by telephone, by fax, by e-mail and via website
Hours: Mon to Fri, 0900 to 1700
Special comments: No visitors.

Links with:
International Union of Biological Sciences (IUBS)
International Union of Geological Sciences (IUGS)

EUROPEAN BANK FOR RECONSTRUCTION AND DEVELOPMENT – BUSINESS INFORMATION CENTRE

Acronym or abbreviation: EBRD

One Exchange Square, London, EC2A 2JN

Tel: 020 7338 7269
Fax: 020 7338 6155
E-mail: stanojes@ebrd.com

Website:
http://www.ebrd.com
Full details of publications.

Enquiries:
Enquiries to: Senior Information Officer

Founded:
1991

Organisation type and purpose:
International organisation.
Financing the economic transition in Central and Eastern Europe and the former Soviet Union.

Subject coverage:
Business information for Central and Eastern Europe and the CIS.

Museum or gallery collection, archive, or library special collection:
Collection of books, periodicals, CD-ROMs and other documents relating to the area of Central and Eastern Europe and the CIS

Trade and statistical information:
Economic and business-related data covering the countries of Central and Eastern Europe and the CIS.

Printed publications:
EBRD Directory of business information sources on Central and Eastern Europe and the CIS (annually, £175)
Order printed publications from: ETM Ltd, PO Box 171, Grimsby, DN35 0TP; tel. 01472 816660; fax 01472 816660; e-mail sales@dataresources.co.uk

Electronic and video publications:
EBRD Directory of business information sources on Central and Eastern Europe and the CIS

Publications list:
Available online and in print

Access to staff:
Contact by letter, by fax and by e-mail.
Appointment necessary. Letter of introduction required.
Hours: Mon to Fri, 0900 to 1700

Access for disabled people:
Toilet facilities
Special comments: Access by lift in Exchange Square and access by lift to Exchange Square from Appold Street

EUROPEAN BEER CONSUMER UNION

Acronym or abbreviation: EBCU

230 Hatfield Road, St Albans, Hertfordshire, AL1 4LW

Tel: 01727 798449
Fax: 01727 867670
E-mail: ebcu@camra.org.uk

Website:
http://www.camra.org.uk

Enquiries:
Enquiries to: Communications Manager
Direct e-mail: iain.loe@camra.org.uk

Founded:
1990

Organisation type and purpose:
International organisation (membership is by subscription), present number of members: 100,000.

Subject coverage:
Beer and brewing. Legislation relating to beer, brewing, sale of alcohol. Historical information on beer and brewing.

Trade and statistical information:
Some statistical information on UK Brewing, less on the rest of Europe.

Printed publications:
Good Beer Guide (annually, pub October)
Variety of guides to pubs in the UK and parts of rest of Europe

Access to staff:
Contact by letter, by telephone and by e-mail.
Appointment necessary.
Hours: Mon to Fri, 0900 to 1700

Access for disabled people:
Parking provided, level entry

EUROPEAN CENTRE FOR MEDIUM-RANGE WEATHER FORECASTS

Acronym or abbreviation: ECMWF

Shinfield Park, Reading, Berkshire, RG2 9AX

Tel: 0118 949 9000
Fax: 0118 986 9450
E-mail: dra@ecmwf.int

Website:
http://www.ecmwf.int/
Weather information.

Enquiries:
Enquiries to: Director
Direct tel: 0118 949 9101

Founded:
1975

Organisation type and purpose:
International organisation, research organisation.

Subject coverage:
Numerical weather prediction in the medium range.

Library catalogue:
All or part available in-house

Printed publications:
Scientific work

Electronic and video publications:
Analysed fields
Observations
Meteorological data

Access to staff:
Contact by letter and by e-mail. Appointment necessary.
Hours: Mon to Fri, 0900 to 1700

Access to building, collection or gallery:
No access other than to staff

EUROPEAN CHRISTIAN MISSION

50 Billing Road, Northampton, NN1 5DH

Tel: 01604 621092
E-mail: ecm.gb@ecmi.org

Website:
http://www.ecmi.org
A large amount of information including vacancies.

Enquiries:
Enquiries to: Information Officer

Founded:
1904

Organisation type and purpose:
International organisation, voluntary organisation, registered charity.

Access to staff:
Contact by letter, by telephone, by e-mail and via website
Hours: Mon to Fri, 0900 to 1700

Access for disabled people:
Parking provided, ramped entry

EUROPEAN COMMISSION – EDINBURGH

Acronym or abbreviation: EC or EU

9 Alva Street, Edinburgh, EH2 4PH

Tel: 0131 225 2058
Fax: 0131 226 4105
E-mail: diana.hart@cec.eu.int

Website:
http://europa.eu.int
The European Union's Server.
http://www.cec.org.uk
UK Representation.
http://www.europe.org.uk
UK Resource Centres.

Enquiries:
Enquiries to: Information Officer

Founded:
1975

Formerly called:
European Economic Community (EEC)

Organisation type and purpose:
International organisation.
Representation of the EC in Scotland.

Subject coverage:
Information on the European Union.

Museum or gallery collection, archive, or library special collection:
Official Publications of the European Community

Trade and statistical information:
Eurostat.

Printed publications:
A very large number of publications including:
Documents (the COM Documents of the European Commission)
Official Journal of the EC
The European Community as a Publisher (1995) (extract from the publications catalogue)
Order printed publications from: The Stationery Office

Publications list:
Available in print

Access to staff:
Contact by letter, by telephone, by fax, by e-mail and via website. Appointment necessary.
Hours: Mon to Fri, 0900 to 1700

Access to building, collection or gallery:
Prior appointment required

EUROPEAN COMMISSION – LONDON

Formal name: European Commission Representation in the United Kingdom

Europe House, 32 Smith Square, London, SW1P 3EU

Tel: 020 7973 1992
Fax: 020 7973 1900/10

Website:
http://europa.eu/index_en.htm
Gateway to information on the European Union policies and institutions. News, answers to key questions, institutions, policies, mailbox for comments and ideas.
http://www.europarl.org.uk/index.htm
Website of the UK office of the European Parliament.
http://ec.europa.eu/unitedkingdom/index_en.htm
Daily update of the latest developments in the EU with regard to policies and programmes, recruitment, EU-related events in the UK, publications lists, etc.

Enquiries:
Enquiries to: Public Diplomacy Unit
Direct e-mail: marguerite-marie.brenchley@ec.europa.eu

Formerly called:
Commission of the European Communities

Organisation type and purpose:
International organisation.
Representation of the European Commission.

Subject coverage:
European Community polices, legislation and documentation.

Information services:
See: http://www.europe.org.uk/info, which brings together the EU information network in the UK.

Trade and statistical information:
Eurostat publications.

Library catalogue:
All or part available in-house and in print

Printed publications:
Free publications on all aspects of EU policies:
http://ec.europa.eu/unitedkingdom/information/publications/index_en.htm
Order printed publications from: See list of agents in the UK at http://publications.europa.eu/others/agents/index_en.htm

Publications list:
Available online and in print

Access to staff:
Contact by letter, by telephone and by fax. Appointment necessary.
Hours: Mon to Fri, 0900 to 1700
Special comments: The Representation in the UK is now supporting a national network of information centres (http://www.europe.org.uk/info) to whom all enquiries should be addressed. Visitors to the library may be referred to the Representation by the information centres, when they are unable to help. Visits are organised strictly by appointment.

Also at:
European Commission
Publications Office of the European Union, 2 rue Mercier, 2985, Luxembourg; tel: 00 352 29291; e-mail: info@publications.europa.eu; website: http://publications.europa.eu/index_en.htm
European Commission
Rue de la Loi 200, 1049, Brussels, Belgium; tel: 00 32 2 235 1111; website: http://ec.europa.eu/index_en.htm
European Commission Office in Northern Ireland
Windsor House, 9–15 Bedford Street, Belfast, BT2 7EG; tel: 028 9024 0708; fax: 028 9024 8241
European Commission Office in Scotland
9 Alva Street, Edinburgh, EH2 4PH; tel: 0131 225 2058; fax: 0131 226 4105

European Commission Office in Wales / Swyddfa'r Comisiwn Ewropeaidd yng Nghymru
2 Caspian Point / 2 Pentir Caspian, Caspian Way / Ffordd Caspian, Cardiff/Caerdydd, CF10 4QQ; tel: 029 2089 5020; fax: 029 2089 5035
European Commission Statistical Office (Eurostat)
Bâtiment Bech, 11 Rue Alphonse Weicker, 2721, Luxembourg; tel: 00 352 43011; website: http://epp.eurostat.ec.europa.eu/portal/page?_pageid=1090,1&_dad=portal&_schema=PORTAL

Links with:
Members of the European Parliament (MEPs)
London Office of the EP
Europe House, 32 Smith Square, London, SW1P 3EU; tel: 020 7227 4300; e-mail: eplondon@europarl.europa.eu; website: http://www.europarl.org.uk/office/TheOfficeMain.htm

EUROPEAN COMPUTER LEASING AND TRADING ASSOCIATION

Formal name: European Computer Leasing and Trading Association
Acronym or abbreviation: ECLAT

1285 Stratford Road, Hall Green, Birmingham, B28 9AJ

Tel: 0121 778 5327
Fax: 0121 778 5924
E-mail: jgsewel@attglobal.net

Website:
http://www.eclat.net
List of members by country and details of ECLAT's conferences.
http://www.ascdi.com
List of members by country and details of ASCDI's conferences.

Enquiries:
Enquiries to: Director General

Founded:
1979

Organisation type and purpose:
Trade association (membership is by qualification, election or invitation), present number of members: 230.
Represents the interests of the computer leasing and trading industry.

Subject coverage:
Specialised knowledge on computer leasing and on purchase and sale of used computers.

Access to staff:
Contact by letter, by telephone, by fax and by e-mail. Appointment necessary. Non-members charged.
Hours: Mon to Fri, 0900 to 1730

Connections with:
Association of Service and Computer Dealers International (ASCDI)
131 NW 1st Avenue, Derray Beach, FL 33444, USA; tel: +561 266 9016; fax: +561 266 9017; e-mail: jmarion@ix.netcom.com

EUROPEAN CONSTRUCTION INSTITUTE

Acronym or abbreviation: ECI

Loughborough University, Sir Frank Gibb Annex, Loughborough, Leicestershire, LE11 3TU

Tel: 01509 223526
Fax: 01509 260118
E-mail: eci@lboro.ac.uk

Website:
http://www.eci-online.org
ECI activities, company profiles, task forces, picture gallery, hot news, conferences/ seminars/ workshops, email addresses, publications.

Enquiries:
Enquiries to: Administrator
Direct tel: 01509 223643

Founded:
1990

Organisation type and purpose:
International organisation, membership association (membership is by subscription), research organisation.
To improve the performance of the European construction industry.

Subject coverage:
Construction in Europe.

Museum or gallery collection, archive, or library special collection:
Business Roundtable (USA) publications
Construction Industry Institute (USA) publications

Printed publications:
ECI News (3 times a year)
Taskforce papers
Construction in Europe (conference papers)
Partnering in the Public Sector
The ECI Guide to Managing Health in Construction
Over 30 publications related to the construction industry

Publications list:
Available in print

Access to staff:
Contact by letter, by telephone, by fax, by e-mail and via website. Appointment necessary.
Hours: Mon to Fri, 0900 to 1730

Has:
over 70 member companies

EUROPEAN COUNCIL OF INFORMATION ASSOCIATIONS

Acronym or abbreviation: ECIA

Aslib, Holywell Centre, 1 Phipp Street, London, EC2A 4PS

Tel: 020 7613 3031
Fax: 020 7613 5080
E-mail: ecia@aslib.com

Website:
http://www.aslib.com/ecia/index.html
ECIA VIEWS.

Enquiries:
Enquiries to: Honorary Secretary
Direct e-mail: roger.bowes@aslib.com
Other contacts: President

Founded:
1979

Formerly called:
WERTID (year of change 1992)

Organisation type and purpose:
International organisation.

Subject coverage:
Management of information.

Printed publications:
ECIA VIEWS (Newsletter)

Access to staff:
Contact by e-mail
Hours: Mon to Fri, 0900 to 1700

Members:
Associação Portuguesa para a Gestao da Informação Edificio (INCITE)
Portugal; e-mail: incite@net.sapo.pt; website: www.incite.pt
Association Belge de Documentation, Belgische Vereniging voor Documentatie (ABD-BVD)
Belgium; e-mail: abdbrd@abd-bvd.be; website: www.abd-bvd.be
Associazione Italiana per la Documentazione Avanzata (AIDA)
Italy; e-mail: aida-cd@inroma.roma; website: www.aidaweb.it

continued overleaf

Deutsche Gesellschaft für
Informationswissenschaft und Informationspraxis
(DGI)
　Germany; e-mail: zentrale@dgi-info.de; website:
　www.dgi-info.de
L'Association des professionnels de l'information
et de la documentation (ADBS)
　France; e-mail: ADBS@adbs.fr; website: www
　.adbs.fr
Sociedad Española de Documentación e
Información Científica (SEDIC)
　Spain; e-mail: sedic@sedic.es; website: www
　.sedic.es
Swedish Association for Information Specialists
(TLS)
　Sweden; e-mail: kansliet@tls.se; website: www
　.tls.se
The Association for Information Management
(ASLIB)
　UK; e-mail: ecia@aslib.com; website: www.aslib
　.com
Tietopalveluseura ry – Finish Society for
Information Services
　Finland; e-mail: info@tietopalveluseura.fi;
　website: www.tietopalveluseura.fi

EUROPEAN COUNCIL OF INTERNATIONAL SCHOOLS

Formal name: European Council of International
Schools
Acronym or abbreviation: ECIS

21 Lavant Street, Petersfield, Hampshire, GU32
3EL

Tel: 01730 268244
Fax: 01730 267914
E-mail: ecis@ecis.org

Website:
http://www.ecis.org
Details of ECIS, links to international schools. Online directory of international schools, job
vacancies and professional development.

Enquiries:
Enquiries to: Executive, Information & Resources

Founded:
1965

Organisation type and purpose:
International organisation, membership
association, present number of members: 515
schools, 400 colleges and universities, suitable for
ages: 3 to 18.
Provides services to international schools
worldwide including: conferences, teacher/senior
administrator recruitment, school accreditation
and publications.

Subject coverage:
Arranges and conducts professional meetings,
publishes directories, newsletters and journals,
assists member schools with finding staff,
evaluates and accredits schools, conducts research
and acts as a consultant, encourages the
professional development of teachers and provides
a link to higher education.

Printed publications:
Most Important Decision (£5 members only)
ECIS Policy Planner (£50 members only)
Sample Contracts for Heads (£5 members only)
Languages & Cultures in English-Language-Based
International Schools (£17 members only)
ECIS Guide to School Evaluation & Accreditation
(6th ed., £25 members only)
The 2002/3 International Schools Directory (£35)
The following three publications are available
through: Sales Dept John Catt Educational Ltd,
Great Glemham, Saxmundham IP17 2DH. Tel:
01728 663666 Fax:01728 663415
The ECIS Higher Education Directory 2003 (£40)
The International Schools Journal (2 times a year,
£15 members)
IS, International School magazine (3 times a year,
£15)

Access to staff:
Contact by letter, by telephone, by fax, by e-mail
and via website
Hours: Mon to Fri, 0830 to 1700

Other offices:
European Council of International Schools
　PO Box 6066, 28080 Madrid, Spain; tel: +34 91
　562 6722; fax: +34 91 745 1310; e-mail:
　ecismadrid@ecis.org
European Council of International Schools
　105 Tuxford Terrace, Basking Ridge, NJ 07920,
　USA; tel: +1 908 903 0552; fax: +1 908 480 9381; e-
　mail: malyecisna@aol.com
European Council of International Schools
　Cumburri IEC, PO Box 367, Kilmore 3764,
　Victoria, Australia; tel: +61 35 781 1351; fax: +61
　35 781 1151

EUROPEAN COUNCIL OF OPTOMETRY AND OPTICS

Acronym or abbreviation: ECOO

61 Southwark Street, London, SE1 0HL

Tel: 020 7928 9269
Fax: 020 7261 0228
E-mail: richardecoo@aop.org.uk

Website:
http://www.ecoo.info

Enquiries:
Enquiries to: Secretary General

Founded:
1992

Formerly called:
GOOMAC, PEG

Organisation type and purpose:
Professional body.

Subject coverage:
Optometry, optics, eyecare, optical appliances, eye
conditions and examinations, co-operation with
ophthalmology.

Access to staff:
Contact by letter
Hours: Mon to Fri, 0900 to 1700

EUROPEAN DESIGN CENTRE, WALSALL COLLEGE OF ARTS AND TECHNOLOGY

St Pauls Street, Walsall, West Midlands, WS1 1XN

Tel: 01922 657000
Fax: 01922 657083
E-mail: j.pearson@walcat.ac.uk

Website:
http://www.walcat.ac.uk/

Enquiries:
Enquiries to: Library Manager
Direct tel: ext 7078

Organisation type and purpose:
training organisation.

Subject coverage:
Engineering: mechanical, production, electronic;
building; business studies; catering; community
care; hair and beauty; robotics, CADCAM; leisure
and tourism; computing; creative arts; design;
performing arts; GCSE; A levels; management;
accounts and law; photography; languages;
humanities; teacher training; counselling; adult
education and return to learn; access to HE; motor
vehicle; science; painting and decorating; interior
design and soft furnishing.

Non-library collection catalogue:
All or part available online

Library catalogue:
All or part available online

Access to staff:
Contact by e-mail
Hours: Term time: Mon to Thu, 0900 to 2200; Fri,
0945 to 1630; Sat, 0930 to 1230, 1300 to 1530.

Vacations: Mon to Fri, 0900 to 1630
Special comments: There is a small charge for
computer usage for non-members.

Access for disabled people:
Parking provided, ramped entry, toilet facilities

EUROPEAN DOCUMENTATION CENTRE – COVENTRY UNIVERSITY

Acronym or abbreviation: EDC

Lanchester Library, Gosford Street, Coventry,
Warwickshire, CV1 5DD

Tel: 024 7688 7541
Fax: 024 7688 7525
E-mail: lbx203@coventry.ac.uk

Website:
http://www.coventry.ac.uk

Enquiries:
Enquiries to: EDC Librarian

Organisation type and purpose:
University library.

Subject coverage:
European Union.

Trade and statistical information:
Eurostats.

Library catalogue:
All or part available online

Access to staff:
Contact by letter, by telephone, by fax, by e-mail,
in person and via website
Hours: Term-time: Mon to Thu, 0830 to 1900; Fri,
0900 to 1715; Sat, Sun, 1300 to 1700
Vacations: Mon to Fri, 0900 to 1700

Access for disabled people:
Level entry, access to all public areas, toilet
facilities, parking

EUROPEAN DOCUMENTATION CENTRE – DURHAM UNIVERSITY

Acronym or abbreviation: EDC

Official Publications Collection, Durham
University Library, Stockton Road, Durham, DH1
3LY

Tel: 0191 334 2944
Fax: 0191 334 2971
E-mail: n.p.davies@durham.ac.uk

Website:
http://www.dur.ac.uk/library/resources/european/
edc

Enquiries:
Enquiries to: European Documentation Officer

Founded:
1969

Organisation type and purpose:
University library.

Subject coverage:
European Communities legislation; preparing
legislation; statistical material, background
information; reports and periodicals; information
on EC grants and loans; UK government
publications in all fields.

Non-library collection catalogue:
All or part available online and in-house

Printed publications:
Documentation notes (occasional series)
Guide

Publications list:
Available in print

Access to staff:
Contact by letter, by telephone and by e-mail.
Appointment necessary.
Hours: Mon to Fri, 0900 to 1700 (staffed)

Special comments: For unstaffed access, see Durham University opening hours online

Access for disabled people:
Level entry, access to all public areas, toilet facilities

EUROPEAN DOCUMENTATION CENTRE – UNIVERSITY OF CAMBRIDGE

Acronym or abbreviation: EDC

Cambridge University Library, West Road, Cambridge, CB3 9DR

Tel: 01223 333138
Fax: 01223 333160
E-mail: wani000@cam.ac.uk

Enquiries:
Enquiries to: Under-Librarian

Founded:
1963

Organisation type and purpose:
University library.

Subject coverage:
All subjects.

Museum or gallery collection, archive, or library special collection:
Council of Europe publications
EU Publications
ECE publications
EFTA publications
NATO publications
Nordic Council publications
OECD publications
OSCE publications
Very many in the rest of the library

Trade and statistical information:
Worldwide collection of statistical abstracts, EC statistics, UN statistics.

Library catalogue:
All or part available online

Access to staff:
Contact by letter, by telephone, by fax and by e-mail. Appointment necessary. Letter of introduction required.
Hours: Mon to Fri, 0930 to 1845; Sat, 0930 to 1245

Access for disabled people:
Parking provided, ramped entry, access to all public areas, toilet facilities

EUROPEAN DOCUMENTATION CENTRE – UNIVERSITY OF DUNDEE

Acronym or abbreviation: EDC

Law Library, Scrymgeour Building, Park Place, Dundee, DD1 4HN

Tel: 01382 384101
Fax: 01382 381019
E-mail: edc-library@dundee.ac.uk

Website:
http://www.dundee.ac.uk/edc
General information on holdings of the EDC and classification list; links to all EU institutions and agencies; links to related and non-EU sites.

Enquiries:
Enquiries to: Senior Assistant Librarian

Founded:
1972

Organisation type and purpose:
University library.
To promote and consolidate studies and research in European Union matters, particularly European legislation; to make the policies of the EU known to citizens.

Subject coverage:
Legislation of the European Union, via the Official Journal and websites. General information on all institutions and agencies of the EU.

Museum or gallery collection, archive, or library special collection:
Official documentation of the institutions of the European Communities, reports and studies

Non-library collection catalogue:
All or part available online

Library catalogue:
All or part available online

Access to staff:
Contact by letter, by telephone, by fax, by e-mail, in person and via website
Hours: Term time: Mon to Fri, 0900 to 1700; Vacations: Mon to Fri, 0900 to 1700

Access to building, collection or gallery:
No prior appointment required

Member organisation of:
European Information Association (EIA)
Central Library, St Peter's Square, Manchester, M2 5PD; tel: 0161 228 3691; fax: 0161 236 6547; e-mail: eia@manchester.gov.uk

Parent body:
University of Dundee
Perth Road, Dundee, DD1 4HN; tel: 01382 383000; fax: 01382 201604; e-mail: university@dundee.ac.uk; website: http://www.dundee.ac.uk

EUROPEAN DOCUMENTATION CENTRE – UNIVERSITY OF ESSEX

Acronym or abbreviation: EDC

Albert Sloman Library, University of Essex, PO Box 24, Colchester, Essex, CO4 3UA

Tel: 01206 873333
Fax: 01206 873598

Website:
http://libwww.essex.ac.uk/
Subject access to Internet resource; connections to other library catalogues and WWW servers; access to NISS, BUBL and a number of databases; text of various library guides.

Enquiries:
Enquiries to: EDC Librarian
Direct tel: 01206 873181
Direct fax: 01206 872289

Founded:
1976

Organisation type and purpose:
University library.

Subject coverage:
Specialised EDC, concentrating on social and economic affairs.

Trade and statistical information:
UK and EC trade statistics.

Library catalogue:
All or part available online

Access to staff:
Contact by letter, by telephone, by fax and by e-mail. Appointment necessary.
Hours: Term time: Mon to Fri, 0900 to 2000; Sat, 0900 to 1800; Sun, 1400 to 1900

Access for disabled people:
Access to all public areas, toilet facilities

EUROPEAN DOCUMENTATION CENTRES

Organisation type and purpose:
European Documentation Centres (EDCs) are set up to stimulate European awareness and the study of Europe in academic institutions. They hold copies of all documentation on the Community legislative process that has been published by the European Commission. In addition they hold

preparatory documents and reports from the Commission, European Parliament and Economic and Social Committee. They do not hold stocks of documents for sale. Some produce guides and bulletins.

Contacts:
Aberdeen
Aberdeen University, Taylor Library, Dunbar Street, Aberdeen, AB9 2UE; tel: 01224 273819; fax: 01224 273819; e-mail: e.a.mackie@abdn.ac.uk
Aberystwyth
University of Wales, The Library, Hugh Owen Building, Penglais Campus, Aberystwyth, SY23 3DZ; tel: 01970 622401; fax: 01970 622404; e-mail: llis@aber.ac.uk
Ashford
Wye College, The Library, Wye, Ashford, Kent, TN25 5AH; tel: 01223 812401 ext 512; fax: 01223 813320; e-mail: w.sage@wye.ac.uk
Bath
Bath University, University Library, Claverton Down, Bath, BA2 7AY; tel: 01225 826826 ext 5594; fax: 01225 826229; e-mail: a.holbrook@bath.ac.uk
Belfast
Queen's University of Belfast, Main Library, Belfast, BT7 1LS; tel: 028 9024 5133 ext 3605; fax: 028 9032 3340; e-mail: a.mcmillan@qub.ac.uk
Birmingham
Birmingham University, Main Library, Edgbaston, Birmingham, B15 2TT; tel: 0121 414 7574 or 6570; fax: 0121 471 4691; e-mail: p.a.robinson@bham.ac.uk
Birmingham
University of Central England in Birmingham, William Kendrick Library, Perry Bar, Birmingham, B42 2SU; tel: 0121 331 5298; fax: 0121 356 2875; e-mail: linda.garratt@uce.ac.uk
Bradford
Bradford University, J B Priestley Library, Richmond Road, Bradford, West Yorkshire, BD7 1DP; tel: 01274 383402; fax: 01274 383398; e-mail: g.l.hudson@bradford.ac.uk
Brighton
University of Sussex, Library Information Services, Falmer, Brighton, East Sussex, BN1 9QL; tel: 01273 678159; fax: 01273 678441; e-mail: library@sussex.ac.uk
Bristol
Bristol University, Wills Memorial Library, Queen's Road, Bristol, BS8 1RJ; tel: 0117 928 7944; fax: 0117 925 1870; e-mail: sue.pettit@bristol.ac.uk
Cambridge
Cambridge University, University Library, West Road, Cambridge, CB3 9DR; tel: 01223 333138; fax: 01223 333160; e-mail: wan@ula.cam.ac.uk
Canterbury
University of Kent, Templeman Library, Canterbury, CT2 7NU; tel: 01227 764000 ext 3111; fax: 01227 823984; e-mail: s.h.carter@ukc.ac.uk
Cardiff
UWCC, The Guest Library, PO Box 430, Cardiff, CF1 3XT; tel: 029 2087 4262; fax: 029 2022 9340; e-mail: edc@cardiff.ac.uk and thomson@cardiff.ac.uk
Colchester
University of Essex, Albert Sloman Library, PO Box 24, Colchester, CO4 3UA; tel: 01206 873181; fax: 01206 872289; e-mail: helenb@essex.ac.uk
Coleraine
University of Ulster, The Library, Cromore Road, Coleraine, Co Londonderry, BT52 1SA; tel: 028 9132 4029; fax: 028 9132 4928; e-mail: p.j.compton@ulst.ac.uk
Coventry
University of Warwick, The Library, Gibbet Hill Road, Coventry, CV4 7AL; tel: 024 7652 3523 ext 2041; fax: 024 7652 4211; e-mail: j.bennett@warwick.ac.uk
Coventry
Coventry University, The Lanchester Library, Much Park Street, Coventry, CV1 2HF; tel: 024 7683 8295; fax: 024 7683 8686; e-mail: lbx029@coventry.ac.uk

continued overleaf

Dundee
  Dundee University, The Law Library, Perth
  Road, Dundee, DD1 4HN; tel: 01382 344102; fax:
  01382 228669; e-mail: a.duncan@dundee.ac.uk
Durham
  Durham University, The University Library,
  Stockton Road, Durham, DH1 3LY; tel: 0191 374
  3041/3044; fax: 0191 374 7481; e-mail: r.I.caddel@
  durham.ac.uk
Edinburgh
  Edinburgh University, Europa Library, Old
  College, South Bridge, Edinburgh, EH8 9YL; tel:
  0131 650 2041; fax: 0131 650 6343; e-mail: kdt@
  festival.ed.ac.uk
Exeter
  Exeter University, Law Library, Amory Building,
  Rennes Drive, Exeter, EX4 4RL; tel: 01392 263356;
  fax: 01392 263196; e-mail: p.c.overy@exeter.ac.uk
Glasgow
  Glasgow University, University Library, Hillhead
  Street, Glasgow, G12 8QE; tel: 0141 330 6722; fax:
  0141 330 4952; e-mail: gxlr30@lib.gla.ac.uk
Guildford
  Surrey University, George Edwards Library,
  Guildford, Surrey, GU2 5XH; tel: 01483 259233;
  fax: 01483 259500; e-mail: s.telfer@surrey.ac.uk
Hull
  Hull University, Brynmor Jones Library,
  Cottingham Road, Hull, HU6 7RX; tel: 01482
  465941; fax: 01482 466205; e-mail: w.m.carroll@
  lib.hull.ac.uk or e.b.davies@lib.hull.ac.uk
Keele
  Keele University, Library, Keele, Staffordshire,
  ST5 5BG; tel: 01782 583283; fax: 01782 711553; e-
  mail: b.g.finnemore@cc.keele.ac.uk
Lancaster
  Lancaster University, The Library, Bailrigg,
  Lancaster, LA1 4YH; tel: 01524 65201; fax: 01524
  63806; e-mail: m.dunne@lancaster.ac.uk
Leeds
  Leeds University, Faculty of Law Library, 20
  Lydon Terrace, Leeds, LS2 9JT; tel: 0113 233 5040;
  fax: 0113 233 5561; e-mail: j.m.porter@leeds.ac.uk
Leeds
  Leeds Metropolitan University, Calverley Street,
  Leeds, LS1 3HE; tel: 0113 283 3126; fax: 0113 283
  3123; e-mail: m.message@lmu.ac.uk
Leicester
  Leicester University, Library, University Road,
  Leicester, LE1 9RH; tel: 0116 252 2044; fax: 0116
  252 2066; e-mail: arsi@leic.ac.uk
London
  London School of Economics and Political
  Science, British Library of Political and Economic
  Science, 10 Portugal Street, London, WC2A 2HD;
  tel: 020 7955 7273 or 7229; fax: 020 7955 7454; e-
  mail: f.m.shipsey@lse.ac.uk
London
  University of London, Queen Mary and
  Westfield College Library, Mile End Road,
  London, E1 4NS; tel: 020 7775 3321; fax: 020 7981
  0028; e-mail: r.d.burns@qmw.ac.uk
Loughborough
  Loughborough University, Pilkington Library,
  Loughborough, Leicestershire, LE11 3TU; tel:
  01509 222352 or 222343; fax: 01509 234806; e-
  mail: l.a.mcgarry@lut.ac.uk
Manchester
  Manchester University, John Rylands University
  Library, Oxford Road, Manchester, M13 9PP; tel:
  0161 275 3770; fax: 0161 273 7488; e-mail: h.j
  .blackhurst@man.ac.uk
Newcastle
  University of Northumbria at Newcastle, The
  City Campus Library, Ellison Place, Newcastle
  upon Tyne, NE1 8ST; tel: 0191 227 4136; fax: 0191
  227 4563; e-mail: maimie.balfour@unn.ac.uk
Norwich
  University of East Anglia, University Library,
  University Plain, Norwich, Norfolk, NR4 7TJ; tel:
  01603 592412; fax: 01603 259490 (Library)
Nottingham
  Nottingham University, Hallward Library,
  Nottingham, NG7 2RD; tel: 0115 951 4579; fax:
  0115 951 4558; e-mail: susan.heaster@nottingham
  .ac.uk

Oxford
  Oxford University, Bodleian Law Library, St
  Cross Building, Oxford, OX1 3UR; tel: 01865
  271463; fax: 01865 271475; e-mail: elizabeth
  .martin@bodley.ox.ac.uk
Portsmouth
  Portsmouth University, The Frewen Library,
  Cambridge Road, Portsmouth, PO1 2ST; tel: 023
  9284 3239; fax: 023 9284 3233; e-mail: mayfield@
  libr.port.ac.uk
Reading
  Reading University, The Library, Whiteknights,
  PO Box 223, Reading, RG6 6AE; tel: 0118 931
  8782; fax: 0118 931 2335; e-mail: vlsedc@reading
  .ac.uk
Salford
  Salford University, The Library, Academic
  Information Servcies, Salford, M5 4WT; tel: 0161
  745 5846; fax: 0161 745 5888; e-mail: j.m.wilson@
  als.salford.ac.uk
Sheffield
  Sheffield Hallam University, The Library, Pond
  Street, Sheffield, S1 1WB; tel: 0114 253 2126; fax:
  0114 253 2125; e-mail: g.h.wills@shu.ac.uk
Southampton
  Southampton University, Hartley Library,
  Southampton, SO9 5NH; tel: 023 8059 3451; fax:
  023 8059 3939; e-mail: rfy@soton.ac.uk
Wolverhampton
  Wolverhampton University, Robert Scott Library,
  St Peter's Square, Wolverhampton, West
  Midlands, WV1 1RH; tel: 01902 322300; fax:
  01902 322668; e-mail: a.edwards@wlv.ac.uk

EUROPEAN FEDERATION OF FOUNDATION CONTRACTORS

Acronym or abbreviation: EFFC

Forum Court, 83 Copers Cope Road, Beckenham,
Kent, BR3 1NR

Tel: 020 8663 0948
Fax: 020 8663 0949
E-mail: effc@effc.org

Website:
http://www.effc.org

Enquiries:
Enquiries to: Secretary

Founded:
1988

Organisation type and purpose:
International organisation, trade association
(membership is by qualification), present number
of members: 17 countries, 350 companies.

Access to staff:
Contact by letter, by telephone, by fax and by e-
mail
Hours: Mon to Fri, 0900 to 1700

EUROPEAN FITTINGS MANUFACTURERS ASSOCIATION

Acronym or abbreviation: EFMA

55 Bryanston Street, London, W1H 7AA

Tel: 020 7868 8930
Fax: 020 7868 8819
E-mail: efma@coppercouncil.org

Enquiries:
Enquiries to: Secretary

Formerly called:
European Capillary Fittings Manufacturers
Association (ECFMA)

Organisation type and purpose:
International organisation, trade association,
present number of members: 4.

Access to staff:
Contact by letter, by telephone, by fax and by e-
mail. Appointment necessary. Access for members
only.
Hours: Mon to Fri, 0900 to 1700

EUROPEAN FLEXIBLE INTERMEDIATE BULK CONTAINER ASSOCIATION

Acronym or abbreviation: EFIBCA

18 Wellesley Road, Colchester, Essex, CO3 3HF

Tel: 01206 575584
Fax: 01206 575584
E-mail: efibca@aspects.net

Website:
http://www.efibca.com

Enquiries:
Enquiries to: Director General

Founded:
1983

Organisation type and purpose:
Trade association (membership is by qualification),
present number of members: 36.

Subject coverage:
Flexible intermediate bulk containers.

Printed publications:
Safe Use of Flexible Intermediate Bulk Containers
  (FIBCs, Issue 2, 2002, £5)

Access to staff:
Contact by letter, by telephone, by fax and by e-
mail
Hours: Mon to Fri, 0900 to 1700

EUROPEAN GENERAL GALVANIZERS ASSOCIATION

Acronym or abbreviation: EGGA

Maybrook House, 97 Godstone Road, Caterham,
Surrey, CR3 6RE

Tel: 01883 331277
Fax: 01883 331287
E-mail: mail@egga.com

Website:
http://www.egga.com
Newsletter and information

Enquiries:
Enquiries to: Director

Organisation type and purpose:
Trade association.

Subject coverage:
Galvanizing.

Printed publications:
Conference proceedings vols available
International Galvanizing

Access to staff:
Contact by letter, by fax and by e-mail
Hours: Mon to Fri, 0830 to 1630

EUROPEAN GUILD

Acronym or abbreviation: Euroguild

Media House, 11b High Street, Sandbach,
Cheshire, CW11 1HH

Tel: 01270 753133
Fax: 01270 753444
E-mail: europeanguild@tesco.net

Enquiries:
Enquiries to: Administrator
Direct tel: 01270 753444

Founded:
1988

Formerly called:
European Guild of Media and Marketing,
European Guild of Sales and Marketing

Organisation type and purpose:
International organisation, membership
association (membership is by subscription),
service industry, training organisation,
consultancy, research organisation.

Support to develop new projects in Europe with PR, VT production and in rare cases sponsorship, TV, radio, newspapers, tourism attractions, music, art.

Subject coverage:
Radio development, applications for licence etc, design and production of tourist attractions, voice/over production (in-house), VT production, public relations, tourism development.

Printed publications:
Various available on request

Electronic and video publications:
Tape, Disk, CD-ROM, Video for purchase

Access to staff:
Contact by letter, by telephone, by fax and by e-mail. Letter of introduction required.
Hours: Mon to Fri, 0930 to 1700
Special comments: A charge of £10 per hour or 17 Euros may apply for certain assistance.

Access to building, collection or gallery:
Prior appointment required

EUROPEAN INFORMATION ASSOCIATION

Acronym or abbreviation: EIA

Central Library, St Peter's Square, Manchester, M2 5PD

Tel: 0161 228 3691
Fax: 0161 236 6547
E-mail: eia@libraries.manchester.gov.uk

Website:
http://www.eia.org.uk
Information about EIA's products and services. Includes up-to-date news about the EU and a currency converter.

Founded:
1980

Formerly called:
Association of European Documentation Centre Librarians (year of change 1991)

Organisation type and purpose:
Membership association (membership is by subscription), present number of members: 500, registered charity (charity number 294502).
To assist information workers dealing with European information to network, share experience and train. To improve EU information provision.

Subject coverage:
The European Union, its policies and legislative process.

Publications list:
Available online and in print

Access to staff:
Contact by letter, by telephone, by fax, by e-mail and via website. Access for members only.
Hours: Mon to Fri, 0900 to 1700
Special comments: Please phone before personal visits.

EUROPEAN INSTITUTE OF GOLF COURSE ARCHITECTS

Acronym or abbreviation: EIGCA

Meadow View House, Tannery Lane, Bramley, Surrey, GU5 0AJ

Tel: 01483 891831
Fax: 01483 891846
E-mail: info@eigca.org

Website:
http://www.eigca.org
Golf course architecture.

Enquiries:
Enquiries to: Executive Officer

Founded:
2000

Created by the merger of:
British Institute of Golf Course Architects (BIGCA), Association Française des Architectes de Golf (AFAG), European Society of Golf Architects (ESGA) (year of change 2000)

Formerly called:
British Association of Golf Course Architects (BAGCA)

Organisation type and purpose:
International organisation, advisory body, professional body (membership is by subscription, qualification, election or invitation), present number of members: 133, training organisation, consultancy.

Subject coverage:
Design of golf courses.

Information services:
The Librarian is happy to help with any enquiries relating to golf course architecture.

Museum or gallery collection, archive, or library special collection:
The EIGCA Library contains some 800 books and a dozen or so journals on golf course architecture and related subjects. Of particular interest is the collection of golf club histories generally produced to mark a club's centenary, which now numbers over 300 titles.

Non-library collection catalogue:
All or part available online

Library catalogue:
All or part available online

Printed publications:
Information leaflets

Electronic and video publications:
E-mail newsletter
Order electronic and video publications from: the website

Access to staff:
Contact by letter, by telephone, by fax, by e-mail and via website. Appointment necessary.
Hours: Mon to Fri, 0930 to 1430

Access to building, collection or gallery:
Prior appointment required

EUROPEAN LEAD SHEET INDUSTRY ASSOCIATION

Acronym or abbreviation: ELSIA

c/o 17A Welbeck Way, London, W1G 9YJ

Tel: 020 7499 8422
Fax: 020 7493 1555
E-mail: enq@elsia.org

Website:
http://www.elsia-web.org

Enquiries:
Enquiries to: Administrator

Founded:
1985

Organisation type and purpose:
Trade association.

Subject coverage:
Applications and specifications of rolled lead sheet in the construction industry.

Access to staff:
Contact by letter, by telephone, by fax, by e-mail and via website. Appointment necessary.
Hours: Mon to Fri, 0900 to 1700

EUROPEAN LEISURE SOFTWARE PUBLISHERS ASSOCIATION

Acronym or abbreviation: ELSPA

Station Road, Offenham, Evesham, Worcestershire, WR11 8JJ

Tel: 01386 830642
Fax: 01386 833871

E-mail: info@elspa.com

Website:
http://www.elspa.com

Enquiries:
Enquiries to: Deputy Director General
Direct tel: 01386 835811
Direct e-mail: press@ukie.info

Organisation type and purpose:
Trade association.

Subject coverage:
Publishing and development of computer and video games.

Trade and statistical information:
Sales data for computer and video games.

Printed publications:
European Leisure Software Yearbook (available to purchase)

Access to staff:
Contact by letter, by telephone, by fax and by e-mail
Hours: Mon to Fri, 0900 to 1700

EUROPEAN LIQUID WATERPROOFING ASSOCIATION

Acronym or abbreviation: ELWA

Fields House, Gower Road, Haywards Heath, West Sussex, RH16 4PL

Tel: 01444 417458
Fax: 01444 415616
E-mail: info@elwassociation.org.uk

Website:
http://www.elwassociation.org.uk
List of members.

Enquiries:
Enquiries to: Secretary

Founded:
1979

Formerly called:
Bituminous Roof Coatings Manufacturers Association; European Liquid Roofing Association

Organisation type and purpose:
Trade association.
Seeks to raise the level of awareness of the technical and financial benefits of specifying liquid waterproofing systems and to establish product and installation standards.

Subject coverage:
Bituminous and polymer-based waterproofing membranes, codes of practice, installation, specification and application.

Printed publications:
Code of Practice – Liquid Waterproofing Membranes (free of charge)

Access to staff:
Contact by letter, by telephone, by fax, by e-mail and via website
Hours: Mon to Fri, 0900 to 1700

Affiliated to:
Flat Roofing Alliance (FRA)
Fields House, Gower Road, Haywards Heath, West Sussex, RH16 4PL; tel: 01444 440027; fax: 01444 415616

EUROPEAN MARKETING SYSTEMS

Acronym or abbreviation: EMS

100 New Kings Road, London, SW6 4LX

Tel: 020 7736 0350
E-mail: ems@emsbase.co.uk

Website:
http://www.emsbase.co.uk

Enquiries:
Enquiries to: Managing Director

continued overleaf

Founded:
1991

Organisation type and purpose:
Service industry, consultancy.
Database agency for corporate marketing.

Subject coverage:
Corporate data for marketing to the UK and
Europe, Central and Eastern Europe, energy and
environmental industries and financial sectors,
telecoms and IT sectors, government and EU across
Europe.

**Museum or gallery collection, archive, or library
special collection:**
News extracts on Central and Eastern Europe
(1989 to date)

Electronic and video publications:
E-LIST – 12,000 contacts involved in e-commerce
CITY LIST & OFFSHORE – 16,000 financial and
banking contacts in Europe
EASTBASE – database of 15,000 contacts trading in
or with Central and Eastern Europe
ENERGY – 8000 contacts in oil, gas, renewable,
nuclear & energy industries, carbon exchange,
NGOs & regulators
EUROBASE – companies and organisations that
are active on a national or transnational scale,
use English as a commercial language, are of a
size or standing to be essential commercial
prospects
EUROPEAN GOVERNMENT – database of over
20,000 Ministries, Embassies, EU and public
offices
TELEBASE – database of 10,000 IT/Telecoms
contacts in the commercial sector
The Green Route (EUROGREEN) – database of
29,000 organisations with an interest in
environmental issues

Publications list:
Available in print

Access to staff:
Contact by letter, by telephone, by e-mail and via
website. Appointment necessary.
Hours: Mon to Fri, 0900 to 1800 (24-hr
answerphone)

Subsidiary body:
EPIC books

EUROPEAN MOVEMENT
(SCOTTISH COUNCIL)

12B Cumberland Street, South East Lane,
Edinburgh, EH3 6RU

Tel: 0131 557 9790
Fax: 0131 557 9790
E-mail: scotland@euromove.org.uk

Enquiries:
Enquiries to: National Organiser

Founded:
1990

Organisation type and purpose:
International organisation, membership
association (membership is by subscription),
present number of members: 430, voluntary
organisation.
Independent, cross-party, membership
organisation which believes in European unity and
seeks to ensure that Scotland's interests are
safeguarded and developed as Europe evolves.

Subject coverage:
The European Union, Europe, information and
activities for schools and universities. Visiting
speakers including senior European figures. Study
visits to Europe. Annual conference and dinner.
Links with other national and international
councils. Regular newsletters and information
packs.

Access to staff:
Contact by letter, by telephone, by fax and by e-
mail
Hours: Tue to Thu, 0900 to 1600

EUROPEAN ORTHODONTIC
SOCIETY

Acronym or abbreviation: EOS

Flat 20, 49 Hallam Street, London, W1W 6JN

Tel: 020 7637 0367
Fax: 020 7637 0367
E-mail: eoslondon@aol.com

Enquiries:
Enquiries to: Honorary Secretary

Founded:
1907

Organisation type and purpose:
International organisation, professional body
(membership is by subscription), registered charity
(charity number 238836), training organisation,
research organisation.

Subject coverage:
Orthodontics, orthodontic services in Europe.

Printed publications:
European Journal of Orthodontics (6 times a year,
OUP)

Electronic and video publications:
Asksam list of orthodontic literature

Publications list:
Available in print

Access to staff:
Contact by letter, by telephone, by fax and by e-
mail
Hours: Mon to Fri, 0900 to 1700

EUROPEAN PARLIAMENT UK
OFFICE

2 Queen Anne's Gate, London, SW1H 9AA

Tel: 020 7227 4300
Fax: 020 7227 4302
E-mail: eplondon@europarl.europa.eu

Website:
http://www.europarl.org.uk
http://www.europarl.europa.eu
EUROPARL database.

Enquiries:
Enquiries to: Librarian
Direct fax: 020 7227 4301

Organisation type and purpose:
European institution, European Parliament press
and information office.

Subject coverage:
Reports, debates and minutes of the European
Parliament, EP activities in Committee and
elsewhere, election results and systems for the EP
elections.

**Museum or gallery collection, archive, or library
special collection:**
EP reports from 1979, debates and minutes from
1973

Printed publications:
The European Parliament and Business (2003)
The Future Enlargement of the European Union
(2002)
The European Parliament and the Environment
(2002)
The European Parliament and Young People (2002)
The European Parliament and Your MEPs (2003)
EU MAP: European elections 10 June 2004 (2002)
The Eight Scottish MEPs and the European
Parliament (1999)
The Right to Petition the European Parliament

Electronic and video publications:
The European Parliament and Business (2003)
The Future Enlargement of the European Union
(2002)
The European Parliament and the Environment
(2002)
The European Parliament and Young People (2002)
The European Parliament and Your MEPs (2003)
EU MAP: European elections 10 June 2004 (2002)

The Right to Petition the European Parliament

Publications list:
Available online and in print

Access to staff:
Contact by letter, by telephone, by fax, by e-mail
and in person
Hours: Mon to Fri, 1000 to 1300, 1400 to 1730

EUROPEAN PHENOLIC FOAM
ASSOCIATION

Acronym or abbreviation: EPFA

Tournai Hall, Evelyn Woods Road, Aldershot,
Hampshire, GU11 2LL

Tel: 01252 357837
Fax: 01252 357831
E-mail: admin@epfa.org.uk

Website:
http://www.epfa.org.uk

Enquiries:
Enquiries to: Honorary Secretary

Founded:
before 1989

Formerly called:
Phenolic Foam Manufacturers Association (PFMA)

Organisation type and purpose:
Trade association, present number of members: 8.
Members all share an interest in phenolic foam
products, either as producers or as providers of
raw materials.

Subject coverage:
Phenolic foam in insulation applications, its use
based on the technical data available especially
that relating to performance in fire.

Printed publications:
Several data sheets on the use of phenolic foam

Publications list:
Available online and in print

Access to staff:
Contact by letter, by telephone, by fax, by e-mail
and via website
Hours: Mon to Fri, 0900 to 1700

EUROPEAN PIANO TEACHERS'
ASSOCIATION, UK LIMITED

Acronym or abbreviation: EPTA UK

35 The Warren, Burgess Hill, West Sussex, RH15
0DU

Tel: 08456 581054
Fax: 08456 581054
E-mail: admin@epta-uk.org

Website:
http://www.epta-uk.org
Membership, Piano Professional, events.

Enquiries:
Enquiries to: Administrator
Other contacts: Chairman for policy matters.

Founded:
1978

Organisation type and purpose:
International organisation, membership
association (membership is by election or
invitation), registered charity (charity number
293698), suitable for ages: 6+.

Subject coverage:
Piano teaching and performance.

**Museum or gallery collection, archive, or library
special collection:**
Extensive collection of audio and video tapes,
books and other printed matter available for
reference by members only

Printed publications:
Members' Handbook (annually, free to members,
others £4 per copy)

Piano Professional (3 times a year, free to members, others £3.75 per issue)

Electronic and video publications:
Membership list (for purchase, members only)

Publications list:
Available in print

Access to staff:
Contact by letter, by telephone, by fax and by e-mail
Hours: Mon to Fri, 0900 to 1700

Access to building, collection or gallery:
Prior appointment required

Has:
31 Regional Organisers

Members reference collection:
Piano Teachers Information Centre
London College of Music, St Mary's Road, Ealing, London, W5 5RF; tel: 020 8231 2648

Parent body:
European Piano Teachers' Association
Secretary, 34 Carver Road, London, SE24 9LT; tel: 020 7274 6821; fax: 020 7737 5015

EUROPEAN POLICY FORUM LIMITED

125 Pall Mall, London, SW1Y 5EA

Tel: 020 7839 7565
Fax: 020 7839 7339
E-mail: epfltd@compuserve.com

Website:
http://www.epfltd.org

Enquiries:
Enquiries to: President

Founded:
1992

Organisation type and purpose:
Research organisation.
International research institute.

Printed publications:
For purchase only

Publications list:
Available in print

Access to staff:
Contact by letter, by telephone, by fax, by e-mail and via website. Appointment necessary.
Hours: Mon to Fri, 0900 to 1700

Access to building, collection or gallery:
No prior appointment required

EUROPEAN PUBLIC INFORMATION RELAYS

Organisation type and purpose:
Based in public libraries to provide the general public with access to information about EU policies and programmes.

England East Midlands:
Chesterfield
tel: 01246 209292
Derby
tel: 01332 255398
Grimsby
tel: 01472 323600
Leicester
tel: 0116 255 6699
Lincoln
tel: 01522 549160
Matlock
Derbyshire; tel: 01629 580000 ext 6578
Northampton
tel: 01604 30404
Nottingham
tel: 0115 941 2121
Oakham
Rutland; tel: 01572 723654

Scarborough
tel: 01724 860161

England Eastern:
Bedford
tel: 01234 350931
Cambridge
tel: 01223 712017
Chelmsford
tel: 01245 492758
Dunstable
tel: 01582 477073
Hatfield
tel: 01707 281558
Ipswich
tel: 01473 583705
King's Lynn
tel: 01553 772568 or 761393
Luton
tel: 01582 454580
Norwich
Norfolk; tel: 01603 215255
Peterborough
tel: 01733 348343

England Greater London:
Barking
tel: 020 8517 8666
Battersea
tel: 020 8871 7467
Bexley Heath
tel: 020 8301 5151
Brixton
tel: 020 7926 1067
Bromley
Kent; tel: 020 8460 9955 ext 250
City
tel: 020 7638 8215
Croydon
tel: 020 8760 5400
Ealing
tel: 020 8567 3656
Elephant & Castle
tel: 020 7708 0516
Enfield
tel: 020 8443 1701
Hackney
tel: 020 8525 2576
Hammersmith
tel: 020 8576 5053
Harringay
tel: 020 8365 1155
Harrow
tel: 020 8424 1055/6
Hendon
tel: 020 8359 2883
Highbury
tel: 020 7619 6931
Ilford
tel: 020 8478 7145 ext 222
Kensington
tel: 020 7937 2542
Kingston
tel: 020 8547 6425
Lewisham
tel: 020 8297 9430
Marylebone
tel: 020 7641 1039
Morden
tel: 020 8545 4089
Richmond
tel: 020 8940 5529
Romford
Essex; tel: 01708 772393/4
Stratford
tel: 020 8519 6346
Sutton
Surrey; tel: 020 8770 4785
Swiss Cottage
London; tel: 020 7413 6527
Uxbridge
tel: 01895 250603
Walthamstow
tel: 020 8520 3017
Wembley
Middlesex; tel: 020 8937 3500
Westminster
tel: 020 7641 2034
Woolwich
tel: 020 8312 5750

England North East:
Altrincham
Cheshire; tel: 0161 912 5923
Ashton-under-Lyne
tel: 0161 342 2031
Darlington
tel: 01325 462034
Durham
tel: 0191 383 4231
Gateshead
Tyne & Wear; tel: 0191 477 3478
Hartlepool
tel: 01429 272905
Middlesbrough
tel: 01642 263364
Morpeth
tel: 01670 512385
Newcastle upon Tyne
tel: 0191 261 0691
North Shields
tel: 0191 200 5424
South Shields
tel: 0191 427 1818 ext 2133
Sunderland
tel: 0191 514 8435

England North West:
Birkenhead
tel: 0151 652 6106
Bolton
Lancashire; tel: 01204 522173
Crosby
tel: 0151 928 6487/8
Ellesmere Port
tel: 0151 356 7606
Knowsley
tel: 0151 443 3738
Liverpool
tel: 0151 225 5435
Manchester
tel: 0161 234 1996
Oldham
tel: 0161 911 4643
Preston
Lancashire; tel: 01772 404010
Salford
tel: 0161 793 3016
Southport
tel: 0151 934 2119
St Helens
Merseyside; tel: 01744 456989/51
Stockport
tel: 0161 474 4524
Warrington
tel: 01925 442889
Wigan
tel: 01942 827619/27
Workington
Cumbria; tel: 01900 325170/77

England South East:
Aylesbury
tel: 01296 383252
Bracknell
tel: 01344 423149
Brighton
East Sussex; tel: 01273 296969
Camberley
tel: 01276 683626
Hastings
tel: 01424 716481
Maidenhead
tel: 01628 625657
Maidstone
Kent; tel: 01622 696503/511
Milton Keynes
tel: 01908 835008
Newbury
tel: 01635 40972
Newport
Isle of Wight; tel: 01983 823800
Oxford
tel: 01865 810182
Reading
Berkshire; tel: 0118 923 3234
Slough
Berkshire; tel: 01753 535166
Southampton
tel: 023 8083 2958

continued overleaf

Worthing
Sussex; tel: 01903 212414

England South West:
Bristol
tel: 0117 929 9148
Dorchester
Dorset; tel: 01305 224448
Exeter
tel: 01392 384206
Gloucester
tel: 01452 425027
Plymouth
Devon; tel: 01752 305906
Poole
Dorset; tel: 01202 671496
Swindon
Wiltshire; tel: 01793 463240
Taunton
Somerset; tel: 01823 336354
Trowbridge
Wiltshire; tel: 01225 713727
Truro
Cornwall; tel: 01872 272702
Yate
Bristol; tel: 01454 865818

England West Midlands:
Birmingham
tel: 0121 235 4545/6
Coventry
tel: 024 7683 2325
Dudley
tel: 01384 815554/560
Kidderminster
tel: 01562 512900
Nuneaton
tel: 024 7638 4027
Shrewsbury
Shropshire; tel: 01743 255380
Solihull
tel: 0121 704 6974
Stafford
tel: 01785 278351
Stoke-on-Trent
tel: 01782 238431
Walsall
tel: 01922 653110
West Bromwich
tel: 01902 322300
Wolverhampton
tel: 01902 312026

England Yorkshire:
Barnsley
South Yorkshire; tel: 01226 773935
Beverley
tel: 01482 885081
Bradford
West Yorkshire; tel: 01274 383402
Doncaster
tel: 01302 734320
Halifax
tel: 01422 392631/2
Huddersfield
tel: 01484 221967
Hull
tel: 01482 883025
Leeds
tel: 0113 247 8282
Northallerton
North Yorkshire; tel: 01609 776202
Rotherham
tel: 01709 823614
Scarborough
North Yorkshire; tel: 01723 364285
Sheffield
tel: 0114 273 4736

Northern Ireland:
Ballymena
tel: 028 2532 3456
Ballynahinch
tel: 028 9756 6400
Belfast
tel: 028 9024 3233
Omagh
tel: 028 8224 4821
Portadown
tel: 028 3833 5247

Scotland:
Aberdeen
tel: 01224 652534
Alloa
tel: 01259 722262
Ardrossan
tel: 01294 469137
Ayr
tel: 01292 282109
Bathgate
tel: 01506 776335
Bearsden
tel: 0141 943 0121
Carrick
tel: 01292 288820
Clydebank
tel: 0141 952 1416 or 8765
Clydesdale
tel: 01555 661144
Cumbernauld
tel: 01236 725664
Cummock & Doon
tel: 01290 422111
Cupar
tel: 01334 653722 ext 111
Dumbarton
tel: 01389 763129
Dumfries
tel: 01387 253820
Dundee
tel: 01382 434336
Dunfermline
tel: 01383 723661
Dunoon
tel: 01436 679567
East Kilbride
tel: 01355 220046
Eastwood
tel: 0141 638 6511
Edinburgh
tel: 0131 225 5584
Elgin
tel: 01343 542746
Falkirk
tel: 01324 503605/08
Forfar
tel: 01307 461460
Galashiels
tel: 01896 752512
Giffnock
tel: 0141 544 4976
Glasgow
G3; tel: 0141 287 2850
Glasgow
G2; tel: 0141 621 3424
Glenrothes
tel: 01592 755866
Greenock
tel: 01475 726211
Haddington
tel: 01620 828202
Hamilton
tel: 01698 452403
Inverness
tel: 01463 235713
Kilmarnock
tel: 01563 526401
Kirkcaldy
tel: 01592 412879
Kirkintilloch
tel: 0141 776 8090
Kirkwall
Orkney; tel: 01856 873166
Lanark
tel: 01555 661144
Lerwick
Shetlands; tel: 01595 693868
Loanhead
tel: 0131 225 5584
Mephil
tel: 01333 592470
Monklands
tel: 01236 424150 or 434847
Moray
tel: 01343 544475
Motherwell
tel: 01698 251311

Oldmeldrum
tel: 01651 872707
Paisley
tel: 0141 889 2360
Perth
tel: 01738 477060
Selkirk
tel: 01750 20842
Stepps
tel: 0141 304 1800
Stirling
tel: 01786 432106
Stornoway
Lewis; tel: 01851 703064

Wales:
Barry
tel: 01446 735722
Blackwood
tel: 01495 223345
Bodlondeb
tel: 01492 860101
Bridgend
tel: 01656 767451
Caernarfon
tel: 01286 679465
Cardiff
tel: 029 2038 2116
Cwnbran
tel: 01633 867584
Ebbw Vale
tel: 01495 303069
Llanelli
tel: 01554 773538
Llangefni
tel: 01248 752092
Merthyr Tydfil
tel: 01685 723057
Mold
tel: 01352 704400
Neath
tel: 01639 764230
Newport
tel: 01633 211376
Rhyl
tel: 01745 353814
Swansea
tel: 01792 655521
Wrexham
tel: 01978 261932

EUROPEAN REFERENCE CENTRES

Organisation type and purpose:
The European Reference Centres (ERCs) hold
collections of EC documents.

Other addresses:
Aberystwyth
European Liaison Office, University College of
Wales Aberystwyth, Laura Place, Aberystwyth,
SY23 3AX; tel: 01970 622401; fax: 01970 623364
Brighton
Brighton Central Library, Reference Library and
Information Service, Church Street, Brighton,
East Sussex, BN1 2UE; tel: 01273 601197; fax:
01273 695882
Chalfont St Giles
Buckinghamshire College of Higher Education,
Library, Newlands Park, Chalfont St Giles,
Buckinghamshire, HP8 4AD; fax: 01494 874441
Chelmsford
Anglia Polytechnic University, Victoria Road
South, Chelmsford, Essex, CM1 1LL; tel: 01245
493131 ext 3757; fax: 01245 490935
Edinburgh
National Library of Scotland, George IV Bridge,
Edinburgh, EH1 1EW; tel: 0131 650 2041; fax:
0131 667 9780
Exmouth
The European Reference Centre, University of
Plymouth Library, Exmouth Campus, Douglas
Avenue, Exmouth, Devon, EX8 2AT; tel: 01395
255352
Halifax
Calderdale College, Francis Street, Halifax, West
Yorkshire, HX1 3UZ; tel: 01422 358221 ext 2117

Hatfield
Hertfordshire University, College Lane, Hatfield, Hertfordshire, AL10 9AD; tel: 01707 84678; fax: 01707 284670
Ipswich
Suffolk County Reference Library, Northgate Street, Ipswich, Suffolk, IP1 3DE; tel: 01473 583705; fax: 01473 583700
London
Thames Valley University, Ealing Campus, St Mary's Road, Ealing, London, W5 5RF; tel: 020 8231 2246; fax: 020 8231 2631
Middlesbrough
Teesside University, Borough Road, Middlesbrough, Cleveland, TS1 3BA; tel: 01642 218123; fax: 01642 342067
Northampton
Nene College, Boughton Green Road, Moulton Park, Northampton, NN2 7AL; tel: 01604 715000; fax: 01604 720636
Preston
University of Central Lancashire, Library and Resources Service, St Peter's Square, Preston, Lancashire, PR1 2TQ; tel: 01772 53191/22141
Reading
Reading University, Bulmershe Library, Woodlands Avenue, Reading, RG6 1HY; tel: 0118 931 8651
Sheffield
Sheffield University, Crookesmoor Library, Crookesmoor Building, PO Box 598, Sheffield, S10 1FL; tel: 0114 276 8555 ext 6779; fax: 0114 275 4670
Stirling
Stirling University, Library, Stirling, FK9 4LA; tel: 01786 467227; fax: 01786 466866
Swansea
University College of Swansea, Natural Sciences Library, Singleton Park, Swansea, SA2 8PP; tel: 01792 205678 ext 4037
Wrexham
European Reference Centre, North East Wales Institute of Higher Education, Information Services, Plas Coch, Mold Lane, Wrexham, Clwyd, LL11 2AW; tel: 01978 293261 or 293237; fax: 01978 293254

EUROPEAN REGIONS AIRLINE ASSOCIATION

Acronym or abbreviation: ERAA

The Baker Suite, Fairoaks Airport, Chobham, Woking, Surrey, GU24 8HX

Tel: 01276 856495
Fax: 01276 857038
E-mail: info@eraa.org

Website:
http://www.eraa.org
Background information on ERA, statistics, press releases, fleet data, presentations and briefings, publications content descriptions. Member contact details and how to join. Calendar of events, members news.

Enquiries:
Enquiries to: Corporate Communications Manager
Direct e-mail: lesley.shepherd@eraa.org
Other contacts: Director General

Founded:
1980

Formerly called:
European Regional Airline Association

Organisation type and purpose:
Trade association.
To protect and promote the interests of regional airlines throughout Europe.
To be the principal body representing the interests of organisations involved in air transport in Europe's regions.

Subject coverage:
Airlines, air safety issues, operations, maintenance, infrastructure, environmental issues, air transport policy.

Trade and statistical information:
Traffic statistics of European regional airlines and airports (ERA members only).

Printed publications:
ERA Yearbook (reference guide and contact details of members)
Performance (statistical publication, quarterly)
Regional International (newsletter, monthly)

Publications list:
Available online

Access to staff:
Contact by letter, by telephone, by fax, by e-mail and via website
Hours: Mon to Fri, 0800 to 1730

EUROPEAN RELAY CENTRES

Made up of:
European Documentation Centres
European Public Information Relays
European Reference Centres

EUROPEAN RESOURCE CENTRES FOR SCHOOLS & COLLEGES

Central Bureau for Educational Visits and Exchanges, 10 Spring Gardens, London, SW1A 2BN

Tel: 020 7389 4004

Organisation type and purpose:
To provide teachers and pupils with information on Europe, and to support the development of the European dimension in the curriculum.

Museum or gallery collection, archive, or library special collection:
Extensive stocks of directories, journals, books and brochures on Europe, the EU and European issues

Printed publications:
Brochures on EU institutions, EU countries, and statistical information (free)

Contacts:
East Anglia (ACER)
The Association of Colleges in the Eastern Region, Merlin Place, Milton Road, Cambridge, CB4 4DP; tel: 01223 424022; fax: 01223 423389
East Midlands
Leicestershire Comenius Centre, Quorn Hall, Meynell Road, Quorn, Leicestershire, LE12 8BG; tel: 01509 416950; fax: 01509 416993
London and the Home Counties
Kent County Council Education Department, Springfield, Maidstone, Kent, ME14 2LJ; tel: 01622 605704; fax: 01622 605704
London and the Home Counties
Wheathampstead Education Centre (drop-in centre only), Butterfield Road, Wheathampstead, St Albans, Hertfordshire, AL4 8PY
London and the Home Counties
Colchester Curriculum Development Centre (drop-in centre only, telephone to arrange a visit), Acacia Avenue, Greenstead, Colchester, CO4 3TQ; tel: 01206 863839
London and the Home Counties
Central Bureau (written and telephone enquiries only), 10 Spring Gardens, London, SW1A 2BN; tel: 020 7389 4697 or 4723; fax: 020 7389 4426
London and the Home Counties (CiLT)
Centre for Information on Language Teaching and Research, (drop-in centre only), 20 Bedfordbury, London, WC2N 4LB; tel: 020 7379 5110
North East
European Information and Education Centre, John Smith House, 1 South View, Jarrow, NE32 5JP; tel: 0191 420 1711/428 2436; fax: 0191 489 0643
North West
European Information Unit (drop-in centre only), Central Library, St Peter's Square, Manchester, M2 5PD

North West
Liverpool Quality Assurance Service, Dulcie Cottages, Riverside Road, Liverpool, L19 3QN; tel: 0151 225 8110; fax: 0151 494 2846
Southern
West Sussex County Council, Education Department, County Hall, Chichester, PO19 1RF; tel: 01243 777578; fax: 01243 777229
Southern
International Education Office, The Hucclecote Centre, Churchdown Lane, Hucclecote, Gloucester, GL3 3QN; tel: 01452 427204 or 427270; fax: 01452 427204
Wales
Ysgol Leithoedd Modern, School of Modern Languages, Prifysgol Cymru, Bangor, Gwynedd, LL57 2DG; tel: 01248 383874; fax: 01248 382551
Wales
National Comenius Centre of Wales, WJEC, 245 Western Avenue, Cardiff, CF5 2YX; tel: 029 2026 5043; fax: 029 2057 6201
West Midlands
Matthew Boulton College, 3rd Floor, Magnolia House, 73 Conybere Street, Birmingham, B12 0YL; tel: 0121 446 3400; fax: 0121 446 3401
Yorkshire & Humberside
Elmete Professional Development Centre, Elmete Lane, Leeds, LS8 2LJ; tel: 0113 214 4072; fax: 0113 214 4069
Yorkshire & Humberside
Hull University, Curriculum Development, Brynmor Jones Library, Cottingham Road, Hull, HU6 7RX; tel: 01482 466843; fax: 01482 466839

Incorporates the:
UK Centre for European Education Partners Overseas

Parent body:
British Council

EUROPEAN SCHOOL OF OSTEOPATHY

Formal name: Osteopathic Education and Research Limited
Acronym or abbreviation: ESO

Boxley House, Boxley, Kent, ME14 3DZ

Tel: 01622 671558
Fax: 01622 662165
E-mail: library@eso.ac.uk

Website:
http://www.eso.ac.uk

Enquiries:
Enquiries to: Library Supervisor

Founded:
1973

Formerly called:
Ecole Européenne d'Ostéopathie (EEO)

Organisation type and purpose:
Registered charity. College of higher education.

Subject coverage:
Osteopathy and other manual and alternative medical therapies.

Library catalogue:
All or part available in-house

Access to staff:
Contact by letter, by telephone, by fax and by e-mail. Appointment necessary.
Hours: Mon to Fri, 0900 to 1700
Special comments: No loans to non-members.

Also at:
European School of Osteopathy Clinic
104 Tonbridge Road, Maidstone, Kent, ME16 8SL; tel: 01622 685913; fax: 01622 661812

EUROPEAN STUDIES PROGRAMME

The Southern Education and Library Board, 3 Charlemont Place, The Mall, Armagh, BT61 9AX

Tel: 028 3751 2247

continued overleaf

Fax: 028 3751 2285
E-mail: office@esp.dnet.co.uk

Website:
http://www.european-studies.org

Enquiries:
Enquiries to: Information Officer

Founded:
1986

Formerly called:
European Studies (Ireland and Great Britain)
Project

Organisation type and purpose:
Membership association (membership is by
election or invitation), present number of
members: 500 schools, suitable for ages: 11 to 18.
European Studies is a joint partnership between
the Dept of Education NI and Dept of Education
ROI promoting joint study and communication
among students and teachers in 20 different
jurisdications, aiming to promote mutal
understanding, awareness and tolerance in the
youth of contemporary Europe.

Subject coverage:
Various units of study/topics in both the junior and
senior programmes have been designed to assist
students in examining not only areas of shared
interest today, but also areas of conflict in the past.
They are intended to broaden the student's
knowledge and understanding of their own place
and their relationship to others in the Europe of
today.

Publications list:
Available in print

Access to staff:
Contact by letter, by telephone, by fax, by e-mail
and via website
Hours: Mon to Fri, 0900 to 1700

Access to building, collection or gallery:
Prior appointment required

Access for disabled people:
Ramped entry

EUROPEAN-ATLANTIC GROUP

Acronym or abbreviation: E-AG

4 St Paul's Way, Finchley, London, N3 2PP

Tel: 020 8632 9253
Fax: 020 8343 3532
E-mail: info@eag.org.uk

Website:
http://www.eag.org.uk

Enquiries:
Enquiries to: Director

Founded:
1954

Organisation type and purpose:
Registered charity (charity number 274898).
Provides a regular forum in the United Kingdom
for informed discussion between European and
Atlantic countries.
Discusses problems and possibilities for better
economic, strategic and political co-operation with
each other and with the rest of the world.
Disseminates authoritative information concerning
the work of international organisations, such as the
Council of Europe, the North Atlantic Treaty
Organization, the Organisation for Economic Co-
operation and Development, the European Union,
the World Trade Organization and the
Organization for European Security and Co-
operation.

Subject coverage:
Economic, strategic and political co-operation
between European and Atlantic countries, and
with the rest of the world.

Printed publications:
European-Atlantic Journal
Hitler and King Boris of Bulgaria
Order printed publications from: E-AG office

Publications list:
Available online

Access to staff:
Contact by letter, by telephone, by fax and by e-
mail. Appointment necessary.

EURYDICE UNIT FOR ENGLAND, WALES AND NORTHERN IRELAND

Acronym or abbreviation: Eurydice at NFER

NFER, The Mere, Upton Park, Slough, Berkshire,
SL1 2DQ

Tel: 01753 637036
Fax: 01753 531458
E-mail: eurydice@nfer.ac.uk

Website:
http://www.nfer.ac.uk/eurydice

Formerly called:
Education Policy Information Centre (EPIC
Europe) (year of change 1998)

Organisation type and purpose:
International organisation, research organisation.
Eurydice is part of the European Union's Lifelong
Learning Programme.

Subject coverage:
Education policy throughout the European Union,
EFTA/EEA states.

Printed publications:
Education in the News (current awareness
  bulletin)
International Review of Curriculum and
  Assessment Frameworks Internet Archive
  (INCA) (http://www.inca.org.uk)
Occasional briefing papers on specific policy
  themes, either covering the countries of the
  Eurydice Network or England, Wales and
  Northern Ireland
Factsheets
The Eurydice Network Eurybase, the European
  database on education systems, a series of
  education indicators and a range of comparative
  studies on education in Europe
Order printed publications from: Dissemination Unit,
Eurydice Unit for England, Wales and Northern
Ireland, The Mere, Upton Park, Slough, Berkshire,
SL1 2DQ; online from the Eurydice European Unit
(http://www.eurydice.org). Details of how to order
printed publications are also on the website.

Access to staff:
Contact by letter, by telephone and by e-mail
Hours: Mon to Fri, 0915 to 1715
Special comments: Service restricted to national and
local education policymakers.

Links with:
Eurydice European Unit (and National Units in 31
European countries)
  website: http://eacea.ec.europa.eu/education/
  eurydice/index_en.php

Parent body:
National Foundation for Educational Research
tel: 01753 574123; fax: 01753 691632; website:
http://www.nfer.ac.uk

EVANGELICAL ALLIANCE

Acronym or abbreviation: EA

Whitefield House, 186 Kennington Park Road,
London, SE11 4BT

Tel: 020 7207 2100
Fax: 020 7207 2150
E-mail: info@eauk.org

Website:
http://www.eauk.org
Information on EA projects, activities and
resources. Databases of church and organisational
members.

Enquiries:
Enquiries to: Information Officer

Direct tel: 020 7207 2110

Founded:
1846

Organisation type and purpose:
Membership association (membership is by
subscription), present number of members: 38,000
individuals, 3,000 Churches, 700 organisations,
registered charity (charity number 212325).
National para-church body representing the
concerns of more than 1m. Christians from over a
dozen denominations to the state, society and the
wider Church.

Subject coverage:
Evangelical Christian activity in Britain.
Information on the views and beliefs of
Evangelicals across the United Kingdom.

**Museum or gallery collection, archive, or library
special collection:**
19th-century documents of the Evangelical
  Alliance; uncatalogued collection

Printed publications:
IDEA (magazine, 6 times a year, free to members)

Publications list:
Available online and in print

Access to staff:
Contact by letter, by telephone, by fax, by e-mail
and via website. Appointment necessary.
Hours: Mon, Wed, Thu, 0900 to 1600

Access to building, collection or gallery:
Please book to arrange appointment

Access for disabled people:
Level entry, toilet facilities

Also at:
Evangelical Alliance Northern Ireland
  Downview House, 440 Shore Road,
  Newtownabbey, BT37 9RU; tel: 028 9029 2266;
  fax: 028 9029 2277; e-mail: nireland@eauk.org
Evangelical Alliance Scotland
  Challenge House, 29 Canal Street, Glasgow, G4
  0AD; tel: 0141 332 8700; fax: 0141 332 8704; e-
  mail: scotland@eauk.org
Evangelical Alliance Wales
  20 High Street, Cardiff, CF10 1PT; tel: 029 2022
  9822; fax: 029 2022 9741; e-mail: wales@eauk.org;
  cymru@eauk.org

Links with:
European Evangelical Alliance
World Evangelical Alliance

EVANGELICAL LIBRARY

Acronym or abbreviation: EL

5/6 Gateway Mews, Ringway, Bounds Green,
London, N11 2UT

Tel: 020 8362 0868
E-mail: stlibrary@zen.co.uk

Website:
http://www.evangelical-library.org.uk

Enquiries:
Enquiries to: Librarian
Other contacts: Treasurer (for advice on donations)

Founded:
1945

Organisation type and purpose:
Membership association (membership is by
subscription), present number of members: 1,100,
research organisation.
Lending, reference and research library.

Subject coverage:
Evangelical faith, hymnology, revivals, reformers,
Puritans, denominational and biographical history.

**Museum or gallery collection, archive, or library
special collection:**
Journals from 1766
Manuscripts of unpublished letters, etc.
Robinson Collection of Puritan works
Slides – Bible scene slide tours

Non-library collection catalogue:
All or part available in print

Library catalogue:
All or part available online

Printed publications:
Annual Lecture
In Writing (twice a year)
Evangelical Library Lectures are available dating from 1983, including:
A Glorious Heritage (R. Oliver, 1997)
Lex Rex, the Law and the Prince (D. Searl, 2000)
The Ecumenical Century and Evangelical Responses (H. R. Jones, 1998)
Reversal or Betrayal? Evangelicals and Socio-political Involvement (M. Tinker, 1998)
The Glory of Christ – B. B. Warfield on Jesus (C. Trueman, 2001)

Publications list:
Available in print

Access to staff:
Contact by letter, by telephone, by e-mail, in person and via website. All charged.
Hours: Mon to Sat, 1000 to 1700

Access to building, collection or gallery:
No prior appointment required
Hours: Mon to Sat, 1000 to 1700

EVELYN OLDFIELD UNIT

London Voluntary Sector Resource Centre, 356 Holloway Road, London, N7 6PA

Tel: 020 7700 8213
Fax: 020 7700 8136
E-mail: administrator@evelynoldfield.co.uk

Website:
http://www.evelynoldfield.co.uk

Founded:
1994

Organisation type and purpose:
Established by a consortium of funding bodies (including the City Parochial Foundation, Thames Telethon, London Borough Grants, the Refugee Working Party and the Refugee Council) to develop specialist support for refugee organisations to enable them to tackle the pressing needs of the communities that they served.

EVENT SUPPLIER AND SERVICES ASSOCIATION

Acronym or abbreviation: ESSA

ESSA House, Uplands Business Park, Blackhorse Lane, London, E17 5QJ

Tel: 0845 122 1880
Fax: 020 8523 5204
E-mail: info@essa.uk.com

Website:
http://www.essa.uk.com

Enquiries:
Direct e-mail: paula.ripoll@essa.uk.com

Created by the merger of:
British Exhibition Contractors Association (BECA) and Association of Exhibition Contractors (AEC) (year of change 2008)

Organisation type and purpose:
Trade association.

Subject coverage:
Employment, legislation, health and safety, quality assurance.

Constituent member of:
CBI

EVESHAM LIBRARY

Oat Street, Evesham, Worcestershire, WR11 4PJ

Tel: 01905 822722
Fax: 01386 765855

E-mail: eveshamlib@worcestershire.gov.uk

Website:
http://www.worcestershire.gov.uk/libraries

Enquiries:
Enquiries to: Library Manager

Organisation type and purpose:
Public library.

Subject coverage:
General; local history.

Museum or gallery collection, archive, or library special collection:
Barnard Bequest (local history)

Non-library collection catalogue:
All or part available online

Library catalogue:
All or part available online

Microform publications:
Evesham Journal 1860–present

Access to staff:
Contact by letter, by telephone, by fax, by e-mail and in person. Appointment necessary.
Hours: Mon, Wed, Fri, 0930 to 1730; Tue, Thu, 0930 to 2000; Sat, 0930 to 1700

Access to building, collection or gallery:
Hours: As above

Access for disabled people:
Hours: As above

Parent body:
Worcestershire County Council Cultural Services

EVESHAM TOURIST INFORMATION AND ALMONRY HERITAGE CENTRE

Almonry Heritage Centre, Abbey Gate, Evesham, Worcestershire, WR11 4BG

Tel: 01386 446944
Fax: 01386 442348
E-mail: tic@almonry.ndo.co.uk

Website:
http://www.almonryevesham.org

Enquiries:
Enquiries to: Tourist Information and Heritage Centre Manager

Founded:
1957

Organisation type and purpose:
Local government body, museum, suitable for ages: all.
Heritage and Tourist Information Centre.

Subject coverage:
Tourist information housed in the local heritage centre with its collection of archaeology and local history of the Evesham area, displays relating to the Battle of Evesham (1265), Evesham Abbey (701–1540) and the crafts and history of the Vale, civic regalia of the former Evesham Borough and artefacts belonging to the former Evesham Abbey, display of Anglo-Saxon jewellery and weapons found on a burial site just outside the town.

Printed publications:
A selection of books is available from the Heritage Centre, including:
Abbey and Parish Churches
Battle of Evesham
Battle of Worcester
Evesham Official Guide 2002 (every 3–4 years)
Evesham Pocket Guide and Map (every 2–3 years)
The Almonry Museum (guide to building, 1975)

Publications list:
Available in print

Access to staff:
Contact by letter, by telephone, by fax, by e-mail, in person and via website
Hours: Mon to Sat, 1000 to 1700; Sun, 1400 to 1700
Special comments: Closed Sun, in Nov, Dec, Jan and Feb, and for 2 weeks at Christmas and New Year.

Access for disabled people:
Level entry

Parent body:
Evesham Town Council
Community Contact Centre, Abbey Road, Evesham, Worcs, WR11 4SB; tel: 01386 47070; fax: 01386 423811; e-mail: townclerk@ eveshamtowncouncil.gov.uk

EXEMPLAS BUSINESS INTELLIGENCE

Acronym or abbreviation: EXEMPLAS

45 Grosvenor Road, St Albans, Hertfordshire, AL1 3AW

Tel: 01727 813813
Fax: 01727 813404
E-mail: info@exemplas.com

Website:
http://www.exemplas.com

Enquiries:
Enquiries to: Information Manager
Direct e-mail: ClareN@exemplas.com

Founded:
1994

Organisation type and purpose:
Advisory body, research organisation.
Information and advice service.
Designed to improve business competitiveness through an outstanding range and quality of business information, advice and services to Hertfordshire, UK and international firms.

Subject coverage:
Business, science and technology, intellectual property, pharmaceuticals, current affairs, management and products.

Library catalogue:
All or part available in-house

Access to staff:
Contact by letter, by telephone, by fax, by e-mail and in person
Hours: Mon, Wed to Fri, 0900 to 1700; Tue, 0900 to 1600

Links with:
Hertfordshire Chamber of Commerce and Industry
Hertfordshire County Council
Hertfordshire Learning and Skills Council
University of Hertfordshire

EXERCISE, MOVEMENT AND DANCE PARTNERSHIP

Acronym or abbreviation: EMDP

1 Grove House, Foundry Lane, Horsham, West Sussex, RH13 5PL

Tel: 01403 266000
Fax: 01403 266111
E-mail: office@emdp.org

Website:
http://www.emdp.org.uk

Enquiries:
Enquiries to: Support Administrator
Direct e-mail: sara@emdp.org

Founded:
2006

Created by the merger of:
the Keep Fit Association, the Fitness League and the Medau Society (1952)

Organisation type and purpose:
Professional body.

Subject coverage:
Medau rhythmic movement.

Printed publications:
Annual Report and Constitution
Medau Rhythmic Movement (Society handbook)
The Medau Approach to Piano Improvisation

continued overleaf

Access to staff:
Contact by letter, by telephone, by fax and by e-mail. Access for members only.
Hours: Term time: 0930 to 1500

Links with:
Medau College
Coburg

EXETER CATHEDRAL LIBRARY

Diocesan House, Palace Gate, Exeter, Devon, EX1 1HX

Tel: 01392 272894, Library; 01392 495954, Archives
Fax: 01392 285986
E-mail: library@exeter-cathedral.org.uk

Website:
http://www.exeter-cathedral.org.uk
Description of content and facilities.

Enquiries:
Enquiries to: Librarian
Other contacts: Assistant Librarian

Founded:
11th century

Organisation type and purpose:
Cathedral library.

Subject coverage:
Theological subjects, in early printed books, tracts etc. Early printed works on travel, law, literature, linguistics, history, local history, history of medicine, bibliography.

Museum or gallery collection, archive, or library special collection:
Cathedral archives and manuscripts
Collection of tracts (Civil War period)
Cook Collection (early foreign language material, 19th-century linguistics)
Exeter Book of Anglo-Saxon poetry c965–75
Exon Domesday 1086
Glass Collection and Exeter Medical Library (early medicine and science)
Harington Collection (theology, history, 16th to 19th century)
Manuscript books, 10th century onwards
Printed books, 15th century onwards, including a large proportion of early imprints

Non-library collection catalogue:
All or part available in-house

Library catalogue:
All or part available in-house

Printed publications:
The library and archives of Exeter Cathedral, by L J Lloyd and Audrey M Erskine, 3rd edn (Exeter 2004)

Microform publications:
Most library manuscript material available on microfilm (this does not apply to archives)

Access to staff:
Contact by letter, by telephone, by e-mail and in person
Hours: Library: Mon to Fri, 1400 to 1700
Archives: Mon to Wed, 1400 to 1700, by appointment
Special comments: Casual visitors restricted to exhibition area; browsing not permitted.

Archives jointly administered and financed by the:
Dean and Chapter of Exeter and the Devon Record Office
   Devon Record Office, Great Moor House, Bitton Road, Sowton, Exeter, EX2 7NL; tel: 01392 384253 (DRO); fax: 01392 384256 (DRO); e-mail: devrec@devon.gov.uk

Parent body:
Dean and Chapter of Exeter Cathedral
   Cathedral Office, 1 The Cloisters, Exeter, EX1 1HS; tel: 01392 255573; fax: 01392 285986; e-mail: admin@exeter-cathedral.org.uk

EXETER CENTRAL LIBRARY

Castle Street, Exeter, Devon, EX4 3PQ

Tel: 01392 384206
Fax: 01392 384208
E-mail: exeter.central.library@devon.gov.uk

Website:
http://www.devon.gov.uk/library
Range of services, contacts, opening hours, library catalogue, community information, local studies database.

Enquiries:
Enquiries to: Group Librarian (South and East)
Direct tel: 01392 384222

Organisation type and purpose:
Local government body, public library.
The Central Library for South and East Devon of the Devon Library & Information Services, houses the Westcountry Studies Library.

Subject coverage:
General; music and drama, West Country local history, business information, careers, official publications.

Museum or gallery collection, archive, or library special collection:
British Standards
Drama Collection (play sets)
HMSO collection (selective subscription from 1975)
Pocknell Collection (early books on shorthand)
Pre-1800 Book Collection (2,000 volumes)

Trade and statistical information:
Keynote market research reports, UK business monitors, government trade statistics.

Library catalogue:
All or part available online

Printed publications:
Community Information Booklets

Access to staff:
Contact by letter, by telephone, by fax, by e-mail, in person and via website
Hours: Mon, Tue, Thu, Fri, 0930 to 1900; Wed 1000 to 1700; Sat 0930 to 1600; Sun 1100 to 1430

Access for disabled people:
Ramped entry, access to all public areas, toilet facilities

EXETER CHAMBER OF COMMERCE & INDUSTRY

10 Southernhay West, Exeter, Devon, EX1 1JG

Tel: 01392 431133
Fax: 01392 278804
E-mail: enquiries@exeterchamber.co.uk

Website:
http://www.exeterchamber.co.uk
Full membership directory, application form, details of subscriptions, events, links to other sites of interest.

Enquiries:
Enquiries to: Administrator

Founded:
1992

Organisation type and purpose:
Trade association (membership is by subscription), present number of members: over 450.

Subject coverage:
Business information, trade and business contacts.

Printed publications:
Membership list (continually updated, £25+VAT)

Access to staff:
Contact by letter, by telephone, by fax, by e-mail and via website. Appointment necessary.
Hours: Mon to Fri, 0900 to 1730

EXETER CITY CENTRE CONSORTIUM

PO Box 209, Exeter, Devon, EX1 1YJ

Tel: 01392 494980

Enquiries:
Enquiries to: Administrator

Founded:
1991

Organisation type and purpose:
Trade association (membership is by subscription), present number of members: 80.
To represent the interest of members; to promote Exeter City Centre by whatever means with intention of improving the prosperity of business dependent upon Exeter City Centre; to work with others for the enhancement of the city centre environment. To provide the Christmas illuminations each year. To provide and run the Storewatch Radio System.

Subject coverage:
City centre improvement.

Access to staff:
Contact by letter, by telephone and by e-mail
Hours: Mon to Fri, 0900 to 1700

EXETER CITY COUNCIL

Civic Centre, Paris Street, Exeter, Devon, EX1 1JN

Tel: 01392 277888
Fax: 01392 265265

Website:
http://www.exeter.gov.uk
All council services and city information.

Enquiries:
Enquiries to: Communications Manager
Direct tel: 01392 265319
Direct fax: 01392 265247
Direct e-mail: mandy.pearse@exeter.gov.uk

Organisation type and purpose:
Local government body.

Subject coverage:
Local government.

Printed publications:
Exeter Citizen (council newspaper, quarterly)

Access to staff:
Contact by letter, by telephone, by fax and by e-mail
Hours: Mon to Fri, 0900 to 1700

Access for disabled people:
Parking provided, ramped entry, access to all public areas, toilet facilities

EXETER HEALTH LIBRARY

Acronym or abbreviation: EHL

Peninsula Medical School Building, Royal Devon and Exeter NHS Foundation Trust, Barrack Road, Exeter, Devon, EX2 5DW

Tel: 01392 406800
Fax: 01392 406728
E-mail: medlib@exeter.ac.uk

Website:
http://www.exeter.ac.uk/library/eml

Enquiries:
Enquiries to: Library Manager

Organisation type and purpose:
NHS/Medical School library.

Subject coverage:
Medicine, healthcare.

Museum or gallery collection, archive, or library special collection:
Collection of pre-19th century medical books (housed in Exeter Cathedral Library)

Non-library collection catalogue:
All or part available online

Library catalogue:
All or part available online

Access to staff:
Contact by letter, by telephone, by fax, by e-mail, in person and via website
Hours: Mon to Fri, 0830 to 1730

Parent body:
Royal Devon and Exeter NHS Foundation Trust
Barrack Road, Exeter EX2 5DW

EXMOOR NATIONAL PARK AUTHORITY

Exmoor House, Dulverton, Somerset, TA22 9HL

Tel: 01398 323665
Fax: 01398 323150
E-mail: info@exmoor-nationalpark.gov.uk

Website:
http://www.exmoor-nationalpark.gov.uk
Information about National Park Authority and Exmoor area.

Enquiries:
Enquiries to: Head of Education and Interpretation
Other contacts: External Relations Manager for media and general enquiries

Founded:
1954

Organisation type and purpose:
Local government body, planning authority, statutory body.
Statutory purposes of the National Park are to conserve and enhance the natural beauty, wildlife and cultural heritage of the area. To promote opportunities for the understanding and enjoyment of the park's special qualities. To seek to foster the economic and social well being of the communities within the National Park without incurring significant expenditure in so doing. The Authority is also the planning authority for Exmoor.

Subject coverage:
Exmoor, its natural history, history, culture, access, recreation and tourist facilities.

Information services:
3 National Park Centres.

Education services:
Residential outdoor education centre, sleeps 40.

Services for disabled people:
Easy access trails.

Museum or gallery collection, archive, or library special collection:
Books, maps and photographs of Exmoor, including aerial photography

Printed publications:
Exmoor Visitor (newspaper, free)
National Park Management Plan
National Park Local Plan
Park Life (newspaper, free)
Various technical, educational and visitor publications
Walking Guides, General Interest
FILEXMOOR: an information pack about Exmoor National Park, written especially for students at GCSE level but of interest to anyone wanting to know more about the Park (10 Files 60p each or £6 the set in a presentation folder, plus p&p) (available on line)
QUESTEX: information about Exmoor National Park Authority, written especially for students at A level but of interest to anyone wanting to know more about management issues (6 Files 60p each plus p&p) (educational publications are downloadable from the website)
Order printed publications from: Centre Head, National Park Centre, Dulverton TA22 9EX, tel: 01398 323841

Publications list:
Available online and in print

Access to staff:
Contact by letter, by telephone, by fax, by e-mail and via website. Appointment necessary.
Hours: Mon to Thu, 0900 to 1700; Fri, 0900 to 1600

Access for disabled people:
Parking provided, ramped entry, toilet facilities, lift to committee room

Member of:
UK Association of National Park Authorities (ANPA)
126 Bute Street, Cardiff, CF10 5LE; tel: 02920 499966; e-mail: enquiries@anpa.gov.uk

National Park Centre:
ENPA
Fore Street, Dulverton, TA22 3EX; tel: 01398 323841; e-mail: npcdulverton@exmoor-nationalpark.gov.uk

EXMOOR SOCIETY

Parish Rooms, Rosemary Lane, Dulverton, Somerset, TA22 9DP

Tel: 01398 323335
Fax: 01398 323335
E-mail: exmoorsociety@yahoo.co.uk

Website:
http://www.exmoorsociety.org.uk
General information about the society, history of the society, items taken from Newsletter and Annual Report.

Enquiries:
Enquiries to: Secretary

Founded:
1959

Organisation type and purpose:
Membership association (membership is by subscription), present number of members: 2200, voluntary organisation, registered charity (charity number 245761).
Conservation.

Subject coverage:
Conservation of Exmoor.

Museum or gallery collection, archive, or library special collection:
Archives from Roger Miles including:
Forestry Commission Reports
NPC Reports
Alfred Vowles Photographic Archive

Non-library collection catalogue:
All or part available in-house

Library catalogue:
All or part available in-house

Printed publications:
Annual Report
Newsletter
Exmoor Bibliography (£3.50)
Exmoor Review (annually, £3.60)
Index of Exmoor Review (£3.95)
Smuggling on Exmoor (£5, a one-off print run, copies available)

Access to staff:
Contact by letter, by telephone, by fax, by e-mail and in person
Hours: Tue to Thu, 0900 to 1600

EXMOUTH LIBRARY

40 Exeter Road, Exmouth, Devon, EX8 1PS

Tel: 01395 272677
Fax: 01395 271426
E-mail: exmouth.library@devon.gov.uk

Website:
http://www.devon.gov.uk/libraries

Enquiries:
Enquiries to: Library Manager

Founded:
1946

Organisation type and purpose:
Local government body, public library.
Part of the Devon Library & Information Services.

Subject coverage:
General, Exmouth local history.

Museum or gallery collection, archive, or library special collection:
Exmouth local history

Trade and statistical information:
A selection of standard printed sources.

Library catalogue:
All or part available online

Microform publications:
Exmouth Journal (1869–1995)

Access to staff:
Contact by letter, by telephone, by e-mail, in person and via website
Hours: Mon, Tue, Thu, Fri, 0930 to 1900; Wed, 0930 to 1300; Sat, 0930 to 1600. First Fri of the month, open at 1030 (staff training)

Access for disabled people:
Ramped entry

Parent body:
Devon County Council, Devon Library & Information Services
Great Moor House, Sowton, Exeter, EX2 7NL; tel: 01392 384315; fax: 01392 384316; e-mail: devlibs@devon.gov.uk

EXPORT CREDITS GUARANTEE DEPARTMENT

Acronym or abbreviation: ECGD

PO Box 2200, 2 Exchange Tower, Harbour Exchange Square, London, E14 9GS

Tel: 020 7512 7000
Fax: 020 7512 7649
E-mail: help@ecgd.gsi.gov.uk

Website:
http://www.ecgd.gov.uk
Information on products and services, lines of credit, country cover.

Enquiries:
Enquiries to: ECGD Help Desk
Direct tel: 020 7512 7887

Founded:
1919

Organisation type and purpose:
National government body.
Government department.
UK's official export credit agency.

Subject coverage:
Export credit insurance for UK exporters, overseas investment insurance, export finance guarantees for banks.

Printed publications:
Annual Review and Resource Accounts
Global Exporter-The Official ECGD Yearbook
ECGD News – customer newsletter (quarterly)
ECGD Customer Charter
ECGD's Business Principles
Guides to Products:
Buyer Credit Finance Guarantees
Supplier Credit Finance Guarantees
Overseas Investment Insurance
One-Stop-Shop
Credit Terms
Lines of Credit
Project Financing Scheme
Bond Insurance Policy
Export Insurance Policy
Claims and Recoveries
Recourse
Debt Conversion Scheme

Access to staff:
Contact by letter, by telephone, by fax, by e-mail and via website
Hours: Mon to Fri, 0800 to 1800

Responsible to the:
Secretary of State for Trade and Industry

EXTEND EXERCISE TRAINING LTD

Formal name: Movement to Music for the over Sixties and the Less Able of Any Age
Acronym or abbreviation: EXTEND

2 Place Farm, Wheathampstead, Hertfordshire, AL4 8SB

Tel: 01582 832760
Fax: 01582 832760
E-mail: admin@extend.org.uk

Website:
http://www.extend.org.uk

Enquiries:
Enquiries to: Head Office Senior Administrator
Other contacts: Director of Training, Assistant Administrator

Founded:
1976

Organisation type and purpose:
Registered charity (charity number 802498), training organisation.
Provides recreational movement to music for the over sixties and for the less able of any age.
To promote good health and enhance the quality of life through stimulating physical and mental health, increasing mobility and independence, improving strength, stamina, posture and coordination and to overcoming loneliness and isolation.

Subject coverage:
Recreational movement to music, recreational rehabilitation, use of music and rhythm, diet and nutrition.

Information services:
Details of how to train as an Extend Teacher and contact a teacher for a nearby class.

Services for disabled people:
Provision of exercise classes.

Printed publications:
Leaflets (free)

Access to staff:
Contact by letter, by telephone, by fax, by e-mail and via website. Appointment necessary. Access for members only.
Hours: Mon to Fri, 0900 to 1500

EYECARE TRUST, THE

Acronym or abbreviation: EIS

PO Box 804, Aylesbury, Buckinghamshire, HP20 9DF

Tel: 0845 129 5001
Fax: 0845 129 5001
E-mail: info@eyecaretrust.org.uk

Website:
http://www.eye-care.org.uk

Enquiries:
Enquiries to: Membership Secretary
Direct e-mail: pr@eyecaretrust.org.uk
Other contacts: Administrator

Founded:
2001

Formerly called:
Eyecare Information Bureau (ECIB), Optical Information Council (OIC); Eyecare Information Service (EIS) (year of change 2001)

Organisation type and purpose:
National organisation, advisory body, membership association (membership is by subscription), present number of members: 500, voluntary organisation, registered charity (charity number 1086146).
Public relations and promotions for the whole of optics.

Subject coverage:
All aspects of eyes and optics.

Trade and statistical information:
Statistics relating to the optical sector.

Printed publications:
Individual leaflets (free of charge to the public, bulk orders to members only)

Electronic and video publications:
CD-ROM – available to EIS 2000 members, health authority hospitals and other healthcare organisations and companies

Publications list:
Available online and in print

Access to staff:
Contact by letter, by telephone, by fax, by e-mail and via website
Hours: Mon to Fri, 1000 to 1600

Members:
Association of British Dispensing Opticians (ABDO)
Association of Contact Lens Manufacturers (ACLM)
Association of Optometrists (AOP)
British College of Optometrists (BCO)
Federation of Manufacturing Opticians (FMO)
Federation of Ophthalmic and Dispensing Opticians (FODO)

FABIAN SOCIETY

11 Dartmouth Street, London, SW1H 9BN

Tel: 020 7227 4900
Fax: 020 7976 7153
E-mail: info@fabian-society.org.uk

Website:
http://www.fabians.org.uk
Recent publications, events, conferences.

Enquiries:
Enquiries to: Membership Secretary
Direct e-mail: members@fabian-society.org.uk
Other contacts: Editor

Founded:
1884

Organisation type and purpose:
Membership association (membership is by subscription), present number of members: 6,700, research organisation, publishing house.
Senior Think Tank for the Labour Party and the oldest socialist society affiliated to the Labour Party.

Subject coverage:
Politics, current affairs, social policy and economics.

Publications list:
Available online and in print

Access to staff:
Contact by letter, by telephone, by fax, by e-mail and via website. Appointment necessary.
Hours: Mon to Fri, 0930 to 1300 and 1400 to 1730

FACULTY OF CREATIVE ARTS LIBRARY, UNIVERSITY OF THE WEST OF ENGLAND, BRISTOL

Acronym or abbreviation: UWE, Bristol

Bower Ashton Campus, Kennel Lodge Road, Bristol, BS3 2JT

Tel: 0117 328 4750
Fax: 0117 328 4745
E-mail: library.sca@uwe.ac.uk

Website:
http://www.uwe.ac.uk/library

Enquiries:
Enquiries to: Campus/Faculty Librarian
Direct tel: 0117 328 4731

Founded:
1992

Formerly called:
Bristol Polytechnic (year of change 1992)

Organisation type and purpose:
University library.

Subject coverage:
Art and design, media studies, cinema films.

Museum or gallery collection, archive, or library special collection:
Cinema films (video and DVD format)
Collection of slides
Collection of artists' books
Exhibition catalogues

Library catalogue:
All or part available online

Access to staff:
Contact by letter, by telephone, by fax and by e-mail. Appointment necessary.
Hours: Mon to Fri, 0900 to 1700

Member organisation of:
ARLIS (UK and Eire)

FACULTY OF DENTAL SURGERY

Acronym or abbreviation: FDS RCSEng

Royal College of Surgeons of England, 35–43 Lincoln's Inn Fields, London, WC2A 3PN

Tel: 020 7869 6810
Fax: 020 7869 6816
E-mail: fds@rcseng.ac.uk

Website:
http://www.rcseng.ac.uk/public/fds/fds.htm

Enquiries:
Enquiries to: Administrative Assistant

Founded:
1947

Organisation type and purpose:
International organisation, advisory body, professional body (membership is by subscription, qualification, election or invitation), present number of members: 4,222, registered charity, training organisation.

Subject coverage:
Postgraduate dental education and training, and oral and maxillofacial surgery.

Museum or gallery collection, archive, or library special collection:
Odontological collection

Non-library collection catalogue:
All or part available in-house

Publications list:
Available online

Access to staff:
Contact by e-mail
Hours: Mon to Fri, 0900 to 1700

Access to building, collection or gallery:
Prior appointment required

Access for disabled people:
Parking provided

FACULTY OF FAMILY PLANNING AND REPRODUCTIVE HEALTH CARE

Acronym or abbreviation: FFPRHC

27 Sussex Place, Regent's Park, London, NW1 4RG

Tel: 020 7724 5681
Fax: 020 7723 5333
E-mail: journal@ffprhc.org.uk

Enquiries:
Enquiries to: Secretary

Founded:
1993

Organisation type and purpose:
Professional body (membership is by qualification), registered charity (charity number 1019969), training organisation.
Training for medical professionals (doctors).

Subject coverage:
All fields of family planning and reproductive health.

Printed publications:
Journal of Family Planning and Reproductive Health Care (quarterly)
Order printed publications from: Journal of Family Planning and Reproductive Healthcare at the main address
Subscriptions/purchasing, Professional, Managerial & Healthcare Publications Ltd., PO Box 100, Chichester, West Sussex, PO18 8HD, tel: 01243 576444, fax: 01243 576456, e-mail: admin@pmh.uk.com

Electronic and video publications:
Journal of Family Planning and Reproductive Health Care

Access to staff:
Access for members only.
Hours: Mon to Fri, 0900 to 1700

Parent body:
Royal College of Obstetricians and Gynaecologists at the same address

FAIR ISLE BIRD OBSERVATORY TRUST

Acronym or abbreviation: FIBOT

Fair Isle Bird Observatory, Fair Isle, Shetland, ZE2 9JU

Tel: 01595 760258
Fax: 01595 760258 (phone first)
E-mail: fairisle.birdobs@zetnet.co.uk

Website:
http://www.fairislebirdobs.oc.uk

Enquiries:
Enquiries to: Warden
Other contacts: Administrator for office business.

Founded:
1948

Organisation type and purpose:
Registered charity, research organisation.
Ornithological research and holiday accommodation.

Subject coverage:
Seabird monitoring and migration studies at Fair Isle Bird Observatory. Accommodation for paying guests/visitors to Observatory/Isle.

Museum or gallery collection, archive, or library special collection:
Richard Richardson Library

Printed publications:
Fair Isle Bird Observatory Report
Order printed publications from: Fair Isle Bird Observatory Reports

Access to staff:
Contact by letter, by telephone, by e-mail, in person and via website
Hours: Any time, any day.

Access to building, collection or gallery:
Prior appointment required
Special comments: Open to visitors end April to end October.

FAIR ORGAN PRESERVATION SOCIETY

Acronym or abbreviation: FOPS

43 Woolmans, Fullers Slade, Milton Keynes, Buckinghamshire, MK11 2BA

Tel: 01908 263707
Fax: 01908 263707

Website:
http://www.fops.org/

Enquiries:
Enquiries to: Membership Secretary
Direct e-mail: membership@fops.org

Founded:
1958

Organisation type and purpose:
Membership association (membership is by subscription), present number of members: 900 in 13 countries.
Promotion and encouragement of interest in, and the preservation of, fairground organs and mechanical musical instruments.

Subject coverage:
Fairground organs, Dutch and German street organs, Belgian dance organs.

Museum or gallery collection, archive, or library special collection:
Documentary archive held within the National Fairground Archive at Sheffield University

Printed publications:
The Key Frame (journal, quarterly, free to members, back issues for sale)
Pocket Book of Coming Events (annually, free to members)
On Display

Access to staff:
Contact by letter, by telephone, by fax, by e-mail and via website
Hours: Answerphone out of office hours

FALKIRK COLLEGE OF FURTHER AND HIGHER EDUCATION

Grangemouth Road, Falkirk, Strathclyde, FK2 9AD

Tel: 01324 403045
Fax: 01324 403046
E-mail: library@falkirkcollege.ac.uk

Enquiries:
Enquiries to: Librarian

Founded:
1963

Organisation type and purpose:
College of further education.

Subject coverage:
Automobile, electrical, electronic, mechanical, and plant engineering, construction and building, food technology, catering, health, social care, business studies, office services, leisure management, sport and recreation, computer studies, art and design, environmental management.

Library catalogue:
All or part available in-house

FALKIRK COUNCIL ARCHIVES

Callendar House, Callendar Park, Falkirk, FK1 1YR

Tel: 01324 503778
Fax: 01324 503771
E-mail: callendar.house@falkirk.gov.uk

Website:
http://www.falkirk.gov.uk/archives.htm
Finding aids for archives collections; collections browser (museum and archives collections); information on depositing records, using the archives and resources for schools.

Enquiries:
Enquiries to: Archivist
Direct tel: 01324 503779
Other contacts: Archives Assistants

Founded:
1992

Organisation type and purpose:
Local government body.

Subject coverage:
Local government administration.

Museum or gallery collection, archive, or library special collection:
Local authority records, including Falkirk Burgh 1803–1975, Grangemouth Burgh 1872–1975, Bo'ness Burgh, Denny & Dunipace Burgh 1833–

1975, Stirling County District Councils 1930–1975, West Lothian County District Councils 1930–1975, parish councils and parochial boards; Falkirk District Council, 1975–1995 and Falkirk Council, 1995 to present
Photograph collection, over 43,000 images of local places, events and people
Records of local businesses, organisations, trade unions, professional associations, churches, families and estates
Small reference library

Non-library collection catalogue:
All or part available online and in-house

Access to staff:
Contact by letter, by telephone, by fax, by e-mail and in person
Hours: Mon to Fri, 1000 to 1230 and 1330 to 1700
Special comments: Closed on local public holidays.

Access to building, collection or gallery:
No prior appointment required
Hours: Mon to Sat, 1000 to 1700

Access for disabled people:
Parking available, level entry, access to all public areas, toilet facilities

Parent body:
Falkirk Council

FALKIRK COUNCIL LIBRARY SERVICE

Victoria Buildings, Queen Street, Falkirk, FK2 7AF

Tel: 01324 506800
Fax: 01324 506801
E-mail: library.support@falkirk.gov.uk

Website:
http://www.falkirk.gov.uk/services/community/library_services/library_services.aspx

Enquiries:
Enquiries to: Principal Librarian (Support Services)
Direct tel: 01324 506804
Direct e-mail: shona.hill@falkirk.gov.uk

Founded:
1996

Organisation type and purpose:
Local government body, public library.

Subject coverage:
General, local history.

Non-library collection catalogue:
All or part available online and in-house

Library catalogue:
All or part available online and in-house

Printed publications:
Current awareness bulletin for local government (weekly)
The following publications are available at all libraries and museums:
A History of Falkirk
A series of handy guides of various historical trails in the district: Bo'ness Town Trail, 2,000 years of History: a guided trail for Kinneil Estate
Annals of a Country Parish: old days and ways in Bothkennar Parish (a transcript of the Kirk of Sessions Minutes of Bothkennar Parish 172241)
Bo'ness: a glimpse of the past
Bonnybridge in Bygone Days
Corsets in Stripeside (personal memoirs of the Denny and Dunipace area)
Edinburgh and Glasgow Union Canal (a history of the development of the canal)
Falkirk's Yesterdays
Grangemouth: Two Towns
Grangemouth's Modern History
Happy Valley: memories of Laurieston
Heroes Departed: Falkirk District during the First World War
Histories of some of the towns and villages, written by local authors including:
Larbert and Stenhousemuir
Maps, including Falkirk District Map, reprints of early Ordnance Survey Maps and street guides
Miscellaneous books and accounts

continued overleaf

Old photographs, including:
Pits, Pints and Poverty: an account of the village of
    Standburn
Polmont and the Braes
Redding Pit Disaster: an illustrated account
Select Bibliography and Source Guide to the
    Romans in Falkirk District
Selection of local postcards/greetings cards and
    maps
Shieldhill: a glimpse of the past
Symington and the Charlotte Dundas (concise
    illustrated booklet on William Symington and
    the building of this steamship in Grangemouth)
Target Falkirk: Falkirk District in the Second World
    War
The Dear Auld Hame: Changing Scenes in Falkirk
    District
The first and second statistical accounts giving
    descriptions of parishes in Falkirk District in the
    18th and 19th centuries
To Labour All Our Lives: Old Photographs of
    Working Lives in Falkirk District
Travelling Through Time: Transport in Falkirk
    District
Vale of Bonny: The history and the legend
Order printed publications from: Library Support,
Victoria Buildings, Queen Street, Falkirk, FK2 7AF,
tel: 01324 506800

Publications list:
Available online and in print

Access to staff:
Contact by letter, by telephone, by fax, by e-mail,
in person and via website
Hours: Mon to Fri, 0900 to 1700

FALKLAND ISLANDS
GOVERNMENT OFFICE

Acronym or abbreviation: FIGO

Falkland House, 14 Broadway, London, SW1H
0BH

Tel: 020 7222 2542
Fax: 020 7222 2375
E-mail: rep@falklands.gov.fk

Website:
http://www.falklands.gov.fk
http://www.visitorfalklands.com
Tourism information.

Enquiries:
Enquiries to: Representative

Founded:
1983

Organisation type and purpose:
National government body.
To provide an information source and trade links
in the United Kingdom. Point of contact for UK
Parliament.

Subject coverage:
All aspects relating to the government,
development of trade, tourism and travel to the
Falklands. Dissemination of all information of a
general nature in connection with the Falklands.

Trade and statistical information:
General and specific information on trade to and
from the Islands.

Printed publications:
Falkland Islands... Sustaining a Secure Future (free
    brochure)
Falklands Focus (free newsheet published twice a
    year)
Tourism and Holiday Brochures (free)
Brochures and leaflets (free)
Order printed publications from: Falkland Islands
Government Office, Falkland House, 14 Broadway,
Westminster, London, SW1H 0BH

Electronic and video publications:
The Modern Falklands (free DVD)
Order electronic and video publications from: Falkland
Islands Government Office, Falkland House, 14
Broadway, Westminster, London, SW1H 0BH

Publications list:
Available in print

Access to staff:
Contact by letter, by telephone, by fax, by e-mail,
in person and via website
Hours: Mon to Fri, 0900 to 1300 and 1400 to 1730

Access to building, collection or gallery:
Prior appointment required
Hours: Mon to Fri, 0900 to 1300 and 1400 to 1730

Links with:
Falkland Islands Development Corporation
    Shackleton House, Davis Street East, Stanley,
    Falkland Islands, FIQQ 1ZZ; tel: +500 27211; fax:
    +500 27210; e-mail: develop@fidc.co.fk; website:
    http://www.fidc.co.fk
Falkland Islands Tourist Board
    Jetty Visitor Centre, Stanley, Falkland Islands,
    FIQQ 1ZZ; tel: +500 22215; fax: +500 22619; e-
    mail: jettycentre@horizon.co.fk; website: http://
    www.visitorfalklands.com

Parent body:
Falkland Islands Government
    The Secretariat, Stanley, Falkland Islands, FIQQ
    1ZZ; tel: +500 27242; fax: +500 27109; e-mail:
    lbrownlee@sec.gov.fk

FAMILIES NEED FATHERS

134–146 Curtain Road, London, EC2A 3AR

Tel: 020 7613 5060
Fax: 020 7739 3410
E-mail: fnf@fnf.org.uk

Website:
http://www.fnf.org.uk

Enquiries:
Enquiries to: Secretary

Founded:
1974

Organisation type and purpose:
Membership association (membership is by
subscription), present number of members: 3000,
voluntary organisation, registered charity (charity
number 276899).
Support group, self-help society and pressure
group to change and improve the present legal
process and to eliminate unnecessary and
protracted legal conflict.
Keeping children in contact with both parents after
separation or divorce.
Promoting shared-parenting.

Printed publications:
For the Sake of the Children – FNF guide to shared
    parenting (Secker S)
Fatherhood Reclaimed (Burgess A)
Psychological Research on Fathering (Russan S)
Booklets
Leaflets

Publications list:
Available online and in print

Access to staff:
Contact by telephone, by e-mail and via website
Hours: Mon to Fri, 0900 to 1700

FAMILY AND COMMUNITY
HISTORICAL RESEARCH SOCIETY

Formal name: Family and Community Historical
Research Society Limited
Acronym or abbreviation: FACHRS

Fir Trees, 12 Fryer Close, Chesham, Bucks, HP5
1RD

E-mail: honsec@fachrs.org.uk

Website:
http://www.fachrs.com

Enquiries:
Enquiries to: Hon. Sec.

Organisation type and purpose:
Membership organisation (membership by
subscription), registered charity (charity number
3965865).
To promote and communicate research in family
and community history within a scholarly
framework.

Printed publications:
Journal (2 times a year)
Newsletter
Swing Unmasked (book)
Breaking New Ground (book)
Order printed publications from: website: http://
www.fachrs.com

Access to staff:
Contact by letter, by e-mail and via website

FAMILY FUND

Unit 4, Alpha Court, Monks Cross Drive,
Huntington, York, YO32 9WN

Tel: 01904 621115\ Minicom no. 01904 658085
Fax: 01904 652625
E-mail: info@familyfund.org.uk

Website:
http://www.familyfund.org.uk

Enquiries:
Enquiries to: Information Officer
Direct tel: 0845 130 4542

Founded:
1973

Formerly called:
Family Fund (year of change 1994)

Organisation type and purpose:
Registered charity (charity number 1053866).
To ease the stress on families who care for severely
disabled children under 16, by providing grants
related to the care of the child.

Subject coverage:
Families with disabled children.

Printed publications:
After 16 – What's New? (free to young disabled
    people)
Family Fund leaflet and application form (in
    English, large print and other languages)

Publications list:
Available online and in print

Access to staff:
Contact by letter, by telephone, by fax, by e-mail
and via website
Hours: Mon to Fri, 0900 to 1700

FAMILY HISTORY SOCIETY OF
CHESHIRE

Acronym or abbreviation: FHSC

Little Trees, Gawsworth Road, Gawsworth,
Macclesfield, SK11 9RA

Tel: 01625 426173
E-mail: info@fhsc.org.uk

Website:
http://www.fhsc.org.uk

Enquiries:
Enquiries to: Secretary

Founded:
1969

Organisation type and purpose:
Membership association (membership is by
subscription), present number of members: 3,000,
voluntary organisation, registered charity (charity
number 515168), suitable for ages: all.
To promote interest in family history research in
Cheshire by organising monthly meetings of the 18
local groups, hosting conferences, open days, and
publishing transcriptions and indexes of local
records.

Subject coverage:
Family history in Cheshire.

Museum or gallery collection, archive, or library special collection:
Over 2,000 books and magazines, and exchange journals from other family history societies
Many films of Cheshire Parish Registers and Bishop's Transcripts
Microfiche of the IGI, GRO BMD 1837 to 1900
1881 Census on CD-ROM

Library catalogue:
All or part available in-house

Printed publications:
A large number of printed, microfiche and CD publications including:
Cheshire Ancestor (quarterly, members)
1841 Census Index Birkenhead
1841 Census Index Northwich
1851 Census Index Stockport, Macclesfield, Wilmslow, Runcorn, Northwich, Congleton, Nantwich, Chester, Wirral, Birkenhead
Order printed publications from: Family History Society of Cheshire, 91 Stretford House, Chapel Lane, Stretford, Manchester, M32 9AY

Microform publications:
Monumental inscriptions (over 150 graveyards)
1841 Census Index Birkenhead & Tranmere
1861 Census Index Nantwich
Register transcriptions
Members' Interests
Pigot's Directory of Cheshire 1830 and 1834
Order microform publications from: Family History Society of Cheshire
10 Daleswood Avenue, Whitefield, Manchester, M45 7WP tel: 0161 766 5997

Electronic and video publications:
CDs (both own and bought in) including parish registers, old maps, books and various collections of data
Order electronic and video publications from: 10 Daleswood Avenue, Whitefield, Manchester, M45 7WP tel: 0161 766 5997

Publications list:
Available online and in print

Access to staff:
Contact by letter, by telephone, by e-mail and via website
Hours: Mon to Fri, 0900 to 1700

Access to building, collection or gallery:
No prior appointment required; non-members please tel: 01625 599722,
Hours: Library: Mon to Fri, 1000 to 1600
Special comments: Library and Research Centre, Festival Hall, Alderley Edge, Cheshire; Mon to Fri, 1000 to 1600.
Members only and joining facility.

Access for disabled people:
Please tel: 01625 599722, Mon to Fri, 1000 to 1600

Has local groups in:
Alsager, Altrincham, Bebington, Birkenhead, Bramhall, Chester, Congleton, Crewe, Dukinfield, Macclesfield, Middlesex, Nantwich, Northwich, Runcorn, Stockton Heath, Tarporley, Wallasey, West Kirby

FAMILY WELFARE ASSOCIATION

Acronym or abbreviation: FWA

501–505 Kingsland Road, Dalston, London, E8 4AU

Tel: 020 7254 6251
Fax: 020 7249 5443
E-mail: fwa.headoffice@fwa.org.uk

Enquiries:
Enquiries to: Chief Executive

Founded:
1869

Formerly called:
Charity Organisation Society (year of change 1946)

Organisation type and purpose:
Registered charity, voluntary organisation (charity number 264713).
Support for families, children and others in need.

Subject coverage:
Educational grants advice for students/potential students, who are ineligible for statutory grants. Information and advice to people requiring help through various services in certain areas.

Museum or gallery collection, archive, or library special collection:
Archives of Charity Organisation Society and the Family Welfare Association held by London Metropolitan Archives

Publications list:
Available in print

Access to staff:
Contact by letter
Hours: Mon to Fri, 0900 to 1700

FANY (PRVC)

Formal name: FANY (Princess Royal's Volunteer Corps)

TA Headquarters, 95 Horseferry Rd, London, SW1P 2DY

Tel: 020 7976 5459
Fax: 020 7630 8019
E-mail: hq@fany.org.uk

Website:
http://www.fany.org.uk
Details of the organisation, current events, history, publications, recruitment.

Enquiries:
Enquiries to: Adjutant

Founded:
1907

Organisation type and purpose:
Voluntary organisation, suitable for women aged: 18 to 45.
To serve the country in peace and war; volunteer Emergency Response units providing support to the City of London and Metropolitan Police in Major Incidents and to the British Army as required, particularly in the protection of the capital against terrorism.

Subject coverage:
Provides emergency response teams of women able to cope in a variety of circumstances.

Museum or gallery collection, archive, or library special collection:
Archive documents and photographs, WWI, WWII and to the present day

Non-library collection catalogue:
All or part available online

Access to staff:
Contact by letter, by telephone, by fax, by e-mail and via website. Appointment necessary. Letter of introduction required.
Hours: Mon to Thu, 0900 to 1800

Access to building, collection or gallery:
Prior appointment required

FAREHAM COLLEGE

Bishopsfield Road, Fareham, Hampshire, PO14 1NH

Tel: 01329 815200
Fax: 01329 822483

Website:
http://www.fareham.ac.uk

Enquiries:
Enquiries to: Learning Resources Coordinator
Direct tel: 01329 815322
Direct e-mail: catherine.stevenson@fareham.ac.uk

Founded:
1969

Organisation type and purpose:
College of education, suitable for ages: 16+.

Subject coverage:
Full time A-level, BTEC Introductory, First, BTEC National Diplomas, NVQs Levels1, 2 and 3, Entry Level Certificates, VRQ and City and Guilds.

Non-library collection catalogue:
All or part available online and in-house

Library catalogue:
All or part available online and in-house

Access to staff:
Contact by letter, by telephone, by e-mail and in person
Hours: Mon, 0830 to 1700; Tue to Thu, 0830 to 1900; Fri, 0830 to 1630

Access for disabled people:
Parking provided, ramped entry, access to all public areas, toilet facilities

FARM ANIMAL WELFARE COUNCIL

Acronym or abbreviation: FAWC

Area 5A, 9 Millbank, c/o Nobel House, 17 Smith Square, London, SW1P 3JR

Tel: 020 7238 5192
Fax: 020 7238 3169
E-mail: fawcsecretariat@defra.gsi.gov.uk

Website:
http://www.fawc.org.uk
About FAWC, its membership, current work and publications.

Enquiries:
Enquiries to: Secretary
Other contacts: Assistant Secretaries

Founded:
1979

Organisation type and purpose:
Advisory body to Government; membership is by Ministerial appointment. FAWC's membership includes farmers, researchers, consumers, animal welfarists and veterinarians.
To keep under review welfare of farm animals and to advise the Government of legislative or other changes.

Subject coverage:
Farm animal welfare: studies on farm assurance schemes, cloning, broiler breeders, outdoor pigs, farmed fish, laying hens and dairy cattle have been completed. Other areas addressed include sheep, turkeys, wild boar, ostriches, broilers and transport.

Museum or gallery collection, archive, or library special collection:
Reports on all subject coverage

Printed publications:
FAWC Annual Review and all Reports
Government Animal Welfare Codes (available free from MAFF Publications)
Order printed publications from: MAFF Publications, London, SE99 7TP; tel: 0645 556000

Publications list:
Available online

Access to staff:
Contact by letter, by telephone, by fax and by e-mail
Hours: Mon to Fri, 0900 to 1700

Access to building, collection or gallery:
No access other than to staff

Parent body:
Department for Environment, Food and Rural Affairs

FARM STAY (UK) LIMITED

Acronym or abbreviation: FSUK

continued overleaf

National Agricultural Centre, Stoneleigh Park, Kenilworth, Warwickshire, CV8 2LZ

Tel: 024 7669 6909
Fax: 024 7669 6930
E-mail: admin@farmstayuk.co.uk

Website:
http://www.farmstayuk.co.uk
Comprehensive information for every member, including colour photos and interactive website with search mechanism throughout the UK.

Enquiries:
Enquiries to: Chief Executive
Other contacts: Office Manager for administrative queries, requests for information, promotional material.

Founded:
1983

Formerly called:
Farm Holiday Bureau (UK) Limited (FHB) (year of change 2000)

Organisation type and purpose:
National organisation, membership association (membership is by qualification), present number of members: 1000.
Self-funding Agricultural Cooperative. Producing a full colour brochure promoting members' businesses.

Subject coverage:
Farm-based holiday accommodation; information for farmers and customers; farm and rural tourism; tourism markets.

Printed publications:
Open Gate (newsletter, quarterly for members)
Stay On A Farm (guide to over 1000 farms, free)

Access to staff:
Contact by letter, by telephone, by fax, by e-mail and via website. Appointment necessary.
Hours: Mon to Fri, 0900 to 1700

Access to building, collection or gallery:
No prior appointment required

FARMDATA LIMITED

Westertown, Rothienorman, Inverurie, Aberdeenshire, AB51 8US

Tel: 01467 671457
Fax: 01467 671448
E-mail: sales@farmdata.co.uk

Website:
http://www.farmdata.co.uk
Full information on the company and its services.

Enquiries:
Enquiries to: Information Officer

Founded:
1978

Organisation type and purpose:
Service industry.

Access to staff:
Contact by letter, by telephone, by fax, by e-mail and via website
Hours: Mon to Fri, 0900 to 1700

FARNHAM CASTLE INTERNATIONAL BRIEFING & CONFERENCE CENTRE

Farnham Castle, Farnham, Surrey, GU9 0AG

Tel: 01252 721194
Fax: 01252 719277
E-mail: info@farnhamcastle.com

Website:
http://www.farnhamcastle.com
Latest news about the centre, full details of range of training programmes plus conference, meeting and event facilities.

Enquiries:
Enquiries to: Sales Manager

Direct tel: 01252 720418
Direct e-mail: lroberts@farnhamcastle.com
Other contacts: Client Services Administrator

Founded:
1953

Formerly called:
Centre for International Briefing (CIB) (year of change 2001)

Organisation type and purpose:
International organisation, registered charity (charity number 313648), training organisation. Not for profit organisation offering intercultural awareness training, international assignment briefings, business briefings for people proposing to live and work overseas.

Subject coverage:
Briefings on any country, including current economics, politics, the people and their social and business culture, the business environment, social and domestic conditions, constructive and efficient conducting of verbal and non-verbal communications, agreements, discussions, negotiations; practical aspects of moving overseas; information on leisure and recreation, health, education and security. Business briefings for home-based international personnel. Intercultural workshops and repatriation programmes.

Printed publications:
Brochure about programmes

Access to staff:
Contact by letter, by telephone, by fax, by e-mail, in person and via website. Appointment necessary.
Hours: Mon to Fri, 0900 to 1700

FASHION MUSEUM, BATH – STUDY FACILITIES

The Assembly Rooms, Bennett Street, Bath, BA1 2QH

Tel: 01225 477754
E-mail: fashion_enquiries@bathnes.gov.uk

Website:
http://www.fashionmuseum.co.uk
Includes information about the fashion research facilities.

Founded:
1974

Formerly called:
Fashion Research Centre (year of change 2007)

Organisation type and purpose:
Museum's study facilities.

Subject coverage:
History of fashionable dress.

Information services:
24-hour information line tel: 01225 477867

Special visitor services:
To book a reading space or a study table, tel: 01225 477754 or e-mail: fashion_enquiries@bathnes.gov.uk

Museum or gallery collection, archive, or library special collection:
Designated collection of historical and contemporary fashionable dress, mostly 18th- to 20th-century, archives

Non-library collection catalogue:
All or part available in-house

Library catalogue:
All or part available in-house

Printed publications:
Fashion Museum Treasures (Scala Publishers, 2009)
Order printed publications from: Fashion Museum Shop, email: museumshop_enquiries@bathnes.gov.uk

Access to staff:
Contact by telephone and by e-mail
Hours: Mon to Fri, 0930 to 1700
Special comments: Closed on public holidays.

Access to building, collection or gallery:
Hours: Mon to Sun, 1030 to 1700
Special comments: Closed 25 and 26 Dec.

Access for disabled people:
Study facilities are on the first floor of the Assembly Rooms, so access may be difficult for those with limited mobility; telephone the Study Facilities to discuss individual requirements.

Parent body:
Bath and North East Somerset Council Heritage Services Division

FATHER HUDSON'S SOCIETY

Coventry Road, Coleshill, Birmingham, B46 3ED

Tel: 01675 434 000
E-mail: enquiries@fatherhudsons.org.uk

Website:
http://www.fatherhudsons.org.uk
Details of all services provided; community-based projects; Origin services.

Founded:
1902

Formerly called:
Birmingham Diocesan Rescue Society for the Protection of Homeless and Friendless Catholic Children (year of change 1984)

Organisation type and purpose:
A registered charity (number 512992).
The Social Care Agency of the Roman Catholic Archdiocese of Birmingham, covering the counties of Staffordshire, Worcestershire, West Midlands, Warwickshire and Oxfordshire.
Offers services to children, young people, adults and families in need, without favour or discrimination, in order to improve their quality of life.

Subject coverage:
Provides adult residential and day care, adoption and fostering services, and community projects.

Information services:
Origin Services providing information from over a hundred years of archive records regarding personal origins to all those who, as children, were involved with Father Hudson's becuase of being adopted, in care, or part of child migration schemes.

Access to staff:
Contact by letter, by telephone and by e-mail

FAVERSHAM SOCIETY

Fleur de Lis, 10–13 Preston Street, Faversham, Kent, ME13 8NS

Tel: 01795 534542
Fax: 01795 533261
E-mail: ticfaversham@btconnect.com.

Website:
http://www.faversham.org/society
Full details of the centre and the society.

Enquiries:
Enquiries to: Honorary Director

Founded:
1977

Organisation type and purpose:
Membership association, present number of members: 1000, voluntary organisation, registered charity (charity number 250945).
The Society is run by 100% voluntary effort for the good of the area. It is completely independent and open to all sharing its interests.

Subject coverage:
History of Faversham area, including the port of Faversham, and industries; family history in Faversham area, history of explosives industry.

Special visitor services:
Networker (officer), Tourist Information Centre

Museum or gallery collection, archive, or library special collection:
Museum, gallery, two libraries

Non-library collection catalogue:
All or part available in-house

Library catalogue:
All or part available in-house

Printed publications:
Faversham Papers: some 100 monographs about the area, including:
The History of Faversham
The Foundation of Faversham Abbey
The War Years 1939–1945 in Faversham and District
Faversham Stone Trail
Changing Landlords, the Annexation of the Maison Dieu to St John's College, Cambridge
Faversham Studies including:
Faversham and District Bibliography, Primary Sources (7 Volumes, Hyde P)
Faversham and District Bibliography, Secondary Sources (Hyde P)
Sittingbourne Papers: produced by the Faversham Society for the Sittingbourne Society

Electronic and video publications:
Several DVDs and CDs
Order electronic and video publications from: above address

Publications list:
Available online and in print

Access to staff:
Contact by letter, by telephone, by fax, by e-mail, in person and via website
Hours: Mon to Sat, 1000 to 1600; Sun, 1000 to 1300

Access to building, collection or gallery:
Hours: Mon to Sat, 1000 to 1600; Sun, 1000 to 1300

Access for disabled people:
Available over most of complex
Hours: Mon to Sat, 1000 to 1600; Sun, 1000 to 1300

Manages the:
Chart Gunpowder Mills
Westbrook Walk, Faversham

Manages the:
Fleur de Lis Heritage Centre
at the same address

Manages the:
Maison Dieu Museum
Ospringe Street, Faversham

FEDERATION AGAINST COPYRIGHT THEFT LIMITED

Acronym or abbreviation: FACT

7 Victory Business Centre, Worton Road, Isleworth, Middlesex, TW7 6DB

Tel: 020 8568 6646
Fax: 020 8560 6364
E-mail: contact@fact-uk.org.uk

Enquiries:
Enquiries to: Director General
Direct e-mail: eddy.leviten@fact-uk.org.uk
Other contacts: Company Secretary

Founded:
1983

Organisation type and purpose:
National organisation, membership association (membership is by subscription, election or invitation), present number of members: 20. Private company.

Subject coverage:
Copyright protection of motion pictures.

Access to staff:
Contact by letter and by e-mail
Hours: Mon to Fri, 0900 to 1700

Affiliated to:
Motion Picture Association

FEDERATION AGAINST SOFTWARE THEFT

Acronym or abbreviation: FAST

York House, 18 York Road, Maidenhead, Berkshire, SL6 1SF

Tel: 01628 622121
Fax: 01628 760355
E-mail: fast@fast.org

Website:
http://www.fast.org.uk
Information on software piracy and the activities of The Federation.

Enquiries:
Enquiries to: Public Relations Manager
Other contacts: Account Manager for membership.

Founded:
1984

Organisation type and purpose:
National organisation, advisory body, trade association, membership association (membership is by subscription), present number of members: 150.

Subject coverage:
Software control and management, auditing, the law governing software copyright, forensic examination of counterfeits, software piracy.

Printed publications:
Audit pack – Audit services contact list (free)
Computer crime – A guide for enforcement authorities (free)
FASTtalk (newsletter, quarterly)
Information pack (free)

Access to staff:
Contact by letter, by telephone, by fax, by e-mail and via website
Hours: Mon to Fri, 0900 to 1700

Access to building, collection or gallery:
Prior appointment required

Access for disabled people:
Parking provided, ramped entry, level entry, toilet facilities

FEDERATION OF BAKERS

Acronym or abbreviation: FoB

6 Catherine Street, London, WC2B 5JW

Tel: 020 7420 7190
Fax: 020 7379 0542

Website:
http://www.bakersfederation.org.uk
FoB and the baking industry, resources and events, health and safety

Founded:
1942

Organisation type and purpose:
Membership association, represents the interests of the UK's largest baking companies who manufacture sliced and wrapped bread, bakery snacks and other bread products. The Federation has 7 member companies running 44 bakeries in the United Kingdom.
To deliver professional services to members and other users of its services to an excellent standard and in genuine partnership with all stakeholders; this may be in the provision of advice, training or leadership in health and safety, or in a representational role lobbying on technical issues or promoting the consumption of bread through PR work.

Subject coverage:
Bread baking industry.

Information services:
Annual conference presentations available on website.

Printed publications:
Fact Sheets, Reports and Industry Guidance documents
Order printed publications from: website

Electronic and video publications:
Fact Sheets, Reports and Industry Guidance documents
Press releases
Order electronic and video publications from: website

Publications list:
Available online

Access to staff:
Contact by letter, by telephone and by fax

FEDERATION OF BRITISH AQUATIC SOCIETIES

Acronym or abbreviation: FBAS

2 Cedar Avenue, Wickford, Essex, SS12 9DT

Tel: 01268 472095
E-mail: chris@cheswright.freeserve.co.uk

Enquiries:
Enquiries to: General Secretary

Founded:
1938

Organisation type and purpose:
Membership association (membership is by subscription), voluntary organisation.
Central governing body for all UK aquarist clubs.

Subject coverage:
All fields of aquatics associated with fishkeeping: coldwater, tropical, marine; the environment, keeping, breeding and showing of fish; fish diseases and cures.

Printed publications:
Details of Clubs around Country
Fishworld (magazine, quarterly, £5 p.a.)
Publications on all subjects given above
Order printed publications from: Merchandising Officer, FBAS
28 The Mall, Binstead, Isle of Wight, PO33 3SF, tel: 01983 566810

Publications list:
Available in print

Access to staff:
Contact by fax
Hours: Telephone after 1800

FEDERATION OF BRITISH ARTISTS

Acronym or abbreviation: FBA

17 Carlton House Terrace, London, SW1Y 5BD

Tel: 020 7930 6844
Fax: 020 7839 7830
E-mail: press@mallgalleries.com

Website:
http://www.mallgalleries.org.uk

Enquiries:
Enquiries to: Secretary
Other contacts: Marketing and Communications Officer

Founded:
1961

Organisation type and purpose:
Membership association (membership is by election or invitation), present number of members: 600, voluntary organisation, registered charity (charity number 200048). Federation of voluntary art societies (see list).
The FBA promotes the visual arts in Britain and is the umbrella organisation for nine autonomous national art societies.

Subject coverage:
Arranging art exhibitions in the Mall Galleries, London SW1, advice on commissioning portraits or other art work, visual arts by contemporary artists, past and present society members.

Museum or gallery collection, archive, or library special collection:
Catalogues of previous exhibitions

continued overleaf

Non-library collection catalogue:
All or part available in print

Printed publications:
Catalogues of exhibitions for each art society
Newsletter

Access to staff:
Contact by letter, by telephone, by fax, by e-mail
and via website
Hours: Mon to Fri, 0930 to 1700

Access to building, collection or gallery:
Prior appointment required
Hours: Mon to Fri, 0930 to 1700

Access for disabled people:
Toilet facilities, stair lift
Special comments: Stair lift.

Links with:
FBA Friends Society
   contact through the FBA
Hesketh Hubbard Art Society
   contact through the FBA
Mall Galleries
   contact through the FBA
New English Art Club
   contact through the FBA
Pastel Society
   contact through the FBA
Royal Institute of Oil Painters
   contact through the FBA
Royal Institute of Painters in Watercolours
   contact through the FBA
Royal Society of British Artists
   contact through the FBA
Royal Society of Marine Artists
   contact through the FBA
Royal Society of Portrait Painters
   contact through the FBA
Society of Wildlife Artists
   contact through the FBA

FEDERATION OF BRITISH BONSAI SOCIETIES

Acronym or abbreviation: FOBBS

17 Woodland Park, Ynystawe, Swansea, West
Glamorgan, SA6 5AR

Tel: 01792 845659
E-mail: ukbonsai@ntlworld.com

Website:
http://www.fobbs.co.uk
Details of clubs, events, advice, gallery.
http://uk.geocities.com/fobbs_uk

Enquiries:
Enquiries to: General Secretary

Founded:
1982

Organisation type and purpose:
Membership association (membership is by
subscription), voluntary organisation, registered
charity.

Subject coverage:
Bonsai and bonsai clubs, national bonsai collection,
bonsai traders, bonsai events.

**Museum or gallery collection, archive, or library
special collection:**
National Bonsai Collection at Birmingham
   Botanical Gardens

Printed publications:
Newsletter (once every other month)
Membership List (annual)

Access to staff:
Contact by letter, by telephone, by e-mail and via
website
Hours: Any reasonable time

Affiliated to:
Friends of the National Bonsai Collection
   (Charitable trust); tel: 0121 378 4837; fax: 0121
   311 1912

FEDERATION OF BRITISH HAND TOOL MANUFACTURERS

Acronym or abbreviation: FBHTM

c/o Manufacturing Technologies Association

Tel: 020 7298 6400
Fax: 020 7298 6430
E-mail: info@britishtools.co.uk

Website:
http://www.britishtools.co.uk

Enquiries:
Enquiries to: Secretary

Organisation type and purpose:
Trade association.

Subject coverage:
Engineers' cutting tools industry, exhibition and
export activities, publicity for the industry.

Links with:
British Hardmetal and Engineers' Cutting Tool
Association (BHECTA)

Member organisation of:
European Cutting Tools Association (ECTA)

FEDERATION OF BRITISH HAND TOOL MANUFACTURERS

Acronym or abbreviation: FBHTM

c/o Manufacturing Technologies Association, 62
Bayswater Road, London, W2 3PS

Tel: 020 7298 6400
Fax: 020 7298 6430
E-mail: info@britishtools.co.uk

Website:
http://www.britishtools.co.uk

Enquiries:
Enquiries to: Secretary

Organisation type and purpose:
Trade association.

Subject coverage:
British hand tool manufacturing industry,
exhibition and export activity, publicity for the
industry.

Member organisation of:
Comité Européen d'Outillage (CEO – European
Hand Tool Committee)

Member organisations:
Construction Fixings Association
   website: http://www.fixingscfa.co.uk

FEDERATION OF BUILDING SPECIALIST CONTRACTORS

Acronym or abbreviation: FBSC

Unit 9 Lakeside Industrial Estate, Stanton
Harcourt, Oxfordshire OX29 5SL

Tel: 01865 883557
Fax: 01865 884467
E-mail: enquiries@fbsc.org.uk

Website:
http://www.fbsc.org.uk/

Enquiries:
Enquiries to: Membership Secretary

Organisation type and purpose:
Trade association (membership is by subscription).

Subject coverage:
Details of member companies covering a wide
range of specialist trades in the building industry.

Access to staff:
Contact by letter, by telephone, by fax and by e-
mail
Hours: Mon to Fri, 0900 to 1700

Access to building, collection or gallery:
No prior appointment required

Member of:
Construction Confederation

FEDERATION OF BURIAL AND CREMATION AUTHORITIES

Acronym or abbreviation: FBCA

41 Salisbury Road, Carshalton, Surrey, SM5 3HA

Tel: 020 8669 4521

Website:
http://www.fbca.org.uk
Details of services offered by the Federation along
with relevant guides, code of practice, etc.

Enquiries:
Enquiries to: Secretary
Direct e-mail: fbcasec@btconnect.com

Founded:
1924

Formerly called:
Federation of British Cremation Authorities (year
of change 2006)

Organisation type and purpose:
Trade association and technical advisory service.

Subject coverage:
All matters connected with the management and
operation of cemeteries and crematoria.

Printed publications:
Resurgam (journal, quarterly)
Technical booklets/leaflets

Access to staff:
Contact by letter, by telephone, by fax, by e-mail
and via website
Hours: Mon to Fri, 0900 to 1700

FEDERATION OF CHILDREN'S BOOK GROUPS

Acronym or abbreviation: FCBG

2 Bridge Wood View, Horsforth, Leeds, West
Yorkshire, LS18 5PE

Tel: 0113 258 8910
E-mail: info@fcbg.org.uk

Website:
http://www.fcbg.org.uk

Enquiries:
Enquiries to: National Secretary

Founded:
1968

Organisation type and purpose:
Membership association (membership is by
subscription), present number of members: 30
book groups, plus individual and professional
members, voluntary organisation, registered
charity (charity number 268289).
To promote enjoyment and interest in children's
books and reading.

Subject coverage:
Children's booklists, book group details and
locations, children's book award information,
annual conference details.

Printed publications:
Various current free booklists
Pick of the Year booklists

Access to staff:
Contact by letter, by telephone, by e-mail and via
website
Hours: Mon to Fri, 0900 to 1700

FEDERATION OF CITY FARMS AND COMMUNITY GARDENS

Acronym or abbreviation: FCFCG

The Green House, Hereford Street, Bedminster,
Bristol, BS3 4NA

Tel: 0117 923 1800
Fax: 0117 923 1900
E-mail: admin@farmgarden.org.uk

Website:
http://www.farmgarden.org.uk

News and events, farms and gardens in the UK, start your own, young people.

Enquiries:
Enquiries to: Director
Other contacts: Information Officer

Founded:
1980

Formerly called:
National Federation of City Farms (NFCF) (year of change 1999)

Organisation type and purpose:
Membership association (membership is by subscription), present number of members: 398 projects and affiliates, registered charity (charity number 294494).
To promote community development and advance education in animal husbandry and gardening.

Subject coverage:
Farming and gardening in urban areas, legal requirements for setting up a charity or company limited by guarantee, community management of a voluntary project.

Museum or gallery collection, archive, or library special collection:
Teacher Resource Centre

Library catalogue:
All or part available in-house

Printed publications:
Various reports and information packs including:
Annual Review (free)
Community Garden Starter Pack (£6)
Compost Box
Members' newsletter (members only)
Public Newsletter (2 a year, free)

City Farm Starter Pack (£6)
Child Protection Guidelines (£2.00)
Good Practice Case Studies pack (£6)

Publications list:
Available in print

Access to staff:
Contact by letter, by fax and by e-mail.
Appointment necessary.
Hours: Mon to Fri, 0900 to 1700

Access to building, collection or gallery:
No prior appointment required

Access for disabled people:
Ramped entry, access to all public areas, toilet facilities
Hours: Mon to Fri, 0900 to 1700

Member farms and gardens:
More than 350 in the UK

Member of:
Black Environment Network
Council for Environmental Education
European Federation of City Farms
National Council for Voluntary Organisations
NCVCCO

FEDERATION OF CLOTHING DESIGNERS AND EXECUTIVES

Acronym or abbreviation: FCDE

56 Eden Park Avenue, Beckenham, Kent, BR3 3HW

Tel: 020 8650 5429
Fax: 020 8663 0073
E-mail: maggiewatts@compuserve.com

Website:
http://www.ntu.ac.uk/fas/fcde/index.htm

Enquiries:
Enquiries to: General Secretary

Founded:
1935

Formerly called:
Federation of Clothing Designers and Production Managers

Organisation type and purpose:
Trade association (membership is by election or invitation).
Improving knowledge and skills of members by technical meetings and conventions.

Subject coverage:
Technical information on clothing manufacturing in the areas of pattern technology, design, clothing and manufacturing techniques on all types of outerwear.

Access to staff:
Contact by letter, by telephone, by fax, by e-mail and via website. Non-members charged.
Hours: Mon to Fri, 0900 to 1700

Branches in:
London, Manchester, The Midlands, and Nottingham

FEDERATION OF COCOA COMMERCE LTD

Acronym or abbreviation: FCC

Cannon Bridge House, 1 Cousin Lane, London, EC4R 3XX

Tel: 020 7379 2884
Fax: 020 7379 2389
E-mail: fcc@liffe.com

Website:
http://www.cocoafederation.com
Home page.

Enquiries:
Enquiries to: Chief Executive
Direct tel: 020 7379 2882

Founded:
1929

Organisation type and purpose:
International organisation, trade association.

Subject coverage:
Cocoa trading.

Access to staff:
Contact by letter, by telephone, by fax, by e-mail and via website
Hours: Mon to Fri, 0900 to 1700

FEDERATION OF COMMUNICATION SERVICES LIMITED

Acronym or abbreviation: FCS

Burnhill Business Centre, Provident House, Burrell Row, High Street, Beckenham, Kent, BR3 1AT

Tel: 020 8249 6363
Fax: 0844 870 5927
E-mail: fcs@fcs.org.uk

Website:
http://www.fcs.org.uk

Enquiries:
Enquiries to: Chief Executive

Founded:
1981

Organisation type and purpose:
National organisation, trade association (membership is by subscription), present number of members and associates: 360, manufacturing industry, service industry.
Mobile and telecoms services communication trade association.

Subject coverage:
Mobile communications, telecommunications, radio communications.

Printed publications:
FCS Annual Report
FCS Bulletin

Access to staff:
Contact by e-mail and via website. Appointment necessary.

Hours: Mon to Fri, 0900 to 1730

Access to building, collection or gallery:
No access other than to staff

FEDERATION OF ECONOMIC DEVELOPMENT AUTHORITIES

Acronym or abbreviation: FEDA

7 Franklin's Yard, Fossgate, York, YO1 9TN

Tel: 01904 670534
Fax: 01904 670536
E-mail: feda@btconnect.com

Enquiries:
Enquiries to: Director

Founded:
1943

Organisation type and purpose:
Membership association (membership is by subscription), present number of members: local authorities in the UK.

Subject coverage:
Economic development issues in relation to impact on local authorities.

Printed publications:
FEDA (journal)

Access to staff:
Contact by letter, by telephone, by fax and by e-mail
Hours: Mon to Fri, 0930 to 1730

FEDERATION OF ENGINE RE-MANUFACTURERS

Acronym or abbreviation: FER

59 Mewstone Avenue, Wembury, Plymouth, PL9 OJT

Tel: 01752 863681
Fax: 01752 863682
E-mail: ferm@btinternet.com

Website:
http://www.fer.co.uk/

Enquiries:
Enquiries to: Director

Founded:
1938

Organisation type and purpose:
Trade association.

Subject coverage:
Re-manufacture of internal combustion engines.

Printed publications:
List of members (and associates)
Newsletter (monthly)

Access to staff:
Contact by letter
Hours: Mon to Fri, 0900 to 1700

FEDERATION OF ENVIRONMENTAL TRADE ASSOCIATIONS

Acronym or abbreviation: FETA

2 Waltham Court, Milley Lane, Hare Hatch, Reading, Berkshire, RG10 9TH

Tel: 0118 940 3416
Fax: 0118 940 6258
E-mail: info@feta.co.uk

Website:
http://www.feta.co.uk

Enquiries:
Enquiries to: Director-General

Organisation type and purpose:
Trade association.

continued overleaf

Subject coverage:
Building services, heating, ventilating, air
conditioning and refrigeration.

Printed publications:
Directories
Fact sheets, particularly on energy efficiency
Product, specification and services directories

Publications list:
Available online and in print

Access to staff:
Contact by letter, by telephone, by fax and by e-mail
Hours: Mon to Thu, 0830 to 1630; Fri, 0830 to 1600

Member organisations:
British Flue and Chimney Manufacturers'
Association (BFCMA)
 at same address
British Refrigeration Association (BRA)
 at same address
Chilled Beam and Ceiling Association (CBCA)
 at same address
Fan Manufacturers Association (FMA)
 at same address
Heat Pump Association (HPA)
 at same address
Heating, Ventilating and Air-Conditioning
Manufacturers' Association (HEVAC)
 at same address
Hose Manufacturers' and Suppliers' Association
(HMSA)
 at same address
Residential Ventilation Association (RVA)
 at same address
Smoke Control Association (SCA)
 at same address

FEDERATION OF FAMILY HISTORY SOCIETIES

Acronym or abbreviation: FFHS

PO Box 8857, Lutterworth, Leicestershire, LE17 9BJ

Tel: 01455 203133
E-mail: info@ffhs.org.uk

Website:
http://www.ffhs.org.uk
Latest news from the family history world, list of
member societies.

Enquiries:
Enquiries to: Administrator

Founded:
1974

Organisation type and purpose:
International organisation, trade association,
membership association (membership is by
subscription), present number of members: 200,
registered charity (charity number 1038721),
suitable for all ages.

Subject coverage:
Family history, local history, genealogy, heraldry,
demography, historical research.

**Museum or gallery collection, archive, or library
special collection:**
Archive collection of member societies, not open to
 public

Printed publications:
Really Useful Leaflet includes list of member
 societies
Information leaflets

Electronic and video publications:
National Burial Index Version 3 (CD-ROM, £30)

Access to staff:
Contact by letter, by telephone, by e-mail and via
website
Hours: Mon to Fri, 0900 to 1700

Access to building, collection or gallery:
No access other than to staff

FEDERATION OF HOLISTIC THERAPISTS

Acronym or abbreviation: FHT

18 Shakespeare Business Centre, Hathaway Close,
Eastleigh, Hampshire, SO50 4SR

Tel: 0844 875 2022
Fax: 023 8062 4399
E-mail: info@fht.org.uk

Website:
http://www.fht.org.uk
Membership criteria and benefits.

Enquiries:
Enquiries to: Chief Executive
Other contacts: Marketing Manager for information
about International Therapist Magazine –
advertising, editorial etc.

Founded:
1962

Formerly called:
International Federation of Health and Beauty
Therapists

Organisation type and purpose:
International organisation, professional body
(membership is by qualification), present number
of members: 18,000.
Oldest and largest professional association for the
health and beauty industry. Publishers of the
International Therapist Journal.
Services to members, teachers and employers,
advisory and information service to health and
beauty employers and to the media regarding the
nature of the work, to arrange insurance and
provide a code of practice for hygiene in salons
and clinics.

Subject coverage:
Health and beauty including physical treatment
through massage, colour, sports and beauty
therapy, aromatherapy, reflexology. All aspects of
health and beauty therapy including employment.

Printed publications:
Many publications restricted to members, also:
Code of Practice for Hygiene in Beauty Salons and
 Clinics (£4.95 plus p&p)
Essential Business Guide for Therapists (updated
 yearly)
International Therapist (journal, 6 times a year)

Access to staff:
Contact by letter, by telephone, by fax, by e-mail
and via website
Hours: Mon to Fri, 0900 to 1700
Special comments: No visitors in person.

Founder member of the industry lead body:
Health and Beauty Therapy Training Board

Links with:
Association of Therapy Lecturers
Federation of Professional Sugaring
fraternal organisations in many overseas countries
Health and Beauty Employers Federation
International Council of Health, Fitness and Sports
Therapists
International Council of Holistic Therapists
International Federation of Health and Beauty
Therapists

FEDERATION OF INDEPENDENT DETECTORISTS

Acronym or abbreviation: FID

Detector Lodge, 44 Heol Dulais, Birchgrove,
Swansea, West Glamorgan, SA7 9LT

Tel: 07866 914253
Fax: 07866 914253
E-mail: hon.sec.fid@detectorists.net

Website:
http://www.fid.newbury.net
Information, photographs, free recovery service,
application form for joining, etc.

Enquiries:
Enquiries to: Honorary Secretary

Direct tel: 01635 522578

Founded:
1982

Organisation type and purpose:
International organisation, membership
association, voluntary organisation.
A lobby on behalf of the members' interests;
information service to the press, media, parliament
and local authorities.

Subject coverage:
The recreational use of metal detectors.

Printed publications:
Bulletin (quarterly, members only)
Leaflets, press releases (from time to time)

Electronic and video publications:
Internet Access (Detectorists.net, CD-ROM or
 online)

Access to staff:
Contact by letter, by telephone, by e-mail and via
website
Hours: Mon to Fri, 0900 to 1700

Affiliated to:
Detector Information Group
Heritage 2100
Heritage for All

Also at:
Press and Public Relations Officer, Federation of
Independent Detectorists
 61 Newtown Road, Newbury, Berkshire, RG14
7BU; tel: 01635 522578

Member organisation of:
Standing Conference of European Metal Detecting

FEDERATION OF IRISH SOCIETIES

Acronym or abbreviation: FIS

52 Camden Square, London, NW1 9XB

Tel: 020 7916 2725
Fax: 020 7916 2753

Enquiries:
Enquiries to: Administrator

Founded:
1973

Organisation type and purpose:
National organisation, membership association
(membership is by qualification), present number
of members: 100, voluntary organisation, research
organisation.
Representation of the Irish community in Britain.

Subject coverage:
Information relative to the Irish Community in
Britain.

Printed publications:
Alcohol and Disadvantage amongst the Irish in
 England, Larry Harrison and Roy Carr-Hill
 (£4.95 plus 80p p&p)
Developing Community Response: the Service
 Needs of the Irish Community in Britain, Ute
 Kowarzik (£4.95 plus £1 p&p)
Elderly Irish People in London: A Profile (Tilki M,
 £4 plus 75p p&p)
FIS Directory of Membership Organisations
 (voluntary organisations, £15; Statutory and
 commercial organisations, £40)
Index of Member Organisations (free, sae)
Irish Community Services: Meeting Diverse Needs
 (Kowarzik A, £4.95 plus £1 p&p)
Report of the Irish Pensioners Conference: October
 1997 (£3 plus 75p p&p)
Report on the Needs of Irish Agencies: to assist
 Development, Seán Hutton (£4.95 plus £1 p&p)
The Health of the Irish in Britain: The Report of a
 Community Conference (£5 plus 75p p&p)
The Irish Community: Discrimination and the
 Criminal Justice System (£1 p&p)
The Irish in Britain: An Annotated Bibliography on
 Health and Related Issues (£5 plus 75p p&p)

Order printed publications from: Community Administrative Assistant, Federation of Irish Societies
tel: 020 7916 2729, fax: 020 7916 2753

Publications list:
Available in print

Access to staff:
Contact by letter, by telephone and by fax
Hours: Mon to Fri, 0900 to 1700

FEDERATION OF LICENSED VICTUALLERS ASSOCIATIONS

Acronym or abbreviation: FLVA

128 Bradford Road, Brighouse, West Yorkshire, HD6 4AU

Tel: 01484 710534
Fax: 01484 718647
E-mail: admin@flva.co.uk

Website:
http://www.flva.co.uk

Founded:
1992

Organisation type and purpose:
Professional body, trade association.
To provide help and advice to licensed victuallers.

Subject coverage:
All aspects of the licensing trade, up-to-date legislation of employment law, health and safety, food and hygiene.

Printed publications:
Publications available free to members
Food Safety, General Food Hygiene Regulations 1995 (Guidance notes)
Helping Hand for the Licensed Trade (business plan)
Publicans Guide to the Health and Safety at Work Act

Access to staff:
Contact by letter, by telephone, by fax and by e-mail
Hours: Mon to Fri, 0900 to 1700

FEDERATION OF LONDON YOUTH CLUBS

Acronym or abbreviation: The Fed; London Youth

Bridge House, Bridge House Quay, Prestons Road, London, E14 9QA

Tel: 020 7537 2777
Fax: 020 7537 7072
E-mail: hello@londonyouth.org.uk

Enquiries:
Enquiries to: Chief Executive

Founded:
1887

Formed by the merger of:
London Federation of Clubs for Young People (LFCYP), London Union of Youth Clubs (LUYC) (year of change 1999)

Formerly called:
London Federation of Boys Clubs (LFBC) (year of change 1994–1999)

Organisation type and purpose:
Voluntary organisation, registered charity (charity number 303324).
Youth work.

Subject coverage:
Youth work in London since 1887.

Access to staff:
Contact by letter, by fax and by e-mail
Hours: Mon to Fri, 0900 to 1700

Access for disabled people:
Parking provided

Other locations at:
Hindleap Warren
   Wych Cross, Forest Row, East Sussex, RH18 5JS; tel: 01342 822625; fax: 01342 822913; e-mail: hindleap@londonyouth.org.uk
Woodrow High House
   Cherry Tree Lane, Amersham, Buckinghamshire, HP7 0QG; tel: 01494 433531; fax: 01494 431391; e-mail: woodrow@londonyouth.org.uk

FEDERATION OF MASTER BUILDERS

Acronym or abbreviation: FMB

Gordon Fisher House, 14–15 Great James Street, London, WC1N 3DP

Tel: 020 7242 7583
Fax: 020 7404 0296

Website:
http://www.fmb.org.uk
Details about the Federation of Master Builders and pages for members only.

Enquiries:
Enquiries to: Information Officer

Founded:
1941

Organisation type and purpose:
Trade association.

Subject coverage:
Building industry; all aspects affecting the building employer; health and safety, employment law, product and manufacturer traces, contract law, EC law, technical.

Trade and statistical information:
Quarterly state of trade survey (based on response from members).

Library catalogue:
All or part available in-house

Printed publications:
Master Builder (magazine, monthly)
Regional Yearbook (available to members, local authorities and public libraries only)
Factsheets on various topics (members only)
Small Works Contract

Publications list:
Available in print

Access to staff:
Contact by letter
Hours: Mon to Fri, 0900 to 1700
Special comments: Not open to the public, no loan facilities.

Member of:
European Builders Confederation

With the:
Transport and General Workers Union formed the Building & Allied Trades Joint Industrial Council

FEDERATION OF MULTIPLE SCLEROSIS THERAPY CENTRES

Bradbury House, 155 Barkers Lane, Bedford, MK41 9RX

Tel: 01234 325781
Fax: 01234 365242
E-mail: info@ms-selfhelp.org

Website:
http://www.ms-selfhelp.org

Enquiries:
Enquiries to: Administrator
Other contacts: Chairman

Founded:
1994

Formerly called:
ARMS (Multiple Sclerosis Research) Limited

Organisation type and purpose:
Statutory body, voluntary organisation, registered charity.

70 centres provide therapy information and support to Multiple Sclerosis sufferers.

Subject coverage:
Multiple sclerosis, self-help disease management, support and information, treatment by professional therapists, support for carers of people with MS, information on MS for the general public.

Printed publications:
Diet Booklet
Information booklet
Long term results on Hyperbaric oxygen
Recipe booklet

Publications list:
Available online and in print

Access to staff:
Contact by letter, by telephone, by fax, by e-mail and via website. Appointment necessary.
Hours: Mon to Fri, 1000 to 1600

Access for disabled people:
Parking provided, ramped entry, access to all public areas, toilet facilities

FEDERATION OF OILS, SEEDS AND FATS ASSOCIATIONS LIMITED

Acronym or abbreviation: FOSFA

20 St Dunstans Hill, London, EC3R 8NQ

Tel: 020 7283 5511
Fax: 020 7623 1310
E-mail: contact@fosfa.org

Website:
http://www.fosfa.org

Enquiries:
Enquiries to: Chief Executive

Organisation type and purpose:
International organisation, trade association.

Subject coverage:
Oil seed and animal, vegetable and margarine oils and fats; HPS groundnuts; trading conditions; analysis, sampling and specification.

Access to staff:
Access for members only.
Hours: Mon to Fri, 0900 to 1700

Associated with:
National Farmers' Union
UK Agricultural Supply Trade Association

Incorporating the:
Incorporated Oil Seed Association
London Copra Association
London Oil and Tallow Trades Association
Seed, Oil, Cake and General Produce Association

Liaison with:
over 50 kindred organisations throughout the world

FEDERATION OF OPHTHALMIC AND DISPENSING OPTICIANS

Acronym or abbreviation: FODO

199 Gloucester Terrace, London, W2 6LD

Tel: 020 7298 5151
Fax: 020 7298 5111
E-mail: helen@fodo.com

Website:
http://www.fodo.com

Founded:
1985

Formerly called:
Guild of British Dispensing Opticians (year of change 1985)

Organisation type and purpose:
Membership association (membership is by subscription), registered charity (charity number 368950).

continued overleaf

Subject coverage:
Optical practice and dispensing, sources of optics, training, memberships.

Printed publications:
Careers leaflet for people interested in studying optics
Optics at a Glance (annually)

Access to staff:
Contact by letter and by telephone
Hours: Mon to Fri, 0900 to 1700
Special comments: By letter in the first instance.

FEDERATION OF PATIDAR ASSOCIATIONS

Patidar House, 22 London Road, Wembley, Middlesex, HA9 7EX

Tel: 020 8795 1648
Fax: 020 8795 1648
E-mail: info@patidars.org

Website:
http://www.patidars.org

Enquiries:
Enquiries to: Honorary Secretary
Other contacts: President

Founded:
November 1976

Organisation type and purpose:
Membership association (membership is by subscription), present number of members: 13 organisations, voluntary organisation, registered charity (charity number 1076284), suitable for ages: 2 to 25.
Drop-in centre for elderly; performing arts classes; yoga; youth club.

Subject coverage:
Nursery; day centre for elderly; performing arts classes (Bhart Natyam, Kathak, folk dances, music); yoga; Bollywood dance; sitar

Access to staff:
Contact by letter, by telephone and by e-mail
Hours: Mon to Fri, 1000 to 1800

Access to building, collection or gallery:
Hours: Mon to Sun, 0800 to 2200

Access for disabled people:
Hours: Mon to Fri, 1000 to 1400

FEDERATION OF PILING SPECIALISTS

Acronym or abbreviation: FPS

Forum Court, 83 Copers Cope Road, Beckenham, Kent, BR3 1NR

Tel: 020 8663 0947
Fax: 020 8663 0949
E-mail: fps@fps.org.uk

Website:
http://www.fps.org.uk

Enquiries:
Enquiries to: Executive Secretary

Organisation type and purpose:
Trade association.

Subject coverage:
Ground engineering, foundation and pile construction techniques, ground improvement.

Access to staff:
Contact by letter, by telephone, by fax and by e-mail
Hours: Mon to Fri, 0900 to 1700

Member organisation of:
European Federation of Foundation Contractors (EFFC)
Ground Forum
National Specialist Contractors Council (NSCC)

FEDERATION OF PLASTERING AND DRYWALL CONTRACTORS

Acronym or abbreviation: FPDC

1st Floor, 8–9 Ludgate Square, London, EC4M 7AS

Tel: 020 7634 9480
Fax: 020 7248 9263
E-mail: membership@fpdc.org

Website:
http://www.fpdc.org

Enquiries:
Enquiries to: Director
Other contacts: Administrator

Founded:
1942

Formerly called:
Dry Lining and Partition Association, National Federation of Plastering Contractors (year of change 1990)

Incorporates the:
London Master Plasterers Association (year of change 1997)

Organisation type and purpose:
Trade association.

Subject coverage:
Plastering and drywall construction.

Printed publications:
Specifiers Guide

Publications list:
Available online

Access to staff:
Contact by letter, by telephone and by fax
Hours: Mon to Fri, 0930 to 1715

Member of:
National Specialist Contractors Council (NSCC)
tel: 020 7608 5090; fax: 020 7608 5081

FEDERATION OF RECORDED MUSIC SOCIETIES LIMITED

Acronym or abbreviation: FRMS

FRMS Secretary, 18 Albany Road, Hartshill, Stoke-on-Trent, ST4 6BB

Tel: 01782 251460
E-mail: secretary@thefrms.co.uk

Website:
http://www.thefrms.co.uk
A description of the functions of the Federation, plus the annual programme content of many of the member societies.

Enquiries:
Enquiries to: Secretary

Founded:
1936

Formerly called:
National Federation of Gramophone Societies

Organisation type and purpose:
Voluntary organisation, present number of members: 205 affiliated societies with members numbering 11,000.

Subject coverage:
Organisation, establishment and conduct of recorded music societies, reproducing equipment, copyright and related subjects applying to gramophone records and all forms of tape, audio matters in general.

Printed publications:
Bulletin (2 times a year)

Access to staff:
Contact by letter, by telephone and by e-mail
Hours: Any time

FEDERATION OF SMALL BUSINESSES

Acronym or abbreviation: FSB

2 Catherine Place, London, SW1E 6HF

Tel: 020 7592 8100
Fax: 020 7828 5919
E-mail: press@fsb.org.uk

Website:
http://www.fsb.org.uk
Small business issues.

Enquiries:
Enquiries to: Head of Public Affairs
Direct tel: 020 7592 8112
Direct e-mail: stephen.alambritis@fsb.org.uk
Other contacts: Press Office

Founded:
1974

Formerly called:
National Federation of Self-Employed and Small Businesses (year of change 1990)

Organisation type and purpose:
Trade association, membership association (membership is by subscription), present number of members: 215,000.
To represent the small business sector in the UK.

Subject coverage:
Small business issues.

Trade and statistical information:
Statistics on small businesses.

Printed publications:
First Voice (national magazine, 6 times a year, free to members)
Voice (regional magazine, 6 times a year, free to members)

Access to staff:
Contact by letter, by telephone and by e-mail.
Appointment necessary. Access for members only.
Hours: Mon to Fri, 0900 to 1700

Access to building, collection or gallery:
Prior appointment required

Links with:
ESBA – European Small Business Alliance

FEDERATION OF THE RETAIL LICENSED TRADE NORTHERN IRELAND

Acronym or abbreviation: FRLT

91 University Street, Belfast, BT7 1HP

Tel: 028 9032 7578
Fax: 028 9032 7578
E-mail: enquiries@ulsterpubs.com

Website:
http://www.ulsterpubs.com
Licensed trade information for members and public. Online details of some members.

Enquiries:
Enquiries to: Chief Executive

Founded:
1872

Organisation type and purpose:
Trade association (membership is by subscription, qualification), present number of members: 1200, training organisation.

Subject coverage:
Licensing legislation and statistics relating to Northern Ireland. Licensed trade training.

FEDERATION OF ZOOLOGICAL GARDENS OF GREAT BRITAIN AND IRELAND

Acronym or abbreviation: FZGB

Regent's Park, London, NW1 4RY

Tel: 020 7586 0230
Fax: 020 7722 4427
E-mail: fedzoo@zsl.org

Website:
http://www.zoofederation.org.uk

Enquiries:
Enquiries to: Administrator
Other contacts: Director, Conservation Co-ordinator

Founded:
1966

Formerly called:
National Federation of Zoological Gardens of
Great Britain and Ireland

Organisation type and purpose:
Professional body, membership association
(membership is by subscription, qualification,
election or invitation), present number of
members: 61, registered charity (charity number
248553).
The Federation of Zoos, the principal professional
body representing the zoo community in Britain
and Ireland, is a conservation, education and
scientific wildlife charity dedicated to the
maintenance of the world's biodiversity, the
welfare of animals in zoos and the advancement of
scientific knowledge.
The Federation achieves its objectives through:
conservation breeding programmes and support
for projects in the wild; inspiring an understanding
of the natural world through environmental
education; and non-invasive scientific studies of
animals.

Subject coverage:
Data concerning zoos in the UK and including
details of species stocked, breeding schemes,
education service, conservation projects; zoo
legislation; zoo standards and management;
careers in zoos.

Printed publications:
Annual Report
Literature on careers in zoos
Management Guidelines for Zoo Animals (series,
ten titles, prices vary)
Veterinary Guidelines for Felids (£5 members, £10
non-members)
Zoo Federation News (newsletter, 3 times a year,
members and associates only)
Codes of Practice:
Notes for Inspectors (invertebrate collections,
£2.75)
Euthanasia of Invertebrates (£1.75)
Hazardous Invertebrates (£4)

Electronic and video publications:
Management Guidelines for Zoo Animals (series,
disc, five titles, prices vary)
Database of Browse used in Federation Zoos (CD-
ROM with Microsoft Access Database and Word
file with information regarding poisonous plants

Publications list:
Available in print

Access to staff:
Contact by letter, by fax, by e-mail, in person and
via website. Appointment necessary. Access for
members only. Non-members charged.
Hours: Mon to Fri, 0900 to 1700

Access for disabled people:
Parking provided, ramped entry, access to all
public areas, toilet facilities

A member of:
European Association of Zoos and Aquaria
(EAZA)
    tel: + 31 20 5200 753; fax: + 31 20 5200 754; e-mail:
    corinne.bos@ndvzoos
World Conservation Union (IUCN)
    tel: +22 999 00 01; fax: +22 999 00 02
World Zoo Organisation (IUDZG)
    (The Secrtariat is currently moving from the US
    to the UK)

Has:
66 Member Collections (list available, £15) and 63
Associates
    tel: 020 7586 0230; fax: 020 7722 4427; e-mail:
    fedzoo@zsl.org

Members:
Amazon World
    Watery Lane, Newchurch, Isle of Wight, PO36
    0LX; tel: 01983 867122; fax: 01983 868560; e-mail:
    amaozonworld@dialstart.net
Aquarium & Vivarium, National Museums &
Galleries on Merseyside
    Liverpool Museum, William Brown Street,
    Liverpool, L3 8EN; tel: 0151 207 0001; fax: 0151
    478 4390
Banham Zoo Ltd
    The Grove, Banham, Norfolk, NR16 2HE; tel:
    01953 887771; fax: 01953 888445; website: http://
    www.banhamzoo.co.uk
Battersea Park Children's Zoo
    Battersea Park, London, SW11 4NJ; tel: 020 8871
    7540; fax: 020 7350 0477
Birdland
    Rissington Road, Bourton-on-the-Water,
    Cheltenham, Gloucestershire, GL54 2BN; tel:
    01451 820480; fax: 01451 822398; e-mail: sb
    .birdland@virgin.net
Birdworld
    Holt Pound, Farnham, Surrey, GU10 4LD; tel:
    01420 22140; fax: 01420 23715; website: http://
    www.birdworld.co.uk
Blackpool Zoo Park
    East Park Drive, Stanley Park, Blackpool,
    Lancashire, FY3 8PP; tel: 01253 830830; fax:
    01253 830800; e-mail: zookeeper@blackpool-zoo
    .freeserve.co.uk
Brent Lodge Park Animal Centre
    Brent Lodge Park, Church Road, Hanwell,
    London, W7 3BP; tel: 020 8758 5019; fax: 020
    8840 4244
Bristol, Clifton & West of England Zoological
Society
    Bristol Zoo Gardens, Clifton, Bristol, BS8 3HA;
    tel: 0117 974 7300; fax: 0117 973 6814; e-mail:
    information@bristolzoo.org.uk; website: http://
    www.bristolzoo.org.uk
Butterfly & Wildlife Park
    Long Sutton, Spalding, Linclonshire, PE12 9LE;
    tel: 01406 363833; fax: 01406 363182; e-mail:
    butterflypark@hotmail.com
Camperdown Wildlife Centre
    Camperdown Country Park, Coupar Angus
    Road, Dundee, DO2 4TF, and education
    department; tel: 01382 432661; fax: 01382 432660
Chester Zoo
    North of England Zoological Society, Caughall
    Road, Upton-by-Chester, Cheshire, CH2 1LH;
    tel: 01244 380280; fax: 01244 371273; e-mail: f
    .jaques@chesterzoo.co.uk; website: http://www
    .chesterzoo.co.uk
Chestnut Centre Conservation Park
    Castleton Road, Chapel-en-le-Frith, Derbyshire,
    SK23 0QS; tel: 01298 814099; fax: 01298 816213
City of Belfast Zoo
    Antrim Road, Newtownabbey, Co Antrim, BT36
    7PN; tel: 028 9077 6277; fax: 028 9037 0578;
    website: http://www.belfastzoo.co.uk
Colchester Zoo
    Maldon Road, Stanway, Colchester, Essex, CO3
    5SL; tel: 01206 331292; fax: 01206 331392; e-mail:
    colchester.zoo@btinternet.com; website: http://
    www.colchester-zoo.co.uk
Cotswold Wild Life Park
    Burford, Oxfordshire, OX18 4JW; tel: 01993
    823006; fax: 01993 823807
Curraghs Wildlife Park
    Ballaugh, Isle of Man, IN7 5EA; tel: 01624
    897323; fax: 01624 897327
Drusillas Zoo Park
    Alfriston, East Sussex, BN26 5QS; tel: 01323
    870656; fax: 01323 870846; e-mail: drusilla@
    drusilla.demon.co.uk
Dublin Zoo
    Zoological Society of Ireland, Phoenix Park,
    Dublin, 8, Republic of Ireland; tel: 00 353 1 677
    1425; fax: 00 353 1 677 1660; website: http://www
    .dublinzoo.ie
Dudley and West Midlands Zoological Society Ltd
    Dudley Zoo, 2 The Broadway, Dudley, DY1 4QB;
    tel: 01384 215300; fax: 01384 456048; e-mail:
    marketing@dudleyzoo.org.uk

Durrell Wildlife Conservation Trust
    Jersey Zoo, Les Augres Manor, Trinity, Jersey, JE3
    5BF; tel: 01534 860000; fax: 01534 860001; e-mail:
    jerseyzoo@durrell.org
East Midlands Zoological Society Ltd
    Twycross Zoo Park, Norton-juxta-Twycross,
    Atherstone, Warwickshire, CV9 3PX; tel: 01827
    880250; fax: 01827 880700; e-mail: twycross.zoo@
    btinternet.com
Edinburgh Zoo
    Royal Zoological Society of Scotland, 134
    Corstorphine Road, Edinburgh, EH12 6TS; tel:
    0131 334 9171 (press 0 for operator); fax: 0131 316
    4050; e-mail: amanda@edinburghzoo.org.uk;
    website: http://www.edinburghzoo.org.uk
Exmoor Zoological Park
    Bratton Fleming, Barnstaple, North Devon, EX31
    4SG; tel: 01598 763352; fax: 01598 763352
Fota Wildlife Park
    Zoological Society of Ireland, Carrigtwohill, Co
    Cork, Republic of Ireland; tel: 00 353 21 812 678;
    fax: 00 353 21 812 744; e-mail: fota@indigo.ie
Gatwick Zoo
    Russ Hill, Charlwood, Surrey, RH6 0EG; tel:
    01293 862312; fax: 01293 862550
Harewood Bird Garden
    Harewood House, Harewood, Leeds, LS17 9LQ;
    tel: 0113 288 6238; fax: 0113 288 6784; e-mail:
    birdgdn@harewood.org; website: http://www
    .harewood.org
Hawk Conservancy
    Weyhill, Andover, Hampshire, SP11 8DY; tel:
    01264 773850; fax: 01264 773772; website: http://
    www.hawk-conservancy.org
Highland Wildlife Park
    Royal Zoological Society of Scotland, Kincraig,
    Kingussie, Inverness-shire, PH21 1NL; tel: 01540
    651270; fax: 01540 651236; e-mail: wildlife@rzss
    .org.uk; website: http://www.kincraig.com/
    wildlife
Kirkleatham Owl Centre
    Kirkleatham Village, Redcar, TS10 5NW; tel:
    01642 480512; fax: 01642 492790; e-mail: stan@
    kirk58.freeserve.co.uk; website: http://www
    .jillsowls.co.uk
Knowsley Safari Park
    Prescot, Merseyside, L34 4AN; tel: 0151 430 9009;
    fax: 0151 426 3677; website: http://www
    .knowsley.com
Lakeland Wildlife Oasis
    Hale, Milnthorpe, Cumbria, LA7 7BW; tel: 01539
    563027; e-mail: wildlifeoasis@hotmail.com
Linton Zoological Gardens
    Hadstock Road, Linton, Cambridgeshire, CB1
    6NT; tel: 01223 891308; fax: 01223 891308
London Zoo
    Zoological Gardens, Regent's Park, London,
    NW1 4RY, tel: 020 7449 6551 education
    department; tel: 020 7722 3333; fax: 020 7586
    5743; website: http://www.zsl.org
Lotherton Hall Bird Garden
    Towton Road, Near Aberford, Leeds, LS25 3EB;
    tel: 0113 281 3723
Manor House Wildlife and Leisure Park
    St Florence, Tenby, Dyfed, SA70 8RJ; tel: 01646
    651201; fax: 01646 651201
Marwell Zoological Park
    Colden Common, Winchester, Hampshire, SO21
    1JH; tel: 01962 777407; fax: 01962 777511; e-mail:
    marwel@marwell.org.uk
Mole Hall Wildlife Park
    Widdington, Saffron Walden, Essex, CB11 3SS;
    tel: 01799 540400; fax: 01799 540400; e-mail:
    molehall@aol.com
National Birds of Prey Centre
    Newent, Gloucestershire, GL18 1JJ; tel: 01531
    821581; fax: 01531 821389; e-mail: jpj@nbpc
    .demon.co.uk
Newquay Zoo
    Trenance Park, Newquay, Cornwall, TR7 2LZ;
    tel: 01637 873342; fax: 01637 851318; e-mail:
    mark@newquayzoo.demon.co.uk
Owl Centre
    Muncaster Castle, Ravenglass, Cumbria, CA18
    1RQ; tel: 01229 717393; fax: 01229 717107

continued overleaf

Paignton Zoo Environmental Park
Totnes Road, Paignton, Devon, TQ4 7EU; tel:
01803 697500; fax: 01803 523457; e-mail: amy@
paigntonzoo.demon.co.uk
Palacerigg Country Park
Cumbernauld, G67 3HU; tel: 01236 720047; fax:
01236 458271; e-mail: pccreception@northlan.gw
.uk
Paradise Wildlife Park
White Stubbs Lane, Broxbourne, Hertfordshire,
EN10 7QA; tel: 01992 470490; fax: 01992 440525;
website: http://www.pwpark.com
Shaldon Wildlife Trust Ltd
Ness Drive, Shaldon, Devon, TQ14 0HP; tel:
01626 872234; fax: 01626 872234; website: http://
www.the-zoo.demon.co.uk
Southport Zoo and Conservation Trust
Princes Park, Southport, Merseyside, PR8 1RX;
tel: 01704 538102; fax: 01704 548102; e-mail:
100534.35@compuserve.com
Suffolk Wildlife Park
Whites Lane, Kessingland, Lowestoft, Suffolk,
NR33 7TF; tel: 01502 740291; fax: 01953 888427;
website: http://www.suffolkwildlifepark.co.uk
Thrigby Hall Wildlife Gardens
Thrigby Hall, Filby, Great Yarmouth, Norfolk,
NR29 3DR; tel: 01493 369477; fax: 01493 368256
Tilgate Nature Centre
Tilgate Park, Crawley, West Sussex, RH10 5PQ;
tel: 01293 521168; fax: 01293 533981
Tropical World
Canal Gardens, Roundhay Park, Leeds, LS8 1DF;
tel: 0113 266 1850; fax: 0113 237 0077
Welsh Mountain Zoo
Zoological Society of Wales, Colwyn Bay, Clwyd,
LL28 5UY; tel: 01492 532938; fax: 01492 530498;
e-mail: welshmountainzoo@enterprise.net
Whipsnade Wild Animal Park
Zoological Society of London, Dunstable,
Bedfordshire, LU6 2LF; tel: 01582 872171; fax:
01582 872649; e-mail: nick.lindsay@zsl.org;
website: http://www.zsl.org
Wildfowl & Wetland Trust
Mill Road, Arundel, West Sussex, BN18 9PB; tel:
01903 883355; fax: 01903 884834; e-mail: wwt
.arundel@virgin.net; website: http://www.wwt
.org.uk
Wildfowl & Wetland Trust
District 15, Washington, Tyne & Wear, NE38 8LE;
tel: 0191 416 5454; fax: 0191 416 5801; website:
http://www.wwt.org.uk
Wildfowl & Wetland Trust
Martin Mere, Fish Lane, Burscough, Ormskirk,
Lancashire, L40 0TA; tel: 01704 895181; fax:
01704 892343; website: http://www.wwt.org.uk
Wildfowl & Wetland Trust
Slimbridge, Gloucestershire, GL2 7BT; tel: 01453
890333; fax: 01453 890827; website: http://www
.wwt.org.uk
Wildfowl & Wetland Trust
Canolfan Llanelli Centre, Penclacwydd,
Llwynhendy, Llanelli, Dyfed, SA14 9SH; tel:
01554 741087; website: http://www.wwt.org.uk
Wildfowl & Wetland Trust
Castle Espie, Ballydrain Road, Comber, Co
Down, BT23 6EA; tel: 028 9187 4146; fax: 028
9187 3857; website: http://www.wwt.org.uk
Woburn Safari Park
Woburn, Bedfordshire, MK17 9QN; tel: 01525
290407; fax: 01525 290489; e-mail: WobSafari@
aol.com
Yorkshire Dales Falconry and Conservation Centre
Crows Nest, Near Giggleswick, Settle, North
Yorkshire, LA2 8AS; tel: 01729 822832 Direct
01729 825164 Information; fax: 01729 825160

FEED THE MINDS

Park Place, 12 Lawn Lane, London, SW8 1UD

Tel: 020 7582 3535
Fax: 020 7735 7617
E-mail: info@feedtheminds.org

Website:
http://www.feedtheminds.org

Enquiries:
Enquiries to: Administrator

Founded:
1964

Organisation type and purpose:
Registered charity (charity number 291333).
An ecumenical Christian organisation that
supports education in the world's poorest regions.

Printed publications:
Annual Report
Feed the Minds News (twice a year)

Access to staff:
Contact by letter, by telephone, by fax and by e-
mail. Appointment necessary.
Hours: Mon to Fri, 0900 to 1700

Constituent bodies:
22 agencies and mission societies from Anglican,
Baptist, Catholic, Methodist and Reformed
backgrounds

Links with:
Council of Churches for Britain and Ireland
United Society for Christian Literature
at the same address

Member organisation of:
Churches' Commission on Mission
World Association for Christian Communication
(WACC)

FELINE ADVISORY BUREAU

Acronym or abbreviation: FAB

Taeselbury, High Street, Tisbury, Wiltshire, SP3
6LD

Tel: 01747 871872
Fax: 01747 871873
E-mail: information@fabcats.org

Website:
http://www.fabcats.org
Information on the Feline Advisory Bureau, future
meetings and conferences, information on cat care,
including behaviour and disease, catteries, etc.
http://www.web.ukonline.co.uk/fab
Information on International Society of Feline
Medicine.

Enquiries:
Enquiries to: Chief Executive

Founded:
1958

Organisation type and purpose:
Advisory body, membership association
(membership is by subscription), present number
of members: 3,000, registered charity (charity
number 1117342), suitable for ages: adults,
publishing house.
To provide information on the health and welfare
of cats.

Subject coverage:
Disease, treatment, management and welfare of
the feline species, particularly the domestic cat.
Information on design, construction and
management of boarding catteries and rescue
facilities. Approved Boarding Cattery listing.
Boarding Cattery Information Service: constructing
and management of boarding catteries. Advice to
owners on all feline problems, behavioural or
sickness, and general cat care.

Access to staff:
Contact by letter, by telephone, by fax, by e-mail
and via website
Hours: Mon to Fri, 0900 to 1700

Constituent bodies:
Central Fund for Feline Studies

Subsidiary body:
Boarding Cattery Information Service

Supports the:
International Society of Feline Medicine (ESFM)

FELL & ROCK CLIMBING CLUB
OF THE ENGLISH LAKE DISTRICT

Acronym or abbreviation: FRCC

Library, Lancaster University Library, Bailrigg,
Lancaster, LA1 4YH

Tel: 01524 65201

Enquiries:
Enquiries to: Honorary Librarian

Founded:
1907

Organisation type and purpose:
Climbing club library housed in the University
Library.

Subject coverage:
Fell walking and rock climbing, particularly in the
English Lake District; protection of the amenities of
the District; mountaineering in other parts of Great
Britain, the Alps, the Himalayas, and other great
ranges.

**Museum or gallery collection, archive, or library
special collection:**
Himalayan Journal
Journals of Alpine Club, American and Canadian
Alpine Clubs
Journals of FRCC, Climbers' Club, Scottish
Mountaineering Club, etc

Printed publications:
Catalogue of Maps
Catalogue of the Library (2nd ed., 1987)
FRCC Guide Books (rock climbing guides to the
English Lake District)

Access to staff:
Contact by letter
Hours: Mon to Fri, 0900 to 1700

FELL RUNNERS ASSOCIATION

Acronym or abbreviation: FRA

8 Leygate View, New Mills, High Peak, SK22 3EF

Tel: 01663 746476

Website:
http://www.fellrunner.org.uk
News, forums, joining details and form, race
details, results, internationals, juniors,
championships and library.

Enquiries:
Enquiries to: General Secretary
Direct e-mail: alan.brentnall@btinternet.com

Founded:
1970

Organisation type and purpose:
National organisation, membership association
(membership is by subscription), present number
of members: 7,000.
Governing body of the sport in England.

Subject coverage:
Fell running in the British Isles.

Printed publications:
Annual Handbook and Fixtures Calendar
The Fellrunner (magazine, 3 times a year, free of
charge, available to FRA members only)

Publications list:
Available in print

Access to staff:
Contact by letter, by telephone and by e-mail
Hours: Mon to Fri, 0900 to 1700

FELLOWSHIP OF CHRISTIAN
MOTORCYCLISTS

Acronym or abbreviation: FCM

6 St Anne's Close, Formby, Liverpool, L37 7AX

Tel: 01704 875828
E-mail: info@fcm-bikers.org.uk

Website:
http://www.fcm-bikers.org.uk
Fellowship home page, membership, information

Enquiries:
Enquiries to: Chairman

Founded:
1976

Organisation type and purpose:
Membership association (membership is by subscription), present number of members: 120.

Printed publications:
Transmission (monthly newsletter, members, and enquirers on application)

Access to staff:
Contact by letter
Hours: Mon to Fri, 0900 to 1700

FELLOWSHIP OF INDEPENDENT EVANGELICAL CHURCHES

Acronym or abbreviation: FIEC

39 The Point, Market Harborough, LE16 7QU

Tel: 01858 434540
Fax: 01858 411550
E-mail: admin@fiec.org.uk

Website:
http://www.fiec.org.uk
Resource information helpful to churches.

Enquiries:
Enquiries to: Administrator
Direct e-mail: rod@fiec.org.uk
Other contacts: Office Manager, tel: 01858 411551

Founded:
1922

Organisation type and purpose:
Advisory body, registered charity (charity number 263354).
Association of churches, ministers and Christian workers.

Subject coverage:
Church related practical issues, evangelism, pastoral care guidance.

Printed publications:
Churches Handbook
Together (magazine, 2 times a year)
FIEC Directory

Access to staff:
Contact by letter, by telephone, by fax, by e-mail and via website
Hours: Mon to Fri, 0900 to 1700

Access for disabled people:
Hours: Mon to Fri, 0900 to 1700
Special comments: Ground floor only

Affiliated to:
Affinity
PO Box 246, Bridgend, CF31 9FD; tel: 01656 646152; fax: info@affinity.org.uk; website: www.affinity.org.uk

FELLOWSHIP OF MAKERS AND RESEARCHERS OF HISTORICAL INSTRUMENTS

Acronym or abbreviation: FoMRHI

c/o Lewis Jones, London Metropolitan University, 41 Commercial Road, London, E1 1LA

E-mail: ljones@lgu.ac.uk

Website:
http://www.hrinstruments.demon.co.uk/fomrhi.html

Enquiries:
Enquiries to: Honorary Secretary

Founded:
1975

Organisation type and purpose:
Learned society (membership is by subscription).

Subject coverage:
Reconstruction of early musical instruments (from the Stone Age to about 1900, but mostly from the Middle Ages to 1800 or so), conservation and restoration of instruments of the same periods.

Printed publications:
Annual List of Members
FoMRHI Quarterly (for members)

Access to staff:
Contact by letter and by e-mail
Hours: Mon to Fri, 0900 to 1700

FELLOWSHIP OF POSTGRADUATE MEDICINE

Acronym or abbreviation: FPM

12 Chandos Street, London, W1G 9DR

Tel: 020 7636 6334
Fax: 020 7436 2535
E-mail: admin@fpm-uk.org

Website:
http://www.fpm-uk.org
Continuing Medical Education and original articles

Enquiries:
Enquiries to: Administrator

Organisation type and purpose:
Learned society (membership is by election or invitation), present number of members: c. 50, registered charity (charity number 313355).
Medical education and publishing.

Subject coverage:
Postgraduate medical education.

Access to staff:
Contact by letter and by e-mail
Hours: Tue, Wed and Thu, 1000 to 1730

FELLOWSHIP OF ST ALBAN AND ST SERGIUS

Acronym or abbreviation: FSASS

1 Canterbury Road, Oxford, OX2 6LU

Tel: 01865 552991
Fax: 01865 316700
E-mail: gensec@sobornost.org

Website:
http://www.sobornost.org

Enquiries:
Enquiries to: General Secretary
Other contacts: Treasurer for subscription enquiries.

Founded:
1928

Organisation type and purpose:
Membership association (membership is by subscription), present number of members: 1218, registered charity (charity number 245112).
To promote understanding between Western and Eastern Christian churches.

Subject coverage:
Information on the Orthodox Churches in the British Isles, information on the unity between Christians of East and West.

Museum or gallery collection, archive, or library special collection:
Small orthodoxy and theological library with emphasis on Russian Church Studies

Printed publications:
Newsletter (quarterly)
Sobornost, incorporating Eastern Churches Review (journal, 2 times a year)
Various studies supplementary to Sobornost/ECR

Microform publications:
Sobornost (available on microfiche from UMI)

Publications list:
Available online and in print

Access to staff:
Contact by letter, by telephone, by e-mail and via website
Hours: Mon to Fri, 0900 to 1300

Access to building, collection or gallery:
Prior appointment required
Special comments: Library open to members of the Fellowship.

FEMINIST LIBRARY RESOURCE AND INFORMATION CENTRE

Acronym or abbreviation: FLRIC

5 Westminster Bridge Road, London, SE1 7XW

Tel: 020 7928 7789
E-mail: feministlibrary@beeb.net

Website:
http://www.genesis.ac.uk
Archive collection description

Enquiries:
Enquiries to: Information Officer

Founded:
1975

Formerly called:
Women's Research and Resource Centre (year of change 1982)

Organisation type and purpose:
Membership association (membership is by subscription), voluntary organisation, registered charity (charity number 272410).

Subject coverage:
Women, feminism, black women, lesbians, disabled women and women's studies.

Museum or gallery collection, archive, or library special collection:
Archive material relating to second wave women's movement (WLM) 1970s
Women's Liberation Movement – Archives
Extensive journals collection from UK and around the world
10,000 books, 1500 journals, 1200 articles, 9000 pamphlets and ephemera

Library catalogue:
All or part available in-house

Printed publications:
Newsletter (quarterly)

Access to staff:
Contact by letter and by telephone. Appointment necessary.
Hours: Tue, 1100 to 2000; Wed, 1500 to 2000; Sat, 1400 to 1700

FENCING CONTRACTORS ASSOCIATION

Acronym or abbreviation: FCA

Hillside Grange, Warren Road, Trellech, Monmouth, Gwent, NP25 4PQ

Tel: 07000 560722
Fax: 01600 860614
E-mail: info@fencingcontractors.org

Website:
http://www.fencingcontractors.org

Enquiries:
Enquiries to: Chief Executive

Founded:
1942

Organisation type and purpose:
Trade association.

Subject coverage:
All types of fencing and gates including vehicle restraint systems and electric security fencing.

Museum or gallery collection, archive, or library special collection:
British Standards Parts – 1722 fences
FCA Code of Practice (PAS 48)
Publicly available specification (PAS 47) for electric fences

Printed publications:
List of members

continued overleaf

Access to staff:
Contact by letter, by telephone, by fax and by e-mail
Hours: Mon to Fri, 0900 to 1700

Access to building, collection or gallery:
Prior appointment required
Hours: Mon to Fri, 0900 to 1700

Access for disabled people:
Parking provided, ramped entry, access to all public areas, toilet facilities

Connections with:
Association of Safety Fencing Contractors (ASFC)
As main address
Electric Security Fencing Federation (ESFF)
As main address

FERFA: THE RESIN FLOORING ASSOCIATION

16 Edward Road, Farnham, Surrey, GU9 8NP

Tel: 01252 714250

Website:
http://www.ferfa.org.uk

Enquiries:
Enquiries to: Secretary

Founded:
1969

Organisation type and purpose:
Trade association (membership is by subscription and election), present number of members: 85.
Represents UK manufacturers, contractors and associated companies involved in industrial resin flooring systems and surface preparation.

Subject coverage:
UK manufacturers, contractors and associated companies involved in industrial resin flooring systems and surface preparation.

Printed publications:
Publishes a range of guidance notes (all available free online)
Guide to the specification and application of synthetic resin floors
Guide to the selection of synthetic resin floors
Osmosis in resin flooring
Static controlled flooring
Chemical resistance of resin flooring
Assessing the slip resistance of resin floors
Installing resin flooring systems onto substrates with a high moisture content
Cleaning resin floors
Guide to PPE for use with in situ resin floors and floor preparation (downloadable in A4 format or as a printed free pocket guide)
Guide to seamless resin terrazzo
Flowable polymer screeds as underlayments for resin floor finishes
Order printed publications from: PPE booklet available from FeRFA, 16 Edward Road, Farnham, Surrey GU9 8NP; tel: 01252 714250

Publications list:
Available online and in print

Access to staff:
Contact by letter, by telephone, by fax, by e-mail and via website
Hours: Mon to Fri, 0900 to 1700

Access to building, collection or gallery:
By appointment only

FERRARI OWNERS' CLUB OF GREAT BRITAIN

Acronym or abbreviation: FOCGB

14 Lynn Road, Snettisham, King's Lynn, Norfolk, PE31 7PT

Tel: 01485 544500
Fax: 01485 544515
E-mail: foc.info@btconnect.com

Website:
http://www.ferrariownersclub.co.uk

General information regarding club, its activities and membership.

Enquiries:
Enquiries to: General Secretary

Founded:
1967

Organisation type and purpose:
Membership association (membership is by subscription, qualification).
To provide events, activities, information and news for Ferrari owners and enthusiasts.

Subject coverage:
Club activities including Ferrari competition, racing, sprints and hillclimb, concours events, international Ferrari events and activity, Ferrari cars old and new, technical guidance through established outlets, market trend, advertising outlets and publications.

Museum or gallery collection, archive, or library special collection:
Club library and OC register of cars

Printed publications:
Ferrari (quarterly, colour)
Ferrari News (magazine, 6 times a year, black and white)

Access to staff:
Contact by letter, by telephone, by fax and by e-mail
Hours: Mon to Fri, 0900 to 1700

FIBRE CEMENT MANUFACTURERS' ASSOCIATION LIMITED

Acronym or abbreviation: FCMA

ATSS House, Station Road East, Stowmarket, Suffolk, IP14 1RQ

Tel: 01449 676053
Fax: 01449 770028
E-mail: fcma@ghyllhouse.co.uk

Enquiries:
Enquiries to: Secretary General
Other contacts: Chairman

Founded:
1985

Formerly called:
Asbestos Cement Manufacturers Association

Organisation type and purpose:
Trade association.

Subject coverage:
Manufacture of fibre cement building products; technical development; health and safety, occupational training.

Access to staff:
Contact by letter, by telephone, by fax and by e-mail
Hours: Mon to Fri, 0900 to 1700

Access to building, collection or gallery:
No access other than to staff

Member of:
CBI
NFRC

FIBREOPTIC INDUSTRY ASSOCIATION

Acronym or abbreviation: FIA

The Manor House, Buntingford, Hertfordshire, SG9 9AB

Tel: 01763 273039
Fax: 01763 273255
E-mail: jane@fiasec.demon.co.uk

Website:
http://www.fia-online.co.uk
Wide ranging information on fibre optic industry and members' products and services.

Enquiries:
Enquiries to: Secretary

Founded:
1990

Organisation type and purpose:
Trade association (membership is by subscription), present number of members: 200.
Technology-based trade association for the fibre optics industry.

Subject coverage:
Fibre optics, data communications, telecommunications.

Printed publications:
FIA Guide to Training
Guide to Members' Products and Services
Membership pack
Newsletter

Publications list:
Available online

Access to staff:
Contact by letter, by telephone, by fax, by e-mail and via website
Hours: Mon to Fri, 0930 to 1630

FIELD

Formal name: Foundation for International Environmental Law and Development

3 Endsleigh Street, London, WC1H 0DD

Tel: 020 7872 7200
Fax: 020 7388 2826
E-mail: field@field.org.uk

Website:
http://www.field.org.uk/
Information on FIELD's four main programme areas, RECIEL and Internships.

Enquiries:
Enquiries to: Administrator
Direct e-mail: clare.duckney@field.org.uk
Other contacts: Director for Project Co-ordinator and fundraising.

Founded:
1989

Formerly called:
Centre for International Environment Law (CIEL) (year of change 1989)

Organisation type and purpose:
Advisory body, registered charity (charity number 802934), training organisation, research organisation.
To promote the progressive development of EU and international law through research, teaching, training and publishing.

Subject coverage:
Environmental law related to climate and energy; trade, environment and sustainable development; international courts and tribunals; biological diversity and marine resources, international law and sustainable development and EC environmental law.

Museum or gallery collection, archive, or library special collection:
Field Brochure/Folder
FIELD in Brief
RECIEL Journal

Printed publications:
Review of European Community & International Environmental Law RECIEL (quarterly, pub. Blackwell)
Numerous books, reports and papers include:
Principles of International Environmental Law, Principles of Policy, Institution and Compliance
Environmental Priorities for the World Trading System

Publications list:
Available online and in print

Access to staff:
Contact by letter, by telephone, by fax, by e-mail and via website
Hours: Mon to Fri, 0900 to 1700

Access to building, collection or gallery:
No access other than to staff

Connections with:
IUCN
World Conservation for Nature

FIELD STUDIES COUNCIL

Acronym or abbreviation: FSC

Preston Montford, Montford Bridge, Shrewsbury, Shropshire, SY4 1HW

Tel: 01743 852100
Fax: 01743 852101
E-mail: fsc.headoffice@field-studies-council.org

Enquiries:
Enquiries to: Chief Executive
Other contacts: Education Officer for advice, courses, INSET.

Founded:
1943

Formerly called:
Council for the Promotion of Field Studies

Organisation type and purpose:
Membership association (membership is by subscription), registered charity (charity number 313364), suitable for ages: 4 to adult.
Educational charity.
Environmental understanding for all.

Subject coverage:
Biology, botany, geography, ecology, environment, environmental auditing, natural history, photography, birds, butterfly safaris, archaeology, walking, painting, crafts.

Printed publications:
Annual Report
Field Studies Journal (annually)
Over 500 publications, charts and studies
  including:
Adult and Family Course Programmes
Discover Your National Parks (educational
  resource pack, £15)
Identification guides
Synopses of the British Fauna
The Outdoor Classroom – for schools and colleges
The AIDGAP (Aids to Identification in Difficult
  Groups of Animals & Plants) Project publications
Order printed publications from: Postal Sales Officer,
FSC Publications
at the same address, tel: 01743 850370

Publications list:
Available in print

Access to staff:
Contact by telephone, by fax and by e-mail.
Appointment necessary.
Hours: Mon to Fri, 0900 to 1700

FIELDEN-CEGOS LIMITED

The Towers, Towers Business Park, Wilmslow Road, Didsbury, Manchester, M20 2FZ

Tel: 0161 445 2426
Fax: 0161 446 2051
E-mail: customerservices@fielden-cegos.co.uk

Website:
http://www.fielden-cegos.co.uk
Training courses and in-company services, access to our international partners.

Enquiries:
Enquiries to: Course Registrar
Direct e-mail: jeremy.blain@cegos.co.uk

Founded:
1949

Formerly called:
Fielden House Limited (year of change 1989)

Organisation type and purpose:
Training organisation, consultancy.
Management training centre.

Subject coverage:
Management development, supervisory training, trainer training, health and safety, administrative/ secretarial, personnel/H.R., supply chain management, quality management, consultancy, sales, marketing.

Printed publications:
Courses Directory (annually)

Electronic and video publications:
Course Directory (CD-ROM, free of charge)

Access to staff:
Contact by letter, by telephone, by fax, by e-mail and via website
Hours: Mon to Fri, 0900 to 1700

Subsidiary of:
CEGOS
  France

FIELDS IN TRUST

Acronym or abbreviation: FIT

2D Woodstock Studios, 36 Woodstock Grove, London, W12 8LE

Tel: 020 8735 3380
Fax: 020 8735 3397
E-mail: info@fieldsintrust.org

Website:
http://www.fieldsintrust.org/
http://www.npfa.co.uk/

Enquiries:
Enquiries to: Director

Founded:
1925

Formerly called:
National Playing Fields Association (NPFA) (year of change 2007)

Organisation type and purpose:
Advisory body, membership association (membership is by subscription), registered charity (charity number 306070), consultancy, publishing house.

Subject coverage:
Playing fields, their establishment, conservation and development.

Printed publications:
Impact Absorbing Surfaces for Children's
  Playgrounds
Floodlighting
Insurance and Children's Play
The New European Play Safety Standards
The NPFA Cost Guides – Play and Sport
The Six Acre Standard
Playground Management and Safety
Great Playtimes Games Kit
Playground Markings
Order printed publications from: Publications
Department, NPFA
tel: 020 7833 5360, fax: 020 7833 5365, e-mail:
publications@npfa.co.uk

Publications list:
Available online and in print

Affiliated to:
National Council for Voluntary Organisations

Also at:
Midland Sports Centre
  Cromwell Lane, Coventry, CV4 8AS; tel: 024
  7669 4517; fax: 024 7669 4614; e-mail: fields@npfa
  .co.uk
NPFA Cymru
  2 Queen Street, Cardiff, CF10 2BU; tel: 029 2035
  3030; fax: 029 2035 3039; e-mail: cymru@npfa.co
  .uk
NPFA Scotland
  20 Queen Street, Edinburgh, EH2 1JX; tel: 0131
  225 5763

FIFE COUNCIL

Fife House, North Street, Glenrothes, Fife, KY7 5LT

Tel: 01592 414141\ Minicom no. 01592 414201
Fax: 01592 414142

Enquiries:
Enquiries to: Co-ordination Assistant
Direct tel: 01592 413991
Direct fax: 01592 413939

Founded:
1 April 1996

Organisation type and purpose:
Local government body.

FIFE COUNCIL LIBRARIES & MUSEUMS

Formal name: Fife Council Libraries Arts and Museums

LAM Headquarters, East Fergus Place, Kirkcaldy, Fife, KY1 1XT

Tel: 01592 583204
E-mail: libraries.museums@fife.gov.uk

Website:
http://www.fifedirect.org.uk/libraries
Service delivery and access information and associated links.

Enquiries:
Enquiries to: Service Manager, Libraries Arts and Museums
Other contacts: Administration Officer

Founded:
1883

Created by the merger of:
Libraries & Museums Service with Cultural Partnerships and Events Team (year of change 2010)

Organisation type and purpose:
Public Libraries & Museums.
Has a network of 54 libraries, 10 museums, 2 heritage sites and hundreds of access points in schools, sheltered housing complexes and homes, bringing enjoyment, learning and enlightenment to all of Fife's citizens.

Subject coverage:
Libraries provide a gateway to the world of information and cultural resources, offer leisure reading and learning support on the local doorstep, open the door further with free membership, free internet access and free requests, and stock, conserve and exploit family and local history resources.
Museums collect, document, conserve and interpret objects and materials relating to Fife, encourage others to take an interest in and preserve Fife's heritage, make the objects and their history accessible, and maximise the learning potential of the collections for adults and children.

Museum or gallery collection, archive, or library special collection:
Genealogical material
Local newspapers (microfilm and hard copy)
Local studies collection Fife
Natural, social and industrial artefacts and
  photographs relating to Fife
Art Gallery – focusing on Scottish artists

Trade and statistical information:
General trades directories.

Non-library collection catalogue:
All or part available online and in-house

Library catalogue:
All or part available online

Publications list:
Available in print

Access to staff:
Contact by letter, by telephone, by e-mail and in person
Hours: Mon to Fri, 0900 to 1700

continued overleaf

Access to building, collection or gallery:
No prior appointment required
Hours: Hours vary between locations

Access for disabled people:
Access varies between locations

Parent body:
Fife Council
Fife House, North Street, Glenrothes; tel: 0845
155 0000; e-mail: fife.council.fife.gov.uk; website:
http://fifedirect.org.uk

FIFE COUNCIL LIBRARIES – EAST AREA

Library Headquarters, County Buildings, St
Catherine Street, Cupar, Fife, KY15 4TA

Tel: 01334 412737
Fax: 01334 412941

Enquiries:
Enquiries to: Libraries Information Services Co-
ordinator

Formerly called:
North East Fife District Libraries (year of change
1996)

Organisation type and purpose:
Local government body, public library.

Subject coverage:
Local history of East Fife area and St. Andrews,
local agriculture and fisheries, genealogical records
relating to North East Fife, community
information.

Non-library collection catalogue:
All or part available in-house

Printed publications:
City of St Rule
Family history sources in North East Fife 1989
Fife Pictorial and Historical (A H Millar, 2 vol.
reprint of 1895 original)
Local history collections in North East Fife 1989
Reminiscences of golf – St Andrews Links (maybe
out of print)
The Shores of Fife (W Ballingal, reprint of 1872
edition)

Publications list:
Available in print

Access to staff:
Contact by letter, by telephone and by fax
Hours: Mon to Fri, 0900 to 1700

Parent body:
Fife Council

FIFE COUNCIL MUSEUMS WEST

Acronym or abbreviation: FCMW

Museum HQ, Dunfermline Museum, Viewfield
Terrace, Dunfermline, Fife, KY12 7HY

Tel: 01383 313838
Fax: 01383 313837
E-mail: lesley.botten@fife.gov.uk

Founded:
1996

Formerly called:
Dunfermline District Museum and Small Gallery
(year of change 1997)

Organisation type and purpose:
Local government body, museum, suitable for
ages: all.
Headquarters of Fife Council Museums West.

Subject coverage:
Local history and archaeology; 19th and 20th
century luxury linen damask weaving industry
history; costume; coal mining; of the west Fife area.

**Museum or gallery collection, archive, or library
special collection:**
Comprehensive collection of machinery, designs
and products from the luxury damask linen and
silk industry of 19/20th century Dunfermline

Access to staff:
Contact by letter, by telephone, by fax and by e-
mail. Appointment necessary.
Hours: Mon to Fri, 0900 to 1700

Access to building, collection or gallery:
Prior appointment required

Access for disabled people:
Ramped entry, level entry

Branch museums:
Dunfermline Museum
Viewfield Terrace, Dunfermline, Fife, KY12 7HY
Inverkeithing Museum
The Friary, Queen Street, Inverkeithing
Pittencrieff House Museum
Pittencrieff Park, Dunfermline
St. Margaret's Cave (Dunfermline)

Parent body:
Fife Council

FIFE FAMILY HISTORY SOCIETY

Acronym or abbreviation: FFHS

Glenmoriston, Durie Street, Leven, Fife, KY8 4HF

E-mail: via website

Website:
http://www.fifefhs.org
Links to other sites and searchable databases.
Publications for sale, and Society information.

Enquiries:
Enquiries to: Secretary

Founded:
1989

Organisation type and purpose:
Membership association (membership is by
subscription), voluntary organisation, registered
charity.

Access to staff:
Hours: Mon to Fri, 0900 to 1700

Access to building, collection or gallery:
Hours: Mon to Fri, 0900 to 1700

Chairman:
Fife Family History Society
Hallfield, Blebo Craigs, Cupar, KY15 5UQ

FILM DISTRIBUTORS' ASSOCIATION LIMITED

22 Golden Square, London, W1F 9JW

Tel: 020 7437 4383
Fax: 020 7734 0912
E-mail: info@fda.uk.net

Website:
http://www.launchingfilms.com

Enquiries:
Enquiries to: Chief Executive

Founded:
1915

Formerly called:
Society of Film Distributors Limited (SFD) (year of
change 2001)

Organisation type and purpose:
Trade association.

Subject coverage:
UK Film distribution.

Electronic and video publications:
Guide to UK Film Distribution (online via website)

Publications list:
Available online

Access to staff:
Contact by letter, by telephone, by fax, by e-mail
and via website
Hours: Mon to Fri, 0930 to 1730

FILMLINK

Acronym or abbreviation: FL

South Way, Leavesden, Hertfordshire, WD25 7LZ

Tel: 01923 495051
Fax: 01923 333007
E-mail: nfl@herts-filmlink.co.uk

Enquiries:
Enquiries to: Centre Administrator

Founded:
1996

Formed from:
South West Herts Business Partnership (SWHBP);
Herts Film Link (HFL) (year of change 1996)

Formerly called:
Business Link Hertfordshire, South West Herts
Centre

Organisation type and purpose:
Advisory body.
A film and television commission office.

Subject coverage:
Filmlink is the point of contact for all film enquiries
in the county. Services include location searching,
location library, private and public authority
liaison, production guide to the county.

Trade and statistical information:
200 location enquiries processed a month. 40
shooting days a month.

Printed publications:
Filmlink (magazine)
The Production Guide

Access to staff:
Contact by e-mail
Hours: Mon to Fri, 0800 to 1800

Access to building, collection or gallery:
No prior appointment required
Special comments: No prior appointment required
for locations library.

FILTON COLLEGE LEARNING RESOURCE CENTRE

Filton Avenue, Filton, Bristol, BS34 7AT

Tel: 0117 931 2121
Fax: 0117 931 2233

Website:
http://www.filton.ac.uk

Enquiries:
Enquiries to: Learning Resources Manager

Founded:
1960

Organisation type and purpose:
Suitable for ages: 16+.
Library.

Subject coverage:
A Level subjects; foundation degrees; national and
first diplomas.

Library catalogue:
All or part available online

Access to staff:
Contact by letter, by telephone, by fax and by e-
mail
Hours: Mon to Thu, 0830 to 1930; Fri, 0830 to 1630

Access to building, collection or gallery:
Prior appointment required
Hours: Mon to Thu, 0830 to 1930; Fri, 0830 to 1630

Access for disabled people:
Parking provided, ramped entry, toilet facilities

FINANCE AND LEASING ASSOCIATION

Acronym or abbreviation: FLA

2nd Floor, Imperial House, 15–19 Kingsway,
London, WC2B 6UN

Tel: 020 7836 6511
Fax: 020 7420 9655
E-mail: info@fla.org.uk

Website:
http://www.fla.org.uk

Enquiries:
Enquiries to: Head of Government Affairs
Direct tel: 020 7420 9654
Direct e-mail: edward.simpson@fla.org.uk

Founded:
1992

Formerly called:
Finance Houses Association (FHA) (year of change 1992)

Incorporates the former:
Equipment Leasing Association (ELA) (year of change 1992)

Organisation type and purpose:
Trade association.

Subject coverage:
The FLA is the trade association for companies offering business finance and leasing, consumer credit and motor finance in the UK, and holds information on all of these subjects.

Trade and statistical information:
Asset finance and leasing, business finance, consumer credit, motor finance.

Printed publications:
Lending Code 2006
Business Finance Code
Final demand: debt and mental health
Repaying Your Loan Early
Your Credit Decision Explained
FLA Good Practice Guidelines for Second Charge Mortgages – Helping Customers with Payment Difficulties
Why should I check the history of a motor vehicle?
FLA Annual Review
Code of Practice Annual Report
Key Facts
Campaigning for You
FLA Manifesto
FLA Briefing for Parliamentary Candidates

Publications list:
Available online

Access to staff:
Contact by letter, by telephone, by fax and by e-mail
Hours: Mon to Fri, 0900 to 1700

Access to building, collection or gallery:
No access other than to staff

Access for disabled people:
Ramped entry

FINANCIAL OMBUDSMAN SERVICE

South Quay Plaza, 183 Marsh Wall, London, E14 9SR

Tel: 020 7964 1000
Fax: 020 7964 1001
E-mail: enquiries@financial-ombudsman.org.uk

Website:
http://www.financial-ombudsman.org.uk

Formed by the merger of:
Banking Ombudsman (BO), Building Societies Ombudsman (BSO), Insurance Ombudsman Bureau (IOB), Investment Ombudsman Bureau (IOB), Office of the Investment Ombudsman (OIO)

Organisation type and purpose:
Statutory body.
Set up by law to help settle individual disputes between consumers and financial firms.

Subject coverage:
Banking, insurance, pensions, savings and investments, credit cards and store cards, loans and credit, hire purchase and pawnbroking, financial advice, stocks, shares, unit trusts and bonds.

Printed publications:
Ombudsman News (monthly newsletter)
Your Complaint and the Ombudsman leaflet
Information about the services is available in a range of languages, publications can also be produced in Braille or large print or on audiotape.

Electronic and video publications:
Annual Review
Guide for complaint handlers
Your Complaint and the Ombudsman

Publications list:
Available online and in print

Access to staff:
Contact by letter, by telephone, by fax, by e-mail and via website
Hours: Mon to Fri, 0900 to 1700

FINANCIAL SERVICES AUTHORITY, THE

Acronym or abbreviation: FSA

25 The North Colonnade, London, E14 5HS

Tel: 020 7066 1000
Fax: 020 7066 1097

Website:
http://www.fsa.gov.uk
An introduction to the FSA, the Central Register, information for investors, enforcement information, publications and press releases, investor alerts.

Enquiries:
Enquiries to: Public Enquiry Officer

Founded:
1986

Formerly called:
Securities and Investments Board (SIB), date of change, October 1997

Incorporating the former:
Building Societies Commission (BSC), Friendly Societies Commission (FSC), date of change, December 2001

Organisation type and purpose:
Statutory body.
Financial services regulation and investor protection.

Subject coverage:
Financial services regulation.

Publications list:
Available in print

Access to staff:
Contact by letter and by telephone
Hours: Mon to Fri, 0900 to 1700

FINANCIAL SERVICES COMPENSATION SCHEME

Acronym or abbreviation: FSCS

7th Floor, Lloyds Chambers, 1 Portsoken Street, London, E1 8BN

Tel: 020 7892 7300
Fax: 020 7892 7301
E-mail: enquiries@fscs.org.uk

Website:
http://www.fscs.org.uk
Full guide to the Scheme for consumers, claimants and industry.

Enquiries:
Enquiries to: Customer Services Team
Other contacts: Head of Communications for press enquiries.

Founded:
Dec 2001

Formerly called:
Deposit Protection Board (DPB), Investors Compensation Scheme (ICS), Policyholders Protection Board (PPB) (year of change 2001)

Organisation type and purpose:
Statutory body.
FSCS is a final safety net for customers of authorised financial services firms. It compensates consumers if an authorised firm is unable to pay claims against it. The Scheme covers deposits, insurance and investments.

Subject coverage:
Set up under the Financial Services and Markets Act (FSMA) 2000.

Printed publications:
Annual Report and Accounts
How to Claim
How We Can Help (consumer guide)
What to do if You're not Happy (guide to FSCS complaints' procedure)
Do's and Don'ts for Investors
Outlook (industry newsletter)

Publications list:
Available online and in print

Access to staff:
Contact by letter, by telephone, by fax and by e-mail. Appointment necessary.
Hours: Mon to Fri, 0900 to 1700

Access to building, collection or gallery:
No access other than by appointment

Access for disabled people:
Access to all public areas

Independent but accountable to:
FSA

FINANCIAL SERVICES SKILLS COUNCIL

51 Gresham Street, London, EC2V 7HQ

Tel: 020 7216 7366
Fax: 020 7216 7370
E-mail: info@fssc.org.uk

Website:
http://www.fssc.org.uk

Enquiries:
Enquiries to: Sector Support Executive
Direct e-mail: info@fsnto.org

Formerly called:
Banking Industry Training and Development Council (BITDC), BBS NTO, IRFS NTO, FS NTO

Organisation type and purpose:
Sector Skills Council.

Subject coverage:
Labour market information for the financial services sector.

Printed publications:
See website
Order printed publications from: e-mail: www.fssc.org.uk

Electronic and video publications:
See website

Publications list:
Available online

Access to staff:
Contact by e-mail and via website
Hours: Mon to Fri, 0900 to 1700

Access to building, collection or gallery:
No access other than to staff

Access for disabled people:
Access to all public areas

FINE ART SOCIETY PLC

Acronym or abbreviation: FAS

continued overleaf

148 New Bond Street, London, W1S 2JT

Tel: 020 7629 5116
Fax: 020 7491 9454
E-mail: art@faslondon.com

Website:
http://www.faslondon.com
Current and future exhibitions and current stock.

Enquiries:
Enquiries to: Information Officer

Founded:
1876

Organisation type and purpose:
Service industry, art gallery.
Art dealers.

Subject coverage:
Dealers in 19th and 20th century fine and
contemporary arts.

Museum or gallery collection, archive, or library special collection:
Past and present exhibition catalogues held by
Victoria and Albert Museum National Art
Library

Printed publications:
Past and current exhibition catalogues available for
sale

Access to staff:
Contact in person
Hours: Mon to Fri, 1000 to 1800; Sat, 1000 to 1300
Special comments: Closed Saturdays in August.

FINE ART TRADE GUILD

16–18 Empress Place, London, SW6 1TT

Tel: 020 7381 6616
Fax: 020 7381 2596
E-mail: info@fineart.co.uk

Website:
http://www.fineart.co.uk
Directory of members, services, publications, code
of practice, etc.

Enquiries:
Enquiries to: Managing Director
Other contacts: Editor, Art Business Today (for wide
industry knowledge and insight)

Founded:
1910

Formerly called:
The Printsellers Association; broadened scope to
become the Fine Art Trade Guild (year of change
1910)

Organisation type and purpose:
International organisation, trade association
(membership is by subscription), present number
of members: 1,000, service industry, manufacturing
industry, publishing house.

Subject coverage:
Pictures, print publishing, limited-edition prints,
picture framing industry.

Museum or gallery collection, archive, or library special collection:
Archives of limited edition prints

Printed publications:
Art Business Today (magazine, 5 times a year)
Various industry-related books

Access to staff:
Contact by letter, by telephone, by fax, by e-mail
and via website. Appointment necessary.
Hours: Mon to Fri, 0930 to 1730

FINISHING PUBLICATIONS LIMITED

105 Whitney Drive, Stevenage, Hertfordshire, SG1
4BL

Tel: 01438 745115
Fax: 01438 364536

E-mail: finpubs@compuserve.com

Website:
http://www.finishingpublications.com
http://www.surfacequery.com
Searchable database with some 130,000 technical
abstracts

Enquiries:
Enquiries to: Manager

Founded:
1964

Organisation type and purpose:
Publishing house.

Subject coverage:
Surface engineering and treatment, metal finishing,
electroplating, anodizing, etching, pickling,
plating, printed circuit board fabrication, effluent
treatment for these industries. Books relating to St
Ives and its literary/artistic community

Museum or gallery collection, archive, or library special collection:
In-house Metal-Finishing Library (UK, USA,
German serials, books)

Trade and statistical information:
Statistical information available from in-house
database (costs, market size, etc).

Non-library collection catalogue:
All or part available online

Printed publications:
Coating and Surface Treatment Systems for Metals:
A Comprehensive Guide to Selection (J.
Edwards, £80)
Handbook of Effluent Treatment and Recycling for
the Metal Finishing Industry (L. Hartinger, 2nd
edn, £120)
History of Medicine, Surgery and Dentistry: Patent
Abridgements 1620 to 1866 (facsimile)
I'll Raise the Wind Tomorrow: A Biography of
Arthur Caddick (D. Calvert)
Bactericidal and Oligodynamic Action of Silver
and Copper in Hygiene, Medicine and Water
Treatment (Landau, et al)
Plating and Electroplating of Metals: History and
Patent Abridgements, 1617 to 1866 (facsimile)
For other titles, see website

Electronic and video publications:
Cradle of Inventions (CD-ROM Database of British
Patent Titles 1616–1890)
Defects in Aluminium Anodising (CD-ROM
troubleshooting guide)
Defects in Plated Zinc Diecastings (CD-ROM
troubleshooting guide)
Electroplating Defects and Troubleshooting (CD-
ROM)
The Art of Sven Berlin (CD-ROM photo gallery)
Surface Energy and Cleanliness Testing by Wetting
Methods (CD-ROM)

Publications list:
Available online

Access to staff:
Contact by letter, by telephone, by fax, by e-mail
and via website. Appointment necessary.
Hours: Mon to Fri, 0900 to 1700

Access for disabled people:
Parking provided, level entry

FIRA INTERNATIONAL LTD

Formal name: Furniture Industry Research
Association
Acronym or abbreviation: FIRA

Maxwell Road, Stevenage, Hertfordshire, SG1 2EW

Tel: 01438 777700
Fax: 01438 777800
E-mail: info@fira.co.uk

Website:
http://www.fira.co.uk
FIRA activities, Industry news, Members access to
journals. List of publications available to all.

Enquiries:
Enquiries to: Technical Advisors

Organisation type and purpose:
FIRA International is acknowledged as the UK
centre of excellence for furniture research, testing,
consultancy and information who provides a suite
of products and services to a number of global
businesses.

Subject coverage:
Furniture design and manufacturing methods,
tests for furniture materials and complete items of
furniture, upholstery, standards, environmental
issues, ergonomics, flammability, fault
investigations, market research and marketing,
consultancy in product costing, factory layout etc,
machinery and material selection, statistics for the
industry.

Printed publications:
FIRA Newsletter, Members Quarterly Review,
research and technical journals
Statistical digests/market survey reports UK and
European furniture statistics

Publications list:
Available online

Access to staff:
Contact by letter, by telephone and by fax. Access
for members only.
Hours: Mon to Fri, 0900 to 1700

Access to building, collection or gallery:
No access other than to staff

FIRE BRIGADE SOCIETY

Acronym or abbreviation: FBS

17 Kinsbourne Way, Southampton, SO19 6HB

Website:
http://www.firebrigadesociety.freeserve.co.uk/fbs/
welcome.htm

Enquiries:
Enquiries to: General Secretary

Founded:
1963

Organisation type and purpose:
International organisation, membership
association (membership is by subscription).
Voluntary association.

Subject coverage:
Fire service, past, present and future.

Access to staff:
Contact by letter
Hours: Mon to Fri, 0900 to 1700

FIRE BRIGADES UNION

Acronym or abbreviation: FBU

Bradley House, 68 Coombe Road, Kingston upon
Thames, Surrey, KT2 7AE

Tel: 020 8541 1765
Fax: 020 8546 5187
E-mail: office@fbu.org.uk

Website:
http://www.fbu.org.uk

Enquiries:
Enquiries to: General Secretary

Founded:
1918

Organisation type and purpose:
Trade union, present number of members: 51,600.

Subject coverage:
Fire services.

Printed publications:
Journal (monthly)

Access to staff:
Contact by letter, by telephone, by e-mail and via
website
Hours: Mon to Fri, 0900 to 1700

Access to building, collection or gallery:
Prior appointment required

Affiliated to:
TUC

FIRE FIGHTING VEHICLE MANUFACTURERS ASSOCIATION

Acronym or abbreviation: FFVMA

Forbes House, Halkin Street, London, SW1X 7DS

Tel: 020 7344 9232
Fax: 020 7235 7112
E-mail: cford@smmt.co.uk

Website:
http://www.smmt.co.uk
Brief outline.

Enquiries:
Enquiries to: Director

Founded:
1972

Organisation type and purpose:
Trade association.

Subject coverage:
Legislation and standards regarding fire appliances and associated vehicles and equipment.

Trade and statistical information:
UK Vehicle Registration Statistics.

Access to staff:
Contact by letter, by telephone, by fax and via website. Appointment necessary.
Hours: Mon to Fri, 0900 to 1700

Affiliated to the:
Society of Motor Manufacturers & Traders (SMMT)
tel: 020 7235 7000; fax: 020 7235 7112

FIRE INDUSTRY ASSOCIATION

Acronym or abbreviation: FIA

Thames House, 29 Thames Street, Kingston Upon Thames, Surrey, KT1 1PH

Tel: 020 8549 5855
Fax: 020 8547 1564
E-mail: info@fia.uk.com

Website:
http://www.fia.uk.com/

Enquiries:
Enquiries to: General Manager
Other contacts: Committee Secretary

Created by the merger of:
the Fire Extinguishing Trades Association (FETA) and the British Fire Protection Systems Association (BFPSA)

Organisation type and purpose:
Trade association.

Subject coverage:
Development, manufacture and specialist distribution of fire extinguishers of all types, portable fire fighting equipment fillings.

Printed publications:
Guide to the Servicing of Portable fire
    extinguishers and hose reels (purchase)
List of Members (free)

Access to staff:
Contact by letter, by telephone and by fax
Hours: Mon to Fri, 0900 to 1700

Affiliated to, and premises and secretarial services shared with, the:
Association of British Fire Trades (ABFT)
British Approvals for Fire Equipment (BAFE)
Fire Industry Confederation (FIC)

FIRE MARK CIRCLE

44 Kings Road, East Sheen, London, SW14 8PF

Tel: 020 8878 7123

Fax: 020 8878 7123
E-mail: saunders_mj@hotmail.com

Website:
http://www.firemarkcircle.fsnet.co.uk
Information on fire marks, on the history of fire marks and fire insurance, information on meetings and auctions.

Enquiries:
Enquiries to: Honorary Secretary

Founded:
1934

Organisation type and purpose:
Learned society.
For persons interested in the origin and history of fire insurance companies, their fire marks, fire brigades and all that pertains to the past of fire insurance.

Subject coverage:
History of fire insurance and fire-fighting.

Printed publications:
FMC News

Publications list:
Available in print

Access to staff:
Contact by letter, by telephone, by fax, by e-mail and via website
Hours: Mon to Fri, 0900 to 1700

FIRE SERVICE COLLEGE

Acronym or abbreviation: FSC

Moreton-in-Marsh, Gloucestershire, GL56 0RH

Tel: 01608 812050
Fax: 01608 812048
E-mail: library@fireservicecollege.ac.uk

Website:
http://www.fireservicecollege.ac.uk

Enquiries:
Enquiries to: Library Manager
Direct e-mail: jmason@fireservicecollege.ac.uk
Other contacts: Customer Services for enquiries

Organisation type and purpose:
National government body, training organisation, Government agency.
Training personnel from UK fire service and industry in fire, fire safety and related subjects.

Subject coverage:
Fire and emergency, technology, engineering, safety, operational aspects and disaster management, related subjects and history of the Fire Service.

Museum or gallery collection, archive, or library special collection:
Archives of Fire Service History
Fire Journal from first issue
Library of over 80,000 books

Non-library collection catalogue:
All or part available online

Library catalogue:
All or part available online, in-house and in print

Access to staff:
Contact by letter, by telephone, by fax, by e-mail and via website. Appointment necessary.
Hours: Mon to Thu, 0900 to 1700; Fri, 0900 to 1400

Access to building, collection or gallery:
No public access

FIRE SERVICE PRESERVATION GROUP

Acronym or abbreviation: FSPG

50 Old Slade Lane, Iver, Buckinghamshire, SL0 9DR

Website:
http://www.f-s-p-g.org
Group and membership details.

Enquiries:
Enquiries to: Membership Secretary

Founded:
1968

Organisation type and purpose:
Membership association (membership is by subscription), present number of members: 1200.
Preservation of all types of fire appliances and equipment.

Subject coverage:
Fire appliances and equipment, equipment of the NFS and AFS, equipment dating back to the formation of the Fire Brigades, clothing spare parts, hand pumps, horse-drawn appliances and extinguishers, legislation and registration of appliances.

Museum or gallery collection, archive, or library special collection:
Library of books and reference manuals

Printed publications:
Handbook (annually, members)
Off the Run (newsletter, monthly, members)

Access to staff:
Contact by letter and via website
Hours: Mon to Fri, 0900 to 1700

Member of:
Federation of British Historic Vehicle Clubs (FBHVC)

FIRST DIVISION ASSOCIATION

Acronym or abbreviation: FDA

2 Caxton Street, London, SW1H 0QH

Tel: 020 7343 1111
Fax: 020 7343 1105
E-mail: head-office@fda.org.uk

Website:
http://www.fda.org.uk
FDA services, FDA contacts, current news, about the FDA.
http://www.fda.org.uk/members
FDA members area (restricted access).

Enquiries:
Enquiries to: General Secretary

Founded:
1919

Formerly called:
Association of First Division Civil Servants (FSA) (year of change 2001)

Organisation type and purpose:
Professional body, trade union (membership is by subscription), present number of members: 11,000.

Subject coverage:
Civil Service; modernising government; freedom of information.

Printed publications:
Public Service Magazine

Publications list:
Available online

Access to staff:
Contact by letter, by telephone, by fax, by e-mail and via website
Hours: Mon to Fri, 0900 to 1700

Access to building, collection or gallery:
Prior appointment required

Affiliated to the:
Trades Union Congress (TUC)

FIRST KEY

Oxford Chambers, Oxford Place, Leeds, West Yorkshire, LS1 3AX

Tel: 0113 244 3898
Fax: 0113 243 2541
E-mail: information@firstkeyleeds.com or admin@firstkeyleeds.com

continued overleaf

Website:
http://www.first-key.co.uk

Enquiries:
Enquiries to: Administrator

Founded:
1984

Organisation type and purpose:
Voluntary organisation, registered charity (charity number 289552).
To improve the life chances of young people leaving public care, through training, advice, consultancy.

Subject coverage:
Young people leaving public care.

Printed publications:
Publications include:
A Study of Black Young People Leaving Care 1987
Education 'Looked After'
National Standards in Leaving Care
The Children Act 1989
The Children Act Aftercare One Year On
Training Issues for Organisations Working with Care-leavers
Whatever Next?

Publications list:
Available in print

Access to staff:
Contact by letter, by telephone, by fax and by e-mail. Appointment necessary.
Hours: Mon to Fri, 1000 to 1600

Other addresses:
First Key
London Voluntary Sector Resource Centre, 356 Holloway Road, London, N7 6PA; tel: 020 7700 8130; fax: 020 7700 8174; e-mail: admin@firstkeylondon.com
First Key
Room 14 Koco Building, Unit 15, The Arches, Spon End, Coventry, CV1 3JQ; tel: 02476 716259; fax: 02476 677554; e-mail: information@firstkeycoventry.com

FIRST STEPS TO FREEDOM

Acronym or abbreviation: FSTF

PO Box 476, Newquay, TR7 1WQ

Tel: 0845 120 2916
E-mail: first.steps@btconnect.com

Website:
http://www.first-steps.org

Enquiries:
Enquiries to: Secretary

Founded:
1991

Organisation type and purpose:
Membership association (membership is by subscription), present number of members: 1,400, voluntary organisation, registered charity (charity number 1006837).
To offer help, advice and support to those suffering from stress-related disorders such as phobias, panic attacks and Obsessive Compulsive Disorder

Subject coverage:
Generalised anxiety disorder (GAD), phobias, compulsive disorders
FSTF offers a confidential helpline, practical advice, telephone self-help groups, one-to-one telephone counselling and befriending, leaflets, self-help booklets and videos.

Printed publications:
Advice for carers on phobias, panic attacks and Obsessive Compulsive Disorder
Booklets on Obsessive and Compulsive Disorder, Bulimia and Panic Attacks
Fact sheets on a range of phobias

Electronic and video publications:
Audio tapes; relaxation tapes
What you really need to know about (series covering stress, depression, anxiety, etc.; videos)

Yoga (beginners, intermediate and advanced; videos)

Publications list:
Available online and in print

Access to staff:
Contact by letter, by telephone, by fax, by e-mail and via website
Hours: Helpline, daily, 1000 to 2200

Links with:
Queen Elizabeth's Hospital
Department of Psychiatry, Welwyn Garden City, Hertfordshire

Member organisation of:
Telephone Helplines Association

FIRST STOP CENTRE

29 Bocking End, Braintree, Essex, CM7 9AE

Tel: 01376 346535
E-mail: via website

Website:
http://www.firststopcentre.org.uk
About First Stop and its services.

Founded:
1990

Organisation type and purpose:
Registered charity (charity number 803170).
To relieve the condition of disadvantaged persons in mid-Essex experiencing difficulties with homelessness, joblessness, substance misuse, physical and mental health and related problems, or learning disabilities by the provision of support services; to assist such persons in maintaining normal relationships with and within the community in which they reside.

Subject coverage:
Services include a drop-in centre open to all ages and backgrounds, where staff can help with many issues such as form-filling, housing, employment and debts; a free needle exchange; basic skills education, free, for numeracy and literacy; a formal counselling service for individuals and couples; a postal holding address for those that are homeless or do not have a secure mailing address. Help is offered for any adult in need of help in a crisis.

Education services:
Free-of-charge basic skills training for numeracy and literacy.

Electronic and video publications:
Leaflets:
Main
Counselling
Needle exchange
Anger and anxiety
Basic skills education
Postal holdings
Order electronic and video publications from:
Download from website

Publications list:
Available online

Access to staff:
Contact by letter, by telephone, in person and via website
Hours: Mon, Tue, Thu, Fri, 1030 to 1330
Special comments: Answer machine service out of hours.

Access to building, collection or gallery:
Hours: Drop-in centre (incl. needle exchange): Mon, Tue, Thu, Fri, 1030 to 1330
Special comments: Other activities take place outside these core hours, including basic skills education, counselling, anger and anxiety groups.

FISHERIES RESEARCH SERVICES MARINE LABORATORY LIBRARY

Acronym or abbreviation: FRS

PO Box 101, 375 Victoria Road, Aberdeen, AB11 9DB

Tel: 01224 876544
Fax: 01224 295309

Website:
http://www.marlab.ac.uk

Enquiries:
Enquiries to: Librarian
Direct tel: 01224 295391
Direct e-mail: k.mutch@marlab.ac.uk

Organisation type and purpose:
Research organisation.
Executive Agency of the Scottish Office.

Subject coverage:
Marine biology, oceanography, fisheries, fishing methods and gear, pollution and aquaculture, marine ecology, fish diseases, sonar.

Museum or gallery collection, archive, or library special collection:
Ogilvie Collection on diatomaceae

Non-library collection catalogue:
All or part available in-house

Library catalogue:
All or part available in-house

Printed publications:
FRS Annual Report and Accounts
Aquaculture Information Series (irregular, on sale)
Library: Weekly Contents of Recent Journals
Scottish Fisheries Information Pamphlets
Scottish Fisheries Research Reports

Publications list:
Available online

Access to staff:
Contact by letter, by telephone, by fax and by e-mail. Appointment necessary. Non-members charged.
Hours: Mon to Thu, 0900 to 1700; Fri, 0900 to 1630
Special comments: Charges made for photocopying.

Access for disabled people:
Toilet facilities

Branch library at the:
Freshwater Fisheries Laboratory
Pitlochry

Parent body:
Scottish Executive Environment and Rural Affairs Department (SEERAD)

FISHERIES SOCIETY OF THE BRITISH ISLES

Acronym or abbreviation: FSBI

Martineau Johnson , No. 1 Colmore Square, Birmingham, B4 6AA

Tel: 0870 763 1487
E-mail: membership@fsbi.org.uk

Website:
http://www.fsbi.org.uk/

Enquiries:
Enquiries to: Secretary
Direct e-mail: secretary@fsbi.org.uk

Founded:
1967

Organisation type and purpose:
Learned society.

Subject coverage:
Scientific aspects of freshwater and marine fisheries, fish biology.

Printed publications:
Journal of Fish Biology (monthly)

Access to staff:
Contact by letter, by telephone, by fax, by e-mail and via website
Hours: Mon to Fri, 0900 to 1700

FITNESS INDUSTRY ASSOCIATION

Acronym or abbreviation: FIA

Castlewood House, 77–91 New Oxford Street, London, WC1A 1PX

Tel: 020 7420 8560
Fax: 020 7420 8561

Website:
http://www.fia.org.uk

Enquiries:
Enquiries to: Executive Director
Direct e-mail: davidstalker@fia.org.uk

Founded:
1990

Organisation type and purpose:
A not-for-profit organisation and trade body that represents the interests of members in the health and fitness industry across the UK, currently represents over 2,800 operators in the public and private sectors, as well as 250 supplier organisations, including multi-site operators, individual local gyms, and many leading suppliers.
Regularly responds to government consultations, publishes research and engages with the political community.

Subject coverage:
Collective purchasing; professional development seminars and events to develop staff and share best practice; community engagement programmes; government campaigns; sponsoring opportunities.

Electronic and video publications:
FIA State of the Industry Report
Press announcements
Fact sheets
Order electronic and video publications from: Website

Access to staff:
Contact by letter, by telephone, by fax and via website

Runs the following government-funded programmes:
MoreActive4Life, Fit For the Future, active school, go, active at work

FITNESS WALES

1B Clarke Street, Cardiff, CF5 5AL

Tel: 029 2057 5155
Fax: 029 2056 8886
E-mail: enquiries@fitnesswales.co.uk

Enquiries:
Enquiries to: Director
Other contacts: Manager for general enquiries.

Founded:
1966

Organisation type and purpose:
Training organisation.
Governing Body of Exercise and Fitness.
To promote exercise and physical fitness and to monitor standards in the fitness sector in Wales.

Subject coverage:
Training opportunities to teach exercise and fitness. Qualifications needed in fitness industry (national standards). Registration of fitness instructors. Fitness events in Wales.

Printed publications:
Diary Update
Fitness Focus

Access to staff:
Contact by letter, by telephone, by fax, by e-mail, in person and via website
Hours: Mon to Fri, 0900 to 1700

FITZWILLIAM COLLEGE LIBRARY

Storey's Way, Cambridge, CB3 0DG

Tel: 01223 332042
Fax: 01223 477976
E-mail: library@fitz.cam.ac.uk

Website:
http://www.fitz.cam.ac.uk/library

Enquiries:
Enquiries to: Librarian

Founded:
1963

Organisation type and purpose:
University department or institute.
College library.

Subject coverage:
Some specialisation in international law.

Non-library collection catalogue:
All or part available online

Library catalogue:
All or part available online

Access to staff:
Contact by letter, by telephone, by fax, by e-mail and via website. Appointment necessary.
Hours: Mon to Fri, 0900 to 1700

FITZWILLIAM MUSEUM

Library, Trumpington Street, Cambridge, CB2 1RB

Tel: 01223 332900
Fax: 01223 332923
E-mail: fitzmuseum-enquiries@lists.cam.ac.uk

Website:
http://www.fitzmuseum.cam.ac.uk

Enquiries:
Enquiries to: Librarian
Other contacts: Keeper of Manuscripts and Printed Books

Organisation type and purpose:
Museum, university department or institute.

Subject coverage:
The collection is valuable for its form rather than subject coverage: illuminated manuscripts, music manuscripts and printed music, autograph letters, rare books of all periods, art reference works, literary manuscripts, fine arts and antiquities.

Museum or gallery collection, archive, or library special collection:
Collections include:
Most of music and some of the other manuscript material on microfilm
Music by Patrick Hadley, MacFarren, Handel
William Hayley papers
W. S. Blunt papers

Non-library collection catalogue:
All or part available online and in print

Library catalogue:
All or part available online

Printed publications:
Biennial Report
Catalogues of the collections
Newsletter (3 times a year)

Microform publications:
Microfilm, photographs available for purchase via Photographic Sales Officer

Access to staff:
Contact by letter, by telephone, by e-mail and in person. Appointment necessary. Letter of introduction required.
Hours: Tue to Fri, 1000 to 1200 and 1330 to 1630
Special comments: Access restrictions apply only to the users of curatorial materials (i.e. manuscripts and rare books). Introductory letter required for use of special collections.

Access to building, collection or gallery:
No access other than to staff
Hours: Tue to Fri, 1000 to 1200 and 1330 to 1630

Parent body:
University of Cambridge

FLAG INSTITUTE

38 Hill Street, Mayfair, London, W1J 5NS

Website:
http://www.flaginstitute.org

Enquiries:
Enquiries to: Editor

Founded:
1971

Organisation type and purpose:
Voluntary organisation.

Subject coverage:
Flags and related emblems both historical and modern, with particular reference to national flags, flag protocol and usage, flag design, the publication of flag information in various formats, charts and information packs.

Museum or gallery collection, archive, or library special collection:
Country by country flag dossiers
Frederick Warne collection
John Sharpe Collection of flag books
Library of flag books, charts and pictures
Louis Loynes Collection of flag paintings and drawings

Trade and statistical information:
Information on the flag trade (manufacture and distribution) in Britain and abroad.

Printed publications:
Flagmaster (quarterly)
Pamphlets on design, protocol, terminology

Publications list:
Available in print

Access to staff:
Contact by letter and via website. All charged.
Hours: Mon to Fri, 1000 to 1800

Member of:
Fédération Internationale des Associations Vexillologiques

FLINTSHIRE COUNTY COUNCIL

County Hall, Mold, Flintshire, CH7 6NB

Tel: 01352 752121
E-mail: info@flintshire.gov.uk

Website:
http://www.flintshire.gov.uk

Enquiries:
Enquiries to: Corporate Communications Manager

Founded:
1996

Organisation type and purpose:
Local government body.

Access to staff:
Contact by letter, by telephone, by fax, by e-mail, in person and via website
Hours: Mon to Fri, 0830 to 1700

FLINTSHIRE HISTORICAL SOCIETY

Flintshire Record Office, The Old Rectory, Hawarden, Flintshire, CH5 3NR

Tel: 01244 532414
Fax: 01244 538344

Enquiries:
Enquiries to: Honorary Secretary
Direct tel: 01745 332220

Founded:
1911

Organisation type and purpose:
Learned society (membership is by subscription), present number of members: 280 individual, 38 corporate, registered charity (charity number 218288).

Subject coverage:
History and archaeology of the historical county of Flintshire.

Printed publications:
Journal (irregular, vols 1 to 37)

continued overleaf

Order printed publications from: Flintshire Records Office

Publications list:
Available in print

Access to staff:
Contact by letter and by telephone. Non-members charged.
Hours: Mon to Fri, 0900 to 1700

FLINTSHIRE LIBRARY AND INFORMATION SERVICE

Library Headquarters, County Hall, Mold, Flintshire, CH7 6NW

Tel: 01352 704400
Fax: 01352 753662
E-mail: libraries@flintshire.gov.uk

Website:
http://www.flintshire.gov.uk/libraries

Enquiries:
Enquiries to: Head of Libraries, Culture & Heritage

Founded:
1996

Organisation type and purpose:
Local government body, public library.

Subject coverage:
Arthurian legend, Wales and Welsh literature, general public reference service.

Museum or gallery collection, archive, or library special collection:
Arthurian Legend Collection
Local history collection
Daniel Owen Museum
Mold Gold Cape replica
Buckley pottery museum collection

Library catalogue:
All or part available online

Printed publications:
Arthurian Catalogue
Facsimile Limited Edition Reprints of Local Study Items
Order printed publications from: As above

Access to staff:
Contact by letter, by telephone, by fax, by e-mail, in person and via website
Hours: Mon to Fri, 0900 to 1700

Access for disabled people:
At Library HQ: parking provided, ramped entry, toilet facilities, lift

FLINTSHIRE MUSEUM SERVICE

County Hall, Mold, Flintshire, CH7 6NW

Tel: 01352 704409
Fax: 01352 753662
E-mail: museums@flintshire.gov.uk

Website:
http://www.flintshire.gov.uk

Enquiries:
Enquiries to: Principal Museums Officer
Direct e-mail: deborah.seymour@flintshire.gov.uk

Founded:
1996

Formerly called:
Clwyd County Museum Service (year of change 1996)

Organisation type and purpose:
Local government body.
Local authority museum service.

Subject coverage:
The support of local culture and history.

Museum or gallery collection, archive, or library special collection:
Flintshire historical artefacts

Non-library collection catalogue:
All or part available in-house

Access to staff:
Contact by letter, by telephone, by fax, by e-mail and via website. Appointment necessary.
Hours: Mon to Fri, 0900 to 1700

Access to building, collection or gallery:
No prior appointment required

Branch museums:
Buckley Library and Heritage Centre
  The Precinct, Buckley, Flintshire, CH7 2EF; tel: 01244 549210; e-mail: museums@flintshire.gov.uk; website: http://www.flintshire.gov.uk
Mold Library and Museum
  Earl Road, Mold, Flintshire, CH7 1AP; tel: 01352 754791; e-mail: museums@flintshire.gov.uk; website: http://www.flintshire.gov.uk

Links with:
Greenfield Valley Heritage Park
  Greenfield, Holywell, CH8 7GH; tel: 01352 714172; e-mail: info@greenfieldvalley.com; website: http://www.greenfieldvalley.com

FLINTSHIRE RECORD OFFICE

Acronym or abbreviation: FRO

The Old Rectory, Hawarden, Flintshire, CH5 3NR

Tel: 01244 532364
Fax: 01244 538344
E-mail: archives@flintshire.gov.uk

Website:
http://www.flintshire.gov.uk/archives

Enquiries:
Enquiries to: Searchroom
Other contacts: Conservator for conservation enquiries

Founded:
1951

Formerly called:
Flintshire Record Office (year of change 1974);
Clwyd Record Office (year of change 1996)

Organisation type and purpose:
Local government body.
Archives, conservation, records management.

Subject coverage:
All aspects of the history of Flintshire from 12th to 20th century, official, public and deposited records for Flintshire and North East Wales.

Museum or gallery collection, archive, or library special collection:
Family papers of W. E. Gladstone

Non-library collection catalogue:
All or part available online and in-house

Library catalogue:
All or part available in-house

Printed publications:
Annual Report
Buckley in Archive Photographs
Flintshire in Archive Photographs
Guide to the Parish Records of Clwyd
Handlist of Chapel Registers (list of all records in the record office, £2.50 incl. p&p)
Handlist of the Denbighshire Quarter Sessions Records (2 vols, 1647–1971)
Handlist of the Grosvenor (Halkyn) MSS (lead and coal mining in north-east Wales, £9.70 incl. p&p)
Introductory Leaflet (free)
List of Parish Registers
Mold in Archive Photographs
Reproduction old postcards, posters, maps and prints
Sources for the Genealogist

Electronic and video publications:
Bygone Flintshire (CD-ROM)
Mr Gladstone (CD-ROM)

Access to staff:
Contact by letter, by telephone, by fax, by e-mail and via website. Appointment necessary.

Access to building, collection or gallery:
Hours: Mon to Thu, 0900 to 1645; Fri, 0900 to 1615; documents not produced between 1200 and 1330
Special comments: CARN Reader's Ticket required; can be issued on production of proof of ID with address and signature.

Access for disabled people:
Parking provided, level entry

Constituent part of:
Flintshire County Council
  tel: 01352 752121; website: http://www.flintshire.gov.uk

FLOUR ADVISORY BUREAU LIMITED

Acronym or abbreviation: FAB

21 Arlington Street, London, SW1A 1RN

Tel: 020 7493 2521
Fax: 020 7493 6785

Website:
http://www.grainchain.com
http://www.fabflour.co.uk

Enquiries:
Enquiries to: Head of Communications / Communications Assistant
Direct e-mail: fab@nabim.org.uk

Founded:
1956

Organisation type and purpose:
Trade association.
A central source of information on matters relating to bread and flour in the UK.

Subject coverage:
Generic information on wheat, flour and bread; usage, recipes, educational material, nutritional information and market trends.

Education services:
See website.

Printed publications:
Literature for schools and consumers on wheat, flour and bread

Access to staff:
Contact by letter, by telephone, by fax, by e-mail and via website
Hours: Mon to Fri, 0900 to 1700

Public relations arm of the:
National Association of British and Irish Millers (NABIM)
  at the same address

FLOWERS & PLANTS ASSOCIATION

Acronym or abbreviation: F&PA

266 Flower Market, New Covent Garden Market, London, SW8 5NB

Tel: 020 7738 8044
Fax: 020 7738 8083
E-mail: press-office@flowers.org.uk

Website:
http://www.flowers.org.uk
Information on the association, flowers and plants industry, healthy house plants, seasonal pages, trend information, care advice.
http://www.tryflowers.org.uk

Enquiries:
Enquiries to: Chief Executive

Founded:
1984

Organisation type and purpose:
Trade association (membership is by subscription), present number of members: 200 companies.
Promotion of fresh cut flowers and indoor pot plants.

Subject coverage:
Commercially grown cut flowers, commercially grown pot plants (indoor), statistical data on market; care advice; product information; general related topics of interest.

Trade and statistical information:
Statistics for members only.
Data on cut flower market.
Data on pot plants market.

Printed publications:
Advertising point of sale material (members only)
Booklets and leaflets on flowers and plants
Factsheets on flowers & plants
Flowers & Plants Association News (quarterly, members)
Postcards of indoor flowers & plants
Posters of indoor flowers & plants
Trend information

Access to staff:
Contact by letter, by telephone, by fax, by e-mail and via website. Appointment necessary. Non-members charged.
Hours: Mon to Fri, 0900 to 1700
Special comments: Certain information is available to members only.

FOCUS

10 Great Pulteney Street, London, W1F 9NB

Tel: 020 3214 0100
Fax: 020 3214 0126

Website:
http://www.focusnet.co.uk
Description of our services, online service is on a separate URL and is available by subscription only.

Enquiries:
Enquiries to: Director

Founded:
1984

Still trading and formed from:
Property Intelligence Limited (year of change 2004)

Organisation type and purpose:
Service industry, research organisation.
Provides information on commercial properties UK-wide.

Subject coverage:
Commercial properties in the UK; socioeconomic and geo-demographic data on major UK towns, 17 million property records, 1 million deals, 900 retailers' requirements, 2.1 million occupiers, 7 town reports, planning details, auction information, property history, rating information, office availability, office requirements.

Museum or gallery collection, archive, or library special collection:
Company prospectuses
Property journals
Property company and fund reports
Press releases

Printed publications:
Agency League Tables
Newsletter
Auction Guide Analysis
Retail Demand Report
London Office Market Report

Electronic and video publications:
FOCUS online database

Access to staff:
Contact by letter, by telephone, by fax, by e-mail and via website. Appointment necessary. All charged.
Hours: Mon to Fri, 0830 to 1800

Access for disabled people:
Ramped entry, toilet facilities
Special comments: Ramped Entry

Connections with:
Scottish Property Network Limited
26 New Street, Paisley, PA1 1YB; tel: 0141 561 7300; fax: 0141 561 7319; e-mail: info@ scottishproperty.co.uk

FOLKESTONE LIBRARY, MUSEUM AND SASSOON GALLERY

2 Grace Hill, Folkestone, Kent, CT20 1HD

Tel: 01303 850123\ Minicom no. 01303 240258
Fax: 01303 242907

Enquiries:
Enquiries to: Librarian
Direct tel: 01303 256710
Direct fax: 01303 256710
Direct e-mail: janet.adamson@kent.gov.uk
Other contacts: (1) Information Officer (2) Heritage Officer for (1) reference (2) local studies.

Founded:
1888

Organisation type and purpose:
Local government body, museum, art gallery, public library, suitable for ages: all.

Subject coverage:
General and local information, including Channel Tunnel, local and family history.

Museum or gallery collection, archive, or library special collection:
Heritage Room, historical records, maps, photographs and newspapers for Folkestone and the Shepway area
Bishop's Transcripts and Archdeacon's Transcripts and Parish Registers for many parishes (microfilm)
Census enumerator's returns for 1841–1891 for Shepway and Capel-le-Ferne
Photographic collection
Map collection
Newspapers

Printed publications:
Creed's, Sinnock's, Pike's, Parson's and Kelly's Directories 1871–1938 (microfiche)

Access to staff:
Contact by letter, by telephone, by fax, by e-mail and in person
Hours: Mon, Tue, Thu, 0930 to 1800; Fri, 0930 to 1900; Sat, Wed, 0930 to 1700

Access for disabled people:
Level entry, access to all public areas, toilet facilities

Part of:
Kent County Council, Education and Libraries Department

FOLLY FELLOWSHIP

Acronym or abbreviation: F/F

7 Inch's Yard, Market Street, Newbury, Berkshire, RG14 5DP

Tel: 01635 42864
E-mail: andrew@follies.fsnet.co.uk

Website:
http://www.follies.org.uk

Enquiries:
Enquiries to: Secretary
Other contacts: Membership Secretary

Founded:
1988

Organisation type and purpose:
International organisation, learned society (membership is by subscription), registered charity (charity number 1002646).
To protect, preserve and promote follies, grottoes and garden buildings.

Subject coverage:
Architectural follies, grottoes and landscape buildings in the United Kingdom and worldwide.

Museum or gallery collection, archive, or library special collection:
Picture and photographic library

Printed publications:
Follies (quarterly, £5 incl. back copies from 1988)
Follies Journal (annually, £10.50)
Order printed publications from: e-mail: membership@follies.org.uk

Electronic and video publications:
Foll-e (monthly e-bulletin, free to anyone requesting copies)

Access to staff:
Contact by letter, by telephone, by e-mail and via website. Appointment necessary.
Hours: Mon to Fri, 0900 to 1700

FOOD AND DRINK FEDERATION

Acronym or abbreviation: FDF

6 Catherine Street, London, WC2B 5JJ

Tel: 020 7836 2460
Fax: 020 7836 0580
E-mail: generalenquiries@fdf.org.uk

Website:
http://www.fdf.org.uk
Information about FDF and the food manufacturing industry.

Enquiries:
Enquiries to: Information Manager

Formerly called:
Food Manufacturers Federation

Organisation type and purpose:
Trade association.

Subject coverage:
UK food manufacturing industry.

Electronic and video publications:
A list of publications is available from the website

Publications list:
Available online

Access to staff:
Contact by letter, by telephone, by fax, by e-mail and via website. Access for members only.
Hours: Mon to Fri, 0930 to 1730
Special comments: Visitors not normally permitted.

European link is the:
CIAA

Members:
Association of Cereal Food Manufacturers
British Pasta Products Association
British Starch Industry Association
Cereal Ingredient Manufacturers' Association
Frozen and Chilled Potato Processors' Association
tel: 0131 229 9415
Infant & Dietetic Foods Association
Margarine and Spreads Association
National Association of Cider Makers
Potato Processors' Association
tel: 0131 229 9415
Seasoning and Spice Association
UK Association of Manufacturers of Bakers' Yeast
UK Preserves Manufacturers' Association
UK Tea Association

FOOD COMMISSION

94 White Lion Street, London, N1 9PF

Tel: 020 7837 2250
Fax: 020 7837 1141
E-mail: enquiries@foodcomm.org.uk

Website:
http://www.foodcomm.org.uk

Enquiries:
Enquiries to: Information Officer

Founded:
1990

Formerly called:
London Food Commission (year of change 1990)

continued overleaf

Organisation type and purpose:
Registered charity, voluntary organisation (charity number 1000358), consultancy, research organisation.
Consumer watchdog, campaigning for better food.

Subject coverage:
Food policy, food labelling, irradiation, claims, nutrition and health, food composition analysis, agriculture and the environment, pesticides, contaminants, food adulteration, baby foods, genetic engineering, advertising.

Museum or gallery collection, archive, or library special collection:
Books, magazines and press cuttings

Printed publications:
The Food Magazine (quarterly)
The Nursery Food Book (£10.99 inc. p&p)
Healthy Eating for Babies and Children (£6.99 inc. £1 p&p)
The Food Our Children Eat (£8.99 inc. £1 p&p)
More than Rice and Peas (£17.50 in. £2.50 p&p)
Poor Expectations – Poverty and Undernourishment in Pregnancy (£5.50 inc. 50p p&p)
Food Irradiation (£6.50 in. £1 p&p)
Fast Food Nation (£9.99 inc. p&p)
The Shopper's Guide to Organic Food (£8.99 inc. £1 p&p)
GM Free – A shopper's guide to genetically modified food (£5.70 inc. p&p)
Various Photocopied Reports available from the Food Commission

Publications list:
Available online and in print

Access to staff:
Contact by letter, by telephone and by fax. Appointment necessary.
Hours: Mon to Fri, 1030 to 1800

Subsidiary body:
Food Additives Campaign Team
Food Commission Research Charity
Food Irradiation Campaign

FOOD STORAGE AND DISTRIBUTION FEDERATION

Acronym or abbreviation: FSDF

7 Diddenham Court, Lamb Wood Hill, Grazeley, Reading, Berkshire, RG7 1JQ

Tel: 0118 988 4468
Fax: 0118 988 7035
E-mail: info@fsdf.org.uk

Website:
http://www.fsdf.org.uk

Enquiries:
Enquiries to: Chief Executive

Founded:
1911

Formerly called:
Cold Storage and Distribution Federation (CSDF);
National Cold Storage Federation

Organisation type and purpose:
Trade association (membership is by subscription).

Subject coverage:
All aspects of controlled storage and distribution including operations temperature, health and safety, legislative aspects, fire, construction and related food processing acts.

Printed publications:
Directory (every 2 years, £35, free to members)
Fire Risk Assessment Guide (£17)
Guide to Safety in the Use of Pallets, Pallet Converters, Palletainers and Racking (£18)
Guide to Storage and Handling of Frozen Foods (£12)
Guide to the Management and Control of Fire Risks in Temperature Controlled Structures of the Refrigerated Food Industry (£43)
Technical papers and briefs as required – apply for details

Publications list:
Available in print

Access to staff:
Contact by letter, by telephone, by fax and by e-mail. Appointment necessary.
Hours: Mon to Fri, 0900 to 1700

Affiliated to:
Refrigerated Food Industry Confederation (RFIC)

Associated European and International links:
European Cold Storage and Logistics Association (ECSLA)
European Consortium for the Responsible Application of Refrigerants
International Association of Cold Store Contractors

FOODSERVICE CONSULTANTS SOCIETY INTERNATIONAL

Acronym or abbreviation: FCSI

Bourne House, Horsell Park, Woking, Surrey, GU21 4LY

Tel: 01483 761122
Fax: 01483 751991
E-mail: admin@fcsi.org.uk

Website:
http://www.fcsi.org.uk

Enquiries:
Enquiries to: Administrator

Founded:
1970

Formerly called:
SCHMC; Society of Catering and Hotel Management Consultants (year of change 1996)

Organisation type and purpose:
International organisation, professional body.

Subject coverage:
Market research, design and planning facilities, catering and hotel systems and procedures, recruitment, equipment, human resources, all related to hotel and catering industry.

Access to staff:
Contact by letter, by telephone, by fax and by e-mail. Appointment necessary.
Hours: Mon to Fri, 0900 to 1700

Parent body:
Foodservices Consultants Society International Suite 201, 304 West Liberty Street, Louisville, KY 40202 – 3068, USA; tel: +1 502 589 3783; fax: +1 502 589 3602; e-mail: fcsi@fcsi.org

FOOTBALL ASSOCIATION

Acronym or abbreviation: FA

25 Soho Square, London, W1D 4FA

Tel: 020 7745 4545
Fax: 020 7745 4546
E-mail: info@the-fa.org

Website:
http://www.fa.premier.com
Official site of the FA Carling Premiership.

Enquiries:
Enquiries to: Chief Executive

Founded:
1863

Organisation type and purpose:
Membership association.
To promote the sport of association football.

Subject coverage:
Football: coaching, competitions, refereeing and registrations.

Printed publications:
Soccer Referee's Manual
The Winning Formula (official coaching manual)
FA Handbook
FA News (quarterly)
FA Yearbook
Laws of Association Football

Weekly Bulletin (fixtures and results)
Order printed publications from: FACA Resources
tel: 0113 279 1395, fax: 0113 231 9606

Publications list:
Available in print

Access to staff:
Contact by letter, by telephone, by fax and by e-mail. Appointment necessary.
Hours: Mon to Fri, 0900 to 1700

Affiliated to:
FIFA
UEFA
World and European governing bodies

Has:
42,000 affiliated clubs

Other address:
Football Association
62 Lancaster Mews, London, W2 3QG

FOOTBALL ASSOCIATION OF WALES

Acronym or abbreviation: FAW

11–12 Neptune Court, Vanguard Way, Cardiff, CF24 5PJ

Tel: 029 2043 5830
Fax: 029 2049 6953
E-mail: info@faw.co.uk

Website:
http://www.faw.org.uk
Welsh football, cup competitions, international teams, news, handbook, discipline, clubs, fixtures and events, player registrations, ticket information, hospitality, welfare.

Enquiries:
Enquiries to: Secretary General

Founded:
1876

Organisation type and purpose:
Governing body for association football in Wales.

Subject coverage:
In addition to its administration responsibilities for football in Wales also has responsibility for running the 8 international teams, A, U21, U19, U17, Semi-Professional, Womens, Women's U19 and Women's U17.

Electronic and video publications:
FAW Official Handbook
Order electronic and video publications from:
Download from website

Access to staff:
Contact by letter, by telephone, by fax and by e-mail

Constituent part of:
International Football Association Board (with FIFA, The FA, SFA and IFA)

Member organisation of:
FIFA
UEFA

FOOTBALL LICENSING AUTHORITY

Acronym or abbreviation: FLA

27 Harcourt House, 19 Cavendish Square, London, W1G 0PL

Tel: 020 7491 7191
Fax: 020 7491 1882
E-mail: fla@flaweb.org.uk

Website:
http://www.flaweb.org.uk
Statutory Remit, publications and links to relevant sites.

Enquiries:
Enquiries to: Office Manager

Founded:
1990

Organisation type and purpose:
Statutory body.
Application of Safety of Sports Ground Act 1975 amended and Football Spectators Act 1989.

Subject coverage:
Safety of sports grounds and spectators, accommodation including seating, terracing and accommodation for spectators with disabilities.

Printed publications:
Accessible Stadia
Concourses
Control Rooms

Electronic and video publications:
Publications available online at website for free download:
Annual Report
Exercise Planning
Safety Certification
Briefing / Debriefing
Contingency Planning

Access to staff:
Contact by letter, by telephone, by fax and by e-mail. Appointment necessary.
Hours: Mon to Fri, 0900 to 1700

Parent body:
Department for Culture, Media and Sport (DCMS) Sport and Recreation Division, 2–4 Cockspur Street, London, SW1Y 5DY; tel: 020 7211 6200; e-mail: enquiries@culture.gov.uk; website: www .cluture.gov.uk

FORCE

Formal name: FORCE (Friends of the Oncology and Radiotherapy Centre) Cancer Charity

FORCE Cancer Support Centre, Corner House, Barrack Road, Exeter, EX2 5DW

Tel: 01392 406151 (patient suppport)
E-mail: support@forcecancercharity.co.uk

Website:
http://www.forcecancercharity.co.uk
The charity and its services, events.

Enquiries:
Enquiries to: Information Manager
Direct tel: 01392 406151
Other contacts: Support Information Assistant

Founded:
1987

Organisation type and purpose:
Registered charity (charity number 296884).
Cancer charity.
Provides a relaxed and comfortable environment where people can seek information and discuss their needs with experienced staff and also meet other Centre users and talk with trained volunteers.

Subject coverage:
Finances improvements in patient care through research, the purchase of advanced equipment and a Cancer Support and Information Centre located in the grounds of the RD&E Hospital.

Information services:
Benefits advice service, run in partnership with the Citizens Advice Bureau.

Museum or gallery collection, archive, or library special collection:
Library of leaflets, helpful articles, books to borrow and audio-visual materials, as well as guided internet access

Electronic and video publications:
Newsletter
Order electronic and video publications from:
Download from website

Access to staff:
Contact by letter, by telephone, by e-mail, in person and via website
Hours: Benefits advice service appointments: Thu

FORD 400E OWNERS CLUB

1 Maltings Farm Cottages, Witham Road, White Notley, Witham, Essex, CM81 1SE

E-mail: sandy@thames400e.freeserve.co.uk

Enquiries:
Enquiries to: Membership Secretary

Founded:
1991

Organisation type and purpose:
Membership association (membership is by subscription), present number of members: 120.

Subject coverage:
Ford medium commercial vehicle range 1957–1965, 400E models.

Museum or gallery collection, archive, or library special collection:
Sales and technical literature

Printed publications:
Newsletter/Magazine (6 times a year, members only)

Access to staff:
Contact by letter and by e-mail. Appointment necessary.
Hours: Telephone: Mon and Fri only, 1900 to 2100.

FORD CORSAIR OWNERS' CLUB

Acronym or abbreviation: FCOC

4 Bexley Close, Hailsham, East Sussex, BN27 1NH

Tel: 01323 840655
E-mail: checkleylizandray@yahoo.co.uk

Website:
http://www.fordcorsairownersclub.co.uk
Details of club and membership form.

Enquiries:
Enquiries to: Membership Secretary
Direct tel: 01634 272232

Founded:
1985

Organisation type and purpose:
Membership association (membership is by subscription), present number of members: 130.

Subject coverage:
Technical advice for Ford Corsair cars.

Access to staff:
Contact by letter, by telephone, by e-mail and via website
Hours: Mon to Fri, 0900 to 1700; Sat and Sun, 1000 to 2000

FORD EXECUTIVE OWNERS REGISTER

3 Shanklin Road, Stonehouse Estate, Coventry, Warwickshire, CV3 4EE

Tel: 024 7651 1822

Enquiries:
Enquiries to: Information Officer

Founded:
1985

Organisation type and purpose:
Membership association (membership is by subscription).
Classic car club.

Subject coverage:
Classic Car Club, cars included are Ford Cortina 1600E, Ford Cortina 2000E, Ford Corsair 2000E, Ford Capri 3000E, Ford Escort 1300E, Ford Zodiac Executive.

Printed publications:
Free to membership

Publications list:
Available in print

Access to staff:
Contact by letter and by telephone
Hours: Mon to Fri, 0900 to 1700

FORD MADOX FORD SOCIETY

Department of English, The Open University, Walton Hall, Milton Keynes, Buckinghamshire, MK7 6AA

Tel: 01908 653453
Fax: 01908 653750
E-mail: s.j.haslam@open.ac.uk

Website:
http://www.open.ac.uk/Arts/fordmadoxford -society

Enquiries:
Enquiries to: Chair
Direct e-mail: p.skinner370@btinternet.com (Treasurer)
Other contacts: Treasurer

Founded:
1996

Organisation type and purpose:
International organisation, learned society, present number of members: c. 140, voluntary organisation, registered charity.
Provides information on and generates research into Ford Madox Ford. Co-ordinates conferences and publications.

Subject coverage:
Ford Madox Ford, modernism, research/ conferences.

Printed publications:
Journal of FMF Studies (annually since 2002, for purchase direct or to members)
Annual newsletter

Publications list:
Available online

Access to staff:
Contact by letter, by telephone, by fax, by e-mail and via website
Hours: Any reasonable time

Access to building, collection or gallery:
No access other than to staff

Links with:
Joseph Conrad Society

FORD MK II INDEPENDENT OC INTERNATIONAL

173 Sparrow Farm Drive, Feltham, Middlesex, TW14 0DG

Tel: 020 8384 3559
Fax: 020 8890 3741
E-mail: brian.enticknap@mypostoffice.co.uk

Enquiries:
Enquiries to: President

Founded:
1988

Organisation type and purpose:
Membership association, present number of members: 500.
Motor vehicle authenticator for RAC and MSA.

Subject coverage:
All aspects, and information on the Ford MKII Consul, Zephyr, Zodiac; technical advice; modification; classic car meetings and rallies, national and international.

Museum or gallery collection, archive, or library special collection:
Original parts books
Workshop manuals

Printed publications:
Newsletter (6 times a year, members)

Access to staff:
Contact by letter, by telephone and by fax
Hours: Mon to Fri, 0900 to 2100

continued overleaf

Officially recognised by:
DVLA
  Swansea
Ford Motor Company

FORD MODEL 'T' REGISTER OF GB

195 Bradford Road, Riddlesden, Keighley, West Yorkshire, BD20 5JR

Tel: 01535 607978
E-mail: jma195@aol.com

Website:
http://www.t-ford.co.uk

Enquiries:
Enquiries to: Secretary

Founded:
1960

Organisation type and purpose:
Advisory body, membership association, voluntary organisation.

Subject coverage:
Register of Model T Ford vehicles, help with such and supply of parts; magazine; events held throughout the year.

Printed publications:
T Topics (magazine, quarterly, non-members £3.50)
Order printed publications from: The Secretary

Publications list:
Available in print

Access to staff:
Contact by letter, by telephone, by e-mail and via website
Hours: Mon to Fri, 1730 to 2100

FORD MOTOR COMPANY LIMITED

Eagle Way, Brentwood, Essex, CM13 3BW

Tel: 01277 253000

Enquiries:
Enquiries to: Secretary

Founded:
1928

Organisation type and purpose:
Manufacturing industry.
The principal activity in which the Company is engaged is the manufacture and sale of motor vehicles and components.

Subject coverage:
Motor vehicle manufacture; industrial engines; parts and accessories.

Access to staff:
Contact by letter
Hours: Mon to Fri, 0900 to 1700

FORECAST INTERNATIONAL/DMS INC

Templehurst House, 48 New Street, Chipping Norton, Oxfordshire, OX7 5LJ

Tel: 01608 643281
Fax: 01608 641159
E-mail: hawk@hawk.co.uk

Website:
http://www.hawk.co.uk
Internet home page: List of contents, company capabilities, news highlights, newsletters.

Enquiries:
Enquiries to: Managing Director

Founded:
1975

Organisation type and purpose:
Research organisation, publishing house.

Subject coverage:
Aircraft maintenance, budget, funding, commercial aircraft, commercial inventories, contractors, electronics, avionics, emerging technologies, gas turbines, military aircraft, military inventories, military vehicles, missiles, ordnance, munitions, power systems, space systems and satellites, component and niche market analysis.

Museum or gallery collection, archive, or library special collection:
Library containing hardcopy and CD-ROM formats for market intelligence for aerospace, defence, electronics, power systems and transportation industries

Trade and statistical information:
Production forecasts and analysis for aerospace, weapons systems, power systems, naval systems, electronic systems, US defence budget including inventories and product life cycle analysis.

Electronic and video publications:
CD-ROM/online based market intelligence services (£1595 each, £35,000 full set) covering:
Aerospace Systems Group
Geo-Political and Economic Group
Electronics Group
Weapons Systems Group
Naval Systems Group

Publications list:
Available in print

Access to staff:
Contact by telephone, by fax, by e-mail and via website
Hours: Mon to Fri, 0900 to 1700

Head office:
Forecast International/DMS
  22 Commerce Road, Newtown, Connecticut, 06470, USA

FOREIGN AND COMMONWEALTH OFFICE

Acronym or abbreviation: FCO

Downing Street, London, SW1A 2AL

Tel: 020 7270 3925
Fax: 020 7270 3270
E-mail: library.historical@fco.gov.uk

Enquiries:
Enquiries to: Librarian
Other contacts: Head of Library Enquiry Services; e-mail library.current@fco.gov.uk for current affairs

Formerly called:
Colonial Office (CO), Commonwealth Relations Office (CRO); Foreign Office (FO) (year of change '968)

Organisation type and purpose:
National government body.

Subject coverage:
International relations, international law, diplomacy and politics, history, administration, economics and laws of overseas countries.

Museum or gallery collection, archive, or library special collection:
Historic Collections of books of the former colonial and foreign offices
Photographic Collection mainly of Commonwealth countries and former UK Colonies
Portraits of Diplomats and Colonial Governors, places and events c. 1850 to current

Non-library collection catalogue:
All or part available in-house

Access to staff:
Contact by letter, by telephone and by e-mail. Appointment necessary.
Hours: Mon to Fri, 0900 to 1700

Access to building, collection or gallery:
Prior appointment required

Access for disabled people:
Ramped entry, toilet facilities

FOREIGN AND COMMONWEALTH OFFICE – KNOWLEDGE AND LEARNING CENTRE

Acronym or abbreviation: FCO

Room G6, Building 17, Hanslope Park, Hanslope, Milton Keynes, Buckinghamshire, MK19 7BH

Tel: 01908 515960
Fax: 01908 515943

Website:
http://www.fco.gov.uk
Summary of FCO services, functions, ministers, structure and main contact points, includes FCO travel advice on foreign travel.

Enquiries:
Enquiries to: Librarian
Other contacts: Librarian (London address) for non-central-government enquiries to FCO's main library in first instance.

Organisation type and purpose:
National government body.
Support and IT services for the FCO at home and abroad.

Subject coverage:
Hanslope Park Knowledge and Learning Centre is an information unit and open learning centre primarily serving FCO staff based on site. Stock is available for loan to other central government departments and agencies. Other enquirers are requested to contact the main FCO library in London, in the first instance, or consult the FCO's website, www.fco.gov.uk, for advice on foreign travel.

Non-library collection catalogue:
All or part available in-house

Printed publications:
Order printed publications from: Stationery Office Ltd (formerly HMSO)

Access to staff:
Contact by letter, by telephone and by fax. Appointment necessary.
Hours: Mon to Fri, 0830 to 1630

Access to building, collection or gallery:
Prior appointment required

Other address:
Foreign and Commonwealth Office (FCO)
  Library, Room E213, King Charles Street, London, SW1A 2AH; tel: 020 7270 3925; fax: 020 7270 3270/3682

FOREIGN AND COMMONWEALTH OFFICE – TRAVEL ADVICE UNIT

Acronym or abbreviation: TAU

Consular Directorate, Old Admiralty Building, Whitehall, London, SW1A 2PA

Tel: 0845 850 2829
Fax: 020 7008 0155

Website:
http://www.fco.gov.uk/
Travel advice notices, do's and don'ts, consular services abroad.

Enquiries:
Enquiries to: Travel Advice Clerk

Organisation type and purpose:
National government body, advisory body.

Subject coverage:
Up-to-date travel advice on threats to personal safety, arising from political unrest, lawlessness, violence, natural disasters, epidemics, anti-British demonstrations and aircraft safety, is given to help British travellers avoid trouble when overseas.

Printed publications:
Backpackers and Independent Travellers
British Consular Services Abroad (for ordering fax: 01444 246620)
Checklist for travellers

Death Overseas
Travellers' Tips
Dual Nationality
In Prison Abroad
International Child Abduction
Victims of Crime Abroad

Access to staff:
Contact by letter, by telephone, by fax and by e-mail. Appointment necessary.
Hours: Mon to Fri, 0930 to 1600

FOREIGN PRESS ASSOCIATION IN LONDON

Acronym or abbreviation: FPA

25 Northumberland Avenue, London, WC2N 5AP

Tel: 020 7930 0445
E-mail: briefings@foreign-press.org.uk

Website:
http://www.foreign-press.org.uk
Press briefings, conferences, annual FPA Media Awards, membership information.

Enquiries:
Enquiries to: Director
Direct e-mail: christopherwyld@foreign-press.org.uk

Founded:
1888

Organisation type and purpose:
International organisation, professional body (membership is by annual subscription), present number of members: 450.
Professional body/club for foreign journalists based in the UK.

Subject coverage:
Foreign media in the UK.

Printed publications:
Weekly online bulletin of events and useful information for journalists

Access to staff:
Contact by telephone and by e-mail
Hours: Mon to Fri, 0900 to 1800

Links with:
Commonwealth Club
25 Northumberland Avenue; tel: 02077669200; e-mail: events@thercs.org; website: http://www.thercs.org

FORENSIC SCIENCE SERVICE LIMITED

Acronym or abbreviation: FSS

Information Services, Forensic Science Service, 109 Lambeth Road, London, SE1 7LP

Fax: 020 7160 4651
E-mail: info.services.enquiry.desk@fss.pnn.police.uk

Website:
http://www.forensic.gov.uk
Information on the Forensic Science Service.

Enquiries:
Enquiries to: Library Services Manager

Founded:
1967

Organisation type and purpose:
Government-owned company.
Provides scientific support in the investigation of crime.

Subject coverage:
All aspects of forensic science, including serology, DNA profiling and immunology, analysis of chemicals, drugs, pesticides and trace elements, toxicology, document examination and fingerprint enhancement.
General scientific techniques applied to the analysis of small quantities of drugs, paint, glass, metals, body fluids, etc; the investigation, at the scene and in the laboratory, of cases of known and suspected arson; metallurgic problems such as mechanical failures; the restoration of erased identification numbers on stolen car engines and other property; the analysis of physical evidence arising from traffic offences such as tyre examinations and the mathematical analysis of vehicle accidents; grouping systems on dried blood and body secretions; DNA profiling; high-performance liquid chromatography techniques applied to drugs and lubricating oils; gas liquid chromatography for the analysis of drugs, blood-alcohol, the routine screening of drugs and extracts in toxicological analysis, hydrocarbons (petrol, paraffin, diesel etc) and other solvents; use of scanning electron microscopy for identification of very small particles; examination, analysis and identification of synthetic fibres and fibres of living origin (plant and animal); identification of bullets found at scenes, bullet and cartridge-case comparisons and the examination of firearms; examination of forged and altered documents using non-destructive techniques, such as infra-red and ultra-violet light, and the comparison of handwriting and typewriting; use of specialised photographic techniques at crime scenes and of items examined at the laboratory for the enhancement of fingerprints and other marks, blood patterns and the location of body fluids.

Museum or gallery collection, archive, or library special collection:
Analytic Data on Drugs and Chemicals
Forensic Science Bibliographic Database (FORS)
Shoeprint Collection in kind, photographs and documents
Sidelamp and Headlamp Collection
Vehicle Paint and Tyre Data

Non-library collection catalogue:
All or part available online

Library catalogue:
All or part available in-house

Printed publications:
FORSight – The Forensic Abstracts Journal (12 times a year, prices on request)
Annual Report (also available on website)
Forensic Science Thesaurus (prices on request)
Restricted Internal Research Reports
Order printed publications from: Library Services Manager; e-mail: info.services.enquiry.desk@fss.pnn.police.uk

Electronic and video publications:
FORS, a comprehensive online database (prices on request) on forensic science, 70,000 records from 1900 sources. Covers toxicology, firearms, fingerprints, forensic medicine, DNA profiling, etc.
Order electronic and video publications from: Library Services Manager; e-mail: info.services.enquiry.desk@fss.pnn.police.uk

Access to staff:
Contact by letter, by fax, by e-mail and via website. Non-members charged.
Hours: Mon to Fri, 1000 to 1600

Laboratories at:
Chepstow, Wetherby, Chorley, Huntingdon and Birmingham

FORENSIC SCIENCE SOCIETY

Acronym or abbreviation: FSSoc

Clarke House, 18A Mount Parade, Harrogate, North Yorkshire, HG1 1BX

Tel: 01423 506068
Fax: 01423 566391
E-mail: president@forensic-science-society.org.uk

Website:
http://www.forensic-science-society.org.uk

Enquiries:
Enquiries to: Secretary

Founded:
1959

Organisation type and purpose:
Learned society (membership is by subscription), present number of members: 2300, registered charity (charity number 205992), publishing house.
To advance the study, application and standing of forensic science and to facilitate co-operation among persons interested in forensic science throughout the world.

Subject coverage:
Forensic sciences, pathology and medicine, forensic chemistry and biology, forensic serology, forensic science in connection with textiles, tyres, metallurgy, photographs and marks; forensic identification, handwriting and documents examination, explosion investigation, firearms and ballistics, aspects of alcohol.

Printed publications:
Science and Justice (quarterly)
World List of Forensic Science Laboratories, Interfaces (newsletter – quarterly)

Access to staff:
Contact via website
Hours: Mon to Fri, 0900 to 1700

FORESIGHT

28 The Paddock, Godalming, Surrey, GU7 1XD

Tel: 01483 427839
Fax: 01483 427668

Website:
http://www.foresight-preconception.org.uk

Enquiries:
Enquiries to: Chairman

Founded:
1978

Formerly called:
Foresight, The Association for the Promotion of Preconceptual Care

Organisation type and purpose:
Registered charity (charity number 279160).

Subject coverage:
Preparing couples for pregnancy.

Library catalogue:
All or part available in print

Printed publications:
Planning a Healthy Baby (Barnes B and Bradley S G)
The Hyperactive Child, what the family can do (Barnes B and Colquhoun I)
Preparation for Pregnancy: an Essential Guide (Bradley S G and Bennett N)
The Foresight Wholefood Cookbook (Jervis N and Jervis R)
Order printed publications from: Resource Centre, Foresight
Mead House, Littlemead Estate, Alfold Road, Cranleigh, Surrey, GU6 8ND, tel: 01483 548071

Publications list:
Available in print

Access to staff:
Contact by letter, by telephone, by fax and in person. Appointment necessary.
Hours: Mon to Fri, 0900 to 1700
Special comments: Organisation works almost always by letter/telephone etc.

Access to building, collection or gallery:
Prior appointment required

Access for disabled people:
Parking provided, ramped entry

FOREST

Formal name: Freedom Organisation for the Right to Enjoy Smoking Tobacco

Sheraton House, Castle Park, Cambridge, CB3 0AX

Tel: 01223 370156
E-mail: contact@forestonline.org

continued overleaf

Website:
http://www.forestonline.org/

Enquiries:
Enquiries to: Media Enquiries
Direct tel: 07774 781840

Founded:
1979

Organisation type and purpose:
National organisation, membership association
(membership is by subscription), voluntary
organisation.
To promote equal rights for smokers of tobacco,
and those who wish to accommodate them.

Subject coverage:
Smoking, a sensible smoking policy and different
aspects of the smoking debate.

Printed publications:
A range of publications on:
Taxation and economics, rights and free choice,
children, restrictions, health and environmental,
tobacco smoke and the work-place
Free Choice (journal, 4 times a year)
Smoking and Its Enemies
FOREST : Smoking in the workplace : Consultancy
Pack

Publications list:
Available online and in print

Access to staff:
Contact by letter, by telephone, by fax, by e-mail
and via website. Appointment necessary.
Hours: Mon to Fri, 0930 to 1730

Access to building, collection or gallery:
No prior appointment required

FOREST HEATH DISTRICT COUNCIL

College Heath Road, Mildenhall, Suffolk, IP28 7EY

Tel: 01638 719000
Fax: 01638 716493
E-mail: info@forest-heath.gov.uk

Website:
http://www.forest-heath.gov.uk

Enquiries:
Enquiries to: Public Relations Manager

Organisation type and purpose:
Local government body.

Access to staff:
Contact by letter, by telephone, by fax, by e-mail,
in person and via website
Hours: Mon to Fri, 0900 to 1700

Access for disabled people:
Parking provided, level entry, toilet facilities

FOREST OF DEAN RAILWAY LIMITED

Formal name: T/A Dean Forest Railway Company
Limited
Acronym or abbreviation: DFR

Forest Road, Lydney, GL15 4ET

Tel: 01594 843423 (information line, recorded times
& dates of services)
E-mail: infodfr@btconnect.com

Website:
http://www.dfr.co.uk

Enquiries:
Enquiries to: Commercial Director
Direct tel: 01594 845840
Direct e-mail: membership@dfr.co.uk
Other contacts: DFR Society – Membership
Applications

Founded:
1970

Formerly called:
Dean Forest Railway Preservation Society

Organisation type and purpose:
Operators of the Dean Forest Railway Co. Ltd and
Dean Forest Railfreight Ltd.

Subject coverage:
Dean Forest Railway is a predominantly steam-
powered standard gauge tourist heritage railway
operating between Parkend and Lydney Junction.
It is adjacent, and connected, to Railtrack. The
railway is the sole surviving remnant of the Severn
and Wye Railway. The headquarters at Norchard
are on the site of the former West Gloucestershire
Power Station and Norchard Colliery. Railway
artefacts plus a working telephone system.

Printed publications:
Colour brochure/timetable (annual, free, please
enclose a sae)
Order printed publications from: Dean Forest Railway
Co. Ltd at the above address

Electronic and video publications:
Norchard/Dean Forest Railway (video, £10.95 plus
p&p)
Order electronic and video publications from: Dean
Forest Railway Co. Ltd at the above address

Access to staff:
Contact by letter. Appointment necessary.
Hours: 1100 to 1600; longer opening hours when
trains are running

Access to building, collection or gallery:
No prior appointment required
Hours: Museum and gift shop: daily, except
Christmas Day and Boxing Day, 1100 to 1600
Special comments: Longer opening hours when
trains are running.

Access for disabled people:
Parking provided, ramped entry, toilet facilities
Hours: As above
Special comments: Access to shop, station, etc. only
at Norchard.

FORESTRY AND TIMBER ASSOCIATION

Formal name: Association of Timber Growers and
Forestry Professionals Ltd
Acronym or abbreviation: FTA

5 Dublin Street Lane South, Edinburgh, EH1 3PX

Tel: 0131 538 7111
Fax: 0131 538 7222
E-mail: info@forestryandtimber.org

Enquiries:
Enquiries to: Chief Executive

Founded:
1957

Formed from:
Ulster Timber Growers Organisation (UTGA)
(year of change 2001); Association of Professional
Foresters (APF), Timber Growers Association
(TGA) (year of change 2002)

Organisation type and purpose:
Membership association (membership is by
subscription), present number of members: 2500.

FORESTRY COMMISSION

Silvan House, 231 Corstorphine Road, Edinburgh,
EH12 7AT

Tel: 0131 334 0303
Fax: 0131 334 3047
E-mail: enquiries@forestry.gsi.gov.uk

Website:
http://www.forestry.gov.uk

Enquiries:
Enquiries to: Information Officer

Founded:
1919

Organisation type and purpose:
National government body.

Subject coverage:
Forestry.

Publications list:
Available online and in print

Access to staff:
Contact by letter, by telephone, by fax, by e-mail
and in person. Appointment necessary.
Hours: Mon to Fri, 0900 to 1700

Access for disabled people:
Parking provided, ramped entry, access to all
public areas, toilet facilities

Also at:
Forestry Commission England
England National Office, 620 Bristol Business
Park, Coldharbour Lane, Bristol, BS16 1EJ; tel:
0117 906 6000; fax: 0117 931 2859
Forestry Commission Scotland
Silvan House, 231 Corstorphine Road,
Edinburgh, EH12 7AT; tel: 0131 334 0303; fax:
0131 334 3047
Forestry Commission Wales
Welsh Assembly Government, Rhodfa Padarn,
Llanbadarn Fawr, Aberystwyth, Ceredigion,
SY23 3UR; tel: 0300 068 0300; fax: 0300 068 0301

FORESTRY COMMISSION LIBRARY

Forest Research, Alice Holt Lodge, Wrecclesham,
Farnham, Surrey, GU10 4LH

Tel: 01420 22255
Fax: 01420 23653
E-mail: library@forestry.gsi.gov.uk

Website:
http://www.forestry.gov.uk
Directory of addresses of Forestry Commission
offices in Great Britain, background information on
recreation, the forest industry, education,
woodland management and forestry policy and
research.

Enquiries:
Enquiries to: Librarian
Direct e-mail: research.info@forestry.gsi.gov.uk

Founded:
1919

Organisation type and purpose:
National government body, research organisation.

Subject coverage:
Forestry in temperate regions; arboriculture
(information provided by the Arboricultural
Advisory and Information Service).

Non-library collection catalogue:
All or part available in-house

Library catalogue:
All or part available in-house

Printed publications:
Bulletins, handbooks, field books, guidelines,
information notes, practice notes, research notes,
technical notes
Local Forestry Commission offices issue local trail
guides and other publications
Order printed publications from: Forestry
Commission Publications, PO Box 501, Leicester,
LE94 0AA; tel: 0844 991 6500; fax: 0844 991 6501; e-
mail forestry@mrm.co.uk

Electronic and video publications:
Tree Doctor (CD-ROM, £38)
Order electronic and video publications from: Disease
and Diagnostic Advisory Service, Forest Research,
Alice Holt Lodge, Wrecclesham, Farnham, Surrey,
GU10 4LH; e-mail tree.doctor@forestry.gsi.gov.uk

Publications list:
Available online

Access to staff:
Contact by letter, by telephone, by fax and by e-
mail. Appointment necessary. All charged.
Hours: Mon to Thu, 0900 to 1700; Fri, 0900 to 1630

Access to building, collection or gallery:
As Library

Hours: Mon to Thu, 0900 to 1700; Fri, 0900 to 1630

Access for disabled people:
Level entry, toilet facilities

Also at:
Forestry Commission Public Enquiries Service
231 Corstorphine Road, Edinburgh, EH12 7AT;
tel: 0131 334 0303; fax: 0131 334 3047; e-mail:
enquiries@forestry.gsi.gov.uk
Public Enquiry Line
tel: 0845 FORESTS (0845 367 3787)
Tree Helpline
tel: 09065 161147 (£1.50 per minute)

FORESTRY CONTRACTING ASSOCIATION

Acronym or abbreviation: FCA

Dalfling, Blairdaff, Inverurie, Aberdeenshire, AB51 5LA

Tel: 01467 651368
Fax: 01467 651595
E-mail: members@fcauk.com

Website:
http://www.fcauk.com
General background information on the
Association and membership benefits.

Enquiries:
Enquiries to: Executive Director
Direct e-mail: gordon@fcauk.com
Other contacts: Membership Services

Founded:
1992

Organisation type and purpose:
Trade association.

Subject coverage:
All forestry matters; training, running a business,
insurance, finance, health and safety and other
legislation, wood fuel and biomass.

Printed publications:
FCA News (quarterly)
FCA Directory of Members (yearly)

Electronic and video publications:
Best Business Practice CD-ROM – Free to members

Access to staff:
Contact by letter, by telephone, by fax, by e-mail
and via website. Appointment necessary.
Hours: Mon to Fri, 0900 to 1700

FORGOTTEN RACING CLUB

Acronym or abbreviation: FRC

Hillside, Holt Road, Hackney, Matlock,
Derbyshire, DE4 2QD

Tel: 01629 733898

Enquiries:
Enquiries to: Membership Secretary

Founded:
1986

Formerly called:
Forgotten Era Racing Club

Organisation type and purpose:
Membership association.

Subject coverage:
Racing motorcycles predominantly from the
period 1963 to 1986, their restoration and use.

Printed publications:
Club magazine (6 times a year, free to members)

Access to staff:
Contact by letter and by telephone
Hours: Evenings and weekends

FORK LIFT TRUCK ASSOCIATION

Manor Farm Buildings, Lasham, Alton,
Hampshire, GU34 5SL

Tel: 01256 381441
Fax: 01256 381735
E-mail: mail@fork-truck.org.uk

Enquiries:
Enquiries to: Chief Executive

Founded:
1992

Formerly called:
Fork Truck Hire Association; Fork Truck
Association

Organisation type and purpose:
Trade Association.

Subject coverage:
Fork lift trucks.

Non-library collection catalogue:
All or part available online

Publications list:
Available online and in print

Access to staff:
Contact by letter, by telephone, by fax and via
website. Appointment necessary.
Hours: Mon to Fri, 0900 to 1700

FORTRESS STUDY GROUP

Acronym or abbreviation: FSG

6 Lanark Place, London, W9 1BS

Tel: 0020 7286 5512

Website:
http://www.fsgfort.com

Enquiries:
Enquiries to: Honorary Secretary

Founded:
1975

Organisation type and purpose:
Learned society (membership is by subscription),
registered charity (charity number 288790).
To advance the education of the public in the study
of all aspects of fortifications and their armaments,
especially works constructed to mount or resist
artillery.

Subject coverage:
Fortification since the introduction of artillery.

Printed publications:
Casemate (newsletter, 3 times a year)
Fort (journal, annually)

Access to staff:
Contact by letter, by telephone and by e-mail
Hours: Evenings

Affiliated to:
International Fortress Council

FORUM FOR THE BUILT ENVIRONMENT

Acronym or abbreviation: FBE

35 Hayworth Road, Sandiacre, Nottingham, NG10 5LL

Tel: 0115 949 0641
Fax: 0115 949 1664

Website:
http://www.fbe-org.co.uk

Enquiries:
Enquiries to: Chief Executive
Direct e-mail: phil.laycock@fbe-org.co.uk

Founded:
1946

Organisation type and purpose:
Learned society.
Multi-professional society for all engaged in
construction.
Construction networking.

Subject coverage:
There are 154 technical advice panels covering a
very wide range of building and civil engineering,
and related subjects, including acoustics, asphalt
technology, bridge construction, building
construction and maintenance, ceramics, contract
law and procedure, demolition, district and group
heating, drainage, gas engineering and technology,
geodetic engineering, lift installation, materials
handling, testing and purchasing, piling,
quarrying, sewerage technology, timber
technology.

Printed publications:
Annual Lectures Awards
Journal (2 times a year)
Newsletter (10 times a year)
Register of members
Technical papers

Access to staff:
Contact by letter, by telephone, by fax and by e-
mail. Appointment necessary.
Hours: Mon to Fri, 0900 to 1730

Has:
19 regional UK branches and overseas
representation

FORUM OF PRIVATE BUSINESS

Acronym or abbreviation: The Forum

Ruskin Chambers, Drury Lane, Knutsford,
Cheshire, WA16 6HA

Tel: 01565 634467
Fax: 0870 241 9570
E-mail: info@fpb.org

Website:
http://www.fpb.org
Advice, guidance, offers, events, benefits, research,
news, how to join, links.

Enquiries:
Enquiries to: Research Projects Manager
Other contacts: Media and PR Manager

Founded:
1977

Organisation type and purpose:
Business support organisation (SMEs), research
organisation.
Parliamentary representative body for SMEs.

Subject coverage:
Structure and needs of UK small businesses,
concerns and priorities of SME problems, financial,
administrative and legal; research on specific
issues, bank/SME relationships, late payment, legal
identities, crime, ISO and others.

**Museum or gallery collection, archive, or library
special collection:**
Reports, consultation responses and research on
SME-related topics

Trade and statistical information:
Quarterly report on current SME issues and
longitudinal survey research on specific
concerns, detailed academic reports on
specialised areas (banking, etc.).

Printed publications:
Reports on specific issues (£75–£500)
Press releases (free)
Business Insight – quarterly magazine (free to
members)
Referendum quarterly newsletter (free to
members)
Employment Guide (£175–£320; discounted rates
for members)
Health and Safety Guide (£105–£210; discounted
rates for members)

Electronic and video publications:
Weekly eNewsletter (free to members)
Monthly eNewsletter (free to subscribers)

Access to staff:
Contact by letter, by telephone, by fax and by e-
mail. Appointment necessary.

continued overleaf

Hours: Mon to Fri, 0900 to 1730

Access to building, collection or gallery:
Appointment required

FOSTERING NETWORK

Acronym or abbreviation: tFN

87 Blackfriars Road, London, SE1 8HA

Tel: 020 7620 6400; Infoline: 020 7261 1884
Fax: 020 7620 6401
E-mail: info@fostering.net

Website:
http://www.fostering.net

Enquiries:
Enquiries to: Information Officer

Founded:
1974

Formerly called:
National Foster Care Association (NFCA) (year of change 2001)

Organisation type and purpose:
Membership association (membership is by subscription), voluntary organisation, registered charity (charity number 280852), training organisation, consultancy, research organisation, publishing house.
To improve the quality of life for all children in foster care.

Subject coverage:
Foster care, including allowances for foster carers, dealing with difficult behaviour, dealing with allegations of abuse, after-care needs of young people, needs of foster children with disabilities, needs of teenagers in foster care.

Information services:
E-mail and telephone information service – deals with general fostering enquiries.

Museum or gallery collection, archive, or library special collection:
Foster Care Resource Centre

Trade and statistical information:
One of the largest collections of resources relating to foster care in the UK.

Library catalogue:
All or part available online

Printed publications:
A large selection of books, papers and reports, including:
Booklets on aspects of being a foster carer
Foster Care (magazine, quarterly)
Leaflets on all aspects of becoming a foster carer
Research reports
Training materials
Policy guidelines
Leaving Care
Practical Guides for Carers
Order printed publications from: website: http://www.fosteringresources.co.uk

Electronic and video publications:
DVDs on aspects of foster care

Publications list:
Available online and in print

Access to staff:
Contact by letter, by telephone, by fax, by e-mail, in person and via website. Appointment necessary.
Hours: Infoline: Mon to Fri, 1000 to 1600
Special comments: Appointments to use the Foster Care Resource Centre are necessary to ensure library and information staff are available.

Access to building, collection or gallery:
By appointment with the Information Officer
Hours: Office: Mon to Thu, 0900 to 1700; Fri, 0900 to 1630

Constituent bodies:
The Fostering Network Northern Ireland
Unit 10, 40 Montgomery Road, Belfast, BT6 9HL; tel: 028 9070 5056; fax: 028 9079 9215; e-mail: ni@fostering.net

The Fostering Network Scotland
Ingram House, 2nd Floor, 227 Ingram Street, Glasgow, G1 1DA; tel: 0141 204 1400; fax: 0141 204 6588; e-mail: scotland@fostering.net
The Fostering Network Wales
1 Caspian Point, Pierhead Street, Cardiff Bay, CF10 4DQ; tel: 029 2044 0940; fax: 029 2044 0941; e-mail: wales@fostering.net

Member organisations:
Almost all local authorities in the UK

FOUNDATION FOR ASSISTIVE TECHNOLOGY

Acronym or abbreviation: FAST

12 City Forum, 250 City Road, London, EC1V 8AF

Tel: 020 7253 3303
Fax: 020 7253 5990
E-mail: info@fastuk.org

Website:
http://www.fastuk.org
Online Database of over 700 organisations involved with research projects, research-related publications and assistive technology events, news information and links to other sites.
User Forum, a list of people who use assistive technology who are willing to participate in research and development projects.
Annual Parliamentary Report outlining assistive technology research and development funded by the government.

Enquiries:
Enquiries to: Administrator
Direct e-mail: pat@fastuk.org

Some services taken over from:
Disability Information Trust (DIT) (year of change 2001)

Organisation type and purpose:
National organisation, registered charity (charity number 1061636).
The Foundation for Assistive Technology (FAST) is an independent networking organisation funded by the Department of Health. We will:
- enable you to contact other people active in the Assistive Technology research and development community via our database which contains information on over 1500 organisations and individuals.
- keep you up to date and act as a signpost to useful and related information about research and development activity in Assistive Technology.

Subject coverage:
Assistive Technology.

Printed publications:
Each month FAST produces a bulletin for the AT Forum with breaking news and updates. FAST produces the annual RAPID Report on Research and Development in Assistive Technology. FAST is also commissioned by the Department of Health to produce an annual parliamentary report which provides the DoH with an overview of the outcomes of research and development funded by Government.

Access to staff:
Contact by e-mail and via website
Hours: Mon to Fri, 0900 to 1700
Special comments: Online service.

FOUNDATION FOR CREDIT COUNSELLING

Formal name: Consumer Credit Counselling Service
Acronym or abbreviation: CCCS

2 Ridgmount Street, London, WC1E 7AA

Tel: 020 7636 5214
Fax: 020 7580 0016
E-mail: mhurlston@hurlstons.com

Enquiries:
Enquiries to: Chairman

Other contacts: (1) Public Relations Officer; (2) Chief Executive Operations for (1) political, media; (2) technical.

Founded:
1993

Also:
CCCS Scotland

Organisation type and purpose:
Registered charity.

Subject coverage:
Consumer debt.

Trade and statistical information:
Data on levels of enquiries and debts.

Printed publications:
Statistical Yearbook 2005

Access to staff:
Contact by e-mail
Hours: Mon to Fri, 0900 to 1700

Access to building, collection or gallery:
No access other than to staff

Other addresses:
Customer Access
Merrion Centre, Leeds; tel: 0800 138 1111; 0800 138 DEBT
Foundation for Credit Counselling
Merrion Centre, Leeds; tel: 0800 138 1111; 0800 138 DEBT

FOUNDATION FOR EDUCATION AND RESEARCH IN CHILD BEARING

27 Walpole Street, London, SW3 4QS

Tel: 020 7730 2800
Fax: 020 7730 0710

Enquiries:
Enquiries to: Information Officer

Founded:
1972

Organisation type and purpose:
Registered charity (charity number 262318).

Subject coverage:
Prevention of handicaps of perinatal origin.

Printed publications:
The Prevention of Preterm Birth (Wynn M and A, £3 direct plus p&p)
The Prevention of Handicap of Perinatal Origin (Wynn, M and A, £2 direct plus p&p)
Nutrition Counselling in the Prevention of Low Birth Weight (Wynn M and A, 40p direct plus p&p)
Some Consequences of Induced Abortion to Children Born Subsequently (Wynn M and A, 60p direct plus p&p)
Prevention of Handicap of Early Pregnancy Origin: some evidence for the value of good health before conception (Wynn M and A, £5 direct plus p&p)

Access to staff:
Contact by letter, by telephone and by fax.
Appointment necessary.
Hours: Mon to Fri, 0900 to 1700

FOUNDATION FOR THE STUDY OF INFANT DEATHS

Acronym or abbreviation: FSID

11 Belgrave Road, London, SW1V 1RB

Tel: 020 7802 3200
E-mail: office@fsid.org.uk

Website:
http://www.fsid.org.uk
Information on research presently funded and previous funded work summaries.
Information available, support/in memory page, education/risk cot death, advert for project grants and research fellowships.

Enquiries:
Enquiries to: Communications Officer

Founded:
1971

Organisation type and purpose:
Voluntary organisation, registered charity (charity number 262191), research organisation.
Library holding SIDS articles and related topics.
To raise funds for research, to support families whose baby has died suddenly and unexpectedly, to disseminate information about cot death and infant health to health professionals and the general public.

Subject coverage:
Research into cot death and sudden infant death, information for bereaved families and for professionals who may have to deal with this, general information on infant health and care. The scope of FSID is all infant deaths, not just cot death.

Information services:
Helpline, tel 020 7233 2090, e-mail helpline@fsid.org.uk.

Printed publications:
List of leaflets, booklets and books
Newsletter (twice a year)
BabyZone (free)
TravelZone (free)
Reduce the Risk of Cot Death (free)
Selected reference list of articles relevant to health education and welfare
Selected reference list of published articles on research into causes and prevention of cot deaths, management of unexpected infant death, and counselling of bereaved parents

Electronic and video publications:
Video films:
Sudden Infant Deaths: Words Can't Describe How You Feel (£20, or £30 with workbook)

Publications list:
Available in print

Access to staff:
Contact by letter, by telephone, by fax, by e-mail and via website. Appointment necessary.
Hours: Mon to Fri, 0900 to 1700

FOUNDATION FOR WOMEN'S HEALTH RESEARCH AND DEVELOPMENT

Acronym or abbreviation: FORWARD

Suite 2.1, Chandelier Building, 2nd Floor, 8 Scrubs Lane, London, NW10 6RB

Tel: 020 8960 4000
Fax: 020 8960 4014
E-mail: forward@forwarduk.org.uk

Website:
http://www.forwarduk.org.uk

Enquiries:
Enquiries to: Administrator

Founded:
1985

Organisation type and purpose:
International organisation, voluntary organisation, registered charity (charity number 292403), suitable for ages: all, consultancy, research organisation.
Leading voluntary organisation in the UK campaigning against FGM. Provision of training and education to women affected by FGM, and for health, social work, education and child protection professionals.

Subject coverage:
Minority health issues with focus on African women and children's reproductive and sexual health. Female genital mutilation (FGM) in the UK and Africa.

Printed publications:
Information pack (free on request with sae)

Islamic Ruling on Male and Female Circumcision (World Health Organisation, 1996, £3 plus p&p)
Child Protection and Female Genital Mutilation (Hedley R and Darkenoo E, £4.50 plus p&p)
A Report of the Conference on FGM – Moving Forward (£4 plus p&p)
Possessing the Secret of Joy (Walker A, £5 plus p&p)

Publications list:
Available in print

Access to staff:
Contact by letter, by telephone, by fax and by e-mail
Hours: Mon to Fri, 0900 to 1700

FOUNDRY EQUIPMENT AND SUPPLIERS ASSOCIATION

Acronym or abbreviation: FESA

Queensway House, 2 Queensway, Redhill, Surrey, RH1 1QS

Tel: 01737 768611
Fax: 01737 855469

Website:
http://www.fesa.org.uk

Enquiries:
Enquiries to: Secretary
Direct tel: 01737 855280
Direct e-mail: marywhite@uk.dmgworldmedia.com

Founded:
1925

Organisation type and purpose:
Trade association (membership is by subscription), present number of members: 34.

Access to staff:
Contact by letter
Hours: Mon to Fri, 0800 to 1300

Access to building, collection or gallery:
No access other than to staff

FOUNTAIN SOCIETY, THE

26 Binney Street, London, W1K 5BL

Tel: 020 7355 2002 ansaphone
Fax: 020 7355 2002

Website:
http://www.fountainsoc.org.uk

Enquiries:
Enquiries to: Chairman
Direct tel: 01306 883874
Direct fax: 01306 883874
Direct e-mail: knowlsonpm@cix.co.uk
Other contacts: Projects Officer

Founded:
1986

Organisation type and purpose:
International organisation, membership association (membership is by subscription), present number of members: 320, voluntary organisation, registered charity (charity number 292778).

Subject coverage:
Conservation and restoration of fountains of aesthetic merit for public enjoyment, promotion of the provision of fountains in new developments and the restoration of cascades and waterfalls.

Museum or gallery collection, archive, or library special collection:
Bibliography available to members

Printed publications:
Creating a Fountain?

Access to staff:
Contact by letter, by telephone, by fax, by e-mail and via website
Hours: Mon to Fri, 0900 to 1700

FPA

Formal name: Family Planning Association

50 Featherstone Street, London, EC1Y 8QU

Tel: 020 7608 5240
Fax: 0845 123 2349
E-mail: library.information@fpa.org.uk

Website:
http://www.fpa.org.uk
fpa services, projects and publications. Also information on methods of contraception, STIs, family planning and GYN Clinics.

Enquiries:
Direct tel: 020 7923 5228

Founded:
1930

Organisation type and purpose:
Membership association (membership is by subscription), voluntary organisation, registered charity (charity number 250187).
To advance the sexual health and reproductive rights and choices of all people throughout the United Kingdom.

Subject coverage:
Family planning, contraception, sexual health, fertility control, unplanned pregnancy, sexually transmitted infections, sex education.

Museum or gallery collection, archive, or library special collection:
Archives of the Family Planning Association, 1920–1977 (held at the Wellcome Institute for the History of Medicine, Contemporary Medical Archives Centre, London)

Library catalogue:
All or part available in-house

Printed publications:
Books for professionals, leaflets for consumers on contraception and sexually transmitted infections, booklets for young people on periods, puberty, growing up, pregnancy and abortion
Factsheets available singly
Order printed publications from: fpa Direct
50 Featherstone Street, London, EC1Y 8QU

Electronic and video publications:
Talking to Your Kids About Sex (video)
Sex, Storks and Gooseberry Bushes: Talking to Children about Sex (video)
How Much How Soon – teaching sex in primary schools (video)
The Fairy Godfather (video)
Challenging Homophobia (video)

Publications list:
Available in print

Access to staff:
Contact by letter, by telephone, by fax and by e-mail. Appointment necessary.
Hours: Mon to Fri, 0900 to 1700

Access to building, collection or gallery:
Prior appointment required

Access for disabled people:
Level entry, toilet facilities

Other offices:
fpa Cymru
Greenhouse, Trevelyan Terrace, Bangor, Gwynedd, LL57 1AX; tel: 01248 353534; fax: 01248 371138
fpa Cymru
Suite D1, Canton House, 435–451 Cowbridge Road East, Cardiff, CF5 1JH; tel: 029 2064 4034; fax: 029 2064 4306
fpa Northern Ireland
2nd Floor, Northern Counties Building, Custom House Street, Derry, BT48 6AE; tel: 028 7126 0016; fax: 028 7136 1254
fpa Northern Ireland
113 University Street, Belfast, BT7 1HP; tel: 028 9032 5488; fax: 028 9031 2212
fpa Scotland
Unit 10, Firhill Business Centre, 76 Firhill Road, Glasgow, G20 7BA; tel: 0141 576 5088; fax: 0141 576 5006

FRAGILE X SOCIETY

Rood End House, 6 Stortford Road, Great
Dunmow, Essex, CM6 1DA

Tel: 01371 875100
E-mail: info@fragilex.org.uk

Website:
http://www.fragilex.org.uk

Enquiries:
Enquiries to: National Contact
Direct tel: 01371 875100
Direct fax: 01371 859915

Founded:
1990

Organisation type and purpose:
Registered charity (charity number 1003981).
To provide support, information and advice to
families whose children and adult relatives have
fragile X syndrome; offers national support and
information, telephone helplines on education
statementing, benefits and epilepsy, family-link
members, family conferences and reports, access to
latest research, free UK family membership of the
society, free attendance at society conferences.
Fragile X shows itself in a wide range of difficulties
with learning and development delay, as well as
social, language, attentional, emotional and
behavioural problems.

Subject coverage:
Fragile X is the second most common cause of
inherited learning disabilities.

Printed publications:
What is Fragile X?
Fragile X Syndrome: An Introduction
Fragile X Syndrome: An Introduction to
    Educational Needs
Issues of Diagnosis and Treatment
Titles relating to genetics, carriers and siblings
Titles relating to behavioural and cognitive
    functioning, education, adolescence and
    adulthood
Titles relating to treatment, health and family
    experiences
Newsletter

Electronic and video publications:
DVD and video

Publications list:
Available online and in print

Access to staff:
Contact by letter, by telephone, by e-mail and via
website
Hours: Mon to Fri, 0900 to 1700

FRAME

Formal name: Fund for the Replacement of Animals
in Medical Experiments

Russell & Burch House

Tel: 0115 958 4740
Fax: 0115 950 3570
E-mail: frame@frame.org.uk

Website:
http://www.frame.org.uk
The charity's aims and work, the Three Rs
approach to the problem, information resources.

Enquiries:
Enquiries to: Communications Officer
Direct e-mail: info@frame.org.uk; science@frame.org
.uk

Founded:
1969

Organisation type and purpose:
Registered as a national charity (charity number
259464).
FRAME believes that the current scale of animal
experimentation is unacceptable, but recognises
that the immediate abolition of all laboratory
animal use is not possible. Its long-term goal is the
total elimination of the need for any laboratory
animal procedures, through the development,

validation and acceptance of replacement
alternative methods. Until this goal is reached,
FRAME supports efforts to reduce the numbers of
animals used, through better experimental design
and data analysis, and to refine procedures, so that
the suffering of any animals necessarily used is
minimised. Supports research at the University of
Nottingham, primarily within the FRAME
Alternatives Laboratory and the Molecular
Toxicology Group.

Subject coverage:
The Three Rs approach to this problem:
Replacement, Reduction and Refinement.

Information services:
Online information of relevance to laboratory
technicians, statisticians and scientists who are
actively engaged in animal experimentation or
developing alternatives to using animals in
medical experiments.

Education services:
FRAME scientists give talks to school students or
to other groups interested in the use of animals in
science (limited to the Nottinghamshire area).

Electronic and video publications:
A series of leaflets on various topics concerned
    with animal experimentation and how it can be
    Replaced, Reduced or Refined. The leaflets are
    aimed at A level and first year undergraduate
    students and aim to offer a simple, but scientific,
    introduction to the topics.
Order electronic and video publications from:
Download from website

Publications list:
Available online

Access to staff:
Contact by letter, by telephone, by fax and by e-
mail

FRANCIS BACON RESEARCH TRUST

Acronym or abbreviation: FBRT

Old Rick Barn, Mill Lane, Shenington, Oxfordshire,
OX15 6NB

Tel: 01295 678623
E-mail: secretary@fbrt.org.uk

Website:
http://www.fbrt.org.uk

Enquiries:
Enquiries to: Secretary
Direct e-mail: sarah@fbrt.org.uk

Founded:
1980

Organisation type and purpose:
International organisation, membership
association (membership is by subscription),
training organisation, consultancy, research
organisation.
Educational charity.

Subject coverage:
Study of the life and works of Sir Francis Bacon
and of all those associated with him, and to make
known and further the Great Instauration... a
worldwide scheme intended to create
understanding between peoples in which
illumined peace be acquired; ancient wisdom and
traditions, the wisdom of Shakespeare.

Printed publications:
Programme of Events (annually)
Publication Brochure (annually)
A range of books (prices vary), including:
Shakespeare Enigma
Building Paradise
Francis Bacon: Herald of New Age

Publications list:
Available in print

Access to staff:
Contact by letter, by telephone, by e-mail and via
website. Appointment necessary. Non-members
charged.
Hours: Mon to Fri, 1000 to 1700

FRANCIS BRETT YOUNG SOCIETY

Acronym or abbreviation: FBY Society

92 Gower Road, Halesowen, West Midlands, B62
9BT

Tel: 0121 422 8969

Website:
http://www.fbysociety.co.uk
Information on Society's activities.

Enquiries:
Enquiries to: Chairman
Direct e-mail: michael.hall10@gmail.com

Founded:
1978

Organisation type and purpose:
Learned society (membership is by subscription),
present number of members: 210, registered
charity (charity number 1075904).
Literary society.
To provide opportunities for members to meet,
correspond, and to share the enjoyment of the
author's works.

Subject coverage:
Life and literary works of Francis Brett Young.

Printed publications:
Journal (2 times a year, for members)

FRANCIS-BARNETT OWNERS CLUB

Acronym or abbreviation: FBOC

307 Lower Hillmorton Road, Rugby, Warwickshire,
CV21 4AD

Tel: 01788 544909
E-mail: mrs.eileen.lloyd@virgin.net

Website:
http://www.francis-barnett.freeserve.co.uk

Enquiries:
Enquiries to: Secretary

Founded:
1986

Organisation type and purpose:
Company limited by guarantee, registered in
England and Wales, no. 4750767 (membership is
by subscription), present number of members: 550.
To encourage ownership, use and preservation of
Francis-Barnett motorcycles.

Subject coverage:
All models of Francis Barnett motor cycles
produced by that company in Coventry from 1919
until the demise of AMC (AJS, Matchless, Norton)
in the late 1960s.

**Museum or gallery collection, archive, or library
special collection:**
A library of model information manuals and
    spares lists for most models

Non-library collection catalogue:
All or part available in print

Library catalogue:
All or part available in print

Printed publications:
The Directory (magazine, quarterly, members only)

Access to staff:
Contact by letter
Hours: Mon to Fri, 0900 to 1700
Special comments: There are no full-time staff.

Registered office:
at the same address

FRANCO-BRITISH COUNCIL

16–18 Strutton Ground, London, SW1P 2HP

Tel: 020 7976 8380
Fax: 020 7976 8181
E-mail: fbc@cix.co.uk

Website:
http://www.francobritishcouncil.org.uk

Enquiries:
Enquiries to: Secretary General

Founded:
1972

Organisation type and purpose:
International organisation, membership
association (membership is by election or
invitation), registered charity.
Promoting Franco-British relations.

Printed publications:
Meeting Reports from 1992–2001, in English (£5
each) recent titles:
Transatlantic Relations (1999)
Transport Policy (1999)
Social Exclusion: Jobs for Young (2000)
Film industry: A Day in June (2000); Arts Funding
(2000)
Policing (2000)
Truancy and Exclusion from School (2001)
Peacekeeping and International Crisis
Management (2001)
Report: Crossing the Channel (2001)
What do we Want from Europe? (2001)
Commonwealth and Francophonie (2002)
Food and Bio-engineering (2002)

Publications list:
Available online and in print

Access to staff:
Contact by letter, by telephone, by fax and by e-
mail
Hours: Tue to Thu, 0930 to 1730

FREE CHURCHES' GROUP

Acronym or abbreviation: FCG

Churches Together in England, 27 Tavistock
Square, London, WC1H 9HH

Tel: 020 7539 8131
Fax: 020 7529 8134
E-mail: freechurch@cte.org.uk

Website:
http://www.cte.org.uk

Enquiries:
Enquiries to: Secretary
Direct tel: 020 7387 8413
Other contacts: Health Care Chaplaincy

Founded:
1940

Organisation type and purpose:
Voluntary organisation.
Representative body for Free Church opinion.

Subject coverage:
Free Church tradition and opinion, Free Church
and ecumenical relations.

Access to staff:
Contact by letter, by telephone, by fax and by e-
mail. Appointment necessary.
Hours: Mon to Fri, 0900 to 1700

Access to building, collection or gallery:
No access other than to staff

Also at:
Free Church Education Unit
27 Tavistock Square, London WC1H 9HH; tel:
020 7529 8131; fax: 020 7529 8134; e-mail: sarah
.lane@cte.org.uk

Members:
Afro Westindian United Council of Churches
(AWUCOC)
tel: 020 8888 9427; fax: 020 8888 2877

Baptist Union of Great Britain (BUGB)
tel: 01235 517700; fax: 01235 517715; e-mail:
baptistuniongb@baptist.org.uk
Baptist Union of Wales
tel: 01792 655468; fax: 01792 469489
Congregational Federation
tel: 0115 911 1460; fax: 0115 911 1462; e-mail:
michael.heaney@congregational.org.uk
Council of African and Afro-Caribbean Churches
(UK) (CAAC-UK)
tel: 020 7582 4209, Work: 020 7620 4444
Countess of Huntingdon's Connexion
tel: 0118 933 2569; e-mail: brianbrendabaldwin@
talk21.com
Fellowship of Churches of Christ
tel: 0121 373 7942; fax: 0121 373 7942; e-mail:
hazelwilson@bigfoot.com
Free Church of England
tel: 01273 845092; fax: 01273 845092; e-mail:
rtal799@aol.com
Independent Methodist Churches
tel: 01942 223526; fax: 01942 227768; e-mail:
resourcecentre@imcgb.org.uk
Methodist Church
tel: 020 7486 5502; fax: 020 7467 5226; e-mail:
conferenceoffice@methodistchurch.org.uk
Moravian Church
tel: 020 8883 3409/1912; fax: 020 8365 3371
New Testament Church of God
tel: 01604 643311/645944; fax: 01604 790254
Old Baptist Union
tel: 01625 422404; fax: 01625 422404
Presbyterian Church of Wales
tel: 029 2049 4913; fax: 029 2046 4293
Salvation Army
tel: 020 7367 4614; fax: 020 7367 4718; e-mail:
webmajor@salvationarmy.org.uk
Undeb yr Annibynwyr Cymraeg (Union of Welsh
Independents)
tel: 01792 652542/467040; fax: 01792 650647; e-
mail: tyjp@tyjp.co.uk
United Reformed Church in the United Kingdom
tel: 020 7916 2020; fax: 020 7916 2021; e-mail:
david.cornick@urc.org.uk
Wesleyan Reform Union
tel: 0114 272 1938; fax: 0114 272 1965; e-mail:
john@wesleyan-reform.freeserve.co.uk

FREIGHT TRANSPORT ASSOCIATION LIMITED

Acronym or abbreviation: FTA

Hermes House, 157 St John's Road, Tunbridge
Wells, Kent, TN4 9UZ

Tel: 01892 526171
Fax: 01892 534989
E-mail: enquiries@fta.co.uk

Website:
http://www.fta.co.uk/
General FTA information.
http://supplychain.fta.co.uk/
Series of communication platforms on logistics
issues.

Enquiries:
Enquiries to: Director of Communications
Direct tel: 01892 552255
Direct fax: 01892 552323
Direct e-mail: jtanner@fta.co.uk
Other contacts: Media Relations Manager

Founded:
1889

Formerly called:
Traders Road Transport Association (year of
change 1969)

Organisation type and purpose:
Trade association.

Subject coverage:
Freight transport, including transport law, costs
and rates, statistics, education and training, vehicle
maintenance, international transport, shipping,
hazardous cargoes.

Printed publications:
Freight (magazine, monthly)

FTA Yearbook of Road Transport Law
Miscellaneous Reports

Access to staff:
Contact by letter, by telephone, by fax, by e-mail
and via website
Hours: Mon to Fri, 0900 to 1700

Includes the:
British Shippers Council

FRENCH CHAMBER OF COMMERCE IN GREAT BRITAIN

Acronym or abbreviation: FCCGB

21 Dartmouth Street, Westminster, London, SW1H
0BP

Tel: 020 7304 4040
Fax: 020 7304 7034
E-mail: jpintore@ccfgb.co.uk

Website:
http://www.ccfgb.co.uk

Enquiries:
Enquiries to: Public Relations Manager
Direct tel: 020 7304 7017
Direct e-mail: atassi@ccfgb.co.uk

Founded:
1883

Organisation type and purpose:
Membership association (membership is by
subscription), present number of members: c. 550,
consultancy.
Chamber of Commerce.
Increase Franco-British trade.

Subject coverage:
Publications for settling in France or Great Britain
as an individual or a professional.

**Museum or gallery collection, archive, or library
special collection:**
Databases of French companies in the UK and
British companies in France, exporters/importers
in the UK and France
Directories of members of the French Chamber

Printed publications:
Info (magazine)
chamber@work (newsletter)
Cross the Channel – Control your Tax
Cross Channel Transport Directory
Doing Business with France
Guide des affaires en GB
Guide pratique des Français en GB
Le registre des investissements français au
Royaume-Uni
Make yourself at Home in France
Setting up a small business in France
The Franco-British Trade Directory 2001–2002
(annually)

Electronic and video publications:
List of French investments in the UK (disk, paper,
labels, database)
List of members (CD-ROM, labels, book)

Publications list:
Available online and in print

Access to staff:
Contact by letter and by e-mail. Appointment
necessary.
Hours: Mon to Fri, 0900 to 1700

Access to building, collection or gallery:
Prior appointment required

Access for disabled people:
Level entry

FRENCH EMBASSY – CULTURAL DEPARTMENT

23 Cromwell Road, London, SW7 2EL

Tel: 020 7073 1300
Fax: 020 7073 1320
E-mail: cultural@ambafrance.org.uk

continued overleaf

Website:
http://www.institut_francais.org.uk/lb_about.htm

Enquiries:
Enquiries to: Cultural Counsellor

Organisation type and purpose:
Diplomatic mission.

Subject coverage:
Education in France; studies in France; teaching in France; sport exchanges; theatre; cinema; literature and publishing; music; dance; concerts and recitals; art exhibitions in France and Great Britain.

Library catalogue:
All or part available online

Printed publications:
Le Français en tête (poster)
Institut français (programme)

Electronic and video publications:
French video clips

Access to staff:
Contact by letter, by fax and by e-mail
Hours: Mon to Fri, 0900 to 1700

Other addresses:
Institut Français
17 Queensberry Place, London, SW7 2DT; tel: 020 7073 1350; fax: 020 7073 1355; e-mail: box .office@ambafrance.org.uk

FRENCH EMBASSY – SCIENCE AND TECHNOLOGY DEPARTMENT

6 Cromwell Place, London, SW7 2JN

Tel: 020 7073 1380
Fax: 020 7073 1390
E-mail: info@ambascience.co.uk

Website:
http://www.ambascience.co.uk
Online information.

Enquiries:
Enquiries to: Information Officer
Other contacts: Counsellor for Science and Technology

Organisation type and purpose:
National government body.
Embassy.

Subject coverage:
French and English research in: humanities and social sciences, chemical sciences, life sciences, sciences of the universe, physical sciences and mathematics, engineering sciences, information sciences and technology, medicine – health.

Non-library collection catalogue:
All or part available in-house

Library catalogue:
All or part available in-house

Printed publications:
A monthly review of the Press (free)
Vade-mecum of Research Funding (free)
Publications making analysis and taking stock of situations (free)

Electronic and video publications:
A monthly review of the Press (online)
Vade mecum of Research Funding (online)
Publications making analysis and taking stock of situations (online)

Publications list:
Available online and in print

Access to staff:
Contact by letter, by telephone, by fax and by e-mail
Hours: Mon to Fri, 0900 to 1730

Parent body:
Ministère des affaires étrangères et européennes (French Ministry for Foreign and European Affairs)
Paris, France

FRENCH INSTITUTE

Acronym or abbreviation: IFE

13 Randolph Crescent, Edinburgh, EH3 7TT

Tel: 0131 225 5366
Fax: 0131 220 0648
E-mail: library@ifecosse.org.uk

Website:
http://www.ifecosse.org.uk
Catalogue online.

Enquiries:
Enquiries to: Librarian

Founded:
1946

Organisation type and purpose:
International organisation, membership association (membership is by subscription).
To promote French language and culture.

Subject coverage:
French language and culture, for adults and children, contemporary France, French cinema, documentary exhibitions.

Museum or gallery collection, archive, or library special collection:
Books: 20,000 volumes, mostly in French, relating to various aspects of French life and culture
Videos and DVDs: 1,100 films and documentary films with or without subtitles; 962 films of French cinema from classics to recent productions; 747 documentary films on a diversity of topics related to contemporary France
CDs: talking books, classical, contemporary, popular music and jazz; 1,000 CDs of popular music from traditional chanson to current trends
CD-ROMs: 200 CD-ROMs for adults and children including many games
Newspapers and magazines: 50 titles on a wide range of topics to suit everyone including daily papers
Reference: many dictionaries and encyclopaedic books.

Non-library collection catalogue:
All or part available online and in-house

Library catalogue:
All or part available in-house

Access to staff:
Contact by letter, by telephone, by fax, by e-mail, in person and via website. Appointment necessary.
Hours: Mon, 1400 to 1830; Tue to Fri, 0930 to 1830; Sat, 0930 to 1300

Access to building, collection or gallery:
No access other than to staff
Hours: Mon to Fri, 0930 to 1830; Sat, 0930 to 1300

FRESHWATER BIOLOGICAL ASSOCIATION

Acronym or abbreviation: FBA

The Ferry House, Far Sawrey, Ambleside, Cumbria, LA22 0LP

Tel: 015394 42468
Fax: 015394 46914
E-mail: info@fba.org.uk

Website:
http://www.fba.org.uk

Enquiries:
Enquiries to: Librarian
Direct e-mail: library@fba.org.uk

Founded:
1929

Organisation type and purpose:
International organisation, learned society (membership is by subscription), registered charity (charity number 214440), research organisation.
The Freshwater Biological Association is an independent body that conducts research into all aspects of freshwater science, usually by awarding grants and studentships.

Subject coverage:
Limnology, freshwater biology (hydrobiology), freshwater algae, microbiology, fish, invertebrates, physics and chemistry of lakes and rivers.

Museum or gallery collection, archive, or library special collection:
Fritsch Collection of illustrations of the freshwater algae

Non-library collection catalogue:
All or part available online, in-house and in print

Library catalogue:
All or part available online, in-house and in print

Printed publications:
Annual Report
Freshwater Forum
Keys for the Identification of Freshwater Organisms
Scientific and occasional publications (A5 booklets)
Special publications
Blue-Green Algae (colour poster, 12 photos plus notes, £2 plus p&p)

Microform publications:
Order microform publications from: Fritsch Collection

Electronic and video publications:
Order electronic and video publications from: see website: http://www.freshwaterlife.org

Publications list:
Available online and in print

Access to staff:
Contact by letter, by telephone, by fax, by e-mail and via website. Appointment necessary. Non-members charged.
Hours: Mon to Fri, 0900 to 1700

FRIENDS OF ANIMALS LEAGUE

Acronym or abbreviation: Foal Farm

Foal Farm, Jail Lane, Biggin Hill, Kent, TN16 3AX

Tel: 01959 572386
Fax: 01959 572386
E-mail: info@foalfarm.org.uk

Website:
http://www.foalfarm.org.uk

Enquiries:
Enquiries to: Customer Services Manager
Direct tel: 01959 572386

Founded:
1960

Organisation type and purpose:
Voluntary organisation, registered charity (charity number 201654).
Animal rescue and re-homing centre.

Subject coverage:
Care of sick, distressed or unwanted animals; restoring them to health; organisation and functioning of an animal sanctuary.

Printed publications:
Foal Farm News (3 times a year, posted to members, available at the centre to visitors)

Access to staff:
Contact by letter
Hours: Mon, Wed, Thu, Fri, Sat, Sun, 1400 to 1700

Access for disabled people:
Toilet facilities

Member organisation of:
The Association of British Dogs' and Cats' Homes

FRIENDS OF BIRZEIT UNIVERSITY

Acronym or abbreviation: FoBZU

1 Gough Square, London, EC4A 3DE

Tel: 020 7832 1340
Fax: 020 7832 1349
E-mail: director@fobzu.org

Website:
http://www.fobzu.org

Information regarding relevant subjects mentioned.

Enquiries:
Enquiries to: Development Director

Founded:
1978

Organisation type and purpose:
Registered charity (charity number 1114343).
To support education at Birzeit University and its right to academic freedom. Birzeit University is the leading Palestinian University on the West Bank.

Subject coverage:
Palestinian higher education; human rights violations affecting university community; projects (development/education); workcamps; Arabic and Social Science courses for internationals at Birzeit University.

Printed publications:
Occasional e-mail reports on Palestinian higher education

Access to staff:
Contact by letter, by telephone, by fax and by e-mail. Appointment necessary.
Hours: Mon to Thurs, 0930 to 1730

FRIENDS OF CATHEDRAL MUSIC

Acronym or abbreviation: FCM

27 Old Gloucester Street, London, WC1N 3XX

Tel: 0845 644 3721
E-mail: info@fcm.com.uk

Website:
http://www.fcm.org.uk
Details about the Association and its activities and publications.

Enquiries:
Enquiries to: General Secretary

Founded:
1956

Organisation type and purpose:
Membership association (membership is by subscription), present number of members: 2500, voluntary organisation, registered charity (charity number 285121).

Subject coverage:
Details and times of choral services at cathedrals and collegiate establishments in the UK.

Printed publications:
Cathedral Music (annually, free to members)
Singing in Cathedrals (published in association with the British Tourist Authority)

Access to staff:
Contact by letter and by e-mail
Hours: Mon to Fri, 0900 to 1700

FRIENDS OF CONSERVATION

Acronym or abbreviation: FOC

Southcombe Business Centre, 11–12 Southcombe Street, London, W14 0RA

Tel: 020 7348 3408
E-mail: focinfo@aol.com

Website:
http://www.foc-uk.com

Enquiries:
Enquiries to: Director

Founded:
1989

Organisation type and purpose:
Registered charity (charity number 328176).
The FOC is a registered charity, with offices in the UK, USA and Kenya, that aims to protect endangered species and habitats.

Subject coverage:
Conservation education, habitat conservation, wildlife monitoring, forestry projects, community projects for local people and tourist education world-wide.

Printed publications:
Various brochures and newsletters

Access to staff:
Contact by letter and by e-mail
Hours: Mon to Fri, 0900 to 1700

FRIENDS OF ENGLISH NATIONAL OPERA

London Coliseum, St Martin's Lane, London, WC2N 4ES

Tel: 020 7845 9420
Fax: 020 7845 9272
E-mail: friends@eno.org

Enquiries:
Enquiries to: Membership Administrator
Direct tel: 020 7845 9441
Direct e-mail: rreiss@eno.org

Organisation type and purpose:
Membership association, registered charity (charity number 257210).
Supporting English National Opera.

Subject coverage:
Current activities of English National Opera.

Access to staff:
Contact by letter, by telephone, by fax and by e-mail
Hours: Mon to Fri, 1000 to 1800

FRIENDS OF REAL LANCASHIRE

1 Belvidere Park, Great Crosby, Lancashire, L23 0SP

Tel: 0151 928 2770
E-mail: csd@forl.co.uk

Website:
http://www.forl.co.uk
Information about the campaign, and information about the true identity of Lancashire.

Enquiries:
Enquiries to: Chairman
Direct tel: 01539 535507 (membership)
Direct e-mail: janet.m.ainsworth@btinternet.com (membership)
Other contacts: Membership Secretary

Founded:
1992

Organisation type and purpose:
Membership association (membership is by subscription), voluntary organisation.
To promote the true identity of the traditional county of Lancashire.

Subject coverage:
The true identity of the traditional county of Lancashire.

Printed publications:
Newsletters (3 times a year, sent to members)
The Lancastrian (magazine, annually, sent to members)
OS Map of Lancashire – County Palatine of Lancaster

Access to staff:
Contact by letter, by telephone and by e-mail
Hours: Sun to Sat, 0900 to 1700, and evenings

Member organisation of:
Association of British Counties

FRIENDS OF THE EARTH

26–28 Underwood Street, London, N1 7JQ

Tel: 020 7490 1555
Fax: 020 7490 0881
E-mail: info@foe.co.uk

Website:
http://www.foe.co.uk
Information about Friends of the Earth, campaign updates, nearest local group, international news.

Enquiries:
Enquiries to: Supporter Information Team

Founded:
1971

Organisation type and purpose:
Membership association (membership is by subscription), voluntary organisation, registered charity (charity number 281681), research organisation.
Environmental group, largely funded by subscriptions, donations and grants.

Subject coverage:
Environmental issues in general, climate change, natural resources, environmental justice and green economics.

Printed publications:
Earthmatters (magazine, three issues a year, members)
A large selection of publications on the following topics: climate change, pollution, transport, corporate accountability, biodiversity and habitats, energy, renewables, waste, recycling and packaging, resource use, sustainable development, international policy, trade, environmental justice.
Order printed publications from: Information Service, Friends of the Earth, 26–28 Underwood St, London, N1 7JQ

Publications list:
Available online and in print

Access to staff:
Contact by letter, by telephone, by fax, by e-mail and via website
Hours: Mon to Fri, 0900 to 1700

Also at:
Friends of the Earth Membership Services
56–58 Alma Street, Luton, Bedfordshire, LU1 2PH; tel: 020 7490 1555; e-mail: info@foe.co.uk; website: http://www.foe.co.uk

FRIENDS OF THE ELDERLY

Friends of the Elderly, 40–42 Ebury Street, London, SW1W 0LZ

Tel: 020 7730 8263
Fax: 020 7259 0154
E-mail: enquiries@fote.org.uk

Website:
http://www.fote.org.uk
Mission and services.

Founded:
1905

Organisation type and purpose:
Registered charity (number 226064).
Supports older people, particularly those in need due to frailty, isolation or lack of adequate resources, by providing high quality caring services, personalised to the needs of the individual, integrated with local communities and dedicated to promoting the independence, well-being, dignity and peace of mind of each person with whom it works.

Subject coverage:
Provides direct services including residential care homes, nursing homes and dementia care homes. Its day clubs, home support, home visiting, telephone befriending and grant-giving services help older people live independently at home.

Access to staff:
Contact by letter, by telephone, by fax and by e-mail

FRIENDS OF THE LAKE DISTRICT

Acronym or abbreviation: FLD

continued overleaf

Murley Moss, Oxenholme Road, Kendal, Cumbria,
LA9 7SS

Tel: 01539 720788
Fax: 01539 730355
E-mail: info@fld.org.uk

Website:
http://www.fld.org.uk
Information on the organisation.

Enquiries:
Enquiries to: Executive Director
Direct e-mail: andrew-forsyth@fld.org.uk
Other contacts: Communications officer

Founded:
1934

Organisation type and purpose:
Membership association, present number of
members: 7,100, voluntary organisation, registered
charity (charity number 11000759), conservation
and landscape society.
To promote and organise concerted action for the
protection and conservation of the landscape and
natural beauty of the Lake District and the County
of Cumbria.

Subject coverage:
Subjects relating to conservation and protection of
landscape and natural beauty in the Lake District
National Park and Cumbria, representations to
planning authorities, and policies on access,
tourism, development pressures, roads, transport,
agriculture, forestry.

**Museum or gallery collection, archive, or library
special collection:**
Library of books, documents and photographs
(including slides)

Printed publications:
Conserving Lakeland (magazine, Summer and
Winter)
Annual Report

Access to staff:
Appointment necessary.
Hours: Mon to Fri, 0900 to 1700

Affiliated to:
CPRE
128 Southwark Street, London, SE1 0SW; tel: 020
7981 2800; fax: 020 7981 2899; e-mail: info@cpre
.org.uk; website: www.cpre.org.uk

Represents:
Council for the Protection of Rural England
(CPRE) in Cumbria

FRIENDS OF THE NATIONAL
LIBRARIES

Acronym or abbreviation: FNL

c/o Department of MSS, British Library, 96 Euston
Road, London, NW1 2DB

Tel: 0207 412 7559
E-mail: secretary@fnlmail.org.uk

Website:
http://www.friendsofnationallibraries.org.uk

Enquiries:
Enquiries to: Honorary Secretary

Founded:
1931

Organisation type and purpose:
Membership association (membership is by
subscription), present number of members: 723,
registered charity (charity number 313020).
To give grants for the purchase of printed books,
manuscripts and archives by libraries and other
institutions that provide public access within the
United Kingdom.

Subject coverage:
Raising of funds to save rare books and
manuscripts for national and local institutions.

Printed publications:
Annual Report (members)

Access to staff:
Contact by letter, by telephone and via website
Hours: 24-hour answerphone
Special comments: Voicemail only.

FRIENDS OF THE PEAK DISTRICT

The Stables, 22A Endcliffe Crescent, Sheffield,
South Yorkshire, S10 3EF

Tel: 0114 2665822
Fax: 0114 2685514
E-mail: mail@friendsofthepeak.org.uk

Website:
http://www.friendsofthepeak.org.uk
Latest news about campaigning work to safeguard
Peak District landscapes.

Enquiries:
Enquiries to: Communications Officer
Direct e-mail: liz@friendsofthepeak.org.uk
Other contacts: Office Manager

Founded:
1924

Organisation type and purpose:
Local charity.
Campaigning work to safeguard Peak District
landscapes.

Subject coverage:
Peak District.

Printed publications:
Peak Power – report on micro hydro in the Peak
District
Peakland Guardian magazine (published twice a
year)
Annual review
Order printed publications from: Downloadable at:
http://www.friendsofthepeak.org.uk

Access to staff:
Contact by letter, by telephone, by fax, by e-mail
and via website. Appointment necessary.
Hours: Mon to Fri, 1000 to 1600

Access to building, collection or gallery:
Please make appointment

Access for disabled people:
Ramped entry

Links with:
Campaign to Protect Rural England (CPRE)
128 Southwark Street London SE1 0SW; tel: 020
7981 2800

Member organisation of:
Campaign for National Parks
6–7 Barnard Mews, London, SW11 1QU; tel: 020
7924 4077; website: http://www.cnp.org.uk

FRIENDS OF UCLH

Ground floor, University College London Hospital,
250 Euston Road, London, NW1 2PG

Tel: 0845 155 5000 extn 73038
E-mail: friendsuclh@uclh.nhs.uk

Website:
http://www.uclh.nhs.uk/Charities+at+UCLH/
Friends+at+UCLH
Aims, news, recent projects.

Founded:
2005

Created by the merger of:
Leagues of Friends of four major London hospitals

Organisation type and purpose:
A Registered Charity (No 266669).
To help the hospital, its patients and staff by
providing facilities and amenities which are not
available from the National Health Service. This
covers many items which cannot otherwise be
afforded.

Subject coverage:
Grant requests from various wards and
departments in the hospital.

Access to staff:
Contact by letter, by telephone and by e-mail

Links with:
University College London Hospitals NHS
Foundation Trust (UCLH)
250 Euston Road, London, NW1 2PG; tel: 0845
1555 000

FRISKY REGISTER

Graces Cottage, Tregagle, Monmouth, Gwent,
NP25 4RZ

Tel: 01600 860420
Fax: 01600 860420

Enquiries:
Enquiries to: Registrar

Founded:
1974

Organisation type and purpose:
Membership association.
Car register.

Subject coverage:
The restoration of the Frisky car, engines, body,
chassis, electrics, history, components.

**Museum or gallery collection, archive, or library
special collection:**
Maintenance manuals
Press releases
Technical information, handbooks, engine books,
article reprints

Printed publications:
General Frisky literature

Access to staff:
Contact by letter, by telephone and by fax.
Appointment necessary.
Hours: Mon to Fri, 0900 to 1700

FRONTIER: THE SOCIETY FOR
ENVIRONMENTAL EXPLORATION

Acronym or abbreviation: Frontier

50–52 Rivington Street, London, EC2A 3QP

Tel: 020 7613 2422
Fax: 020 7613 2992
E-mail: info@frontier.ac.uk

Website:
http://www.frontier.ac.uk
Information about Frontier's research overseas,
publications list, gap year and volunteering
opportunities.

Enquiries:
Enquiries to: Marketing Manager
Direct e-mail: marketing@frontier.ac.uk

Founded:
1989

Organisation type and purpose:
International organisation, voluntary organisation,
training organisation, research organisation.
To conduct development projects and conservation
research in Fiji, Nepal, Peru, Tibet, Guatemala,
India, Tanzania, Madagascar, Cambodia and
Nicaragua. To provide opportunities for volunteers
to carry out conservation work and obtain tropical
field experience.

Subject coverage:
Conservation and environmental research,
development of natural resources, volunteer work
abroad, teaching, community development,
language courses.

Printed publications:
Information brochure
Various technical reports

Publications list:
Available online and in print

Access to staff:
Contact by letter, by telephone, by fax, by e-mail
and via website

Hours: Mon to Fri, 0930 to 1730
Special comments: No visits without appointment.

Branches:
Frontier–Cambodia
  PO Box 1275, General Post Office, Phlauv 13,
  Phnom Penh, Cambodia; tel: +855 23 221 163
Frontier–Costa Rica
  c/o Amigos de Osa, Apartido 54, 8203 Puerto
  Jiménez Golfito, Costa Rica; tel: +506 87562183
Frontier–Madagascar
  BP 413, Tulear 1 Zone Portuaire, Madagascar; tel:
  +261 20 94 430 38
Frontier–Tanzania
  PO Box 9473, Dar es Salaam, Tanzania; tel: +255
  22 2780063; fax: +255 22 2780063; e-mail:
  frontier@raha.com

FRS FRESHWATER LABORATORY

Formal name: Fisheries Research Service Freshwater
Laboratory
Acronym or abbreviation: FRS FL

Faskally, Pitlochry, Perthshire, PH16 5LB

Tel: 01224 294408 or 01796 472060
Fax: 01796 473523
E-mail: FL_Library@marlab.ac.uk

Website:
http://www.frs-scotland.gov.uk

Enquiries:
Enquiries to: Librarian

Founded:
1948

Organisation type and purpose:
National government body, research organisation.

Subject coverage:
Salmonid ecology, salmon fisheries, coarse fish,
freshwater biology, fish biology, environmental
chemistry (inorganic), fisheries science,
environmental pollution, fish culture, aquaculture.

**Museum or gallery collection, archive, or library
special collection:**
The Library is the only government research
  library in Great Britain which is devoted to the
  subject of freshwater fisheries

Trade and statistical information:
Statistical Bulletin: Scottish Salmon and Sea Trout
  Catches.

Library catalogue:
All or part available in-house

Printed publications:
Scottish Fisheries information pamphlets
Scottish Fisheries research reports
FRS information leaflets
Scottish Annual Fish Farms Production Survey
Scottish Annual Shellfish Farms Production Survey
Order printed publications from:
ML_Library@marlab.ac.uk

Publications list:
Available online

Access to staff:
Contact by letter, by telephone, by fax, by e-mail
and via website. Appointment necessary.
Hours: Mon to Fri, 0900 to 1700

Access to building, collection or gallery:
Hours: Mon to Fri, 0900 to 1700

Constituent part of:
FRS Marine Laboratory Library
  375 Victoria Road, Aberdeen, AB11 9DB; tel:
  01224 876544; fax: 01224 295309; e-mail:
  ML_Library@marlab.ac.uk; website: www.frs
  -scotland.gov.uk

FULL TIME MOTHERS

PO Box 43690, London, SE22 9WN

Tel: 020 8653 8786
Fax: 020 8761 6574
E-mail: fulltimemothers@hotmail.com

Website:
http://www.fulltimemothers.org

Enquiries:
Enquiries to: Chairman

Founded:
1990

Organisation type and purpose:
Membership association (membership is by
subscription, election or invitation).
To promote understanding of the child's need for a
full-time mother, enhance the status and self
esteem of mothers at home, campaign for changes
in the tax and benefits system and in employment
policies to give women a chance to be full-time
mothers.

Subject coverage:
The voice of the mother at home; information or
quotes on: caring for children; mothers at home;
childcare; tax and benefits relative to the family;
psychology of the child; isolation and self-esteem
of mothers; general motherhood; family-friendly
employment policies.

Printed publications:
Newsletter (quarterly, for members)

Access to staff:
Contact by letter, by telephone and by e-mail
Hours: Mon to Fri, 0900 to 1700

Affiliated to:
Fédération des Femmes au Foyer (FEFAF)

FURNITURE HISTORY SOCIETY

Acronym or abbreviation: FHS

1 Mercedes Cottages, St John's Road, Haywards
Heath, West Sussex, RH16 4EH

Tel: 01444 413845
Fax: 01444 413845
E-mail: furniturehistorysociety@hotmail.com

Website:
http://www.furniturehistorysociety.org
Aims, membership, publications, activities
(lectures, visits, tours).

Enquiries:
Enquiries to: Membership Secretary and
Publications Officer
Direct e-mail: brian.austen@zen.co.uk

Founded:
1966

Organisation type and purpose:
International organisation, learned society
(membership is by subscription), present number
of members: 1,700.
International learned society dedicated to the
study and publication of research on the history of
furniture and furnishings.

Subject coverage:
All aspects of the history of furniture and
furnishings of all periods, especially that of Europe
and North America.

Printed publications:
Furniture History (journal, annually, £18 members,
  £30 non-members)
Newsletter (quarterly, members only)
A Bibliography of the Printed Works of the late
  John Forrest Hayward (£2.50 inc. p&p)
Dictionary of Edinburgh Wrights and Furniture
  Makers 1660–1840 (Bamford F, £20 inc. p&p)
Index to the Dictionary of English Furniture
  Makers 1660–1840 (Evans A, £20 inc. p&p)
Irish Furniture (ed Austen, B, £8.95)
Pictorial Dictionary of Marked London Furniture
  1700–1840 (Gilbert C, £29 members, £45 non-
  members)
The London Furniture Trade 1700–1870 (Kirkham
  P, £20 inc. p&p)
The Life of the Author, Johnson T (Simon, £8.95
  inc. p&p)
Directory of English Furniture Makers (Beard &
  Gilbert, £49 members, £75 non-members)

Makers, Dealers and Collectors Studies in Honour
  of Geoffrey de Bellaigue (£24.95 inc. p&p)
John Stafford of Bath and his 'Interior Decorations'
  (Simon S. Jervis £6.95 inc p&p)
Order printed publications from: Furniture History
Society, via website, post, telephone, fax, or email

Publications list:
Available online and in print

Access to staff:
Contact by letter, by telephone, by fax, by e-mail,
in person and via website. Appointment necessary.
Hours: Telephone calls accepted 0800 to 2200, Sun
to Sat

FUTURES AND OPTIONS ASSOCIATION

Acronym or abbreviation: FOA

2nd Floor, 36–38 Botolph Lane, London, EC3R 8DE

Tel: 020 7929 0081
Fax: 020 7621 0223

Website:
http://www.foa.co.uk
FOA, membership, regulation, operational
services, training, events.

Organisation type and purpose:
The principal European association for the futures
and options industry, representing its interests in
the public and regulatory domain.
Membership includes banks, financial institutions,
brokers, commodity trade houses, energy market
participants, fund managers, exchanges, clearing
houses, systems providers, lawyers, accountants,
consultants.

Subject coverage:
Principally concerned with financial and
commodity exchange-traded derivatives markets,
but also addresses related issues arising in other
markets (e.g. OTC markets) or issues that have a
cross-sectoral impact. In such cases, it liaises, as
appropriate, with other affected trade associations.

Education services:
Provides a variety of training courses to
supplement core activities and provide a
benchmark in industry best practice.

Electronic and video publications:
Press releases
Order electronic and video publications from:
Download from website

Access to staff:
Contact by letter, by telephone, by fax and via
website

Member organisation of:
European Parliamentary Financial Services Forum
(EPFSF)
  Brussels
Industry Advisory Group of the Associate
Parliamentary Group (APG) on Wholesale
Financial Markets and Services

GALLOWAY CATTLE SOCIETY OF GREAT BRITAIN & IRELAND

15 New Market Street, Castle Douglas,
Kirkcudbrightshire, DG7 1HY

Tel: 01556 502753
Fax: 01556 502753
E-mail: info@gallowaycattlesociety.co.uk

Enquiries:
Enquiries to: Secretary

Founded:
1877

Organisation type and purpose:
Trade association (membership is by subscription),
present number of members: 450, registered
charity (charity number CR 36927).

continued overleaf

Registration and promotion of beef cattle known as Galloway. Galloway cattle are found throughout the world and, whilst they have their own societies, this society is considered the parent body by many.

Subject coverage:
History of Galloway Cattle. Pedigrees held of all registered Galloway Cattle in Britain and Ireland.

Printed publications:
Breed Journal (free to all members)

Access to staff:
Contact by letter, by telephone and by fax
Hours: Wed, Fri, 0930 to 1630

GALPIN SOCIETY

37 Townsend Drive, St. Albans, Hertfordshire, AL3 5RF

E-mail: administrator@galpinsociety.org

Website:
http://www.galpinsociety.org
Membership – how to join. Contents of journals only.

Enquiries:
Enquiries to: Administrator
Other contacts: Editor for publications & contributions to them.

Founded:
1946

Organisation type and purpose:
International organisation, learned society (membership is by subscription), present number of members: 900, registered charity (charity number 306012).
The study of development, history, construction and use of musical instruments.

Subject coverage:
History, construction, development and use of musical instruments.

Museum or gallery collection, archive, or library special collection:
The Society's archives (for members only)
Documents relating to the history of the Society (for members only)

Printed publications:
Galpin Society Journal (annually, on sale to non-members at subscription rate)
Membership list (members only)
Newsletter (3 times a year, for members only)

Electronic and video publications:
Index to volumes XXI-XXV on discs

Publications list:
Available online and in print

Access to staff:
Contact by letter and by e-mail

GAMBICA ASSOCIATION LIMITED

Formal name: Association for Instrumentation, Control, Automation & Laboratory Technology

Broadwall House, 21 Broadwall, London, SE1 9PL

Tel: 020 7642 8080
Fax: 020 7642 8096
E-mail: assoc@gambica.org.uk

Website:
http://www.gambica.org.uk
Includes general information on the Association, details of members and Association groups, including hot links to member company sites. Latest updates and details of publications are available to download or order.

Enquiries:
Enquiries to: Executive Secretary
Direct e-mail: schenery@gambica.org.uk

Founded:
1915

Formerly called:
Association for the Laboratory Supply Industry (ALSI), British Instrument Control and Automation Manufacturers (BIMCAM), Control and Automation Manufacturers Association (CAMA), Scientific Instrument Manufacturers Association (SIMA); British Laboratory Ware Association (BLWA) (year of change 1991); BWLA Limited (year of change 2001)

Organisation type and purpose:
Trade association.

Subject coverage:
Instrumentation, control, automation and laboratory technology, sources of supply, etc.

Printed publications:
Association Guide
Technical Guides
Technical Reports
Orgalime General Conditions and Model Forms

Publications list:
Available online

Access to staff:
Contact by letter, by fax, by e-mail and via website
Hours: Mon to Thu, 0900 to 1700; Fri, 0900 to 1545

Member organisation of:
European Association of Optical and Scientific Instrument Manufacturers (EUROM)
ORGALIME

Secretaries of:
EROM II Optics, Lasers and Laboratory Instrumentation

GAMBLERS ANONYMOUS (UK)

Acronym or abbreviation: GA

PO Box 5382 London W1A 6SA

Tel: 020 7384 3040
E-mail: info@gamblersanonymous.org.uk

Website:
http://www.gamblersanonymous.org.uk

Enquiries:
Enquiries to: Secretary
Direct e-mail: info@gamblersanonymous.org.uk

Organisation type and purpose:
Voluntary organisation.
A self-help fellowship of compulsive gamblers.

Subject coverage:
Group therapy and advice on the best ways to stop gambling.

Non-library collection catalogue:
All or part available in-house

Library catalogue:
All or part available in-house

Printed publications:
Helping Agencies leaflets
Newsletter (monthly)

Access to staff:
Contact by telephone
Hours: 24-hour helpline

Links with:
GAM-ANON, for wives and/or relatives of the compulsive gambler

GAMCARE

Formal name: National Association for Gambling Care, Educational Resources and Training

2nd floor, 7–11 St John's Hill, Clapham Junction, London, SW11 1TR

Tel: 020 7801 7000
Fax: 020 7801 7033
E-mail: director@gamcare.org.uk

Website:
http://www.gamcare.org.uk

Enquiries:
Enquiries to: Business Administrator
Other contacts: Chairman

Founded:
1990

Formerly called:
UK Forum on Young People and Gambling (UKF) from 1990 to 1997

Organisation type and purpose:
Membership association (membership is by subscription), present number of members: 100, registered charity (charity number 1060005), suitable for ages: all.
Friends Association, National Centre for information.

Subject coverage:
Gambling, information, advice and practical help in relation to the social impact of gambling, damage done by such activities, strategies to reduce potential and actual harm to young people.

Trade and statistical information:
Statistical information on gambling, particularly in relation to the number of calls to the Helpline
Information on social impact of gambling in the UK.

Printed publications:
Books and booklets providing advice and guidance in working with problem gamblers
A Certain Bet – Exploring Gambling (£15 plus £3 p&p)
Range of leaflets addressing issues of people and gambling
Quit Compulsive Gambling (Gordon Moody, £5.99 plus 50p p&p)
Working with Young Problem Gamblers: Guidelines to Practice (£3.50 plus 30p p&p)

Electronic and video publications:
Videos

Publications list:
Available in print

Access to staff:
Contact by letter, by telephone, by fax, by e-mail and via website. Appointment necessary.
Hours: Helpline: Mon to Fri, 1000 to 2200; Sat, 1000 to 1800; Sun, 1800 to 2200

Affiliated to:
European Association for the Study of Gambling
Society for Study of Gambling
Youth Access

GAME AND WILDLIFE CONSERVATION TRUST

Acronym or abbreviation: GWCT

Burgate Manor, Fordingbridge, Hampshire, SP6 1EF

Tel: 01425 652381
Fax: 01425 655848
E-mail: info@gwct.org.uk

Website:
http://www.gwct.org.uk

Enquiries:
Enquiries to: Librarian
Direct tel: 01425 651019
Direct e-mail: library@gwct.org.uk

Founded:
1931

Formerly called:
Game Conservancy Trust (year of change 2007)

Organisation type and purpose:
Registered charity (charity number 1112023), research organisation.

Subject coverage:
Game management and conservation; habitat requirements; problems imposed by intensive farming methods on wildlife populations; predators, upland wildlife; advises government and other decision makers on wildlife policy.

Printed publications:
Annual Review
Magazine (3 times a year)
Order printed publications from: Membership
Department, Game and Wildlife Conservation
Trust, Burgate Manor, Fordingbridge, SP6 1EF

Access to staff:
Contact by letter, by telephone, by fax, by e-mail
and via website. Appointment necessary.
Hours: Mon to Fri, 0900 to 1700

Access to building, collection or gallery:
Library facilities only
Hours: Mon to Fri, 0900 to 1700
Special comments: By appointment only.

Constituent bodies:
Game and Wildlife Conservation Trust Trading Ltd

GANDHI FOUNDATION

Acronym or abbreviation: GF

c/o G. Paxton, 87 Barrington Drive, Glasgow, G4
9ES

Tel: 0845 313 8419
E-mail: contact@gandhifoundation.org

Website:
http://www.gandhifoundation.org

Enquiries:
Enquiries to: Administrator
Other contacts: The Editor, The Gandhi Way (e-mail
gpaxton@phonecoop.coop)

Founded:
1983

Organisation type and purpose:
International organisation, membership
association (membership is by subscription),
voluntary organisation, registered charity (charity
number 292629).

Subject coverage:
Spreading Gandhian principles through multifaith
celebration, annual summer gathering, annual
lectures, Peace Award, seminars and conferences,
AGM and workshops, newsletter.

Printed publications:
The Gandhi Way (quarterly)

Access to staff:
Contact by letter, by telephone, by e-mail, in
person and via website. Appointment necessary.

GARAGE EQUIPMENT ASSOCIATION LIMITED

Acronym or abbreviation: GEA

2–3 Church Walk, Daventry, Northamptonshire,
NN11 4BL

Tel: 01327 312616
Fax: 01327 312606
E-mail: john@gea-ltd.demon.co.uk

Website:
http://www.gea.co.uk
Directory of members by product.

Enquiries:
Enquiries to: Administrator

Founded:
1945

Organisation type and purpose:
Trade association.

Subject coverage:
Garage equipment selection, design, layout,
distribution, installation and importation.

**Museum or gallery collection, archive, or library
special collection:**
Trade catalogues dating back to 1950s and 1960s

Printed publications:
An Introduction to Air Conditioning (£15)
Code of Practice 1996 (£13.50)
The World of Emissions (£13.50)

The World of Waveforms (£14.50)
OBD & Diagnosis After The Code (£16, update
£3.50)

Publications list:
Available in print

Access to staff:
Contact by letter, by telephone, by fax, by e-mail
and in person
Hours: Mon to Fri, 0830 to 1300 and 1400 to 1700

Affiliated to:
Aftermarket Association Liaison Group (AALG)

GARDEN HISTORY SOCIETY

Acronym or abbreviation: GHS

70 Cowcross Street, London, EC1M 6EJ

Tel: 020 7608 2409
Fax: 020 7490 2974
E-mail: enquiries@gardenhistorysociety.org

Website:
http://www.gardenhistorysociety.org

Enquiries:
Enquiries to: Chairman

Founded:
1965

Organisation type and purpose:
International organisation, learned society. Also
statutory consultee on planning applications
affecting listed historic designed landscapes. The
Society's aims are to promote the study of the
history of gardening, landscape gardening and
horticulture in all its aspects; to promote the
protection and conservation of historic parks,
gardens and designed landscapes, and to promote
and advise on their conservation; and to encourage
the creation of new parks, gardens and designed
landscapes.

Subject coverage:
Garden history, landscape design, architectural
features, horticultural use of plants, conservation.

**Museum or gallery collection, archive, or library
special collection:**
The Society's library is housed at King's Manor
Library, University of York and Department of
Art History, University of Bristol.

Non-library collection catalogue:
All or part available online

Library catalogue:
All or part available online

Printed publications:
Bibliography (online)
Garden History (journal, twice a year)
Newsletter (twice a year)
Order printed publications from: Back issues
department

Publications list:
Available online

Access to staff:
Contact by letter, by telephone, by fax and by e-
mail. Appointment necessary.
Special comments: Staff work part time

Access to building, collection or gallery:
Special comments: Appointment necessary

GARDEN INDUSTRY MANUFACTURERS ASSOCIATION (1999) LIMITED

Acronym or abbreviation: GIMA

225 Bristol Road, Edgbaston, Birmingham, B5 7UB

Tel: 0121 446 5213
Fax: 0121 446 5215
E-mail: info@gima.org.uk

Website:
http://www.gima.org.uk

Enquiries:
Enquiries to: Director
Direct tel: 01428 712513
Direct fax: 01428 712513
Direct e-mail: marshpr1@aol.com

Founded:
1999

Known as:
Garden Products Association (GPA)

Organisation type and purpose:
Trade association.

Subject coverage:
Trade specific information made available to
members.

Access to staff:
Access for members only.
Hours: Mon to Fri, 0900 to 1700

Access to building, collection or gallery:
No access other than to staff

Secretariat:
British Hardware Federation (BHF)
tel: 0121 446 6688; fax: 0121 446 5215

GATESHEAD COLLEGE

Formal name: Gateshead College Library

Quarryfield Road, Baltic Business Quarter,
Gateshead, Tyne and Wear, NE8 3BN

Tel: 0191 490 2306; 0191 490 2289
Fax: 0191 490 2313
E-mail: library.manager@gateshead.ac.uk

Website:
http://www.gateshead.ac.uk

Enquiries:
Enquiries to: Customer Services Officers
Direct tel: 0191 490 2249
Direct e-mail: library@gateshead.ac.uk

Founded:
1956

Formerly called:
Gateshead College Learning Centre, Gateshead
College Library and Resources Unit, Centre 4...
Knowledge

Organisation type and purpose:
College of further education. Suitable for ages: 16
upwards.

Subject coverage:
General subjects spread over wide range of
qualifications including some higher education.

Library catalogue:
All or part available online

Access to staff:
Contact by letter, by telephone, by fax and by e-
mail. Appointment necessary. All charged.
Hours: Mon to Thu, 0830 to 2000; Fri, 1000 to 1630

Access for disabled people:
Pay and display parking provided, ramped entry,
toilet facilities, internal lifts for access to floors

GATESHEAD LIBRARIES AND ARTS

Central Library, Prince Consort Road, Gateshead,
Tyne and Wear, NE8 4LN

Tel: 0191 433 8400
Fax: 0191 433 8424
E-mail: libraries@gateshead.gov.uk

Website:
http://www.gatesheadlibraries.com
Gateshead libraries online service with access to
the library catalogue, a wide variety of online
resources including streamed music, encyclopedias
and newspapers, plus local history information
and and archive of over 4,000 photographs.
http://www.gateshead.gov.uk
The Gateshead Council website with information
about all council services.

continued overleaf

http://isee.gateshead.gov.uk
Access Gateshead's local history photograph
collection – over 4,000 photographs available
online.

Enquiries:
Enquiries to: Head of Libraries and Arts
Direct e-mail: annborthwick@gateshead.gov.uk
Other contacts: Principal Library Manager

Founded:
1885

Organisation type and purpose:
Local government body, public library.

Subject coverage:
Reading, readers' groups, local history, heritage,
tourism, learning, children's library, community
rooms, music, film, internet access, wi-fi.

**Museum or gallery collection, archive, or library
special collection:**
Gateshead Local Studies collection including:
Brockett Collection of items relating to Gateshead
 in the 1830s
Oxberry Collection of Local History relating to
 Gateshead and Felling
Local Newspapers from 1711
Collection relating to the General Strike, including
 several national newspapers for 1926
Suffragette publications
Collection of reports and magazines on women
 workers
Felling Collection of Joan Hewitt
Maughan collection on Ryton and Blaydon.

Non-library collection catalogue:
All or part available online

Library catalogue:
All or part available online

Printed publications:
Gateshead Live events guide
Various local history publications, including:
Cinemas of Gateshead
Crossing the Tyne
Making an Angel

Electronic and video publications:
Talking Newspaper (free to residents in Gateshead,
 outside subscriptions) from AIRS service

Access to staff:
Contact by letter, by telephone, by fax, by e-mail,
in person and via website
Hours: Mon, Tue, Thu and Fri, 0900 to 1900; Wed,
0900 to 1700; Sat, 0900 to 1300

Access to building, collection or gallery:
Hours: Mon, Tue, Thu and Fri, 0900 to 1900; Wed,
0900 to 1700; Sat, 0900 to 1300

Access for disabled people:
Wheelchair accessible parking provided, ramped
entry, level entry, access to all public areas, toilet
facilities, staff with signing skills
Hours: Mon, Tue, Thu and Fri, 0900 to 1900; Wed,
0900 to 1700; Sat, 0900 to 1300

Links with:
BALTIC: The Centre for Contemporary Art
The Sage Gateshead

Parent body:
Gateshead Council

GAUGE AND TOOL MAKERS' ASSOCIATION

Acronym or abbreviation: GTMA

3 Forge House, Summerleys Road, Princes
Risborough, Buckinghamshire, HP27 9DT

Tel: 01844 274222
Fax: 01844 274227
E-mail: gtma@gtma.co.uk

Website:
http://www.gtma.co.uk

Enquiries:
Enquiries to: Executive Manager
Other contacts: Business Manager for technical
enquiries.

Founded:
1942

Organisation type and purpose:
Trade association.

Subject coverage:
Gauge and toolmaking, precision machining, rapid
prototyping, metrology.

Printed publications:
Buyers Guide (annually)
Newsletter (quarterly)
World Class Standards
Deeds of Apprenticeship
Pentamode – Code of Practice for the Plastics
 Industry

Access to staff:
Contact by telephone, by fax and by e-mail
Hours: Mon to Fri, 0900 to 1700

GB-RUSSIA SOCIETY, THE

Formal name: GB-Russia Society, The

24 Maida Avenue, London, W2 1ST

Website:
http://www.gbrussia.org

Enquiries:
Enquiries to: Secretary
Other contacts: Via online form at website
www.gbrussia.org

Organisation type and purpose:
Registered charity (charity number 1105296)

Printed publications:
Journal (3 times a year)

Access to staff:
Contact by letter, by e-mail and via website

GEDLING BOROUGH COUNCIL

Civic Centre, Arnot Hill Park, Arnold,
Nottingham, NG5 6LU

Tel: 0115 901 3901\ Minicom no. 0115 901 3935
Fax: 0115 901 3921

Enquiries:
Enquiries to: Public Relations Manager
Direct tel: 0115 901 3801
Direct fax: 0115 901 3807
Direct e-mail: carolyn.iwanowski@gedling.gov.uk

Founded:
1974

Organisation type and purpose:
Local government body.

Printed publications:
Borough Guide (free)
Business Directory (free)
Committee Reports (various, free)
Flyer (civic newspaper, free)
Planning Handbook (free)

Access to staff:
Contact by letter
Hours: Mon to Thu, 0845 to 1715; Fri, 0845 to 1645

Access for disabled people:
Parking provided, level entry, access to all public
areas, toilet facilities

GEM MOTORING ASSIST

Acronym or abbreviation: GEM

Station Road, Forest Row, East Sussex, RH18 5EN

Tel: 01342 825676
Fax: 01342 824847
E-mail: info@motoringassist.com

Website:
http://www.motoringassist.com

Enquiries:
Enquiries to: Chief Executive
Direct e-mail: david.williams@motoringassist.com

Founded:
1932

Formerly called:
Company of Veteran Motorists (year of change
1983)

Organisation type and purpose:
Membership association.
Promotion of road safety, provision of motoring
services to members.

Subject coverage:
Promotion of road safety, motoring law, motoring
technology, motor insurance and claims.

Information services:
Advice given on Road Safety and Motoring
matters

Printed publications:
Good Motoring (magazine, 4 times a year)
Various safety orientated leaflets

Publications list:
Available online

Access to staff:
Contact by letter, by telephone, by e-mail and via
website. Appointment necessary.
Hours: Mon to Fri, 0900 to 1700

Access to building, collection or gallery:
By invitation only

GEMMOLOGICAL ASSOCIATION AND GEM TESTING LABORATORY OF GREAT BRITAIN

Acronym or abbreviation: GAGTL

27 Greville Street (Saffron Hill Entrance), London,
EC1N 8TN

Tel: 020 7404 3334 or 020 7405 3351
Fax: 020 7404 8843
E-mail: gagtl@btinternet.com

Website:
http://www.gagtl.ac.uk/gagtl

Enquiries:
Enquiries to: Director
Other contacts: Director of Education for member of
Council of Management.

Founded:
1908

Formed by the merger of:
Gem Testing Laboratory of Great Britain (1925),
Gemmological Association of Great Britain (1908)
(year of change 1990)

Organisation type and purpose:
Professional body, service industry, suitable for
ages: 16+, training organisation, publishing house.
Gemmological education, with gem testing and
grading services.

Subject coverage:
Gemmology, gemstones, diamonds, pearls, gem
minerals, gem materials, gem identification, gem
testing methods and equipment, gemmological
education.

Non-library collection catalogue:
All or part available in-house

Library catalogue:
All or part available in-house

Printed publications:
Gem and Jewellery News (joint publication with
 Society of Jewellery Historians, quarterly)
Journal of Gemmology (quarterly)

Access to staff:
Contact by telephone, by e-mail and via website
Hours: Mon to Fri, 0900 to 1700

Access to building, collection or gallery:
Prior appointment required

Wholly owned subsidiary:
Gemmological Instruments Limited, which sells
gemmological books and instruments
 tel: 020 7404 3334; fax: 020 7404 8843; e-mail:
 gagtl@btinternet.com

GENDER TRUST

Formal name: Gender Trust Association
Acronym or abbreviation: GT

Community Base, 113 Queens Road, Brighton, BN1 3XG

Tel: 0845 231 0505 (helpline, Mon to Fri, 1000 to 2200, Sat and Sun, 1300 to 2200)
E-mail: info@gendertrust.org.uk

Website:
http://www.gendertrust.org.uk

Enquiries:
Enquiries to: Project Manager
Direct tel: 01273 234024
Other contacts: Administrator

Founded:
1990

Organisation type and purpose:
National organisation, registered charity (charity number 1088150).
To support any adult affected by gender identity issues, throughout the United Kingdom.

Subject coverage:
Gender identity, gender dysphoria, transsexuality.

Printed publications:
GT News (quarterly, for members)
The GT Guide
Sex Reassignment Surgery: A Patient's Guide
Standards of Care for Gender Identity Disorders (6th edn)
Recommendations and Guidelines for Employees
An Employer's Guide to Transition in the Workplace (2nd edn)
Various information sheets

Publications list:
Available online and in print

Access to staff:
Contact by letter, by telephone, by e-mail and via website. Appointment necessary.
Hours: Tue to Thu, 0900 to 1700

GENERAL CONFERENCE OF THE NEW CHURCH

Swedenborg House, 20 Bloomsbury Way, London, WC1A 2TH

Tel: 020 7229 9340
Fax: 01206 302932

Enquiries:
Enquiries to: Chief Executive
Direct tel: 01206 303800
Other contacts: Treasurer (for financial matters)

Founded:
1789

Organisation type and purpose:
Registered charity (charity number 253206).
Free Church organisation.
Propagation of the Christian teachings of Emanuel Swedenborg (1688–1772).

Subject coverage:
Faith and doctrines of the New Church (Swedenborgian) and the history of the organisation; life and teaching of Emanuel Swedenborg.

Museum or gallery collection, archive, or library special collection:
Archives and records of the General Conference of the New Church and individual congregations of the organisation
Works of Emanuel Swedenborg

Non-library collection catalogue:
All or part available in-house

Library catalogue:
All or part available in-house

Printed publications:
Lifeline (monthly, except Jan and Jul)

List of books published by related organisations from: New Church House, 34 John Dalton Street, Manchester, M2 6LE
Outlook (quarterly)
Year Book (annually)
Order printed publications from: North of England New Church House, 34 John Dalton Street, Manchester, M2 6LE; tel: 0161 834 4192

Electronic and video publications:
Some audio and video tapes are available

Publications list:
Available in print

Access to staff:
Contact by letter, by telephone and by e-mail. Appointment necessary.
Hours: Mon to Fri, 0900 to 1700

Chief Executive:
General Conference of the New Church
59 Campernell Close, Brightlingsea, Colchester, Essex, CO7 0PP; tel: 01206 303800; fax: 01206 303800; e-mail: michael.hindley@ generalconference.org.uk

Close links with:
Swedenborg Society
20 Bloomsbury Way, London, WC1A 2TH; tel: 020 7405 7986

Organisation is made up of:
23 churches in the UK and 8 groups

Treasurer:
General Conference of the New Church
42 Hillside, Findern, Derby, DE65 6AZ; tel: 01283 702764; e-mail: nigel.sutton@generalconference .org.uk

GENERAL CONSUMER COUNCIL FOR NORTHERN IRELAND

Elizabeth House, 116 Holywood Road, Belfast, BT4 1NY

Tel: 028 9067 2488\ Minicom no. 028 9067 2488
Fax: 028 9065 7701
E-mail: info@consumercouncil.org.uk

Website:
http://www.consumercouncil.org.uk
Information about the Council and its work, press releases issued by the Council.
http://www.consumerline.org
Advice on consumer rights across a wide range of issues.

Enquiries:
Enquiries to: Chief Executive

Founded:
1985

Formed from:
Northern Ireland Consumer Council, Transport Users Committee (year of change 1985)

Organisation type and purpose:
Advisory body, statutory body, professional body, membership association, present number of members: 14, research organisation.
The General Consumer Council is Northern Ireland's official consumer organisation, set up by the Government in 1985.
Membership is by open competition.
To promote and safeguard the interests of consumers in Northern Ireland.

Subject coverage:
Consumer affairs generally, food, energy, electricity, coal, natural gas, transport, consumer education.

Printed publications:
Variety of leaflets and information packs on consumer affairs available online or on application to the Council, including:
Annual Report
Burning Issues – Consumers and Coal (1997)
Consumers in the Dark – Rights, Redress and Proficiency (1999)
Consumer Education Manifesto (2000)
Equality Scheme 2001

Hungry for Change (2001)
The Transport Trap (2001)
Taking Taxis (1997)
Top Tips for cutting car insurance costs (leaflet)
Transport Watchdog (2000)
What's on my Record? (leaflet)
What's Wrong with Walking? (1997)

Electronic and video publications:
Of Consuming Interest (video, 1998)

Publications list:
Available online and in print

Access to staff:
Contact by letter, by telephone, by fax, by e-mail and in person
Hours: Mon to Fri, 0900 to 1700

Access for disabled people:
Access to all public areas, toilet facilities

Affiliated to:
BEUC – the European Consumer organization

GENERAL COUNCIL AND REGISTER OF NATUROPATHS

Acronym or abbreviation: GCRN

1 Green Lane Avenue, Street, Somerset, BA16 0QS

Tel: 01458 840072
E-mail: admin@naturopathy.org.uk

Website:
http://www.naturopathy.org.uk

Enquiries:
Enquiries to: Secretary

Founded:
1964

Organisation type and purpose:
Professional body (membership is by qualification).
To register suitably qualified practitioners, to enforce a code of professional conduct and maintain educational standards.

Subject coverage:
Naturopathy, natural medicine, alternative medicine, complementary medicine.

Printed publications:
Naturopathic medicine (leaflet, free for C5 sae)
Register of Practitioner Members (£3.00)

Access to staff:
Contact by letter, by telephone, by e-mail and via website
Hours: Mon to Fri, 0900 to 1300

Links with:
British Naturopathic Association

GENERAL COUNCIL OF THE BAR OF ENGLAND AND WALES

Acronym or abbreviation: Bar Council

289–293 High Holborn London WC1V 7HZ

Tel: 020 7242 0082
Fax: 020 7831 9217

Website:
http://www.barprobono.org.uk
Legal advice for charities and voluntary organisations.
http://www.barcouncil.org.uk
Work of the Bar Council.

Enquiries:
Enquiries to: Library/Registry Officer
Direct e-mail: library@barcouncil.org.uk

Founded:
1894

Formerly called:
Senate of the Inns of Court and the Bar

continued overleaf

Organisation type and purpose:
National organisation, professional body
(membership is by qualification), present number
of members: 20,000.
Central governing body of the profession of the Bar
of England and Wales.
Regulation of the profession and promotion of the
interests of barristers.

Subject coverage:
Barristers' profession in England and Wales;
official records of names and addresses of
practising barristers. Provision of legal services by
barristers; information on entry to the profession;
recruiting information; complaints against
barristers.

Printed publications:
Bar Directory
Career at the Bar
Code of Conduct for the Bar of England and Wales
Counsel (magazine, by subscription only)

Access to staff:
Contact by letter, by telephone, by fax and by e-
mail
Hours: Mon to Fri, 0900 to 1700

Access to building, collection or gallery:
Prior appointment required

Access for disabled people:
Ramped entry, toilet facilities

Other departments:
Complaints Department
Northumberland House, 303/306 High Holborn,
London, WC1V 7JZ
Education and Training Departments
2–3 Cursitor Street, London, EC4A 1NE; tel: 020
7440 4002 (Complaints) 020 7440 4000 (Education
& Training); fax: 020 7440 4001

GENERAL DENTAL COUNCIL

Acronym or abbreviation: GDC

37 Wimpole Street, London, W1G 8DQ

Tel: 0845 222 4141 (Typetalk calls accepted)
Fax: 020 7224 3294
E-mail: information@gdc-uk.org

Website:
http://www.gdc-uk.org
Information on all aspects of the GDC's role and
work, including searchable dentists and dental
care professionals registers and specialist lists.
Information for dental professionals on applying
for GDC registration. Information for the public on
what to do if there is a problem with a dental
professional.

Founded:
1956

Organisation type and purpose:
Statutory body.
The General Dental Council's purpose is to protect
the public by regulating dental professionals in the
UK.
Registers qualified professionals; sets standards of
dental practice and conduct; assures the quality of
dental education; ensures professionals keep up to
date with developments in their profession; helps
patients with complaints about a dental
professional; and works to strengthen patient
protection.

Subject coverage:
All aspects of the dental profession: regulation,
registration, qualifications, education,
undergraduate training and continuing
professional development, specialist training in
oral surgery, surgical dentistry, endodontics,
periodontics, prosthodontics, restorative dentistry,
dental public health, orthodontics, paediatric
dentistry, oral medicine, oral microbiology, oral
pathology and dental and maxillofacial radiology.

Printed publications:
All publications are available from website:
Continuing Professional Development for Dentists
Continuing Professional Development for DCPs

The First Five Years
Developing the Dental Team
GDC Gazette
GDC Annual Report and Accounts 2009
Smile
Going abroad for your dental care?
Advice for those who employ dental professionals
How to report a dental professional to us
Standards for dental professionals
Student Fitness to Practise
How we check the quality of dental education and
training

Electronic and video publications:
All publications can be downloaded from the
website

Publications list:
Available online

Access to staff:
Contact by letter, by telephone, by fax, by e-mail,
in person and via website
Hours: Mon to Fri, 0900 to 1700

GENERAL FEDERATION OF TRADE UNIONS

Acronym or abbreviation: GFTU

Headland House, 308–312 Grays Inn Road,
London, WC1X 8DP

Tel: 0207 520 8340
Fax: 0207 520 8350
E-mail: gftuhq@gftu.org.uk

Website:
http://www.gftu.org.uk

Enquiries:
Enquiries to: General Secretary

Founded:
1899

Organisation type and purpose:
Trade union.

Subject coverage:
Services, education and research for trade unions.

Printed publications:
Federation News

Access to staff:
Contact by letter
Hours: Mon to Fri, 0900 to 1700

GENERAL OPTICAL COUNCIL

Acronym or abbreviation: GOC

41 Harley Street, London, W1G 8DJ

Tel: 020 7307 3939
Fax: 020 7436 3525
E-mail: goc@optical.org

Website:
http://www.optical.org
Access to the Opticians Registers; overview of the
Council's work; how to make a complaint about
your optician; news; GOC publications, events and
consultations; careers information; hearings section
with explanations of the hearings process, plus
details on sanctions and outcomes from past
hearings; FAQs; information for GOC registrants;
legislation.

Enquiries:
Enquiries to: Registrar and Chief Executive

Founded:
1958

Organisation type and purpose:
The GOC is the regulator for the optical
professions in the UK. Its purpose is to protect the
public by promoting high standards of education
and conduct amongst opticians. The Council
currently registers around 23,500 optometrists,
dispensing opticians, student opticians and optical
businesses.

Subject coverage:
It holds: statutory registers of all those registered
and fit to practise, train, or carry out optical
business; information relating to education and
training prior to registration; advice on the
application of the Opticians Act 1989; information
on professional conduct.

Information services:
Opticians registers – an online statutory register of
all optometrists and dispensing opticians who are
registered and fit to practise in the UK.

Education services:
Careers information available.

Trade and statistical information:
Data on the number and distribution of registered
opticians.

Printed publications:
Annual Report
Bulletin newsletter
Careers factsheet
Opticians Handbook
GOC Stakeholder Update

Electronic and video publications:
Data on registered opticians available at cost in
electronic form

Publications list:
Available online

Access to staff:
Contact by letter, by telephone, by fax, by e-mail
and via website. Appointment necessary.
Hours: Mon to Thur, 0900 to 1700; Fri, 0900 to 1645

Access to building, collection or gallery:
Hours: Mon to Thur, 0900 to 1700; Fri, 0900 to 1645

Access for disabled people:
Ramp available; please call or email in advance

GENERAL OSTEOPATHIC COUNCIL

Acronym or abbreviation: GOsC

Osteopathy House, 176 Tower Bridge Road,
London, SE1 3LU

Tel: 020 7357 6655
Fax: 020 7357 0011
E-mail: info@osteopathy.org.uk

Website:
http://www.osteopathy.org.uk

Enquiries:
Enquiries to: Osteopathic Information Service
Direct tel: Extn 242

Founded:
1993

Organisation type and purpose:
Statutory body.
To regulate, promote and develop the profession of
osteopathy.

Subject coverage:
Osteopathy.

Trade and statistical information:
Osteopathic profession.

Printed publications:
The Osteopath Magazine (apply direct for
subscriptions)

Access to staff:
Contact by letter, by telephone, by fax, by e-mail
and via website
Hours: Mon to Fri, 0900 to 1700

GENERAL REGISTER OFFICE (NORTHERN IRELAND)

Formal name: Northern Ireland Statistics and
Research Agency
Acronym or abbreviation: NISRA

Oxford House, 49–55 Chichester Street, Belfast,
BT1 4HL

Tel: 028 9025 2000
Fax: 028 9025 2044
E-mail: grostats.nisra@dfpni.gov.uk

Website:
http://www.nisra.gov.uk
General information.
http://www.groni.gov.uk

Enquiries:
Enquiries to: Assistant Registrar General
Direct tel: 028 9025 2033
Direct e-mail: annette.gilkeson@dfpni.gov.uk

Founded:
1922

Organisation type and purpose:
National government body.
Central government department.

Subject coverage:
Statistics on births, deaths, marriages, divorces and population.

Museum or gallery collection, archive, or library special collection:
Birth, death and marriage statistics from 1922
Divorce statistics from 1983

Printed publications:
Registrar General's Annual Report
Registrar General's Quarterly Returns

Access to staff:
Contact by letter, by telephone, by fax, by e-mail, in person and via website. All charged.
Hours: Mon to Fri, 0930 to 1600

Access to building, collection or gallery:
Hours: Mon to Fri, 0930 to 1700

GENERAL REGISTER OFFICE FOR SCOTLAND

Acronym or abbreviation: GROS

New Register House, Edinburgh, EH1 3YT

Tel: 0131 334 0380
Fax: 0131 314 4400
E-mail: records@gro-scotland.gsi.gov.uk

Website:
http://www.gro-scotland.gov.uk
http://www.scotlandspeople.gov.uk

Enquiries:
Enquiries to: Registrar General

Founded:
1855

Organisation type and purpose:
National government body.

Subject coverage:
Registration of births, deaths, marriages, civil partnerships, divorces, dissolution of civil partnerships, adoptions, still-births, gender-recognition, change of name in Scotland, census of population of Scotland, vital and population statistics for Scotland, law governing marriage in Scotland, NHS Central Register for Scotland.

Museum or gallery collection, archive, or library special collection:
Old parish registers of births, deaths and marriages (1553–1854)
Records of the decennial censuses of the population of Scotland (1841–1901 are open to the public)
Statutory registers of births, deaths, marriages, still-births, adoptions, civil partnerships and divorces

Trade and statistical information:
Population, census and vital events data for Scotland.

Non-library collection catalogue:
All or part available online and in-house

Library catalogue:
All or part available in-house

Printed publications:
Annual Report of the Registrar General for Scotland
Census reports
Civil Parish Maps Index
Population Estimates Scotland
Registrar General's Preliminary Return
Registrar General's Quarterly Statistics
Jock Tamson's Bairns: a history of the records of the General Register Office for Scotland (£1)

Electronic and video publications:
Small area statistics (census, CD-ROM)

Publications list:
Available online and in print

Access to staff:
Contact by letter, by telephone, by fax, by e-mail and in person. All charged.
Hours: Mon to Fri, 0900 to 1630
Special comments: Disabled persons can be accompanied by a helper.
Orders accepted by post or fax or by credit card on direct tel: 0131 314 4411, but not by e-mail.

Access for disabled people:
Ramped entry, toilet facilities

Also at:
General Register Office for Scotland
    Ladywell House, Edinburgh, EH12 7TF; tel: 0131 334 0380; fax: 0131 314 4344; e-mail: customer@gro-scotland.gsi.gov.uk

Branches:
Census, Population Statistics, Corporate Services, Vital Events and National Health Service Central Register
    Ladywell House, Corstorphine, EH12 7TF; tel: 0131 334 0380

Part of the devolved:
Scottish Administration under the Scotland Act 1998

Scottish counterpart of the:
Identity and Passport Service in England and Wales

GENERAL TEACHING COUNCIL FOR SCOTLAND

Acronym or abbreviation: GTC Scotland

Clerwood House, 96 Clermiston Road, Edinburgh, EH12 6UT

Tel: 0131 314 6000
Fax: 0131 314 6001
E-mail: gtcs@gtcs.org.uk

Website:
http://www.gtcs.org.uk
General information about the Council. Email contacts to staff members,

Enquiries:
Enquiries to: Chief Executive
Other contacts: (1) Exceptional Admissions Secretary; (2) Communications Officer for all enquiries about registration from outwith Scotland and for press enquiries and enquiries of a general nature.

Founded:
1965

Organisation type and purpose:
National organisation, advisory body, statutory body, professional body (membership is by qualification), present number of members: 83,000. Regulatory body for the teaching profession in Scotland. Registration with the Council is required for teaching in local authority and independent schools in Scotland.

Subject coverage:
Teaching in Scotland, accreditation of teacher education courses in Scotland, probationary teaching service.

Trade and statistical information:
Certain limited statistics on numbers of teachers registered with the Council, including applications under EC directive 89/48 (mutual recognition of professional qualifications).

Printed publications:
Probationer Teacher Support (separate packs for Primary/Nursery and Secondary)
The Assessment of Probationer Teachers: Guidance for Headteachers and those concerned with the management of probationers (separate packs for Primary/Nursery and Secondary)
Welcome to Teaching for First Year Probationer Teachers
Teaching Scotland (newspaper, 4 times a year)
Quadrennial Review and Accounts
Various leaflets and information packs relating to the work of the Council, including its role in supervising the support and assessment of probationer teachers (most available free of charge)

Electronic and video publications:
Various videos available for purchase

Access to staff:
Contact by letter, by telephone, by fax, by e-mail and via website. Appointment necessary.
Hours: Mon to Thu, 0900 to 1645; Fri, 0900 to 1530

Access for disabled people:
Ramped entry, access to all public areas, toilet facilities

GENERAL TEACHING COUNCIL FOR WALES

Acronym or abbreviation: GTCW

4th Floor, Southgate House, Wood Street, Cardiff, CF10 1EW

Tel: 029 2055 0350
Fax: 029 2055 0360
E-mail: information@gtcw.org.uk

Website:
http://www.gtcw.org.uk

Enquiries:
Enquiries to: Deputy Chief Executive
Direct e-mail: hayden.llewellyn@gtcw.org.uk

Founded:
2000

Organisation type and purpose:
Professional body.

Subject coverage:
Information concerning registered teachers.

Printed publications:
Annual Statistics Digest
Order printed publications from:
publications@gtcw.org.uk

Access to staff:
Contact by letter, by telephone, by fax, by e-mail, in person and via website
Hours: Mon to Fri, 0900 to 1700

Access to building, collection or gallery:
Prior appointment required

Access for disabled people:
Access to all public areas

GENETICS SOCIETY

Acronym or abbreviation: GENSOC

Wallace Building, Roslin BioCentre, Roslin, Midlothian, EH25 9PS

Tel: 0131 200 6391
Fax: 0131 200 6394
E-mail: christine.crees@genetics.org.uk

Website:
http://www.genetics.org.uk
Genetics Society website.

Enquiries:
Enquiries to: Executive Officer

continued overleaf

Founded:
1919

Organisation type and purpose:
Learned society (membership is by subscription), present number of members: 2,000, registered charity (charity number 261062).

Subject coverage:
Genetics.

Printed publications:
Genes and Development (monthly)
Heredity (monthly)
Newsletter

Access to staff:
Contact by letter, by telephone, by fax and by e-mail

GENOME DAMAGE & STABILITY CENTRE

Acronym or abbreviation: GDSC

Science Park Road, University of Sussex, Falmer, Brighton, East Sussex, BN1 9RQ

Tel: 01273 678123
Fax: 01273 678121
E-mail: qhfa1@sussex.ac.uk

Website:
http://www.biols.susx.ac.uk/gdsc
Research centre.

Enquiries:
Enquiries to: Director
Direct e-mail: gdsc@sussex.ac.uk
Other contacts: Centre Administrator

Founded:
2001

Organisation type and purpose:
National government body, university department or institute, research organisation.

Subject coverage:
The GDSC is a research centre investigating the responses of cells to genome damage and their relationship to cancer and other aspects of human disease. The purpose-built laboratories, funded by the Joint Infrastructure Fund (JIF), the Wolfson Foundation and the University, are located adjacent to the School of Life Sciences and provide a dynamic and collaborative environment for carrying out state-of-the-art research. Much of this research is supported by the Medical Research Council via a Centre Development Grant and Programme Grants. The Centre currently houses ten research groups.

Printed publications:
Available through scientific journals

Access to staff:
Contact by telephone, by fax, by e-mail and via website. Appointment necessary.
Hours: Mon to Fri, 0900 to 1700

Access to building, collection or gallery:
Prior appointment required
Hours: Mon to Fri, 0900 to 1700

Access for disabled people:
Ramped entry, toilet facilities

Parent body:
Sussex University
   Falmer, Brighton, BN1 9RH; tel: 01273 606755; website: http://www.sussex.ac.uk

GEOGRAPHICAL ASSOCIATION

Acronym or abbreviation: GA

160 Solly Street, Sheffield, South Yorkshire, S1 4BF

Tel: 0114 296 0088
Fax: 0114 296 7176
E-mail: info@geography.org.uk

Website:
http://www.geographyshop.org.uk
Online joining facilities and publication sales

http://www.geography.org.uk
General information and members-only access

Founded:
1893

Organisation type and purpose:
Membership association (membership is by subscription), present number of members: 7,000, voluntary organisation, registered charity (charity number 313129), publishing house.
Resource centre for the teaching of geography.

Subject coverage:
The teaching of geography, its promotion nationally and in schools.

Printed publications:
GA Magazine (incorporating GA News) (termly)
Geography (termly)
Primary Geographer (termly)
Teaching Geography (termly)
Core resources for teaching geography in all phases of education
Order printed publications from:
sales@geography.org.uk

Publications list:
Available online and in print

Access to staff:
Contact by letter, by telephone, by fax, by e-mail, in person and via website. Appointment necessary.
Hours: Mon to Fri, 0900 to 1700

GEOGRAPHY OUTDOORS

Formal name: Geography Outdoors: the centre supporting field research, exploration and outdoor learning

Royal Geographical Society (with IBG), 1 Kensington Gore, London, SW7 2AR

Tel: 020 7591 3030
Fax: 020 7591 3031
E-mail: go@rgs.org

Website:
http://www.rgs.org/go

Enquiries:
Enquiries to: Head of Expeditions and Fieldwork
Direct e-mail: s.winser@rgs.org

Founded:
1980

Formerly called:
Royal Geographical Society and Young Explorer's Trust; Expedition Advisory Centre (year of change 2006)

Organisation type and purpose:
Advisory body, registered charity, suitable for ages: university undergraduates and adult leaders and teachers, training organisation, publishing house.
Information, training and advice for those planning expeditions and field research overseas.

Subject coverage:
Scientific expeditions and adventure travel overseas: planning, fieldwork, equipment, safety, medicine; logistics of operating in tropical, desert and arctic environments; environmental information, training.

Museum or gallery collection, archive, or library special collection:
Expedition reports dating back to 1965

Non-library collection catalogue:
All or part available online

Library catalogue:
All or part available in-house

Printed publications:
Expedition Planners' Handbook and Directory
Fieldwork Guides (9 titles)
Expedition Manuals
Logistics and Safety Manuals (6 titles)
Oxford Handbook of Expedition and Wilderness Medicine (2008, £28.95)
Tropical Forest Expeditions (2001, £12)
Polar Expeditions (2001, £12)
Reference books and pamphlets (6 titles)

Sources of Information for Independent and Overland Travellers (2000, £5)
Creating a University Exploration Society (1999, £2.50)

Electronic and video publications:
Joining an Expedition (annually)
Order electronic and video publications from: http://www.rgs.org/JE

Publications list:
Available online and in print

Access to staff:
Contact by letter, by telephone, by fax, by e-mail and via website. Appointment necessary.
Hours: Mon to Fri, 0900 to 1700

Access to building, collection or gallery:
Prior appointment required
Hours: Mon to Fri, 1100 to 1700

Access for disabled people:
Ramped entry, toilet facilities

Office of the:
Royal Geographical Society (with IBG)
   tel: 020 7591 3000; fax: 020 7591 3001; e-mail: info@rgs.org

GEOLOGICAL CURATORS GROUP

Acronym or abbreviation: GCG

Natural History Division, National Museum of Ireland, Merrion St, Dublin 2, Republic of Ireland

Tel: +353 87 122 1967
E-mail: mparkes@museum.ie

Website:
http://www.geocurator.org

Enquiries:
Enquiries to: Secretary

Founded:
1974

Organisation type and purpose:
Professional body.
To improve the status of geology in museums and the standard of geological curation in general.

Subject coverage:
All aspects of geology in museums; protection/care of collections; collecting; display; conservation; history; research, etc.

Printed publications:
A Directory of British Geological Museums (May 1994)
Coprolite (newsletter, 3 times a year)
Guidelines for the Curation of Geological Materials 1985
The Geological Curator (journal, 2 times a year)

Access to staff:
Contact by letter, by e-mail and via website
Hours: Mon to Fri, 0900 to 1700

Affiliated to:
Geological Society of London

GEOLOGICAL SOCIETY

Burlington House, Piccadilly, London, W1J 0BG

Tel: 020 7434 9944
Fax: 020 7439 8975
E-mail: enquiries@geolsoc.org.uk

Website:
http://www.geolsoc.org.uk

Enquiries:
Enquiries to: Science & Communications Officer
Direct e-mail: sarah.day@geolsoc.org.uk
Other contacts: Librarian (for bibliographical enquiries, tel: 020 7432 0999)

Founded:
1807

Incorporates the former:
Institution of Geologists

Organisation type and purpose:
Learned society, professional body (membership is by qualification, election or invitation), present number of members: 8,800, registered charity (charity number 210161), publishing house.
To serve the science and profession of geology in the UK.

Subject coverage:
Geology and allied sciences.

Museum or gallery collection, archive, or library special collection:
Murchison Letters and Diaries
Rare Book Collection

Library catalogue:
All or part available online and in-house

Printed publications:
Annual Review
Geoscientist (12 times a year)
Journal of the Geological Society (6 times a year)
Memoirs
Petroleum Geoscience (4 times a year)
Quarterly Journal of Engineering Geology
Special Publications
Order printed publications from: Geological Society Publishing House, Unit 7, Brassmill Lane, Bath, Somerset, BA1 3JN; tel: 01225 445046; fax: 01225 442836; e-mail: http://bookshop.geolsoc.org.uk

Publications list:
Available online and in print

Access to staff:
Contact by letter, by fax, by e-mail and via website. Appointment necessary. Non-members charged.
Hours: Mon to Fri, 0930 to 1730
Special comments: Charges made to non-members for use of the Library and information.

Has:
23 specialist groups and joint associations

GEOLOGISTS' ASSOCIATION

Acronym or abbreviation: GA

Burlington House, Piccadilly, London, W1V 9AG

Tel: 020 7434 9298
Fax: 020 7287 0280
E-mail: geol.assoc@btinternet.com

Website:
http://www.geologist.demon.co.uk

Enquiries:
Enquiries to: Executive Secretary

Founded:
1858

Organisation type and purpose:
Learned society (membership is by election or invitation), present number of members: 2000, registered charity (charity number 233199), suitable for ages: 18+.

Subject coverage:
Geological sciences.

Printed publications:
Circular (monthly)
Proceedings (quarterly)
Geological Guides mainly districts of the UK but also places abroad such as Iceland, Jamaica and Mallorca
London Illustrated Geological Walks (two books, Robinson E, £3.95 each)

Access to staff:
Contact by letter, by telephone, by fax, by e-mail and via website
Hours: Mon to Fri, 0930 to 1600

GEORGE ELIOT FELLOWSHIP

71 Stepping Stones Road, Coventry, Warwickshire, CV5 8JT

Tel: 024 7659 2231

Enquiries:
Enquiries to: Honorary Secretary

Founded:
1930

Organisation type and purpose:
Membership association (membership is by subscription, election or invitation), present number of members: 600, voluntary organisation, registered charity (charity number 1054060).
Literary society to promote interest in George Eliot.

Subject coverage:
George Eliot's life, works, family and friends.

Printed publications:
George Eliot Review (annually, £10 plus p&p)
Pitkin Guide to George Eliot (£3.50 plus p&p)
Little Sister (£1 plus p&p)
Story of the George Eliot Fellowship (£2.50 plus p&p)
Those Of Us Who Loved Her: The men in George Eliot's life (£7.50 plus p&p)
Magazine (annually)
Newsletter (quarterly)

Electronic and video publications:
Two 60 minute cassettes of readings from George Eliot's novels by Gabriel Woolf

Publications list:
Available in print

Access to staff:
Contact by letter and by telephone
Hours: Mon to Fri, 0900 to 2200

Affiliated to the:
Alliance of Literary Societies
22 Belmont Grove, Havant, Hampshire, PO9 3PU; tel: 01705 475855; fax: 01705 788842; e-mail: rosemary@sndc.demon.co.uk

Branches at:
George Eliot Fellowship
2006–13–212 Yamakuni, Yashiro-Cho, Kato-Gun, Hyogo 673–1421, Japan
George Eliot Fellowship
PO Box 10167, Springfield, MO 65808–0167, USA

GEORGE MACDONALD SOCIETY, THE

9 Medway Drive, Forest Row, East Sussex, RH18 5NU

Tel: 01342 823859
Fax: 01342 823859
E-mail: macdonald-society@britishlibrary.net

Website:
http://www.george-macdonald.com
General on MacDonald.
http://www.gmsociety.org.uk
All MacDonald Society matters.

Enquiries:
Enquiries to: Honorary Secretary
Other contacts: Membership Secretary for membership enquiries.

Founded:
1981

Organisation type and purpose:
Membership association (membership is by subscription), present number of members: 190, registered charity.
Literary society.

Subject coverage:
All matters connected with the Victorian writer, lecturer and preacher George MacDonald.

Library catalogue:
All or part available in-house

Printed publications:
North Wind (journal, annually)
Orts (newsletter, quarterly)
Order printed publications from: The George MacDonald Society, 18 Tapanhall Road Fernhill Heath, Worcester, WR3 7TR, tel: 01905 453214, fax: 01905 453214, e-mail: terryandrachel@puzzlejug.co.uk

Access to staff:
Contact by letter, by telephone, by fax and by e-mail
Hours: Any reasonable time

Other addresses:
The George MacDonald Society
The Library, King's College, Strand, London, WC2R 2LS

GEORGE PADMORE INSTITUTE

Acronym or abbreviation: GPI

76 Stroud Green Road, Finsbury Park, London, N4 3EN

Tel: 020 7272 8915
Fax: 020 7281 4662

Website:
http://www.georgepadmoreinstitute.org

Organisation type and purpose:
A registered charity (no. 1003001) offering an archive, an educational resource and a research centre.

Subject coverage:
The black community of Caribbean, African and Asian descent in Britain and continental Europe.

GEORGIAN GROUP

6 Fitzroy Square, London, W1T 5DX

Tel: 0871 750 2936
Fax: 0871 750 2937
E-mail: office@georgiangroup.org.uk

Website:
http://www.georgiangroup.org.uk
Publications list, membership information and forms, some casework reports, events and study days information.

Enquiries:
Enquiries to: Secretary

Founded:
1937

Organisation type and purpose:
Voluntary organisation, registered charity (charity number 209934).
National amenity society.

Subject coverage:
Conservation of Georgian architecture, 1700–1840; advice to owners and public authorities; uses to which such buildings can be adapted.

Non-library collection catalogue:
All or part available in-house and in print

Library catalogue:
All or part available in-house

Printed publications:
Georgian Group Guides: a series of 16 short illustrated guides on windows, doors, paint colour etc
Georgian Group Journal 1991–2001
Rescued or Ruined? (1999): Dealing with enabling development
Symposia proceedings, including Georgian Vernacular 1995
Squanderous and Lavish Profusion
The Picturesque in Late Georgian England

Publications list:
Available online and in print

Access to staff:
Contact by letter, by telephone, by fax and by e-mail
Hours: Mon to Fri, 0930 to 1730

Liaison with:
20th Century Society
English Heritage
Society for the Protection of Ancient Buildings
Victorian Society

GERMAN HISTORICAL INSTITUTE LONDON

Acronym or abbreviation: GHIL

17 Bloomsbury Square, London, WC1A 2NJ

Tel: 020 7309 2050
Fax: 020 7309 2055
E-mail: ghil@ghil.ac.uk

Website:
http://www.ghil.ac.uk

Enquiries:
Enquiries to: Librarian
Direct tel: 020 7309 2022; 020 7309 2019
Direct e-mail: library@ghil.ac.uk
Other contacts: Head Librarian

Founded:
1975

Organisation type and purpose:
Research organisation.
Academic institute.

Subject coverage:
German history and politics (apart from the library,
the Institute's staff of German historians are
experts in various periods of German and English
history from the late Middle Ages onwards).

**Museum or gallery collection, archive, or library
special collection:**
75,000 vols, including microforms
200 current periodicals on German and English
history
German and English newspapers

Library catalogue:
All or part available online

Printed publications:
Annual Lectures
Bulletin (twice a year)
Vols in the English series of publications
Vols in the German series of publications
Order printed publications from: For English
publications: Oxford University Press, Great
Clarendon Street, Oxford, OX2 6DP; tel. 01865
556767; fax 01865 556646
For German publications: Oldenbourg,
Rosenheimerstrasse 145, 81671 Munich, Germany;
tel. +49 8945 0510

Publications list:
Available online and in print

Access to staff:
Contact by letter, by telephone, by fax, by e-mail,
in person and via website

Access to building, collection or gallery:
No prior appointment required (but check on
website for short notice closures)
Hours: Mon, Tue, Wed and Fri, 1000 to 1700; Thu,
1000 to 2000
Special comments: Readers' tickets required
(photograph and proof of address needed), free
access, reference only.

Links with:
Partner institutes in Rome, Paris, Washington,
Warsaw, Moscow, Tokyo, Beirut, Istanbul

Parent body:
Stiftung Geisteswissenschaftliche Institute im
Ausland
  Rheinallee 6, 53173 Bonn, Germany; e-mail:
  dgia@stiftung-dgia.de; website: http://www
  .stiftung-dgia.de

GERMAN NATIONAL TOURIST OFFICE

Acronym or abbreviation: GNTO

PO Box 2695, London, W1A 3TN

Tel: 020 7317 0908
Fax: 020 7317 0917
E-mail: gntolon@d-z-t.com

Website:
http://www.germany-tourism.de
General and tourist information on Germany.

http://www.germany-christmas-market.org.uk
Dedicated information on German Christmas
Markets.

Enquiries:
Enquiries to: Information Officer

Founded:
1951

Organisation type and purpose:
National government body.
National tourist office.
Promotion of Germany as a travel destination.

Subject coverage:
Information on travel to and within Germany,
including list of tour operators, accommodation
lists, tourist information, events, conferences and
fairs in Germany.

**Museum or gallery collection, archive, or library
special collection:**
Picture library (online at http://www.images-
dzt.de)

Trade and statistical information:
Data on travel and tourism from the UK and
Ireland to Germany.
Data on the German travel industry (incoming
only).

Printed publications:
Printed products available through a mailing
house
Approximately 500 brochures on various areas and
subjects
Posters

Publications list:
Available online and in print

Access to staff:
Contact by letter, by telephone, by fax, by e-mail
and via website
Hours: Mon to Fri, 0900 to 1700
Special comments: Telephone hours are 1000 to 1600.
No counter service.

Access to building, collection or gallery:
No access other than to staff

Branches:
30 branch offices world-wide and representative
agencies world-wide

Parent body:
Head Office (GNTB)
  German National Tourist Board, Beethoven str
  69, 60325 Frankfurt am Main, Germany; tel: +49
  69 974640; fax: +49 69 751903; e-mail: info@d-z-t
  .com

GERMAN-BRITISH CHAMBER OF INDUSTRY & COMMERCE

16 Buckingham Gate, London, SW1E 6LB

Tel: 020 7976 4100
Fax: 020 7976 4101
E-mail: mail@ahk-london.co.uk

Website:
http://www.germanbritishchamber.co.uk

Enquiries:
Enquiries to: PA to Director General

Founded:
1971

Formerly called:
German Chamber of Industry & Commerce in the
UK (year of change 1993)

Organisation type and purpose:
Chamber of Commerce.

Subject coverage:
Promotion of trade and investment between
Germany and the United Kingdom.
Specialist groups: membership, events, business
information, legal, business partner search,
marketing services, business promotion, trade
fairs, VAT refund, green dot.

Publications list:
Available online and in print

Access to staff:
Contact by letter, by telephone, by fax, by e-mail,
in person and via website. Appointment necessary.
Non-members charged.
Hours: Mon to Fri, 0900 to 1700

GERMANISCHER LLOYD INDUSTRIAL SERVICES (UK) LIMITED

Acronym or abbreviation: GLIS (UK)

Enterprise Court, Gapton Hall, Great Yarmouth,
Norfolk, NR31 0ND

Tel: 01493 442112
Fax: 01493 444365
E-mail: glocb-great.yarmouth@gl-group.com

Website:
http://www.ocbgl.com
General details of Company divisions.

Enquiries:
Enquiries to: Company Secretary

Founded:
1976

Organisation type and purpose:
Professional body.

Subject coverage:
Verification services – i.e. oilrigs, offshore and
onshore structures etc.

Printed publications:
Offshore Health and Safety
The Guide to the Law and Practice

Publications list:
Available in print

Access to staff:
Contact by letter
Hours: Mon to Fri, 0900 to 1700

Main shareholding company:
Germanischer Lloyd AG

GFK NOP

Ludgate House, 245 Blackfriars Road, London, SE1
9UL

Tel: 020 7890 9000
Fax: 020 7890 9001
E-mail: ukinfo@gfk.com

Website:
http://www.gfknop.co.uk

Enquiries:
Enquiries to: Chief Executive

Founded:
1957

Organisation type and purpose:
Market Research organisation.

Subject coverage:
automotive, business, consumer (including CPR,
travel, new media), financial services, healthcare,
media, mystery shopping, technology, social
Research, omnibus surveys.

Access to staff:
Contact by letter, by telephone, by fax, by e-mail
and via website. Appointment necessary.
Hours: Mon to Fri, 0930 to 1730

Access for disabled people:
Access to all public areas

Affiliated to:
MRS, GfK Group

GIBRALTAR GOVERNMENT

Acronym or abbreviation: GIB

Arundel Great Court, 179 Strand, London, WC2R
1EH

Tel: 020 7836 0777
Fax: 020 7240 6612
E-mail: info@gibraltar.gov.uk

Website:
http://www.gibraltar.gov.uk

Enquiries:
Enquiries to: Director
Direct fax: 020 7240 6612

Formerly called:
Gibraltar Tourist Board

Organisation type and purpose:
National government body.
Information office.

Subject coverage:
Gibraltar: all subjects including political, tourism, finance, trade and industry, property, conferences, stamps, ship repair, ship registry, yacht facilities etc.

Museum or gallery collection, archive, or library special collection:
Picture library

Library catalogue:
All or part available online

Printed publications:
Gibraltar government publications (produced when required)
Main tourism brochure (annually, October)

Electronic and video publications:
Videos

Publications list:
Available online and in print

Access to staff:
Contact by letter, by telephone, by fax, by e-mail and via website
Hours: Mon to Fri, 0900 to 1700

Access to building, collection or gallery:
No prior appointment required

Access for disabled people:
Level entry

Other address:
Gibraltar Government
6 Convent Place, Gibraltar; tel: + 350 70071; fax: + 350 76396; e-mail: govscc@gibnet.gi

GIFTED CHILDREN'S INFORMATION CENTRE

Acronym or abbreviation: GCIC

Hampton Grange, 21 Hampton Lane, Solihull, West Midlands, B91 2QJ

Tel: 0121 705 4547
Fax: 0121 705 4547
E-mail: petercongdon@blueyonder.co.uk

Website:
http://www.ukselfhelp.info/giftedchildren

Enquiries:
Enquiries to: Director

Founded:
1978

Organisation type and purpose:
Advisory body, suitable for ages: all, consultancy, publishing house.

Subject coverage:
Gifted children; dyslexic children and adults; left-handed individuals; attention deficit and hyperactivity disorder; Asperger's Syndrome.

Museum or gallery collection, archive, or library special collection:
Books and guides on the above subjects

Printed publications:
Books and guides on gifted children, thinking skills, Dyslexia, ADHD and left-handed children
Computer educational software
Teaching packs for parents and teachers

Publications list:
Available in print

Access to staff:
Contact by letter, by telephone and by fax. Appointment necessary.
Hours: 24-hour service

Connections with:
British Dyslexia Association
Dyslexia Information Centre
Dyslexia Institute
Irlen Institute
at the same address
National Association for Gifted Children (NAGC)

GIFTWARE ASSOCIATION

Acronym or abbreviation: GA

Federation House, 10 Vyse Street, Birmingham, B18 6LT

Tel: 0121 236 2657
Fax: 0121 236 3921
E-mail: enquiries@ga-uk.org

Website:
http://www.ga-uk.org
Events and seminars, product finder, membership.

Organisation type and purpose:
Membership organisation, the trade association for the UK gift and home industry.
Represents companies from across the gift and home industry – manufacturers, designers, wholesalers, importers, exporters, retailers (independents, multiples and online), from sole traders to major plcs.

Subject coverage:
UK gift and home industry.

Access to staff:
Contact by letter, by telephone, by fax and by e-mail

Constituent part of:
British Jewellery Giftware and Finishing Federation
at the same address

GILBERT AND SULLIVAN SOCIETY

7–20 Hampden Gurney Street, London, W1H 5AX

Enquiries:
Enquiries to: Honorary Secretary

Founded:
1924

Organisation type and purpose:
Membership association (membership is by subscription), registered charity (charity number 1062970).

Subject coverage:
The operas of Gilbert and Sullivan, their lives and their other works.

Museum or gallery collection, archive, or library special collection:
Society library held at the Barbican music library, London

Printed publications:
Gilbert and Sullivan News (3 times a year, free to members, on sale to non-members)

Access to staff:
Contact by letter
Hours: Mon to Fri, 0900 to 1700

Affiliated societies throughout the:
English speaking world

GILERA APPRECIATION SOCIETY

Acronym or abbreviation: GAS

Fox House, Moor Road, Langham, Colchester, Essex, CO4 5NR

Tel: 01206 272737

Fax: 01206 273064
E-mail: ged@fox-house.freeserve.co.uk

Website:
http://www.gilera.com
History of the Gilera marque, text and photographs for downloading and a search facility, links to other Gilera-related sites.

Enquiries:
Enquiries to: Information Officer

Founded:
1982

Formerly called:
Gilera Owners Club (GOC) (year of change 1987)

Organisation type and purpose:
Voluntary organisation.

Subject coverage:
History, and technical assistance on all models of the Gilera motorcycle from the earliest in 1909 until the final models in 1993; contemporary articles, road tests, manuals, sources of spare parts and relevant information appropriate to Gilera.

Museum or gallery collection, archive, or library special collection:
Sales brochures, handbooks, workshop manuals
Spare parts lists, exploded diagrams, contemporary magazine road tests, period b/w photographs

Non-library collection catalogue:
All or part available online and in-house

Library catalogue:
All or part available in-house

Printed publications:
Classic Bike
Classic Motorcycle Legends
International Classic Racer
The Classic Motorcycle

Electronic and video publications:
History of Gilera (CD-ROM)
Gilera 90th Anniversary in Arcore, Italy and Parades around Monza captured on video (VHS only)

Access to staff:
Contact by letter, by telephone, by e-mail and via website
Hours: Mon to Fri, 0900 to 2230 via telephone

Affiliated to:
Italian Motorcycle Owners Club
34 Pictor Road, Fairfield, Buxton, SK17 7TB; tel: 01298 79899

GILGAL SOCIETY

PO Box 53515, London, SE19 2TX

E-mail: info@gilgalsoc.org

Website:
http://www.gilgalsoc.org
About the Gilgal Society and routes to all other pages, including publications.
http://www.circinfo.com
Gilgal Publications online plus links to many related pages from other information suppliers.

Enquiries:
Enquiries to: Information Officer

Founded:
1988

Organisation type and purpose:
Voluntary organisation, publishing house, not-for-profit publisher.
Provision of accurate, medically approved, information regarding male sexual health, with special reference to circumcision.

Subject coverage:
Male genital health with special reference to circumcision.

Information services:
Medically approved information about male circumcision for all ages.

continued overleaf

Printed publications:
Have You Heard About the Benefits of
Circumcision? (A Guide for Men and Teens)
Circumcision: A Guide for Parents
Sex and Circumcision: What Every Woman Needs
to Know
Preparation and After-Care for Circumcision
(Infant or Child or Teen/Adult)
List of Possible Circumcisers (UK or Rest of World)
All About Being Circumcised (for 7–10-year-olds)
Glossary of Terms Related to Circumcision and the
Genital Organs
Myths, Lies and Half-Truths about Male
Circumcision
Parental Rights, Parental Duties
Questions Young People Ask About Male
Circumcision
Questions Girls Ask about Male Circumcision
Principal Methods of Male Circumcision
Adult Circumcision Account
Benefits of Male Circumcision
Circumcision – A Guide to a Decision
Order printed publications from: website: http://
www.gilgalsoc.org/sterlingorder.html

Electronic and video publications:
Adult Circumcision (video)
Ritual and Other Circumcisions (video)
Order electronic and video publications from: website:
http://www.gilgalsoc.org/sterlingorder.html

Publications list:
Available online and in print

Access to staff:
Contact by letter, by e-mail and via website.
Appointment necessary.
Hours: Daily, 0900 to 2000
Special comments: No direct access, no opening
hours.

Access to building, collection or gallery:
No access other than to staff

GILLETTE ADVANCED
TECHNOLOGY CENTRE UK

460 Basingstoke Road, Reading, Berkshire, RG2
0QE

Tel: 0118 987 5222
Fax: 0118 975 2822

Enquiries:
Enquiries to: Library and Information Services
Manager

Formerly called:
Gillette Research & Development Laboratory (year
of change 2002)

Organisation type and purpose:
Research organisation.

Subject coverage:
Shaving devices, toiletries, writing instruments.

Access to staff:
Contact by letter, by fax and by e-mail
Hours: Mon to Fri, 0800 to 1600

Access to building, collection or gallery:
No access other than to staff

Subsidiary of:
Gillette Company, USA

GIN AND VODKA ASSOCIATION

Formal name: Gin and Vodka Association of Great
Britain
Acronym or abbreviation: GVA

Cross Keys House, Queen Street, Salisbury,
Wiltshire, SP1 1EY

Tel: 01722 415892
Fax: 01722 415840
E-mail: gva@ginvodka.org.uk

Website:
http://www.ginvodka.org.

Enquiries:
Enquiries to: Director-General

Founded:
1991

Created by the merger of:
Gin Rectifiers and Distillers Association, and
Vodka Trade Association

Organisation type and purpose:
Trade association.

Subject coverage:
Gin and vodka industries; neutral alcohol industry,
specific regulations in sector, nationally and
internationally.

Trade and statistical information:
Data on UK gin and vodka industries, data on EC
spirits industry.

Printed publications:
Annual Report

Access to staff:
Contact by fax and by e-mail
Hours: Mon to Fri, 0900 to 1700

GINGERBREAD

255 Kentish Town Road, London, NW5 2LX

Tel: 0808 802 0925 (helpline); 020 7428 5400 (office)
Fax: 020 7482 4851
E-mail: info@gingerbread.org.uk

Website:
http://www.gingerbread.org.uk

Enquiries:
Enquiries to: Helpline.

Founded:
1918

Created by the merger of:
One Parent Families, and Gingerbread (year of
change 2007)

Organisation type and purpose:
Voluntary organisation, registered charity (charity
number 230750).
Campaigning and lobbying organisation.

Subject coverage:
Single parent families with reference to poverty,
social security, welfare rights, housing and
homelessness, equality of women, family law,
divorce, pregnancy and parenthood, child care.

Printed publications:
Annual Report
Publications (free to single parents) include:
- Help with reaching agreement when a
relationship ends
- Action when a relationship ends
- Claiming income support and child tax credits for
single parents who are not working or work
under 16 hours a week
- Claiming jobseeker's allowance for single parents
who are not working or work under 16 hours per
week
- Changing your child's name
- Child with additional needs
- Contact between your child and their other
parent
- Child maintenance tips
- Making arrangements for child maintenance
- Financial help for single parents who are not
working due to ill health
- Money for further education
- Sources of financial help
- Flexible new deal
- Getting legal help
- Money for high education students
- Help with household bills
- Holidays for single parents
- Housing options for single parents
- Financial help during maternity and adoption
- Help with moving into work
- Money matters
- Money sense
- Information for dads or mums who live apart
from their children
- Parental responsibility: rights and responsibility
for parents who live apart
- Residence: where a child normally lives

- Tax credits when your circumstances change
- Benefits and Tax credits if you work 16+ hours
- Money for teenage parents magazine
- Children with challenging behaviour

Publications list:
Available online and in print

Access to staff:
Contact by telephone
Hours: Mon to Fri, 0900 to 1700, Wed 0900 to 2000

Access to building, collection or gallery:
No access other than to staff

GIRLGUIDING SCOTLAND

16 Coates Crescent, Edinburgh, EH3 7AH

Tel: 0131 226 4511
Fax: 0131 220 4828
E-mail: administrator@girlguiding-scot.org.uk

Founded:
1910

Formerly called:
Guide Association Scotland; The Girl Guide
Association (Scotland) (year of change 1995)

Organisation type and purpose:
Helps girls to reach their potential through
programme of activities.

Subject coverage:
Guiding in Scotland.

Access to staff:
Contact by letter, by telephone and by fax.
Appointment necessary.
Hours: Mon to Fri, 0900 to 1700

Also at:
The Guide Association Scotland
Netherurd House, Blyth Bridge, West Linton,
EH46 7AQ; tel: 01968 682208; fax: 01968 682371

GIRLGUIDING UK

17–19 Buckingham Palace Road, London, SW1W
0PT

Tel: 020 7834 6242
Fax: 020 7828 8317
E-mail: chq@girlguding.org.uk

Website:
http://www.girlguiding.org.uk

Enquiries:
Enquiries to: Receptionist

Founded:
1910

Formerly called:
Guide Association; Girl Guides Association (year
of change 1994)

Organisation type and purpose:
Membership organisation, present number of
members: 575,000, voluntary organisation,
registered charity (charity number 306016).
Voluntary Interdenominational International
Uniformed Movement for Girls.

Subject coverage:
Guide training, outdoor pursuits, skills training,
service to community.

**Museum or gallery collection, archive, or library
special collection:**
Archives from 1910 to date
Books, documents, badges, uniforms,
photographs, exhibits

Non-library collection catalogue:
All or part available in-house

Library catalogue:
All or part available in-house

Printed publications:
Guiding Magazine
The Rainbows Annual
The Brownie Annual

Training books, handbooks, history books, activity books for all ages, etc.
Order printed publications from: The Guide Association, Trading Service, Atlantic Street, Broadheath, Altrincham, Cheshire, WA14 5EQ, tel: 0161 941 2237, fax: 0161 941 6326, e-mail: tradings@ girlguiding.org.uk

Publications list:
Available in print

Access to staff:
Contact by letter, by telephone, by fax, by e-mail and via website. Appointment necessary.
Hours: Mon to Fri, 0900 to 1700

Access to building, collection or gallery:
Prior appointment required
Hours: Archives: Mon to Fri, 1000 to 1600

Access for disabled people:
Ramped entry, access to all public areas, toilet facilities

Links with:
Scout Association

GIRLS' BRIGADE ENGLAND AND WALES, THE

Acronym or abbreviation: GB (England and Wales)

PO Box, 129 Broadway, Didcot, Oxfordshire, OX11 8XN

Tel: 01235 510425
Fax: 01235 510429
E-mail: admin@girlsbrigadeew.org.uk

Website:
http://www.girlsbrigadeew.org.uk

Enquiries:
Enquiries to: National Director

Founded:
1965

Formerly called:
Girls' Brigade of Ireland, Girls' Guildry, Girls' Life Brigade (year of change 1965)

Organisation type and purpose:
International organisation, membership association, registered charity (charity number 206655).
Christian youth organisation.

Subject coverage:
Children and youth issues; Duke of Edinburgh Award scheme; Christian teaching.

Museum or gallery collection, archive, or library special collection:
History of organisation – bound copies of GB Chronicle since 1900

Printed publications:
Annual Report
The View

Access to staff:
Contact by letter, by telephone, by fax, by e-mail, in person and via website. Appointment necessary.
Hours: Mon to Fri, 0900 to 1700

Affiliated to:
The Girls' Brigade Ireland
The Girls' Brigade N Ireland
The Girls' Brigade Scotland

GIRLS' FRIENDLY SOCIETY

Acronym or abbreviation: GFS Platform

GFS Platform, Unit 2, Angel Gate, 326 City Road, London EC1V 2PT

Tel: 020 7837 9669
E-mail: annualreport@gfsplatform.org.uk

Website:
http://www.gfsplatform.org.uk
General.

Enquiries:
Enquiries to: Director

Founded:
1875

Formerly called:
Girls' Friendly Society and Townsend Fellowship

Organisation type and purpose:
Membership association (membership is by subscription), present number of members: 1000, voluntary organisation, registered charity (charity number 1054310).

Subject coverage:
Parish-based work with girls and women. Youth and community work with women.

Museum or gallery collection, archive, or library special collection:
Girls' Friendly Society Archives from 1875

Printed publications:
Leaflets
Newsletter (2 times a year)

Access to staff:
Contact by letter, by telephone, by fax and by e-mail. Appointment necessary.
Hours: Mon to Fri, 0900 to 1700

Member of:
Anglican Voluntary Societies Forum
National Council for Voluntary Organisations
National Council for Voluntary Youth Services

GLAMORGAN ARCHIVES

Glamorgan Archives, Clos Parc Morgannwg, Leckwith, Cardiff, CF11 8AW

Tel: 029 2087 2200
E-mail: glamro@cardiff.gov.uk

Website:
http://www.glamro.gov.uk
Basic information, opening hours, location, main collections, leaflets, photocopying order forms, educational resources.

Founded:
1939

Formerly called:
Glamorgan Record Office (year of change 2010)

Organisation type and purpose:
Local government body.
Serving the authorities of Bridgend, Caerphilly, Cardiff, Merthyr Tydfil, Rhondda Cynon Taff and the Vale of Glamorgan.

Subject coverage:
History of Glamorgan.

Museum or gallery collection, archive, or library special collection:
Records of:
Glamorgan Quarter Sessions, Petty Sessions
Glamorgan County Council, Mid Glamorgan County Council, South Glamorgan County Council, Urban and district councils, boroughs
Local boards of health, burial boards, highway boards
Coroners, Poor Law unions, hospitals, police, vehicle licensing
Port of Cardiff Shipping Registers, crew agreements (Cardiff-registered ships)
Land tax assessments, registers of electors, schools and education
Business and industry (including iron companies – Dowlais Iron Company, Rhymney Iron Company, etc. and records of the South Wales Coalfield)
Estates, families and individuals
Maps and plans
Parish records for Glamorgan parishes in the Diocese of Llandaff
Civil Parishes
Non-conformist chapels and churches
Jewish synagogues and individuals
Quaker records for Wales
Societies and associations
Political records
Manorial records
Pictorial records

Non-library collection catalogue:
All or part available in-house

Printed publications:
Books on local history
Reproduction maps, engravings, watercolours, posters, documents

Publications list:
Available online and in print

Access to staff:
Contact by letter, by telephone, by e-mail and in person. Appointment necessary.
Hours: Mon, 1300 to 1700; Tue to Fri 0900 to 1700
Every 2nd Sat of the month, 0900 to 1200
Every 3rd Mon of the month, 1700 to 2000
Special comments: Closed Bank Holidays.

GLASGOW & WEST OF SCOTLAND FAMILY HISTORY SOCIETY

Acronym or abbreviation: G&WSFHS

Unit 13, 32 Mansfield Street, Glasgow, G11 5QP

Tel: 0141 339 8303

Website:
http://www.gwsfhs.org.uk
Subscription rates, details of services and facilities.

Enquiries:
Enquiries to: Librarian
Other contacts: Publications Secretary (for details of publications)

Founded:
1977

Organisation type and purpose:
Membership association (membership is by subscription), present number of members: 1,750–2,000, voluntary organisation, registered charity (charity number SC 010866), research organisation.
To promote the study of family history, particularly in Glasgow and the west of Scotland.

Subject coverage:
Genealogical research in Glasgow and the west of Scotland i.e. Argyll, Ayrshire, Bute, Dunbartonshire, Lanarkshire, Renfrewshire and Stirlingshire (part).

Non-library collection catalogue:
All or part available online and in-house

Library catalogue:
All or part available online and in-house

Printed publications:
See website for full list of publications

Microform publications:
1851 Census indexes for Old Monkland (microfiche, £7.50 per set, plus p&p)
Index to births and marriages in the Glasgow Herald in 1851 (fiche, £3.50 per set, plus p&p)
Index to deaths in the Glasgow Herald in 1851 (fiche, £4.50 per set, plus p&p)
1851 Census Index, Glasgow City East (12 fiche, £11 plus p&p)
1851 Census Index, Glasgow City West (11 fiche, £10 plus p&p)
1851 Census index for Renfrewshire (10 microfiches Set 1, £9; 15 microfiches Set 2, £12 plus p&p)
1851 Glasgow Herald – Index to Births, Marriages and Deaths (3 fiche, £3.50 plus p&p)

Electronic and video publications:
CD-ROM: 1851 Census Indexes for Lanarkshire, Dumbartonshire & Glasgow.
Burial indexes for Glasgow High Church & Govan

Publications list:
Available online and in print

Access to staff:
Contact by letter, by telephone and in person.
Access for members only.
Hours: Tue, Sat, 1400 to 1630; Thu, 1000 to 2030
Special comments: Only members have access to the research facilities.

continued overleaf

Access to building, collection or gallery:
No prior appointment required
Hours: Tue, Sat, 1400 to 1630; Thu, 1000 to 2030
Special comments: Members only.

Member of:
Scottish Association of Family History Societies
e-mail: longerlive@tiscali.co.uk

GLASGOW ARCHAEOLOGICAL SOCIETY

Acronym or abbreviation: GAS

Flat 1–2, 27 Kirkland Street, Glasgow, G22 6SY

Tel: 0141 287 3625

Website:
http://www.glasarchsoc.org.uk

Enquiries:
Enquiries to: Secretary
Direct tel: 0141 945 0447 (evenings)
Direct e-mail: james_mearns@yahoo.co.uk

Founded:
1856

Organisation type and purpose:
Learned society (membership is by subscription),
present number of members: 350.
Encouragement of interest and research in
archaeology, especially in the West of Scotland.

Subject coverage:
Archaeology, architecture, archives.

Printed publications:
Newsletter (3 times a year)
Scottish Archaeological Journal (2 times a year)

Publications list:
Available in print

Access to staff:
Contact by letter, by telephone, by e-mail and via
website
Hours: Mon to Fri, 0900 to 1700

Member of:
Council for Scottish Archaeology

GLASGOW ASSOCIATION FOR MENTAL HEALTH

Acronym or abbreviation: GAMH

St. Andrews by the Green, 33 Turnbull Street,
Glasgow, G1 5PR

Tel: 0141 552 5592
E-mail: info@gamh.org.uk

Website:
http://www.gamh.org.uk
Information on GAMH and changes to services

Enquiries:
Enquiries to: Advice and Resource Centre

Founded:
1979

Organisation type and purpose:
Membership association (membership is by
subscription), voluntary organisation, registered
charity (charity number SCO 11684).
Advice and resource centre.

Subject coverage:
Mental health in Glasgow, community-based
services, befriending home support, advocacy,
equalities project.

Printed publications:
Leaflets on the work of the Association and
services provided

Access to staff:
Contact by letter, by telephone, by fax, by e-mail
and via website. Appointment necessary.
Hours: Office 0900 to 1700, Fir, 0900 to 1630; Advice
and Resource Centre Tue, Fri, 1000 to 1600

Access for disabled people:
Parking provided, level entry, toilet facilites

Citywide services:
Advice and Resource Centre
tel: 0141 552 5592; e-mail: info@gamh.org.uk
Advocacy Matters
tel: 0141 559 5491; e-mail: advocacy@gamh.org
.uk
Carers Support Project
tel: 0141 429 7593; e-mail: carers@gamh.org.uk
Homeless Support Project
tel: 0141 554 6200; e-mail: homelesssupport@
gamh.org.uk
Supported Living Project
tel: 0141 429 6307; e-mail: supportedliving@
gamh.org.uk

Services in North and East Glasgow:
Active Outreach Team
tel: 0141 554 6200; e-mail: activeoutreach@gamh
.org.uk
Housing Support Project – East
tel: 0141 564 1206; e-mail: hspeast@gamh.org.uk
Housing Support Project – North
tel: 0141 587 1018; e-mail: hspnorth@gamh.org
.uk
North and East Community Project
tel: 0141 558 0943; e-mail: northeast@gamh.org
.uk
Scotia Clubhouse
tel: 0141 556 7766; e-mail: scotiaclubhouse@gamh
.org.uk

Services in South Glasgow:
Housing Support Project – South
tel: 0141 433 9393; e-mail: hspsouth@gamh.org
.uk
South Community Project
tel: 0141 423 0408; e-mail: south@gamh.org.uk
Young Carers Southside
tel: 0141 424 1708; e-mail: youngcarers@gamh
.org.uk

Services in West Glasgow:
Housing Support Project – West
tel: 0141 579 0013; e-mail: hspwest@gamh.org.uk
West Community Project
tel: 0141 357 2570; e-mail: west@gamh.org.uk
Young Carers Riverside
tel: 0141 424 1708; e-mail: youngcarers@gamh
.org.uk

GLASGOW CALEDONIAN UNIVERSITY LIBRARY IN THE SALTIRE CENTRE

Acronym or abbreviation: GCU

70 Cowcaddens Road, Glasgow, G4 0BA

Tel: 0141 273 1000
Fax: 0141 273 1000

Website:
http://www.gcal.ac.uk/library
General library information, contacts and external
links.

Enquiries:
Enquiries to: Director of Library Services
Direct tel: 0141 273 1180

Founded:
1992

Formed by the merger of:
Glasgow Polytechnic, Queen's College, Glasgow

Organisation type and purpose:
University library.

Subject coverage:
Biology, building and surveying, business
administration, computer studies, economics,
engineering, finance and accounting, health and
nursing studies, law and public administration,
management, mathematics, ophthalmic optics,
optometry and vision science, psychology, risk and
financial services, social sciences, social work,
hospitality and leisure, consumer studies,
physiotherapy, radiography, podiatry, nutrition,
orthoptics and occupational therapy.

Museum or gallery collection, archive, or library special collection:
Norman and Janey Buchan collection (left-wing
politics)
David Donald collection (left-wing politics)
Gallacher Memorial Library (left-wing politics)
Sandy Hobbs collection
George H Johannes collection (South Africa, ANC,
struggle against apartheid)
William Kemp collection (left-wing politics)
John Lenihan collection
Norrie McIntosh collection (left-wing politics)
Jim Milligan collection (left-wing politics)
Queen's College collection (home economics,
domestic science)
Samuel Stewart collection (left-wing politics)
Michael Scott collection (left-wing politics)
Scottish and Northern Book Distribution Centre
Limited collection (alternative politics, pressure
groups)

Library catalogue:
All or part available online

Printed publications:
Library Guides for students and staff and website

Publications list:
Available in print

Access to staff:
Letter of introduction required. Non-members
charged.
Hours: Mon to Thu, 0830 to 2100; Fri, 0830 to 1700;
Sat, Sun, 1000 to 1800

Access for disabled people:
Parking provided, access to all public areas, toilet
facilities

GLASGOW CITY COUNCIL

City Chambers, George Square, Glasgow, G2 1DU

Tel: 0141 287 2000
Fax: 0141 287 5666
E-mail: pr@glasgow.gov.uk

Website:
http://www.glasgow.gov.uk

Enquiries:
Enquiries to: Public Relations Manager
Direct tel: 0141 287 0901
Direct fax: 0141 287 0904

Founded:
April 1996

Organisation type and purpose:
Local government body, statutory body.
Local government.

Subject coverage:
Local government services.

Printed publications:
Glasgow (magazine, 6 times a year)
City Insider (staff magazine, monthly)

Publications list:
Available online and in print

Access to staff:
Contact by letter, by telephone, by e-mail and via
website
Hours: Mon to Fri, 0900 to 1700

GLASGOW COLLEGE OF NAUTICAL STUDIES

Library, 21 Thistle Street, Glasgow, G5 9XB

Tel: 0141 565 2582
Fax: 0141 565 2599
E-mail: resources@gcns.ac.uk

Website:
http://www.gcns.ac.uk
General college information.

Enquiries:
Enquiries to: Librarian
Direct e-mail: m.scalpello@gcns.ac.uk

Founded:
1969

Organisation type and purpose:
Suitable for ages: 16+.
Further education college.

Subject coverage:
Maritime studies, marine engineering,
telecommunications, instrumentation and control,
nautical science, social science, social care, sport
and leisure, beauty therapy, child care, drama,
professional writing.

Non-library collection catalogue:
All or part available in-house

Library catalogue:
All or part available online

Printed publications:
Library Guide

Access to staff:
Contact by letter, by telephone, by fax, by e-mail,
in person and via website
Hours: Term time: Mon, Tue, Thu, 0830 to 1930;
Wed, Fri, 0830 to 1630
Vacations: Mon to Fri, 0830 to 1630

Links with:
Glasgow Colleges Librarians Group (GCLG)

GLASGOW COUNCIL ON ALCOHOL

Acronym or abbreviation: GCA

Seventh Floor, Newton House, 457 Sauchiehall
Street, Glasgow G2 3LG

Tel: 0141 353 1800
Fax: 0141 353 1030
E-mail: email@thegca.org.uk

Website:
www.thegca.org.uk

Enquiries:
Enquiries to: Director

Founded:
1965

Organisation type and purpose:
Voluntary organisation, registered charity (charity
number SCO 14501).
The aim of GCA is to reduce alcohol abuse in the
community of Greater Glasgow.

Subject coverage:
Counselling, education and advice on alcohol and
alcohol abuse.

Access to staff:
Contact by letter, by telephone, by fax and in
person
Hours: Mon to Thu, 0900 to 2030; Fri, 0900 to 1645

Access for disabled people:
Toilet facilities

Affiliated to:
Alcohol Focus Scotland
2nd Floor, 166 Buchanan Street, Glasgow, G1
2NH; tel: 0141 333 9677; fax: 0141 333 1606; e-
mail: enquiries@alcohol-focus-scotland.org.uk

GLASGOW INTERNATIONAL JAZZ FESTIVAL

Formal name: Royal Bank Glasgow Jazz Festival
Acronym or abbreviation: GIJF

81 High Street, Glasgow, G1 1NB

Tel: 0141 552 3552
Fax: 0141 552 3592
E-mail: glasgow@jazzfest.co.uk

Website:
http://www.jazzfest.co.uk

Enquiries:
Enquiries to: Director
Direct e-mail: olive@jazzfest.co.uk

Founded:
1987

Organisation type and purpose:
Annual jazz festival organiser.
To present the best of international jazz and jazz
related music.

Subject coverage:
Jazz and blues.

**Museum or gallery collection, archive, or library
special collection:**
Photographic library
Previous festival programmes

Printed publications:
Brochure (pub in May)

Publications list:
Available online and in print

Access to staff:
Contact by letter, by telephone, by fax, by e-mail
and via website
Hours: Mon to Fri, 1000 to 1700

GLASGOW LIBRARIES, INFORMATION & LEARNING

Mitchell Library, North Street, Glasgow, G3 7DN

Tel: 0141 287 2999
Fax: 0141 287 2815
E-mail: lil@csglasgow.org

Website:
http://www.glasgowlibraries.org
New site under construction.

Enquiries:
Enquiries to: Head of Libraries and Archives
Direct tel: 0141 287 5114
Direct fax: 0141 287 5151
Other contacts: Information Services Manager for
specific remit for Mitchell Library.

Founded:
1877

Formerly called:
Glasgow City Libraries and Archives

Organisation type and purpose:
Local government body.
Public reference library.

Subject coverage:
General and business information, newspapers,
philosophy, religion, social sciences, language,
literature, science, technology, arts, recreation,
music, history and topography, particularly
Scottish, Glasgow collection.

**Museum or gallery collection, archive, or library
special collection:**
Andrew Bain Memorial Collection (4000 vols local
history)
Archives (records of the City of Glasgow)
Armour Donation (3600 vols German literature)
Bell Collection (450 pamphlets, Scottish Union)
British Standards (complete set)
Clem Edwards Donation (2000 vols Labour
Movement)
Cumming Pamphlets (185 pamphlets, Scottish
religion and education – 19th century)
Dante Collection (216 vols)
Donald Purchase (400 vols shorthand)
E A Reynolds Collection (711 vols Rationalist
literature)
E J Thomson Collection (500 vols Scottish
topography)
Forrester Pamphlets (500 pamphlets, religion –
19th century)
Gardyne Collection (1800 vols Scottish poetry)
Glasgow Collection (20,000 vols)
Gourlay Donation (1042 vols India)
Graham Collection (local history)
Henderson Purchase (2800 vols Celtic languages)
Hillhouse Purchase (300 vols draughts)
Inverclyde Donation (Inverclyde Family albums,
etc.)
J H Thomson Collection (1230 vols Covenanting
history)

Jenkins Donation (500 vols Spain)
Jervise Collection (1300 vols provincial poets of
Scotland)
Kidson Collection (9000 vols 18th century popular
music)
Lipton Collection (Sir Thomas Lipton albums, etc.)
McClelland Donation (350 vols phrenology)
Moncrieff Mitchell Collection (3000 vols and 100
prints, local history)
Moody Manners Collection (2900 vols vocal and
orchestral opera scores)
Morgan Collection (6000 vols pure and applied
science)
Morrison Collection (7000 vols theology)
New Church Collection (2000 vols)
North British Locomotive Company Collection
(10,000 items)
Patent Specifications (5,000,000 UK, US, European)
Private Press Collection (1600 vols)
R L Stevenson Collection (200 vols)
Reid Collection (850 vols angling)
Reid Donation (134 vols Social Credit)
Russell-Fergus Collection (20 vols history of the
harp)
Scottish Poetry Collection (15,000 vols including
4000 vols on Robert Burns)
Scouler Collection (2000 vols science and
philosophy, 16th to 19th centuries)
Slains Castle Collection (3100 vols theology,
literature, travel, 16th to 18th centuries)
Smeal Collection (117 vols anti-slavery)
Trade Unions Collection (2500 vols)
UK and Scottish Newspapers
UK patents and specifications
United Nations Collection (10,000 vols)
Wallace and Bruce Collection (310 vols)
Whitton Bequest (347 vols botany, horticulture,
etc.)
William ('Crimea') Simpson Collection (103 items)
Wotherspoon Collection (41 vols Clyde
steamships)

Trade and statistical information:
A wide selection of trade and statistical
information, including market research reports,
is available in the business information and
social sciences sections.

Non-library collection catalogue:
All or part available in-house

Library catalogue:
All or part available in-house

Printed publications:
Books on the history, social and literary life of the
area including:
City of the Dead – the story of Glasgow's Southern
Necropolis (Hutt C, £4.99)
Glasgow Illustrated (Fairful-Smith G, £7.99)
Imagining a City, 20th Century Glasgow Writing (a
catalogue, Burgess M, £3.99)
Queen's Park, Historical & Heritage Walk
(Marshall I and Smith R, £2.99)
The King's Grocer. The Life of Sir Thomas Lipton
(Crampsey B, £9.99)
The Seeing Eye (Oliver G, £9.99)
West of Scotland Census Returns and Old
Parochial Registers (Escott A, 50p)
Order printed publications from: Stock control
at the same address, tel: 0141 287 2812, fax: 0141
287 2815

Publications list:
Available in print

Access to staff:
Contact by letter, by telephone, by fax, by e-mail
and in person
Hours: Mon to Thu, 0900 to 2000; Fri, Sat, 0900 to
1700
Archives: Mon to Thu, 0930 to 1645; Fri, 0930 to
1600; or by appointment

Access for disabled people:
Parking provided, toilet facilities
Special comments: Parking by prior arrangement via
duty librarian.
Level entry via Kent Road.

GLASGOW METROPOLITAN COLLEGE

230 Cathedral Street, Glasgow, G1 2TG

Tel: 0141 566 1664
Fax: 0141 566 1666
E-mail: tony.donnelly@glasgowmet.ac.uk

Website:
http://www.glasgowmet.ac.uk/library
Catalogue, subject-focused guides to electronic, e-book and book collections, copyright and other guides.

Enquiries:
Enquiries to: Chief Librarian
Direct tel: 0141 566 1550

Founded:
2005

Created by the merger of:
Glasgow College of Food Technology (f. 1972) and Glasgow College of Building and Printing (year of change 2005)

Organisation type and purpose:
Further Education.

Subject coverage:
Construction, design, ESOL, commmunication and media, printing, sports science, tourism, health and safety, food technology, food science, food processing, hospitality and catering, professional cookery, travel and tourism.

Library catalogue:
All or part available online

Access to staff:
Contact by letter, by telephone, by fax, by e-mail, in person and via website. Appointment necessary. Non-members charged.
Hours: Term time: Mon to Wed, 0800 to 1930; Thu, 1000 to 1700; Fri, 0800 to 1700.
Vacation: Mon to Fri, 0900 to 1600

Access for disabled people:
Parking provided, ramped entry, access to all public areas, toilet facilities

Links with:
Glasgow Caledonian University (GCU)
Cowcaddens Road, Glasgow, G4 0BA

GLASGOW MUSEUMS

Culture & Leisure Services, 20 Trongate, Glasgow, G1 5ES

Tel: 0141 271 8310
Fax: 0141 271 8354
E-mail: museums@cls.glasgow.gov.uk

Website:
http://www.glasgowmuseums.com
Links to all the related museums and galleries

Enquiries:
Enquiries to: Director
Direct tel: 0141 287 2600
Other contacts: Marketing Officer

Founded:
1901

Formerly called:
Glasgow Museums and Art Galleries

Organisation type and purpose:
Local government body, museum, art gallery, suitable for all ages.
Glasgow Museums is the corporate title for Glasgow City Council, Culture & Leisure Services, Museums Service, and administers Glasgow's 12 municipal museums and art galleries.

Subject coverage:
The subjects covered by the twelve museums of Glasgow include art, history, British history, worldwide ethnography, sociology, natural history, history of science, history of transport, religious history and content and conservation science.

Information services:
Selective dissemination services; The Open Museum Department lends objects and displays to community groups in Glasgow and Strathclyde. Glasgow Museums offers touring exhibitions to venues in UK and elsewhere. For Museum Education Department tel: 0141 276 9368.

Special visitor services:
Tape recorded guides, materials and/or activities for children.

Education services:
Group education facilities.

Trade and statistical information:
Glasgow's municipal art and design collections of over 1 million objects, a substantial proportion of which relate to the City's artistic, cultural, political and social history.

Non-library collection catalogue:
All or part available in print

Printed publications:
Variety of publications including:
Patterns of Childhood: Samplers from Glasgow Museums (£9.99)
One Million Days in China (£6.99)
Guide to the Museum of Transport (£5.99)
Guide to Provand's Lordship (£5.99)
Millet to Matisse – 19th century painting from Kelvingrove Art Gallery (£35)
Art Treasures of Kelvingrove (£7.99)
Glasgow's Spitfire (£12.99)
What Do You Want to Say? Communicating through Exhibitions – a Guide for Community Groups (free)
Annual Benchmarking Report (free)
I Knew I Was Painting for My Life – Holocaust Artworks of Marianne Grant (£5)
Glasgow's Hidden Treasure – Charles Rennie Mackintosh's Ingram Street Tearooms (£5.99)
Preview Magazine (free of charge)
Glasgow Art Gallery and Museum: The Buildings and the Collections (£6.95)
Guide to the Museum of Transport (£2.95)
The Burrell Collection: a guide (£6.95)
The People's Palace and Glasgow Green (E King, £3.99)
The St Mungo Museum of Religious Life and Art (M O'Neill, £4.99)
The Strike of the Glasgow Weavers (E King, £1.65)
Order printed publications from: Marketing Department, Culture and Leisure Services, Martyrs' School, Parson Street, Glasgow, G4 0PX

Publications list:
Available online and in print

Access to staff:
Contact by letter, by telephone, by fax and by e-mail. Appointment necessary.
Hours: Mon to Thu, Sat, 1000 to 1700; Fri, Sun, 1100 to 1700

Access to building, collection or gallery:
Prior appointment required

Access for disabled people:
Parking provided, level entry, access to all public areas, toilet facilities

Museums and Galleries:
Burrell Collection
2060 Pollokshaws Road, Glasgow, G43 1AT; tel: 0141 287 2550; fax: 0141 287 2597
Fossil Grove
Victoria Park, Glasgow, G14 1BN; tel: 0141 287 2000
Gallery of Modern Art (GoMA)
Royal Exchange Square, Glasgow, G1 3AH; tel: 0141 229 1996; fax: 0141 204 5316
Glasgow Museums Resource Centre (GMRC)
200 Woodhead Road, Nitshill, Glasgow, G53 7NN; tel: 0141 276 9300; fax: 0141 276 9305
Kelvingrove Art Gallery & Museum
Argyle Street, Glasgow, G3 8AG; tel: 0141 287 2699; fax: 0141 287 2690
Martyrs' School (by appointment only)
Parson Street, Glasgow, G4 0PX; tel: 0141 553 2557; fax: 0141 271 8354

McLellan Galleries (currently closed)
270 Sauchiehall Street, Glasgow, G2 3EH; tel: 0141 565 4137; fax: 0141 565 4111
Museum of Transport
1 Bunhouse Road, Glasgow, G3 8DP; tel: 0141 287 2720; fax: 0141 287 2692
Open Museum
Glasgow Museums Resource Centre, 200 Woodhead Road, Nitshill, Glasgow, G53 7NN; tel: 0141 276 9368; fax: 0141 276 9305
People's Palace and Winter Gardens
Glasgow Green, Glasgow, G40 1AT; tel: 0141 271 2951; fax: 0141 271 2960
Pollok Country Park, Pollok House (Managed by The National Trust for Scotland)
Pollok Country Park, 2060 Pollokshaws Road, Glasgow, G43 1AT; tel: 0141 616 6410; fax: 0141 616 6521; website: www.nts.org.uk
Provand's Lordship
3 Castle Street, Glasgow, G4 0RB; tel: 0141 552 8819; fax: 0141 552 4744
Scotland Street School Museum
225 Scotland Street, Glasgow, G5 8QB; tel: 0141 287 0500; fax: 0141 287 0515
St Mungo Museum of Religious Life and Art
2 Castle Street, Glasgow, G4 0RH; tel: 0141 553 2557; fax: 0141 552 4744

Parent body:
Glasgow City Council, Culture and Leisure Services
20 Trongate, Glasgow, G1 5ES; tel: 0141 287 4350; fax: 0141 287 5558

GLASGOW PHILHARMONIC MALE VOICE CHOIR

c/o John McFarlane, 5 Chapelton Avenue, Bearsden, Glasgow, G61 2RE

Tel: 0141 586 5195
E-mail: john.mcfarlane4@ntlworld.com

Website:
http://www.glasphilmvc.org.uk

Enquiries:
Enquiries to: General Secretary

Founded:
1925

Organisation type and purpose:
Membership association (membership is by subscription), present number of members: 60.

Subject coverage:
Male voice choral singing.

Museum or gallery collection, archive, or library special collection:
Large library of male voice music, now accommodated in the Mitchell Library, Glasgow

Non-library collection catalogue:
All or part available in-house

Access to staff:
Contact by letter, by e-mail and via website
Hours: daily, before 2200

GLASGOW SCHOOL OF ART

Acronym or abbreviation: GSA

Library, 167 Renfrew Street, Glasgow, G3 6RQ

Tel: 0141 353 4500
Fax: 0141 353 4670
E-mail: c.nicholson@gsa.ac.uk

Website:
http://www.gsa.ac.uk/library
Access information, details of collections, on line catalogue.

Enquiries:
Enquiries to: Head of Learning Resources
Direct tel: 0141 353 4550
Other contacts: Archivist for extensive archives of GSA and of art and design generally.

Founded:
1845

Organisation type and purpose:
University library.
Art college library.

Subject coverage:
Fine art and design, architecture, art history.

Museum or gallery collection, archive, or library special collection:
Books, exhibition catalogues, newspaper cuttings and other documents relating to the history of the School, its staff and students
Glasgow School of Art Archives
Hill and Adamson Collection of photographic calotypes and carbon prints

Library catalogue:
All or part available online

Access to staff:
Contact by letter, by telephone and by e-mail. Non-members charged.
Hours: Term Time: Mon to Thu, 0930 to 1945; Fr, 0930 to 1645
Vacations: Mon to Fri, 0930 to 1645

Access for disabled people:
Ramped entry, toilet facilities,

GLASGOW WOMEN'S LIBRARY

Acronym or abbreviation: GWL

15 Berkeley Street, Glasgow, G3 7BW

Tel: 0141 248 9969
E-mail: info@womenslibrary.org.uk

Website:
http://www.womenslibrary.org.uk

Founded:
1991

Organisation type and purpose:
A registered charity (charity number SC029881) and a registered company (number 178507), maintaining a lending library, archive collections and historical artifacts.

Subject coverage:
Women's lives, histories and achievements.

Education services:
Lifelong Learning Programme, Adult Literacy and Numeracy Project and a Black and Minority Ethnic Women's Project.

Non-library collection catalogue:
All or part available online

Library catalogue:
All or part available online

Access to staff:
Contact by letter, by telephone, by e-mail, in person and via website
Hours: Mon to Fri, 0930 to 1700

Access to building, collection or gallery:
Pending major refurbishment of new premises, the majority of the collection is in storage and access is limited.
Hours: Mon to Fri, 0930 to 1700

Access for disabled people:
Please contact the Library about accessibility

GLASSFIBRE REINFORCED CONCRETE ASSOCIATION

Acronym or abbreviation: GRCA

c/o The Concrete Society, Riverside House, 4 Meadows Business Park, Station Approach, Blackwater, Camberley, Surrey, GU17 9AB

Tel: 01276 607140
Fax: 01276 607141
E-mail: enquiries@grca.org.uk

Website:
http://www.grca.co.uk
General information on GRC, list of members, industry news, technical information.

Enquiries:
Enquiries to: Adviser

Founded:
1975

Organisation type and purpose:
International organisation, advisory body, trade association (membership is by subscription). Technical database for GRC industry.
Creation of CEN standards and representation on non-UK trade associations, relevant to the CRC (GFRC) industry.

Subject coverage:
Technical advice and sourcing of suppliers of glassfibre reinforced concrete.

Printed publications:
GRC In Action
Practical Design Guide
Proceedings of biennial Congresses since 1977
Register of Members
Technical information
Test Methods
Order printed publications from: The Concrete Bookshop, Riverside House, 4 Meadows Business Park, Station Approach, Blackwater, Camberley, Surrey, GU17 9AB; tel: 01276 607140; fax: 01276 607141; e-mail: enquiries@concretebookshop.com; website: http://www.concretebookshop.com

Electronic and video publications:
GRC Practical Fixing Guide Parts 1 & 2
Order electronic and video publications from: The Concrete Bookshop

Publications list:
Available online and in print

Access to staff:
Contact by letter, by telephone, by fax, by e-mail and via website. Appointment necessary.
Hours: Mon to Fri, 0900 to 1700

Access to building, collection or gallery:
No prior appointment required

Administered by:
The Concrete Society
Riverside House, 4 Meadows Business Park, Station Approach, Blackwater, Camberley, Surrey, GU17 9AB; tel: 01276 607140; fax: 01276 607141; website: http://www.concrete.org.uk

GLAXOSMITHKLINE

North Lonsdale Road, Ulverston, Cumbria, LA12 9DR

Tel: 01229 582261
Fax: 01229 482282

Enquiries:
Enquiries to: Technical Information Officer
Direct tel: 01229 482232
Direct fax: 01229 482257

Formerly called:
Glaxo Wellcome Operations

Organisation type and purpose:
Manufacturing industry, research organisation.

Subject coverage:
Pharmaceutical development and production.

GLAXOSMITHKLINE, RESEARCH AND DEVELOPMENT

New Frontiers Science Park (North), Third Avenue, Harlow, Essex, CM19 5AW

Tel: 01279 622000
Fax: 01279 622100

Website:
http://www.gsk.com
General GlaxoSmithKline information. No information on the library.

Enquiries:
Enquiries to: Librarian

Formerly called:
Beecham Pharmaceuticals Research Division, SmithKline Beecham Pharmaceuticals, Research and Development

Organisation type and purpose:
Research organisation.

Subject coverage:
Organic chemistry, pharmacology, neurosciences.

Non-library collection catalogue:
All or part available in-house

Library catalogue:
All or part available in-house

Access to staff:
Contact by letter and by e-mail
Hours: Mon to Fri, 0900 to 1700

Access to building, collection or gallery:
No access other than to staff
Special comments: No access to library.

Subsidiary of:
GlaxoSmithKline

GLOBAL EDUCATION MILTON KEYNES

Acronym or abbreviation: GEMK

Priory Rise School, Bronte Avenue, Tattenhoe Park, Milton Keynes, MK4 3GE

Tel: 01908 505777
E-mail: info@gemk.org.uk

Website:
http://www.gemk.org.uk

Enquiries:
Enquiries to: Information Officer
Other contacts: Centre Co-ordinator

Founded:
1980

Formerly called:
Milton Keynes World Development Education Centre (year of change 2001)

Organisation type and purpose:
Charitable company (charity number 1086858; company number 4102062), training organisation, resource centre.
Public education in the field of sustainability, global issues and world development.

Subject coverage:
Materials for teachers and community workers on world development issues, e.g. food, water, population, India, Ghana, Tanzania, schools-linking, recycling and disability, sustainable development and citizenship.

Special visitor services:
Resource Centre with loan facility for members.

Education services:
Provides support for Sustainable Schools, Global Schools, Sustainable Communities and for teachers and others seeking to bring a global dimension to their work.

Museum or gallery collection, archive, or library special collection:
Everyday items from India, Ghana, Tanzania
Recycled items commonly made in Ghana and Zambia

Printed publications:
Annual Report (free)
Commonwealth Common Waste (now available online)
When Chemistry Goes Bang! Primary School Musical to help teachers tackle the Preventing Violent Extremism Agenda (available autumn 2010)

Electronic and video publications:
Compelling Learning Day Toolkit on Sustainable Communities (aimed at secondary schools)

Access to staff:
Contact by letter, by telephone and by e-mail. Appointment necessary.

continued overleaf

Hours: By appointment; restricted availability in the school holidays

Links with:
Development Education Association
CAN Mezzanine 32–36 Loman Street London
SE1 0EH; tel: 020 7922 7930; fax: 020 7922 7929;
e-mail: dea@dea.org.uk

GLOBAL SCHOOL PARTNERSHIPS

Acronym or abbreviation: GSP

British Council, 10 Spring Gardens, London, SW1A 2BN

Tel: 020 7389 4031
Fax: 020 7389 4426
E-mail: globalschools@britishcouncil.org

Website:
http://www.dfid.gov.uk/globalschools.htm

Enquiries:
Enquiries to: Marketing, Sales and Communications Manager
Direct e-mail: andrea.mason@britishcouncil.org

Founded:
2003

Organisation type and purpose:
Registered charity.

Printed publications:
Partners in Learning: A Guide to Successful Global School Partnerships

Electronic and video publications:
Partners in Learning (.pdf format)
One World, One People (DVD)
The Partnership Journey (DVD)
Order electronic and video publications from: Website:
http://www.difid.gov.uk/globalschools

Publications list:
Available in print

Access to staff:
Contact by letter, by telephone, by fax and by e-mail
Hours: Mon to Fri, 0900 to 1730

Constituent part of:
British Council

GLOSCAT

Formal name: Gloucestershire College of Arts and Technology

Princess Elizabeth Way, Cheltenham, Gloucestershire, GL51 7SJ

Tel: 01242 532000
Fax: 01242 532196
E-mail: info@gloscat.ac.uk

Website:
http://www.gloscat.ac.uk
GLOSCAT Learning Centres – opening hours, staff, services.

Enquiries:
Enquiries to: Librarian
Direct tel: 01242 532185

Organisation type and purpose:
College of further education.

Subject coverage:
Cheltenham site: bakery, beauty therapy, business studies, caring, catering, clerical, computing, GCSEs, hairdressing, home economics, hotels, languages, leisure studies, science, secretarial, textiles, tourism.
Brunswick site: building studies, construction, design, electronic communication engineering, electronic engineering, manufacturing engineering, motor vehicles, surveying.

Library catalogue:
All or part available in-house

Access to staff:
Contact by letter, by telephone, by fax, by e-mail and via website

Hours: Mon to Fri, 0900 to 1700

Access to building, collection or gallery:
No prior appointment required
Hours: Cheltenham: term time: Mon, Wed, Thu, 0830 to 2000; Tue 0930 to 2000; Fri, 0830 to 1700
Brunswick: term time: Mon, Wed, Thu, 0830 to 2000; Tue 0930 to 2000; Fri, 0830 to 1700; Sat, 1015 to 1345
Both sites, vacations: Mon to Fri, 0900 to 1700
Special comments: Reference only.

Access for disabled people:
Level entry, access to all public areas, toilet facilities

Other site at:
GLOSCAT
Brunswick Campus, Brunswick Road, Gloucester, GL1 1HU; tel: 01452 426530; fax: 01452 426531

GLOUCESTER CITY COUNCIL

North Warehouse, The Docks, Gloucester, GL1 2EP

Tel: 01452 522232
Fax: 01452 396140
E-mail: thecouncil@gloucester.gov.uk

Website:
http://www.gloucester.gov.uk

Enquiries:
Enquiries to: Head of Communications and Marketing
Direct tel: 01452 396133
Direct fax: 01452 396334

Organisation type and purpose:
Local government body.

Subject coverage:
Local government services.

Access to staff:
Contact by letter, by telephone, by fax, by e-mail, in person and via website. Appointment necessary.
Hours: Mon to Fri, 0830 to 1700

GLOUCESTER LIBRARY

Brunswick Road, Gloucester, GL1 1HT

Tel: 01452 426979\ Minicom no. 01452 426975
Fax: 01452 521468

Website:
http://www.gloscc.gov.uk/pubserv/gcc/clams
Gloucestershire and its heritage; individual library pages.

Enquiries:
Enquiries to: Librarian

Founded:
1900

Organisation type and purpose:
Public library.

Non-library collection catalogue:
All or part available online and in-house

Library catalogue:
All or part available in-house

Access to staff:
Contact by letter, by telephone, by fax, by e-mail, in person and via website
Hours: Mon, Tue, Thu, 1000 to 1930; Wed, Fri, 1000 to 1700; Sat, 0900 to 1300

Access for disabled people:
Access to all public areas, toilet facilities

Parent body:
Gloucestershire County Library, Arts and Museum Service
Quayside House, Shire Hall, Gloucester, GL1 2HY

GLOUCESTERSHIRE ARCHIVES

Acronym or abbreviation: GA

Clarence Row, Alvin Street, Gloucester, GL1 3DW

Tel: 01452 425295
Fax: 01452 426378
E-mail: archives@gloucestershire.gov.uk

Website:
http://www.gloucestershire.gov.uk/archives
All archive catalogues online

Enquiries:
Enquiries to: Head of Information Management and Archives
Other contacts: Customer Services Manager (for specific historical enquiries)

Founded:
1936

Formerly called:
Gloucestershire Record Office (year of change 2006)

Incorporates the former:
Gloucestershire Collection (local studies collection) (year of change 2005)

Organisation type and purpose:
Local government body.
An amalgamation of the County Record Office, the Gloucester Diocesan Archives and the Gloucester City Archives; also houses the Victoria History of Gloucestershire and the Gloucester Local Studies Collection.
Aims to preserve locally generated historical records of the county and all its communities dating from earliest times to the present day. The documents are kept in strong-rooms at the Record Office but ownership is retained by depositors.

Subject coverage:
Local history and topography of Gloucestershire and all its towns and parishes; biography, demography, genealogy, history of churches, landed estates, organisations, businesses, charities within the county; contribution of Gloucestershire to regional and national history.

Museum or gallery collection, archive, or library special collection:
Archives of: the diocese of Gloucester, Gloucestershire County Council and its predecessors, all district councils and predecessor town and borough councils, City of Gloucester, boroughs of Tewkesbury and Cheltenham, also nonconformist churches, charities, schools, businesses and antiquarian collections
Many family collections including St Aldwyn, Lloyd-Baker, Bathurst, Hicks-Beach, Beaufort, Blathwayt, Codrington, Sherborne
Gloucestershire Local Studies Collection

Non-library collection catalogue:
All or part available online and in-house

Microform publications:
Microfilm of any document to order
Microfiche of parish registers for sale

Publications list:
Available online and in print

Access to staff:
Contact by letter, by telephone, by fax, by e-mail, in person and via website
Hours: Tue, Wed, Fri, 0900 to 1700; Thu, 0900 to 1830; Sat, 0900 to 1300

Access for disabled people:
Access to all public areas

Also at:
Gloucestershire Archives
Shire Hall Record Centre, Westgate Street, Gloucester, GL1 2TG; tel: 01452 425289

Parent body:
Gloucestershire County Council
Community and Adult Care Directorate

GLOUCESTERSHIRE LIBRARIES & INFORMATION

Quayside House, Shire Hall, Gloucester, GL1 2HY

Tel: 0845 230 5420
Fax: 01452 452042
E-mail: libraryhelp@gloucestershire.gov.uk

Website:
http://www.gloucestershire.gov.uk/libraries
http://www.searchourshelves.gloucestershire.gov
.uk/TalisPrism/

Enquiries:
Enquiries to: Ask Us Enquiry Service.
Direct tel: 0845 230 5421
Direct e-mail: ask@gloucestershire.gov.uk

Organisation type and purpose:
Local government body, public library.
Library headquarters, there are 39 libraries in the
County.

Subject coverage:
General reference, business information,
Gloucestershire local studies & family history,
Gloucestershire arts and crafts.

Information services:
Ask Us Enquiry Service offers information support
by phone, e-mail, letter and website form. The Ask
us service supports reference services in all
Gloucestershire Libraries.
Gloucester library holds the Europe Direct service
and official publications collection. Cheltenham
also has a reference collection, including Art
collection.

Education services:
Library Services for Education, tel: 01452 427240

Services for disabled people:
For the visually impaired; for the hearing
impaired.

**Museum or gallery collection, archive, or library
special collection:**
Art Collection – Cheltenham
Europe Direct – Gloucester
Cheltenham Local & Family History Library
Tewkesbury, Stroud, Cirencester, Stow on the Wold
& Cinderford Libraries all have Local & Family
history collections.

Trade and statistical information:
From Ask Us Enquiry Service.

Non-library collection catalogue:
All or part available online

Access to staff:
Contact by letter, by telephone, by fax, by e-mail
and via website
Hours: Mon to Fri, 0900 to 1700

Parent body:
Gloucestershire County Council

Strategic libraries at:
Cheltenham, Cinderford, Cirencester, Gloucester,
Stroud and Tewkesbury

GLOUCESTERSHIRE LOCAL HISTORY COMMITTEE

Community House, 15 College Green, Gloucester,
GL1 2LZ

Tel: 01452 528491
Fax: 01452 528493
E-mail: glosrcc@grcc.org.uk

Website:
http://www.gloshistory.org.uk
Titles of articles in Gloucestershire History 1987 to
date
List of Gloucestershire Local History speakers
Current local history societies' meetings

Enquiries:
Enquiries to: Secretary

Founded:
1948

Organisation type and purpose:
Voluntary organisation.

Subject coverage:
Local history and archaeology of Gloucestershire,
local history and activities within Gloucestershire.

Printed publications:
Gloucestershire History (annually)
Local History Newsletter (annually, free with
  above)

Access to staff:
Contact by letter, by telephone, by fax and by e-
mail
Hours: 0900 to 1700

Constituent part of:
Gloucestershire Rural Community Council
(GRCC)

GLUED LAMINATED TIMBER ASSOCIATION

Formal name: Glued Laminated Timber Association
– GLULAM
Acronym or abbreviation: GLTA

Chiltern House, Stocking Lane, Hughenden Valley,
High Wycombe, Buckinghamshire, HP14 4ND

Tel: 01494 565180
Fax: 01494 565487
E-mail: sales@glulam.co.uk

Website:
http://www.glulam.co.uk
Technical and pictorial information, list of
members and their contact details.

Enquiries:
Enquiries to: Secretary

Founded:
1987

Organisation type and purpose:
Trade association (membership is by subscription),
present number of members: 6.
To promote the awareness and use of glued
laminated timber in the UK.

Printed publications:
Publications free, available from the secretariat

Electronic and video publications:
Publications available to download from our
  website

Access to staff:
Contact by letter, by telephone, by fax, by e-mail
and via website
Hours: Mon to Fri, 0900 to 1700
Special comments: Visitors not normally received by
secretariat.

GLYNDWR UNIVERSITY

Library, Postal Point 22L, Glyndwr Univeristy,
Mold Road, Wrexham, LL11 2AW

Tel: 01978 293338
Fax: 01978 293435
E-mail: enquirydesk@glyndwr.ac.uk

Website:
http://www.glyndwr.ac.uk
Information about Glyndwr and its services.

Enquiries:
Enquiries to: Library Services Manager
Other contacts: University Librarian

Founded:
2008

Formerly called:
North East Wales Institute of Higher Education
(year of change 2008)

Organisation type and purpose:
University library, suitable for ages: 18+.

Subject coverage:
Creative industries, computing, engineering,
education, art and design, health, sciences, social
work, business and management, humanities.

Library catalogue:
All or part available online

Access to staff:
Contact by letter, by telephone, by fax, by e-mail
and in person

Hours: Term time: Mon to Thu, 0845 to 2100; Fri,
0845 to 1700; Sat, 1000 to 1700
Vacation: Mon to Fri, 0845 to 1200

Access for disabled people:
Parking provided, level entry, toilet facilities

GMB

22–24 Worple Road, Wimbledon, London, SW19
4DD

Tel: 020 8947 3131
Fax: 020 8944 6552
E-mail: info@gmb.org.uk

Website:
http://www.gmb.org.uk/

Enquiries:
Enquiries to: General Secretary

Founded:
1889

Formerly called:
FTAT, National Union of Tailor and Garment
Workers (NUTGW); General & Municipal Workers
(GMW) (year of change 1987)

Organisation type and purpose:
Trade union (membership is by subscription),
present number of members: 600,000, voluntary
organisation.

Subject coverage:
Industrial relations, collective bargaining,
employment law, occupational pensions, health
and safety at work, job education, work study.

**Museum or gallery collection, archive, or library
special collection:**
Agreements on wages and conditions of work with
  companies where GMB is recognised (accessible
  to public only by special arrangement)

Printed publications:
Bargaining Brief (information service to members)
Booklets, covering the above subjects (TOPICS)
Action (journal)

Publications list:
Available in print

Access to staff:
Contact by letter and by fax
Hours: Mon to Fri, 0900 to 1700

Access for disabled people:
Parking provided, ramped entry, access to all
public areas, toilet facilities

Affiliated to:
The Labour Party
Trades Union Congress

GO! SIGN

Formal name: Go! Sign – Christ in the Deaf
Community

E-mail: via website

Website:
http://www.gosign.org.uk
Aims and activities.

Founded:
1998

Organisation type and purpose:
Registered charity dedicated to serving the
spiritual and social needs of deaf people, their
families and friends.
To advance the Christian faith, particularly
amongst deaf people, to support deaf people, to
promote full participation for deaf people in their
communities.

Subject coverage:
GRACE programme:
- Growth in the network of deaf Christian groups,
leaders, churches, fellowship and individuals.
- Renewal and spiritual growth through training,
support, events and conferences.

continued overleaf

- Access to information promoting deaf Christian issues, support and service provisions.
- Churches: strengthening members through deaf spiritual awareness, network support and equipping.
- Evangelism via drama shows, video resources and training.

Education services:
Summer school.

Electronic and video publications:
Magazine (quarterly)
e-News (occasional e-mail)
Order electronic and video publications from: Website

Access to staff:
Contact via website

GOETHE-INSTITUT

Library, 50 Princes Gate, Exhibition Road, London, SW7 2PH

Tel: 020 7596 4040
Fax: 020 7594 0230
E-mail: library@london.goethe.org

Website:
http://www.goethe.de
http://www.goethe.de/ins/gb/lon/inz/bib/enindex
.htm

Enquiries:
Enquiries to: Information Officer

Organisation type and purpose:
International organisation.
Cultural organisation.

Subject coverage:
Germany: general information on all aspects, German books with some English translations covering all fields in the arts, history, humanities and social sciences, language, emphasis on German literature, contemporary history, art and language.

Library catalogue:
All or part available online and in-house

Printed publications:
Catalogue of DVDs and videos

Access to staff:
Contact by letter, by telephone, by fax, by e-mail, in person and via website
Hours: Mon to Thu, 1300 to 1830; Sat, 1300 to 1700

Links with:
Goethe-Institut München
    Dachauer Strasse 122, München, D-80637, Germany

GOETHE-INSTITUT GLASGOW, GERMAN CULTURAL INSTITUTE

3 Park Circus, Glasgow, G3 6AX

Tel: 0141 332 2555
Fax: 0141 343 1656
E-mail: library@glasgow.goethe.org

Website:
http://www.goethe.de/glasgow
Language and cultural programmes, general library and cultural information, online catalogue.

Enquiries:
Enquiries to: Librarian
Other contacts: Language Office (for language courses in Glasgow and Germany, scholarships for Scottish teachers of German and seminars)

Founded:
1973

Formerly called:
Goethe-Institut Inter Nationes; Goethe-Institut (year of change 2001)

Organisation type and purpose:
International organisation.
Promotion of the German language at all levels of education and of international cultural co-operation, library and information service.

Subject coverage:
German language, literature, culture and teaching.

Museum or gallery collection, archive, or library special collection:
Library, books, videos, cassettes, CD-ROMs, DVDs, CDs

Non-library collection catalogue:
All or part available online and in-house

Library catalogue:
All or part available online and in-house

Printed publications:
Library acquisitions lists (once or twice a year, free)
Prospectus of the language programme (2 times a year, free)

Access to staff:
Contact by letter, by telephone, by fax, by e-mail, in person and via website
Hours: Language Department: Mon to Thu, 1000 to 1700; Fri, 1000 to 1500
Library & Information Service: Mon, 1600 to 18.30; Tue,Thu, 1200 to 1830; Wed, 1200 to 2000; Sat, 1000 to 1330
Special comments: A membership fee is applicable for borrowing rights. Reference use of the library is free.
Full: £20 annually, £14 monthly.
Concession (students, unemployed, senior citizens: £14 annually, £10 monthly).
Membership for Goethe-Institut students is free.
Concessionary membership for members of the Alliance Française de Glasgow.

Access for disabled people:
There are steps into the building

Headquarters address:
Goethe-Institut
    Zerntrale München, München, D-80637, Germany

GOFAL CYMRU

26 Dunraven Place, Bridgend, CF31 1JD

Tel: 01656 647722
E-mail: centraloffice@gofalcymru.org.uk

Website:
http://www.gofalcymru.org.uk
The charity and its work, news, leaflets.

Founded:
1990

Organisation type and purpose:
A mental health registered charity (charity number 1000889) with nearly 20 years experience of service provision. Currently working across 11 counties in Wales, Gofal Cymru provides innovative support and advice to people experiencing mental ill health.

Subject coverage:
The services Gofal Cymru provides assist service users with various aspects of daily life including applying for benefits, tenancy issues, health appointments, advocacy, daily living skills, accessing work and training, debt management and budgeting, crisis prevention, advice in accessing suitable housing, and liaison with other health professionals such as CPNs, CMHT, GPs and psychiatrists. Its services range from supported housing for people unable to live independently to tenancy support for people who already have a home but require assistance and support to maintain and retain their tenancy.

Electronic and video publications:
Leaflets in English and in Welsh on such topics as tenancy support, supported/shared housing, work preparation, out-of-hours support, the Gateway project – Newport,
housing support and advice

Publications list:
Available online

Access to staff:
Contact by letter, by telephone and by e-mail

Branches:
Offices in Swansea, Neath Port Talbot, Bridgend, Rhondda Cynon Taff, Vale of Glamorgan, Blaenau Gwent, Caerphilly and Merthyr, Cardiff, Torfaen and Newport

GOLD COCKEREL BOOKS

Kennerleigh, Crediton, Devon, EX17 4RS

Tel: 01363 866750
Fax: 01363 866750

Website:
http://www.goldcockerelbooks.co.uk
List and description of books.

Enquiries:
Enquiries to: Director

Founded:
1987

Organisation type and purpose:
Research organisation, publishing house.

Subject coverage:
Poultry history, poultry breeding, old breeds of hens, ducks, geese, turkeys, poultry health, and small holding and countryside.

Printed publications:
Gold Cockerel series of practical books, 29 titles as at Aug 2010, see website: http:// www.goldcockerelbooks.co.uk for titles

Publications list:
Available in print

Access to staff:
Contact by letter, by telephone, by fax, by e-mail and via website
Hours: Mon to Fri, 0900 to 1700

GOLDSMITHS

Formal name: Goldsmiths' College

Library, University of London, Lewisham Way, New Cross, London, SE14 6NW

Tel: 020 7919 7171
Fax: 020 7919 7165
E-mail: library@gold.ac.uk

Website:
http://www.goldsmiths.ac.uk
College and departmental information.

Enquiries:
Enquiries to: Librarian
Direct tel: 020 7919 7150

Founded:
1891

Organisation type and purpose:
University library.

Subject coverage:
Anthropology, education, music, social sciences, creative arts, humanities.

Museum or gallery collection, archive, or library special collection:
A L Lloyd Collection of European and North American Folk Music
Ewan MacColl and Peggy Seeger collection
Centre for Russian Music collection
Serge Prokofiev Archive
Women's Art Library
LIFT Living Archive
Bush collection
Stevens collection
Deac Rossell collection
Angus Fairhurst collection
John Thomas collection
Glen Baxter collection
Artist's books and ephemera collections
Constance Howard Centre for Textiles collections

Non-library collection catalogue:
All or part available online and in-house

Library catalogue:
All or part available online

Publications list:
Available online

Access to staff:
Contact by letter, by telephone, by fax and by e-mail. Appointment necessary.
Hours: Term time and Christmas and Easter holidays: Mon to Fri, 0915 to 2045; Sat and Sun, 1130 to 1700
Summer holidays: Mon to Fri, 0915 to 1645; Sat, 1130 to 1700; Sun closed
Special comments: No access for visitors to computers (except the library catalogue), audiovisual collections or to electronic databases.

Access to building, collection or gallery:
No prior appointment required

Access for disabled people:
Level entry, access to all public areas, toilet facilities

College of the:
University of London

GOLF FOUNDATION

Foundation House, The Spinney, Hoddesdon Road, Stanstead Abbotts, Hertfordshire, SG12 8GF

Tel: 01920 876200
Fax: 01920 876211

Website:
http://www.golf-foundation.org
History of Golf Foundation; details of all development initiatives, coaching activities and tournaments.

Enquiries:
Enquiries to: Executive Director
Direct e-mail: hayley@golf-foundation.org

Founded:
1952

Organisation type and purpose:
Registered charity (charity number 285917). Junior Golf Development.
To promote and develop junior golf for young people in full-time education.

Subject coverage:
Coaching and tournaments for junior golfers. Development initiatives for grass roots junior golf.

Printed publications:
Annual Report
Don't Be A Golf Menace (free)
Golf Rules in Brief (free)
Taking up Golf (£4.99)
Junior Golf Matters (newsletter)

Publications list:
Available in print

Access to staff:
Contact by letter, by telephone, by fax and by e-mail
Hours: Mon to Fri, 0900 to 1700

GONVILLE AND CAIUS COLLEGE

Library, Cambridge, CB2 1TA

Tel: 01223 332419
E-mail: library@cai.cam.ac.uk

Website:
http://www.cai.cam.ac.uk/college/library/index.php
History of library and details of service; all aspects of college activities covered.

Enquiries:
Enquiries to: College Librarian

Founded:
1349

Organisation type and purpose:
University library.
College library.

Subject coverage:
Broad-based; covers most subjects taught within the University Tripos; some post-graduate and research level material.

Museum or gallery collection, archive, or library special collection:
15,000 early-printed books
900 medieval and later manuscripts
Music manuscripts, e.g. Charles Wood, Patrick Hadley
Venn manuscripts

Library catalogue:
All or part available online

Microform publications:
Microfilms of manuscripts are available for purchase
Order microform publications from: College Librarian

Electronic and video publications:
Digital images derived from manuscripts and early-printed books are available for purchase
Order electronic and video publications from: College Librarian

Access to staff:
Contact by letter, by telephone, by e-mail and via website. Appointment necessary. Letter of introduction required.
Hours: Mon to Fri, 0930 to 1245 and 1415 to 1645

GOOD GARDENERS ASSOCIATION

Acronym or abbreviation: GGA

4 Lisle Place, Wotton-under-Edge, Gloucestershire, GL2 7AZ

Tel: 01453 520322
E-mail: info@goodgardeners.org.uk

Enquiries:
Enquiries to: Secretary General
Other contacts: Soil Scientist

Founded:
1961

Organisation type and purpose:
International organisation, membership association (membership is by subscription), voluntary organisation, registered charity (charity number 255300), suitable for ages: adults.
To teach the 'No Dig' method of growing fruit and vegetables on natural soil for the nutritional benefits that this provides in the maintenance of health worldwide.

Subject coverage:
Organics, soil fertility – nature's way, soil science, organic marketing, community supported agriculture, composting, nutrition, health from plant-orientated foods.

Printed publications:
Newsletter (quarterly)
Variety of booklets and leaflets

Publications list:
Available in print

Access to staff:
Contact by letter, by telephone and by e-mail. Access for members only. Non-members charged.
Hours: Mon to Fri, 0900 to 1700

GOOD SCHOOLS GUIDE

Acronym or abbreviation: GSG

3 Craven Mews, London, SW11 5PW

Tel: 020 7801 0191
Fax: 0870 052 4067
E-mail: editor@goodschoolsguide.co.uk

Website:
http://www.goodschoolsguide.co.uk
The Good Schools Guide online in its entirety (for subscribers), comprehensive UK educational data analysis covering exams, catchment data,

university entrance (for subscribers), searches, advice and links (mostly free), reviewed book list (free).

Enquiries:
Enquiries to: Editor

Founded:
1985

Organisation type and purpose:
Consultancy, research organisation, publishing house.
Describes United Kingdom schools and international schools worldwide as they really are, advising parents on them through the web and one-to-one; provides information on schools and schooling over the internet and in printed form.

Subject coverage:
Primary and secondary schools in the United Kingdom, both private and state; international schools worldwide.

Information services:
The Good Schools Guide Advice Service offers parents one-to-one consultations on school choice.

Trade and statistical information:
School examination and other statistics.

Printed publications:
The Good Schools Guide (15th edn, Lucas Publications, 2010)
The Good Schools Guide – Special Educational Needs (3rd edn, Lucas Publications, 2008)
Uni in the USA (1st edn, Lucas Publications, 2005)
11+ English: A Parent's Toolkit (1st edn, Lucas Publications, 2004)
Order printed publications from: e-mail: orders@goodschoolsguide.co.uk

Electronic and video publications:
The Good Schools Guide (online)
The Good Schools Guide International (online)
Order electronic and video publications from: website: http://www.goodschoolsguide.co.uk

Access to staff:
Contact by letter, by telephone, by fax, by e-mail, in person and via website. Appointment necessary.
Hours: Mon to Fri, 0900 to 1700

Administers:
The Good Schools Guide International website: http://www.gsgi.co.uk

Parent body:
Lucas Publications Ltd

GOOLE LOCAL STUDIES LIBRARY

Carlisle Street, Goole, East Riding of Yorkshire, DN14 5DS

Tel: 01405 762187
Fax: 01405 768329
E-mail: gooleref.library@eastriding.gov.uk

Enquiries:
Enquiries to: Librarian

Organisation type and purpose:
Public library.

Subject coverage:
Collections on Goole and the surrounding area, local family history resources.

Museum or gallery collection, archive, or library special collection:
2500 books covering Goole and the historic East, North and West Ridings of Yorkshire
Collections of books and 3000 photographs

Non-library collection catalogue:
All or part available online and in-house

Library catalogue:
All or part available online

Access to staff:
Contact by letter, by telephone, by fax, by e-mail and in person
Hours: Mon, Wed, 1000 to 1900; Tue, Thu, Fri, 1000 to 1700; Sat, 0900 to 1300

continued overleaf

Access to building, collection or gallery:
No prior appointment required
Special comments: For detailed enquiries preferable to advise staff beforehand.
Prior appointment required for booking microform readers.

Access for disabled people:
Level entry
Special comments: Lift to Local Studies Library on first floor.

Parent body:
East Riding of Yorkshire Council

GORDON KEEBLE OWNERS CLUB

26 Burford Park Road, Kings Norton, Birmingham, B38 8PB

Tel: 0121 459 8700
Fax: 0121 459 9587

Enquiries:
Enquiries to: Secretary

Founded:
1970

Organisation type and purpose:
Membership association (membership is by subscription).

Subject coverage:
The Gordon Keeble car marque parts availability, location of cars.

Access to staff:
Contact by letter, by telephone and by fax.
Appointment necessary.
Hours: Mon to Fri, 0900 to 1700

GOSPORT BOROUGH COUNCIL

Town Hall, Gosport, Hampshire, PO12 1EB

Tel: 023 9258 4242
Fax: 023 9251 1279
E-mail: enquiries@gosport.gov.uk

Website:
http://www.gosport.gov.uk
Development opportunities, business pages, tourism and leisure, council services and information, events list.

Enquiries:
Enquiries to: Marketing Manager
Direct tel: 023 9254 5258
Direct fax: 023 9254 5238

Organisation type and purpose:
Local government body.

Subject coverage:
Local government.

Access to staff:
Contact by letter, by fax and by e-mail.
Appointment necessary.
Hours: Mon to Fri, 0900 to 1700

GOSS COLLECTORS CLUB

22 Littlebrook Gardens, Cheshunt, Hertfordshire, EN8 8QQ

Tel: 01992 627033
E-mail: registrar@gosscollectorsclub.org

Website:
http://www.gosschina.com
Brief description of the club and its activities.
http://www.gosscollectorsclub.org

Enquiries:
Enquiries to: Registrar
Direct e-mail: auctionsecretary@gosscollectorsclub.org
Other contacts: Auction Secretary for enquiries re the postal auction.

Founded:
1970

Organisation type and purpose:
International organisation, membership association (membership is by subscription).

Subject coverage:
The works of William Henry Goss, Goss china collecting and identification, associated heraldry.

Museum or gallery collection, archive, or library special collection:
Various collection of books, documents, etc., including comprehensive slide bank, held by archivist (available to members only)

Printed publications:
The Goss Hawk Magazine (monthly, free to members)

Access to staff:
Contact by letter, by telephone, by e-mail and via website
Hours: Up to 2100

GOVERNING COUNCIL OF THE CAT FANCY, THE

Acronym or abbreviation: GCCF

4–6 Penel Orlieu, Bridgwater, Somerset, TA6 3PG

Tel: 01278 427575
E-mail: GCCF_CATS@compuserve.com

Website:
http://www.gccfcats.org
Information on GCCF.

Enquiries:
Enquiries to: Secretary

Founded:
1910

Organisation type and purpose:
Voluntary organisation.
Council made up of affiliated Cat Clubs.
Registration body for pedigree cats.

Subject coverage:
Pedigree cats breeds, shows and cat clubs.

Museum or gallery collection, archive, or library special collection:
Cat registration records from 1910
Own records 1910 onwards

Trade and statistical information:
Analysis of cats registered.

Printed publications:
Free leaflets
Guides, stud books, lists of shows, clubs, judges etc

Publications list:
Available in print

Access to staff:
Contact by letter, by telephone, by e-mail and via website. Appointment necessary.
Hours: Mon to Fri, 0900 to 1700

GOVERNMENT ACTUARY'S DEPARTMENT

Acronym or abbreviation: GAD

Finlaison House, 15–17 Furnival Street, London, EC4A 1AB

Tel: 020 7211 2600
Fax: 020 7211 2650
E-mail: enquiries@gad.gov.uk

Website:
http://www.gad.gov.uk
Population projections; quinquennial review of social security scheme; departmental contacts.

Enquiries:
Enquiries to: Director
Direct tel: 020 7211 2620
Other contacts: Directing Actuary (for advice on pensions)

Founded:
1919

Organisation type and purpose:
National government body, consultancy. Central government department. Actuarial and financial consultancy.

Subject coverage:
Demography (including national population projections), survey of occupational pension schemes, social security projection, public sector pensions.

Printed publications:
Annual Report
Departmental Report
Occupational Pensions Schemes Survey 2000
Pension Provision in Britain (1994)
Quinquennial Review of National Insurance Fund (1999)
Report by the Government Actuary on the drafts of the Social Security Benefits Up-rating order 1999 and the Social Security (contributions) (Re-rating and National Insurance Fund Payments) Order 1999
Resource Accounts
Review of Certain Contracting-out Terms (1996)
1996-based National Population Projections
2000-based Projections of Population
Order printed publications from: Publications Officer, Government Actuary Department; tel: 020 7211 2620; fax: 020 7211 2650; e-mail: marilyn.estrick@gad.gov.uk

Access to staff:
Contact by letter, by fax and by e-mail
Hours: Mon to Fri, 0900 to 1700

GOVERNMENT COMMUNICATIONS HEADQUARTERS

Acronym or abbreviation: GCHQ

Open Source Library and Information Services, Room B2g, Hubble Road, Cheltenham, Gloucestershire, GL51 0EX

Tel: 01242 221491 ext. 32538
Fax: 01242 709002
E-mail: library@gchq.gsi.gov.uk

Enquiries:
Enquiries to: Librarian

Organisation type and purpose:
National government body.

Subject coverage:
Telecommunications, electronic engineering, mathematics, computer applications, communications security, linguistics.

Library catalogue:
All or part available in-house

Access to staff:
Contact by letter, by telephone, by fax and by e-mail
Hours: Mon to Fri, 0900 to 1700

Access to building, collection or gallery:
No access other than to staff

GOWER PUBLISHING LIMITED

Gower House, Croft Road, Aldershot, Hampshire, GU11 3HR

Tel: 01252 331551
Fax: 01252 344405
E-mail: info@gowerpub.com

Website:
http://www.gowerpub.com
Full online catalogue of publications, training books and links to sister companies.

Enquiries:
Enquiries to: Customer Service Manager

Founded:
1967

Organisation type and purpose:
Publishing house. Academic, business and professional publishing.

Subject coverage:
Business, management, personal skills, specialist areas of business activity, information management, training.

Printed publications:
101 Ideas to Help You be a Better Manager (£25, pub Gower)
Dictionary of Marketing (£60, Gower Press)
Economic Bulletin (monthly, £150 a year, German Institute for Economic Research)
European Design Guide (£45, pub. Gower)
Handbook of Food Additives: An International Guide to 7500 Products (book and disc)
Handbook of International Credit Management (£70, pub. Gower)
ISO 14000 and ISO 9000 – Feb 96 (£39.50, pub. Gower)
Sources of European Economic and Business Information (£125, pub. Gower)
World Index of Economic Forecasts (£125, pub. Gower)
Librarianship and Information Management publications (see publications list)
Order printed publications from: Bookpoint Limited, Gower Publishing Direct Sales
130 Milton Park, Abingdon, Oxon, OX14 4SB, tel: 01235 827730, fax: 01235 400454, e-mail: orders@bookpoint.co.uk

Electronic and video publications:
Gardners Chemical Synonyms and Trade Names Electronic Handbook (£170, on CD-ROM)
Industrial Surfactants Electronic Handbook (£195, on CD-ROM)
Plastic and Rubber Electronic Handbook (£170, on CD-ROM)

Publications list:
Available online and in print

Access to staff:
Contact by letter, by telephone, by fax, by e-mail and via website
Hours: Mon to Fri, 0900 to 1700

Access to building, collection or gallery:
Prior appointment required

Parent body:
Ashgate Group Publishing Limited
  at the same address

Subsidiary body:
Dartmouth Press
Scolar Press
Variorum Press

GRADUATE PROSPECTS LTD

Formal name: Higher Education Careers Services Unit
Acronym or abbreviation: HECSU

Prospects House, Booth Street East, Manchester, M13 9EP

Tel: 0161 277 5200
Fax: 0161 277 5210
E-mail: enquiries@prospects.ac.uk

Website:
http://www.prospects.ac.uk/

Enquiries:
Enquiries to: Marketing Communications Manager

Formerly called:
Central Services Unit for Graduate Careers and Appointments Services

Subject coverage:
Graduate trends and predictions, graduate training, graduate salaries, university output, college output, graduate supply and demand, postgraduate training, higher education careers services.

Trade and statistical information:
Statistics on the graduate recruitment market.

Publications list:
Available online

Access to staff:
Contact by letter, by telephone, by fax and by e-mail
Hours: Mon to Fri, 0900 to 1700

Access to building, collection or gallery:
No access other than to staff

Access for disabled people:
Parking provided, ramped entry, level entry, access to all public areas, toilet facilities

Commercial subsidiary of the:
Higher Education Careers Services Unit (HECSU)

Jointly owned by:
Universities UK and the Guild HE

Publishing house for the:
Association of Graduate Careers Advisory Services (AGCAS)

GRADUATE SCHOOL OF EUROPEAN AND INTERNATIONAL STUDIES

Acronym or abbreviation: GSEIS

University of Reading, Whiteknights, PO Box 218, Reading, Berkshire, RG6 2AA

Tel: 0118 931 8378
Fax: 0118 975 5442
E-mail: gseis@reading.ac.uk

Website:
http://www.rdg.ac.uk/AcaDepts/ce/GSEIS/home.html

Enquiries:
Enquiries to: Secretary

Founded:
1960

Formerly called:
GSEIS

Organisation type and purpose:
University department or institute, research organisation.

Subject coverage:
Postgraduate teaching and training in the fields of European and international studies, international security studies, political theory and public ethics, governance and international law and world order, diplomacy.

Library catalogue:
All or part available in-house

Printed publications:
A regular series of Discussion Papers on European and International Social Science Research and occasional papers
Monographs, Occasional Papers, Research papers, etc
Publicity material including the Graduate School's Booklist
University of Reading series on Europe and International Studies (published in association with the Macmillan Press)

Publications list:
Available in print

Access to staff:
Contact by telephone and by e-mail
Hours: Mon to Fri, 1000 to 1600

Access for disabled people:
Ramped entry, access to all public areas

GRAHAM GREENE BIRTHPLACE TRUST

17 North Road, Berkhamsted, Hertfordshire, HP4 3DX

Tel: 01442 866694
E-mail: secretary@grahamgreenebt.org

Website:
http://www.grahamgreenebt.org

Frequent information about the Trust and its annual festival.

Enquiries:
Enquiries to: Secretary

Founded:
1997

Organisation type and purpose:
International organisation, membership association (membership is by subscription), present number of members: 200, voluntary organisation, registered charity (charity number 1064839).

Subject coverage:
Life and works of Graham Greene.

Museum or gallery collection, archive, or library special collection:
Archive and Specialist Library

Library catalogue:
All or part available in print

Printed publications:
Newsletter (quarterly)
Occasional Papers (£2, £2.50 if posted)
Other publications as listed on website

Electronic and video publications:
The Voice of Graham Greene (CD-ROM, £10, incl p&p)
Many Festival talks available on video/CD

Publications list:
Available online and in print

Access to staff:
Contact by letter, by telephone, by e-mail and via website. Appointment necessary.
Hours: Sun to Sat, 0900 to 2100
Special comments: Answerphone out of hours.

GRAIN AND FEED TRADE ASSOCIATION

Acronym or abbreviation: GAFTA

GAFTA House, 6 Chapel Place, Rivington Street, London, EC2A 3SH

Tel: 020 7814 9666
Fax: 020 7814 8383
E-mail: post@gafta.com

Website:
http://www.gafta.com
Membership information, list of publications, courses, some categories of membership, membership fees.

Enquiries:
Enquiries to: Director-General

Organisation type and purpose:
International organisation, trade association (membership is by subscription), present number of members: more than 1,000.

Subject coverage:
Grain, animal feedstuffs, pulses and rice, contracts, arbitration, trade policy.

Publications list:
Available online

Access to staff:
Contact by letter, by e-mail and via website
Hours: Mon to Fri, 0900 to 1700

Access to building, collection or gallery:
Prior appointment required

Access for disabled people:
Level entry, toilet facilities

GRANTFINDER LIMITED

Enterprise House, Carlton Road, Worksop, Nottinghamshire, S81 7QF

Tel: 01909 501200
Fax: 01909 501225
E-mail: enquiries@grantfinder.co.uk

continued overleaf

Website:
http://www.grantfinder.co.uk
Fully searchable grantfinder database with option to store and later retrieve project profiles. Update and Newsflash facilities available to keep up-to-date with new funding schemes and up-coming deadlines.

Enquiries:
Enquiries to: Managing Director

Founded:
1985

Organisation type and purpose:
Consultancy, research organisation, publishing house, providers of information on grants.

Subject coverage:
Information on grants, aids and incentives available from the UK Government and European Community to organisations in the public, private and voluntary sectors.

Printed publications:
Grantfinder profiled publication
Grantfinder Report

Electronic and video publications:
Grantfinder

Access to staff:
Contact by e-mail and via website. All charged.
Hours: Mon to Fri, 0900 to 1730

GRAPHIC ENTERPRISE SCOTLAND

Acronym or abbreviation: GES

112 George Street, Edinburgh, EH2 4LH

Tel: 0131 220 4353
Fax: 0131 220 4344
E-mail: info@graphicenterprisescotland.org

Website:
http://www.graphicenterprisescotland.org

Enquiries:
Enquiries to: Director

Founded:
1910

Formerly called:
Society of Master Printers of Scotland (SMPS) (year of change 1991); Scottish Print Employers Federation (SPEF) (year of change 2009)

Organisation type and purpose:
Trade association (membership is by subscription).

Subject coverage:
Employee relations; training; health and safety; commercial information.

Access to staff:
Contact by letter, by telephone and by fax. Appointment necessary.
Hours: Mon to Fri, 0900 to 1700

Links with:
Intergraf (International Confederation for Printing and Allied Industries)

GRAPHICAL, PAPER AND MEDIA UNION

Acronym or abbreviation: GPMU

Birmingham and West Midlands Branch, Union House, 9 William Street North, Birmingham, B19 3QH

Tel: 0121 236 2963 or 8860
Fax: 0121 233 1731
E-mail: gpmuwestmidlands@btclick.com

Website:
http://www.gmpu.org.uk

Enquiries:
Enquiries to: Branch Secretary

Formerly called:
Birmingham Typographical Society (year of change 1995)

Organisation type and purpose:
Trade union (membership is by subscription), present number of members: 8000.

Subject coverage:
Information on general print, finishings, graphics, lithography, flexography, silk screen. Electronic and digital generations, employment legislation, health and safety, pension information, state benefits, welfare advice.

Access to staff:
Contact by letter, by telephone, by fax and in person
Hours: Mon to Fri, 0900 to 1700

Affiliated to:
Graphical, Paper and Media Union
  Keys House, Bromham Road, Bedford; tel: 01234 351521; fax: 01234 270580; website: www.gpmu.org.uk

GRAY CANCER INSTITUTE

Acronym or abbreviation: GLCRT

PO Box 100, Mount Vernon Hospital, Northwood, Middlesex, HA6 2JR

Tel: 01923 828611
Fax: 01923 835210
E-mail: wardman@gci.ac.uk

Website:
http://www.gci.ac.uk

Enquiries:
Enquiries to: Deputy Director

Founded:
1955

Organisation type and purpose:
Registered charity, research organisation. Research into cancer.

Subject coverage:
Experimental cancer therapy, especially with radiation; tumour biology; tumour kinetics; tumour vasculature; radiation physics; radiation chemistry; radiation biology; neutrons; X-rays; radiation sources.

Museum or gallery collection, archive, or library special collection:
Fowler-Scott Library of books and journals related to cancer research and biological effects of radiation

Printed publications:
Papers and books published

Publications list:
Available in print

Access to staff:
Contact by letter, by telephone and by e-mail. Letter of introduction required.
Hours: Mon to Fri, 0900 to 1700

Access to building, collection or gallery:
Prior appointment required

GRAY'S INN LIBRARY

Formal name: The Honourable Society of Gray's Inn

The Honourable Society of Gray's Inn, 5 South Square, Gray's Inn, London, WC1R 5ET

Tel: 020 7458 7822
Fax: 020 7458 7850
E-mail: library.information@graysinn.org.uk

Website:
http://www.graysinnlibrary.org.uk

Enquiries:
Enquiries to: Librarian
Other contacts: Archivist (for historical material)

Founded:
c. 15th century

Organisation type and purpose:
Legal library.

Museum or gallery collection, archive, or library special collection:
Core collection of 60,000 vols on all aspects of the the law, but specifically entertainment and sport, IT and communications law, and the law of education
Manuscripts (medieval to 19th century)

Library catalogue:
All or part available online

Access to staff:
Contact by letter, by telephone, by fax and by e-mail. Access for members only. Letter of introduction required.

Access to building, collection or gallery:
Hours: Student and Legal terms: Mon to Fri, 0900 to 2000; holidays: see website for details
Special comments: Open to all barrister and student mems of Gray's Inn and barrister mems of all Inns of Court; other researchers by appointment with the Librarian

Access for disabled people:
Wheelchair lift
Hours: Telephone for assistance and advice

GRAYS CENTRAL LIBRARY

Orsett Road, Grays, Essex, RM17 5DX

Tel: 01375 413973
Fax: 01375 385504
E-mail: grays.library@thurrock.gov.uk

Website:
http://www.thurrock.gov.uk/libraries
General library details, council and community information, online reference sources.

Enquiries:
Enquiries to: Librarian
Direct tel: 01375 413977

Organisation type and purpose:
Local government body, public library.

Subject coverage:
General, local studies.

Museum or gallery collection, archive, or library special collection:
Museum

Non-library collection catalogue:
All or part available online

Library catalogue:
All or part available online

Access to staff:
Contact by letter, by telephone, by fax, by e-mail, in person and via website
Hours: Mon, Tue, Thu, 1000 to 1900; Wed, Fri, Sat, 1000 to 1700

Access to building, collection or gallery:
No access other than to staff

Access for disabled people:
Parking provided, access to all public areas, toilet facilities

Constituent part of:
Thurrock Libraries

GREAT BRITAIN POSTCARD CLUB

34 Harper House, St James Crescent, London, SW9 7LW

Tel: 020 7771 9404

Enquiries:
Enquiries to: Executive Director

Founded:
1961

Organisation type and purpose:
Membership association.

Subject coverage:
Postcard collecting throughout the world, ephemera under 100 subjects.

Printed publications:
Postcard World (journal, 6 times a year, £10)

Access to staff:
Contact by letter
Hours: Mon to Fri, 0900 to 1700

GREAT BRITAIN RACQUETBALL FEDERATION

Acronym or abbreviation: GBRF

78 Suffolk Drive, Rendlesham, Woodbridge, Suffolk, IP12 2TP

Tel: 01394 461069
E-mail: aburrow.newman@btinternet.com

Enquiries:
Enquiries to: General Secretary

Founded:
1984

Organisation type and purpose:
National government body, membership association (membership is by subscription), voluntary organisation, suitable for ages: 8+. Promote the game of racquetball and racquetball education.

Subject coverage:
Racquetball rules, regulations, court specifications.

Access to staff:
Contact by letter and by telephone
Hours: Mon to Fri, 0900 to 1700

Affiliated to:
European Racquetball Federation
International Racquetball Federation

GREAT BRITAIN WHEELCHAIR BASKETBALL ASSOCIATION

Acronym or abbreviation: GBWBA

GBWBA Office, Suite B, Technology Centre, Epinal Way, Loughborough, Leicestershire, LE11 3GE

Tel: 01509 631671
Fax: 01509 631672
E-mail: office@gbwba.org.uk

Website:
http://www.gbwba.org.uk

Enquiries:
Enquiries to: Chief Executive
Direct e-mail: c.bethel@gbwba.org.uk ; info@gbwba.org.uk
Other contacts: League Secretary, Chairman, General Secretary

Founded:
1973

Organisation type and purpose:
Membership association (membership is by subscription), present number of members: over 700, registered charity (charity number 298045). National governing body for the sport.

Subject coverage:
All matters relating to the sport of wheelchair basketball in Great Britain.

Museum or gallery collection, archive, or library special collection:
Records of Association, member clubs, registered players and officials etc

Printed publications:
Coaching Award Manuals (Coaching Assistant Award and Coach Award)
Handbook (annual)
Information Pack
List of members and clubs
Rebound (newsletter, 2 times a year)
e-Zene (4 times a year)

Electronic and video publications:
Basic Coaching (video)
Introducing Wheelchair Basketball (video)

Publications list:
Available in print

Access to staff:
Contact by letter, by telephone, by fax, by e-mail and via website. Appointment necessary.
Hours: Mon to Fri, 0900 to 1700
Special comments: Not after 2200.

Affiliated to:
International Wheelchair Basketball Federation (IWBF)
  IWBF Secretariat, 108–109 Watson Street, Winnipeg, Manitoba, Canada, R2P 2E1; tel: (204) 632 6475; e-mail: iwbfpresident@aol.com

GREAT BRITAIN-SASAKAWA FOUNDATION

Acronym or abbreviation: GBSF

Dilke House, 1 Malet Street, London, WC1E 7JN

Tel: 020 7436 9042
E-mail: gbsf@gbsf.org.uk

Website:
http://www.gbsf.org.uk

Enquiries:
Enquiries to: Chief Executive

Founded:
1984

Organisation type and purpose:
Registered charity (charity number 290766). To improve relations between the United Kingdom and Japan by promoting a deeper understanding between the peoples of both nations. Awards grants to organisations for cultural events, youth exchanges, Japanese language/studies and academic research collaboration.

Subject coverage:
Promotion of Anglo-Japanese understanding.

Publications list:
Available in print

Access to staff:
Contact by letter and by e-mail
Hours: Mon to Fri, 0900 to 1700

Also at:
Great Britain-Sasakawa Foundation
  The Nippon Foundation Building 4F, 1–2-2 Akasaka, Tokyo, 107–0052, Japan; tel: +81 3 6229 5465; fax: +81 3 6229 5467; e-mail: gbsf@spf.or.jp

GREAT WESTERN AIR AMBULANCE

Appeals Office, Eastwood Park Training and Conference Centre, Falfield, Wotton under Edge, Gloucestershire, GL12 8DA

Tel: 0303 444 4999; 0845 838 8492
E-mail: info@greatwesternairambulance.org.uk

Website:
http://www.greatwesternairambulance.com

Founded:
2008

Organisation type and purpose:
Registered charity (charity number 1121300). The provision of a sustainable Helicopter Emergency Medical Service (HEMS) within the area covered by the Great Western Ambulance Service NHS Trust.

Subject coverage:
Covering the counties of Avon, Gloucestershire, North Somerset and Wiltshire, an area of 3,000 sq. km and serving a resident population of 2.2m. people, together with a transient and visiting population, heavy industrial sector, and sporting and leisure activity, the service helps to provide a fully effective and integrated road and air response emergency medical system that meets best practice response standards and outcomes for patients.

Access to staff:
Contact by letter, by telephone and by e-mail
Hours: Appeals Office: Mon to Fri, 0830 to 11.40

GREAT WESTERN SOCIETY LIMITED

Acronym or abbreviation: GWS

Didcot Railway Centre, Didcot, Oxfordshire, OX11 7NJ

Tel: 01235 817200
Fax: 01235 510621
E-mail: didrlyc@globalnet.co.uk

Website:
http://www.didcotrailwaycentre.org.uk

Enquiries:
Enquiries to: Secretary

Founded:
1961

Organisation type and purpose:
Membership association (membership is by subscription), voluntary organisation, registered charity (charity number 272616), museum.

Subject coverage:
Great Western Railway.

Non-library collection catalogue:
All or part available online and in print

Printed publications:
Didcot Railway Centre Guidebook (irregular)
Great Western Echo (quarterly, to members)

Access to staff:
Contact by letter, by telephone, by e-mail and via website
Hours: Mon to Fri, 0900 to 1700

Affiliated to:
Heritage Railway Association
Transport Trust

GREAT YARMOUTH CENTRAL LIBRARY

Tolhouse Street, Great Yarmouth, Norfolk, NR30 2SH

Tel: 01493 844551/842279
Fax: 01493 857628
E-mail: yarmouth.lib@norfolk.gov.uk

Website:
http://www.library.norfolk.gov.uk

Enquiries:
Enquiries to: Librarian

Organisation type and purpose:
Local government body, public library.

Subject coverage:
General, history and current information on Great Yarmouth and East Norfolk including newspaper cuttings; backfiles of local newspapers on microfilm, illustrations, maps etc; herring fishing, town walls and rows (narrow passageways), Dickens, Nelson, local genealogical information.

Museum or gallery collection, archive, or library special collection:
Francis Frith collection of photographs of Great Yarmouth and East Norfolk early/mid twentieth century
Herbert Tinkler MSS (early 20th century entertainments in Great Yarmouth)
W A S Wynne Collection (history of SE Norfolk and NE Suffolk)
William de Castre MSS (early 20th century writings and indexes on Great Yarmouth and Caister)
Yallop collection of glass plate negatives of Great Yarmouth Victorian/Edwardian era

Printed publications:
Family history resources available at Great Yarmouth Library
Parish Registers held at Great Yarmouth Library

continued overleaf

The Local Studies Collection at Great Yarmouth Library

Parent body:
Norfolk Library and Information Service

Part of:
Anglian Libraries Information Exchange Scheme

GREATER GLASGOW & CLYDE VALLEY TOURIST BOARD

11 George Square, Glasgow, G2 1DY

Tel: 0141 204 4480
Fax: 0141 204 4772
E-mail: enquiries@seeglasgow.com

Website:
http://www.seeglasgow.com
Information about the Greater Glasgow & Clyde Valley area for visitors and travel trade.

Enquiries:
Enquiries to: Director
Other contacts: (i) Marketing Manager; (ii) Manager for (1) Leisure Tourism (2) Convention Bureau.

Organisation type and purpose:
Statutory body, membership association (membership is by subscription), present number of members: 700+.
Destination marketing organisation.

Subject coverage:
Information on the Greater Glasgow Clyde Valley area for visitors, i.e. accommodation information, things to see and do and assistance to tour operators and travel trade, e.g. itinerary planning.

Trade and statistical information:
Statistics relating to visitors to the Greater Glasgow & Clyde Valley Area.

Printed publications:
Accommodation Guide (free)
Essential Guide (free)
Visitor Guide (free)
Touring Route Guide (free)

Electronic and video publications:
CD-ROM of Images (for travel trade only, free)
Destination Video (for travel trade only, free)

Publications list:
Available online

Access to staff:
Contact by letter, by telephone, by fax, by e-mail, in person and via website. Appointment necessary.
Hours: Mon to Fri, 0900 to 1700
Special comments: Seasonal weekend opening for tourist information offices.

Access for disabled people:
Toilet facilities

GREATER LONDON ACTION ON DISABILITY

Acronym or abbreviation: GLAD

336 Brixton Road, London, SW9 7AA

Tel: 020 7346 5800\ Minicom no. 020 7326 4554
Fax: 020 7346 8844

Enquiries:
Enquiries to: Information Officer
Direct tel: 020 7346 5819
Other contacts: Head of Policy for information on disability equality, training and DDA training.

Formerly called:
Greater London Association of Disabled People (GLAD) (year of change 1999)

Organisation type and purpose:
Membership association (membership is by subscription, qualification), voluntary organisation, registered charity (charity number 293158), training organisation.
Centre of network of affiliated disability organisations throughout Greater London.

Subject coverage:
All non-medical disability issues such as access, aids, benefits, education, employment, holidays, housing, leisure and sport.

Printed publications:
All publications are available in large print, in Braille
BOADICEA (newsletter, 6 times a year for disabled women £4 individuals, £7 organisations)
Disability Update (current awareness bulletin and abstracting service, fortnightly, £35 voluntary organisations, £45 statutory and commercial)
London Disability News (newsletter, 10 times a year, £8 individuals, £12 organisations, also on cassette and in large print)
Who we are and what we do (leaflet free with 27p sae)
Directory of Greater London Borough Disability Organisations (2002, £25)
Self-Advocacy Training Packs
Ethnicity and Disability: Moving towards equity in service
Disabled Women and Safety

Electronic and video publications:
All publications are available on audio cassette or by e-mail

Publications list:
Available online and in print

Access to staff:
Contact by letter, by telephone, by fax and by e-mail. Appointment necessary.
Hours: Information line: Mon, Wed, Fri, 1330 to 1630

Access for disabled people:
Parking provided, ramped entry, access to all public areas, toilet facilities

Links with:
Alliance of Disability Advice and Information Providers
British Council of Disabled People
London Voluntary Service Council (LVSC)
National Council for Voluntary Organisations
National Information Forum
Rights Now!
Royal Association for Disability and Rehabilitation (RADAR)

GREATER LONDON AUTHORITY INFORMATION SERVICES

City Hall, The Queen's Walk, London, SE1 2AA

Tel: 020 7983 4455
Fax: 020 7983 4674
E-mail: isinfo@london.gov.uk

Website:
http://www.london.gov.uk

Founded:
2000

Organisation type and purpose:
Local government body, research organisation.
GLA Information Services is a specialist library and provides information services for urban and social policy planners.

Subject coverage:
Planning and transport, business, the economy, labour market, education and training, health, housing and social exclusion, equalities policy, environment, culture, governance, police and community safety.

Museum or gallery collection, archive, or library special collection:
Library collection includes more than 250,000 books, reports and journal articles (including grey literature), and 500 regular periodicals and statistical series.

Non-library collection catalogue:
All or part available in-house

Library catalogue:
All or part available in-house

Printed publications:
Community Safety and Crime Bulletin (monthly)
Culture Bulletin (monthly)
Daily Information Bulletin
Economic and Business Bulletin (fortnightly)
Environment News (fortnightly)
Local Management and Finance (fortnightly)
Planning and Transport News (fortnightly)
Social Policy, Housing and Health Bulletin (fortnightly)
Urban Abstracts (monthly)

Electronic and video publications:
Urbaline database; Urbadoc database (contributor); Social Policy and Practice database (contributor)

Publications list:
Available online and in print

Access to staff:
Appointment necessary. Non-members charged.
Hours: Mon to Fri, 0930 to 1700

Access for disabled people:
Lift and ramp entry, toilet facilities

GREATER LONDON FUND FOR THE BLIND

12 Whitehorse Mews, 37 Westminster Bridge Road, London, SE1 7QD

Tel: 020 7620 2066
Fax: 020 7620 2016
E-mail: info@glfb.org.uk

Website:
http://www.glfb.org.uk

Enquiries:
Enquiries to: Information Officer

Founded:
1921

Organisation type and purpose:
Registered charity (charity number 1074958).

Subject coverage:
The visually impaired.

Access to staff:
Contact by letter, by telephone, by fax, by e-mail and in person. Appointment necessary.
Hours: Mon to Fri, 0915 to 1715

Member organisations:
Clarity: Employment for Blind People
Croydon Voluntary Association for the Blind
Kingston-upon-Thames Association for the Blind
MertonVision
Metropolitan Society for the Blind
SeeAbility
Surrey Association for Visual Impairment
Sutton Association for the Blind
The Middlesex Association for the Blind

GREATER MANCHESTER CENTRE FOR VOLUNTARY ORGANISATION

Acronym or abbreviation: GMCVO

St Thomas Centre, Ardwick Green North, Manchester, M12 6FZ

Tel: 0161 277 1000
Fax: 0161 273 8296
E-mail: gmcvo@gmcvo.org.uk

Website:
http://www.gmcvo.org.uk
GMCVO services; conference facilities; resource units on transport, access to services and rural issues; conferences and lectures; management and leadership training; consultancy; monthly news digest; bi-monthly policy briefing; print and design service.

Enquiries:
Enquiries to: Policy and Information Officer

Founded:
1975

Organisation type and purpose:
Voluntary organisation.
To strengthen the voluntary and community sector, build bridges with other sectors and influence local and national policy.

Printed publications:
Digest (monthly news round-up, £10 p.a.)
Issues (bi-monthly policy briefing, £30 p.a.)

Access to staff:
Contact by letter, by telephone, by fax, by e-mail and via website. Appointment necessary.
Hours: Phone lines open Mon to Fri, 0900 to 1700

Access for disabled people:
Ramped entry, toilet facilities

Member of:
National Association for Voluntary and Community Action
National Council for Voluntary Organisations
Voluntary Sector North West

GREATER MANCHESTER COUNTY RECORD OFFICE (WITH MANCHESTER ARCHIVES)

Acronym or abbreviation: GMCRO

56 Marshall Street, New Cross, Manchester, M4 5FU

Tel: 0161 832 5284
Fax: 0161 839 3808
E-mail: archiveslocalstudies@manchester.gov.uk

Website:
http://www.gmcro.co.uk

Enquiries:
Enquiries to: County Archivist

Founded:
1976

Organisation type and purpose:
Local government body.
Archive service, storage, reprographics, conservation.

Subject coverage:
Industrial and business records of Greater Manchester county, family and estate records, probate and registration indexes. Family history, public records, maps, newspapers, documentary photography archive, records of Greater Manchester County Council, societies, organisations and trade unions in Greater Manchester.

Museum or gallery collection, archive, or library special collection:
Archives relating to Greater Manchester Region from 1197 to modern day
Photographs – documentary photography archive
Photographs – Manchester Ship Canal Collection

Non-library collection catalogue:
All or part available online and in-house

Access to staff:
Contact by letter, by telephone, by fax, by e-mail, in person and via website

Access to building, collection or gallery:
Hours: Mon, Tue, Thu and Fri, 0900 to 1700; Wed, closed; 2nd and 4th Sat, 0900 to 1700
Special comments: CARN ticket required; essential to book a place in the searchroom in advance; essential to reserve archives in advance (2 working days' notice for on-site collections; 2 weeks' notice for off-site collections).

Access for disabled people:
Access to all public areas
Special comments: Private study room available for those with special access requirements.

Administers:
From Jun 2010, provides access to Manchester Archives' collections (during closure of Manchester Central Library for refurbishment) alongside GMCRO's own collections

Parent body:
Managed by Manchester City Council on behalf of Association of Greater Manchester Authorities (AGMA)

GREEK NATIONAL TOURISM ORGANISATION

Acronym or abbreviation: EOT/GNTO

4 Conduit Street, London, W1S 2DJ

Tel: 020 7495 9300
Fax: 020 7495 4057
E-mail: info@gnto.co.uk

Website:
http://www.visitgreece.gr
Useful information for tourists.
http://www.tourist-offices.org.uk
General information on Greece and its towns and cities, historical information.
http://www.antor.com/greece
Useful information for tourists.

Enquiries:
Enquiries to: Information Officer

Organisation type and purpose:
International organisation, national government body.

Subject coverage:
All forms of tourism to Greece including mainland and islands, special interest and conferences, information regarding transport, accommodation, tour operators, local festivals and cultural events.

Printed publications:
Brochures, posters, maps, general information, bus and ferry timetables, tour operator lists and special events

Microform publications:
Slides, photographs

Electronic and video publications:
Videos, CD-ROM

Access to staff:
Contact by letter, by telephone, by fax, by e-mail and in person
Hours: Mon to Thu, 0930 to 1700; Fri, 0930 to 1630

Access for disabled people:
Level entry

Headquarters address:
EOT
Tsocha 7, Athens, Greece; tel: +30 210 8707000; e-mail: info@gnto.gr; website: http://www.visitgreece.gr

GREEN PARTY

1a Waterlow, London, N19 5NJ

Tel: 020 7272 4474
Fax: 020 7272 6653
E-mail: office@greenparty.org.uk

Website:
http://www.greenparty.org.uk
General information about Green Party and current work.

Enquiries:
Enquiries to: Chair of the Executive
Other contacts: Head of Office

Founded:
1973

Formerly called:
People (year of change 1975); Ecology Party (year of change 1985)

Organisation type and purpose:
Political party.

Subject coverage:
Green politics, party policies.

Printed publications:
Green Activist (4 times a year, members only)

Green World: party newspaper (4 times a year, free to members)
Information booklets, briefing sheets, posters, election materials etc

Access to staff:
Contact by letter, by telephone, by e-mail and via website. Appointment necessary.
Hours: Mon to Fri, 0900 to 1700

GREENPEACE UK

Canonbury Villas, London, N1 2PN

Tel: 020 7865 8100
Fax: 020 7865 8200
E-mail: info@uk.greenpeace.org

Website:
http://www.greenpeace.org.uk
Information on campaigns, membership, press releases, photograph and video archives.

Enquiries:
Enquiries to: Information Officer

Founded:
1977

Organisation type and purpose:
International organisation.
Environmental campaigning.

Subject coverage:
Global warming, toxic waste, civil nuclear, nuclear disarmament, renewable energy, ancient forests, oceans.

Printed publications:
Briefing Sheets
Children's poster factsheets
Greenpeace Business (magazine, bi-monthly, subscription)
Connect (newsletter, subscription)
Greenpeace reports under the headings; atmosphere and energy, forests, toxins, nuclear, genetic engineering, oceans.

Electronic and video publications:
Video Lending Library:
Frontline Videos 1993–2004
Rainbow Warrior Promo

Publications list:
Available in print

Access to staff:
Contact by letter, by telephone, by fax, by e-mail and via website
Hours: Mon to Fri, 0900 to 1700

Parent body:
Greenpeace Environmental Trust at the same address

GREENWICH COMMUNITY COLLEGE LEARNING RESOURCES CENTRE

95 Plumstead Road, Plumstead, London, SE18 7DQ

Tel: 020 8488 4813
Fax: 020 8488 4899
E-mail: lib-help@gcc.ac.uk

Website:
http://www.gcc.ac.uk
Course details, open learning details.

Enquiries:
Enquiries to: Learning Resources Service Manager

Formerly called:
Woolwich & Greenwich Community College Learning Resource Service; Greenwich Community College, Woolwich College (year of change 1998)

Organisation type and purpose:
College of education learning resources centre.

Subject coverage:
General.

continued overleaf

Non-library collection catalogue:
All or part available online

Library catalogue:
All or part available online and in-house

Access to staff:
Contact by letter, by telephone and by fax
Hours: Mon to Fri, 0900 to 1700

Access for disabled people:
Level entry, toilet facilities, lift access

GREENWICH HERITAGE CENTRE

Artillery Square, Royal Arsenal, Woolwich, SE18 4DX

Tel: 020 8854 2452
E-mail: heritage.centre@greenwich.gov.uk

Website:
http://www.greenwich.gov.uk/greenwich/
leisureculture/historyandheritage/heritagecentre
Guide to the Heritage Centre and its resources.

Enquiries:
Enquiries to: Search Room

Founded:
2003

Created by the merger of:
London Borough of Greenwich's Borough Museum and Local History Library

Organisation type and purpose:
Museum, library and archive for exhibitions, research and education.

Subject coverage:
The history of the area now designated the London Borough of Greenwich.

Museum or gallery collection, archive, or library special collection:
Museum objects relating to the archaeology, social and natural history of the area
Paintings and drawings collection
Books, pamphlets, periodicals manuscripts, maps and illustrations relating to the people, topography and history of the area
Official repository of the records of the London Borough of Greenwich and its predecessors

Non-library collection catalogue:
All or part available in-house

Library catalogue:
All or part available in-house

Printed publications:
Sugar, Spices and Human Cargo: an early Black History of Greenwich (Anim-Addo J, 1996)
Free for All (Watson J and Gregory W, 1993)
In the Meantime: a Book on Greenwich (Watson J and Gregory K, 1988)
Woolwich Reviewed (Watson J, 1986)

Access to staff:
Contact by letter, by telephone, by fax, by e-mail and in person
Hours: Tue to Sat, 0900 to 1700

Access to building, collection or gallery:
Open to the public
Hours: Tue to Sat, 0900 to 1700

Access for disabled people:
Full access
Hours: Tue to Sat, 0900 to 1700

Parent body:
Greenwich Council
tel: 020 8854 8888

GREENWICH LIBRARY AND INFORMATION SERVICE

Woolwich Reference Library, Calderwood Street, Woolwich, London, SE18 6QZ

Tel: 020 8921 5748
Fax: 020 8316 1545
E-mail: reference.library@greenwich.gov.uk

Website:
http://www.greenwich.gov.uk

Enquiries:
Enquiries to: Librarian
Direct tel: 020 8921 5749

Founded:
1965

Organisation type and purpose:
Local government body, public library.

Subject coverage:
Metropolitan Special Collection in the following fields: recreation; indoor and outdoor games and sports; dancing (excluding ballet); official books of most sports associations.

Museum or gallery collection, archive, or library special collection:
Greenwich Local History and Archives Collection (history, topography and archaeology, at the Greenwich Heritage Centre)
Metropolitan Special Collection (recreation, sports) at Library Headquarters, Plumstead Library

Non-library collection catalogue:
All or part available online

Library catalogue:
All or part available online

Printed publications:
Enquiries to Greenwich Heritage Centre
Photographic reproductions of local material (to order)
Range of local history prints, postcards and publications
Order printed publications from: Greenwich Heritage Centre, Artillery Square, Royal Arsenal, Woolwich, SE18 4DX. tel: 020 8854 2452, fax: 020 8854 2490

Access to staff:
Contact by letter, by telephone, by fax, by e-mail, in person and via website

Access to building, collection or gallery:
No prior appointment required

Constituent bodies:
Library and Information Service

Headquarters address:
Greenwich Library and Information Service
c/o Plumstead Library, High Street, Plumstead, London, SE18 1JL; tel: 020 8317 4466; fax: 020 8317 4868

Links with:
Greenwich Heritage Centre
Building 41, Royal Arsenal, Woolwich, SE18 6SP; tel: 020 8854 2452; e-mail: heritage.centre@ greenwich.gov.uk; website: http://www .greenwich.gov.uk

Parent body:
Greenwich Council, Culture and Community Services
tel: 020 8854 8888

GREEVES RIDERS ASSOCIATION

Acronym or abbreviation: GRA

4 Longshaw Close, North Wingfield, Chesterfield, Derbyshire, S42 5QR

Tel: 01246 853846

Enquiries:
Enquiries to: Membership Secretary

Founded:
1984

Organisation type and purpose:
Membership association.

Subject coverage:
Information on all Greeves motor-cycles, technical, for restoration, parts supply, clarification of models and month of manufacture.

Access to staff:
Contact by letter and by telephone
Hours: Mon to Fri, 1800 to 2100

GREYFACE DARTMOOR SHEEP BREEDERS ASSOCIATION

Acronym or abbreviation: DSBA

c/o Biscombe Hill Farm, Churchstanton, Taunton, Somerset, TA3 7PZ

E-mail: info@greyface-dartmoor.org.uk

Website:
http://www.greyface-dartmoor.org.uk

Enquiries:
Enquiries to: Secretary

Founded:
1909

Organisation type and purpose:
Membership association (membership is by subscription), present number of members: 220, registered charity (charity number 266083).
Sheep Breeding Association (Greyface Dartmoor).

Subject coverage:
Sheep breeding.

Access to staff:
Contact by letter, by telephone, by fax, by e-mail and via website
Hours: Evenings preferred

GROUDLE GLEN RAILWAY

29 Hawarden Avenue, Douglas, Isle of Man, IM1 4BP

Tel: 01624 622138 (evenings only); 01624 670453 (weekends only)
E-mail: lbeard@manx.net

Enquiries:
Enquiries to: Honorary Secretary

Founded:
1982

Organisation type and purpose:
Membership association (membership is by subscription), present number of members: 700, voluntary organisation, registered charity (charity number Isle of Man No. 406).
Restoration and operation of a narrow gauge railway.

Subject coverage:
Railway restoration and operation of a 2ft gauge line with steam and diesel locomotives over 3/4 mile track.

Printed publications:
Magazine (quarterly, to members)
History of the Groudle Glen Railway

Access to staff:
Contact by letter. Appointment necessary.
Special comments: No access to staff.

Access for disabled people:
Special comments: Please telephone for advice before your visit.

Affiliated to:
Isle of Man Steam Railway Supporters Association at the same address

GROWTH THROUGH TRAINING (GTT) LIMITED

Formal name: Growth Through Training (GTT) Ltd
Acronym or abbreviation: GTT Ltd

55 Curlew Drive, Chippenham, Wiltshire, SN14 6YG

Tel: 01249 661231
Fax: 01249 447442
E-mail: csimons@dircon.co.uk

Enquiries:
Enquiries to: Managing Director

Founded:
1985

Organisation type and purpose:
Organisational and human resource development,
consultancy.
Management Development, Investors in People
practitioners.

Subject coverage:
Organisational development, management
development training. Investors in People
consultancy, counselling at work.

Printed publications:
Effective Communication Skills for Managers (C
Simons and B Naylor-Stables, Cassell Sep 1997,
ISBN 0 304 331201, hardback; 0 304 33125,
paperback)

Access to staff:
Contact by letter, by telephone, by fax and by e-
mail. Appointment necessary.
Hours: Any reasonable time

GRUBB INSTITUTE

Formal name: Grubb Institute of Behavioural
Studies Limited

Cloudesley Street, London, N1 0HU

Tel: 020 7278 8061
Fax: 020 7278 0728
E-mail: info@grubb.org.uk

Website:
http://www.grubb.org.uk

Enquiries:
Enquiries to: Executive Director

Founded:
1969

Organisation type and purpose:
Registered charity (charity number 313460),
training organisation, consultancy, research
organisation.

Subject coverage:
Analysis of organisation: theory, including
organisational behaviour, group dynamics,
systems psychology, religious behaviour;
applications in the following fields: leadership and
organisation of institutions, the educational
process in secondary and higher education,
industrial organisation and structure, management
in central and local government agencies, religious
institutions in society, community service and
voluntary organisations, probation and after-care,
prisons and penal establishments, transition from
childhood to adult life, management training,
group and inter-group relations, unemployment.

Printed publications:
List of published work up to 2008
Reports and Occasional Papers
Order printed publications from: Publications
Secretary, e-mail: purchases@grubb.org.uk

Publications list:
Available online and in print

Access to staff:
Contact by letter, by telephone, by fax, by e-mail
and via website. Appointment necessary.
Hours: Mon to Fri, 0900 to 1730

GS1 UK

10 Maltravers Street, London, WC2R 3BX

Tel: 020 7655 9000
Fax: 020 7681 2290
E-mail: info@gs1uk.org

Website:
http://www.gs1uk.org
Information to assist the understanding and use of
e-commerce, article numbering, bar coding,
electronic data interchange.

Enquiries:
Enquiries to: Chief Executive
Direct e-mail: suraya.adnan@gs1uk.org
Other contacts: Director, Business Development, for
marketing issues.

Founded:
1976

Organisation type and purpose:
Advisory body, trade association (membership is
by subscription), present number of members:
16,000 members, training organisation.
Trusted source of the best standards for business
data and the best practices for electronic
commerce.
The system provides the foundation for improved
supply chain management and electronic trading.

Subject coverage:
Best practice code for doing business electronically
across the extended enterprise. One-stop
organisation for help and advice on electronic
commerce to UK organisations. Supports and
promulgates EAN UCC standards, and electronic
commerce standards. Strong lobbying position on
behalf of 'UK plc'.

Library catalogue:
All or part available in-house

Printed publications:
The following publications are for members only:
General EAN UCC Specifications
Migration to Better Business Practice
EDIFACTS Manuals
Tradcoms (TDI) Manual
Brochures, information and advice titles for easy
reference

Electronic and video publications:
Edifacts Manuals (CD-ROM)
Producing Quality Barcodes (CD-ROM

Publications list:
Available in print

Access to staff:
Contact by letter, by fax, by e-mail and via
website
Hours: Mon to Fri, 0900 to 1700

Access to building, collection or gallery:
Prior appointment required

Access for disabled people:
Parking provided, ramped entry

Affiliated to:
International Article Numbering Association (EAN
Int)
tel: + 32 2 2271020; fax: + 32 2 2271021

Founder member of:
EAN

GUARDIAN NEWS & MEDIA LTD

Acronym or abbreviation: GNM

Research & Information, The Guardian, Kings
Place, 90 York Way, London N1 9GU

E-mail: richard.nelsson@guardian.co.uk

Website:
http://www.guardian.co.uk

Enquiries:
Enquiries to: Information Manager

Organisation type and purpose:
Publishing house.
Media.

GUILD OF AID FOR GENTLEPEOPLE

Acronym or abbreviation: The Guild

10 St Christopher's Place, London, W1U 1 HZ

Tel: 020 7935 0641
Fax: 0207 486 0128
E-mail: thead@pcac.org.uk

Enquiries:
Enquiries to: Assistant Secretary

Founded:
1904

Organisation type and purpose:
National organisation, voluntary organisation,
registered charity (charity number 31/BEN).
Providing assistance to those of gentle birth and
good education.

Subject coverage:
Financial assistance to people of gentle birth and
good education who have fallen into poverty.

Information services:
General.

Education services:
Education and further education.

Printed publications:
Annual Report (free)

Access to staff:
Contact by letter, by telephone, by fax and by e-
mail
Hours: Mon to Fri, 0930 to 1700

Access to building, collection or gallery:
No access other than to staff

Affiliated to:
Professional Classes Aid Council
administered from the same address; tel: as
above

GUILD OF AIR PILOTS AND AIR NAVIGATORS

Acronym or abbreviation: GAPAN

Cobham House, 9 Warwick Court, Gray's Inn,
London, WC1R 5DJ

Tel: 020 7404 4032
Fax: 020 7404 4035
E-mail: gapan@gapan.org

Website:
http://www.gapan.org

Enquiries:
Enquiries to: Clerk

Founded:
1929

Organisation type and purpose:
Professional body (membership is by subscription,
qualification, election or invitation), present
number of members: 1650, voluntary organisation,
suitable for ages: 17+.
Livery company of the City of London.
To promote air safety and aviation knowledge.

Subject coverage:
Air safety, aircrew licensing and training, technical
developments in aviation and the allocation of
flying scholarships and awards.

Access to staff:
Contact by letter, by fax, by e-mail and in person.
Appointment necessary.
Hours: Mon to Fri, 0900 to 1700

GUILD OF ALL SOULS

Acronym or abbreviation: GAS

Royal London House, 22–25 Finsbury Square,
London, EC2A 1DX

Tel: 020 7920 6468
Fax: 01371 831430
E-mail: contact@guildofallsouls.org.uk

Website:
http://www.guildofallsouls.org.uk

Enquiries:
Enquiries to: General Secretary

Founded:
1873

Organisation type and purpose:
Membership association (membership is by
subscription), present number of members: 1,800,
registered charity (charity number 240234).
Religious guild and patron of 40 livings.

continued overleaf

Museum or gallery collection, archive, or library special collection:
40 Advowson documents (some dating back to the 18th century)

Printed publications:
Order printed publications from: e-mail: contact@guildofallsouls.org.uk, or postal address

Publications list:
Available online

Access to staff:
Contact by letter, by telephone, by fax, by e-mail, in person and via website. Appointment necessary. Access for members only.
Hours: Mon and Thu, 1030 to 1500

GUILD OF ANTIQUE DEALERS AND RESTORERS

Acronym or abbreviation: GADAR

111 Belle Vue Road, Shrewsbury, Shropshire, SY3 7NJ

Tel: 01743 271852

Enquiries:
Enquiries to: Membership Secretary
Other contacts: Chairman

Founded:
1989

Organisation type and purpose:
Advisory body, learned society, professional body, trade association (membership is by subscription), present number of members: 300, consultancy, research organisation.
Advice to trade and public regarding restoration of furniture, ceramics, glass, silver, paintings, etc.

Subject coverage:
All restoration to antiques. Information regarding courses on restoration. Valuations for probate and insurance.

Museum or gallery collection, archive, or library special collection:
Reference books on all aspects of restoration and antiques

Printed publications:
Newsletter (quarterly, to members)

Access to staff:
Contact by letter, by telephone and in person
Hours: Mon and Fri, 0930 to 1700; 24-hour answering service

Access to building, collection or gallery:
Prior appointment required

GUILD OF ARCHITECTURAL IRONMONGERS

Acronym or abbreviation: GAI

8 Stepney Green, London, E1 3JU

Tel: 020 7790 3431
Fax: 020 7790 8517
E-mail: info@gai.org.uk

Website:
http://www.gai.org.uk
Membership, standards, technical.

Enquiries:
Enquiries to: Chief Executive

Founded:
1961

Organisation type and purpose:
International organisation, trade association (membership is by subscription), present number of members: 400, service industry.

Subject coverage:
Architectural ironmongery and industry training.

Printed publications:
Manuals on hinges, locks, fittings etc

Publications list:
Available in print

Access to staff:
Contact by letter, by fax, by e-mail and via website
Hours: Mon to Fri, 0900 to 1700

GUILD OF BRITISH BUTLERS, ADMINISTRATORS AND PERSONAL ASSISTANTS

12 Little Bornes, Alleyn Park, Dulwich, London, SE21 8SE

Tel: 020 8670 5585
Fax: 020 8670 0055

Website:
http://www.ivorspencer.com

Enquiries:
Enquiries to: Chief Executive
Direct tel: 020 8670 5585

Founded:
1981

Organisation type and purpose:
Professional body, voluntary organisation, training organisation.

Subject coverage:
Controlling large households; banqueting; purchasing for large parties; training staff for service in hotels and private households; organisation of Royal and State banquets world-wide.

Access to staff:
Contact by letter, by telephone and by fax
Hours: Mon to Fri, 0900 to 1700

Links with:
Ivor Spencer School for Butler Administrators at the same address

GUILD OF BUILDERS AND CONTRACTORS

Crest House, 102–104 Church Road, Teddington, Middlesex, TW11 8PY

Tel: 020 8977 1105
Fax: 020 8943 3151
E-mail: info@buildersguild.co.uk

Website:
http://www.BuildersGuild.co.uk

Enquiries:
Enquiries to: Director General

Founded:
1992

Organisation type and purpose:
National organisation, trade association (membership is by subscription, election or invitation), present number of members: 1700.

Subject coverage:
Building.

Access to staff:
Contact by letter, by telephone, by fax and by e-mail
Hours: Mon to Fri, 0930 to 1600

Access to building, collection or gallery:
No access other than to staff

Access for disabled people:
Parking provided

GUILD OF CHURCH MUSICIANS

Acronym or abbreviation: GCM

Hillbrow, Godstone Road, Bletchingley, Surrey, RH1 4PJ

Tel: 01883 743168
E-mail: JohnMusicsure@orbix.co.uk

Enquiries:
Enquiries to: General Secretary

Founded:
1888

Formerly called:
Incorporated Guild of Church Musicians (IGCM) (year of change 1988)

Organisation type and purpose:
International organisation, professional body (membership is by election or invitation), present number of members: 700, registered charity, suitable for ages: all, training organisation.
Examining body for Archbishop's Certificate in Church Music and Fellowship of the Guild of Church Musicians, and the Archbishop's Certificate in Public Worship.

Subject coverage:
Church music; administration of Archbishops' Certificates in Church Music and Public Worship, associate and fellowship examinations.

Non-library collection catalogue:
All or part available in print

Library catalogue:
All or part available in-house

Printed publications:
Guild Year Book
Laudate (magazine, 3 times a year)

Access to staff:
Contact by letter, by telephone, by e-mail and via website. Appointment necessary.
Hours: Mon to Fri, 0930 to 1800

Liaison with the:
Royal School of Church Music

Other addresses:
St Katharine Cree Church
86 Leadenhall Street, London, EC3; tel: 020 7283 5733

GUILD OF DISABLED HOMEWORKERS

23 Fountain Street, Nailsworth, Gloucestershire, GL6 0BL

Tel: 01453 835623
Fax: 01453 835623
E-mail: godcl@tiscali.co.uk

Enquiries:
Enquiries to: Membership Secretary

Founded:
1972

Subject coverage:
Homeworking for the disabled.

Access to staff:
Contact by letter, by telephone, by fax and by e-mail
Hours: Mon to Fri, 0930 to 1630

Access for disabled people:
Ramped entry

GUILD OF FOOD WRITERS

The Administrator, 255 Kent House Road, Beckenham, Kent, BR3 1JQ

Tel: 020 8659 0422
E-mail: guild@gfw.co.uk

Website:
http://www.gfw.co.uk

Enquiries:
Enquiries to: Administrator

Founded:
1984

Organisation type and purpose:
Professional body, membership association (membership is by subscription, election or invitation), present number of members: 390.

Publications list:
Available online

Access to staff:
Contact by letter, by telephone, by e-mail and via website
Hours: Mon to Fri, 0900 to 1700

GUILD OF FREEMEN OF THE CITY OF LONDON

PO Box 1202, Kingston upon Thames, Surrey, KT2 7XB

Tel: 020 8541 1435
Fax: 020 8541 1455
E-mail: clerk@guild-freemen-london.co.uk

Website:
http://www.guild-freemen-london.co.uk

Enquiries:
Enquiries to: The Clerk

Founded:
1908

Organisation type and purpose:
Membership association (membership is by subscription, qualification, election or invitation), present number of members: 2,500.
Guild, whose Patron is The Lord Mayor of the City of London. Membership restricted to individuals having the freedom of the City of London.
To bring together Freemen of the City of London, for the purposes of Charity, Benevolence, Education and Social Activities.

Subject coverage:
History of Guild of the Freemen of the City of London and current information.

Printed publications:
History of Guild (£20)
Leaflet about Guild (free)
Annual Journal (£5)
Order printed publications from: The Clerk

Access to staff:
Contact by letter, by telephone, by fax, by e-mail and via website
Hours: Mon to Fri, 0900 to 1700

GUILD OF GLASS ENGRAVERS

Acronym or abbreviation: GGE

87 Nether Street, London, N12 7NP

Tel: 020 8446 4050
Fax: 020 8446 4050
E-mail: enquiries@gge.org.uk

Website:
http://www.gge.org.uk

Enquiries:
Enquiries to: Secretary

Founded:
1975

Organisation type and purpose:
International organisation, membership association (membership is by subscription), present number of members: 300, voluntary organisation, registered charity (charity number 1016162).

Subject coverage:
Glass engraving; methods, the copper wheel lathe, the hand-held stylus, acid etch, electrically driven hand-held drill.

Museum or gallery collection, archive, or library special collection:
Images of Fellows' and Associate Fellows' engraved glass, books, slides, DVDs on different techniques of glass engraving

Printed publications:
Annual Report available on request
Membership and suppliers lists (members only)
Annual Newsletter available to purchase
Tri monthly Newsletters(available to members of the Guild only)

Order printed publications from: e-mail: enquiries@gge.org.uk; tel: 0208 0446 4050

Electronic and video publications:
Images of Fellows' and Associate Fellows' engraved glass, books, slides, DVDs on different techniques of glass engraving
Order electronic and video publications from: website: http://www.gge.org.uk

Publications list:
Available online and in print

Access to staff:
Contact by letter, by telephone, by e-mail and via website
Hours: Mon, 0930 to 1530; Tue, 0930 to 1530; Wed, 0930 to 1430

GUILD OF INTERNATIONAL PROFESSIONAL TOASTMASTERS

12 Little Bornes, Alleyn Park, Dulwich, London, SE21 8SE

Tel: 020 8670 5585
Fax: 020 8670 0055

Website:
http://www.ivorspencer.com

Enquiries:
Enquiries to: Life President
Direct tel: 020 8670 8424

Founded:
1992

Formerly called:
Guild of Professional Toastmasters (year of change 1992)

Organisation type and purpose:
Advisory body, professional body.

Subject coverage:
Organisation of functions of all types, including Royal events, in the UK and abroad; award of Best Speaker of the Year.

Access to staff:
Contact by letter and by telephone
Hours: Mon to Fri, 0900 to 1700

Links with:
Guild of Professional After Dinner Speakers

GUILD OF MACE-BEARERS

C/o The Mayor's Parlour, The Town Hall, Katharine Street, Croydon, CR9 1XW

Tel: 020 8760 5764
Fax: 020 8633 9517
E-mail: guildclerk.pa@virgin.net

Enquiries:
Enquiries to: Guild Clerk

Founded:
1933

Organisation type and purpose:
National organisation, membership association (membership is by subscription), present number of members: 350.

Subject coverage:
Ceremonial activities, protocol matters and advice, toastmastering duties, chauffeuring duties.

Access to staff:
Contact by fax and by e-mail
Hours: Monday to Friday, 0900 to 1700

GUILD OF NATUROPATHIC IRIDOLOGISTS INTERNATIONAL

Acronym or abbreviation: GNI Int

94 Grosvenor Road, London, SW1V 3LF

Tel: 020 7821 0255
Fax: 020 7821 0255
E-mail: info@gni-international.org

Website:
http://www.gni-international.org
History, mechanics and illustration on iridology. Situations vacant, events etc. Register.

Enquiries:
Enquiries to: Vice President and Registrar
Other contacts: Managing Director, General Secretary

Founded:
1993

Formerly called:
Holistic Health Consultancy and College (year of change 1993); British Register of Iridologists (MBRI) (year of change 1997); UK College of Clinical Iridologists (year of change 1999)

Organisation type and purpose:
International organisation, advisory body, professional body (membership is by qualification), present number of members: 120 + 84 Licentiates + 62 Student members, training organisation, research organisation.
Now the UK's only umbrella body for iridologists. Affiliates 11 training colleges.

Subject coverage:
Iridology, naturopathic medicine, herbal medicine, nutrition.

Museum or gallery collection, archive, or library special collection:
Iridiagnosis (Kritzer, J Maskel MD, original manuscript)
Prospectuses re Accredited Training Courses
Teaching Models
EU & US Iridology Books

Trade and statistical information:
Data on recognised professional training courses, events and post-graduate training dates and venues.

Non-library collection catalogue:
All or part available in print

Library catalogue:
All or part available in-house

Printed publications:
Course Material for Holistic Health College: 19 modules over 2 years (£150 per module)
Prospectus re training courses (send £2 in stamps)
Pupillotonia and Pupil Manifestations by Peter Bradbury
Register of Professionally Qualified Practitioners
Register and Information pack (send large sae)
Code of Ethics
Constitution
Newsletters (2 times a year)

Electronic and video publications:
1998 International Iridology Symposium
Videos: Aloe Vera, ME, Herbal Dispensaries Management (on hire only)

Publications list:
Available online and in print

Access to staff:
Contact by letter, by telephone, by fax, by e-mail and in person. Appointment necessary. Access for members only.
Hours: Mon to Wed, 0900 to 1700; Thu and Fri, 0800 to 1100
Special comments: Telephone Monday to Wednesday only.

Access to building, collection or gallery:
Prior appointment required

Access for disabled people:
Access to all public areas, toilet facilities

GUILD OF ONE-NAME STUDIES

Acronym or abbreviation: GOONS

Box G, 14 Charterhouse Buildings, Goswell Road, London, EC1M 7BA

Tel: 0800 011 2182
E-mail: guild@one-name.org

continued overleaf

Website:
http://www.one-name.org

Enquiries:
Enquiries to: Secretary
Direct e-mail: Apply for membership online at the Guild website

Founded:
1979

Organisation type and purpose:
International organisation, membership association (membership is by subscription), present number of members: 2,500, registered charity (charity number 802048). Furtherance of family history.

Subject coverage:
Study of surnames.

Information services:
Members supply information about the registered surname that they are studying. Register of names available on website.

Education services:
Techniques for one-name (surname) study available in the Forum, Journal, Seminars, Help Desk (see website for more details).

Printed publications:
Information brochures
Journal of One-Name Studies
Register of One-Name Studies

Publications list:
Available in print

Access to staff:
Contact by letter, by telephone, by e-mail and via website
Hours: 24 hours

GUILD OF PHOTOGRAPHERS (UNITED KINGDOM)

Acronym or abbreviation: GWP

59 Fore Street, Trowbridge, Wiltshire, BA14 8ET

Tel: 01225 760088
Fax: 01225 759159
E-mail: info@gwp-uk.co.uk

Website:
http://www.gwp-uk.co.uk
Advice on choosing a wedding photographer. Listing of qualified members.

Enquiries:
Enquiries to: Administrator

Founded:
1988

Formerly called:
Guild of Wedding Photographers UK (year of change 1999)

Organisation type and purpose:
Membership association (membership is by subscription), present number of members: 1200, service industry, suitable for ages: 18+, training organisation.
Training, qualifying and marketing services for photographers engaged in wedding and portrait photography.

Subject coverage:
Photography at weddings and other similar social functions in the UK and overseas.

Printed publications:
Big Marketing Ideas for Wedding Photographers (monthly, members only)
How to Choose Your Wedding Photographer booklet (free to members of the public)
News Sheet (monthly, members only)
Wedding Photography Today (monthly, members only)

Electronic and video publications:
Training Videos (available to members)

Publications list:
Available in print

Access to staff:
Contact by letter, by telephone, by fax, by e-mail and via website
Hours: Mon to Fri, 0900 to 1730

GUILD OF PROFESSIONAL VIDEOGRAPHERS

Acronym or abbreviation: GPV

11 Telfer Road, Coventry, Warwickshire, CV6 3DG

Tel: 024 7627 2548
Fax: 024 7627 2548
E-mail: info@professional-videographers.co.uk

Website:
http://www.professional-videographers.co.uk

Enquiries:
Enquiries to: General Secretary

Founded:
1991

Organisation type and purpose:
Advisory body, trade association (membership is by subscription, qualification), present number of members: 215, training organisation.

Subject coverage:
Information concerning copyright law. Investigations into new equipment available. Widespread international freelance videographers available for work.

Access to staff:
Contact by letter, by telephone, by fax, by e-mail, in person and via website
Hours: Mon to Fri, 0900 to 1700

GUILD OF PSYCHOTHERAPISTS, THE

47 Nelson Square, London, SE1 0QA

Tel: 020 8540 4454
E-mail: guild@psycho.org.uk

Website:
http://www.psycho.org.uk
Prospectus and events.

Enquiries:
Enquiries to: Administrator

Founded:
1974

Organisation type and purpose:
Professional body, registered charity, training organisation.

Subject coverage:
All aspects of training in psychoanalytic psychotherapy leading to UKCP registration. Referrals to psychoanalytic psychotherapists.

Printed publications:
List of Practitioners
Prospectus

Access to staff:
Contact by letter
Hours: Mon to Fri, 0900 to 1700

Member of:
UK Council for Psychotherapy
Psychoanalytic and Psychodynamic Psychotherapy Section, 167–169 Great Portland Street, London, WIN 5FB; tel: 020 7436 3002; fax: 020 7436 3013; e-mail: ukcp@psychotherapy.org.uk

GUILD OF REGISTERED TOURIST GUIDES

Guild House, 52D Borough High Street, London, SE1 1XN

Tel: 020 7403 1115
Fax: 020 7378 1705
E-mail: guild@blue-badge.org.uk

Website:
http://www.visitbritain.com
http://www.blue-badge.org.uk

Enquiries:
Enquiries to: Office Manager

Founded:
1950

Formerly called:
Guild of Guide Lecturers (GGL) (year of change 1995)

Organisation type and purpose:
National organisation, advisory body, membership association (membership is by subscription, qualification), present number of members: 1800, voluntary organisation.
The Guild is the national professional association for tourist board registered guides in the United Kingdom.
It represents 1800 guides in England, Northern Ireland, Scotland, Wales, Jersey and the Isle of Man, who between them speak 38 different languages.

Subject coverage:
Tourism, guide training, organisation of tours, sources of information for tourist guides and tour operators, tourist guides, the languages spoken, special interests offered.

Printed publications:
Guide Post (newsletter, monthly)
Subscriber's Bulletin (newsletter, monthly)
The Guild Directory – Annual List of Registered Guides
The Guide's Guides

Publications list:
Available online and in print

Access to staff:
Contact by letter, by telephone, by fax, by e-mail and via website. Appointment necessary.
Hours: Mon to Fri, 0900 to 1700

Member of:
Federation of European Guides
London and Regional Tourist Boards
World Federation of Tourist Guides

GUILD OF TAXIDERMISTS

Acronym or abbreviation: GOT

Glasgow Museums Resource Centre, 200 Woodhead Road, South Nitshill, Glasgow, G53 7NN

Tel: 0141 276 9445/9311
Fax: 0141 276 9305

Enquiries:
Enquiries to: Honorary Secretary
Direct e-mail: james.dickinson@lancashire.gov.uk

Founded:
1976

Organisation type and purpose:
International organisation, membership association (membership is by subscription), present number of members: 210, voluntary organisation, museum, suitable for ages: all, training organisation, consultancy.

Subject coverage:
Taxidermy and natural history display work.

Museum or gallery collection, archive, or library special collection:
Photograph library plus slide collection covering many techniques

Printed publications:
Careers in taxidermy (free)
Information sheets on the purpose and work of the Guild (free)
Newsletter/journal (annually)

Access to staff:
Contact by letter, by telephone, by fax, by e-mail and in person. Appointment necessary.
Hours: Mon to Fri, 0900 to 1700

Member organisation of:
European Taxidermy Federation
at the same address

GUILD OF TRAVEL AND TOURISM

Suite 193 Temple Chambers, 3–7 Temple Avenue,
London, EC4Y 0DB

Tel: 020 7583 6333
E-mail: nigel.bishop@traveltourismguild.com

Website:
http://www.traveltourismguild.com

Enquiries:
Enquiries to: Chief Executive
Other contacts: International Development Director

Founded:
1994

Organisation type and purpose:
Travel industry trade association.

Printed publications:
The E-Travel Business

Access to staff:
Contact by e-mail

Branches:
Guild of Travel and Tourism Asia Chapter in Hong
Kong
e-mail: steven.ballantyne@traveltourismguild
.com

GUILDFORD BOROUGH COUNCIL

Millmead House, Millmead, Guildford, Surrey,
GU2 4BB

Tel: 01483 505050
Fax: 01483 444444

Website:
http://www.guildford.gov.uk/

Enquiries:
Enquiries to: Chief Executive

Organisation type and purpose:
Local government body.

Printed publications:
About Guildford

Access to staff:
Contact by letter, by telephone, by fax, by e-mail
and in person
Hours: Mon to Fri, 0900 to 1700

Access to building, collection or gallery:
Mon to Wed, 0830 to 1700; Thu, 0830 to 2000; Fri,
0830 to 1630

Access for disabled people:
Parking spaces, lift, stair-lift

Parent body:
Surrey County Council

GUILDFORD COLLEGE OF FURTHER AND HIGHER EDUCATION

Stoke Park, Guildford, Surrey, GU1 1EZ

Tel: 01483 448611
Fax: 01483 448606

Website:
http://www.guildford.ac.uk

Enquiries:
Enquiries to: Librarian
Direct e-mail: dmarshall@guildford.ac.uk

Organisation type and purpose:
Further Education College.

Subject coverage:
Health, social studies, education, mathematics,
engineering, catering, management, business
studies, computing, travel and tourism, geography,
sport, leisure, media studies, art, graphic, printing,
science, construction, humanities.

Library catalogue:
All or part available in-house

Printed publications:
Guides to the Library
List of Journals (annually)
New Additions to Stock (selective)

Access to staff:
Contact by letter, by telephone, by e-mail, in
person and via website
Hours: Term time: Mon to Thu, 0830 to 2000; Fri,
0830 to 1700; Sat, 1000 to 1300

Access for disabled people:
Toilet facilities
Special comments: Lift available

GUILDFORD INSTITUTE

Ward Street, Guildford, Surrey, GU1 4LH

Tel: 01483 562142
Fax: 01483 451034
E-mail: info@guildford-institute.org.uk

Website:
http://www.guildford-institute.org.uk

Enquiries:
Enquiries to: Manager

Founded:
1834

Organisation type and purpose:
The Guildford Institute is registered in England
and Wales as a company limited by guarantee
(company number 6571640; registered charity
number 1125031). Educational institute and library.
Membership organisation (membership by
subscription).

Subject coverage:
A selection of the latest fiction and non-fiction and
a unique local history collection.

**Museum or gallery collection, archive, or library
special collection:**
Library of 13,000 vols, newspapers, periodicals,
local history books, ephemera, photographs,
prints and drawings relating to the history,
people, antiquities and topography of Guildford
and the county of Surrey.
The institutional archive is held by the Surrey
History Service: 130 Goldsworth Road, Woking,
Surrey, GU21 1ND

Printed publications:
Journal (2 times a year; free to members)
Courses and events brochure (3 times per year)

Access to staff:
Contact by letter, by telephone, by e-mail and in
person. Non-members charged.
Hours: Tue to Fri, 1000 to 1500; Sat, 1000 to 1300
Special comments: Library closed Mon.

GUILDHALL LIBRARY

Aldermanbury, London, EC2V 7HH

Tel: 020 7332 1868/1870
Fax: 020 7600 3384
E-mail: guildhall.library@cityoflondon.gov.uk

Website:
http://www.cityoflondon.gov.uk/guildhalllibrary

Enquiries:
Enquiries to: Guildhall Librarian

Founded:
1828

Organisation type and purpose:
Local government body, public library.

Subject coverage:
London history, English topography, local
societies, historical horology, historical technology,
clockmaking, maritime history, cookery, wine
trade, genealogy, parliamentary and statutory
materials, business history, English law reports,
history of shorthand.

**Museum or gallery collection, archive, or library
special collection:**
Acts (public, private and local)
Antiquarian Horological Society Library
Clockmakers' Company Library
Alfred Cock Collection (Thomas More)
English Law Reports from the 17th century
onwards
Fletchers' Company Library (archery)
Gardeners' Company Library
Gresham College Collection (early music)
Elizabeth David Collection (food and wine)
Institute of Masters of Wine Library
International Genealogical Index (microfiche)
compiled by the Church of Jesus Christ of the
Latter-Day Saints: British Isles and Ireland
International Wine and Food Society Library
Charles Lamb Society Collection
Lloyds Marine Collection
Sir Thomas More Collection
Parliamentary Papers from 1801
Public Record Office Publications
André Simon Collection (food and wine)
Stock Exchange Reports and Prospectuses c.1824–
1964
Pepys Collection
Wilkes Collection (John Wilkes and 18th-century
radical history)

Library catalogue:
All or part available online and in-house

Printed publications:
City of London Parish Registers
Facsimiles of Early London Maps
Greater London Parish Registers
Gresham Music Library Catalogue
City Livery Companies and Related Organisations
A Guide to Genealogical Sources in the Guildhall
Library
A Guide to Lloyd's Marine Collection at Guildhall
Library
A Hand List of Business Archives at Guildhall
Library
A Hand List of Non-conformist, Roman Catholic,
Jewish and Burial Ground Registers at Guildhall
Library
Mediaeval Guildhall of London (1974)
London Buildings and Sites: A Guide for
Researchers in Guildhall Library
Historic Trade Directories in Guildhall Library

Publications list:
Available in print

Access to staff:
Contact by letter, by telephone, by fax, by e-mail
and in person

Access to building, collection or gallery:
No prior appointment required
Hours: Mon to Sat, 0930 to 1700
Special comments: Closed on Sat before Bank
Holidays.

Access for disabled people:
Lift entry, access to all public areas, toilet facilities

Parent body:
City of London Corporation

GUILDHALL SCHOOL OF MUSIC AND DRAMA

Acronym or abbreviation: GSMD

Silk Street, Barbican, London, EC2Y 8DT

Tel: 020 7382 7178
Fax: 020 7786 9378
E-mail: library@gsmd.ac.uk

Website:
http://www.gsmd.ac.uk

continued overleaf

Enquiries:
Enquiries to: Senior Librarian
Direct tel: 020 7382 7174
Direct e-mail: keaton@gsmd.ac.uk
Other contacts: Deputy Librarian

Founded:
1880

Organisation type and purpose:
Suitable for ages: 18+ (HE).
Conservatoire of music and drama.

Subject coverage:
Music, drama.

Museum or gallery collection, archive, or library special collection:
Alkan Society Collection (material on or by Charles Alkan)
Appleby Collection of guitar music
Goossens Collection of oboe music
Harris Opera Collection
Lute Society Collection of art reproductions depicting early instruments
Merrett Collection of double bass music
Westrup Library of music and books on music

Non-library collection catalogue:
All or part available in-house

Library catalogue:
All or part available in-house

Printed publications:
Various guides to the library

Access to staff:
Contact by letter, by telephone, by e-mail and in person. Appointment necessary.
Hours: Mon to Fri, 0900 to 1900

Access to building, collection or gallery:
Prior appointment required

Parent body:
Corporation of London

GUILDHE

20 Tavistock Square, Woburn House, London, WC1H 9HB

Tel: 020 7387 7711
Fax: 020 7387 7712
E-mail: business@guildhe.ac.uk

Website:
http://www.guildhe.ac.uk

Enquiries:
Enquiries to: PA to Chief Executive
Direct tel: 020 7529 8795

Founded:
1978

Formerly called:
Standing Conference of Principals (year of change 2006)

Organisation type and purpose:
National organisation, membership association (membership is by subscription), registered charity (charity number 1012218), research organisation.

Subject coverage:
Higher education issues relating specially to colleges of higher education in England and Northern Ireland.

Publications list:
Available online

Access to staff:
Contact by letter, by telephone, by fax, by e-mail and via website
Hours: Mon to Fri, 0900 to 1700

GUN TRADE ASSOCIATION LIMITED

Acronym or abbreviation: GTA

PO Box 43, Tewkesbury, Gloucestershire, GL20 5ZE

Tel: 01684 291868
Fax: 01684 291864
E-mail: enquiries@guntradeassociation.com

Website:
http://www.gtaltd.co.uk

Enquiries:
Enquiries to: Director
Direct e-mail: john@guntradeassociation.com

Founded:
1912

Organisation type and purpose:
Trade association.
Represents all sectors of the British sporting gun and allied trades.

Subject coverage:
The manufacture, supply and legitimate use of firearms and ammunition, the law relating to the above.

Printed publications:
Newsletter (4 times a year, members only)
Occasional publications

Access to staff:
Contact by letter, by telephone, by fax and by e-mail
Hours: Mon to Fri, 0900 to 1700

Access to building, collection or gallery:
No access to building.

Member organisation of:
British Shooting Sports Council
European Association for the Civil Commerce of Weapons
Standing Conference on Countryside Sports
World Forum on the Future of Sport Shooting Activities

GURKHA WELFARE TRUST

2nd floor, Cross Keys House, PO Box 2170, 22 Queen Street, Salisbury, SP2 2EX

Tel: 01722 323955
Fax: 01722 343119
E-mail: staffassistant@gwt.org.uk

Website:
http://www.gwt.org.uk
Information on Gurkhas and on the welfare trust.

Founded:
1969

Organisation type and purpose:
Registered charity (charity number 1103669).
Founded to support Gurkha soldiers and/or dependents and widows of soldiers who had served in World War II, but did not qualify for an army pension.
To relieve poverty and distress among Gurkha veterans of the Crown and their dependents.
Supports Gurkhas through welfare pensions, a first class medical scheme, hardship grants, emergency aid, community projects, and education grants to the dependants of retired Gurkhas.

Subject coverage:
The Trust distributes funds in Nepal and responds to welfare needs as they arise in the UK.
It supports around 10,000 welfare pensioners in Nepal. Most are in their 80s and are totally reliant on the Trust for a dignified comfortable old age.
Increasing numbers of Gurkhas will settle in the UK and the Trust is ready to respond. As the lead charity for Gurkha welfare, it has a co-ordinating role for helping those in need in the UK and other service charities. However, its firm focus remains Nepal and 10,000 veterans who will spend their final days in the mountain villages.

Electronic and video publications:
Recipes, audio and videos
Newsletter (via e-mail)
Order electronic and video publications from:
Download from website

Publications list:
Available online

Access to staff:
Contact by letter, by telephone, by fax, by e-mail and in person. Appointment necessary.
Hours: By appointment

Grant in aid funding from:
Ministry of Defence

Links with:
The Gurkha Museum
Peninsula Barracks, Romsey Road, Winchester, SO23 8TS; tel: 01962 843659; fax: 01962 877597; e-mail: curator@thegurkhamuseum.co.uk; website: http://www.thegurkhamuseum.co.uk

GUT TRUST

Unit 5, 53 Mowbray Street, Sheffield, S3 8EN

Tel: 0114 272 3253
E-mail: info@theguttrust.org

Website:
http://www.theguttrust.org

Enquiries:
Enquiries to: Membership Officer

Founded:
1991

Formerly called:
IBS Network (year of change 2007)

Organisation type and purpose:
Membership association (membership is by subscription), voluntary organisation, registered charity (charity number 1057563).
A self-help organisation.
To inform, support and educate those with IBS.

Subject coverage:
Irritable bowel syndrome.

Museum or gallery collection, archive, or library special collection:
Art Works: entries to Living with IBS competition (2000, 2001)
Assorted books on IBS
Gut Reaction Journal (issue 1 to date)

Non-library collection catalogue:
All or part available in-house

Printed publications:
A Complete Guide to Relief from IBS (C. Dancey and S. Backhouse)
Fact Sheets (direct)
Gut Reaction (journal, quarterly, free to members, direct, back issues available)
Order printed publications from: A Complete Guide To Relief, order from IBS, Robinson Publishing, 7 Kensington Church Court, London, W8 4SP

Electronic and video publications:
Feeling Better Relaxed (CD)

Publications list:
Available online and in print

Access to staff:
Contact by letter, by telephone, by e-mail and via website
Hours: Office: Mon to Fri, 1000 to 1500
Helpline: Tue and Thu, 1930 to 2130

Access to building, collection or gallery:
Prior appointment required

GUYANA HIGH COMMISSION

3 Palace Court, Bayswater Road, London, W2 4LP

Tel: 020 7229 7684
Fax: 020 7727 9809
E-mail: ghc.1@ic24.net

Enquiries:
Enquiries to: First Secretary

Organisation type and purpose:
National body of the Republic of Guyana.
Guyana's diplomatic representation.

Subject coverage:
Political, social, economic and cultural aspects of Guyana.

Access to staff:
Contact by letter, by telephone, by fax and by e-mail
Hours: Office Hours: Mon to Fri, 0930 to 1730
Consular Matters: Mon to Fri, 0930 to 1430

GUYS' AND ST THOMAS' POISONS UNIT, GUY'S AND ST THOMAS' NHS FOUNDATION TRUST

Acronym or abbreviation: GTPU

Mary Sheridan House, Guy's Hospital, Great Maze Pond, London, SE1 9RT

Tel: 020 7188 0600
Fax: 020 7188 0700
E-mail: guyspoisons@gstt.nhs.uk

Website:
http://www.medtox.co.uk

Organisation type and purpose:
Poisons centre; part of Guy's and St Thomas' NHS Foundation Trust.

Subject coverage:
Medical toxicology.

Information services:
Poisons information service.

Library catalogue:
All or part available in-house

Access to staff:
Contact by letter, by telephone, by fax, by e-mail and via website. Appointment necessary.
Hours: Mon to Fri, 0930 to 1730

Access to building, collection or gallery:
24 hours' notice required
Hours: Mon to Fri, 0930 to 1730
Special comments: Researchers and NHS staff only.

Links with:
Guy's and St Thomas' NHS Foundation Trust
  St Thomas' Hospital, Lambeth Palace Road, London, SE1 7EH; tel: 020 7188 7188; website: http://www.guysandstthomas.nhs.uk

GWE BUSINESS WEST LTD

Emlyn Square, Swindon, SN1 5BP

Tel: 01275 373373
Fax: 01275 370 706
E-mail: info@gwebusinesswest.co.uk

Website:
http://www.gwebusinesswest.co.uk
Details of a range of business support (inc training, workspace, venue hire) and Chamber of Commerce services provided by or via GWE Business West Ltd.

Enquiries:
Enquiries to: Receptionist

Founded:
2008

Created by the merger of:
Great Western Enterprise (GWE) Ltd and Business West (year of change 2008)

Organisation type and purpose:
Business support and chamber membership

Subject coverage:
Bath and Bristol Chambers of Commerce; office space to let; virtual office services; meeting room hire; conferencing facilities and venue hire; business training (courses and bespoke); mentoring; international trade advice and support; event management; networking; business advice; business workshops; business information.

Printed publications:
What's On
Business I
Update Magazine

Access to staff:
Contact via website

Branches:
Bristol Chamber of Commerce
  Leigh Court, Abbey Meads, Bristol, BS8 3RA; tel: 01275 373373; website: http://www.gwebusinesswest.co.uk
Business Link (Berkshire)
  The Crossbow Centre, Crossbow House, 40 Liverpool Road, Slough, Berkshire, SL1 4QZ; tel: 0845 600 9006; website: http://www.gwebusinesswest.co.uk

Links with:
Bath Chamber of Commerce
  16 Abbey Churchyard, Bath, BA1 1PB; website: http://www.gwebusinesswest.co.uk
Business Link (South West)
  Leigh Court, Abbey Meads, Bristol, BS8 3RA; tel: 0845 600 9006; website: http://www,gwebusinesswest.co.uk

GWENT LOCAL HISTORY SOCIETY

Ty Derwen, Church Road, Newport, NP19 7EJ

Tel: 01633 241564
E-mail: karen.vowles@gavowales.org.uk

Website:
http://www.gavowales.org.uk/gwent_local_history/index.htm

Enquiries:
Enquiries to: Secretary

Founded:
1954

Organisation type and purpose:
Voluntary organisation.
Provides forum for local history societies within Gwent.

Subject coverage:
Gwent local history.

Printed publications:
Gwent Local History journal (2 times a year)

Access to staff:
Contact by letter, by telephone, by fax and by e-mail
Hours: Mon to Fri, 0900 to 1700

Member of:
British Association of Local History

GWENT RECORD OFFICE

Acronym or abbreviation: GRO

County Hall, Cwmbran, Newport, Gwent, NP44 2XH

Tel: 01633 644886
Fax: 01633 648382
E-mail: gwent.records@torfaen.gov.uk

Founded:
1939

Formerly called:
Monmouthshire Record Office (year of change 1974)

Organisation type and purpose:
Local government body.
County record office.

Subject coverage:
Public records; manorial and tithe records; turnpike trusts; highways boards; health and services records; estate and family records; church parochial records etc.

Museum or gallery collection, archive, or library special collection:
Archive

Non-library collection catalogue:
All or part available in-house

Printed publications:
Guides to Research (on selected subjects)

Access to staff:
Contact by letter, by telephone, by fax, by e-mail, in person and via website
Hours: Tue to Thu, 0930 to 1700; Fri, 0930 to 1600

Access for disabled people:
Hours: Tue to Thu, 0930 to 1700; Fri, 0930 to 1600

Host authority:
Torfaen County Borough Council
  Civic Centre, Pontypool, Torfaen, NP4 6YB; tel: 01495 762200; fax: 01495 755513; website: www.torfaen.gov.uk

Parent body:
Gwent Joint Records Committee

GWENT WILDLIFE TRUST

16 White Swan Court, Monmouth, Gwent, NP25 3NY

Tel: 01600 715501
Fax: 01600 715832
E-mail: gwentwildlife@cix.co.uk

Website:
http://www.wildlifetrust.org.uk

Enquiries:
Enquiries to: Chairman

Organisation type and purpose:
Membership association (membership is by subscription), present number of members: 2500, voluntary organisation.
Aims to protect and enhance wildlife sites in Gwent.

Subject coverage:
Conservation management, species protection, site protection and enhancement, ecological surveying, advice and education, trust nature reserves, Gwent wildlife.

Trade and statistical information:
Species recording, site recording.

Printed publications:
Wild about Gwent (newsletter, Jan, May and Sep)

Affiliated to:
RSNC and Wildlife Trusts Partnership

Education Centre:
Gwent Wildlife Trust
  Festival Park, Ebbw Vale, NP23 6UF; tel: 01495 305289

GWYNEDD ARCHIVES & MUSEUMS SERVICE

Victoria Dock, Caernarfon, Gwynedd

Tel: 01286 679095
Fax: 01286 679637
E-mail: archives.caernarfon@gwynedd.gov.uk

Website:
http://www.gwynedd.gov.uk/archives

Enquiries:
Enquiries to: Archivist

Organisation type and purpose:
County Record Office.

Subject coverage:
Usual county archive collection with particular strengths in the industrial (quarrying), maritime and estate records.

Education services:
Group education facilities, resources for Key Stages 1 and 2 and 3.

Non-library collection catalogue:
All or part available online and in-house

Publications list:
Available online

Access to staff:
Contact by telephone, by fax, by e-mail and in person
Hours: Closed Mon; Tue, Thu, Fri, 0930 to 1230 and 1330 to 1700; Wed, 0930 to 1230 and 1330 to 1900

continued overleaf

Access to building, collection or gallery:
No prior appointment required
Hours: Closed Mon; open Tue, Thu, Fri, 0930 to 1230 and 1330 to 1700; Wed, 0930 to 1230 and 1330 to 1900
Special comments: CARN readers ticket required. Appointment advised for microfiche and microfilm readers

Access for disabled people:
Level entry, access to all public areas, toilet facilities

Other address:
Gwynedd Archives
   Dolgellau Area Record Office

GWYNEDD COUNTY COUNCIL

Development Directorate, Culture and Leisure, County Offices, Caernarfon, Gwynedd, LL55 1SH

Tel: 01286 672255
Fax: 01286 677347
E-mail: celf@gwynedd.gov.uk

Website:
http://www.gwynedd.gov.uk
County information, arts information, archive lists, library catalogue.

Enquiries:
Enquiries to: Assistant Director: Culture

Founded:
1996

Formerly called:
Arfon Borough Council, Dwyfor District Council, Gwynedd County Council, Meirionydd District Council (year of change 1996)

Organisation type and purpose:
Local government body, museum, art gallery, public library, suitable for ages: 4 to 18. Archives, arts organisation.

Subject coverage:
General reference materials, local history, county archives, artefacts.

Museum or gallery collection, archive, or library special collection:
County archives collections
European Community publications
Local history collections
Maritime records, including Lloyd's Registers, Lloyd's Lists, registers, crew lists and log books
Reports, Hansard etc of Welsh Assembly
Welsh periodicals and local newspapers

Non-library collection catalogue:
All or part available online and in-house

Library catalogue:
All or part available online

Printed publications:
Maritime Wales (annually)
Series of lectures, picture books, postcards etc

Access to staff:
Contact by letter, by telephone, by fax, by e-mail and in person
Hours: Mon to Fri, 0900 to 1700; late nights to 1900
Library also Sat, 1000 to 1300

Access to building, collection or gallery:
No access other than to staff

Other addresses:
Archives and Museum Service
   County Offices, Caernarfon, Gwynedd; tel: 01286 679093; fax: 01286 679637; e-mail: archifau@gwynedd.gov.uk
County Library Headquarters
   Allt Pafiliwn, Caernarfon, Gwynedd; tel: 01286 679465; fax: 01286 671137; e-mail: llyfrgell@gwynedd.gov.uk

GYPSUM PRODUCTS DEVELOPMENT LIMITED

Acronym or abbreviation: GPDA

PO Box 35084, London, NW1 4XE

Tel: 020 7935 8532
E-mail: admin@gpda.com

Website:
http://www.gpda.com

Enquiries:
Enquiries to: General Secretary

Founded:
1889

Organisation type and purpose:
Trade association (membership is by subscription).

Subject coverage:
Gypsum product usage (gypsum plaster, plasterboard); mainly in the fields of building and refurbishment.

Printed publications:
Publications on specific areas of gypsum product usage (irregular, free)

Publications list:
Available online

Access to staff:
Contact by letter, by telephone, by fax, by e-mail and via website
Hours: Mon to Fri, 0900 to 1700

Links with:
Construction Products Association
   tel: 020 7323 3770; fax: 020 7323 0307; e-mail: enquiries@constprod.org.uk; website: http://www.constrprod.org.uk
Eurogypsum (European Gypsum Industry Association)
   tel: +32 2 521 3890; e-mail: info@eurogypsum.org; website: http://www.eurogypsum.org

GYPSY COUNCIL, THE

Acronym or abbreviation: NGC

Greenacres Caravan Park, Common Lane, Hapsford, Frodsham, Cheshire, WA6 0JS

Tel: 01928 723138
Fax: 01928 723138

Enquiries:
Enquiries to: President

Founded:
1966

Formerly called:
National Gypsy Council (NGC)

Organisation type and purpose:
Voluntary organisation.
Membership restricted to Gypsies as defined in legislation.

Subject coverage:
Site provision for travellers, including information of site facilities, design and management; statistical information on numbers of Gypsy families in England, Wales and Scotland; existing sites and sites needed; movement of travellers; development and diversity of the travelling community in Britain; Gypsies and government policy; Gypsies and local government; Gypsy education; new age travellers, hippies.

Printed publications:
Annual Report
Gipsy Sites and Planning: an Objective Criticism of the DOE Circular 1/94 (no 2/94)
Practical Proposals for Gypsy/Traveller Law Reform (a discussion paper 1997)
Responses to government policies and documents including
Response to the Criminal Justice and Public Order Bill
Romano Drom (Gypsy News, back issues)

Publications list:
Available in print

Access to staff:
Contact by letter, by telephone and by fax
Hours: Mon to Fri, 0900 to 1700

Links with:
Romani Kris (West European Gypsy Council)

H C STARCK LIMITED

Acronym or abbreviation: HCST

UK Sales Office, Aizlewood's Mill, Nursery Street, Sheffield, S3 8GG

Tel: 0114 282 3158
E-mail: malcolm.greaves@hcstarck.com

Website:
http://www.hcstarck.com

Founded:
1969

Organisation type and purpose:
International organisation, manufacturing industry.

Subject coverage:
Refractory metals; corrosion-resistant metals e.g. tantalum, titanium, tungsten, hastelloy, zirconium, molybdenum, nickel and nickel alloys.

Printed publications:
Order printed publications from: HC Starck Inc
e-mail: Website: www.hcstarck.com

Publications list:
Available online

Access to staff:
Contact by letter, by telephone, by fax, by e-mail and via website. Appointment necessary.
Hours: Mon to Fri, 0900 to 1700

Access to building, collection or gallery:
Prior appointment required

Subsidiary of:
H C Starck Inc (HCSI)
   45 Industrial Place, Newton, MA 0241–1951, USA; tel: 00 1 617 630 5800; fax: 00 1 617 630 5919; website: www.hcstarck.com

UK production site:
H C Starck Limited
   1 Harris Road, Calne, Wiltshire, SN11 9PT; tel: 01249 822122; fax: 01249 823800

H G WELLS SOCIETY, THE

Acronym or abbreviation: HGWS

56 Riseholme Road, Gainsborough, Lincolnshire, DN21 1YT

E-mail: stevemclean_7@hotmail.com

Website:
http://hgwellsusa.50megs.com

Enquiries:
Enquiries to: General Secretary

Founded:
1960

Organisation type and purpose:
International organisation, learned society.
To promote and encourage an interest in, and appreciation of, the life, work and thought of H G Wells.

Subject coverage:
The life and work of Herbert George Wells (1866–1946).

Printed publications:
The Wellsian (annually)
The H G Wells Newsletter (quarterly)

Access to staff:
Contact by letter
Hours: Mon to Fri, 0900 to 1700

HABERDASHERS' COMPANY, THE

Formal name: Worshipful Company of Haberdashers

Haberdashers' Hall, 18 West Smithfield, London, EC1A 9HQ

Tel: 020 7246 9988
Fax: 020 7246 9989
E-mail: enquiries@haberdashers.co.uk

Website:
http://www.haberdashers.co.uk

Enquiries:
Enquiries to: The Clerk

Founded:
1448

Organisation type and purpose:
Membership association (membership is by election or invitation).
City of London Livery Company.

Access to staff:
Contact by letter, by telephone, by fax and by e-mail

HACKNEY ARCHIVES

43 De Beauvoir Road, London, N1 5SQ

Tel: 020 7241 2886
E-mail: archives@hackney.gov.uk

Website:
http://www.hackney.gov.uk/ca-archives
Guide.

Founded:
1965

Organisation type and purpose:
Local government body.
Record office.

Non-library collection catalogue:
All or part available online, in-house and in print

Library catalogue:
All or part available online and in-house

Publications list:
Available online and in print

Access to staff:
Contact by letter, by telephone, by e-mail and via website
Hours: Tue to Thu, 0930 to 1300 and 1400 to 1730; Fri, 0930 to 1300; Sat, 1000 to 1300 and 1400 to 1630

Access for disabled people:
Ramped entry
Special comments: Car park is restricted to permit holders (residential and staff).

HACKNEY HORSE SOCIETY

Fallowfields, Little London, Heytesbury, Warminster, Wiltshire, BA12 0ES

Tel: 01985 840717
Fax: 01985 840616
E-mail: admin@hackney-horse.org.uk

Website:
http://www.hackney-horse.org.uk

Enquiries:
Enquiries to: Secretary General

Organisation type and purpose:
Membership association.
Breed Society.

Subject coverage:
Breeding of hackney horses and ponies.

Museum or gallery collection, archive, or library special collection:
Stud Books from 1884
Year Books from 1967

Printed publications:
Newsletter (3 times a year, members)
Stud Books (every 3 years)

Links with:
British Horse Society

HAEMOPHILIA SOCIETY

3rd Floor, Chesterfield House, 385 Euston Road, London, NW1 3AU

Tel: 020 7380 0600
Fax: 020 7387 8220
E-mail: info@haemophilia.org.uk

Website:
http://www.haemophilia.org.uk

Enquiries:
Enquiries to: Information Officer
Direct e-mail: dan@haemophilia.org.uk

Founded:
1950

Organisation type and purpose:
Membership association (membership is by subscription), registered charity (charity number 288260).

Subject coverage:
Haemophilia and related bleeding disorders, treatment and care, education, employment, welfare benefits, HIV, hepatitis C.

Printed publications:
HQ (4 times a year)
Essentials of Haemophilia Care
Haemophilia and Schools
Introduction to Haemophilia (4th ed.)
Living with Haemophilia (Dr P Jones)
Reports and booklets, etc
Safer Sex Guide

Publications list:
Available online and in print

Access to staff:
Contact by letter, by telephone, by fax, by e-mail and via website
Hours: Mon to Fri, 0900 to 1700

Affiliated to:
European Haemophilia Consortium
World Federation of Haemophilia

HAIG HOMES

Formal name: Douglas Haig Memorial Homes

Alban Dobson House, Green Lane, Morden, Surrey, SM4 5NS

Tel: 020 8685 5777
Fax: 020 8685 5778
E-mail: haig@haighomes.org.uk

Website:
http://www.haighomes.org.uk
How to apply, locations of properties, information for tenants.

Founded:
1929

Incorporates the former:
Housing Association for Officers' Families (HAOF)

Organisation type and purpose:
Established as a charitable trust.
To provide housing assistance to ex-Service people and/or their dependants. Currently this object is achieved by letting homes at affordable rents. To be considered for housing, applicants must have a British Armed Forces connection and be in housing need.

Subject coverage:
The Association has over 1,300 houses, flats, maisonettes and bungalows throughout the UK, built mostly in the 1930s, 1950s and 1990s.

Electronic and video publications:
Annual report
Newsletter (3 a year)
Order electronic and video publications from:
Download from website

Access to staff:
Contact by letter, by telephone, by e-mail and via website
Hours: Mon to Fri, 0900 to 1700
Out of office hours: answerphone

HAIR AND BEAUTY INDUSTRY AUTHORITY (HABIA)

Acronym or abbreviation: HABIA

Fraser House, Nether Hall Road, Doncaster, South Yorkshire, DN7 2PH

Tel: 0845 230 6080
Fax: 01302 623171
E-mail: info@habia.org

Website:
http://www.habia.org
Provides information about HABIA and training and education issues relating to Hairdressing and Beauty Therapy.
http://www.qualifications.org
http://www.salon.org.uk

Enquiries:
Enquiries to: Reception
Other contacts: Entry to the Workforce Manager for specific training, careers and education information.

Founded:
January 1997

Formed from:
Beauty Industry Authority (BIA), Hairdressing Training Board (HTB), Hairdressing Training Board Scotland

Formerly called:
Health and Beauty Therapy Training Board (HBTTB)

Organisation type and purpose:
Advisory body.
Lead body.

Subject coverage:
Hairdressing and beauty therapy.

Trade and statistical information:
Data on UK hairdressing and beauty industry.

Non-library collection catalogue:
All or part available online

Printed publications:
Extensive selection of books on all aspects of hairdressing and beauty

Publications list:
Available online and in print

Access to staff:
Contact by letter, by telephone, by fax, by e-mail and via website. Appointment necessary.
Hours: Mon to Thu, 0830 to 1700; Fri, 0830 to 1530

Access to building, collection or gallery:
No access other than to staff

Links to:
City & Guilds
2 Giltpur Street, London, EC1A 9DD; tel: 020 7294 2468
Thomson Learning

HAIRDRESSING COUNCIL

Acronym or abbreviation: HC

30 Sydenham Road, Croydon, Surrey, CRO 2EF

Tel: 020 8760 7010
Fax: 020 8688 5372
E-mail: registrar@haircouncil.org.uk

Website:
http://www.haircouncil.org.uk

Enquiries:
Enquiries to: Registrar

Founded:
1964

Organisation type and purpose:
Statutory body.
Maintains state register of qualified hairdressers.

Subject coverage:
Hairdressing profession and industry; details of State Registered Hairdressers who are properly trained and qualified (to NVQ Hairdressing

continued overleaf

Certificate level). Details of personnel on state register; what to do in the event of a bad or unsatisfactory hairdressing experience.

Printed publications:
Hairdresser (quarterly, available to non-registered stylists at £3 plus p&p)
Handbook of Hairdressers (lists every state registered hairdresser alphabetically and by location, much useful information, £14.95 incl. p&p)

Publications list:
Available online

Access to staff:
Contact by telephone, by fax, by e-mail and via website
Hours: Mon to Fri, 0900 to 1600

Access to building, collection or gallery:
No access other than to staff

Links with:
The Guild of Hairdressers
The National Hairdressers Federation
Union of Shop Distributive and Allied Workers

Member organisations:
Association of Hairdressing Teachers in Colleges of Further Education
British Medical Association
Hairdressing Employers' Association
individuals include Members of Parliament, teachers, trichologists and other experts
Institute of Trichologists
Royal College of Physicians

HAKLUYT SOCIETY

Map Library, British Library, 96 Euston Road, London, NW1 2DB

Tel: 01428 641850
E-mail: office@hakluyt.com

Website:
http://www.hakluyt.com

Enquiries:
Enquiries to: Administrator

Founded:
1846

Organisation type and purpose:
Learned society (membership is by subscription), present number of members: 1,800, registered charity (charity number 313168).

Subject coverage:
Original narratives of important and historical voyages, travels, expeditions and other geographical records.

Non-library collection catalogue:
All or part available online

Printed publications:
Scholarly editions of records of voyages, travels and geographical material
First Series (100 vols, 1847–1898, out of print)
Second Series (81 vols, 1899 to date, some out of print)
Third Series (21 vols, 2002 to date)
Extra Series (46 vols to date, some out of print)
Order printed publications from: Publishers, Ashgate Ltd (non-members)

Microform publications:
First Series (microfilm)
Second series (microfilm of early vols)
Extra Series (vols 1–12, microfiche)
Order microform publications from: University Publications of America, UPA

Publications list:
Available online and in print

Access to staff:
Contact by e-mail and via website

HALIFAX ANTIQUARIAN SOCIETY

356 Oldham Road, Sowerby Bridge, Halifax, HX6 4QU

Tel: 01422 823966
E-mail: anne@boothwoodnook.fsnet.co.uk

Website:
http://www.halifaxhistory.org.uk

Enquiries:
Enquiries to: Secretary

Founded:
c. 1900

Organisation type and purpose:
Learned society (membership is by subscription), present number of members: c. 300, voluntary organisation.

Subject coverage:
History of Parish of Halifax.

Museum or gallery collection, archive, or library special collection:
Books and documents re Parish of Halifax

Library catalogue:
All or part available in-house

Printed publications:
Transactions since 1901
Back Numbers to 1901 (if available, from Publications Officer)
Order printed publications from: Publications Officer, Halifax Antiquarian Society, 6 Baker Fold, Raglan Street, Halifax, HX1 5TX

Publications list:
Available online

Access to staff:
Contact by letter, by telephone and via website

HALL-CARPENTER ARCHIVES

Acronym or abbreviation: HCA

Archives Division, Library of the London School of Economics and Political Science, 10 Portugal Street, London, WC2A 2HD

Tel: 020 7955 7223
E-mail: document@lse.ac.uk

Website:
http://www2.lse.ac.uk/library/archive/holdings/lesbian_and_gay_archives.aspx
Outline of the collection and link to the online catalogue.

Organisation type and purpose:
An archive of gay activism in Britain including the archives of LGBT organisations and activists, newspapers and magazines from the gay press, and series of ephemera from campaigns and individuals.

Subject coverage:
Gay activism in Britain.

Museum or gallery collection, archive, or library special collection:
Archive collection

Non-library collection catalogue:
All or part available online

Access to staff:
Contact by letter, by telephone, by e-mail, in person and via website. Appointment necessary.
Hours: Term-time and Easter vacation: Mon to Thu, 1000 to 2000; Fri, 1000 to 1700; Sat, 1100 to 1800
Special comments: Opening hours differ on public holidays and around Easter and Christmas; please contact for further details.

HALLMARK IP LIMITED

1 Pemberton Row, London. EC4A 3BG

Tel: 020 3102 9000
Fax: 020 3102 9001
E-mail: info@hallmark-ip.com

Website:
http://www.hallmark-ip.com

Enquiries:
Enquiries to: Company Secretary
Other contacts: Senior Attorney

Founded:
1886

Formerly called:
Trade Mark Owners Association Limited (year of change 2004)

Organisation type and purpose:
Service industry, trade mark attorneys.

Subject coverage:
Advisers into the availability for use and registration of trade marks, designs and copyright; attorneys obtaining rights in trade marks, continued protection of those marks, including through renewal of trade mark registrations, and subsequent enforcement of trade mark rights; design protection, including searching, registration, renewal and enforcement of design rights; copyright protection and enforcement; all throughout the UK, EU and worldwide.

Access to staff:
Contact by letter, by telephone, by fax, by e-mail, in person and via website
Hours: Mon to Fri, 0800 to 1800

Links with:
Nucleus Limited
John Loftus House, Summer Road, Thames Ditton, Surrey, KT7 0RD; tel: 020 8398 9133; fax: 020 8398 8785; e-mail: enquiries@nucleus.co.uk; website: http://www.nucleus.co.uk

HAMBLETON DISTRICT COUNCIL

Civic Centre, Stone Cross, Northallerton, North Yorkshire, DL6 2UU

Tel: 0845 1211 555
Fax: 01609 767228
E-mail: info@hambleton.gov.uk

Website:
http://www.hambleton.gov.uk
Information on district council services; tourism, including The World of James Herriot; leisure facilities.

Enquiries:
Enquiries to: Chief Executive
Other contacts: Press Officer for press enquiries.

Organisation type and purpose:
Local government body.

Subject coverage:
Local government services.

Access to staff:
Contact by letter, by telephone, by fax, by e-mail and in person
Hours: Mon to Fri, 0900 to 1700

Access to building, collection or gallery:
No access other than to staff
Hours: The World of James Herriott:
Mar to Oct, 1000 to 1800 (last admission 1700)
Nov to Feb, 1000 to 1700 (last admission 1600)

Access for disabled people:
Parking provided, level entry, toilet facilities

Administers:
The World of James Herriot
23 Kirkgate, Thirsk, North Yorkshire, YO7 1PL; tel: 01845 524234; fax: 01845 525333

HAMMERSMITH AND FULHAM ARCHIVES AND LOCAL HISTORY CENTRE

The Lilla Huset, 191 Talgarth Road, London, W6 8BJ

Tel: 020 8741 5159
E-mail: archives@lbhf.gov.uk

Website:
http://www.lbhf.gov.uk

Enquiries:
Enquiries to: Archivist

Founded:
1992

Organisation type and purpose:
Local government body.
Combined record office and local history library.

Subject coverage:
Local history of Hammersmith and Fulham, family history sources for Hammersmith and Fulham, records of Hammersmith and Fulham Council and its predecessors, deposited archives of local organisations and individuals.

Museum or gallery collection, archive, or library special collection:
Special Collections:
William Morris
Kelmscott Press
A. P. Herbert
White City Exhibitions
Sir William Bull
Cecil French Bequest of pictures (British art of the late 19th and early 20th centuries, especially Sir Edward Burne-Jones)
Old Ordnance Survey Maps and other maps
Old postcards and photographs
Old local newspapers
Topographical collection of paintings and prints of the Borough
Books and pamphlets
Archives relating to the history of the Borough

Non-library collection catalogue:
All or part available in-house

Library catalogue:
All or part available in-house

Printed publications:
Books, Godfrey reproduction maps, postcards and greetings cards
Publications on the history of the area

Publications list:
Available in print

Access to staff:
Contact by letter, by telephone, by e-mail and in person

Access to building, collection or gallery:
Hours: Mon, 0930 to 1630; Tue, 0930 to 1945; Thu, 0930 to 1630; closed Wed and Fri; 2nd and 4th Sat in month (excluding bank holiday weekends), 0930 to 1630

Access for disabled people:
Parking provided, level entry, access to all public areas, toilet facilities

Parent body:
London Borough of Hammersmith and Fulham
Hammersmith Town Hall, King Street, London, W6 9JU; tel: 020 8748 3020

HAMMERSMITH AND FULHAM LIBRARIES

Hammersmith Library, Shepherds Bush Road, London, W6 7AT

Tel: 020 8753 3813
Fax: 020 8753 3815
E-mail: info@haflibs.org.uk

Website:
http://www.lbhf.gov.uk
For information about our service.

Enquiries:
Enquiries to: Head of Library Services

Organisation type and purpose:
Local government body, public library.

Subject coverage:
English law, United Kingdom government publications, EC Public Information Relay at Hammersmith library, theology, fine art at Fulham Library.

Museum or gallery collection, archive, or library special collection:
Audio Collections: Mendelssohn, Vaughan Williams, Jazz composers HP-JEF, British poetry, Folk music of Iran, Iraq, Lebanon, Syria and Jordan
Doves Press (Archive Centre)
Early Children's Books
Special Fiction Collection: Authors CRI-DEL

Library catalogue:
All or part available online and in-house

Printed publications:
Before Windrush: the early Black presence in Hammersmith & Fulham (2000)
Hammersmith and Fulham: the twentieth century, 1999
Instant Past: old Hammersmith in pictures
Life in Fulham: old Fulham in pictures, 1984

Access to staff:
Contact by letter, by telephone, by fax and in person
Hours: Fulham and Hammersmith Libraries: Mon, Tue, Thu, 0930 to 2000; Wed, Fri, Sat, 0930 to 1700; Sun, 1315 to 1700

Branch libraries:
Askew Road Library
    87–91 Askew Road, London, W12 9AS; tel: 020 8753 3863
Barons Court Library
    North End Crescent, London, W14 8TG; tel: 020 8753 3888
Fulham Library
    598 Fulham Road, London, SW6 5NX; tel: 020 8753 3879; fax: 020 7736 3741
Hammersmith Library
    Shepherds Bush Road, London, W6 7AT; tel: 020 8753 3827; fax: 020 8753 3815
Sands End Library
    The Community Centre, 59–61 Broughton Road, London, SW6 2LA; tel: 020 8753 3885
Shepherds Bush Library
    7 Uxbridge Road, London, W12 8LJ; tel: 020 8753 3842; fax: 020 8740 1712

Member of:
Art Reference Libraries Information Service (ARLIS)
Association of British Theological and Philosophical Libraries
British and Irish Association of Law Librarians
Greater London Audio Specialisation Scheme
International Association of Music Libraries

Participates in:
Joint Fiction Reserve Scheme
LASER Special Collections Scheme

HAMPSHIRE AND WIGHT TRUST FOR MARITIME ARCHAEOLOGY

Acronym or abbreviation: HWTMA

Room W1/95, National Oceanography Centre, Empress Dock, Southampton, SO14 3ZH

Tel: 023 8059 3290
Fax: 023 8059 3052
E-mail: info@hwtma.org.uk

Website:
http://www.hwtma.org.uk

Organisation type and purpose:
A charitable organisation that relies on grants, donations and assistance in kind.

Subject coverage:
British maritime archaeology, with emphasis on Hampshire, the Isle of Wight and adjacent areas.

Education services:
Education and outreach programme. Educational display at the Underwater Archaeology Centre at Fort Victoria. Public lectures and talks.

HAMPSHIRE ARCHIVES AND LOCAL STUDIES

Acronym or abbreviation: HALS

Hampshire Record Office, Sussex Street, Winchester, Hampshire, SO23 8TH

Tel: 01962 846154; textline 0808 100 2484
Fax: 01962 878681
E-mail: enquiries.archives@hants.gov.uk

Website:
http://www.hants.gov.uk/record-office

Enquiries:
Enquiries to: Archivist

Founded:
1947

Created by the merger of:
Hampshire Record Office and Hampshire Local Studies Service (year of change 2008)

Organisation type and purpose:
Local government body.

Subject coverage:
Records relating to Hampshire and Hampshire families, includes records of local government (Quarter Sessions, County Council, civil, parish, etc.), Church of England, individuals, families, businesses, societies, chapels, schools, etc.

Museum or gallery collection, archive, or library special collection:
Archives relating to Hampshire and Hampshire families
Wessex Film and Sound Archive – film, video and audio tapes from the wider Wessex region
Local Studies collection of books, pamphlets, periodicals and other printed materials

Non-library collection catalogue:
All or part available in-house

Library catalogue:
All or part available online and in-house

Printed publications:
History curriculum resource packs and videos (for schools)
Hampshire Record Series (by subscription or purchase of individual vols)
Portsmouth Record Series including: Maps of Portsmouth before 1801, Royal Charters 1194–1974 (by subscription or purchase of individual vols)
Hampshire Papers and Maps
Leaflets
Education Services Newsletter (annually)
Guides to Sources (30)

Microform publications:
Directories, will index, parish registers, Phillimore's Hampshire Marriage Registers

Electronic and video publications:
Videos for schools

Publications list:
Available online and in print

Access to staff:
Contact by letter, by telephone, by fax, by e-mail, in person and via website
Hours: Mon to Fri, 0900 to 1900; Sat, 0900 to 1600

Access for disabled people:
Parking provided, level entry, access to all public areas, toilet facilities

HAMPSHIRE COUNTY COUNCIL LIBRARY AND INFORMATION SERVICE, BASINGSTOKE LIBRARY

1920 Westminster House, Festival Place, Basingstoke, Hampshire, RG21 7LS

Tel: 0845 603 5631
Fax: 01256 470666
E-mail: basingstoke.library@hants.gov.uk

Website:
http://libcat.hants.gov.uk
Library catalogue.

continued overleaf

http://www3.hants.gov.uk/library/reference-online
.htm
For customers with Hampshire Library
membership cards.

Enquiries:
Enquiries to: Library Officer

Organisation type and purpose:
Local government public library.

Subject coverage:
General and local history.

**Museum or gallery collection, archive, or library
special collection:**
Jane Austen Collection
Local History Collection

Trade and statistical information:
General trade directories and statistical volumes

Library catalogue:
All or part available online

Microform publications:
Local newspaper, 1878 to date
Hants Trade Directories
Census for Basingstoke and Deane, 1891, 1901
1881 Census Index
Parish Registers for Basingstoke and Deane
IGI 1988
IGI 1992 (Hampshire, Wiltshire and Berkshire)
Wills Index 1853–1943
GRO Index (incomplete)

Access to staff:
Contact by letter, by fax, by e-mail and in person
Hours: During normal opening hours
Special comments: If specific member of staff
required, please make arrangments in advance.

Access to building, collection or gallery:
Hours: Mon, Tue, Wed and Fri 0930 to 1900; Thu
0930 to 1730; Sat 0930 to 1600; Sun 1100 to 1700

Access for disabled people:
Level entry
Special comments: Lift to Library on first floor.

Links with:
Basingstoke Citizens Advice Bureau
  at same address, first floor

Parent body:
Hampshire County Council

HAMPSHIRE COUNTY COUNCIL MUSEUMS SERVICE HEADQUARTERS

Chilcomb House, Chilcomb Lane, Winchester,
Hampshire, SO23 8RD

Tel: 01962 826700
Fax: 01962 869836
E-mail: musmga@hants.gov.uk

Website:
http://www.hants.gov.uk/museums
Overview and introduction to Hampshire County
Council Museums Service, including specialist and
community museums, collections and
conservation; searchable database of parts of the
collection.

Enquiries:
Enquiries to: Senior Keeper of Printed and
Topographical Collections
Direct e-mail: gill.arnott@hants.gov.uk

Founded:
1944

Organisation type and purpose:
Local government body.
The museums headquarters houses administration,
documentation, and the conservation workshops
that assist the work of the specialist and
community museums operated by Hampshire
County Council but also has a role in supporting
museums across the South East Region.

Subject coverage:
Collections are subdivided into six subject
disciplines under a Senior Keeper: Archaeology;
Decorative Arts, including ceramics and historic
textiles and dress and the childhood collections;
Natural Science, including geology; Printed and
Topographical Collections, including historic
photographs; Social History; and Transport and
Technology. Each discipline holds relevant
reference material which is available for
examination by appointment.

Special visitor services:
Researchers welcome by appointment with
relevant Keepers.

**Museum or gallery collection, archive, or library
special collection:**
Archaeological site archives
Blair Collection (entomologist's notes)
Thornycroft archive relating to vehicle
  manufacture in Basingstoke
Small collection of material relating to William
  Curtis, Botanist of Alton
Tasker Collection (steam machinery, engineering
  drawings, archives and plans)
Paintings by WH Allen (searchable online)
Tichborne Archive (image database searchable
  online, documents shared with Hampshire
  Records Office)

Non-library collection catalogue:
All or part available in-house

Library catalogue:
All or part available in-house

Access to staff:
Contact by letter, by telephone, by fax, by e-mail
and in person. Appointment necessary.
Hours: Mon to Fri, 0900 to 1630

Access to building, collection or gallery:
Hours: Mon to Fri, 0900 to 1630

Access for disabled people:
Special comments: Access only to part of the site.

Branch museums:
Aldershot Military Museum
  Queens Avenue, Aldershot, Hampshire, GU11
  2LG; tel: 0845 603 5635
Allen Gallery
  Church Street, Alton, Hampshire, GU34 2BW;
  tel: 0845 603 5635
Andover Museum & Museum of the Iron Age
  6 Church Close, Andover, Hampshire, SP10 1DP;
  tel: 0845 603 5635
Basing House
  Redbridge Lane, Basing, Basingstoke,
  Hampshire, RG24 7HB; tel: 0845 603 5635
Bursledon Windmill
  Windmill Lane, Bursledon, Southampton, SO31
  8BG; tel: 0845 603 5635
Curtis Museum
  High Street, Alton, Hampshire, GU34 1BA; tel:
  0845 603 5635
Eastleigh Museum
  25 High Street, Eastleigh, Hampshire, SO50 5LF;
  tel: 0845 603 5635
Gosport Discovery Centre
  Walpole Road, Gosport, Hampshire, PO12 1NS;
  tel: 023 9258 8035; fax: 023 9250 1951
Milestones: Hampshire's Living History Museum
  Leisure Park, Churchill Way West, Basingstoke,
  Hampshire, RG21 6YR; tel: 0845 603 5635
Red House Museum
  Quay Road, Christchurch, Hampshire, BH23
  1BU; tel: 0845 603 5635
Rockbourne Roman Villa
  Rockbourne, Fordingbridge, Hampshire, SP6
  3PG; tel: 0845 603 5635
SEARCH
  50 Clarence Road, Gosport, Hampshire, PO12
  1BU; tel: 0845 603 5635
St Barbe Museum
  New Street, Lymington, Hampshire, SO41 9BH;
  tel: 01590 676969; fax: 01590 679997
Westbury Manor Museum
  84 West Street, Fareham, Hampshire, PO16 0JJ;
  tel: 0845 603 5635

Willis Museum & Sainsbury Gallery
  Old Town Hall, Market Place, Basingstoke,
  Hampshire, RG21 7QD; tel: 0845 603 5635

Parent body:
Hampshire County Council

HAMPSHIRE COUNTY LIBRARY, WINCHESTER DISCOVERY CENTRE

Jewry Street, Winchester, Hampshire, SO23 8SB

Tel: 01962 873600
E-mail: winchester.discoverycentre@hants.gov.uk

Enquiries:
Enquiries to: Library Manager

Organisation type and purpose:
Local government body, public library.
To provide information to all who live, work and
study in the county of Hampshire.

Subject coverage:
General.

**Museum or gallery collection, archive, or library
special collection:**
Comprehensive collection of broadsheet
  newspapers from 1979 onward on microfilm and
  CD-ROM
Official publications from 1972

Trade and statistical information:
Statistics collection including all relevant official
  publications (UK) and selected EC and UN
  publications; trade directories collection covering
  the United Kingdom.

Non-library collection catalogue:
All or part available online

Library catalogue:
All or part available online

Access to staff:
Contact by letter, by telephone, by fax, by e-mail
and in person
Hours: Mon to Fri, 0900 to 1900; Sat, 0900 to 1700;
Sun 1000 to 1600

HAMPSHIRE FIELD CLUB AND ARCHAEOLOGICAL SOCIETY

Acronym or abbreviation: Hants Field Club

14 Smeeton Road, Lee On The Solent, Gosport,
Hampshire, PO13 8LH

Tel: 01202 408376
E-mail: martin.goodchild@baesystems.com

Website:
http://www.fieldclub.hants.org.uk

Enquiries:
Enquiries to: General Secretary

Founded:
1885

Organisation type and purpose:
Learned society (membership is by subscription),
present number of members: 611, registered
charity (charity number 243773).

Subject coverage:
Archaeology, local history, natural history,
industrial archaeology, geology, landscape and
historical buildings of Hampshire.

**Museum or gallery collection, archive, or library
special collection:**
Library in the Southampton University Library
  Archives
Photographic Collection in the Hampshire Record
  Office

Printed publications:
Archaeology Monographs (9 to date)
New Forest Section Annual Report
Newsletters of the Sections (2 times a year)
Proceedings of the Hampshire Field Club and
  Archaeological Society (Hampshire Studies)
  (annually)

Access to staff:
Contact by letter and by e-mail
Hours: Mon to Fri, 0900 to 1700

Member of:
Council for British Archaeology

HAMPSHIRE LIBRARY AND INFORMATION SERVICE

Library and Information Service Headquarters, 56 Moorside Place, Moorside Road, Winchester, SO23 7FZ

Tel: 01962 826688
Fax: 01962 856615
E-mail: library@hants.gov.uk

Website:
http://www.hants.gov.uk/library
Over 250,000 pages of information about clubs, societies, voluntary organisations, health resources, council minutes, education, business advice, leisure and tourism.

Enquiries:
Enquiries to: Head of Operations

Organisation type and purpose:
Local government body, public library.

Subject coverage:
General; business information, local government information service, naval studies, railways, military history, aeronautics.

Museum or gallery collection, archive, or library special collection:
British Standards
Local Studies Collections
Aeronautics Collection (Farnborough)
Military Collection (Aldershot)
Naval Collection (Gosport)
Railway Collection (Winchester)

Trade and statistical information:
Published United Kingdom, European Union and world trade directories, statistical series and marketing information.

Non-library collection catalogue:
All or part available online

Library catalogue:
All or part available online

Printed publications:
Various user guides to services

Access to staff:
Contact by letter, by telephone, by fax, by e-mail, in person and via website
Hours: Mon to Fri, 0900 to 1700

Access for disabled people:
Parking provided, level entry

Branch libraries:
include Basingstoke, Fareham, Farnborough and Winchester

Member organisation of:
European RELAY Network

Parent body:
Hampshire County Council
tel: 01962 841841

HAMPSHIRE LIBRARY AND INFORMATION SERVICE – FARNBOROUGH

Acronym or abbreviation: HLIS

Farnborough Library, Pinehurst, Farnborough, Hampshire, GU14 7JZ

Tel: 01252 513838
Fax: 01252 511149
E-mail: CLNOREF@Hants.gov.uk

Website:
http://www.hants.gov.uk/library/

Enquiries:
Enquiries to: Information and Lifelong Learning Librarian

Organisation type and purpose:
Local government body, public library.

Subject coverage:
General; business and aviation; local studies for Farnborough area.

Museum or gallery collection, archive, or library special collection:
Aviation and aerospace
British standards (online)
Local Studies: books, maps, photographs, news cuttings, periodicals etc for Farnborough and surrounding area

Trade and statistical information:
UK and other official, unofficial statistics.
Trade and business directories.
Company reports.

Library catalogue:
All or part available online and in-house

Access to staff:
Contact by letter, by telephone, by fax, by e-mail, in person and via website
Hours: Mon, Tue, Thu, Fri, 0930 to 1900; Wed, 0930 to 1700; Sat, 0930 to 1600

Access for disabled people:
Parking provided, level entry, access to all public areas

HANNAH RESEARCH INSTITUTE

Acronym or abbreviation: HRI

Kirkhill, St Quivox, Ayr, KA6 5HL

Tel: 01292 674000
Fax: 01292 674005
E-mail: e.barbour@hannah.ac.uk

Website:
http://www.hri.sari.ac.uk

Enquiries:
Enquiries to: Librarian
Direct tel: 01292 674116

Founded:
1928

Organisation type and purpose:
Consultancy, research organisation.

Subject coverage:
Biological research, biochemistry, molecular biology, integrative biology, biological science and technology, food research, food science and technology, physical chemistry.

Printed publications:
Hannah Research Institute Yearbook (includes list of publications, annually)
Visitors Guide

Access to staff:
Contact by telephone. Appointment necessary.
Hours: Mon to Fri, 0900 to 1700

Connections with:
University of Glasgow

Funded by:
Scottish Office Agriculture, Environment and Fisheries Department

Research programme agreed in consultation with the:
Agricultural and Food Research Council
Biotechnology and Biological Sciences Research Council

HANSEL FOUNDATION

Broadmeadows, Symington, Ayrshire, KA1 5PU

Tel: 01563 830340
E-mail: info@hansel.org.uk

Website:
http://www.hansel.org.uk
Services, jobs, supporting Hansel.

Founded:
1962

Organisation type and purpose:
Registered Scottish charity (charity number SCO 01514).
To help people with disabilities have a future that is interesting, meaningful and fulfilling. Supports people in finding and keeping work, building their own social lives, living in their own homes, planning their own futures, getting the kind of support they want, to do the things they want to do.

Subject coverage:
Services include: residential accommodation and supported living; individual support; short breaks; support towads employment; and the Fairway Project, which helps with the transition to adult life.

Printed publications:
Who Cares Wins (Chisholm, A., former Chairman of Hansel Foundation, autobiography, £12 incl. p&p, proceeds to the Foundation)
Order printed publications from: Hansel Foundation, tel: 10563 830340

Access to staff:
Contact by letter, by telephone, by e-mail and via website

HARINGEY ARCHIVE SERVICE

Bruce Castle Museum, Lordship Lane, London, N17 8NU

Tel: 020 8808 8772
Fax: 020 8808 4118
E-mail: museum.services@haringey.gov.uk

Enquiries:
Enquiries to: Local History Officer

Organisation type and purpose:
Local government body, museum.

Subject coverage:
Archives and local history of the present local authority (Borough of Haringey) and its predecessors (Tottenham, Wood Green and Hornsey).
Collections of maps, photographs, postcards, 1841 to 1891 census returns on 35mm microfilm for Tottenham, Wood Green and Hornsey, newspapers, directories.

Non-library collection catalogue:
All or part available in-house

Access to staff:
Contact by letter and by telephone. Appointment necessary.
Hours: Wed to Fri, 1300 to 1645; alternate Sat, 1300 to 1645
Special comments: Appointment required.

HARINGEY LIBRARIES, ARCHIVES AND MUSEUM SERVICE

Wood Green Central Library, High Road, Wood Green, London, N22 6XD

Tel: 020 8489 2700
Fax: 020 8489 2722

Website:
http://www.haringey.gov.uk
Library news, opening hours, what's on, links, contact us.

Enquiries:
Enquiries to: Head of Library Services
Other contacts: Principal Librarian Systems and Support Services for Head of Bibliographic Computer Services.

Formerly called:
Haringey Library Services

Organisation type and purpose:
Local government body, public library.

Subject coverage:
General; instrumental recitals and the works of Telemann (under the Greater London Audio Subject Specialisation scheme GLASS).

continued overleaf

Information services:
Enquiries desk; Online information services, printed information

Museum or gallery collection, archive, or library special collection:
Public health engineering under the LASCRA specialisation
Heath Robinson Collection (at Wood Green Library)

Non-library collection catalogue:
All or part available online

Library catalogue:
All or part available online

Printed publications:
Connections by Sylvia Caldecott
How Things Were
Lost Houses of Haringey

Access to staff:
Contact by letter, by telephone, by fax, by e-mail and in person. Appointment necessary.
Hours: Central Library: Mon to Fri, 0900 to 1900; Sat, 0900 to 1700; Sun, 1200 to 1600 (Wood Green only)
Special comments: Contact other branch libraries for information regarding opening times and disabled access facilities.

Access to building, collection or gallery:
No access other than to staff
Hours: Central Library: Mon to Fri, 0700 to 1930; Sat, 0700 to 1730; Sun, 1100 to 1630
Special comments: Staff only or by appointment before usual opening hours

Access for disabled people:
Level entry, access to all public areas, toilet facilities, lift
Hours: Central Library: Mon to Fri, 0900 to 1900; Sat, 0900 to 1700; Sun, 1200 to 1600 (Wood Green only)

Branch libraries:
Alexandra Park
  Alexandra Park Road, London, N22 7UJ; tel: 020 8883 8553
Coombes Croft
  Tottenham High Road, London; tel: 020 8348 3443
Highgate
  Shepherd's Hill, London, N6 5QT; tel: 020 8348 3443
Hornsey
  Haringey Park, London, N8 9JA; tel: 020 8489 1427
Marcus Garvey
  Tottenham Green Leisure Centre, 1 Philip Lane, London, N15 4JA; tel: 020 8489 5350
Muswell Hill
  Queens Avenue, London, N10 3PE; tel: 020 8883 6734
St Ann's
  Cissbury Road, London, N15 5PU; tel: 020 8800 4390
Stroud Green
  Quernomore Road, London, N4 4QR; tel: 020 8348 4363

Parent body:
London Borough of Haringey Education Service
  Civic Centre, High Road, Wood Green, London, N22 7UJ; tel: 020 8849 0000 (ask for Education Services)

HARLEIAN SOCIETY

Formal name: Harleian Society Incorporated 1902, The

College of Arms, Queen Victoria Street, London, EC4V 4BT

Tel: 020 7236 7728
Fax: 020 7248 6448
E-mail: info@harleian.org.uk

Website:
http://harleian.org.uk

Enquiries:
Enquiries to: Honorary Secretary

Founded:
1869

Organisation type and purpose:
Learned society (membership is by subscription), present number of members: 280, registered charity (charity number 253659), publishing house.

Subject coverage:
Transcribing, printing and publishing of the Heraldic Visitations of the counties of England and Wales and other unpublished manuscripts relating to genealogy, family history and heraldry.

Printed publications:
Over 200 publications, see website: http://harleian.org.uk

Publications list:
Available online and in print

Access to staff:
Contact by letter, by telephone, by fax and by e-mail
Hours: Mon to Fri, 0900 to 1700

HARLOW COLLEGE

Velizy Avenue, Town Centre, Harlow, Essex, CM20 3LH

Tel: 01279 868000
Fax: 01279 868260

Enquiries:
Enquiries to: Learning Resources Centre Manager

Organisation type and purpose:
College of further education.

Subject coverage:
Education, catering, art, hairdressing, floristry, engineering, construction, journalism, social care, social sciences, business, secretarial, computing, performing arts, mathematics, sciences, leisure and community.

Library catalogue:
All or part available in-house

Printed publications:
Booklists on request
Guide to the Library (annual)
Subject guides (infrequent)

Access to staff:
Contact by letter and by telephone. Appointment necessary. Access for members only.
Hours: Mon to Fri, 0900 to 1700

HARLOW DISTRICT COUNCIL

Town Hall, Harlow, Essex, CM20 1HJ

Tel: 01279 446611\ Minicom no. 01279 446026
Fax: 01279 446767
E-mail: postroom@harlow.gov.uk

Website:
http://www.harlow.gov.uk/community/info
List of community groups to join etc.
http://www.harlow.gov.uk/harlow_council/index.htm
Harlow Council.
http://www.harlow.gov.uk
Information on Harlow.

Enquiries:
Enquiries to: Chief Executive

Founded:
1974

Formerly called:
Harlow Development Corporation Commission for New Towns, Harlow District Council (year of change 1974)

Organisation type and purpose:
Local government body.
Provision of services to local people.

Subject coverage:
Social, economic, historic or local government related information specific to Harlow.

Museum or gallery collection, archive, or library special collection:
Archive held at Harlow Study Centre and the Museum of Harlow

Printed publications:
Range of printed products including:
Business Directory (£10)
Harlow Guide (free)
Harlowlife (magazine, once every other month, free)
Numerous free leaflets etc

Access to staff:
Contact by letter, by telephone, by fax, by e-mail and via website. Appointment necessary.
Hours: Mon to Fri, 0830 to 1700

Access for disabled people:
Ramped entry

Other sites:
Details available on request

HARPER ADAMS UNIVERSITY COLLEGE LIBRARY

Newport, Shropshire, TF10 8NB

Tel: 01952 820280
Fax: 01952 814783

Website:
http://www.harper-adams.ac.uk
Information about the college.

Enquiries:
Enquiries to: Library Service Manager
Direct tel: 01952 815220
Direct fax: 01952 815391
Direct e-mail: kgreaves@harper-adams.ac.uk

Founded:
1901

Organisation type and purpose:
research organisation.

Subject coverage:
Animal production (sheep, cattle, pigs, poultry), crop production (cereals, potatoes, sugar beet, grass, oilseeds), farm management; agricultural economics and policy, agricultural marketing, agricultural engineering, rural land and estate management, the environment.

Museum or gallery collection, archive, or library special collection:
18th, 19th and early 20th century agricultural books and journals
Library of the National Institute of Poultry Husbandry
Sir Edward Brown Library (18th, 19th and early 20th century poultry books)

Non-library collection catalogue:
All or part available in-house

Library catalogue:
All or part available online

Printed publications:
College Farm Guide (annually)
College Farm Report (fortnightly)
Learning Resources Guide (annually)
Silcock Fellowship for Livestock Research Reports (irregular)
Temperton Fellowship for Poultry Research Reports (irregular)

Access to staff:
Contact by letter, by telephone and in person
Hours: Term time: Mon to Fri, 0900 to 2200, Sat and Sun, 1000 to 1700
Outside Term time: Mon to Fri, 0900 to 1700
Special comments: Charges for external borrowers.

HARRIS MANCHESTER COLLEGE LIBRARY

Mansfield Road, Oxford, OX1 3TD

Tel: 01865 271016
Fax: 01865 271012
E-mail: librarian@hmc.ox.ac.uk

Website:
http://www.hmc.ox.ac.uk
Information about the College and the Library.

Enquiries:
Enquiries to: Fellow Librarian
Direct tel: 01865 281472
Other contacts: Library Assistant

Founded:
1786

Formerly called:
Manchester Academy (year of change 1786);
Manchester College (year of change 1803);
Manchester New College (year of change 1840);
Manchester College (year of change 1889)

Incorporates the former:
Harris Manchester College (year of change 1996)

Organisation type and purpose:
A college library of the University of Oxford.

Subject coverage:
Church history; Protestant Reformation in Europe
and Great Britain (radical sects); dissenting church
history in Britain; Socinianism in Europe and
Britain; 19th-century Unitarian Church history in
Great Britain and the USA.
Provision of undergraduate and graduate reading
for University of Oxford degrees.

Services for disabled people:
Collection is accessible to all visitors through
service delivery.

**Museum or gallery collection, archive, or library
special collection:**
Carpenter Library of Comparative (World)
Religions
Manuscripts and printed notes of lectures in
Dissenting Academies
Manuscripts collections, especially letters of 19th-
and 20th-century Unitarians
Old Library (pre-1800, especially Enlightenment
and nonconformist authors)
Sociniana
Tract Collection (pamphlets, etc. on politics and
dissent, 1500–1914)
Unitariana

Non-library collection catalogue:
All or part available online and in print

Library catalogue:
All or part available online

Printed publications:
A Catalogue of the Manuscripts of Harris
Manchester College, Oxford (ed. D. Porter, the
College, 1998)
Truth, Liberty, Religion: Essays Celebrating 200
Years of Manchester College (ed. B. Smith,
Oxford, the College 1986, £5 plus p&p)
Order printed publications from: e-mail: librarian@
hmc.ox.ac.uk

Access to staff:
Contact by letter, by telephone, by fax, by e-mail,
in person and via website. Appointment necessary.
Letter of introduction required.
Hours: Mon to Fri, 0900 to 1630
Special comments: Library is also closed during
College closure.
Vacations: library may be closed due to staff
holidays.

Access to building, collection or gallery:
Hours: Mon to Fri, 0900 to 1630

Access for disabled people:
Ramped entry
Special comments: A reading room is available on
the ground floor and staff will fetch items for
individuals, e.g. parts of the old catalogue, books,
periodicals, anything within reason; toilet facilities:
doorway is very narrow.

Member organisation of:
Association of British Theological and
Philosophical Libraries

University of Oxford
website: http://www.ox.ac.uk

HARRIS TWEED AUTHORITY

Acronym or abbreviation: HTA

6 Garden Road, Stornoway, Isle of Lewis, HS1 2QJ

Tel: 01851 702269
Fax: 01851 702600
E-mail: enquiries@harristweed.org

Website:
http://www.harristweed.org

Enquiries:
Enquiries to: Chief Executive

Founded:
1909

Organisation type and purpose:
Statutory body, trade association (membership is
invitation), present number of members: 10.
Harris Tweed certification body.

Subject coverage:
Harris Tweed industry.

Education services:
information packs

Trade and statistical information:
Marketing and certification of Harris Tweed.

Printed publications:
Booklets on the manufacture, etc. of Harris Tweed

Electronic and video publications:
CD available

Access to staff:
Contact by letter, by telephone, by fax, by e-mail,
in person and via website. Appointment necessary.
Hours: Mon to Thu, 0900 to 1700; Fri, 0900 to 1200

HARROW LIBRARY SERVICE

PO Box 4, Civic Centre, Harrow, Middlesex, HA1
2UU

Tel: 020 8424 1059
Fax: 020 8424 1971
E-mail: library@harrow.gov.uk

Enquiries:
Enquiries to: Interim Head of Service – Library
Services
Direct tel: 020 8424 1055/1056 (for general
information and local history enquiries)
Other contacts: Principal Librarian (Reference and
Information Services)

Organisation type and purpose:
Local government body, public library.

Subject coverage:
General, architecture and building, civil
engineering, town and country planning and the
local history of Harrow and Middlesex. Also a
section on family history and genealogy in general
(eg IGI, 1881 Census for England and Wales on
file).

Library catalogue:
All or part available online

Branch libraries:
Bob Lawrence Library
  6–8 North Parade, Mollison Way, Edgware, HA8
  5QH; tel: 020 8952 4140; e-mail: boblawrence
  .library@harrow.gov.uk
Civic Centre Library
  Central Reference Library, Station Road, Harrow,
  HA1 2UU; tel: 020 8424 1055/6 (enquiries); 020
  8424 1051 (renewals); e-mail: civiccentre.library@
  harrow.gov.uk
Gayton Library (Central Lending Library and main
music library)
  Garden House, 5 St John's Road, Harrow,
  Middlesex, HA1 2EE; tel: 020 8427 6012 or 8986;
  e-mail: gayton.library@harrow.gov.uk

Hatch End Library
  Uxbridge Road, Hatch End, HA5 4EA; tel: 020
  8428 2636; e-mail: hatchend.library@harrow.gov
  .uk
Kenton Library
  Kenton Lane, Kenton, HA3 8UJ; tel: 020 8907
  2463; e-mail: kenton.library@harrow.gov.uk
Local History Library
  e-mail: localhistory.library@harrow.gov.uk
North Harrow Library
  429–433 Pinner Road, North Harrow, HA1 4HN;
  tel: 020 8427 0611; e-mail: northharrow.library@
  harrow.gov.uk
Pinner Library
  Marsh Road, Pinner, HA5 5NQ; tel: 020 8866
  7827; e-mail: pinner.library@harrow.gov.uk
Rayners Lane Library
  Imperial Drive, Rayners Lane, HA2 7HJ; tel: 020
  8866 9185; e-mail: raynerslane.library@harrow
  .gov.uk
Roxeth Library
  Northolt Road, South Harrow, HA2 8EQ; tel: 020
  8422 0809; e-mail: roxeth.library@harrow.gov.uk
Stanmore Library
  8 Stanmore Hill, Stanmore, HA7 3BQ; tel: 020
  8954 9955; e-mail: stanmore.library@harrow.gov
  .uk
Wealdstone Library
  Wealdstone Centre, 38–40 High Street,
  Wealdstone, HA3 7AE; tel: 020 8420 9333; e-
  mail: wealdstone.library@harrow.gov.uk

HARTLEPOOL CENTRAL LIBRARY

Reference and Information Service, 124 York Road,
Hartlepool, TS26 9DE

Tel: 01429 263778
Fax: 01429 283400
E-mail: infodesk@hartlepool.gov.uk

Website:
http://www.hartlepool.gov.uk
Description of library service, library catalogues

Enquiries:
Enquiries to: Reference manager

Founded:
1895

Organisation type and purpose:
Public library.

Subject coverage:
All subjects, specialist coverage: local studies,
family history, local organisations database.

**Museum or gallery collection, archive, or library
special collection:**
William Gray and Co – Ships Particulars Books
  1872 to 1941
Luke Blumer and Son – Shipbuilders and Ship
  Repairs Accounts 1853 to 1868
Music scores
Family History Collection
Local Studies Collection
Map Collection – local area and port
Photograph Collection – local area

Library catalogue:
All or part available online and in-house

Access to staff:
Contact by letter, by telephone, by fax, by e-mail,
in person and via website
Hours: Mon to Thu, 0930 to 1900; Fri to Sat, 0930 to
1700; Sun, 1130 to 1530

Access to building, collection or gallery:
No prior appointment required
Hours: Mon to Thu, 0930 to 1900; Fri to Sat, 0930 to
1700; Sun, 1130 to 1530

Access for disabled people:
Level entry, access to all public areas, toilet
facilities

HARVEIAN SOCIETY OF LONDON

11 Chandos Street, Cavendish Square, London,
W1M 0EB

continued overleaf

Tel: 020 7580 1043
Fax: 020 7580 5793

Enquiries:
Enquiries to: Executive Secretary

Founded:
1831

Organisation type and purpose:
Learned society (membership is by election or invitation), present number of members: 330, registered charity.

Subject coverage:
Medicine in general, history of medicine.

Museum or gallery collection, archive, or library special collection:
Archives of Society

Access to staff:
Contact by letter and by fax
Hours: Mon to Fri, 0900 to 1700

HASTINGS REFERENCE LIBRARY

Brassey Institute, 13 Claremont, Hastings, East Sussex, TN34 1HE

Tel: 0345 608 0195
Fax: 01424 724698
E-mail: library.hastings.ref@eastsussex.gov.uk

Website:
http://www.eastsussex.gov.uk/libraries

Enquiries:
Enquiries to: Information and Local Studies Librarian

Organisation type and purpose:
Local government body, public library.

Subject coverage:
General reference material; large local studies collection including photographs, newspapers, maps (especially Hastings, with some Sussex).

Museum or gallery collection, archive, or library special collection:
Brassey Collection (material by, about, and relating to Thomas, 1st Earl Brassey, and his family)

Library catalogue:
All or part available online and in-house

Access to staff:
Contact by letter, by telephone, by fax, by e-mail and in person
Hours: Mon, 0930 to 1800; Tue, Thu, 0930 to 1830; Wed, 0930 to 1300; Fri, 1030 to 1830; Sat, 0930 to 1700; Sun, closed

Access for disabled people:
Access to all public areas

Parent body:
East Sussex Libraries

HAUGHTON INTERNATIONAL FAIRS

15 Duke Street, St James's, London, SW1Y 6DB

Tel: 020 7389 6555
Fax: 020 7389 6556
E-mail: info@haughton.com

Website:
http://www.haughton.com

Enquiries:
Enquiries to: Public Relations Manager

Founded:
1989

Organisation type and purpose:
Organiser of international fine art and antiques fairs, including the International Fine Art & Antique Dealers Show, and Art Antiques London.

Subject coverage:
Art and antiques from all periods and countries, including pictures, sculpture, furniture, ceramics, jewellery, silver, manuscripts, textiles, ethnographica.

Museum or gallery collection, archive, or library special collection:
Catalogues of past fairs

Printed publications:
Catalogues for International Ceramics Fair and Seminar (hardback) and New York international fairs (softback)

Access to staff:
Contact by letter, by telephone, by fax and by e-mail
Hours: Mon to Fri, 1000 to 1800

Access for disabled people:
Yes

HAVANT BOROUGH COUNCIL

Acronym or abbreviation: HBC

Civic Offices, Civic Centre Road, Havant, Hampshire, PO9 2AX

Tel: 023 9247 4174\ Minicom no. 023 9244 6602
Fax: 023 9248 0263
E-mail: customer.services@havant.gov.uk

Website:
http://www.havant.gov.uk

Enquiries:
Enquiries to: Public Relations Manager
Direct tel: 023 9244 6420
Direct fax: 023 9244 6490

Founded:
1974

Organisation type and purpose:
Local government body.

Subject coverage:
All matters relating to local government issues within the Borough of Havant.

Printed publications:
Borough Guide
Community Strategy
Best Value Plan Summary
Council Magazine (quarterly)

Access to staff:
Contact by letter, by telephone, by fax, by e-mail and in person
Hours: Mon to Fri, 0900 to 1700

Access for disabled people:
Parking provided, level entry, access to all public areas, toilet facilities

HAVERFORDWEST PUBLIC LIBRARY

Dew Street, Haverfordwest, Pembrokeshire, SA61 1SU

Tel: 01437 765244
Fax: 01437 767092
E-mail: haverfordwestlibrary@pembrokeshire.gov.uk

Enquiries:
Enquiries to: Librarian
Direct tel: 01437 775248
Other contacts: Principal Librarian (for main contacts for all County libraries)

Organisation type and purpose:
Public library.

Subject coverage:
General reference. Local studies of Pembrokeshire including: a multi-format collection relating to the people/places/events/subjects connected to the County of Pembrokeshire, past and present.

Museum or gallery collection, archive, or library special collection:
Francis Green Genealogical Collection covering the prominent families of Cardiganshire, Carmarthenshire and Pembrokeshire at the turn of the century

Library catalogue:
All or part available online

Printed publications:
The History and Antiquities of St Davids (£12.00)
Burton Parish, Pembrokeshire (£1.00)
Rosemarket: A Village Beyond Wales (£1.00)
When the Poppies Bloom Again, Pembrokeshire and the Great War (£5.00)
Solva; an introduction to village life and guide to the walks (£1.00)
Glandwr School in the 18th and 19th Centuries (£1.00)
History of Jeffreyston Parish Church (£0.30)
End of the line: a history of Neyland (£7.00)
Neyland and Llanstadwell in old postcards (£3.00)
A Proud Centenary; Neyland in 1900 (£3.00)
The Pembroke Yeomanry (£0.99)
Fishguard and Goodwick in old postcards (£3.00)
Pembrokeshire County History Vol 3 (£25.00)
Order printed publications from: Local Studies Librarian, County Library, Dew St. Haverfordwest, SA61 1SU

Publications list:
Available in print

Access to staff:
Contact by letter, by telephone, by fax, by e-mail and in person
Hours: Mon, Wed, Thu, 0930 to 1700; Tue, Fri, 0930 to 1900; Sat 0930 to 1300

Access for disabled people:
Parking provided, toilet facilities, customer lift

Branch libraries:
Crymych Library
    Preseli School, Crymych, SA41 3QF; tel: 01239 832092; e-mail: crymychlibrary@pembrokeshire.gov.uk
Fishguard Library
    Town Hall, The Square, Fishguard, SA65 9HA; tel: 01437 776638; e-mail: fishguardlibrary@pembrokeshire.gov.uk
Milford Haven Library
    Cedar Court, Milford Haven, SA73 3LS; tel: 01437 771888; e-mail: milfordhavenlibrary@pembrokeshire.gov.uk
Narberth Library
    St James Street, Narberth, SA67 7BU; tel: 01437 775650; e-mail: narberthlibrary@pembrokeshire.gov.uk
Newport Library
    Bank House, Bridge Street, Newport, SA42 0TB; tel: 01239 821169; e-mail: newportlibrary@pembrokeshire.gov.uk
Neyland Library
    St Clements Road, Neyland, SA73 1SH; tel: 01437 775131; e-mail: neylandlibrary@pembrokeshire.gov.uk
Pembroke Dock Library
    Water Street, Pembroke Dock, SA72 6DW; tel: 01437 775825; e-mail: pembrokedocklibrary@pembrokeshire.gov.uk
Pembroke Library
    Commons Road, Pembroke, SA71 4EA; tel: 01437 776454; e-mail: pembrokelibrary@pembrokeshire.gov.uk
Saundersfoot Library
    Regency Hall, Saundersfoot, SA69 9NG; tel: 01834 813958; e-mail: saundersfootlibrary@pembrokeshire.gov.uk
St Davids Library
    City Hall, High Street, St Davids, SA62 6SD; tel: 01437 721170; e-mail: stdavidslibrary@pembrokeshire.gov.uk
Tenby Library
    Greenhill House, Tenby, SA70 7LB; tel: 01834 843934; fax: 01834 843934; e-mail: tenbylibrary@pembrokeshire.gov.uk

Headquarters address:
County Library
  Dew Street, Haverfordwest, SA61 1SU; tel: 01437
  775244; fax: 01437 769218; e-mail:
  haverfordwestlibrary@pembrokeshire.gov.uk

HAVERGAL BRIAN SOCIETY

Acronym or abbreviation: HBS

39 Giles Coppice, Gipsy Hill, Upper Norwood,
London, SE19 1XF

Tel: 020 8761 8134
E-mail: damian_rees@yahoo.com

Website:
http://www.havergalbrian.org

Enquiries:
Enquiries to: Secretary

Founded:
1974

Organisation type and purpose:
Membership association (membership is by
subscription, election or invitation), present
number of members: 200, registered charity
(charity number 275793).
To promote public knowledge of the work of
William Havergal Brian (1876–1972) and, to this
end, to support and sponsor its publication,
performance and recording.

Subject coverage:
Havergal Brian (1876–1972): the composer and his
work.

**Museum or gallery collection, archive, or library
special collection:**
Havergal Brian Society Archive in the University of
Keele

Printed publications:
Complete Piano Works (price £11)
Havergal Brian's Gothic Symphony (Two Studies,
  price £10)
Havergal Brian on Music, vol. 1 British Music (first
  of six vols, 1986, published with Toccata Press;
  vol. 2 to be published 2008–09)
Information leaflet with Discography,
  Bibliography, Society's Aims and Objects
Newsletter (6 times a year, free to members)

Access to staff:
Contact by letter, by telephone, by e-mail and via
website

HAVERING COLLEGE OF FURTHER AND HIGHER EDUCATION

Acronym or abbreviation: HCFHE

Ardleigh Green Road, Hornchurch, Essex, RM11
2LL

Tel: 01708 455011; minicom no. 01708 462735
Fax: 01708 462758
E-mail: lrcag@havering-college.ac.uk

Website:
http://www.havering-college.ac.uk
General information.
http://svrautolib.havering-college.ac.uk/opac/
opacreq.dll/new
Library catalogue.

Enquiries:
Enquiries to: Head of Learning Centres
Direct tel: 01708 462831; 01708 462758 (Library)
Direct e-mail: astrande@havering-college.ac.uk

Founded:
1948

Organisation type and purpose:
Library of a college of further and higher
education.

Subject coverage:
Art; design; hairdressing; beauty therapy;
graphics; media production; business studies;
management; accountancy; health services

administration; motor vehicle engineering;
mechanical engineering; electrical engineering;
electronic engineering; computer studies; robotics;
humanities; mathematics; science; secretarial and
office studies; social services; social work; nursery
nursing; teacher education; catering, youth work.

Non-library collection catalogue:
All or part available online

Library catalogue:
All or part available online

Access to staff:
Contact by letter, by telephone, by fax and by e-
mail
Hours: Ardleigh Green Site: Mon to Thu, 0830 to
1900; Fri, 1000 to 1700
Quarles Site: Mon to Thu, 0830 to 1900; Fri, 1000 to
1700

Access for disabled people:
Parking provided, ramped entry, access to all
public areas, toilet facilities

Branch libraries:
Quarles Campus
  Harold Hill, Romford, Essex; tel: 01708 462759;
  e-mail: jforsyth@havering-college.ac.uk

HAWK AND OWL TRUST

Acronym or abbreviation: HOT

c/o Zoological Society of London, Regent's Park,
London, NW1 4RY

Tel: 01626 334864
Fax: 01626 334864
E-mail: hawkandowl@aol.com

Website:
http://www.hawkandowl.org
general information on the Trust and education
services at the Education Centre.

Enquiries:
Enquiries to: Chairman
Direct tel: 01761 462017
Direct fax: 01761 462017
Other contacts: The Hawk and Owl Trust
Membership Secretary: for administration of the
Trust's Adopt a Box scheme, and issues periodic
reports to subscribers.

Founded:
1969

Formerly called:
The Hawk Trust

Organisation type and purpose:
Membership association (membership is by
subscription), present number of members: c. 2500,
voluntary organisation, registered charity (charity
number 1058565), suitable for all ages, research
organisation.
The conservation of birds of prey in the wild and
their habitat.

Subject coverage:
Conservation of the barn owl and all birds of prey
in the wild, nestboxes and habitat creation. The
Law and Planning Regulations concerning birds of
prey, particularly building regulations affecting
barn owls.

**Museum or gallery collection, archive, or library
special collection:**
Slide and picture library

Trade and statistical information:
Barn Owl road casualties survey.
Urban Peregrine Falcon survey.

Printed publications:
Barn Owl (Newsletter of Barn Owl Conservation
  Network, 2 times a year)
Boxes, Baskets and Platforms, Artificial Nest Sites
  for Owls and Other Birds of Prey
Peregrine (Newsletter of Hawk & Owl Trust, 2
  times a year)
The Barn Owl in the British Isles, its Past, Present
  and Future
The Barn Owl, The Farmer's Friend, Needs a
  Helping Hand

Order printed publications from: Publications Officer,
The Hawk and Owl Trust Publications
PO Box 530, Windlesham, GU20 6XZ, e-mail:
hawkowlpub@tiscali.co.uk

Publications list:
Available in print

Access to staff:
Contact by letter, by telephone, by fax, by e-mail
and via website
Hours: Mon to Fri, 0900 to 1700

Adopt a Box:
Adopt a Box
  2 Mill Walk, Wheathampstead, AL4 8DT; tel:
  01582 832182; fax: 01582 832182; e-mail:
  hawkandowltrust@aol.com

Education Officer:
The Hawk and Owl Trust
  Exhibition and education parties at the
  Education Centre, Chalfont St Giles,
  Buckinghamshire, HP8 4AB; tel: 01494 876262;
  fax: 01494 876262; e-mail: hoteducation@tesco
  .net

Member of:
Birdlife International

Membership Secretary:
The Hawk and Owl Trust
  11 St Mary's Close, Abbotskerswell, Newton
  Abbot, Devon, TQ12 5QF; tel: 01626 334864; fax:
  01626 334864; e-mail: hawkandowl@aol.com

Other addresses:
Education Officer
  c/o Chiltern Open Air Museum, Newland Park,
  Gorelands Lane, Chalfont St Giles, HP8 4AB; tel:
  01494 876262; fax: 01494 876262; e-mail:
  hoteducation@tesco.net
The Hawk and Owl Trust National Conservation
and Education Centre
The HOT Barn Owl Conservation Network
  National Coordinator, c/o Sheepdrove Trust,
  Sheepdrove Organic Farm Centre, Lambourn,
  Berkshire, RG17 7UU; tel: 01488 674727; fax:
  01488 72677

HAWTHORNS URBAN WILDLIFE CENTRE

Acronym or abbreviation: The Hawthorns

The Hawthorns, Southampton Common,
Southampton, SO15 7NN

Tel: 023 8067 1921; minicom no. 023 8067 8079
Fax: 023 8067 6859
E-mail: lin.hand@southampton.gov.uk

Website:
http://www.southampton.gov.uk/s-leisure/
parksgreenspaces/thehawthorns

Enquiries:
Enquiries to: Southampton City Council Natural
Environment Manager
Direct e-mail: hawthorns.wildlife.centre@
southampton.gov.uk

Founded:
1980

Organisation type and purpose:
Local government body.
Urban wildlife centre.
Urban nature conservation displays, events,
education and information.

Subject coverage:
Biological records, wildlife information, urban
habitat management, cafe.

Information services:
Displays, expert staff, walks and talks.

Special visitor services:
Room hire, cafe.

Education services:
Education officer.

Services for disabled people:
Centre fully accessible.

continued overleaf

Access to staff:
Contact by letter, by telephone, by fax, by e-mail, in person and via website. Appointment necessary.
Hours: Mon to Fri, 1000 to 1700; Sat, Sun, 1200 to 1600

Access for disabled people:
Access to all public areas

Also at:
Natural Environment Unit, Southampton City Council
    As main address; tel: As main numbers

Parent body:
Neighbourhoods, Southampton City Council
    Civic Centre, Southampton, SO14 7LP; tel: 023 8022 3855; website: http://www.southampton .gov.uk

HAYDN SOCIETY OF GREAT BRITAIN

2 Hindley Hall, Stocksfield, Northumberland, NE43 7RY

Tel: 01661 842167
E-mail: d.mccaldin@lancaster.ac.uk

Website:
http://www.haydnsocietyofgb.com

Enquiries:
Enquiries to: Director

Founded:
1979

Organisation type and purpose:
Learned society (membership is by subscription).

Subject coverage:
Music of Joseph Haydn and his contemporaries, all matters concerning Haydn performances and research.

Printed publications:
Journal (annually, ISSN 1350–1267)

Electronic and video publications:
Haydn and Schubert Masses (Meridian and Duo 89003 commercially available or direct mail from Haydn Society, CD or cassette)
Haydn Nelson Mass, The Storm, Missa Brevis in F (Meridian CDE 84393 commercially available or from the Haydn Society)
Haydn Divertimenti – Scherzi & Notturni (HS 1020 commercially available or from the Haydn Society)

Access to staff:
Contact by letter, by telephone, by e-mail and via website. Appointment necessary.
Hours: Mon to Fri, 0900 to 1700

Links with:
Similar societies world-wide

HCPT – THE PILGRIMAGE TRUST

Acronym or abbreviation: HCPT

Oakfield Park, 32 Bilton Rd, Rugby, Warwickshire, CV22 7HQ

Tel: 01788 564646; minicom: 01788 564642
Fax: 01788 564640
E-mail: hq@hcpt.org.uk

Website:
http://www.hcpt.org.uk
The trust and its pilgrimages, information for parents and carers on how to be involved.

Founded:
1956

Organisation type and purpose:
Registered charity (number 281074).
Organises trips to Lourdes for over 7,000 people each year.

Subject coverage:
Annually takes almost 2,000 children to Lourdes from the UK, Ireland and increasingly from other countries. The children have a wide range of physical and mental disabilities, or are physically and emotionally deprived or neglected. Cared for by voluntary helpers, including doctors, nurses and chaplains, most of whom pay for themselves, the total size of the Easter Pilgrimage is now about 5,000; the largest pilgrimage from the UK and Ireland and probably the largest children's pilgrimage from any country. The holiday pilgrimage is centred around the international shrine of Our Lady of Lourdes and gives children, aged 7–18, with many types of disability or special needs, the opportunity to experience a really stimulating and highly enjoyable group holiday. From HCPT grew the Hosanna House Trust, which was the response to a request from young adults for an opportunity to experience a similar holiday to that of the children. Today, Hosanna House, the Trust's residential centre just outside Lourdes in Bartres, takes nearly 2,000 pilgrims in groups of 40 to 50, many of whom have disabilities or special needs. These guests stay for a week between Easter and November.

Museum or gallery collection, archive, or library special collection:
Online photo gallery, film library and music

Printed publications:
Trust News
Order printed publications from: e-mail: trust.news@ hcpt.org.uk

Electronic and video publications:
HCPT 2008 Mission Booklet
Hosanna House History (pdf sample)
50 Years of HCPT (sample)
Easter leaflet
Bartrès Villa leaflet
Hosanna House leaflet
Legacy leaflet
Payroll giving leaflet
A variety of fact sheets
Order electronic and video publications from:
Download from website

Publications list:
Available online

Access to staff:
Contact by letter, by telephone, by fax and by e-mail

HDRA

Formal name: Henry Doubleday Research Association

Ryton Organic Gardens, Ryton-on-Dunsmore, Coventry, Warwickshire, CV8 3LG

Tel: 024 7630 3517
Fax: 024 7663 9229
E-mail: enquiry@hdra.org.uk

Website:
http://www.hdra.org.uk
General organic gardening.

Enquiries:
Enquiries to: Chief Executive

Founded:
1958

Organisation type and purpose:
International organisation, membership association (membership is by subscription), present number of members: 30,000, registered charity (charity number 298104), suitable for ages: all, consultancy, research organisation.
Research, education, promotion of environmentally friendly organic gardening, farming and food.

Subject coverage:
Organic gardening, organic horticulture, organic farming, organic food, recycling, composting, reafforestation, organic catering and retailing.

Museum or gallery collection, archive, or library special collection:
Organic gardening and farming book collection library and scientific papers

Trade and statistical information:
Data on organic techniques in the UK and overseas.
Data on reafforestation tree species in developing countries.

Printed publications:
The Organic Gardening Catalogue 2000
Organic Handbook Series
Step by Step Organic Gardening Series
The Encyclopedia of Organic Gardening
A Simple Guide to Organic Gardening
Growing Vegetables from Seed
Order printed publications from: The Organic Gardening Catalogue – Retail, Chase Organics Ltd River Dene Estate, Molesey Road, Hersham, Surrey, KT12 4RG, tel: 01932 253666, fax: 01932 252707

Electronic and video publications:
An Introduction to Organic Gardening (video)

Access to staff:
Contact by letter, by telephone, by fax, by e-mail, in person and via website
Hours: Mon to Fri, 0900 to 1700

Access for disabled people:
Parking provided, access to all public areas, toilet facilities

Other addresses:
Yalding Organic Gardens
    Benover Lane, Yalding, Maidstone, Kent, ME18 6EX; tel: 01622 814650; fax: 01622 814650

HEADMASTERS' AND HEADMISTRESSES' CONFERENCE

Acronym or abbreviation: HMC

12 The Point, Rockingham Road, Market Harborough, Leicestershire, LE16 7QU

Tel: 01858 469059
Fax: 01858 469532
E-mail: hmc@hmc.org.uk

Enquiries:
Enquiries to: Secretary
Other contacts: Chairman

Founded:
1869

Formerly called:
Headmasters' Conference

Organisation type and purpose:
Professional body, trade union.

Subject coverage:
Independent education; boarding; curriculum matters; professional development of members and members' schools; school sport; community service.

Printed publications:
Conference and Common Room (3 times a year)

Access to staff:
Contact by letter, by telephone and by e-mail
Hours: Mon to Fri, 0900 to 1700

HEADWAY – THE BRAIN INJURY ASSOCIATION

Bradbury House, 190 Bagnall Road, Old Basford, Nottingham, NG6 8SF

Tel: 0115 924 0800
Fax: 0115 958 4446
E-mail: enquiries@headway.org.uk

Website:
http://www.headway.org.uk
Information on brain injury. Access to our services across the UK and Channel Islands. Specialist solicitors list for brain injury claims. Information for professionals.

Enquiries:
Enquiries to: Helpline
Direct tel: Helpline tel: 0115 924 0800 / 0808 800 2244 (freephone)

Direct e-mail: helpline@headway.org.uk

Founded:
1979

Organisation type and purpose:
National organisation, voluntary organisation, registered charity (charity number 1025852). Community services for people with head injuries. We have over 100 local groups around the UK. Over half run Headway House day care centres. Contact details of local groups are available from us where we can also provide straightforward information on many aspects of head injury.

Subject coverage:
Head injury; traumatic brain damage and its physical and psychological outcome; help and support of survivors and their families.

Printed publications:
Booklets
Headway News (quarterly, members)
Leaflets
What is Head Injury
Know Someone Who Has Had a Head Injury

Microform publications:
Brain Injury: The Way Forward (video)

Publications list:
Available online and in print

Access to staff:
Contact by letter, by telephone, by fax, by e-mail and via website
Hours: Mon to Fri, 0900 to 1700 (helpline)

HEALING TRUST

Formal name: NFSH Charitable Trust Ltd

21 York Road, Northampton, NN1 5QG

Tel: 01604 603247
Fax: 01604 603534
E-mail: via website

Website:
http://www.thehealingtrust.org.uk
Healing, careers in healing, accessing a healer, training, workshops and continuing professional development, events, support groups, research, membership, shop.

Founded:
1954

Organisation type and purpose:
A registered charity (number 1094702), membership organisation (membership is by subscription).
Spiritual healing.
To raise the standards and awareness of healing in the UK and overseas.

Subject coverage:
National standards of training delivered by accredited trainers; a minimum 2 years' training period with national standards of final assessment; professional code of conduct, disciplinary procedures, professional insurance; over 50 Healing Centres throughout the UK, staffed by volunteer members; accreditation of independent voluntary centres that meet Healing Trust standards.

Printed publications:
In Touch Magazine (quarterly, free to members, £21 annnually to Friends)
Energy Healing – The Practical Workbook (£15.00)
Hands on Healing for Pets (£11.00)
Punk Science (£11.99)
Sacred Healing (£18.30)
The Animal Healer (£8.00)
The Big Book of the Soul (£16.00)
The Field (£9.50)
The Frog and the Wizard (£11.50)
Order printed publications from: Website

Publications list:
Available online

Access to staff:
Contact by letter, by telephone, by fax and via website

HEALTH AND SAFETY EXECUTIVE

Acronym or abbreviation: HSE

Rose Court, 2 Southwark Bridge, London, SE1 9HS

Tel: 020 7717 6000
Fax: 020 7717 6134
E-mail: public.enquiries@hse.gov.uk

Website:
http://www.hse.gov.uk

Enquiries:
Enquiries to: Manager Site Services

Founded:
1975

Organisation type and purpose:
National government body.

Subject coverage:
Occupational health and safety policy.

Printed publications:
Order printed publications from: HSE Books, PO Box 1999, Sudbury, Suffolk, CO10 2WA, tel: 01787 881165, fax: 01787 313995, e-mail: via http://www.hsebooks.co.uk

Publications list:
Available in print

Access to staff:
Contact by letter, by telephone, by fax, by e-mail and via website. Appointment necessary.
Hours: Mon to Fri, 0900 to 1700

Access for disabled people:
Level entry
Department of Transport, Local Government and the Regions

HEALTH AND SAFETY EXECUTIVE – ELECTRICAL EQUIPMENT CERTIFICATION SERVICE

Acronym or abbreviation: EECS

Harpur Hill, Buxton, Derbyshire, SK17 9JN

Tel: 01298 28000
Fax: 01298 28244
E-mail: baseefa.info.eecs@hsl.gov.uk

Website:
http://www.baseefa.com
Information relating to services provided by EECS. Guidance on safety in hazardous areas and certification. List of EECS publications.

Enquiries:
Enquiries to: Director
Other contacts: Product Certification Support Team

Founded:
1926

Formerly called:
British Approvals Service for Electrical Equipment in Flammable Atmosphere (BASEEFA) (year of change 1987)

Organisation type and purpose:
National government body.
Government certification body, Electrical Equipment Certification Service (EECS) of the Health and Safety Executive.
Testing and Certification of explosion protected electrical equipment. Safety in hazardous areas.

Subject coverage:
Explosion protection (eg flameproof, intrinsic safety), equipment and systems for use in hazardous areas, flammable and explosive atmospheres, European conformity and directives, certification, testing, quality assurance, repairs.

Printed publications:
Publications include:
BASEEFA Technical Rules (£10)

Designers Guide – Intrinsic Safety for Group II Equipment (1994, £35)
Designers Guide – Intrinsic Safety for Mining Equipment (P001–1993, £35)
EECS Newsletter (3 times a year, free)
Electrical Equipment Certification Service Appeals Procedure (P002–2000, free)
Quality Assurance Guide (1998, free)
Type Examination Guide (1998, free)
Verification Guide (1998, free)

Publications list:
Available online and in print

Access to staff:
Contact by letter, by telephone, by fax, by e-mail and via website. Appointment necessary.
Hours: Mon to Thu, 0900 to 1700; Fri, 0900 to 1630

Parent body:
Department of the Environment

HEALTH AND SAFETY EXECUTIVE – INFORMATION SERVICES

Acronym or abbreviation: HSE

Caerphilly Business Park, Caerphilly, CF83 3GG

Tel: 0845 345 00 55
Fax: 0845 4089566
E-mail: hse.infoline@natbrit.com

Website:
http://www.hse.gov.uk
Information on the structure and functioning of the HSE is given together with information on the latest developments from within the HSE and the full text of HSE's free leaflets.

Enquiries:
Enquiries to: Public Enquiry Point

Organisation type and purpose:
National government body.

Subject coverage:
Occupational health and safety, particularly medical, chemical and technical information..

Printed publications:
Order printed publications from: HSE Books
PO Box 1999, Sudbury, Suffolk, CO10 2WA, tel: 01787 881165, fax: 01787 313995, e-mail: http://www.hsebooks.co.uk

Publications list:
Available online and in print

Access to staff:
Contact by letter, by telephone, by fax, by e-mail and via website
Hours: Mon to Fri, 0830 to 1700

Other address:
Health and Safety Executive

Parent body:
Department for Work and Pensions

HEALTH AND SAFETY LABORATORY

Acronym or abbreviation: HSL

Information Centre, Health & Safety Laboratory, Harpur Hill, Buxton, Derbyshire, SK17 9JN

Tel: 01298 218000
Fax: 01298 218635
E-mail: hslinfo@hsl.gov.uk

Website:
http://www.hsl.gov.uk

Enquiries:
Enquiries to: Information Centre Manager
Direct tel: 01298 218218

Organisation type and purpose:
Research laboratory in the field of occupational health and safety.

continued overleaf

Subject coverage:
Occupational health, hygiene and safety, engineering, human factors, analytical and biological sciences, fire and explosion safety, risk sciences.

Library catalogue:
All or part available in-house

Printed publications:
Annual report, research reports, newsletters
Order printed publications from: Health and Safety Laboratory, Information Centre, Harpur Hill, Buxton, Derbyshire, SK17 9JN

Electronic and video publications:
Research reports
Order electronic and video publications from: website: http://www.hse.gov.uk

Publications list:
Available online

Access to staff:
Contact by letter, by telephone, by fax, by e-mail and via website
Hours: Mon to Fri, 0930 to 1530

Parent body:
Health and Safety Executive
Redgrave Court, Merton Road, Bootle, Merseyside, L20 7HS; tel: 0151 951 9000; website: http://www.hse.gov.uk

HEALTH CARE LIBRARIES

Cairns Library, John Radcliffe Hospital, Headington, Oxford, OX3 9DU

Tel: 01865 221936
Fax: 01865 221941
E-mail: hcl-library@bodleian.ox.ac.uk

Website:
http://www.bodleian.ox.ac.uk/medicine

Enquiries:
Enquiries to: Head of Health Care Libraries

Formerly called:
Oxford Postgraduate Medical Library (year of change 1973); Cairns Library (year of change 2002); Institute of Health Sciences Library (year of change 2002)

Organisation type and purpose:
University library, library of the Faculty of Clinical Medicine, University of Oxford.
Also serves as an information source for NHS staff in the Oxford Radcliffe Hospitals Trust and the Oxfordshire Primary Care Trust.

Subject coverage:
Health care including clinical medicine, nursing, physiotherapy, radiography and other paramedical subjects. Satellite libraries have specialities in cancer, diabetes, neurosciences, gerontology, public health medicine and statistics.

Library catalogue:
All or part available online

Access to staff:
Contact by letter, by telephone, by fax and by e-mail. Appointment necessary.

Access to building, collection or gallery:
No access other than to staff
Hours: 24 hours
Special comments: Members only.

Access for disabled people:
Access to all public areas
Special comments: Ramped or level entry – varies on different sites.

Also at:
Knowledge Centre
University of Oxford Old Road Campus Research Building, Headington, Oxford, OX3 7DQ; tel: 01865 221936; fax: 01865 289406; e-mail: hcl-library@bodleian.ox.ac.uk; website: http://www.bodleian.ox.ac.uk/medicine

Links with:
University of Oxford
Wellington Square, Oxford, OX1 2JD; tel: 01865 270001

HEALTH DEVELOPMENT AGENCY

Acronym or abbreviation: HDA

Holborn Gate, 330 High Holborn, London, WC1V 7BA

Tel: 020 7430 0850
Fax: 020 7061 3390
E-mail: communications@hda-online.org.uk

Website:
http://www.hda.nhs.uk/
Health Development Agency
http://www.foodpovertyprojects.org.uk/
Food poverty projects database
http://www.hda.nhs.uk/evidence/
HDA Evidence Base
http://www.healthaction.nhs.uk/
Health Action website and knowledge management service
http://healthpromis.hda-online.org.uk/
HealthPromis database
http://www.hiagateway.org.uk/
Health Impact Assessment Gateway
http://www.quick.org.uk
Quality Information Checklist, designed for use in educational settings.
http://www.phel.gov.uk/
Public Health electronic Library
http://www.social-action.org.uk/sarp/
SARP – Provides details of the social action research projects in Nottingham and Salford, set up to find out how social interventions can contribute to the promotion of health and the reduction of inequalities.
http://www.ohn.gov.uk
Our Healthier Nation.
http://www.hda.nhs.uk/nurseeducators/
Support for Nurse Educators
http://www.wiredforhealth.gov.uk
National Healthy School Standard
http://www.welltown.gov.uk
For Key Stage 1
http://www.galaxy-h.gov.uk
For Key Stage 2
http://www.lifebytes.gov.uk
For Key Stage 3
http://www.mindbodysoul.gov.uk
For Key Stage 4

Enquiries:
Enquiries to: Director of Marketing & Communications
Direct tel: 020 7061 3110
Direct e-mail: jfrench@hda-online.org.uk

Founded:
April 2000

Formerly called:
Health Education Council (HEC); Health Education Authority (HEA) (year of change 2000)

Organisation type and purpose:
Statutory body; research and review organisation; evidence-based practice;
Special Health Authority within the NHS; the HDA's functions will transfer to the National Institute for Clinical Excellence from April 2005

Subject coverage:
Accidents, alcohol, black and minority ethnic groups, breastfeeding, cancer, children, communities, coronary heart disease, diet, drugs, evaluation, evidence, health impact assessment, health improvement, health inequalities, HIV/AIDS and sexual health, local strategic partnerships, management and strategies, men's health, mental health, National Healthy School Standard, health needs assessment, nutrition, obesity, older people, physical activity, pregnancy, primary care, public health, research and review, smoking, surveys, transport, women's health, workplace health, young people

Printed publications:
Health Development Today (magazine, 6 times a year)
Health Development Agency Annual Report
Health Development Agency Delivery Plan (annual)
Health Development Agency Impact Report (annual)
HDA Catalogue which includes selected HEA titles
All HDA publications are available for download from the HDA website
Order printed publications from: Health Development Agency
PO Box 90, Wetherby, Yorkshire, LS23 7EX, tel: 0870 121 4194, fax: 0870 121 4195, e-mail: hda@twoten.press.net

Publications list:
Available online and in print

Access to staff:
Contact by letter, by telephone, by e-mail and via website. Appointment necessary.
Hours: Mon to Fri, 0900 to 1700

Access to building, collection or gallery:
No access other than to staff

Access for disabled people:
Level entry, access to all public areas

HEALTH FOOD MANUFACTURERS' ASSOCIATION

Acronym or abbreviation: HFMA

63 Hampton Court Way, Thames Ditton, Surrey, KT7 0LT

Tel: 020 8398 4066
Fax: 020 8398 5402
E-mail: pviner@hfma.co.uk

Website:
http://www.hfma.co.uk

Enquiries:
Enquiries to: Director
Direct e-mail: denise@hfma.co.uk

Founded:
1965

Part of the now disbanded:
British Health Food Trade Association (year of change 1991)

Organisation type and purpose:
Trade association (membership is by subscription), present number of members: 150, manufacturing industry, consultancy.

Subject coverage:
Health foods, homoeopathic, herbal, dietetic products etc, food supplements, alternative medicines, natural beauty products, other health-related matters, import, export, labelling regulations etc.

Printed publications:
Health foods, homoeopathic, herbal, dietetic products etc

Access to staff:
Contact by letter, by telephone, by fax and by e-mail. Access for members only.
Hours: Mon to Fri, 0900 to 1700

HEALTH FOR ALL NETWORK (UK) LTD

Acronym or abbreviation: HFAN (UK)

New Century House, 52 Tithebarn Street, Liverpool, L2 2SR

Tel: 0151 231 4283
Fax: 0151 231 4209
E-mail: ukhfan@livjm.ac.uk

Website:
http://independent.livjm.ac.uk/healthforall/

Enquiries:
Enquiries to: Office Manager

Direct e-mail: a.boyd@livjm.ac.uk

Founded:
1989

Formerly called:
United Kingdom Healthy Cities Network (year of change 1991); United Kingdom Health for All Network (year of change 1995)

Organisation type and purpose:
Membership association (membership is by subscription), present number of members: 450, registered charity (charity number 1062376), suitable for ages: all, training organisation.

Subject coverage:
Information on health for all, healthy cities, work and health, public policy.

Printed publications:
Action for Health in Cities (1994, £2 plus p&p)
Annual Report
Newsletter – Network News
Our Cities Our Future
Full Resource Pack
HFA Starter Pack (M Halliday, 1993, £7 plus p&p)
Community Participation in HFA Pack (1993, £3 plus p&p)
Community Health Needs Assessment (1993, £3 plus p&p)

Publications list:
Available in print

Access to staff:
Contact by letter, by telephone, by fax and by e-mail
Hours: Mon to Fri, 0900 to 1700

HEALTH MANAGEMENT LIBRARY AND INFORMATION SERVICE

Health Management Library, Scottish Health Service Centre, Crewe Road South, Edinburgh, EH4 2LF

Tel: 0131 275 7760
Fax: 0131 315 2369
E-mail: nss.hmlibrary@nhs.net

Website:
http://www.healthmanagementonline.co.uk
NHS Scotland's largest collection of healthcare management information.

Enquiries:
Enquiries to: Librarian
Direct e-mail: hmlibrary@nhs.net

Founded:
1965

Formerly called:
Common Services Agency – Management Education and Training Division (MET), Scottish Health Service Management Development Group (MDG); NHS in Scotland Development Group (DG) (year of change 1998)

Organisation type and purpose:
National government body. Library and information service for NHS in Scotland staff.

Subject coverage:
National Health Service, health services planning, administration, management, social welfare.

Library catalogue:
All or part available online and in-house

Printed publications:
Library Current Awareness Bulletin (monthly)
Periodicals List (annually)

Publications list:
Available online and in print

Access to staff:
Contact by letter, by telephone, by fax, by e-mail, in person and via website
Hours: Mon to Thu, 0830 to 1700; Fri, 0830 to 1630

Access to building, collection or gallery:
No prior appointment required

Access for disabled people:
Ramped entry

Constituent part of:
NHS National Services Scotland
  Gyle Square, 1 South Gyle Crescent , Edinburgh, EH12 9EB; tel: 0131 275 6000

HEALTH PROFESSIONS COUNCIL

Acronym or abbreviation: HPC

Park House, 184 Kennington Park Road, London, SE11 4BU

Tel: 020 7582 0866
Fax: 020 7820 9684

Website:
http://www.hpc-uk.org

Enquiries:
Enquiries to: Registrar & Chief Executive

Founded:
2002

Formerly called:
Council for Professions Supplementary to Medicine (CPSM) (year of change 2002)

Organisation type and purpose:
Statutory body.
Independently regulating 13 health professions. Protection of the public.

Subject coverage:
Matters related to courses approved for state registration of arts therapists, chiropodists, dieticians, medical laboratory scientific officers, occupational therapists, orthoptists, orthotists, prosthetists, physiotherapists and radiographers; clinical scientists; paramedics; speech and language therapists; operating department practitioners.

Museum or gallery collection, archive, or library special collection:
Registers of the professions of chiropody, dietetics, medical laboratory sciences, occupational therapy, orthoptics, physiotherapy and radiography

Trade and statistical information:
Data on numbers of professionals registered including those registered under European directives on mutual recognition of academic qualifications.

Printed publications:
Annual Register listing state-registered personnel in each of the professions
Annual Report
Public/Patient Leaflet
Consultation Document

Access to staff:
Contact by letter, by telephone, by fax and in person
Hours: Mon to Fri, 0900 to 1700

Access to building, collection or gallery:
Hours: Mon to fri, 0900 to 1700

Access for disabled people:
Access to all public areas, toilet facilities
Hours: Mon to Fri, 0900 to 1700

HEALTH PROMOTION AGENCY FOR NORTHERN IRELAND

Acronym or abbreviation: HPANI

18 Ormeau Avenue, Belfast, BT2 8HS

Tel: 028 9031 1611
Fax: 028 9031 1711
E-mail: info@hpani.org.uk

Website:
http://www.healthpromotionagency.org.uk
http://www.drugsalcohol.info
Regional website, drugs and alcohol information for health professionals.
http://mindingyourhead.info

Information to promote and increase understanding of good mental health.
http://www.up-2-you.net
Information on health risks of drugs, alcohol and smoking for young people aged 11–14.
http://www.breastfedbabies.org
To provide information on breastfeeding for mothers and health professionals.

Enquiries:
Enquiries to: Finance & Administration Manager
Other contacts: Resources Manager for availability of published resources and information

Founded:
1990

Organisation type and purpose:
Advisory body, statutory body.
Special Agency of the Department of Health, Social Services and Public Safety.
To make health a top priority for everyone in Northern Ireland. Summarised under the following broad headings: policy development and advice; research, information and analysis; public and professional information; training and professional development; corporate business services.

Subject coverage:
Information on health promotion related issues, including campaigns, research and training, topic information on alcohol and drugs, smoking, physical activity, nutrition and oral health, children and young people, mental health, social health, breastfeeding, Healthy Schools, Health Promoting Hospitals, Health Promoting Workplaces. The Confidential Enquiry into Maternal and Child Health (CEMACH) aims to improve the health of mothers, babies and children by carrying out confidential enquiries on a nationwide basis and widely disseminating the findings and recommendations.

Printed publications:
A range of resources providing health promotion information including research reports, leaflets, booklets
Annual Report
Annual Research and Evaluation Reviews
Inform (newsletter, 6 times a year)

Publications list:
Available online

Access to staff:
Contact by letter, by telephone, by fax, by e-mail and via website
Hours: Mon to Thurs, 0900 to 1700; Fri, 0900 to 1630
Special comments: Enquiries welcome from health professionals, members of the public should contact the central health promotion resource service of their local Health and Social Services Board area.

Access for disabled people:
Ramped entry, access to all public areas, toilet facilities

HEALTH PROTECTION AGENCY

Acronym or abbreviation: HPA

Porton Down, Salisbury, Wiltshire, SP4 0JG

Tel: 01980 612711
Fax: 01980 612818
E-mail: porton.library@hpa.org.uk

Website:
http://www.hpa.org.uk

Enquiries:
Enquiries to: Librarian

Founded:
1979

Formerly called:
Centre for Applied Microbiology and Research (year of change 2004)

Organisation type and purpose:
National government body, research organisation.
Non-departmental public body.

continued overleaf

Public health research and production of biopharmaceuticals.

Subject coverage:
Infectious diseases; immunology; vaccine research and production; emergency response; molecular biology; therapeutic products; pathogens; virology

Library catalogue:
All or part available in-house

Access to staff:
Contact by letter, by telephone, by fax and by e-mail
Hours: Mon to Fri, 0900 to 1700

Access to building, collection or gallery:
No access other than to staff

Constituent part of:
Department of Health

HEALTH PROTECTION AGENCY – CENTRE FOR INFECTIONS

Acronym or abbreviation: HPA

61 Colindale Avenue, London, NW9 5EQ

Tel: 020 8327 7616
Fax: 020 8200 7875

Website:
http://www.hpa.org.uk

Enquiries:
Enquiries to: Library enquiries
Direct e-mail: colindale.library@hpa.org.uk

Founded:
2003

Organisation type and purpose:
National government body

Subject coverage:
Infectious diseases, medical microbiology and virology, vaccination, microbiological aspects of public health, microbiology of food and water.

Information services:
Reference only, by prior appointment only

Library catalogue:
All or part available online and in-house

Access to staff:
Contact by letter. Appointment necessary.
Hours: Mon to Fri, 0930 to 1700
Special comments: Prior appointment required

Access to building, collection or gallery:
Prior appointment required
Hours: Mon to Fri, 0930 to 1700

HEALTH PROTECTION AGENCY – CENTRE FOR RADIATION, CHEMICAL AND ENVIRONMENTAL HAZARDS

Acronym or abbreviation: HPA CRCE

Chilton, Didcot, Oxfordshire, OX11 0RQ

Tel: 01235 831600
Fax: 01235 833891
E-mail: david.perry@hpa.org.uk

Website:
http://www.hpa.org.uk/
Description of Health Protection Agency, its work and publications.

Enquiries:
Enquiries to: Librarian
Direct tel: 01235 822649

Founded:
2005

Formerly called:
National Radiological Protection Board

Organisation type and purpose:
National government body, research organisation. Government body established by statute to give advice on health effects of radiation, chemicals.

Subject coverage:
Radiological protection, biological and medical effects of ionising radiations, cytogenetics, health hazards posed by chemical exposures, health effects of non-ionising radiations; radioactivity in consumer protection; radioactivity in the natural environment and environmental modelling; radioactivity in man, dosimetry; training in radiological protection; epidemiology; medical physics.

Museum or gallery collection, archive, or library special collection:
ICRP, NCRP, ICRU, IAEA safety series, IARC Monographs and Scientific Publications

Library catalogue:
All or part available in-house

Printed publications:
Annual Report
Consultative Documents (occasional)
Documents of the Health Protection Agency Series B: Radiation, Chemical and Environmental Hazards (formal advice, irregular)
Information Sheets and booklets
Living with Radiation (booklet)
Technical Reports (HPA-RP series)
Chemical Hazards & Poisons Report

Electronic and video publications:
All recent publications available electronically (online)

Publications list:
Available online

Access to staff:
Contact by letter, by fax and by e-mail.
Appointment necessary.
Hours: Mon to Thu, 0815 to 1700; Fri, 0815 to 1600

Access to building, collection or gallery:
Prior appointment required

Access for disabled people:
Ramped entry, toilet facilities

Also at:
HPA Occupational Services
  Leeds
HPA Radiation and Environmental Monitoring Scotland
  Glasgow

HEALTH PROTECTION AGENCY – MYCOLOGY REFERENCE LABORATORY

Acronym or abbreviation: HPA MRL

Myrtle Road, Kingsdown, Bristol, BS2 8EL

Tel: 0117 929 1326
Fax: 0117 922 6611

Enquiries:
Enquiries to: Director

Founded:
1946

Organisation type and purpose:
National government body, service industry.

Subject coverage:
Maintenance of the National Collection of Pathogenic Fungi, identification of fungi isolated from clinical sources.

Museum or gallery collection, archive, or library special collection:
National Collection of Pathogenic Fungi

Non-library collection catalogue:
All or part available online and in print

Access to staff:
Contact by letter, by telephone and by fax
Hours: Mon to Fri, 0900 to 1700

Access to building, collection or gallery:
Prior appointment required

HEALTH SCOTLAND LIBRARY

NHS Health Scotland, The Priory, Canaan Lane, Edinburgh, EH10 4SG

Tel: 0131 536 5581
Fax: 0131 536 5502
E-mail: nhs.healthscotland-library@nhs.net

Website:
http://www.healthscotland.com/resources/library

Enquiries:
Enquiries to: Library Services Manager
Direct tel: 0131 536 5578
Direct e-mail: juliagreen@nhs.net

Formerly called:
Health Promotion Library Scotland (year of change 2003)

Organisation type and purpose:
Library service for people interested in health improvement who live and/or work in Scotland.

Subject coverage:
Health improvement, health promotion and public health.

Library catalogue:
All or part available online

Printed publications:
Health Scotland publications are listed on Health Scotland website.
Library produces a bi-monthly bulletin on a range of health improvement topics and several topic-specific monthly current awareness alerts
Order printed publications from: e-mail: nhs.healthscotland-library@nhs.net

Publications list:
Available online

Access to staff:
Contact by letter, by telephone, by fax, by e-mail, in person and via website
Hours: Mon to Thu, 0900 to 1630; Fri, 0900 to 1600

Access to building, collection or gallery:
Hours: Mon to Thu, 0900 to 1630; Fri, 0900 to 1600

Also at:
NHS Health Scotland
  Woodburn House, Canaan Lane, Edinburgh, EH10 4SG; tel: 0131 536 5500; fax: 0131 536 5501

HEALTH SERVICES MANAGEMENT CENTRE

Acronym or abbreviation: HSMC

School of Social Policy, University of Birmingham, Park House, 40 Edgbaston Park Road, Birmingham, B15 2RT

Tel: 0121 414 7060
Fax: 0121 414 7051

Website:
http://www.bham.ac.uk/hsmc/library
General information on services, access to catalogue and to list of journal holdings.

Enquiries:
Enquiries to: Librarian

Founded:
1972

Organisation type and purpose:
University department or institute, consultancy. Education and research in the field of health service management.

Subject coverage:
Health services management, quality in health services management, primary health care overseas.

Library catalogue:
All or part available online

Printed publications:
Discussion papers, research reports, handbook series, project reports, working papers and other publications

Order printed publications from: B. Earp, Health Services Management Centre, The University of Birmingham, Park House, 40 Edgbaston Park Road, Birmingham, B15 2RT, tel: 0121 414 2976, e-mail: b.earp@bham.ac.uk

Publications list:
Available online and in print

Access to staff:
Appointment necessary.
Hours: Mon to Fri, 0900 to 1700

HEALTHLINK WORLDWIDE

The Grayston Centre, 28 Charles Square, London, N1 6HT

Tel: 020 7250 6950
Fax: 020 7324 4740
E-mail: info@healthlink.org.uk

Website:
http://www.healthlink.org.uk
http://www.asksource.info
An international information support centre containing databases of resources relating to health, disability and development; organisations around the world that work on related issues; and distributors of free and low-cost information on these topics.

Enquiries:
Enquiries to: Programme Manager Knowledge Sharing
Direct e-mail: source@ich.ucl.ac.uk

Founded:
1977

Organisation type and purpose:
Voluntary organisation, registered charity (charity number 274260).
Non-governmental organisation.

Subject coverage:
Primary healthcare in developing countries, information management, information production, disability-related issues in developing countries.

Museum or gallery collection, archive, or library special collection:
Reference collection of materials on primary healthcare and disability in developing countries

Library catalogue:
All or part available online

Printed publications:
One-off publications including directories, 'how-to' manuals, and briefing papers
Order printed publications from: Programme Manager Knowledge Sharing

Electronic and video publications:
Database available online

Publications list:
Available online and in print

Access to staff:
Contact by letter, by telephone, by fax and by e-mail. Appointment necessary. All charged.
Hours: Mon to Fri, 0900 to 1700

Access for disabled people:
Lift at entrance, toilet facilities

HEARING AID COUNCIL, THE

70 St Mary Axe, London, EC3A 8BD

Tel: 020 3102 4030
Fax: 020 3102 4476
E-mail: hac@thehearingaidcouncil.org.uk

Website:
http://www.thehearingaidcouncil.org.uk

Enquiries:
Enquiries to: Registrar

Founded:
1968

Organisation type and purpose:
Statutory body, professional body.
To regulate trade practices in the private sector of dispensing hearing aids.

Subject coverage:
Examination and registration of hearing aid dispensers.

Printed publications:
Code of Practice (free)
Regulating the Sale of Hearing Aids (free)

Access to staff:
Contact by letter, by telephone, by fax, by e-mail and via website. Appointment necessary.
Hours: Mon to Fri, 0830 to 1730

HEARING CONCERN

95 Gray's Inn Road, London, WC1X 8TX

Tel: 020 7440 9871
Fax: 020 7440 9872
E-mail: info@hearingconcern.org.uk

Website:
http://www.hearingconcern.org.uk
Factsheets, news, services, links.

Enquiries:
Enquiries to: Director

Founded:
1947

Formerly called:
British Association of the Hard of Hearing

Organisation type and purpose:
National organisation, membership association (membership is by subscription, election or invitation), present number of members: 4416, voluntary organisation, registered charity (charity number 223322).

Subject coverage:
Hearing loss, lip reading, noise, vocational and welfare matters, aids to hearing, assistive aids for the deaf, loop systems, education.

Trade and statistical information:
Numbers of Hearing Impaired people in the UK stands at 8.4 million.

Printed publications:
Hearing Concern Magazine (quarterly)
Books
Leaflets on medical matters such as tinnitus, dizziness, otosclerosis, Ménières disease
Technical leaflets on hearing and communication aids with lists of manufacturers of equipment
Choosing a Hearing Aid
Facing up to Hearing Loss in Later Life
Lipreading
You and Your Hearing Aid

Publications list:
Available online and in print

Access to staff:
Contact by letter, by telephone, by fax, by e-mail, in person and via website. Appointment necessary.
Hours: Mon to Fri, 0900 to 1700

Access to building, collection or gallery:
Prior appointment required

Access for disabled people:
Parking provided, ramped entry, toilet facilities

Affiliated to:
Disability Alliance

HEARING DOGS FOR DEAF PEOPLE

The Grange, Wycombe Road, Saunderton, Princes Risborough, Buckinghamshire, HP27 9NS

Tel: 01844 348 100 (voice and minicom)
Fax: 01844 348 101 info@hearingdogs.org.uk
E-mail: info@hearingdogs.org.uk

Website:
http://www.hearingdogs.co.uk

Enquiries:
Enquiries to: Managing Director
Other contacts: Client Secretary for applying for a hearing dog.

Founded:
1982

Formerly called:
Hearing Dogs for the Deaf (year of change 1997)

Organisation type and purpose:
National organisation, registered charity (charity number 293358).

Subject coverage:
Hearing Dogs for Deaf People aims to offer greater independence, confidence and security to deaf people by providing dogs trained to alert them to chosen everyday sounds. Hearing dogs are free to deaf applicants.

Printed publications:
Favour (magazine)

Access to staff:
Contact by letter, by telephone, by fax, by e-mail and via website. Appointment necessary.
Hours: Mon to Fri, 0900 to 1700

Access to building, collection or gallery:
Prior appointment required

Access for disabled people:
Parking provided, ramped entry, level entry, toilet facilities

Other addresses:
Hearing Dogs for Deaf People
 29 Craigiehall Crescent, West Freelands, Erskine, Renfrewshire, PA8 7DD; tel: 0141 812 6542
Hearing Dogs for Deaf People
 12 Main Street, Crawfordsburn, Bangor, Co Down, BT19 1JE; tel: 028 9185 3669
Hearing Dogs for Deaf People
 The Beatrice Wright Training Centre, Hull Road, Cliffe, North Yorkshire, YO8 7NG
Hearing Dogs for Deaf People
 The Grange, Wycombe Road, Saunderton, Buckinghamshire, HPP27 9NS

HEART RESEARCH UK

Acronym or abbreviation: HRUK

Suite 12D, Joseph's Well, Leeds, West Yorkshire, LS3 1AB

Tel: 0113 234 7474
Fax: 0113 297 6208
E-mail: mail@heartresearch.org.uk

Website:
http://www.heartresearch.org.uk

Enquiries:
Enquiries to: National Director
Direct e-mail: info@heartresearch.org.uk
Other contacts: Grant Administrator

Founded:
1967

Formerly called:
National Heart Research Fund (year of change 2005)

Organisation type and purpose:
Registered charity (charity number 1044821), research organisation.

Subject coverage:
Prevention, treatment and cure of heart disease

Information services:
e-mail: info@heartresearch.org.uk.

Education services:
e-mail: lifestyle@heartresearch.org.uk.

Printed publications:
Pulse Newsletter & Healthy Heart Lifestyle Leaflets
Order printed publications from: Lifestyle Department or Richard Gledhill

continued overleaf

Access to staff:
Contact by letter, by telephone, by fax, by e-mail and via website. Appointment necessary.
Hours: Mon to Thu, 0900 to 1700; Fri 0900 to 1600

Access for disabled people:
Parking provided

Branches:
Heart Research UK in the Midlands
 Lee House, 6a Highfield Road, Edgbaston, Birmingham, B15 3ED; tel: 0121 454 1799; fax: 0121 454 1799; e-mail: midlands@heartresearch .org.uk; website: www.heartresearch.org.uk

HEAT PUMP ASSOCIATION

Acronym or abbreviation: HPA

2 Waltham Court, Milley Lane, Hare Hatch, Reading, Berkshire, RG10 9TH

Tel: 0118 940 3416
Fax: 0118 940 6258
E-mail: info@feta.co.uk

Website:
http://www.feta.co.uk

Enquiries:
Enquiries to: Commercial Manager

Founded:
1994

Organisation type and purpose:
Trade association.

Subject coverage:
The benefits and proper use of heat pumps and heat pump technology.

Access to staff:
Contact by letter, by telephone, by fax and by e-mail
Hours: Mon to Thu, 0830 to 1630; Fri, 0830 to 1600

Member organisation of:
Federation of Environmental Trade Associations

HEAT TRANSFER & FLUID FLOW SERVICE

Acronym or abbreviation: HTFS

Hyprotech UK Ltd, Harwell International Business Centre, Gemini Building, Fermi Avenue, Didcot, Oxfordshire, OX11 0QR

Tel: 01235 448330
Fax: 01235 448350
E-mail: htfs@hyprotech.com

Website:
http://www.htfs.com
Description of products and services available.

Enquiries:
Enquiries to: Administrator

Founded:
1968

Organisation type and purpose:
International organisation, research organisation.

Subject coverage:
Heat transfer; condensation; boiling; evaporation; general fluid flow; cryogenic fluids; combustion; heat transfer in nuclear reactors, design of heat exchangers and furnaces.

Electronic and video publications:
HTFS Heatflo database (web page)

Access to staff:
Contact by fax, by e-mail and via website
Hours: Mon to Fri, 0900 to 1700

Links with:
Hyprotech Ltd
 Canada
National Engineering Laboratory

HEATHER SOCIETY

c/o Tippitiwitchet Cottage, Hall Road, Outwell, Wisbech, Cambridgeshire, PE14 8PE

Tel: 01945 774077
Fax: [indirect] 01449 711220
E-mail: theheathersociety@phonecoop.coop

Website:
http://www.heathersociety.org.uk
General information on heathers. Listing of heathers commercially available. Heather-garden design.

Enquiries:
Enquiries to: Administrator
Other contacts: Chairman; Treasurer; Secretary; Registrar

Founded:
1963

Organisation type and purpose:
International organisation, membership association (membership is by subscription), present number of members: 250, registered charity in England & Wales (charity number 261407).
International Registration Authority for cultivars of heathers.

Subject coverage:
Growing and propagation of heathers; nomenclature and identification; availability of individual cultivars in commerce.

Museum or gallery collection, archive, or library special collection:
Heather Society slide library (free access to members)

Printed publications:
Bulletin (3 times a year)
Heather: yearbook of The Heather Society (annual)
Everyone can grow heathers

Publications list:
Available online

Access to staff:
Contact by letter, by telephone and by e-mail

Affiliated to:
Royal Horticultural Society

Links with:
Dutch, North American and German Heather Societies

HEATHERSLAW LIGHT RAILWAY COMPANY LTD

Ford Forge, Heatherslaw, Etal, Cornhill on Tweed, Northumberland, TD12 4TJ

Tel: 01890 820244; 01890 820317
E-mail: info@heatherslawlightrailway.co.uk

Website:
http://www.heatherslawlightrailway.co.uk

Enquiries:
Enquiries to: Managing Director

Founded:
1988

Organisation type and purpose:
Service industry.

Subject coverage:
Operation of a light railway.

Printed publications:
Leaflet (free, direct)

Access to staff:
Contact by letter, by telephone, by e-mail and via website
Hours: Sun to Sat, 0900 to 1700

Subsidiary company:
Errol Hut Smithy
 Letham Hill, Etal, Cornhill-on-Tweed, Northumberland; tel: 01890 820317

HEBRIDEAN SHEEP SOCIETY

Knox Mill, Knox Mill Lane, Harrogate, North Yorkshire, HG3 2AE

Tel: 01423 507741
E-mail: info@hebrideansheep.org.uk

Enquiries:
Enquiries to: General Secretary

Founded:
1986

Formerly called:
Hebridean Sheep Breeders' Group (year of change 1994)

Organisation type and purpose:
Membership association (membership is by subscription), present number of members: 230.
Sheep Breed Society.
Registration authority for Hebridean Sheep in UK.

Access to staff:
Contact by letter, by telephone, by fax and by e-mail
Hours: Mon to Fri, 0900 to 1700

Affiliated to:
National Sheep Association (NSA)
 Sheep Centre, Malvern, Worcestershire

HEBRON TRUST

12 Stanley Avenue, Norwich, Norfolk, NR7 0BE

Tel: 01603 439905
Fax: 01603 700799
E-mail: info@hebrontrust.org.uk

Website:
http://www.hebrontrust.co.uk
Content for individuals who are interested in rehabilitation for themselves, but also for professionals, concerned friends, family and others who want to learn more about Hebron Trust.

Founded:
1993

Organisation type and purpose:
Registered charity (number 1020095), voluntary organisation.
Provides a safe, nurturing and intensively supportive community environment in which to rehabilitate from drug and alcohol dependency and the life-dominating problems that serious substance misuse can cause.

Subject coverage:
Residential rehabilitation for up to 10 women aged 18–65 who share the common goal of recovery.

Access to staff:
Contact by letter, by telephone, by fax and by e-mail

HELP ADVISORY CENTRE

Acronym or abbreviation: HAC

57 Portobello Road, London, W11 3DB

Tel: 020 7221 9974

Website:
http://www.helpcounselling.com

Enquiries:
Enquiries to: Administrator
Direct tel: 020 7221 7914

Founded:
1968

Organisation type and purpose:
Voluntary organisation.
Counselling centre.

Subject coverage:
Counselling, psychotherapy, communication skills, career direction, assertiveness, sexuality, life choices, life changes.

Access to staff:
Contact by letter and by telephone
Hours: Mon to Fri, 1100 to 1830

Connections with:
Virgin Co Limited
120 Campden Hill Road, London, W8 7AR

HELP FOR HEROES

Acronym or abbreviation: H4H

Steynings House, Summerlock Approach,
Salisbury, Wilts, SP2 7RJ

Website:
http://www.helpforheroes.org.uk
The charity, its projects, events and fundraisers,
news, FAQs, online shop.

Founded:
2007

Organisation type and purpose:
Registered charity (number 1120920) helping
wounded Servicemen and women.
To promote and protect the health of those who
have been wounded whilst serving in the Armed
Forces by making grants to purchase equipment
for their rehabilitation; to make grants to other
charities that assist members of the Armed Forces
and their dependents.

Subject coverage:
Current grants policy is to look for strategic
partners that are developing the rehabilitation
infrastructure required by those Servicemen and
women injured in the line of duty, both in action
and in more general service. Mindful of the work
of other service charities, H4H currently restricts
its grant making to supporting those affected by
the current conflicts, i.e since 11th Sept 2001.

Access to staff:
Contact by letter, by telephone and via website

Also at:
Help for Heroes Donations Office
 Unit 6, Aspire Business Centre, Ordnance Road,
 Tidworth, Hants, SP9 7QD; tel: 0845 673 1760;
 01980 846 459
Help for Heroes Trading Company Ltd (H4HT) – a
wholly owned trading subsidiary
 14 Parker's Close, Downton Business Centre,
 Salisbury, Wiltshire, SP5 3RB; tel: 01725 513212

HELP THE AGED

207–221 Pentonville Road, London, N1 9UZ

Tel: 020 7278 1114
Fax: 020 7278 1116
E-mail: info@helptheaged.org.uk

Website:
http://www.helptheaged.org.uk
Information on Help the Aged and issues of
concern to senior citizens.

Enquiries:
Other contacts: Policy Officer for awareness of local
government policies.

Founded:
1961

Organisation type and purpose:
Voluntary organisation, registered charity (charity
number 272786).
To free disadvantaged older people from poverty,
isolation, and neglect.
To campaign for change in government policy, to
undertake research into the needs of older people,
and to provide local services in communities across
the UK and overseas.

Subject coverage:
Age-related issues: demographics, welfare and
disability benefits, community care, housing,
residential care, health issues, home safety and
security and more. Help the Aged cannot provide
information on international or development
issues – refer to Help Age International.

Printed publications:
Advice leaflets under the headings: financial,
housing and home safety, health (free)

Other publications, some charged some free:
 independence of older people, transport, income
 and pensions, health and care, housing and
 homelessness, rural issues and poetry.

Electronic and video publications:
Be Strong, Be Steady (video)
Step to the Future (DVD, video)

Publications list:
Available in print

Access to staff:
Contact by letter, by telephone, by fax and by e-
mail
Hours: Mon to Fri, 0900 to 1700

Access to building, collection or gallery:
No access other than to staff

Other addresses:
Help the Aged Northern Ireland
 Ascot House, Shaftesbury Square, Belfast, BT2
 7DB; tel: 028 9023 0666; fax: 028 9024 8183
Help the Aged Scotland
 11 Granton Square, Edinburgh, EH5 1HX; tel:
 0131 551 6331; fax: 0131 551 5415
Help the Aged Wales
 12 Cathedral Road, Cardiff, CF11 9LJ; tel: 029
 2034 6550; fax: 029 2039 0898; e-mail:
 infocymru@helptheaged.org.uk

Part of:
Help Age International Network which currently
has 16 members

HEMEL HEMPSTEAD CENTRAL LIBRARY

Combe Street, Hemel Hempstead, Hertfordshire,
HP1 1HJ

Tel: 01438 737333
Fax: 01442 404660
E-mail: hemelhempstead.library@hertscc.gov.uk

Website:
http://www.hertslib.hertscc.gov.uk
Stock catalogue for county and community
information database.

Enquiries:
Enquiries to: Librarian

Organisation type and purpose:
Public library.

Library catalogue:
All or part available online

Access to staff:
Contact by letter, by telephone, by fax, by e-mail
and in person
Hours: Mon, Thu, Fri, 0930 to 2000; Tue, 1030 to
2000; Wed, 0930 to 1300; Sat, 0930 to 1600
Special comments: Reference library and local
statistics collection on first floor, but no lift.

Access to building, collection or gallery:
No access other than to staff
Hours: Mon, Thu, Fri, 0930 to 2000; Tue, 1030 to
2000; Wed, 0930 to 1300; Sat, 0930 to 1600

Links with:
Community Information Department
 Hertfordshire County Council, County Hall,
 Hertford, SG13 8DE; tel: 01438 737333; fax:
 01442 555614; e-mail: cidb@hertscc.gov.uk

HENLEY BUSINESS SCHOOL

Formal name: Henley Business School at the
University of Reading

Greenlands, Henley-on-Thames, Oxfordshire, RG9
3AU

Tel: 01491 571454
Fax: 01491 571635
E-mail: arc@henley.com

Website:
http://www.henley.reading.ac.uk

Enquiries:
Enquiries to: Librarian

Direct tel: 01491 418823

Founded:
1945

Formerly called:
Henley Management College; Administrative Staff
College

Organisation type and purpose:
Business School

Subject coverage:
Accounting, banking, business studies, currency,
economics, industrial relations, management,
marketing, office management and practice,
operational research, personnel recruitment and
management, production management and
control, sales management, information
management, statistics.

**Museum or gallery collection, archive, or library
special collection:**
Papers of Colonel L. F. Urwick

Access to staff:
Contact by letter, by telephone and by e-mail.
Appointment necessary. Access for members only.
Letter of introduction required.
Hours: Mon to Fri, 0830 to 2130; Sat, 0900 to 1900;
Sun, 1000 to 1800

Access to building, collection or gallery:
Special comments: Reference only

HENRY GEORGE FOUNDATION OF GT BRITAIN LIMITED

Acronym or abbreviation: Henry George Foundation

212 Piccadilly, London, W1J 9HG

Tel: 020 7917 1899
Fax: 020 7917 1899

Website:
http://www.henrygeorge.org.uk
About HGF and the progressive forum; books
published; events; ideas; links.

Enquiries:
Enquiries to: Secretary

Formerly called:
Economic and Social Science Research Association
(ESSRA)

Organisation type and purpose:
Membership association, present number of
members: 500, registered charity (charity number
259194), suitable for ages: 18+, research
organisation, publishing house.
To promote a greater understanding of ways of
improving the tax system to the benefit of the
whole community.

Subject coverage:
Economic theory; tax developments worldwide;
history of the Georgist movement with archives;
history of land tax and its implementation around
the world.

Library catalogue:
All or part available in-house

Printed publications:
Land & Liberty (journal, quarterly)
Books on economics and related subjects

Publications list:
Available in print

Access to staff:
Contact by letter, by telephone, by fax, by e-mail
and via website. Appointment necessary.
Hours: Mon to Fri, 0930 to 1700

Access to building, collection or gallery:
Prior appointment required

HENRY MOORE FOUNDATION

Dane Tree House, Perry Green, Much Hadham,
Hertfordshire, SG10 6EE

Tel: 01279 843333
Fax: 01279 843647

continued overleaf

Website:
http://www.henry-moore-fdn.co.uk

Founded:
1977

Organisation type and purpose:
A registered charity with the aim of advancing the education of the public by the promotion of their appreciation of the fine arts, and in particular of the works of Henry Moore.

Museum or gallery collection, archive, or library special collection:
Elmwood Library, specialising in Henry Moore studies
Henry Moore Archive
Henry Moore Image Archive of photographs recording the artist's life and works
Henry Moore Bibliography online

HENRY WATSON MUSIC LIBRARY

Central Library, St Peter's Square, Manchester, M2 5PD

Tel: 0161 234 1976
Fax: 0161 234 1961
E-mail: music@libraries.manchester.gov.uk

Website:
http://www.manchester.gov.uk/libraries/central/hwml/index.htm
Web pages.

Enquiries:
Enquiries to: Music Co-ordinator

Founded:
1899

Organisation type and purpose:
Local government body, public library.

Subject coverage:
Printed and manuscript music and the literature of music (principally classical music).

Museum or gallery collection, archive, or library special collection:
Early printed music (2000 items)
Newman Flower Collection (Handel)
Collection of orchestral and choral music (for hire)
C18 Italian manuscripts

Library catalogue:
All or part available in-house

Printed publications:
George Frideric Handel: The Newman Flower Collection in the Henry Watson Music Library (A D Walker, 1972)

Microform publications:
Microfilm available for all rare or unique items in stock

Access to staff:
Contact by letter, by telephone, by fax, by e-mail, in person and via website
Hours: Mon to Thu, 0900 to 2000; Fri to Sat, 0900 to 1700

Access to building, collection or gallery:
No prior appointment required

Access for disabled people:
Ramped entry, toilet facilities

Parent body:
Manchester City Council

HENRY WILLIAMSON SOCIETY

7 Monmouth Road, Dorchester, Dorset, DT1 2DE

Tel: 01305 264092
E-mail: zseagull@aol.com

Website:
http://www.henrywilliamson.co.uk

Enquiries:
Enquiries to: General Secretary

Founded:
1980

Organisation type and purpose:
Learned society (membership is by subscription), present number of members: 500, registered charity (charity number 288168).
To encourage interest in and a deeper understanding of the life and work of the writer, Henry Williamson.

Museum or gallery collection, archive, or library special collection:
Archive at Exeter University

Printed publications:
Publications available for purchase
Order printed publications from: Publications Manager, Henry Williamson Society
14 Nethergrove, Longstanton, Cambridge, CB4 5EL, tel: 01954 200598, e-mail: john@camnews.net

Publications list:
Available in print

Access to staff:
Contact by letter, by telephone and by e-mail
Hours: Mon to Fri, 0900 to 2000

Other addresses:
Membership Secretary
16 Doran Drive, Redhill, Surrey, RH1 6AX; e-mail: mm@misterman.freeserve.co.uk

HENSHAWS SOCIETY FOR BLIND PEOPLE

Acronym or abbreviation: hsbp

John Derby House, 88–92 Talbot Road, Old Trafford, Manchester, M16 0GS

Tel: 0161 872 1234
Fax: 0161 848 9889
E-mail: info@hsbp.co.uk

Website:
http://www.hsbp.co.uk
General information, services and events

Enquiries:
Enquiries to: Chief Executive

Founded:
1837

Organisation type and purpose:
Voluntary organisation, registered charity (charity number 221888).
Registered social landlord.

Subject coverage:
Visual impairment and related issues.

Museum or gallery collection, archive, or library special collection:
Minute books and Annual Reports of the Society since 1837
Early minute books are housed at the John Rylands' Library, Manchester

Printed publications:
Annual Report and Accounts
General factsheets
Information packs
Leaflets about the services provided

Electronic and video publications:
Sex, Eyes and Audiotape – everything you had to see to know about HIV (tape, a health education information resource for people with visual impairment)

Publications list:
Available in print

Access to staff:
Contact by letter, by telephone, by fax and by e-mail. Appointment necessary.
Hours: Mon to Fri, 0900 to 1630

Access to building, collection or gallery:
No appointment necessary but staff members may not always be available if apppointment not made in advance.

Access for disabled people:
Ramped entry, access to all public areas, toilet facilities, talking lift, loop system.

Now incorporating the:
Manchester and Salford Blind Aid Society

Other addresses:
Community Services North & West Yorkshire
50 Bond End, Knaresborough, North Yorkshire, HG5 9AL; tel: 01423 541888; fax: 01423 541889
Harrogate Community Housing
50 Bond End, Knaresborough, North Yorkshire, HG5 9AL; tel: 01423 541888; fax: 01423 541889
Henshaws Arts and Craft Centre
Bond End, Knaresborough, North Yorkshire, HG5 9AL; tel: 01423 541888; fax: 01423 541889
Henshaws College
Bogs Lane, Harrogate, North Yorkshire, HG1 4ED; tel: 01423 886451; fax: 01423 885095
Henshaws Training & Professional Development Centre
John Derby House, 88/92 Talbot Road, Old Trafford, Manchester, M16 0GS; tel: 0161 872 1234; fax: 0161 848 9889
Merseyside Resource Centre
Wellington Buildings, The Strand, Liverpool, L2 0PP; tel: 0151 227 1226; fax: 0151 236 3641
Old Trafford Resource Centre
John Derby House, 88–92 Talbot Road, Old Trafford, Manchester, M16 0GS; tel: 0161 872 1234; fax: 0161 848 9889
Patient Support Service
Manchester Royal Eye Hospital, Manchester; tel 0161 276 5515

Works with:
Liverpool Workshops and Birkenhead Society for the Blind

HENTY SOCIETY

205 Icknield Way, Letchworth, Hertfordshire, SG6 4TT

Tel: 01462 671357
E-mail: davidwalmsley@hentysociety.org

Enquiries:
Enquiries to: Honorary Secretary

Founded:
1977

Organisation type and purpose:
International organisation, learned society (membership is by subscription), present number of members: 120.
To further knowledge of the life and work of George Alfred Henty (1832–1902), special correspondent, The Standard newspaper, writer of books for boys and young people.

Subject coverage:
19th-century children's literature.

Printed publications:
Occasional lists available from Honorary Secretary

Access to staff:
Contact by letter and by telephone
Hours: Mon to Fri, 0900 to 1800
Special comments: This society is run by volunteers from their own homes.

HER MAJESTY'S INSPECTORATE FOR EDUCATION AND TRAINING IN WALES

Acronym or abbreviation: Estyn

Anchor Court, Keen Road, Cardiff, CF24 5JW

Tel: 029 2044 6446
Fax: 029 2044 6448
E-mail: enquiries@estyn.gsi.gov.uk

Website:
http://www.estyn.gov.uk

Enquiries:
Enquiries to: Her Majesty's Chief Inspector of Education and Training in Wales
Direct tel: 029 2044 6475
Direct fax: 029 2044 6531
Direct e-mail: chief-inspector@estyn.gsi.gov.uk
Other contacts: Communications Team

Founded:
1992

Organisation type and purpose:
National government body.
Non-ministerial government department in Wales.

Subject coverage:
Inspects quality and standards in education and training in Wales, including: nursery schools and settings that are maintained by, or receive funding from, local education authorities (LEAs); primary schools; secondary schools; special schools; pupil-referral units; independent schools; further education; adult community-based learning; youth support services; LEAs; teacher education and training; work-based learning; careers companies; and the education, guidance and training elements of Department for Work and Pensions-funded training programmes.
Estyn also provides advice on quality and standards in education and training in Wales to the National Assembly for Wales and others, and makes public good practice based on inspection evidence.

Access to staff:
Contact by letter, by telephone, by fax, by e-mail and via website. Appointment necessary.
Hours: Mon to Fri, 0900 to 1700

Access to building, collection or gallery:
Hours: Mon to Fri, 0900 to 1700

Also at:
Estyn
Broncoed House, Broncoed Business Park, Mold, Flintshire; tel: 029 2044 6319

HERALDRY SOCIETY

53 Hitchin Street, Baldock, Hertfordshire, SG7 6AQ

Tel: 01462 892062
Fax: 01462 491262
E-mail: honsecheraldrysociety@googlemail.com

Enquiries:
Enquiries to: Honorary Secretary

Founded:
1947

Organisation type and purpose:
International organisation, learned society (membership is by subscription), present number of members: 1,000, registered charity (charity number 241456), suitable for ages: all.
Specialist library, special facilities available to members at Society of Antiquaries, London and Chetham Library, Manchester.
Study of Heraldry.

Subject coverage:
Heraldry, armoury, chivalry, genealogy.

Museum or gallery collection, archive, or library special collection:
Library on heraldry, for use of members only
Special facilities available to members at Society of Antiquaries, London and Chetham Library, Manchester.

Printed publications:
Heraldry Gazette (quarterly newsletter, members only)
Coat of Arms (quarterly)

Publications list:
Available in print

Access to staff:
Contact by letter, by telephone, by fax and by e-mail
Hours: Mon to Fri, 0900 to 1700
Special comments: No premises for visits.

HERALDRY SOCIETY OF SCOTLAND

25 Craigentinny Crescent, Edinburgh, EH7 6QA

Website:
http://www.heraldry-scotland.co.uk

Enquiries:
Enquiries to: Treasurer

Founded:
1977

Organisation type and purpose:
Learned society (membership is by subscription), present number of members: 400.

Subject coverage:
Scottish heraldry; the Heraldic Executive in Scotland; use of heraldry in Scottish art and architecture; Scottish heraldic families; ceremonial in Scotland; the Order of the Thistle; the Order of Baronets of Nova Scotia.

Printed publications:
The Double Tressure (annually)

Publications list:
Available in print

Access to staff:
Contact by letter

HERB SOCIETY

Sulgrave Manor, Sulgrave, Banbury, Oxfordshire, OX17 2SD

Tel: 01295 768899
Fax: 01295 768069
E-mail: herbs@herbsociety.org.uk

Website:
http://www.herbsociety.co.uk

Enquiries:
Enquiries to: Administrator

Founded:
1927

Organisation type and purpose:
Membership association (membership is by subscription).

Subject coverage:
Herbs and herbal matters with emphasis on medicinal aspects, cultivation, uses and history.

Printed publications:
Herbarium (4 times a year)
Herbs Magazine (4 times a year)

Publications list:
Available in print

Access to staff:
Contact by letter, by telephone, by fax, by e-mail, in person and via website
Hours: Mon to Fri, 0900 to 1700

Access to building, collection or gallery:
No prior appointment required

Access for disabled people:
Parking provided, level entry, access to all public areas, toilet facilities

HERBERT HOWELLS SOCIETY

32 Barleycroft Road, Welwyn Garden City, Hertfordshire, AL8 6JU

Tel: 01707 335315
E-mail: andrew.millinger@virgin.net

Enquiries:
Enquiries to: Honorary Secretary

Founded:
1987

Organisation type and purpose:
Membership association (membership is by subscription), present number of members: 300.

Subject coverage:
The Society exists to promote the performance, publication and recording of the works of Herbert Howells.

Access to staff:
Contact by letter, by telephone and by e-mail.
Appointment necessary.

Hours: Any reasonable time, answerphone available

Branches:
Herbert Howells Society, North American Branch
Dr Jane Gamble; e-mail: drjanegamble@aol.com

HEREFORD CATHEDRAL LIBRARY AND ARCHIVES

The Cathedral, Hereford, HR1 2NG

Tel: 01432 374225/6
Fax: 01432 374220
E-mail: library@herefordcathedral.org

Website:
http://www.herefordcathedral.org

Enquiries:
Enquiries to: Librarian
Other contacts: Archivist

Founded:
c. 12th century

Organisation type and purpose:
Registered charity, research organisation.
Ecclesiastical library.

Subject coverage:
Religion and theology, ecclesiastical history, history of Hereford Cathedral, local history, rare books and manuscripts, medieval maps ecclesiastical art and architecture, sacred (and some secular) music, including manuscripts of the 18th and 19th centuries.

Museum or gallery collection, archive, or library special collection:
1,500 books (manuscripts and printed) chained to early 17th-century presses
229 medieval manuscripts, from the 8th to the early 16th centuries (microfilmed)
30,000 archives of the Dean and Chapter, dating from the 9th to 20th centuries (some microfilmed)
All Saints Chained Library (over 300 vols, 15th to 18th centuries, chained to early 18th-century presses)
Manuscript and printed music, 18th to 20th centuries (c. 350 vols)
Over 3,000 pre-1801 printed books, including 56 incunabula, 10,000 books published post-1800 on subjects listed above, many borrowable

Non-library collection catalogue:
All or part available online, in-house and in print

Library catalogue:
All or part available online and in-house

Printed publications:
Catalogue of the Manuscripts of Hereford Cathedral Library (R. A. B. Mynors and R. M. Thomson, 1993)
Mappa Mundi and the Chained Library (J. Williams, 1999)

Microform publications:
Microfilms of the medieval manuscripts and some archive documents (positive copies can be ordered from the negatives) and some Hereford-related material in other collections

Access to staff:
Contact by letter, by telephone, by fax, by e-mail, in person and via website

Access to building, collection or gallery:
Hours: Reading Room: Tue and Thu, 1000 to 1600; open other times by prior appointment

Access for disabled people:
Level entry, access to all public areas, toilet facilities

Parent body:
Dean and Chapter of Hereford
tel: 01432 374200; e-mail: office@herefordcathedral.org; website: http://www.herefordcathedral.org
Hereford Mappa Mundi Trustees

HEREFORD CATTLE SOCIETY

Hereford House, 3 Offa Street, Hereford, HR1 2LL

Tel: 01432 272057
Fax: 01432 377529
E-mail: postroom@herefordcattle.org

Website:
http://www.herefordcattle.org

Enquiries:
Enquiries to: The Secretary

Founded:
1878

Organisation type and purpose:
National organisation, membership association (membership is by election or invitation), registered charity.

Subject coverage:
Hereford cattle.

HEREFORDSHIRE COLLEGE OF TECHNOLOGY – HEREFORD CAMPUS

Acronym or abbreviation: HCT

Folly Lane, Hereford, HR1 1LS

Tel: 01432 352235
Fax: 01432 365395
E-mail: enquiries@hct.ac.uk

Website:
http://www.hct.ac.uk
Information on the college and the courses on offer, details of the student support services, what students feel about HCT and where they go afterwards.

Enquiries:
Enquiries to: Learning Resources Manager
Direct tel: 01432 365470
Direct e-mail: lrc@hct.ac.uk
Other contacts: LRC Co-ordinator

Founded:
1974

Formerly called:
Herefordshire Technical College (year of change 1992)

Organisation type and purpose:
College of further and higher education.

Subject coverage:
Construction, business studies, caring, hospitality, tourism and leisure, engineering, farriery, blacksmithing, art and design, education, humanities, computing, agriculture, forestry, animal care, horticulture, sports, outdoor education.

Library catalogue:
All or part available in-house

Access to staff:
Contact by letter, by telephone, by fax, by e-mail and in person
Hours: Mon to Thu, 0830 to 2030; Fri, 0830 to 1630

Access to building, collection or gallery:
By prior arrangement with LRC staff

Access for disabled people:
Parking provided, disabled access, toilet facilities

HEREFORDSHIRE COLLEGE OF TECHNOLOGY – HOLME LACY CAMPUS

Holme Lacy, Hereford, HR2 6LL

Tel: 01432 870316
Fax: 01432 870566
E-mail: enquiries@hct.ac.uk

Website:
http://www.hct.ac.uk/
College prospectus.

Enquiries:
Enquiries to: Learning Resources Manager

Founded:
1963

Formerly called:
Herefordshire College of Agriculture

Incorporates the former:
Holme Lacy College (part of the Pershore Group of Colleges) (year of change 2007)

Organisation type and purpose:
Suitable for ages: 16+.
Land based further education.

Subject coverage:
Agriculture, horticulture, forestry, small animal care, equine studies, gamekeeping, floristry, environmental studies, sustainability, organic agriculture, leisure, recreation, business studies.

Museum or gallery collection, archive, or library special collection:
Workman collection of forestry-related material

Non-library collection catalogue:
All or part available in-house

Library catalogue:
All or part available in-house

Access to staff:
Contact by letter, by telephone and by fax.
Appointment necessary.
Hours: Open in term time only
Special comments: Reduced hours during college holidays as posted.

Access for disabled people:
Parking provided, ramped entry, toilet facilities
Special comments: Access to all areas of the library.

HEREFORDSHIRE FAMILY HISTORY SOCIETY

Acronym or abbreviation: HFHS

6 Birch Meadow, Gosmore Road, Clehonger, Hereford, HR2 9RH

Tel: 01981 250974
E-mail: prosser_brian@hotmail.com

Website:
http://www.rootsweb.com/~ukhfhs
Web page for the society.

Enquiries:
Enquiries to: Secretary General

Founded:
1980

Organisation type and purpose:
Membership association (membership is by subscription), present number of members: 900, voluntary organisation, registered charity (charity number 517785).
Family history society with particular reference to Herefordshire.

Subject coverage:
General family history enquiries.

Library catalogue:
All or part available in-house

Printed publications:
Order printed publications from: Publication Officer, Herefordshire FHS
79 College Road, Hereford, HR1 1ED

Publications list:
Available online and in print

Access to staff:
Contact by letter, by telephone, by e-mail and via website
Hours: Mon to Fri, 0900 to 1700

Access for disabled people:
Parking provided

HEREFORDSHIRE LIBRARIES

Stock Unit, Herefordshire Libraries, Shirehall, Hereford, HR1 2HY

Tel: 01432 261570
Fax: 01432 260744
E-mail: libraries@herefordshire.gov.uk

Website:
http://www.herefordshire.gov.uk/libraries

Enquiries:
Enquiries to: Principal Libraries Officer
Direct tel: 01432 260557

Founded:
1998

Formerly called:
Hereford and Worcester County Libraries (year of change 1998)

Organisation type and purpose:
Local government body, public library.

Subject coverage:
Local studies, particularly history of the old county of Hereford; apple and pear cultivation; cidermaking; beekeeping.

Museum or gallery collection, archive, or library special collection:
Hopton Collection (local history, crosses)
Pilley Collection (local history, general and religious history, especially of the 19th century)
Alfred Watkins and F. C. Morgan Collections of photographic glass slides and negatives

Non-library collection catalogue:
All or part available in-house

Library catalogue:
All or part available online and in-house

Access to staff:
Contact by letter, by telephone, by fax and in person. Appointment necessary.
Hours: Mon to Fri, 0900 to 1700

Constituent bodies:
Woolhope Naturalists' Field Club

Parent body:
Herefordshire Council
Brockington, 35 Haford Road, Hereford, HR1 1SH; tel: 01432 260044; fax: 01432 340189; website: http://www.herefordshire.gov.uk

HEREFORDSHIRE RECORD OFFICE

Acronym or abbreviation: HRO

Harold Street, Hereford, HR1 2QX

Tel: 01432 260750
Fax: 01432 260066
E-mail: archives@herefordshire.gov.uk

Website:
http://www.herefordshire.gov.uk/archives

Founded:
1958

Organisation type and purpose:
Local government body.
Record office.

Subject coverage:
All aspects of local and family history.

Museum or gallery collection, archive, or library special collection:
Hereford photographic survey

Printed publications:
Information leaflets about various aspects of the service (free)

Access to staff:
Contact by letter, by telephone, by fax, by e-mail, in person and via website

Access to building, collection or gallery:
Hours: Mon, 0915 to 1645; Tue to Fri, 0915 to 1645; Wed, 1000 to 1645; second Sat in each month, 0915 to 1645

Special comments: CARN Readers ticket needed for all records, ticket issued on production of identification of name and address. Searchers wishing to use microfilm readers should book in advance. Access to parish registers as well as some other heavily used material is normally only by microform.

Access for disabled people:
Special comments: Lift, automatic doors, adapted furniture, large-print and Braille leaflets

HERIOT-WATT UNIVERSITY – ARCHIVE, RECORDS MANAGEMENT AND MUSEUM SERVICE

Acronym or abbreviation: ARMMS

Riccarton, Edinburgh, EH14 4AS

Tel: 0131 541 3219
E-mail: archive@hw.ac.uk

Website:
http://www.hw.ac.uk/archive

Enquiries:
Enquiries to: Archivist

Founded:
1821

Incorporates the former:
Heriot-Watt became a university by royal charter in 1966, but its origins go back to the Edinburgh School of Arts, the first mechanics institute, founded in 1821.

Organisation type and purpose:
University museum and archive.

Subject coverage:
Collecting is governed by the University Acquisition and Disposal Policy. The university collects objects, works of art and archives in all formats including electronic and digital media. Collecting policy is focused on: the origins and development of Heriot-Watt University, its teaching and research activities, the achievements of its staff, students and other people associated with it, its links with business and industry and its campuses at Edinburgh, Galashiels, Orkney and Dubai; the history of Riccarton, home of the Edinburgh campus, and its communities; Scottish textile heritage and its development over four centuries from the paisley shawl to the Vivienne Westwood kilt; works of art, especially artists of the Edinburgh School, from Raeburn to Blackadder.

Museum or gallery collection, archive, or library special collection:
The Museum and Archive at the Edinburgh campus contains archives, plans, photographs, objects and works of art relating to the history of Heriot-Watt University and its predecessors – Heriot-Watt College (1885–1966) and The School of Arts and Watt Institution & School of Arts (1821–1885). Related collections include archives of Leith Nautical College and records relating to the engineering firm of Boulton and Watt.
Other collections relate to the history of the Edinburgh campus at Riccarton including estate records dating back to the 15th century. There was a strong connection between the estate and the local communities of Currie, Balerno and Juniper Green and images and archives are also held relating to the history of these communities including images of paper and snuff mills on the Water of Leith.
Works of art include portraits of the Gibson-Craig family by Sir Henry Raeburn, paintings by artists of the Edinburgh School such as Elizabeth Blackadder and John Bellany and sculptures including James Watt by Peter Slater and A Stone for the Whales by Stan Wilson.
The Textile Collection held at the Scottish Borders Campus in Galashiels is a unique resource for the history of Scottish textiles from the mid-18th century to the present. Highlights include business records and pattern books from Borders

mills; fabrics and apparel from designer and artist Bernat Klein; furnishing fabrics from Donald Brothers of Dundee; Paisley shawls, highland dress, tartan and costume. The Collection also includes records of textile professional education from the first classes provided by the Galashiels Manufacturers Corporation in 1883 to the Galashiels Combined Technical College (1889–1909), South of Scotland Combined Technical College (1909–1922), Scottish Woollen Technical College (1922–1968), Scottish College of Textiles (1968–1998) and Heriot-Watt University School of Textiles and Design (1998 to date).

Non-library collection catalogue:
All or part available online and in-house

Printed publications:
Heriot-Watt University: Two Centuries of learning: your guide to the University's heritage
Heriot-Watt University: Art and Academia: your guide to the art collection
Heriot-Watt University: a place to discover: your guide to the Edinburgh campus
Heriot-Watt University: an illustrated history by Patrick O'Farrell
Order printed publications from: Corporate Communications, George Heriot Wing, Heriot-Watt University, Edinburgh EH14 4AS; website: http://www.hw.ac.uk/ppr/index.htm; e-mail: pr@hw.ac.uk

Publications list:
Available online

Access to staff:
Contact by letter, by telephone, by e-mail, in person and via website. Appointment necessary.
Hours: Mon to Fri, 0900 to 1700
Special comments: By appointment.

Access to building, collection or gallery:
No prior appointment required

HERIOT-WATT UNIVERSITY – SCOTTISH BORDERS CAMPUS

Netherdale, Galashiels, Selkirkshire, TD1 3HF

Tel: 01896 892185
Fax: 01896 758965 (Campus Reception)
E-mail: servicedesk@sbc.hw.ac.uk

Website:
http://www.hw.ac.uk/sbc/library
Information service.

Enquiries:
Enquiries to: Campus Librarian
Direct tel: 01896 892155
Direct e-mail: sbclibhelp@hw.ac.uk
Other contacts: Further Education Liaison Librarian

Founded:
1922

Formerly called:
Scottish Woollen Technical College (year of change 1968); Scottish College of Textiles (year of change 1998)

Organisation type and purpose:
University department or institute.

Subject coverage:
Art, business, clothing, chemistry, computing, design, fashion, management, marketing, textiles.

Information services:
Enquiry Service for staff and students of Borders College and Heriot-Watt University.

Museum or gallery collection, archive, or library special collection:
The Co-operative College Collection at Heriot-Watt University, includes periodicals, books and pamphlets about the Co-operative Movement

Library catalogue:
All or part available online

Access to staff:
Contact by letter, by telephone, by e-mail, in person and via website. Appointment necessary.
Hours: Mon to Fri, 0900 to 1645

Access for disabled people:
Parking provided, ramped entry, access to all public areas, toilet facilities

Constituent part of:
Heriot-Watt University

HERIOT-WATT UNIVERSITY LIBRARY

Riccarton, Edinburgh, EH14 4AS

Tel: 0131 451 3577
Fax: 0131 451 3164
E-mail: libhelp@hw.ac.uk

Website:
http://www.hw.ac.uk/library
Home page and extensive pointers to relevant subject resources.
http://hwlibrary.wordpress.com
The Library blog (called 'spineless?') for news and articles of interest, etc.

Enquiries:
Enquiries to: Librarian
Direct tel: 0131 451 3570
Other contacts: University Archivist

Founded:
1821

Organisation type and purpose:
University library.

Subject coverage:
Librarianship and information science, history of the university, biological sciences, psychology, economics, modern European languages, building, chemical, civil, electrical, mechanical, offshore and petroleum engineering, physics, chemistry, mathematics, statistics, electronics, computer science.

Museum or gallery collection, archive, or library special collection:
History of the University
James Watt
Sir Robert Blair MSS

Non-library collection catalogue:
All or part available online

Library catalogue:
All or part available online

Access to staff:
Contact by letter, by telephone, by fax, by e-mail, in person and via website
Hours: Mon to Fri, 0900 to 2145; Sat and Sun 1000 to 2000 (term time)

Access to building, collection or gallery:
No prior appointment required

Branch campuses:
Dubai Campus
    Dubai Academic City, PO Box 294345, Dubai, United Arab Emirates; tel: +971 4 3616999; fax: +971 4 3604800; e-mail: dubaienquiries@hw.ac.uk
Scottish Borders Campus
    Galashiels, TD1 3HF; tel: 01896 892185; e-mail: sbclibhelp@hw.ac.uk

HERITAGE ENGINEERING

22 Carmyle Avenue, Glasgow, G32 8HJ

Tel: 0141 763 0007
Fax: 0141 763 0583

Enquiries:
Enquiries to: Marketing Manager
Direct e-mail: sales@heritageengineering.com

Founded:
1991

Organisation type and purpose:
Consultancy, research organisation.
Restoration of historical artifacts.

continued overleaf

Subject coverage:
Cast and wrought iron founders; ships; trains; trams; machinery; bandstands and park furniture; architectural metal work.

Access to staff:
Contact by letter, by telephone, by fax and by e-mail. Appointment necessary.

Connected with:
The Industrial Heritage Company Limited
tel: 0141 763 0007; fax: 0141 763 0583; e-mail: indherco@aol.com

HERITAGE HUB

Formal name: Scottish Borders Archive and Local History Centre

Kirkstile, Hawick, TD9 0AE

Tel: 01450 360699
E-mail: archives@scotborders.gov.uk

Website:
http://www.heartofhawick.co.uk/heritagehub

Organisation type and purpose:
Local government body, archive and local history.

Subject coverage:
Local history of the Scottish Borders.

Museum or gallery collection, archive, or library special collection:
Andrew Lang Collection
Census returns 1841–1901
IGI
Index to christenings and marriages in the pre-1855 old parish records for each county in Scotland (microfiche)
Information about and original records from pre-1975 counties of Roxburghshire, Berwickshire, Peeblesshire, Selkirkshire
James Hogg Collection
Local business records
Local newspapers (microfilm)
Maps and plans
Postcards
Pre-1855 parish records covering the counties of Roxburghshire, Berwickshire, Peebleshire, Selkirkshire
Sir Walter Scott Collection

Non-library collection catalogue:
All or part available in-house

Access to staff:
Contact by letter, by telephone, by e-mail, in person and via website
Hours: Mon, Fri, 1000 to 1645; Tue, Thu, 1000 to 1945; Wed, closed (pre-booked tours only); Sat 1000 to 1300 and 1400 to 1645
Special comments: Access to some collections may be covered by data protection legislation.

Access for disabled people:
disabled parking spaces, accessible building

Parent body:
Scottish Borders Council

HERITAGE LOTTERY FUND

Acronym or abbreviation: HLF

7 Holbein Place, London, SW1W 8NR

Tel: 020 7591 6000; minicom no. 020 7591 6255
Fax: 020 7591 6001
E-mail: enquire@hlf.org.uk

Website:
http://www.hlf.org.uk

Enquiries:
Enquiries to: Information Team
Direct tel: 020 7591 6042
Direct fax: 020 7591 6271

Founded:
1993

Organisation type and purpose:
Non-departmental public body. Distributes funds raised through the National Lottery. Grants are given to projects that help people to learn about, look after and celebrate heritage.

Subject coverage:
Invests in every part of heritage, including museums, parks, historic places, archaeology, natural environment and cultural traditions.

Trade and statistical information:
Statistics on grants awarded.

Electronic and video publications:
Application guidance documents
Annual reports
Order electronic and video publications from: Online

Publications list:
Available online

Access to staff:
Contact by letter, by telephone, by fax, by e-mail and via website. Appointment necessary.
Hours: Mon to Fri, 0930 to 1730

Access to building, collection or gallery:
Prior appointment required (if parking required)
Hours: Mon to Fri, 0930 to 1730

Access for disabled people:
Parking provided, ramped entry, access to all public areas, toilet facilities

Administered by:
The Trustees
National Heritage Memorial Fund; tel: 020 7591 6000; fax: 020 7591 6001; e-mail: enquire@hlf.org.uk

Also at:
Heritage Lottery Fund (HLF)
Hodge House, Guildhall Place, Cardiff, CF10 1DY; tel: 029 2034 3413; fax: 029 2034 3427; e-mail: wales@hlf.org.uk
Heritage Lottery Fund (HLF)
51–53 Adelaide Street, Belfast, BT2 8FE; tel: 028 9031 0120; fax: 028 9031 0121; e-mail: northernireland@hlf.org.uk
Heritage Lottery Fund (HLF)
28 Thistle Street, Edinburgh, EH2 1EN; tel: 0131 225 9450; fax: 0131 225 9454; e-mail: scotland@hlf.org.uk
Heritage Lottery Fund (HLF)
Terrington House, 13–15 Hills Road, Cambridge, CB2 1NL; tel: 01223 224870
Heritage Lottery Fund (HLF)
Chiltern House, St Nicholas Court, 25–27 Castle Gate, Nottingham, NG1 7AR; tel: 0115 934 9050
Heritage Lottery Fund (HLF)
St Nicholas Building, St Nicholas Street, Newcastle upon Tyne, NE1 1RF; tel: 0191 255 7570; fax: 0191 255 7571; e-mail: northeastcontact@hlf.org.uk
Heritage Lottery Fund (HLF)
9th Floor, 82 King Street, Manchester, M2 4WQ; tel: 0161 831 0850
Heritage Lottery Fund (HLF)
7 Holbein Place, London, SW1W 8NR; tel: 020 7591 6171; e-mail: southeastengland@hlf.org.uk
Heritage Lottery Fund (HLF)
Trinity Court, Southernhay East, Exeter, EX1 1PG; tel: 01392 223950; e-mail: southwest@hlf.org.uk
Heritage Lottery Fund (HLF)
Bank House, 8 Cherry Street, Birmingham, B2 5AL; tel: 0121 616 6870; e-mail: westmidlands@hlf.org.uk
Heritage Lottery Fund (HLF)
Carlton Tower, 34 St Paul's Street, Leeds, LS1 2QB; tel: 0113 388 8030; fax: 0113 388 8031; e-mail: y&hdevelopment@hlf.org.uk

HERITAGE RAILWAY ASSOCIATION

Acronym or abbreviation: HRA

10, Hurdeswell, Long Hanborough, Witney, Oxfordshire, OX29 8DH

Tel: 01993 883384

Fax: 01993 883384
E-mail: john.crane@hra.gb.com

Website:
http://www.heritagerailways.com
Details of organisation and of many members who operate heritage railways, railway centres or tramways.

Enquiries:
Enquiries to: Press Officer
Other contacts: Managing Director

Founded:
1996

Created by the merger of:
Association of Independent Railways (AIR); Association of Railway Preservation Societies Limited (ARPS) (year of change 1996)

Organisation type and purpose:
Advisory body, trade association (membership is by subscription), present number of members: 800, service industry, voluntary organisation, training organisation, consultancy, research organisation. National representation of preserved railways, railway museums and tramways.

Subject coverage:
Preserved railways, details of locomotives, rolling stock, operating and maintenance equipment, setting up and operating railway preservation organisations.

Printed publications:
Guide to Steam Trains in the British Isles (send sae)
Bi-monthly newsletters, Annual Report, Information Papers (on request)
Journal (quarterly)

Publications list:
Available in print

Access to staff:
Contact by letter, by telephone, by fax and by e-mail
Hours: Mon to Fri, 0900 to 1700
Special comments: Not by overnight fax.

Also at:
Managing Director, Heritage Railway Association (HRA)
8 Ffordd Dyfrig, Tywyn, Gwynedd, LL36 9EH; tel: 01654 710344

Member organisation of:
Association of Independent Museums
European Federation of Museum and Tourist Railways (FEDECRAIL)
Heritage Alliance
Institution of Railway Operators
International Association of Transport and Communication Museums (IATM)
UKinbound

HERPES VIRUSES ASSOCIATION

Acronym or abbreviation: HVA, SPHERE

41 North Road, London, N7 9DP

Tel: helpline: 0845 123 2305; office: 020 7607 9661
Fax: on request
E-mail: marian@herpes.org.uk

Website:
http://www.herpes.org.uk
Patient-run website with clearly and sensitively written information on all aspects of herpes simplex.

Enquiries:
Enquiries to: Director
Other contacts: Administrator

Founded:
1985

Organisation type and purpose:
Registered charity.

Subject coverage:
Facial and genital herpes simplex, herpes zoster, shingles and other types of herpes viruses: research on drug trials, alternative treatments, psychological aspects of simplex.

Museum or gallery collection, archive, or library special collection:
Articles from media and medical press re herpes viruses

Non-library collection catalogue:
All or part available online

Library catalogue:
All or part available online, in-house and in print

Printed publications:
6-page booklet (£2.50, including postage)
Journal (quarterly, free to members)
Leaflets (free to members)

Electronic and video publications:
Video (£5)

Publications list:
Available online and in print

Access to staff:
Contact by letter, by e-mail and via website.
Appointment necessary.
Hours: Mon to Fri, 1000 to 2000
Special comments: Please phone helpline number not office number. Fax number available on request.

HERTFORD COLLEGE LIBRARY

Catte Street, Oxford, OX1 3BW

Tel: 01865 279400
E-mail: susan.griffin@hertford.ox.ac.uk

Enquiries:
Enquiries to: Librarian
Direct tel: 01865 279409

Organisation type and purpose:
University department or institute, College library of the University of Oxford.

Subject coverage:
General, mainly for first degree course but with some provision for graduates; old library (16th to 18th centuries largely) in general subjects, but topography, science, theology, history and classics predominate.

Museum or gallery collection, archive, or library special collection:
Gilbert Library (geography)
Seiffert Bequest (German language and linguistics)

Non-library collection catalogue:
All or part available online and in-house

Library catalogue:
All or part available online and in-house

Access to staff:
Contact by letter, by telephone, by e-mail and in person. Appointment necessary. Letter of introduction required.
Hours: Mon to Fri, 0900 to 1530

HERTFORD REGIONAL COLLEGE

Ware Centre, Scotts Road, Ware, Hertfordshire, SG12 9JF

Tel: 01992 411400
Fax: 01992 411885
E-mail: library@hertreg.ac.uk

Website:
http://www.hrc.ac.uk
College website, general information and information on library.
http://colleges.herts.ac.uk
Library catalogue, joint one with other Hertfordshire college libraries.

Enquiries:
Enquiries to: Head of Library and Learning Services
Direct tel: 01992 411977
Direct fax: 01992 411978
Direct e-mail: smaskell@hrc.ac.uk

Founded:
1991

Formerly called:
East Herts College, Ware College (year of change 1991)

Organisation type and purpose:
College of further education.

Subject coverage:
Child care, art and design, catering, hairdressing, beauty therapy, business studies, adult literacy, social care, computer studies, engineering, drama, media studies, leisure and tourism, information technology, special needs, management studies.

Library catalogue:
All or part available online

Access to staff:
Contact by letter, by telephone, by fax and by e-mail. Appointment necessary.
Hours: Term time: Mon to Thu, 0845 to 1930; Fri, 0845 to 1640
Vacations: Mon to Fri, 1000 to 1300 and 1400 to 1600

Access to building, collection or gallery:
No access other than to staff
Hours: Term time: Mon to Thu, 0900 to 1930; Fri, 0900 to 1640
Vacations: Mon to Fri, 1000 to 1300 and 1400 to 1600
Special comments: Reference use only for non staff or students.

Access for disabled people:
Parking provided, level entry

Other addresses:
Hertford Regional College
Broxbourne Centre, Broxbourne, Turnford, Hertford, EN10 6AF; tel: 01992 411400; fax: 01992 411650

HERTFORDSHIRE ARCHIVES AND LOCAL STUDIES

Acronym or abbreviation: HALS

County Hall, Hertford, SG13 8EJ

Tel: 01438 737333 (customer service centre – ask for archives/local studies)
Fax: 01992 555113
E-mail: hertsdirect@hertscc.gov.uk

Website:
http://www.hertsdirect.org/hals

Founded:
1895

Formerly called:
Hertfordshire Local Studies; Hertfordshire Record Office (HRO) (year of change 1997)

Organisation type and purpose:
Local government body.
Archive, record office, local studies library.

Subject coverage:
Hertfordshire: history; family history; local history; geography; topography and environment.

Museum or gallery collection, archive, or library special collection:
Manuscripts: estate collections: Cowper of Panshanger; Lytton of Knebworth; Grimston of Gorhambury
Ebenezer Howard papers
Photographs: John Dickinson; Stingemore collection

Non-library collection catalogue:
All or part available online and in-house

Library catalogue:
All or part available online

Access to staff:
Contact by letter, by telephone, by fax, by e-mail, in person and via website

Access to building, collection or gallery:
No prior appointment required

Hours: Mon and Wed, 0900 to 1730; Tue, 1000 to 1930; Thu, 0900 to 1930; Fri, 0900 to 1700; Sat, 0900 to 1300

Access for disabled people:
Parking provided, ramped entry, access to all public areas, toilet facilities

HERTFORDSHIRE FAMILY AND POPULATION HISTORY SOCIETY

30 Blenheim Way, Stevenage, Hertfordshire, SG2 8TE

E-mail: secretary@hertsfhs.org.uk

Website:
http://www.hertsfhs.org.uk

Enquiries:
Enquiries to: Honorary Secretary

Founded:
1977

Organisation type and purpose:
Membership association (membership is by subscription), present number of members: 1,000, voluntary organisation, registered charity (charity number 285008), suitable for all ages.
To further the education of family history within the ancient county of Hertfordshire.

Subject coverage:
Genealogy, family history, militia history, monumental inscription recording, hobbies, Hertfordshire.

Printed publications:
Directory of Members' Interests
Hertfordshire People (journal, quarterly, free to members, £1 plus 35p per issue)
Hertfordshire Strays: Out of Area and Late Baptisms (6 vols)
Herts People (index to surnames)
Monumental Inscriptions (68 vols to date for specific locations, a few in microfiche)
Special Publications:
Transported Beyond the Seas
Fleet Marriages of Hertfordshire People to 1754
Hertfordshire Settlement Certificates
Militia Lists, over 110 booklets listing the names of men aged between 18 and 45 in respect of liability for military service from 1757 to about 1805
Order printed publications from: Booksales Officer, Hertfordshire Family and Population History Society, 56 Dalkeith Road, Harpenden, Hertfordshire, AL5 5PW

Microform publications:
Militia Lists (113 vols to date for specific areas, microfiche and booklet)

Publications list:
Available online and in print

Access to staff:
Contact by letter, by e-mail and via website
Hours: Mon to Fri, 0900 to 1700
Special comments: Please enclose an sae or two international reply coupons for a reply to a letter.

Access to building, collection or gallery:
Special comments: Library open for members.

Member organisation of:
Federation of Family History Societies

HERTFORDSHIRE MULTIPLE SCLEROSIS THERAPY CENTRE

Acronym or abbreviation: HMSTC

Unit 30, Campus Five, Letchworth, Hertfordshire, SG6 2JF

Tel: 01462 684214
Fax: 01462 487172
E-mail: info@hertsmstherapy.org.uk

Website:
http://www.hertsmstherapy.org.uk
Description of centre and its facilities.

continued overleaf

Enquiries:
Enquiries to: Manager

Founded:
1983

Formerly called:
North Hertfordshire Friends of Arms (year of change 1994)

Organisation type and purpose:
Membership association (membership is by subscription), present number of members: 250, registered charity (charity number 299524).
To provide useful therapies, advice and support to people with MS in Hertfordshire.

Subject coverage:
Hyperbaric oxygen therapy, physiotherapy, yoga, aromatherapy, reflexology, counselling, dietary advice, chiropody/podiatry.

Printed publications:
Welcome pack (for prospective members, descriptive brochure)

Access to staff:
Contact by letter, by telephone, by fax, by e-mail and in person
Hours: Mon to Fri, 0900 to 1700

Access for disabled people:
Parking provided, ramped entry, toilet facilities

HERTFORDSHIRE NATURAL HISTORY SOCIETY

Acronym or abbreviation: HNHS

32 Mandeville Road, Hertford, SG13 8JQ

Tel: 01992 586150

Website:
http://www.hnhs.org

Enquiries:
Enquiries to: President
Direct e-mail: apreynolds22@hotmail.com

Founded:
1875

Organisation type and purpose:
Voluntary organisation, registered charity (charity number 218418).

Subject coverage:
Strengths at present are in botany, mammals, birds, geology, mycology, entomology, amphibians and reptiles, arachnology.

Museum or gallery collection, archive, or library special collection:
Pryor Bequest (valuable collection of rare old botanical books, held at University College under special storage conditions)

Printed publications:
Newsletter (twice a year, free to members)
Herts Naturalist Transactions have been issued regularly since 1875, currently one part is issued annually as the Bird Report and a second part of non-bird material each year when available (free to members)

Access to staff:
Contact by letter, by telephone and by e-mail
Hours: Mon to Fri, 0900 to 1700

Affiliated to:
Hertfordshire Geological Society

Includes the:
Hertfordshire Bird Club
Hertfordshire Dragonfly Group
Hertfordshire Mammal Group

HERTFORDSHIRE VISUAL ARTS FORUM

Acronym or abbreviation: HVAF

PO Box 894, St Albans, Hertfordshire AL1 9EG

E-mail: enquiries@hvaf.org.uk

Website:
http://www.hvaf.org.uk
List of members, members' gallery, press releases.

Enquiries:
Enquiries to: Public Relations Manager
Other contacts: Membership Secretary for membership.

Founded:
1990

Organisation type and purpose:
Membership association (membership is by subscription), present number of members: 250, voluntary organisation.
Develop appreciation of visual arts in Hertfordshire.

Subject coverage:
Visual arts: painting, sculpture, crafts, ceramics.

Printed publications:
Leaflet (free, direct)

Access to staff:
Contact by letter
Hours: Mon to Fri, 0900 to 1700

HESKETH OWNERS CLUB

97 Oakdale Avenue, Stanground, Peterborough, Cambridgeshire, PE2 8TE

Enquiries:
Enquiries to: Secretary

Founded:
1982

Organisation type and purpose:
International organisation, membership association (membership is by subscription), present number of members: 52.
Provide a contact point for people interested in Hesketh motorcycles.

Subject coverage:
Hesketh motorcycle, buying, selling, spares, mechanical and club services.

Museum or gallery collection, archive, or library special collection:
Large archive of material and technical information available within the club

Printed publications:
Club magazine (members)

Access to staff:
Contact by letter
Hours: Mon to Fri, 0900 to 2100

Affiliated to:
British Motorcyclists Federation

HEWLETT-PACKARD CDS

Formal name: Hewlett-Packard Customer Delivery Services
Acronym or abbreviation: HP CDS

Imperium Level 1, West Wing, Imperial Way, Reading RG2 0TD

Tel: 01189 227600
Fax: 01189 227601
E-mail: enquiries@synstar.com

Website:
http://www.synstar.com

Enquiries:
Enquiries to: Manager

Founded:
2004

Incorporates the former:
Synstar plc

Organisation type and purpose:
Service industry.

Subject coverage:
Business continuity services, computer disaster recovery, mid-range systems and PC networks, mobile recovery, business recovery, business continuity planning, services and consultancy.
Business availability services: business continuity, networking, lifecycle and data management and computer services.

Trade and statistical information:
Business continuity services throughout UK and Europe.

Electronic and video publications:
Strategy – Business Continuity Planning Software

Access to staff:
Contact by letter, by telephone, by fax and by e-mail
Hours: Mon to Fri, 0900 to 1730

Subsidiary of:
Hewlett-Packard

HEWLETT-PACKARD LABORATORIES

Acronym or abbreviation: HPLB

Filton Road, Stoke Gifford, Bristol, BS34 8QZ

Fax: 0117 3128964
E-mail: bl@hplb.hpl.hp.com

Website:
http://www.hpl.hp.com/techreports/index.html
Hewlett-Packard Laboratories Technical Report Series.
http://www.uk.hpl.hp.com
Hewlett-Packard Laboratories external home page

Enquiries:
Enquiries to: Information Services

Founded:
1984

Organisation type and purpose:
International organisation, research organisation.

Subject coverage:
Computing and telecommunications, networks and network security. Also e-services and personal appliances.

Trade and statistical information:
Hewlett Packard Laboratories Technical Report Series.

Printed publications:
Order printed publications from: Via website

Publications list:
Available online and in print

Access to staff:
Contact by letter and by e-mail
Hours: Mon to Fri, 0900 to 1700
Special comments: Services outside HPLB very limited, therefore quick reference questions only please.

HEXHAM LIBRARY

Queen's Hall, Beaumont Street, Hexham, Northumberland, NE46 3LS

Tel: 01434 652488
Fax: 01434 652474
E-mail: mmason@northumberland.gov.uk

Enquiries:
Enquiries to: Senior Librarian
Other contacts: Assistant Librarian for local history enquiries.

Formerly called:
Tynedale Area Library; West Area Library (year of change 1992); Hexham Group Library (year of change 1996); West Group Library (year of change 1998)

Organisation type and purpose:
Local government body, public library.

Subject coverage:
General, Hexham and Northumberland local history.

Museum or gallery collection, archive, or library special collection:
Brough Local Studies Collection
Census Returns (microfilm)
Electoral rolls, 1832 to 1950 (microfilm)
Local newspapers, 1864 to date (microfilm)
Parish Register transcripts
Photographs
Trades Directories

Library catalogue:
All or part available in-house

Printed publications:
Family History in Hexham Library: a guide to source material in the Brough Local Studies Collection (1996, 50p)
Border Reivers Booklist: an introduction to Hexham's Collections (1997, 30p)

Access to staff:
Contact by letter, by telephone, by fax and in person
Hours: Mon, Fri, 0930 to 1930; Tue, Wed, 0930 to 1700; Thu, closed; Sat, 0930 to 1230

Parent body:
Northumberland County Amenities Division

HEYDAY

Astral House, 1268 London Road London SW16 4ER

Tel: 0845 888 4444
E-mail: memberservices@heyday.org.uk

Website:
http://www.heyday.org.uk/
Membership benefits, campaigning activity, general news, press releases.

Enquiries:
Enquiries to: Public Relations Manager

Founded:
1988

Formerly called:
Association of Retired and Persons Over Fifty (ARP/O50) (year of change 2006)

Organisation type and purpose:
Membership association (membership is by subscription), present number of members: 107,000, suitable for ages: 50+.

Subject coverage:
Legislation affecting the retired and over 50s. Attitudes to all aspects of retirement including, finance, health, leisure and legislation as available.

Trade and statistical information:
The members of the Association provide access to a research and consumer based data collection facility.

Printed publications:
GOODTIMES, incorporating Association News (magazine, membership and news-stand)
Membership Handbook

Access to staff:
Contact by telephone, by fax, by e-mail and via website
Hours: Mon to Fri, 0930 to 1730

Also at:
Heyday
PO Box 87, Oakengates, TF3 3WT

HFT

Formal name: The Home Farm Trust

Merchants House, Wapping Road, Bristol, BS1 4RW

Tel: 0117 930 2600
Fax: 0117 922 5938
E-mail: marketing@hft.org.uk

Website:
http://www.hft.org.uk

Enquiries:
Enquiries to: Marketing Manager

Founded:
1962

Formerly called:
The Home Farm Trust

Organisation type and purpose:
Registered charity (charity number 313069). Services for adults with learning disabilities.

Subject coverage:
Provision of residential and other services for people with learning disabilities which develop their potential and sustain their rights.

Printed publications:
Today Magazine (2 times a year, free)
Annual Report and Accounts
Christmas Catalogue
Annual Review (yearly, free)

Electronic and video publications:
Communication Training Video (£58.75)
Out and About

Access to staff:
Contact by letter, by telephone, by fax, by e-mail, in person and via website. Appointment necessary.
Hours: Mon to Fri, 0900 to 1700

Access to building, collection or gallery:
Hours: Mon to Fri, 0900 to 1700

Access for disabled people:
Hours: Mon to Fri, 0900 to 1700

Parent body:
HFT Trading Limited
at the same address

HI KENT

18 Brewer Street, Maidstone, Kent, ME14 1RU

Tel: 01622 691151\ Minicom no. 01622 691151
Fax: 01622 672436
E-mail: enquiries@hikent.org.uk

Website:
http://www.hikent.org.uk
Services provided by organisation and general information on deafness.

Enquiries:
Enquiries to: Information Officer
Direct e-mail: d.lewis@hikent.org.uk

Founded:
1986

Formerly called:
Hi Kent Association (year of change 1995)

Organisation type and purpose:
Membership association (membership is by subscription), present number of members: 72, registered charity (charity number 1052036). Information and resource centre for hearing impaired.

Subject coverage:
Assistive equipment for deaf people, sign language, deaf awareness, tinnitus.

Museum or gallery collection, archive, or library special collection:
Factsheets on assistive equipment for deaf people
Information sheets on deafness
Books and videos provided by Kent County Council Arts and Libraries for loan in Kent only on deaf subjects

Non-library collection catalogue:
All or part available in-house

Library catalogue:
All or part available in-house

Printed publications:
Fact and information sheets

Access to staff:
Contact by letter, by telephone, by fax, by e-mail and in person
Hours: Mon to Fri, 0900 to 1700

Access for disabled people:
Ramped entry, toilet facilities

Other addresses:
Hi Kent
East Kent Centre, 46 Northgate, Canterbury, Kent, CT1 1BE; tel: 01227 760046; fax: 01227 760068; e-mail: jon.lambert@kent.gov.uk
Hi Kent Medway Centre
Audiology Unit, Medway Maritime Hospital, Windmill Road, Gillingham, Kent, ME7 5NY; tel: 01634 825043; e-mail: l.dray@hikent.org.uk

Works in partnership with:
Kent County and Medway Council Social Services

HIGH COMMISSION OF THE REPUBLIC OF NAMIBIA

6 Chandos Street, London, W1G 9LU

Tel: 020 7636 6244
Fax: 020 7637 5694

Enquiries:
Enquiries to: Information Officer
Other contacts: (1) First Secretary (2) Commercial Counsellor (3) Tourism Attaché (4) Counsellor for (1) educational/cultural matters (2) trade and investment in Namibia (3) geography and history of Namibia (4) passports/visas.

Organisation type and purpose:
National government body.

Subject coverage:
Any enquiry relating directly to Namibia, whether political, cultural, historical, geographical or economic; trade and investment information; tourism and travel information; diplomatic and consular matters, including enquiries about visa/passports; more generalised information on Africa and the Commonwealth.

Trade and statistical information:
Statistical documents and reports from the respective ministries of the Government of Namibia. For specific enquiries regarding trade and investment contact the Commerical Counsellor.

Access to staff:
Contact by letter, by telephone, by fax and in person
Hours: Mon to Fri, 0900 to 1700

Parent body:
Ministry of Foreign Affairs, Information and Broadcasting
Government Offices (4th Floor), Robert Mugabe Avenue, Private Bag 13347, Windhoek, Namibia; tel: +26461 282 9111; fax: +26461 22 3937

HIGH COMMSSION FOR THE REPUBLIC OF CYPRUS

13 St James' Square, London, SW1Y 4LB

Tel: 020 73214100
Fax: 020 7321 4167
E-mail: cyphclondon@dial.pipex.com

Website:
http://www.cyprus.gov.cy
Official website of the Republic of Cyprus, general information about the country of Cyprus, information on government and independent services, overseas and repatriated Cypriots, business in Cyprus, news, links to other Cyprus-related websites.
http://www.mfa.gov.cy
Website of the Cyprus Ministry of Foreign Affairs, information on Cyprus question, Cyprus and the European Union, foreign policy issues, also information for overseas and repatriated Cypriots and consular information, news.

continued overleaf

Enquiries:
Enquiries to: Press Counsellor
Direct tel: 020 7321 4141/3
Direct fax: 020 7321 4165
Direct e-mail: presscounsellor@chclondon.org.uk
Other contacts: Consular General (tel: 020 7321 4101, for Consular matters)

Organisation type and purpose:
National government body.
Embassy and Consulate. Diplomatic.

Subject coverage:
General information about Cyprus (press and office information).
Consular enquiries (Consulate).

Library catalogue:
All or part available in-house

Printed publications:
Various subject publications are available free of charge from Press and Information Office
General
Political/The Cyprus Problem
Cyprus and the European Union
Business/Economy
Others which include: Filming in Cyprus, and Cyprus in Figures (published by the Statistical Office of Cyprus)
Leaflets
Cyprus Tourism Organisation
University of Cyprus
Maps

Electronic and video publications:
The following are available free of charge from Press and Information Office:
Cyprus 2000 (CD-ROM)
Cyprus History and Culture (CD-ROM)

Access to staff:
Contact by letter, by telephone, by fax and by e-mail
Hours: Mon to Fri, 0900 to 1630
Consulate Public Hours: Mon to Fri, 0930 to 1300

Links with:
Cyprus Tourism Organisation
17 Hanover Street, London, W1S 1YP; tel: 020 7569 8800; fax: 020 7499 4935; e-mail: informationcto@btconnect.com; website: http://www.visitcyprus.org.cy
Cyprus Trade Centre
13 St James' Square, London, SW1Y 4LB; tel: 020 7321 4146; e-mail: cytradecentreuk@btinternet.com

Parent body:
Ministry of Foreign Affairs of Cyprus
Dem Severis Avenue, Nicosia 1447, Cyprus; tel: + 357 22 300713; fax: + 37 7 22 665313; website: http://www.mfa.gov.cy

HIGH SHERIFFS' ASSOCIATION OF ENGLAND & WALES

PO Box 21, Heritage House, Baldock, Herts SG7 5SH

Tel: 01462 896688
Fax: 01462 896677
E-mail: secretary@highsheriffs.com

Enquiries:
Enquiries to: Honorary Secretary

Founded:
1971

Organisation type and purpose:
Membership association (membership is by election or invitation).
To promote and strengthen the Office of High Sheriff in England and Wales.

Subject coverage:
History and current activities of High Sheriffs in the Counties of England and Wales, relating to ceremonial matters. The prevention of crime and particularly juvenile crime through National Crimebeat, and debt and money management through DebtCred, both of which are charities established by the Association.

Printed publications:
The High Sheriff (magazine, 2 times a year)

Access to staff:
Contact by letter, by fax and by e-mail.
Appointment necessary.
Hours: Mon to Fri, 0900 to 1700

HIGHBURY COLLEGE LEARNING CENTRE

Cosham, Portsmouth, Hampshire, PO6 2SA

Tel: 023 9231 3213
Fax: 023 9237 1972
E-mail: library@highbury.ac.uk

Enquiries:
Enquiries to: Librarian

Formerly called:
Highbury Technical College

Organisation type and purpose:
Suitable for ages: 16+ further education.
College of technology.

Subject coverage:
Building, hospitality and catering, business and management studies, social welfare, leisure and tourism, electrical and electronic engineering, mechanical engineering.

Library catalogue:
All or part available in-house

Access to staff:
Contact by letter, by telephone, by fax, by e-mail and in person
Hours: Term time; Mon to Thu, 0900 to 2100; Fri, 0930 to 1700
Vacations; Mon to Thu, 0900 to 1700; Fri, 0900 to 1630

Access for disabled people:
Access to all public areas

HIGHER EDUCATION FUNDING COUNCIL FOR ENGLAND

Acronym or abbreviation: HEFCE

Northavon House, Coldharbour Lane, Bristol, BS16 1QD

Tel: 0117 931 7317
Fax: 0117 931 7203
E-mail: hefce@hefce.ac.uk

Website:
http://www.hefce.ac.uk

Enquiries:
Enquiries to: Knowledge Centre Manager
Direct tel: 0117 931 7438
Direct fax: 0117 931 7082
Direct e-mail: s.roberts@hefce.ac.uk

Founded:
1993

Created by the merger of:
Polytechnics and Colleges Funding Council (PCFC), Universities Funding Council (UFC) (year of change 1993)

Formerly called:
University Grants Committee (UGC) (year of change 1988)

Organisation type and purpose:
The HEFCE is a non-departmental public body set up under the Further and Higher Education Act 1992. Its primary role is to distribute public funding for teaching and research and related activities in universities and colleges in England.

Subject coverage:
Funding for higher education in England.

Museum or gallery collection, archive, or library special collection:
Books and documents related to the subject of higher education

Library catalogue:
All or part available in-house

Printed publications:
Order printed publications from: Some publications are available by post; all publications available via http://www.hefce.ac.uk/pubs

Publications list:
Available online

Access to staff:
Contact by letter, by telephone, by fax, by e-mail and via website
Hours: Mon to Fri, 0900 to 1700

Access to building, collection or gallery:
There is no public access

HIGHER EDUCATION FUNDING COUNCIL FOR WALES

Acronym or abbreviation: HEFCW

Linden Court, The Orchards, Ilex Close, Llanishen, Cardiff, CF14 5DZ

Tel: 029 2076 1861
Fax: 029 2076 3163

Website:
http://www.elwa.ac.uk
Information on HEFCW, copies of HEFCW circulars, news sheets, and other publications.

Enquiries:
Enquiries to: Clerk to the Council
Direct e-mail: info@elwa.ac.uk

Founded:
1992

Organisation type and purpose:
National government body.
Non-departmental government body.
The Council is responsible for the administration of funds made available by the Welsh Assembly Government in support of the provision of higher education and the undertaking of research in higher education institutions in Wales.

Subject coverage:
Funding for higher education in Wales. Student enrolment in Wales. Council funding for research in Welsh higher education institutions.

Printed publications:
Annual Report
Corporate Plan
Operational Plan

Electronic and video publications:
Other circulars and publications available online

Publications list:
Available online and in print

Access to staff:
Contact by letter, by telephone and by e-mail
Hours: Mon to Fri, 0900 to 1700

Access to building, collection or gallery:
No access other than to staff, prior appointment required

Access for disabled people:
Parking provided, ramped entry

Parent body:
National Assembly for Wales
Higher Education Division, Cathays Park, Cardiff, CF10 3NQ; tel: 029 2082 5111

HIGHER EDUCATION STATISTICS AGENCY

Acronym or abbreviation: HESA

95 Promenade, Cheltenham, Gloucestershire, GL50 1HZ

Tel: 01242 255577
Fax: 01242 211122
E-mail: www@hesa.ac.uk

Website:
http://www.hesa.ac.uk

access to HOLIS (HESA on-line information system): an interactive information system allowing interrogation of datasets by users. Also details of data collected by HESA, and relevant publications.

Enquiries:
Enquiries to: Data Provision Manager

Founded:
1993

Organisation type and purpose:
Registered charity (charity number 1039709). HESA is the official agency for the collection, analysis and dissemination of quantitative information about higher education.

Subject coverage:
Statistics of students and staff at all UK universities in six main record areas: undergraduates, postgraduates, first destinations of graduates, staff and short courses, finance.

Museum or gallery collection, archive, or library special collection:
Microfiche library of all statistical analyses produced 1972–1993 (in addition to original computerised database for same period)

Printed publications:
Higher Education Management Statistics (annually, also CD-ROM)
Reference Volume: Students in Higher Education Institutions (annually, £33 hardcopy, £35+VAT CD-ROM)
Research Datapack 1: Ethnicity (£120 hardcopy including disc)
Research Datapack 2: Entry Qualifications in HE (£120 hardcopy including disc)
Research Datapack 3: Course Results (£120 hardcopy including disc)
Research Datapack 4: First Destinations (£120 hardcopy including disc)
Research Datapack 5: Disability (£120 hardcopy including disc)
Research Datapack 6: Overseas Students (£120 hardcopy including disc)
Research Datapack 7: Regional Issues (£120 hardcopy including disc)
Research Datapack 8: Ethnicity in Higher Education (£120 hardcopy including disc)
Research Datapack 9: Academic Staff in Higher Education (£120 hardcopy including disc)
Research Datapack 10: Non-credit-bearing Courses in Higher Education (£120 hardcopy including disc)
Research Datapack 11: Ethnicity of Students 1999/2000 (£150 plus VAT, CD-ROM)

Publications list:
Available in print

Access to staff:
Contact by letter, by telephone, by fax, by e-mail and via website
Hours: Mon to Thu, 0830 to 1700; Fri, 0830 to 1600

HIGHGATE LITERARY AND SCIENTIFIC INSTITUTION

Acronym or abbreviation: HLSI

11 South Grove, Pond Square, Highgate, London, N6 6BS

Tel: 020 8340 3343
Fax: 020 8340 5632
E-mail: librarian@hlsi.net

Website:
http://www.hlsi.net

Enquiries:
Enquiries to: Librarian
Direct tel: 020 8340 3343 (option 3)

Founded:
1839

Organisation type and purpose:
Membership association (membership is by subscription), voluntary organisation, lending library.

Subject coverage:
Literature; biography; the arts; fiction; local history.

Museum or gallery collection, archive, or library special collection:
Highgate local history and archives
John Betjeman
Samuel Taylor Coleridge
London local history

Non-library collection catalogue:
All or part available in-house

Library catalogue:
All or part available in-house

Access to staff:
Contact by letter, by telephone, by fax, by e-mail and in person. Appointment necessary. Letter of introduction required.
Hours: Tue to Fri, 1000 to 1700; Sat, 1000 to 1600

Access to building, collection or gallery:
Hours: Tue to Fri, 1000 to 1700; Sat, 1000 to 1600
Special comments: Closed for one week at Christmas and Easter, three weeks in August.

Links with:
Association of Independent Libraries
website: http://www.independentlibraries.co.uk

HIGHLAND FAMILY HISTORY SOCIETY

Acronym or abbreviation: HFHS

Suite 4, Third Floor, Albyn House, 37a Union Street, Inverness, IV1 1QA

E-mail: jdurham@highlandfhs.org.uk

Website:
http://www.highlandfhs.org.uk
http://www.genfair.com
Publications and membership

Enquiries:
Enquiries to: Honorary Secretary
Direct e-mail: abethune@highlandfhs.org.uk

Founded:
1981

Organisation type and purpose:
Membership association (membership is by subscription).

Subject coverage:
Genealogy, parish records, census returns, monumental inscriptions.

Printed publications:
Order printed publications from: Public Library at Farraline Park, Genfair
via http://www.genfair.com

Publications list:
Available online and in print

Access to staff:
Contact via website. Access for members only.
Hours: Tue only, 1000 to 1630

Access for disabled people:
Lift to third floor

HIGHLAND LIBRARIES

Formal name: The Highland Council. Education, Culture & Sport Service

31A Harbour Road, Inverness, IV1 1UA

Tel: 01463 235713
Fax: 01463 236986
E-mail: libraries@highland.gov.uk

Website:
http://www.highland.gov.uk/leisureandtourism/libraries
Connect with Highland Libraries through e-mail or social networking sites. Find out about new library collections, library news and events, discover a range of electronic reference resources, and find out what's happening in your community. Become a fan, follow and engage with your Highland Library online.

Enquiries:
Enquiries to: Library and Information Services Co-ordinator
Other contacts: Senior Librarian, Information Co-ordinator

Founded:
1975

Organisation type and purpose:
Local government body, public library.

Subject coverage:
General; specialised sections include local history, genealogy.

Information services:
The Highland Council's Library and Information Service forms part of the Education Culture and Sport Service and operates through a network of joint and separate School, Community, Mobile Libraries and online services.

Museum or gallery collection, archive, or library special collection:
Held at Inverness:
Fraser Mackintosh Collection (local history, law and literature)
Gaelic Society of Inverness Library (Gaelic language and culture)
Highland Family History Society Library (extensive local history and genealogy collections)
Kirk Session Library (antiquarian interest)
Held at Wick:
John Mowat Collection (local history of Caithness and northern Scotland)

Non-library collection catalogue:
All or part available online and in-house

Library catalogue:
All or part available online and in-house

Access to staff:
Contact by letter, by telephone, by fax, by e-mail and in person. Appointment necessary.
Hours: Mon to Fri, 0800 to 1700

Access to building, collection or gallery:
No prior appointment required
Hours: Mon to Fri, 0800 to 1700

Access for disabled people:
Level entry

Parent body:
The Highland Council
Education, Culture and Sport Service, Council Buildings, Glenurquhart Road, Inverness IV3 5NX; tel: 01463 702000; fax: 01463 711177; website: http://www.highland.gov.uk

HIGHLANDS & ISLANDS ENTERPRISE

Acronym or abbreviation: HIE

Cowan House, Inverness Retail & Business Park, Inverness, IV2 7GF

Tel: 01463 234171
Fax: 01463 244469
E-mail: hie.general@hient.co.uk

Website:
http://www.hie.co.uk

Enquiries:
Enquiries to: Librarian
Direct tel: 01349 868971
Direct fax: 01349 868944
Direct e-mail: library@hient.co.uk

Founded:
1991

Organisation type and purpose:
National government body.
HIE is a government-sponsored development agency.
Economic and social development in the Highlands and Islands of Scotland.

continued overleaf

Subject coverage:
Business information, Highlands and Islands of Scotland, regional and industrial development, training, primary industries, fisheries, fish farming, land use, tourism, transport, community co-operatives, agriculture, renewable energy.

Library catalogue:
All or part available in-house

Printed publications:
HIE Report & Accounts (annually)

Access to staff:
Contact by letter, by telephone, by fax, by e-mail, in person and via website. Appointment necessary. Access for members only.
Hours: Mon to Fri, 0900 to 1700

Access to building, collection or gallery:
Prior appointment required

Access for disabled people:
Parking provided, level entry, toilet facilities

HILL TAYLOR DICKINSON

20–30 Irongate House, Duke's Place, London, EC3A 7HX

Tel: 020 7283 9033
Fax: 020 7283 1144
E-mail: library@htd-london.com

Enquiries:
Enquiries to: Library and Information Manager

Organisation type and purpose:
Solicitors.

Subject coverage:
Law: shipping, insurance, company and commercial, litigation, property, taxation, probate.

Member of:
British and Irish Association of Law Librarians (BIALL)

HILLCLIMB & SPRINT ASSOCIATION LIMITED

Spring Cottage, Gaydon Road, Bishops Itchington, Warwickshire, CV47 2QX

Tel: 01926 612432
Fax: 01926 612432

Enquiries:
Enquiries to: Membership Secretary
Direct tel: 01926 424609
Direct fax: 01926 424609

Founded:
1955

Organisation type and purpose:
Membership association (membership is by subscription), present number of members: 1000. Motor sport association whose members compete in speed hillclimb and sprint meetings.

Subject coverage:
Speed hillclimb and sprint car racing.

Printed publications:
Magazine (covers all aspects of the sport across the country, 6 times a year)

Access to staff:
Contact by letter, by telephone and by fax
Hours: Mon to Fri, 1800 to 2100; not weekends

HILLINGDON BOROUGH LIBRARIES

Central Library, 14–15 High Street, Uxbridge, Middlesex, UB8 1HD

Tel: 01895 250600
Fax: 01895 239794
E-mail: clibrary@lbhill.gov.uk or clibrary@hillingdon.gov.uk

Website:
http://www.hillingdon.gov.uk

London Borough of Hillingdon site includes library information pages.

Enquiries:
Enquiries to: Librarian
Direct tel: 01895 250603
Direct fax: 01895 811164

Organisation type and purpose:
Local government body, public library.

Subject coverage:
General; history of Hillingdon, Middlesex and surrounding areas.

Museum or gallery collection, archive, or library special collection:
Government Publications (SSS except for SI's)

Trade and statistical information:
All current HMSO statistical series.

Printed publications:
Local history monographs

Access to staff:
Contact by letter, by telephone, by fax, by e-mail, in person and via website
Hours: Mon to Fri, 0900 to 1700

Access to building, collection or gallery:
No access other than to staff
Hours: Mon, Tue, Thu, 0930 to 2000; Wed, 0930 to 1730; Fri, 1000 to 1730; Sat, 0930 to 1600

Access for disabled people:
Level entry, access to all public areas, toilet facilities

HILLINGDON FAMILY HISTORY SOCIETY

20 Moreland Drive, Gerrards Cross, Buckinghamshire, SL9 8BB

Tel: 01753 885602
E-mail: gillmay@dial.pipex.com

Website:
http://www.hfhs.co.uk
Information about the Society; programme for the year; publications.
http://www.rootsweb.com/~enghfhs
Information about the Society; programme for the year; publications.

Enquiries:
Enquiries to: Honorary Secretary

Founded:
1987

Organisation type and purpose:
Membership association (membership is by subscription).

Subject coverage:
Family history and genealogy with particular reference to the London Borough of Hillingdon.

Museum or gallery collection, archive, or library special collection:
Collection of genealogical books, journals, CD-ROMs and microforms available to members

Non-library collection catalogue:
All or part available online

Library catalogue:
All or part available online

Printed publications:
Journal (quarterly, members)

Microform publications:
Church School, Ickenham (1873–1929)
Middlesex Sessions Records (Hillingdon extracts)
Monumental Inscriptions: St Mary's, Harefield; Holy Trinity, Northwood; St Laurence, Cowley; St Martin's, West Drayton.
St Giles' parish registers
Ickenham baptisms, marriages, and burials

Publications list:
Available online and in print

Access to staff:
Contact by letter, by telephone and by e-mail

Hours: Mon to Fri, 0900 to 1700; evenings and weekends

Member of:
Federation of Family History Societies

HILLINGDON LOCAL STUDIES, ARCHIVES AND MUSEUMS

Central Library, 14–15 High Street, Uxbridge, Middlesex, UB8 1HD

Tel: 01895 250702
Fax: 01895 811164
E-mail: archives@hillingdon.gov.uk

Website:
http://www.hillingdon.gov.uk/heritage
Council information.

Enquiries:
Enquiries to: Local Studies and Archives Manager
Direct e-mail: ccotton@hillingdon.gov.uk
Other contacts: Assistant Archivist

Founded:
1922

Formerly called:
Hillingdon Local Heritage Service; London Borough of Hillingdon Libraries (year of change 1991)

Organisation type and purpose:
Museum, public library, archives.

Subject coverage:
Local and family history of the Hillingdon area.

Education services:
School visits and talks.

Museum or gallery collection, archive, or library special collection:
Challoner Collection of Uxbridge photographs
Gazette newspaper photographs 1920 to 1950
Minet Archives, deeds, etc. of Minet Properties in Hayes

Non-library collection catalogue:
All or part available online

Library catalogue:
All or part available online

Printed publications:
Hillingdon Cultural Activities and Libraries Service has published several books and leaflets on local history and local walks of general interest, including:
Gregory King's Harefield; an English village in the 1690s (Cuthbertson E, 1992, £4.90)
The Goodliest Place in Middlesex; a history of the ancient parish of Ruislip from the Domesday Book to modern times (Bowlt E, 1989, £8.50)
The History of Heathrow (Sherwood P, 2nd ed, 1993, £4.50)

Publications list:
Available online and in print

Access to staff:
Contact by letter, by telephone, by fax, by e-mail and in person
Hours: Mon, 0930 to 2000; Tue, Wed, Thu, 1300 to 1730; Fri, 1000 to 1230 and 13.30 to 17.30; Sat, 0930 to 1200 and 1300 to 1600

Access to building, collection or gallery:
Local Studies is located within the Central Library Uxbridge
Hours: Mon, Tue, Thu, 0930 to 2000; Wed, 0930 to 1730; Fri, 1000 to 1730; Sat 0930 to 1600; Sun, 1230 to 1630

Access for disabled people:
Access to all public areas, toilet facilities

HILLMAN COMMER & KARRIER CLUB

Acronym or abbreviation: HCKC

Capri House, Walton-on-Thames, Surrey, KT12 2LY

Tel: 01932 269109
Fax: 01932 269109

Enquiries:
Enquiries to: Chairman

Founded:
1989

Organisation type and purpose:
International organisation, membership association (membership is by subscription), present number of members: 1,600 approx, voluntary organisation.

Subject coverage:
Hillman, Commer and Karrier and other Rootes built vehicles, mechanical and technical information, insurance, registration, restoration.

Museum or gallery collection, archive, or library special collection:
Books, manuals, technical information, magazines, etc. relevant to Hillman, Commer, Karrier and Rootes vehicles

Library catalogue:
All or part available in-house

Printed publications:
ARVO News
HCKC News

Publications list:
Available in print

Access to staff:
Contact by letter and by fax
Hours: Mon to Fri, 0900 to 1700

Access to building, collection or gallery:
No prior appointment required

Parent body:
Association of Rootes Vehicle Owners

HINCKLEY & BOSWORTH BOROUGH COUNCIL

Council Offices, Argents Mead, Hinckley, Leicestershire, LE10 1BZ

Tel: 01455 238141
Fax: 01455 251172

Website:
http://www.hinckley-bosworth.gov.uk

Enquiries:
Enquiries to: Chief Executive

Organisation type and purpose:
Local government body.

Subject coverage:
Local government services.

Printed publications:
Councillors Guide (councillors, local services, A–Z of council services)

Access to staff:
Contact by letter and by fax
Hours: Mon to Fri, 0900 to 1700

Health authority:
Leicestershire, Northamptonshire and Rutland Health Authorities

Local education authority:
Leicestershire Local Education Authority

HIRE ASSOCIATION EUROPE

Acronym or abbreviation: HAE

2 Holland Road West, Waterlinks, Birmingham, B6 4DW

Tel: 0121 380 4600
Fax: 0121 333 4109
E-mail: mail@hae.org.uk

Website:
http://www.hae.org.uk
Membership.

Enquiries:
Enquiries to: Managing Director

Founded:
1971

Organisation type and purpose:
International organisation, trade association, membership association (membership is by subscription), present number of members: 1000. Membership body for hire equipment shops.

Subject coverage:
Small plant and tool hire equipment, hire of equipment for leisure, catering, fencing and portable sanitation, training and safety supplies to the hire industry, audiovisual and powered access hire.

Trade and statistical information:
Turnover and employment statistics.

Printed publications:
Executive Hire News (magazine, 10 times a year)
Hire Standard
Safety Manuals
Technical Safety Handling leaflets

Publications list:
Available in print

Access to staff:
Contact by letter, by telephone, by fax and via website. Appointment necessary.
Hours: Mon to Fri, 0900 to 1700

Access to building, collection or gallery:
No prior appointment required
Hours: Mon to Fri, 0900 to 1700

Subsidiary body:
Executive Hire News

HISTORIC COMMERCIAL VEHICLE SOCIETY

Acronym or abbreviation: HCVS

Iden Grange, Cranbrook Road, Staplehurst, Kent, TN12 0ET

Tel: 01580 892929
Fax: 01580 893227
E-mail: hcvs@btinternet.com

Website:
http://www.hcvs.co.uk
Society details, events, magazine, insurance service.

Enquiries:
Enquiries to: Membership Secretary

Founded:
1958

Organisation type and purpose:
International organisation, national organisation, membership association (membership is by subscription), present number of members: 3500, registered charity (charity number 271123).

Subject coverage:
Historic commercial vehicles.

Library catalogue:
All or part available in-house

Access to staff:
Contact by letter, by telephone, by fax, by e-mail and via website
Hours: Mon to Fri, 0900 to 1700

Access to building, collection or gallery:
No access other than to staff
Special comments: Prior appointment required for library research (situated in Cardiff)

HISTORIC FARM BUILDINGS GROUP

Acronym or abbreviation: HFBG

c/o Museum of English Rural Life, University of Reading, PO Box 229, Whiteknights, Reading, Berkshire, RG6 6AG

Tel: 0118 931 8663
Fax: 0118 975 1264
E-mail: r.d.brigden@reading.ac.uk

Website:
http://www.chelt.ac.uk/ccru/hfbg
Information about the group, contacts and newsletter

Enquiries:
Enquiries to: Secretary

Founded:
1985

Organisation type and purpose:
Learned society.

Subject coverage:
History of old farm buildings.

Printed publications:
Annual Journal

Access to staff:
Contact by letter and by e-mail
Hours: Mon to Fri, 0900 to 1700

HISTORIC HOUSES ASSOCIATION

Acronym or abbreviation: HHA

2 Chester Street, London, SW1X 7BB

Tel: 020 7259 5688
Fax: 020 7259 5590
E-mail: info@hha.org.uk

Website:
http://www.hha.org.uk

Enquiries:
Enquiries to: Executive Secretary

Founded:
1973

Organisation type and purpose:
Membership association (membership is by subscription).

Subject coverage:
Preservation for the future of historic houses, parks, gardens and places of interest in Britain; pressure for a long-term policy based on private ownership.

Printed publications:
Historic House (HHA Journal, 4 times a year for members)
Technical manuals
Yearbook (for members only)

Access to staff:
Contact by letter, by telephone, by fax, by e-mail and via website
Hours: Mon to Fri, 0900 to 1700

Access to building, collection or gallery:
Prior appointment required

Affiliated to:
European Union of Historic Houses Association

Close liaison with:
British Tourist Authority
Cadw Welsh Historic Monuments
Department of National Heritage
English Heritage
Historic Scotland
National Trust
National Trust for Scotland

HISTORIC LOTUS REGISTER

Acronym or abbreviation: HLR

Badgers Farm, Short Green, Winfarthing, Diss, Norfolk, IP22 2EE

Tel: 01953 860508

Enquiries:
Enquiries to: Honorary Secretary

Founded:
1974

Organisation type and purpose:
International organisation (membership is by subscription), present number of members: 1000, voluntary organisation.
Motor club.

continued overleaf

Subject coverage:
Historic Lotus cars manufactured prior to 1961, preservation and research.

Museum or gallery collection, archive, or library special collection:
Lotus factory records

Printed publications:
Newsletter (quarterly)

Access to staff:
Contact by letter and by telephone
Hours: Mon to Sun 0900 to 2000

HISTORIC SCOTLAND

Acronym or abbreviation: HS

Technical Conservation Research and Education Group, Resource Centre, Longmore House, Salisbury Place, Edinburgh, EH9 1SH

Tel: 0131 668 8600
Fax: 0131 668 8699
E-mail: hs.website@scotland.gsi.gov.uk

Website:
http://www.historic-scotland.gov.uk

Enquiries:
Enquiries to: Resource Centre Manager
Direct tel: 0131 668 8642
Direct fax: 0131 668 8669
Direct e-mail: lisa.nicholson@scotland.gsi.gov.uk

Founded:
1991

Organisation type and purpose:
National government body, statutory body.

Subject coverage:
Information on historic buildings and monuments under the guardianship of Scottish Ministers, architecture, archaeology, conservation and the environment.

Museum or gallery collection, archive, or library special collection:
Resource Centre of 3,500 items, comprising printed and mixed media covering all aspects of built heritage – archaeology, architecture, history, conservation and related areas. This includes specialist and general journals concerning the built environment and Historic Scotland publications on specialist conservation techniques, which also include conservation of artistic works.
Separate Historic Scotland Library of 10,000 books, 2,000 reports and pamphlets, 170 periodicals, Historic Scotland guidebooks and reports
Separate photographic library of 50,000 slides of ancient monuments

Non-library collection catalogue:
All or part available online, in-house and in print

Library catalogue:
All or part available in-house

Printed publications:
A range of publications are available in the following categories:
Technical advices notes; research reports; conference proceedings and abstracts on subjects relating to the built environment and other conservation related areas.

Electronic and video publications:
CD-ROMs, DVDs, videos relating to the technical aspect of conservation

Publications list:
Available online and in print

Access to staff:
Contact by letter, by telephone, by fax, by e-mail, in person and via website. Appointment necessary.
Hours: Mon to Fri, 1000 to 1600

Access to building, collection or gallery:
Prior appointment required

Access for disabled people:
Parking provided, ramped entry, toilet facilities

Constituent part of:
Scottish Executive Education Department
tel: 0131 668 8600

HISTORIC SOCIETY OF LANCASHIRE AND CHESHIRE

Acronym or abbreviation: HSLC

Flat 4, 3 Bramhall Road, Waterloo, Liverpool, L22 3XA

Tel: 0151 920 8213
E-mail: rch2949@yahoo.co.uk

Website:
http://www.hslc.org.uk

Enquiries:
Enquiries to: Secretary

Founded:
1848

Organisation type and purpose:
Learned society (membership is by subscription), registered charity (charity number 224825).

Subject coverage:
Local history of Lancashire and Cheshire.

Museum or gallery collection, archive, or library special collection:
Society's collections held at Liverpool Record Office, but see website as Record Office closed for major rebuilding work: http:// www.liverpool.gov.uk/libraries

Library catalogue:
All or part available online

Printed publications:
Transactions (annually, together with the Occasional Series vols, for the past 150 years)
Back numbers of the Transactions and offprints
Order printed publications from: Publications Officer, Historic Society of Lancashire and Cheshire, c/o School of History, 9 Abercromby Square, Liverpool, L69 7WZ; tel: 0151 428 4121

Publications list:
Available in print

Access to staff:
Contact by letter and by e-mail
Hours: Mon to Fri, 0900 to 1700

HISTORIC SPORTS CAR CLUB

Acronym or abbreviation: HSCC

Silverstone Circuit, Silverstone, Towcester, Northamptonshire, NN12 8TN

Tel: 01327 858400
Fax: 01327 858500
E-mail: office@hscc.org.uk

Enquiries:
Enquiries to: Executive Director

Founded:
1966

Organisation type and purpose:
International organisation, membership association (membership is by subscription), present number of members: 850.
Organiser of historic car race meetings and championships.
Appointed to coordinate European Championship for pre 1985 F1 cars by the FIA, now a major club.

Subject coverage:
History of, and information regarding, historic motor racing.

Museum or gallery collection, archive, or library special collection:
Large archive of historic motor racing books and magazines dating back to 1940s

Printed publications:
HSCC News (magazine, 6 times a year)

Access to staff:
Contact by letter, by telephone, by fax, by e-mail, in person and via website. Appointment necessary.
Hours: Mon to Fri, 0900 to 1700

Affiliated to:
RACMSA

HISTORIC VOLKSWAGEN CLUB

5 Gresley Close, Sutton Coldfield, West Midlands, B75 5HT

Tel: 0121 308 3693
E-mail: nigel.wallace@virgin.net

Website:
http://www.historicvws.org.uk

Enquiries:
Enquiries to: Membership Secretary

Founded:
1974

Organisation type and purpose:
Membership association (membership is by subscription), voluntary organisation.
Provides a focal point for owners and enthusiasts of pre-1967 (Aug) Volkswagen vehicles. Provides technical information, spares location and historical information for members and others.

Subject coverage:
Technical, historical, diary dates for gatherings of enthusiasts relating to Volkswagen products manufactured prior to August 1967.

Printed publications:
The Historic Volkswagen (4 times a year)

Access to staff:
Contact by letter, by telephone, by e-mail and via website
Hours: Mon to Fri, evenings only

HISTORICAL ASSOCIATION

Acronym or abbreviation: HA

59A Kennington Park Road, London, SE11 4JH

Tel: 020 7735 3901
Fax: 020 7582 4989
E-mail: enquiry@history.org.uk

Website:
http://www.history.org.uk

Enquiries:
Enquiries to: Membership Secretary

Founded:
1906

Organisation type and purpose:
Membership association (membership is by subscription), registered charity (charity number 1120261).
Subject teaching association.

Subject coverage:
General information on all areas of history, history teaching, careers in history.

Museum or gallery collection, archive, or library special collection:
The following collections not open to the public:
Bound copies Annual Bulletin of Historical Literature, 1907 to date
Bound copies of History, 1912 to date

Printed publications:
The following publications are available direct, for purchase:
Books on Teaching History to 5 to 18 year olds
Bulletin of Historical Literature (annually)
History (3 times a year)
Short bibliographies on specific periods of history
Teaching History (4 times a year)
Primary History (3 times a year)

Publications list:
Available online and in print

Access to staff:
Contact via website
Hours: Mon to Fri, 1000 to 1700

HISTORICAL METALLURGICAL SOCIETY LIMITED

Acronym or abbreviation: HMS

c/o The Institute of Materials, Minerals and Mining, 1 Carlton House Terrace, London, SW1Y 5DB

Tel: 01792 233223

Website:
nttp://hist-met.org./ad_index.html
Archaeometallurgical datasheets.
http://hist-met.org/hmspub.htm
Publications.
http://hist-met.org/resources.html
Resources for historians.
http://hist-met.org/hm_index.html
Journal Contents.
http://hist-met.org
Membership information, journal contents, meetings information.

Enquiries:
Enquiries to: General Secretary
Direct fax: 01792 233223
Direct e-mail: hon-sec@hist-met.org

Founded:
1979

Organisation type and purpose:
Learned society.

Subject coverage:
Metallurgical history and archaeometallurgy.

Museum or gallery collection, archive, or library special collection:
A collection of miscellaneous documents relating to metallurgical history. Includes the Charles Blick Archive, mainly conservation of metallurgical sites
A miscellaneous collection of largely metallurgical books, some scarce, mostly out of date

Non-library collection catalogue:
All or part available online

Library catalogue:
All or part available online

Printed publications:
Conference Proceedings such as Boles and Smelt Mills
Historical Metallurgy
Metals and the Sea
Order printed publications from: Publications Officer, 22 Windley Crescent, Darley Abbey, Derbyshire, DE3 1BZ, tel: 01332 553430, e-mail: brian.read2@ ntlworld.com

Electronic and video publications:
Disk based index for Historical Metallurgy (not yet complete)

Publications list:
Available online

Access to staff:
Contact by letter, by telephone, by fax and by e-mail
Hours: Mon to Fri, 0900 to 2200

Affiliated to:
Institute of Materials, Minerals aand Mining

HISTORICAL MODEL RAILWAY SOCIETY

Acronym or abbreviation: HMRS

c/o The Midland Railway Centre, Butterley Station, Ripley, Derbyshire, DE5 3QZ

Tel: 01773 745959
Fax: 01773 745959
E-mail: studycentre-manager@hmrs.org.uk

Website:
http://www.hmrs.org.uk

Enquiries:
Enquiries to: Museum and Study Centre Manager

Founded:
1950

Organisation type and purpose:
Membership association (membership is by subscription),
present number of members: 2500, registered charity (charity number 273110), research organisation.
Educational organisation.

Subject coverage:
Railways of Britain and the Commonwealth: all aspects from their invention to the present day.

Museum or gallery collection, archive, or library special collection:
Library of railway books and periodicals including some non-published documents of railway companies
Photographic library of over 50,000 items

Non-library collection catalogue:
All or part available online and in-house

Library catalogue:
All or part available online and in-house

Publications list:
Available online and in print

Access to staff:
Contact by letter, by fax, by e-mail and via website
Hours: Mon to Fri, 0900 to 1700

HISTORY OF ADVERTISING TRUST

Acronym or abbreviation: HAT Archive

HAT House, 12 Raveningham Centre, Raveningham, Norwich, NR14 6NU

Tel: 01508 548623
Fax: 01508 548478
E-mail: enquiries@hatads.org.uk

Website:
http://www.hatads.org.uk
Major brand advertising, research papers, journals, historical collections, educational resources to colleges, e-learning for Diploma courses, collections storage, rescue and preservation of UK brand heritage.

Enquiries:
Enquiries to: General Manager
Direct tel: 01508 548623
Direct fax: 01508 548478
Direct e-mail: enquiries@hatads.org.uk
Other contacts: Curator or CEO

Founded:
1976

Organisation type and purpose:
HAT Archive is a registered charity (no. 276194) that seeks to collect and preserve the UK's advertising heritage and to make it available for research and study for all. Its research and study facilities allow academics and students to search more than 3 million items of advertising, marketing and media, including over 50,000 TV commercials from 1955 to today.

Subject coverage:
Advertising in the United Kingdom from the early 1800s to the present day. ·

Information services:
Curator, General Manager, Knowledge Officer.

Special visitor services:
Michael Cudlipp Research and Study Centre.

Education services:
AD:Mission education project for 14–19-year-olds for e-learning, creative media (Diploma).

Services for disabled people:
Ground floor only, disabled access and toilet facilities.

Museum or gallery collection, archive, or library special collection:
Archive of UK advertising

Non-library collection catalogue:
All or part available online, in-house and in print

Library catalogue:
All or part available in-house

Printed publications:
Advertising in Britain, a History; 30 years of Television, a history
Order printed publications from: HAT Archive

Electronic and video publications:
Order electronic and video publications from: HAT Archive

Access to staff:
Contact by letter, by telephone, by fax, by e-mail and via website. Appointment necessary.
Hours: Mon to Fri, 0900 to 1700
Special comments: Not weekends.

Access to building, collection or gallery:
By appointment
Hours: Mon to Thu, 0900 to 1700
Special comments: Not weekends.

Access for disabled people:
Ground floor, disabled toilets, disabled entry access
Hours: No restrictions

HISTORY OF ADVERTISING TRUST ARCHIVE

Acronym or abbreviation: HAT Archive

HAT House, 12 Raveningham Centre, Raveningham, Norwich, Norfolk, NR14 6NU

Tel: 01508 548623
Fax: 01508 548478
E-mail: enquiries@hatads.org.uk

Website:
http://www.hatads.org.uk

Enquiries:
Enquiries to: General Manager
Other contacts: Chief Executive; Curator

Founded:
1976

Organisation type and purpose:
Registered charity (no. 276194), educational trust and research organisation. National archive of UK advertising and brand communication. Aims to rescue, collect and preserve the industry's archives and best work and to make it available to all.

Subject coverage:
The history of advertising and brand communications 1800-present day, including advertising agencies; advertising controls; clubs and organisations; corporate and retail marketing; designers and creatives; professional interest bodies; special collections; TV commercials (over 70,000) 1950s to present.

Information services:
Research and information service.

Special visitor services:
Study visits by appointment only

Education services:
Education services will be available in 2009

Museum or gallery collection, archive, or library special collection:
Specialist library of over 6,000 books
Large collections of proofs, posters, original artwork, market research and company records (see website for details)

Trade and statistical information:
Over 130 advertising and marketing industry journal titles; published industry statistics and surveys; market research and trends; selected titles of consumer magazines.

Non-library collection catalogue:
All or part available in-house

continued overleaf

Library catalogue:
All or part available in-house

Printed publications:
Advertising in Britain, A History (T. A. Nevett)
British Television Advertising: The first 30 years (B. Henry)
HAT News (quarterly newsletter)
Journal of Advertising History
HAT Annual Report and Financial Statements
Calendars, postcards, etc.
Order printed publications from:
enquiries@hatads.org.uk

Electronic and video publications:
Vintage TV commercial compilations (DVD, to order)
Order electronic and video publications from:
enquiries@hatads.org.uk

Publications list:
Available online and in print

Access to staff:
Contact by letter, by telephone, by fax, by e-mail, in person and via website. Appointment necessary. All charged.
Hours: Mon to Fri, 0900 to 1700

Access to building, collection or gallery:
Study visits by appointment only
Hours: Mon to Fri, 0900 to 1700
Special comments: Closed public holidays and weekends. UK student research visits free of charge.

Access for disabled people:
Parking provided, level entry, access to all public areas, toilet facilities

HISTORY OF EDUCATION SOCIETY

Faculty of Education, Health and Social Care, University of Winchester, Sparkford Road, Winchester, Hampshire, SO22 4NR

Tel: 01962 827125
Fax: 01962 827479
E-mail: stephanie.spencer@winchester.ac.uk

Website:
http://www.historyofeducation.org.uk
General; membership; details of society's conferences and seminars; links to other societies for history of education and related sites.

Enquiries:
Enquiries to: Secretary

Founded:
1967

Organisation type and purpose:
Learned society (membership is by subscription), present number of members: 300, registered charity (charity number 1055764).

Subject coverage:
History of education, its study and teaching.

Printed publications:
History of Education Journal (6 times a year)
History of Education Society Researcher (2 times a year)
Order printed publications from: HEJ: order through Taylor and Francis
History of Education Society Researcher: contact Secretary

Access to staff:
Contact by letter, by e-mail and via website
Hours: Mon to Fri, 0900 to 1700

Member organisation of:
International Standing Conference for the History of Education

HISTORY OF PARLIAMENT TRUST

15 Woburn Square, London, WC1H 0NS

Tel: 020 7862 8800
Fax: 020 7255 1442
E-mail: s.macquire@histparl.ac.uk

Website:
http://www.ihrinfo.ac.uk
Role of history, publications, list of staff.

Enquiries:
Enquiries to: Administrator
Other contacts: Director

Founded:
1951

Organisation type and purpose:
Registered charity, research organisation.

Subject coverage:
History of Parliament.

Printed publications:
The History of Parliament: The Commons – 1386–1421 (Roskell J S et al, 4 volumes, £275)
The History of Parliament: The House of Commons – 1509–1558 (ed Bindoff S T, 3 volumes, £120)
The History of Parliament: The House of Commons – 1558–1603 (ed Hasler P W, 3 volumes, £120)
The History of Parliament: The House of Commons – 1660–1690 (ed Henning B D, 3 volumes £120)
The History of Parliament: The House of Commons – 1715–1754 (ed Sedgwick R, 2 volumes £90)
The History of Parliament: The House of Commons – 1754–1790 (eds Namier L and Brooks J, 3 volumes £120)
The History of Parliament: The House of Commons – 1790–1820 (ed Thorne R G, 5 volumes £225)
Order printed publications from: Available from, Sutton Publishing
Phoenix Mill, Far Thrupp, Stroud, Gloucestershire, GL5 2BU, tel: 01453 731114, fax: 01453 731117

Electronic and video publications:
The History of Parliament (all 23 volumes, CD-ROM, pub Cambridge University Press, 1998)

Publications list:
Available in print

Access to staff:
Contact by letter and by e-mail
Hours: Mon to Fri, 0900 to 1700

Access to building, collection or gallery:
No prior appointment required

HM LAND REGISTRY

Acronym or abbreviation: HMLR

32 Lincoln's Inn Fields, London, WC2A 3PH

Tel: 020 7917 8888
Fax: 020 7955 0110
E-mail: enquiries.pic@landreg.gov.uk

Website:
http://www.landreg.gov.uk
Information on the works of the Land Registry. Annual Report and Accounts. Residential property price report.

Enquiries:
Enquiries to: Librarian
Direct tel: 020 7917 8888 ext 4800
Other contacts: Agency Customer Service Manager

Founded:
1862

Organisation type and purpose:
National government body.
HM Land Registry is a government executive agency and trading fund.
It aims to: maintain and develop a stable and effective land registration system throughout England and Wales; guarantee title to registered estates and interests in land; provide ready access to up-to-date and guaranteed land information.

Subject coverage:
Mapping of all the property boundaries, change of ownership of property, and land registration system in England and Wales, granting of legal title on behalf of the Crown, provides ready access to up-to-date and guaranteed information.

Trade and statistical information:
Quarterly Residential Property Price Report (published free) on property prices in England and Wales, detailing average prices and volume of sales broken down by property type, counties and London Boroughs.

Printed publications:
Annual Report
Practice advice leaflets (free)
Public relations leaflets (free)
Residential Property Price Report (quarterly, free)

Electronic and video publications:
Residential Property Price Report (on disc, £10)

Publications list:
Available in print

Access to staff:
Contact by letter, by telephone, by fax, by e-mail, in person and via website. All charged.
Hours: Mon to Fri, 0900 to 1700

Access to building, collection or gallery:
No prior appointment required

District Land Registries:
Birkenhead (Old Market) District Land Registry\
For registered land titles in Merseyside and Staffordshire and Stoke-on-Trent
Old Market House, Hamilton Street, Birkenhead, Merseyside, CH41 5FL; tel: 0151 473 1110; fax: 0151 473 0251
Birkenhead (Rosebrae) District Land Registry\ *For registered land titles in Cheshire and the London Boroughs of Kensington and Chelsea, and Hammersmith and Fulham*
Rosebrae Court, Woodside Ferry Approach, Birkenhead, Merseyside, CH41 5FL; tel: 0151 472 0666; fax: 0151 472 6789
Coventry District Land Registry\ *For registered land titles in West Midlands and Worcestershire districts of Wychavon, Bromsgrove and Redditch*
Leigh Court, Torrington Avenue, Tile Hill, Coventry, CV4 9XZ; tel: 024 7686 0860; fax: 024 7686 0021
Croydon District Land Registry\ *For registered land titles in London Boroughs of Bexley, Bromley, Merton, Croydon and Sutton*
Sunley House, Bedford Park, Croydon, CR9 3LE; tel: 020 8781 9100; fax: 020 8781 9110
Durham (Bolden House) District Land Registry\ *For registered land titles in Cumbria and Surrey*
Bolden House, Wheatlands Way, Pity Me, Durham, DH1 5GJ; tel: 0191 301 2345; fax: 0191 301 2300
Durham District Land Registry\ *For registered land titles in Durham, Hartlepool, Middlesbrough, Northumberland, Redcar and Cleveland, Stockton-on-Tees and Tyne & Wear*
Southfield House, Southfield Way, Durham, DH1 5TR; tel: 0191 301 3500; fax: 0191 301 0020
Gloucester District Land Registry\ *For registered land titles in Berkshire, Bristol, Gloucestershire, Oxfordshire, South Gloucestershire and Warwickshire*
Twyver House, Bruton Way, Gloucester, GL1 1DQ; tel: 01452 511111; fax: 01452 510050
Harrow District Land Registry\ *For registered land titles in Barnet, Brent, Camden, City of London, City of Westminster, Harrow, Inner & Middle Temples and Islington*
Lyon House, Lyon Road, Harrow, Middlesex, HA1 2EU; tel: 020 8235 1181; fax: 020 8862 0176
Hull District Land Registry\ *For registered land titles in Kingston upon Hull, Lincolnshire, Norfolk, North East Lincolnshire and Suffolk*
Earle House, Portland Street, Hull, Humberside, HU2 8JN; tel: 01482 223244; fax: 01482 224278
Lancashire District Land Registry\ *For registered land titles in Blackburn with Darwen, Blackpool and Lancashire*
Wrea Brook Court, Lytham Road, Warton, Preston, Lancashire, PR4 1TE; tel: 01772 836700; fax: 01772 836970

Leicester District Land Registry\ Leicester District Land Registry\ *For registered land titles in Buckinghamshire, Northamptonshire, Daventry and Leicestershire*
  Westbridge Place, Leicester, LE3 5DR; tel: 0116 265 4000; fax: 0116 265 4008
Lytham District Land Registry\ *For registered land titles in Greater Manchester*
  Birkenhead House, East Beach, Lytham St Annes, Lancashire, FY8 5AB; tel: 01253 840001; fax: 01253 840013
Nottingham (East) District Land Registry\ *For registered land titles in Nottinghamshire, South Yorkshire*
  Robins Wood Road, Nottingham, NG8 3RQ; tel: 0115 906 5353; fax: 0115 936 0036
Nottingham (West) District Land Registry\ *For registered land titles in Derbyshire and West Yorkshire*
  Chalfont Drive, Nottingham, NG8 3RN; tel: 0115 935 1166; fax: 0115 935 0038
Peterborough District Land Registry\ *For registered land titles in Bedfordshire, Cambridgeshire, Essex*
  Touthill Close, City Road, Peterborough, Cambridgeshire, PE1 1XN; tel: 01733 288288; fax: 01733 280022
Plymouth District Land Registry\ *For registered land titles in Bath and North East Somerset, Cornwall, Devon, Isles of Scilly, North Somerset and Somerset*
  Plumer House, Tailyour Road, Crownhill, Plymouth, PL6 5HY; tel: 01752 636000; fax: 01752 636161
Portsmouth District Land Registry\ *For registered land titles in East Sussex, Isle of Wight, West Sussex and Hampshire*
  St Andrew's Court, St Michael's Road, Portsmouth, PO1 2JH; tel: 023 9276 8888; fax: 023 9276 8768
Stevenage District Land Registry\ *For registered land titles in Hertfordshire and the London Boroughs of Barking & Dagenham, Enfield, Hackney, Havering, Newham, Redbridge, Tower Hamlets and Waltham Forest*
  Brickdale House, Swingate, Stevenage, Hertfordshire, SG1 1XG; tel: 01438 788888; fax: 01438 780107
Swansea District Land Registry\ *For registered land titles in Hereford & Worcester and the London Boroughs of Ealing, Hillingdon, Hounslow and Haringey*
  Ty Bryn Glas, High Street, Swansea, SA1 1PW; tel: 01792 458877; fax: 01792 473236
Telford District Land Registry\ *For registered land titles in Shropshire and the London Boroughs of Greenwich, Kingston Upon Thames, Lambeth, Lewisham, Richmond Upon Thames, Southwark and Wandsworth*
  Parkside Court, Hall Park Way, Telford, Shropshire, TF3 4LR; tel: 01952 290355; fax: 01952 290356
The Land Registry for Wales\ *For registered land in the principality of Wales*
  Ty Cwm Tawe, Phoenix Way, Llansamlet, Swansea, SA7 9FQ; tel: 01792 355000; fax: 01792 355055
Tunbridge Wells District Land Registry\ *For registered land titles in Kent*
  Forest Court, Forest Road, Tunbridge Wells, Kent, TN2 5AQ; tel: 01892 510015; fax: 01892 510032
Weymouth District Land Registry\ *For registered land titles in Dorset, Wiltshire, South Somerset and Mendip*
  1 Cumberland Drive, Weymouth, Dorset, DT4 9TT; tel: 01305 363636; fax: 01305 363646
York District Land Registry\ *For registered land titles in North Yorkshire, York and East Riding of Yorkshire*
  James House, James Street, York, YO1 3YZ; tel: 01904 450000; fax: 01904 450086

Parent body:
Lord Chancellor's Department

Subsidiary body:
23 District Land Registries in England and Wales

HM NAUTICAL ALMANAC OFFICE

Acronym or abbreviation: HMNAO

UK Hydrographic Office, Admiralty Way, Taunton, Somerset, TA1 2DN

Tel: 01823 337900
Fax: 01823 335396
E-mail: hmnao@ukho.gov.uk

Website:
http://www.hmnao.com
Contact information, details of publications, samples of our products, details of forthcoming astronomical events.

Enquiries:
Enquiries to: UKHO Helpdesk
Direct tel: 01823 723366
Direct fax: 01823 251816
Direct e-mail: helpdesk@ukho.gov.uk

Founded:
1831

Organisation type and purpose:
National government body, professional body.

Subject coverage:
Astronomy, navigation, land surveying using astronomy, astronomical phenomena, astronomical data, calendarial information, prayer times, first sighting of new moon, forensic astronomy, historical astronomy, astronomical software, astronomical data in various forms, e.g. camera-ready, floppy disc, e-mail and electronic.

Printed publications:
The Nautical Almanac (annually)
The Astronomical Almanac (annually)
Astronomical Phenomena (annually)
The UK Air Almanac (annually)
The Star Almanac for Land Surveyors (annually)
Rapid Sight Reduction Tables for Navigation (every five years)
NavPac and Compact Data 2006–2010 (every five years)
Planetary and Lunar Coordinates 2001–2020 (every 20 years)
Order printed publications from: UK Hydrographic Office Admiralty Brand Distributor Network: http://www.admiraltyshop.co.uk

Electronic and video publications:
The Star Almanac for Land Surveyors (annually)
NavPac and Compact Data 2006–2010 (every five years)

Publications list:
Available in print

Access to staff:
Contact by letter, by telephone, by fax, by e-mail and via website
Hours: Mon to Fri, 0800 to 1600

Links with:
Astronomical Applications Department
  US Naval Observatory, 3450 Massachusetts Avenue NW, Washington, DC 20392–5420, USA; tel: +1 (202) 762 1617; fax: +1 (202) 762 1612; website: http://aa.usno.navy.mil

Parent body:
UK Hydrographic Office
  Admiralty Way, Taunton, Somerset, TA1 2DN; tel: 01823 337900; 01823 251816 (helpdesk); e-mail: helpdesk@ukho.gov.uk; website: http://www.ukho.gov.uk

HOLBORN LIBRARY

32–38 Theobalds Road, London, WC1X 8PA

Tel: 020 7974 6354
Fax: 020 7974 6356

Website:
http://www.camden.gov.uk
Catalogue access via a link

Enquiries:
Enquiries to: Group Manager

Organisation type and purpose:
Local government body, public library.

Subject coverage:
General fiction and non-fiction. online databases (including Ancestry, Lexis)

Non-library collection catalogue:
All or part available online

Library catalogue:
All or part available online

Access to staff:
Contact by letter, by telephone, by fax, in person and via website
Hours: Mon, Thu, 1000 to 1900; Tue, Fri, 1000 to 1800; Wed, 1000 to 1800; Sat, 1000 to 1700

Access for disabled people:
Ramped entry, access to all public areas, toilet facilities

Parent body:
London Borough of Camden, Culture and Environment Directorate

HOLIDAY CENTRES ASSOCIATION

Acronym or abbreviation: HCA

The Coppice, Rowe Close, Bideford, Devon, EX39 5XX

Tel: 01237 421 347
Fax: 01273 421 347
E-mail: holidaycentres@aol.com

Website:
http://www.holidaycentres.com

Enquiries:
Enquiries to: Chief Executive

Founded:
1936

Formerly called:
National Association of Holiday Centres

Organisation type and purpose:
Trade association.
Represents the majority of United Kingdom holiday centres and villages.

Subject coverage:
Tourism, holiday centres and villages.

Trade and statistical information:
Data on the holiday centre sector of the tourist industry.

Printed publications:
Membership list

Access to staff:
Appointment necessary.
Hours: Mon to Fri, 0900 to 1700

HOLISTIC HEALTH COLLEGE

Acronym or abbreviation: HHC

94 Grosvenor Road, London, SW1V 3LF

Tel: 020 7834 3579
Fax: 020 7821 0255

Website:
http://www.gni-international.org
Further information.

Enquiries:
Enquiries to: General Secretary
Other contacts: Registrar

Founded:
1992

Formed from:
Holistic Health Consultancy (year of change 1983)

Formerly called:
Holistic Health Consultancy and College (year of change 1992)

continued overleaf

Organisation type and purpose:
International organisation, training organisation, research organisation.

Subject coverage:
Iridology, herbal medicine, nutrition, naturopathy and homoeopathy.

Library catalogue:
All or part available in-house

Printed publications:
Naturopathic Iridology (course material 18 modules at £150 per module)
Intensive Iridology (course material for practitioners only, 6 modules at £110 per module plus £90 registration, total £750)
Prospectus

Electronic and video publications:
Aloe Vera and Aids (video)
Videos on ME treatments and iridiology (hire only)

Publications list:
Available in print

Access to staff:
Contact by letter and by telephone. Appointment necessary.
Hours: Mon to Wed, 0900 to 1700; Thu and Fri, 0800 to 1100

Access for disabled people:
Access to all public areas, toilet facilities

Affiliated to:
Association of Master Herbalists
Holden Natural Health Centre, The Bield, Lewes Road, Forest Row, East Sussex, RH18 5AF; tel: 01342 826899; fax: 01342 826896; e-mail: kelly@holclinic.com
General Naturopathic Council Limited
255 Lavender Hill, London, SW11 1JD; tel: 020 7498 9966; e-mail: maraia.harewood@btconnect.com
Guild of Naturopathic Iridologists International at the same address; tel: 020 7821 0255; fax: 020 7821 0255; e-mail: info@gni_international.org

Connections with:
Holistic Health Consultancy
at the same address; tel: 020 7834 3579; fax: 020 7821 0255

Parent body:
Institute of Complementary Medicine
PO Box 194, London, SE16 1QZ; tel: 020 7237 5165; fax: 020 7237 5175

HOLLYCOMBE STEAM AND WOODLAND GARDEN SOCIETY

Iron Hill, Midhurst Road, Liphook, Hampshire, GU30 7LP

Tel: 01428 724900
Fax: 01428 723682
E-mail: hollycombe@talk21.com

Website:
http://www.hollycombe.co.uk
Details of museum, Description of artefacts. Open days, exhibits. Up-to-date news.

Enquiries:
Enquiries to: Information Officer

Founded:
1971

Organisation type and purpose:
Membership association (membership is by subscription), present number of members: 150, voluntary organisation, registered charity, museum, suitable for ages: all.
Operates Hollycombe Steam Collection, a working steam power museum of national importance in the UK. Open to the public as advertised.

Subject coverage:
History and application of steam power to transport, agriculture, fairground, marine, industry. Shown working when open.

Printed publications:
Museum Guide Book

Publicity leaflet

Electronic and video publications:
Fairground Organ Tapes (available for purchase)

Access to staff:
Contact by letter, by telephone, by fax, by e-mail, in person and via website
Hours: Office: Mon to Fri, 0900 to 1700

Access to building, collection or gallery:
No prior appointment required
Hours: Collection open to public: Sun and Public holidays; Easter to mid Oct; daily late Jul to late Aug, 1200 to 1700
Special comments: Admission charge published. Prior appointment is required when closed to the public.

Access for disabled people:
Parking provided, level entry, toilet facilities
Special comments: Access to most areas.

HOLLYHOCK SOCIETY, ENGLAND, SCOTLAND AND WALES

5 Clarence Road, Cheltenham, Gloucestershire, GL52 2AY

Tel: 01242 2621459

Subject coverage:
Propagation and cultivation of hollyhocks.

Non-library collection catalogue:
All or part available online

HOLSTEIN UK

Acronym or abbreviation: HUK

Scotsbridge House, Scots Hill, Rickmansworth, Hertfordshire, WD3 3BB

Tel: 01923 695200
Fax: 01923 770003
E-mail: info@holstein-uk.org

Website:
http://www.holstein-uk.org
Latest sire and dam information; full ancestry records; hall of fame; press releases and news.

Enquiries:
Enquiries to: Chief Executive

Founded:
1909

Formed by the merger of:
British Holstein Society (BHS), Holstein-Friesian Society (HFS) (year of change 1999)

Formerly called:
British Friesian Cattle Society (BFCS) (year of change 1986)

Organisation type and purpose:
Membership association (membership is by subscription).
Cattle breed society.
Registration and promotion of the Holstein and Friesian breeds in the United Kingdom.

Subject coverage:
Holstein breed history and present day facts and figures related to the breeding of Holstein cows; bull proofs, cow indexes. Ancestry details, production and conformation records and genetic indexes for production and conformation for over 4 million animals.

Printed publications:
Holstein Journal (6 times a year)

Access to staff:
Contact by letter, by telephone, by fax, by e-mail and via website. Appointment necessary.
Hours: Mon to Fri, 0900 to 1700

Member of:
European Confederation of Black and White Breed Societies
World Holstein Friesian Federation

HOME ACCIDENT PREVENTION NORTHERN IRELAND

Nella House, Dargan Crescent, Belfast, BT3 9JP

Tel: 028 9050 1160
Fax: 028 9050 1164

Website:
http://www.rospa.co.uk

Enquiries:
Enquiries to: Executive Secretary

Founded:
1965

Formerly called:
Northern Ireland Home Accident Prevention Council; Northern Ireland Home Safety Council (year of change 1997)

Organisation type and purpose:
Advisory body, voluntary organisation.

Subject coverage:
Accident prevention in and around the home.

Museum or gallery collection, archive, or library special collection:
Variety of information on accidents and accident prevention

Printed publications:
ROSPA material (charges made)
Various leaflets (available free of charge)

Access to staff:
Contact by letter, by telephone, by fax, by e-mail and in person. Appointment necessary.
Hours: Closed, 1300 to 1400

Access to building, collection or gallery:
No prior appointment required

Parent body:
Royal Society for the Prevention of Accidents (ROSPA)
tel: 028 9050 1160; fax: 028 9050 1164

HOME DECORATION RETAILERS ASSOCIATION

Acronym or abbreviation: HDRA

BHF Group, 225 Bristol Road, Edgbaston, Birmingham B5 7UB

Tel: 0121 446 6688
Fax: 0121 446 5215
E-mail: membership@bhfgroup.co.uk

Enquiries:
Enquiries to: Company Secretary

Founded:
1955

Formerly called:
Wallpaper, Paint and Wallcovering Retailers Association (WPWRA); Wallcovering, Fabric and Décor Retailers Association Limited (WFDRA) (year of change 1995)

Organisation type and purpose:
Advisory body, trade association (membership is by subscription), present number of members: 750, publishing house.
To promote the wellbeing of the independent home decorating specialist retailer.

Subject coverage:
Home décor trade market, decorating materials, DIY materials, paint, wall coverings, co-ordination of decorative materials, design, fabrics, home furnishings.

Trade and statistical information:
Data on home décor trade products.

Printed publications:
Gold Décor Directory (annually)
Home Décor and Furnishings (magazine, 6 times a year)

Access to staff:
Contact by letter, by telephone, by fax and by e-mail
Hours: Mon to Fri, 0900 to 1700

Affiliated to:
Trade and Professional Alliance (TPA)

Division of:
The British Hardware Federation (BHF)

HOME MISSION DESK

Acronym or abbreviation: HMD

39 Eccleston Square, London. SW1V 1BX

Tel: 020 7901 4818
E-mail: homemission@cbcew.org.uk

Website:
http://www.catholicchurch.org.uk
Website for the Catholic Church in England and
Wales.
http://www.life4seekers.co.uk
Website for those seeking information about
Catholic life and beliefs.

Enquiries:
Enquiries to: Home Mission Advisor

Formerly called:
Catholic Missionary Society (year of change 2003);
Catholic Agency to Support Evangelisation (year
of change 2009)

Organisation type and purpose:
To support Catholic communities and individuals
to engage in mission in England and Wales.

Printed publications:
Evangelisation Directory

Publications list:
Available online

Access to staff:
Contact by letter, by telephone and by e-mail.
Appointment necessary.
Hours: Mon to Fri, 0900 to 1700

Access to building, collection or gallery:
Prior appointment required

HOME OFFICE: INFORMATION AND LIBRARY TEAM, INFORMATION MANAGEMENT SERVICE, SHARED SERVICES DIRECTORATE

Formal name: Information Services Centre
Acronym or abbreviation: ISC

Information Services Centre, Lower Ground Floor,
Seacole Building, 2 Marsham Street, London,
SW1P 4DF

Tel: 020 7035 6699
E-mail: informationservicescentre@homeoffice.gsi
.gov.uk

Website:
http://www.homeoffice.gov.uk

Founded:
1782

Organisation type and purpose:
National government body, central government
departmental library.

Subject coverage:
Social sciences, especially parliamentary
publications; community relations; criminal law;
criminology; immigration and nationality; police;
security; drugs; citizenship.

Trade and statistical information:
The Home Office publishes a range of statistical
data such as probation statistics and statistical
bulletins. Many other statistics are published on
behalf of the Home Office by The Stationery
Office (e.g. criminal statistics).

Printed publications:
Criminal Statistics England and Wales
HM Inspectorate of Constabulary reports
UKBA reports
HM Inspectorate of Probation Reports

Order printed publications from: Direct
Communications Unit, 2 Marsham Street, London,
SW1P 4DF; tel: 020 7035 4848; fax: 020 7035 4745; e-
mail: public.enquiries@homeoffice.gsi.gov.uk

Access to staff:
Appointment necessary.
Hours: Mon to Thu, 0900 to 1730; Fri 0900 to 1700
Special comments: Access only for Home Office staff
and staff of other government agencies, by prior
appointment; no access to members of the public.

HOMEOPATHY COLLEGE

Acronym or abbreviation: THC

454 Hagley Road West, Quinton, Birmingham, B68
0DL

Tel: 0121 423 1913
E-mail: admin@homoeopathytraining.co.uk

Website:
http://www.homoeopathytraining.co.uk
General information about homeopathy and
training to be a homeopath.

Enquiries:
Enquiries to: Principal
Direct e-mail: enquirer@homoeopathytraining.co.uk

Founded:
1988

Formerly called:
College of Practical Homeopathy, Midlands (year
of change 2006)

Organisation type and purpose:
Training organisation.
Training professional homeopathic practitioners.

Subject coverage:
Homeopathy.

Access to staff:
Contact by letter, by telephone, by e-mail, in
person and via website. Appointment necessary.
Hours: Mon, Tue, Wed, Thu, 0930 to 1630

Access to building, collection or gallery:
Prior appointment required
Hours: Mon, Tue, Wed, Thu, 0930 to 1630

HOMERTON COLLEGE LIBRARY

Homerton College, Hills Road, Cambridge, CB2
8PH

Tel: 01223 507259

Enquiries:
Enquiries to: Librarian

Organisation type and purpose:
College library

Subject coverage:
All subjects taken for the Cambridge Tripos

**Museum or gallery collection, archive, or library
special collection:**
Children's Literature Collection

Non-library collection catalogue:
All or part available in-house

Library catalogue:
All or part available in-house

Access to staff:
Contact by letter, by telephone, by e-mail and in
person. Appointment necessary. Non-members
charged.

Access to building, collection or gallery:
Hours: Term time: Mon to Fri, 0900 to 1700
Vacations: 1000 to 1700 (please telephone first)
Special comments: Closed to general public

Constituent part of:
University of Cambridge

HOMERTON HOSPITAL NEWCOMB LIBRARY

Formal name: Homerton University Hospital NHS
Foundation Trust Newcomb Library

Homerton Row, London, E9 6SR

Tel: 020 8510 7751
Fax: 020 8510 7281
E-mail: newcomb.library@homerton.nhs.uk

Website:
http://www.homerton.nhs.uk/education/
11573611372688.html
Information re library services, opening hours,
library staff.
Links to electronic journals, databases, etc.

Enquiries:
Enquiries to: Library Manager
Direct e-mail: isabel.cantwell@homerton.nhs.uk

Formerly called:
Hackney Hospital Medical Library (year of change
1986)

Organisation type and purpose:
Multidisciplinary hospital library.

Subject coverage:
Medicine and allied subjects.

Library catalogue:
All or part available online

Printed publications:
Bibliographies of selected subjects
Journals List (annual)
Library Guide (annual)
New Books List (6 times a year)

Access to staff:
Contact by letter, by telephone, by fax, by e-mail
and via website. Appointment necessary. Letter of
introduction required.
Hours: Mon, 1100 to 2000; Tue to Fri, 0900 to 2000
Special comments: Staff availability permitting.

Links with:
London Strategic Health Authority
Nursing Union List of Journals

Member organisation of:
London Health Libraries
London Regional Library Scheme
Psychiatric Libraries Co-operative Scheme

HOMES FOR SCOTLAND

Acronym or abbreviation: SHBA

Forsyth House, 93 George Street, Edinburgh, EH2
3EJ

Tel: 0131 243 2595
Fax: 0131 243 2596
E-mail: info@homesforscotland.co.uk

Website:
http://www.homesforscotland.co.uk

Enquiries:
Enquiries to: Manager
Other contacts: Manager, Marketing and
Development

Founded:
Early 1980s

Formerly called:
Scottish Building Employers Federation (SBEF)
(year of change 1985); Scottish House-Builders
Association (SHBA) (year of change 2001)

Organisation type and purpose:
Trade association.

Subject coverage:
House building.

Trade and statistical information:
Research and produce surveys etc on house
building industry and economic factors affecting
it in Scotland.

continued overleaf

Access to staff:
Contact by letter, by telephone, by fax and by e-mail
Hours: Mon to Fri, 0900 to 1700

HONDA OWNERS CLUB (GB)

35 Mortimer Way, North Baddesley, Hampshire, SO52 9NE

Website:
http://www.hoc.org.uk

Enquiries:
Enquiries to: Secretary Classic

Founded:
1961

Organisation type and purpose:
Membership association (membership is by subscription), present number of members: 6000, voluntary organisation.

Subject coverage:
Honda motor cycles, insurance, discounts, help and advice.

Printed publications:
Golden Wing (magazine)
Magazine (once every two months, issued with membership)

Access to staff:
Contact by letter
Hours: Mon to Fri, 0900 to 1700

Subsidiary body:
Honda Owners Club (GB)
  Classic Section

HONG KONG TOURISM BOARD

Acronym or abbreviation: HKTB

6 Grafton Street, London, W1S 4EQ

Tel: 020 7533 7100
Fax: 020 7533 7111
E-mail: lonwwo@hktb.com

Website:
http://www.discoverhongkong.com
Tourist information on Hong Kong.

Enquiries:
Enquiries to: Regional Director

Founded:
1957

Organisation type and purpose:
National government body, statutory body, trade association (membership is by qualification), present number of members: 350.
Tourism board.
National tourist office.

Subject coverage:
Tourist information on Hong Kong.

Printed publications:
Travellers Guide to Hong Kong (free of charge)

Access to staff:
Contact by letter, by telephone, by fax, by e-mail and in person
Hours: Mon to Fri, 0930 to 1730

Location:
Hong Kong Tourism Board
  Citicorp Centre, 18 Whitfield Road, North Point, Hong Kong; tel: 00 852 2807 6543; fax: 00 852 2806 0303

HONOURABLE COMPANY OF MASTER MARINERS

Acronym or abbreviation: HCMM

HQS Wellington, Temple Stairs, Victoria Embankment, London, WC2R 2PN

Tel: 020 7836 8179
Fax: 020 7240 3082
E-mail: info@hcmm.org.uk

Website:
http://www.hcmm.org.uk

Enquiries:
Enquiries to: Clerk to the Company
Direct e-mail: clerk@hcmm.org.uk

Founded:
1926

Organisation type and purpose:
Professional body (membership is by qualification, election or invitation).
City of London Livery Company.

Education services:
School visits programme for KS1 and KS2.

Library catalogue:
All or part available in print

Printed publications:
The Floating LIvery Hall – An Introduction

Access to staff:
Contact by letter, by telephone and by e-mail
Hours: Mon to Fri, 0900 to 1700

Access to building, collection or gallery:
No prior appointment required

HONOURABLE SOCIETY OF GRAY'S INN

8 South Square, Gray's Inn, London, WC1R 5ET

Tel: 020 7458 7800
Fax: 020 7458 7801

Enquiries:
Enquiries to: Administration Secretary

Organisation type and purpose:
Professional body.

Subject coverage:
Legal education, records, professional conduct etc (in conjunction with the Council of Legal Education and the General Council of the Bar).

Printed publications:
Graya

Access to staff:
Contact by telephone
Hours: Mon to Fri, 1000 to 1600

HONOURABLE SOCIETY OF LINCOLN'S INN

Library, Holborn, London, WC2A 3TN

Tel: 020 7242 4371
Fax: 020 7404 1864
E-mail: library@lincolnsinn.org.uk

Website:
http://www.lincolnsinn.org.uk
The Inn's homepage, includes information on the library.
http://www.lincolnsinnlibrary.org.uk
Library catalogue (for the bulk of the printed collections, but excluding some pamphlets and tracts, early continental law, superseded Commonwealth legislation).

Enquiries:
Enquiries to: Librarian

Founded:
pre 1470

Organisation type and purpose:
Professional body.
Library of an Inn of Court.

Subject coverage:
Law, including the laws of the Commonwealth countries, legal history. Genealogical information and biographical information on past members and other barristers.

Museum or gallery collection, archive, or library special collection:
Continental legal dissertations (6000 items, 17th and 18th centuries)

Manuscripts (medieval and later, including the Hale Collection)
Parliamentary Papers 1800 to date
Roman, Canon and Foreign law (15th to 19th century)
Tracts and pamphlets (15,000 items, 16th to 19th century)

Library catalogue:
All or part available online

Access to staff:
Contact by letter, by telephone, by fax and by e-mail. Appointment necessary. Letter of introduction required.
Hours: Mon to Fri, 0900 to 2000; Aug to mid-Sep, 0930 to 1800
Special comments: Current legal collection not available to the public or litigants in person. Genealogical enquiries by email or letter only.

Access for disabled people:
Level entry
Special comments: Parking by prior arrangement.

HONOURABLE SOCIETY OF THE INNER TEMPLE

The Library, Inner Temple, London, EC4Y 7DA

Tel: 020 7797 8217/8/9
Fax: 020 7583 6030
E-mail: library@innertemple.org.uk

Website:
http://www.innertemplelibrary.org.uk
Library services; history of the Inner Temple and library; Inns of Court libraries union lists; AccessToLaw (links).

Enquiries:
Enquiries to: Deputy Librarian

Founded:
1500

Organisation type and purpose:
Professional body.

Subject coverage:
Law of the United Kingdom and Commonwealth countries.

Museum or gallery collection, archive, or library special collection:
Barrington manuscripts (57 vols)
Inner Temple Records (39 vols)
Miscellaneous manuscripts (211 vols)
Mitford manuscripts (79 vols)
Petyt manuscripts (386 vols)

Non-library collection catalogue:
All or part available in print

Library catalogue:
All or part available online

Printed publications:
Catalogue of manuscripts
Guide to catalogues and indexes
Guides to Internet services & CD-ROM databases
Readers' Guide
Student Guide
Transcripts of judicial proceedings: guide to sources

Access to staff:
Contact by letter, by telephone, by fax, by e-mail and via website. Appointment necessary.
Hours: Term time: Mon to Thu, 0900 to 2000; Fri, 0900 to 1900
Vacations: Mon to Fri, 0900 to 1730
Special comments: Non-members by letter only.

Member of:
Aslib
BIALL
CILIP
NAG
UKSG

HONOURABLE SOCIETY OF THE MIDDLE TEMPLE

Acronym or abbreviation: Middle Temple

Library, Middle Temple Lane, London, EC4Y 9BT

Tel: 020 7427 4830
Fax: 020 7427 4831
E-mail: library@middletemple.org.uk

Website:
http://www.middletemplelibrary.org.uk

Enquiries:
Enquiries to: Keeper of the Library

Founded:
1641

Organisation type and purpose:
Learned society.
Library of an Inn of Court.

Subject coverage:
Law and legal material covering the United Kingdom, Ireland, European Union and its member states, and the USA.

Services for disabled people:
Lift access to all floors

Museum or gallery collection, archive, or library special collection:
16th- and 17th-century tracts
Archives of the Inn and its members
Phillimore Collection (legal)
Incunabula
John Donne's Library
Robert Ashley's Collection
Ecclesiastical law collection
USA law collection
Capital punishment collection

Non-library collection catalogue:
All or part available in print

Library catalogue:
All or part available online

Printed publications:
Library catalogue 1914 and 1925 supplement (out of print)
Register of Admissions to the Honourable Society of the Middle Temple, 1500–1975 (5 vols, published in 1949 and 1977)
Register of Admissions to the Honourable Society of the Middle Temple, 1976–1989 (vol. 6, out of print)
Middle Templars' Associations with America (Sir Lynden Macassey)
Middle Temple Hall, An Architectural Appreciation (Michael G. Murray)
Middle Temple Hall, Four Centuries of History (Joseph Dean)
The Middle Temple Bench Book (vol. 3, 19821998)
Order printed publications from: Library

Publications list:
Available in print

Access to staff:
Contact by letter, by telephone, by fax and by e-mail. Appointment necessary. Non-members charged.

Access to building, collection or gallery:
Hours: Term time: Mon to Thu, 0900 to 2000; Fri, 0900 to 1900; one Sat in every four, 1000 to 1700
Vacations: Mon to Fri, 0900 to 1730
Special comments: Open to all members of the Bar and Middle Temple students. Bone fide researchers admitted by prior appointment, at the discretion of the Librarian.

HOPE UK

25F Copperfield Street, London, SE1 0EN

Tel: 020 7928 0848
Fax: 020 7401 3477
E-mail: m.watson@hopeuk.org

Website:
http://www.hopeuk.org

Information about Hope UK's services as well as drug and alcohol prevention advice.

Enquiries:
Enquiries to: Business Manager

Founded:
1855

Formerly called:
UK Band of Hope Union (year of change 1995)

Organisation type and purpose:
Registered charity in England, Wales and Scotland (England and Wales: 1044475; Scotland: SC040550); national voluntary organisation with membership; company limited by guarantee (number 3022470)
To prevent drug and alcohol-related harm to children and young people.

Subject coverage:
Hope UK is a drug education charity working from a Christian basis. Its mission is to provide accurate information that enables children and young people to consider their attitudes to alcohol and drugs. It supports parents, teachers and youth leaders with quality resources, speakers and training events. Children and young people are at the centre of its work and it encourages positive peer influence and the ability to choose healthy options in the prevention of the abuse of alcohol, tobacco and other drugs.

Education services:
Hope UK provides drug and alcohol awareness sessions for children and young people as well as those with responsibility for them (eg, parents and youth workers). Two two-day courses accredited with the Open College Network are also available for youth and family workers.

Museum or gallery collection, archive, or library special collection:
The Liversey Collection, University of Central Lancashire, Lambeth Palace Library, London SE1 7JU

Printed publications:
Parents' Action Plan
Take the Test (alcohol awareness leaflet)
in the know (booklet about alcohol)

Publications list:
Available online and in print

Access to staff:
Contact by letter, by telephone, by fax, by e-mail, in person and via website
Hours: Mon to Fri, 0900 to 1700
Special comments: 24-hour answerphone.

Access to building, collection or gallery:
Parking limited as in central London – congestion charge applies

Affiliated to:
Drug Education Forum
Evangelical Alliance

Member organisation of:
DrugScope
National Council for Voluntary Organisations (NCVO)
National Council for Voluntary Youth Services (NCVYS)

HORDER CENTRE

St Johns Road, Crowborough, East Sussex, TN6 1XP

Tel: 01892 665577
Fax: 01892 662142
E-mail: info@hordercentre.co.uk

Website:
http://www.hordercentre.co.uk

Enquiries:
Enquiries to: Main Reception

Founded:
1954

Organisation type and purpose:
Service industry, registered charity (charity number 1046624).

Charitable and specialist hospital.
To offer help, advice and hospital services for people with arthritis and musculo-skeletal conditions.

Subject coverage:
Medical unit offering total comprehensive care and attention to patients with arthritis and musculo-skeletal conndition, requiring medical treatment, surgical intervention or rehabilitation, major joint reconstruction surgery.

Printed publications:
Annual Report
Information brochures

Access to staff:
Contact by letter, by telephone and by e-mail. Appointment necessary.
Hours: Mon to Fri, 0900 to 1700

Access for disabled people:
Parking provided, ramped entry, toilet facilities

HORSES AND PONIES PROTECTION ASSOCIATION

Acronym or abbreviation: HAPPA

Taylor Building, Shores Hey Farm, Black House Lane, Briercliffe, Nr Burnley, BB10 3QU

Tel: 01282 455992
Fax: 01282 451992
E-mail: enquiries@happa.org.uk

Website:
http://www.happa.org.uk

Enquiries:
Enquiries to: General Secretary
Other contacts: Association Secretary

Founded:
1937

Organisation type and purpose:
National organisation, membership association (membership is by subscription), present number of members: 5,000, registered charity (charity number 1085211).
Equine welfare.

Subject coverage:
Horse care and welfare; prosecuting horse cruelty cases; investigation of complaints re neglect and ill treatment of equines.

Printed publications:
Annual report (May)
Autumn newsletter and gift catalogue (Sep)
Leaflets on horsecare
Photographs of cruelty cases involving horses
Spring newsletter (Feb)

Access to staff:
Contact by letter, by telephone, by fax, by e-mail, in person and via website
Hours: Mon to Thu, 0900 to 1700; Fri, 0900 to 1600

HORSHAM DISTRICT COUNCIL

Park House, North Street, Horsham, West Sussex, RH12 1RL

Tel: 01403 215100
Fax: 01403 262985
E-mail: contact@horsham.gov.uk

Website:
http://www.horsham.gov.uk
District Council services and information about the Horsham district.

Enquiries:
Enquiries to: Communications Manager
Direct tel: 01403 215549
Direct e-mail: richard.morris@horsham.gov.uk

Founded:
1974

Organisation type and purpose:
Local government body.

continued overleaf

Subject coverage:
District Council services.

Printed publications:
Business directory
Council magazine (twice yearly)
Other Council publications

Electronic and video publications:
Business and Economic development (video)

Access to staff:
Contact by letter, by telephone, by fax and by e-mail
Hours: Mon to Thu, 0840 to 1720; Fri, 0840 to 1620

Access to building, collection or gallery:
No access other than to staff, no prior appointment required, prior appointment required

Access for disabled people:
Parking provided, ramped entry, level entry, access to all public areas, toilet facilities

HORTICULTURAL DEVELOPMENT COMPANY

Acronym or abbreviation: HDC

Bradbourne House, East Malling, West Malling, Kent, ME19 6DZ

Tel: 01732 848383
Fax: 01732 848498
E-mail: hdc@hdc.org.uk

Website:
http://www.hdc.org.uk
Information on the HDC, Council and staff members, press releases, calendar of events, research and crop protection information (members only).

Enquiries:
Enquiries to: Communication Manager

Founded:
1986

Organisation type and purpose:
Non-Departmental Public Body.
Statutory levy body.

Subject coverage:
Horticulture.

Printed publications:
Newsletter (10 times a year)

Publications list:
Available online and in print

Access to staff:
Contact by letter, by telephone and by e-mail.
Appointment necessary.
Hours: Mon to Fri, 0900 to 1700

Sponsoring department:
Department for Environment, Food and Rural Affairs
  Nobel House, 17 Smith Square, London, SW1P 3JR; tel: 020 7238 6000

HORTICULTURE RESEARCH INTERNATIONAL

Acronym or abbreviation: HRI

Wellesbourne, Warwickshire, CV35 9EF

Tel: 01789 470382
Fax: 01789 470552

Website:
http://www.hri.ac.uk

Enquiries:
Enquiries to: Business Development
Direct tel: 01789 470440
Direct fax: 01789 472069

Founded:
1990

Organisation type and purpose:
University department or institute, research organisation.

The administrative headquarters, centre for strategic science and annual crops research, research and development organisation.

Subject coverage:
Horticulture, botany, soil science, plant physiology, plant biochemistry, pesticides, weed control, entomology, plant pathology, biometrics, vegetable crops. Edible fungi, field vegetables, fruit, industrial crops, ornamentals, protected crops, tropical crops, crop production/agronomy, pest and disease control, environment, plant breeding, post-harvest technology, propagation and seed technology.

Museum or gallery collection, archive, or library special collection:
Historical books on horticulture
Vegetable gene bank

Printed publications:
Annual Report (which also lists all publications by the staff) (£15)

Access to staff:
Contact by letter, by telephone and by fax
Hours: Mon to Fri, 0900 to 1700

Affiliated to:
DEFRA

Has:
some 500 staff sited at five locations, two of which have extensive libraries

Other addresses:
Development research on field vegetables and bulbs
  Willington Road, Kirton, Boston, Lincolnshire, PE20 1EJ; tel: 01205 723477; fax: 01205 722922
Development research on glasshouse crops, nursery stock, micropropagation and soft fruit
  Lymington, Hampshire, SO41 0LZ; tel: 01590 673341; fax: 01590 671553
Hops research
  Department of Hop Research, Wye College, Wye, Ashford, Kent, TN25 5AH; tel: 01233 812179; fax: 01233 813126
Horticultural Research International Efford
Horticultural Research International Kirton
Horticultural Research International Wye

HOSPICE INFORMATION

Help the Hospices, Hospice House, 34–44 Britannia Street, London, WC1X 9JG

Tel: 0870 903 3903
Fax: 020 7278 1021
E-mail: info@hospiceinformation.info

Website:
http://www.hospiceinformation.info
Statistical information, e-mail news bulletin, listings of educational and job opportunities, advice.

Enquiries:
Enquiries to: Information Officer
Direct e-mail: m.hodson@helpthehospices.org.uk

Founded:
1977

Organisation type and purpose:
International organisation, membership association (membership is by subscription), present number of members: 1,000, voluntary organisation, registered charity (charity number 1014851).
Hospice Information is a joint venture between St Christopher's Hospice and Help the Hospices. It is a world-wide resource for professionals and the public that encourages sharing of information and experience amongst those involved in palliative care.

Subject coverage:
Hospice and palliative care services in the UK and overseas; care of people with advanced cancer, motor neurone disease, AIDS; research and education; nursing, medical, social work and other

health professional material related to terminal and palliative care; pastoral care, bereavement issues and ethical aspects.

Printed publications:
Booklist (a very large number of titles)
eChoices (listing of courses and conferences, quarterly and on website)
Directory of Hospice and Palliative Care Services in the UK and Ireland (annually)
Fact sheets on hospice services
Hospice Information Bulletin (newsletter, quarterly)
Hospice Worldwide (directory of overseas hospices and palliative care)
Job Opportunities (listing of job vacancies, on website)
Several e-mail newsletters on UK and international hospice and palliative care

Electronic and video publications:
Palliative Care Worldwide Links: database of palliative care practitioners and services having professional links with overseas hospices
News Bulletin (online)

Publications list:
Available online and in print

Access to staff:
Contact by letter, by telephone, by fax, by e-mail, in person and via website. Appointment necessary
Hours: Mon to Fri, 0900 to 1700

Also at:
St Christopher's Hospice
  51–59 Lawrie Park Road, London, SE26 6DZ; fax: 020 8776 9345; e-mail: info@stchristophers.org.uk

Parent body:
Help the Hospices

HOSPITAL CHAPLAINCIES COUNCIL

Acronym or abbreviation: HCC

Church House, Great Smith Street, London, SW1P 3NZ

Tel: 020 7898 1892
Fax: 020 7898 1891

Website:
http://www.nhs-chaplaincy-spiritualcare.org.uk/

Enquiries:
Enquiries to: Administrator

Organisation type and purpose:
Advisory body, training organisation.

Subject coverage:
Responsible to the General Synod of the Church of England for Anglican Hospital Chaplaincy, HCC relates to the Department of Health and NHS administration, assisting trusts in the selection, appointment and training of Healthcare Chaplains and co-operating with other Christian denominations and other faiths and traditions in promoting the highest standards of spiritual care for patients, relatives and staff.

Printed publications:
Guidelines and information leaflets for healthcare chaplains available on request
Directory of Whole-Time Hospital Chaplains & Chaplains' Assistants in the United Kingdom (£5 inc. p&p)

Publications list:
Available in print

Access to staff:
Contact by letter, by telephone, by e-mail and via website
Hours: Mon to Fri, 0930 to 1730

Close liaison with:
Department of Health

Co-operates with:
Health Care Chaplaincy Boards of the Roman Catholic Church

Hospital Chaplaincy Boards of the Free Church Federal Council

Member of:
Churches Committee for Hospital Chaplaincy

HOSPITAL CONSULTANTS AND SPECIALISTS ASSOCIATION

Acronym or abbreviation: HCSA

Kingsclere Road, Overton, Basingstoke, Hampshire, RG25 3JA

Tel: 01256 771777
Fax: 01256 770999
E-mail: conspec@hcsa.com

Website:
http://www.hcsa.com

Enquiries:
Enquiries to: Advisory Service Manager
Other contacts: Administrative Director.

Founded:
1945

Organisation type and purpose:
Trade union, present number of members: 3100.

Access to staff:
Contact by letter, by telephone, by fax and by e-mail. Appointment necessary.
Hours: Mon to Thu, 0900 to 1700; Fri, 0900 to 1630

Access to building, collection or gallery:
Prior appointment required

Access for disabled people:
Parking provided, ramped entry

HOSTELLING INTERNATIONAL NORTHERN IRELAND

Acronym or abbreviation: YHANI

22–32 Donegal Road, Belfast, BT12 5JN

Tel: 028 9032 4733
Fax: 028 9031 5889
E-mail: info@hini.org.uk

Website:
http://www.hini.org.uk

Enquiries:
Enquiries to: General Secretary

Founded:
1931

Organisation type and purpose:
International organisation, membership association (membership is by subscription), registered charity.
To provide budget priced accommodation for travellers.

Subject coverage:
Hostelling in Northern Ireland; knowledge, love and use of the countryside; preservation of the countryside; maintenance of rights-of-way.

Printed publications:
Accommodation Leaflet

Access to staff:
Contact by letter, by telephone and by fax
Hours: Mon to Fri, 0900 to 1700

HOTEL AND CATERING INTERNATIONAL MANAGEMENT ASSOCIATION

Acronym or abbreviation: HCIMA

191 Trinity Road, London, SW17 7HN

Tel: 020 8772 7400
Fax: 020 8772 7500
E-mail: library@hcima.org.uk

Website:
http://www.hcima.org.uk/
Homepage.

Enquiries:
Enquiries to: Director of ITS Services

Founded:
1971

Organisation type and purpose:
Professional body.
Management in all sectors of industry; examining body.

Subject coverage:
Hotels; restaurants; caterers; hospitals; school meals; staff; welfare; civic and industrial catering etc; hotel and catering industry abroad; research; tourism.

Printed publications:
HCIMA Hospitality Yearbook
Hospitality (formerly HCIMA Journal; 10 times a year)

Electronic and video publications:
WHATT (Worldwide Hospitality and Tourist Trends) (online at www.whatt.net)

Publications list:
Available in print

Access to staff:
Contact by letter, by telephone, by fax and by e-mail
Hours: Mon to Fri, 0900 to 1700
Special comments: Non-members can use the service, by appointment only, for a charge.

HOUNSLOW LIBRARY NETWORK

Acronym or abbreviation: HLN

Centre Space, 24 Treaty Centre, High Street, Hounslow, Middlesex, TW3 1ES

Tel: 020 8583 4545
Fax: 020 8583 4595

Website:
http://www.cip.org.uk

Enquiries:
Enquiries to: Strategic Library Manager (IT and Electronic Resources)
Direct tel: 020 8583 4623
Direct fax: 020 8583 4719
Other contacts: Borough Librarian

Organisation type and purpose:
Local government body, public library.

Subject coverage:
International or foreign affairs (to 1985): relations, policy, diplomacy etc; parliaments; legislative assemblies; political parties and the party systems; party organisation and tactics. Local history. Geology (from 1985).

Museum or gallery collection, archive, or library special collection:
Chiswick Press Collection (19th century)
GLASS Collection (Debussy, Wagner, Jazz)
GLASS: Greater London Audio Specialisation Scheme Collection (spoken word; American literature)
Laser Collection (international or foreign affairs 1976–1984 and geology from 1985)
Layton Collection (English historical and topographical antiquarian material, 16th to 19th centuries)

Library catalogue:
All or part available in-house

Printed publications:
Local history publications

Access to staff:
Contact by telephone, by fax and in person
Hours: Mon to Sat, 0930 to 1730

Access for disabled people:
Parking provided

Has links with:
Community Initiative Partnerships (CIP) Centrespace, Treaty Centre, High Street, Hounslow, Middlesex, TW3 1FS
Other Libraries in London Borough of Hounslow, including Chiswick Library and Feltham Library

HOUSE OF BEAULY LIMITED

Station Road, Beauly, Invernessshire, IV4 7EH

Tel: 01463 782578
Fax: 01463 782409
E-mail: info@houseofbeauly.com

Website:
http://www.houseofbeauly.com

Enquiries:
Enquiries to: Operations Manager

Founded:
1991

Organisation type and purpose:
Visitor centre, retail.

Subject coverage:
Scottish crafts, giftware and traditional textiles, marketing and retailing of crafts.

Access to staff:
Contact by letter, by telephone, by fax, by e-mail, in person and via website. Appointment necessary.
Hours: Mon to Fri, 0900 to 1700

HOUSE OF COMMONS INFORMATION OFFICE

Acronym or abbreviation: HCIO

House of Commons, Westminster, London, SW1A 2TT

Tel: 020 7219 4272
Fax: 020 7219 5839
E-mail: hcinfo@parliament.uk

Website:
http://www.parliament.uk
Enquiries on the proceedings, membership and history of the House of Commons.

Founded:
1978

Organisation type and purpose:
Information office.

Subject coverage:
All matters concerning the work, history and membership of the House of Commons and Parliamentary publications.

Printed publications:
APRILL (Access to Parliamentary Resources and Information in London Libraries)
Education Sheets and Wallcharts
House of Commons Library Documents and some 68 Factsheets on a variety of subjects including historical matters, procedures and members
Services of the HCIO (leaflet)

Publications list:
Available in print

Access to staff:
Contact by letter, by telephone, by fax and by e-mail
Hours: Mon to Thu, 0900 to 1800; Fri, 0900 to 1630

HOUSE OF LORDS INFORMATION

House of Lords, London, SW1A 0PW

Tel: 020 7219 3107
Fax: 020 7219 0620
E-mail: hlinfo@parliament.uk

Website:
http://www.parliament.uk
Full text of bills and Hansard. Information on the work of the House, its membership and all Select Committee Reports.

continued overleaf

Enquiries:
Enquiries to: Head of Enquiry Services

Organisation type and purpose:
National government body.
One of the Houses of Parliament.

Information services:
Information Office

Special visitor services:
Tours Office

Education services:
Education Service

Services for disabled people:
Black Rod's Office

Museum or gallery collection, archive, or library special collection:
Parliamentary archives

Printed publications:
Several publications on the membership, work, attendance and history of the House (details on request)

Electronic and video publications:
See also website

Access to staff:
Contact by letter, by telephone, by fax, by e-mail and via website
Hours: When the House of Lords is sitting: Mon to Thu, 1000 to 1800; Fri, 1000 to 1600
Recess: 1000 to 1600

HOUSE OF LORDS LIBRARY

House of Lords, London, SW1A 0PW

Tel: 020 7219 5242 or 5433
Fax: 020 7219 6396
E-mail: hllibrary@parliament.uk

Enquiries:
Enquiries to: Librarian

Founded:
1826

Organisation type and purpose:
Private library for members of the House of Lords.

Subject coverage:
All matters concerning the House of Lords, parliament, parliamentary publications, British government, administration and politics, as well as the law of England and Wales, and of Scotland.

Museum or gallery collection, archive, or library special collection:
Collections of pamphlets made by Lords Truro and Farnham in the 19th century
Lord Truro's collection of English lawbooks
Peel Tracts (c. 2,000 pamphlets chiefly concerning 18th-century Ireland)

Library catalogue:
All or part available in-house

Access to staff:
Contact by letter, by telephone, by fax and by e-mail
Hours: Mon to Fri, 0930 to 1730
Special comments: No facilities for personal enquiries.

HOUSEBUILDER PUBLICATIONS

Acronym or abbreviation: HBP

Housebuilder Media Ltd, Byron House, 7–9 St. James's Street, London, SW1A 1EE

Tel: 020 7960 1630
Fax: 020 7960 1631

Website:
http://www.house-builder.co.uk
Back issues, news online, jobs online, subscription information, etc.
http://www.hbmedia.co.uk/

Enquiries:
Enquiries to: Publishing Manager

Direct tel: 020 7608 5128
Direct e-mail: ben.roskrow@hbmedia.co.uk
Other contacts: Editor

Founded:
1955

Organisation type and purpose:
National organisation, trade association (membership is by subscription), publishing house.

Subject coverage:
New housing development, new homes marketing, housing economics, building products information.

Trade and statistical information:
UK data on new homes.

Non-library collection catalogue:
All or part available in-house

Library catalogue:
All or part available in-house

Printed publications:
On subscription if not member of HBF or NHBC

Publications list:
Available online

Access to staff:
Contact by letter, by telephone, by fax, by e-mail and via website
Hours: Mon to Fri, 0900 to 1700

Access to building, collection or gallery:
No access other than to staff

Access for disabled people:
Parking provided

Connections with:
House Builders Federation (HBF)
  tel: 020 7608 5199

HOUSING OMBUDSMAN SERVICE

Acronym or abbreviation: HOS

81 Aldwych, London, WC2B 4HN

Tel: 020 7421 3800
Fax: 020 7831 1942
E-mail: info@housing-ombudsman.org.uk

Website:
http://www.ihos.org.uk

Enquiries:
Other contacts: Deputy Ombudsman (for handling complaints); Casework Manager (for deposit disputes)

Founded:
1997

Organisation type and purpose:
National organisation, membership association (membership is by subscription), present number of members: 2,300.
To investigate complaints made by tenants against member landlords who are either RSLs or private landlords.

Subject coverage:
Housing, complaints handling, dispute resolution.

Printed publications:
Various publications available free of charge

Publications list:
Available online and in print

Access to staff:
Contact by letter, by telephone, by fax, by e-mail and via website
Hours: Mon to Fri, 0900 to 1700

Access to building, collection or gallery:
Prior appointment required

Access for disabled people:
Toilet facilities, lift.

HOUSMAN SOCIETY

80 New Road, Bromsgrove, Worcestershire, B60 2LA

Tel: 01527 874136
E-mail: info@housman-society.co.uk

Website:
http://www.housman-society.co.uk
Basic information, index of journals, book list.

Enquiries:
Enquiries to: Chairman
Direct tel: 01527 878586

Founded:
1974

Organisation type and purpose:
Learned society, present number of members: 280 (charity number 1001107), literary society.
Exists to promote knowledge and appreciation of the work of A. E. Housman. Also promotes the causes of literature and poetry in general. Sponsors an annual Housman lecture at the Hay Festival.

Subject coverage:
A. E. Housman and his family, his writings, poetry and life.

Museum or gallery collection, archive, or library special collection:
Books published by the society

Printed publications:
Housman Society Journal (£4)
Housman's Places (£7.99)
The Westerly Wanderer (£8.95)
Unkind to Unicorns (2nd ed, £7.50 paperback, £25 limited edition hardback)
Soldier I wish you well (9.50)
Three Bromsgrove Poets (£7.50)
The Name and Nature of Poetry (£5.00)
Westminster Abbey Testimonials (£5.00)
Inseparable Siblings (£10.00)
Order printed publications from: 80 New Road, Bromsgrove, Worcs, B60 2LA; e-mail: info@housman-society.co.uk

Publications list:
Available in print

Access to staff:
Contact by letter, by telephone, by e-mail and via website
Hours: Mon to Fri, 0900 to 1700

HOVERCRAFT CLUB OF GREAT BRITAIN

Formal name: HoverClub of Great Britain Ltd.
Acronym or abbreviation: HCGB

PO Box 328, Bolton, Lancashire, BL6 4RR

Tel: 01204 841248
E-mail: info@hovercraft.co.uk

Website:
http://www.hovercraft.co.uk
Events, membership, sales, information, bulletin board (for technical information) and certain publications downloads.
http://www.hoverclub.org.uk
Cruising and Recreation Club – related to HCGB.

Enquiries:
Enquiries to: Information Officer
Direct e-mail: gordon.taylor61@hotmail.com
Other contacts: Secretary; Archivist (for historical information)

Founded:
1966

Organisation type and purpose:
Membership association, voluntary organisation, suitable for ages: all.

Subject coverage:
Construction and use of lightweight sporting hovercraft, history of light hovercraft development, details of manufacturers past and present, personalities in hovercraft.

Information services:
See website or telephone for details.

Education services:
By request to Secretary.

Services for disabled people:
By request.

Museum or gallery collection, archive, or library special collection:
Archives include historical information on light hovercraft, history, development, club, people, manufacturers, etc.

Non-library collection catalogue:
All or part available in-house

Printed publications:
Cruising Hovercraft Construction Regulations (£4)
A Guide to Model Hovercraft (£6)
Hover Humour (£1.50)
Hovercraft – The Constructors Guide (£17)
Light Hovercraft (12 issues, £25 annually)
National Hovercraft Competition Regulations (£4)
New Racing Driver Handbook (£4)
Racing Hovercraft Construction Regulations (£4)
Order printed publications from: Publications Officer, Po Box 328, Bolton, BL6 4FP

Electronic and video publications:
Hovercraft Construction Regulations (CD-ROM £12.95, purchase direct from Information Office)
Hovercraft Video (£9.99)
Order electronic and video publications from: As above

Publications list:
Available online and in print

Access to staff:
Contact by letter, by telephone, by e-mail, in person and via website. Appointment necessary.
Hours: Mon to Sat, 0900 to 1700

Access to building, collection or gallery:
No prior appointment required
Hours: By arrangement

Also at:
Archivist, Hovercraft Club of Great Britain Limited 29 Mytton View, Clitheroe, Lancashire, BB7 5AZ; tel: 01200 426689; e-mail: gordon.taylor61@ hotmail.com

HOVERCRAFT MUSEUM TRUST

Argus Gate, Daedalus site, Chark Lane, off Broom Way, Lee-on-Solent, Gosport, Hampshire, PO13 9NY

Tel: 023 9255 2090
E-mail: enquiries@hovercraft-museum.org

Website:
http://www.hovercraft-museum.org
2,000 pages and pictures.

Enquiries:
Enquiries to: Trustee
Direct tel: 023 9260 1310 (for TV and film enquiries)
Direct e-mail: wjacobs@supanet.com

Founded:
1988

Organisation type and purpose:
Learned society (membership is by subscription), registered charity, museum, suitable for ages: all, consultancy.

Subject coverage:
Application of the air cushion principle; hovercraft applications in materials handling, civil engineering and medicine; ferries, transport, leisure, military.

Education services:
School visits at £100 per class.

Museum or gallery collection, archive, or library special collection:
Early papers and books on the hovercraft principle, papers and proceedings, videos, photographs, films and slides
SRNI log book
2 Cross-Channel SRN4 Hovercraft
Many early historic craft – last of types
Last SRNS and many pioneer vehicles
A collection of 60 hovercraft, and over 5,000 books, pictures, etc.

Non-library collection catalogue:
All or part available in-house and in print

Library catalogue:
All or part available in-house and in print

Printed publications:
Hovercraft Museum Newsletter

Electronic and video publications:
Set of 10 dvds (£15 each)

Publications list:
Available online and in print

Access to staff:
Contact by letter, by telephone, by e-mail, in person and via website. Appointment necessary. Non-members charged.
Hours: Any time
Special comments: Library access, by appointment.

Access to building, collection or gallery:
Prior appointment required
Hours: By appointment only or on open /show days

Access for disabled people:
Parking provided, level entry, toilet facilities

HOVERCRAFT SEARCH AND RESCUE UK

Acronym or abbreviation: HSR-UK

2 Park Court, Pyrford Road, West Byfleet, Surrey, KT14 6SD

Tel: 01932 340492
E-mail: info@hsr-uk.org

Website:
http://www.hsr-uk.org

Founded:
1997

Organisation type and purpose:
Registered charity (charity number 1061801). Specialist search and rescue services.

Access to staff:
Contact by letter, by telephone and by e-mail
Hours: Mon to Fri, 0900 to 1700

HOWARD LEAGUE FOR PENAL REFORM

Formal name: The Howard League for Penal Reform

1 Ardleigh Road, London, N1 4HS

Tel: 020 7249 7373
Fax: 020 7249 7788
E-mail: info@howardleague.org

Website:
http://www.howardleague.org

Enquiries:
Enquiries to: Director

Organisation type and purpose:
Voluntary organisation, registered charity (charity number 251926).
To promote penal reform by evidence to government committees, working parties, public education and campaigning.

Subject coverage:
Criminal justice, prison reform, penal history and alternatives to prison.

Library catalogue:
All or part available online

Printed publications:
Annual Report
The Howard newspaper (ISSN 1753–7134)
The Howard Journal of Criminal Justice (quarterly)
A number of Howard League Reports and books on the subject of criminal justice (full list available on the website: http:// www.howardleague.org) including a number of publications available to download

Electronic and video publications:
Video: Wake Up, Slop Out, Banged Away Again

Publications list:
Available online

Access to staff:
Contact by telephone. Appointment necessary.
Hours: Mon to Fri, 0900 to 1700

HOWELL HARRIS MUSEUM

Coleg Trefeca, Brecon, Powys, LD3 0PP

Tel: 01874 711423
Fax: 01874 712212
E-mail: colegtrefeca@ebcpcw.org.uk

Website:
http://www.trefeca.org.uk/
Historical and general outline of work of the college.
http://www.ebcpcw.org.uk
General information regarding Presbytarian Church of Wales including Coleg Trefeca.

Enquiries:
Enquiries to: Manager

Founded:
1752

Organisation type and purpose:
Registered charity (charity number 258456), museum, historic building, house or site, suitable for ages: 8+.
Christian training, retreat and conference centre and museum.

Subject coverage:
The Welsh Methodist revival by means of an audiovisual presentation. Artefacts include the Trefeca 'Family' period. Also features contacts with English Methodists such as Wesley, Whitefield and the Countess of Huntingdon.
Library on Welsh Methodist history and related subjects, in English and Welsh, historic Grade II listed building (1752 onwards), extensive training, retreat and conference programme.

Information services:
Library available for reference (for conditions see Access above)

Special visitor services:
Guided tours, materials and/or activities for children.

Education services:
Resources for Key Stages 1 and 2, 3, 4 and Further or Higher Education.

Services for disabled people:
For the hearing impaired; displays and/or information at wheelchair height.

Museum or gallery collection, archive, or library special collection:
Electrifying Machine. 1763
Howell Harris Preaching Chair/Pulpit. Field Pulpit. ca. 1741
Joseph Harris' Telescope (recorded the transit of Venus over sun – experiment presented to Royal Society) 1761
Pulpit from the Countess of Huntingdon's College, Trefeca
Turrett clock and bell. Rose drums of Yew. 1754 added to house, restored by Barometer Shop, Leominster, 1999
Swords and guns. Brecknock Militia ('Seven Year's War', 1756)
Books published by Treveka Press 1756–1800

Non-library collection catalogue:
All or part available in-house

Library catalogue:
All or part available in-house

Printed publications:
There was a man sent . . . A short history of Howell Harris and the Methodist revival (£1.25)
Treveka 1714–1964 (Davies G, £1.75)

continued overleaf

Access to staff:
Contact by letter, by telephone, by fax and by e-mail. Appointment necessary.
Hours: Daily, 0900 to 1600

Access to building, collection or gallery:
Prior appointment required
Hours: Daily, 0900 to 1600
Special comments: Other times strictly by appointment only.
Dec to Feb: closed Sat, Sun.
Closed Good Friday to Easter Tuesday and Christmas.

Access for disabled people:
Parking provided, ramped entry, toilet facilities
Special comments: Access to museum area by chair lift.
Access to historic house involves one step.

Parent body:
Presbyterian Church of Wales (PCW EBC)
Tabernacle Chapel, 81 Merthyr Road, Whitchurch, Cardiff, CF14 1DD; tel: 029 2062 7465; fax: 029 2061 6188; e-mail: swyddfa.office@ebcpcw.org.uk; website: http://www.ebcpcw.org.uk

HPI LIMITED

Formal name: Hire Purchase Information Limited

Dolphin House, New Street, Salisbury, Wiltshire, SP1 2PH

Tel: 01722 422422, Consumer Service; 412888, Trade Service
Fax: 01722 412746

Website:
http://www.hpi.co.uk
Car fraud detection database.

Enquiries:
Enquiries to: Director
Direct tel: 01722 413434

Founded:
1938

Organisation type and purpose:
Service industry.
Information provider on high value mobile assets.
Business to business and consumer services.
Vehicle identity checks, written-off vehicle register, outstanding finance register and other information on used vehicles.

Subject coverage:
Information on used vehicles for motor trade, motor auctions, finance and insurance companies by subscription.
Available to consumers by credit card, Switch etc.

Printed publications:
Press material available through Harrison Sadler
Order printed publications from: Harrison Sadler
1 Bridgeman Road, Teddington, TW11 9AJ, tel: 01481 9779132

Access to staff:
Contact by telephone, by fax and by e-mail
Hours: Mon to Sat, 0800 to 2000; Sun, 1000 to 1700
Special comments: On-line information service available 24 hours.

Access for disabled people:
Access to all public areas, toilet facilities

Associate member of:
Finance and Leasing Association (FLA)
Retail Motor Industry Federation (RMIF)

HUDDERSFIELD AND DISTRICT FAMILY HISTORY SOCIETY

Acronym or abbreviation: H&D FHS

'The Root Cellar', 15 Huddersfield Road, Meltham, Holmfirth, HD9 4NJ

Tel: 01484 859229
E-mail: secretary@hdfhs.org.uk

Website:
http://www.hdfhs.org.uk

Enquiries:
Enquiries to: Research Officer
Direct e-mail: research@hdfhs.org.uk

Founded:
1987

Organisation type and purpose:
Membership association (membership is by subscription), present number of members: 1100, registered charity (charity number 702199).
Research into family history.

Subject coverage:
Family history in the metropolitan District of Kirklees including Batley, Colne Valley, Denby Dale, Dewsbury, Huddersfield, Holme Valley, Kirkburton, Meltham, Mirfield and Spen Valley.

Museum or gallery collection, archive, or library special collection:
Reference Library (borrowing facilities for UK members)
Lancashire 1861–1901
Yorkshire 1861–1901
Lincolnshire 1841–1901
Cheshire 1841–1901
Durham 1851–1901
1851 Census – Kirklees only
1851 for Norfolk, Devon, Warwickshire (fiche)
1881 Census England and Wales (microfiche)
1881 Census (CD-ROM)
IGI UK (microfiche)
National Probate Calendars – England and Wales 1858 to 1943 (fiche)
Soldiers Died in WWI (CD-ROM)

Printed publications:
1841 census indices for whole area covered
1851 census indices for whole area covered
Monumental Inscriptions (3 graveyards)
National Burial Indexes 1813–56 are being published in 2000
Parish Register transcriptions (16 parishes, mostly baptisms)
Order printed publications from: Librarian, Huddersfield and District Family History Society, Root Cellar, 15 Huddersfield Road, Meltham, Holmfirth, West Yorkshire, HD9 4NJ

Publications list:
Available online and in print

Access to staff:
Contact by letter, by telephone and by e-mail
Hours: Mon to Fri, 0900 to 1700

Access to building, collection or gallery:
No prior appointment required
Special comments: Tues, 1400 to 1630; Wed, 1000 to 1230 and 1400 to 1630; Thu, 1400 to 1630 and 1930 to 2200

HUDDERSFIELD CENTRAL LIBRARY

Princess Alexandra Walk, Huddersfield, West Yorkshire, HD1 2SU

Tel: 01484 221967
Fax: 01484 221974
E-mail: hudlib.reflib@kirklees.gov.uk

Website:
http://www.kirklees.gov.uk/libraries

Enquiries:
Enquiries to: Senior Reference and Information Services Librarian

Organisation type and purpose:
Local government body, public library.

Subject coverage:
Local history; modern literature in the languages of India, Pakistan and Bangladesh.

Museum or gallery collection, archive, or library special collection:
British Standards, newspaper archives, wide range of hard copy and online reference sources
Family, local authority and other archives

Non-library collection catalogue:
All or part available online and in-house

Library catalogue:
All or part available in-house

Access to staff:
Contact by letter, by telephone, by fax, by e-mail and in person

Parent body:
Kirklees Metropolitan Council

HUDSON LIBRARY

Cathedral & Abbey Church of St Alban, Sumpter Yard, St Albans, Hertfordshire, AL1 1BY

Tel: 01727 830576
Fax: 01727 850944

Enquiries:
Enquiries to: Librarian

Organisation type and purpose:
Registered charity (charity number 280566).

Subject coverage:
Comparative religion, Bible, history of Christianity, theology, philosophy, psychology, sociology, some history and literature, plus local history of Hertfordshire and Bedfordshire, particularly of St Albans City and Abbey.

Museum or gallery collection, archive, or library special collection:
Beardsmore Collection (History of Hertfordshire in book, pamphlet and ephemera)

Library catalogue:
All or part available in-house

Access to staff:
Contact by letter, by telephone and in person
Hours: Mon to Fri, 0900 to 1700

Located in:
St Alban's Abbey Chapter House

Supported by:
Diocese of St Albans and the Cathedral Council

HUGH BAIRD COLLEGE LIBRARY

Balliol Road, Bootle, Merseyside, L20 7EW

Tel: 0151 353 4409
Fax: 0151 353 4409

Website:
http://www.hughbaird.ac.uk/llc/default.asp
Details of library and learning centre service.

Enquiries:
Enquiries to: Learning Resources Manager
Direct tel: 0151 353 4455

Organisation type and purpose:
Suitable for ages: 16+.

Subject coverage:
Art, design and display; hairdressing and beauty therapy; floristry; construction; electrical engineering; business and secretarial studies; education; health and social care; child care; pre-uniform; visual merchandising; GCSE subjects, NVQs, AS, A2, motor vehicle engineering, foundation degrees, travel and tourism, visual merchandising BA (top up).

Library catalogue:
All or part available online and in-house

Access to staff:
Contact by letter, by telephone and via website.
Appointment necessary.
Hours: Mon to Thu, 0845 to 1900; Fri, 0845 to 1600
Vacation Times, contact Library direct, tel: 0151 353 4409
Special comments: Reference library only. Lending facilities to college staff and students enrolled at the College.

Access to building, collection or gallery:
ID card or visitor's pass required

HUGUENOT LIBRARY

UCL, Gower Street, London, WC1E 6BT

Tel: 020 7679 5199
E-mail: library@huguenotsociety.org.uk

Website:
http://www.huguenotsociety.org.uk/library

Enquiries:
Enquiries to: Librarian

Founded:
1885

Organisation type and purpose:
Learned society (membership is by subscription), present number of members: 1,500, registered charity.

Subject coverage:
Huguenot history, general, ecclesiastical, economic, social, art and genealogy.

Museum or gallery collection, archive, or library special collection:
Archives of the French Protestant Hospital and other manuscript material
Huguenot Pedigrees
Library of the French Hospital (La Providence)
Royal Bounty Archives

Library catalogue:
All or part available online and in print

Printed publications:
Huguenot Families (first edn, 1999)
Newsletter
Proceedings of the Huguenot Society of Great Britain and Ireland
Quarto Series of the Huguenot Society of Great Britain and Ireland

Microform publications:
French Protestant Hospital Archives
Quarto series 139
Royal Bounty Archives

Electronic and video publications:
Huguenot Familes (vols 115)
Quarto Series (vols 153)
Order electronic and video publications from: See website for details.

Publications list:
Available online and in print

Access to staff:
Contact by letter, by telephone and by e-mail. Appointment necessary. Non-members charged.
Hours: Tue and Wed, 1000 to 1700

Access to building, collection or gallery:
Hours: Tue and Wed, 1000 to 1700
Special comments: Fee of £10 per day, except for Fellows of the Huguenot Society, undergraduates, or members of UCL.

Access for disabled people:
Hours: Access during opening hours

Administered by:
Huguenot Society of Great Britain and Ireland

Also at:
French Protestant Hospital
Rochester, Kent

HULL & HUMBER CHAMBER OF COMMERCE AND INDUSTRY

34–38 Beverley Rd, Hull, HU3 1YE

Tel: 01482 324976
Fax: 01482 213962
E-mail: info@hull-humber-chamber.co.uk

Website:
http://www.hull-humber-chamber.co.uk
News regarding all the Chamber business support activities.

Enquiries:
Enquiries to: Membership and Business Manager
Direct e-mail: b.massie@hull-humber-chamber.co.uk

Founded:
1837

Organisation type and purpose:
Business support organisation, membership association (membership is by subscription), service industry, training organisation.

Subject coverage:
Export requirements, business information, economic surveys, training seminars, networking events, marketing.

Printed publications:
Business Intelligence Members' magazine
Members' Annual Directory

Access to staff:
Contact by letter, by telephone, by fax, by e-mail, in person and via website
Hours: 0830 to 1700

Also at:
Hull & Humber Chamber of Commerce
Dock Offices, Cleethorpes Road, Grimsby, DN31 3LL; tel: 01472 342981; fax: 01472 349524; e-mail: a.tate@hull-humber-chamber.co.uk; website: http://www.hull-humber-chamber.co.uk

HULL AND HUMBER CHAMBER OF COMMERCE, INDUSTRY AND SHIPPING

34–38 Beverley Road, Hull, East Yorkshire, HU3 1YE

Tel: 01482 324976
Fax: 01482 213962
E-mail: info@hull-humber-chamber.co.uk

Enquiries:
Enquiries to: Information Officer

Founded:
1837

Organisation type and purpose:
Trade association, service industry.

Subject coverage:
Exports, including export documentation.

Printed publications:
Business Intelligence
Humber company directory
Information pack
Quarterly Economic Review

Electronic and video publications:
Who supplies what in EC countries

Access to staff:
Contact by letter, by telephone and by fax.
Appointment necessary.
Hours: Mon to Fri, 0900 to 1700

HULL CITY ARCHIVES

Hull History Centre, Worship Street, Kingston upon Hull, East Yorkshire, HU2 8BG

Tel: 01482 317500
E-mail: hullhistorycentre@hullcc.gov.uk

Website:
http://www.hullhistorycentre.org.uk
http://www.a2a.org.uk
Archive database

Enquiries:
Enquiries to: Archivist

Founded:
1968

Organisation type and purpose:
Local government body.
Hull City Archives collects, preserves and makes available records of Kingston upon Hull City Council and its predecessor bodies back to 1299, as well as collections of records relating to local businesses, societies, charities and families.

Subject coverage:
All aspects of the City of Hull from medieval times to the present day. The holdings are especially strong for the 16th to 17th centuries local government; the built environment and infrastructure (architecture and engineering); the administration of justice in the 19th and 20th centuries; the fishing industry in Hull. Important collections are held relating to maritime history of the Humber Region.

Museum or gallery collection, archive, or library special collection:
Hellyer Bros. Trawler Owners c.1890 to 1975
Hull and Goole Port Sanitary Authority
Thomas Hamling and Co, Trawler Owners c.1890 to 1980
Pease family of Hull and Hesslewood archives C17C20
Borough of Kingston upon Hull 1299 to 1835, records of the Newlands Homes 18212001
Archives:
Archives of the City Council and its predecessors, 1299 to date; local courts 17th to 20th centuries, charities 13th to 19th centuries, churches 19th and 20th centuries, business 19th and 20th centuries, families 18th to 20th centuries
City of Kingston upon Hull 1835 to present

Non-library collection catalogue:
All or part available online and in-house

Library catalogue:
All or part available in-house

Printed publications:
A variety of leaflets describing topics and sources (free)
Guide to the Kingston upon Hull Record Office: Part I Records of Local Authorities whose areas or functions were taken over by the former County Borough of Kingston upon Hull (G W Oxley)

Publications list:
Available online and in print

Access to staff:
Contact by letter, by telephone, by fax, by e-mail, in person and via website. Appointment necessary.
Hours: Tue to Thu, 0900 to 1645; Fri 0900 to 1600
Special comments: Appointments are essential, closure can happen without notice.

Access to building, collection or gallery:
Tue to Thu, 0930 to 1645

Access for disabled people:
By appointment

Parent body:
Kingston upon Hull City Council
The Guildhall, Alfred Gelder Street, Kingston upon Hull, HU1 2AA; tel: 01482 300300

HULL LIBRARIES

Reference and Information Library, Central Library, Albion Street, Hull, East Yorkshire, HU1 3TF

Tel: 01482 223344
Fax: 01482 616858
E-mail: reference.library@hullcc.gov.uk

Website:
http://www.hullcc.gov.uk
http://prismcollect.hullcc.gov.uk
Online library catalogue.

Enquiries:
Enquiries to: Specialist Librarian

Founded:
1901

Organisation type and purpose:
Local government body, public library.

Subject coverage:
In Reference Library: general coverage; family history (national resources).

continued overleaf

In Hull History Centre: the study of Hull and the surrounding area – its history, geology, geography, archaeology and flora and fauna; family history (local resources).

Museum or gallery collection, archive, or library special collection:
In Reference Library: British Standards Online, BvD MINT Company and market research, Lloyd's Register of Ships 1764 to date (with gaps), Napoleon, books published 1741–1759
In Hull History Centre: Andrew Marvell (1621–1678); Deposited records of Forster and Andrews, organ builders of Hull, 1843–1956; Hull City Health Department photographs 1890s to 1930s; whales and whaling; William Wilberforce and slavery; Winifred Holtby (1898–1935) correspondence, cuttings, photographs, publications, etc.; GRO indexes on microfiche 1837 onwards.

Library catalogue:
All or part available online

Access to staff:
Contact by letter, by telephone, by fax, by e-mail, in person and via website
Hours: Mon to Thu, 0930 to 2000; Fri, 0930 to 1730; Sat, 0900 to 1630

Access for disabled people:
Ramped entry, toilet facilities, lift
Special comments: Limited access to Local Studies Library at present.

HULL LOCAL STUDIES LIBRARY

Formal name: Hull History Centre

Hull History Centre, Worship Street, Hull, HU2 8BG

Tel: 01482 317500
E-mail: david.smith@hullcc.gov.uk

Website:
http://www.hullhistorycentre.org.uk

Enquiries:
Enquiries to: Senior Local Studies Librarian

Founded:
1960

Organisation type and purpose:
Local government body, joint local studies library and archive.

Subject coverage:
Family history, the study of Kingston upon Hull and the surrounding area – its history, people, geology, geography, archaeology, flora and fauna.

Museum or gallery collection, archive, or library special collection:
Kingston upon Hull Local Studies Library special collections include:
Amy Johnson correspondence
Andrew Marvell (1621–78)
Deposited records of Forster and Andrews, organ builders of Hull, 1843–1956
Hull City Health Department photographs, 1890s to 1930s
Whales and whaling
William Wilberforce and slavery
Winifred Holtby (1898–1935) correspondence, cuttings, photographs, publications, etc.

Non-library collection catalogue:
All or part available online and in-house

Library catalogue:
All or part available online and in-house

Printed publications:
Hull Through the Ages: The development of Hull through maps and plans (on CDR, also includes two trade directories, a history of Hull and film footage of Amy Johnson, £15.95)
The Centenary Book of Hull (Highgate Publications (Beverley) Ltd, in conjunction with Kingston upon Hull City Libraries, 1997, £12.95, ISBN 09489 29979)

Forgotten Hull: A selection of photographs taken from the Hull Corporation Health Department Collection 1890s–1930s (G. Wilkinson and G. Watkins, Kingston Press, 1999, ISBN 1902039009, out of print)

Access to staff:
Contact by letter, by telephone, by fax, by e-mail, in person and via website

Access to building, collection or gallery:
Hours: Mon and Wed, 0930 to 1945; Tue, Thu and Fri, 0930 to 1730; Sat, 0900 to 1630

Access for disabled people:
Full disabled access, all facilities on ground floor; toilet facilities

Links with:
Hull City Archives
Worship Street, Hull, HU2 8BG; tel: 01482 317500; website: http://www.hullhistorycentre.org.uk
University of Hull Archives
Worship Street, Hull, HU2 8BG; tel: 01482 317500; website: http://www.hullhistorycentre.org.uk

HULTON ARCHIVE

Unique House, 21–31 Woodfield Road, London, W9 2BA

Tel: 020 7266 2662
Fax: 020 7266 3154
E-mail: info@getty-images.com

Website:
http://www.hultonarchive.com
Picture search engine, e-commerce enabled.
http://www.getty-images.com
Library history, agencies, electronic catalogue, CD-ROM data.

Enquiries:
Enquiries to: Sales Manager
Other contacts: Picture enquiries tel no: 0171 266 2662, fax: 0171 266 3154

Founded:
1947

Organisation type and purpose:
International organisation.
Commercial picture lending library.
Sale of reproduction rights for publishing, TV, and advertising, editorial, web usage, sale of prints (photographs, framed or unframed).

Subject coverage:
Over 18 million images covering all subjects from pre-history to 1980s; especially strong on social history, royalty, performing arts, sport, fashion, transport. Engravings, woodcuts, maps, etchings, cartoons etc large colour section.

Museum or gallery collection, archive, or library special collection:
Baron Collection (ballet)
Sasha Collection (theatre)
Keystone Collection
Topical Press Collection (general)
Picture Post Collection (general)
Studo Lisa Collection (royalty)
Evening Standard Collection (general)
Ernst Haas Collection
Slim Aarons Collection (personalities)
Fox Photos (general)
Central Press (general)
Weegee Collection (US crime)
Archive Photographs (general and US)

Non-library collection catalogue:
All or part available online

Printed publications:
HPC press releases
Hulton Catalogues
Seven Ages of Man (Hulton Getty catalogue)
Many books available through book sellers

Access to staff:
Contact by letter, by telephone, by fax, by e-mail and via website. Appointment necessary.
Hours: Mon to Fri, 0915 to 1800

Special comments: Fees chargeable according to usage.

Access to building, collection or gallery:
Prior appointment required
Hours: Mon to Fri, 0930 to 1730

Affiliated to:
British Association of Picture Libraries

Part of:
Getty Images
101 Bayham Street, London, NW1 0FG; tel: 020 7544 3333; fax: 020 7544 3334; e-mail: info@getty-images.com

HUMAN RIGHTS

Acronym or abbreviation: HR

Mariners Hard, High Street, Cley-next-the-Sea, Holt, Norfolk, NR25 7RX

Tel: 01263 740990
Fax: 01263 740990
E-mail: human-rights-society@ukgateway.net

Enquiries:
Enquiries to: Executive Secretary

Founded:
1971

Organisation type and purpose:
Voluntary organisation, registered charity (charity number 262328).

Subject coverage:
Alternatives to euthanasia – i.e. hospice and home care services, relief of pain in terminal illness and other help.

Printed publications:
Newsletter (Human Rights Society)
Pushing the Passing (Human Rights Society)
Reports and leaflets include:
Human Value (Human Rights Society)
The Relief of Pain (Human Rights)
No Right to Play God (Human Rights Society)
Understanding Euthanasia (Human Rights Society)

Electronic and video publications:
A Matter of Death and Life – The Future? (educational video with tutor's notes for purchase direct, Human Rights)

Publications list:
Available in print

Access to staff:
Contact by letter, by telephone, by fax and by e-mail
Hours: Variable hours

Membership body:
Human Rights Society (HRS)
at the same address

HUMANE RESEARCH TRUST

29 Bramhall Lane South, Bramhall, Stockport, SK7 2DN

Tel: 0161 439 8041
Fax: 0161 439 3713
E-mail: info@humaneresearch.org.uk

Website:
http://www.humaneresearch.org.uk
Aims, current and past research, news and events, gift catalogue.

Founded:
late 1950s

Carries out the functions of the former:
Lawson Tait Trust

Organisation type and purpose:
A registered charity (number 267779) encouraging and supporting new medical research that does not include the use of animals, with the objectives of advancing the diagnosis and treatment of disease in humans.

Subject coverage:
The Trust focuses upon human models for human diseases, to the permanent benefit of both people and animals.

Access to staff:
Contact by letter, by telephone, by fax and by e-mail

HUMANE SLAUGHTER ASSOCIATION

Formal name: Humane Slaughter Association and Council of Justice to Animals
Acronym or abbreviation: HSA

The Old School, Brewhouse Hill, Wheathampstead, Hertfordshire, AL4 8AN

Tel: 01582 831919
Fax: 01582 831414
E-mail: info@hsa.org.uk

Website:
http://www.hsa.org.uk

Enquiries:
Enquiries to: Chief Executive & Scientific Director
Other contacts: Technical Director (for technical matters)

Founded:
1911

Organisation type and purpose:
Membership association (membership is by subscription), present number of members: 650, registered charity (charity number 209563), suitable for ages: adults, training organisation, research organisation.
Promotion of humane methods of slaughter and the introduction of reforms in livestock markets (including transport facilities).

Subject coverage:
Welfare of livestock (including birds) destined for slaughter. Training of vets, farmers and slaughtermen in slaughter techniques. Improvements in market facilities. Improvements in transport facilities for livestock. Training of hauliers, stockmen, market staff.

Printed publications:
Fact Sheets
Annual Newsletter
Annual Report
Technical Booklets

Electronic and video publications:
Instructional videos and CD-ROMs: educational on humane slaughter, livestock in transit, handling in markets

Publications list:
Available online and in print

Access to staff:
Contact by letter, by telephone, by fax, by e-mail and via website. Appointment necessary.
Hours: Mon to Fri, 0900 to 1600

Access to building, collection or gallery:
Prior appointment required
Hours: Mon to Fri, 0900 to 1600

HUMBER AND WOLDS RURAL COMMUNITY COUNCIL

Acronym or abbreviation: HWRCC

14 Market Place, Howden, East Yorkshire, DN14 7BJ

Tel: 01430 430904
Fax: 01430 432037
E-mail: info@hwrcc.org.uk

Website:
http://www.hwrcc.org.uk

Enquiries:
Enquiries to: Chief Executive

Founded:
1976

Organisation type and purpose:
Membership association (membership is by qualification), present number of members: approx. 1000, registered charity (charity number 505489), and company limited by guarantee (number 4606085). Administers grants and fosters community development.

Subject coverage:
Rural issues; parish and town council issues; community buildings (eg village halls).

Printed publications:
Humbrella (free)

Access to staff:
Contact by letter, by telephone, by fax and by e-mail. Appointment necessary.
Hours: Mon to Thu, 0900 to 1700; Fri, 0900 to 1630
Special comments: No disabled access but can arrange to meet visitors elsewhere.

HUMBER REGISTER

175 York Road, Broadstone, Dorset, BH18 8ES

Tel: 01202 695937
E-mail: thearmans@googlemail.com

Website:
http://www.humberregister.org.uk

Enquiries:
Enquiries to: Registrar

Founded:
1951

Organisation type and purpose:
Membership association (membership is by subscription), present number of members: 300.

Subject coverage:
All Humber models from 1896 to 1930 plus the inlet over exhaust (i.o.e.) engined cars from 1931 and 1932.

Museum or gallery collection, archive, or library special collection:
Large library, including all known statistical information

Printed publications:
Bulletin (6 times a year, free to members)

Access to staff:
Contact by letter, by telephone and by e-mail
Hours: Any reasonable time

HUNGARIAN CULTURAL CENTRE

Acronym or abbreviation: HCC

10 Maiden Lane, Covent Garden, London, WC2E 7NA

Tel: 020 7240 8448
Fax: 020 7240 4847
E-mail: culture@hungary.org.uk

Website:
http://www.hungary.org.uk

Founded:
1999

Organisation type and purpose:
Associated with Hungary's Ministry of Culture.

Subject coverage:
Hungarian culture and civilisation.

Special visitor services:
Library (open Tue and Thu 1100 to 1900).

HUNGARIAN EMBASSY

35 Eaton Place, London, SW1X 8BY

Tel: 020 7235 5218
Fax: 020 7823 1348
E-mail: office.lon@kum.hu

Website:
http://www.huemblon.org.uk

General information on Hungary, visa and consular information, Hungarian Trade Commission, Hungarian Tourist Office, Hungary, NATO and the EU

Enquiries:
Enquiries to: Information Officer

Organisation type and purpose:
International organisation.

Printed publications:
Fact sheets on Hungary
Hungarian Quarterly
Tourist Brochures

Access to staff:
Contact by letter, by telephone, by fax and via website
Hours: Mon to Thu, 0900 to 1700; Fri, 0900 to 1400
Special comments: Consular Department is open to personal callers Mon to Fri, 0930 to 1200 only.

Other office:
The Hungarian Tourist Office
46 Eaton Place, London, SW1X 8AL; tel: 020 7823 1032; fax: 020 7823 1459
The Hungarian Trade Commission
46 Eaton Place, London, SW1X 8AL; tel: 020 7235 8767; fax: 020 7235 4319

HUNTINGDON LIFE SCIENCES

Acronym or abbreviation: HLS

Woolley Road, Alconbury, Huntingdon, Cambridgeshire, PE28 4HS

Tel: 01480 892000
Fax: 01480 892978

Website:
http://www.huntingdon.com

Enquiries:
Enquiries to: Information Officer

Organisation type and purpose:
International organisation, research organisation, consultancy.

Subject coverage:
Toxicology; environmental science; pathology; pharmacology; microbiology; cell biology; metabolic studies; analytical chemistry; veterinary science.

Library catalogue:
All or part available in-house

Access to staff:
Contact by letter, by telephone and by fax
Hours: Mon to Fri, 0900 to 1700

Access to building, collection or gallery:
No access other than to staff

HUNTINGDONSHIRE ARCHIVES

Acronym or abbreviation: HA

Grammar School Walk, Huntingdon, Cambridgeshire, PE29 3LF

Tel: 01480 375842
E-mail: hunts.archives@cambridgeshire.gov.uk

Website:
http://www.cambridgeshire.gov.uk/archives

Enquiries:
Enquiries to: Senior Archivist

Founded:
1948

Formerly called:
Huntingdonshire County Record Office (year of change 1968); County Record Office, Huntingdon (year of change 2008)

Organisation type and purpose:
Local government body.
Record office.

continued overleaf

Subject coverage:
Local history of Huntingdonshire and to a lesser degree of the Soke of Peterborough, including genealogy and topography.

Museum or gallery collection, archive, or library special collection:
Records of the former Huntingdonshire and Soke of Peterborough County Councils. Deposited official and unofficial records relating to Huntingdonshire, including archdeaconry, parish and borough records and family and estate collections, including those of the Dukes of Manchester of Kimbolton and of the Earls of Sandwich of Hinchingbrooke, c.1200 to 20th century

Non-library collection catalogue:
All or part available online and in-house

Library catalogue:
All or part available online and in-house

Printed publications:
County Archivist's Annual Reports 1974–95
List of inclosure awards and plans (free)
Maps in the County Record Office Huntingdon (£1 plus p&p)
Summary of Sources for Genealogists (free)

Publications list:
Available in print

Access to staff:
Contact by letter, by telephone, by fax, by e-mail and in person

Access to building, collection or gallery:
Hours: Tue, Wed and Thu, 0900 to 1245 and 1345 to 1715; Fri, 0900 to 1245 and 1345 to 1615; second Sat in each month, 0900 to 1200 by appointment
Special comments: CARN ticket required

Access for disabled people:
Stairlift to the first floor public search room

Parent body:
Cambridgeshire County Council, Cambridgeshire Archives and Local Studies
  Shire Hall, Castle Hill, Cambridge; tel: 01223 718131

HUNTINGDONSHIRE LOCAL HISTORY SOCIETY

3 The Lanes, Houghton, Huntingdon, Cambridgeshire, PE28 2BW

Tel: 01480 463007
E-mail: dam.coz@virgin.net

Enquiries:
Enquiries to: Honorary Secretary

Founded:
1957

Organisation type and purpose:
Voluntary organisation, registered charity (charity number 290741).
Local history society.

Subject coverage:
Local history of Huntingdonshire, vernacular architecture.

Printed publications:
Records of Huntingdonshire (annually £3.50, free to members)
Order printed publications from: Hon. Editor, Dr Philip Saunders
Deputy Country Archivist, Cambs. County Record Office, Shire hall, Castle Hill, Cambridge, CB31 0PA, e-mail: philip.saunders@cambridgeshire.gov.uk

Access to staff:
Contact by letter, by telephone and in person
Hours: Mon to Fri, 0900 to 1700, and evenings

Affiliated to:
Cambridge Local History Association

Member of:
British Association for Local History

HUNTINGDONSHIRE REGIONAL COLLEGE

California Road, Huntingdon, Cambridgeshire, PE29 1BL

Tel: 01480 379100
Fax: 01480 379127
E-mail: college@huntingdon.ac.uk

Enquiries:
Enquiries to: Librarian

Organisation type and purpose:
Suitable for ages: 16+.
Further education college.

Subject coverage:
Art, business studies, engineering, photography, general education, hairdressing, beauty therapy, care, IT.

Library catalogue:
All or part available in-house

Access to staff:
Contact by letter and by telephone
Hours: Mon to Fri, 0900 to 1700

Access to building, collection or gallery:
Prior appointment required

HUNTINGTON'S DISEASE ASSOCIATION

Acronym or abbreviation: HDA

Neurosupport Centre, Norton Street, Liverpool, L3 8LR

Tel: 0151 298 3298
Fax: 0151 298 9440
E-mail: info@hda.org.uk

Website:
http://www.hda.org.uk

Enquiries:
Other contacts: 24 regional care advisers around the country

Founded:
1974

Organisation type and purpose:
Membership association, present number of members: 6,000, voluntary organisation, registered charity (charity number 296453).
To provide care, advice, support and education to anyone who is affected by Huntington's Disease.

Subject coverage:
Information for families, carers, and health and social service professionals, to advise and support people with Huntington's Disease.

Printed publications:
Factsheets for sufferers, carers and professionals
All about the Huntington's Disease Association
Huntington's Disease in the Family
Living with Juvenile Huntington's Disease
Physician's Guide to the Management of Huntington's Disease

Electronic and video publications:
Video

Publications list:
Available online and in print

Access to staff:
Contact by letter, by telephone, by fax and by e-mail
Hours: Mon to Fri, 0900 to 1700

HURLINGHAM POLO ASSOCIATION, THE

Acronym or abbreviation: HPA

Manor Farm, Little Coxwell, Faringdon, Oxfordshire, SN7 7LW

Tel: 01367 242828
Fax: 01367 242829
E-mail: enquiries@hpa-polo.co.uk

Website:
http://www.hpa-polo.co.uk
Order form for yearbooks, videos etc, general polo information and list of affiliated clubs.

Enquiries:
Enquiries to: Chief Executive

Founded:
1874

Organisation type and purpose:
National government body, membership association (membership is by subscription), present number of members: 2300, voluntary organisation.
Governing body of the game in the UK and the Commonwealth.

Subject coverage:
Polo.

Library catalogue:
All or part available in-house

Printed publications:
HPA Arena Yearbook (free to members)
HPA Yearbook (free to members)

Electronic and video publications:
Some videos available

Access to staff:
Contact by letter, by telephone, by fax, by e-mail and via website
Hours: Mon to Fri, 0900 to 1700

Access for disabled people:
Parking provided, ramped entry

HYMN SOCIETY OF GREAT BRITAIN AND IRELAND

Acronym or abbreviation: HSGBI

7 Paganel Road, Minehead, Somerset, TA24 5ET

Tel: 01643 703530
Fax: 01643 703530
E-mail: g.wrayford@breathemail.net

Website:
http://www.hymnsocgbi.org

Enquiries:
Enquiries to: Honorary Secretary

Founded:
1936

Organisation type and purpose:
Learned society (membership is by subscription), present number of members: 450.

Subject coverage:
Use of hymns in Christian worship; research in hymnology.

Printed publications:
Bulletin (quarterly)
Combined Index
Hymns and Tunes Indexed
Occasional papers

Access to staff:
Contact by letter, by telephone, by fax and by e-mail
Hours: Mon to Fri, 0900 to 1700

Member of:
Hymn Society in the United States and Canada
International Fellowship of Hymnology (IAH)

HYPERACTIVE CHILDREN'S SUPPORT GROUP

Acronym or abbreviation: HACSG

71 Whyke Lane, Chichester, West Sussex, PO19 7PD

Tel: 01243 539966
E-mail: hyperactive@hacsg.org.uk

Website:
http://www.hacsg.org.uk
Services provided; information on hyperactivity, diet, nutrition and additives.

Enquiries:
Enquiries to: Director

Founded:
1977

Organisation type and purpose:
Membership association, registered charity
(charity number 277643).
Parent support, research & information group.

Subject coverage:
Hyperactivity in children and young people, its
relationship to diet, nutrition, allergy and
environment; organic brain dysfunction.

Printed publications:
Booklist
ADHD, Hyperactive Children: A Guide for Parents
  (£8)
A Professional Pack containing the above
  Handbook and a selection of articles and reprints
  (£10)
Free introductory leaflets
Numerous articles and reprints for sale
Teachers' Pack containing appropriate articles and
  reprints (£6)

Publications list:
Available in print

Access to staff:
Contact by letter, by telephone, by e-mail and via
website
Hours: Mon, Thu, Fri, 1000 to 1200; Wed, 1430 to
1630

Connections with:
Autism Unravelled
British Society for Nutritional Medicine
Foresight Association for Preconceptual Care
Green Network

HYPERION RECORDS LIMITED

PO Box 25, London, SE9 1AX

Tel: 020 8318 1234
Fax: 020 8263 1230
E-mail: info@hyperion-records.co.uk

Website:
http://www.hyperion-records.co.uk
Complete catalogues, distributors, biographies and
photographs, etc.

Enquiries:
Enquiries to: Managing Director

Founded:
1980

Organisation type and purpose:
Publishing house.
Record company (classical CDs).

Subject coverage:
Recording and sale of classical music under the
Hyperion and Helios labels.

Printed publications:
Catalogue (free)

Electronic and video publications:
Over 1000 classical CDs and some cassettes

Publications list:
Available in print

Access to staff:
Contact by letter, by telephone, by fax, by e-mail
and via website
Hours: Mon to Fri, 0930 to 1730

HYPERLIPIDAEMIA EDUCATION & ATHEROSCLEROSIS RESEARCH TRUST UK

Acronym or abbreviation: HEART UK

7 North Road, Maidenhead, Berkshire, SL6 1PE

Tel: 01628 777046
Fax: 01628 628698
E-mail: ask@heartuk.org.uk

Website:
http://www.heartuk.org.uk

Enquiries:
Enquiries to: Nurse Advisor
Direct tel: 0845 450 5988
Other contacts: Dieticians

Founded:
2002

Formerly called:
Familial Hypercholestrolaemia, Familial
Hyperlipidaemia Association

Organisation type and purpose:
Membership association (membership is by
subscription, qualification), present number of
members: 1,300, voluntary organisation, registered
charity (charity number 1003904).
To help people at high risk of coronary heart
disease.

Subject coverage:
Diet, food nutrition and dietetics, lifestyle
management, heart health, dietary and body/blood
fats (lipids), origins of health and disease,
prevention of coronary heart disease, cholesterol,
familial hypercholesterolaemia, familial
hyperlipidaemias.

Printed publications:
Family Heart Digest (4 times a year, £12 a year, free
  to members)
Booklets and leaflets on the following topics and
  others for a small price:
Blood Pressure
Cholesterol
Coronary Heart Disease and Familial
  Hyperlipidaemia
Coronary Heart Disease: a Family Problem
Family Food Guide
Healthy Eating Guide
Lipid Lowering Eating Advice
Lipids and Heart Disease: a Practical Approach
Smoking

Electronic and video publications:
Factsheets were being updated in 2008 and were to
  be available in downloadable format from
  HEART UK website

Publications list:
Available online and in print

Access to staff:
Contact by letter, by telephone, by fax, by e-mail
and via website
Hours: Mon to Fri, 0930 to 1600

Access to building, collection or gallery:
No access other than to staff

I CAN

4 Dyer's Buildings, Holborn, London, EC1N 2QP

Tel: 0845 225 4071
Fax: 0845 225 4072
E-mail: ican@ican.org.uk

Website:
http://www.ican.org.uk
http://www.talkingpoint.org.uk

Enquiries:
Enquiries to: Marketing Officer
Direct e-mail: media@ican.org.uk
Other contacts: Chief Executive

Founded:
1888

Organisation type and purpose:
Registered charity (charity number 210031).
I CAN exists to help children communicate. Our
special focus is children with a communication
disability.

Subject coverage:
I CAN provides a combination of specialist
therapy and education for children with the most
severe and complex disabilities, information for
parents and training and advice for teachers and
other professionals. We also work to ensure that

the needs of these children are taken into account
in all children's policy and carry out research to
find the best ways to support these children.

**Museum or gallery collection, archive, or library
special collection:**
Archives (of 100 years)

Printed publications:
Information Pack (free)

Publications list:
Available in print

Access to staff:
Contact by letter, by telephone, by fax and by e-
mail
Hours: Mon to Fri, 0900 to 1700

Access for disabled people:
Toilet facilities

IA – THE ILEOSTOMY AND INTERNAL POUCH SUPPORT GROUP

Acronym or abbreviation: IA

Peverill House, 1–5 Mill Road, Ballyclare, BT39
9DR

Tel: 0800 018 4724
Fax: 028 9332 4606
E-mail: info@iasupport.org

Website:
http://www.iasupport.org
General information, directory of local groups.

Enquiries:
Enquiries to: National Secretary

Founded:
1956

Organisation type and purpose:
Membership association (membership is by
subscription), present number of members: 10,000,
registered charity (charity number 234472).

Subject coverage:
Ileostomy: care, mutual aid, rehabilitation,
equipment and skin care for those who have had
their colon removed.

Printed publications:
IA Journal (quarterly)
IA Journal Omnibus Edition

Publications list:
Available in print

Access to staff:
Contact by letter, by telephone, by fax, by e-mail
and via website
Hours: Mon to Fri, 0900 to 1700

Affiliated to:
International Ostomy Association, over 59
branches

IAPA

IAPA International Secretariat, Old Chambers, 93–
West Street, Farnham, Surrey, GU9 7EB

Tel: 01252 720810
Fax: 01252 720830
E-mail: admin@iapa.net

Website:
http://www.iapa.net
IAPA, regional groups, areas of expertise,
membership benefits, conferences, news.

Founded:
1979

Organisation type and purpose:
A global association of independent accountancy
and business advisory firms providing accounting,
audit, tax advisory and business consultancy
services. Comprises around 230 member firms
with offices in more than 50 countries.

continued overleaf

To support its members in providing their clients with a diverse range of professional, comprehensive and cost-effective business solutions, regardless of sector or location. IAPA does not itself provide client services.

Subject coverage:
Accounting, audit, tax advisory and business consultancy services.

Access to staff:
Contact by letter, by telephone, by fax and by e-mail

IATEFL

Formal name: International Association of Teachers of English as a Foreign Language

Darwin College, University of Kent, Canterbury, Kent, CT2 7NY

Tel: 01227 824430
Fax: 01227 824431
E-mail: generalenquiries@iatefl.org
Website:
http://www.iatefl.org

Enquiries:
Enquiries to: Executive Officer

Founded:
1967

Organisation type and purpose:
International organisation, membership association (membership is by subscription), present number of members: 4000, voluntary organisation, registered charity (charity number 1090853).

Subject coverage:
The teaching of English to those for whom it is a second language.

Publications list:
Available online and in print

Access to staff:
Contact by letter, by telephone, by fax, by e-mail and in person
Hours: Mon to Fri, 0900 to 1700

IBM UNITED KINGDOM LIMITED

Library (MP 149), Hursley Park, Winchester, Hampshire, SO21 2JN

Tel: 01962 815641
Fax: 01962 818199
E-mail: library@uk.ibm.com
Website:
http://isource.ibm.com/world/index.shtml

Enquiries:
Enquiries to: Librarian

Organisation type and purpose:
Research organisation.

Subject coverage:
Data processing; computers; programming languages; computer applications; visual display units, computer software.

Museum or gallery collection, archive, or library special collection:
IBM Manuals
IBM Technical Reports
IBM History
Computing History

Library catalogue:
All or part available in-house

Access to staff:
Contact by letter, by telephone, by fax and by e-mail
Hours: Mon to Fri, 0900 to 1700

ICAEW

Formal name: The Institute of Chartered Accountants in England and Wales

Chartered Accountants' Hall, Moorgate Place, London, EC2P 2BJ

Tel: 020 7920 8620
Fax: 020 7920 8621
E-mail: library@icaew.com
Website:
http://www.icaew.com/library
http://www.icaew.com

Enquiries:
Enquiries to: Head of Library and Information Services

Founded:
1880

Organisation type and purpose:
National organisation, professional body with international presence.

Subject coverage:
Accountancy, auditing, company law, taxation, management consultancy, financial management, financial services, information technology in accounting.

Museum or gallery collection, archive, or library special collection:
Files of comments on exposure drafts of accounting and auditing standards
Rare Books on book-keeping, 1494–1914

Trade and statistical information:
Accountancy research, technical releases, press releases available on website: http://www.icaew.com

Non-library collection catalogue:
All or part available online

Library catalogue:
All or part available online

Printed publications:
Accountancy (monthly)
Technical Releases (irregular)
Directory of ICAEW Members (annual)
Members' Handbook
Foreign Books on Book-keeping, 1494–1750: a bibliography
Historical Accounting Literature (catalogue)

Electronic and video publications:
Accountancy magazine (monthly, online via http://www.accountancymagazine.com)

Publications list:
Available online

Access to staff:
Contact by letter, by telephone, by fax, by e-mail, in person and via website. Letter of introduction required. Non-members charged.
Hours: Mon to Fri, 0830 to 1800
Special comments: Members of the public may have visiting access by providing a letter of introduction from a member of the ICAEW or by paying a daily fee.

Member organisation of:
Consultative Committee of Accountancy Bodies (CCAB)

ICC – INTERNATIONAL MARITIME BUREAU

Formal name: International Chamber of Commerce – International Maritime Bureau
Acronym or abbreviation: ICC IMB

Cinnabar Wharf, 26 Wapping High Street, London E1W 1NG

Tel: 020 7423 6960
Fax: 020 7423 6961
E-mail: imb@icc-ccs.org
Website:
http://www.icc-ccs.org
The IMB is part of Commercial Crime Services, the anti-crime arm of the ICC.

Enquiries:
Enquiries to: Director
Other contacts: Deputy Director (for piracy)

Founded:
1981

Organisation type and purpose:
International organisation
The ICC–International Maritime Bureau (IMB) is a specialised membership division of the International Chamber of Commerce, the world business organisation. It is recognised by a special resolution of the International Maritime Organisation (IMO). The IMB was set up in 1981 to act as a focal point for the international trading community in the fight against trade fraud and malpractice. Its membership comprises some of the world's leading banks, insurance, shipping and trading companies and all those that have a legitimate interest in international trade.

Subject coverage:
All types of maritime fraud and malpractice, piracy, investigations, cargo loss, document verification, loss prevention and due diligence.

Non-library collection catalogue:
All or part available in-house

Library catalogue:
All or part available in-house

Printed publications:
Commercial Crime International (monthly, £95 a year)
Various books, special reports and guides on matters relating to maritime fraud

Publications list:
Available online and in print

Access to staff:
Contact by telephone, by fax, by e-mail and via website. Appointment necessary. Non-members charged.
Hours: Mon to Fri, 0900 to 1700

Access for disabled people:
Ramped entry

ICE CREAM ALLIANCE LIMITED

Acronym or abbreviation: ICA

3 Melbourne Court, Pride Park, Derby, DE24 8LZ

Tel: 01332 203333
Fax: 01332 203420
E-mail: info@ice-cream.org
Website:
http://www.ice-cream.org
Full Ice Cream Alliance website.

Enquiries:
Enquiries to: Chief Executive Officer
Other contacts: Membership Adviser / Administrator

Founded:
1944

Organisation type and purpose:
Trade Association.

Subject coverage:
Ice cream, equipment and associated materials for manufacture and sale of the product.

Printed publications:
Ice Cream (magazine, monthly, members only, membership £144)
Code of Practice for the Manufacture of Ice Cream (£20.00 plus p&p)
Food Safety Made Easy Level 2 (members: £5.00, non-members: £8.00 plus p&p)
Guide to Safe Handling and Service of Ice Cream (£3.00 plus p&p)
Order printed publications from: Ice Cream Alliance

Publications list:
Available online and in print

Access to staff:
Contact by letter, by telephone, by fax, by e-mail and via website. Appointment necessary. Non-members charged.

Hours: Mon to Thu, 0900 to 1700; Fri, 0900 to 1600

Access to building, collection or gallery:
Appointment required

ICE ERGONOMICS LIMITED

Holywell Building, Holywell Way, Loughborough, Leicestershire, LE11 3UZ

Tel: 01509 283300
Fax: 01509 283360

Website:
http://www.ice.co.uk
Work of ICE and its sub-units.

Enquiries:
Enquiries to: Operations Director
Other contacts: Business Manager for business/financial matters.

Founded:
1970

Organisation type and purpose:
University department or institute, consultancy, research organisation.

Subject coverage:
Ergonomics in the design, development and evaluation of products, procedures, systems and environments, with application to consumer, industrial, commercial, automotive and transport areas. Special skills in occupational safety and health, accident research, and job assessment and allocation for disabled people.

Non-library collection catalogue:
All or part available in-house

Library catalogue:
All or part available in-house

Publications list:
Available in print

Access to staff:
Appointment necessary.
Hours: Mon to Fri, 0900 to 1700

Access to building, collection or gallery:
No prior appointment required

Access for disabled people:
Parking provided, level entry, access to all public areas, toilet facilities

Parent body:
Loughborough University
Ashby Road, Loughborough, Leicestershire, LE11 3TU; tel: 01509 263171

ICE HOCKEY UK

Acronym or abbreviation: IHUK

19 Heather Avenue, Rise Park, Romford, Essex, RM1 4SL

Tel: 020 8732 4505
Fax: 020 8952 9515
E-mail: ihukoffice@yahoo.co.uk

Website:
http://www.icehockeyuk.co.uk
Ice Hockey.

Enquiries:
Enquiries to: Administrator

Founded:
1936

Organisation type and purpose:
National organisation, training organisation. Governing body for ice hockey in UK and Northern Ireland.

Subject coverage:
Ice hockey.

Museum or gallery collection, archive, or library special collection:
Photographs

Access to staff:
Contact by letter, by telephone, by fax, by e-mail, in person and via website
Hours: Mon to Thu, 0900 to 1700; Fri, 0900 to 1600

Access to building, collection or gallery:
No prior appointment required

Affiliated to:
BOA
CCPR
International Ice Hockey Federation (IIHF)
Sports Council

Houses the:
English Ice Hockey Association
Northern Ireland Ice Hockey Association
Scottish Ice Hockey Association

ICON

Formal name: Institute of Conservation

3rd Floor, Downstream Building, 1 London Bridge, London, SE1 9BG

Tel: 020 7785 3805
Fax: 020 7785 3806
E-mail: admin@icon.org.uk

Website:
http://www.icon.org.uk

Enquiries:
Enquiries to: Administrator

Founded:
2005

Organisation type and purpose:
International organisation, professional body, present number of members: 3,000, registered charity (charity number 1049444).

Subject coverage:
All aspects of restoration and conservation of artistic and historic works, glass, ceramics, furniture, stone, easel paintings, wall paintings, books and paper, textiles, metals, stained glass, gilding, historical interiors, natural materials and archaeological objects.

Printed publications:
Icon News (newsletter, 6 times a year, available to members)
The Conservator (annually, available to members and to purchase one year after date of publication)
The Paper Conservator (annually, available to members and to purchase one year after date of publication)

Access to staff:
Contact by letter, by telephone, by fax and by e-mail
Hours: Mon to Fri, 0900 to 1300 (best time to call)

IDOX INFORMATION SERVICE

Acronym or abbreviation: PLANEX

Tontine House, 8 Gordon Street, Glasgow, G1 3PL

Tel: 0141 574 1920
Fax: 0141 248 9433
E-mail: iu@idoxgroup.com

Website:
http://iis.idoxgroup.com

Enquiries:
Enquiries to: Information Services Manager

Founded:
1973

Formerly called:
Planning Exchange (year of change 2002)

Organisation type and purpose:
Subscription-based service, specialising in the development and delivery of products, services and people for information management and knowledge sharing, for both public and private sector clients. Information service in the fields of economic, environmental and social development through a database of bibliographic abstracts, a telephone helpline and document supply.

Subject coverage:
Economic and business development, regeneration, local government, finance and management, education and training, community development, the environment, housing, nature conservation, rural and urban areas, social work, town and country planning, regional development, transport, leisure and tourism

Museum or gallery collection, archive, or library special collection:
All Scottish planning appeal decision letters and reports from January 1976
All Scottish local plans

Non-library collection catalogue:
All or part available online and in-house

Library catalogue:
All or part available online and in-house

Printed publications:
Scottish Planning and Environmental Law (3 times a year)
Bulletin (weekly, part of the IDOX Information Service)

Electronic and video publications:
New Towns Record (DVD)

Access to staff:
Contact by letter, by telephone, by fax, by e-mail, in person and via website. Appointment necessary. Non-members charged.
Hours: Mon to Fri, 0900 to 1700
Special comments: By appointment for members.

IEA COAL RESEARCH

The Clean Coal Centre, Gemini House, 10–18 Putney Hill, London, SW15 6AA

Tel: 020 8780 2111
Fax: 020 8780 1746
E-mail: mail@iea-coal.org.uk

Website:
http://www.iea-coal.org.uk

Enquiries:
Enquiries to: Information Services Group Manager

Founded:
1975

Organisation type and purpose:
International organisation providing information on coal

Subject coverage:
All aspects of coal production and use including coal reserves and exploration, mining, preparation, properties, processing, combustion, transport and handling, waste management, and political, legal, economic, environmental, health and safety aspects.

Library catalogue:
All or part available in-house

Printed publications:
Annual Report
Newsletter (3 times a year)
Profiles (summaries of reports)
Review and assessment reports
About 200 publications on all aspects of the Coal Industry world-wide
Order printed publications from: tel: 020 8789 0111, fax: 020 8789 0111, e-mail: sales@iea-coal.org.uk

Electronic and video publications:
CoalPower (databases of information on over 1,850 coal-fired power stations and 5,000 individual units and related subjects, in over 30 countries, non-members £5,000, members £500, which includes online access)
Coal Abstracts database (over 180,000 abstracts to coal literature, non-members £5,000, members £500pa; after one year non-members £3,000, members £300, education establishments £250 (member countries))

continued overleaf

Publications list:
Available online and in print

Access to staff:
Contact by letter, by telephone, by fax, by e-mail and via website. Appointment necessary. All charged.
Hours: Mon to Fri, 0900 to 1700

Links with:
International Energy Agency (IEA)
2 rue André-Pascal, Paris cedex 16, 75775, France

Member countries:
Austria, Canada, Germany, Italy, Japan, Poland, Republic of Korea, Spain, Sweden, United Kingdom, USA

IEEM

Formal name: Institute of Ecology and Environmental Management

45 Southgate Street, Winchester, Hampshire, SO23 9EH

Tel: 01962 868626
Fax: 01962 868625
E-mail: enquiries@ieem.net

Website:
http://www.ieem.net
Meetings; courses; conferences; membership.

Enquiries:
Enquiries to: Executive Director

Founded:
1991

Organisation type and purpose:
Professional Body

Subject coverage:
Ecology and Environmental Management.

Library catalogue:
All or part available in-house

Printed publications:
Conference Proceedings (£21)
In Practice (quarterly) (£10 each or £30 annually)
Rooting for a Career in Ecology and
    Environmental Management (free for 50p sae)
The Profession of Ecology and Ecological
    Management: what you need to know (1995, £9)
Training Workshops and Events Diary (free for sae)
Guidelines on Ecological Impact Assessment 2006
    (online only)

Publications list:
Available online and in print

Access to staff:
Contact by letter, by telephone, by fax and by e-mail
Hours: Mon to Fri, 0900 to 1700
Special comments: Members only

IEPRC

Formal name: International Electronic Publishing Research Centre Limited

PO Box 83, Leatherhead, Surrey, KT22 7AZ

Tel: 01372 373646
Fax: 01372 379732
E-mail: admin@ieprc.org

Website:
http://www.ieprc.org
Detailed information is for members only.

Enquiries:
Enquiries to: Administrator
Direct tel: 01372 278335
Other contacts: (1) Chief Executive (2) Research Manager (3) Company Secretary for (1) strategic issues (2) research and development (3) finance and administration.

Founded:
1981

Organisation type and purpose:
International organisation, membership association (membership is by subscription, qualification, election or invitation), present number of members: 70 organisations, research organisation.
Voluntary association of international multimedia publishers and related companies.

Subject coverage:
Electronic publishing.

Trade and statistical information:
Information for members only.

Electronic and video publications:
Online/website for members only

Publications list:
Available online

Access to staff:
Contact by letter, by telephone, by fax, by e-mail and via website. Access for members only.
Hours: Telephone is answered from 0800 to 2200, on 01372 278335 outside usual business hours

Access to building, collection or gallery:
No access other than to staff

IFPI

Formal name: International Federation of the Phonographic Industry

IFPI Secretariat, 10 Piccadilly, London, W1J 0DD

Tel: 020 7878 7900
Fax: 020 7878 7950
E-mail: info@ifpi.org

Website:
http://www.ifpi.org

Founded:
1933

Organisation type and purpose:
International organisation, trade association.
Represents producers of sound recordings.

Subject coverage:
Copyright in sound and video recordings, worldwide industry turnover, estimates of piracy of recordings.

Trade and statistical information:
Annual and half yearly sales statistics of the record industry.

Access to staff:
Contact by fax and by e-mail
Hours: Mon to Fri, 0900 to 1730

Access to building, collection or gallery:
Prior appointment required

Consultative status with:
WIPO

IFS SCHOOL OF FINANCE

8th Floor, Peninsular House, 36 Monument Street, London, EC3R 8LJ

Tel: 020 7444 7100
Fax: 020 7444 7109
E-mail: knowledgebank@ifslearning.ac.uk

Website:
http://www.ifslearning.ac.uk
Service for members.

Enquiries:
Enquiries to: KnowledgeBank

Founded:
1879

Organisation type and purpose:
Education. A registered charity.
To provide qualifications and lifelong career support services to those working within the financial services industry and formal education to customers.

Subject coverage:
Financial services, banking, financial education for 14–19 year olds, regulatory qualifications, accountancy, investment, economics, bank history, financial management, risk, e-commerce, financial technology, marketing in financial services, monetary and financial systems, financial services law.

Access to staff:
Contact by letter, by telephone, by fax, by e-mail and via website

IHS

Willoughby Road, Bracknell, Berkshire, RG12 8FB

Tel: 01344 328000
Fax: 01344 328008
E-mail: customer.support@ihs.com

Website:
http://uk.ihs.com
Home page and product demonstration.

Enquiries:
Enquiries to: Information Officer

Founded:
1964

Formerly called:
Technical Indexes Ltd

Organisation type and purpose:
Manufacturing industry.
Producers and distributors of information products on CD-ROM and online formats; registered to ISO 9002 by BSI Quality Assurance.

Subject coverage:
Electronic engineering; process and chemical engineering; engineering components and materials; manufacturing and materials handling; construction and civil engineering; standards for construction industry; standards in health and safety; NATO Stock Numbers; laboratory equipment; British standards; Defence standards and specifications; American industrial and military standards and specifications; Canadian, Japanese and world standards.

Printed publications:
Electronic Engineering Suppliers Guide
Engineering Design and Manufacturing Suppliers
    Guide
Process Engineering Suppliers Guide

Electronic and video publications:
Construction Product Library (CD-ROM)
Engineering Product Library (CD-ROM)
Occupational Health and Safety Information
    Service (CD-ROM and online)
Specify IT (online)
Construction Information Service (online)
British Standards (online)
E4 Data (online)

Publications list:
Available in print

Access to staff:
Contact by letter, by telephone, by e-mail and via website. Appointment necessary.
Hours: Mon to Fri, 0845 to 1645

Links with:
IHS Group – Information Handling Services (IHS Group)
    Colorado, USA

Other address:
RAPIDOC – Hard Copy Supply Division
    Willoughby Road, Bracknell; tel: 01344 861666; fax: 01344 714440; e-mail: rapidoc@techindex.co.uk

IMAGINATE

45a George Street, Edinburgh, EH2 2HT

Tel: 0131 225 8050
Fax: 0131 225 6440
E-mail: info@imaginate.org.uk

Enquiries:
Enquiries to: Chief Executive

Founded:
1989

Organisation type and purpose:
Registered charity, suitable for ages: 3 to 14.
Largest performing arts festival for 3 to 14 year
olds in the UK.

Subject coverage:
Children's Theatre.

Printed publications:
Festival Programme

Access to staff:
Contact by letter, by telephone, by fax and by e-
mail. Appointment necessary. Letter of
introduction required.
Hours: Mon to Fri, 0900 to 1700

IMERYS MINERALS LTD

Par Moor Centre, Par Moor, Par, Cornwall, PL24
2SQ

Tel: 01726 811311
Fax: 01726 811200
E-mail: adrian.mutton@imerys.com

Enquiries:
Enquiries to: Property Surveyor

Organisation type and purpose:
Company producing china clay and ball clay.

Subject coverage:
China clay and ball clay.

Trade and statistical information:
Information service provided to external solicitors
in planning searches associated with house
purchase, land development etc.

Access to staff:
Contact by letter, by telephone and by fax
Hours: Mon to Fri, 0900 to 1700

IMMIGRATION MANAGEMENT &
BUSINESS GROUP

Acronym or abbreviation: IMB Group

75 Cannon Street, London, EC4N 5BN

Tel: 020 7556 7112
Fax: 020 7556 7001
E-mail: admin@immigration.co.uk

Website:
http://www.workpermits.com
http://www.immigration.co.uk

Enquiries:
Enquiries to: General Manager

Founded:
1985

Organisation type and purpose:
Service industry, consultancy.

Subject coverage:
All categories of UK work permit, employment
approval and fast extensions and foreign passport
endorsement.

Publications list:
Available online

Access to staff:
Contact by letter, by telephone, by fax, by e-mail
and via website. Appointment necessary.
Hours: Mon to Fri, 0830 to 1800

Access for disabled people:
Parking provided, ramped entry, toilet facilities

Connections with:
japanese-immigration.com
Same address

IMP CLUB LIMITED

76 Star Lane, Folkestone, CT19 4QQ

Tel: 01438 741917
E-mail: membership@theimpclub.co.uk

Website:
http://www.theimpclub.co.uk

Enquiries:
Enquiries to: Chairman

Founded:
1980

Organisation type and purpose:
Membership association (membership is by
subscription).
Classic Car Club.

Subject coverage:
All Hillman Imp cars and their variants (Singer,
Sunbeam, Commer), Imp-based cars, technical
advice, history, technical services.

**Museum or gallery collection, archive, or library
special collection:**
Broad selection of technical reports and historical
information
Comprehensive collection of photographs, sales
literature and associated memorabilia

Non-library collection catalogue:
All or part available online and in-house

Library catalogue:
All or part available in-house

Printed publications:
Impressions (club magazine, monthly)
Several books relevant to club's interests

Access to staff:
Contact by letter, by telephone, by e-mail and via
website
Hours: Evenings and weekends

Links with:
Association of Rootes Car Clubs

IMPERIAL COLLEGE LONDON –
CENTRAL LIBRARY

Formal name: Imperial College of Science,
Technology and Medicine – Central Library

South Kensington, London, SW7 2AZ

Tel: 020 7594 8820
Fax: 020 7584 8876
E-mail: library@imperial.ac.uk

Website:
http://www.imperial.ac.uk/library

Enquiries:
Enquiries to: Helpdesk

Organisation type and purpose:
University library.

Subject coverage:
Aeronautics; biotechnology; business; chemical
engineering and chemical technology; chemistry;
civil engineering; computing; electrical and
electronic engineering; environment; earth
sciences; geology; history of science; life sciences;
materials; mathematics; mechanical engineering;
medicine; physics.

**Museum or gallery collection, archive, or library
special collection:**
Annan Collection (history of metals, mining and
metallurgy)

Non-library collection catalogue:
All or part available online

Library catalogue:
All or part available online

Printed publications:
The following are available from Archivist:
Pictorial Histories of Imperial College, St Mary's
Hospital Medical School
Imperial College of Science 1945: A History of the
Future
Imperial College School of Medicine
150 Years of the Royal School of Mines

Access to staff:
Contact by letter, by telephone, by fax, by e-mail,
in person and via website. Appointment necessary.
Hours: Please check the website

Access for disabled people:
Access to all public areas, toilet facilities

Branch libraries:
Charing Cross Campus Library
Imperial College London, The Reynolds
Building, St Dunstan's Road, London, W6 8RP;
tel: 020 7594 0755; fax: 020 7594 0851; e-mail:
library@imperial.ac.uk
Chelsea and Westminster Campus Library
Imperial College London, Chelsea and
Westminster Hosptial, Fulham Road, London,
SW10 9NH; tel: 020 8746 8107; e-mail: library@
imperial.ac.uk
Hammersmith Campus Library
Imperial College London, Hammersmith
Hospital, Du Cane Road, London, W12 0NN; tel:
020 8383 3246; fax: 020 8383 2195; e-mail:
library@imperial.ac.uk
Royal Brompton Campus Library
Faculty of Medicine, Royal Brompton Hospital,
Dove House Street, London, SW3 6LY; tel: 020
7351 8150; fax: 020 7351 8117; e-mail: library@
imperial.ac.uk
St Mary's Campus Library
Faculty of Medicine, Norfolk Place, Paddington,
London, W2 1PG; tel: 020 7594 3692; fax: 020
7402 3971 (mark: Attn Library); e-mail: library@
imperial.ac.uk
The Michael Way Library
Silwood Park Campus, Ascot, Berkshire, SL5
7TA; tel: 020 7594 2461; e-mail: library@imperial
.ac.uk

Links with:
Science Museum Library
tel: 020 7942 4242; fax: 020 7942 4243; e-mail:
smlinfo@sciencemuseum.org.uk

IMPERIAL COLLEGE SCHOOL OF
MEDICINE – ST MARY'S CAMPUS
LIBRARY

Formal name: Imperial College of Science,
Technology and Medicine – St Mary's Campus
Library

Norfolk Place, Paddington, London, W2 1PG

Tel: 020 7594 3692
Fax: 020 7402 3971
E-mail: n.palmer@ic.ac.uk

Website:
http://www.lib.ic.ac.uk/depts/stindex.htm

Enquiries:
Enquiries to: Librarian

Founded:
1854

Organisation type and purpose:
University department or institute.
Medical school.

Subject coverage:
Medicine.

Access to staff:
Contact by letter. Letter of introduction required.
Non-members charged.
Hours: Term time: Mon to Fri, 0900 to 2100; Sat,
0900 to 1300
Vacations: Mon to Fri, 0900 to 1900; Sat, closed

Campus of:
Imperial College of Science, Technology and
Medicine

IMPERIAL PRESS

Pantiles, Garth Lane, Knighton, Powys, LD7 1HH

Tel: 01547 520360
E-mail: militarymuseums@tiscali.co.uk

Enquiries:
Enquiries to: Proprietor

continued overleaf

Founded:
1984

Organisation type and purpose:
Publishing house.
Bookseller.

Subject coverage:
Wargaming, military history.

Printed publications:
Cheshire in the Great Civil War (£1.95)
Garrisons of Shropshire in the Civil War (£6.95)
Guide to Military Museums and other places of
    military interest (once every two to three years,
    10th ed., ISBN 1–85674–035–8, £5, Aug 2001)
Liverpool During the Great Civil War (£1.95)

Publications list:
Available in print

Access to staff:
Contact by letter and by telephone
Hours: Mon to Fri, 0900 to 1700

Access to building, collection or gallery:
No access other than to staff

IMPERIAL SOCIETY OF TEACHERS OF DANCING

Acronym or abbreviation: ISTD

Imperial House, 22–26 Paul Street, London, EC2A
4QE

Tel: 020 7377 1577
Fax: 020 7247 8979
E-mail: marketing@istd.org

Website:
http://www.istd.org
Description and illustrations of various dance
faculties within society.

Enquiries:
Enquiries to: Chief Executive

Founded:
1904

Organisation type and purpose:
Professional body, present number of members:
9500, registered charity (charity number 250397),
training organisation.
Dance Examination Board.
The ISTD exists to promote knowledge of dance
and to maintain and improve teaching standards.

Subject coverage:
Ballroom dance, Latin American dance, sequence
dance, disco/freestyle/rock-n-roll dance, classical
ballet, modern theatre dance, tap dance, jazz
dance, national dance, folk dance, classical Greek
dance, South Asian dance, alternative rhythms.

**Museum or gallery collection, archive, or library
special collection:**
Library collection related to dance

Printed publications:
Dance Magazine (4 times a year, £20 or overseas,
    £26)
Examination syllabus requirements
Promotion Brochure

Publications list:
Available in print

Access to staff:
Contact by letter, by telephone, by e-mail and via
website
Hours: Mon to Fri, 0900 to 1700

IMPERIAL TOBACCO LIMITED

Acronym or abbreviation: ITL

PO Box 525, Upton Road, Southville, Bristol, BS99
1LQ

Tel: 0117 963 6636

Website:
http://www.imperial-tobacco.com

Founded:
1996

Organisation type and purpose:
Manufacturing industry.
Tobacco manufacturing.

Subject coverage:
Tobacco industry.

Trade and statistical information:
Tobacco trade volumes.

Library catalogue:
All or part available in-house

Access to staff:
Contact by letter
Hours: Mon to Fri, 0900 to 1700

Access to building, collection or gallery:
No access other than to staff

IMPERIAL WAR MUSEUM

Acronym or abbreviation: IWM

Department of Printed Books, Lambeth Road,
London, SE1 6HZ

Tel: 020 7416 5342
Fax: 020 7416 5246
E-mail: collections@iwm.org.uk

Website:
http://www.iwm.org.uk
Includes Collections Online catalogue and advice
pages on family history research. Historical
enquiries may be submitted to the Collections
Enquiry Service via a webform.

Enquiries:
Enquiries to: Keeper, Department of Printed Books

Founded:
1917

Organisation type and purpose:
Museum, suitable for ages: 16+.

Subject coverage:
Study of conflicts in which British and
Commonwealth forces have been engaged in the
20th century, particularly the two World Wars;
naval, military and air operations; unit records;
social, political, economic and literary aspects of
modern warfare.

**Museum or gallery collection, archive, or library
special collection:**
Over 100,000 books, 25,000 pamphlets, 8,000
    periodical titles, 45,000 maps, and other special
    or ephemera collections, etc.
British, Commonwealth, French, German and
    American unit histories
Pamphlet Collection (wartime propaganda, ration
    books and other ephemera)
United States Strategic Bombing Survey Reports
Women's Activities in the First World War

Non-library collection catalogue:
All or part available online and in-house

Library catalogue:
All or part available online and in-house

Printed publications:
Bibliographies and book lists (on some 500 topics)
Tracing Your Family History – series of guides on
    Army, Navy, RAF and Merchant Navy
A selection of facsimile reprints of official books
    and pamphlets
Order printed publications from: Mail Order, Imperial
War Museum, Duxford Air Field, Cambridge, CB2
4QR; tel. 01223 499348; fax 01223 839688; e-mail
mailorder@iwm.org.uk

Electronic and video publications:
Official History of the Great War – Military
    Operations France and Belgium 1914–1918
    MAPS (CD-ROM, from Naval and Military
    Press)
Imperial War Museum Trench Map (Great War)
    Archive (CD-ROM, from Naval and Military
    Press)

Order electronic and video publications from: Naval
and Military Press; tel. 01825 749494; e-mail order
.dept@naval-military-press.co.uk

Publications list:
Available online

Access to staff:
Contact by letter, by telephone, by fax, by e-mail
and via website. Appointment necessary.
Hours: Telephone access: Mon to Fri, 0900 to 1700

Access for disabled people:
Parking provided, ramped entry, toilet facilities
Special comments: Wheelchair-accessible study area
available during opening hours, by appointment.

Constituent bodies:
Museum Collection Division, Department of Art
    tel: 020 7416 5342; e-mail: collections@iwm.org
    .uk; website: http://collections.iwm.org.uk
Museum Collection Division, Department of
Documents
    tel: 020 7416 5221; e-mail: docs@iwm.org.uk;
    website: http://collections.iwm.org.uk
Museum Collection Division, Department of
Exhibits and Firearms
    tel: 020 7416 5342; e-mail: collections@iwm.org
    .uk; website: http://collections.iwm.org.uk
Museum Collection Division, Photograph Archive
    tel: 020 7416 5333; e-mail: photos@iwm.org.uk;
    website: http://collections.iwm.org.uk
Museum Collection Division, Sound Archive
    tel: 020 7416 5342; e-mail: collections@iwm.org
    .uk; website: http://collections.iwm.org.uk
Museum Collection Division, United Kingdom
National Inventory of War Memorials
    tel: 020 7416 5353; e-mail: memorials@iwm.org
    .uk; website: http://www.ukniwm.org.uk

IMS PRUSSIA COVE

Formal name: International Musicians Seminar,
Prussia Cove
Acronym or abbreviation: IMS

32 Grafton Square, London, SW4 0DB

Tel: 020 7720 9020
Fax: 020 7720 9033
E-mail: rosie@i-m-s.org.uk

Enquiries:
Enquiries to: Administrator

Founded:
1972

Organisation type and purpose:
International organisation, registered charity
(charity number 270204), suitable for ages: 16 to 30.
Music master classes, strings and piano for
advanced international young musicians.

Subject coverage:
Master classes/seminars provide a totally
professional atmosphere and aim to foster the
highest level of advanced study, drawing
inspiration from the mid-European tradition.

Access to staff:
Contact by letter, by telephone, by fax and by e-
mail
Hours: Mon to Fri, 0900 to 1700

INCORE, UNIVERSITY OF ULSTER

Formal name: Institute for Conflict Resolution
Acronym or abbreviation: INCORE

Aberfoyle House, Northland Road, Londonderry,
BT48 7JA

Tel: 028 7137 5500
Fax: 028 7137 5510
E-mail: incore@incore.ulst.ac.uk

Website:
http://www.incore.ulst.ac.uk
Wide variety of information on global conflict and
ethnicity, country guides, thematic guides and
academic data bank.

Enquiries:
Enquiries to: Administrator

Founded:
1991

Organisation type and purpose:
International organisation, membership
association (membership is by election or
invitation), present number of members: 700,
university department or institute, research
organisation.
Promote communication between networks of
international scholars.

Subject coverage:
Ethnic and community conflict, especially in
relation to education, churches, voluntary and
community groups, material conditions; controlled
or regulated conflict; conflict resolution;
international conflict resolution.

**Museum or gallery collection, archive, or library
special collection:**
Collection of Novels relating to the Northern
Ireland Conflict
Collection of Political Ephemera Relating to the
Northern Ireland Conflict

Library catalogue:
All or part available in-house

Printed publications:
From Protagonist to Pragmatist: Political
Leadership in Societies in Transition (Gormley-
Heenan C)
Hope and History: Study on the Management of
Diversity in Northern Ireland (Leonard B)
Community Conflict Skills (Fitzduff M)
Past Imperfect: Dealing with the Past in Northern
Ireland and Societies in Transition (Hamber B)
Researching Violently Divided Societies: Ethical
and Methodological Issues (Edited by Smyth M
and Robinson G)

Publications list:
Available online and in print

Access to staff:
Contact by letter, by telephone, by fax, by e-mail
and via website. Appointment necessary.
Hours: Mon to Fri, 0900 to 1700

Access to building, collection or gallery:
No access other than to staff

Access for disabled people:
Parking provided, level entry

Collaborates with:
Initiative on Conflict Resolution and Ethnicity
(INCORE)

Links with:
Conflict Archive on the Internet (CAIN)

INCORPORATED ASSOCIATION OF ORGANISTS

Acronym or abbreviation: IAO

19 The Poplars, Gosforth, Newcastle upon Tyne,
NE3 4AE

Tel: 0191 285 7303
E-mail: pvc1@btinternet.com

Website:
http://www.iao.org.uk

Enquiries:
Enquiries to: General Secretary

Founded:
1913

Organisation type and purpose:
Membership association (membership is by
subscription), present number of members: 6,000,
registered charity (charity number 269986).

Subject coverage:
Organists and all lovers of the organ and its music.

Printed publications:
Organists' Review

Access to staff:
Contact by letter, by fax and by e-mail
Hours: Mon to Fri, 0900 to 1700

INCORPORATED COUNCIL OF LAW REPORTING FOR ENGLAND AND WALES

Acronym or abbreviation: ICLR

Megarry House, 119 Chancery Lane, London,
WC2A 1PP

Tel: 020 7242 6471
Fax: 020 7831 5247
E-mail: postmaster@iclr.co.uk

Website:
http://www.lawreports.co.uk
Details of publications, current and forthcoming
cases published, student newsletter and special
events.

Enquiries:
Enquiries to: Secretary

Founded:
1865

Organisation type and purpose:
Professional body, registered charity (charity
number 250605), publishing house.
Preparation and publication of reports of judicial
decisions of the superior and appellate courts in
England.

Subject coverage:
Reports (prepared by barristers) of judicial
decisions of the superior and appellate courts in
England.

Printed publications:
The Weekly Law Reports
The Law Reports (monthly)
The Industrial Cases Reports
The Business Law Reports
The Public and Third Sector Law Reports
Consolidated Index (to the Law Reports, the
Weekly Law Reports, the Industrial Cases
Reports and other major series)
Statutes and Public General Acts

Electronic and video publications:
The WLR Daily
Order electronic and video publications from: available
online at http://www.lawreports.co.uk

Publications list:
Available online and in print

Access to staff:
Contact by letter, by telephone, by fax, by e-mail
and via website. Appointment necessary.
Hours: Mon to Fri, 0900 to 1700

Access to building, collection or gallery:
No prior appointment required

INCORPORATED FROEBEL EDUCATIONAL INSTITUTE

Acronym or abbreviation: IFEI

Templeton Priory Lane, London, SW15 5JW

Tel: 020 8878 7546
Fax: 020 8876 2753

Enquiries:
Enquiries to: Secretary

Founded:
1892

Organisation type and purpose:
University department or institute, suitable for
ages: 3 to 16, research organisation.

**Museum or gallery collection, archive, or library
special collection:**
Froebel Education Archive

Printed publications:
Functions and Seminars Brochure, Templeton
House

Access to staff:
Contact by letter, by telephone and by fax.
Appointment necessary.
Hours: Mon to Fri, 0900 to 1700

INCORPORATED PHONOGRAPHIC SOCIETY

Acronym or abbreviation: IPS

Bishopsgate Institute, 230 Bishopsgate, London,
EC2M 4QH

Tel: 020 8684 9984
Fax: 020 8684 9984

Website:
http://www.the-ipa.org.uk

Enquiries:
Enquiries to: Administrator
Direct e-mail: jhdorrington@hotmail.com

Founded:
1872

Organisation type and purpose:
Membership association (membership is by
subscription, qualification).
Examining body for shorthand and typewriting.

Subject coverage:
Pitman's shorthand (otherwise known as
phonography); history of shorthand (not restricted
to Pitman's); history of writing machines (mainly
typewriters).

**Museum or gallery collection, archive, or library
special collection:**
Books about and printed in Pitman shorthand;
books about typewriting

Printed publications:
IPS Journal (quarterly)

Access to staff:
Contact by letter, by telephone, by fax and by e-
mail
Hours: Mon to Fri, 0900 to 1700

INCORPORATED SOCIETY OF MUSICIANS

Acronym or abbreviation: ISM

10 Stratford Place, London, W1C 1AA

Tel: 020 7079 1202
Fax: 020 7408 1538
E-mail: membership@ism.org

Website:
http://www.ism.org
Membership benefits, links to members, music
news, online publications and information.

Enquiries:
Enquiries to: Chief Executive
Other contacts: Head of Professional Development
(for policy development); Head of Legal and
General Services (for casework)

Founded:
1882

Organisation type and purpose:
Professional body, training organisation.

Subject coverage:
Private music teachers, musicians at all stages of
education, solo, ensemble and orchestral
performers, composers and conductors.

Printed publications:
Yearbook
Information sheets on legal guidance, professional
business advice, financial advice, ISM
membership and services, professional
development, professional practice,
recommended minimum rates, careers
information
Music Journal (monthly, free to members, non-
members £3)

continued overleaf

Electronic and video publications:
Registers of Performers and Composers, Musicians in Education and Professional Private Teachers (online at http://www.ism.org)

Publications list:
Available online and in print

Access to staff:
Contact by letter, by telephone, by fax and by e-mail
Hours: Mon to Fri, 0930 to 1730

INDEPENDENT ASSOCIATION OF PREP SCHOOLS

Formal name: IAPS
Acronym or abbreviation: IAPS

11 Waterloo Place, Leamington Spa, Warwickshire, CV32 5LA

Tel: 01926 887833
Fax: 01926 888014
E-mail: iaps@iaps.org.uk

Website:
http://www.iaps.org.uk
Tailored information sections for members, parents and the general public.

Enquiries:
Enquiries to: Association Administrator

Founded:
1892

Organisation type and purpose:
International organisation, professional body, membership association (membership is by election or invitation).

Subject coverage:
Preparatory school education.

Printed publications:
Attain magazine (three times a year – termly)
Order printed publications from: Distribution Manager, Attain Magazine, Chapel Studios, High Street, Moreton-in-Marsh, Gloucestershire, GL56 0AX

Access to staff:
Contact by letter, by telephone, by fax, by e-mail, in person and via website. Appointment necessary.
Hours: Mon to Fri, 0830 to 1700

Access to building, collection or gallery:
Prior appointment required

Member organisation of:
Independent Schools Council
St Vincent House, 30 Orange Street, London, WC2H 7HH; tel: 020 7766 7070; fax: 020 7766 7071; e-mail: office@isc.co.uk; website: http://www.isc.co.uk

INDEPENDENT PANEL OF ARBITRATORS

c/o Retail Motor Industry Federation, 9 North Street, Rugby, Warwickshire, CV21 2AB

Tel: 01788 538317
Fax: 01788 538326

Enquiries:
Enquiries to: Administrator

Organisation type and purpose:
To provide an alternative complaint redress mechanism for motor trade related matters.

Subject coverage:
Independent arbitration on complaints about motor vehicles.

Access to staff:
Contact by letter and by fax
Hours: Mon to Fri, 0900 to 1700

Access to building, collection or gallery:
No access other than to staff

INDEPENDENT POLICE COMPLAINTS COMMISSION

Acronym or abbreviation: IPCC

5th Floor, 90 High Holborn, London, WC1V 6BH

Tel: 08453 002002; mincom: 020 7404 0431
Fax: 020 7404 0430
E-mail: enquiries@ipcc.gsi.gov.uk

Website:
http://www.ipcc.gov.uk

Enquiries:
Enquiries to: Chairman
Direct e-mail: pressoffice@ipcc.gsi.gov.uk

Founded:
1985

Carries out the functions of the former:
Police Complaints Authority (year of change 2004)

Organisation type and purpose:
Statutory body.

Trade and statistical information:
Data on police complaints in England and Wales.

Printed publications:
PCA Annual Report to Parliament (Stationery Office, ISBN 0–10–291037–5, £15.25)
PCA 10 Police Complaints Authority – The first 10 years (HMSO, ISBN 0–11–341146–4, £4.95)
Triennial Review of the PCA 1991–4 (HMSO, ISBN 0–10–239694–9, £5.45)
Free leaflets and summary reports available on request
Custody Officer Training: investing in safety (PCA, ISBN 0–9533157–3, £3.95)
Striking a Balance: the police use of new batons (PCA, ISBN 0–9533157–1–1, £4)
Deaths in Police Custody: reducing the risks (PCA, ISBN 0–9533157–2–X, £5)
One Year On, Deaths in Police Custody: the risks reduced (PCA, ISBN 0–9533157–3–8, £5)
Order printed publications from: For charged publications: Stationery Office, PO Box 276, London, SW8 5DT, tel. 0845 7023474 (for orders), fax: 0870 600 5533, e-mail: book.orders@theso.co.uk

Publications list:
Available in print

Access to staff:
Contact by letter, by telephone, by e-mail and via website. Appointment necessary.
Hours: Complaints against police can be made at any police station or in writing to the PCA

Parent body:
Home Office
Queen Anne's Gate, London, SW1H 9AT

INDEPENDENT PUBLISHERS GUILD

Acronym or abbreviation: IPG

PO Box 93, Royston, Hertfordshire, SG8 5GH

Tel: 01763 247014
Fax: 01763 246293
E-mail: info@ipg.uk.com

Website:
http://www.ipg.uk.com

Enquiries:
Enquiries to: Executive Director
Direct e-mail: bridget@ipg.uk.com

Founded:
1962

Organisation type and purpose:
Trade association (membership is by subscription; present number of members: 310.

Subject coverage:
Publishing.

Electronic and video publications:
website archive of event reports

Access to staff:
Contact by e-mail and via website. Access for members only.
Hours: Variable hours, e-mail is fastest

INDEPENDENT SCHOOLS COUNCIL

Acronym or abbreviation: ISC

St Vincent House, 30 Orange Street, London, WC2H 7HH

Tel: 0845 724 6657
Fax: 020 7766 7071

Website:
http://www.isc.co.uk

Enquiries:
Enquiries to: Senior Information Officer
Direct tel: 020 7766 7067
Direct e-mail: liam.butler@isc.co.uk

Founded:
1973

Organisation type and purpose:
The Independent Schools Council works with its members to promote and preserve the quality, diversity and excellence of UK independent education both at home and abroad.
ISC's core principles are:
- The importance of a strong and diverse independent sector, founded on a belief in adding value for the individual child
- The widening of opportunity for children from all backgrounds to achieve their potential
- Access to Higher Education on merit, with each child treated as an individual, and with transparent information on the admissions process
- The widening of opportunity for parents to choose the best education for their child
- Open access to professional development, on equal terms, for teachers in the maintained and independent sectors
- The widening of opportunities for teachers to gain experience in both the maintained and independent sectors, and the removal of barriers to transfer between the sectors
- Co-operation between the maintained and independent sectors to improve outcomes for all children
- The importance of an independent sector participating fully in the national debate on educational issues.

Subject coverage:
Independent schools.

Access to staff:
Contact by letter, by telephone, by fax, by e-mail and via website
Hours: Mon to Fri, 0900 to 1700

Constituent bodies:
Girls' Schools Association
Governing Bodies Association
Governing Bodies of Girls Schools Association
Headmasters' and Headmistresses' Conference
Incorporated Association of Preparatory Schools
Independent Schools Association Incorporated
Independent Schools Bursars' Association
Society of Headmasters and Headmistresses of Independent Schools

INDEPENDENT SCHOOLS COUNCIL INFORMATION SERVICE

Acronym or abbreviation: ISCis

Grosvenor Gardens House, 35–37 Grosvenor Gardens, London, SW1W 0BS

Tel: 020 7798 1500
Fax: 020 7798 1501
E-mail: info@iscis.uk.net

Website:
http://www.isc.co.uk/
Information about ISCis and its member schools.

Enquiries:
Enquiries to: Press Officer
Direct tel: 020 7766 7067
Direct e-mail: hayley.dunlop@isc.co.uk

Founded:
1972

Organisation type and purpose:
Membership association, present number of
members: 1300 schools, suitable for ages: 1 to 19,
consultancy.
Information service for parents, media,
researchers, academics, government departments
and politicians.

Subject coverage:
Independent schools in the UK, details of nearly
1300 schools, plus statistical surveys and services
for the media and politicians, placement services
for parents overseas who want their children
educated in the UK (below university level).

Trade and statistical information:
Statistical surveys of independent schools in the
UK.

Printed publications:
Annual Census
Handbooks listing member schools, National and
regional, numbers of pupils, fees charged etc
Leaflets on independent education
The ISC Guide to Accredited Independent Schools

Electronic and video publications:
The ISC Guide to Accredited Independent Schools
(CD-ROM, £1.50 UK, £5 EU, and £7.50 rest of
world)

Publications list:
Available in print

Access to staff:
Contact by letter, by telephone, by fax, by e-mail,
in person and via website
Hours: Mon to Fri, 0900 to 1700

Parent body:
Independent Schools Council (ISC)
tel: 020 7798 1590; fax: 020 7798 1591

Sponsored by:
Governing Bodies Association
Governing Bodies of Girls Schools Association
Incorporated Association of Preparatory Schools
Independent Schools Association

INDEPENDENT WASTE PAPER PROCESSORS ASSOCIATION

Acronym or abbreviation: IWPPA

Heritage House, Vicar Lane, Daventry, NN11 4GD

Tel: 01327 703223
Fax: 01327 300612
E-mail: admin@iwppa.co.uk

Enquiries:
Enquiries to: Chief Executive

Founded:
1975

Organisation type and purpose:
Trade association.

Subject coverage:
Waste paper; disposal and recycling.

Access to staff:
Contact by letter and by e-mail
Hours: Mon to Fri, 0900 to 1700

INDEPENDENTAGE (FORMERLY THE ROYAL UNITED KINGDOM BENEFICENT ASSOCIATION)

Acronym or abbreviation: RUKBA

6 Avonmore Road, London, W14 8RL

Tel: 020 7605 4200
Fax: 020 7605 4201
E-mail: charity@independentage.org.uk

Website:
http://www.independentage.org.uk
Information on what IndependentAge does, who
we help, fundraising events, our nursing and
residential homes.

Enquiries:
Enquiries to: Director

Founded:
1863

Organisation type and purpose:
Membership association, registered charity
(charity number 210729).
To help elderly people on very low incomes to stay
in their own homes.

Subject coverage:
Care for elderly or infirm people who have
devoted their personal or professional lives to
others; IndependentAge maintains independence
through the provision of a regular, small additional
income and the practical support of over 1,000
volunteers.
RUKBA also runs three residential and nursing
homes. Help may be available with care home fees.

Printed publications:
Annual Review
Information Leaflets
IndependentAge Family Matters (newsletter)

Access to staff:
Contact by letter, by telephone and by fax
Hours: Mon to Fri, 0900 to 1700

Trustees for:
Universal Beneficent Society
at the same address

INDIA DEVELOPMENT GROUP (UK) LIMITED

Acronym or abbreviation: IDG(UK)

68 Downlands Road, Purley, Surrey, CR8 4JF

Tel: 020 8668 3161
Fax: 020 8660 8541
E-mail: idguk@clara.co.uk

Enquiries:
Enquiries to: Chief Executive
Other contacts: Administrator

Founded:
April 1970

Organisation type and purpose:
Voluntary organisation, registered charity (charity
number 291167), training organisation,
consultancy, research organisation.
To promote economic, social and educational
development of India's rural areas where the
majority of people live, to reverse drift to urban
areas unable to absorb them.

Subject coverage:
Alleviation of poverty and the generation of
income in the backward areas of India.
Development of appropriate technology.

Access to staff:
Contact by letter, by telephone, by fax and by e-
mail
Hours: Mon to Fri, 1000 to 1500

Links with:
Schumacher Institute of Appropriate Technology
Village Melhaur, Chinhat, Lucknow (UP), India

INDIA HOUSE LIBRARY

High Commission of India, India House, Aldwych,
London, WC2B 4NA

Tel: 020 7632 3166
E-mail: info@hcilondon.net

Website:
http://www.meagor.nic.in
General information about India including
newspapers.
http://www.ficci.com

Federation of Indian Chambers of Commerce and
Industry
http://www.culturopedia.com
Treasure house of India's culture and heritage; art,
music, dance, crafts, theatre, language and
literature etc.
http://www.indiagov.nic.in
India facts
http://www.nic.in/
Information on states of India
http://www.ciionline.org.com
Confederation of Indian Industry
http://www.nic.in/ncti
National Centre for Trade Information
http://www.hci.london.net
Information on visas
http://www.mapsofindia.com/maps
Maps
http://www.commin.nic.in
Department of Commerce

Enquiries:
Enquiries to: Librarian

Founded:
ca 1925

Organisation type and purpose:
Governmental body of the Indian Ministry of
External Affairs, New Delhi.

Subject coverage:
India and Indian affairs, mainly from 1950.

**Museum or gallery collection, archive, or library
special collection:**
Indian Central Government Official Publications
from 1950 to approximately 1980 mainly
economic (now in the Brynmor Jones Library,
University of Hull)

Trade and statistical information:
Available from the Economic Department in the
High Commission.

Library catalogue:
All or part available in-house

Printed publications:
Order printed publications from: Publications
Manager, Central News Agency Private Limited
P-23 Connaught Circus, PO Box 374, New Delhi,
110001, India, tel: 00 91 11 3364448, fax: 00 91 11
7526036, e-mail: info@can-india.com

Electronic and video publications:
Karishma – The Wonder that is India (multi-media
CD-ROM, from Delhi or the USA)
Order electronic and video publications from: CD
Division, India High Commission
240 Okala Industrial Estate, Phase III, New Delhi,
110020, fax: 00 91 11 6919073
Multisynic Trends Inc
186 Laauwe Avenue, Wayne, New Jersey, 07470,
USA, fax: 00 1 201 595 8281

Access to staff:
Contact by letter, by telephone and by fax
Hours: Mon to Fri, 0900 to 1700

Access to building, collection or gallery:
By appointment

INDIAN INSTITUTE READING ROOM

Bodleian Library, Broad Street, Oxford, OX1 3BG

Tel: 01865 287300
Fax: 01865 277182
E-mail: indian.institute@bodley.ox.ac.uk

Website:
http://www.ouls.ox.ac.uk/bodley/library/rooms/
iirr
http://www.bodley.ox.ac.uk/oxlip
Oxford Libraries bibliographic and full text
subscription databases

Enquiries:
Enquiries to: Librarian
Direct tel: 01865 277083
Direct e-mail: gillian.evison@bodley.ox.ac.uk

continued overleaf

Organisation type and purpose:
University library.

Subject coverage:
All subjects and languages of South Asia and Tibet, excluding natural sciences; secondary material only for Afghanistan, Burma.

Museum or gallery collection, archive, or library special collection:
Malan Collection
Monier Williams Collection
Whinfield Collection

Non-library collection catalogue:
All or part available online

Library catalogue:
All or part available online

Access to staff:
Contact by letter, by telephone, by fax and by e-mail. Appointment necessary.
Hours: Mon to Fri, 0900 to 1700
Special comments: See details: http://www.ouls.ox.ac.uk/bodley/services/admissions

Access for disabled people:
See details: http://www.ouls.ox.ac.uk/bodley/services/disability

Constituent part of:
Bodleian Library, University of Oxford
  Broad Street, Oxford, OX1 3BG; e-mail: reader .services@ouls.ox.ac.uk; website: http://www .ouls.ox.ac.uk/bodley/home

INDIAN MILITARY HISTORICAL SOCIETY

Acronym or abbreviation: IMHS

33 High Street, Tilbrook, Huntingdon, Cambridgeshire, PE28 0JP

Tel: 01480 860437
E-mail: imhs@mcclenaghan.waitrose.com

Enquiries:
Enquiries to: Honorary Secretary

Founded:
1983

Organisation type and purpose:
International organisation, membership association (membership is by subscription), present number of members: 230, research organisation.

Subject coverage:
History of service units in India both before and after independence, including details of uniforms, medals, badges, buttons and other militaria. These include: Royal Navy, British Army and Royal Air Force units which have served in India; Units of the Honourable East India Company's Army and Marine prior to 1861; the Indian Army subsequent to 1861, including the European Volunteer Corps; the Royal Indian Marine and the Royal Indian Navy; the Army of Nepal and those of the Princely States; the present day Armed Services of India, Pakistan and Bangladesh, including Frontier Corps, Paramilitary and Police Units.

Printed publications:
Four Journals each year for members only (Durbar)

Access to staff:
Contact by letter and by e-mail
Hours: Mon to Fri, 0900 to 1700

INDIAN MOTORCYCLE CLUB OF GB

2 Keswick Drive, Cullercoats, North Shields, Tyne & Wear, NE30 3EW

Tel: 01912 522840
E-mail: jdwright@netcomuk.co.uk

Website:
http://www.indianmotorcycle.co.uk

Enquiries:
Enquiries to: Membership Secretary

Founded:
1989

Organisation type and purpose:
Membership association (membership is by subscription), present number of members: 150.

Subject coverage:
Indian motorcycles manufactured in the USA between 1901 and 1953.

Museum or gallery collection, archive, or library special collection:
Part books and workshop manuals available for use by club members only

Printed publications:
Four magazines a year with interim newsletters, for club members only

Access to staff:
Contact by letter. Access for members only.
Hours: Mon to Fri, 0900 to 1700

INDIVIDUAL TRAVELLERS CO LTD

Acronym or abbreviation: ITC Ltd

Spring Mill, Earby, Barnoldswick, Lancashire, BB94 0AA

Tel: 0845 604 3877
E-mail: itcpno@holidaycottagesgroup.com

Website:
http://www.individualtravellers.com/

Enquiries:
Enquiries to: Director

Founded:
1976

Organisation type and purpose:
Service industry.
Tour operator.

Subject coverage:
Self-catering in France, Italy, Spain and Portugal, New England, Sicily, Corsica, Mallorca.

Printed publications:
Brochures (available free directly or through travel agency)

Publications list:
Available online

Access to staff:
Contact by letter, by telephone, by fax, by e-mail, in person and via website
Hours: Mon to Fri, 0900 to 1730

Access to building, collection or gallery:
No prior appointment required

Links with:
Individual Travellers Spain and Portugal
  tel: 01798 869461; fax: 01798 869343; e-mail: spain@indiv-travellers.com
New England Country Homes
  tel: 01798 869461; fax: 01798 869343; e-mail: newengland@indiv-travellers.com
Vacances en Campagne
  tel: 01798 869461; fax: 01798 869343; e-mail: france@indiv-travellers.com
Vacanze in Italia
  tel: 01798 869461; fax: 01798 869343; e-mail: italy@indiv-travellers.com

INDUSTRIAL CLEANING MACHINE MANUFACTURERS' ASSOCIATION

Acronym or abbreviation: ICMMA

PO Box 12492, Solihull, West Midlands, B91 9AX

Tel: 0121 703 0636
E-mail: icmma@icmma.org.uk

Website:
http://www.icmma.org.uk

Enquiries:
Enquiries to: Director

Founded:
1961

Organisation type and purpose:
Trade association.

Subject coverage:
Manufacture and marketing of industrial cleaning machines.

Access to staff:
Contact by letter and via website
Hours: Mon to Fri, 0900 to 1700

Member of:
BEAMA Ltd

INDUSTRIAL DEVELOPMENT BANGOR (UWB) LIMITED

Acronym or abbreviation: IDB Ltd

University of Wales Bangor, Dean Street, Bangor, Gwynedd, LL57 1UT

Tel: 01248 382749
Fax: 01248 372105
E-mail: enquiries@idb.wales.com

Website:
http://www.idb.wales.com
General information and catalogue.

Enquiries:
Enquiries to: Managing Director
Direct tel: 01248 382748
Direct e-mail: emlyn@idb.wales.com

Founded:
1978

Organisation type and purpose:
Manufacturing industry, consultancy, research organisation.
Engineering company.
Strengthen links between industry and academia.

Subject coverage:
Design and manufacture of specialist electronic instrumentation: in particular, portable simultaneous translation systems, navigation and location by satellite, electrostatic monitors, instrumentation for nuclear and hydro-electric power generation industries.

Printed publications:
Catalogue

Publications list:
Available online and in print

Access to staff:
Appointment necessary.
Hours: Mon to Fri, 0900 to 1700

Access to building, collection or gallery:
Prior appointment required

Access for disabled people:
Parking provided, ramped entry, level entry, access to all public areas

Parent body:
University of Wales Bangor (UWB)

INDUSTRIAL INJURIES ADVISORY COUNCIL

Acronym or abbreviation: IIAC

2nd Floor, Caxton House, Tothill Street, London, SW1H 9NA

Tel: 020 7449 5618
E-mail: iiac@dwp.gsi.gov.uk

Website:
http://www.iiac.org.uk

Enquiries:
Other contacts: Secretary (for formal questions or comment to the Council)

Organisation type and purpose:
Advisory body.

IIAC is an independent body that advises the Secretary of State for Social Security on Industrial Injuries Disablement Benefit.

Subject coverage:
Industrial diseases.

Library catalogue:
All or part available online and in print

Publications list:
Available online and in print

INDUSTRIAL MARKETING RESEARCH ASSOCIATION

Acronym or abbreviation: IMRA

18 St Peters Steps, Brixham, Devon, TQ5 9TE

Tel: 01803 859575

Enquiries:
Enquiries to: Director General
Other contacts: Chairman

Founded:
1963

Organisation type and purpose:
Professional body (membership is by election or invitation).

Subject coverage:
Industrial market research, international marketing research.

Non-library collection catalogue:
All or part available in-house

Library catalogue:
All or part available in-house

Printed publications:
Journal of International Marketing and Marketing Research
Journal of International Selling and Sales Management
Manual of Industrial Market Research (1991)
Symposia Papers (13 titles)

Access to staff:
Contact by letter. Non-members charged.
Hours: Mon to Fri, 0900 to 1700

Access to building, collection or gallery:
No access other than to staff

Member of:
European Council for Industrial Marketing (CEMI)
Industrial Marketing Council (in the UK)
International Marketing Federation

INDUSTRIAL RELATIONS RESEARCH UNIT

Acronym or abbreviation: IRRU

Warwick Business School, University of Warwick, Coventry, CV4 7AL

Tel: 024 7652 4268
Fax: 024 7652 4184
E-mail: val.jephcott@wbs.ac.uk

Website:
http://www2.warwick.ac.uk/fac/soc/wbs/research/irru
Publications and research interests.

Enquiries:
Enquiries to: Director
Direct tel: 024 7652 4272

Founded:
1970

Organisation type and purpose:
University department or institute, research organisation.

Subject coverage:
Industrial relations.

Printed publications:
Warwick Papers in Industrial Relations (IRRU)
Warwick Studies in Industrial Relations (pub Blackwell)

Publications list:
Available online

Access to staff:
Contact by letter, by telephone, by fax, by e-mail and via website
Hours: Mon to Fri, 0900 to 1700

INDUSTRIAL ROPE ACCESS TRADE ASSOCIATION

Acronym or abbreviation: IRATA

Evelyn Woods Road, Aldershot, Hampshire, GU11 2LL

Tel: 01252 357839
Fax: 01252 357831
E-mail: info@irata.org

Website:
http://www.irata.org

Enquiries:
Enquiries to: Administrator
Direct e-mail: wendy@irata.org

Organisation type and purpose:
Trade association, present number of members: 38. Equipment suppliers, trainers and operators involved in rope access for industrial purposes.

Subject coverage:
Equipment suppliers, trainers and operators involved in rope access for industrial purposes.

Printed publications:
Directory of IRATA Members Companies
Colour brochure on rope access
General Requirements for certification of personnel engaged in industrial rope access methods (rev 1998, £40 inc. p&p)
Guidelines on the use of rope access methods
Information sheet on LOLER
Report on Safety Record

Publications list:
Available in print

Access to staff:
Contact by letter, by e-mail and via website
Hours: Mon to Fri, 0900 to 1700

INFERTILITY NETWORK UK

Formal name: Infertility Network UK
Acronym or abbreviation: INUK

114 Lichfield Street, Walsall, West Midlands, WS1 1SZ

Tel: 08701 188088
Fax: 01424 731858

Website:
http://www.issue.co.uk
Information about ISSUE and infertility.
http://www.moretolife.co.uk
Issue initiative.

Enquiries:
Enquiries to: Chief Executive
Other contacts: Chair

Founded:
1976

Organisation type and purpose:
National organisation, membership association (membership is by subscription), present number of members: 3000, voluntary organisation, registered charity (charity number 1099960). Support group.
To help people through the infertility maze with information, counselling and support at regional and national levels.

Subject coverage:
Infertility, treatment, adoption and fostering, alternatives to childlessness, coping and living with childlessness.

Printed publications:
Factsheets
Information pack (free)
Magazine (quarterly)

Electronic and video publications:
Videos (rental or purchase)

Publications list:
Available online and in print

Access to staff:
Contact by letter, by telephone, by fax, by e-mail and via website
Hours: Mon to Fri, 0830 to 1700

Access for disabled people:
Yes

Member of the:
International Federation of Infertility Patient Associations

INFLUENCE DESIGN ASSOCIATES LTD

Influence House, 10 Moorfield Grove, Heaton Moor, Stockport, Cheshire SK4 4BQ

Tel: 0870 228 2272
Fax: 0870 228 2202
E-mail: indulge@influencedesign.com

Website:
http://www.influencedesign.com

Enquiries:
Enquiries to: Administrator
Direct e-mail: info@influencedesign.com
Other contacts: Personal Assistant

Founded:
1992

Organisation type and purpose:
Membership association (membership is by qualification), service industry, consultancy. Design to print and production.

Library catalogue:
All or part available online

Access to staff:
Contact by letter, by fax and by e-mail
Hours: Mon to Fri, 0900 to 1700

INFONORTICS LIMITED

15 Market Place, Tetbury, Gloucestershire, GL8 8DD

Tel: 01666 505772
Fax: 01666 505774
E-mail: contact-1@infonortics.com

Website:
http://www.infonortics.eu

Enquiries:
Enquiries to: Managing Director

Founded:
1988

Organisation type and purpose:
Conference organiser.

Subject coverage:
Information, documentation, chemical information, competitive intelligence, information technology, search engines.

Publications list:
Available online

Access to staff:
Contact by letter, by telephone, by fax, by e-mail and via website
Hours: Mon to Fri, 0900 to 1700

Access to building, collection or gallery:
No access other than to staff

INFORMATION CENTRE, COBHAM TECHNICAL SERVICES

Cleeve Road, Leatherhead, Surrey, KT22 7SA

Tel: 01372 367007
Fax: 01372 367009
E-mail: era.info@cobham.com

continued overleaf

Website:
http://www.cobham.com/technicalservices
Details of ERA capabilities, conferences, publications and information services, electronic commerce service available for the purchasing of ERA publications and booking places at ERA conferences, courses and seminars.

Enquiries:
Enquiries to: Information Officer
Direct fax: 01372 367009
Direct e-mail: era.info@cobham.com

Founded:
1920

Organisation type and purpose:
International organisation, service industry. ERA Technology works at the leading edge of many advanced technologies and provides specialist, technology-based services including design and development, testing, assessment and expert advice. ERA has capabilities in electrical, electronic, software and communications engineering, RF microwave and radar, complex EMC, risk analysis, safety engineering, reliability and failure analysis, plant integrity, micro-electronics and materials technologies.

Subject coverage:
Electrotechnology; computing technology; electrical and electronic engineering; energy conservation; alternative energy; product design and prototype construction; new materials; testing and certification; regulatory compliance; national and international standardisation; explosion hazards; electromagnetic compatibility; servocomponents; electric motors; insulation; cables; radio frequency technology; electromechanical engineering; engineering materials; materials science; failure analysis.

Library catalogue:
All or part available in-house

Printed publications:
Annual report and accounts
Reports List
Safety & EMC (newsletter for designers and suppliers of electrical and electronic products)
RE4view – The Recycling Electrical and Electronic Equipment Environmental Review (newsletter covering developments in the implementation of the WEEE, RoHs, and EuP directives)
Solutions@ERA (newsletter)

Publications list:
Available online and in print

Access to staff:
Contact by letter, by telephone, by fax, by e-mail and via website. Appointment necessary. Non-members charged.
Hours: Mon to Fri, 0900 to 1700
Special comments: Certain services are charged for.

Access to building, collection or gallery:
Prior appointment required

INFORMATION COMMISSIONER'S OFFICE

Acronym or abbreviation: ICO

Wycliffe House, Water Lane, Wilmslow, Cheshire, SK9 5AF

Tel: 01625 545745
Fax: 01625 524510
E-mail: mail@ico.gsi.gov.uk

Website:
http://www.ico.gov.uk
The UK's independent public body set up to promote access to official information and protect personal information by promoting good practice, ruling on eligible complaints, providing information to individuals and organisations, and taking appropriate action when the law is broken.

Enquiries:
Enquiries to: Marketing & Communications Officer

Founded:
1984

Organisation type and purpose:
Statutory body; non-departmental government organisation.
To enforce the Data Protection Act and the Freedom of Information Act.

Subject coverage:
Data Protection Act 1984 and its implications and application. The Freedom of Information Act 2000.

Printed publications:
All publications are free of charge
Be Open . . . Data Protection
CCTV Code of Protection
Freedom of Information – Summary
Media Briefing on the New Law
No Credit? Data Protection
Notification Exemptions and Handbook
The Data Protection Act 1998 An Introduction (available in large print)
Using the Law to Protect Your Information (leaflet)

Electronic and video publications:
Barry's Bad Data Day (video)
Protecting the Plumstones (CD-ROM, educational)
No Credit? Data Protection (tape)
Audit Guide (CD-ROM)

Publications list:
Available online and in print

Access to staff:
Contact by letter, by telephone, by fax, by e-mail, in person and via website
Hours: Mon to Fri, 0900 to 1700

INFORMATION DIRECT

Central Library, Chamberlain Square, Birmingham, B3 3HQ

Tel: 0121 303 4531
Fax: 0121 303 4532
E-mail: information.direct@birmingham.gov.uk

Enquiries:
Enquiries to: Information Officer

Founded:
1989

Organisation type and purpose:
Local government body.
Fee-based business research and enquiry service.

Subject coverage:
Business information, company information, market intelligence, mailing lists, company formations.

Access to staff:
Contact by letter, by telephone, by fax and by e-mail. Appointment necessary. All charged.
Hours: Mon to Fri, 0900 to 1700

Parent body:
Birmingham Library Service

INFORMATION FOR SCHOOL AND COLLEGE GOVERNORS

Acronym or abbreviation: ISCG

Avondale Park School, Sirdar Road, London, W11 4EE

Tel: 020 7229 0200
Fax: 020 7229 0651
E-mail: iscg@governors.fsnet.co.uk

Enquiries:
Enquiries to: Secretary

Founded:
1991

Organisation type and purpose:
Advisory body, research organisation.
An independent research and information service for governors.

Subject coverage:
Current concerns and needs of school and college governors.

Printed publications:
ISCG Manual for Governing Bodies and their Clerks (£10)
Helping Children to Learn (£2.50)
Investing in Ethos (£2.50)
Planning for Improvement (£5)
Parent Pack (£5)
Clerking Matters (new, free with sae)
Admissions Appeals Pack (free)
Exclusion Appeals Pack (free)
ISCG Checklists including: Governors' Visits to Schools
TGA occasional papers including:
Assessment, Recording and Reporting in Schools 1995
Inspection: A Weapon or a Tool
Reviewing the National Curriculum
ISCG Education Leaflets

Publications list:
Available in print

Access to staff:
Contact by letter, by telephone, by fax, by e-mail and via website. Appointment necessary.
Hours: Mon to Fri, 1100 to 1600
Special comments: Answerphone when office closed.

Access to building, collection or gallery:
No access other than to staff

INFORMATION ON TRANQUILLISERS AND ANTIDEPRESSANTS

Acronym or abbreviation: CITA

Cavendish House, Brighton Road, Waterloo, Merseyside, L22 5NG

Tel: 0151 474 9626
Fax: 0151 284 8324

Website:
http://www.citawithdrawal.org.uk
Information about CITA and its work together with information on tranquillisers and their effects. Details of CITA's publications.

Enquiries:
Enquiries to: Administrator

Founded:
1987

Formerly called:
Council for Involuntary Tranquilliser Addiction

Organisation type and purpose:
National organisation, advisory body, voluntary organisation, registered charity (charity number 519334), training organisation.
To provide support, counselling and GP clinics for those withdrawing from involuntary tranquilliser addiction.

Subject coverage:
Sufferers as a result of taking tranquillisers, sleeping pills or anti-depressants, benzodiazepine and tranquilliser withdrawal, anxiety management.

Printed publications:
Information Pack: includes Back to Life book, letter of protocol for GP, further information about CITA (£7.50 inc. p&p)
Information Pack: includes Back to Life book, the cassette tapes, letter of protocol for GP, some further information (£20 inc. p&p)
Alive and Kicking: personal story of addiction to tranquillisers and sleeping pills (£5.50 inc. p&p)
Back to Life: information on tranquilliser addiction and withdrawal (£4.95 inc. p&p)

Electronic and video publications:
Cassettes (£7.50 each inc p&p)

Publications list:
Available in print

Access to staff:
Contact by letter, by telephone and by fax
Hours: Mon to Fri, 1000 to 1300

INFORMATION WORLD REVIEW

Acronym or abbreviation: IWR

Bizmedia Ltd, 80–82 Chiswick High Road, London
W4 1SY

Tel: 020 8995 9345
E-mail: peterw@bizmedia.co.uk

Website:
http://www.iwr.co.uk
Fully searchable information and articles
published by Information World Review.

Enquiries:
Enquiries to: Editor

Founded:
1977

Organisation type and purpose:
Business publisher.

Subject coverage:
Online information retrieval; optical publishing
and storage; artificial intelligence software and
tools.

Publications list:
Available in print

Access to staff:
Contact by letter, by telephone and by e-mail
Hours: Mon to Fri, 0930 to 1730

Parent body:
Bizmedia Ltd

INFOTERRA LTD

Atlas House, 41 Wembley Road, Leicester, LE3
LUT

Tel: 0116 273 2300
Fax: 0116 273 2400
E-mail: info@infoterra-global.com

Website:
http://www.infoterra.co.uk
http://www.geostore.com
Online aerial photography and height data

Organisation type and purpose:
Geo-information products and services

Subject coverage:
Provider of geographic information products and
services, including airborne and satellite data
acquisition, geo-information creation, database
management and outsourced hosting. Provides
geospatial knowledge to companies world-wide.

**Museum or gallery collection, archive, or library
special collection:**
Landsat and Spot satellites UK archive, a complete
   UK collection of photographic proof available
   with an image browse facility
IRS and IKONOS data
Remote Sensing Society Library

Printed publications:
Infoterra Group Brochure
Solutions for Defence and Security
Solutions for Subsidence Risk Management
Geospatial Services for Risk Management
Support for Risk Assessment
GeoStore
Solutions for Network Planning
Land Administration Services
Oil, Gas and Mineral Exploration
Global Seeps
Satellite Imagery data – Nigeria
Solutions for Flood Risk Management
Detailed Mapping of the Environment – Rapid
   Surveyor
Geospatial Services for Civil Engineering

Publications list:
Available online and in print

Access to staff:
Contact by telephone and by e-mail. Appointment
necessary. All charged.
Hours: Mon to Fri, 0900 to 1700

Also at:
Infoterra France SAS
   31 rue des Cosmonautes, 31402 Toulouse, cedex
   4, France; tel: +33 562 19 55 70; fax: +33 562 19 97
   81; e-mail: info@infoterra-global.com; website:
   http://www.infoterra-global.com
Infoterra GmbH
   tel: +49 7545 8 9969; fax: +49 7545 8 5650; e-mail:
   info@infoterra-global.com; website: http://www
   .infoterra-global.com
Infoterra Hungary Kft
   Soroksari ut 48, 7ep, 11.em, 1095 Budapest.
   Hungary; tel: +361 468 3638; fax: +361 468 3640;
   e-mail: info@infoterra-global.com; website:
   http://www.infoterra.co.uk
Infoterra Ltd
   Europa House, The Crescent, Southwood,
   Farnborough. Hampshire. GU14 0NL; tel: 01252
   362000; fax: 01252 375016; e-mail: info@infoterra
   -global.com; website: http://www.infoterra.co.uk

Parent body:
Astrium Limited
   Anchorage Road, Portsmouth, Hampshire, PO3
   5PU; website: http://www.astrium.eads.net

INLAND REVENUE LIBRARY AND INFORMATION SERVICE

1 Parliament Street, London, SW1A 2BQ

Enquiries:
Enquiries to: Librarian

Organisation type and purpose:
National government body.
Government library.

Subject coverage:
Taxation (UK), Hansard, Public General Acts.

Access to staff:
Contact by letter. Appointment necessary.

INLAND WATERWAYS ASSOCIATION

Acronym or abbreviation: IWA

Island House, Moor Road, Chesham, HP5 1WA

Tel: 01494 783453
E-mail: iwa@waterways.org.uk

Website:
http://www.waterways.org.uk

Enquiries:
Enquiries to: Chief Executive
Direct e-mail: lesley.sanders@waterways.org.uk

Founded:
1946

Organisation type and purpose:
Membership association (membership is by
subscription), present number of members: 18,000,
registered charity (charity number 212342).
Campaigning for the retention, restoration,
conservation and development of the inland
waterways for the fullest possible commercial and
recreational use.

Subject coverage:
Restoration, retention and development of inland
waterways in the British Isles, commercial and
recreational use.

**Museum or gallery collection, archive, or library
special collection:**
IWA John Hoap Archive, at Boat Museum,
   Ellesmere Port

Printed publications:
Annual Report
Wide variety of books on life afloat, decoration,
   waterway history and waterway travels
   including:
Guides, maps
Landscape with Figures (L T C Rolt)
Narrow Boat (L T C Rolt, the classic of canal books,
   first published 1944)
Waterways (4 times a year, free to members)

Electronic and video publications:
Various videos – specific and general
Canal Planner (Route planning, CD-ROM for
   Windows 95 or 98)

Publications list:
Available in print

Access to staff:
Contact by letter and by fax
Hours: Mon to Fri, 0830 to 1630

Affiliated to:
Inland Waterways Enterprises Ltd
IWA (Sales) Ltd
Waterway Recovery Group Ltd

INMARSAT

99 City Road, London, EC1Y 1AX

Tel: 020 7728 1777
Fax: 020 7728 1142
E-mail: customer_care@inmarsat.com

Website:
http://www.inmarsat.com/
About Inmarsat, products and services, about
satcoms, contacts.

Enquiries:
Enquiries to: Information Officer
Direct e-mail: john_warehand@inmarsat.com

Founded:
1979

Organisation type and purpose:
Mobile satellite communications operator.

Subject coverage:
Satellite communications and related areas, mobile
communications (land, sea, air), engineering;
electronics, international communications etc.

Non-library collection catalogue:
All or part available in-house

Publications list:
Available online

Access to staff:
Contact by letter and via website. Appointment
necessary. Letter of introduction required.
Hours: Mon to Fri, 0900 to 1700

Access to building, collection or gallery:
Prior appointment required

Access for disabled people:
Level entry, toilet facilities

INNER TEMPLE LIBRARY

Inner Temple, London, EC4Y 7DA

Tel: 020 7797 8217
Fax: 020 7583 6030
E-mail: library@innertemple.org.uk

Website:
http://www.innertemplelibrary.org.uk

Enquiries:
Enquiries to: Librarian and Keeper of Manuscripts
Direct e-mail: mclay@innertemple.org.uk

Founded:
c.1500

Organisation type and purpose:
Legal library.

Information services:
General guides, database guides.

**Museum or gallery collection, archive, or library
special collection:**
70,000 vols on law of the United Kingdom and
   Commonwealth
Petyt Manuscripts (386 volumes)
Barrington Manuscripts (57 vols)
Inner Temple Records (39 vols)
Mitford Collection of Legal Manuscripts (79 vols)
Miscellaneous Manuscripts (211 vols)
Inner Temple Archives (16th century to present)

continued overleaf

Library catalogue:
All or part available online and in-house

Electronic and video publications:
Guides to online databases, CD-ROMs; Current
Awareness [blog]: see http://
innertemplelibrary.wordpress.com; Access to
Law [gateway site]: http://www.accesstolaw.com

Access to staff:
Contact by letter, by telephone, by fax and by e-
mail. Appointment necessary. Access for members
only. Non-members charged.
Hours: Legal terms: Mon to Thu, 0900 to 2000; Fri,
0900 to 1900; every 4th Sat, during legal term time,
in rotation with the other Inns of Court libraries,
1000 to 1700

Access to building, collection or gallery:
Open to all members of the Inns of Court; not open
to the general public (researchers by written
application to the Librarian)

INNERPEFFRAY LIBRARY

Innerpeffray by Crieff, Perthshire, PH7 3RF

Tel: 01764 652819
E-mail: info@@innerpeffraylibrary.co.uk

Website:
http://www.innerpeffraylibrary.co.uk

Enquiries:
Enquiries to: Librarian

Founded:
1680

Organisation type and purpose:
Registered charity (charity number SCO 13843),
museum, research organisation.
Reference library, library museum, first lending
library in Scotland.

Subject coverage:
Wide range of pre-1800 printed books, strong
theological and religious content, natural history,
history, agriculture, gardening, travel etc.

**Museum or gallery collection, archive, or library
special collection:**
Accounts of Library etc
Borrowing Records from 1747 to 1968
3000 books published 1502 AD to 1800 AD
1400 volumes post 1801 AD
David Drummond Collection, 3rd Lord Maderty
d.1692
Robert Hay-Drummond Collection, Archbishop of
York d.1781
Visitor Books

Library catalogue:
All or part available online and in-house

Access to staff:
Contact by letter, by telephone, by e-mail, in
person and via website. All charged.
Hours: Wed to Sat, 1000 to 1645; Sun, 1400 to 1600

INNOVATION NORWAY

Charles House, 5–11 Lower Regent Street, London,
SW1Y 4LR

Tel: 0207 389 8800
Fax: 020 7839 6014
E-mail: london@innovationnorway.no

Website:
http://www.visitnorway.co.uk

Enquiries:
Enquiries to: Consultant
Direct e-mail: marta.dixon@innovationnorway.no

Organisation type and purpose:
National organisation.
Government foundation.

Subject coverage:
Tourism in Norway; hotel accommodation, camp
sites and youth hostels; timetables and local or
regional area brochures; conference facilities; tour
operators; ferry companies and airlines.

Information is sent out on request.

**Museum or gallery collection, archive, or library
special collection:**
Library of photographs and videos (strictly for use
in travel promotion)

Access to staff:
Contact by letter, by telephone, by fax, by e-mail
and via website
Hours: Mon to Fri, 0900 to 1630
Special comments: Open to trade only – not public.

Parent body:
Innovation Norway
PO Box 448, Sentrum, NO-0104, Oslo, Norway;
tel: + 47 22 00 25 00; fax: + 47 22 00 25 01; e-mail:
oslo@innovationnorway.no

INSOLVENCY PRACTITIONERS ASSOCIATION

Acronym or abbreviation: IPA

52–54 Gracechurch Street, London, EC3V 0EH

Tel: 020 7623 5108
Fax: 020 7623 5127
E-mail: secretariat@insolvency-practitioners.org.uk

Website:
http://www.ipa.uk.com

Enquiries:
Enquiries to: Secretary

Founded:
1961

Organisation type and purpose:
Professional body.
Association of 'full-time' insolvency practitioners
(Recognised Professional Body under the
Insolvency Act 1986).

Subject coverage:
Insolvency.

Printed publications:
Examination Syllabus and Course Documentation
Index of Members (annually)

Access to staff:
Contact by letter
Hours: Mon to Fri, 0900 to 1700

Affiliated to:
Insol International
SPI

INSPEC

Michael Faraday House, Six Hills Way, Stevenage,
Hertfordshire, SG1 2AY

Tel: 01438 313311
Fax: 01438 767339
E-mail: inspec@theiet.org

Website:
http://www.theiet.org/publications

Enquiries:
Enquiries to: Managing Director

Organisation type and purpose:
Learned society, professional body (membership is
by qualification), publishing house.
Publishing, information and abstracting service;
department of The Institution of Engineering and
Technology.

Subject coverage:
Physics, electrical engineering, electronics, control
engineering, computing, information technology
and manufacturing, mechanical and production
engineering.

Printed publications:
Computer and Control Abstracts (monthly)
Current Papers in Physics (twice monthly)
Electrical and Electronic Abstracts (monthly)
Key Abstracts (22 titles, monthly)
Physics Abstracts (twice monthly)
Inspec Current Awareness Services

Electronic and video publications:
INSPEC Online
INSPEC Site Licences
INSPEC Data Services

Access to staff:
Contact by letter, by telephone, by fax, by e-mail
and via website
Hours: Mon to Fri, 0900 to 1700

Parent body:
Institution of Engineering and Technology

INSTITUT FRANÇAIS – LA MÉDIATHÈQUE

Formal name: Institut Français du Royaume Uni
Acronym or abbreviation: IFRU

17 Queensberry Place, London, SW7 2DT

Tel: 020 7073 1350
Fax: 020 7073 1363
E-mail: library@ambafrance.org.uk

Website:
http://www.institut-francais.org.uk

Enquiries:
Enquiries to: Librarian
Direct tel: 020 7073 1354

Founded:
1910

Organisation type and purpose:
National government body (membership is by
subscription), present number of members: 4,500,
public library.
French cultural centre.

Subject coverage:
France: humanities, mainly literature, history,
geography, travel guides, but also civilisation,
history, philosophy, religion, social sciences, art,
bibliography and linguistics (books mostly in
French; a few in English).

Education services:
Guided visits to school groups on request and by
appointment.

**Museum or gallery collection, archive, or library
special collection:**
60,000 items (books, audio books, videos, DVDs,
tapes)
French magazines and newspapers
Free French periodicals and special collection
about France Libre and the French Resistance
Denis Saurat's archives

Non-library collection catalogue:
All or part available online, in-house and in print

Library catalogue:
All or part available online, in-house and in print

Printed publications:
Programme of Activities of the Institut Français du
Royaume-Uni
Selected bibliographies

Electronic and video publications:
Video and tape recordings of lectures given at the
Institut (for consultation only)
Order electronic and video publications from:
Conferences on line

Publications list:
Available in print

Access to staff:
Contact by letter, by telephone, by fax, by e-mail,
in person and via website. Appointment necessary
Hours: Tue to Fri, 1200 to 1900; Sat, 1200 to 1800
Children's Section: Tue to Sat, 1400 to 1800
Special comments: Closed 1 week at Christmas and
all of August.

Access to building, collection or gallery:
No prior appointment required
Hours: 1200 to 1900

Access for disabled people:
Access available for disabled, lift
Hours: 1200 to 1900

Also at:
Institut Français
    Language Centre, 14 Cromwell Place, London,
    SW7 2JR; tel: 020 7581 2701; fax: 020 7581 0061;
    e-mail: language-center@ambafrance.org.uk;
    website: http://www.institut-francais.org.uk
Institut Français
    Children's Library, 29 Harrington Road, London
    SW7; tel: 020 7073 1350; fax: 020 7073 1363; e-
    mail: library@ambafrance.org.uk; website: http://
    www.institut-francais.org.uk

INSTITUTE AND FACULTY OF ACTUARIES

Napier House, 4 Worcester Street, Oxford, OX1
2AW

Tel: 01865 268200
Fax: 01865 268211
E-mail: libraries@actuaries.org.uk

Website:
http://www.actuaries.org.uk

Enquiries:
Enquiries to: Librarian
Direct tel: 01865 268208

Founded:
1848

Please select:
Institute of Actuaries
Faculty of Actuaries (year of change 2010)

Organisation type and purpose:
Professional body (membership is by
qualification), present number of members: 16,850.

Subject coverage:
Actuarial science, life assurance, general insurance,
pensions, employee benefits, friendly societies,
social security, investment, demography, mortality,
probability, risk theory, histories of insurance and
life assurance companies.

**Museum or gallery collection, archive, or library
special collection:**
Small photograph collection
Small rare book and manuscript collection

Trade and statistical information:
Demographic statistics, mortality statistics.

Non-library collection catalogue:
All or part available online and in-house

Library catalogue:
All or part available online

Printed publications:
British Actuarial Journal (five a year)
Annals of Actuarial Science
Papers on actuarial subjects
The Actuary (magazine, monthly)
Annals of Actuarial Science (twice a year)
Order printed publications from: Publications Officer

Microform publications:
Actuaries' Investment Index 1928–1962

Electronic and video publications:
List of Members (annually, online only)

Publications list:
Available online and in print

Access to staff:
Contact by letter, by telephone, by fax, by e-mail
and via website. Appointment necessary.

Access to building, collection or gallery:
Hours: Mon to Fri, 0900 to 1700
Special comments: Special collections are housed at
Staple Inn Hall, High Holborn, London, WC1V
&QJ.

Access for disabled people:
Level entry, toilet facilities

Also at:
Institute and Faculty of Actuaries
    Maclaurin House, 18 Dublin Street, Edinburgh,
    EH1 3PP; tel: 0131 240 1311; fax: 0131 240 1313;
    e-mail: libraries@actuaries.org.uk

Institute and Faculty of Actuaries, Staple Inn
    Staple Inn Hall, High Holborn, London, WC1V
    7QJ; tel: 020 7632 2111; e-mail: libraries@
    actuaries.org.uk

Member organisation of:
Groupe Consultatif des Associations d'Actuaires
des Pays des Communautés Européennes

INSTITUTE FOR ADVANCED STUDIES IN THE HUMANITIES

University of Edinburgh, Hope Park Square,
Edinburgh, EH8 9NW

Tel: 0131 650 4671
Fax: 0131 668 2252
E-mail: iash@ed.ac.uk

Website:
http://www.iash.ed.ac.uk/
Information about the Institute, its projects and
fellowships.

Enquiries:
Enquiries to: Director

Founded:
1970

Organisation type and purpose:
University department or institute.
Department of the University of Edinburgh.
To promote scholarship in the Humanities and to
further inter-disciplinary enquiries, by means of
research fellowships, seminars, lectures and
cultural events.

Subject coverage:
All fields of the humanities very widely defined i.e.
all departments of arts faculties, social sciences,
theology, music and law.

**Museum or gallery collection, archive, or library
special collection:**
Small private library available only to elected
    fellows of the Institute or by arrangement

Non-library collection catalogue:
All or part available online

Library catalogue:
All or part available in-house

Printed publications:
Institute Brochure
Occasional papers

Publications list:
Available in print

Access to staff:
Contact by letter, by telephone, by fax, by e-mail
and via website
Hours: Mon to Fri, 0900 to 1700

Parent body:
University of Edinburgh

INSTITUTE FOR ANIMAL HEALTH – COMPTON LABORATORY

Acronym or abbreviation: IAH

Compton, Newbury, Berkshire, RG20 7NN

Tel: 01635 577256
E-mail: compton.library@bbsrc.ac.uk

Website:
http://www.iah.bbsrc.ac.uk

Enquiries:
Enquiries to: IAH Libraries Manager (IAH
Compton & IAH Pirbright Laboratories)
Direct e-mail: chris.gibbons@bbsrc.ac.uk

Organisation type and purpose:
Research organisation.

Subject coverage:
Diseases of economic importance in farm animals
(exotic and endemic), immunology, molecular
biology, veterinary science.

**Museum or gallery collection, archive, or library
special collection:**
Specialist libraries on veterinary science

Library catalogue:
All or part available in-house

Access to staff:
Contact by letter, by telephone, by fax and by e-
mail
Hours: Mon to Thu, 0900 to 1700; Fri, 0900 to 1630

Constituent part of:
Biotechnology and Biological Sciences Research
Council

INSTITUTE FOR ANIMAL HEALTH – PIRBRIGHT LABORATORY

Ash Road, Pirbright, Woking, Surrey, GU24 0NF

Tel: 01483 232441
Fax: 01483 232448
E-mail: pirbright.ill@bbsrc.ac.uk

Website:
http://www.iah.bbsrc.ac.uk

Enquiries:
Enquiries to: Librarian
Direct tel: 01483 231030

Founded:
1925

Organisation type and purpose:
Research organisation.
Houses the World Reference Laboratory for Foot
and Mouth Disease.
Research into infectious diseases of farm animals.

Subject coverage:
Animal virology, particularly foot and mouth
disease and other viruses exotic to the United
Kingdom

**Museum or gallery collection, archive, or library
special collection:**
Collection of reprints on foot and mouth disease
    and other viruses
Database of 100,000 virological references

Library catalogue:
All or part available in-house

Printed publications:
Annual Report with other laboratories of the IAH

Access to staff:
Contact by letter and by e-mail. Appointment
necessary.
Hours: Mon to Fri, 0800 to 1430

Parent body:
Biotechnology and Biological Sciences Research
Council (BBSRC)

INSTITUTE FOR ARCHAEOLOGISTS

Formal name: Institute of Field Archaeologists
Acronym or abbreviation: IfA

SHES, Whiteknights, PO Box 227, Reading, RG6
6AB

Tel: 0118 931 6446
Fax: 0118 931 6448
E-mail: admin@archaeologists.net

Website:
http://www.archaeologists.net

Enquiries:
Enquiries to: Administrative Assistant

Founded:
1982

Organisation type and purpose:
Professional body, present number of members
over 2,800.
To promote professional standards and ethics for
conserving, managing, and understanding
enjoyment of heritage.

continued overleaf

Information services:
Jobs Information Service (JIS)

Printed publications:
Directory of Members
Jobs Information Service Bulletin
The Archaeologist (quarterly)
Professional Practice Papers (occasional)

Publications list:
Available online and in print

Access to staff:
Contact by letter, by telephone, by fax, by e-mail
and via website
Hours: Mon to Fri, 0900 to 1730

INSTITUTE FOR ARTS IN THERAPY AND EDUCATION

Acronym or abbreviation: IATE

2–18 Britannia Row, Islington, London, N1 8PA

Tel: 020 7704 2534
Fax: 020 7704 0171
E-mail: info@artspsychotherapy.org

Website:
http://www.artspsychotherapy.org

Enquiries:
Enquiries to: Manager
Other contacts: Administrator

Founded:
1992

Organisation type and purpose:
Training organisation.

Subject coverage:
Integrative arts psychotherapy training.

Printed publications:
Current prospective

Access to staff:
Contact by letter, by telephone, by e-mail and via
website. Appointment necessary.
Hours: Mon to Fri, 0900 to 1730

Access for disabled people:
Ramped entry, toilet facilities

Full member of the:
United Kingdom Council for Psychotherapy

INSTITUTE FOR COMPLEMENTARY AND NATURAL MEDICINE

Acronym or abbreviation: ICNM

Can-Mezzanine, 32–36 Loman Street, London, SE1
0EH

Tel: 020 7922 7980
Fax: 020 7922 7981
E-mail: info@icnm.org.uk

Website:
http://www.i-c-m.org.uk

Enquiries:
Enquiries to: Information Officer
Other contacts: Research Director

Founded:
1982

Created by the merger of:
Nature Cure Clinic (NCC) and Institute for
Complementary Medicine (ICM) (year of change
2007)

Organisation type and purpose:
Advisory body, learned society (membership is by
qualification), voluntary organisation, registered
charity (charity number 326258).
To provide information on complementary
medicine. To support research into complementary
medicine. To develop professional standards of
practice.

Subject coverage:
Complementary medicine, practitioner training
and qualification, membership of the register,
contacts within the field and comments on the state
and range of the subject, low technology methods
of health care, traditional remedies and health care
methods.

**Museum or gallery collection, archive, or library
special collection:**
A modest library

Non-library collection catalogue:
All or part available in-house

Library catalogue:
All or part available in-house

Printed publications:
Lists of schools and teaching colleges in
complementary medicine
Update for practitioners

Access to staff:
Contact by letter, by telephone and by e-mail
Hours: Mon to Fri, 0930 to 1600
Special comments: Free information to public and
media, fees required from commercial interests.

Access to building, collection or gallery:
Prior appointment required

Parent body:
Healing Research Trust
tel: As for ICNM

INSTITUTE FOR EMPLOYMENT STUDIES

Acronym or abbreviation: IES

Sovereign House, Church Street, Brighton, BN1
1UJ

Tel: 01273 763400
Fax: 01273 763401
E-mail: askies@employment-studies.co.uk

Website:
http://www.employment-studies.co.uk/pubs

Enquiries:
Enquiries to: Communications Manager
Direct e-mail: andy.davidson@employment-studies
.co.uk

Founded:
1969

Formerly called:
Institute of Manpower Studies (year of change
1995)

Organisation type and purpose:
Research organisation.

Subject coverage:
Human resources, labour markets, public
employment policy, training and skills analysis,
careers, equality and diversity in employment,
health and well-being at work.

Printed publications:
Annual Report
IES Reports (more than 100 titles representing the
mainstream of Institute thinking and experience)
HR Insight (2 times a year)
Employment Studies (2 times a year)
Joint publishing with commercial and other
publishers
Order printed publications from: website: http://
www.employment-studies.co.uk/pubs

Publications list:
Available online

Access to staff:
Contact by letter, by telephone, by fax, by e-mail
and via website
Hours: Mon to Fri, 0900 to 1700

Access to building, collection or gallery:
No access other than to staff

INSTITUTE FOR EUROPEAN ENVIRONMENTAL POLICY

Acronym or abbreviation: IEEP

Dean Bradley House, 52 Horseferry Road, London
SW1P 2AG

Tel: 020 7799 2244
Fax: 020 7799 2600
E-mail: central@ieep.eu

Website:
http://www.ieep.org.uk

Enquiries:
Enquiries to: Information Officer
Direct e-mail: aglynn@ieep.eu

Organisation type and purpose:
Voluntary organisation, registered charity (charity
number 802956), consultancy, research
organisation.
Independent body with offices in Bonn, Paris,
London, Brussels and Madrid.

Subject coverage:
EU environmental policy including, environment,
agriculture, water, air pollution, waste, chemicals,
natural resources, fisheries, transport, rural
development and strategic/horizontal issues.

Printed publications:
Manual of Environmental Policy: the EC and
Britain (Haigh N, updated 2 times a year,
available through Elsevier Science)
Various publications, see IEEP website

Publications list:
Available in print

Access to staff:
Contact by letter, by fax, by e-mail and via
website
Hours: Mon to Fri, 0900 to 1700

Brussels Office:
IEEP
18 Avenue des Gaulois, Brussels, B-1040; tel: + 32
2 732 4234/4004

INSTITUTE FOR FISCAL STUDIES

Acronym or abbreviation: IFS

7 Ridgmount Street, London, WC1E 7AE

Tel: 020 7291 4800
Fax: 020 7323 4780
E-mail: mailbox@ifs.org.uk

Website:
http://www.ifs.org.uk

Enquiries:
Enquiries to: External Relations Manager
Direct tel: 020 7291 4850

Founded:
1969

Organisation type and purpose:
Membership association (membership is by
subscription), present number of members: 1,150,
registered charity (charity number 258815);
independent, non-profit-making economic
research organisation.
To encourage debate and disseminate independent
information about all aspects of taxation and
government microeconomic policy. Promotes
effective economic and social policies by
understanding better their impact on individuals,
families, businesses and government finances.

Subject coverage:
Research in the fiscal regime, taxation (but not
individual tax matters), public economic policy,
government expenditure, local and European
activities and international development
economics.

Printed publications:
An extensive selection of publications on the
following topics: corporate behaviour, finance
and tax, econometrics, environment, Europe,
income distribution, indirect taxation and
consumer behaviour, labour supply and wage

determination, local government, pensions and savings, personal taxation and benefits, tax law and administration
Conference proceedings
Fiscal Studies (journal, quarterly)
Research papers
Non-technical reports
Briefing notes
Order printed publications from: e-mail: mailbox@ifs org.uk

Electronic and video publications:
Fiscal Studies (journal, articles, available free after three years, current articles available to subscribing academic institutions or pay-per-view via Wiley-Blackwell: http://www.interscience.wiley.com)
Summaries of all research and short briefing notes (free, online)
Working papers (free, online)
Virtual Economy: an interactive teaching simulation about the economy for A-Level and degree students

Publications list:
Available online

Access to staff:
Contact by letter, by telephone, by fax, by e-mail and via website. Appointment necessary.
Hours: Mon to Fri, 0930 to 1730

Access to building, collection or gallery:
Prior appointment required

Access for disabled people:
Ramped entry, access to all public areas, toilet facilities

INSTITUTE FOR JEWISH POLICY RESEARCH

Acronym or abbreviation: JPR

79 Wimpole Street, London, W1G 9RY

Tel: 020 7935 8266
Fax: 020 7935 3252
E-mail: jpr@jpr.org.uk

Website:
http://www.jpr.org.uk
Newsletters, press releases, summaries of research papers and anti-Semitism in the World Today.
http://www.axt.org.uk

Enquiries:
Enquiries to: Director

Founded:
1941

Organisation type and purpose:
Membership association (membership is by subscription), present number of members: 500, registered charity (charity number 252626), consultancy, research organisation, publishing house.

Subject coverage:
International Jewish affairs, anti-Semitism, race relations, civic society, human rights, neo-Nazism, Israel (domestic issues), the Middle East, migration and refugees, Jewish culture, history of Jewish communities, Jewish communities in Diaspora.

Printed publications:
Recent JPR Publications:
A Community of Communities (Report of the Commission on Representation of the Interests of the British Jewish community, March 2000)
A guide to Jewish television: prospects and possibilities, findings of the JPR Working Party (July 1999)
Combating Holocaust denial through law in the United Kingdom (Report of the J P R Law Panel, 2000)
Cultural Politics and European Jewry (Waterman S, Feb 1999)
Developing Jewish Museums in Europe (Clark D, Feb 1999)
Ethnic and religious questions in the 2001 UK Census of Population: policy recommendations (Kosmin B, Mar 1999)

French edition: Enjeux culturels et judaisme européen (Waterman S, Février 1999)
Governance in the Jewish voluntary sector (Harris M and Rochester C, 2001)
Grant-making trusts in the Jewish sector (Schlesinger E, 2000)
JPR News (newsletter, 3 times a year)
Jews of the 'New South Africa'; highlights of the 1998 national survey of South African Jews, (Kosmin B A, Goldberg J, Shain M and Bruk S, Sep 1999)
North American Conservative Jewish teenagers' attachment to Israel (Keysar A and Kosmin B A, July 1999)
Patterns of Prejudice (quarterly)
The financial resources of the UK Jewish voluntary sector (Halfpenny P and Reid M, 2000)

Electronic and video publications:
Antisemitism and Xenophobia Today (www.axt.org.uk)

Publications list:
Available online and in print

Access to staff:
Contact by letter, by fax, by e-mail and via website
Hours: Mon to Thu, 0930 to 1730

Access to building, collection or gallery:
No access other than to staff

INSTITUTE FOR METROPOLITAN STUDIES

Acronym or abbreviation: IMS

The Bartlett School of The Built Environment, UCL, Gower Street, London, WC1E 8BT

Tel: 020 7243 4205
Fax: 020 7727 5268

Enquiries:
Enquiries to: Chief Executive

Organisation type and purpose:
University department or institute, consultancy, research organisation.

Subject coverage:
Metropolitan studies with particular focus on London.

Printed publications:
A Fresh Start for London (£15, 1992)
London In Prospect (£25, 1991)
The London Factor (£95, 1994)

Access to staff:
Contact by fax. Appointment necessary.
Hours: Mon to Fri, 0900 to 1700

Access for disabled people:
Toilet facilities

Affiliated to:
University College London

INSTITUTE FOR MIDDLE EASTERN AND ISLAMIC STUDIES

Acronym or abbreviation: IMEIS

Al Qasimi Building, Elvet Hill Road, Durham, DH1 3TU

Tel: 0191 334 5660
Fax: 0191 334 5661
E-mail: a.ehteshami@durham.ac.uk

Website:
http://www.dur.ac.uk/~dme0www
Brief introduction to the institute.

Enquiries:
Enquiries to: Director

Founded:
early 1900s

Organisation type and purpose:
University department or institute.
Teaching and research on the Middle East.

Subject coverage:
Extensive information and documentation on all matters related to the Middle East and North Africa, Islam, including Arabic, Persian and Turkish languages, politics, economy and social science of the contemporary Middle East.

Museum or gallery collection, archive, or library special collection:
Middle East Documentation Unit (University Library)
Sudan Archive

Trade and statistical information:
Most relevant Middle East economic statistics.

Printed publications:
Economic Research Papers
Over 60 publications including:
A Bibliography of Saudi Arabia (Stevens J H and King R, 1973, £10)
The Collapse and Reconstitution of Lebanon (Najem J, 1998, £10)
The Condominium Remembered: Proceedings of the Durham Sudan Historical Records Conference 1982
The Egyptian Theatre in the Nineteenth Century (1799–1882)
Urbanisation in the Arabian Peninsula

Publications list:
Available in print

Access to staff:
Contact by letter, by telephone, by fax and by e-mail
Hours: Mon to Fri, 0900 to 1700

Access to building, collection or gallery:
Prior appointment required

Access for disabled people:
Parking provided, level entry

INSTITUTE FOR NATIONALIST AFFAIRS

Acronym or abbreviation: INA

National House, PO Box 83, Tonbridge, Kent, TN9 1YN

Tel: 01732 851259
Fax: 01732 852376
E-mail: mikeeaster@dialstart.net

Enquiries:
Enquiries to: Secretary

Founded:
1987

Organisation type and purpose:
Research organisation.

Subject coverage:
Research into fundamental matters concerning the government of the United Kingdom from the Nationalist viewpoint.

Printed publications:
Institute for Nationalist Affairs (booklet)
Occasional publications

Access to staff:
Contact by letter, by telephone and by e-mail
Hours: Mon to Fri, 0900 to 1700

INSTITUTE FOR OPTIMUM NUTRITION

Acronym or abbreviation: ION

Avalon House, 72 Lower Mortlake Road, Richmond, Surrey, TW9 2JY

Tel: 020 8614 7800
Fax: 0870 979 1133
E-mail: reception@ion.ac.uk

Website:
http://www.ion.ac.uk
About Institute for Optimum Nutrition, services ION provides, contact details for ION staff and department nutrition information.

continued overleaf

Founded:
1984

Organisation type and purpose:
Membership association, registered charity
(charity number 1013084), research organisation.
Independent educational charity.

Subject coverage:
Achieving optimum nutrition and reaching the
highest level of health through nutrition.
To educate both the general public and health
professionals about nutrition and nutritional
therapy.

**Museum or gallery collection, archive, or library
special collection:**
Information List available on request with sae
Library of books, journals and specific research
papers, nutrition and medical related (alternative
and complementary medicine related)

Printed publications:
Optimum Nutrition magazine (ONM) (4 times a
year)
ON Magazine (back issues available, subject to
availability)
ON Magazine Reprints on previous articles
available
ION Factsheet Pack
ION Directory of Nutritional Therapists

Publications list:
Available in print

Access to staff:
Contact by letter, by telephone, by fax, by e-mail
and in person. All charged.
Hours: Mon to Fri, 0900 to 1700

Access to building, collection or gallery:
Prior appointment required
Hours: Mon to Fri, 1000 to 1700
Special comments: Library access to ION members
and ION students only.

INSTITUTE FOR OUTDOOR LEARNING

Acronym or abbreviation: IOL

Plumpton Old Hall, Plumpton, Penrith, Cumbria,
CA11 9NP

Tel: 01768 885800
Fax: 01768 885801
E-mail: institute@outdoor-learning.org

Website:
http://www.outdoor-learning.org
Membership details; insurance details; publication
details; The Source, outdoor providers list.

Enquiries:
Enquiries to: Administrator
Direct e-mail: louise@outdoor-learning.org

Organisation type and purpose:
National organisation, membership association
(membership is by subscription), present number
of members: 1400, registered charity (charity
number 1085697), publishing house.
Supports, develops and promotes the achievement
of learning through purposeful and planned
outdoor education.

Subject coverage:
Careers and qualifications in outdoor education,
safety, insurance for outdoor education, outdoor
training and development; school curriculum and
outdoors, access and environment, urban
adventure, equal opportunities and outdoors,
insurance for outdoor education.

**Museum or gallery collection, archive, or library
special collection:**
Small library of articles and books on all aspects of
outdoor learning

Printed publications:
IOL Newsletter (quarterly)
Horizons (magazine, quarterly)
Outdoor Source Book (once every two years)
Journal of Adventure Education and Outdoor
Learning (annually)

Guide to Careers in the Outdoors (2 times a year)

Publications list:
Available online and in print

Access to staff:
Contact by letter, by telephone, by fax, by e-mail,
in person and via website. Non-members charged.
Hours: Mon to Fri, 0900 to 1600

Access for disabled people:
Parking provided, access to all public areas, toilet
facilities

INSTITUTE FOR PUBLIC POLICY RESEARCH

Acronym or abbreviation: ippr

30–32 Southampton Street, London, WC2E 7RA

Tel: 020 7470 6100
Fax: 020 7470 6111
E-mail: info@ippr.org.uk

Website:
http://www.ippr.org.uk
General information on the institute, particular
information on projects and research, a publication
list.

Enquiries:
Enquiries to: Information Officer

Founded:
1989

Organisation type and purpose:
Registered charity (charity number 800065).

Subject coverage:
Health and social policy, education, economy,
business and public private partnerships, public
and democratic involvement, citizenship and
governence, the digital society.

Printed publications:
Publications available to purchase through an
agency
Order printed publications from: IPPR Orders,
Central Books
99 Wallis Road, London, E9 5LN, tel: 0845 458
9911, fax: 0845 458 9912, e-mail: ippr@centralbooks
.com

Publications list:
Available in print

INSTITUTE FOR SOCIAL AND ECONOMIC RESEARCH

Acronym or abbreviation: ISER

University of Essex, Wivenhoe Park, Colchester,
Essex, CO4 3SQ

Tel: 01206 872957
Fax: 01206 873151
E-mail: iser@essex.ac.uk

Website:
http://www.iser.essex.ac.uk/
General
http://www.iser.essex.ac.uk/pubs/index.php
Publications

Enquiries:
Enquiries to: Enquiries
Direct e-mail: katet@essex.ac.uk
Other contacts: (1) Research Resources Unit
Manager (2) Communications Manager for (1)
library (2) press.

Founded:
1989

Organisation type and purpose:
Research organisation.

Subject coverage:
Household organisation, labour market, income
and wealth, housing, health, socio-economic
values, British Household Panel User Study and
longitudinal studies methodology.

**Museum or gallery collection, archive, or library
special collection:**
The Research Resource Unit (RRU) houses a
collection of survey-related documents to
support the centre's research. The collection
largely consists of 'grey literature'. Outsiders can
use the collection by prior appointment only

Non-library collection catalogue:
All or part available online

Library catalogue:
All or part available online

Printed publications:
ISER Report Series (1 paper, £15 inc. postage UK)
Occasional Paper Series (12 papers cost varies
between £3.50 and £7.50 plus postage)
Technical Paper Series (15 papers, £3.50 each inc.
postage UK)
Working Paper Series (100+ papers, £3.50 each inc
postage UK)

Electronic and video publications:
BHPS data available from ESRC Data Archive,
University of Essex in following specifications:
floppy disk, JANET, online data access service
MIMAS (tel: 01206 872001)

Publications list:
Available online and in print

Access to staff:
Contact by letter, by telephone, by fax and by e-
mail
Hours: Mon to Fri, 0930 to 1600
Special comments: Visitors by prior appointment to
Research Resources Unit.

Access to building, collection or gallery:
Prior appointment required

Access for disabled people:
Level entry, toilet facilities

Partly funded by:
Economic and Social Science Research Council
(ESRC)

INSTITUTE FOR SPORT, PARKS AND LEISURE

Acronym or abbreviation: ISPAL

Abbey House, 1650 Arlington Business Park,
Theale, Reading

Tel: 0844 418 0077
Fax: 0118 929 8001
E-mail: infocentre@ispal.org.uk

Website:
http://www.ispal.org.uk

Enquiries:
Enquiries to: Research and Resources Manager

Founded:
1983

Created by the merger of:
Institute of Leisure and Amenity Management
(ILAM) and NASD (year of change 2006)

Organisation type and purpose:
Professional body.
Professional institute for sport, parks and leisure
managers and aspiring managers.
To improve management in sport, parks and
leisure industry and to enhance the quality of
experience of those undertaking activities within
these sectors.

Subject coverage:
Leisure management, sport, recreation, arts,
tourism, play, countryside, parks and open spaces,
local government.

Non-library collection catalogue:
All or part available online, in-house and in print

Library catalogue:
All or part available online, in-house and in print

Printed publications:
Fact sheets
Policy Position Statements
Bibliographies

Reading Lists
Current Articles Bulletin
Leisure Abstracts and Documentation Service
Order printed publications from: Research and
Resources Manager

Publications list:
Available online and in print

Access to staff:
Contact by letter, by telephone, by fax, by e-mail,
in person and via website. Appointment necessary.
Access for members only. Non-members charged.
Hours: Mon to Fri, 0900 to 1700

Access for disabled people:
Parking provided, level entry, toilet facilities
Special comments: Please notify beforehand.

INSTITUTE FOR THE MANAGEMENT OF INFORMATION SYSTEMS

Acronym or abbreviation: IMIS

5 Kingfisher House, New Mill Road, Orpington,
Kent, BR5 3QG

Tel: 0700 00 23456
Fax: 0700 00 23023
E-mail: central@imis.org.uk

Website:
http://www.imis.org.uk

Enquiries:
Enquiries to: Chief Executive

Organisation type and purpose:
Professional body (membership is by subscription,
qualification), registered charity (charity number
291495).
Examining body.

Subject coverage:
Management of information systems and
information technology for commerce, industry
and general business.

Printed publications:
IMIS Journal (6 times a year)

Access to staff:
Contact by letter, by telephone, by fax, by e-mail
and via website. Appointment necessary.
Hours: Mon to Fri, 0900 to 1700

Connections with:
IMIS Publications Limited
at the same address

INSTITUTE FOR THE STUDY OF THE AMERICAS

Acronym or abbreviation: ISA

University of London, School of Advanced Study,
Senate House, South Block, London WC1E 7HU

Tel: 020 7862 8870
Fax: 020 7862 8886
E-mail: americas@sas.ac.uk

Website:
http://www.americas.sas.ac.uk

Enquiries:
Enquiries to: Information Resources Manager
Direct tel: 020 7862 8501
Direct e-mail: christy.palmer@sas.ac.uk
Other contacts: Latin American Bibliographer (in
librarian's absence)

Founded:
1965

Created by the merger of:
Institute of Latin American Studies (ILAS) with the
Institute of United States Studies (IUSS) (year of
change 2004)

Organisation type and purpose:
University department or institute.

Subject coverage:
Latin America, predominantly humanities and
social sciences.

**Museum or gallery collection, archive, or library
special collection:**
Archive collection (news sources, political party
material)
Bibliography and reference
British Union Catalogue of Latin American
(BUCLA) (author card catalogue, to 1988 closed)
Current affairs and political party ephemera
(1960–)
Nissa Torrents video collection

Non-library collection catalogue:
All or part available online and in-house

Printed publications:
Annual Report
Latin American and Caribbean Studies in the
Humanities and Social Sciences in the
Universities of the United Kingdom (1997)
Guide to Latin American and Caribbean census
material: a bibliography and union list (1990)
Latin American and Carribean library resources in
London: a guide (7th ed., 1997)
Libraries and special collections on Latin America
and the Caribbean: a directory of European
resources (1988, pub Athlone Press)
List of Booksellers dealing in Latin Americana and
Caribbeana (2nd ed., 1987)

Publications list:
Available in print

Access to staff:
Contact by letter, by telephone, by fax, by e-mail,
in person and via website. Letter of introduction
required.
Hours: Mon to Fri, 0930 to 1730
Special comments: Letter of introduction required
for undergraduate students.

Houses the editorial office of the:
Journal of Latin American Studies

Member Institute of:
University of London's School of Advanced Study

Member of:
Red Europea de Información y Documentación
sobre América Latina (REDIAL)

Member organisation of:
Advisory Council on Latin American and Iberian
Information Resources (ACLAIIR)
Seminar on the Acquisition of Latin American
Library Materials (SALALM)

INSTITUTE FOR TRANSPORT STUDIES

Acronym or abbreviation: ITS

University of Leeds, 38–40 University Road, Leeds,
West Yorkshire, LS2 9JT

Tel: 0113 233 5325
Fax: 0113 233 5334
E-mail: m.r.wardman@its.leeds.ac.uk

Website:
http://www.its.leeds.ac.uk

Enquiries:
Enquiries to: Director
Other contacts: Director of Research; Director of
Studies

Founded:
1966

Organisation type and purpose:
University department or institute, consultancy,
research organisation.

Subject coverage:
Public transport and freight economics; road safety
and accident analysis; environmental economics
and evaluation; information technology; surveys
and data capture; transport policy and appraisal;
land use and transport issues; transport demand
management; travel demand forecasting; traffic
management and control; transport network

modelling; transport operations; microsimulation
of traffic behaviour; traffic pollution monitoring
and modelling.

Printed publications:
Annual Report in Traffic Engineering and Control
(March)
Technical Note Series (lists of)
Working Paper Series (lists of)
Order printed publications from: Publications
Secretary, Institute for Transport Studies
at the same address, e-mail: akruk@its.leeds.ac.uk

Access to staff:
Contact by e-mail and via website
Hours: Mon to Fri, 0900 to 1700

Access for disabled people:
Parking provided, ramped entry, toilet facilities

Links with:
Transport Statistics Users' Group (TSUG)
Universities Transport Study Group (UTSG)

Parent body:
University of Leeds

INSTITUTE OF ACOUSTICS

Acronym or abbreviation: IOA

77A St Peter's Street, St Albans, Hertfordshire, AL1
3BN

Tel: 01727 848195
Fax: 01727 850553
E-mail: ioa@ioa.org.uk

Website:
http://www.ioa.org.uk

Enquiries:
Enquiries to: Chief Executive

Founded:
1974

Organisation type and purpose:
International organisation, learned society,
professional body (membership is by qualification,
election or invitation), present number of
members: 2600, registered charity (charity number
267026), publishing house.

Subject coverage:
Acoustics, noise, vibration, ultrasonics.

Library catalogue:
All or part available in-house and in print

Printed publications:
Acoustics Bulletin
Buyers' Guide
Members Register
Proceedings of the Institute

Publications list:
Available online and in print

Access to staff:
Contact by letter, by telephone, by fax, by e-mail,
in person and via website. Appointment necessary.
Hours: Mon to Fri, 0900 to 1700

Links with:
European Acoustics Association (EAA)
International Institute of Noise Control
Engineering (I/INCE)

INSTITUTE OF ADMINISTRATIVE MANAGEMENT

Acronym or abbreviation: IAM

6 Graphite Square, Vauxhall Walk, London, SE11
5EE

Tel: 020 7091 2600
Fax: 020 7091 2619
E-mail: info@instam.org

Website:
http://www.instam.org

Founded:
1915

continued overleaf

Organisation type and purpose:
Established in 1915, the Institute of Administrative Management is the only professional body for both practising and aspiring Administrative Managers. Students and Members are professionals who are responsible for the management of: systems, human resources, communication, information technology, facilities, training and development, finance. The IAM supports managers (and aspiring managers) at all levels, aiming to improve both personal and organisational performance through a systematic approach to professional development.

Subject coverage:
Administrative management, office supervision, business management.

Information services:
Publications relating to the management of business.

Education services:
A wide range of professional qualifications in business management.

Printed publications:
Manager – The British Journal of Administrative Management (monthly, on annual subscription)
Study manuals
Order printed publications from: info@instam.org

Publications list:
Available online

Access to staff:
Contact by letter, by telephone, by fax, by e-mail and via website. Appointment necessary.
Hours: Mon to Fri, 0900 to 1700

INSTITUTE OF ADVANCED LEGAL STUDIES LIBRARY

Acronym or abbreviation: IALS

17 Russell Square, London, WC1B 5DR

Tel: 020 7862 5800
Fax: 020 7862 5770
E-mail: ials@sas.ac.uk

Website:
http://ials.sas.ac.uk
Information about IALS as a whole and IALS Library; access to IALS online catalogue, structured links to electronic legal research resources.

Enquiries:
Enquiries to: Library Administrative Officer
Direct tel: 020 7862 5801

Founded:
1947

Organisation type and purpose:
University department or institute.
Postgraduate legal research, other than Oriental and Eastern European law.

Subject coverage:
Commonwealth Law; US Law; Western European Law; Public International Law.

Museum or gallery collection, archive, or library special collection:
Commonwealth Law; US Law; Western European Law; Public International Law

Non-library collection catalogue:
All or part available online and in-house

Library catalogue:
All or part available online

Printed publications:
IALS Library, list of serials (annually)

Access to staff:
Contact by letter, by telephone, by fax, by e-mail and via website
Hours: Mon to Fri, 0900 to 2000; Sat, 1000 to 1730
Special comments: Please apply to the library for admissions leaflet and subscription rates. There are restrictions, and charges for some users.

Access for disabled people:
Toilet facilities

Member organisation of:
School of Advanced Study of the University of London
   tel: 020 7862 8659; fax: 020 7862 8657; e-mail: school@sas.ac.uk

Parent body:
University of London
   tel: 020 7862 8000

INSTITUTE OF ADVANCED MOTORISTS LIMITED

Acronym or abbreviation: IAM

IAM House, 510 Chiswick High Road, London, W4 5RG

Tel: 020 8996 9600
Fax: 020 8996 9601

Website:
http://www.iam.org.uk

Enquiries:
Enquiries to: Chief Executive

Founded:
1956

Organisation type and purpose:
Membership association (membership is by qualification), present number of members: 110,000, registered charity (charity number 249002), training organisation.
To improve road safety by raising driving standards.

Subject coverage:
Driving standards, driving techniques.

Printed publications:
Motorcycle Roadcraft (£11.99)
Passing Your Advanced Driving Test (£7.99)
Passing Your Advanced Motorcycling Test (£7.99)
Roadcraft (£13.99)

Electronic and video publications:
Advanced Driver Training (CD-ROM single user £41, multi user £103.40)
Roadcraft: An Advanced Driving Course (video, £14.99)
Safer Driving (video, £13.60)
Road Runners plus Road Skills for Life (CD-ROM, £20)
The Advanced Driving Test, Your Licence to Drive (CD-ROM, £29.99)
The Theory Test (CD-ROM, £18)
Top Rider (video, £14.49)

Publications list:
Available in print

Access to staff:
Contact by letter, by telephone and by fax
Hours: Mon to Fri, 0900 to 1700

Subsidiary bodies:
IAM Fleet Training Ltd
   at the same address; tel: 0845 3108311; fax: 020 8996 9701
IAM Group Services Ltd
   at the same address

INSTITUTE OF AGRICULTURAL MANAGEMENT

Acronym or abbreviation: IAgrM

Portbury House, Sheepway, Portbury, Bristol BS20 7TE

Tel: 01275 843825
Fax: 01275 374747
E-mail: cooksleyandco@btconnect.com

Website:
http://www.iagrm.org.uk
Full description of the Institute's activities and services.

Enquiries:
Enquiries to: Director

Founded:
1966

Organisation type and purpose:
Learned society, professional body (membership is by subscription), present number of members: 850, registered charity.

Subject coverage:
Business management in agriculture and associated industries; management techniques; management applications in agriculture.

Education services:
Courses are available in Management and Supervisory Studies (in agriculture and associated subjects).

Printed publications:
Agricultural Management – Reference List of Current Publications (1994, members, £1; non-members £3)
Case Studies in Agricultural & Rural Land Management (2nd ed., 1997)
Courses available in Management and Supervisory Studies (in agriculture and associated subjects, 1997)
Farm management (quarterly, free to members, otherwise on subscription)
Farm managers in 1995 (price on application)
Food – Its Production, Marketing and Consumption (1992, members £10, non-members £11.95, overseas £14)
From FMA to CMA (1993, members £3, others in UK £5, overseas £7)
Institute News (3 times a year)
Leadership & the challenge of developing rural leaders (1998)
The Manager as Farmer – Wisdom from some I have known (1996)
The Manager's Environment (1990, members £5, others in UK £8, overseas £10)

Publications list:
Available online and in print

Access to staff:
Contact by letter, by telephone, by fax, by e-mail and via website. Appointment necessary.
Hours: Mon to Fri, 0900 to 1700
Special comments: The office is manned during office hours. Answerphone at other times.

Links with:
International Farm Management Association

INSTITUTE OF AGRICULTURAL SECRETARIES AND ADMINISTRATORS

Acronym or abbreviation: IAgSA

National Agricultural Centre, Stoneleigh, Kenilworth, Warwickshire, CV8 2LG

Tel: 024 7669 6592
Fax: 024 7641 7937
E-mail: iagsa@iagsa.co.uk

Website:
http://www.iagsa.co.uk
General.

Enquiries:
Enquiries to: General Secretary

Founded:
1967

Organisation type and purpose:
Professional body (membership is by subscription), present number of members: 950

Subject coverage:
Agricultural secretaryship and rural business administration.

Printed publications:
Newsletter (on sale)

Access to staff:
Contact by letter, by telephone, by fax, by e-mail and via website
Hours: Mon to Fri, 0900 to 1700

INSTITUTE OF ALCOHOL STUDIES

Acronym or abbreviation: IAS

Alliance House, 12 Caxton Street, London, SW1H 0QS

Tel: 020 7222 4001
Fax: 020 7799 2510
E-mail: librarian@ias.org.uk

Website:
http://www.ias.org.uk
Current figures and statistics, including fact sheets, news bulletins and links to other sites of interest.
http://www.ias.org.uk/press.htm
IAS press digest's news service

Enquiries:
Enquiries to: Librarian

Founded:
1982

Organisation type and purpose:
National organisation, registered charity, research organisation.
A specialised reference library, which collects information on alcohol-related issues from a wide variety of sources.
To increase the knowledge of alcohol and the social and health cosequences of its misuse.

Subject coverage:
Library on alcohol-related issues with bibliographic database. Alcohol consumption and associated problems; alcohol control policies; social science research and policy studies. Historical archive of temperance-related material.

Museum or gallery collection, archive, or library special collection:
Historical (temperance) material, books, periodicals etc
Modern materials, books, scientific journals etc

Trade and statistical information:
Data and reference material on alcohol consumption and harm principally in the UK.

Library catalogue:
All or part available in-house

Printed publications:
A Great and Growing Evil: The Medical Consequences of Alcohol Abuse (Royal College of Physicians)
A Lot of Bottle (Rutherford D)
Alcohol Policy and the Public Good (Edwards G)
Alcohol Policy and the Public Good – A Guide for Action (A summary)
Alcohol Problems in the Family
Alcohol and the Young (Royal College of Physicians and British Paediatric Association, 1995)
Counterbalancing the Drinks Industry – A Eurocare Report to the European Union on Alcohol Policy
Industrial Pack (Guidelines)
UK Alcohol Alert (journal, quarterly)
The Globe (journal, quarterly)
Order printed publications from: e-mail: sales@ias.org.uk

Publications list:
Available online and in print

Access to staff:
Contact by letter, by telephone, by fax, by e-mail and via website. Appointment necessary.
Hours: Mon to Fri, 0930 to 1600
Special comments: Charges made for photocopies.

Affiliated to:
Alliance House Foundation
at the same address; tel: 020 7222 4001
Eurocare (Alliance of alcohol problems mainly in European Union)
tel: 01480 466766

INSTITUTE OF AMATEUR CINEMATOGRAPHERS

Acronym or abbreviation: IAC

Global House, 1 Ashley Avenue, Epsom, Surrey, KT18 5NY

Tel: 01372 822812
E-mail: admin@theiac.org.uk

Website:
http://www.theiac.org.uk
General information

Enquiries:
Enquiries to: Administrator

Founded:
1932

Organisation type and purpose:
Membership association (membership is by subscription), present number of members: 2000, voluntary organisation, registered charity (charity number 260467).

Subject coverage:
Amateur cinematography.

Museum or gallery collection, archive, or library special collection:
Archive library of amateur films

Printed publications:
Film and Video Maker (6 times a year, for members)

Access to staff:
Contact by letter, by telephone and by e-mail.
Appointment necessary.
Hours: Staffed part-time only

INSTITUTE OF ANIMAL TECHNOLOGY

Acronym or abbreviation: IAT

5 South Parade, Summertown, Oxford, OX2 7JL

E-mail: iat101@btconnect.com

Website:
http://www.iat.org.uk

Enquiries:
Enquiries to: IAT Administrator

Founded:
1950

Organisation type and purpose:
Professional body (membership is by qualification), present number of members: more than 2,200, voluntary organisation.
Advancing and promoting excellence in the care and welfare of animals in science.

Subject coverage:
Laboratory animal technology; animal welfare; animal husbandry; advances in new technology; transgenic technology; seminars and symposiums.

Information services:
Animal technology careers advice and opportunities.

Education services:
Education and qualifications advice.

Printed publications:
Animal Technology & Welfare (Journal, 3 times a year, subscription available to non-members)
Bulletin (monthly, members only)
Membership pack (members only)
Introduction to Animal Technology (reference handbook)
Manual of Animal Technology (reference handbook)
Career as an Animal Technologist (free guide)
Gaining Momentum (IAT brochure free)

Electronic and video publications:
With Care (a series of teaching videos)

Access to staff:
Contact by letter, by e-mail and via website
Hours: Normal working hours

INSTITUTE OF ARCHITECTURAL IRONMONGERS

Acronym or abbreviation: IAI

8 Stepney Green, London, E1 3JU

Tel: 020 7790 3431
Fax: 020 7790 8517
E-mail: info@gai.org.uk

Website:
http://www.iai.uk.com
General information.

Enquiries:
Enquiries to: General Secretary

Founded:
1970

Organisation type and purpose:
Professional body (membership is by qualification).
Parent body, the Guild of Architectural Ironmongers.

Subject coverage:
Architectural ironmongery.

Access to staff:
Contact by letter, by telephone, by fax, by e-mail and via website
Hours: Mon to Fri, 0900 to 1700

INSTITUTE OF ART AND LAW

Acronym or abbreviation: IAL

1–5 Cank Street, Leicester, LE1 5GX

Tel: 0116 253 8888
Fax: 0116 251 1666
E-mail: info@ial.uk.com

Website:
http://www.ial.uk.com

Enquiries:
Enquiries to: Administrator

Founded:
1995

Organisation type and purpose:
International organisation (membership is by subscription).

Subject coverage:
Art, law.

Printed publications:
Museums and the Holocaust (Palmer N)
Commentary on the UNESCO Convention (O'Keefe P)
Commentary on the Unidroit Convention (Prott L)
Art and Taxation: A Guide (Simmonds J)
Cultural Heritage Statutes
Cultural Rights and Wrongs
Art Treasures and War (Kowalski W)
17 Seminar Papers including:
Transacting in Art: General Issues
Title and Time in Art and Antiquity Claims
Copyright: Is your Copying Right?
Recovery of Stolen Looted Works of Art
Art, Law and the Holocaust
Beyond Reasonable Doubt? Art Crime and the Criminal Law

Publications list:
Available online and in print

Access to staff:
Contact by e-mail
Hours: Mon to Fri, 0900 to 1700

Access to building, collection or gallery:
Prior appointment required

INSTITUTE OF ASPHALT TECHNOLOGY, THE

Acronym or abbreviation: IAT

IAT Head Office, Paper Mews Place, 290 High Street, Dorking, Surrey, RH4 1QT

Tel: 01306 742792

continued overleaf

Fax: 01306 888902
E-mail: secretary@instofasphalt.org

Website:
http://www.instofasphalt.org

Enquiries:
Enquiries to: Secretary

Founded:
1966

Organisation type and purpose:
Learned society, professional body (membership is by subscription, election or invitation), present number of members: 1650.
Furtherance of excellence in asphalt technology.

Subject coverage:
Asphalt technology, bitumen, bituminous materials.

Museum or gallery collection, archive, or library special collection:
Past journals and Year Books

Non-library collection catalogue:
All or part available in print

Library catalogue:
All or part available in-house and in print

Printed publications:
Asphalt Technology (journal, 1966 to 1991)
Asphalt Yearbook (1992 to 2005)
IAT Newsletter (1994 to 2002)
Asphalt Professional (6 times a year)

Electronic and video publications:
Sampling Bituminous Materials (video)
Hot Rolled Asphalt Production, Laying and
   Compaction (video)

Access to staff:
Contact by letter, by telephone, by fax, by e-mail and via website
Hours: Mon to Fri, 0900 to 1700

Has:
11 regional branches thoughout the UK and an overseas branch,
   contact Head Office for details

Professional affiliate member of:
The Engineering Council

INSTITUTE OF ASSOCIATION MANAGEMENT

Acronym or abbreviation: IofAM

Venture House, 6 Silver Court, Welwyn Garden City, Hertfordshire, AL7 1TS

Tel: 08456 590 704
E-mail: info@iofam.co.uk

Website:
http://www.iofam.org.uk
Membership, affiliates, research, careers, CPD, events.

Founded:
1933

Formerly called:
Society of Association Executives (year of change 2000); Secretaries Club (year of change prior to 2000)

Organisation type and purpose:
An independent professional body made up of managers and senior staff responsible for the management, development and governance of trade bodies, professional institutes, societies, chambers of commerce, voluntary organisations, charities and other representative groups.
To develop, promote and share best practice for the benefit of IofAM members and all those involved in the governance of associations. To achieve its objectives, the IofAM offers a forum for education, training and development, dissemination of information, networking, and research.

Subject coverage:
Promotes best practice and professional standards in association management and governance; promulgates the role and contribution of

associations in national life and the status and reputation of association management as a profession; provides services of value to members, by delivering information and advice on association management matters through means such as events, networking and member forums.

Access to staff:
Contact by letter, by telephone, by e-mail and via website

INSTITUTE OF AUCTIONEERS AND APPRAISERS IN SCOTLAND

The Rural Centre – Westmains, Ingliston, Newbridge, Midlothian, EH28 8NZ

Tel: 0131 472 4067
Fax: 0131 472 4067
E-mail: iaas@auctioneersscotland.co.uk

Enquiries:
Enquiries to: Executive Secretary
Direct e-mail: iaas@auctioneersscotland.co.uk

Founded:
1926

Organisation type and purpose:
Professional body.

Subject coverage:
Auction of livestock and chattels; urban and rural valuation; urban and rural estate agency; animal welfare; marketing; agricultural arbitration.

Printed publications:
Individual Members catalogues of sales

Access to staff:
Access for members only.
Hours: Mon to Thu, 0900 to 1300

Links with:
European Association of Livestock Markets
Livestock Auctioneers Market Committee for England and Wales

INSTITUTE OF BARRISTERS' CLERKS

Acronym or abbreviation: IBC

289–293 High Holborn, London, WC1V 7HZ

Tel: 020 7831 7144
Fax: 020 7831 7144
E-mail: admin@barristersclerks.com

Website:
http://www.barristersclerks.com
Home page, general information.

Enquiries:
Enquiries to: Administrator

Founded:
1922

Organisation type and purpose:
Membership association (membership is by subscription), present number of members: 810.

Subject coverage:
Work conditions, employment, education.

Access to staff:
Contact by letter, by telephone and by e-mail.
Appointment necessary. Non-members charged.
Hours: Mon to Fri, 0900 to 1700

Access for disabled people:
Toilet facilities
Special comments: Wheelchair access by prior arangement, lift from basement.

INSTITUTE OF BIOLOGICAL, ENVIRONMENTAL AND RURAL SCIENCES

Acronym or abbreviation: IBERS

Aberystwyth University, Gogerddan, Aberystwyth, Ceredigion, SY23 3EB

Tel: 01970 823000

Fax: 01970 828357
E-mail: tns@aber.ac.uk

Website:
http://www.aber.ac.uk/en/ibers

Enquiries:
Enquiries to: Librarian
Direct tel: 01970 823051
Other contacts: Business Manager (for external liaison and research contract enquiries)

Founded:
1919

Formerly called:
IGER – Institute of Grassland and Environmental Research (year of change 2008)

Organisation type and purpose:
University research and teaching institute

Subject coverage:
Grassland, agriculture, environment, cellular and molecular biology, genetic manipulation, plant development, environmental biology, plant physiology and biochemistry, pathology, nitrogen, fixation, plant genetics, forage and cereal breeding, ecology and environmental plant science including agricultural pollution, organic farming, ruminant nutrition and forage conservation, land use including low-input legume-based technology, alternative animals and crop systems.

Museum or gallery collection, archive, or library special collection:
Antiquarian agricultural and botanical collections of books
Flora (British county and overseas), Prof. Harper reprint collection
Gene bank collections of herbage and cereal seeds, and germplasm
Herbarium flora and fauna collection
Pre-1840 books on grassland and agriculture
Works of Sir George Stapledon 1882–1960

Non-library collection catalogue:
All or part available online and in-house

Library catalogue:
All or part available online and in-house

Printed publications:
IBERS Knowledge-based Innovations (annually)
Information leaflets
Technical Advisory Report (irregular, £3)
Order printed publications from: Stapledon Library, Institute of Biological, Environmental and Rural Sciences, Aberystwyth University, Gogerddan, Aberystwyth, Ceredigion, SY23 3EB, Wales; e-mail gogstaff@aber.ac.uk

Publications list:
Available online and in print

Access to staff:
Contact by letter, by telephone, by fax, by e-mail and via website
Hours: Mon to Fri, 0900 to 1700

INSTITUTE OF BIOMEDICAL SCIENCE

Acronym or abbreviation: IBMS

12 Coldbath Square, London, EC1R 5HL

Tel: 020 7713 0214
Fax: 020 7436 4946

Website:
http://www.ibms.org

Enquiries:
Enquiries to: Publications Officer
Direct e-mail: mc@ibms.org

Founded:
1912

Organisation type and purpose:
Professional body, present number of members: 17,500, registered charity (charity number 261926).
To promote and develop biomedical science and its practitioners and to establish and maintain professional standards.

Subject coverage:
Haematology, transfusion science, medical microbiology, virology, clinical chemistry, cellular pathology, immunology, pathology, all other biomedical science disciplines, laboratory administration and management, and laboratory safety.

Printed publications:
The Biomedical Scientist (monthly)
British Journal of Biomedical Science (4 times a year)

Publications list:
Available online and in print

Access to staff:
Contact by letter, by telephone, by fax, by e-mail and via website. Non-members charged.
Hours: Mon to Fri, 0900 to 1700

Access to building, collection or gallery:
No prior appointment required

INSTITUTE OF BIOSCIENCE AND TECHNOLOGY

Cranfield University, Silsoe, Bedfordshire, MK45 4DT

Tel: 01525 863000
Fax: 01525 863001

Website:
http://www.cranfield.ac.uk/ibst
Full details of the Institute of BioScience and Technology.

Enquiries:
Enquiries to: Commercial and Marketing Director
Direct tel: 01525 863168
Direct fax: 01525 863080
Direct e-mail: l.tigwell@cranfield.ac.uk

Founded:
1981

Organisation type and purpose:
University department or institute.
Specialises in contract research, consultancy and postgraduate training, including short courses.

Subject coverage:
Biotechnology, biosensors, environmental biotechnology, food and agricultural biotechnology, analysis of pollutants, medical diagnostics, molecular biology, education in biotechnology, food spoilage, environmental monitoring, oncology, in vitro toxicity testing, advanced imaging, clinical research in in vitro diagnostic assay technology, measurement science and instrumentation, computational intelligence, bioinformatics, process monitoring and integration, systems manufacture, computational chemistry, molecularly-imprinted polymers.

Printed publications:
Publicity brochure
Research papers in national and international journals
Reports

Electronic and video publications:
Reports

Publications list:
Available in print

Access to staff:
Contact by e-mail
Hours: Mon to Fri, 0900 to 1700

Access to building, collection or gallery:
Prior appointment required

INSTITUTE OF BREWING AND DISTILLING

Acronym or abbreviation: IBD

33 Clarges Street, London, W1J 7EE

Tel: 020 7499 8144
Fax: 020 7499 1156
E-mail: enquiries@ibd.org.uk

Website:
http://www.ibd.org.uk

Enquiries:
Enquiries to: Executive Director

Founded:
1886

Organisation type and purpose:
Learned society, present number of members: 4,000, registered charity (charity number 269830).

Subject coverage:
Brewing science.

Museum or gallery collection, archive, or library special collection:
Historical Brewing Science Library (brewing, distilling, malting) now held at Oxford Brookes University

Printed publications:
The Brewer and Distiller International (monthly)
Journal of the Institute of Brewing (quarterly)
IBD Brewing and Distilling Directory (annual)
Past exam papers
General Certificate in Brewing, General Certificate in Distilling, General Certificate in Packaging – Exam Syllabus and CD-ROM of Learning Material
Diploma in Brewing Examination Syllabus
Diploma in Distilling Examination Syllabus
Diploma in Packaging Examination Syllabus
Master Brewer Examination Syllabus
Revision material for examinations

Electronic and video publications:
General Certificate in Brewing, General Certificate in Distilling, General Certificate in Packaging – Exam Syllabus and CD-ROM of Learning Material
Diploma in Brewing Examination Syllabus
Diploma in Distilling Examination Syllabus

Publications list:
Available online and in print

Access to staff:
Contact by letter, by telephone, by fax and by e-mail. Appointment necessary.

Access to building, collection or gallery:
Prior appointment required
Hours: Mon to Fri, 0900 to 1700; closed bank holidays, Christmas and Easter

Links with:
American Society of Brewing Chemists
Brewing, Food and Beverage Industry Suppliers Association (BFBI)
Master Brewers of America Assocation (MBAA)

INSTITUTE OF BUDDHIST STUDIES

PO Box 443, Tring, Hertfordshire, HP23 6PX

Tel: 01442 890882

Enquiries:
Enquiries to: Managing Director
Direct e-mail: ts1@soas.ac.uk

Founded:
1966

Organisation type and purpose:
Learned society (membership is by election or invitation), registered charity (charity number 314166).
Promotion of Buddhist Studies.

Subject coverage:
Buddhism in Asian countries.

Printed publications:
Asceticism in Buddhism and Brahminism (£18.50)
Indo-Tibetan Studies (£25)
Tales of an Old Lama (£14.50)
The Bodhisattvapitaka (40)
The Buddhist Heritage (£20)
The Cult of the Deity Vajrakila (£21)
The Rishukyo (£27)
The Vajrabhairava Tantras (£24)
The Six perfections (£12.50)

Kriyasamgraha (£19.50)
Vajravali of Abhyakaragupta, 2 vols (£50)
The Buddhist Forum
Buddhica Britannica

Publications list:
Available in print

Access to staff:
Contact by letter, by telephone and by e-mail
Hours: Mon to Fri, 0900 to 1700
Special comments: No access to public.

Access to building, collection or gallery:
No access other than to staff

INSTITUTE OF BUILDERS' MERCHANTS

Acronym or abbreviation: IoBM

2 Crab Apple Way, Gamlingay, Sandy, Beds, SG19 3LS

Tel: 01767 650662
E-mail: admin@instbm.co.uk

Website:
http://www.iobm.co.uk

Enquiries:
Enquiries to: Administrator

Founded:
1968

Organisation type and purpose:
Professional body.

Subject coverage:
Building supplies.

Access to staff:
Contact by letter, by telephone and by e-mail
Hours: Mon to Thu, 0900 to 1300

INSTITUTE OF BUSINESS ADVISERS

Acronym or abbreviation: IBA

Response House, Queen Street North, Chesterfield, Derbyshire, S41 9AB

Tel: 01246 453322
Fax: 01246 453300

Website:
http://www.iba.org.uk
Help for small businesses and business advisers, general information on IBA.

Enquiries:
Enquiries to: Chief Executive
Direct e-mail: john.milburn@managers.org.uk
Other contacts: Membership & Communications Manager for membership and small business enquiries.

Founded:
1989

Organisation type and purpose:
Professional body (membership is by qualification, election or invitation), present number of members: 2500.

Subject coverage:
Small and medium enterprises, how to start up and run a small business, business planning, marketing, accounting, exporting, trade credit, raising finance, and all other aspects of small business growth, including related support services, business advisers, business counsellors, business mentors, business trainers and supporting staff.

Printed publications:
Series of information sheets and forms (free to £5) including:
Brief History of the Institute
Code of Conduct – for Professional Business Counsellors and Advisers
Counselling for Enterprise
Training Courses – Accredited Courses and Providers

continued overleaf

Publications list:
Available in print

Access to staff:
Contact by letter, by telephone, by e-mail and via website. Appointment necessary.
Hours: Mon to Fri, 0900 to 1700

Professional Development and Accounts Departments:
IBA
Response House, Queen Street North, Chesterfield, S41 9AB; tel: 01246 453322; fax: 01246 453300; e-mail: info@iba.org.uk

INSTITUTE OF BUSINESS CONSULTING

4th Floor, 2 Savoy Court, Strand, London, WC2R 0EZ

Tel: 020 7497 0580
Fax: 020 7497 0463
E-mail: ibc@ibconsulting.org.uk

Website:
http://www.ibconsulting.org.uk
Services, professional development, purchasing consultancy, national register, news and events.

Founded:
1961

Created by the merger of:
Institute of Management Consultancy (IMC) and Chartered Management Institute (year of change 2005); Institute of Business Advisers (IBA) and the Institute of Management Consultancy (IMC) (year of change 2007)

Formerly called:
Institute of Management Consultants (IMC) (year of change 1990s); Institute of Management Consultancy (IMC) (year of change 2007)

Organisation type and purpose:
The only professional body for all business consultants and advisers. Encompasses the entire profession of consultants and advisers with a membership touching on all areas of the UK economy.
To raise standards of professional practice in support of enhancing business performance. Offers a development path for the profession, supported by high quality online resources and a recognised qualification route.

Subject coverage:
Business and management consultancy.

Access to staff:
Contact by letter, by telephone, by fax and by e-mail

INSTITUTE OF BUSINESS ETHICS

Acronym or abbreviation: IBE

24 Greencoat Place, London, SW1P 1BE

Tel: 020 7798 6040
Fax: 020 7798 6044
E-mail: info@ibe.org.uk

Website:
http://www.ibe.org.uk

Enquiries:
Enquiries to: Director

Founded:
1986

Organisation type and purpose:
Registered charity (charity number 1084014) with mission to encourage high standards of business behaviour based on ethical values. Offers training, research, advice. Membership association (membership is by subscription).

Subject coverage:
Codes of business ethics, business and the environment, management and health of employees, education and business. Ethical aspects of information technology, the teaching of business ethics, reputation risk management, supply chain.

Printed publications:
Applying Codes of Business Ethics
Benefiting Business & the Environment
Business & Society – The Approach of The Faiths
Codes of Ethics & International Business
Company Philosophies & Codes of Business Ethics
Competitive Intelligence
Corporate Uses of Codes of Ethics 2004
Demonstrating Corporate Values
Developing a Code of Business Ethics
Does Business Ethics Pay?
Does Business Ethics Pay? Revisited
Employee Views of Ethics at Work 2008
Employees Health & Organisational Practice
Ethical Aspects of IT
Ethical Business
Ethical Due Diligence
Ethics at Work
Ethics Environment & the Company
Ethics Matters (with CIHE)
GPG 1: Speak Up Procedures
GPG 2: Surveying Staff on Ethical Matters
Illustrative Code of Business Ethics – Updated
Living Up to Our Values
Making Business Ethics Work
Management & the Health of Employees
Marketing Responsibly
Ethics in the Provision and Use of IT for Business
Doing Business in South Korea
Priorities, Practice and Ethics in Small Firms
Risky Business
Setting the Tone
Supplier Relationships in the UK
Takeovers – What ethical considerations should apply?
Taking the Temperature
The Ethics of Influence
The Teaching of Business Ethics
Use of Codes of Ethics in Business
What's all this about Business Ethics
Order printed publications from: website: http://www.ibe.org.uk

Electronic and video publications:
E-learning CD – Introduction to Business Ethics
Order electronic and video publications from: website: http://www.ibe.org.uk

Publications list:
Available online and in print

Access to staff:
Contact by letter, by telephone, by fax and by e-mail. Appointment necessary.
Hours: Mon to Fri, 0900 to 1700

Access to building, collection or gallery:
Appointment required

Partners of:
Caux Round Table

INSTITUTE OF CANCER RESEARCH

Acronym or abbreviation: ICR

15 Cotswold Road, Sutton, Surrey, SM2 5NG

Tel: 020 8643 8901
Fax: 020 7352 6283

Enquiries:
Enquiries to: Librarian
Direct tel: 020 7352 5946
Direct e-mail: press@icr.ac.uk

Organisation type and purpose:
Research organisation.

Subject coverage:
Oncology, cancer.

Library catalogue:
All or part available in-house

Printed publications:
Annual Report (apply secretariat)

Access to staff:
Contact by letter, by telephone, by fax and by e-mail. Appointment necessary. Access for members only.
Hours: Reference only for non-ICR staff

Access to building, collection or gallery:
Prior appointment required

Affiliated to:
University of London

INSTITUTE OF CAREER GUIDANCE

Acronym or abbreviation: ICG

27A Lower High Street, Stourbridge, West Midlands, DY8 1TA

Tel: 01384 376464
Fax: 01384 440830
E-mail: hq@icg-uk.org

Website:
http://www.icg-uk.org

Enquiries:
Enquiries to: Business Development Manager
Direct tel: 01384 445631
Other contacts: Marketing Department

Founded:
1922

Organisation type and purpose:
Advisory body, professional body (membership is by subscription), present number of members: 3500.
Building principles and practice of high quality careers guidance.

Subject coverage:
All aspects of career guidance ware, including connections, careers service, information, advice and guidance partnerships, HE and FE.

Museum or gallery collection, archive, or library special collection:
Archive material on the work of Careers Service

Printed publications:
Career Guidance Today (6 times a year)
PORTICO (Appointment vacancies, fortnightly)
Personal Adviser (magazine, 6 times a year)

Access to staff:
Contact by letter, by telephone, by fax, by e-mail and via website
Hours: Mon to Fri, 0900 to 1700

INSTITUTE OF CARPENTERS

Acronym or abbreviation: IOC

32 High Street, Wendover, Bucks, HP22 6EA

Tel: 0844 879 7696
Fax: 01296 620981
E-mail: info@instituteofcarpenters.com

Website:
http://www.instituteofcarpenters.com
Aims, members' area, careers advice, news, find a professional, master certificate scheme, competitions and awards, exams, who's who.

Enquiries:
Enquiries to: Administrator

Founded:
1890

Organisation type and purpose:
Professional body for skilled woodworkers. Promotes and enhances the role and status of skilled craftsmen and women everywhere; encourages the highest standards of craftsmanship for all working with wood; maintains the best traditions of historic crafts; works to enhance and promote the status of the ancient profession and to

ensure that members and their clients benefit from the superior knowledge and craftsmanship associated with the Institute.

Subject coverage:
Membership open to carpenters, furniture and cabinet makers, boat builders (woodworking skills), joiners, shopfitters, heavy structural post and beam carpenters, wheelwrights, wood carvers, wood turners. Offers technical and practical information and advice, respected qualifications from Foundation through to Fellowship level, specialist service for members. Master Certificate Scheme

Printed publications:
The Cutting Edge (magazine, 6 a year)

Electronic and video publications:
The Cutting Edge (magazine, 6 a year)
Order electronic and video publications from: Back copies available free to members on line

Access to staff:
Contact by letter, by telephone, by fax and by e-mail

INSTITUTE OF CAST METALS ENGINEERS

Acronym or abbreviation: ICME

National Metalforming Centre, 47 Birmingham Road, West Bromwich, Birmingham, B70 6HA

Tel: 0121 601 6979
Fax: 0121 601 6981
E-mail: info@icme.org.uk

Website:
http://www.icme.org.uk

Enquiries:
Enquiries to: Operations Director

Founded:
1904

Organisation type and purpose:
Professional body.

Subject coverage:
Cast metals technology, education, training.

Museum or gallery collection, archive, or library special collection:
Library available, with limited information service

Trade and statistical information:
Summary of statistics.

Printed publications:
Technical books
The Foundryman (journal, monthly)
Order printed publications from: info@icme.org.uk

Publications list:
Available online and in print

Access to staff:
Contact by letter, by telephone, by fax, by e-mail and via website. Appointment necessary.
Hours: Mon to Thu, 0900 to 1700; Fri, 0900 to 1330

Access to building, collection or gallery:
Hours: Mon to Thu, 0900 to 1700; Fri, 0900 to 1330

Access for disabled people:
Fully accessible

Links with:
International Committee of Foundry Technical Associations

INSTITUTE OF CHARTERED ACCOUNTANTS IN ENGLAND AND WALES

Acronym or abbreviation: ICAEW

Chartered Accountants' Hall, Moorgate Place, London, EC2R 6EA

Tel: 020 7920 8100
Fax: 020 7920 0547
E-mail: via website

Website:
http://www.icaew.com
Find a chartered accountant, qualifications, students, members, employers, technical and business topics, library.

Enquiries:
Direct tel: 020 7920 8620 (for library enquiries)
Direct e-mail: library@icaew.com (for library enquiries)

Founded:
1880

Organisation type and purpose:
The largest professional accountancy body in Europe, membership association, offers a number of routes to membership for both trainee and qualified accountants, as well as access to specialist technical and business groups.
Responsible for protecting the public by ensuring that members maintain the highest standards of professional conduct and competence.

Subject coverage:
Accountancy.

Information services:
Library & Information Service located in the Business Centre in Chartered Accountants' Hall; the eLibr@ry provides fast online access to full text online resources for members and registered students; LibCat is the online catalogue of the Institute's Library and Information Service, containing details of over 40,000 books, 50,000 journal articles and other items held in the Library collection.

Museum or gallery collection, archive, or library special collection:
The Library holds an archive of all publicly available books and journals published by the Institute

Library catalogue:
All or part available online

Printed publications:
Accountancy (magazine, monthly, free to members, £84 a year non-members)
For full list of publications, see website
Order printed publications from: website or from Subscriber Services team, tel: 01635 588493

Access to staff:
Contact by letter, by telephone, by fax and via website
Hours: Library & Information Service Enquiry Line: Mon to Thu, 0900 to 1730; Fri, 1000 to 1730

Access to building, collection or gallery:
Hours: Library & Information Service is in autumn 2010 trialling opening from 0800 to 1800

Also at:
11 regional UK offices and 6 overseas offices
ICAEW
    Level 1, Metropolitan House, 321 Avebury Boulevard, Milton Keynes, MK9 2FZ; tel: 01908 248100; fax: 01908 248088

INSTITUTE OF CHARTERED ACCOUNTANTS IN IRELAND

Acronym or abbreviation: ICAI

11 Donegal Square South, Belfast, BT1 5JE

Tel: 028 9032 1600
Fax: 028 9023 0071

Website:
http://www.icai.ie
Full library catalogue (OPAC) and indexed journals (CABIN).

Enquiries:
Enquiries to: Librarian

Organisation type and purpose:
Professional body (membership is by subscription, qualification).

Subject coverage:
Taxation, accountancy, auditing.

Library catalogue:
All or part available online

Access to staff:
Access for members only. Non-members charged.
Hours: Mon to Fri, 0900 to 1700

INSTITUTE OF CHARTERED ACCOUNTANTS OF SCOTLAND

Acronym or abbreviation: ICAS

CA House, 21 Haymarket Yards, Edinburgh, EH12 5BH

Tel: 0131 347 0100
Fax: 0131 347 0105
E-mail: infoservice@icas.org.uk

Website:
http://www.icas.org.uk

Enquiries:
Enquiries to: Information Service Manager
Direct tel: 0131 347 0135
Other contacts: Information Officer

Founded:
1854

Organisation type and purpose:
National organisation, professional body (membership is by subscription, qualification), present number of members: 18,300, training organisation.

Subject coverage:
Accountancy, finance, auditing, taxation, management, company law, company accounts, company information, statutes and law reports.

Museum or gallery collection, archive, or library special collection:
Antiquarian collection on accounting and related topics, 1494–1930, now on deposit in National Library of Scotland but maintained by ICAS
Stock exchange daily official list (SEDOL) 1986 to date (mainly microfiche)

Non-library collection catalogue:
All or part available online

Library catalogue:
All or part available online

Printed publications:
CA Magazine (monthly)
Various books, monographs and research publications
Order printed publications from: Research books, monographs and research publications from the ICAS Research Department or ICAS website
CA Magazine from ICAS or from the CA Magazine website

Publications list:
Available online and in print

Access to staff:
Contact by letter, by telephone, by fax, by e-mail, in person and via website
Hours: Mon to Fri, 0900 to 1700

Access to building, collection or gallery:
Hours: Mon to Fri, 0900 to 1700
Special comments: Limited car parking – please book a space in advance.

Access for disabled people:
Parking provided, access to all public areas

INSTITUTE OF CHARTERED FORESTERS

Acronym or abbreviation: ICF

59 George Street, Edinburgh, EH2 2JG

Tel: 0131 240 1425
Fax: 0131 240 1424
E-mail: icf@charteredforesters.org

Website:
http://www.charteredforesters.org

Enquiries:
Enquiries to: Administrative Officer

continued overleaf

Other contacts: Executive Director (for code of ethics queries)

Founded:
1926

Organisation type and purpose:
Professional body.

Subject coverage:
Amenity planting, arboriculture, tree surveys, farm forestry, timber valuations, forest landscaping, forest management, forest pathology, forest roads planning and construction, forest investment, taxation and economics, harvesting and marketing, integrated stock and site inventory, land use appraisals, environmental assessments, nature conservation, wood-based energy, negotiations on sale and purchase of land and woodlands, poplar cultivation, sawmilling, small woods, training and education, upland forestry, urban forestry.

Printed publications:
Chartered Forester magazine
Forestry: An International Journal of Forest Research
Order printed publications from: e-mail: icf@ charteredforesters.org

Publications list:
Available online and in print

Access to staff:
Contact by letter, by telephone, by fax, by e-mail and via website
Hours: Mon to Fri, 0900 to 1700

INSTITUTE OF CHARTERED SHIPBROKERS

Acronym or abbreviation: ICS

85 Gracechurch Street, London, EC3V 0AA

Tel: 020 7623 1111
Fax: 020 7623 8008
E-mail: info@ics.org.uk

Website:
http://ics.org.uk/

Enquiries:
Enquiries to: Director General
Direct e-mail: membership@ics.org.uk

Organisation type and purpose:
International organisation, professional body.

Subject coverage:
Ship-broking.

Printed publications:
The Shipbroker (quarterly)

Access to staff:
Contact by letter, by telephone, by e-mail and in person
Hours: Mon to Fri, 0900 to 1700

Member of:
Federation of National Associations of Shipbrokers and Agents (FONASBA)
   tel: 020 7628 5559; fax: 020 7588 7836; e-mail: fonasba@ics.org.uk

INSTITUTE OF CHIROPODISTS AND PODIATRISTS

Acronym or abbreviation: IOCP

27 Wright Street, Southport, Merseyside, PR9 0TL

Tel: 01704 546141
Fax: 01704 500477
E-mail: secretary@iocp.org.uk

Website:
http://www.iocp.org.uk

Enquiries:
Enquiries to: General Secretary

Founded:
1955

Organisation type and purpose:
Professional body.

Subject coverage:
Foot care; training in chiropody, podiatry, foot health.

Printed publications:
Career information (supplied for sae)
Podiatry Review (6 times a year, free to members, £25 a year to others in UK, £40 overseas)
Footcare leaflet (£11 per 100)

Access to staff:
Contact by e-mail and via website. Appointment necessary.
Hours: Mon to Thu, 0845 to 1700; Fri, 0900 to 1600

INSTITUTE OF CIVIL DEFENCE AND DISASTER STUDIES

Acronym or abbreviation: ICDDS

2 Grosvenor Gardens, Muswell Hill, London, N10 3TE

Tel: 020 8883 3555

Website:
http://www.icds.org

Enquiries:
Enquiries to: Librarian

Founded:
1938

Organisation type and purpose:
Learned society (membership is by subscription), voluntary organisation, registered charity (charity number 266522).
Educational charity.

Subject coverage:
Civil defence, civil protection, emergency planning, disaster management.

Museum or gallery collection, archive, or library special collection:
Collection on civil defence and emergency planning from 1914 to present day

Printed publications:
Journal (quarterly)
Management Congress 1988
Proceedings of the Fourth International Disaster Study reports

Electronic and video publications:
Video: Hurricane called Camille

Publications list:
Available in print

Access to staff:
Contact by letter
Hours: Mon to Fri, 0900 to 1700

Access to building, collection or gallery:
Prior appointment required

Member of:
International Civil Defence Organization
   10–12 Chemin De Surville, 1213 Petit-Lancy, Geneva, Switzerland

INSTITUTE OF CLASSICAL STUDIES LIBRARY

Acronym or abbreviation: ICS

3rd Floor, Senate House, Malet Street, London, WC1E 7HU

Tel: 020 7862 8709
Fax: 020 7862 8735
E-mail: sue.willetts@sas.ac.uk

Website:
http://icls.sas.ac.uk/library/Home.htm

Enquiries:
Enquiries to: Librarian
Direct tel: 020 7862 8710
Direct fax: 020 7862 8724
Direct e-mail: colin.annis@sas.ac.uk

Founded:
1953

Organisation type and purpose:
University department or institute, Institute of London University and member of the University of London Research Library Services (ULRS).

Subject coverage:
All aspects of classical civilisation, including archaeology, art and architecture, language and literature, history, law, politics, religion, philosophy and science of the Minoan, Mycenaean and Hellenic world, and the Byzantine Empire; also of the early Italic and Etruscan civilisations, and of the Roman Empire to 5th century AD, including Roman Britain.

Museum or gallery collection, archive, or library special collection:
Contains 110,000 monographs and pamphlets and 20,000 bound vols of periodicals
675 current periodicals taken
Slides collection (joint library) of 6,800

Library catalogue:
All or part available online

Printed publications:
Bulletin of the Institute of Classical Studies, plus Supplements
Order printed publications from: Publications Department, Institute of Classical Studies, at the same address; tel. 020 7862 8700; fax 020 7862 8722, e-mail icls.publications@sas.ac.uk

Publications list:
Available online and in print

Access to staff:
Contact by letter, by telephone, by fax, by e-mail and in person. Access for members only.
Hours: Mon to Fri, 0930 to 1800; Sat, 1000 to 1630, term-time, Tue, Wed and Thu, 0930 to 2000

Links with:
Society for the Promotion of Hellenic Studies
   tel: 020 7862 8730; fax: 020 7862 8731; e-mail: office@hellenicsociety.org.uk; website: http:// www.hellenicsociety.org.uk
Society for the Promotion of Roman Studies
   tel: 020 7862 8727; fax: 020 7862 8728; e-mail: office@romansociety.org; website: http://www .romansociety.org

INSTITUTE OF CLERKS OF WORKS AND CONSTRUCTION INSPECTORATE

Formal name: Institute of Clerks of Works and Construction Inspectorate of GB Incorporated
Acronym or abbreviation: ICWCI

Equinox, 28 Commerce Road, Lynchwood, Peterborough, PE2 6LR

Tel: 01733 405160
Fax: 01733 405161
E-mail: info@icwci.org

Website:
http://www.icwci.org

Enquiries:
Enquiries to: Company Secretary
Other contacts: Editor and Event Organiser; Membership Officer

Founded:
1882

Organisation type and purpose:
Professional body.

Subject coverage:
Comprehensive and technical knowledge of the construction process of the built environment, particularly independent inspection of work in process in the construction industry.

Museum or gallery collection, archive, or library special collection:
Journal of the Institute of Clerks of Works from 1883 to the present day, now known as the Institute of Clerks of Works and Construction Inspectorate

Printed publications:
Clerk of Works and Site Inspector Handbook (£32 members, £39.95 non-members)
Directory of Self-Employed, Freelance and Private Practice Clerks of Works (annually, free)
Site Recorder: Journal of the Institute (annually, £35). Postage may differ for overseas postage. Please apply separately.

Access to staff:
Contact by letter, by telephone, by fax, by e-mail, in person and via website
Hours: Mon to Fri, 0900 to 1700

Access to building, collection or gallery:
No access other than to staff

INSTITUTE OF CLINICAL RESEARCH

Acronym or abbreviation: ICR

Institute House, Boston Drive, Bourne End, Buckinghamshire, SL8 5YS

Tel: 0845 521 0056
Fax: 01628 530641
E-mail: resources@icr-global.org

Website:
http://www.icr-global.org
Educational courses, academic courses, seminars, conferences, publications, library and resources, journal CRfocus, mailing and advertising opportunities, CPD, membership

Enquiries:
Enquiries to: Head of Information Services
Direct tel: 01628 536969
Direct e-mail: hkorjonen@icr-global.org
Other contacts: General Manager

Founded:
1978

Organisation type and purpose:
Professional body, training organisation, conference organiser, publisher

Subject coverage:
Pharmaceutical industry and clinical research.

Museum or gallery collection, archive, or library special collection:
Clinical research resources only.

Non-library collection catalogue:
All or part available online, in-house and in print

Library catalogue:
All or part available online

Printed publications:
Clinical Research Focus (journal, 11 times a year)
Series of monographs and smaller publications (c.32 publications)
Order printed publications from: http://www.icr-global.org

Publications list:
Available online and in print

Access to staff:
Contact by letter, by telephone, by fax, by e-mail, in person and via website. Appointment necessary. Access for members only. Letter of introduction required. Non-members charged.

Access to building, collection or gallery:
No prior appointment required for members
Hours: Mon to Fri, 0800 to 1700

INSTITUTE OF COMMERCIAL MANAGEMENT

Acronym or abbreviation: ICM

ICM House, Castleman Way, Ringwood Hants, BH24 3BA

Tel: 01202 490555
Fax: 01202 409666
E-mail: info@icm.ac.uk

Website:
http://www.icm.ac.uk

Enquiries:
Enquiries to: Chief Executive

Founded:
1979

Organisation type and purpose:
A professional body (membership is by qualification), present number of full and student members: 210,000, registered charity (charity number 1045370), suitable for ages: 19+, training organisation, consultancy, research organisation, publishing house.
A QCA/Ofqual accredited UK Examining and Awarding body. Operating in 120 countries, providing advisory and capacity-building services to business schools and colleges;

Subject coverage:
Business and management education, tourism, trade and professional development.

Information services:
Industry news, by sector, from 120 countries.

Education services:
The design, development of business and management programmes from HND to degree levels and the examination and assessment of candidates. The design of CPD programmes for the corporate sector.

Printed publications:
A range of business and management texts

Access to staff:
Contact by letter, by telephone, by fax, by e-mail, in person and via website

Access to building, collection or gallery:
Hours: Mon to Fri, 0900 to 1730

Access for disabled people:
Fully accessible

Links with:
a range of UK and overseas universities for HE progression purposes for student members

INSTITUTE OF COMMONWEALTH STUDIES LIBRARY

Acronym or abbreviation: ICS

University of London, 28 Russell Square, London, WC1B 5DS

Tel: 020 7862 8844
Fax: 020 7862 8820
E-mail: icommlib@sas.ac.uk

Website:
http://catalogue.ulrls.lon.ac.uk
Library catalogue.
http://commonwealth.sas.ac.uk/library.htm
Library homepage.
http://archives.ulrls.lon.ac.uk
Archives catalogue

Enquiries:
Enquiries to: Information Resources Manager

Founded:
1949

Organisation type and purpose:
University library, university department or institute, research organisation.

Subject coverage:
Class, Commonwealth, culture, economics, environment, gender, health, history, human rights, international relations, literature, migration, Pacific, politics, race.
Antigua and Barbuda, Australia, The Bahamas, Bangladesh, Barbados, Belize, Botswana, Brunei Darussalam, Cameroon, Canada, Cyprus, Dominica, Fiji Islands, The Gambia, Ghana, Grenada, Guyana, India, Jamaica, Kenya, Kiribati, Lesotho, Malawi, Malaysia, Maldives, Malta, Mauritius, Mozambique, Namibia, Nauru, New Zealand, Nigeria, Pakistan, Papua New Guinea, Samoa, Seychelles, Sierra Leone, Singapore, Solomon Islands, South Africa, Sri Lanka, St Kitts and Nevis, St Lucia, St Vincent and The

Grenadines, Swaziland, Tanzania, Tonga, Trinidad and Tobago, Tuvalu, Uganda, Vanuatu, Zambia, Zimbabwe.

Museum or gallery collection, archive, or library special collection:
Material on the contemporary history, economics, politics and social aspects of all Commonwealth countries. The collections (200,000 items) include monographs, government publications, research papers, statistical data, census and more than 9,000 periodicals and annual publications. Over 70% of the stock is published in Commonwealth countries
Special Collections or strengths include:
Caribbean, West Indies, including the West India Committee Library and minute books
Australia, New Zealand, the Pacific area, Canada
India, Pakistan, Bangladesh, Sri Lanka
African member countries
National bibliographies
Collection of more than 10,000 documents issued by political parties, pressure groups and trade unions in Commonwealth member countries
A number of important archive collections, including the papers of Ellis Ashmead-Bartlett, Sir Ivor Jennings, Richard Jebb and the West India Committee. Guides to archival materials are available
International Defence and Aid Fund newscutting microfiche archive South Africa, 1975–90 and Namibia, 1975–90

Trade and statistical information:
Trade statistics, census statistics.

Non-library collection catalogue:
All or part available online

Library catalogue:
All or part available online

Printed publications:
Current periodicals list
Guides and publications (in both printed and electronic format), including:
Theses in progress in Commonwealth studies

Publications list:
Available online and in print

Access to staff:
Contact by letter, by telephone, by fax, by e-mail, in person and via website. Letter of introduction required. Non-members charged.

Access to building, collection or gallery:
Hours: Term time: Mon to Fri, 0930 to 1830
Vacations: Mon to Fri, 0930 to 1730
Special comments: ID required. Membership open to all academic and academically related university staff and postgraduates. Undergraduates admitted free of charge.

Member organisation of:
School of Advanced Study and University of London Research Library Services
University of London

INSTITUTE OF CONCRETE TECHNOLOGY

Acronym or abbreviation: ICT

4 Meadows Business Park, Blackwater, Camberley, GU17 9AB

Tel: 01276 607140
Fax: 01276 607141
E-mail: ict@concrete.org.uk

Website:
http://ict.concrete.org.uk
Membership, news, history, structure, contacts, sponsors, convention, events.

Enquiries:
Enquiries to: Executive Officer

Founded:
1972

Organisation type and purpose:
Professional body.

continued overleaf

Subject coverage:
Concrete technology.

Museum or gallery collection, archive, or library special collection:
Institute's own Convention and meeting papers
ACT reports

Non-library collection catalogue:
All or part available online

Printed publications:
Yearbook (£50, contains convention papers)

Publications list:
Available online and in print

Access to staff:
Contact by letter, by telephone, by fax and by e-mail
Hours: Mon to Thurs, 0800 to 1400
Special comments: We do not offer a technical advisory service.

INSTITUTE OF CONFLICT MANAGEMENT

Acronym or abbreviation: ICM

840 Melton Road, Thurmaston, Leicester, LE4 8BN

Tel: 0116 260 6961
Fax: 0116 264 0141
E-mail: icm@association.org.uk

Website:
http://www.conflictmanagement.org
General information

Enquiries:
Enquiries to: Executive Secretary

Founded:
1999

Organisation type and purpose:
National organisation, advisory body, membership association, present number of members: 200+, service industry, age range: higher, training organisation, research organisation.
Regulatory body, membership is by qualification and/or by experience.

Subject coverage:
Education and training in conflict management and other physical and non-physical intervention skills and techniques. Prints and publishes journals, newspapers, periodicals, books and leaflets to advance and inform on subjects connected with the work, theory and practices relating to conflict management, including statistics, scientific investigation and similar subjects. Has established a library and other information bureau for the use of Members and others on all related subjects.

Printed publications:
Newsletter (quarterly)

Electronic and video publications:
Managing Work Related to Violence (CD, published by Employment NTO)

Access to staff:
Contact by letter, by telephone, by fax, by e-mail and via website. Appointment necessary.
Hours: Mon to Fri, 0900 to 1700

Access for disabled people:
Level entry, access to all public areas

INSTITUTE OF CONTEMPORARY ARTS

Acronym or abbreviation: ICA

12 Carlton House Terrace, London, SW1Y 5AH

Tel: 020 7930 0493
Fax: 020 7873 0051
E-mail: info@ica.org.uk

Website:
http://www.ica.org.uk
Events, listings, archive, etc.

Enquiries:
Enquiries to: Administrative Assistant
Other contacts: Education Officer for tel no: 020 7766 1423.

Founded:
1947

Organisation type and purpose:
Membership association, registered charity (charity number 236848), art gallery, suitable for ages: 16+.
Arts Centre.

Subject coverage:
Contemporary cultural activities, including film, theatre, dance and music; events and exhibitions.

Museum or gallery collection, archive, or library special collection:
Pre-1990 collection at the Tate

Electronic and video publications:
1500 audio recordings of lectures
Over 200 videos of art events

Publications list:
Available in print

Access to staff:
Contact by letter, by telephone, by fax, by e-mail and via website. Appointment necessary. Non-members charged.
Hours: Mon to Fri, 1200 to 1930

Access to building, collection or gallery:
No prior appointment required
Hours: Mon to Fri, 1200 to 1930

Subsidiary body:
ICA Projects Ltd

INSTITUTE OF CONTEMPORARY MUSIC PERFORMANCE

Acronym or abbreviation: ICMP

Foundation House, 1A Dyne Road, London, NW6 7XG

Tel: 020 7328 0222
E-mail: enquiries@icmp.co.uk

Website:
http://www.icmp.co.uk

Enquiries:
Enquiries to: Admissions Advisor

Founded:
1985

Formerly called:
Guitar Institute & Basstech

Organisation type and purpose:
Membership association (membership is by subscription), suitable for ages: all, training organisation.
Music school, accredited by Institute of Thames Valley University.

Subject coverage:
Music tuition and career advice for musicians.

Printed publications:
School Prospectus (free from school)

Access to staff:
Contact by letter, by telephone, by fax, by e-mail, in person and via website. Appointment necessary.
Hours: Mon to Fri, 0900 to 1700

Access to building, collection or gallery:
No prior appointment required

Parent body:
University of East London
Docklands Campus, University Way, London, E16 2RD

INSTITUTE OF COST AND EXECUTIVE ACCOUNTANTS

Acronym or abbreviation: ICEA

Akhtar House, 2 Shepherd's Bush Road, London, W6 7PJ

Tel: 020 8749 7126
Fax: 020 8749 7127
E-mail: icea@enta.net

Website:
http://www.icea.enta.net

Enquiries:
Enquiries to: Secretary General
Other contacts: Membership Secretary

Founded:
1958

Organisation type and purpose:
International organisation, professional body (membership is by qualification).
Producing tomorrow's accountant.

Subject coverage:
Accountancy, executive accountancy, financial decision making, management auditing, strategic management.

Non-library collection catalogue:
All or part available online and in-house

Library catalogue:
All or part available in-house

Printed publications:
Executive Accountant (quarterly)
Newsletter

Access to staff:
Contact by letter, by telephone, by fax and by e-mail
Hours: Mon to Fri, 1000 to 1600

Member of:
European Accounting Association and Council for Education in the Commonwealth

INSTITUTE OF COUNSELLING

Acronym or abbreviation: IoC

6 Dixon Street, Glasgow, G1 4AX

Tel: 0141 204 2230
Fax: 0141 221 2841
E-mail: iofcounsel@aol.com

Website:
http://www.collegeofcounselling.com
Online course prospectus.

Enquiries:
Enquiries to: General Manager

Founded:
1985

Organisation type and purpose:
Membership association (membership is by subscription, qualification, present number of members: 600, suitable for ages: adults, training organisation.

Subject coverage:
Counselling, counselling training and bereavement.

Printed publications:
The Living Document (twice a year, members)
Open learning material

Electronic and video publications:
6 training videos (£175 for 6 videos plus manual):
Counselling in Action
Counselling in Perspective
Counselling in Depth
Counselling in Focus
Counselling in Analysis
Counselling in Role Play
Essential Skills of Counselling (series of 8 cassettes £24.95)

Publications list:
Available in print

Access to staff:
Contact by letter, by telephone, by fax, by e-mail, in person and via website. Appointment necessary.
Non-members charged.
Hours: Mon to Fri, 0900 to 1700

Also at:
Institute of Counselling
10 High Street, Bromsgrove, B61 8HQ; tel: 01527
577803; fax: 01527 577803; e-mail: instofcoun@
aol.com

INSTITUTE OF CREDIT MANAGEMENT

Acronym or abbreviation: ICM

The Water Mill, South Luffenham, Oakham,
Leicestershire LE15 8NB

Tel: 01780 722900
Fax: 01780 721333
E-mail: info@icm.org.uk

Website:
http://www.icm.org.uk

Enquiries:
Enquiries to: Chief Executive's Office
Direct tel: 01780 722912
Direct e-mail: ceo@icm.org.uk

Founded:
1939

Organisation type and purpose:
Professional body (membership is by subscription,
qualification, election or invitation), present
number of members: 8,500, registered charity,
training organisation, consultancy, research
organisation.

Subject coverage:
All aspects of credit management.

Printed publications:
Credit Management (journal, monthly)
Comprehensive Credit Management Text and
Reference Book Service. Books available for sale
to members and non-members
Order printed publications from: e-mail: bookshop@
icm.org.uk

Publications list:
Available online

Access to staff:
Contact by letter, by telephone, by fax and by e-
mail. Access for members only.
Hours: Mon to Fri, 0900 to 1700

Member organisation of:
Federation of European Credit Management
Associations (FECMA)

INSTITUTE OF CUSTOMER CARE

Acronym or abbreviation: IOCC

St John's House, Chapel Lane, Westcott, Dorking,
Surrey, RH4 3PJ

Tel: 01306 876210
Fax: 01306 876249

Enquiries:
Enquiries to: Membership Secretary

Founded:
1987

Organisation type and purpose:
Advisory body, membership association
(membership is by subscription), training
organisation, consultancy.

Subject coverage:
Customer care, total quality management, market
research, complaint management, customer
charters, mystery shopping, accreditation,
customer satisfaction indices, quality audits, staff
surveys, networking, benchmarking, training,
facilities management.

Access to staff:
Contact by letter and by telephone. Non-members
charged.
Hours: Mon to Fri, 0900 to 1700

INSTITUTE OF CUSTOMER SERVICE

Acronym or abbreviation: ICS

2 Castle Court, St Peter's Street, Colchester, CO1
1EW

Tel: 01206 571716
E-mail: via website

Website:
http://www.instituteofcustomerservice.com
Research and publications, benchmarking and
accreditation, professional development, case
studies, events.

Founded:
1996

Organisation type and purpose:
The independent, professional membership body
for customer service. Members are more than 300
organisations – from across the private, public and
third sectors – and individuals.
To lead customer service performance and
professionalism; to be the first port of call for every
aspect of customer service, delivering high quality,
tangible benefits to organisations, individuals and
other stakeholders, so that the Institute's customers
can improve their own customers' experiences and
their business performance; to improve customer
service performance and raise the status of people
working directly or indirectly in customer service
roles.

Subject coverage:
Customer service.

Printed publications:
World-class customer service: The what, the why,
the how (£125.00)
Finance (banks) Sector UKCSI Report July 2010
(£200.00)
Order printed publications from: Online shop

Electronic and video publications:
Guidance notes (free)
customerfirst magazine articles (free to members)
Consumer Channel Choice (£25)
Service Excellence = Reputation = Profit (£50.00)
Delivering Service Excellence: The view from the
front-line (£50.00)
Order electronic and video publications from:
Downloadable PDFs, available from website or
online shop

Publications list:
Available online

Access to staff:
Contact by letter, by telephone and via website

INSTITUTE OF DEVELOPMENT STUDIES LIBRARY

Formal name: British Library for Development
Studies
Acronym or abbreviation: BLDS

BLDS, Institute of Development Studies,
University of Sussex, Falmer, Brighton, East
Sussex, BN1 9RE

Tel: 01273 915659
Fax: 01273 621202; 01273 691647
E-mail: blds@ids.ac.uk

Website:
http://www.blds.ids.ac.uk
BLDS catalogue and journal articles database,
covering Europe's largest research collection on
economic and social change in developing
countries; details of/access to BLDS services.
http://www.ids.ac.uk/go/knowledge-services
Access to a range of IDS Knowledge Services,
which include both broad-based services, such as
the development policy, research and practice
information gateway ELDIS, and specialist services
such as BRIDGE (gender), the Governance and
Social Development Resource Centre (GSDRC) and
the Livelihoods Connect Network.
http://www.ids.ac.uk

Details of IDS research, teaching, publishing and
operational programmes.

Founded:
1966

Formerly called:
IDS Library

Organisation type and purpose:
Research / teaching institute library, with a local
role to cater for the information needs of the parent
institution and a wider remit to increase access to
information for development practitioners,
especially those in the global South.
Services to researchers, postgraduate students, and
developing country users.

Subject coverage:
Social, economic, political, technological and
cultural aspects of societal change, primarily in
developing countries. Over 50% of the collection
originates from the global South.

Information services:
Ask a Librarian – helpdesk providing advice on
development-related resources.
BLDS Updates – updates by email or RSS giving
details of the latest acquisitions. These are available
for 24 different subject areas, and 5 regions, and are
produced approximately every 2 weeks.
Document Delivery – the remote supply of scans
or copies of material in the collection. This is
available free of charge to users in developing
countries who are members of GDNet.

Special visitor services:
Visitors can access the collection for reference
purposes free of charge.
External membership, allowing borrowing from
the collection, is offered for a charge.

Services for disabled people:
BLDS will ensure that all who need to use the
collection or services have access to what they need
during their visit.

Non-library collection catalogue:
All or part available online

Library catalogue:
All or part available online

Printed publications:
IDS Bulletin
IDS Discussion Papers
IDS Research Reports
IDS Working Papers
Order printed publications from: via website: http://
www.ids.ac.uk/go/bookshop

Publications list:
Available online and in print

Access to staff:
Contact by letter, by telephone, by fax, by e-mail,
in person and via website
Hours: Mon to Fri, 0900 to 1700

Access to building, collection or gallery:
For all.
Hours: Mon to Fri, 0900 to 1700

Access for disabled people:
For all
Hours: Standard hours
Special comments: Some open book stacks
inaccessible to wheelchair users.

Funded by:
Institute of Development Studies
UK Department for International Development
(DfID)

Parent body:
Institute of Development Studies (IDS)

INSTITUTE OF DIRECT MARKETING

Acronym or abbreviation: IDM

1 Park Road, Teddington, Middlesex, TW11 0AB

Tel: 020 8614 0274
Fax: 020 8614 0246
E-mail: enquiries@theidm.com

continued overleaf

Website:
http://www.theidm.com
Information on membership of the IDM, direct marketing courses, the IDM Certificate and Diploma in Direct Marketing and publications available for purchase via IDM Direct. Index of published information on direct marketing.

Enquiries:
Enquiries to: Information Services Manager
Direct tel: 020 8614 0253
Direct e-mail: juliethilditch@theidm.com

Founded:
1987

Organisation type and purpose:
Professional body (membership is by qualification), present number of members: 5000, registered charity (charity number 1001865), training organisation.

Subject coverage:
Direct marketing.

Museum or gallery collection, archive, or library special collection:
Books, journals, press cuttings, reports

Non-library collection catalogue:
All or part available online and in-house

Library catalogue:
All or part available online and in-house

Printed publications:
A large selection of books is available and includes:
The Interactive and Direct Marketing Guide, IDM, 2002 (3 vols)
Journal of Direct, Data and Digital Marketing Practice (journal, quarterly, also online)

Electronic and video publications:
Absolute Essentials (video series, IDM)

Publications list:
Available online

Access to staff:
Contact by telephone, by fax, by e-mail and via website. Appointment necessary. Non-members charged.
Hours: Mon, Tues, 0930 to 1330; Wed, Thur, 0900 to 1600; Fri, 0900 to 1500

INSTITUTE OF DIRECTORS

Acronym or abbreviation: IoD

116 Pall Mall, London, SW1Y 5ED

Tel: 020 7839 1233
Fax: 020 7321 0145

Website:
http://www.iod.com
Description of IoD's services plus some access to press releases and information briefings.

Enquiries:
Enquiries to: Head of Information and Advsory Services
Direct tel: 020 7451 3100
Direct e-mail: businessinfo@iod.com

Founded:
1903

Organisation type and purpose:
Professional body.

Subject coverage:
Company directors, company law, boardroom practice, business, corporate governance.

Museum or gallery collection, archive, or library special collection:
Company direction collection

Trade and statistical information:
Bi-monthly business opinion survey.

Library catalogue:
All or part available online

Printed publications:
Books, policy papers and topical surveys
Director's Guide Series (23 titles)

Director (monthly)
Director's Handbook
IOD News (monthly)
Order printed publications from: Book Sales, Institute of Directors
116 Pall Mall, London, SW1Y 5ED, tel: 020 7766 8866, fax: 020 7766 8833, e-mail: pubs@iod.com

Access to staff:
Contact via website. Appointment necessary.
Hours: Mon to Fri, 0830 to 1730

Access for disabled people:
Toilet facilities

INSTITUTE OF DOMESTIC HEATING AND ENVIRONMENTAL ENGINEERS

Acronym or abbreviation: IDHEE

Unit 35A, New Forest Enterprise Centre, Chapel Lane, Totton, Southampton, SO40 9LA

Tel: 023 8066 8900
Fax: 023 8066 0888
E-mail: admin@idhee.org.uk

Website:
http://www.idhee.org.uk

Enquiries:
Enquiries to: Chairman
Direct tel: 07973 214574
Direct fax: 023 8081 4756
Direct e-mail: bill.bucknell@idhee.org.uk

Founded:
1964

Organisation type and purpose:
National organisation, professional body (membership is by subscription, qualification), present number of members: 1,026.

Subject coverage:
Domestic heating and environmental engineering.

Publications list:
Available online

Access to staff:
Contact by telephone, by e-mail and via website. Non-members charged.
Hours: Mon to Fri, 0900 to 1700

INSTITUTE OF ECONOMIC AFFAIRS

Acronym or abbreviation: IEA

2 Lord North Street, London, SW1P 3LB

Tel: 020 7799 8900
Fax: 020 7799 2137
E-mail: iea@iea.org.uk

Website:
http://www.iea.org.uk

Enquiries:
Enquiries to: Director General

Founded:
1955

Organisation type and purpose:
Registered charity (charity number CC 235 351), research organisation, publishing house.

Subject coverage:
Political economy, public choice, microeconomics.

Printed publications:
Economic Affairs (4 times a year)
Hobart Papers
IEA Readings
Occasional Papers
Research Monographs

Electronic and video publications:
Videos

Publications list:
Available online and in print

Access to staff:
Contact by letter, by telephone, by fax, by e-mail and via website
Hours: Mon to Fri, 0900 to 1700

INSTITUTE OF ECOTECHNICS

Acronym or abbreviation: IE

24 Old Gloucester Street, Holborn, London, WC1N 3AL

Tel: 020 7405 1824
Fax: 020 7405 1851
E-mail: nelson@biospheres.com

Website:
http://www.ecotechnics.edu

Enquiries:
Enquiries to: Secretary

Founded:
1972

Organisation type and purpose:
International organisation, learned society, training organisation, consultancy, research organisation. Consultant to several businesses managing demonstration projects in varied biomes internationally: Tropic Ventures, Puerto Rico; Savannah Systems Pty Limited, West Australia; RV Heraclitus; Les Marronniers conference centre and Provençal farm, Aix-en-Provence, France; Synergia Ranch, New Mexico, USA.

Subject coverage:
Ecological management, biospheric and closed systems.

Printed publications:
Books in association with Synergetic Press (see website)
Brochure

Access to staff:
Contact by letter, by fax and by e-mail. Appointment necessary.
Hours: Mon to Fri, 0900 to 1700

Access for disabled people:
Ramped entry

INSTITUTE OF EDUCATION

Information Services, 20 Bedford Way, London, WC1H 0AL

Tel: 020 7612 6080
Fax: 020 7612 6093
E-mail: lib.enquiries@ioe.ac.uk

Website:
http://www.ioe.ac.uk/is
Catalogues, archives and special collections.

Enquiries:
Enquiries to: Library Enquiries
Other contacts: Archivist (for access to archives and special collections)

Founded:
1902

Organisation type and purpose:
University department or institute, research organisation.

Subject coverage:
All aspects of education.

Museum or gallery collection, archive, or library special collection:
Largest collection on education in the United Kingdom
Assorted deposited collections and archives

Non-library collection catalogue:
All or part available online, in-house and in print

Library catalogue:
All or part available online and in-house

Printed publications:
Education libraries bulletin (1958–88)
Catalogue of the Comparative Education Library, Institute of Education (and supplement)

Catalogue of the Collection of Education of Tropical Areas

Access to staff:
Contact by letter, by telephone, by fax, by e-mail, in person and via website. Non-members charged.

Access to building, collection or gallery:
Hours: Mon to Thu, 0930 to 2000; Fri, 0930 to 1900; Sat, 0930 to 1700

Access for disabled people:
Level entry, access to all public areas, toilet facilities, lift from Bedford Way

INSTITUTE OF EDUCATIONAL TECHNOLOGY

Acronym or abbreviation: IET

Open University, Walton Hall, Milton Keynes, Buckinghamshire, MK7 6AA

Tel: 01908 655581
Fax: 01908 654173
E-mail: j.taylor@open.ac.uk

Website:
http://iet.open.ac.uk

Enquiries:
Enquiries to: Director

Founded:
1970

Organisation type and purpose:
University department or institute, consultancy, research organisation.
The role of the Institute of Educational Technology is to be a centre of international excellence for the teaching, research and development of educational technology in the service of effective learning.

Subject coverage:
All aspects of distance and open teaching and learning, specialist areas: course design, education and quality assessment, use of media, information technology, multimedia, disabled students.

Trade and statistical information:
National student data on media use and ownership.
National student data on vocational intentions.

Printed publications:
Masters course brochures for MA in Online and Distance Learning

Publications list:
Available in print

Access to staff:
Contact by letter
Hours: Mon to Fri, 0900 to 1700

INSTITUTE OF ELECTROLYSIS, THE

27 Emerson Valley, Milton Keynes, Buckinghamshire, MK4 2AF

Tel: 01908 503161
Fax: 0870 051 3611
E-mail: institute@electrolysis.co.uk

Website:
http://www.electrolysis.co.uk
Information on hair removal, list of members.

Enquiries:
Enquiries to: Administrator

Founded:
1946

Organisation type and purpose:
International organisation, professional body (membership is by qualification), present number of members: 200.

Access to staff:
Contact by letter, by telephone and by e-mail
Hours: Mon to Fri, 0900 to 1700

INSTITUTE OF ENVIRONMENTAL MANAGEMENT & ASSESSMENT

Acronym or abbreviation: IEMA

St Nicholas House, 70 Newport, Lincoln, LN1 3DP

Tel: 01522 540069
Fax: 01522 540090
E-mail: info@iema.net

Website:
http://www.iema.net
General information on the IEMA, how to become a member, activities and new products and services.

Enquiries:
Enquiries to: Chief Executive
Other contacts: Membership Secretary for general membership enquiries.

Founded:
1990

Organisation type and purpose:
National organisation, advisory body, professional body, membership association (membership is by subscription), present number of members: 6500, training organisation, consultancy, research organisation.
To support environmental practitioners in careers by best practice advice in environmental assessment and environmental management, professional development and networking.

Subject coverage:
Sustainability and environmental management in UK industry, commerce and local government. Professional accreditation for environmental professionals; registration for environmental auditors and assessors; registration as Specialist in Land Condition (SiLC); registration for Environmental Impact Assessment (EIA); certification of training; networking and best practice; expert advice and technical support for corporate members.

Printed publications:
The following publications are available direct for purchase or via IEMA website
Best Practice (journal, 2 or 3 times a year)
EIA Guidelines – Baseline Ecological Assessment, Environmental Assessment of Road Traffic, Landscape & Visual Impact Assessment
Practitioner Journals
EIA Yearbook
The Environmentalist (journal, monthly by subscription)
Perspective (journal, participating in environmental decision-making)
Practitioner (journal, managing climate change emission)
Various environmental titles

Electronic and video publications:
Membership information, past journal articles (CD-ROM), Past Journals (CD-ROM)

Publications list:
Available online and in print

Access to staff:
Contact by letter, by telephone, by fax, by e-mail and via website. Appointment necessary.
Hours: Mon to Fri, 0900 to 1700

Access to building, collection or gallery:
Prior appointment required
Hours: Mon to Fri, 0900 to 1700
Special comments: Library available to corporate members only.

Access for disabled people:
Parking provided, toilet facilities
Special comments: Steps up to building

INSTITUTE OF EXPLOSIVES ENGINEERS

Acronym or abbreviation: IExpE

Wellington Hall 289, Cranfield University, Defence Academy of the UK, Shrivenham, Swindon, Wiltshire, SN6 8LA

Tel: 01793 785322
Fax: 01793 785772
E-mail: iexpe@cranfield.ac.uk

Website:
http://www.iexpe.org
Membership, news and events.

Enquiries:
Enquiries to: Secretary

Founded:
1974

Organisation type and purpose:
Professional body, membership association (membership is both by subscription and by qualification).
To represent companies and individuals who use explosives as part of the everyday tools of their trade.
A forum for demolition contractors, explosives manufacturers, underwater specialists, miners, tunnellers, quarrymen, disposal contractors, vibration specialists, oil industry contractors, special effects technicians (pyrotechnicians), firework display operators, police explosives liaison officers, legislators and members of the armed services.

Subject coverage:
Use of explosives in civil engineering (demolition, tunnelling, shaft sinking, land clearance and excavation, underwater rock breaking and excavation) and in quarries and offshore oil operations; recording and interpreting disturbances occasioned by blasting operations.

Printed publications:
Directory of Members (annually)
Explosives Engineering (quarterly)

Access to staff:
Contact by letter, by telephone, by fax and by e-mail

Member organisation of:
European Federation of Explosives Engineers

Professional affiliate of:
Engineering Council UK (ECUK)

INSTITUTE OF EXPORT

Acronym or abbreviation: IoE

Export House, Minerva Business Park, Lynch Wood, Peterborough, Cambridgeshire, PE2 6FT

Tel: 01733 404400
Fax: 01733 404444
E-mail: institute@export.org.uk

Website:
http://www.export.org.uk
Institute's organisation, training courses, support services to exporters, membership news, forums, newsletter.

Enquiries:
Enquiries to: Information Officer

Founded:
1935

Organisation type and purpose:
Professional body (membership is by qualification), registered charity, university department or institute, suitable for ages: Post-school and Mature, training organisation.
Sets and raises standards in International Trade Management and Export Practice through professional qualifications and training.

Subject coverage:
Sources of information on all aspects of international trade and training for exporters, leading to professional qualifications.

Printed publications:
International Trade Today (10 times a year)

Electronic and video publications:
Professional Examinations

Publications list:
Available in print

continued overleaf

Access to staff:
Contact by letter, by telephone, by fax, by e-mail and via website
Hours: Mon to Fri, 0900 to 1700

Access for disabled people:
Parking provided, level entry, toilet facilities

INSTITUTE OF FAMILY THERAPY (LONDON) LIMITED

Acronym or abbreviation: IFT

24–32 Stephenson Way, London, NW1 2HX

Tel: 020 7391 9150
Fax: 020 7391 9169
E-mail: ift@psyc.bbk.ac.uk

Website:
http://www.instituteoffamilytherapy.org.uk

Enquiries:
Enquiries to: Director
Other contacts: Senior Administrator

Founded:
1977

Organisation type and purpose:
Professional body (membership is by qualification), present number of members: 204, voluntary organisation, registered charity (charity number 284858), training organisation, consultancy.

Subject coverage:
Availability of family therapy resources across the country; advice, through appropriate professionals, on specialist subjects relating to the family, such as bereavement, divorce, child abuse, AIDS, adolescent problems, disability and many other issues.

Electronic and video publications:
Lecture video tapes
Hire of video teaching tapes

Publications list:
Available in print

Access to staff:
Contact by letter, by telephone, by fax, by e-mail and via website
Hours: Mon to Thu, 1000 to 1800; Fri, 1000 to 1700 (some evenings)

Affiliated to:
Birkbeck College
London University
National Family Mediation

Member of:
Association of Family Therapy
European Family Therapy Association
UK Council for Psychotherapy
UK Standing Conference for Psychotherapy

INSTITUTE OF FINANCIAL ACCOUNTANTS

Acronym or abbreviation: IFA

Burford House, 44 London Road, Sevenoaks, Kent, TN13 1AS

Tel: 01732 458080
Fax: 01732 455848
E-mail: mail@ifa.org.uk

Website:
http://www.ifa.org.uk

Enquiries:
Enquiries to: Chief Executive

Founded:
1916

Organisation type and purpose:
Professional body.
Examining and qualifying body.

Subject coverage:
All aspects of accountancy, management, company law, data processing, information technology, taxation, economics and general administration.

Printed publications:
Financial Accountant (6 times a year)

Access to staff:
Contact by letter, by telephone, by fax, by e-mail and via website. Appointment necessary.
Hours: Mon to Thu, 0900 to 1700; Fri, 0900 to 1600

Access to building, collection or gallery:
Prior appointment required

Access for disabled people:
Parking provided

Junior body is the:
International Association of Book-Keepers

INSTITUTE OF FINANCIAL PLANNING

Acronym or abbreviation: IFP

Southgate, Whitefriars, Lewins Mead, Bristol, BS1 2NT

Tel: 0117 945 2470
Fax: 0117 929 2214
E-mail: enquiries@financialplanning.org.uk

Website:
http://www.financialplanning.org.uk

Enquiries:
Enquiries to: Chief Executive

Founded:
1986

Organisation type and purpose:
International organisation, professional body (membership is by subscription, qualification), present number of members: 1300, training organisation.
The principle aim of the Institute is to promote the understanding and recognition of the financial planning profession.

Subject coverage:
Personal financial planning and management, business planning.

Museum or gallery collection, archive, or library special collection:
Reference works

Printed publications:
List of qualified members for reference by public, press and trade
Journal (for members, back and current copies)

Electronic and video publications:
Educational tape recordings of presentations made to Institutes' past Annual Conferences (tape, available for purchase, direct)

Access to staff:
Contact by letter, by telephone, by fax, by e-mail and via website
Hours: Mon to Fri, 0915 to 1745

Member of:
International Certified Financial Planner Council

INSTITUTE OF FOOD SCIENCE AND TECHNOLOGY

Acronym or abbreviation: IFST

5 Cambridge Court, 210 Shepherd's Bush Road, London, W6 7NJ

Tel: 020 7603 6316
Fax: 020 7602 9936
E-mail: info@ifst.org

Website:
http://www.ifst.org
Membership, publications, careers information, frequently asked questions, information statements.

Enquiries:
Enquiries to: Team Executive

Founded:
1964

Organisation type and purpose:
Professional body (membership is by qualification), present number of members: 2500, registered charity (charity number 264044).

Subject coverage:
Food Science and Technology.

Museum or gallery collection, archive, or library special collection:
Mounfield Collection of historic books relating to food science and technology (no public access)

Trade and statistical information:
No

Non-library collection catalogue:
All or part available in-house

Printed publications:
Development & Use of Microbiological Criteria for Foods
Food Hygiene Training: A Guide to its Responsible Management
Food Science & Technology, (quarterly, available free to members or on subscription)
Guidelines to Good Catering Practice
Guide to Food Biotechnology
International Journal of Food Science and Technology, IJFST (10 times a year subscription)
Listing of Codes of Practice applicable to Foods
Shelf Life of Foods – Guidelines for its Determination and Prediction
Food & Drink: Good Manufacturing Practice – A Guide to its Responsible Management

Publications list:
Available online and in print

Access to staff:
Contact by letter, by telephone, by fax, by e-mail and via website. Appointment necessary.
Hours: Mon to Fri, 0930 to 1300 and 1400 to 1730

Access to building, collection or gallery:
No access other than to staff

INSTITUTE OF FUNDRAISING

Park Place, 12 Lawn Lane, London, SW8 1UD

Tel: 020 7840 1000
Fax: 020 7840 1001

Website:
http://www.institute-of-fundraising.org.uk/

Enquiries:
Enquiries to: Press Team
Direct e-mail: press@institute-of-fundraising.org.uk

Founded:
1983

Formerly called:
Institute of Charity Fundraising Managers (ICFM)

Organisation type and purpose:
Professional body.

Subject coverage:
Codes of practice, training, advice and techniques for fundraisers.

Museum or gallery collection, archive, or library special collection:
Fundraising in the UK and abroad, targets including trusts and companies

Printed publications:
Various Codes of Practice and Books including:
Code of Practice on Reciprocal Mailing (£2.50)
House to House Collection (£2.50)
Schools Fundraising (£9.95)
The Complete Fundraising Handbook (£12.95)
The Scottish Code of Fundraising Practice (£10)
Fundraising on the Internet (£12.95)
Reference Manual on Payroll Giving (£2.50)

Publications list:
Available online and in print

Access to staff:
Contact by letter, by telephone and by e-mail.
Appointment necessary.
Hours: Mon to Fri, 0900 to 1700

Access to building, collection or gallery:
Prior appointment required
Hours: Mon to Fri, 0900 to 1700

Access for disabled people:
Ramped entry

INSTITUTE OF GROCERY DISTRIBUTION

Acronym or abbreviation: IGD

Grange Lane, Letchmore Heath, Watford, Hertfordshire, WD2 8DQ

Tel: 01923 857141
Fax: 01923 852531
E-mail: igd@igd.com

Website:
http://www.igd.com

Enquiries:
Enquiries to: Database Manager

Founded:
1909

Organisation type and purpose:
Professional body (membership is by subscription), present number of members: 500, registered charity (charity number 105680), training organisation, consultancy, research organisation.

Subject coverage:
Leading source of information and analysis on the UK and European food industry.

Printed publications:
Backhauling & Factory Gate Pricing
Category Management – Which Way Now?
Children's Food – Market Forces & Industry
   Responses
Consumer Watch 2002 – Consumer Attitudes to
   Food & Grocery Issues
Convenience Retailing 2002 – The Market Report
Driving Improvement – Business Case Studies
   Report
Food Consumption 2002 – The one stop guide to
   the food consumer
Global Retailing 2002
Grocery Wholesaling 2002 (annually)
International Retailer Profiles
Order printed publications from: Publications
Department, IGD
at same address, tel: 01923 851925, fax: 01923
852531, e-mail: publications@igd.org.uk

Electronic and video publications:
All printed publications are now available
   electronically

Publications list:
Available in print

Access to staff:
Contact by letter, by telephone, by fax, by e-mail
and via website. Appointment necessary. Non-
members charged.
Hours: Mon to Fri, 0900 to 1700

Access to building, collection or gallery:
Prior appointment required

INSTITUTE OF GROUNDSMANSHIP

Acronym or abbreviation: IOG

28 Stratford Office Village, Walker Avenue, Wolverton Mill East, Milton Keynes, MK12 5TW

Tel: 01908 312511
Fax: 01908 311140
E-mail: iog@iog.org

Website:
http://www.iog.org

Enquiries:
Enquiries to: Chief Executive

Direct e-mail: marketing@iog.org

Founded:
1934

Organisation type and purpose:
Membership association, suitable for ages: 18+, training organisation, consultancy.

Subject coverage:
All matters relating to grass, or turf, in sports amenity or leisure; organiser of the largest trade exhibition for the sports amenity and landscaping industry, IOGSALTEX, held annually at the Royal Windsor Racecourse in September; consultancy service on all aspects of the turf industry.

Printed publications:
Fact Sheets on turf care problems
The Groundsman Magazine (monthly)

Access to staff:
Contact by letter, by telephone, by fax, by e-mail
and via website. Appointment necessary.
Hours: Mon to Fri, 0900 to 1700

Incorporates the:
Association of Landscape Managers

Links with:
FA Technical Pitch Committee
RHS
ROSPA
Sports Council

INSTITUTE OF HEALTH PROMOTION AND EDUCATION

Acronym or abbreviation: IHPE

University Dental Hospital, Higher Cambridge Street, Manchester, M15 6FH

Tel: 0161 275 6610
Fax: 0161 275 6299
E-mail: honsec@ihpe.org.uk

Website:
http://www.ihpe.org.uk

Enquiries:
Enquiries to: Honorary Secretary

Organisation type and purpose:
Professional organisation.

Subject coverage:
Health promotion and education.

Printed publications:
International Journal of Health Promotion and
   Education (quarterly)

INSTITUTE OF HEALTH RECORD INFORMATION & MANAGEMENT

Acronym or abbreviation: IHRIM(UK)

IHRIM(UK) Headquarters, 141 Leander Drive, Rochdale, Lancashire, OL11 2XE

Tel: 01706 868481
Fax: 01706 868481
E-mail: ihrim@zen.co.uk

Enquiries:
Enquiries to: Chief Executive

Founded:
1948

Organisation type and purpose:
International organisation, professional body (membership is by qualification), present number of members: 1000, consultancy.

Subject coverage:
Management of health records – systems and services, health record information management.

Printed publications:
IHRIM(UK) Journal (quarterly)
Health Records Quality Handbook – A self audit
   tool (£35)
Understanding Medical Terminology (£5.50)

Publications list:
Available in print

Access to staff:
Contact by letter, by telephone and by fax.
Appointment necessary. Non-members charged.
Hours: Mon to Fri, 0930 to 1230

INSTITUTE OF HEALTH SCIENCES LIBRARY

Acronym or abbreviation: IHS

Old Road, Headington, Oxford, OX3 7LF

Tel: 01865 226688
Fax: 01865 226619
E-mail: library.enquiries@ihs.ox.ac.uk

Website:
http://www.library.ox.ac.uk
Oxford University libraries

Enquiries:
Enquiries to: Librarian
Direct tel: 01865 226618

Founded:
1996

Organisation type and purpose:
University library.

Subject coverage:
Health Services administration, evidence based medicine, epidemiology, primary care and public health.

Library catalogue:
All or part available online

Access to staff:
Contact by letter, by telephone, by fax and by e-
mail. Non-members charged.
Hours: Mon to Fri, 0900 to 1700

Access for disabled people:
Access to all public areas, toilet facilities
Special comments: Lift to first floor

Parent body:
University of Oxford

INSTITUTE OF HEALTHCARE ENGINEERING & ESTATE MANAGEMENT

Acronym or abbreviation: IHEEM

2 Abingdon House, Cumberland Business Centre, Northumberland Road, Portsmouth, Hampshire, PO5 1DS

Tel: 023 9282 3186
Fax: 023 9281 5927
E-mail: office@iheem.org.uk

Website:
http://www.iheem.org.uk

Enquiries:
Enquiries to: Administration Officer

Founded:
1943

Formerly called:
Hospital of Engineering

Incorporates the former:
X Ray Society

Organisation type and purpose:
Learned society, professional body (membership is by qualification, election or invitation).

Subject coverage:
Hospital engineering, medical equipment, estate management relating to the healthcare sector.

Printed publications:
Journal (monthly)
Order printed publications from: Main address

Access to staff:
Contact by letter, by telephone, by fax, by e-mail
and via website
Hours: Mon to Fri, 0900 to 1700

continued overleaf

Administers:
International Federation of Healthcare Engineering
   website: http://www.ifhe.info

Links with:
Engineering Council

INSTITUTE OF HERALDIC AND GENEALOGICAL STUDIES

Acronym or abbreviation: IHGS

79–82 Northgate, Canterbury, Kent, CT1 1BA

Tel: 01227 768664
Fax: 01227 765617
E-mail: librarian@ihgs.ac.uk

Website:
http://www.ihgs.ac.uk

Enquiries:
Enquiries to: Librarian

Founded:
1961

Organisation type and purpose:
Membership association, registered charity
(charity number 286429), research organisation.
Educational trust; training, study and research
body.

Subject coverage:
Family history, genealogy, heraldry, foreign
heraldry, Coats of Arms, genetic diseases.

Museum or gallery collection, archive, or library special collection:
Catholic Marriage Index (London and Essex)
Complete Collection of Siebmacher's
   Wappenbuchen
Armorial Indexes
Manorial and early heraldic manuscripts
Marriage Indexes not collected elsewhere
Numerous family histories and pedigrees
Pallot Marriage Index (1780–1837, mainly London)
Sources and finding aids of special significance
   including International Genealogical Index and
   other indexes on microfiche; printout services
   available
Special collections for Kent, Sussex, Hampshire,
   London and Middlesex

Non-library collection catalogue:
All or part available in-house

Library catalogue:
All or part available in-house

Printed publications:
Family History (journal)
Guide to Library
Anglo-Norman Armory (C. R. Humphery-Smith,
   1973)
Armigerous Ancestors: an essential guide and
   index to the Herald's Visitations (C. R.
   Humphery-Smith, 1997)
Hugh Revel (C. R. Humphery-Smith, 1994)
Our Family History (C. R. Humphery-Smith)

Microform publications:
Family History Journal Index (Vols 1–5 1962–67,
   microfiche)
The Protestation Returns of Kent 1641/2
   (microfiche)

Publications list:
Available in print

Access to staff:
Contact by letter, by telephone and by e-mail.
Appointment necessary. Non-members charged.
Hours: Mon to Fri, 1000 to 1630

INSTITUTE OF HIGHWAY ENGINEERS

Acronym or abbreviation: IHE

De Morgan House, 58 Russell Square, London,
WC1B 4HS

Tel: 020 7436 7487
Fax: 020 7436 7488

E-mail: information@theihe.org

Website:
http://www.theihe.org

Enquiries:
Enquiries to: Secretary
Direct e-mail: secretary@theihe.org

Founded:
1965

Formerly called:
Institute of Highway Incorporated Engineers (year
of change 2009)

Organisation type and purpose:
Professional body, present number of members:
3,000.

Subject coverage:
Highway engineering; traffic and transportation;
highway maintenance.

Electronic and video publications:
IHIE Engineering Guidelines for Motorcycles
   (2005, CD-ROM)
IHIE Home Zone Design Guidelines (2002, CD-
   ROM)

Publications list:
Available online

Access to staff:
Contact by letter, by telephone, by e-mail and via
website. Appointment necessary.
Hours: Mon to Fri, 0900 to 1700

Member organisation of:
Engineering Council UK

INSTITUTE OF HISTORICAL RESEARCH

Acronym or abbreviation: IHR

University of London, Senate House, Malet Street,
London, WC1E 7HU

Tel: 020 7862 8760
Fax: 020 7862 8762
E-mail: ihr.library@sas.ac.uk

Website:
http://www.history.ac.uk
Institute website, with link to library page.
http://catalogue.ulrls.lon.ac.uk/search~S10
Access to the library's holdings in the catalogue of
the University of London Research Library
Services (ULRLS).

Enquiries:
Enquiries to: Librarian

Founded:
1921

Organisation type and purpose:
University department or institute, postgraduate
institute.

Subject coverage:
History of Western Europe and its expansion
overseas, c. AD450 to the present; imperial and
colonial history; military and naval history;
diplomatic history; history of international
relations.

Library catalogue:
All or part available online

Printed publications:
Historical Research for Higher Degrees in the
   United Kingdom (annually)
Historical Research: Bulletin of the Institute of
   Historical Research (three times a year)
Teachers of History in the Universities of the
   United Kingdom (annually)
Victoria History of the Counties of England (200
   vols published, in progress)
Grants for History (annually)
Order printed publications from: Publications
Manager

Electronic and video publications:
Interviews with Historians (videos)

Publications list:
Available online and in print

Access to staff:
Contact by letter, by telephone, by e-mail and in
person. Appointment necessary.
Hours: Mon to Fri, 0900 to 2045; Sat, 0930 to 1715

Member organisation of:
School of Advanced Study
   University of London, Senate House, Malet
   Street, London, WC1E 7HU; website: http://
   www.sas.ac.uk
University of London Research Library Services
(ULRLS)
   Senate House, Malet Street, London, WC1E 7HU
   website: http://www.ulrls.lon.ac.uk

INSTITUTE OF HORTICULTURE

Acronym or abbreviation: IOH

9 Red Lion Court, London, EC4A 3EF

Tel: 020 7936 5957
Fax: 020 7936 5958
E-mail: ioh@horticulture.org.uk

Website:
http://www.horticulture.org.uk

Enquiries:
Enquiries to: Administration Manager

Founded:
1984

Organisation type and purpose:
Professional body (membership is by
qualification), present number of members: 2,000.

Subject coverage:
All aspects of horticulture, education, training and
career progression in the amenity, commercial,
research and advisory sectors.

Printed publications:
Come into Horticulture (careers booklet)
Conference Proceedings: Micropropagation in
   Horticulture; Managing Gardens for Leisure and
   Profit; Growing with Plastics; Horticultural
   Exploitation of Recent Biological Developments
Courses and Training in Horticulture (for sae)
Directory of Horticultural Consultants
Landscape Plants
The Horticulturist (journal, quarterly)
Trees in the Environment: Their Biology
   Management and Control

Publications list:
Available in print

Access to staff:
Contact by letter, by telephone and by fax.
Appointment necessary.
Hours: Mon to Fri, 0900 to 1700

INSTITUTE OF HOSPITALITY

Trinity Court, 34 West Street, Sutton, Surrey, SM1
1SH

Tel: 020 8661 4900
Fax: 020 8661 4901

Website:
http://www.instituteofhospitality.org
The institute, membership, qualifications,
accreditation, publications, information services,
news, events.
http://moodle.instituteofhospitality.org
The institute's online learning website; includes
five free e-learning modules available to the
general public upon free registration.

Founded:
1971

Created by the merger of:
Hotel and Catering Institute (HCI, created 1949)
and the Institutional Management Association
(IMA, created 1938) (year of change 1971)

Formerly called:
Hotel & Catering International Management
Association (HCIMA) (year of change 2007)

Organisation type and purpose:
A registered educational charity, the professional body for managers – and aspiring managers – working in the hospitality, leisure and tourism industries, a recognised and authoritative international body in the field of accreditation for hospitality, leisure and tourism programmes of learning; has over 10,000 members in the UK, and in more than 100 countries world-wide.
To promote the highest professional standards of management and education in the international hospitality, leisure and tourism industries; to benefit members in their professional and career development, while continuing to improve industry sector standards; to offer support to members throughout their careers in the industry.

Subject coverage:
Covers all sectors of the industry including hotels, contract catering companies, restaurants, pubs and clubs, as well as leisure outlets, theme parks and sports venues. Works closely with all hospitality, leisure and tourism agencies, education and awarding bodies, and government departments, providing an interface between education and industry.

Information services:
Library Staff, tel: 020 8661 4902; e-mail: library@instituteofhospitality.org.

Education services:
Free online learning modules tailored to meet the needs of hospitality and tourism students and professionals.

Museum or gallery collection, archive, or library special collection:
Library and Information Service is a unique collection of resources in the field of hospitality, leisure & tourism (HLT); members have free access

Library catalogue:
All or part available online

Printed publications:
Hospitality (quarterly magazine, £44 annually)

Electronic and video publications:
Hospitality magazine articles available online (free to members)
Management Guides (free to members; non-members may download an order form)
Know-how (bi-monthly CPD newsletter, free to members by e-mail or download from website)

Publications list:
Available online

Access to staff:
Contact by letter, by telephone, by fax and via website

INSTITUTE OF INDIAN CULTURE (BHARATIYA VIDYA BHAVAN)

Formal name: Bharatiya Vidya Bhavan – Institute of Indian Art and Culture
Acronym or abbreviation: BHAVAN

4A Castletown Road, West Kensington, London, W14 9HQ

Tel: 020 7381 3086 or 4608
Fax: 020 7381 8758

Website:
http://www.bhavan.net
Descriptions of activities, products and facilities available for students, members and customers.

Enquiries:
Enquiries to: Executive Director
Other contacts: Academic Director

Founded:
1972

Organisation type and purpose:
International organisation, professional body (membership is by subscription), present number of members: 1220, voluntary organisation,

registered charity (charity number 312879), public library, suitable for ages: 7+, training organisation, research organisation.
To popularise in the UK Indian Art, Archaeology, Languages and Culture in general.

Subject coverage:
Indian philosophy, religion, languages, pilgrimage centres, festivals, calendar dates, music, dance, drama and all things connected with Indian art and culture.

Museum or gallery collection, archive, or library special collection:
Complete writings of Gandhi, Nehru and other Indian writers

Printed publications:
Books on Indian philosophy, art & culture mainly in English, Gujerati, Hindi and Sanskrit

Electronic and video publications:
Audio and video tapes available to purchase directly from us

Publications list:
Available in print

Access to staff:
Contact by letter, by telephone, by fax and in person. Appointment necessary. All charged.
Hours: 0900 to 1900, seven days a week
Special comments: Wheelchair access to ground floor only.

Access to building, collection or gallery:
No prior appointment required
Hours: Mon to Fri, 0900 to 1700
Special comments: Books cannot be borrowed from Bhavani's library.

Bhavan's outreach classes at:
Alperton Community School
Stanley Avenue, off Ealing Road, Wembley, Middlesex, HA0 4JE; tel: 020 7381 3086; fax: 020 7381 8758

Parent body and Head Office:
Bharatiya Vidya Bhavan (BHAVAN)
Munshi Sadan, Kulapati K M Munshi Marg, Chaupatti, Mumbai, Bombay, 400 007, India; tel: 00 91 22 363 0786; fax: 00 91 22 363 0058

INSTITUTE OF INDIRECT TAXATION

Acronym or abbreviation: IIT

Suite G1, The Stables, Station Road West, Oxted, RH5 9EE

Tel: 01883 730658
Fax: 01883 717778
E-mail: enquiries@theiit.org.uk

Website:
http://www.theiit.org.uk
Conferences, membership, VAT compliance diploma, students, benefits, branches

Enquiries:
Enquiries to: Administrator
Direct e-mail: postmaster@theiit.org.uk

Founded:
1991

Organisation type and purpose:
Professional body.

Subject coverage:
Indirect taxes.

Printed publications:
Indirect TaxVoice (9 times a year, available on subscription to non-members)

Access to staff:
Contact by letter, by telephone, by fax, by e-mail and via website. Appointment necessary.
Hours: Mon to Fri, 0900 to 1700

Access to building, collection or gallery:
Mon to Fri, 0900 to 1700

Access for disabled people:
Fully accessible

INSTITUTE OF INTERNAL AUDITORS UK & IRELAND

Acronym or abbreviation: IIA UK & Ireland

13 Abbeville Mews, 88 Clapham Park Road, London, SW4 7BX

Tel: 020 7498 0101
Fax: 020 7978 2492
E-mail: info@iia.org.uk

Website:
http://www.iia.org.uk
Extensive online knowledge centre.

Founded:
1975

Organisation type and purpose:
Professional body (membership is by subscription), present number of members: 6,000.

Subject coverage:
Corporate governance and risk management, internal control and internal auditing (general and computer).

Non-library collection catalogue:
All or part available online and in print

Library catalogue:
All or part available in-house

Printed publications:
Internal Auditing Magazine (monthly)

Publications list:
Available online and in print

Access to staff:
Contact by letter, by telephone, by fax, by e-mail and via website
Hours: Mon to Fri, 0900 to 1700

Affiliated to:
European Confederation of Institutes of Internal Auditing
Institute of Internal Auditors Incorporate, USA

INSTITUTE OF INTERNAL COMMUNICATION

Acronym or abbreviation: IoIC

Suite GA2, Oak House, Woodlands Business Park, Linford Wood, Milton Keynes, MK14 6EY

Tel: 01908 313755
Fax: 01908 313661
E-mail: enquiries@ioic.org.uk

Website:
http://www.ioic.org.uk

Founded:
1949

Formerly called:
British Association of Industrial Editors (year of change 1995); British Association of Communicators in Business Ltd (CiB) (year of change 2010)

Organisation type and purpose:
Professional body (membership is by subscription), present number of members: 1000.

Subject coverage:
Corporate media management and practice.

Electronic and video publications:
IoIC Ezine (electronic monthly magazine)

Access to staff:
Contact by letter, by telephone, by fax and by e-mail

Liaison with:
International Association of Business Communicators
USA

Member of:
Federation of European Industrial Editors Associations

INSTITUTE OF INTERNATIONAL EDUCATION IN LONDON

Acronym or abbreviation: IIEL

Charlton House, Charlton Road, Charlton, London, SE7 8RE

Tel: 020 8331 3100
Fax: 020 8331 3149
E-mail: enquiries@iiel.org.uk

Website:
http://www.iiel.org.uk

Enquiries:
Enquiries to: Course Coordinator
Other contacts: Publicity Coordinator

Founded:
1989

Organisation type and purpose:
International organisation, university department or institute, suitable for ages: 5+, training organisation, consultancy.
Japanese teacher training centre, EFL courses, JFL courses and consultancy on university and college entrance.

Subject coverage:
Japanese language for younger learners (mother tongue Japanese), Japanese teacher training, the study of Japanese as a foreign language, the study of English as a foreign language and entrance to British universities.

Printed publications:
Okina Chikyu (educational bulletin, quarterly)
Prospectus and course information only
Ransho (in-house newsletter)
Study of Japanese Language Teaching (bulletin, annually)

Access to staff:
Contact by letter, by telephone, by fax, by e-mail, in person and via website. Appointment necessary.
Hours: Mon to Fri, 0900 to 1730

Also at:
ICJ – Japan Office
2F Maeda Building, 2–13–2 Suido, Bunkyo-ku, Tokyo, 112–0005, Japan; tel: 00 81 3 5940 0506; fax: 00 81 3 5940 0507; e-mail: info@edu-icj.com

INSTITUTE OF INTERNATIONAL LICENSING PRACTITIONERS

Acronym or abbreviation: IILP

28 Main Street, Mursley, Milton Keynes, MK17 0RT

Tel: 01296 728136
Fax: 01296 720070
E-mail: enquiries@iilp.net

Website:
http://www.iilp.net

Founded:
1969

Organisation type and purpose:
International organisation, professional body (membership is by qualification, election or invitation).
To provide professional licensing assistance to companies requiring technology transfer services; to set professional standards for those engaged in licensing consultancy.

Subject coverage:
Licensing, commercialising invention, technology transfer, distribution agreements, strategic alliances, joint ventures.

Printed publications:
Exploits

Access to staff:
Contact by letter, by telephone, by fax and by e-mail. Non-members charged.
Hours: Mon to Fri, 0800 to 1800

Affiliated to:
Licensing Innovation and Technology Consultants Association (LICTA)
Let 2 Anaweg 25–27, Triesen, FL-9495, Liechtenstein; tel: +41 75 399 1000; fax: +41 75 399 1091; e-mail: enquiries@iilp.net; website: http://www.iilp.net

INSTITUTE OF INVENTORS

Acronym or abbreviation: IoI

19–23 Fosse Way, Ealing, London, W13 0BZ

Tel: 020 8998 3540/6372
E-mail: mikinvent@aol.com

Website:
http://www.instituteofinventors.com

Enquiries:
Enquiries to: President
Direct tel: 020 8998 6372

Founded:
1964

Organisation type and purpose:
International organisation, advisory body, professional body (membership is by subscription), present number of members: 1526, voluntary organisation, university department or institute, consultancy, research organisation.
To advise and assist inventors at all stages of their inventions, evaluation, patenting, prototypes, licence agreements, manufacture and marketing.

Subject coverage:
New inventions, invention research, invention, evaluation, exploitation, patenting, licensing, marketing and sponsorship.

Non-library collection catalogue:
All or part available online

Library catalogue:
All or part available online

Printed publications:
New Invention List (for Business Members only)

Access to staff:
Contact by telephone. Appointment necessary.
Hours: Mon to Sun, 1000 to 1800

INSTITUTE OF IRISH STUDIES

Queen's University Belfast, 8 Fitzwilliam Street, Belfast, BT9 6AW

Tel: 028 9027 3386
Fax: 028 9043 9238
E-mail: irish.studies@qub.ac.uk

Website:
http://www.qub.ac.uk/iis/
Home page, information on research, teaching, fellowship, scholarships and publications.

Enquiries:
Enquiries to: Director
Other contacts: Secretary for enquiries about courses, the work of the Institute etc.

Founded:
1965

Organisation type and purpose:
University department or institute, research organisation, publishing house.

Subject coverage:
Academic research on Ireland, primarily in the humanities.

Printed publications:
Order printed publications from: Institute of Irish Studies
at the same address, tel: 028 9027 3235, fax: 028 9043 9238, e-mail: m.mcnulty@qub.ac.uk

Publications list:
Available online and in print

Access to staff:
Contact by letter and by fax
Hours: Mon to Fri, 0900 to 1700

INSTITUTE OF ISMAILI STUDIES

Acronym or abbreviation: IIS

210 Euston Road, London, NW1 2DA

Tel: 020 7756 2700
Fax: 020 7756 2740
E-mail: info@iis.ac.uk

Website:
http://www.iis.ac.uk
Information about the institute, research, lectures, seminars, study programmes and library collections.

Founded:
1977

Organisation type and purpose:
Research institute, graduate studies, library.
To promote scholarship and learning of Islamic cultures and societies, historical as well as contemporary, Shi'ism in general, Isma'ilism in particular.

Subject coverage:
Islamic studies, especially Shi'ism and Isma'ilism.

Museum or gallery collection, archive, or library special collection:
Library of 25,000 items, including manuscripts (in Arabic, Persian, and Khojki script)

Non-library collection catalogue:
All or part available in-house and in print

Library catalogue:
All or part available online and in-house

Printed publications:
Educational and research publications for specialists, the general public, adult audiences and young people
Occasional papers, monographs, editions, translations, conference proceedings and bibliographical works
Order printed publications from: See website for details: http://www.iis.ac.uk

Publications list:
Available online and in print

Access to staff:
Contact by letter, by telephone, by fax, by e-mail and via website

INSTITUTE OF JEWISH STUDIES

Acronym or abbreviation: IJS

University College London, Foster Court, Gower Street, London, WC1E 6BT

Tel: 020 7679 3520
Fax: 020 7209 1026
E-mail: ijs@ucl.ac.uk

Website:
http://www.ucl.ac.uk/hebrew-jewish/ijs

Organisation type and purpose:
Affiliated with University College London's Department of Hebrew and Jewish Studies, the Institute is dedicated to the promotion of all aspects of Jewish scholarship and civilisation, with the aim of reaching every section of the Jewish community and of the interested non-Jewish public.
Holds public lectures, symposia, seminars and international conferences.

Subject coverage:
Jewish scholarship and civilisation.

INSTITUTE OF LEADERSHIP & MANAGEMENT

Acronym or abbreviation: ILM

Stowe House, Netherstone, Lichfield, Staffordshire, WS13 6TJ

Tel: 01543 251346
Fax: 01543 266811
E-mail: ism@ismstowe.demon.co.uk

Website:
http://www.nebsmgt.co.uk
http://www.i-l-m.com
Under development.
http://www.ismstowe.com
Educational awards. Membership information –
news and press releases. Development is on-going.

Enquiries:
Enquiries to: Information Services Manager
Direct e-mail: info@ismstowe-info.demon.co.uk

Founded:
1947

Organisation type and purpose:
Professional body (membership is by subscription,
qualification), present number of members: 20,000,
registered charity (charity number 248226),
suitable for ages: normally 19+.
Professional institute for front line managers and
supervisors.

Subject coverage:
Accreditation of management courses and NVQ/
SVQs; customer care awards, training support
awards, and world class qualifications,
management and training topics.

Library catalogue:
All or part available in-house

Printed publications:
ISM Mentor (3 times a year)
Modern Management (membership journal, 6
  times a year, free to members)
Learning Together Guides (series) to MCI
  Standards level 3 (workbooks)
Progress (journal, 3 times a year, free to Centres
  and students)
Superseries (published by Pergamon)
See website for other items

Electronic and video publications:
See website

Access to staff:
Contact by letter, by telephone, by fax, by e-mail
and via website. Appointment necessary.
Hours: Mon to Fri, 0830 to 1700

Access to building, collection or gallery:
No access other than to staff
Hours: Mon to Fri, 1000 to 1600

Access for disabled people:
Parking provided, ramped entry, toilet facilities

Second address:
Institute of Leadership & Management
  1 Giltspur Street, London, EC1A 9DD; tel: 020
  7294 3057; fax: 020 7294 2402; e-mail: nebsmgt@
  city-and-guilds.co.uk

INSTITUTE OF LEGAL CASHIERS & ADMINISTRATORS

Acronym or abbreviation: ILCA

146–148 Eltham Hill, Eltham, London, SE9 5DX

Tel: 020 8294 2887
Fax: 020 8859 1682
E-mail: info@ilca.org.uk

Website:
http://www.ilca.org.uk
General information, course information,
publications information

Enquiries:
Enquiries to: Executive Secretary
Other contacts: Editor for press information.

Founded:
1978

Organisation type and purpose:
Professional body (membership is by subscription),
present number of members: 2600, training
organisation, research organisation, publishing
house.
To promote excellence in legal finance and
administration.

Subject coverage:
Legal accounting, financial control, administration,
marketing, personnel management, solicitors'
accounts rules, VAT, law office management,
accounting for legal aid.

Printed publications:
Annual Report and Accounts
Legal Abacus (journal, 6 times a year)
Legal Software

Publications list:
Available in print

Access to staff:
Contact by letter, by telephone, by fax, by e-mail
and via website. Appointment necessary.
Hours: Mon to Fri, 0900 to 1700

Access for disabled people:
Access to all public areas

Chairman:
Institute of Legal Accountants of Ireland
  c/o Wellfield House, Blessington Road, Naas,
  County Kildare, Eire

INSTITUTE OF LEGAL EXECUTIVES

Acronym or abbreviation: ILEX

Kempston Manor, Kempston, Bedford, MK42 7AB

Tel: 01234 841000
Fax: 01234 840989
E-mail: info@ilex.org.uk

Website:
http://www.ilex.org.uk
Introduction to ILEX and how to qualify, members'
news and professional issues.
http://www.legal-executive-recruitment.com
Online recruitment for Legal Executives.
http://www.ilexjournal.com
Interactive journal for members.
http://www.ilexpt.co.uk
Law for non-lawyers.
http://www.ilex-tutorial.ac.uk
Introduction to distance learning and ILEX
Tutorial College.

Enquiries:
Enquiries to: Secretary General
Other contacts: Head of Communications and
Public Relations for press and media enquiries,
articles etc.

Founded:
1963

Organisation type and purpose:
Professional body (membership is by
qualification), present number of members: 22,000.
Examining body.

Subject coverage:
Legal training services, for both lawyers and non-
lawyers, law reform, distance learning.

**Museum or gallery collection, archive, or library
special collection:**
Law Library (members only)

Printed publications:
The Legal Executive (journal, monthly)

Electronic and video publications:
The Virtual Practitioner – Develop legal skills (CD-
  ROM, £30 plus VAT)
Introduction to ILEX (video)
The Journal – on cassette tape for the blind (tape)

Access to staff:
Contact by letter, by telephone, by fax and by e-
mail. Appointment necessary.
Hours: Mon to Fri, 0900 to 1700

Subsidiary bodies:
ILEX Paralegal Training
  tel: 01234 348848; fax: 01234 266557; e-mail: ilex
  .pt@btconnect.com
ILEX Publishing and Advertising
  tel: 01234 845721; fax: 01234 841999; e-mail: ipa@
  legal-executive-journal.co.uk

ILEX Tutorial College
  tel: 01234 841010; fax: 01234 841373

INSTITUTE OF LICENSED TRADE STOCK AUDITORS

Acronym or abbreviation: ILTSA

7 Comely Bank Place, Edinburgh, EH4 1DT

Tel: 0131 315 2600
Fax: 0131 315 4346

Website:
http://www.iltsa.co.uk
Background information, news, stocktakers
(qualified).

Enquiries:
Enquiries to: Secretary
Direct e-mail: secretary@iltsa.co.uk

Founded:
1953

Organisation type and purpose:
National organisation, professional body
(membership is by qualification), present number
of members: c. 400.
The only qualifying body for Stock Auditors
within the licensed trade. The institute is also able
to mediate in disputes concerning stocktaking and
can act in an advisory capacity to any company or
individual who seeks advice.

Subject coverage:
Qualified stocktakers, stocktaking, licensed trade,
training, examinations, legislation affecting trade,
specialist valuations.

Printed publications:
The Stock Auditor (magazine, 12 times a year)
Taking Stock (hard back copy, £15 plus £3 p&p)

Access to staff:
Contact by letter, by telephone, by fax and by e-
mail
Hours: Mon to Fri, 0900 to 1700

INSTITUTE OF MANAGEMENT CONSULTANCY

Acronym or abbreviation: IMC

3rd Floor, 17–18 Haywards Place, London, EC1R
0EQ

Tel: 020 7566 5220
Fax: 020 7566 5230

Website:
http://www.imc.co.uk
Full details of IMC.

Enquiries:
Enquiries to: Chief Executive

Founded:
1962

Organisation type and purpose:
Professional body.
The IMC leads the profession of management
consultancy by qualifying, supporting and
regulating individual management consultants
and providing a forum for all management
consultancy stakeholders.

Subject coverage:
Management consulting practice and careers.

Printed publications:
Annual Report 1999 (from April 2000, free)
Inside Careers Guide to Management Consultancy
Me A Management Consultant (free)
Standard Terms and Conditions of Engagement
  (£20)
Update Newsletter
Professional Consultancy (quarterly)

Publications list:
Available in print

Access to staff:
Contact by letter, by telephone and by fax.

continued overleaf

Appointment necessary.
Hours: Mon to Fri, 0900 to 1700

INSTITUTE OF MANAGEMENT SERVICES

Acronym or abbreviation: IMS

Brooke House, 24 Dam Street, Lichfield, Staffordshire, WS13 6AA

Tel: 01543 266909
Fax: 01543 257848
E-mail: admin@ims-stowe.fsnet.co.uk

Website:
http://www.ims-productivity.com

Enquiries:
Enquiries to: Information Officer

Founded:
1941

Organisation type and purpose:
Professional body, present number of members: 1700.

Subject coverage:
Work study; organisation and methods, business systems, work environment, motivation, information technology; quality management and control; industrial engineering, business process re-engineering.

Printed publications:
Management Services (4 times a year)
Management Services Handbook (2nd ed., 1991)
Student's Compendia
Wealth Creation – The Added Value Concept
Work Measurement

Electronic and video publications:
Activity Sampling
Clerical Work Measurement
Introducing Management Services
Method Study
Profit Improvement & Cost Reduction

Publications list:
Available in print

Access to staff:
Contact by letter, by telephone, by fax, by e-mail and via website. Appointment necessary. Non-members charged.
Hours: Mon to Fri, 0930 to 1445

Links with:
Alliance of Manufacturing and Management Organisations (AMMO)
European Federation of Productivity Services (EFPS)
World Confederation of Productivity Science (WCPS)

INSTITUTE OF MANAGEMENT SPECIALISTS

Acronym or abbreviation: IMS

Warwick Corner, 42 Warwick Road, Kenilworth, Warwickshire, CV8 1HE

Tel: 01926 866623
E-mail: info@group-ims.com

Website:
http://www.group-ims.com

Enquiries:
Enquiries to: Administrative Director

Founded:
1971

Organisation type and purpose:
International organisation, professional body (membership is by subscription, qualification), training organisation, range of professional diploma courses available.

Subject coverage:
Management (general and specialised); administration; technical and computer sciences.

Printed publications:
The Management Specialist (3 times a year)

Access to staff:
Contact by letter, by telephone, by e-mail and via website

Links with:
Institute of Manufacturing and Professional Business and Technical Management
    at the same address
The Academy of Executives and Administrators
    at the same address
The Academy of Multi-Skills
    at the same address

INSTITUTE OF MANUFACTURING

Acronym or abbreviation: IManf

Warwick Corner, 42 Warwick Road, Kenilworth, Warwickshire, CV8 1HE

Tel: 01926 866623
E-mail: info@group-ims.com

Website:
http://www.group-ims.com

Enquiries:
Enquiries to: Administrative Director

Founded:
1978

Organisation type and purpose:
Professional body (membership is by subscription, qualification), training organisation, range of professional diploma courses available.

Subject coverage:
Manufacturing; industry; management – general and specialised; technical and computer sciences; education and training.

Printed publications:
Manufacturing (annually, spring)
Manufacturing Management (annually, autumn)

Access to staff:
Contact by letter, by telephone, by e-mail and via website

Links with:
Institute of Management Specialists and Professional Business and Technical Management
The Academy of Executives and Administrators
The Academy of Multi-Skills

INSTITUTE OF MARINE ENGINEERING, SCIENCE AND TECHNOLOGY

Acronym or abbreviation: IMarEST

80 Coleman Street, London, EC2R 5BJ

Tel: 020 7382 2600
Fax: 020 7382 2670
E-mail: mic@imare.org.uk

Website:
http://www.imare.org.uk
General information on Institute of Marine Engineers, careers and jobs, events and conferences, library catalogue.

Enquiries:
Enquiries to: Manager of Information Centre
Direct tel: 020 7382 2645
Direct e-mail: membership@imarest.org
Other contacts: Manager of Engineering, Science & Technology for technical information regarding marine engineering.

Founded:
1889

Organisation type and purpose:
Learned society, professional body (membership is by qualification), present number of members: 17,000, registered charity (charity number 212992). Promoting the maritime industries.

Subject coverage:
Marine engineering; marine electrical engineering; ocean technology, offshore engineering, naval architecture, shipping, subsea technology.

Non-library collection catalogue:
All or part available online

Printed publications:
Conference Proceedings
Marine Engineers Review (annual subscription £85, members free, 10 times a year)
Maritime IT and Electronics (annual subscription £40, 6 times a year)
The Journal of Offshore Technology (annual subscription £50, members free, 6 times a year)
Transactions Volume 113 (annual subscription £120, members £15)

Electronic and video publications:
International Directory of Maritime Consultants and Technical Services (annual, £59, available on the Web)
Marine Technology Abstracts on CD-ROM (joint venture with British Maritime Technology, available on annual subscription, available on the Web)

Publications list:
Available online and in print

Access to staff:
Contact by letter, by telephone, by fax, by e-mail, in person and via website. All charged.
Hours: Mon to Fri, 0900 to 1700

Access for disabled people:
Ramped entry

INSTITUTE OF MATERIALS, MINERALS AND MINING

Acronym or abbreviation: IOM3

1 Carlton House Terrace, London, SW1Y 5DB

Tel: 020 7451 7300
Fax: 020 7839 1702
E-mail: libraryservices@iom3.org

Website:
http://www.iom3.org/content/library-services
Information about the library services and facilities.
http://www.iom3.org

Enquiries:
Enquiries to: Information and Library Co-ordinator or Information Officer
Direct tel: 020 7451 7360/7324
Direct fax: 020 7451 7406
Direct e-mail: hilda.kaune@iom3.org; frances .perry@iom3.org

Founded:
1869

Organisation type and purpose:
Professional body (membership is by qualification), present number of members: 20,000. The Institute of Materials, Minerals and Mining (IOM3) is a major UK engineering institution, the activities of which encompass the whole materials cycle, from exploration and extraction, through characterisation, processing, forming, finishing and application, to product recycling and land reuse. It exists to promote and develop all aspects of materials science and engineering, geology, mining and associated technologies, mineral and petroleum engineering and extraction metallurgy, as a leading authority in the world-wide materials and mining community.

Subject coverage:
Science and technology of metals, polymers, rubbers, ceramics, composites, wood and packaging; production and use; physics and chemistry of materials and production processes. Economic geology, mining and processing of minerals, non-ferrous extractive metallurgy.

Information services:
Enquiries, referral service, loans, photocopies, literature searches.

Museum or gallery collection, archive, or library special collection:
Historical collection: antiquarian books, biographies, photographs, portraits, technical drawings, artefacts
Special Collection: Bessemer Room and artefacts

Non-library collection catalogue:
All or part available in-house

Library catalogue:
All or part available in-house

Printed publications:
Maney Publishing for the IOM3 publishes a range of books and journals covering many aspects of materials including ceramics, polymers, ironmaking and steelmaking, materials science and technology and the minerals and mining industry
Institute of Materials Editorial Deparment produces and publishes Materials World, Packaging Professional, Clay Technology, Wood Focus, MADE
Order printed publications from: Order Processing Dept, Maney Publishing, Suite 1C, Joseph's Well, Hanover Walk, Leeds, LS3 1AB; tel: 0113 243 2800; fax: 0113 386 8178; e-mail: maney@maney.co.uk

Electronic and video publications:
The Information Team produces IMMAGE (Information on Mining, Metallurgy and Geological Exploration) http://www.iom3.org/immage, which is the world's foremost reference database of abstracts and citations of scientific and engineering literature for the international minerals industry. Covering material published from 1979 to the present, IMMAGE now contains over 105,000 records, with two to three thousand references being added each year.
To produce this high-quality, internationally recognised and reputable database, selection, abstracting and indexing are carried out by experienced and technically qualified staff and the content is indexed with controlled vocabulary and thesaurus terms.

Publications list:
Available online

Access to staff:
Contact by letter, by telephone, by fax, by e-mail, in person and via website. Appointment necessary. Non-members charged.
Hours: Mon to Fri, 0930 to 1700

Also at:
David West Library, Institute of Materials, Minerals and Mining
tel: 020 7451 7360; fax: 020 7451 7406; e-mail: hilda.kaune@iom3.org; frances.perry@iom3.org
Doncaster Regional Office
Danum House, South Parade, Doncaster, DN1 2DY; tel: 01302 320486; fax: 01302 380900
Grantham Centre
The Boiler House, Springfield Business Park, Caunt Road, Grantham, Lincs NG31 7FZ; tel: 01476 513880; fax: 01476 513899
Stoke Regional Office
Shelton House, 12 Stoke Road, Stoke-on-Trent, Staffordshire, ST4 2DR; tel: 01782 221700; fax: 01782 221722

INSTITUTE OF MATHEMATICS AND ITS APPLICATIONS

Acronym or abbreviation: IMA

Catherine Richards House, 16 Nelson Street, Southend-on-Sea, Essex, SS1 1EF

Tel: 01702 354020
Fax: 01702 354111
E-mail: post@ima.org.uk

Website:
http://www.ima.org.uk
Membership, IMA conferences, IMA publications, event and news, mathematics website list.

Enquiries:
Enquiries to: Executive Director

Founded:
1964

Organisation type and purpose:
Professional body, registered charity (charity number 1017777).

Subject coverage:
Mathematics, mathematical education, statistics, applications of mathematics, operational research.

Printed publications:
Extensive range of mathematics and its applications: books, papers, conference proceedings and monographs published on behalf of the IMA
IMA Journal of Applied Mathematics (6 times a year)
IMA Journal of Management Mathematics (quarterly)
IMA Journal of Mathematical Control and Information (quarterly)
Mathematical Medicine and Biology: A Journal of the IMA (quarterly)
IMA Journal of Numerical Analysis (quarterly)
Teaching Mathematics and its Applications: an International Journal of the IMA (quarterly)
Mathematics Today (6 times a year)

Publications list:
Available online and in print

Access to staff:
Contact by letter, by telephone, by fax, by e-mail and via website
Hours: Mon to Fri, 0900 to 1700

INSTITUTE OF MEASUREMENT AND CONTROL

Acronym or abbreviation: INSTMC

87 Gower Street, London, WC1E 6AF

Tel: 020 7387 4949
Fax: 020 7388 8431
E-mail: publications@instmc.org.uk

Website:
http://www.instmc.org.uk
Institute Home Page.

Enquiries:
Enquiries to: Assistant CEO / Communications Manager

Founded:
1944

Organisation type and purpose:
Learned society (membership is by qualification, election or invitation), present number of members: 4,000, registered charity, publishing house.
To promote for the public benefit all aspects of measurement and control technology and its applications.

Subject coverage:
Instrumentation, measurement, control engineering, automation.

Library catalogue:
All or part available in-house

Printed publications:
Instrument Engineers' Yearbook
Measurement and Control (journal, 10 times a year)
Transactions of INSTMC (5 times a year)

Publications list:
Available online and in print

Access to staff:
Contact by letter, by telephone, by fax, by e-mail, in person and via website. Appointment necessary.
Hours: Mon to Fri, 0900 to 1700

Access to building, collection or gallery:
Prior appointment required
Special comments: Library is open to members only.

INSTITUTE OF MEDICAL ILLUSTRATORS

Acronym or abbreviation: IMI

12 Coldbath Square, London, EC1R 5HL

Tel: 0207 837 2846

Website:
http://www.imi.org.uk
Members, news, discussion forum, education, training, careers, standards, law and ethics, national guidelines, awards, jobs, detailed contacts.

Enquiries:
Enquiries to: Hon. Secretary
Direct e-mail: secretary@imi.org.uk

Founded:
1968

Organisation type and purpose:
A rich network of fellow professionals, working together to improve and develop medical illustration by means of conferences, courses and regional meetings.
To promote the role of the medical illustrator as a professional member of a multi-skilled team who offer a range of core clinical illustrative and communication services as part of the healthcare team for the benefit of patients and clients; to strive for the highest professional standards; to support, guide and motivate members to achieve success and personal recognition for the quality of their contribution to the healthcare team; to promote its standards to government, to employers and to potential members; to improve recognition of the profession; to seek national registration of all medical illustrators.

Subject coverage:
Brings together the disciplines of clinical photography, medical art, illustration, graphic design and video within healthcare.

Printed publications:
Journal of Visual Communication in Medicine (quarterly)
IMI News (4 a year)

Electronic and video publications:
Journal of Visual Communication in Medicine (quarterly)
IMI News (4 a year)
Order electronic and video publications from: Free download for members from website

Publications list:
Available online

Access to staff:
Contact by letter, by telephone and by e-mail

Member organisation of:
Committee for the Accreditation of Medical Illustration Practitioners (CAMIP)

INSTITUTE OF METAL FINISHING

Acronym or abbreviation: IMF

Exeter House, 48 Holloway Head, Birmingham, B1 1NQ

Tel: 0121 622 7387
Fax: 0121 666 6316
E-mail: exeterhouse@instituteofmetalfinishing.org

Enquiries:
Enquiries to: Secretary

Organisation type and purpose:
Learned society.
Technical and scientific society; eight regional branches; three technical groups.

Subject coverage:
Metal finishing and all aspects of the surface treatment industry, metal finishing, printed circuits, anodizing, coating, all types of metal protection.

Printed publications:
Information Newsletter (6 times a year)
Reports of Working Parties
Symposia; International conference

continued overleaf

Transactions of the Institute (6 times a year)

INSTITUTE OF MONEY ADVISERS

Acronym or abbreviation: IMA

Stringer House, 34 Lupton Street, Leeds, LS10 2QW

Tel: 0845 094 2384; 0113 270 8444
Fax: 0845 094 2175; 0113 270 2111
E-mail: office@i-m-a.org.uk

Website:
http://www.i-m-a.org.uk
Conferences, membership, branches, training, free seminars, jobs, qualifications, information on debt relief orders, social policy issues, web-based resources for money advisers.

Founded:
2006

Carries out the functions of the former:
Money Advice Association (founded 1984) (year of change 2006)

Organisation type and purpose:
A charitable company, the only professional body acting solely for money advisers in England, Wales and Northern Ireland, current number of members: over 1,400.
To develop professional standards; to provide support services to members; to promote free money advice; to influence policy and practice relating to personal finance.

Subject coverage:
Money and debt advice.

Education services:
Offers free seminars on topics such as Insolvency Options, Managing Legal Advice Cases & Caseloads, and Utilities & Fuel Debt.

Printed publications:
Quarterly Account (journal, free to members, by subscription to non-members)
Order printed publications from: Website

Electronic and video publications:
IMA News (quarterly newsletter)
Order electronic and video publications from:
Download from website

Publications list:
Available online

Access to staff:
Contact by letter, by telephone, by fax and by e-mail
Special comments: IMA is not able to give advice directly to members of the public.

Branches:
15 branches across England and Wales

INSTITUTE OF NATURAL THERAPY

Acronym or abbreviation: INT

PO Box 1418, Dorchester, Dorset, DT1 1YF

Tel: 01305 267069

Website:
http://www.institute-natural-therapy.org.uk
Member list and tutors.

Enquiries:
Enquiries to: General Secretary

Founded:
1991

Organisation type and purpose:
International organisation, advisory body, professional body (membership is by qualification).

Subject coverage:
Hypnotherapy, healing, complementary therapies.

Access to staff:
Contact by letter and by telephone
Hours: Mon to Fri, 0900 to 1700

Patron of:
General Hypnotherapy Standards Council (GHSC)
PO Box 204, Lymington, SO41 6WP; tel: 01590 683770; fax: 01590 683770

INSTITUTE OF NAVAL MEDICINE

Acronym or abbreviation: INM

Alverstoke, Gosport, Hampshire, PO12 2DL

Tel: 023 9276 8101
Fax: 023 9250 4823
E-mail: lib@inm.mod.uk

Enquiries:
Enquiries to: Librarian

Organisation type and purpose:
National government body, training organisation, research organisation.

Subject coverage:
Underwater medicine, survival medicine, habitability, submarine environmental chemistry, heat, cold, toxicology, nuclear medicine and radiological protection, dosimetry, audiology and hearing conservation, submarine medicine, experimental physiology, occupational medicine and hygiene, microbiology, analytical chemistry, medical statistics, health and safety at work, ergonomics, human factors, anthropometry, psychology.

Library catalogue:
All or part available in-house

Printed publications:
Annual Report
Clinical Research Working Party Reports
INM Reports and Technical Memoranda
Journal of the Royal Naval Medical Service

Access to staff:
Contact by letter, by telephone, by fax and by e-mail. Appointment necessary.
Hours: Mon to Fri, 0900 to 1700

Access to building, collection or gallery:
Prior appointment required

Access for disabled people:
Parking provided, level entry, toilet facilities

Part of:
Ministry of Defence, Medical Directorate (Naval)

INSTITUTE OF NAVAL MEDICINE – HISTORIC COLLECTIONS LIBRARY

Acronym or abbreviation: INM H

Alverstoke, Gosport, Hampshire, PO12 2DL

Tel: 023 0276 8238
Fax: 023 9250 4823
E-mail: inm-cs-infohistlib@mod.uk

Website:
http://www.royalnavy.mod.uk/training-and
-people/rn-life/medical-branch/institute-of-naval
-medicine/historic-library
The website gives a basic guide to the library; the e-mail address it cites is at present incorrect.

Enquiries:
Enquiries to: Historic Collections Librarian

Founded:
1948

Formerly called:
Royal Naval Medical School (previously RNMS Clevedon) (year of change 1960s)

Historic Collections installed:
(year of change 2001)

Organisation type and purpose:
National government body.

Subject coverage:
Naval history; history of medicine; history of naval medicine; natural history (small proportion); early printed books (small proportion).

Museum or gallery collection, archive, or library special collection:
Works of James Lind
Dr Robert McKinnal bequest
Dr Leonard Gillespie bequest
Navy List
Health of the Navy
Archive material (incomplete) from former staff of RNHs Haslar and Plymouth; some photographs
Small collection of papers relating to William J. Maillard, VC (1863–1903), holder of the only Royal Naval Medical Service Victoria Cross

Non-library collection catalogue:
All or part available in-house

Library catalogue:
All or part available in-house

Access to staff:
Contact by letter, by telephone, by fax and by e-mail. Appointment necessary.
Hours: Mon to Fri, 1000 to 1730
Special comments: No more than 20 people per group visit.

Access to building, collection or gallery:
Prior appointment required
Hours: Mon to Fri, 1000 to 1600
Special comments: Visitors must call at main gate or arrival.

Access for disabled people:
Parking provided
Hours: Mon to Fri, 1000 to 1600
Special comments: Level entry to main building but steps with rails to collections. Arrangements can be made to view items elsewhere on site.

Historic Collections holdings are in the ownership of::
The Admiralty Library
Naval Historical Branch, PP 20, Main Road, HM Naval Base, Portsmouth, PO1 3LU; tel: 02392 725297; e-mail: cns-nhbal@mod.uk

INSTITUTE OF OCCUPATIONAL MEDICINE

Acronym or abbreviation: IOM

Research Avenue North, Riccarton, Edinburgh, EH14 4AP

Tel: 0870 850 5131
Fax: 0870 850 5132
E-mail: info@iom-world.org

Website:
http://www.iom-world.org

Enquiries:
Enquiries to: Information Officer

Founded:
1969

Organisation type and purpose:
International organisation, service industry, registered charity, consultancy, research organisation.

Subject coverage:
Health, hygiene and safety at work; occupational and environmental health, hygiene and epidemiology; ergonomics; hearing loss; respiratory diseases; asbestos; asbestosis; silica; pneumoconiosis; personal protective equipment.

Printed publications:
Booklets on COSHH and Noise
IOM Research Reports
Research Papers

Publications list:
Available in print

Access to staff:
Contact by letter, by telephone, by fax and by e-mail. Appointment necessary.
Hours: Mon to Fri, 0900 to 1700

INSTITUTE OF OPERATIONS MANAGEMENT

Acronym or abbreviation: IOM

CILT(UK), Earlstrees Court, Earlstrees Road, Corby, Northamptonshire, NN17 4AX

Tel: 01536 740105
Fax: 01536 740101
E-mail: info@iomnet.org.uk

Website:
http://www.iomnet.org.uk
On-line Index to Control, access to IOM Alert.

Enquiries:
Enquiries to: Membership Enquiries
Direct e-mail: members@iomnet.org.uk

Founded:
1969

Organisation type and purpose:
Professional body.
Professional institute for operations and production managers.

Subject coverage:
Production management and control; inventory management; stock control; logistics; supply chain management; materials management; business process re-engineering; advanced planning and scheduling; ERP; MRPII; learn manufacturing; Just-in-Time (JIT).

Museum or gallery collection, archive, or library special collection:
Library of specialised technical books and journals on all aspects of operations management particularly production and inventory control

Library catalogue:
All or part available in-house

Printed publications:
IOM Link (electronic newsletter)
Control (8 issues, free to members, sold to non-members)

Electronic and video publications:
ROME Programme: An internet/CD-ROM distance learning programme, utilising a virtual factory coupled with an interactive handbook (ca. 550 pages)

Publications list:
Available online and in print

Access to staff:
Contact by letter, by telephone, by fax, by e-mail and via website. Appointment necessary. Non-members charged.
Hours: Mon to Thu, 0900 to 1700; Fri, 0900 to 1600
Special comments: Members only may borrow from library.

Access for disabled people:
Parking provided, level entry, access to all public areas, toilet facilities
Hours: Mon to Thu, 0900 to 1700; Fri, 0900 to 1600

INSTITUTE OF OPTOMETRY, THE

56 Newington Causeway, London, SE1 6DS

Tel: 020 7407 4183
Fax: 020 7403 8007
E-mail: admin@ioo.org.uk

Website:
http://www.ioo.org.uk
Details of clinics run, courses and staff.

Enquiries:
Enquiries to: Director of Administration

Founded:
1922

Organisation type and purpose:
Registered charity (charity number 207965).

Subject coverage:
Optometric examination and prescription/treatment for patients, continuing education and training for optometrists, optometric research.

Access to staff:
Contact by letter, by telephone, by fax and by e-mail
Hours: Mon to Thu, 0900 to 2100; Fri, 0900 to 1700

INSTITUTE OF PAPER CONSERVATION

Acronym or abbreviation: IPC

Leigh Lodge, Leigh, Worcester, WR6 5LB

Tel: 01886 832323
Fax: 01886 833688
E-mail: information@ipc.org.uk

Website:
http://www.ipc.org.uk

Enquiries:
Enquiries to: Executive Secretary
Other contacts: Membership Secretary for membership.

Founded:
1976

Organisation type and purpose:
International organisation, professional body (membership is by subscription, qualification), present number of members: 1400, registered charity (charity number 280888), training organisation, publishing house.
Care and repair of artefacts on paper.

Subject coverage:
Training in paper conservation, all types of paper-related materials including books, textiles, globes, wallpaper, archives, maps, works of art, photographs, manuscripts, frames, parchment. Collection care, conservation surveys, disaster planning, storage and preservation.

Museum or gallery collection, archive, or library special collection:
Specialist library at 1 Grove Cottage, St Cross Road, Oxford OX1 3TX

Trade and statistical information:
Data on conservation profession.
Register of accredited book and paper conservators.

Non-library collection catalogue:
All or part available in print

Library catalogue:
All or part available in print

Printed publications:
Conference Papers
Paper Conservator (annually, vols 1–26 1976–2002, £15 each, £25 non-members)
The Care and Repair of Paper Artefacts (leaflet)
Defaced (leaflet)
Guidelines for Conservation Framing (leaflet)

Publications list:
Available online and in print

Access to staff:
Contact by letter, by telephone, by fax and by e-mail
Hours: Mon to Fri, 0915 to 1715

INSTITUTE OF PARALEGAL TRAINING, THE

The Mill, Climping Street, Climping, Littlehampton, West Sussex, BN17 5RN

Tel: 01903 714276
Fax: 01903 713710
E-mail: amanda@ibberson.fsbusiness.co.uk

Enquiries:
Enquiries to: Secretary General

Founded:
1976

Organisation type and purpose:
International organisation, professional body (membership is by qualification, election or invitation), service industry, training organisation.

Access to staff:
Contact by letter, by telephone, by fax and by e-mail
Hours: Mon to Fri, 0900 to 1700

INSTITUTE OF PATENTEES AND INVENTORS

Acronym or abbreviation: IPI

PO Box 39296, London, SE3 7WH

Tel: 0871 226 2091
Fax: 020 8293 5920
E-mail: ipi@invent.org.uk

Website:
http://www.invent.org.uk/
Information on Institute, membership, etc.

Enquiries:
Enquiries to: Secretary

Founded:
1919

Organisation type and purpose:
National organisation, advisory body, professional body, membership association (membership is by subscription), present number of members: 700. A non-profit organisation offering its members advice and guidance on all aspects of inventing from idea conception to innovation and development.

Subject coverage:
National and international patents, registered designs, trade-marks, copyright, the furtherance, protection and exploitation of inventions through to industrial innovation.

Printed publications:
Future and the Inventor (newsletter, quarterly, free to members)
General information pack including publications list of a selection of books available to help the lone inventor (various prices, discounts to members, available free on request)

Publications list:
Available in print

Access to staff:
Contact by letter, by telephone, by fax, by e-mail and via website
Hours: Mon to Fri, 1000 to 1700

INSTITUTE OF PAYROLL PROFESSIONALS

Acronym or abbreviation: IPP

Shelly House, Farmhouse Way, Monkspath, Solihull, West Midlands, B90 4EH

Tel: 0121 712 1000
Fax: 0121 712 1001
E-mail: info@payrollprofession.org

Website:
http://www.payrollprofession.org

Enquiries:
Enquiries to: Marketing Coordinator
Direct tel: 0121 712 1019
Direct e-mail: dawn.baxter@payrollprofession.org

Founded:
1985

Formerly called:
Institute of Payroll and Pensions Management (IPPM) (year of change 2006)

Organisation type and purpose:
The Institute of Payroll Professionals (IPP) is the only membership association for individuals working in payroll and pensions in the UK and has in excess of 5,000 professionals enjoying membership benefits.
In addition, the IPP is the UK's leading provider of qualifications, training and consultancy for payroll, and has a Pensions Faculty responsible for delivering qualifications and membership services to those responsible for public sector pensions.

continued overleaf

Subject coverage:
Membership, training, qualifications, consultancy, specialist interest groups, Payroll Quality Partnership and events for payroll and pensions professionals.

Printed publications:
PayrollProfessional and TPF Insight (10 times a year, free to members)
Order printed publications from: e-mail: info@ payrollprofession.org

Publications list:
Available in print

Access to staff:
Contact by telephone, by fax, by e-mail and via website
Hours: Mon to Thu, 0900 to 1700, Fri 0900 to 1630

Access to building, collection or gallery:
No access other than to staff

INSTITUTE OF PHYSICS

Acronym or abbreviation: IOP

76–78 Portland Place, London, W1B 1NT

Tel: 020 7470 4800
Fax: 020 7470 4848
E-mail: physics@iop.org

Website:
http://www.iop.org
Provides information to physicists at all levels on careers, policy, education projects and opportunities, and much more. It is a key tool to find out about all of IOP's activities in its work to promote physics in the UK and across the world.
http://www.iop.org/publications/index.html
All Institute of Physics publications can be found in this section of the IOP website.

Enquiries:
Enquiries to: Corporate Communications Officer
Direct e-mail: corporatecomms@iop.org

Founded:
1874

Organisation type and purpose:
The Institute of Physics is a scientific charity devoted to increasing the practice, understanding and application of physics.
It has a world-wide membership of more than 37,000 and is a leading communicator of physics-related science to all audiences, from specialists through to government and the general public. Its publishing company, IOP Publishing, is a world leader in scientific publishing and the electronic dissemination of physics.

Subject coverage:
Aspects of physics – pure and applied – in education, industry, government and public sector, and the media.

Printed publications:
Reports, resource packs, policy briefing notes, information brochures, magazines, journals
Order printed publications from: Institute of Physics Publishing

Electronic and video publications:
A range of electronic products

Publications list:
Available online

Access to staff:
Contact by letter, by telephone, by fax, by e-mail and via website
Hours: Mon to Fri, 0900 to 1730

Access for disabled people:
Ramped entry, toilet facilities

Links with:
IOP Publishing
Dirac House, Temple Back, Bristol, BS1 6BE; tel: 0117 929 7481; fax: 0117 929 4318; e-mail: custserv@iop.org; website: http://publishing.iop .org

Member organisation of:
European Optical Society

European Physical Society
International Union of Pure and Applied Physics (IUPAP)
e-mail: admin.iupap@iop.org

INSTITUTE OF PHYSICS AND ENGINEERING IN MEDICINE

Acronym or abbreviation: IPEM

Fairmount House, 230 Tadcaster Road, York, YO24 1ES

Tel: 01904 610821
Fax: 01904 612279
E-mail: office@ipem.ac.uk

Website:
http://www.ipem.ac.uk
IPEM membership, scientific meetings, publications, training schemes and general information.

Enquiries:
Enquiries to: General Secretary

Founded:
1995

Organisation type and purpose:
Professional body (membership is by qualification, election or invitation), registered charity (charity number 1047999), training organisation, publishing house.

Subject coverage:
Physical science as applied to medicine, including radiation protection, radiotherapy, diagnostic radiology, nuclear magnetic resonance, nuclear medicine, ultrasonics, lasers, rehabilitation engineering, physiological measurement, bioengineering, non-ionising radiation.

Printed publications:
Physiological Measurement (4 times a year)
Medical Engineering and Physics (8 times a year)
Physics in Medicine and Biology (journal, fortnightly)
Scientific and Conference Reports

Publications list:
Available online and in print

Access to staff:
Contact by telephone and by fax. Non-members charged.
Hours: Mon to Thu, 0900 to 1700: Fri, 0900 to 1600

Access to building, collection or gallery:
No prior appointment required

INSTITUTE OF PHYSICS PUBLISHING

Acronym or abbreviation: IOP Publishing

Dirac House, Temple Back, Bristol, BS1 6BE

Tel: 0117 929 7481
Fax: 0117 929 4318
E-mail: custserv@iop.org

Website:
http://www.journals.iop.org
Publication list for journals. All journals full text. Many other services such as access to abstracts and multimedia functionality.

Enquiries:
Enquiries to: Managing Director
Direct tel: 0117 930 1144
Direct fax: 0117 920 0775
Direct e-mail: jerry.cowhig@iop.org

Founded:
1874

Organisation type and purpose:
International organisation, learned society, professional body (membership is by subscription, qualification, election or invitation), present number of members: 37,000, registered charity, publishing house.

The Institute, which has its origins in the Physical Society established in 1874, is one of the world's leading publishers in physics and related subjects. Journals go back to 1874 and include several world leaders in their respective fields.
Dissemination of knowledge and education in physics.

Subject coverage:
Physics.

Non-library collection catalogue:
All or part available online

Printed publications:
Journals published in the fields of: Astronomy, Astrophysics, Geophysics; Atomic, Molecular and Plasma Physics; Condensed Matter, Materials Science and Semiconductor Physics; Electronics and Electrical Engineering; Engineering and Technology; Mathematics, Mathematical Physics and Computer Science; Measurement Science, Technology/Sensors and Smart Materials; Medical Physics and Biomedical Engineering; Nuclear and High Energy Physics, Optics and Quantum Optics
Journals relating to: Applied Mathematics and Mathematical Physics; Applied Physics; Atomic Molecular and Optical Physics; Computer Science and Information Processing; Condensed Matter and Materials Science; Measurement Science and Sensors; Medical Physics; Nuclear Physics and Particle Physics; Physics Education, Plasma Physics; Optics

Microform publications:
All journals also available in microfiche form

Electronic and video publications:
All journals also available in electronic format (see Web site)

Publications list:
Available online and in print

Access to staff:
Contact by letter, by telephone, by fax, by e-mail and via website
Hours: Mon to Fri, 0900 to 1700

Access for disabled people:
Ramped entry, access to all public areas, toilet facilities

INSTITUTE OF PLUMBING AND HEATING ENGINEERING

Acronym or abbreviation: IPHE

64 Station Lane, Hornchurch, Essex, RM12 6NB

Tel: 01708 472791
Fax: 01708 448987
E-mail: info@iphe.org.uk

Website:
http://www.iphe.org.uk

Enquiries:
Enquiries to: Editor of Plumbing & Heating Engineering Magazine
Direct tel: 01708 463114
Direct e-mail: carolc@iphe.org.uk

Founded:
1906

Organisation type and purpose:
Professional body (membership is by qualification), present number of members: 12,000, registered charity (charity number 278169), suitable for ages: 18 to 60.
To improve the standards of plumbing in the public interest.

Subject coverage:
Plumbing, heating and allied subjects, names of registered plumbers.

Printed publications:
Plumbing Engineering Services Design Guide (reprinted 2002)
Business Directory of Registered Plumbers
P&HE Magazine (6 times a year)

Electronic and video publications:
Business Directory of Registered Plumbers (CD-ROM)
Annual Directory

Access to staff:
Contact by letter, by telephone, by fax, by e-mail and via website. Appointment necessary.
Hours: Mon to Fri, 0900 to 1700

INSTITUTE OF PRACTITIONERS IN ADVERTISING

Acronym or abbreviation: IPA

44 Belgrave Square, London, SW1X 8QS

Tel: 020 7235 7020
Fax: 020 7245 9904
E-mail: info@ipa.co.uk

Website:
http://www.ipa.co.uk
General information, news, events and publications.

Enquiries:
Enquiries to: Head of Information Systems

Founded:
1917

Organisation type and purpose:
Professional body, trade association (membership is by subscription).

Subject coverage:
Advertising including European and international advertising, marketing, media, public relations, all aspects of communication, and related fields.

Printed publications:
Publications available on the website

Publications list:
Available online and in print

Access to staff:
Contact by letter, by telephone, by fax and by e-mail. Access for members only.
Hours: Mon to Fri, 0900 to 1700
Special comments: IPA members only.

Access for disabled people:
Access to all public areas, toilet facilities

Member organisation of:
Advertising Association
European Association of Communication Agencies (EACA)

INSTITUTE OF PROFESSIONAL ADMINISTRATORS

Acronym or abbreviation: IPA

6 Graphite Square, Vauxhall Walk, London, SE11 5EE

Tel: 020 7091 2606
Fax: 020 7091 7340
E-mail: info@inprad.org

Website:
http://www.inprad.org
Membership, events, learning, knowledge, services.

Founded:
1957

Formerly called:
Private Secretaries Association (year of change 1966); Institute of Qualified Private Secretaries (year of change 2007); Institute of Qualified Professional Secretaries (IQPS) (year of change 2009)

Organisation type and purpose:
Professional body for all administration and office professionals. Membership includes secretaries, PAs, receptionists, general administrators, executive assistants and virtual assistants.
To be the leader in the field of administration and the institute of choice for administrators; to become a strong, professional and well-respected institute

in the UK and overseas; to raise the profile of administration skills in the UK and overseas; to champion quality, good practice and professionalism.

Subject coverage:
Professional administration.

Printed publications:
The Professional Administrator Quarterly (magazine)

Electronic and video publications:
Monthly eNewsletter

Access to staff:
Contact by letter, by telephone, by fax and by e-mail

INSTITUTE OF PROFESSIONAL INVESTIGATORS LIMITED

Acronym or abbreviation: IPI

Runnymede Malthouse, off Hummer Road, Egham, Surrey, TW20 9BD

Tel: 0870 330 8622
Fax: 0870 330 8612
E-mail: admin@ipi.org.uk

Website:
http://www.ipi.org.uk
Courses available, directory of members in private practice, benefits of membership.

Enquiries:
Enquiries to: Secretary General

Founded:
1976

Organisation type and purpose:
Professional body.

Subject coverage:
Investigation services and practice; further education within the profession.

Printed publications:
Directory of Members in Private Practice
Instructional leaflets on subjects relating to investigations practice

Access to staff:
Contact by letter, by telephone, by fax and by e-mail
Hours: Mon to Fri, 1000 to 1600

Access to building, collection or gallery:
No access other than to staff

INSTITUTE OF PROFESSIONAL WILLWRITERS

Acronym or abbreviation: IPW

Trinity Point, New Road, Halesowen, B63 3HY

Tel: 08456 442042
Fax: 08456 442043
E-mail: office@ipw.org.uk

Website:
http://www.ipw.org.uk

Enquiries:
Enquiries to: Office Manager
Other contacts: Chairman for public relations.

Founded:
1991

Organisation type and purpose:
Professional body (membership is by qualification), present number of members: 500, suitable for ages: 18+, training organisation.

Subject coverage:
All aspects of wills and their writing, current members local to enquirer, membership requirements.

Education services:
Willwriting courses

Printed publications:
Code of Practice for Willwriting Profession (free, 2008)
Journal (12 times a year for members and interested persons)
Inheritance Matters (quarterly journal)
Order printed publications from: IPW Accounts

Access to staff:
Contact by letter, by telephone, by fax, by e-mail, in person and via website. Appointment necessary.
Hours: Mon to Fri, 0900 to 1700

INSTITUTE OF PROMOTIONAL MARKETING LTD

Acronym or abbreviation: IPM

70 Margaret Street, London, W1W 8SS

Tel: 020 7291 7730
Fax: 020 7291 7731
E-mail: enquiries@theipm.org.uk

Website:
http://www.theipm.org.uk

Enquiries:
Enquiries to: Chief Executive Officer
Direct e-mail: annies@theipm.org.uk

Founded:
1933

Organisation type and purpose:
Trade association.

Subject coverage:
Promotional marketing.

Access to staff:
Contact by letter, by telephone, by fax, by e-mail and via website
Hours: Mon to Fri, 0900 to 1700

Access to building, collection or gallery:
Prior appointment required
Hours: Mon to Fri, 0900 to 1700

INSTITUTE OF PSYCHIATRY

De Crespigny Park, Denmark Hill, London, SE5 8AF

Tel: 020 7848 0204
Fax: 020 7848 0209
E-mail: iop.library@iop.kcl.ac.uk

Website:
http://www.iop.kcl.ac.uk/iopweb/departments/home/default.aspx?locator=12

Enquiries:
Enquiries to: Librarian

Organisation type and purpose:
University department or institute.

Subject coverage:
Psychiatry, psychology, neurology and neuroscience, psychopharmacology, genetics and genomics.

Museum or gallery collection, archive, or library special collection:
Guttmann-Maclay Collection of psychotic art
Henry Maudsley Collection of historic books in psychiatry
Mayer-Gross Collection of historic texts in European psychiatry

Non-library collection catalogue:
All or part available online

Library catalogue:
All or part available in-house

Printed publications:
Maudsley Monographs series
Maudsley Discussion papers (11 titles)

Publications list:
Available in print

continued overleaf

Access to staff:
Contact by letter, by telephone, by e-mail and via website. Appointment necessary. Non-members charged.
Hours: Mon to Fri, 0900 to 2000; Term time: Sat, 1000 to 1700; Summer vacation: Sat, 1000 to 1500.

Parent body:
King's College London

INSTITUTE OF PSYCHOANALYSIS

Formal name: British Psychoanalytical Society
Acronym or abbreviation: BPAS

112A Shirland Road, London, W9 2EQ

Tel: 020 7563 5000
Fax: 020 7563 5001
E-mail: ginette@goulston-lincoln.com

Website:
http://www.psychoanalysis.org.uk

Enquiries:
Enquiries to: Institute Manager

Founded:
1919

Organisation type and purpose:
Professional body (membership is by qualification), present number of members: 510, registered charity (charity number 212330), training organisation.
The training organisation for psychoanalysis in Britain, also treats patients in The London Clinic of Psychoanalysis at the same addess.

Subject coverage:
Psycho-analysis.

Museum or gallery collection, archive, or library special collection:
Archives

Non-library collection catalogue:
All or part available in-house

Library catalogue:
All or part available in-house

Printed publications:
International Journal of Psycho-analysis

Electronic and video publications:
PEP CD-ROM

Access to staff:
Contact by letter, by telephone, by fax, by e-mail and in person. Appointment necessary. Non-members charged.
Hours: Mon to Fri, 0930 to 1730

Access to building, collection or gallery:
Appointment required
Hours: Mon to Fri, 0930 to 1730; Sat and Sun, closed
Special comments: Archives, apply to the Honorary Archivist for access.

Access for disabled people:
Ramped entry, toilet facilities

Member organisation of:
International Psycho-Analytical Association

INSTITUTE OF PSYCHOSEXUAL MEDICINE

Acronym or abbreviation: IPM

12 Chandos Street, Cavendish Square, London, W1G 9DR

Tel: 020 7580 0631
Fax: 020 7580 0631
E-mail: admin@ipm.org.uk

Enquiries:
Enquiries to: Administrator
Other contacts: Referrals Secretary

Founded:
1974

Organisation type and purpose:
National organisation, professional body (membership is by subscription), present number of members: 450, registered charity (charity number 298172), university department or institute, training organisation.
Referral service.
Refers members of the public to psychosexual doctors.

Subject coverage:
Training for doctors in the field of psychosexual medicine (sexual difficulties and related marital or psychosomatic problems); training over 2 years for Diploma from Institute of Psychosexual Medicine and at 4 years for membership of Institute of Psychosexual Medicine.

Trade and statistical information:
List of doctors qualified in the field of psychosexual medicine and able to receive referrals through our referrals secretary.

Printed publications:
Institute of Psychosexual Medicine Journal available to total membership of IPM three times a year

Publications list:
Available online and in print

Access to staff:
Contact by letter, by telephone, by fax, by e-mail and via website
Hours: Mon to Fri, 0900 to 1700
Special comments: Answerphone also. Prefer sae from those wanting list of doctors.

INSTITUTE OF PSYCHOSYNTHESIS

65A Watford Way, London, NW4 3AQ

Tel: 020 8202 4525
Fax: 020 8202 6166
E-mail: institute@psychosynthesis.org

Website:
http://www.psychosynthesis.org
Information on training and booklist for training.

Enquiries:
Enquiries to: Administration

Founded:
1973

Organisation type and purpose:
Membership association, training organisation.
Psychology, coaching, counselling and psychotherapy training, low cost clinic open to members of the public.

Subject coverage:
Psychotherapy and counselling, coaching, psychology.

Printed publications:
Some books available to purchase, contact direct for pricing

Publications list:
Available online

Access to staff:
Contact by letter, by telephone, by e-mail and via website. Appointment necessary.
Hours: Mon to Fri, 1000 to 1700
Special comments: Appointments for the clinic are made in advance.

Access to building, collection or gallery:
Prior appointment required
Hours: Mon to Fri, 0700 to 2100

Access for disabled people:
There is a staircase

Member of:
British Association for Counselling and Psychotherapy (BACP)
European Association for Psychotherapy
European Mentoring and Coaching Council
United Kingdom Council for Psychotherapy (UKCP)

INSTITUTE OF PUBLIC LOSS ASSESSORS

Acronym or abbreviation: IPLA

Coughtry House, 112–116 Broad Street, Chesham, Bucks, HP5 3ED

Tel: 01494 793370
E-mail: jdturberville@tiscali.co.uk

Enquiries:
Enquiries to: General Secretary

Founded:
1963

Organisation type and purpose:
Professional body.
To represent the interests of professional loss assessors in their dealings with their clients.

Subject coverage:
Loss assessment, preparation, submission and negotiation of all types of statutory and insurance claims on behalf of the public and corporate bodies.

Printed publications:
List of members (in return for A5 sae)

Access to staff:
Contact by letter and by telephone
Hours: Mon to Fri, 0900 to 1700

INSTITUTE OF PUBLIC RIGHTS OF WAY AND ACCESS MANAGEMENT

Acronym or abbreviation: IPROW

PO Box 78, Skipton, North Yorkshire, BD23 4UP

Tel: 07000 782318
Fax: 07000 782318
E-mail: iprow@iprow.co.uk

Website:
http://www.iprow.co.uk

Enquiries:
Enquiries to: Executive Officer

Founded:
1986

Organisation type and purpose:
Professional body.

Subject coverage:
Public rights of way, outdoor access management.

Printed publications:
Waymark (journal)
Order printed publications from: e-mail: iprow@iprow.co.uk

Publications list:
Available in print

Access to staff:
Contact by letter, by e-mail and via website
Hours: Mon to Fri, 0900 to 1700

Access to building, collection or gallery:
No access

INSTITUTE OF PYRAMIDOLOGY

Acronym or abbreviation: IOP

108 Broad Street, Chesham, Buckinghamshire, HP5 3ED

Tel: 01494 771774
E-mail: 101234.1734@compuserve.com

Enquiries:
Enquiries to: Director

Founded:
1940

Organisation type and purpose:
International organisation, membership association (membership is by subscription), voluntary organisation, research organisation.

Subject coverage:
Pyramidology: study of the Great Pyramid of Egypt; books on pyramidology.

Printed publications:
Pyramid Quarterly

Access to staff:
Contact by letter, by telephone and by e-mail
Hours: Mon to Fri, 0900 to 1700

INSTITUTE OF QUARRYING

7 Regent Street, Nottingham, NG1 5BS

Tel: 0115 941 1315
Fax: 0115 948 4035
E-mail: mail@quarrying.org

Website:
http://www.quarrying.org

Enquiries:
Enquiries to: The Secretary
Direct tel: 0115 945 3880
Direct e-mail: lyn.bryden@quarrying.org
Other contacts: Membership Co-ordinator

Founded:
1917

Organisation type and purpose:
Professional body (membership is by qualification), present number of members: 5,000 world-wide, 3,000 UK, registered charity.

Subject coverage:
Quarrying.

Printed publications:
Technical Handbooks include:
Sand and Gravel Production (Littler A & Millburn S £35)
Crushing and Screening (Rothery K, £25)
Explosives in Quarrying (Cordon J & Christie I, £35)
Safety and Legislation (Darlow E C, £25)
Environmental Management (Edited by Smith MR & Watkins MS, £35)
Asphalt Production (Jervis DE ,£35)
Order printed publications from: 7 Regent Street, Nottingham, NG1 5BS; tel: 0115 945 3880

Publications list:
Available online and in print

Access to staff:
Contact by letter, by telephone, by fax and by e-mail
Hours: Mon to Fri, 0900 to 1700

INSTITUTE OF RACE RELATIONS

Acronym or abbreviation: IRR

2–6 Leeke Street, London, WC1X 9HS

Tel: 020 7837 0041
Fax: 020 7278 0623
E-mail: info@irr.org.uk

Website:
http://www.irr.org.uk

Founded:
1958

Organisation type and purpose:
Registered charity (charity number 223989), research organisation.
Educational charity.

Subject coverage:
Race and minority group relations; racism; imperialism; Third World issues.

Library catalogue:
All or part available in-house

Printed publications:
Annual Report
European Race Bulletin (ed. Fekete, quarterly, £7.50)
Race and Class (quarterly, £7)
Broadsheet on racism in Britain
Educational pamphlets

European Race Audit Bulletin
Race Relations Abstracts
Order printed publications from: IRR

Electronic and video publications:
HomeBeats: Struggles for Racial Justice (CD-ROM)

Publications list:
Available in print

Access to staff:
Contact by telephone and by e-mail. Appointment necessary.
Hours: Mon to Thu, 1000 to 1300 and 1400 to 1700 (hours may be restricted)
Special comments: Access at librarian's discretion.

INSTITUTE OF REFRACTORIES ENGINEERS

Formal name: Institute of Refractories Engineers
Acronym or abbreviation: IRE

General Secretary and Treasurer, Joan Royd Cottage, Penistone, Sheffield, S36 9DA

Tel: 01226 762578
Fax: 01226 762673
E-mail: secretary@ireng.org

Website:
http://ireng.org/
All activities of Institute, developments in refractories engineering and contacts with other professional institutes.

Enquiries:
Enquiries to: General Secretary
Direct e-mail: alanhey@ireng.org
Other contacts: Treasurer

Founded:
1961

Organisation type and purpose:
Learned society (membership is by qualification, election or invitation), present number of members: 1500.

Subject coverage:
Refractories – manufacture and use, research and development, education and training.

Printed publications:
Guide to Good Practice for Installation of Monolithics
The Refractories Engineer (6 times a year)

Publications list:
Available in print

Access to staff:
Contact by letter, by telephone, by fax, by e-mail and via website
Hours: Mon to Fri, 0900 to 1700

INSTITUTE OF REFRIGERATION

Acronym or abbreviation: IOR

Kelvin House, 76 Mill Lane, Carshalton, Surrey, SM5 2JR

Tel: 020 8647 7033
Fax: 020 8773 0165
E-mail: ior@ior.org.uk

Website:
http://www.ior.org.uk

Enquiries:
Enquiries to: Secretary

Founded:
1899

Organisation type and purpose:
Learned society (membership is by subscription).

Subject coverage:
Refrigeration and air conditioning.

Museum or gallery collection, archive, or library special collection:
Reference library at Cambridge Refrigeration Technology

Non-library collection catalogue:
All or part available online

Publications list:
Available online

Access to staff:
Contact by letter, by telephone, by fax, by e-mail and via website. Appointment necessary.
Hours: Mon to Fri, 0900 to 1700

Links with:
Cambridge Refrigeration Technology

INSTITUTE OF REVENUES, RATING AND VALUATION

Acronym or abbreviation: IRRV

41 Doughty Street, London, WC1N 2LF

Tel: 020 7831 3505
Fax: 020 7831 2048
E-mail: enquiries@irrv.org.uk

Website:
http://www.irrv.org.uk
Background information on the Institute.

Founded:
1882

Organisation type and purpose:
Local government body, professional body.

Subject coverage:
Local taxation and property valuation issues including: Council Tax (Council Tax benefits, banding, enforcement), housing benefits, non-domestic rates.

Printed publications:
Details of magazines, guides and books available at website www.irrv.org.uk
Order printed publications from: Communications Manager

Electronic and video publications:
Note: all prices excl. VAT:
Benefit Legislation Infobase (£300, updates £195)
Council Tax Legislation Infobase (£300, updates £195)
NNDR Legislation Infobase (£300, updates £195)
Rating Cases Infobase (£300, updates £195)

Publications list:
Available online and in print

Access to staff:
Contact by letter, by fax and by e-mail. Appointment necessary.
Hours: Mon to Fri, 0900 to 1700

Access to building, collection or gallery:
Prior appointment required

Represents:
over 6000 local authority revenues and benefits officers
private valuers and officers from appellate bodies

INSTITUTE OF RISK MANAGEMENT

Acronym or abbreviation: IRM

Lloyds Avenue House, 6 Lloyds Avenue, London, EC3N 3AX

Tel: 020 7709 9808
Fax: 020 7709 0716
E-mail: enquiries@irmgt.co.uk

Website:
http://www.theIRM.org

Enquiries:
Enquiries to: Executive Director
Other contacts: Examinations Officer, Membership Officer

Founded:
1986

continued overleaf

Organisation type and purpose:
International organisation, advisory body, professional body (membership is by subscription, qualification), present number of members: 1700, research organisation.
To provide a diploma in risk management.

Subject coverage:
Business organisation and finance, occupational health and safety, public sector, finance, physical risk, liability exposures, contingency and disaster, risk analysis, business organisation and finance, local authority risk management, health sector.

Printed publications:
Annual Report
Inform (journal, 6 times a year)
Reading List
The Risk Management Series (books)

Electronic and video publications:
Introduction to Risk Management (video, VHS version, £99 plus VAT; NTSC, version £150 plus VAT)

Publications list:
Available in print

Access to staff:
Contact by letter, by telephone, by fax and by e-mail. Appointment necessary.
Hours: Mon to Fri, 0900 to 1700

INSTITUTE OF ROAD SAFETY OFFICERS

Acronym or abbreviation: IRSO

Pin Point, 1–2 Rosslyn Crescent, Harrow, Middlesex, HA1 2SB

Tel: 0870 010 4442
Fax: 0870 333 7772
E-mail: irso@dbda.co.uk

Website:
http://www.irso.org.uk

Enquiries:
Enquiries to: Executive Secretary
Direct tel: 01202 262051
Direct fax: 01202 262091
Direct e-mail: k.saunders@poole.gov.uk
Other contacts: National Secretary

Founded:
1971

Organisation type and purpose:
Professional body (membership is by subscription), training organisation.
Mainly local government officers.

Subject coverage:
Road safety; education, training and publicity, engineering and enforcement.

Trade and statistical information:
Accident statistics.

Printed publications:
Inroads (quarterly)

Access to staff:
Contact by letter, by telephone and by fax. Appointment necessary.
Hours: Mon to Fri, 0900 to 1700

Access to building, collection or gallery:
No access other than to staff

INSTITUTE OF ROOFING

Acronym or abbreviation: IoR

24 Weymouth Street, London, W1N 3FA

Tel: 020 7436 0103
Fax: 020 7637 5215

Website:
http://www.instituteofroofing.org.uk

Enquiries:
Enquiries to: Director
Direct fax: 020 7636 1287
Direct e-mail: info@instituteofroofing.org.uk

Founded:
1980

Organisation type and purpose:
Professional body (membership is by qualification).

Subject coverage:
Education within the roofing industry.

Access to staff:
Contact by letter, by telephone, by fax, by e-mail and via website
Hours: Tue, Wed, Thu, 1000 to 1500

Access to building, collection or gallery:
Prior appointment required

INSTITUTE OF SOUND AND COMMUNICATIONS ENGINEERS

Acronym or abbreviation: ISCE

PO Box 7966, Reading, Berkshire, RG6 7WY

Tel: 0118 954 2175
Fax: 0118 954 2175
E-mail: ros@isce.org.uk

Website:
http://www.isce.org.uk
The institute, events, membership information and services, members' pages, training, engineering notes, situations wanted and vacant.

Enquiries:
Enquiries to: Secretariat Manager

Founded:
1948

Organisation type and purpose:
Membership association (membership is by subscription), an independent institute, the specialist learned society for sound and communications engineers.
To unite those professionally engaged in the sound, video, communications, entertainment lighting and staging industries; to maintain and to raise technical standards throughout the profession; to disseminate technical and professional information through the publication of papers and by means of conferences, seminars and training courses; to promote educational and training programmes for those seeking advancement in the profession and to assist career development and continuing professional development within the industry; to promote the advancement and application of science and technology within the profession in the interests of society at large; to present the institute as an authoritative and influential professional body, representing trained, qualified and experienced practitioners within the profession; to establish and maintain a code of conduct in professional activities, embodying high ethical standards and concern for the environmental and sociological impacts of professional activities; to protect and promote the interests of members, collectively and individually.

Subject coverage:
Sound and communications engineering.

Electronic and video publications:
Engineering Notes (some files available to members only)
Order electronic and video publications from:
Download from website

Access to staff:
Contact by letter, by telephone, by fax and by e-mail

INSTITUTE OF SOUND AND VIBRATION RESEARCH

Acronym or abbreviation: ISVR

The University, Southampton, SO17 1BJ

Tel: 023 8059 2294
Fax: 023 8059 3190
E-mail: mzs@isvr.soton.ac.uk

Website:
http://www.isvr.soton.ac.uk

Enquiries:
Enquiries to: Director

Founded:
1963

Organisation type and purpose:
University department or institute, consultancy, research organisation.

Subject coverage:
Acoustics; structural dynamics; audiology; fluid dynamics; signal processing; active control; subjective acoustics; human response to vibration automotive engineering; instrumentation; random process analysis; human response to noise and vibration; hearing conservation; urban planning and noise; vibration engineering and control; machinery noise and vibration, signal processing, etc.

Museum or gallery collection, archive, or library special collection:
Literature on the human response to vibration

Non-library collection catalogue:
All or part available online

Library catalogue:
All or part available online

Printed publications:
Annual Report (listings and summary of research projects, staff publications)

Publications list:
Available online and in print

Access to staff:
Contact by letter, by telephone, by fax and by e-mail
Hours: Mon to Fri, 0900 to 1700

Access to building, collection or gallery:
Prior appointment required

Access for disabled people:
Parking provided, ramped entry, toilet facilities

Links with:
ISVR Consultancy Service
tel: 023 8059 2162; e-mail: djf@isvr.soton.ac.uk

INSTITUTE OF SPORT AND RECREATION MANAGEMENT

Acronym or abbreviation: ISRM

Sir John Beckwith Centre for Sport, Loughborough University, Loughborough, Leicestershire, LE11 3TU

Tel: 01509 226474
Fax: 01509 226475
E-mail: ralphriley@isrm.co.uk

Website:
http://www.isrm.co.uk
ISRM courses, media releases, ISRM information service, publications, recreation magazine, ISRM vacancy service.

Enquiries:
Enquiries to: Chief Executive

Founded:
1921

Organisation type and purpose:
Membership association (membership is by qualification), present number of members: 2300, registered charity (charity number 250902).
Educational Charity.
National professional body for sport and recreation facility management and operation.

Subject coverage:
Management and operation of public baths and recreation facilities, education and training.

Printed publications:
ISRM Conference Papers
ISRM Publications leaflet, listing Publications/Posters/Codes of Practice for Management and Operation

Recreation (magazine, 10 times a year)
Energy Conservation in Sports Centres and
    Swimming Pools
Guidance Documents for Risk Assessment
ISRM Integrated Management System
The Operation of Giant Waterslides
The Safe Use and Operation of Bouncy Castles

Electronic and video publications:
Training Videos

Publications list:
Available online and in print

Access to staff:
Contact by letter, by telephone, by fax and by e-
mail
Hours: Mon to Fri, 0830 to 1630

INSTITUTE OF SPORTS AND EXERCISE MEDICINE

Acronym or abbreviation: ISEM

30 Devonshire Street, London, W1G 6PU

Tel: 020 7288 5310
E-mail: d.patterson@ucl.ac.uk

Website:
http://www.fsem.co.uk

Enquiries:
Enquiries to: Secretary

Founded:
1965

Organisation type and purpose:
Learned society, professional body, registered
charity (charity number 313301).
To encourage postgraduate medical research,
teaching and treatment in all aspects of sports
medicine.

Subject coverage:
Sports and Exercise Medicine.

Access to staff:
Contact by letter, by fax and by e-mail
Hours: Mon to Fri, 0900 to 1700
Special comments: No access – co-ordinating centre
only.

Access to building, collection or gallery:
No access other than to staff

INSTITUTE OF SPRING TECHNOLOGY LIMITED

Acronym or abbreviation: IST

Henry Street, Sheffield, South Yorkshire, S3 7EQ

Tel: 0114 276 0771
Fax: 0114 252 7997
E-mail: ist@ist.org.uk

Website:
http://www.ist.org.uk

Enquiries:
Enquiries to: Information Manager .
Direct tel: 0114 252 7982
Direct e-mail: mom@ist.org.uk

Founded:
1945

Formerly called:
Spring Research and Manufacturers' Association
(SRAMA) (year of change 1997)

Organisation type and purpose:
Trade association (membership is by subscription),
present number of members: 300, research
organisation.

Subject coverage:
Spring technology; design study and investigation
of failures in springs and materials; technical,
contract, testing and inspection services including
SEM facilities; training; relevant British and foreign
standards.

Information services:
Technical information on all aspects of spring
technology – free to members, chargeable to non-
members

Education services:
Training Courses on all aspects of spring
technology – including tailored in-house

Printed publications:
Facilities and Services leaflets
Directory of British Spring Manufacturers
    (occasional)
Membership Directory
Newsletter (quarterly)
Research Reports and Index thereto
Spring Design Guides

Electronic and video publications:
Spring design and validation software
Spring Material Selector (CD-ROM)

Publications list:
Available in print

Access to staff:
Contact by letter, by telephone, by fax and by e-
mail. Appointment necessary. Non-members
charged.
Hours: Mon to Thu, 0800 to 1630; Fri, 0800 to 1500

INSTITUTE OF SWIMMING POOL ENGINEERS LIMITED

Acronym or abbreviation: ISPE

PO Box 3083, Norwich NR6 7YL

Tel: 01603 499959
Fax: 01603 499959

Enquiries:
Enquiries to: General Secretary

Founded:
1978

Organisation type and purpose:
Professional body (membership is by qualification,
election or invitation), present number of
members: 850, training organisation, publishing
house.
Membership also by direct application.
Professional membership, education and training
to those in the swimming pool industry.

Subject coverage:
All aspects of engineering related to swimming
pools.

Printed publications:
Home Study Course – filtration, construction,
    water chemistry and pool heating
ISPE Magazine (4 times a year, free to members)
Update (Swimming Pool Industry Directory and
    Specifier, £25 plus p&p)
Quick reference guide (£10 plus p&p)
Market Survey (£15 plus p&p)
Technical papers include the following plus 16
    other titles:
Disinfection Fundamentals (Turk J, Marks C and
    Reid R, £9 plus p&p)
Modern Pool Water Testing Technology (Shute G,
    £13 plus £2 p&p)
Water Treatment for Pool Operators (Lamb J, £10
    plus p&p)

Publications list:
Available in print

Access to staff:
Contact by letter, by telephone, by fax and by e-
mail
Hours: Mon to Fri, 0900 to 1700

INSTITUTE OF THE MOTOR INDUSTRY

Acronym or abbreviation: IMI

Fanshaws, Brickendon, Hertford, SG13 8PQ

Tel: 01992 511521
Fax: 01992 511548

E-mail: imi@motor.org.uk

Website:
http://www.motor.org.uk
Training and education programmes; details of
membership of IMI; book list; Institute news,
publications.

Enquiries:
Enquiries to: Director of Marketing
Direct e-mail: kellysh@motor.org.uk
Other contacts: Director of Communications

Founded:
1920

Organisation type and purpose:
International organisation, professional body,
present number of members: 26,000.

Subject coverage:
Professional guidance for individuals in the retail
motor industry, including information on training
and education and qualifications in all sectors.

Printed publications:
Motor Industry Management (magazine, 10 times
    a year, UK subscription £35)
Text Books, including:
Engines, Electronics and Related Systems (3rd ed,
    2001)
Maintenance and Repair of Road Vehicles (3rd ed,
    2001)
Transmission, Chassis and Related Systems (2001)
Vehicle Maintenance Service Replacement (2001)
Motor Trade Administration and Organisation
Motor Trade Management and Finance
Motor Trade Law

Electronic and video publications:
Autodata on CD-ROM

Publications list:
Available in print

Access to staff:
Contact by letter, by telephone, by fax, by e-mail
and via website
Hours: Mon to Fri, 0900 to 1700

Access to building, collection or gallery:
Prior appointment required
Hours: Mon to Fri, 0900 to 1700

INSTITUTE OF TRADE MARK ATTORNEYS

Acronym or abbreviation: ITMA

Outer Temple, 222–225 Strand, London, WC2R
1BA

Tel: 020 7101 6090
Fax: 020 7101 6099
E-mail: tm@itma.org.uk

Website:
http://www.itma.org.uk
Brochures, careers leaflets, fact sheets and
membership list.

Enquiries:
Enquiries to: Chief Executive
Other contacts: Public Relations Manager (for press
enquiries, presentations)

Founded:
1934

Organisation type and purpose:
Professional body (membership is by subscription,
election or invitation), present number of
members: 1,500.

Subject coverage:
Trade marks and allied matters.

Printed publications:
Brochures and careers leaflets
Information Circular (members only)
Membership list
Newsletter (monthly, members only)
Fact sheets

Electronic and video publications:
as above

continued overleaf

Access to staff:
Contact by letter, by telephone, by fax and by e-mail
Hours: Mon to Fri, 0900 to 1700

INSTITUTE OF TRAFFIC ACCIDENT INVESTIGATORS

Acronym or abbreviation: ITAI

Column House, London Road, Shrewsbury, SY2 6NN

Tel: 08456 212066
Fax: 08456 212077
E-mail: admin@itai.org

Website:
http://www.itai.org
Detailed contacts, practitioners list, CPD approved list, events, conference, technical papers, education and CPD.

Founded:
1988

Organisation type and purpose:
A registered charity (number 1014784), professional body for traffic accident investigators. Membership includes forensic scientists, academics, specialist police officers, consultant investigators, engineers, vehicle assessors, lawyers, doctors and others; overseas membership has representatives from across the world.
To promote the free and open exchange of knowledge between those involved in the field of investigating road traffic accidents, and through this, enhance expertise; to represent the interests of the profession in a collective way by arranging field days, lectures, seminars and other educational forums.

Subject coverage:
Provides a forum for communication, education, representation and regulation in the field of traffic accident investigation. The Institute is committed to encouraging and, where possible, assisting with research programmes in connection with vehicles and roads.

Printed publications:
IMPACT (magazine, 3 a year, free to members, available to purchase to non-members)
CONTACT (newsletter, 6 a year, free to members)

Access to staff:
Contact by letter, by telephone, by fax and by e-mail

INSTITUTE OF TRANSACTIONAL ANALYSIS

Acronym or abbreviation: ITA

Broadway House, 149–151 St Neots Road, Hardwick, Cambridge, CB23 7QJ

Tel: 01954 212468
Fax: 01954 212468
E-mail: admin@ita.org.uk

Website:
http://www.ita.org.uk
Practitioners, training establishments, TA training in general, TA 101 dates and much more.

Organisation type and purpose:
Institute for practitioners of Transactional Analysis. Committed to effective personal and professional relationships. Advice is available on training and TA practice from ITA committees and council; Contractual Trainees, CTAs, PT/STAs or T/STAs may be included in the ITA Register of Practitioners provided certain criteria are met.

Subject coverage:
Transactional Analysis – a theory of personality that offers a range of models that can be used to understand communication and relationships.

Electronic and video publications:
ITA News (quarterly newsletter)
EATA Newsletter (3 a year)

ITA Psychotherapy Training Handbook
Order electronic and video publications from:
Download from website

Access to staff:
Contact by letter, by telephone, by fax and by e-mail

INSTITUTE OF TRANSLATION AND INTERPRETING

Acronym or abbreviation: ITI

Fortuna House, South Fifth Street, Milton Keynes, Buckinghamshire, MK9 2PQ

Tel: 01908 325250
Fax: 01908 325259
E-mail: info@iti.org.uk

Website:
http://www.iti.org.uk
Organisation description and activities, online directory of members, events calendar.

Enquiries:
Enquiries to: Office Administrator

Founded:
1986

Organisation type and purpose:
Professional body (membership is by qualification), present number of members: c. 3,000, training organisation.

Subject coverage:
Translation and interpreting.

Printed publications:
ITI Bulletin (6 times a year)

Publications list:
Available in print

Access to staff:
Contact by letter, by telephone, by fax and by e-mail. Appointment necessary.
Hours: Mon to Fri, 0900 to 1730

Access to building, collection or gallery:
No access other than to staff

Member organisation of:
Fédération Internationale des Traducteurs (FIT)
63 rue La Fontaine, 75016 Paris, France; website: http://www.fit-ift.org

INSTITUTE OF TRANSPORT ADMINISTRATION

Acronym or abbreviation: IoTA

The Old Studio, 25 Greenfield Road, Westoning, Bedfordshire, MK45 5JD

Tel: 01525 634940
Fax: 01525 750016
E-mail: director@iota.org.uk

Website:
http://www.iota.org.uk

Enquiries:
Enquiries to: Director

Founded:
1944

Organisation type and purpose:
Professional body, present number of members: 2,500.

Subject coverage:
Transport management and operations.

Printed publications:
Guides to Careers and Membership (free for schools)
Transport Management (journal, 6 times a year, free to members, others on subscription)

Access to staff:
Contact by letter, by telephone, by fax, by e-mail and via website. Appointment necessary.
Hours: Mon to Fri, 0900 to 1600

INSTITUTE OF TRAVEL AND TOURISM

Acronym or abbreviation: ITT

PO Box 217, Ware, Hertfordshire, SG12 8WY

Tel: 0870 770 7960
Fax: 0870 770 7961

Website:
http://www.itt.co.uk

Enquiries:
Enquiries to: Chairman
Direct e-mail: press@itt.co.uk

Founded:
1956

Organisation type and purpose:
Professional body (membership is by qualification), present number of members: 3200.

Subject coverage:
Education and training in the travel and tourism industry.

Printed publications:
Careers Pack
ITT Bulletin (quarterly)
Year Book (annually)

Access to staff:
Contact by letter, by telephone, by fax and by e-mail. Appointment necessary.
Hours: Mon to Fri, 0900 to 1730

Access for disabled people:
Level entry, toilet facilities

INSTITUTE OF TRICHOLOGISTS

Ground floor office, 24 Langroyd Road, London, SW17 7PL

Tel: 0845 604 4657
Fax: 01722 741380
E-mail: admin@trichologists.org.uk

Website:
http://www.trichologists.org.uk
The institute, trichology, ethics, training, membership, information on hair conditions, clinics in UK and overseas, news, events.

Founded:
1902

Organisation type and purpose:
Professional association for trichologists, the largest provider of trichology training in Europe, and the longest established body of its type.

Subject coverage:
Advice and treatment for hair loss, scalp problems, hair texture problems, hair restoration, wigs, extensions, weaving, chemotherapy hair loss and many more hair- and scalp-related issues.

Access to staff:
Contact by letter, by telephone, by fax and by e-mail

INSTITUTE OF VEHICLE ENGINEERS

Acronym or abbreviation: IVehE

31 Redstone Farm Road, Birmingham, B28 9NU

Tel: 0121 778 4354
Fax: 0121 702 2615
E-mail: info@ivehe.org

Website:
http://www.ivehe.org

Enquiries:
Enquiries to: Executive Director
Direct e-mail: james@ivehe.org

Founded:
1881

Organisation type and purpose:
Professional body.

Subject coverage:
Manufacturing section of the vehicle industry, original equipment.

Museum or gallery collection, archive, or library special collection:
Library of books on historic automobiles and carriages

Printed publications:
Vehicle Technology (journal, 4 times a year)

Access to staff:
Contact by letter, by telephone, by fax, by e-mail and via website
Hours: Mon to Fri, 0900 to 1700

Access to building, collection or gallery:
No access other than to staff, prior appointment required

INSTITUTE OF VIDEOGRAPHY

Acronym or abbreviation: IOV

PO Box 625, Loughton, IG10 3GZ

Tel: 0845 741 3626; 020 8502 3817
Fax: 020 8508 9211
E-mail: info@iov.co.uk

Website:
http://www.iov.co.uk
Information and news, microsites and zones, training and education, products and services.
http://www.videoskills.net
The Core Competencies of Videography

Founded:
1985

Organisation type and purpose:
A UK-registered, not-for-profit limited company (number 2623169), professional body for those involved in video production.
To establish and maintain videography as a recognised profession; to establish the IOV as the leading body in professional videography; to establish recognised qualifications and training in videography; to provide members with a commercial advantage over non-members; to promote videography as an effective business tool; to promote videography as an art form; to promote videography as an archive medium; to promote the IOV's Code of Practice; to promote qualified members of the IOV.

Subject coverage:
Professional video production.

Access to staff:
Contact by letter, by telephone, by fax and by e-mail

INSTITUTE OF VITREOUS ENAMELLERS

Acronym or abbreviation: IVE

39 Sweetbriar Way, Heath Hayes, Cannock, Staffs, WS12 2UST

Tel: 01543 450596
Fax: 08700 941237
E-mail: info@ive.org.uk

Website:
http://www.ive.org.uk

Enquiries:
Enquiries to: Secretary General

Founded:
1934

Incorporates:
The Vitreous Enamel Association (VEA, founded in 1956 as the Vitreous Enamel Development Council; name changed in 1995)

Organisation type and purpose:
Trade association.
Represent the vitreous enamel industry by presentations to the public, industry and education also control the cleaner scheme – approval of cleaners for vitreous enamel.

Subject coverage:
Nature and uses of vitreous enamel finishes.

Printed publications:
How to Clean Vitreous Enamel
List of cleaning products for use on vitreous enamel
Vitreous Enamel – A Performance Guide (1984, for sale)

Electronic and video publications:
Videos: Part 1 for architects, designers and engineers; parts 2 and 3 for domestic use (1991, for purchase)

Access to staff:
Contact by letter, by telephone, by fax and by e-mail. Appointment necessary.
Hours: Mon to Fri, 0900 to 1700

Access to building, collection or gallery:
No prior appointment required

Affiliated to:
British Cookware Manufacturers Association

Parent body:
The Institute of Vitreous Enamel (IVE)

INSTITUTE OF WATER

Acronym or abbreviation: IWater

4 Carlton Court, Team Valley, Gateshead, Tyne and Wear, NE11 0AZ

Tel: 0191 422 0088
Fax: 0191 422 0087
E-mail: info@instituteofwater.org.uk

Website:
http://www.instituteofwater.org.uk

Enquiries:
Enquiries to: Chief Executive
Direct e-mail: lynn@instituteofwaternrg.uk

Founded:
1945

Organisation type and purpose:
Membership association (membership is by subscription), present number of members: 1,700.

Subject coverage:
Water industry.

Printed publications:
Institute of Water Journal (journal, quarterly, free to members, £30 annual subscription in UK; £50 annual subscription overseas)

Access to staff:
Contact by letter, by telephone, by fax, by e-mail and via website. Appointment necessary.
Hours: Mon to Fri, 0900 to 1700

INSTITUTE OF WOMEN'S HEALTH

Acronym or abbreviation: IWH

PO Box 9010, Leicester, LE1 8BX

Tel: 0116 255 2100
E-mail: instituteofwomenshealth@yahoo.co.uk / info@iwhealth.co.uk

Website:
http://www.iwhealth.co.uk

Enquiries:
Enquiries to: Trustee

Founded:
1999

Organisation type and purpose:
Registered charity (charity number 1065037/0), suitable for ages: Adults, training organisation.
To provide information and education on subject of menopause and related issues so that women feel able to make informed health choices.

Subject coverage:
Menopause; osteoporosis; other gynaecological issues.
Management Therapies: hormone replacement therapy, lifestyle aspects, complementary therapy.

Museum or gallery collection, archive, or library special collection:
Textbooks, leaflets, videos, audio tapes, journals on subject areas covered

Non-library collection catalogue:
All or part available in-house

Printed publications:
Leaflets on subject areas (individually free, in bulk 10/50 leaflets charge)

Access to staff:
Contact by letter, by telephone, by e-mail and in person. Appointment necessary.
Hours: Wed, Thu, 1000 to 1400

Access for disabled people:
Parking provided, level entry, toilet facilities

INSTITUTION OF AGRICULTURAL ENGINEERS

Acronym or abbreviation: IAgrE

The Bullock Building, University Way, Cranfield, Bedford, MK43 0GH

Tel: 01234 750876
Fax: 01234 751319
E-mail: secretary@iagre.org

Website:
http://www.iagre.org

Enquiries:
Enquiries to: Chief Executive
Direct e-mail: crw@iagre.org

Founded:
1938

Organisation type and purpose:
Professional body.

Subject coverage:
Agricultural engineering; agricultural machinery; agriculture, horticulture, forest engineering; engineering for amenity areas; engineering for food storage and handling; food process engineering; environmental engineering; renewable energy.

Printed publications:
Landwards (IAgrE journal, 4 times a year, £52 a year)

Microform publications:
Conference proceedings, The Agricultural Engineer including the former Soil and Water (microfiche)

Electronic and video publications:
AgEng 2000 (CD-ROM)
Forest Engineering Group Symposia 1989–2000 (CD-ROM)

Access to staff:
Contact by letter, by telephone, by fax, by e-mail and in person
Hours: Mon to Fri, 0830 to 1630

Affiliated to:
Engineering Council (UK)

Links with:
European Society of Agricultural Engineers

INSTITUTION OF ANALYSTS AND PROGRAMMERS

Acronym or abbreviation: IAP

Charles House, 36 Culmington Road, London, W13 9NH

Tel: 020 8567 2118
Fax: 020 8567 4379
E-mail: dg@iap.org.uk

Website:
http://www.iap.org.uk/iapdg

Enquiries:
Enquiries to: Secretary

Founded:
1981

continued overleaf

Organisation type and purpose:
Professional body.
The Institution is Britain's leading specialised professional organisation for computer programmers and systems analysts.

Subject coverage:
Advice on matters relating to training and career development in the IT industry.

Printed publications:
Register of Consultants (a booklet listing qualified and experienced computer programmers and/or analysts who have passed the Institute's selection procedures)

Electronic and video publications:
Register of Consultants (disc)

Access to staff:
Contact by telephone and by e-mail
Hours: Mon to Fri, 0900 to 1700

INSTITUTION OF CIVIL ENGINEERING SURVEYORS

Acronym or abbreviation: ICES

Dominion House, Sibson Road, Sale, Cheshire, M33 7PP

Tel: 0161 972 3100
Fax: 0161 942 3118
E-mail: ices@ices.org.uk

Website:
http://www.ices.org.uk
General information with reference to civil engineering surveying, routes to membership, information about ICES.

Enquiries:
Enquiries to: Administrator

Founded:
1972

Organisation type and purpose:
Advisory body, professional body (membership is by qualification, election or invitation), present number of members: 4,000, registered charity, suitable for ages: 18+.
Qualifying body for engineering and quantity surveyors involved with civil engineering.

Subject coverage:
Construction, commercial management including: quantity surveying, project management, estimating, construction law, construction economics, planning, procurement engineering. Geospacial Engineering surveying including: land surveying, engineering surveying, hydrographic surveying, remote sensing, cartography, geographical information systems, photogrammetry.

Printed publications:
Civil Engineering Surveyor (journal, monthly, free to members)
Information literature free to schools, employers, students etc
Various technical publications

Publications list:
Available in print

Access to staff:
Contact by letter, by telephone, by fax, by e-mail and via website
Hours: Mon to Fri, 0830 to 1700

Access for disabled people:
Parking provided, access to all public areas, toilet facilities

Associated institution of the:
Institution of Civil Engineers

Member of:
Construction Industry Council
International Federation of Surveyors
Survey and Mapping Alliance

Wholly owned marketing and publications company is:
SURCO Limited

INSTITUTION OF CIVIL ENGINEERS

Acronym or abbreviation: ICE

1 Great George Street, Westminster, London, SW1P 3AA

Tel: 020 7222 7722
Fax: 020 7976 7610
E-mail: library@ice.org.uk

Website:
http://www.ice.org.uk

Enquiries:
Enquiries to: Head Knowledge Transfer
Direct tel: 020 7665 2252
Other contacts: Archivist (for access for archives)

Founded:
1818

Organisation type and purpose:
Learned society.
Qualifying body.

Subject coverage:
Civil engineering and related theoretical and applied sciences; civil engineering, building, construction; concrete, iron, steel and timber in structures; geotechnical engineering; public health engineering; hydrology and hydraulics; municipal engineering; history of technology; transport, environment.

Museum or gallery collection, archive, or library special collection:
18th- and 19th-century pamphlets
Archives of Council of Engineering Institutions
Archives of Institution of Civil Engineers
Archives of Institution of Municipal Engineers
Archives of Smeatonian Society
B L Vulliamy Horological Library
Films, videos and photographic collections
Gibb Collection
J G James Collection
Mackenzie Collection
MSS of Telford, Smeaton, the Rennies, Brunel and other early civil engineers

Non-library collection catalogue:
All or part available online, in-house and in print

Library catalogue:
All or part available online

Printed publications:
Advances in Cement Research (quarterly)
Conference publications
Geotechnique (quarterly)
Ground Engineering (monthly)
Magazine of Concrete Research
NEC International (monthly)
New Civil Engineer (weekly)
Nuclear Energy (6 times a year)
Offshore Engineer (monthly)
Proceedings (10 parts, quarterly)
Key facts pamphlets (annual, free of charge)

Electronic and video publications:
Audio visual catalogue (£2)

Publications list:
Available online and in print

Access to staff:
Contact by letter, by telephone, by fax, by e-mail, in person and via website. Appointment necessary. Access for members only. Letter of introduction required. Non-members charged.
Hours: Mon to Fri, 0915 to 1730
Special comments: Charges made to all users for certain services.

Houses the:
British Dam Society
British Geotechnical Association
British Hydrological Society
British Tunnelling Society
Central Dredging Association – British Section
European Council of Civil Engineers
International Association for Hydraulic Research – British Section
International Commission on Irrigation and Drainage – British Section (ICID)

International Navigation Association – British Section (PIANC)
Nuclear Institute
Offshore Engineering Society
Railway Civil Engineers Association
Society for Earthquake and Civil Engineering Dynamics (SECED)
Transport Planning Society
Wind Engineering Society

INSTITUTION OF DIESEL AND GAS TURBINE ENGINEERS

Acronym or abbreviation: IDGTE

Bedford Heights, Manton Lane, Bedford, MK41 7PH

Tel: 01234 214340
Fax: 01234 355493
E-mail: enquiries@idgte.org

Website:
http://www.idgte.org/

Enquiries:
Enquiries to: Secretary

Founded:
1913

Organisation type and purpose:
International organisation, learned society (membership is by subscription, qualification), present number of members: 700.
The institution is devoted to the advancement of diesel and gas engines, gas turbines and related products and technology.

Subject coverage:
Diesel engines and gas turbines.

Printed publications:
Technical papers (6 times a year, for members; on sale to non-members)

Electronic and video publications:
Annual Working Cost and Operational Report (available on disk, for sale to members and non-members)

Publications list:
Available in print

Access to staff:
Contact by letter, by telephone, by fax, by e-mail and via website
Hours: Mon to Fri, 0900 to 1700

Access to building, collection or gallery:
Prior appointment required

INSTITUTION OF ENGINEERING AND TECHNOLOGY

Acronym or abbreviation: IET

Savoy Place, London, WC2R 0BL

Tel: 020 7240 5461
Fax: 020 7240 8467
E-mail: libdesk@theiet.org

Website:
http://www.theiet.org
The IET; publishing; news; education and careers; events; membership; engineering policy; communities; research; links to archives, library and publications pages.

Enquiries:
Enquiries to: Librarian
Direct tel: 020 7344 5461
Direct fax: 020 7344 8467
Direct e-mail: jcoupland@theiet.org
Other contacts: Archivist

Founded:
1871

Created by the merger of:
Institution of Electrical Engineers (IEE) and Institution of Incorporated Engineers (IIE) (year of change 2006)

Organisation type and purpose:
International organisation, learned society (membership is by subscription, qualification), present number of members: 150,000, registered charity (charity number 211014), publishing house. Qualifying body.

Subject coverage:
Electrical, electronic and control engineering, computer science, information technology, manufacturing, engineering, telecommunications.

Information services:
Technical and business research service.

Special visitor services:
PC access and wi-fi.

Museum or gallery collection, archive, or library special collection:
Silvanus Thompson Memorial Collection (rare books and manuscripts)
Sir Francis Ronalds Collection (19th-century rare books and manuscripts on electricity)

Trade and statistical information:
Small collection of market reports

Non-library collection catalogue:
All or part available online

Library catalogue:
All or part available online

Printed publications:
A large range of books, abstract publications, journals, symposia proceedings, etc. (see also INSPEC), including:
Books (some 150 current titles; about 20 new titles a year)
Electronics Letters (fortnightly)
Power Engineering Journal (6 times a year)
Proceedings of the IEE (10 bi-monthly parts)
Ships Regulations
Wiring Regulations
Order printed publications from: Publications Sales, IET, PO Box 96, Stevenage, Hertfordshire, SG1 2SD; tel. 01438 767328; fax 01438 742792; e-mail sales@theiet.org

Electronic and video publications:
CD-ROMs, online services, tape services
Order electronic and video publications from:
Publications Sales, IET, PO Box 96, Stevenage, Hertfordshire, SG1 2SD; tel. 01438 767328; fax 01438 742792; e-mail sales@theiet.org

Publications list:
Available online and in print

Access to staff:
Contact by letter, by telephone, by fax, by e-mail, in person and via website. Non-members charged.
Hours: Mon to Fri, 0900 to 1700

Access to building, collection or gallery:
No prior appointment required
Hours: Mon to Fri, 0900 to 1700

Access for disabled people:
Ramped entry, toilet facilities

Also at:
IET
  Michael Faraday House, Six Hills Way, Stevenage, Hertfordshire, SG1 2AY; tel: 01438 313311; fax: 01438 313465; e-mail: postmaster@theiet.org; website: http://www.theiet.org

Subsidiary:
Inspec
  Michael Faraday House, Six Hills Way, Stevenage, SG1 2AY; tel: 01438 767540; fax: 01438 742840; e-mail: inspec@theiet.org; website: http://www.theiet.org/inspec

INSTITUTION OF ENGINEERING DESIGNERS

Acronym or abbreviation: IED

Courtleigh, Westbury Leigh, Westbury, Wiltshire, BA13 3TA

Tel: 01373 822801
Fax: 01373 858085

E-mail: ied@ied.org.uk

Enquiries:
Enquiries to: Secretary

Founded:
1945

Organisation type and purpose:
Professional body (membership is by qualification, election or invitation), present number of members: 5300, registered charity (charity number 269879).

Subject coverage:
Engineering design, engineering drawing, design, design education.

Printed publications:
Conference proceedings, etc
Engineering Designer (6 times a year)
Guide to Engineering Design Courses in the UK

Access to staff:
Contact by letter, by telephone, by fax, by e-mail and via website
Hours: Mon to Fri, 0900 to 1700

Nominated body of the:
Engineering Council
  tel: 020 7240 7891

INSTITUTION OF ENVIRONMENTAL SCIENCES

Acronym or abbreviation: IES

PO Box 16, Bourne, Lincolnshire, PE10 9FB

Tel: 01778 394846
Fax: 01778 394846
E-mail: ies-uk@breathemail.net

Website:
http://www.greenchannel.com/ies

Enquiries:
Enquiries to: Honorary Secretary

Founded:
1971

Organisation type and purpose:
Professional body.

Subject coverage:
Environmental science including ecology, pollution, public health, urban problems, genetic effects, climatic effects, effects of technology and transport.

Printed publications:
Environmental Careers Handbook (£9.95)
Environmental Scientist (6 times a year, £4 per copy)
IES leaflet (free)
Monographs (occasional)
Proceedings (2 times a year)

Access to staff:
Contact by letter and by e-mail
Hours: Mon to Fri, 0900 to 1700

INSTITUTION OF FIRE ENGINEERS

Acronym or abbreviation: IFE

London Road, Moreton-in-Marsh, Gloucestershire, GL56 0RH

Tel: 01608 812580
Fax: 01608 812581
E-mail: info@ife.org.uk

Website:
http://www.ife.org.uk
General information, and publications

Enquiries:
Enquiries to: Membership Officer
Direct e-mail: gill.haynes@ife.org.uk

Organisation type and purpose:
Professional body (membership is by subscription).

Subject coverage:
Fire engineering.

Printed publications:
Fire Prevention and Fire Engineers Journal (monthly)

Access to staff:
Contact by letter, by telephone, by fax, by e-mail and via website. Appointment necessary.
Hours: Mon to Fri, 0900 to 1700

Part of:
Federation of British Fire Organisations

INSTITUTION OF GAS ENGINEERS AND MANAGERS

Acronym or abbreviation: IGEM

IGEM House, High Street, Kegworth, Derbyshire, DE74 2DA

Tel: 0844 375 4436
Fax: 01509 678198
E-mail: general@igem.org.uk

Website:
http://www.igem.org.uk
General information on IGEM plus specific information on publications, membership, journal, library, etc.

Enquiries:
Enquiries to: Librarian

Founded:
1863

Organisation type and purpose:
Professional body, registered charity (charity number 214011).

Subject coverage:
Gas engineering, manufacture, transmission and distribution, gas utilisation, natural gas, LNG, gas by-products, gas industry administration and personnel, gas industry history.

Library catalogue:
All or part available in-house

Printed publications:
Communications Series – technical publications, subjects include: transmission and distribution practice, safety recommendations, gas measurement, utilisation procedures, gas legislation guidance
Gas International, Engineering and Management (10 times a year)
Recommendations for Transmission, Distribution, Safety, Measurement and Environmental Practice

Publications list:
Available online and in print

Access to staff:
Contact by letter, by telephone, by fax, by e-mail and via website. Appointment necessary. Non-members charged.
Hours: Mon to Fri, 0900 to 1700

Member organisation of:
Engineering Council
International Gas Union

INSTITUTION OF HIGHWAYS AND TRANSPORTATION

Acronym or abbreviation: IHT

6 Endsleigh Street, London, WC1H 0DZ

Tel: 020 7387 2525
Fax: 020 7387 2808
E-mail: iht@iht.org

Website:
http://www.iht.org
IHT activities, staff contacts, publications.

Enquiries:
Enquiries to: Chief Executive
Other contacts: Director of Technical Affairs for technical enquiries.

Founded:
1930

continued overleaf

Organisation type and purpose:
Learned society, registered charity (charity number 267321).

Subject coverage:
Highways and transportation infrastructure, planning and design for: roads, traffic, light rail, safety, disabled access, environment.

Printed publications:
IHT Guidelines including – Transport in the Urban Environment (1997, £49)
Guidelines – Safety Audit of Highways (1996, £15)
Alan Brant Seminar Papers 1995, 1996, 1997, 1998 and 1999 (£10 each)
Cycle Audit and Cycle Review (1998, £25 UK)
Highways and Transportation (monthly, free to members or on subscription)
Operational Management of the Highway Network (1997, £10)
Planning for Public Transport in Development (1999)
Rural Safety Management (1999, £25)

Electronic and video publications:
Guidelines – Transport in the Urban Environment (CD-ROM, 1997, £49)
Code of Pracice for Highways Maintenance (CD-ROM, £85 UK)
The Environmental Management of Highways (CD-ROM, 2001, £45 UK)
Providing for Journey on Foot (CD-ROM, £29 UK)
Rural Safety Management (CD-ROM, £25 UK)

Publications list:
Available in print

Access to staff:
Contact by letter, by telephone, by fax, by e-mail and via website. Appointment necessary.
Hours: Mon to Fri, 0930 to 1700
Special comments: Access difficult for those with mobility handicaps.

Access to building, collection or gallery:
No prior appointment required
Hours: Library: Mon to Fri, 0930 to 1700
Special comments: Not open if meeting in library.

Close professional cooperation with the:
Institute of Highways Incorporated Engineers (IHIE)

INSTITUTION OF LIGHTING ENGINEERS

Acronym or abbreviation: ILE

Lennox House, 9 Lawford Road, Rugby, Warwickshire, CV21 2DZ

Tel: 01788 576492
Fax: 01788 540145
E-mail: info@ile.co.uk

Website:
http://www.ile.co.uk
Regional information, technical reports, events, contacts, news, jobs.

Enquiries:
Enquiries to: Chief Executive
Other contacts: Technical Services Manager for technical advice.

Founded:
1924

Organisation type and purpose:
National organisation, professional body (membership is by qualification), present number of members: 2075, registered charity (charity number 268547), suitable for ages: all, training organisation, research organisation, publishing house.
To promote excellence in lighting.

Subject coverage:
All aspects of lighting, particularly exterior including street, sports, flood, emergency, tunnel lighting.

Museum or gallery collection, archive, or library special collection:
Small library

Library catalogue:
All or part available in-house

Printed publications:
Guidance Notes for the Reduction of Light Pollution (1997)
Lighting Journal (6 times a year, free to members)
Technical reports
A Practical Guide to the Procurement of Street Lighting Projects through the Private Finance Initiative (1999)
Lighting and Crime (1999)
A Guide for Crime and Disorder Reduction through a Public Lighting Strategy (1999)
Appraising the use of Remote Monitoring and Switching Technology in Street Lighting Services (1999)

Electronic and video publications:
Lighting Video
Brightness of Illuminated Advertisements (CD-ROM)

Publications list:
Available online and in print

Access to staff:
Contact by letter, by telephone, by fax, by e-mail and via website. Appointment necessary. Non-members charged.
Hours: Mon to Fri, 0900 to 1700

Access to building, collection or gallery:
Prior appointment required

Nominated body of the:
Engineering Council

INSTITUTION OF MECHANICAL ENGINEERS

Acronym or abbreviation: IMechE

1 Birdcage Walk, Westminster, London, SW1H 9JJ

Tel: 020 7222 7899; 020 7973 1274 (information and library service)
Fax: 020 7222 4557
E-mail: library@imeche.org

Website:
http://www.imeche.org

Enquiries:
Enquiries to: Manager
Direct fax: 020 7222 8762
Other contacts: Archivist (for access to archives)

Founded:
1847

Organisation type and purpose:
Professional body (membership is by subscription, qualification), registered charity (charity number 206882).
To create a natural home for all involved in mechanical engineering science that commands high regard in the community, whose members' expert views are sought on all important, relevant issues, and to membership of which every mechanical engineer aspires.

Subject coverage:
Mechanical engineering and related fields: tribology, solid mechanics and machine systems, energy, materials, manufacturing technology and design, combustion engines, environmental engineering, offshore engineering, pressurised systems, aerospace and automotive engineering, maritime engineering, power engineering, railway engineering.

Museum or gallery collection, archive, or library special collection:
Archives of: Institution of Mechanical Engineers, Institution of Locomotive Engineers, Institution of Automobile Engineers
Manuscripts of: George Stephenson and Robert Stephenson; James Nasmyth; David Joy; FW Lanchester; Christopher Hinton; Joseph Whitworth; Livesey, Henderson and Company; many others
Library contains technical papers dating back to 1847

ESDU Data Sheets
More than 200 professional and trade journals, over 122,000 vols of books, some of which date back to the foundation of the Institution
American Society of Automotive Engineers, SAE, pre-prints

Non-library collection catalogue:
All or part available online and in-house

Library catalogue:
All or part available online

Printed publications:
International Journal of Engine Research (6 a year)
Automotive Engineer (11 a year)
Journal of Strain Analysis for Engineering Design (8 a year)
List of Current Periodicals (ILS)
Proceedings of the Institution (separate papers, 14 parts as follows)
Part A Journal of Power and Energy (8 a year)
Part B Journal of Engineering Manufacture (12 a year)
Part C Journal of Mechanical Engineering Science (monthly)
Part D Journal of Automobile Engineering (monthly)
Part E Journal of Process Mechanical Engineering (quarterly)
Part F Journal of Rail and Rapid Transit (quarterly)
Part G Journal of Aerospace Engineering (6 a year)
Part H Journal of Engineering in Medicine (8 a year)
Part I Journal of Systems and Control Engineering (8 a year)
Part J Journal of Engineering Tribology (8 a year)
Part K Journal of Multi-body Dynamics (quarterly)
Part L Journal of Materials: Design and Applications (quarterly)
Part M Journal of Maritime Environment (quarterly)
Part N Journal of Nanoengineering and Nanotechnology (quarterly)
Part O Journal of Risk and Reliability (twice a year)
Professional Engineering (twice a month)
Order printed publications from: Professional Engineering Publishing, 1 Birdcage Walk, London, SW1H 9JJ

Electronic and video publications:
Full text of current journal proceedings available online for members only

Publications list:
Available online and in print

Access to staff:
Contact by letter, by telephone, by fax, by e-mail, in person and via website. Appointment necessary.

Access to building, collection or gallery:
No prior appointment required
Hours: Mon to Fri, 0915 to 1730
Special comments: Loans available to members only. Some services charged.

Access for disabled people:
Access to all public areas, toilet facilities
Special comments: Lift

INSTITUTION OF NUCLEAR ENGINEERS

Acronym or abbreviation: INucE

Allan House, 1 Penerley Road, London, SE6 2LQ

Tel: 020 8698 1500 or 4750
Fax: 020 8695 6409
E-mail: inuce@lineone.net

Website:
http://www.inuce.co.uk
General, conferences and seminars, application for membership

Enquiries:
Enquiries to: General Secretary
Other contacts: President

Founded:
1959

Organisation type and purpose:
Learned society, professional body.

Subject coverage:
Peaceful aspects of nuclear technology; nuclear engineering in relation to other disciplines, electronic/nuclear, mechanical/nuclear, nuclear physics, nuclear mathematics.

Printed publications:
Nuclear Engineer (6 times a year)

Microform publications:
Microfiche
Order microform publications from: UMI, Bell and Howell Co
300 N Zeeb Road, Ann Arbor, MI 48106–1346, USA

Publications list:
Available in print

Access to staff:
Contact by letter, by telephone, by fax, by e-mail and via website. Appointment necessary.
Hours: Mon to Fri, 0830 to 1700

Affiliated to:
The Engineering Council

Member society of the:
European Nuclear Society

INSTITUTION OF OCCUPATIONAL SAFETY AND HEALTH

Acronym or abbreviation: IOSH

The Grange, Highfield Drive, Wigston, Leicestershire, LE18 1NN

Tel: 0116 257 3100
Fax: 0116 257 3101
E-mail: enquiries@iosh.co.uk

Website:
http://www.iosh.co.uk
Information about IOSH; magazine style update feature; chat forum for occupational safety and health professionals; abstracts; technical information.

Enquiries:
Enquiries to: Publishing and Media Assistant

Founded:
1945

Organisation type and purpose:
Learned society, professional body (membership is by qualification), present number of members: 33,000, registered charity (charity number 210981), training organisation, publishing house.

Subject coverage:
Occupational safety, health and hygiene; training; legislation; environmental management.

Printed publications:
Policy and Practice in Health and Safety (twice a year)
The Safety and Health Practitioner (monthly, published by CMP Information)
Principles of Health and Safety at Work (7th UK edn)
Principles of Health and Safety at Work (Int'l edn)
Protect Your People and Your Business: the Practical One-stop Health and Safety Toolkit
Questioning Performance: the Director's Essential Guide to Health, Safety and the Environment
Health and Safety: Risk Management
Health and Safety: Hazardous Agents
Essentials of Environmental Management
Workplace Ergonomics

Publications list:
Available in print

Access to staff:
Contact by letter, by telephone, by fax, by e-mail, in person and via website
Hours: Mon to Fri, 0900 to 1700

IOSH has:
regional branches in the UK and Ireland and a number of special interest groups

INSTITUTION OF STRUCTURAL ENGINEERS

Acronym or abbreviation: IStructE

11 Upper Belgrave Street, London, SW1X 8BH

Tel: 020 7235 4535
Fax: 020 7235 4294
E-mail: mail@istructe.org

Website:
http://www.istructe.org

Enquiries:
Enquiries to: Manager, Library and Information Services
Direct tel: 020 7201 9105
Direct fax: 020 7201 9118
Direct e-mail: library@istructe.org

Founded:
1908

Formerly called:
Concrete Institute (year of change 1922)

Organisation type and purpose:
Learned society.

Subject coverage:
Structural engineering, defined as the science and art of designing and making with economy and elegance, buildings, bridges, frames and other similar structures so that they can safely resist the forces to which they may be subjected.

Information services:
Library service for IStructE members

Library catalogue:
All or part available online

Printed publications:
The Structural Engineer (23 times a year)
Structural use of glass in buildings (1999)
Temporary demountable structures: guidance on procurement, design and use (2nd edn, 1999)
Subsidence of low-rise buildings (2nd edn, 2000)
Inspection of underwater structures (2001)
Guidance for the use of computers for engineering design calculations (2002)
Design recommendations for multi-storey and underground car parks (2002)
Safety in tall buildings and other buildings of large occupancy (2002)
Manual for the design of reinforced concrete building structures (2nd edn, 2002)
Introduction to the fire safety engineering of structures (2003)
Expert evidence: a guide for expert witnesses and their clients (2nd edn, 2003)
Design and construction of deep basements including cut-and-cover structures (2004)
Manual for the design of plain masonry in building structures (2nd edn, 2005)
Standard method of detailing structural concrete: a manual for best practice (3rd edn, 2006)
Manual for the design of concrete building structures to Eurocode 2 (2006)
Temporary demountable structures: guidance on procurement, design and use (2007)
Guide to the advanced fire safety engineering of structures (2007)
The operation and maintenance of bridges access gantries and runways (2nd edn, 2007)
Manual for the design of timber building structures to Eurocode 5 (2007)
Manual for the design of plain masonry in building structures to Eurocode 6 (2008)
Guide to surveys and inspections of buildings and associated structures (2008)
Manual for the design of steelwork building structures (3rd edn, 2008)
Order printed publications from: Publications Department, at the same address

Publications list:
Available online and in print

Access to staff:
Contact by letter, by telephone, by fax, by e-mail, in person and via website. Access for members only.
Hours: Mon to Fri, 0930 to 1730
Special comments: Prior appointment required for non-members

Access to building, collection or gallery:
Prior appointment required for non-members
Hours: Mon to Fri, 0930 to 1730

Access for disabled people:
Ramp available

Constituent bodies:
Standing Committee on Structural Safety (SCOSS)

Member organisation of:
Construction Industry Council
EC (UK)

INSTOCK FOOTWEAR SUPPLIERS ASSOCIATION

Acronym or abbreviation: IFSA

Marlow House, Churchill Way, Fleckney, Leicester, LE8 8UD

Tel: 0116 240 3232
Fax: 0116 240 2762

Enquiries:
Enquiries to: Information Officer

Organisation type and purpose:
National organisation, trade association, membership association (membership is by subscription), present number of members: 8.

Subject coverage:
Footwear wholesaling in the UK.

Access to staff:
Contact by letter, by telephone and by fax
Hours: Mon to Fri, 0900 to 1700

Access to building, collection or gallery:
No access other than to staff

Affiliated to:
Federation of Wholesale and Industrial Distributors and the Footwear Distributors

INSULATED RENDER AND CLADDING ASSOCIATION

Acronym or abbreviation: INCA

Royal London House, 22–25 Finsbury Square, London, EC2A 1DX

Tel: 0844 249 0040
Fax: 0844 249 0042
E-mail: info@inca.org.uk

Website:
http://www.inca-ltd.org.uk

Enquiries:
Enquiries to: Information Officer

Founded:
1983

Organisation type and purpose:
Advisory body, trade association (membership is by qualification), present number of members: 60.

Subject coverage:
Insulated render and cladding for solid or defective walled housing/buildings.

Trade and statistical information:
UK insulated render and cladding market sales figures.

Printed publications:
Advisory literature
Insulated Render and Cladding: Specifiers and Property Owners' Briefing (free)
The Industry Insurance Guarantee Scheme (free)
Members List incorporating Register of Installers (free)
Register of Systems (free)
Code of Practice for Approved Applicators (free)

continued overleaf

Code of Practice for Approved Systems (free)

Publications list:
Available online

Access to staff:
Contact by letter, by telephone, by fax, by e-mail
and via website
Hours: Mon to Fri, 0900 to 1700

INSULATION AND ENVIRONMENTAL TRAINING TRUST LIMITED

Acronym or abbreviation: IETTL

TICA House, Allington Way, Yarm Road Business
Park, Darlington, Co Durham, DL1 4QB

Tel: 01325 466704
Fax: 01325 487691
E-mail: enquiries@tica-acad.co.uk

Enquiries:
Enquiries to: Director

Organisation type and purpose:
Registered charity, training organisation.

Subject coverage:
Industry training in insulation and asbestos
removal.

Access to staff:
Contact by letter, by fax and by e-mail
Hours: Mon to Thu, 0830 to 1700; Fri, 0830 to 1530

Access to building, collection or gallery:
Prior appointment required

Access for disabled people:
Parking provided

Affiliated to:
Insulation & Environmental Training Agency
(IETA)
 tel: 01325 466704; fax: 01325 487691; e-mail:
 enquiries@tica-acad.co.uk
Thermal Insulation Contractors Association (TICA)
 tel: 01325 466704; fax: 01325 487691; e-mail:
 enquiries@tica-acad.co.uk

INSURANCE INSTITUTE OF LONDON

Acronym or abbreviation: IIL

5th Floor, 20 Aldermanbury, London, EC2V 7HY

Tel: 020 7600 1343
Fax: 020 7600 6857
E-mail: iil.london@cii.co.uk

Website:
http://www.iilondon.co.uk

Founded:
1907

Organisation type and purpose:
Professional body.
To raise the professional knowledge of those
working in insurance in the London Market.

Subject coverage:
Insurance industry.

Printed publications:
The London Journal – an annual publication
London Institute Centenary Souvenir Booklet
 (June 2007)
Research Studies including:
208B – Construction Insurance (December 1999)
228A – Professional Indemnity Insurance
 (September 2010)
234A – Directors' and Officers' Liability Insurance
 (April 2010)
237 – Insuring Industrial and Process Machinery
 (May 2000)
240 – Marine Insurance in the Former Soviet Union
 (July 1999)
244 – Developments in Excess of Loss Reinsurance
 (May 2000)
249 – Business Continuity (December 2007)

253 – Run-off Management and Commutations in
 Practice (December 2006)
254 – Insurance of Revenue for Projects under
 Construction (September 2003)
256 – Insuring aspects of E-commerce (June 2009)
258 – War Risks and Terrorism (October 2007)
259 – Insuring Privately Financed Projects
 (November 2009)
Order printed publications from: website: http://
www.iilondon.co.uk

Publications list:
Available online and in print

Access to staff:
Contact by letter, by telephone, by fax, by e-mail,
in person and via website. Appointment necessary.
Hours: Mon to Thu, 0900 to 1700; Fri, 0900 to 1645

Parent body:
Chartered Insurance Institute
 at the same address

INTER FAITH NETWORK FOR THE UK

8A Lower Grosvenor Place, London, SW1W 0EN

Tel: 020 7931 7766
Fax: 020 7931 7722
E-mail: ifnet@interfaith.org.uk

Website:
http://www.interfaith.org.uk
General information, online publications, annual
reviews.

Enquiries:
Enquiries to: Director

Founded:
1987

Organisation type and purpose:
Voluntary organisation, registered charity (charity
number 1068934).

Subject coverage:
Information and contacts for Britain's faith
communities at national and local level; advice and
information on inter faith matters.

Printed publications:
Inter Faith Update (newsletter, 3 times a year)
Building Good Relations with People of Different
 Faiths and Beliefs
Connect: Different Faiths Shared Values
Inter Faith Organisations in the UK: A Directory
Local Inter Faith Activity in the UK: A Survey
The Quest for Common Values
The Local Inter Faith Guide
Inter Faith Week 2009: A Report and Evaluation

Publications list:
Available online and in print

Access to staff:
Contact by letter, by telephone, by fax, by e-mail
and via website. Appointment necessary.
Hours: Mon to Fri, 0930 to 1730

Access to building, collection or gallery:
Prior appointment required

INTER-CREDIT INTERNATIONAL

Formal name: Inter-Credit International Ltd

4th Floor, South Point House, 321 Chase Road,
Southgate, London, N14 6JT

Tel: 020 8482 4444
Fax: 020 8482 4455
E-mail: collection@intercred.com

Website:
http://www.intercred.com/

Enquiries:
Enquiries to: Managing Director

Founded:
1971

Organisation type and purpose:
Service industry.

National and international debt recovery agency
and credit reference agency.

Subject coverage:
Credit scoring.

INTERACT READING SERVICE

Room 8, Victoria Charity Centre, 11 Belgrave
Road, London SW1V 1RB

Tel: 020 7931 6458
E-mail: info@interactreading.org

Website:
http://www.interactreading.org
How and where the service operates, news and
events, stroke information.

Founded:
2000

Organisation type and purpose:
A registered charity (number 1080046).
Uniquely provides a professional, live, interactive
reading service for stroke patients in hospitals and
stroke clubs.

Subject coverage:
Over 200 professional actors visiting hospitals
across London and in 6 regions of the UK and over
40 stroke clubs in London and the South East. In
the hospitals the actors mainly read on a one-to-
one basis at the patient's bedside. The Stroke Club
readings are performance based; the reader
performs a programme and reads to the whole
group.
InterAct actors are professionally trained. They
work for InterAct when not working in theatre,
radio, film and television.

Access to staff:
Contact by letter, by telephone and by e-mail

INTERACTIVE

Unit 2B07, London South Bank University,
Technopark, 90 London Road, London, SE1 6LN

Tel: 020 7717 1699
E-mail: info@interactive.uk.net

Website:
http://www.interactive.uk.net

Enquiries:
Enquiries to: Office Co-ordinator

Founded:
1981

Organisation type and purpose:
Membership association (membership is by
subscription, election or invitation), voluntary
organisation, registered charity (charity number
1055683), suitable for ages: all, training
organisation.
To develop sporting and recreational opportunities
for all disabled people including those with
learning disabilities, physical impairments, visual
impairments and deaf people.

Subject coverage:
Sporting and recreational activities for disabled
people, training programmes, equipment.

Publications list:
Available online

Access to staff:
Contact by letter, by telephone, by fax, by e-mail
and via website. Appointment necessary.
Hours: Mon to Fri, 0900 to 1700

Access for disabled people:
Parking provided, ramped entry, toilet facilities

INTERCONTINENTAL CHURCH SOCIETY

Acronym or abbreviation: ICS

1 Athena Drive, Tachbrook Park, Warwick, CV34
6NL

Tel: 01926 430347
Fax: 01926 888092
E-mail: enquiries@ics-uk.org

Website:
http://www.ics-uk.org

Enquiries:
Enquiries to: General Manager

Founded:
1823

Formerly called:
Colonial and Continental Church Society (year of change 1861); Commonwealth and Continental Church Society (year of change 1958)

Organisation type and purpose:
Membership association (membership is by subscription), present number of members: 830, voluntary organisation, registered charity (charity number 1072584).
ICS, an evangelical Anglican mission society, supports the ministry of English-speaking, international congregations in several continents, ministers to holidaymakers in Europe and the Mediterranean.

Subject coverage:
English-language church services abroad.

Printed publications:
Directory of English-speaking Churches Abroad (2010, £4)
ICS News (4 times a year, minimum annual donation £15)

Access to staff:
Contact by letter, by telephone, by fax, by e-mail and via website
Hours: Mon to Fri, 0930 to 1700

Access to building, collection or gallery:
No access other than to staff

Access for disabled people:
Level entry

Links with:
Partnership for World Mission (PWM)
Church House, 27 Great Smith Street, London, SW1P 3AZ; tel: 020 7898 1328

INTERMEDIATE TECHNOLOGY DEVELOPMENT GROUP LIMITED

Acronym or abbreviation: ITDG

The Schumacher Centre for Technology and Development, Bourton Hall, Bourton on Dunsmore, Rugby, Warwickshire, CV23 9QZ

Tel: 01926 634400
Fax: 01926 634401
E-mail: enquiries@practicalaction.org.uk

Website:
http://www.itdg.org

Enquiries:
Enquiries to: Information Officer
Direct e-mail: carolr@itdg.org.uk

Founded:
1966

Organisation type and purpose:
International organisation, registered charity (charity number 247257).
An international development agency working at the cutting edge of sustainable community development through country offices in Africa, Asia and South America.
To build the technical skills of poor people in developing countries, enabling them to improve the quality of their lives and that of future generations.

Subject coverage:
Appropriate technology, low-cost and small-scale manufacturing processes suitable for the developing countries, in agriculture, water supply and sanitation, building materials and construction, energy, transport, food production, food processing, mining and small industries.

Museum or gallery collection, archive, or library special collection:
Books on appropriate technologies and grey literature

Printed publications:
Books on all aspects of the work of the group
Annual Report
Small World (magazine)
Waterlines (quarterly)
Order printed publications from: IT Publications
103–105 Southampton Row, London, WC1B 4HH, tel: 020 7436 9761, fax: 020 7436 2013, e-mail: itpubs@itpubs.org.uk

Publications list:
Available in print

Access to staff:
Contact by letter, by telephone, by fax, by e-mail and via website. Appointment necessary.
Hours: Mon to Fri, 0900 to 1700

INTERNATIONAL ACCOUNTING STANDARDS BOARD

Acronym or abbreviation: IASB

1st Floor, 30 Cannon Street, London, EC4M 6XH

Tel: 020 7246 6410
Fax: 020 7246 6411
E-mail: iasb@iasb.org.uk

Website:
http://www.iasb.org.uk
Details of the organisation, structure, aims and publications.

Enquiries:
Enquiries to: Secretary General
Other contacts: Publications Director

Founded:
1973

Organisation type and purpose:
Accountancy regulatory body.
To formulate international accounting standards and to promote their use worldwide.

Subject coverage:
International accounting standards.

Printed publications:
IASC's Annual review (for purchase)
IASC Update (for purchase)
IASC Insight (quarterly newsletter, all three on subscription £120)
International Accounting Standards (for purchase)
Exposure Drafts of proposed International Accounting Standards (for purchase)
Hedge Accounting (£10)
Order printed publications from: Publications Department, IASB
tel: 020 7427 5927, fax: 020 7353 0562

Electronic and video publications:
International Accounting Standards (CD-ROM)

Publications list:
Available online and in print

Access to staff:
Contact by letter and by telephone
Hours: Mon to Fri, 0900 to 1700
Special comments: Access for members only.

Access to building, collection or gallery:
No access other than to staff

INTERNATIONAL ACUPUNCTURE ASSOCIATION OF PHYSICAL THERAPISTS

Acronym or abbreviation: IAAPT

Hilltop, Benjamin Road, High Wycombe, Buckinghamshire, HP13 6SR

Tel: 01494 451295
Fax: 01494 451295
E-mail: merianmum@hotmail.com

Enquiries:
Enquiries to: UK Representative
Direct e-mail: merianmum@hotmail.com

Founded:
1991

Organisation type and purpose:
Professional body.

Subject coverage:
Acupuncture and physiotherapy.

Printed publications:
Meridian Worldwide – in-house newsletter

Access to staff:
Contact by letter and by fax
Hours: Unrestricted

Affiliated to:
World Confederation for Physical Therapy (WCPT)

Links with:
Acupuncture Association of Chartered Physiotherapists (AACP)

INTERNATIONAL AESTHETICIENNES

International Beauty Therapy Examination Board, Bache Hall, Bache Hall Estate, Chester, Cheshire, CH2 1BR

Tel: 01244 376539
Fax: 01244 373571
E-mail: info@iabeauty.com

Website:
http://www.iabeauty.com

Enquiries:
Enquiries to: Secretary

Founded:
1979

Organisation type and purpose:
International organisation, professional body (membership is by subscription, qualification).

Subject coverage:
Beauty, body and electrolysis, examinations, Membership with or without insurance.

Electronic and video publications:
Open Learning
Training videos and syllabus for purchase

Access to staff:
Contact by letter, by telephone, by fax and by e-mail
Hours: Sat, 0900 to 1700

INTERNATIONAL AFRICAN INSTITUTE

Acronym or abbreviation: IAI

SOAS, Thornhaugh Street, Russell Square, London, WC1H 0XG

Tel: 020 7898 4429
Fax: 020 7898 4410
E-mail: iai@soas.ac.uk

Website:
http://www.internationalafricaninstitute.org

Enquiries:
Enquiries to: Secretary

Founded:
1926

Organisation type and purpose:
International organisation, learned society (membership is by election or invitation), present number of members: 27, registered charity (charity number 1084798), research organisation, publishing house.
The International African Institute has been the foremost international association engaged in encouraging the study of African society and disseminating the results of research. Its prime objective is to facilitate communication between scholars within the continent and Africans

continued overleaf

throughout the world on issues that are of direct relevance to the peoples of this region. It achieves this objective through its publication programme, seminars, African and non-African scholars; and projects which are concerned with the infrastructure for learning and research in Africa.

Subject coverage:
Communications between scholars in Africa and elsewhere, African societies and cultures.

Printed publications:
Africa (quarterly)
Africa Bibliography (annually)
African Issues (series, published with James
   Currey Publishers)
Classics in African Anthropology (published with
   James Currey Publishers)
International Africa (library series published with
   Edinburgh University Press)
Readings in African Arguments (series, published
   with Zed Books)
Order printed publications from: Edinburgh
University Press
22 George Square, Edinburgh, EH8 9LF
James Currey Publisher
73 Botley Road, Oxford, OX2 0BS

Publications list:
Available online and in print

Access to staff:
Contact by e-mail
Hours: Mon to Fri, 0900 to 1700

INTERNATIONAL AIRLINE PASSENGERS ASSOCIATION

Acronym or abbreviation: IAPA

Advertiser House, 19 Bartlett Street, South Croydon, Surrey, CR2 6TB

Website:
http://www.iapa.com
About IAPA, benefits of membership.

Founded:
1960

Formerly called:
Airways Club (year of change 1982)

Organisation type and purpose:
Membership association.
To represent the interests of frequent air travellers by providing them with special discounts on items such as hotel accommodation, car rental and insurance, in addition to protecting and promoting their rights as airline passengers.
Works in partnership with major companies world-wide to bring the best deals possible to members.

Subject coverage:
Offers a range of services, from guaranteeing the 'best available rate' on key hotel chains and savings on car rental reservations, to a market-leading range of specialist insurance products for members; also provides a range of travel-planning services, helps members save money on mobile phone bills when travelling, and represents their interests as a frequent flyer to industry and government bodies.

Access to staff:
Contact by letter, by telephone, by fax and by e-mail
Hours: London Membership Services: Mon to Fri, 0800 to 2000; Sat and public hols, 0900 to 1700; Sun and Dec 25, closed

Also at:
Membership Services, IAPA
   PO Box 380, Croydon, Surrey, CR9 2ZQ; tel: 020
   8681 6555; fax: 020 8681 0234; e-mail: info
   .london@iapa.com
Membership Services, IAPA
   PO Box 700188, Dallas, TX 75370–0188, USA; tel:
   +1 972 404 9980; toll-free in USA/Canada/Mexico:
   800 821 4272; fax: +1 972 233 5348; toll-free in
   USA/Canada/Mexico: 800 647 4272; e-mail: info
   .dallas@iapa.com

Membership Services, IAPA
   GPO Box 9200, Hong Kong; tel: +852 2528 4263;
   fax: +852 2865 6891; e-mail: info.hongkong@iapa
   .com

Constituent part of:
Priority Travel Group

INTERNATIONAL ALUMINIUM INSTITUTE

Acronym or abbreviation: IAI

New Zealand House, Haymarket, London, SW1Y 4TE

Tel: 020 7930 0528
Fax: 020 7321 0183
E-mail: iai@world-aluminium.org

Website:
http://www.world-aluminium.org

Enquiries:
Enquiries to: Secretary General

Founded:
1972

Organisation type and purpose:
International organisation, trade association, membership association (membership is by qualification), present number of members: 22. International association of the primary aluminium industry.

Subject coverage:
Aluminium industry; aluminium products; energy requirements; statistics, developments; environmental health and safety.

Trade and statistical information:
Information and statistics are available on the website.

Publications list:
Available online

Access to staff:
Contact by letter, by telephone, by fax and by e-mail
Hours: Mon to Fri, 0900 to 1700

INTERNATIONAL ARTIST MANAGERS' ASSOCIATION

Acronym or abbreviation: IAMA

23 Garrick Street, Covent Garden, London, WC2E 9BN

Tel: 020 7379 7336
Fax: 020 7379 7338
E-mail: info@iamaworld.com

Website:
http://www.iamaworld.com
Publications.

Enquiries:
Enquiries to: Chief Executive

Founded:
1954

Organisation type and purpose:
International organisation, membership association (membership is by election or invitation), present number of members: 230.

Subject coverage:
Artist management, concert promotion (classical music).

Printed publications:
Directory of Artists (online)
Quarterly Newsletter (free to members)

Publications list:
Available online and in print

Access to staff:
Contact by letter, by telephone, by fax, by e-mail and via website
Hours: Mon to Fri, 0930 to 1730

INTERNATIONAL ASSOCIATION OF BOOK-KEEPERS

Acronym or abbreviation: IAB

Burford House, 44 London Road, Sevenoaks, Kent, TN13 1AS

Tel: 01732 458080
Fax: 01732 455848
E-mail: mail@iab.org.uk

Website:
http://www.ifa.org.uk
http://www.iab.org.uk
Membership information, course syllabus, etc.

Enquiries:
Enquiries to: Chief Executive

Founded:
1973

Organisation type and purpose:
Professional body.
Examining body.

Subject coverage:
All aspects of book-keeping and accountancy.

Printed publications:
Financial Accountant (6 times a year)
International Book-keeper (6 times a year)

Access to staff:
Contact by letter, by telephone, by fax, by e-mail and via website. Appointment necessary.
Hours: Mon to Fri, 0900 to 1700

Parent body:
Institute of Financial Accountants
   Burford House, 44 London Road, Sevenoaks,
   Kent, TN13 1AS; tel: 01732 458080; fax: 01732
   455848; e-mail: mail@ifa.org.uk

INTERNATIONAL ASSOCIATION OF CLASSIFICATION SOCIETIES

Acronym or abbreviation: IACS

6th Floor, 36 Broadway, London, SW1H 0BH

Tel: 020 7976 0660
Fax: 020 7808 1100
E-mail: permsec@iacs.org.uk

Website:
http://www.iacs.org.uk
General information on classification, IACS and its members, publications lists and downloadable publications.

Enquiries:
Enquiries to: Permanent Secretary
Other contacts: Principal Technical Officer for technical enquiries.

Founded:
1992

Organisation type and purpose:
International organisation, membership association (membership is by qualification), present number of members: 11, voluntary organisation, registered charity, research organisation.
Trade association representing the world's 11 largest classification societies.

Subject coverage:
Ship classification; vessel surveys; vessel repairs; vessel hull and essential engineering systems; international maritime conventions and regulations; safety at sea; prevention of marine pollution.

Trade and statistical information:
IACS member societies classify the hull and essential engineering systems of over 90% of the world's merchant fleet by tonnage on behalf of well over 100 sovereign states worldwide.

Printed publications:
Bulk Carriers: Guidelines for Survey Assessment
   and Repair of Hull Structures (£22 inc. p&p)
Guidelines for the Inspection and Maintenance of
   Double Hull Tanker Structures (£35 plus p&p)
IACS Brochure, free

IACS Unified Requirements (£250 plus p&p)

Electronic and video publications:
IACS Unified Requirements (CD-ROM, £250 plus p&p)

Publications list:
Available online

Access to staff:
Contact by letter, by telephone, by fax, by e-mail and via website. Appointment necessary.
Hours: Mon to Fri, 0900 to 1700

Access to building, collection or gallery:
Prior appointment required

Access for disabled people:
Level entry

Also at:
IACS QSCS OPS
Suite 2, Orchard House, 51–67 Commercial Road, Southampton, SO15 1GG; tel: 023 8021 1369; e-mail: qscs.ops@iacs.org.uk

Links with:
European Association of Classification Societies (EURACS)

Member organisations:
American Bureau of Shipping
ABS Plaza, 16855 Northchase Drive, Houston, TX 77060, USA; tel: +1 281 877 6000; fax: +1 281 877 6001; e-mail: abs-worldhq@eagle.org
Bureau Veritas
Paris, France; tel: +33 1 42 91 52 91; fax: +33 1 42 91 52 93; e-mail: veristarinfo@bureauveritas.com
China Classification Society
Beijing, China; tel: +86 10 5811 2288; fax: +86 10 5811 2811; e-mail: ccs@ccs.org.cn
Det Norske Veritas
Hovik, Norway; tel: +47 67 57 99 00; fax: +47 67 57 99 11; e-mail: iacs@dnv.com
Germanischer Lloyd
Hamburg, Germany; tel: +49 40 36 14 90; fax: +49 40 36 14 9200; e-mail: headoffice@gl-group.com
Indian Register of Shipping
Mumbai, India; tel: +91 22 2570 3627; fax: +91 22 2570 3611; e-mail: ho@irclass.org
Korean Register of Shipping
Taejon, Korea; tel: +82 42 869 9114; fax: +82 42 862 6011; e-mail: krsiacs@krs.co.kr
Lloyd's Register of Shipping
London; tel: 020 7709 9166; fax: 020 7488 4796; e-mail: lloydsreg@lr.org
Nippon Kaiji Kyokai
Tokyo, Japan; tel: +81 3 3230 1201; fax: +81 3 3230 3524; e-mail: xad@classnk.or.jp
Register of Shipping (Russia)
St Petersburg, Russia; tel: +7 812 312 3569; fax: +7 812 312 3569; e-mail: 004@rs-head.spb.ru
Registro Italiano Navale
Genova, Italy; tel: +39 010 53 851; fax: +39 010 59 1877; e-mail: info@rina.org

INTERNATIONAL ASSOCIATION OF HYDROGEOLOGISTS

Acronym or abbreviation: IAH

PO Box 9, Kenilworth, Warwickshire, CV8 1JG

Tel: 01926 450677
Fax: 01926 856561
E-mail: iah@iah.org

Website:
http://www.iah.org
Information on the Association publications, information on hydrogeology.

Enquiries:
Enquiries to: Secretary General

Founded:
1956

Organisation type and purpose:
International organisation, professional body (membership is by subscription), present number of members: 3500.

Subject coverage:
Hydrogeology, groundwater, role in developing countries.

Printed publications:
Hydrogeology (journal, pub Springer Verlag)
International Contributions to Hydrogeology (book series, pub Balkerna, Rotterdam)

Electronic and video publications:
Newsletter (online)

Publications list:
Available online

Access to staff:
Contact by letter, by fax, by e-mail and via website
Hours: Irregular

Affiliated to:
International Union of Geological Sciences

INTERNATIONAL ASSOCIATION OF INSTITUTES OF NAVIGATION

Acronym or abbreviation: IAIN

Royal Institute of Navigation, 1 Kensington Gore, London, SW7 2AT

Tel: 020 7591 3130
Fax: 020 7591 3131
E-mail: prentpage@aol.com

Website:
http://www.rin.org.uk/iain/frame1.htm

Enquiries:
Enquiries to: Secretary General
Direct tel: 01444 232405
Direct fax: 01444 232405

Organisation type and purpose:
International organisation.
Coordinating and consulting body of 19 national institutes of navigation throughout the world.

Subject coverage:
Navigation by land, sea, air and in space.

Printed publications:
Newsletter

Electronic and video publications:
Newsletter available via website

Access to staff:
Contact by letter, by fax, by e-mail and via website
Hours: Mon to Fri, 0900 to 1700

Members are the institutes of navigation of:
Arab States, Argentine, Austria, Australia, Czech Republic, China, France, Germany, Italy, Japan, Korea, Netherlands, Nordic States, Poland, Russia, Spain, Switzerland, UK, USA
Tel and fax numbers and e-mail address on IAIN website (http://www.rin.org.uk/iain/frame1.htm)

INTERNATIONAL ASSOCIATION OF MUSIC LIBRARIES, ARCHIVE AND DOCUMENTATION CENTRES (UNITED KINGDOM BRANCH)

Acronym or abbreviation: IAML (UK & Irl)

Website:
http://www.iaml-uk-irl.org

Founded:
1953

Organisation type and purpose:
International organisation, professional body (membership is by subscription, election or invitation), present number of members: 295.
Voluntary association in liaison with the Chartered Institute of Library Information Professionals.
Promotes music libraries and supports anyone working in music libraries or related fields.

Subject coverage:
Music bibliography and librarianship.

Museum or gallery collection, archive, or library special collection:
A collection of books and magazines about music librarianship is held at the Department of Music, University of Oxford

Library catalogue:
All or part available online and in print

Printed publications:
BRIO (journal, 2 times a year)
British Union Catalogue of Music Periodicals (BUCOMP2)
First Stop for Music (2001)
Working with Music in Libraries
Library and Information Plan for Music (1993)
Newsletter (2 times a year)
The Availability of Printed Music in Great Britain (1988)
Music Sets Survey (1997)
Access to Music (2003)
Concert Programmes in the UK and Ireland (2003)
Order printed publications from: Publications Officer, IAML (UK & Irl), County Library Headquarters, Walton Street, Aylesbury, Buckinghamshire, HP20 1UU, tel: 01296 382266, fax: 01296 382274, e-mail: mroll@buckscc.gov.uk

Publications list:
Available online

Access to staff:
Contact by letter, by telephone, by fax, by e-mail and in person. Appointment necessary.
Hours: Mon to Fri, 0900 to 1700

Links with:
Chartered Institute of Library and Information Professionals

INTERNATIONAL ASSOCIATION OF TOUR MANAGERS

Acronym or abbreviation: IATM

397 Walworth Road, London, SE17 2AW

Tel: 020 7703 9154
Fax: 020 7703 0358
E-mail: iatm@iatm.co.uk

Website:
http://www.iatm.co.uk

Enquiries:
Enquiries to: General Manager

Founded:
1962

Organisation type and purpose:
Trade association, membership association (membership is by subscription).

Subject coverage:
Tour management.

Printed publications:
IATM Newsletter, Annual Membership handbook

Access to staff:
Contact by letter, by telephone, by e-mail and via website
Hours: Mon to Fri, 0900 to 1430

Access to building, collection or gallery:
No access other than to staff

Member organisation of:
American Society of Travel Agents (ASTA)
website: http://www.asta.org
European Tour Operators Association (ETOA)
Weighhouse Street, London; e-mail: http://www.etoa.org
European Travel and Tourism Action Group (ETAG)
website: http://www.etag-euro.org

INTERNATIONAL AUTISTIC RESEARCH ORGANISATION – AUTISM RESEARCH LIMITED

Acronym or abbreviation: IARO

continued overleaf

49 Orchard Avenue, Shirley, Croydon, Surrey, CR0
7NE

Tel: 020 8777 0095
Fax: 020 8776 2362
E-mail: iaro@autismresearch.wanadoo.co.uk

Website:
http://www.iaro.org.uk

Enquiries:
Enquiries to: Director
Other contacts: Secretary

Founded:
1981

Organisation type and purpose:
International organisation, membership
association (membership is by subscription),
present number of members: 300+, voluntary
organisation, registered charity (charity number
802391), research organisation.
Information body.
To encourage research into autism and to
disseminate the useful results of such research.
Information provision and awareness-raising of
scientific research into autism.

Subject coverage:
Information in autism and the latest research.

Education services:
Medical research only.

Printed publications:
Newsletter
An Essential Facts Leaflet for Carers, Persons with
Autism and Professionals (free)
Research papers (nominal fee)
Asperger's Syndrome Symptoms (10p)
Asperger's Language, Cognition, Behaviour (10p)
Genetic Information (80p)

Publications list:
Available in print

Access to staff:
Contact by letter, by telephone, by fax and by e-
mail
Hours: Mon to Fri, 0900 to 1700
Special comments: By appointment only.
Charges made to non-members for printed
matters.

Access to building, collection or gallery:
Prior appointment required

Access for disabled people:
Special comments: No wheelchair access.

Networking:
Autism Research Review International
4182 Adams Avenue, San Diego, CA 92116, USA;
tel: (619) 281 7165; fax: (619) 563 6840; website:
http://www.AutismResearchInstitute.com
Autism Society of America
7910 Woodmont Avenue, Suite 300, Bethesda,
Maryland 20814–3067, USA; tel: (301) 657 0881;
fax: (301) 657 0869; website: http://www.autism
-society.org
Autistik (Autism Society of the Czech Republic)
Estonia Autistic Society
Tartu EE2400, Estonia
Indiana Research Centre, Indiana University,
Indiana Institute on Disability Community,
Indiana's Centre for Excellence on Disability
2853 East Tenth Street, Bloomington, IN 74708–
2696, USA; tel: (812) 855 6508; fax: (812) 855
9630; e-mail: cbow-man@indianna.edu

INTERNATIONAL BAR
ASSOCIATION

Acronym or abbreviation: IBA

10th Floor, 1 Stephen St, London, W1T 1AT

Tel: 020 7691 6868
Fax: 020 7691 6544
E-mail: via website

Website:
http://www.ibanet.org

IBA, committees, task forces, bar associations,
conferences, Human Rights Institute, publications,
membership, education, charitable foundations,
online shop.

Founded:
1947

Organisation type and purpose:
A global organisation of international legal
practitioners, bar associations and law societies.
Membership of more than 40,000 individual
lawyers and 197 bar associations and law societies
spanning all continents.
To promote an exchange of information between
legal associations world-wide; to support the
independence of the judiciary and the right of
lawyers to practise their profession without
interference.
Influences the development of international law
reform and shapes the future of the legal
profession throughout the world; provides support
of human rights for lawyers world-wide through
its Human Rights Institute; has considerable
expertise in providing assistance to the global legal
community.

Subject coverage:
International law and the legal profession globally;
human rights.

Printed publications:
Thousands of IBA publications available,
including:
9 journals and magazines
Books
Over 50 specialist committee newsletters
Conference papers
Guides and free materials
Order printed publications from: Online shop
(discount for members)

Publications list:
Available online

Access to staff:
Contact by letter, by telephone, by fax and via
website
Hours: Mon to Fri, 0900 to 1730

Also at:
Latin America office
Rua Helena, 170–cjs 141–142, 04552–050 Sao
Paulo/SP, Brazil; tel: +55 11 3044 1456; fax: +55 11
3044 0803
Middle East office
Dubai International Financial Centre, Office 15,
L3, B4 Gate Village Business Centre, PO Box
113355, Sheikh Zayed Road, Dubai, UAE; tel:
+971 4 401 9563; fax: +971 4 401 9990

Links with:
IBA Human Rights Institute (IBAHRI)

INTERNATIONAL BEE RESEARCH
ASSOCIATION

Acronym or abbreviation: IBRA

16 North Road, Cardiff, CF10 3DY

Tel: 029 2037 2409
Fax: 056 0113 5640
E-mail: mail@ibra.org.uk

Website:
http://www.ibra.org.uk

Enquiries:
Enquiries to: Executive Director
Direct e-mail: jonessl@ibra.org.uk

Founded:
1949

Organisation type and purpose:
International organisation, learned society,
membership association (membership is by
subscription), present number of members: 395,
registered charity (charity number 209222),
museum, consultancy, publishing house.
Library; Research Data Collection.
The world information service for bee science and
beekeeping.

Subject coverage:
Apiculture; bees (all species, but especially
honeybees); substances used by bees; plants
foraged by bees; bee products and their uses;
pollination by bees and other insects; pests and
diseases of bees; history of beekeeping; beekeeping
development programmes in the Third World.

**Museum or gallery collection, archive, or library
special collection:**
Apis Library, Morland, Manley and Essinger
Collections
Eva Crane Library (over 40,000 publications)
Historical and Contemporary Beekeeping Material
Picture Collection

Non-library collection catalogue:
All or part available in-house and in print

Library catalogue:
All or part available in-house

Printed publications:
A selected list:
Anatomy and Dissection of the Honeybee (1994)
Beeswax and Propolis for Pleasure and Profit
(1997)
Bee World Index 1919–49
Bibliography of Tropical Apiculture (1978)
British Bee Books: a Bibliography 1500–1976
Bumble Bees for Pleasure and Profit (1995)
Dictionary of Beekeeping Terms with Allied
Scientific Terms (in several vols, each
multilingual)
Garden Plants Valuable to Bees
Habitat Management for Wild Bees and Wasps
(1998)
Honey and Healing (2001)
Journal of Apicultural Research (quarterly, from
1962)
The New Varroa Handbook (2007)
The Rock Art of Honey Hunters (2001)
Varroa Fight The Mite (1996)
Form and Function in the Honey Bee (2003)
Bibliography of Commonwealth Apiculture (2005)
Making a Beeline (2003)
Eva Crane – Bee Scientist (2008)
Field Notes on Queen Rearing (2008)
Buzz Extra (newsletter/magazine, quarterly, 2003–
2005)
Bee World (quarterly journal from 1919)
Colour Guide to Pollen Loads of the Honey Bee
(2006)
Order printed publications from: IBRA Bookshop, 16
North Road, Cardiff, CF10 3DY; website: http://
www.ibra.org.uk/shop

Microform publications:
Index to Apicultural Abstracts 1950–83 (on
microfiche)

Electronic and video publications:
Available on CD:
Apicultural Abstracts, various year ranges and
topics
Journal of Apicultural Research, various themes
spanning the last 10 years
The IBRA Historical Collection – an Overview
(2005)
The IBRA Collection – Protective Clothing for
Beekeepers (2006)
The IBRA Historical Collection – Skeps and Skep-
making accessories (2007)
Beekeeping of a Bygone Era (2010)
Order electronic and video publications from: IBRA
Bookshop, 16 North Road, Cardiff, CF10 3DY;
website: http://www.ibra.org.uk/shop

Publications list:
Available online and in print

Access to staff:
Contact by letter, by telephone, by fax, by e-mail,
in person and via website. Appointment necessary.
Non-members charged.
Hours: Mon to Fri, 1000 to 1600

Access to building, collection or gallery:
Contact before visiting
Hours: Mon to Fri, 1000 to 1600

Access for disabled people:
Limited access (stairs, no lift, parking difficult), but most information offered online or by telephone

Links with:
International Union for Biological Sciences
Bat. 442, Université Paris Sud 11, 91405 Orsay Cedex, France; tel: +33 1 69 15 50 27; e-mail: secretariat@iubs.org; website: http://www.iubs.org
National Library of Wales
Aberystwyth; tel: 01970 632800; fax: 01790 615709; website: http://www.llgc.org.uk

INTERNATIONAL BIBLE STUDENTS ASSOCIATION

Watch Tower House, The Ridgeway, London, NW7 1RN

Tel: 020 8906 2211
Fax: 020 8371 0051

Website:
http://www.watchtower.org
http://www.jw-media.org

Enquiries:
Enquiries to: Public Relations Manager
Direct e-mail: opi@wtbts.org.uk

Founded:
1914

Organisation type and purpose:
International organisation, membership association (membership is by qualification), present number of members: Britain: 133,900, world-wide: 7,313,173, voluntary organisation, registered charity (charity number IBSA: 216647; Watch Tower: 1077961), publishing house.
To promote understanding of the Bible and its message. Bible based educational work.

Subject coverage:
Comprehensive Bible education (free).

Printed publications:
Awake! (monthly)
The Watchtower (semi-monthly)
See official website for other publications

Electronic and video publications:
Organized to Share the Good News – Our Whole Association of Brothers (DVD)
The Bible A Book of Fact and Prophecy (DVD)
Others available, contact for details

Publications list:
Available online and in print

Access to staff:
Contact by letter and by telephone
Hours: Mon to Fri, 0800 to 1200 and 1300 to 1700

Connections with:
Watch Tower Bible and Tract Society of Pennsylvania
25 Columbia Heights, Brooklyn, NY 11201, USA; tel: +1 718 560 5000

INTERNATIONAL BIOGRAPHICAL CENTRE

Acronym or abbreviation: IBC

Melrose Press Limited, St Thomas Place, Ely, Cambridgeshire, CB7 4GG

Tel: 01353 646600
Fax: 01353 646601
E-mail: tradesales@melrosepress.co.uk

Website:
http://www.melrosepress.co.uk
Publication schedule and title information.

Enquiries:
Enquiries to: Chief Executive

Organisation type and purpose:
Publishing house.

Subject coverage:
Publishers of biographical reference books in areas such as music, literature, medicine, the arts in general.

Printed publications:
Dictionary of International Biography (31st ed, 2004, £160)
The World Who's Who of Women (14th ed, 1997, £135)
Who's Who in Asia and the Pacific Nations (4th ed, 1999, £95)

Publications list:
Available in print

Access to staff:
Contact by letter, by telephone, by fax and by e-mail
Hours: Mon to Fri, 0900 to 1700

INTERNATIONAL BOATBUILDING TRAINING COLLEGE

Acronym or abbreviation: IBTC

Sea Lake Road, Oulton Broad, Lowestoft, Suffolk, NR32 3LQ

Tel: 01502 569663
Fax: 01502 500661
E-mail: ibtc@globalnet.co.uk

Website:
http://www.htk.co.uk/ibtc

Enquiries:
Enquiries to: Managing Director
Other contacts: Course Secretary for general.

Founded:
1974

Organisation type and purpose:
Service industry, training organisation.
Provision of practical training in boatbuilding skills.

Subject coverage:
Boatbuilding, boatyard and marine management.

Access to staff:
Contact by letter, by telephone, by fax, by e-mail and via website. Appointment necessary.
Hours: Mon to Fri, 0830 to 1630

Access for disabled people:
Parking provided, ramped entry, toilet facilities

Parent body:
Broadblue Limited
At the same address

INTERNATIONAL CAMELLIA SOCIETY

Acronym or abbreviation: ICS

UK Region, 41 Galveston Road, London, SW15 2RZ

Tel: 020 8870 6884
Fax: 020 8874 4633
E-mail: patricia_short@btconnect.com

Website:
http://www.camellia-ics.org
A variety of information, articles, etc.

Enquiries:
Enquiries to: Honorary Secretary

Founded:
1962

Organisation type and purpose:
International organisation, membership association (membership is by subscription).

Subject coverage:
History, nomenclature, cultivation, propagation, exhibition and arrangement of camellias; trial grounds (2 in England, 1 in Scotland, 1 in N Ireland).

Printed publications:
International Journal (annually, free to members)

UK Region Newsletter (2–3 times a year, free to members)

Access to staff:
Contact by letter, by telephone, by fax and by e-mail
Hours: Mon to Fri, 0900 to 1700

INTERNATIONAL CENTRE FOR BIRDS OF PREY

Acronym or abbreviation: ICBP

Great Boulsdon, Newent, Gloucestershire, GL18 1JJ

Tel: 01531 820285/821581
E-mail: jpj@icbp.org

Website:
http://www.icbp.org
All information on the centre, courses, membership.

Enquiries:
Enquiries to: Director
Direct tel: 01531 820286
Direct e-mail: info@icbp.org

Founded:
1967

Formerly called:
The Falconry Centre, The National Birds of Prey Centre

Organisation type and purpose:
Public facility, open seven days a week, ten months of the year. Suitable for ages: all, research and conservation organisation.
Conservation through education, captive breeding and research.

Subject coverage:
Information on birds of prey and owls, welfare and management, captive breeding, education on them, research projects, hunting with them.

Information services:
Courses on falconry, training birds of prey, demonstration training, PWLO training.

Special visitor services:
Three flying demonstrations daily.

Education services:
Group education facilities.

Printed publications:
Amazing Birds of Prey (Parry-Jones J, pub. Dorling Kindersley)
The Really Useful Owl Guide (Parry-Jones J, pub. TFH Kingdom)
Eye Witness Eagle (Parry-Jones J, pub. Dorling Kindersley)
Falconry-care, Captive Breeding & Conservation (Parry-Jones J, pub. David & Charles)
Training Birds of Prey (Parry-Jones J, pub. David & Charles)
Understanding Owls (Parry-Jones J, pub. David & Charles)

Electronic and video publications:
DVDs on training diurnal birds of prey for falconry, owls, captive breeding

Access to staff:
Contact by letter, by telephone and by e-mail
Hours: Open to public Feb to Nov, Mon to Sun

Access to building, collection or gallery:
Ten months of the year
Hours: 1030 to 1730
Special comments: Closed December and January.

Access for disabled people:
Parking provided, ramped entry, level entry, access to all public areas, toilet facilities

Links with:
200 international connections

INTERNATIONAL CENTRE FOR CONSERVATION EDUCATION

Acronym or abbreviation: ICCE

continued overleaf

Brocklebank House, Butts Lane, Woodmancote, Cheltenham, Gloucestershire, GL52 9QH

Tel: 01242 674839
Fax: 01242 674839
E-mail: icce@brocklebank.plus.com

Website:
http://www.icce.org.uk

Enquiries:
Enquiries to: Executive Director
Direct e-mail: enquiries@icce.org.uk

Founded:
1984

Organisation type and purpose:
International organisation, registered charity (charity number 289468), consultancy, publishing house.
Environmental education. To promote greater understanding of global environmental issues and sustainable development.

Subject coverage:
Environmental education and development of resources for all levels.

Museum or gallery collection, archive, or library special collection:
Books, games and packs
Environmental photolibrary

Printed publications:
Primary education resource material
Secondary education resource material

Microform publications:
Slide packs (to purchase)

Electronic and video publications:
CD-ROMs
Photo library/Imagebank
Videos

Publications list:
Available online and in print

Access to staff:
Contact by letter, by telephone and by e-mail
Hours: Mon to Fri, 0900 to 1700

INTERNATIONAL CENTRE FOR DISTANCE LEARNING

Acronym or abbreviation: ICDL

Open University, Library and Learning Resources Centre, Walton Hall, Milton Keynes, Buckinghamshire, MK7 6AA

Tel: 01908 659001
Fax: 01908 653571
E-mail: lib-help@open.ac.uk

Website:
http://lcdlit.open.ac.uk

Founded:
1983

Organisation type and purpose:
University department or institute.
Documentation Centre.
Documentation centre specialising in distance education across the world.

Subject coverage:
Distance education encompassing all disciplines and all education levels.

Museum or gallery collection, archive, or library special collection:
Approximately 15,000 printed items; books, journals, conference papers, research reports, dissertations and other types of literature, all relating to the theory and practice of distance education
Distance education library

Non-library collection catalogue:
All or part available online

Library catalogue:
All or part available online and in-house

Access to staff:
Contact by letter, by telephone, by fax, by e-mail, in person and via website
Hours: Helpdesk enquiries by e-mail, telephone, webchat, web form, fax, letter – Mon to Thu, 0900 to 2000; Fri, Sat, 0900 to 1700; Sun, 1200 to 1700

Access to building, collection or gallery:
Staff and students only
Hours: Mon to Thu, 0830 to 1830; Fri 0830 to 1700

Access for disabled people:
Parking provided, level entry, toilet facilities

Parent body:
Open University

INTERNATIONAL CENTRE FOR PROTECTED LANDSCAPES

Acronym or abbreviation: ICPL

8E, Cefn Llan Science Park, Aberystwyth, Ceredigion, SY23 3AH

Tel: 01970 622620
Fax: 01970 622619
E-mail: icpl@protected-landscapes.org

Website:
http://www.protected-landscapes.org

Enquiries:
Enquiries to: Executive Director

Founded:
1991

Organisation type and purpose:
Training organisation, consultancy, research organisation.
To promote the concept of integrated conservation and development especially in relation to protected areas, through professional training, higher education, research and consultancy.

Subject coverage:
Protected areas and landscapes, integrated conservation and development.

Library catalogue:
All or part available in-house

Publications list:
Available in print

Access to staff:
Contact by letter, by telephone, by fax, by e-mail and via website. Appointment necessary.
Hours: Mon to Fri, 0900 to 1700

Access to building, collection or gallery:
Prior appointment required

Access for disabled people:
Parking provided, ramped entry, access to all public areas, toilet facilities

Member of:
The World Conservation Union (IUCN)

INTERNATIONAL CENTRE FOR RESEARCH IN ACCOUNTING

Acronym or abbreviation: ICRA

The Management School, University of Lancaster, Lancaster, LA1 4YX

Tel: 01524 593632
Fax: 01524 847321
E-mail: p.pope@lancaster.ac.uk

Enquiries:
Enquiries to: Director

Founded:
1971

Organisation type and purpose:
Registered charity (charity number 501487), research organisation.

Subject coverage:
Accountancy, particularly the financial reporting practices of companies and their regulation and standard-setting processes, corporate governance, derivative products.

Printed publications:
ICRA Occasional Paper Series

Electronic and video publications:
Corporate governance and board quality databases

Access to staff:
Contact by letter, by telephone, by fax and by e-mail
Hours: Mon to Fri, 0900 to 1700

Links with:
Lancaster University

INTERNATIONAL CENTRE FOR TECHNICAL RESEARCH LIMITED

Acronym or abbreviation: ICTR

Unit 1A Crusader House, 249–289 Cricklewood Broadway, London, NW2 6NX

Tel: 020 8450 8383
Fax: 020 8452 3366
E-mail: info@reictr.com

Enquiries:
Enquiries to: Chairman
Other contacts: Director

Founded:
1981

Organisation type and purpose:
International organisation, university department or institute, consultancy.

Subject coverage:
A non-profit-making organisation aimed at the transfer of technology to third world countries via consultancy, education and conferences.

Access to staff:
Contact by letter, by fax and by e-mail
Hours: Mon to Fri, 0900 to 1700

Access for disabled people:
Ramped entry, level entry, access to all public areas

INTERNATIONAL CHAMBER OF COMMERCE (UNITED KINGDOM)

Acronym or abbreviation: ICC UK

12 Grosvenor Place, London, SW1X 7HH

Tel: 020 7838 9363
Fax: 020 7235 5447
E-mail: richardbate@iccorg.co.uk

Website:
http://www.iccbookshop.com

Enquiries:
Enquiries to: Director

Founded:
1920

Organisation type and purpose:
International organisation, membership association (membership is by subscription), present number of members: 350.

Printed publications:
A range of publications on arbitration and settlement of disputes, banking practice, commerce and transport, marketing and advertising
Reference works, reports and studies

Publications list:
Available in print

Access to staff:
Contact by letter, by telephone, by fax and by e-mail. Appointment necessary.
Hours: Mon to Fri, 0900 to 1700

INTERNATIONAL CHAMBER OF SHIPPING

Acronym or abbreviation: ICS

Carthusian Court, 12 Carthusian Street, London, EC1M 6EZ

Tel: 020 7417 8844
Fax: 020 7417 8877
E-mail: ics@marisec.org

Website:
http://www.marisec.org
ISC home page
http://www.marisec.org/pubs
Publication list

Enquiries:
Enquiries to: Secretary General

Founded:
1921

Organisation type and purpose:
International organisation, trade association, membership association, publishing house.

Subject coverage:
International shipping, safe ship operations e.g. tanker safety, helicopter and ship operations, prevention of drug trafficking.

Printed publications:
Model Ballast Management Plan (2nd ed 2000)
On Board Training Record Books
Personal Training and Service Record Books
Order printed publications from: Marisec Publications at the same address, e-mail: publications@marisec org

Publications list:
Available online and in print

Access to staff:
Contact by letter, by telephone, by fax and by e-mail
Hours: Mon to Fri, 0900 to 1700

Has consultative status with the:
International Maritime Organization
Various inter-governmental organisations

Members are the:
General Council of British Shipping
National shipowners' associations in 34 countries

INTERNATIONAL CHILDCARE TRUST

Acronym or abbreviation: ICT

Development House, 56–64 Leonard Street, London EC2A 4LT

Tel: 020 7065 0970
Fax: 020 7065 0971
E-mail: info@ict-uk.org

Website:
http://www.ict-uk.org

Enquiries:
Enquiries to: CEO

Founded:
1982

Organisation type and purpose:
International organisation, registered charity. Eradicate poverty and protect the basic rights of children and young people anywhere in the world who are in condition of need, hardship or distress, by preventing and relieving sickness and advancing their education.

Subject coverage:
The charity develops partnerships with local people and organisations according to their needs and in accordance with their culture. The Trust never funds other projects.

Electronic and video publications:
CD-ROM available

Access to staff:
Contact by letter, by telephone, by fax, by e-mail and via website

Hours: Mon to Fri, 0900 to 1700

Links with:
BOND
CSC

INTERNATIONAL CLEMATIS SOCIETY

Acronym or abbreviation: ICIS

3 Cuthberts Close, Waltham Cross, Hertfordshire, EN7 5RB

Tel: 01992 636524
E-mail: clematis@clematisinternational.com

Website:
http://www.clematisinternational.com

Enquiries:
Enquiries to: Secretary

Founded:
1984

Organisation type and purpose:
International organisation, membership association (membership is by subscription), present number of members: 275.

Subject coverage:
Clematis, cultivation and propagation.

Printed publications:
Clematis International (annually)
Newsletter (twice a year)

Access to staff:
Contact by letter, by telephone, by e-mail and via website
Hours: Mon to Fri, 0900 to 1700

INTERNATIONAL COCOA ORGANISATION

Acronym or abbreviation: ICCO

Commonwealth House, 1–19 New Oxford Street, London, WC1A 1NU

Tel: 020 7400 5050
Fax: 020 7421 5500
E-mail: info@icco.org

Website:
http://www.icco.org

Enquiries:
Enquiries to: Information Officer
Direct e-mail: library@icco.org

Founded:
1973

Organisation type and purpose:
International organisation.
Intergovernmental organisation.

Subject coverage:
Cocoa, economics, production and processing.

Trade and statistical information:
Statistics: production and consumption.

Printed publications:
Annual Report
Bulletin of Cocoa Statistics (quarterly)
ICCO World Cocoa Directory
Cocoa and Chocolate in Brazil
Cocoa Consumption in the Russian Federation
Country studies of Cocoa Production and Cocoa
  Consumption (irregular)

Publications list:
Available online and in print

Access to staff:
Contact by letter, by telephone, by fax, by e-mail and via website. Appointment necessary.
Hours: Library: 0900 to 1700 by appointment

Affiliated to:
UNCTAD

INTERNATIONAL COLLEGES OF ISLAMIC SCIENCES

Acronym or abbreviation: ICIS

Unit 1A Crusader House, 249–289 Cricklewood Broadway, London, NW2 6NX

Tel: 020 8450 8383
Fax: 020 8452 3366
E-mail: Registrar@IslamicColleges.com

Enquiries:
Enquiries to: Chairman
Other contacts: Registrar

Founded:
1990

Organisation type and purpose:
International organisation, registered charity (charity number 802651), university department or institute.
Education.

Subject coverage:
Islamic higher education.

Printed publications:
Islamic University Journal (quarterly, annual subscription £40)

Publications list:
Available in print

Access to staff:
Contact by letter, by telephone and by fax
Hours: Mon to Fri, 1000 to 1730

Parent body:
International Centre for Technical Research
  tel: 020 8450 8383; fax: 020 8452 3366

INTERNATIONAL COMMISSION ON ZOOLOGICAL NOMENCLATURE

Acronym or abbreviation: ICZN

The Natural History Museum, Cromwell Road, London, SW7 5BD

Tel: 020 7942 5653
E-mail: iczn@nhm.ac.uk

Website:
http://www.iczn.org

Enquiries:
Enquiries to: Scientific Administrator
Other contacts: Executive Secretary

Founded:
1895

Organisation type and purpose:
International organisation (membership is by election or invitation), present number of members: 28.
International Commission for the furtherance of stability and universality in the nomenclature of animals.

Subject coverage:
Zoological nomenclature, maintenance and interpretation of the International Code of Zoological Nomenclature, rulings on particular problems.

Printed publications:
Bulletin of Zoological Nomenclature (journal, quarterly)
Towards Stability in the Names of Animals (1995)
International Code of Zoological Nomenclature (4th edn, 1999)
Official lists and indexes of names and works in zoology (1987)
Official lists and indexes of names and works in zoology – Supplement 1986–2001

Access to staff:
Contact by letter and by e-mail
Hours: Mon to Fri, 0900 to 1700

Links with:
International Union of Biological Sciences

INTERNATIONAL COMMITTEE FOR THE CONSERVATION OF THE INDUSTRIAL HERITAGE

Acronym or abbreviation: TICCIH

Chygarth, 5 Beacon Terrace, Camborne, Cornwall, TR14 7BU

Tel: 01209 612142
Fax: 01209 612142
E-mail: stuartbsmith@chygarth.co.uk

Website:
http://www.mnactec.com/ticcih
http://www.ticcih.org

Enquiries:
Enquiries to: Secretary

Founded:
1978

Organisation type and purpose:
International organisation, membership association (membership is by subscription), present number of members: 500, registered charity (charity number 1079809).
To promote the preservation and interpretation of industrial sites throughout the world.

Subject coverage:
International co-operation in the preservation, conservation, investigation, documentation, research and presentation of industrial heritage, promotion of education in these matters. This includes the physical remains of the industrial past, such as landscapes, sites, structures, plant, equipment, products and other fixtures and fittings, as well as the documentation, consisting of both verbal and graphic material, and memories and opinions of the people involved.

Printed publications:
Bulletin (quarterly)

Publications list:
Available in print

Access to staff:
Contact by letter, by telephone, by fax, by e-mail and via website
Hours: Mon to Fri, 0900 to 1700

Links with:
ICOMOS
tel: +33 145 67 6770; fax: +33 145 66 0622; e-mail: secretariat@icomos.org
National representatives and correspondents in 49 countries

INTERNATIONAL COMPLIANCE ASSOCIATION

Acronym or abbreviation: ICA

Wrens Court, 52–54 Victoria Road, Sutton Coldfield, Birmingham, B72 1SX

Tel: 0121 362 7747
Fax: 0121 240 3002
E-mail: ica@int-comp.org

Website:
http://www.int-comp.org
Qualifications, ICA world-wide, membership, events, bookshop, job zone.

Organisation type and purpose:
Professional body for compliance practitioners world-wide.
To advance knowledge and learning in the field of anti-money laundering, financial crime prevention and compliance practice; to develop the skills, expertise and standing of anti-money laundering, financial crime prevention and compliance professionals worldwide; to undertake research and to make representation of a technical nature to regulatory and governmental bodies and other agencies in order to promote greater understanding of the benefits of compliance, financial crime prevention and anti-money laundering practice; to develop an effective and coherent approach to the prevention of money laundering, financial crime and the mitigation of regulatory compliance risk; to establish and maintain standards for professionals through education, training and examination programmes; to promote and enhance the ICA Code of Ethics, by encouraging business to be conducted with integrity, diligence and professionalism; to promote courses, conferences and meetings as a mechanism to discuss, exchange information and enhance understanding of international issues in the field; to provide a forum for members to develop professional and working relationships within the industry and with related professions and organisations.

Subject coverage:
Anti-money laundering, financial crime prevention and compliance practice.

Access to staff:
Contact by letter, by telephone, by fax and by e-mail

Also at:
Dubai Office
Dubai International Financial Centre, Centre of Excellence, The Gate Village, Building 2, Level 3, PO Box 506745, Dubai; tel: +971 4 4019310; e-mail: info@ictmiddleeast.com
Singapore Office
10 Shenton Way, 12–01 MAS Building, Singapore 079117; tel: +65 6500 0010; fax: +65 6327 9618; e-mail: enquiries@int-comp.org

INTERNATIONAL COUNCIL FOR SELF-ESTEEM

Acronym or abbreviation: ICSE

5 Ferry Path, Cambridge, CB4 1HB

Tel: 01223 365351
Fax: 01223 365351
E-mail: esteemhere@aol.com

Website:
http://www.murraywhite-selfesteem.co.uk

Enquiries:
Enquiries to: UK Representative

Founded:
1990

Organisation type and purpose:
International organisation, learned society, present number of countries in membership: 70.
To promote concept of self-esteem and its significance; facilitates the co-ordination of self-esteem activities throughout the world.

Subject coverage:
Self-esteem in homes, schools and organisations, behaviour issues.

Printed publications:
Details of workshops and talks: a range of photocopiable resources and CD-ROMs
Magic Circles: Self-esteem for Everyone through Circle Time (Murray White, Sage Publications, London, 2009, £25)
Raising Self-Esteem, 50 Activities (Murray White, Pearson, Cambridge, £26)
Picture This for Families (Murray White, Sage Publications, London)

Publications list:
Available online and in print

Access to staff:
Contact by letter, by telephone, by e-mail, in person and via website. Appointment necessary.
Hours: Mon to Fri, 0900 to 1700

INTERNATIONAL COUNCIL OF TANNERS

Acronym or abbreviation: ICT

Leather Trade House, Kings Park Road, Moulton Park, Northampton, NN3 6JD

Tel: 01604 679999
Fax: 01604 679998
E-mail: sec@tannerscouncil.org

Website:
http://www.tannerscouncilict.org

Enquiries:
Enquiries to: Secretary
Direct tel: 01604 679917

Founded:
1926

Organisation type and purpose:
International organisation.

Subject coverage:
Leather production and related activities.

Trade and statistical information:
Surveys of production and relevant information eg environmental regulations normally restricted to members.

Printed publications:
International Glossary of Leather Terms

Access to staff:
Contact by letter, by fax and by e-mail
Hours: Mon to Fri, 0900 to 1700

INTERNATIONAL COUNCIL ON MONUMENTS AND SITES UK

Acronym or abbreviation: ICOMOS-UK

70 Cowcross Street, London, EC1M 6EJ

Tel: 020 7566 0031
Fax: 020 7566 0045
E-mail: admin@icomos-uk.org

Website:
http://www.icomos.org/uk

Enquiries:
Enquiries to: The Secretary

Founded:
1965

Organisation type and purpose:
International organisation, advisory body, membership association (membership is by subscription), present number of members: 250, voluntary organisation, registered charity (charity number 1057254).

Subject coverage:
Preservation and management of monuments and historic sites.

Printed publications:
Publications List available on request

Publications list:
Available online and in print

Access to staff:
Contact by letter and by fax
Hours: Irregular, dependent on part-time staff

Links with:
ICOMOS International Secretariat
49–51 rue de la Fédération, 75015 Paris, France

INTERNATIONAL CRAFT AND HOBBY FAIR LIMITED

Acronym or abbreviation: ICHF Ltd

Dominic House, Seaton Road, Christchurch, Dorset, BH23 5HW

Tel: 01425 272711
Fax: 01425 279369
E-mail: info@ichf.co.uk

Website:
http://www.ichf.co.uk

Enquiries:
Enquiries to: Manager

Founded:
1976

Organisation type and purpose:
Service industry.
Exhibition Organisers.

Subject coverage:
Crafts and hobbies, design and technology, needlecraft.

Printed publications:
Lists of UK exhibitions

Access to staff:
Contact by letter, by telephone, by fax, by e-mail and via website
Hours: Mon to Fri, 0900 to 1700
Special comments: All listings, addresses and exhibiting companies are held solely for ICHF use only.

INTERNATIONAL CREMATION FEDERATION

Acronym or abbreviation: ICF

Van Stolkweg 29A, 2585 JN, The Hague, The Netherlands

Tel: +31 70 351 8836
Fax: +31 70 351 8827
E-mail: keizer@facultatieve.com

Website:
http://www.int-ciem-fed.org

Enquiries:
Enquiries to: Secretary-General

Founded:
1937

Organisation type and purpose:
International organisation, advisory body, registered charity.
The provision of a central, international, source of help, advice and information to all those interested or involved in any aspect of cremation.

Subject coverage:
All aspects of cremation.

Trade and statistical information:
International cremation statistics, cremation figures and details of cremation societies throughout the world.

Printed publications:
Pharos International (journal, quarterly, for sale)

Access to staff:
Contact by letter, by telephone, by fax and by e-mail
Hours: Mon to Fri, 0900 to 1700

INTERNATIONAL DANCE TEACHERS' ASSOCIATION

Acronym or abbreviation: IDTA

International House, 76 Bennett Road, Brighton, East Sussex, BN2 5JL

Tel: 01273 685652
Fax: 01273 674388
E-mail: info@idta.co.uk

Website:
http://www.idta.co.uk

Enquiries:
Enquiries to: General Secretary
Other contacts: Administration Officer

Founded:
1903

Organisation type and purpose:
International organisation, professional body (membership is by qualification), present number of members: 6000, service industry, suitable for ages: all.
Awarding body.

Subject coverage:
Dance (social and theatre); statistics related to dance; amateur tests in dance.

Museum or gallery collection, archive, or library special collection:
History of Dance

Printed publications:
Dance Teacher (monthly)
Dancing Year Book (£15)
Freestyle (£10)
Rock 'n' Roll (£10)
Technique of Ballroom Dancing (£16 inc. p&p)
Technique of Latin Dancing (£17 inc. p&p)
Technique of Theatre Dance (£17 including binder)
The Story of British Popular Dancing (£11 inc. p&p)
Order printed publications from: IDTA Sales Ltd – International Sales
at the same address, tel: 01273 608583

Electronic and video publications:
Ballroom Dancing (video)
Freestyle, Latin and Salsa (video, for sale)
Various Dance Music (CD-ROM)
Various Dance Videos
Various Theatre Dance Subjects (CD-ROM)
Various Theatre Dance Subjects (video)

Publications list:
Available online and in print

Access to staff:
Contact by letter, by fax, by e-mail and via website
Hours: Mon to Fri, 0900 to 1700

Access to building, collection or gallery:
No access other than to staff

Affiliated to:
British Council of Ballroom Dancing
Central Council of Physical Recreation

Member of:
Council for Dance Education and Training
Stage Dance Council International
13 Braemar Road, Fallowfield, Manchester, M14 6PQ

INTERNATIONAL FEDERATION OF ACTORS

Acronym or abbreviation: FIA

Guild House, Upper St Martin's Lane, London, WC2H 9EG

Tel: 020 7379 0900
Fax: 020 7379 8260
E-mail: office@fia-actors.com

Website:
http://www.fia-actors.com

Enquiries:
Enquiries to: General Secretary

Founded:
1952

Organisation type and purpose:
Trade union.
Representation of 100 performers' unions in 75 countries.

Subject coverage:
FIA provides four main services to member unions: representation at the various international organisations as an accredited non-governmental organisation; defence of the artistic freedom of performers; union development; information exchange.

Printed publications:
FIA Focus (2–3 times a year)

Access to staff:
Contact by letter, by telephone, by fax and by e-mail. Appointment necessary.
Hours: Mon to Fri, 0900 to 1700

INTERNATIONAL FEDERATION OF AROMATHERAPISTS

Acronym or abbreviation: IFA

7B Walpole Court, Ealing Green, Ealing, London W5 5ED

Tel: 020 8567 2243
Fax: 020 8840 9288

E-mail: office@ifaroma.org

Website:
http://www.ifaroma.org/

Enquiries:
Enquiries to: Public Relations Manager
Direct e-mail: office@ifarom.org
Other contacts: Chairperson

Founded:
1985

Organisation type and purpose:
International organisation, professional body, registered charity (charity number 327290).
Registration of courses.

Subject coverage:
Aromatherapy, aromatherapy training, registered courses.

Museum or gallery collection, archive, or library special collection:
Aromatherapy books
Lists of members and courses

Printed publications:
Aromatherapy Times (quarterly, £15 UK, £18 Europe)
Directory of Members Registered with IFA (£2.50)
Directory of Training Courses Registered with IFA (£2.50)

Access to staff:
Contact by letter, by telephone and by fax
Hours: Mon to Fri, 0900 to 1700
Special comments: Charges for some services.

Affiliated to:
ICM
Unit 15, Tavern Quay, Commercial Centre, Rope Street, London, SE16 1TX

Member of:
Aromatherapy Organisations Council
PO Box 19834, London, SE25 6LB

INTERNATIONAL FEDERATION OF BUSINESS AND PROFESSIONAL WOMEN

Acronym or abbreviation: IFBPW

PO Box 568, Horsham, West Sussex, RH13 9ZP

Tel: 01403 739343
Fax: 01403 734432
E-mail: members@bpwintl.com

Website:
http://www.bpwintl.com
Background / history, international executive and contacts, headquarters and director contact details, diary dates of future activities, membership enquiries and general information.

Enquiries:
Enquiries to: Director
Other contacts: International President

Founded:
1930

Organisation type and purpose:
International organisation, membership association (membership is by subscription), present number of members: 38,000, voluntary organisation, registered charity.
International non-governmental organisation.
Promote the status of women.

Subject coverage:
Business and professional women and all issues relating to achieving equal status for women in political, economic and civil spheres of society.

Printed publications:
Newsletter (monthly)
Biography of Founder
First part history of IFBPW plus a variety of other publications
Part II of History of BPW International (IFBPW)

Publications list:
Available in print

continued overleaf

Access to staff:
Contact by letter, by telephone, by fax, by e-mail, in person and via website. Appointment necessary.
Hours: Mon to Fri, 0900 to 1700

Subsidiary regional groups:
Africa
Asia and Pacific
Europe
Latin America and Spanish-speaking West Indies
North America and non-Spanish-speaking West Indies

INTERNATIONAL FEDERATION OF GYNAECOLOGY AND OBSTETRICS

Acronym or abbreviation: FIGO

70 Wimpole Street, London, W1G 8AX

Tel: 020 7224 3270
Fax: 020 7935 0736
E-mail: figo@figo.org

Website:
http://www.figo.org

Enquiries:
Enquiries to: Secretariat
Other contacts: Secretary General

Founded:
1954

Organisation type and purpose:
International organisation, membership association (membership is by subscription), present number of members: 103 national societies. Non-governmental organisation.

Subject coverage:
Obstetrics and gynaecology.

Printed publications:
International Journal of Gynaecology and Obstetrics (monthly, on subscription)
Newsletter (members only)
Report on Gynaecological Cancer

Publications list:
Available online

Access to staff:
Contact by letter, by telephone, by fax, by e-mail, in person and via website
Hours: Mon to Fri, 0900 to 1700

Cooperation with:
19 non-governmental organisations involved in women and children's health

Incorporated in Geneva, its title is the:
Fédération Internationale de Gynécologie et d'Obstétrique

INTERNATIONAL FEDERATION OF INSPECTION AGENCIES

Formal name: International Federation of Inspection Agencies Limited
Acronym or abbreviation: IFIA

22 Great Tower Street, London, EC3R 5HE

Tel: 020 7283 1001 / 020 7280 3200
Fax: 020 7626 4416

Enquiries:
Enquiries to: Director General
Direct e-mail: secretariat@ifia-federation.org

Founded:
1982

Organisation type and purpose:
Trade association.

INTERNATIONAL FEDERATION OF PROFESSIONAL AROMATHERAPISTS

Acronym or abbreviation: IFPA

82 Ashby Road, Hinckley, Leicestershire, LE10 1SN

Tel: 01455 637987
Fax: 01455 890956
E-mail: admin@ifparoma.org

Website:
http://www.ifparoma.org

Enquiries:
Enquiries to: Administrator
Other contacts: Membership Secretary (for membership enquiries)

Founded:
2002

Organisation type and purpose:
International organisation, professional body, membership association (membership is by subscription, qualification), present number of members: 1,959, registered charity (charity number 1091325).

Subject coverage:
Aromatherapy, qualified therapists, educational standards.

Printed publications:
In Essence (journal, quarterly)

Access to staff:
Contact by letter, by telephone, by fax, by e-mail and via website
Hours: Mon to Fri, 0900 to 1700

Access for disabled people:
Parking provided, level entry, toilet facilities

Subsidiary body:
48 accredited schools throughout the UK and overseas

INTERNATIONAL FERTILISER SOCIETY

Acronym or abbreviation: IFS

PO Box 4, York, YO32 5YS

Tel: 01904 492700
Fax: 01904 492700
E-mail: secretary@fertiliser-society.org

Website:
http://www.fertiliser-society.org

Enquiries:
Enquiries to: Secretary

Founded:
1947

Organisation type and purpose:
International organisation, learned society, professional body.

Subject coverage:
Scientific, technical, economic and environmental aspects of the production, marketing, distribution, use and application of fertilisers and crop nutrients.

Museum or gallery collection, archive, or library special collection:
Complete proceedings of the Society from 1947 (foundation) to date (approx 670)
Complete set of papers written by Dr George Cooke FRS

Library catalogue:
All or part available online

Printed publications:
Proceedings of the Society (irregular, £12.50)

Publications list:
Available online

Access to staff:
Contact by letter, by telephone, by fax, by e-mail and via website
Hours: Mon to Fri, 0900 to 1700

INTERNATIONAL FOOD INFORMATION SERVICE

Acronym or abbreviation: IFIS

Lane End House, Shinfield Road, Shinfield, Reading, Berkshire, RG2 9BB

Tel: 0118 988 3895
Fax: 0118 988 5065
E-mail: ifis@ifis.org

Website:
http://www.foodsciencecentral.com
The latest food science news; hot topics of interest to food scientists; the latest news regarding IFIS product developments; information on IFIS products and services and purchasing of IFIS books and journals.

Enquiries:
Enquiries to: Head of Marketing & Sales

Founded:
1968

Organisation type and purpose:
International organisation, service industry, registered charity (charity number 1068176), publishing house.
International co-operative organisation.
Information, products and services to the food science, food technology and human nutrition sectors.

Subject coverage:
Food science, food technology and human nutrition – all aspects, including biotechnology, food safety and toxicology, food psychology, sensory analysis, novel foods, pet foods, economics, all commodities (meat, fish, etc.), standards and patents relating to food, legislation, engineering and packaging.

Printed publications:
FoodInfo (newsletter, free)
Food Science and Technology Abstracts (FSTA) (monthly)
FSTA™ Thesaurus Eighth Edition (in print and electronic formats)
IFIS Dictionary of Food Science and Technology Second Edition
Food Science and Technology Bulletin: Functional Foods (subscription, purchase individual reviews)
FSTA in print (monthly, annual subscription)
Serial Publications Scanned for FSTA (free)

Electronic and video publications:
FSTA is available online via: FSTA Direct™, SilverPlatter, Ovid SP, the Web of Knowledge, EBSCOhost, Datastar, Dialog and STN. Other tailored services available include FSTA Custom Alerts™ and FSTA™ One time search

Access to staff:
Contact by letter, by telephone, by fax, by e-mail and via website. Appointment necessary.
Hours: Mon to Fri, 0900 to 1700

Sponsored by:
CAB International
Deutsche Landwirtschafts-Gesellschaft Germany
Institute of Food Technologists (IFT) USA

INTERNATIONAL FRIENDSHIP LEAGUE, BRITISH SECTION

Acronym or abbreviation: IFL

Head Office, 3 Creswick Road, Acton, London, W3 9HE

Website:
http://www.ifl-peacehaven.co.uk

Enquiries:
Enquiries to: Chairman

Founded:
1931

Organisation type and purpose:
Membership association (membership is by subscription), voluntary organisation.

Subject coverage:
International friendship and understanding by services of home hospitality, pen friends, entertaining and helping overseas visitors.

Printed publications:
Friendship News

Access to staff:
Contact by letter
Hours: Mon to Fri, 0900 to 1700
Special comments: By letter only, except in connection with the Guest House.

Affiliated to:
United Nations Association

Includes the:
IFL Pen Friend Service (Overseas)
   3 Creswick Road, Acton, London, W3 9HE
International Guest House
   Peace Haven, 3 Creswick Road, Acton, London, London, W3 9HE; tel: 020 8752 0055; fax: 020 8752 0066; e-mail: ifl-peacehaven@tiscali.co.uk

Parent body:
IFL Head Office
   3 Creswick Road, Acton, London, W3 9HE

INTERNATIONAL FUND FOR ANIMAL WELFARE

Acronym or abbreviation: IFAW

87–90 Albert Embankment, London, SE1 7UD

Tel: 020 7587 6700
Fax: 020 7587 6720

Website:
http://www.ifaw.org
Information on the IFAW and its work.

Enquiries:
Enquiries to: Public Relations Manager
Direct tel: 020 7587 6708
Direct fax: 020 7587 6718
Direct e-mail: lkey@ifaw.org

Founded:
1969

Organisation type and purpose:
International organisation, present number of members: 2 million worldwide.
Conservation organisation.

Subject coverage:
Animal welfare, conservation.

Museum or gallery collection, archive, or library special collection:
Picture and video library
Digital picture library

Printed publications:
Animal Update (quarterly, free)
Report: Is the fox a pest? (£5)
Report: How will a ban on hunting affect the British fox population? (£5)
Annual Report

Electronic and video publications:
Video of the IFAW's campaigning work
Digital photo library

Access to staff:
Contact by letter, by telephone, by fax, by e-mail and via website
Hours: Mon to Fri, 0900 to 1730

Access to building, collection or gallery:
Prior appointment required

Parent body:
IFAW
   International headquarters, 411 Main Street, Yarmouth Port, MA 02675, USA; tel: 00 1 508 744 2076; fax: 00 1 508 744 2079

INTERNATIONAL GLACIOLOGICAL SOCIETY

Acronym or abbreviation: IGS

Scott Polar Research Institute, Lensfield Road, Cambridge, CB2 1ER

Tel: 01223 355974
Fax: 01223 354931
E-mail: igsoc@igsoc.org

Website:
http://www.igsoc.org

Enquiries:
Enquiries to: Secretary-General
Other contacts: Assistant to Secretary-General

Founded:
1936

Organisation type and purpose:
International organisation, learned society (membership is by subscription), present number of members: 700, registered charity (charity number 231043).
To facilitate communication and information exchange between all individuals having a scientific, practical or general interest in any aspect of snow and ice.

Subject coverage:
Glaciology, cryosphere, atmospheric ice, avalanches, chemistry of ice and snow, floating ice, glacial geology, glaciers, ground ice, ice, ice and climate, ice cores, icebergs, permafrost, physics of ice and snow, sea ice, snow, Antarctica, Greenland.

Museum or gallery collection, archive, or library special collection:
Book, documents and manuscripts on various aspects of glaciology

Printed publications:
Journal of Glaciology
Annals of Glaciology
Books
Ice (news bulletin)

Publications list:
Available online and in print

Access to staff:
Contact by letter, by telephone, by fax and by e-mail. Appointment necessary.
Hours: Mon to Fri, 0830 to 1630

INTERNATIONAL GLAUCOMA ASSOCIATION

Acronym or abbreviation: IGA

Woodcote House, 15 Highpoint Business Village, Henwood, Ashford, Kent, TN24 8DH

Tel: 01233 648164
Fax: 01233 648179
E-mail: info@iga.org.uk

Website:
http://www.glaucoma-association.com

Enquiries:
Enquiries to: Head of Marketing & PR
Direct tel: 01233 648169
Direct e-mail: s.zerbib@iga.org.uk
Other contacts: CEO

Founded:
1974

Organisation type and purpose:
International organisation (membership is by subscription), present number of members: 6,000, charity registered in England and Wales (charity number 274681) and Scotland (charity number SCO41550). Seeks to raise awareness of glaucoma, to promote research related to early diagnosis and treatment, and to provide support to patients and all those who care for them.

Subject coverage:
Glaucoma, its diagnosis, treatment and research.

Information services:
Sightline (tel. 01233 648170), Mon to Fri, 0930 to 1700

Trade and statistical information:
Glaucoma prevalence information, high-risk categories and groups.

Non-library collection catalogue:
All or part available online

Printed publications:
Newsletter (for members, quarterly)
Booklets:
Glaucoma: A Guide
Glaucoma: A Greater Understanding
Glaucoma in Babies and Children
Ocular Hypertension Guide
Dry Eye Syndrome: A Guide
Numerous specialised pamphlets relating to aspects of glaucoma

Publications list:
Available online and in print

Access to staff:
Contact by letter, by telephone, by fax, by e-mail and via website. Appointment necessary.
Hours: Mon to Fri, 0930 to 1700

Access to building, collection or gallery:
Prior appointment required

Links with:
International Agency for the Prevention of Blindness

INTERNATIONAL GRAINS COUNCIL

Acronym or abbreviation: IGC

One Canada Square, Canary Wharf, London, E14 5AE

Tel: 020 7513 1122
Fax: 020 7513 0630
E-mail: igc-fac@igc.org.uk

Website:
http://www.igc.org.uk

Enquiries:
Enquiries to: Executive Director

Founded:
1949

Organisation type and purpose:
International organisation, present number of members: 26 governments including the European Community. Intergovernmental commodity organisation, administers the Grains Trade Convention of the International Grains Agreement 1995 and provides administrative services for the Food Aid Convention of the IGA.
To further international cooperation in trade in grains, to promote the expansion of grains trade, to contribute to the stability of the international grain market, and to enhance food security.

Subject coverage:
Statistics and general information on wheat and coarse grains, market developments; long-term and short-term outlook for world grain economy, grain production, use, consumption, stocks, trade and prices; review of national grain policies and their effects; grain handling and transportation, including ocean freight rates; international co-operation and wheat agreements, food aid shipments.

Trade and statistical information:
Details of international trade in wheat, wheat flour and coarse grains, excepting Intra-EC.

Non-library collection catalogue:
All or part available online

Printed publications:
Grain Market Report (11 times a year), weekly Grain Market Indicators
Report of the Council (annually)
Report on Food Aid Shipments (annually)
Wheat and coarse grains shipments (annually)
World Grain Statistics (annually) (this and all titles are for sale)

Publications list:
Available online and in print

Access to staff:
Contact by letter, by fax and by e-mail.

continued overleaf

Appointment necessary. Non-members charged.
Hours: Mon to Fri, 0900 to 1730

INTERNATIONAL GRAPHOLOGY ASSOCIATION

Acronym or abbreviation: IGA

Stonedge, Dunkerton, Bath, BA2 8AS

Tel: 01761 437809
Fax: 01761 432572
E-mail: ljw@graphology.org.uk

Website:
http://www.graphology.org.uk
Information about graphology, analyses, research, etc.

Enquiries:
Enquiries to: Director

Founded:
1983

Organisation type and purpose:
Professional body, suitable for ages: adults, consultancy, research organisation.
International professional society.
Provision of training and examination in graphology. Undertaking research.

Subject coverage:
Graphology; handwriting; analysis for personality assessment.

Museum or gallery collection, archive, or library special collection:
Handwriting samples

Printed publications:
Journal (quarterly, free to members or by subscription to non-members)
Books, monographs and combined papers on graphology including:
Personality in Handwriting
Graphologists Dictionary
Evaluation Guide

Publications list:
Available in print

Access to staff:
Contact by letter, by telephone, by fax, by e-mail, in person and via website. Appointment necessary.
Hours: Mon to Fri, 0900 to 1700

INTERNATIONAL GUILD, BUTLER ADMINISTRATORS AND PERSONAL ASSISTANTS

12 Little Bornes, Alleyn Park, Dulwich, London, SE21 8SE

Tel: 020 8670 5585
Fax: 020 8670 8424

Website:
http://www.ivorspencer.com

Enquiries:
Enquiries to: Chief Executive

Founded:
1981

Organisation type and purpose:
Professional body.

Subject coverage:
Butler administrators and personal assistants.

Access to staff:
Contact by letter, by telephone, by fax, by e-mail and via website
Hours: Mon to Fri, 0900 to 1700

INTERNATIONAL HEALTH AND BEAUTY COUNCIL

Acronym or abbreviation: IHBC

c/o VTCT, 3rd Floor, Eastleigh House, Market Street, Eastleigh, Hampshire, SO50 9FD

Tel: 023 8068 4500
Fax: 023 8065 1493
E-mail: info@vtct.org.uk

Website:
http://www.vtct.org.uk

Enquiries:
Enquiries to: Information Officer
Other contacts: Head of Quality Assurance for training centres as opposed to individual enquiries.

Founded:
1962

Organisation type and purpose:
International organisation.
Awarding body – service sector (beauty therapy).

Subject coverage:
All aspects of health and beauty, qualification and training.

Education services:
Courses are provided at more than 400 centres in the UK, mostly Colleges of Further Education.

Museum or gallery collection, archive, or library special collection:
Photographs of treatments

Printed publications:
List of centres providing training in health and beauty therapy, also available on our website

Access to staff:
Contact by letter
Hours: Mon to Fri, 0900 to 1700
Special comments: No visitors in person.

Affiliated to:
Action for Lifelong Learning Limited
tel: 01243 842064; fax: 01243 842489; e-mail: info@vtct.org.uk
Vocational Awards International Limited
tel: 01243 842064; fax: 01243 842489; e-mail: info@vtct.org.uk

Subsidiary of:
Vocational Training Charitable Trust (VTCT)
tel: 023 8068 4500; fax: 023 8065 1493; e-mail: info@vtct.org.uk

INTERNATIONAL HOSPITAL FEDERATION

Acronym or abbreviation: IHF

46–48 Grosvenor Gardens, London, SW1W 0EB

Tel: 020 7881 9222
Fax: 020 7881 9223
E-mail: 101662.1262@compuserve.com

Website:
http://www.hospitalmanagement.net

Enquiries:
Enquiries to: Director General

Organisation type and purpose:
International organisation, voluntary organisation.
Dependent non-governmental association.

Subject coverage:
Planning and management of hospitals and health services.

Printed publications:
Hospital International Newsletter (quarterly)
Hospital Management International (yearbook)
New World Health (year book)
Occasional books and papers
World Hospitals and Health Services (3 times per annum)

Access to staff:
Contact by letter, by telephone, by fax, by e-mail and via website
Hours: Mon to Fri, 0900 to 1700

Collaboration with:
Kings Fund Library

Official liaison with the:
International Council of Nurses
World Health Organization
World Medical Association

INTERNATIONAL HOUSE

Acronym or abbreviation: IH

106 Piccadilly, London, W1V 9FL

Tel: 020 7518 6900
Fax: 020 7518 6941
E-mail: info@ihlondon.co.uk

Website:
http://www.international-house.org
http://www.ihlondon.com

Enquiries:
Enquiries to: Director

Founded:
1953

Organisation type and purpose:
Professional body, training organisation.

Access to staff:
Contact by letter, by telephone, by fax, by e-mail, in person and via website. Appointment necessary.
Hours: Mon to Fri, 0900 to 1700

INTERNATIONAL IMMIGRATION ADVISORY SERVICES

65 Kingsway, Manchester, M19 2LL

Tel: 0161 224 1973
Fax: 0161 224 4449
E-mail: intias@hotmail.com

Enquiries:
Enquiries to: Principal
Direct tel: 07785 541375

Founded:
1991

Organisation type and purpose:
Consultancy.

Subject coverage:
International immigration, nationality and law.

Access to staff:
Contact by letter, by telephone, by fax and by e-mail. Appointment necessary. All charged.
Hours: Mon to Fri, 0900 to 1730; Sat, 1030 to 1400

Access to building, collection or gallery:
No prior appointment required

Access for disabled people:
Level entry, toilet facilities

INTERNATIONAL INSTITUTE FOR CONSERVATION OF HISTORIC AND ARTISTIC WORKS

Acronym or abbreviation: IIC

6 Buckingham Street, London, WC2N 6BA

Tel: 020 7839 5975
Fax: 020 7976 1564
E-mail: iic@iiconservation.org

Website:
http://www.iiconservation.org
Membership, publications, congress.

Enquiries:
Enquiries to: Executive Secretary

Founded:
1950

Organisation type and purpose:
International organisation, membership association, registered charity (charity number 209677).

Subject coverage:
Conservation of heritage.

Printed publications:
Archaeological Conservation and its Consequences (Preprints of the IIC Copenhagen Congress 1996, members £20, non-members £40)
Case Studies in the Conservation of Stone and Wall Paintings (Preprints of the IIC Bologna Congress 1986, members £20, non-members £40)

Conservation of Far Eastern Art (Preprints of the IIC Kyoto Congress 1988, members £20, non-members £40)

Conservation of the Iberian and Latin American Cultural Heritage (Preprints of the IIC Madrid Congress 1992, members £20, non-members £40)

Painting Techniques: History, Materials and Studio Practice (Contributions to the IIC Dublin Congress 1998, members £25, non-members £40)

Preventive Conservation: Practice, Theory & Research (Preprints of the IIC Ottawa Congress 1992, members £20, non-members £40)

Tradition and Innovation: Advances in Conservation (Contributions to the IIC Melbourne Congress 2000, members £25, non-members £40)

Works of Art on Paper, Books, Documents and Photographs: Techniques and Conservation (Contributions to the IIC Baltimore Congress 2002, members £25, non-members £40)

Modern Art: New Museums (Contributions to the IIC Bilbao Congress 2004, members £25, non-members £40)

The Object in Context: Crossing Conservation Boundaries (Contributions to the IIC Munich Congress 2006, members £25, non-members £40)

Conservation and Access (Contributions to the IIC London Congress 2008, members £25, non-members £40)

News in Conservation (prices and availability on application)

Reviews in Conservation (prices and availability on application)

Studies in Conservation (prices and availability on application)

Publications list:
Available online and in print

Access to staff:
Contact by letter, by telephone, by fax, by e-mail and via website. Access for members only.

INTERNATIONAL INSTITUTE FOR ENVIRONMENT AND DEVELOPMENT

Acronym or abbreviation: IIED

3 Endsleigh Street, London, WC1H 0DD

Tel: 020 7388 2117
Fax: 020 7388 2826
E-mail: iied@iied.org

Website:
http://www.iied.org
General information, publication list, participation database.

Enquiries:
Enquiries to: Information Officer
Direct e-mail: info@iied.org

Founded:
1971

Organisation type and purpose:
Registered charity (charity number 800066), research organisation.
Promotion of sustainable patterns of world development.

Subject coverage:
Natural resources, human settlements, governance, climate change, sustainable markets.

Non-library collection catalogue:
All or part available online

Printed publications:
Annual Report
Drylands – Haramata (quarterly newsletter in English and French)
Environment and Urbanisation (journal, twice a year)
Environmental Economics – Discussion Paper Series
Participatory Learning and Action Notes
List of publications available on website

Electronic and video publications:
For details of DVDs and CD-ROMs see website:
http://www.iied.org

Publications list:
Available online and in print

Access to staff:
Contact by letter, by telephone, by fax and by e-mail
Hours: Mon to Fri, 0900 to 1700

Also at:
International Institute for Environment and Development
4 Hanover Street, Edinburgh, EH2 2EN; tel: 0131 624 7040

INTERNATIONAL INSTITUTE FOR STRATEGIC STUDIES

Acronym or abbreviation: IISS

13–15 Arundel Street, London, WC2R 3DX

Tel: 020 7379 7676
Fax: 020 7836 3108
E-mail: iiss@iiss.org

Website:
http://www.iiss.org

Enquiries:
Enquiries to: Librarian
Direct tel: 020 7395 9122
Direct e-mail: library@iiss.org

Founded:
1958

Organisation type and purpose:
International organisation, membership association (membership is by subscription), research organisation.

Subject coverage:
Nuclear issues; arms control, agreements, negotiations and possibilities; regional security issues (worldwide); armed forces of the world; current conflict situations; non-military aspects of national security (economic, demography, scarce resources, environment, etc.).

Information services:
Library

Museum or gallery collection, archive, or library special collection:
Subject files from 1958

Trade and statistical information:
Data on holdings of weapons (by system) for all countries of the world.

Non-library collection catalogue:
All or part available online and in-house

Library catalogue:
All or part available online and in-house

Printed publications:
Adelphi Papers (Monograph Series, approximately 8 a year)
Strategic Survey – Annual retrospective of the year's political and military trends (annually)
Survival (6 a year, subscription student rate)
The Military Balance – Inventory of the world's armed forces (annually)
Order printed publications from: Journals Customer Services, Taylor and Francis, Cheriton House, North Way, Andover, Hampshire, SP10 5BE; tel: 020 7017 5544; fax: 020 7017 4760; e-mail: journals.orders@tandf.co.uk or book.orders@routledge.co.uk

Electronic and video publications:
Russian Regional Perspectives online
Strategic Comments (10)

Publications list:
Available online and in print

Access to staff:
Contact by letter, by telephone, by fax, by e-mail, in person and via website. Non-members charged.

Access to building, collection or gallery:
No prior appointment required
Hours: Institute: Mon to Fri, 0900 to 1800
Library: Mon to Fri, 1000 to 1700

INTERNATIONAL INSTITUTE OF COMMUNICATIONS

Acronym or abbreviation: IIC

Regent House, 24–25 Nutford Place, London W1H 5YN

Tel: 020 7723 7210
Fax: 020 7723 6982
E-mail: enquiries@iicom.org

Website:
http://www.iicom.org

Enquiries:
Enquiries to: Projects Executive

Founded:
1968

Organisation type and purpose:
Membership association.
Global forum for communications.

Subject coverage:
Communications; copyright; all aspects of telecommunication; all aspects of broadcasting, radio, television, multimedia; satellite communications; development in its political, social, cultural, economic spheres; regulatory side of above topics/subjects.

Museum or gallery collection, archive, or library special collection:
Regulatory and legislative materials, e.g. acts, statutes, bills, etc. on broadcasting and telecommunications, principally in Europe but increasingly outside Europe

Trade and statistical information:
Telecom voice traffic flows, television flows.

Printed publications:
Intermedia (journal, 5 times a year, £175 p.a.)

Publications list:
Available in print

Access to staff:
Contact by letter, by telephone, by fax and by e-mail. Appointment necessary.
Hours: Mon to Fri, 0930 to 1730

INTERNATIONAL INSTITUTE OF HEALTH AND HOLISTIC THERAPIES

Acronym or abbreviation: IIHHT

VTCT, 3rd Floor, Eastleigh House, Upper Market Street, Eastleigh, Hampshire, SO50 9FD

Tel: 023 8068 4500
Fax: 023 8065 1493
E-mail: info@vtct.org.uk

Website:
http://www.vtct.org.uk

Enquiries:
Enquiries to: Information Officer
Direct e-mail: recordsoffice@vtct.org.uk
Other contacts: Head of Quality Assurance for training centres as opposed to individual enquiries.

Founded:
1962

Organisation type and purpose:
International organisation. International education organisation. Provides qualifications in holistic, health, fitness and complementary therapies.

Subject coverage:
Body massage, aromatherapy, reflexology.

Education services:
Courses are provided at Centres across the UK, primarily in Colleges of Further Education.

continued overleaf

Printed publications:
List of centres providing courses for qualifications in the above fields (free) also available on our website

Access to staff:
Contact by letter
Hours: Mon to Fri, 0900 to 1700
Special comments: No visitors in person.

Affiliated to:
Action for Lifelong Learning Limited
  tel: 01243 842064; fax: 01243 842489; e-mail: info@vtct.org.uk
Vocational Awards International Limited
  tel: 01243 842064; fax: 01243 842489; e-mail: info@vtct.org.uk

Subsidiary of:
Vocational Training Charitable Trust (VTCT)
  tel: 023 8668 4500; fax: 023 8064 1493; e-mail: info@vtct.org.uk

INTERNATIONAL INSTITUTE OF RISK AND SAFETY MANAGEMENT

Acronym or abbreviation: IIRSM

70 Chancellors Road, London, W6 9RS

Tel: 020 8600 5536/7/8/9
Fax: 020 8741 1349
E-mail: enquiries@iirsm.org

Website:
http://www.iirsm.org

Enquiries:
Enquiries to: Organising Secretary

Founded:
1975

Organisation type and purpose:
International organisation, professional body (membership is by qualification), registered charity (charity number 269326).
The institute's main objective is to advance public education in accident prevention and occupational health in industry.

Subject coverage:
General safety; safety management; principles of risk management; international organisations.

Printed publications:
Health & Safety Managers Newsletter: Includes listing of professional vacancies (11 times a year, free to members)
IIRSM Update (as and when required)
Safety Management Magazine of British Safety Council (11 times a year)
Safety Management, by Tony Corfield, IIRSM/ISM (1988)

Access to staff:
Contact by letter, by telephone, by fax, by e-mail and via website. Access for members only.
Hours: Mon to Fri, 0900 to 1700

Affiliated to:
British Safety Council
  tel: 020 8741 1231; fax: 020 8741 4555

INTERNATIONAL INSTITUTE OF SPORTS THERAPY

Acronym or abbreviation: IIST

VTCT, 3rd Floor, Eastleigh House, Upper Market Street, Eastleigh, Hampshire, SO50 9FD

Tel: 023 8068 4500
Fax: 023 8065 1493
E-mail: info@vtct.org.uk

Website:
http://www.vtct.org.uk

Enquiries:
Enquiries to: Information Officer
Direct e-mail: recordsoffice@vtct.org.uk
Other contacts: Head of Quality Assurance for training centres as opposed to individual enquiries.

Founded:
1962

Organisation type and purpose:
International organisation.
Provision of qualifications in fitness and sport therapies.

Subject coverage:
All aspects of health, fitness and sports therapy and especially centres providing training in these subjects. Largest Awarding Body in this sector, courses are provided across the UK, primarily in Colleges of Further Education.

Museum or gallery collection, archive, or library special collection:
Photographs of treatments

Printed publications:
List of approved centres providing above qualification in the above fields (free) also on the website

Access to staff:
Contact by letter
Hours: Mon to Fri, 0900 to 1700
Special comments: No visitors in person.

Affiliated to:
Action for Lifelong Learning Limited
  tel: 01243 842064; fax: 01243 842489; e-mail: info@vtct.org.uk
Vocational Awards International Limited
  tel: 01243 842064; fax: 01243 842489; e-mail: info@vtct.org.uk

Susidiary of:
Vocational Training Charitable Trust (VTCT)
  tel: 023 8068 4500; fax: 023 8065 1493; e-mail: info@vtct.org.uk

INTERNATIONAL INTELLIGENCE ON CULTURE

Acronym or abbreviation: IIC

4 Baden Place, Crosby Row, London, SE1 1YW

Tel: 020 7403 6454
Fax: 020 7403 2009

Enquiries:
Enquiries to: Information Officer
Direct tel: 020 7403 7001

Founded:
1994

Organisation type and purpose:
Independent company specialising in cultural policy analysis and intelligence; consultancy; research; project management; training; and advisory and information services with an international cultural dimension.
To provide a comprehensive range of services and respond to the needs of the international cultural sector.

Subject coverage:
Policy intelligence, consultancy, research, project management, training, information and advice services for the international cultural sector.

Printed publications:
Arts Networking Europe
On the Road – the start up guide to touring the arts in Europe (1995)
To Travel, Hopefully! A guide to travel grant opportunities (rev 1998)
Order printed publications from: Library and Publications, Arts Council of England
4 Great Peter Street, London, SW1P 3NQ, tel: 020 7973 6931, fax: 020 7973 6590, e-mail: enquiries@artscouncil.org.uk

Publications list:
Available in print

Access to staff:
Contact by letter, by telephone, by fax and by e-mail
Hours: Mon to Fri, 0930 to 1730; please call to check opening times of enquiry service, which are subject to change

Special comments: Offices are not open for drop-in services.

Funded by:
Irish Arts Council

Links with:
Arts Council of Scotland
Arts Council of Wales
British Film Institute
Crafts Council
Cultural Information and Research Centres Liaison in Europe (CIRCLE)
Museum and Galleries Commission

INTERNATIONAL INTERFAITH CENTRE

Acronym or abbreviation: IIC

17 Courtiers Green, Clifton Hampden, Abingdon, Oxon, OX14 3EN

E-mail: iic@interfaith-centre.org

Website:
http://www.interfaith-centre.org
Information about the IIC and other relevant interfaith contacts and resources.

Founded:
1993

Organisation type and purpose:
International organisation, registered charity, consultancy, research organisation.
To facilitate interreligious encounter and dialogue.

Subject coverage:
Religion, interreligious issues, interfaith issues, projects, conferences, contacts and research, courses, videos.

Museum or gallery collection, archive, or library special collection:
Interfaith and religious journals from around the world

Printed publications:
IIC newsletter
Directory of Faith Communities in Oxford
Order printed publications from: Main address

Electronic and video publications:
Faith and Interfaith DVD, interviews with various people from different faiths, countries, cultures
Order electronic and video publications from: e-mail: iic@interfaith-centre.org

Publications list:
Available online

Access to staff:
Contact by letter, by e-mail and via website

INTERNATIONAL LABOUR ORGANISATION

Acronym or abbreviation: ILO

International Labour Office, Millbank Tower, 21–24 Millbank, London, SW1P 4QP

Tel: 020 7828 6401
Fax: 020 7233 5925
E-mail: london@ilo.org

Website:
http://www.ilo.org/london

Enquiries:
Enquiries to: Manager, Publications/Information Unit
Direct e-mail: brett@ilo.org

Founded:
1919

Organisation type and purpose:
International organisation.
The UN specialised agency concerned with work and employment issues.

Subject coverage:
International labour standards; labour statistics; management; workers' education; women and work; industrial relations; migrant labour; labour administration; employment and conditions of work; labour legislation; human rights; freedom of association; training, retraining and rehabilitation; safety and health.

Museum or gallery collection, archive, or library special collection:
All ILO publications and documents since its establishment in 1919

Printed publications:
CIS Abstracts (8 times a year, on safety and health)
ILO Catalogue of Safety Publications
Projects currently in progress (continuously)

Publications list:
Available online and in print

Access to staff:
Contact by letter, by telephone, by fax and by e-mail. Appointment necessary.
Hours: Mon to Fri, 1000 to 1300 and 1400 to 1630

Head Office:
International Labour Office
Geneva 22, CH 211, Switzerland; tel: + 41 22 799 6111; fax: + 41 22 799 8577; e-mail: communication@ilo.org; website: http://www.ilo.org

Works with:
International Centre for Occupational Safety and Health (CIS)

INTERNATIONAL LANGUAGE (IDO) SOCIETY OF GREAT BRITAIN

Acronym or abbreviation: ILSGB

24 Nunn Street, Leek, Staffordshire, ST13 8EA

Tel: 01538 381491

Website:
http://www.users.aol.com/idolinguo

Enquiries:
Enquiries to: Honorary Secretary

Founded:
1913

Organisation type and purpose:
Membership association.

Subject coverage:
The international language IDO.

Printed publications:
Various books in and about the language

Publications list:
Available in print

Access to staff:
Contact by letter and by telephone
Hours: Mon to Fri, 0900 to 1700

Affiliated to:
International Uniono por la Lingo Internaciona at the same address

INTERNATIONAL LASER CLASS ASSOCIATION

PO Box 26, Falmouth, Cornwall, TR11 3TN

Tel: 01326 315064
Fax: 01326 318968
E-mail: office@laserinternational.org

Website:
http://www.laserinternational.org

Enquiries:
Enquiries to: Executive Secretary

Organisation type and purpose:
International organisation.

Subject coverage:
Sailing laser class boats.

Access to staff:
Contact by e-mail and via website
Hours: Mon to Fri, 0900 to 1730

INTERNATIONAL LAW ASSOCIATION

Acronym or abbreviation: ILA

Charles Clore House, 17 Russell Square, London, WC1B 5DR

Tel: 020 7323 2978
Fax: 020 7323 3580
E-mail: info@ila-hq.org

Website:
http://www.ila-hq.org
Full homepage: history, activities, branches, committees, newsletters, etc.

Enquiries:
Enquiries to: Secretary

Founded:
1873

Organisation type and purpose:
International organisation, learned society (membership is by subscription, election or invitation), registered charity (charity number 249637).

Subject coverage:
Space law, international monetary law, maritime neutrality, international human rights law and practice, water resources law, coastal state jurisdiction over marine pollution, international commercial arbitration, legal aspects of sustainable development, refugee procedures, legal aspects of inter-country adoption and protection of the family, the formation of customary international law, international securities regulation, cultural heritage law, international law in national courts, regional economic development law, arms control and disarmament law, feminism and international law, extradition and human rights, international civil and commercial litigation, international trade law, Islamic law and international law, internally displaced persons, aspects of the law of state succession, diplomatic protection of persons and property, accountability of international organisations.

Publications list:
Available in print

Access to staff:
Contact by letter, by telephone, by fax and by e-mail. Appointment necessary.
Hours: Mon to Thu, 0900 to 1700

Has:
50 branches world-wide

INTERNATIONAL LEAD AND ZINC STUDY GROUP

Acronym or abbreviation: ILZSG

2 King Street, London, SW1Y 6QL

Tel: 020 7484 3300
Fax: 020 7930 4635
E-mail: root@ilzsg.org

Website:
http://www.ilzsg.org

Enquiries:
Enquiries to: Information Officer

Founded:
1959

Organisation type and purpose:
International organisation, research organisation.

Subject coverage:
Lead and zinc.

Trade and statistical information:
International trade and world situation in lead and zinc, including movements of stocks and prices.

Printed publications:
Lead and Zinc Statistics – Monthly Bulletin
Lead and Zinc New Mine and Smelter Projects
Various reports and conference proceedings including:
Principal Uses of Lead and Zinc
Recycling Lead and Zinc into the 21st Century (2 vols, July 1995)
World Directory: Lead and Zinc Mines and Primary Metallurgical Works (5th ed, July 1994)
World Directory: Primary and Secondary Lead Plants (1997)
World Directory: Primary and Secondary Zinc Plants (1997)

Publications list:
Available in print

Access to staff:
Contact by letter and via website
Hours: Mon to Fri, 0900 to 1700

Founded in 1959 by the:
United Nations

INTERNATIONAL LEAD ASSOCIATION

Acronym or abbreviation: ILA

17A Welbeck Way, London, W1G 9YJ

Tel: 020 7499 8422
Fax: 020 7493 1555
E-mail: enq@ila-lead.org

Website:
http://www.ila-lead.org

Enquiries:
Enquiries to: Director

Founded:
1946

Organisation type and purpose:
Trade association.

Subject coverage:
Building, batteries, coatings, environment, health and safety, extraction, refining and production, noise insulation, economics and statistics.

Non-library collection catalogue:
All or part available online

Library catalogue:
All or part available online

Printed publications:
Technical leaflets, brochures, books

Electronic and video publications:
Videos

Publications list:
Available online

Access to staff:
Contact by letter, by telephone, by fax, by e-mail and via website. Appointment necessary.
Hours: Mon to Fri, 0930 to 1715

INTERNATIONAL MARINE CONTRACTORS ASSOCIATION

Acronym or abbreviation: IMCA

52 Grosvenor Gardens, London, SW1W 0AU

Tel: 020 7824 5520
Fax: 020 7824 5521
E-mail: imca@imca-int.com

Website:
http://www.imca-int.com

Enquiries:
Enquiries to: Chief Executive

Founded:
1995

Organisation type and purpose:
International organisation, trade association (membership is by subscription), present number of members: 530, service industry.

continued overleaf

Subject coverage:
Offshore, marine and underwater engineering companies.

Printed publications:
Wide variety of publications (prices vary):
AODC documents
Complete collection of all AODC, IMCA (excluding Marine Division) and DMAC Guidance Notes and Codes of Practice
Diving Medical Advisory Committee (DMAC) documents
DPVOA and IMCA Marine Division documents
IMCA Diving Division documents
IMCA ROV Division documents
Log books
Pocket safety cards and safety posters
Careers material
Order printed publications from: via website

Electronic and video publications:
Various CDs and DVDs

Publications list:
Available online and in print

Access to staff:
Contact by letter, by telephone, by fax, by e-mail, in person and via website. Appointment necessary.
Hours: Mon to Fri, 0900 to 1700

Access to building, collection or gallery:
No prior appointment required

INTERNATIONAL MARITIME ORGANIZATION

Acronym or abbreviation: IMO

4 Albert Embankment, London, SE1 7SR

Tel: 020 7735 7611
Fax: 020 7587 3210
E-mail: info@imo.org

Website:
http://www.imo.org

Enquiries:
Enquiries to: Head, Public Information Services
Direct tel: 020 7587 3153

Founded:
1959

Organisation type and purpose:
International organisation.
To promote safety and security at sea and to prevent pollution of the sea from ships.

Subject coverage:
Prevention of marine pollution, safety at sea, security, IMO conventions, technical co-operation.

Museum or gallery collection, archive, or library special collection:
Maritime Knowledge Centre: houses a complete collection of IMO publications, IMO meetings documents in English, French and Spanish (some reports in Russian, Chinese and Arabic)
UN documents related to the maritime world

Trade and statistical information:
Casualty statistics, marine pollution, maritime transport, safety of life at sea.

Non-library collection catalogue:
All or part available online

Library catalogue:
All or part available online

Printed publications:
IMO Library Acquisitions List (quarterly)
IMO Library Current Awareness Bulletin (fortnightly)
IMO News (quarterly)
International Shipping and World Trade – Facts and Figures
Available free to bona fide organisations
Order printed publications from: Publishing Services

Electronic and video publications:
International Maritime Dangerous Goods Code (IMDG Code; CD-ROM and diskettes, for sale)

IMO VEGA database (for identification of applicable IMO requirements, CD-ROM, for sale)
See Catalogue, video on IMO
Order electronic and video publications from: Publishing Services

Publications list:
Available online and in print

Access to staff:
Contact by letter, by telephone, by fax, by e-mail and via website. Appointment necessary.
Hours: Mon to Fri, 0900 to 1700
Special comments: Closed for Christmas.

Access to building, collection or gallery:
Prior appointment required

Access for disabled people:
Toilet facilities

Parent body:
United Nations

INTERNATIONAL MOHAIR ASSOCIATION

Acronym or abbreviation: IMA

10–12 The Grove, Ilkley, West Yorkshire, LS29 9EG

Tel: 01943 817149
Fax: 01943 817150
E-mail: info@int-mohair.com

Website:
http://www.int-mohair.com
Members lists, care and properties of mohair, the angora goat, sales information, promotional items, links, forum, what's new, contact.

Enquiries:
Enquiries to: Manager

Founded:
1974

Organisation type and purpose:
Trade association.
To promote, advance and protect the interests of its members and their manufactured mohair products.

Subject coverage:
Mohair.

Printed publications:
Mohair – A Review of Its Properties, Processing and Applications (Dr Lawrence Hunter, programme manager at the CSIR, Port Elizabeth, South Africa, £50 plus p&p)

Access to staff:
Contact by letter, by telephone, by fax, by e-mail and via website. Appointment necessary.
Hours: Mon to Thu, 0930 to 1230

INTERNATIONAL NETWORK FOR THE AVAILABILITY OF SCIENTIFIC PUBLICATIONS

Acronym or abbreviation: INASP

58 St. Aldates, Oxford, OX1 1ST

Tel: 01865 249909
Fax: 01865 251060
E-mail: inasp@inasp.info

Website:
http://www.inasp.info
Newsletters, leaflets, programme information. Full text electronic publishing, reader and other reference markers and guidebooks.

Enquiries:
Enquiries to: Director

Founded:
1992

Organisation type and purpose:
International organisation.
Charity.

INASP is a programme of the International Council for Science (ICSU). It aims to improve worldwide access to information.

Subject coverage:
Information about research publication and access, information about library and book development in developing and transitional countries.

Printed publications:
Newsletter (3 times a year)

Electronic and video publications:
Newsletter (3 times a year)
Directories
Monographs

Publications list:
Available online

Access to staff:
Contact by letter, by telephone, by fax, by e-mail and via website. Appointment necessary.
Hours: Mon to Fri, 0900 to 1700

INTERNATIONAL OIL POLLUTION COMPENSATION FUNDS

Acronym or abbreviation: IOPC Funds

Portland House, Bressenden Place, London, SW1E 5PN

Tel: 020 7592 7100
Fax: 020 7592 7111
E-mail: info@iopcfund.org

Website:
http://www.iopcfund.org

Enquiries:
Enquiries to: Information Officer

Founded:
1978

Organisation type and purpose:
International organisation.
The International Oil Pollution Compensation Funds are two intergovernmental organisations which provide compensation for oil pollution damage resulting from spills of persistent oil from tankers.

Subject coverage:
Oil pollution compensation.

Publications list:
Available online

Access to staff:
Contact by letter, by telephone, by fax, by e-mail and via website. Appointment necessary.
Hours: Mon to Fri, 0900 to 1730

Access to building, collection or gallery:
Prior appointment required

Access for disabled people:
Access to all public areas

INTERNATIONAL ORDER OF KABBALISTS

Acronym or abbreviation: IOK

6 Oakwood, 62 King Charles Road, Surbiton, Surrey, KT5 8QR

Fax: 020 8390 5604
E-mail: iokoffice@yahoo.com

Website:
http://www.internationalorderofkabbalists.com

Enquiries:
Enquiries to: Secretary

Founded:
1969

Organisation type and purpose:
Membership association (membership is by subscription).

Subject coverage:
The Kabbalah, related occult and esoteric subjects.

Printed publications:
Aromatics in Ritual and Therapeutics (J. Sturzaker)
Gemstones and their Occult Powers (J. Sturzaker)
Kabbalistic Aphorisms (J. Sturzaker)
Meaning, Dangers and Purpose of Ritual (M.
Defries)
The Twelve Rays (J. Sturzaker)
Colour and Kabbalah (J. Sturzaker and D. L.
Sturzaker)
A Practical Guide to Symbolism (J. Sturzaker)
Booklets and study papers

Publications list:
Available online and in print

Access to staff:
Contact by letter, by fax, by e-mail and via
website
Hours: Mon to Fri, 0900 to 1700

INTERNATIONAL OTTER SURVIVAL FUND

Acronym or abbreviation: IOSF

7 Black Park, Broadford, Isle of Skye, IU49 9DE

Tel: 01471 822487
Fax: 01471 822487
E-mail: iosf@otter.org

Website:
http://www.otter.org
Wildlife charity helping the 13 species of otters
worldwide.

Enquiries:
Enquiries to: Director
Direct e-mail: grace@otter.org

Founded:
1993

Organisation type and purpose:
Registered charity (charity number SC003875).
Wildlife conservation.

Subject coverage:
Otter ecology and conservation, wildlife, wild
animal care and treatment.

Education services:
School trips and talks.

Non-library collection catalogue:
All or part available in print

Library catalogue:
All or part available online and in print

Printed publications:
Otter News
Otters in Britain
Otter Journal, 2007
Otter Road Mortalities

Electronic and video publications:
Videos for sale

Publications list:
Available online and in print

Access to staff:
Contact by letter, by telephone, by fax, by e-mail
and via website. Appointment necessary.
Hours: Mon to Fri, 0900 to 1700

Access to building, collection or gallery:
Prior appointment required

Access for disabled people:
Parking provided

INTERNATIONAL PEN

9–10 Charterhouse Buildings, Goswell Road,
London, EC1M 7AT

Tel: 020 7253 4308
Fax: 020 7253 5711
E-mail: intpen@dircon.co.uk

Website:
http://www.oneworld.org/internatpen

Enquiries:
Enquiries to: Administrative Secretary

Direct e-mail: frank.geary@internationalpen.org.uk
Other contacts: Administrative Assistant for
subscriptions, general information.

Founded:
1921

Organisation type and purpose:
International organisation, professional body,
voluntary organisation, registered charity (charity
number 1010627).
Non-governmental organisation.
PEN originally stood for Poets, Essayists,
Novelists, but now membership is open to all
writers.

Subject coverage:
Literature as common currency between nations;
freedom of expression and free press; origins and
history of International PEN; positions of banned,
imprisoned or otherwise mistreated writers.

Printed publications:
Pen International (magazine, 2 times a year, £8 or
$13 a year)

Access to staff:
Contact by letter, by telephone, by fax and by e-
mail
Hours: Mon to Fri, 1030 to 1800

Access to building, collection or gallery:
No access other than to staff

In consultative relation with:
UNESCO

Other addresses:
132 centres in 95 countries throughout the world
including:
English Centre
   152–156 Kentish Town Road, London, NW1
   9QB; tel: 020 7267 9444
International PEN
International PEN
International PEN
Scottish Centre
   c/o Greenleaf Editorial, 126 West Princess Street,
   Glasgow, G4 9DB
Welsh Centre
   80 Plymouth Road, Gwynneth Street, Penarth,
   CF64 5DL

INTERNATIONAL PESTICIDE APPLICATION RESEARCH CENTRE

Acronym or abbreviation: IPARC

Imperial College at Silwood Park, Sunninghill,
Ascot, Berkshire, SL5 7PY

Tel: 020 7594 2234
Fax: 020 7594 2450
E-mail: g.matthews@imperial.ac.uk

Website:
http://www.bio.ic.ac.uk/staff/gamat/matthews.htm

Enquiries:
Enquiries to: Information Officer

Founded:
1955

Formerly called:
Overseas Spraying Machinery Centre

Organisation type and purpose:
University department or institute, consultancy,
research organisation.

Subject coverage:
Pest management, particularly equipment needed
for effective and safe application of pesticides. This
includes vector control as well as agriculture.

**Museum or gallery collection, archive, or library
special collection:**
Pesticide application equipment with emphasis on
   that which is manually carried or operated

Access to staff:
Contact by e-mail

INTERNATIONAL PHONETIC ASSOCIATION

Acronym or abbreviation: IPA

Centre for Language & Communication Studies,
Arts Building, Trinity College, Dublin, Dublin 2,
Republic of Ireland

Tel: 00 353 1 608 1348
Fax: 00 353 1 677 2694
E-mail: anichsid@tcd.ie

Website:
http://www.arts.gla.ac.uk/IPA/ipa.html

Enquiries:
Enquiries to: Treasurer

Founded:
1886

Organisation type and purpose:
International organisation, learned society
(membership is by subscription), present number
of members: 900.

Subject coverage:
Phonetics and phonology; the International
Phonetic Alphabet.

Printed publications:
Available to purchase, direct

Access to staff:
Contact by letter, by telephone, by fax, by e-mail
and via website
Hours: Mon to Fri, 0900 to 1700

INTERNATIONAL POWERED ACCESS FEDERATION LIMITED

Acronym or abbreviation: IPAF

Bridge End Business Park, Milnthorpe, LA7 7RH

Tel: 015395 62444
Fax: 015395 64686
E-mail: info@ipaf.org

Website:
http://www.ipaf.org
Services available from IPAF, industry news,
details of IPAF approved training scheme and
location of training centres.

Enquiries:
Enquiries to: Managing Director

Founded:
1983

Organisation type and purpose:
International organisation, trade association
(membership is by subscription), training
organisation.
To represent the interests of the mobile elevating
work platform industry on an international basis.

Subject coverage:
Powered access equipment.

**Museum or gallery collection, archive, or library
special collection:**
British, EC, US, Canadian Standards for powered
   access equipment (on mobile elevated) work
   platforms

Printed publications:
IPAF Guide to Mast Climbing Work Platforms
Mobile Elevating Work Platform Operators Safety
   Guide

Access to staff:
Contact by letter, by telephone, by fax, by e-mail
and via website. Appointment necessary. Non-
members charged.
Hours: Mon to Fri, 0900 to 1700

INTERNATIONAL PRIMATE PROTECTION LEAGUE (UK)

Acronym or abbreviation: IPPL

166 Gilmore Road, London, SE13 5AE

Tel: 020 8297 2129

continued overleaf

Fax: 020 8297 2099
E-mail: enquiries@ippl-uk.org

Website:
http://www.ippl-uk.org

Enquiries:
Enquiries to: Conservation and Welfare Officer

Founded:
1976

Subject coverage:
Protection of primates.

Printed publications:
Monkey Tales (newsletter, 3 times a year)

Access to staff:
Contact by letter, by telephone, by e-mail and via
website. Appointment necessary. Letter of
introduction required.
Hours: Mon to Fri, 0900 to 1700

Access to building, collection or gallery:
Prior appointment required

INTERNATIONAL PSYCHOANALYTICAL ASSOCIATION

Acronym or abbreviation: IPA

Broomhills, Woodside Lane, London, N12 8UD

Tel: 020 8446 8324
Fax: 020 8445 4729
E-mail: ipa@ipa.org.uk

Website:
http://www.ipa.org.uk

Enquiries:
Enquiries to: Membership Secretary

Founded:
1908

Organisation type and purpose:
Professional body, membership association
(membership is by subscription), present number
of members: 12,000.

Subject coverage:
Psychoanalysis.

Printed publications:
4 series:
Contemporary Freud
Controversies in Psychoanalytic Ideas and
　Applications
International Psychoanalysis Library
Psychoanalysis
Order printed publications from: Karnac Books

Publications list:
Available online

Access to staff:
Contact by e-mail
Hours: Mon to Fri, 0900 to 1700

INTERNATIONAL RECORDS MANAGEMENT TRUST

Acronym or abbreviation: IRMT

Suite 14/15, 88–90 Hatton Garden, London EC1N
8PN

Tel: 020 7831 4101
Fax: 020 7831 6303
E-mail: info@irmt.org

Website:
http://www.irmt.org
Overview of the work of the IRMT; access to free
downloads of educational material and assessment
tools.

Founded:
1989

Organisation type and purpose:
To develop new strategies for managing public
sector records, through consultancy, education and
research.
Registered charity (charity number 3477376).

Subject coverage:
Records management, archives, education,
consultancy.

Access to staff:
Contact by letter, by telephone, by fax and by e-
mail
Hours: 1000 to 1730

INTERNATIONAL SAFETY COUNCIL

21 Tilton Road, Borough Green, Sevenoaks, Kent,
TN15 8RS

Tel: 01732 886581
E-mail: smitht@nsc.org

Website:
http://www.nsc.org
Safety information; environmental health.

Enquiries:
Enquiries to: Executive Director

Founded:
1913

Organisation type and purpose:
International organisation.
Non-profitmaking public service organisation
holding consulting status with the United Nations.

Subject coverage:
Health and Safety: occupational, home and
community, public, transportation.

Trade and statistical information:
Worldwide accident statistics.

Non-library collection catalogue:
All or part available online

Library catalogue:
All or part available online and in print

Printed publications:
A variety of subject areas is covered by the large
selection of published material, and includes:
Accident Prevention, Security Management,
Incident Investigation, Safety & Health
Management, Environmental Management,
Industrial Hygiene, Ergonomics, Fleet Safety
Management, Aviation Ground Safety, Defensive
Driving, Attitudinal Dynamics, First Aid, CPR,
AED and Oxygen Administration, Baby and
Child CPR, Best Practice Case Studies in Health
and Safety.

Publications list:
Available online and in print

Access to staff:
Contact by letter, by telephone, by e-mail and via
website
Hours: Mon to Fri, 0900 to 1700

Also at:
International Safety Council
　1121 Spring Lake Drive, Itasca, Illinois, USA; tel:
　00 1 630 285 1121; fax: 00 1 630 285 1613; e-mail:
　smitht@nsc.org; website: http:.//www.nsc.org

Parent body:
National Safety Council (USA)
　1121 Spring Lake Drive, Itasca, Illinois, USA; tel:
　00 1 708 285 1121; fax: 00 1 708 285 1613

INTERNATIONAL SCHOOL OF LONDON

Acronym or abbreviation: ISL

139 Gunnersbury Avenue, London, W3 8LG

Tel: 020 8992 5823
Fax: 020 8993 7012
E-mail: mail@islondon.com

Website:
http://www.islondon.com

Enquiries:
Enquiries to: Development Officer

Founded:
1972

Organisation type and purpose:
Education

Subject coverage:
Primary and secondary education; international
baccalaureate; ESL, intensive English; home
languages taught.

Access to staff:
Contact by letter, by telephone, by fax, by e-mail
and via website
Hours: Mon to Fri, 0800 to 1800

Access to building, collection or gallery:
Prior appointment required
Hours: Mon to Fri, 0800 to 1700

INTERNATIONAL SEISMOLOGICAL CENTRE

Acronym or abbreviation: ISC

Pipers Lane, Thatcham, Newbury, Berkshire, RG19
4NS

Tel: 01635 861022
Fax: 01635 872351
E-mail: admin@isc.ac.uk

Website:
http://www.isc.ac.uk

Enquiries:
Enquiries to: Director
Other contacts: Administration Officer for
publication sales.

Founded:
1964

Organisation type and purpose:
International organisation, consultancy, research
organisation.
Collection, collation, analysis and publication of
world earthquake data.

Subject coverage:
Seismology; world earthquakes.

**Museum or gallery collection, archive, or library
special collection:**
Complete sets of seismological journals and other
historical published matter

Printed publications:
Bibliography of Seismology (2 times a year, now
　discontinued)
Bulletin of ISC (monthly, 2 years in arrears of
　event)
Felt and Damaging Earthquakes, 1976–90
　(annually, now discontinued)
Information brochure
Regional Catalogues of Earthquakes (2 times a
　year, 2 years in arrears)

Electronic and video publications:
The following Bulletins of ISC, are on CD-ROM for
　purchase
Bulletin of ISC 1964 to 1977
Bulletin of ISC 1978 to 1985
Bulletin of ISC 1986 to 1991
Bulletin of ISC 1992 to 1993
Bulletin of ISC 1994 to 1995
Bulletin of ISC 1996
Bulletin of ISC 1997
Bulletin of ISC 1998
Bulletin of ISC 1999

Access to staff:
Contact by e-mail
Hours: Mon to Fri, 0900 to 1700

Links with:
UNESCO
　Paris, France
WMO
　Geneva

INTERNATIONAL SHAKESPEARE ASSOCIATION

Acronym or abbreviation: ISA

Shakespeare Centre, Henley Street, Stratford-upon-
Avon, Warwickshire, CV37 6QW

Tel: 01789 201840
Fax: 01789 294911
E-mail: isa@shakespeare.org.uk

Website:
http://www.shakespeare.org.uk
Under 'Education'.

Enquiries:
Enquiries to: Executive Secretary

Founded:
1974

Organisation type and purpose:
International organisation, learned society
(membership is by subscription), present number
of members: 600.

Subject coverage:
Shakespearean research, publication, translation
and performance, initiation and planning of
international Shakespeare congresses.

**Museum or gallery collection, archive, or library
special collection:**
Archive of the International Shakespeare
Association and books donated to it are
deposited in the Shakespeare Centre Library at
the same address

Printed publications:
Newsletter (annual)
Occasional papers
Proceedings of the ISA Congresses (every 5 years)

Publications list:
Available in print

Access to staff:
Contact by letter, by telephone, by fax and by e-
mail
Hours: Mon to Fri, 0900 to 1700

INTERNATIONAL SHEEP DOG SOCIETY, THE

Acronym or abbreviation: ISDS

Clifton House, 4a Goldington Road, Bedford,
MK40 3NF

Tel: 01234 352672
Fax: 01234 348214
E-mail: office@isds.org.uk

Website:
http://www.isds.org.uk
Information about the Society, general information
and articles about sheepdog trialling and Border
Collies, and details of UK trials and results.

Enquiries:
Enquiries to: Chief Executive

Founded:
1906

Organisation type and purpose:
Membership association (membership is by
subscription), present number of members: 5000,
registered charity (charity number 209009).
To maintain a breed register (Stud Book) for
working sheepdogs as represented by the Border
Collie, organise the major UK National and World
Sheepdog trials, and provide a range of member
services.

Subject coverage:
Sheepdog trialling in the UK.

**Museum or gallery collection, archive, or library
special collection:**
Breed records for ISDS registered dogs

Printed publications:
Stud Books from 1985 (for purchase)
Newsletters (issued to members)
Introductory material available to enquirers

Access to staff:
Contact by letter, by telephone, by fax and by e-
mail. Access for members only.
Hours: Mon to Fri, 0900 to 1700

Access to building, collection or gallery:
No access other than to staff

INTERNATIONAL SOCIETY FOR SOIL MECHANICS AND GEOTECHNICAL ENGINEERING

Acronym or abbreviation: ISSMGE

City University London, Northampton Square,
London, EC1V 0HB

Tel: 020 7040 8154
Fax: 020 7040 8832
E-mail: secretariat@issmge.org

Website:
http://www.issmge.org

Enquiries:
Enquiries to: Secretary General

Organisation type and purpose:
International organisation, professional body.

Subject coverage:
Soil mechanics, foundation engineering,
geotechnical engineering, environmental
geotechnics.

Printed publications:
Conference Proceedings
Lexicon
Report on Penetration Testing
Report on Pile Testing

Access to staff:
Contact by e-mail and via website

INTERNATIONAL SOCIETY FOR TRENCHLESS TECHNOLOGY

Acronym or abbreviation: ISTT

15 Belgrave Square, London, SW1X 8PS

Tel: 020 850 9119
Fax: 020 850 7447
E-mail: info@istt.com

Website:
http://www.istt.com
Inter-active site giving full details of the Society's
activities.

Enquiries:
Enquiries to: Executive Secretary
Other contacts: Membership Secretary for
alternative contact.

Founded:
1986

Organisation type and purpose:
International 'not for profit' professional
organisation, membership is by subscription,
present number of members: 3500, registered
charity (charity number 295274).
ISTT aims to promote and increase the use of
trenchless technology worldwide. Trenchless
technology is for the installation and maintenance
of underground utility services with minimum
surface excavation. Trenchless technology has been
accepted by the United Nations Environment
Programme
(UNEP) as an Environmentally Sound Technology
for supporting its sustainability initiatives

Subject coverage:
Information on the various types of trenchless
technology for the installation, renovation and
repair of pipeline systems under ground in order
to minimise excavation and environmental
damage.

Trade and statistical information:
World data on the use of trenchless technology and
advice on the latest techniques.

Library catalogue:
All or part available online

Printed publications:
Trenchless Technology Research (once every 4
months, pub Elsevier Oxford)
Trenchless Technology International (bi-monthly,
Benjamin Media, USA)

Electronic and video publications:
Trenchless Technology Database (CD-ROM,
purchase, direct)

Publications list:
Available online

Access to staff:
Contact by letter, by fax, by e-mail, in person and
via website
Hours: Mon to Fri, 0900 to 1700

Access to building, collection or gallery:
Belgrave Square is the registered address only. The
staff are home based using the internet. For contact
use Fax or Email

INTERNATIONAL STAR REGISTRY

Acronym or abbreviation: ISR

23–28 Penn Street, London, N1 5DL

Tel: 020 7684 4444
Fax: 020 7684 4443
E-mail: orion@starregistry.co.uk

Website:
http://www.international-star-registry.org
Information on how to name a star.

Enquiries:
Enquiries to: Public Relations Manager

Founded:
1991

Organisation type and purpose:
International organisation, service industry.
Name-a-star service. Naming a star in the heavens
as a gift idea.

Subject coverage:
Astronomy, naming stars in the heavens.

**Museum or gallery collection, archive, or library
special collection:**
Your Place in the Cosmos, volumes I to V
Register of International Star Registry star names
worldwide, 1979–1999

Printed publications:
Package of commemorative documents issued
when a star is named
Information packs (free)

Access to staff:
Contact by letter, by telephone, by fax, by e-mail
and via website
Hours: Mon to Fri, 0900 to 1700

Access to building, collection or gallery:
Prior appointment required

Has:
16 offices worldwide

INTERNATIONAL STEEL TRADE ASSOCIATION

Acronym or abbreviation: ISTA

Broadway House, Tothill Street, Westminster,
London, SW1H 9NQ

Tel: 020 7799 2662
Fax: 020 7799 2468
E-mail: hbailey@steeltrade.co.uk

Website:
http://www.steeltrade.co.uk

Enquiries:
Enquiries to: Director

Founded:
1969

Organisation type and purpose:
Trade association.

Subject coverage:
International iron and steel trade.

Access to staff:
Access for members only.
Hours: Mon to Fri, 0930 to 1730

INTERNATIONAL STUDENTS HOUSE

Acronym or abbreviation: ISH

1 Park Crescent, London, W1B 1SH

Tel: 020 7631 8300
Fax: 020 7631 8307
E-mail: info@ish.org.uk

Website:
http://www.ish.org.uk

Founded:
1965

Organisation type and purpose:
To provide housing and social facilities for overseas students.

Subject coverage:
Welfare advice service for overseas students.

Printed publications:
The International Students A-Z Guide to London
The International Students A-Z Guide to Great Britain

Access to staff:
Contact by letter, by telephone, by fax, by e-mail and via website. Appointment necessary.
Hours: 24-hour access

Access for disabled people:
Parking provided, level entry, toilet facilities

INTERNATIONAL SUGAR ORGANIZATION

Acronym or abbreviation: ISO

1 Canada Square, Canary Wharf, Docklands, London, E14 5AA

Tel: 020 7513 1144
Fax: 020 7513 1146
E-mail: exdir@isosugar.org

Website:
http://www.isosugar.org
Details of publications.

Enquiries:
Enquiries to: Executive Director
Direct e-mail: info@isosugar.org

Founded:
1937

Organisation type and purpose:
International organisation.

Subject coverage:
Statistics on production, consumption, exports and imports of sugar in all countries of the world.

Printed publications:
MECAS Series, including:
MECAS (07)18 Outlook for the White Sugar Premium after the EU Sugar Reform
MECAS (07)17 Government Biofuels Policy and Sugar Crops: Outlook to 2015
MECAS (07)16 Import Dynamics and World Sugar Prices
Proceedings of Previous ISO seminars and workshops
Full list at: http://www.isosugar.org/ publications.htm
Order printed publications from: Publications division, tel: 020 7715 9436; e-mail: publications@isosugar.org; or via website

Electronic and video publications:
CD: 2007: International Conference – Egypt – Proceedings (£175)
CD: 2005: International Conference – Egypt – Proceedings (£150)

Publications list:
Available online and in print

Access to staff:
Contact by letter, by telephone, by fax and by e-mail
Hours: Mon to Fri, 0930 to 1730

Access to building, collection or gallery:
Prior appointment required

The agreement (ISA) is under the auspices of:
UNCTAD
Geneva

INTERNATIONAL SUPPORT VESSEL OWNERS ASSOCIATION

Acronym or abbreviation: ISOA

12 Carthusian Street, London, EC1M 6EZ

Tel: 020 7417 8844
Fax: 020 7417 8877
E-mail: isoa@marisec.org

Enquiries:
Enquiries to: Assistant Secretary

Founded:
1985

Organisation type and purpose:
Shipping association.
Common forum for discussion of issues specific to the offshore industry, in particular international support vessel owners.

Access to staff:
Contact by letter, by telephone, by fax and by e-mail
Hours: Mon to Fri, 0900 to 1700

INTERNATIONAL SWAMINARAYAN SATSANG ORGANISATION

Acronym or abbreviation: ISSO

ISSO Central Office, 72 Colmer Road, Streatham, London, SW16 5JS

Tel: 020 8830 0771
Fax: 020 8830 0804
E-mail: info@swaminarayan.info

Website:
http://www.isso-europe.org
The Swaminarayan Sampraday explained with details of branches.

Enquiries:
Enquiries to: General Secretary

Founded:
1990

Organisation type and purpose:
International organisation, learned society, registered charity.
Religious Hindu organisation specialising in the Swaminarayan Faith/Sect.

Subject coverage:
Information from authentic sources on the Swaminarayan Sect of Hinduism.

Museum or gallery collection, archive, or library special collection:
References available through published and unpublished documents on the way of life in Gujarat, India about 200 years ago

Printed publications:
Large choice of publications in English, Gujarati, Hindi
Order printed publications from: International Swaminarayan Satsang Organisation
e-mail: central@issa.org.uk

Electronic and video publications:
Exploring Shikshapatri – Understanding God's word via a multimedia CD-ROM
Inauguration of Temples – The Vedic Way (video, for purchase)
Swaminarayan Nagar – The Swaminarayan Way (video, for purchase)

Access to staff:
Contact by letter, by fax and by e-mail.
Appointment necessary.
Hours: Mon to Fri, 0900 to 1700

Associate temple:
Swaminarayan Temples
37 Forradsgatan, Mariestad, S-54235, Sweden; tel: 00 46 501 12473; e-mail: sweden@isso.org.uk

Parent body:
Shree Swaminarayan Temple
Kalupur Ahmedabad, Gujarat, 380 001, India; tel: 00 91 79 213 6818; fax: 00 91 79 745 2145; e-mail: info@swaminarayan.info

Swaminarayan Temples in:
Leicester
139–141 Loughborough Road, Leicester, LE4 5LQ; tel: 0116 2666 210; fax: 0116 2666 210; e-mail: leicester@isso.org.uk
London
72 Colmer Road, London, SW16 5SZ; tel: 020 8679 8050; e-mail: streatham@isso.org.uk

INTERNATIONAL TABLE TENNIS FEDERATION

Acronym or abbreviation: ITTF

Chemin de la Roche 11, Renens/Lausanne, 1020, Switzerland

Tel: 00 41 21 340 70 90
Fax: 00 41 21 340 70 99
E-mail: ittf@ittf.com

Website:
http://www.ittf.com
Competition results, ranking lists, approved equipment list, rules, archives, museum, press releases.

Enquiries:
Enquiries to: Executive Director

Founded:
1926

Organisation type and purpose:
International organisation.
Governing body of the sport.

Subject coverage:
Table tennis.

Printed publications:
ITTF Directory
ITTF Handbook
ITTF Handbook for Match Officials
ITTF Rules Booklet
Table Tennis Illustrated (6 times a year)
ITTF News

Publications list:
Available online and in print

Access to staff:
Contact by letter, by telephone, by fax, by e-mail and via website. Appointment necessary.
Hours: Mon to Fri, 0900 to 1700

Access to building, collection or gallery:
Prior appointment required

Access for disabled people:
Access to all public areas

Other offices:
ITTF
1125 Colonel by Drive, Ontario, K1S 5RI, Canada; tel: 00 1 613 7332468; fax: 00 1 613 7334603; e-mail: ittf@ittf.com
Marketing Division & President's Office,

INTERNATIONAL TANKER OWNERS POLLUTION FEDERATION LIMITED

Acronym or abbreviation: ITOPF

1 Oliver's Yard, 55 City Road, London, EC1Y 1HQ

Tel: 020 7566 6999
Fax: 020 7566 6950
E-mail: central@itopf.com

Website:
http://www.itopf.com

Information about ITOPF's history, staffing, technical services and publications, plus general information on tanker spills (including statistics), clean-up techniques, compensation arrangements, etc.

Enquiries:
Enquiries to: Information Officer
Direct e-mail: deborahansell@itopf.com

Founded:
1968

Organisation type and purpose:
International organisation, membership association.
ITOPF offers a broad range of technical and information services in the field of spill response, damage assessment, claims analysis and contingency planning to its shipowner members and associates, their pollution insurers and other groups worldwide.

Subject coverage:
Regulations and insurance aspects of oil and chemical spills from ships; organisation and contingency planning for spill clean-up; clean-up equipment and techniques; environmental effects of marine pollution; environmental planning.

Museum or gallery collection, archive, or library special collection:
Trade literature covering all types of spill clean-up equipment
Books, journal articles, conference papers on oil pollution from tankers and related topics

Library catalogue:
All or part available in-house

Printed publications:
Annual Review
Handbook
Ocean Orbit – annual newsletter (free)
Response to Marine Oil Spills (also available in French, Spanish, Japanese and Korean) 1987
Technical Information Papers (12 titles)

Publications list:
Available in print

Access to staff:
Contact by letter, by telephone, by fax, by e-mail and via website. Appointment necessary.
Hours: Mon to Fri, 0900 to 1700

INTERNATIONAL TEA COMMITTEE LIMITED

Acronym or abbreviation: ITC

1 Carlton House Terrace, London, SW1Y 5DB

Tel: 020 7839 5090
E-mail: info@inttea.com

Website:
http://www.inttea.com/

Enquiries:
Enquiries to: Executive Assistant
Direct e-mail: rumi.ali@inteacom.globalnet.co.uk

Organisation type and purpose:
Membership association.
Statistical secretariat for tea throughout the world.

Subject coverage:
Tea statistics for producing, consuming countries; acreage; world auction prices; imports, exports, consumption, supply and absorption.

Trade and statistical information:
Statistics for tea going back over 60 years.

Printed publications:
Annual Bulletin of Statistics
Monthly Statistical Summary
World Tea Statistics 1910–1990

Access to staff:
Contact by letter, by telephone, by fax, by e-mail and via website
Hours: Mon to Fri, 0830 to 1630

INTERNATIONAL THEATRE INSTITUTE LIMITED

Acronym or abbreviation: ITI

ITI @ Goldsmiths College, University of London, Lewisham Way, New Cross, London, SE14 6NW

Tel: 020 7919 7276
Fax: 020 7919 7277
E-mail: iti@gold.ac.uk

Website:
http://iti.gold.ac.uk

Enquiries:
Enquiries to: Administrator

Founded:
1948

Organisation type and purpose:
International organisation, membership association (membership is by subscription), registered charity (charity number 295092). Non-governmental organisation under the auspices of UNESCO. To facilitate networking and exchange of information, produce events and play an active role in promoting cultural exchange.

Subject coverage:
Theatre, dance and music theatre. Facilitates international contacts, research and networking in the performing arts. (Members may also approach any of the 95 centres worldwide.)

Museum or gallery collection, archive, or library special collection:
Archive containing performing arts books, journals, directories, scripts, reviews and funding information from around the world

Printed publications:
Transcripts of seminars and conferences
Information bulletin (quarterly, free to members)
International Theatre Institute books and directories

Publications list:
Available in print

Access to staff:
Contact by letter, by telephone, by fax and by e-mail. Appointment necessary. Access for members only.
Hours: Mon to Fri, 0930 to 1730
Special comments: Open 2 days per week.

Access to building, collection or gallery:
No prior appointment required

Has:
95 national centres around the world

Secretariat of the:
ITI
Paris

Works in liaison with:
AICT (critics)
AITA (amateur theatre)
ASSITEJ (young people's theatre)
FIA (actors federation)
FIRT (arts research)
OISTAT (scenographers and technicians)
SIBMAS (libraries and museums)
UNIMA (puppeteers)

INTERNATIONAL THERAPY EXAMINATION COUNCIL

Acronym or abbreviation: ITEC

4 Heathfield Terrace, London, W4 4JE

Tel: 020 8994 4141
Fax: 020 8994 7880
E-mail: info@itecworld.co.uk

Website:
http://www.itecworld.co.uk
Range of pages on qualifications; colleges registered; how to get information; books and teaching materials.

Enquiries:
Enquiries to: Director

Founded:
1973

Organisation type and purpose:
International awarding body for therapy qualifications.
Provides a syllabus and examinations for professional vocational qualifications in beauty, complementary and sports therapies.

Subject coverage:
ITEC provide an independent examination system for the beauty, therapy, health, sport and leisure industries, and complementary therapies.

Printed publications:
ITEC News Bulletin
ITEC Registration Pack
ITEC Syllabus

Publications list:
Available online and in print

Access to staff:
Contact by letter, by telephone, by fax and by e-mail. Appointment necessary.
Hours: Mon to Fri, 0900 to 1700

Parent body:
ITEC Professionals
at the same address; tel: 020 8994 7856; fax: 020 8994 7880; e-mail: professionals@itecworld.co.uk

INTERNATIONAL TRANSPORT WORKERS' FEDERATION

Acronym or abbreviation: ITF

49–60 Borough Road, London, SE1 1DR

Tel: 020 7403 2733
Fax: 020 7357 7871
E-mail: mail@itf.org.uk

Website:
http://www.itfglobal.org

Enquiries:
Enquiries to: General Secretary
Direct tel: 020 7940 9257
Direct fax: 020 7407 0319
Direct e-mail: hawke_jenny@itf.org.uk

Founded:
1896

Organisation type and purpose:
Trade union.
International trade union federation.
Provides a wide range of support and advice for its affiliated unions.

Subject coverage:
Transport industry and trade unionism.

Museum or gallery collection, archive, or library special collection:
19th and 20th century trade union history (held by Warwick University)

Library catalogue:
All or part available in-house

Printed publications:
About the ITF (leaflet, 2001, available in many languages)
Globalising Solidarity Manual (2002)
Women Transporting the World (2002)
Human Rights are Workers' Rights (2002)
Transport International (quarterly, from mid 2000)
Various other current subject publications which include: Education, Women, Seafarers/Fisheries, Agreements, Ports, Railways/Road and Urban Transport, Civil Aviation

Electronic and video publications:
Some of the following videos are available in other languages:
A Seafarer's Tale (video, 2000)
Flags for Sale (video, 1998)
Global Mariner (video, 2000)
The Voyage of the Global Mariner (4 videos, 2000/ 2001)
Life at Sea (CD-ROM, 1999)

continued overleaf

Publications list:
Available in print

Access to staff:
Contact by letter and by e-mail. Appointment necessary.
Hours: Mon to Fri, 0900 to 1700

Access to building, collection or gallery:
Prior appointment required

Access for disabled people:
Ramped entry

INTERNATIONAL TREE FOUNDATION

Acronym or abbreviation: ITF

Sandy Lane, Crawley Down, Crawley, West Sussex, RH10 4HS

Tel: 01342 717300
Fax: 01342 718282
E-mail: info@internationaltreefoundation.org

Website:
http://www.internationaltreefoundation.org

Enquiries:
Enquiries to: Information Officer

Founded:
1924

Organisation type and purpose:
Membership and supporter association (membership is by subscription), present number of members: 3000, registered charity (charity number 1106269).
To protect and plant trees worldwide.

Subject coverage:
Tree planting, tree care, tree protection, in UK and overseas.

Printed publications:
Trees (journal, annually)

Electronic and video publications:
eBulletins (bi-monthly)

Access to staff:
Contact by letter, by telephone, by fax, by e-mail and via website
Hours: Mon to Fri, 0900 to 1630

Access to building, collection or gallery:
No access other than to staff

INTERNATIONAL UNDERWRITING ASSOCIATION

Formal name: International Underwriting Association of London
Acronym or abbreviation: IUA

London Underwriting Centre, 3 Minster Court, Mincing Lane, London, EC3R 7DD

Tel: 020 7617 4444
Fax: 020 7617 4440
E-mail: info@iua.co.uk

Website:
http://www.lirma.co.uk
General background and Association news.
http://www.iua.co.uk
An interactive website including information about the IUA London Market, membership, current projects, press updates, events, contact details and downloadable publications.

Enquiries:
Enquiries to: Chief Executive
Direct tel: 020 7617 4446
Direct e-mail: michelle.bolton@iua.co.uk
Other contacts: Press & PR Manager for general enquiries.

Founded:
1998

Organisation type and purpose:
Trade association.

For ordinary members, central accounting and processing of insurance and reinsurance contracts, also central settlement of claims. Representation and research provision.

Subject coverage:
International insurance, reinsurance; reinsurance statistics; earthquake studies, bodily injury awards trends, regulation, claims, marine insurance and reinsurance, aviation, eRisks and industry clauses.

Museum or gallery collection, archive, or library special collection:
Master copy of all publications and information relevant to members held

Trade and statistical information:
Reports of information meetings and seminars, annual membership statistics, earthquakes hazard atlas, reports of forum meetings, marine statistics, eLondon company market statistics, UK Bodily Injury Studies.

Printed publications:
Annual Report and Accounts
EMU – What it means to the London Market
Earthquake studies (irregular)
IUA Digest (for members only)
IUMI Marine & Casualty Statistics
Information bulletins (hardcopies and on disk)
Reinsurance Statistics
Summary of Indirect Taxation on Insurance
   Contracts in Europe
Risk Today
The London Insurance Market
UK Bodily Injury Awards Study 1 & 2
The Rating of Pro-rata Treaties
World @ Risk
Weather Studies
Order printed publications from: Publications Distribution Manager, IUA
3 Minster Court, Mincing Lane, London, EC3R 7DD, tel: 020 7617 5443, fax: 020 7617 9440, e-mail: anthony.dickinson@iua.co.uk

Electronic and video publications:
Competition Act (CD-ROM)
eRisk – The New Frontier (CD-ROM)
FSA's Impact on Senior Management (CD-ROM)
Reinsurance Clauses (CD-ROM)

Publications list:
Available in print

Access to staff:
Contact by letter, by telephone, by fax, by e-mail and via website
Hours: Mon to Fri, 0900 to 1700

Access to building, collection or gallery:
Prior appointment required

Access for disabled people:
Ramped entry, access to all public areas, toilet facilities

INTERNATIONAL VISUAL COMMUNICATION ASSOCIATION

Acronym or abbreviation: IVCA

19 Pepper Street, Glengall Bridge, Docklands, London, E14 9RP

Tel: 020 7512 0571
Fax: 020 7512 0591
E-mail: info@ivca.org

Website:
http://www.ivca.org

Enquiries:
Enquiries to: Information Officer
Direct e-mail: davecomley@ivca.org

Founded:
1988/89

Organisation type and purpose:
International organisation, advisory body, trade association.
Provides collective voice for the business communication industry, and products and services to benefit membership.

Subject coverage:
Business communications, industry and products, film and video.

Trade and statistical information:
Data on the UK business communications industry.

Printed publications:
A Guide to Copyright
Commissioning a Programme
IVCA Business Media Handbook
IVCA Update (newsletter, monthly)
The Case Study Booklet

Publications list:
Available online

Access to staff:
Contact by letter, by telephone, by e-mail and via website
Hours: Mon to Fri, 0930 to 1730

Access to building, collection or gallery:
Prior appointment required

Parent body:
Independent Television Association Limited (ITVA)

INTERNATIONAL VOLUNTARY SERVICE

Acronym or abbreviation: IVS GB

Thorn House, 5 Rose Street, Edinburgh, EH2 2PR

Tel: 0131 243 2745
Fax: 0131 243 2747
E-mail: info@ivsgb.org

Website:
http://www.ivsgb.org

Enquiries:
Enquiries to: Administrator

Founded:
1931

Organisation type and purpose:
International organisation (British branch), voluntary organisation, registered charity.

Subject coverage:
Opportunities for short-term and long-term voluntary work throughout Britain and the world.

Printed publications:
Annual Listing
International Voluntary Service
Short-term projects
Long-term projects

Publications list:
Available online

Access to staff:
Contact by letter, by telephone, by fax, by e-mail, in person and via website
Hours: Mon to Fri, 0900 to 1700

Parent body:
Service Civil International (SCI)
   A worldwide movement

INTERNATIONAL VOLUNTARY SERVICE (NORTH)

Acronym or abbreviation: IVS

Castlehill House, 21 Otley Road, Leeds, West Yorkshire, LS6 3AA

Tel: 0113 230 4600
Fax: 0113 230 4610
E-mail: info@ivsgb.org

Website:
http://www.ivsgbn.demon.co.uk

Enquiries:
Enquiries to: Regional Co-ordinator
Direct e-mail: info@ivsgb.org
Other contacts: National Fundraiser

Founded:
1931

Organisation type and purpose:
International organisation, national organisation, voluntary organisation, registered charity (charity number 275424).
To promote peace, justice and international understanding through voluntary work.

Subject coverage:
Information on over 700 international work camps, on opportunities for short and medium term volunteering for British volunteers in Europe, North America, CIS, North Africa, Japan and Australia.

Printed publications:
Information Leaflets
Interactions (newsletter, quarterly)
Workcamp Listing (annually, published April)

Access to staff:
Contact by letter and by e-mail
Hours: Mon to Fri, 0900 to 1700

Other addresses:
IVS – Scotland
7 Upper Bow, Edinburgh, EH1 2JN; tel: 0131 226 6722; fax: 0131 226 6723; e-mail: ivsgbscot@ivsgbscot.demon.co.uk
IVS – South
Old Hall, East Bergholt, Colchester, CO7 6TQ; tel: 01206 298215; fax: 01206 299043; e-mail: ivsgbsouth@ivsgbsouth.demon.co.uk

Parent body:
Service Civil International (SCI)

INTERNATIONAL WATER ASSOCIATION

Acronym or abbreviation: IWA

12 Alliance House, Caxton Street, London, SW1H 0QS

Tel: 020 7654 5500
Fax: 020 7654 5555
E-mail: water@iwahq.org

Website:
http://www.iwahq.org
Membership, events, key programmes, publications and specialist technical groups.

Enquiries:
Enquiries to: Executive Director

Founded:
1965

Organisation type and purpose:
International organisation, professional body, membership association (membership is by subscription), registered charity (charity number 1076690).
Global reference point and network for water professionals.

Subject coverage:
Wastewater treatment processes, water reuse, impact of pollutants on water bodies; water suppliers nationally and worldwide.

Non-library collection catalogue:
All or part available online

Printed publications:
Reference Books
European Commission Research Reports
Scientific and Technical Reports
Water21 (magazine, 6 times a year)
Water Research (journal, 20 times a year, original research papers)
Water Science and Technology (journal, 24 times a year, original research papers)
Water Science and Technology: Water Supply (journal, 6 times a year)
Journal of Hydroinformatics (journal, 4 times a year)
Journal of Water and Health (journal, 4 times a year)
Journal of Water and Climate Change (journal, 4 times a year)
Journal of Water Supply: Research and Technology-AQUA (journal, 8 times a year)
Hydrology Research (journal, 6 times a year)

Water Policy (journal, 6 times a year)
Journal of Water, Sanitation and Hygiene for Development (journal, 4 times a year)
Water Practice and Technology (online journal, 4 times a year)
Water Asset Management International (newsletter, 4 times a year)
Water Utility Management International (newsletter, 4 times a year)
Yearbook and Directory of Members
Order printed publications from: website: http://www.iwapublishing.com; Distributor: Portland Customer Services, Commerce Way, Colchester, CO2 8HP, UK; tel: 01206 796351; fax: 01206 799331; e-mail: sales@portland-services.com

Publications list:
Available online and in print

Access to staff:
Contact by letter and by e-mail
Hours: Mon to Fri, 0900 to 1700

Access to building, collection or gallery:
Prior appointment required

Affiliated to:
World Health Organisation

Non-governmental organisation of:
The United Nations

INTERNATIONAL WHALING COMMISSION

Acronym or abbreviation: IWC

The Red House, 135 Station Road, Impington, Cambridge, CB24 9NP

Tel: 01223 233971
Fax: 01223 232876
E-mail: secretariat@iwcoffice.org

Website:
http://www.iwcoffice.org

Enquiries:
Enquiries to: Editor

Founded:
1946

Organisation type and purpose:
International organisation, membership association, present number of members: 81 member nations.
Conservation of whales and regulation of whaling.

Subject coverage:
Whales, whaling, population, biology, resource management, ecosystem management, genetics, statistical surveys, whale catch and sightings database.

Non-library collection catalogue:
All or part available in print

Printed publications:
Annual Reports, Journal of Cetacean Research and Management, Special Issues (all available, priced)
Basic Documents (convention, schedule)
Free information leaflets
Journal of Cetacean Research and Management
Special Issues on various whaling topics
Order printed publications from: PA to the Secretary, IWC

Electronic and video publications:
Published and unpublished scientific documents on bibliographical database

Publications list:
Available online and in print

Access to staff:
Contact by letter, by telephone, by fax, by e-mail and via website. Appointment necessary.
Hours: Mon to Fri, 0900 to 1700
Special comments: Dependent upon availability of staff.

Access to building, collection or gallery:
Prior appointment required
Hours: Mon to Fri, 0900 to 1700

Access for disabled people:
Parking provided, ramped entry
Special comments: Level access on ground floor.

INTERNATIONAL WILDLIFE COALITION TRUST

Acronym or abbreviation: IWCT

141A High Street, Edenbridge, Kent, TN8 5AX

Tel: 01732 866955
Fax: 01732 966995
E-mail: iwcuk@iwcmail.demon.co.uk

Website:
http://www.iwctk9.co.uk

Enquiries:
Enquiries to: Director

Founded:
1987

Organisation type and purpose:
International organisation, voluntary organisation, registered charity (charity number 1035381).

Subject coverage:
Animal welfare.

Publications list:
Available online and in print

Access to staff:
Contact by letter, by telephone, by fax, by e-mail, in person and via website. Appointment necessary.
Hours: Mon to Fri, 0900 to 1700

Access to building, collection or gallery:
Prior appointment required

INTERNATIONAL WINE & FOOD SOCIETY

Acronym or abbreviation: IWFS

9 Fitzmaurice Place, Berkeley Square, London, W1J 5JD

Tel: 020 7495 4191
Fax: 020 7495 4172
E-mail: sec@iwfs.org

Enquiries:
Enquiries to: Executive Director
Other contacts: Membership Administrator

Founded:
1933

Organisation type and purpose:
International organisation, membership association (membership is by subscription), present number of members: 7500.
Educational and social.

Subject coverage:
Every aspect of wine and cookery, gastronomy.

Museum or gallery collection, archive, or library special collection:
Library is situated in Guildhall Public Library, City of London

Printed publications:
Monographs Series
Quarterly Newsletters of European, North American and Asian Pacific Membership

Publications list:
Available in print

Access to staff:
Contact by letter, by telephone, by fax and by e-mail. Appointment necessary. Non-members charged.
Hours: Mon to Fri, 1000 to 1630
Special comments: Membership card required.

Also:
140 local branches worldwide

INTERNATIONAL YOUTH FOUNDATION OF GREAT BRITAIN

Acronym or abbreviation: IYF

6a Pont Street, London, SW1X 9EL

Tel: 020 7235 7671
Fax: 020 7235 7370
E-mail: info@euyo.org.uk

Website:
http://www.euyo.org.uk

Enquiries:
Enquiries to: Secretary General

Founded:
1978

Organisation type and purpose:
International organisation, registered charity (charity number 281420).

Subject coverage:
Youth orchestras, choirs, ballet, opera, folk and youth bands, formation and development of national youth orchestras, music and education in the European Union.

Printed publications:
Annual brochure and programme

Access to staff:
Contact by letter, by telephone, by fax and by e-mail
Hours: Mon to Fri, 0930 to 1730

Under its auspices is the:
European Union Youth Orchestra (EUYO)
at the same address; tel: 020 7235 7671; fax: 020 7235 7370; e-mail: info@euyo.org.uk

INTERNATIONAL ZEN ASSOCIATION (UNITED KINGDOM)

Acronym or abbreviation: IZAUK

91–93 Gloucester Road, Bristol, BS7 8AT

Tel: 0117 942 4347

Website:
http://www.izauk.org

Enquiries:
Enquiries to: Information Officer

Founded:
1986

Organisation type and purpose:
Registered charity (charity number 296285).
Spiritual and religious practice.

Subject coverage:
Soto Zen Buddhism.

Printed publications:
Book list (available on request)
Leaflet (available on request)

Access to staff:
Contact by letter, by telephone, by e-mail and in person
Hours: By arrangement

Branches:
10 subsidiary groups in the United Kingdom, in Bristol, Manchester, London, Leeds, Norwich, Oxford, Brighton and Wells-next-the-Sea

Member organisation of:
Association Zen Internationale
175 rue de Tolbiac, Paris, 75013, France

INTERPAVE, THE PRECAST CONCRETE PAVING AND KERB ASSOCIATION

60 Charles Street, Leicester, LE1 1FB

Tel: 0116 253 6161
Fax: 0116 251 4568
E-mail: info@paving.org.uk

Website:
http://www.paving.org.uk

Enquiries:
Enquiries to: Secretary

Organisation type and purpose:
Trade association.

Subject coverage:
Precast concrete paving flags, block paving and kerbs.

Library catalogue:
All or part available online

Printed publications:
Literature Pack (free)
The Structural Design of Heavy Duty Pavements for Ports and Other Industries

Publications list:
Available online

Access to staff:
Contact by letter, by telephone, by fax and by e-mail. Appointment necessary.
Hours: Mon to Fri, 0900 to 1700

Member organisation of:
British Precast Concrete Federation

INVENSYS APV

23 Gatwick Road, Crawley, West Sussex, RH10 9JB

Tel: 01293 527777
Fax: 01293 552640

Website:
http://www.apv.co.uk

Enquiries:
Enquiries to: Marketing Manager
Direct tel: 01293 574380

Founded:
1910

Organisation type and purpose:
International organisation.
Company.
Provision of components, process engineering, automation and service to the food, drink, pharmaceutical and healthcare industries.

Subject coverage:
Design, production, installation and technical know-how of food, liquid food and pharmaceutical engineering processes. Provision of automation solutions to the above industries.

Access to staff:
Contact by letter, by telephone and by fax.
Appointment necessary.
Hours: Mon to Fri, 0900 to 1700

Access for disabled people:
Ramped entry

Parent body:
Invensys plc
Invensys House, Carlisle Place, London, SW1P 1BX; tel: 020 7834 3848; fax: 020 7834 3879

INVERCLYDE LIBRARIES

Central Library, Clyde Square, Greenock, Renfrewshire, PA15 1NA

Tel: 01475 712323
Fax: 01475 712339
E-mail: library.central@inverclyde.gov.uk

Website:
http://www.inverclyde.gov.uk/Libraries

Enquiries:
Enquiries to: Librarian

Organisation type and purpose:
Local government body, public library.

Subject coverage:
General, local history.

Museum or gallery collection, archive, or library special collection:
Watt Library (local history, 18th and 19th century publications)

Library catalogue:
All or part available online and in-house

Access to staff:
Contact by letter, by telephone, by fax, by e-mail and in person
Hours: Mon, Tue, Thu, 0930 to 1900; Fri, 0930 to 1700; Wed, 0930 to 1300; Sat, 1000 to 1300

INVESTMENT MANAGEMENT ASSOCIATION

Acronym or abbreviation: IMA

65 Kingsway, London, WC2B 6TD

Tel: 020 7831 0898
Fax: 020 7831 9975
E-mail: ima@investmentuk.org

Website:
http://www.investmentuk.org

Enquiries:
Enquiries to: Head of Communications

Founded:
1959

Created by the merger of:
Association of Unit Trusts and Investment Funds (AUTIF) and Fund Managers Association (FMA) (year of change 2002)

Formerly called:
Unit Trust Association

Organisation type and purpose:
Trade association (membership is by subscription) for asset management companies. Affiliate membership for service providers to asset management companies.

Subject coverage:
Unit trusts, open-ended investment companies (OEICs), ISAs, investment, saving, pensions, markets.

Museum or gallery collection, archive, or library special collection:
Historical statistics

Trade and statistical information:
UK data on asset management, unit trusts OEIC and ISA sales data.

Printed publications:
Introducing Investment (booklet)
Introducing IMA (corporate brochure)
Factsheets, including:
Ethical Investment Funds
Investing in ISAs
Monthly Savings
Investment Funds and Tax
IMA Pocket Guide
Child Trust Fund
Enabling Choice in Retirement
Annual Asset Management in the UK Survey

Publications list:
Available online and in print

Access to staff:
Contact by letter, by telephone and by e-mail
Hours: Mon to Fri, 0900 to 1700

Access to building, collection or gallery:
No access other than to staff

INVESTOR RELATIONS SOCIETY

Acronym or abbreviation: IRS

Bedford House, 3 Bedford Street, London, WC2E 9HD

Tel: 020 7379 1763
Fax: 020 7240 1320
E-mail: enquiries@irs.org.uk

Website:
http://www.ir-soc.org.uk

The society, members' zone, news, publications, professional development, careers, events, conference, best practice, find a service provider.

Enquiries:
Enquiries to: General Manager

Founded:
1980

Organisation type and purpose:
The UK's professional body for investor relations practitioners. Has almost 600 members from corporates and consultancies from across the UK, Europe and beyond and includes the majority of the FTSE 100 and a healthy representation from the FTSE 250.
To promote best practice in investor relations; to support the professional development of its members; to represent their views to regulatory bodies, the investment community and government; and to act as a forum for issuers and the investment community.

Subject coverage:
The communication of information and insight between a company and the investment community. This process enables a full appreciation of the company's business activities, strategy and prospects and allows the market to make an informed judgement about the fair value and appropriate ownership of a company.

Electronic and video publications:
IR Society Bulletin (weekly)
Informed (quarterly journal)
Order electronic and video publications from:
Download from website

Publications list:
Available online

Access to staff:
Contact by letter, by telephone, by fax and by e-mail

Member organisation of:
Global Investor Relations Network (GIRN)

IOP: THE PACKAGING SOCIETY

Acronym or abbreviation: IOP

Springfield House, Springfield Business Park, Grantham, Lincolnshire, NO31 7BG

Tel: 01476 514590
Fax: 01476 514591
E-mail: iop@pi2.org.uk

Website:
http://www.iop.co.uk
Full range of Institute of Packaging's products and services.

Enquiries:
Enquiries to: Head of Education, Training & Development
Direct tel: 01664 502150
Direct e-mail: gordon-stewart@iop.co.uk

Founded:
1947

Organisation type and purpose:
Professional body, present number of members: 3500, registered charity (charity number 295762), consultancy, publishing house.
Supports courses at Brunel and Loughborough Universities.
To promote packaging and provide education and training in packaging technology.

Subject coverage:
Packaging technology, packaging and the environment, legislation, packaging education and qualification, packaging publications, overseas contacts and exhibitions.

Museum or gallery collection, archive, or library special collection:
Reference library dedicated to packaging, packaging technology and related topics. Includes British Standards, periodicals and technical conference papers in addition to text books

Trade and statistical information:
Details of overseas trade exhibitions related to packaging and grants available to firms.

Printed publications:
Fundamentals of Packaging Technology
Packaging – The Facts (schools)

Electronic and video publications:
Open This End (video for schools)

Access to staff:
Contact by letter, by telephone, by fax, by e-mail and via website. Appointment necessary.
Hours: Mon to Fri, 0900 to 1700
Special comments: Three steps up to front door.

Secretariat for the:
Packaging Federation
at the same address
Pressure Sensitive Manufacturers Association
at the same address

IP FEDERATION

Acronym or abbreviation: IPF

Fifth Floor, 63–66 Hatton Garden, London, EC1N 8LE

Tel: 020 7242 3923
Fax: 020 7242 3924
E-mail: admin@ipfederation.com

Website:
http://www.ipfederation.com

Enquiries:
Enquiries to: Administrator

Founded:
1920

Organisation type and purpose:
Membership association (membership is by subscription, qualification), present number of members: 50, manufacturing industry, service industry.
Spokesman for industry on intellectual property (patents, trade marks, designs and copyright).

Subject coverage:
Industry views on trade marks, patents, copyright and industrial designs.

Access to staff:
Contact by letter, by telephone and by e-mail
Hours: Mon to Fri, 0900 to 1700

IP3

Formal name: Institute of Paper, Printing and Publishing

Runnymede Malthouse, off Hummer Road, Egham, Surrey, TW20 9BD

Tel: 0870 330 8625
Fax: 0870 330 8615
E-mail: info@ip3.org.uk

Website:
http://www.ip3.org.uk/

Enquiries:
Enquiries to: Information Officer

Founded:
2004

Created by the merger of:

Organisation type and purpose:
Professional body.

Printed publications:
Annual Lecture Booklet (free to members)
Calculations Booklet (£6 inc. p&p, to non-members)

Manual of Paper Trading (£44.50 inc. p&p, to non-members)
Paper Today (member magazine, quarterly, free to members)
Paper Samples Book (£25 inc. p&p, to non-members)
Yearly Prospectus (free)

Access to staff:
Contact by telephone, by fax and by e-mail
Hours: Mon to Fri, 0900 to 1700

IPSEA

Formal name: Independent Parental Special Education Advice
Acronym or abbreviation: IPSEA

Hunters Court, Debden Road, Saffron Walden, Essex, CB11 4AA

Tel: 01799 582030 (admin. only); 0800 018 4016 (main helpline)

Website:
http://www.ipsea.org.uk
Lots of useful, free resources for parents seeking the right education for their child with SEN/disability.

Enquiries:
Enquiries to: Administrator
Direct tel: 01394 384711
Direct fax: 01394 446577

Organisation type and purpose:
Voluntary organisation.

Subject coverage:
IPSEA offers free and independent advice and support to parents of children with special educational needs including, free advice on LEAs' legal duties towards children with SEN, free home visits where necessary, free support and possible representation for those parents appealing to the Special Educational Needs Tribunal, and free second opinions on a child's needs and the provision required to meet those needs.

Printed publications:
Sent Ahead – a parents guide to the Special Educational Needs Tribunal
Taking Action – your child's right to special educational provision

Publications list:
Available in print

Access to building, collection or gallery:
No prior appointment required

IPSOS MORI

Formal name: Ipsos MORI
Acronym or abbreviation: MORI

79–81 Borough Road, London, SE1 1FY

Tel: 020 7347 3000
Fax: 020 7347 3800

Website:
http://www.mori.com/pubinfo/articles.htm

Enquiries:
Enquiries to: Marketing Executive
Direct e-mail: patricia.ifejika@mori.com
Other contacts: Head of Communications Department

Founded:
October 2005

Organisation type and purpose:
International organisation, research organisation. Full market research agency.

Subject coverage:
Specialist knowledge of over 40 specialist business areas, including financial, corporate image, employee, leisure and tourism and social research.

Printed publications:
Publication list available on-line or via the marketing department. All free of charge

continued overleaf

Order printed publications from: Marketing
Department

Electronic and video publications:
Corporate video available free of charge

Publications list:
Available online

Access to staff:
Contact by telephone and by e-mail
Hours: Mon to Fri, 0830 to 1800

Other addresses:
Ipsos MORI
 Kings House, Kymberley Road, Harrow, HA1
 1PT; tel: 020 8861 8000; fax: 020 8861 5515

IPSWICH INSTITUTE

Reading Room and Library, 15 Tavern Street,
Ipswich, Suffolk, IP1 3AA

Tel: 01473 253992
E-mail: library@ipswichinstitute.org.uk

Enquiries:
Enquiries to: Executive Secretary

Founded:
1824

Organisation type and purpose:
Membership association (membership is by
subscription), present number of members: 2400,
registered charity (charity number 304772).
Private subscription library with reading room
having 9000 books.
To advance the education of the inhabitants of
Ipswich and neighbourhood.

Subject coverage:
Fiction and non-fiction books, talking tapes,
newspapers, magazines.

Access to staff:
Contact by letter, by telephone and by e-mail.
Appointment necessary.
Hours: Mon to Fri, 0900 to 1700; Sat, 0900 to 1600

Access to building, collection or gallery:
No prior appointment required
Special comments: Membership organisation – one
visit acceptable prior ro membership.

Also at:
Ipswich Institute
 13 Tower Street, Ipswich, Suffolk, IP1 3PG; tel:
 01473 253992

Member of:
Association of Independent Libraries
 Leeds Library, 18 Commercial Street, Leeds, LS1
 6AL; website: www.independentlibraries.co.uk

IQEA LIMITED

Formal name: Improving the Quality of Education
for All

Sycamores, Holebottom Road, Todmorden,
Lancashire, OL14 8DD

Tel: 01706 839274
Fax: 01706 839274
E-mail: admin@iqea.com

Website:
http://www.iqea.com
Background information on the project and current
details of research being undertaken.

Enquiries:
Enquiries to: Managing Director
Direct tel: 07920 449247
Other contacts: IQEA Co-ordinator for details about
schools involved in the project

Founded:
2002

Organisation type and purpose:
International organisation, advisory body, learned
society (membership is by election or invitation),
present number of members: 100 schools,

university department or institute, suitable for
ages: primary and secondary, training
organisation, consultancy, research organisation.
School Improvement Network.
To support school improvement efforts locally,
nationally and internationally. The key purpose is
to enhance the quality of student learning and
achievement.

Subject coverage:
The quality of education in primary and secondary
schools.

Library catalogue:
All or part available in-house and in print

Printed publications:
Many papers in professional publications

Access to staff:
Contact by letter, by telephone, by fax, by e-mail,
in person and via website. Appointment necessary.
Non-members charged.
Hours: Mon to Fri, 0900 to 1700

Access to building, collection or gallery:
No public access

IRAN SOCIETY

2 Belgrave Square, London, SW1X 8PJ

Tel: 020 7235 5122
Fax: 020 7259 6771
E-mail: info@iransociety.org

Website:
http://www.iransociety.org

Enquiries:
Enquiries to: Honorary Secretary

Organisation type and purpose:
Membership association (membership is by
subscription, election or invitation), present
number of members: 350, voluntary organisation
(charity number 248678).
Promotes the study of Iran, its peoples and culture
and particularly aims to advance education
through the study of language, literature, art,
history, religion, antiquities, usages, institutions
and customs of Iran.

Subject coverage:
Iran (excluding contemporary politics).

Access to staff:
Contact by letter, by telephone, by fax, by e-mail
and via website
Hours: Wed to Fri, 0930 to 1700

IRISH COUNCIL OF CHURCHES & THE IRISH INTER-CHURCH MEETING

Acronym or abbreviation: ICC & IICM

48 Elmwood Avenue, Belfast, BT9 6AZ

Tel: 028 9066 3145
Fax: 028 9066 4160
E-mail: info@irishchuches

Website:
http://www.irishchurches.org
Resources, news, photos, links.

Enquiries:
Enquiries to: Administrator

Founded:
1922

Organisation type and purpose:
National organisation, registered charity (charity
number XN 48617).
Church body.

Subject coverage:
Information on Irish ecumenism.

Publications list:
Available online and in print

Access to staff:
Contact by letter, by telephone, by fax, by e-mail
and in person
Hours: Mon to Fri, 0900 to 1700

IRISH FOOTBALL ASSOCIATION

Acronym or abbreviation: IFA

20 Windsor Ave, Belfast BT9 6EG

Tel: 028 9066 9458
E-mail: info@irishfa.com

Website:
http://www.irishfa.com
News, results, fixtures for all Irish league clubs and
competitions, updated tables, weekly newsletter,
interactive section.

Enquiries:
Enquiries to: General Secretary
Other contacts: President

Founded:
1880

Merged with:
the Irish Football League (IFL, founded 1890) (year
of change 2003)

Organisation type and purpose:
Sporting body.

Subject coverage:
Soccer in Northern Ireland, Irish league clubs.

Access to staff:
Contact by letter, by telephone, by fax and by e-
mail
Hours: Mon to Fri, 0900 to 1700

IRISH LINEN GUILD

c/o Riverside Factory, Victoria Street, Lurgan,
Craigavon, County Armagh, BT67 9DU

E-mail: info@irishlinen.co.uk

Website:
http://www.irishlinen.co.uk
Information on all aspects of the Irish Linen
Industry.

Enquiries:
Enquiries to: Director
Other contacts: Webmaster

Founded:
1928

Organisation type and purpose:
Professional body, membership association
(membership is by qualification), present number
of members: 6.
Promotion of Irish linen.

Subject coverage:
History and production of Irish linen, sourcing
Irish linen products including yarn, fabric and
household textiles. Information about current
manufacturers and suppliers.

Electronic and video publications:
Copyright to: The Wee Blue Blossom (1944),
 Directed by John Alderson
Others include:
Irish Symphony (1952)
Irish and Elegant (1957)
To Last a Lifetime (1961)
Looking in on Irish Linen (1968)

Publications list:
Available in print

Access to staff:
Contact by letter, by e-mail and via website

IRISH SEA FORUM

Acronym or abbreviation: ISF

Oceanography Laboratories, The University of
Liverpool, Liverpool, L69 3BX

Tel: 0151 794 4089

Fax: 0151 794 4099
E-mail: d.f.shaw@liv.ac.uk

Website:
http://www.liv.ac.uk/

Enquiries:
Enquiries to: Director
Other contacts: Administrative Officer for all
information about Irish Sea Forum.

Founded:
1992

Organisation type and purpose:
Membership association (membership is by
subscription), present number of members: 95,
voluntary organisation.
Non-profit making organisation operating within
the University of Liverpool; liaison with industry
and commerce, voluntary and statutory
organisations, and educational establishments on
all shores of the Irish Sea, individual membership
welcomed from those wishing to support the
purpose of the Forum.
To bring together those who are interested in the
enhancement of the environmental health of the
Irish Sea and its coastal features and estuaries, and
the sustainable development of its resources.

Subject coverage:
All aspects of environmental management
pertaining to the Irish Sea.

Printed publications:
Irish Sea Forum, Seminar Series (available from
Irish Sea Forum, Administrator, 3 times a year)
Irish Sea Group reports (1990) vols 1–4

Publications list:
Available in print

Access to staff:
Contact by letter, by telephone, by fax, by e-mail
and via website. Appointment necessary.
Hours: Mon to Fri, 0900 to 1700

Access to building, collection or gallery:
No prior appointment required

IRISH TEXTS SOCIETY

Acronym or abbreviation: ITS

Royal Bank of Scotland, Drummonds Branch, 49
Charing Cross, Admiralty Arch, London, SW1A
2DX

Website:
http://www.ucc.ie/locus/ITS.html

Enquiries:
Enquiries to: Secretary
Direct e-mail: shuttonseanfile@aol.com
Other contacts: Honorary Treasurer; email
burnsfarm@iol.ie for book orders, membership
queries/ applications.

Founded:
1898

Organisation type and purpose:
Learned society (membership is by subscription),
publishing house.

Subject coverage:
Irish language, history; texts and translations;
poetry and prose.

**Museum or gallery collection, archive, or library
special collection:**
The archives of the Society are in the Library of
University College Cork, Ireland

Printed publications:
57 titles; new volume approximately each year;
subsidiary publications series, proceedings of
annual ITS/UCC Seminar
A guide to the archives is contained in Pádraig ó
Riain Ed. Irish Texts Society: The First Hundred
Years (ITS, 1998)
ITS Newsletter (members only)

Publications list:
Available in print

Access to staff:
Contact by letter and by e-mail
Hours: Mon to Fri, 0900 to 1700

Connections with:
ITS/UCC Seminar (annually)
website: www.ucc.ie/locus/its.html

IRM UK STRATEGIC IT TRAINING LIMITED

Acronym or abbreviation: IRM UK

Bishops Walk House, 19–23 High Street, Pinner,
Middlesex, HA5 5PJ

Tel: 020 8866 8366
Fax: 020 8866 7966
E-mail: customerservice@irmuk.co.uk

Website:
http://www.irmuk.co.uk

Enquiries:
Enquiries to: Managing Director
Direct e-mail: jeremy.hall@irmuk.co.uk

Founded:
1999

Organisation type and purpose:
Service industry, training organisation.

Subject coverage:
Seminars and conferences on business process
management, enterprise architecture, data
management, software development, value-driven
IT, mastering the requirements process, project
management, information quality.

Electronic and video publications:
Conference Documentation as follows, plus p&p
per copy £10 UK, £20 Europe or £30 rest of the
world:
Europe's Most Authoritative Data Management
and Information Quality Conferences 2001, 2002,
2003, 2004 (£300 a year on CD)
Harnessing E-Business to Empower the 21st
Century Energy Company (£200)
Enterprise Architecture Conference Europe 2001,
2002, 2003, 2004 (£250 a year on CD)
Global Business Process Forum 2004 (£300 on CD)

Access to staff:
Contact by letter, by telephone, by fax, by e-mail
and via website. Appointment necessary.
Hours: Mon to Fri, 0900 to 1700

Access to building, collection or gallery:
No access other than to staff

Access for disabled people:
Access to all public areas

IRONBRIDGE GORGE MUSEUM TRUST

Acronym or abbreviation: Ironbridge Gorge
Museums

Coach Road, Coalbrookdale, Telford, Shropshire,
TF8 7DQ

Tel: 01952 433522
Fax: 01952 433204
E-mail: info@ironbridge.org.uk

Website:
http://www.ironbridge.org.uk

Enquiries:
Enquiries to: Head of Marketing
Direct e-mail: marketing@ironbridge.org.uk

Founded:
1967

Organisation type and purpose:
Registered charity (charity number 503717-R),
museum, suitable for ages: 5+.

Subject coverage:
A series of museums and monuments which
capture the stories of Britain's Industrial
Revolution. Ten museums covering six square
miles of East Shropshire coalfields.

Information services:
Library available for reference (for conditions see
Access above). Educational and school visits, tel:
01952 433970 or e-mail:
education@ironbridge.org.uk. Group visits:
telephone, or e-mail: visits@ironbridge.org.uk.

Special visitor services:
Guided tours, materials and/or activities for
children.

Education services:
Group education facilities, resources for Key
Stages 1 and 2, 3, 4 and Further or Higher
Education.

Services for disabled people:
For the visually impaired; for the hearing
impaired; displays and/or information at
wheelchair height.

**Museum or gallery collection, archive, or library
special collection:**
Collection on the life and works of Thomas Telford
Elton Collection (paintings, prints, book,
pamphlets and memorabilia relating to the
history of the Industrial Revolution)

Non-library collection catalogue:
All or part available online, in-house and in print

Library catalogue:
All or part available online

Printed publications:
Educational publications
Site specific guidebooks available to purchase
Souvenir Guide which covers all main sites
Various books which cover site subject matter,
available on request
Order printed publications from: Mail Order
Department

Electronic and video publications:
Souvenir Video

Access to staff:
Contact by letter, by fax and by e-mail
Hours: Mon to Fri, 0900 to 1700

Access for disabled people:
Parking provided, ramped entry, toilet facilities
Special comments: Sites vary, access guides available
on request.

Historic Site:
Blists Hill Victorian Town
Broseley Pipeworks
Coalport China Museum
Enginuity
Ironbridge Gorge Museum Trust
Jackfield Tile Museum
Museum of Iron
Museum of the Gorge
Tar Tunnel
The Darby Houses
The Iron Bridge and Tollhouse
The Merrythought Teddy Bear Shop and Museum

Links with:
Association for Industrial Archaeology

Maintains the:
Blists Hill Open Air Museum
Broseley Pipeworks Museum
Coalbrookdale Museum of Iron and Furnace
Coalport China Museum
Jackfield Tile Museum
Long Warehouse which houses the Ironbridge
Institute and the Museum library and archives
Museum of the Gorge

Manages:
Ironbridge Institute

Secretariat of the:
Association for Industrial Archaeology (AIA)

IRONBRIDGE GORGE MUSEUM TRUST – MUSEUM LIBRARY

Coach Road, Coalbrookdale, Telford, Shropshire,
TF8 7DQ

Tel: 01952 432141
Fax: 01952 432237

continued overleaf

E-mail: library@ironbridge.org.uk

Website:
http://www.ironbridge.org.uk

Enquiries:
Enquiries to: Librarian and Information Officer

Founded:
1968

Organisation type and purpose:
Registered charity, suitable for ages: 16+.
Private library. Courses at the Library run from
Birmingham University.

Subject coverage:
Industrial history, particularly East Shropshire
Coalfield; history of technology; museology.

Education services:
Group education facilities, resources for Further or
Higher Education.

Non-library collection catalogue:
All or part available in-house

Library catalogue:
All or part available in-house

Access to staff:
Contact by letter, by telephone, by fax and by e-
mail. Appointment necessary.
Hours: Mon to Fri, 0900 to 1700

Access to building, collection or gallery:
Prior appointment required
Hours: Mon to Fri, 0930 to 1700

Access for disabled people:
Toilet facilities
Special comments: Many stairs, access to ground
floor only and not to library itself. Staff happy to
assist disabled users, please telephone for
information.

Links with:
Birmingham University

IRONBRIDGE INSTITUTE

Ironbridge Gorge Museum Trust, Coalbrook,
Telford, Shropshire, TF8 7DX

Tel: 01952 432751
Fax: 01952 435937
E-mail: j.p.fletcher@bham.ac.uk

Website:
http://www.ironbridge.bham.ac.uk

Enquiries:
Enquiries to: Administrator

Founded:
1980

Organisation type and purpose:
University department or institute.
Postgraduate training and professional
development.

Subject coverage:
All aspects of the industrial past, industrial
archaeology, management of heritage resources
(museums, historic buildings, townscapes and the
natural environment).

**Museum or gallery collection, archive, or library
special collection:**
Elton Collection
Telford Collection

Access to staff:
Contact by letter, by telephone, by fax, by e-mail
and in person
Hours: Mon to Fri, 0900 to 1700

Managed jointly by the:
Institute of Archaeology and Antiquity
   The University of Birmingham
Ironbridge Gorge Museum Trust

ISBA

Formal name: ISBA – The Voice of British
Advertisers

Langham House, 1B Portland Place, London, W1B
1PN

Tel: 020 7291 9020
Fax: 020 7291 9030
E-mail: answers@isba.org.uk

Website:
http://www.isba.org.uk
All information about ISBA, our activities and
services.

Enquiries:
Enquiries to: Director of Marketing Services
Other contacts: Director of Membership
Development

Founded:
1900

Organisation type and purpose:
Membership association (membership is by
subscription), present number of members: over
310 companies.
Non-profit making organisation representing
advertisers to the Government, media, agencies
and other organisations.
ISBA acts as a catalyst encouraging advertisers to
join forces, debate and take action on any issue
affecting market communications.

Subject coverage:
Advertising in the UK and overseas; voluntary
controls; legislation: terms and conditions of
business in all advertising media; public relations;
direct marketing; sales promotion.

Printed publications:
Annual Report
Best Practice Guides, codes, research reports, etc
British Advertisers – Advancing the Nation's
   Prosperity (2001 Update)
Glossary of Advertising Media Terms (1996
   Update)
Guide to Sponsorship Evaluation (1998)
Parliamentary Guide to Advertising (2000)
The Internet – A Practical Guide for Marketers
   (1999)

Publications list:
Available in print

Access to staff:
Contact by letter, by fax, by e-mail and via
website
Hours: Mon to Fri, 0900 to 1730

Associated with:
Advertising Association (AA)
World Federation of Advertising and the
Advertisers (WFA)

ISI (EUROPE, MIDDLE-EAST AND AFRICA)

Formal name: Institute for Scientific Information
Acronym or abbreviation: ISI

Thomson Reuters, 77 Hatton Garden, London,
EC1N 8JS

Tel: 020 7433 4000
Fax: 020 7433 4001

Website:
http://scientific.thomson.com/isi/
Latest news, corporate information.
http://www.isinet.com/emea
Support and training materials in English,
German, Spanish

Enquiries:
Enquiries to: Press Office
Direct tel: 020 7433 4691
Direct e-mail: eoin.bedford@thomsonreuters.com

Founded:
1958 (USA)

Organisation type and purpose:
Service industry, research organisation.

Subject coverage:
Produces multidisciplinary and scientific
information tools for the international research
community. ISI's databases link the researcher to
the world's scholarly literature through its indexes
of bibliographic information and cited references.
Areas covered include all areas of pure and
applied sciences, social sciences, arts and
humanities.

Printed publications:
Arts and Humanities Citation Index (twice yearly
   and annually, 5 year cumulations)
Biotechnology Citation Index
Chemistry Citation Index
Current Contents (weekly, 7 editions: Life Sciences;
   Agriculture, Biology & Environmental Sciences;
   Engineering, Computing & Technology; Arts &
   Humanities; Clinical Medicine; Physical,
   Chemical & Earth Sciences; Social & Behavioural
   Sciences)
Index to Scientific and Technical Proceedings
   (monthly and annual cumulations)
Index to Scientific Book Contents
Index to Scientific Reviews
Index to Social Sciences and Humanities
   Proceedings
Materials Science Citation Index
Neuroscience Citation Index
Science Citation Index (6 times a year and annual,
   5-year and 10-year cumulations))
Social Sciences Citation Index (2 times a year and
   annual, 5-year and 10-year cumulations)

Microform publications:
Journal Citation Reports

Electronic and video publications:
BIOSIS Previews
CAB Abstracts
Current Contents Connect
Derwent Innovations Index
Journal Citation Reports
Web of Knowledge
Web of Science (3 indexes – SCIE, SSCI and AHCI)

Publications list:
Available online and in print

Access to staff:
Contact by letter, by telephone, by fax, by e-mail
and via website
Hours: Mon to Fri, 0900 to 1730

Access to building, collection or gallery:
Prior appointment required

Access for disabled people:
Toilet facilities

Other addresses for ISI:
ISI (Australia & New Zealand) (ISI)
   100 Harris Street, Pyrmont, NSW 2009, Australia;
   tel: +61 (2) 8587 7948; fax: +61 (2) 8587 7848; e-
   mail: asiainfo@isinet.com
ISI (Japan) (ISI)
   Thomson Corporation KK, Palaceside Building
   5F, 1–1-1 Hitotsubashi, Chiyoda-ku, Tokyo, 100-
   0003, Japan; tel: +81 3 5218 6530; fax: +81 3 5218
   6536; e-mail: jpinfo@isinet.com (inquiries)
ISI (North America, Latin America and Caribbean)
   (ISI)
   3501 Market Street, Philadelphia, PA 19104, USA;
   tel: +1 215 386 0100; fax: +1 215 386 2911; e-mail:
   sales@isinet.com
ISI (People's Republic of China) (ISI)
   Room 1291/1292 Pana Tower, #128 Zhi Chun
   Road, Hai Dan District, Beijing, 100086, PR
   China; tel: +86 10 8261 1504; fax: +86 10 6257
   8045; e-mail: chinainfo@isinet.com
ISI (Republic of Korea) (ISI)
   10FL Daenong Building, 33–1 Mapo-dong,
   Mapo-ku, Seoul, 121–708, Republic of Korea; tel:
   +82 2 711 3412; fax: +82 2 711 3520; e-mail:
   koreainfo@isinet.com
ISI (South/South East Asia, Hong Kong & Taiwan)
   (ISI)
   6 Battery Road #29–03, Standard Chartered Bank
   Building, Singapore, 049909; tel: +65 6879 4118;
   fax: +65 6223 2634; e-mail: asianinfo@isinet.com
   (inquiries)

Subsidiary of:
ISI
   3501 Market Street, Philadelphia, PA 19104, USA;
   tel: +1 215 386 0100; fax: +1 215 386 2911; e-mail:
   sales@isinet.com

ISLAMIC CULTURAL CENTRE

London Central Mosque, 146 Park Road, London,
NW8 7RG

Tel: 020 7724 3363
Fax: 020 7724 0493
E-mail: islamic200@aol.com

Website:
http://www.islamicculturalcentre.co.uk

Enquiries:
Enquiries to: Director-General

Founded:
1977

Organisation type and purpose:
Place of worship and for cultural activities.
Information point for the religion of Islam, facility
provider for Muslim community and advice to
government, local authorities, statutory bodies and
voluntary organisations.

Subject coverage:
Islam, religion, culture, history (modern and
ancient), Arabic language, art and heritage.

**Museum or gallery collection, archive, or library
special collection:**
Numerous books, documents in Arabic, Urdu,
 Farsi etc on the religion of Islam, history, culture
 etc

Printed publications:
Books and pamphlets
Islamic Quarterly (academic journal)
Bookshop leased to private company

Electronic and video publications:
Cassette and CDs of the Holy Quran (available for
 purchase)

Access to staff:
Contact by letter, by telephone, by fax, by e-mail
and in person. Appointment necessary.
Hours: Mon to Fri, 0900 to 1700
Special comments: No filming or press interviews
without prior arrangement.

Access to building, collection or gallery:
No prior appointment required
Special comments: Prior appointment required for
media.

Access for disabled people:
Parking provided, ramped entry, level entry, access
to all public areas, toilet facilities

ISLAND HISTORY TRUST

Dockland Settlement, 197 East Ferry Road,
London, E14 3BA

Tel: 020 7987 6041
E-mail: eve@islandhistory.org.uk

Website:
http://www.islandhistory.org.uk

Founded:
1980

Organisation type and purpose:
A community history project dedicated to
recording and preserving the history of London's
Isle of Dogs.

Subject coverage:
History of the Isle of Dogs.

Information services:
Family history on Isle of Dogs.

Special visitor services:
Access to photograph collections.

Education services:
Resources for schools.

**Museum or gallery collection, archive, or library
special collection:**
Local photographs and ephemera

Non-library collection catalogue:
All or part available in-house

Library catalogue:
All or part available in-house

Printed publications:
Island History News (a newsletter)
The Isle of Dogs A Brief History Volumes One and
 Two
A Child's History of the Isle of Dogs
Order printed publications from: above address

Access to staff:
Contact by letter, by telephone, by e-mail and in
person. Appointment necessary.
Hours: Tue to Thu, 0900 to 1700

Access to building, collection or gallery:
Hours: Tue, Wed and 1st Sun of the month, 1330 to
1630; at other times by appointment

Access for disabled people:
Major events only

ISLE OF AXHOLME FAMILY HISTORY SOCIETY

Acronym or abbreviation: IofAFHS

Colywell, 43 Commonside, Westwoodside, nr
Doncaster, DN9 2AR

Tel: 01427 752692
E-mail: secretary@axholme-fhs.org.uk

Website:
http://www.axholme-fhs.org.uk
Information about the society.

Enquiries:
Enquiries to: Honorary Secretary
Other contacts: Vice Chairman
(webmaster@axholme-fhs.org.uk)

Founded:
1988

Organisation type and purpose:
Membership association (membership is by
subscription), present number of members: 261,
voluntary organisation, research organisation.
To assist people with an ancestry or an interest in
the 12 parishes of the Isle of Axholme.

Subject coverage:
Family history in the 12 Lincolnshire parishes west
of the River Trent, i.e. the Isle of Axholme.

**Museum or gallery collection, archive, or library
special collection:**
Transcriptions of Parish Registers, Census Returns
Local historical matters in booklets, CD-ROMs and
 floppy disks pertaining to the Isle of Axholme

Library catalogue:
All or part available in-house

Printed publications:
Monumental Inscriptions (16 churches and
 cemeteries)
Parishes Registers (separate volumes, 51 for
 baptisms, 45 for marriages and 46 for burials)
Bishop's Transcripts for Luddington, Keadby with
 Althorpe
Census 1851–1901 all parishes, 1871–1891 Crowle
The Isle of Axholme before Vermuyden (Thirsk J)
The Crowle Poor Law Rate Book 1857
Order printed publications from: J Oliver, 17B West
 End Road, Epworth, Doncaster, DN9 1LA

Electronic and video publications:
Marriage Indexes (disc) for Amcotts, Belton,
 Epworth, Crowle, Haxey, Keadby with Althorpe,
 Luddington, Owston Ferry, Wroot, West
 Butterwick and Eastoft
Crowle Churchwarden's Accounts 1790–1812 (CD-
 ROM)
Order electronic and video publications from: Isle of
 Axholme Family History Society, Alberma,
 Luddington Road, Garthorpe, Isle of Axholme,
 Lincolnshire, DN17 4RU; e-mail: interests@
 axholme-fhs.org.uk

Publications list:
Available online and in print

Access to staff:
Contact by letter, by telephone, by e-mail, in
person and via website
Hours: Daily, 1000 to 2200

Access to building, collection or gallery:
4th Thu in month, except Aug and Dec
Hours: 0700 to 2100

Access for disabled people:
Yes
Hours: 1830 to 2130

ISLE OF MAN CIVIL REGISTRY

The Registries, Deemsters Walk, Bucks Road,
Douglas, Isle of Man, IM1 3AR

Tel: 01624 687039
Fax: 01624 685237
E-mail: civil@registry.gov.im

Enquiries:
Enquiries to: Registrar

Organisation type and purpose:
Manx government body.

Subject coverage:
Isle of Man Records of birth, death and marriage
registrations, parish records of baptisms, marriages
and burials pre-1878 (Church of England).

Printed publications:
Chief Registrar's Annual Report (contains a wide
 range of population statistics)

Access to staff:
Contact by letter, by telephone, by fax, by e-mail
and in person
Hours: Mon to Fri, 0900 to 1300 and 1400 to 1700

Access to building, collection or gallery:
No prior appointment required

Access for disabled people:
Parking provided, level entry, access to all public
areas, toilet facilities

ISLE OF MAN DEPARTMENT OF TOURISM AND LEISURE

Sea Terminal Buildings, Douglas, Isle of Man, IM1
2RG

Tel: 01624 686801
Fax: 01624 686800
E-mail: tourism@gov.im

Website:
http://www.visitisleofman.com

Enquiries:
Enquiries to: Tourist Information Manager
Direct tel: 01624 686851
Direct fax: 01624 627443
Direct e-mail: steve.dawson@gov.im

Organisation type and purpose:
National government body.
Promotion of tourism and leisure.

Subject coverage:
Promotion of tourism in the Isle of Man.

Printed publications:
Isle of Man Holiday Guide
Various free tourist leaflets; saleable publications
 list on request

Publications list:
Available online and in print

Access to staff:
Contact by letter, by telephone, by fax, by e-mail
and in person
Hours: Winter: Mon to Fri, 0915 to 1700
Summer: Daily, 0915 to 1900

Access for disabled people:
Parking provided, level entry, toilet facilities

ISLE OF MAN PUBLIC RECORD OFFICE

Acronym or abbreviation: IOMPRO

Unit 40a, Spring Valley Industrial Estate, Braddan, Douglas, Isle of Man, IM2 2QS

Tel: 01624 693569
Fax: 01624 613384
E-mail: public.records@registry.gov.im

Website:
http://www.gov.im/registries/publicrecords
General information.

Enquiries:
Enquiries to: Public Records Officer

Founded:
1992

Organisation type and purpose:
National government body, statutory body.
Record office.

Subject coverage:
History of public administration in the Isle of Man.

Museum or gallery collection, archive, or library special collection:
Records of the Isle of Man Government and other public bodies, particularly 20th century

Access to staff:
Contact by letter, by telephone, by fax and by e-mail. Appointment necessary.
Hours: Mon to Thurs, 0900 to 1300 and 1400 to 1730; Fri, 0900 to 1300 and 1400 to 1700

Access to building, collection or gallery:
If opening hours are difficult, please contact staff to discuss alternative arrangements
Hours: Thu, 0930 to 1300, and 1400 to 1700; Fri, 0930 to 1300 and 1400 to 1630

Parent body:
Isle of Man Government
  General Registry

ISLE OF MAN TRANSPORT

Banks Circus, Douglas, Isle of Man, IM1 5PT

Tel: 01624 663366
Fax: 01624 663637
E-mail: info@busandrail.dtl.gov.im

Enquiries:
Enquiries to: Director

Founded:
1873

Organisation type and purpose:
National government body, service industry.
Government transport undertaking bus and rail, public transport operator.

Subject coverage:
Public transport on the Isle of Man: railway, bus, tram network and workshops.

Printed publications:
Railway leaflets and transport timetables (free)

Access to staff:
Contact by letter, by telephone, by fax and by e-mail
Hours: Mon to Fri, 0900 to 1700

Access to building, collection or gallery:
No access other than to staff

Access for disabled people:
Toilet facilities

Connections with:
Isle of Man Government
  Department of Tourism & Leisure, Sea Terminal, Douglas, Isle of Man

Constituent bodies:
Isle of Man Bus Service
Isle of Man Railway
Manx Electric Railway
Snaefell Mountain Railway

ISLE OF WIGHT ARCHAEOLOGY AND HISTORIC ENVIRONMENT SERVICE

County Archaeological Centre, 61 Clatterford Road, Carisbrooke, Newport, Isle of Wight, PO30 1NZ

Tel: 01983 823810

Website:
http://www.iwight.com/living_here/planning/archaeology

Organisation type and purpose:
A local government body which advises individuals, organisations and the local planning authority on managing, preserving and understanding archaeological remains on the Isle of Wight.

Subject coverage:
Archaeology and history of the Isle of Wight.

Museum or gallery collection, archive, or library special collection:
Sites and Monuments Record (SMR), a computerised database cataloguing archaeological information, complemented by documentary archives and historic maps, aerial photographs and an archaeological library; access is by prior appointment only

ISLE OF WIGHT CHAMBER OF COMMERCE, TOURISM AND INDUSTRY

Acronym or abbreviation: IWCCTI

Mill Court, Furrlongs, Newport, Isle of Wight, PO30 2AA

Tel: 01983 520777
Fax: 01983 554555
E-mail: chamber@iwchamber.co.uk

Website:
http://www.iwchamber.co.uk
Island business magazine, internet directory of Island businesses, general business information.

Enquiries:
Enquiries to: Membership Officer
Direct tel: 01983 554541

Founded:
1910

Organisation type and purpose:
Membership association.

Subject coverage:
A chamber of commerce for Isle of Wight businesses, business advice and support, export documentation service.

Museum or gallery collection, archive, or library special collection:
All relevant business support books, Croner, etc.

Printed publications:
Island Business (monthly magazine)
Membership Directory

Access to staff:
Contact by e-mail
Hours: Mon to Fri, 0900 to 1700

Access to building, collection or gallery:
Prior appointment required

Access for disabled people:
Parking provided

ISLE OF WIGHT COLLEGE

Medina Way, Newport, Isle of Wight, PO30 5TA

Tel: 01983 526631
Fax: 01983 521707
E-mail: library@iwcollege.ac.uk

Website:
http://www.iwcollege.ac.uk

Enquiries:
Enquiries to: Learning Resources Centre Manager

Direct tel: 01983 550789
Direct e-mail: bev.vaughan@iwcollege.ac.uk

Founded:
1954

Organisation type and purpose:
College of further education, 6th form and higher education.

Subject coverage:
Horticulture, health and community studies, crafts, education, computer studies, engineering, construction, business studies, management, office skills, adult education, travel and tourism, local history, composites, marine engineering, fitness, fashion, performing arts, animal care, A-levels in hospitality and catering.

Library catalogue:
All or part available online

Access to staff:
Contact by letter, by telephone, by e-mail and via website. Appointment necessary. Access for members only.
Hours: Term-time: Mon to Thu, 0855 to 1930; Fri 1000 to 1700.
Vacations: Mon to Fri, 0900 to 1400.
Special comments: Use of learning resources centre for reference only unless College student. IT facilities available only to College students and staff.

Access for disabled people:
Blue badge-friendly site: park anywhere as long as parked safely and blue badge displayed; lift between floors

ISLE OF WIGHT LIBRARIES – REFERENCE LIBRARY

Lord Louis Library, Orchard Street, Newport, Isle of Wight, PO30 1LL

Tel: 01983 823800
Fax: 01983 825972
E-mail: reflib@postmaster.co.uk

Enquiries:
Enquiries to: Reference Librarian

Organisation type and purpose:
Local government body, public library.

Subject coverage:
General, Isle of Wight and related areas, local history, maritime history, local geology and archaeology, European Information Relay, family history.

Museum or gallery collection, archive, or library special collection:
Isle of Wight local collection
Maritime collection

Library catalogue:
All or part available in-house

Printed publications:
Local Clubs and Societies List

Access to staff:
Contact by letter, by telephone, by fax, by e-mail and in person
Hours: Mon to Wed and Fri, 0930 to 1730; Thu, 1000 to 2000; Sat, 0900 to 1700; Sun, 1000 to 1600

Access for disabled people:
Ramped entry, level entry, access to all public areas

Links with:
County Library Headquarters
  Parkhurst Road, Newport, Isle of Wight, PO30 5TX; tel: 01983 825717; fax: 01983 528047

ISLE OF WIGHT LIBRARY SERVICE

Library Headquarters, 5 Mariners Way, Somerton Industrial Estate, Cowes, Isle of Wight, PO31 8PD

Tel: 01983 203880

Website:
http://www.iwight.gov.uk/thelibrary
Library service website, transactional based.

Enquiries:
Enquiries to: Head of Libraries and Information Services

Founded:
1904

Organisation type and purpose:
Local government body, public library, suitable for ages: all.

Subject coverage:
General, Isle of Wight and related areas.

Museum or gallery collection, archive, or library special collection:
Isle of Wight, music scores, maritime history

Non-library collection catalogue:
All or part available in-house

Access to staff:
Contact by letter, by telephone, by fax, by e-mail and in person
Hours: Mon to Fri, 0900 to 1700

Access to building, collection or gallery:
Prior appointment required

Access for disabled people:
Ramped entry, access to all public areas

ISLE OF WIGHT RECORD OFFICE

26 Hillside, Newport, Isle of Wight, PO30 2EB

Tel: 01983 823820/823821
Fax: 01983 823820
E-mail: record.office@iow.gov.uk

Website:
http://www.iwight.com/library/record_office
Basic information about range of records held by office.
http://www.a2a.pro.gov.uk
National database comprising online catalogues (some of which relate to Isle of Wight).

Enquiries:
Enquiries to: County Archivist

Founded:
1961

Organisation type and purpose:
Local government body.
To preserve archives relating to Isle of Wight and make them available to the public for research purposes.

Subject coverage:
Local history and genealogy relating to Isle of Wight.

Museum or gallery collection, archive, or library special collection:
Numerous including:
Records of parish churches, nonconformist churches, estates, businesses, local government, schools, hospitals
Census returns, newspapers, copy wills, photographs and maps

Non-library collection catalogue:
All or part available online and in-house

Access to staff:
Contact by letter, by telephone, by fax, by e-mail, in person and via website
Hours: Mon, 0930 to 1225 and 1300 to 1700; Tue to Fri, 0900 to 1225 and 1300 to 1700
Special comments: Appointment necessary to view material held on microfilm/fiche.

Access for disabled people:
Parking provided
Special comments: Telephone Record Office to reserve a parking space. Access to building is possible for wheelchairs, but assistance required.

ISLES OF SCILLY WILDLIFE TRUST

Acronym or abbreviation: IOSWT

Carn Thomas, St Mary's, Isles of Scilly, TR21 0PT

Tel: 01720 422153
Fax: 01720 422153
E-mail: enquiries@ios-wildlifetrust.org.uk

Website:
http://www.ios-wildlifetrust.org.uk

Founded:
1986

Formerly called:
Isles of Scilly Environmental Trust (year of change 2001)

Organisation type and purpose:
Membership association (membership is by subscription), registered charity (charity number 293512), conservation.

Subject coverage:
Wildlife habitat management, satellite environmental records centre, visitor centre.

Printed publications:
Leaflets
Membership magazine (joint with Cornwall Wildlife Trust)
Order printed publications from: the office or the website

Publications list:
Available online and in print

Access to staff:
Contact by letter, by telephone, by fax, by e-mail and in person. Appointment necessary.
Hours: Mon, Tue and Fri, 1000 to 1600; by appointment for other times

Links with:
The Wildlife Trust (UK Office)
The Kiln, Waterside, Mather Road, Newark, Nottinghamshire, NG24 1WT; tel: 01636 677711; fax: 01636 670001

ISLINGTON ARCHAEOLOGY AND HISTORY SOCIETY

Formal name: Islington Archaeology and History Society

8 Wynyatt Street, EC1V 7HU

Tel: 020 7833 1541

Website:
http://www.iahs.org.uk

Founded:
1975

Organisation type and purpose:
Membership association (membership by subscription).
To arrange lectures, visits and courses in relation to the archaeology and history of the London Borough of Islington.
To publish work on the archaeology and history of the Borough.
To cooperate with local government bodies and other agencies in matters of planning and development within the Borough in order to record and protect Islington's sites which are of archaeological and historical importance.

Printed publications:
Newsletter (4 times per year)

Access to staff:
Contact by letter and by telephone

ISLINGTON LIBRARY AND HERITAGE SERVICES

Central Library, 2 Fieldway Crescent, Islington, London, N5 1PF

Tel: 020 7527 6900
Fax: 020 7527 6902

E-mail: library.informationunit@islington.gov.uk

Website:
http://www.islington.gov.uk/Education/LocalHistory
http://www.islington.gov.uk/libraries
Library services, opening hours, local history, learning centres, and the Islington Museum, plus links to the library catalogue and online Directory of Local Services.

Enquiries:
Enquiries to: Information Manager
Direct tel: 020 7527 6922
Direct fax: 020 7527 6926
Direct e-mail: john.smith@islington.gov.uk
Other contacts: Central Reference Librarian (tel: 020 7527 6931)

Organisation type and purpose:
Local government body, public library service.

Subject coverage:
General, local community information, photography and local history of Islington.

Information services:
Online local information directory, online resources – general and business, European information, reference and information library.

Services for disabled people:
Adaptive hardware and software in all branches, but especially at Central Reference Library.

Museum or gallery collection, archive, or library special collection:
Local History Archive
Joe Orton Book Jacket Collection
Local history archives
Sadlers Wells Collection (at Finsbury library)
Sickert Collection

Trade and statistical information:
General collection of trade directories and statistical information.

Library catalogue:
All or part available online

Printed publications:
Local information fact sheets, e.g. halls for hire, community groups, etc.
Guide to the local history collections
Local history publications and reprints including books, postcards, maps and prints
Subject booklists
Order printed publications from: Central Reference Library, at the same address; tel: 020 7527 6931; fax: 020 7527 6939; e-mail: centralref.library@islington.gov.uk

Publications list:
Available in print

Access to staff:
Contact by letter, by telephone, by fax, by e-mail, in person and via website. Appointment necessary.

Access for disabled people:
All buildings fully accessible

Branch libraries:
Archway Library
Hamlyn House, Highgate Hill, London, N19 5PH; tel: 020 7527 7820; e-mail: archway.library@islington.gov.uk
Finsbury Library
245 St. John Street, London, EC1V 4NB; tel: 020 7527 7960; e-mail: finsbury.library@islington.gov.uk
John Barnes Library
275 Camden Road, London, N7 0JN; tel: 020 7527 7900; e-mail: johnbarnes.library@islington.gov.uk
Lewis Carroll Children's Library
180 Copenhagen Street, London, N1 0ST; tel: 020 7527 7936; e-mail: lewiscarroll.library@islington.gov.uk
Mildmay Library
21–23 Mildmay Park, London, N1 4NA; tel: 020 7527 7880; e-mail: mildmay.library@islington.gov.uk

continued overleaf

N4 Library
26 Blackstock Road, London, N4 2DW; tel: 020 7527 7800; e-mail: n4.library@islington.gov.uk
North Library
Manor Gardens, London, N7 6JX; tel: 020 7527 7840; e-mail: north.library@islington.gov.uk
South Library
115–117 Essex Road, London, N1 2SL; tel: 020 7527 7860; e-mail: south.library@islington.gov.uk
West Library
Bridgeman Road, London, N1 1BD; tel: 020 7527 7920; e-mail: west.library@islington.gov.uk

Branch museums:
Islington Museum
245 St John Street, London, EC1V 4NB; tel: 020 7527 3235; e-mail: islington.museum@islington .gov.uk

Branches:
First Steps Learning Centre
Central Library, 2 Fieldway Crescent, London, N5 1PF; tel: 020 7527 7002; e-mail: sineadgannon@isonline.org
Islington Computer Skills Centre
Finsbury Library, 245 St. John Street, London, EC1V 4NB; tel: 020 7713 6593; e-mail: info@ icskills.co.uk
Islington Local History Centre
Finsbury Library, 245 St. John Street, London, EC1V 4NB; tel: 020 7527 7988; e-mail: local .history@islington.gov.uk

ISMITHERS RAPRA

Formal name: Smithers Rapra Technology Limited

Shawbury, Shrewsbury, Shropshire, SY4 4NR

Tel: 01939 250383
Fax: 01939 251118
E-mail: publications@ismithers.net

Website:
http://www.ismithers.net
Website giving access to full range of services and products.
http://www.polymer-books.com
Comprehensive online bookstore for the plastics and rubber industries.

Enquiries:
Direct e-mail: cparkinson@ismithers.net
Founded:
1920

Organisation type and purpose:
Independent plastics and rubber consultancy; technology and information services; membership association (membership is by subscription); research organisation; publishing house.

Subject coverage:
Rubber, plastics and allied fields, synthesis and applications design, additives, processing, properties and testing, market information, chemical resistance, industrial hazards, thermal transition, trade names, adhesives, standards and specifications.

Museum or gallery collection, archive, or library special collection:
Porritt and Dawson Collection (on rubbers and plastics)

Non-library collection catalogue:
All or part available online

Library catalogue:
All or part available online

Printed publications:
Cellular Polymers (6 times a year)
Polymers and Polymer Composites (8 times a year)
International Polymer Science and Technology (monthly)
Progress in Rubber, Plastics and Recycling Technology (quarterly)
Polymers for Renewable Resources (quarterly)
Order printed publications from: Publications Sales

Publications list:
Available online and in print

Access to staff:
Contact by letter, by telephone, by fax, by e-mail and via website. Appointment necessary. Access for members only. All charged.
Hours: Mon to Fri, 0800 to 1645

Access to building, collection or gallery:
Prior appointment required

ISO/BIZZARRINI CLUB

47 St Margarets Road, Twickenham, Middlesex, TW1 2LL

Tel: 020 8891 6663
E-mail: iso.bizz@tesco.net

Website:
http://www.burstow0.demon.co.uk

Enquiries:
Enquiries to: Secretary

Founded:
1988

Organisation type and purpose:
Membership association.

Subject coverage:
All aspects (spares, technical and encouragement) of owning and maintaining an ISO or Bizzarrini car.

Access to staff:
Contact by letter, by telephone and by e-mail
Hours: Mon to Fri, 0900 to 1700

ISRAEL GOVERNMENT TOURIST OFFICE

Acronym or abbreviation: IGTO

UK House, 180 Oxford Street, London, W1D 1NN

Tel: 020 7299 1111
Fax: 020 7299 1112
E-mail: info@igto.co.uk

Website:
http://www.thinkisrael.com

Enquiries:
Enquiries to: Office Manager and PA
Direct tel: 020 7299 1100

Organisation type and purpose:
National government body.
National government tourist office.
To advertise, sell and promote Israel as a destination for winter sun holidays, pilgrimages, vacations, birdwatching, hiking, etc.

Subject coverage:
Holidays in Israel, pilgrimages and Holy Land tours, hotel lists, traveller information, trade information and Israel events.

Museum or gallery collection, archive, or library special collection:
Feature article library
Photograph and slide library (CD-ROM)
Video library (DVD)

Trade and statistical information:
Data on number of visitors to Israel from United Kingdom and world-wide.
Statistics and data on different type of visitors ie how many arrive as pilgrims, birdwatchers, holiday, etc.

Printed publications:
All promotional literature is free and available, including maps, posters, videos, slide and window displays

Access to staff:
Contact by letter, by telephone, by fax and by e-mail
Special comments: By appointment only

Parent body:
Israel Ministry of Tourism
Jerusalem

ISRAELI EMBASSY

2 Palace Green, London, W8 4QB

Tel: 020 7957 9500
Fax: 020 7957 9555
E-mail: info-sec@london.mfa.gov.il

Website:
http://london.mfa.gov.il

Enquiries:
Enquiries to: Information Officer

Organisation type and purpose:
National government body.

Access to staff:
Contact by letter, by telephone, by fax and by e-mail
Hours: Mon to Thu, 0900 to 1800; Fri, 0900 to 1400

Also at:
Israeli Embassy
15a Old Court Place, London, W8 4PL

ISSB LIMITED

Formal name: Iron and Steel Statistics Bureau

1 Carlton House Terrace, London, SW1Y 5DB

Tel: 020 7343 3900
Fax: 020 7343 3901
E-mail: info@issb.co.uk

Website:
http://www.issb.co.uk
Various.

Organisation type and purpose:
To provide statistical information on the steel industry and trade in steel and related products including raw materials.

Subject coverage:
International steel statistics.

Trade and statistical information:
World data on steel production.

Printed publications:
UK Iron and Steel Industry: Annual Statistics (£175)
International Steel Statistics Country Books 2001 (£190 per country, £2600 for complete series)
World Steel Exports – All Qualities 2001 (£650)
World Steel Statistics Monthly (£950)

Access to staff:
Contact by letter, by telephone, by fax, by e-mail and via website. All charged.
Hours: Mon to Fri, 0900 to 1700

Subsidiary company of:
UK Steel Association
Broadway House, Tothill Street, London, SW1H 9NQ; tel: 020 7222 7777; fax: 020 7222 3531; e-mail: enquiries@uksteel.org.uk

ITALIAN CULTURAL INSTITUTE

39 Belgrave Square, London, SW1X 8NX

Tel: 020 7235 1461
Fax: 020 7235 4618
E-mail: library.icilondon@esteri.it

Website:
http://www.bibliowin.it/iic/ICLN
Online library catalogue.
http://www.icilondon.esteri.it

Founded:
1950

Organisation type and purpose:
National government body, membership association (membership is by subscription).
The cultural office of the Italian Embassy.
To promote Italian culture in the United Kingdom.

Subject coverage:
General and language studies in Italy; education in Italy; bursaries; music and arts; exhibitions; study qualifications; Italy and events of Italian interest.

Museum or gallery collection, archive, or library special collection:
Dante Collection
Italian contemporary fiction and poetry
Good collection of videos especially Italian Cinema

Library catalogue:
All or part available online

Access to staff:
Contact by letter, by telephone, by fax, by e-mail, in person and via website. Appointment necessary.
Hours: By appointment only; flexible times and dates, but normally Mon to Fri, 1030 to 1330 and 1430 to 1800

ITRI INNOVATION LTD

Unit 3, Curo Park, Frogmore, St. Albans, Hertfordshire, AL2 2DD

Tel: 01727 875544
Fax: 01727 871341
E-mail: info@itri.co.uk

Website:
http://www.lead-free.org
Lead-free soldering – news, events, technical information, etc.
http://www.itri-innovation.com
Tin and its uses, facilities, Member information, etc.

Enquiries:
Enquiries to: Information Officer
Direct e-mail: jeremy.pearce@itri.co.uk; tony .wallace@itri.co.uk

Founded:
1932

Formerly called:
Tin Technology Ltd (year of change 2008)

Organisation type and purpose:
Membership association (membership is by subscription), present number of members: 75, research organisation.

Subject coverage:
Tin and its alloys and compounds, and their applications, solder and soldering, tin and tin alloy plating, pewter, bearing metals, whitemetals, tin in cast iron, organo-tins and other tin chemicals, fire retardants, non-toxic ammunition, lead-free wheel weights.

Museum or gallery collection, archive, or library special collection:
40,000 published papers on tin from 1932 – on microfiche

Trade and statistical information:
Tin – production information and statistics.

Non-library collection catalogue:
All or part available online and in-house

Electronic and video publications:
Technical publications on tin technology (CD-ROM and online)

Publications list:
Available in print

Access to staff:
Contact by letter, by telephone, by fax, by e-mail and via website. Appointment necessary. Non-members charged.
Hours: Mon to Fri, 0900 to 1645

Access to building, collection or gallery:
Prior appointment required

Access for disabled people:
Parking provided, ramped entry, toilet facilities
ITRI Ltd
 Unit 3, Curo Park, Frogmore, St Albans, Hertfordshire, AL2 2DD

IWSC: THE WOOD TECHNOLOGY SOCIETY

Formal name: IWSc: The Wood Technology Society, a Division of the Institute of Materials, Minerals and Mining
Acronym or abbreviation: IWSc

! Carlton House Terrace, London, SW1Y 5DB

Tel: 0207 451 7415
Fax: 0207 839 1702
E-mail: efi.fragkou@iom3.org; duncan.king@iom3 .org

Website:
http://www.iom3.org/content/wood-technology

Enquiries:
Enquiries to: Executive Advisor, Wood Technology
Direct tel: 07795 561057

Founded:
1955

Organisation type and purpose:
Professional body (membership is by qualification, election or invitation), present number of members: 1,400, registered charity.

Subject coverage:
The study of timber and wood-based materials.

Information services:
Enquiries, loan available to members, referral service.

Special visitor services:
Please contact the Library prior to a visit to make an appointment.

Museum or gallery collection, archive, or library special collection:
Library consists of approximately 300 text books, directories and Journal of the The Institute of Wood Science and Wood Focus

Library catalogue:
All or part available in-house

Printed publications:
From 2010: International Wood Products Journal, formerly the Journal of the Institute of Wood Science, refereed papers – biannual publication, published by Maney Publishing on behalf of the Wood Technology Society of the Institute of Materials, Minerals and Mining
Wood Focus (magazine, three times a year, subscription £25, available online only)

Access to staff:
Contact by letter, by telephone, by fax, by e-mail and via website. Appointment necessary.
Hours: Mon to Fri, 0900 to 1700

J S PUBLICATIONS

PO Box 505, Newmarket, Suffolk, CB8 7TF

Tel: 01638 561590
Fax: 01638 560924
E-mail: ukrew@jspubs.com

Website:
http://www.jspubs.com

Enquiries:
Enquiries to: Customer Services Manager

Founded:
1988

Organisation type and purpose:
Publishing house.

Subject coverage:
Publishers of the UK Register of Expert Witnesses, the UK's largest and longest established database of vetted expert witnesses. Recognised by the UK legal profession and various Government bodies, the Register provides a listing of individuals who are both expert in their own field and qualified to give expert evidence in court and write expert reports connected with litigation. Also available is a full range of support services for both instructing

solicitors (e.g. assistance in locating a specific expert) and experts themselves (newsletters/factsheets/helpline).

Printed publications:
UK Register of Expert Witnesses (including electronic version, annually, £110 plus VAT)

Electronic and video publications:
UK Register of Expert Witnesses (on disc and CD-ROM, available free to registered users of printed product)

Access to staff:
Contact by letter, by telephone, by fax, by e-mail and via website
Hours: Mon to Fri, 0900 to 1700

JACOB SHEEP SOCIETY

14 Mortimer Road, Kenilworth, Warwickshire, CV8 1FR

Tel: 01923 855393
Fax: 01923 855393
E-mail: valhunt@jacobsheep.freeserve.co.uk

Enquiries:
Enquiries to: Secretary

Founded:
1979

Organisation type and purpose:
Membership association (membership is by subscription), present number of members: 763, registered charity.
Sheep Breed Society.

Access to staff:
Contact by letter, by telephone and by e-mail
Hours: Mon to Fri, 0930 to 1500

Links with:
National Sheep Association (NSA)
 Malvern, Worcestershire

JAGUAR ENTHUSIASTS' CLUB

Acronym or abbreviation: JEC

Abbeywood Office Park, Emma Chris Way, Filton, Bristol, BS34 7JU

Tel: 01179 698186
Fax: 01179 791863
E-mail: jechq@btopenworld.com

Website:
http://www.jec.org.uk
Full information on the club and its activities.

Enquiries:
Enquiries to: General Manager
Direct e-mail: graham.searle@btinternet.com

Founded:
1984

Organisation type and purpose:
Membership association.
To maintain and promote interest in Jaguar Cars.

Subject coverage:
History of Jaguar cars, technical information, insurance, specialist tools, parts, rallies and shows, books and accessories, specialist guide.

Printed publications:
Magazine (monthly, members)

Access to staff:
Contact by letter, by telephone, by fax, by e-mail, in person and via website
Hours: Mon to Fri, 0800 to 1700

JAMAICA TRADE COMMISSION

Formal name: Jamaica Promotions Corporation
Acronym or abbreviation: JAMPRO

1 Prince Consort Road, London, SW7 2BZ

Tel: 020 7584 8894
Fax: 020 7823 9886
E-mail: jamprouk@investjamaica.com

continued overleaf

Website:
http://www.investjamaica.com

Enquiries:
Enquiries to: Trade Commissioner

Organisation type and purpose:
International organisation, national government body, manufacturing industry, service industry. Investment; trade; promotion.

Subject coverage:
Trade and investment information in Jamaica.

Access to staff:
Contact by letter, by telephone, by fax, by e-mail and via website. Appointment necessary.
Hours: Mon to Fri, 0930 to 1700

JANE AUSTEN SOCIETY

20 Parsonage Rd, Henfield, W. Sussex, BNS 9JG

Tel: 01273 494210
E-mail: hq@jasoc.org.uk

Website:
http://www.janeaustensociety.org.uk
History of the Society, publications, regional groups in the UK, subscriptions, education, biography.

Enquiries:
Enquiries to: Honorary Secretary

Founded:
1940

Organisation type and purpose:
Learned society (membership is by subscription), present number of members: 1700 UK, 350 overseas, registered charity (charity number 1040613).

Subject coverage:
Life and works of Jane Austen, the Austen family, English literature, Georgian history and female novelists of the 18th and 19th century.

Museum or gallery collection, archive, or library special collection:
Collection of documents, books and memorabilia held at Jane Austen's house and museum at Chawton, Hampshire; tel or fax: 01420 83626

Publications list:
Available online and in print

Access to staff:
Contact by letter, by telephone and by e-mail
Hours: Mon to Fri, 0900 to 1700

Branches:
10 branches in the UK and overseas societies in Australia, Canada, the USA, and Japan

JANE'S INFORMATION GROUP

Acronym or abbreviation: Jane's

Sentinel House, 163 Brighton Road, Coulsdon, Surrey, CR5 2YH

Tel: 020 8700 3700
Fax: 020 8763 1006

Website:
http://www.janes.com/
Company and product details. Subscriptions to specific products.
http://catalogue.janes.com
Full online list of publications.

Enquiries:
Enquiries to: PR Manager
Direct tel: 020 8700 3745
Direct e-mail: amanda.castle@janes.com

Founded:
1898

Organisation type and purpose:
International organisation, publishing house. Publishers of defence, transport and law enforcement information to governments, militaries, businesses and universities worldwide.

Subject coverage:
Technical specifications, quantities, details of manufacturers and users of defence, aerospace and law enforcement, terrorism and security as well as transportation equipment; geopolitical and strategic information. Also analysis and consulting services are offered in all mentioned areas.

Museum or gallery collection, archive, or library special collection:
Back numbers of Jane's Yearbooks

Non-library collection catalogue:
All or part available online and in print

Printed publications:
Online services, magazines, directories, yearbooks (over 40 titles)
Jane's International Defence Review
Jane's Airport Review
Jane's Defence Weekly
Jane's Intelligence Review
Jane's Police Review
Jane's Intelligence Digest
Jane's Islamic Affairs Analyst
Jane's Terrorism and Security Monitor
Jane's Foreign Report

Microform publications:
Jane's Fighting Ships
Jane's All the World's Aircraft
Jane's World Railways

Electronic and video publications:
All products are available via CD-ROM, Internet (online), in html. Some email services

Publications list:
Available online and in print

Access to staff:
Contact by letter, by telephone, by fax, by e-mail and via website. Appointment necessary. All charged.
Hours: Mon to Fri, 0900 to 1700

Access to building, collection or gallery:
Prior appointment required

Access for disabled people:
Parking provided, level entry, access to all public areas, toilet facilities

Parent body:
The Woodbridge Company Limited

JANSSEN-CILAG LIMITED

PO Box 79, Saunderton, High Wycombe, Buckinghamshire, HP14 4HJ

Tel: 01494 567444
Fax: 01494 567445
E-mail: medinfo@janssen-cilag.co.uk

Website:
http://www.janssen-cilag.co.uk
General and specific information on Company's product portfolio.

Enquiries:
Enquiries to: Information Officer

Organisation type and purpose:
Trade association, research organisation.

Subject coverage:
Pharmaceutical medicine: gastroenterology, antifungals, anaesthesia, drug safety, psychiatry, pain, neurology.

Part of:
Johnson and Johnson

JAPAN FOUNDATION

Formal name: Kokusai Koryu Kikin (in Japanese)

Russell Square House, 10–12 Russell Square, London, WC1B 5EH

Tel: 020 7436 6695
Fax: 020 7323 4888
E-mail: info@jpf.org.uk

Enquiries:
Enquiries to: Assistant Programme Officer

Founded:
1972

Organisation type and purpose:
Promotion of Japanese culture overseas through various grant programmes.

Subject coverage:
Japanese culture, enquiries may be referred to the appropriate organisations.

Museum or gallery collection, archive, or library special collection:
Reference books

Printed publications:
Japan Foundation News (Japanese)
Japan Foundation Newsletter
Japan Foundation Japanese Language Centre News

Access to staff:
Contact by letter, by telephone, by fax, by e-mail and in person. Appointment necessary.
Hours: Mon to Fri, 0930 to 1730

Parent body:
Japan Foundation (Kokusai Koryu Kikin)
Ark Mori Building, 1 12 32 Akasaka, Minato-ku, Tokyo, 107, Japan

JAPAN NATIONAL TOURIST ORGANIZATION

Acronym or abbreviation: JNTO

Heathcoat House, 20 Savile Row, London, W1S 3PR

Tel: 020 7734 9638
Fax: 020 7734 4290
E-mail: info@jnto.co.uk

Website:
http://www.jnto.go.jp
Japan travel updates, news, regional tourism information, maps, festivals and events, budget travel tips, accommodation directories.

Enquiries:
Enquiries to: Public Relations Manager
Other contacts: Deputy Director

Founded:
1953

Organisation type and purpose:
National government body.
Tourist office.
Promoting Japan as a business and leisure travel destination. Offering information and advice to people planning to visit Japan.

Subject coverage:
All areas of travel to and within Japan including transport (rail, air, ferry, bus), accommodation, attractions, resorts, places to visit, package holidays and tours, travelling on a budget, food, shopping, climate etc; festivals, events, conventions, conferences and exhibitions in Japan, conference and convention facilities; other information.

Museum or gallery collection, archive, or library special collection:
Films, videos and slides

Trade and statistical information:
Statistics on number of visitors to Japan (by country and purpose of visit) and on number of Japanese overseas travellers.

Non-library collection catalogue:
All or part available in-house

Printed publications:
Range of tourist information pamphlets, accommodation guides and maps available free of charge
Japan: Your Guide
Travel Manual (updated annually, for agents and tour operators)

Publications list:
Available in print

Access to staff:
Contact by telephone, by fax, by e-mail and in person
Hours: Mon to Fri, 0930 to 1730
Special comments: Closed on some Japanese National Holidays.

Links with:
Asia Travel Marketing Association
Association of National Tourist Office Representatives
Pacific Asia Travel Association

Parent body:
Japan National Tourist Organization
2–10–1 Yuraku-cho, Chiyoda-ku, Tokyo, 100, Japan

JAPAN SOCIETY OF THE UK

Formal name: Japan Society of the UK

Swire House, 59 Buckingham Gate, London, SW1E 1AJ

Tel: 020 7828 6330
Fax: 020 7828 6331
E-mail: info@japansociety.org.uk

Website:
http://www.japansociety.org.uk/

Enquiries:
Enquiries to: Office Director
Direct e-mail: john.toppon@japansociety.org.uk

Founded:
1891

Organisation type and purpose:
Membership organisation and information service. To enhance Anglo-Japanese relations with the aim of providing a better mutual understanding of the cultures, societies and businesses of Japan and the United Kingdom.
Registered charity (charity number 1063952)

Subject coverage:
Anglo-Japanese relations

Museum or gallery collection, archive, or library special collection:
Library of 6,000 vols

Library catalogue:
All or part available online

Access to staff:
Contact by letter, by telephone, by fax, by e-mail and via website. Appointment necessary.

Access to building, collection or gallery:
Special comments: Library: Wed, 1400 to 1700; Fri, 1200 to 1500

JAPANESE CHAMBER OF COMMERCE AND INDUSTRY IN THE UNITED KINGDOM

Acronym or abbreviation: JCCI

5th Floor, Salisbury House, 29 Finsbury Circus, London, EC2M 5QQ

Tel: 020 7628 0069
Fax: 020 7374 2280
E-mail: chamber@jcci.org.uk

Website:
http://www.jcci.org.uk

Enquiries:
Enquiries to: Manager (Research and PR)

Founded:
1959

Organisation type and purpose:
Trade association (membership is by subscription). Chamber of Commerce for Japanese companies in the United Kingdom.

Subject coverage:
Japanese commercial interests in the United Kingdom; United Kingdom trade with Japan.

Access to staff:
Contact by letter, by telephone, by fax and by e-mail. Appointment necessary.
Hours: Mon to Fri, 0930 to 1230 and 1330 to 1730

Access to building, collection or gallery:
Prior appointment required

JAPANESE CONSULATE-GENERAL

2 Melville Crescent, Edinburgh, EH3 7HW

Tel: 0131 225 4777
Fax: 0131 225 4828

Website:
http://www.edinburgh.uk.emb-japan.go.jp

Enquiries:
Enquiries to: Consul-General

Founded:
1991

Organisation type and purpose:
Diplomatic Mission.

Subject coverage:
Information relating to Japan (information section), passports, visas, etc. (consular section).

Printed publications:
Selected publications on various aspects of Japanese life (available from Information Section)

Access to staff:
Contact by letter, by telephone and by fax. Appointment necessary.
Hours: Mon to Fri, 0930 to 1300 and 1430 to 1730

Parent body:
Ministry for Foreign Affairs
Tokyo, Japan

JAPANESE EMBASSY

Acronym or abbreviation: JICC

Japan Information and Cultural Centre, 101–104 Piccadilly, London, W1V 9FN

Tel: 020 7465 6500
Fax: 020 7465 6546
E-mail: info@embjapan.org.uk

Website:
http://www.embjapan.org.uk

Enquiries:
Enquiries to: Information Officer

Organisation type and purpose:
National government body.

Subject coverage:
All cultural aspects of Japan, lists of specialised companies or organisations for specific requests.

Museum or gallery collection, archive, or library special collection:
Small library (no appointment necessary, open to the public, Mon to Fri, 0930 to 1245 and 1430 to 1700)
Slide, video and artefact collections for schools and organisation (apply in writing, free of charge)

Trade and statistical information:
Basic statistics on culture, population and economy.

Printed publications:
Varied depending on availability (no charge)

Access to staff:
Contact by letter, by telephone, by fax, by e-mail and via website. Appointment necessary.
Hours: Mon to Fri, 0930 to 1300 and 1430 to 1700
Special comments: Slides, videos etc only to organisations not individuals; does not provide tourist information.

JENNIFER TRUST FOR SPINAL MUSCULAR ATROPHY

Acronym or abbreviation: JTSMA

Elta House, Birmingham Road, Stratford-upon-Avon, Warwickshire, CV37 0AQ

Tel: 01789 267520
Fax: 01789 268371
E-mail: jennifer@jtsma.org.uk

Website:
http://www.jtsma.org.uk

Enquiries:
Enquiries to: Information Officer

Founded:
1985

Organisation type and purpose:
National organisation, membership association (membership is by subscription), present number of members: 1,500, voluntary organisation, registered charity (charity number 1106815), research organisation.
The Jennifer Trust is a support group offering information, advice and friendship to those affected or involved with spinal muscular atrophy. Subscription is free.

Subject coverage:
Information and advice on issues relating to living with spinal muscular atrophy.

Library catalogue:
All or part available in print

Printed publications:
Newsletter (quarterly) 'Inspirations'
Information sheets available free of charge to families and adults with the condition
JTSMA General Information Leaflet
Severe SMA Information Booklet, Type II, Type III, Adult onset
JTSMA Library Book List

Publications list:
Available online and in print

Access to staff:
Contact by letter, by telephone, by fax, by e-mail and via website
Hours: Mon to Fri, 0900 to 1700

Access to building, collection or gallery:
Portable ramps

Access for disabled people:
Portable ramps

JEROME K JEROME SOCIETY

Acronym or abbreviation: JKJ Society

Tony Gray, Fraser Wood, Mayo & Pinson, 15 Lichfield Street, Walsall, West Midlands, WS1 1TS

Tel: 01922 627077
Fax: 01922 721065
E-mail: tonygray@jkj.demon.co.uk

Website:
http://www.jeromekjerome.com

Enquiries:
Enquiries to: Honorary Secretary
Direct tel: 07801 788532

Founded:
1984

Organisation type and purpose:
Learned society (membership is by subscription), present number of members: 150, registered charity (charity number 517057).
To stimulate interest in Jerome's works; access to the author's birthplace in Belsize House, Bradford St, Walsall.

Subject coverage:
Life and works of Jerome Klapka Jerome (1859–1927), novelist and playwright.

Printed publications:
Idle Thoughts (magazine, 2 times a year)

continued overleaf

Idle Thoughts on Jerome K Jerome (hb book of the best of Idle Thoughts published to celebrate the 150th anniversary of JKJ's birth).
Order printed publications from: Order the hb book from e-mail: jeremy@jeremynicholas.com or idlethoughts@jeromekjerome.com

Access to staff:
Contact by letter, by fax, by e-mail and via website
Hours: Mon to Fri, 0900 to 1700

Access to building, collection or gallery:
By prior appointment with Yvette Fletcher, tel: 01922 633214
Hours: Mon to Fri, 0900 to 1700, subject to prior appointment

JERSEY ARCHIVE

Clarence Road, St Helier, Jersey, JE2 4JY, Channel Islands

Tel: 01534 833300
Fax: 01534 833101
E-mail: archives@jerseyheritage.org

Website:
http://www.jerseyheritage.org
General introduction to services, online searchable catalogue of all holdings.

Founded:
1993

Organisation type and purpose:
Archive or Record Office.

Subject coverage:
The written history of Jersey.

Museum or gallery collection, archive, or library special collection:
The Jersey Archive collects and preserves the records of the States of Jersey, States Committees and Departments, The Royal Court, The Lieutenant Governor, parishes, churches, businesses, societies and individuals relating to the Island.

Non-library collection catalogue:
All or part available online and in-house

Printed publications:
A Glossary for the Historian of Jersey (Aubin C N, 1997, £9.95)

Access to staff:
Contact by letter, by telephone, by fax, by e-mail and in person
Hours: Tue to Thu, 0900 to 1700; last Thu of month, 0900 to 1900

Access to building, collection or gallery:
No prior appointment required

Access for disabled people:
Full disabled access, parking provided, level entry, toilet facilities
Special comments: Hearing Loop; lift to Reading Rooms.

Links with:
Jersey Heritage Trust
Jersey Museum, The Weighbridge, St Helier, Jersey, JE2 3NF, Channel Islands; tel: 01534 633300; fax: 01534 633301

JERSEY LIBRARY

Halkett Place, St Helier, Jersey, JE2 4WH, Channel Islands

Tel: 01534 448700
Fax: 01534 448730
E-mail: je.library@gov.je

Website:
http://www.gov.je/library

Enquiries:
Enquiries to: Chief Librarian

Founded:
1743

Organisation type and purpose:
Public library.

Subject coverage:
Channel Islands bibliography and history, geography, archaeology, particularly the Bailiwick of Jersey.

Museum or gallery collection, archive, or library special collection:
17th- and 18th-century belles lettres and religion
Falle Collection

Library catalogue:
All or part available online and in-house

Access to staff:
Contact by letter, by telephone, by fax, by e-mail and in person
Hours: Mon, Wed, Thu, Fri, 0930 to 1730; Tue, 0930 to 1930; Sat, 0930 to 1600

Access for disabled people:
Level entry, access to all public areas, toilet facilities

JERSEY TOURISM

Liberation Square, St Helier, Jersey, JE1 1BB, Channel Islands

Tel: 01534 500700
Fax: 01534 500899
E-mail: info@jersey.com

Organisation type and purpose:
National government body.

Subject coverage:
Jersey.

Publications list:
Available online

Access to staff:
Contact by e-mail
Hours: Mon to Fri, 0900 to 1700

Access for disabled people:
Ramped entry

JESUS COLLEGE OLD LIBRARY

Jesus College, Cambridge, CB5 8BL

Tel: 01223 339405
Fax: 01223 324910

Website:
http://www.jesus.cam.ac.uk
Introduction to Old Library.

Enquiries:
Enquiries to: Keeper or Assistant Keeper of the Old Library
Direct tel: 01223 339427
Direct e-mail: sch1000@hermes.cam.ac.uk (Keeper)
Other contacts: archives@jesus.cam.ac.uk; f.willmoth@jesus.cam.ac.uk (Assistant Keeper)

Founded:
c.1500

Formerly called:
The Library, Jesus College (year of change 1912)

Organisation type and purpose:
Historic library of a college of University of Cambridge .

Subject coverage:
Subjects directly related to University studies prior to 1900, especially theology, classics, mathematics and law.

Information services:
Queries by post, telephone or e-mail will be answered; e-mailers please give postal address.

Museum or gallery collection, archive, or library special collection:
Medieval manuscripts
Military Books of the 16th–18th centuries
Malthus Collection, deriving from T. R. Malthus (1766–1834) and his relatives

Non-library collection catalogue:
All or part available in print

Library catalogue:
All or part available in-house

Access to staff:
Contact by letter and by e-mail. Appointment necessary. Letter of introduction required.
Hours: Mon, Tue, Thu, Fri, 1000 to 1300 and 1415 to 1700
Special comments: The Assistant Keeper shares her time between the Old Library and the College Archives (tel: 01223 339439).

Access to building, collection or gallery:
Prior appointment required

Access for disabled people:
Disabled access can be provided, but is slow to operate

JETRO LONDON

Formal name: Japan External Trade Organisation
Acronym or abbreviation: JETRO

Japan Trade Centre, MidCity Place, 71 High Holborn, London, WC1V 6AL

Tel: 020 7421 8300
Fax: 020 7421 0009
E-mail: ldnresearch@jetro.go.jp

Website:
http://www.jetro.go.jp/uk
Details of JETRO London's activities.
http://www.jetro.go.jp
Head Office, Tokyo.

Enquiries:
Enquiries to: Information Officer

Founded:
1958

Organisation type and purpose:
International organisation.
Japanese government-related trade promotion organisation.

Subject coverage:
Promotion of trade between Japan and the UK.

Trade and statistical information:
Statistics related to Japan.

Library catalogue:
All or part available in-house

Printed publications:
Access to Japan's Import Market: 35 different product reports
Focus Japan (periodical, monthly)
JETRO Marketing Series
Directory for Doing Business in Japan
Directory of Japanese-Affiliated Companies in Asia (with CD-ROM)
Directory of Japanese-Affiliated Companies in USA and Canada
Directory of Japanese-Affiliated Companies in the EU (with CD-ROM)
A Guide to Investment in Japan
Human Resource Management Guidebook
Japan Trade Directory (annually, with CD-ROM)
Japanese Lifestyles
New Technology Japan (monthly
Setting up Enterprises in Japan
Specifications and Standards for Food, Food Additives, etc. under the Food Sanitation Law
Numerous publications (many free) providing information to companies wishing to export to, and/or set up in, the Japanese market
Order printed publications from: Japan External Trade Organisation, 2–5 Toranomon 2-chome, Minato-ku, Tokyo, 105–8466, Japan; tel: +81 3 3582 5511; fax: +81 3 3587 0219
OCS Tokyo (door-to-door delivery service), 2–9 Shibaura, Minato-ku, Tokyo, 108–8701, Japan; tel: +81 3 5476 8131; fax: +81 3 3453 8091
Public Relations Department (for advice first), JETRO London; tel: 020 7470 4700; fax: 020 7491 7570

Electronic and video publications:
Video catalogue

Publications list:
Available online and in print

Access to staff:
Contact by letter and by fax. Appointment necessary.
Hours: Mon to Fri, 0930 to 1230 and 1330 to 1730
Special comments: If contacting by fax, give full address as reply is by letter.

Access to building, collection or gallery:
Prior appointment required
Hours: Mon to Fri, 0930 to 1230 and 1400 to 1630

Funded by:
Ministry of Economy, Trade and Industry, Japan

JEWEL & ESK COLLEGE

Acronym or abbreviation: JEC

Edinburgh Campus, 24 Milton Road East,
Edinburgh, EH15 2PP

Tel: 0131 344 7000
Fax: 0131 344 7001
E-mail: pmccafferty@jec.ac.uk

Website:
http://www.jec.ac.uk
College web entry of course and college information.

Enquiries:
Enquiries to: Marketing Officer
Direct tel: 0131 344 7199
Direct e-mail: marketing@jec.ac.uk

Founded:
1987

Formerly called:
Jewel & Esk Valley College (year of change 2007)

Organisation type and purpose:
Local government body, suitable for ages: 12+,
training organisation.
Further Education College.

Subject coverage:
Business and management studies, office systems and administration, hairdressing and hospitality, caring studies, video production studies, educational support, computing and music, general education, mathematics and science, electronic engineering, electrical engineering, building, manufacturing, plant and instrumentation, sport and leisure, safety and first aid.

Information services:
tel: 0131 344 7152

Special visitor services:
tel: 0131 344 7405

Education services:
tel: 0131 344 7166

Services for disabled people:
tel: 0131 344 7405

Non-library collection catalogue:
All or part available online, in-house and in print

Library catalogue:
All or part available online and in-house

Printed publications:
College Prospectus (annually)

Electronic and video publications:
College promotional video 8 mins
Food hygiene and handling 35 mins (REHIS approved)
Both available direct from college, or food video also through REHIS, can be supplied in any format
College Prospectus (CD-ROM)

Publications list:
Available online and in print

Access to staff:
Contact by letter, by telephone, by fax, by e-mail, in person and via website

Hours: Mon to Fri, 0830 to 1630

Access to building, collection or gallery:
No prior appointment required
Hours: Edinburgh Campus: Mon, Fri, 0845 to 1630,
Tue, Wed, Thu, 0845 to 1930
Midlothian Campus: Mon to Fri, 0845 to 1630

Access for disabled people:
Parking provided, ramped entry, level entry, access to all public areas, toilet facilities

Also at:
Jewel & Esk College
Midlothian Campus, 46 Dalhousie Road,
Dalkeith, Midlothian, EH22 3FR; tel: 0131 344
7000; e-mail: info@jevc.ac.uk

Parent body:
Lothian Region Department of Education

JEWELLERY DISTRIBUTORS' ASSOCIATION

Acronym or abbreviation: JDA

Federation House, 10 Vyse Street, Birmingham,
B18 6LT

Tel: 0121 237 1100
Fax: 0121 236 3921
E-mail: secretariat@jda.org.uk

Website:
http://www.jda.org.uk

Enquiries:
Enquiries to: Manager

Founded:
1947

Organisation type and purpose:
Trade association (membership is by subscription).
The Jewellery Distributors Association is the national trade body for distributors and wholesalers of precious and fashion jewellery.

Subject coverage:
Product – fashion and precious jewellery.

Publications list:
Available in print

Access to staff:
Contact by letter, by telephone, by fax, by e-mail and in person
Hours: Mon to Fri, 0900 to 1700

Access for disabled people:
Parking provided, ramped entry, level entry, access to all public areas, toilet facilities
Special comments: Lift.

Parent body:
British Jewellery and Giftware Federation Limited at the same address; tel: 0121 236 2657; fax: 0121 236 3921

JEWISH BLIND AND DISABLED

Acronym or abbreviation: JBD

35 Langstone Way, London, NW7 1GT

Tel: 020 8371 6611
Fax: 020 8371 4225
E-mail: info@jbd.org

Website:
http://www.jbd.org

Founded:
1969

Organisation type and purpose:
National organisation, voluntary organisation, registered charity (charity number 259480).

Subject coverage:
Welfare services, particularly sheltered housing, for Jewish blind or disabled people, couples or families.

Printed publications:
Newsletter
Diary
Appeal Leaflets

Braille Cards
Moon Cards

Access to staff:
Contact by letter, by telephone, by fax, by e-mail and via website
Hours: Mon to Thu, 0905 to 1730; Fri, 0905 to 1400

Access for disabled people:
Parking provided, ramped entry, level entry, access to all public areas, toilet facilities

JEWISH CARE

Stuart Young House, 221 Golders Green Road,
London, NW11 9DQ

Tel: 020 8922 2000\ Minicom no. 020 8922 2233
Fax: 020 8922 1998
E-mail: info@jcare.org

Enquiries:
Enquiries to: Reception
Direct tel: 020 8922 2000
Direct fax: 020 8922 1998

Founded:
1990

Organisation type and purpose:
Voluntary organisation, registered charity (charity number 802559).
Voluntary association.
Provides a wide range of social services for the Jewish Community living in Greater London and the South East.

Subject coverage:
Information on all Jewish Care Resource Centres including: residential homes, day centres, social services, home care, specialist services, including services for people who are mentally ill, physically disabled, visually impaired, as well as Holocaust survivors and refugees.

Museum or gallery collection, archive, or library special collection:
Archive material on Jewish Welfare Board and Jewish Blind Society dating back to 1819 held at University of Southampton

Printed publications:
Annual Report (since 1859)
Careline (in-house magazine)
Information pack
Volunteer News

Access to staff:
Contact by letter
Hours: Mon to Fri, 0900 to 1730

Access to building, collection or gallery:
Prior appointment required

Access for disabled people:
Level entry, toilet facilities

Affiliated to:
Central Council for Jewish Social Service

Trustees for:
Relief of the Jewish Poor Registered

JEWISH EAST END CELEBRATION SOCIETY

Acronym or abbreviation: JEECS

PO Box 57317, London, E1 3WG

E-mail: enquiries@jeecs.org.uk

Website:
http://www.jeecs.org.uk

Organisation type and purpose:
A registered charity (no. 1107714), with membership by subscription, which focuses on Jewish life and culture in the East End of London, documenting past Jewish life and preserving the area's Jewish heritage, and reinvigorating and supporting current Jewish life through education, events, publications and good relations with other cultures represented in the area.

continued overleaf

Subject coverage:
Jewish life and culture in the East End of London.

Printed publications:
Newsletter

JEWISH EDUCATION BUREAU

Acronym or abbreviation: JEB

8 Westcombe Avenue, Leeds, West Yorkshire, LS8 2BS

Tel: 0345 567 40 70
Fax: 0844 873 1046
E-mail: jeb@jewisheducationbureau.co.uk

Website:
http://www.jewisheducationbureau.co.uk
Workshops, local Jewish history, presentations in schools and colleges.

Enquiries:
Enquiries to: Director
Direct e-mail: rabbi@jewisheducationbureau.co.uk

Founded:
1974

Organisation type and purpose:
Consultancy.
Promotes the study of Judaism as a world religion in British schools and colleges through religious education, multicultural education and the humanities.

Subject coverage:
Judaism; anti-Semitism, especially the Holocaust; Israel.

Education services:
Visits to schools and colleges; visits to synagogues arranged.

Museum or gallery collection, archive, or library special collection:
Collection of books on the Holocaust, Women, Stories, Inter-Faith Dialogue, Anglo-Jewry

Library catalogue:
All or part available in print

Access to staff:
Contact by telephone and by e-mail. Appointment necessary. All charged.
Hours: Mon to Fri, 0900 to 1700

Links with:
Consultation of Northern Religious Education Centres
Professional Council for Religious Education

JEWISH HISTORICAL SOCIETY OF ENGLAND

Acronym or abbreviation: JHSE

33 Seymour Place, London, W1H 5AP

Tel: 020 7723 5852
Fax: 020 7723 5852
E-mail: info@jhse.org

Website:
http://www.jhse.org

Enquiries:
Enquiries to: Administrator
Other contacts: Board of Deputies of British Jews for general Jewish queries.

Founded:
1893

Organisation type and purpose:
International organisation, learned society (membership is by subscription), present number of members: 720, registered charity (charity number 217331).

Subject coverage:
Anglo-Jewish history.

Museum or gallery collection, archive, or library special collection:
Library is the Mocatta Library which is now the University College London, Jewish Studies Library

Printed publications:
List of Works (some 42 titles)
Miscellanies (13 parts)
Transactions (40 vols)

Access to staff:
Contact by letter, by telephone, by fax and by e-mail. Appointment necessary.
Hours: Answerphone service
Special comments: 15 hours weekly, on various days

Links with:
Anglo-Jewish Archives

JEWISH MARRIAGE COUNCIL

Acronym or abbreviation: JMC

23 Ravenshurst Avenue, London, NW4 4EE

Tel: 020 8203 6311
Fax: 020 8203 8727
E-mail: info@jmc-uk.org

Enquiries:
Enquiries to: Director

Founded:
1946

Organisation type and purpose:
National organisation, voluntary organisation, registered charity (charity number 1078723). Recognised by the Lord Chancellor's Department, Office of the Chief Rabbi and local authorities.

Subject coverage:
Marriage preparation, guidance and counselling; family and individual counselling, divorce counselling, marriage bureau and divorce advisory service, mediation service.

Printed publications:
Annual Report (copies available free of charge)

Publications list:
Available in print

Access to staff:
Contact by letter, by telephone, by fax and by e-mail
Hours: Mon to Fri, 0935 to 1730
Special comments: Closes at 1400 on Fridays in winter.

Access for disabled people:
Ramped entry

Branch office:
Jewish Marriage Council (JMC)
  Nicky Alliance Centre, 85 Middleton Road, Manchester, M8 4JY; tel: 0161 740 5764

JEWISH MUSIC INSTITUTE

Acronym or abbreviation: JMI

SOAS, University of London, PO Box 232, Harrow, Middlesex, HA1 2NN

Tel: 020 8909 2445
Fax: 020 8909 1030
E-mail: jewishmusic@jmi.org.uk

Website:
http://www.jmi.org.uk

Enquiries:
Enquiries to: Director
Other contacts: Events Co-ordinator

Founded:
1983

Formerly called:
Jewish Music Heritage Trust

Organisation type and purpose:
An independent, non-religious arts organisation with charitable status, based at the University of London's School of Oriental and African Studies

(SOAS) and working closely with the School's Department of Music and the SOAS library. The institute documents, preserves and teaches all aspects of the Jewish musical heritage, and presents that heritage to the public, supporting university courses and running workshops, summer schools, regular classes and outreach projects. Aims to provide an international focus for study and musicianship through such initiatives as the International Forum for Suppressed Music, the International Forum for Yiddish Culture and the Forum for the Promotion of Arab-Jewish Dialogue through Music.

Subject coverage:
All aspects of the Jewish musical heritage, including liturgical, classical, ethnic and folk music and music suppressed by the Nazi and Soviet regimes.

Special visitor services:
Bands for Weddings and Parties.

Education services:
Summer schools, regular classes and outreach projects.

Museum or gallery collection, archive, or library special collection:
Library of recordings, books, manuscripts and scores in all genres of Jewish music, dating from the Middle Ages to the present

Access to staff:
Contact by letter, by fax, by e-mail and via website

JOCKEY CLUB

151 Shaftesbury Avenue, London, WC2H 8AL

Tel: 020 7189 3800
Fax: 020 7189 3801
E-mail: info@thejockeyclub.co.uk

Website:
http://www.thejockeyclub.co.uk

Enquiries:
Enquiries to: Public Relations Officer

Founded:
1752

Organisation type and purpose:
National organisation (membership is by election or invitation).
Regulatory body for horseracing in Great Britain. To set and maintain standards for racing, to support the British Horseracing Board in administering and developing the best interests of horseracing and breeding.

Subject coverage:
Safety and welfare of horse and rider, licensing individuals and racecourses, and compiling and applying rules of racing.

Access to staff:
Contact by letter, by telephone, by fax and by e-mail
Hours: Mon to Fri, 0900 to 1700

JODRELL BANK OBSERVATORY

Jodrell Bank, Lower Withington, Macclesfield, Cheshire, SK11 9DL

Tel: 01477 571321
Fax: 01477 571618

Website:
http://www.jb.man.ac.uk
Information on research activities.

Enquiries:
Enquiries to: Public Relations Manager

Founded:
1957

Organisation type and purpose:
University department or institute, research organisation.

Subject coverage:
Astronomy; radio astronomy techniques, radio telescope design and control, low noise receive-systems, long and short baseline interferometry; signal processing and computing techniques; galactic structure; hydrogen line observations; radio sources and source surveys and identifications; pulsars; radio stars; active galactic nuclei; radio galaxies; quasars; cosmic microwave background.

Access to staff:
Contact by letter
Hours: Mon to Fri, 0900 to 1700

Part of:
Department of Physics and Astronomy, University of Manchester

JOHANN STRAUSS SOCIETY OF GREAT BRITAIN

12 Bishams Court, Church Hill, Caterham, Surrey, CR3 6SE

Tel: 01883 349681
E-mail: strauss.sec@btinternet.com

Enquiries:
Enquiries to: Honorary Secretary

Founded:
1964

Organisation type and purpose:
Learned society (membership is by subscription), present number of members: 550, voluntary organisation.
Musical appreciation society.

Subject coverage:
History of the Strauss Family and their music, performance and recording of lesser-known works of the Strauss Family and their Viennese contemporaries.

Printed publications:
Newsletter (6 times a year, members)
Vienna Music (journal, twice yearly)

Access to staff:
Contact by letter and by telephone
Hours: Mon to Fri, 0900 to 1700

Affiliated to other:
Johann Strauss Societies in Vienna, France, Germany, Italy, Japan, Poland, Southern Africa, Sweden, Australia, Romania, Czech Republic and Slovak Republic

JOHN BUCHAN SOCIETY

Acronym or abbreviation: JBSoc

The Toft, 37 Waterloo Road, Lanark, ML11 7QH

Tel: 01555 662103
E-mail: glennismac2000@yahoo.co.uk

Website:
http://www.johnbuchansociety.co.uk

Enquiries:
Enquiries to: Honorary Secretary

Founded:
1979

Organisation type and purpose:
Learned society, voluntary organisation.
To promote a wider understanding and appreciation of the life and works of John Buchan and to support the John Buchan Centre at Broughton, near Peebles.

Non-library collection catalogue:
All or part available in-house

Printed publications:
Journal (2 times a year)
Newsletter twice yearly

Access to staff:
Contact by letter, by telephone and by e-mail.
Access for members only.
Hours: Mon to Fri, 0900 to 1700

JOHN CABOT CITY TECHNOLOGY COLLEGE

Formal name: John Cabot City Technology College Bristol Trust
Acronym or abbreviation: John Cabot CTC

Woodside Road, Kingswood, South Gloucestershire, BS15 8BD

Tel: 0117 976 3000
Fax: 0117 976 0630
E-mail: info@cabot.ac.uk

Website:
http://www.cabot.ac.uk
Full description of college operation and multiple hot links.

Enquiries:
Enquiries to: Principal

Founded:
1993

Organisation type and purpose:
Suitable for ages: 11 to 19.
Independent state maintained secondary school.

Subject coverage:
Specialist education in maths, science and technology.

Printed publications:
Annual prospectus

Access to staff:
Contact by letter
Hours: Hire of facilities out of hours

JOHN CLARE SOCIETY

9 The Chase, Ely, Cambridgeshire, CB6 3DR

Tel: 01353 668438 (evenings)

Website:
http://vzone.virgin.net/linda.curry/jclare
For information about the John Clare Society.
http://human.ntu.ac.uk/clare.html
Bibliography, chronology, selection of articles related to Clare and current information on Clare events.
http://www.johnclare.org.uk
General information, book sales, membership information, events and useful links

Enquiries:
Enquiries to: Honorary Secretary
Other contacts: Chairman for website, e-mail, linked to university.

Founded:
1981

Organisation type and purpose:
International organisation, learned society (membership is by subscription), present number of members: 650, voluntary organisation.

Subject coverage:
Promoting the study of the life and works of John Clare, poet (1793–1864).

Museum or gallery collection, archive, or library special collection:
None owned by the Society but note:
Manuscripts and books (at Northampton Central Reference Library)
Manuscripts (the largest collection at Peterborough Museum)

Printed publications:
A Descriptive Catalogue of the John Clare Collection on Peterborough Museum and Art Gallery
John Clare, Flower Poems (ed Kovesi S)
Cumulative Index of Journals 1982–2001
For John Clare: an anthology of verse (selected and edited by John Lucas)
John Clare – Love Poems (ed Kovesi S)
John Clare, the Northamptonshire Poet (ed Carr)
John Clare, The Poet and the Place (Moyse P, contact peter.moyse@amserve.com)
The John Clare Society Journal (annually)
The John Clare Society Newsletter (quarterly)

The Life and Times of John Clare

Publications list:
Available online and in print

Access to staff:
Contact by letter and by telephone
Hours: Mon to Fri, 0900 to 1700
Special comments: Enquiries by letter enclosing sae please.

Autonomous affiliate:
John Clare Society of North America
Executive Director, Department of English, University of Maryland, Baltimore County, Baltimore, MD21250, USA; tel: 00 1 410 455 2164

Member of:
The Alliance of Literary Societies
Hon. Secretary, 71 Stepping Stones Road, Coventry, CV5 8JT

JOHN FROST NEWSPAPERS

Formal name: John Frost Newspapers Limited

22B Rosemary Avenue, Enfield, Middlesex, EN2 0SS

Tel: 020 8366 1392/0946
Fax: 020 8366 1379
E-mail: andrew@johnfrostnewspapers.com

Website:
http://www.johnfrostnewspapers.co.uk
Summary of holdings.
http://www.johnfrostnewspapers.com

Enquiries:
Enquiries to: Archivist

Founded:
1965

Organisation type and purpose:
Research organisation.
In depth files on crime, royalty, war, politics, pop.

Subject coverage:
UK and overseas newspapers reporting outstanding events since 1640 – political, economy, royalty, disasters. crime, sport, war, etc.

Museum or gallery collection, archive, or library special collection:
100,000 press cuttings reporting historic and outstanding events, from 1640 to present day
100,000 newspapers: British and overseas

Printed publications:
Pamphlet available on request

Publications list:
Available online and in print

Access to staff:
Contact by letter, by telephone and by fax.
Appointment necessary.
Hours: Mon to Fri, 0900 to 1700

Access to building, collection or gallery:
Prior appointment required

Access for disabled people:
Toilet facilities

Also at:
John Frost Newspapers
8 Monks Avenue, New Barnet, Hertfordshire, EN5 1DB; tel: 020 8440 3159

JOHN INNES CENTRE AND SAINSBURY LABORATORY

Acronym or abbreviation: JIC

Norwich Research Park, Colney, Norwich, Norfolk, NR4 7UH

Tel: 01603 450000
Fax: 01603 450045

Website:
http://www.jic.bbsrc.ac.uk
John Innes Centre homepage.

Enquiries:
Enquiries to: Librarian

continued overleaf

Direct e-mail: jic.library@bbsrc.ac.uk
Other contacts: Archivist for Historical Collections
Librarian.

Founded:
1994

Organisation type and purpose:
Registered charity (charity number 223852),
research organisation.

Subject coverage:
Mostly at postgraduate level and above, currently
includes classical botany, horticulture, crop plants,
plant breeding, classical and molecular plant
genetics, plant genome mapping, plant
biochemistry, physiology and cell biology, plant
virology and pathology and plant biotechnology.
In addition, we hold material on microbial genetics
(notably Streptomyces and Rhizobium), nitrogen
fixation and enzymology, bioinorganic chemistry,
history of genetics, history of plant sciences.

**Museum or gallery collection, archive, or library
special collection:**
Cyril Darlington Library
History of Genetics Library
John Innes reprint collection and archives
John Innes Trustees' collection of rare botanical
books
William Bateson Library and letters

Non-library collection catalogue:
All or part available online and in print

Library catalogue:
All or part available in-house

Printed publications:
Annual Report
Proceedings: John Innes Symposia

Access to staff:
Contact by telephone and by e-mail. Appointment
necessary. Non-members charged.
Hours: Mon to Fri, 0900 to 1700

Access to building, collection or gallery:
Prior appointment required

Grant-aided by:
Biotechnology and Biological Sciences Research
Council (BBSRC)

JOHN INNES MANUFACTURERS ASSOCIATION

Acronym or abbreviation: JIMA

PO Box 8, Department M14/A, Harrogate, North
Yorkshire, HG2 8XB

Tel: 01423 879208
Fax: 01423 870025
E-mail: info@johninnes.info

Website:
http://www.johninnes.info

Enquiries:
Enquiries to: Secretary and PR Officer

Founded:
1977

Organisation type and purpose:
Trade association.

Subject coverage:
Loam-based potting mixes and related growing
media for both amateur gardening and
professional growers in the United Kingdom.

Printed publications:
Benefits of Loam-Based Composts (leaflet, free)
18 Technical data and information sheets series
(free) including
TDS1 The History of John Innes Composts
TDS2 Formulation of John Innes Composts
TDS4 Grades and Application of JI Composts
TDS5 Storage of John Innes Composts
TDS6 How to Use John Innes Composts
TDS7 What Compost Do I Use? – That is the
question!
TDS10 Registered Manufacturers of John Innes
TDS16 John Innes for Planters, Tubs and Window
Boxes

TDS14 John Innes Ericaceous Compost
TDS17 JIMA Quality Control Specifications

Publications list:
Available online and in print

Access to staff:
Contact by letter, by telephone, by fax and by e-
mail. Appointment necessary.
Hours: Mon to Fri, 0900 to 1800

JOHN LEWIS PARTNERSHIP

171 Victoria Street, London, SW1E 5NN

Tel: 020 7828 1000

Website:
http://www.waitrose.com
Transactional ISP information site – Waitrose
supermarkets.
http://www.johnlewis.com
Transactional information site – John Lewis
department stores.
http://www.johnlewispartnership.co.uk
Corporate site – John Lewis Partnership.

Enquiries:
Enquiries to: Manager, Business Information
Direct tel: 020 7592 6219
Direct fax: 020 7592 6294
Direct e-mail: business_information@johnlewis.co
.uk

Organisation type and purpose:
Service industry.
Retail business run on co-operative principles.

Subject coverage:
Retailing; industrial democracy.

Trade and statistical information:
Weekly trading figures for John Lewis plc are
published in The Gazette of the John Lewis
Partnership and on the corporate website.

Library catalogue:
All or part available in-house

Access to staff:
Appointment necessary.
Hours: Mon to Fri, 0900 to 1700

Access to building, collection or gallery:
Prior appointment required

JOHN MEADE FALKNER SOCIETY

Acronym or abbreviation: JMF Soc

Greenmantle, Main Street, Kings Newton,
Melbourne, Derbyshire, DE73 8BX

Tel: 01332 865315
E-mail: nebuly@hotmail.co.uk

Website:
www.johnmeadefalknersociety.co.uk

Enquiries:
Enquiries to: Honorary Secretary

Founded:
1999

Organisation type and purpose:
Learned society (membership is by subscription),
present number of members: 56, voluntary
organisation.
To promote the appreciation and study of John
Meade Falkner's life, times and works.

Library catalogue:
All or part available in-house

Printed publications:
Journal (annually)
Newsletters
Order printed publications from: Honorary Secretary

Publications list:
Available online

Access to staff:
Contact by letter, by telephone, by e-mail and via
website
Hours: Mon to Fri, 0900 to 1700

JOHN RYLANDS UNIVERSITY LIBRARY OF MANCHESTER

Acronym or abbreviation: JRULM

Oxford Road, Manchester, M13 9PP

Tel: 0161 275 3751
Fax: 0161 273 7488

Website:
http://www.manchester.ac.uk/library
General library information and access to the
catalogue of the John Rylands University Library
as well as other external information collections.

Enquiries:
Enquiries to: Administrator
Direct tel: 0161 306 1938
Direct e-mail: lisa.donnelly@manchester.ac.uk
Other contacts: Subject and Information Services
(tel: 0161 275 3751); Publications Enquiries (tel:
0161 275 3749)

Founded:
1851

Created by the merger of:
Manchester University Library and the John
Rylands Library

Organisation type and purpose:
University library.

Subject coverage:
American studies, ancient history, archaeology,
architecture, astronomy, audiology, biological
sciences, Celtic studies, chemistry, classical studies,
computer science, dentistry, drama, earth sciences,
education, engineering, English, European studies,
French, geography, German, health services
administration, history, history of art, history of
science and medicine, Italian, law, linguistics,
materials science, mathematics, medicine,
metallurgy, Middle Eastern studies, military
studies, music, nursing, palaeontology, pharmacy,
philosophy, physics, planning and landscape,
polymer science, Portuguese, psychotherapy, radio
astronomy, religious studies, Russian, Spanish,
theology.

**Museum or gallery collection, archive, or library
special collection:**
Anti-Slavery (Raymond English Collection; H G
Wilson Pamphlet Collection)
Architecture (Archives of the Manchester Society
of Architects; Archives of the Society of
Architectural Historians of GB)
British Standards
Celtic Studies (Strachan Celtic Books; Katharine
Tynan Collection)
Childrens' Literature (Alison Uttley Books and
Papers; Vera Southgate Booth Collection;
Marmion Collection)
Church and Society (Audenshaw Collection;
William Temple Collection)
Dante Collection
Drama: see Theatre and Drama
Early Printed Books (Spencer, Aldine, Christie and
Bullock Collections)
Education for Special Needs (Deaf Education
Collection; Hester Adrian Collection; Hilliard
Collection)
English Historians (Papers of E A Freeman, James
Tait and T F Tout)
English Literature (George Bellairs, Elizabeth
Gaskell, L P Hartley, Howard Spring and Thrale-
Piozzi MSS)
Esperanto Collection
European Communities Collection (European
Documentation Centre)
Family Muniments (Bagshawe, Bromley-
Davenport, Cornwall-Legh, Ducie, Dunham
Massey, Legh of Lyme, Tabley and Warburton)
French Studies (Victor Hugo Correspondence;
Mazarinades Pamphlets; French Revolution
Collection; Alexandre Dumas, père, collection)
Geography (Manchester Geographical Society
Collection; Map Collection)
German Studies (Peter Huchel Collection)
Health and Safety Collection
History of Astronomy (Archives of Zdenek Kopal,
Bernard Lovell; Jodrell Bank Collection)

History of Chemistry (Papers of John Dalton and H
   E Roscoe; Partington Collection)
History of Medicine (Manchester Medical Society
   Collection)
Industrial and Commercial History (Archives of
   Bolton Cotton Spinners, Thomas Botfield and
   Co., McConnel and Kennedy, Oldham Textile
   Employers and Owen Owens)
Journalism (Guardian Archives; Papers of W P
   Crozier, Alastair Hetherington, P J Monkhouse
   and C P Scott; Newspaper Collection)
Judaica (Moses Gaster Collection including
   Genizah Fragments; Haskalah and Marmorstein
   Collections)
Local History (Cheshire, Lancashire and
   Derbyshire Family Muniment Collections)
Manchester Museum Collection
Manchester University Archives
Military Studies (Clinton, Auchinleck and Dorman
   O'Gowan Papers; World War I Collection)
NASA and NIST Deposit Library
Near Eastern Book and MSS Collections (especially
   Arabic and Persian)
Nonconformity (Methodist Archives;
   Congregational College, Northern Baptist
   College and Unitarian College Collections;
   Papers of T W Manson and Thomas Raffles)
Official Publications (British and International
   Organisations)
Oriental Book and MSS Collections
Papyri (Arabic, Coptic, Greek, Hieratic and
   Hieroglyphic)
Philosophy (Papers of Samuel Alexander and
   Robert Adamson)
Political Economy (W S Jevons Papers)
Political Parties (Labour Party Newscuttings and
   Pamphlets)
Pre-Raphaelites (Papers of Holman Hunt and John
   Ruskin)
Private Press Books (eg Kelmscott)
Russian History (eg Alexis Aladin Papers)
Spectral and Technical Data Collection
Sport (Brockbank Cricket Collection)
Suffragette Collections
Theatre and Drama (Papers of Basil Dean, Stephen
   Joseph, C E Montague and A N Monkhouse; G L
   Brook, Annie Horniman and Allardyce Nicoll
   Collections)
Transport (e.g. Kenneth Brown and T J Edmondson
   Railway Collections)
United Nations Deposit Library
Western Medieval MSS (especially Latin, English
   and French)

Printed publications:
Publications: for sale
Bulletin of the John Rylands University Library of
   Manchester, including off-prints and indexes (list
   available)
Catalogues of certain special collections:
   manuscript and printed book collections
Commercial microfilm and facsimile publications
   (listed in Publications in Print 1993, pp. 68–71)
Exhibition catalogues
John Rylands Research Institute Prospectus
Research Guides
Slides: Treasures from the John Rylands University
   Library

Provides headquarters for the:
John Rylands Research Institute
Manchester Bibliographical Society
Manchester Medical Society

JOHNSON MATTHEY TECHNOLOGY CENTRE

Acronym or abbreviation: JMTC

Blounts Court, Sonning Common, Reading,
Berkshire, RG4 9NH

Tel: 0118 924 2000
Fax: 0118 924 2254

Website:
http://www.matthey.com
General, divisional and product information for
Johnson Matthey.

Founded:
1817

Organisation type and purpose:
Manufacturing industry, research organisation.
Serving the Catalysts and Chemicals, and Precious
Metals Divisions of Johnson Matthey plc.

Subject coverage:
Platinum group metals; gold; base metals;
inorganic chemistry; materials science; catalysis;
pollution control; fuel cells; electrochemistry

**Museum or gallery collection, archive, or library
special collection:**
London Collection (books c. 1850 to early 1900s on
history of London)

Printed publications:
Platinum (annually)
Platinum Metals Review (quarterly)

Access to staff:
Contact by telephone and by fax
Hours: Mon to Fri, 0900 to 1700

JOINT ASSOCIATION OF CLASSICAL TEACHERS

Acronym or abbreviation: JACT

Senate House, Malet Street, London, WC1E 7HU

Tel: 020 7862 8719
Fax: 020 7255 2297
E-mail: office@jact.org

Website:
http://www.jact.org
General information about JACT.

Enquiries:
Enquiries to: Administrator

Founded:
1961

Organisation type and purpose:
Professional body, registered charity (charity
number 313165).

Subject coverage:
Teaching of Classics (Greek, Latin, classical
civilisation and ancient history) at all levels;
bibliographic and teaching aids.

Printed publications:
Journal of Classics Teaching (3 times a year)
Omnibus (2 times a year)

Microform publications:
Filmstrips

Access to staff:
Contact by letter, by telephone, by fax, by e-mail
and in person. Appointment necessary.
Hours: Tues to Fri, 1000 to 1700

JOINT COUNCIL FOR LANDSCAPE INDUSTRIES

Acronym or abbreviation: JCLI

c/o The Landscape Institute, 6/8 Barnard Mews,
London, SW11 1QU

Tel: 020 7350 5200
Fax: 020 7350 5201

Enquiries:
Enquiries to: Secretary
Direct e-mail: paull@landscapeinstitute.org
Other contacts: Committee Services Officer

Organisation type and purpose:
National organisation.
Umbrella body for the landscape industry.

Subject coverage:
Co-ordinates views of member organisations and
represents those members in all matters of
common interest and concerns at all levels,
including Local and National Government and
internationally represents British Landscape
interests and promotes and encourages greater
public interest.

Printed publications:
Order printed publications from: The Landscape
Institute

Publications list:
Available in print

Access to staff:
Contact by letter, by telephone, by fax and by e-
mail
Hours: Mon to Fri, 0900 to 1700

Connections with:
Arboricultural Association (AA)
British Association of Landscape Industries (BALI)
Horticultural Trades Association (HTA)
Institute of Leisure and Amenity Management
(ILAM)
Landscape Institute (LI)
National Farmers Union (NFU)

JOINT COUNCIL FOR QUALIFICATIONS

Sixth Floor, 29 Great Peter Street, London, SW1P
3LW

Tel: 020 7638 4132
Fax: 020 7374 4343
E-mail: info@jcq.org.uk

Website:
http://www.jcq.org.uk
Publications, examination results, statistics.

Enquiries:
Enquiries to: Office Manager

Founded:
2004

Organisation type and purpose:
Membership association (membership is by
election or invitation), suitable for ages: 11 to 19.

Library catalogue:
All or part available online

Printed publications:
Access Arrangements, Reasonable Adjustments
   and Special Consideration: General and
   Vocational Qualifications – 1 September 2010 to
   31 August 2011
General and Vocational Qualifications: General
   Regulations for Approved Centres – 1 September
   2010 to 31 August 2011
General, Vocational and Diploma Qualifications:
   Instructions for conducting examinations – 1
   September 2010 to 31 August 2011
GCSE specifications and Principal Learning units
   within Diploma Qualifications: Instructions for
   conducting controlled assessments – 1
   September 2010 to 31 August 2011
Order printed publications from: See list of Member
Awarding Bodies

Publications list:
Available online

Access to staff:
Contact by letter, by fax and by e-mail
Hours: Mon to Fri, 0900 to 1700

Member Awarding Body:
Assessment and Qualifications Alliance
   Stag Hill House, Guildford, Surrey, GU2 7XJ; tel:
   01483 506506
Edexcel
   One90 High Holborn, London, WC1V 7BH; tel:
   0844 576 0025
Northern Ireland Council for the Curriculum
Examinations and Assessment
   29 Clarendon Road, Belfast, BT1 3BG; tel: 028
   9026 1200
OCR
   Syndicate Buildings, 1 Hills Road, Cambridge,
   CB1 2EU; tel: 01223 553998
Scottish Qualifiations Authority
   The Optima Building, 58 Robertson Street,
   Glasgow G2 8DQ
The City and Guilds London Institute
   1 Giltspur Street, London, EC1A 9DD

continued overleaf

WJEC/CBAC
245 Western Avenue, Cardiff, CF5 2YX; tel: 02920 265000

JOINT COUNCIL FOR THE WELFARE OF IMMIGRANTS

Acronym or abbreviation: JCWI

115 Old Street, London, EC1V 9RT

Tel: 020 7251 8708
Fax: 020 7251 8707
E-mail: info@jcwi.org.uk

Website:
http://www.jcwi.org.uk

Enquiries:
Enquiries to: Office Manager
Direct e-mail: info@jcwi.org.uk
Other contacts: Training Officer (for training)

Founded:
1967

Organisation type and purpose:
Membership association (membership is by subscription), present number of members: 1,000, voluntary organisation, training organisation, campaign organisation, publishing house.
1,000 affiliated organisations and individuals; mainly black and ethnic minority organisations, advice agencies, community relations councils, local authorities, solicitors.
Immigration Law advice and training agency.

Subject coverage:
Immigration, nationality and refugee law and practice.

Information services:
Fee telephone advice service for the public, Wed 1100 to 1300.

Special visitor services:
Two solicitors providing legally-funded help; representation at competitive rates for individuals who do not qualify for public funding.

Printed publications:
JCWI Bulletin (quarterly)
A small number of books, leaflets and briefings including:
JCWI Immigration Nationality & Refuge Law Handbook (2006)
See website for further updates

Publications list:
Available online and in print

Access to staff:
Contact by letter, by telephone, by fax and by e-mail. Appointment necessary.
Hours: Mon to Fri, 0900 to 1700

Access for disabled people:
Ramped entry, toilet facilities

JOINT EDUCATIONAL TRUST

Acronym or abbreviation: JET

6–8 Fenchurch Buildings, London, EC3M 5HT

Tel: 020 3217 1100
Fax: 020 3217 1110
E-mail: admin@jetcharity.org

Website:
http://www.jetcharity.org

Enquiries:
Enquiries to: Director

Founded:
1971

Organisation type and purpose:
Registered charity (charity number 313218), suitable for ages: 7 to 13.

Subject coverage:
Suitable schools for vulnerable children with social need, not educational need.

Printed publications:
Order printed publications from: JET, free of charge

Access to staff:
Contact by letter, by telephone, by fax, by e-mail and via website
Hours: Mon to Fri, 0900 to 1700

Access to building, collection or gallery:
No access other than to staff

Access for disabled people:
Access to all public areas, toilet facilities

JOINT INDUSTRY BOARD FOR THE ELECTRICAL CONTRACTING INDUSTRY

Acronym or abbreviation: JIB

Kingswood House, 47–51 Sidcup Hill, Sidcup, Kent, DA14 6HP

Tel: 020 8302 0031
Fax: 020 8309 1103

Website:
http://www.jib.org.uk
Including the Handbook.

Enquiries:
Enquiries to: Chief Executive

Founded:
1968

Organisation type and purpose:
Membership association (membership is by qualification), present number of members: 27,000. Implements national wage agreement and working rules in the electrical contracting industry.

Subject coverage:
Wage rates and terms and conditions of employment for hourly paid employees in the electrical contracting industry.

Printed publications:
Health and Safety Handbook (£4)
Handbook (annual, £5)

Electronic and video publications:
Electronic version of the Handbook can be downloaded from the web site

Access to staff:
Contact by letter
Hours: Mon to Fri, 0900 to 1700

JOINT LIBRARY OF THE HELLENIC AND ROMAN SOCIETIES

3rd Floor, Senate House, Malet Street, London, WC1E 7HU

Tel: 020 7862 8709
Fax: 020 7862 8735

Website:
http://icls.sas.ac.uk/library/Home.htm

Enquiries:
Enquiries to: Librarian
Direct tel: 020 7862 8710
Direct fax: 020 7862 8724
Direct e-mail: colin.annis@sas.ac.uk

Founded:
1950

Organisation type and purpose:
Private Library combined with Institute of Classical Studies Library.

Subject coverage:
All aspects of classical civilisation, including archaeology, art and architecture, language and literature, history, law, politics, religion, philosophy and science relating to the Minoan, Mycenaean, Ancient Greek and early Byzantine World, and also to early Italic and Etruscan civilisations, and to the Roman World from the beginning of the 5th century AD (including Roman Britain).

Museum or gallery collection, archive, or library special collection:
110,000 monographs and pamphlets
20,000 bound volumes of periodicals
6,800 slides
675 current periodicals taken

Library catalogue:
All or part available online

Printed publications:
Britannia (available to members as part of the subscription; available for purchase to non-members)
Journal of Hellenic Studies (available to members as part of the subscription; available for purchase to non-members)
Journal of Roman Studies (available to members as part of the subscription; available for purchase to non-members)
Order printed publications from: Secretary, Hellenic Society, at the same address, tel: 020 7862 8730; fax: 020 7862 8731; e-mail: office@hellenicsociety.org.uk
Secretary, Roman Society, at the same address, tel: 020 7862 8727; fax: 020 7862 8728; e-mail: office@romansociety.org

Publications list:
Available online and in print

Access to staff:
Contact by letter, by telephone, by fax, by e-mail and in person. Access for members only.
Hours: Mon to Fri, 0930 to 1800
Term time: Tue, Wed and Thu, 0930 to 2000; Sat, 1000 to 1630; closed Sat during August

Combined with:
Institute of Classical Studies Library (ICS)

JOINT NATURE CONSERVATION COMMITTEE

Acronym or abbreviation: JNCC

Monkstone House, City Road, Peterborough, Cambridgeshire, PE1 1JY

Tel: 01733 562626
Fax: 01733 555948
E-mail: communications@jncc.gov.uk

Website:
http://www.jncc.gov.uk
Work of JNCC, news and information, online catalogue and the list of available JNCC reports, together with forthcoming publications, online publications such as the Annual Report and Corporate Plan.

Founded:
1991

Organisation type and purpose:
Advisory body.
Responsible to the UK Government for research and advice on nature conservation at both UK and international levels, on behalf of the Countryside Council for Wales, Natural England, Scottish Natural Heritage, and the Council for Nature Conservation and the Countryside (Northern Ireland); the Committee also includes independent members.

Subject coverage:
Nature conservation

Printed publications:
Corporate Plans
Wide variety of books on birds, coasts, earth science, habitat, herpetofauna, invertebrates, land use, mammals, marine life, plants and pollution.
Annual Reports from 1991 onwards
Order printed publications from: NHBS, 2–3 Wills Road, Totnes, Devon, TQ9 5XN, tel: 01803 865913, fax: 01803 865280, e-mail: nhbs@nhbs.co.uk

Publications list:
Available online and in print

Access to staff:
Contact by letter, by telephone, by fax, by e-mail and via website. Appointment necessary.
Hours: Mon to Thu, 0830 to 1700; Fri, 0830 to 1630

Also at:
JNCC (Aberdeen Office)
  Dunnet House, 7 Thistle Place, Aberdeen, AB10
  1UZ; tel: 01224 655704; fax: 01224 621488; e-
  mail: communications@jncc.gov.uk; website:
  http://www.jncc.gov.uk

JOINT SERVICES COMMAND & STAFF COLLEGE LIBRARY

Acronym or abbreviation: JSCSC

Faringdon Road, Watchfield, Shrivenham,
Wiltshire, SN6 8TS

Tel: 01793 788236
Fax: 01793 788281
E-mail: library.jscsc@defenceacademy.mod.uk

Enquiries:
Enquiries to: Librarian

Founded:
1997

Organisation type and purpose:
National government body, central government
establishment.
Military staff training college.

Subject coverage:
Air power, aviation (military), modern warfare,
historical warfare, defence policy and studies,
NATO, Warsaw Pact countries, international
affairs, communications skills, management
techniques, Armed Forces, sea power, Royal Navy,
navies, land warfare, British Army, armies and
Royal Air Force, leadership, campaign studies.

**Museum or gallery collection, archive, or library
special collection:**
Extensive archive of British military documents
  and books dating back to the 18th Century

Library catalogue:
All or part available online and in-house

Printed publications:
Reader's Guides, Bibliographies
Order printed publications from: e-mail: ibrary.jscsc@
defenceacademy.mod.uk

Access to staff:
Contact by letter, by telephone, by fax and by e-
mail. Appointment necessary.
Hours: Mon to Fri, 0800 to 1800

Access to building, collection or gallery:
Prior appointment required
Hours: Mon to Fri, 0800 to 1800

Access for disabled people:
Access to all public areas

Parent body:
Ministry of Defence

JONES LANG LASALLE

22 Hanover Square, London, W1A 2BN

Tel: 020 7493 6040
Fax: 020 7399 5818

Website:
http://www.joneslanglasalle.co.uk

Enquiries:
Enquiries to: Information Manager
Direct e-mail: infodesk@en.jll.com

Founded:
1999

Organisation type and purpose:
Consultancy.

Subject coverage:
Real estate.

Printed publications:
Central London Market Report (4 times a year)
Office Service Charges (annually)
Property Index (quarterly)

Publications list:
Available online and in print

Access to staff:
Contact by letter and by e-mail
Hours: Mon to Fri, 0900 to 1730

Access to building, collection or gallery:
No access other than to staff

JORDAN INFORMATION BUREAU

Acronym or abbreviation: JIB

6 Upper Phillimore Gardens, London, W8 7HB

Tel: 020 7937 9499
Fax: 020 7937 6741
E-mail: info@jiblondon.com

Website:
http://www.jordanembassyuk.gov.jo
Tourism, economic, news, contacts, general
information, weekly publications.

Enquiries:
Enquiries to: Director
Other contacts: Information Officer

Founded:
1992

Organisation type and purpose:
Part of Diplomatic Mission.
Press, media and information section.

Subject coverage:
General information about Jordan, history, politics,
economy, culture, social life, and the Middle East
Peace process.

**Museum or gallery collection, archive, or library
special collection:**
Library containing information on Jordan and the
  Middle East

Printed publications:
General information on Jordan

Electronic and video publications:
Some video information (available for loan only)
CD-ROM on Jordan

Access to staff:
Contact by letter, by telephone, by fax, by e-mail
and via website
Hours: Mon to Fri, 0900 to 1600

Access to building, collection or gallery:
No prior appointment required

Connections with:
Embassy of The Hashemite Kingdom of Jordan
  6 Upper Phillimore Gardens, London, W8 7HB

JORDANS LIMITED

21 St Thomas Street, Bristol, BS1 6JS

Tel: 0117 923 0600
Fax: 0117 923 0063
E-mail: businessinformation@jordans.co.uk

Website:
http://www.jordans.co.uk

Enquiries:
Enquiries to: Customer Service Administrator
Direct tel: 0117 918 1283
Direct e-mail: denise_sebastian@jordans.co.uk
Other contacts: Customer Services Administrator
for purchase of data, or for quotations.

Founded:
1898

Organisation type and purpose:
Registration agents, law agents.
Business information provider.
Publishing house, printers and stationers.

Subject coverage:
Company financial information including
information for marketing, credit checking,
performance analysis, status reports, money-
laundering report, official filings at Companies
House.

Trade and statistical information:
Industry sector reports: financial analysis of
  companies by industry region, size, growth etc.

Printed publications:
Financial Reports
Top 10,000 privately owned companies

Electronic and video publications:
Amadeus: financial database of top 200,000
  European companies on CD/DVD-ROM and
  internet
A wide variety of reports on disc
FAME (Financial Analysis Made Easy) Database
  on CD/DVD-ROM and internet (2.5m UK and
  Irish cos)
Jordan Company Database of 2,000 plcs holding
  more than 0.15% shares
Shareholder Information on disc
Jordanwatch for financial profiles and image-link
  (online)
KYC (Know Your Client) money-laundering data
  (online)

Publications list:
Available online and in print

Access to staff:
Contact by letter, by telephone, by fax, by e-mail,
in person and via website. Appointment necessary.
Hours: Mon to Fri, 0900 to 1700

Other addresses:
Jordans Limited
  20–22 Bedford Row, London, WC1R 4JS; tel: 020
  7400 3333; fax: 020 7400 3366
Jordans Limited
  44 Whitchurch Road, Cardiff, CF4 3UQ; tel: 029
  2037 1901; fax: 029 2038 2342
Oswalds
  24 Great King Street, Edinburgh, EH3 6QN; tel:
  0131 557 6966; fax: 0131 556 2917

Parent body:
West of England Trust Limited
  21 St Thames Street, Bristol, BS1 6JS

JOSEPH ROWNTREE FOUNDATION

Acronym or abbreviation: JRF

The Homestead, 40 Water End, York, YO30 6WP

Tel: 01904 629241
Fax: 01904 620072
E-mail: info@jrf.org.uk

Website:
http://www.jrf.org.uk
Corporate information, summaries of research
supported by the Foundation in the form of
'Findings', from 1998: list of current research
supported by the Foundation.

Enquiries:
Enquiries to: Information Services Officer
Direct tel: extn 243
Direct e-mail: janet.mccullough@jrf.org.uk

Founded:
1904

Formerly called:
Joseph Rowntree Village Trust (year of change
1959); Joseph Rowntree Memorial Trust (year of
change 1990)

Organisation type and purpose:
Endowed foundation, funding large, UK-wide
research and development programme.
Housing Association.

Subject coverage:
Housing research; social policy; social care;
poverty; drugs and alcohol; housing associations;
New Earswick (model village); Rowntree family
history.

**Museum or gallery collection, archive, or library
special collection:**
Archive at Borthwick Institute, University of York

Library catalogue:
All or part available in-house

continued overleaf

Printed publications:
Over 500 books and reports published since 1989
including:
Death in Britain: How Local Mortality Rates Have
Changed: 1950s–1990s
Findings (reports of projects)
Report of the Independent Working Group on
Drug Consumption Rooms
Meeting Part M and designing lifetime homes
Monitoring poverty and social exclusion: 2005
Poverty and Social Exclusion in Britain
Search (2 or 3 times a year)
People in Low-Paid Informal Work: Need not
Greed
'Planned' Teenage Pregnancy: Views and
Experiences of Young People from Poor and
Disadvantaged Backgrounds
Order printed publications from: York Publishing
Services, 64 Hallfield Road, Layerthorpe, York,
YO3 7XQ; tel. 01904 430033; fax 01904 430868

Electronic and video publications:
see website

Publications list:
Available online and in print

Access to staff:
Contact by letter, by telephone, by fax and by e-
mail. Appointment necessary.
Hours: Mon to Fri, 0900 to 1230 and 1400 to 1700

Access to building, collection or gallery:
Prior appointment required

Links with:
Joseph Rowntree Housing Trust
The Garth, White Rose Avenue, New Earswick,
YO32 4TZ

JOSEPHINE BUTLER SOCIETY

Acronym or abbreviation: JBS

4 The Hedges, Maidstone, Kent, ME14 2JW

Tel: 01622 679630

Website:
http://www.jbs.webeden.co.uk

Enquiries:
Enquiries to: Honorary Correspondence Secretary

Founded:
1869

Organisation type and purpose:
Membership association (membership is by
subscription), present number of members: 90,
voluntary organisation.

Subject coverage:
Objects: to promote a high and equal standard of
morality and sexual responsibility for men and
women in public opinion, law and practice. To
secure the abolition of state regulation of
prostitution internationally and prevent all forms
of exploitation of prostitutes by third parties. To
examine existing and proposed legislation on all
matters connected with prostitution, and to
promote social, legal and administrative reform,
the law as it affects prostitutes and related subjects
e.g. kerb crawling, sexual offences etc. Combating
the traffic in persons (known in the past as the
White Slave Trade).

**Museum or gallery collection, archive, or library
special collection:**
Main JBS collection is held at the Women's Library,
London; smaller collection at the Durham
University Library, Durham

Library catalogue:
All or part available online

Printed publications:
News and Views (magazine, annually)
Occasional papers

Access to staff:
Contact by letter and by telephone
Hours: Mon to Fri, 0900 to 1700

Links with:
Anti-Slavery Society
tel: 020 7924 9555; fax: 020 7738 4110; e-mail:
antislavery@gn.apc.orb
Church Army
tel: 020 8318 1226
Church of England Board for Social Responsibility
tel: 020 7222 9011
Council for Voluntary Services
Fawcett Society
tel: 020 7628 4441; fax: 020 7628 2865; e-mail:
fawcett@gn.apc.org; website: http://www.gn.apc
.org/fawcett
Human Rights Network
International Abolitionist Federation
France; e-mail: b.amont@libertysurf.fr
International Alliance of Women
tel: 612 6568 6239 (Australia)
International Council of Women
tel: 00 331 47 42 19 40; fax: 00 331 42 66 26 23
(France); e-mail: icw_cif@wanadoo.fr
Minority Rights Group
tel: 020 7978 9498
Mothers Union
tel: 020 7222 5533
National Council of Women of Great Britain
tel: 020 7354 2395; fax: 020 7354 9214; website:
http://www.cerbernet.co.uk/ncwgb/
Salvation Army
tel: 020 7332 0022; fax: 020 7236 6272
Wellclose Trust
tel: 01823 325 632

JOSIAH WEDGWOOD & SONS LIMITED

Barlaston, Stoke-on-Trent, Staffordshire, ST12 9ES

Tel: 01782 204141
Fax: 01782 204666

Website:
http://www.wedgwood.co.uk
Company history, product information, visitor
centre, events, company magazine, gift ideas.

Enquiries:
Enquiries to: Public Relations Manager
Direct tel: 01782 282516
Direct fax: 01782 204433
Direct e-mail: andrew.stanistreet@wedgwood.com

Founded:
1759

Organisation type and purpose:
Manufacturing industry, museum.

Subject coverage:
Manufacturing processes of fine bone china and
earthenware, company history from 1759.

**Museum or gallery collection, archive, or library
special collection:**
Museum of ceramics and manuscripts

Access to staff:
Contact by letter, by fax and by e-mail
Hours: Mon to Fri, 0900 to 1700

JOZEF PILSUDSKI INSTITUTE OF RESEARCH LIMITED

Historical Institute, 238–240 King Street, London,
W6 0RF

Tel: 020 8748 6197
Fax: 020 8748 6197
E-mail: instytut@pilsudski.org.uk

Enquiries:
Enquiries to: General Secretary
Direct tel: 020 8579 3823

Founded:
1947

Organisation type and purpose:
Learned society (membership is by election or
invitation), present number of members: 140,
registered charity, museum, research organisation.
Reference library.

Historical research into the recent history of Poland
in relation to work and deeds of Jozef Pilsudski.

Subject coverage:
The Struggle for Polish independence before and
during World War I, political and military events
during the years of independence 1918–1939 and
organisation of Polish State.

**Museum or gallery collection, archive, or library
special collection:**
Archives of documents, manuscripts and
photographs (mostly in Polish)
Militaria Library related to recent history of Poland
before 2nd World War
Museum of personal objects of Marshal Pilsudski

Non-library collection catalogue:
All or part available in-house

Library catalogue:
All or part available in-house

Printed publications:
Over 40 publications in Polish includes the
following:
Jozef Pilsudski – Korespondencja 1914–1917 (£10)
Niepodleglosc 17 volumes (for sale)

Publications list:
Available in print

Access to staff:
Contact by letter, by telephone, by fax, by e-mail
and in person
Hours: Tue and Thu, 1000 to 1700; or by
appointment

Access for disabled people:
Ramped entry

JUDGE INSTITUTE OF MANAGEMENT

University of Cambridge, Trumpington Street,
Cambridge, CB2 1AG

Tel: 01223 339700
Fax: 01223 339701
E-mail: enquiries@jims.cam.ac.uk

Website:
http://www.jims.cam.ac.uk
Information about the institute and links to
research and workshop papers.

Enquiries:
Enquiries to: Communications Manager
Direct tel: 01223 388608
Direct fax: 01223 766920
Direct e-mail: press-publicity@jims.cam.ac.uk

Founded:
1990

Organisation type and purpose:
University Business School.

Subject coverage:
Management studies, Business and Management.

Trade and statistical information:
Market and Company Information.

Non-library collection catalogue:
All or part available online

Library catalogue:
All or part available online

Printed publications:
Working Papers
Order printed publications from: Publications
Secretary
As main address

Electronic and video publications:
Working Papers – current year

Publications list:
Available online and in print

Access to staff:
Contact by letter, by telephone, by fax, by e-mail
and via website
Hours: Mon to Fri, 0900 to 1700

Access to building, collection or gallery:
No access other than to staff

Access for disabled people:
Parking provided, level entry, access to all public areas, toilet facilities

Links with:
Cambridge Business Research Centre (CBRC)
Cambridge Entrepreneurship Centre
CMI
Management Studies Group
  Department of Engineering, University of Cambridge
Massachusetts Institute of Technology (MIT)

JUNIOR CHAMBER INTERNATIONAL LONDON

Formal name: Junior Chamber International (JCI) London
Acronym or abbreviation: JCI

33 Queen Street, London, EC4R 1AP

Tel: 020 7203 1951

Website:
http://www.jcilondon.org.uk
Junior Chamber International (JCI) is a dynamic, global organisation for people in their 20s and 30s. It creates positive change by developing the leaders of the future. It delivers innovative and exciting programmes, enhancing citizenship, fellowship and self-development, leading to sustainable success in members' lives and organisations and in society. Members can go to inspiring seminars, fun conferences and meet new friends from all over the world. JCI London has 130 members from more than 30 different nationalities. Members are active and responsible citizens and future leaders. JCI London is the largest JCI chamber in the UK with members representing several major corporations in Greater London as well as being self-employed entrepreneurs.

Enquiries:
Enquiries to: President
Direct e-mail: solveig.malvik@gmail.com

Founded:
1953

Formerly called:
Junior Chamber of Commerce for London (year of change 2004)

Organisation type and purpose:
International organisation (membership is by election or invitation), present number of members: 135, voluntary organisation, suitable for ages: 18 to 40, training organisation.
Part of a worldwide organisation dedicated to developing the business and managerial skills of the future business leaders of our communities.

Subject coverage:
Concentrates on 5 areas: international, business networking, community projects, leadership development and management opportunities.

Access to staff:
Contact by letter, by telephone and by e-mail
Hours: Mon to Fri, preferably evenings

Affiliated to:
British Junior Chamber, which is affiliated to Junior Chamber International

Headquarters address:
British Junior Chamber (BJC)
12 Regent Place, Rugby, Warwickshire, CV21 2PM; tel: 01788 572795; fax: 01788 542091; e-mail: 1007633171@compuserve.com

JUPITER OWNERS' AUTO CLUB

Acronym or abbreviation: JOAC

Redbrook, 6 Rudhall Meadow, Ross-on-Wye, Herefordshire, HR9 7AW

Tel: 01989 767 815

E-mail: davehkennedy@wyenet.co.uk

Website:
http://www.jowettjupiter.co.uk
Information with many images (free to use) on the Jowett Jupiter sports car; historical information and current and recent usage of this important classic car.

Enquiries:
Enquiries to: Membership Secretary
Direct tel: 01273 843457
Direct e-mail: ghis@jowettjupiter.co.uk

Founded:
1962

Organisation type and purpose:
Membership association (membership is by subscription), present number of members: 220. Club for owners of Jowett Jupiter Cars 1950–54.

Subject coverage:
About 900 Jowett Jupiters were built from 1950 to 1954 – many still survive and we aim to keep these interesting and rare collectible cars on the road and restored.

Access to staff:
Contact by letter, by e-mail and via website
Hours: Mon to Fri, 0900 to 1700

JUSTICE

59 Carter Lane, London, EC4V 5AQ

Tel: 020 7329 5100
Fax: 020 7329 5055
E-mail: admin@justice.org.uk

Website:
http://www.justice.org.uk
Overview of Justice's work, news of legal events and issues, copies of briefings and information on reports.

Enquiries:
Enquiries to: Director
Other contacts: Legal Officer

Founded:
1957

Organisation type and purpose:
Membership association (membership is by subscription), present number of members: 2000, voluntary organisation, registered charity (charity number 1058580).
An international non-governmental organisation concerned with promoting observance of the Rule of Law, law reform and the legal protection of Human Rights.

Subject coverage:
Law reform, rule of law, access to justice, human rights in UK and EU.

Museum or gallery collection, archive, or library special collection:
Archive material 1990-.
ICJ reports
Justice reports and memoranda

Printed publications:
Justice Bulletin (Spring, Summer and Autumn, free to members)
Reports on criminal law, civil and family law, administrative and public laws and the legal aid system
Criminal Justice Reform Briefings

Publications list:
Available in print

Access to staff:
Contact by letter
Hours: Mon to Fri, 0930 to 1730

British Section of the:
International Commission of Jurists Geneva

JUSTICE FOR ALL VACCINE-DAMAGED CHILDREN

Acronym or abbreviation: JVDC

Erin's Cottage, Fussell's Buildings, Whiteway Road, Bristol, BS5 7QY

Tel: 0117 955 7818

Enquiries:
Enquiries to: Secretary
Other contacts: Justice and Basic Support for MMR vaccine damage.

Founded:
1981

Organisation type and purpose:
Voluntary organisation.
To ensure the safer manufacture of vaccines, that all medical personnel are aware of the Vaccine Damage Payments Act (1979), that all adverse reactions are reported to the Committee on Safety of Medicines.

Subject coverage:
Compensation for vaccine-damaged children.

Access to staff:
Contact by telephone
Hours: Mon to Sun, 0900 to 2100 telephone only

Also at:
Justice for all Vaccine-Damaged Children
  99 Hendris Road, Kirkcaldy, Fife, KY2 5DB

Other vaccine damage groups:
Justice, Awareness, Basic Support (JABS)
  1 Gawsworth Road, Golbourne, Warrington, Cheshire, WA3 3RF; tel: 01942 713565
The Informed Parent
  PO Box 870, Harrow, Middlesex; tel: 020 8861 1022
Victims of Vaccination Support Group
  27 Malcolm Grove, Rednal, Birmingham, BH5 9BS; tel: 0121 2437759

JUVENILE DIABETES RESEARCH FOUNDATION

Acronym or abbreviation: JDRF

19 Angel Gate, City Road, London, EC1V 2PT

Tel: 020 7713 2030
Fax: 020 7713 2031
E-mail: info@jdrf.org.uk

Website:
http://www.jdrf.org.uk

Enquiries:
Enquiries to: Director of Communications

Founded:
1986

Organisation type and purpose:
National organisation, registered charity in England and Wales (No. 295716) and in Scotland (No. SC040123).
To find a cure for diabetes through the support of research. To provide information about the progress of research.

Printed publications:
Type 1 Discovery Magazine and T1 Kids Magazine
Order printed publications from: website: http://www.jdrf.org.uk

Access to staff:
Contact by letter, by telephone, by fax, by e-mail and via website
Hours: Mon to Fri, 0900 to 1730
Special comments: 3rd floor – lift access.

Access to building, collection or gallery:
Prior appointment required

Affiliated to:
The Juvenile Diabetes Foundation International
  120 Wall Street, New York, USA; website: http://www.jdrf.org

continued overleaf

Also at:
JDRF Scotland
  JDRF c/o Subsea 7, Greenwell Base, Greenwell
  Rd, East Tullos Industrial Estate, Aberdeen,
  AB12 3AX; tel: 0151 709 5533; website: http://
  www.jdrf.org
JDRF South West
  2 Berkeley Square, Clifton, Bristol; tel: 0117
  9452491
JDRF West Midlands
  Suite 32 Fifth Floor, Queensgate, 121 Suffolk
  Street, Queensway, Birmingham, B1 1LX; tel:
  0121 685 7102

JVC PROFESSIONAL EUROPE LTD.

Acronym or abbreviation: JVC

JVC House, JVC Business Park, 12 Priestley Way,
London, NW2 7BA

Tel: 020 8208 6200
Fax: 020 8208 6260
E-mail: sales@jvcpro.co.uk

Website:
http://www.jvcpro.co.uk
Latest JVC news, product information and user
stories for both the professional video and CCTV
markets.

Enquiries:
Enquiries to: Sales Manager
Direct tel: 020 8208 6204

Founded:
1988

Organisation type and purpose:
Manufacturing industry.
UK marketing and distribution of JVC professional
broadcast, display and security products.

Subject coverage:
Manufacturer of professional video equipment,
projection, displays, 3D, CCTV and security.

Printed publications:
HIGHWAY and MONITOR magazines
Order printed publications from: e-mail: marketing@
jvcpro.co.uk

Publications list:
Available online

Access to staff:
Contact by letter, by telephone, by e-mail and via
website
Hours: Mon to Fri, 0900 to 1730

Access to building, collection or gallery:
Hours: Mon to Fri, 0900 to 1700

Access for disabled people:
Ramped entry, toilet facilities

KAPUSTIN SOCIETY, THE

9 Burnside Close, Twickenham, Middlesex, TW1
1ET

Tel: 020 8287 5518
Fax: 020 8287 5518
E-mail: KapustinSoc@blueyonder.co.uk

Website:
http://www.trg.ed.ac.uk

Enquiries:
Enquiries to: Secretary

Founded:
2002

Organisation type and purpose:
Learned society, membership association
(membership is by subscription).

Subject coverage:
Music of Nikolai Kapustin (1937-).

Printed publications:
Photocopies of most solo piano and some chamber
  music scores
Projected Bulletin

Access to staff:
Contact by letter, by telephone, by fax and by e-
mail. Appointment necessary.
Hours: Mon to Fri, 0900 to 1700

Access to building, collection or gallery:
Prior appointment required

Access for disabled people:
Parking provided, level entry, toilet facilities

KARMANN GHIA OWNERS' CLUB (GB)

13 Hilltop Road, Toms Lane, Kings Langley,
Hertfordshire, WD4 8NS

Tel: 01923 263658
E-mail: john@jfigg.freeserve.co.uk

Enquiries:
Enquiries to: General Secretary

Founded:
1982

Organisation type and purpose:
National organisation.

Subject coverage:
Karmann Ghia motorcars, sale of cars, insurance
benefits, club events, national related events,
international events, specialist services.

**Museum or gallery collection, archive, or library
special collection:**
History of the manufacture of the car
Service and repair data

Access to staff:
Contact by letter, by telephone and by e-mail
Hours: Mon to Fri, 0900 to 1700

KATE SHARPLEY LIBRARY

Acronym or abbreviation: KSL

BM Hurricane, London, WC1N 3XX

E-mail: info@katesharpleylibrary.net

Website:
http://www.katesharpleylibrary.net
Introduction. Online version of bulletin, details of
publications, wants list, book reviews and online
documents

Enquiries:
Enquiries to: Information Officer

Founded:
1979

Organisation type and purpose:
Voluntary organisation, research organisation,
publishing house.
To research and publish materials on anarchist
history especially in areas that have been ignored
or misrepresented by academic experts.

Subject coverage:
Anarchism; anarcho-syndicalism; council
communism; Labour Movement; Libertarian
socialism; revolutionary industrial unionism
(Industrial Workers of the World); situationism;
Spanish Civil War and Resistance; Syndicalism.

**Museum or gallery collection, archive, or library
special collection:**
The Library covers Anarchist, Syndicalist,
  Libertarian Socialist, Situationist and Council
  Communist books, pamphlets and periodicals in
  all languages
Various archive collections including Albert
  Meltzer papers (Anarchism)

Non-library collection catalogue:
All or part available in-house

Library catalogue:
All or part available in-house

Printed publications:
Please send an sae for up to date list
KSL Bulletin of the Kate Sharpley Library
  (quarterly)

The Anarchist resistance to Franco, Biographical
  notes (£2)
British Syndicalism: Pages from Labour History
  (Brown T, £1)
Mayday and Anarchism (2004, £3)
Prisoners and Partisans: Italian Anarchists in the
  struggle against Fascism (1999, £3)
Revolutionary activism: The Spanish Resistance in
  context (Alberola O, Millán A, Zambrana J, £3)
Unknown Heroes : Biographies of Anarchist
  Resistance Fighters (2005, £3)
The Walsall Anarchists (£1)
With The Poor People Of The Earth : A Biography
  Of Doctor John Creaghe of Sheffield & Buenos
  Aires (2004, £3)
Yiddish Anarchist Bibliography (1998, £7.50)

Publications list:
Available online and in print

Access to staff:
Contact by letter, by e-mail and via website.
Appointment necessary.

Other address:
Kate Sharpley Library (KSL)
  PMB 820, 242S Channing Way, Berkeley,
  California, CA 94704, USA

KEELE UNIVERSITY LIBRARY

Keele, Staffordshire, ST5 5BG

Tel: 01782 733535
Fax: 01782 734502
E-mail: libhelp@keele.ac.uk

Website:
http://www.keele.ac.uk/depts/li

Founded:
1949

Organisation type and purpose:
University Library.

Subject coverage:
American studies; English; history; music;
philosophy; economics; history; education;
biological sciences; pharmacology; management;
chemistry; communication and neuroscience;
computer science; geology; mathematics; physics;
medicine; geography; international relations;
industrial relations; law; politics; criminology;
social gerontology; psychology; social policy;
social work; physiology; sociology; social
anthropology.

**Museum or gallery collection, archive, or library
special collection:**
Arnold Bennett Collection
Sneyd Papers (Sneyd family of Keele Hall 1600
  onwards)
Spode Papers

Trade and statistical information:
European Documentation Centre

Printed publications:
Guides and leaflets regularly updated

Access to staff:
Contact by letter, by telephone, by fax and by e-
mail
Hours: Term time: Mon to Fri, 0850 to 2200; Sat,
0930 to 2200; Sun, 1000 to 2200
Vacations: please enquire

Access for disabled people:
Accessible, via entrance on ground floor

Member organisation of:
SCONUL Access
Society of College, National and University
Libraries

KEEP BRITAIN TIDY

Elizabeth House, The Pier, Wigan, Lancashire,
WN3 4EX

Tel: 01942 612621
Fax: 01942 824778
E-mail: enquiries@keepbritaintidy.org

Website:
http://www.keepbritaintidy.org
Keep Britain Tidy – anti litter campaigns, environmental education programmes, information, research.

Enquiries:
Enquiries to: Public Information Officer
Direct tel: 01942 612602

Founded:
1961

Formerly called:
Keep Britain Tidy Group (year of change 1987); EnCams (year of change 2009)

Organisation type and purpose:
Voluntary organisation, registered charity (charity number 1071737), consultancy. Independent national agency for the improvement of the quality of local environments.

Subject coverage:
Local Environmental Quality and associated anti-social behaviour, Cleaner Safer Greener Network, Eco-Schools Programme, Green Flag for Parks, Quality Coast Award and Blue Flag Awards.

Museum or gallery collection, archive, or library special collection:
Documents, posters, printed materials, leaflets, etc.

Non-library collection catalogue:
All or part available online, in-house and in print

Library catalogue:
All or part available in-house

Printed publications:
Campaigning materials
Education leaflets and packs
Information leaflets
Newsletter
Research reports and summaries

Publications list:
Available online

Access to staff:
Contact by letter, by telephone, by fax, by e-mail, in person and via website. Access for members only.
Hours: Mon to Fri, 0700 to 1900

Access to building, collection or gallery:
Only one Central Services Office
Hours: Mon to Fri, 0700 to 1900

Access for disabled people:
Access to all public areas, toilet facilities

KEIGHLEY & DISTRICT FHS

2 The Hallows, Shann Park, Keighley, West Yorkshire, BD20 6HY

Tel: 01535 672144
E-mail: suedaynes@hotmail.co.uk

Website:
http://www.kdfhs.org.uk

Enquiries:
Enquiries to: Honorary Secretary
Other contacts: Administration and Programme Secretary

Founded:
1986

Organisation type and purpose:
Membership association (membership is by subscription), present number of members: 300, voluntary organisation.
To exchange information, ideas regarding individual family histories and discuss research problems.

Subject coverage:
Family history in the Keighley and District Area, which includes: Bingley to the east, west to Kildwick, Skipton and the Aire Valley, and the villages of the Worth Valley, Haworth, Oakworth, Oxenhope, etc.

Non-library collection catalogue:
All or part available in-house

Library catalogue:
All or part available in-house

Printed publications:
An extensive list of monumental inscriptions, parish registers and transcripts is given online
Order printed publications from: Publications Secretary, 13 King Edward Street, Sutton in Craven, Keighley, West Yorkshire, BD20 7ET; e-mail: a.thorley171@btinternet.com

Publications list:
Available online and in print

Access to staff:
Contact by letter, by e-mail and via website. Appointment necessary. Access for members only.
Hours: Mon to Fri, 0900 to 1700

Access to building, collection or gallery:
at Keighley Public Library, Local Studies Library on 1st floor
Hours: Mon to Fri, 0900 to 1900; Sat, 0900 to 1700
Special comments: Access to Society's reference library for members only on sight of membership card.

Access for disabled people:
Use Albert Street entrance and lift to 1st floor
Hours: Mon to Fri, 0900 to 1900; Sat, 0900 to 1700

Links with:
Federation of Family History Societies
Artillery House, 15 Byron Street, Manchester, M3 4PF; e-mail: admin@ffhs.org.uk

Membership Secretary:
Keighley & District FHS
3 Walton Street, Skipton, North Yorkshire, BD23 2QX; website: sjp03tiscali.co.uk

KELVEDON HATCH SECRET BUNKER

Brentwood, Essex, CM14 5TL

Tel: 01277 364883
Fax: 01277 365260
E-mail: bunker@sapar.demon.co.uk

Website:
http://www.japar.demon.co.uk

Enquiries:
Enquiries to: Managing Director

Founded:
1994

Organisation type and purpose:
Nuclear bunker.

Subject coverage:
Cold War bunker built in 1952 for government.

Access to staff:
Contact by letter, by fax, by e-mail and via website
Hours: Mar to Oct, Mon to Fri, 1000 to 1600; Sat and Sun, 1000 to 1700
Nov to Feb, Thu to Sun, 1000 to 1600
Special comments: Charge for admission.

Access for disabled people:
Parking provided, toilet facilities
Special comments: Limited entry.

KENNEL CLUB

Formal name: The Kennel Club

1–5 Clarges Street, Piccadilly, London, W1J 8AB

Tel: 0844 770 5235
Fax: 020 7518 1058

Website:
www.thekennelclub.org.uk/library
Library services, catalogue.
http://www.dogimages.org.uk
Photo library.
http://www.thekennelclub.org.uk/gallery
Art collection.

Enquiries:
Enquiries to: Library and Collections Manager

Direct tel: 020 7518 1009
Direct fax: 020 7518 1045
Direct e-mail: library@thekennelclub.org.uk

Founded:
1873

Organisation type and purpose:
Membership association (membership is by election or invitation).
To promote in every way the general improvement of dogs.

Subject coverage:
Dogs: choice, care, training, breeding, health, welfare, showing, obedience, agility, working and field trials, pedigree dog registration.

Museum or gallery collection, archive, or library special collection:
Books, archive, photographs, artwork, ephemera, etc.

Library catalogue:
All or part available online

Printed publications:
Guides to Showing and Judging
Kennel Club Breed Records Supplement (quarterly)
Kennel Club Stud Book (annually)
Kennel Club Yearbook
Kennel Gazette (monthly)
Rescue Directory
The Kennel Club's Illustrated Breed Standards

Electronic and video publications:
Footage of Crufts and Discover Dogs available for purchase

Publications list:
Available online

Access to staff:
Contact by letter, by telephone, by e-mail, in person and via website
Hours: Mon to Fri, 0930 to 1630

Access to building, collection or gallery:
Prior appointment required
Hours: Library: Mon to Fri, 0930 to 1630

Access for disabled people:
Ground floor, no steps, accessible bathroom

KENSINGTON AND CHELSEA (ROYAL BOROUGH) LIBRARY

Formal name: Royal Borough of Kensington and Chelsea
Acronym or abbreviation: RBKC

Central Library, Phillimore Walk, London, W8 7RX

Tel: 020 7937 3010
Fax: 020 7361 2976
E-mail: libraries@rbkc.gov.uk

Website:
http://www.rbkc.gov.uk/leisureandlibraries/libraries.aspx

Enquiries:
Enquiries to: Head of Library Service
Other contacts: Head of Service

Founded:
1965

Organisation type and purpose:
Local government body, public library.

Subject coverage:
General, biography and genealogy, customs and folklore.

Museum or gallery collection, archive, or library special collection:
Kensington and Chelsea local history and current information
Records of the Chelsea Arts Club 1890–1974

Non-library collection catalogue:
All or part available in-house

Library catalogue:
All or part available online and in-house

continued overleaf

Publications list:
Available in print

Access to staff:
Contact by letter, by telephone, by fax, by e-mail, in person and via website
Hours: Mon, Tue, Thu, Fri, 0930 to 2000; Wed, Sat, 0930 to 1700; Sun 1300 to 1700

KENT AND EAST SUSSEX RAILWAY

Acronym or abbreviation: K&ESR

Tenterden Town Station, Tenterden, Kent, TN30 6HE

Tel: 01580 765155
Fax: 01580 765654
E-mail: enquiries@kesr.org.uk

Website:
http://www.kesr.org.uk

Enquiries:
Enquiries to: Commercial Manager
Other contacts: Bookings and Administration Secretaries for general information and bookings.

Founded:
1971

Organisation type and purpose:
Voluntary organisation, registered charity. Preserved steam railway operating between Tenterden, Kent and Bodiam, East Sussex.

Access to staff:
Contact by letter, by telephone, by fax and by e-mail
Hours: Mon to Fri, 0900 to 1700
Special comments: Trains run approximately 190 days per year – please telephone for timetable details.

Access for disabled people:
Parking provided, ramped entry, level entry, toilet facilities

KENT ARCHAEOLOGICAL SOCIETY

Acronym or abbreviation: KAS

The Museum, St Faith's Street, Maidstone, Kent, ME14 1LH

E-mail: secretary@kentarchaeology.org.uk

Website:
http://www.kentarchaeology.org.uk

Enquiries:
Enquiries to: Librarian
Direct tel: 01795 472218
Direct fax: 01795 472218
Direct e-mail: dr.fh.panton@grove-end-tunstall
.fsnet.co.uk; secretary@kentarchaeol
Other contacts: Hon Gen Sec

Founded:
1857

Organisation type and purpose:
Learned society, present number of members: c. 1,300, voluntary organisation, registered charity (charity number 2243382), suitable for ages: all, training organisation, research organisation, publishing house.
To promote the study and publication of archaeology and history in all their branches, especially within the ancient county of Kent. Library open (on request to Hon. Librarian) to bona fide non-members, lectures, training.

Subject coverage:
Fieldwork; vernacular architecture, historic buildings and churches; place names; visual records; local history.

Museum or gallery collection, archive, or library special collection:
Extensive collections on history, etc., Kent, runs of County, National (UK) and overseas (Western Europe) publications on archaeological,
genealogical, numismatic, place names, ecclesiastical records, etc.; manuscript material held by Kent County Council Archives, Centre for Kentish Studies

Non-library collection catalogue:
All or part available online

Library catalogue:
All or part available online and in-house

Printed publications:
Archaeologia Cantiana (one or more volumes annually)
Newsletter (quarterly)
Research and records volumes

Publications list:
Available in print

Access to staff:
Contact by letter, by telephone and by e-mail. Appointment necessary. Letter of introduction required.
Hours: Members: Mon to Sat, 1000 to 1630; Sun, 1100 to 1600 (other times by appointment) on production of membership card and signing of visitors book
Non-members: by appointment with Hon. Librarian

KENT COUNTY COUNCIL LIBRARIES AND ARCHIVES

Acronym or abbreviation: KCC Libraries and Archive

County Central Library, Springfield, Maidstone, Kent, ME14 2LH

Tel: 01622 696511
Fax: 01622 696494
E-mail: libraries@kent.gov.uk

Website:
http://www.kent.gov.uk/libraries

Enquiries:
Enquiries to: Information Services Team
Direct tel: 01622 696438
Direct fax: 01622 696445
Direct e-mail: libraries.informationservices@kent
.gov.uk

Organisation type and purpose:
Public library

Museum or gallery collection, archive, or library special collection:
Wide range of online databases
Canterbury Cathedral and City, archives
Centre for Kentish Studies, archives
East Kent Archives

Library catalogue:
All or part available online and in-house

Publications list:
Available online

Access to staff:
Contact by letter, by telephone, by fax, by e-mail, in person and via website

Access to building, collection or gallery:
Hours: Mon to Fri, 0900 to 1800; Sat, 0900 to 1700; check branch libraries online

Branch libraries:
Ashford Library
    Church Road, Ashford, TN23 1QX; tel: 01233 620649; fax: 01233 620295
Canterbury Library
    18 High Street, Canterbury, CT1 2JF; tel: 01227 463608; fax: 01227 768338
Dartford Library
    Central Park, Dartford; tel: 01322 221133; fax: 01322 278271
Dover Discovery Centre
    Market Square, Dover, CT16 1PH; tel: 01304 204241; fax: 01304 225914
Folkestone Library
    2 Grace Hill, Folkestone, CT20 1HD; tel: 01303 850123; fax: 01303 242907

Gravesend Library
    Windmill Street, Gravesend, DA12 1BE; tel: 01474 352758; fax: 01474 320284
Margate Library
    Thanet Gateway, Cecil Square, Margate, CT9 1RE; tel: 01843 223626; fax: 01843 293015
Sevenoaks Library
    Buckhurst Lane, Sevenoaks, TN13 1LQ; tel: 01732 453118; fax: 01732 742682
Sittingbourne Library
    Central Avenue, Sittingbourne, ME10 4AH; tel: 01795 476545; fax: 01795 428376
Tonbridge Library
    Avebury Avenue, Tonbridge, TN9 1TG; tel: 01732 352754; fax: 01732 358300
Tunbridge Wells Library
    Mount Pleasant Road, Tunbridge Wells, TN1 1NS; tel: 01892 522352; fax: 01892 514657

Member organisation of:
Association of Local Government Information Services
Chartered Institute of Librarians and Information Professionals (CILIP)
European Public Information Centre Network (EPIC)
International Association of Music Librarian
Kent Information and Libraries Network

KENT FAMILY HISTORY SOCIETY

Acronym or abbreviation: KFHS

Bullockstone Farm, Bullockstone Road, Herne Bay, Kent, CT6 7NL

Tel: 01227 363030
E-mail: kristn@globalnet.co.uk

Website:
http://www.kfhs.org.uk
Details of the society, recent publications with prices and ordering information.

Enquiries:
Enquiries to: Secretary

Founded:
1974

Organisation type and purpose:
International organisation, membership association (membership is by subscription), present number of members: 3500, voluntary organisation.
To promote interest in family history research in Kent.

Subject coverage:
Family history in Kent, including the diocese of Canterbury and part of the Rochester diocese.

Library catalogue:
All or part available in-house

Microform publications:
Approximately 2000 microfiche publications including:
New Members' Interest Directory up to December 2001
Complete Listing of Microfiche Publications, November 2001
Order microform publications from: Kent Family History Society
41 The Street, Kennington, Ashford, Kent, TN24 9HD

Electronic and video publications:
Some publications online

Publications list:
Available in print

Access to staff:
Contact by letter, by e-mail and via website. Non-members charged.
Hours: Mon to Fri, 0900 to 1700

KENT INSTITUTE OF ART AND DESIGN AT MAIDSTONE

Acronym or abbreviation: KIAD

Oakwood Park, Oakwood Road, Maidstone, Kent,
ME16 8AG

Tel: 01622 757286
Fax: 01622 621100
E-mail: librarymaid@kiad.ac.uk

Website:
http://www.kiad.ac.uk
Prospectus, student and staff work, exhibition
information etc, library catalogue.

Enquiries:
Enquiries to: Head of Library and Learning
Resources
Direct e-mail: vcrane@kiad.ac.uk

Founded:
1988

Organisation type and purpose:
Suitable for ages: 18+.
College of higher and further education.
Art, design and architecture education.

Subject coverage:
Fine art, architecture, fashion design, interior
design, graphic design, film and video,
photography, jewellery and precious metalwork,
ceramics, illustration.

**Museum or gallery collection, archive, or library
special collection:**
Early printed books and books from private
presses
Slide Collection

Library catalogue:
All or part available online

Access to staff:
Contact by letter. Appointment necessary. Letter
of introduction required.
Hours: Mon to Fri, 0900 to 1900

Location:
Kent Institute of Art and Design
New Dover Road, Canterbury, Kent, CT1 3AN;
tel: 01227 769371; fax: 01227 817500; e-mail:
librarycant@kiad.ac.uk
Kent Institute of Art and Design
Fort Pitt, Rochester, Kent, ME1 1DZ; tel: 01634
830022; fax: 01634 820300; e-mail: libraryroch@
kiad.ac.uk

KENT WILDLIFE TRUST

Tyland Barn, Sandling, Maidstone, Kent, ME14
3BD

Tel: 01622 662012
Fax: 01622 671390
E-mail: kentwildlife@cix.co.uk

Website:
http://www.kentwildlife.org.uk
Describes Kent Wildlife Trust, its work and how
people can help.

Enquiries:
Enquiries to: Director

Founded:
1958

Organisation type and purpose:
Membership association (membership is by
subscription), present number of members: 13,000,
registered charity (charity number 239992).
One of 46 county wildlife trusts.
To secure a better future for the native wildlife of
Kent.

Subject coverage:
Wildlife conservation in Kent.

Printed publications:
Please enquire

Access to staff:
Contact by letter, by telephone, by fax and by e-
mail
Hours: Mon to Fri, 0900 to 1700

Parent body:
The Wildlife Trust

KERRIER DISTRICT COUNCIL

Dolcoath Avenue, Camborne, Cornwall, TR14 8SX

Tel: 01209 614000
Fax: 01209 614491
E-mail: kerrierdc@kerrier.gov.uk

Enquiries:
Enquiries to: Chief Executive
Other contacts: Marketing & Public Relations
Officer for press/media enquiries.

Organisation type and purpose:
Local government body.

Subject coverage:
Local government services.

Printed publications:
A-Z of Council Services
Various departmental publications including:
Holiday Guide
Planning and Building Control Handbook
Civic Magazine
Kerrier Coast to Coast
Annual Performance (update)
Best Value Performance Plan
Order printed publications from: Marketing & Public
Relations Officer, Kerrier District Council
at the same address, tel: 01209 614000, fax: 01209
614494, e-mail: marketing@kerrier,gov,uk

Access to staff:
Contact by letter, by telephone, by fax and by e-
mail
Hours: Mon to Fri, 0900 to 1700

Access to building, collection or gallery:
Prior appointment required
Hours: 0845 to 1715
Special comments: No prior appointment required
for Revenues and Benefits

Access for disabled people:
Parking provided, level entry, toilet facilities

KESTON INSTITUTE

PO Box 752, Oxford, OX1 9QF

E-mail: admin@keston.org.uk

Website:
http://www.keston.org.uk

Founded:
1970

Organisation type and purpose:
Registered charity (charity number 314103).

Subject coverage:
Keston promotes religious freedom and studies
religious affairs in the postcommunist and
communist world. Its unique archive and library
are now housed at Baylor University, Texas, USA.

Access to staff:
Contact by letter and by e-mail

KETTERING BOROUGH COUNCIL

Municipal Offices, Bowling Green Road, Kettering,
Northamptonshire, NN15 7QX

Tel: 01536 410333
Fax: 01536 532424
E-mail: customerservices@kettering.gov.uk

Website:
http://www.kettering.gov.uk
Community information, democratic information,
leisure information, business information.

Enquiries:
Direct e-mail: media@craftscouncil.org.uk

Organisation type and purpose:
Local government body.

Subject coverage:
Information on the Borough of Kettering.

Education services:
via Northamptonshire County Council, tel: 01604
236236.

Services for disabled people:
via Northamptonshire County Council, tel: 01604
236236.

Printed publications:
Various information leaflets

Publications list:
Available online and in print

Access to staff:
Contact by letter, by telephone, by fax, by e-mail,
in person and via website. Appointment necessary.
Hours: Mon to Fri, 0830 to 1730; Sat, 0900 to 1300

Access for disabled people:
Parking provided, toilet facilities
Special comments: Access to all public areas

KEYGRAPHICA

Acronym or abbreviation: Keygraphica

PO Box 1381, Rugby, Warwickshire, CV21 2ZF

Tel: 01788 536389
Fax: 01788 550152
E-mail: keygraphica@assocnbureau.demon.co.uk

Enquiries:
Enquiries to: Secretary

Organisation type and purpose:
Trade association.

Subject coverage:
Artwork; photographic facilities; toolmaking;
anodising; etching; plating; litho and screen
printing; paint spraying; laminating; press work;
die cutting; stamping-embossing; casting; machine
engraving; injection moulding; standards.

KIDDERMINSTER LIBRARY

Market Street, Kidderminster, Worcestershire,
DY10 1AD

Tel: 01562 824500
Fax: 01562 512907
E-mail: kidderminsterlib@worcestershire.gov.uk

Website:
http://www.worcestershire.gov.uk/homepage.htm
County internet providing information on national
and local government, local clubs and community
groups, tourism, leisure and cultural activities.

Enquiries:
Enquiries to: Information Officer

Founded:
1855

Organisation type and purpose:
International organisation, membership
association (membership is by subscription), public
library, consultancy, research organisation.

Subject coverage:
General, including music; local studies on
Kidderminster and nearer parts of Salop in
particular, Worcestershire and Shropshire in
general; carpets and textiles.

**Museum or gallery collection, archive, or library
special collection:**
Carpet and Textile Collection
Local History Collection (Worcestershire and
Salop)

Non-library collection catalogue:
All or part available online

Printed publications:
Carpet and Textile Collection List (irregular)
Current Events (monthly)
Library guides and booklists and guides to the
Local Collection
Local Societies List (2 times a year)

Access to staff:
Contact by letter, by telephone, by fax, by e-mail,
in person and via website
Hours: Mon, Fri, 0930 to 1730; Tue,Wed, Thu, 0930
to 2000; Sat 0930 to 1730

continued overleaf

Access for disabled people:
Access to all public areas, toilet facilities

Library of the:
Worcestershire County Libraries

KIDS

6 Aztec Row, Berners Road, London, N1 0PW

Tel: 020 7359 3635
Fax: 020 7359 3520
E-mail: enquiries@kids.org.uk

Website:
http://www.kids.org.uk

Enquiries:
Enquiries to: Information Officer

Founded:
1970

Formerly called:
Kids Active, HAPA

Organisation type and purpose:
Membership association, registered charity
(charity number 275936).
Working with disabled children, young people and
their families.

Subject coverage:
KIDS is the leading national voice for the policy
and practice of inclusive play. This is undertaken
by promoting inclusive play nationwide via
training, consultancy and publications, and by
providing play opportunities on seven adventure
playgrounds in London. KIDS works with disabled
children and their families. KIDS works in
partnership with parents to provide services which
aim to meet the full range of children's needs,
including educational, social, developmental and
emotional. These services include early years
education, play and leisure facilities, family
support, and advice.

Printed publications:
Newsletter (2 times a year)

Microform publications:
Photographs, slides

Publications list:
Available online and in print

KIDSCAPE

2 Grosvenor Gardens, London, SW1W 0DH

Tel: 020 7730 3300
Fax: 020 7730 7081
E-mail: contact@kidscape.org.uk

Website:
http://www.kidscape.org.uk
Child safety and anti-bullying information,
information and online purchase of publications
and resources, training information.

Enquiries:
Enquiries to: Director

Founded:
1984

Organisation type and purpose:
Registered charity (charity number 326864),
training organisation, research organisation.

Subject coverage:
Child protection, anti-bullying.

Information services:
Parents' anti-bullying helpline: 08451 205 204 (Mon
to Fri, 1000 to 1600)

Printed publications:
Booklets & leaflets (one copy available with sae
and 6 loose first class stamps)
Books
Posters
Order printed publications from: website: http://
www.kidscape.org.uk/shop

Electronic and video publications:
DVDs for purchase about child protection and
bullying
Order electronic and video publications from: website:
http://www.kidscape.org.uk/shop

Publications list:
Available online

Access to staff:
Contact by letter, by telephone, by fax, by e-mail,
in person and via website. Appointment necessary.
Hours: Mon to Fri, 1000 to 1600

KILVERT SOCIETY

30 Bromley Heath Avenue, Downend, Bristol, BS16
6JP

Tel: 0117 957 2030
E-mail: via website

Website:
http://www.communigate.co.uk/here/
kilvertsociety
Information on the Revd Francis Kilvert and The
Kilvert Society.

Enquiries:
Enquiries to: Honorary Secretary
Other contacts: Membership Secretary (for enquiries
from prospective new members)

Founded:
1948

Organisation type and purpose:
Learned society (membership is by subscription),
present number of members: 646, voluntary
organisation.
To foster an interest in the Reverend Francis
Kilvert, his work, his diary, and the countryside he
loved.

Subject coverage:
Rev Francis Kilvert and his Diary.

**Museum or gallery collection, archive, or library
special collection:**
At Radnorshire Museum, Llandrindod Wells

Non-library collection catalogue:
All or part available in-house

Printed publications:
Kilvert's Kathleen Mavoureen (Farmery E and
Taylor R B, £3)
Francis Kilvert (Lockwood D, 1990, £6.60)
Journal (2 times a year)
The Bevan-Dew Extracts
Who Was Who in Kilvert's Diary (£13)
Order printed publications from: Publications Officer,
Kilvert Society Publications, Tregothnan, Pentrosfa
Crescent, Llandrindod Wells, Powys, LD1 5NW;
tel: 01597 822062

Publications list:
Available in print

Access to staff:
Contact by letter, by telephone and via website
Hours: Mon to Fri, 0900 to 2100
Special comments: No personal callers.

Access to building, collection or gallery:
No prior appointment required

Also at:
Membership Secretary, Kilvert Society
Seend Park Farm, Semington, Trowbridge,
Wiltshire, BA14 7LH

KING'S COLLEGE LIBRARY

King's College, Cambridge, CB2 1ST

Tel: 01223 331232
Fax: 01223 331891
E-mail: library@kings.cam.ac.uk

Website:
http://library.kings.cam.ac.uk

Enquiries:
Enquiries to: Librarian
Direct tel: 01223 331337

Other contacts: Archivist for modern manuscripts
and college archives only; Rowe Music Librarian
for the music collection.

Organisation type and purpose:
University department or institute.

Subject coverage:
Academic subjects, incorporating a music library.

**Museum or gallery collection, archive, or library
special collection:**
English books printed before 1800
Incunabula
Keynes Library (English literature, including 17th
century plays; manuscripts by and concerning
Isaac Newton; works of a number of authors
important in the history of thought. The Newton
Manuscripts are available on microfilm in the
University Library; modern Literary Papers in
the fields of 20th century art, literature and
economics including Rupert Brooke, E.M.
Forster, T.S. Eliot and members of the
Bloomsbury group. Papers of Economists (J.M.
Keynes, J.M. Robinson, Richard Kahn, Nicholas
Kaldor))
College's own administrative records, 11th – 21st
centuries.
Rowe Music Library (collected works and scores;
strong in 18th century music, especially Handel)

Non-library collection catalogue:
All or part available online, in-house and in print

Library catalogue:
All or part available online and in-house

Access to staff:
Contact by letter, by telephone, by fax, by e-mail,
in person and via website. Appointment necessary.
Access for members only. Letter of introduction
required.
Hours: Mon to Fri, 0900 to 1730

KING'S COLLEGE LONDON INFORMATION SERVICES CENTRE AT WESTON EDUCATION CENTRE

Cutcombe Road, London, SE5 9RJ

Tel: 020 7848 5541/2
Fax: 020 7848 5550

Website:
http://www.kcl.ac.uk/iss/library/denmark.html

Enquiries:
Enquiries to: Information Services Centre Manager
Direct tel: 020 7848 5554
Direct e-mail: david.crossinggum@kcl.ac.uk

Organisation type and purpose:
University library, NHS Trust

Subject coverage:
Clinical medicine and dentistry, health services,
biomedical sciences.

**Museum or gallery collection, archive, or library
special collection:**
Historical texts

Library catalogue:
All or part available online

Access to staff:
Contact by letter, by telephone, by fax and by e-
mail. Appointment necessary. Access for members
only.
Hours: Mon to Fri, 0830 to 2100; Sat, 0930 to 1730;
Sun, 1100 to 1900

Parent body:
King's College London
Strand, London, WC2R 2LS

KING'S COLLEGE LONDON – MAUGHAN LIBRARY AND INFORMATION SERVICES CENTRE

Chancery Lane, London, WC2R 1LR

Tel: 020 7848 2424
Fax: 020 7848 2277
E-mail: issenquiry@kcl.ac.uk

Website:
http://www.kcl.ac.uk/iss

Enquiries:
Enquiries to: Site Services Manager
Direct e-mail: vivien.robertson@kcl.ac.uk

Founded:
1829

Organisation type and purpose:
University library.

Subject coverage:
American studies, Australian studies, Byzantine and modern Greek, classics, cultural and creative industries, digital culture and technology, English, European studies, film studies, French, geography, German, history, linguistics, music, philosophy, Portuguese and Brazilian studies, Spanish and Spanish-American studies, theology and religious studies, war studies, law (including the Institute of Taxation's Tony Arnold Library), medical ethics, computer science, engineering, mathematics and physics

Museum or gallery collection, archive, or library special collection:
Adam Collection (20th-century poetry, Romanian and French literature)
Box Collection (Hebrew and Old Testament studies)
Carnegie Collection of British Music (early 20th-century British music)
Cohn Collection (German and Swiss Law)
De Beer Collection (works on or about Charles Darwin)
Early Science Collection (science and technology mainly 1800–1915)
Foreign and Commonwealth Office Historical Collection (European diplomatic history, British colonial history, voyages and travels, international law and relations)
Glaessner Collection (history of the German Democratic Republic)
Guy's Hospital Medical School Historical Collection (medicine pre-1900)
Guy's Hospital Physical Society Collection (science and pre-1900 medicine)
H. G. Adler Collection (history of the Holocaust)
Hamilton Collection (military history and poetry)
Institute for the Study and Treatment of Delinquency Collection (the causes of crime and the punishment, treatment and rehabilitation of offenders)
Institute of Psychiatry Historical Collection (psychology and psychiatry)
Jeremy Adler Collection (poetry and German literature)
Kantorowicz Collection (German literature and Juadaica)
King's College School of Medicine and Dentistry (pre-1900 medicine)
Marsden Collection (philology, early Bibles, voyages and travels)
Maurice Collection (19th-century military history)
Mottram Collection (English and American literature)
Rainbow Collection (liturgical music)
Rare Books Collection (mostly pre-1801 items in a wide range of subjects, including, science, classics, travel, theology, Portuguese studies, Greece and the eastern Mediterranean)
Ratcliff Collection (liturgy and church history)
Relton Collection (ecclesiastical history and Christian dogmatic theology)
Ruggles Gates Collection (genetics, eugenics, botany)
Skeat and Furnivall Collection (Old and Middle English, Elizabethan literature, linguistics, philology)
St Thomas's Hospital Historical Medical Collection (medicine)
Stebbing Collection (marine zoology)
Wheatstone Collection (physics, telegraphy)

Non-library collection catalogue:
All or part available online and in-house

Library catalogue:
All or part available online

Access to staff:
Contact by letter, by telephone, by fax and by e-mail. Non-members charged.
Hours: Term time: Mon to Thur, 0830 to 2030; Fri, 0830 to 1730; Sat, 0930 to 1730; Sun, 1100 to 1900; check website for vacation opening hours

Access to building, collection or gallery:
Hours: Term time: Mon to Fri, 0830 to 2200; Sat, 0930 to 1730; Sun, 1100 to 1900; check website for vacation opening hours

Access for disabled people:
Ramps to entrance, lifts provide access to most of building, induction loops at service desks

Constituent part of:
University of London

KING'S COLLEGE LONDON – NEW HUNT'S HOUSE INFORMATION SERVICES CENTRE

Guy's Campus, London, SE1 1UL

Tel: 020 7848 6740
Fax: 020 7848 6743
E-mail: andrew.baster@kcl.ac.uk

Website:
http://www.kcl.ac.uk

Enquiries:
Enquiries to: Manager

Founded:
1903

Organisation type and purpose:
University library.

Subject coverage:
Medical and related sciences, medical librarianship and information work, dental science, history of medicine.

Museum or gallery collection, archive, or library special collection:
Historical collection of printed books
Books by Guy's Men 19th and 20th Centuries

Library catalogue:
All or part available online

Printed publications:
Readers' Guides

Access to staff:
Contact by letter, by telephone, by fax and by e-mail. Appointment necessary.
Hours: Term time: Mon to Fri, 0900 to 2045, Sat, 0900 to 1645
Vacations: Mon to Fri, 0900 to 1900

Member of:
South Thames Regional Library and Information Service

Other addresses:
King's College London
   Warner Dental Library

Parent body:
University of London

KING'S COLLEGE LONDON – ST THOMAS' HOUSE INFORMATION SERVICES CENTRE

Acronym or abbreviation: KCL

Westminster Bridge Road, London, SE1 7EH

Tel: 020 7188 3740
Fax: 020 7188 8358
E-mail: issenquiry@kcl.ac.uk

Website:
http://www.kcl.ac.uk/iss

Enquiries:
Enquiries to: NHS Information Specialist
Direct tel: 020 7188 3744

Direct e-mail: sarah.lawson@kcl.ac.uk

Founded:
1903

Organisation type and purpose:
University library, NHS Trust.

Subject coverage:
Medicine, health care, history of medicine.

Museum or gallery collection, archive, or library special collection:
History of St Thomas' Hospital
Printed books and manuscripts on medicine and related sciences

Library catalogue:
All or part available online

Access to staff:
Contact by letter, by telephone, by fax, by e-mail, in person and via website. Access for members only.
Hours: Term time: Mon to Fri, 0900 to 1700

Member organisation of:
London Health Libraries network
   website: http://www.londonlinks.nhs.uk

KING'S COLLEGE LONDON – STAMFORD STREET INFORMATION SERVICES CENTRE

Acronym or abbreviation: KCL

Franklin-Wilkins Building, 150 Stamford Street, London, SE1 8WA

Tel: 020 7848 4498
Fax: 020 7848 4290
E-mail: peter.walsh@kcl.ac.uk

Website:
http://www.kcl.ac.uk

Enquiries:
Enquiries to: Manager

Founded:
1829

Organisation type and purpose:
University library.

Subject coverage:
Education, life sciences, management, nutrition, nursing, pharmacy.

Museum or gallery collection, archive, or library special collection:
Listed under the Strand Campus entry

Library catalogue:
All or part available online

Access to staff:
Contact by letter and by telephone
Hours: Mon to Fri, 0900 to 2100; Sat, 0930 to 1730

Also at:
Director of Library Services (no library at this address)
   King's College London, London, WC2R 2LS; tel: 020 7848 2139; fax: 020 7848 1777; website: http://www.kcl.ac.uk/depsta/iss/servicesindex.html
Information Services Centre
   New Hunt's House, Guys Hospital, St Thomas Street, London, SE1 9RT; tel: 020 7848 6600; fax: 020 7848 6743; website: http://www.kcl.ac.uk/depsta/iss/sites/guys/topguys.html
Information Services Centre
   Franklin-Wilkins Building, 150 Stamford Street, London, SE1 9NN; tel: 020 7848 4378; website: http://www.kcl.ac.uk/depsta/iss/sites/waterloo/topwaterloo.html
King's College London
   Strand, London, WC2R 2LS
Library and Information Services Centre
   Chancery Lane, London, WC2A 1LR; tel: 020 7848 2424; fax: 020 7848 2277; website: http://www.kcl.ac.uk/depsta/iss/sites/chancery/index.html

continued overleaf

Medical Library
  Weston Education Centre, Cutcombe Road,
  London, SE5 9JP; tel: 020 7848 5541; fax: 020 7848
  5550; website: http://www.kcl.ac.uk/depsta/iss/
  sites/denmarkhill/topdenmarkhill.ht
Medical Library
  St Thomas' Hospital, Lambeth Palace Road,
  London, SE1 7EH; tel: 020 7928 9292 ext 2367;
  fax: 020 7401 3932; website: http://www.kcl.ac
  .uk/depsta/iss/sites/stthomas/topthomas.html

KING'S FUND

11–13 Cavendish Square, London, W1G 0AN

Tel: 020 7307 2400
Fax: 020 7307 2801

Website:
http://www.kingsfund.org.uk

Enquiries:
Enquiries to: Chief Executive
Other contacts: Director of Corporate Affairs

Founded:
1897

Organisation type and purpose:
Registered charity (charity number 207401),
training organisation, research organisation.
To promote good health in London, to reduce
inequalities in health, to promote the benefits of
diversity, to involve the public in health
policymaking and to break down boundaries
between organisations working for health.

Subject coverage:
Health care (not clinical medicine), grant making,
training and education, social care and policy and
public health.

**Museum or gallery collection, archive, or library
special collection:**
Health Services library; reports and journals in
health and social care

Printed publications:
Reports of Studies dealing with subjects such as;
acute care, carers, community care, ethics and
consensus, health and race, health services
management, inequalities in health, learning
difficulties, London, medical education, medical
technology, mental health, nursing, patient
choice, physical disability, primary health care,
user view and surveys
Order printed publications from: King's Fund
Bookshop, at the same address; tel: 020 7307 2591;
e-mail: bookshop@kingsfund.org.uk

Publications list:
Available online and in print

Access to staff:
Contact by letter, by telephone and in person
Hours: Mon to Fri, 0900 to 1700

Access to building, collection or gallery:
No prior appointment required

Access for disabled people:
Parking provided, level entry, access to all public
areas, toilet facilities

KING'S FUND INFORMATION AND LIBRARY SERVICE

Formal name: The King's Fund

11–13 Cavendish Square, London, W1G 0AN

Tel: 020 7307 2568
Fax: 020 7307 2805
E-mail: library@kingsfund.org.uk

Website:
http://www.kingsfund.org.uk
Provides the latest information about The King's
Fund's work, projects, publications and research
findings, explains how to attend one of the Fund's
education and leadership development
programmes and gives details of venue hire.

Enquiries:
Enquiries to: Librarian

Founded:
1897

Organisation type and purpose:
Registered charity.
To improve the health of, and health care for,
Londoners.

Subject coverage:
Health care policy, social care policy, planning,
organisation and management, leadership;
hospital and community-based health services in
the UK.

**Museum or gallery collection, archive, or library
special collection:**
350 current serial titles
30,000 items including grey literature
Collection of NHS Policy Reports (earliest 1897)
Department of Health Circulars
King's Fund Publications
WHO – Regional Office for Europe Publications

Non-library collection catalogue:
All or part available online and in-house

Library catalogue:
All or part available online and in print

Printed publications:
Reading lists on popular topics (available free on
  the web)

Electronic and video publications:
HMIC (online) comprising databases of the King's
  Fund Library and the Department of Health
Current Awareness Bulletin (weekly, online, free)
News alert on health policy issues (twice-weekly,
  by e-mail, free)

Publications list:
Available online and in print

Access to staff:
Contact by letter, by telephone, by fax, by e-mail,
in person and via website
Hours: Mon, Tue, Thu, Fri, 0930 to 1730; Wed, 1100
to 1730

Access for disabled people:
Level entry, access to all public areas, toilet
facilities

KING'S LYNN LIBRARY

London Road, King's Lynn, Norfolk, PE30 5EZ

Tel: 01553 772568 or 761393
Fax: 01553 769832
E-mail: kings.lynn.lib@norfolk.gov.uk

Website:
http://www.library.norfolk.gov.uk
Norfolk electronic library, library catalogue,
information about services provided by Norfolk
Libraries, local information.

Enquiries:
Enquiries to: Manager
Other contacts: Community Librarian

Founded:
1904

Organisation type and purpose:
Local government body, public library.

Subject coverage:
General, history of King's Lynn and West Norfolk.

**Museum or gallery collection, archive, or library
special collection:**
St Margaret's Library Collection (founded 1631)
St Nicholas' Library Collection (founded 1617)
Stanley Library Collection (founded 1854)
Medical, historical, religious and travel works of
  15th to 19th centuries

Non-library collection catalogue:
All or part available in-house

Library catalogue:
All or part available online

Access to staff:
Contact by letter, by telephone, by fax, by e-mail
and in person

Hours: Mon to Fri, 0900 to 1700

Access for disabled people:
Ramped entry

Parent body:
Norfolk County Council Library and Information
Service

KINGSTON LIBRARIES

Kingston Library, Fairfield Road, Kingston upon
Thames, Surrey, KT1 2PS

Tel: 020 8547 6400
Fax: 020 8547 6401

Website:
http://www.kingston.gov.uk/Enjoying/Libraries/
default.htm
Library catalogue, community information,
opening hours, library services, online reference.

Enquiries:
Enquiries to: Head of Library Services
Direct tel: 020 8547 6413
Direct fax: 020 8547 6426
Direct e-mail: jo.gloyn@rbk.kingston.gov.uk
Other contacts: Information Librarian

Founded:
1902

Organisation type and purpose:
Local government body, public library.

Subject coverage:
General, English literature, fine arts, statistics, non-
HMSO and HMSO government publications.

Library catalogue:
All or part available online

Access to staff:
Contact by letter, by telephone, by fax and by e-
mail. Appointment necessary.
Hours: Mon, 0930 to 1900; Tue and Fri, 0930 to
1730; Wed, closed; Thu, 0930 to 2000; Sat, 0900 to
1730

Access for disabled people:
Ramped entry, access to all public areas

Parent body:
Royal Borough of Kingston upon Thames

KINGSTON UNIVERSITY

Information Services, Penrhyn Road, Kingston
upon Thames, Surrey, KT1 2EE

Tel: 020 8547 2000
Fax: 020 8417 2111
E-mail: library@kingston.ac.uk

Website:
http://www.kingston.ac.uk/library
Addresses, opening hours, subject coverage,
catalogues.

Enquiries:
Enquiries to: Director of Information Services

Organisation type and purpose:
University library.

Subject coverage:
Business, law, chemistry, pharmacy, life sciences,
mathematics, computer science, surveying, civil,
mechanical, production and aeronautical
engineering, geography, geology, art and design,
architecture, performing art, social sciences,
economics, history, English, education, healthcare
studies.

**Museum or gallery collection, archive, or library
special collection:**
Iris Murdoch Collections, Vane Ivanovic Library,
  Sheridan Morley Theatre Collection

Non-library collection catalogue:
All or part available online

Library catalogue:
All or part available online

Printed publications:
Library guides

Access to staff:
Contact by letter, by telephone, by e-mail, in person and via website
Hours: Mon to Fri, 0900 to 1700
Special comments: Please see website for full details.

Access to building, collection or gallery:
Special comments: Visitors are advised to carry identification.

KINGSTON UPON HULL CITY LIBRARIES

Hull Central Library, Albion Street, Hull, East Yorkshire, HU1 3TF

Tel: 01482 223344
Fax: 01482 616858
E-mail: rosemary.reed@hullcc.gov.uk

Website:
http://www.hullcc.gov.uk/libraries
General information on the library departments, council, local interest, libraries and museums, business.

Enquiries:
Enquiries to: Librarian
Direct e-mail: reference.library@hullcc.gov.uk

Founded:
1903

Organisation type and purpose:
Local government body, public library.

Subject coverage:
General, food technology, fish and fishing industry, paint and organic chemicals, edible oils, ports, pharmaceuticals, building industry, business information, reference enquiries, literature, arts, religion.

Museum or gallery collection, archive, or library special collection:
British Standards
Lloyds Registers (1760 to present day)
Napoleon
Regimental histories

Trade and statistical information:
Range of statistical information, market research info.

Non-library collection catalogue:
All or part available in-house

Library catalogue:
All or part available online

Publications list:
Available online and in print

Access to staff:
Contact by letter, by telephone, by fax, by e-mail, in person and via website
Hours: Mon to Thu, 0930 to 2000; Fri 0930 to 1730; Sat 0900 to 1630

Access to building, collection or gallery:
Hours: Mon to Thu, 0930 to 2000; Fri 0930 to 1730; Sat 0900 to 1630

Access for disabled people:
Ramped entry, toilet facilities

Branch libraries:
1 central and 16 branch libraries

KIPLING SOCIETY

6 Clifton Road, London, W9 1SS

Tel: 020 7286 0194
Fax: 020 7286 0194
E-mail: jmkeskar@btinternet.com

Website:
http://www.kipling.org.uk

Enquiries:
Enquiries to: Honorary Secretary
Other contacts: Honorary Librarian (for the library)

Founded:
1927

Organisation type and purpose:
Learned society (membership is by subscription), registered charity (charity number 278885).

Subject coverage:
Life, works and associations of Rudyard Kipling 1865–1936; 5 meetings annually in central London with guest speakers.

Museum or gallery collection, archive, or library special collection:
Library of books on and by R Kipling

Library catalogue:
All or part available online and in-house

Printed publications:
The Kipling Journal (quarterly, from 1927 onwards)

Access to staff:
Contact by letter, by telephone, by fax, by e-mail and via website
Hours: Mon to Fri, 0900 to 1700
Special comments: Library open to members only, by appointment.

Access to building, collection or gallery:
No prior appointment required

Library housed at:
City University
    Northampton Square, London; tel: 020 7359 2464

Representative in:
USA and Australia

KIRKLEES COLLEGE – HUDDERSFIELD CENTRE

Acronym or abbreviation: KC

Library, New North Road, Huddersfield, West Yorkshire, HD1 5NN

Tel: 01484 536521
Fax: 01484 511885

Website:
http://www.huddcoll.ac.uk

Enquiries:
Enquiries to: Librarian
Direct e-mail: libraryenquiries@kirkleescollege.ac.uk

Created by the merger of:
Huddersfield Technical College and Dewsbury College (year of change 2008)

Subject coverage:
Business studies, catering, engineering, science, construction, computing, music, social work, leisure and recreation, motor vehicle technology, education and training, art and design, hairdressing, animal care sciences.

Library catalogue:
All or part available online and in-house

Electronic and video publications:
CD-ROMs, videos, DVDs, Shibboleth access to databases, journals

Access to staff:
Contact by letter, by telephone, by fax, by e-mail and in person. Appointment necessary.
Hours: Mon to Thu, 0845 to 2000; Fri, 0845 to 1600

Access for disabled people:
Parking provided, level entry, access to all public areas, toilet facilities
Special comments: Lifts for disabled

KIRKLEES METROPOLITAN BOROUGH COUNCIL

Cultural Services Headquarters, Red Doles Lane, Huddersfield, West Yorkshire, HD2 1YF

Tel: 01484 226300
Fax: 01484 226342

Website:
http://www.kirkleesmc.gov.uk

Enquiries:
Enquiries to: Head of Service
Other contacts: (1) Assistant Head of Service (2) Assistant Head of Service for (1) libraries and information service (2) community history, arts and town halls.

Organisation type and purpose:
Local government body, museum, art gallery, public library.

Subject coverage:
Local government services.

Library catalogue:
All or part available in-house

Printed publications:
Publications include:
Happy Inspiration: the story of Castle Hill and its Tower (Bywater H)
Heritage of Huddersfield (Schofield I)
History of the Huddersfield Fire Brigade (Smith C)
Huddersfield: A Most Handsom Town (Haigh E A H)
Oakwell Hall
Three in a Bed: memories of a Dewsbury lass (Braybrook I)
Order printed publications from: Bibliographical Services, at the same address, tel: 01484 226374, fax: 01484 226342, e-mail: julie.peel@kirkleesmc.gov.uk

Publications list:
Available in print

Access to staff:
Contact by letter, by telephone, by fax, by e-mail, in person and via website
Hours: Mon to Fri, 0900 to 1700

KITE SOCIETY OF GREAT BRITAIN

Acronym or abbreviation: KSGB

PO Box 2274, Great Horkesley, Colchester, Essex, CO6 4AY

Tel: 01206 271489
Fax: 01206 271489
E-mail: info@thekitesociety.org.uk

Website:
http://www.thekitesociety.org.uk

Enquiries:
Enquiries to: General Secretary

Founded:
1979

Organisation type and purpose:
Membership association.

Subject coverage:
Kite design, kite groups, kite events, kite shops, kite-flying.

Printed publications:
Kite Design Booklets
Kite Material Suppliers Booklet
Kitefliers Handbook
The Kiteflier (newsletter, quarterly)

Access to staff:
Contact by letter, by telephone, by fax and by e-mail
Hours: Mon to Fri, 0900 to 1700

Has:
most local kite groups as affiliates

KNITTING & CROCHET GUILD OF GREAT BRITAIN

PO Box 4421, Kidderminster, Worcestershire, DY11 6YW

E-mail: info@knitting-and-crochet-guild.org.uk

Website:
http://www.knitting-and-crochet-guild.org.uk

continued overleaf

Enquiries:
Direct e-mail: info@knitting-and-crochet-guild.org.uk

Organisation type and purpose:
A registered national educational charity (no. 01113468).

Subject coverage:
Knitting and crochet.

Museum or gallery collection, archive, or library special collection:
Library of books, periodicals and patterns
Collection of garments, samples, domestic knitting machines, yarns, tools and ephemera from the past two hundred years

KNITTING INDUSTRIES' FEDERATION

Acronym or abbreviation: KIF

12 Beaumanor Road, Leicester, LE1 5XY

Tel: 0116 266 3332
Fax: 0116 266 3335
E-mail: directorate@knitfed.co.uk

Enquiries:
Enquiries to: Director

Founded:
1942

Organisation type and purpose:
Trade association (membership is by subscription), present number of members: 300, manufacturing industry.

Subject coverage:
Industrial relations, trade policy, government lobbying, environment, health and safety statistics.

Trade and statistical information:
Knitstats – comprehensive summary of knitting industry statistics.

Printed publications:
Industry Analysis 1993 to 1997 (£75)
Knitstats (£50)

Access to staff:
Contact by letter, by telephone, by fax and by e-mail. Appointment necessary. Non-members charged.
Hours: Mon to Fri, 0900 to 1700

Access to building, collection or gallery:
No prior appointment required

A sector of the:
British Clothing Industry Association Limited

KNOWSLEY LIBRARY SERVICE

Huyton Library, Civic Way, Huyton, Knowsley, Merseyside, L36 9GD

Tel: 0151 443 3738
Fax: 0151 443 3739
E-mail: huyton.lending.library@knowsley.gov.uk

Website:
http://history.knowsley.gov.uk
Local history of Knowsley Borough and its townships including text, images, maps, town trails, audio clips, etc.
http://www.knowsley.gov.uk
Information on Knowsley Metropolitan Borough Council, including libraries.

Enquiries:
Enquiries to: Information Services Manager

Organisation type and purpose:
Local government body, public library.

Subject coverage:
General and local history.

Museum or gallery collection, archive, or library special collection:
Local history of Knowsley Metropolitan Borough

Library catalogue:
All or part available online

Printed publications:
Archive Photography Series – Huyton with Roby
Archive Photography Series – Kirkby and Knowsley
Huyton and Roby: A History of The Townships
Inns of Prescot and Whiston
Tracing your Family History in the Knowsley Area at Huyton Library
Whiston: A Young Person's Guide

Publications list:
Available in print

Access to staff:
Contact by letter, by telephone, by fax, by e-mail, in person and via website
Hours: Mon to Fri, 0915 to 1900; Sat, 1000 to 1600; Sun, 1200 to 1600

Access for disabled people:
Parking provided, ramped entry, level entry, access to all public areas, toilet facilities

KODÁLY INSTITUTE OF BRITAIN

Acronym or abbreviation: KIB

Queen's Gate School, 133 Queen's Gate, London, SW7 5LE

Tel: 020 7823 7371 or 020 7589 3056
Fax: 020 7584 7691

Enquiries:
Enquiries to: Administrator
Other contacts: Director

Founded:
1994

Organisation type and purpose:
International organisation, professional body (membership is by subscription), present number of members: 150, training organisation.
Music education/training for adults using the Kodály concept.

Subject coverage:
Principles and practice of the Kodály concept.

Printed publications:
The Kodály Way to Music, Book 1 by Cecilia Vajda (book for purchase)
The Kodály Way to Music, Book 2 by Cecilia Vajda (book for purchase)

Electronic and video publications:
Early Childhood Music Education (video for hire)
Musicianship Training at Key Stage 2 (video for hire)
Musicianship Training at Key Stage 3 (video, for purchase)
Series of five Musicianship Training (cassettes, for purchase)
Sing and Play – The Kodály Way (cassette for purchase)
The Kodály Concept (video for purchase)

Publications list:
Available in print

Access to staff:
Contact by letter, by telephone and by fax. Appointment necessary.
Hours: Mon to Sun, 0900 to 2200

Parent body:
International Kodály Society
Budapest, Hungary

Subsidiary:
Liszt Academy of Music
Budapest

KOREA NATIONAL TOURISM ORGANIZATION

Acronym or abbreviation: KNTO

3rd Floor, New Zealand House, Haymarket, London, SW1Y 4TE

Tel: 020 7321 2535
Fax: 020 7321 0876
E-mail: london@mail.knto.or.kr

Website:
http://www.tour2korea.com

Enquiries:
Enquiries to: Director
Other contacts: Marketing Manager

Founded:
1960

Organisation type and purpose:
National government body.
Tourist office.
To promote travel and tourism to South Korea.

Subject coverage:
Tourism in Korea.

Printed publications:
Available free, directly – generally

Publications list:
Available online

Access to staff:
Contact by letter, by telephone, by fax, by e-mail, in person and via website. Appointment necessary. Access for members only.
Hours: Mon to Fri, 0900 to 1700

Access to building, collection or gallery:
Hours: Mon to Fri, 0900 to 1700

Access for disabled people:
Access to all public areas

Has:
over 50 overseas branches

KPMG

20 Farringdon Street, London, EC4A 4PP

Tel: 020 7311 1000
Fax: 020 7311 3311

Enquiries:
Enquiries to: Tax Librarian
Direct tel: 020 7311 3970
Direct fax: 020 7311 3886
Direct e-mail: john.ridgley@kpmg.co.uk

Organisation type and purpose:
Accounting and management consultancy.

Subject coverage:
Accountancy; auditing; company law; corporate finance; taxation; management in many countries and various industries.

Non-library collection catalogue:
All or part available in-house

Access to staff:
Contact by telephone, by fax and by e-mail. Appointment necessary. Access for members only.
Hours: Mon to Fri, 0930 to 1730

Access to building, collection or gallery:
No prior appointment required

LA LECHE LEAGUE (GREAT BRITAIN)

Acronym or abbreviation: LLLGB

PO Box 29, West Bridgford, Nottingham, NG2 7NP

Tel: 0845 456 1866; 0115 981 5599
E-mail: lllgb@wsds.co.uk

Website:
http://www.laleche.org.uk
About the organisation and its services.
http://www.lllbooks.org.uk
Publications and how to order them.

Enquiries:
Enquiries to: Administrator

Founded:
1973

Organisation type and purpose:
Membership association (membership is by subscription), present number of members: 1,000, registered charity (charity number 283771).

To provide information, help and support to mothers wanting to breastfeed.

Subject coverage:
Breastfeeding.

Non-library collection catalogue:
All or part available online and in print

Printed publications:
The Womanly Art of Breastfeeding (6th ed, 465pp, £14.99)
Breastfeeding Your Premature Baby (Gotsch G, 56pp, £6.99)
Books and leaflets on breastfeeding and family life including:
The Breastfeeding Answer Book (Mohrbacher N and Stock J, 2nd ed, 608pp, £48)
Order printed publications from: LLL Books Ltd, PO Box 29, West Bridgford, Nottingham, NG2 7NP

Publications list:
Available online and in print

Access to staff:
Contact by letter and by telephone
Hours: 24-hour helpline
Office admin: Mon to Fri, 0900 to 1800

Access to building, collection or gallery:
No access other than to staff

Also at:
LLLGB
  Administrative Office, PO Box 29, West Bridgford, Nottingham, NG2 7NP; tel: 0115 945 5772

LABAN CENTRE LONDON

Formal name: Laban Centre for Movement and Dance Limited

14–18 Creekside, Deptford, London, SE8 3DZ

Tel: 020 8692 4070 ext 120
Fax: 020 8694 8749
E-mail: library@laban.co.uk

Website:
http://www.laban.co.uk

Enquiries:
Enquiries to: Librarian

Organisation type and purpose:
Registered charity (charity number 801973), suitable for ages: 18+.

Subject coverage:
Practical and academic education in dance and movement, all kinds of dance: ballet, contemporary, social, theatre, community, dance therapy and related subjects e.g. anatomy, music, psychology, scenography, dance notation, Rudolf Laban, dance medicine, Pilates, European Tanz theatre.

Museum or gallery collection, archive, or library special collection:
Grey Literature
Laban Collection (Laban's work in Germany, 1920–1930s) – microfiche
Other printed and audio visual materials
Peter Williams Collection (books, photographs, manuscripts etc, 1930–1995)
Peter Brinson Collection (sociology, education, working archive of 'Ballet for All')
Shirley Wynn Collection (historical dance, notation)

Non-library collection catalogue:
All or part available in-house

Library catalogue:
All or part available in-house

Printed publications:
Book List – see website
Dance Theatre Journal (4 times a year)

Publications list:
Available online

Access to staff:
Contact by letter, by telephone, by fax, by e-mail, in person and via website. Appointment necessary. Non-members charged.
Hours: Term time: Mon, Wed & Thu, 0900 to 2000; Tue, 0900 to 1930; Fri, 0900 to 1700; Sat, 1030 to 1430
Vacations: Mon to Fri, 0900 to 1700

LABAN GUILD FOR MOVEMENT AND DANCE

5/24 Westcote Road, Reading, Berkshire, RG30 2DE

Tel: 0118 961 6903

Enquiries:
Enquiries to: Secretary

Founded:
1946

Organisation type and purpose:
International organisation, membership association (membership is by subscription), present number of members: 400, registered charity, voluntary organisation (charity number 266435).
To promote and advance the study of Laban based movement and dance. Provides a resource for its members within which they can experience teaching, development, exchange of information and a sense of identity. Promotes the development of movement as an art form, the study of human movement, particularly recognising the contribution made by the late Rudolf Laban.

Printed publications:
Magazine (quarterly)

Access to staff:
Contact by letter
Hours: Mon to Fri, 0900 to 1700

LABORATORY ANIMAL SCIENCE ASSOCIATION

Acronym or abbreviation: LASA

PO Box 3993, Tamworth, Staffordshire, B78 3QU

Tel: 01827 259130
Fax: 01827 259188
E-mail: lasa@globalnet.co.uk

Website:
http://www.lasa.co.uk

Enquiries:
Enquiries to: Secretary

Organisation type and purpose:
Learned society (membership is by subscription). Advancement of care, welfare and use of animals and replacement where appropriate.

Subject coverage:
Animal welfare, refinement in animal studies, alternatives to animal use, education, training in laboratory animal science, laboratory animal health, regulatory controls over uses of laboratory animals, laboratory animal genetics, laboratory animal nutrition, toxicology tests, management of laboratory animal units.

Printed publications:
Newsletter (quarterly, members only)
Laboratory Animals (quarterly)

Publications list:
Available in print

Access to staff:
Contact by letter, by telephone, by fax and by e-mail
Hours: Mon to Fri, 0900 to 1700

Affiliated to:
Federation of European Laboratory Animal Science Associations (FELASA)

LABOUR PARTY

Eldon House, Regent Centre, Newcastle Upon Tyne, NE3 3PW

Tel: 08705 900 200

Website:
http://www.labour.org.uk/

Organisation type and purpose:
Internal resource centre of a political party.

Subject coverage:
Social sciences, especially politics, labour history.

Museum or gallery collection, archive, or library special collection:
Archives of the Labour Party held at National Museum of Labour History, 103 Princess Street, Manchester M1 6DD, Tel no: 0161 228 7212

Access to staff:
Contact by letter, by telephone, by fax and by e-mail
Hours: No access

LABOUR RELATIONS AGENCY

Acronym or abbreviation: LRA

Head Office, 2–8 Gordon Street, Belfast, BT1 2LG

Tel: 028 9032 1442\ Minicom no. 028 9023 8411
Fax: 028 9033 0827
E-mail: info@lra.org.uk

Website:
http://www.lra.org.uk

Enquiries:
Enquiries to: Director
Other contacts: (1) Director (Corporate Services) (2) Director (Advisory Services) (3) Director (Conciliation and Arbitration)

Founded:
1976

Organisation type and purpose:
Statutory body.
Provides mediation, arbitration, conciliation and advisory services to employers, trade unions etc and issues codes of practice on employment relations matters.

Subject coverage:
Joint consultative and negotiating machinery, employment relations legislation, internal relations and communications, grievance, disciplinary, dismissal and redundancy procedures, trade union recognition, terms and conditions of employment, recruitment, selection and induction, payment systems and job evaluation, manpower planning, labour turnover and absenteeism, employment relations research, training, maternity provisions and legislation, equality legislation.

Printed publications:
Annual Reports
Codes of Practice; Research Reports; Advisory Guides
Information Notes Series covering various employment relations topics
Review of Employment Topics (peer-reviewed journal 1993 to 1997)

Publications list:
Available online and in print

Access to staff:
Contact by letter, by telephone, by fax, by e-mail and in person. Appointment necessary.
Hours: Mon to Fri, 0900 to 1700

Access to building, collection or gallery:
No prior appointment required

Access for disabled people:
Ramped entry, level entry, access to all public areas, toilet facilities
Special comments: Parking provided at head office.

continued overleaf

Regional Office:
Labour Relations Agency
1–3 Guildhall Street, Londonderry, BT48 6BJ; tel:
028 7126 9639; fax: 028 7126 7729; e-mail: lra@
dnet.co.uk

LACE GUILD

Formal name: The Lace Guild

The Hollies, 53 Audnam, Stourbridge, West
Midlands, DY8 4AE

Tel: 01384 390739
Fax: 01384 444415
E-mail: hollies@laceguild.org

Website:
http://www.laceguild.demon.co.uk
Home page with links to: About the Guild; Craft of
Lace; Lace magazine; events; publications;
suppliers.

Enquiries:
Enquiries to: Administrative Officer; Accounts
Officer
Other contacts: Headquarters staff (for availability
on a daily basis)

Founded:
1976

Organisation type and purpose:
International organisation, national organisation,
membership association (membership is by
subscription), present number of members: 5,000
approx, voluntary organisation, registered charity
(charity number 274397), museum, suitable for
ages: all.
Accredited museum (number RD 1950).
The role of The Lace Guild is to promote
understanding and appreciation of all aspects of
lace and lacemaking.

Subject coverage:
All aspects of lace including: history (social and
technical); making of all English and most
European bobbin, needle and craft laces;
equipment and materials; publications; exhibitions;
courses.

**Museum or gallery collection, archive, or library
special collection:**
Collections of lace and lace-related artefacts,
including patterns, tools, materials, sample
books
Comprehensive library of books, magazines (from
around the world), photographs, documents and
study folios covering every aspect of lace

Non-library collection catalogue:
All or part available in-house

Library catalogue:
All or part available online and in print

Printed publications:
Information leaflets
Instruction books
Magazine and Newsletter (quarterly, members)
Patterns and Pattern books
Young Lacemakers Magazine

Publications list:
Available online and in print

Access to staff:
Contact by letter, by telephone, by fax, by e-mail
and via website. Appointment necessary.
Hours: Mon to Fri, 0900 to 1600

Access to building, collection or gallery:
Prior appointment required
Hours: Mon to Fri, 0900 to 1600

LACROSSE SCOTLAND

Tel: 07764 943053
E-mail: president@lacrossescotland.com

Website:
http://www.lacrossescotland.com
Various teams, where to play, history and rules of
the game, news.

To view upcoming events and matches either click
on the Events Calendar icon on the right, or
navigate to the individual team pages.

Enquiries:
Enquiries to: President
Other contacts: Membership Secretary

Organisation type and purpose:
Governing body for lacrosse in Scotland.

Subject coverage:
All aspects of lacrosse in Scotland from schools to
international fixtures.

Access to staff:
Contact by telephone and by e-mail

LADIES EUROPEAN TOUR

Acronym or abbreviation: LET

The Old Hall, Dorchester Way, Macclesfield,
Cheshire, SK10 2LQ

Tel: 01625 611444
Fax: 01625 610406
E-mail: mail@ladieseuropeantour.com

Website:
http://www.ladieseuropeantour.com
Profile of players, information on tournaments,
results and money list, press releases.

Enquiries:
Enquiries to: Executive Director

Founded:
1988

Organisation type and purpose:
Professional Sports Body.

Subject coverage:
Women's professional golf.

Printed publications:
Yearly Tour Guide listing top players with profiles

Access to staff:
Contact by letter, by fax, by e-mail and via
website. Appointment necessary.
Hours: Mon to Fri, 0900 to 1700

LADIES' GOLF UNION

Acronym or abbreviation: LGU

The Scores, St Andrews, Fife, KY16 9AT

Tel: 01334 475811
Fax: 01334 472818
E-mail: info@lgu.org

Website:
http://www.lgu.org

Enquiries:
Enquiries to: CEO

Founded:
1893

Organisation type and purpose:
Membership association.

Subject coverage:
Ladies' amateur golf from 1893.

**Museum or gallery collection, archive, or library
special collection:**
Photograph albums 1893–1929
Records of British ladies' golf since 1893

Printed publications:
Handbook (annually, February)
eNews

Access to staff:
Contact by letter, by telephone, by fax, by e-mail
and via website
Hours: Mon to Fri, 0900 to 1700

LAKE DISTRICT NATIONAL PARK
AUTHORITY

Acronym or abbreviation: LDNPA

Murley Moss Business Park, Oxenholme Road,
Kendal, Cumbria, LA9 7RL

Tel: 01539 724555\ Minicom no. 01539 731263
Fax: 01593 740822
E-mail: hq@lake-district.gov.uk

Website:
http://www.lake-district.gov.uk

Enquiries:
Enquiries to: Communications Manager
Direct tel: 01539 792683
Direct fax: 01539 740822
Direct e-mail: mick.casey@lake-district.gov.uk

Founded:
1951

Organisation type and purpose:
Local government body, membership association
(membership is by election or invitation), present
number of members: 26, service industry.
To conserve and enhance natural beauty, wildlife
and cultural heritage of the National Park, promote
opportunities for understanding and enjoyment of
its special qualities, seeking to foster economic and
social well-being of its local communities.

Subject coverage:
Information on the National Park: access,
conservation, landscape, historic sites, buildings
etc, farming, mining and quarrying, traffic and
parking, tourism. Local community, control of
development.

Printed publications:
Lake District National Park Management Plan (£1
    plus p&p)
Lake District National Park Local Plan (£16.50 plus
    p&p)
Cumbria and Lake District Joint Structure Plan
    (£10 plus p&p)
Other specific area management plans
Repairing Upland Path Erosion (£19.95 plus p&p)
The Caravan and Tent Guide (99p plus p&p)

Publications list:
Available online and in print

Access to staff:
Contact by letter, by telephone, by fax, by e-mail
and via website. Appointment necessary.
Hours: Mon to Thu, 0900 to 1700; Fri, 0900 to 1645

Access for disabled people:
Parking provided, level entry, toilet facilities

Member of:
Association of National Park Authorities (ANPA)
    Ponsford House, Moretonhampstead, Newton
    Abbot, Devon, TQ13 8NL; tel: 01647 440245
Federation of Nature and National Parks of Europe

LAKELAND DIALECT SOCIETY

Acronym or abbreviation: LDS

Gale View, Main Street, Shap, Penrith, Cumbria,
CA10 3NH

Tel: 01931 716386
E-mail: lakespeak@aol.com

Website:
http://www.lakelanddialectsociety.org

Enquiries:
Enquiries to: Honorary Secretary
Other contacts: Vice President and Editor, tel: 01931
715359

Founded:
1939

Organisation type and purpose:
Membership association (membership is by
subscription), present number of members: 300,
voluntary organisation.

Subject coverage:
The Cumbrian dialect in general, its origins and its
use today.

Museum or gallery collection, archive, or library special collection:
Small collection of Cumbrian dialect literature, minute books and papers of the Society (held in Carlisle Library, Globe Lane, Carlisle). May be viewed by arrangement

Printed publications:
Annual Journal (free to members and on sale to the general public, £1.50)
Lakeland Treasury – the works of Lance Porter (£5.50)

Electronic and video publications:
Lakeland Gems 73 minutes of stories, poems and songs in dialect (CD, £11.50, audio tape, £5.50 inc p&p)

Access to staff:
Contact by letter, by telephone, by e-mail, in person and via website
Hours: Mon to Fri, 0900 to 1800
Special comments: Evenings after 1945 hours.

Access to building, collection or gallery:
No prior appointment required

Internal links with:
Cumberland Women's Institute
Yorkshire Dialect Society
Librarian, School of English, University of Leeds, Leeds, LS2 9JT

LAMBETH ARCHIVES DEPARTMENT

Minet Library, 52 Knatchbull Road, London, SE5 9QY

Tel: 020 7926 6076
Fax: 020 7926 6080

Enquiries:
Enquiries to: Archivist

Organisation type and purpose:
Local government body, public library.
Record office.
To preserve and make accessible the records of the London Borough of Lambeth, its predecessors, and the records of Lambeth people and places.

Subject coverage:
Records of the London Borough of Lambeth and its predecessors; deposited records of local Lambeth organisations; local history and topography of Lambeth and the old county of Surrey; manorial records; estate records; business records.

Museum or gallery collection, archive, or library special collection:
Crystal Palace Collection (books, programmes, cuttings)
South London Theatres Collection (playbills and programmes)
Surrey Collection
Vauxhall Gardens Collection (playbills, cuttings, songbooks, manuscripts)
Woolley Collection of Doulton and other stoneware

Printed publications:
Born & Bred – Tracing your Lambeth family history
Clapham
Guide to Lambeth Archives
Lambeth Stoneware
Lambeth's Open Spaces
Short Guide to the Surrey Collection
St Luke, West Norwood, 1825–1975
Story of Norwood

Publications list:
Available in print

Access to staff:
Contact by letter, by telephone, by fax, by e-mail and in person. Appointment necessary.
Hours: Mon to Fri, 0900 to 1700

Access for disabled people:
Ramped entry

Parent body:
London Borough of Lambeth

LAMBETH PALACE LIBRARY

London, SE1 7JU

Tel: 020 7898 1400
Fax: 020 7928 7932
E-mail: lpl.staff@lpl.c-of-e.org.uk

Website:
http://www.lambethpalacelibrary.org
Conditions of access, hours of opening, etc; holdings guide; research guides; catalogue of printed books online; reprographics; Friends of the Library.

Enquiries:
Enquiries to: Librarian

Founded:
1610

Organisation type and purpose:
Academic Research Library.

Subject coverage:
Ecclesiastical history, particularly of the Church of England; general history; palaeography; early printing; art history; American colonial history; bibliography; genealogy; topography.

Museum or gallery collection, archive, or library special collection:
Archives of the Province of Canterbury, including marriage allegations, wills, Court of Arches, etc
Incunables (200)
Manuscripts from 9th century to present (4000)
Papers of the Archbishops of Canterbury from the 16th century
Papers of the Bishops of London, including extensive collections concerning colonial America and the West Indies from the 17th century
Papers of the Commonwealth, Earls of Shrewsbury, Anthony Bacon, George Carew (Earl of Totnes), Commissioners for Building 50 New Churches (Queen Anne Churches)
Papers of societies etc, within the Church of England, Anglo-Continental Society, Christian Faith Society, Church of England Temperance Society, Church Union, Clergy Orphan Corporation, Confraternity of the Blessed Sacrament etc
Papers of statesmen and bishops, Gladstone, Selborne, Bishops G K A Bell, A C Headlam, E J Palmer, C Wordsworth etc
Printed books collection (approximately 200,000 items)
Prints collection (church topography and portraits)
Records of Lambeth Conferences, from 1867
Records of the Incorporated Church Building Society (19th and 20th centuries, 16,000 originals and database)
Registers of foreign churches, Basra, Khartoum, Shanghai, Shantung
Registers of the Archbishops of Canterbury, from 13th century
Sion College collection (manuscripts and printed books pre 1850)
STC Titles (3500)

Non-library collection catalogue:
All or part available online, in-house and in print

Library catalogue:
All or part available in-house

Printed publications:
Annual Report
List of catalogues of some of the Collections (leaflet, available from the Lambeth Palace Library)

Microform publications:
Filming facilities for some material (for purchase directly)
Some material commercially available through publishing house. Please enquire

Publications list:
Available in print

Access to staff:
Contact by letter, by telephone, by fax and in person. Letter of introduction required.
Hours: Mon to Fri, 1000 to 1700

Special comments: Closed for 10 days at Christmas and Easter.

Access for disabled people:
Parking, bathroom facilities, ramp, hearing induction loop.

Funded by:
Church Commissioners for England (Church of England)

LAMBRETTA CLUB GB

Acronym or abbreviation: LCGB

8 Trent Close, Rainhill, Prescot, Merseyside, L35 9LD

Tel: 0151 426 9839
Fax: 0151 426 9839
E-mail: lcgb2@blueyonder.co.uk

Website:
http://www.lcgb.co.uk

Enquiries:
Enquiries to: General Secretary
Direct tel: 07966 265588 (Mobile)

Founded:
1953

Organisation type and purpose:
International organisation, membership association.
To further the interests of Lambretta enthusiasts worldwide.

Subject coverage:
Everything for the Lambretta enthusiast from shows, events, competition, technical information, DVLA approved for registration problems.

Museum or gallery collection, archive, or library special collection:
Various books and manuals relevant to Lambretta

Printed publications:
Club magazine (free to members)
A wide range of products bearing the club's logo (for sale)

Electronic and video publications:
Various Lambretta videos and DVD's

Access to staff:
Contact by letter, by telephone, by fax and by e-mail
Hours: Mon to Fri, 0930 to 1730
Special comments: Contact by fax, 0930 to 1730, mark for the attention of Kev Walsh.

LANARK LIBRARY

Lindsay Institute, 16 Hope Street, Lanark, ML11 7LZ

Tel: 01555 661144
E-mail: lanark.ref@library.s-lanark.org.uk

Website:
http://www.southlanarkshire.gov.uk
General information regarding public library service.

Enquiries:
Enquiries to: Reference Library Supervisor

Founded:
1914

Organisation type and purpose:
Local government body, public library.

Subject coverage:
Reference and local history.

Museum or gallery collection, archive, or library special collection:
William Smellie Collection (mainly 18th-century midwifery, obstetrics, gynaecology)
Robert Owen Collection (co-operative movement, New Lanark)
Coalburn Collection (330 images of a coal mining village c. 1880–1930)

continued overleaf

Poster Collection (200 posters of local events, including circuses, visiting shows, sports and civic functions)

Image Collection 3,271 items – mainly local views, people and events, but with a proportion of South Seas images (121 items inc. New Zealand, Samoa etc.), Algiers & environs (79 items) and a collection of 'Moral Tales' (98 items) [Includes Coalburn Collection]

Library catalogue:
All or part available in-house

Access to staff:
Contact by letter, by telephone, by e-mail and in person
Hours: Mon, 0915 to 1930; Tue and Thu, 0915 to 2000; Wed and Sat, 0915 to 1700; Fri, 0930 to 1930

Access to building, collection or gallery:
Public access during opening hours

Access for disabled people:
To ground and second floors only. No disabled access to upper-floor IT suite. However, Internet access is also available on second floor.

LANCASHIRE AND CHESHIRE ANTIQUARIAN SOCIETY

Acronym or abbreviation: LCAS

59 Malmesbury Road, Cheadle Hulme, Cheadle, Cheshire, SK8 7QL

Tel: 0161 439 7202
E-mail: morrisgarratt@sky.com

Website:
http://www.landcas.org.uk

Enquiries:
Enquiries to: Honorary Secretary

Founded:
1883

Organisation type and purpose:
Learned society (membership is by subscription), present number of members: 320, suitable for all ages

Subject coverage:
Interests are broad, encompassing national and local events and all historical aspects of the life and topography of the region. Current fields of study include archaeology, both traditional and industrial; architecture and the arts; social and economic history, particularly religious and educational developments; the history of trade, trades and transport; and the history of institutions and local government.

Museum or gallery collection, archive, or library special collection:
Library books, chiefly relating to the north-west of England, (c.1,600 vols)

Library catalogue:
All or part available in print

Printed publications:
Transactions (almost annually since 1883; 103 vols to date)
Offprints of many papers in the Transactions are available separately

Publications list:
Available online

Access to staff:
Contact by letter, by telephone, by e-mail and via website
Hours: Mon to Fri, 0930 to 1630 (Portico Library)

Access to building, collection or gallery:
No access other than to staff
Special comments: Library housed in Manchester Central Library. Members may request library tickets.

Also at:
c/o Portico Library
57 Mosley Street, Manchester, M2 3HY; tel: 0161 236 6785
Honorary Membership Secretary (subscriptions)
3 Syddal Crescent, Bramhall, Stockport

LANCASHIRE COUNTY LIBRARY AND INFORMATION SERVICE

Harris Library, Market Square, Preston, Lancashire, PR1 2PP

Tel: 01772 532676
Fax: 01772 555527
E-mail: harris.enquiries@lancashire.gov.uk

Website:
http://www.lancashire.gov.uk/libraries
Home page with general information on the library service.

Founded:
1879

Organisation type and purpose:
Local government body, public library.

Subject coverage:
Business information, commerce, standards, general information in social studies and humanities fields, community history, genealogy, market research reports

Museum or gallery collection, archive, or library special collection:
Dr. Shepherd Library of mostly 18th- and 19th-century books of medical, general and historical interest
Francis Thompson Collection (poetry)
Local Studies – Lancashire
Spencer Collection of Children's Books
Stocks Massey Music Library (Burnley Central Library)

Non-library collection catalogue:
All or part available online

Library catalogue:
All or part available online

Printed publications:
Family History in Preston
Special collections in the Harris Library, Preston

Access to staff:
Contact by letter, by telephone, by fax, by e-mail and in person
Hours: Mon, Wed, Fri, 0930 to 1930; Tue, Thu, Sat, 0930 to 1700; Sun, 1100 to 1600

Access for disabled people:
Ramped entry, lift

Parent body:
Lancashire County Council

LANCASHIRE COUNTY MUSEUM SERVICE

Stanley Street, Preston, Lancashire, PR1 4YP

Tel: 01772 534061
Fax: 01772 534079
E-mail: museums.enquiries@lancashire.gov.uk

Website:
http://www.lancsmuseums.gov.uk

Enquiries:
Enquiries to: Marketing Assistant

Founded:
1983

Organisation type and purpose:
Local government body, suitable for ages: all. Administrative body for the local government museums.

Subject coverage:
The subjects covered by the museums of Lancashire include: military history, local history, social history, maritime history, textile machinery, art, fine art, childhood collections, geology, natural science and conservation.

Access to staff:
Contact by letter, by telephone, by fax, by e-mail and via website
Hours: Mon to Fri, 0900 to 1700

Access for disabled people:
Ramped entry, access to all public areas, toilet facilities

Museums, Galleries or Historic Sites:
Fleetwood Museum
Queens Terrace, Fleetwood, Lancashire, FY7 6BT; tel: 01253 876621; fax: 01253 878088; e-mail: fleetwood.museum@lancashire.gov.uk
Gawthorpe Hall
Padiham, Nr Burnley, BB12 8UA; tel: 01282 771004; fax: 01282 770178; e-mail: gawthorpe.hall@lancashire.gov.uk
Helmshore Mills Textile Museum
Holcombe Road, Helmshore, Rossendale, Lancashire, BB4 4NP; tel: 01706 226459; fax: 01706 218554; e-mail: helmshore.museum@lancashire.gov.uk
Judges' Lodgings
Church Street, Lancaster, LA1 1YS; tel: 01524 32808; e-mail: judges.lodgings@lancashire.gov.uk
Lancaster Castle
Shire Hall, Castle Parade, Lancaster, LA1 1YJ; tel: 01524 64998; fax: 01524 847914
Lancaster City Museum
Market Square, Lancaster, LA1 1HT; tel: 01524 64637; fax: 01524 841692; e-mail: lancaster.citymuseum@lancashire.gov.uk
Lancaster Cottage Museum
15 Castle Hill, Lancaster, LA1 1HT; tel: 01524 64637; fax: 01524 841692
Lancaster Maritime Museum
Custom House, St. George's Quay, Lancaster, LA1 1RB; tel: 01524 382264; fax: 01524 841692
Museum of Lancashire
Stanley Street, Preston, PR1 4YP; tel: 01772 534075; fax: 01772 534079
Queen Street Mill
Harle Skye, Burnley, Lancashire, BB10 2HX; tel: 01282 412555; fax: 01282 430220; e-mail: queenstreet.mill@lancashire.gov.uk
Rossendale Museum
Whitaker Park, Rawtenstall, Rossendale, BB4 6RE; tel: 01706 244682; fax: 01706 250037; e-mail: rossendalemuseum@lancashire.gov.uk

Parent body:
Lancashire County Council
County Hall, Preston, Lancashire

LANCASHIRE RECORD OFFICE

Acronym or abbreviation: LRO

Bow Lane, Preston, Lancashire, PR1 2RE

Tel: 01772 533039
Fax: 01772 533050
E-mail: record.office@ed.lancscc.gov.uk

Website:
http://www.a2a.org.uk
Some catalogues available.
http://www.archives.lancashire.gov.uk

Enquiries:
Enquiries to: County Archivist

Founded:
1940

Organisation type and purpose:
Local government body.
County Record Office.
Providing archive services to Lancashire, Blackburn with Darwen, and Blackpool.

Subject coverage:
Historical primary source material relating to all aspects of life and society in Lancashire, 12th century to present day.

Museum or gallery collection, archive, or library special collection:
Lancashire Local Studies Library
8 miles of archives, too extensive to specify
For listings see Guide to Lancashire Record Office and Guide to Lancashire Record Office, a Supplement 1977–1989

Non-library collection catalogue:
All or part available online and in-house

Library catalogue:
All or part available online and in-house

Printed publications:
Guide to Lancashire Record Office 1940–1976
(£3.00 plus p&p)
Guide to Lancashire Record Office, A supplement
1977–1989 (£3.00 plus p&p)
Note: both publications can be bought together for
£5.00 plus p&p

Microform publications:
Copy material can be purchased in certain
instances

Electronic and video publications:
Finding Folk: A Handlist of Genealogical Sources
(online)

Publications list:
Available online and in print

Access to staff:
Contact by letter, by telephone, by fax, by e-mail,
in person and via website
Hours: Mon, Wed, Fri, 0900 to 1700; Tue, 0900 to
2030; Thu, 1000 to 1700
Open 2nd Sat of each month (except holiday
weekends), 1000 to 1600
Special comments: County Archives Research
Network (CARN) ticket required (can be issued on
production of an acceptable ID).

Access to building, collection or gallery:
No access other than to staff

Access for disabled people:
Parking provided, access to all public areas, toilet
facilities
Special comments: Disabled persons' lift.

Provides archive services for unitary councils:
Blackpool Council and Blackburn with Darwen
Council

LANCASHIRE TEACHING HOSPITALS NHS FOUNDATION TRUST

Library and Information Service, Royal Preston
Hospital, Sharoe Green Lane, Preston, Lancashire,
PR2 9HT

Tel: 01772 522763
Fax: 01772 523491
E-mail: mandy.beaumont@lthtr.nhs.uk

Website:
www.lancsteachinghospitals.nhs.uk

Enquiries:
Enquiries to: Knowledge and Library Services
Manager
Direct e-mail: libraryRPH@lthtr.nhs.uk

Organisation type and purpose:
National government body.
Health library.
Multiprofessional library.

Subject coverage:
Medicine, health sciences, NHS management,
nursing, general practice.

Library catalogue:
All or part available in-house

Printed publications:
A-Z Guide to the Library (subject guide)
Clinical Librarian Service
Guide to the Library (pamphlet)
Journal Holdings (booklet)
Library Bulletin

Publications list:
Available online

Access to staff:
Contact by letter, by telephone, by fax, by e-mail,
in person and via website. Appointment necessary.
All charged.
Hours: Wed, Fri, 0900 to 1700; Mon, Tue, Thu, 0900
to 1900

Member of:
British Medical Association (BMA)
Library and Information Health Network
Northwest (LIHNN)
Royal College of Surgeons

LANCASHIRE TEXTILE MANUFACTURERS' ASSOCIATION

Acronym or abbreviation: LTMA

4 St Andrew's Street, Blackburn, Lancashire, BB1
8AE

Tel: 01254 580248
Fax: 01254 580248
E-mail: enquiries@ltma.co.uk

Website:
http://ltma.co.uk
Profile, services, events, directory of member
organisations.

Enquiries:
Enquiries to: Secretary
Direct e-mail: s.walsh@ltma.co.uk

Founded:
1850

Organisation type and purpose:
A non-profit making trade organisation, the
operating costs of which are met by an annual levy
on members who are drawn from an area
encompassing Cumbria, Lancashire, Greater
Manchester and West Yorkshire.
To provide practical and up-to-date help and
advice on any problem that its textile industry
member companies may face; to act as a first point
of contact for sales or supply enquiries from third
parties; to promote the benefits to the regional
economy of a strong and healthy textile industry.

Subject coverage:
Services to member organisations: a
comprehensive industrial relations service,
including assistance in resolving disputes; advice
on employment law, training and health and safety
matters; district negotiations on wages, conditions
of service and holidays; interpretation and
implementation of both local and national
agreements; commercial and economic
information; seminars on subjects of special
interest to members; information on grant aid as
and when available from both central and local
government and the EU; a bi-annual survey of
wage levels within the industry; assistance with
legally required employment documentation;
representation at employment tribunals if
necessary; assistance in drafting company policy
documents.

Printed publications:
Members' Newsletter (monthly)

Access to staff:
Contact by letter, by telephone, by fax, by e-mail
and via website

Member organisation of:
United Kingdom Fashion and Textiles Association

LANCASTER CENTRAL LIBRARY

Market Street, Lancaster, LA1 1HY

Tel: 01524 580700
Fax: 01524 580709
E-mail: lancaster.library@lancscc.gov.uk

Website:
http://www.lancashire.gov.uk/libraries/
librarydetails/libsearch1.asp?name=Lancaster

Enquiries:
Enquiries to: Librarian
Other contacts: District Manager; Community
History Manager

Founded:
1932

Organisation type and purpose:
Public library.

Subject coverage:
General, local history.

Information services:
Information Desk, Quick Reference, Online
Reference Library.

Education services:
Heritage Centre (local, community and family
history).

Trade and statistical information:
via the Online Reference Library accessible to
library members.

Non-library collection catalogue:
All or part available online

Library catalogue:
All or part available online

Access to staff:
Contact by letter, by telephone, by fax, by e-mail,
in person and via website
Hours: Mon to Wed and Fri, 0930 to 1700; Thu, 0930
to 1900; Sat, 0930 to 1600

LANCASTER CITY COUNCIL

Town Hall, Lancaster, LA1 1PJ

Tel: 01524 582000\ Minicom no. 01524 582175
Fax: 01524 582161
E-mail: customerservices@lancaster.gov.uk

Website:
http://www.lancaster.gov.uk/
Information about the area; council services; useful
links.

Enquiries:
Enquiries to: Chief Executive

Founded:
1974

Organisation type and purpose:
Local government body.

Subject coverage:
Public and local information about services
available within the Lancaster district.

**Museum or gallery collection, archive, or library
special collection:**
Various public records relating to the Lancaster
district

Printed publications:
Information leaflets and brochures
Public documents including the electoral register
and committee agenda minutes

Access to staff:
Contact by letter, by telephone, by fax, by e-mail,
in person and via website
Hours: Mon to Fri, 0845 to 1715

LANCASTER CITY MUSEUMS

Market Square, Lancaster, LA1 1HT

Tel: 01524 64637
Fax: 01524 841692
E-mail: lancaster.citymuseum@mus.lancsoc.gov.uk

Website:
http://www.lancsmuseum.gov.uk
Brief history, opening hours, brief details of
collections.

Founded:
1923

Organisation type and purpose:
Local government body, museum, suitable for
ages: 5+.

Subject coverage:
King's Own Royal Regiment, maritime history,
archaeology, local history, social history, costume,
numismatics, fine art, decorative art, transport,
military history.

Information services:
Guided tours on request.

Special visitor services:
Guided tours, materials and/or activities for
children.

continued overleaf

Education services:
Group education facilities, resources for Key
Stages 1 and 2, 3, 4 and Further or Higher
Education.

Services for disabled people:
For the visually impaired; displays and/or
information at wheelchair height.

**Museum or gallery collection, archive, or library
special collection:**
Archive and library relating to the King's Own
    Royal Regiment (Lancaster) (inc important MSS)

Printed publications:
Exhibition lists (annually)
Local history publications (21 titles), irregular
    additions, for sale
Museum guidebooks (2) for sale
Subject leaflets (12, irregular additions, for sale)

Access to staff:
Contact by letter, by telephone, by fax, by e-mail,
in person and via website. Appointment necessary.
Hours: Mon to Sat, 1000 to 1700
Special comments: Prior appointment required.

Access to building, collection or gallery:
No prior appointment required
Hours: Mon to Sat, 1000 to 1700
Special comments: Closed Christmas and New Year.

Access for disabled people:
Ramped entry, access to all public areas

**Comprises 3 local Government Museums and a
trustee museum:**
King's Own Regimental Museum

Museum sites:
City Museum
    same address
Cottage Museum
    15 Castle Hill, Lancaster
Lancaster Maritime Museum
    St George's Quay, Lancaster, LA1 1RB; tel: 01524
    64637; fax: 01524 841692; e-mail: awhite@
    lancaster.gov.uk

Parent body:
Lancaster City Council
    at the same address

Supported by:
Friends of Lancaster City Museum
    at the same address

LANCASTER UNIVERSITY
LIBRARY

Bailrigg, Lancaster, LA1 4YH

Tel: 01524 592536
Fax: 01524 63806/65719
E-mail: library@lancaster.ac.uk

Website:
http://www.libweb.lancs.ac.uk
Library home page.
http://cat.lib.lancs.ac.uk
Library catalogue.

Enquiries:
Enquiries to: Librarian
Direct e-mail: c.powne@lancaster.ac.uk

Founded:
1963

Organisation type and purpose:
University library.

Subject coverage:
Usual fields of university study, science and
technology, social sciences, business studies,
humanities.

**Museum or gallery collection, archive, or library
special collection:**
Beetham Vestry Library
Burnley Grammar School Collection (rare books,
    17th and 18th centuries)
Business Histories
European Documentation Centre
Ford Railway Collection
Headlam-Morley Religious pamphlets

Jack Hylton Archive
Legal History Collection
Library of the Fell and Rock Climbing Club of the
    English Lake District
Patten Second World War Pamphlet Collection
Preston Library (Cartmel Priory)
Quaker Collection
Redlich Collection (music)
Socialist Collection

Trade and statistical information:
Numerous holdings, including government
publications, to support the teaching and
research of the Economics Department and
Management School.

Library catalogue:
All or part available online

Electronic and video publications:
Numerous library guides covering most library
    subject areas, functions and services
Order electronic and video publications from: Available
through web pages

Access to staff:
Contact by letter, by telephone, by fax, by e-mail
and in person. Non-members charged.
Hours: Term time & Easter Vacation: Mon, Tue,
Thu, 0845 to 2400; Wed, 0930 to 2400; Fri, 0845 to
2200; Sat, 1000 to 1800; Sun, 1000 to 2100.
Summer & Christmas Vacations: Mon, Tue, Thu,
0845 to 2200, Wed, 0930 to 2200, Fri, 0845 to 1700,
Sat, 1000 to 1700; Sun, closed
Special comments: Term time and Easter Vacation:
Reference services only Mon to Fri, 2200 to 2400;
Sun, 1000 to 2100.
Summer & Christmas Vacations: Reference services
only Sat, 1300 to 1700.

Parent body:
Lancaster University
    Bailrigg, Lancaster, LA1 4YW; tel: 01524 65201;
    fax: 01524 846243

LANDCRAB OWNERS CLUB
INTERNATIONAL LIMITED

Acronym or abbreviation: LOCI

5 Rolston Avenue, Huntington, York, YO31 9JD

Tel: 01904 620125 (evenings only)

Website:
http://www.landcrab.net

Enquiries:
Enquiries to: Chairman
Other contacts: Spares Secretary, Historian

Founded:
1988

Organisation type and purpose:
Membership association (membership is by
subscription), voluntary organisation.

Subject coverage:
Austin Morris Wolseley 1800 and 2200s, from 1964
to 1975 (ADO 17): advice; spares; interest and
exhibitions of these vehicles.

Non-library collection catalogue:
All or part available in-house

Library catalogue:
All or part available in-house

Printed publications:
Club magazine

Access to staff:
Contact by letter and by telephone
Hours: Telephone: evenings only

Has:
Local groups

Member of:
Federation of British Historic Vehicle Clubs
(FBHVC)
    PO Box 2506, Henfield, West Sussex; tel: 01273
    495051

LANDLIFE

National Wildflower Centre, Court Hey Park,
Liverpool, L16 3NA

Tel: 0151 737 1819
Fax: 0151 737 1820
E-mail: info@landlife.org.uk

Website:
http://www.landlife.org.uk
Charitable activities, trading activities, National
Wildflower Centre.

Enquiries:
Enquiries to: Administrator
Other contacts: Chief Executive

Founded:
1975

Organisation type and purpose:
National organisation, voluntary organisation,
registered charity (charity number 290510).
Landlife is a charity taking action for a better
environment by creating new opportunities for
wildlife and encouraging people to enjoy them.

Subject coverage:
Wildflower landscaping and gardening, creative
conservation consultancy service, environmental
advice for community groups and schools, derelict
land reclamation techniques and research, sales of
wildflower seed, plants and publications.

Library catalogue:
All or part available online and in print

Printed publications:
Annual Report
Newsletter (members)
Wildflower seed and plant catalogue (free,
    gardeners and trade)
Wildflowers Work, creative conservation
    techniques (£12.50)
How to make Wildflower Habit Gardens (16pp full
    colour, £2)

Publications list:
Available online and in print

Access to staff:
Contact by letter, by telephone, by fax and by e-
mail. Appointment necessary.
Hours: Mon to Fri, 0900 to 1700

Access for disabled people:
Parking provided, ramped entry, toilet facilities

Links with:
National Wildflower Centre
    (Landlife's Millennium project); tel: 0151 737
    1819; fax: 0151 737 1820; e-mail: info@nwc.org
    .uk
UK MAB Urban Forum
Urban Wildlife Partnership
Wildlife Trusts

Trading subsidiary:
Landlife Wildflowers Limited
    tel: 0151 737 1819; fax: 0151 737 1820; e-mail:
    info@wildflower.org.uk

LANDMARK INFORMATION
GROUP

7 Abbey Court, Eagle Way, Sowton, Exeter, Devon,
EX2 7HY

Tel: 01392 441700
Fax: 01392 441709

Website:
http://www.landmark-information.co.uk
Company site.
http://www.promap.co.uk
http://www.home-envirosearch.com
Product information.
http://www.old-maps.co.uk
First edition Ordnance Survey maps.

Enquiries:
Enquiries to: Customer Services

Founded:
1995

Organisation type and purpose:
Service industry.
Suppliers of environmental risk information, current and historical mapping.

Subject coverage:
Environmental risk management, digital mapping, contaminated land, previous land use, current land use.

Museum or gallery collection, archive, or library special collection:
Digital historical maps (with OS)
Environmental information database

Printed publications:
Envirocheck
Envirosearch Commercial
Envirosearch Residential
Promap
Sitecheck
Site Search

Electronic and video publications:
Envirocheck
Promap Envirosearch

Access to staff:
Contact by letter, by telephone, by fax, by e-mail and via website
Hours: Mon to Fri, 0900 to 1700

Access to building, collection or gallery:
No access other than to staff
Hours: Mon to Fri, 0900 to 1700

Access for disabled people:
Level entry, toilet facilities

Other address:
Landmark Information Group
3rd Floor, Challanger House, 42 Adler Street, London, E1 1EE; tel: 020 7958 4999; fax: 020 7958 4981; e-mail: mailbox@landmark-information.co.uk
Prodat Systems plc
Northpoint House, Highlands Lane, Henley on Thames, Oxon, RG9 4PR; tel: 01491 413030; fax: 01491 413031; e-mail: sales@promap.co.uk

Parent body:
Daily Mail and General Trust Group (DMGT)
Northcliffe House, 2 Derry Street, Kensington, London, W8 5TT

LANDMARK TRUST

Shottesbrooke, Maidenhead, Berkshire, SL6 3SW

Tel: 01628 825920
Fax: 01628 825417

Website:
http://www.landmarktrust.org.uk

Enquiries:
Enquiries to: Public Relations Manager

Founded:
1965

Organisation type and purpose:
Registered charity in England and Wales (charity number 243312) and Scotland (charity number SC039205).
Building preservation charity.

Subject coverage:
Restoration of historic buildings for self-catering holidays all year round.

Museum or gallery collection, archive, or library special collection:
A picture library of all Landmarks.

Printed publications:
Handbook (approximately once every two years)
Legacy leaflets and brochures (occasional)
Newsletter (2 times a year)
Price List (annually)

Access to staff:
Contact by letter
Hours: Mon to Fri, 0900 to 1700

LANDS TRIBUNAL FOR SCOTLAND

Acronym or abbreviation: LTS

George House, 126 George Street, Edinburgh, EH2 4HH

Tel: 0131 271 4350
Fax: 0131 271 4399
E-mail: mailbox@lands-tribunal-scotland.org.uk

Website:
http://www.lands-tribunal-scotland.org.uk

Enquiries:
Enquiries to: Clerk to the Tribunal
Other contacts: Depute Clerk

Founded:
1971

Organisation type and purpose:
Judicial body.
Various jurisdictions relating to valuation of land in Scotland.

Subject coverage:
Discharge and variation of title conditions; determination of disputed compensation (eg following compulsory purchase); disputed valuations for tax purposes (eg assessment for ratings); appeals against Keeper of the Registers of Scotland and disputes arising from Tenants' Rights legislation in relation to tenants' right to buy.

Access to staff:
Contact by letter, by telephone, by fax, by e-mail and in person
Hours: Mon to Thu, 0900 to 1700; Fri, 0900 to 1600

Access to building, collection or gallery:
Hours: as above

Access for disabled people:
Hours: as above

LANDSCAPE INSTITUTE

Acronym or abbreviation: LI

Charles Darwin House, 12 Roger Street, London, WC1N 2JU

Tel: 020 7685 2640
Fax: 020 7685 2641
E-mail: lesleym@landscapeinstitute.org

Website:
http://www.landscapeinstitute.org

Founded:
1929

Organisation type and purpose:
Professional body.
To promote the highest standard of professional service in the application of the arts and sciences of landscape architecture, management and science.

Subject coverage:
Landscape design, management, conservation or restoration.

Printed publications:
Directory of Registered Landscape Practices (annually)
Landscape (12 times a year)
A range of titles covering all aspects of landscape architecture

Publications list:
Available online

Access to staff:
Contact by letter, by telephone, by fax and by e-mail
Hours: Mon to Fri, 0900 to 1700

Access to building, collection or gallery:
No prior appointment required
Hours: Library: Mon to Fri, 0900 to 1700

Member of:
Construction Industry Council
International Federation of Landscape Architects (IFLA)
World Conservation Union (IUCN)

LANDSCAPE RESEARCH GROUP LTD

Acronym or abbreviation: LRG

PO Box 1482, Oxford, OX4 9DN, UK

E-mail: admin@landscaperesearch.org

Website:
http://www.landscaperesearch.org.uk

Enquiries:
Enquiries to: Administrator

Founded:
1967

Organisation type and purpose:
International organisation, learned society (membership is by subscription), voluntary organisation, registered charity (charity number 287610).

Subject coverage:
Landscape: aesthetics, design, management, conservation, perception, assessment, planning; landscape and the arts; landscape, literature and ecology.

Printed publications:
Conference Reports (for purchase directly)
Landscape Research (journal, 6 a year, for purchase directly or via publishing house)
Landscape Research Extra (newsletter, 3 a year, for purchase directly)

Access to staff:
Contact by letter and by e-mail
Hours: Mon to Fri, 0900 to 1700

LANGHOLM LIBRARY

The Library Buildings, High Street, Langholm, Dumfries & Galloway, DG13 0DJ

Enquiries:
Enquiries to: Chairman

Founded:
1800

Organisation type and purpose:
Voluntary organisation, registered charity (charity number SCO 11403).

Library catalogue:
All or part available in-house

Access to staff:
Contact by letter. Appointment necessary.
Hours: Tue, Fri, 1000 to 1200; Thu, 1900 to 2100

LANGTON MATRAVERS LOCAL HISTORY AND PRESERVATION SOCIETY

Acronym or abbreviation: LMLHPS

Barton, The Hyde, Langton Matravers, Swanage, Dorset, BH19 3HE

Tel: 01929 423168

Website:
http://www.langtonia.org.uk

Enquiries:
Enquiries to: Membership Secretary
Direct tel: 01929 421481
Direct e-mail: localhistory@langtonia.org.uk
Other contacts: Publicity Officer, tel: 01929 422218

Founded:
1971

Organisation type and purpose:
Learned society (membership is by subscription), registered charity (charity number 272407), museum.
To research and publish local history.

Subject coverage:
Local history, family history, local industries.

continued overleaf

Museum or gallery collection, archive, or library special collection:
Genealogical charts, transcripts of parish registers, memorial inscriptions, national census returns, etc.
Local history library

Non-library collection catalogue:
All or part available in-house

Library catalogue:
All or part available in-house

Publications list:
Available online and in print

Access to staff:
Contact by letter, by telephone, by e-mail, in person and via website
Hours: Mon to Fri, 0900 to 1700

Access to building, collection or gallery:
No prior appointment required
Hours: Apr 1 to Sept 30: Mon to Sat, 1000 to 1200 and 1400 to 1600
Special comments: Or by appointment.

Access for disabled people:
Parking provided, level entry, access to all public areas

Parent body for:
Langton Matravers Museum
at the same address

LANTERNHOUSE

Formal name: Lanternhouse International

Lanternhouse, The Ellers, Ulverston, Cumbria, LA12 0AA

Tel: 01229 581127; minicom no. 01229 587146
Fax: 01229 581232
E-mail: welcome@lanternhouse.org

Website:
http://www.lanternhouse.org

Enquiries:
Enquiries to: Communications Co-ordinator

Organisation type and purpose:
International organisation, registered charity (charity number 265461), art gallery, suitable for ages: all, consultancy, research organisation, publishing house.
Artist-led company pioneering the arts of celebration and ceremony.

Subject coverage:
Arts of celebration.

Special visitor services:
Guided tours.

Education services:
Group education facilities.

Printed publications:
The Dead Good Funerals Book (£9.50 plus p&p)
The Dead Good Guide to Namings & Baby Welcoming Ceremonies (£7.50 plus p&p)
The Dead Good Time Capsule Book (£6.95 plus p&p)
Engineers of the Imagination (£12.99 plus p&p)
Eyes on Stalks (£14.99 plus p&p)

Access to staff:
Contact by letter, by telephone, by fax, by e-mail and via website. Appointment necessary.
Hours: Mon to Fri, 0900 to 1700

Access for disabled people:
Parking provided, level entry, access to all public areas, toilet facilities

LARGS AND NORTH AYRSHIRE FAMILY HISTORY SOCIETY

c/o Bogriggs Cottage, Carlung, West Kilbride, Ayrshire, KA23 9PS

Tel: 01294 823690

Website:
http://www.lnafhs.freeyellow.com

Enquiries:
Enquiries to: General Secretary

Founded:
1988

Organisation type and purpose:
Membership association, present number of members: 140.
Family history society.

Subject coverage:
Advice in family history research sources.

Library catalogue:
All or part available in-house

Access to staff:
Contact by letter and by telephone
Hours: Mon to Fri, 0900 to 1700

LASA

3rd Floor, Universal House, 88 Wentworth Street, London, E1 7SA

Tel: 020 7377 2748
Fax: 020 7247 4725
E-mail: info@lasa.org.uk

Website:
http://www.lasa.org.uk
http://www.rightsnet.org.uk
Welfare rights information for advice workers.
http://www.multikulti.org.uk
Information on debt, housing, immigration and asylum, employment, education, health, welfare benefits and racism in 12 community languages.
http://ictknowledgebase.org.uk
The knowledgebase is designed to help community and voluntary sector organisations access the benefits of information technology.
http://www.suppliersdirectory.org.uk
The Suppliers Directory connects voluntary and community sector organisations and registered adult social care providers in England with suppliers of ICT products and services.
http://ukriders.lasa.org.uk
Circuit Riders are voluntary sector technology development and support workers, each of whom supports a caseload of organisations in the same way that a development worker might.
http://ictchampion.lasa.org.uk
Championing ICT in London's voluntary and community sector.

Founded:
1984

Formerly called:
London Advice Services Alliance (year of change 2010)

Organisation type and purpose:
Voluntary organisation, registered charity, training organisation, consultancy, research organisation.

Subject coverage:
Research and consultancy into advice service provision and development; training to advice workers on welfare rights; IT consultancy and advice to voluntary sector; website services and case management software.

Printed publications:
Review (on subscription, £19 voluntary sector, £24 others)
Computanews (free to download)
Computanews Factsheets including:
Buying IT (£5)
Managing IT (£5)
Networks (£5)
Project Management (free)

Electronic and video publications:
AIMS, Enquiry Recording and Case Management (software)
rightsnet.org.uk – information on welfare benefits

Publications list:
Available online

Access to staff:
Contact by letter, by telephone, by fax, by e-mail and via website

Hours: Mon to Fri, 0930 to 1700
Special comments: Charges for major undertakings such as consultancies and research.

Access to building, collection or gallery:
Mon to Fri, 0900 to 1700

LATIN MASS SOCIETY

11–13 Macklin Street, London, WC2B 5NH

Tel: 020 7404 7284
Fax: 020 7831 5585
E-mail: info@latin-mass-society.org

Website:
http://www.latin-mass-society.org

Enquiries:
Enquiries to: Secretary

Founded:
1965

Organisation type and purpose:
Learned society, registered charity.

Subject coverage:
Preservation and restoration of the Tridentine Rite of Mass in the Catholic Church,
restoration of the church's treasury of liturgical music, esp. Gregorian chant.

Printed publications:
Newsletter (quarterly, for members)
The Plain Man's Guide to the Traditional Rite of Holy Mass
Simplicissimus: a New Approach to Learning the Latin of the Traditional Roman Missal
ORDO (annually)

Electronic and video publications:
DVDs of i) High Mass, Low Mass and Benediction; ii) High Mass and Conference at Westminster Cathedral – celebrant Cardinal Castrillon Hoyos; iii) High Mass at the Basilica of St Mary Major Rome

Publications list:
Available online and in print

Access to staff:
Contact by letter, by telephone, by fax, by e-mail, in person and via website
Hours: Mon to Fri, 0930 to 1700

Access to building, collection or gallery:
Hours: Mon to Fri, 0930 to 1700
Special comments: Entryphone only.

Access for disabled people:
Lift

Affiliated to:
Una Voce International
44 Queensway, Shotley Bridge, Consett, Co. Durham, DH8 0RZ

LAUTERPACHT CENTRE FOR INTERNATIONAL LAW

Acronym or abbreviation: LCIL

5 Cranmer Road, Cambridge, CB3 9BL

Tel: 01223 335358
Fax: 01223 300406
E-mail: admin@rcil.cam.ac.ul

Website:
http://lcil.law.cam.ac.uk

Enquiries:
Enquiries to: Administrator

Founded:
1983

Organisation type and purpose:
University department or institute.

Subject coverage:
Public international law.

Printed publications:
Order printed publications from: Cambridge University Press

Edinburgh Building, Shaftesbury Road,
Cambridge, CB2 2RU

Publications list:
Available online

Access to staff:
Contact by letter, by e-mail and via website
Hours: Mon to Fri, 0900 to 1700

Access to building, collection or gallery:
No prior appointment required

LAVENDER LINE LIMITED

Isfield Station, Isfield, Uckfield, East Sussex, TN22
5XB

Tel: 01825 750515

Website:
http://www.lavender-line.co.uk
General and specific information about the Line,
facilities available and special events

Enquiries:
Enquiries to: Secretary

Founded:
1992

Organisation type and purpose:
Registered charity (charity number 1010085),
museum.

Subject coverage:
Preservation and running a railway.

**Museum or gallery collection, archive, or library
special collection:**
Steam engines, steam crane, main line and
industrial diesel locomotives, some running and
some in the course of restoration and repair

Non-library collection catalogue:
All or part available online

Access to staff:
Contact by letter, by telephone and in person
Hours: Mon to Fri, 0900 to 1700

Access for disabled people:
Parking provided, ramped entry
Special comments: Not suitable for the severely
disabled

LAW CENTRES FEDERATION

Acronym or abbreviation: LCF

PO Box 65836, London, EC4P 4FX

Tel: 020 7842 0720
Fax: 020 7842 0721
E-mail: info@lawcentres.org.uk

Website:
http://www.lawcentres.org.uk
Information about Law Centres, their work, and
LCF's work.

Enquiries:
Enquiries to: Office Manager

Founded:
1978

Organisation type and purpose:
Voluntary organisation.
Representative body for the national network of
Law Centres.

Subject coverage:
Information about Law Centres generally, how
they originated, what they do, how to set one up,
how to develop existing services; their place in the
provision of legal services; whereabouts of Law
Centres and the areas of legal advice in which they
specialise.

Printed publications:
Legal and Advice Services A Pathway out of Social
   Exclusion
LCF 2007 Annual Report
Law Centres Federation Promoting Access to
   Justice
Law Centres Providing Access to Justice

What is a Law Centre?
Access to Justice Series 1999:
History and Funding of Law Centres
A New Deal for Social Justice
Law Centres and Local Government
Law Centres in the Community
Law Centres A Quality Service
Law Centres in the Digital Age
Law Centres Working Together
Working for a Law Centre
List of Law Centres

Access to staff:
Contact by letter, by telephone, by fax, by e-mail
and via website
Hours: Mon to Fri, 1000 to 1700

Branches:
Avon and Bristol Law Centre
   2 Moon Street, Bristol, BS2 8QE; tel: 0117 924
   8662; fax: 0117 924 8020; e-mail: mail@ablc
   .demon.co.uk; website: http://www
   .avonandbristollawcentre.org.uk
Barnet Law Service (Law Centre)
   9 Bell Lane, London, NW4 2BP; tel: 020 8203
   4141; fax: 020 8203 8042; e-mail: admin@
   barnetlaw.org.uk; website: http://www
   .barnetlaw.co.uk
Battersea Law Centre (part of South-West London
Law Centres)
   125 Bolingbroke Grove, London, SW11 1DA; tel:
   020 7585 0716; fax: 020 7585 0718; e-mail:
   solicitors@battersealawcentre.fsnet.co.uk
Birmingham Law Centre
   Dolphin House, 54 Coventry Road, Birmingham,
   B10 0RX; tel: 0121 766 7466; fax: 0121 766 8860;
   e-mail: admin@birminghamlawcentre.org.uk;
   website: http://www.birminghamlawcentre.org
   .uk
Bradford Law Centre
   31 Manor Row, Bradford, West Yorkshire, BD1
   4PS; tel: 01274 306617; fax: 01274 390939; e-mail:
   enquiries@bradfordlawcentre.co.uk
Brent Community Law Centre
   389 High Road, Willesden, London, NW10 2JR;
   tel: 020 8451 1122; fax: 020 8830 2462; e-mail:
   brentlaw@brentlaw.org.uk
Bury Law Centre
   8 Bank Street, Bury, BL9 0DL; tel: 0161 272 0666;
   fax: 0161 272 0031; e-mail: info@burylawcentre
   .co.uk; website: http://www.burylawcentre.co.uk
Cambridge House Law Centre
   131 Camberwell Road, Camberwell, London,
   SE5 0HF; tel: 020 7358 7000; fax: 0845 305 2160;
   e-mail: info@ch1889.org; website: http://www
   .ch1889.org/lawcentre/
Camden Community Law Centre
   2 Prince of Wales Road, London, NW5 3LG; tel:
   020 7284 6510; fax: 020 7267 6218; e-mail:
   admin@cclc.org.uk; website: http://www.cclc.org
   .uk
Cardiff Law Centre
   41–42 Clifton Street, Cardiff, CF24 1LS; tel: 029
   2049 8117; fax: 029 2049 7118; e-mail: cardiff
   .lawcentre@dial.pipex.com
Central London Law Centre
   14 Irving Street, London, WC2H 7AF; tel: 020
   7839 2998; fax: 020 7839 6158; website: http://
   www.londonlawcentre.org.uk
Chesterfield Law Centre
   44 Park Road, Chesterfield, Derbyshire, S40 1XZ;
   tel: 01246 550674; fax: 01246 551069; e-mail: clc@
   chesterfieldlawcentre.org.uk; website: http://
   www.chesterfieldlawcentre.org.uk
Coventry Law Centre
   Oakwood House, St Patricks Road Entrance,
   Coventry, CV1 2HL; tel: 024 7622 3053; fax: 024
   7622 8551; e-mail: enquiries@covlaw.org.uk;
   website: http://www.covlaw.org.uk
Cross Street Law Centre
   4 Cross Street, Erith, Kent, DA8 1AB; tel: 020
   8311 0555; fax: 01322 331 073; website: http://
   www.tmlc.org.uk
Croydon and Sutton Law Centre (part of South
West London Law Centres)
   79 Park Lane, London, CRO 1JG; tel: 020 8667
   9226; fax: 020 8662 8079

Cumbria Law Centre
   8 Spencer Street, Carlisle, CA1 1BG; tel: 01228
   515129; fax: 01228 515819; e-mail: reception@
   comlaw.co.uk; website: http://www
   .communitylaw.org.uk
Derby Community Legal Advice Centre
   Stuart House, Green Lane, Derby, DE1 1RS; tel:
   01332 295711; fax: 01332 228701; e-mail: advice@
   citizensadviceandlawcentre.org; website: www
   .derbylawcentre.org
Devon Law Centre
   Frobisher House, 64–66 Ebrington Street,
   Plymouth, Devon, PL4 9AQ; tel: 01752 519794;
   fax: 01752 519795; e-mail: information@
   devonlawcentre.org.uk; website: http://www
   .devonlawcentre.org.uk
Gloucester Law Centre
   75–81 Eastgate Street, Gloucester, GL1 1PN; tel:
   01452 423492; fax: 01452 387594; e-mail: admin@
   gloucesterlawcentre.co.uk; website: http://www
   .gloucesterlawcentre.co.uk
Greenwich Community Law Centre
   187 Trafalgar Road, London, SE10 9EQ; tel: 020
   8853 2550; fax: 020 8858 5253; e-mail: info@gclc
   .co.uk
Hackney Community Law Centre
   8 Lower Clapton Road, London, E5 0PD; tel: 020
   8985 8364; fax: 020 8533 2018; e-mail: info@hclc
   .org.uk; website: http://www.hclc.org.uk
Hammersmith and Fulham Law Centre
   142–144 King Street, London, W6 0QU; tel: 020
   8741 4021; fax: 020 8741 1450; e-mail: hflaw@
   hflaw.ogr.uk
Harehills and Chapletown Law Centre
   263 Roundhay Road, Leeds, LS8 4HS; tel: 0113
   249 1100; fax: 0113 235 1185; e-mail: admin@
   leedslawcentre.org.uk
Haringey Law Centre
   Ground Floor, 7 Holcombe Road, Tottenham,
   London, N17 9AA; tel: 020 8808 5354; fax: 020
   8801 1516; e-mail: tottenhamlawcentre@tiscali.co
   .uk
Hillingdon Law Centre
   12 Harold Avenue, Hayes, Middlesex, UB3 4QW;
   tel: 020 8561 9400; fax: 020 8756 0837; e-mail:
   info@hillingdonlawcentre.co.uk; website: http://
   www.hillingdonlaw.org.uk
Hounslow Law Centre
   51 Lampton Road, Hounslow, Middlesex, TW3
   1JG; tel: 020 8570 9505; fax: 020 8572 0730; e-
   mail: info@hounslowlawcentre.org.uk; website:
   http://www.hounslowlawcentre.org.uk
Isle of Wight Law Centre
   Exchange House, St Cross Lane, Newport, Isle of
   Wight, PO30 5BZ; tel: 01983 524715; fax: 01983
   522606; e-mail: iowlc@iowlc.org.uk
Islington Law Centre
   161 Hornsey Road, London, N7 6DU; tel: 020
   7607 2461; fax: 020 7700 0072; e-mail: info@
   islingtonlaw.org.uk; website: http://www
   .islingtonlaw.org.uk
Kingston and Richmond Law Centre (part of South
West London Law Centres)
   Siddeley House, 50 Canbury Park Road,
   Kingston, KT2 6LX; tel: 020 8547 2882; fax: 020
   8547 2350
Kirklees Law Centre
   Units 11/12, Empire House, Wakefield Old Road,
   Dewsbury, West Yorkshire, WF12 8DJ; tel: 01924
   439829; fax: 01924 868140; e-mail: manager@
   kirkleeslc.org.uk
Lambeth Law Centre
   Unit 4, The Co-op Centre, 11 Mowll Street,
   London, SW9 6BG; tel: 020 7840 2000; fax: 020
   7820 8303; e-mail: admin@lambethlawcentre.org
Law Centre (Northern Ireland)
   Western Area Office, 9 Clarendon Street,
   Londonderry, BT48 7EP; tel: 028 7126 2433; fax:
   028 7126 2343; e-mail: admin.derry@
   lawcentreniwest.org; website: http://www
   .lawcentreni.org
Law Centre (Northern Ireland)
   124 Donegall Street, Belfast, BT1 2GY; tel: 028
   9024 4401; fax: 028 9023 6340; e-mail: admin
   .belfast@lawcentreni.org; website: http://www
   .lawcentreni.org

continued overleaf

Luton Law Centre
6th Floor, Cresta House, Alma Street, Luton, Bedfordshire, LU1 2PL; tel: 01582 481000; fax: 01582 482581; e-mail: admin@lutonlawcentre.org.uk

Merton Law Centre (part of South West London Law Centres)
112 London Road, Morden, Surrey, SM4 5AX; tel: 020 8543 4069; fax: 020 8542 3814

Newcastle Law Centre
1st floor, 1 Charlotte Square, Newcastle Upon Tyne, NE1 4XF; tel: 0191 230 4777; fax: 0191 233 0295; e-mail: info@newcastlelawcentre.co.uk

North Kensington Law Centre
74 Golborne Road, London, W10 5PS; tel: 020 8969 7473; fax: 020 8968 0934; e-mail: info@nklc.co.uk; website: http://www.nklc.co.uk

North Manchester Law Centre
Harpurhey District Centre, off Rochdale Road, Harpurhey, Manchester, M9 4DH; tel: 0161 205 5040; fax: 0161 205 8654; e-mail: info@nmlc.org.uk; website: http://www.nmlc.org.uk

Nottingham Law Centre
119 Radford Road, Nottingham, NG7 5DU; tel: 0115 978 7813; fax: 0115 979 2969; e-mail: enquiries@nottinghamlawcentre.org.uk; website: http://www.nottinghamlawcentre.org.uk

Oldham Law Centre
First Floor, Archway House, Bridge Street, Oldham, OL1 1ED; tel: 0161 627 0925; fax: 0161 620 3411; e-mail: admin@oldhamlawcentre.org

Paddington Law Centre
439 Harrow Road, London, W10 4RE; tel: 020 8960 3155; fax: 020 8968 0417; e-mail: paddingtonlaw@btconnect.com

Plumstead Community Law Centre
105 Plumstead High Street, London, SE18 1SB; tel: 020 8855 9817; fax: 020 8316 7903

Rochdale Law Centre
15 Drake Street, Rochdale, OL16 1RE; tel: 01706 657766; fax: 01706 346588; e-mail: info@rochdalelawcentre.org.uk; website: http://www.rochdalelawcentre.org.uk

Saltley and Nechells Law Centre
2 Alum Rock Road, Saltley, Birmingham, B8 1JB; tel: 0121 328 2307; fax: 0121 327 7486; e-mail: snlc@snlc.co.uk

Sheffield Law Centre
1st Floor, Waverley House, 10 Joiner Street, Sheffield, S3 8GW; tel: 0114 273 1888; fax: 0114 273 7778; e-mail: post@slc.org.uk; website: http://www.slc.org.uk

South Manchester Law Centre
584 Stockport Road, Manchester, M13 0RQ; tel: 0161 225 5111; fax: 0161 225 0210; e-mail: admin@smlc.org.uk; website: http://www.smlc.org.uk

South West London Law Centre
101a Tooting High Street, London, SW17 0SU; tel: 020 8767 2777; fax: 020 8767 2711; website: www.swllc.org.uk

Southwark Law Centre
Hanover Park House, 14–16 Hanover Park, Peckham, London, SE15 5HG; tel: 020 7732 2008; fax: 020 7732 2034

Springfield Law Centre
Springfield Hospital, 61 Glenburnie Road, London, SW17 7DJ; tel: 020 8767 6884; fax: 020 8767 6996; e-mail: info@springfieldlawcentre.org.uk

Streetwise Community Law Centre
1–3 Anerley Station Road, Penge, London, SE20 8PY; tel: 020 8778 5854; fax: 020 8776 9392

Surrey Law Centre
34–36 Chertsey Street, Guildford, Surrey, GU1 4HD; tel: 01483 215000; fax: 01483 750770; e-mail: info@surreylawcentre.org; website: www.surreycommunity.info/surreylawcentre/

Tower Hamlets Law Centre
214 Whitechapel Road, London, E1 1BG; tel: 020 7247 8998; fax: 020 7247 9424; e-mail: info@thlc.co.uk; website: http://www.thlc.co.uk

Trafford Law Centre
4th Floor, John Darby House, 88–92 Talbot Road, Old Trafford, Manchester, M16 0GS; tel: 0161 872 3669; fax: 0161 872 2208; e-mail: admin@traffordlawcentre.org.uk; website: www.traffordlawcentre.org.uk

Vauxhall Law and Information Centre
Vauxhall Training and Enterprise Centre, Silvester Street, Liverpool, L5 8SE; tel: 0151 482 2001; fax: 0151 207 4948

Wandsworth and Merton Law Centre (part of the South-West London Law Centres)
101a Tooting High Street, London, SW17 0SU; tel: 020 8767 2777; fax: 020 8767 2711; e-mail: info@swllc.org.uk

Warrington Law Centre
The Boultings, Winwick Street, Warrington, Cheshire, WA2 7TT; tel: 01925 258360; fax: 01925 637668; e-mail: admin@warringtonlawcentre.com; website: http://www.warringtonlawcentre.org

Wiltshire Law Centre
Temple House, 115–118 Commercial Road, Swindon, Wiltshire, SN1 5PL; tel: 01793 486926; fax: 01793 432193; e-mail: info@wiltslawcentre.co.uk; website: http://www.wiltslawcentre.org.uk

Wythenshawe Law Centre
260 Brownley Road, Wythenshawe, Manchester, M22 5EB; tel: 0161 498 0905/6; fax: 0161 498 0750; e-mail: info@wlawcentre.co.uk

Links with:
Scottish Association of Law Centres
c/o Renfrewshire Law Centre, 65–71 George Street, Paisley, PA1 2JY; tel: 0141 561 7266; fax: 0141 944 7605; e-mail: jonsalc@hotmail.co.uk; website: vwww.scotlawcentres.blogspot.com

Member organisations:
AIRE Advice on Individual Rights in Europe
Third Floor, 17 Red Lion Square, London, WC1R 4QH; tel: 020 7831 3850; fax: 020 7404 7760; e-mail: aire@binternet.com

Castlemilk Law and Money Advice Centre
155 Castlemilk Drive, Castlemilk, Glasgow, G45 9AD; tel: 0141 634 0313; fax: 0141 634 1944; e-mail: mail@castlemilklawcentre.co.uk

Disability Law Service
Ground Floor, 39–45 Cavell Street, London, E1 2BP; tel: 020 7791 9800 (Minicom 020 7791 9801); fax: 020 7791 9802; e-mail: advice@dls.org.uk; website: www.dls.org.uk

EarthRights solicitors
36 Town Street, Thaxted, Essex, CM6 2LA; tel: 01371 831936; e-mail: jd1@earthrights.org.uk; website: http://www.earthrights.org.uk

Ethnic Minorities Law Centre
41 St. Vincent Place, 2nd Floor, Glasgow, G1 2ER; tel: 0141 204 2888; fax: 0141 204 2006; e-mail: admin@emlc.org.uk; website: www.emlc.org.uk

Free Legal Advice Centre (Ireland)
13 Lower Dorset Street, Dublin 1, Ireland; tel: +353 1874 5690; fax: +353 1874 5320; e-mail: info@flac.ie; website: www.flac.ie

Govan Law Centre (Associate Member)
47 Burleigh Street, Govan, Glasgow, GS1 3LB; tel: 0141 440 2503; fax: 0141 445 3934; e-mail: mail@govanlc.com

Greater Manchester Immigration Aid Unit
1 Delaunays Road, Crumpsall Green, Manchester, M8 4QS; tel: 0161 740 7722; fax: 0161 740 5172; e-mail: gmaiau@ein.org.uk

Mary Ward Legal Centre
26–27 Boswell Street, London, WC1N 3JZ; tel: 020 7831 7079; fax: 020 7831 5431; e-mail: enquiries@marywardlegal.org.uk; website: wwww.marywardlegal.org.uk

LAW COMMISSION

Steel House, 11 Tothill Street, London, SW1H 9LJ

Tel: 020 3334 0200
Fax: 020 3334 0201
E-mail: chief.executive@lawcommission.gsi.gov.uk

Website:
http://www.lawcom.gov.uk
Contains the most recent reports and consultation papers.

Enquiries:
Enquiries to: Librarian
Direct tel: 020 3334 0220
Direct fax: 020 3334 0202
Direct e-mail: library@lawcommission.gsi.gov.uk

Other contacts: Chief Executive

Founded:
1965

Organisation type and purpose:
Statutory body, law reform body for England & Wales.

Subject coverage:
Law, programmes of the Law Commission.

Library catalogue:
All or part available in-house

Printed publications:
Annual Report (includes outline of yearly progress and list of publications)
Law under Review: list of law reform projects (on website)
Programmes of Law Reform (3 issues)
Reports and Consultation Papers on law reform proposals
Reports on proposals for the consolidation or repeal of statute law
Order printed publications from: The Stationery Office

Publications list:
Available online

Access to staff:
Contact by letter, by telephone and by e-mail
Hours: Open to the staff of the Commission 24 hours a day
Special comments: No public access.

Parent body:
Ministry of Justice

LAW SOCIETY LIBRARY

Formal name: Law Society of England and Wales

113 Chancery Lane, London, WC2A 1PL

Tel: 0870 606 2511; 020 7320 5972
Fax: 020 7831 1687
E-mail: library@lawsociety.org.uk

Website:
http://www.lawsociety.org.uk/library
Information about collections and services, research guides;link to online catalogue and indexes to legal information, legal news items.

Founded:
1825

Organisation type and purpose:
Professional body.
Professional society for solicitors in England and Wales.

Subject coverage:
Law: UK including England, Scotland, Wales, Northern Ireland; Eire; and European Union; Channel Islands; Isle of Man.

Information services:
The library runs a document delivery service and a parliamentary debates research service.

Museum or gallery collection, archive, or library special collection:
Over 43,000 vols of material dating back to the 13th century, comprising practitioner textbooks (current and previous edns), public legislation (up-to-date and historical), private and local legislation, law reports, parliamentary material, journals and legal encyclopaedias (current and previous edns).
Historical collections (trials, legal history, history of solicitors' profession, archives)
Mendham Collection of religious books (on loan to Canterbury Cathedral Library)
Parliamentary papers, 1801 onwards (on microfiche)

Non-library collection catalogue:
All or part available in print

Library catalogue:
All or part available online

Printed publications:
Publishes over 100 titles

LCIA arbitration rules and schedule of costs, LCIA mediation procedure, mediation schedule of fees and expenses, introductory brochure, membership leaflet and details of forthcoming events.

Enquiries:
Enquiries to: Registrar
Other contacts: Manager – Membership & Conferences for membership or conference enquiries.

Founded:
1892

Organisation type and purpose:
The expert and cost-effective administration of arbitration and ADR worldwide, under LCIA and other rules and procedures.

Subject coverage:
International commercial dispute resolution.

Printed publications:
Arbitration International and LCIA Newsletter
LCIA Arbitration Rules and Schedule of Costs (free of charge)
LCIA Mediation Procedure and Schedule of Fees and Expenses (free of charge)
LCIA Introductory Brochure (free of charge)
LCIA Membership/Services Leaflet (free of charge)

Access to staff:
Contact by letter, by telephone, by fax, by e-mail and via website. Appointment necessary.
Hours: Mon to Fri, 0900 to 1700

Access to building, collection or gallery:
No access other than to staff
Hours: Mon to Fri, 1000 to 1700
Special comments: No smoking or eating in the library.

LE VELO CLUB LIMITED

74 Warwick Avenue, Quorn, Loughborough, Leicestershire, LE12 8HE

Tel: 01509 554230
E-mail: davidfbod@yahoo.co.uk

Website:
http://www.leveloclub.org.uk

Enquiries:
Enquiries to: Honorary Secretary

Founded:
1983

Organisation type and purpose:
Membership association (membership is by subscription), present number of members: 1,300. To promote enjoyment, riding and restoration of LE, Valiant, Vogue and Viceroy motorcycles.

Subject coverage:
Technical and historical information on LE Velo motorcycle and its derivatives.

Museum or gallery collection, archive, or library special collection:
Extensive collection of original drawings (now on CD-ROM)

Non-library collection catalogue:
All or part available online

Printed publications:
Magazine (6 times a year, members)

Access to staff:
Contact by letter, by e-mail and via website
Hours: Mon to Fri, 0900 to 1700

LEA-FRANCIS OWNERS' CLUB

Acronym or abbreviation: LFOC

French's, Long Wittenham, Abingdon, Oxfordshire, OX14 4QQ

Tel: 01865 407515

Website:
http://www.lfoc.org
Club officers and services listed; events notified; history of the marque and models summarised.

Enquiries:
Enquiries to: General Secretary
Direct e-mail: secretary@lfoc.org
Other contacts: Membership Secretary for applications to join

Founded:
1953

Organisation type and purpose:
International organisation, membership association (membership is by subscription), present number of members: 340.
Factory records and histories of individual vehicles, technical details and information on the repair and maintenance of most models.
Preservation and use of Lea-Francis vehicles.

Subject coverage:
History of all Lea-Francis products, production history, racing history, as well as history of individual vehicles, technical information on all models.

Information services:
Full records of all Lea-Francis products

Museum or gallery collection, archive, or library special collection:
Catalogues, information sheets, brochures and other sales literature issued by Lea-Francis Cars
Technical literature and handbooks for most models

Printed publications:
The LeaFlet (magazine, 6 times a year, free to members)
Lea-Francis Owners' Club Jubilee Book 2003

Electronic and video publications:
Video of 1995 Centenary Rally

Access to staff:
Contact by letter, by telephone, by e-mail and via website
Hours: Mon to Sun, 0900 to 2200

Access to building, collection or gallery:
No access other than to staff

LEAD SHEET ASSOCIATION

Acronym or abbreviation: LSA

Unit 10, Archers Park, Branbridges Road, East Peckham, Tonbridge, Kent, TN12 5HP

Tel: 01622 872432
Fax: 01622 871649
E-mail: info@leadsheetassociation.org.uk

Website:
http://www.leadsheetassociation.org.uk
Outline of LSA services.

Enquiries:
Enquiries to: Administrator
Other contacts: General Manager

Founded:
1926

Organisation type and purpose:
Trade association (membership is by subscription, election or invitation), manufacturing industry, training organisation, consultancy.

Subject coverage:
Technical advice and training on the specification and use of rolled lead sheet in the construction industry.

Museum or gallery collection, archive, or library special collection:
All relevant industry publications

Trade and statistical information:
Confidential industry statistics not for general release.

Printed publications:
Rolled Lead Sheet: The Complete Manual

Publications list:
Available online and in print

Access to staff:
Contact by letter, by telephone, by fax, by e-mail and via website. Appointment necessary.
Hours: Mon to Fri, 0900 to 1700

LEAD SMELTERS AND REFINERS ASSOCIATION

Acronym or abbreviation: LSRA

c/o 17a Welbeck Way, London, W1G 9YJ

Tel: 020 7499 8422
Fax: 020 7493 1555
E-mail: enq@ldaint.org

Enquiries:
Enquiries to: General Secretary

Organisation type and purpose:
Trade association.

Subject coverage:
Smelting and refining of lead.

Trade and statistical information:
Confidential – not generally available.

Access to staff:
Contact by letter, by telephone and by fax
Hours: Mon to Fri, 0900 to 1700

LEADHILLS AND WANLOCKHEAD RAILWAY

The Station, Leadhills, Lanarkshire, ML12 6XP

Tel: 01555 662963
E-mail: secretary@leadhillsrailway.co.uk

Website:
http://www.leadhillsrailway.co.uk

Enquiries:
Enquiries to: Secretary
Other contacts: Publicist (e-mail: davidwinpenny@hotmail.com)

Founded:
1983

Organisation type and purpose:
Membership association (membership is by subscription), voluntary organisation.

Subject coverage:
Railway preservation.

Special visitor services:
Train service Sat and Sun during May to Sept

Education services:
Museum in shop

Non-library collection catalogue:
All or part available online

Printed publications:
The Leadhills and Wanlockhead Light Railway (the original branch line, 1901–38, 64pp illustrated, £5)
Leaflet about industrial heritage available

Access to staff:
Contact by letter, by telephone, by e-mail and via website. Appointment necessary.
Hours: Mon to Fri, 0900 to 1700

Access to building, collection or gallery:
Hours: Sat and Sun, 1000 to 1700

Access for disabled people:
Access to building, but restricted access on train

LEAGUE AGAINST CRUEL SPORTS LIMITED

Acronym or abbreviation: LACS

83–87 Union Street, London, SE1 1SG

Tel: 020 7403 6155
Fax: 020 7403 4532

Website:
http://www.league.uk.com
Information about the campaign to ban hunting.

Enquiries:
Enquiries to: Information Officer
Direct e-mail: press@league.org.uk
Other contacts: PA to Chief Executive

Founded:
1924

Organisation type and purpose:
National organisation, membership association (membership is by subscription), voluntary organisation.
Company.
To campaign to end cruel sports and to protect threatened animals.

Subject coverage:
Hunting of wild animals with dogs, hare coursing, shooting, wildlife protection and conservation.

Trade and statistical information:
Information on hunted animals and on cruel sports.

Printed publications:
Wildlife Guardian (quarterly, free to members)
A Brush with Conscience
Care for the Wild
Draghunting – A family sport
Falconry in Britain
How to Make a Wildlife Garden
Rearing Pheasants for Shoots
Uncivil Liberties
The Red Fox: Friend or Foe?
The Tradition of Staghunting on Exmoor & the Quantocks
Wildlife Protection

Publications list:
Available online and in print

Access to staff:
Contact by letter, by telephone, by fax and by e-mail
Hours: Mon to Fri, 0900 to 1700

LEAGUE FOR THE EXCHANGE OF COMMONWEALTH TEACHERS

Acronym or abbreviation: LECT

Commonwealth House, 7 Lion Yard, Tremadoc Road, London, SW4 7NQ

Tel: 0870 770 2636
Fax: 0870 770 2637
E-mail: info@lect.org.uk

Website:
http://www.lect.org.uk

Enquiries:
Enquiries to: Director
Direct e-mail: anna.tomlinson@lect.org.uk

Founded:
1901

Organisation type and purpose:
International organisation, membership association, present number of members: 2500, registered charity.

Subject coverage:
Education in the Commonwealth including information about international professional D+V for teachers.

Electronic and video publications:
Newsletter (email)
Library of research reports on overseas visits undertaken (via website)

Access to staff:
Contact by letter, by telephone, by fax, by e-mail, in person and via website
Hours: Mon to Fri, 0900 to 1700

LEARNING & SKILLS COUNCIL LONDON NORTH

Acronym or abbreviation: LSC London North

Dunmayne House, 1 Fox Lane, Palmers Green, London, N13 4AB

Tel: 0845 019 4158
Fax: 020 8882 5931

Enquiries:
Enquiries to: Customer Services

Founded:
1991

Organisation type and purpose:
Statutory body, training organisation.
Organisation and strategic funding of post-16 education (excluding higher education) in London North area.

Subject coverage:
Information available for youth programmes, adult training and initiatives, business services, information for employers/employees. Special projects including equal opportunities policies, special needs provision, childcare, capacity building for voluntary sector, and other ongoing projects.

Printed publications:
Social and Economic Assessment
Skills and Employer Survey Reports
Needs Analysis

Publications list:
Available in print

Access to staff:
Contact by letter, by telephone, by fax and in person
Hours: Mon to Fri, 0900 to 1700

Access to building, collection or gallery:
No access other than to staff

Access for disabled people:
Parking provided, level entry, access to all public areas, toilet facilities

LEARNING AND SKILLS COUNCIL SOUTH EAST

Princes House, 53 Queens Road, Brighton, BN1 3XB

Tel: 01273 783555
Fax: 01273 783507
E-mail: info@lsc.gov.uk

Website:
http://www.lsc.gov.uk/regions/SouthEast/

Enquiries:
Enquiries to: Marketing and PR Manager
Direct tel: 01329 228502

Founded:
2001

Organisation type and purpose:
Local government body, service industry.
Comprises five local Councils.
Post-16 learning and education.

Subject coverage:
Support for post-16 and education.

Trade and statistical information:
Labour and market economic information for Hampshire.

Access to staff:
Contact by letter, by telephone and by fax
Hours: Mon to Fri, 0900 to 1700

LEARNING AND SKILLS COUNCIL THAMES VALLEY

Acronym or abbreviation: LSC

LSC South East, Pacific House, Imperial Way, Reading, RG2 0FT

Tel: 0845 019 4147
Fax: 0118 908 2109
E-mail: SE-ESFCo-financing@lsc.gov.uk

Website:
http://www.lsc.gov.uk
Information about our mission, what we do, contact details, publications.

Enquiries:
Enquiries to: Regional ESF Administrator
Direct tel: 01273 783614

Founded:
2001

Organisation type and purpose:
National government body, national organisation, service industry, training organisation.
To plan and fund all post-16 training and education, except higher education.
To raise participation and attainment through high quality education and training which puts learners first.

Subject coverage:
Investors in people, training, National Vocational Qualification, local labour market, workforce development, modern apprenticeship, Foundation Apprenticeship, adult learning, schools, college, 6th forms, ESF funding, management development.

Museum or gallery collection, archive, or library special collection:
Various business and grants databases

Printed publications:
Investors in People
Modern Apprenticeships
Strategic Plan 2002–2005
Workforce Development

Access to staff:
Contact by letter, by telephone, by fax, by e-mail and via website
Hours: Mon to Fri, 0900 to 1700

Access to building, collection or gallery:
No access other than to staff

Access for disabled people:
Parking provided, ramped entry, toilet facilities

Funded by:
Central Government

National Office:
Learning and Skills Council
Cheylesmore House, Quinton Road, Coventry, CV1 2WT; tel: 024 7670 3241; fax: 024 7686 3100; e-mail: nationalinfo@lsc.gov.uk

LEARNING AND SKILLS DEVELOPMENT NETWORK

Acronym or abbreviation: LSN

Fifth Floor, Holborn Centre, 120 Holborn, London, EC1N 2AD

Tel: 0845 071 0800
E-mail: enquiries@lsneducation.org.uk

Website:
http://www.lsneducation.org.uk/
http://www.lsda.org.uk

Enquiries:
Enquiries to: Information Officer
Other contacts: Communications Managerr, tel no: 020 7840 5360 for press and PR.

Founded:
1995

Formerly a part of:
the Learning and Skills Development Agency (year of change 2006)

Organisation type and purpose:
National development agency, educational organisation.
Research for the further education sector.

Subject coverage:
Information for education managers on aspects of post-16 further education which relate to: developing competence, curriculum and staff management, curriculum planning and management, equal opportunities, flexible learning, provision for adults, new technologies, European links, governors, quality issues, key skills, professional development, vocational learning and research for the post-16 sector.

continued overleaf

Non-library collection catalogue:
All or part available in-house

Printed publications:
Briefing (newsletter)
A wide range of reports, papers, bulletins, books
and other publications

Publications list:
Available online and in print

Access to staff:
Contact by letter, by telephone, by fax, by e-mail
and via website. Appointment necessary.
Hours: Mon to Fri, 0900 to 1700

Access to building, collection or gallery:
Prior appointment required

LEARNING AND TEACHING SCOTLAND

Acronym or abbreviation: LTS

The Optima, 58 Robertson Street, Glasgow, G2
8DU

Tel: 0141 282 5000
Fax: 0141 282 5050
E-mail: enquiries@ltscotland.org.uk

Website:
http://www.ltscotland.org.uk

Enquiries:
Enquiries to: Senior Communications and
Information Officer
Direct e-mail: t.wallace@ltscotland.org.uk

Founded:
2000

Organisation type and purpose:
Executive non-departmental public body
sponsored by Scottish Government, Learning and
Teaching Scotland is the main organisation for the
development and support of the Scottish
curriculum, combining expertise in the curriculum
0–18 with advice on the use of ICT in education.

Subject coverage:
LTS is responsible for leading and supporting
improvement in the delivery of education for
children and young people; working closely with a
wide range of partner organisations to share
interesting innovative practice; providing advice,
support, resources and staff development, which
can enhance the quality of learning and teaching;
playing a key role in all major developments in
Scottish education; moving education forward in
partnership with key stakeholders.

Library catalogue:
All or part available in-house

Printed publications:
Over 200 publications on aspects of education and
subjects in the curriculum
Annual review
Order printed publications from: Learning and
Teaching Scotland, Distribution Centre, 7 Tom
Johnston Road, West Pitkerro, Dundee, DD4 8XD

Publications list:
Available online

Access to staff:
Contact by letter, by telephone, by fax, by e-mail,
in person and via website. Appointment necessary.
Hours: Mon to Fri, 0845 to 1645

Funded by:
Scottish Government

LEARNING CENTRE LIBRARY

Walsall Hospitals NHS Trust, Manor Hospital,
Moat Road, Walsall, West Midlands, WS2 9PS

Tel: 01922 656628
Fax: 01922 656220
E-mail: kaljinder.dhanda@walsallhospitals.nhs.uk

Enquiries:
Enquiries to: Librarian

Founded:
1970

Organisation type and purpose:
NHS hospital library.

Subject coverage:
Medical information.

Information services:
Multi-disciplinary collection of medical and
healthcare textbooks covering undergraduate and
postgraduate. Split across two sites.

Special visitor services:
All staff and students on placement or working for
Walsall Hospitals NHS Trust and Walsall Teaching
Primary Care Trust, including members of other
Base libraries. Reference only to non-members.

Non-library collection catalogue:
All or part available online

Library catalogue:
All or part available online

Access to staff:
Access for members only. Non-members charged.
Hours: Mon to Fri, 0900 to 1700

Access for disabled people:
Ground floor access.

LEARNING ON SCREEN

Enquiries:
Enquiries to: Administrator

Founded:
1968

Organisation type and purpose:
International organisation, trade association
(membership is by subscription), present number
of members: 150, registered charity (charity
number 325081-R).
Members are concerned with the production and
use of materials for learning and training. They
include broadcasters, producers, universities,
colleges and schools.

Subject coverage:
Uses of screen-based media in education and
training, selection of video equipment for
education and training, production of material for
education and training, research into the
effectiveness of screen-based material for learning
and training, television in distance learning.

Printed publications:
Screen Seen (magazine, quarterly)

Access to staff:
Contact by letter, by telephone, by e-mail and via
website. Appointment necessary.
Hours: Mon to Fri, 0830 to 1600

Recognised by the:
Department for Education and Employment
Scottish Education Department
Welsh Education Office

LEARNING THROUGH LANDSCAPES

Acronym or abbreviation: LTL

Third Floor, Southside Offices, The Law Courts,
Winchester, Hampshire, SO23 9DL

Tel: 01962 846258
Fax: 01962 869099
E-mail: schoolgrounds-uk@ltl.org.uk

Website:
http://www.ltl.org.uk
Projects, membership, benefits of becoming
members, publications list.

Enquiries:
Enquiries to: Information Officer

Founded:
1990

Organisation type and purpose:
Registered charity.

To improve the quality of school grounds.

Subject coverage:
School grounds.

Museum or gallery collection, archive, or library special collection:
Around 1000 documents on school grounds
projects and associated organisations

Library catalogue:
All or part available in-house

Printed publications:
A Guide to the Management and Maintenance of
School Grounds (£10.95)
Developing School Grounds Toolkit (video,
management guide and photocopiable material)
The Challenge of an Urban School Site (£10.95)
In the School Grounds Series (KS1 and KS2):
Arts in the School Grounds (£8.99)
English in the School Grounds (£7.95)
Geography in the School Grounds (£8.99)
Mathematics in the School Grounds (£7.95)
Science in the School Grounds (£7.95)
Trees in the School Grounds (£6.95)
Order printed publications from: Southgate
Publishers Limited
The Square, Sandford, Crediton, Devon, EX17
4LW, tel: 01363 776888, fax: 01363 776889

Electronic and video publications:
3 videos available for purchase
Seating in the School Grounds (CD-ROM)

Publications list:
Available in print

Access to staff:
Contact by letter, by telephone, by fax, by e-mail
and via website. Appointment necessary.
Hours: Mon to Fri, 0900 to 1700
Special comments: Charges for some services.

LEATHER CONSERVATION CENTRE

University Campus, Boughton Green Road,
Moulton Park, Northampton, NN2 7AN

Tel: 01604 719766
E-mail: lcc@northampton.ac.uk

Website:
http://www.leatherconservation.org

Enquiries:
Enquiries to: Head of Conservation

Founded:
1978

Organisation type and purpose:
Registered charity (charity number 276485).

Subject coverage:
Conservation and analysis of historical leather,
history of leather manufacture.

Museum or gallery collection, archive, or library special collection:
Reference collection of leather types

Printed publications:
Conservation of Leathercraft and Related Objects
(ICOM, 1992, £15)
Parchment: The physical and chemical
characteristics of parchment and the materials
used in its conservation (£12.50)
Surface Coatings for Binding Leathers (£10)
Order printed publications from: Above address

Publications list:
Available online and in print

Access to staff:
Contact by letter, by telephone and by e-mail.
Appointment necessary.
Hours: Mon to Fri, 0900 to 1700

Associate member of:
British Leather Confederation

Member organisation of:
Historic Houses Association

LEATHERHEAD FOOD INTERNATIONAL

Acronym or abbreviation: LFI

Randalls Road, Leatherhead, Surrey, KT22 7RY

Tel: 01372 376761
Fax: 01372 386228
E-mail: help@lfra.co.uk

Website:
http://www.leatherheadfood.com/lfi

Enquiries:
Enquiries to: Business Manager, Library and Electronic Information
Direct tel: 01372 822279
Direct fax: 01372 822268
Direct e-mail: library@lfra.co.uk

Organisation type and purpose:
Scientific and information services for the international food industry

Subject coverage:
Food science and technology, nutrition, sensory analysis, analytical chemistry, food microbiology, food hygiene, food toxicology.

Printed publications:
Majority of publications are confidential to members
Market Reports
Food Legislation Surveys
Literature Surveys
Research Reports
Scientific and Technical Surveys
Technical Circulars
Order printed publications from: http://www.leatherheadfood.com/lfi/submenu.asp?section=11§ionname=Bookshop

Electronic and video publications:
FoodlineWeb Science database (food science and technology)
FoodlineWeb Market database (market and product intelligence)
FoodlineWeb Legal database (additives legislation)
FoodlineWeb News database (food industry news)
Global Food Markets (reports on international food markets and trends)
Regulatory Manuals (UK, EU and International)
Order electronic and video publications from: http://services.leatherheadfood.com/foodline/subscribe.aspx

Publications list:
Available online

Access to staff:
Contact by letter, by telephone, by fax, by e-mail, in person and via website. Access for members only. Non-members charged.
Hours: Mon to Fri, 0830 to 1730
Special comments: Non-members at the discretion of the Librarian.

LEBANESE EMBASSY

21 Kensington Palace Gardens, London, W8 4QN

Tel: 020 7229 7265
Fax: 020 7243 1699
E-mail: emb.leb@btinternet.com

Enquiries:
Enquiries to: Ambassador's Secretary

Organisation type and purpose:
National government body.
Embassy.
The issue of visas and passports, and actions as power of attorney (Consular Section).

Subject coverage:
Lebanon; its economy and tourism.

Printed publications:
Lebanon – 59 Years of Independence

Access to staff:
Contact by letter, by telephone, by fax and in person. Appointment necessary.
Hours: Mon to Fri, 0900 to 1530

Parent body:
Ministry for Foreign Affairs
Beirut, Lebanon

LEBRECHT MUSIC AND ARTS PHOTO LIBRARY

3 Bolton Road, London, NW8 0RJ

Tel: 020 7625 5341
Fax: 020 7625 5341
E-mail: pictures@lebrecht.co.uk

Website:
http://www.lebrecht.co.uk
http://www.authorpictures.co.uk

Enquiries:
Enquiries to: Director

Founded:
1992

Organisation type and purpose:
Consultancy, research organisation.
Picture library.
Supply of arts and music pictures to commercial clients from the world's largest specialist music archive, with access to over 8m. arts pictures.

Subject coverage:
Lebrecht Music & Arts Picture Library consists of three specialist libraries, covering music (classical, rock, pop, jazz, opera, ballet), literature (authors, manuscripts, fictional heroes, theatre, book covers, illustrations, literary arts), and history through fine arts (especially strong on Russian, French, Italian and English art).

Museum or gallery collection, archive, or library special collection:
New York Public Library (Performing Arts division)
Alan Bush Foundation
Kurt Weill Foundation
Martinu Archives
Royal Academy of Music Collection of Images
Ben Uri Russian Collection

Non-library collection catalogue:
All or part available online, in-house and in print

Library catalogue:
All or part available online and in-house

Publications list:
Available online

Access to staff:
Contact by letter, by telephone, by fax, by e-mail and via website. Appointment necessary.
Hours: Mon to Fri, 0900 to 1730

LEEDS (SOUTH) METHODIST CIRCUIT OFFICE

Trinity House, Lodge Lane, Leeds, West Yorkshire, LS11 6LR

Tel: 0113 271 6641

Enquiries:
Enquiries to: Superintendent Minister
Other contacts: Circuit Minister

Founded:
18th Century

Organisation type and purpose:
Voluntary organisation.
Church organisation.

Subject coverage:
Methodist Churches in South Leeds.

Access to staff:
Contact by letter, by telephone and by e-mail
Hours: Mon to Fri, 0900 to 1700

LEEDS CITY LIBRARIES – BUSINESS AND PATENT INFORMATION SERVICES

Acronym or abbreviation: BAPIS

Central Library, Calverley Street, Leeds, LS1 3AB

Tel: 0113 247 8266
Fax: 0113 247 8268
E-mail: piu@leeds.gov.uk

Website:
http://www.businessandpatents.org
Factsheets, information and useful links for anyone starting up or growing a business.
http://www.bapisleeds.blogspot.com
News and events.
http://www.leedsinventorsgroup.blogspot.com
News and events for inventors.

Enquiries:
Enquiries to: Manager
Other contacts: Librarian

Incorporates the former:
Patent Information Unit and Information for Business (year of change 2004)

Organisation type and purpose:
Local government body, public library.

Subject coverage:
All aspects of business, commerce, statistics, company information, market research, job-seeking, intellectual property (ip) trademarks, patents registered designs and copyright.

Information services:
Tailored marketing lists, enquiry service, patent and trademarks searching and information on IP

Museum or gallery collection, archive, or library special collection:
British Standards
Company Information
D & B KBE
MINT, FAME
KeyNote Market Research
Mintel Market Research
Marquesa
DWPI
Derwent Innovations Index
GPI
Trade Marks
Patent information
Leeds Inventors Group

Library catalogue:
All or part available online and in-house

Printed publications:
Information handouts on its services
Separate sheets on company information, mailing lists, copyright in music, copyright in photography
Top 700 companies in Leeds
Order printed publications from: e-mail: piu@leeds.gov.uk

Access to staff:
Contact by letter, by telephone, by fax, by e-mail, in person and via website
Hours: Mon to Fri, 0900 to 1700; Sat, 1000 to 1300
Special comments: Phone to make an appointment for a one-to-one consultation on IP.

Access to building, collection or gallery:
Hours: Mon to Wed, 0900 to 2000; Thu and Fri, 0900 to 1700; Sat, 1000 to 1700; Sun, 1300 to 1700

Access for disabled people:
Ramped entry, toilet facilities, lift

LEEDS COLLEGE OF TECHNOLOGY

Acronym or abbreviation: LCOT

Cookridge Street, Leeds, West Yorkshire, LS2 8BL

Tel: 0113 297 6300\ Minicom no. 0113 297 6470
Fax: 0113 297 6301

Enquiries:
Enquiries to: Librarian
Direct tel: 0113 297 6353
Direct e-mail: library@leeds-lcot.ac.uk

Organisation type and purpose:
Suitable for ages: 16+.
Further education college.

continued overleaf

Subject coverage:
Engineering, manufacturing, computing, business, media studies, health and social care.

Library catalogue:
All or part available online

Access to staff:
Contact by letter, by telephone, by fax, by e-mail and in person
Hours: Mon to Thu, 0830 to 2030; Fri, 0830 to 1630
Special comments: Letter of introduction required for non LCOT students.

Access for disabled people:
Ramped entry, access to all public areas, toilet facilities
Special comments: Above disabled facilities for Central Site only.

Also at:
Leeds College of Technology
   East Street, Leeds, LS2 8PH; tel: 0113 297 7272; fax: 0113 297 7273
Leeds College of Technology
   Westland Road, Leeds, LS11 5SB; tel: 0113 297 9400; fax: 0113 297 9401

LEEDS INDUSTRIAL MUSEUM

Armley Mills, Canal Road, Armley, Leeds, West Yorkshire, LS12 2QF

Tel: 0113 263 7861
Fax: 0113 224 4365
E-mail: neil.dowlan@leeds.gov.uk

Website:
http://www.leeds.gov.uk
Web page covering areas of collections.
http://www.leeds.gov.uk/tourinfo/attract/museums/armley/index.html
Armley Mills homepage.
http://www.leeds.gov.uk/tourinfo/events/lmg_arm.html
Events listings.

Enquiries:
Enquiries to: Curator
Direct tel: 0113 224 4372
Direct e-mail: amy.jenkinson@leeds.gov.uk

Founded:
1982

Organisation type and purpose:
Local government body, professional body, museum.
Museum holding information on Leeds' industrial history.

Subject coverage:
Leeds industrial history, printing, photography, cinematography, engineering, textiles, ready-made clothing, locomotive building, cranes, transport (road rollers, etc.).

Information services:
Library available for reference by appointment (for conditions see Access).

Special visitor services:
Materials and/or activities for children.

Museum or gallery collection, archive, or library special collection:
Working exhibits include:
1904 Spinning Mule
Ploughing engine, mill engine, steam locomotive
1920s cinema
Archives of photographs/documents relating to Leeds Industries

Non-library collection catalogue:
All or part available in-house

Library catalogue:
All or part available in-house

Printed publications:
Guide Book
Building Sights (Beesley I, commissioned by Museum)

Access to staff:
Contact by letter, by telephone, by fax, by e-mail, in person and via website. Appointment necessary.
Hours: By appointment only, Tues 1100 to 1630; Wed 0900 to 1630; Thu, 0900 to 1400

Access to building, collection or gallery:
Museum Opening Hours
Hours: Tues to Sat, 1000 to 1700; Sun, 1300 to 1400

Access for disabled people:
Parking provided, ramped entry, toilet facilities
Special comments: Access to most areas; touch trail; lift to all floors.

Parent body:
Director of Museums and Galleries
   Leeds City Council, Leisure Services Department, Museums & Galleries Division, Leeds Town Hall, Leeds, West Yorkshire

LEEDS LIBRARY

18 Commercial Street, Leeds, LS1 6AL

Tel: 0113 245 3071
Fax: 0113 245 1191
E-mail: enquiries@theleedslibrary.org.uk

Website:
http://www.theleedslibrary.org.uk

Enquiries:
Enquiries to: Librarian

Founded:
1768

Organisation type and purpose:
Independent subscription library (company number 5577905; charity number 1114386).

Museum or gallery collection, archive, or library special collection:
Library of 135,000 items
Civil War pamphlets
Reformation Tracts

Library catalogue:
All or part available online and in print

Printed publications:
The Dial (newsletter, occasional)

Access to staff:
Contact by letter, by telephone, by fax, by e-mail and via website. Appointment necessary. Letter of introduction required.
Hours: Mon to Fri, 0900 to 1700; 1st Sat of the month, 0930 to 1300

LEEDS LIBRARY AND INFORMATION SERVICES

Central Library, Municipal Buildings, Calverley Street, Leeds, West Yorkshire, LS1 3AB

Tel: 0113 247 6016
Fax: 0113 247 4222
E-mail: enquiry.express@leeds.gov.uk

Website:
http://www.leeds.gov.uk/libraries
Local history, family history, online reference resources, library catalogue, library events, enquiries.

Enquiries:
Enquiries to: Manager

Organisation type and purpose:
Local government body, public library.

Subject coverage:
Business and company information, patents information, local history (Leeds and Yorkshire) also general information service covering all other subjects; separate Art and Music Libraries; Research Library.

Museum or gallery collection, archive, or library special collection:
Art Library:
Gillow Archives (business archives of Gillow Furniture Company)

Kitson Collection (early English watercolours and Rembrandt etchings)
Leeds pottery (including Pattern Books)
Sanderson Collection (19th-century fashion plates and periodicals)
Music Library:
Scores and cassettes, compact discs
Taphouse Collection (17th- and 18th-century music and books on music)
Business and Research Library:
British Standards
Gascoigne Collection (military and naval history)
Gott Bequest (early gardening books)
HMSO publications
Leeds Philatelic Society Library
Local History Collection (Leeds and Yorkshire)
Extensive archive of Leeds Theatre materials, including posters, indexed by actor, theatre, play, author, etc.
Porton Collection (Judaica)
Private press and early printed books
Yorkshire Ramblers Club Library (mountaineering, speleology)

Non-library collection catalogue:
All or part available in-house

Library catalogue:
All or part available in-house

Access to staff:
Contact by letter, by telephone, by fax and by e-mail
Hours: Mon, Tue, Wed, 0900 to 2000; Thu, Fri, 0900 to 1700; Sat, 1000 to 1700; Sun, 1300 to 1700

Access for disabled people:
Level entry, toilet facilities

LEEDS MEDICAL INFORMATION

Acronym or abbreviation: LMI

University of Leeds, Leeds, West Yorkshire, LS2 9JT

Tel: 0113 343 5552
Fax: 0113 343 5568
E-mail: lmi@leeds.ac.uk

Website:
http://www.leeds.ac.uk/lmi/
http://www.leeds.ac.uk/lmi/publications.html
List of all publications which can then be accessed from this page.

Enquiries:
Enquiries to: Manager
Direct tel: 0113 343 4381
Direct e-mail: n.v.king@leeds.ac.uk

Founded:
1974

Organisation type and purpose:
University library.
Academic publishing unit and information consultancy; based at the University of Leeds.

Subject coverage:
Clinical cancer (oncology), cancer; palliative care

Printed publications:
Mitomycin-C Update (quarterly)
Progress in Palliative Care (6 times a year)

Access to staff:
Contact by letter, by telephone, by fax and by e-mail
Hours: Mon to Fri, 0900 to 1700

Parent body:
University of Leeds

LEEDS METROPOLITAN UNIVERSITY

City Campus Library, Leslie Silver Building, Woodhouse Lane, Leeds, West Yorkshire, LS1 3HE

Tel: 0113 812 5956
E-mail: j.norry@leedsmet.ac.uk

Website:
http://libraryonline.leedsmet.ac.uk

Guide to libraries, subject guides, service information, library catalogue, access to electronic services.

Enquiries:
Enquiries to: Director of Libraries and Learning Innovation
Direct tel: 0113 812 1000
Direct e-mail: infodesk.lc@leedsmet.ac.uk

Organisation type and purpose:
University library services.

Subject coverage:
Accounting and finance; art, design, film, TV and photography; architecture; landscape design; business studies, management, law; health and science; hospitality management; engineering; social sciences; computing and information systems; education; languages; sport science; sport and leisure; tourism; construction; quantity surveying; civil engineering; environmental health; urban development.

Museum or gallery collection, archive, or library special collection:
Collection of the West Yorkshire Society of Architects
European Documentation Centre

Non-library collection catalogue:
All or part available online

Library catalogue:
All or part available online

Access to staff:
Contact by letter, by telephone, by e-mail, in person and via website. Non-members charged.
Hours: Term time: Mon to Thu, 0830 to 2000; Fri, 0830 to 1900; Sat, 1000 to 1600; Sun, 1000 to 1800
Special comments: Restrictions on accessing online information services apply. Charges made for borrowing.

Branch libraries:
Headingley Library
James Graham Building, Beckett Park, Leeds, LS6 3HF; tel: 0113 812 1000

LEEDS TRINITY UNIVERSITY COLLEGE

Library, Brownberrie Lane, Horsforth, Leeds, West Yorkshire, LS18 5HD

Tel: 0113 283 7100
Fax: 0113 283 7200
E-mail: n.goodfellow@leedstrinity.ac.uk

Website:
http://www.leedstrinity.ac.uk/services/library/Pages/default.aspx
Brief details of Library services. Access to Library catalogue.

Enquiries:
Enquiries to: Librarian
Direct tel: 0113 283 7246

Founded:
1966

Organisation type and purpose:
University library.

Subject coverage:
Education; communication and media studies; business and management; social and environmental studies: psychology; English, French and Spanish language and literature; economics; history; music; sport, health and leisure; sociology; theology; public media; journalism.

Museum or gallery collection, archive, or library special collection:
Yorkshire Local History Collection

Library catalogue:
All or part available online

Access to staff:
Contact by letter, by telephone and by e-mail
Hours: Mon to Fri, 0900 to 1700

Access to building, collection or gallery:
No access other than to staff
Hours: Term time: Mon to Thu, 0830 to 2045; Fri, 0830 to 1745; Sat, 1300 to 1645; Sun, 1400 to 2045

Affiliated to:
University of Leeds

LEEK GROWERS' ASSOCIATION

Acronym or abbreviation: TLGA

133 Eastgate, Louth, Lincolnshire, LN11 9QG

Tel: 01507 602427
Fax: 01507 607165
E-mail: crop.association@pvga.co.uk

Website:
http://www.british-leeks.co.uk

Enquiries:
Enquiries to: Membership Secretary

Founded:
1980s

Organisation type and purpose:
National organisation, trade association.

Subject coverage:
Leeks.

Access to staff:
Contact by letter, by telephone, by fax and by e-mail
Hours: Mon to Fri, 0900 to 1700

LEGAL ACTION GROUP

Formal name: LAG Education and Service Trust Limited
Acronym or abbreviation: LAG

242 Pentonville Road, London, N1 9UN

Tel: 020 7833 2931
Fax: 020 7837 6094
E-mail: lag@lag.org.uk

Website:
http://www.lag.org.uk
Policy, comment, publications and training courses.

Enquiries:
Enquiries to: Director

Founded:
1972

Organisation type and purpose:
Voluntary organisation, registered charity (charity number 265703).
Solicitors, barristers, advisers, academics, students and others, concerned to improve legal services to the community.

Subject coverage:
Legal services, legal profession, social welfare, law, penal affairs and crime.

Printed publications:
Legal Action (monthly magazine)
Community Care Law reports (quarterly)
Books include:
Employment Law (T. Lewis, 2009, £35)
Defending Suspects at Police Stations (E. Cape with J. Luqmani, 2006, £52)
Support for Asylum-Seekers (S. Willman et al, 2009, £45.00)

Publications list:
Available online and in print

Access to staff:
Contact by e-mail and via website. Appointment necessary.
Hours: Mon to Fri, 1000 to 1700

LEGAL SERVICES OMBUDSMAN

3rd Floor, Sunlight House, Quay Street, Manchester, M3 3JZ

Tel: 0161 839 7262 / Lo-call 0845 601 0794

Fax: 0161 832 5446
E-mail: lso@olso.gsi.gov.uk

Website:
http://www.olso.org

Enquiries:
Enquiries to: Information Officer

Founded:
1990

Subject coverage:
Deals with complaints about the behaviour and quality of service of solicitors if the Solicitors Complaints Bureau has failed to provide satisfaction.

Printed publications:
Annual reports, leaflets.

Access to staff:
Contact by letter, by telephone, by fax and by e-mail
Hours: Mon to Fri, 0900 to 1630

Access to building, collection or gallery:
No prior appointment required

Access for disabled people:
Level entry

LEICESTER CENTRAL LEARNING AND INFORMATION LIBRARY

Bishop Street, Leicester, LE1 6AA

Tel: 0116 299 5401
Fax: 0116 299 5444
E-mail: central.reference@leicester.gov.uk

Website:
http://www.leicester.gov.uk/libraries

Enquiries:
Enquiries to: Manager
Direct e-mail: michael.lewis@leicester.gov.uk
Other contacts: Duty Officer

Founded:
1905

Formerly called:
Reference and Information Library (year of change 2007)

Organisation type and purpose:
Public library.

Subject coverage:
General public library subject coverage.

Museum or gallery collection, archive, or library special collection:
Stretton Collection of of books and memorabilia relating to British railway development from the late 19th century
Stretton railway collection

Trade and statistical information:
Small collection of UK government statistics.

Non-library collection catalogue:
All or part available in-house

Library catalogue:
All or part available online

Access to staff:
Contact by letter, by telephone, by fax, by e-mail, in person and via website
Hours: Mon to Thu, 0930 to 1900; Fri, 0900 to 1700; Sat, 0900 to 1600

Access to building, collection or gallery:
Hours: as for access to staff

Access for disabled people:
Disabled access door and ramp, lift access to first floor
Hours: as for access to staff

LEICESTER CENTRAL LENDING LIBRARY

54 Belvoir Street, Leicester, LE1 6QG

Tel: 0116 299 5402

continued overleaf

Fax: 0116 299 5434
E-mail: artsl203@leicester.gov.uk

Enquiries:
Enquiries to: Manager

Organisation type and purpose:
Public library.

Access to staff:
Contact by letter, by telephone, by fax, by e-mail
and in person
Hours: Mon to Thu, 0930 to 1900; Fri, 0930 to 1700;
Sat, 0900 to 1600

Access to building, collection or gallery:
No prior appointment required

Access for disabled people:
Ramped entry

LEICESTER CITY COUNCIL

New Walk Centre, Welford Place, Leicester, LE1
6ZG

Tel: 0116 254 9922
Fax: 0116 254 5531

Website:
http://www.demontforthall.co.uk
http://www.leicester.gov.uk
http://www.leicestermuseums.ac.uk
http://www.leicesterspark.co.uk
http://www.leicester-env-city.org.uk

Enquiries:
Enquiries to: Chief Executive

Organisation type and purpose:
Local government body.

LEICESTER LONGWOOL SHEEP BREEDERS ASSOCIATION

Acronym or abbreviation: LLSBA

Driffield Agricultural Society, The Showground,
Kelley Thorpe, Driffield, East Yorkshire, YO25
9DN

Tel: 01377 257494
Fax: 01377 257464
E-mail: office@driffieldshow.co.uk

Website:
http://www.stockmaster.co.uk
Breeds of livestock with contact details.

Enquiries:
Enquiries to: Secretary

Founded:
1883

Organisation type and purpose:
Membership association (membership is by
subscription), present number of members: 81.
Breed society.

Printed publications:
Flock Book (purchase to non-members)

Publications list:
Available online

Access to staff:
Contact by letter, by telephone, by fax, by e-mail
and in person
Hours: Mon to Fri, 0900 to 1700

Connected with:
National Sheep Association (NSA)
Rare Breeds Survival Trust (RBST)

LEICESTER YMCA ADVICE & SUPPORT CENTRE

Acronym or abbreviation: YASC

Y Advice and Support Centre, The Dawn Centre,
Conduit Street, Leicester, LE2 0JN

Tel: Homeless Support: 0116 221 2787
Fax: 0116 221 2785
E-mail: via website

Website:
http://www.leicesterymca.co.uk/homeless-support
.php
The Y Advice and Support Centre and its services
for the homeless.
http://www.leicesterymca.co.uk
Full range of leicester YMCA services.

Organisation type and purpose:
Drop-in centre for homeless people, based in
Leicester city centre, close to the train station.

Subject coverage:
Practical help, such as breakfast, emergency food
parcels where possible, access to toilets, showers,
washing facilities and toiletries, free laundry
facilities for rough sleepers, a change of clothes,
access to telephone for non-personal calls. Advice
and information: help finding accommodation in
emergency or longer term, welfare benefits advice
and assistance, advice on managing debt,
information and signposting to specialist drugs
and alcohol agencies, a year-round health
promotion programme, specialist mental health
advice, help establishing identification. Education
and activities: the day centre delivers a wide range
of activities including home economics, IT, arts and
diversity, creative writing, photography and jobs
club. The sessions identify interests and
capabilities, focussing on personal development,
building on self-esteem personal achievements.
Medical Services: a full range of health services is
accessible via YASC, provided by The Homeless
Primary Healthcare Service. Psychologists and
mental health practitioners are also provided by
Leicestershire Partnership NHS Trust.

Access to staff:
Contact by letter, by telephone, by fax, in person
and via website
Hours: Mon to Fri, 0800 to 1600
Special comments: No appointment is necessary.

Access to building, collection or gallery:
Hours: Mon to Fri, 0800 to 1600

LEICESTERSHIRE ARCHAEOLOGICAL AND HISTORICAL SOCIETY

Acronym or abbreviation: LAHS

The Guildhall, Leicester, LE1 5FQ

E-mail: rjb16@le.ac.uk

Website:
http://le.ac.uk/lahs

Enquiries:
Enquiries to: Webmaster

Founded:
1855

Organisation type and purpose:
International organisation, national organisation,
learned society (membership is by subscription),
registered charity.

Subject coverage:
Archaeology; local history; Leicestershire
vernacular architecture; history of Leicester and
Leicestershire.

**Museum or gallery collection, archive, or library
special collection:**
Local History and Archaeology Library

Library catalogue:
All or part available online and in-house

Printed publications:
Leicestershire Historian (annually)
Transactions of the Society (annually)
Newsletter (2 times a year)
Order printed publications from: website: http://
www.le.ac.uk/publications/orderform.html

Publications list:
Available online

Access to staff:
Contact by letter and by e-mail
Hours: Mon to Fri, 0900 to 1700

LEICESTERSHIRE CHAMBER OF COMMERCE

Acronym or abbreviation: LCCI

1 Mill Lane, Leicester, LE2 7HU

Tel: 0116 247 1800
Fax: 0116 247 0430
E-mail: leics@chamberofcommerce.co.uk

Website:
http://www.chamberofcommerce.co.uk

Enquiries:
Enquiries to: Chief Executive

Founded:
1860

Organisation type and purpose:
Membership association (membership is by
subscription), present number of members: 1,500,
manufacturing industry, service industry.

Subject coverage:
International trade services, training, general
employment information, business networking
events.

Printed publications:
Chamber News, Business Issues

Access to staff:
Contact by letter, by telephone, by e-mail and via
website. Appointment necessary. Access for
members only.
Hours: Mon to Fri, 0900 to 1630

Access to building, collection or gallery:
Prior appointment required

LEICESTERSHIRE COUNTY COUNCIL

Acronym or abbreviation: LLIS

Libraries & Information Service, County Hall,
Glenfield, Leicester, LE3 8SS

Tel: 0116 265 7372
Fax: 0116 265 7370

Website:
http://www.leics.gov.uk/libraries

Enquiries:
Enquiries to: Chief Librarian
Other contacts: Head of Library Services for
Education for Library Services for Education/
Schools.

Organisation type and purpose:
Local government body, statutory body, public
library.

Subject coverage:
General; Leicestershire.

**Museum or gallery collection, archive, or library
special collection:**
Hunting Collection at Melton Mowbray Library

Library catalogue:
All or part available online

Printed publications:
Local History Material
Order printed publications from: Publicity and
Promotions Officer, Leicestershire Libraries and
Information Service
County Hall, tel: 0116 265 7386, fax: 0116 265 7370

Publications list:
Available in print

Access to staff:
Contact by letter, by telephone, by fax, by e-mail,
in person and via website
Hours: Mon to Fri, 0900 to 1700

Other addresses:
Library Services for Education
   929–931 Loughborough Road, Rothley, Leicester,
   LE7 7NH; tel: 0116 267 8000; fax: 0116 267 8039;
   e-mail: gwillars@leics.gov.uk

LEICESTERSHIRE LIBRARY SERVICES

Acronym or abbreviation: LLS

County Hall, Glenfield, Leicester, LE3 8SS

Tel: 0116 305 7015
Fax: 0116 305 6960
E-mail: libraries@leics.gov.uk

Website:
http://www.leics.gov.uk/libraries

Enquiries:
Enquiries to: Head of Library Services
Other contacts: Local Government Information Librarian

Organisation type and purpose:
Local government body, statutory body, public library.

Subject coverage:
General, Leicestershire.

Museum or gallery collection, archive, or library special collection:
Hunting collection at Melton Mowbray library

Library catalogue:
All or part available online

Printed publications:
Local history material

Publications list:
Available in print

Access to staff:
Contact by letter, by telephone, by fax, by e-mail, in person and via website
Hours: Mon to Fri, 0900 to 1700

Parent body:
Leicestershire County Council

LEICESTERSHIRE MUSEUMS SERVICE

County Hall, Glenfield, Leicester, LE3 8RA

Tel: 0116 265 6783
Fax: 0116 264 5820
E-mail: museums@leics.gov.uk

Website:
http://www.leics.gov.uk/museums

Enquiries:
Enquiries to: Director

Organisation type and purpose:
Local government body, museum.
Headquarters of Leicestershire Museums.

Subject coverage:
Coal mining

Museum or gallery collection, archive, or library special collection:
Library of coal-mining at Snibston Museum, Coalville

Non-library collection catalogue:
All or part available in-house

Access to staff:
Contact by letter, by telephone, by fax, by e-mail, in person and via website. Appointment necessary.
Hours: Mon to Fri, 0900 to 1630

Access to building, collection or gallery:
Prior appointment required

Access for disabled people:
Parking provided, toilet facilities

LEISURE AND OUTDOOR FURNITURE ASSOCIATION

Acronym or abbreviation: LOFA

113 Worcester Road, Chichester, PO19 5EE

Tel: 01243 839593
Fax: 01243 839467
E-mail: info@lofa.com

Website:
http://www.lofa.com
Products, members list, guide to types of garden furniture, news, code of practice.

Enquiries:
Enquiries to: Secretary

Founded:
1967

Organisation type and purpose:
Membership and trade association for companies that manufacture garden furniture, barbecues, hammocks, parasols or soft furnishings in the UK or are an exclusive or non-exclusive distributor, holding stocks in the UK, or a non-UK based company with a subsidiary or an exclusive representative, operating in the UK.

Subject coverage:
LOFA members supply an extensive selection of garden and leisure furniture in a range of materials including all types of wood, cane, cast and wrought metal, plastic and resin, and lightweight tubular metal.

Electronic and video publications:
Press releases
Order electronic and video publications from:
Download from website

Publications list:
Available online

Access to staff:
Contact by letter, by telephone, by fax and by e-mail

LEISURE DATABASE COMPANY, THE

33 Bedford Street, Covent Garden, London, WC2E 9EJ

Tel: 020 7379 3197
Fax: 020 7379 0898

Website:
http://www.theleisuredatabase.com
Company services.

Enquiries:
Enquiries to: Managing Director
Direct tel: 020 7395 6171
Other contacts: Director, Sales and Subscriptions for sales enquiries.

Founded:
1981

Organisation type and purpose:
Research organisation.
Commercial information company.
Providing the country's leading database of sports, health and fitness provision.

Subject coverage:
Sports provision, health and fitness.

Trade and statistical information:
Sport facilities charges in London.
Data on Leisure Facility Management: UK-wide.
Data on health and fitness clubs: UK-wide.
Data on public sector sports provision: UK-wide.

Printed publications:
State of the Health & Fitness Industry (annually)
Sports Facility Charges in the London Boroughs

Electronic and video publications:
Private Health Clubs UK Dataset
Local Authority Sports Venues

Publications list:
Available in print

Access to staff:
Contact by letter, by telephone, by fax and by e-mail
Hours: Mon to Fri, 0900 to 1800

LEISURE, CULTURE AND LIFELONG LEARNING

Libraries and Heritage Central Library, Lichfield Street, Walsall, West Midlands, WS1 1TR

Tel: 01922 653110
Fax: 01922 654013
E-mail: librarycentref@walsall.gov.uk

Website:
http://www.walsall.gov.uk/libraries

Enquiries:
Enquiries to: Information Officer

Founded:
1906

Organisation type and purpose:
Local government body, public library.

Subject coverage:
Tourist information, clubs and societies relating to Walsall, business information, council information, European information.

Museum or gallery collection, archive, or library special collection:
Guardian 1990–, KBE–Current, Social Trends, Times 1990– (CD-ROMs)

Non-library collection catalogue:
All or part available online

Library catalogue:
All or part available online

Printed publications:
Local Organisations Directory
How to contact your Walsall Councillor
Periodical catalogue
Tourist information for Walsall
Walsall information guides – listing clubs, societies and local organisations in Walsall

Access to staff:
Contact by letter, by telephone, by fax, by e-mail and in person
Hours: Mon to Fri, 0900 to 1700

Member organisation of:
Black Country Libraries in Partnership

LEO BAECK COLLEGE LIBRARY

Acronym or abbreviation: LBC

Sternberg Centre for Judaism, 80 East End Road, London, N3 2SY

Tel: 020 8349 5610
Fax: 020 8349 5619
E-mail: library@lbc.ac.uk

Website:
http://www.lbc.ac.uk
General information and online catalogue.

Enquiries:
Enquiries to: Librarian
Direct e-mail: annette.boeckler@lbc.ac.uk

Founded:
1956

Organisation type and purpose:
International organisation, registered charity (charity number 209777), suitable for ages: postgraduate.
Academic Judaica Library with 60,000 volumes, 40 periodicals.
Rabbinic training and Jewish college.

Subject coverage:
Jewish studies.

Information services:
Academic Judaica Library with 60.000 volumes, 40 periodicals.

Education services:
Offers Rabbinic studies, Jewish Adult learning, GCSE exams, lectures, Shiurim, MA and Advanced Diploma courses, Early Years courses in Jewish education

continued overleaf

Museum or gallery collection, archive, or library special collection:
Library: 30,000 books, pamphlets, etc.

Library catalogue:
All or part available online

Printed publications:
Annual diary
A selection of Jewish Educational material
Book Series
European Judaism (learned journal, twice yearly)
Shalom Batsheva (a girl's life during the war; price £4.50)

Electronic and video publications:
Jewish Heritage Video (intermediate age, lower secondary, four videos for £15)
The Western Wall Video (Jerusalem, the city of three great faiths; price £7.50)

Publications list:
Available online and in print

Access to staff:
Appointment necessary.
Hours: Mon to Fri, 0900 to 1700

LEONARD CHESHIRE

Head Office, 66 South Lambeth Road, London, SW8 1RL

Tel: 020 3242 0200
Fax: 020 3242 0250
E-mail: info@lcdisability.org

Website:
http://www.leonard-cheshire.org
Information on Leonard Cheshire's services and activities.

Enquiries:
Enquiries to: Information Resources Officer

Founded:
1948

Organisation type and purpose:
Voluntary organisation.
To provide choice and opportunity to people with disabilities, emphasising the right of the individual to decide how he or she wants to live.

Subject coverage:
Operating in 55 countries worldwide. It promotes the care, general well-being and rehabilitation of people with physical and learning disabilities. In the UK the Foundation comprises 85 Cheshire Homes offering a range of care services, including full-time residential care, respite and day care and short-stay holiday breaks. Some of these also offer accommodation for full or semi-independent living with all the advantages of separate housing combined with 24 hour help close at hand if needed. In addition, there are a growing number of Care at Home Services (37 in 1993) which provide personal care and undertake day to day tasks for people with disabilities in their own homes.

Museum or gallery collection, archive, or library special collection:
Personal Collection of Founder, Group Captain Leonard Cheshire VC, available in hardcopy, microform; also audiovisual and photographs available
Administrative Archive of organisations he founded: Leonard Cheshire, Ryder-Cheshire and World Memorial Fund

Non-library collection catalogue:
All or part available in-house

Printed publications:
Variety of leaflets and reports (free)
International Services Directory
Leonard Cheshire Service Directory
The Hidden World (Cheshire L)
Still the Candle Burns (Beslievre J)
Rydale Pilgrimage (52 prints of Yorkshire churches with personal impressions, history and architecture, Goodall D)

Electronic and video publications:
Enabling Ordinary Lives (video, free plus £3.95 for p&p)
Database of services available

Publications list:
Available in print

Access to staff:
Contact by letter, by telephone, by fax, by e-mail and via website
Hours: Mon to Fri, 0900 to 1700

Access to building, collection or gallery:
Prior appointment required

Access for disabled people:
Parking provided, level entry, access to all public areas, toilet facilities

LEONARD CHESHIRE DISABILITY ARCHIVE

Leonard Cheshire Disability Archive Centre, Newlands House, Main Street, Netherseal, DE12 8DA

Tel: 01283 763951
Fax: 01283 763951
E-mail: archive@lcdisability.org

Website:
http://www.lcdisability.org/?lid=21
http://www.leonard-cheshire.org

Enquiries:
Enquiries to: Honorary Secretary
Other contacts: Archivist

Founded:
1948

Organisation type and purpose:
International organisation, voluntary organisation, registered charity (charity number 218186).
The archive of The Leonard Cheshire Foundation. The parent body The Leonard Cheshire Foundation offers services to people with disabilities.

Subject coverage:
Leonard Cheshire (the man), Group Captain Lord Cheshire of Woodhall, VC OM DSO DFC.
Leonard Cheshire Foundation's work; Ryder-Cheshire Foundation's work; services for people with disabilities provided by these organisations.

Non-library collection catalogue:
All or part available in-house

Printed publications:
Order printed publications from: National Information Officer, Leonard Cheshire, 30 Millbank, London, SW1P 4QD; tel: 020 7802 8200

Electronic and video publications:
Enabling Ordinary Lives – details, aims and scope of Leonard Cheshire – Outlines products and services (CD-ROM and tape)

Access to staff:
Contact by letter, by telephone and by fax.
Appointment necessary.
Hours: Mon to Fri, 0900 to 1700
Special comments: Some material on restricted access.

Access to building, collection or gallery:
No prior appointment required

Other address:
Leonard Cheshire Disability
66 South Lambeth Road, London, SW8 1RL; tel: 020 3242 0200; fax: 020 3242 0250

LEPRA HEALTH IN ACTION

Acronym or abbreviation: LEPRA

28 Middleborough, Colchester, CO1 1TG

Tel: 01206 216732
Fax: 01206 762151
E-mail: lepra@leprahealthinaction.org

Website:
http://www.leprahealthinaction.org
LEPRA Health in Action is a medical development charity restoring health, hope and dignity to people affected by diseases of poverty, including leprosy, lymphatic filariasis, malaria, TB and HIV/AIDS.

Enquiries:
Enquiries to: Information Officer
Direct e-mail: irenea@leprahealthinaction.org
Other contacts: Communications Officer; Direct Marketing Officer

Founded:
1924

Formerly called:
British Leprosy Relief Association (year of change 2008)

Organisation type and purpose:
Registered charity (number 213251 in England and Wales and SC039715 in Scotland).
Restoring health, hope and dignity to people affected by leprosy and other diseases of poverty.

Subject coverage:
Health education, advocacy, research into treatment of diseases of poverty.

Printed publications:
Leprosy Review (quarterly: Mar, Jun, Sep, Dec, £45 per year, or £12 per issue)
Order printed publications from: website: http://www.leprahealthinaction.org/category/information/leprosy-review

Publications list:
Available online

Access to staff:
Contact by letter, by telephone, by fax, by e-mail, in person and via website
Hours: Mon to Fri, 0900 to 1700

Access for disabled people:
Disabled Access

Subsidiary body:
LEPRA India
Post Box 1518, Krishnapuri Colony, West Marredpally, Secunderabad, 500 026, India; tel: +91 040 44586060 / 27802139 / 27807314; fax: +91 040 27801391; e-mail: info@leprahealthinaction.in; website: https://leprasociety.org

LEPROSY MISSION INTERNATIONAL

Acronym or abbreviation: TLM

80 Windmill Road, Brentford, Middlesex, TW8 0QH

Tel: 020 8326 6767
Fax: 020 8326 6777
E-mail: friends@tlmint.org

Website:
http://www.leprosymission.org
Information on organisation and the disease of leprosy; national office contacts.

Enquiries:
Enquiries to: Communications Manager
Other contacts: Director for Knowledge Management

Founded:
1874

Organisation type and purpose:
International organisation, voluntary organisation, registered charity.
To minister in the name of Jesus Christ to people affected by leprosy.

Subject coverage:
Leprosy (Hansen's disease), historical, medical, current field work.

Museum or gallery collection, archive, or library special collection:
Library of Leprosy-related books and archive of organisation

Archive photographs dating from 1890s to present
TLM's annual reports (dating back to early 1900s)

Printed publications:
Magazines and information packs for general
public
Books sold through TLM Trading Catalogue

Publications list:
Available in print

Access to staff:
Contact via website. Appointment necessary.
Hours: Mon to Fri, 0900 to 1700

Access for disabled people:
Parking provided, ramped entry, level entry, access
to all public areas, toilet facilities

Also at:
Leprosy Mission England and Wales (includes The
Channel Islands and The Isle of Man)
 Goldhay Way, Orton Goldhay, Peterborough,
 Cambridgeshire, PE2 5GZ; tel: 01733 370505; fax:
 01733 404880; e-mail: post@tlmew.org.uk;
 website: http://www.leprosymission.org.uk
Leprosy Mission Northern Ireland
 Lagan House, 2A Queens Road, Lisburn, BT27
 4TZ; tel: 028 9038 1842; e-mail: info@tlm-ni.org;
 website: http://www.tlm-ni.org
Leprosy Mission Scotland
 Suite 2, Earlsgate Lodge, Livilands Lane, Stirling,
 FK8 2BG; tel: 01786 449266; e-mail: office@
 tlmscotland.org.uk; website: http://www
 .tlmscotland.org.uk

Member organisation of:
Global Connections
 Whitefield House, 186 Kennington Park Road,
 London, SE11 4BT; tel: 020 7207 2157; 020 8133
 2958; website: http://www.globalconnections.co
 .uk
International Federation of Anti-Leprosy
Associations (ILEP)
 234 Blythe Road, London, W14 0HJ

LESOTHO HIGH COMMISSION

7 Chesham Place, London, SW1X 8HN

Tel: 020 7235 5686
Fax: 020 7235 5023
E-mail: lhc@lesotholondon.org.uk

Website:
http://www.lesotholondon.org.uk

Enquiries:
Enquiries to: First Secretary
Other contacts: First Secretary, Information Officer

Founded:
1966

Organisation type and purpose:
International organisation, national government
body.
Diplomatic mission.

Subject coverage:
Lesotho.

Access to staff:
Contact by letter, by telephone, by fax, by e-mail
and via website. Appointment necessary.
Hours: Mon to Fri, 0900 to 1245 and 1400 to 1600

Access to building, collection or gallery:
No access other than to staff

LEUKAEMIA & LYMPHOMA RESEARCH

Acronym or abbreviation: L&LR

43 Great Ormond Street, London, WC1N 3JJ

Tel: 020 7405 0101
Fax: 020 7405 3139
E-mail: info@llresearch.org.uk

Website:
http://www.llresearch.org.uk

Enquiries:
Enquiries to: Clinical Information Specialist

Direct tel: 020 7269 9060
Direct e-mail: kcampbell@llresearch.org.uk

Founded:
1960

Formerly called:
Leukaemia Research Fund, Leukaemia Research

Organisation type and purpose:
National organisation, voluntary organisation,
registered charity (charity number 216032),
research organisation.
Improving treatment, finding cures and causes of
leukaemia, lymphoma, myeloma, myelodysplasia,
myeloproliferative disorders and aplastic anaemia.

Subject coverage:
Leukaemia, acute leukaemia in children, coping
with childhood leukaemia, acute lymphoblastic
leukaemia, acute myeloid leukaemia, chronic
myeloid leukaemia, bone marrow and stem cell
transplantation, the lymphomas, multiple
myeloma, myelodysplastic syndromes, aplastic
anaemia, dictionary of leukaemia and related
diseases, chronic lymphocytic leukaemia, less
common disorders related to leukaemia,
myeloproliferature disorders.

Information services:
Information on leukaemia, lymphoma, myeloma
and related conditions

Special visitor services:
None

Services for disabled people:
None

Printed publications:
Abstracts of Research Workshops
Annual Guest Lectures
Annual Review
Booklets and leaflets on each of the several types of
 leukaemia, lymphoma, myeloma and related
 conditions (free)
Newsletters
Proceedings of International Symposia

Publications list:
Available online and in print

Access to staff:
Contact by letter, by telephone, by fax, by e-mail,
in person and via website
Hours: Mon to Fri, 0930 to 1645

Access to building, collection or gallery:
No public access

Member organisation of:
UK Co-ordinating Committee for Cancer Research,
Cancer Campaigning Group

LEUKAEMIA CARE SOCIETY

2 Shrubbery Avenue, Worcester, WR1 1QH

Tel: 01905 330003 or Care Line: 0800 1696680
Fax: 01905 330090
E-mail: enquiries@leukaemiacare.org.uk

Website:
http://www.leukaemiacare.org.uk

Enquiries:
Enquiries to: Network Operations Manager
Direct e-mail: Dawn.knott@leukaemiacare.org.uk

Founded:
1967

Organisation type and purpose:
Voluntary organisation, registered charity (charity
number 259483).

Subject coverage:
Information about leukaemia and allied blood
disorders, friendship, support and practical help
for sufferers and their relatives, caravan holidays,
limited financial assistance.

Printed publications:
Brochure and leaflets (free)
Newsletter (free, 2 times a year)

Access to staff:
Contact by letter, by telephone, by fax, by e-mail
and via website. Appointment necessary.
Hours: 0900 to 1630
Special comments: Telephone diversion outside
office hours.

LEUKAEMIA RESEARCH UNIT

Centre for Adult Leukaemia, Hammersmith
Hospital/Imperial College, Du Cane Road,
London, W12 0NN

Tel: 020 8383 3238
Fax: 020 8740 9679

Enquiries:
Enquiries to: Chairman

Founded:
1988

Organisation type and purpose:
Professional body, university department or
institute.

Subject coverage:
Leukaemia.

Printed publications:
Order printed publications from: Chairman,
Department of Haematology
Imperial College School of Medicine,
Hammersmith Hospital, Du Cane Road, London,
W12 0NN

LEWIS CARROLL SOCIETY

Acronym or abbreviation: LCS

50 Lauderdale Mansions, Lauderdale Road,
London, W9 1NE

E-mail: markrichards@aznet.co.uk

Website:
http://lewiscarrollsociety.org.uk

Enquiries:
Enquiries to: Chairman

Founded:
1969

Organisation type and purpose:
International organisation, learned society
(membership is by subscription), present number
of members: 450, registered charity (charity
number 266239), suitable for all ages.

Subject coverage:
Charles Dodgson: life and works (Lewis Carroll).

Printed publications:
Bandersnatch (newsletter, quarterly)
Lewis Carroll Review (reviewing journal,
 occasional)
The Carrollian (journal, half-yearly)

Publications list:
Available online and in print

Access to staff:
Contact by letter, by e-mail and via website
Hours: Mon to Fri, 0900 to 1700

LEWISHAM LOCAL HISTORY AND ARCHIVES CENTRE

Lewisham Library, 199–201 Lewisham High Street,
London, SE13 6LG

Tel: 020 8314 8509/8501
Fax: 020 8297 1169
E-mail: local.studies@lewisham.gov.uk

Website:
http://www.lewisham.gov.uk

Enquiries:
Enquiries to: Archivist

Founded:
1960

continued overleaf

Organisation type and purpose:
Local government body, public library.
Archives.
Archive and local studies service for the London Borough of Lewisham.

Subject coverage:
London Borough of Lewisham; history.

Museum or gallery collection, archive, or library special collection:
Archives of the Borough and predecessor authorities, and of organisations within the Borough
Local studies material relating to the Borough
Small museum collection

Non-library collection catalogue:
All or part available online and in-house

Library catalogue:
All or part available online and in-house

Publications list:
Available online and in print

Access to staff:
Contact by letter, by telephone, by fax, by e-mail and in person
Hours: Mon, 1000 to 1700; Fri, Sat, 0900 to 1700; Tue and Thu, 0900 to 2000
Special comments: Appointments advised.

Access for disabled people:
Access to all public areas

Parent body:
London Borough of Lewisham
  London, SE6

LEWISHAM REFERENCE LIBRARY

199–201 Lewisham High Street, London, SE13 6LG

Tel: 020 8297 9430
Fax: 020 8314 8556
E-mail: reference.library@lewisham.gov.uk

Website:
http://www.lewisham.gov.uk
Information about Lewisham as a local authority.

Enquiries:
Enquiries to: Reference Librarian

Organisation type and purpose:
Local government body, public library.

Subject coverage:
Arts, humanities and social sciences, specialist holding at Library Service Bookstore, Hither Green Lane, London SE13 6TJ: biology.

Library catalogue:
All or part available in-house

Access to staff:
Contact by telephone, by e-mail and in person
Hours: Mon, 1000 to 2000; Tue, Thu, 0900 to 2000; Wed, Fri, 0900 to 1800; Sat, 0900 to 1700; Sun, 1300 to 1600

Access for disabled people:
Parking provided, level entry, access to all public areas, toilet facilities

Member organisation of:
South East Area Libraries Information Service

LGC

Formal name: LGC

Queens Road, Teddington, Middlesex, TW11 0LY

Tel: 020 8943 7000
Fax: 020 8943 2767
E-mail: info@lgc.co.uk

Website:
http://www.lgc.co.uk

Enquiries:
Enquiries to: Client Services

Organisation type and purpose:
International organisation, statutory body, service industry, training organisation, consultancy, research organisation.

Subject coverage:
Analytical chemistry, methods of analysis: wines, soft drinks, spirits, beer, sugar composites, foods, pesticide formulations and residues, drug analysis, radionuclides in water, water analysis, environmental analysis and advice, contaminated land analysis, background information on a wide variety of products, including plastics, chemicals, hydrocarbon and essential oils, safety and health, analytical quality control and certified reference materials, lifesciences (DNA services) and analytical molecular biology.

Library catalogue:
All or part available in-house

Printed publications:
Annual Report
Corporate Brochure
Annual Review of the Government Chemist

Publications list:
Available in print

Access to staff:
Contact by letter, by telephone, by fax and by e-mail
Hours: Mon to Fri, 0900 to 1730

Access to building, collection or gallery:
No access other than to staff

LIBERAL DEMOCRATS

4 Cowley Street, London, SW1P 3NB

Tel: 020 7222 7999
Fax: 020 7799 2170
E-mail: libdems@cix.co.uk

Website:
http://www.libdems.org.uk

Enquiries:
Enquiries to: Information Officer
Direct tel: 020 7227 1385

Organisation type and purpose:
Membership association (membership is by subscription), present number of members: 90,000.
Political party.

Subject coverage:
Party policy, party structure and organisation, party history.

Museum or gallery collection, archive, or library special collection:
Liberal Party archive held at London School of Economics and Political Science Library, Houghton Street, London, WC2A 2AE
SDP archive held at Albert Sloman Library, University of Essex

Printed publications:
Handbook and Directory
Liberal Democrat News (weekly, on subscription)
Policy papers, policy briefings, annual report
Order printed publications from: Liberal Democrat Publications
4 Cowley Street, London, SW1P 3NB, tel: 020 7222 7999, fax: 020 7799 2170, e-mail: ld-membservs@cix.co.uk

Publications list:
Available in print

Access to staff:
Contact by letter, by telephone, by fax, by e-mail and via website
Hours: Mon to Fri, 0930 to 1730

Full member of the:
Federation of European Liberal Democrat and Reform Parties (ELDR)
  Building Leo (D2), 55C rue Wiertz, Brussels, B-1047, Belgium; tel: + 322 284 3169; fax: + 322 231 1907

Liberal International (LI)
  1 Whitehall Place, London, SW1A 2HE; tel: 020 7839 5905; fax: 020 7925 2685; e-mail: worldlib@cix.co.uk

Other addresses:
Liberal Democrats, Wales
  Bay View House, 102 Bute Street, Cardiff, CF1 6AD; tel: 029 2031 3400; fax: 029 2031 3401; e-mail: ldwales@cix.co.uk
Scottish Liberal Democrats
  4 Clifton Terrace, Edinburgh, EH12 5DR; tel: 0131 337 2314; fax: 0131 337 3566; e-mail: scotlibdem@cix.co.uk; website: www.scotlibdems.org.uk

LIBERAL INTERNATIONAL

Acronym or abbreviation: LI

1 Whitehall Place, London, SW1A 2HD

Tel: 020 7839 5905
Fax: 020 7925 2685
E-mail: all@liberal-international.org

Website:
http://www.liberal-international.org
The official homepage of more than 83 liberal parties and youth organisations worldwide.

Enquiries:
Enquiries to: Secretary General
Other contacts: (1) Programme Officer (2) Political Assistant for (1) specific information about member parties (2) specific information about member parties and general information.

Founded:
1947

Organisation type and purpose:
International organisation.
A global network of Liberals as well as the world union of Liberal parties. It acts as a platform and political meeting point and represents its member parties. The main goal of the organisation is the promotion of Liberal values.

Subject coverage:
International liberalism, human rights, democratisation, tolerance, freedom and an economy based on market principles.

Museum or gallery collection, archive, or library special collection:
Basic documents on liberal ideology

Printed publications:
A Sense of Liberty: The History of Liberal International
Giovanni Malagodi
Liberalism in the World (annual)
London Aerogramme (6 times a year)
Reports and brochures
The Local Politics Toolbox
Various Leaflets

Access to staff:
Contact by letter, by telephone, by fax, by e-mail and via website. Access for members only.
Hours: Mon to Fri, 0900 to 1700

Access to building, collection or gallery:
No access other than to staff

LIBERAL JUDAISM

The Montagu Centre, 21 Maple Street, London, W1T 4BE

Tel: 020 7580 1663
Fax: 020 7631 9838
E-mail: montagu@liberaljudaism.org

Website:
http://www.liberaljudaism.org

Enquiries:
Enquiries to: Office Manager
Direct tel: 020 7631 9822
Direct e-mail: s.o'dwyer@liberaljudaism.org

Founded:
1902

Organisation type and purpose:
International organisation, membership association (membership is by subscription), present number of members: over 9,000, voluntary organisation, registered charity (charity number 236590), publishing house.
National organisation of synagogues.

Subject coverage:
Progressive Judaism in Great Britain, education, Liberal Judaism.

Printed publications:
Books and prayer books
From Belsen to Buckingham Palace (Oppenheimer P)
Judaism for Today
On Being Jewish (Neuberger J)
The Illuminated Haggadah
The People's Bible
Liberal Judaism: A Judaism for the 21st Century
Liberal Judaism: The First 100 Years
Order printed publications from: Liberal Judaism, at the same address; e-mail: books@liberaljudaism .org

Electronic and video publications:
How to do Seder (tape and booklet)
This is Liberal Judaism (CD-Rom)

Publications list:
Available online and in print

Access to staff:
Contact by letter, by fax, by e-mail and in person
Hours: Mon to Thu, 0900 to 1700; Fri, 0900 to 1500

Access to building, collection or gallery:
No access other than to staff

Affiliated to:
World Union for Progressive Judaism

LIBERTARIAN ALLIANCE

Acronym or abbreviation: LA

Suite 35, 2 Lansdowne Mews, Mayfair, London, W1J 6HL

Tel: 07956 472199
E-mail: sean@libertarian.co.uk

Website:
http://www.libertarian.co.uk

Enquiries:
Enquiries to: Director

Founded:
1965

Organisation type and purpose:
Voluntary organisation, publishing house.
Political organisation, radical pro-free market and civil libertarian group.

Subject coverage:
Libertarian issues, civil and economic liberties, free market economics, data base on scholars, scholarship and organisations in these areas.

Museum or gallery collection, archive, or library special collection:
Photographs of leading contemporary and historical Libertarian and Classical Liberal scholars and writers

Printed publications:
Irregular notes, guides, and other publications covering:
Political notes
Philosophical notes
Legal notes
Cultural notes
Historical notes
Sociological notes
Foreign Policy Perspectives
Libertarian Fictions, etc.

Publications list:
Available online and in print

Access to staff:
Contact by letter, by telephone and by e-mail. Appointment necessary.

Hours: Mon to Fri, 0900 to 1700

Affiliated to:
International Society for Individual Liberty
Libertarian International
Liberty: The National Council for Civil Liberties

Subsidiary body:
British Association of Libertarian Feminists

LIBERTY

Formal name: National Council for Civil Liberties

21 Tabard Street, Borough, London, SE1 4LA

Tel: 020 7403 3888
Fax: 020 7407 5354
E-mail: info@liberty-human-rights.org.uk

Website:
http://www.liberty-human-rights.org.uk
Campaigns and lobbying; human rights test cases; policy; events and legal training; lawyers for liberty.

Enquiries:
Enquiries to: Information Officer

Founded:
1934

Organisation type and purpose:
National organisation, membership association (membership is by subscription), present number of members: 7000.
Commissions and publishes research, and runs the Civil Liberties Library.

Subject coverage:
Civil liberties, especially administration of justice, children's rights, women's rights and sex discrimination, race discrimination, discrimination against homosexuals, police powers, official secrecy and freedom of information, privacy; Bill of Rights; human rights, prisoners' rights, academic freedom, securing services, Northern Ireland, public order, policing, criminal justice.

Museum or gallery collection, archive, or library special collection:
Collection of publications since the foundation in 1934

Library catalogue:
All or part available in-house

Printed publications:
Civil Liberty (newsletter, quarterly)
Judging Inequality (book)
Bibliography of Civil Liberties Teaching Material
Bibliographies from the database
Annual Report, covering current research and education projects

Publications list:
Available in print

Access to staff:
Contact by letter. Appointment necessary. All charged.
Hours: Mon to Fri, 1000 to 1300 and 1400 to 1730

Affiliated to:
International League for Human Rights

Charitable arm is the:
Civil Liberties Trust

Established by members of, and shares premises with, the:
National Council of Civil Liberties

LIBRARY AND MUSEUM OF FREEMASONRY

Formal name: Library and Museum Charitable Trust of the United Grand Lodge

Freemasons' Hall, Great Queen Street, London, WC2B 5AZ

Tel: 020 7395 9251
Fax: 020 7404 7418
E-mail: libmus@ugle.org.uk

Website:
http://www.freemasonry.london.museum

Enquiries:
Enquiries to: Director
Other contacts: Librarian f(or research queries)

Founded:
1996

Organisation type and purpose:
Professional body, registered charity (charity number 1058497), museum.
Research library.

Subject coverage:
Freemasonry, historical record and information, extensive library and artefact collection.

Non-library collection catalogue:
All or part available in-house

Library catalogue:
All or part available in-house

Access to staff:
Contact by letter, by telephone, by fax and in person. All charged.
Hours: Mon to Fri, 1000 to 1700

LIBRARY CAMPAIGN

22 Upper Woburn Place, London, WC1H 0TB

Tel: 0845 450 5946
Fax: 0845 450 5946
E-mail: librarycam@aol.com

Website:
http://www.librarycampaign.com

Enquiries:
Enquiries to: Secretary

Founded:
1984

Organisation type and purpose:
Registered Charity (England and Wales no. 1102634), national organisation, advisory body, membership association (membership is by subscription), present number of members: 600, voluntary organisation.
Charitable aims: to advance the lifelong education of the public by the promotion, support, assistance and improvement of libraries, and through the activities of friends and user groups; to be the national voice of users of library services through a network of local groups; to co-ordinate a network of Friends of Library Groups.

Subject coverage:
Information on local user groups for libraries, where they are and how to start a group.

Printed publications:
Handbook for Library Friends and User Groups
The Library Campaigner (journal, 2–3 a year)
Various leaflets

Access to staff:
Contact by letter, by telephone and by e-mail
Special comments: 24-hour answerphone. The Campaign is run by volunteers

Access to building, collection or gallery:
None – address is accommodation address only

Member organisations:
Has approximately 40 local organisations

LIBRARY OF AVALON

Acronym or abbreviation: LOA

Rear Courtyard, Above 2–4 High Street, Glastonbury, Somerset, BA6 9DU

Tel: 01458 832759
E-mail: librarian@libraryofavalon.org.uk

Website:
http://www.libraryofavalon.org.uk
Book catalogue, general information.

Enquiries:
Enquiries to: Honorary Secretary

continued overleaf

Other contacts: Events Co-ordinator for Library of Avalon annual short story and poetry competition

Founded:
1988

Organisation type and purpose:
Membership association (membership is by subscription), present number of members: 109, voluntary organisation, registered charity (charity number 1065014).

Subject coverage:
Arthurian and related subjects; earth mysteries; history and archaeology; alternative and complementary medicine; psychology, personal development, social psychology; astrology; occult and esoteric thought and studies, including magical practice and theory; mythology; comparative religion including paganism; eastern religion and philosophy; Glastonbury.

Museum or gallery collection, archive, or library special collection:
A selection of magazines on paganism and earth mysteries (reference only)
Book catalogue held on database (title, author and publisher details only, no text)
Wessex research group collection
Willem Koppejan collection
Rilko collection

Non-library collection catalogue:
All or part available online and in-house

Library catalogue:
All or part available in-house

Publications list:
Available online

Access to staff:
Contact by letter, by telephone, by e-mail, in person and via website
Hours: Mon, Wed, Thu, 1330 to 1630; Tue, 1100 to 16.30; Fri, 1200 to 1700; Sat, 1200 to 1600; Sun (most; tel. to check), 1200 to 1500
Special comments: Specialist library open to the public with reading room, but only members may take publications out of the building.

Access to building, collection or gallery:
Hours: as above

Access for disabled people:
Ramped entry

LIBRARY RESEARCH AGENCY

Burberry, Devon Road, Salcombe, Devon, TQ8 8HJ

Tel: 01548 842769
Fax: 01548 842536

Enquiries:
Enquiries to: Managing Director

Founded:
1983

Organisation type and purpose:
Public library, university library, university department or institute, research organisation.

Subject coverage:
Research in French, German, Russian, Serbo-Croat, Bulgarian languages, from major libraries, cryptology, cryptanalysis.

Access to staff:
Contact by letter, by telephone and by fax
Hours: Mon to Fri, 0900 to 1700

LICENSED TAXI DRIVERS ASSOCIATION

Acronym or abbreviation: LTDA

LTDA Taxi House, Woodfield Road, London, W9 2BA

Tel: 020 7286 1046
Fax: 020 7286 2494
E-mail: via website

Website:
http://www.ltda.co.uk
Benefits of membership, campaigns.

Organisation type and purpose:
Trade association for licensed taxi drivers.

Subject coverage:
Offers legal representation, leisure discounts, tax investigations, insurance.

Access to staff:
Contact by letter, by telephone, by fax and via website

LICHFIELD DISTRICT COUNCIL

District Council House, Frog Lane, Lichfield, Staffordshire, WS13 6YU

Tel: 01543 308000; minicom no. 01543 308078
Fax: 01543 309899
E-mail: enquiries@lichfielddc.gov.uk

Enquiries:
Enquiries to: Chief Executive

Founded:
1974

Organisation type and purpose:
Local government body.

Subject coverage:
All functions of the local authority; planning, economic development, leisure and environmental health.

Access to staff:
Contact by letter, by telephone and by fax.
Appointment necessary.
Hours: Mon to Fri, 0845 to 1715

Access for disabled people:
Parking provided, ramped entry, toilet facilities

LICHFIELD RECORD OFFICE

Acronym or abbreviation: LRO

The Friary, Lichfield, Staffordshire, WS13 6QG

Tel: 01543 510720
Fax: 01543 510716
E-mail: lichfield.record.office@staffordshire.gov.uk

Website:
http://www.staffordshire.gov.uk/archives/lich.htm

Enquiries:
Enquiries to: Area Archivist

Founded:
1959

Organisation type and purpose:
Local government body. To preserve and make available archives of the diocese of Lichfield and archives created in, and/or relating to, the city of Lichfield and the town of Burton upon Trent and their surrounding areas.

Subject coverage:
Ecclesiastical, social, economic and political history of the diocese and City of Lichfield and of Burton upon Trent; genealogy.

Non-library collection catalogue:
All or part available online, in-house and in print

Printed publications:
Directly for purchase

Publications list:
Available online and in print

Access to staff:
Contact by letter, by telephone, by fax, by e-mail and in person. Appointment necessary.

Access to building, collection or gallery:
Hours: Mon, Tue, Wed and Fri, 0930 to 1700; Thu, 1130 to 1900; 2nd Sat of each month, 0930 to 1230
Special comments: Some records closed for 30 or more years from latest date.

Branches:
Staffordshire Record Office
Eastgate Street, Stafford; tel: 01785 278379; e-mail: staffordshire.record.office@staffordshire
.gov.uk
Stoke on Trent Archives
tel: 01782 238420; e-mail: stoke.archives@stoke
.gov.uk

Parent body:
Staffordshire and Stoke on Trent Archive Service

LIDDELL HART CENTRE FOR MILITARY ARCHIVES

Acronym or abbreviation: LHCMA

King's College London, Strand, London, WC2R 2LS

Tel: 020 7848 2015
Fax: 020 7848 2760
E-mail: archives.web@kcl.ac.uk

Website:
http://www.kcl.ac.uk/iss/archives
Summary guides to all collections, detailed catalogues of main collections.

Enquiries:
Enquiries to: Director of Archives and Information Management

Founded:
1964

Subject coverage:
Archive repository for the papers of senior defence personnel, authors and commentators on international security and defence policy, with the scope of the holdings ranging from high-level defence policy and strategic planning, to the command of individual units in the field in almost every major campaign in which British troops have fought from 1900 to present day. Additional material on the history of science and journalism, and the study of racial interaction and colonial administration.

Museum or gallery collection, archive, or library special collection:
The Centre holds the papers of over 700 senior defence personnel, including:
Sir Basil Liddell Hart (1895–1970)
FM Lord Alanbrooke (1883–1993)
FM Lord Allenby (1861–1936)
ACM Sir Robert Brooke-Popham (1878–1953)
Sir Arthur Bryant (1899–1985)
Sir Frank Cooper (1922–2002)
Maj-Gen. J. F. C. Fuller (1878–1966)
Gen. Sir Ian Hamilton (1853–1947)
Gen. Lord Ismay (1887–1965)
Gen. Sir Richard O'Connor (1889–1981)
FM Lord Milne (1866–1948)
FM Sir Archibald Montgomery-Massingberd (1871–1947)
FM Sir William Robertson (1860–1933)
Gen. Sir Hugh Stockwell (1903–1986)
Television documentary archives include:
The Nuclear Age (1989)
The Death of Yugoslavia (1995)
The Washington Version (1992) (Gulf War)
The Fall of the Wall (1994)

Non-library collection catalogue:
All or part available online

Access to staff:
Contact by letter, by telephone, by fax, by e-mail and via website. Appointment necessary. Letter of introduction required.
Hours: Mon to Fri, 0930 to 1730

Access for disabled people:
Level entry, toilet facilities

LIFE

LIFE House, 1 Mill Street, Leamington Spa, Warwickshire, CV31 1ES

Tel: 01926 421587
Fax: 01926 336497

E-mail: info@lifecharity.org.uk

Website:
http://www.lifecharity.org.uk

Enquiries:
Enquiries to: Trustee
Other contacts: Research Officer

Founded:
1970

Organisation type and purpose:
Voluntary organisation, registered charity.
Opposed to all direct abortion and offering free
practical help to women with unplanned
pregnancies. Counselling before and after abortion.
Accommodation for homeless pregnant women.

Subject coverage:
Abortion, pregnancy, birth, counselling after
abortion, housing single mothers, infertility,
fertility control, infertility treatment, school talks
and study days.

Printed publications:
A wide range of leaflets about different aspects of
abortion and 'Life' issues
LIFE News (journal, four times a year)

Electronic and video publications:
Life in the Millennium
Life, what it does and why
Whose choice is it anyway? (video, £15)

Access to staff:
Contact by letter, by telephone, by fax, by e-mail
and via website
Hours: Mon to Fri, 0900 to 1700

LIFE EDUCATION CENTRES

Acronym or abbreviation: LEC

1st Floor, 53–56 Great Sutton Street, London, EC1V
0DG

Tel: 020 7490 3210
Fax: 020 7490 3610

Website:
Information on LEC.

Enquiries:
Enquiries to: Director of Research
Direct e-mail: enquiries@lifeeducation.org.uk

Founded:
1979

Organisation type and purpose:
Registered charity (charity number 800727),
suitable for ages: 3 to 15, training organisation,
publishing house.
Drug prevention charity for children, schools and
families.

Subject coverage:
Drug prevention (theory, research), drug
information (effects etc), evaluation of drug
prevention programmes.

**Museum or gallery collection, archive, or library
special collection:**
Drug prevention and research: books, reports,
journals, newspaper clippings

Trade and statistical information:
Statistical information on drug use (especially
youth).
Data on prevention programme effects (especially
LEC).

Printed publications:
Being Yourself: A Teenage Pregnancy Prevention
Pack
Body System Posters
Day of the Dinosaur: introduction for 9–12 year
olds to HIV studies
Harold the Giraffe Activity Books, Songbook and
Cassette
How to Talk to Your Child About Drugs: The Life
Education Parents' Guide
Taking Care; An HIV/AIDS Pack for Teaching 10–
12 year olds
Order printed publications from: Publications
Manager, Life Education Centres

at the same address

Electronic and video publications:
Ozone (CD-ROM)
You Make the Difference (LEC's Video guide for
parents and carers)
Harold's Greatest Hits (cassette)

Publications list:
Available in print

Access to staff:
Contact by letter, by telephone and by fax
Hours: Mon to Fri, 0900 to 1700

Parent body:
Life Education International (LEI)

LIFETIME MANAGEMENT OF
MATERIALS ADVISORY SERVICE

Acronym or abbreviation: LMM

National Physical Laboratory, Hampton Road,
Teddington, Middlesex, TW11 0LW

Tel: 020 8943 6142
E-mail: lmm@npl.co.uk

Website:
http://www.npl.co.uk/npl/lmmt/aqueous/
about_ncs.html

Enquiries:
Enquiries to: Executive Secretary
Direct tel: 020 8943 6179

Founded:
1975

Formerly called:
National Corrosion Service (year of change 2007)

Organisation type and purpose:
Advisory body, consultancy, research organisation.
The United Kingdom's gateway to corrosion,
materials expertise and advice.

Subject coverage:
Corrosion control and prevention; design and
selection of materials; coating systems; cathodic
protection; environmental factors; failure analysis
and investigations.

Printed publications:
Avoidance of Corrosion in Plumbing Systems
(free)
Guide to Stress Corrosion Cracking
Guide to Bimetallic Corrosion
Corrosion in Pumps and Valves
Checklist for Corrosion Control
Protection of Structural Steelwork

Publications list:
Available online and in print

Access to staff:
Contact by letter, by telephone, by fax, by e-mail
and via website. Appointment necessary.
Hours: Mon to Fri, 0900 to 1700

Constituent part of:
Serco Group plc
Serco House, 16 Bartley Wood Business Park,
Hook, Hants, RG27 9UY

LIFT AND ESCALATOR INDUSTRY
ASSOCIATION

Acronym or abbreviation: LEIA

33–34 Devonshire Street, London, W1G 6PY

Tel: 020 7935 3013
Fax: 020 7935 3321
E-mail: enquiries@leia.co.uk

Enquiries:
Enquiries to: Director

Founded:
1997

Organisation type and purpose:
Trade association, present number of members: c.
150.

Subject coverage:
Lifts, escalators, passenger conveyors, safety,
design and standardisation.

Access to staff:
Contact by letter, by telephone and by fax
Hours: Mon to Fri, 0900 to 1700

Member of:
Specialist Engineering Contractors Group

LIFTING EQUIPMENT ENGINEERS
ASSOCIATION

Acronym or abbreviation: LEEA

3 Osprey Court, Kingfisher Way, Hinchingbrooke
Business Park, Huntingdon, Cambridgeshire, PE29
6FN

Tel: 01480 432801
Fax: 01480 436314
E-mail: mail@leea.co.uk

Website:
http://www.leea.co.uk
About the LEEA, What's new, membership list,
publications, benefits of membership, how to join
the LEEA, member information (password).

Enquiries:
Enquiries to: Chief Executive

Founded:
1944

Organisation type and purpose:
Trade association.

Subject coverage:
Lifting equipment.

Library catalogue:
All or part available online and in-house

Printed publications:
Code of Practice for the Safe Use of Lifting
Equipment (2006 ed, £135)
Lifting Equipment – A User's Pocket Guide (£8)
Lifting Engineers Handbook (£20)
Hand Chain Blocks and Lever Hoists in the ofshore
Environment (£15)
Membership List (2 times a year, free)
Newsletter

Publications list:
Available online and in print

Access to staff:
Contact by letter, by telephone, by fax and by e-
mail. Appointment necessary. Access for members
only.
Hours: Mon to Fri, 0830 to 1700

LIGHTING ASSOCIATION

Formal name: The Lighting Association Ltd
Acronym or abbreviation: LA

Stafford Park 7, Telford, Shropshire, TF3 3BQ

Tel: 01952 290905
Fax: 01952 290906
E-mail: enquiries@lightingassociation.com

Website:
http://www.lightingassociation.com
Wide range of information available covering
membership and services.

Enquiries:
Enquiries to: Marketing Communications Manager

Founded:
1939

Organisation type and purpose:
Trade Association.

Subject coverage:
Product and lighting company sourcing, technical
information, regulations, lighting manufacture,
distribution and assembly.

Printed publications:
Buyers Guide (annually)
Diary (with member companies)

continued overleaf

President's Report (annually)

Electronic and video publications:
Monthly Newsletter
Order electronic and video publications from: Weekley
Newsletters

Access to staff:
Contact by letter, by telephone, by e-mail and via
website. Appointment necessary.
Hours: Mon to Fri, 0900 to 1700

LINACRE COLLEGE LIBRARY

St Cross Road, Oxford, OX1 3JA

Tel: 01865 271650
Fax: 01865 271668
E-mail: library@linacre.oc.ac.uk

Website:
http://www.linacre.ox.ac.uk/it-and-library/Library

Enquiries:
Enquiries to: Assistant Librarian
Direct tel: 01865 271661

Founded:
1962

Organisation type and purpose:
University library.

Subject coverage:
Small coverage in all disciplines.

**Museum or gallery collection, archive, or library
special collection:**
Ryle Collection (early 20th-century philosophy in
England)

Library catalogue:
All or part available online

Access to staff:
Contact by e-mail
Hours: Mon to Fri, 0900 to 1700

Access to building, collection or gallery:
No prior appointment required
Special comments: Access is restricted to members of
Linacre College.

Access for disabled people:
Toilet facilities

Constituent part of:
University of Oxford

LINCOLN CATHEDRAL LIBRARY

Minster Yard, Lincoln, LN2 1PX

Tel: 01522 561640
Fax: 01522 561641
E-mail: librarian@lincolncathedral.com

Website:
http://www.lincolncathedral.com

Enquiries:
Enquiries to: Librarian

Founded:
1092

Organisation type and purpose:
Cathedral library.

Subject coverage:
Early printed books (especially 17th century);
cathedrals (especially Lincoln); ecclesiastical
history and architecture; liturgy.

**Museum or gallery collection, archive, or library
special collection:**
3,000 17th-century pamphlets and Broadsides
E. J. Willson Collection (architectural drawings)
John Wilson Library (17th- and 18th-century
theological works)
Medieval manuscripts
19th-century Religious Tracts
Pre-1800 printed books
Post-medieval manuscripts

Non-library collection catalogue:
All or part available online

Printed publications:
Library publications are issued through Lincoln
Cathedral Publications
Pamphlets about the history, architecture and art of
the Cathedral

Publications list:
Available in print

Access to staff:
Contact by letter. Appointment necessary. Letter
of introduction required.
Hours: Mon, Tue, 1000 to 1230 and 1400 to 1600

Access to building, collection or gallery:
No access other than to staff
Hours: Exhibition open April to October: Mon to
Fri, 1300 to 1500; Sat, 1100 to 1500; closed Sun

Links with:
Lincoln Record Society
Lincoln Cathedral Library, Minster Yard, Lincoln,
LN2 1PX; tel: 01522 561640; e-mail: secretary@
lincoln-record-society.org.uk; website: http://
www.lincoln-record-society.org.uk

LINCOLN CITY COUNCIL

City Hall, Beaumont Fee, Lincoln, LN1 1DB

Tel: 01522 881188
Fax: 01522 521736

Website:
http://www.lincoln-info.org.uk

Enquiries:
Enquiries to: Policy Officer
Direct tel: 01522 873384
Direct e-mail: nicola.desforges@lincoln.gov.uk

Organisation type and purpose:
Local government body.

Subject coverage:
Local government services.

Access to staff:
Contact by letter, by telephone, by fax and by e-
mail
Hours: Mon to Fri, 0900 to 1700

LINCOLN COLLEGE LIBRARY

Lincoln College, Turl Street, Oxford, OX1 3DR

Tel: 01865 279831
E-mail: library@lincoln.ox.ac.uk

Website:
http://www.lincoln.ox.ac.uk/index.php?page=
welcome+to+the+library

Enquiries:
Enquiries to: Librarian

Founded:
1427

Organisation type and purpose:
University department or institute.

Subject coverage:
General.

**Museum or gallery collection, archive, or library
special collection:**
Senior library of rare books and college archives

Access to staff:
Contact by letter and by e-mail. Access for
members only.
Hours: Mon to Fri, 0900 to 1700

Constituent part of:
University of Oxford

LINCOLN LONGWOOL SHEEP
BREEDERS ASSOCIATION

Lincolnshire Showground, Grange-de-Lings,
Lincoln, LN2 2NA

Tel: 01522 511395
Fax: 01552 520345
E-mail: lincolnlongwool@lineone.net

Enquiries:
Enquiries to: Secretary
Direct tel: 01522 730033

Organisation type and purpose:
Membership association (membership is by
subscription), present number of members: 90
approx, registered charity (charity number
215539).

Subject coverage:
Lincoln longwool sheep.

Access to staff:
Contact by letter, by telephone, by fax and by e-
mail
Hours: Mon to Fri, 0900 to 1700

LINCOLN RECORD SOCIETY

Acronym or abbreviation: LRS

Lincoln Cathedral Library, Minster Yard, Lincoln,
LN2 1PX

Tel: 01522 561640
Fax: 01522 561641
E-mail: treasurer@lincoln-record-society.org.uk

Website:
http://www.lincoln-record-society.org.uk

Enquiries:
Enquiries to: Honorary Secretary

Founded:
1910

Organisation type and purpose:
Learned society.

Subject coverage:
History of the ancient county and diocese of
Lincoln.

Printed publications:
Annual Report
Some 100 record texts relating to the ancient
county and diocese of Lincoln (issued either
annually or bi-annually, free to subscribers and
available for purchase by non-members)

Publications list:
Available online and in print

Access to staff:
Contact by letter and by e-mail
Hours: Mon to Fri, 0900 to 1700

Links with:
Society for Lincolnshire History and Archaeology
The Survey of Lincoln

LINCOLN RED CATTLE SOCIETY

Showground, Grange-de-Lings, Lincoln, LN2 2NA

Tel: 01522 511395
Fax: 01522 520345
E-mail: info@lincolnredcattlesociety.co.uk

Website:
http://www.lincolnredcattlesociety.co.uk

Enquiries:
Enquiries to: Secretary

Founded:
1896

Organisation type and purpose:
Membership association (membership is by
subscription), present number of members: 120
approx, registered charity (charity number
215662).

Access to staff:
Contact by letter, by telephone and by fax
Hours: Mon to Fri, 0900 to 1700

LINCOLN'S INN LIBRARY

The Honourable Society of Lincoln's Inn, The
Treasury Office, Lincoln's Inn, London, WC2A 3TL

Tel: 020 7242 4371
Fax: 020 7404 1864

E-mail: library@lincolnsinn.org.uk

Website:
http://www.lincolnsinn.org.uk/lib_gen.asp

Enquiries:
Enquiries to: Librarian
Direct tel: 020 7693 5160
Direct e-mail: librarian@lincolnsinn.org.uk

Founded:
c. 15th century

Organisation type and purpose:
Legal library.

Museum or gallery collection, archive, or library special collection:
150,000 vols of English law, Commonwealth law and Parliamentary papers
Hale Manuscripts
Black Books (Inn records, 1422 to present)

Non-library collection catalogue:
All or part available in print

Library catalogue:
All or part available online

Access to staff:
Contact by letter, by telephone, by fax, by e-mail and via website. Appointment necessary. Access for members only.
Hours: Normal: Mon to Fri, 0900 to 2000; every 4th Sat, by rotation with other Inns of Court libraries, 1000 to 1700
Aug to mid-Sept: Mon to Fri, 0930 to 1800

Access to building, collection or gallery:
Open to all members of the Inn and all barristers with chambers in the Inn and their pupils. Barristers who are not members and have chambers elsewhere are welcome to use the Library for material not held by their own Inn, but may not borrow. Solicitors may use the library as last resort only. Other researchers by appointment.

LINCOLN-ZEPHYR OWNERS CLUB

22 New North Road, Hainault, Ilford, Essex, IG6 2XG

Tel: 020 8500 4039

Website:
http://www.lzoc.org
Membership details, information on Lincoln-Zephyrs.

Enquiries:
Enquiries to: Information Officer

Founded:
1968

Subject coverage:
Lincoln-Zephyr cars.

Access to staff:
Contact by letter and by telephone
Hours: Mon to Fri, 0900 to 1700

LINCOLNSHIRE ARCHIVES

Acronym or abbreviation: LA

St Rumbold Street, Lincoln, LN2 5AB

Tel: 01522 782040 (search room bookings), 526204 (enquiries)
Fax: 01522 530047
E-mail: lincolnshire_archive@lincolnshire.gov.uk

Website:
http://www.lincolnshire.gov.uk/archives
Information about Lincolnshire Archives and services; list of convicts transported to Australia 1788–1840 (with document references).

Enquiries:
Enquiries to: Site Coordinator

Founded:
1948

Organisation type and purpose:
Local government body.
Record office.

Subject coverage:
History of the historical County and the ancient Diocese of Lincoln; rights of way; boundary delineation; family history; local and village history; school and university projects; leisure and general interest, research, educational research, official and legal enquiries.

Museum or gallery collection, archive, or library special collection:
Business records
Ecclesiastical records
Estate and family records
Foster Library (local history, national, historical and archaeological journals)
Local authority and public records

Non-library collection catalogue:
All or part available online and in-house

Library catalogue:
All or part available online and in-house

Microform publications:
All deposited Lincoln Diocese Parish Registers on microfilm and fiche

Publications list:
Available online and in print

Access to staff:
Contact by letter, by telephone, by fax, by e-mail, in person and via website. Appointment necessary.
Hours: Tue to Sat, 1000 to 1600; Mon, closed
Special comments: Reader Ticket (apply in person).

Access for disabled people:
Parking provided, level entry, access to all public areas, toilet facilities

Incorporated within the service is the:
Lincoln Diocesan Record Office

Parent body:
Lincolnshire County Council

LINCOLNSHIRE LIBRARY SERVICE

Education and Cultural Services Directorate, County Offices, Newland, Lincoln, LN1 1YL

Tel: 01522 782010
Fax: 01522 516137
E-mail: library.support@lincolnshire.gov.uk

Website:
http://www.lincolnshire.gov.uk
County council information, community information, database 20,000 screens includes 'What's On', health advice, education.

Enquiries:
Enquiries to: Customer Services
Direct e-mail: customer_services@lincolnshire.gov.uk

Founded:
1974

Organisation type and purpose:
Local government body, public library.

Subject coverage:
General, music and drama, education, local government and management, agriculture, foreign languages, medicine, Tennyson, literature, local studies.

Museum or gallery collection, archive, or library special collection:
Abell Collection (local studies, 90 scrapbooks) at Central Library, Lincoln
Armitage Collection (drainage of the county) at Central Library, Lincoln
Banks Collection (Sir Joseph Banks collection of letters, manuscripts and drawings on Lincolnshire and Lincolnshire churches) at Central Library, Lincoln
Binnal Collection (Louth and Lincolnshire) at Louth Library
Exley Collection (Lincolnshire) at Central Library, Lincoln
Goulding Collection (Lincolnshire and Louth) at Louth Library
Lincolnshire illustrations index

Medical Library at Lincoln County Hospital
Medical Library at Pilgrim Hospital, Boston
Newcombe Library (17th- and early 18th-century theology, philosophy and history) at Grantham Library
Newton Collection (material by and about Sir Isaac Newton) at Lincoln Central and Grantham Libraries
Pye Collection (Grimsby and Cleethorpes district) at Central Library, Lincoln
Ross Collection (Lord Monson's collection on Lincoln and Lincolnshire villages) at Central Library, Lincoln
Tennyson Research Collection
Wheeler Collection (drainage of the Fens and the building of the port of Boston) at Boston Library
DVDs, music CDs

Non-library collection catalogue:
All or part available online

Library catalogue:
All or part available online

Publications list:
Available in print

Access to staff:
Contact by letter, by telephone, by fax, by e-mail and via website. Appointment necessary.
Hours: Mon to Fri, 0900 to 1700

Access for disabled people:
Level entry

Constituent bodies:
Tennyson Research Centre

Parent body:
Lincolnshire County Council
County Offices, Newland, Lincoln

LINCOLNSHIRE TOURIST GUIDES ASSOCIATION

Winterbourne, Church Lane, Tathwell, Louth, Lincolnshire, LN11 9SR

Tel: 01507 604717
E-mail: jrbh@btinternet.com

Enquiries:
Enquiries to: Booking Officer

Founded:
1985

Organisation type and purpose:
Tourist guides association.

Subject coverage:
Guided walks and tours, talks on all aspects of Lincolnshire's heritage.

Access to staff:
Contact by letter, by telephone and by e-mail
Hours: Mon to Fri, 0900 to 1700

LINDE MATERIAL HANDLING (UK) LTD

Kingsclere Road, Basingstoke, Hampshire, RG21 6XJ

Tel: 01256 342000
Fax: 01256 342923
E-mail: enquiries@linde-mh.co.uk

Website:
http://www.linde-mh.co.uk/

Enquiries:
Enquiries to: Public Relations Officer

Founded:
1943

Formerly called:
Lansing Linde Limited (year of change 2003)

Organisation type and purpose:
Manufacturing industry.

continued overleaf

Subject coverage:
Materials handling using industrial trucks, including freight, warehousing, high density storage; fork truck operation and maintenance; rental and leasing.

Printed publications:
Technical data sheets and catalogues

Access to staff:
Contact by letter, by telephone and by fax
Hours: Mon to Fri, 0900 to 1700

Access to building, collection or gallery:
No prior appointment required

LINEN HALL LIBRARY

17 Donegall Square North, Belfast, BT1 5GB

Tel: 028 9032 1707
Fax: 028 9043 8586
E-mail: info@linenhall.com

Website:
http://www.linenhall.com
Guide to library collections, online catalogue, information of events, details of publications, membership and gift shop.

Enquiries:
Enquiries to: Librarian

Founded:
1788

Organisation type and purpose:
Registered charity.
Independent subscription library.

Subject coverage:
Irish (especially Ulster) local history and biography, Irish bibliography, Irish genealogy, Belfast printed books, political literature and general subjects.

Museum or gallery collection, archive, or library special collection:
Belfast printed book collection
Genealogical collection
Irish newspaper and periodical collection
Irish postcard collection
Kennedy collection of Ulster poetry
Northern Ireland political collection
Theatre and Performing Arts Archive

Non-library collection catalogue:
All or part available online

Library catalogue:
All or part available online and in-house

Printed publications:
The Library publishes a selection of books and prints linked to the collections and of Irish interest

Microform publications:
Northern Ireland political literature on microfiche; phase 1 periodicals 1966–1989

Electronic and video publications:
Troubled Images (CD-ROM)

Publications list:
Available online and in print

Access to staff:
Contact by letter, by telephone, by fax, by e-mail, in person and via website
Hours: Mon to Fri, 0930 to 1730; Sat, 0930 to 1300

Access to building, collection or gallery:
No prior appointment required

Access for disabled people:
Access to all public areas, toilet facilities

LINK CENTRE FOR DEAFENED PEOPLE

Acronym or abbreviation: LINK

19 Hartfield Road, Eastbourne, East Sussex, BN21 2AR

Tel: 01323 638230\ Minicom no. 01323 739998

Fax: 01323 642968
E-mail: info@linkdp.org

Website:
http://www.linkdp.org

Enquiries:
Enquiries to: Helpdesk

Founded:
1972

Organisation type and purpose:
Voluntary organisation, registered charity.
Rehabilitation for deafened adults.

Subject coverage:
Care and welfare of adults with severe or total irreversible deafness or severe progressive deafness not compensated by hearing aids, sudden deafness, speech conservation, speech-reading, lipreading, counselling, rehabilitation, advice and help to family or companion of the sufferer, self-management of deafness, psychosocial rehabilitation.

Publications list:
Available online and in print

Access to staff:
Contact by letter, by telephone, by fax and by e-mail. Appointment necessary.
Hours: Mon to Fri, 0900 to 1700

Access for disabled people:
Ramped entry, access to all public areas, toilet facilities
Special comments: Loop available.

LINK PICTURE LIBRARY

78 Dorien Road, London, SW20 8EJ

Tel: 020 8540 0187; mobile 07947 884517
E-mail: library@linkpicturelibrary.com

Website:
http://www.linkphotographers.com

Enquiries:
Enquiries to: Librarian

Founded:
1982

Organisation type and purpose:
Commercial picture library and photography service.

Subject coverage:
Photographic collections covering many aspects of China, India and South Africa. Able to source images from contributing liaison agents.

Information services:
Specialist image collection from China, India and South Africa

Library catalogue:
All or part available in-house

Access to staff:
Contact by telephone, by e-mail and via website.
Appointment necessary.
Hours: Irregular, but constant monitoring of e-mail

Access to building, collection or gallery:
Appointment required

Links with:
Dinodia Picture Library (India), Fotoe (China) and multiple sources in South Africa

LINNEAN SOCIETY OF LONDON

Burlington House, Piccadilly, London, W1J 0BF

Tel: 020 7434 4479
Fax: 020 7287 9364
E-mail: lynda@linnean.org

Website:
http://www.linnean.org

Enquiries:
Enquiries to: Librarian
Other contacts: Deputy Librarian (for IT queries)

Founded:
1788

Organisation type and purpose:
Learned society (membership is by election or invitation), present number of members: 3,000, registered charity.
Promote taxonomy in all its branches.

Subject coverage:
Anthropology; natural history; evolutionary biology; botany; zoology; taxonomy; history of science.

Museum or gallery collection, archive, or library special collection:
Correspondence and manuscripts of 18th- and 19th-century naturalists
J. E. Smith Collection
J. Insch Tea Library
Linnaean Collection

Non-library collection catalogue:
All or part available online

Library catalogue:
All or part available online

Printed publications:
Biological Journal (monthly)
Botanical Journal (monthly)
Catalogue of Manuscripts, parts I to IV
Symposia
Synopses of British Fauna
Zoological Journal (monthly)
Order printed publications from: Office Manager

Publications list:
Available online and in print

Access to staff:
Contact by letter, by telephone, by fax, by e-mail, in person and via website. Appointment necessary.
Hours: Mon to Fri, 1000 to 1700
Special comments: Letter of introduction required for manuscript access only.

Access to building, collection or gallery:
No prior appointment required

Links with:
Institute of Biology
International Association of Plant Taxonomists

LIST AND INDEX SOCIETY

Acronym or abbreviation: L&I

The National Archives, Kew, Richmond-upon-Thames, Surrey, TW9 4DU

Tel: 020 8876 3444
Fax: 020 8392 5286
E-mail: listandindexsociety@nationalarchives.gov.uk

Enquiries:
Enquiries to: Secretary

Founded:
1965

Organisation type and purpose:
Learned society (membership is by subscription).

Subject coverage:
To publish and provide Public Record Office search room lists and indexes, coverage – public records from 13th to 20th centuries.

Printed publications:
Typed catalogue of the society's publications is available on request

Publications list:
Available in print

Access to staff:
Contact by letter, by fax and by e-mail
Hours: Mon to Fri, 0900 to 1700

Affiliated to:
Public Record Office

LISTENING BOOKS

12 Lant Street, London, SE1 1QH

Tel: 020 7407 9417
Fax: 020 7403 1377
E-mail: info@listening-books.org.uk

Website:
http://www.listening-books.org.uk

Enquiries:
Enquiries to: Membership Services Officer

Organisation type and purpose:
Membership association (membership is by
subscription), present number of members:
12,000+, voluntary organisation, registered charity
(charity number 264221).

Subject coverage:
A postal and digital audiobook library service for
people who cannot read or hold a book in the
usual way, due to illness, disability or special
education needs.

Library catalogue:
All or part available online and in print

Printed publications:
Annual Report
Newsletter and leaflet

Publications list:
Available in print

Access to staff:
Contact by letter, by telephone, by fax, by e-mail
and via website
Hours: Mon to Fri, 0900 to 1700

Access to building, collection or gallery:
Prior appointment required

LISTER INSTITUTE OF PREVENTIVE MEDICINE

PO Box 1083, Bushey, Hertfordshire, WD23 9AG

Tel: 01923 801886
Fax: 01923 801886
E-mail: secretary@lister-institute.org.uk

Website:
http://www.lister-institute.org.uk
History of the Institute and details of the
Fellowship scheme. Research examples included.

Enquiries:
Enquiries to: Secretary

Founded:
1891

Organisation type and purpose:
Registered charity (charity number 206271).
Promoting biomedical excellence in the UK
through the support of research projects with
implications for preventive medicine.

Subject coverage:
Biomedical research in the UK within research
institutions.

Printed publications:
Lister Institute of Preventive Medicine – A concise
history

Access to staff:
Contact by letter, by telephone, by fax, by e-mail
and via website
Hours: Mon to Fri, 0930 to 1700

Access to building, collection or gallery:
No access other than to staff

LISU

Loughborough University, Loughborough,
Leicestershire, LE11 3TU

Tel: 01509 635680
Fax: 01509 635699
E-mail: lisu@lboro.ac.uk

Website:
http://www.lboro.ac.uk/departments/dis/lisu

Enquiries:
Enquiries to: Director

Formerly called:
Library and Information Statistics Unit (year of
change 2004)

Organisation type and purpose:
Library and information statistics unit. Research
organisation, publishing house, consultancy.

Subject coverage:
Regular publication of average prices of academic
books in the United Kingdom and the USA.
Surveys and statistics of public, academic, special
and school librarians and information centres in
the United Kingdom and Europe.

Printed publications:
Average Prices of Academic Books (UK & USA,
annual)
Who else writes like? A readers' guide to fiction
Who next? A children's guide to fiction
LISU Annual Library Statistics: featuring a 10-year
trend analysis (discontinued)
Public Library Materials Fund and Budget Survey
(discontinued)
A Survey of Library Services to schools and
children in the UK (discontinued)
Occasional papers

Electronic and video publications:
LAMPOST (Libraries, Archives, Museums,
Publishing Online Statistics Tables)
Online version of Who else writes like...? at: http://
www.whoelsewriteslike.com
Order electronic and video publications from: see
website

Publications list:
Available online and in print

Access to staff:
Contact by letter, by telephone, by fax, by e-mail
and via website. Appointment necessary.
Hours: Mon to Fri, 0900 to 1700

Constituent part of:
Loughborough University
Department of Information Science

LISZT SOCIETY, THE

9 Burnside Close, Twickenham, Middlesex, TW1
1ET

Tel: 020 8287 5518
Fax: 020 8287 5518
E-mail: LisztSoc@blueyonder.co.uk

Enquiries:
Enquiries to: Secretary

Founded:
1950

Organisation type and purpose:
Learned society.
To encourage, and promote enjoyment in and
appreciation of the music of Liszt, to draw
attention to live performances or recordings, to
encourage research into his compositions and life
and the exchange of views and information about
them.

Subject coverage:
Music of Franz (Ferenc) Liszt, 1811–1886: his life,
times, influence and contemporaries.

Printed publications:
Journal (annually)
Music scores
Newsletters (quarterly)
Order printed publications from: Hardie Press (for
scores)
details from the Society

Access to staff:
Contact by letter, by telephone, by fax and by e-
mail. Appointment necessary.
Hours: Mon to Sun, 0800 to 2200

Access to building, collection or gallery:
Prior appointment required

Access for disabled people:
Parking provided, level entry, toilet facilities

Connections with:
Liszt Societies Worldwide

LITERARY & PHILOSOPHICAL SOCIETY OF NEWCASTLE UPON TYNE

23 Westgate Road, Newcastle upon Tyne, NE1 1SE

Tel: 0191 232 0192
Fax: 0191 261 4494
E-mail: library@litandphil.org.uk

Website:
http://www.litandphil.org.uk

Enquiries:
Enquiries to: Librarian

Founded:
1793

Organisation type and purpose:
Learned society (membership is by subscription),
present number of members: 1200, registered
charity (charity number 528069).
Private subscription library.

Subject coverage:
The humanities with older scientific and
technological material of particular importance to
the region, plus local collections relating to
Northumberland and Durham, 19th century
periodicals.

**Museum or gallery collection, archive, or library
special collection:**
Joseph Crawhall collection
Douglas W Dickenson collection for the history of
the Northern Architectural Association
Manuscripts and other documents recording the
history of the Society
Northern Arts manuscript collection
Pamphlets and tracts from 19th century onwards
Rosner collection of books, periodicals and reports
on Town Planning
Wesley Historical Society collection relating to
Methodism in the North East
Range of 19th century periodicals

Printed publications:
Annual Reports
Occasional publications of notable lectures
Literary and Philosophical Society Bicentenary
Lecture 1993 (Philipson J, £15 plus £1.50 p&p)
The History of the Literary and Philosophical
Society of Newcastle upon Tyne vol. II 1896–1989
(£15 plus £1.50 p&p)
Sir Joseph Wilson Swan FRS (Chirnside RC, 75p)
Reverend William Turner: dissent and reform in
Georgian Newcastle upon Tyne (Harbottle S T L,
Northern Universities Press, £20; £17.50 to non-
members)

Access to staff:
Contact by letter, by telephone, by fax, by e-mail
and in person. Appointment necessary.
Hours: Mon to Fri, 0930 to 1900; Tue, 0930 to 2000;
Sat, 0930 to 1300

LITTLE ROYALTY

2 Ninehams Gardens, Caterham, Surrey, CR3 5LP

Tel: 020 8660 3738

Enquiries:
Enquiries to: Manager

Founded:
1997

Organisation type and purpose:
Service industry.

Subject coverage:
Restoration of soft toys damaged by owners and
time, in as authentic a manner possible. Also
completion of unfinished needlework projects
including cross stitch kits, tapestries and dressmaking projects.

continued overleaf

Access to staff:
Contact by letter and by telephone
Hours: Mon to Fri, 0900 to 1700
Special comments: Please send an sae for price list.

LIVERPOOL & SW LANCASHIRE FAMILY HISTORY SOCIETY

Acronym or abbreviation: L&SWLFHS

6 Kirkmore Road, Liverpool, L18 4QN

E-mail: patchwork34@waitrose.com

Website:
http://www.liverpool-genealogy.org.uk
Outline of the society, contact addresses, publications.

Enquiries:
Enquiries to: General Secretary

Founded:
1976

Organisation type and purpose:
Learned society (membership is by subscription), present number of members: 2,050, registered charity (charity number 512908).
To provide educational facilities for the study of family history in the area, to transcribe, index, and wherever possible publish relevant material, and to provide links with other similar societies.

Subject coverage:
Family history and genealogy in the area of the ancient County of Lancashire known as the Hundred of West Derby.

Printed publications:
Wide range of books concerning Lancashire, Leigh, Liverpool, St Helens, Warrington and Wigan areas
The Liverpool Historian (journal, quarterly)
1851 Census of Liverpool Inner Districts (34 vols)
1851 Census of Liverpool Outer Districts (over 30 vols)
Order printed publications from: Publications Officer, Liverpool & SW Lancashire Family History Society, 9 Manor Road, Lymm, Cheshire, WA13 0AY; tel: 01925 755469; e-mail: joe.griffiths@lineone.net

Microform publications:
Wide range of microfiche register transcriptions and census indexes

Electronic and video publications:
1851 Census of Liverpool index (CD-ROM)

Publications list:
Available online and in print

Access to staff:
Contact by letter
Hours: Mon to Fri, 0900 to 1700

Local groups covering:
Liverpool, Leigh & District, Southport
Widnes, Skelmersdale & Upholland, Warrington

LIVERPOOL ASSOCIATION OF DISABLED PEOPLE

Acronym or abbreviation: LAD

Lime Court Centre, Upper Baker Street, Liverpool, L6 1NB

Tel: 0151 263 8366\ Minicom no. 0151 260 3187
Fax: 0151 263 1855
E-mail: ladisabled@freenetname.co.uk

Website:
http://www.ladisabled.co.uk

Enquiries:
Enquiries to: Manager

Founded:
1966

Organisation type and purpose:
Advisory body, membership association (membership is by subscription), voluntary organisation.

Subject coverage:
Campaigns for civil and welfare rights of disabled people.

Printed publications:
Contact (magazine)

Access to staff:
Contact by letter, by telephone, by fax and by e-mail. Appointment necessary.
Hours: Mon to Thu, 0900 to 1700; Fri, 0900 to 1630

Access for disabled people:
Parking provided, level entry, access to all public areas, toilet facilities

Member of:
BCODP
FIAC

LIVERPOOL CHAMBER OF COMMERCE AND INDUSTRY

Number One, Old Hall Street, Liverpool, L3 9HG

Tel: 0151 227 1234
Fax: 0151 236 0121
E-mail: chamber@liverpoolchamber.org.uk

Website:
http://www.liverpoolchamber.org.uk
Description of facilities and services.

Enquiries:
Enquiries to: Infopool Agent
Direct tel: 0845 145 1115
Direct fax: 0845 145 1116
Direct e-mail: infopool@liverpoolchamber.org.uk

Founded:
1850

Organisation type and purpose:
Membership association.
Delivering accredited services for members and other businesses which improve their profit and increase their efficiency. Providing opportunities for contact and trade between members. Representing members' needs and views at local, national and international levels. Work in partnership with other organisations to improve the prosperity of the region.

Subject coverage:
Mailing lists, company information, financial information, product sourcing, market research, grant searches, employment law, pay statistics, local economic surveys, international trade, trade missions (inward and outward), international market awareness events, European funding schemes, transnational links, Ordnance Survey (large and small scale mapping), The Stationery Office, British Standards, Health and Safety Agency, original research.

Museum or gallery collection, archive, or library special collection:
Reference library, over 700 directories, electronic sources

Printed publications:
Directory of Members (annually, free to members)
Export Matters (10 times a year, not Aug or Dec, free)
Liverpool Packet (6 times a year, free to members)
Greater Merseyside Quarterly Economic Survey (available at www.merseysidebusinessservey.org.uk, free)
North West Chambers of Commerce Directory (includes Liverpool Chamber of Commerce members, annually, free to members)

Access to staff:
Contact by letter, by telephone, by fax, by e-mail, in person and via website
Hours: Mon to Fri, 0900 to 1700

Access for disabled people:
Ramped entry, access to all public areas, toilet facilities

LIVERPOOL CHARITY AND VOLUNTARY SERVICES

Acronym or abbreviation: LCVS

14 Castle Street, Liverpool, L2 0NJ

Tel: 0151 236 7728
Fax: 0151 258 1153
E-mail: info@lcvs.org.uk

Website:
http://www.lcvs.org.uk

Enquiries:
Enquiries to: Chief Executive

Founded:
1909

Organisation type and purpose:
Professional body, voluntary organisation, registered charity (charity number 223485).

Subject coverage:
The information and advisory service is for and about the voluntary sector, and includes charity law, charity registration, sources of funding, management, the workings of government, local, central and European.

Museum or gallery collection, archive, or library special collection:
Small library of information relating to voluntary organisations and charities archive material

Printed publications:
Liverpool Link (news magazine, 10 times a year)
Take it From Here – A Handbook of Social Services on Merseyside (annual directory)
Merseyside Directory of Grant Making Trusts (once every 2 years)
Liverpool Community Network Newsletter (6 times a year)

Publications list:
Available in print

Access to staff:
Contact by letter, by telephone, by fax, by e-mail and via website
Hours: Mon to Fri, 0900 to 1700

LIVERPOOL HOPE UNIVERSITY

Hope Park, Liverpool, L16 9JD

Tel: 0151 291 2001
Fax: 0151 291 2037
E-mail: taylorl@hope.ac.uk

Website:
http://www.hope.ac.uk/library

Enquiries:
Enquiries to: Director of Library and Learning Support
Direct tel: 0151 251 3528
Other contacts: Head of Library Service

Founded:
1844

Formerly called:
Liverpool Hope University College; Liverpool Institue of Higher Education (LIHE)

Organisation type and purpose:
Suitable for ages: 18+.

Subject coverage:
Information technology; media; creative and performing arts; psychology; theology; sociology; social work; physical education; business and management; law; politics; art; music; literature; geography; tourism; education; history; children's fiction; science; environmental science; sport; drama.

Museum or gallery collection, archive, or library special collection:
Gradwell Collection, theology
Picton Collection, theology
National Ex-Church of England Society, religious education
Radcliffe Library from Liverpool Cathedral and St Aidans, theology

Professor Andrew F. Walls African-Asian
   Christianity Collection
Archbishop Stuart Blanch (1918–94)

Library catalogue:
All or part available online

Access to staff:
Contact by letter, by telephone, by fax, by e-mail
and via website. Appointment necessary.
Hours: Term time: Mon, Thu, 0900 to 1845; Fri, 0900
to 1645; Sun, 1400 to 1645 (see website for details)

Access to building, collection or gallery:
Special comments: University ID card or signing in
required.

Access for disabled people:
Parking provided, level entry, access to all public
areas, toilet facilities, lift

LIVERPOOL INSTITUTE FOR PERFORMING ARTS

Acronym or abbreviation: LIPA

Mount Street, Liverpool, L1 9HF

Tel: 0151 330 3000
Fax: 0151 330 3131
E-mail: k.odonoghue@lipa.ac.uk

Website:
http://www.lipa.ac.uk

Enquiries:
Enquiries to: Director of Information Services and
Technical Support
Direct tel: 0151 330 3250

Founded:
1990

Organisation type and purpose:
Membership association, present number of
members: 620, university library, suitable for ages:
18+.
Degree-awarding body, Liverpool John Moores
University.

Subject coverage:
Performing arts, sound technology, performance
design, acting, dance, music, enterprise
management, community arts.

Library catalogue:
All or part available in-house

Access to staff:
Contact by letter, by telephone, by fax, by e-mail
and via website. Appointment necessary.
Hours: Mon to Fri, 0900 to 1700

LIVERPOOL JOHN MOORES UNIVERSITY – AVRIL ROBARTS LEARNING RESOURCE CENTRE

Acronym or abbreviation: LJMU

79 Tithebarn Street, Liverpool, L2 2ER

Tel: 0151 231 4022
Fax: 0151 231 4479

Website:
http://www.ljmu.ac.uk/lea
For all the University Learning Resource Centres.
http://www.ljmu.ac.uk/lea/avril
Information on Avril Robarts Learning Resource
Centre including opening hours.

Enquiries:
Enquiries to: Principal Information Officer
(Operations)
Direct e-mail: c.haddock@ljmu.ac.uk

Organisation type and purpose:
University department or institute.
Learning resource centre.

Subject coverage:
Sciences, engineering, health and applied social
sciences.

Library catalogue:
All or part available online

Printed publications:
Numerous publications including guides to the
service, course materials, fact sheets, subject
literature guides and user guides

Publications list:
Available online and in print

Access to staff:
Contact by letter, by fax and by e-mail
Hours: Mon to Thu, 0900 to 2100; Fri, 0930 to 1700;
Sat, Sun, 1000 to 1600

Access for disabled people:
Disabled access available

LIVERPOOL JOHN MOORES UNIVERSITY – LIBRARY AND STUDENT SUPPORT

Acronym or abbreviation: LJMU

Aldham Robarts Learning Resource Centre, Mount
Pleasant Campus, Maryland Street, Liverpool, L3
5UZ

Tel: 0151 231 3544
Fax: 0151 231 3113
E-mail: m.melling@ljmu.ac.uk

Website:
http://www.ljmu.ac.uk/lea

Enquiries:
Enquiries to: Director of Learning and Information
Services

Organisation type and purpose:
University Library.

Subject coverage:
Art and design; fashion; business; management;
law; civil, mechanical, electrical and electronic
engineering; surveying; architecture; natural
sciences; health; humanities; social sciences; sport
and recreation; librarianship; computing; home
economics; languages; education; social work.

**Museum or gallery collection, archive, or library
special collection:**
Everyman Theatre Archive
Frankie Vaughan Collection of Scores and Parts
Jon Savage Punk Collection
Liddle Hart Collection on Fashion
Stafford Beer Collection
Cold War Collection
Barry Miles Archive

Library catalogue:
All or part available online

Printed publications:
Catalogue of the Liddle Hart Collection
Union List of Legal Materials held in Liverpool,
1985

Publications list:
Available in print

Access to staff:
Contact by letter, by telephone, by fax, by e-mail
and via website. Appointment necessary. Non-
members charged.
Hours: Mon to Fri, 0900 to 1700

LIVERPOOL LIBRARIES AND INFORMATION SERVICES

Formal name: City of Liverpool Libraries and
Information Services (Dept)

Central Library, William Brown Street, Liverpool,
L3 8EW

Tel: 0151 233 5835/36\ Minicom no. 0151 233 5850
Fax: 0151 233 5886
E-mail: refbt.central.library@liverpool.gov.uk

Website:
http://www.liverpool.gov.uk/libraries
Description of services.

Enquiries:
Enquiries to: Head of Libraries and Information
Services

Direct tel: 0151 233 6346
Direct fax: 0151 233 6399
Other contacts: Team Leader, Services to Business
for main contact for business information services.

Founded:
1852

Organisation type and purpose:
Local government body, public library.
Reorganised into three departments; information
services, lending services, record office and family
history services.

Subject coverage:
All subject fields are covered, including: arts and
recreation; government, law, economics, transport,
business information, statistics; librarianship,
religion, philosophy, sociology and education;
language, literature, history and topography; local
studies; science and technology, including
computers, health and safety, medicine,
engineering, patents and standards, publications of
British Government and International
organisations.

**Museum or gallery collection, archive, or library
special collection:**
British Government publications
Carl Rosa Opera Collection
Earl of Derby Papers
Complete set of BSI
Parish Registers and other church records
European Union documents
H F Hornby bequest and other rare book
   collections consisting of c. 12,000 manuscripts,
   finely printed and illustrated books and fine
   bindings; c. 8000 etchings, engravings and
   woodcuts; c. 75,000 bookplates
Historical Collection of Childrens' books
Liverpool City Council Archives and a wide range
   of deposited archives
Merseyside County Council, Merseyside
   Development Corporation and joint authority
   archives
Melly Papers
Moore Papers
Norris Papers
Patent specifications, including Patent Co-
   operation Treaty, European, US and GB (on CD-
   ROM)
Roscoe Papers
UN and WHO collection
Walter Crane Collection

Trade and statistical information:
Wide range of official and commercial statistical
publications, including UK government, EU,
UN, Mintel and Keynote market research
reports.

Non-library collection catalogue:
All or part available in-house

Library catalogue:
All or part available in-house

Publications list:
Available in print

Access to staff:
Contact by letter, by telephone, by fax, by e-mail
and in person
Hours: Mon to Thu, 0900 to 1800; Fri, 0900 to 1800;
Sat, 0900 to 1700; Sun, 1200 to 1600

Access for disabled people:
Parking provided, ramped entry, toilet facilities
Special comments: IT equipment and software
available for disabled customers – Contact services
to Disabled People Unit, 0151 233 5865

Parent body of:
LADSIRLAC
   tel: 0151 233 5825; fax: 0151 233 5886; e-mail: stb
   .central.library@liverpool.gov.uk
Liverpool Record Office and Family History
Service
   tel: 0151 233 5817; fax: 0151 233 5886; e-mail:
   recoffice.central.library@liverpool.gov.uk

LIVERPOOL MEDICAL INSTITUTION

Acronym or abbreviation: LMI

114 Mount Pleasant, Liverpool, L3 5SR

Tel: 0151 709 9125
Fax: 0151 707 2810
E-mail: library@lmi.org.uk

Website:
http://www.lmi.org.uk

Enquiries:
Enquiries to: Librarian

Founded:
1779

Organisation type and purpose:
Learned society (membership is by election or invitation), present number of members: 1200, registered charity (charity number 210112).

Subject coverage:
History of medicine.

Museum or gallery collection, archive, or library special collection:
Historical Collection of medical books

Non-library collection catalogue:
All or part available in-house and in print

Library catalogue:
All or part available in-house

Printed publications:
Catalogue of Books in the Liverpool Medical Institution Library to the end of the Nineteenth Century, 1968
History of the Liverpool Medical Institution (J A Shepherd, 1979)

Access to staff:
Contact by letter, by telephone, by fax, by e-mail and via website. Appointment necessary. Access for members only. Letter of introduction required. Non-members charged.
Hours: Mon to Fri, 0930 to 1730

Access to building, collection or gallery:
Prior appointment required

Access for disabled people:
Parking provided, ramped entry, level entry, access to all public areas, toilet facilities

LIVERPOOL RECORD OFFICE AND LOCAL HISTORY SERVICE

Liverpool Libraries Satellite Service, Unit 33, Wellington Employment Park South, Dune's Way, Liverpool, L5 9ZS

Tel: 0151 233 5817
Fax: 0151 233 5824
E-mail: recoffice.central.library@liverpool.gov.uk

Website:
http://www.liverpool.gov.uk
Brief details of the service under libraries.
http://www.liverpool.gov.uk/archives
Archives catalogue, images, publications, information leaflets.

Enquiries:
Enquiries to: Manager

Founded:
1850

Organisation type and purpose:
Local government body, public library.

Subject coverage:
Local history, family history, primarily City of Liverpool, but some more general material for Merseyside and Lancashire and Cheshire.

Museum or gallery collection, archive, or library special collection:
Archives and local studies materials on all aspects of the City's history

Non-library collection catalogue:
All or part available online and in-house

Library catalogue:
All or part available online and in-house

Printed publications:
Handlists:
Church of England Parish Registers and Records (rev Sep 1999)
Roman Catholic Parish Records
Cemetery and Burial Records
Non-Conformist Churches
Maps:
Map of Church of England Parishes
Plan of Liverpool (Eyes J, June 1765)
Map of Liverpool (Tallis J, 1851)
Liverpool in 1859 (Isaac J R)
Leaflets:
Liverpool Record Office, Local Studies and Family History Service, general information
Merseyside Record Office, general guide
Liverpool Record Office Information Leaflets: series of guides to sources

Microform publications:
Order microform publications from: Microform Academic Publishers

Electronic and video publications:
Archive photographs with archive film footage (CD-ROM)
Order electronic and video publications from: North West Film Archive

Publications list:
Available online and in print

Access to staff:
Contact by letter, by telephone, by fax, by e-mail, in person and via website. Appointment necessary.
Hours: Mon to Sat, 0930 to 1700

Access to building, collection or gallery:
Hours: Tue to Sat, 0930 to 1630
Special comments: By appointment only, minimum 24-hours' notice.

Access for disabled people:
Ramped entry, toilet facilities

LIVERPOOL SCHOOL OF TROPICAL MEDICINE

Pembroke Place, Liverpool, L3 5QA

Tel: 0151 708 9393
Fax: 0151 708 8733
E-mail: robbinsv@liverpool.ac.uk

Enquiries:
Enquiries to: Director
Other contacts: (1) Librarian (2) Secretary LATH for (1) library and publications (2) Liverpool Associates in Tropical Health Limited.

Founded:
1898

Organisation type and purpose:
Registered charity (charity number 222655), university department or institute, research organisation.

Subject coverage:
Human health in tropical and developing countries; tropical community health; management in primary health care; health information systems, health education and promotion; clinical tropical medicine; tropical paediatrics and child health; maternal health; parasitology, medical entomology; immunology and molecular biology as applied to tropical medicine; veterinary parasitology; epidemiology and statistics.

Museum or gallery collection, archive, or library special collection:
Archive collection on all aspects of the School's history
Dawes Parasitology Collection
Library of some 40,000 volumes
Reference collections of trypanosomes of man and animals
Rodent malaria parasites and Leishmania

Printed publications:
Annals of Tropical Medicine and Parasitology (6 times a year)
Annals of Tropical Paediatrics (quarterly)
Annual Report
Prospectus

Publications list:
Available in print

Access to staff:
Contact by letter, by telephone, by fax, by e-mail and via website. Appointment necessary.
Hours: Mon to Fri, 0900 to 1700

Affiliated to:
University of Liverpool

Subsidiary body:
Liverpool Associates in Tropical Health (LATH)

LIVING STREETS

Acronym or abbreviation: PA

3rd Floor, 31–33 Bondway, London, SW8 1SJ

Tel: 020 7820 1010
Fax: 020 7820 8208
E-mail: info@pedestrians.org.uk

Website:
http://www.pedestrians.org.uk

Enquiries:
Enquiries to: Director

Founded:
1929

Organisation type and purpose:
National organisation, membership association (membership is by subscription), present number of members: 1400, voluntary organisation, registered charity (charity number 206006), suitable for ages: all.
Living Streets is a national charity working to create streets and public spaces that people on foot can use and enjoy.

Subject coverage:
Statistical, legal, parliamentary, local government, town planning, highway and traffic engineering, and medical aspects of walking with special regard for its safety and convenience.

Museum or gallery collection, archive, or library special collection:
Association archives

Printed publications:
Walk (members magazine, 3 times per annum)
Annual Report
Living Streets – Action Manifesto (free of charge)
Schools Resource Pack
The School Run: Blessing or Blight?
Taking the Stategy Step
Walk to School (leaflet)

Publications list:
Available online and in print

Access to staff:
Contact by letter, by telephone, by fax, by e-mail and via website
Hours: Mon to Fri, 0930 to 1730

Affiliated to:
Federation of Europe Pedestrians Associations
International Federation of Pedestrians

Local contacts:
Countrywide

LLANELLI LIBRARY

Vaughan Street, Llanelli, Carmarthenshire, SA15 3AS

Tel: 01554 773538
Fax: 01554 750125
E-mail: libraries@carmarthenshire.gov.uk

Enquiries:
Enquiries to: Manager

Founded:
1860

Organisation type and purpose:
Local government body, public library.

Subject coverage:
General.

Museum or gallery collection, archive, or library special collection:
1800 coal mine plans
Collection of manuscripts
Theodore Nichol Collection

Non-library collection catalogue:
All or part available in-house

Library catalogue:
All or part available online and in-house

Printed publications:
Local history publications

Publications list:
Available online and in print

Access to staff:
Contact by letter, by telephone, by fax and in person
Hours: Mon to Fri, 0900 to 1700

Access to building, collection or gallery:
No access other than to staff

Access for disabled people:
Ramped entry, access to all public areas, toilet facilities
Special comments: Lift to first floor.

LLANGEFNI LIBRARY

Lon y Felin, Llangefni, Anglesey, LL77 7RT

Tel: 01248 752908
Fax: 01248 752999
E-mail: jrtlh@ynysmon.gov.uk

Website:
http://www.ynysmon.gov.uk
Isle of Anglesey County Council corporate web-site.

Enquiries:
Enquiries to: Manager

Founded:
1996

Organisation type and purpose:
Local government body, public library.

Subject coverage:
Local history, the Isle of Anglesey.

Museum or gallery collection, archive, or library special collection:
Local studies collection – Isle of Anglesey

Non-library collection catalogue:
All or part available in-house

Library catalogue:
All or part available online

Access to staff:
Contact by letter, by telephone, by fax, by e-mail and in person
Hours: Mon to Fri, 0900 to 1700

Access to building, collection or gallery:
No prior appointment required

Access for disabled people:
Parking provided, level entry, access to all public areas, toilet facilities

Parent body:
Isle of Anglesey County Council
Library, Information and Archives Services

LLOYD'S REGISTER OF SHIPPING

71 Fenchurch Street, London, EC3M 4BS

Tel: 020 7709 9166
Fax: 020 7488 4796

Website:
http://www.lr.org
Details of organisation.

Enquiries:
Enquiries to: Information Officer & Archivist
Direct tel: 020 7423 2077
Direct fax: 020 7423 2039
Direct e-mail: lloydsreg@lr.org

Founded:
1760

Organisation type and purpose:
International organisation, advisory body, statutory body, service industry, training organisation, consultancy, research organisation, publishing house.
Classification Society and Independent Inspection Agency.

Subject coverage:
Ships: classification, specification and advisory service, international conventions, Register Book (full details of all known merchant ships of the world over 100 tons), statistics, technical records; offshore services: certification and classification in connection with steel and concrete, submersibles and underwater habitats, welding, linepipe etc; land-based industry: rail, nuclear power stations, thermal and hydro-electric power stations, oil refineries and chemical plants, freight containers, and general engineering; other services include yachts, cargo gear, docks etc; instrumentation; refrigeration and cold stores; mass-produced machinery; computer services; offshore rigs.

Museum or gallery collection, archive, or library special collection:
Complete set of the Lloyd's Register Statistical Tables from 1878 to date
Complete set of the Lloyd's Register of Ships from 1764 to date
Complete set of the Lloyd's Register of Yachts from 1878 to 1980
Complete set of the Lloyd's Register Casualty Return 1890 to date

Trade and statistical information:
Shipping statistics 1878 to date.
Casualty (shipping) information from 1890 to date.
Shipping Information (Specific Ships) 1764 to date.
Shipowners 1876 to date.
Yachts 1904 to 1980.
Shipbuilders 1886 to date.

Non-library collection catalogue:
All or part available in-house

Library catalogue:
All or part available in-house

Printed publications:
Rules and Regulations for the Classification of Ships
Other publications can be found at http://www.webstore.lr.org
Information about titles now published by IHS Fairplay can be found at http://www.ihsfairplay.com
Order printed publications from: Lloyd's Register 71 Fenchurch Street, London, EC3M 4BS; e-mail rules@lr.org

Electronic and video publications:
Electronic shipping information available on CD-ROM
The Ultimate Guide to Ships (CD-ROM)
Rules and Regulations for the classification of ships (CD-ROM)

Publications list:
Available online

Access to staff:
Contact by letter, by telephone, by fax, by e-mail, in person and via website. Appointment necessary. All charged.
Hours: Mon to Fri, 0930 to 1200 and 1300 to 1630
Special comments: Closed on public holidays and between Christmas and New Year.

Access for disabled people:
Access to all public areas, toilet facilities
Special comments: Entry to building by lift; prior notice appreciated but not necessary.

LOCAL AUTHORITIES COORDINATORS OF REGULATORY SERVICES

Acronym or abbreviation: LACORS

Local Government House, Smith Square, London, SW1P 3HZ

Tel: 020 7665 3888
Fax: 020 7665 3887
E-mail: info@lacors.gov.uk

Website:
http://www.lacors.gov.uk
General information on organisation. Detailed information by subscription (details on web)

Enquiries:
Enquiries to: Executive Director

Founded:
1978

Organisation type and purpose:
Local government statutory body.

Subject coverage:
Food, trading standards, health and safety, animal health and welfare, environmental protection, private-sector housing, licensing and gambling

Publications list:
Available in print

Access to staff:
Contact by letter, by telephone, by fax, by e-mail and via website
Hours: Mon to Fri, 0900 to 1700

Access to building, collection or gallery:
Prior appointment required

Access for disabled people:
Ramped entry

LOCAL AUTHORITY ACTION FOR SOUTHERN AFRICA

Acronym or abbreviation: LAACTSA

c/o Glasgow City Council, DRS, 229 George Street, Glasgow, G1 1QU

Tel: 0141 287 8665
Fax: 0141 287 9958
E-mail: john.mcfadden@drs.glasgow.gov.uk

Enquiries:
Enquiries to: Membership Secretary

Founded:
1995

Organisation type and purpose:
Local government body, advisory body, membership association (membership is by subscription), present number of members: 60 UK Councils, training organisation, consultancy, research organisation.
Supporting development and democracy in post-apartheid South Africa.

Subject coverage:
Local government in Southern Africa (South Africa and other countries within SADC – Angola, Mozambique, Zambia, Zimbabwe, Tanzania, DRC, Lesotho, Namibia, Swaziland, Botswana, Malawi, Seychelles and Mauritius). British local government links with Southern Africa.

Printed publications:
2001 Special Report

Access to staff:
Contact by letter, by fax and by e-mail
Hours: Wed to Fri, 1000 to 1800

continued overleaf

Sister organisation:
Action for Southern Africa (ACTSA)
231 Vauxhall Bridge Road, London, SW1V 1EH;
tel: 020 3263 2001; fax: 020 7931 9398; e-mail:
info@actsa.org

Special interest group of:
Local Government Association LGA (LGIB)

LOCAL AUTHORITY CATERERS ASSOCIATION

Acronym or abbreviation: LACA

Bourne House, Horsell Park, Woking, Surrey,
GU21 4LY

Tel: 01483 766777
Fax: 01483 751991
E-mail: admin@laca.co.uk

Website:
http://www.laca.co.uk

Enquiries:
Enquiries to: Administrator

Founded:
1991

Organisation type and purpose:
Professional body.
Providers of catering services and supplies to
education, social services, leisure and civil catering.

Subject coverage:
Catering with local authorities, including
education, welfare, civic, leisure; development of
school meals services.

Trade and statistical information:
Data on uptake of school meals.
Data on volume of purchasers in local authority
catering.

Printed publications:
Handbook (annually)
List of Information on Provision of Services
List of Members
Newsletter (quarterly)
Survey of School Meals

Access to staff:
Contact by letter, by telephone, by fax and by e-
mail
Hours: Mon to Fri, 0900 to 1700

LOCAL GOVERNMENT ASSOCIATION

Acronym or abbreviation: LGA

Local Government House, Smith Square, London,
SW1P 3HZ

Tel: 020 7664 3000
Fax: 020 7664 3030
E-mail: info@local.gov.uk

Website:
http://www.local.gov.uk/association

Enquiries:
Enquiries to: LGconnect

Founded:
1997

Organisation type and purpose:
Local government body.
The national voice for local authorities in England
and Wales, speaking for 350 local authorities
representing 50m. people.

Subject coverage:
Local government in England and Wales, policy
including finance, education, libraries, economic
development, social services, transport, leisure,
housing, tourism, contracts, environment,
personnel, police, fire, consumer protection, health,
etc.

**Museum or gallery collection, archive, or library
special collection:**
Policy and structure issues; review team; finance;
economic development, tourism and leisure;
legal and parliamentary; planning, transport,
environment and housing

Printed publications:
Checklist of circulars (weekly, members only)
First (weekly)
Other publications available on the following
topics: best value, development, drugs,
education, environment, equal opportunities,
finance, highways, housing, leisure and tourism,
management, planning, police, quality, social
services, surveys and research, and transport
Order printed publications from: LG Connect,
Publication Sales, Local Government House, Smith
Square, London, SW1P 3HZ; tel: 020 7664 3000

Publications list:
Available online

Access to staff:
Contact by letter, by telephone, by fax and by e-
mail
Hours: Mon to Fri, 0900 to 1700

Autonomous Welsh arm replaces the:
Assembly of Welsh Counties
Committee of Welsh Districts

LOCAL GOVERNMENT BOUNDARY COMMISSION FOR SCOTLAND

Thistle House, 91 Haymarket Terrace, Edinburgh,
EH12 5HD

Tel: 0131 538 7510
Fax: 0131 538 7511
E-mail: secretariat@scottishboundaries.gov.uk

Website:
http://www.lgbc-scotland.gov.uk
Information on the boundaries of local government
areas in Scotland and their electoral wards, and on
reviews of those boundaries.

Enquiries:
Enquiries to: Secretary

Founded:
1973

Organisation type and purpose:
Statutory body. Advisory non-departmental public
body, constituted under the Local Government
(Scotland) Act 1973, reporting to the Scottish
Government.

Subject coverage:
Local government boundaries.

Printed publications:
Reports on electoral and administrative area
reviews
Order printed publications from: The Secretary

Electronic and video publications:
Reports available from website as PDF files

Publications list:
Available online

Access to staff:
Contact by letter, by telephone, by fax, by e-mail
and via website
Hours: Mon to Fri, 0900 to 1700

LOCAL GOVERNMENT BOUNDARY COMMISSION FOR WALES

Acronym or abbreviation: LGBCW

1st Floor, Caradog House, 1–6 St Andrews Place,
Cardiff, CF10 3BE

Tel: 029 2039 5031
Fax: 029 2039 5250
E-mail: lgbc.wales@wales.gsi.gov.uk

Website:
http://www.lgbc-wales.gov.uk

Enquiries:
Enquiries to: Secretary

Founded:
1972

Organisation type and purpose:
National government body.
A statutory body that reviews local government
electoral and boundary arrangements in Wales.

Subject coverage:
The work of the LGBCW involves local
government electoral and boundary reviews in
Wales since 1972.

**Museum or gallery collection, archive, or library
special collection:**
All reports published and related working files and
maps

Printed publications:
Reports (free, distributed to local authorities and
other interested parties on publication, members
of the public may write for copies or call by
appointment)

Publications list:
Available online and in print

Access to staff:
Contact by letter, by telephone, by fax and by e-
mail. Appointment necessary.
Hours: Mon to Fri, 0800 to 1630

Parent body:
National Assembly for Wales
Cathays Park, Cardiff, CF10 3NQ

LOCAL GOVERNMENT INTERNATIONAL BUREAU

Acronym or abbreviation: LGIB

Local Government House, Smith Square, London,
SW1P 3HZ

Tel: 020 7664 3100
Fax: 020 7664 3128
E-mail: enquiries@lgib.gov.uk

Website:
http://www.lgib.gov.uk
Information about LGIB; information about UK
delegation to Committee of the Regions; on-line
database of European Information Service 1997-;
access to European Twinning market.

Enquiries:
Enquiries to: Public Relations Manager
Direct tel: 020 7664 3112
Other contacts: Twinnings Officer for information
about town twinning and local authority
international links.

Founded:
1988

Organisation type and purpose:
International organisation, local government body,
national organisation, professional body
(membership is by qualification), present number
of members: 500.
European and International Affairs Unit of the
Local Government Association and Welsh Local
Government Association. LGIB also represents
Northern Ireland Local Government Association.
Funded from the local government revenue
support grant.

Subject coverage:
European policy and legislation as it affects UK
local government, European information of
interest to local government, details of
international representation by UK local
government, projects and funding, development
cooperation, information on international linking
(eg town twinning).

**Museum or gallery collection, archive, or library
special collection:**
Committee of the Regions papers
EU legislation and policy

Library catalogue:
All or part available online

Printed publications:
Publications include:
Special Reports on Committee of the Regions, EU Budget, Brussels Offices, International local government links
European Information Service (EIS, 10 times a year) 2001–02 subscription £290 a year, discount for UK local authorities (£145)
Leaflet on the Work of the Bureau
Linking News (5 times a year)

Electronic and video publications:
EIS Online – access to 5 year archive of European Information Service, available as part of EIS subscription

Publications list:
Available online and in print

Access to staff:
Contact by letter, by telephone, by fax, by e-mail and via website
Hours: Mon to Fri, 0900 to 1700
Special comments: No visitors as no library facilities.

British member of the:
Council of European Municipalities and Regions (CEMR)
International Union of Local Authorities (IULA)

Other addresses:
Brussels Office
Rue d'Arlon 22, 1050 Brussels, Belgium; tel: 00 32 2 502 3680; fax: 00 32 2 502 4035; e-mail: brussels.office@lgib.org

Parent body:
Local Government Association

LOCAL GOVERNMENT OMBUDSMAN

Formal name: Commission for Local Adminstration in England

10th Floor, Millbank Tower, Millbank, London, SW1P 4QP

Tel: 020 7217 4620
Fax: 020 7217 4621
E-mail: advice@lgo.org.uk

Website:
http://www.lgo.org.uk
Most publications, including annual reports, annual accounts, annual reviews to councils, digest of cases, guidance notes, leaflet on how to complain, complaint statistics, recent investigation reports, and recent customer satisfaction survey reports.

Enquiries:
Enquiries to: LGO Advice Team
Direct tel: 0300 061 0614
Direct fax: 024 7682 0001

Founded:
1974

Organisation type and purpose:
Statutory body.

Subject coverage:
Local Government Ombudsmen investigate complaints of injustice arising from maladministration by local authorities and certain other bodies. They look into complaints about most council services, including social care and privately arranged care. The objective is to secure, where appropriate, satisfactory redress for complainants and better administration for the authorities. The Ombudsmen have the power to examine files of local authorities and to interview officers and members. The authority must consider an Ombudsman's report and recommendations and notify him/her of the action it intends to take.

Museum or gallery collection, archive, or library special collection:
All investigation reports

Library catalogue:
All or part available in-house

Printed publications:
Complained to the council? Still not satisfied? (in large print, Braille and on CD, free)
Annual Report (free up to 10 copies)
Digest of cases for 1996, 1997, 1998, 1999, 2000, 2001, 2002/03, 2003/04, 2004/05, 2005/06, 2006/07 (free up to 5 copies)
Guidance on good practice – a series of 3 titles (free up to 5 copies)
Order printed publications from: Communications Assistant, Local Government Ombudsman, at the same address; tel: 020 7217 4683; fax: 020 7217 4621; e-mail: t.davey@lgo.org.uk

Publications list:
Available online and in print

Access to staff:
Contact by letter, by telephone, by fax and by e-mail. Appointment necessary.
Hours: Mon to Fri, 0900 to 1700
Special comments: Personal callers by appointment only.

Access to building, collection or gallery:
No prior appointment required
Hours: Mon to Fri, 0900 to 1700

Access for disabled people:
Ramped entry, toilet facilities

Also at:
Local Government Ombudsman
The Oaks No. 2, Westwood Way, Westwood Business Park, Coventry, CV4 8JB; tel: 024 7682 0000; fax: 024 7682 0001
Local Government Ombudsman
Beverley House, 17 Shipton Road, York, YO30 5FZ; tel: 01904 380200; fax: 01904 380269

LOCAL GOVERNMENT REFORM SOCIETY

Acronym or abbreviation: LGRS

14 Princes Avenue, Bognor Regis, West Sussex, PO21 2DY

Tel: 01243 863726

Enquiries:
Enquiries to: General Secretary
Other contacts: Information Officer

Founded:
1960

Organisation type and purpose:
International organisation, voluntary organisation.
Non-profit-making organisation.
Radical reform of local government to guarantee real democratic and public trustee basis.

Subject coverage:
History of local government and its reform, private bills relating to local government, corruption in local government, maladministration, reform of individual authorities, rating reform and use of the local referendum.

Printed publications:
Newsletter
Research Papers
Seminar Study Reports

Access to staff:
Contact by letter
Hours: Mon to Fri, 0900 to 1700

LOCAL STUDIES CENTRE

Central Library, Northumberland Square, North Shields, Tyne and Wear, NE30 1QA

Tel: 0191 643 5270
Fax: 0191 200 6118
E-mail: local.studies@northtyneside.gov.uk

Website:
http://www.northtyneside.gov.uk/libraries/index.htm

Enquiries:
Enquiries to: Librarian

Founded:
1974

Organisation type and purpose:
Local government body.
Archive.

Subject coverage:
Contains printed sources dealing with people and organisations in or from the present North Tyneside Borough, past, present and future. There is also a collection of local photographs.

Museum or gallery collection, archive, or library special collection:
Shields Daily News 1864–

Non-library collection catalogue:
All or part available online and in-house

Library catalogue:
All or part available online and in-house

Access to staff:
Contact by letter, by telephone, by fax, by e-mail and in person

Access for disabled people:
Level entry, lift, access to all public areas, toilet facilities

Links with:
North Tyneside Council

LONDON 21 SUSTAINABILITY NETWORK

Unit LS2, The Kensington Charity Centre, Fourth Floor, Charles House, 375 Kensington High Street, W14 8QH

Tel: 020 7471 6795
Fax: 020 7471 6796
E-mail: office@london21.org

Website:
http://www.london21.org
Community projects in London.

Enquiries:
Enquiries to: Coordinator
Direct e-mail: vinciane.rycroft@london21.org

Founded:
1998

Organisation type and purpose:
Voluntary organisation.
Network.
To promote, support and network community-based action for a greener, healthier London; to engage communities and individuals with local sustainability issues.

Subject coverage:
Information on organisations and projects regarding sustainability and Agenda 21 in Greater London and community initiatives. Channels for policy formation and information exchange.

Access to staff:
Contact by letter, by telephone and by e-mail.
Access for members only.
Hours: Monday to Fri, 0930 to 1700

LONDON ACADEMY OF DRESSMAKING AND DESIGN

Acronym or abbreviation: LADD

18 Dobree Avenue, Willesden, London, NW10 2AE

Tel: 020 8451 7174
Fax: 020 8459 7927
E-mail: info@londonacademy.com

Website:
http://www.londonacademy.com
A world famous academic institution with a long and proud record of achievement. 50 fashion courses, covering basic to advanced designing, from children's to adults; short and long courses – the Academy has a flexible course structure to ensure a suitable programme to suit students' interests, aspirations and time.

continued overleaf

Enquiries:
Enquiries to: Principal Designer

Founded:
1969

Organisation type and purpose:
Dressmaking, design & fashion college.

Subject coverage:
Advanced designing in ladies' and children's wear, bridal wear, fashion drawing, draping, bead and silk embroidery, grading, soft furnishing, millinery, swim wear and lace appliqué; senior diploma, basic and advanced diploma, basic foundation diploma.

Printed publications:
Prospectus

Access to staff:
Contact by letter, by telephone, by fax, by e-mail, in person and via website. Appointment necessary.
Hours: Mon to Fri, 0930 to 1730

LONDON AND MIDDLESEX ARCHAEOLOGICAL SOCIETY

Acronym or abbreviation: LAMAS

Museum of London, London Wall, London, EC2Y 5HN

Tel: 020 7814 5734
Fax: 020 7600 1058
E-mail: jkeily@museumoflondon.org.uk

Website:
http://www.lamas.org.uk

Enquiries:
Enquiries to: Hon. Secretary

Founded:
1855

Organisation type and purpose:
Membership association (membership is by subscription), present number of members: 666, voluntary organisation, registered charity (charity number 267552).
To further the study of archaeology, local history and the historic buildings of the London area and to publish the results of such research; to encourage public interest in those areas and so promote preservation of historic buildings, ancient monuments and other remains of historic or archaeological interest.

Subject coverage:
History and archaeology of London and the London area; preservation of historic buildings in this area.

Museum or gallery collection, archive, or library special collection:
Books and periodicals

Library catalogue:
All or part available in-house

Printed publications:
Newsletter (quarterly)
Special Papers (occasional)
Transactions (annually)

Publications list:
Available online

Access to staff:
Contact by letter, by telephone, by e-mail and via website
Hours: Mon to Fri, 0900 to 1700

Access to building, collection or gallery:
Prior appointment required
Special comments: Members only

Links with:
about 50 local societies in London

Member organisation of:
Council for British Archaeology

LONDON ASSOCIATION OF PRIMAL PSYCHOTHERAPISTS

Acronym or abbreviation: LAPP

West Hill House, 6 Swains Lane, London, N6 6QU

Tel: 020 7267 9616 / 020 7482 4212
Fax: 020 7485 7957
E-mail: info@lapp.org

Website:
http://www.lapp.org

Enquiries:
Enquiries to: General Secretary

Founded:
1990

Organisation type and purpose:
Professional body (membership is by qualification, election or invitation), present number of members: 55, voluntary organisation.

Subject coverage:
Psychotherapy.

Access to staff:
Contact by letter, by telephone, by fax, by e-mail and via website. Appointment necessary. Non-members charged.
Hours: Mon to Fri, 0900 to 1900; Sat

Affiliated to:
The United Kingdom Council for Psychotherapy (UKCP)
  tel: 020 7436 3002

LONDON BAPTIST ASSOCIATION

Acronym or abbreviation: LBA

235 Shaftesbury Avenue, London, WC2H 8EP

Tel: 020 7692 5592
Fax: 020 7692 5593
E-mail: lbaoffice@londonbaptist.org.uk

Website:
http://www.londonbaptist.org.uk

Enquiries:
Enquiries to: Secretary

Founded:
1865

Organisation type and purpose:
Membership association (membership is by election or invitation), registered charity.

Subject coverage:
Baptist churches in Greater London.

Museum or gallery collection, archive, or library special collection:
Records of statistics, ministers, locations of Baptist Churches in Greater London, 1865 onwards

Printed publications:
Annual Directory

Access to staff:
Contact by letter, by fax and by e-mail
Hours: Mon to Fri, 0900 to 1700

Affiliated to:
Baptist Union of Great Britain

LONDON BEREAVEMENT NETWORK

Acronym or abbreviation: LBN

356 Holloway Road, London, N7 6PA

Tel: 020 7700 8134
Fax: 020 7700 8146
E-mail: info@bereavement.org.uk

Website:
http://www.bereavement.org.uk

Enquiries:
Enquiries to: Director
Other contacts: Chairperson

Founded:
1993

Organisation type and purpose:
Membership association (membership is by qualification), present number of members: 115, voluntary organisation, registered charity (charity number 1077215).
Membership is by subscription and qualification. To refer bereaved members of the public in the Greater London area on to their local bereavement support service. To offer training, information and support to staff and volunteers of members services.

Subject coverage:
Bereavement, bereavement counselling and the training of volunteer counsellors.

Museum or gallery collection, archive, or library special collection:
A reference library of journals and periodicals on bereavement and voluntary sector. Issues available to staff and volunteers of member services only
Small lending library of books, videos and audio tapes
Small library of books, periodicals, tapes and videos on bereavement counselling available to members

Printed publications:
Annual Report
Leaflet

Access to staff:
Contact by letter, by telephone, by fax, by e-mail and via website
Hours: Mon to Fri, 0900 to 1700
Special comments: Answerphone outside office hours.

Umbrella body for the:
bereavement support services across London

LONDON BEREAVEMENT RELIEF SOCIETY

175 Tower Bridge Road, London, SE1 2AH

Tel: 020 7407 7585
Fax: 020 7403 6711

Enquiries:
Enquiries to: Information Officer

Founded:
1823

Organisation type and purpose:
Registered charity (charity number 208260).

Subject coverage:
Financial relief in relation to bereavement.

Printed publications:
Annual Report
Leaflet about the Society

Access to staff:
Contact by letter
Hours: Mon to Fri, 0900 to 1700

LONDON BOROUGH OF BARKING AND DAGENHAM

Civic Centre, Dagenham, Essex, RM10 7BN

Tel: 020 8592 4500\ Minicom no. 020 8227 2685
Fax: 020 8595 3758
E-mail: jbufton@barking-dagenham.gov.uk

Website:
http://www.barking-dagenham.gov.uk

Enquiries:
Enquiries to: Chief Executive

Organisation type and purpose:
Local government body.

Subject coverage:
Council.

Access to staff:
Contact by letter, by telephone, by fax, by e-mail and via website

Hours: Mon to Fri, 0900 to 1700

Access for disabled people:
Parking provided, ramped entry

LONDON BOROUGH OF BARNET ARCHIVES AND LOCAL STUDIES CENTRE

80 Daws Lane, Mill Hill, London, NW7 4SL

Tel: 020 8959 6657
E-mail: library.archives@barnet.gov.uk

Website:
http://www.earl.org.uk/familia
Genealogical sources.
http://www.hmc.gov.uk
Deposited lists, RHMC.
http://www.barnet.gov.uk/localstudies

Enquiries:
Enquiries to: Local Studies Manager

Founded:
1965

Organisation type and purpose:
Local government body, public library.

Subject coverage:
All aspects of local study for the area of the
London Borough of Barnet.
Records of predecessor authorities.

Non-library collection catalogue:
All or part available online and in-house

Access to staff:
Contact by letter, by telephone, by e-mail, in
person and via website. Appointment necessary.
Hours: Tue, Wed, Fri, 0930 to 1630; Thu, 1300 to
1900

LONDON BOROUGH OF BEXLEY CENTRAL LIBRARY AND LOCAL STUDIES

Townley Rd, Bexleyheath, DA6 7HJ

Tel: 020 8303 7777
Fax: 020 8304 7058
E-mail: libraries@bexley.gov.uk

Website:
http://elibrary.bexley.gov.uk/rooms
Library website.

Founded:
1899

Organisation type and purpose:
Local government body, public library.

Subject coverage:
Public library service. Local collections.

**Museum or gallery collection, archive, or library
special collection:**
Local studies collections

Non-library collection catalogue:
All or part available online

Library catalogue:
All or part available online

Printed publications:
A range of local history titles including:
Bexley Deneholes (Le Gear R F)
Family History in Bexley (Reilly L)
Hall Place (Shaw J C M and Scott. M)
Medieval Bexley (Du Boulay F R H)
Story of Barnehurst (Thomas E O)
Order printed publications from: Bexley Local Studies
and Archives Centre, Central Library, Townley
Road, Bexleyheath, Kent, DA6 7HJ; tel: 020 8303
7777

Publications list:
Available online and in print

Access to staff:
Contact by letter, by telephone, by fax, by e-mail
and in person. Appointment necessary.
Hours: Dependent on service

Access for disabled people:
Access to all public areas

Branches:
Bexley Village, Blackfen, Bostall, Crayford, Erith,
North Heath, Sidcup, Slade Green, Thamesmead,
Upper Belvedere, Welling
See website

Headquarters address:
Bexley Libraries, Arts and Archives
Footscray Offices, Maidstone Road, Sidcup,
Kent, DA14 5HS.; e-mail: libraries@bexley.gov
.uk

LONDON BOROUGH OF CAMDEN

Camden Town Hall, Judd Street, London, WC1H
9JE

Tel: 020 7278 4444
Fax: 020 7974 3210
E-mail: info@camden.gov.uk

Website:
http://cindex.camden.gov.uk
http://www.camden.gov.uk

Enquiries:
Enquiries to: Chief Executive
Direct e-mail: emily.banfield@camden.gov.uk

Organisation type and purpose:
Local government body.

Subject coverage:
Camden Council services and referral to other local
services.

Library catalogue:
All or part available online

Printed publications:
Annual Report
A-Z of Council Services
Camden Citizen (newspaper, monthly, free)

Access to staff:
Contact by letter, by telephone, by fax, in person
and via website
Hours: Mon to Fri, 0900 to 1700

Other address:
Camden Information Services
Crowndale Centre, 218 Eversholt Street, London,
NW1 1BD; tel: 020 7974 1656; fax: 020 7974 1566;
e-mail: camdeninformationservices@camden.gov
.uk

LONDON BOROUGH OF CAMDEN – LEISURE AND COMMUNITY SERVICES DEPARTMENT

Crowndale Centre, 216–218 Eversholt Street,
London, NW1 1DE

Tel: 020 7974 4001
Fax: 020 7974 1615

Enquiries:
Enquiries to: Librarian
Direct e-mail: david.jones@camden.gov.uk

Founded:
1965

Organisation type and purpose:
Public library.

Subject coverage:
General public library service, philosophy and
psychology.

**Museum or gallery collection, archive, or library
special collection:**
Kate Greenaway collection of early children's
books
Special collections on philosophy and psychology

Non-library collection catalogue:
All or part available online and in-house

Library catalogue:
All or part available online

Publications list:
Available online

Access to staff:
Contact by letter, by telephone, by fax, by e-mail,
in person and via website
Hours: Mon to Fri, 0900 to 1700

Access to building, collection or gallery:
No access other than to staff
Hours: Central Reference Library: Mon, Thu, 1000
to 1900; Tue, Wed, Fri, 1000 to 1800; Sat, 1000 to
1700

Access for disabled people:
Level entry, toilet facilities

Also at:
Central Reference Library
Swiss Cottage, 88 Avenue Road, London, NW3
3HA; tel: 020 7974 6522; fax: 020 7974 6505

LONDON BOROUGH OF ENFIELD – ENFIELD TOWN LIBRARY

66 Church Street, Enfield, Middlesex, EN2 6AX

Tel: 020 8379 8341
Fax: 020 8379 8331
E-mail: central.library@enfieldgov.uk

Website:
http://www.enfield.gov.uk/library
Library homepage, local information.
http://www.enfield.gov.uk/24hourlibrary
Virtual Library, online study and information
resources.
http://www.enfield.gov.uk/localinformation
Local information sheets, lists of groups, societies,
etc. in Enfield.
http://en-gb.facebook.com/pages/Enfield-Library
-and-Museum-Service/125768384131910
Follow Enfield Library and Museum Service on
Facebook.
https://twitter.com/enfieldlibrary
Follow Enfield Libraries on Twitter.

Enquiries:
Enquiries to: Librarian
Direct e-mail: central.reference.library@enfield.gov
.uk
Other contacts: Local History Librarian (tel: 020
8379 2724)

Founded:
1908

Organisation type and purpose:
Local government body, public library.

Non-library collection catalogue:
All or part available online

Library catalogue:
All or part available online and in-house

Access to staff:
Contact by letter, by telephone, by fax, by e-mail,
in person and via website
Hours: Enfield Town Library: Mon, Tue, Thu & Sat,
0930 to 2000; Wed & Fri, 0930 to 1730; please check
for all other libraries

Branch libraries:
Bowes Road Library
Bowes Road, London, N11 1BD; tel: 020 8379
1707; e-mail: bowesroadlibrary@yahoo.co.uk
Bullsmoor Library
Kempe Road, Enfield, Middlesex, EN1 1QS; tel:
020 8379 1723; e-mail: bullsmoor.library@enfield
.gov.uk
Enfield Highway Library
258 Hertford Road, Enfield, Middlesex, EN3
5BN; tel: 020 8379 1710; e-mail: enfield.highway
.library@enfield.gov.uk
Fore Street Library
109–111 Fore Street, Edmonton, N18 2XF; tel:
020 8379 1717; e-mail: weir.hall.library@enfield
.gov.uk
John Jackson Library
Agricola Place, Enfield, Middlesex, EN1 1DW;
tel: 020 8379 1709; e-mail: bush.hill.library@
enfield.gov.uk
Oakwood Library
185–187 Bramley Road, Enfield, Middlesex, N14
4XA; tel: 020 8379 1711; e-mail: oakwood
.library@enfield.gov.uk

continued overleaf

Ponders End Library
College Court, High Street, Enfield, Middlesex,
EN3 4EY; tel: 020 8379 1712; e-mail: ponders.end
.library@enfield.gov.uk
Winchmore Hill Library
Greens Lane, Winchmore Hill, London, N21
3AP; tel: 020 8379 1718; e-mail: winchmore.hill
.library@enfield.gov.uk

Main libraries:
Edmonton Green Library
36–44 South Mall, Edmonton, London, N9 0TN;
tel: 020 8379 2600; e-mail: edmonton.green
.library@gov.uk
Ordnance Road Library
645 Hertford Road, Enfield, Middlesex, EN3
6ND; tel: 020 8379 1725/6; e-mail: ordnance.road
.library@enfield.gov.uk
Palmers Green Library
Broomfield Lane, Palmers Green, London, N13
4EY; tel: 020 8379 2711; e-mail: palmers.green
.library@enfield.gov.uk
Ridge Avenue Library
Ridge Avenue, Winchmore Hill, London, N21
2RH; tel: 020 8379 1714/5; e-mail: ridge.avenue
.library@enfield.gov.uk
Southgate Circus Library
High Street, Southgate, London, N14 6BP; tel:
020 8350 1124; e-mail: southgate.circus.library@
enfield.gov.uk

LONDON BOROUGH OF
HAVERING LIBRARY SERVICE

Central Library, St Edwards Way, Romford, Essex,
RM1 3AR

Tel: 01708 432393
Fax: 01708 432391
E-mail: informationservices.library@havering.gov
.uk

Website:
http://www.havering.gov.uk

Enquiries:
Enquiries to: Information Services Manager
Other contacts: Borough Library Manager

Founded:
1965

Organisation type and purpose:
Local government body, public library.

Subject coverage:
General reference material, central government
publications, European information, local history.

**Museum or gallery collection, archive, or library
special collection:**
Local studies

Non-library collection catalogue:
All or part available online, in-house and in print

Library catalogue:
All or part available online and in print

Printed publications:
Making of Emerson Park (£4.95)
Hornchurch and the New Zealand connection (£5)
A history of Havering-Atte-Bower (£5.95)
A short history of Stubbers (£2.95)
Childhood memories of Hornchurch (£1.50)
From country to cockney (£4.95)
History of Queen's Theatre, Hornchurch (£2.95)
Victoria County History, Romford and Hornchurch
(£4.50)

Publications list:
Available in print

Access to staff:
Contact by letter, by telephone, by fax and by e-
mail. Appointment necessary.
Hours: Mon, 1000 to 2000; Tue to Fri, 0900 to 2000;
Sat, 0900 to 1600

Parent body:
London Borough of Havering
(Romford) Town Hall, Romford, Essex, RM1
3BD; tel: 01708 434343

LONDON BOROUGH OF
HOUNSLOW

Acronym or abbreviation: LBH

The Civic Centre, Lampton Road, Hounslow,
Middlesex, TW3 4DN

Tel: 020 8583 2000
Fax: 020 8583 2598
E-mail: information.ced@hounslow.gov.uk

Website:
http://www.lbhounslow.gov.uk

Enquiries:
Enquiries to: Customer Services Manager
Direct tel: 020 8583 2590
Direct fax: 020 8583 2592

Founded:
1965

Organisation type and purpose:
Local government body.

Subject coverage:
Council information, council tax, refuge, planning,
environmental education, leisure services, housing,
councillors, groups, societies, organisations,
charities and advice-givers.

Access to staff:
Contact by letter, by telephone, by fax, by e-mail,
in person and via website. Appointment necessary.
Hours: Mon to Thu, 0845 to 1700; Fri, 0845 to 1645

Access for disabled people:
Parking provided, ramped entry, access to all
public areas, toilet facilities

LONDON BOROUGH OF
LEWISHAM

Lewisham Town Hall, Catford, London, SE6 4RU

Tel: 020 8695 6000
Fax: 020 8314 5659

Website:
http://www.lewisham.gov.uk

Enquiries:
Enquiries to: Chief Executive
Direct e-mail: barry.quirk@lewisham.gov.uk

Organisation type and purpose:
Local government body.

Subject coverage:
Local government services.

Access to staff:
Contact by letter, by telephone, by fax, by e-mail
and in person
Hours: Mon to Fri, 0900 to 1700

Access to building, collection or gallery:
No prior appointment required

Access for disabled people:
Parking provided, ramped entry, level entry, access
to all public areas, toilet facilities

LONDON BOROUGH OF
LEWISHAM – LIBRARY SERVICE

1st Floor, Town Hall Chambers, Rushey Green,
Catford, London, SE6 4RU

Tel: 020 8314 8024
Fax: 020 8314 3229

Enquiries:
Enquiries to: Librarian

Organisation type and purpose:
Local government body, public library.

Subject coverage:
General, local studies.

Non-library collection catalogue:
All or part available in-house

Access to staff:
Contact by letter, by telephone, by fax and in
person

Hours: Varies from library to library

Libraries at:
Blackheath Village Library
3–4 Blackheath Grove, London, SE3 0DD; tel:
020 8852 5309
Catford Library
Laurence House, Catford, London, SE6 4RU; tel:
020 8314 6399; fax: 020 8314 1110
Crofton Park Library
Brockley Road, London, SE4 2AF; tel: 020 8692
1683
Downham Library
Moorside Road, Downham, London, BR1 5EP;
tel: 020 8698 1475
Forest Hill Library
Dartmouth Road, London, SE23 3HZ; tel: 020
8699 2065; fax: 020 8699 8296
Grove Park Library
Somertrees Avenue, London, SE12 0BX; tel: 020
8857 5794
Lewisham Library
199–201 Lewisham High Street, London, SE13
6LG; tel: 020 8297 9677, minicom 8369; fax: 020
8297 1169
Lewisham Reference Library
199–201 Lewisham High Street, London, SE13
6LG; tel: 020 8297 9430; fax: 020 8297 1169
Local Studies Centre
199–201 Lewisham High Street, London, SE13
6LG; tel: 020 8297 0682; fax: 020 8297 1169
Manor House Library
Old Road, Lee, London, SE13 5SY; tel: 020 8852
0357
New Cross Library
283/5 New Cross Road, London, SE14 6AS; tel:
020 8694 2534
Sydenham Library
Sydenham Road, London, SE26 5SE; tel: 020
8778 7563
Torridon Road Library
Torridon Road, Catford, London, SE6 1RQ; tel:
020 8698 1590
Wavelengths Library
Griffin Street, Deptford, London, SE8 4RJ; tel:
020 8694 2535; fax: 020 8694 9652

LONDON BOROUGH OF TOWER
HAMLETS

Mulberry Place, 5 Clove Crescent, London, E14
2BG

Tel: 020 7364 5000
Fax: 020 7364 4296

Website:
http://www.towerhamlets.gov.uk/

Enquiries:
Enquiries to: Press Office

Organisation type and purpose:
Local government body.

LONDON BUDDHIST CENTRE

Acronym or abbreviation: LBC

51 Roman Road, Bethnal Green, London, E2 0HU

Tel: 0845 458 4716
Fax: 0871 433 5995
E-mail: info@lbc.org.uk

Website:
http://www.lbc.org.uk
http://www.londonbuddhistcentre.com

Enquiries:
Enquiries to: Centre Director
Other contacts: Assistant Centre Director

Founded:
1978

Organisation type and purpose:
International organisation, voluntary organisation,
registered charity.
Religious centre.

Subject coverage:
Buddhism, the Western Buddhist Order;
meditation, yoga, Tai Chi, acupuncture, alternative
health, Alexander Technique, osteopathy,
reflexology, shiatsu, homoeopathy, naturopathy,
nutritional therapy, medical herbalism, massage,
kinesiology, hypnotherapy, polarity therapy, reiki,
counselling and psychotherapy.

Museum or gallery collection, archive, or library special collection:
Book, video and audio-tape library

Printed publications:
A concise history of Buddhism
Introducing Buddhism
Newsletter
Change Your Mind
Many other books on Buddhism
Order printed publications from: Books, Windhorse
Publications, 11 Park Road, Birmingham, B13 8AB,
tel: 0121 449 9997, e-mail: shantavira@compuserve
.com

Electronic and video publications:
Clear Vision (series of videos)
Dharmachakra Tapes and CD-ROMs
Order electronic and video publications from: Audio
Artefacts, Dharmachakra, 3 Coral Park, Henley
Road, Cambridge, CB1 3EA, tel: 01223 516821, e-
mail: orders@dharmachakra.freeserve.co.uk
Visual Artefacts, Clearvision Trust, 16–20 Turner
Street, Northern Quarter, Manchester, M4 1DZ, tel:
0161 839 9579, fax: 0161 839 4815, e-mail:
clearvision@clear-vision.org

Publications list:
Available in print

Access to staff:
Contact by letter, by telephone, by fax, by e-mail,
in person and via website. Appointment necessary.
Hours: Mon to Fri, 1000 to 1700

Access to building, collection or gallery:
No prior appointment required
Hours: Mon to Fri, 1000 to 1700

Centre of the:
Friends of the Western Buddhist Order (FWBO)
30 Chantry Road, Birmingham, B13 8AL; tel:
0121 449 3700; fax: 0121 449 3780; e-mail:
communications@fwbo.org; website: http://
www.fwbo.org/

Has:
22 public centres in UK and retreat centres and
smaller groups, also centres abroad

LONDON BUDDHIST VIHARA

Dharmapala Building, The Avenue, Chiswick,
London, W4 1UD

Tel: 020 8995 9493
Fax: 020 8994 8130
E-mail: london.vihara@virgin.net

Website:
http://www.londonbuddhistvihara.org

Enquiries:
Enquiries to: Secretary
Other contacts: Head Monk

Founded:
1926

Organisation type and purpose:
Voluntary organisation.
Religious institution.
To spread knowledge of Buddhism.

Subject coverage:
General Buddhism, specialising in the Theravada
tradition; teaching of Pali and Sinhala languages
(the latter to GCSE); meditation.

Museum or gallery collection, archive, or library special collection:
Buddhist scriptures written in Pali language on Ola
leaves (palm leaves)
Reference Library (over 3500 titles) of books in
English, Pali, Sinhalese, Burmese and many
European languages

Library catalogue:
All or part available in-house

Printed publications:
Information sheets
Samadhi (magazine, quarterly)
Newsletter

Access to staff:
Contact by letter, by telephone, by fax, by e-mail
and in person
Hours: 0900 to 2100, seven days a week

Access to building, collection or gallery:
No access other than to staff

Access for disabled people:
Ramped entry, access to all public areas, toilet
facilities

Managers:
Maha Bodhi Society of Sri Lanka

Owned by:
Anagarika Dharmapala Trust (Sri Lanka)

LONDON BUSINESS SCHOOL

Acronym or abbreviation: LBS

Sussex Place, Regent's Park, London, NW1 4SA

Tel: 020 7262 5050
Fax: 020 7724 7875

Website:
http://www.london.edu/library/
London Business School library catalogue
including details of working papers and
accessions.

Enquiries:
Enquiries to: Librarian
Other contacts: Information Service Manager for
enquiries about fee-based business research.

Organisation type and purpose:
University department or institute.

Subject coverage:
Management and business management;
education; international business; marketing;
market data; production; finance; company
financial data; accounting; economics and
economic forecasting; industries; operational
research; statistics; computers and data processing;
Europe.

Museum or gallery collection, archive, or library special collection:
Corporate Library: annual reports of about 8000
British, European, North American, and Asian
Pacific companies
Market Research Reports

Library catalogue:
All or part available online

Printed publications:
Serials Holdings lists (twice a year, £15)
London Classification of Business Studies
Thesaurus (revised ed. Feb 1998)

Access to staff:
Non-members charged.
Hours: Mon to Fri, 0900 to 1700

Access for disabled people:
Level entry, toilet facilities

Affiliated to:
University of London

Other addresses:
London Business School Information Service (Fee
based)
tel: 020 7723 3404; fax: 020 7706 1897; e-mail:
infoserve@london.edu

LONDON CENTRE FOR FASHION STUDIES

Acronym or abbreviation: LCFS

Bradley Close, 8 White Lion Street, Islington,
London, N1 9PF

Tel: 020 7713 1991
Fax: 020 7713 1997
E-mail: learnf@shion.demon.co.uk

Website:
http://www.fashionstudies.co.uk
http://www.fashion.studies.com
Details of full and part time courses.

Enquiries:
Enquiries to: Director

Founded:
1991

Organisation type and purpose:
University department or institute, suitable for
ages: 18+, training organisation, consultancy,
publishing house.
Independent fashion school.

Subject coverage:
Fashion: pattern technology, pattern grading
techniques, grading and dress modelling, fashion
business, marketing, merchandising, production,
teacher training – fashion teachers.

Printed publications:
Grading for the Fashion Industry
Pattern Cutting and Making Up
Pattern Cutting and Making Up for Outerwear
Fashions
The Art of Dress Modelling

Electronic and video publications:
The Art of Dress Modelling (video, series 1 and 2)
The Art of Jacket Pattern Cutting (video, series 3)

Publications list:
Available in print

Access to staff:
Contact by letter, by telephone, by fax, by e-mail,
in person and via website
Hours: Open some evenings

In partnership with:
Middlesex University

LONDON CENTRE FOR PSYCHOTHERAPY

Acronym or abbreviation: LCP

32 Leighton Road, London, NW5 2QE

Tel: 020 7482 2002
Fax: 020 7482 4222

Website:
http://www.lcp-psychotherapy.org.uk

Enquiries:
Enquiries to: Chairman

Founded:
1973

Organisation type and purpose:
Professional body (membership is by subscription,
qualification), present number of members: 200,
registered charity (charity number 267244),
training organisation.

Subject coverage:
Psychotherapy.

Access to staff:
Contact by letter, by telephone, by e-mail and via
website
Hours: Mon to Fri, 1000 to 1600

Access to building, collection or gallery:
Prior appointment required

LONDON CHAMBER OF COMMERCE AND INDUSTRY

Acronym or abbreviation: LCCI

33 Queen Street, London, EC4R 1AP

Tel: 020 7248 4444
Fax: 020 7489 0391
E-mail: lc@londonchamber.co.uk

Website:
http://www.londonchamber.co.uk

continued overleaf

Outline of services offered. Details of events and press releases.

Enquiries:
Enquiries to: Information Officer
Direct e-mail: info@londonchamber.co.uk

Founded:
1881

Organisation type and purpose:
Membership association (membership is by subscription), present number of members: 3500.
To help London businesses succeed by promoting their interests and expanding their opportunities as members of a worldwide business network.

Subject coverage:
Business information in the broadest sense, company information, market information, economic and financial data, suppliers of goods and services, occupational; Euro Information Centre, European legislation.

Trade and statistical information:
Activities on the London Economy. European statistics.

Printed publications:
Annual Review of the London Economy (subscribers only)
Directory of Members (free to members)
Quarterly Economic Report and Survey (subscribers only)

Access to staff:
Contact by letter, by telephone, by fax, by e-mail, in person and via website. Non-members charged.
Hours: Mon to Fri, 0900 to 1730

Access to building, collection or gallery:
No prior appointment required for members
Hours: Mon to Fri, 0900 to 1730
Special comments: Access free to members only; no access to non-members.

Access for disabled people:
Level entry, toilet facilities

LONDON CHAMBER OF COMMERCE AND INDUSTRY EXAMINATIONS BOARD

Acronym or abbreviation: LCCIEB

Athena House, 112 Station Road, Sidcup, Kent, DA15 7BJ

Tel: 020 8302 0261
Fax: 020 8302 4169
E-mail: enquiries@ediplc.com

Website:
http://www.lccieb.com

Enquiries:
Enquiries to: General Manager – Sales and Marketing

Founded:
1887

Organisation type and purpose:
International organisation, registered charity.
Examinations board and business related NVQ awarding body.

Subject coverage:
LCCIEB offers a wide range of qualifications both timetabled and on demand. English and International Languages, Information Technology, Secretarial and Business Administration, Customer Service and Marketing, Finance, Travel and Tourism and a wide range of business-related NVQs.

Publications list:
Available online and in print

Access to staff:
Contact by letter, by telephone, by fax, by e-mail and via website
Hours: Mon to Fri, 0900 to 1700

Access to building, collection or gallery:
No access other than to staff

LONDON CHAMBER PLAYERS

Acronym or abbreviation: LCP

PO Box 84, London, NW11 8AL

Tel: 020 8455 6799
Fax: 020 8455 6799
E-mail: london-players@excite.com

Enquiries:
Enquiries to: Director
Direct fax: 020 8455 6799

Founded:
1979

Organisation type and purpose:
Registered charity, suitable for ages: children, adults
Musical performances.

Subject coverage:
Music, music education

Access to staff:
Contact by letter, by telephone, by fax and by e-mail. Appointment necessary.
Hours: Mon to Fri, 0930 to 1730

Access to building, collection or gallery:
Prior appointment required

LONDON CITY PRESBYTERIAN CHURCH

St Botolph-without-Aldersgate, Aldersgate Street, London, EC1A 4EU

Website:
http://www.londonfreechurch.org.uk
Service times, history of building.

Enquiries:
Enquiries to: Information Officer
Direct e-mail: davidtastrain@ntlworld.com

Formerly called:
Free Church of Scotland; Cole Abbey Presbyterian Church (year of change c. 2003)

Organisation type and purpose:
Membership association (membership is by qualification), voluntary organisation, registered charity.

Subject coverage:
History and present activities of Reformed and Presbyterian Churches.

Access to staff:
Contact by letter, by telephone, by fax and via website
Hours: Mon to Fri, 0900 to 1700

Access to building, collection or gallery:
Prior appointment required

LONDON CLEARING HOUSE LIMITED, THE

Acronym or abbreviation: LCH

Aldgate House, 33 Aldgate High Street, London, EC3N 1EA

Tel: 020 7426 7000
Fax: 020 7426 7001

Website:
http://www.lch.com

Enquiries:
Enquiries to: Corporate Communications Director
Direct tel: 020 7426 7234
Direct fax: 020 7426 7665
Direct e-mail: matchm@lch.co.uk

Founded:
1888

Organisation type and purpose:
International organisation, present number of members: 116, service industry.
To clear contracts traded on London's major exchanges. Clearing house for LCH Repoclear – Interbank trades in European Government Repos; Clearing house for LCH Swapclear – Interbank

interest rate swaps. Clearing house for LCH Equity Clear – equities traded on the London Stock Exchange's SETS system.

Subject coverage:
Risk management, clearing, settlement.

Printed publications:
Market Protection (free)
Rules, Regulations and Procedures (free, available on-line)
Understanding London Span (free, available on-line)
Order printed publications from: Member Liaison Department
at the same address

Publications list:
Available in print

Access to staff:
Contact by telephone, by fax, by e-mail and via website
Hours: Mon to Fri, 0930 to 1730

LONDON COLLEGE OF COMMUNICATION

Acronym or abbreviation: LCC

Information Services: Library, Elephant and Castle, London, SE1 6SB

Tel: 020 7514 8026
Fax: 020 7514 6597
E-mail: libraryenquiries@lcc.arts.ac.uk

Website:
http://www.arts.ac.uk/library

Enquiries:
Other contacts: Information Services Librarian (for access to the Library)

Organisation type and purpose:
University department or institute.

Subject coverage:
Art and design; fine art; graphic design; animation; printing and publishing; film and video; journalism; media; photography.

Museum or gallery collection, archive, or library special collection:
Printing Historical Collection – The Art of the Western Book

Zine collection

Library catalogue:
All or part available online

Printed publications:
Information guides in major subject areas

Access to staff:
Contact by letter and by e-mail. Appointment necessary.
Hours: Mon to Thu, 0930 to 2015; Fri, 0930 to 1745; Sat, 1000 to 1545
Vacation opening times: please telephone to confirm

Constituent part of:
University of the Arts London

LONDON COLLEGE OF FASHION LIBRARY

20 John Princes Street, London, W1G 0BJ

Tel: 020 7514 7453/7455
Fax: 020 7514 7580

Website:
http://www.linst.ac.uk/library

Enquiries:
Enquiries to: Chief Librarian
Direct tel: 020 7514 7518

Subject coverage:
Fashion, design, clothing manufacture, embroidery, hairdressing, beauty therapy, costume history, textile history, footwear and accessories.

Museum or gallery collection, archive, or library special collection:
Clothing Institute Special Collection on historic tailoring
Fashion Photographs
Hairdressers Journal (bound volumes 1882 to the present; unique in the world)
History of Costume Collection

Access to staff:
Appointment necessary.
Hours: Mon to Thu, 0930 to 2015; Fri, 1000 to 1715

Constituent college of the:
London Institute

Other address:
Cordwainers at The London College of Fashion
182 Mare Street, London, E8 3RE

LONDON COLLEGE OF MASSAGE

Acronym or abbreviation: LCM

16 Bramley Court, Wickham Street, Kent, DA16 3DG

Tel: 020 3259 0000
E-mail: training@londoncollegeofmassage.co.uk

Website:
http://www.massagelondon.com

Enquiries:
Enquiries to: Director

Founded:
1987

Organisation type and purpose:
Training organisation.
Clinic.

Subject coverage:
Massage training and treatments; complementary health; anatomy and physiology; remedial and sports massage and other related postgraduate courses.

Museum or gallery collection, archive, or library special collection:
Dissertations relating to massage therapy

Printed publications:
Home Health Massage (Kavanagh W, pub Hamlyn)
The massage manual (Fiona Harrold, pub Headline)

Electronic and video publications:
Basic Massage (Pickwick video PV2256)

Publications list:
Available in print

Access to staff:
Contact by letter, by telephone, by fax and by e-mail. Appointment necessary.
Hours: Mon to Fri, 1100 to 1900

Affiliated to:
British Complementary Medicine Association
9 Soar Lane, Leicester, LE3 5DE; tel: 0116 242 5406; fax: 0116 242 5496
British Massage Therapy Council
17 Rymers Lane, Oxford, OX4 3JU; tel: 01865 774123; fax: 01865 774123
Institute of Complementary Medicine
PO Box 194, London, SE16 1QZ; tel: 020 7237 5165; fax: 020 7237 5175

LONDON COLLEGE OF OSTEOPATHIC MEDICINE/ OSTEOPATHIC ASSOCIATION CLINIC

Acronym or abbreviation: LCOM

8–10 Boston Place, London, NW1 6QH

Tel: 020 7262 1128
Fax: 020 7723 7492

Enquiries:
Enquiries to: Administrator

Founded:
1946

Organisation type and purpose:
Registered charity (charity number 209713), suitable for ages: post-graduates, training organisation.
Postgraduate college training (qualified doctors only) in Osteopathy, charity clinic for osteopathic patients.

Printed publications:
Directory of members

Access to staff:
Contact by letter, by telephone and by fax.
Appointment necessary.
Hours: Mon to Fri, 0930 to 1645

LONDON COLLEGE OF TRADITIONAL ACUPUNCTURE AND ORIENTAL MEDICINE

Acronym or abbreviation: LCTA

60 Ballards Lane, Finchley, London, N3 2BU

Tel: 020 8371 0820
Fax: 020 8371 0830
E-mail: college@lcta.com

Website:
http://www.lcta.com
Course information.

Enquiries:
Enquiries to: Course Administrator

Founded:
1992

Organisation type and purpose:
Training organisation.

Subject coverage:
Professional training in acupuncture, oriental herbal medicine, tui na massage, nutrition and medical qi gong.

Printed publications:
Prospectus (free)
Dragons Tale (newsletter)

Access to staff:
Contact by letter, by telephone, by fax, by e-mail and via website. Appointment necessary.
Hours: Mon to Sun, 0900 to 1730

LONDON CYCLO-CROSS ASSOCIATION

Acronym or abbreviation: LCCA

25 Lenham Road, Platt Heath, Kent, ME17 2NY

Tel: 01622 850533
E-mail: MondSBarry@aol.com

Website:
http://www.britishcycling.org.uk

Enquiries:
Enquiries to: General Secretary
Direct tel: 020 8662 3963

Organisation type and purpose:
Voluntary organisation.
Cyclo-cross racing.

Subject coverage:
Sport, cycling, mountain biking, competition, cyclo-cross.

Access to staff:
Contact by letter, by telephone, by e-mail and via website
Hours: Mon to Fri, 0900 to 1700

Parent body:
British Cycling
Stuart Street, Manchester, M11 4DQ; tel: 0870 871 2000; fax: 0870 871 2001; e-mail: cyclo-cross@ britishcycling.org.uk; website: www .britishcycling.org.uk

LONDON DISTRICT SURVEYORS ASSOCIATION

Acronym or abbreviation: LDSA

c/o Building Control Officer, London Borough of Merton, Merton Civic Centre, London Road, Morden, Surrey, SM4 5DX

Tel: 020 8545 3121
Fax: 020 8543 6085
E-mail: trevor.mcintosh@merton.gov.uk

Website:
http://www.londonbuildingcontrol.org
Contacts, history, publications, regulations, frequently asked questions.

Enquiries:
Enquiries to: Honorary Secretary

Founded:
1987

Organisation type and purpose:
Professional body (membership is by election or invitation), present number of members: 33.
An organisation of the Heads of the Building Control service in all the 32 London Boroughs and the City of London.
To further the profession and be a vehicle for achieving uniformity; to collate and disseminate information and to co-operate with similar bodies; to promote training and continuing professional development; to petition, confer with and promote deputations to government and other public or professional bodies; to guide the building control offices in London with up-to-date, expert advice to achieve uniformity of interpretation and operation of the Building Regulations.

Subject coverage:
Commitees include those dealing with the following subjects: electrical and mechanical; career development and training; management and legislation; publications and seminars; safety at sports grounds; fire safety and means of escape; licensing; technical and foundations; LANTAC; and marketing. IT working party and benchmark forum.

Museum or gallery collection, archive, or library special collection:
Minutes of general meetings, policy decisions, questions and information

Printed publications:
National Directory of Development Services – Listing Local Authorities & Contact Names (1997)
Level of Service – Recommended Level of Service for the Building Control Function (1999)
Enforcement Procedures – Building Regulations Practical Guidance (1995)
Risk Assessment – Management of Health & Safety at Work
Technical Standards for Places of Entertainment (2001)
Model National Standard Conditions for Places of Entertainment (2002)
Fire Safety Guides (2 documents, 1990–1997)
Safety of Sports Grounds (8 documents, 1990–1999)
Foundations No 1 – Guidance Notes for the Design of Bored Straight Shafted Piles in London Clay (2000)
Order printed publications from: LDSA Publications
From: LABC Contact details above

Electronic and video publications:
Some publications are available on disc

Publications list:
Available online and in print

Access to staff:
Contact by letter, by e-mail and via website
Hours: Mon to Fri, 0900 to 1700

continued overleaf

A region of the:
District Surveyors Association (of England &
Wales) (DSA)
  c/o LABC Services, Third floor, 66 South
  Lambeth Road, London, SW8 1RL; tel: 0844 561
  6136; fax: 01625 435076; e-mail: info@labc.uk
  .com; website: http://www.labc.uk.com

Liaison with bodies such as:
London Fire and Emergency Planning Authority
(LFEPA)
  8 Albert Embankment, London, SE1 7SD; tel: 020
  7587 2000; e-mail: info@london-fire.gov.uk

LONDON DOUGLAS MOTOR CYCLE CLUB LIMITED

Acronym or abbreviation: LDMCC

48 Standish Avenue, Stoke Lodge, Patchway,
Bristol, BS34 6AG

Tel: 01454 898185

Website:
http://www.douglasmotorcycles.co.uk
Club history, activities and contact address, online
application form.

Enquiries:
Enquiries to: Membership Secretary
Direct e-mail: via website

Founded:
1928

Organisation type and purpose:
Membership association (membership is by
subscription), present number of members: 1,100.

Subject coverage:
Douglas motor cycles manufactured at
Kingswood, Bristol 1907–1957; spares service for
pre-war and post-war machines; marque specialist
providing technical information on most models; a
register of all Douglas machines known to the club
throughout the world providing a source of
information for identification and dating; machine
transfers and badges.

**Museum or gallery collection, archive, or library
special collection:**
Archive of technical information

Printed publications:
The New Conrod (magazine, 6 times a year, club
  members only)

Access to staff:
Contact by letter
Hours: Mon to Fri, 0900 to 1700

Affiliated to:
Auto Cycle Union under title of 'LDMCC' as 'Non-
Territorial Club'

LONDON ELECTRONICS COLLEGE

Acronym or abbreviation: LEC

20 Penywern Road, London, SW5 9SU

Tel: 020 7373 8721
Fax: 020 7244 8733
E-mail: contact@lec.org.uk

Website:
http://www.lec.org.uk

Enquiries:
Enquiries to: Principal

Founded:
1892

Organisation type and purpose:
Independent further and higher education.

Subject coverage:
Electronics, TV and video, telecommunications,
microprocessors, software, IT, computer systems,
networks.

Access to staff:
Appointment necessary.
Hours: Mon to Fri, 0900 to 1700

LONDON FERTILITY CENTRE

Formal name: London Fertility Centre Ltd
Acronym or abbreviation: LFC

Cozens House, 112a Harley Street, London, W1G
7JH

Tel: 020 7224 0707
Fax: 020 7224 3102
E-mail: info@lfc.org.uk

Website:
http://www.lfc.org.uk
Information on LFC and treatments offered.

Enquiries:
Enquiries to: Information Officer
Other contacts: General Manager.

Founded:
1990

Formerly called:
London Gynaecology and Fertility Centre Ltd
(year of change 2010)

Organisation type and purpose:
Assisted conception, IVF and gynaecology

Subject coverage:
Gynaecology and fertility.

Printed publications:
The following available free, direct:
Information Packs
Patient Information Leaflets
Price Lists

Access to staff:
Contact by letter, by telephone, by fax, by e-mail
and via website
Hours: Mon to Fri, 0900 to 1730; Sat, Sun, 0900 to
1600

Access for disabled people:
Ramped entry, toilet facilities

Parent body:
Spire Healthcare
  120 Holborn, London

LONDON FIRE AND EMERGENCY PLANNING AUTHORITY

Acronym or abbreviation: LFEPA

Room 520, Hampton House, 20 Albert
Embankment, London, SE1 7SD

Tel: 020 7587 2000
Fax: 020 7587 6086
E-mail: libraryservices@london-fire.gov.uk

Website:
http://www.london-fire.gov.uk

Enquiries:
Enquiries to: Library Information Resources Centre
Manager
Direct tel: 020 7587 6340

Founded:
1983

Organisation type and purpose:
Local government body.
Responsible for running London Fire Brigade and
providing emergency planning in London.

Subject coverage:
Fire protection, fire fighting, fire prevention,
chemical hazards, history of fire fighting,
emergencies.

Access to staff:
Contact by letter, by telephone, by fax and via
website. Appointment necessary.
Hours: Mon to Fri, 0900 to 1700

Also known as:
London Fire Brigade

Member organisation of:
Fire Information Group (an information exchange
co-operative in the fire and loss prevention field)

LONDON GREEN BELT COUNCIL

4A Paddock Way, Fenny Stratford, Milton Keynes,
MK2 2NB

Tel: 07794 592924
E-mail: info@londongreenbeltcouncil.org.uk

Website:
http://www.londongreenbeltcouncil.org.uk

Enquiries:
Enquiries to: Honorary Secretary

Founded:
1954

Organisation type and purpose:
Grouping of organisations with an interest in
preserving and promoting the Green Belt. No
individual members.

Subject coverage:
Green Belts, and particularly the Metropolitan
Green Belt.

Member organisations:
Campaign to Protect Rural England
Local amenity societies
Open Spaces Society
Parish councils
Ramblers Association

LONDON GYMNASTICS FEDERATION

Acronym or abbreviation: LGF

4 Victoria Road, Chingford, London, E4 6BZ

Tel: 020 8529 1142
Fax: 020 8529 1142
E-mail: lgf@longym.freeserve.co.uk

Website:
http://www.longym.freeserve.co.uk
General information plus links to find further
information.

Enquiries:
Enquiries to: General Secretary

Organisation type and purpose:
Membership association (membership is by
subscription), present number of members: 65
clubs, 11,000 members, voluntary organisation.
Governing body of the sport for London.

Subject coverage:
Gymnastics, pre-school, boys, girls, adults, special
needs, competitive and recreational, all
information regarding gymnastic clubs in the
Greater London area, gymnastic coaching courses,
gymnastic competitions and events.

Printed publications:
Regional newsletter (6 times a year, £10 a year)

Access to staff:
Contact by telephone, by fax, by e-mail and via
website
Hours: Mon to Fri, 0900 to 1700

Parent body:
British Gymnastics Association (BG)
  tel: 01952 820330

LONDON HAZARDS CENTRE

Acronym or abbreviation: LHC

Hampstead Town Hall Centre, 213 Haverstock
Hill, London, NW3 4QP

Tel: 020 7794 5999
Fax: 020 7794 4702
E-mail: mail@lhc.org.uk

Website:
http://www.lhc.org.uk
Bibliographic and full-text databases for
subscribers and affiliates.

Enquiries:
Enquiries to: The Advice Worker
Other contacts: Information Officer

Founded:
1984

Organisation type and purpose:
Advisory body, membership association
(membership is by subscription), voluntary
organisation, registered charity (charity number
1981088), training organisation, consultancy,
research organisation, publishing house.
Work with tenants associations and workplace
safety representatives.

Subject coverage:
Work-related ill health, occupational health and
safety law, health and safety in the workplace and
the community.

Printed publications:
Chemical Hazards Handbook 1999 (£15 plus p&p)
Factsheets (contact the Centre for current list)
Fluorescent Lighting: A health hazard overhead
 (£5 plus p&p)
Hard Labour: Stress, ill-health and hazardous
 employment practices (1994, £6.95 plus p&p)
Practical handbooks on health and safety in the
 workplace and community, including:
RSI Hazards Handbook (1996, £12 plus p&p)
Sick Building Syndrome – causes, effects and
 control (1990, £4.50 plus p&p)
The Asbestos Hazards Handbook (1995, £12 plus
 p&p)
The Daily Hazard (newspaper, members)
VDU Work and the Hazards to Health (1993, £6.50
 plus p&p)

Publications list:
Available online and in print

Access to staff:
Contact by letter, by telephone, by fax, by e-mail
and via website
Hours: Mon, Tue, Thu, Fri, 1000 to 1200 and 1400 to
1700
Special comments: Charges to professional
organisations, solicitors, media, etc. Free service
only to Londoners.

Access to building, collection or gallery:
No prior appointment required

Connections with:
London Hazards Centre Trust Ltd
 at the same address

LONDON INSTITUTE FOR CONTEMPORARY CHRISTIANITY

Acronym or abbreviation: LICC

St Peters Church, Vere Street, London, W1G 0DQ

Tel: 020 7399 9555
Fax: 020 7399 9556
E-mail: mail@licc.org.uk

Website:
http://www.licc.org.uk
Work of LICC, articles, publications, events,
courses.

Enquiries:
Enquiries to: Executive Director

Founded:
1982

Organisation type and purpose:
Registered charity (charity number 286102),
training organisation. Christian adult education.

Subject coverage:
The relevance and application of the Bible and the
Christian faith in today's world, application of
biblical teaching to contemporary issues and
everyday life.

Printed publications:
Magazines (quarterly, free to applicants)
Workwise (electronic magazine)
Email newsletter on Biblical reflection and
 contemporary culture (2 times per week)

Electronic and video publications:
Audio tapes of lectures (available for sale)
Catalogue available on request

Access to staff:
Contact by letter, by telephone, by fax, by e-mail
and in person
Hours: Mon to Fri, 0900 to 1700

LONDON INVESTMENT BANKING ASSOCIATION

Acronym or abbreviation: LIBA

6 Frederick's Place, London, EC2R 8BT

Tel: 020 7796 3606
Fax: 020 7796 4345
E-mail: liba@liba.org.uk

Website:
http://www.liba.org.uk

Enquiries:
Enquiries to: Secretary

Organisation type and purpose:
Trade association (membership is by subscription).

Subject coverage:
Investment banking and securities industry in the
United Kingdom including corporate finance, asset
management and securities trading, and the
regulation thereof.

**Museum or gallery collection, archive, or library
special collection:**
Book of Prospectuses, June 1939 to August 1984
Issuing House Year Book from 1939 to 1987
Prospectuses on UK companies to 6 June 1939
Times (later Extel)

Printed publications:
Annual Report

Access to staff:
Contact by letter and by e-mail
Hours: Mon to Fri, 0930 to 1730

Access to building, collection or gallery:
No access other than to staff

LONDON IRISH CENTRE

50–52 Camden Square, London, NW1 9XB

Tel: 020 7916 2222
Fax: 020 7916 2638
E-mail: info@londonirishcentre.org

Website:
http://www.londonirishcentre.org

Enquiries:
Enquiries to: Director

Founded:
1954

Organisation type and purpose:
Advisory body, voluntary organisation, registered
charity (charity number 221172), training
organisation, research organisation.

Subject coverage:
Welfare, culture and social events.

Information services:
Advice and support; social and cultural activities.

Education services:
Various classes.

Access to staff:
Contact by letter, by telephone, by fax, by e-mail,
in person and via website
Hours: Mon to Fri, 0900 to 1700

Access to building, collection or gallery:
Hours: 0900 to 2200

Access for disabled people:
Lift assistance

LONDON JEWISH CULTURAL CENTRE

Ivy House, 94–96 North End Road, London, NW11
7SX

Tel: 020 8457 5000

E-mail: admin@ljcc.org.uk

Website:
http://www.ljcc.org.uk

Organisation type and purpose:
A registered charity (no. 1081014) and company
limited by guarantee (no. 3811133), funded by
donors, benefactors and supporters and by income
generated from courses and events.

Subject coverage:
Jewish history, life and learning, languages, current
affairs, music, literature, art and film.

Education services:
Day and evening courses in Jewish history, life and
learning, languages, current affairs, music,
literature, art and film, and outreach courses to the
wider community. Holocaust and Anti-racism
Education Department.

**Museum or gallery collection, archive, or library
special collection:**
Archive of Jewish-related feature and
 documentary film

LONDON LESBIAN & GAY SWITCHBOARD

Acronym or abbreviation: LLGS

PO Box 7324, London, N1 9QS

Tel: 020 7837 7324 (helpline); 020 7689 8501
(minicom)
Fax: 020 7837 7300
E-mail: admin@llgs.org.uk

Website:
http://www.llgs.org.uk
London Lesbian & Gay Switchboard (LLGS)
provides an information, support and referral
service for lesbians, gay men, bisexual and trans
people, and anyone who needs to consider issues
around their sexuality.

Enquiries:
Enquiries to: Administrator
Direct tel: 020 7837 6768

Founded:
1974

Organisation type and purpose:
Voluntary organisation, registered charity (charity
number 296193).
To provide information and advice to lesbians, gay
men, bisexual and trans people, and to anyone
with questions about sexuality.

Subject coverage:
Sexual health, legal advice and information, for all
callers around lesbian, gay, bisexual and
transgender issues (LGBT).

Publications list:
Available online and in print

Access to staff:
Contact by letter, by telephone, by fax, by e-mail
and via website

Access to building, collection or gallery:
No access other than to staff and volunteers

Links with:
Telephone Helplines Association (THA)

LONDON LIBRARY

14 St James's Square, London, SW1Y 4LG

Tel: 020 7930 7705
Fax: 020 7766 4766
E-mail: membership@londonlibrary.co.uk

Website:
http://www.londonlibrary.co.uk

Enquiries:
Enquiries to: Librarian

Founded:
1841

continued overleaf

Organisation type and purpose:
Membership association (membership is by
subscription), present number of members: 7,000,
registered charity (charity number 312175).
Independent subscription library (lending and
reference).

Subject coverage:
Extensive collection of books and periodicals in
English and all major European languages within
the arts and humanities with particular strengths
in literature, history and related subjects. Good
representation of fine and applied art, architecture,
bibliography, philosophy, religion, topography and
travel, with some coverage of the social sciences.

**Museum or gallery collection, archive, or library
special collection:**
Heron-Allen Collection (on Omar Khayyam)
Higginson Collection (books on hunting and field
sports)

Non-library collection catalogue:
All or part available online

Access to staff:
Contact by letter, by telephone, by fax, by e-mail
and via website. Appointment necessary. Access
for members only. Letter of introduction required.
All charged.
Hours: Mon to Wed, 0930 to 1930; Thu to Sat, 0930
to 1730

LONDON LIBRARY & INFORMATION DEVELOPMENT UNIT

Acronym or abbreviation: LLIDU

20 Guildford Street, London, WC1N 1DZ

Tel: 020 7692 3389
Fax: 020 7692 3393
E-mail: ldnlidu@llidu.ac.uk

Website:
http://www.londonlinks.ac.uk
Supports access to electronic information for
librarians and healthcare professionals.

Enquiries:
Enquiries to: Head of Unit
Other contacts: Unit Co-ordinator

Founded:
April 2001

Organisation type and purpose:
NHS health care library information network; 50
library service points offering a range of services.
The Unit is a strategic and advisory body working
closely with Workforce Development
Confederations and other stakeholders and
professional colleagues to co-ordinate and develop
library and information services for all NHS staff in
line with national policy guidance.

Subject coverage:
Strategic advice on library and information
services to support NHS staff.

Electronic and video publications:
Union List of Serials and Regional Documents
Database (CD-ROM)

Publications list:
Available online

Access to staff:
Contact by telephone, by fax, by e-mail and via
website
Hours: Mon to Fri, 0900 to 1700

Access to building, collection or gallery:
Prior appointment required

Affiliated to:
London Department of Postgraduate Medical &
Dental Education
NHS London Region

LONDON MARATHON

Formal name: The Flora London Marathon

PO Box 1234, London, SE1 8RZ

Tel: 020 7620 4117
Fax: 020 7620 4208

Website:
http://www.london-marathon.co.uk

Enquiries:
Enquiries to: Administrator

Organisation type and purpose:
Registered charity (charity number 283813).
Organisation of sporting events.

Access to staff:
Contact by letter, by telephone and by fax
Hours: Mon to Fri, 0900 to 1700

Access to building, collection or gallery:
No access other than to staff

LONDON MATHEMATICAL SOCIETY

Acronym or abbreviation: LMS

De Morgan House, 57–58 Russell Square, London,
WC1B 4HS

Tel: 020 7637 3686
Fax: 020 7323 3655
E-mail: lms@lms.ac.uk

Website:
http://www.lms.ac.uk

Enquiries:
Enquiries to: Executive Secretary

Founded:
1865

Organisation type and purpose:
Learned society.

Subject coverage:
Mathematics.

**Museum or gallery collection, archive, or library
special collection:**
Photographs of academic mathematicians from
1865 onwards to the present

Printed publications:
Publications direct through a publishing house
Order printed publications from: Oxford University
Press

Electronic and video publications:
via our website

Publications list:
Available online and in print

Access to staff:
Contact by letter, by telephone, by fax and by e-
mail
Hours: Mon to Fri, 0930 to 1700

Access to building, collection or gallery:
Prior appointment required

LONDON MEDIEVAL SOCIETY

Acronym or abbreviation: LMS

The Colloquia Secretary, 3 Rothwell Street,
London, NW1 8YH

Tel: 020 7722 1040
E-mail: thodgsonjones@googlemail.com

Website:
http://www.the-lms.org

Enquiries:
Enquiries to: Membership Secretary
Direct e-mail: r.ellis@qmul.ac.uk

Founded:
1946

Organisation type and purpose:
Learned society (membership is by subscription),
present number of members: 20, voluntary
organisation.

Subject coverage:
Literature and language relating to the medieval
European vernaculars and to medieval Latin;
historical and cultural context of medieval Europe.

Access to staff:
Contact by letter, by telephone and by e-mail
Hours: Mon to Fri, 0900 to 1700

LONDON MENNONITE CENTRE

Formal name: London Mennonite Centre

14 Shepherds Hill, Highgate, London N6 5AQ

Tel: 020 8340 8775
Fax: 020 8341 6807
E-mail: lmc@menno.org.uk
previous

Website:
http://www.menno.org.uk

Organisation type and purpose:
To embody Mennonite and Anabaptist ideas and
insights within the wider church and cultivate
Christian discipleship as a whole way of life.

Subject coverage:
Mennonites, Anabaptism and Christianity.

**Museum or gallery collection, archive, or library
special collection:**
Library of Anabaptism, Mennonite history and
theology, Radical Reformation, Amish and
Hutterites.

Access to staff:
Contact by letter, by telephone, by fax, by e-mail,
in person and via website
Hours: Mon to Fri, 0900 to 1700

LONDON METROPOLITAN ARCHIVES

Acronym or abbreviation: LMA

40 Northampton Road, London, EC1R 0HB

Tel: 020 7332 3820
Fax: 020 7833 9136
E-mail: ask.lma@cityoflondon.gov.uk

Website:
http://www.cityoflondon.gov.uk/archives/lma
A guide to the holdings and access information.

Enquiries:
Enquiries to: Assistant Director (Heritage)

Founded:
1965

Organisation type and purpose:
Local government body.
Record office.

Subject coverage:
London County Council, Greater London Council,
Metropolitan Board of Works, Middlesex County
Council, London local government, education,
health, topography, the built environment,
philanthropy, transport, parish and diocesan
administration, history of medicine, City of
London Corporation.

**Museum or gallery collection, archive, or library
special collection:**
100 kilometres of archives including:
Local government
Ecclesiastical
Health
Family
Business
Manorial and other records
Prints and drawings (over 40,000 items) including:
Harben Bequest
John Burns Collection
Hanslip Fletcher Studio Collection
110,000 printed monographs
London Directories (from 1744)
London local government publications and
minutes

350,000 photographs forming a visual record of the history and topography of London, from the late 19th century to the 1980s, schools, housing, transport, parks, bridge, public buildings, private and historic buildings and houses, street scenes, including:
Whiffin Collection
Olney Collection
Morris Collection
Over 10,000 maps and plans
Archives of the Family Welfare Association
Books and pamphlets of the Charity Organisation Society to 1946
London Library of John Burns (19th-century LCC Councillor)
London Topographical Library
London Vestry and District Board Reports 1855–1900
Minute books of the Charity Organisation Society to 1946
Microfilmed archives on charities from 1869

Non-library collection catalogue:
All or part available online and in-house

Library catalogue:
All or part available online and in-house

Printed publications:
Information leaflets on the holdings (free with sae)
We Think You Ought to Go (£5)

Publications list:
Available in print

Access to staff:
Contact by letter, by telephone, by fax, by e-mail, in person and via website
Hours: Mon, Wed, Fri, 0930 to 1645; Tue, Thu, 0930 to 1930; selected Sat, please enquire for details

Parent body:
City of London
Guildhall, PO Box 270, London, EC2P 2EJ; tel: 020 7606 3030

LONDON METROPOLITAN POLYMER CENTRE

Acronym or abbreviation: LMPC

London Metropolitan University, Holloway Road, London, N7 8DB

Tel: 020 7133 2248
Fax: 020 7133 2184
E-mail: polymers@londonmet.ac.uk

Website:
http://www.londonmet.ac.uk/polymers
Information on the London Metropolitan University including the London Metropolitan Polymer Centre.

Enquiries:
Enquiries to: Business Development Manager
Direct tel: 020 7133 2189
Direct e-mail: alison.green@londonmet.ac.uk
Other contacts: Adam Bradley for information on short courses and training.

Founded:
1896

Organisation type and purpose:
University department or institute, training organisation, consultancy, research organisation. short courses, distance learning programmes.
To provide education, training, consultancy and research for the UK and International Polymer and allied industries.

Subject coverage:
Polymer materials and composites, polymer processing, mould and die design, injection moulding, extrusion, blown film, blow moulding, thermo vacuum forming, materials testing and characterisation, industrial studies, training, education, short courses, distance learning programmes, consultancy, research.

Trade and statistical information:
Information on polymer materials and processing.

Printed publications:
Information booklets
Distance Learning Programmes
Order printed publications from: Business Development Manager

Electronic and video publications:
Distance Learning Programmes

Publications list:
Available online and in print

Access to staff:
Contact by letter, by telephone, by fax, by e-mail and via website. Appointment necessary.
Hours: Mon to Fri, 0900 to 1700
Special comments: Voice Mail active out of hours.

Access for disabled people:
Ramped entry, toilet facilities

LONDON METROPOLITAN UNIVERSITY

31 Jewry Street, London, EC3N 2EY

Tel: 020 7423 0000

Website:
http://www.londonmet.ac.uk/library

Enquiries:
Enquiries to: Help Desk at any of the sites who will refer on if necessary

Founded:
1896

Organisation type and purpose:
Suitable for ages: 18+.

Subject coverage:
Business, environment, social studies, science, computing, engineering, humanities, teaching. Art and design: cabinet making, design studies, design for disability, fine arts, furniture design, production and history, interior design, jewellery, media studies, musical instrument technology, photography, silversmithing.
Management, accountancy, economics, financial services, law, shipping and transport, civil aviation, computing and information systems, psychology.

Museum or gallery collection, archive, or library special collection:
European Documentation Centre
TUC Library Collections
Workers Educational Association Archive

Library catalogue:
All or part available online

Access to staff:
Contact by letter and by telephone
Hours: Mon to Fri, 0900 to 1700

Other addresses:
London Metropolitan University
Commercial Road ILRC, 41–71 Commercial Road, London, E1 1LA; tel: 020 7320 1863; fax: 020 7320 1862
London Metropolitan University
Moorgate Library, 84 Moorgate, London, EC2M 6SQ; tel: 020 7320 1561; fax: 020 7320 1565
London Metropolitan University
City Campus, Calcutta House Library, Old Castle Street, London, E1 7NT; tel: 020 7320 1000; fax: 020 7320 1177
London Metropolitan University
Ladbroke House Library, Highbury Grove, London, N5 2AD; tel: 020 7133 5149; fax: 020 7133 5100
London Metropolitan University
Holloway Road Learning Centre, 236–250 Holloway Road, London, N7 6PP; tel: 020 7133 2442; fax: 020 7133 2066

LONDON NARROW BOAT ASSOCIATION

Acronym or abbreviation: LNBA

Battlebridge Moorings, Wharfdale Road, London, N1 9UY

Tel: 07970 799032

Enquiries:
Enquiries to: Secretary

Founded:
1978

Organisation type and purpose:
Membership association (membership is by election or invitation), voluntary organisation. Waterways campaigning.

Subject coverage:
Moorings in London area.

Access to staff:
Contact by letter

Members of:
Aylesbury Canal Society (ACS)
Canal Basin, Walton Street, Aylesbury, HP21 7QG
Inland Waterways Association (IWA)
Island House, Moor Road, Chesham, HPS 1WA

LONDON NATURAL HISTORY SOCIETY

Acronym or abbreviation: LNHS

21 Green Way, Frinton-on-Sea, Essex, CO13 9AL

Tel: 01255 674678
Fax: 01255 674678

Website:
http://www.users.globalnet.co.uk~lnhsweb

Enquiries:
Enquiries to: Secretary

Founded:
1858

Organisation type and purpose:
Learned society (membership is by subscription).

Subject coverage:
Natural history of the London area, research and identification of species, observation and conservation, botany, ecology, entomology, geology, ornithology.

Museum or gallery collection, archive, or library special collection:
Library is housed at Imperial College of Science, Technology and Medicine, Central Libraries

Printed publications:
Books on breeding birds, flora and butterflies of the London area
London Bird Report (annually)
London Naturalist (annually)
Newsletters (for members, 6 times a year)

Access to staff:
Contact by letter
Hours: Mon to Fri, 0900 to 1700

LONDON PLAYING FIELDS FOUNDATION

Acronym or abbreviation: LPFF

73 Collier Street, London, N1 9BE

Tel: 0845 026 2292
E-mail: enquiries@lpff.org.uk

Website:
http://www.lpff.org.uk
All about the LPFF

Enquiries:
Enquiries to: Chief Executive
Other contacts: Operations Director

Founded:
1890

Organisation type and purpose:
Registered charity, voluntary organisation (charity number 302925).

continued overleaf

The main charity for the provision, protection and promotion of playing fields in Greater London.

Subject coverage:
Managing sports facilities within the Greater London area, including football, cricket, rugby, hockey and tennis, for the use of local communities, especially the young, the elderly, the disabled and the disadvantaged.

Printed publications:
Annual Report
Newsletter (2 a year)
Centenary history 1890–1990

Access to staff:
Contact by letter, by telephone, by fax, by e-mail and via website. Appointment necessary.
Hours: Mon to Fri, 0900 to 1730

LONDON RECORD SOCIETY

PO Box 691, Exeter, EX1 9PH

E-mail: londonrecordsoc@btinternet.com

Website:
http://www.londonrecordsociety.org.uk
General information and list of publications.

Enquiries:
Enquiries to: Honorary Secretary
Other contacts: Honorary Editor (for book proposals)

Founded:
1964

Organisation type and purpose:
Learned society, registered charity.
Publishing society.
To publish editions of primary sources for London history.

Subject coverage:
Primary sources and archives on the history of London.

Printed publications:
Cartulary of Holy Trinity, Aldgate (1971)
London Viewers and their certificates, 1508–1588 (1989)
Chamber accounts of the 16th century (1984)
Church in London, 1375–1392 (1977)
Commissions for building 50 new churches (1986)
Committees for Repeal of the Test and Corporation minutes, 1786–1790, 1827–1828 (1978, out of print)
Joshua Johnson's Letterbook, 1771–4 (1979)
Justice in 18th Century Hackney (1991)
Letters of John Paige, London Merchant, 1648–58 (1984)
London and Middlesex Chantry Certificate, 1548 (1980)
London and Middlesex Published Records (1970, out of print)
London Assize of Nuisance, 1301–1401: a calendar (1973)
London Bridge: selected accounts, 1381–1547 (1995)
London Consistory Court Wills, 1492–1547 (1967)
London Consistory Court Depositions, 1586–1611 (1997)
London debating societies, 1776–1799 (1994)
London Eyre of 1244 (1970) now o/p
London Eyre of 1276 (1976)
London Inhabitants within the Walls, 1695 (1966)
London Politics, 1713–1713 (1981)
London Pollbooks, 1713 (1981)
London Possessory Assizes: a calendar (1965)
London Radicalism, 1830–1843 (1970)
London Viewers and their certificates 1508–1588 (1989)
Port and Trade of Early Elizabethan London (1972)
Records of St Andrew Hubbard, 1454–1560 (1999)
Register of the Fraternity of the Trinity and SS. Fabian and Sebastian in the Church of St Botolph (1982)
Richard Hutton's complaints book (1987)
Scriveners Company Common Paper, 1357–1628; continuation to 1678 (1968, out of print)
Settlement and bastardy examinations of St Luke, Chelsea, 1730–66 (1999)

Spanish Company (1973, out of print)
Survey of documentary sources for property holding in London before the Great Fire (1985)
The overseas trade of London, 1480–1481 (1990)
Trinity House of Deptford: transactions, 1609–35 (1983)
Two Calvinistic Methodist Chapels, 1743–1811 (1975)
Two Tudor subsidy assessment rolls, 1541 and 1582 (1993)
Westminster Abbey charters, 1066 to c. 1214 (1988)
Selected Letters of William Freeman (2002)
Checklist of Unpublished Diaries by Londoners and Visitors (2003)
The English Fur Trade in the Later Middle Ages (2nd ed, 2003)
The Bede Roll of the Parish Clerks' Company (2 vols, 2004)
The Estate and Household Accounts of William Worsley, Dean of St Paul's Cathedral, 1479–97 (2004)
A Woman in Wartime London: the Diary of Kathleen Tipper, 1941–45 (2006)
Prisoners' Letters to the Bank of England, 1781–1827 (2007)
The Apprenticeship of a Mountaineer: Edward Whymper's London Diary 1855–59 (2008)
The Pinners' and Wiresellers' Book 1462–1511
Some vols can be viewed via the British History Online website
Order printed publications from: website: http://www.londonrecordsociety.org.uk

Publications list:
Available online and in print

Access to staff:
Contact by letter, by e-mail and via website. Appointment necessary.

LONDON RETAIL MEAT TRADERS LIMITED

Acronym or abbreviation: LRMTA

Gate 27, Central Markets, Smithfield, London, EC1A 9EB

Tel: 020 8248 0732
Fax: 020 8329 1463

Enquiries:
Enquiries to: Secretary

Founded:
1926

Organisation type and purpose:
National organisation, trade association (membership is by election or invitation), present number of members: 350, service industry.

Subject coverage:
Meat retailing, small scale meat processing, training.

Access to staff:
Contact by letter, by telephone and by fax
Hours: Mon to Thu, 0800 to 1500

Affiliated to:
National Federation of Meat & Food Traders Tunbridge Wells, Kent, TN1 1YW; tel: 01892 541412; fax: 01892 535462; e-mail: INFO@ NFMFT.co.uk

Members include:
local butchers associations

LONDON SCHOOL OF HYGIENE AND TROPICAL MEDICINE

Acronym or abbreviation: LSHTM

Keppel Street, London, WC1E 7HT

Tel: 020 7927 2276
Fax: 020 7927 2273
E-mail: library@lshtm.ac.uk

Website:
http://www.lshtm.ac.uk/as/library/libintro.htm

Founded:
1899

Organisation type and purpose:
University department or institute.
Postgraduate medical school.

Subject coverage:
Environmental health, epidemiology, human nutrition, medical microbiology, entomology, parasitology, medical statistics, population studies and demography, tropical medicine, public health, health policy, the health of developing countries and international health.

Museum or gallery collection, archive, or library special collection:
Historical collection (books on public health and tropical medicine)
Manson Collection (papers of Sir Patrick Manson)
Reece Collection (on vaccination)
Ross Archives (papers of Sir Ronald Ross)

Non-library collection catalogue:
All or part available online

Library catalogue:
All or part available online and in print

Printed publications:
Annual Report
Health Policy and Planning (quarterly, pub. OUP)
Tropical Medicine and International Health (6 times a year, pub. Blackwell's)

Access to staff:
Contact by letter, by telephone, by e-mail and via website
Hours: Mon to Fri, 0930 to 1730

Access for disabled people:
Ramped entry, toilet facilities

Parent body:
University of London

LONDON SCHOOL OF JOURNALISM LIMITED

Acronym or abbreviation: LSJ

126 Shirland Road, London, W9 2BT

Tel: 020 7289 7777
Fax: 020 7432 8141
E-mail: info@lsjournalism.com

Website:
http://www.home-study.com
Details of all courses and terms etc.
http://www.lsj.org
Details of all courses and terms, etc.

Enquiries:
Enquiries to: Administrator
Direct tel: 020 7432 8140
Direct fax: 020 7432 8140
Direct e-mail: enquiries@lsjournalism.com
Other contacts: Director of Studies for tutorial course information.

Founded:
1921

Organisation type and purpose:
Training organisation. Training by distance learning. Postgraduate attendance courses.

Subject coverage:
Training for news journalism, freelance writing and creative writing, both by distance learning and by attendance classes.

Printed publications:
General Prospectus (free, available on request)

Access to staff:
Contact by letter, by telephone, by fax, by e-mail and via website. Appointment necessary.
Hours: Mon to Fri, 1000 to 1630
Special comments: Times may vary, telephone in advance.

Member of:
(OLF) (ABCC)
Association of British Correspondence Colleges

(OLF) (ABCC) (ODLQC)
Open and Distance Learning Quality Council

LONDON SCHOOL OF PUBLISHING

Acronym or abbreviation: LSP

David Game House, 69 Notting Hill Gate, London, W11 3JS

Tel: 020 7221 3399
Fax: 020 7243 1730
E-mail: lsp@easynet.co.uk

Website:
http://www.publishing-school.co.uk
Training programmes and courses.

Enquiries:
Enquiries to: Course Director
Other contacts: Courses Co-ordinator

Founded:
1983

Organisation type and purpose:
Training organisation.
Training courses that run in the evening on a part time basis. Courses run in Feb, Oct and May – some day courses available.
To provide training courses and programmes for graduates who wish to enter the publishing industry, as well as for those who are in the early stages of their publishing careers, or those who wish to change career paths.

Subject coverage:
Training in: editing (book and magazine), feature writing, picture research, QuarkXpress, Photoshop, HTML, Dreamweaver, magazine subediting, writing for the Web.

Education services:
Training in publishing.

Printed publications:
Prospectuses (detailing training programmes)

Publications list:
Available online and in print

Access to staff:
Contact by telephone and by e-mail
Hours: Mon to Fri, 0930 to 1830
Special comments: No weekend access.

Access to building, collection or gallery:
Hours: Mon to Fri, 0900 to 18,30

Access for disabled people:
Access to all public areas
Hours: Mon to Fri, 0900 to 1800

Links with:
London School of Public Relations
National Union of Journalists (NUJ)

LONDON SCHOOL OF THEOLOGY

Acronym or abbreviation: LSt

Green Lane, Northwood, Middlesex, HA6 2UW

Tel: 01923 456190
Fax: 01923 456001
E-mail: library@lst.ac.uk

Website:
http://www.lst.ac.uk
Information on the college and its courses; Christian
comment on current issues; book and film reviews by faculty members.

Enquiries:
Enquiries to: Librarian
Direct tel: 01923 456192
Direct e-mail: a.linfield@lst.ac.uk
Other contacts: Library Administrator for routine enquiries.

Founded:
1943

Organisation type and purpose:
Suitable for ages: 18+.

To prepare students for Christian ministry and to further the academic
study and research of theology.

Subject coverage:
Theology, predominant emphasis is on Christian theology but also Islamics collection in process of ongoing development.

Museum or gallery collection, archive, or library special collection:
Papers of Dr Donald Guthrie (not yet catalogued or otherwise organised)

Library catalogue:
All or part available online and in-house

Access to staff:
Contact by letter, by telephone, by fax, by e-mail, in person and via website. Appointment necessary. Non-members charged.
Hours: Mon to Fri, 0900 to 1700
Special comments: If at all possible visitors are encouraged to visit during vacations as space in the library is in heavy demand during term time.

Associated college of:
Brunel University

Subsidiary body:
Centre for Islamic Studies
LST Postgraduate School of Theology

LONDON SOCIETY

Mortimer Wheeler House, 46 Eagle Wharf Road, London, N1 7ED

Tel: 020 7253 9400
E-mail: info@londonsociety.org.uk

Website:
http://www.londonsociety.org.uk

Enquiries:
Enquiries to: Administrator

Founded:
1912

Organisation type and purpose:
National organisation, membership association (membership is by subscription), registered charity (charity number 206270).
Advancing the practical improvement and artistic development of London.

Subject coverage:
Ancient and modern London, history, architecture and planning, improvement and enhancement of London by the efforts of its citizens, the environment, visits to places of interest within Greater London.

Museum or gallery collection, archive, or library special collection:
Library; 3,000 books, 100 maps, housed in the Museum of London (Mortimer Wheeler House)

Library catalogue:
All or part available online

Printed publications:
Journal (twice a year, free to members)

Access to staff:
Contact by letter, by telephone and by e-mail.
Appointment necessary.
Hours: Wed and Fri, 0900 to 1630

Links with:
Europa Nostra
Green Belt Council

LONDON SOUTH BANK UNIVERSITY – ENGINEERING, SCIENCE AND THE BUILT ENVIRONMENT

103 Borough Road, London, SE1 OAA

Tel: 020 7815 8320
Fax: 020 7815 8366

Website:
http://www.lsbu.ac.uk/esbe/

Library guide, helpsheets, catalogue, staff contacts.

Enquiries:
Enquiries to: Faculty Administrative Officer
Direct e-mail: teidyk@lsbu.ac.uk
Other contacts: Information Advisers

Organisation type and purpose:
University library, university department or institute.

Subject coverage:
Architecture; town planning; built environment law; land and building economics; estate management; construction; civil engineering.

Museum or gallery collection, archive, or library special collection:
Reference collection on architectural theory, history, practice and related crafts and technology, 17th-20th centuries (particularly strong 1717–1759 and 1880–1920)

Library catalogue:
All or part available online

Access to staff:
Contact by letter, by telephone and by fax
Hours: Term time: Mon, Tue, Thu, 0830 to 2100; Wed, Fri, 0830 to 1900
Vacations: 0900 to 1700
Special comments: Non-members must apply for reference facilities in writing.

Access to building, collection or gallery:
No prior appointment required
Special comments: In term time, unless a member of the M25 Group. In vacation, any university students may have reference access on production of current ID card.

Access for disabled people:
Toilet facilities
Special comments: Main floor of library accessible by lift, gallery level by arrangement.

LONDON SOUTH BANK UNIVERSITY – LIBRARY

103 Borough Road, London, SE1 0AA

Tel: 020 7815 6607
Fax: 020 7261 1865
E-mail: postmaster@vax.sbu.ac.uk

Website:
http://www.sbu.ac.uk/lioa

Enquiries:
Enquiries to: Director of Learning Information Services
Direct tel: 020 7815 6601
Direct fax: 020 7815 6699
Direct e-mail: john.akeroyd@sbu.ac.uk

Organisation type and purpose:
University library.

Subject coverage:
Business studies; accountancy; management; finance; public sector studies; chemical engineering; electrical engineering; electronics; mathematics and computing; mechanical and production engineering; environmental engineering; bakery; building technology, practice and management; civil and structural engineering; transportation; land economics; multi-environment; architecture; law; humanities; nursing; health services; occupational hygiene; sociology; biotechnology; social policy; education; town planning.

Museum or gallery collection, archive, or library special collection:
Architectural books 1717–1740, 1790–1830, 1880–1920
Building manuals, directories and patents 1750 to date

Printed publications:
Annual Report

continued overleaf

Access to staff:
Contact by letter. Appointment necessary. Letter of introduction required.
Hours: Mon to Fri, 0900 to 2100

LONDON SOUTH BANK UNIVERSITY – SYSTEMS AND LEARNING TECHNOLOGIES

Acronym or abbreviation: LSBU – SALT

103 Borough Road, London, SE1 0AA

Tel: 020 7815 6668

Website:
http://www1.lsbu.ac.uk/clsd/itsupport

Enquiries:
Enquiries to: Team Leader

Founded:
1982

Organisation type and purpose:
University department or institute, consultancy, research organisation.

Access to staff:
Contact by letter, by telephone, by fax, by e-mail, in person and via website. Appointment necessary.
Hours: Mon to Fri, 0900 to 1700

Access to building, collection or gallery:
Prior appointment required

Access for disabled people:
Access to all public areas

Constituent part of:
Centre for Learning Support and Development

LONDON SUBTERRANEAN SURVEY ASSOCIATION

Acronym or abbreviation: LSSA

98 Cambridge Gardens, London, W10 6HS

Tel: 020 8968 1360
E-mail: wolstan-dixie@hotmail.co.uk

Enquiries:
Enquiries to: Secretary

Founded:
1968

Organisation type and purpose:
Learned society (membership is by election or invitation).

Subject coverage:
Man-made or used underground space or constructions in London and their effect on surface development.

Museum or gallery collection, archive, or library special collection:
Books, maps, pamphlets, grey literature, press cuttings, videos, photographs, illustrations

Non-library collection catalogue:
All or part available in-house

Library catalogue:
All or part available in-house

Access to staff:
Contact by letter, by telephone and by e-mail. Non-members charged.
Hours: Mon to Fri, 1000 to 1700

Links with:
Subterranea Britannica

LONDON SYMPHONY ORCHESTRA LIMITED

Acronym or abbreviation: LSO

Barbican Centre, London, EC2Y 8DS

Tel: 020 7588 1116
Fax: 020 7374 0127
E-mail: admin@lso.co.uk

Website:
http://www.lso.co.uk
Book tickets for concerts, order LSO Live CDs, artist features and interviews, news and information

Enquiries:
Enquiries to: Head of Marketing
Direct fax: 020 7638 4578

Founded:
1904

Organisation type and purpose:
International organisation, registered charity (charity number 232391).
Orchestra, arts organisation.

Subject coverage:
Orchestra, music, classical music, arts.

Museum or gallery collection, archive, or library special collection:
LSO Archives, photographs, publicity material including programmes

Printed publications:
LSO News
The LSO at 90 (Stewart A)
Leaflet; LSO Education – Projects for Primary Schools, Secondary Schools, Special Needs; daytime concerts for schools and families
Living Music: The London Symphony Orchestra Magazine (free to members)
Season brochures; Spring, Summer and Autumn

Electronic and video publications:
LSO Live, the LSO's own record label, plus classical recordings for major record companies and film sound tracks

Publications list:
Available in print

Access to staff:
Contact by letter, by telephone, by fax, by e-mail and via website. Appointment necessary.
Hours: Mon to Fri, 0930 to 1800

Other address:
LSO St Luke's
UBS & LSO Music Education Centre, 161 Old Street, London, EC1V 9NJ; tel: 020 7588 1116; fax: 020 7384 0127; e-mail: swales@lso.co.uk

LONDON TANKER BROKERS' PANEL LIMITED

Acronym or abbreviation: LTBP

Copenhagen House, 5–10 Bury Street, London, EC3A 5AT

Tel: 020 7456 6600
Fax: 020 7456 6601
E-mail: ltbp@worldscale.co.uk

Website:
http://www.ltbp.co.uk

Enquiries:
Enquiries to: Managing Director

Founded:
1953

Organisation type and purpose:
Consultancy.

Subject coverage:
Oil tanker freight rates, AFRA (average freight rate assessment), time charter rates, assessment of freight consideration for tankers.

Museum or gallery collection, archive, or library special collection:
Tanker freight rates

Printed publications:
Monthly statistics (on subscription only)

Publications list:
Available in print

Access to staff:
Contact by letter, by telephone, by fax and by e-mail. Appointment necessary.
Hours: Mon to Fri, 0900 to 1700

LONDON THAMES GATEWAY FORUM OF VOLUNTARY AND COMMUNITY ORGANISATIONS

Acronym or abbreviation: LTGF

The Brady Centre, 192 Hanbury Street, London, E1 5HU

Tel: 020 7377 1822
Fax: 020 7247 5637
E-mail: mail@ltgf.co.uk

Website:
Under development.

Enquiries:
Enquiries to: Information Officer
Other contacts: Director, Regeneration for planning and regeneration.

Founded:
1975

Organisation type and purpose:
Membership association (membership is by qualification), present number of members: 506, voluntary organisation.

Subject coverage:
Geography, sociology and politics of urban change in the London Thames Gateway area and the inner city generally, environment, regeneration issues.

Non-library collection catalogue:
All or part available in-house

Library catalogue:
All or part available in-house

Printed publications:
Amongst many are:
Docklands Forum Annual Review
Docklands Forum – 20th Anniversary Publication
Conservation in Dockland – Old buildings in a changing environment (Calvocoressi P, 1990, £1.50)
Docklands Redevelopment – A Moral Dimension (Bishop of Stepney, £5)
Heliports (1997, £7.50)
Housing and the Regeneration of Docklands (£4)
Proposed Exhibition Centre in the Royal Victoria Dock (1997, £4)
Urban Clearway (1997, £5)
Urban Regeneration. Partnerships for Success (1997, £3.50)
Breaking Barriers & Bridging the Gap, Achieving Social Inclusion (1999)
Your Plan Your Future, Getting to grips with your UDP and Its Review (1999)
A Community Vision for the Thames Gateway London (1999)
Urban Sustainable Development, The Policy Context and Use of Indicators, in Developing and Assessing Initiatives (1999)
London Thames Gateway Forum Annual Report
Newsletters 2000-
Membership Survey Report 2001

Publications list:
Available online and in print

Access to staff:
Contact by letter, by telephone, by fax and by e-mail. Appointment necessary.
Hours: Mon to Fri, 1000 to 1800

Access to building, collection or gallery:
No access other than to staff, prior appointment required
Hours: Mon to Fri, 1000 to 1800

Access for disabled people:
Parking provided, ramped entry, toilet facilities
Special comments: Need to pre-check for parking space.

LONDON THEOLOGICAL SEMINARY

Acronym or abbreviation: LTS

104 Hendon Lane, London, N3 3SQ

Tel: 020 8346 7587
E-mail: admin@ltslondon.org

Website:
http://www.ltslondon.org

Enquiries:
Enquiries to: Administrator

Founded:
1977

Organisation type and purpose:
Registered charity. Training for Christian ministry.

Subject coverage:
Theology.

Museum or gallery collection, archive, or library special collection:
Dr Martyn Lloyd-Jones' Library

Library catalogue:
All or part available in-house

Access to staff:
Contact by letter and by e-mail
Hours: Mon to Fri, 0900 to 1700

LONDON TOPOGRAPHICAL SOCIETY

Acronym or abbreviation: LTS

Southgate, 7 Linden Avenue, Dorchester, Dorset, DT1 1EJ

Tel: 01305 261548
E-mail: patfrazer@yahoo.co.uk

Website:
http://www.topsoc.org

Enquiries:
Enquiries to: Honorary Secretary

Founded:
1880

Organisation type and purpose:
Learned society (membership is by subscription), present number of members: 1,100.
To publish material relating to the study of London topography.

Subject coverage:
London topography, maps, prints and views.

Printed publications:
Annual publications (books, maps, views – free to members; available for purchase by non-members)
London Topographical Record (journal every 5 years – free to members; available for purchase by non-members)
Newsletters (twice a year; free to members)
Order printed publications from: Honorary Treasurer, Flat 13, 13 Tavistock Place, London, WC1H 9SH

Publications list:
Available online and in print

Access to staff:
Contact by letter and by e-mail
Hours: No access.

LONDON TRAVELWATCH

Formal name: London Transport Users' Committee

6 Middle Street, London, EC1A 7JA

Tel: 020 7505 9000
Fax: 020 7505 9003
E-mail: info@londontravelwatch.org.uk

Website:
http://www.londontravelwatch.org.uk

Enquiries:
Enquiries to: Chief Executive
Direct e-mail: jo.debank@londontravelwatch.org.uk
Other contacts: Casework Team

Founded:
2000

Organisation type and purpose:
National government body, advisory body, statutory body, membership association, present number of members: 21.

Statutory consumer watchdog.
Acts as an appeals body considering suggestions and complaints concerning the service.
To represent the interests of transport provided, procured or licensed by Transport for London, Heathrow Express, Eurostar and the national railways in and around London.

Subject coverage:
Matters relating to public transport in and around London; problems faced by people using public transport in and around London.

Museum or gallery collection, archive, or library special collection:
An extensive library of transport related material
The Cullen inquiry into the Ladbroke Grove Rail crash (transcript)
The Uff inquiry into the Southall Rail crash (transcript)
The Fennell inquiry into the Kings Cross Fire (transcript)
The Hidden inquiry into the Clapham Junction Rail crash (transcript)

Trade and statistical information:
Data on users' comments, complaints and suggestions.

Publications list:
Available online

Access to staff:
Contact by letter, by telephone, by fax, by e-mail and in person. Appointment necessary.
Hours: Mon to Fri, 0900 to 1700

Access for disabled people:
Wheelchair access, hearing loop

LONDON UNDERGROUND RAILWAY SOCIETY

Acronym or abbreviation: LURS

54 Brinkley Road, Worcester Park, Surrey, KT4 8JF

Tel: 020 8330 1855

Website:
http://www.lurs.org.uk
General information about the Society.

Enquiries:
Enquiries to: Secretary

Founded:
1961

Organisation type and purpose:
Membership association (membership is by subscription), present number of members: 900, voluntary organisation.

Subject coverage:
All aspects of London's underground railways, past, present and future.

Museum or gallery collection, archive, or library special collection:
Cartographic Collection
Chandos Papers
Photographic Collection
Sound and Vision Collection

Printed publications:
Specialised books published by the Society are now out of print. Books written about the Underground, many written by members, are now published by commercial houses specialising in public transport subjects
Underground News (monthly)

Access to staff:
Contact by letter
Hours: Mon to Fri, any reasonable time

LONDON VIDEO TRADE ASSOCIATION

314 Walworth Road, London, SE17 2NA

Tel: 020 7703 3081
Fax: 020 7703 3081

Enquiries:
Enquiries to: Secretary

Founded:
1982

Organisation type and purpose:
Trade association (membership is by qualification), present number of members: 44.
Help and advice to video shops.

Subject coverage:
Video trade.

Access to staff:
Contact by letter, by telephone, by fax and in person
Hours: Mon to Fri, 1030 to 1800

Access for disabled people:
Ramped entry

LONDON VOLUNTARY SERVICE COUNCIL

Acronym or abbreviation: LVSC

356 Holloway Road, London, N7 6PA

Tel: 020 7700 8107
Fax: 020 7700 8108
E-mail: info@lvsc.org.uk

Website:
http://www.lvsc.org.uk

Enquiries:
Enquiries to: Resource Officer
Direct tel: 020 7700 8192

Organisation type and purpose:
Voluntary organisation, registered charity (charity number 276886).

Subject coverage:
Social policy affecting London's voluntary sector, organisational support for London's voluntary sector, information on London's voluntary sector.

Museum or gallery collection, archive, or library special collection:
Over 5000 items related to London's voluntary and community sector including general information and organisational development information.
Access to Funderfinder by appointment.

Library catalogue:
All or part available in-house

Printed publications:
Publications include (prices inc. p&p):
Avoiding the wastepaper basket (1996)
Just about Managing – effective management for voluntary organisations and community groups
Voluntary But Not Amateur – a guide to the law for voluntary organisations and community groups
Voluntary Voice (subscription, voluntary organisations 1–5 staff £18, voluntary organisations 6+ staff £21, individuals £30, other organisations £30)
LVSC's Annual Report

Publications list:
Available in print

Access to staff:
Contact by letter, by telephone, by fax, by e-mail and in person
Hours: Varies for different services

LONDON WILDLIFE TRUST

Skyline House, 200 Union Street, London, SE1 0LX

Tel: 020 7261 0447
Fax: 020 7261 0538
E-mail: enquiries@wildlondon.org.uk

Website:
http://www.wildlondon.org.uk

Enquiries:
Enquiries to: Education Co-ordinator

Founded:
1981

continued overleaf

Organisation type and purpose:
Membership association (membership is by subscription), registered charity (charity number 283895).
The London Wildlife Trust fights to sustain and enhance London's wildlife habitats to create a city richer in wildlife.

Subject coverage:
Wildlife, urban wildlife, site protection and management, environmental education and training.

Museum or gallery collection, archive, or library special collection:
Environmental education publications

Printed publications:
Create a School Wildlife Garden
Enviroscope
Gardening for Wildlife
Literally Wild: Wildlife Text for Literacy Hour
RiverWATCH
The Cycle of Wood
The Habitat Pack
The Wildlife Action Pack
Wildlife Facts Leaflets
Wild Seasons

Publications list:
Available in print

Access to staff:
Contact by letter, by telephone, by fax, by e-mail and via website. Appointment necessary.
Hours: Mon to Fri, 0930 to 1730

Access to building, collection or gallery:
No prior appointment required

Affiliated to:
Wildlife Watch .

Manages:
57 sites across London

Part of:
Wildlife Trusts

LONG DISTANCE WALKERS' ASSOCIATION LIMITED

Acronym or abbreviation: LDWA

Bellevue, Princes Street, Ulverston. LA12 7NB

E-mail: secretary@ldwa.org.uk

Website:
http://www.ldwa.org.uk

Enquiries:
Enquiries to: General Secretary
Other contacts: Long Distance Path Information Officer f(or information about long distance paths and routes)

Founded:
1972

Organisation type and purpose:
Membership association (membership is by subscription), present number of members: 6,500, voluntary organisation, recognised governing body.
To further the interests of those who enjoy long distance walking.

Subject coverage:
Long distance walking, paths and trails.

Museum or gallery collection, archive, or library special collection:
Details of over 600 walks and trails etc are held

Printed publications:
Details of Walks/Trails
Guidelines for Walking Events (£1.50)
Trailwalkers Handbook (£18.95)
Strider (journal, 3 times a year, free to members)
Order printed publications from: Merchandising Officer, Long Distance Walkers' Association
2 Sandy Lane, Beeston, Nottinghamshire, NG9 3GS; tel: 0115 922 1849

Access to staff:
Contact by letter, by e-mail and via website

Affiliated to:
European Ramblers Association
Ramblers Association
Scottish Rights of Way Society
Sports Council

LOTTERIES COUNCIL

2 Regan Road, Moira, Swadlincote, Derbyshire, DE12 6DS

Tel: 01925 710880
Fax: 01925 710880
E-mail: judith@lotteriescouncil.co.uk

Website:
http://www.lotteriescouncil.co.uk

Enquiries:
Enquiries to: Secretary
Other contacts: Executive Officer

Founded:
1979

Organisation type and purpose:
Trade association, present number of members: 145.

Subject coverage:
Management of lotteries; accounting procedures; requirements under the Lotteries and Amusements Act 1976, and the National Lotteries Act 1993, etc.; history of lotteries in the UK; lottery regulations.

Printed publications:
Annual Conference Report and Annual General Meeting
Code of Conduct booklet
Lottery Magazine (quarterly)
The Acts Combined (brings together in one booklet the Laws on Lotteries to Date)

Access to staff:
Contact by letter, by telephone, by fax and by e-mail
Hours: Mon to Fri, 0900 to 1700

Other addresses:
Executive Officer
21 Bristow Close, Great Sankey, Warrington, WA5 8EU; tel: 01925 710880; fax: 01925 710880

LOTUS SEVEN CLUB

Formal name: Lotus Seven Club of Great Britain

PO Box 777, Haywards Heath, West Sussex, RH16 2YA

Tel: 07000 572582
Fax: 07000 572582
E-mail: memsec@lotus7club.co.uk

Website:
http://www.lotus7club.co.uk

Enquiries:
Enquiries to: Membership Secretary

Founded:
1985

Organisation type and purpose:
International organisation, membership association, present number of members: 3000.

Subject coverage:
Lotus Seven from 1957 to 1973 and the Caterham Seven from 1973 to date.

Museum or gallery collection, archive, or library special collection:
Video lending library (members only)
Original Lotus Seven Specifications

Printed publications:
Low Flying (magazine, monthly, free to members)

Access to staff:
Contact by letter, by telephone, by fax, by e-mail and via website
Hours: Mon to Fri, 0900 to 1700

LOUGHBOROUGH UNIVERSITY – DEPARTMENT OF INFORMATION SCIENCE

Acronym or abbreviation: DIS

Epinal Way, Loughborough, Leicestershire, LE11 3TU

Tel: 01509 223051
Fax: 01509 223053
E-mail: dis@lboro.ac.uk

Website:
http://www.lboro.ac.uk/departments/dis

Enquiries:
Enquiries to: Head of Department
Direct tel: 01509 223065

Founded:
1972

Organisation type and purpose:
University department or institute.

Subject coverage:
Exploitation of business information; database design and development; marketing library and information services; development of expert systems for library and information services; archives and records management; conservation of materials; communications and information networks; intellectual property law; distance learning in library and information education; information skills; cataloguing and bibliographic control of materials; library planning, information, dissemination, strategic planning, electronic document delivery, electronic journals/publishing.

Museum or gallery collection, archive, or library special collection:
Mary Ward Collection of children's literature
Parish Libraries of Ashby de la Zouch and Loughborough (on deposit)

Trade and statistical information:
A range of statistical and related data as accumulated through various research projects and studies (including that of LISU).

Non-library collection catalogue:
All or part available in-house

Printed publications:
Prospectuses on departmental activities – teaching, research and consultancy

Access to staff:
Contact by letter, by telephone, by fax and by e-mail. Appointment necessary.
Hours: Mon to Fri, 0900 to 1700

Access for disabled people:
Parking provided, ramped entry, access to all public areas, toilet facilities

Constituent bodies:
Higher Education Academy Information and Computer Science Study Centre
tel: 01509 635708; fax: 01509 223053; e-mail: a.s .mcnab@lboro.ac.uk
Library and Information Statistics Unit (LISU)
tel: 01509 635680; fax: 01509 635699; e-mail: c .creaser@lboro.ac.uk

LOUGHBOROUGH UNIVERSITY – UNIVERSITY LIBRARY

Loughborough, Leicestershire, LE11 3TU

Tel: 01509 222360
Fax: 01509 223993
E-mail: library@lboro.ac.uk

Website:
http://www.lboro.ac.uk/library

Enquiries:
Enquiries to: Service Development Manager
Direct tel: 01509 222355
Direct e-mail: j.g.walton@lboro.ac.uk

Organisation type and purpose:
University library.

Subject coverage:
Art; business studies; design and technology; economics; English and drama; European studies; geography; human sciences; information studies; management; social sciences; chemical engineering; chemistry; civil engineering; computer studies; electrical and electronic engineering; human biology; ergonomics; materials technology; mathematics; mechanical engineering; physics; transport technology; manufacturing engineering; sports science.

Non-library collection catalogue:
All or part available online

Library catalogue:
All or part available online

Access for disabled people:
Parking provided, level entry, access to all public areas, toilet facilities

Links with:
LISU

LOUTH NATURALISTS' ANTIQUARIAN AND LITERARY SOCIETY

Acronym or abbreviation: LNALS

The Museum, 4 Broadbank, Louth, Lincolnshire, LN11 0EQ

Tel: 01507 601211
E-mail: louthmuseum@btconnect.com

Website:
http://www.louth.org.uk

Enquiries:
Enquiries to: Manager

Founded:
1884

Organisation type and purpose:
Learned society (membership is by subscription), present number of members: 205, registered charity (charity number 504370), museum, publishing house.

Subject coverage:
Local history relating to Louth and district.

Museum or gallery collection, archive, or library special collection:
Architectural Drawings of James Fowler, FRIBA, 1828–92, architect of Louth
Paintings by Peter DeWint
Works of Thomas Wilkinson Wallis, 1821–1903, internationally known woodcarver
Louth-made flat-weave carpets
Brick making
1920 Louth flood interpretation
Domestic and commercial bygones

Printed publications:
The Louth Flood
William Brown and the Louth Panorama
The Story of Hubbards Hills
The Lincolnshire Rising 1536
Tales of a Lincolnshire Parson
Louth House of Correction (Prison history)
Recollections of a Lincolnshire Miller
Lincolnshire Stuff (Wool industry-based fiction)
Withern – The story of a Lincolnshire parish
Birds of Louth
Billy Paddison of Soloby
Adam Eve and Louth Carpets
Order printed publications from: Louth Museum, 4 Broadbank, Louth, LN11 0EQ; tel. 01507 601211

Access to staff:
Contact by letter, by telephone, by e-mail and in person. Appointment necessary. Non-members charged.

Access to building, collection or gallery:
No prior appointment required
Hours: April to October: Tue to Sat, 1000 to 1600

Access for disabled people:
Fully accessible

Member organisation of:
Lincoln Record Society
Society for Lincolnshire History and Archaeology

LP GAS ASSOCIATION

Acronym or abbreviation: LPGA

Unit 14, Bow Court, Fletchworth Gate, Burnsall Road, Coventry, CV5 6SP

Tel: 024 7667 2108
E-mail: mail@lpga.co.uk

Website:
http://www.lpga.co.uk

Enquiries:
Enquiries to: Director General

Founded:
1970

Organisation type and purpose:
Professional body, trade association (membership is by subscription), present number of members: 180.

Subject coverage:
Liquefied petroleum gas, safety, standards, distribution, storage, handling and utilisation, LPG cylinders, hoses, vessels and systems.

Museum or gallery collection, archive, or library special collection:
Codes of practice for the LP Gas Industry

Printed publications:
Codes of Practice (30 titles)
Guides

Publications list:
Available online and in print

Access to staff:
Contact by letter, by telephone, by fax, by e-mail and via website
Hours: Mon to Thu, 0830 to 1700; Fri, 0830 to 1630

Member of:
Association Européen des Gas de Petrole Lingfiés (AEGPL)

LSE LIBRARY

London School of Economics and Political Science (LSE), 10 Portugal Street, London, WC2A 2HD

Tel: 020 7955 7229
Fax: 020 7955 7454
E-mail: library@lse.ac.uk

Website:
http://www.library.lse.ac.uk
Library home page and link to on-line catalogue.

Enquiries:
Enquiries to: Director of Library Services
Other contacts: Archivist

Founded:
1896

Organisation type and purpose:
University library.

Subject coverage:
Accounting; anthropology; climate change; economics; geography; government; history; industrial relations; law; philosophy; politics; population studies; psychology; social administration; sociology; statistics.

Museum or gallery collection, archive, or library special collection:
Archives and private papers on recent political, social and economic history, social anthropology and the history of the London School of Economics; including papers of the Liberal Party, the Independent Labour Party, John Stuart Mill, Beatrice and Sidney Webb, Fabian Society, William Beveridge, George Lansbury, Hugh Dalton, Walter Citrine, Bronislaw Malinowski, C A R Crosland and the Hall-Carpenter Archives of lesbian and gay activism

Collections of rare books on political, economic and social subjects from the 16th century to the present day
The Library is a depository for the United Nations, the United States Government and is a European Documentation Centre
A large collection of publications from intergovernmental organisations and national governments world-wide, with particular emphasis on statistics

Non-library collection catalogue:
All or part available online

Library catalogue:
All or part available online

Printed publications:
Annual Report
Various free guides to the Library

Access to staff:
Contact by letter, by telephone, by fax, by e-mail, in person and via website. Non-members charged.
Hours: Core hours: Mon to Fri, 0900 to 2000
Hours vary throughout year, full details on website
Special comments: Charges to commercial/business users.
Letter of introduction required in certain circumstances.

Access for disabled people:
Level entry, access to all public areas, toilet facilities

Parent body:
London School of Economics and Political Science

LUBRICANTS UK LIMITED

Castrol Technology Centre, Whitchurch Hill, Pangbourne, Reading, Berkshire, RG8 7QR

Tel: 0118 984 3311
Fax: 0118 976 5536
E-mail: toomeym@castrol.com

Website:
http://www.castrol.com
Castrol's home page. Information about our automotive, marine and industrial lubricants range, the origins of synthetic and mineral oils, company history, information about Castrol's sponsorship.

Enquiries:
Enquiries to: Librarian
Direct tel: 0118 976 5396

Founded:
1899

Organisation type and purpose:
Research organisation.
Research and development on lubricants, greases, antifreeze, hydraulic fluids etc.

Subject coverage:
Lubrication, tribology, greases, antifreeze, hydraulic fluids.

Library catalogue:
All or part available in-house

Access to staff:
Contact by letter, by telephone, by fax and by e-mail. Appointment necessary.
Hours: Mon to Fri, 0900 to 1700

Parent body:
BP plc
Britannic House, 1 Finsbury Circus, London, EC2M 7BA

LUDLOW MUSEUM RESOURCE CENTRE

Ludlow Museum Resource Centre, 7–9 Parkway, Ludlow, Shropshire, SY8 2PG

Tel: 01584 813665
Fax: 01584 813666
E-mail: llmrc@shropshire.gov.uk

continued overleaf

Website:
http://www.shropshire.gov.uk/museums.nsf

Organisation type and purpose:
Museum.
Formed in 1833 as a museum.

Subject coverage:
History of Ludlow including its archaeology and geology.

Museum or gallery collection, archive, or library special collection:
Geological, biological, social history collections

Non-library collection catalogue:
All or part available in-house

Library catalogue:
All or part available in-house

Access to staff:
Contact by letter, by telephone, by fax, by e-mail and in person. Appointment necessary.
Hours: Mon to Fri, 0900 to 1700

Access to building, collection or gallery:
Prior appointment required

Access for disabled people:
Parking nearby

Also at:
Ludlow Museum
Castle Street, Ludlow. SY8 1AS; tel: 01584 878765; e-mail: ludlow.museum@shropshire.gov.uk

LUPUS UK

St James House, Eastern Road, Romford, Essex, RM1 3NH

Tel: 01708 731251
Fax: 01708 731252
E-mail: headoffice@lupusuk.org.uk

Website:
http://www.lupusuk.org.uk

Enquiries:
Enquiries to: Administrator
Other contacts: Director

Founded:
1990

Organisation type and purpose:
Registered charity.
Fund-raising for medical research into cure and treatment for lupus; publicity and information.

Subject coverage:
Systemic lupus erythematosus, its nature, treatment and research; support for sufferers from the disease.

Printed publications:
Factsheets (free with sae)
Coping with Lupus (£12.50)
Lupus: Everything You Need To Know (£10.50)
The Lupus Book (£13.50)
Lupus Diagnosis and Treatment (£5.00)
Hughes Syndrome, A Patient's Guide (£3.00)
Living with Lupus from Eleven (£6.50)
Lupus: a guide for patients (£3)
A Patients' Guide to Lupus (£5.99)
Your First 100 Questions (£3.00)
Talking About Lupus (£7.99)
The Butterfly Traveller (£12.00)
Coping & Living with Lupus (£2.00)
The Facts – Lupus (second edition) (£9.99)
The Brain and Other Animals (£5.99)
Posters and leaflets

Publications list:
Available online and in print

Access to staff:
Contact by letter, by telephone, by fax, by e-mail and in person
Hours: Mon to Fri, 0900 to 1700

LUTON CENTRAL LIBRARY

St Georges Square, Luton, Bedfordshire, LU1 2NG

Tel: 01582 547418
Fax: 01582 547461
E-mail: referencelibrary@lutonculture.com

Website:
http://www.lutonlibraries.co.uk

Enquiries:
Enquiries to: Director of Libraries
Direct tel: 01582 547422
Direct e-mail: jean.george@lutonculture.com
Other contacts: Central Library Manager (for administration of building and services); Principal Librarian (for information services, adult/young people services)

Organisation type and purpose:
Charitable trust, public library.

Subject coverage:
General, and the history of Luton.

Museum or gallery collection, archive, or library special collection:
Workshop manual collection
Local studies collection, focusing on Luton

Non-library collection catalogue:
All or part available in-house

Library catalogue:
All or part available online

Printed publications:
Luton: collection of old photographs, by Mark Stubbs
Luton Local Studies material

Electronic and video publications:
Luton Celebrates: 50 years of history (video)

Access to staff:
Contact by letter, by telephone, by fax, by e-mail, in person and via website
Hours: Mon, 1100 to 1900; Tue to Thu, 0900 to 1900; Fri, 0900 to 1700; Sat, 0930 to 1600; Sun, 1000 to 1600

Branch libraries:
Leagrave Library
Marsh Road, Luton, Bedfordshire, LU3 2NL; tel: 01582 556650; fax: 01582 556651
Lewsey Library
Landrace Road, Luton, Bedfordshire, LU4 0SW; tel: 01582 696094; fax: 01582 696094
Marsh Farm Library
Purley Centre, Luton, Bedfordshire, LU3 3SR; tel: 01582 574803; fax: 01582 574803
Stopsley Library
Hitchin Road, Luton, Bedfordshire, LU2 7UG; tel: 01582 706368; fax: 01582 706368
Sundon Park Library
Hill Rise, Luton, Bedfordshire, LU3 3EE; tel: 01582 574573; fax: 01582 574573
Wigmore Library
Wigmore Lane, Luton, Bedfordshire, LU3 8DJ; tel: 01582 706340; fax: 01582 706340

Member organisation of:
European Public Information Relay

Parent body:
Luton Cultural Services Trust
LCST HQ, 4th floor, Luton Central Library, St Georges Square, Luton, LU1 2NG; tel: 01582 547470; fax: 01582 547461; website: http://www.lutonculture.com

LUTYENS TRUST

Goddards, Abinger Common, Dorking, Surrey, RH5 6JH

Tel: 01306 730487

Website:
http://www.lutyenstrust.org.uk

Enquiries:
Enquiries to: Honorary Secretary

Founded:
1984

Organisation type and purpose:
Learned society (membership is by subscription), present number of members: 350, registered charity (charity number 326776).
The Lutyens' Trust is an educational charity that acts as a source of information and help on the care and maintenance of the works of Sir Edwin Lutyens.
To protect the spirit and substance of the work of Sir Edwin Lutyens OM.

Subject coverage:
Historical and technical information on the buildings designed by Edwin Lutyens in 1889–1944.

Museum or gallery collection, archive, or library special collection:
Goddards, a Lutyens house. Though still owned by the Lutyens Trust, it is managed by the Landmark Trust

Printed publications:
Newsletter

Access to staff:
Appointment necessary.
Hours: Mon to Fri, 0900 to 1700
Special comments: Open Wed afternoon between Apr and Sept; appointments to be made with The Landmark Trust.

Access to building, collection or gallery:
Prior appointment required

Goddards transferred to the:
Landmark Trust

LUXEMBOURG EMBASSY

Formal name: Ambassade du Grand-Duché de Luxembourg à Londres

27 Wilton Crescent, London, SW1X 8SD

Tel: 020 7235 6961
Fax: 020 7235 9734

Enquiries:
Enquiries to: Counsellor
Direct e-mail: londres.amb@mae.etat.lu

Organisation type and purpose:
Embassy/Consulate.

Subject coverage:
Luxembourg: its history, political system, geography, economy, taxation, statistics, cultural life, education, commerce.

Museum or gallery collection, archive, or library special collection:
Memorials (Journal Officiel du Grand-Duché de Luxembourg), 3 series A, B and C covering laws, regulations and administration, company information

Access to staff:
Contact by letter and by e-mail. Appointment necessary.
Hours: Mon to Fri, 0900 to 1700

LUXEMBOURG TOURIST OFFICE

Sicilian House, Sicilian Avenue, London, WC1 1QH

Tel: 020 7434 2800
Fax: 020 7430 1773
E-mail: tourism@luxembourg.co.uk

Website:
http://www.luxembourg.co.uk

Enquiries:
Enquiries to: Director

Founded:
1954

Organisation type and purpose:
National government body.

Subject coverage:
Luxembourg (the country and city).

Trade and statistical information:
General statistics on Luxembourg.

Printed publications:
Available free of charge (return sae appreciated):
Camping guides
General brochures and maps
Hotel lists

Electronic and video publications:
Pictures, photographs (CD-ROM and online)

Access to staff:
Contact by letter, by telephone, by fax, by e-mail, in person and via website
Hours: Mon to Fri, 1000 to 1700

Access to building, collection or gallery:
Hours: Mon to Fri, 1000 to 1700

Access for disabled people:
Level entry, lift
Special comments: Lift.

LYMPHOMA ASSOCIATION

Acronym or abbreviation: LA

PO Box 386, Aylesbury, Buckinghamshire, HP20 2GA

Tel: 01296 619400
Fax: 01296 619400
E-mail: information@lymphomas.org.uk

Website:
http://www.lymphomas.org.uk
Details of Association's services and how to contact the Helpline.

Enquiries:
Enquiries to: Chief Executive
Direct tel: 0808 808 5555 (Helpline)

Founded:
1986

Organisation type and purpose:
Advisory body, membership association (membership is by subscription), present number of members: 2,000+ (charity number 1068395), training organisation.
Provides information and emotional support for patients with Hodgkin Lymphoma and non-Hodgkin Lymphoma and their families.

Subject coverage:
Lymphomas, Hodgkin Lymphoma, non-Hodgkin Lymphoma, diagnosis, treatment, chemotherapy, radiotherapy, coping with disease and treatment, local support groups, patient-to-patient links, buddy links.

Museum or gallery collection, archive, or library special collection:
DVDs, CDs, loan collection

Printed publications:
Comprehensive literature available (free)

Publications list:
Available online and in print

Access to staff:
Contact by letter, by telephone, by fax, by e-mail and via website
Hours: Mon to Thu, 0900 to 1800; Fri, 0900 to 1700

LYMPHOMA RESEARCH TRUST

Trustees Department, 5th Floor East, 250 Euston Road, London, NW1 2PG

Tel: 020 7380 9931
E-mail: hannah.jetuah@uclh.nhs.uk

Website:
http://www.lymphoma-research-trust.org.uk
Aims, news, contacts, small grants scheme.

Founded:
1973

Organisation type and purpose:
A registered charity (number 263424).

Strives to improve the life expectancy and quality of life of patients with Hodgkin's Lymphoma and non-Hodgkin's Lymphoma. Supports research into the treatment of lymphoma. Makes grants to medical researchers at the Lymphoma Trials Office who organise clinical trials and operate a database with over 18,000 patients on it.

Subject coverage:
The database contains details of patients' treatments and annual follow-ups, and provides a valuable record of the outcome of different treatments for lymphomas. The clinical trials assess whether new treatments work better than existing ones, and test different combinations of treatments to see which are most effective. The information gained from these trials improves knowledge of lymphoma and enables patients to be treated more effectively.

Access to staff:
Contact by letter, by telephone and by e-mail

Links with:
University College London Hospitals NHS Foundation Trust (UCLH)
    250 Euston Road, London, NW1 2PG; tel: 0845 1555 000

MAARA

Formal name: Midlands Asthma and Allergy Research Association

7 Stadium Business Court, Millennium Way, Pride Park, Derby, DE24 8HP

Tel: 01162 479888
Fax: 01162 479888
E-mail: enquiries@maara.org

Website:
http://www.maara.org
Medical website gives extensive help and information on asthma and allergy and also gives detailed information on the services, charity and supports.

Enquiries:
Enquiries to: General Manager

Founded:
1968

Organisation type and purpose:
Rregistered charity (charity number 257131).
Concerned with funding research into asthma and other allergies, runs an information service and is renowned for aerobiological research.
Main aim is to fund research into the cause and treatment of asthma and allergy.

Subject coverage:
Information on asthma and other allergic conditions, aerobiology, patient education, pollen and spore levels, pollen forecasts, anaphylaxis.

Trade and statistical information:
Aerobiological data.

Printed publications:
Leaflets on allergic conditions
MAARA Newsletter (annually)
Aerobiology research publications

Publications list:
Available online

Access to staff:
Contact by letter, by telephone, by fax, by e-mail, in person and via website. Appointment necessary.
Hours: Mon to Fri, 0900 to 1630

Branches:
MAARA
    PO Box 1057, Leicester, LE2 3GZ; tel: 01162 479888; e-mail: eva.day@virgin.net

MACAULAY LAND USE RESEARCH INSTITUTE

Acronym or abbreviation: Macaulay Institute

Craigiebuckler, Aberdeen, AB15 8QH

Tel: 01224 395000
Fax: 01224 395010
E-mail: l.robertson@macaulay.ac.uk

Website:
http://www.macaulay.ac.uk

Enquiries:
Enquiries to: Librarian
Direct e-mail: e.mackenzie@macaulay.ac.uk

Founded:
1987

Organisation type and purpose:
Research organisation.

Subject coverage:
Soil science; crop suitability; land use; hill farming; plant physiology; peat and forest soils; forestry; environmental conservation and pollution; land reclamation; drainage; water research.

Library catalogue:
All or part available in-house

Printed publications:
Annual Report
Land capability for agriculture maps
Land use maps
Soil maps
Soil Survey of Scotland (HMSO, Edinburgh; in continuation) consists of monographs and soil maps

Publications list:
Available in print

Access to staff:
Contact by letter, by telephone, by fax, by e-mail and via website. Appointment necessary.
Hours: Mon to Thu, 0900 to 1700; Fri, 0900 to 1600

Access to building, collection or gallery:
Prior appointment required

Access for disabled people:
Parking provided, level entry, access to all public areas, toilet facilities

Grant administered by the:
Scottish Government

MACCLESFIELD BOROUGH COUNCIL

Town Hall, Macclesfield, Cheshire, SK10 1AH

Tel: 01625 500500\ Minicom no. 01625 500321
Fax: 01625 504203

Website:
http://www.macclesfield.gov.uk
Economic profile, tourism, general information about the borough.

Enquiries:
Enquiries to: Public Relations Manager
Direct tel: 01625 504165
Direct fax: 01625 504155

Founded:
1974

Organisation type and purpose:
Local government body.

Subject coverage:
Services and amenities of the local borough council.

Access to staff:
Contact by letter, by telephone, by fax and by e-mail. Appointment necessary.
Hours: Mon to Thu, 0845 to 1700; Fri, 0845 to 1630

Access for disabled people:
Parking provided, ramped entry, toilet facilities

MACECORP LIMITED

Acronym or abbreviation: AIIT

Somers House, 1 Somers Road, Reigate, Surrey, RH2 9DU

Tel: 01737 224427
Fax: 01737 224428

continued overleaf

E-mail: mcl@aiit.demon.co.uk

Website:
http://www.aiit.com/
Information on the company, its products and services, including multiclient studies, databases and newsletters.

Enquiries:
Enquiries to: Managing Director
Other contacts: Senior Consultant for Research Head.

Founded:
1985

Organisation type and purpose:
International organisation, advisory body, professional body, consultancy, research organisation.
IT and telecommunications management consultancy.

Subject coverage:
IT, telecommunications, market research, business strategy, market positioning, IT budgeting, and resourcing, partnership search, product/vendor/objective analyses, support and training in product launch, information services, temporary experts.

Trade and statistical information:
European telecommunications spend statistics, voice resale markets in Europe, key European and International IT activities.

Printed publications:
Market Analyzer newsletter (monthly)
Topics of the Month

Publications list:
Available in print

Access to staff:
Contact by letter, by telephone, by fax, by e-mail and via website. Appointment necessary.
Hours: Mon to Fri, 0900 to 1800

Access to building, collection or gallery:
Prior appointment required

Associates in:
France, Germany, Ireland, Italy, Netherlands, Belgium, Spain, Sweden and USA

MACMILLAN CANCER RELIEF

39 Albert Embankment, London, SE1 7UQ

Tel: 020 7340 7840\ Minicom no. 0808 808 0121
Fax: 020 7840 7841
E-mail: cancerline@macmillan.org.uk

Website:
http://www.macmillan.org.uk

Enquiries:
Enquiries to: Corporate Communications Assistant
Direct tel: 020 7840 7817
Direct e-mail: oplummer@macmillan.org.uk

Founded:
1911

Organisation type and purpose:
Voluntary organisation, registered charity (charity number 261017).
Helps to provide expert care and practical and emotional support for people living with cancer, including families, friends and carers. In order to achieve this it raises funds for specialist Macmillan nurses and doctors, builds vitally needed treatment centres, provides grants for patients with financial difficulties, offers training and resources to cancer self-help and support groups, and provides a range of information locally and nationally.

Subject coverage:
General information on help for cancer patients, applications for financial grants accepted from health professionals on behalf of cancer patients, domiciliary nursing care for cancer patients.

Museum or gallery collection, archive, or library special collection:
Cancer information

Printed publications:
Help is There (details of over 40 cancer support and care charities in the UK)
The Cancer Guide
Information leaflets about Macmillan Cancer Relief's Services:
All About Macmillan
Macmillan Nurses
Macmillan Information Services
Macmillan Patient Grants
Macmillan Doctors
Information leaflets:
Common Breast Problems
Breast Cancer: How to Help Yourself
Gynaecological Cancers: How to Help Yourself
Staying Well: Gynaecological Health
No Time to Draw Breath: What Every Smoker Should Know
Breathing Easier

Microform publications:
A Presentation on Macmillan Cancer Relief (slide set describing the service)

Publications list:
Available online and in print

Access to staff:
Contact by letter, by telephone, by fax, by e-mail and via website
Hours: Mon to Fri, 0930 to 1930

Affiliated to:
BACUP
Breast Cancer Care
British Colostomy Association
CancerLink
National Association of Laryngectomee Clubs

MACULAR DISEASE SOCIETY

Acronym or abbreviation: MDS

PO Box 1870, Andover, Hampshire, SP10 9AD

Tel: 01264 350551
Fax: 01264 350558
E-mail: info@maculardisease.org

Website:
http://www.maculardisease.org

Enquiries:
Enquiries to: Information
Direct tel: helpline: 0845 241 2041

Founded:
1987

Subject coverage:
Macular disease, sight impairment, low vision aids, emotional support.

Museum or gallery collection, archive, or library special collection:
Information material (booklets, pamphlets, etc., free on request via helpline)

Trade and statistical information:
Data on sight impairment.

Printed publications:
Side View (4 times a year, large print and audiotape)
Digest annually
Booklets (various)

Access to staff:
Contact by letter, by telephone, by fax and by e-mail
Hours: Mon to Fri, 0900 to 1700

Access to building, collection or gallery:
No access other than to staff

MADE-UP TEXTILES ASSOCIATION LIMITED

Acronym or abbreviation: MUTA

42 Heath Street, Tamworth, Staffordshire, B79 7JH

Tel: 01827 52337
Fax: 01827 310827
E-mail: associations@compuserve.com

Website:
http://www.muta.org.uk

Enquiries:
Enquiries to: Administrator

Founded:
1919

Organisation type and purpose:
Trade association.

Subject coverage:
The making-up industry of heavy industrial textiles into marquees, tarpaulins, covers, sails, tents etc.

Printed publications:
Industrial Textiles (trade magazine, quarterly)
Members Trade Directory

Publications list:
Available online

Access to staff:
Contact by letter, by telephone, by fax, by e-mail and via website
Hours: Mon to Fri, 0900 to 1700

MAG (UK)

Formal name: Motorcycle Action Group

PO Box 750, Warwick, CV34 9FU.

Tel: 01926 844064
Fax: 01926 844065
E-mail: mag-hq@mag-uk.org

Website:
http://www.mag-uk.org
Main information.

Enquiries:
Enquiries to: General Secretary
Direct e-mail: nich.brown@mag-uk.org

Founded:
1973

Organisation type and purpose:
National organisation, membership association (membership is by subscription), present number of members: 10,000 Individual, plus 40,000 via club affiliation, lobbying and campaigning organisation on behalf of motorcyclists' rights, voluntary organisation, consultancy, research organisation, publishing house.
Representative lobby group for motorcyclists, i.e. user group, service organisation, multiple member benefits.

Subject coverage:
Motorcycle user-related information.

Museum or gallery collection, archive, or library special collection:
Motorcycle-related archive, mostly hard copy, PC-indexed

Trade and statistical information:
Some statistical source data from outside bodies, government, etc.

Non-library collection catalogue:
All or part available online and in print

Library catalogue:
All or part available online and in print

Printed publications:
The Road (magazine, A4 format, 6 times a year, free to members direct, on request to non-members £1.99)
Network (12 times a year to national MAG representatives, clubs and interested parties)

Access to staff:
Contact by letter, by telephone, by fax, by e-mail and via website. Access for members only. Non-members charged.
Hours: Mon to Fri, 0900 to 1700

Access to building, collection or gallery:
Prior appointment required

Affiliated to:
Federation of European Motorcyclists Associations (FEMA)
Rue Des Champs 62, 1040 Brussels, Belgium; tel: +32 2 736 9407; fax: +32 2 736 9401; e-mail: info@fema-online.eu; website: http://www.fema-online.eu

MAGDALEN COLLEGE

Library and Archives, Oxford, OX1 4AU

Tel: 01865 276045
Fax: 01865 276057
E-mail: library@magd.ox.ac.uk

Website:
http://www.magd.ox.ac.uk/college_life/libraries_and_archives.shtml

Enquiries:
Enquiries to: Librarian
Other contacts: Archivist, tel: 01865 276088 for archives queries

Founded:
1458

Organisation type and purpose:
College library and archives.

Subject coverage:
All taught subjects; college-related archives.

Museum or gallery collection, archive, or library special collection:
Gibbard Bequest 1608 (medical books)
Goodyer Bequest 1664 (botanical books)
Throckmorton Bequest 1626 (continental books)

Non-library collection catalogue:
All or part available in-house

Library catalogue:
All or part available online

Printed publications:
Magdalen College Occasional Papers (series)
Magdalen Poets (2000), Hidden Magdalen (2008), History of Magdalen College (2008) (books)
Order printed publications from: Home Bursar's Office, Magdalen College, Oxford OX1 4AU

Publications list:
Available online

Access to staff:
Contact by letter, by telephone, by e-mail and via website. Appointment necessary.
Hours: Mon to Fri, 0900 to 1700

Access to building, collection or gallery:
Members only, or by appointment

MAGIC CIRCLE, THE

Centre for the Magic Arts, 12 Stephenson Way, London, NW1 2HD

Tel: 020 7387 2222
Fax: 020 7387 5114
E-mail: prattmsm@hotmail.com

Website:
http://www.themagiccircle.co.uk
General information about the Magic Circle.

Enquiries:
Enquiries to: Secretary
Direct tel: 01707 654971
Direct fax: 01707 654971

Founded:
1905

Organisation type and purpose:
Membership association (membership is by subscription, qualification, election or invitation), present number of members: 1400.

Subject coverage:
Art of magic, magical inventions and presentations.

Access to staff:
Contact by letter, by telephone and by fax
Hours: Mon to Fri, 0900 to 1700

MAGIC LANTERN SOCIETY

Acronym or abbreviation: MLS

South Park, Galphay Road, Kirkby Malzeard, Ripon, North Yorkshire, HG4 3RX

Tel: 01765 658485
Fax: 01765 658485
E-mail: lmh.smith@magiclanternsocy.demon.co.uk

Website:
http://www.magiclantern.org.uk
All information about the society.

Enquiries:
Enquiries to: Honorary Secretary

Founded:
1976

Organisation type and purpose:
Learned society (membership is by subscription), present number of members: 400.

Subject coverage:
All aspects of pre-cinema optical entertainment.

Printed publications:
Journal
Short-run, high quality books occasionally published
Newsletter (quarterly)

Publications list:
Available in print

Access to staff:
Contact by letter, by telephone, by fax, by e-mail and via website
Hours: Mon to Fri, 0900 to 1700

MAGISTRATES' ASSOCIATION

Acronym or abbreviation: MA

28 Fitzroy Square, London, W1T 6DD

Tel: 020 7387 2353
Fax: 020 7383 4020
E-mail: communications@magistrates-association.org.uk

Website:
http://www.magistrates-association.org.uk
The Magistrates' Association – the voice of the magistracy – representing, informing, consulting, training and supporting the magistracy in England and Wales. Providing advice and information about magistrates and magistrates' courts.

Enquiries:
Enquiries to: Communications Director (for media and public relation enquiries, information enquiries)
Direct e-mail: information@magistrates-association.org.uk

Founded:
1920

Organisation type and purpose:
Membership association.
To advise and represent magistrates in England and Wales.

Subject coverage:
All matters of relevance to the lay magistracy.

Museum or gallery collection, archive, or library special collection:
A small library of law books relating to magistrates' courts and the magistracy

Library catalogue:
All or part available in-house

Printed publications:
Annual Report
Journal (monthly)

Access to staff:
Contact by letter, by telephone, by fax, by e-mail, in person and via website. Appointment necessary.
Access for members only.
Hours: Mon to Fri, 0915 to 1700

Access to building, collection or gallery:
Prior appointment required

Hours: Mon to Fri, 0930 to 1700

Access for disabled people:
Very limited – toilets accessible only via stairs

MAHARISHI FOUNDATION

Beacon House, Willow Walk, Woodley Park, Skelmersdale, Lancs, WN8 6UR

Tel: 01695 728847
E-mail: reception@maharishi-european-sidhaland.org.uk

Website:
http://www.maharishi.co.uk

Enquiries:
Enquiries to: Administrator
Direct tel: 020 7937 3353
Direct fax: 020 7376 9625

Founded:
1975

Organisation type and purpose:
Registered charity (charity number 270157). Educational charity.
To advance the education of the public by establishing, conducting and maintaining an institution of higher education; and by offering such courses of instruction to the public as will promote the mental and creative development of the individual.

Subject coverage:
Transcendental meditation, Maharishi's Vedic Science, Maharishi's Vedic approach to health, Maharishi's integrated system of education, Maharishi Ayur Veda, Maharishi Jyotish, Maharishi Sthapatya Ved, Maharishi Gandharva Ved.

Printed publications:
The Cosmic Computer (£20)
Perfect Blood Pressure Naturally (2001, £6.99)
Bhagavad Gita (paperback, £12.99)
Science of Being (paperback, £16)
Transcendental Meditation (Roth R, £12)
The TM Book (Denniston D, £11)
The Crime Vaccine (£15)
Neurophysiology of Enlightenment (£13)
Enlightened Management (£11)
Success from Within (£11)
Growing Up Enlightened (£13)
Self-Recovery: Treating Addictions (£24)
Key to Kingdom of Heaven (£4.95)
Order printed publications from: Maharishi Ayur-Veda Products, FREEPOST 5128, Skelmersdale, Lancashire, WN8 6BR, tel: 01695 51015, fax: 01695 50517

Electronic and video publications:
Maharishi Ayurveda Introductory Video (£5)
Bhagavad Gita (audio book, £60)
Science of Being (audio book, £70)
Maharishi at Lake Louise (video, £50)
A Promise for the Family of Man (video, £48)
Maharishi on Government (video, £38)
Maharishi's Lecture at the Harvard Law Forum (video, £38)
Maharishi on Education (video, £38)
Maharishi at the Royal Albert Hall (video, £48)
Maharishi Sthapatya Veda – Architecture in Harmony with Natural Law (video 30mins, £22)
The Physics of Flying (£39)
Is Consciousness the Unified Field? (£39)

Publications list:
Available online and in print

Access to staff:
Contact by letter, by telephone, by fax, by e-mail and via website
Hours: Mon to Fri, 1000 to 1700

Affiliated to:
Maharishi University of Natural Law at the same address

National Enquiry Office:
Beacon House
Woodley Park, Skelmersdale, Lancashire, WN8 6UR; tel: 01695 51213

MAIDENHEAD LIBRARY

St Ives Road, Maidenhead, Berkshire, SL6 1QU

Tel: 01628 796969
Fax: 01628 796971
E-mail: maidenhead.library@rbwm.gov.uk

Website:
http://www.rbwm.gov.uk

Enquiries:
Enquiries to: Librarian

Organisation type and purpose:
Local government body, registered charity, public library.

Library catalogue:
All or part available online

Access to staff:
Contact by letter, by telephone, by fax, by e-mail, in person and via website
Hours: Mon and Wed, 0930 to 1700; Tue and Thu, 0930 to 2000; Fri, 0930 to 1900; Sat, 0930 to 1600

Access for disabled people:
Ramped entry, access to all public areas, toilet facilities
Special comments: Parking opposite in the road, unreserved.

Parent body:
Royal Borough of Windsor and Maidenhead

MAIDSTONE & TUNBRIDGE WELLS NHS TRUST

Acronym or abbreviation: MTW

The Library, Kent & Sussex Hospital, Mount Ephraim, Tunbridge Wells, Kent, TN4 8AT

Tel: 01892 632384
Fax: 01892 531975
E-mail: gm.e.mtw-tr.library@nhs.net

Enquiries:
Enquiries to: Library & Information Services Manager
Direct tel: ext 2384
Other contacts: Site Librarian

Founded:
1974

Organisation type and purpose:
Education (NHS).

Subject coverage:
General surgery, otolaryngology, general practice, general medicine, trauma and orthopaedics.

Non-library collection catalogue:
All or part available online

Access to staff:
Appointment necessary. Non-members charged.
Hours: Mon to Fri, 0900 to 1700

Access to building, collection or gallery:
Prior appointment required

Access for disabled people:
Level entry, access to all public areas, toilet facilities

Member of:
Health Libraries Network

MAIDSTONE BOROUGH COUNCIL

Maidstone House, King Street, Maidstone, Kent, ME15 6JQ

Tel: 01622 602000
Fax: 01622 692246
E-mail: customercare@maidstone.gov.uk

Website:
http://www.maidstone.gov.uk

Enquiries:
Enquiries to: Chief Executive

Founded:
1974

Organisation type and purpose:
Local government body.

Subject coverage:
Local government services.

Publications list:
Available online and in print

Access to staff:
Contact by letter, by telephone, by fax, by e-mail, in person and via website
Hours: Mon to Thu, 0830 to 1700; Fri, 0830 to 1630

Access for disabled people:
Parking provided, level entry, toilet facilities

MAJOR CONTRACTORS GROUP

Acronym or abbreviation: MCG

55 Tufton Street, London, SW1P 3QL

Tel: 020 7227 4505
Fax: 020 7227 4506
E-mail: enquiries@mcg.org.uk

Website:
http://www.mcg.org.uk/

Enquiries:
Enquiries to: Director

Founded:
July 1996

Organisation type and purpose:
Trade association (membership is by election or invitation), present number of members: 23.

Subject coverage:
Construction industry.

Access to staff:
Contact by letter and by e-mail
Hours: Mon to Fri, 0900 to 1700

Member of:
Construction Confederation

MAKING MUSIC

Formal name: National Federation of Music Societies
Acronym or abbreviation: NFMS

2–4 Great Eastern Street, London, EC2A 3NW

Tel: 020 7422 8280
Fax: 020 7422 8299
E-mail: info@makingmusic.org.uk

Website:
http://www.makingmusic.org.uk

Enquiries:
Enquiries to: Communications Manager
Direct e-mail: sarah.robinson@makingmusic.org.uk

Founded:
1935

Organisation type and purpose:
Membership association (membership is by subscription), present number of members: 2,650, registered charity (charity number 249219), training organisation, research organisation. Making Music provides members with services and information to aid them in their voluntary activities.

Subject coverage:
Forming and running amateur music groups in the voluntary sector e.g. choirs, orchestras, music clubs, steel bands, jazz groups, classical Indian etc.

Non-library collection catalogue:
All or part available online and in print

Printed publications:
Highnotes (3 times a year)
Information sheets and How to Guides available in print

Electronic and video publications:
Information sheets and How to Guides available online
iNotes and regional e-bulletins

Repertoire service
Music Exchange service

Access to staff:
Contact by letter, by telephone, by fax, by e-mail and via website
Hours: Mon to Fri, 1000 to 1800

Affiliated to:
Association of British Orchestras
Incorporated Society of Musicians
Music Education Council (MEC)
National Campaign for the Arts
National Music Council of Great Britain
Voluntary Arts Network
World Federation of Amateur Orchestras

MALACOLOGICAL SOCIETY OF LONDON

Acronym or abbreviation: The Malsoc

Central Science Laboratory, Sand Hutton, York YO10 4JW

Tel: 01904 462349
E-mail: vasiliki@flari.fsnet.co.uk

Website:
http://www.malacsoc.org.uk/index.html

Enquiries:
Enquiries to: Honorary Secretary

Founded:
1893

Organisation type and purpose:
Learned society.

Subject coverage:
Molluscan biology, applied malacology, zoology, marine biology, snail culture, slugs and snails in agriculture, ecology, biochemistry, parasitology.

Printed publications:
The Malacologist (newsletter, twice a year)
Journal of Molluscan Studies (quarterly, pub. OUP)
Supplements to the Journal (17 titles to date of which numbers 6–17 are currently available)
Order printed publications from: Oxford University Press
Great Clarendon Street, Oxford, OX2 6DP, tel: 01865 267907, e-mail: jnlorders@oup.co.uk

Access to staff:
Contact by letter, by fax and by e-mail
Hours: Mon to Fri, 0900 to 1700

MALAYSIAN INDUSTRIAL DEVELOPMENT AUTHORITY

Acronym or abbreviation: MIDA

17 Curzon Street, London, W1J 5HR

Tel: 020 7493 0616
Fax: 020 7493 8804
E-mail: midalon@btconnect.com

Website:
http://www.mida.gov.my
Investment opportunities in Malaysia's manufacturing sector.

Enquiries:
Enquiries to: Director

Founded:
1967

Organisation type and purpose:
National government body.
Malaysian Government body.
Promotes inward investment into Malaysia's manufacturing sector.

Subject coverage:
Investment opportunities in Malaysia's manufacturing sector.

Printed publications:
Malaysia Your Profit Centre in Asia
Investment in the Manufacturing Sector: Policies, Incentives and Facilities
The Cost of Doing Business in Malaysia

The Functions of MIDA
Why Malaysia
Map of Malaysia

Publications list:
Available in print

Access to staff:
Contact by letter, by telephone, by fax, by e-mail
and in person
Hours: Mon to Fri, 0900 to 1700

Headquarters:
Malaysian Industrial Development Authority
(MIDA)
Plaza Sentral, Jalan Stesen Sentral 5, KL Sentral,
50470 Kuala Lumpur, Malaysia; tel: +60 3 2267
3633; fax: +60 3 2274 7970; e-mail: promotion@
mida.gov.my

MALONE SOCIETY

c/o Dr C. Richardson, School of English, University
of Kent, Canterbury, CT2 7NX

Tel: 01227 824656
E-mail: c.t.richardson@kent.ac.uk

Website:
http://ies.sas.ac.uk/malone/index.htm

Enquiries:
Enquiries to: Orders Secretary

Founded:
1906

Organisation type and purpose:
International organisation, learned society
(membership is by subscription), present number
of members: 650, registered charity (charity
number 1027048).
To make accessible materials for the study of
English drama up to 1642 by editing and
publishing dramatic texts and related documents.

Subject coverage:
English drama up to 1642.

Printed publications:
Over 150 books published, most still in print.
Available via annual subscription (£15 or
equivalent), or (recent titles) from Manchester
University Press, or (older titles) by direct
application.
Order printed publications from: Orders Secretary, at
the same address

Publications list:
Available online

Access to staff:
Contact by letter, by telephone and by e-mail
Hours: Mon to Fri, 0900 to 1700

Access to building, collection or gallery:
No access other than to staff

MALTA TOURIST OFFICE

Malta House, 36–38 Piccadilly, London, W1J 0LD

Tel: 020 7292 4900
Fax: 020 7734 1880
E-mail: office.uk@visitmalta.com

Website:
http://www.visitmalta.com

Enquiries:
Enquiries to: Director
Direct e-mail: john.montague@visitmalta.com

Organisation type and purpose:
National government body.
Tourist office.

Subject coverage:
General tourist information.

Trade and statistical information:
Number of tourists to Malta.
Percentage of countries visiting Malta.

Library catalogue:
All or part available in-house

Printed publications:
Malta brochure, brochures on Valleta, Mdina,
Gozo, hotel guides
Religion historic sites, events

Electronic and video publications:
Videos on Malta

Access to staff:
Contact by letter, by telephone, by fax, by e-mail,
in person and via website. Appointment necessary.
Hours: Mon to Fri, 0900 to 1700

Access for disabled people:
Level entry

Parent body:
Malta Tourism Authority
Merchants Str, Valletta, Malta; tel: 00 356 2122
4444; fax: 00 356 2122 0401; e-mail: info@
visitmalta.com

MALTSTERS ASSOCIATION OF GREAT BRITAIN

Acronym or abbreviation: MAGB

31B Castlegate, Newark, Nottinghamshire, NG24
1AZ

Tel: 01636 700781
Fax: 01636 701836
E-mail: info@magb.org.uk

Website:
http://www.malt.info.com
http://www.ukmalt.com

Enquiries:
Enquiries to: Executive Director

Founded:
1827

Organisation type and purpose:
Trade association.

Subject coverage:
Malting.

Access to staff:
Contact by letter, by telephone and by fax
Hours: Mon to Fri, 0900 to 1700

MALVERN LIBRARY

Graham Road, Malvern, Worcestershire, WR14
2HU

Tel: 01905 822722
Fax: 01684 892999
E-mail: malvernlib@worcestershire.gov.uk

Website:
http://www.worcestershire.gov.uk
County-wide information service web site
(includes information on all county council
services, with links to many useful web sites).

Founded:
1905

Organisation type and purpose:
Local government body, public library.

Subject coverage:
General, local history of Malvern.

**Museum or gallery collection, archive, or library
special collection:**
Local Studies Collection, including a substantial
collection of illustrations

Non-library collection catalogue:
All or part available in-house

Library catalogue:
All or part available online

Access to staff:
Contact by letter, by telephone, by fax, by e-mail
and in person. Appointment necessary.
Hours: Mon, Fri, 0900 to 1730; Tue to Thu, 0900 to
2000; Sat, 0900 to 1730; Sun, closed

Access to building, collection or gallery:
No prior appointment required

Hours: Mon, Fri, 0900 to 1730; Tue to Thu, 0900 to
2000; Sat, 0900 to 1730
Special comments: Sun, closed. Closed on Bank
holidays, Good Friday and over Christmas.

Access for disabled people:
Parking provided, ramped entry

Constituent part of:
Worcestershire County Council
County Hall, Spetchley Road, Worcester, WR5
2NP; tel: 01905 763763; fax: 01905 766244; e-
mail: kkirk@worcestershire.gov.uk

MAMMAL SOCIETY

3 The Carronades, New Road, Southampton, SO14
0AA

Tel: 023 8023 7874
Fax: 023 8063 4726
E-mail: enquiries@mammal.org.uk

Website:
http://www.mammal.org.uk

Enquiries:
Enquiries to: Office Manager

Founded:
1954

Organisation type and purpose:
Membership association (membership is by
subscription), present number of members: 2,000,
voluntary organisation, registered charity (charity
number 278918).
To protect British mammals, halt the decline of
threatened species and advise on all issues
affecting British mammals.

Subject coverage:
British mammals, their biology, conservation,
ecology, management, distribution and status, and
methods of study.

Printed publications:
Books, guides and occasional publications
including:
Mammals of the British Isles, Handbook 4th Edn
A Review of British Mammals (latest population
estimates and review of their conservation status,
1995, £16.40)
British Mammal Fact Sheet Series
Mammal News (newsletter)
Mammal Review (journal, quarterly, free to
members)
Mammalaction News (for teenagers)

Publications list:
Available online

Access to staff:
Contact by letter, by telephone, by fax, by e-mail
and via website
Hours: Mon to Fri, 0900 to 1700

Access to building, collection or gallery:
No access other than to staff

Member organisation of:
IUCN

MAN B&W DIESEL LIMITED, PAXMAN

Paxman Works, PO Box 8, Colchester, Essex, CO1
2HW

Tel: 01206 795151
Fax: 01206 797869
E-mail: mike-johnson@manbwltd.com

Enquiries:
Enquiries to: Information Officer
Direct tel: 01206 875508
Direct e-mail: mike.johnson@alstom.ind.com

Founded:
1865

Organisation type and purpose:
Trade association.

continued overleaf

Subject coverage:
General engineering, diesel engines, design and manufacture.

Library catalogue:
All or part available in-house

Access to staff:
Contact by letter, by telephone, by fax and by e-mail. Appointment necessary. Letter of introduction required.
Hours: Mon to Thu, 0900 to 1700; Fri, 0900 to 1600

MANAGEMENT CONSULTANCIES ASSOCIATION

Acronym or abbreviation: MCA

49 Whitehall, London, SW1A 2BX

Tel: 020 7321 3990
Fax: 020 7321 3991
E-mail: mca@mca.org.uk

Website:
http://www.mca.org.uk

Enquiries:
Enquiries to: Deputy Director
Direct tel: 020 7321 3993
Direct e-mail: lydia.waliszak@mca.org.uk

Founded:
1956

Organisation type and purpose:
Trade association (membership is by qualification), present number of members: 39.

Subject coverage:
Management consulting, selection of management consultants, statistics relating to members' earnings, career guidance, case studies, journal and reports on management issues.

Trade and statistical information:
Members' earnings broken down by type or consultancy work performed and industry.

Printed publications:
Annual Report
Careers in Management Consulting
Statement of Best Practice
MCA Journal
MCA Think Tank Reports

Access to staff:
Contact by letter, by telephone, by fax, by e-mail and via website. Appointment necessary.
Hours: Mon to Fri, 0900 to 1700

Access to building, collection or gallery:
Prior appointment required

Member of:
Federation of European Management
Consultancies Associations
3/4/5 Avenue des Arts, Brussels, B-1210, Belgium; tel: +32 2 250 0650; fax: +32 2 250 0651; e-mail: feaco@feaco.org

MANCHESTER AND LANCASHIRE FAMILY HISTORY SOCIETY

Acronym or abbreviation: M&LFHS

Clayton House, 59 Piccadilly, Manchester, M1 2AQ

Tel: 0161 236 9750
Fax: 0161 237 3812
E-mail: office@mlfhs.org.uk

Website:
http://www.mlfhs.org.uk
General information about the Society. Mail order book list and order form. Membership details and application form.

Enquiries:
Enquiries to: General Secretary

Founded:
1964

Organisation type and purpose:
Membership association (membership is by subscription), present number of members: 3,200, registered charity (charity number 515599).

Subject coverage:
Genealogy, heraldry and local history.

Library catalogue:
All or part available in-house

Printed publications:
1851 Census Indexes (59 volumes)
Irish in 1861 Census
Publications of the Bolton & District Branch

Microform publications:
Unfilmed 1851 Census Transcripts
Oldham Area Burial Transcripts
Indexes to Army Deserters

Electronic and video publications:
Scots in E & W 1851 Census (CD-ROM)
Manchester City Battalions Book of Honour (CD-ROM)

Publications list:
Available online and in print

Access to staff:
Contact by letter, by telephone, by fax, by e-mail, in person and via website
Hours: Mon, Fri, 1015 to 1300; Tue, Thu, 1015 to 1600

Branches:
Anglo Scottish Branch
Bolton & District Branch
Irish Ancestry Branch
Oldham & District Branch

MANCHESTER ARTS LIBRARY

Central Library, St Peter's Square, Manchester, M2 5PD

Tel: 0161 234 1974
Fax: 0161 234 1961
E-mail: arts@libraries.manchester.gov.uk

Website:
http://www.manchester.gov.uk/libraries

Enquiries:
Enquiries to: Arts Coordinator

Founded:
1852

Organisation type and purpose:
Local government body, public library.

Subject coverage:
Art and design in general, costume and fashion, town planning, architecture, decorative arts, antiques, interiors, textiles, ceramics, sculpture, drawing and painting, graphics, photography, cinema, radio and TV, theatre, dance, sport and recreation.

Museum or gallery collection, archive, or library special collection:
18th and 19th century sales catalogues
Local Theatre Material Collection (estimated 30,000 items, from mid-18th century to present day)
News Chronicle Photograph Collection (52 boxes, mainly 1940–60 costume accessories)
Many important 19th century periodicals. Videos and DVDs of classic films.

Access to staff:
Contact by letter, by telephone, by fax, by e-mail, in person and via website
Hours: Mon to Thu, 1000 to 2000; Fri, Sat, 1000 to 1700

Access for disabled people:
Ramped entry, lift, toilet facilities
Special comments: Limited parking; access to most areas; staff will assist with access to lifts etc as required.

MANCHESTER BUSINESS SCHOOL

Acronym or abbreviation: MBS

Booth Street West, Manchester, M15 6PB

Tel: 0161 275 6507
Fax: 0161 275 6505
E-mail: kkirby@man-mbs.ac.uk

Website:
http://www.mbs.ac.uk

Enquiries:
Enquiries to: Information and Services Manager
Direct tel: 0161 275 6499
Other contacts: Head of Business Information Service for an information brokerage to companies on a fee paying basis.

Founded:
1965

Organisation type and purpose:
University department or institute.

Subject coverage:
Management science and education, marketing, production, finance, personnel management, economics, operations research, accounting, computing, statistics, business and companies information, market data.

Museum or gallery collection, archive, or library special collection:
Business and management journals, both printed and electronic
20,000 books

Trade and statistical information:
Collection of UK and other official statistics – OECD, European Union, UN, ILO.
Also various trade association statutes.

Printed publications:
Research Reports
Working Papers

Access to staff:
Contact by letter, by telephone, by fax and by e-mail. Non-members charged.
Hours: Term time: Mon to Fri, 0830 to 2030; Sat, 0930 to 1700
Vacations: Mon to Fri, 1000 to 1700
Special comments: The library is open to members of MBS and post-graduates and staff of other Manchester Universities. Researchers from other universities may use the library for reference purposes, by arrangement. All other users are charged an access fee.

Faculty of:
Business Administration, University of Manchester, but separately funded

Member of:
Manchester Federal School of Business and Management

MANCHESTER CENTRAL LIBRARY

St Peter's Square, Manchester, M2 5PD

Tel: 0161 234 1900 \ Minicom no. 0161 234 1984
Fax: 0161 234 1963

Organisation type and purpose:
Public library.

MANCHESTER CENTRAL LIBRARY – SOCIAL SCIENCES LIBRARY

St Peter's Square, Manchester, M2 5PD

Tel: 0161 234 1983 \ Minicom no. 0161 234 1983/4
Fax: 0161 234 1927
E-mail: socsci@libraries.manchester.gov.uk

Website:
http://www.manchester.gov.uk/libraries
Information about the Central Library and district libraries.

Enquiries:
Enquiries to: Librarian

Founded:
1852

Organisation type and purpose:
Public library.

Subject coverage:
Bibliography, philosophy, religion, social sciences, home economics, archaeology, geography, history, biography within subject areas indicated.

Museum or gallery collection, archive, or library special collection:
18th and 19th century pamphlets
National Newspapers (on microfilm)
Parish Registers and related genealogical material
Parliamentary papers
Private Press books

Access to staff:
Contact by letter, by telephone, by fax, by e-mail, in person and via website
Hours: Mon to Thu, 1000 to 2000; Fri and Sat, 1000 to 1700

Access for disabled people:
Ramped entry

MANCHESTER CENTRE FOR REGIONAL HISTORY

Acronym or abbreviation: MCRH

Department of History and Economic History, Manchester Metropolitan University, Room 103, Geoffrey Manton Building, Rosamond Street West, Manchester, M15 6LL

Tel: 0161 247 6491
E-mail: c.horner@mmu.ac.uk

Website:
http://www.mcrh.mmu.ac.uk

Founded:
1998

Organisation type and purpose:
Research centre of Manchester Metropolitan University.

Subject coverage:
History of Manchester and the northwest of England.

Printed publications:
Manchester Region History Review (journal)

MANCHESTER CITY GALLERIES

Mosley Street, Manchester, M2 3JL

Tel: 0161 235 8888 \ Minicom no. 0161 235 8893
Fax: 0161 235 8899
E-mail: cityart@mcrl.poptel.org.uk

Website:
http://www.cityartgalleries.org.uk

Enquiries:
Enquiries to: Administration

Founded:
1882

Organisation type and purpose:
Local government body, art gallery, historic building, house or site, suitable for ages: all. Administrative body for the Manchester City Art Galleries and Museums.

Subject coverage:
Fine and decorative art from antiquity to present day; costume, picture, decorative art, and costume restoration.

Special visitor services:
Guided tours, tape recorded guides, materials and/ or activities for children.

Education services:
Group education facilities, resources for Key Stages 1 and 2, 3, 4 and Further or Higher Education.

Museum or gallery collection, archive, or library special collection:
20th century British Paintings
Assheton-Bennett Collection of English silver and 17th century Dutch painting
Old Masters
Pre-Raphaelites
Thomas Greg Collection of English pottery

Non-library collection catalogue:
All or part available online, in-house and in print

Printed publications:
Concise Catalogue of British Paintings (2 vols)
Foreign Paintings
Large selection of printed items eg posters, prints, postcards, greetings cards etc
Other catalogues of temporary exhibitions
Pre-Raphaelite Paintings

Access to staff:
Contact by letter, by telephone and via website.
Appointment necessary.
Hours: Mon to Fri, 0900 to 1700

Galleries and historic houses:
Gallery of Costume
 Platt Hall, Wilmslow Road, Rusholme, Manchester, M14 5LL; tel: 0161 224 5217; fax: 0161 256 3278
Heaton Hall
 Heaton Park, Prestwich, Manchester, M25 5SW; tel: 0161 773 1231
Manchester Art Gallery
 Mosley Street, Manchester, M2 3JL; tel: 0161 235 8888; fax: 0161 235 8899
Queen's Park Conservation Studio
 Queen's Park, Rochdale Road, Harpurhey, Manchester, M9 5SH; tel: 0161 205 2645; fax: 0161 205 6164
Wythenshawe Hall
 Wythenshaw Park, Northenden, Manchester, M23 0AB; tel: 0161 998 2331

Parent body:
Manchester City Council
 website: www.manchester.gov.uk

MANCHESTER GEOGRAPHICAL SOCIETY

Acronym or abbreviation: MGS

Meadowbank, Ringley Road, Radcliffe, Manchester, M26 1FW

Tel: 0161 723 1433
E-mail: paulhindle@talktalk.net

Website:
http://www.mangeogsoc.org.uk

Enquiries:
Enquiries to: Honorary Secretary

Founded:
1884

Organisation type and purpose:
Learned society, registered charity (charity number 1134626), runs lecture series, research organisation, publishing house.
To encourage the study of geography at all levels.

Subject coverage:
Geography.

Museum or gallery collection, archive, or library special collection:
Library – held by John Rylands University Library of Manchester

Library catalogue:
All or part available online and in print

Printed publications:
Library catalogue
The Manchester Geographer (1980–93)
The North West Geographer (1997–2000)

Electronic and video publications:
North West Geography (free online journal, 2001 to date)
Order electronic and video publications from: website: http://www.mangeogsoc.org.uk/nwgeog.htm

Publications list:
Available online

Access to staff:
Contact by letter, by telephone, by e-mail and via website

MANCHESTER LANGUAGE AND LITERATURE LIBRARY

Central Library, St Peter's Square, Manchester, M2 5PD

Tel: 0161 234 1972
Fax: 0161 234 1963
E-mail: lang_lit@libraries.manchester.gov.uk

Website:
http://www.manchester.gov.uk/libraries/central/langlit/index.htm
General guide to department e-resources.

Enquiries:
Enquiries to: Librarian

Founded:
1852

Organisation type and purpose:
Local government body, public library.

Subject coverage:
Language; literature; folklore.

Museum or gallery collection, archive, or library special collection:
Alexander Ireland Collection (works by or relating to Charles and Mary Lamb, William Hazlitt, Leigh Hunt, Thomas and Jane Carlyle, Ralph W Emerson)
Bellot Chinese Collection
Brontë Collection
Coleridge Collection
de Quincey Collection
Elizabeth Gaskell Collection
Foreign library (lending collection of literature in 28 languages)
Index of local translators
James L Hodson Collection
Language courses on tape for loan (72 languages)
Literature and criticism on cassette
Manchester Ballad and Chapbook Collections
Videos of literary interest

Non-library collection catalogue:
All or part available in-house

Access to staff:
Contact by letter, by telephone, by fax, by e-mail and in person
Hours: Mon to Thu, 0900 to 2000; Fri, 0900 to 1700; Sat, 0900 to 1700

MANCHESTER LAW LIBRARY

Formal name: Manchester Incorporated Law Library Society
Acronym or abbreviation: MILLS

14 Kennedy Street, Manchester, M2 4BY

Tel: 0161 236 6312
Fax: 0161 236 6119
E-mail: librarian@manchester-law-library.co.uk

Website:
http://www.manchester-law-library.co.uk

Enquiries:
Enquiries to: Librarian

Founded:
1820

Organisation type and purpose:
Membership association.
Subscription Library for practising barristers, solicitors and in-house lawyers.

Subject coverage:
All aspects of law likely to be of interest to practising lawyers.

continued overleaf

Museum or gallery collection, archive, or library special collection:
nominate reports and local and personal acts from 1837

Library catalogue:
All or part available in-house

Access to staff:
Contact by letter, by telephone, by fax, by e-mail and in person. Access for members only. All charged.

Access to building, collection or gallery:
Hours: Mon to Fri, 0900 to 1700
Special comments: members only

MANCHESTER METROPOLITAN UNIVERSITY – DEPARTMENT OF INFORMATION AND COMMUNICATIONS

Geoffrey Manton Building, Rosamond Street West, off Oxford Road, Manchester, M15 6LL

Fax: 0161 247 6351
E-mail: infcomms-hums@mmu.ac.uk

Website:
http://www.hlss.mmu.ac.uk/infocomms/
Course details, research information, contact details.

Enquiries:
Enquiries to: Executive assistant, HLSS

Organisation type and purpose:
University department or institute.

Subject coverage:
Library and information education and research.

Access to staff:
Contact by letter, by telephone, by fax, by e-mail and via website. Appointment necessary.
Hours: Mon to Fri, 0900 to 1700

Access for disabled people:
Parking provided, level entry, access to all public areas, toilet facilities

MANCHESTER METROPOLITAN UNIVERSITY – UNIVERSITY LIBRARY

All Saints Building, Grosvenor Square, Oxford Road, Manchester, M15 6BH

Tel: 0161 247 3096
Fax: 0161 247 6349
E-mail: lib-website@mmu.ac.uk

Website:
http://www.mmu.ac.uk/services/library
Information about services, access to catalogue and to other Web resources.

Enquiries:
Enquiries to: Librarian
Direct e-mail: c.harris@mmu.ac.uk

Founded:
1992

Organisation type and purpose:
University library.

Subject coverage:
Art and design; business studies; clothing technology; education; finance and accounting; health sciences; home economics; hotel and catering studies; humanities; languages; law; librarianship; management; media studies; music; psychology; science; social science; speech pathology; sports science and technology.

Museum or gallery collection, archive, or library special collection:
Artists Archives, including Barnet Freedman, Rigby Graham, Paul Hogarth
Book Design Collection (12,000 items including 1000 artists' books)
Children's Book Collection (3000 items, 19th and 20th century books and periodicals)

Cotton Collection (history of 20th century cotton trade)
Historical collection of books on cookery and household management from the 17th to mid-20th century
Laura Seddon Collection of Victorian and Edwardian greeting cards
Local Studies (3000 items)
Manchester Society of Architects' Library (books on 18th and 19th century architecture)
Morten-Dandy Collection (19th century children's fiction, textbooks, readers and picture books)
Nonesuch Press (250 items)
Sir Harry Page Collection of Victorian Ephemera

Library catalogue:
All or part available online

Printed publications:
Illustrated Exhibition Catalogues mostly related to the Library's Book Design collection

Access to staff:
Contact by letter, by e-mail and via website. Appointment necessary.
Hours: Mon to Fri, 0900 to 1630

MANCHESTER ROOM@CITY LIBRARY

Acronym or abbreviation: MALS

The Manchester Room@City Library, Elliot House, 151 Deansgate, Manchester, M3 3WD

Tel: 0161 234 1979
E-mail: archiveslocalstudies@manchester.gov.uk

Website:
http://www.manchester.gov.uk/libraries/arls
Main webpage.
http://www.images.manchester.gov.uk
Print Collection webpage.

Enquiries:
Enquiries to: Archives & Local Studies Officer
Direct tel: 0161 234 1960
Direct e-mail: r.bond@manchester.gov.uk

Founded:
1991

Organisation type and purpose:
Local government body, public library.
Local studies service for City of Manchester.

Subject coverage:
Political, economic, religious, educational and historical development of Manchester and the region.

Museum or gallery collection, archive, or library special collection:
Print Collection (approx. 145,000 items, prints, photographs, postcards, etc.) of which 77,000 available in digital form
Microform collections:
Census Returns (Manchester 1841–1901)
Directories of Manchester, 1772–1969
Local Newspapers from early 18th century
Parish Registers (large collection, Manchester, Cheshire and Lancashire)

Non-library collection catalogue:
All or part available online, in-house and in print

Library catalogue:
All or part available online and in-house

Printed publications:
Municipal Palace: a bibliography on the construction and opening of Manchester Town Hall, 1877 (1977)
Peterloo 1819: a portfolio of contemporary documents (1975)
Peterloo: a bibliography (1969)
Manchester Wartime Memories (2006; book, CD)
Selection of reproduction maps, 1800–1876
Selection of reproduction posters, mainly 18th century
Various information sheets

Microform publications:
Women's Suffrage Collection (30 Microfilms, available from Adam Matthew Publications, 8 Oxford Street, Marlborough, Wilts, SN8 1AP)
Parish Register – subject to permission (microfilm, details on archives section of website)

Access to staff:
Contact by letter, by telephone, by fax, by e-mail, in person and via website
Hours: Mon to Thu, 0900 to 2000; Fri and Sat, 0900 to 1700

Access for disabled people:
Disabled entrance on Jacksons Row; lift available.

Parent body:
Manchester City Council
Town Hall, Manchester, M60 2LA; tel: 0161 234 5000; website: http://www.manchester.gov.uk

MANIPULATION ASSOCIATION OF CHARTERED PHYSIOTHERAPISTS

Acronym or abbreviation: MACP

Chartered Society of Physiotherapy, 14 Bedford Row, London, WC1R 4ED

Tel: 01202 706161
E-mail: admin@macpweb.org

Website:
http://www.macpweb.org
Details of organisation, benefits of membership, directory of members, guidance papers.

Enquiries:
Enquiries to: Administrator

Founded:
1967

Organisation type and purpose:
Professional body (membership is by qualification), present number of members: 1,100, training organisation.
To maintain and further develop clinical excellence in neuro-musculoskeletal physiotherapy which will be of benefit to the current and future needs of both the profession and the general public.

Subject coverage:
Physiotherapy, manual therapy, manipulation, neuro-musculoskeletal physiotherapy.

Printed publications:
Manual Therapy (6 times a year, pub. Churchill Livingstone)
Order printed publications from: Manual Therapy, Churchill Livingstone Marketing, Robert Stevenson House, 1–3 Baxter's Place, Leith Walk, Edinburgh, EH1 3AF; tel: 0800 801 405

Publications list:
Available online

Access to staff:
Contact by letter, by telephone, by e-mail and via website
Hours: Mon to Fri, 0900 to 1700

Constituent part of:
Chartered Society of Physiotherapy
14 Bedford Row, London, WC1R 4ED; tel: 020 7366 6666; fax: 020 7306 6611

MANORIAL SOCIETY OF GREAT BRITAIN

Acronym or abbreviation: MSGB

104 Kennington Road, London, SE11 6RE

Tel: 020 7735 6633
Fax: 020 7582 7022
E-mail: manorial@msgb.co.uk

Website:
http://www.msgb.co.uk
Website with information on the Society and sales. Titles in upcoming auctions.

Enquiries:
Enquiries to: Chairman

Direct tel: 020 7582 1588

Founded:
1906

Organisation type and purpose:
International organisation, learned society
(membership is by election or invitation), research
organisation, publishing house.

Subject coverage:
Holders and addresses of feudal titles; legal
research into title; holders and addresses of British
peerage and baronetage; publishers; conference
and exhibitions (all historical) organisers. Sale price
of titles sold ranges from £5,000 to £30,000: 80%
UK, most of rest Europe and US.

**Museum or gallery collection, archive, or library
special collection:**
Historical, topographical and genealogical library
Paper file on 4,500 manors and feudal baronies.
  Not available to general public

Printed publications:
List available on application

Electronic and video publications:
Due in 2011

Publications list:
Available in print

Access to staff:
Contact by letter, by telephone, by fax and by e-
mail. Appointment necessary.
Hours: Mon to Fri, 1000 to 1700
Special comments: No members of the public, except
by appointment.

Access to building, collection or gallery:
Prior appointment required

Access for disabled people:
No disabled access

Affiliated to:
English Manor Register Ltd
  As above; tel: 020 7735 6633; fax: 020 7582 1588
Institute of Constitutional research
  As above; tel: 020 7735 6633; fax: 020 7582 1588
Manorial Auctioneers Limited
  As above; tel: 020 7582 1588; fax: 020 7582 7022;
  e-mail: manorial@msgb.co.uk
Smith's Peerage Limited
  tel: 020 7735 6633; fax: 020 7582 7022; e-mail:
  manorial@msgb.co.uk

MANUFACTURING
TECHNOLOGIES ASSOCIATION

Acronym or abbreviation: MTA

62 Bayswater Road, London, W2 3PS

Tel: 020 7298 6413
E-mail: mta@mta.co.uk

Website:
http://www.mta.org.uk

Enquiries:
Enquiries to: Marketing Manager
Direct e-mail: bromige@mtta.co.uk

Founded:
1919

Organisation type and purpose:
Trade association.
Representing metal-cutting and metal-forming
manufacturers.

Subject coverage:
Information supplied on: statistics, education and
training, technical assistance, i.e: CE marks,
standards. public relations, relevant exhibitions in
the United Kingdom and abroad, trade missions,
distributor and agent information, market sector
reports, meetings, presentations, publications,
industry representation.

Trade and statistical information:
A full range of data on machine tool users and
  suppliers.

Printed publications:
British Machine Tools and Equipment (annually,
  free of charge)
Electrical Equipment of Machine Tools
Machine Tool Enterprise (quarterly, free)
Machine Tool Statistics (annually, for sale)
Safety Codes of Practice for Machine Tools and
  Robots
Standards and booklets

Electronic and video publications:
Manufacturers (CD-ROM)
Importers (CD-ROM)

Publications list:
Available in print

Access to staff:
Contact by letter, by telephone, by fax, by e-mail
and via website. Non-members charged.
Hours: Mon to Fri, 0900 to 1700

Access to building, collection or gallery:
No access other than to staff
Special comments: Prior appointment required for
access to library.

MANX NATIONAL HERITAGE
LIBRARY AND ARCHIVES

Acronym or abbreviation: MNH

Manx Museum and National Trust, Kingswood
Grove, Douglas, Isle of Man, IM1 3LY

Tel: 01624 648000
Fax: 01624 648001
E-mail: enquiries@mnh.gov.im

Website:
http://www.gov.im/mnh

Enquiries:
Enquiries to: Librarian-Archivist

Founded:
1886

Organisation type and purpose:
National government body, registered charity
(charity number 603), museum, art gallery, public
library, research organisation.
National reference library and archives of the Isle
of Man.

Subject coverage:
Manx studies, particularly history, archaeology,
folklore, natural history and art, all aspects of
Manx heritage, politics, international relations,
economy, peoples, music, etc., 12th century to
present.

Special visitor services:
Film theatre, restaurant, galleries.

**Museum or gallery collection, archive, or library
special collection:**
Family Papers of the Derby and Atholl Families,
  relating to their Lordship of the Isle of Man
Manx Government Records, 1417 to the present

Printed publications:
Bibliography of the literature of the Isle of Man,
  vol. I 1933, vol. II 1939
Guides and handbooks
Guides to branch museums
History of the Isle of Man
Journal of the Manx Museum
Order printed publications from: Website

Electronic and video publications:
See website

Publications list:
Available in print

Access to staff:
Contact by letter, by telephone, by fax, by e-mail
and in person
Hours: Mon to Sat, 1000 to 1700

Access to building, collection or gallery:
Hours: Mon to Sat, 1000 to 1700

Access for disabled people:
Disabled access to all floors
Hours: Mon to Sat, 1000 to 1700

MAPLE SOCIETY

The Membership Secretary, 12 Rustens Manor
Road, Wymondham, Norfolk, NR18 0NH

Enquiries:
Enquiries to: Membership Secretary
Other contacts: Chairman for technical information.

Founded:
1991

Organisation type and purpose:
International organisation, membership
association (membership is by subscription),
present number of members: 152.
To dispense information on and facilitate the study
of Maples.

Subject coverage:
Cultivation and after care, indentification,
historical information of Maple species and
'Japanese Maples'.

Printed publications:
The Newsletter (quarterly, to members, free;
  otherwise by subscription)

Access to staff:
Contact by letter and by telephone

MARENDAZ SPECIAL CAR
REGISTER

c/o 107 Old Bath Road, Cheltenham,
Gloucestershire, GL53 7DA

Enquiries:
Enquiries to: Registrar

Founded:
1971

Organisation type and purpose:
Register.

Subject coverage:
Marendaz Special cars, technical information,
historical data, photographs.

Access to staff:
Contact by letter

MARGARINE AND SPREADS
ASSOCIATION

Acronym or abbreviation: MSA

6 Catherine Street, London, WC2B 5JJ

Tel: 020 7836 2460
Fax: 020 7379 5735
E-mail: jhowarth@fdf.org.uk

Website:
http://www.margarine.org.uk
History, chemistry, manufacturing, nutrition and
health and uses of margarine and spreads

Enquiries:
Enquiries to: Secretary General
Direct tel: 020 7420 7121 (direct)

Founded:
1966

Organisation type and purpose:
Trade association (membership is by subscription,
qualification, election or invitation), present
number of members: 9, manufacturing industry.

Subject coverage:
The UK margarine and spread industry, including
the history and chemistry of margarine and
spreads and how they are manufactured. Nutrition
and health information relating to the role played
by fats in the diet. Specialist area: all legislation
pertaining to food.

Trade and statistical information:
Production statistics and value.

Printed publications:
Brochure – Lifting the lid, spreading the word,
  raising the standards

continued overleaf

Access to staff:
Contact by letter, by telephone, by fax, by e-mail and via website. Appointment necessary.
Hours: Mon to Fri, 0930 to 1730

Links with:
International Federation of Margarine Associations (IFMA)
International Margarine Association of the countries of Europe (IMACE)

Member of:
The Food and Drink Federation

MARGERY KEMPE SOCIETY, THE

1 Auckland Road, London, SW11 1EW

Tel: 020 7924 5868

Enquiries:
Enquiries to: Honorary Treasurer

Founded:
1999

Organisation type and purpose:
National organisation, learned society (membership is by subscription), present number of members: 15.
To encourage and facilitate study of Margery Kempe, late medieval female piety.

Subject coverage:
Margery Kempe.

Printed publications:
Newsletter (members only)
Bibliography (members only)

Access to staff:
Contact by letter
Hours: Mon to Fri, 0900 to 1700

MARIA MONTESSORI INSITITUTE AMI

Formal name: Maria Montessori Training Organisation
Acronym or abbreviation: MMI

26 Lyndhurst Gardens, London, NW3 5NW

Tel: 020 7435 3646
Fax: 020 7431 8096
E-mail: info@mariamontessori.org

Website:
http://www.mariamontessori.org
Details on courses that train adults to work with children in the Montessori approach to education.

Founded:
1952

Organisation type and purpose:
Registered charity (charity number 313087).
Training adults to work with children using the Montessori approach to education.
Also runs 5 Montessori schools in London.

Subject coverage:
Institute that trains people in the Montessori approach to education, specialising in children under six years old (AMI International Diploma on completion).

Printed publications:
Training Course Prospectus

Access to staff:
Contact by letter, by telephone, by fax and by e-mail. Appointment necessary.
Hours: Mon to Fri, 0900 to 1600

Links with:
Association Montessori Internationale (AMI) Koninginneweg 161, 1075 CN Amsterdam, Netherlands; tel: +31 206 798932; fax: +31 206 767341; e-mail: ami@xs4all.nl; website: http://www.montessori-ami.org

MARINE CONSERVATION SOCIETY

Acronym or abbreviation: MCS

9 Gloucester Road, Ross-on-Wye, Herefordshire, HR9 5BU

Tel: 01989 566017
Fax: 01989 567815
E-mail: info@mcsuk.org

Website:
http://www.mcsuk.org
http://www.goodbeachguide.co.uk
http://www.adoptabeach.org.uk

Enquiries:
Enquiries to: Communications Officer

Founded:
1983

Organisation type and purpose:
Professional body, membership association (membership is by subscription), registered charity (charity number 1004005).
The UK's national charity for the protection of the marine environment and its wildlife.

Subject coverage:
Water quality, coastal zone management, marine debris, fisheries, marine wildlife, toxins in the marine environment, coral reefs.

Museum or gallery collection, archive, or library special collection:
Marine environment and marine wildlife photographic library
Transparencies available for use under licence and fee

Trade and statistical information:
Annual Beachwatch Report (sources and quantity of UK beach litter).
Good Beach Guide (Recommended UK beaches where bathing water quality is considered safe to use).

Library catalogue:
All or part available in-house

Printed publications:
The Good Fish Guide Marine Conservation Magazine
Beachwatch Report
Information Packs on: Coral Reef Conservation; Marine Species; Marine Habitats; Pollution; Sea Empress
Marine Conservation – The UK Action Guide
No Take Zones – A Realistic Tool for Fisheries Management
School Curriculum Packs
The Good Beach Guide
The Species Directory (British Isles and Surrounding Areas)

Publications list:
Available online and in print

Access to staff:
Contact by letter, by telephone, by fax, by e-mail and via website
Hours: Mon to Fri, 0900 to 1700

Access to building, collection or gallery:
No prior appointment required
Special comments: Members only.

Also at:
Marine Conservation Society
3 Coates Place, Edinburgh, EH3 7AA; tel: 0131 226 6360; fax: 0131 226 2391; e-mail: mcs.scotland@care4free.net

MARINE ENGINE AND EQUIPMENT MANUFACTURERS ASSOCIATION

Acronym or abbreviation: MEEMA

56 Braycourt Avenue, Walton-on-Thames, Surrey, KT12 2BA

Tel: 01932 224910
Fax: 01932 224910

E-mail: bcbaali@aol.com

Website:
http://www.bmif.co.uk

Enquiries:
Enquiries to: Secretary

Founded:
1960

Organisation type and purpose:
Trade association, present number of members: 75.

Subject coverage:
For UK companies within the British Marine Industries Federation who have a common interest in the manufacture or distribution and retail sales of marine engines and related equipment, including personal watercraft.

Access to staff:
Contact by letter, by telephone, by fax and by e-mail
Hours: Mon to Fri, 0900 to 1700

Affiliated to:
British Marine Industries Federation
tel: 01784 473377; fax: 01784 439678; e-mail: bmif@bmif.co.uk

MARINE LEISURE ASSOCIATION

Acronym or abbreviation: MLA

General Secretary, Marine Leisure Association, Burrwood, 24 Peterscroft Avenue, Southampton, SO40 7AB

Tel: 023 8029 3822
Fax: 023 8029 3888
E-mail: info@marineleisure.co.uk

Website:
http://www.marineleisure.co.uk

Enquiries:
Enquiries to: General Secretary

Founded:
1964

Formerly called:
Association of Bonded Sailing Companies, National Federation of Sea Schools, Yacht Charter Assocation (year of change 2005)

Organisation type and purpose:
Trade association for training, charter and holidays.
Formed to offer the general public better protection, guidance and advice. A Group Association within the BMF (British Marine Federation), representing MLA Members' views within the BMF Council. All members are expected to abide by both the MLA Code of Conduct and the BMF Code of Practice. Has representation on various National Committees to safeguard interests of Members and the general public.

Subject coverage:
Marine leisure industry.

Trade and statistical information:
Statistics on the marine leisure industry including participation, economic benefits, labour market assessment, tourism and industry assessment.

Printed publications:
MLA Bareboat Charter Agreement, MLA Skippered Charter Agreement and MLA Management Charter Agreement available for sale; a discounted price is available for multiple purchases
Annual membership brochure containing a full A-Z membership listing together with guidance information on training, charter and holidays worldwide

Access to staff:
Contact by letter, by telephone, by fax, by e-mail and via website. Appointment necessary.
Hours: Mon to Fri, 0900 to 1700

Parent body:
British Marine Federation (BMF)
tel: 01784 473377; fax: 01784 439678; e-mail:
info@britishmarine.co.uk; website: http://www
.britishmarine.co.uk

MARINE SOCIETY, THE

202 Lambeth Road, London, SE1 7JW

Tel: 020 7261 9535
Fax: 020 7401 2537
E-mail: enq@marine-society.org

Website:
http://www.marine-society.org
Details of services and activities.

Enquiries:
Enquiries to: Director

Founded:
1756

Organisation type and purpose:
Voluntary organisation, registered charity (charity
number 313013), training organisation.
Education, training and welfare of seafarers.

Subject coverage:
Merchant Navy, Royal Navy, careers at sea,
seafaring.

**Museum or gallery collection, archive, or library
special collection:**
All above Records held at National Maritime
Museum
British Ship Adoption Society (from 1936)
Incorporated Thames Nautical Training College
(from 1862)
Marine Society Records (from 1756)
Seafarers Education Service (from 1919)

Printed publications:
General Publications on the Society (free)
Schools posters and Project material on Marine
subjects (price on application)
The Seafarer (quarterly, £10 p.a.)

Access to staff:
Contact by letter, by telephone, by fax, by e-mail,
in person and via website
Hours: Mon to Fri, 0900 to 1700

Access to building, collection or gallery:
Prior appointment required

Access for disabled people:
Parking provided, ramped entry

MARITIME AND COASTGUARD AGENCY

Acronym or abbreviation: MCA

Spring Place, 105 Commercial Road, Southampton,
SO15 1EG

Tel: 023 8032 9100\ 0870 600 6505 (Infoline)
Fax: 023 8032 9122
E-mail: infoline@mcga.gov.uk

Website:
http://www.mcga.gov.uk
Work of MCA, publications, flagging-in, contact
list, contingency plan.

Enquiries:
Enquiries to: Publications Manager
Direct tel: 023 8032 9401
Direct e-mail: mca_mic@mcga.gov.uk

Founded:
1998

Organisation type and purpose:
National Government Agency.

Subject coverage:
Civil maritime search and rescue, maritime safety,
major oil spillages and other hazardous substances
at sea from ships, civil maritime emergencies,
safety advice and assistance to local authorities,
and port and harbour authorities, merchant
shipping, carriage by sea of dangerous goods,
hovercraft and high speed craft legislation, safety

of navigation and related topics, ownership of
items found in or on the shores of the sea or any
tidal water.

Trade and statistical information:
National and international fleet and accident
statistics.

Printed publications:
Codes of Practice (available from TSO)
Consolidated List of M Notices (available from
TSO, £120)
MSN, MGN & MIN – Mail Marketing (Scotland)
Also available on MCA website

Access to staff:
Contact by letter, by telephone, by fax, by e-mail
and via website. Appointment necessary.
Hours: Mon to Fri, 0900 to 1700

Access for disabled people:
Level entry, toilet facilities

Executive Agency of:
Department of Transport

Other addresses:
Branches throughout the UK

MARITIME INFORMATION ASSOCIATION

Acronym or abbreviation: MIA

The Marine Society, 202 Lambeth Road, London,
SE1 7JW

Website:
http://www.maritime-information.org

Enquiries:
Enquiries to: Honorary Secretary

Founded:
1977

Organisation type and purpose:
Professional body (membership is by subscription).
Forum for those active in maritime information,
with regular visits, an annual conference and
opportunities to network.

Subject coverage:
Marine technology; shipping; shipbuilding; marine
engineering and telecommunications; maritime
law and economics; maritime history; ports; cargo
handling; fisheries; offshore activities (not marine
biology or life sciences).

Printed publications:
List of Members (for members only)
Marine Information: a guide to libraries and
sources of information in the UK (4th ed., 2004,
£25)

Access to staff:
Contact by fax

MARKET RESEARCH SOCIETY

Acronym or abbreviation: MRS

15 Northburgh Street, London, EC1V 0JR

Tel: 020 7490 4911
Fax: 020 7490 0608
E-mail: info@mrs.org.uk

Website:
http://www.mrs.org.uk
Information on MRS, including training,
qualifications, products and events.

Founded:
1946

Organisation type and purpose:
Professional body.

Subject coverage:
Methodology of market research; market research
industry.

Non-library collection catalogue:
All or part available online and in-house

Library catalogue:
All or part available online and in-house

Printed publications:
International Journal of Market Research
MRS Conference Proceedings
Occupation Groupings: A Job Directory
Research (monthly)
Research Buyer's Guide
Range of guidelines on market research

Electronic and video publications:
Research Buyer's Guide
Order electronic and video publications from: http://
www.rbg.org.uk

Publications list:
Available online

Access to staff:
Contact by letter, by telephone, by fax, by e-mail
and via website. Access for members only.
Hours: Mon to Fri, 1000 to 1700

MARKETING GUILD, THE

Regency House, Westminster Place, York Business
Park, York, YO26 6RW

Tel: 01904 520820
Fax: 01904 520899
E-mail: help@marketing-guild.com

Website:
http://www.marketing-guild.com
Marketing ideas and free sample reports.

Enquiries:
Enquiries to: Managing Director

Founded:
1986

Organisation type and purpose:
Professional body (membership is by subscription),
present number of members: 1400, service
industry.
Marketing ideas and support for professional and
service businesses.

Subject coverage:
Marketing and sales information, ideas and
strategies.

Printed publications:
Strategic Marketing (newsletter)
Marketing Insider
Marketing in Action

Electronic and video publications:
Encyclopaedia of marketing strategies with
support manuals (Argosy CD software)
Audio cassettes and training

Publications list:
Available online and in print

Access to staff:
Contact by letter, by telephone and by e-mail.
Non-members charged.
Hours: Mon to Fri, 0900 to 1700

Connected with and at the same address as the:
Internet Marketing Guild

MARKS AND CLERK

Sussex House, 83–85 Mosley Street, Manchester,
M2 3LG

Tel: 0161 236 2275
Fax: 0161 236 5846
E-mail: manchester@marks-clerk.com

Website:
http://www.marks-clerk.com
Details of UK and International offices, history of
the firm, information service on all aspects of
intellectual property.

Enquiries:
Enquiries to: Information Manager
Direct tel: 0161 233 5803

Founded:
1887

Organisation type and purpose:
Service industry.

continued overleaf

Professional firm of patent and trade mark agents.

Subject coverage:
Patents; trade marks; designs; copyright; licensing; intellectual property; technology licensing, litigation.

Access to staff:
Contact by letter, by telephone, by fax and by e-mail. Appointment necessary.
Hours: Mon to Fri, 0900 to 1700

MARLOWE SOCIETY

Chairman, 27 Melbourne Court, Randolph Avenue, London, W9 1BJ

E-mail: valerie.colin-russ@marlowe-society.org

Website:
http://www.marlowe-society.org
Society news, membership details, meetings and events, Marlowe's life, education, works, reference books.

Enquiries:
Enquiries to: Membership Secretary
Other contacts: See website

Founded:
1955

Organisation type and purpose:
International organisation, learned society (membership is by subscription), present number of members: 200, registered charity (charity number 1075418).
To promote interest and research into Christopher Marlowe, Elizabethan poet/dramatist.

Subject coverage:
Christopher Marlowe's life and works; his associates; his contribution to the growth of secular drama; life in the Tudor period; contemporary dramatists, particularly those influenced by Marlowe. A memorial in Poets Corner, Westminster Abbey 2002.

Museum or gallery collection, archive, or library special collection:
Library – visit by appointment only

Non-library collection catalogue:
All or part available online

Library catalogue:
All or part available online

Printed publications:
Newsletter (periodically; free to members)
Occasional booklets – most recently a 'Marlowe Guide'

Publications list:
Available online

Access to staff:
Contact by letter, by telephone, by fax, by e-mail and via website. Appointment necessary.
Hours: Mon to Fri, 0900 to 1700

MARTIN CENTRE FOR ARCHITECTURAL AND URBAN STUDIES

University of Cambridge, Department of Architecture, 6 Chaucer Road, Cambridge, CB2 2EB

Tel: 01223 331700
Fax: 01223 331701

Website:
http://www.arct.cam.ac.uk

Enquiries:
Enquiries to: Publications Officer
Direct e-mail: mc@arct.cam.ac.uk

Founded:
1967

Organisation type and purpose:
University department or institute, research organisation.

Subject coverage:
Environmental design, architectural acoustics, energy conservation, Third World planning and construction technology, building in earthquake areas, computer-aided design.

Museum or gallery collection, archive, or library special collection:
British New Towns collection

Printed publications:
Annual Report
Occasional reports and working papers

Access to staff:
Contact by letter, by telephone and by fax
Hours: Mon to Fri, 0900 to 1700

Within the:
Cambridge University Department of Architecture

MARX MEMORIAL LIBRARY

37A Clerkenwell Green, London, EC1R 0DU

Tel: 020 7253 1485
Fax: 020 7251 6039
E-mail: info@marx-memorial-library.org

Website:
http://www.marx-memorial-library.org

Enquiries:
Enquiries to: Librarian

Founded:
1933

Organisation type and purpose:
National organisation, membership association (membership is by subscription), registered charity (charity number 270309), historic building, house or site.
Independent subscription library.
To provide materials for the study of Marxism, socialism and history of working class movements.

Subject coverage:
Marxist classics, philosophy, economics, political theory, labour and trade union history, social conditions and movements, early socialist thought (radical, chartist, etc.), international working class movement), socialist countries, Spanish Civil War, US Labor Movement, peace.

Museum or gallery collection, archive, or library special collection:
BSP and SDF pamphlets
Daily Worker and Morning Star (bound vols)
General Strike
International Brigade – Spanish Civil War (International Brigade Archive)
J. D. Bernal Peace Movement Library (books and documents from the libraries of Prof. J. D. Bernal and Ivor Montagu)
James Klugman Collection (books, pamphlets and tracts mainly of the Chartist and early British Labour Movement, and ceramics)
John Williamson American Labour History Collection
May Day
Photograph library
Spanish War and International Brigade Collection
US labour and socialist history 1920–70s

Printed publications:
Bulletin (2 times a year)
Spanish War and International Brigade catalogue (3 vols)

Microform publications:
BSP and SDF Pamphlets, Daily Worker 1938–1941
Inprecorr to be read on site
International Brigade Memorial Archive (Collection up to 1986, available from Mindata Ltd Bath)

Electronic and video publications:
Videos of Library lectures
Videos and CD-ROM of library history, present and future

Access to staff:
Contact by letter, by telephone, by fax, by e-mail and in person. Appointment necessary. Access for members only.
Hours: Mon to Thu, 1300 to 1800 (visitors 1300 to 1400, or by appointment)

Access for disabled people:
Ramped entry
Special comments: Access to ground floor. Books brought to desk on ground floor for readers unable to reach first floor reading room.

MARY ROSE TRUST

Acronym or abbreviation: PORMR

College Road, HM Naval Base, Portsmouth, Hampshire, PO1 3LX

Tel: 023 9275 0521
Fax: 023 9287 0588
E-mail: mail@maryrose.org

Website:
http://www.maryrose.org

Founded:
1979

Organisation type and purpose:
Museum, research organisation, tourist attraction. Registered Charity Number 277503; Registered Company Number 1415654 England; VAT Registration Number GB 339 0628 49.
Designated as an Outstanding Collection and MLA Accredited Museum.
Objectives: to find, record, excavate, raise, bring ashore, preserve, publish, report on and display for all time in Portsmouth the Mary Rose. To establish, equip and maintain a museum or museums in Portsmouth to house the Mary Rose and related or associated material. To promote and develop interest, research and knowledge relating to the Mary Rose and all matters relating to the underwater cultural heritage. All for the education and benefit of the nation.

Subject coverage:
Henry VIII's warship Mary Rose, launched in 1511, social and maritime history of the Tudor period, evolution of the wooden ship in the late medieval period, conservation and care of material excavated from wet sites, archaeology and underwater technology.

Museum or gallery collection, archive, or library special collection:
The Mary Rose (the only recovered 16th-century warship) together with the excavated military, domestic and personal artefacts, ecofacts and human remains.
Excavation archive.
Photographic library for hire.

Non-library collection catalogue:
All or part available online

Printed publications:
The Archaeology of the Mary Rose (vols 1–5)
Annual Reports
Leaflets and fact sheets
Firstwatch

Electronic and video publications:
Video for hire

Publications list:
Available online

Access to staff:
Contact by letter, by telephone, by e-mail and via website. Appointment necessary.
Hours: Mon to Fri, 1000 to 1700
Special comments: The Trust is located in an operational Naval Base. MoD security restrictions may apply.

Constituent bodies:
Mary Rose Society and Mary Rose Information Group
c/o The Mary Rose Trust, College Road, HM Naval Base, Portsmouth, Hampshire, PO1 3LX; tel: 023 9275 0521; fax: 023 9287 0588; e-mail: mail@maryrose.org

MASTER CARVERS' ASSOCIATION

Unit 2, 15B Vandyke Road, Leighton Buzzard, Beds, LU7 3HG

Tel: 01525 851594
Fax: 01525 851594
E-mail: info@mastercarvers.co.uk

Website:
http://www.mastercarvers.co.uk
Information about the Association and showcase of members work.

Enquiries:
Enquiries to: Honorary Secretary

Founded:
1897

Organisation type and purpose:
Trade association.
Promotion and protection of the interests of stone carving, woodcarving and modelling generally, and of the members of the association in particular.

Subject coverage:
Wood and stone carving; architectural furniture, restoration, ecclesiastical, heraldic, conservation, apprenticeship; rates of wages and conditions of service; modelling.

Printed publications:
List of Members and their specialist crafts

Access to staff:
Contact by letter, by telephone, by fax and by e-mail. Appointment necessary.
Hours: Mon to Fri, 0900 to 1700

MASTER LOCKSMITHS ASSOCIATION

Acronym or abbreviation: MLA

5D Great Central Way, Woodford Halse, Daventry, Northamptonshire, NN11 3PZ

Tel: 01327 262255
Fax: 01327 262539
E-mail: enquiries@locksmiths.co.uk

Website:
http://www.locksmiths.co.uk/

Enquiries:
Enquiries to: Chief Executive Officer

Founded:
1958

Organisation type and purpose:
Advisory body, professional body, trade association, training organisation, consultancy.

Subject coverage:
Physical security, mechanical security, locks, safes, vehicle security, access systems, training, consultancy, expert witness, product testing, keycutting, bolts.

Museum or gallery collection, archive, or library special collection:
Collection of books on locksmithing – reference purposes and for use by members only

Printed publications:
Keyways (magazine, 6 times a year, members)
Lists of Trade Division Members

Access to staff:
Contact by letter, by telephone, by fax and by e-mail. Appointment necessary. Letter of introduction required.
Hours: Mon to Fri, 0830 to 1700

Affilated to:
Associated Locksmiths of Ireland

Affilated to:
Associated Locksmiths of America
European Locksmiths Federation

Subsidiary body:
British Locksmiths Institute
MLA Trade Division

MASTER PHOTOGRAPHERS ASSOCIATION OF GREAT BRITAIN

Acronym or abbreviation: MPA

Hallmark House, 1 Chancery Lane, Darlington, Co Durham, DL1 5QP

Tel: 01325 356555
Fax: 01325 357813
E-mail: mpa@mpauk.com

Website:
http://www.mpauk.com

Enquiries:
Enquiries to: Chief Executive

Founded:
1952

Organisation type and purpose:
Trade association.

Subject coverage:
Association for full-time professional photographers.

Access to staff:
Contact by letter, by telephone, by fax, by e-mail and via website
Hours: Mon to Fri, 0900 to 1700

MASTERFOODS EDUCATION CENTRE

Acronym or abbreviation: MEC

4 Bedford Square, London, WC1B 3RA

Tel: 020 7255 1100
Fax: 020 7631 0602

Website:
http://www.pet-educationresources.co.uk
Free worksheets to download for teaching literacy, numeracy, science and PSHE & Citizenship for Key Stages 1 and 2. Pets are the theme of the resources.

Enquiries:
Enquiries to: Public Relations Manager
Direct e-mail: mec@uk.grayling.com

Founded:
1971

Organisation type and purpose:
Suitable for ages: 4 to 11.

Subject coverage:
Resource material for schools about pets and responsible pet ownership; putting pets onto the National Curriculum in schools – applicable to Key Stages 1 and 2.

Printed publications:
Packs, posters, stories, leaflets

Publications list:
Available online and in print

Access to staff:
Contact by letter, by telephone, by fax and by e-mail
Hours: Mon to Fri, 0900 to 1700

MASTERS OF DEERHOUNDS ASSOCIATION

Acronym or abbreviation: MDHA

Bilboa House, Dulverton, Somerset, TA22 9DW

Tel: 01398 323475

Enquiries:
Enquiries to: Honorary Secretary

Founded:
1951

Organisation type and purpose:
Membership association.
Governing body of packs of hounds hunting wild deer in Great Britain.

Subject coverage:
Conservation and control of the last remaining sizeable herd of red deer in England, hunting wild deer with recognised packs of hounds.

Printed publications:
Pamphlets relevant to deer hunting (available on request)

Access to staff:
Contact by letter and by telephone
Hours: Mon to Fri, 0900 to 1700

MASTIC ASPHALT COUNCIL

Acronym or abbreviation: MAC

PO Box 77, Hastings, East Sussex, TN35 4WL

Tel: 01424 814400
Fax: 01424 814446
E-mail: masphaltco@aol.com

Website:
http://www.masticasphaltcouncil.co.uk

Enquiries:
Enquiries to: Director

Founded:
1948

Organisation type and purpose:
Trade association.

Subject coverage:
Information on the use of Mastic Asphalt with member lists and insurance backed guarantees.

Museum or gallery collection, archive, or library special collection:
Technical guide on the application of mastic asphalt. Information regarding codes of practice and British Standards

Publications list:
Available in print

Access to staff:
Contact by letter, by telephone, by fax, by e-mail and via website. Appointment necessary.
Hours: Mon to Fri, 0900 to 1700

Access to building, collection or gallery:
Prior appointment required

Member of:
National Specialist Contractors Council (NSCC)

MATERIALS HANDLING ENGINEERS ASSOCIATION

Acronym or abbreviation: MHEA

2B Hills Lane, Ely, Cambridgeshire, CB6 1AY

Tel: 01353 666298
Fax: 01353 666298
E-mail: pw@mhea.co.uk

Website:
http://www.mhea.co.uk

Enquiries:
Enquiries to: Secretary
Other contacts: Chairman of Technical Committee for technical or publications.

Founded:
1938

Organisation type and purpose:
Trade association.

continued overleaf

Subject coverage:
The UK Centre for technical and commercial excellence regarding the manufacture and use of bulk and continuous materials handling equipment.

Printed publications:
Guide to the Design of Transfer Chutes & Chute Linings (2002)
Recommended Practice for Troughed Belt Conveyors (available for purchase)

Publications list:
Available in print

Access to staff:
Contact by letter, by telephone, by fax, by e-mail and via website
Special comments: Charges to non-members if justified.

Access to building, collection or gallery:
No access other than to staff

MATERIALS SCIENCE LIBRARY

Formal name: University of Cambridge Department of Materials Science and Metallurgy Library

New Museums Site, Pembroke Street, Cambridge, CB2 3QZ

Tel: 01223 334300 (dept); 01223 334318 (library)
Fax: 01223 334567 (dept)
E-mail: library@msm.cam.ac.uk

Website:
http://www.msm.cam.ac.uk/library

Enquiries:
Enquiries to: Librarian

Organisation type and purpose:
University department or institute.

Subject coverage:
Materials science, metallurgy, access to external library services.

Museum or gallery collection, archive, or library special collection:
Department's Ph.D and M.Phil theses

Library catalogue:
All or part available online

Access to staff:
Contact by letter, by telephone, by fax, by e-mail and in person. Appointment necessary.
Hours: During library office hours, Mon to Fri, 0900 to 1500
Special comments: Single member of staff. Please make appointment before any special journey to the library. Library may be unstaffed in particular on Fri in vacations.

Access to building, collection or gallery:
For members of the department and external visitors.
Hours: 24 hours for members of the department; Mon to Fri, 0900 to 1500 for others
Special comments: Very restricted parking. Parking on site only by special arrangement.

Access for disabled people:
Access to library on 4th floor via user-operated lifts

MATHEMATICAL ASSOCIATION

Acronym or abbreviation: MA

259 London Road, Leicester, LE2 3BE

Tel: 0116 221 0013
Fax: 0116 212 2835
E-mail: office@m-a.org.uk

Website:
http://www.m-a.org.uk

Enquiries:
Enquiries to: Senior Administrator
Direct e-mail: senioradministrator@m-a.org.uk

Founded:
1871

Organisation type and purpose:
Membership association (membership is by subscription), registered charity (charity number 313281).
To support and improve the teaching of mathematics.

Subject coverage:
Mathematics and the teaching of mathematics.

Museum or gallery collection, archive, or library special collection:
Library housed in Leicester University Library

Library catalogue:
All or part available in-house

Printed publications:
Books, reports covering infant years to 6th form for pupils and teachers including:
Mathematical Gazette (termly)
Mathematics in School (5 times a year)
Mathematical Pie (termly)
Primary Mathematics (termly)
Equals (termly)
Symmetry Plus+ (termly)
The MA News (termly)

Publications list:
Available online and in print

Access to staff:
Contact by letter, by telephone, by fax, by e-mail, in person and via website
Hours: Mon to Fri, 0900 to 1700

Access to building, collection or gallery:
No prior appointment required

Affiliated to:
JMC

MATHEMATICS RESEARCH CENTRE

Acronym or abbreviation: MRC

University of Warwick, Coventry, Warwickshire, CV4 7AL

Tel: 024 7652 8317
Fax: 024 7652 3548
E-mail: mrc@maths.warwick.ac.uk

Website:
http://www.maths.warwick.ac.uk/research

Enquiries:
Enquiries to: Secretary

Founded:
1968

Organisation type and purpose:
University department or institute, research organisation.
Symposium and conference organisation in mathematics.

Subject coverage:
Mathematics.

Access to staff:
Contact by e-mail. Appointment necessary.
Hours: Mon to Fri, 0900 to 1600

Associated with:
Mathematics Department, University of Warwick

MATRA ENTHUSIASTS CLUB UK

Acronym or abbreviation: MEC UK

Flat 6 Woodlands Court, Woodlands Road, Harrow, Middlesex, HA1 2RU

Tel: 020 8861 1035
E-mail: roy@matraclub.org.uk

Website:
http://www.matraclub.org.uk

Enquiries:
Enquiries to: Membership Secretary
Direct tel: 01509 852974
Direct e-mail: philipjowen@yahoo.co.uk

Founded:
1983

Organisation type and purpose:
International organisation, membership association (membership is by subscription), present number of members:100.

Subject coverage:
Technical and historical information on Matra cars from 1964 to 2002, including DJet, M530, Bagheera, Rancho, Murena, Espace, Avantime.

Museum or gallery collection, archive, or library special collection:
Most books and magazines in English and French about Matra automobiles or containing road tests or reports of related products

Printed publications:
A5 Magazine (6 times a year, members)

Access to staff:
Contact by telephone, by e-mail and via website
Hours: Telephone, daily, 1700 to 2100

Links with:
French, Belgian and other European clubs and the North American Matra Register

MCC LIBRARY

Formal name: Marylebone Cricket Club Library

Lord's Cricket Ground, St John's Wood, London, NW8 8QN

Tel: 020 7616 8559
Fax: 020 7616 8659
E-mail: mcclibrary@mcc.org.uk

Website:
http://www.lords.org/history/mcc-library

Enquiries:
Enquiries to: Research Officer

Founded:
1787

Organisation type and purpose:
Membership association (membership is by election or invitation), historic building, house or site.
Private Cricket Club.

Subject coverage:
History of cricket, modern cricket, scores and statistics, real tennis, some other sports, history of Lord's and the MCC.

Museum or gallery collection, archive, or library special collection:
Early cricket books and bats
Sir George Allen scrapbooks

Non-library collection catalogue:
All or part available in-house

Library catalogue:
All or part available in-house

Access to staff:
Contact by letter, by telephone, by e-mail and via website. Appointment necessary.
Hours: Mon to Thu, 1000 to 1700; Fri, 1000 to 1600
Special comments: Open Sat and Sun by arrangement on cricket days.

Access to building, collection or gallery:
Prior appointment required

Access for disabled people:
Special comments: Library is accessed only by stairs.

MCDOUGALL TRUST

Formal name: Arthur McDougall Fund

6 Chancel Street, London, SE1 0UX

Tel: 020 7620 1080
Fax: 020 7928 1528
E-mail: admin@mcdougall.org.uk

Website:
http://www.mcdougall.org.uk

Small charity supppporting study and research in political science, especially electoral studies.

Enquiries:
Enquiries to: Executive Secretary
Other contacts: Chairman (for formal correspondence)

Founded:
1948

Organisation type and purpose:
Voluntary organisation, registered charity (charity number 212151), research organisation, publishing house.
To advance study and knowledge of economic and political science, especially electoral science and methods of election and government of representative organisations of all kinds.

Subject coverage:
All aspects of elections including electoral law and practice, voting systems, electoral reform, proportional representation, election monitoring, election campaigns, balloting in organisations of all kinds, representation and democracy, political science, suffrage.

Information services:
Enquiries in writing preferred.

Special visitor services:
Visitors by prior appointment.

Museum or gallery collection, archive, or library special collection:
2,500 books and 2,500 pamphlets
Early pamphlets on PR in Britain, USA, Australia, including Charles Dodgson
Papers of Lord Courtney of Penwith and Dr J. F. S. Ross
Pamphlets donated by H. R. Droop
Extensive press cuttings and other printed material from mid-19th century on electoral reform, proportional representation, suffrage and related issues
Reports on various recent international election observation missions

Trade and statistical information:
Electoral statistics relating to elections in the United Kingdom and elsewhere.

Non-library collection catalogue:
All or part available in-house

Library catalogue:
All or part available in-house

Printed publications:
Annual Report
Representation: Journal of Representative Democracy (ISSN: 0034–4893), in association with Taylor & Francis.
Twelve Democracies: Electoral Systems in the European Community (Enid Lakeman, out-of-print)
Comparative Electoral Systems (Robert A. Newland)
Order printed publications from: Executive Secretary, McDougall Trust

Access to staff:
Contact by letter, by telephone, by fax and by e-mail. Appointment necessary. Letter of introduction required.
Hours: Mon to Fri, 1000 to 1700
Special comments: By arrangement only.

Access for disabled people:
Toilet facilities
Special comments: Wheelchair stair climber (Victorian building).

Constituent bodies:
Lakeman Library for Electoral Studies
6 Chancel Street, London, SE1 OUX; tel: 020 7620 1080; fax: 020 7928 1528; website: http://www.mcdougall.org.uk

Links with:
Electoral Reform Society (Library holding includes ERS archives)
tel: 020 7620 1080; fax: 020 7928 1528; e-mail: admin@mcdougall.org.uk; website: http://www.mcdougall.org.uk

MCTIMONEY CHIROPRACTIC ASSOCIATION

Acronym or abbreviation: MCA

Crowmarsh Gifford, Wallingford, Oxfordshire, OX10 8DJ

Tel: 01491 829211
Fax: 01491 829492
E-mail: admin@mctimoney-chiropractic.org

Website:
http://www.mctimoneychiropractic.org
Information on chiropractic treatment and practitioner location.

Enquiries:
Enquiries to: Administrator
Other contacts: Executive Liaison Officer

Founded:
1979

Organisation type and purpose:
Professional association, training and research organisation.

Subject coverage:
McTimoney Chiropractic, education, training and information.

Trade and statistical information:
Membership and subject information data.

Printed publications:
Practitioner Directory
Human Chiropractic LFLT
Animal Chiropractic LFLT
Inhouse Magazine

Access to staff:
Contact by letter, by telephone, by fax and by e-mail. Appointment necessary. Non-members charged.
Hours: Mon to Fri, 0900 to 1700

MDC EVALUATIONS

Unit 4, Greenways Business Park, Bellinger Close, Chippenham, Wiltshire, SN15 1BN

Tel: 01249 467272
Fax: 01249 467273
E-mail: enquiry@mdcevaluations.co.uk

Website:
http://www.mdcevaluations.co.uk
Information on UK dairy industry. PTAs, statistics, bull/cow lists, publications.

Enquiries:
Enquiries to: PA to Technical Director

Founded:
2002

Subject coverage:
Predicted transmitting abilities for dairy bulls and cows in UK.
Genetic trends in UK dairy industry.
Industry statistics (UK dairy industry).
Technical information on UK evaluation system for dairy bulls and cows.

Trade and statistical information:
Statistics on UK dairy industry.

Non-library collection catalogue:
All or part available online

Printed publications:
Breed Books
Fact Sheets
Statistics Books
Technical Bulletin
Various publications free of charge, direct or website

Publications list:
Available online

Access to staff:
Contact by letter, by telephone, by fax, by e-mail and via website
Hours: Mon to Fri, 0900 to 1700

MDF THE BIPOLAR ORGANISATION

Acronym or abbreviation: MDF

Castle Works, 21 St Georges Road, London, SE1 6ES

Tel: 08456 340540
Fax: 020 7793 2639
E-mail: mdf@mdf.org.uk

Website:
http://www.mdf.org.uk
Books, factsheets.

Enquiries:
Enquiries to: Administrator

Founded:
1984

Organisation type and purpose:
National organisation, membership association (membership is by subscription), present number of members: 4,000, voluntary organisation, registered charity (charity number 293340).

Subject coverage:
Mental health, manic depression, self-help group support, drug treatment, self-management.

Non-library collection catalogue:
All or part available online and in print

Library catalogue:
All or part available online

Printed publications:
Information pack (free)
Leaflets, factsheets, books
Pendulum (journal, quarterly)

Publications list:
Available in print

Access to staff:
Contact by letter, by telephone, by fax, by e-mail and via website
Hours: Mon to Fri, 0900 to 1700

ME ASSOCIATION

Formal name: Myalgic Encephalopathy Association
Acronym or abbreviation: MEA

7 Apollo Office Court, Radclive Road, Gawcott, Buckinghamshire, MK18 4DF

Tel: 01280 818968
E-mail: meconnect@meassociation.org.uk

Website:
http://www.meassociation.org.uk
News, lots of editorial content and lists, updated several times a day.

Enquiries:
Enquiries to: Publicity Manager
Direct tel: 01406 370293
Direct e-mail: tbritton02@yahoo.com

Founded:
1976

Organisation type and purpose:
Registered Charity Number 801279. The MEA is a campaigning national charity that provides information and support to an estimated 240,000 people in the United Kingdom with ME/Chronic Fatigue Syndrome, their families and carers. This is provided through a quarterly magazine, literature, education and training. It also runs ME Connect, the United Kingdom's premier helpline for people with ME/CFS. The charity supports research into the physical nature and cause of ME via The MEA Ramsay Research Fund.

Subject coverage:
Myalgic encephalopathy (ME) information, support, education and training.

Information services:
Telephone helpline: 0844 576 5326, open daily, 1000 to 1200 and 1400 to 1600 and 1900 to 2100

Non-library collection catalogue:
All or part available online and in print

continued overleaf

Library catalogue:
All or part available online and in print

Printed publications:
ME Essential magazine (quarterly, to members)
Extensive list of leaflets (available online)
Order printed publications from: Buckinghamshire office; tel. 01280 818968; e-mail meconnect@ meassociation.org.uk

Publications list:
Available online and in print

Access to staff:
Contact by letter, by telephone, by e-mail, in person and via website
Hours: Mon to Fri, 0930 to 1630

Also at:
The ME Association, Publicity, Communications and PR
   60 Broadgate, Weston, Spalding, PE12 6HY; tel: 01406 370293; e-mail: tbritton02@yahoo.com

MÉDECINS SANS FRONTIÈRES

Acronym or abbreviation: MSF

67–74 Saffron Hill, London, EC1N 8QX

Tel: 020 7404 6600
Fax: 020 7404 4466
E-mail: office@london.msf.org

Website:
http://www.msf.org

Enquiries:
Enquiries to: Public Information Administrator
Direct tel: 020 7404 6600
Other contacts: (1) Fundraising Administrator (2) Recruitment Assistant for (1) donation enquiries (2) recuitment enquiries.

Founded:
1971

Organisation type and purpose:
International organisation, voluntary organisation, registered charity (charity number 1026588).
To provide medical emergency relief to victims of disaster worldwide.

Subject coverage:
Humanitarian and medical aid, emergency relief.

Printed publications:
Dispatches (newsletter, quarterly, free)
International Activity Report (annually)
Order printed publications from: Médecins Sans Frontières
8 Rue Saint Sabin, Paris Cedex 11, 75544, France, tel: 00 33 1 40 21 29 29, fax: 00 33 1 48 06 68 68, e-mail: office@paris.msf.org

Access to staff:
Contact by letter, by telephone, by fax, by e-mail and via website. Appointment necessary.
Hours: Mon to Fri, 0900 to 1800
Special comments: No wheelchair access.

International office:
Médecins Sans Frontières
   39 Rue de la Tourelle, Brussels, B-1040, Belgium; tel: 00 32 2 280 18 81; fax: 00 32 2 280 01 73

MEDIATION UK

Alexander House, Telephone Avenue, Bristol, BS1 4BS

Tel: 0117 904 6661
Fax: 0117 904 3331
E-mail: enquiry@mediationuk.org.uk

Website:
http://www.mediation.org.uk
Basic information, publications and conferences, training opportunities, services list, information about mediation.

Enquiries:
Enquiries to: Director

Founded:
1984

Organisation type and purpose:
National organisation, membership association (membership is by subscription), present number of members: 503, registered charity (charity number 1019275).
Network of projects, organisations and individuals interested in mediation and constructive conflict resolution; umbrella organisation for mediation schemes in the UK.
Mediation UK is a national charity which represents and promotes mediation within local communities. It has a membership of 170 registered services throughout the UK which offer mediation to parties in dispute. The majority of these services are free to the user, and a national helpline exists to direct the public to their nearest mediation service. Services specialise in one or more areas including neighbour disputes, school bullying, and victim/offender mediation. Mediation UK also supports mediation within the workplace, and sectors like the health service. Mediation UK is actively involved in encouraging the establishment of new mediation services around the country, as well as ensuring mediation services adhere to quality standards and guidelines.

Subject coverage:
Mediation and constructive conflict resolution, including neighbour disputes and community mediation; victim/offender mediation; conflict resolution and mediation in schools; other conflict resolution projects; training in mediation and conflict resolution skills.

Printed publications:
Annual Report
Information sheets, occasional papers
Introductory Leaflet
Mediation (magazine, for sale)
Training Manual in Community Mediation Skills
Conflict Resolution Peer Mediation in Schools – A Directory of Services and Training
The Rough Guide to Restorative Justice and the Crime & Disorder Act
Mediation Works
Victor/Offender Mediation Pack

Electronic and video publications:
Some printed material available in fully accessible formats

Publications list:
Available in print

Access to staff:
Contact by letter, by telephone, by fax, by e-mail and via website. Appointment necessary.
Hours: Mon to Fri, 0900 to 1700

Also at:
Mediation Wales
   1 The Spa Centre, Station Crescent, Llandrindod Wells, Powys, LD1 5BB; tel: 01597 829100

MEDIAWATCH–UK

3 Willow House, Kennington Road, Ashford, Kent, TN24 0NR

Tel: 01233 633936
Fax: 01233 633836
E-mail: info@mediawatchuk.org

Website:
http://www.mediawatchuk.org

Enquiries:
Enquiries to: Director

Founded:
1965

Organisation type and purpose:
National organisation, membership association (membership is by subscription), voluntary organisation.
Campaigning for good media standards and effective reform of the law on obscenity.

Subject coverage:
Mass media, broadcasting, programme standards, obscene publications.

Printed publications:
Brochure (free on request)
Mediawatch–UK News (3 times a year, formerly The Viewer and Listener)
Children and the Media: how best to protect children and respond to harmful influences in the media (£1)
Order printed publications from: Mediawatch–UK

Access to staff:
Contact by letter, by telephone, by fax, by e-mail and in person. Appointment necessary.
Hours: Mon to Fri, 0930 to 1730

MEDICAL ADVISORY SERVICE

Acronym or abbreviation: MAS

PO Box 3087, London, W4 4ZP

Tel: 020 8994 9874 (general medical)

Website:
http://www.medicaladvisoryservice.org.uk

Enquiries:
Enquiries to: Director
Direct tel: 020 8995 8503 (admin. only)
Direct fax: 020 8995 3275 (admin. only)

Founded:
1986

Organisation type and purpose:
Registered charity (charity number 295953).

Subject coverage:
General medical helpline to the public.

Printed publications:
A Guide to a good night's sleep (included in a general sleep information pack)
Order printed publications from: Medical Advisory Service, PO Box 3087, London, W4 4ZP

Publications list:
Available in print

Access to staff:
Contact by letter and by telephone
Hours: Mon to Sun, 1800 to 2000

Links with:
Sleep Matters
   PO Box 3087, London, W4 4ZP; tel: 020 8994 9874

MEDICAL ADVISORY SERVICES FOR TRAVELLERS ABROAD

Acronym or abbreviation: MASTA

29 Harley Street, London, W1G 9QR

Tel: 09068 224100 Travellers Healthline
Fax: 020 7323 5843
E-mail: rattewell@masta.org

Website:
http://www.masta.org
Travel health information.

Enquiries:
Enquiries to: Medical Director

Founded:
1984

Organisation type and purpose:
Advisory body, professional body, service industry, training organisation, research organisation.

Subject coverage:
Health risks for travellers abroad; information is maintained on 230 countries, and 84 conditions and diseases that affect travellers in varying living conditions. Healthcare items catalogue for travellers.

Printed publications:
Health briefs sent by 1st class post for any journey requested via Travellers Healthline 09068 224100
Order printed publications from: Travellers Healthline
tel: 09068 224100

Publications list:
Available in print

Access to staff:
Contact by telephone, by e-mail and via website
Hours: 24-hour helpline

Associated with:
Boots Travel Clinics
MASTA Travel Clinics

Sales and Marketing & Technical:
MASTA
Moorfield Road, Yeadon, Leeds, LS19 7BN; tel: 0113 238 7500

MEDICAL COUNCIL ON ALCOHOL, THE

Acronym or abbreviation: MCA

4 St Andrew's Place, Regent's Park, London, NW1 4LB

Tel: 020 7487 4445
Fax: 020 7935 4479
E-mail: mca@medicouncilalcol.demon.co.uk

Website:
http://www.medicouncilalcol.demon.co.uk

Enquiries:
Enquiries to: Administrative Secretary

Founded:
1967

Organisation type and purpose:
Professional body (membership is by subscription), present number of members: 370, voluntary organisation, registered charity (charity number 265242).
Devoted to improving medical understanding of alcohol-related problems, their prevention and treatment.

Subject coverage:
Alcohol and alcoholism: medical aspects and facilities for dealing with the problem.

Museum or gallery collection, archive, or library special collection:
Information on alcohol in relation to health including education of medical students on alcohol

Trade and statistical information:
Morbidity and mortality statistics.

Printed publications:
Alcohol Abuse Detection (leaflet)
Alcohol and Alcoholism (journal, 6 times a year)
Alcohol and Health Handbook for Nurses, Midwives and Health Visitors
Alcoholism (newsletter for general practitioners, 6 times a year)
Drinking Diary
Handbook: Alcohol and Health
Hazardous Drinking Handbook for General Practitioners
Problem Drinking at Work Notes for the Occupational Physician
Taking Care of Alcohol Issues at Work (for small businesses)
You, Your Patients and Alcohol (for 1st year medical students)

Publications list:
Available in print

Access to staff:
Contact by letter, by telephone, by fax and by e-mail. Appointment necessary.
Hours: Mon to Fri, 0930 to 1630

MEDICAL DEFENCE UNION LIMITED

Acronym or abbreviation: MDU

230 Blackfriars Road, London, SE1 8PJ

Tel: 020 7202 1500
Fax: 020 7202 1666

Website:
http://www.the-mdu.com

Enquiries:
Enquiries to: Librarian
Direct e-mail: media@the-mdu.com

Founded:
1885

Organisation type and purpose:
Membership association (membership is by subscription), service industry.

Subject coverage:
Medical negligence, litigation, ethics.

Non-library collection catalogue:
All or part available online

Access to staff:
Access for members only.
Hours: Mon to Wed, 1030 to 1730

Access to building, collection or gallery:
Prior appointment required

Access for disabled people:
Parking provided

MEDICAL FOUNDATION FOR THE CARE OF VICTIMS OF TORTURE

111 Isledon Road, London, N7 7JW

Tel: 020 7697 7777
Fax: 020 7697 7799
E-mail: info@torturecare.org.uk

Website:
http://www.torturecare.org.uk

Enquiries:
Enquiries to: Information Officer

Founded:
1986

Organisation type and purpose:
Registered charity (charity number 1000340).
The Medical Foundation aims to provide survivors of torture in the UK with medical treatment, practical assistance and psychotherapeutic support, document evidence of torture, provide training for health professionals working with torture survivors, educate the public and decision-makers about torture and its consequences, ensure that Britain honours its international obligations towards asylum-seekers and refugees.

Subject coverage:
Medical foundation providing survivors of torture in the UK with medical treatment, social assistance and psychotherapeutic support, documentation of evidence of torture, education of the public and decision-makers about torture and its consequences.

Museum or gallery collection, archive, or library special collection:
Library

Non-library collection catalogue:
All or part available in-house and in print

Library catalogue:
All or part available in-house

Printed publications:
Evidence of torture: A study of Pakistani torture survivors coming to the UK (Salinsky M, 2001, £3)
Guidelines for the examination of survivors of torture, (Forrest D and Hutton F, 2nd ed, 2000, £3)
Caught in middle: A study of Tamil torture survivors coming to the UK from Sri Lanka (2000, £3)
Lives under threat: A study of Sikhs coming to the UK from Punjab (Forrest D, Salinsky M, Verity Smith S, Carroll S, 2nd ed, 1999, £3)
Staying alive by accident: torture survivors from Turkey in the UK (Salinsky M, Miller C, 1999, £3)
Zaire: A torture State (Porta C, 1998, £5)
Rape as a Method of Torture: Peel M (2004, £18 inc. p&p)

Mental Health Services in Kosovo, Bolderson H and Simpson K (2004, £5)
Right First Time? Home Office Asylum Interviewing and Reasons for Refusal Letters, Smith E (2004, £5)
Every Morning, Just Like Coffee: Torture in Cameroon, Ball O (2002, £3)
Extensive selection of papers written by Medical Foundation Staff
All publications are charged to cover the costs of production and postage

Publications list:
Available online and in print

Access to staff:
Contact by letter and by telephone
Hours: Mon to Fri, 0900 to 1830

Access to building, collection or gallery:
Prior appointment required
Hours: Mon to Fri, 1000 to 1700

Access for disabled people:
Ramped entry, lift, toilet facilities

MEDICAL INDEMNITY REGISTER

Acronym or abbreviation: MIR

PO Box 44375, London, SW19 8WA

Tel: 020 8739 0066
Fax: 020 8739 0077
E-mail: malpractice@btconnect.com

Website:
http://www.medicalindemnity.com
Medical negligence insurance, PL + EL insurance, D&O cover.

Enquiries:
Enquiries to: Registrar

Founded:
1990

Organisation type and purpose:
Advisory body, medical malpractice insurance for individuals and companies, present number of members: 2,000, training organisation.

Subject coverage:
Pre-hospital life support (PHLS), medical malpractice and public liability insurance.

Information services:
Quarterly Newsletter, M.I.R. NEWS.

Education services:
First Aid and EMT training.

Non-library collection catalogue:
All or part available online

Printed publications:
M.I.R. News (quarterly)

Publications list:
Available online and in print

Access to staff:
Contact by letter, by telephone, by fax, by e-mail and via website. Access for members only. Non-members charged.
Hours: Mon to Fri, 0900 to 1700

Access to building, collection or gallery:
No access other than to staff

Insurers:
Marketform Limited

MEDICAL PRACTITIONERS' UNION

Acronym or abbreviation: MPU

128 Theobald's Road, London, WC1X 8TN

Tel: 020 3371 2013
E-mail: carol.english@unitetheunion.org

Founded:
1914

Organisation type and purpose:
Trade union.

continued overleaf

Subject coverage:
Medico-politics; National Health Service, industrial relations, equal opportunities.

Printed publications:
MPU Newsletter
Salaried Service, Threat or Opportunity?
The Future of Primary Care

Publications list:
Available in print

Access to staff:
Contact by letter and by e-mail

Section of:
Unite
  tel: 020 7611 2500; website: http://www
  .unitetheunion.org

MEDICAL PROTECTION SOCIETY

Acronym or abbreviation: MPS

Granary Wharf House, Leeds, LS11 5PY

Tel: 0845 605 4000
Fax: 0113 241 0500
E-mail: info@mps.org.uk

Website:
http://www.medicalprotection.org/uk
About the Medical Protection Society; contact information; medico-legal advice; publications; case reports, educational services.

Enquiries:
Enquiries to: Library & Information Manager
Direct tel: 0113 241 0615
Direct e-mail: tony.albrow@mps.org.uk

Founded:
1892

Organisation type and purpose:
International organisation, advisory body, professional body (membership is by subscription), service industry.
MPS is the leading provider of comprehensive professional indemnity and expert advice to doctors, dentists and health professionals around the world. It is a mutual, not-for-profit medical defence organisation, offering more than 265,000 members help with legal and ethical problems that arise from their professional practice. This includes clinical negligence claims, complaints, medical council inquiries, legal and ethical dilemmas, disciplinary procedures, inquests and fatal accident inquiries. MPS is not an insurance company. The benefits of membership are discretionary.

Subject coverage:
Medico-legal matters.

Printed publications:
Casebook (journal, 3 times a year, UK and various overseas editions) plus various other medico-legal-themed factsheets and booklets
Order printed publications from: Publications free to members and freely available on website

Publications list:
Available online

Access to staff:
Contact by letter, by telephone, by fax, by e-mail and via website. Appointment necessary. Access for members only.
Hours: Mon to Fri, 0800 to 1630

Access for disabled people:
Access to all public areas, toilet facilities

Also at:
Medical Protection Society
  33 Cavendish Square, London, W1G 0PS; tel: 0845 605 4000; e-mail: info@mps.org.uk

MEDICAL RESEARCH COUNCIL CANCER DIVISION, MRC CLINICAL TRIALS UNIT

Acronym or abbreviation: MRC CTU

222 Euston Road, London, NW1 2DA

Tel: 020 7670 4700
Fax: 020 7670 4818
E-mail: contact@ctu.mrc.ac.uk

Website:
http://www.ctu.mrc.ac.uk
Information about the office, current trials, news, methodology, meta-analysis, IT, UK register of trials, links.

Enquiries:
Enquiries to: Information Officer
Direct tel: 020 7670 4737
Direct e-mail: ch@ctu.mrc.ac.uk

Founded:
1977

Organisation type and purpose:
Membership association, present number of members: 80, research organisation.
The conduct of multi-centre clinical trials in the treatment of HIV, cancer, and associated research.

Subject coverage:
To design, conduct and analyse clinical trials in cancer in most solid tumour sites, mainly on behalf of the MRC.
To undertake teaching, supervisory, editorial and refereeing work.
The Cancer Division is a member of the editorial boards of various journals including the British Medical Journal, British Cancer Journal, Clinical Oncology etc.
The Cancer Division is the UK editorial office for the journal Statistics in Medicine.

Printed publications:
Various publications are available, listed in the Annual Report

Publications list:
Available online and in print

Access to staff:
Contact by letter, by fax, by e-mail and via website. Appointment necessary.
Hours: Mon to Fri, 0900 to 1700

Parent body:
Medical Research Council
  Head Office, 20 Park Crescent, London, W1N 4AL; tel: 020 7636 5422

MEDICAL RESEARCH COUNCIL – COGNITION AND BRAIN SCIENCES UNIT

Acronym or abbreviation: MRC–CBU

15 Chaucer Road, Cambridge, CB2 7EF

Tel: 01223 355294
Fax: 01223 359062

Website:
http://www.mrc-cbu.cam.ac.uk
Staff and research details.

Founded:
1944

Formerly called:
MRC Applied Psychology Unit (year of change 1997)

Organisation type and purpose:
Research organisation.

Subject coverage:
Fundamental human psychological functions in domains such as attention, memory, language and emotion. Clinical implications for patient therapy and rehabilitation.

Non-library collection catalogue:
All or part available online

Library catalogue:
All or part available in-house

Publications list:
Available online

Access to staff:
Contact by letter and by e-mail. Appointment necessary.
Hours: Mon to Fri, 0900 to 1700

Access to building, collection or gallery:
No access other than to staff

Access for disabled people:
Parking provided, ramped entry, toilet facilities

MEDICAL RESEARCH COUNCIL – HARWELL

Harwell, Didcot, Oxfordshire, OX11 0RD

Tel: 01235 841000 extn 1121
Fax: 01235 841200
E-mail: m.bulman@har.mrc.ac.uk

Website:
http://www.har.mrc.ac.uk/initial.html

Enquiries:
Enquiries to: Librarian

Organisation type and purpose:
Research organisation.

Subject coverage:
Mammalian genetics, particularly mouse genetics.

Library catalogue:
All or part available online

Access to staff:
Contact by telephone and by e-mail. Appointment necessary.
Hours: Mon to Fri, 0900 to 1700

MEDICAL SOCIETY OF LONDON

11 Chandos Street, London, W1M 0EB

Tel: 020 7580 1043
Fax: 020 7580 5793

Enquiries:
Enquiries to: Registrar

Founded:
1773

Organisation type and purpose:
Learned society (membership is by election or invitation), registered charity.

Subject coverage:
Medicine and the history of medicine.

Printed publications:
Transactions of the Medical Society of London

Access to staff:
Contact by letter. Appointment necessary.
Hours: Mon to Fri, 0900 to 1700

MEDICAL WOMEN'S FEDERATION

Acronym or abbreviation: MWF

Tavistock House North, Tavistock Square, London, WC1H 9HX

Tel: 020 7387 7765
Fax: 020 7388 9216
E-mail: admin.mwf@btconnect.com

Website:
http://www.medicalwomensfederation.org.uk

Enquiries:
Enquiries to: Honorary Secretary

Founded:
1917

Organisation type and purpose:
Membership association (membership is by subscription), present number of members: c.1,500, voluntary organisation, registered charity (charity number 261820).

Subject coverage:
Careers for women doctors working on a full- or part-time basis.

Museum or gallery collection, archive, or library special collection:
Archives on history of women in medicine (now on permanent loan to the Wellcome Institute on the History of Medicine)

Printed publications:
Medical Woman (newsletter)

Access to staff:
Contact by letter, by telephone, by fax, by e-mail and via website
Hours: Mon to Fri, 0900 to 1700

Access to building, collection or gallery:
Prior appointment required

Links with:
Medical Womens' International Association

MEDICINES AND HEALTHCARE PRODUCTS REGULATORY AGENCY

Acronym or abbreviation: MHRA

Information Centre, 10th Floor, Market Towers, 1 Nine Elms Lane, London, SW8 5NQ

Tel: 020 7084 2000
Fax: 020 7084 2353
E-mail: info@mhra.gsi.gov.uk

Website:
http://www.mhra.gov.uk
MHRA home page describing the organisation and giving contact names and numbers.

Enquiries:
Enquiries to: Central Enquiry Point, Information Centre
Direct e-mail: florence.palmer@mhra.gsi.gov.uk

Founded:
1989

Created by the merger of:
Medicines Control Agency (MCA) and Medical Devices Agency (MDA) (year of change 2003)

Organisation type and purpose:
National government body, statutory body. Executive Agency of the Department of Health. Regulatory body for human medicines and devices in the UK.

Subject coverage:
Safeguarding public health by ensuring that medicines and medical devices work, and are acceptably safe.

Museum or gallery collection, archive, or library special collection:
British National Formulary 1947 to date
British Pharmaceutical Codex 1923 to date
British Pharmacopoeia 1898 to date
Data Sheet Compendiums 1974 to date

Non-library collection catalogue:
All or part available online

Library catalogue:
All or part available online

Publications list:
Available online

Access to staff:
Contact by letter, by telephone, by fax and by e-mail
Hours: Mon to Fri, 0900 to 1700
Special comments: A private information centre serving MHRA staff, only open to researchers as a last resort.

Executive agency of:
Department of Health

MEDIEVAL SETTLEMENT RESEARCH GROUP

Acronym or abbreviation: MSRG

c/o Dr Neil Christie, School of Archaeology and Ancient History, University of Leicester, Leicester, LE1 7RH

Tel: 0116 252 2617
Fax: 0116 252 5005
E-mail: njc10@leicester.ac.uk

Website:
http://www.britarch.ac.uk/msrg
Introduction to the Group, forthcoming events, list of publications, grants and prizes, contact details, policy statement.

Enquiries:
Enquiries to: Honorary Secretary
Other contacts: Treasurer (for membership); Editor (for publications); President

Founded:
1986

Created by the merger of:
Medieval Village Research Group (MVRG, founded 1952) and the Moated Sites Research Group (founded 1971) (year of change 1986)

Organisation type and purpose:
Learned society (membership is by subscription), registered charity (charity number 801634), research organisation.
To advance knowledge of rural settlements of all kinds, particularly those of the 5th to 16th centuries. To publish an annual journal, Medieval Settlement Research, to help disseminate research, finds, and debates.

Subject coverage:
Medieval manors and moats; English, Welsh and some Continental rural settlement studies, especially for the 5th to 16th centuries.

Museum or gallery collection, archive, or library special collection:
The Library is held as part of the Marc Fitch Library, The University of Leicester – for information contact Prof. C. Dyer, School of English Local History, The University of Leicester
The former MVRG sites archive is held on the MSRG's behalf by the National Monuments Record in Swindon (English Heritage). Archive has a computerised index

Printed publications:
Annual Journal (free to members)
Bibliography of Moated Sites
Indexes to Volumes Annual Report
Policy Statement on Medieval Rural Settlements (1996; revised 2006)
Seasonal Settlement (1995)
Order printed publications from: Annual journal

Publications list:
Available online and in print

Access to staff:
Contact by letter, by telephone, by fax, by e-mail and via website. Appointment necessary.
Hours: Mon to Fri, 0900 to 1700

Affiliated to:
Council for British Archaeology (CBA)
St Mary's House, 66 Bootham, York, YO30 7BZ; tel: 01904 671417; fax: 01904 671384; e-mail: archaeology@csi.com; website: http://www.britarch.ac.uk
Society for Medieval Archaeology (SMA)
website: http://www.socmedarch.org

MEDITERRANEAN ASSOCIATION TO SAVE THE SEA TURTLES

Acronym or abbreviation: MEDASSET

c/o 24 Park Towers, 2 Brick Street, London, W1J 7DD

Tel: 020 7629 0654
Fax: 020 7629 0654
E-mail: medasset@medasset.org

Website:
http://www.medasset.org
MEDASSET's website
http://www.euroturtle.org

EuroTurtle – a Mediterranean Sea Turtle Biology & Conservation website for Science and Education is a result of collaboration between King's College, Taunton and MEDASSET – the Mediterranean Association to Save the Sea Turtles.

Enquiries:
Enquiries to: Communications Officer
Direct tel: +30 210 3613572
Direct fax: +30 210 3613572

Founded:
1988

Organisation type and purpose:
An international not-for-profit environmental NGO registered as a charity (charity number 1077649) and private company in the UK and as a Non Profit Organisation in Greece.
MEDASSET plays an active role in the study and conservation of sea turtles and their habitats throughout the Mediterranean, through scientific research, environmental education, political lobbying and raising public awareness.The organisation has been a Partner to the Mediterranean Action Plan (MAP) of UNEP and a Permanent Observer-member of the Bern Convention at the Council of Europe since 1988.

Museum or gallery collection, archive, or library special collection:
Videos, CDs, slides, newspaper cuttings
Holds an extensive list of related publications, technical reports, papers, etc.

Non-library collection catalogue:
All or part available online and in-house

Library catalogue:
All or part available in-house

Printed publications:
Posters, leaflets and brochures relevant to sea turtle conservation
Environmental Education Kit for teachers and students
Order printed publications from: http://www.medasset.org

Electronic and video publications:
Return to Origin (TV spot)
Turkey's Sea Turtles in Trouble (short documentary)
Rights of distribution of Greek edition of Turtles in Trouble (short animation film)

Publications list:
Available online and in print

Access to staff:
Contact by letter, by telephone, by fax, by e-mail and via website. Appointment necessary. Letter of introduction required.
Hours: Mon to Fri, 0900 to 1700
Special comments: Telephone first for access hours.

Also at:
MEDASSET Greece
1(c) Licavitou Street, Athens 10672, Greece; tel: +30 210 3613572; +30 210 3640389; fax: +30 210 3613572; e-mail: medasset@medasset.gr; website: http://www.medasset.gr

MEDITERRANEAN GARDEN SOCIETY UK BRANCH

Acronym or abbreviation: MGS UK

Baldocks, Chiddingstone Causeway, Tonbridge, TN11 8JX

Tel: 01892 870880
E-mail: hma@clara.net

Website:
http://www.mediterraneangardensociety.org
Garden/plant information, details/history of society, membership details, articles, photographs, etc.

Enquiries:
Enquiries to: Chairman

Founded:
1995

continued overleaf

Organisation type and purpose:
International organisation, membership association (membership is by subscription), present number of members: 2,500, voluntary organisation.
To promote understanding and interest in Mediterranean plants and gardening and water-wise gardening.

Subject coverage:
The society provides a forum for members on any related Mediterranean garden/plant topics.

Printed publications:
Journal (quarterly)

Also at:
MGS
Sparoza, PO Box 14, 190 02 Peania, Greece

MEDWAY ARCHIVES AND LOCAL STUDIES CENTRE

Acronym or abbreviation: MALSC

Clocktower Building, Civic Centre, Strood, Rochester, Kent, ME2 4AU

Tel: 01634 332714/332095
Fax: 01634 297060
E-mail: malsc@medway.gov.uk

Website:
http://cityark.medway.gov.uk
Piece-level database of archives stock organised in folders, sub-folders and flat html files according to provenance and structure of collections, comprising descriptions of documents. Imagebase of selected collections. Imagebase of parish records.
http://libcat.medway.gov.uk/cgi-bin/vps2_viewpoint.sh
Library catalogue.

Enquiries:
Enquiries to: Borough Archivist
Other contacts: Local Studies Librarians (for local studies stock)

Founded:
1990

Organisation type and purpose:
Local government body, public library (reference only).
Archives.

Subject coverage:
Archives: Rochester City Council, Rochester upon Medway City Council, Hoo Rural District Council, Chatham Borough Council, Rochester City Council, Gillingham Borough Council, Strood Rural District Council, parish councils for north west Kent, state school and school board records (Medway Council area), Rochester Cathedral, Hawkins' Hospital (Chatham), Rochester Dickens' Fellowship, Watts' Charity (Rochester), St. Bartholomew's Hospital (Rochester/Chatham), Foord Almshouses (Rochester), Earls of Darnley of Cobham Hall, Best family of Boxley and Chatham, Winget Ltd (Strood), Blaw Knox Ltd (Rochester), Dove, Phillips and Pett Ltd (Strood and Rochester), Rogers, Stevens and Chance (Chatham), Winch and Winch (Chatham), Church of England parishes (Rochester Archdeaconry area), Methodist Church Medway Towns Circuit, Chatham Memorial Synagogue (Rochester), Unitarian Church (Chatham), Congregational Church (Clover Street, Chatham), Medway Conservancy Board, Medway Navigation Company, Port of Rochester shipping registers and crew lists, Medway and Swale Dock Labour Board, Rochester Book Society, Rochester and District Natural History Society, Dickens' Country Protection Society, Old Roffensian Society (Rochester), City of Rochester Society, King's School (Rochester), Sir Joseph Williamson's Mathematical School (Rochester)
Local studies: Dickens' collection, naval collection, local history, Medway Council area and Kent topography, Kent periodicals, census, IGI, GRO Index, public access computers, CD-Roms, OS

maps, electoral registers, telephone and street directories, local area newspapers and parish register index fiche.

Education services:
Outreach programme and educational local history packs by arrangement.

Museum or gallery collection, archive, or library special collection:
Dickens collection
IGI
Naval collection
Usual local authority archive stock

Trade and statistical information:
Census.

Non-library collection catalogue:
All or part available online and in print

Library catalogue:
All or part available online and in-house

Printed publications:
Archive and Local Studies Leaflets (free)

Microform publications:
Films and microfiche by arrangement

Electronic and video publications:
Public access computers, People's Network, Ancestry (library edition)

Access to staff:
Contact by letter, by telephone, by fax, by e-mail, in person and via website. Appointment necessary.
Hours: Mon, Tues,Thu, Fri, 0900 to 1700; Sat, 0900 to 1600; Wed, closed
Special comments: CARN reader's ticket for archives.

Access for disabled people:
Parking provided, level entry, wheelchair access to all public areas, toilet facilities, loop system, screen reader software, evac chair

Parent body:
Medway Council
Directorate of Regeneration and Community Services; tel: 01634 306000; fax: 01634 732848; website: http://www.medway.gov.uk

MEDWAY COUNCIL

Medway Libraries, c/o Chatham Library, Gun Wharf, Dock Road, Chatham, Kent, ME4 4TX

Tel: 01634 337799
Fax: 01634 337800
E-mail: chatham.library@medway.gov.uk

Website:
http://www.medway.gov.uk/libraries
https://medway.spydus.co.uk

Enquiries:
Enquiries to: Librarian

Founded:
1998

Organisation type and purpose:
Local government body, public library.

Subject coverage:
Business information, European information, UK Online Centre, archives, local studies

Library catalogue:
All or part available online

Access to staff:
Contact by letter, by telephone, by fax, by e-mail and in person
Hours: Mon, Wed and Fri, 0900 to 1800; Tue, 1000 to 1900; Thu, 0900 to 1900; Sat, 0900 to 1700

Access to building, collection or gallery:
No prior appointment required

Also at:
Medway Archives and Local Studies Centre
Clocktower Building, Civic Centre, Strood, ME2 4AU; tel: 01634 332714; fax: 01634 297060; e-mail: local.studies@medway.gov.uk; website: http://cityarc.medway.gov.uk

Member organisation of:
UK Online Centre

MEDWAY LIBRARY, INFORMATION & MUSEUM SERVICE

Civic Centre, Strood, Rochester, Kent, ME2 4AU

Tel: 01634 306000

Website:
http://cityark.medway.gov.uk
Archives database.
http://libcat.medway.gov.uk
Library catalogue.

Enquiries:
Enquiries to: Librarian
Direct tel: 01634 843589
Direct fax: 01634 827976
Direct e-mail: chatham.library@medway.gov.uk
Other contacts: Reference, Archives, Local Studies Manager for reference, local studies and archives.

Founded:
1998

Organisation type and purpose:
Local government body, public library.

Subject coverage:
Local studies and archives, business information.

Museum or gallery collection, archive, or library special collection:
See Leaflets

Non-library collection catalogue:
All or part available online

Library catalogue:
All or part available online

Printed publications:
Order printed publications from: Chatham Reference Library
Riverside, Chatham, Kent, ME4 4SN, e-mail: chatham.library@medway.gov.uk

Access to staff:
Contact by letter, by telephone, by fax, by e-mail, in person and via website
Hours: Various

Other address:
Chatham Library
Riverside, Chatham, Kent, ME4 4SN; tel: 01634 843589; fax: 01634 827976; e-mail: chatham .library@medway.gov.uk
Medway Archives and Local Studies Centre
Clocktower Building, Civic Centre, Strood, ME2 4AU; tel: 01634 332714
Medway Library Information and Museum Service, Education and Leisure
Civic Centre, Strood, Kent, ME2 4AU; tel: 01634 306000; fax: 01634 332756

MEET A MUM ASSOCIATION

Acronym or abbreviation: MAMA

National MAMA Office, 7 Southcourt Road, Linslade, Leighton Buzzard, Beds LU7 2QF

Tel: 0845 120 6162

Website:
http://www.mama.co.uk/

Enquiries:
Enquiries to: Manager
Direct e-mail: jeanette@mama.co.uk
Other contacts: Helpline Administrator for listing details.

Founded:
1979

Organisation type and purpose:
National organisation, membership association (membership is by subscription), registered charity (charity number 283271).
National charity.

Subject coverage:
Support for mums or mums-to-be with post-natal depression or a feeling of isolation.

Non-library collection catalogue:
All or part available in-house

Printed publications:
Publications are available, for a small fee, on related subjects including:
Postnatal illness
The effects of a new baby on the family
Difficulties faced by women following childbirth
How to support a women with PNI
Plus leaflets and factsheets for mothers on panic attacks, relaxation techniques and notes for carers (free)

Publications list:
Available online and in print

Access to staff:
Contact by letter, by telephone, by e-mail and via website
Hours: Mon to Fri, 1000 to 1530

Access to building, collection or gallery:
No prior appointment required

Has:
over 35 local groups throughout the UK

MEETINGS INDUSTRY ASSOCIATION

Acronym or abbreviation: MIA

PO Box 515, Kelmarsh, Northampton, NN6 9XW

Tel: 0845 230 5508
Fax: 0845 230 7708
E-mail: info@mia-uk.org

Website:
http://www.mia-uk.org
About MIA, directory of AIM accredited members, research, how to join, news, jobs, academy of training programmes.

Enquiries:
Enquiries to: Chief Executive
Direct e-mail: janee@mia-uk.org

Founded:
1990

Organisation type and purpose:
Membership and professional association for all organisations involved in the meetings industry for the UK & Ireland. Its own accreditation scheme, AIM, is the only meetings industry standard endorsed by VisitBritain, Visit England, Visit Wales, Meeting Professionals International and the Association of British Professional Conference Organisers.
To encourage improvement of service and facilities offered by the UK meetings industry through the sharing of best practice and the setting of standards.

Subject coverage:
The meetings industry.

Education services:
Learning and Development Academy training courses (see website).

Electronic and video publications:
MIA conducts regular research of the UK conference market (all sent via e-mail in pdf format, free to members, for sale to non-members, for prices see website)
Order electronic and video publications from: tel: 0845 230 5508; e-mail: sarahp@mia-uk.org

Publications list:
Available online

Access to staff:
Contact by letter, by telephone, by fax and by e-mail

MELTON BOROUGH COUNCIL

Council Offices, Nottingham Road, Melton Mowbray, Leicestershire, LE13 0UL

Tel: 01664 502502
Fax: 01664 410283

Website:
http://www.melton.gov.uk

Enquiries:
Enquiries to: Public Relations Manager
Direct tel: 01664 502385

Organisation type and purpose:
Local government body.

Access to staff:
Contact by letter, by telephone and by fax
Hours: Mon to Fri, 0900 to 1700

MEN OF THE STONES

Acronym or abbreviation: MOS

Beech Croft, Weston-under-Lizard, Shifnal, Shropshire, TF11 8JT

Tel: 01952 850269
Fax: 01952 850269
E-mail: mltebbutt@lineone.net

Enquiries:
Enquiries to: Chairman
Direct tel: 07980 63118 (mobile)
Other contacts: Honorary Secretary

Founded:
1947

Organisation type and purpose:
Learned society, membership association (membership is by subscription), present number of members: 465, registered charity (charity number 229497).
A society advocating the use of stone and other natural and local building materials, for encouraging craftsmanship and preserving good architectural qualities.

Subject coverage:
Architecture and good buildings of all periods; conservation, preservation, repair; use and re-use of stone and other natural and local materials; constructional arts and crafts of architecture, including stone masonry, sculpture, carving; gilding; pargetting, wrought iron and cast lead work, stone roof slating.

Printed publications:
Annual Report (members only)
Yearbook and Directory (free to members, £5 others)

Access to staff:
Contact by letter, by telephone and by e-mail
Hours: Mon to Fri, 0900 to 1700

Affiliated to:
Ancient Monuments Society
English Heritage (West Midlands Region)
tel: 0121 625 6820
Georgian Group
Society for the Protection of Ancient Buildings

Links with:
Collyweston Stone Slaters Trust
Orton Trust Stonemasonry Training Centre

MENINGITIS RESEARCH FOUNDATION

Midland Way, Thornbury, Bristol, BS35 2BS

Tel: 01454 281811
Fax: 01454 281094
E-mail: info@meningitis.org

Website:
http://www.meningitis.org

Enquiries:
Enquiries to: Head of Communications and Campaigns
Direct e-mail: harpinderc@meningitis.org

Founded:
1989

Organisation type and purpose:
Registered charity (charity number 1091105).

Subject coverage:
Meningitis Research Foundation funds vital scientific research into the prevention, detection and treatment of meningitis and septicaemia – the blood poisoning form of the disease. Raises awareness of the diseases, and offers support through in-depth information and befriending to those affected.

Museum or gallery collection, archive, or library special collection:
General Public – Symptoms Literature
Health Professionals – Diagnosis guidelines and treatment protocols, and photo library

Library catalogue:
All or part available online

Printed publications:
Various publications available free of charge (however, Meningitis Reasearch Foundation is a registered charity and welcomes donations to help to continue vital work)

Electronic and video publications:
Awareness (video)
Symptoms Information (tapes)

Publications list:
Available online and in print

Access to staff:
Contact by letter, by telephone, by fax and by e-mail
Hours: Mon to Fri, 0900 to 1700; 24-hour Helpline: 0808 800 3344

Access for disabled people:
Parking provided, toilet facilities

Other addresses:
Meningitis Research Foundation
63 Lower Gardiner Street, Dublin 1, Republic of Ireland; tel: +353 1 819 6931; fax: +353 1 819 6931; e-mail: meningitis@iol.ie
Meningitis Research Foundation
133 Gilmore Place, Edinburgh, EH3 9PP; tel: 0131 228 3322; fax: 0131 221 0300; e-mail: info@scotland-meningitis.org.uk
Meningitis Research Foundation
71 Botanic Avenue, Belfast, BT7 1JL; tel: 028 9032 1283; fax: 028 9032 1284; e-mail: info@meningitis-ni.org

MENTAL HEALTH FOUNDATION

Acronym or abbreviation: MHF

9th Floor, Sea Containers House, 20 Upper Ground, London, SE1 9QB

Tel: 020 7803 1101
Fax: 020 7803 1111
E-mail: mhf@mhf.org.uk

Website:
http://www.mentalhealth.org.uk
Home page, frames based website.

Enquiries:
Enquiries to: Head of Information
Direct tel: 020 7802 0315
Direct e-mail: press@mhf.org.uk

Founded:
1949

Organisation type and purpose:
Registered charity (charity number 801130).
Mental Health Foundation incorporating the Foundation for People with Learning Disabilities, is the leading UK charity working in mental health and learning disabilities.
With pioneering research and community projects we aim to improve the support available for people with mental health problems and people with learning disabilities.

continued overleaf

Subject coverage:
Mental health, learning disabilities, mental illness, depression, anxiety, dementia, manic depression, schizophrenia, stress therapy, psychiatry, psychology, user movement, attention deficit, conduct disorder, eating disorder.

Printed publications:
The Mental Health Foundation has a comprehensive booklist including:
Because You Care (Dr K Hinchliffe and Dr G Livingstone, 1994, free for A5 sae, bulk orders 50p per booklet)
Challenging Behaviour – What We Want to Know (Sep 1995, £7)
Chinese Mental Health Issues in Britain: Perspectives form the Chinese Mental Health Association (1997, £9)
Citizens Advice Bureaux Service for People with Mental Health Problems
Creating Community Care: Report of the Mental Health Foundation Inquiry into Community Care for People with Severe Mental Illness (Sep 1994, £9.50)
Don't Forget Us. Services for Children with Learning Disabilities and Severe Challenging Behaviour (1997, £12)
Healing Minds (Wallcraft J, July 1998, £12)
Helping You Cope: A Guide to Starting and Stopping Tranquillisers and Sleeping Tablets (1994, free for A5 sae, bulk orders 40p per booklet)
Knowing Our Own Minds (Faulkner A, Feb 1997, £15)
Legal Issues Arising for the Care, Control and Safety of Children with Learning Disabilities who also Present Severe Challenging Behaviour (Professor C Low, June 1994)
Mental Health Care: A Guide for Housing Workers (June 1995, £7)
Nowhere Else to Go (Fleischmann P and Wigmore J, July 2000, £9.99)
Strategies for Living: The Research Report (Mar 2000, £22.50)
The Fundamental Facts: All the Latest Facts and Figures on Mental Illness (Bird L, Feb 1999, £15)
Too Many for the Road (1996, £10)

Electronic and video publications:
Restoring the Balance – a self-help CD-ROM designed for people with mild to moderate anxiety and depression
Peer Support (video)

Publications list:
Available online and in print

Access to staff:
Contact by letter, by telephone, by fax, by e-mail and via website
Hours: Mon to Fri, 0900 to 1700 plus Dial & Listen Service

Other address:
Mental Health Foundation – Scotland Office 24 St George's Square, Glasgow, G2 1EG; tel: 0141 572 0125; fax: 0141 572 0246; e-mail: scotland@mhf.org .uk

MENTAL HEALTH MEDIA

Acronym or abbreviation: MHM

The Resource Centre, 356 Holloway Road, London, N7 6PA

Tel: 020 7700 8171
Fax: 020 7686 0959

Website:
http://www.mhmedia.com

Enquiries:
Enquiries to: Director
Direct tel: 020 7700 8131

Founded:
1983

Organisation type and purpose:
Voluntary organisation, registered charity (charity number 286467), training organisation, consultancy, research organisation.

A charity working with the media, statutory and voluntary organisations and service users to break down the stigma of mental distress.

Subject coverage:
Mental health and distress, wellbeing, stress and stress management, ability and disability, community care, coping with bereavement, cultural identity and racism, women and well-being, counselling and psychotherapy, learning difficulties, sexuality, child abuse, advocacy, housing, video production and working with the media.

Electronic and video publications:
Behind the Behaviour
Behind the Symptoms
Friends & Family
Insight in Mind
Mannki Baat
Myths about Madness
Testimony
Working Partners
What Women Want
Open Up Anti-Discrimination Toolkit: Challenging Discrimination in Everyday Life
Fired Up

Publications list:
Available in print

Access to staff:
Contact by letter, by telephone, by fax and by e-mail. Appointment necessary.
Hours: Mon to Fri, 0900 to 1800

MENTAL WELFARE COMMISSION FOR SCOTLAND

Acronym or abbreviation: MWC

K Floor, Argyle House, 3 Lady Lawson Street, Edinburgh, EH3 9SH

Tel: 0131 222 6111
Fax: 0131 222 6112
E-mail: enquiries@mwcscot.org.uk

Website:
http://www.mwcscot.org.uk

Enquiries:
Enquiries to: Communications Manager

Founded:
1960

Organisation type and purpose:
Statutory body.

Subject coverage:
Mental welfare.

Museum or gallery collection, archive, or library special collection:
Mental Health Law
Reports and Grey Literature (relating to Mental Health)
Small collection of reference books and some journal titles

Library catalogue:
All or part available in-house

Printed publications:
Annual reports
Inquiry reports
Good Practice Evidence

Publications list:
Available online

Access to staff:
Contact by letter, by telephone, by fax, by e-mail and via website
Hours: Mon to Fri, 0900 to 1700

Access to building, collection or gallery:
Prior appointment required

Access for disabled people:
Access to all public areas

MENZIES CENTRE FOR AUSTRALIAN STUDIES

Acronym or abbreviation: MCAS

King's College London, The Australia Centre, Strand, London, WC2B 4LG

Tel: 020 7557 7160
Fax: 020 7240 8292
E-mail: menzies.centre@kcl.ac.uk

Website:
http://www.kcl.ac.uk/menzies

Enquiries:
Enquiries to: Head

Founded:
1982

Organisation type and purpose:
University department or institute.

Subject coverage:
Australian tertiary education; Australian literature, poetry and drama; international relations, history, politics, art, film; Australian scholarships and fellowships administered by MCAS.

Museum or gallery collection, archive, or library special collection:
Australia House Library (old Australian High Commission Library)
Files of Britain-Australia Bicentennial Committee

Non-library collection catalogue:
All or part available online

Printed publications:
Conference papers (3 titles in hard copy)
Newsletter (twice a year, free, all available in hard copy and on web)
Special lectures (available on web and in hard copy)
London Papers and Working Papers of seminars (available on web and in hard copy; variable number produced each year)

Publications list:
Available online and in print

Access to staff:
Contact by letter, by telephone, by fax and by e-mail. Appointment necessary.
Hours: Mon to Fri, 1000 to 1700
Special comments: Secretarial staff answer telephone enquiries; academic staff available for comment and research advice on Australian subjects. Access to Australia House library collection with permission from MCAS.

Access to building, collection or gallery:
Prior appointment required

Constituent part of:
King's College London, University of London

Funded by:
The Australian Government

Links with:
Sir Robert Menzies Memorial Foundation

MERCEDES-BENZ CLUB LIMITED

18 Viga Road, Winchmore Hill, London, N21 1HJ

Tel: 07071 818868

Website:
http://www.mercedes-benzownersclub.co.uk

Enquiries:
Enquiries to: Director and Membership Secretary
Direct e-mail: vharris@mercedes-benzownersclub .co.uk

Founded:
1952

Organisation type and purpose:
Membership association (membership is by subscription), present number of members: 8000.

Subject coverage:
Mercedes-Benz cars.

Museum or gallery collection, archive, or library special collection:
Library of books and documents covering Mercedes-Benz cars from 1884 to the present

Printed publications:
Gazette (monthly, members only)

Access to staff:
Contact by e-mail and via website
Hours: Mon to Fri, 0900 to 1700

MERCHANT TAYLORS' COMPANY

Formal name: Guild of Merchant Taylors of the Fraternity of St John Baptist in the City of London

Merchant Taylors' Hall, 30 Threadneedle Street, London, EC2R 8JB

Tel: 020 7450 4440
Fax: 020 7450 4499
E-mail: livery@merchant-taylors.co.uk

Website:
http://www.merchant-taylors.co.uk

Founded:
1327

Organisation type and purpose:
Membership association (membership is by election or invitation).
City of London Livery Company.

Access to staff:
Contact by letter, by telephone, by fax, by e-mail and via website

MERCK, SHARP AND DOHME RESEARCH LABORATORIES

Acronym or abbreviation: MSDRL

Hertford Road, Hoddesdon, Hertfordshire, EN11 9BU

Tel: 01992 467272
Fax: 01992 451075
E-mail: externalaffairs_uk@merck.com

Website:
http://www.msd-uk.com/
Website for the site.
http://www.merck.com
Website for Global Company.

Enquiries:
Enquiries to: Literature Resources Associate
Direct tel: 01279 440131
Direct fax: 01279 440667

Founded:
1983

Organisation type and purpose:
International organisation.
Research division of multinational pharmaceutical company.

Subject coverage:
Medicinal and organic chemistry; diseases of central nervous system; pharmacology; biochemistry.

Non-library collection catalogue:
All or part available in-house

Library catalogue:
All or part available in-house

Printed publications:
Merck Index
Merck Manual
Order printed publications from: Public Affairs Department, Merck and Co Inc
Whitehouse Station, New Jersey, 08889–0100, USA, tel: 00 1 908 423 1000

Access to staff:
Contact by letter and by e-mail
Hours: Mon to Fri, 0900 to 1700
Special comments: Not open to the public.

Links with:
Merck & Co Inc
Whitehouse Station, One Merck Drive, PO Box 100, Whitehouse Station, NJ 08889–0100, USA

MERIONETH HISTORICAL AND RECORD SOCIETY

Acronym or abbreviation: MHRS

Bryn Bedd, Nantgwynant, Caernarfon, Gwynedd, LL55 4NL

Tel: 01766 890550
E-mail: brynbedd@ukonline.co.uk

Enquiries:
Enquiries to: Hon. Membership Secretary

Founded:
1939

Organisation type and purpose:
Learned society (membership is by subscription), present number of members: 318, voluntary organisation.

Subject coverage:
History, geography and literature of Merioneth.

Printed publications:
Annual journal
History of Merioneth Vol II 'The Middle Ages'

Access to staff:
Contact by letter, by telephone and by e-mail

MERRIST WOOD CAMPUS

Worplesdon, Guildford, Surrey, GU3 3PE

Tel: 01483 884000
Fax: 01483 884001
E-mail: mwinfo@guildford.ac.uk

Website:
http://www.guildford.ac.uk
Home page, details of courses, new, special events.

Enquiries:
Enquiries to: Learner Services
Direct tel: 01483 884040

Founded:
1945

Organisation type and purpose:
Suitable for ages: 16+.
College of the land-based industries.

Subject coverage:
Arboriculture, horticulture, countryside, practical habitat management, small-scale farming, plant production, garden design, landscape construction, equine studies, animal care, greenkeeping and sports turf management, professional floristry, golf studies, bespoke training, public services

Printed publications:
Prospectus and course details available on request

Access to staff:
Contact by letter, by telephone, by fax, by e-mail, in person and via website
Hours: Mon to Fri, 0900 to 1700

MERSEY TELEVISION GROUP, THE

Formal name: Mersey Television Independent Television Company
Acronym or abbreviation: Mersey Television

Campus Manor, Childwall Abbey Road, Liverpool, L16 0JP

Tel: 0151 722 9122
Fax: 0151 722 6839
E-mail: admin@merseytv.com

Website:
http://www.merseytv.com
http://www.connect.org.uk/brookside
Brookside.
http://www.connect.org.uk/eastenders
Eastenders.
http://www.andover.org.uk/shaun/emmerdale.htm
Emmerdale.
http://www.brookside.com
http://www.hollyoaks.com

Enquiries:
Enquiries to: Administrator

Founded:
1982

Organisation type and purpose:
Television production company.

Subject coverage:
Television programmes and production.

Access to staff:
Contact by letter
Hours: Mon to Fri, 0900 to 1700

Access to building, collection or gallery:
No access other than to staff
Special comments: This area is a closed site.

MERSEYSIDE INDUSTRIAL HERITAGE SOCIETY

Acronym or abbreviation: MIHS

Merseyside Maritime Museum, Albert Dock, Liverpool, L3 4AQ

Tel: 0151 478 4402
Fax: 0151 478 4590

Enquiries:
Enquiries to: Secretary

Founded:
1964

Organisation type and purpose:
Learned society.

Subject coverage:
Industrial archaeology and history, particularly of Merseyside; history of public services, docks, railways, canals, manufacturing industries, buildings, trades, chemical industry, transport, power generation, mining and quarrying.

Museum or gallery collection, archive, or library special collection:
Site Record Cards (held by Merseyside Archaeological Service, tel: 0151 478 4258)

Printed publications:
Bulletin (monthly)
Occasional publications
A Guide to Merseyside's Industrial Past

Publications list:
Available in print

Works closely with:
Merseyside Maritime Museum (part of National Museums and Galleries on Merseyside)
Albert Dock, Liverpool, L3 4AQ; tel: 0151 207 0001

MERSEYSIDE RECORD OFFICE

Liverpool Libraries Satellite Service, Unit 33, Wellington Employment Park South, Dunes Way, Liverpool, L5 9ZS

Tel: 0151 233 5817
Fax: 0151 233 5824
E-mail: recoffice.central.library@liverpool.gov.uk

Enquiries:
Enquiries to: Archivist

Founded:
1974

Organisation type and purpose:
Local government body.
Record office.

continued overleaf

Subject coverage:
Merseyside County Council, residuary body and joint authority records; Liverpool, Southport and Wirral coroners; some hospital records; some nonconformist church records; some business records; social agencies, e.g. League of Welldoers.

Non-library collection catalogue:
All or part available in-house

Printed publications:
Brief general information leaflet (free)

Access to staff:
Contact by letter, by telephone, by fax, by e-mail and in person. Appointment necessary.
Hours: Mon to Sat, 0900 to 1700
Special comments: Search fee for written enquiries requiring research.
Proof of identity required, including address.

Access to building, collection or gallery:
Hours: Tue to Sat, 0930 to 1630
Special comments: Appointment only, minimum 24 hours' notice.

Access for disabled people:
Ramped entry, toilet facilities

MERTHYR TYDFIL COUNTY BOROUGH COUNCIL

Acronym or abbreviation: MTCBC

Civic Centre, Castle Street, Merthyr Tydfil, Mid Glamorgan, CF47 8AN

Tel: 01685 725000
Fax: 01685 722146
E-mail: customer.care@merthyr.gov.uk

Website:
http://www.merthyr.gov.uk

Enquiries:
Enquiries to: Public Relations Manager
Direct tel: 01685 725166
Direct fax: 01685 374397
Direct e-mail: public.relations@merthyr.gov.uk

Founded:
1996

Organisation type and purpose:
Local government body.

Subject coverage:
Local government, education, social services, community services, technical services, local government finance.

Library catalogue:
All or part available online, in-house and in print

Publications list:
Available online and in print

Access to staff:
Contact by letter, by telephone, by fax, by e-mail and via website. Appointment necessary.
Hours: Mon to Thu, 0830 to 1700; Fri, 0830 to 1630

MERTHYR TYDFIL PUBLIC LIBRARIES

Central Library, High Street, Merthyr Tydfil, Mid Glamorgan, CF47 8AF

Tel: 01685 723057
Fax: 01685 370690
E-mail: library.services@merthyr.gov.uk

Enquiries:
Enquiries to: Librarian

Founded:
1935

Organisation type and purpose:
Local government body, public library.

Subject coverage:
Local history collection, the borough of Merthyr Tydfil, 19th century iron and steel industry, coal mining in South Wales, Quakerism, Aberfan and the 1966 disaster.

Museum or gallery collection, archive, or library special collection:
Aberfan Tribunal Report
Photographic collection – Borough of Merthyr Tydfil
Welsh ballads

Non-library collection catalogue:
All or part available online and in print

Library catalogue:
All or part available online and in-house

Printed publications:
Local history booklets illustrated with old photographs
Books on local history including:
History of the Hamlet of Gellideg
Merthyr Boat Boy (Thomas C et al, £7.50)
The Dowlais Ironworks
The Merthyr Tydfil and District Naturalists' Society – Historic Taf Valleys (vols 2 & 3, £6 each)
The Merthyr Tydfil Historical Society – Merthyr Historian vols 5 to 12

Electronic and video publications:
Oral History video recordings – available directly

Publications list:
Available in print

Access to staff:
Contact by letter, by telephone, by fax, by e-mail and in person
Hours: Mon, Fri, 0900 to 1800; Tue, 0900 to 1900; Wed, Thurs, 0900 to 1730

Access to building, collection or gallery:
No access other than to staff

Access for disabled people:
Ramped entry

MERTON COLLEGE LIBRARY

Merton College, Oxford, OX1 4JD

Tel: 01865 276380
Fax: 01865 276361
E-mail: library@admin.merton.ox.ac.uk

Website:
http://www.lib.ox.ac.uk/libraries/libcats.html
Bibliographic records of current holdings and of pre-1800 imprints.

Enquiries:
Enquiries to: Librarian

Founded:
1264

Organisation type and purpose:
University department or institute, college library of the University of Oxford

Subject coverage:
General, no special fields.

Museum or gallery collection, archive, or library special collection:
Max Beerbohm Collection
F H Bradley Collection
Brenchley Collection of printed materials by T S Eliot
Medieval manuscripts
Merton College Archives
Merton Blackwell Collection of archival material relating to Sir Basil Blackwell and Blackwells booksellers and publishers

Non-library collection catalogue:
All or part available online and in-house

Library catalogue:
All or part available online and in-house

Access to staff:
Contact by letter, by telephone, by fax and by e-mail. Appointment necessary.
Hours: Mon to Fri, 0900 to 1700

Access to building, collection or gallery:
Prior appointment required

MERTON LIBRARIES AND HERITAGE SERVICES

12th Floor, Merton Civic Centre, London Road, Morden, Surrey, SM4 5DX

Tel: 020 8545 3783
Fax: 020 8545 3237
E-mail: ingrid.lackajis@merton.gov.uk

Website:
http://www.merton.gov.uk
Information about Merton.
http://www.merton.gov.uk/libraries
Libraries in Merton.

Enquiries:
Enquiries to: Head of Library and Heritage Services
Direct tel: 020 8545 3770
Direct e-mail: library.enquiries@merton.gov.uk

Organisation type and purpose:
Local government body, museum, public library.

Subject coverage:
General and local studies: at Morden Library; William Morris, Horatio Nelson: at Wimbledon Library; business and European information: at Morden Library; Merton Local Studies Centre.

Museum or gallery collection, archive, or library special collection:
The following are all in Local Studies Centre:
Carters Tested Seeds Collection at Morden
Simpson Papers at Morden
Tom Francis Picture Collection (transparencies) at Morden

Non-library collection catalogue:
All or part available online and in-house

Library catalogue:
All or part available online and in-house

Printed publications:
Local history publications

Access to staff:
Contact by letter, by telephone, by fax, by e-mail and in person. Appointment necessary.
Hours: Variable hours – please contact for details

Access to building, collection or gallery:
Appointment required

Parent body:
London Borough of Merton, Community and Housing Department
Merton Civic Centre, London Road, Morden, Surrey, SM4 5DX; website: http://www.merton.gov.uk

MESEMB STUDY GROUP

Formal name: Mesembryanthemum Study Group
Acronym or abbreviation: MSG

Brenfield, Bolney Road, Ansty, West Sussex, RH17 5AW

Tel: 01444 459151
Fax: 01444 454061
E-mail: msg@cactus-mall.com

Website:
http://www.mesemb.org/index.html
Sample bulletin pages, membership information, links, index of bulletin information.

Enquiries:
Enquiries to: Honorary Secretary

Founded:
1985

Organisation type and purpose:
International organisation, membership association (membership is by subscription).

Subject coverage:
Study of plants of the family mesembryanthemaceae.

Printed publications:
MESEMB Study Group Bulletin (quarterly, ISSN 0955 8276)

Publications list:
Available in print

Access to staff:
Contact by letter, by telephone, by fax, by e-mail and via website. Appointment necessary.
Hours: Mon to Fri, 0900 to 1700

Access to building, collection or gallery:
Prior appointment required

Access for disabled people:
Level entry

MESSERSCHMITT OWNERS CLUB

Acronym or abbreviation: MOC

169 Coulsdon Road, Coulsdon, Surrey, CR5 1EG

Tel: 01527 61826
E-mail: andrew.woolley@fmrservices.co.uk

Website:
http://www.messerschmitt.co.uk
Kabinews on-line.

Enquiries:
Enquiries to: General Secretary

Founded:
1956

Organisation type and purpose:
Membership association.

Subject coverage:
Preservation of Messerschmitt/Fend vehicles and historic technical data relating to their design, specific vehicle information, given chassis numbers etc.

Museum or gallery collection, archive, or library special collection:
Refer to Messerschmitt Foundation of Great Britain, 0121 744 2615

Printed publications:
Kabinews (magazine, monthly)

Access to staff:
Contact by letter and by e-mail
Hours: Mon to Fri, 0900 to 1700

Affiliated to:
Messerschmitt Club Deutschland eV

MET OFFICE – EDINBURGH

Saughton House, Broomhouse Drive, Edinburgh, EH11 3XQ

Tel: 0131 528 7319
Fax: 0131 244 8389
E-mail: metlib@metoffice.gov.uk

Website:
http://www.metoffice.gov.uk

Enquiries:
Enquiries to: Archive Information Officer

Founded:
1854

Organisation type and purpose:
National government body.
Public record office.

Subject coverage:
Meteorology, climatology.

Museum or gallery collection, archive, or library special collection:
Weather records for Scotland

Non-library collection catalogue:
All or part available in-house

Library catalogue:
All or part available online

Access to staff:
Contact by letter, by telephone, by fax and by e-mail. Appointment necessary.
Hours: Mon to Fri, 0930 to 1600

Access for disabled people:
Yes
Hours: Mon to Fri, 0930 to 1600

Branch of:
National Meteorological Library
Met Office, FitzRoy Road, Exeter, Devon, EX1 3PB; tel: 0870 900 0100; fax: 0870 900 5050; e-mail: enquiries@metoffice.gov.uk

MET OFFICE – EXETER

FitzRoy Road, Exeter, Devon, EX1 3PB

Tel: 01392 885680
Fax: 01392 885681
E-mail: enquiries@metoffice.gov.uk

Website:
http://www.metoffice.com

Enquiries:
Enquiries to: Press Officer
Direct tel: 01392 886655
Direct e-mail: pressoffice@metoffice.gov.uk
Other contacts: Library Information Officer tel: 01344 854841/856694; Archive Manager tel: 01344 855960

Founded:
1854

Organisation type and purpose:
National government body.
Government Agency (Trading Fund).
The UK's National Met Service providing advice on the world's weather and natural environment to private and public sector customers.

Subject coverage:
Meteorology, climatology and most aspects of atmospheric and related sciences, application and meteorological information to weather-sensitive activities and planning, fundamental research in meteorology and professional training.

Museum or gallery collection, archive, or library special collection:
Original weather records (4.5 km of shelves) archived under the terms of the Public Records Act
Rare and historical books and pamphlets on meteorology and climatology held in conjunction with the Royal Meteorological Society

Printed publications:
Annual Report and Accounts
Commercial Publications (market sector/product specific)
HMSO Sectional List No. 37
Marine Observer (quarterly)
Records Act
Science & Technical Review
Scientific Papers and other Reports

Access to staff:
Contact by telephone
Hours: By telephone to Customer Centre – 24 hours
Special comments: National Meteorological Library and Archives open to the general public.

Access for disabled people:
Parking provided, ramped entry, toilet facilities

Trading arm of the:
Ministry of Defence

METAL PACKAGING MANUFACTURERS ASSOCIATION

Acronym or abbreviation: MPMA

The Stables, Tintagel Farm, Sandhurst Road, Wokingham, Berkshire, RG40 3JD

Tel: 01189 788433
Fax: 01189 788433
E-mail: enquiries@mpma.org.uk

Website:
http://www.mpma.org.uk
List of members and products manufactured.
Information on how cans are made. Statistics and press information.

Enquiries:
Enquiries to: Director

Founded:
1977

Organisation type and purpose:
Trade association.

Subject coverage:
Metal packaging; cans, tins, and other containers and closures.

Trade and statistical information:
UK statistics.

Access to staff:
Contact by e-mail
Hours: Mon to Fri, 0900 to 1700

Access to building, collection or gallery:
No access other than to staff

METALFORMING MACHINERY MAKERS ASSOCIATION LIMITED

Acronym or abbreviation: MMMA

The Cottage, Down End, Hook Norton, Oxfordshire, OX15 5LW

Tel: 01608 737129
Fax: 01295 253333
E-mail: enquiries@mmma.org.uk

Website:
http://www.mmma.org.uk
Details on Association and its services, member pages, member products and services.

Enquiries:
Enquiries to: Secretary

Founded:
1949

Organisation type and purpose:
Trade association.

Subject coverage:
Metal forming machinery trade.

Printed publications:
Handbook (free)

Access to staff:
Contact by letter, by telephone, by fax and by e-mail
Hours: Mon to Fri, 0900 to 1700

Member of:
METCOM

METALS INDUSTRY SKILLS & PERFORMANCE LIMITED

5–6 Meadowcourt, Amos Road, Sheffield, South Yorkshire, S9 1BX

Tel: 0114 244 6833
Fax: 0114 256 2855
E-mail: enquiries@metskill.co.uk

Website:
http://www.metskill.co.uk

Enquiries:
Enquiries to: Director, Marketing and Communications
Direct e-mail: d.vinall@metskill.co.uk

Founded:
1990

Organisation type and purpose:
Membership association (membership is by subscription), present number of members: 90 companies, training organisation, consultancy.
To raise the profile, quality and effectiveness of training, to contribute to the competitive success of the UK steel industry, to influence the training field.

Subject coverage:
All types of education, training, qualifications and skills for the steel and metals industries.

Trade and statistical information:
An analysis of steel industry skills.
Workforce Development Plan.

continued overleaf

Electronic and video publications:
Steel Industry Modern Apprenticeship (video)
Steel Industry NVQs (video)
Steel Industry Production NVQs (CD-ROM)

Publications list:
Available in print

Access to staff:
Contact by letter, by telephone, by fax, by e-mail
and via website. Appointment necessary.
Hours: Mon to Fri, 0900 to 1700

Access to building, collection or gallery:
Prior appointment required

Access for disabled people:
Parking provided, level entry, toilet facilities

Also at:
Metals Industry Skills and Performance Limited
Suite 15, Vision Point, Vaughan Trading Estate,
Sedgely Road East, Tipton, West Midlands, DY4
7UJ; tel: 0121 521 5511/5512/5513; fax: 0121 521
5510; e-mail: enquiries@metskill.co.uk

Has a division:
Metals Industry Competitive Enterprise (MICE)
e-mail: enquiries@metalsindustry.co.uk

Parent body:
UK Steel Association

METAMORPHIC ASSOCIATION

Acronym or abbreviation: MA

PO Box 32368, London, SW17 8YB

Tel: 0870 770 7984
Fax: 020 8672 5951
E-mail: metamorphicassoc@aol.com

Website:
http://www.metamorphicassociation.org.uk
Listing of events such as workshops, exhibitions
and open days. Lists of practitioners and teachers,
UK and international. Materials that can be
ordered from the Association including books,
videos etc. General information.

Enquiries:
Enquiries to: Director

Founded:
1979

Organisation type and purpose:
Membership association (membership is by
qualification), present number of members: 500+,
registered charity (charity number 326525),
training organisation.

Subject coverage:
Teaching and practice of the Metamorphic
Technique for self-healing and personal growth.

Printed publications:
Information Pack
Metamorphosis: Journal of the Metamorphic
Association
The Metamorphic Technique – Principles and
Practice (book)

Electronic and video publications:
Video and audio cassette

Publications list:
Available online and in print

Access to staff:
Contact by letter, by telephone, by fax, by e-mail
and in person. Appointment necessary.
Hours: Mon to Fri, 0930 to 1730

METANOIA INSTITUTE

13 North Common Road, Ealing, London, W5 2QB

Tel: 020 8579 2505
Fax: 020 8832 3070
E-mail: info@metanoia.ac.uk

Website:
http://www.metanoia.ac.uk

Enquiries:
Enquiries to: General Manager

Founded:
1994

Organisation type and purpose:
Membership association (membership is by
subscription), present number of members: 1000,
registered charity (charity number 1050175),
suitable for ages: adults, training organisation.
Training in counselling, psychotherapy and
counselling psychology – part-time.

Subject coverage:
Training in counselling, psychotherapy and
counselling psychology with optional academic
awards validated by Middlesex University at BA,
MSc, Masters, Doctorate level.

Library catalogue:
All or part available in-house

Printed publications:
Newsletter (quarterly for members)

Access to staff:
Contact by letter, by telephone, by fax, by e-mail,
in person and via website
Hours: Mon to Fri, 0900 to 1700
Special comments: Training at weekends 0930 to
1730.

Access to building, collection or gallery:
No prior appointment required
Hours: Mon to Fri, 0900 to 1700
Special comments: Trainees only at weekends.

Access for disabled people:
Ramped entry, toilet facilities

METEOROLOGICAL OFFICE

Weather Centres/Climate Offices:
Aberdeen Weather Centre
Lime Street, Aberdeen, AB11 5FJ; tel: 01224
210574; fax: 01224 210575
Belfast Climate Offices
32 College Street, Belfast, BT1 6BQ; tel: 028 9032
8457; fax: 028 9032 8457
Belfast Weather Centre
Meteorological Office, Belfast International
Airport, Belfast, BT29 4AB; tel: 028 9442 2339;
fax: 028 9445 4091
Birmingham Weather Centre
2040 The Crescent, Birmingham Business Park,
Birmingham, B37 7YE; tel: 0121 717 0575; fax:
0121 717 0577
Bristol Weather Centre
8th Floor, The Gaunt's House, Denmark Street,
Bristol, BS1 5DH; tel: 0117 927 9298; fax: 0117
927 9060
Cardiff Weather Centre
Southgate House, Wood Street, Cardiff, CF1
1EW; tel: 029 2039 7020; fax: 029 2039 0435
Glasgow Weather Centre
Wallace House, 220 St Vincent Street, Glasgow,
G2 5QD; tel: 0141 248 3451; fax: 0141 303 0101
Leeds Weather Centre
Oak House, Park Lane, Leeds, LS3 1EL; tel: 0113
245 1990; fax: 0113 2457760
London Weather Centre
127 Clerkenwell Road, London, EC1R 5DB; tel:
020 7242 3663; fax: 020 7404 4314
Manchester Weather Centre
Applicon House, Exchange Street, Stockport,
Cheshire, SK3 0ER; tel: 0161 477 1060; fax: 0161
476 0714
Newcastle Weather Centre
Portman House, Portland Road, Newcastle upon
Tyne, NE2 1AQ; tel: 0191 232 3808; fax: 0191 261
4965
Norwich Weather Centre
Rouen House, Rouen Road, Norwich, Norfolk,
NR1 1RB; tel: 01603 660779; fax: 01603 623531
Scottish Climate Office
Wallace House, 220 St Vincent Street, Glasgow,
G2 5QD; tel: 0141 303 0110; fax: 0141 303 0101
Southampton Weather Centre
160 High Street, Southampton, SO14 2BT; tel: 023
8022 8844; fax: 023 8022 8846

METHODIST ARCHIVES AND RESEARCH CENTRE

Acronym or abbreviation: JRULM

John Rylands University Library of Manchester,
Deansgate, Manchester, M3 3EH

Tel: 0161 834 5343 or 6765
Fax: 0161 834 5574
E-mail: peter.nockles@man.ac.uk

Website:
http://rylibweb.man.ac.uk/data1/dg/text/method
.html
General information, listings, collections, guides,
including some content of publication guides, e.g.,
to special collections, and catalogues, manuscript
and picture gallery, on-line exhibitions, Methodist
internet links.

Enquiries:
Enquiries to: Methodist Librarian

Organisation type and purpose:
University library.

Subject coverage:
Methodist church archives, Methodist history,
women's studies, family history, chapel history,
popular religion, social history, Methodist
theology, Wesley family.

**Museum or gallery collection, archive, or library
special collection:**
Books, letters, diaries, printed works of John
Wesley
Collection of Class Tickets and Circuit Plans
Diaries (some 80 volumes, of prominent
Methodists)
General pamphlet literature, 1562–1933 (6000
items)
Letters of Methodist Ministers (50,000 items)
Pamphlet literature of the Methodist Movement
(600 items)
Percy Collection (nucleus of a collection of hymn
books, some 3000)
Papers of John and Mary Fletcher, 43 boxes of
manuscripts

Printed publications:
Newsletter
Bulletin of the JRULM

Publications list:
Available in print

Access to staff:
Contact by letter, by telephone, by fax, by e-mail
and via website. Appointment necessary.
Hours: Mon to Fri, 1000 to 1730; Sat, 1000 to 1300
Special comments: E-mail or letter are preferred.

METHODIST MISSIONARY SOCIETY

Acronym or abbreviation: MMS

Methodist Church House, 25 Marylebone Road,
London, NW1 5JR

Tel: 020 7486 5502
Fax: 020 7467 3761
E-mail: helpdesk@methodistchurch.org.uk

Enquiries:
Enquiries to: Archivist
Direct tel: 020 7467 5166

Founded:
1818

Organisation type and purpose:
Registered charity (charity number Exception
Order No 180/1996).

Subject coverage:
Missionary work overseas since 1786.

**Museum or gallery collection, archive, or library
special collection:**
Records of British Methodist Missionary Work
(including photographs) from late 18th century
to 1945, world-wide cover and on microfiche
Later accessions continue to be made available,
19th century publications held with archives

Printed publications:
Detailed inventories in typescript of a large part of the Archives
Guide to the Archives (available free, from the publisher, to those who intend to order parts of the Archives on microfiche)

Microform publications:
Microfiche for purchase through publishing house

Access to staff:
Contact by letter. Letter of introduction required.
Hours: Mon to Thu, 0900 to 1700

Archives are held at the:
Special Collections Reading Room
  The Library, School of Oriental and African Studies, Thornhaugh Street, Russell Square, London, WC1H 0XG; tel: 020 7691 3347

METROPOLITAN BOROUGH OF BURY

Acronym or abbreviation: Bury Metro

Town Hall, Knowsley Street, Bury, Lancashire, BL9 0SW

Tel: 0161 253 5000
Fax: 0161 253 5079
E-mail: b.hargreaves@bury.gov.uk

Website:
http://www.bury.gov.uk
A to Z of services, list and details of all councillors, facts and figures on Bury Metro.

Enquiries:
Enquiries to: Information Officer

Founded:
1974

Organisation type and purpose:
Local government body (membership is by election or invitation), present number of members: 51.

Subject coverage:
Local government services.

Publications list:
Available in print

Access to staff:
Contact by letter, by telephone, by fax, by e-mail and via website. Appointment necessary.
Hours: Mon to Fri, 0900 to 1700

Access for disabled people:
Parking provided, ramped entry, level entry, access to all public areas, toilet facilities

METROPOLITAN BOROUGH OF DONCASTER

Acronym or abbreviation: DMBC

2 Priory Place, Doncaster, South Yorkshire, DN1 1BN

Tel: 01302 734444
Fax: 01302 734040

Website:
http://www.doncaster.gov.uk
Community website and information relating to Council, its services and councillors.

Enquiries:
Enquiries to: Chief Executive
Other contacts: Press and Public Relations Manager for media, public relations.

Founded:
1974

Organisation type and purpose:
Local government body.

Subject coverage:
Doncaster Borough, local authority matters.

Access to staff:
Contact by letter, by telephone, by fax and by e-mail

Hours: Mon to Fri, 0900 to 1700

Access to building, collection or gallery:
No prior appointment required

METROPOLITAN BOROUGH OF KNOWSLEY

Municipal Buildings, Archway Road, Huyton, Merseyside, L36 9YU

Tel: 0151 489 6000
Fax: 0151 443 3507
E-mail: knowsley@connect.org.uk

Website:
http://www.knowsley.gov.uk
general information and services.

Enquiries:
Enquiries to: Chief Executive
Direct tel: 0151 443 3772
Direct fax: 0151 443 3030
Direct e-mail: steve.gallagher@knowsley.gov.uk

Founded:
1974

Organisation type and purpose:
Local government body.

Subject coverage:
Local government services.

Printed publications:
Borough Guide
Knowsley Street Atlas
Who's Who in Knowsley

Electronic and video publications:
Bubble reef (CD-ROM)
Community Information Programme (CD-ROM)
Invest in Knowsley (CD-ROM)
Knowsley Wood (CD-ROM)
Lifeskills (CD-ROM)
Pixel (CD-ROM)

Access to staff:
Contact by letter, by telephone, by fax, by e-mail and via website
Hours: Mon to Fri, 0900 to 1700

Access to building, collection or gallery:
No access other than to staff

Access for disabled people:
Parking provided, level entry, toilet facilities

METROPOLITAN BOROUGH OF WIGAN

Acronym or abbreviation: Wigan Council

Town Hall, PO Box 36, Library Street, Wigan, Lancashire, WN1 1NN

Tel: 01942 244991
Fax: 01942 827451

Website:
http://www.wiganmbc.gov.uk
A to Z of services, internal telephone directory, press releases, and description of Council, etc.

Enquiries:
Enquiries to: Chief Executive
Direct tel: 01942 827001

Founded:
1246

Organisation type and purpose:
Local government body.

Subject coverage:
Local government services, all aspects of the lives of 310,000 citizens from architects to gravediggers.

Trade and statistical information:
Census details and demographic analyses, employment figures and resource procurement advice.

Non-library collection catalogue:
All or part available in-house

Library catalogue:
All or part available in-house

Printed publications:
The A to Z of Council Services
Wigan Borough Guide
Introducing Wigan Council
Wigan Town Trail
Leigh Town Trail

Publications list:
Available in print

Access to staff:
Contact by letter, by telephone, by fax, by e-mail and in person
Hours: Mon to Fri, 0900 to 1700

Access to building, collection or gallery:
No access other than to staff

Access for disabled people:
Ramped entry, access to all public areas, toilet facilities

METROPOLITAN POLICE ECONOMIC SPECIALIST CRIME OCU

Acronym or abbreviation: MPS Specialist Crime OCU

67–73 Buckingham Gate, London, SW1E 6BE

Tel: 020 7230 1212
Fax: 020 7230 1133

Enquiries:
Enquiries to: Grade 9
Direct tel: 020 7230 1220
Direct e-mail: fraud.alert@met.police.uk

Organisation type and purpose:
National government body.

Access to staff:
Contact by letter
Hours: Mon to Fri, 0900 to 1700

METROPOLITAN SOCIETY FOR THE BLIND

Acronym or abbreviation: MSB

Lantern House, 102 Bermondsey Street, London, SE1 3UB

Tel: 020 7403 6184
Fax: 020 7234 0708
E-mail: enquiries@msb.gb.com

Enquiries:
Enquiries to: Secretary

Founded:
1834

Subject coverage:
The MSB assists blind and partially sighted residents of 12 Inner London Boroughs and the City of London.

Access to staff:
Contact by letter, by telephone, by fax and by e-mail
Hours: Mon to Fri, 0930 to 1600

Access for disabled people:
Level entry, access to all public areas, toilet facilities

MG OCTAGON CAR CLUB

Unit 1–3, Parchfields Farm, Trent Valley, Rugeley, Staffordshire, WS15 3HB

Tel: 01889 574666
Fax: 01889 574555
E-mail: harry@mgoctagoncarclub.com

Website:
http://www.mgoctagoncarclub.com

Enquiries:
Enquiries to: Secretary

Founded:
1969

continued overleaf

Organisation type and purpose:
International organisation, membership association (membership is by subscription). Caters for Pre-56 MGs only.

Subject coverage:
Pre-1956 MG parts, literature and publications, advise and assistance, valuations.

Museum or gallery collection, archive, or library special collection:
Chassis files, workshop manuals, parts lists, hand books

Printed publications:
Bulletin (monthly)

Publications list:
Available online and in print

Access to staff:
Contact by letter, by telephone, by fax, by e-mail and via website. Appointment necessary.
Hours: Mon to Fri, 0900 to 2200

MG OWNERS' CLUB

Octagon House, 1 Over Road, Swavesey, Cambridgeshire, CB24 4QZ

Tel: 01954 231125
Fax: 01954 232106
E-mail: mginfo@mgownersclub.co.uk

Website:
http://www.mgownersclub.co.uk
Technical archive, forthcoming events, local area meeings, photo gallery, on-line regalia sales, worldwide contacts, on-line membership application, classified cars and spares adverts, race championship news, scrolling MG news feed, MG model history.
http://www.mgocspares.co.uk
Full on-line range of MG spares & accessories
http://www.mgocworkshop.co.uk
Comprehensive coverage of the MG Owners' Club Workshop facility that undertakes all mechanical and bodywork repair with MG Rover trained technicians.

Enquiries:
Enquiries to: Secretary

Founded:
1973

Organisation type and purpose:
Membership association (membership is by subscription), present number of members: 30,000. To assist all owners of MG motor cars to run and maintain their vehicles at reasonable cost.

Subject coverage:
MG motor cars from 1920s to present day.

Trade and statistical information:
Full technical support service available for members, by telephone, email, written enquiry, fax, for all MG models.
Full range of spares available for visitors and on mail order, competitive specialist insurance scheme.

Printed publications:
Enjoying MG (magazine, monthly on subscription)
Recommended supplier directory
Buying MG guide
Other technical publications

Electronic and video publications:
Full electronic version of monthly magazine on-line for subscribing members

Access to staff:
Contact by letter, by telephone, by fax, by e-mail, in person and via website
Hours: Mon to Fri, 0900 to 1730; Sat, 1000 to 1300

Access for disabled people:
Parking provided, ramped entry, toilet facilities

MG OWNERS' CLUB (NORTHERN IRELAND)

Acronym or abbreviation: MGOC(NI)

17 Meadowlands, Newtownabbey, Co Antrim, BT37 0VL

Tel: 028 9086 2807
E-mail: samone@btinternet.com

Website:
http://www.mgocni.co.uk

Enquiries:
Enquiries to: Secretary

Founded:
1981

Organisation type and purpose:
Membership association.

Subject coverage:
The MG car in Northern Ireland.

Access to staff:
Contact by letter and by e-mail
Hours: Mon to Fri, 0900 to 1700

Affiliated to:
MGOC, Swavesey

MI-21 WORLD METAL INDEX

Acronym or abbreviation: MI-21 WMI

Sheffield Libraries, Archives and Information, Central Library, Surrey Street, Sheffield, South Yorkshire, S1 1XZ

Tel: 0114 273 4714; 0114 273 4744
Fax: 0114 275 7405
E-mail: wmi@sheffield.gov.uk

Website:
http://www.sheffield.gov.uk/worldmetalindex
http://www.mi-21.com

Enquiries:
Enquiries to: Information LIbrary Officer

Organisation type and purpose:
Local government body.
Information service.

Subject coverage:
The World Metal Index is the key to a unique collection of standards and specifications, trade literature and technical journals on both ferrous and non-ferrous metals. Over 200,000 individual metal grades are included, both current and historical. Together with Namtec and TWI, MI-21 World Metal Index provides in-depth information and technical support services. 20,000 datasheets currently available online by subscription. Access to remaining 180,000 as well as additonal resources and services of WMI is by telephone, fax and e-mail.
24-hour access to search the database by grade name, trade name, chemical and mechanical properties.
Information on metal properties, heat treatment, working, fabrication, welding, machining, corrosion, fatigue, creep and rupture properties.

Information services:
Metals identification service; metals information service.

Museum or gallery collection, archive, or library special collection:
National standards and specifications: BS, BSEN, BSENISIO, ASTM, AMS, DIN, AFNOR, UNI; emerging producer nations' standards, e.g. China

Trade and statistical information:
Trade literature collection from metal producers and suppliers.

Access to staff:
Contact by letter, by telephone, by fax, by e-mail and via website. Appointment necessary. All charged.
Hours: Mon to Fri, 0930 to 1630

Links with:
National Metals Technology Centre (Namtec)
Swinden House, Moorgate Road, Rotherham, South Yorkshire, S60 3AR; tel: 01709 724990; fax: 01709 724999; e-mail: info@namtec.co.uk; website: http://www.namtec.co.uk

MID DEVON DISTRICT COUNCIL

The Great House, 1 St Peter Street, Tiverton, Devon, EX16 6NY

Tel: 01884 255255\ Minicom no. 01884 255294
Fax: 01884 258852

Enquiries:
Enquiries to: Public Relations Co-ordinator
Direct e-mail: communications@middevon.gov.uk

Organisation type and purpose:
Local government body.

Subject coverage:
Provision of local services ranging from planning to recycling.

Publications list:
Available in print

Access to staff:
Contact by letter, by telephone, by fax, by e-mail and in person
Hours: Mon to Thu, 0900 to 1700; Fri, 0900 to 1630

MID SUFFOLK DISTRICT COUNCIL

Council Offices, 131 High Street, Needham Market, Suffolk, IP6 8DL

Tel: 01449 720711\ Minicom no. 01140 727120
Fax: 01449 721946

Website:
http://www.mid-suffolk-dc.gov.uk

Enquiries:
Enquiries to: Publicity and Information Officer
Direct tel: 01449 727193
Direct fax: 01449 727187
Direct e-mail: elizabeth.woolnough@midsuffolk.co.uk

Organisation type and purpose:
Local government body.

Access to staff:
Contact by letter, by telephone and by fax
Hours: Mon to Fri, 0900 to 1700

MIDDLE EAST CENTRE LIBRARY AND ARCHIVES

Acronym or abbreviation: MEC

St Antony's College, Woodstock Road, Oxford, OX2 6JF

Tel: 01865 284700
Fax: 01865 311475
E-mail: mastan.ebtehaj@sant.ox.ac.uk

Website:
http://www.sant.ox.ac.uk/areastudies/middle-east.shtml
The Centre's web page with links to the library and archives.

Enquiries:
Enquiries to: Librarian
Direct tel: 01865 284764
Other contacts: Archivist, tel 01865 284706, email debbie.usher@sant.ox.ac.uk

Organisation type and purpose:
University department or institute.
Regional centre of postgraduate college of Oxford University.

Subject coverage:
Modern history, politics, international affairs and economics of the Middle East.

Museum or gallery collection, archive, or library special collection:
Papers of many Middle East diplomats

Access to staff:
Contact by letter, by fax and by e-mail.
Appointment necessary. Access for members only.
Letter of introduction required.
Hours: Mon to Fri, 0930 to 1245 and 1345 to 1715

Includes the:
Middle East Centre
tel: 01865 284764

MIDDLE EAST LIBRARIES COMMITTEE (UK)

Acronym or abbreviation: MELCOM(UK)

The Library, School of Oriental and African Studies, University of London, Thornhaugh Street, Russell Square, London, WC1H 0XG

Tel: 020 7898 4152
Fax: 020 7436 3844
E-mail: lis-middleeast@mailbase.ac.uk

Website:
http://www.ex.ac.uk/melcom/

Enquiries:
Enquiries to: Secretary
Direct tel: 020 7323 6099
Direct e-mail: pc7@soas.ac.uk

Founded:
1967

Organisation type and purpose:
Voluntary organisation, university department or institute.
Libraries having substantial Middle East collections, and of individuals in the UK concerned with collecting, organising and making available materials on the Middle East.

Subject coverage:
Middle Eastern studies from the rise of Islam to the present; Islamic studies; Arabic, Persian and Turkish studies.

Museum or gallery collection, archive, or library special collection:
Collections are held by most of the member libraries; notable are those of Cambridge University Library; Middle East Centre, St Antony's College Oxford; Durham University Library; British Library Oriental Collections; London University School of Oriental and African Studies Library; John Rylands University Library of Manchester; Exeter University Library and The Bodleian Library, Oxford Documents are held by the Documentation Unit, Centre for Middle Eastern and Islamic Studies, University of Durham and the Documentation Unit, Centre for Arab Gulf Studies, University of Exeter; Selly Oak Colleges Library, Birmingham; Edinburgh University Library

Printed publications:
Arab Islamic Bibliography, 1977
Arabic Biographical Dictionaries, 1987
Bibliographical Guide to Iran, 1982
Books From the Arab World: a guide to selection and acquisition, 1988
Collections in British Libraries on Middle Eastern and Islamic Studies, 1982
Introductory Guide To Middle Eastern and Islamic Bibliography, 1990
Middle East and Islam: a bibliographical introduction, (1979 and Supplement, 1977–83, 1986)
Middle East Materials in United Kingdom and Irish Libraries: a directory, 1982
Middle Eastern photographic collections in the United Kingdom, 1989
Official Publications on the Middle East: a selective guide to the statistical sources, 1985
Periodicals in Turkish and Turkic Languages: a union list of holdings in UK Libraries, 1993
The Intifada: a bibliography of books and articles 1987–1992, 1993

Union Catalogue of Arabic Serials and Newspapers in British Libraries, 1977
Union Catalogue of Persian Serials and Newspapers in British Libraries, 1985
Order printed publications from: Joppa Books Limited
68 High Road, Byfleet, Surrey, KT14 7QL, tel: 01932 336777, fax: 01932 348881, e-mail: joppa@dial.pipex .com

Publications list:
Available online

Access to staff:
Contact by e-mail
Hours: Mon to Fri, 0900 to 1700

Affiliated to:
British Society for Middle Eastern Studies

MIDDLE TEMPLE LIBRARY

Formal name: The Honourable Society of the Middle Temple Library

Middle Temple Lane, London, EC4Y 9BT

Tel: 020 7427 4830
Fax: 020 7427 4831
E-mail: library@middletemple.org.uk

Website:
http://www.middletemplelibrary.org.uk

Enquiries:
Enquiries to: Keeper of the Library

Founded:
1641

Organisation type and purpose:
Legal library.

Subject coverage:
Law.

Museum or gallery collection, archive, or library special collection:
150,000 vols of mainly English law
Law Reports
Government publications
Ecclesiastical Collection
Rare Books Collection
EU Collection
American Collection
Capital Punishment Collection
Middle Temple Archive (administrative, financial, membership and property records of the Inn since 1501)

Non-library collection catalogue:
All or part available in-house

Library catalogue:
All or part available online

Access to staff:
Contact by letter, by telephone, by fax and by e-mail. Appointment necessary. Access for members only. Non-members charged.
Hours: Term time: Mon to Thu, 0900 to 2000; Fri, 0900 to 1900; every fourth Sat in rotation with the other Inns of Court Libraries, 1000 to 1700

Access to building, collection or gallery:
Private library for use by members of the four Inns of Court. Enquiries under special circumstances from non-members, for whom access is strictly by appointment. Visits for research by appointment only.
Hours: Term time: Mon to Thu, 0900 to 2000; Fri, 0900 to 1900. Vacation time: Mon to Fri, 0900 to 1730

Access for disabled people:
Wheelchair ramp at library entrance; lift to all floors

MIDDLESBROUGH LIBRARIES AND INFORMATION

Central Library, Victoria Square, Middlesbrough, TS1 2AY

Tel: 01642 729001

Fax: 01642 729954
E-mail: reference_library@middlesbrough.gov.uk

Website:
http://www.middlesbrough.gov.uk
Middlesbrough Borough Council website.
Information on all departments, including the public library service.

Enquiries:
Enquiries to: Reference Librarian

Organisation type and purpose:
Local government body, public library.

Subject coverage:
All areas covered, local history of Middlesbrough and surrounding area, North Yorkshire and South Durham.

Museum or gallery collection, archive, or library special collection:
Dickie Collection (maritime subjects)
William Kelly Collection (mostly theological works and bibles)
All major national newspapers published in England from 1990 to 1996 on CD-ROM
North Eastern Daily Gazette, Middlesbrough, 1869 to present (microfilm); Times, 1785 to present, many other local and national newspapers

Library catalogue:
All or part available online

Printed publications:
Leaflets on the Library's services

Access to staff:
Contact by letter, by telephone, by fax, by e-mail and in person. Appointment necessary.
Hours: Mon, Tue, Thu, 0930 to 1900; Wed, Fri, Sat, 0930 to 1700

Comprises:
11 libraries

Links with:
other Teesside Archives

MIDDLESEX UNIVERSITY

Learning Resources, The Sheppard Library, The Burroughs, London, NW4 4BT

Tel: 020 8411 5234
Fax: 020 8362 5163
E-mail: via website

Website:
http://www.lr.mdx.ac.uk/
Front page to various library services including the catalogue.

Enquiries:
Enquiries to: Director of Learning Resources and University Librarian

Founded:
1973

Organisation type and purpose:
University library.

Subject coverage:
Accountancy and finance; business; mathematics; business studies; management; marketing; economics; computing science; product design; geography; pollution; art and design; interior design; humanities; law; sociology and social policy; social work; psychology; criminology; architecture and interior design; education; performance arts (music, dance, drama); computer graphics; flood hazard research; hotel catering and tourism management; psychology; robotics; transport planning and management; teacher training; education; nursing; health studies.

Museum or gallery collection, archive, or library special collection:
Runnymede Trust Library
Black Theatre Forum Archive
Bernie Grant Archive
Hall-Carpenter Archive (jointly held with BLPES), a national lesbian and gay archive, 40,000 items of press cuttings

continued overleaf

Non-library collection catalogue:
All or part available online

Library catalogue:
All or part available online

Access to staff:
Contact by letter, by telephone, by fax, by e-mail
and via website. Appointment necessary. Letter of
introduction required. Non-members charged.
Hours: Hours vary (term time only) by campus,
within: Mon to Thu, 0900 to 2000; Fri, 0900 to 1800;
Sat, 1100 to 1700

Access to building, collection or gallery:
Hours: Mon to Thu, 0830 to 2200; Fri, 0830 to 2000;
Sat, 1100 to 1700

Access for disabled people:
Parking provided
Special comments: Access arrangements vary at each
campus.

Campuses at:
Archway
    10 Highgate Hill, London, N19 5ND
Cat Hill
    Barnet, Hertfordshire, EN4 8HT; tel: 020 8411
    5042
Hendon
    The Burroughs, London, NW4 4BT
Trent Park
    Bramley Road, London, N14 4YZ

MIDLAND RAILWAY CENTRE

Butterley Station, Ripley, Derbyshire, DE5 3QZ

Tel: 01773 747674
Fax: 01773 570721
E-mail: information@midlandrailwaycentre.co.uk

Enquiries:
Enquiries to: Manager

Founded:
1969

Organisation type and purpose:
Membership association (membership is by
subscription), present number of members: 1200,
voluntary organisation, registered charity (charity
number 502278), museum, training organisation.

Subject coverage:
Railway history, demonstration signal box,
Victorian railwayman's church. 3.5 mile heritage
railway, Golden Valley Light Railway (2ft gauge),
Butterley Park Miniature Railway (3.5 and 5 in
gauges), model railways.

**Museum or gallery collection, archive, or library
special collection:**
Archive of railway books, records and
    photography
Collection of railway equipment, mainly Midland
    Railway, its predecessors and successors
Princess Royal Class Locomotive Trust Depot
Midland Diesel Group collection of main line
    diesel power
Stationary Power Gallery

Printed publications:
The Wyvern (quarterly magazine)
Guide
Stockbook

Access to staff:
Contact by letter, by telephone and by fax.
Appointment necessary.
Hours: Mon to Fri, 0900 to 1700

Access to building, collection or gallery:
Prior appointment required
Hours: Static display: daily, 1000 to 1615
Closed Christmas Day

Access for disabled people:
Parking provided, toilet facilities

Affiliated to:
Midland Railway Enterprises plc
Midland Railway Trust

MIDLANDS AGRICULTURAL
INFORMATION GROUP

Acronym or abbreviation: MidAIG

Warwickshire College, Moreton Morrell Centre,
Moreton Morrell, Warwick, CV35 9BL

Tel: 01926 318278
Fax: 01926 318300

Enquiries:
Enquiries to: Membership Secretary
Direct e-mail: librarymm@warksccl.ac.uk

Founded:
1982

Organisation type and purpose:
Voluntary organisation.
An informal group of information services
personnel who meet annually with an informal
network to assist each other professionally –
interlibrary co-operation.

Subject coverage:
Generally land-based industries: agriculture,
horticulture, conservation of natural resources,
food science and applied biology, equine industry,
small animal care, arboriculture, construction,
greenkeeping.

Access to staff:
Contact by letter, by telephone, by fax and by e-
mail. Appointment necessary.
Hours: Mon to Thu, 0830 to 2200; Fri, 0830 to 1700;
Sat, 1000 to 1600
Vacations: Mon to Fri, 0915 to 1645

Access to building, collection or gallery:
Prior appointment required

Access for disabled people:
Level entry, access to all public areas, toilet
facilities

Members are:
Librarians and information professionals and other
staff in libraries and information services with an
agricultural/land-based industry related subject
area or interest

MIDLANDS CLUB CRICKET
CONFERENCE

Acronym or abbreviation: MCCC

65 Tilesford Close, Monkspath, Solihull, West
Midlands, B90 4YF

Tel: 0121 744 6746; 07890 739489
E-mail: murray.ali@gmail.com

Website:
http://www.mccc.co.uk

Enquiries:
Enquiries to: Honorary Secretary

Founded:
1947

Organisation type and purpose:
Membership association, voluntary organisation.

Subject coverage:
All matters relating to cricket.

Printed publications:
Newsletter (quarterly, free to members, for sale to
    non-members)
Year book (free to members, for sale to non-
    members)

Access to staff:
Contact by letter, by telephone, by e-mail and via
website
Hours: Mon to Fri, 0900 to 2100

MIDLOTHIAN COUNCIL

Midlothian House, Buccleuch Street, Dalkeith,
Midlothian, EH22 1DN

Tel: 0131 270 7500\ Minicom no. 0131 271 3610
Fax: 0131 271 3050

Website:
http://www.midlothian.gov.uk
Information on Midlothian Council and links to
related websites.
http://www.earl.org.uk/partners/midlothian/index
.html
Information on libraries only.

Enquiries:
Enquiries to: Communication Manager
Direct tel: 0131 271 3425
Direct fax: 0131 271 3536
Direct e-mail: Susan.Whiteford@midlothian.gov.uk

Founded:
1996

Organisation type and purpose:
Local government body.

Subject coverage:
Information about council services available to the
people of Midlothian, and how to access them.

Library catalogue:
All or part available in-house

Printed publications:
Midlothian News (free to all householders in
    Midlothian)
Business News (free to Midlothian business
    community)

Publications list:
Available online

Access to staff:
Contact by letter, by e-mail and via website
Hours: Mon to Fri, 0930 to 1530

Access to building, collection or gallery:
No prior appointment required

MIDLOTHIAN COUNCIL LIBRARY
SERVICES

Library Headquarters, 2 Clerk Street, Loanhead,
Midlothian, EH20 9DR

Tel: 0131 271 3980
Fax: 0131 440 4635
E-mail: library.hq@midlothian.gov.uk

Website:
http://www.midlothian.gov.uk/library

Enquiries:
Enquiries to: Library Services Manager
Direct tel: 0131 271 3970
Direct e-mail: alan.reid@midlothian.gov.uk

Founded:
1996

Organisation type and purpose:
Local government body, public library.

Subject coverage:
General, local history of Midlothian.

**Museum or gallery collection, archive, or library
special collection:**
Black Collection (Penicuik historical interest)
Midlothian Council Archive

Library catalogue:
All or part available online

Printed publications:
The Dalkeith Tolbooth and Market Cross (D R
    Smith, £5)
Publications on local subjects include:
Early Railways of the Lothians (Worling M J, £3:95)
From Rosewell to the Rhondda (£2.95)
Mauricewood Disaster (Donaldson A B, £2.95)
Midlothian Gravestones (Donaldson I, £6.95)
Music of Midlothian (booklet and cassette)
The Prisoners at Penicuik – French and Other
    Prisoners of War 1803–1814 (MacDougall I,
    £3.95)
New Statistical Account of Midlothian (3 volumes)
The Origins of Street Names in Dalkeith
    (Williamson M G, £6.99)

Electronic and video publications:
Newtongrange Silver Band Play Variations (CD
    and cassette)

Music of Midlothian (cassette)
The Midlothian 2000 CD-ROM (£15)
Scottish Brewers Silver Band, Newtongrange (CD
  and cassette)

Publications list:
Available online and in print

Access to staff:
Contact by letter, by telephone, by fax, by e-mail
and via website. Appointment necessary.
Hours: Mon to Thu, 0900 to 1700; Fri, 0900 to 1530
Special comments: Opening hours vary, contact
individual branch.

Access for disabled people:
Parking provided, ramped entry, toilet facilities

Branch libraries:
Bonnyrigg Library
  31 Polton Street, Bonnyrigg, Midlothian, EH19
  3HB; tel: 0131 663 6762; fax: 0131 654 9019; e-
  mail: bonnyrigg.library@midlothian.gov.uk
Dalkeith Library
  White Hart Street, Dalkeith, Midlothian, EH22
  1AE; tel: 0131 663 2083; fax: 0131 654 9029; e-
  mail: dalkeith.library@midlothian.gov.uk
Danderhall Library
  1a Campview, Danderhall, Midlothian, EH22
  1QD; tel: 0131 663 9293; e-mail: danderhall
  .library@midlothian.gov.uk
Gorebridge Library
  98 Hunterfield Road, Gorebridge, Midlothian,
  EH23 4TT; tel: 01875 820630; fax: 01875 823657;
  e-mail: gorebridge.library@midlothian.gov.uk
Loanhead Library
  George Avenue, Loanhead, Midlothian, EH20
  9HD; tel: 0131 440 0824; e-mail: loanhead
  .library@midlothian.gov.uk
Local Studies Library
  2 Clerk Street, Loanhead, Midlothian, EH20 9DR;
  tel: 0131 271 3976; fax: 0131 440 4635; e-mail:
  local.studies@midlothian.gov.uk
Mayfield Library
  Stone Avenue, Mayfield, Dalkeith, Midlothian,
  EH22 5PB; tel: 0131 663 2126; e-mail: mayfield
  .library@midlothian.gov.uk
Newtongrange Library
  St David's, Newtongrange, Midlothian, EH22
  4LG; tel: 0131 663 1816; fax: 0131 654 1990; e-
  mail: newtongrange.library@midlothian.gov.uk
Penicuik Library
  The Penicuik Centre, Carlops Road, Penicuik
  EH26 9EP; tel: 01968 664050; fax: 01968 679408;
  e-mail: penicuik.library@midlothian.gov.uk
Roslin Library
  9 Main Street, Roslin, Midlothian, EH25 9LD; tel:
  0131 448 2781; e-mail: roslin.library@midlothian
  .gov.uk
Woodburn Library
  Dalkeith Leisure Centre, 6 Woodburn Road,
  Dalkeith, Midlothian, EH22 2AR; tel: 0131 654
  4323; e-mail: woodburn.library@midlothian.gov
  .uk

Parent body:
Midlothian Council
  Midlothian House, Buccleuch Street, Dalkeith,
  Midlothian, EH22 1DJ; tel: 0131 270 7500; fax:
  0131 271 3050; e-mail: enquiries@midlothian.gov
  .uk

MIGRAINE ACTION

Acronym or abbreviation: MA

27 East Street, Leicester, LE1 6NB

Tel: 0116 275 8317
Fax: 0116 254 2023
E-mail: info@migraine.org.uk

Website:
http://www.migraine.org.uk
Packed with information on migraine and other
headache disorders. It also features the latest
migraine news, event details, research information
and fundraising news. There is also an interactive
web and 'ask the expert' forum where migraineurs
can share their experiences and management tips
with like-minded individuals.
http://www.migraine.org.uk/youngmigraineurs

Migraine Action has 3 age-specific websites
especially created for children affected by
migraine, which can all be accessed here. There is
an accompanying 17-piece information resource
pack for parents / carers, teachers, school nurses
and young migraineurs themselves.

Founded:
1958

Organisation type and purpose:
Migraine Action is the UK's leading charity
dedicated to individuals affected by migraine. It is
a registered charity that aims to bridge the gap
between the migraineur and the medical world by
providing information on all aspects of the
condition and its management.
It strives to provide an excellent patient-led,
compassionate and empathetic support
community for individuals affected by migraine. It
has as its main aims:
1. To provide information and friendly, positive
reassurance, understanding and encouragement to
migraine sufferers and their families.
2. To encourage and support research and
investigation into migraine, its causes, diagnosis,
prevention and treatment.
3. To gather and pass on information about
treatments available for the control and relief of
migraine and to facilitate an exchange of
information on the subject.
Migraine Action is funded entirely by donations
and members' subscriptions. UK membership
gives access to a telephone, postal and e-mail
information and a support line, a quarterly
newsletter, access to booklets and information on
the website, and regular updates from research
studies and trials. UK enhanced membership
additionally provides access to the web and 'Ask
the Expert' forums, as well as access to booklets,
online reports and regular communications from
Migraine Action on related subjects.

Subject coverage:
Has a wide range of information booklets available
on migraine, including preventative and acute
treatments, migraine triggers, stress management,
complementary therapies, and migraine in
children and young people.

Information services:
Dedicated telephone helpline: 0116 275 8317, to
give information and advice to migraineurs and
those affected by migraine.

Education services:
Migraine education days held throughout the UK.
These give migraineurs the opportunity to meet
with others affected in their area, hear from experts
in the field, and learn more about Migraine
Action's work on their behalf.

Printed publications:
Challenging Migraine (quarterly newsletter; gives
  updates on treatments, research and Migraine
  Action's work, and also shares members'
  experiences and tips)
Over 100 leaflets produced on various aspects of
  migraine
Order printed publications from: Visit our online shop
for a full list of leaflets: http://
www.migraine.org.uk/shop; tel: 0116 275 8317; e-
mail: info@migraine.org.uk

Publications list:
Available online

Access to staff:
Contact by letter, by telephone, by fax, by e-mail
and via website. Appointment necessary.
Hours: Mon to Fri, 0900 to 1700

Access to building, collection or gallery:
Hours: Mon to Fri, 0900 to 1700

Access for disabled people:
Parking provided, ramped entry, toilet facilities

MIGRAINE TRUST

55–56 Russell Square, London, WC1B 4HP

Tel: 020 7436 1336

Fax: 020 7436 2880
E-mail: info@migrainetrust.org

Website:
http://www.migrainetrust.org
Information about migraine, other headaches and
their management, latest news, upcoming events,
how to support the Trust and get involved, how to
contact the Trust.

Enquiries:
Enquiries to: Information and Enquiry Service
Direct tel: 020 7462 6601

Founded:
1965

Organisation type and purpose:
National organisation, registered charity (charity
number 1081300).
The Migraine Trust is the health and medical
research charity for migraine in the United
Kingdom. It is committed to funding and
promoting research, raising awareness and
providing information.

Subject coverage:
An Information and Enquiry Service is available
for questions people may have about migraine,
other headaches and their management. All
information is based on the best available
evidence.
The Migraine Trust produces a range of fact sheets
and information packs covering such issues as
medication, specialist clinics, young migraine
sufferers and managing migraine in the workplace.

Information services:
Information and Enquiry Service –for questions
about migraine, other headaches and their
management; tel: 020 7462 6601; e-mail:
info@migrainetrust.org.

Printed publications:
Migraine News (three times per year) journal sent
  to supporters.
The Migraine Trust produces a range of fact sheets
  and information packs covering such issues as
  medication, specialist clinics, keeping a diary,
  trigger factors, young migraine sufferers and
  managing migraine in the workplace.
Order printed publications from: website: http://
www.migrainetrust.org/C2B/document_tree/
ViewADocument.asp?ID=99&CatID=93

Publications list:
Available online and in print

Access to staff:
Contact by letter, by telephone, by fax, by e-mail
and via website
Hours: Answerphone before 0900 and after 1700

MIGRANTS RESOURCE CENTRE

24 Churton Street, London, SW1V 2LP

Tel: 020 7834 2505

Website:
http://www.migrantsresourcecentre.org.uk

Organisation type and purpose:
The Centre works with migrants and refugees from
all over the world, providing assistance and advice
and helping to enable full participation in British
society.

Information services:
Online Centre.
Legal Advice Team at: Derry House, Penfold
Street, London, NW8 8HJ; tel: 0845 241 0961

MILITARY HERALDRY SOCIETY

The Cloth Insignia Research and Collectors Society,
Windyridge, 27 Sandbrook, Ketley, Telford,
Shropshire, TF1 5BB

Tel: 01952 270221

Website:
http://www.militaryheraldrysociety.co.uk

continued overleaf

Enquiries:
Enquiries to: Publicity Officer
Direct tel: 01952 270221
Direct e-mail: billbowbagins@hotmail.com

Founded:
1951

Organisation type and purpose:
International organisation, membership
association (membership is by subscription),
present number of members: 320, research
organisation.
Collecting.

Subject coverage:
Research and study of military cloth insignia
(formation signs, shoulder titles, regimental and
unit flashes, skill-at-arms and similar cloth items).

Printed publications:
Formation Sign (journal, quarterly)

Access to staff:
Contact by letter, by telephone and by e-mail

MILITARY VEHICLE TRUST

Acronym or abbreviation: MVT

General Secretary, Meadowhead Cottage,
Beaumaris Avenue, Blackburn, Lancashire, BB2
4TP

Tel: 01254 202253
E-mail: gensec@mvt.org.uk

Website:
http://www.mvt.org.uk

Enquiries:
Enquiries to: Membership Secretary
Direct tel: 0845 475 1941
Direct e-mail: membershipsec@mvt.org.uk

Founded:
1968

Organisation type and purpose:
Membership association, registered charity.
Contact with owners of all ex-military vehicles to
share information and give advice on preservation,
and to provide details of club activities. Vehicle
verification service. Shop. Monitoring of new
legislation to ensure continuing use of preserved
vehicles.

Subject coverage:
Preservation and restoration of historic military
vehicles.

**Museum or gallery collection, archive, or library
special collection:**
Vehicle manual library (for the use of members)

Library catalogue:
All or part available online

Printed publications:
Windscreen (magazine, quarterly, for members)
Green Sheet (newsletter, 6 a year, for members)

Access to staff:
Contact by letter, by telephone, by e-mail and via
website
Hours: Evenings and weekends, up to 2100

MILTON KEYNES & NORTH BUCKS CHAMBER OF COMMERCE

Acronym or abbreviation: MKCOC

World Trade Center @ The Hub, 9 Rillaton Walk,
Central Milton Keynes, MK9 2FZ

Tel: 01908 259000
Fax: 01908 246799
E-mail: enquiry@mk-chamber.co.uk

Website:
http://www.mk-chamber.co.uk
Information about the organisation.

Enquiries:
Enquiries to: Information Services Manager
Direct tel: 01908 259433

Founded:
1995

Organisation type and purpose:
Membership association (membership is by
subscription), present number of members: over
1400.
Business Link brings together a wide range of
support services for growing businesses in Milton
Keynes. Part of a national network it is committed
to improving the competitiveness of UK Industry
and Commerce.

Subject coverage:
International trade, Europe desk, business
information (local, UK and worldwide).

**Museum or gallery collection, archive, or library
special collection:**
Business and trade directories, reference books
CD-ROM and online databases

Trade and statistical information:
International trade department covers export and
import worldwide.
Milton Keynes and North Bucks Economic survey.

Printed publications:
Opportunity

Access to staff:
Contact by letter, by telephone, by fax and by e-
mail. Appointment necessary. All charged.
Hours: Mon to Fri, 0900 to 1700

Access to building, collection or gallery:
Prior appointment required

Affiliated to:
Association of British Chambers of Commerce
Business Link

Parent body:
Milton Keynes and North Buckinghamshire
Chamber of Commerce

MILTON KEYNES COLLEGE LEARNING RESOURCES CENTRE

Chaffron Way Campus, Woughton Campus West,
Leadenhall West, Milton Keynes,
Buckinghamshire, MK6 5LP

Tel: 01908 684444\ Minicom no. 01908 684401
Fax: 01908 684399

Enquiries:
Enquiries to: Learning Resources Manager
Direct tel: 01908 684429

Organisation type and purpose:
Suitable for ages: 16+.

Subject coverage:
Business, administrative, secretarial subjects, social
care; non-advanced engineering (electrical,
electronic, mechanical, motor vehicle), hospitality
and catering, beauty therapy, sport and leisure and
general education, art and design.

Library catalogue:
All or part available in-house

Access to staff:
Contact by letter, by telephone, by fax and in
person
Hours: Term time: Mon to Thu; 0900 to 2000; Fri,
1000 to 1600
Vacations: hours will differ

Other addresses:
Bletchley Centre
 Sherwood Drive, Bletchley, Milton Keynes,
 Buckinghamshire, MK3 6DR; tel: 01908 684444;
 fax: 01908 684199

MILTON KEYNES COUNCIL

Acronym or abbreviation: MKC

Civic Offices, 1 Saxon Gate East, Milton Keynes,
Buckinghamshire, MK9 3HG

Tel: 01908 691691\ Minicom no. 01908 252727
Fax: 01908 252456

Enquiries:
Enquiries to: Public Relations Manager

Founded:
1997

Organisation type and purpose:
Local government body.

Subject coverage:
Local government services.

MILTON KEYNES LEARNING CITY LIBRARIES NETWORK

Open University Library, Walton Hall, Milton
Keynes, Buckinghamshire, MK7 6AA

Tel: 01908 653254
Fax: 01908 653571

Website:
http://www.mkweb.co.uk/mk-libraries-network
http://www.mkinspire.org.uk

Enquiries:
Enquiries to: Chairman
Direct e-mail: n.whitsed@open.ac.uk
Other contacts: Secretary

Founded:
2004

Formerly called:
Beds & Bucks Information Plan (BBi)

Organisation type and purpose:
Collaboration of local libraries.
To facilitate and encourage the use of all major
libraries in the Milton Keynes area by everyone
who lives, works, or studies in Milton Keynes.

Subject coverage:
Education, health, co-operative training.

Non-library collection catalogue:
All or part available online

Library catalogue:
All or part available online

Electronic and video publications:
Electronic products all web-based

Publications list:
Available online

Access to staff:
Contact by letter, by telephone, by fax, by e-mail
and via website. Appointment necessary.

MIND (THE MENTAL HEALTH CHARITY)

Formal name: National Association for Mental
Health

Granta House, 15–19 Broadway, Stratford,
London, E15 4BQ

Tel: 020 8519 2122
Fax: 020 8522 1725
E-mail: contact@mind.org.uk

Website:
http://www.mind.org.uk

Enquiries:
Enquiries to: Administrator
Direct tel: 020 8215 2235
Direct fax: 020 8215 2468
Direct e-mail: k.field@mind.org.uk

Founded:
1945

Organisation type and purpose:
Membership association (membership is by
subscription), voluntary organisation, registered
charity (charity number 219830).

Subject coverage:
Mental health, mental illness, the mental health
services, service provision, especially community
care, rights of service recipients, legislation,
treatments, sources of therapy, voluntary
associations, housing, women; employment.

Non-library collection catalogue:
All or part available online, in-house and in print

Library catalogue:
All or part available in-house

Printed publications:
Benefits and Employment (7 titles)
Care in the Community (13 titles)
Drugs and Treatment (20 titles)
Fact sheets, reading lists, books, reports
Making Sense Series (6 titles)
Openmind Magazine (6 times a year)

Publications list:
Available online and in print

Access to staff:
Contact by letter, by telephone, by fax, by e-mail
and via website. Appointment necessary.
Hours: Mon to Fri, 0915 to 1715

Access to building, collection or gallery:
No prior appointment required

Branch at:
Mind Cymru
  3rd Floor, Quebec House, Castlebridge Road
  East, Castlebridge, Cardiff, CF11 9AB; tel: 029
  2039 5123

MINERAL INDUSTRY RESEARCH ORGANISATION

Acronym or abbreviation: MIRO

Concorde House, Trinity Park, Solihull,
Birmingham, West Midlands, B37 7UQ

Tel: 0121 635 5225
Fax: 0121 635 5226
E-mail: mail@miro.co.uk

Website:
http://www.miro.co.uk

Enquiries:
Enquiries to: Administrator

Founded:
1972

Organisation type and purpose:
Membership association (membership is by
subscription), present number of members: 70,
consultancy, research organisation.
To organise collaborative research projects.

Subject coverage:
Geosciences, mineral exploration; mining, mineral
processing, metal refining, recycling and
environmental issues.

**Museum or gallery collection, archive, or library
special collection:**
The Stan Nelmes Collection – a collection of books,
  journals and reports of interest to those in the
  metallurgical industry dating from 1903 to 1990,
  66 titles in total

Non-library collection catalogue:
All or part available online and in print

Library catalogue:
All or part available online and in print

Printed publications:
Publications include:
Quarry Reclamation
Mixing and Dewatering in the Mineral Industry
TRAWMAR (Targeted Research Action on Waste
  Minimisation and Recycling) (2000)
Technical Review Series including:
Pressure Hydrometallurgy – A Review
REMINDER (A Review and Evaluation of Minerals
  Industry Databases of Environmental
  References)
Treatment Options for Waste Products from
  Metallurgical Operations
The use of Micro Organisms in the Minerals and
  Metals Industries (Vol 1 1991, Vol 2 1995, Vol 3
  2000)
Order printed publications from: Administrator,
MIRO

Electronic and video publications:
A Technical Framework for Mine Closure Planning
  (CD-ROM)
Impurity Control and Removal in Extractive
  Metallurgy (CD-ROM)
SOLVEX solvent extraction database (disk)
The use of Micro Organisms in the Minerals and
  Metals Industries (Vols 2 and 3) (CD-ROM)
Pressure Hydrometallurgy: A Review (CD-ROM)
TRAWMAR (Targeted Research Action on Waste
  Minimisation and Recycling) Workshop
  Proceedings, 1998, 1999, 2000 (CD-ROM)

Publications list:
Available online and in print

Access to staff:
Contact by letter, by telephone, by fax, by e-mail
and via website
Hours: Mon to Fri, 0900 to 1700

Access to building, collection or gallery:
Prior appointment required

Access for disabled people:
Ramped entry, access to all public areas, toilet
facilities

Member of:
Association of Independent Research and
Technology Organisations (AIRTO)
Mining Association of the United Kingdom

MINERALOGICAL SOCIETY OF GREAT BRITAIN AND IRELAND

Acronym or abbreviation: MinSoc

41 Queen's Gate, London, SW7 5HR

Tel: 020 7584 7516
Fax: 020 7823 8021
E-mail: info@minersoc.org

Website:
http://www.minersoc.org.uk
Membership, publications, events, conferences,
special interest groups, shop, education.

Enquiries:
Enquiries to: Executive Secretary
Direct e-mail: kevin@minersoc.org

Founded:
1876

Organisation type and purpose:
National organisation, learned society, registered
charity (charity number 233706), publishing house.

Subject coverage:
Mineralogy, petrology, geochemistry,
crystallography and environmental science.

Library catalogue:
All or part available online

Printed publications:
Elements (6 times a year)
Clay Minerals (quarterly)
Mineralogical Magazine (bi-monthly)

Electronic and video publications:
Clay Minerals
Mineralogical Magazine (available online)
MINABS (online)

Publications list:
Available online and in print

Access to staff:
Contact by letter, by telephone, by fax, by e-mail
and via website. Appointment necessary.
Hours: Mon to Fri, 0900 to 1700

Access to building, collection or gallery:
Prior appointment required
Hours: Mon to Fri 0900 to 1700
Special comments: Library housed at Kingston
University.

MINERALS ENGINEERING SOCIETY

Acronym or abbreviation: MES

2 Ryton Close, Blyth, Worksop, Nottinghamshire,
S81 8DN

Tel: 01909 591940
Fax: 01909 591940
E-mail: hon.sec.mes@lineone.net

Website:
http://www.mineralsengineering.org

Enquiries:
Enquiries to: Honorary Secretary

Founded:
1958

Organisation type and purpose:
Learned society.

Subject coverage:
Minerals engineering; mineral processing; coal
preparation.

Printed publications:
MQR Magazine (10 times a year)
Minerals Engineering Handbook
Symposia Handbooks

Access to staff:
Contact by letter, by telephone, by fax and by e-
mail
Hours: Mon to Fri, 0700 to 2200

MINI MARCOS OWNERS CLUB

Acronym or abbreviation: MMOC

28 Meadow Road, Claines, Worcester, WR3 7PP

Tel: 01905 458533
E-mail: roger@minimarcos.plus.com

Website:
http://www.minimarcos.org.uk

Enquiries:
Enquiries to: Secretary

Founded:
1977

Organisation type and purpose:
International organisation, membership
association (membership is by subscription).

Subject coverage:
History and development of Mini Marcos and Mini
Jem cars, history of Kingfisher Sprint cars.

Printed publications:
Club Magazine (including back issues)
Club Technical Manual
Order printed publications from: Publications Officer,
Mini Marcos Owners Club, 16 Townfield, Kidford,
Billingshurst, West Sussex, RH14 0LZ

Publications list:
Available online

Access to staff:
Contact by letter, by telephone, by e-mail, in
person and via website
Hours: Evenings and weekends

Links with:
RACMSA

MINI OWNERS CLUB

Formal name: National Mini Owners Club

15 Birchwood Road, Boley Park, Lichfield,
Staffordshire, WS14 9UN

Tel: 01543 257956
Fax: 01543 257956
E-mail: nmoc@yahoo.com

Website:
http://www.miniownersclub.co.uk
Club information and other Mini related
information.

Enquiries:
Enquiries to: Secretary

Founded:
1979

continued overleaf

Organisation type and purpose:
Membership association (membership is by subscription).

Subject coverage:
Mini cars, technical advice.

Access to staff:
Contact by letter, by telephone, by fax, by e-mail and via website
Hours: Mon to Sun, 0900 to 2100

MINIATURE AFV ASSOCIATION

Formal name: Miniature Armoured Fighting Vehicles Association
Acronym or abbreviation: MAFVA

45 Balmoral Drive, Holmes Chapel, Cheshire, CW4 7JQ

Tel: 01477 535373
Fax: 01477 535892
E-mail: mafvahq@aol.com

Website:
http://www.mafva.net

Enquiries:
Enquiries to: Honorary Secretary

Founded:
1965

Organisation type and purpose:
International organisation, membership association (membership is by subscription), present number of members: 7,500, voluntary organisation.
Collection and dissemination of information on military vehicles and equipment.

Subject coverage:
Armoured fighting vehicles and other military equipment, arms, materials and accoutrements from World War I to date; scale models and information, markings, colour schemes, badges and insignia.

Information services:
Available to members.

Museum or gallery collection, archive, or library special collection:
Collection of military insignia (particularly cloth) of the British Army, British Indian Army and Army Cadet Force, 1914 to date: quantity several thousand
Vehicle markings and colour schemes

Non-library collection catalogue:
All or part available in-house

Printed publications:
Branch newsletters (Dragon, etc.)
Tankette (6 a year)
Order printed publications from: Honorary Secretary

Electronic and video publications:
Index of Tankette Magazine Vol. 1 to 34 (floppy disk, £1)

Publications list:
Available online and in print

Access to staff:
Contact by letter, by telephone, by fax, by e-mail, in person and via website. Appointment necessary. Non-members charged.
Hours: Daily

Access to building, collection or gallery:
Prior appointment required

MINISTRY OF DEFENCE – TECHNICAL INFORMATION CENTRE ROYAL ENGINEERS

Acronym or abbreviation: TICRE

Chetwynd Barracks, Chilwell, Nottingham, NG9 5HA

Tel: 0115 957 2310
Fax: 0115 957 2294

Enquiries:
Enquiries to: Librarian
Direct tel: 0115 957 2309

Founded:
1979

Organisation type and purpose:
National government centre, of the Ministry of Defence.
To provide technical information for the Corps of Royal Engineers.

Subject coverage:
Civil, mechanical and electrical engineering, construction, fortifications.

Library catalogue:
All or part available in-house

Printed publications:
In-house publications only

Access to staff:
Contact by letter, by telephone and by fax. Appointment necessary.
Hours: Mon to Thu, 0800 to 1630; Fri, 0800 to 1330

Access to building, collection or gallery:
Prior appointment required
Hours: Mon to Thu, 0800 to 1630; Fri, 0800 to 1330

MINISTRY OF DEFENCE INFORMATION AND LIBRARY SERVICE – GLASGOW

Acronym or abbreviation: MOD

Room 1410, Kentigern House, 65 Brown Street, Glasgow, G2 8EX

Tel: 0141 224 2500
Fax: 0141 224 2257

Enquiries:
Enquiries to: Librarian
Direct tel: 0141 224 2501

Organisation type and purpose:
National government body.
Central government department.

Subject coverage:
Defence policy, armed forces, public administration, management, computing and information science, health and safety, standards, military science and engineering.

Museum or gallery collection, archive, or library special collection:
Full set of British standards on CD-ROM

Library catalogue:
All or part available in-house

Access to staff:
Appointment necessary.
Hours: Mon to Fri, 0900 to 1700

Branch of the:
Ministry of Defence Information and Library Service, Whitehall Library

MINISTRY OF DEFENCE INFORMATION AND LIBRARY SERVICE – WHITEHALL INFORMATION AND LIBRARY CENTRE

Acronym or abbreviation: MOD

Ground Floor, Zone D, Main Building, Whitehall, London, SW1A 2HB

Tel: 020 7218 4445
Fax: 020 7218 5413
E-mail: cio-svcslibrary-office@mod.uk

Website:
http://www.mod.uk

Organisation type and purpose:
National government body.

Subject coverage:
Defence policy, organisation, strategy and technology; politics, government and international relations; management; computers; public administration.

Library catalogue:
All or part available in-house

Access to staff:
Contact by letter. Appointment necessary.
Hours: Mon to Fri, 0830 to 1630

MINISTRY OF JUSTICE

Acronym or abbreviation: MoJ

1st Floor, Tower, 102 Petty France, London, SW1H 9AJ

Tel: 020 3334 3000
E-mail: moj.library@justice.gsi.gov.uk

Website:
http://www.justice.gov.uk
http://www.hmprisonservice.gov.uk
http://www.hmcourts-service.gov.uk

Founded:
2009

Created by the merger of:
Department of Constitutional Affairs and parts of Home Office Library (year of change 2009)

Incorporates the former:
Prison Service HQ Library, which became part of Home Office Library (year of change 2003)

Organisation type and purpose:
Government department.

Subject coverage:
Prisons, penology, criminal justice, civil justice, courts, human rights, law, constitutional reform, devolution.

Museum or gallery collection, archive, or library special collection:
Publications by MoJ and predecessor departments

Trade and statistical information:
see MoJ website.

Library catalogue:
All or part available in-house

Electronic and video publications:
see websites

Access to staff:
Access for members only.
Hours: Mon to Fri, 0900 to 1700
Special comments: MoJ Library is a library of last resort for departmental publications only.

MINTEL INTERNATIONAL GROUP

18–19 Long Lane, London, EC1A 9PL

Tel: 020 7606 4533
Fax: 020 7606 5932

Website:
http://www.cior.com
List of publications and services, contents pages, prices, ordering information.

Enquiries:
Enquiries to: Director

Founded:
1972

Organisation type and purpose:
Research organisation.
Global information provider.

Subject coverage:
Retailing, retailers, retail trade and retail topics in the UK and Europe, retailers based elsewhere but with a presence in the European market, global cross border activity.

Museum or gallery collection, archive, or library special collection:
Specialist retailing library and files (including historical information)

Extensive files on individual retail companies and operations, UK, Europe especially
Retail sector information
Retail statistical data

Trade and statistical information:
Retail trade data by country, by sector, data on cross-border retailing and retailers.

Printed publications:
Retail Reports and Database Service on over 30 topics, many sectors and on the UK, Europe and US
Consumer Product Market Surveys across Europe, Providing: market size, market shares, consumption patterns, distribution (£150)
European Retail Statistics – 17 Countries (£195)

Electronic and video publications:
Euro-RETAILNET (online database, 3000 company profiles, updated daily, from £1500)

Publications list:
Available in print

Access to staff:
Contact by letter, by telephone, by fax and in person
Hours: Mon to Fri, 0900 to 1730

Other locations:
Chicago; Frankfurt; Sydney; Belfast; Los Angeles

MINTEL INTERNATIONAL GROUP LIMITED

18–19 Long Lane, London, EC1A 9HE

Tel: 020 7606 4533
Fax: 020 7606 5932
E-mail: enquiries@mintel.com

Website:
http://www.mintel.com

Enquiries:
Enquiries to: Head of Marketing
Direct e-mail: stevec@mintel.com

Founded:
1972

Organisation type and purpose:
Research organisation.
Consumer research publisher.

Subject coverage:
Pan-European studies, FMCG (fast moving consumer goods) markets, food and drink, retail industry, leisure industry, personal finance industry, new products, company profiles, consumer research, life styles, business to business, Irish, industrial.

Trade and statistical information:
Comprehensive market data on all UK consumer, European and Industrial markets.

Printed publications:
European intelligence
Finance intelligence (annually)
Industrial intelligence
Irish intelligence
Leisure intelligence (annually)
Market intelligence (annually)
Retail intelligence (annually)
Special Reports (annually)
US Consumer Research

Publications list:
Available in print

Access to staff:
Contact by telephone, by e-mail and via website
Hours: Mon to Fri, 0900 to 1700

Affiliated to:
Chartered Institute of Marketing

MIRA LIMITED

Formal name: Motor Industry Research Association

Watling Street, Nuneaton, Warwickshire, CV10 0TU

Tel: 024 7635 5000
Fax: 024 7635 5355
E-mail: enquiries@mira.co.uk

Website:
http://www.mira.co.uk/aic
General information about MIRA as well as access to MIRA databases.

Enquiries:
Enquiries to: Information Officer
Direct tel: 024 7635 5275
Direct fax: 024 7635 5036

Founded:
1946

Organisation type and purpose:
Consultancy, research organisation.

Subject coverage:
Automobile engineering; problems applicable to motor vehicles including noise, vibration, comfort, safety and air pollution.

Trade and statistical information:
World data on automotive industry.

Printed publications:
Automobile Abstracts (monthly)
Automotive Business Index (weekly)
Bibliographies and information searches

Publications list:
Available online and in print

Access to staff:
Contact by e-mail and via website. Appointment necessary. Non-members charged.
Hours: Mon to Fri, 0900 to 1600

European agent for the:
Japan Society of Automotive Engineers Review

MISCARRIAGE ASSOCIATION

c/o Clayton Hospital, Northgate, Wakefield, West Yorkshire, WF1 3JS

Tel: 01924 200799
Fax: 01924 298834
E-mail: info@miscarriageassociation.org.uk

Website:
http://www.miscarriageassociation.org.uk

Enquiries:
Enquiries to: Administrator

Founded:
1982

Organisation type and purpose:
Registered charity (charity number 1076829).
Has a network of over 200 volunteer telephone contacts and 50 support groups in the UK.
To provide support and information for all on the subject of pregnancy loss.

Subject coverage:
Management and understanding of miscarriage in hospitals and the community.

Printed publications:
Basic Information Pack
We are sorry you have had a miscarriage (introductory leaflet)
Blighted Ovum
Ectopic Pregnancy
About the Cervical Stitch
Miscarriage: Guidelines for good practice

Publications list:
Available online and in print

Access to staff:
Contact by letter, by telephone, by fax, by e-mail and via website
Hours: Mon to Fri, 0900 to 1600

MISSING PEOPLE

284 Upper Richmond Road West, London, SW14 7JE

Tel: 020 8392 4545
E-mail: services@missingpeople.org.uk

Website:
http://www.missingpeople.org.uk

Enquiries:
Enquiries to: Co-founders (for senior management)

Founded:
1992

Organisation type and purpose:
National organisation, registered charity (charity number 1020419).
Offers a lifeline for the 250,000 people who run away and go missing each year. For those left behind, it searches and provides specialised support to end the heartache and confusion.

Subject coverage:
Missing persons.

Special visitor services:
Helpline: 0500 700 700; Message Home, 0800 700 740: 24-hr freefone service to help missing adults reach advice and support and to reconnect with their family or carers via a message or a 3-way call; Runaway Helpline, 0808 800 7070: national, free and confidential 24-hr service for anyone who has run away from home or care, or been forced to leave home.

Printed publications:
Newsletter (quarterly)
General information leaflets

Access to staff:
Contact by letter, by telephone, by e-mail and via website
Hours: 24-hour service

Also at:
Message Home
at the same address; tel: 020 8392 4559; e-mail: services @missingpeople.org.uk
Runaway Helpline
at the same address; tel: 020 8392 4559; e-mail: services @missingpeople.org.uk

MISSIO

Formal name: Also known as Pontifical Mission Societies

23 Eccleston Square, London, SW1V 1NU

Tel: 020 7821 9755
Fax: 020 7630 8466
E-mail: director@missio.org.uk

Website:
http://www.missio.org.uk

Enquiries:
Enquiries to: Director

Founded:
1833

Formerly called:
Pontifical Mission Societies (year of change 2009)

Organisation type and purpose:
Registered charity (charity number 1056651).
Support of the Catholic Church in mission areas.

Printed publications:
Mission Today, Mission Tomorrow, Mission Outlook

Access to staff:
Contact by letter, by e-mail and via website
Hours: Mon to Fri, 0900 to 1700

MISSION AVIATION FELLOWSHIP (UK)

Acronym or abbreviation: MAF (UK)

Castle House, Castle Hill Avenue, Folkestone, Kent, CT20 2TN

Tel: 0845 8509505
Fax: 01303 852800
E-mail: supporter.relations@maf-uk.org

Enquiries:
Enquiries to: Chief Executive

continued overleaf

Founded:
1947

Organisation type and purpose:
International organisation, registered charity (charity number 1064598).
Providing aviation and technical support to church, mission and relief agencies in the developing world.

Subject coverage:
Speakers and presentations of the work on Mission Aviation Fellowship are available on request.

Printed publications:
MAF News (magazine, quarterly, available on request free of charge)

Electronic and video publications:
Videos of operational work overseas available by request

Access to staff:
Contact by letter, by telephone, by fax and by e-mail. Appointment necessary.
Hours: Mon to Fri, 0900 to 1700

Branches:
Mission Aviation Fellowship
29 Canal Street, Glasgow, G4 0AD; tel: 0141 332 5222; fax: 0141 332 5222; e-mail: maf-scot.off@maf-uk.org

Member organisation of:
Evangelical Alliance
Global Connections

MISSION TO SEAFARERS, THE

St Michael Paternoster Royal, College Hill, London, EC4R 2RL

Tel: 020 7248 5202
Fax: 020 7248 4761
E-mail: general@missiontoseafarers.org

Website:
http://www.missiontoseafarers.org
Information about where we work and what we do.

Enquiries:
Enquiries to: Public Relations Officer

Organisation type and purpose:
Voluntary organisation, registered charity (charity number 212432).
The Mission to Seafarers, a world mission agency of the Anglican church, cares for the welfare of seafarers of all nationalities and faiths in ports around the world.

Subject coverage:
Seafarers' conditions and welfare.

Museum or gallery collection, archive, or library special collection:
Selected archive material of The Mission to Seafarers and activities

Printed publications:
The Sea (newspaper for seafarers, every other month issued via centres and mailing list, subscription £1.50 per annum, 6 issues)
Flying Angel News (newspaper, three time a year for members/supporters, subscription £2 per annum, 3 issues)

Access to staff:
Contact by letter, by telephone, by fax, by e-mail and via website. Appointment necessary.
Hours: Mon to Fri, 0900 to 1700

Access to building, collection or gallery:
Prior appointment required

Members of:
International Christian Maritime Association (ICMA)
Herald House, 15 Lambs Passage, London EC1Y 8TQ, UK; tel: 020 7256 9216; fax: 020 7256 9217; e-mail: icma.secgen@btconnect.com; website: www.icma.as

MISSIONARY INSTITUTE LONDON

Acronym or abbreviation: MIL

Holcombe House, The Ridgeway, London, NW7 4HY

Tel: 020 8906 1893
Fax: 020 8906 4937
E-mail: mil@mdx.ac.uk

Enquiries:
Enquiries to: Librarian
Other contacts: Secretary for enquiries about courses.

Founded:
1969

Organisation type and purpose:
Registered charity (charity number 269713), university department or institute.

Subject coverage:
Theology, missiology, church history, social anthropology.

Library catalogue:
All or part available in-house

Access to staff:
Contact by letter, by fax and by e-mail
Hours: Mon to Fri, 0900 to 1700

Access to building, collection or gallery:
Prior appointment required
Hours: Mon to Fri, 0900 to 1700
Special comments: No loans to non-registered students.

Access for disabled people:
Parking provided, level entry

MKI CORTINA OWNERS CLUB

The Membership Secretary, 51 Studley Rise, Trowbridge, BA14 0PD

Tel: 01225 763888
E-mail: info@mk1cortina.com

Website:
http://www.mk1cortina.com
History of club, application form, bulletin board – cars for sale, spares, online order form.

Enquiries:
Enquiries to: Membership Secretary
Direct e-mail: alison-membership@blueyonder.co.uk

Founded:
1982

Organisation type and purpose:
Membership association (membership is by subscription), present number of members: 1100, voluntary organisation.
Car club.

Subject coverage:
Ford Cortina MkI car events, spares sourcing, legislation, insurance.

Printed publications:
Newsletter (members)

Publications list:
Available in print

Access to staff:
Contact by letter, by telephone, by fax, by e-mail and via website
Hours: Mon to Fri, 1800 to 2130

MND SCOTLAND

Formal name: Scottish Motor Neurone Disease Association

76 Firhill Road, Glasgow, G20 7BA

Tel: 0141 945 1077
Fax: 0141 945 2578
E-mail: info@mndscotland.org.uk

Website:
http://www.mndscotland.org.uk

Enquiries:
Enquiries to: Information Officer – Librarian

Founded:
1981

Organisation type and purpose:
Voluntary organisation, registered charity (charity number SCO 02662).
Aims to ensure that people with motor neurone disease secure the care and support they need. Activites: a network of MND Care Team Specialists throughout Scotland; specialist equipment loan service; family information evenings, library and information service; study days for health and social care professionals; small grants to individuals in need; counselling service; holiday caravan; welfare and benefits service.

Subject coverage:
Motor neurone disease/amyotrophic lateral sclerosis; palliative care; carers; bereavement; disability issues; carers' issues; community care; complementary medicine; health care; charity management.

Information services:
Library and Information Service for patients/families, and health and social care professionals.

Education services:
MND Study Days for health professionals.

Library catalogue:
All or part available online

Printed publications:
Aware (quarterly newsletter)
Annual Report
Factsheets
Many publications downloadable from website

Publications list:
Available online and in print

Access to staff:
Contact by letter, by telephone, by fax, by e-mail, in person and via website
Hours: Mon to Fri, 0900 to 1700; out-of-hours answerphone
Special comments: Information Officer works part-time, so appointment necessary.

Access to building, collection or gallery:
No prior appointment required
Hours: Mon to Fri, 0900 to 1700
Special comments: Library: by appointment only.

Access for disabled people:
Parking provided, level entry, toilet facilities, fully accessible

Links with:
International Alliance of MND/ALS Associations
Scottish Health Information Network (SHINE) website: http://www.shinelib.org.uk
Scottish Health Libraries Catalogue (SHELCAT) website: http://www.shelcat.org

MOBILISE

Formal name: Mobilise Organisation

National Headquarters, Ashwellthorpe, Norwich, Norfolk, NR16 1EX

Tel: 01508 489449
Fax: 01508 488173
E-mail: enquiries@mobilise.info

Website:
http://www.mobilise.info
Mobilise is the UK's leading disabled motorists and campaigning organisation.
Mobilise gives a clear lead in the fight to improve mobility and access and to put an end to discrimination and segregation. It campaigns at national and local government level and works closely with other organisations such as Motability and the Department for Transport where it makes its voice heard and listened to. Information on all aspects of mobility is available directly from the office or via monthly magazine. Various discounts

are available to members on ferry concessions and motoring products. Membership: single £16, joint £21 per year.

Enquiries:
Enquiries to: Information Officer

Founded:
2005

Created by the merger of:
Disabled Drivers' Association and Disabled Drivers' Motor Club (year of change 2005)

Organisation type and purpose:
Membership, campaigning charity (membership is by subscription, qualification), present number of members: 20,000, voluntary organisation, registered charity (charity number 1111826). Membership: single, £16, joint, £21.

Subject coverage:
Mobility benefits and queries, assessment centres, licensing problems, car/vehicle insurance for disabled people, car acquisition and adaptation, holidays, ferry concessions, legislation on transport and parking.

Information services:
Brief information services for non-members; members are entitled to unlimited access to Information Officers who will take up case work, help with appealing against parking tickets, etc.

Services for disabled people:
Provides case work for members, help with appealing against parking tickets, acts on behalf of members by contacting local authorities, etc.

Museum or gallery collection, archive, or library special collection:
Archive of Magic Carpet magazines (bound vols) dating back to foundation in 1948, which form a valuable historical resource

Printed publications:
Mobilise monthly magazine
A range of leaflets: VAT relief on motor vehicles adapted for disabled people, Blue Badge, Parking in London, Returning to driving, Ferry concessions, Toll concessions, Guide to mobility vehicles. Leaflets are free to members, £10 for all leaflets to non-members.

Publications list:
Available in print

Access to staff:
Contact by letter, by telephone, by fax, by e-mail, in person and via website
Hours: Mon to Fri, 0900 to 1700
Special comments: Answerphone outside office hours.

Access to building, collection or gallery:
Fully accessible

Access for disabled people:
Parking provided, level entry, access to all public areas, toilet facilities

Branches:
30 local groups

MOBILITY INFORMATION SERVICE – TELFORD

Acronym or abbreviation: MIS

20 Burton Close, Dawley, Telford, TF4 2BX

Tel: 01743 340269
E-mail: mis@nmcuk.freeserve.co.uk

Website:
http://www.mis.org.uk

Enquiries:
Enquiries to: Chief Officer
Other contacts: Information Officer f(or general information on mobility matters)

Founded:
1979

Organisation type and purpose:
International organisation, voluntary organisation, registered charity (charity number 1085593). Provides mobility information to disabled people in order to help them attain independence.

Subject coverage:
Information on all aspects of mobility.

Museum or gallery collection, archive, or library special collection:
Hamilton Index
Handynet database
Rehadat

Non-library collection catalogue:
All or part available online and in-house

Printed publications:
Adaptions for the Disabled Driver: definitive listing of driver adaptions and specialist suppliers (£3.95 inc. p&p)
The Disabled Passenger (£3.95 inc. p&p)

Publications list:
Available online and in print

Access to staff:
Contact by letter, by telephone, by e-mail and via website
Hours: Tue, Fri, 1030 to 1530

Access to building, collection or gallery:
No public access

Access for disabled people:
No public access

MOD ADMIRALTY LIBRARY

Naval Historical Branch, No. 24 Store, PP 20, Main Road, HM Naval Base, Portsmouth, PO1 3LU

Tel: 023 9272 5297
Fax: 023 9272 4003
E-mail: cnsnhbal@a.dii.mod.uk

Enquiries:
Enquiries to: Admiralty Librarian

Founded:
1809

Organisation type and purpose:
National government body.
Historical Library.

Subject coverage:
History of the Royal Navy, with particular reference to administration, policy, doctrine, operations, strategy, tactics, hydrography, naval aviation, signalling and gunnery.

Museum or gallery collection, archive, or library special collection:
Approximately 180,000 vols and 100,000 pamphlets, in process of being catalogued
Catalogue of manuscripts and some printed charts searchable on the National Museum of the Royal Navy website
Historical collections of the Royal Naval Medical Services held at the Institute of Naval Medicine.

Library catalogue:
All or part available online, in-house and in print

Printed publications:
The following out-of-print catalogues will in due course be replaced by an online database:
Admiralty Library. Subject Catalogue of Printed Books, Part 1. Historical Section (London HMSO, 1912)
Admiralty Library. Subject Catalogue of Printed Books, Part 2. Law Section (London HMSO, 1915)
Catalogue of the Naval Library, Ministry of Defence, London (5 vols, Boston, MA, G. K. Hall, 1967)

Access to staff:
Contact by letter, by telephone, by fax, by e-mail and in person. Appointment necessary.
Hours: Tue to Thu, 1000 to 1645

Access to building, collection or gallery:
Appointment necessary

Hours: Tue to Thu, 1000 to 1700

Access for disabled people:
Access to all public areas, toilet facilities. Reserved parking space adjacent to building

Branches:
Admiralty Library, Portsmouth
No. 12 Store, PP 64, Semaphore Tower Road, HM Naval Base, Portsmouth, PO1 JNH; tel: 023 9272 3795; fax: 023 9272 3942; e-mail: library@nmrn .org.uk; website: http://www.royalnavalmuseum .org
Historical Library
Institute of Naval Medicine, Crescent Road, Alverstoke, Gosport, Hampshire, PO12 2DL; tel: 023 9276 8238; fax: 023 9250 4823; e-mail: inm-cs -infohistlib@mod.uk; website: http://www .royalnavy.mod.uk/training-and-people/rn-life/ medical-branch/institute-of-naval-medicine

Constituent part of:
Naval Historical Branch (NHB)
No. 24 Store, PP 20, Main Road, HM Naval Base, Portsmouth PO1 3LU; tel: 02392 725300; fax: 02392 724003

MODEL YACHTING ASSOCIATION

Acronym or abbreviation: MYA

Five Oaks, Church Lane, Oakley, Bedfordshire, MK43 7RU

Tel: 01234 822408
E-mail: m.clifton@easynet.co.uk

Website:
http://www.radiosailing.org.uk
Racing calendar; results; clubs; general information; links.

Enquiries:
Enquiries to: Information Officer
Direct tel: 01789 751800
Direct e-mail: graham.reeves@virgin.net

Founded:
1911

Organisation type and purpose:
Membership association.
National sporting authority.

Subject coverage:
Competitive sailing of wind-powered models; design, construction, operation of model yachts; locations of affiliated clubs; history of the sport.

Museum or gallery collection, archive, or library special collection:
Comprehensive reference library of printed books and magazines since 1879
Minutes and other administrative records of the MYA since 1931

Printed publications:
Acquaints (individual members and affiliated clubs, 4 times a year)
Rating Rules for Model Yachts
Year Book

Publications list:
Available in print

Access to staff:
Contact by letter, by telephone and by e-mail
Hours: Mon to Fri, 0900 to 2100

Associated with:
Central Council for Physical Recreation
International Sailing Federation (Radio Sailing Division) (ISAF/RSD)
Royal Yachting Association

MODERN CHURCHPEOPLE'S UNION

Acronym or abbreviation: MCU

MCU Office, 9 Westward View, Liverpool, Merseyside, L17 7EE

Tel: 0845 345 1909
E-mail: office@modchurchunion.org

continued overleaf

Website:
http://www.modchurchunion.org

Enquiries:
Enquiries to: Administrator

Founded:
1898

Organisation type and purpose:
Learned society (membership is by subscription),
present number of members: 700, voluntary
organisation, registered charity (charity number
281573).

Subject coverage:
Church affairs, especially Church of England;
theology; philosophy of religion; ethics.

Printed publications:
Modern Believing (4 times a year)
The Contemporary Challenge of Modernist
  Theology
The New Liberalism: Faith for the Third
  Millennium
Hastings Rashdall: Bibliography of the Published
  Writings

Publications list:
Available online

Access to staff:
Contact by letter, by telephone, by e-mail and via
website. Appointment necessary.
Hours: Mon to Fri, 0900 to 1500

MODERN HUMANITIES RESEARCH ASSOCIATION

Acronym or abbreviation: MHRA

1 Carlton House Terrace, London, SW1Y 5AF

E-mail: mail@mhra.org.uk

Website:
http://www.mhra.org.uk
Publications and activities.

Enquiries:
Enquiries to: Honorary Secretary

Founded:
1918

Organisation type and purpose:
International organisation, learned society,
registered charity.

Subject coverage:
Modern and medieval languages and literatures,
including English.

Printed publications:
Annual Bibliography of English Language and
  Literature
Austrian Studies
MHRA Annual Bulletin
MHRA Bibliographies
MHRA Critical Texts
MHRA Style Guide
MHRA Texts and Dissertations
Modern Language Review (quarterly)
Oxford German Studies (jointly with Maney
  Publishing)
Legenda (jointly with Maney Publishing)
Portuguese Studies (biannual)
Publications of the MHRA
Slavonic and East European Review (quarterly)
Year's Work in Modern Language Studies
Yearbook of English Studies (biannual)
MHRA Translations

Electronic and video publications:
Annual Bibliography of English Language and
  Literature (online)
MHRA Working Paper in the Humanities
University Theses in Russian, Soviet, and East
  European Studies 1907 – A Bibliographical
  Database of Research in the British Isles

Publications list:
Available online and in print

Access to staff:
Contact by letter and by e-mail. Appointment
necessary.

MODERN PENTATHLON ASSOCIATION OF GREAT BRITAIN, THE

Acronym or abbreviation: MPAGB

Norwood House, University of Bath, Claverton
Down, Bath, BA2 7AY

Tel: 01225 386808
Fax: 01225 386995
E-mail: admin@mpagb.org.uk

Website:
http://www.mpagb.org.uk
About association, athletes, clubs calendar, links
with other sports and federations.

Enquiries:
Enquiries to: Administration Officer

Founded:
1948

Organisation type and purpose:
Membership association (membership is by
subscription), present number of members: 1500,
voluntary organisation.
Governing body and co-ordinating authority.

Subject coverage:
Modern pentathlon – compilation of five sports:
fencing, swimming, shooting, running and riding;
biathlon, triathlon, tetrathlon, pentathlon,
coaching, events.

Printed publications:
Broadsheet (3 times a year, members)
Modern Pentathlon Rule Book (£5.50 plus p&p)

Access to staff:
Contact by letter, by telephone, by fax, by e-mail
and via website
Hours: Mon to Fri, 0900 to 1700

MOLE VALLEY DISTRICT COUNCIL

Pippbrook, Dorking, Surrey, RH4 1SJ

Tel: 01306 885001\ Minicom no. 01372 819094
Fax: 01306 876821
E-mail: information@molevalley.gov.uk

Website:
http://www.molevalley.gov.uk

Enquiries:
Enquiries to: Communications Officer
Direct tel: 01306 879113
Other contacts: communications@molevalley.gov.uk

Founded:
1974

Organisation type and purpose:
Local government body.

Subject coverage:
Local authority services, Mole Valley district
including the main towns of Dorking and
Leatherhead.

Trade and statistical information:
Data on area and population.

Printed publications:
Mole Valley District Guide – A guide to towns and
  countryside around Dorking and Leatherhead
Mole Valley street map
Various information leaflets relating to Mole Valley
  services and amenities
Walking in Mole Valley (series of 20)

Access to staff:
Contact by letter, by telephone, by fax, by e-mail
and in person
Hours: Mon to Fri, 0830 to 1700; helpline open
same hours

Parent body:
Surrey County Council
  County Hall, Penrhyn Road, Kingston upon
  Thames, KT1 2DN; tel: 020 8541 8800; fax: 020
  8541 9005

MONEYFACTS PUBLICATIONS

Formal name: Moneyfacts Group plc

Moneyfacts House, 66–70 Thorpe Road, Norwich,
Norfolk, NR1 1BJ

Tel: 01603 476476
Fax: 01603 476477
E-mail: enquiries@moneyfacts.co.uk

Enquiries:
Enquiries to: Librarian

Founded:
1988

Organisation type and purpose:
Research organisation, publishing house.

Subject coverage:
Mortgage, savings, pensions, investments, and
business finance information.

Trade and statistical information:
UK mortgage, savings and investment rates,
  offshore mortgage and savings rates, business
  finance data, data on life, pensions and unit trust
  products.

Printed publications:
Business Moneyfacts: Guide to Business Finance
  (monthly, £87.50 annual subscription)
Life & Pensions Moneyfacts (monthly, £88.50,
  annual subscription)
Moneyfacts: Guide to Savings and Mortgage Rates
  (monthly, £89.50 annual subscription)

Publications list:
Available in print

Access to staff:
Contact by letter, by telephone and by fax. All
charged.
Hours: Mon to Fri, 0900 to 1700

Access for disabled people:
Parking provided, ramped entry

MONMOUTHSHIRE COUNTY COUNCIL

County Hall, Croesyceiliog, Cwmbran, Gwent,
NP44 2XH

Tel: 01633 644644
Fax: 01633 644666

Website:
http://www.monmouthshire.gov.uk

Enquiries:
Enquiries to: Communication Officer
Direct tel: 01633 644402
Direct e-mail: paulaskyrme@monmouthshire.gov
.uk

Founded:
1996

Organisation type and purpose:
Local government body.

Subject coverage:
Local government services, background to
Monmouthshire.

**Museum or gallery collection, archive, or library
special collection:**
The former Gwent County Record Office and
  Archives hold all records and collections

Printed publications:
Order printed publications from: Community Spirit
(residents' newspaper)

Access to staff:
Contact by letter, by telephone, by fax and by e-
mail. Appointment necessary.
Hours: Fri, 0900 to 1600

Access to building, collection or gallery:
By appointment

Access for disabled people:
Parking provided, level entry, toilet facilities

MONMOUTHSHIRE LIBRARIES AND INFORMATION SERVICE

Acronym or abbreviation: MLIS

Chepstow Library, Manor Way, Chepstow, NP16 5HZ

Tel: 01291 635730
Fax: 01291 635736
E-mail: infocentre@monmouthshire.gov.uk

Website:
http://www.monmouthshire.gov.uk/leisure/
libraries
http://libraries.monmouthshire.gov.uk
Community information database.

Enquiries:
Enquiries to: Principal Librarian

Founded:
1996

Organisation type and purpose:
Local government body, public library.

Subject coverage:
Local studies, historical Monmouthshire, advice and self-help information.

Museum or gallery collection, archive, or library special collection:
Chepstow Collection (material pertaining to Chepstow, donated by the Chepstow Society in 1952 and housed in Chepstow Library)

Trade and statistical information:
Welsh Assembly Government collection at Chepstow.

Non-library collection catalogue:
All or part available online

Library catalogue:
All or part available online

Publications list:
Available in print

Access to staff:
Contact by letter, by telephone, by fax, by e-mail, in person and via website

Access to building, collection or gallery:
Hours: Hours vary from site to site

Access for disabled people:
Ramped entry

Branch libraries:
Abergavenny Library
  Baker Street, Abergavenny, NP7 5BD; tel: 01873 735980; fax: 01873 735985; e-mail: abergavennylibrary@monmouthshire.gov.uk
Caldicot Library
  Woodstock Way, Caldicot, NP26 4DB; tel: 01291 426425; fax: 01291 426426; e-mail: caldicotlibrary@monmouthshire.gov.uk
Chepstow Library and Information Centre
  Manor Way, Chepstow, NP16 5HZ; tel: 01291 635730; fax: 01291 635736; e-mail: chepstowlibrary@monmouthshire.gov.uk
Gilwern Library
  Gilwern Community Education Centre and Library, Common Road, Gilwern; tel: 01873 833055; fax: 01873 833055; e-mail: gilwernlibrary@monmouthshire.gov.uk
Monmouth Library
  Rolls Hall, Whitecross Street, Monmouth, NP25 3BY; tel: 01600 775215; fax: 01600 775218; e-mail: monmouthlibrary@monmouthshire.gov.uk
Usk Library
  18A Maryport Street, Usk, NP15 1AE; tel: 01291 674925; fax: 01291 674924; e-mail: usklibrary@ monmouthshire.gov.uk

Parent body:
Monmouthshire County Council
  tel: 01633 644644; fax: 01633 644545

MONTESSORI SOCIETY AMI (UK)

26 Lyndhurst Gardens, London, NW3 5NW

Tel: 020 7435 7874
E-mail: info@montessori-uk.org

Website:
http://www.montessori-uk.org

Enquiries:
Enquiries to: Honorary Secretary

Founded:
1935

Organisation type and purpose:
National organisation, professional body, membership association (membership is by subscription), present number of members: 300, voluntary organisation.
To spread the ideas of child development and philosophy set out by Dr Maria Montessori to parents and others concerned with children.

Subject coverage:
Montessori system of education, child development, location of Montessori schools, training, training courses recognised by AMI, apparatus, supply information, Montessori literature.

Printed publications:
Book list containing publications by and about Maria Montessori
Introducing Montessori
Direction (magazine)

Electronic and video publications:
Montessori in Action: Learning for Life (video)
Order electronic and video publications from: see book order form

Publications list:
Available in print

Access to staff:
Contact by letter, by telephone and by e-mail.
Appointment necessary. Letter of introduction required.
Hours: Mon to Fri, 0900 to 1630
Special comments: Answerphone for other times.

Affiliated to:
Association Montessori Internationale (AMI)
  tel: + 31 20 679 8932; fax: + 31 20 676 7341; e-mail: ami@xs4all.nl; website: http://www.montessori -ami.org

MONUMENTAL BRASS SOCIETY

c/o H. M. Stuchfield, Lowe Hill House, Stratford St Mary, Suffolk, CO7 6JX

Tel: 01206 337239
Fax: 01206 861852
E-mail: martinstuchfield@btconnect.com

Website:
http://www.mbs-brasses.co.uk

Founded:
1887

Organisation type and purpose:
Learned society.

Subject coverage:
Preservation of monumental brasses, indents of lost brasses and incised slabs.

Printed publications:
Bulletin (3 times a year)
Portfolio (occasional, 5 or 6 plates of brasses and incised slabs)
Transactions (annually)

Access to staff:
Contact by letter, by fax and by e-mail
Hours: Mon to Fri, 0900 to 1700

MOOR GREEN

Formal name: Moor Green (Brain Injury Rehabilitation Centre)
Acronym or abbreviation: Moor Green

Moseley Hall Hospital, Alcester Road, Moseley, Birmingham, B13 8JL

Tel: 0121 442 3400
Fax: 0121 442 3420
E-mail: Liz.wright@sbcht.wmids.nhs.uk

Enquiries:
Enquiries to: Clinical Manager

Founded:
1967

Organisation type and purpose:
National Health Service.
To provide out-patient rehabilitation following brain injury. Assessment for services and equipment etc. To provide information, advice, counselling, loan equipment and special services.

Subject coverage:
Rehabilitation of people who have suffered head injuries (middle to late stage treatment).

Museum or gallery collection, archive, or library special collection:
Literature on Brain injury

Printed publications:
Moor Green leaflets

Access to staff:
Contact by letter, by telephone and by fax.
Appointment necessary.
Hours: Mon to Fri, 0900 to 1700

Links with:
West Midlands Rehabilitation Centre
  Oak Tree Lane, Selly Oak, Birmingham, B29 6JA

MORAVIAN CHURCH IN GREAT BRITAIN

Moravian Church House, 5–7 Muswell Hill, London, N10 3TJ

Tel: 020 8883 3409
Fax: 020 8365 3371
E-mail: moravianchurchhouse@btinternet.com

Website:
http://www.moravian.org.uk

Enquiries:
Enquiries to: General Secretary
Other contacts: Archivist for visits to the archives and library.

Founded:
1457

Organisation type and purpose:
International organisation, present number of members: 2000, voluntary organisation, registered charity.
Christian church.
To worship God and spread the gospel.

Subject coverage:
History, doctrine and practices of the Moravian Church in the UK and overseas.

Museum or gallery collection, archive, or library special collection:
Manuscript diaries and letters from the 18th and 19th centuries relating to the growth and work of the Church, especially in West Indies and Labrador
Numerous letters from John Wesley to Moravian leaders

Printed publications:
Various hymn and prayer books
Over 40 publications including:
Baptism and Confirmation certificates
Church Order of the Unitas Fratrum
Customs and Practices of the Moravian Church
History of the Moravian Church
Moravian Mission in Labrador

Publications list:
Available online and in print

Access to staff:
Contact by letter, by telephone and by e-mail.
Appointment necessary.
Hours: Mon to Fri, 0930 to 1700

MORAY COUNCIL DEPARTMENT OF EDUCATIONAL SERVICES

Council Offices, High Street, Elgin, Moray, IV30 1BX

Tel: 01343 543451
Fax: 01343 563478
E-mail: campbea@moray.gov.uk

Website:
http://www.moray.gov.uk

Enquiries:
Enquiries to: Libraries and Museums Manager
Direct tel: 01343 563398
Other contacts: Principal Librarian

Organisation type and purpose:
Local government body, public library.

Subject coverage:
General, local history of Moray, Nairn and Banffshire, family history.

Museum or gallery collection, archive, or library special collection:
Archives of preceding and current local authorities
Falconer Papers
Local history collection
Local newspapers on microfilm
Microfilm records of births, marriages and deaths and early census returns
Wittet and Doig Collection of 10,000 architectural plans, 1828–1900

Non-library collection catalogue:
All or part available online

Library catalogue:
All or part available online

Printed publications:
A Flannel Sark an Vik (1999)
Churches of Moray (1981)
Elgin Past and Present (1980, revised 1995)
Laich O'Moray Past and Present (1985)
Tar Atween Yer Taes (1999)
The Lintie O'Moray (facsimile of 1984 edn)
Order printed publications from: Principal Librarian (Central Services), Elgin Library, Cooper Park, Elgin, Morayshire, IV30 1BX; tel: 01343 562607; fax: 01343 562630; e-mail: elgin.library@moray.gov.uk

Publications list:
Available online

Access to staff:
Contact by letter, by telephone, by fax, by e-mail and in person
Hours: Mon to Fri, 0845 to 1700

Member organisation of:
European Information Relay
Scottish Library and Information Council

MORAY COUNCIL LOCAL HERITAGE SERVICE

Old East End School, Institution Road, Elgin, Moray, IV30 1RP

Tel: 01343 569011
E-mail: heritage@moray.gov.uk

Website:
http://www.moray.org/heritage/roots.html
http://www.moray.org/heritage/index.html

Enquiries:
Enquiries to: Local Heritage Officer

Founded:
1996

Organisation type and purpose:
Local government body, research organisation.

Subject coverage:
Sources relating to Moray including archives, books, maps, newspapers and genealogical records.

Education services:
Resources for Further or Higher Education.

Non-library collection catalogue:
All or part available in-house

Library catalogue:
All or part available in-house

Access to staff:
Contact by letter, by telephone, by e-mail, in person and via website

Access to building, collection or gallery:
No prior appointment required
Hours: Mon, Wed, Thu, Fri, 1000 to 1700; Tue, 1000 to 2000; Sat, 1000 to 1200

Access for disabled people:
Access to all public areas

MORDEN LIBRARY

Merton Civic Centre, London Road, Morden, Surrey, SM4 5DX

Tel: 020 8545 4040\ Minicom no. 020 8946 1136
Fax: 020 8545 4037
E-mail: morden.library@merton.gov.uk

Enquiries:
Enquiries to: Library and Service Manager
Direct tel: 020 8545 3775
Direct e-mail: di.reynolds@merton.gov.uk

Founded:
1960

Organisation type and purpose:
Local government body, public library.

Subject coverage:
General, local history covering the area of Merton London Borough and its predecessor authorities.

Museum or gallery collection, archive, or library special collection:
Collection of Catalogues etc from Carters Tested Seeds
Lord Nelson
Simpson Papers
Tom Francis Collection of photographic negatives
William Morris, books, pictures and other material

Non-library collection catalogue:
All or part available in-house

Library catalogue:
All or part available in-house

Printed publications:
Various local history publications including:
Paradise Merton: the story of Nelson and the Hamiltons at Merton Place (Philip Rathbone, £2.50)
William Morris at Merton (David Saxby, £3.95)

Publications list:
Available in print

Access to staff:
Contact by letter, by telephone, by fax, by e-mail and in person
Hours: Mon, Tues, Thurs, Fri, 0930 to 1900; Wed, 0930 to 1300; Sat, 0930 to 1700

Access to building, collection or gallery:
No prior appointment required

Access for disabled people:
Parking provided, level entry, access to all public areas, toilet facilities

Also at the same address:
Merton Local Studies Centre
  tel: 020 8545 3239

Parent body and at the same address:
London Borough of Merton, Merton Library Service

MOREDUN RESEARCH INSTITUTE

Pentlands Science Park, Bush Loan, Penicuik, Midlothian, EH26 0PZ

Tel: 0131 445 5111
Fax: 0131 445 6235
E-mail: library@mri.sari.ac.uk

Website:
http://www.mri.sari.ac.uk

Enquiries:
Enquiries to: Librarian

Founded:
1920

Organisation type and purpose:
Research organisation.

Subject coverage:
Veterinary aspects of bacteriology, microbiology, pathology, molecular biology, parasitology, immunology, virology, especially relating to ruminants and particularly sheep.

Non-library collection catalogue:
All or part available in-house

Library catalogue:
All or part available in-house

Printed publications:
Annual List of Papers by Institute Staff
Annual Report

Access to staff:
Contact by telephone and by e-mail. Appointment necessary.
Hours: Mon to Fri, 0850 to 1715

Access to building, collection or gallery:
Prior appointment required

Access for disabled people:
Level entry

Funded by:
Scottish Executive Environment and Rural Affairs Department

Links with:
BBSRC

Parent body:
Moredun Foundation

MORLEY COLLEGE

Formal name: Morley College (1993) Limited

61 Westminster Bridge Road, London, SE1 7HT

Tel: 020 7928 8501
Fax: 020 7928 4074
E-mail: enquiries@morleycollege.ac.uk

Website:
http://www.morleycollege.ac.uk

Enquiries:
Enquiries to: Library Manager
Direct tel: 020 7450 9229

Organisation type and purpose:
Registered charity.
Adult education.

Subject coverage:
Music, art, languages (self tuition courses), social studies, literature, theatre, exercise and health, self tuition wordprocessing, spreadsheets etc, courses, multimedia.

Access to staff:
Contact by letter, by telephone, by e-mail and in person. Appointment necessary. Access for members only.
Hours: Term time: Mon to Thu, 1100 to 2000; Fri, 1100 to 1900

MOROCCAN NATIONAL TOURIST OFFICE

Formal name: Moroccan National Tourist Office
Acronym or abbreviation: MNTO

205 Regent Street, London, W1B 4HB

Tel: 020 7437 0073
Fax: 020 7734 8172
E-mail: mnto@btconnect.com

Website:
http://www.tourism-in-morocco.com

Enquiries:
Enquiries to: Director
Other contacts: Information Officer for information relevant to tourism in Morocco.

Founded:
1916

Organisation type and purpose:
National government body.
Morocco's official tourist representation, under the jurisdiction of the Moroccan Tourism Ministry. The main objective of the MNTO is to promote Morocco abroad as a distinctive destination choice for tourism.

Subject coverage:
Tourist information and advice for Morocco.

Museum or gallery collection, archive, or library special collection:
Maps
Posters
Slides (are kept in our office library)

Trade and statistical information:
Information is obtainable from the Moroccan Embassy on 020 7581 5001, contact the Economic Attaché.

Printed publications:
List of contacts for tour operators and travel agents
Tourist literature (free of charge, direct)
Promotional material in brochures, guides and posters

Electronic and video publications:
Documentaries on video
Various Hotel Properties in Morocco (Video and CD-ROM)

Publications list:
Available in print

Access to staff:
Contact by letter, by telephone, by fax, by e-mail and in person. Appointment necessary.
Hours: Mon to Fri, 0900 to 1730

Parent body:
Moroccan National Tourist Office, Rabat, Morocco
31 Angle Rue Oued Fès Avenue, Al Abtal-Agdal-Rabat, Morocco; tel: 00 2123 7 681531/32/33; fax: 00 2123 7 777437 or 681527; e-mail: visitmorocco@onmt.org.ma

MORRAB LIBRARY

Morrab House, Morrab Gardens, Penzance, Cornwall, TR18 4DA

Tel: 01736 364474

Website:
http://www.morrablibrary.co.uk

Enquiries:
Enquiries to: Librarian
Other contacts: Chairman (for committee decisions)

Founded:
1818

Organisation type and purpose:
Membership association (membership is by subscription).
Independent library.

Subject coverage:
General: all subjects, particularly history, English literature, theology, art. Special collections; Cornish collections; archival holdings, mostly Cornish; photographic archive (West Cornwall).

Museum or gallery collection, archive, or library special collection:
Stock of 50,000 books
Dawson Collection: Napoleana, Peers of the Realm
Photographic archive
Borlase manuscripts

Non-library collection catalogue:
All or part available in-house

Library catalogue:
All or part available in-house

Access to staff:
Contact by letter, by telephone, by e-mail and in

person. Appointment necessary. Non-members charged.
Hours: Tue to Fri, 1000 to 1600; Sat, 1000 to 1300
Special comments: Appointment necessary for archives.

MORRIS COWLEY & OXFORD OWNERS CLUB

Acronym or abbreviation: MCOC

202 Chantry Gardens, Southwick, Trowbridge, Wiltshire, BA14 9QX

Tel: 01225 766800

Enquiries:
Enquiries to: Secretary

Founded:
1979

Organisation type and purpose:
Membership association (membership is by subscription).
To supply parts to classic vehicle owners, clubs etc.

Subject coverage:
General information which appertains to the Morris Cowley, Oxford and Isis range of vehicles (built 1954–60); spares availability, costing and cars for sale. Also information/membership for owners of Hindustan Ambassadors.

Printed publications:
The Cowley News (magazine, quarterly, members)

Access to staff:
Contact by letter, by telephone and in person
Hours: Mon to Fri, 0900 to 2100, and weekends

MORRIS FEDERATION

Acronym or abbreviation: MF

Corner Cottage, 2 Lower Street, Sproughton, Ipswich, IP8 3AA

Tel: 01473 742334
E-mail: archive@morrisfed.org

Website:
http://www.morrisfed.org

Enquiries:
Enquiries to: Archive Officer
Direct e-mail: archive@morrisfed.org

Founded:
1975

Formerly called:
Women's Morris Federation

Organisation type and purpose:
Membership association (membership is by subscription), present number of members: 420, voluntary organisation.
To promote Morris Dancing.

Subject coverage:
Morris dancing, sword dancing, mumming.

Museum or gallery collection, archive, or library special collection:
Archive of Morris material

Non-library collection catalogue:
All or part available in-house and in print

Library catalogue:
All or part available in-house

Printed publications:
Information Leaflet (on request)
Newsletter (quarterly)
Order printed publications from: Jenny Everett, MF Treasurer, Corner Cottage, 2 Lower Street, Sproughton, Ipswich IP8 3AA

Publications list:
Available in print

Access to staff:
Contact by letter, by telephone and by e-mail. Appointment necessary. Access for members only. All charged.
Hours: Mon to Sun, 1800 to 2000

Access to building, collection or gallery:
Prior appointment required

Also at:
FeeLock (MF Secretary)
28 Fairstone Close, Hastings, Sussex, TN35 5EZ; tel: 01424 436052; e-mail: sec@morrisfed.org

Links with:
English Folk Dance & Song Society
tel: 020 7485 2206; fax: 020 7284 0534
Morris Ring
Open Morris
Sword Dance Union

MORRIS MARINA / ITAL DRIVERS' CLUB

Acronym or abbreviation: MIDC

12 Nithsdale Road, Liverpool, L15 5AX

Enquiries:
Enquiries to: Membership Secretary

Founded:
1984

Formerly called:
Morris Marina Owners' Club (year of change 1986)

Organisation type and purpose:
International organisation, membership association (membership is by subscription), present number of members: 5.
To assist owners and enthusiasts of Morris Marina and Ital cars and their derivatives to restore, maintain, preserve and operate the cars.

Subject coverage:
Maintenance, preservation and restoration of Morris Marina and Ital cars; historical and production information on Morris Marina and Ital cars.

Museum or gallery collection, archive, or library special collection:
Technical reference library; workshop manuals, parts lists, magazine articles, etc., register

Printed publications:
Last of The Line (newsletter, 6 times a year)
Something for Everyone, 3 vols
Alternative Parts Numbers List
Order printed publications from: J G Lawson at above address

Electronic and video publications:
Something for Everyone (120,000 word book available on disk)

Publications list:
Available in print

Access to staff:
Contact by letter. Appointment necessary. Access for members only.
Hours: Mon to Fri, 0900 to 1700

Links with:
Sun-Tor Register
35 Walkerith Road, Morton, Gainsborough, Lincolnshire, DN21 3DA

MORRIS MARINA OWNERS CLUB AND MORRIS ITAL REGISTER

39 Portley Road, Dawley, Telford, Shropshire, TF4 3JW

Tel: 01952 504900
E-mail: ajmmarina@aol.com

Enquiries:
Enquiries to: General Secretary
Other contacts: Life President, Chairman

Founded:
1985

Organisation type and purpose:
Membership association (membership is by subscription), present number of members: 450.

continued overleaf

Subject coverage:
Morris Marina and Morris Ital, saloon, coupe, estate, van, pickup, caravanette and motor caravan versions marketed and produced worldwide.

Museum or gallery collection, archive, or library special collection:
Information collected and held by members, brochures, workshop manuals, road test reports, press release information

Printed publications:
Marina Matters (magazine, quarterly)

Access to staff:
Contact by letter, by telephone and by e-mail
Hours: Mon to Fri, 0900 to 1700

MORRIS MINOR OWNERS CLUB LIMITED

8 Castings Road, Sir Francis Ley Industrial Estate, Derby, DE23 8YL

Tel: 01332 291675
Fax: 01332 290661
E-mail: andrew.booth@morrisminoroc.co.uk

Website:
http://www.morrisminoroc.co.uk
Club information.

Enquiries:
Enquiries to: Membership Administrator
Other contacts: Magazine Editor for magazine entries.

Founded:
1976

Organisation type and purpose:
Membership association (membership is by subscription), present number of members: 13,500.

Subject coverage:
General information on all Morris Minor cars manufactured between 1948 and 1971.

Printed publications:
Magazine (6 times a year, members)

Access to staff:
Contact by letter, by telephone, by fax, by e-mail and via website
Hours: Mon to Fri, 0900 to 1700. 24-hour answerphone

MORTAR INDUSTRY ASSOCIATION

Acronym or abbreviation: MIA

156 Buckingham Palace Road, London, SW1W 9TR

Tel: 020 7730 8194
Fax: 020 7730 4355
E-mail: james@qpa.org

Website:
http://www.mortar.org.uk
Datasheets for download, general information.

Enquiries:
Enquiries to: Secretary

Founded:
1971

Organisation type and purpose:
Trade association.
To promote the use of all factory made mortars, to further this it maintains an interest in and actively promotes masonry construction in the wider sense.

Subject coverage:
Factory made mortars for constructing brickwork, blockwork and stonework, external render, internal plaster and paving mortar.

Printed publications:
Data sheets (various topics)
Benefits (brochure)

Electronic and video publications:
Video

Publications list:
Available in print

Access to staff:
Contact by letter, by telephone, by fax, by e-mail and via website
Hours: Mon to Fri, 0900 to 1700

Founder member of:
Masonry Society

Parent body:
Quarry Products Association (QPA)
at the same address

MOTABILITY

Warwick House, Roydon Road, Harlow, Essex, CM19 5PX

Tel: 0845 456 4566
Fax: 01279 632000

Website:
http://www.motability.co.uk
A step by step guide to the Motability scheme.

Enquiries:
Enquiries to: Customer Helpline

Founded:
1977

Organisation type and purpose:
Registered charity, charity number 299745.
The Motability Scheme is the UK's leading car scheme for disabled people providing affordable, convenient, trouble-free motoring to 430,000 disabled customers and their families. Powered wheelchairs and scooters can also be financed using the scheme. Motability also provides financial assistance to customers who would otherwise be unable to afford the mobility solution they need.

Subject coverage:
Cars and powered wheelchairs, for recipients of the higher rate mobility component of DLA (Disability Living Allowance), or the war pensioners' mobility supplement.

Printed publications:
Leaflets and brochures
Lifestyle (magazine)

Electronic and video publications:
DVDs

Access to staff:
Contact by letter, by telephone and by fax
Hours: Mon to Fri, 0845 to 1715

Access for disabled people:
Parking provided, access to all public areas, toilet facilities

MOTHERS' UNION

Mary Sumner House, 24 Tufton Street, London, SW1P 3RB

Tel: 020 7222 5533
Fax: 020 7227 9736
E-mail: marketing@themothersunion.org

Website:
http://www.themothersunion.org

Enquiries:
Enquiries to: Head of Marketing
Other contacts: Communications Officer

Founded:
1876

Organisation type and purpose:
International organisation, voluntary organisation, registered charity.
To strengthen and preserve marriage and Christian family life.

Subject coverage:
Family and marriage-related subjects, role and status of women overseas, law reform, the media, prayer and spirituality.

Museum or gallery collection, archive, or library special collection:
Committee and administrative archives, founder's correspondence
Set of MU periodicals

Non-library collection catalogue:
All or part available online and in print

Library catalogue:
All or part available online

Printed publications:
Books, leaflets, prayers and services
Order printed publications from: email: marketing@themothersunion.org

Publications list:
Available online and in print

Access to staff:
Contact by letter, by telephone, by fax, by e-mail, in person and via website
Hours: Mon to Fri, 0900 to 1800

Links with:
66 dioceses in the British Isles and 27 provinces of the Anglican Communion worldwide

MOTO GUZZI CLUB GB

Acronym or abbreviation: MGCGB

Mole Cottage, 26 The Crescent, The Wells, Epsom, Surrey, KT18 7LL

Tel: 01372 724681
Fax: 01372 724681

Website:
http://www.motoguzzigb.com

Enquiries:
Enquiries to: General Secretary

Founded:
1976

Organisation type and purpose:
Membership association (membership is by subscription), present number of members: 3000.

Subject coverage:
All aspects of Moto Guzzi motorcycle ownership; discounts, technical advice, local club branches, social events, continental touring, factory visits, deals on insurance and valuation service, DVLA approved for marque requests.

Printed publications:
Gambalunga (magazine, 6 times a year)

Access to staff:
Contact by letter, by telephone and by fax
Hours: Mon to Fri, 1800 to 2000

Parent body:
British Motorcycle Federation

MOTOR CARAVANNERS' CLUB

Formal name: The Motor Caravanners' Club Limited

22 Evelyn Close, Twickenham, Middlesex, TW2 7BN

Tel: 020 8893 3883
Fax: 020 8893 8324
E-mail: info@motorcaravanners.eu

Website:
http://www.motorcaravanners.eu
Details of club membership and club activities, diary of club events available via links to group web pages.

Enquiries:
Enquiries to: Executive Secretary

Founded:
1961

Organisation type and purpose:
Membership association (membership is by subscription), present number of members: 15,000.

Subject coverage:
Leisure & holiday camping activities, motor caravans, motor homes, RV's, DIY conversions, UK touring, European touring, technical information, legislation interpretation.

Library catalogue:
All or part available in print

Printed publications:
Only to club members

Publications list:
Available in print

Access to staff:
Contact by letter, by telephone, by fax, by e-mail and via website
Hours: Mon to Thu, 0900 to 1700; Fri, 0900 to 1400

Member organisation of:
Fédération Internationale de Camping et de Caravanning (FICC)

MOTOR CYCLE INDUSTRY ASSOCIATION LIMITED

Acronym or abbreviation: MCI

Starley House, Eaton Road, Coventry, Warwickshire, CV1 2FH

Tel: 0870 070 6242
Fax: 0870 070 3291
E-mail: motorcycling@mcia.co.uk

Website:
http://www.mcia.co.uk
Corporate website.

Enquiries:
Enquiries to: Marketing Manager
Direct tel: 0870 330 7813
Direct fax: 0870 070 3292
Direct e-mail: press@mcia.co.uk

Founded:
1910

Organisation type and purpose:
Trade association.

Subject coverage:
Structure of the UK motor cycle industry, manufacture, technical and legislative information, imports, accessories, market statistics.

Trade and statistical information:
Data on import and export production, vehicles in use and registrations by type and capacity of mopeds and motorcycles.

Printed publications:
Annual Report
Bespoke Industry Statistics
Members List
Statistics Digest (monthly)
Various Industry Publications

Publications list:
Available in print

Access to staff:
Contact by letter, by fax and by e-mail
Hours: Mon to Fri, 0900 to 1700

Subsidiary and at the same address is:
Motorcycle Industry Exhibitions (MCIE)

MOTOR CYCLING CLUB LIMITED

Acronym or abbreviation: MCC

20 Old Shipyard Centre, West Bay, Bridport, Dorset, DT6 4HG

Tel: 01308 420706
E-mail: johnaley@portwrinkle.fsnet.co.uk

Website:
http://www.themotorcyclingclub.org.uk

Enquiries:
Enquiries to: Secretary General

Founded:
1901

Organisation type and purpose:
Membership association (membership is by subscription), present number of members: 1050. Motor club.
Organisation of motoring events, particularly classic trials for motorcycles and cars.

Access to staff:
Contact by letter, by telephone, by e-mail and via website
Hours: Day or Evening
Special comments: No personal callers.

MOTOR INSURANCE REPAIR RESEARCH CENTRE

Acronym or abbreviation: MIRRC/Thatcham

Colthrop Way, Thatcham, Berkshire, RG19 4NR

Tel: 01635 868855
Fax: 01635 871346
E-mail: enquiries@thatcham.org

Website:
http://www.NCSR.co.uk
Security web site
http://www.thatcham-orangepages.info
Crash repair directory (October 2002)
http://www.ncwr.co.uk
head restraint ratings
http://www.thatcham.org
Main Thatcham web site

Enquiries:
Enquiries to: Public Relations Manager
Direct tel: 01635 294829
Direct fax: 01635 861862
Direct e-mail: lesley@thatcham.org
Other contacts: Research and Operations Director for research or engineering enquiry.

Founded:
1969

Organisation type and purpose:
Training organisation, consultancy, research organisation, publishing house.
Sponsored by Motor Insurance Companies and Lloyds Syndicates.

Subject coverage:
Vehicle body repair, cost control and standards improvement.

Printed publications:
Available on subscription:
Paint Cost Guide
Repair booklets
Special Reports
Thatcham Newsletters
Order printed publications from: Subscriptions Department, MIRRC/Thatcham
Colthrop Way, Thatcham, Berkshire, RG19 4NR

Microform publications:
Many video recordings on repair techniques and crash testing (for purchase)

Electronic and video publications:
General Thatcham Introduction (CD-ROM)
eScribe – Crash repair methods & terms
TPA – Parts Price Analysis
TPG – Summary Parts Prices
TPS – Parts Prices
TTS – Repair Times
TVIS – Vehicle Identification (CD-ROM)

Access to staff:
Contact by letter, by telephone, by fax, by e-mail and via website. Appointment necessary.
Hours: Mon to Thu, 0830 to 1630; Fri, 0830 to 1545

Access for disabled people:
Parking provided, toilet facilities

Sponsored by:
Lloyds Syndicates
Motor insurance companies

MOTOR INSURERS' BUREAU

Acronym or abbreviation: MIB

Linford Wood House, 6–12 Capital Drive, Milton Keynes, Buckinghamshire, MK14 6XT

Tel: 01908 830001
Fax: 01908 671660
E-mail: enquiries@mib.org.uk

Enquiries:
Enquiries to: Finance Director

Founded:
1946

Organisation type and purpose:
International organisation, membership association (membership is by qualification).
To compensate victims of uninsured/untraceable drivers. United Kingdom's green card bureau.

Subject coverage:
Green card matters. Compensation from uninsured and untraced accidents.

Access to staff:
Contact by letter, by telephone and by fax
Hours: Mon to Fri, 0900 to 1700

MOTOR NEURONE DISEASE ASSOCIATION

Acronym or abbreviation: MND Association

PO Box 246, Northampton, NN1 2PR

Tel: 01604 250505
Fax: 01604 624726
E-mail: enquiries@mndassociation.org

Website:
http://www.mndassociation.org

Enquiries:
Enquiries to: Information Services Coordinator

Founded:
1979

Organisation type and purpose:
Voluntary organisation, registered charity.

Subject coverage:
Management, research and symptoms of motor neurone disease; care of patients, including information, compiled by professionals, for medical and paramedical staff; equipment, including loan service.

Museum or gallery collection, archive, or library special collection:
Unpublished reports on Motor Neurone Disease

Printed publications:
Annual Review
Basic and specific leaflets (available upon request)
Leaflets for professional use
Thumb Print (magazine, quarterly)

Publications list:
Available in print

Access to staff:
Contact by letter, by telephone, by fax, by e-mail and via website
Hours: Mon to Fri, 0900 to 1700

Member and Secretariat of:
International Alliance of ALS/MND Associations

Member of:
Association of Medical Research Charities
Neurological Alliance

MOTOR SPORTS ASSOCIATION

Formal name: The Royal Automobile Club Motor Sports Association Limited
Acronym or abbreviation: MSA

Motor Sports House, Riverside Park, Colnbrook, Slough, Berkshire, SL3 0HG

Tel: 01753 765000
Fax: 01753 682938
E-mail: msa_mail@compuserve.com

Website:
http://www.msauk.org
Website ordering of publications.

791

continued overleaf

Enquiries:
Enquiries to: Communications Manager
Other contacts: Corporate Executive (for media, PR, etc.)

Founded:
1979

Organisation type and purpose:
Statutory body.
Governing body of motor car sport in Great Britain and Northern Ireland.

Subject coverage:
Motor car sport, racing, rallying, autotests and trials, grasstrack, historic cars, karting, technical and medical administration, safety; fire precautions.

Printed publications:
MSA Kart Book (£3 a year)
FIA Yearbook of Automobile Sport (£50 a year)
FIA Yearbook of Karting Sport (£22 a year)
Motor Sport Club News (monthly, £40 a year)
MSA Motor Sports Directory (£3 a year)
Motorsports Now! (newsletter, quarterly, £40 a year)
MSA Officials' Yearbook (£5 a year)
MSA Yearbook (including regulations, £20 a year)
MSA Go Motorsport (£3 a year)
Order printed publications from: Data Base Controller

Electronic and video publications:
Kart Yearbook (CD-ROM, £25)
MSA Yearbook (CD-ROM)
MSA Officials Yearbook (CD-ROM)

Publications list:
Available online and in print

Access to staff:
Contact via website. Appointment necessary.
Hours: Mon to Fri, 0900 to 1730

Access for disabled people:
Access to all public areas, toilet facilities

Has:
17 regional associations

MOUNT SAINT BERNARD ABBEY LIBRARY

Coalville, Leicestershire, LE67 5UL

Tel: 01530 832298 or 832022
Fax: 01530 814608
E-mail: mountsaintbernard@btinternet.com

Enquiries:
Enquiries to: Librarian

Founded:
1835

Organisation type and purpose:
Registered charity (charity number 211004).

Subject coverage:
All aspects of theology, specialising in monasticism and patrology.

Museum or gallery collection, archive, or library special collection:
Recusant literature from the 16th-17th centuries
Two 12th century manuscripts

Access to staff:
Contact by letter, by telephone, by fax and by e-mail
Hours: Mon to Fri, 0900 to 1700

Access to building, collection or gallery:
No access other than to staff, prior appointment required

MOUNTAIN LEADER TRAINING SCOTLAND

Acronym or abbreviation: MLTS

Glenmore, Aviemore, Inverness-shire, PH22 1QU

Tel: 01479 861248
Fax: 01479 861249
E-mail: smltb@aol.com

Website:
http://www.mltscotland.org
Course dates; registration forms; Winter Mountain Leader Award documentation.

Enquiries:
Enquiries to: Executive Secretary

Founded:
1964

Scottish Mountain Leader Training Board formed from:
Scottish Sports Council

Organisation type and purpose:
National government body, training organisation.

Subject coverage:
All aspects of training and assessment of those involved in leading groups hill walking, mountaineering and climbing in the United Kingdom.

Access to staff:
Contact by letter, by telephone, by fax, by e-mail and in person. Appointment necessary.
Hours: Mon to Fri, 0900 to 1700

MOUNTAIN RESCUE COUNCIL

Acronym or abbreviation: MRC

69 Werneth Road, Glossop, Derbyshire, SK13 6NF

Tel: 01457 869506
Fax: 01457 869506

Enquiries:
Enquiries to: Honorary Secretary

Founded:
1930

Organisation type and purpose:
Voluntary organisation (charity number 222596).
Representative body dealing with mountain rescue in England and Wales.

Subject coverage:
Search and rescue of people in mountainous or wild places; assistance to statutory bodies with off-road incidents.

Printed publications:
History of the Mountain Rescue Committee
Mountain and Cave Rescue (handbook, annually)

Microform publications:
Mountain Rescue films (distributed by National Audio-Visual Aids Library)

Access to staff:
Contact by letter and by telephone
Hours: Mon to Fri, 0900 to 1700

Some support from the:
Department of Health and Social Security
Home Office

MOVEMENT FOR REFORM JUDAISM

Sternberg Centre for Judaism, 80 East End Road, Finchley, London, N3 2SY

Tel: 020 8349 5640
Fax: 020 8349 5699
E-mail: admin@reformjudaism.org.uk

Website:
http://www.reformjudaism.org.uk

Enquiries:
Enquiries to: Public Relations Manager
Direct tel: 020 8349 5689

Organisation type and purpose:
Registered charity (charity number 250060).
Religious body.

Subject coverage:
All matters relating to the practices of Reform Judaism.

Museum or gallery collection, archive, or library special collection:
Leo Baeck College Rabbinical seminary and library

Printed publications:
Annual Report
Manna Journal (quarterly, £15 a year)

Access to staff:
Contact by letter, by telephone, by fax, by e-mail and via website. Appointment necessary.
Hours: Mon to Thu, 0930 to 1700; Fri, 0930 to 1500, excluding Jewish Holy Days

Access for disabled people:
Parking provided, toilet facilities

Links with:
42 synagogues throughout the United Kingdom

MRC

Formal name: Medical Research Council

Head Office, 20 Park Crescent, London, W1B 1AL

Tel: 020 7636 5422
Fax: 020 7436 6179
E-mail: corporate@headoffice.mrc.ac.uk

Website:
http://www.mrc.ac.uk/
List of research establishments, detailed information about current research supported by MRC, research support schemes, research career opportunities, schools programme, research and the public, commercial ventures, latest MRC research news.

Enquiries:
Enquiries to: Information Officer
Direct e-mail: corporate@headoffice.mrc.ac.uk

Founded:
1913

Organisation type and purpose:
Research organisation.
To promote the balanced development of medical and related biological research and to advance knowledge that will lead to the maintenance and improvement of human health.

Subject coverage:
Medical and scientific research. Cannot give personal medical advice.

Printed publications:
Annual Report (annually, autumn)
Ethics Series
Field Reviews
Research in Focus (issues of topical interest eg cancer, ageing, stem cell therapy)
MRC/NIAS GCSE Worksheets
MRC Research Updates 1995–1999
Strategic Plan (annually, late spring)

Electronic and video publications:
Most publications available directly on website

Publications list:
Available in print

Access to staff:
Contact by letter, by telephone, by fax, by e-mail and via website
Hours: Mon to Fri, 0900 to 1700

MRC HUMAN GENETICS UNIT

Formal name: Medical Research Council Human Genetics Unit
Acronym or abbreviation: MRC HGU

Crewe Road, Edinburgh, EH4 2XU

Tel: 0131 332 2471
Fax: 0131 467 8456
E-mail: library@hgu.mrc.ac.uk or siobhan.marron@hgu.mrc.ac.uk

Website:
http://www.hgu.mrc.ac.uk/
Home page.

Enquiries:
Enquiries to: Librarian
Direct tel: 0131 467 8420

Founded:
1913

Organisation type and purpose:
Research Organisation.

Subject coverage:
Human genetics; cancer genetics; population genetics; gene therapy; molecular biology, mouse genetics developmental biology; molecular cytogenetics; chromosome structure; yeast molecular genetics; bioinformatics.

Museum or gallery collection, archive, or library special collection:
MRC Human Genetics Unit reprints by unit staff, 1948 to the present

Non-library collection catalogue:
All or part available in-house

Library catalogue:
All or part available in-house

Printed publications:
Annual Report of the Library (free)
Journals Holdings of the Unit (free)
Publications List of staff papers (annually)

Publications list:
Available in print

Access to staff:
Contact by letter, by telephone, by fax, by e-mail and in person. Appointment necessary.
Hours: Mon to Fri, 0845 to 1645

MRC HUMAN NUTRITION RESEARCH

Acronym or abbreviation: MRC HNR

Elsie Widdowson Laboratory, Fulbourn Road, Cambridge, CB1 9NL

Tel: 01223 426356
Fax: 01223 437515
E-mail: susan.jones@mrc-hnr.cam.ac.uk

Website:
http://www.mrc-hnr.cam.ac.uk
Mission statement, nutrition communication/consultancy, seminars, details of research publications, library information.

Enquiries:
Enquiries to: Librarian

Founded:
1998

Incorporates the former:
MRC Dunn Nutrition Unit (year of change 1998)

Organisation type and purpose:
Advisory body, research organisation.
Collaborative centre.

Subject coverage:
HNR is a Medical Research Council unit which exists to advance knowledge of the relationships between human nutrition and health by providing a national centre of excellence for the measurement and interpretation of biochemical, functional and dietary indications of nutritional status and health.

Museum or gallery collection, archive, or library special collection:
Library of nutrition publications
Archival material

Trade and statistical information:
Nutrition information.

Non-library collection catalogue:
All or part available in-house

Library catalogue:
All or part available in-house

Publications list:
Available online

Access to staff:
Contact by telephone, by fax, by e-mail and via website. Appointment necessary.
Hours: Mon to Fri, 1030 to 1330 and 1400 to 1530

Access to building, collection or gallery:
Special comments: Reference only

Access for disabled people:
Parking provided, level entry, access to all public areas, toilet facilities

Links with:
Addenbrooke's Hospital
Cambridge; tel: 01223 245151; website: http://www.addenbrookes.org.uk
University of Cambridge
tel: 01223 337733; website: http://www.cam.ac.uk

Parent body:
Medical Research Council
20 Park Crescent, London, W1B 1AL; tel: 020 7636 5422; fax: 020 7436 6179; website: http://www.mrc.ac.uk

MRC INSTITUTE OF HEARING RESEARCH

University Park, University of Nottingham, Nottingham, NG7 2RD

Tel: 0115 922 3431
Fax: 0115 951 8503
E-mail: enquiries@ihr.mrc.ac.uk

Website:
http://www.ihr.mrc.ac.uk
Epidemiology and public health.

Enquiries:
Enquiries to: Information Officer
Other contacts: Unit Manager

Founded:
1977

Organisation type and purpose:
Research organisation.

Subject coverage:
Auditory Processessing Disorder, hereditary deafness, neural representation of complex sounds, assessment of cochlear function in humans, auditory perception, hearing disability, rehabilitation and benefit from hearing aids, cochlear implants, service delivery and rehabilitation, clinical studies of tinnitus, epidemiological and public health aspects of hearing disorders, causes, consequences and management of middle-ear disease.

Printed publications:
Annual Report
List of Journals held in Library
Publication Report listed under eight themes: hereditary deafness; auditory neurophysiology; peripheral auditory function in humans; central auditory function; hearing disability; rehabilitation and benefit from hearing aids; cochlear implantation; epidemiology and public health; causes, consequences and treatment of middle-ear disease
A variety of well-specified clinical procedures and test procedures plus equipment or software to support their use

Electronic and video publications:
Toy Test illustrates administration of the McCormick Toy Discrimination Toy Test (video)
Glue Ear (video)
CD-ROMs that include test materials.

Publications list:
Available online

Access to staff:
Contact by letter, by fax, by e-mail and via website
Hours: Mon to Fri, 0900 to 1700

Parent body:
Medical Research Council
tel: 020 7636 5422; fax: 020 7436 6179

MS TRUST

Formal name: Multiple Sclerosis Trust

Spirella Building, Bridge Road, Letchworth Garden City, Hertfordshire, SG6 4ET

Tel: 01462 476700
Fax: 01462 476710
E-mail: info@mstrust.org.uk

Website:
http://www.mstrust.org.uk
Information on all aspects of the MS Trust's work, information, education, research, fundraising, campaigns.

Founded:
1993

Formerly called:
MS Research Trust (year of change 2001)

Organisation type and purpose:
Charity working with and for the 100,000 people in the United Kingdom with multiple sclerosis (MS), to enable them to live their lives to the full. Provides information, education for health professionals, research into better management of MS, support for anyone affected by MS.

Subject coverage:
Multiple sclerosis: information on all aspects of the disease, especially the management of symptoms.

Information services:
Information for anyone affected by multiple sclerosis, either personally or professionally. Publications, newsletters and personal enquiry service.

Education services:
Education courses for health and social care professionals working with people with MS.

Printed publications:
Wide range of publications,see website: http://www.mstrust.org.uk/publications
Order printed publications from: tel: 01462 476700; e-mail: info@mstrust.org.uk; website: http://www.mstrust.org.uk/publications; or by post

Electronic and video publications:
MS Together (DVD for recently diagnosed)
Move It For MS (DVD of exercises, £1)
Order electronic and video publications from: tel: 01462 476700; e-mail: info@mstrust.org.uk; website: http://www.mstrust.org.uk/publications; or by post

Publications list:
Available online and in print

Access to staff:
Contact by letter, by telephone, by fax, by e-mail and via website
Hours: Mon to Fri, 0900 to 1700; answerphone outside office hours

Access to building, collection or gallery:
No access other than to staff

MSD BIOLOGICS (UK) LTD

PO Box 2, Billingham, Cleveland, TS23 1YN

Tel: 01642 363511
Fax: 01642 364463

Enquiries:
Enquiries to: Librarian
Direct tel: 01642 364484

Founded:
1999

Formerly called:
Avecia Biologics, Avecia Biotechnology, Avecia Lifescience Molecules, Zeneca Lifescience Molecules, ICI Bio Products (year of change 2010)

Organisation type and purpose:
Research organisation.

Subject coverage:
Healthcare, bioscience.

Access to staff:
Contact by letter, by telephone and by fax
Hours: Mon to Fri, 0900 to 1700

continued overleaf

Parent body:
Merck Sharp & Dohme (Holdings) Limited
Hertford Road, Hoddesdon, Hertfordshire, EN11
9BU

MSI MARKETING RESEARCH FOR INDUSTRY

Acronym or abbreviation: MSI

Viscount House, River Lane, Saltney, Chester,
Cheshire, CH4 8RH

Tel: 01244 681186
Fax: 01244 681457
E-mail: enquiries@msi-marketingresearch.co.uk

Enquiries:
Enquiries to: Managing Director
Other contacts: Sales and Marketing Co-ordinator
for marketing purposes.

Founded:
1980

Organisation type and purpose:
Consultancy, research organisation.

Subject coverage:
Market research across wide range of sectors;
principally covering non-consumer markets such
as industrial, engineering and construction
markets.

Printed publications:
Market Research Reports (over 150 titles, list
available) under the headings: Construction &
Building Products, Distribution, Engineering
Components, Electrical Components &
Telecommunications, Environmental, Service
Markets, Packaging & Paper, Metals &
Metalworking Industry, Transportation &
Infrastructure, Utilities & Process Industries,
Security & Heating, Healthcare, Industrial
Services, Marketing Presentations
Marketing Surveys Index (10 times a year)

Electronic and video publications:
MSI reports available online

Publications list:
Available in print

Access to staff:
Contact by letter, by telephone, by fax and by e-
mail. Appointment necessary.
Hours: Mon to Fri, 0900 to 1700

MULLARD SPACE SCIENCE LABORATORY

Acronym or abbreviation: MSSL

Department of Space and Climate Physics,
University College London, Holmbury St Mary,
Dorking, Surrey, RH5 6NT

Tel: 01483 274111
Fax: 01483 278312

Website:
http://www.mssl.ucl.ac.uk/

Enquiries:
Enquiries to: Director

Organisation type and purpose:
University department or institute, research
organisation.

Subject coverage:
X-ray astronomy; solar X-ray studies;
magnetospheric studies; earth remote sensing for
climate and geodetic studies.

Publications list:
Available online and in print

Also at:
Department of Space and Climate Physics
University College London, Gower Street,
London, WC1E 6BT; tel: 020 7679 2000

MULTI-FAITH CENTRE

Formal name: The Multi-Faith Centre at the
University of Derby
Acronym or abbreviation: MFC

University of Derby, Kedleston Road, Derby, DE22
1GB

Tel: 01332 591285
E-mail: mfc@derby.ac.uk

Website:
http://www.multifaithcentre.org

Enquiries:
Enquiries to: Centre Director

Founded:
1999

Organisation type and purpose:
Registered charity (charity number 1087140),
university department or institute, research
organisation.
Information on world religious traditions and
commitments, and inter-faith and multi-faith
initiatives.

Subject coverage:
Religious organisations in the United Kingdom,
religions, statistics, demographics, inter-faith
relations.

Museum or gallery collection, archive, or library special collection:
Collection of questionnaires underlying the
publication, Religions in the UK: A multi-faith
directory
Directories of many UK religious organisations
Ephemera from many religious organisations

Trade and statistical information:
Data on religious organisations in the UK, data on
religious statistics.

Non-library collection catalogue:
All or part available in-house

Library catalogue:
All or part available in-house

Printed publications:
Religions in the UK: Directory (2007 edn: £30.00
incl. p&p)
Order printed publications from: the Multi-Faith
Centre at the University of Derby

Access to staff:
Contact by letter, by telephone, by e-mail and via
website. Appointment necessary.
Hours: Mon to Fri, 0900 to 1700

Access to building, collection or gallery:
Prior appointment required

MULTIPLE BIRTHS FOUNDATION

Acronym or abbreviation: MBF

Hammersmith House – Level 4, Queen Charlotte's
& Chelsea Hospital, Du Cane Road, London, W12
0HS

Tel: 020 8383 3519
Fax: 020 8383 3041
E-mail: mbf@imperial.nhs.uk

Website:
http://www.multiplebirths.org.uk

Enquiries:
Enquiries to: Administrator

Founded:
1988

Organisation type and purpose:
Registered charity (charity number 1094546).
To offer professional support for families with
multiple births as well as advice and training to
medical, educational and other professionals
involved in their care.

Subject coverage:
Multiple births.

Museum or gallery collection, archive, or library special collection:
Library and resource centre of books, journals,
articles and videos relating to multiple births

Printed publications:
Are They Identical? Zygosity Determination
Feeding Twins, Triplets and More
Preparing for Twins and Triplets (E Bryan, 1996,
£2.50)
Guidelines for Professionals (Bryan E, Denton J
and Hallett F):
Bereavement
Facts about Multiple Births
Infertility New Choices – New Dilemmas
Multiple Pregnancy
Twins & Multiple Births
Twins, Triplets and More

Publications list:
Available online and in print

Access to staff:
Contact by letter, by telephone and by e-mail
Hours: Mon to Fri, 0900 to 1700

MULTIPLE SCLEROSIS INTERNATIONAL FEDERATION

Acronym or abbreviation: MSIF

3rd Floor, Skyline House, 200 Union Street,
London, SE1 0LX

Tel: 020 7620 1911
Fax: 020 7620 1922
E-mail: info@msif.org

Website:
http://www.msif.org

Enquiries:
Enquiries to: Chief Executive

Founded:
1967

Organisation type and purpose:
International organisation, membership
association (membership is by subscription,
qualification, election or invitation), present
number of members: 42 autonomous national
member societies, voluntary organisation,
registered charity.
Coordinating the work of national MS societies
worldwide.

Subject coverage:
The full integration of people with MS,
international development, coordination and
furthering of the work of national MS societies
worldwide, scientific research and educational
information relating to MS; development of
existing societies.

Printed publications:
MS in focus (journal, twice yearly)
Annual Review
Order printed publications from: email: info@msif.org

Access to staff:
Contact by letter, by telephone, by fax, by e-mail
and via website. Appointment necessary.
Hours: Mon to Fri, 0930 to 1730

Access for disabled people:
Parking provided, ramped entry, access to all
public areas, toilet facilities

Member organisations:
42 national MS societies

MULTIPLE SCLEROSIS RESOURCE CENTRE

Acronym or abbreviation: MSRC

7 Peartree Business Centre, Peartree Road,
Stanway, Colchester, Essex, CO3 0JN

Tel: 01206 505444
Fax: 01206 505449
E-mail: themsrc@yahoo.com

Website:
http://www.msrc.co.uk
Comprehensive site for anyone affected by
Multiple Sclerosis.

Enquiries:
Enquiries to: Office Manager
Direct tel: 01206 505453
Direct fax: 01206 505449
Direct e-mail: info@msrc.co.uk
Other contacts: Counsellors for counselling – 24 Hr
Telephone Counselling 0800 783 0518.

Founded:
1993

Subject coverage:
Offers support to those affected by MS,
information helpline, support counselling, referal
to other agencies, publications.

Printed publications:
New Pathways, magazine, once every other
    month)
All 21 Leaflets (available free, direct)
The Multiple Sclerosis Resource Centre A-Z Guide
    to Complementary Therapies (Graham J and
    Pulling F, 2000, £12.50)
Eating & MS – Information & Recipes (£6.95)
Emotional Reactions to MS (Revised 1994, £4)
Multiple Sclerosis Pregnancy & Parenthood
    (Graham J, 1996, £7.75)

Publications list:
Available in print

Access to staff:
Contact by letter, by telephone, by fax, by e-mail,
in person and via website. Appointment necessary.
Hours: Mon to Fri, 0900 to 1700

Access for disabled people:
Parking provided, ramped entry

MULTIPLE SCLEROSIS SOCIETY

Formal name: Multiple Sclerosis Society of Great
Britain and Northern Ireland
Acronym or abbreviation: MSS

MS National Centre, 372 Edgware Road,
Cricklewood, London, NW2 6ND

Tel: 020 8438 0700
Fax: 020 8438 0701
E-mail: info@mssociety.org.uk

Website:
http://www.mssociety.org.uk
Extensive website including details of current
activities/services/publications, and access to
online library database, which includes many full-
text publications aimed at a lay audience.

Enquiries:
Enquiries to: Information Officer
Direct tel: 020 8438 0799
Direct e-mail: infoteam@mssociety.org.uk
Other contacts: Information Officers

Founded:
1953

Organisation type and purpose:
The Society is a registered charity (charity number
207495), which offers support to all those affected
by MS. To this end it funds MS research, provides
information, grants (financial assistance),
education and training on MS. It produces
numerous publications on MS and runs a
freephone specialist Helpline.

Subject coverage:
Research into the cause and cure of multiple
sclerosis, issues relating to all those affected by
multiple sclerosis.

Information services:
Enquiry line and library.

Services for disabled people:
Services available.

**Museum or gallery collection, archive, or library
special collection:**
Oliver Ball Library

Library catalogue:
All or part available online

Printed publications:
Publications (free of charge, donations are
    welcome) include:
What is MS? (booklet)
Just diagnosed (booklet)
MS Essentials – 28 booklets on all aspects of MS
MS Matters (magazine, six times a year)
Standards of Healthcare for People with MS
Order printed publications from: website: http://
www.mssociety.org.uk/publications

Electronic and video publications:
Video (for loan only)

Publications list:
Available online and in print

Access to staff:
Contact by letter, by telephone, by fax, by e-mail,
in person and via website
Hours: Mon to Fri, 0900 to 1700

Access to building, collection or gallery:
No prior appointment required
Hours: Mon to Fri, 0900 to 1700

Access for disabled people:
Parking provided, ramped entry, toilet facilities
Hours: Mon to Fri, 0900 to 1700

Affiliated to:
Multiple Sclerosis International Federation (MSIF)

Branches:
Multiple Sclerosis Society in Scotland
    Ratho Park, 88 Glasgow Road, Ratho Station,
    Newbridge, EH28 8PP; tel: 0131 335 4050; fax:
    0131 335 4051; e-mail: enquiries@
    mssocietyscotland.org.uk; website: http://www
    .mssocietyscotland.org.uk
Multiple Sclerosis Society Northern Ireland
    34 Annadale Avenue, Belfast, BT7 3JJ; tel: 028
    9080 2802; e-mail: info@mssocietyni.co.uk;
    website: http://www.mssocietyni.co.uk
Multiple Sclerosis Society Wales/Cymru
    Temple Court, Cathedral Road, Cardiff, CF11
    9HA; tel: 029 2078 6676; fax: 029 2078 6677; e-
    mail: mscymruwales@mssociety.org.uk; website:
    http://www.mssociety.org.uk/wales

MURRAY EDWARDS COLLEGE

Rosemary Murray Library, Murray Edwards
College, Huntingdon Road, Cambridge, CB3 0DF

Tel: 01223 762202
Fax: 01223 763110
E-mail: library@murrayedwards.cam.ac.uk

Website:
http://www.murrayedwards.cam.ac.uk/exploring/
rosemarymurraylibrary/rosemarymurraylibrary

Enquiries:
Enquiries to: Librarian

Founded:
1954

Formerly called:
New Hall (year of change 2008)

Organisation type and purpose:
College library.

Subject coverage:
All Tripos subjects and those of the special
collections.

**Museum or gallery collection, archive, or library
special collection:**
Bequests of Eleonora Duse, Elizabeth Rawson,
    classics and ancient history, and Dorothy Gabe
    French
Women's studies

Library catalogue:
All or part available in-house

Printed publications:
Women's Art at New Hall (catalogue)
New Hall 1954–1972: The making of a college

Access to staff:
Appointment necessary. Access for members only.
Hours: Mon to Fri, 0900 to 1700

Access for disabled people:
Level entry, toilet facilities

Parent body:
University of Cambridge

MUSCULAR DYSTROPHY CAMPAIGN

Acronym or abbreviation: MDC

61 Southwark Street, London, SE1 0HL

Tel: 020 7803 4800; 020 7401 3495
Fax: 020 7401 3495
E-mail: info@muscular-dystrophy.org

Website:
http://www.muscular-dystrophy.org
Information on neuromuscular disorders and the
Group.

Enquiries:
Enquiries to: Information Officer

Founded:
1959

Organisation type and purpose:
Voluntary organisation, registered charity (charity
number 205395).
Medical research.
Support and care.

Subject coverage:
Neuromuscular conditions, muscular dystrophy,
aids and equipment, research.

Printed publications:
Annual Report
Annual Review
Target MD (4 times a year)

Publications list:
Available in print

Access to staff:
Contact by letter, by telephone and by fax
Hours: Mon to Fri, 0900 to 1700

Member organisation of:
European Alliance of Neuromuscular Disorders
Associations (EADMA)

MUSEUM OF ADVERTISING & PACKAGING

Albert Warehouse, The Docks, Gloucester, GL1
2EH

Tel: 01452 302309

Website:
http://www.themuseum.co.uk

Enquiries:
Enquiries to: Curator

Founded:
1984

Organisation type and purpose:
Museum.

Subject coverage:
Advertising, packaging and social history 1850 to
present.

**Museum or gallery collection, archive, or library
special collection:**
Television commercial programmes
The Robert Opie Collection (300,000 items relating
    to the history of the consumer society)

MUSEUM OF ENGLISH RURAL LIFE

Acronym or abbreviation: MERL

University of Reading, Redlands Road, Reading,
RG1 5EX

continued overleaf

Tel: 0118 378 8660
Fax: 0118 378 5632
E-mail: merl@reading.ac.uk

Website:
http://www.reading.ac.uk/merl
Museum website and online catalogue.

Enquiries:
Enquiries to: Librarian
Other contacts: Archivist for archive and
photographic enquiries.

Founded:
1951

Organisation type and purpose:
Museum, university department or institute,
research organisation.

Subject coverage:
Agricultural and rural history including history of
agricultural engineering, and food manufacturing
and processing industries, agricultural societies,
history of environmental organisations, rural
industries, farm implements, craft tools, machines,
domestic equipment; agricultural museology.

**Museum or gallery collection, archive, or library
special collection:**
Book collections:
NIRD and Milk Marketing Board Collection
  (Dairying); Nuptown House and Fussell
  Collections (pre-1850 agriculture and
  agricultural history); Edgar Thomas Collection
  (agricultural research papers)
Archive collections:
Records of agricultural engineering, processing
  and seed production firms; records of
  agricultural co-operatives and organisations;
  records of countryside and rural affairs
  organisations; farm records collection; records
  relating to crafts and rural industries;
  agricultural research papers
Photographic collections:
Local collections; press collections (including
  'Farmers Weekly' and 'Farmer and Stockbreeder'
  Archives); countryside and environment
  collections; farm machinery and engineering
  collections; film and video collections

Trade and statistical information:
Agricultural statistics.
Food consumption and expenditure statistics.

Non-library collection catalogue:
All or part available online and in-house

Library catalogue:
All or part available online

Access to staff:
Contact by letter, by telephone, by fax, by e-mail,
in person and via website. Appointment necessary.
Hours: Mon to Fri, 0900 to 1700

Access to building, collection or gallery:
Hours: Museum: Tue to Fri, 0900 to 1700; Sat and
Sun, 1400 to 1630
Reading Room, for access to library and archives:
Mon to Fri, 0900 to 1700

Parent body:
University of Reading

MUSEUM OF LONDON
DOCKLANDS

Library and Archives, Museum of London
Docklands, No 1 Warehouse, West India Quay,
Hertsmere Road, London, E14 4AL

Tel: 020 7001 9844
Fax: 020 7001 9801

Website:
http://www.museumoflondon.org.uk/docklands

Enquiries:
Enquiries to: General Enquiries
Direct e-mail: info.docklands@museumoflondon
.org.uk

Founded:
1984

Organisation type and purpose:
Museum, historic building, house or site, suitable
for ages: 5+.

Subject coverage:
The history and development of the Port of
London from 1770 to date, including the current
regeneration of London's Docklands, the enclosed
docks and riverside wharves, the docks and river,
cargo handling, dock trades, dock police, dock
equipment, labour history of the docks, tools and
equipment used in the docks.

**Museum or gallery collection, archive, or library
special collection:**
20,000 photographs of docks and river
British Ports Authority archive covering the port
  transport industry nationally from 1911–1975
Coal Meter's Society archive c. 1750 to c. 1980
Data on the registered dock labour force in London
  (1950–1988)
Data on the trade of the port of London (1800 to
  the present)
Docklands Forum archive 1975–1995
Historic films of docks 1921–1970
Port of London Authority records 1909 to date
  (historic records only, i.e. non-operational)
Records of the Corporation of London River
  Thames Committee (1770–1857) and the Thames
  Conservators (1857–1909)
The surviving business records of the private dock
  companies operating on the Thames (1799–1909)

Trade and statistical information:
Data on the trade of the Port of London (1800 to the
present).
Data on the registered dock labour force in London
1950–1988.

Non-library collection catalogue:
All or part available in-house

Library catalogue:
All or part available in-house

Printed publications:
Dockland Life: historic and social history 1860–
  1970 (for sale)
Gateway to the East (for sale)
Liquid History: the first 50 years of the PLA (for
  sale)
Order printed publications from: website: http://
www.museumoflondonshop.co.uk

Electronic and video publications:
City of Ships (1938) (DVD, for sale)
Waters of Time (1951) (DVD, for sale)
Royal River (1929/1953) (DVD, for sale)
Thames Port (1970s) (DVD, for sale)
Order electronic and video publications from: http://
www.museumoflondonshop.co.uk

Access to staff:
Contact by letter, by telephone, by fax, by e-mail,
in person and via website. Appointment necessary.
Hours: Mon to Fri, 1030 to 1630

Access for disabled people:
Parking provided, ramped entry, access to all
public areas, toilet facilities, dedicated disabled
persons' lift
Special comments: Dedicated disabled persons lift

Branch museums:
Museum of London Docklands
  at same address

Funded by:
Corporation of London (COL) and Department for
Culture, Media and Sport (DCMS)

Parent body:
Museum of London
  150 London Wall, London, EC2Y 5HN; tel: 020
  7001 9844; e-mail: info@museumoflondon.org
  .uk; website: http://www.museumoflondon.org
  .uk

MUSEUM OF THE HISTORY OF
EDUCATION

Leeds University, Parkinson Court, Leeds, West
Yorkshire, LS2 9JT

Tel: 0113 233 4665/4545
Fax: 0113 233 4529

Website:
http://education.leeds.ac.uk/edu/inted/museum
.htm

Enquiries:
Enquiries to: Curator

Founded:
1951

Organisation type and purpose:
Museum.
University collection and centre for research and
publication.

Subject coverage:
History of education and educational
administration.

**Museum or gallery collection, archive, or library
special collection:**
Board of Education files 1939–1945
Educational artefacts
Library of the history of education
Pupil exercise books
West Riding County Council Education Committee
  Minutes 1904–1974 and other documents

Printed publications:
Catalogue 1980
Educational Administration and History
  Monographs (list available from the Museum)
Journal of Educational Administration and History
  (2 times a year)

Access to staff:
Contact by letter and by telephone. Appointment
necessary.
Hours: Mon, Wed, Fri, 1330 to 1630; Thu, 1330 to
1630; Tue closed

Access to building, collection or gallery:
Prior appointment required
Special comments: The museum is closed for staff
and public holidays and when in use by students.
Prior booking of visits advised.

Access for disabled people:
Ramped entry

MUSEUMS ASSOCIATION

Acronym or abbreviation: MA

24 Calvin Street, London, E1 6NW

Tel: 020 7426 6970
Fax: 020 7426 6961
E-mail: info@museumsassociation.org

Website:
http://www.museumsassociation.org
Details of conferences, training events, MA
membership, publications and updates on
museum news.

Enquiries:
Enquiries to: Information
Direct tel: 020 7426 6950

Founded:
1889

Organisation type and purpose:
Professional body, registered charity (charity
number 313024).

Subject coverage:
Museums, particularly professional matters and
training.

Printed publications:
Museums Journal (monthly)
Museums Yearbook
Museum Services Directory

Electronic and video publications:
Museum Practice (3 times a year)

Publications list:
Available online and in print

Access to staff:
Contact by letter, by telephone, by fax, by e-mail
and via website. Appointment necessary.

Hours: Mon to Fri, 0900 to 1700

Access to building, collection or gallery:
Hours: Mon to Fri, 0900 to 1700

MUSEUMS GALLERIES SCOTLAND

Acronym or abbreviation: MGS

1 Papermill Wynd, McDonald Road, Edinburgh EH7 4QL

Tel: 0131 550 4100
Fax: 0131 550 4139
E-mail: inform@museumsgalleriesscotland.org.uk

Website:
http://www.museumsgalleriesscotland.org.uk
Information about Museums Galleries Scotland and museums and galleries in Scotland.

Enquiries:
Enquiries to: Research Manager

Founded:
1964

Formerly called:
Scottish Museums Council

Organisation type and purpose:
National organisation, membership association, present number of members: 200+, registered charity (charity number SCO 15593).
MGS is the membership organisation for museums and galleries in Scotland.

Subject coverage:
Museums/galleries as applied to Scotland.

Museum or gallery collection, archive, or library special collection:
General information on Scottish museums and galleries

Trade and statistical information:
Data on the number and nature of museums in Scotland.

Library catalogue:
All or part available in-house

Access to staff:
Contact by letter, by telephone, by fax, by e-mail and via website
Hours: Mon to Fri, 0900 to 1700

MUSEUMS, LIBRARIES AND ARCHIVES COUNCIL

Acronym or abbreviation: MLA

Grosvenor House, 14 Bennetts Hill, Birmingham, B2 5RS

Tel: 0121 345 7300
Fax: 0121 345 7303
E-mail: info@mla.gov.uk

Website:
http://www.mla.gov.uk

Enquiries:
Direct e-mail: john.harrison@mla.gov.uk

Founded:
2000

Organisation type and purpose:
To connect people and change lives through museums, libraries and archives; to increase and sustain participation; to put museums, libraries and archives at the heart of national, regional and local life; to establish a world class and sustainable sector and put it on the best footing for the future; to lead sector strategy and policy development.

Subject coverage:
Museums, libraries and archives

Access to staff:
Contact by letter, by telephone, by fax, by e-mail and via website

Regional 'Renaissance' programmes:
East Midlands, East of England, London, North East, North West, South East, South West, West Midlands, Yorkshire

MUSHROOM GROWERS' ASSOCIATION

Acronym or abbreviation: MGA

2 St Paul's Street, Stamford, Lincolnshire, PE9 2BE

Tel: 01780 766888
Fax: 01780 766558
E-mail: carolyn@snowcapmushrooms.co.uk

Enquiries:
Enquiries to: Secretary to the Association

Founded:
1945

Organisation type and purpose:
Trade association (membership is by subscription).

Subject coverage:
Mushroom cultivation.

Printed publications:
Mushroom Journal (monthly)

Access to staff:
Contact by letter
Hours: Mon to Fri, 0900 to 1700

Specialist branch of the:
National Farmers' Union

MUSIC EDUCATION COUNCIL

Acronym or abbreviation: MEC

54 Elm Road, Hale, Altrincham, Cheshire, WA15 9QP

Tel: 0161 928 3085
Fax: 0161 929 9648
E-mail: ahassan@easynet.co.uk

Website:
http://www.mec.org.uk
Information about MEC, current work and projects, members and links.

Enquiries:
Enquiries to: Professional Officer

Organisation type and purpose:
Membership association (membership is by subscription), present number of members: 168 corporate, 70 individual, registered charity (charity number 270004).
Umbrella body for music education and training.

Subject coverage:
Music education.

Printed publications:
Newsletter (6 times a year)

Access to staff:
Contact by letter, by telephone, by fax and by e-mail
Hours: Mon to Fri, 0900 to 1700

Acts as UK's representative body on:
International Society for Music Education

MUSIC IN HOSPITALS

Acronym or abbreviation: MiH

Case House, 85–89 High Street, Walton-on-Thames, Surrey, KT12 1DZ

Tel: 01932 260810
Fax: 01932 224123
E-mail: info@musicinhospitals.org.uk

Website:
http://www.musicinhospitals.org.uk

Enquiries:
Enquiries to: Chief Executive

Founded:
1948

Organisation type and purpose:
Registered charity (charity number 1051659).

Subject coverage:
Provides live concerts in hospitals, hospices, nursing homes, day centres throughout the United Kingdom. These are given by carefully selected professional musicians who are chosen not only for their high standard of musicianship, but also for their ability to relate to the most confused, apathetic or ill and to involve them in the performance.

Printed publications:
Annual Report

Access to staff:
Contact by letter, by telephone, by fax and by e-mail
Hours: Mon to Fri, 0830 to 1700

Also at:
Music in Hospitals – Northwest
  RNCM , 124 Oxford Road, Manchester, M13 9RD; tel: 0161 907 5387; fax: 0161 273 7611
Music in Hospitals Scotland
  10 Forth Street, Edinburgh, EH1 3LD; tel: 0131 556 5848; fax: 0131 556 0225
Welsh Office
  25 Ystrad Drive, Johnstown, Carmarthen, SA31 3PG; tel: 01267 242981; fax: 0167 242981

MUSIC MASTERS' AND MISTRESSES' ASSOCIATION

Acronym or abbreviation: MMA

Wayfaring, Smithers Lane, East Peckham, Tonbridge, Kent, TN12 5HT

Tel: 01622 871576
Fax: 01622 871576
E-mail: mma.admin@ntlworld.com

Enquiries:
Enquiries to: Administrator

Organisation type and purpose:
Membership association.

Subject coverage:
Teaching of music in schools.

Printed publications:
Directory of Members
Journal (3 times a year, members)
Music Awards at Independent Senior Schools (annual guide to music scholarships)

Access to staff:
Contact by letter, by telephone, by fax and by e-mail
Hours: Mon to Fri, 0900 to 1700

MUSICAL BOX SOCIETY OF GREAT BRITAIN

Acronym or abbreviation: MBSGB

PO Box 373, Welwyn, AL6 0WY

E-mail: mail@mbsgb.org.uk

Website:
http://www.mbsgb.org.uk
General information about the Society and how to join.

Enquiries:
Enquiries to: Secretary

Founded:
1962

Organisation type and purpose:
International organisation, membership association (membership is by subscription), voluntary organisation.
Collectors, museums, restorers.
To promote the preservation, restoration and enjoyment of mechanical music.

Subject coverage:
Mechanical music, technical details, history, restoration and repair, dealers and auctioneers, authors.

continued overleaf

Museum or gallery collection, archive, or library special collection:
Society Archives

Printed publications:
Books and booklets
Music Box (quarterly, members)
Tune Sheet Book
The Organette Book

Publications list:
Available in print

Access to staff:
Contact by letter, by e-mail and via website
Hours: Mon to Fri, 0900 to 1700

MUSICIANS' UNION

Acronym or abbreviation: MU

60–62 Clapham Road, London, SW9 0JJ

Tel: 020 7582 5566
Fax: 020 7582 9805
E-mail: info@musiciansunion.org.uk

Website:
http://www.musiciansunion.org.uk

Enquiries:
Enquiries to: Deputy General Secretary

Founded:
1893

Organisation type and purpose:
Trade union (membership is by subscription), present number of members: 31,000.

Subject coverage:
Music, rates for musicians, contract advice.

Printed publications:
Musician (quarterly)

Access to staff:
Contact by letter, by fax and via website
Hours: 1000 to 1730

Access to building, collection or gallery:
Prior appointment required

Also at:
Musicians' Union
 40 Canal Street, Manchester, M1 3WD; tel: 0161 236 1764; fax: 0161 236 0159
Musicians' Union
 11 Sandyford Place, Glasgow, G3 7NB; tel: 0141 248 3723; fax: 0141 204 3510
Musicians' Union
 Benson House, Lombard Street, Birmingham, B12 0QN; tel: 0121 622 3870; fax: 0121 622 5361
Musicians' Union
 131 St Georges Road, Bristol, BS1 5UW; tel: 0117 926 5438; fax: 0117 925 3729

MUSLIM EDUCATIONAL TRUST

Acronym or abbreviation: MET

130 Stroud Green Road, London, N4 3RZ

Tel: 020 7272 8502
Fax: 020 7281 3457
E-mail: info@muslim-ed-trust.org.uk

Website:
http://www.muslim-ed-trust.org.uk

Enquiries:
Enquiries to: Director
Other contacts: Assistant Director and Sales Manager.

Founded:
1966

Organisation type and purpose:
Registered charity (charity number 313192), suitable for ages: 4 to 18, publishing house. Educational charity.

Subject coverage:
Muslim, Islamic education in a non-Muslim country; religious education for Muslim children; Islamic studies.

Printed publications:
British Muslims and Schools (Sarwar G, 1994, £2.50)
Islam: a brief guide (Sarwar G, 15th ed., 2003, free)
Islam: Beliefs and Teachings (Sarwar G, 7th ed., 2003, £6.50 inc. p&p)
Islam for Younger People (Sarwar G, 4th ed., 2003, £3 inc. p&p)
Issues in Islamic Education: a collection of twelve essays (1996, £3.75 inc. p&p)
Posters (A2, colour, laminated, £2 inc. p&p)
Parents and Children in Islam
5 Basic Duties of Islam
3 Most Sacred Places of Islam
How to make Wudu and How to Perform Salah
Prophets of Allah
Islamic Manners
Reflect (magazine for young Muslims, 3 times a year)
Sex Education – The Muslim Perspective (Sarwar G, 4th ed., 2004, £3.75 inc. p&p)
The beginner's Book of Salah (Sarwar G, 6th ed. £3 inc. p&p)
What does Islam say? (Hewitt I, 4th ed., 2004, £3.75 inc. p&p)

Publications list:
Available online and in print

Access to staff:
Contact by letter, by telephone and by fax. Appointment necessary.
Hours: Mon to Fri, 0900 to 1700

Affiliated to:
Religious Education Council of UK and Eire
 CEM, Royal Buildings, Victoria Street, Derby, DE1 1GW; tel: 01332 296655; fax: 01332 343253

MUSLIM WOMEN'S WELFARE ASSOCIATION

425 Lea Bridge Road, London, E10 7EA

Tel: 020 8539 7478
Fax: 020 8539 7478

Enquiries:
Enquiries to: Co-ordinator

Founded:
1983

Access to staff:
Contact by letter, by telephone, by fax and in person
Hours: Mon to Fri, 1000 to 1530

Access to building, collection or gallery:
No access other than to staff

Access for disabled people:
Level entry

MUSLIM WORLD LEAGUE

46 Goodge Street, London, W1T 4LU

Tel: 020 7636 7568
Fax: 020 7637 5034
E-mail: mwl@webstar.com.uk

Enquiries:
Enquiries to: Deputy Director

Founded:
1982

Organisation type and purpose:
International organisation, registered charity (charity number 290098).
To help the community in educational, cultural and religious matters.

Subject coverage:
Information about the problems, rights, duties etc concerning the Muslim Community in UK and Eire.

Library catalogue:
All or part available in-house

Access to staff:
Contact by letter, by telephone, by fax, by e-mail and in person. Appointment necessary. Letter of introduction required.
Hours: Mon to Fri, 1030 to 1600

Access to building, collection or gallery:
No prior appointment required

Links with:
Muslim World League (MWL)
 PO Box 537, Makkah, Saudi Arabia; tel: 00 9662 560 0919; fax: 00 9662 560 1267/560 1319; e-mail: mul@aol.com
Supreme Council of Mosques
 Makkah, Saudi Arabia

MVRA LIMITED

Glenfield Business Park, Philips Road, Blackburn, Lancashire, BB1 5QH

Tel: 0870 458 3051
Fax: 0870 458 3149
E-mail: info@mvra.com

Website:
http://www.mvra.com

Enquiries:
Enquiries to: Managing Director
Direct e-mail: enquiry@mvra.com
Other contacts: Membership Services Manager for membership.

Founded:
1988

Subject coverage:
Motor industry, accident management, quality repairers, quality body and mechanical garages/repairers.

Trade and statistical information:
Data covering all aspects of the motor industry.

Access to staff:
Contact by letter, by telephone and by e-mail
Hours: Closed Bank Holidays

Access to building, collection or gallery:
Mon to Fri, 0900 to 1700

Access for disabled people:
Parking provided, toilet facilities

MYCOBACTERIUM REFERENCE UNIT

Acronym or abbreviation: MRU

Public Health Laboratory, King's College Hospital (Dulwich), East Dulwich Grove, London, SE22 8QF

Tel: 020 8693 1312
Fax: 020 8346 6477

Website:
http://www.phls.co.uk

Enquiries:
Enquiries to: Director

Organisation type and purpose:
National government body, research organisation.

Subject coverage:
Laboratory diagnosis of tuberculosis and other mycobacterial diseases in man and animals; identification and sensitivity testing of mycobacteria; advice on treatment of such diseases. Basic research into host pathogen interactions and the epidemiology of mycobacterial diseases.

Access to staff:
Contact by letter and by fax
Hours: Mon to Fri, 0900 to 1715

Links to:
Public Health Laboratory Service (PHLS)
 61 Colindale Avenue, London, NW9

MYCOLOGY REFERENCE CENTRE

Department of Microbiology, University of Leeds, Leeds, West Yorkshire, LS2 9JT

Tel: 0113 233 5600/1
Fax: 0113 233 5640

Website:
http://www.leeds.ac.uk/mbiology/res/mycol/mrl
.htm
Services, research, interests.

Enquiries:
Enquiries to: Clinical Scientist

Organisation type and purpose:
Diagnostic medical laboratory.

Subject coverage:
Diseases of man and animals caused by infection with fungi; allergy to fungi; examination of cultures; tissue section; serological and molecular tests; antifungal assays.

Access to staff:
Contact by letter, by telephone and by fax. All charged.
Hours: Mon to Fri, 0900 to 1700
Special comments: Posting of samples subject to Royal Mail regulations.

Parent bodies:
Leeds Teaching Hospitals NHS Trust
    Leeds, LS1 3EX
University of Leeds
    Leeds, LS2 9JT

MYFANWY TOWNSEND MELANOMA RESEARCH FUND

6 Manor Road, East Grinstead, West Sussex, RH19 1LR

Tel: 01342 322508
E-mail: harry@melanoma-fund.co.uk

Website:
http://www.melanoma-fund.co.uk
About the fund, events, Melanoma Awareness Week, fact sheet.

Founded:
c. 2000

Organisation type and purpose:
Registered charity (number 1085969).
To raise awareness and publicise the deadly nature of malignant melanoma and diagnostic signs and precautions that should be taken, to educate about the disease, to fund research to find a cure, to make diagnosis more readily available (e.g. through free walk-in clinics).

Subject coverage:
Melanoma.

Special visitor services:
Melanoma Awareness Week, annually in June.

Access to staff:
Contact by letter, by telephone and by e-mail

NACELL

Formal name: National Advisory Centre on Early Language Learning

c/o CILT, the National Centre for Languages, 20 Bedfordbury, London, WC2N 4LB

Tel: 020 7379 5101
Fax: 020 7379 5082

Website:
http://www.nacell.org.uk

Enquiries:
Enquiries to: Information Officer
Direct e-mail: primarylanguages@cilt.org.uk

Organisation type and purpose:
NACELL is a Department for Education and Skills Initiative to promote and develop the provision and quality of Modern Foreign Language learning in the Primary sector.

NACELL is coordinated by CILT, the National Centre for Languages. National organisation, registered charity (charity number 313938), public library, university department or institute, suitable for ages: all.

Subject coverage:
Early language learning, primary languages, teaching foreign languages to young children (under 11s).

Non-library collection catalogue:
All or part available online and in-house

Library catalogue:
All or part available online and in-house

Printed publications:
Order printed publications from: Central Books Ltd 99 Wallis Road, London, E9 5LN, tel: 0845 4589910, e-mail: mo@centralbooks.com

Publications list:
Available online and in print

Access to staff:
Contact by letter, by telephone, by fax, by e-mail, in person and via website
Hours: Term time, Mon, Tue, Thu, Fri, 1030 to 1700; Wed, 1030 to 2000; Sat, 1000 to 1300:
Vacations, Mon to Fri, 1030 to 1700

Access to building, collection or gallery:
No prior appointment required
Hours: Term time, Mon, Tue, Thu, Fri, 1030 to 1700; Wed, 1030 to 2000; Sat, 1000 to 1300:
Vacations, Mon to Fri, 1030 to 1700

Access for disabled people:
Toilet facilities

Parent body:
CILT, the National Centre for Languages
    at the same address

NACRO, THE CRIME REDUCTION CHARITY

Formal name: Nacro

159 Clapham Road, London, SW9 0PU

Tel: 020 7840 6464
Fax: 020 7840 6420
E-mail: helpline@nacro.org.uk

Website:
http://www.nacro.org.uk

Enquiries:
Enquiries to: Resettlement Helpline Officer

Founded:
1966

Organisation type and purpose:
To reduce crime by giving disadvantaged people – offenders and those at risk of offending – a positive stake in society. Provides direct services (education and employment, housing, youth projects, advice), and consultancy and training services. Runs a resettlement helpline to give advice and information to ex-offenders, their family and friends and others around issues such as housing and employment.

Subject coverage:
Resettlement services for ex-offenders, Rehabilitation of Offenders Act 1974, special needs housing, employment, training, education, youth crime, crime and criminal justice (especially prisons), mentally disordered offenders, community safety, race and criminal justice.

Printed publications:
Wide range of reports, practical guides, leaflets and briefing papers on the subjects listed

Publications list:
Available online

Access to staff:
Contact by letter, by telephone, by fax and by e-mail
Hours: Mon to Fri, 0900 to 1700

NAFAS

Formal name: National Association of Flower Arrangement Societies

Osborne House, 12 Devonshire Square, London, EC2M 4TE

Tel: 020 7247 5567
Fax: 020 7247 7232
E-mail: flowers@nafas.org.uk

Website:
http://www.nafas.org.uk
Events, courses and publications.

Enquiries:
Enquiries to: Administrator

Founded:
1959

Organisation type and purpose:
Membership association, present number of members: 100,000, registered charity (charity number 289038), suitable for ages: 8+.
Education charity.
To promote the art and teaching of flower arranging.

Subject coverage:
Flower arranging.

Library catalogue:
All or part available in-house

Printed publications:
The Flower Arranger (magazine)
Instruction leaflets

Publications list:
Available in print

Access to staff:
Contact by letter, by telephone, by fax, by e-mail and via website. Appointment necessary.
Hours: Mon to Fri, 0900 to 1700

Access to building, collection or gallery:
Prior appointment required

Affiliated to:
Royal Horticultural Society

NAMIBIA HIGH COMMISSION

Formal name: High Commission for the Republic of Namibia

6 Chandos Street, London, W1G 9LU

Tel: 020 7636 6244
Fax: 020 7687 5694

Website:
http://www.namibhc.org.uk
The official website of the Namibia High Commission, London: copious information on Namibia, particularly with regard to tourism and trade; full details of all consular matters, with downloadable forms for visa applications; useful links to other websites related to Namibia.

Enquiries:
Enquiries to: Information Officer
Direct e-mail: info@namibiahc.org.uk
Other contacts: First Secretary for Political Affairs and Trade; First Secretary for Commonwealth Affairs and Education; First Secretary for Consular Matters

Organisation type and purpose:
National government body, national organisation. Protocol and bilateral relations between Namibia and the UK, consular enquiries (visas, work permits, passports). Tourism departments, political, economic, trade and educational links between Namibia and the UK.

Subject coverage:
General enquiries regarding geography, wildlife and environment of Namibia; Namibian cultures and customs; economic and political affairs; education and other matters. Contact names and addresses of individuals and organisations in Namibia can be provided.

continued overleaf

Information services:
All enquiries regarding Namibia: politics, economy, trade, education, tourism, wildlife and environment.

Education services:
The High Commission encourages twinning links between UK and Namibian schools, and will assist with school visits to Namibia.

Museum or gallery collection, archive, or library special collection:
Outside Namibia, the most comprehensive collection of materials relating to Namibian history and culture is held at: Namibia Resource Centre, Basler Afrika Bibliographien, PO Box 2037, 4001, Basel, Switzerland

Trade and statistical information:
The Commercial Attaché can answer most enquiries, and help establish commercial relationships with Namibian companies.

Printed publications:
A variety of printed material is available from the Commercial Attaché
For tourist information and brochures contact the Consular Secretary

Access to staff:
Contact by letter, by telephone, by fax, by e-mail, in person and via website. Appointment necessary.
Hours: Mon to Fri, 0900 to 1300 and 1400 to 1700
Special comments: Excepting Namibian and UK public holidays.

NAPO

4 Chivalry Road, Battersea, London, SW11 1HT

Tel: 020 7223 4887
Fax: 020 7223 3503
E-mail: info@napo.org.uk

Website:
http://www.napo.org.uk

Enquiries:
Enquiries to: Information Manager

Founded:
1912

Organisation type and purpose:
Professional body, trade union, present number of members: 9,500.
Trade union and professional association for Family Court and probation staff.

Subject coverage:
Probation Service, criminal justice system, Family Court Service.

Printed publications:
Napo News (monthly)
Probation Journal (quarterly)

Access to staff:
Contact by letter, by telephone, by fax, by e-mail and via website. Appointment necessary.
Hours: Mon to Fri, 0900 to 1700

Access to building, collection or gallery:
Prior appointment required

NAPOLEONIC SOCIETY

Formal name: Napoleonic Society of Great Britain

157 Vicarage Road, Leyton, London, E10 5DU

Tel: 020 8539 3876
Fax: 020 8539 3876
E-mail: keys@fsmail.net

Enquiries:
Enquiries to: Secretary

Founded:
1969

Organisation type and purpose:
Learned society.

Subject coverage:
Napoleon. French and Napoleonic history 1769–1945.

Non-library collection catalogue:
All or part available in-house

Library catalogue:
All or part available in-house

Printed publications:
Napoleon (occasional bulletin)

Access to staff:
Contact by letter, by telephone, by fax and by e-mail. Appointment necessary.
Hours: Mon to Sat, 1100 to 1900

Access for disabled people:
Limited access

NASPCS

Formal name: National Advisory Service for Parents of Children with a Stoma

51 Anderson Drive, Valley View Park, Darvel, Ayrshire, KA17 0DE

Tel: 01560 322024
E-mail: john@stoma.freeserve.co.uk

Enquiries:
Enquiries to: Chairman

Founded:
1986

Organisation type and purpose:
National organisation, membership association, present number of members: 650 families, voluntary organisation, registered charity (charity number 327922).
National advisory service for parents of incontinent children and children with a stoma. Membership is free.
To provide a contact and information service for parents, on the practical day-to-day management of a child with either a colostomy, ileostomy or urostomy.

Subject coverage:
Bladder and bowel incontinence, ileostomy, urostomy, colostomy, Hirschsprung's disease, imperforate anus, cloacal exstrophy, exompholus, prune belly syndrome, Vater syndrome, ectopia vesicae, colonic/intestinal neuronal dysplasia and gastroschisis.

Printed publications:
My Child Has Hirschsprung's Disease (free)
Beating Sneaky Poo (free)
Our Special Children – A practical guide to stoma care in babies and young children (free)
Newsletter (quarterly)
8 information sheets (free)
ACE Procedure – A guide for nurses (free)
My Child Has An Imperforate Anus (free)
Breaking the Taboo – Support leaflet of young people (free)

Publications list:
Available in print

Access to staff:
Contact by letter, by telephone and by e-mail
Hours: Mon to Fri, 0900 to 1700

Access to building, collection or gallery:
No access other than to staff

Members of:
International Ostomy Association

Membership Secretary:
NASPCS
Maran Bank, Main Street, Glenfarg, Tayside, PH2 9NT; tel: 01577 830661

Northern Ireland Representative:
NASPCS
11 Earlford Heights, Doagh Road, Newtownabbey, Belfast, BT36 8WZ; tel: 01232 837972

NASUWT THE TEACHERS UNION

Hillscourt Eductaion Centre, Rose Hill, Rednal, Birmingham, B45 8RS

Tel: 0121 453 6150
Fax: 0121 457 6208/9
E-mail: nasuwt@mail.nasuwt.org.uk

Website:
http://www.nasuwt.org.uk

Founded:
1919

Organisation type and purpose:
Professional body, trade union, present number of members: 280,000.

Subject coverage:
Salaries, superannuation and conditions of service of UK teachers; education in the UK; primary and secondary school education; teacher training and education; equality.

Printed publications:
Refer to website for complete information
Various information updates
Order printed publications from: website: http://www.nasuwt.org.uk

Publications list:
Available online

Access to staff:
Contact by letter, by telephone, by fax, by e-mail and via website. Appointment necessary.
Hours: Mon to Fri, 0830 to 1730

Affiliated to:
Education International
European Trade Union Committee for Education
Federation of Professional Workers
Irish Congress of Trade Unions
National Foundation for Educational Research
Scottish Trades Union Congress
Trades Union Congress
Welsh Trades Union Congress

Headquarters address:
NASUWT
Hillscourt Education Centre, Rosehill, Rednal, Birmingham, B45 8RS; tel: 0121 453 6150; fax: 0121 457 6208/9; e-mail: nasuwt@mail.nasuwt.org.uk; website: http://www.nasuwt.org.uk

NATIONAL 39/45 MILITARY VEHICLE GROUP

9 Cordelia Way, Rugby, Warwickshire, CV22 6JU

Tel: 01788 812250

Enquiries:
Enquiries to: Treasurer

Founded:
1972

Organisation type and purpose:
Membership association, voluntary organisation, research organisation.

Subject coverage:
Restoration of World War II Allied and Axis military vehicles and equipment, uniforms, memoirs, archives; film advice and vehicle supply; vehicle date verification.

Museum or gallery collection, archive, or library special collection:
Archive photographs and drawings of airborne vehicle modifications
British and American military vehicle numbers

Printed publications:
Club Magazine (quarterly)

Access to staff:
Contact by letter and by telephone
Hours: Telephone after 1800

NATIONAL ACCESS & SCAFFOLDING CONFEDERATION

Acronym or abbreviation: NASC

4th Floor, 12 Bridewell Place, London EC4V 6AP

Tel: 020 7822 7400
Fax: 020 7822 7401

E-mail: enquiries@nasc.org.uk

Website:
http://www.nasc.org.uk

Enquiries:
Enquiries to: Director

Founded:
1943

Organisation type and purpose:
Trade association.

Subject coverage:
All aspects of scaffolding; technical information, safety, suppliers and contractors.

Printed publications:
Yearbook
Technical and safety guidance notes

Publications list:
Available in print

Access to staff:
Contact by letter, by telephone and by fax
Hours: Mon to Fri, 0900 to 1700

Member of:
National Specialist Contractors Council (NSCC)

NATIONAL ACQUISITIONS GROUP

Acronym or abbreviation: NAG

12–14 King Street, Wakefield, WF1 2SQ

Tel: 01924 383010
Fax: 01924 383010
E-mail: nag1@btconnect.com

Website:
http://www.nag.org.uk

Enquiries:
Enquiries to: Administrator

Founded:
1986

Organisation type and purpose:
Professional body, membership association (membership is by subscription), present number of members: 481.
Bringing together those concerned in library acquisitions, publishers, booksellers, system suppliers and librarians (public, academic, special, etc.).

Subject coverage:
Library acquisitions and collections management in the United Kingdom and the Republic of Ireland, technological developments, producers, suppliers and libraries.

Printed publications:
Taking Stock (journal, twice a year)
The Tender Guide (2005)
Guidelines to Servicing – Part 1: Books
Value to Libraries of Special Services
Public Library Stock Management
Order printed publications from: same address

Electronic and video publications:
NAG News, Servicing Guidelines, Supply Specification, Directory of Acquisitions Librarians 2008
Order electronic and video publications from: As part of membership benefits or from the Group

Publications list:
Available online and in print

Access to staff:
Contact by letter, by telephone, by fax, by e-mail and via website

Access to building, collection or gallery:
Hours: Mon to Fri, 0900 to 1700

Access for disabled people:
Special comments: Steep stairs in old building

Links with:
CILIP
7 Ridgmount Street, London, WC1E 7AE; tel: 020 7255 0500; website: http://www.cilip.org.uk

NATIONAL AEROSPACE LIBRARY

Acronym or abbreviation: NAL

The Hub, Fowler Avenue, IQ Farnborough, Hants, GU14 7JP.

Tel: 01252 701038 ; 01252 701060
E-mail: hublibrary@aerosociety.com

Website:
http://www.aerosociety.com

Enquiries:
Enquiries to: Librarian

Founded:
2007

Incorporates the former:
Library of the Royal Aeronautical Society

Organisation type and purpose:
Learned society, registered charity (charity number 313708).

Subject coverage:
Aeronautics, astronautics, aerospace engineering, aerospace history, space, air law, air power, air transport, guided flight, aerospace propulsion, flight testing, avionics, rotorcraft, aviation medicine, piloting, aerodynamics, aircraft maintenance, aircraft structures and materials. An extensive collection of material relating to the development and recent technical advances in aeronautics, aviation and aerospace technology from the earliest times through to current operations and technology.

Museum or gallery collection, archive, or library special collection:
30,000 books, 1,000 periodical titles, 40,000 technical reports, 100,000 photographs, 200 current journal titles
Extensive collection (in excess of 200,000) of aviation photographs, glass lantern slides and lithographs
Books, letters, papers and manuscripts of early pioneers, including:
Major B. F. S. Baden-Powell (1860–1937)
Sir George Cayley (1773–1857)
C. G. Grey (1875–1953)
Lawrence Hargrave (1850–1915)
John Stringfellow (1799–1883)
Katharine Wright (1874–1929)
Orville Wright (1871–1948)
Wilbur Wright (1867–1912)
F. S. Barnwell (1880–1938, Design notebooks)
Various papers relating to the long history of the Society
Cuthbert-Hodgson Collection (ballooning and early aeronautical material)
Maitland Airship Collection
Poynton Collection (early ballooning, etc.)
Air Ministry/Ministry of Aircraft Production Air Publications
Air Accidents Investigations Branch Reports
Advisory Committee for Aeronautics/Aeronautical Research Council (ARC) technical reports
Society of British Aircraft Constructors/Aerospace Companies (SBAC) Minutes 1916–2000
The Air Pilot/UK Aeronautical Information Publication (AIP) August 1948–1999

Library catalogue:
All or part available online

Printed publications:
Aerospace International (monthly)
The Aeronautical Journal (monthly)
The Aerospace Professional (monthly)
Proceedings of Conferences
Publications Index 1897–1977
The National Aerospace Library (B. Riddle, 2007, £4.00)
Letters of the Wright Brothers: Letters of Wilbur, Orville and Katharine Wright in the Royal Aeronautical Society Library (ed. Brian Riddle and Colin Sinnott, 2003)
Pioneers of Flight Exhibition Programme (B. Riddle, 2003)

Access to staff:
Contact by letter, by telephone, by e-mail, in person and via website

Hours: Tues to Fri, 1000 to 1600

Administered by:
Royal Aeronautical Society
4 Hamilton Place, London, W1J 7BQ; tel: 0207 499 3515; website: www.aerosociety.com

NATIONAL AIDS TRUST

Acronym or abbreviation: NAT

New City Cloisters, 196 Old Street, London, EC1V 9FR

Tel: 020 7814 6767
Fax: 020 7216 0111
E-mail: info@nat.org.uk

Website:
http://www.nat.org.uk
Work of the organisation.
http://www.worldaidsday.org
World Aids Day.

Founded:
1988

Organisation type and purpose:
National organisation, voluntary organisation, registered charity (charity number 297977).
The National Aids Trust's (NAT) vision is a world in which people living with HIV are treated as equal citizens with respect, dignity and justice, are diagnosed early and receive the highest standards of care, and in which everyone knows how and is able to protect themselves and others from HIV infection.
All the Trust's work is focussed on achieving four strategic goals:
- Effective HIV prevention in order to halt the spread of HIV
- Early diagnosis of HIV through ethical, accessible and appropriate testing
- Equitable access to treatment, care and support for people living with HIV
- Eradication of HIV-related stigma and discrimination

Subject coverage:
Policy; World Aids Day; employers' initiatives; special projects.

Museum or gallery collection, archive, or library special collection:
Art of Awareness Collection: 100 framed images created depicting AIDS awareness, various media

Library catalogue:
All or part available in-house

Printed publications:
Available free and for purchase, direct

Electronic and video publications:
Specific videos available direct

Publications list:
Available online and in print

Access to staff:
Contact by letter, by telephone, by fax, by e-mail and via website. Appointment necessary.
Hours: Mon to Fri, 0900 to 1700

Access to building, collection or gallery:
No prior appointment required

NATIONAL ANIMAL WELFARE TRUST

Acronym or abbreviation: NAWT

Tyler's Way, Watford By-pass, Watford, Hertfordshire, WD25 8WT

Tel: 020 8950 0177
Fax: 020 8420 4454
E-mail: watford@nawt.org.uk

Website:
http://www.nawt.org.uk

Enquiries:
Enquiries to: Chief Executive

continued overleaf

Founded:
1971

Organisation type and purpose:
Registered charity, voluntary organisation (charity number 1090499).
Rescue and rehoming of unwanted animals.

Subject coverage:
Animal rescue and rehoming.

Printed publications:
NAWT Centre leaflets
NAWT News (2 times a year)

Access to staff:
Contact by letter, by telephone, by fax, by e-mail, in person and via website
Hours: Administration: Mon to Fri, 0900 to 1700; Rescue Centres: Watford, 1100 to 1500; Langport (Somerset), 1100 to 1530; Cornwall, 1300 to 1600; Berkshire, 1100 to 1600

Access for disabled people:
Parking provided, ramped entry, access to all public areas, toilet facilities

Other addresses:
National Animal Welfare Trust
 Heaven's Gate Farm, West Henley, Langport, Somerset, TA10 9BE; tel: 01458 252656; fax: 01458 253806
National Animal Welfare Trust
 Trindledown Farm, Wantage Lane, Great Shefford, Newbury, Berkshire, RG17 7DQ; tel: 01488 638584; fax: 01488 638141
National Animal Welfare Trust
 Wheal Alfred Farm, Wheal Alfred Road, Hayle, Cornwall, TR27 5JT; tel: 01736 756005

NATIONAL ANKYLOSING SPONDYLITIS SOCIETY

Acronym or abbreviation: NASS

Unit 0.2, One Victoria Villas, Richmond upon Thames, Surrey, TW9 2GW

Tel: 020 8948 9117
E-mail: admin@nass.co.uk

Website:
http://www.nass.co.uk
Guidebook for patients, forum, members section, newsletters, charity news, fundraising news, shop

Enquiries:
Enquiries to: Administrator

Founded:
1976

Organisation type and purpose:
Registered charity (charity number 272258). NASS is a membership charity which gives information and support to people with ankylosing spondylitis. Has about 100 branches in the United Kingdom.

Subject coverage:
Ankylosing spondylitis.

Printed publications:
Guidebook for Patients (free)
Newsletter (twice yearly)
Car Driving with Ankylosing Spondylitis

Electronic and video publications:
Exercise (DVD)

Publications list:
Available online and in print

Access to staff:
Contact by letter, by telephone, by e-mail and via website
Hours: Mon to Fri, 0930 to 1730

Access to building, collection or gallery:
No public access

Links with:
Ankylosing Spondylitis International Federation at the same address

NATIONAL ANTI-HUNT CAMPAIGN

Acronym or abbreviation: NAHC

PO Box 66, Stevenage, SG1 2TR

Tel: 01442 240246
Fax: By arrangement

Website:
http://www.liberation-mag.org.uk/nahc.htm

Enquiries:
Enquiries to: Information Officer
Direct e-mail: info@savethepigeons.org

Founded:
1992

Organisation type and purpose:
Membership association (membership is by subscription), voluntary organisation.
Peaceful legal campaigning against all hunting with dogs.

Subject coverage:
All areas relating to hunting with hounds, legal problems with hunt trespass etc.

Printed publications:
Free leaflets and factsheets are available on all aspects of hunting

Access to staff:
Contact by letter, by telephone, by fax and by e-mail
Hours: Mon to Fri, 0900 to 1700

NATIONAL ARCHIVES

Formal name: The National Archives
Acronym or abbreviation: TNA

Kew, Richmond, Surrey, TW9 4DU

Tel: 020 8876 3444; minicom no. 020 8392 9198
E-mail: http://www.nationalarchives.gov.uk/contact/form

Website:
http://www.nationalarchives.gov.uk
Information about The National Archives, access to online catalogues and digitised public records, online bookshop, ordering copies of records, and contact information. Website includes global search facility, for searches across a number of different catalogues. Also includes access to Your Archives, a wiki, where users can contribute knowledge of archival sources.
http://www.nationalarchives.gov.uk/catalogue
Catalogue descriptions of over 10m. documents held by The National Archives.

Founded:
1838

Created by the merger of:
Public Record Office (PRO) and Historical Manuscripts Commission (HMC); (The Office of Public Sector Information was incorporated in 2006) (year of change 2004)

Organisation type and purpose:
National government body, government department and executive agency under the Secretary of State for Justice.
National Archive Office.

Subject coverage:
As the official archive for England, Wales and the central UK government, The National Archives holds records ranging from parchment and paper scrolls through to digital files and archived websites. Increasingly, these records are being put online, making them universally accessible. The collection covers the British Isles, the territories that formed the British Empire and the countries of the Commonwealth.
The National Archives is at the heart of information policy, setting standards and supporting innovation in information and records management across the UK, providing advice on opening up and encouraging the re-use of public sector information. Through its efforts in

promoting best practice in information management, it looks to ensure the survival of today's information for the future.

Education services:
See website: http://www.nationalarchives.gov.uk/teachers.

Museum or gallery collection, archive, or library special collection:
The collections are too numerous to specify (documents number many millions, and currently cover 100 miles of shelving)
Famous documents include the Domesday Book, Shakespeare's will, the Log of HMS Victory, World Wars documents

Non-library collection catalogue:
All or part available online

Library catalogue:
All or part available online

Printed publications:
Research guides available free of charge on website
Many published sources available including:
First World War Army Service Records
Army Records: a guide for family historians
Census: the expert guide
Naval Records for Genealogists
Tracing Your Ancestors

Publications list:
Available online and in print

Access to staff:
Contact by letter, by telephone, by fax, by e-mail, in person and via website
Hours: Mon, Fri, 0900 to 1700; Tue, Thu, 0900 to 1900; Wed, 1000 to 1700; Sat, 0930 to 1700

Access to building, collection or gallery:
Access during open hours. A reader's ticket is required for access to orginal documents. A ticket can be obtained free of charge by bringing proof of identity and proof of address. A list of suitable identification documents is on the website at: http://www.nationalarchives.gov.uk/registration
Hours: Mon, Fri, 0900 to 1700; Tue, Thu, 0900 to 1900; Wed, 1000 to 1700; Sat, 0930 to 1700

Access for disabled people:
Parking provided, level entry, access to all public areas, toilet facilities; for more information see website: http://www.nationalarchives.gov.uk/visit/disabled.htm?source=ddmenu_visit7

NATIONAL ARCHIVES OF SCOTLAND

Acronym or abbreviation: NAS

HM General Register House, 2 Princes Street, Edinburgh, EH1 3YY

Tel: 0131 535 1314
Fax: 0131 535 1360
E-mail: enquiries@nas.gov.uk

Website:
http://www.nas.gov.uk

Enquiries:
Enquiries to: Keeper of the Records of Scotland

Founded:
1789

Organisation type and purpose:
National government body, statutory body.
Record office and archive.
Repository for the public and legal records of Scotland, accepts many local and private archives for which it is felt to be the most suitable repository.

Subject coverage:
Scottish affairs, history, topography, law, genealogy.

Museum or gallery collection, archive, or library special collection:
Administrative records of pre-Union Scotland, registers of central and local courts of law, public registers of property rights and legal documents, local and church records and private archives (computerised database for some)
Records of Scottish parliament and government departments, nationalised industries, maps and plans, and business records

Non-library collection catalogue:
All or part available online, in-house and in print

Library catalogue:
All or part available online and in-house

Printed publications:
A Proper Repository: the building of General Register House
The Guide to the National Archives of Scotland
Tracing Your Scottish Ancestors: The Official Guide
Tracing Scottish Local History
Leaflet on the records (free)

Electronic and video publications:
Scottish Archives for Schools (CD-ROMs)

Publications list:
Available online and in print

Access to staff:
Contact by letter, by telephone, by fax, by e-mail and in person
Hours: Mon to Fri, 0900 to 1700

Access for disabled people:
For wheelchair users and people with mobility impairments disabled parking is available within the car park off West Register Street. Note this parking is limited and it is recommended an appointment is made. Access to the building can be made via either a ramp or disabled lift adjacent to the car park. Disabled toilet facilities are available on all floors.

NATIONAL ART LIBRARY

Acronym or abbreviation: NAL

Victoria and Albert Museum, Cromwell Road, South Kensington, London, SW7 2RL

Tel: 020 7942 2400
Fax: 020 7942 2394 or 2401
E-mail: nal.enquiries@vam.ac.uk

Website:
http://www.vam.ac.uk/nal
Information on services, holdings, events and current news.

Enquiries:
Enquiries to: Deputy Keeper
Direct tel: 020 7942 2562
Direct e-mail: j.meriton@vam.ac.uk
Other contacts: Head of Information Services, e-mail: m.flynn@vam.ac.uk

Founded:
1837

Organisation type and purpose:
National organisation, art gallery, historic building, house or site.
National Art Library, open to the public, research library.

Subject coverage:
Architecture, fine and applied art and design of all periods and western countries, as well as Indian, Islamic and Far Eastern; prints, drawings, paintings; modern art; design; sculpture; metalwork; book production and the art of the book (bindings, illustration, fine printing); history of art; crafts; history of printing; history of costume; private presses; photography; artists' books; comics; children's books; calligraphy; manuscript illumination; heraldry; interior design; furniture and woodwork; ceramics and glass; textiles and dress; museums and museology; Beatrix Potter; Natalia Goncharova; Mikhail Larionov.

Museum or gallery collection, archive, or library special collection:
The General Collection contains: 1,000,000 books, 2,000 current periodical titles, 9,000 closed periodical titles, 60,000 exhibition catalogues, 300 illuminated manuscripts, 50,000 sales catalogues, 20,000 information files, literature from international exhibitions
Archives, artists' books, letters and manifestos, books using innovative technology or structure, books with notable dustjackets, calligraphy, children's books, comics and graphic novels, documentary manuscripts, early printed books, ephemera and jobbing printing, fine and noteworthy bindings and printing, illuminated manuscripts, modern book and magazine design, typography, writing and lettering books
Artists' Books
Exhibition Catalogues
Sales Catalogues
Trade Literature
The Special Collections are varied and include:
19th-century Periodicals
Clements Collection of armorial bindings
Cole Collection: diaries, notebooks, correspondence and books of Sir Henry Cole
Forster Collection: English literature and history 16th to 19th centuries (including manuscripts of Charles Dickens)
Dyce Collection: literature and theatre, Britain and Europe 16th to 19th centuries
Harrod Collection: 19th-century illustrated books
Hole Bequest: 17th- and 18th-century literature
Hutton Bequest: works on fencing, swordsmanship, weapons and self-defence
Jobbing Printing Collection: material from the 1920s, 1930s and 1960s
Jones Collection: literature and works relating to art and manufacturing
Osbert Lancaster Collection: comic art, humour
Larionov Collection: work by Larionov and Goncharova, theatre and opera in Europe (especially Russia and France)
Liberty and Company Printed Catalogues Collection
Linder Bequest and Collection: Beatrix Potter drawings, watercolours, manuscripts and letters (held at Blythe House)
Guy Little Bequest: children's books
Mediaeval Manuscripts
Osman-Gidal Collection: photojournalism
Pinto Bequest: directories relating to London and the provinces
Piot Collection: fairs and festivals
Queen Mary's Collection of children's books (held at Blythe House)
Rakoff Collection: comics and graphic novels
Renier Collection (held at Blythe House)
Weale Collection: part of the working library of W H James Weale, Keeper of the National Art Library, 1890–1899

Library catalogue:
All or part available online

Printed publications:
Following publications describe parts of the Library's Special Collections:
Art of the book (James Bettley, ed., 2001)
Beatrix Potter: the V & A collection (A S Hobbs and J I Whalley, 1985)
Bookbindings (Harthan J P, 3rd ed., 1985)
Bookbindings and rubbings of bindings in the National Art Library, South Kensington Museum, (W H Weale, 1894–1898, 2 volumes)
Fine Illustrations in Western European Printed Books (T M MacRobert, 1969)
From Manet to Hockney: modern artists illustrated books (C Hogben and R Watson, 1985)
From the 1890s to the 1980s: fashion periodicals (1988)
Islamic Bookbindings in the Victoria and Albert Museum (D Haldane, 1983)
Series of booklets on modern British private presses
The History of the Illustrated Book (Harthan J P, 1981)
The Universal Penman: a survey of western calligraphy from the Roman period (Whalley J I, 1980)

Publications list:
Available online

Access to staff:
Contact by letter, by telephone, by fax, by e-mail, in person and via website
Hours: Tue, Wed, Thu, Sat, 1000 to 1730; Fri, 1000 to 1830
Special comments: Closed Bank Hol weekends, Christmas to New Year (except for 1 day) and two weeks' annual stocktaking in Aug. (check website for full details of closures).
All users must register after showing means of identification, access with readers' tickets only; visitors by prior appointment for reserved materials.

Access to building, collection or gallery:
No prior appointment required
Hours: Sun to Sat, 1000 to 1745; Fri, 1000 to 2200 (selected galleries remain open after 1800)
Special comments: Closed 24, 25 & 26 Dec.

Access for disabled people:
Parking provided, ramped entry, toilet facilities
Special comments: 4 parking bays for vehicles with stickers for disabled people, next to the Exhibition Road entrance.

Parent body:
Victoria and Albert Museum

Subsidiary body:
Archive of Art and Design
23 Blythe Road, London, W14 0QF; tel: 020 7603 1514; fax: 020 7602 0980; e-mail: archive@vam.ac.uk; website: http://www.vam.ac.uk/resources/archives

NATIONAL ASSEMBLY FOR WALES

Library, New Crown Building, Cathays Park, Cardiff, CF10 3NQ

Tel: 029 2082 5449 or 823683
Fax: 029 2082 5508

Website:
http://www.wales.gov.uk

Enquiries:
Enquiries to: Librarian
Direct tel: 029 2082 3362

Founded:
1999

Organisation type and purpose:
National government body.

Subject coverage:
Local government; housing; education; health and social services; public finance and administration; law; libraries and museums; agriculture; economic planning; land use; transport and highways; tourism; ancient monuments; national parks; water; environment.

Trade and statistical information:
Welsh statistics.

Library catalogue:
All or part available in-house

Printed publications:
Many titles including:
Current Information Bulletins (7 titles)
Digest of Welsh Historical Statistics
Digest of Welsh Statistics
Health Statistics, Wales
List of Welsh Official Publications (monthly and annually)
Statistics of Education and Training in Wales
Order printed publications from: website: http://www.wales.gov.uk

Publications list:
Available online

Access to staff:
Appointment necessary.
Hours: Mon to Fri, 0900 to 1700

Access to building, collection or gallery:
By appointment

NATIONAL ASSOCIATION FOR CHILDREN OF ALCOHOLICS

Acronym or abbreviation: NACOA

PO Box 64, Fishponds, Bristol, BS16 2UH

Tel: 0117 924 8005; 0800 358 3456 (helpline)
Fax: 0117 942 2928
E-mail: helpline@nacoa.org.uk

Website:
http://www.nacoa.org.uk

Enquiries:
Enquiries to: Administrator
Other contacts: Chief Executive

Founded:
1990

Organisation type and purpose:
Advisory body, membership association, registered charity (charity number 1009143), research organisation.
To raise the public consciousness to the needs of children of alcoholics, educate professionals as to their specific needs, provide advice, information and fellowship and promote research.

Subject coverage:
Information and advice on children of alcoholics for professionals and client group; other resources available, suggested reading.

Printed publications:
Leaflets for children of alcoholics and professionals (free), including:
Information for Children of Alcoholics
Some Mums and Dads Drink Too Much or Use Drugs (and poster)
A Guide for Schools: Children of Alcoholics in the Classroom
If a child of an alcoholic or addict comes to you
If you think someone in your family drinks too much or uses drugs
NACOA Annual Report
NACOA News
Suggested Reading List

Publications list:
Available online and in print

Access to staff:
Contact by letter, by telephone, by fax and by e-mail
Hours: Administration: Mon to Fri, 1000 to 1600
Helpline: Mon, Fri, 1000 to 1900; Tues, Wed, Thu, 1000 to 2100; Sat, 1000 to 1500

NATIONAL ASSOCIATION FOR COLITIS AND CROHN'S DISEASE

Acronym or abbreviation: NACC

4 Beaumont House, Sutton Road, St Albans, Hertfordshire, AL1 5HH

Tel: 01727 830038 (admin); 844296 (information)
Fax: 01727 862550
E-mail: nacc@nacc.org.uk

Website:
http://www.nacc.org.uk
Information about Colitis and Crohn's, and about the organisation. Contact details for overseas organisations.

Enquiries:
Enquiries to: Director
Direct tel: 01727 734479
Other contacts: PA to Director

Founded:
1979

Organisation type and purpose:
Membership association (membership is by subscription), present number of members: 28,000, voluntary organisation (charity number 282732).

Subject coverage:
Inflammatory bowel diseases, colitis, Crohn's disease, support of sufferers and their families.

Printed publications:
Newsletters, booklets, etc. (members)

Some information sheets available to non-members

Electronic and video publications:
Talkabout Colitis (video, Linkward Productions)
Talkabout Crohn's Disease (video, Linkward Productions)

Access to staff:
Contact by letter, by telephone, by fax, by e-mail and via website
Hours: Mon to Fri, 0900 to 1700

Has:
65 area groups in the UK

NATIONAL ASSOCIATION FOR ENVIRONMENTAL EDUCATION (UK)

Acronym or abbreviation: NAEE (UK)

University of Wolverhampton, Walsall Campus, Gorway Road, Walsall, West Midlands, WS1 3BD

Tel: 01922 631200
E-mail: info@naee.org.uk

Website:
http://www.naee.org.uk

Enquiries:
Enquiries to: National Coordinator
Other contacts: CoChair

Founded:
1968

Organisation type and purpose:
Membership association (membership is by subscription), registered charity, suitable for ages: all, early years to university.
Offers guidance and assistance in the delivery of environmental education for sustainable development within the formal education sector.

Subject coverage:
Environmental education in schools.

Printed publications:
Environmental Education (journal, 3 times a year)
Occasional papers
Practical guides
Resource pack

Publications list:
Available in print

Access to staff:
Contact by letter, by telephone, by e-mail, in person and via website. Appointment necessary.
Hours: Thu

Access to building, collection or gallery:
Prior appointment required
Special comments: Please telephone for details.

Access for disabled people:
Parking provided

Links with:
Environmental Education Advisers Association
Field Studies Council

NATIONAL ASSOCIATION FOR GIFTED CHILDREN

Acronym or abbreviation: NAGC

Suite 14, Challenger House, Sherwood Drive, Bletchley, Milton Keynes, Buckinghamshire, MK3 6DP

Tel: 0870 7703217
Fax: 0870 7703219
E-mail: amazingchildren@nagcbritain.org.uk

Website:
http://www.nagcbritain.org.uk
Information in identification, support and education of gifted and able children.

Enquiries:
Enquiries to: Director
Other contacts: Education Consultants

Founded:
1965

Organisation type and purpose:
National organisation, membership association (membership is by subscription), present number of members: 2500, voluntary organisation, registered charity (charity number 313182), suitable for ages: 0 to 20, training organisation, consultancy, research organisation, publishing house.
To support gifted children, their families and schools concerned with their education and welfare.

Subject coverage:
Identification of gifted children, education of gifted children, local branches and helpful contacts (where available).

Museum or gallery collection, archive, or library special collection:
Books on gifted children and their needs

Printed publications:
Help with Bright Children
Intelligence
Newsletter
The Social, Educational and Emotional Needs of Gifted Children

Publications list:
Available in print

Access to staff:
Contact by letter, by telephone, by fax, by e-mail, in person and via website. Appointment necessary. All charged.
Hours: Helpline: Mon, Wed, Thu, Fri, 0930 to 1430
Visitors: Mon to Fri, 0900 to 1630
Special comments: Charges made for training and consultancy, free access to Helpline.

Access to building, collection or gallery:
Prior appointment required

Access for disabled people:
Access to all public areas

Member of:
National Children's Bureau
Telephone Helplines Association

NATIONAL ASSOCIATION FOR LITERATURE DEVELOPMENT

Acronym or abbreviation: NALD

PO Box 49657, London, N8 7YZ

E-mail: director@nald.org

Website:
http://www.nald.org

Enquiries:
Enquiries to: Co-ordinator
Direct e-mail: steve@inck.fsnet.co.uk

Organisation type and purpose:
National organisation, membership association (membership is by subscription), present number of members: 144.

Subject coverage:
Networking and professional development information for literature development sector.

Electronic and video publications:
E-Newsletter (fortnightly to members)

Publications list:
Available online

Access to staff:
Contact by letter, by telephone, by e-mail, in person and via website
Hours: Mon to Fri, 0900 to 1700

Access to building, collection or gallery:
No access other than to staff

NATIONAL ASSOCIATION FOR PASTORAL CARE IN EDUCATION

Acronym or abbreviation: NAPCE

c/o Institute of Education, University of Warwick, Coventry, Warwickshire, CV4 7AL

Tel: 024 7652 3810
Fax: 024 7652 4110
E-mail: base@napce.org.uk

Website:
http://www.napce.org.uk
About NAPCE: People, purpose, role etc; journal information; online purchase and membership; publication; conference, workshop information; useful links: pastoral, training, education general.

Enquiries:
Enquiries to: Base Administrator
Other contacts: Chairman for press contact.

Founded:
1982

Organisation type and purpose:
International organisation, membership association (membership is by subscription), present number of members: 1500, registered charity (charity number 291295), training organisation, research organisation, publishing house.

Subject coverage:
Pastoral care in schools and colleges, personal-social education, effective learning.

Museum or gallery collection, archive, or library special collection:
Small collection of materials on bullying

Printed publications:
Journal of Pastoral Care in Education
Broadsheets on topical issues:
Children and Bereavement, Death and Loss: what can the school do?
Developing Effective Links with Parents
From Head of Year to Year Curriculum Coordinator?
Governors and Pastoral Care
Improving School Behaviour
Learning about Learning
PSE and the Whole Curriculum
Quality Review in Pastoral Care
Reducing School Bullying: What Works?
Refugee children in school
Staff development Resources:
Reclaiming Pastoral Care
Targeting Strategies
The Value of Pastoral Care & PSE?
Tutor Review
Tutoring for Learning
Whole-School PSE: Policy and Practice

Microform publications:
Journal of Pastoral Care in Education (Blackwell)

Electronic and video publications:
Staff Development Resources (on disk)

Publications list:
Available online and in print

Access to staff:
Contact by letter, by telephone, by fax, by e-mail and via website. Appointment necessary.
Hours: Mon to Fri, 0900 to 1330

Chairman:
National Association for Pastoral Care in Education

NATIONAL ASSOCIATION FOR PATIENT PARTICIPATION

Acronym or abbreviation: N.A.P.P.

10 Rosegarth Avenue, Aston, Sheffield, S26 2DD

Tel: 0114 2874035
Fax: 0114 2874035
E-mail: enquire@napp.org.uk

Website:
http://www.napp.org.uk
General information about patient and public involvement in health. Pointers to more specific information.

Enquiries:
Enquiries to: Hon Secretary

Founded:
1977

Organisation type and purpose:
National organisation, membership association (membership is by subscription), voluntary organisation, registered charity (charity number 292157).
Promotes patient participation in primary health care at local GPs surgeries, health centres.
Promotes and supports patient's participation in their own primary health care with their GPs through a network of regional representatives.
N.A.P.P. is the patient's participation voice at meetings and conferences organised by NHS and health organisations.

Subject coverage:
Practical advice, guidance and information to affiliated patients groups who are located in local surgeries. Experienced help provided in setting up patients' groups and network potential via affiliation.

Printed publications:
Members' Handbook for affiliated patients' groups
Newsletter (quarterly)
Information Pack for those interested in forming a group

Publications list:
Available in print

Access to staff:
Contact by letter, by telephone, by fax, by e-mail and via website
Hours: 24 hours (answerphone)
Special comments: Volunteers work from home.

Regular contact with:
BMA Events
Kings Fund Conferences
NCVO Affiliation
Patient Liaison Committee of the Royal College of General Practitioners

Representation on:
Doctor Patient Partnership
UK Patients' Forum

NATIONAL ASSOCIATION FOR PREMENSTRUAL SYNDROME

Acronym or abbreviation: NAPS

41 Old Road, East Peckham, Kent TN12 5AP

Tel: 0870 777 2178
E-mail: contact@pms.org.uk

Website:
http://www.pms.org.uk

Enquiries:
Enquiries to: Chief Executive

Founded:
1984

Organisation type and purpose:
Advisory body, membership association (membership is by subscription), voluntary organisation, registered charity (charity number 289901), research organisation.

Subject coverage:
Premenstrual syndrome, postnatal depression and tension.

Museum or gallery collection, archive, or library special collection:
Bibliographical research database available to professional members

Printed publications:
Understanding PMS
Information Pack
N.A.P.S. News
Premenstrual Syndrome – A Clinical Review

Publications list:
Available online and in print

Access to staff:
Contact by letter, by telephone, by e-mail and via website
Hours: 24-hour information line

NATIONAL ASSOCIATION FOR PRIMARY EDUCATION

Acronym or abbreviation: NAPE

Nape National Office, Moulton College, Moulton, Northampton, NN3 7RR

Tel: 01604 647646
Fax: 01604 647660
E-mail: nationaloffice@nape.org.uk

Website:
http://www.nape.org.uk
Information about NAPE and its activities.

Enquiries:
Enquiries to: Honorary Secretary
Direct tel: 01865 890281
Other contacts: Press & Information Officer (for comments on policy and educational news)

Founded:
1980

Organisation type and purpose:
International organisation, national organisation, advisory body, membership association (membership is by subscription, election or invitation), present number of members: 200,000 covered by group membership, voluntary organisation, registered charity (charity number 289645), suitable for ages: birth to 13, training organisation, consultancy, research organisation.
To promote high quality education for every child from birth to 13 years.

Subject coverage:
Primary education, funding of schools, class sizes, current issues in education as they arise, e.g. OfSTED inspections, teacher stress/morale, inclusion, home/school partnership, workload, teacher shortage, classroom assistant issues.

Printed publications:
NAPE Publications include:
Newsbrief
The Numbers Game (Alexander P, £2.25)
Current Home and School Council publications
In His Own Words (Schiller C, £5.95)
New Childhood (journal, 2 times a year, free to members)
Shining in the Sun (poems by children from NAPE Poetry competition 1995)
Why am I Starting School? (Backbone Productions)
Home and School Council Publications include:
Children Can Enjoy Writing Stories (Taylor G, £2)
Choosing and Using Books for Children (Inglis J, £1.50)
Parents & Reading (Tibertius S, £2)
Spelling: a Visual Approach (Cripps C and Bushell R, £2)

Electronic and video publications:
Starting School (video, Marks & Spencer)

Publications list:
Available in print

Access to staff:
Contact by letter, by telephone, by fax, by e-mail and via website. Appointment necessary.
Hours: Mon to Fri, 0900 to 1330
Special comments: School terms only.

NATIONAL ASSOCIATION FOR SPECIAL EDUCATIONAL NEEDS, THE

Acronym or abbreviation: NASEN

NASEN House, 4–5 Amber Business Village, Amber Close, Amington, Tamworth, Staffordshire, B77 4RP

Tel: 01827 311500
Fax: 01827 313005
E-mail: welcome@nasen.org.uk

continued overleaf

Website:
http://www.nasen.org.uk
Information on publications, courses, journals, membership, consultation documents, press releases, policy gathering forum.

Enquiries:
Enquiries to: Honorary General Secretary

Founded:
1992

Organisation type and purpose:
National organisation, membership association (membership is by subscription), present number of members: 11,200, service industry, voluntary organisation, registered charity (charity number 1007023), suitable for ages: mainly KS1, KS2 and KS3, training organisation, research organisation, publishing house.
NASEN aims to promote the education, training, advancement and development of all those with special educational needs.

Subject coverage:
Development of children and young people with special educational needs, education, welfare, treatment, rehabilitation, equal opportunities.

Printed publications:
British Journal of Special Education (journal, quarterly)
Behaviour series
Language development
Literacy handbooks
Mathematics handbooks
Other handbooks
Special! (magazine, termly)
Staff development series
Support for Learning (journal, quarterly)
Teachers and Parents: Together for Reading

Electronic and video publications:
CD-ROM for purchase through NASEN

Publications list:
Available online and in print

Access to staff:
Contact by letter, by telephone, by fax, by e-mail, in person and via website. Appointment necessary.
Hours: Mon to Fri, 0900 to 1700

Access to building, collection or gallery:
Prior appointment required

Access for disabled people:
Parking provided, ramped entry, toilet facilities

NATIONAL ASSOCIATION FOR THE RELIEF OF PAGET'S DISEASE

Acronym or abbreviation: NARPD

323 Manchester Road, Walkden, Worsley, Manchester, M28 3HH

Tel: 0161 799 4646
Fax: 0161 799 6511
E-mail: director@paget.org.uk

Website:
http://www.paget.org.uk

Enquiries:
Enquiries to: Director

Founded:
1973

Organisation type and purpose:
Membership association (membership is by subscription), present number of members: 2400, registered charity (charity number 266071).
To offer information and support for those suffering from Paget's Disease. To raise awareness of the disease to the medical profession and the public at large. To encourage and assist research.

Subject coverage:
Information on research into the cause, prevention, treatment and cure of Paget's Disease of the bone, and support for sufferers and their families.

Printed publications:
General Information for patients suffering from Paget's Disease of Bone (free)
Paget's Disease of Bone – Its Nature and Management (A Guide for Patients) (free)
The Treatment of Paget's Disease of Bone (free)
Newsletter (quarterly, members)

Publications list:
Available in print

Access to staff:
Contact by letter, by telephone, by fax, by e-mail and via website. Appointment necessary.
Hours: Mon to Fri, 0900 to 1700

Access to building, collection or gallery:
Prior appointment required

Access for disabled people:
Parking provided

Links with:
Paget's Disease Foundation of America
Paget's Disease Support Group
 New Zealand

NATIONAL ASSOCIATION FOR THE TEACHING OF ENGLISH

Acronym or abbreviation: NATE

50 Broadfield Road, Sheffield, South Yorkshire, S8 0XJ

Tel: 0114 255 5419
Fax: 0114 255 5296
E-mail: info@nate.org.uk

Website:
http://www.nate.org.uk

Enquiries:
Enquiries to: Director

Founded:
1963

Organisation type and purpose:
NATE is the UK's professional body for all those involved in English education from pre-school to university. It is a membership organisation. NATE supports effective teaching and learning, keeps teachers informed about current developments and provides them with a voice at a national level.
NATE welcomes as members anyone who works in, or has an interest in, English education at any level.
The association is run on a voluntary basis through elected executive and council committees.
The association has a range of committees and standing working parties that address current concerns, disseminate knowledge and ideas, promote the work of the association and seek to represent the views of the association to national bodies, local education authorities, the DCSF, OFSTED, QCDA and Examination Boards.
The association conducts research into the teaching of English.
NATE is an active member of the International Federation of the Teachers of English where it seeks to share the experience of English teachers in the UK and learn from teachers in diverse parts of the world.

Subject coverage:
Teaching of English through all age ranges.

Printed publications:
English in Education (academic journal)
NATE News (newsletter)
English Drama Media (professional journal)
NATE Classroom (magazine)
Order printed publications from: website: http://www.nate.org.uk

Publications list:
Available online and in print

Access to staff:
Contact by letter, by telephone, by fax and by e-mail. Appointment necessary.
Hours: Mon to Fri, 0830 to 1700

Is organised into:
14 Regions in the UK

Member organisation of:
College of Teachers
International Federation for the Teaching of English

NATIONAL ASSOCIATION FOR VOLUNTARY AND COMMUNITY ACTION

Acronym or abbreviation: NAVCA

The Tower, 2 Furnival Square, Sheffield, South Yorkshire, S1 4QL

Tel: 0114 278 6636
Fax: 0114 278 7004
E-mail: navca@navca.org.uk

Website:
http://www.navca.org.uk

Enquiries:
Enquiries to: Policy and Communications Officer

Founded:
1991

Formerly called:
National Association of Councils for Voluntary Service

Organisation type and purpose:
National organisation, membership association (membership is by qualification). National voice of local third sector infrastructure in England. Members work with 164,000 local third sector groups and organisations that provide community services, regenerate neighbourhoods, promote volunteering and tackle discrimination in partnership with local public bodies.

Subject coverage:
Information on management of voluntary organisations, contacts in local infrastructure organisations and councils for voluntary service, setting up and managing voluntary organisations.

Printed publications:
See website http://www.navca.org.uk/publications

Publications list:
Available online and in print

Access to staff:
Contact by letter, by telephone, by fax and by e-mail. Appointment necessary.
Hours: Mon to Fri, 0900 to 1700

Access to building, collection or gallery:
Prior appointment required

Access for disabled people:
Access to all public areas, toilet facilities

Member of:
National Council for Voluntary Organisations (NCVO)
Volunteering England

Subsidiary bodies:
364 local third sector infrastructure organisations in England

NATIONAL ASSOCIATION OF ADULT PLACEMENT SERVICES

Acronym or abbreviation: NAAPS

6 The Cotton Exchange, Old Hall Street, Liverpool, L3 9LQ

Tel: 0151 227 3499
Fax: 0151 236 3590

Website:
http://naaps.org.uk

Enquiries:
Enquiries to: Co-ordinator
Direct e-mail: jackie@naaps.org.uk

Founded:
1992

Organisation type and purpose:
National organisation, membership association
(membership is by subscription), present number
of members: 1500+, voluntary organisation,
registered charity (charity number 1019231).
To promote and develop adult placement services
as a resource within the community.

Subject coverage:
Adult placement.

Access to staff:
Contact by letter, by telephone and by fax
Hours: Mon to Fri, 0900 to 1700

NATIONAL ASSOCIATION OF AGRICULTURAL CONTRACTORS

Acronym or abbreviation: NAAC

Samuelson House, 62 Forder Way, Hampton,
Peterborough, PE7 8JB

Tel: 0845 644 8750
Fax: 01733 352806
E-mail: jill.hewitt@naac.co.uk

Website:
http://www.naac.co.uk

Enquiries:
Enquiries to: Chief Executive

Founded:
1893

Organisation type and purpose:
Trade association.

Subject coverage:
Contract services to agriculture and allied land-
based industries including crop protection and
spraying, whole farm and whole crop contracting,
vegetation control, mobile seed cleaning and
processing, cultivating and harvesting of all UK
crops.

Printed publications:
NAAC Newsletter (members)
Contracting Bulletin

Access to staff:
Contact by letter, by telephone, by fax, by e-mail
and via website
Hours: Mon to Fri, 0900 to 1700

NATIONAL ASSOCIATION OF BANK & INSURANCE CUSTOMERS

Acronym or abbreviation: NABIC

PO Box 15, Caldicot, Newport, Gwent, NP26 5YD

Tel: 0845 123 5002
Fax: 0845 123 5002
E-mail: webmaster@lemonaid.net

Website:
http://www.lemonaid.net
Information, advice and general background to
NABIC and its activities.

Enquiries:
Enquiries to: Information Officer
Other contacts: Chief Executive for press comment,
member query or complaint.

Founded:
1991

Organisation type and purpose:
International organisation, membership
association (membership is by subscription),
present number of members: 25,000, training
organisation, consultancy, research organisation.
To protect and promote the interests of private and
commercial users of bank and insurance services
through information, education and mediation
processes. To build a detailed database of
procedures and abuses.

Subject coverage:
Banking, insurance, legal representation, customer
complaints, recalculation of bank statements to
find errors, business planning services, business
planning software and customer service standards.

**Museum or gallery collection, archive, or library
special collection:**
Database of queries and complaints and standard
responses

Trade and statistical information:
Data on the frequency and type of bank and
insurance disputes.

Printed publications:
Ad hoc reports on technical matters
Banking Charter
Datasheets on a variety of topics (free to members)
Occasional newsletter (free to members)

Electronic and video publications:
Business Planning Software

Access to staff:
Contact by letter, by telephone, by fax, by e-mail
and via website
Hours: Mon to Fri, 0900 to 1700

Links with:
ADICAE
　Spain
ADOSBEF
　Italy
AFUB
　France
AIC
　USA
CONSUMENT and GELDZAKEN
　Holland
European Union of Financial Service Users
　contact via NABIC

NATIONAL ASSOCIATION OF BRITISH MARKET AUTHORITIES

Acronym or abbreviation: NABMA

13 Moor Road, Wigan, Lancashire, WN5 8DN

Tel: 01942 203797
Fax: 01942 205885
E-mail: nabma@nabma.com

Website:
http://www.nabma.com
List of member authorities, news and events for
public, members only secured area for members of
this Association.

Enquiries:
Enquiries to: General Secretary

Founded:
1919

Organisation type and purpose:
Local government body, membership association.

Subject coverage:
Organisation and operation by local authorities of
markets of all kinds including open retail markets,
market halls, wholesale fruit, vegetable, flower,
fish and meat markets; livestock markets; public
abattoirs, and pleasure fairs.

Printed publications:
Annual Conference Report including conference
　papers
Rules

Access to staff:
Contact by letter, by telephone and by fax
Hours: Mon to Fri, 0900 to 1700

Member of:
European Association of Livestock Markets
World Union of Wholesale Markets

NATIONAL ASSOCIATION OF CHILD CONTACT CENTRES

Acronym or abbreviation: NACCC

Minerva House, Spaniel Row, Nottingham, NG1
6EP

Tel: 0845 4500280
Fax: 0845 4500420
E-mail: contact@naccc.org.uk

Website:
http://www.naccc.org.uk

Enquiries:
Enquiries to: Administrator
Other contacts: Chief Executive for matters of policy
as opposed to administration.

Organisation type and purpose:
Registered charity (charity number 1003868).
To promote safe child contact within a national
framework of 325 Child Contact Centres

Subject coverage:
Neutral meeting places where children of
separated families can spend time with one or both
parents, and sometimes other family members, in a
safe and comfortable environment when there is
no viable alternative.

Printed publications:
General information leaflet
Ben's Story, An Introduction to Child Contact
　Centres (for children £2.50)
Lily's Story, An Introduction to Child Contact
　Centres for the Very Young (£2.50)
NACCC Manual (available only to members)
NACCC Directory of Member Centres, includes
　referral details, opening times etc (available only
　to members)

Electronic and video publications:
NACCC Training Video (£30 non-members
　outright purchase, £10 members outright
　purchase, £5 members only 2 week hire charge)

Publications list:
Available online

NATIONAL ASSOCIATION OF CHIMNEY SWEEPS

Acronym or abbreviation: NACS

Unit 15, Emerald Way, Stone Business Park, Stone,
Staffordshire, ST15 0SR

Tel: 01785 811732
Fax: 01785 811712
E-mail: nacs@chimneyworks.co.uk

Website:
http://www.nacs.org.uk

Enquiries:
Enquiries to: Administrator

Founded:
1982

Organisation type and purpose:
Trade association.

Subject coverage:
Chimney sweeping and chimneys in general.

Library catalogue:
All or part available in-house

Printed publications:
Code of practice
Chimney Journal (trade magazine, Apr, Aug, Dec)
Heat your Home Safely (leaflet)
List of members

Access to staff:
Contact by letter, by telephone, by fax and by e-
mail
Hours: Mon to Fri, 0800 to 1600

Access to building, collection or gallery:
Prior appointment required

Access for disabled people:
Parking provided, level entry

Links with:
HETAS
　tel: 01242 513747; fax: 01242 513747; e-mail:
　billk@albionmillshouse.freeserve.co.uk

continued overleaf

NACE
tel: 01773 599095; fax: 01773 599195; e-mail:
info@nace.org.uk
NFA
tel: 0121 200 2100; fax: 0121 200 1306

Member of:
European Federation of Chimney Sweeps
(ESCHFO)
tel: +49 2241 340713; fax: +49 2241 340710; e-mail:
ziv-kelz-quadt@schornsteinfeger.de

NATIONAL ASSOCIATION OF CHOIRS

Acronym or abbreviation: NAC

Fig Tree House, 9 The Green, Glinton,
Peterborough, Cambridgeshire, PE6 7JN

Tel: 01733 252464
Fax: 01733 252464
E-mail: gensecnac@gensecnac.force9.co.uk

Website:
http://www.ukchoirsassoc.co.uk
Details of all member choirs, officers, services
provided, links to suppliers, etc.

Enquiries:
Enquiries to: General Secretary

Founded:
1920

Organisation type and purpose:
Voluntary organisation.

Subject coverage:
Study and performance of choral music, choral
societies and choirs.

Printed publications:
News and Views (newsletter, quarterly)
Year Book

Publications list:
Available in print

Access to staff:
Contact by letter, by telephone, by fax, by e-mail
and via website
Hours: Any day up to 2200

Affiliated to:
British Federation of Music Festivals

Member of:
British Federation of Youth Choirs
National Choral Advisory Body

NATIONAL ASSOCIATION OF CITIZENS ADVICE BUREAUX

Acronym or abbreviation: NACAB

Myddelton House, 115–123 Pentonville Road,
London, N1 9LZ

Tel: 020 7833 2181 (Admin only)
Fax: 020 7833 4371 (Admin only)

Website:
http://www.nacab.org.uk
To find your nearest CAB.
http://www.adviceguide.org.uk
For CAB information online.

Enquiries:
Enquiries to: Communications Assistant

Founded:
1939

Organisation type and purpose:
National organisation, advisory body, voluntary
organisation, registered charity.
To provide information and advice on any topic.

Subject coverage:
Debt and consumer, social security, employment,
housing, property and land, family and personal,
administration of justice, taxes and duties, local
information, health, national and international
travel, transport and holidays, education,
immigration and nationality, communication and
leisure.

Printed publications:
Annual Report
CAB News (annually)
Evidence Papers (list available)

Access for disabled people:
Parking provided, level entry, access to all public
areas, toilet facilities
Special comments: Myddleton House only.

Affiliated to:
Advice Services Alliance
National Council for Voluntary Organisations

Has:
approximately 1300 CABs throughout the country

Links with:
Citizens Advice Scotland

NATIONAL ASSOCIATION OF CLINICAL TUTORS UK

Acronym or abbreviation: NACT UK

Norfolk House East, 499 Silbury Boulevard, Milton
Keynes, MK2 9AH

Tel: 01908 488033
Fax: 01296 715255
E-mail: office@nact.org.uk

Website:
http://www.nact.org.uk
Support for members involving Postgraduate
Medical Education.

Enquiries:
Enquiries to: Chairman

Founded:
1969

Organisation type and purpose:
Professional body.

Subject coverage:
Postgraduate medical education; career
counselling in medicine; educational techniques
related to postgraduate medicine.

Printed publications:
Directory of Postgraduate Medical Centres

Access to staff:
Contact by letter, by telephone, by fax and by e-
mail. Appointment necessary. Access for members
only.
Hours: Mon to Fri, 0900 to 1700

NATIONAL ASSOCIATION OF COMMERCIAL FINANCE BROKERS

Acronym or abbreviation: NACFB

3 Silverdown Office Park, Fair Oak Close, Exeter,
Devon, EX5 2UX

Tel: 01392 440040
Fax: 01392 363931
E-mail: admin@nacfb.org.uk

Website:
http://www.nacfb.org
Find a broker, become a member, news and events,
legal and compliance, press centre, member centre.

Founded:
1992

Organisation type and purpose:
The UK's trade body for business finance brokers.
To raise standards of proper professional practice
in the commercial broker industry.

Subject coverage:
Commercial finance, leasing and asset finance,
vehicle finance. NACFB has established complaints
and disciplinary procedures designed to eliminate
unacceptable working practices amongst its
members; it aims to protect its members and their
clients against restrictive practices within the
industry; in the interests of members and their
clients, the NACFB monitors legislation and makes
representations to the government and regulators;

it furthers the principles of good practice by
seeking to work with kindred associations and
interest groups, and by providing education and
training for its members and their employees.

Electronic and video publications:
Downloadable brochures – general brochures such
as application forms and brochures from
previous events the Association has run
NACFB Templates – such as model Terms of
Business agreement
Fact Sheets – information on some key areas of
commercial finance
Member Magazines – the NACFB's own quarterly
magazine
Order electronic and video publications from: Website;
accessible only by members

Publications list:
Available online

Access to staff:
Contact by letter, by telephone, by fax and by e-
mail

NATIONAL ASSOCIATION OF CYCLE TRADERS LIMITED

Acronym or abbreviation: ACT

31a High Street, Tunbridge Wells, Kent, TN1 1XN

Tel: 01892 526081
Fax: 01892 544278
E-mail: info@actsmart.biz

Website:
http://www.act-bicycles.com

Enquiries:
Enquiries to: Information Officer

Founded:
1920

Organisation type and purpose:
Trade association.

Subject coverage:
Cycle safety and standards, cycle mechanics
accreditation scheme, cycle retailing, technical
information.

Printed publications:
Newsletter (quarterly, members)

Access to staff:
Contact by letter, by e-mail and via website
Hours: Mon to Fri, 0900 to 1700

NATIONAL ASSOCIATION OF DEAFENED PEOPLE

Acronym or abbreviation: NADP

PO Box 50, Amersham, Buckinghamshire, HP6
6XB

Tel: 0845 055 9663
Fax: 01305 262591
E-mail: enquiries@nadp.org.uk

Website:
http://www.nadp.org.uk

Enquiries:
Enquiries to: Honorary Secretary

Founded:
1984

Organisation type and purpose:
Membership association (membership is by
subscription), present number of members: 300,
voluntary organisation, registered charity (charity
number 294922).
To provide a network of information and support
for deafened people.

Subject coverage:
Increasing public awareness of the needs and
problems of deafened people; the promotion of an
improvement in the rehabilitation, education,
training, re-training and employment
opportunities available for deafened people.

Printed publications:
Introduction to Cochlear Implants (3rd edn, £5 inc
p&p)
Network (newsletter, quarterly, members only)
Tips on how to Communicate with deaf people
(individual copies free, bulk supplies available at
£15 per 100 copies.)
NADP Information Booklet (covers a wide range of
issues, £7.50 inc p&p, also available as pdf
download.)
Order printed publications from: Postal or e-mail
address shown above

Publications list:
Available online and in print

Access to staff:
Contact by letter, by fax, by e-mail and via
website

Access to building, collection or gallery:
No access to office

NATIONAL ASSOCIATION OF DECORATIVE & FINE ARTS SOCIETIES

Acronym or abbreviation: NADFAS

NADFAS House, 8 Guilford Street, London,
WC1N 1DT

Tel: 020 7430 0730
Fax: 020 7242 0686
E-mail: enquiries@nadfas.org.uk

Website:
http://www.nadfas.org.uk

Enquiries:
Enquiries to: PA to Chairman & Chief Executive

Founded:
May 1968

Organisation type and purpose:
International organisation, membership
association (membership is by subscription),
present number of members: 88,000, registered
charity (charity number 263487), art gallery.
Arts educational charity.
Volunteer-led cultivation, appreciation and study
of the decorative and fine arts, and giving aid to
the preservation of national artistic heritage for the
benefit of the general public.

Subject coverage:
Decorative and fine arts. NADFAS is an arts
educational organisation based on leisure interests
rather than careers. It consists of member societies
that meet on a monthly basis for lectures, and
organises visits to places of historic interest and
museums. In addition members carry out
voluntary work in museums, historic houses and
churches.

Printed publications:
NADFAS News (magazine, 2 times a year)
Inside Churches (£9.95 or £6.67 to trade)
Order printed publications from: Manager, NADFAS
Enterprises
at the same address

Access to staff:
Contact by letter, by telephone and by e-mail
Hours: Mon to Fri, 0930 to 1730

Access to building, collection or gallery:
No prior appointment required

Has:
320 societies in the UK, 22 in Australia and 9 in
Europe

Head Office:
National Association of Decorative & Fine Arts
Societies (NADFAS)
  at the same address

NATIONAL ASSOCIATION OF EDUCATIONAL INSPECTORS, ADVISERS AND CONSULTANTS

Acronym or abbreviation: NAEIAC

Woolley Hall, Woolley, Wakefield, West Yorkshire,
WF4 2JR

Tel: 01226 383428
Fax: 01226 383427
E-mail: naeiac@gemsoft.co.uk

Website:
http://www.naeiac.co.uk
Membership information, services provided.

Enquiries:
Enquiries to: General Secretary

Founded:
1918

Organisation type and purpose:
National organisation, professional body, trade
union (membership is by subscription).

Subject coverage:
Education from pre-school to higher education:
curriculum, management, inspection and advice.

Printed publications:
Briefing
Business Register Directory
Information Bulletin

Access to staff:
Contact by letter, by telephone, by fax, by e-mail
and via website
Hours: Mon to Thu, 0830 to 1700; Fri, 0830 to 1630

Representation on:
Soulbury Committee

NATIONAL ASSOCIATION OF FARRIERS, BLACKSMITHS AND AGRICULTURAL ENGINEERS

Acronym or abbreviation: NAFBAE

Avenue B, 10th Street, National Agricultural
Centre, Stoneleigh, Kenilworth, Warwickshire,
CV8 2LG

Tel: 02476 696595
Fax: 02476 696708
E-mail: nafbaehq@nafbae.org.uk

Enquiries:
Enquiries to: Membership Secretary
Other contacts: National Organiser

Founded:
1904

Organisation type and purpose:
National organisation, trade association
(membership is by subscription).

Access to staff:
Contact by letter, by telephone, by fax and by e-
mail. Access for members only.
Hours: Mon to Fri, 0900 to 1700

Access to building, collection or gallery:
No prior appointment required

NATIONAL ASSOCIATION OF FUNERAL DIRECTORS

Acronym or abbreviation: NAFD

618 Warwick Road, Solihull, West Midlands, B91
1AA

Tel: 0845 230 1343
Fax: 0121 711 1351
E-mail: info@nafd.org.uk

Website:
http://nafd.org.uk

Enquiries:
Enquiries to: Chief Executive Officer

Founded:
1905

Organisation type and purpose:
Trade association, present number of members:
3272.

Subject coverage:
All aspects of the funeral profession.

Printed publications:
Careers in the Funeral Service
Code of Practice
Independent Chairman's Report of the Disciplinary
  Committee
Funeral Arbitration Scheme

Access to staff:
Contact by letter, by telephone, by fax, by e-mail,
in person and via website
Hours: Mon to Fri, 0900 to 1700

Access to building, collection or gallery:
No prior appointment required

Access for disabled people:
Parking provided

NATIONAL ASSOCIATION OF GOLDSMITHS OF GREAT BRITAIN AND IRELAND

Acronym or abbreviation: NAG

78A Luke Street, London, EC2A 4XG

Tel: 020 7613 4445
Fax: 020 7613 4450
E-mail: nag@jewellers-online.org

Website:
http://www.jewellers-online.org

Enquiries:
Enquiries to: Information Manager
Direct e-mail: information@jewellers-online.org

Founded:
1894

Organisation type and purpose:
Trade association (membership is by subscription,
election or invitation), present number of
members: 1,000 companies, training organisation,
consultancy, publishing house.
To provide services, support, education and
information to best encourage professionalism in
the retail jewellery industry.

Subject coverage:
All aspects of the jewellery industry; history,
materials, gems, gold, silver, retail, valuations.

Printed publications:
The Jeweller Magazine
Order printed publications from: NAG switchboard

Publications list:
Available in print

Access to staff:
Contact by letter, by fax, by e-mail and via
website. Appointment necessary. Access for
members only.
Hours: Mon to Fri, 0900 to 1700

NATIONAL ASSOCIATION OF HEALTH WORKERS FOR TRAVELLERS

Acronym or abbreviation: NAHWT

Balsall Heath Health Centre, 43 Edward Road,
Balsall Heath, Birmingham, B12 9LB

Tel: 0121 446 2300
Fax: 0121 446 5936
E-mail: joanne.davis@hobtpct.nhs.uk

Enquiries:
Enquiries to: Secretary

Founded:
1992

Subject coverage:
Health care relating to Travellers and Gypsies in
Britain.

Access to staff:
Contact by letter, by fax and by e-mail
Hours: Mon to Wed, 0900 to 1700

Access to building, collection or gallery:
No access other than to staff

continued overleaf

Links with:
Community Practioners and Health Visitors
Association
40 Bermondsey Street, London, SE1 3UD; tel: 020
7939 7000; fax: 020 7403 2976

NATIONAL ASSOCIATION OF INDEPENDENT TRAVEL AGENTS

Acronym or abbreviation: NAITA

79–80 Margaret Street, London, W1W 8TA

Tel: 020 7323 3408
Fax: 020 7323 5189
E-mail: naita@advantage4travel.com

Website:
http://www.advantage4travel.com

Enquiries:
Enquiries to: Manager
Direct e-mail: debbiew@advantage4travel.com
Other contacts: Membership Co-ordinator for
membership enquiries.

Founded:
1978

Organisation type and purpose:
National organisation, trade association
(membership is by subscription), present number
of members: 904.
Commercial and Marketing Consortia (Travel).
To enhance, from a commercial and marketing
viewpoint, the business and professionalism of our
members (independent travel agents in the UK)
and help maximise their profitability.

Subject coverage:
Travel trade consortia for independent travel
agents in the UK, offering commercial and
marketing support, to include signage, window
decals, hanging banners, late availability board,
tactical campaigns, monthly magazine and
supplier-led promotions, together with a
professional sales development team offering
expert advice and support to all members.

Access to staff:
Contact by letter, by telephone, by fax, by e-mail
and via website. Appointment necessary.
Hours: Mon to Fri, 0830 to 1800

Trading as:
Advantage Travel Centres
38 Anderston Quay, Glasgow, G3 8BX; tel: 0141
248 3466; fax: 0141 248 5170; e-mail: glasgow@
advantage4travel.com

NATIONAL ASSOCIATION OF KARATE AND MARTIAL ART SCHOOLS NATIONAL GOVERNING BODY

Acronym or abbreviation: NAKMAS National
Governing Body

PO Box 262, Herne Bay, Kent, CT6 9AW

Tel: 01227 370055
Fax: 01227 37005
E-mail: info@nakmas.org.uk6

Website:
http://www.nakmas.org.uk
Information on different forms of martial arts,
insurance, black belt register, publications, events.

Enquiries:
Enquiries to: Chair
Direct e-mail: joe.ellis@nakmas.org.uk

Founded:
1992

Organisation type and purpose:
A non-funded national governing body for martial
arts with over 73,000 members within the UK.
An independent publisher with offices in Kent and
Buckinghamshire.

Subject coverage:
Traditional and modern martial arts.

Printed publications:
In Touch (members' magazine)
Stay Safe (welfare magazine)

Access to staff:
Contact by letter, by telephone, by fax and by e-
mail
Hours: Mon to Thu, 0900 to 1600; Fri, 0900 to 1500

Member organisation of:
Central Council of Physical Recreation (CCPR)

NATIONAL ASSOCIATION OF LADIES' CIRCLES

Formal name: National Association of Ladies'
Circles of Great Britain and Ireland
Acronym or abbreviation: NALC

Marchesi House, 4 Embassy Drive, Edgbaston,
Birmingham, B15 1TP

Tel: 0121 456 0304
E-mail: headquarters@ladies-circle.org.uk

Website:
http://www.ladies-circle.org.uk

Enquiries:
Enquiries to: Association Secretary

Founded:
1936

Organisation type and purpose:
National organisation, membership association
(membership is by subscription), present number
of members: 6500, voluntary organisation.

Subject coverage:
Charities, fund-raising, community service,
women's issues, family issues.

Printed publications:
The Circler (twice a year, April and September, free
to members)

Access to staff:
Contact by letter, by telephone, by fax, by e-mail
and via website
Hours: Mon to Fri, 0900 to 1700

Affiliated to:
Ladies Circle International
at the same address

NATIONAL ASSOCIATION OF LARYNGECTOMEE CLUBS

Acronym or abbreviation: NALC

Lower Ground Floor, 152 Buckingham Palace
Road, London, SW1W 9TR

Tel: 020 7730 8585
Fax: 020 7730 8584
E-mail: info@laryngectomy.org.uk

Website:
http://www.laryngectomy.org.uk

Enquiries:
Enquiries to: Association Secretary

Founded:
1976

Organisation type and purpose:
National organisation, membership association,
present number of members: 97 clubs with 5,000
members, voluntary organisation, registered
charity (charity number 273635).
National Association with clubs situated
throughout the UK for those who have undergone
a laryngectomy operation, their family and friends.

Subject coverage:
Rehabilitation of laryngectomee patients,
availability of speech aids and medical supplies.

Printed publications:
NALC pamphlet
NATO Alphabet, pocket card
Professional Care, pack of 3 leaflets
Living with a Laryngectomy, pack of 4 leaflets
Emergency card
Information pamphlet

Clan (newsletter, quarterly)
Work of the Association (pamphlet)
Stoma care pamphlet
Resources pamphlet
Resuscitation pamphlet
NALC Handbook

Electronic and video publications:
LIFE, Laryngectomy Information for First Aid and
Emergency Treatment (video)
Talking it Through (video)
Nursing and Laryngectomee Care (video)

Publications list:
Available in print

Access to staff:
Contact by letter, by telephone, by fax, by e-mail
and via website. Appointment necessary.
Hours: Mon to Thu, 0900 to 1630; Fri, 0900 to 1600

Links with:
Macmillan Cancer Support
National associations in various countries

NATIONAL ASSOCIATION OF LICENSED PARALEGALS

Acronym or abbreviation: NALP

3.08 Canterbury Court, 1–3 Brixton Road, London,
SW9 6DE

Tel: 020 3176 0900
Fax: N/A
E-mail: info@nationalparalegals.co.uk

Website:
http://www.nationalparalegals.com/nalp.htm
NALP is recognised as an awarding organisation
by Ofqual, the regulator of qualifications in
England, offering accredited and recognised
professional paralegal courses and qualifications
for a career in the field of law.

Enquiries:
Enquiries to: Chief Executive
Other contacts: Business Development Manager,
Membership

Founded:
1987

Organisation type and purpose:
Self-regulatory and professional body, suitable for
ages: 18+. Educational, training and career
development organisation.

Subject coverage:
Career guidance for paralegals, qualifications by
examination and otherwise for paralegals, training
for career progression, seminars, workshops and
courses on legal subjects.

Printed publications:
Printed Course Material

Access to staff:
Contact by letter, by telephone, by e-mail and via
website. Appointment necessary.
Hours: Mon to Fri, 0930 to 1730

Access to building, collection or gallery:
Prior appointment required
Hours: Mon to Fri, 0900 to 1800

Access for disabled people:
Hours: Mon to Fri, 0930 to 1730

NATIONAL ASSOCIATION OF LOCAL COUNCILS

Acronym or abbreviation: NALC

109 Great Russell Street, London, WC1B 3LD

Tel: 020 7637 1865
Fax: 020 7436 7451
E-mail: nalc@nalc.gov.uk

Website:
http://www.nalc.gov.uk

Enquiries:
Enquiries to: Deputy Chief Executive

Founded:
1947

Organisation type and purpose:
Local government body, membership association.

Subject coverage:
Any matter to do with small scale local
government, particularly rural, legal and financial.

**Museum or gallery collection, archive, or library
special collection:**
A complete law library

Printed publications:
Booklets and leaflets (32 titles, some free)
Conduct of Parish Meetings
Local Council Review (quarterly)
Powers and Constitution of Local Councils
Standing Orders and Chairmanship

Access to staff:
Contact by letter, by fax and by e-mail.
Appointment necessary.
Hours: Mon to Fri, 0900 to 1700

Access to building, collection or gallery:
No access other than to staff

NATIONAL ASSOCIATION OF MASTER BAKERS

Acronym or abbreviation: NAMB

21 Baldock Street, Ware, Hertfordshire, SG12 9DH

Tel: 01920 468061
Fax: 01920 461632
E-mail: namb@masterbakers.co.uk

Website:
http://www.masterbakers.co.uk

Enquiries:
Enquiries to: Chief Executive

Founded:
1887

Organisation type and purpose:
Trade association.

Subject coverage:
Bread, flour and confectionery.

**Museum or gallery collection, archive, or library
special collection:**
Copies of Bakers' Review from 1887 to present day

Printed publications:
Bakers' Review (monthly)
Handbook and Buyers Guide (annually)

NATIONAL ASSOCIATION OF MASTER LETTER CARVERS

Acronym or abbreviation: NAMLC

c/o NAMM, Castle Mews, Rugby, CV21 2XL

Tel: 01788 542264
Fax: 01788 542276
E-mail: enquiries@namm.org.uk

Enquiries:
Enquiries to: Honorary Secretary

Founded:
1920

Organisation type and purpose:
Trade association, present number of members: 50,
consultancy.
Publication of list of members. Setting
recommended prices.

Subject coverage:
Hand-carved lettering in stone and wood,
memorials, monuments, etc.

**Museum or gallery collection, archive, or library
special collection:**
History of Association
Minutes since 1920

Printed publications:
Introduction to the Association

Access to staff:
Contact by letter and by telephone
Hours: Mon to Fri, 0900 to 1700

NATIONAL ASSOCIATION OF MEMORIAL MASONS

Acronym or abbreviation: NAMM

1 Castle Mews, Rugby, CU21 2XL

Tel: 01788 542264
Fax: 01788 542276
E-mail: enquiries@namm.org.uk

Website:
http://www.namm.org.uk

Enquiries:
Enquiries to: National Executive Officer

Founded:
1907

Organisation type and purpose:
Trade association (membership is by subscription).

Subject coverage:
All matters relating to natural stone memorials,
standards in the trade, training.

Printed publications:
Choosing a Memorial
List of Members
Newsletter
Code of Working Practice
Order printed publications from: National
Association of Memorial Masons, as above

Access to staff:
Contact by letter, by telephone, by fax and by e-
mail
Hours: Mon to Fri, 0900 to 1700

Associate member of:
Council of British Funeral Services
Institute of Cemetery and Crematorium
Management

NATIONAL ASSOCIATION OF MINING HISTORY ORGANISATIONS

Acronym or abbreviation: NAMHO

Peak District Mining Museum, The Pavilion,
Matlock Bath, Derbyshire, DE4 3NR

Tel: 01629 583834

Website:
http://www.namho.org

Enquiries:
Enquiries to: Honorary Secretary

Founded:
1979

Organisation type and purpose:
National organisation, learned society
(membership is by election or invitation), present
number of members: 75, voluntary organisation,
registered charity (charity number 297301).
Representative body for mining history.

Subject coverage:
Mining history; past and present mining in the UK;
access policy and legislation thereon; conservation
and display of artefacts; production of codes of
practice on research techniques.

Printed publications:
Archival Research
Codes of Practice (free on receipt of sae)
Exploration (leaders)
Exploration (novices)
Guidelines for the Leisure Use of Mines
Mineral collection
Mining Heritage Guide
Removal of Artefacts

Access to staff:
Contact by letter and by telephone
Hours: Mon to Fri, 0900 to 1700
Special comments: SAE required for reply.

Member of:
National Caving Association
Momomark House, 27 Old Gloucester Street,
London, WC1N 3XX

NATIONAL ASSOCIATION OF MUSIC EDUCATORS

Acronym or abbreviation: NAME

Gordon Lodge, Snitterton Road, Matlock,
Derbyshire, DE4 3LZ

Tel: 01629 760791
E-mail: musiceducation@name.org.uk

Website:
http://www.name.org.uk

Enquiries:
Enquiries to: Business Manager

Founded:
1996

Organisation type and purpose:
Company limited by guarantee, registered charity.

Subject coverage:
Music education.

Printed publications:
Information Bulletins (£1.50)
Composing in the Classroom (£7)
Rites of Passage (£11)
Ideas In Music Out (£8)
Bluebirds and Crows (£8)
Ways into Music (£11)
No Need for Words (£11)
Music and the Power of Partnerships (£11)
Ways into Music (£11)
Sound Progress (£11)
Order printed publications from: NAME Business
Manager
at same address

Publications list:
Available online and in print

Access to staff:
Contact by letter, by telephone, by e-mail and via
website
Hours: Mon to Fri, 0900 to 1700

NATIONAL ASSOCIATION OF PENSION FUNDS

Acronym or abbreviation: NAPF

NIOC House, 4 Victoria Street, London, SW1H
0NX

Tel: 020 7808 1300
Fax: 020 7222 7585
E-mail: jane.dawson@napf.co.uk

Website:
http://www.napf.co.uk
Full details of the NAPF Press Office, including
releases, speeches, articles, publications and other
services.

Enquiries:
Enquiries to: Public Relations Manager
Other contacts: Press Officer

Founded:
1923

Organisation type and purpose:
Trade association.

Subject coverage:
All aspects of occupational pensions, both benefits
and investments.

Printed publications:
Policy Watch (monthly)
NAPF News (4 times a year)
Leaflets and other pensions material
NAPF Annual Survey of Occupational Pension
Schemes (£120 members, £160 non-members)
Series of guides, leaflets and handbooks for
pension funds and others in the pensions
industry

continued overleaf

Electronic and video publications:
Interactive introduction to the NAPF (CD-ROM, free)

Publications list:
Available online and in print

Access to staff:
Contact by letter, by telephone, by fax, by e-mail and via website. Appointment necessary.
Hours: Mon to Fri, 0915 to 1715

NATIONAL ASSOCIATION OF POULTRY SUPPLIERS

1 Belgrove, Tunbridge Wells, Kent, TN1 1YW

Tel: 01892 541412
Fax: 01892 535462
E-mail: naps@nfmft.co.uk

Enquiries:
Enquiries to: Secretary
Direct e-mail: graham@nfmft.co.uk

Organisation type and purpose:
National organisation, trade association (membership is by subscription).

Subject coverage:
All aspects of wholesale poultry trade.

Access to staff:
Contact by letter, by telephone and by fax
Hours: Mon to Fri, 0900 to 1700

NATIONAL ASSOCIATION OF PRISON VISITORS

Acronym or abbreviation: NAPV

29 Kimbolton Road, Bedford, MK40 2PB

Tel: 01234 359763
Fax: 01234 359763

Enquiries:
Enquiries to: General Secretary

Founded:
1924

Organisation type and purpose:
National organisation, membership association (membership is by subscription), present number of members: 1400, voluntary organisation, suitable for ages: 21 to 70.

Subject coverage:
Concern and friendship for, and visits to, people in prison.

Printed publications:
Newsletter (2 times a year)

Access to staff:
Contact by letter, by telephone and by fax
Hours: Mon to Fri, 0900 to 1700

NATIONAL ASSOCIATION OF PUBLIC GOLF COURSES

Acronym or abbreviation: NAPGC

12 Newton Close, Redditch, Worcestershire, B98 7YR

Tel: 01527 542106
Fax: 01527 455320
E-mail: eddiemitchell@blueyonder.co.uk

Website:
http://www.napgc.org.uk

Enquiries:
Enquiries to: Secretary

Founded:
1927

Organisation type and purpose:
Voluntary organisation.
Specially for the cohesion of golf clubs formed on public golf courses.

Subject coverage:
Golf club and course management authority integration, national golf tournaments for public course clubs.

Printed publications:
Year Book

Links with:
English Golf Union
Royal & Ancient Golf Club of St Andrews

NATIONAL ASSOCIATION OF ROUND TABLES OF GREAT BRITAIN AND IRELAND

Acronym or abbreviation: RTBI

Marchesi House, 4 Embassy Drive, Edgbaston, Birmingham, B15 1TP

Tel: 0121 456 4402
Fax: 0121 456 4185
E-mail: hq@roundtable.org.uk

Website:
http://www.roundtable.org.uk
Home page.

Founded:
1927

Organisation type and purpose:
Membership association (membership is by election or invitation), present number of members: 5,500
Fellowship.

Subject coverage:
Community service, normally within local Table area.

Printed publications:
TM

Access to staff:
Contact by letter, by telephone, by fax, by e-mail and via website
Hours: Mon to Fri, 0900 to 1700

Access for disabled people:
Access to all public areas

NATIONAL ASSOCIATION OF SCHOOLMASTERS AND UNION OF WOMEN TEACHERS

Acronym or abbreviation: NASUWT

Northern Ireland Centre, Ben Madigan House, Edgewater Office Park, Edgewater Road, Belfast, BT3 9JQ

Tel: 028 9078 4480
Fax: 028 9078 4489
E-mail: rc-nireland@mail.nasuwt.org.uk

Website:
http://www.northern-ireland.nasuwt.org.uk
Professional and trade union information.

Enquiries:
Enquiries to: Regional Organiser (Northern Ireland)

Founded:
1962

Organisation type and purpose:
National organisation, trade union (membership is by subscription), present number of members: 11,100 in NI.

Subject coverage:
All matters pertaining to school teachers.

Non-library collection catalogue:
All or part available online and in print

Library catalogue:
All or part available online and in print

Printed publications:
Teaching Today
Platform

Access to staff:
Contact by letter, by telephone, by fax, by e-mail and via website

Hours: Mon to Fri, 0830 to 1730

Access to building, collection or gallery:
Prior appointment required
Hours: Mon to Fri, 0830 to 1730

Access for disabled people:
Parking provided, access to all public areas, toilet facilities

Parent body:
National Association of Schoolmasters and Union of Women Teachers
Rose Hill, Rednal, Birmingham, B45 8RS; tel: 0121 453 6150; fax: 0121 457 6208/9; e-mail: nasuwt@mail.nasuwt.org.uk

NATIONAL ASSOCIATION OF SESSIONAL GPS

Acronym or abbreviation: NASGP

PO Box 188, Chichester, West Sussex, PO19 2FP

Fax: 01243 536428
E-mail: info@nanp.org.uk

Website:
http://www.nasgp.org.uk

Enquiries:
Enquiries to: Chief Executive

Founded:
1997

Organisation type and purpose:
National organisation, membership association (membership is by subscription), present number of members: 2500, voluntary organisation. Independent voluntary organisation of non-principal general practitioners, such as locums and assistants, who work in the NHS, to improve status and welfare of its members.

Subject coverage:
Non-principal general practitioners in the NHS.

Publications list:
Available online

Access to staff:
Contact by letter, by fax, by e-mail and via website
Hours: Mon to Fri, 0900 to 1700

NATIONAL ASSOCIATION OF SHOPFITTERS

Acronym or abbreviation: NAS

NAS House, 411 Limpsfield Road, The Green, Warlingham, Surrey, CR6 9HA

Tel: 01883 624961
Fax: 01883 626841
E-mail: nas@clara.net

Website:
http://www.shopfitters.org
Members list, membership benefits, general information.

Enquiries:
Enquiries to: Director

Founded:
1919

Organisation type and purpose:
Trade association.

Subject coverage:
Shopfitting.

Printed publications:
Annual Report and Directory
Guide to Controlling Risks to Health in the Shopfitting Industry
Shopfitters' Guide to CDM Regulations
ShopSpec (annually, pub Nexus Media Limited)
Code of Practice on Safe Erection of Hoardings etc

Publications list:
Available online and in print

Access to staff:
Contact by letter, by telephone, by fax, by e-mail and via website
Hours: Mon to Fri, 0900 to 1700

Affiliated to:
International Shopfitters Organisation

Houses the:
Automatic Door Suppliers Association

NATIONAL ASSOCIATION OF STEEL STOCKHOLDERS

Acronym or abbreviation: NASS

First Floor, The Citadel, 190 Corporation Street, Birmingham, B4 6QD

Tel: 0121 200 2288
Fax: 0121 236 7444
E-mail: info@nass.org.uk

Website:
http://www.nass.org.uk

Enquiries:
Enquiries to: Director-General

Founded:
1928

Organisation type and purpose:
Trade association.

Subject coverage:
United Kingdom steel stockists and suppliers.

Printed publications:
Annual Report
List of Members
NASS News
Safety Guidelines (£100)
Steel and its Distribution (£10)
Safe Delivery and Unloading of Steel Products
Order printed publications from: e-mail: info@nass.org.uk

Electronic and video publications:
Industry Video (£150)
Safe Delivery and Unloading of Steel Products (downloadable)
Order electronic and video publications from: e-mail: info@nass.org.uk

Access to staff:
Contact by letter, by telephone, by fax, by e-mail and via website
Hours: Mon to Fri, 0900 to 1700

NATIONAL ASSOCIATION OF SWIMMING CLUBS FOR THE HANDICAPPED

Acronym or abbreviation: NASCH

The Willows, Mayles Lane, Wickham, Hampshire, PO17 5ND

Tel: 01329 833689
E-mail: naschswim-willows@yahoo.co.uk

Website:
http://www.nasch.org.uk

Enquiries:
Enquiries to: Administrator

Founded:
1965

Organisation type and purpose:
Membership association (membership is by subscription), present number of members: 101, registered charity (charity number 247772).

Subject coverage:
Swimming for the handicapped, including swimming aids, hoists and other equipment, tuition, formation of clubs, insurance, and the Distance Award (incentive) scheme. Regional and national swimming galas.

Printed publications:
Free booklets
Lifting and Handling
Medical Considerations
Swimming and Epilepsy
Teaching Disabled People to Swim (series of 2 booklets)
Order printed publications from: Administrator

NATIONAL ASSOCIATION OF TEACHERS OF DANCING

Acronym or abbreviation: NATD

Bateman House, 44–47 The Broadway, Thatcham, Newbury, Berkshire, RG19 3HP

Tel: 01635 868888
Fax: 01635 872301
E-mail: info@natd.org.uk

Website:
http://www.natd.org.uk

Enquiries:
Enquiries to: General Secretary

Founded:
1906

Organisation type and purpose:
Membership association (membership is by subscription), training organisation.

Subject coverage:
Dance teaching.

Access to staff:
Contact by letter, by telephone, by fax, by e-mail and via website
Hours: Mon to Fri, 0830 to 1600

Access to building, collection or gallery:
No access other than to staff

NATIONAL ASSOCIATION OF THE LAUNDERETTE INDUSTRY LIMITED

Acronym or abbreviation: NALI

146 Welling Way, Welling, Kent, DA16 2RS

Tel: 020 8856 9798
Fax: 020 8856 9394

Enquiries:
Enquiries to: Secretary

Organisation type and purpose:
Trade association.

Subject coverage:
Launderettes and coin-operated dry cleaners.

Printed publications:
Launderette and Cleaning World (quarterly, members only)
What Every Launderette Owner Should Know (£5.50 inc. p&p)

Access to staff:
Contact by letter, by telephone and by fax
Hours: Mon to Fri, 0900 to 1700

NATIONAL ASSOCIATION OF TOOL DEALERS

Acronym or abbreviation: NATD

225 Bristol Road, Edgbaston, Birmingham, B5 7UB

Tel: 0121 446 6688
Fax: 0121 446 5215
E-mail: natd@bhfgroup.demon.co.uk

Enquiries:
Enquiries to: Managing Director

Founded:
1899

Organisation type and purpose:
Trade association.
Representation of members interests to government and others.

Subject coverage:
Hand and power tools.

Printed publications:
Hardware Today

Member of:
BHF Group

NATIONAL ASSOCIATION OF TOY AND LEISURE LIBRARIES

Acronym or abbreviation: NATLL

1A Harmood Street, London, NW1 8DN

Tel: 020 7428 2281
Fax: 020 7428 2281
E-mail: admin@playmatters.co.uk

Website:
http://www.natll.org.uk

Enquiries:
Enquiries to: Helpline
Direct tel: 020 7428 2286
Direct e-mail: helpline@playmatters.co.uk

Founded:
1967

Organisation type and purpose:
National organisation, membership association (membership is by subscription), present number of members: 500 toy libraries, 2 leisure libraries, voluntary organisation, registered charity (charity number in England and Wales 270291 and in Scotland SCO39458), suitable for ages: Toy Library – 0 to 12, usually extended for children with special needs; Leisure Libraries – adults with special needs and their families, training organisation.
The national body for toy and leisure libraries throughout the United Kingdom. Toy libraries lend good quality, carefully chosen toys to all families with young children, including children with special needs. They offer a befriending, supportive service to parents and carers. NATLL offers help, advice, information support and training for people setting up and running toy and leisure libraries; offers a range of publications on running toy libraries, toys and play; organises training courses for the voluntary and statutory sectors; offers Quality Assurance Scheme 'Quality Play Matters' to member toy libraries; has contracts with: the Department for Education to deliver services under Every Child Matters, the Scottish Executive, the Welsh Assembly and a number of local authorities.

Subject coverage:
Toy libraries; leisure libraries; toys and play, particularly for children with special needs; learning through play, recreational activities for adults with additional needs.

Information services:
Helpline, website, publications.

Special visitor services:
Outreach Workers in selected areas of the UK.

Education services:
Training, quality assurance.

Services for disabled people:
Toy libraries offer loan of specialist toys and equipment, multi-sensory experiences and support to families of children with special needs.

Museum or gallery collection, archive, or library special collection:
Good Toy Guide
Play Matters magazine

Printed publications:
Play Matters Magazine (formerly ARK; journal, quarterly for members. From 2010, an e-magazine only available to members online)
Books and leaflets include:
Good Toy Guide (annually) suspended for 2010
Guide to Choosing and Using Musical Instruments (2001)
Nuts and Bolts: Setting up a Toy Library (2003)
Nytiau a Boltau (Welsh version of Nuts and Bolts)
Play Matters for Adults Too (1999)
More Playsense Activity Cards

continued overleaf

Quality PlayMatters Workbook
The really useful guide to involving volunteers
Toy Care
Starting Out (out of print, 2010)
Special Needs Supplies (2000)
Starting a Toy Library in School (1999)
Switch into Action (2000)
Toys and Play in Child Development (1995)
Games Pack for Extended Schools
Let's Make Cookery Bags
Let's Make Maths Bags
Order printed publications from: website; mail order
from HQ

Electronic and video publications:
Play Helps Video
Order electronic and video publications from: website;
mail order from HQ

Publications list:
Available online and in print

Access to staff:
Contact by letter, by telephone, by fax, by e-mail
and via website. Appointment necessary.
Hours: Mon to Fri, 0900 to 1700
Special comments: Please send A4 sae.

Access to building, collection or gallery:
Prior appointment required

Access for disabled people:
Fully acccessible

Also at:
National Association of Toy and Leisure Libraries
Gilmerton Community Centre, 4 Drum Street,
Edinburgh, EH17 8QG; tel: 0131 664 2746; fax:
0131 664 2753; e-mail: natll.scotland@
playmatters.co.uk
National Association of Toy and Leisure Libraries
(in Wales)
Suite 11, 65 Penarth Road, Cardiff, CF10 5DL; tel:
029 2023 0047; e-mail: walesadmin@playmatters
.co.uk

Member organisation of:
International Toy Library Association
website: http://www.itla-toylibraries.org
NCVCCO
NCVO
VOLCUF

NATIONAL ASSOCIATION OF WIDOWS

Acronym or abbreviation: NAW

48 Queens Road, Coventry, Warwickshire, CV1
3EH

Tel: 024 7663 4848
E-mail: info@nawidows.co.uk

Website:
http://www.nawidows.co.uk
The website is being updated and is currently a
holding site.

Enquiries:
Enquiries to: Administrator

Founded:
1971

Organisation type and purpose:
National organisation (membership is by
subscription), present number of members: 3000,
voluntary organisation, registered charity (charity
number 1096896).
Run by widows for widows; providing friendship
and support with local branches throughout the
country; Head Quarters membership is also
available for widows who have no local contact.

Printed publications:
Newsletter (2 times a year)
Information Sheets (free) include:
Widowed mothers and their children
Disability Support
Solo Holidays
Social activities and volunteering
Helpful Books

Access to staff:
Contact by letter, by telephone and by e-mail
Hours: Mon , Tues, Thu, Fri, 0900 to 1600

Access to building, collection or gallery:
No prior appointment required

Access for disabled people:
Lift

NATIONAL ASSOCIATION OF WOMEN PHARMACISTS

Acronym or abbreviation: NAWP

c/o The Royal Pharmaceutical Society of Great
Britain, 1 Lambeth High Street, London, SE1 7JN

E-mail: enquiries@nawp.org.uk

Website:
http://www.nawp.org.uk

Enquiries:
Enquiries to: Honorary Secretary
Direct tel: 01296 712568
Direct e-mail: renatainglis@hotmail.com

Founded:
1905

Organisation type and purpose:
Professional body (membership is by subscription,
qualification), present number of members: 300.

Subject coverage:
Pharmacy, academic, hospital, community,
industrial; returners, continuing education.

**Museum or gallery collection, archive, or library
special collection:**
Early records and newsletters held in the Archives
of the Royal Pharmaceutical Society of Great
Britain

Printed publications:
Newsletter (3 times a year, members)

Access to staff:
Contact by telephone, by e-mail and via website
Hours: 24-hour access

Links with:
Royal Pharmaceutical Society of Great Britain
1 Lambeth High Street, Lambeth, London, SE1
7JN

Member organisation of:
Standing Conference of Women Returners
Network
Standing Conference of Women's Organisations

NATIONAL ASSOCIATION OF WOMEN'S CLUBS

Acronym or abbreviation: NAWC

5 Vernon Rise, King's Cross Road, London, WC1X
9EP

Tel: 020 7837 1434
Fax: 020 7713 0727

Enquiries:
Enquiries to: Administrator
Other contacts: National Secretary

Founded:
1935

Organisation type and purpose:
Registered charity, voluntary organisation (charity
number 273397).
To advance education and recreation or leisure
time occupation for women in the interests of
social welfare.

Subject coverage:
Assistance in running or opening new clubs for
women to provide education and recreation.

**Museum or gallery collection, archive, or library
special collection:**
Minutes of meetings, photographs

Printed publications:
Annual Report

Education, Friendship and Fun – a History of
NAWC
Newsletters (members)

Access to staff:
Contact by letter, by telephone and by fax
Hours: Mon to Fri, 0930 to 1630

Affiliated to:
National Council of Women of Great Britain

Member of:
Women's National Commission

NATIONAL ASSOCIATION OF YOUTH ORCHESTRAS

Acronym or abbreviation: NAYO

Central Hall, West Tollcross, Edinburgh, EH3 9BP

Tel: 0131 221 1927
Fax: 0131 229 2921
E-mail: admin@nayo.org.uk

Website:
http://www.nayo.org.uk
General information on NAYO.

Enquiries:
Enquiries to: General Manager
Other contacts: Administrator

Founded:
1961

Organisation type and purpose:
Voluntary organisation, registered charity (charity
number 281493).
To represent youth orchestras throughout the UK
and to foster their development.

Subject coverage:
Youth orchestral work: training, performance
repertoire, organisation and maintenance, touring,
international exchanges, courses; Edinburgh and
Glasgow Festivals of British Youth Orchestras;
European Youth Music Week, Allianz Cornhill
Musical Insurance Youth Orchestra Awards,
Allianz Cornhill Musical Insurance Conducting
Prize/Seminar.

**Museum or gallery collection, archive, or library
special collection:**
Marion Semple Weir Library of Chamber Music

Library catalogue:
All or part available online, in-house and in print

Printed publications:
Full Orchestra (newsletter, 3 times a year)
General leaflet (annually)
Leaflet from European Youth Music Week
Directory of Youth and Student Orchestras
Child Protection Guidelines

Access to staff:
Contact by letter, by telephone, by fax, by e-mail
and via website. Appointment necessary.
Hours: Mon to Fri, 0900 to 1700

Access to building, collection or gallery:
Prior appointment required

Affiliated to:
Association of British Orchestras
Edinburgh Festival Fringe
European Association of Youth Orchestras
Incorporated Society of Musicians
Music Education Council
Voluntary Arts Network

NATIONAL ASSOCIATION OF YOUTH THEATRES

Acronym or abbreviation: NAYT

The Arts Centre, Vane Terrace, Darlington, Co
Durham, DL3 7AX

Tel: 01325 363330
Fax: 01325 363313
E-mail: nayt@btconnect.com

Website:
http://www.nayt.org.uk

Enquiries:
Enquiries to: Management Assistant

Founded:
1982

Organisation type and purpose:
NAYT works with over 1,000 groups and individuals to support the development of youth theatre activity through information and support services, advocacy, training, participation and partnerships. Registration is free and open to any group or individual using theatre techniques in their work with young people, outside of formal education. Registered charity (charity number 1046042).

Subject coverage:
Youth theatre provision, practice and location in the United Kingdom, public and national support.

Printed publications:
Youth Theatre Now (quarterly magazine)
State of the Sector (twice-yearly journal)
Excellent and Inclusive documents (self-assessment toolkit)

Access to staff:
Contact by letter, by telephone and by e-mail.
Appointment necessary.
Hours: Mon to Fri, 0900 to 1700

Access to building, collection or gallery:
Prior appointment required

Funded by:
Arts Council England
Department for Education
The D'Oyly Carte Charitable Trust

NATIONAL AUDIT OFFICE

Acronym or abbreviation: NAO

157–197 Buckingham Palace Road, London, SW1W 9SP

Tel: 020 7798 7000
Fax: 020 7798 7894
E-mail: enquiries@nao.gsi.gov.uk

Website:
http://www.nao.org.uk

Enquiries:
Enquiries to: Library Enquiries Desk
Direct tel: 020 7798 7264

Organisation type and purpose:
Statutory body.
Audit of centrally funded bodies and government departments.

Subject coverage:
Value for Money and Financial Audit Reports (relating to centrally funded bodies and government departments).

Information services:
Regularly updated press notices, corporate information, full text of reports 1999/2000 parliamentary session to present (all online).

Printed publications:
Annual Report

Access to staff:
Contact by letter, by telephone and by fax.
Appointment necessary.
Hours: Mon to Fri, 0900 to 1700

Access to building, collection or gallery:
Prior appointment required

NATIONAL AURICULA & PRIMULA SOCIETY (SOUTHERN)

67 Warnham Court Road, Carshalton Beeches, Surrey, SM5 3ND

E-mail: lawrencew67@googlemail.com

Website:
http://www.southernauriculaprimula.org

Enquiries:
Enquiries to: Honorary Secretary

Founded:
1876

Organisation type and purpose:
Learned society (membership is by subscription).

Subject coverage:
Breeding and cultivation of auriculas, primroses, polyanthus, and all primula species and hybrids, their exhibition and history.

Printed publications:
Newsletter
Year Book

Access to staff:
Contact by letter and by e-mail
Hours: Mon to Fri, 0900 to 1700

Affiliated to:
Royal Horticultural Society

Has a:
Midland and West Section
Northern Section

NATIONAL AUTISTIC SOCIETY

Acronym or abbreviation: NAS

393 City Road, London, EC1V 1NG

Tel: 020 7833 2299; 0845 070 4004 (Autism Helpline)
Fax: 020 7833 9666
E-mail: nas@nas.org.uk

Website:
http://www.autism.org.uk

Enquiries:
Enquiries to: Information Centre
Direct tel: 020 7903 3599
Direct e-mail: info@nas.org.uk

Founded:
1962

Organisation type and purpose:
National organisation, membership association (membership is by subscription), present number of members: 19,000, voluntary organisation, registered charity (charity number 269425).

Subject coverage:
Autism; The Autism Helpline provides impartial and confidential information, advice and support for people with an autistic spectrum disorder, their families and professionals.

Information services:
Enquiry service, document delivery.

Museum or gallery collection, archive, or library special collection:
Library of books, journals, videos
Database of 25,000 records online at http://www.autism.org.uk/autismdata

Non-library collection catalogue:
All or part available online

Library catalogue:
All or part available online

Printed publications:
Communication (journal, quarterly, members)
Numerous publications on all aspects of autism and Asperger syndrome
Order printed publications from: Central Books Ltd, 99 Wallis Road, London, E9 5LN; tel. 0845 458 9911; fax 0845 458 9912; e-mail nas@centralbooks.com

Electronic and video publications:
Videos
Autism Update (via login on website, 6 times a year, £14.99)
Titles in Autism (via login on website, 6 times a year, £14.99)

Publications list:
Available online and in print

Access to staff:
Contact by letter, by telephone, by fax, by e-mail and via website
Hours: Mon to Fri, 0930 to 1700

Access to building, collection or gallery:
Prior appointment required
Hours: Mon to Fri, 1000 to 1600

Access for disabled people:
Parking provided, ramped entry, toilet facilities

NATIONAL AUTOCYCLE AND CYCLEMOTOR CLUB LTD

Acronym or abbreviation: NACC

7 St. Nicholas Road, Copmanthorpe, York, YO23 3UX

Tel: 01904 704373
E-mail: info@thebuzzingclub.co.uk

Website:
http:// www.thebuzzingclub.co.uk

Founded:
1981

Organisation type and purpose:
International organisation, membership association (membership is by subscription), present number of members: 1,800. Library covering machines for which the club caters. Aims to promote interest, restoration and use of all autocycles, cyclemotors and mopeds under 100cc.

Subject coverage:
Restoration and preservation of autocycles, cyclemotors and mopeds under 100cc marque enthusiasts, help and advice, library, transfers, etc. Certified machine dating. Authorised by the DVLA to approve V.765 applications for the retention or original registration marks and age-related registration numbers.

Museum or gallery collection, archive, or library special collection:
Parts lists, manuals, road tests, sales cats, etc.

Non-library collection catalogue:
All or part available in-house

Library catalogue:
All or part available in-house

Printed publications:
Buzzing (magazine, 6 times a year, free to members)
Fact and advice sheets
Library booklet of literature held

Publications list:
Available in print

Access to staff:
Contact by letter, by telephone, by e-mail and via website
Hours: 0900 to 2100
Special comments: By telephone, e-mail or letter to the Chairman; please enclose sae for reply.

Access to building, collection or gallery:
No access other than to staff

NATIONAL BED FEDERATION

Acronym or abbreviation: NBF

High Corn Mill, Chapel Hill, Skipton, North Yorkshire, BD23 1NL

Tel: 0845 055 6406
Fax: 0845 055 6407
E-mail: info@bedfed.org.uk

Website:
http://www.bedfed.org.uk

Enquiries:
Enquiries to: Administrator
Other contacts: PR Consultant for media and consumer enquiries

Founded:
1912

Organisation type and purpose:
Trade association (membership is by subscription), present number of members: 72, manufacturing industry.

continued overleaf

To represent UK manufacturers of beds and mattresses and their suppliers.

Subject coverage:
Beds and mattresses in the UK market.

Printed publications:
Consumer leaflets (free):
The Good-night Guide for Children
The Sleep Good Feel Good Guide
The Bed Buyers Guide
Back In Bed – A bed guide for people with back problems

Publications list:
Available online

Access to staff:
Contact by letter, by telephone, by fax, by e-mail and via website
Hours: Mon to Fri, 0900 to 1700

NATIONAL BEEF ASSOCIATION

Acronym or abbreviation: NBA

Mart Centre, Tyne Green, Hexham, NE46 3SG

Tel: 01434 601005
Fax: 01434 601008
E-mail: info@nationalbeefassociation.com

Website:
http://www.nationalbeefassociation.com/

Enquiries:
Enquiries to: General Secretary

Founded:
1998

Organisation type and purpose:
Trade association (membership is by subscription), present number of members: 3000, voluntary organisation.
Umbrella organisation to help the cattle industry.

Access to staff:
Contact by letter, by telephone and by e-mail
Hours: Mon to Fri, 0900 to 1700

NATIONAL BENEVOLENT INSTITUTION

Acronym or abbreviation: NBI

Peter Hervé House, Eccles Court, Tetbury, Gloucestershire, GL8 8EH

Tel: 01666 505500
Fax: 01666 503111
E-mail: office@nbi.org.uk

Website:
http://www.nbi.org.uk

Enquiries:
Enquiries to: Welfare Officer
Direct tel: 01666 505200
Direct e-mail: welfare@nbi.org.uk

Founded:
1812

Organisation type and purpose:
Registered charity (number 212450).
Financial assistance for the elderly in need.
Residential nursing home in Tetbury, Gloucestershire. Self-contained flats in Old Windsor & Tetbury.

Subject coverage:
Geriatrics.

Access to staff:
Contact by letter, by telephone, by fax, by e-mail, in person and via website. Appointment necessary.
Hours: Mon to Fri, 1000 to 1600

NATIONAL BLOOD AUTHORITY

Acronym or abbreviation: NBA

Oak House, Reeds Crescent, Watford, Hertfordshire, WD24 4QN

Tel: 01923 486800

Fax: 01923 486801

Website:
http://www.blood.co.uk
NBS website.

Enquiries:
Enquiries to: Head of Corporate Communications
Direct tel: 0113 214 8734
Direct fax: 0113 214 8736
Direct e-mail: jim.moir@nbs.nhs.uk

Organisation type and purpose:
National government body.
Part of the National Health Service.
Control of collection, processing and distribution of blood and blood products in England.

Subject coverage:
Collection, processing, testing and distribution of blood products in England from voluntary unpaid donors.

Access to staff:
Contact by letter. Appointment necessary.
Hours: Mon to Fri, 0900 to 1700

Links with:
Northern Ireland Blood Transfusion Service
Scottish National Blood Transfusion Service
Welsh Blood Service

National Blood Service Centres:
NBS Birmingham Blood
  Vincent Drive, Edgbaston, Birmingham, B15 2DG; tel: 0121 253 4000; fax: 0121 253 4005
NBS Brentwood
  Crescent Drive, Brentwood, Essex, CM15 8DP; tel: 01277 306000; fax: 01227 306132
NBS Bristol
  Southmead Road, Bristol, BS10 5ND; tel: 0117 991 2000; fax: 0117 991 2002
NBS Cambridge
  Long Road, Cambridge, CB2 2PT; tel: 01223 548000; fax: 01223 548114
NBS Lancaster
  Royal Lancaster Infirmary, Ashton Road, Lancaster, LA1 4GT; tel: 01524 306250; fax: 01524 306273
NBS Leeds
  Bridle Path, Leeds, LS15 7TW; tel: 0113 214 8600; fax: 0113 214 8737
NBS Liverpool
  West Derby Street, Liverpool, L7 8TW; tel: 0151 551 8800; fax: 0151 551 8896
NBS Manchester
  Plymouth Grove, Manchester, M13 9LL; tel: 0161 251 4200; fax: 0161 251 4331
NBS Newcastle
  Holland Drive, Newcastle upon Tyne, NE2 4NQ; tel: 0191 219 4400; fax: 0191 219 4505
NBS North London
  Colindale Avenue, London, NW9 5BG; tel: 020 8258 2700; fax: 020 8258 2970
NBS Oxford
  John Radcliffe Hospital, Headington, Oxford, OX3 9DU; tel: 01865 447900; fax: 01865 447915
NBS Plymouth
  Derriford Hospital, Derriford Road, Plymouth, PL6 8DH; tel: 01752 617815; fax: 01752 617806
NBS Sheffield
  Longley Lane, Sheffield, S5 7JN; tel: 0114 203 4800; fax: 0114 203 4911
NBS South Thames
  75 Cranmer Terrace, London, SW17 0RB; tel: 020 8258 8300; fax: 020 8258 8453
NBS Southampton
  Coxford Road, Southampton, SO16 5AF; tel: 023 8029 6700; fax: 023 8029 6760

Other addresses:
Bio Products Laboratory
  Dagger Lane, Elstree, Hertfordshire, WD6 3BX; tel: 020 8258 2200; fax: 020 8258 2601

NATIONAL BOTANIC GARDEN OF WALES, THE

Acronym or abbreviation: NBGW

Llanarthne, Carmarthenshire, SA32 8HG

Tel: 01558 668768

Fax: 01558 668933
E-mail: reception@gardenofwales.org.uk

Website:
http://www.gardenofwales.org.uk
Garden guide, news and events information, pricing and opening hours, directions.

Enquiries:
Enquiries to: Executive Director for Development

Founded:
2000

Organisation type and purpose:
International organisation, registered charity (charity number 1036354), research organisation.

Subject coverage:
Botanic garden.

Access to staff:
Contact by letter, by telephone, by fax and by e-mail
Hours: Summer, Mon to Sun, 1000 to 1800
Winter, Mon to Sun, 1000 to 1630

Access for disabled people:
Parking provided, level entry, access to all public areas, toilet facilities

NATIONAL CAMPAIGN FOR FIREWORK SAFETY

Acronym or abbreviation: NCFS

118 Long Acre, London, WC2E 9PA

Tel: 020 7836 6703
Fax: 020 7836 6703

Website:
http://www.cgsystems.co.uk/ncfs
http://www.firework.co.uk/ncfp
CG Systems.

Enquiries:
Enquiries to: Director

Founded:
1969

Organisation type and purpose:
International organisation, national organisation, membership association (membership is by subscription), present number of members: 370,000, voluntary organisation, registered charity, research organisation.
To amend the 1875 and 1976 firework laws; to introduce legislation restricting fireworks to holders of licences over 18 for properly organised firework displays and a national training scheme.
To promote history and education on the subject.

Subject coverage:
International firework legislation, history of fireworks, education and technical training, films and documentaries.

Trade and statistical information:
Firework accident statistics.

Non-library collection catalogue:
All or part available in-house

Library catalogue:
All or part available online and in print

Printed publications:
Information sheets (£1)
Reports (£5)

Microform publications:
Safety films

Access to staff:
Contact by letter, by telephone, by fax and by e-mail. Appointment necessary. Non-members charged.
Hours: Mon to Fri, 0900 to 1800
Special comments: Not weekends except 15 October to 10 November.

Access to building, collection or gallery:
No access other than to staff, prior appointment required

Links with:
Age Concern

Cats Protection League
CBI
Fire Brigades Union
Institute of Trading Standards Offices
London Fire & Civil Defence Authority
National Canine Defence League
National Federation of Retirement Pensioners
Royal College of Nursing
RSPCA
TUC
UK Noise Association (UKNA)

Other addresses:
NCFS Manchester
 19 Plummer Avenue, Cholton, Manchester, M21
 2FU
NCFS Northumberland
 53 Longstone Close, Bradwell, Northumberland,
 NE67 5BS

NATIONAL CAMPAIGN FOR NURSERY EDUCATION

Formal name: The National Campaign for Real
Nursery Education
Acronym or abbreviation: NCNE

Membership Secretary, Tachbrook Nursery School,
Aylesford Street, London, SW1V 3RT

E-mail: ncrne@yahoo.co.uk

Website:
http://www.ncne.co.uk

Enquiries:
Enquiries to: Membership Secretary
Direct e-mail: head@tachbrooknursery.co.uk

Founded:
1965

Organisation type and purpose:
Membership association (membership is by
subscription), service industry, suitable for ages: 3
to 5.
Campaign Group.
To campaign for the expansion of state-funded
nursery education, and to defend existing
provision.

Subject coverage:
Necessity of education for two years before
statutory school age, extension and protection of
the provision of education.

Printed publications:
Defending and Promoting State Nursery
 Education
Four Year Olds in Reception Classes
Newsletters and papers on current issues
 concerned with nursery education
The Importance of the Local Education Authority
 Nursery School
When Should Your Child Start School?
What is Nursery Education?

Access to staff:
Contact by letter
Hours: Mon to Fri, 0900 to 1700

NATIONAL CARAVAN COUNCIL LIMITED

Acronym or abbreviation: NCC

Catherine House, Victoria Road, Aldershot,
Hampshire, GU11 1SS

Tel: 01252 318251
Fax: 01252 322596
E-mail: info@nationalcaravan.co.uk

Website:
http://www.nationalcaravan.co.uk
List of NCC members, products and services
provided.

Enquiries:
Enquiries to: Director General

Founded:
1939

Organisation type and purpose:
Trade association (membership is by subscription),
present number of members: 500.
Representative body.

Subject coverage:
Centre of information on all aspects of the caravan
industry providing an advisory service on
technical legislation, regulation and commercial
matters.

Non-library collection catalogue:
All or part available online

Printed publications:
Annual Report
The Business (quarterly magazine)
Various other NCC industry and consumer
 publications

Access to staff:
Contact by letter, by telephone, by fax, by e-mail
and via website. Access for members only. Letter
of introduction required.
Hours: Mon to Fri, 0900 to 1700

NATIONAL CARE ASSOCIATION

Acronym or abbreviation: NCHA

45–49 Leather Lane, London, EC1N 7TJ

Tel: 020 7831 7090
Fax: 020 7831 7040
E-mail: info@nca.gb.com

Website:
http://www.nca.gb.com

Enquiries:
Enquiries to: Chief Executive

Founded:
1981

Organisation type and purpose:
Trade association.

Subject coverage:
Community care, social security, residential care,
nursing home care.

Publications list:
Available in print

Access to staff:
Contact by letter, by telephone, by fax and by e-
mail. Appointment necessary.
Hours: Mon to Fri, 0900 to 1700

Access to building, collection or gallery:
Prior appointment required

Access for disabled people:
Access to all public areas

Subsidiary body:
National Care Homes Association Commercial
Limited

NATIONAL CARPET CLEANERS ASSOCIATION

Formal name: Carpet Cleaners Association Ltd
Acronym or abbreviation: NCCA

62C London Road, Oadby, Leicestershire, LE2 5DH

Tel: 0116 271 9550
Fax: 0116 271 9588
E-mail: admin@ncca.co.uk

Website:
http://www.ncca.co.uk
About NCCA, emergency cleaning tips, directory
of accredited cleaners, training, news and events.

Founded:
1968

Organisation type and purpose:
A non-profit-making body, the only nationally
recognised trade association dedicated to the
cleaning of carpets, hard flooring, upholstery,
curtains and other soft furnishings.

The principal objective is the establishment and
maintenance of minimum standards within the
carpet and upholstery cleaning industry, with the
dual aim of safeguarding the reputation of the
industry and protecting its customers, whether in
the domestic or commercial sphere.

Subject coverage:
Cleaning of all types of flooring and soft
furnishings; hard floor restoration; rug cleaning
and repair; leather furniture cleaning and
restoration; carpet and fabric repair; fabric and
fibre protection; curtain cleaning; carpet fitting; fire
and flood restoration.

Education services:
Comprehensive compulsory training programme
for members, plus advanced courses, workshops,
branch meetings, technical roadshows and other
events.

Access to staff:
Contact by letter, by telephone, by fax and by e-
mail

NATIONAL CATALOGUING UNIT FOR THE ARCHIVES OF CONTEMPORARY SCIENTISTS

Acronym or abbreviation: NCUACS

University of Bath, Claverton Down, Bath, BA2
7AY

Tel: 01225 383522
Fax: 01225 386229
E-mail: lispbh@bath.ac.uk

Website:
http://www.bath.ac.uk/ncuacs
Information about the role of the NCUACS and
work completed.

Enquiries:
Enquiries to: Director

Founded:
1973

Carries out the functions of the former:
Contemporary Scientific Archives Centre (year of
change 1987)

Organisation type and purpose:
Research organisation.
Locating, cataloguing and finding places of
permanent deposit for the manuscript papers of
eminent contemporary British scientists and
engineers.

Subject coverage:
Professional and personal papers and
correspondence of distinguished UK scientists and
engineers deceased since c. 1950; scientific source
material; cataloguing such material.

Printed publications:
Catalogues of complete collections (lists of
 catalogues available)
Progress Reports (2 times a year)

Publications list:
Available online

Access to staff:
Contact by letter and by e-mail
Hours: Mon to Fri, 0900 to 1700

Access to building, collection or gallery:
No access other than to staff

NATIONAL CENTRE FOR EARLY MUSIC

Acronym or abbreviation: NCEM

St Margaret's Church, Walmgate, York, YO1 9TL

Tel: 01904 658338
Fax: 01904 612631
E-mail: info@ncem.co.uk

Website:
http://www.ncem.co.uk

continued overleaf

Organisation type and purpose:
Administered by the York Early Music Foundation, registered charity no. 1068331, certificate of incorporation 3499629. Offers conference and recording facilities and performances of early music. Hosts the York Early Music Festival and the Beverley and East Riding Early Music Festival.

Education services:
Year-round community and education programme.

Access for disabled people:
The Centre is flat-floored throughout, making it accessible for wheelchair users. There are two designated disabled parking places in the adjacent car park, an entrance ramp and disabled toilet facilities

NATIONAL CENTRE FOR EATING DISORDERS

Acronym or abbreviation: NcfeD

54 New Road, Esher, Surrey, KT10 9NU

Tel: 0845 838 2040
Fax: 01372 469550
E-mail: admin@ncfed.com

Website:
http://www.eating-disorders.org.uk
About the organisation, treatments and training.

Enquiries:
Enquiries to: Information Officer

Founded:
1984

Organisation type and purpose:
Professional body, training organisation, consultancy.
Treatment service for eating disorders and weight problems. Training for counselling skills in eating disorders.

Subject coverage:
Compulsive or binge eating, bulimia nervosa, anorexia, obesity, slimming pill abuse, body image problems and therapies for eating problems.

Printed publications:
Factsheets available on all aspects of eating disorders
A contemporary assessment of Bulimia Nervosa
A contemporary assessment of Anorexia Nervosa
Does Eating Rule Your Life?

Publications list:
Available online and in print

Access to staff:
Contact by letter, by telephone, by e-mail and via website. Appointment necessary.
Hours: Mon to Fri, 0900 to 1700

Access to building, collection or gallery:
Prior appointment required

Affiliated to:
up to 60 individual therapists nationwide receiving referrals from head office

NATIONAL CENTRE FOR SOCIAL RESEARCH

35 Northampton Square, London, EC1V 0AX

Tel: 020 7250 1866
Fax: 020 7250 1524
E-mail: info@natcen.ac.uk

Website:
http://www.natcen.ac.uk
Information about the Centre's research and publications.

Enquiries:
Enquiries to: Information Officer
Direct e-mail: linda.maynard@natcen.ac.uk

Founded:
1969

Organisation type and purpose:
Registered charity, research organisation.

Subject coverage:
Social research, especially social policy surveys and survey methodology.

Printed publications:
National Centre publications covering the following subjects:
Crime and Socio-Legal Studies
Education and Lifetime Learning
Ethnic Minority Research
Health
Labour Market Studies
Methodology
Political and Electoral Behaviour
Social Attitudes
Social Security

Publications list:
Available online

Access to staff:
Contact by letter, by telephone, by fax and by e-mail
Hours: Mon to Fri, 0900 to 1700

Access to building, collection or gallery:
No access other than to staff
Special comments: Only to consult the National Centre Publications.

NATIONAL CENTRE FOR TRAINING AND EDUCATION IN PROSTHETICS AND ORTHOTICS

Acronym or abbreviation: NCTEPO

Curran Building, 131 St James' Road, Glasgow, G4 0LS

Tel: 0141 548 3814
Fax: 0141 552 1283
E-mail: h.smart@strath.ac.uk

Website:
http://www.recal.org.uk
Description of all RECAL products and services. Subscription access to RECAL Bibliographical Database.

Enquiries:
Enquiries to: Information Officer
Direct tel: 0141 548 3814
Direct fax: 0141 552 1283
Direct e-mail: h.smart@strath.ac.uk

Founded:
1978

Organisation type and purpose:
University department or institute.
University of Strathclyde Centre, having an internationally used library and information service.

Subject coverage:
Prosthetics and orthotics, related physical medicine and rehabilitation engineering.

Non-library collection catalogue:
All or part available online

Printed publications:
RECAL Current Awareness
RECAL Bibliographic Database
RECAL Thesaurus

Electronic and video publications:
RECAL Bibliographic Database (CD-ROM and on-line)

Access to staff:
Contact by letter, by telephone, by fax and by e-mail. Appointment necessary.
Hours: Mon to Fri, 0900 to 1700

Access to building, collection or gallery:
No prior appointment required

Parent body:
University of Strathclyde
tel: 0141 552 4400

NATIONAL CENTRE FOR YOUNG PEOPLE WITH EPILEPSY

Acronym or abbreviation: NCYPE

St Piers Lane, Lingfield, Surrey, RH7 6PW

Tel: 01342 832243
Fax: 01342 834639
E-mail: info@ncype.org.uk

Website:
http://www.ncype.org.uk
The starting point to find out about the NCYPE and get information on services for young people with epilepsy, including education, treatment, assessment, rehabilitation and care.

Enquiries:
Enquiries to: Media and Communications Officer
Direct tel: Extn 310
Direct e-mail: kohaire@ncype.org.uk
Other contacts: Admissions Co-ordinator (for further information about admission to the NCYPE)

Founded:
1897

Organisation type and purpose:
National organisation, voluntary organisation, registered charity (charity number 311877), suitable for ages: 5 to 25.
The NCYPE is the major provider of specialised services for young people with epilepsy in the UK. It provides education, treatment, assessment, rehabilitation and care to young people with epilepsy and other complex neurological disorders in partnership with Great Ormond Street Hospital for Children NHS Trust. It provides residential medical care and education for children and young people with epilepsy and other complex special needs.

Subject coverage:
Multidisciplinary team-working between many different experts, medical consultants, teachers, nurses, therapists, psychologists, carers and skilled support staff supports the many different needs of students and helps each individual achieve their true potential.

Printed publications:
Leaflets and brochures
Research project information may be made available
Order printed publications from: Marketing Development Officer, NCYPE, tel: 01342 832243

Access to staff:
Contact by letter, by telephone, by fax, by e-mail and via website. Appointment necessary. Letter of introduction required.
Hours: Mon to Fri, 0830 to 1700

Access to building, collection or gallery:
Prior appointment required

Access for disabled people:
Parking provided, toilet facilities

Member organisation of:
Association of National Specialist Colleges
Joint Epilepsy Council for Great Britain and Ireland
National Association of Independent and Non-maintained Special Schools
National Association of Special Schools

Partnership with:
Great Ormond Street Hospital for Children NHS Trust

NATIONAL CHEMICAL EMERGENCY CENTRE

Acronym or abbreviation: NCEC

AEA, The Gemini Building, Fermi Avenue, Harwell, Didcot, Oxon OX11 0QR

Tel: 0870 190 6621
Fax: 0870 190 6614
E-mail: ncec@aeat.com

Website:
http://www.the-ncec.com
Information on products and services as well as free resources.
http://www.aeat.com
Parent company website – AEA, an award-winning environmental consultancy.

Enquiries:
Enquiries to: Manager

Founded:
1973

Organisation type and purpose:
The UK's National Chemical Emergency Centre – operating within AEA Technology as a commercial company providing products, services and advice to public and private sector organisations worldwide.

Subject coverage:
Safety data sheet management, COSHH, REACH, GHS/CLP, chemical legislation consultancy, chemical emergency response, chemical hazards database, chemical health and safety, chemical risk management, training.

Printed publications:
Hazchem scale cards (available for purchase, direct), Emergency Action Code List 2009 (the 2011 list will be published)

Electronic and video publications:
Chemical Hazard Database – Chemdata – for PC or Windows Mobile Device. Contains information on in excess of 38,000 chemicals

Access to staff:
Contact by letter, by telephone, by fax, by e-mail and via website
Hours: Mon to Fri, 0800 to 1630 (for non-emergency calls)
Special comments: 24-hour emergency information service provided to public emergency services and industry.

NATIONAL CHILDREN'S CENTRE

Brian Jackson House, New North Parade, Huddersfield, West Yorkshire, HD1 5JP

Tel: 01484 519988
Fax: 01484 435150
E-mail: nfo@nccuk.org.uk

Enquiries:
Enquiries to: Chief Executive

Founded:
1975

Organisation type and purpose:
Registered charity.

Subject coverage:
Child care, education, families from overseas, training young people, addressing offending, school truancy, homeless families, family support, parent training.

Museum or gallery collection, archive, or library special collection:
Brian Jackson archive, contains manuscripts, printed works on social and political history, child care issues and educational issues

Printed publications:
1st Age Brochure
Annual Reports
Future Parenthood Paper
Reports on 4 National Conferences on the Chinese Community in Great Britain

Access to staff:
Contact by letter, by telephone and by fax
Hours: Mon to Fri, 0900 to 1700

Access for disabled people:
Ramped entry, level entry, access to all public areas, toilet facilities

NATIONAL CHRYSANTHEMUM SOCIETY

Acronym or abbreviation: NCS

c/o Mr. Peter Fraser, 317 Plessey Road, Blyth, Northumberland, NE24 3L J

Tel: 01670 353580
E-mail: peter@fpeter.fsnet.co.uk

Website:
http://www.ncsuk.info/index.htm

Enquiries:
Enquiries to: Membership Secretary

Founded:
1846

Organisation type and purpose:
International organisation, advisory body, membership association (membership is by subscription), present number of members: 4000, voluntary organisation, registered charity (charity number 248484), suitable for ages: 10+, consultancy.
British registry office for chrysanthemums.
To promote the growing of chrysanthemums.

Subject coverage:
Chrysanthemum cultivation, pest and disease control, literature.

Printed publications:
List (some 12 titles) available from the Society including:
Bulletin (spring and autumn, free to members, £3 each)
Manual (regular update, £14.95)
Year Book (free to members, £5 others)
Other specialised publications

Electronic and video publications:
Videos

Publications list:
Available in print

Access to staff:
Contact by letter, by telephone, by fax and in person
Hours: Mon to Fri, 0900 to 1700

Access to building, collection or gallery:
Prior appointment required

Access for disabled people:
Access to all public areas, toilet facilities

Affiliated to:
Royal Horticultural Society

Has:
6 regional groups, South, West, Midland, North, Welsh, Scottish, access via main office

NATIONAL CHURCHES TRUST

31 Newbury Street, London, EC1A 7HU

Tel: 020 7600 6090
Fax: 020 7796 2442
E-mail: info@nationalchurchestrust.org

Website:
http://www.nationalchurchestrust.org
Information for donors and grant applicants.

Enquiries:
Enquiries to: Office Manager
Other contacts: Grants Manager (for applications for funding)

Founded:
1953

Formerly called:
Historic Churches Preservation Trust (year of change 2007)

Organisation type and purpose:
National organisation, registered charity (charity number 1119845).

A charity that offers financial assistance to Christian churches of any recognised denomination for essential fabric repairs and alteration such as entrances/kitchens/toilets to allow community use of the building.

Subject coverage:
Churches, chapels and meeting houses in the UK.

Information services:
Information for those seeking funding for repair/ alteration to church buildings

Printed publications:
Annual Review, Magazine
Historic Churches (review)
Order printed publications from: Friends (£20 joining fee) receive the above free of charge

Access to staff:
Contact by letter, by telephone, by fax, by e-mail and via website
Hours: Mon to Fri, 0930 to 1730

Access to building, collection or gallery:
No access other than to staff

NATIONAL CO-OPERATIVE ARCHIVE

Co-operative College, Holyoake House, Hanover Street, Manchester, M60 0AS

Tel: 0161 246 2925
Fax: 0161 246 2946
E-mail: archive@co-op.ac.uk

Website:
http://www.archive.coop
National Co-operative Archive at the Co-operative College, information, bibliographies, etc.

Enquiries:
Enquiries to: Archivist
Direct e-mail: gillian@co-op.ac.uk

Founded:
1869

Formerly called:
Co-operative Union Archive (year of change 2000); Co-operative College Archive (year of change 2000)

Organisation type and purpose:
National Co-operative Archive is home to a wide array of records relating to the history of the world-wide co-operative movement.

Subject coverage:
History of the British co-operative movement; contemporary co-operative developments and issues; overseas co-operative movements; history of the labour movement in Britain; co-operative leaders and social reformers; co-operation; co-operative history nationally and internationally; co-operative society history and histories; co-operative film archive; co-operative archive; international economic development; centre for alternative industrial and technological systems archive; co-operative oral history archive.

Museum or gallery collection, archive, or library special collection:
Christian Socialists: books, pamphlets and periodicals
Co-operative Society histories and rule books
Co-operative Society pamphlets, 1830 to date
MS Collection of E O Greening correspondence and documents (11,000 items)
MS Collection of G J Holyoake correspondence and documents, 1835–1903 (4000 items)
MS Collection of Robert Owen correspondence and documents, 1820 onwards (3000 items)
Rare 19th century books, newspapers and periodicals on co-operation and social reform
CAITS Archive
Midlands Co-operative Society Archive
Co-operative Group South East, South Midlands and Northern Region Co-operative Archive
Co-operative Youth Movements
National Co-operative Film Archive
Co-operative Oral History Archive
Periodicals

continued overleaf

Non-library collection catalogue:
All or part available online, in-house and in print

Printed publications:
Holdings lists for special collections
Co-operative Commemorative Plateware
Co-operative Congress Special Papers
Co-operative Education
Co-operative Party
Co-operative Periodicals
Co-operative Plays and Sketches
Co-operative Production
Co-operative Society Histories
Co-operative Society Rules
Co-operative Women's Guild
Co-operative Youth
Dividend & Check Systems
Edward Owen Greening
Edward Vansittart Neale
George Jacob Holyoake
Historical Periodicals
National Co-operative Film Archive
National Co-operative Oral History Archive
National Guild of Co-operators
Philatelic Collection
Robert Owen
Rochdale Pioneers
Order printed publications from: Available on request

Access to staff:
Contact by letter, by telephone, by fax, by e-mail
and via website. Appointment necessary.
Hours: Mon to Fri, 1000 to 1700

Access to building, collection or gallery:
Hours: Mon to Fri, 1000 to 1700
Special comments: By appointment.

Access for disabled people:
As above

Governing body:
Co-operative Heritage Trust
5th Floor, New Century House, Corporation
Street, Manchester M60 4ES; e-mail: cht@co-op
.ac.uk; website: http://www.co-operativeheritage
.coop

Member organisation of:
Co-operatives UK
Euro-co-op
International Co-operative Alliance

NATIONAL COASTWATCH INSTITUTION

HeadQuarters, Unit 26 Basepoint Business Centre,
Exeter, EX2 8LB

Tel: 0300 111 1202; 0845 460 1202
E-mail: info@nci.org.uk

Website:
http://www.nci.org.uk/contact
The Institution, its history, its work, news, online
shop.

Founded:
1994

Organisation type and purpose:
Registered charity (charity number 1045645),
voluntary organisation.
Established to restore a visual watch along UK
shores after many small coastguard stations were
closed. Each station assists in the protection and
preservation of life at sea and around the UK
coastline. Currently over 40 NCI stations are fully
operational and manned by over 1,700 volunteers
keeping watch around the British Isles from
Cornwall in the South West to Wearside in the
North East.

Subject coverage:
While high technology and sophisticated systems
are aids to improved safety, a computer cannot
spot a distress flare, an overturned boat or a
yachtsman or fisherman in trouble. Other
vulnerable activities like diving, wind surfing and
canoeing are made safer with visual surveillance.
NCI watchkeepers provide the eyes and ears along
the coast, monitoring radio channels and
providing a listening watch in poor visibility. They

are trained to deal with emergencies, offering a
variety of skills and experience, and full training by
the NCI ensures that high standards are met. Over
170,000 hours of organised coastal surveillance are
completed each year, all at no cost to the public.

Information services:
Printable map of NCI stations; useful information
for mariners and walkers; guide for potential new
stations.

Printed publications:
Watchkeeper (quarterly magazine)

Access to staff:
Contact by letter, by telephone, by e-mail and via
website

NATIONAL COLLECTION OF TYPE CULTURES

Acronym or abbreviation: NCTC

Health Protection Agency Centre for Infections, 61
Colindale Avenue, London, NW9 5EQ

Tel: 020 8327 6704
Fax: 020 8205 7483
E-mail: hpacultures@hpa.org.uk

Website:
http://www.hpacultures.org.uk
Information on NCTC and its parent organisation.

Enquiries:
Direct tel: 01980 612512
Direct fax: 01980 611315

Founded:
1920

Organisation type and purpose:
Research organisation.
Maintaining and supplying cultures of
authenticated bacteria of medical/veterinary
interest.

Subject coverage:
Microbiology, especially medical/veterinary;
reference strains of bacteria for particular usage
(taxonomic), antibiotic assay, teaching, controls for
bacteriological tests; freeze-drying; mycoplasmas;
plasmid-bearing strains; availability of cultures in
other culture collections (UK and abroad).

**Museum or gallery collection, archive, or library
special collection:**
Early works on bacteriology, etc.

Non-library collection catalogue:
All or part available online

Printed publications:
Catalogue of the NCTC (PHLS) (8th edn, 1994)

Access to staff:
Contact by letter, by telephone, by fax, by e-mail
and via website
Hours: Mon to Fri, 0900 to 1700

Access to building, collection or gallery:
Prior appointment required

Access for disabled people:
Parking provided, ramped entry, level entry, access
to all public areas, toilet facilities

European Resource Centre for:
Plasmids

Links with:
European Culture Collection Organisation
World Federation for Culture Collections

Member organisation of:
United Kingdom National Culture Collection
(UKNCC)

Parent body:
Health Protection Agency

NATIONAL COLLEGE OF HYPNOSIS AND PSYCHOTHERAPY

Acronym or abbreviation: NCHP

PO Box 5779, Loughborough, LE12 5ZF

Tel: 01509 881477
E-mail: enquiries@nchp.org.uk

Website:
http://www.hypnotherapyuk.net

Enquiries:
Enquiries to: Administrator

Founded:
1977

Organisation type and purpose:
Hypno-psychotherapy training.

Subject coverage:
Hypno-psychotherapy.

Access to staff:
Contact by letter, by telephone, by fax, by e-mail,
in person and via website. Appointment necessary.
Hours: Mon to Fri, 0900 to 1700

Access to building, collection or gallery:
Prior appointment required

Access for disabled people:
Level entry

Links with:
UK Council for Psychotherapy (UKCP)
2nd Floor, Edward House, 2 Wakley Street,
London, EC1V 7LT; tel: 0870 167 2131; website:
http://www.psychotherapy.org.uk

NATIONAL COMPUTING CENTRE LIMITED

Formal name: National Computing Centre
Acronym or abbreviation: NCC

Oxford House, Oxford Road, Manchester, M1 7ED

Tel: 0161 228 6333
Fax: 0161 242 2499
E-mail: info@ncc.co.uk

Website:
http://www.ncc.co.uk
Generally on products and services, but also
specific information for members.

Enquiries:
Enquiries to: Marketing Manager
Direct tel: 0161 242 2146
Direct e-mail: Michael.Dean@ncc.co.uk
Other contacts: IT Manager/Director

Founded:
1966

Organisation type and purpose:
National organisation, membership association
(membership is by subscription), present number
of members: 1300, research organisation.
Promotes the most effective use of IT.

Subject coverage:
IT: all aspects of computing in UK and
internationally.

Non-library collection catalogue:
All or part available online

Printed publications:
IT User Survey
Salary and Staff Issues in IT Survey (annually)
Security Breaches Survey

Electronic and video publications:
Centrelink
Filetab

Publications list:
Available online and in print

Access to staff:
Contact by letter, by telephone, by fax, by e-mail
and via website. Appointment necessary. Non-
members charged.
Hours: Mon to Fri, 0900 to 1700

Access to building, collection or gallery:
Prior appointment required

Access for disabled people:
Access to all public areas

NATIONAL CONSUMER CREDIT FEDERATION

Acronym or abbreviation: NCCF

98–100 Holme Lane, Sheffield, South Yorkshire, S6 4JW

Tel: 0114 234 8101
Fax: 0114 234 5459
E-mail: nccf@talk21.com

Enquiries:
Enquiries to: General Secretary

Founded:
1927

Organisation type and purpose:
Trade association (membership is by subscription).

Subject coverage:
Consumer credit.

Printed publications:
Code of Practice
Newsletter

Access to staff:
Contact by letter, by telephone and by fax
Hours: Mon to Fri, 0930 to 1630

NATIONAL CONSUMER FEDERATION

Acronym or abbreviation: NCF

24 Hurst House, Penton Rise, London, WC1X 9ED

Tel: 020 7837 8545
Fax: 020 7837 8545
E-mail: secretary@ncf.info

Website:
http://www.ncf.info

Enquiries:
Enquiries to: Honorary Secretary

Founded:
2001

Organisation type and purpose:
Voluntary organisation.
Co-ordinates the activities of local consumer groups and represents the views of consumers to government and business.

Subject coverage:
Consumer affairs, consumer law, food.

Printed publications:
Consumer News (quarterly, on subscription)

Electronic and video publications:
News sheet (monthly, online)

Access to staff:
Contact by letter, by telephone, by fax, by e-mail and via website. Non-members charged.
Hours: Mon to Fri, 0900 to 1200; outside office hours, by e-mail

NATIONAL CORRESPONDENCE CHESS CLUB

81 Surrey Street, Norwich, NR1 3PG

Tel: 01603 491199
E-mail: simoncarer@aol.com

Enquiries:
Enquiries to: Chairman

Founded:
1932

Organisation type and purpose:
National organisation (membership is by subscription).
Postal Chess Club.

Subject coverage:
Correspondence chess.

Access to staff:
Contact by letter and by e-mail
Hours: Any reasonable time.

Affiliated to:
British Postal Chess Federation
e-mail: norman.king2@virgin.net

NATIONAL COUNCIL FOR DRAMA TRAINING

Acronym or abbreviation: NCDT

5 Tavistock Place, London, WC1H 9SS

Tel: 020 7387 3650
Fax: 020 7681 4733
E-mail: ncdt@lineone.net

Website:
http://www.ncdt.co.uk

Enquiries:
Enquiries to: Executive Secretary

Founded:
1976

Organisation type and purpose:
National government body, professional body, registered charity.
Accreditation body maintaining standards at professional drama schools.

Subject coverage:
List of courses in professional, vocational actor and stage management training accredited by the NCDT.

Non-library collection catalogue:
All or part available online

Printed publications:
List of accredited courses in the UK

Publications list:
Available online and in print

Access to staff:
Contact by letter, by telephone, by fax, by e-mail and via website
Hours: Mon to Fri, 0930 to 1730

Access to building, collection or gallery:
No access other than to staff

Members of the organisation are:
BBC
British Actors Equity
Channel 4
Conference of Drama Schools
Society of London Theatre
Theatre Management Association

NATIONAL COUNCIL FOR SCHOOL SPORT

Acronym or abbreviation: NCSS

c/o RFU National Centre for Schools and Youth, Castlecroft Stadium, Castlecroft Road, Wolverhampton, West Midlands, WV3 8NA

Tel: 01902 380302
Fax: 01902 380311
E-mail: info@ncss.org.uk

Website:
http://www.ncss.org.uk

Enquiries:
Enquiries to: Honorary Secretary

Founded:
1948

Organisation type and purpose:
Membership association (membership is by subscription, election or invitation), present number of members: 31, voluntary organisation.
To co-ordinate the work of the National School Sports Associations. To represent the views of members to government departments, National Sports Associations, local education authorities and wherever else necessary.

Subject coverage:
School sports organisations – governing and regional bodies details of activities staged with participation and spectator figures, general details

and participation in sports in schools, coaching development plans for sports. International schools activities.
Sports activities of children (5 to 18 years), administration of school sport at national and local level, formation of new associations in sports where none exists.

Printed publications:
National Council for School Sport Handbook (annually)
Information leaflets and other documents
Official Journal (6 times a year)

Access to staff:
Contact by letter and by e-mail
Hours: Mon to Fri, 0900 to 1700

Executive Officer:
National Council for School Sport
95 Boxley Drive, West Bridgford, Nottinghamshire, NG2 7GN; tel: 0115 923 1229; e-mail: schoolsport@ntlworld.com

NATIONAL COUNCIL FOR THE DIVORCED AND SEPARATED

Acronym or abbreviation: NCDS

National Secretary, c/o 101 Anson Road, Southtown, Great Yarmouth, Norfolk, NR31 0EG

Tel: 07041 478120
E-mail: info@ncds.org.uk

Enquiries:
Enquiries to: Honorary Secretary

Organisation type and purpose:
Membership association (membership is by qualification), present number of members: 10,000, voluntary organisation.
A means of meeting people in, or who have been in, a situation similar to their own, giving opportunity for a social life again.

Subject coverage:
All aspects relating to separation and divorce.

Printed publications:
NCDS News (quarterly)

Access to staff:
Contact by letter, by telephone, by e-mail and via website
Hours: Mon to Sat, 0900 to 2000

Has:
6 Regional Clubs and several non-regional branches

NATIONAL COUNCIL FOR THE TRAINING OF JOURNALISTS

Acronym or abbreviation: NCTJ

The New Granary, Station Road, Newport, Saffron Walden, Essex, CB11 3PL

Tel: 01799 544014
Fax: 01799 544015
E-mail: info@nctj.com

Website:
http://www.nctj.com
Careers advice, etc. Details of courses, colleges/ universities, etc.

Founded:
1951

Organisation type and purpose:
National organisation, awarding body, learned society, registered charity (charity number 1026685), training organisation.
Training and examining organisation.
To advance the education and training of trainee journalists and press photographers.

Subject coverage:
Careers and training in journalism, at college/ university, by distance learning.

Trade and statistical information:
UK newspaper industry's own training scheme for journalists.

continued overleaf

Printed publications:
Textbooks, shorthand CDs, past examination
papers, distance learning courses.
Order printed publications from: Online shop

Electronic and video publications:
e-journalism news

Publications list:
Available online

Access to staff:
Contact by letter, by telephone, by fax, by e-mail
and via website. Appointment necessary.
Hours: Mon to Fri, 0900 to 1700

Access for disabled people:
Parking provided, access to all public areas

Wholly-owned trading company:
NCTJ Training Ltd
   tel: 01799 544014; fax: 01799 544015; e-mail:
   info@nctj.com

NATIONAL COUNCIL FOR VOLUNTARY ORGANISATIONS

Acronym or abbreviation: NCVO

Regent's Wharf, 8 All Saints Street, London, N1
9RL

Tel: 020 7713 6161
Fax: 020 7713 6300
E-mail: ncvo@ncvo-vol.org.uk

Website:
http://www.ncvo-vol.org.uk/publications
Publications information.
http://www.ncvo-vol.org.uk
General information.

Founded:
1919

Organisation type and purpose:
Membership association (membership is by
subscription, qualification), present number of
members: 8,300 voluntary organisations, voluntary
organisation, registered charity (charity number
225922).
NCVO champions the cause of voluntary
organisations and works to increase their
effectiveness.

Subject coverage:
Voluntary organisations and their response to
current social issues; resources for voluntary
organisations; interests and independence of such
organisations; current legislation; government
funding and its efficient use; trustee and
governance issues; relationship of sector with
business and public sectors, rural aspects.

Trade and statistical information:
Data on voluntary sector issues, eg: size of sector,
   profiling of areas of work.

Printed publications:
Wide range of publications. Full list at http://
   www.ncvo-vol.org.uk/publications
Engage magazine
Order printed publications from: Website: http://
www.ncvo-vol.org.uk/publications
Tel: 0800 279 8798
In person: at NCVO reception (see address above)

Publications list:
Available online

Access to staff:
Contact by letter, by telephone, by fax, by e-mail
and via website
Hours: Mon to Fri, 0900 to 1700

Access for disabled people:
Level entry, toilet facilities

NATIONAL COUNCIL FOR VOLUNTARY YOUTH SERVICES

Acronym or abbreviation: NCVYS

3rd Floor, Lancaster House, 33 Islington High
Street, London, N1 9LH

Tel: 020 7278 1041
Fax: 020 7833 2491
E-mail: mail@ncvys.org.uk

Website:
http://www.ncvys.org.uk
Description of the organisation, news,
publications, work areas, etc.

Enquiries:
Enquiries to: Communication Officer
Direct tel: 020 7253 1010

Founded:
1936

Organisation type and purpose:
National organisation, membership association
(membership is by subscription), present number
of members: 144, voluntary organisation,
registered charity (charity number 281632).
Representing about 160 National Voluntary Youth
Organisations and Local and Regional Councils for
Voluntary Youth Services. Provides support
information and representation to a national
network of youth organisations.

Subject coverage:
Voluntary youth services and social issues
affecting young people; child protection; equal
opportunities, diversity, youth participation.

Printed publications:
In The Service of Youth: A History of NCVYS
   (book, £7.50, free to members)
Out of Harm's Way: A Survey of Child Protection
   Policy and Practice in National Voluntary Youth
   Organisations (Smith D R, 1999, £7.50 statutory/
   commercial, £4.50 voluntary, £3.50 members)
The NCVYS Voluntary Youth Sector Infrastructure
   Project (Wright L and Jeffs L, 1999, £7.50
   statutory/commercial, £4.50 voluntary, £3.50
   members)
Annual Directory
Network (magazine, quarterly, free to members or
   £20 a year)
NCVYS Facts Sheet: a concise guide to NCVYS and
   its purpose

Publications list:
Available online and in print

Access to staff:
Contact by letter, by telephone, by fax, by e-mail
and via website. Appointment necessary. Non-
members charged.
Hours: Mon to Fri, 0900 to 1700

NATIONAL COUNCIL OF PAKISTANI ORGANISATIONS (UK)

Acronym or abbreviation: NCOPO

103 Wexham Close, Luton, Bedfordshire, LU3 3TX

Tel: 01582 598394
Fax: 01582 618335
E-mail: mshafikhan@hotmail.com

Enquiries:
Enquiries to: Chairman

Founded:
1982

Organisation type and purpose:
National organisation, advisory body, learned
society (membership is by qualification), voluntary
organisation, consultancy.
To guide and support organisations and
individuals as and when needed for their
development in the community in every respect of
their life. Also to help in social, welfare and
cultural development, legal matters, and
encourage integration of Pakistani community into
the host community.

Subject coverage:
All aspects of Pakistan as a country and Pakistani
culture in general.

Access to staff:
Contact by letter, by telephone and by fax

Hours: Any reasonable time

Access to building, collection or gallery:
Prior appointment required

NATIONAL COUNCIL OF VOLUNTARY CHILD CARE ORGANISATIONS

Acronym or abbreviation: NCVCCO

Unit 25 Angel Gate, City Road, London, EC1V 2PT

Tel: 020 7833 3319
Fax: 020 7833 8637
E-mail: office@ncvcco.org

Website:
http://www.ncvcco.org/

Enquiries:
Enquiries to: Information Officer
Direct e-mail: ian@ncvcco.org

Founded:
1942

Organisation type and purpose:
Membership association (membership is by
subscription), present number of members: 110,
voluntary organisation, registered charity (charity
number 1044239).
To assist the work of English child care charities.

Subject coverage:
Child care particularly in the voluntary sector;
residential care of children, day care of children,
family support within communities, fostering and
adoption, funding for voluntary child care groups,
European initiatives including child care and
funding.

**Museum or gallery collection, archive, or library
special collection:**
Small library on child care and the voluntary sector
   (for members' use only)

Printed publications:
Magnet (bulletin, monthly)
Outlook (journal, quarterly)

Publications list:
Available in print

Access to staff:
Contact by letter, by telephone, by fax and by e-
mail
Hours: Mon to Fri, 0900 to 1700

Access to building, collection or gallery:
Prior appointment required

Member of:
European Forum for Child Welfare
International Forum for Child Welfare

NATIONAL COUNCIL OF WOMEN OF GREAT BRITAIN

Acronym or abbreviation: NCW

36 Danbury Street, London, N1 8JU

Tel: 020 7354 2395
Fax: 01325 367378

Enquiries:
Enquiries to: President

Founded:
1895

Organisation type and purpose:
National organisation, membership association
(membership is by subscription), present number
of members: 1000 plus 70 affiliated societies,
voluntary organisation, registered charity.
To improve the quality of life for all, and to
encourage the effective participation of women in
the life of the nation.

Subject coverage:
Arts, consumer affairs, education, health, housing,
international affairs, mass media, scientific
development, social welfare, status and
employment of women and transport.

Museum or gallery collection, archive, or library special collection:
Minutes of Meetings 1890 to date, working papers etc
NCW archives
Publications and reports produced by NCW

Printed publications:
New News (newsletter, 4 times a year)
Many reports on matters of concern and women's issues
Responses to government consultation papers (published quarterly)
Securing Our Future, Women and Economics of Later Life

Publications list:
Available online and in print

Access to staff:
Contact by letter, by telephone and by e-mail
Hours: Mon to Fri, 0900 to 1700

Access to building, collection or gallery:
No prior appointment required
Special comments: Pre 1980 archive deposited with London Record Office.

Access for disabled people:
Level entry

Has:
70 affiliated organisations

Member of:
International Council of Women

NATIONAL DAY NURSERIES ASSOCIATION

Acronym or abbreviation: NDNA

Oak House, Woodvale Road, Brighouse, West Yorkshire, HD6 4AB

Tel: 0870 774 4244
Fax: 0870 774 4243
E-mail: info@ndna.org.uk

Website:
http://www.ndna.org.uk
Home page.
http://www.ndna.org.uk/publications
Publications listing.

Enquiries:
Enquiries to: Membership Officer
Direct e-mail: jacqui.smith@ndna.org.uk

Founded:
1991

Organisation type and purpose:
Membership association (membership is by subscription), present number of members: 2300, registered charity (charity number 1078275).
A national childcare charity that is dedicated to the provision, support and promotion of high quality care and education for all children in the early years.

Subject coverage:
Advice, support and training to help nurseries deliver quality early years education and care.

Printed publications:
Starting a Day Nursery (£25)
Policy and Procedures Pack (£100, £50 NDNA members)
Nutrition, Serving Food & Oral Health (£10)
Recruitment and Selection Pack (£100, £50 NDNA members)
NDNA Nursery Cookbook (£10)
Working in a Day Nursery video (£10)

Publications list:
Available online and in print

Access to staff:
Contact by letter, by telephone, by fax and by e-mail. Appointment necessary.
Hours: Mon to Fri, 0900 to 1700

NATIONAL DEAF CHILDREN'S SOCIETY (NDCS)

Acronym or abbreviation: NDCS

15 Dufferin Street, London, EC1Y 8UR

Tel: 0808 800 8880 (freephone helpline, voice and text)
Fax: 020 7251 5020
E-mail: helpline@ndcs.org.uk

Website:
http://www.ndcs.org.uk

Founded:
1944

Organisation type and purpose:
NDCS is an organisation of families, parents and carers providing emotional and practical support through a freephone helpline, a network of trained support workers, a wide range of other support services and publications, and a website.

Subject coverage:
Childhood deafness, audiology, technology for deaf children, benefits for deaf children, education and communication.

Printed publications:
Fact sheets and guides on issues around childhood deafness including:
Audiology and Health
Communication
State Benefits and Disability Living Allowance
Information in Community Languages
Education
Technology

Publications list:
Available in print

Access to staff:
Contact by letter, by telephone, by fax and by e-mail. Appointment necessary.
Hours: Mon to Fri, 0900 to 1700
Special comments: Helpline: Mon to Fri, 0930 to 1700; Sat 0930 to 1200.

Access to building, collection or gallery:
Prior appointment required

Access for disabled people:
Level entry, access to all public areas, toilet facilities, loop system in meeting room

Also at:
NDCS Northern Ireland
  Wilton House, 5 College Square North, Belfast, BT1 6AR; tel: 028 9031 3170 (voice and text); fax: 028 9031 3170
NDCS Scotland
  Second Floor, Empire House, 131 West Nile Street, Glasgow, G1 2RX; tel: 0141 354 7850 (voice and text); fax: 0141 331 2780; e-mail: ndcs.scotland@ndcs.org.uk
NDCS Wales
  4 Cathedral Road, Cardiff, CF11 9LJ; tel: 029 20373474; minicom: 029 20232739; fax: 029 20379800; e-mail: ndcswales@ndcs.org.uk

Branches:
120 local deaf children's societies

Member organisation of:
Deaf Accord

NATIONAL DEBTLINE

Acronym or abbreviation: NDL

Tricorn House, 51–53 Hagley Road, Edgbaston, Birmingham, B16 8TP

Tel: 0808 808 4000
Fax: 0121 410 6230
E-mail: via website: http://www.nationaldebtline.co.uk

Website:
http://www.nationaldebtline.co.uk

Enquiries:
Direct tel: 0121 410 6251/2

Founded:
1987

Organisation type and purpose:
Voluntary organisation, registered charity (charity number 1099506).
Telephone helpline for debt.

Subject coverage:
National telephone helpline for people with debt problems; covers all aspects of dealing with debt issues, e.g: repossession, magistrates court, county court and high court procedures, negotiations with creditors, bankruptcy, consumer credit, benefits and income maximisation. National Debtline can also assist callers who wish to set up a debt management plan (DMP), a debt relief order (DRO) or an individual voluntary arrangement (IVA) to deal with their debts.

Museum or gallery collection, archive, or library special collection:
Library of relevant publications to money advice work including some legislation and case reports, books and periodicals

Library catalogue:
All or part available in-house

Printed publications:
Self-help packs, including:
Dealing with your debts (£5),
Dealing with your Debts: Scotland (£5).
Fact sheets: England and Wales (38 items, £2 each, £40 per set).
Scotland Fact sheets (26 items, £2 each, or £25 per set).
Free to callers in debt. Charges made to agencies.
Order printed publications from: National Debtline

Publications list:
Available online and in print

Access to staff:
Contact by letter, by telephone, by fax, by e-mail and via website
Hours: Mon to Fri, 0900 to 2100; Sat, 0930 to 1300
Special comments: 24-hour voicemail service.

A project of:
Money Advice Trust
  21 Garlick Hill, London, EC4V 2AU; website: http://www.moneyadvicetrust.org

NATIONAL DEPOSIT FRIENDLY SOCIETY LIMITED

Acronym or abbreviation: NDFS

4–5 Worcester Road, Clifton, Bristol, BS8 3JL

Tel: 0117 973 9003
Fax: 0117 974 1367
E-mail: @nationaldeposit.co.uk

Website:
http://www.nationaldeposit.co.uk
Products and services.

Enquiries:
Enquiries to: Information Officer

Founded:
1868

Organisation type and purpose:
National organisation, service industry.
Friendly Society – provision of life assurance, investments, sickness, accident and medical insurance for members.

Access to staff:
Contact by letter and by e-mail
Hours: Mon to Fri, 0900 to 1700

Access to building, collection or gallery:
Prior appointment required

NATIONAL DISABILITY ARTS FORUM

Acronym or abbreviation: NDAF

Website:
http://www.ndaf.org
Information about disability arts.

continued overleaf

Enquiries:
Enquiries to: Director

Founded:
1990

Organisation type and purpose:
National organisation, membership association, registered charity.

Subject coverage:
Disability arts, arts and disability.

Museum or gallery collection, archive, or library special collection:
Disability Arts Database, UK and Europe; UK Arts Access Database

Printed publications:
e-Newsletter (weekly, free)

Publications list:
Available online

Access to staff:
Contact by letter, by telephone, by fax, by e-mail and in person. Appointment necessary.
Hours: Mon to Fri, 0900 to 1700

Access to building, collection or gallery:
No access other than to staff

Also at:
National Disability Arts Forum

NATIONAL DOG TATTOO REGISTER

PO Box 5720, Harwich, Essex, CO12 3SY

Tel: 01255 552455
Fax: 01255 552412

Subject coverage:
Identification of individual dogs by marking with tattoo. Register of marked dogs makes tracing of individual dogs possible.

Access to staff:
Contact by letter, by telephone and by fax
Hours: Access seven days a week

NATIONAL EARLY MUSIC ASSOCIATION

Acronym or abbreviation: NEMA

137 Preston Road, Wembley, HA9 8NW

Tel: 020 8904 1076
Fax: 020 8723 7787
E-mail: mark@nema-uk.org

Website:
http://www.nema-uk.org

Enquiries:
Enquiries to: Administrator

Founded:
1981

Organisation type and purpose:
International organisation, membership association (membership is by subscription), present number of members: 350, voluntary organisation, registered charity (charity number 297300).

Subject coverage:
Mediaeval, renaissance, baroque music; singing; dance; instrument makers; early music in education; amateur and professional music making; societies concerned with early music and dance; promotion of conferences and workshops.

Printed publications:
Early Music Yearbook, incorporates directory of instrument makers and players (annually)
Magazine (twice a year)
Early Music Performer

Publications list:
Available online

Access to staff:
Contact by letter, by telephone, by fax and by e-mail
Hours: Mon to Fri, 0900 to 1700

NATIONAL ECZEMA SOCIETY

Acronym or abbreviation: NES

Hill House, Highgate Hill, London, N19 5NA

Tel: 020 7281 3553 (Business only); 0800 0891122 (Helpline)
Fax: 020 7281 6395
E-mail: helpline@eczema.org

Website:
http://www.eczema.org
Information, fundraising and membership.

Enquiries:
Direct tel: 0207 281 3553
Other contacts: Helpline for advice, 0800 to 2000

Founded:
1975

Organisation type and purpose:
Registered charity (charity number 1009671). To help those affected by eczema to make informed choices through information, advice and support. Campaign to raise awareness and understanding of eczema. To run continuous research programme to gather the facts about eczema and its treatment. To provide education and training to spread awareness amongst the medical profession and general public. Organises fundraising to support the work of the charity.

Subject coverage:
Management and care of eczema; details of research into eczema treatments and advice on products suitable for people with eczema, information on complementary therapy treatments.

Printed publications:
Range of booklets and information sheets, some free
Exchange – members' journal (quarterly, free to members, £5 to non-members)

Publications list:
Available online and in print

Access to staff:
Contact by letter, by telephone, by fax, by e-mail and via website
Hours: Mon to Fri, 0800 to 2000 (helpline staff only)

Access to building, collection or gallery:
No access other than to staff

NATIONAL EDUCATIONAL VIDEO LIBRARY

Acronym or abbreviation: NEVL

Arfon House, Bontnewydd, Caernarfon, Gwynedd, LL54 7UN

Tel: 01286 676001
Fax: 01286 676001
E-mail: tryfannevl@aol.com

Website:
Being reconstructed and will contain the catalogue list of library.

Enquiries:
Enquiries to: Manager

Founded:
1997

Organisation type and purpose:
International organisation, professional body, suitable for ages: Keystage 1 to 4 and Further Education.
Sale of films, video and multimedia kits; film to video transfer.

Subject coverage:
Educational and training material available on history, geography, business studies, technology, sport science, biology, mathematics, home economics, arts and crafts, social studies and teacher education.

Library catalogue:
All or part available in-house

Publications list:
Available in print

Access to staff:
Contact by letter, by telephone and by fax
Hours: Mon to Fri, 0900 to 1700

Parent body:
Tryfan Audio Visual Services (TAVS)
tel: 01286 676001; e-mail: tryfanav@aol.com

NATIONAL ELECTRONIC AND VIDEO ARCHIVE OF THE CRAFTS

Acronym or abbreviation: NEVAC

University of the West of England – Bristol, School of Creative Arts, Bower Ashton Campus, Kennel Lodge Road, off Clanage Road, Bristol, BS3 2JT

Tel: 0117 328 4746
E-mail: matthew.partington@uwe.ac.uk

Website:
http://www.media.uwe.ac.uk/nevac

Organisation type and purpose:
Aims to gather and digitise interviews with people engaged in crafts.

Subject coverage:
Crafts and craftsmen.

NATIONAL ENDOMETRIOSIS SOCIETY

Suite 50, Westminster Palace Gardens, 1–7 Artillery Row, London, SW1P 1RR

Tel: 020 7222 2781
Fax: 020 7222 2786
E-mail: nes@endo.org.uk

Website:
http://www.endo.org.uk
General information about endometriosis and about the Society.

Enquiries:
Enquiries to: Chief Executive
Other contacts: Office Manager

Founded:
1981

Organisation type and purpose:
Membership association (membership is by subscription), present number of members: 2600, voluntary organisation, registered charity (charity number 1035810).

Subject coverage:
Endometriosis, support for sufferers.

Printed publications:
Please contact the Society for a full list of publications

Publications list:
Available in print

Access to staff:
Contact by letter, by telephone, by fax and in person
Hours: Mon to Fri, 0900 to 1700
Special comments: Helpline, some mornings, most evenings, some afternoons

NATIONAL ENERGY ACTION

Acronym or abbreviation: NEA

St Andrew's House, 90–92 Pilgrim Street, Newcastle upon Tyne, NE1 6SG

Tel: 0191 261 5677

Fax: 0191 261 6496
E-mail: info@nea.org.uk

Website:
http://www.nea.org.uk

Enquiries:
Enquiries to: Library Manager

Founded:
1981

Organisation type and purpose:
Registered charity (charity number 290511).
To develop policies and practices to tackle the
heating and insulation problems of low-income
households through improvements in energy
efficiency.

Subject coverage:
Fuel poverty, energy efficiency.

Printed publications:
Energy Action (journal, quarterly)
Demonstration Project Reports
Policy Reports
Training, educational and technical publications
Good Practice Briefings
Publications for school children, nursery to Key
    Stage 4

Publications list:
Available in print

Access to staff:
Contact by letter, by telephone, by fax and by e-
mail. Appointment necessary.
Hours: Mon to Thu, 0930 to 1630; Fri, 0930 to 1600

NATIONAL ENERGY
FOUNDATION

Acronym or abbreviation: NEF

Davy Avenue, Knowlhill, Milton Keynes,
Buckinghamshire, MK5 8NG

Tel: 01908 665555
E-mail: nef@natenergy.org.uk

Website:
http://www.natenergy.org.uk
Energy efficiency (mainly domestic).
http://www.greenergy.org.uk
Renewable energy.
http://www.powered.org.uk
Renewable energy kits for schools.
http://www.solar-schools.org.uk
Schools' renewable energy advice, visits.

Enquiries:
Enquiries to: Deputy Director
Other contacts: Manager, NEF Renewables for
information about Renewable Energy.

Founded:
1988

Organisation type and purpose:
National organisation (membership is by election
or invitation), registered charity (charity number
298951).
Encouraging the sustainable use of energy.

Subject coverage:
Energy efficiency, renewable energy.

Printed publications:
Leaflets on Renewable Energy and Energy
    Efficiency (available free of charge)

Electronic and video publications:
Understanding Energy (CD-ROM, available
    through publishing house, Anglia Multimedia)

Access to staff:
Contact by letter, by telephone, by e-mail and via
website. Appointment necessary.
Hours: Mon to Fri, 0900 to 1700

Access to building, collection or gallery:
Prior appointment required

Access for disabled people:
Level entry, access to all public areas, toilet
facilities

NATIONAL EQUINE DEFENCE
LEAGUE

Oaktree Farm, Wetheral Shields, Wetheral, Carlisle,
Cumbria, CA4 8JA

Tel: 01228 560082
Fax: 01228 560985

Enquiries:
Enquiries to: Organising Secretary

Founded:
1909

Organisation type and purpose:
Membership association (membership is by
subscription), voluntary organisation, registered
charity (charity number 280700).

Subject coverage:
Animal welfare matters.

Printed publications:
Annual Report
Many leaflets dealing with several aspects of
    welfare

Publications list:
Available in print

Access to staff:
Contact by letter, by telephone, by fax and in
person
Hours: Mon to Sat, 0930 to 1730

Access for disabled people:
Parking provided, ramped entry, toilet facilities

NATIONAL EXAMINATION
BOARD IN OCCUPATIONAL
SAFETY AND HEALTH

Acronym or abbreviation: NEBOSH

Dominus Way, Meridian Business Park, Leicester,
LE19 1QW

Tel: 0116 263 4700
Fax: 0116 282 4000
E-mail: info@nebosh.org.uk

Website:
http://www.nebosh.org.uk

Enquiries:
Enquiries to: Information Officer

Founded:
1979

Organisation type and purpose:
Examination board.

Subject coverage:
The NEBOSH National General Certificate in
Occupational Health and Safety.
The NEBOSH National Diploma in Occupational
Health and Safety.
The NEBOSH Specialist Diploma in Environmental
Management.
The NEBOSH National Certificate in Construction
Safety and Health.
The NEBOSH International General Certificate in
Occupational Safety and Health.
The NEBOSH Certificate in Fire Safety and Risk
Management.

Printed publications:
NEBOSH National Diploma Series:
Past Examination Question Papers for the
    NEBOSH National Diploma (£2.50 per unit)
Examiners Reports for the NEBOSH National
    Diploma (£8.50 each)
NEBOSH Specialist Diploma in Environmental
    Management:
Syllabus for the NEBOSH Specialist Diploma (£13)
Past Examination Question Papers (£2.50 each)
Examiners Reports (£6 each)
Guide to the NEBOSH National General Certificate
    (£12)
Plus numerous other publications

Publications list:
Available online and in print

Access to staff:
Contact by letter, by telephone, by fax, by e-mail
and via website
Hours: Mon to Fri, 0900 to 1700

Access for disabled people:
Parking provided, level entry, toilet facilities

NATIONAL EXHIBITORS
ASSOCIATION

Acronym or abbreviation: NEA

29A Market Square, Biggleswade, Bedfordshire,
SG18 8AQ

Tel: 01767 316255
Fax: 01767 316255
E-mail: peter.cotterell@eou.org.uk

Website:
http://www.seoevent.co.uk

Enquiries:
Enquiries to: Information Officer

Founded:
1988

Organisation type and purpose:
Trade association.

Access to staff:
Contact by letter, by telephone and by fax
Hours: Mon to Fri, 0900 to 1700

NATIONAL EXTENSION COLLEGE

Acronym or abbreviation: NEC

The Michael Young Centre, Purbeck Road,
Cambridge, CB2 2HN

Tel: 01223 400200
Fax: 01223 400399
E-mail: info@nec.ac.uk

Website:
http://www.nec.ac.uk
The latest information on distance learning courses
and open learning services for all areas of
education and training.
http://www.nec.ac.uk/resources
NEC's online Guide to Courses and Resources
Catalogue.

Enquiries:
Enquiries to: Customer Relations Manager
Direct tel: 0800 389 2839
Direct fax: 01223 400321
Other contacts: Customer Relations Adviser

Founded:
1963

Began trading as part of:
Learning Skills Network (LSN) (year of change
2010)

Organisation type and purpose:
Registered charity (charity number 1113456),
suitable for ages: all.
Providers of open and distance learning materials.

Subject coverage:
Open learning resources for the following areas; A
level, GCSE, IGCSE, language and
communications skills, learning and study skills,
numeracy and literacy skills, IT user skills, foreign
language skills, NVQs in accounting and
administration, marketing, vocational and
professional skills, training, IT and office skills,
small business development, voluntary work, care
and childcare NVQs, caring and health,
counselling and guidance, staff development,
resource development, leisure and general interest.
Home Study courses in the following areas: GCSE,
IGCSE and A level, book-keeping and accounting,
management and professional skills, personal
development, business skills, office skills, childcare
and early years.

Printed publications:
Guide to Courses (GCSE, A Level, etc.)
Resources Catalogue

continued overleaf

A wide range of titles covering: general education, GCSEs, IGCSEs and A Levels, professional skills, book-keeping and accounting, business and management, online skills development, childcare training

Electronic and video publications:
Key Skills Collection CD-ROM
The Learning Guide

Publications list:
Available online and in print

Access to staff:
Contact by letter, by telephone, by fax, by e-mail, in person and via website. Appointment necessary.
Hours: Mon to Fri, 0900 to 1700

Access to building, collection or gallery:
No access other than to staff

Access for disabled people:
Parking provided, toilet facilities

Trades as part of:
Learning Skills Network (LSN)
Fifth Floor, Holborn Centre, 120 Holborn, London, EC1 2AD

NATIONAL EYE RESEARCH CENTRE

Acronym or abbreviation: NERC

Bristol Eye Hospital, Lower Maudlin Street, Bristol, BS1 2LX

Tel: 0117 929 0024
Fax: 0117 925 1421
E-mail: nerc-charity@bris.ac.uk

Website:
http://www.nerc.co.uk
Description of the charity, details from annual report including accounts.

Enquiries:
Enquiries to: Director

Founded:
1986

Organisation type and purpose:
Registered charity (charity number 294087), research organisation.
Research into eye diseases and eye disabilities, and the prevention of blindness.

Subject coverage:
Research projects being funded into the causes and treatment of eye disease and disabilities of the eye, and the prevention of blindness.

Printed publications:
Annual Report

Access to staff:
Contact by letter, by telephone, by fax and by e-mail. Appointment necessary.
Hours: Mon to Fri, 0900 to 1700

Other addresses:
National Eye Research Centre (Yorkshire) (NERC(Y))
Eye Department, Leeds General Infirmary, Leeds, LS2 9NS; tel: 0113 292 2837; fax: 0113 292 2837; e-mail: nercy.lgi@leedsth.nhs.uk

Subsidiary body:
Corneal Support Group
Rotary Eye Bank Campaign

NATIONAL FAMILY MEDIATION

Acronym or abbreviation: NFM

4 Barnfield Hill, Exeter, Devon, EX1 1SR

Tel: 01392 271610
Fax: 01392 271945
E-mail: general@nfm.org.uk

Website:
http://www.nfm.org.uk

Enquiries:
Enquiries to: Administrator

Direct fax: 020 7838 5994
Other contacts: Communications Manager (for press enquiries)

Founded:
1991

Organisation type and purpose:
Registered charity (charity number 1074796).
A service with over 50 branches throughout the United Kingdom.

Subject coverage:
Provision of assistance to separating or divorcing parents in making joint decisions regarding children, finance and property, family mediation, separation and divorce.

Printed publications:
Annual Report

Access to staff:
Contact by letter, by telephone, by e-mail and via website
Hours: Mon to Fri, 0900 to 1630

Branches:
African-Caribbean Family Mediation Service (Lambeth, Lewisham, Wandsworth, Southwark)
2–4 St John's Crescent, Brixton, London, SW9 7LZ; tel: 020 7737 2366; fax: 020 7733 0637; e-mail: donna@acfms.org
Berkshire FMS (Reading, Newbury and Wokingham)
Third Floor, 160–163 Friar Street, Reading, RG1 1HE; tel: 0118 957 1159; fax: 0118 958 4755; e-mail: roger@berksfm.fsnet.co.uk
Birmingham and District FMS (Birmingham, Solihull, Walsall)
First Floor, Coleridge Chambers, 177 Corporation Street, Birmingham, B4 6RG; tel: 0121 233 1999; fax: 0121 233 3399; e-mail: bdfm@netcomuk.co.uk
Boys and Girls Welfare Society Mediation Services (Cheshire)
Goss Chambers, Goss Street, Chester, CH1 2BG; tel: 01244 400658; fax: 01244 343751; e-mail: cms.bgws@virgin.net
Bristol FMS (Avon and South Gloucestershire)
25 Hobbs Lane, Bristol, BS1 5ED; tel: 0117 929 2002; fax: 0117 929 9312; e-mail: mediation@bfmbristol.co.uk
Cambridge and District FMS (Cambridge, Huntingdon and surrounding areas)
Essex House, 71 Regent Street, Cambridge, CB2 1AB; tel: 01223 576308; fax: 01223 576309; e-mail: contact@cfadc.freeserve.co.uk
Central Middlesex Family Mediation (Harrow, Ealing, Hillingdon, Brent)
Civic Centre Complex, Station Road, Harrow, London, HA1 2HX; tel: 020 8427 2076; fax: 020 8861 3471; e-mail: familymediation@ukf.net
Chiltern FMS (Amersham, Watford, Aylesbury)
1 King George V Road, Amersham, Buckinghamshire, HP6 5TT; tel: 01494 732782; fax: 01494 732782
Cleveland FMS (Cleveland and neighbouring areas)
St Mary's Centre, 82–90 Corporation Road, Middlesbrough, Cleveland, TS1 2RW; tel: 01642 222967; fax: 01642 210782; e-mail: clevelandfms@compuserve.com
Coventry and Warwickshire FMS
Suite 11, Koco Building, The Arches, Spon End, Coventry, CV1 3QJ; tel: 024 7671 7109; fax: 024 7671 7119; e-mail: cw.fms@virgin.net
Cumbria FMS
Stricklandgate House, 92 Stricklandgate, Kendal, LA9 4PU; tel: 01539 733705; fax: 01539 733705; e-mail: nwcfms@mail.nch.org.uk
Derbyshire FMS
NCH Action for Children, 32a Newbold Road, Chesterfield, North Derbyshire, S41 7PH; tel: 01246 277422; fax: 01246 277363; e-mail: mddfmp@mail.nch.org.uk
Durham and Darlington Family Mediation (County Durham and Darlington)
First Floor, 72–76 North Road, Durham City, DH1 4SQ; tel: 0191 386 5418; fax: 0191 386 3057; e-mail: nedadfm@mail.nch.org.uk

Exeter and District FMS (Exeter and East Devon)
49 Polsloe Road, Exeter, EX1 2DT; tel: 01392 410529; e-mail: nfmexeter@eurobell.co.uk
Eye to Eye Mediation (Inner London Probation Area)
NCH Action for Children, 231 Camberwell New Road, London, SE5 0TH; tel: 020 7701 1114 or 703 2532; fax: 020 7703 6129; e-mail: inetem@mail.nch.org.uk
Family Mediation (Hull) (Kingston upon Hull, East Yorkshire, North and North-East Lincolnshire)
34 Bishop Lane, Hull, HU1 1PA; tel: 01482 329740; fax: 01482 323991; e-mail: dorothy@familymediation.karoo.uk
Family Mediation (North Wiltshire) (West and North Wiltshire, parts of Berkshire, Gloucestershire, Oxon)
34 Milton Road, Swindon, Wiltshire, SN1 5JA; tel: 01793 527285; fax: 01793 420532; e-mail: admin@familymediation.fsnet.co.uk
Family Mediation Centre (Greater Manchester)
21 Knowsley Street, Bury, Lancashire, BL9 0ST; tel: 0161 797 9910; fax: 0161 763 9311; e-mail: nwfmsgm@mail.nch.org.uk
Family Mediation Service (North West Yorkshire) (Harrogate, Craven and Richmondshire, Hambleton)
13 Dragon Parade, Harrogate, North Yorkshire, HG1 5BZ; tel: 01423 525156; fax: 01423 520983; e-mail: fmsnwy@lineonline.net
Family Mediation Service (Northumberland and Tyneside FMS) (Newcastle, Gateshead, North Tyneside, Northumberland)
NCH, MEA House, Ellison Place, Newcastle upon Tyne, NE1 8XS; tel: 0191 261 9212; fax: 0191 233 0634; e-mail: nenatfms@mail.nch.org.uk
Family Mediation Service Cardiff
42 Cardiff Street, Cardiff, CF10 2GE; tel: 029 2022 9692; fax: 029 2039 9505
Gloucestershire Family Mediation
PO Box 95, Gloucester, GL1 3YG; tel: 01452 411843; fax: 01452 418441; e-mail: gfm@mediation.fsbusiness.co.uk
Gwent Mediation Service
NCH, 66 Lower Dock Street, Newport, NP20 1EF; tel: 01633 263 065; fax: 01633 222743; e-mail: wagms@mail.nch.org.uk
Hampshire FMS (Hampshire and Isle of Wight)
58d High Street, Cosham, Portsmouth, PO6 3AG; tel: 023 9243 3388; fax: 023 9243 3358; e-mail: admin@hantsmed.org.uk
Herefordshire FMS (Herefordshire and surrounding area)
Second Floor, Berrows Business Centre, Hereford, HR1 2HE; tel: 01432 264087/277996; fax: 01432 351993; e-mail: herefordshire@familymediation.fslife.co.uk
Hertfordshire and Essex FMS (West Essex and parts of Hertfordshire)
Sewell House, 349 The Hides, Harlow, Essex, CM20 3QY; tel: 01279 426749; fax: 01279 426749; e-mail: hefms@dial.pipex.com
Hertfordshire FMS
62–72 Victoria Street, St Albans, Hertfordshire, AL1 3XH; tel: 01727 839300; fax: 01727 839123; e-mail: admin@hertsfms.fsnet.co.uk
Jersey Family Mediation
2 Charles House, Charles Street, St Helier, Jersey, JE2 4SF; tel: 01534 734980; fax: 01534 619945; e-mail: relate.jersey@jerseymail.co.uk
Kent FMS
6 Park Road, Sittingbourne, Kent, ME10 1DR; tel: 01795 429689; fax: 01795 476949; e-mail: familymediation.kent@virgin.net
Lancashire FMS
19 Ribblesdale Place, Preston, Lancashire, PR1 3NA; tel: 01772 204248; fax: 01772 204246; e-mail: mediation@lfms.net
Lincolnshire FMS
Claxlete House, 62 Clasketgate, Lincoln, LN2 1JZ; tel: 01522 575700; fax: 01522 575700; e-mail: lfms@lincs-ln2.freeserve.co.uk
Mediation in Divorce (South West London)
13 Rosslyn Road, East Twickenham, London, TW1 2AR; tel: 020 8891 6860; fax: 020 8891 3107; e-mail: admin@mediationindivorce.co.uk

Merseyside FMS
5a Swiss Road, Liverpool, L6 3AT; tel: 0151 260 9155; fax: 0151 260 0548; e-mail: mediation@pss .org.uk
Milton Keynes Family Mediation (Milton Keynes, North Buckinghamshire, North Hertfordshire and Bedfordshire)
City Counselling Centre, 320 Saxon Gate West, Central Milton Keynes, Buckinghamshire, MK9 2ES; tel: 01908 231293; fax: 01908 690211; e-mail: familymediationmk@talk21.com
Norfolk FMS
Charing Cross Centre, 17–19 St John Maddermarket, Norwich, Norfolk, NR2 1DL; tel: 01603 620 588; fax: 01603 620 588; e-mail: norfolk .fammed@lineone.net
North Devon FMS
The Castle Centre, Castle Street, Barnstaple, Devon, EX31 1DR; tel: 01270 321888; fax: 01271 321888; e-mail: ndfms@lineone.net
North London FMS (Barnet, Haringey, Hertsmere and Enfield)
267 Ballards Lane, Finchley, London, N12 8NR; tel: 020 8343 9899; fax: 020 8445 6603; e-mail: nlmed@email.com
North Staffordshire FMS (Stafford, Stoke and North Staffordshire)
Winton House, Stoke Road, Stoke-on-Trent, Staffordshire, ST4 2RN; tel: 0845 602 0301/01782 416111; fax: 01782 416444; e-mail: nsfms@ hotmail.com
Northamptonshire FMS
49 York Road, First Floor, Northampton, NN1 5QJ; tel: 01604 636651; fax: 01604 637313; e-mail: familymediation@excite.co.uk
Northern Ireland Family Mediation Service
76 Dublin Road, Belfast, BT2 7HP; tel: 028 9032 2914; fax: 028 9315 298
Nottinghamshire Children and Families Mediation Service (FAME)
3 Pelham Court, Pelham Road, Nottingham, NG5 1AP; tel: 0115 985 8855; fax: 0115 962 3606; e-mail: mj@famenottingham.fsbusiness.co.uk
Oxfordshire FMS
First Floor, 125 London Road, Headington, Oxford, OX3 9HZ; tel: 01865 741781; fax: 01865 744393; e-mail: oxmedserv@aol.com
Peterborough and District FMS
61 Broadway, Peterborough, Cambridgeshire, PE1 1SY; tel: 01733 347353; fax: 01733 347353; e-mail: pfms@tinyonline.co.uk
Plymouth Mediation (Plymouth and District)
St Peter's Centre, 18 Harwell Street, Plymouth, PL1 5BA; tel: 01752 312121; fax: 01752 312123; e-mail: plymed@dial.pipex.com
Salisbury and District FMS (Salisbury, South Wiltshire, North Dorset, North West Hampshire)
24b St Edmund's Church Street, Salisbury, Wiltshire, SP1 1EF; tel: 01722 332936; fax: 01722 332936; e-mail: fms@southwilts.nda.co.uk
Scarborough and District FMS
1 Westbourne Grove, Scarborough, North Yorkshire, YO11 2DJ; tel: 01723 507775; fax: 01723 507775; e-mail: manager@sdfms.fsnet.co .uk
Shropshire Family Mediation
65 Withywood Drive, Malinslee, Telford, Shropshire, TF3 2HU; tel: 01952 520091; fax: 01952 520092; e-mail: shropshire.mediation1@ virgin.net
Somerset FMS
The Myrtle Tree, 34 Bridge Street, Taunton, Somerset, TA1 1UD; tel: 01823 352013; fax: 01823 352013; e-mail: mary@relate-somerset.org.uk
South Essex FMS
29 Harcourt Avenue, Southend-on-Sea, Essex, SS2 6HT; tel: 01702 436466; fax: 01702 431173; e-mail: mediation.southessexrelate@virgin.net
South Staffordshire FMS (South Staffordshire, Cannock, Lichfield, Tamworth)
33 Park Road, Cannock, Staffordshire, WS11 1JN; tel: 01543 572600; fax: 01543 579390; e-mail: ssfmscannock@hotmail.com
South Yorkshire FMS
Queen's Building, 55 Queen Street, Sheffield, S1 2DX; tel: 0114 275 2227; fax: 0114 275 3996; e-mail: user@syfm.fsnet.co.uk

South-East London Family Mediation Bureau (Bexley, Bromley, Croydon and surrounding areas)
5 Upper Park Road, Bromley, Kent, BR1 3HN; tel: 020 8460 4606; fax: 020 8466 6572; e-mail: info@familymediationlondon.org.uk
Sunderland and South Tyneside FMS (Sunderland, Washington, Houghton-le-Spring, South Shields, Jarrow)
54 John Street, Sunderland, Tyne and Wear, SR1 1QH; tel: 0191 514 3849; fax: 0191 514 2481; e-mail: sastfms@aol.com
Surrey FMS
316 High Street, Dorking, Surrey, RH4 1QX; tel: 01306 741777; fax: 01306 741383; e-mail: surreyfms@cs.com
Sussex FMS (East and West Sussex)
Garton House, 22 Stanford Avenue, Brighton, East Sussex, BN1 6DD; tel: 01273 550563; fax: 01273 555412; e-mail: sxfms@supanet.com
Thames Valley FMS (South Buckinghamshire, East Berkshire, High Wycombe, Slough, Windsor and Bracknell)
Windsor Magistrates Court, Side Entrance, Alma Road, Windsor, Berkshire, SL4 3HD; tel: 01753 830770; fax: 01753 830770; e-mail: thames@ valleyfm.fsnet.co.uk
The FMS-Institute of Family Therapy (Central London and North West)
24–32 Stephenson Way, London, NW1 2HX; tel: 020 7391 9150; fax: 020 7391 9169; e-mail: ift@ psyc.bbk.ac.uk
West Yorkshire FMS (Bradford, Wakefield, Dewsbury, Halifax, Huddersfield, Leeds)
31 Manor Road, Bradford, West Yorkshire, BD1 4PS; tel: 01274 732768 or 0845 419403; fax: 01274 730115; e-mail: wyfamilymed@netscapeonline.co .uk
Worcestershire FMS
14 Castle Street Street, Worcester, WR1 3ZB; tel: 01905 610925; fax: 01905 619526; e-mail: worcester@familymediation.fsbusiness.co.uk
York FMS (York, Selby, parts of Ryedale and Hambleton)
The Old Coach House, Grange Garth, York, YO10 4BS; tel: 01904 646068; fax: 01904 646068; e-mail: yorkfms@care4free.net

Links with:
Dorset Relate
8 Maumbury Road, Dorchester, Dorset, DT1 1QW; tel: 01305 751781; fax: 01305 751781; e-mail: general@dorsetfamilymediation.co.uk
Leicester Relate
83 Aylestone Road, Leicester, LE2 7LL; tel: 0116 254 1149
North East London FMS (Ilford, Romford, Barking and Dagenham)
Relate Office, Althorne Way, Dagenham, Essex, RM10 7AY; tel: 020 8593 6827; fax: 020 8593 8111; e-mail: nel_mediation@talk21.com
North Wales FMS (Colwyn Bay, Rhyl, Bangor)
Eryl Wen, Eryl Place, Llandudno, LL30 2TX; tel: 01492 870876; fax: 01492 870846

NATIONAL FARMERS' UNION

Acronym or abbreviation: NFU

Agriculture House, Stoneleigh Park, Stoneleigh, Warwickshire, CV8 2TZ

Tel: 024 7685 8500
Fax: 024 7685 8501
E-mail: nfu@nfu.org.uk

Website:
http://www.nfu.org.uk

Enquiries:
Enquiries to: Press Officer
Direct tel: 020 7331 7295
Direct fax: 020 7331 7370
Direct e-mail: sharon.hockley@nfu.org.uk
Other contacts: Director General; President for general management; 'politics'.

Founded:
1908

Organisation type and purpose:
Trade association (membership is by subscription), present number of members: 135,000.
Representing farmers and growers in England and Wales.
To provide farmers and growers with professional and technical services.

Subject coverage:
Policy, economic, legal and other material relating to agriculture, horticulture, land use, agricultural trade and statistics, livestock and crop production.

Museum or gallery collection, archive, or library special collection:
British Farmer, NFU Magazine, NFU Business NFU yearbooks since 1910

Trade and statistical information:
UK Agricultural (June census) statistics from 1866.
Agricultural statistics from 1940.
Household food consumption survey from 1940.

Printed publications:
Annual Report
National and Regional NFU journals available on subscription

Publications list:
Available online

Access to staff:
Contact by letter, by telephone, by fax and by e-mail. Appointment necessary. Non-members charged.
Hours: Archives held in out-of-town store, 48 hours notice needed for retrieval

Access to building, collection or gallery:
No access other than to staff

Affiliated to:
CBI
European Federation of Farmers' Organisations (COPA)
International Chamber of Commerce (ICC)
International Federation of Agricultural Producers (IFPA)

Has:
8 regional offices, HQ outstations and approximately 400 local branches

NATIONAL FEDERATION OF 18 PLUS GROUPS OF GB

Acronym or abbreviation: 18 PLUS

8–10 Church Street Chamber, Church Street, Newent, Gloucestershire, GL18 1PP

Tel: 01531 821210
Fax: 01531 821474
E-mail: office@18plus.org.uk

Website:
http://www.18plus.org.uk
History of 18 Plus, 18 Plus group programmes, links to member group pages, other email contacts.

Enquiries:
Enquiries to: Administrator
Other contacts: Honorary General Secretary

Founded:
1941

Organisation type and purpose:
Membership association (membership is by subscription), present number of members: 1,200, voluntary organisation, suitable for ages: 18 to 35, training organisation.
A social activities organisation for young adults wishing to make friends and take part in a wide range of activities.

Subject coverage:
Social group, personal development training and a variety of activities.

Printed publications:
Information pack for membership enquiries (free of charge on receipt of name and postal address)

continued overleaf

Access to staff:
Contact by letter, by telephone, by fax, by e-mail and via website
Hours: 24-hour answerphone

NATIONAL FEDERATION OF ANGLERS

Acronym or abbreviation: NFA

Halliday House, Egginton Junction, Hilton, Derbyshire, DE65 6GU

Tel: 01283 734735
Fax: 01283 734799
E-mail: office@nfahq.freeserve.co.uk

Enquiries:
Enquiries to: Administration Manager

Founded:
1903

Organisation type and purpose:
Voluntary organisation.
Governing body of coarse angling.

Subject coverage:
Fisheries and fishing; coarse fishing; problems of pollution, water abstraction and land drainage, fishery protection; research; competitions, sponsored events.

Printed publications:
NFA Booklet
NFA Codes
NFA Rules and Constitution

Access to staff:
Contact by letter and by e-mail
Hours: Mon to Fri, 0900 to 1700

Member of:
Confédération Internationale de la Pêche Sportive (CIPS)

NATIONAL FEDERATION OF BUILDERS

Acronym or abbreviation: NFB

B&CC Building Manor Royal, Crawley, West Sussex, RH10 9QP

Tel: 08450 578160
Fax: 08450 578161
E-mail: marketing @builders.org.uk

Website:
http://builders.org.uk/

Enquiries:
Direct e-mail: paul.smith@citypress.co.uk

Organisation type and purpose:
Trade association.

Subject coverage:
Building companies, SMEs.

NATIONAL FEDERATION OF DEMOLITION CONTRACTORS LIMITED

Acronym or abbreviation: NFDC LTD

Resurgam House, 1a New Road, The Causeway, Staines, Middlesex, TW18 3DH

Tel: 01784 456799
Fax: 01784 461118
E-mail: info@demolition-nfdc.com

Website:
http://www.demolition-nfdc.com
List of members and federation officers.

Enquiries:
Enquiries to: National Secretary
Direct e-mail: howard@demolition-nfdc.com

Founded:
1941

Organisation type and purpose:
Trade association.

Subject coverage:
General demolition, demolition of mass and reinforced concrete structures, chimney demolition, dangerous structures, machinery dismantling, shoring, site clearance and excavation, demolition by licensed explosives engineers, asbestos stripping and disposal, thermic boring, plant hire, supplies of hardcore, sale of reclaimed building materials.

Printed publications:
Demolition and Dismantling (journal, quarterly)
List of Members
NFDC Yearbook
The First Fifty Years (history of the federation 1941–91)

Electronic and video publications:
Voice of the Industry (video)

Access to staff:
Contact by letter, by telephone, by fax, by e-mail and via website. Appointment necessary.
Hours: Mon to Fri, 0900 to 1700

Access for disabled people:
Parking provided

Founder member of:
European Demolition Association
tel: + 31 30 259 8330; fax: + 31 30 259 8600; e-mail: eda@eda-demolition.com

NATIONAL FEDERATION OF FISH FRIERS LIMITED

Acronym or abbreviation: NFFF

New Federation House, 4 Greenwood Mount, Meanwood, Leeds, West Yorkshire, LS6 4LQ

Tel: 0113 230 7044
Fax: 0113 230 7010
E-mail: mail@federationoffishfriers.co.uk

Website:
http://www.federationoffishfriers.co.uk

Enquiries:
Enquiries to: Review Manager
Direct tel: 0113 230 7009
Other contacts: General Secretary

Founded:
1913

Organisation type and purpose:
Trade association, present number of members: 2500, training organisation.
Looks after the interests of fish friers throughout the United Kingdom.

Subject coverage:
Covers interests of the members of the fish frying trade; fish, potatoes and other cooking ingredients, frying and refrigeration equipment, health and safety issues.

Printed publications:
Fish Friers Review (journal, to members, annual subscription £41.52)

Access to staff:
Contact by letter, by telephone, by fax, by e-mail and via website. Appointment necessary.
Hours: Mon to Fri, 0900 to 1630

NATIONAL FEDERATION OF MEAT AND FOOD TRADERS, THE

Acronym or abbreviation: NFMFT

1 Belgrove, Tunbridge Wells, Kent, TN1 1YW

Tel: 01892 541412
Fax: 01892 535462
E-mail: info@nfmft.co.uk

Enquiries:
Enquiries to: Chief Executive

Founded:
1888

Organisation type and purpose:
Trade association.

Subject coverage:
Represents the interests of member independent retail butchers in England and Wales.

Printed publications:
Food Trader (journal, monthly)
Essential Business Guide (annual guide to regulations)

Access to staff:
Contact by letter, by telephone, by fax and by e-mail. Appointment necessary. Access for members only. Letter of introduction required.
Hours: Mon to Fri, 0900 to 1715

NATIONAL FEDERATION OF ROOFING CONTRACTORS LIMITED

Acronym or abbreviation: NFRC

24 Weymouth Street, London, W1G 7LX

Tel: 020 7436 0387
Fax: 020 7637 5215
E-mail: info@nfrc.co.uk

Website:
http://www.nfrc.co.uk
Product matrix by category of all NFRC associate members with a keyword selector.
Product and service matrices search for roofers by area and discipline.

Enquiries:
Enquiries to: Secretary
Other contacts: (1) Membership Secretary (2) Public Relations Executive for (2) media, publications information.

Founded:
1893

Organisation type and purpose:
Trade association.

Subject coverage:
Technical roofing information, insurance schemes, education and training in roofing, product and application standards, health and safety.

Printed publications:
Householders Guide to Flat Roofing
NFRC Directory
Roofing & Cladding in Windy Conditions
Safety Passport
Technical Bulletins
UPDATE (magazine, monthly)

Electronic and video publications:
The NFRC Guide to Quality Roofing (disk)

Publications list:
Available online and in print

Access to staff:
Contact by letter, by telephone, by fax, by e-mail and via website. Appointment necessary.
Hours: Mon to Fri, 0900 to 1700

Member of:
National Specialist Contractors Council (NSCC)
Carthusian Court, 12 Carthusian Street, London, EC1M 6EZ; tel: 0870 429 6351; fax: 0870 429 6352

NATIONAL FEDERATION OF SUBPOSTMASTERS

Acronym or abbreviation: NFSP

Evelyn House, 22 Windlesham Gardens, Shoreham-by-Sea, West Sussex, BN43 5AZ

Tel: 01273 452324
Fax: 01273 465403
E-mail: nfsp@subpostmasters.org.uk

Website:
http://www.subpostmasters.org.uk

Enquiries:
Enquiries to: Information Officer

Founded:
1897

Organisation type and purpose:
National organisation, trade association, trade union (membership is by subscription), present number of members: 14,000.
Certificated independent trade union recognised by The Post Office to represent subpostmasters.

Subject coverage:
Post office management.

Access to staff:
Contact by letter and by telephone
Hours: Mon to Fri, 0900 to 1700

Access to building, collection or gallery:
No access other than to staff

NATIONAL FEDERATION OF TERRAZZO MARBLE & MOSAIC SPECIALISTS

Acronym or abbreviation: NFTMMS

PO Box 2843, London, W1A 5PG

Tel: 0845 609 0050
Fax: 0845 607 8610
E-mail: dslade@nftmms.org

Website:
http://www.nftmms.org
Details of activities and services, list of members.

Enquiries:
Enquiries to: Secretary

Founded:
1933

Organisation type and purpose:
Trade association (membership is by election or invitation), present number of members: 40.

Subject coverage:
Technical advice on the laying of terrazzo, mosaic and marble; granite; limestone; investigation of complaints; inspection and reports on work, application etc.

Printed publications:
Members list
Technical specifications to complement British Standards
General Federation Brochure

Access to staff:
Contact by letter, by telephone, by fax and by e-mail
Hours: Mon to Fri, 0900 to 1700

NATIONAL FEDERATION OF THE BLIND OF THE UNITED KINGDOM

Acronym or abbreviation: NFBUK

Sir John Wilson House, 215 Kirkgate, Wakefield, West Yorkshire, WF1 1JG

Tel: 01924 291313
Fax: 01924 200244
E-mail: nfbuk@nfbuk.org

Website:
http://www.nfbuk.org

Enquiries:
Enquiries to: Honorary General Secretary
Other contacts: Public Relations Officer for information.

Founded:
1947

Organisation type and purpose:
Membership association (membership is by subscription), present number of members: 2000, registered charity, voluntary organisation (charity number 236629).
Campaigning organisation.

Subject coverage:
The real needs of the blind and partially-sighted from their perspective e.g. a safer environment, obstructions in pavements, and the particular needs of the deafblind.

Printed publications:
Publications are available both free and for purchase
Information is also available in print and braille

Electronic and video publications:
2 videos are available for purchase
Information is also available on tape and disk

Publications list:
Available in print

Access to staff:
Contact by letter, by telephone, by fax and by e-mail
Hours: Mon, Tue, Thu, Fri, 0900 to 1600; Wed, closed

NATIONAL FEDERATION OF WOMEN'S INSTITUTES

Acronym or abbreviation: NFWI

104 New Kings Road, Fulham, London, SW6 4LY

Tel: 020 7371 9300
Fax: 020 7736 3652
E-mail: gensec@nfwi.org.uk

Website:
http://www.thewi.org.uk

Enquiries:
Enquiries to: General Secretary

Founded:
1915

Organisation type and purpose:
Membership association (membership is by subscription), present number of members: 205,000, voluntary organisation, registered charity.

Subject coverage:
Rural affairs, current and public affairs, particularly on environment and issues of concern to women, health, social welfare, employment, standards of life, home economics, music and drama, education, crafts, sport.

Museum or gallery collection, archive, or library special collection:
The Women's Library, Old Castle Street, London E1

Printed publications:
Annual Report
WI Life (magazine, 8 times a year)
WI Books (various titles)

Publications list:
Available in print

Access to staff:
Contact by letter, by telephone, by fax, by e-mail and via website
Hours: Mon to Fri, 0900 to 1700

Access for disabled people:
None

Also at:
Denman College
    Marcham, Abingdon, Oxfordshire, OX13 6NW; tel: 01865 391991; fax: 01865 391966; e-mail: info@denman.org.uk
NFWI Wales Office (NFWI)
    19–21 Cathedral Road, Cardiff, CF1 9LJ; tel: 02920 221712; fax: 02920 387236

NATIONAL FEDERATION OF WOMEN'S INSTITUTES – WALES

Acronym or abbreviation: NFWI–Wales

19 Cathedral Road, Cardiff, CF11 9HA

Tel: 029 2022 1712
Fax: 029 2038 7236
E-mail: walesoffice@nfwi-wales.org.uk

Website:
http://www.womens-institute.org.uk

Enquiries:
Enquiries to: Head of Wales Office

Other contacts: Administrative/Public Affairs Officer (for preliminary enquiries)

Founded:
1915

Organisation type and purpose:
Membership association (membership is by subscription), present number of members: 20,000, voluntary organisation, registered charity (charity number 803793), suitable for ages: 16+.
The National Federation of Women's Institutes offers opportunities for all women to enjoy friendship, to learn, to widen their horizons, and together to influence local, national and international affairs.

Non-library collection catalogue:
All or part available online

Publications list:
Available in print

Access to staff:
Contact by letter, by telephone and by e-mail
Hours: Mon to Fri, 0900 to 1700

Branches:
13 Federation offices throughout Wales

NATIONAL FILM AND TELEVISION SCHOOL

Acronym or abbreviation: NFTS

Beaconsfield Studios, Station Road, Beaconsfield, Buckinghamshire, HP9 1LG

Tel: 01494 671234
Fax: 01494 674042
E-mail: info@nfts.co.uk

Website:
http://www.nfts.co.uk
Full course descriptions for full-time and short courses, information about fees, financial support available and how to apply. Facility to apply online. Online prospectus. Clips from student films, news and other information about the NFTS.

Enquiries:
Enquiries to: Registrar
Direct tel: 01494 731425

Founded:
1971

Formerly called:
National Film School (year of change 1982)

Organisation type and purpose:
National organisation, suitable for ages: postgraduate, training organisation.

Subject coverage:
Information about MA and Diploma courses in directing (animation, documentary or fiction), cinematography, composing for film and television, digital post-production, editing, producing, producing and directing television entertainment, production design, production management, screenwriting, script development, SFX/VFX, sound design, sound recording

Electronic and video publications:
Prospectus (free, online)

Access to staff:
Contact by letter, by telephone, by fax, by e-mail, in person and via website. Appointment necessary.
Hours: Mon to Fri, 0930 to 1730

Access for disabled people:
Parking provided, level entry, toilet facilities
Hours: During NFTS opening hours
Special comments: Most areas accessible. Special arrangements can be made for individual requirements, preferably give advance notice

Links with:
ShortCourses@NFTS
    at Beaconsfield Studios; tel: 01494 677903; fax: 01494 678708; e-mail: shortcourses@nfts.co.uk; website: http://www.nfts.co.uk

NATIONAL FILM BOARD OF CANADA

Acronym or abbreviation: NFB

Canada House, Trafalgar Square, London, SW1Y 5BJ

Tel: 020 7258 6480
Fax: 020 7258 6532
E-mail: london@nfb.ca

Website:
http://www.nfb.ca
About the NFB and its productions.

Enquiries:
Enquiries to: Sales Representative
Direct tel: 020 7258 6482
Direct e-mail: s.swan@nfb.ca

Founded:
1939

Organisation type and purpose:
Film production and distribution.

Subject coverage:
Film and video production and distribution.

Museum or gallery collection, archive, or library special collection:
Collection of 17,000 titles, mainly documentaries and animation (includes educational programmes)

Printed publications:
NFB Annual Report
NFB Productions

Electronic and video publications:
Videos available for purchase through NFB London office or through its UK distributors

Access to staff:
Contact by letter, by telephone, by fax, by e-mail and via website
Hours: Mon to Fri, 1000 to 1800

NATIONAL FILM THEATRE

Acronym or abbreviation: NFT

South Bank Centre, Belvedere Road, Waterloo, London, SE1 8XT

Tel: 020 7928 3535
Fax: 020 7815 1419
E-mail: nft@bfi.org.uk

Website:
http://www.bfi.org.uk/nft50
http://www.bfi.org.uk/nft

Enquiries:
Enquiries to: Press and Marketing Department

Founded:
1952

Organisation type and purpose:
Cinema.

Subject coverage:
Film and video information related to its own screening.

Printed publications:
NFT 50: A celebration of 50 years of the National Film Theatre researched and written by Allen Eyles (£5)

Electronic and video publications:
Education resource materials (for purchase, from the museum's education department)

Access to staff:
Contact by letter, by telephone, by fax, by e-mail and via website
Hours: Mon to Fri, 1000 to 1800

Access for disabled people:
Parking provided, level entry, toilet facilities

Parent body:
British Film Institute
21 Stephen Street, London, W1P 1PL

NATIONAL FIREPLACE ASSOCIATION

Formal name: Stove and Fireplace Advice
Acronym or abbreviation: SAFA

PO Box 583, High Wycombe, HP15 6XT

Tel: 0845 643 1901
Fax: 0870 130 6747
E-mail: advice@stoveandfireplaceadvice.org.uk

Website:
http://www.stoveandfireplaceadvice.org.uk
Advice on choosing fires, stoves and fireplaces for end users, building industry professionals and architects; advice on complaints.

Enquiries:
Enquiries to: Director

Founded:
2007

Organisation type and purpose:
Trade association.
Promotional body for the fire and fireplace industry; promotion to the end user.

Subject coverage:
Fireplaces, open fires, stoves, roomheaters and fuels (solid fuel, gas, natural and LPG).

Publications list:
Available online and in print

Access to staff:
Contact by telephone, by fax, by e-mail and via website
Hours: Mon to Fri, 0900 to 1700

Also at:
Fire (PR) Service
PO Box 583, Holmer Green, High Wycombe, Buckinghamshire, HP15 6XT; tel: 01494 711430; fax: 0870 130 6747; e-mail: peterhealy@fireplacepr.force9.co.uk

NATIONAL FOREST COMPANY

Enterprise Glade, Bath Yard, Bath Lane, Swadlincote, Derbyshire, DE12 6BD

Tel: 01283 551211
Fax: 01283 552844
E-mail: enquiries@nationalforest.org

Website:
http://www.nationalforest.org
Full information on the National Forest

Founded:
1995

Organisation type and purpose:
Government-funded company.
Creating a new multipurpose forest in the Midlands (Leicestershire, Derbyshire, Staffordshire).

Subject coverage:
Grants for woodland creation, forestry investment and sponsorship opportunities in the National Forest.

Printed publications:
Newsletter (2 times a year)
Visitor Guide
Food Guide
Walks and Site Guides

Publications list:
Available online and in print

Access to staff:
Contact by letter and by e-mail
Hours: Mon to Fri, 0900 to 1700

NATIONAL FOUNDATION FOR EDUCATIONAL RESEARCH

Chestnut House, Tawe Business Village, Phoenix Way, Enterprise Park, Llansamlet, Swansea, West Glamorgan, SA7 9LA

Tel: 01792 459800

Fax: 01792 797815
E-mail: scya@nfer.ac.uk

Website:
http://www.nfer.ac.uk

Enquiries:
Enquiries to: Information Officer
Other contacts: Head of NFER Welsh Unit

Founded:
1946

Organisation type and purpose:
Registered charity (charity number 313392), suitable for ages: 3 to 100, research organisation. Education research – independent charity. NFER conducts independent and objective research through external sponsors and customers. Through its own resources conducts evaluations and surveys and develops tests and assessment materials. NFER Welsh unit at Swansea also specialises in Welsh language research.

Subject coverage:
Education and training.

Access to staff:
Contact by letter, by telephone and by fax
Hours: Mon to Fri, 0900 to 1700

Access for disabled people:
Parking provided

Main office:
National Foundation for Educational Research (NFER)
The Mere, Upton Park, Slough, SL1 2DQ; tel: 01753 574123

NATIONAL FOX WELFARE SOCIETY

Acronym or abbreviation: NFWS

135 Higham Road, Rushden, Northamptonshire, NN10 6DS

Tel: 01933 411996
Fax: 01933 397324
E-mail: natfox@ntlworld.com

Website:
http://www.nfws.org.uk/
http://www.mange.org.uk
Information on the occurrence and treatment of sarcoptic mange.

Enquiries:
Enquiries to: Any Co-ordinator

Founded:
1993

Organisation type and purpose:
National organisation, membership association (membership is by subscription), voluntary organisation.
Animal welfare society providing advice and practical assistance on all fox-related issues.

Subject coverage:
All fox-related subjects, behaviour, rescue, advice, help with treatment for injuries and/or mange.

Printed publications:
Information pack available on request (A4 sae with large-letter stamp)
Vulpine Observer (members only, £12 per annum)
Foxwatching – in the Shadow of the Fox (£7.99 plus 75p p&p)
Urban Foxes (£9.99 plus £1 p&p)
Unearthing the Urban Fox (£4.95 plus 50p p&p)

Publications list:
Available in print

Access to staff:
Contact by letter, by telephone, by e-mail and via website
Hours: Mon to Fri, 1000 to 1800
Special comments: 24 hours, 365 days a year for emergencies.

Access to building, collection or gallery:
No access other than to staff

NATIONAL GALLERIES OF SCOTLAND

Press and Information Department, Dean Gallery Lodge, Belford Road, Edinburgh, EH4 3DS

Tel: 0131 624 6200
Fax: 0131 343 3250

Website:
http://www.nationalgalleries.org

Enquiries:
Enquiries to: Press and Information Assistant
Direct tel: 0131 624 6332
Direct e-mail: pressinfo@nationalgalleries.org

Founded:
1859

Organisation type and purpose:
Art gallery.

Subject coverage:
Provision of information on the National Gallery of Scotland, Scottish National Gallery of Modern Art, Scottish National Portrait Gallery and Dean Gallery.

Printed publications:
Order printed publications from: Publications Department, National Galleries of Scotland, Dean Gallery, Belford Road, Edinburgh, EH4 3DS, tel: 0131 624 6256/6259/6261, fax: 0131 315 2963, e-mail: publications@nationalgalleries.org

Publications list:
Available online and in print

Access to staff:
Contact by letter, by telephone and by e-mail
Hours: Mon to Sun, 1000 to 1700

Access to building, collection or gallery:
No prior appointment required
Hours: Mon to Sun, 1000 to 1700

Access for disabled people:
Access to all public areas, toilet facilities

Also at:
Duff House
 Banff, Banffshire, AB45 2SX; tel: 01261 818181; fax: 01261 818181; e-mail: duff.house@ aberdeenshire.gov.uk; website: http://www .duffhouse.com
National Gallery of Scotland
 The Mound, Edinburgh, EH2 2EL; tel: 0131 624 6200; fax: 0131 220 0917; e-mail: nginfo@ nationalgalleries.org; website: http://www .nationalgalleries.org
Paxton House
 Berwick-upon-Tweed, Berwickshire, TD15 1SZ; tel: 01289 386291; fax: 01289 386660; e-mail: info@paxtonhouse.com; website: http://www .paxtonhouse.co.uk
Scottish National Gallery of Modern Art
 75 Belford Road, Edinburgh, EH4 3DR; tel: 0131 624 6200; fax: 0131 343 2802; e-mail: gmainfo@ nationalgalleries.org; website: http://www .nationalgalleries.org
Scottish National Portrait Gallery
 1 Queen Street, Edinburgh, EH2 1JD; tel: 0131 624 6200; fax: 0131 558 3691; e-mail: pginfo@ nationalgalleries.org; website: http://www .nationalgalleries.org
The Dean Gallery
 73 Belford Road, Edinburgh, EH4 3DS; tel: 0131 624 6200; fax: 0131 343 2802; e-mail: deaninfo@ nationalgalleries.org; website: http://www .nationalgalleries.org

NATIONAL GALLERY

Technical Library, Scientific Department, Trafalgar Square, London, WC2N 5DN

Tel: 020 7747 2400 ext 2829
Fax: 020 7839 3897

Website:
http://www.nationalgallery.org.uk

Enquiries:
Enquiries to: Technical Librarian

Direct tel: 020 7747 2829

Founded:
1950

Organisation type and purpose:
National government body, museum, art gallery, research organisation.
Art museum departmental library. Non-Governmental Departmental Body.

Subject coverage:
Materials, techniques and history of painting, particularly of European easel painting from c. 1300 to 1900, scientific examination of works of art, climate control for works of art, safe exhibition and storage conditions.

Museum or gallery collection, archive, or library special collection:
Eastlake Collection of early books and manuscripts on materials and techniques of painting, and other arts and crafts (part)

Printed publications:
National Gallery Technical Bulletin (£19.95, published by the National Gallery with contributions from the Scientific and Conservation Departments, annually)
Order printed publications from: National Gallery Company Limited
St Vincent House, 30 Orange Street, London, WC2H 7HH, tel: 020 7281 9080

Publications list:
Available online and in print

Access to staff:
Contact by letter, by telephone and by fax
Hours: Mon to Fri, 0930 to 1730
Special comments: No enquiries in person.

Access to building, collection or gallery:
National Gallery hours, daily, 1000 to 1800 except Wed, 1000 to 2100

Access for disabled people:
Lift
Hours: Mon to Fri, 1000 to 1730

NATIONAL GAS ARCHIVE, THE

Unit 1, Europa Court, Europa Boulevard, Warrington, WA5 7TN

Tel: 01925 425740
Fax: 01925 425748
E-mail: archive@uk.ngrid.com

Website:
http://www.gasarchive.org
History of gas industry, scope of collections, facilities.

Enquiries:
Enquiries to: Archivist

Founded:
1995

Organisation type and purpose:
National organisation.

Subject coverage:
Gas history, technical and engineering history, chemical industry.

Non-library collection catalogue:
All or part available online, in-house and in print

Library catalogue:
All or part available in-house

Access to staff:
Contact by letter, by telephone, by fax, by e-mail and via website. Appointment necessary.
Hours: Mon to Fri, 0900 to 1700

Access to building, collection or gallery:
Prior appointment required

Access for disabled people:
Parking provided, level entry, toilet facilities

Connections with:
National Grid

NATIONAL GERBIL SOCIETY

Acronym or abbreviation: NGS

373 Lynmouth Avenue, Morden, Surrey, SM4 4RY

Tel: 020 8241 8942
Fax: 0870 1600 845
E-mail: jackie@gerbils.co.uk

Website:
http://www.gerbils.co.uk
A broad range of information relating to the society, the care of gerbils and jirds, information of general interest relating to gerbils and jirds.

Enquiries:
Enquiries to: Honorary Secretary

Founded:
1970

Organisation type and purpose:
National organisation, membership association (membership is by subscription), present number of members: 80, suitable for ages: all.
To promote the keeping of gerbils and jirds as exhibition animals and as pets, and to promote education about gerbils and how to keep them.

Subject coverage:
Information on the keeping and healthcare etc of all species of gerbils and jirds.

Printed publications:
Newsletter (quarterly, members only)
Yearbook (members only)

Access to staff:
Contact by letter, by telephone and by e-mail
Hours: Telephone only, Mon to Fri, 1800 to 2200

NATIONAL GOVERNORS' ASSOCIATION

Acronym or abbreviation: NGA

36 Great Charles Street, Birmingham B3 3JY

Tel: 0121 237 3780
Fax: 0121 233 1323
E-mail: governorhq@nga.org.uk

Website:
http://www.nga.org.uk
Information about National Governors' Association, its activities, conferences, members, etc. Consultation documents and responses forum.

Enquiries:
Enquiries to: Administrator

Founded:
2006

Created by the merger of:
the National Governors' Council (NGC) and the National Association of School Governors (NASG)

Organisation type and purpose:
National organisation, membership association (membership is by qualification), voluntary organisation, registered charity (charity number 1070331), suitable for ages: nursery to 18.
The national voice for school governing bodies, members are local associations of governing bodies.
Promoting the education and welfare of children and the high standards of schools through the effectiveness of governing bodies.

Subject coverage:
Matters relating to school governance.

Printed publications:
Trigger packs for new governors

Access to staff:
Contact by letter, by telephone, by fax, by e-mail and via website
Hours: Mon to Fri, 0900 to 1700

NATIONAL HAIRDRESSERS' FEDERATION

Acronym or abbreviation: NHF

continued overleaf

One Abbey Court, Fraser Road, Priory Business Park, Bedford, MK44 3WH

Tel: 0845 345 6500
Fax: 01234 838875
E-mail: enquiries@nhf.info

Enquiries:
Enquiries to: General Secretary

Founded:
1942

Organisation type and purpose:
National organisation, trade association (membership is by subscription), present number of members: 7500, service industry.
Advance, defend, promote, protect and represent the interests of hairdressing salon owners in every possible way.

Subject coverage:
Matters affecting hairdressers' employment, independent contractors in salons, management of hairdressing business.

Printed publications:
Chain Renting in Hairdressing Salons
Independent Contractor Agreements
Headline News (6 times a year)
Setting Up Your Own Salon

Access to staff:
Contact by letter, by telephone, by fax and by e-mail. Appointment necessary.
Hours: Mon to Fri, 0900 to 1700

Access to building, collection or gallery:
No access other than to staff

Affiliated to:
Coiffure Europe
   Godierserf 400 Huizen, PO Box 212, Huizen, 1270 AE Huizen, The Netherlands; tel: 00 31 35 525 9200; fax: 00 31 35 526 3786
Organisation Mondiale de la Coiffure
   1–3 Place de la Bourse, F75082, Paris, Cedex 02, France; tel: 00 33 1 42 61 59 09; fax: 00 33 1 42 61 66 83; e-mail: omcoif@wanadoo.fr

NATIONAL HAMSTER COUNCIL

Acronym or abbreviation: NHC

PO Box 4, Llandovery, SA20 0ZH

Tel: 01550 720127
E-mail: peter@towyvale.com

Website:
http://www.hamsters-uk.org
Information on hamster keeping, details of NHC affiliated clubs, details of forthcoming shows.

Enquiries:
Enquiries to: Secretary
Direct tel: 01793 764450
Direct e-mail: rosiehams@yahoo.co.uk

Founded:
1949

Organisation type and purpose:
Membership association.
Governing body of the hamster fancy in the UK. Represents the interests of all concerned with the keeping, exhibiting and/or breeding of all species of hamsters.

Subject coverage:
Hamsters.

Access to staff:
Contact by letter, by telephone, by e-mail and via website
Hours: Mon to Fri, 0900 to 1700

NATIONAL HEART FORUM

Acronym or abbreviation: NHF

Tavistock House South, Tavistock Square, London, WC1H 9LG

Tel: 020 7383 7638
Fax: 020 7387 2799

E-mail: nhf-post@heartforum.org.uk

Website:
http://www.heartforum.org.uk

Enquiries:
Enquiries to: Administrative Co-ordinator
Direct e-mail: dan.french@heartforum.org.uk
Other contacts: Deputy Chief Executive (for press, media, general)

Founded:
1989

Formerly called:
National Forum for the Prevention of Coronary Heart Disease

Organisation type and purpose:
Membership association (membership is by election or invitation), present number of members: 50 organisations, registered charity (charity number 803286).

Subject coverage:
Influencing the prevention of heart disease and associated chronic diseases

Information services:
Free weekly e-news briefing service by subscription: e-mail briefings@heartforum.org.uk

Printed publications:
Annual Review (free)
At Least Five a Day: Strategies to increase vegetable and fruit consumption (£19.99)
Looking to the Future: Making coronary heart disease an epidemic of the past (£22.50)
Physical activity: An agenda for action (£5)
Preventing coronary heart disease: The role of antioxidants, vegetables and fruit (£19.99)
Preventing coronary heart disease in primary care: The way forward (£7.95)
Social Inequalities in CHD (£19.95)
Order printed publications from: Enquire at NHF office for availability

Publications list:
Available in print

Access to staff:
Contact by letter, by telephone, by fax, by e-mail and via website. Appointment necessary.
Hours: Mon to Fri, 0900 to 1730

Access to building, collection or gallery:
Appointment required

NATIONAL HERITAGE LIBRARY

313–315 Caledonian Road, London, N1 1DR

Tel: 020 7609 9639
E-mail: marg_mcniel@o2.co.uk

Enquiries:
Enquiries to: Director

Founded:
1971

Organisation type and purpose:
Membership association (membership is by subscription), suitable for ages: all.
A vast, comprehensive educational reference collection covering every aspect of what there is to see throughout the landscape and culture of the British Isles.

Subject coverage:
Everything there is to see throughout the landscape and culture of the British Isles: every kind of arts, cultural, environmental, historical and sporting site. Every facet of past and present social history, including: education, social welfare, public buildings, commerce, transport and travel, industry both past and present, alternative technology, religions, farming, historical buildings.

Museum or gallery collection, archive, or library special collection:
Books and maps, and extensive fieldwork research and photographic recording by the Founder-Director since the 1960s including over 120,000 photographs in colour, recording a vast range of

sites, including many unique photographs of buildings important in their country's social history that have since been demolished

Non-library collection catalogue:
All or part available in-house

Library catalogue:
All or part available in-house

Printed publications:
Fieldguides covering the other countries and regions of the British Isles
Fieldguide to Wales
Fieldguide to Ireland

Access to staff:
Contact by letter. Appointment necessary.
Hours: Open by prior appointment

Access to building, collection or gallery:
Prior appointment required

Access for disabled people:
Parking provided, level entry

NATIONAL HERITAGE MEMORIAL FUND

Acronym or abbreviation: NHMF

7 Holbein Place, London, SW1W 8NR

Tel: 020 7591 6000
Fax: 020 7591 6001
E-mail: enquire@hlf.org.uk

Website:
http://www.hlf.org.uk

Enquiries:
Enquiries to: Information Officer
Direct tel: 020 7591 6042/3/5

Founded:
1980

Organisation type and purpose:
Non-departmental public body.

Printed publications:
Application pack

Publications list:
Available online and in print

Access to staff:
Contact by letter, by telephone, by fax, by e-mail and via website. Appointment necessary.
Hours: Mon to Fri, 0900 to 1730

Access to building, collection or gallery:
Prior appointment required
Hours: 0930 to 1730

Access for disabled people:
Parking provided, ramped entry, access to all public areas, toilet facilities

NATIONAL HOME IMPROVEMENT COUNCIL

Acronym or abbreviation: NHIC

Carlyle House, 235 Vauxhall Bridge Road, London, SW1V 1EJ

Tel: 020 7828 8230
Fax: 020 7828 0667
E-mail: info@nhic.org.uk

Website:
http://www.nhic.org.uk

Enquiries:
Enquiries to: Director

Founded:
1975

Organisation type and purpose:
Advisory body, trade association, research organisation, consultancy.

Subject coverage:
Condition of housing stock, market research on home improvement, attitude research to home improvement.

Library catalogue:
All or part available online

Access to staff:
Contact by letter, by telephone, by fax and by e-mail
Hours: Mon to Fri, 0900 to 1700

Established the:
NHIC Educational Trust in 1980 to further its aims

NATIONAL HOSPITAL DEVELOPMENT FOUNDATION

Formal name: The National Hospital for Neurology and Neurosurgery Development Foundation

National Hospital, PO Box 123, Queen Square, London, WC1N 3BG

Tel: 020 7829 8724
Fax: 020 7676 2068
E-mail: theresa.dauncey@uclh.nhs.uk

Enquiries:
Enquiries to: Director

Founded:
1984

Organisation type and purpose:
Registered charity (charity number 290173).

Subject coverage:
Neurology and neurosurgery.

Access to staff:
Contact by letter, by telephone, by fax, by e-mail and via website
Hours: Mon to Fri, 0900 to 1700

NATIONAL HOSPITAL FOR NEUROLOGY AND NEUROSURGERY DEVELOPMENT FOUNDATION

Acronym or abbreviation: NHDF

Box 123, Queen Square, London, WC1N 3BG

Tel: 020 7829 8724
Fax: 020 7676 2068

Website:
http://www.uclh.nhs.uk/Charities+at+UCLH/
National+Hospital+Development+Foundation
Events, contacts.

Enquiries:
Enquiries to: Chief Executive
Direct e-mail: theresa.dauncey@uclh.nhs.uk

Founded:
c. 2000

Organisation type and purpose:
Registered charity (number 290173).
The charity dedicated to raising funds for cutting edge equipment, buildings and research for The National Hospital for Neurology and Neurosurgery of UCL Hospitals which, together with the Institute of Neurology, is a world-wide leader in the research and treatment of brain disorders.

Subject coverage:
Neurological conditions, either from birth, through injury, or a slowly developing illness that occurs later in life., including multiple sclerosis (MS), brain and spinal cancer, epilepsy, Parkinson's disease, stroke, Alzheimer's disease and head injury.

Electronic and video publications:
Newsletter (2 a year)

Publications list:
Available online

Access to staff:
Contact by letter, by telephone, by fax and by e-mail

Links with:
University College London Hospitals NHS
Foundation Trust (UCLH)
250 Euston Road, London, NW1 2PG; tel: 0845 1555 000

NATIONAL HOUSEWIVES ASSOCIATION

Acronym or abbreviation: NHA

30 Tollgate, Bretton, Peterborough, Cambridgeshire, PE3 9XA

Tel: 01733 333138

Enquiries:
Enquiries to: Chairman

Founded:
1973

Organisation type and purpose:
National organisation, voluntary organisation.
Aims to put forward the voice of the housewife on matters that are of concern to them. Campaigning for Elderly Residential Homes not to be closed.

Subject coverage:
Consumer affairs.

Printed publications:
Newsletter to members
Special Reports as required

Access to staff:
Contact by letter and by telephone
Hours: Mon to Fri, 0900 to 1700

Links with:
Consumers in European Community Group (This is being taken over by NCC)
London Food Commission
Ministry of Agriculture, Fisheries and Food
National Consumer Council
Potato Marketing Board
Soil Association
Women's Farming Union

NATIONAL HOUSING FEDERATION

Acronym or abbreviation: NHF

Lion Court, 25 Procter Street, London WC1V 6NY

Tel: 020 7067 1010
Fax: 020 7067 1011

Website:
http://www.housing.org.uk

Enquiries:
Enquiries to: Communications Officer
Direct e-mail: NickF@housing.org.uk

Founded:
1935

Organisation type and purpose:
Voluntary organisation.
Central representative body for social housing providers in England.

Subject coverage:
Housing associations, research and training.

Printed publications:
Directory of Members
Training brochure
A large range of publications on social housing including:
Equality in housing: a code of practice
Maintenance and the Law: a guide for housing associations
Neighbourhood renewal funding streams 2002: at a glance guide
Race equality: a framework for review and action
Countdown to rent restructuring: seven steps to implementation
A question-and-answer guide for tenants: the future of housing association rents

Publications list:
Available online and in print

East Midlands Office:
National Housing Federation
2A High Street, Wellingborough, Northampton, NN8 4HR; tel: 01933 440191; fax: 01933 224499

North West Region:
National Housing Federation
City Point, 701 Chester Road, Stretford, Manchester, M32 0RW; tel: 0161 848 8132; fax: 0161 858 8134

South East Region:
National Housing Federation
3rd Floor, Phoenix Building, 32 West Street, Brighton, East Sussex, BN1 2RT; tel: 01273 777445; fax: 01273 721807

NATIONAL ICE SKATING ASSOCIATION OF THE UNITED KINGDOM

Acronym or abbreviation: NISA

Grains Building, High Cross Street, Hockley, Nottingham, NG1 3AX

Tel: 0115 988 8060
Fax: 0115 988 8061
E-mail: via website

Website:
http://www.iceskating.org.uk
Find a rink or club, competitions, news, events, Skate UK flagship learn-to-skate programme.

Founded:
1879

Formerly called:
National Skating Association (year of change 1990)

Organisation type and purpose:
The governing body responsible for figure skating and short track speed in the United Kingdom.
To promote, encourage and to further the growth of skating as a sport and a leisure activity.

Subject coverage:
Ice skating.

Electronic and video publications:
Bulletins

Access to staff:
Contact by letter, by telephone, by fax and via website

Affiliates:
Northern Ireland Ice Skating Association (NIISA)

NATIONAL INFORMATION FORUM

33 Highshore Road, London, SE15 5AF

Tel: 020 7708 5943

Website:
http://www.nif.org.uk

Enquiries:
Enquiries to: Director

Founded:
1981

Organisation type and purpose:
Advisory body, membership association (membership is by election or invitation), voluntary organisation, registered charity (charity number 1099335).
Encourages provision of information to disabled people and others seriously disadvantaged by lack of information.

Subject coverage:
Provision of information to disabled people and carers and others disadvantaged by lack of information, particularly asylum seekers and refugees.

Information services:
Via website

Printed publications:
Alf Morris (biography)
Order printed publications from: Postal address

continued overleaf

Electronic and video publications:
Regular e-mail news briefings
Order electronic and video publications from: Postal
address

Publications list:
Available online

Access to staff:
Contact by letter and by telephone
Hours: Mon to Fri, 0900 to 1700
Special comments: Staff cannot respond to
individual problems.

Access to building, collection or gallery:
No public access

NATIONAL INSTITUTE FOR BIOLOGICAL STANDARDS AND CONTROL

Formal name: National Institute for Biological
Standards and Control – a Centre of the Health
Protection Agency
Acronym or abbreviation: NIBSC

Blanche Lane, South Mimms, Potters Bar,
Hertfordshire, EN6 3QG

Tel: 01707 641000
Fax: 01707 646845
E-mail: library@nibsc.hpa.org.uk

Website:
http://www.nibsc.ac.uk

Enquiries:
Enquiries to: Information Services Manager
Direct e-mail: anita.brewer@nibsc.hpa.org.uk

Organisation type and purpose:
Research organisation.
National control and standardisation laboratory
for biologicals used in medicine; operates as one of
eight European control authorities for testing of
biologicals.

Subject coverage:
Standardisation and control of antisera, bacterial
and viral vaccines, blood products, enzymes and
hormones, AIDS, biochemistry, chemistry,
haematology, endocrinology, microbiology,
immunobiology, virology, electronmicroscopy.

**Museum or gallery collection, archive, or library
special collection:**
Publications on biological standards

Library catalogue:
All or part available online

Printed publications:
Annual Report
Catalogue of Biological Standards and Reference
   Materials
Corporate Plan
Processing Biological Reference Materials

Access to staff:
Appointment necessary.
Hours: Mon to Fri, 0900 to 1700

Funded by:
Department of Health

NATIONAL INSTITUTE FOR CAREERS EDUCATION AND COUNSELLING

Acronym or abbreviation: NICEC

Sheraton House, Castle Park, Cambridge, CB3 0AX

Tel: 01223 460277
Fax: 01223 311708
E-mail: nicec@crac.org.uk

Website:
http://www.crac.org.uk/nicec

Enquiries:
Enquiries to: Chair

Founded:
1975

Organisation type and purpose:
Registered charity (charity number 313164),
consultancy, research organisation.
Careers.
To develop theory, enhance practice and inform
policy in the field of careers.

Subject coverage:
Theory, policy and practice in careers guidance and
career development.

**Museum or gallery collection, archive, or library
special collection:**
CRAC/NICEC library is now held at the Library,
University of London Institute of Education, 20
Bedford Way, London WC1H 0AL and at the
Library, University of Derby, Kedleston Road,
Derby DE22 1GB

Library catalogue:
All or part available online

Printed publications:
NICEC Journal (3 times a year, subscription £27,
   international £40)
NICEC Project Reports
CRAC/NICEC Conference Briefings (free with sae)
NICEC Briefings (free with sae)
NICEC Research Reports Consult online catalogue

Publications list:
Available online and in print

Access to staff:
Contact by letter, by telephone, by fax and by e-
mail
Hours: Mon to Fri, 0900 to 1700

Access to building, collection or gallery:
Prior appointment required

Sponsored by:
Careers Research and Advisory Centre (CRAC)

NATIONAL INSTITUTE FOR MEDICAL RESEARCH

Formal name: MRC National Institute for Medical
Research
Acronym or abbreviation: NIMR

The Ridgeway, Mill Hill, London, NW7 1AA

Tel: 020 8816 2228
Fax: 020 8816 2230
E-mail: library@nimr.mrc.ac.uk

Website:
http://www.nimr.mrc.ac.uk
Summaries of research activities of each division,
publications, library services, essays on biomedical
topics.

Enquiries:
Enquiries to: Librarian

Founded:
1913

Organisation type and purpose:
Research organisation.
Research Council Institute.
To undertake a broad spectrum of basic medical
research.

Subject coverage:
Molecular biology, biochemistry, parasitology,
virology, neuroscience, embryology, immunology,
cell biology, developmental biology, basic
biomedical sciences, structural biology,
bioinformatics.

**Museum or gallery collection, archive, or library
special collection:**
NIMR Archives
MRC Publications

Library catalogue:
All or part available online

Printed publications:
Influenza Bibliography
Mill Hill Essays
Research Opportunities

Access to staff:
Contact by letter, by telephone and by e-mail.
Appointment necessary. Access for members only.
Letter of introduction required.
Hours: Mon to Fri, 0900 to 1700

Access to building, collection or gallery:
Prior appointment required
Special comments: Intending visitors should write,
requesting permission from the Institute Director.

Constituent part of:
Medical Research Council (MRC)
   20 Park Crescent, London; tel: 020 7636 5422; fax:
   020 7436 6179

NATIONAL INSTITUTE OF ADULT CONTINUING EDUCATION (ENGLAND AND WALES)

Acronym or abbreviation: NIACE

21 De Montfort Street, Leicester, LE1 7GE

Tel: 0116 204 4200
Fax: 0116 285 4514

Website:
http://www.niace.org.uk
Information on National Institute of Adult
Continuing Education publications and
conferences, etc.

Organisation type and purpose:
National organisation, voluntary organisation,
registered charity (charity number 2603322),
suitable for ages: 19+, consultancy.

Subject coverage:
Adult and continuing education, community
education, education for the disadvantaged, the
unemployed and the elderly.

Publications list:
Available online and in print

Access to staff:
Contact by letter, by telephone, by e-mail and via
website
Hours: Mon to Fri, 0900 to 1700

Access to building, collection or gallery:
Prior appointment required
Hours: Mon to Fri, 0900 to 1700

Access for disabled people:
Level entry, toilet facilities

Also at:
NIACE Dysgu Cymru (Welsh Office)
   35 Cathedral Road, Cardiff, CF11 9HB; tel: 029
   2037 0900; fax: 029 2037 0909; e-mail: enquiries@
   niacedc.org.uk

Associated body:
Basic Skills Agency

NATIONAL INSTITUTE OF APPLIED POLAROLOGY RESEARCH

Acronym or abbreviation: NIAPR

6 Beechvale, Hillview Road, Woking, Surrey, GU22
7NS

Enquiries:
Enquiries to: Director of Research

Founded:
1938

Organisation type and purpose:
Advisory body, research organisation.

Subject coverage:
Applied research in polarology; research into
polarological-analytical methodologies for
detecting savantism within the dormant 85% of
brain tissue; application research for detecting
savantism within large groups of individuals in
employment, education, hospitals, prisons,
sporting and entertainment arenas and by census;
research into polarogenesis methodology for
creating and developing savantism by mental

polarisational-operational research, and by neural and cardiac stimulation from polar-physiotherapy; polar-psychology research to encourage incipient generation of brilliant ideas, inventions, talents and knowledge.

Printed publications:
Reprints of research papers, following journal publication

Access to staff:
Contact by letter
Hours: Mon to Fri, 0900 to 1700

Links with:
British Polarographic Research Institute
Institute of Pure Polarology Research
National Centres for Polarological and Polarographic Operational Research
Polarographic Society
UK Polarosciences Research Establishment
Departments of Pure and Applied Polarology

Parent body:
British Polarological Research Society (BPRS)
6 Beechvale, Hillview Road, Woking, Surrey, GU22 7NS

NATIONAL INSTITUTE OF CARPET AND FLOORLAYERS

Acronym or abbreviation: NICF

4C St Mary's Place, The Lace Market, Nottingham, NG1 1PH

Tel: 0115 958 3077
Fax: 0115 941 2238
E-mail: info@nicfltd.org.uk

Website:
http://www.nicfltd.org.uk

Founded:
1979

Organisation type and purpose:
Trade association.

Subject coverage:
Carpets of all types, carpet fitting, resilient floorcoverings, wood, laminate.

Museum or gallery collection, archive, or library special collection:
Carpet manufacturers, their products and types

Access to staff:
Contact by letter, by telephone, by fax, by e-mail and via website
Hours: Mon to Fri, 0900 to 1700

NATIONAL INSTITUTE OF CONDUCTIVE EDUCATION

Acronym or abbreviation: NICE

Cannon Hill House, 14 Russell Road, Moseley, Birmingham, B13 8RD

Tel: 0121 449 1569
Fax: 0121 449 1611
E-mail: foundation@conductive-education.org.uk

Website:
http://www.conductive-education.org.uk

Enquiries:
Enquiries to: HR Officer
Direct e-mail: mskerrett@conductive-education.org.uk

Founded:
1986

Organisation type and purpose:
Membership association (membership is by subscription), registered charity (charity number 295873).

Subject coverage:
Conductive education, Hungary, special educational needs, Parkinson's disease, cerebral palsy, stroke, head injury, disability issues.

Museum or gallery collection, archive, or library special collection:
Conductive education – all aspects and all media

Non-library collection catalogue:
All or part available in-house

Printed publications:
Recent Advances in Conductive Education (journal, 2 times a year)
The Conductor (magazine, quarterly)
Adult Conductive Education (Brown M and Mikula Toth A, pub Stanley Thornes Publishing, £18.50 plus £1.28 (p&p))
A Different Outlook (Read J, £5 plus £1.25 p&p)
Conductive Education 1987–1992: the transitional years (Read J, £6.95 plus £1.10 p&p)
Dina: A Mother Practises Conductive Education (English Edition, Akos K and M, £11.95 plus £1.10 p&p)
Last year in Jerusalem (Sutton A, £5 plus £1.25 p&p)
Memoirs of the Beginning of Conductive Pedagogy and András Peto (Forrai J, £10.95 plus £1.39 p&p)
Maria Hari on Conductive Pedagogy (Maguire, G. and Sutton, A. £10 plus £1.00 p&p)
Looking Back and Looking Forwards (Maguire, G. and Nanton, R. £10 plus £1.00 p&p)
Order printed publications from: Librarian

Publications list:
Available online and in print

Access to staff:
Contact by letter, by telephone, by fax, by e-mail, in person and via website. Appointment necessary. Non-members charged.
Hours: Mon to Fri, 0900 to 1700

Access to building, collection or gallery:
Hours: Mon to fri, 0900 to 1600 during term time only

Access for disabled people:
Parking provided, level entry, access to all public areas, toilet facilities

NATIONAL INSTITUTE OF ECONOMIC AND SOCIAL RESEARCH

Acronym or abbreviation: NIESR

2 Dean Trench Street, Smith Square, London, SW1P 3HE

Tel: 020 7222 7665
Fax: 020 7654 1900
E-mail: library@niesr.ac.uk

Website:
http://www.niesr.ac.uk
Staff and publications information, latest quarterly review overview, discussion papers in full text.

Enquiries:
Enquiries to: Librarian
Direct tel: 020 7654 1907
Other contacts: Communications Officer (for press/publication enquiries)

Founded:
1938

Organisation type and purpose:
Research organisation.

Subject coverage:
Economic conditions in the United Kingdom and the world; economic forecasting; education and training; employment.

Information services:
For NIESR research staff only.

Museum or gallery collection, archive, or library special collection:
Runs of international and foreign statistics difficult to find elsewhere

Library catalogue:
All or part available in-house

Printed publications:
Annual Report
National Institute Economic Review (quarterly)

Publications list:
Available online

Access to staff:
Contact by e-mail. Appointment necessary. Letter of introduction required.
Hours: Mon to Fri, 0930 to 1730

NATIONAL INSTITUTE OF MEDICAL HERBALISTS LIMITED

Acronym or abbreviation: NIMH

Elm House, 54 Mary Arches Street, Exeter, Devon, EX4 3BA

Tel: 01392 426022
Fax: 01392 498963
E-mail: info@nimh.org.uk

Website:
http://www.nimh.org.uk

Enquiries:
Enquiries to: Information Officer

Founded:
1864

Organisation type and purpose:
Professional body, training organisation, research organisation.

Subject coverage:
Herbs, use of herbs in treatment of disease, how medical herbalists work, training in medical herbalism, pharmacology of plant medicines.

Printed publications:
Herbal Medicine: for a naturally healthy life (leaflet)
Register of Practitioners (annually, send sae with stamps to the value of 250g Large Letter)

Access to staff:
Contact by letter, by telephone, by fax and by e-mail
Hours: Mon, Fri, 1000 to 1600; Tue, Wed, Thu, 0930 to 1530

NATIONAL INSULATION ASSOCIATION LIMITED

Acronym or abbreviation: NIA

2 Vimy Court, Vimy Road, Leighton Buzzard, Beds, LU7 1FG

Tel: 08451 636363
Fax: 01525 854918
E-mail: info@nationalinsulationassociation.org.uk

Website:
http://www.nationalinsulationassociation.org.uk/

Enquiries:
Enquiries to: Press Officer (Evolution PR Ltd)
Direct e-mail: nia@evolution-pr.co.uk

Founded:
1975

Organisation type and purpose:
Trade association (membership is by subscription), present number of members: 130.

Subject coverage:
Cavity wall insulation; loft insulation; draught proofing; insulated thermal linings

Trade and statistical information:
United Kingdom injected cavity wall insulation market.

Printed publications:
Advisory literature (free)
Register of members

Access to staff:
Contact by letter, by telephone, by fax, by e-mail and via website
Hours: Mon to Fri, 0900 to 1700

NATIONAL JOINT COUNCIL FOR THE MOTOR VEHICLE RETAIL AND REPAIR INDUSTRY

Acronym or abbreviation: NJCMVR&RI

201 Great Portland Street, London, W1W 5AB

Tel: 01788 538309
Fax: 01788 538335

Enquiries:
Enquiries to: Secretary
Direct tel: 01892 664353
Direct e-mail: coryton@supanet.com
Other contacts: Joint Secretary representing the trade unions interests.

Founded:
1943

Organisation type and purpose:
Membership association (membership is by qualification), service industry.
Negotiating and dispute resolving body.

Subject coverage:
Terms and conditions of employment in the industry.

Printed publications:
NJC Handbook
NJC Resolution
Order printed publications from: Business Stationery, Retail Motor Industry Federation
Unit C, Brewery Industrial Estate, Wenlock Road, London, N1 7TA, tel: 020 7307 3429, fax: 020 7490 4197

Access to staff:
Contact by letter, by telephone and by fax
Hours: Mon to Fri, 0900 to 1700

NATIONAL KIDNEY FEDERATION

Acronym or abbreviation: NKF

The Point, Coach Road, Shireoaks, Worksop, Nottinghamshire, S81 8BW

Tel: 01909 544999
Fax: 01909 481723
E-mail: nkf@kidney.org.uk

Website:
http://www.kidney.org.uk

Enquiries:
Enquiries to: Chairman
Other contacts: Chief Executive

Founded:
1978

Organisation type and purpose:
National organisation, membership association (membership is by subscription), present number of members: 25,000, voluntary organisation, registered charity (charity number 278616).

Subject coverage:
Care of persons suffering from kidney failure – medical, social and psychological aspects, treatment options, availability of renal services, issues in transplantation, representation of patients' interests to government.

Library catalogue:
All or part available online, in-house and in print

Printed publications:
Adult Polycystic Kidney Disease
Anaemia in Kidney Failure
Introduction to Haemodialysis
Introduction to Peritoneal Dialysis
Newsletter (quarterly)
Role of the National Kidney Federation
Sexual Relationships in Kidney Failure
Skin Care in Renal Transplant Patients
There are now in excess of 200 leaflets available

Publications list:
Available online and in print

Access to staff:
Contact by letter, by telephone, by fax, by e-mail, in person and via website

Hours: Mon to Fri, 0900 to 1700

Access for disabled people:
Hours: Mon to Fri, 0900 to 1700

Affiliated to:
CEAPIR
European Kidney Federation (CEAPIR)

NATIONAL LANDLORDS' ASSOCIATION

Acronym or abbreviation: NLA

22–26 Albert Embankment, London, SE1 7TS

Tel: 020 7840 8900
Fax: 0871 247 7535
E-mail: mail@landlords.org.uk

Website:
http://www.landlords.org.uk
Information for the landlord of residential property.

Enquiries:
Enquiries to: Head of External Relations
Direct tel: 020 7840 8904
Direct e-mail: simon.gordon@landlords.org.uk

Founded:
1973

Formerly called:
Small Landlords Association (year of change 2004)

Organisation type and purpose:
Trade association (membership is by subscription), voluntary organisation.
To protect and promote the interests of the individual private landlord of residential property.

Subject coverage:
Landlord and tenant matters, residential property, the Housing Acts and 1977 Rent Act.

Printed publications:
Journal
The UK Landlord
Various information sheets for members

Access to staff:
Contact by letter, by telephone, by e-mail and via website. Access for members only. All charged.
Hours: Mon to Fri, 0900 to 1700

NATIONAL LIBRARY OF SCOTLAND

Acronym or abbreviation: NLS

George IV Bridge, Edinburgh, EH1 1EW

Tel: 0131 623 3700
Fax: 0131 623 3701
E-mail: enquiries@nls.uk

Website:
http://www.nls.uk
http://www.nls.ac.uk/catalogues/index.html
Library catalogue and other online resources.

Enquiries:
Enquiries to: Head of Access and Enquiries
Other contacts: Director of Collections and Research (for access to manuscript, rare book, music and map collections)

Founded:
1682

Organisation type and purpose:
Non-departmental public body.
British legal deposit library since 1710.
To acquire, preserve and make available the printed, manuscript and digital record of Scotland's culture.

Subject coverage:
The national reference collection in Scotland of printed material in English and for the humanities; all European and Western languages. The foreign scientific periodicals of the Royal Society of Edinburgh were recently taken over to complement British scientific periodicals received by legal deposit. Extensive coverage of printed materials of Scottish relevance. Manuscript collection relates mainly to Scottish history and literature and activities of Scots, at home and abroad.
Map collection: extensive collection of current and recent atlases and maps of all areas; large historical collection, especially maps of Scotland.
Music collection: classical music of all periods, historical Scottish collection, popular music received by legal deposit.
Scottish Screen Archive.

Information services:
Enquire of Head of Information Systems

Special visitor services:
Enquire of Head of Access and Enquiries

Education services:
Enquire of Head of External Relations

Services for disabled people:
Enquire of Head of Access and Enquiries

Museum or gallery collection, archive, or library special collection:
Astorga Collection (Hispanic)
Balfour Collection (Handel)
Birkbeck Collection (printing and typography)
Blaikie Collection (Jacobite movement)
Blair Collection (Scottish Gaelic and Celtic)
Blairs Collection (theology)
British Architectural Library of unpublished manuscripts in microform
Bute Collection (English plays)
Campbell of Islay (Scottish Gaelic and Celtic)
Christie's Pictorial Archive in microform
Combe Collection (phrenology)
Cowan Collection (theology)
Crawford Collection (German theses and programmata)
Early Scottish Book Collections (Rosebery, Lauriston Castle, Ferguson)
Dieterichs Collection (early German theses and programmata)
Dowden Collection (theology)
Early English Newspapers in microform
Ferguson Collection (early Scottish books)
Glen Collection (Scottish music)
Graham Brown Collection (Alps and mountaineering)
Gray Collection (theology)
Haxton Collection (theology)
Hew Morison Collection (Scottish Gaelic and Celtic)
Hopkinson Collections (Berlioz and Verdi)
Incunabula Collection
Ingli's Collection (Scottish music)
John Murray Archive (manuscript archive of John Murray publishing house)
Jolly Collection (theology)
Labour History Collection
Lauriston Castle Collection (early Scottish books)
Lloyd Collection (Alps and mountaineering)
Lyle Collection (ships and shipping)
Macadam Collection (baking and confectionery)
McCurdy Collection (Leonardo da Vinci)
McDonald Collection (colour slides of town planning)
Maclure Collection (French Revolution)
Maitland Thomson (English plays)
Marischal Collection (Scottish maps)
Murdoch Henderson Collection (Scottish music)
Newman Collection (road-books)
Ossian Collection
Protestant Institute Collection (theology)
Rosebery Collection (early Scottish books)
Scottish Screen Archive
Tait Collection (civil engineering)
Thomason Tracts Collection in microform
Thorkelin Collection (Scandinavian and Icelandic)
Townley Collection (7,500 postcards on early 20th-century topography and railways)
Warden Collection (Arctic and Antarctic exploration)

Non-library collection catalogue:
All or part available online and in print

Library catalogue:
All or part available online

Printed publications:
Annual Report
Catalogue of Manuscripts vols 1–8
Catalogues of exhibitions

Microform publications:
Catalogue of Manuscripts vol. 1 on microfiche

Publications list:
Available online

Access to staff:
Contact by letter, by fax, by e-mail, in person and via website
Hours: Main Reading Room: Mon, Tue, Thu, Fri, 0930 to 2030; Wed, 1000 to 2030; Sat, 0930 to 1300
Map Reading Room: Mon, Tue, Thu, Fri, 0930 to 1700; Wed, 1000 to 1700; Sat, 0930 to 1300

Also at:
Map Reading Room
   33 Salisbury Place, Edinburgh, EH9 1SL; tel: 0131 226 4531
Scottish Screen Archive
   39–41Montrose Avenue, Hillington Park, Glasgow G52 4LA; tel: 0845 366 4600; e-mail: ssaenquiries@nls.uk; website: http://ssa.nls.uk

NATIONAL LIBRARY OF WALES

Llyfrgell Genedlaethol Cymru, Aberystwyth, Ceredigion, SY23 3BU

Tel: 01970 632800
Fax: 01970 615709
E-mail: holi@llgc.org.uk

Website:
http://www.llgc.org.uk
Extensive details of services and collections, virtual exhibitions and some access to databases.

Enquiries:
Enquiries to: Librarian
Direct tel: 01970 632805
Direct fax: 01970 632886
Direct e-mail: mdn@llgc.org.uk

Founded:
1907

Organisation type and purpose:
National government body.
Entitled to privileges under the Copyright Acts.

Subject coverage:
General reference material, specialising in printed, manuscript and graphic material relating to Wales and other Celtic countries.

Museum or gallery collection, archive, or library special collection:
Archives of Welsh Churches
Arthuriana
Bourdillon Collection of medieval French romance
Court of Great Sessions records
Egyptology Collection
Estate records
Geoff Charles Photographic Collection
Gregynog and other private presses
H I Bell Collection on papyrology
Howell Lloyd Davies Collection of dictionaries and grammars
Papers of eminent Welsh scholars and literary figures
Political papers of Lloyd George, Clement Davies, Desmond Donnelly, James Griffiths, etc
Pre-1858 Welsh ecclesiastical probate records
Sidney Hartland Collection of ethnology and folklore
Sir John Williams Collection
Thomas Stanford Collections of incunabula including Euclid
Tithe maps relating to Wales

Printed publications:
A Bibliography of Wales
Handlist of Manuscripts in the National Library of Wales
National Library of Wales Journal
Order printed publications from: Marketing Department, The National Library of Wales

at the same address, tel: 01970 632858, fax: 01970 615709

Publications list:
Available online and in print

Access to staff:
Contact by letter, by telephone, by fax, by e-mail and in person
Hours: Mon to Fri, 0930 to 1800; Sat, 0930 to 1700
Special comments: Closed Bank holidays. Closed first full week in Oct.

NATIONAL LIFE STORIES

Acronym or abbreviation: NLS

British Library, 96 Euston Road, London, NW1 2DB

Tel: 020 7412 7404
Fax: 020 7412 7441
E-mail: nls@bl.uk

Website:
http://www.bl.uk/oralhistory
Information about oral history collections at the British Library.
http://www.bl.uk/nls
Information about National Life Stories projects.
http://www.cadensa.bl.uk
Catalogue of all Sound Archive collections, including oral history and National Life Stories collections.

Enquiries:
Enquiries to: Archive Assistant
Other contacts: Oral History Curator

Founded:
1987

Organisation type and purpose:
Registered charity (charity number 327571), research organisation.
Collecting and archiving oral histories.

Subject coverage:
Oral history.

Museum or gallery collection, archive, or library special collection:
C409 City Lives
C410 Living Memory of the Jewish Community
C466 Artists' Lives
C467 Architects' Lives
C468 Fawcett Collection
C532 Lives in Steel
C736 Legal Lives
C821 Food: From Source to Salespoint
C872 Book Trade Lives
C960 Crafts Lives
C963 Lives in the Oil Industry
C1007 An Oral History of the Post Office
C1015 Oral History of Wolff Olins
C1029 Down to Earth: An Oral History of British Horticulture
C1173 Oral History of British Theatre Design
C1276 Authors' Lives
C1316 The Legacy of the English Stage Company
C1364 An Oral History of the Water Industry
C1367 An Oral History of Barings
C1379 An Oral History of British Science

Non-library collection catalogue:
All or part available online

Library catalogue:
All or part available online

Printed publications:
City Lives (C. Courtney and P. Thompson, Methuen)
Voices of the Holocaust Education Pack (booklet and tapes)
The British Book Trade: An Oral History (Sue Bradley, BL publications)
Order printed publications from: British Library bookshop; tel. 020 7412 7735

Electronic and video publications:
Lives in Steel (CD-ROM and tape)
Connecting Lines: Artists Talk About Drawing (audio CD and online).

Access to staff:
Contact by letter, by telephone, by fax and by e-mail. Appointment necessary.
Hours: Mon to Fri, 0900 to 1700

Access for disabled people:
Ramped entry, access to all public areas, toilet facilities
Special comments: Parking spaces for disabled people are in Midland Road.

NATIONAL LITERACY TRUST

Acronym or abbreviation: NLT

68 South Lambeth Road, London, SW8 1RL

Tel: 020 7587 1842
Fax: 020 7587 1411
E-mail: contact@literacytrust.org.uk

Website:
http://www.literacytrust.org.uk

Founded:
1993

Organisation type and purpose:
Voluntary organisation, registered charity.
Raise literacy standards and encourage more reading and writing for pleasure.

Subject coverage:
Literacy news and initiatives; policy summaries and responses; research summaries

Printed publications:
Support materials for professionals
Order printed publications from: via website

Electronic and video publications:
Research papers and policy responses (online)

Publications list:
Available online

Access to staff:
Contact by letter, by telephone, by fax, by e-mail and via website
Hours: Mon to Fri, 0900 to 1700

Constituent bodies:
Reading Champions
   website: http://www.readingchampions.org.uk
Reading Connects
   website: http://www.readingconnects.org.uk
Reading is Fundamental, UK
   website: http://www.rif.org.uk
Reading the Game
   website: http://www.readingthegame.org.uk
Talk To Your Baby
   website: http://www.talktoyourbaby.org.uk

NATIONAL LOTTERY COMMISSION

Acronym or abbreviation: NLC

101 Wigmore Street, London, W1U 1QU

Tel: 020 7016 3400
Fax: 020 7016 3401
E-mail: publicaffairs@natlotcomm.gov.uk

Website:
http://www.natlotcomm.gov.uk

Enquiries:
Enquiries to: Communications Officer
Direct e-mail: c.wotherspoon@natlotcomm.gov.uk

Founded:
1999

Formerly called:
Oflot (year of change 1999)

Organisation type and purpose:
National government body.
Non-departmental public body (NDPB).
Regulator of the National Lottery.

Subject coverage:
The National Lottery, regulation, gambling.

continued overleaf

Trade and statistical information:
Quarterly Lottery sales data, and quarterly returns to good causes.

Printed publications:
Annual Report, operator performance reports
Order printed publications from: e-mail: publicaffairs@natlotcomm.gov.uk

Electronic and video publications:
Research into under-16s' lottery play, internet use and gambling behaviours
Research into women's gambling behaviours, and randomness of draw-based games
Order electronic and video publications from: website: http://www.natlotcomm.gov.uk; publicaffairs@natlotcomm.gov.uk

Access to staff:
Contact by letter, by telephone, by fax, by e-mail, in person and via website. Appointment necessary.
Hours: Mon to Fri, 0900 to 1700

Access for disabled people:
Access to all public areas, toilet facilities

Parent body:
DCMS
2–4 Cockspur Street, London, SW1Y 5DH; tel: 020 7211 6200; fax: 020 7211 6201; e-mail: enquiries@culture.gov.uk; website: http://www.culture.gov.uk

NATIONAL MARKET TRADERS' FEDERATION

Acronym or abbreviation: NMTF

Hampton House, Hawshaw Lane, Hoyland, Barnsley, South Yorkshire, S74 0HA

Tel: 01226 749021
Fax: 01226 740329
E-mail: enquiries@nmtf.co.uk

Website:
http://www.nmtf.co.uk

Enquiries:
Enquiries to: Chief Executive Officer

Founded:
1899

Organisation type and purpose:
National organisation, trade association (membership is by subscription), present number of members: 34,000.

Subject coverage:
Retail markets in the UK; market law.

Museum or gallery collection, archive, or library special collection:
Documents of the Royal Commission on Market Rights and Tolls (1891)

Printed publications:
Federation Newsletter (Fed News) (6 times a year, members)

Access to staff:
Contact by letter, by telephone, by fax, by e-mail and via website
Hours: Mon to Fri, 0900 to 1700

Access to building, collection or gallery:
Hours: Mon to Fri, 0900 to 1700

Access for disabled people:
Parking provided, ramped entry, toilet facilities
Hours: Mon to Fri, 0900 to 1700

Affiliated to:
Retail Markets Alliance (RMA)
World Union of Wholesale Markets (WUWM)

NATIONAL MEDIATION CENTRE

Acronym or abbreviation: NMC

23 St James Gardens, Swansea, West Glamorgan, SA1 6DY

Tel: 01792 469626
Fax: 01792 650642
E-mail: mediation@dispute.co.uk

Enquiries:
Enquiries to: Chief Executive

Founded:
1995

Organisation type and purpose:
International organisation, national organisation, professional body, service industry, training organisation.
Provider of mediation service.

Subject coverage:
Dispute resolution, mediation.

Access to staff:
Contact by letter, by telephone, by fax and by e-mail
Hours: Mon to Fri, 0900 to 1700

NATIONAL MEMORIAL ARBORETUM

Croxall Road, Alrewas, Burton-on-Trent, Staffordshire, DE13 7AR

Tel: 01283 792333
Fax: 01283 792034
E-mail: info@thenma.org.uk

Website:
http://www.thenma.org.uk

Founded:
2001

Organisation type and purpose:
National organisation, registered charity (charity number 1043992).

Subject coverage:
Tree planting, tree collections, Armed Service contacts, educational visits, conference and events facilities.

Special visitor services:
Group visits welcomed by prior arrangement.

Education services:
School visits welcomed by prior arrangement.

Museum or gallery collection, archive, or library special collection:
FEPOW Memorial Building

Printed publications:
Guidebook, map, walks leaflets, case studies book
Order printed publications from: tel: 01283 792333

Access to staff:
Contact by letter, by telephone, by fax, by e-mail, in person and via website. Appointment necessary.
Hours: Daily, 0900 to 1700

Access to building, collection or gallery:
Hours: Daily, 0900 to 1700; closed Christmas Day

Access for disabled people:
Parking provided, level entry, toilet facilities

Constituent part of:
The Royal British Legion
48 Pall Mall, London, SW1Y 5JY; tel: 020 7973 7207

NATIONAL METEOROLOGICAL LIBRARY AND ARCHIVE

Acronym or abbreviation: Met Office Library

Fitzroy Road, Exeter, EX1 3PB

Tel: 01392 884841
Fax: 01392 885681
E-mail: metlib@metoffice.gov.uk

Website:
http://www.metoffice.com/corporate/library/index.html

Enquiries:
Enquiries to: Information Officer
Direct tel: 01392 360987 (Archive Manager)
Other contacts: Archive Manager

Founded:
1870

Organisation type and purpose:
National government body, learned society, public library. Specialist meteorological records and publications.
To provide public access to official meteorological records and the comprehensive meteorological library.

Subject coverage:
Meteorology, climatology and most aspects of atmospheric and related sciences; original weather reports; summaries and published books, articles and pamphlets; approximately 3m. items, from 16th century to date.

Museum or gallery collection, archive, or library special collection:
Library and archive collections of the Meteorological Office; books, documents and photographs
Original weather records archived under the terms of Public Records Act
Rare and historical books and pamphlets on meteorology and climatology held in conjunction with the Royal Meteorological Society

Non-library collection catalogue:
All or part available online

Library catalogue:
All or part available online and in-house

Microform publications:
Microfiche available to read

Publications list:
Available online

Access to staff:
Contact by letter, by telephone, by fax and by e-mail. Appointment necessary.

Access to building, collection or gallery:
Hours: Mon to Fri, 0830 to 1630 (archive, 1000 to 1800); closed bank holidays

Access for disabled people:
Ramped entry, toilet facilities

Constituent part of:
Met Office, Ministry of Defence
tel: 0870 900 0100; e-mail: enquiries@metoffice.gov.uk; website: http://www.metoffice.gov.uk

NATIONAL MUSEUM OF SCIENCE AND INDUSTRY

Constituent bodies:
National Museum of Photography, Film and Television
National Railway Museum
Science Museum
Science Museum Library

NATIONAL MUSEUM WALES

Acronym or abbreviation: NMGC/NMGW

Library, Cathays Park, Cardiff, CF10 3NP

Tel: 029 2057 3202
E-mail: library@museumwales.ac.uk

Website:
http://www.nmgw.ac.uk
Website for the museum as a whole.

Enquiries:
Enquiries to: Librarian

Founded:
1907

Organisation type and purpose:
National government body, museum, art gallery. Established by royal charter.

Subject coverage:
Archaeology; art; botany; geology; industrial archaeology; zoology; museum science; architecture; private press; in particular, the special interests of Wales in those subjects.

Museum or gallery collection, archive, or library special collection:
Library of the Cambrian Archaeological
Association
Library of the Cardiff Naturalists Society
Tomlin Collection (conchology)
Vaynor Collection (astronomy, travels)
Willoughby Gardner Collection (early books on
natural history)

Non-library collection catalogue:
All or part available online, in-house and in print

Library catalogue:
All or part available in-house

Printed publications:
What's On (quarterly listing of events)
Annual Report
Publications on Museum collections and related
topics

Publications list:
Available in print

Access to staff:
Contact by letter, by telephone, by e-mail and via
website. Appointment necessary.
Hours: Tue to Fri, 1000 to 1700

Access for disabled people:
Parking provided, ramped entry, toilet facilities

Funded by:
National Assembly for Wales

Parent body:
National Museum Wales

NATIONAL MUSEUMS AND GALLERIES OF WALES

Constituent parts:
Big Pit National Mining Museum of Wales
Blaenafon, Torfaen, NP4 9XP; tel: 01495 790311;
fax: 01495 792618; e-mail: bigpit@nmgw.ac.uk
Museum of the Welsh Woollen Industry
Museum of Welsh Life
St Fagans, Cardiff, CF5 6XB; tel: 029 2057 3500;
fax: 029 2057 3490
National Museum & Gallery Cardiff
Cathays Park, Cardiff, CF1 3NP; tel: 029 2039
7951; fax: 029 2037 3219
Roman Legionary Museum
High Street, Caerleon, NP6 1AE; tel: 01633
423134; fax: 01633 422869
Segontium Roman Museum
Beddgelert Road, Caernarfon, Gwynedd, LL55
2LN; tel: 01286 675625; fax: 01286 678416
Turner House Gallery
Plymouth Road, Penarth, South Glamorgan,
CF64 3DM; tel: 029 2070 8870
Welsh Industrial and Maritime Museum
Welsh Slate Museum
Gilfach Ddu, Llanberis, Gwynedd, LL55 4TY; tel:
01286 870630; fax: 01286 871906

NATIONAL MUSEUMS OF SCOTLAND

Acronym or abbreviation: NMS

Chambers Street, Edinburgh, EH1 1JF

Tel: 0131 247 4137 (library enquiries); 0131 247 4219
(museum enquiries)
Fax: 0131 247 4819 (general); 0131 247 4311 (
library)
E-mail: info@nms.ac.uk

Website:
http://www.nms.ac.uk
General site for the National Museums of Scotland,
including details of current exhibitions, collections
and departments of the constituent museums.
Includes details of the library collections, services
and access arrangements.

Enquiries:
Enquiries to: Librarian
Direct tel: 0131 247 4042
Direct fax: 0131 220 4819

Other contacts: Librarian (for specific enquiries); PR
& Marketing Assistant

Organisation type and purpose:
Registered charity (charity number SC 011130),
museum.
Non-departmental public body – NDPB.

Subject coverage:
Decorative arts; archaeology; ethnography; history,
especially Scottish; geology; zoology; history of
science and technology; museology and museum
conservation; military history, especially of the
Scottish regiments.
The Museum of Scotland tells for the first time the
history of Scotland – its land, its people, and their
achievements – through the incomparable national
collections. The collections include that started by
the Society of Antiquaries in 1781 and continued in
the former Museum of Antiquities.

Information services:
Library available for reference (for conditions see
Access above), online searching, CD-ROM based
services, bibliography compilation, selective
dissemination services.

Special visitor services:
Guided tours.

Education services:
Group education facilities, resources for Key
Stages 1 and 2, 3, 4 and further or higher
education.

Services for disabled people:
For the visually impaired; for the hearing
impaired.

Museum or gallery collection, archive, or library special collection:
J A Harvie-Brown manuscripts, library and reprint
collections (natural history)
Society of Antiquaries of Scotland manuscripts and
archives
The Duke of Cumberland's Papers (microfilm)
W S Bruce manuscripts (natural history)
William Jardine manuscripts (natural history)
Book stock: 80,000 on arts, 30,000 on science, 800
current periodicals

Non-library collection catalogue:
All or part available in-house

Library catalogue:
All or part available in-house

Printed publications:
Guides to permanent and temporary exhibitions
Highlight (leaflet, free)
National Museums of Scotland Annual Reports
Publications list available on website: http://
shop.nms.ac.uk/categories/Books/Museum-
books
Order printed publications from: NMS Publishing,
Royal Museum, Chambers Street, Edinburgh, EH1
1JF; tel: 0131 247 4026; fax: 0131 247 4012; e-mail:
publishing@nms.ac.uk

Electronic and video publications:
Investigating the Lewis Chess Pieces (CD-ROM)

Publications list:
Available online and in print

Access to staff:
Contact by letter, by telephone, by fax, by e-mail
and via website. Appointment necessary.
Hours: Royal Museum Library: Mon to Fri, 1000 to
1300 and 1400 to 1700
National War Museum of Scotland Library: Tue,
1000 to 1230, or by appointment

Access for disabled people:
Access to all public areas, toilet facilities
Special comments: Level entry at the Museum of
Scotland.

Also at:
National War Museum of Scotland
Edinburgh Castle
Museum of Scotland
Chambers Street

Branch museums:
Museum of Flight
East Fortune Airfield, East Lothian; tel: 01620
880308; fax: 01620 880355; e-mail: info@nms.ac
.uk
Museum of Scottish Country Life
Wester Kittochside, East Kilbride, G76 9HR; tel:
01355 224181; fax: 01355 571290; e-mail: info@
nms.ac.uk
National War Museum of Scotland
Edinburgh Castle, Edinburgh, EH1 2NG; tel:
0131 225 7534; fax: 0131 225 3848; e-mail:
library@nms.ac.uk
Royal Museum & Museum of Scotland
Chambers Street, Edinburgh, EH1 1JF; tel: 0131
247 4219/4422; fax: 0131 220 4819; e-mail: info@
nms.ac.uk or library@nms.ac.uk
Shambellie House
New Abbey, Dumfriesshire; tel: 01387 850375;
fax: 01387 850461; e-mail: info@nms.ac.uk

The library also includes the collection of the former:
Museum of Antiquities Library

NATIONAL MUSIC AND DISABILITY INFORMATION SERVICE

Acronym or abbreviation: NMDIS

7 Tavern Street, Stowmarket, Suffolk, IP14 1PJ

Tel: 01449 673990
Fax: 01449 673994
E-mail: info@soundsense.org

Website:
http://www.soundsense.org

Enquiries:
Enquiries to: NMDIS Officer

Founded:
1978

Organisation type and purpose:
Advisory body, membership association,
registered charity (charity number 1080918).
To provide information and advice on music and
disability.

Subject coverage:
Music and disability and anything connected with
these areas. Information covers music for any
purpose, in education, therapy, performance,
recreation, leisure, rehabilitation, palliative care
etc.

Museum or gallery collection, archive, or library special collection:
Resource centre holds textbooks, journals, articles,
music, videos and cassettes on music and
disability

Printed publications:
A range of titles in the following categories:
Careers information
Music and disability
All about community music
SoundSense events and conference reports
SoundSense response and evidence papers
One-handed Scores
Funding
Music on the Internet (and where to find it) (1998,
£17.95)
Music for Nursery and Young Children (1993,
£3.60)

Publications list:
Available online and in print

Access to staff:
Contact by letter, by telephone, by fax, by e-mail
and via website
Hours: Mon to Fri, 0900 to 1700

Access to building, collection or gallery:
Prior appointment required

Access for disabled people:
Parking provided
Special comments: Please advise and we will do
utmost to provide access.

NATIONAL MUSIC COUNCIL

Acronym or abbreviation: NMC

60–62 Clapham Road, London, SW9 0JJ

Tel: 0870 909 2621
Fax: 0870 706 5329
E-mail: info@nationalmusiccouncil.org.uk

Website:
http://www.nationalmusiccouncil.org.uk

Enquiries:
Enquiries to: Administrator

Founded:
1953

Organisation type and purpose:
Membership association (membership is by
subscription), present number of members: 33,
registered charity (charity number 239178).
National forum.

Subject coverage:
Music; the encouragement of development of all
British musical activities. Issues facing those
working in music in the United Kingdom.

Printed publications:
A Sound Performance – the economic value of
music to the United Kingdom (out of print)

Electronic and video publications:
Annual Report 2006–07 (online)
Counting the Notes – the economic value of music
to the United Kingdom (online)
Sounding out the Future – post education and
training in the UK music industry (online)

Publications list:
Available online

Access to staff:
Contact by letter, by telephone, by fax and by e-
mail. Appointment necessary.
Hours: Mon to Fri, 0900 to 1700

NATIONAL NEIGHBOURHOOD WATCH ASSOCIATION

Acronym or abbreviation: NNWA

Schomberg House, 80–82 Pall Mall, London, SW1Y
5HF

Tel: 020 7772 3348
Fax: 020 7662 3513
E-mail: info@neighbourhoodwatch.net

Website:
http://www.neighbourhoodwatch.net

Enquiries:
Enquiries to: Director General
Direct e-mail: john.howell@dia.pipex.com

Founded:
1982

Organisation type and purpose:
Registered charity (charity number 1049584).

Subject coverage:
Establishment and best practice of Neighbourhood
Watch, community safety and crime prevention in
relation to Neighbourhood Watch activities.

Printed publications:
Annual Review
Factsheets on particular topics
Information pack
National Directory of Neighbourhood Watch
contacts (police only)
National Neighbourhood Watch Association
Newspaper (NNWA News)

Publications list:
Available online

Access to staff:
Contact by letter, by telephone, by fax, by e-mail
and via website. Appointment necessary. Letter of
introduction required.
Hours: Mon to Fri, 0900 to 1700

Access to building, collection or gallery:
Prior appointment required

Access for disabled people:
Level entry

NATIONAL NEWPIN

Sutherland House, 35 Sutherland Square,
Walworth, London, SE17 3EE

Tel: 020 7358 5900
Fax: 020 7701 2660
E-mail: nationalnewpin@talk21.com

Website:
http://www.newpin.org.uk

Enquiries:
Enquiries to: Information Officer

Founded:
1982

Organisation type and purpose:
International organisation, voluntary organisation,
registered charity (charity number 1022931).
To help parents with children under 6.

Subject coverage:
Helps parents under stress break the cyclical effect
of destructive family behaviour. Through a
network of local centres, expectant mothers,
parents, carers and children are offered a unique
opportunity to achieve positive changes in their
lives and relationships based on respect, support,
equality and empathy. The work focuses on
alleviating maternal depression and other mental
distress.

Access to staff:
Contact by letter, by telephone, by fax, by e-mail,
in person and via website. Appointment necessary.
Hours: Mon to Fri, 0900 to 1700

Centres at:
Chesterfield NEWPIN
10 & 11 The Villas, Walton Hospital,
Chesterfield, Derbyshire, S40 3HN; tel: 01246
552867; fax: 01246 558747
Deptford NEWPIN
Deptford Mission, 1 Creek Road, Deptford,
London, SE8 3BT; tel: 020 8694 6052; e-mail:
centre@deptfordnewpin.freeserve.co.uk
Feltham NEWPIN
Hunter House, Highfields Road, Highfields
Estate, Feltham, Middlesex, TW13 4DL; tel: 020
8893 1716; fax: 020 8893 1377
Foyle NEWPIN
18–19 Jasmine Court, Waterside, Derry, BT47
2DZ; tel: 0150 434 4477; fax: 0150 434 4477; e-
mail: foyle.newpin@virgin.net
Greenwich and Lewisham NEWPIN
1–4 Bissextile House, Bliss Crescent, Lewisham,
London, SE13 7RH; tel: 020 8694 0201; fax: 020
8694 0201
Hoxton NEWPIN
St John's Centre, 85 Pitfield Street, London, N1
6NP; tel: 020 7739 9196; e-mail: centre@
hoxtonnewpin.freeserve.co.uk
Newham NEWPIN
Mayflower Centre, Vincent Street, Canning
Town, London, E16 1LZ; tel: 020 7473 6688; fax:
020 7473 6688
NEWPIN
10–12 Rathmullan Drive, Rathcoole,
Newtonabbey, BT37 9NF; tel: 028 9086 6622; fax:
028 9086 6722; e-mail: centre@rathcodenewpin
.freeserve.co.uk
NEWPIN
160 Wincobank Avenue, Sheffield, S5 6BB; tel:
0114 256 1533
St Paul's NEWPIN
St Paul's Centre, Rossmore Road, London, NW1
6NJ; tel: 020 7724 6765
Sutton NEWPIN
204 Thornton Road, St Helier Estate, Carshalton,
Surrey, SM5 1NF; tel: 020 8646 8604
Tower Hamlets NEWPIN
Bancroft Green, Hadleigh Close, London, E1
4LH; tel: 020 7423 9656

Walworth NEWPIN
35 Sutherland Square, London, SE17 3EE; tel: 020
7703 5271
Wandsworth NEWPIN
Patmore Centre, Patmore Street, London, SW8
4JD; tel: 020 7622 2750; fax: 020 7622 7338

NATIONAL NUCLEAR LABORATORY

Acronym or abbreviation: NNL

Information Retrieval Service (IRS), B709,
Springfields Works, Salwick, Preston, Lancashire,
PR4 0XJ

Tel: 01772 764884
Fax: 01772 762385
E-mail: louise.collins@nnl.co.uk

Enquiries:
Enquiries to: Information Officer

Formerly called:
AEA Technology, Northern Research Laboratories,
NSTS, Nexia Solutions

Organisation type and purpose:
Research organisation.
Government.

Subject coverage:
Nuclear fuel technology; industrial research.

Library catalogue:
All or part available online and in-house

Publications list:
Available in print

Access to staff:
Contact by letter, by telephone and by e-mail
Hours: Mon to Fri, 0900 to 1700

NATIONAL OCEANOGRAPHIC LIBRARY

Acronym or abbreviation: NOCS

National Oceanography Centre, University of
Southampton – Waterfront Campus, European
Way, Southampton, SO14 3ZH

Tel: 023 8059 6111
Fax: 023 8059 6115
E-mail: nol@noc.soton.ac.uk

Website:
http://www.soton.ac.uk/library/about/nol

Enquiries:
Enquiries to: Head of Information Services
Direct e-mail: mias@noc.soton.ac.uk

Founded:
1995

Organisation type and purpose:
University department or institute, consultancy,
research organisation.

Subject coverage:
Ocean and earth sciences: marine chemistry,
biology, geology, geophysics and physics, ocean
engineering, associated ocean instrumentation for
deep oceans and shallow seas, air-sea interaction,
waves, currents, sea levels, coastal oceanography,
water mass dynamics,
seabed topography, sediment mobility, deep ocean,
biological organisms etc., terrestrial geology,
palaeontology

**Museum or gallery collection, archive, or library
special collection:**
Discovery Collection, British Marine Science
Archives

Non-library collection catalogue:
All or part available online

Library catalogue:
All or part available online

Printed publications:
Annual Report
Reports Series

Electronic and video publications:
Marine, Freshwater and Oceanographic Resources
(CD-ROM/Internet)

Publications list:
Available online and in print

Access to staff:
Contact by letter, by telephone, by fax, by e-mail
and via website. Appointment necessary. Non-
members charged.
Hours: Mon to Fri, 0900 to 1700

Access to building, collection or gallery:
Prior appointment required

Access for disabled people:
Access to all public areas

Parent bodies (joint):
Natural Environment Research Council; and
University of Southampton

NATIONAL OFFICE ANIMAL HEALTH (NOAH)

Acronym or abbreviation: NOAH

3 Crossfield Chambers, Gladbeck Way, Enfield,
Middlesex, EN2 7HF

Tel: 020 8367 3131
Fax: 020 8363 1155
E-mail: noah@noah.co.uk

Website:
http://www.noah.co.uk
http://www.noahcompendium.co.uk
http://www.pethealthinfo.org.uk

Enquiries:
Enquiries to: Communications Manager

Founded:
1986

Organisation type and purpose:
National organisation, trade association
(membership is by subscription).
NOAH represents the UK animal medicine
industry: its aim is to promote the benefits of safe,
effective, quality medicines for the health and
welfare of all animals.

Subject coverage:
Animal medicines and issues relating to the animal
medicine industry. The production of healthy food
from healthy animals and the role of animal
medicines (including antibiotics, vaccines,
antiparasite products). Medicines for companion
animals. How animal medicines are approved, and
their use controlled. The Code of Practice for the
Promotion of Animal Medicines.

Trade and statistical information:
Summary data on the animal medicine market in
the UK (ex-manufacturers' prices).

Printed publications:
NOAH Compendium of Data Sheets for Animal
Medicines (published annually)
Animal Medicine Record Book (in conjunction
with Animal Health Distributors' Association)
Poisoning in Veterinary Practice

Electronic and video publications:
Pet Health Information (at: http://
www.pethealthinfo.org.uk)
Online version of the NOAH Compendium of Data
Sheets for Animal Medicines (at: http://
www.noahcompendium.co.uk)
NOAH News (electronic newsletter for NOAH
members only)

Publications list:
Available online and in print

Access to staff:
Contact by letter, by fax, by e-mail and via
website
Hours: Mon to Fri, 0900 to 1700
Special comments: Electronic contact preferred.

Access to building, collection or gallery:
No access other than to staff

Associated body of:
Pet Health Council (PHC)
website: http://www.pethealthcouncil.co.uk

Member organisation of:
Animal Medicines Training Regulatory Authority
(AMTRA)
website: http://www.amtra.org.uk
Farming and Countryside Education (FACE)
website: http://www.face-online.org.uk
IFAH – Europe
website: http://www.ifaheurope.org
IFAH (International Federation for Animal Health)
website: http://www.ifahsec.org
Pet Advisory Committee (PAC)
website: http://www.petadvisory.org.uk
Responsible Use of Medicines in Agriculture
Alliance (RUMA)
website: http://www.ruma.org.uk

Trustee of:
National Pet Month
website: http://www.nationalpetmonth.org.uk

NATIONAL OPERATIC AND DRAMATIC ASSOCIATION

Acronym or abbreviation: NODA

58–60 Lincoln Road, Peterborough, PE1 2RZ

Tel: 0870 770 2480
Fax: 0870 770 2490
E-mail: info@noda.org.uk

Website:
http://www.noda.org.uk

Enquiries:
Enquiries to: Chief Executive

Founded:
1899

Organisation type and purpose:
Membership association (membership is by
subscription), present number of members: 2500
societies, 3000 individuals, registered charity
(charity number 254640).
Servicing amateur theatre societies.

Subject coverage:
Pantomime agency; sales of sheet music; rehearsal
material for plays; musicals, operettas, operas and
pantomimes at discounts to members; insurance
for amateur theatre, help and advice.

**Museum or gallery collection, archive, or library
special collection:**
Collection of vocal scores (some first editions)
Rehearsal material at discounts to members
Sheet music

Printed publications:
Area bulletins
NODA National News (quarterly)
NODA Pantomimes and reference books

Publications list:
Available online

Access to staff:
Contact by letter, by telephone, by fax, by e-mail
and via website. Appointment necessary.
Hours: Mon to Fri, 0900 to 1700
Special comments: Non-members by special
arrangement.

Access to building, collection or gallery:
Prior appointment required

NATIONAL ORGANISATION OF ASIAN BUSINESSES

Acronym or abbreviation: NOAB

East End House, Kenrick Way, West Bromwich,
West Midlands, B71 4EA

Tel: 0121 553 1999
Fax: 0121 525 6565
E-mail: tonydeep@eastendfoods.co.uk

Enquiries:
Enquiries to: Manager

Founded:
1993

Organisation type and purpose:
Voluntary organisation.

Subject coverage:
Representation of the interests of Asian businesses
at a national level.

Access to staff:
Contact by letter, by telephone, by fax and by e-
mail
Hours: Mon to Fri, 0900 to 1700

Access for disabled people:
Parking provided, ramped entry, toilet facilities

NATIONAL OSTEOPOROSIS SOCIETY

Camerton, Bath, BA2 0PJ

Tel: 01761 471771 (Switchboard); 0845 450 0230
(Helpline)
Fax: 01761 471104
E-mail: info@nos.org.uk

Website:
http://www.nos.org.uk

Enquiries:
Enquiries to: Information Centre

Founded:
1986

Organisation type and purpose:
Membership association (membership is by
subscription), voluntary organisation, registered
charity (charity number 1102712 in England and
Wales and SC 039755 in Scotland).

Subject coverage:
Information on treatment and prevention of
osteoporosis for the general public and the medical
professions, hormone replacement therapy (HRT),
the menopause.

Information services:
Information Centre

Education services:
Education Officer

Printed publications:
Series of booklets and information sheets
Order printed publications from: Information Centre

Publications list:
Available online and in print

Access to staff:
Contact by letter, by telephone, by fax, by e-mail,
in person and via website. Appointment necessary.
Hours: Mon to Fri, 0900 to 1600; Helpline: Mon to
Fri, 0900 to 1700

Access to building, collection or gallery:
Prior appointment required

Access for disabled people:
Parking provided, level entry, toilet facilities

Affiliated to:
Association of Medical Research Charities
European Foundation for Osteoporosis
Long-term Medical Conditions Alliance
National Council of Women of Great Britain

NATIONAL OUTDOOR EVENTS ASSOCIATION

Acronym or abbreviation: NOEA

PO Box 4495, Wells, BA5 9AS

Tel: 01749 674 531
E-mail: secretary@noea.org.uk

Website:
http://www.noea.org.uk
General information.

Enquiries:
Enquiries to: General Secretary

continued overleaf

Founded:
1979

Organisation type and purpose:
Trade association.

Subject coverage:
General and technical information on the world of outdoor events for clients and suppliers, basic standards and codes of practice, hazards and risk assessment, statutory requirements.

Printed publications:
NOEA Code of practice for outdoor events (£20, revised addendum, £5)
NOEA Yearbook

Publications list:
Available in print

Access to staff:
Contact by letter, by telephone and by e-mail
Hours: Mon to Fri, 0900 to 1700

Access to building, collection or gallery:
No access other than to staff

Access for disabled people:
Level entry

NATIONAL PARK HOMES COUNCIL

Acronym or abbreviation: NPHC

Catherine House, Victoria Road, Aldershot, Hampshire, GU11 1SS

Tel: 01252 336092
Fax: 01252 322596
E-mail: info@nationalcaravan.co.uk

Website:
http://www.theparkhome.net
List of members, products and services provided.

Enquiries:
Enquiries to: Director General

Founded:
1983

Organisation type and purpose:
Membership association (membership is by subscription), present number of members: 150. Representative body for residential park homes industry, manufacturers, park operators and specialist products and services suppliers.

Subject coverage:
Centre of information on all aspects of the park homes industry.
Gold Shield Ten Year Warranty Scheme.
Quality Award Scheme.

Publications list:
Available in print

Access to staff:
Contact by letter, by telephone, by fax, by e-mail and via website
Hours: Mon to Fri, 0900 to 1700

NATIONAL PEST TECHNICIANS ASSOCIATION

Acronym or abbreviation: NPTA

NPTA House, Hall Lane, Kinoulton, Nottingham, NG12 3EF

Tel: 01949 81133
Fax: 01949 823905
E-mail: officenpta@aol.com

Website:
http://www.npta.org.uk

Enquiries:
Enquiries to: Administrator

Founded:
1993

Organisation type and purpose:
Professional body.

Subject coverage:
Pest control.

Printed publications:
Today's Technician (quarterly, free to members)

Publications list:
Available online and in print

Access to staff:
Contact by letter, by telephone, by fax, by e-mail and via website. Appointment necessary.
Hours: Mon to Fri, 0900 to 1700

NATIONAL PHARMACY ASSOCIATION

Acronym or abbreviation: NPA

Mallinson House, 38–42 St Peter's Street, St Albans, Hertfordshire, AL1 3NP

Tel: 01727 832161
Fax: 01727 840858
E-mail: npa@npa.co.uk

Website:
http://www.npa.co.uk

Enquiries:
Enquiries to: Information Operations Manager
Direct tel: 01727 858687 (ext. 3207)
Direct fax: 01727 795902
Direct e-mail: s.garner@npa.co.uk

Founded:
1921

Organisation type and purpose:
Trade association.

Subject coverage:
Community pharmacy; prescription and other medicines.

Museum or gallery collection, archive, or library special collection:
Foreign pharmacopoeias

Printed publications:
Annual Report
Information leaflets
In Touch magazine (monthly)

Access to staff:
Contact by letter, by telephone, by fax and by e-mail. Access for members only. Non-members charged.
Hours: Mon to Fri, 0900 to 1800; Sat, 0900 to 1300

NATIONAL PHILATELIC SOCIETY

Acronym or abbreviation: NPS

c/o The British Postal Museum & Archive, Freeling House, Phoenix Place, London WC1X 0DL

Tel: 020 7239 2571
E-mail: nps@ukphilately.org.uk/nps

Website:
http://ukphilately.org.uk

Enquiries:
Enquiries to: General Secretary
Direct e-mail: nps@ukphilately.org.uk

Founded:
1899

Organisation type and purpose:
International organisation, membership association (membership is by subscription), present number of members: 4,700, philatelic library, suitable for ages: 14+, publishing house. Non-profit-making society.

Subject coverage:
Philately, postal history, stamp collecting and related hobby material.

Museum or gallery collection, archive, or library special collection:
Collection of forged stamps
Library of philatelic and postal history works, philatelic journals
Reference collection of philatelic archive material

Library catalogue:
All or part available online and in-house

Printed publications:
Stamp Lover (6 times a year, £2 per issue)

Access to staff:
Contact by letter and by telephone
Hours: Tue, Wed, Thu, 1100 to 1615; and 2nd Sat in each month

Access to building, collection or gallery:
No prior appointment required
Hours: Tue, Wed, Thu, 1100 to 1615; and 2nd Sat in each month

NATIONAL PHYSICAL LABORATORY

Acronym or abbreviation: NPL

Queens Road, Teddington, Middlesex, TW11 0LW

Tel: 020 8977 3222
Fax: 020 8943 6458
E-mail: enquiry@npl.co.uk

Website:
http://www.npl.co.uk
About NPL, measurement advice, units of measurement, news and events, services, getting together, scientific centres, vacancies.

Enquiries:
Enquiries to: National Physical Laboratory Helpline
Direct tel: 020 8943 6880
Direct e-mail: susan.evans@npl.co.uk

Founded:
1900

Organisation type and purpose:
National organisation, consultancy, research organisation.
UK national standards laboratory.
Development of highly accurate measurement techniques and their application for industry and government.

Subject coverage:
National and international standards, physics and engineering, including electrical and optical standards and standards of radioactivity and measurement of ionizing radiations, physical acoustics and noise, application of computers and information technology, engineering materials, environmental metrology, measurement and calibration, research and development, knowledge transfer.

Printed publications:
Annual Review
Points of Contact (information on the work of NPL's specialist teams with their contact details, also details of clubs and training services)
Specialist books and booklets (HMSO)
Technical reports and memoranda

Access to staff:
Contact by letter, by telephone, by fax, by e-mail and via website
Hours: Mon to Fri, 0900 to 1700

Operated on behalf of the:
Department of Trade and Industry by NPL Management Limited
a wholly owned subsidiary of Serco Group plc

NATIONAL PIERS SOCIETY

Acronym or abbreviation: NPS

4 Tyrrell Road, South Benfleet, Essex, SS7 5DH

Tel: 01268 757291
Fax: 020 7483 1902
E-mail: pjredditch@msn.com

Website:
http://www.piers.co.uk

Enquiries:
Enquiries to: Honorary Secretary
Other contacts: Chairman

Founded:
1976

Organisation type and purpose:
Learned society (membership is by subscription), voluntary organisation, research organisation.

Subject coverage:
Piers: construction, history, uses, development, architecture, maintenance, grant-aid, assessment and surveying, construction materials, design, engineering, shipping associations, attractions (eg theatres); pier tramways and railways.

Museum or gallery collection, archive, or library special collection:
Copies of most books covering piers, their construction and history; various documents, information files, photographs, drawings and souvenirs

Printed publications:
Piers (journal, quarterly to members)
Reports (irregularly)
Order printed publications from: Piers Information Bureau
3 Withburn Close, Upton, Wirral, L49 6QH, tel: 0151 606 0595

Publications list:
Available in print

Access to staff:
Contact by letter, by telephone, by fax and by e-mail
Hours: Mon to Fri, 0900 to 1700

Links with:
British Association of Leisure Parks, Piers and Attractions
Paddle Steamer Preservation Society

NATIONAL PIGEON ASSOCIATION

Acronym or abbreviation: NPA

Bridge Villa, Main Street, Pollington, Goole, East Yorkshire, DN14 0DW

Tel: 01405 869516
Fax: 01405 869516
E-mail: tracey@edwardspm.fsnet.co.uk

Website:
http://www.zyworld.com/NPA/index.htm
Secretary, activities, costs, dovecote package, found pigeons, breed clubs, championship shows.

Enquiries:
Enquiries to: Secretary

Organisation type and purpose:
Membership association (membership is by subscription), present number of members: 856, voluntary organisation.
For breeding and exhibition of fancy pigeons.

Subject coverage:
Feeding, rearing, management and exhibition of fancy pigeons in general, with advice on sources of further information. Contacts supplied for specialist breed clubs.

Printed publications:
Dovecote Designs and Package (price on request)
Feathered World (magazine, Winckley Publishing, Preston for poultry and fancy pigeons)
Instruction booklet for beginners
Send stamp with request

Electronic and video publications:
An Introduction to Fancy Pigeons (video, £12.50, £14 inc p&p from Secretary or Feathered World)

Access to staff:
Contact by letter and by telephone
Hours: Mon to Fri, 0900 to 1700

Access to building, collection or gallery:
No access other than to staff

Rings and lost birds:
The Ring Distributor
Bridge Villa, Main Street, Pollington, Goole, DN14 0DW; tel: 01405 869516

NATIONAL POISONS INFORMATION SERVICE (CARDIFF CENTRE)

Acronym or abbreviation: NPIS

Gwenwyn Ward, Llandough Hospital, Penarth, Cardiff, CF64 2XX

Tel: 029 2071 5013
Fax: 029 2070 4357
E-mail: poison.information@cardiffandvale.wales.nhs.uk

Enquiries:
Enquiries to: Manager

Founded:
1963

Organisation type and purpose:
Welsh Office service.
Advice on poisonings by all routes, to medical personnel only.

Subject coverage:
Specialist information on all types of poisoning, clinical toxicology; pharmacology.

Publications list:
Available in print

Access to staff:
Contact by letter, by telephone, by fax and by e-mail
Hours: 24-hour service, 365 days a year
Special comments: Not a public access service.

Part of:
National Poisons Information Service

NATIONAL POISONS INFORMATION SERVICE, EDINBURGH CENTRE

Acronym or abbreviation: NPIS Edinburgh / SPIB

Scottish Poisons Information Bureau, Royal Infirmary, Edinburgh, EH16 4SA

Tel: 0131 242 1383
Fax: 0131 242 1387
E-mail: spib@luht.scot.nhs.uk

Website:
http://www.toxbase.org
http://www.show.scot.nhs.uk/spib

Enquiries:
Enquiries to: Manager
Other contacts: Information Officer

Founded:
1963

Organisation type and purpose:
Advisory body.
Poisons information for medical professionals.

Subject coverage:
Toxicology, poisons information, chemicals.

Information services:
Clinical toxicology management advice for registered NHS users

Access to staff:
Contact by letter, by telephone, by fax, by e-mail and via website
Hours: Mon to Fri, 0800 to 2000
Special comments: Medical profession only.

NATIONAL POLICE LIBRARY

Formal name: National Policing Improvement Agency
Acronym or abbreviation: NPIA

NPIA, Bramshill, Hook, Hampshire, RG27 0JW

Tel: 01256 602650
Fax: 01256 602285
E-mail: library@npia.pnn.police.uk

Website:
http://www.npia.police.uk

Enquiries:
Enquiries to: Chief Librarian
Direct tel: 01256 602227

Founded:
1948

Formerly called:
National Police Training (year of change 1993); Centrex (year of change 2007)

Organisation type and purpose:
NPIA provides and supports a range of products and services that underpins its commitment to improving policing priorities in: personal development and HR; systems and IT services; science and forensics; operational policing services; programmes for improvement and research; identification resources and databases

Subject coverage:
Police-related subjects, criminal justice, management.

Museum or gallery collection, archive, or library special collection:
Annual Report of HM Inspectors of Constabulary, 1858 to date
Police and Constabulary Almanac, 1858 to date
Police Journal, 1928 to date
Police Review, 1893 to date

Library catalogue:
All or part available online and in-house

Printed publications:
Monthly list of additions to stock (electronic format only)

Access to staff:
Contact by letter, by telephone, by fax, by e-mail, in person and via website. Appointment necessary. Letter of introduction required. Non-members charged.
Hours: Mon to Thu, 0830 to 1700; Fri, 0830 to 1600

Access for disabled people:
Restricted access

Parent body:
National Policing Improvement Agency
tel: 01256 602100

NATIONAL PONY SOCIETY

Acronym or abbreviation: NPS

Willingdon House, 102 High Street, Alton, Hampshire, GU34 1EN

Tel: 01420 88333
Fax: 01420 80599

Enquiries:
Enquiries to: Secretary

Founded:
1893

Organisation type and purpose:
Membership association.

Subject coverage:
Training for stud assistant's qualification, British Riding Pony Stud Book registration, native breeds, showing competitions, sales, welfare of ponies, training of judges.

Printed publications:
National Pony Society Review (annually)
Stud Book and Register of Riding Ponies

Representation on:
Association of British Equine Societies
British Show Pony Society
Councils of the British Horse Society
Joint Measurement Board
NASTA
National Equine Welfare Council

NATIONAL PORTAGE ASSOCIATION

Acronym or abbreviation: NPA

continued overleaf

Kings Court, 17 School Road, Hall Green,
Birmingham, B28 8JG

Tel: 0121 244 1807
Fax: 0121 244 1801
E-mail: info@portage.org.uk

Website:
http://www.portage.org.uk

Enquiries:
Enquiries to: Administrator
Direct e-mail: administrator@portage.org.uk

Founded:
1976

Organisation type and purpose:
Voluntary organisation, registered charity (charity
number 1087865), company limited by guarantee
(company number 4165317).
Educational organisation.

Subject coverage:
Support for families caring for children with
special needs by promoting and supporting
portage educational home visiting services.

Printed publications:
Code of Practice and Ethical Guidelines
NPA Leaflet
Values Statement
Leaflets are also available in Urdu, Bengali and
Punjabi
Staff Safety

Publications list:
Available online and in print

Access to staff:
Contact by letter, by telephone, by fax, by e-mail
and via website
Hours: Office hours

NATIONAL PORTRAIT GALLERY

Acronym or abbreviation: NPG

Heinz Archive and Library, St Martin's Place,
London, WC2H 0HE

Tel: 020 7321 6617
Fax: 020 7306 0056
E-mail: arc@npg.org.uk

Website:
http://www.npg.org.uk

Enquiries:
Enquiries to: Head of Archive and Library
Direct tel: 020 7321 6617
Direct fax: 020 7306 0056
Direct e-mail: archiveenquiry@npg.org.uk

Founded:
1856

Organisation type and purpose:
National body, history and art gallery, suitable for
all ages. Heinz Archive and library.
Founded in 1856 to collect portraits of men and
women who have made and are continuing to
make a significant contribution to the history and
culture of Britain. Portraits from the collection are
on display in locations around the country.

Subject coverage:
British portraits and portrait artists, 1400s to
present day.

Information services:
Library available for reference by appointment Tue
to Fri, 1000 to 1700; consultation service Wed 1400
to 1700.

**Museum or gallery collection, archive, or library
special collection:**
Unparalleled collection of British portraiture,
comprising primary collection of portraits in all
media and reference collections of portrait
photographs and prints and drawings
Collection of approximately 600,000 reproductions
and illustrations of portraits held in public and
private collections worldwide, arranged in
separate 'sitter' and 'artist' files; extensive index
to portraits reproduced or cited in publications

Collection of artists' sitter books, account books,
correspondence and papers, and research papers
relating to portrait artists
Institutional records of the Gallery, including
acquisition, conservation, exhibition and
administrative records

Non-library collection catalogue:
All or part available online, in-house and in print

Library catalogue:
All or part available online and in-house

Printed publications:
Annual reports (1858 to present)
Catalogue of Seventeenth-Century Portraits (CUP,
1963)
Complete Illustrated Catalogue (2004)
Early Georgian Portraits (HMSO, 1977)
Early Victorian Portraits (HMSO, 1974)
Later Stuart Portraits (HMSO, 2009)
Mid-Georgian Portraits (2004)
National Portrait Gallery: an architectural history
(2000)
National Portrait Gallery: an illustrated guide
(revised edn, 2000)
National Portrait Gallery Collection (1988)
Regency Portraits (1985)
Tudor and Jacobean Portraits (HMSO, 1969;
National Portrait Gallery, 1997)
Various: exhibitions catalogues
Various: thematic monographs

Microform publications:
Scharf notebooks

Publications list:
Available online and in print

Access to staff:
Contact by letter, by telephone and by e-mail.
Appointment necessary.

Access to building, collection or gallery:
Access to Heinz Archive and Library by
appointment only.
Hours: Reference: Tue to Fri, 1000 to 1700;
consultation service: Wed, 1400 to 1700
Special comments: Access to Heinz Archive and
Library by appointment only.

Access for disabled people:
Ramped entry, toilet facilities

Also at:
Beningbrough Hall
Beningbrough, York, North Yorkshire, YO30
1DD; tel: 01904 472027; website: http://www
.nationaltrust.org.uk/main/w
-beningbroughhallandgardens
Bodelwyddan Castle
Bodelwyddan, Rhyl, Denbighshire, LL18 5YA;
tel: 01745 584060; fax: 01745 584563; website:
http://www.bodelwyddan-castle.co.uk
Gawthorpe Hall
Padiham, nr Burnley, Lancashire, BB12 8UA; tel:
01282 771004; website: http://www.nationaltrust
.org.uk/main/w-gawthorpehall
Montacute House
Montacute, Somerset, TA15 6XP; tel: 01935
823289; website: http://www.nationaltrust.org
.uk/main/w-vh/w-visits/w-findaplace/w
-montacute

NATIONAL REGISTER OF PERSONAL TRAINERS

Acronym or abbreviation: NRPT

16 Borough High Street, London, SE1 9QG

Tel: 0870 200 6010
Fax: 020 7407 9225
E-mail: info@nrpt.co.uk

Website:
http://www.nrpt.co.uk
Details on trainers, training companies and why a
personal trainer could be good for you.

Enquiries:
Enquiries to: Managing Director
Direct tel: 020 7407 9223
Direct e-mail: will@nrpt.co.uk

Founded:
1992

Organisation type and purpose:
National organisation, membership association
(membership is by subscription), service industry.

Subject coverage:
Personal fitness trainers across the UK, information
about personal training and personal training
companies.

Access to staff:
Contact by letter, by telephone and by fax. All
charged.
Hours: Mon to Fri, 0900 to 1700

Access to building, collection or gallery:
Prior appointment required

NATIONAL REGISTER OF WARRANTED BUILDERS

Acronym or abbreviation: NRWB

4 Brooklands Avenue, Cambridge, CB2 2BB

Tel: 01223 508407
Fax: 01223 300848
E-mail: registrar@fmb.org.uk

Website:
http://www.fmb.org.uk

Enquiries:
Enquiries to: Registrar

Founded:
1980

Organisation type and purpose:
Trade association (membership is by subscription,
qualification), present number of members: 3000.

Access to staff:
Contact by letter and by e-mail
Hours: Mon to Fri, 0900 to 1700

Links to:
Federation of Master Builders (FMB)
14–15 Great James Street, London, WC1N 3DP

NATIONAL RIFLE ASSOCIATION/ NATIONAL SHOOTING CENTRE LIMITED

Acronym or abbreviation: NRA

Bisley Camp, Brookwood, Woking, Surrey, GU24
0PB

Tel: 01483 797777
Fax: 01483 797285
E-mail: info@nra.org.uk

Website:
http://www.nra.org.uk

Enquiries:
Enquiries to: Chief Executive
Direct tel: ext 126
Direct e-mail: elaine.buttle@nra.org.uk
Other contacts: Membership Secretary for
membership enquiries.

Founded:
1860

Organisation type and purpose:
International organisation, membership
association (membership is by subscription),
present number of members: 5500, registered
charity, suitable for ages: all.
Governing body of full-bore rifle and pistol
shooting in the UK. Central body for affiliated
schools and 1000 shooting clubs and associations.

Subject coverage:
Full-bore rifle and pistol shooting, marksmanship,
rules and regulations in competition shooting,
construction of new ranges.

**Museum or gallery collection, archive, or library
special collection:**
Archives since the Association's foundation in 1860
Museum of historic fire arms and memorabilia

Printed publications:
NRA Journal (quarterly)
NRA Rifle and Pistol Coaching Notes
NRA Rules of Full-bore Shooting (annually)

Access to staff:
Contact by letter, by telephone, by fax and by e-mail
Hours: Mon to Fri, 0900 to 1700

Member of:
British Shooting Sports Council
Great Britain Target Shooting Federation

NATIONAL RIVERS AUTHORITY

Acronym or abbreviation: NRA

Regional Offices:
Anglian Region
  Kingfisher Home, Goldhay Way, Orton Goldhay, Peterborough, Cambridgeshire, PE2 0ZE; tel: 01733 371811; fax: 01733 231840
North West Region
  PO Box 432, Warrington, WA4 1HH
North West Region
  Richard Fairclough House, Knutsford Road, Warrington, WA4 1HG; tel: 01925 53999; fax: 01925 415961
North West Region
  Road Three, Winsford Industrial Estate, Winsford, CW7 3SL
North West Region
  Abbotsfield Road, Reginald Road Industrial Estate, St Helens, WA9 4HU
North West Region
  Chertsey Hill, London Road, Carlisle, CA1 2QX
North West Region
  Holme Road, Bamber Hill, Preston, PR5 6BP
Northumbria & Yorkshire Region
  Eldon House, Regent Centre, Gosforth, Newcastle upon Tyne, NE3 3UB; tel: 0191 213 0266 or 284 5069
Northumbria & Yorkshire Region
  21 Park Square South, Leeds, LS1 2QG; tel: 0113 244 0191; fax: 0113 246 1889
Severn Trent Region
  Sapphire East, 550 Streetsbrook Road, Solihull, Birmingham, B91 9QT; tel: 0121 711 2324; fax: 0121 711 5824
Severn Trent Region
  PO Box 299, Shrewsbury, Shropshire, SY3 8WD
Severn Trent Region, Upper Severn Area
  Hafren House, Welshpool Road, Shelton, Shrewsbury, Shropshire, SY3 8BB
South Western Region
  Manley House, Kestrel Way, Exeter, EX2 7LQ; tel: 01392 444000; fax: 01392 444238
South Western Region, Bridgewater Office
  Rivers House, East Quay, Bridgwater, Somerset, TA6 4YS; tel: 01278 457333; fax: 01278 452985
Southern Region
  Portfield Depot, Oving Road, Chichester, PO20 6AG
Southern Region
  Guildbourne House, Chatsworth Road, Worthing, West Sussex, BN11 1LD; tel: 01903 820692; fax: 01903 821832
Southern Region
  Southern Region Laboratory, 4 The Meadows, Waterberry Drive, Waterlooville, PO7 7XX
Southern Region
  20 Manners View, Newport, Isle of Wight, PO30 5FA
Southern Region
  Ladymead, Guildford, GU1 1BZ
Thames Region
  Isis House, Howbery Park, Wallingford, Oxfordshire, OX10 8BD
Thames Region
  3rd Floor, Kings Meadow House, Kings Meadow Road, Reading, RG1 8DG; tel: 0118 953 5000; fax: 0118 950 0388
Welsh Region
  Rivers House, St Mellons Business Park, St Mellons, Cardiff, CF3 0LT; tel: 029 2077 0088; fax: 029 2079 8555

NATIONAL ROLLER HOCKEY ASSOCIATION OF ENGLAND LTD

Acronym or abbreviation: NRHA

82 Greenfield Road, Farnham, Surrey, GU9 8TQ

Tel: 07702 503383
Fax: 01252 723635
E-mail: gail-whattingham@tinyonline.co.uk

Website:
http://www.nrha.co.uk

Enquiries:
Enquiries to: Public Relations Manager
Other contacts: General Secretary; Archive Historian

Founded:
1912

Organisation type and purpose:
Statutory body, membership association, present number of members: 1,500.
Governing body of the sport.

Subject coverage:
Club addresses, organisation of taster courses; help with development and coaching, courses on coaching for all coaches and referees to international standard.

Non-library collection catalogue:
All or part available in print

Printed publications:
ABC of Roller Hockey
Basic Roller Hockey
Coaching manuals
Roller Hockey (newsletter, quarterly)
Roller Hockey Goalkeeping
The Early Years of English Roller Hockey 1884–1914 (R. Pout)

Electronic and video publications:
Videos

Access to staff:
Contact by letter, by telephone, by fax, by e-mail and via website
Hours: Mon to Fri, 0900 to 1700

Links with:
British Skater Hockey Association
European Committee of Roller Skating (CERS)
International Federation of Roller Skating (FIRS)
National Skating Association
Sport England

Member organisation of:
Central Council of Physical Recreation

NATIONAL SCHIZOPHRENIA FELLOWSHIP (SCOTLAND)

Acronym or abbreviation: NSF(S)

6 Newington Business Centre, Dalkeith Road Mews, Edinburgh, EH16 5GA

Tel: 0131 662 4359
Fax: 0131 662 2289
E-mail: info@nsfscot.org.uk

Website:
http://www.nsfscot.org.uk
Information on mental illness, such as schizophrenia, and the work of NSF(Scotland).

Enquiries:
Enquiries to: Information Officer

Founded:
1984

Organisation type and purpose:
Membership association (membership is by subscription), present number of members: 500, voluntary organisation, registered charity (charity number SCO 13649).

Subject coverage:
Mental illness, particularly schizophrenia.

Library catalogue:
All or part available in-house

Printed publications:
Particularly children's booklets, see website for details

Publications list:
Available online and in print

Access to staff:
Contact by letter, by telephone, by fax, by e-mail and in person
Hours: Mon to Fri, 0900 to 1700

Access for disabled people:
Level entry

NATIONAL SCHOOLS SEVENS

Acronym or abbreviation: NSS

PO Box 52, East Peckham, Tonbridge, Kent, TN12 5ZP

Tel: 01622 871170
Fax: 01622 873426
E-mail: ns7s@btinternet.com

Website:
http://www.armyns7.co.uk
Format, draw, accommodation list, all relevant information for forthcoming tournaments.

Enquiries:
Enquiries to: Tournament Organisers

Founded:
1939

Organisation type and purpose:
National organisation.
Rugby Union Tournament for schools.
To provide a first class Rugby Union Tournament for Schools aged 13 to 18.

Subject coverage:
Seven-a-side rugby union in schools.

Printed publications:
Tournament Programme (available from Tournament Organisers from 1st March, annually)

Access to staff:
Contact by letter, by telephone, by fax, by e-mail and via website
Hours: Sun to Sat, 0900 to 1700

Access for disabled people:
Toilet facilities

NATIONAL SCREEN AND SOUND ARCHIVE OF WALES

Acronym or abbreviation: NSSAW

The National Library of Wales, Aberystwyth, SY23 3BU

Tel: 01970 632828
Fax: 01970 632544
E-mail: agssc@llgc.org.uk

Website:
http://archif.com

Founded:
2001

Organisation type and purpose:
National archive.

Subject coverage:
Films, television programmes, videos, sound recordings and music relating to Wales and the Welsh.

Special visitor services:
Viewing and listening services.

Museum or gallery collection, archive, or library special collection:
Incorporates the collections of:
Wales Film and Television Archive
National Library of Wales' Sound and Moving Image collection

Access to building, collection or gallery:
Hours: Mon to Fri, 1000 to 1700

NATIONAL SECULAR SOCIETY

Acronym or abbreviation: NSS

25 Red Lion Square, London, WC1R 4RL

Tel: 020 7404 3126
Fax: 0870 762 8971
E-mail: enquiries@secularism.org.uk

Website:
http://www.secularism.org.uk

Enquiries:
Enquiries to: Administrator

Founded:
1866

Organisation type and purpose:
Campaigning organisation (membership is by subscription), voluntary organisation.

Subject coverage:
Secular humanism; atheism; civil liberties; rational education; freethought history.

Museum or gallery collection, archive, or library special collection:
C Bradlaugh MP – papers at Bishopsgate Library, Liverpool Street, London EC2

Library catalogue:
All or part available in-house

Printed publications:
Bulletin (3 times a year)
Annual Report
Newsline (weekly email newsletter)

Access to staff:
Contact by letter, by telephone, by e-mail and via website. Appointment necessary.
Hours: Mon to Fri, 0900 to 1700

Access to building, collection or gallery:
Prior appointment required

Affiliates of:
Abortion Rights; Amnesty International; European Humanist Federation; International Humanist and Ethical Union; Liberty; Network for Peace.
International Humanist and Ethical Union

NATIONAL SHEEP ASSOCIATION

Acronym or abbreviation: NSA

The Sheep Centre, Malvern, Worcestershire, WR13 6PH

Tel: 01684 892661
Fax: 01684 892663
E-mail: enquiries@nationalsheep.org.uk

Enquiries:
Enquiries to: Chief Executive

Founded:
1892

Organisation type and purpose:
Membership association (membership is by subscription), present number of members: 12,000, registered charity (charity number 249255).
Agricultural Organisation.
Representative body for sheep farmers.

Subject coverage:
Sheep and the UK sheep industry.

Printed publications:
British Sheep Book (every 3/4 years, breeds of sheep found in Britain including imported breeds)
Sheep Farmer (6 times a year, members only)

Access to staff:
Contact by letter. Appointment necessary.
Hours: Mon to Fri, 0900 to 1700

NATIONAL SMALL-BORE RIFLE ASSOCIATION

Acronym or abbreviation: NSRA

Lord Roberts Centre, Bisley Camp, Brookwood, Woking, Surrey, GU24 0NP

Tel: 01483 485500
Fax: 01483 476392
E-mail: info@nsra.co.uk

Website:
http://www.nsra.co.uk

Enquiries:
Enquiries to: Information Officer
Direct tel: 01483 485505
Direct e-mail: jpage@nsra.co.uk

Founded:
1901

Organisation type and purpose:
Membership association (membership is by subscription), present number of members: 15,500, voluntary organisation, registered charity (charity number 215468).
Governing body for small-bore rifle and pistol shooting, and air rifle and air pistol shooting, and match crossbow shooting.

Subject coverage:
Rifle, pistol small-bore target shooting; air rifle, air gun (.177 calibre) target shooting; match crossbow shooting; range construction, firearms legislation, sale of ammunition, guns and equipment to members.

Printed publications:
Rifleman (quarterly)
Firearm Law
Gun Law
NSRA Rules
Successful Pistol Shooting
Successful Rifle Shooting

Electronic and video publications:
Videos on shooting air rifles, pistol and small-bore rifles

Publications list:
Available in print

Access to staff:
Contact by letter, by telephone, by fax, by e-mail and in person. Access for members only.
Hours: Mon to Fri, 0900 to 1700

Access to building, collection or gallery:
No prior appointment required

Member of:
British Olympic Association
British Shooting Sports Council
Great Britain Target Shooting Federation
International Shooting Sport Federation

NATIONAL SOCIETY FOR EDUCATION IN ART AND DESIGN

Acronym or abbreviation: NSEAD

3 Mason's Wharf, Corsham, Wiltshire, SN13 9FY

Tel: 01225 810134
Fax: 01225 812730
E-mail: johnsteers@nsead.org

Website:
http://www.nsead.org
News, resources, publications, forum, H&S, ICT, professional development.

Enquiries:
Enquiries to: Office Manager
Direct e-mail: info@nsead.org

Founded:
1888

Formerly called:
Society of Art Masters, National Society for Art Education

Organisation type and purpose:
Learned society, trade union (membership is by subscription), present number of members: 2,000, publishing house.

Subject coverage:
Art and design in education across all education sectors; careers in art and design; international and national contacts in field of art and design education.

Information services:
Employment, professional development, art and design education.

Special visitor services:
Archives by appointment.

Education services:
Extensive – see http://www.nsead.org.

Trade and statistical information:
Data on art education development throughout the world via the International Society for Education in Art.

Printed publications:
A Guide to Courses and Careers in Art, Craft and Design
A range of some 80 books from Key Stage 1 to Research
Start Primary Magazine
International Journal of Art and Design Education (3 times a year)
NSEAD Newsletter (6 times a year)

Publications list:
Available online and in print

Access to staff:
Contact by letter, by telephone, by fax, by e-mail and via website. Appointment necessary.
Hours: Mon to Fri, 0900 to 1700

Access to building, collection or gallery:
Hours: Mon to Fri, 0900 to 1700

Access for disabled people:
Hours: Mon to Fri, 0900 to 1700

Member organisation of:
International Society for Education in Art

NATIONAL SOCIETY FOR EPILEPSY

Acronym or abbreviation: NSE

Chesham Lane, Chalfont St Peter, Buckinghamshire, SL9 0RJ

Tel: 01494 601300; 01494 601400 (Helpline)
Fax: 01494 871927

Website:
http://www.epilepsysociety.org.uk/forprofessionals
Professional website, collection of articles
http://www.epilepsysociety.org.uk
Copies of leaflets and fact sheets.

Enquiries:
Enquiries to: Epilepsy Information Services Administrator
Direct tel: 01494 601392
Direct fax: 01494 601337

Founded:
1892

Organisation type and purpose:
National organisation (membership is by subscription), voluntary organisation, registered charity (charity number 206186), training organisation, research organisation.
To provide long-term and respite residential care for adults with epilepsy, to research into, and provide assessment and treatment services for, adults with epilepsy, to raise public awareness and understanding, to provide information, training and other support to people with epilepsy and their carers.

Subject coverage:
Epilepsy; help for people with epilepsy, residential homes, treatment, care and rehabilitation, research, diagnosis, support and management.

Non-library collection catalogue:
All or part available online

Printed publications:
Epilepsy information card and wallet (1 copy free, thereafter 20p each)
Fact sheets and leaflets (5 copies free, thereafter 10p for each factsheet and 20p each leaflet)
Order printed publications from: Order on line or tel. for an information list

Electronic and video publications:
DVD Packs:
Administration of Rectal Diazepam: training package for professionals (£10) and an information DVD for parents/carers (£8)
Epilectic Seizures – a 35 min video/DVD explaining functions of brain and showing genuine seizures (£60)
About Epilepsy – information pack for adults with mild to moderate learning disabilities (9 booklets, £2.50)

Publications list:
Available online and in print

Access to staff:
Contact by letter and by telephone
Hours: Mon to Fri, 0900 to 1700
Special comments: Helpline open Mon to Fri, 1000 to 1600.

Access for disabled people:
Level entry, access to all public areas, toilet facilities

Affiliated to:
National Hospital of Neurology and Neurosurgery

NATIONAL SOCIETY FOR PHENYLKETONURIA

Formal name: National Society for Phenylketonuria (United Kingdom)
Acronym or abbreviation: NSPKU

PO Box 26642, London, N14 4ZF

Tel: 020 8364 3010
Fax: 0845 004 8341
E-mail: info@nspku.org

Website:
http://www.nspku.org
Information about phenylketonuria and the work of NSPKU. Online copies of many of the Society's leaflets and booklets.

Enquiries:
Enquiries to: Administrator

Founded:
1973

Organisation type and purpose:
Registered charity (charity number 273670).

Subject coverage:
Help and advice for people with PKU, their families and carers.

Printed publications:
Dietary booklets (£1.50 to £2)
Leaflets and booklets for PKUs, their families, teachers, GPs and employers (small charge)
News and Views (magazine, quarterly, £1)
Order printed publications from: Administrator, at above address

Publications list:
Available online and in print

Access to staff:
Contact by letter, by telephone and by e-mail
Hours: 24 hours

NATIONAL SOCIETY FOR RESEARCH INTO ALLERGY

Acronym or abbreviation: NSRA

2 Armadale Close, Hollycroft, Hinckley, Leicestershire, LE10 0SZ

Tel: 01455 250715
E-mail: eunicerose@talktalk.net

Website:
http://all-allergy.org

Enquiries:
Enquiries to: Honorary Secretary
Other contacts: Honorary Vice-Chairperson (tel: 01455 291294)

Founded:
1980

Organisation type and purpose:
Advisory body, membership association (membership is by subscription), voluntary organisation, registered charity (charity number 32608).
Aims to see allergy and intolerance accepted and for there to be adequate, effective and safe treatment within the NHS. To assist and impart information to GPs, hospital doctors, and members of other caring and teaching professions, as well as sufferers.

Subject coverage:
Eczema, asthma, urticaria, hyperactivity, irritable bowel syndrome, Crohn's disease, migraine, arthritis, airborne allergy, ME, post-viral syndrome, PIMS and any other allergy or sensitivity, determination of allergy, medically backed diets, substitute foods, hyperventilation, criminal behaviour, thyroid problems.

Information services:
For people suffering or needing to know more about all aspects of allergy/intolerance.

Printed publications:
Allergy and Intolerance in Babies and Small Children (£2)
Anaphylaxis information leaflet (£1)
Crime Busting (£1)
Enzyme Potentiated Desensitisation (£1)
Enzyme Potentiated Desensitisation: Rules for people having this form of treatment (£5)
Hyperactivity (booklet, £2)
Hyperventilation (booklet, £2)
Is it Something You Ate?: allergy exclusion diets that really work (£5, free to members)
List of research projects
Reaction (magazine, 3 times a year, members)
Recipe Book (£5, free to members)

Publications list:
Available in print

Access to staff:
Contact by letter, by telephone, by e-mail and in person. Appointment necessary.
Hours: Mon to Fri, 0900 to 1700

NATIONAL SOCIETY OF ALLIED AND INDEPENDENT FUNERAL DIRECTORS

Acronym or abbreviation: SAIF

SAIF Business Centre, 3 Bullfields, Sawbridgeworth, Hertfordshire, CM21 9DB

Tel: 0845 230 6777
Fax: 01279 726300
E-mail: info@saif.org.uk

Website:
http://www.saif.org.uk
Membership listing and information about the society.

Enquiries:
Enquiries to: Administration Manager
Direct e-mail: linda@saif.org.uk

Founded:
1989

Organisation type and purpose:
Trade association (membership is by subscription), present number of members: over 1,000.

Subject coverage:
All aspects of the UK funeral service.

Access to staff:
Contact by letter, by telephone, by fax and by e-mail
Hours: Mon to Fri, 0900 to 1700

NATIONAL SOCIETY OF ALLOTMENT AND LEISURE GARDENERS LIMITED

Acronym or abbreviation: NSALG

O'Dell House, Hunters Road, Corby, Northamptonshire, NN17 5JE

Tel: 01536 266576
Fax: 01536 264509
E-mail: natsoc@nsalg.org.uk

Enquiries:
Enquiries to: General Secretary

Founded:
1930

Organisation type and purpose:
Membership association (membership is by subscription), present number of members: 80,000, voluntary organisation.
National representative body.
Represents the interests of allotment holders.

Subject coverage:
Horticulture and gardening; interpretation of allotments legislation; environmental planning and development; preparation of leases and tenancy agreements.

Trade and statistical information:
Allotment survey.

Printed publications:
Allotment and Leisure Gardeners (quarterly, members free)

Access to staff:
Contact by letter, by telephone and by fax
Hours: Mon to Fri, 0900 to 1700

Affiliated to:
International League of Leisure Gardens

NATIONAL SOCIETY OF MASTER THATCHERS

Acronym or abbreviation: NSMT

20 The Laurels, Tetsworth, Thame, Oxfordshire, OX9 7BH

Tel: 01844 281568
Fax: 01844 281568
E-mail: nsmt@bigfoot.com

Website:
http://www.nsmt.hypermart.net

Enquiries:
Enquiries to: Secretary

Founded:
1963

Organisation type and purpose:
Trade association (membership is by qualification), present number of members: 80, voluntary organisation.

Subject coverage:
Thatching.

Printed publications:
How to select your thatched roof
The NSMT: its aims its functions

Access to staff:
Contact by letter and by e-mail
Hours: Evenings and weekends

NATIONAL SOIL RESOURCES INSTITUTE

Acronym or abbreviation: SSLRC

Cranfield University, Silsoe, Bedfordshire, MK45 4DT

continued overleaf

Tel: 01525 863242
Fax: 01525 863253

Website:
http://www.silsoe.cranfield.ac.uk/nsri
General capability information. Downloadable
details of the datasets available

Enquiries:
Enquiries to: Development Manager
Direct tel: 01525 863263
Direct e-mail: t.mayr@cranfield.ac.uk

Founded:
2001

Organisation type and purpose:
Consultancy, research organisation.

Subject coverage:
Soils and land use, crop suitability, suitability of
land for a wide range of uses, chemical and
physical properties of soils, environmental risk
assessment and pollution control.

Non-library collection catalogue:
All or part available in-house and in print

Printed publications:
Soil books and maps; national, by region and local,
    large and small scale
Technical and research reports
Order printed publications from: Publications Officer,
National Soil Resources Institute
at the same address, tel: 01525 863242, fax: 01525
863253, e-mail: e.m.paynter@cranfield.ac.uk

Electronic and video publications:
Digital versions of the 1:250,000 scale National Soil
    Map plus soil property data sets
NSI Profile, NSI Site and NSI Elements; data at
    each intersect on a 5-kilometre grid across
    England and Wales
Soil type interpretation
Software

Publications list:
Available online and in print

Access to staff:
Contact by letter, by telephone, by fax, by e-mail
and via website. Appointment necessary.
Hours: Mon to Fri, 0900 to 1700

Access to building, collection or gallery:
Prior appointment required

Access for disabled people:
Level entry, toilet facilities

Other addresses:
National Soil Resources Institute
    NSRI, North Wyke, Okehampton, Devon, EX20
    2SB; tel: 01837 89188; fax: 01837 82139
National Soil Resources Institute
    NSRI, The Innovation Centre, York Science Park,
    Heslington, York, YO10 5DG; tel: 01904 435220;
    fax: 01904 435221
National Soil Resources Institute
    NSRI, Cambria House, 29, Newport Road,
    Cardiff, CF24 0TP; tel: 07775 865701

Parent body:
Cranfield University

NATIONAL SPECIALIST CONTRACTORS COUNCIL

Acronym or abbreviation: NSCC

Carthusian Court, 12, Carthusian Street, London,
EC1M 6EZ

Tel: 0870 429 6351
Fax: 0870 429 6352
E-mail: enquiries@nscc.org.uk

Website:
http://www.nscc.org.uk/index2.htm

Enquiries:
Enquiries to: Director

Founded:
1994

Organisation type and purpose:
Trade association.
Umbrella association representing the interests of
trade associations in the construction industry.

Subject coverage:
Contractors and sub-contractors in the specialist
sector and trade sector of construction.

Access to staff:
Contact by letter, by telephone and by fax
Hours: Mon to Fri, 0900 to 1700

Has:
28 member organisations

NATIONAL SPIRITUAL ASSEMBLY OF THE BAHA'IS OF THE UNITED KINGDOM

Acronym or abbreviation: NSA UK

National Baha'i Centre, 27 Rutland Gate, London,
SW7 1PD

Tel: 020 7584 2566
Fax: 020 7584 9402
E-mail: secretariat@bahai.org.uk

Website:
http://bahainews-uk.info
Blog of news from and about the Baha'i
community in the UK and elsewhere.
http://www.bahai.org.uk
Information about the Baha'i Faith and links to
international, national and local Baha'i websites.
http://www.bahaibooks.org.uk
Online catalogue and sales of primary and
secondary Baha'i literature.

Enquiries:
Enquiries to: Office of Public Information
Direct e-mail: opi@bahai.org.uk

Founded:
1923

Organisation type and purpose:
Elected governing council of UK Baha'i
community, registered charity (charity number
250851).
Religious charity.

Subject coverage:
The Baha'i Faith – its history, teachings, national
and international standing, including its
accreditation with the United Nations.

**Museum or gallery collection, archive, or library
special collection:**
Afnan Trust Library (by appointment only)

Printed publications:
A wide range of titles on all aspects of Baha'i
    teachings and life available
Order printed publications from: The Coordinator,
Baha'i Books UK, 5 Station Approach, Oakham,
Rutland, LE15 6QW; tel: 01572 722780; fax: 01572
724280; e-mail: sales@books.bahai.org.uk

Electronic and video publications:
Audio-visual materials, CDs and DVDs
Order electronic and video publications from: Baha'i
Books UK (as above)

Publications list:
Available online and in print

Access to staff:
Contact by letter, by telephone, by fax, by e-mail,
in person and via website. Appointment necessary.
Hours: Mon to Fri, 0930 to 1700

Access to building, collection or gallery:
Hours: Mon to Fri, 0930 to 1700

Access for disabled people:
Lift, toilet facilities
Special comments: Lift does not reach top floor of
Baha'i Centre.

NATIONAL STOOLBALL ASSOCIATION

Formal name: Stoolball England

Acronym or abbreviation: SE

53 Kings Road, Horsham, West Sussex, RH13 5PP

Tel: 01403 252419
E-mail: kr.price@homecall.co.uk

Website:
http://www.stoolball.org.uk
History of stoolball, rules of the game, mini
stoolball, pitch dimensions, newsletter, match
fixtures and results, what's on.

Enquiries:
Enquiries to: Honorary Secretary
Other contacts: Insurance Officer (for personal
accident and public liability); tel: 01293 772469;
mail leddy@tiscali.co.uk; Sales Officer (for stoolball
equipment); tel: 01403 252419; e-mail: kr.price@
homecall.co.uk

Founded:
1979

Organisation type and purpose:
Advisory body, voluntary organisation.
Recognised governing body of stoolball.

Subject coverage:
All enquiries about stoolball.

**Museum or gallery collection, archive, or library
special collection:**
Archive records from 1880–1950 held at Barbican
    Museum, Lewes, Sussex; appointment needed
    for inspection

Printed publications:
History of Stoolball; Stoolball Coaching Manual

Electronic and video publications:
DVD, Let's Play Stoolball (£20.50)
Coaching Pack (2 DVDs) (£24.95)
Order electronic and video publications from:
Honorary Secretary

Publications list:
Available online and in print

Access to staff:
Contact by letter, by telephone, by e-mail and via
website
Hours: Any reasonable time, answerphone
available

Access to building, collection or gallery:
Prior appointment required

Access for disabled people:
Parking provided

NATIONAL SWEET PEA SOCIETY

Acronym or abbreviation: NSPS

8 Wolseley Road, Parkstone, Poole, Dorset, BH12
2DP

Tel: 01202 734088
E-mail: bg.bulstrode@btinternet.com

Website:
http://www.sweetpeas.org.uk

Enquiries:
Enquiries to: Secretary

Founded:
1900

Organisation type and purpose:
Membership association, registered charity.

Subject coverage:
Breeding, cultivation, development of lathyrus
odoratus (sweet pea) and other lathyrus species;
exhibiting and garden decoration.

**Museum or gallery collection, archive, or library
special collection:**
All publications, since the formation of the Society
in 1901

Printed publications:
Yearbook
Enjoy Sweet Peas (handbook)
Spring and Autumn Bulletins

Access to staff:
Contact by letter and by telephone. Access for members only.
Hours: Mon to Fri, 0900 to 1700

Affiliated to:
Royal Horticultural Society

NATIONAL SYMPHONY ORCHESTRA

Formal name: National Symphony Orchestra of London
Acronym or abbreviation: NSO

177 John Ruskin Street, London, SE5 0PQ

Tel: 020 7703 3148
Fax: 020 7703 5334
E-mail: enquiries@nso.co.uk

Website:
http://www.nso.co.uk
History of the NSO, personnel, current activities.

Enquiries:
Enquiries to: Artistic Director

Founded:
1940

Organisation type and purpose:
Symphony orchestra.

Subject coverage:
Music, arts, entertainment.

Electronic and video publications:
Wide range of CD-ROMs available from major record shops

Access to staff:
Contact by letter, by telephone, by e-mail and in person
Hours: Mon to Fri, 0900 to 1700

NATIONAL TAXI ASSOCIATION

Acronym or abbreviation: NTA

5 Clifton Hill, Brighton, East Sussex, BN1 3HL

Tel: 01273 729403
Fax: 01273 728122
E-mail: enquiries@brighton-streamline.co.uk

Website:
http://www.brighton-streamline.co.uk

Enquiries:
Enquiries to: Administrator

Founded:
1967

Organisation type and purpose:
National organisation, trade association (membership is by subscription).

Subject coverage:
Taxi cabs.

Access to staff:
Contact by letter and by e-mail
Hours: Mon to Fri, 0900 to 1700

NATIONAL THEATRE

Acronym or abbreviation: NT

Upper Ground, London, SE1 9PX

Tel: 020 7452 3000 box office; 020 7452 3333 stage door/admin\ Minicom no. 020 7452 3009
Fax: 020 7452 3030 box office

Website:
http://www.nationaltheatre.org.uk
Information about current and forthcoming productions and general information on the National.

Enquiries:
Enquiries to: Information Officer
Direct tel: 020 7452 3400

Founded:
1963

Organisation type and purpose:
Registered charity (charity number 224223).
The National Theatre is central to the creative life of the country. In its three theatres on the South Bank in London, it presents an eclectic mix of new plays and classics, with seven or eight productions in repertory at any one time. It aims constantly to re-energise the great traditions of the British stage and to expand the horizons of audiences and artists alike. It aspires to reflect in its repertoire the diversity of the culture. At its Studio, the National offers a space for research and development of the NT's stages and the theatre as a whole. Through the NT Education Department, tomorrow's audiences are addressed. Through an extensive programme of Platform performances, backstage tours, foyer music, exhibitions, and free outdoor entertainment it recognises that the theatre does not begin and end with the rise and fall of the curtain. And by touring, the National shares its work with audiences in the UK and abroad.

Subject coverage:
World drama; free exhibitions and live music; platform performances and events; education and community outreach work; theatre backstage tours; bookshop; bars and restaurants.

Non-library collection catalogue:
All or part available online

Printed publications:
Platform papers
Programmes
Books
Collections of Transcripts
Leaflets
Supporters & Education Newsletter
Order printed publications from: National Theatre Bookshop
At the address above, tel: 020 7452 3456, e-mail: bookshop@nationaltheatre.org.uk

Access to staff:
Contact by letter, by telephone and by fax
Hours: Foyers: Mon to Sat, 1000 to 2300; Box Office: Mon to Sat, 1000 to 2000

Access for disabled people:
Parking provided, ramped entry, access to all public areas, toilet facilities
Special comments: Audio-described and sign language interpreted performances.

NATIONAL TORTOISE CLUB OF GREAT BRITAIN & TORTOISE HELPLINE

2 Laith Close, Cookridge, Leeds, West Yorkshire, LS16 6LE

Tel: 0113 267 7587

Enquiries:
Enquiries to: Chairman / Founder

Founded:
1970

Organisation type and purpose:
International organisation, advisory body, membership association, voluntary organisation, consultancy.
Advisory service UK and Europe; funded entirely by Founders.
Permanent sanctuary to any tortoise, on request, free.

Subject coverage:
All aspects of the needs of tortoises and box tortoises (often incorrectly called turtles) throughout the year; health and sickness, diet, hibernation, breeding, care and well-being of all species.

Information services:
Free helpline.

Education services:
Founder accepts invitations to appear on TV and radio.

Printed publications:
Care sheet by experts (at small cost)

Access to staff:
Contact by letter and by telephone
Hours: Mon to Fri, 0900 to 1700
Special comments: Enclose an sae for reply, donations appreciated. If messages left on answerphone no calls back made without assurance that reversed charges will be accepted.

NATIONAL TRACTION ENGINE TRUST

Acronym or abbreviation: NTET

153 Micklefield Road, High Wycombe, Buckinghamshire, HP13 7HA

Tel: 01494 521727
Fax: 01494 521727
E-mail: suejackson@themutual.net

Enquiries:
Enquiries to: Secretary General

Founded:
1954

Organisation type and purpose:
Membership association (membership is by subscription), voluntary organisation, registered charity.
Most local steam groups with similar aims are affiliated.

Subject coverage:
History of engines and their manufacturers, as well as up-to-date information as to repairs, spares and information about traction engine rallies each year, for organisers and the general public, preservation and operation of steam driven traction engines.

Printed publications:
Steaming (quarterly, free to members)

Access to staff:
Contact by letter, by telephone, by fax and by e-mail
Hours: Mon to Fri, 0900 to 1700

NATIONAL TROLLEYBUS ASSOCIATION

Acronym or abbreviation: NTA

24 Heath Farm Road, Ferndown, Dorset, BH22 8JW

Website:
http://www.trolleybus.co.uk/nta

Enquiries:
Enquiries to: Editor
Direct e-mail: cisgar@btinternet.com
Other contacts: editor.tm@btinternet.com

Founded:
1963

Organisation type and purpose:
Membership association.
To produce publications relating to trolleybuses and to preserve trolleybuses (five of which are currently owned).

Subject coverage:
Description of present day trolleybus operation, new vehicle developments, system histories, comprehensive worldwide trolleybus news with maps and illustrations.

Museum or gallery collection, archive, or library special collection:
H Brearley, photographic collection
R F Mack, photographic collection

Trade and statistical information:
Statistics on all aspects of trolleybuses and trolleybus systems.
Information on new vehicles, technical developments, etc.

Printed publications:
Trolleybus Magazine (6 times a year)

Publications list:
Available online

continued overleaf

Access to staff:
Contact by letter and by e-mail
Hours: Mon to Fri, 0900 to 1700

Affiliated to:
Trolleybus Museum Company Ltd

Also at:
Membership Enquiries, National Trolleybus
Association
2 St John's Close. Claines, Worcester, WR3 7PT

Subsidiary for publication sales:
Autumn Reach
The Close, St Ives, Ringwood, BH24 2PE

NATIONAL TRUST

Formal name: National Trust for Places of Historic
Interest or Natural Beauty
Acronym or abbreviation: NT

36 Queen Anne's Gate, London, SW1H 9AS

Tel: 020 7222 9251
Fax: 020 7222 5097
E-mail: enquiries@thenationaltrust.org.uk

Website:
http://www.nationaltrust.org.uk
Includes a section dedicated to providing online
access to information about their holdings, which
include buildings, collections, libraries and
archives

Enquiries:
Enquiries to: Director General
Other contacts: Customer Care Manager for general
enquiries.

Founded:
1895

Organisation type and purpose:
National organisation, membership association
(membership is by subscription), present number
of members: 2.9 million, voluntary organisation,
registered charity (charity number 205846),
museum, historic building, house or site, suitable
for ages: all, research organisation, publishing
house.
Membership is the principal means by which the
NT is supported, but access to its services is not
restricted to members.
The National Trust preserves places of historic
interest or natural beauty for all to enjoy, now and
forever.

Subject coverage:
Conservation of buildings and land of historic
interest or natural beauty held in perpetuity for the
nation, inalienably. History of the National Trust.
Visitor management, sustainability, policy issues
etc.

**Museum or gallery collection, archive, or library
special collection:**
Details may be found in the Trust's handbook and
on the website
Some country houses contain antiquarian libraries
for which the central catalogue is still in the
development stage. All these collections are
managed and accessed by different
arrangements, many of which are local to the
property itself

Printed publications:
Magazine (3 times a year, members)
Properties List (every 5 years)
National Trust Handbook (annually)
Books related to the properties eg architecture and
horticulture, and cooking and children's stories
(sold in National Trust Shops and good
bookshops)
Guide books to practically every property open to
the public (available at the properties or from
Reception at 36 Queen Anne's Gate)
The Lake District: a resource book for teachers
Books for children include:
The Investigating Series: 12 titles connected to Key
Stages 2 and 3 of the National Curriculum
The Mud Pack Series, conservation in England,
Wales and Northern Ireland
See website for complete list

Electronic and video publications:
National Trust British Countryside (CD-ROM,
from Anglia Multimedia, tel 01603 615151,
£29.99)
Timeline: Trust houses brought to life

Publications list:
Available online and in print

Access to staff:
Contact by letter, by telephone, by fax, by e-mail,
in person and via website
Hours: Mon to Fri, 0900 to 1700

Other addresses:
Learning Community and Volunteering Office
Rowan House, Kembrey Park, Swindon,
Wiltshire, SN2 6UG; tel: 0870 609 5383
National Trust Conservation Directorate
33 Sheep Street, Cirencester, Gloucestershire,
CL7 1RQ; tel: 0870 609 5382
National Trust Enterprises
The Stable Block, Heywood House, Westbury,
Wiltshire, BA13 4NA; tel: 0870 609 5381
National Trust for Scotland
Wemyss House, 28 Charlotte Square, Edinburgh,
EH2 4ET; tel: 0131 243 9300
National Trust Office for Northern Ireland
Rowallane House, Saintfield, Ballynahinch, Co
Down, BT24 7LH; tel: 028 9751 0721; fax: 028
9751 1242
National Trust Office for Wales
Trinity Square, Llandudno, LL30 2DE; tel: 01492
860123; fax: 01492 860233
National Trust Theatre Projects
The National Trust, Sutton House, 2 & 4
Homerton High Street, Hackney, London, E9
6JQ; tel: 020 8986 0242
The National Trust Membership Department
PO Box 39, Bromley, Kent, BR1 3XL; tel: 020 8466
6824

Regional Offices:
National Trust, Devon & Cornwall
Killerton House, Broadclyst, Exeter, Devon, EX5
3LE; tel: 01392 881691; fax: 01392 881954
National Trust, Devon & Cornwall
Lanhydrock, Bodmin, Cornwall, PL30 4DE; tel:
01208 74281; fax: 01208 77887
National Trust, East Anglia (Bedfordshire,
Cambridgeshire, Essex, part of Hertfordshire,
Norfolk & Suffolk)
The Dairy House, Ickworth, Suffolk, IP29 5QE;
tel: 0870 609 5388; fax: 01284 736066
National Trust, East Midlands (Derbyshire,
Leicestershire, S Lincolnshire, Northamptonshire,
Nottinghamshire & Rutland)
Clumber Park Stableyard, Worksop,
Nottinghamshire, S80 3BE; tel: 01909 486411;
fax: 01909 486377
National Trust, North West (Cheshire, Cumbria,
Greater Manchester & Lancashire, Merseyside)
The Hollens, Grasmere, LA22 9QZ; tel: 0870 609
5391; fax: 015394 35353
National Trust, South East (East Sussex, Kent,
Surrey & West Sussex)
Polesden Lacey, Dorking, Surrey, RH5 6BD; tel:
01372 453401; fax: 01372 452023
National Trust, Thames & Solent (Berkshire,
Buckinghamshire, Hampshire, part of
Hertfordshire, Isle of Wight, Greater London &
Oxfordshire)
Hughenden Manor, High Wycombe,
Buckinghamshire, HP14 4LA; tel: 01494 528051;
fax: 01494 463310
National Trust, Wessex (Bristol/Bath, Dorset,
Gloucestershire, Somerset & Wiltshire)
Eastleigh Court, Bishopstrow, Warminster,
Wiltshire, BA12 9HW; tel: 01985 843600; fax:
01985 843624
National Trust, West Midlands (Birmingham,
Hereford, Shropshire, Staffordshire, Warwickshire
& Worcestershire)
Attingham Park, Shrewsbury, Shropshire, SY4
4TP; tel: 01743 708100; fax: 01743 708150
National Trust, Yorkshire & North East (Co
Durham, Newcastle & Tyneside, Northumberland)
Scots' Gap, Morpeth, Northumberland, NE61
4EG; tel: 01670 774691; fax: 01670 774317

National Trust, Yorkshire & North East (Yorkshire,
Teesside & N Lincolnshire)
Goddards, 27 Tadcaster Road, York, YO24 1GG;
tel: 01904 702021; fax: 01904 771970

NATIONAL TRUST (DEVON &
CORNWALL REGIONAL OFFICES)
– BODMIN

Formal name: National Trust for Places of Historic
Interest or Natural Beauty
Acronym or abbreviation: NT

Lanhydrock, Bodmin, Cornwall, PL30 4DE

Tel: 01208 74281
Fax: 01208 77887
E-mail: enquiries@thenationaltrust.org.uk

Website:
http://www.nationaltrust.org.uk
Information about the National Trust properties,
opening times and facilities, special events,
educational information.

Enquiries:
Enquiries to: Customer Service Manager

Founded:
1895

Organisation type and purpose:
National organisation, independently owned,
membership association (membership is by
subscription), registered charity (charity number
205846), historic building, house or site, suitable
for ages: all.

Subject coverage:
Administration and management of Trust sites in
the region.
The preservation and upkeep of places of historic
interest and natural beauty in Cornwall.

Publications list:
Available online and in print

Links with:
Trevithick Trust
Trevithick Road, Pool, Redruth, Cornwall, TR15
3NP; tel: 01209 210900; e-mail: info@
trevithicktrust.com

National Trust Sites:
Antony House
Torpoint, Plymouth, PL11 2QA; tel: 01752 812191
Cornish Mines & Engines
Trevithick Road, Pool, Redruth, Cornwall, TR15
3NP; tel: 01209 210900
Cotehele House
St. Dominick, Saltash, Cornwall, PL30 5AD; tel:
01579 351346; e-mail: cctlce@smtp.ntrust.org.uk
Godolphin Estate
Lizard Countryside Office, Helston, Cornwall;
tel: 01326 562882
Lanhydrock House
Cornwall; tel: 01208 73320; e-mail: clhlan@smtp
.ntrust.org.uk
Lawrence House Museum
9 Castle Street, Launceston, Cornwall, PL15 8BA;
tel: 01566 773277
Levant Steam Engine
Trewellard, Pendeen, St Just, Cornwall; tel: 01736
786156
St Michael's Mount
Marazion, Penzance, Cornwall, TR17 0EF; tel:
01736 710507 / 710233; e-mail: godolphin@manor
-office.co.uk
Tintagel Old Post Office
Fore Street, Tintagel, Cornwall, PL34 0DB; tel:
01840 770024
Trerice Manor House
Kestle Mill, Newquay, Cornwall, TR8 4PG; tel:
01637 875404

NATIONAL TRUST (DEVON &
CORNWALL REGIONAL OFFICES)
– EXETER

Formal name: National Trust for Places of Historic
Interest or Natural Beauty

Acronym or abbreviation: NT

Killerton House, Broadclyst, Exeter, Devon, EX5 3LE

Tel: 01392 881691
Fax: 01392 881954
E-mail: enquiries@thenationaltrust.org.uk

Website:
http://www.nationaltrust.org.uk
Information about the National Trust properties, opening times and facilities, special events, educational information, and publications.

Enquiries:
Enquiries to: Service Supporter Manager

Founded:
1895

Organisation type and purpose:
National organisation, independently owned, membership association (membership is by subscription), registered charity (charity number 205846), historic building, house or site, suitable for ages: Lifelong.
Administration and management of Trust sites in Devon.

Subject coverage:
The preservation and upkeep of places of historic interest and natural beauty in Devon.

Non-library collection catalogue:
All or part available in-house

Library catalogue:
All or part available in-house

Publications list:
Available online and in print

Access to staff:
Contact by letter, by telephone, by fax, by e-mail, in person and via website
Hours: Sun to Sat, 0900 to 1700

Access to building, collection or gallery:
Hours: Generally 1100 to 1700, but please check before visit

National Trust sites:
A La Ronde
  Summer Lane, Exmouth, Devon, EX8 5BD; tel: 01395 265514
Arlington Court
  Arlington, Barnstaple, Devon, EX31 4LP; tel: 01271 850296; fax: 01271 850711
Bradley House
  Totnes Road, Newton Abbot, Devon, TQ12 6BN; tel: 01626 354513
Buckland Abbey
  Yelverton, Devon, PL20 6EY; tel: 01822 853607; fax: 01822 855448
Castle Drogo
  Drewsteignton, Exeter, Devon, EX6 6PB; tel: 01647 433306; fax: 01647 433186
Clyston Mill
  Killerton, Broadclyst, Exeter, Devon, EX5 3EW; tel: 01392 462425
Coleton Fishacre House
  Coleton, Brownstone Road, Kingswear, Dartmouth, Devon, TQ6 0EQ; tel: 01803 752466
Compton Castle
  Marldon, Paignton, Devon, TQ3 1TA; tel: 01803 875740
Finch Foundary Museum of Rural Industry
  Sticklepath, Okehampton, Devon, EX20 2NW; tel: 01837 840046
Killerton House
  Broadclyst, Exeter, Devon, EX5 3LE; tel: 01392 881345
Knightshayes Court
  Bolham, Tiverton, Devon, EX16 7RQ; tel: 01884 254665
Loughwood Meeting House
  Dalwood, Axminster, Devon, EX13 7DU; tel: 01392 881691; fax: 01392 881954
Marker's Cottage
  Killerton, Broadclyst, Exeter, Devon, EX5 3HR; tel: 01392 461546
Newhall Equestrian Centre
  Killerton, Broadclyst, Exeter, Devon, EX5 3LW; tel: 01392 462453

Old Bakery, Manor Mill and Forge
  Branscombe, Seaton, Devon, EX12 3DB; tel: 01297 680333
Overbeck's Museum and Gardens
  Sharpitor, Salcombe, Devon, 01548 842893; tel: 01548 842893
Saltram House
  Plympton, Plymouth, Devon, PL7 1UH; tel: 01752 333500; fax: 01752 336474
Shute Barton
  Shute, Axminster, Devon, EX13 7PT; tel: 01297 34692
Watersmeet House
  Watersmeet Road, Lynmouth, Devon, EX35 6NT; tel: 01598 753348

NATIONAL TRUST (EAST MIDLANDS REGIONAL OFFICE)

Formal name: National Trust for Places of Historic Interest or Natural Beauty
Acronym or abbreviation: NT

Clumber Park Stableyard, Worksop, Nottinghamshire, S80 3BE

Tel: 01909 486411
Fax: 01909 486377
E-mail: enquiries@thenationaltrust.org.uk

Website:
http://www.nationaltrust.org.uk
Information about the National Trust properties, opening times and facilities, special events, educational information, and publications.

Enquiries:
Enquiries to: Customer Service Manager

Founded:
1895

Organisation type and purpose:
National organisation, independently owned, membership association (membership is by subscription), registered charity (charity number 205846), historic building, house or site, suitable for ages: Lifelong.
Administration and management of Trust sites in the East Midlands.

Subject coverage:
The preservation and upkeep of places of historic interest and natural beauty in Derbyshire, Leicestershire, South Lincolnshire, Northamptonshire, Nottinghamshire and Rutland.

Publications list:
Available online and in print

Access to staff:
Contact by letter, by telephone, by fax, by e-mail, in person and via website
Hours: Mon to Fri, 0900 to 1700

National Trust sites:
Belton House
  Belton, Grantham, Lincolnshire, NG32 2LS; tel: 01476 566116; e-mail: belton@smpt.ntrust.org.uk
Calke Abbey
  Ticknall, Derbyshire; tel: 01332 863822; e-mail: ecbxxx@smpt.ntrust.org.uk
Canons Ashby House
  Canons Ashby, Daventry, Northamptonshire, NN1 6SD; tel: 01327 860044; fax: 01327 860168; e-mail: canonsashby@ntrust.org.uk
Grantham House
  Castle Gate, Grantham, Lincolnshire, NG31 6SS; tel: 01909 486411 (Regional Office)
Gunby Hall
  Gunby, Spilsby, Lincolnshire, PE23 5SS; tel: 01909 486411 (Regional Office)
Hardwick Hall
  Doe Lea, Chesterfield, Derbyshire, S44 5QJ; tel: 01246 850430
Kedleston Hall
  Kedleston, Derby, DE22 5JH; tel: 01332 842191; fax: 01332 841972; e-mail: kedlestonhall@ntrust.org.uk

Lyveden New Bield
  Oundle, Peterborough, Northamptonshire, PE8 5AT; tel: 01832 205358; e-mail: lyvedennewbield@ntrust.org.uk
Mr Straws House
  7 Blyth Grove, Worksop, Nottinghamshire, S81 0JG; tel: 01909 482380; e-mail: estxxx@smtp.ntrust.org.uk
Museum of Childhood
  Sudbury Hall, Sudbury, Ashbourne, Derbyshire, DE6 5HT; tel: 01283 585305
Priest's House
  39 Church Street, Easton on the Hill, Stamford, Northamptonshire, PE9 3LL; tel: 01909 486411 (Regional Office)
Stainsby Mill
  c/o Hardwick Hall, Doe Lea, Chesterfield, Derbyshire, S44 5QJ; tel: 01246 850430; e-mail: ehwxxx@smtr.ntrust.org.uk
Staunton Harold Church
  Staunton Harold, Ashby-de-la-Zouch, Leicestershire; tel: 01332 863822; fax: 01332 865272; e-mail: stauntonharold@ntrust.org.uk
Sudbury Hall
  Sudbury, Ashbourne, Derbyshire, DE6 5HT; tel: 01283 585305
Tattershall Castle
  Tattershall, Lincoln, LN4 4LR; tel: 01526 342543; e-mail: tattershallcastle@ntrust.org.uk
The Workhouse
  Upton Road, Southwell, Nottinghamshire, NG25 0PT; tel: 01636 817250
Whitegates Cottage
  Gunby Hall Estate, Mill Lane, Bratoft, Spilsby, Lincolnshire; tel: 01909 486411 (Regional Office)
Woolsthorpe Manor
  23 Newton Way, Woolsthorp-by-Colsterworth, Grantham, Lincolnshire, NG33 5NR; tel: 01476 860338

NATIONAL TRUST (EAST OF ENGLAND REGIONAL OFFICE)

Formal name: National Trust for Places of Historic Interest or Natural Beauty
Acronym or abbreviation: NT

Westley Bottom, Bury St Edmunds, Suffolk, IP33 3WD

Tel: 01284 747500
Fax: 01284 747506
E-mail: enquiries@thenationaltrust.org.uk

Website:
http://www.nationaltrust.org.uk
Information about the National Trust properties, opening times and facilities, special events, educational information, and publications.

Enquiries:
Enquiries to: Customer Service Manager

Founded:
1895

Organisation type and purpose:
National organisation, independently owned, membership association (membership is by subscription), registered charity (charity number 205846), historic building, house or site, suitable for ages: Life long.
Administration and management of Trust sites in East Anglia.

Subject coverage:
The preservation and upkeep of places of historic interest and natural beauty in Bedfordshire, Cambridgeshire, Essex, part of Hertfordshire, Norfolk and Suffolk.

Publications list:
Available online and in print

Access to staff:
Contact by letter, by telephone, by fax, by e-mail, in person and via website
Hours: Mon to Fri, 0900 to 1700

continued overleaf

National Trust sites:
Anglesey Abbey, Gardens and Lode Mill
  Quy Road, Nr Lode, Cambridge, CB5 9EJ; tel:
  01223 811200; e-mail: aayusr@ntrust.org.uk
Blickling Hall
  Blickling, Norwich, Norfolk, NR11 6NF; tel:
  01263 738030; e-mail: blickling@ntrust.org.uk
Bourne Mill
  Bourne Road, Colchester, Essex, CO2 8RT; tel:
  01206 572422
Coggeshall Grange Barn
  Grange Hill, Coggeshall, Colchester, Essex, CO6
  1RE; tel: 01376 562226
Elizabethan House Museum
  4 South Quay, Great Yarmouth, Norfolk, NR30
  2QH; tel: 01493 855746; fax: 01493 745459
Felbrigg Hall
  Felbrigg, Norwich, Norfolk, NR11 8PR; tel:
  01263 837444; e-mail: afgusr@smtp.ntrust.org.uk
Guildhall of Corpus Christi
  Market Place, Sudbury, Suffolk, CO10 9QZ; tel:
  01787 247646; e-mail: almjtg@smtp.ntrust.org.uk
Horsey Windpump
  Horsey, Great Yarmouth, Norfolk, NR29 4EF; tel:
  01493 393904 (on open days); e-mail: horsey@
  ntrust.org.uk
Houghton Mill
  Houghton, Huntingdon, Cambridgeshire, PE28
  2EZ; tel: 01480 301494
Ickworth House, Park & Garden
  Horringer, Bury St Edmunds, Suffolk, IP29 5QE;
  tel: 01284 735270
Melford Hall
  Long Melford, Sudbury, Suffolk, CO10 9AA; tel:
  01787 880286; e-mail: amdklx@smtp.ntrust.org
  .uk
Oxburgh Hall
  Oxborough, Kings Lynn, Nofolk, PE33 9PS; tel:
  01366 328258; fax: 01366 328066; e-mail: aohusr@
  smtp.ntrust.org.uk
Paycocke's
  West Street, Coggeshall, Colchester, Essex, CO6
  1NS; tel: 01376 561305
Peckover House
  North Brink, Wisbech, Cambridgeshire, PE13
  1JR; tel: 01945 583463; e-mail: aprigix@smtp
  .ntrust.org.uk
Ramsey Abbey Gatehouse
  Abbey School, Ramsey, Huntingdon,
  Cambridgeshire, PE17 1DH; tel: 0870 609 5388
Shaw's Corner
  Ayot St Lawrence, Welwyn Garden City,
  Hertfordshire, AL6 9BX; tel: 01438 820307; e-
  mail: shawscorner@ntrust.org.uk
Suffolk Horse Museum
  The Market Hill, Woodbridge, Suffolk, IP12 4LP;
  tel: 01394 380643
Sutton Hoo
  Woodbridge, Suffolk; tel: 01394 389700
Theatre Royal
  Westgate Street, Bury St Edmunds, Suffolk, IP33
  1QR; tel: 01284 769505
Wimpole Hall
  Arrington, Royston, Hertfordshire, SG8 0BW; tel:
  01223 207257; fax: 01223 207383; e-mail:
  aweusr@smtp.org.uk

NATIONAL TRUST (NORTH WEST REGIONAL OFFICE)

Formal name: National Trust for Places of Historic
Interest or Natural Beauty
Acronym or abbreviation: NT

The Hollens, Grasmere, Cumbria, LA22 9QZ

Tel: 015394 35599
Fax: 015394 35353
E-mail: enquiries@thenationaltrust.org.uk

Website:
http://www.nationaltrust.org.uk

Enquiries:
Enquiries to: Customer Service Manager

Founded:
1895

Organisation type and purpose:

National organisation, independently owned,
membership association (membership is by
subscription), registered charity (charity number
205846), historic building, house or site, suitable
for ages: life-long.

Administration and management of Trust sites in
the North West region.

Subject coverage:
The preservation and upkeep of places of historic
interest and natural beauty in Cheshire, Cumbria,
Greater Manchester and Lancashire, Merseyside.

Publications list:
Available online and in print

Access to staff:
Contact by letter, by telephone, by fax, by e-mail,
in person and via website
Hours: Mon to Fri, 0900 to 1700

National Trust sites:
20 Forthlin Road
  Liverpool, L24 1YP; tel: 0151 427 7231
  (bookings); e-mail: 20forthlinroad@ntrust.org.uk
Beatrix Potter Gallery
  Main Street, Hawkshead, Ambleside, Cumbria,
  LA22 0NS; tel: 015394 36355; fax: 015394 36187;
  e-mail: beatrixpottergallery@ntrust.org.uk
Cartmel Gatehouse Heritage Centre
  Cavendish Street, Cartmel, Grange-over-Sands,
  Cumbria, LA11 6QA; tel: 015395 36874; fax:
  015395 36636; e-mail: cartmelpriory@ntrust.org
  .uk
Dunham Massey
  Altrincham, Greater Manchester, Cheshire,
  WA14 4SJ; tel: 0161 941 1025; fax: 0161 929 7508;
  e-mail: dunhammassey@ntrust.org.uk
Gawthorpe Hall
  Padiham, Burnley, Lancashire, BB12 8UA; tel:
  01282 771004; fax: 01282 770178; e-mail:
  gawthorpehall@ntrust.org.uk
Hill Top
  Near Sawrey, Ambleside, Cumbria, LA22 0LF;
  tel: 015394 36269; fax: 015394 36188; e-mail:
  hilltop@ntrust.ofg.uk
Little Moreton Hall
  Congleton, Cheshire, CW12 4SD; tel: 01260
  272018; e-mail: littlemoretonhall@ntrust.org.uk
Lyme Park
  Disley, Stockport, Cheshire, SK12 2NX; tel: 01663
  762023; fax: 01663 765035; e-mail: lymepark@
  ntrust.org.uk
Nether Alderley Mill
  Congleton Road, Nether Alderley, Macclesfield,
  Cheshire, SK10 4TW; tel: 01625 584412; e-mail:
  netheralderleymill@ntrust.org.uk
Quarry Bank Mill and Styal Estate
  Quarry Bank Road, Styal, Wilmslow, Cheshire,
  SK9 4LA; tel: 01625 527468; fax: 01625 539267; e-
  mail: quarrybankmill@ntrust.org.uk
Rufford Old Hall
  Rufford, Ormskirk, Lancashire, L40 1SG; tel:
  01704 821254; fax: 01704 821254; e-mail:
  ruffordhall@ntrust.org.uk
Sizergh Castle and Garden
  Sizergh, Kendal, Cumbria, LA8 8AE; tel: 01539
  560070; fax: 015395 61621; e-mail: ntrust@
  sizerghcastle.fsnet.co.uk
Speke Hall
  The Walk, Liverpool, L24 1XD; tel: 0151 427
  7231; fax: 0151 427 9860; e-mail: spekehall@
  ntrust.org.uk
Tatton Park
  Knutsford, Cheshire, WA16 6QN; tel: 01625
  534400; fax: 01625 534403; e-mail: tatton@
  cheshire.gov.uk
Townend
  Troutbeck, Windermere, Cumbria, LA23 1LB; tel:
  01539 432628; e-mail: townend@ntrust.org.uk
Wordsworth House
  Main Street, Cockermouth, Cumbria, CA13 9RX;
  tel: 01900 824805; fax: 01900 824805; e-mail:
  wordsworthhouse@ntrust.org.uk

NATIONAL TRUST (SOUTH EAST REGIONAL OFFICE)

Formal name: National Trust for Places of Historic
Interest or Natural Beauty
Acronym or abbreviation: NT

Polesden Lacey, Dorking, Surrey, RH5 6BD

Tel: 01372 453401
Fax: 01372 452023
E-mail: se.enquiries@nationaltrust.org.uk

Website:
http://www.nationaltrust.org.uk
Information about the National Trust properties,
opening times and facilities, special events,
educational information, and publications.

Enquiries:
Enquiries to: Reception

Founded:
1895

Organisation type and purpose:
National organisation, independently owned,
membership association (membership is by
subscription), registered charity (charity number
205846), historic building, house or site, suitable
for ages: Life long.
Administration and management of Trust sites in
the South East region.

Subject coverage:
The preservation and upkeep of Trust properties of
historic interest and natural beauty in East Sussex,
Kent, Surrey and West Sussex.

Publications list:
Available online and in print

Access to staff:
Contact by letter, by telephone, by fax, by e-mail,
in person and via website
Hours: Mon to Fri, 0900 to 1700

National Trust sites:
Alfriston Clergy House
  The Tye, Alfriston, Polegate, East Sussex, BN26
  5TL; tel: 01323 870001; fax: 01323 871318; e-mail:
  alfriston@nationaltrust.org.uk
Bateman's
  Bateman's Lane, Burwash, Etchingham, East
  Sussex, TN19 7DS; tel: 01435 882302; fax: 01435
  882811; e-mail: batemans@nationaltrust.org.uk
Bodiam Castle
  Bodiam, Robertsbridge, East Sussex, TN32 5UA;
  tel: 01580 830436; fax: 01580 830398; e-mail:
  bodiamcastle@nationaltrust.org.uk
Chartwell
  Mapleton Road, Westerham, Kent, TN16 1PS; tel:
  01732 868381; fax: 01732 868193; e-mail:
  chartwell@nationaltrust.org.uk
Clandon Park
  West Clandon, Guildford, Surrey, GU4 7RQ; tel:
  01483 222482; fax: 01483 223479; e-mail:
  clandonpark@nationaltrust.org.uk
Claremont Landscape Garden
  Portsmouth Road, Esher, Surrey, KT10 9JG; tel:
  01372 467806; e-mail: claremont@nationaltrust
  .org.uk
Emmetts Garden
  Ide Hill, Sevenoaks, Kent, TN14 6AY; tel: 01732
  751509; e-mail: emmetts@nationaltrust.org.uk
Hatchlands Park
  East Clandon, Guildford, Surrey, GU4 7RT; tel:
  01483 222482; fax: 01483 223176; e-mail:
  hatchlands@nationaltrust.org.uk
Ightham Mote
  Ivy Hatch, Sevenoaks, Kent, TN15 0NT; tel:
  01732 810378; fax: 01732 811029; e-mail:
  ighthammote@nationaltrust.org.uk
Knole
  Sevenoaks, Kent, TN15 0RP; tel: 01732 462100;
  fax: 01732 465528; e-mail: knole@nationaltrust
  .org.uk
Lamb House
  West Street, Rye, East Sussex, TN31 7ES; e-mail:
  lambhouse@nationaltrust.org.uk
Monk's House
  Rodmell, Lewes, East Sussex, BN7 3HF; e-mail:
  monkshouse@nationaltrust.org.uk

Nymans
Handcross, nr Haywards Heath, West Sussex, RH17 6EB; tel: 01444 405250; e-mail: nymans@ nationaltrust.org.uk

Oakhurst Cottage
Hambledon, Godalming, Surrey, GU8 4HF; e-mail: oakhurstcottage@nationaltrust.org.uk

Petworth House
Church Street, Petworth, West Sussex, GU28 0AE; tel: 01798 342207; fax: 01798 342963; e-mail: petworth@nationaltrust.org.uk

Polesden Lacey
Great Bookham, Dorking, Surrey, RH5 6BD; tel: 01372 452048; fax: 01372 452023; e-mail: polesdenlacey@nationaltrust.org.uk

Quebec House
Quebec Square, Westerham, Kent, TN16 1TD

River Wey & Godalming Navigations and Dapdune Wharf
Dapdune Wharf, Wharf Road, Guildford, Surrey, GU1 4RR; tel: 01483 561389; fax: 01483 531667; e-mail: riverwey@nationaltrust.org.uk

Scotney Castle Garden and Estate
Lamberhurst, Tunbridge Wells, Kent, TN3 8JN; tel: 01892 893868; fax: 01892 890110; e-mail: scotneycastle@nationaltrust.org.uk

Shalford Mill
Shalford, Guildford, Surrey, GU4 8BS; tel: 01483 561389; e-mail: shalfordmill@nationaltrust.org.uk

Sheffield Park Garden
Sheffield Park, East Sussex, TN22 3QX; tel: 01825 790231; e-mail: sheffieldpark@nationaltrust.org.uk

Sissinghurst Castle Garden
Sissinghurst, Cranbrook, Kent, TN17 2AB; tel: 01580 710700; fax: 01580 710702; e-mail: sissinghurst@nationaltrust.org.uk

Smallhythe Place
Smallhythe, Tenterden, Kent, TN30 7NG; tel: 01580 762334; fax: 01580 762334; e-mail: smallhytheplace@nationaltrust.org.uk

South Foreland Lighthouse
The Front, St Margaret's Bay, Dover, Kent, CT15 6HP; tel: 01304 852463; fax: 01304 215484; e-mail: southforeland@nationaltrust.org.uk

Standen
West Hoathly Road, East Grinstead, West Sussex, RH19 4NE; tel: 01342 323029; fax: 01342 316424; e-mail: standen@nationaltrust.org.uk

Uppark House
South Harting, Petersfield, GU31 5QR; tel: 01730 825415; fax: 01730 825873; e-mail: uppark@ nationaltrust.org.uk

Wakehurst Place
Ardingly, Haywards Heath, West Sussex, RH17 6TN; tel: 01444 894066; fax: 01444 894069; e-mail: wakehurst@kew.org

Winkworth Arboretum
Hascombe Road, Godalming, Surrey, GU8 4AD; tel: 01483 208477; e-mail: winkwortharboretum@ nationaltrust.org.uk

NATIONAL TRUST (THAMES AND SOLENT REGIONAL OFFICE)

Formal name: National Trust for Places of Historic Interest or Natural Beauty
Acronym or abbreviation: NT

Hughenden Manor, High Wycombe, Buckinghamshire, HP14 4LA

Tel: 01494 755500
Fax: 01494 463310
E-mail: enquiries@thenationaltrust.org.uk

Website:
http://www.nationaltrust.org.uk

Enquiries:
Enquiries to: Marketing and Supporter Development Manager
Direct tel: 01494 755550

Founded:
1895

Organisation type and purpose:
National organisation, independently owned, membership association (membership is by subscription), registered charity (charity number 205846), historic building, house or site, suitable for ages: life-long.
Administration and management of Trust sites in the Thames and Solent region.

Subject coverage:
The preservation and upkeep of places of historic interest and natural beauty in Berkshire, Buckinghamshire, Hampshire, part of Hertfordshire, Isle of Wight, Greater London and Oxfordshire.

Publications list:
Available online and in print

Access to staff:
Contact by letter, by telephone, by fax, by e-mail, in person and via website
Hours: Mon to Fri, 0900 to 1700

National Trust sites:
2 Willow Road
2 Willow Road, Hampstead, London, NW3 1TH; tel: 020 7435 6166; e-mail: 2willowroad@ nationaltrust.org.uk

Basildon Park
Lower Basildon, Reading, Berkshire, RG8 9NR; tel: 0118 984 3040; e-mail: basildonpark@ nationaltrust.org.uk

Boarstall Tower
Boarstall, Aylesbury, Buckinghamshire, HP18 9UX; tel: 01844 239339

Buscot Old Parsonage
Buscot, Faringdon, Oxfordshire, SN7 8DQ; tel: 01793 7622209; e-mail: buscot@nationaltrust.org.uk

Buscot Park
Buscot, Faringdon, Oxfordshire, SN7 8BU; tel: 01367 240786; fax: 01367 241794; e-mail: estbuscot@aol.com

Carlyle's House
24 Cheyne Row, Chelsea, London, SW3 5HL; tel: 020 7352 7087; fax: 020 7352 5108; e-mail: carlyleshouse@nationaltrust.org.uk

Claydon House
Middle Claydon, Near Buckingham, Buckinghamshire, MK18 2EY; tel: 01296 730349; fax: 01296 738511; e-mail: claydon@nationaltrust.org.uk

Cliveden
Taplow, Maidenhead, Buckinghamshire, SL6 0JA; tel: 01628 605069; fax: 01628 669461; e-mail: cliveden@nationaltrust.org.uk

Eastbury Manor House
Eastbury Square, Barking, IG11 9SN; tel: 020 8724 1002; fax: 020 8724 1003; e-mail: eastburyhouse@lbbd.gov.uk

Fenton House
Windmill Hill, Hampstead, London, NW3 6RT; tel: 020 7435 3471; e-mail: fentonhouse@ nationaltrust.org.uk

Greys Court
Rotherfield Greys, Henley-on-Thames, Oxfordshire, RG9 4PG; tel: 01491 628529; fax: 01491 628935; e-mail: greyscourt@nationaltrust.org.uk

Hinton Ampner
Bramdean, Alresford, Hampshire, SO24 0LA; tel: 01962 771305; fax: 01962 793101; e-mail: hintonampner@nationaltrust.org.uk

Hughenden Manor Estate
Hughenden Valley, High Wycombe, Buckinghamshire, HP14 4LA; tel: 01494 755573; fax: 01494 474284; e-mail: hughenden@ nationaltrust.org.uk

Long Crendon Court House
Long Crendon, Aylesbury, Buckinghamshire, HP18 9AN; tel: 01494 528051; fax: 01280 822850

Mottisfont Abbey
Mottisfont, Romsey, Hampshire, SO51 0LP; tel: 01794 340757; fax: 01794 341492; e-mail: mottisfontabbey@nationaltrust.org.uk

Needles Old Battery
West Highdown, Totland, Isle of Wight, PO39 0JH; tel: 01983 754772

Old Town Hall, Newtown
Newtown, Newport, Isle of Wight, PO30 4PA; tel: 01983 531785

Rainham Hall
The Broadway, Rainham, Essex, RM13 9YN; tel: 020 7447 6605

Sandham Memorial Chapel
Harts Lane, Burghclere, Newbury, Hampshire, RG20 9JT; tel: 01635 278394; fax: 01635 278394; e-mail: sandham@nationaltrust.org.uk

Sutton House
2/4 Homerton High Street, Hackney, London, E9 6JQ; tel: 020 8986 2264; e-mail: suttonhouse@ nationaltrust.org.uk

The Vyne
Sherborne St John, Basingstoke, Hampshire, RG24 9HL; tel: 01256 883858; fax: 01256 881720; e-mail: thevyne@nationaltrust.org.uk

Waddesdon Manor
Waddesdon, Aylesbury, Buckinghamshire, HP18 0JH; tel: 01296 653226; fax: 01296 653212; e-mail: waddesonmanor@nationaltrust.org.uk

West Wycombe Park
West Wycombe, Buckinghamshire, HP14 3AJ; tel: 01494 513569

NATIONAL TRUST (WESSEX REGIONAL OFFICE)

Formal name: National Trust for Places of Historic Interest or Natural Beauty
Acronym or abbreviation: NT

Bishopstrow, Warminster, Wiltshire, BA12 9HW

Tel: 01985 843600
Fax: 01985 843624
E-mail: enquiries@thenationaltrust.org.uk

Website:
http://www.nationaltrust.org.uk
Information about the National Trust properties, opening times and facilities, special events, educational information, and publications.

Enquiries:
Enquiries to: Customer Service Manager

Founded:
1895

Organisation type and purpose:
National organisation, independently owned, membership association (membership is by subscription), registered charity (charity number 205846), historic building, house or site, suitable for ages: Life long.
Administration and management of Trust sites in the Wessex region.

Subject coverage:
The preservation and upkeep of places of historic interest and natural beauty in Bristol/Bath, Dorset, Gloucestershire, Somerset and Wiltshire.

Publications list:
Available online and in print

Access to staff:
Contact by letter, by telephone, by fax, by e-mail, in person and via website
Hours: Mon to Fri, 0900 to 1700

National Trust sites:
Avebury
Barn Gallery, High Street, Avebury, Marlborough, Wiltshire, SN8 1RF; tel: 01672 539494; e-mail: avebury@ntrust.org.uk

Barrington Court
Barrington, Ilminster, Somerset, TA19 0NQ; tel: 01460 241938; fax: 01460 241938; e-mail: barringtoncourt@ntrust.org.uk

Bath Assembly Rooms
Bennett Street, Bath, BA1 2QH; tel: 01225 477789

Chedworth Roman Villa
Yanworth, Cheltenham, Gloucestershire, GL54 3LJ; tel: 01242 890256

Clevedon Court
Tickenham Road, Clevedon, Somerset, BS21 6QU; tel: 01275 872257

continued overleaf

Coleridge Cottage
  35 Lime Street, Nether Stowey, Bridgwater,
  Somerset, TA5 1NQ; tel: 01278 732662
Corfe Castle
  West Street, Corfe Castle, Wareham, Dorset,
  BH20 5EZ; tel: 01929 481294
Dunster Castle
  Dunster, Minehead, Somerset, TA24 6SL; tel:
  01643 821314; fax: 01643 823000; e-mail:
  wdugen@smtp.ntrust.org.uk
Dyrham Park
  Dyrham, Chippenham, SN14 8ER; tel: 01179
  372501; e-mail: dyrhampark@ntrust.org.uk
Great Chalfield Manor
  Melksham, Wiltshire, SN12 8NJ; tel: 01225
  782239; fax: 01225 783379
Hardy's Cottage
  Higher Bockhampton, Dorchester, Dorset, DT2
  8QL; tel: 01305 262366
Horton Court
  Horton, Chipping Sodbury, Bristol, BS17 6QR;
  tel: 01249 730141
King John's Hunting Lodge
  Axbridge, Somerset, BS26 2AP; tel: 01934 732012
Kingston Lacy
  Wimbourne, Dorset, BH21 4EA; tel: 01202
  883402
Kingston Lacy
  Wimbourne, Dorset, BH21 4EA; tel: 01202
  883402; fax: 01202 882402
Lacock Abbey and Fox Talbot Museum
  Lacock, Chippenham, Wiltshire, SN15 2LG; tel:
  01249 730227
Little Clarendon House
  Dinton, Salisbury, Wiltshire, SP3 5DZ; tel: 01985
  843600 (Regional Office)
Lodge Park House
  Aldsworth, Cheltenham, Gloucestershire, GL54
  3PP; tel: 01450 844130; fax: 01451 844131; e-mail:
  lodgepark@ntrust.org.uk
Lytes Cary Manor
  nr Charlton Mackrell, Somerton, Somerset, TA11
  7HU; tel: 01985 224471; e-mail: lytescarymanor@
  ntrust.org.uk
Max Gate
  Alington Avenue, Dorchester, Dorset, DT1 2AA;
  tel: 01305 262538; fax: 01305 250978
Mompesson House
  The Close, Salisbury, Wiltshire, SP1 2EL; tel:
  01722 335659; fax: 01722 321559; e-mail:
  mompessonhouse@ntrust.org.uk
Montacute House
  Montacute, Somerset, TA15 6XP; tel: 01935
  823289; e-mail: montacute@ntrust.org.uk
Newark Park
  Ozleworth, Wotton under Edge, Gloucestershire,
  GL12 7PZ; tel: 01453 842644
Philipps House and Ditton Park
  Ditton, Salisbury, Wiltshire, SP3 5HH; tel: 01985
  843600 (Regional Office)
Snowshill Manor
  Snowshill, Broadway, Gloucestershire, WR12
  7JU; tel: 01386 852410; fax: 01386 852410; e-mail:
  snowshillmanor@ntrust.org.uk
Stonehenge Down
  Amesbury, Salisbury, Wiltshire, SP4 7DE; tel:
  01980 624715 (Infoline)
Stourhead House
  Stourton, Warminster, Wiltshire, BA12 6QD; tel:
  01747 841152
Westwood Manor
  Westwood, Bradford on Avon, Wiltshire, BA15
  2AF; tel: 01225 863374
White Mill
  Sturminster Marshall, Wimborne, Dorset, BH21
  4BX; tel: 01258 858051

NATIONAL TRUST (YORKSHIRE & NORTH EAST REGIONAL OFFICES) – MORPETH

Formal name: National Trust for Places of Historic
Interest or Natural Beauty
Acronym or abbreviation: NT

Scots' Gap, Morpeth, Northumberland, NE61 4EG

Tel: 01670 774691

Fax: 01670 774317
E-mail: enquiries@thenationaltrust.org.uk

Website:
http://www.nationaltrust.org.uk
Information about the National Trust properties,
opening times and facilities, special events,
educational information, and publications.

Enquiries:
Enquiries to: Communications Marketing Manager
Direct tel: 07500 993500
Direct e-mail: eve.jackson@nationaltrust.org.uk

Founded:
1895

Organisation type and purpose:

National organisation, independently owned,
membership association (membership is by
subscription), registered charity (charity number
205846), historic building, house or site, suitable
for ages: Life long.

Administration and management of Trust sites in
the North East.

Subject coverage:
The preservation and upkeep of Trust properties of
historic interest and natural beauty in Co Durham,
Newcastle and Tyneside, Northumberland.

Publications list:
Available online and in print

Access to staff:
Contact by letter, by telephone, by e-mail, in
person and via website
Hours: Mon to Fri, 0900 to 1700

Access to building, collection or gallery:
Hours: Mon to Fri, 0900 to 1700

National Trust sites:
Cherryburn
  Station Bank, Mickley, Stocksfield,
  Northumberland, NE43 7DD; tel: 01661 843276;
  e-mail: cherryburn@nationaltrust.org.uk
Cragside House
  Rothbury, Morpeth, Northumberland, NE65
  7PX; tel: 01669 620333; fax: 01669 620066; e-mail:
  cragside@nationaltrust.org.uk
Dunstanburgh Castle
  Craster, Alnwick, Northumberland; tel: 01665
  576231
George Stephenson's Birthplace
  Street House, Wylam, Newcastle upon Tyne,
  Northumberland, NE41 8BP; tel: 01661 853457;
  fax: 01670 774317
Gibside
  nr Rowlands Gill, Burnopfield, Newcastle upon
  Tyne, Tyne & Wear, NE16 6BG; tel: 01207 542255;
  fax: 01207 542255; e-mail: gibside@nationaltrust
  .org.uk
Hadrian's Wall & Housesteads Roman Fort
  Bardon Mill, Hexham, Northumberland, NE47
  6NN; tel: 01434 344363 (EH Custodian)
Lindisfarne Castle
  Holy Island, Berwick-upon-Tweed,
  Northumberland, TD15 2SH; tel: 01289 389244;
  fax: 01289 389349; e-mail: lindisfarne@
  nationaltrust.org.uk
Ormesby Hall
  Ormesby, Middlesbrough, Cleveland, TS7 9AS;
  tel: 01642 324188; fax: 01642 300937; e-mail:
  ormesbyhall@nationaltrust.org.uk
Souter Lighthouse
  Coast Road, Whitburn, Sunderland, Tyne and
  Wear, SR6 7NH; tel: 0191 529 3161; Infoline tel:
  01670 773966; fax: 0191 529 0902; e-mail: souter@
  nationaltrust.org.uk
Wallington
  Cambo, Morpeth, Northumberland, NE6 4AR;
  tel: 01670 773967 (Infoline); fax: 01670 774420; e-
  mail: wallington@nationaltrust.org.uk
Washington Old Hall
  The Avenue, District 4, Washington Village,
  Washington, Tyne and Wear, NE38 7LE; tel: 0191
  416 6879; fax: 0191 416 2065; e-mail: washington
  .oldhall@nationaltrust.org.uk

NATIONAL TRUST (YORKSHIRE & NORTH EAST REGIONAL OFFICES) – YORK

Formal name: National Trust for Places of Historic
Interest or Natural Beauty
Acronym or abbreviation: NT

Goddards, 27 Tadcaster Road, York, YO24 1GG

Tel: 01904 702021
Fax: 01904 771970
E-mail: enquiries@thenationaltrust.org.uk

Website:
http://www.nationaltrust.org.uk
Information about the National Trust properties,
opening times and facilities, special events,
educational information, and publications.

Enquiries:
Enquiries to: Marketing & Supporter Development
Manager
Direct e-mail: yne.customerservice@nationaltrust
.org.uk

Founded:
1895

Organisation type and purpose:
National organisation, independently owned,
membership association (membership is by
subscription), registered charity (charity number
205846), historic building, house or site, suitable
for ages: Life long.
Administration and management of Trust sites in
Yorkshire & the North East.

Subject coverage:
The preservation and upkeep of Trust properties of
historic interest and natural beauty in Yorkshire,
Teesside and North Lincolnshire.

Publications list:
Available online and in print

Access to staff:
Contact by letter, by telephone, by fax, by e-mail,
in person and via website
Hours: Mon to Fri, 0900 to 1700

National Trust sites:
Beningbrough Hall
  Beningbrough, York, YO30 1DD; tel: 01904
  472027; fax: 01904 470002; e-mail:
  beningbrough@nationaltrust.org.uk
East Riddlesden Hall
  Bradford Road, Keighley, West Yorkshire, BD20
  5EL; tel: 01535 607075; fax: 01535 691462; e-mail:
  eastriddlesden@nationaltrust.org.uk
Fountains Abbey & Studley Royal
  Fountains, Ripon, North Yorkshire, HG4 3DY;
  tel: 01765 608888; fax: 01765 601002; e-mail:
  fountainsenquiries@nationaltrust.org.uk
Mount Grace Priory
  Osmotherley, Northallerton, North Yorkshire,
  DL6 3JG; tel: 01609 883494
Nostell Priory
  Doncaster Road, Wakefield, West Yorkshire, WF4
  1QE; tel: 01924 863892; fax: 01924 866846; e-mail:
  nostellpriory@nationaltrust.org.uk
Nunnington Hall
  Nunnington, York, YO62 5UY; tel: 01439 748283;
  fax: 01439 748284; e-mail: nunningtonhall@
  nationaltrust.org.uk
Treasurer's House
  Minster Yard, Chapter House Street, York, YO1
  7JL; tel: 01904 624247; fax: 01904 647372; e-mail:
  treasurershouse@nationaltrust.org.uk
Yorkshire Coast
  Old Coastguard Station, The Dock, Robin Hood's
  Bay, Whitby, North Yorkshire, YO22 4SJ; tel:
  01947 885900; e-mail: yorkshirecoast@
  nationaltrust.org.uk

NATIONAL TRUST FOR SCOTLAND

Acronym or abbreviation: NTS

28 Charlotte Square, Edinburgh, EH2 4ET

Tel: 0131 243 9300
Fax: 0131 243 9301

E-mail: information@nts.org.uk

Website:
http://www.nts.org.uk
Information about the National Trust for Scotland properties, opening times and facilities, special events, educational information, and publications.

Enquiries:
Enquiries to: Archivist
Direct tel: 0131 243 9524
Direct e-mail: swilson@nts.org.uk

Founded:
1931

Organisation type and purpose:
Independently owned, membership association (membership is by subscription), registered charity (charity number SCO07410), suitable for ages: all. Conservation of sites which have significance for the natural or built heritage of Scotland.

Subject coverage:
Practical aspects of conserving and making available to the public, with information and visitor services, country houses, small buildings, gardens, battlefields, and countryside and all places of natural beauty or historic or architectural interest in Scotland.

Museum or gallery collection, archive, or library special collection:
Archives of the National Trust for Scotland (1931-current) and some collections of family papers associated with some of our properties
A small reference library

Non-library collection catalogue:
All or part available in-house

Library catalogue:
All or part available in-house

Printed publications:
Annual Report
Architecture and Interiors
Corporate Brochure
Corporate Plan
Educational publications relating to the properties
Guidebooks, brochures and leaflets to Trust properties
Heritage Scotland (magazine, quarterly)
Resource packs
Scotland's Gardens Scheme Handbook 1999

Publications list:
Available in print

Access to staff:
Contact by letter, by telephone, by fax and by e-mail
Hours: Mon to Fri, 0930 to 1630
Special comments: Limited disabled access.

Other locations:
National Trust for Scotland (London Office)
19 Cockspur Street, London, SW1Y 5BL; tel: 020 7321 5765; fax: 020 7389 0758
National Trust for Scotland (North America)
One Boston Place, Fifth Floor, Boston, MA 02108, USA; tel: 00 1 617 619 3631; e-mail: nationaltrustforscotland@mediaone.net

Regional Offices:
Highlands and Islands Regional Office (North)
Balnain House, 40 Huntly Street, Inverness, IV3 5HR; tel: 01463 232034; fax: 01463 732620
Highlands and Islands Regional Office (South)
Lochvoil House, Dunuraran Road, Oban, PA34 4NE; tel: 01631 570000; fax: 01631 570011
National Trust for Scotland (North-East Region)
The Stables, Castle Fraser, Sauchen, Inverurie, Aberdeenshire, AB51 7LD; tel: 01463 232034; fax: 01463 732620
National Trust for Scotland (South Region)
Northgate House, 32 Northgate, Peebles, EH45 8RS; tel: 01721 722502; fax: 01721 726000
National Trust for Scotland (West Region)
Greenbank House, Flenders Road, Clarkston, Glasgow, G76 8RB; tel: 0141 616 2266; fax: 0141 616 0550

NATIONAL TRUST FOR SCOTLAND (NORTH-EAST REGION)

Acronym or abbreviation: NTS

The Stables, Castle Fraser, Sauchen, Inverurie, Aberdeenshire, AB51 7LD

Tel: 01330 833225
Fax: 01330 833666

Website:
http://www.nts.org.uk

Enquiries:
Enquiries to: Public Affairs Manager
Direct tel: 01330 833559
Direct e-mail: glovie@nts.org.uk

Founded:
1931

Organisation type and purpose:
National organisation, independently owned, membership association (membership is by subscription), registered charity (charity number SCO 07410), suitable for ages: all. Administration and management of Trust sites in Perthshire, Angus, Aberdeen & Grampian.

Subject coverage:
Heritage, conservation and environmental projects.

Publications list:
Available in print

Access to staff:
Contact by letter, by telephone and by fax
Hours: Mon to Fri, 0900 to 1700

National Trust for Scotland sites:
Angus Folk Museum
Kirkwynd, Glamis, Forfar, Angus, DD8 1RT; tel: 01307 840288
Barry Water Mill
Barry, Carnoustie, Angus, DD7 7RJ; tel: 01241 856761
Castle Fraser
Sauchen, Inverurie, Aberdeenshire, AB51 7LD; tel: 01330 833463; fax: 01330 833819
Craigievar Castle
Alford, Aberdeenshire, AB33 8JF; tel: 013398 83635; fax: 013398 83280
Crathes Castle, Garden & Estate
Banchory, Aberdeenshire, AB31 5QJ; tel: 01330 844525; fax: 01330 844797; e-mail: crathes@nts.org.uk
Drum Castle, Garden & Estate
Drumoak, Banchory, Aberdeenshire, AB31 5EY; tel: 01330 811204; fax: 01330 811962; e-mail: drum-castle@nts.org.uk
Dunkeld
Ell Shop, The Cross, Dunkeld, Perthshire, PH8 0AN; tel: 01350 727460; e-mail: dunkeld@nts.org.uk
Dunkeld and The Hermitage
Dunkeld, Perthshire; tel: 01350 728641 (Ranger Office); fax: tel/fax 01796 473233 (Killiecrankie Visitor Centre)
Finavon Doocot
Finavon, Angus
Fyvie Castle
Fyvie, Turriff, Aberdeenshire, AB53 8JS; tel: 01651 891266; fax: 01651 891107
Haddo House
Ellon, Aberdeenshire, AB41 7EQ; tel: 01651 851440; fax: 01651 851888; e-mail: haddo@nts.org.uk
House of Dun
Montrose, Angus, DD10 9LQ; tel: 01674 810264; fax: 01674 810722; e-mail: houseofdun@nts.org.uk
J M Barrie's Birthplace
9 Brechin Road, Kirriemuir, Angus, DD8 4BX; tel: 01575 572646
Killiecrankie Visitor Centre
Pitlochry, Perth & Kinross, PH16 5LG; tel: 01796 473233; e-mail: killiecrankie@nts.org.uk
Leith Hall, Garden & Estate
Huntly, Aberdeenshire, AB54 4NQ; tel: 01464 831216; fax: 01464 831594; e-mail: leithhall@nts.org.uk

Museum of Farming Life
Pitmedden Garden, Ellon, Aberdeenshire, AB41 0PD; tel: 01651 842352; fax: 01651 843 188; e-mail: sburgess@nts.org.uk
Pitmedden Garden
Ellon, Aberdeenshire, AB41 7PD; tel: 01651 842352; fax: 01651 843188

Parent body:
National Trust for Scotland
28 Charlotte Square, Edinburgh, EH2 4ET; tel: 0131 243 9300; fax: 0131 243 9301; e-mail: information@nts.org.uk

NATIONAL TRUST FOR SCOTLAND (SOUTH REGION)

Acronym or abbreviation: NTS

Northgate House, 32 Northgate, Peebles, Borders, EH45 8RS

Tel: 01721 722502
Fax: 01721 726000
E-mail: information@nts.org.uk

Website:
http://www.nts.org.uk
Information about the National Trust for Scotland properties, opening times and facilities, special events, educational information, and publications.

Enquiries:
Enquiries to: Director
Direct e-mail: dmcallister@nts.org.uk

Founded:
1931

Organisation type and purpose:
Independently owned, membership association (membership is by subscription), registered charity (charity number SCO 07410), suitable for ages: all.

Subject coverage:
Specific information on its own properties and sites also conservation, environmental issues and heritage.
Administration and management of Trust sites in Dumfries and Galloway, Scottish Borders, Edinburgh and The Lothians, and Fife.

Trade and statistical information:
Tourist, visitor attractions, building conservation.

Access to staff:
Contact by letter, by telephone, by fax and by e-mail. Appointment necessary.
Hours: Mon to Fri 0900 to 1700

National Trust for Scotland sites:
Balmerino Abbey
Balmerino, Fife
Broughton House
12 High Street, Kirkcudbright, Dumfries & Galloway, DG6 4JX; tel: 01557 330437; e-mail: broughtonhouse@nts.org.uk
Caiy Stane
Caiystane View, Edinburgh
Falkland Palace
Falkland, Cupar, Fife, KY15 7BU; tel: 01337 857397; fax: 01337 857980; e-mail: falklandpalace@nts.org.uk
Georgian House
7 Charlotte Square, Edinburgh, EH2 4DR; tel: 0131 226 3318; e-mail: thegeorgianhouse@nts.org.uk
Gladstone's Land
477B Lawnmarket, Edinburgh, EH1 2NT; tel: 0131 226 5856; fax: 0131 226 4851
Hill of Tarvit Mansion House & Gardens
Cupar, Fife, KY15 5PB; tel: 01334 653127
House of the Binns
Linlithgow, West Lothian, EH49 7NA; tel: 01506 834255; e-mail: houseofthebinns@nts.org.uk
Kellie Castle and Garden
Pittenweem, Anstruther, Fife, KY10 2RF; tel: 01333 720271; fax: 01333 720326
Newhailes
Newhailes Road, Musselburgh, East Lothian, EH21 6RY; tel: 0131 665 1546

continued overleaf

No 28 Charlotte Square
  Edinburgh, EH2 4ET; tel: 0131 243 9300; fax:
  0131 243 9339
Preston Mill and Phantassie Doocot
  East Linton, East Lothian, EH40 3DS; tel: 01620
  860426
Robert Smail's Printing Works
  7–9 High Street, Inverleithen, Borders, EH44
  6HA; tel: 01896 830206; e-mail: smails@nts.org
  .uk
Royal Burgh of Culross
  Culross, Fife, KY12 8JH; tel: 01383 880359; fax:
  01383 882675
Threave
  Castle Douglas, Dumfries & Galloway, DG7 1RX;
  tel: 01556 502575; fax: 01556 502683; e-mail:
  threave@nts.org.uk

Parent body:
National Trust for Scotland
  Wemyss House, 28 Charlotte Square, Edinburgh,
  EH2 4ET; tel: 0131 243 9300; fax: 0131 243 9301;
  e-mail: information@nts.org.uk

NATIONAL TRUST FOR SCOTLAND (WEST REGION)

Acronym or abbreviation: NTS

Greenbank House, Flenders Road, Clarkston,
Glasgow, G76 8RB

Tel: 0141 616 2266
Fax: 0141 616 0550
E-mail: kcarr@nts.org.uk

Website:
http://www.nts.org.uk

Enquiries:
Enquiries to: Public Relations Officer
Other contacts: Regional Director (for policy)

Founded:
1931

Organisation type and purpose:
National organisation, membership association,
present number of members: 246,000, voluntary
organisation, registered charity (charity number
SCO 07410), suitable for ages: all.

Subject coverage:
Specific information on the properties, also
conservation and environmental issues,
particularly in this region of Scotland.
Administration and management of Trust sites in
Ayrshire and Arran, Greater Glasgow and Clyde
Valley and Cental Scotland.

Museum or gallery collection, archive, or library special collection:
Many collections appropriate to individual
  properties (details on request)

Trade and statistical information:
Tourist, visitor attractions, building conservation.

Printed publications:
Full colour guide books to many properties
NTS Annual Report (free)
NTS Guide to Over 100 Properties
NTS Handbook
Publications under the following headings:
Architecture and Interiors
Birthplaces, Industrial and Social History
Garden Books, Guides and leaflets
Maps and Charts
Mountains, Islands and Countryside
Walks and Trails

Electronic and video publications:
Wide variety of films, slides and videos for sale
  and hire, including:
A Sampling of Scotland
Britain: Kingdom of the Sea
Countryside in Trust (slides and notes)
Fair Isle – The Happy Island
Gardens in Trust (slides and notes)
House of Dun ... no more handsome and
  convenient a house of the bigness in all the
  ancient Kingdom
Scotland a Heritage

Scotland in Trust (slides and notes)
St Kilda Story
The Tenement House, Glasgow
The Work of the Weavers

Publications list:
Available in print

Access to staff:
Contact by letter, by telephone, by fax, by e-mail
and via website
Hours: Mon to Fri, 0900 to 1700

National Trust for Scotland sites:
Alloa Tower
  Alloa Park, Alloa, FK10 1PP; tel: 01259 211701;
  fax: 01259 218744
Bannockburn Heritage Centre
  Glasgow Road, Bannockburn, Stirling, FK7 0LJ;
  tel: 01786 812664; fax: 01786 810892
Batchelors' Club
  Sandgate Street, Tarbolton, South Ayrshire, KA5
  5RB; tel: 01292 541940
Black Hill
  Lanark, South Lanarkshire
Brodick Castle Garden and Country Park
  Brodick, Isle of Arran; tel: 01770 302202; fax:
  01770 302312; e-mail: brodick@nts.org.uk
Culzean Castle and Country Park
  Maybole, South Ayrshire, KA19 8LE; tel: 01655
  884455; fax: 01655 884503; e-mail: culzean@nts
  .org.uk
David Livingstone Centre
  165 Station Road, Glasgow, South Lanarkshire,
  G72 9BT; tel: 01698 8231140; fax: 01698 821424
Holmwood House
  61–63 Netherlee Road, Cathcart, Glasgow, G44
  3YG; tel: 0141 637 2129; fax: 0141 637 2129; e-
  mail: holmwood@nts.org.uk
Hutchesons' Hall
  158 Ingram Street, Glasgow, G1 1EJ; tel: 0141 552
  8391; fax: 0141552 7031; e-mail: hutchesonshall@
  nts.org.uk
Menstrie Castle
  Castle Street, Menstrie, Clackmannanshire
Moirlanich Longhouse
  Near Killin, Stirling
Museum of Scottish Country Life
  Wester Kittochside, East Kilbride, G76 9HR; tel:
  01355 224181; fax: 01355 571290
Pollok House
  Pollok Country Park, 2060 Pollokshaws Road,
  Glasgow, G43 1AT; tel: 0141 616 6410; fax: 0141
  616 6521; e-mail: pollokhouse@nts.org.uk
Souter Johnnie's Cottage
  Main Road, Kirkoswald, Ayrshire, KA19 8HY;
  tel: 01655 760603
Tenement House
  145 Buccleuch Street, Garnethill, Glasgow, G3
  6QN; tel: 0141 333 0183; e-mail: tenementhouse@
  nts.org.uk
The Hill House
  Upper Colquhoun Street, Helensburgh, G849AJ;
  tel: 01436 673900; fax: 01436 674685
The Pineapple
  North of Airth, Falkirk; tel: 01324 831137
Weaver's Cottage
  Shuttle Street, The Cross, Kilbarchan,
  Renfrewshire, PA10 2JG; tel: 01505 705588

Parent body:
National Trust for Scotland
  Wemyss House, 28 Charlotte Square, Edinburgh,
  EH2 4ET; tel: 0131 243 9300; fax: 0131 243 9301;
  e-mail: information@nts.org.uk

NATIONAL TRUST FOR SCOTLAND HIGHLANDS AND ISLANDS OFFICE (NORTH)

Acronym or abbreviation: NTS

Balnain House, 40 Huntly Street, Inverness, IV3
5HR

Tel: 01463 232034
E-mail: information@nts.org.uk

Website:
http://www.nts.org.uk

Enquiries:
Enquiries to: Director

Organisation type and purpose:
Independently owned, membership association
(membership is by subscription), voluntary
organisation, registered charity, suitable for ages:
all.

Subject coverage:
Specific information on its own properties and sites
also conservation, environmental issues and
heritage.
Administration and management of Trust sites in
Ross-shire, Inverness, Nairn, Moray and The Black
Isle, and Northern Islands.

National Trust for Scotland sites:
Balmacara Estate
  Lochalsh House (NTS), Balmacara, Kyle, Ross-
  shire, IV40 8DN; tel: 01599 566359; e-mail:
  balmacara@nts.org.uk
Boath Doocot
  Auldearn, Nairn, Moray
Brodie Castle
  Brodie, Forres, Moray, IV36 2TE; tel: 01309
  641371; fax: 01309 641600; e-mail: brodiecastle@
  nts.org.uk
Culloden Moor Visitors Centre
  Culloden Moor, Inverness, Highland, IV2 5EU;
  tel: 01463 790607; fax: 01463 794294; e-mail:
  rmackenzie@nts.org.uk
Strome Castle
  Ross-shire

Parent body:
National Trust for Scotland

NATIONAL TRUST FOR SCOTLAND HIGHLANDS AND ISLANDS OFFICE (SOUTH)

Acronym or abbreviation: NTS

Lochvoil House, Dunuaran Road, Oban, Argyll,
PA34 4NE

Tel: 01631 570000
Fax: 01631 570011
E-mail: information@nts.org.uk

Website:
http://www.nts.org.uk
Information about the National Trust for Scotland
properties, opening times and facilities, special
events, educational information, and publications.

Enquiries:
Enquiries to: Director

Organisation type and purpose:
Registered charity (charity number SCO 07410),
suitable for ages: all.
Administration and management of Trust sites in
Argyll & Lochaber and West Coast Islands.

Subject coverage:
Heritage, conservation and environmental projects.
Administration and management of Trust sites in
Argyll and Lochaber, and West Coast Islands.

Access to staff:
Contact by letter, by telephone, by fax and by e-
mail. Appointment necessary.
Hours: Mon to Fri, 0900 to 1700

National Trust for Scotland sites:
Glencoe and Dalness
  The National Trust for Scotland Visitor Centre,
  Glencoe, Argyll, PH49 4LA; tel: 01855 811729;
  fax: 01855 811772; e-mail: glencoe@nts.org.uk
Glenfinnan Monument
  National Trust for Scotland Information Centre,
  Glenfinnan, Highland, PH37 4LT; tel: 01397
  722250; e-mail: glenfinnan@nts.org.uk

Parent body:
National Trust for Scotland
  28 Charlotte Square, Edinburgh, EH2 4ET; tel:
  0131 243 9300; fax: 0131 243 9301; e-mail:
  information@nts.org.uk

NATIONAL TRUST MIDLANDS (WEST)

Formal name: National Trust for Places of Historic Interest or Natural Beauty
Acronym or abbreviation: NT

Attingham Park, Shrewsbury, Shropshire, SY4 4TP

Tel: 01743 708100
Fax: 01743 708150
E-mail: enquiries@thenationaltrust.org.uk

Website:
http://www.nationaltrust.org.uk
Information about the National Trust properties, opening times and facilities, special events, educational information, and publications.

Enquiries:
Enquiries to: Customer Service Manager

Founded:
1895

Organisation type and purpose:
National organisation, independently owned, membership association (membership is by subscription), registered charity (charity number 205846), historic building, house or site, suitable for ages: all.
Administration and management of Trust sites in the West Midlands.

Subject coverage:
The preservation and upkeep of Trust properties of historic interest and natural beauty in Birmingham, Herefordshire, Shropshire, Staffordshire, Warwickshire and Worcestershire.

Publications list:
Available online and in print

Access to staff:
Contact by letter, by telephone, by e-mail, in person and via website
Hours: Mon to Fri, 0900 to 1700

National Trust sites:
Attingham Hall
  Attingham Park, Shrewsbury, Shropshire, SY4 4TP; tel: 01743 709203; fax: 01743 708175; e-mail: attingham@nationaltrust.org.uk
Baddesley Clinton Hall
  Rising Lane, Baddesley Clinton Village, Knowle, Solihull, West Midlands, B93 0DQ; tel: 01564 783294; fax: 01564 782706; e-mail: baddesleyclinton@nationaltrust.org.uk
Benthall Hall
  Broseley, Shropshire, TF12 5RX; tel: 01952 882159; e-mail: benthall@nationaltrust.org.uk
Berrington Hall
  Leominster, Herefordshire, HR6 0DW; tel: 01568 615721; fax: 01568 613263; e-mail: berrington@.nationaltrust.org.uk
Brockhampton House and Estate
  Bringsty, Worcester, WR6 5TB; tel: 01885 482077; e-mail: brockhampton@nationaltrust.org.uk
Charlecote Park
  Warwick, CV35 9ER; tel: 01789 470277; fax: 01789 470544; e-mail: charlecotepark@nationaltrust.org.uk
Croft Castle & Parkland
  Leominster, Herefordshire, HR6 9PW; tel: 01568 780246; e-mail: croftcastle@nationaltrust.org.uk
Dudmaston Hall
  Quatt, Bridgnorth, Shropshire, WV15 6QN; tel: 01746 780866 (Dudmaston Estate); fax: 01746 780744; e-mail: dudmaston@nationaltrust.org.uk
Farnborough Hall
  Banbury, OX17 1DU; tel: 01295 690002; e-mail: farnboroughhall@nationaltrust.org.uk
Greyfriars
  Friar Street, Worcester, WR1 2LZ; tel: 01905 23571; e-mail: greyfriars@nationaltrust.org.uk
Hanbury Hall
  School Road, Hanbury, Droitwich, Worcestershire, WR9 7EA; tel: 01527 821214; fax: 01527 821251; e-mail: hanburyhall@nationaltrust.org.uk
Morville Hall
  Morville, Bridgnorth, Shropshire, WV16 5NB; tel: 01743 708100 (Regional Office); e-mail: morvillehall@nationaltrust.org.uk

Moseley Old Hall
  Moseley Old Hall Lane, Fordhouses, Wolverhampton, West Midlands, WV10 7HY; tel: 01902 782808; e-mail: moseleyoldhall@nationaltrust.org.uk
Packwood House
  Lapworth, Solihull, West Midlands, B94 6AT; tel: 01564 783294; fax: 01564 782706; e-mail: packwood@nationaltrust.org.uk
Sunnycroft
  200 Holyhead Road, Wellington, Telford, Shropshire, TF1 2DR; tel: 01952 242884; e-mail: sunnycroft@nationaltrust.org.uk
Upton House & Gardens
  Near Banbury, Oxfordshire, OX15 6HT; tel: 01295 670266; e-mail: uptonhouse@nationaltrust.org.uk
Wall Roman Site (Letocetum)
  Wall, Lichfield, Staffordshire, WS14 0AW; tel: 01543 480768; e-mail: letocetum@nationaltrust.org.uk
Wightwick Manor
  Wightwick Bank, Wolverhampton, West Midlands, WV6 8EE; tel: 01902 761108 (Infoline); fax: 01902 764663; e-mail: wightwickmanor@nationaltrust.org.uk
Wilderhope Manor
  Longville, Much Wenlock, Shropshire, TF13 6EG; tel: 01694 771363; e-mail: wilderhopemanor@nationaltrust.org.uk

NATIONAL TRUST OFFICE FOR NORTHERN IRELAND

Rowallane House, Saintfield, Ballynahinch, Co Down, BT24 7LH

Tel: 020 9751 0721
Fax: 028 9751 1242

Website:
http://www.ntni.org.uk

Enquiries:
Enquiries to: Manager

Organisation type and purpose:
National organisation, membership association (membership is by subscription), registered charity (charity number 205846), suitable for ages: all.
The preservation and upkeep of places of historic interest or natural beauty.

Subject coverage:
The conservation of places of historic interest or natural beauty in Northern Ireland.

Access to staff:
Contact by letter, by telephone, by fax and by e-mail
Hours: Mon to Fri, 0900 to 1700

Other Trust sites:
Ardress House
  64 Ardress Road, Portadown, Co Armagh, BT62 1SQ; tel: 028 3885 1236; fax: 028 3885 1236; e-mail: ardress@nationaltrust.org.uk
Castle Coole
  Enniskillen, Co Fermanagh, BT74 6JY; tel: 028 6632 2690; fax: 028 6632 5665; e-mail: castlecoole@nationaltrust.org.uk
Castle Ward
  Strangford, Downpatrick, Co Down, BT30 7LS; tel: 028 4488 1204; fax: 028 4488 1729; e-mail: castleward@nationaltrust.org.uk
Derrymore House
  Bessbrook, Newry, Co Armagh, BT35 7EF; tel: 028 3083 8361; e-mail: derrymore@nationaltrust.org.uk
Florence Court
  Enniskillen, Co Fermanagh, BT92 1DB; tel: 028 6634 8249; fax: 028 6634 8873; e-mail: florencecourt@nationaltrust.org.uk
Gray's Printing Press
  49 Main Street, Strabane, Co Tyrone, BT82 8AU; tel: 028 7188 0055; fax: 028 7188 0055
Hezlett House
  107 Sea Road, Castlerock, Coleraine, Co Londonderry, BT51 4TW; tel: 028 7084 8567; fax: 028 2073 1582; e-mail: hezletthouse@nationaltrust.org.uk

Mount Stewart House, Garden and Temple of the Winds
  Newtownards, Co Down, BT22 2AD; tel: 028 4278 8387; fax: 028 4278 8569; e-mail: mountstewart@nationaltrust.org.uk
Patterson's Spade Mill
  Templepatrick, Co Antrim, BT39 0AP; tel: 028 9443 3619; fax: 028 9443 9713; e-mail: patterson@nationaltrust.org.uk
Rowallane Garden
  Saintfield, Ballynahinch, Co Down, BT24 7LH; tel: 028 9751 0131; fax: 028 9751 1242; e-mail: rowallane@nationaltrust.org.uk
Springhill
  20 Springhill Road, Moneymore, Magherafelt, Co Londonderry, BT45 7NQ; tel: 028 8674 8210; fax: 028 8674 8210; e-mail: springhill@nationaltrust.org.uk
The Argory
  Moy, Dungannon, Co Tyrone, BT71 6NA; tel: 028 8778 4753; fax: 028 8778 9598; e-mail: argory@nationaltrust.org.uk
Wellbrook Beetling Mill
  20 Wellbrook Street, Corkhill, Cookstown, Co Tyrone, BT80 9RY; tel: 028 8674 8210/8675 1735; fax: 028 8675 1735; e-mail: wellbrook@nationaltrust.org.uk

NATIONAL TRUST OFFICE FOR WALES

Acronym or abbreviation: NT

Trinity Square, Llandudno, LL30 2DE

Tel: 01492 860123
Fax: 01492 860233
E-mail: ntwales@nt.org.uk

Website:
http://www.nt.org.uk

Enquiries:
Enquiries to: Marketing Manager

Organisation type and purpose:
National organisation, independently owned, membership association (membership is by subscription), registered charity (charity number 205846), suitable for ages: all.
The preservation and upkeep of places of historic interest or natural beauty.

Subject coverage:
Places of Historic Interest or Natural Beauty.

Access to staff:
Contact by letter, by telephone, by fax, by e-mail and via website
Hours: Mon to Fri, 0900 to 1700

Other Trust sites:
Aberconwy House
  Castle Street, Conwy, Gwynedd, LL32 8AY; tel: 01492 592246
Aberdulais Falls and Turbine House
  Aberdulais, Neath, West Glamorgan, SA10 8EU; tel: 01639 636674; e-mail: gaberd@smtp.ntrust.org
Chirk Castle
  Chirk, Wrexham, Clwyd, LL14 5AF; tel: 01691 777701; e-mail: gcwmsn@smtp.ntrust.org.uk
Conwy Suspension Bridge
  Conwy, Gwynedd, LL32 8LD; tel: 01492 573282
Dinefwr
  Llandeilo, SA19 6RT; tel: 01558 825912; e-mail: gdrcsh@smtp.ntrust.org.uk
Dolaucothi Gold Mines
  Pumsaint, Llanwrda, Carmarthenshire, SA19 8US; tel: 01558 650177; e-mail: gdoest@smtp.ntrust.org.uk
Erddig Hall
  Wrexham, Clwyd, LL13 0YT; tel: 01978 355314 (info 01978 315151); e-mail: geroff@smtp.ntrust.org.uk
Llanerchaeron
  Aberaeron, Ceredigion, SA48 8DG; tel: 01545 570200; e-mail: glnest@smtp.ntrust.org.uk
Penrhyn Castle
  Bangor, Gwynedd, LL57 4HN; tel: 01248 353084; fax: 01248 371281

continued overleaf

Plas Newydd
Llanfairpwll, Anglesey, Gwynedd, LL61 6DQ;
tel: 01248 714795; e-mail: ppnmsn@smtp.ntrust
.org.uk
Plas Yn Rhiw
Rhiw, Pwllheli, Gwynedd, LL53 8AB; tel: 01758
780219; e-mail: gprmet@smtp.ntrust.org.uk
Powis Castle & Garden
Welshpool, Powys, SY21 8RF; tel: 01938 551920;
e-mail: ppcmsn@smtp.ntrust.org.uk
Tudor Merchant's House
Quay Hill, Tenby, Pembrokeshire, SA70 7BX; tel:
01834 842279
Ty Mawr Wybrnant
Penmachno, Betws-y-Coed, Conwy, LL25 0HJ;
tel: 01690 760213
Ty'n-Y-Coed Uchaf
Penmachno, Betws-y-Coed, Conwy, LL24 0PS;
tel: 01690 760229

NATIONAL TRUST THEATRE

Sutton House, 2–4 Homerton High Street,
Hackney, London, E9 6JQ

Tel: 020 8986 0242
Fax: 020 8985 2343

Website:
http://www.nationaltrust.org.uk/learning

Enquiries:
Enquiries to: Administrator
Direct e-mail: learning@nationaltrust.org.uk

Founded:
1977

Organisation type and purpose:
Registered charity (charity number 205846),
suitable for ages: all.

**Museum or gallery collection, archive, or library
special collection:**
Stage Costumes – mainly Tudor and Victorian

Printed publications:
The War Child – WW2 drama resource book
(available for purchase)

Access to staff:
Contact by letter, by telephone, by fax and by e-
mail. Appointment necessary.
Hours: Mon to Fri, 0930 to 1730

Access to building, collection or gallery:
Prior appointment required

Access for disabled people:
Toilet facilities
Hours: Mon to Fri, 0930 to 1730
Special comments: No lift to upper floors.

Also at:
The National Trust Learning
Rowan, Kembrey Park, Swindon, SN2 6UG

NATIONAL TYRE DISTRIBUTORS
ASSOCIATION

Acronym or abbreviation: NTDA

8 Temple Square, Aylesbury, Buckinghamshire,
HP20 2QH

Tel: 08449 670707
Fax: 01296 488675
E-mail: info@ntda.co.uk

Website:
http://www.ntda.co.uk

Enquiries:
Enquiries to: Director

Founded:
1936

Organisation type and purpose:
Trade association.

Subject coverage:
Tyres, the tyre industry and fast fit products in the
United Kingdom.

Trade and statistical information:
Market Monitor (monthly).

Printed publications:
COSHH Manual (£10)
Directory of Members & Yearbook (£25)
Health and Safety Policy Manual (£30)
Technical Manual (£30)
The UK Tyre Market Report 2001 (£175)

Access to staff:
Contact by letter, by fax and by e-mail
Hours: Mon to Fri, 0900 to 1700

NATIONAL UNION OF
KNITWEAR, FOOTWEAR AND
APPAREL TRADES

Acronym or abbreviation: KFAT

55 New Walk, Leicester, LE1 7EB

Tel: 0116 255 6703
Fax: 0116 254 4406
E-mail: headoffice@kfat.org.uk

Website:
http://www.kfat.org.uk
Membership, policy and press statements.

Enquiries:
Enquiries to: General Secretary
Other contacts: (1) Research and Press Officer (2)
Deputy General Secretary for (1) press enquiries (2)
general enquiries.

Founded:
1991

Organisation type and purpose:
Trade union, present number of members: 30,000.

Subject coverage:
Industrial relations issues for the knitwear,
footwear, leather, hosiery, and apparel industries.

Printed publications:
KFAT News (3 times a year)

Access to staff:
Contact by letter and by e-mail
Hours: Mon to Fri, 0900 to 1700

Access to building, collection or gallery:
No prior appointment required

Affiliated to:
General Federation of Trade Unions
International Textile Garment and Leather Workers
Federation
Labour Party
Trades Union Congress

NATIONAL UNION OF
RESIDENTS ASSOCIATIONS

Acronym or abbreviation: NURA

20 Park Drive, Romford, Essex, RM1 4LH

Tel: 01708 749119
Fax: 01708 736213
E-mail: info@ian-henry.com

Enquiries:
Enquiries to: Chairman

Founded:
1927

Organisation type and purpose:
Voluntary organisation.
Co-ordinating body of ratepayers, residents and
kindred.

Subject coverage:
Interests of ratepayers; economical local
government administration, finance, transport and
public utilities; non-party politics in local
government.

Printed publications:
A Simple Guide to Planning Applications (£5.25
plus 50p postage)

Access to staff:
Contact by letter, by telephone, by fax and by e-
mail
Hours: Sat, Sun, 0900 to 1900

Access to building, collection or gallery:
No access other than to staff

NATIONAL UNION OF STUDENTS

Formal name: National Union of Students
Acronym or abbreviation: NUS

2nd Floor, Centro 3, Mandela Street, London, NW1
0DY

Tel: 0871 221 8221
Fax: 0871 221 8222
E-mail: nusuk@nus.org.uk

Website:
http://www.nusonline.co.uk

Enquiries:
Enquiries to: National Secretary

Founded:
1922

Organisation type and purpose:
National organisation, membership association
(membership is by subscription, qualification),
present number of members: 650, voluntary
organisation, training organisation, research
organisation, publishing house.
To represent the interests of students' unions and
students in the United Kingdom.

Subject coverage:
All aspects of student and students' union life.

Printed publications:
NUS Directory

Publications list:
Available online and in print

Access to staff:
Contact by letter, by telephone, by fax, by e-mail
and via website. Appointment necessary. Non-
members charged.
Hours: Mon to Fri, 0900 to 1700
Special comments: Parking by advance notice.

Access for disabled people:
Ramped entry, toilet facilities
Special comments: Parking provided by
appointment.

NATIONAL UNION OF TEACHERS

Acronym or abbreviation: NUT

Hamilton House, Mabledon Place, London, WC1H
9BD

Tel: 020 7388 6191
Fax: 020 7387 8458

Website:
http://www.teachers.org.uk
Union policy documents, consultation documents
e.g., user comments on recent Government White
and Green papers and consultative papers.
Teachers' salary scales and conditions of service,
health and safety, regional map and addresses of
Union regional offices, membership application
forms, Union newsletters e.g., NUT News.

Enquiries:
Enquiries to: Information Officer
Direct tel: 020 7380 4713
Direct e-mail: j.friedlander@nut.org.uk

Founded:
1870

Organisation type and purpose:
Trade union (membership is by subscription),
present number of members: 314,174.

Subject coverage:
Education.

Museum or gallery collection, archive, or library special collection:
Archives now at Modern Records Centre, Warwick University, Coventry CV4 7AL, tel: 01203 524219
Government publications since 1816
NUT Annual Reports, 1871 to the present
Schoolmaster (now the Teacher), No. 1 (January 1872-)
Union publications since its inception in 1870

Non-library collection catalogue:
All or part available online and in print

Printed publications:
Pamphlets are available from Despatch, Education, Membership and Communications Departments

Access to staff:
Contact by letter, by telephone, by fax and by e-mail. Appointment necessary.
Hours: Mon to Fri, 0900 to 1700
Special comments: Quick reference enquiries, and access to NUT documentation only for members and others.

Access to building, collection or gallery:
No prior appointment required

Affiliated to:
Trades Union Congress
tel: 020 7636 4030; fax: 020 7636 0632; e-mail: info@tuc.org.uk

NATIONAL VINTAGE TRACTOR AND ENGINE CLUB

Acronym or abbreviation: NVTEC

c/o B. Chester, National Chairman, Low Moor Farm, Marton-le-Moor, Ripon, North Yorkshire, HG4 5AR

Tel: 01765 603418
E-mail: brianchester@tiscali.co.uk

Website:
http://www.nvtec.co.uk

Founded:
1965

Organisation type and purpose:
Membership association (membership is by subscription), present number of members: 5800.

Subject coverage:
History of agricultural vehicles, machines, hand tools and all associated equipment.

Museum or gallery collection, archive, or library special collection:
Workshop manuals and sales literature

Printed publications:
Vaporising (magazine, quarterly, members only)

Access to staff:
Contact by letter, by telephone, by fax and by e-mail
Hours: Mon to Fri, 0900 to 2200

Affiliated to:
National Traction Engine Trust

Archivist:
National Vintage Tractor and Engine Club Waylode, Tetbury Road, Old Sodbury, Bristol, BS17 6RJ; tel: 01454 313305

Has:
33 groups of NVTEC throughout England and Wales with another 25 separate clubs affiliated

NATIONAL WAITING LIST HELPLINE

Acronym or abbreviation: NWLH

St Margaret's House, 21 Old Ford Road, London, E2 9PL

Tel: 020 8983 1133
Fax: 020 8983 1553

Enquiries:
Enquiries to: Information Manager
Direct tel: 020 8983 1225

Direct e-mail: info@collegeofhealth.org.uk

Founded:
1991

Organisation type and purpose:
Advisory body, registered charity.

Subject coverage:
Waiting lists for patients waiting for NHS treatment or surgery.

Trade and statistical information:
Data on the length of waiting lists in England by hospital and surgical speciality.

Electronic and video publications:
Licence available for website access

Access to staff:
Contact by telephone
Hours: Mon, Thu, 1100 to 1900; Fri, 1100 to 1700

Access to building, collection or gallery:
No access other than to staff

Parent body:
College of Health

NATIONAL WATER SPORTS TRAINING CENTRE

Isle of Cumbrae, Millport, Ayrshire, KA28 0HQ

Tel: 01475 530757
Fax: 01475 530013
E-mail: cumbraecentre@sportscotland.org.uk

Website:
http://www.nationalcentrecumbrae.org.uk
Brochure.

Enquiries:
Enquiries to: Principal

Founded:
1974

Organisation type and purpose:
National government body, advisory body, registered charity, training organisation.

Subject coverage:
Specialist knowledge of all watersports: all aspects of sailing, kayaking and sub-aqua.

Printed publications:
Brochure

Access to staff:
Contact by letter, by telephone, by fax and in person. Appointment necessary.
Hours: Any reasonable time

Managed by:
SportScotland

NATIONAL WEIGHTS AND MEASURES LABORATORY

Acronym or abbreviation: NWML

Stanton Avenue, Teddington, Middlesex, TW11 0JZ

Tel: 020 8943 7272
Fax: 020 8943 7270
E-mail: info@nwml.gov.uk

Website:
http://www.nwml.gov.uk

Enquiries:
Enquiries to: General Receptionist
Other contacts: Heads of Units, Measuring Instruments Certification Unit, Metrology and Quality Unit, Legal Metrology Policy Unit, Business Support

Founded:
1987

Organisation type and purpose:
National government body.
Executive Agency.

Subject coverage:
Legal metrology in the United Kingdom; examination and approval of new weighing and measuring equipment to be used for trade, calibration, testing and certification, training.

Printed publications:
Annual Reports and Accounts
NWML Now! (twice a year)
Information leaflets and notes for guidance

Electronic and video publications:
MID Certificates, UK National Certificates, NAWI and EEC Certificates for Type Approval of instruments (online)

Publications list:
Available in print

Access to staff:
Contact by letter, by telephone, by fax, by e-mail and via website. Appointment necessary.
Hours: Mon to Fri, 0900 to 1700

Links with:
International Organisation of Legal Metrology
tel: 020 8943 7274
OIML Publications, Bureau International de Métrologie Légale (BIML)
11 rue Turgot, Paris 75009, France; tel: +33 1 48 78 12 82; fax: +33 1 42 82 17 27

Parent body:
Department for Innovation, Universities and Skills Kinsgate House, 66–74 Victoria Street, London, SW1E 6SW; tel: 020 7215 5555; e-mail: info@dius .gsi.gov.uk; website: http://www.dius.gov.uk

NATIONAL WILDFLOWER CENTRE

Court Hey Park, Roby Road, Liverpool, L16 3NA

Tel: 0151 738 1913
E-mail: info@nwc.org.uk

Website:
http://www.wildflower.co.uk

Founded:
2001

Organisation type and purpose:
A registered charity (no. 1078314). Visitor centre set in Victorian Court Hey Park.

Subject coverage:
Wild flowers.

Education services:
Educational facilities.

NATIONAL WOMEN'S REGISTER

Acronym or abbreviation: NWR

23 Vulcan House, Vulcan Road North, Norwich, Norfolk, NR6 6AQ

Tel: 0845 450 0287
Fax: 01603 407003
E-mail: office@nwr.org.uk

Website:
http://www.nwr.org.uk

Enquiries:
Enquiries to: Administrator
Direct fax: 01442 401657
Direct e-mail: dodkins@ntlworld.com
Other contacts: Communications Co-ordinator (for publicity)

Founded:
1960

Organisation type and purpose:
Membership association (membership is by subscription), registered charity (charity number 295198).

Subject coverage:
Organisation for women only; discussion groups to expand horizons, make new friends, explore new interests, lively conversation and informal discussion.

continued overleaf

Museum or gallery collection, archive, or library special collection:
NWR archive held at The Women's Library

Printed publications:
Newsletter (2 times a year, members)
Magazine – The Register (2 times a year, members)
Annual Review (once a year, members)

Access to staff:
Contact by letter, by telephone, by fax, by e-mail and via website
Hours: Mon, Tue, Thu, 0930 to 1615; Wed, 0900 to 1430

Branches:
National organisations in Australia, Netherlands, South Africa and Zimbabwe
subsidiary groups in Europe

NATIONAL YOUTH AGENCY

Eastgate House, 19–23 Humberstone Road, Leicester, LE5 3GJ

Tel: 0116 242 7350
Fax: 0116 242 7444
E-mail: nya@nya.org.uk

Website:
http://www.nya.org.uk
Information on the work of NYA.

Enquiries:
Enquiries to: Reception
Direct fax: 0116 285 3775
Direct e-mail: info@nya.org.uk

Organisation type and purpose:
Registered charity (charity number 1035804).
Specified public body.
A resource agency in informal social education.

Subject coverage:
The work of the youth service statutory and voluntary, major issues affecting the lives of young people, the curriculum for informal social and health education, education and training initiatives, community involvement and participation, counselling and information for young people, training in youth work.

Museum or gallery collection, archive, or library special collection:
Archive material on intermediate treatment
Archive material on the Youth Service
Educational kits and games
Videos

Non-library collection catalogue:
All or part available online

Printed publications:
Youth Policy Update (10 times a year)
Hear By Right
Quality Mark
Order printed publications from: Sales Department, tel: 0116 285 3709; fax: 0116 285 3777; e-mail: sales@nya.org.uk

Publications list:
Available online and in print

Access to staff:
Contact by letter, by telephone, by e-mail and via website. Appointment necessary.
Hours: Mon to Thu, 0900 to 1730; Fri, 0900 to 1700

Access for disabled people:
Level entry, toilet facilities
Special comments: Disabled lift into NYA library available.

Funded by:
in part through the Local Government Association

NATIONAL YOUTH JAZZ ORCHESTRA OF GREAT BRITAIN

Acronym or abbreviation: NYJO

11 Victor Road, Harrow, Middlesex, HA2 6PT

Tel: 020 8863 2717
Fax: 020 8863 8685

E-mail: bill.ashton@virgin.net
Website:
http://www.classical-artists.com/nyjo
Aims, date sheet (concerts), recordings, how to contact.

Enquiries:
Enquiries to: Musical Director

Founded:
1965

Organisation type and purpose:
National organisation, membership association (membership is by qualification, election or invitation), registered charity (charity number 274578), suitable for ages: up to 25.
Provides an opportunity for gifted young musicians to meet together and play big band jazz to a very high standard. Enables young musicians to gain experience of working to professional standards in major concert venues.

Subject coverage:
All aspects of the National Youth Jazz Orchestra of Great Britain. Becoming a participating musician, obtaining recordings, concert dates, becoming a friend.

Printed publications:
News from NYJO (magazine, quarterly, £10 voluntary donation, includes catalogue of recordings on CD, cassette, vinyl and videos)

Access to staff:
Contact by letter, by telephone, by fax, by e-mail and via website
Hours: Mon to Fri, 0900 to 1700
Special comments: No callers in person.

Access to building, collection or gallery:
No access other than to staff

NATIONAL YOUTH ORCHESTRAS OF SCOTLAND

Acronym or abbreviation: NYOS

13 Somerset Place, Glasgow, G3 7JT

Tel: 0141 332 8311
Fax: 0141 332 3915
E-mail: info@nyos.co.uk

Website:
http://www.nyos.co.uk

Enquiries:
Enquiries to: Chief Executive

Founded:
1979

Organisation type and purpose:
Membership association (membership is by subscription), present number of members: 360, suitable for ages: 8 to 28.
Classical and Jazz orchestras.
To provide top class education and performance experience.

Subject coverage:
Orchestral training, development of youth musicians in Scotland, orchestral music, chamber music, jazz music, professional tuition.

Electronic and video publications:
CD NYOS001 (The National Youth Orchestra of Scotland)
CD NYOS002 (Camerata Scotland)
CD NYOS003 (Camerata Scotland)
CD NYOS004 (The National Youth Orchestra of Scotland)
CD NYOS005 (The National Youth Jazz Orchestra of Scotland)
CD NYOS006 (The National Youth Orchestra of Scotland)

Access to staff:
Contact by letter, by telephone, by fax and by e-mail
Hours: Mon to Fri, 0930 to 1730

Member of:
Association of British Orchestras
European Federation of National Youth Orchestras

National Association of Youth Orchestras
National Federation of Music Societies
World Federation of Amateur Orchestras

Subsidiary body:
Camerata Scotland (NYOS Chamber Orchestra)
National Children's Orchestra of Scotland
National Youth Jazz Orchestra of Scotland
National Youth Orchestra of Scotland
NYOS Futures
NYOS Strings

NATIONAL YOUTH THEATRE OF GREAT BRITAIN

Acronym or abbreviation: NYT

443 Holloway Road, London, N7 6LW

Tel: 020 7281 3863
Fax: 020 7281 8246
E-mail: info@nyt.org.uk

Enquiries:
Enquiries to: General Manager
Other contacts: Development Manager for sponsorship and donations.

Founded:
1956

Organisation type and purpose:
Voluntary organisation, registered charity (charity number 306075), suitable for ages: 13 to 21.

Access to staff:
Contact by letter, by telephone, by fax, by e-mail and via website
Hours: Mon to Fri, 1000 to 1800

Access for disabled people:
Parking provided, level entry, access to all public areas, toilet facilities

NATURAL DEATH CENTRE

12A Blackstock Mews, London, N4 2BT

Tel: 0871 288 2098
Fax: 020 7354 3831
E-mail: contact@naturaldeath.org.uk

Website:
http://www.naturaldeath.org.uk
Online access to Natural Death Handbook, Before and After, Creative Endings, Sooner or Later books, discussions of death and dying, bereavement, alternative funerals etc, woodland burial grounds, mail order coffins, good undertakers, etc.

Enquiries:
Enquiries to: Director
Direct e-mail: susan@naturaldeath.org.uk

Founded:
1991

Organisation type and purpose:
Voluntary organisation, registered charity, research organisation, publishing house.

Subject coverage:
Death, dying, cardboard coffins, cheap coffins, shrouds, helpful undertakers, crematoria, funeral suppliers, funeral directors, befriending network for those with critical illness, green burial grounds, green, or family-organised funerals.

Printed publications:
Natural Death Handbook (£5.50 inc. p&p)
How to Organise an Inexpensive funeral e-mail (£10)
Set of forms: Living Will; Advance Funeral Wishes; Death Plan (for £7 donation)
Sooner or Later
Progressive Endings
After Life
Ways to Go Naturally

Electronic and video publications:
Publications available as pdfs

Access to staff:
Contact by letter, by telephone, by fax and by e-mail. Appointment necessary.
Hours: Mon to Fri, 1100 to 1400

Also at the same address:
Association of Natural Burial Grounds

Links with:
Befriending Network

NATURAL ENGLAND

3rd Floor, Touthill Close, City Road, Peterborough, PE1 1XN

Tel: 0300 060 0910
E-mail: library@naturalengland.org.uk

Website:
http://www.naturalengland.org.uk

Enquiries:
Enquiries to: Information and Library Services

Founded:
2006

Created by the merger of:
English Nature, the landscape, access and recreation elements of the Countryside Agency, and the environmental land management functions of the Rural Development Service (year of change 2006)

Organisation type and purpose:
Advisory body, statutory body.
Natural England aims to conserve and enhance the natural environment, for its intrinsic value, the wellbeing and enjoyment of people and the economic prosperity that it brings.

Subject coverage:
Natural England has been charged with the responsibility to ensure that England's unique natural environment including its land, flora and fauna, freshwater and marine environments, geology and soils are protected and improved. It also has responsibility for helping people enjoy, understand and access the natural environment.

Printed publications:
Wide range of printed materials (browse the publications catalogue online)

Publications list:
Available online and in print

Access to staff:
Contact by letter, by telephone, by fax, by e-mail and via website
Hours: Mon to Thu, 0900 to 1700; Fri, 0900 to 1630

Access to building, collection or gallery:
Prior appointment required

Access for disabled people:
Ramped entry

Headquarters address:
Natural England
1 East Parade, Sheffield, S1 2ET; tel: 0114 241 8920; fax: 0114 241 8921; e-mail: enquiries@naturalengland.org.uk; website: http://www.naturalengland.org.uk

NATURAL ENVIRONMENT RESEARCH COUNCIL

Acronym or abbreviation: NERC

Polaris House, North Star Avenue, Swindon, Wiltshire, SN2 1EU

Tel: 01793 411500
Fax: 01793 411501
E-mail: requests@nerc.ac.uk

Website:
http://www.nerc.ac.uk
NERC Home page includes the NERC mission, environmental issues, NERC contacts, funding routes, training and careers.

Enquiries:
Enquiries to: Information Officer

Founded:
1965

Organisation type and purpose:
Research organisation.
The Natural Environment Research Council (NERC) is the leading body in the UK for research, survey, monitoring and training in the environmental sciences. NERC funds research in universities and in its own centres, surveys and units.

Subject coverage:
Science policy, science and technology, natural environment.

Printed publications:
NERC Annual Report
Planet Earth (quarterly journal)

Publications list:
Available online

Access to staff:
Contact by letter, by telephone, by fax and by e-mail
Hours: Mon to Fri, 0900 to 1700

Centre for Coastal and Marine Science, incorporating the following institutes:
Dunstaffnage Marine Laboratory
PO Box 3, Oban, Argyll, PA34 4AD; tel: 01631 562244; fax: 01631 565518
Plymouth Marine Laboratory
Prospect Place, Plymouth, PL1 3DH; tel: 01752 633100; fax: 01752 633101
Proudman Oceanographic Laboratory
Bidston, Birkenhead, L43 7RA; tel: 0151 653 8633; fax: 0151 653 6269

Centre for Ecology & Hydrology, incorporating the following institutes:
Institute of Freshwater Ecology
The Ferry House, Far Sawrey, Ambleside, Cumbria, LA22 0LP; tel: 01539 442468; fax: 01539 446914
Institute of Hydrology
Maclean Building, Crowmarsh Gifford, Wallingford, Oxfordshire, OX10 8BB; tel: 01491 838800; fax: 01491 692424
Institute of Terrestrial Ecology
Monks Wood, Abbots Ripton, Huntingdon, PE28 2LS; tel: 01487 773381; fax: 01487 773467
Institute of Virology and Environmental Microbiology
Mansfield Road, Oxford, OX1 3SR; tel: 01865 281630; fax: 01865 281696

NERC Centres and Surveys:
British Antarctic Survey
High Cross, Madingley Road, Cambridge, CB3 0ET; tel: 01223 221400; fax: 01223 362616
British Geological Survey
Kingsley Dunham Centre, Keyworth, Nottingham, NG12 5GG; tel: 0115 936 3100; fax: 0115 936 3200
Southampton Oceanography Centre
(a joint venture between NERC and the University of Southampton), Empress Dock, Southampton, SO14 3ZH; tel: 023 8059 6666; fax: 023 8059 6032

NATURAL HISTORY MUSEUM

Acronym or abbreviation: NHM

Cromwell Road, London, SW7 5BD

Tel: 020 7942 5000
Fax: 020 7942 5559
E-mail: library@nhm.ac.uk

Website:
http://www.nhm.ac.uk/research-curation/library/index.html
Description of each library, including the Museum Archives, with contact details: provides access to the library catalogue; link to main museum home page; lists admissions, opening hours and services provided in the library.
http://www.nhm.ac.uk
Main museum home page.

Enquiries:
Enquiries to: Librarian
Other contacts: Specialist Library and Information Services, see below.

Founded:
1881

Organisation type and purpose:
International organisation, national government body, museum, public library, suitable for ages: all, training organisation, research organisation.

Subject coverage:
Botany; biodiversity; entomology; geography, expeditions and travel; mineralogy; museum techniques; oceanography; ornithology; palaeontology; parasitology; physical anthropology; tropical medicine; zoology; environmental studies.

Information services:
Library available for reference (for conditions, see Access), online searching, bibliography compilation, selective dissemination services. Helpline available, tel: 020 7942 5460 information line; field study tours; study days for teachers and museum professionals.

Special visitor services:
Guided tours.

Services for disabled people:
Hearing loop, displays and/or information at wheelchair height.

Museum or gallery collection, archive, or library special collection:
Albert Gunther (zoology)
Day Library (natural history dealers)
John Murray (oceanography)
Joseph Banks (natural history, note-books, etc. from Cook's first voyage around the world)
Linnaeus Collection (binomial nomenclature system in classification; works on plants and animals)
Richard Owen (anatomy)
Robert Brown (botany, including material from the Australian expedition 1801–1805)
Sloane (natural history and collection of curiosities and artefacts of c. 1753. Sloane's collection was the foundation of the British Museum)
Sowerby (natural history, especially botany; the family were artists and publishers)
Sydney Parkinson (natural history; drawings)
Tweeddale Library (zoology)
Walsingham (entomology)
Walter Rothschild (zoology)

Library catalogue:
All or part available online

Printed publications:
A large number of publications on the above subjects including:
Bulletin of the Natural History Museum: Botany series, Entomology series, Geology series, Zoology series
Catalogue of the Books and Manuscripts, Maps and Drawings in the British Museum (Natural History)
Catalogue of the Works of Linnaeus
List of Serials of the Natural History Museum
Monographs, handbooks, guide books including:
Coral Fish (Pitkin L)
Crystals (2nd edn, Cressey G and Mercer I F)
From the Beginning (Edwards K and Rosen B)
Gold (Herrington R J et al)
Lichens (Purvis W et al)
Nature's Connections – An Exploration of Natural History (McGirr N)
Snakes (Stafford P)
The Deep Sea (Rice T)
Volcanoes (2nd edn, van Rose S and Mercer I F)

Publications list:
Available online and in print

Access to staff:
Contact by letter, by telephone, by fax, by e-mail and via website. Appointment necessary.
Hours: Mon to Fri, 1000 to 1630

continued overleaf

Access for disabled people:
Access to all public areas, toilet facilities

Branch museums:
Zoological Museum Library
   Tring, Hertfordshire; tel: 020 7942 6159

Other libraries:
Botany Library
   tel: 020 79425685; e-mail: botlib@nhm.ac.uk
Earth Sciences Library
   tel: 020 7942 5476; e-mail: earthscilib@nhm.ac.uk
Entomology Library
   tel: 020 7942 5751; e-mail: entlib@nhm.ac.uk
General and Zoology Libraries
   tel: 020 7942 5460; e-mail: genlib@nhm.ac.uk
Ornithological and Rothschild Libraries
   Akeman Street, Tring, Hertfordshire, HP23 6AP;
   tel: 020 7942 6158; fax: 020 7942 6150; e-mail:
   ornlib@nhm.ac.uk

NATURAL HISTORY SOCIETY OF NORTHUMBRIA

Acronym or abbreviation: NHSN

Great North Museum, Hancock, Barras Bridge,
Newcastle upon Tyne, NE2 4PT

Tel: 0191 232 6386
Fax: 0191 232 2177
E-mail: nhsn@ncl.ac.uk

Website:
http://www.nhsn.ncl.ac.uk

Enquiries:
Enquiries to: The Secretary
Other contacts: The Archivist

Founded:
1829

Organisation type and purpose:
Learned society (membership is by subscription),
advisory body, present number of members: 850,
voluntary organisation, registered charity,
museum, publishing house.

Subject coverage:
Natural history of Northumberland and Durham,
with particular reference to geology, ornithology,
entomology, mammalia and botany; also Farne
Islands ecology.

Information services:
Library Information, tel: 0191 222 3555

**Museum or gallery collection, archive, or library
special collection:**
The library of the NHSN houses a large natural
   history archive, which includes the
   internationally important Thomas Bewick
   collection of watercolour and pencil drawings
Special collection of early natural history books
   from late 18th to 19th century

Non-library collection catalogue:
All or part available in-house

Library catalogue:
All or part available in-house

Printed publications:
Farne Island Bird Report (annually, free to
   members; on sale to general public)
Flora of Northumberland
Bulletin (3 times a year, to members)
Transactions of Natural History Society of
   Northumbria (annually, free to members; on sale
   to general public)
The following are published as part of the
   Transactions, but on sale to general public:
Red Data Book for Northumberland
Robson's Geology of North East England
The Many Faces of Bewick

Publications list:
Available online and in print

Access to staff:
Contact by letter, by telephone, by fax, by e-mail
and in person
Hours: Mon to Fri, 1000 to 1300
Special comments: Library: open to the public.

Archives and Special Collections: by prior
appointment.

Access to building, collection or gallery:
No prior appointment required
Hours: 1000 to 1700

Access for disabled people:
Yes
Hours: 1000 to 1700

NATURAL SCIENCES COLLECTIONS ASSOCIATION

Acronym or abbreviation: NatSCA

Natural History Museum, Cromwell Road,
London, SW7 5BD

Tel: 020 7942 5196
E-mail: pab@nhm.ac.uk

Website:
http://natsca.info

Enquiries:
Enquiries to: Chair

Founded:
2003

Incorporates the former:
Biology Curators Group (year of change 1975);
Natural Sciences Conservation Group (year of
change 1995)

Organisation type and purpose:
National organisation, advisory body, professional
body, membership association (membership is by
subscription), voluntary organisation.
To promote: the care, knowledge and use of
natural sciences collections and their conservation;
and museum-based, natural sciences-related
activities.

Subject coverage:
The acquisition, long-term care and use of natural
sciences collections. The propagation of natural
sciences information to a wide range of users, and
the promotion of natural sciences.

Trade and statistical information:
Nature, content and possible use of museum-based
   natural sciences collections, as well as many non-
   museum-based collections.

Printed publications:
NatSCA News

Publications list:
Available online

Access to staff:
Contact by letter, by telephone, by e-mail, in
person and via website. Appointment necessary.
Hours: Mon to Fri, 0900 to 1700

NATURE IN ART TRUST

Wallsworth Hall, Main A38, Twigworth,
Gloucester, GL2 9PA

Tel: 01452 731422
Fax: 01452 730937
E-mail: ninart@globalnet.co.uk

Website:
http://www.nature-in-art.org.uk
Current special exhibitions/courses/artist in
residence. Group/school visit details and booking
forms. Overview of the collection, events listing,
contacts, email facility.

Enquiries:
Enquiries to: Director

Founded:
1982

Organisation type and purpose:
Registered charity (charity number 1000553),
museum, art gallery.
Registered with the Museum and Galleries
Commission No 935.

Subject coverage:
All aspects of art inspired by nature, through the
ages; the use of art in environmental and
conservation education, and contacts with
contemporary artists from the UK and abroad.

**Museum or gallery collection, archive, or library
special collection:**
The Trust owns and manages Nature in Art, the
   world's first museum dedicated exclusively to art
   inspired by nature, it includes:
Work of any media of international stature, scope
   and appeal
Work spanning 1500 years collected from over 60
   countries
Small library containing slide collection and
   reference collection

Printed publications:
Nature in Art Magazine (quarterly, free to
   members)
Nature in Art – 300 years of Wildlife Paintings (£35
   or £14.96 paper-backed)

Access to staff:
Contact by letter, by telephone, by fax, by e-mail
and via website. Appointment necessary.
Hours: Tue to Sun, 1000 to 1700; closed Mon, and
December 24/25/26

Access to building, collection or gallery:
No prior appointment required
Special comments: Appointment required for the
library, but not for the gallery etc.

Access for disabled people:
Parking provided, ramped entry, access to all
public areas, toilet facilities

Affiliated to:
Area Museums Council for the South West
Gloucestershire Museums Group
Museums Association
Natur and Kunst (Germany)

NATURIST FOUNDATION

Sheepcote Lane, Orpington, Kent, BR5 4ET

Tel: 01689 871200
E-mail: natfound@hotmail.co.uk

Website:
http://www.naturistfoundation.org

Enquiries:
Enquiries to: General Secretary
Other contacts: Trustees

Founded:
1948

Organisation type and purpose:
Registered charity, voluntary organisation (charity
number 271420).

Subject coverage:
Naturist recreational facilities locally and
throughout the United Kingdom

Access to staff:
Contact by letter, by telephone, by e-mail and via
website
Hours: Mon, Thu, Fri, Sat and Sun, 0930 to 1700

Links with:
Central Council for British Naturism
International Naturist Federation

Member organisation of:
ASA
Kent County Playing Fields Association
RLSS

NAUTICAL INSTITUTE

202 Lambeth Road, London, SE1 7LQ

Tel: 020 7928 1351
Fax: 020 7401 2817
E-mail: pubs@nautinst.org

Website:
http://www.nautinst.org

Information on the Institute, its books and publications.

Enquiries:
Enquiries to: Chief Executive
Direct e-mail: sec@nautinst.org

Founded:
1972

Organisation type and purpose:
Professional body, registered charity (charity number 1002462).
To promote high standards of competence at sea and in the management of maritime operations

Subject coverage:
Navigation, seamanship, maritime operations.

Printed publications:
Books on (seagoing) Command, Work of the Harbour Master, Work of the Nautical Surveyor; pilotage; management of safety
Conference Proceedings
Monographs on various aspects of nautical science
Seaways (members' journal, monthly)

Electronic and video publications:
CD-ROMs for selected publications

Publications list:
Available online and in print

Access to staff:
Contact by letter, by telephone, by fax, by e-mail and via website. Appointment necessary.
Hours: Mon to Fri, 0900 to 1700

Access to building, collection or gallery:
No access other than to staff

NAVY RECORDS SOCIETY

Acronym or abbreviation: NRS

Pangbourne College, Pangbourne, Berkshire, RG8 8LA

E-mail: honsec@navyrecords.org.uk

Website:
http://navyrecords.org.uk

Enquiries:
Enquiries to: Honorary Secretary
Other contacts: Membership Secretary

Founded:
1893

Organisation type and purpose:
International organisation, learned society (membership is by subscription), present number of members: 725, registered charity (charity number 210836).
Publication of naval texts.

Subject coverage:
Naval history of Britain, as recorded in documents and published in some 150 volumes since 1893; the series includes the papers of famous naval commanders as well as statesmen and administrators of the Royal Navy; virtually every campaign in which the Navy has fought from the 15th century is covered; other subjects are: naval administration, shipbuilding and victualling, manning the fleet, everyday life at sea, naval songs, health of seamen, signals, fighting instructions, maritime law and piracy, naval brigades, Naval Air Service.

Non-library collection catalogue:
All or part available online and in print

Printed publications:
Over 150 titles, including:
British Naval Documents 1204–1960 (ed. J. B. Hattendorf, et al)
Naval Administration, 1715–1750 (D. A. Baugh)
The Navy of the Lancastrian Kings: Accounts and Inventories of William Soper, Keeper of the King's Ships 1422–1427 (S. Rose)
The Royal Navy in the Mediterranean, 1915–1918 (ed. P. G. Halpern)
State Papers relating to the Defeat of the Spanish Armada, Anno 1588 (2 vols)

The Battle of the Atlantic and Signals Intelligence: U-boat Situations and Trends, 1941–1945 (ed. D. Syrett)
The Cunningham Papers: Vol I The Mediterranean Fleet, 1939–1942 (ed. M. Simpson)
The Channel Fleet and the Blockade of Brest, 1793–1801 (ed. R. A. Morriss)
The Submarine Service, 1900–1918 (ed. N. Lambert)

Publications list:
Available in print

Access to staff:
Contact by letter, by e-mail and via website
Hours: Mon to Fri, 0900 to 1700

NCB

Formal name: National Children's Bureau

8 Wakley Street, Islington, London EC1V 7QE

Tel: 020 7843 6000
Fax: 020 7843 6007
E-mail: library@ncb.org.uk

Website:
http://www.ncb.org.uk/library

Enquiries:
Enquiries to: Head of Library and Information Service
Direct tel: 020 7843 6008

Founded:
1963

Organisation type and purpose:
Registered charity (charity number 2633796).

Subject coverage:
Children and young people including children in care, children's services, child protection, adolescence, children's rights and participation, crime and youth justice, disability and special educational needs, PSHE and sex education, HIV/AIDS, family law, family and parenting, child health, child psychology, poverty and social exclusion, early childhood, play.

Library catalogue:
All or part available online

Printed publications:
NCB produce a wide range of books, journals and newsletters (publications lists available)
ChildData Abstracts (monthly)
Children in the News (weekly)
Children & Young People Now (weekly, members)
Childstats (quarterly digest of statistics)
Highlights (8 times a year)
Lists of research projects
Reviews of literature and research

Electronic and video publications:
ChildData
Order electronic and video publications from: website: http://www.ncb.org.uk/childdata

Publications list:
Available online and in print

Access to staff:
Contact by telephone, by e-mail, in person and via website. Appointment necessary. Non-members charged.
Hours: Mon to Fri, 1000 to 1700
Special comments: Enquiry line: 1000 to 1200 and 1400 to 1600.

Access for disabled people:
Parking provided, level entry, toilet facilities
Special comments: Parking available on request.

Administers:
Council for Disabled Children
tel: 020 7843 6334; fax: 020 7278 9512

Links with:
Children in Scotland
tel: 0131 228 8484
Children in Wales
tel: 029 2034 2434

NCDL

Formal name: National Canine Defence League

17 Wakley Street, London, EC1V 7RQ

Tel: 020 7837 0006
Fax: 020 7833 2701
E-mail: info@ncdl.org.uk

Website:
http://www.ncdl.org.uk
General information on the Charity and its services – access to factsheets which can be downloaded/printed.

Enquiries:
Enquiries to: Information Officer
Direct tel: 020 7833 7657
Direct e-mail: victoria.horsley@ncdl.org.uk

Founded:
1891

Organisation type and purpose:
Voluntary organisation, registered charity (charity number 227523).
To protect and defend all dogs, rehabilitation and re-homing of stray and abandoned dogs, no healthy dog is ever destroyed.

Subject coverage:
Dog legislation, welfare and control, in particular rescue and care of stray dogs.

Museum or gallery collection, archive, or library special collection:
Annual Reports from the start of the League in 1897, old photos

Printed publications:
Annual Report
Newsletter (3 times a year)
Information leaflets and factsheets including:
Basic dog training
How to be a good dog owner
Routine Healthcare
The History of the NCDL
The NCDL Ruff Guide to Behaviour Problems
Which Puppy (a guide on how to buy a puppy)

Publications list:
Available in print

Access to staff:
Contact by letter, by telephone, by fax, by e-mail and via website. Appointment necessary.
Hours: Mon to Fri, 0900 to 1645

Member of:
Association of British Dogs and Cats Homes (ABDCH)
The Secretary, ABDCH, Battersea Dogs Home, 4 Battersea Park Road, London, SW8 4AA

Rehoming Centres at:
NCDL Ballymena
Fairview, 60 Teeshan Road, Ballymena, Co Antrim, BT43 5PN; tel: 028 2565 2977; fax: 028 2565 8463
NCDL Bridgend
Tondu Road, Bridgend, Mid Glamorgan, CF31 4LH; tel: 01656 652771; fax: 01656 647495
NCDL Canterbury
Radfall Road, Chestfield, Whitstable, Kent, CT5 3ER; tel: 01227 792505; fax: 01227 793988
NCDL Darlington
Hill House Farm, Sadberge, Co Durham, DL2 1SL; tel: 01325 333114; fax: 01325 333048
NCDL Dumfries
Dovecotewell, Glencaple, Dumfriesshire, DG1 4RH; tel: 01387 770346; fax: 01387 770242
NCDL Evesham
89 Pitcher's Hill, Wickhamford, Evesham, Worcesterhire, WR11 6RT; tel: 01386 830613; fax: 01386 832617
NCDL Ilfracombe
Hazeldene, West Down, Ilfracombe, Devon, EX34 8NU; tel: 01271 812709; fax: 01271 814098
NCDL Kenilworth
Honiley, Kenilworth, Warwickshire, CV8 1NP; tel: 01926 484398; fax: 01926 484196
NCDL Leeds
Eccup Lane, Adel, Leeds, LS16 8AL; tel: 0113 261 3194; fax: 0113 230 0886

continued overleaf

NCDL Merseyside
  Whiston Lane, Huyton, Liverpool, L36 6HP; tel:
  0151 480 0660; fax: 0151 480 6176
NCDL Newbury
  Plumb's Farm, Hamstead Marshall, Newbury,
  Berkshire, RG20 0HR; tel: 01488 658391; fax:
  01488 657211
NCDL Roden
  Roden Lane Farm, Roden, Telford, Shropshire,
  TF6 6BP; tel: 01952 770225; fax: 01952 770416
NCDL Salisbury
  45 Amesbury Road, Newton Tony, Wiltshire, SP4
  0HW; tel: 01980 629 634; fax: 01980 629 706
NCDL Shoreham
  Brighton Road, Shoreham-by-Sea, West Sussex,
  BN43 5LT; tel: 01273 452576; fax: 01273 440856
NCDL Snetterton
  North Farm Kennels (Snetterton), North End
  Road, Snetterton, Norfolk, NR16 2LD; tel: 01953
  498377; fax: 01953 498325
NCDL West Calder
  Bentyhead, Hartwood Road, West Calder, West
  Lothian, EH55 8LE; tel: 01506 873459; fax: 01506
  873275

NCS COLOUR CENTRE

71 Ancastle Green, Henley-on-Thames,
Oxfordshire, RG9 1TS

Tel: 01491 411717
Fax: 01491 411231
E-mail: info@ncscolour.co.uk

Website:
http://www.ncscolour.co.uk
Explanation of the NCS System. Details of
products and services, free online CPD seminars,
case studies, FAQs, glossary. Details of and links to
NCS Partners (manufacturers that use NCS). Links
to Worldwide NCS Colour Centres.

Enquiries:
Enquiries to: Customer Services

Founded:
1997

Organisation type and purpose:
Service industry, training organisation,
consultancy.
To advise on and supply Natural Colour System
standards in manufacturing, architecture and
design.

Subject coverage:
Use of the NCS – Natural Colour System®©in
manufacturing, architecture, design, research,
education.

Education services:
Teacher's Guide, including range of individual
exercises for teaching colour skills. NCS
accreditation courses.

Non-library collection catalogue:
All or part available online

Library catalogue:
All or part available online

Printed publications:
NCS Atlas and other colour collections
NCS Educational Material
Colour Choices: A Practitioner's Gude to Colour
  Scheming and Design by Berit Bergström
Colour scales of traditional pigments by Karin
  Fridell Anter & Ake Svedmyr
Nature's Colour Palette: Inherent colours of
  vegetation, stones and ground by Karin Fridell
  Anter & Ake Svedmyr
Other NCS research publications listed on website
Order printed publications from: website: http://
www.ncscolour.co.uk; tel: 01491 411717

Electronic and video publications:
NCS Navigator (free online colour design
  application)
NCS Palette (Mac and PC), NCS Palette AutoCAD
  (PC)
NCS Measurement program (computer software
  for manufacturers and universities)

Order electronic and video publications from: website:
http://www.ncscolour.co.uk; tel: 01491 411717

Publications list:
Available online and in print

Access to staff:
Contact by letter, by telephone, by fax, by e-mail
and via website. Appointment necessary.
Hours: Mon to Fri, 0900 to 1730

Parent body:
NCS Colour AB
  PO Box 49022, 100 28, Stockholm, Sweden

NCT

Alexandra House, Oldham Terrace, London, W3
6NH

Tel: 0300 330 0770 (enquiry line); 0844 243 6000 extn
2315 (library)
Fax: 0844 243 6001
E-mail: library@nct.org.uk

Website:
http://www.nct.org.uk
http://www.nctshop.co.uk
NCT shop.

Enquiries:
Enquiries to: Information Officer and Librarian

Founded:
1956

Formerly called:
National Childbirth Trust (year of change 2008)

Organisation type and purpose:
Membership association (membership is by
subscription), registered charity (charity number
801395).
To offer information and support in pregnancy,
childbirth and early parenthood. We aim to give
every parent the chance to make informed choices.

Subject coverage:
Pregnancy, childbirth, first year of parenthood,
maternity care, breastfeeding, homebirth,
caesarean.

**Museum or gallery collection, archive, or library
special collection:**
Archive of NCT materials and other relevant
  materials – books, videos, films, slides

Non-library collection catalogue:
All or part available in-house

Library catalogue:
All or part available online and in-house

Printed publications:
Wide variety of books and booklets, information
  sheets
Order printed publications from: NCT Shop, 239
Shawbridge Street, Glasgow, G43 1QN; tel: 0845
8100 100; fax: 0845 8100 120; e-mail: contactus@
nctshop.co.uk

Electronic and video publications:
DVDs and CDs
Order electronic and video publications from: NCT
shop

Publications list:
Available online and in print

Access to staff:
Contact by letter, by telephone, by fax and by e-
mail. Appointment necessary. Letter of
introduction required. Non-members charged.
Hours: Mon to Fri, 0900 to 1700
Special comments: Library and information service
is mainly for use of members.

Access for disabled people:
Parking provided
Special comments: Restricted wheelchair access to
library.

Branches:
across the United Kingdom

NEATH PORT TALBOT COUNTY BOROUGH COUNCIL

Civic Centre, Port Talbot, West Glamorgan, SA13
1PJ

Tel: 01639 686868
Fax: 01639 763444
E-mail: contactus@npt.gov.uk

Website:
http://www.npt.gov.uk
Guide to county, borough and council information.

Founded:
1996

Organisation type and purpose:
Local government body.

Access to staff:
Contact by letter, by telephone, by fax, by e-mail
and via website. Appointment necessary.
Hours: Mon to Fri, 0900 to 1700

Also at:
Civic Centre Neath
  Neath; tel: 01639 686868; fax: 01639 763444

NEIL MUNRO SOCIETY, THE

8 Briar Road, Kirkintilloch, Glasgow, G66 3SA

Tel: 0141 776 4280
Fax: 0141 776 4280
E-mail: brian@bdosborne.fsnet.co.uk

Website:
http://www.neilmunro.co.uk

Enquiries:
Enquiries to: Secretary

Founded:
1996

Organisation type and purpose:
Learned society (membership is by subscription),
present number of members: 180, voluntary
organisation.

Subject coverage:
Life and work of Neil Munro (1863–1930) Scottish
novelist, poet, critic and journalist.

**Museum or gallery collection, archive, or library
special collection:**
Archival Collection of books, MSS relating to Neil
  Munro held by Royal College of Physicians and
  Surgeons of Glasgow on behalf of Society.

Non-library collection catalogue:
All or part available online

Printed publications:
Paragraph (magazine, 2 times a year, supplied as
  part of membership package)

Access to staff:
Contact by letter, by telephone, by e-mail and via
website
Hours: Mon to Fri, 0900 to 1700

Access to building, collection or gallery:
Prior appointment required
Hours: Mon to Fri, 0900 to 1700
Special comments: Archive held by Royal College of
Physicians and Surgeons of Glasgow.

NEL

Formal name: National Engineering Laboratory

East Kilbride, Glasgow, G75 0QU

Tel: 01355 220222
Fax: 01355 272999
E-mail: info@nel.uk

Website:
http://www.nel.uk
National Engineering Laboratory services and
activities.

Enquiries:
Enquiries to: Information Officer

Founded:
1947

Organisation type and purpose:
Service industry, consultancy, research organisation.

Subject coverage:
Fluid power engineering, heat exchangers, heat transfer, offshore engineering, physical properties of liquids and gases, pumps, software, structural analysis and testing, turbo machinery, control of noise and vibration in machinery.

Printed publications:
Conference and Symposia Proceedings (for sale, apply to Events Co-ordinator)

Access to staff:
Contact by letter, by fax, by e-mail and via website
Hours: Mon to Fri, 0900 to 1700

Business of the:
TÜV Suddeutschland Group

NERINE AND AMARYLLID SOCIETY

Acronym or abbreviation: NAAS

2 The Grove, Ickenham, Uxbridge, Middlesex, UB10 8QH

Tel: 01895 464694
Fax: 0870 0529321
E-mail: roger.beauchamp@btinternet.com

Website:
http://www.nerine.org.uk

Enquiries:
Enquiries to: Secretary

Founded:
1997

Organisation type and purpose:
National organisation, membership association (membership is by subscription), present number of members: 140.
For the study, dissemination and collection of all information concerning all genera within the family Amaryllidaceae and closely associated families.

Subject coverage:
All aspects of all genera in the family Amaryllidaceae.

Printed publications:
Journal (three times a year)

Publications list:
Available in print

Access to staff:
Contact by letter, by telephone, by fax and by e-mail

NESCOT (NORTH EAST SURREY COLLEGE OF TECHNOLOGY)

Reigate Road, Ewell, Epsom, Surrey, KT17 3DS

Tel: 020 8394 3055
Fax: 020 8394 3030
E-mail: lrc@nescot.ac.uk

Enquiries:
Enquiries to: Library Services Manager

Founded:
1954

Subject coverage:
Biology, building and construction, health and social care, business and computing, art, design, photography, performing arts.

Library catalogue:
All or part available online

Access to staff:
Contact by letter, by telephone, by fax, by e-mail and in person

Hours: Term time: Mon, Wed, 0830 to 1800; Tue, Thu, 0830 to 1930; Fri, 0830 to 1700
Vacations: Mon to Fri, 0900 to 1700 (unless otherwise stated)

Access to building, collection or gallery:
No prior appointment required
Hours: Advance notification preferred

Access for disabled people:
Parking provided, ramped entry, access to all public areas, toilet facilities

NETHERLANDS – BRITISH CHAMBER OF COMMERCE

307–308 High Holborn, London, WC1V 7LS

Tel: 020 7405 1358
Fax: 020 7405 1689
E-mail: nbcc@btinternet.com

Website:
http://www.nbcc.co.uk

Enquiries:
Enquiries to: Manager
Direct fax: 020 7831 4831

Founded:
1891

Organisation type and purpose:
International organisation, advisory body, membership association (membership is by subscription), present number of members: 300, consultancy.
Chamber of Commerce.
To provide information on Anglo-Dutch trade.

Subject coverage:
Anglo-Dutch trade.

Printed publications:
See publications list

Electronic and video publications:
Information supplied on request

Publications list:
Available online and in print

Access to staff:
Contact by letter, by telephone, by fax, by e-mail, in person and via website. Appointment necessary. Non-members charged.
Hours: Mon to Fri, 0900 to 1700

Other addresses:
Netherlands – British Chamber of Commerce NZ Voorburgwal 328L, 1012 RW, Amsterdam, The Netherlands; tel: + 31 20 421 7040; fax: + 31 20 421 7003; e-mail: nbccnl@btinternet.com

NETWORK 81

1–7 Woodfield Terrace, Chapel Hill, Stansted, Essex, CM24 8AJ

Tel: 0845 077 4055
Fax: 0845 077 4057
E-mail: network81@btconnect.com

Website:
http://www.network81.org

Enquiries:
Enquiries to: Administrator
Other contacts: National Development Manager

Founded:
1986

Organisation type and purpose:
Voluntary organisation, registered charity (charity number 1061950).

Subject coverage:
Help, support and advice for parents of children with special educational needs through the assessment and statementing process; 1996 Education Act, Part IV, code of practice.

Printed publications:
Parents Guide (£8.50)

Publications list:
Available online

Access to staff:
Contact by letter, by telephone, by fax, by e-mail and via website
Hours: Mon to Fri, 0900 to 1500
Special comments: Helpline: 1000 to 1300.

NEUROFIBROMATOSIS ASSOCIATION

Quayside House, 38 High Street, Kingston on Thames, KT1 1HL

Tel: 020 8439 1234
Fax: 020 8439 1200
E-mail: nfa@zetnet.co.uk

Website:
http://www.nfauk.org.uk

Enquiries:
Enquiries to: General Secretary
Other contacts: Helpline: 0845 602 4173 (Mon, Thu, 0900 to 1600; Tue, 0900 to 1200)

Founded:
1982

Organisation type and purpose:
Membership association (membership is by subscription), present number of members: 2300, registered charity (charity number 1078790).
To provide help and support to those affected, their families & friends.

Subject coverage:
Information on neurofibromatosis for GPs and health visitors, patients and carers, public; access to consultants via medical advisory board; data for researchers (subject to ethical controls); information on learning difficulties in Nf.

Printed publications:
Annual Report
Newsletter (3 times a year)
Introduction booklet (free)
Fact sheets (free)

Electronic and video publications:
Neurofibromatosis
Order electronic and video publications from: see website

Publications list:
Available online

Access to staff:
Contact by letter, by telephone, by fax and by e-mail
Hours: Mon to Fri, 0900 to 1700

Connections with:
Genetic Interest Group (GIG)
International Neurofibromatosis Association
LMCA Neurological Alliance

NEW ALLIANCE

PO Box 13199, London, SW6 6ZU

Tel: 020 7385 9757
E-mail: info@newalliance.org.uk

Website:
http://www.newalliance.org.uk/contact.htm
http://www.newalliance.org.uk

Enquiries:
Enquiries to: Campaign Manager
Other contacts: Treasurer for donations, legacies

Founded:
1997

Organisation type and purpose:
Learned society, voluntary organisation, consultancy, research organisation, publishing house, campaigning group.
Educating business and the public about the alternatives to European Union membership.

continued overleaf

Subject coverage:
European Union, defence, policing, criminal justice and legal issues, constitution, taxation, business legislation, employment policy, regional policy, the Euro, economic and monetary union, environment, motoring, agriculture, ID cards, referendum issues, BBC coverage, public consultations, metrication.

Non-library collection catalogue:
All or part available online, in-house and in print

Printed publications:
Animal welfare
Newsletters (sent to registered supporters)
Fact sheets on European Union topics:
Alternatives to EU membership
Defence
Policing
Taxation
Business legislation
Employment policy
Regional policy
The euro
Economic and monetary union
Environment
Motoring
Agriculture
ID Cards
Referendum legislation
The Treaty of Nice
BBC coverage
Metrication
Constitution
Criminal justice & legal issues

Electronic and video publications:
Fast Index online via website
Order electronic and video publications from: Can be supplied via electronic and paper media to schools and recognised research institutions

Publications list:
Available online

Access to staff:
Contact by letter, by telephone, by e-mail and via website
Hours: Mon to Sun, 0900 to 2100

Access to building, collection or gallery:
No access other than to staff

Affiliated organisation:
National Referendum Campaign

Affiliated to:
Statewatch

NEW COLLEGE LIBRARY

Holywell Street, Oxford, OX1 3BN

Tel: 01865 279580
Fax: 01865 279590
E-mail: library@new.ox.ac.uk

Website:
http://www.new.ox.ac.uk/The_Library

Enquiries:
Enquiries to: Librarian
Direct e-mail: naomi.vanloo@new.ox.ac.uk

Founded:
1379

Organisation type and purpose:
University college library.

Subject coverage:
Subjects studied by undergraduates in the University of Oxford; the subjects covered by the special collections listed.

Museum or gallery collection, archive, or library special collection:
Archives collection since the foundation of the College
Medieval manuscripts
Early printed books
Papers of Lord Milner (Bodley deposit)
Seton-Watson Collection (Eastern Europe)

Library catalogue:
All or part available online and in-house

Printed publications:
New College Oxford 1379–1979 (J. Buxton and P. Williams, OUP, 1979)
Archives of New College Oxford (F. W. Steer, Phillimore, 1974)

Microform publications:
Microfilms of medieval manuscripts

Access to staff:
Contact by letter, by telephone and by e-mail.
Appointment necessary. Access for members only.
Letter of introduction required.
Hours: Mon to Fri, 0900 to 1700

Access to building, collection or gallery:
Hours: Mon to Fri, 0930 to 1245 and 1415 to 1645

Constituent part of:
University of Oxford

NEW ENGLISH ART CLUB

Acronym or abbreviation: NEAC

17 Carlton Terrace, London, SW1Y 5BD

Tel: 020 7930 6844
Fax: 020 7930 7830
E-mail: press@mallgalleries.com

Website:
http://www.mallgalleries.org.uk

Enquiries:
Enquiries to: Secretary
Other contacts: Marketing and Communications Officer

Founded:
1885

Organisation type and purpose:
Membership association (membership is by election or invitation), present number of members: 84, registered charity (charity number 295780).
To foster and promote the art of draftsmanship and observation.

Printed publications:
NEAC catalogues available during the annual exhibition

Access to staff:
Contact by letter, by telephone, by fax and by e-mail. Appointment necessary.
Hours: Mon to Fri, 0930 to 1700

Access to building, collection or gallery:
No access other than to staff

Access for disabled people:
Stair lift, toilet facilities
Special comments: Stair lift

Links with:
Federation of British Artists
17 Carlton House Terrace, London, SW17 5BD; tel: 020 7930 6844; fax: 020 7839 7830

NEW FOREST PONY BREEDING AND CATTLE SOCIETY

Acronym or abbreviation: NFPB & CS

The Corner House, Ringwood Road, Brausgoe, Hampshire, BH23 8AA

Tel: 01425 672775
Fax: 01425 672775
E-mail: info@newforestpony.com

Website:
http://newforestpony.com

Enquiries:
Enquiries to: Curator

Founded:
1938

Organisation type and purpose:
Membership association (membership is by subscription), present number of members: 1200, registered charity (charity number 1064746).
Breed society.

Conserve and promote New Forest ponies.

Subject coverage:
New Forest ponies.

Museum or gallery collection, archive, or library special collection:
Stud book back numbers

Printed publications:
A Celebration of New Forest Ponies (available from office, £14.95 plus £2 p&p)
Leaflet
Newsletter (2 times a year)
Stud Book (annually)

Access to staff:
Contact by letter, by telephone, by fax and by e-mail. Appointment necessary.
Hours: Telephone: 0830 to 0930 and evenings

Chairman:
New Forest Pony Breeding and Cattle Society Randalls Farm, Burley Street, Ringwood, Hampshire; tel: 01425 402459; e-mail: forestpony@enterprise.net

Daughter New Forest Pony Societies in the:
Netherlands, France, Belgium, Sweden, Finland, Germany, N America and Australia

Member of:
National Pony Society

NEW IMPERIAL OWNERS' ASSOCIATION

Acronym or abbreviation: NIOA

2 Maes-Y-Garreg, Llansantffraid, Powys. SY22 6BD

Tel: 01691 828098
Fax: 01691 828098
E-mail: info@newimperial.co.uk

Website:
http://www.newimperial.co.uk

Enquiries:
Enquiries to: Honorary Secretary

Founded:
1987

Organisation type and purpose:
International organisation, membership association (membership is by subscription), present number of members: 280.
Historic motorcycle club.

Subject coverage:
Information about New Imperial motor cycles manufactured in Birmingham between 1901 and 1939.

Printed publications:
New Imp News (quarterly, free, members only)

Access to staff:
Contact by letter, by telephone, by fax and by e-mail. Appointment necessary.
Hours: Daily, 0900 to 2200

Links with:
Federation of British Historic Vehicle Clubs tel: 01865 400845; fax: 01865 400845; e-mail: secretary@fbhvc.co.uk

NEW INTERNATIONALIST

Acronym or abbreviation: NI

55 Rectory Road, Oxford, OX4 1BW

Tel: 01865 811400
Fax: 01865 793152
E-mail: ni@newint.org

Website:
http://www.newint.org

Enquiries:
Enquiries to: Administrator

Founded:
1972

Organisation type and purpose:
Publishing house.

Subject coverage:
Global political and social stories.

Printed publications:
New Internationalist (magazine, 11 issues a year, £32.85 a year)

Access to staff:
Contact by letter and by e-mail
Hours: Mon to Fri, 0930 to 1730

NEW PRODUCERS ALLIANCE

Acronym or abbreviation: NPA

9 Bourlet Close, London, W1W 1PB

Tel: 020 7580 2480
Fax: 020 7580 2484
E-mail: queries@npa.org.uk

Website:
http://www.npa.org.uk
Information on the film industry and NPA activities and special additional online section restricted to members.

Enquiries:
Enquiries to: Administrator

Founded:
1993

Organisation type and purpose:
National organisation, membership association (membership is by subscription), present number of members: c. 1000, registered charity (charity number 1059200), training organisation. Training and information for film makers.

Subject coverage:
Film production, development and distribution.

Museum or gallery collection, archive, or library special collection:
Reference books and magazines relating to the film industry

Non-library collection catalogue:
All or part available online

Publications list:
Available online

Access to staff:
Contact by letter, by telephone, by fax, by e-mail and via website. Appointment necessary.
Hours: Mon to Fri, 0900 to 1700

NEW ZEALAND HIGH COMMISSION

New Zealand House, 80 Haymarket, London, SW1Y 4TQ

Tel: 020 7930 8422
Fax: 020 7839 4580
E-mail: aboutnz@newzealandhc.org.uk

Website:
http://www.nzembassy.com/uk
General information for New Zealanders in the United Kingdom and Republic of Ireland.

Organisation type and purpose:
New Zealand Government Representative.

Subject coverage:
Limited general information e.g. not on immigration; research and development in government, industry, universities, institutes and associations.

Access to staff:
Contact by letter, by telephone, by fax, by e-mail and via website
Hours: Mon to Fri, 0900 to 1700

Access to building, collection or gallery:
Prior appointment required

Access for disabled people:
Ramped entry

Parent body:
Ministry of Foreign Affairs and Trade
Private Bag 18–901, Wellington, New Zealand

NEW ZEALAND IMMIGRATION SERVICE

Mezzanine Floor, New Zealand House, 80 Haymarket, London, SW1Y 4TE

Tel: 0906 9100 100
Fax: 020 7973 0370

Website:
http://www.immigration.govt.nz

Organisation type and purpose:
International organisation.

Subject coverage:
Emigration to New Zealand.

Access to building, collection or gallery:
No prior appointment required
Hours: Mon to Fri, 1000 to 1545

NEWBURY LIBRARY

The Wharf, Newbury, Berkshire, RG14 5AU

Tel: 01635 519900
Fax: 01635 519906
E-mail: newburylibrary@westberks.gov.uk

Website:
http://www.westberks.gov.uk/libraries

Enquiries:
Enquiries to: Librarian

Organisation type and purpose:
Local government body, public library.

Subject coverage:
General public library material, Newbury and West Berkshire local history.

Museum or gallery collection, archive, or library special collection:
West Berkshire local history collection

Library catalogue:
All or part available online

Access to staff:
Contact by letter, by telephone, by fax, by e-mail, in person and via website
Hours: Mon, Tue, Thu, 0900 to 1900; Wed, Fri, 0900 to 1700; Sat, 0930 to 1600

Access to building, collection or gallery:
Hours: Mon, Tue, Thu, 0900 to 1900; Wed, Fri, 0900 to 1700; Sat, 0930 to 1600

Access for disabled people:
Level entry, access to all public areas, toilet facilities

Parent body:
West Berkshire District Council
Council Offices, Market Street, Newbury, RG14 5LD; tel: 01635 42400; fax: 01635 519392; website: http://www.westberks.gov.uk

NEWCASTLE COLLEGE LIBRARY SERVICES

Rye Hill Campus, Scotswood Road, Newcastle upon Tyne, NE4 7SA

Tel: 0191 200 4020
Fax: 0191 200 4100
E-mail: thelibrary@ncl-coll.ac.uk

Website:
http://ncl-coll.ac.uk
General information relating to Newcastle College.

Enquiries:
Enquiries to: Head of Library Services
Direct tel: 0191 200 4017

Subject coverage:
Engineering, construction, art and design, food industries, computing, business studies, information technology, music, performing arts, humanities, science, hotel and catering management, leisure, childcare, social welfare, training/education, local studies.

Museum or gallery collection, archive, or library special collection:
Local collection

Library catalogue:
All or part available online

Printed publications:
Prospectus

Access to staff:
Contact by letter, by telephone, by fax and by e-mail. Appointment necessary.
Hours: Mon to Fri, 0900 to 1700

NEWCASTLE LIBRARIES

City Library, New Bridge Street, Newcastle upon Tyne, NE1 8AX

Tel: 0191 277 4100
Fax: 0191 277 4137
E-mail: tony.durcan@newcastle.gov.uk

Enquiries:
Enquiries to: Head of Culture, Libraries and Lifelong Learning
Direct tel: 0191 211 5383
Direct fax: 0191 211 5602
Direct e-mail: tony.durcan@newcastle.gov.uk
Other contacts: City Libraries' Manager

Founded:
1880

Organisation type and purpose:
Local government body, public library.

Subject coverage:
Local studies for city and region; general reference collections; genealogy, local and national; patents; business information; community information.

Museum or gallery collection, archive, or library special collection:
Auty-Hastings Collection of glass plate negatives and prints, 1890–1920 (local scenes)
British Standards, Full Set (CD-ROM)
British, European, American and PCT Patent specifications
C. P. Taylor Collection (playwrights' manuscripts)
Clark Music Library (concert programmes, theatre playbills, c.1880–1920, with indexes in the care of the Local History Librarian)
Gibsone's Conches (over 20,000 watercolour paintings of conch shells bought for the City in 1889)
Local studies illustrations collection c.70,000 items
Newspapers 1707 to date
Northern Playwrights Collection
Patents collection (UK, Europe, USA, Japan)
Seymour Bell Collection (plans and charts of the sea)
Thomas Bewick Collection (the 18th-century engraver's books and blocks, Pease Bequest)
Thomlinson Collection (16th- to 18th-century books)
Tyneside Unidentified Flying Objects Society Collection

Non-library collection catalogue:
All or part available in-house

Library catalogue:
All or part available online

Printed publications:
A large range of books on local history

Publications list:
Available in print

Access to staff:
Contact by letter, by telephone, by fax, by e-mail, in person and via website
Hours: Mon, Thu, 0900 to 2000; Tue, Wed, Fri, Sat, 0900 to 1700

Access for disabled people:
Ramped entry, automatic doors at main entrance, toilet facilities

Parent body:
City of Newcastle Upon Tyne, Chief Executive's Office Directorate

NEWCASTLE UNIVERSITY

Robinson Library, Back Jesmond Road West,
Newcastle upon Tyne, NE2 4HQ

Tel: 0191 222 7662
Fax: 0191 222 6235
E-mail: lib-readerservices@newcastle.ac.uk

Website:
http://www.ncl.ac.uk/library

Enquiries:
Enquiries to: Librarian
Direct tel: 0191 222 7674; 0191 222 7671 (Special
Collections Librarian)
Direct e-mail: wayne.connolly@newcastle.ac.uk
Other contacts: Special Collections Librarian

Founded:
1963

Organisation type and purpose:
University library.

Subject coverage:
Accounting and finance, management, economics,
geography, politics, sociology and anthropology,
architecture, planning, English (literature and
linguistics), fine art, modern languages, music,
archaeology, classics, history, religious studies,
museum studies, medicine, dentistry, speech,
psychology, education, law, agriculture and
biological sciences (including marine), chemical
engineering, civil engineering, electrical
engineering, marine technology, mechanical
materials and manufacturing engineering,
chemistry, physics, statistics, computing science,
geomatics, mathematics (applied, pure and
engineering).

**Museum or gallery collection, archive, or library
special collection:**
Collections include:
Barry MacSweeney Papers (poetry)
Catherine Cookson Collection
Chapbooks and Broadsides (many of these
chapbooks are available on microfilm)
C. V. Stanford Collection (musical manuscripts)
Gertrude Bell Collection (history and archaeology
of the Middle East)
Lady Plowden Papers (education)
Library of Japanese science and technology
Merz Collection (mathematics and philosophy)
Pybus Collection (medical history)
Robert White Collection (English literature, Border
history and Antiquities)
Robinson Collection (multilingual rare books
covering exploration, literature and music)
Runciman Papers (early 20th-century politics)
Shefton Collection (Greek archaeology)
Sid Chaplin Papers (literature)
Trevelyan Papers (19th- and 20th-century arts,
literature and politics)
UK Government publications
Victorian Collection (literature)
Wallis Collection (mathematics)

Non-library collection catalogue:
All or part available online

Library catalogue:
All or part available online

Access to staff:
Contact by letter, by telephone, by fax, by e-mail
and in person. Appointment necessary. Non-
members charged.
Hours: Term time: Mon to Fri, 0900 to 2100; Sat and
Sun 1000 to 1730.
Vacations: variable, see website or telephone

Access for disabled people:
Parking provided, level entry, toilet facilities

NEWHAM ASIAN WOMEN'S PROJECT

Acronym or abbreviation: NAWP

661 Barking Road, Plaistow, London, E13 9EX

Tel: 020 8472 0528
Fax: 020 8503 5673

E-mail: info@nawp.org

Website:
http://www.nawp.org
Details of all services and contact information.

Founded:
1987

Organisation type and purpose:
Registered charity (charity number 1001834).
Specialist domestic violence service for Asian
women. Also provides consultations and research
relating to relevant proposed and existing
legislation.

Subject coverage:
Offers advice service, counselling support, refuge
for women and children, a sexual health,
exploitation and abuse project, education and
training (extended to all Black and Minority ethnic
women), and specialist support services for young
Asian women who are vulnerable to self-harm and
suicide in the East London area. NAWP does not
provide emergency assistance.

Information services:
Rights-based advice and information services; free
confidential legal advice and assistance.

Education services:
English language and other mainstream
educational support, and vocational courses.

Library catalogue:
All or part available online

Electronic and video publications:
Annual Report
Self Harm Information (leaflet, available in
English, Bengali, Hindi, Punjabi and Urdu)
NAWP Directory
ESOL leaflet
Advice Surgery leaflet
A variety of training events leaflets and newsletters
Responses and consultations to proposed and
current legislation
Order electronic and video publications from:
Downloadable from website

Publications list:
Available online

Access to staff:
Contact by letter, by telephone, by fax, by e-mail
and in person
Hours: Mon to Fri, 0930 to 1730
Access to legal adviser or solicitor: drop-in sessions
Mon, 1000 to 1200; Tue, 1700 to 1900; appointments
only Wed, 1230 to 1330; Thu, 1400 to 1600

Access to building, collection or gallery:
Hours: Mon to Fri, 0930 to 1730

NEWLIFE FOUNDATION FOR DISABLED CHILDREN

Newlife Centre, Hemlock Way, Cannock,
Staffordshire, WS11 7GF

Tel: 01543 462777
Fax: 01543 468999
E-mail: info@newlifecharity.co.uk

Website:
http://www.newlifecharity.co.uk

Enquiries:
Enquiries to: Chief Executive

Founded:
1991

Formerly called:
Birth Defects Foundation; Happy Birthday Appeal

Organisation type and purpose:
Registered charity (charity number 1001817).

Subject coverage:
Birth defects.

Printed publications:
Publications available free of charge

Publications list:
Available online and in print

Access to staff:
Contact by letter, by telephone, by fax, by e-mail,
in person and via website. Appointment necessary.
Hours: Helpline: Mon to Fri, 0930 to 1900; Sat, 0930
to 1700
Office: Mon to Fri, 0930 to 1700

Access for disabled people:
Parking provided, level entry, access to all public
areas, toilet facilities

NEWMAN UNIVERSITY COLLEGE

Library, Genners Lane, Bartley Green,
Birmingham, B32 3NT

Tel: 0121 476 1181
Fax: 0121 476 1196
E-mail: library@newman.ac.uk

Website:
http://www.newman.ac.uk

Enquiries:
Enquiries to: Librarian

Founded:
1968

Organisation type and purpose:
University College.

Subject coverage:
Counselling, creative arts, drama, early childhood
education and care, education in general, English
language, English literature, history, IT, initial
teacher education, management, media, physical
education, psychology, religious education, sports
science, theology, West Midlands history.

**Museum or gallery collection, archive, or library
special collection:**
West Midlands history – books, pamphlets,
photographs

Library catalogue:
All or part available online

Access to staff:
Contact by letter, by telephone, by fax, by e-mail
and via website
Hours: Mon, Tue, Thu, 0845 to 2100; Wed, 0945 to
2100; Fri, 0845 to 1700; Sat, 1000 to 1500

Access to building, collection or gallery:
Special comments: Access to the Library is usually
available, when both the Library and main
Newman reception are open. Occasionally, due to
unforeseen circumstances, it is necessary to amend
these hours at short notice, so it is recommended to
call the Library prior to a visit.

Research degrees validated by:
Leicester University

NEWPORT AND GWENT CHAMBER OF COMMERCE AND INDUSTRY

Acronym or abbreviation: ngb2b

Unit 30, The Orion Suite, Enterprise Way,
Newport, Gwent, NP20 2AQ

Tel: 01633 222664
Fax: 01633 222301
E-mail: info@ngb2b.org.uk

Website:
http://www.ngb2b.co.uk
Activities and services of organisations, benefits to
business

Enquiries:
Enquiries to: International Trade Manager
Direct e-mail: jennifer@ngb2b.org.uk

Founded:
1867

Organisation type and purpose:
Membership association (membership is by
election or invitation).

Subject coverage:
Material sourcing, financial references, EC legislation, national legislation, export documentation, certificates of origin, VAT legislation, local affairs, available grants via Welsh Office, local developments, infogrants, inforules, training courses. Information and product sourcing, training and seminars, exporting, certificates of origin, networking, commercial services, databases, newsletters, marketing services, credit checks, Chambersign, representation.

Museum or gallery collection, archive, or library special collection:
HMSO Customs and Tariffs
Local business directories
Overseas national directories
Parliamentary and EC year books
Croner's Reference Books (various titles)

Printed publications:
Newsletter (6 times a year, all local businesses and subscribers)
Business in Wales (monthly)
South Wales Business Directory (annually)

Publications list:
Available in print

Access to staff:
Contact by letter, by telephone, by fax, by e-mail, in person and via website
Hours: Mon to Fri, 0900 to 1200, 1300 to 1700

Access to building, collection or gallery:
Prior appointment required

Access for disabled people:
Parking provided, toilet facilities

Affiliated organisations:
Chepstow Chamber of Commerce & Tourism
Gwent Business Women's Network
Monmouth District Chamber of Commerce
Newport Business Club
Newport Chamber of Trade
Royal Forest of Dean Business and Professional Club

NEWPORT CITY COUNCIL

Civic Centre, Newport, Gwent, NP20 4UR

Tel: 01633 656656
Fax: 01633 232537

Website:
http://www.newport.gov.uk
Enquiries:
Enquiries to: Managing Director
Founded:
1996

Organisation type and purpose:
Local government body.

Subject coverage:
Newport.

Trade and statistical information:
Newport inward investment.

Printed publications:
Community Plan (annual, free)
Economic Development Annual Report (free)

Access to staff:
Contact by letter, by telephone and by fax.
Appointment necessary.
Hours: Mon to Fri, 0830 to 1630

NEWPORT COMMUNITY LEARNING AND LIBRARIES

Central Library, John Frost Square, Newport, Gwent, NP20 1PA

Tel: 01633 656656
Fax: 01633 414705
E-mail: central.library@newport.gov.uk

Website:
http://www.newport.gov.uk/libraries

Enquiries:
Enquiries to: Librarian

Organisation type and purpose:
Public library.

Subject coverage:
Local history; local Chartism, general reference, family history.

Services for disabled people:
Wheelchair available, hearing loops.

Museum or gallery collection, archive, or library special collection:
Arthur Machen Collection (local author)
Haines Collection (local history)
Phillips Collection (mainly private press books and the arts)
Mrs Delany's Letters (local history)

Non-library collection catalogue:
All or part available online and in-house

Library catalogue:
All or part available online

Access to staff:
Contact by letter, by telephone, by fax, by e-mail and in person
Hours: Mon to Fri, 0900 to 1800; Sat, 0900 to 1600

Access for disabled people:
Level entry, toilet facilities

Parent body:
Continuing Learning and Leisure
Newport County City Council

NEWQUEST (HERALD & TIMES) LTD

Formal name: Scottish Media Group Newspapers

200 Renfield Street, Glasgow, G2 3QB

Tel: 0141 302 7000
Fax: 0141 302 7383
E-mail: ian.watson@glasgow.newsquest.co.uk

Enquiries:
Enquiries to: Information Officer
Direct e-mail: newslib@glasgow.newsquest.co.uk

Founded:
1783

Organisation type and purpose:
Service industry, publishing house.
Newspaper publisher.

Subject coverage:
Current affairs, sport, arts.

Museum or gallery collection, archive, or library special collection:
Extensive Photo Collection (c. 5 million)

Printed publications:
The (Glasgow) Herald
Sunday Standard (ceased 1983)
Sunday Herald
Evening Times

Microform publications:
All titles available on Microfilm

Electronic and video publications:
Herald and Sunday Herald (CD-ROM)

Publications list:
Available online

Access to staff:
Contact by letter, by fax and by e-mail.
Appointment necessary. All charged.
Hours: Mon to Fri, 0900 to 1700

Access to building, collection or gallery:
Prior appointment required

Access for disabled people:
Parking provided, level entry, toilet facilities

NEWS INTERNATIONAL NEWSPAPERS LIMITED

Information Services, 1 Viginia Street, London, E98 1ES

Tel: 020 7782 6000
E-mail: info@newsint.co.uk

Website:
http://www.newsinternational.co.uk/

Enquiries:
Enquiries to: Information Services Manager
Direct tel: 020 7782 6398
Direct fax: 020 7782 3650

Organisation type and purpose:
Newspaper publishing.

Access to staff:
Contact by letter. Appointment necessary. Non-members charged.
Hours: Mon to Fri, 0900 to 1700

Access to building, collection or gallery:
Prior appointment required

Access for disabled people:
Ramped entry, toilet facilities

Subsidiary of:
News Corporation
website: www.newscorp.com

NEWSPAPER PUBLISHERS ASSOCIATION LIMITED

Acronym or abbreviation: NPA

8th Floor, St Andrew's House, 18–20 St Andrew Street, London, EC4A 3AY

Tel: 020 7636 7014
Fax: 020 7631 5119
E-mail: lynne_anderson@newspapersoc.org.uk

Enquiries:
Direct tel: 020 7931 3806
Direct e-mail: Guy.Black@telegraph.co.uk

Founded:
1906

Organisation type and purpose:
Trade association.
National newspapers.

Subject coverage:
Distribution, advertising, marketing, newsprint.

Access to staff:
Appointment necessary.
Hours: Mon to Fri, 0900 to 1700

NEWSPAPER SOCIETY, THE

Acronym or abbreviation: NS

Bloomsbury House, 74–77 Great Russell Street, London, WC1B 3DA

Tel: 020 7636 7014
Fax: 020 7631 5119
E-mail: ns@newspapersoc.org.uk

Website:
http://www.newspapersoc.org.uk/new-reports/
publications/a-zpublications.html
Publications
http://www.newspapersoc.org.uk.
Facts and figures about the regional press, case studies/research, circulation/readership figures, links/planning aids.

Enquiries:
Enquiries to: Communications Executive
Direct fax: 020 7580 7167
Direct e-mail: lisa_mccarthy@newspapersoc.org.uk

Founded:
1836

Organisation type and purpose:
Trade association (membership is by subscription, qualification), present number of members: 327.
Represents the regional and local press in the UK.

continued overleaf

Subject coverage:
All information relating to Britain's regional press: including training, technical, industrial relations, legal and government matters, advertising sales and distribution, free newspapers, research, editorial readership, newspapers in education, press regulation and promotion.

Electronic and video publications:
A wide variety of publications available online, including:
Ad Control News
Barcoding and the Regional Press 2000 (pdf)
Consumers Choice IV Pocket Book 2000
Focus on ... regional newspapers and retailing terms 2000 (pdf)
Headlines
Intelligence News
NS News
Parliamentary & European Brief
Production Journal
Regional Press Fact Book – Sep 2001 (pdf)
Renaissance of Regional Nations 2000
Reporting Restrictions in the Crown Court (2000)
Reporting Restrictions in the Magistrates Court 2001
UK Automotive Industry 1999
UK Property Market

Publications list:
Available online

Access to staff:
Contact by letter, by fax and by e-mail
Hours: Mon to Fri, 0900 to 1700

Member of:
European Newspaper Publishers' Association
International Federation of Newspaper Publishers
Newspaper Conference

NEWSROOM, GUARDIAN AND OBSERVER ARCHIVE AND VISITOR CENTRE

60 Farringdon Road, London, EC1R 3GA

Tel: 020 7886 9898
Fax: 020 7490 8359
E-mail: newsroom@guardian.co.uk

Website:
http://www.guardian.co.uk/newsroom

Enquiries:
Enquiries to: Centre Administrator

Organisation type and purpose:
To preserve and promote the histories and values of the Guardian, The Observer and Guardian Unlimited through archive, education and exhibitions.

Subject coverage:
Newspapers

Museum or gallery collection, archive, or library special collection:
Individual collections (correspondence, diaries, notebooks, original sketches and photographs):
Jane Bown (Observer photographer)
WP Crozier (editor of the Guardian 1932–44)
Richard Fry (financial editor of the Guardian 1939–65)
Jean Stead (home news editor 1969–78 and reporter)
Donald Trelford (editor of the Observer 1975–93)
Corporate records:
The Guardian Archive (1968 to present)
The Observer Archive (1917 to present)
Newspaper holdings:
Guardian Weekly (1920–1949, 1972-current)
Guardian Commercial (1920–1939)
Observer magazine (1964–1994)
Bound volumes of the original newspapers are held but for preservation reasons surrogates are used where available.

Electronic and video publications:
Order electronic and video publications from:
Guardian (14 July 1984 to present)
Observer (3 January 1993 to present)

Access to staff:
Contact by letter, by telephone, by fax, by e-mail, in person and via website
Hours: Mon to Fri, 1000 to 1700

NEXUS INSTITUTE

119 University Street, Belfast, BT7 1HP

Tel: 028 9032 6803
Fax: 028 9032 5623
E-mail: info@nexusinstitute.org

Website:
http://www.nexusinstitute.org
Information on organisation, training, jobs, services.

Enquiries:
Enquiries to: Manager

Founded:
1984

Organisation type and purpose:
Voluntary organisation, registered charity (charity number XN 46002), training organisation.
Counselling.
For adult survivors of sexual abuse.

Subject coverage:
Field of sexual abuse, counselling of sexual abuse survivors, counsellor training.

Printed publications:
Annual Report (available free with postage paid)
Book of Survivor Poems (£2)

Access to staff:
Contact by letter, by telephone and by e-mail.
Appointment necessary. All charged.
Hours: Mon to Thu, 0900 to 1700; Fri, 0900 to 1600
Special comments: Evening appointments available by arrangement.

Other branches:
Nexus Institute
    38 Clarendon Street, Londonderry, BT48 7ET
Nexus Institute
    6 Portmore Street, Portadown, BT62 3NG
Nexus Institute
    104 Irvinestown Road, Enniskillen, BT74 6DN

NFU SCOTLAND

Acronym or abbreviation: NFUS

Rural Centre, West Mains, Ingliston, Newbridge, Midlothian, EH28 8LT

Tel: 0131 472 4000
Fax: 0131 472 4010
E-mail: webmaster@nfus.org.uk

Website:
http://www.nfus.org.uk

Enquiries:
Enquiries to: Chief Executive

Founded:
1913

Organisation type and purpose:
Professional body (membership is by subscription), voluntary organisation.
Represents the political interests of the Scottish agricultural, horticultural and crofting industries and acts as a professional association for Scottish farmers, growers and crofters.

Subject coverage:
Cereals, fish farming, horticulture, legal, labour and technology matters, livestock, milk, potatoes, poultry, publicity, animal health and welfare, crofting, pigs, environment, landlord/tenant, parliamentary.

Printed publications:
The Scottish Farming Leader (house magazine, circulation 12,000, 12 times a year)
Variety of other booklets (irregular)

Access to staff:
Contact by letter and by fax
Hours: Mon to Fri, 0900 to 1700

NGS PICTURE LIBRARY

Formal name: National Galleries of Scotland Picture Library

National Galleries of Scotland, Scottish National Gallery of Modern Art, 75 Belford Road, Edinburgh, EH4 3DS

Tel: 0131 624 6258; 0131 624 6260
Fax: 0131 623 7135
E-mail: picture.library@nationalgalleries.org

Website:
http://www.nationalgalleries.org

Organisation type and purpose:
National organisation, art gallery, public library.

Subject coverage:
Brings together the works in all the collections of the National Galleries of Scotland including photographs and slides; material depicting the work of artists from the Renaissance to the present day, including the major painters, and a wide variety of subjects, media and styles.

Non-library collection catalogue:
All or part available online, in-house and in print

Library catalogue:
All or part available online, in-house and in print

Printed publications:
A comprehensive list of NGS publications can be found at: http://www.nationalgalleries.org/research/page/7:3790
Order printed publications from: website: http://www.nationalgalleries.org/shop/online/8:398/category/575

Publications list:
Available online and in print

Access to staff:
Contact by letter, by telephone, by fax, by e-mail and via website. Appointment necessary.
Hours: Mon to Fri, 0900 to 1700

Access to building, collection or gallery:
No prior appointment required
Hours: Daily, 1000 to 1700; Thu to 1900
Special comments: Closed 25, 26 December; open 1 January, 1200 to 1700

Access for disabled people:
Access to all public areas, toilet facilities

Parent body:
National Galleries of Scotland
    Belford Road, Edinburgh, EH4 3DR; tel: 0131 624 6200; fax: 0131 623 7126; e-mail: enquiries@nationalgalleries.org; website: http://www.nationalgalleries.org

NGS: GARDENS OPEN FOR CHARITY

Formal name: National Gardens Scheme
Acronym or abbreviation: NGS

Hatchlands Park, East Clandon, Guildford, Surrey, GU4 7RT

Tel: 01483 211535
Fax: 01483 211537
E-mail: ngs@ngs.org.uk

Website:
http://www.ngs.org.uk
Ordering publications.

Enquiries:
Enquiries to: Marketing Communications Manager
Direct tel: 01483 213900
Direct e-mail: cmorley@ngs.org.uk

Founded:
1927

Organisation type and purpose:
Voluntary organisation, registered charity (charity number 1112664).

Subject coverage:
Approximately 3,700 mainly privately owned gardens in England and Wales are opened to the public on behalf of the NGS each year, in order to raise money for good causes.

Printed publications:
The Yellow Book 2007 (£8.99 inc. p&p)
Order printed publications from: Website

Publications list:
Available online

Access to staff:
Contact by letter, by telephone, by fax, by e-mail and via website
Hours: Mon to Fri, 0900 to 1700

Fund-raising body for:
Arthritis Research UK
Crossroads Care
Gardeners' Royal Benevolent Society
Help the Hospices
Local charities nominated by garden owners
Macmillan Cancer Support
Marie Curie Cancer Care
National Trust Careership Scheme
Perennial (Gardeners' Royal Benevolent Society)
Queens Nursing Institute
Royal Gardeners' Orphan Fund

NHBC

Formal name: National House Building Council

Buildmark House, Chiltern Avenue, Amersham, Buckinghamshire, HP6 5AP

Tel: 0870 2414302
Fax: 01494 735201
E-mail: mediaenquiries@nhbc.co.uk

Website:
http://www.nhbc.co.uk
Register of builders, building new homes, building your own home, consultancy services, press, site map, factsheets, statistics.

Enquiries:
Enquiries to: Head of Corporate Communications
Direct tel: 01494 735262
Other contacts: Media Manager (for company information)

Founded:
1936

Organisation type and purpose:
National organisation, professional body, present number of members: 17,000 registered builders, a non-profit-distributing company limited by guarantee.
Independent standard-setting body for the UK house-building industry.
Aims to improve standards of new homes in the UK, benchmark best practice and work with builders to raise standards and protect homeowners.

Subject coverage:
NHBC sets standards for the building of new homes in the UK. It raises standards by providing new home warranty and insurance services for home buyers, setting construction standards for new homes and inspecting at key stages, registering builders and being a service provider of health and safety, training and engineering services.

Trade and statistical information:
New house-building statistics, e.g. UK new home starts and completions, UK average daily sales, new home prices.

Printed publications:
Publications available free and also for purchase
NHBC Rules
Guide to your New Home
Solo for Self Build Guide

Publications list:
Available in print

Access to staff:
Contact by letter, by telephone and by e-mail.
Appointment necessary.
Hours: Mon to Fri, 0900 to 1730

Access to building, collection or gallery:
Prior appointment required
Hours: Mon to Fri, 0900 to 1730

Access for disabled people:
Parking provided, level entry

Also at:
Belfast, Edinburgh, Droitwich, London, Milton Keynes and York
Addresses available on website pages

NHS EDUCATION FOR SCOTLAND

22 Queen Street, Edinburgh, EH2 1JX

Tel: 0131 226 7371
Fax: 0131 225 9970
E-mail: enquiries@nes.scot.nhs.uk

Website:
http://www.nes.scot.nhs.uk

Enquiries:
Direct tel: 0131 220 8603
Other contacts: Corporate Services Manager

Founded:
2002

Organisation type and purpose:
National government body, statutory body, training organisation.
Oversight of postgraduate education of doctors, dentists, clinical psychologists, midwives, nurses, and allied health professions.

Subject coverage:
Postgraduate medical and dental education in Scotland.

Access to staff:
Contact by letter, by telephone and by e-mail
Hours: Mon to Fri, 0900 to 1730

Access for disabled people:
Level entry, toilet facilities

Accountable to the:
Scottish Executive

NHS ESTATES, INFORMATION CENTRE

Department of Health, 1 Trevelyan Square, Boar Lane, Leeds, West Yorkshire, LS1 6AE

Tel: 0113 254 7070
Fax: 0113 254 7167
E-mail: nhs.estates@doh.gov.uk

Website:
http://www.nhsestates.gov.uk/
publications_guidance/index.asp

Enquiries:
Enquiries to: Information Officer

Organisation type and purpose:
National government body.
To enable optimum use of the estates for better healthcare.

Subject coverage:
Health estate management, Health buildings and facilities design, Health technical advice on building components, access to Department of Health Library database, fire and safety design – Health buildings, estate policy advice Health estate.

Museum or gallery collection, archive, or library special collection:
Archival Health buildings directorate publications
Collection of audiovisual material – slides, photographs of hospital building projects (various stages)
Very old departmental circulars and letters

Non-library collection catalogue:
All or part available in-house

Library catalogue:
All or part available in-house

Printed publications:
Various HMSO and NHS Estates publications include:
Design and Briefing: General, Health Building Notes (HBN)
Operational: Firecode, Health Guidance Notes (HGN), Health Technical Memoranda (HTM), Model Engineering Specifications (MES)
Strategic: Commissioning, Concode, Energy, Water & Waste, Environment, Estatecode, Estate Strategy, Facilities Management, Miscellaneous
NHS Estates Policy and Initiatives & General Quarterly Briefing
Order printed publications from: HMSO, PO Box 276 London, SW8 5DT, tel: 0870 600 5522, fax: 0870 600 5533

Electronic and video publications:
Building Better Healthcare 2 (CD-ROM)

Publications list:
Available online and in print

Access to staff:
Contact by telephone, by e-mail and via website.
Appointment necessary.
Hours: Mon to Thu, 0830 to 1730; Fri, 0830 to 1700

Access for disabled people:
Ramped entry, access to all public areas, toilet facilities
Special comments: Parking provided upon request.

Parent body:
Department of Health

NIAB

Formal name: National Institute of Agricultural Botany

Huntingdon Road, Cambridge, CB3 0LE

Tel: 01223 342200
Fax: 01223 277602
E-mail: info@niab.com

Website:
http://www.niab.com
Guide to NIAB services.

Founded:
1919

Organisation type and purpose:
Membership association (membership is by subscription), present number of members: 2500, registered charity, research organisation.

Subject coverage:
Variety testing of most agricultural and horticultural crops (except fruit), choice of variety, seed certification, seed testing procedures, botanical description of varieties, plant pathology, plant science research.

Museum or gallery collection, archive, or library special collection:
Seed catalogues (1900-)

Printed publications:
The following publications available for purchase
Biennial Report
Seed identification
Pocket Guides to Crop Varieties
Plant Genetic Resources (journal, 3 times a year)

Publications list:
Available online and in print

Access to staff:
Contact by letter, by telephone, by e-mail, in person and via website. Appointment necessary.
Access for members only. Non-members charged.
Hours: Mon to Thu, 0900 to 1700; Fri, 0900 to 1645
Special comments: Association members only.

Access to building, collection or gallery:
No prior appointment required

continued overleaf

Access for disabled people:
Ramped entry, toilet facilities

Includes the:
Official Seed Testing Station for England and Wales
at the same address

NICKEL INSTITUTE

Acronym or abbreviation: NI

The Holloway, Alvechurch, Birmingham, B48 7QB

Tel: 01527 584777
Fax: 01527 585562
E-mail: birmingham@nickelinstitute.org

Website:
http://www.nickelinstitute.org
All publications available.

Enquiries:
Enquiries to: European Director
Other contacts: Technical Director

Founded:
1957

Organisation type and purpose:
International organisation, present number of members: 15 industrial members, consultancy.
Market development organisation, offering expert advice in the form of published information and discussion with consultants.
To support, sustain and defend worldwide use of nickel and its alloys.

Subject coverage:
Oil and gas industry, marine offshore industry, electroplating and electroforming, welding, casting and foundry, chemical, environmental, all as applied to nickel and its alloys (especially stainless steel).

Museum or gallery collection, archive, or library special collection:
Computer databases
Technical publications on nickel and its alloys
Videos

Non-library collection catalogue:
All or part available online

Library catalogue:
All or part available online

Printed publications:
Nickel (3 times a year)
Technical information and advice to anyone concerned with nickel and its alloys – designers, specifiers, engineers, architects, manufacturers etc (almost 1000 publications in catalogue, all free)

Electronic and video publications:
Fresh Approaches to Mold Steel Selection (video)
Stainless Steel: The Effective Solution (video)

Publications list:
Available online and in print

Access to staff:
Contact by letter, by telephone, by fax, by e-mail and in person. Appointment necessary.
Hours: Mon to Fri, 0900 to 1700
Special comments: By prior appointment

Access for disabled people:
Special comments: By prior appointment

Has:
offices in 8 countries

Head office:
NI
55 University Avenue, Suite 1801, Toronto, Ontario, M5T 2H7, canada; tel: +1 416 591 7999; fax: +1 416 591 7987; e-mail: ni_toronto@nickelinstitute.org; website: www.nickelinstitute.org

NIELSEN BOOK

3rd Floor, Midas House, 62 Goldsworth Road, Woking, Surrey, GU21 6LQ

Tel: 01483 712200
Fax: 01483 712201
E-mail: libraries.book@nielsen.com

Website:
http://www.nielsenbook.co.uk
A company profile, plus details of BookData's full range of library services.

Enquiries:
Enquiries to: Head of Data Sales – Libraries
Direct e-mail: paul.dibble@nielsen.com
Other contacts: Library Executive

Founded:
2002

Formerly called:
Book Data, Whitaker Information Services, First Edition (year of change 2002)

Organisation type and purpose:
Data partner for the book industry, playing a pivotal role within the industry and offering a comprehensive source of bibliographic data and associated services in the United Kingdom.
Working with publishers large and small, data is collected from 60,000 publishers in over 70 countries. Over 12m. titles are held and millions of changes are made annually to ensure that the most timely, accurate and comprehensive data is available.

Subject coverage:
Bibliographic data, acquisitions, search and discovery, cataloguing, ordering and promotion.

Electronic and video publications:
A range of services for libraries and library suppliers worldwide:
BookData Online
BookData MARC and Multimedia (data feed of MARC records)
BookScan for Libraries
LibScan (measuring library issues)
BookNet EDI
BookData Enrich

Publications list:
Available online

Access to staff:
Contact by letter, by telephone, by fax, by e-mail, in person and via website. Appointment necessary.
Access for members only.
Hours: Mon to Fri, 0900 to 1700

Access to building, collection or gallery:
Prior appointment required

Access for disabled people:
Parking provided, disabled lift, toilet facilities

NIGERIAN HIGH COMMISSION

Nigeria House, 9 Northumberland Avenue, London, WC2N 5BX

Tel: 020 7839 1244
Fax: 020 7839 8746

Website:
http://www.nigeriahighcommissionuk.com

Enquiries:
Enquiries to: Librarian
Direct tel: ext 279 or 303
Other contacts: Head of Chancery for official government statements.

Founded:
1960

Organisation type and purpose:
National government body.

Subject coverage:
Federal government of Nigeria matters e.g. history, economics, laws etc.
Tourist information.

Library catalogue:
All or part available in-house

Printed publications:
The Nigerian (newsletter, published in-house)

Access to staff:
Contact by letter, by telephone and by fax.
Appointment necessary.
Hours: Library: Mon to Fri, 1000 to 1700
Offices: Mon to Fri, 0900 to 1700

Access to building, collection or gallery:
Prior appointment required

Consular Section:
Nigerian High Commission
56–57 Fleet Street, London, EC4; tel: 020 7353 3776

NISSAN INSTITUTE OF JAPANESE STUDIES

University of Oxford, 27 Winchester Road, Oxford, OX2 6NA

Tel: 01865 274570
Fax: 01865 274574
E-mail: secretary@nissan.ox.ac.uk

Website:
http://www.nissan.ox.ac.uk
Basic information about the Nissan Institute.

Enquiries:
Enquiries to: Secretary

Founded:
1981

Organisation type and purpose:
University institute.
To promote the study of modern and contemporary Japan within the University of Oxford.

Subject coverage:
The modern history, politics, economy, international relations, society and education systems of Japan.

Museum or gallery collection, archive, or library special collection:
See Bodleian Japanese Library (separate institution from the Nissan Institute)

Printed publications:
Nissan Institute Occasional Papers (35 papers published, 1986–2004; enquiries to the Secretary, Nissan Institute)
Nissan Institute/Routledge Japanese Studies Series (66 titles published 1986–2006; available through bookshops)

Access to staff:
Contact by letter, by fax, by e-mail and via website. Appointment necessary.
Hours: Mon to Fri, 0900 to 1230 and 1400 to 1645
Special comments: Primarily university access.

Access for disabled people:
Ramped entry, lift

Parent body:
University of Oxford

NO PANIC

Formal name: National Organisation for Phobias, Anxiety Neurosis Information and Care

93 Brands Farm Way, Randlay, Telford, Shropshire, TF3 2JQ

Tel: 01952 590005
Fax: 01952 270962
E-mail: ceo@nopanic.org.uk

Website:
http://www.nopanic.org.uk

Enquiries:
Enquiries to: Chief Executive

Founded:
1991

Organisation type and purpose:
International organisation, membership association (membership is by subscription), present number of members: 2,500, voluntary organisation, registered charity (charity number 1018184).
The relief and rehabilitation of people suffering from anxiety disorders.

Subject coverage:
Sufferers and carers of anxiety disorders caused by panic attacks, phobias, obsessive/compulsive disorders and tranquilliser withdrawal.

Library catalogue:
All or part available online and in print

Printed publications:
Leaflets on a variety of anxieties and phobias, including general anxiety disorder, panic, darkness, dogs, cats, crane flies, bees, birds, spiders, driving, weather and injections
Newsletter (6 a year, members only)
Any Question – The most asked questions about phobias (K. Sell, £4.90)
Counselling –How to help others (K. Sell, £3.50)
Helpful Hints for Phobics (G. Marsden, £2)
Me and My Phobia – How sufferers tackled their phobias (K. Sell, £6.60)
No Panic – A practical guide to managing panic and phobia (K. Gournay, £9.50)
O.C.D. Carers' Questions Answered – All you want to know about O.C.D. (K. Sell, £2.30)
Stress Management – A guide to coping with stress (K. Gournay, £6.95)
To Thine Own Self Be True (S. Holmes, £6.95)

Electronic and video publications:
Agoraphobia and Panic (DVD)
Muscle Relaxation (CD
New Horizons, Agoraphobia Recovery (CD)
New Horizons, Carers Support (CD)
New Horizons, Obsessive/Compulsive Disorder (CD)
New Horizons, Panic Attacks/Anxiety (CD)
Obsessive/Compulsive Disorder (DVD)
Social Phobia (DVD)
Vomit (DVD)
Weather Sound Effects (CD)

Publications list:
Available online and in print

Access to staff:
Contact by letter, by telephone and by fax.
Appointment necessary.
Hours: Mon to Fri, 0900 to 1700

NOC LIBRARY (GIRDLESTONE MEMORIAL)

Nuffield Orthopaedic Centre, National Health Service Trust, Headington, Oxford, OX3 7LD

Tel: 01865 738147
Fax: 01865 738146
E-mail: library@noc.nhs/uk

Website:
http://noclibrary.com
Induction, Athens information, all library documentation, current awareness, literature searching, PubMed links, historical collection, enquiries.

Enquiries:
Enquiries to: Library and Information Services Manager

Organisation type and purpose:
NHS Library.

Subject coverage:
Orthopaedics, orthopaedic engineering (bio-mechanics), rehabilitation, rheumatology, metabolic disease of bone, orthopaedic and trauma nursing.

Museum or gallery collection, archive, or library special collection:
Small collection of early orthopaedic texts

Non-library collection catalogue:
All or part available in-house

Library catalogue:
All or part available online

Access to staff:
Contact by letter, by telephone, by fax, by e-mail, in person and via website
Hours: 0830 to 1700

Access to building, collection or gallery:
24-hour card access for members

Access for disabled people:
Level entry, access to all public areas

Links with:
South Central Strategic Health Authority
website: http://www.nesc.nhs.uk
University of Oxford
Nuffield Department of Orthopaedic, Rheumatology and Musculoskeletal Sciences

NOISE ABATEMENT SOCIETY

Acronym or abbreviation: NAS

44 Grand Parade, Brighton, East Sussex, BN2 9QA

Tel: 01273 682223
Fax: 01273 682223
E-mail: info@noise-abatement.org

Website:
http://www.noiseabatementsociety.com

Enquiries:
Enquiries to: Director
Direct e-mail: info@noise-abatement.org

Founded:
1959

Organisation type and purpose:
National organisation, membership association (membership is by subscription), voluntary organisation, registered charity (charity number 272040), research organisation.
To reduce noise from all sources.

Subject coverage:
Noise abatement in all fields.

Printed publications:
Newsletter

Access to staff:
Contact by letter, by telephone, by fax, by e-mail, in person and via website. Appointment necessary.
Access for members only.
Hours: Mon to Fri, 0900 to 1600

Access to building, collection or gallery:
No access other than to staff

Affiliated to:
International Association Against Noise

NORDOFF ROBBINS LONDON CENTRE

2 Lissenden Gardens, London, NW5 1PQ

Tel: 020 7267 4496
Fax: 020 7267 4369
E-mail: admin@nordoff-robbins.org.uk

Website:
http://www.nordoff-robbins.org.uk
Information about music therapy and services provided by Nordoff Robbins across the UK; information about education programmes including short courses, Masters degree music therapy training and PhD programme; information about research in music therapy; information about getting involved in Nordoff Robbins fundraising.

Enquiries:
Enquiries to: Administrator

Founded:
1980

Please select:
Nordoff-Robbins Music Therapy Centre (year of change 2009)

Organisation type and purpose:
National Headquarters of Nordoff Robbins charity (RCN 280960), which provides music therapy services and music and health projects nationally, and education and training in and about music therapy, and undertakes research in music therapy. Music therapy clinic, music therapy training degree course, research department.

Subject coverage:
Music therapy; music and health.

Information services:
Comprehensive music therapy library open to the general public by arrangement.

Museum or gallery collection, archive, or library special collection:
Comprehensive music therapy library open to the general public by arrangement

Library catalogue:
All or part available in-house

Printed publications:
Brochures, leaflets, newsletters, annual reports, research dissertations, books
Order printed publications from: e-mail: admin@nordoff-robbins.org.uk

Electronic and video publications:
Promotional DVD
Order electronic and video publications from: e-mail: admin@nordoff-robbins.org.uk

Publications list:
Available in print

Access to staff:
Contact by telephone and via website.
Appointment necessary.
Hours: Mon to Fri, 0900 to 1700

Access to building, collection or gallery:
Prior appointment required
Hours: Mon to Fri, 0900 to 1630; Sat, 0900 to 1500
Special comments: Telephone before coming. Library for reference only.

Access for disabled people:
Ramped entry, toilet facilities

Links with:
City University London (validating partner for training programmes)
Northampton Square, London, EC1V 0HB; tel: 020 7040 5060; e-mail: enquiries@city.ac.uk; website: http://www.city.ac.uk

NORFOLK & NORWICH MILLENNIUM LIBRARY

The Forum, Millennium Plain, Norwich, Norfolk, NR2 1AW

Tel: 01603 774774
Fax: 01603 774705
E-mail: millennium.lib@norfolk.gov.uk

Website:
http://www.library.norfolk.gov.uk
Summary of services provided by the Norfolk Library and Information Service, with links to pages giving more information on some of them.

Enquiries:
Enquiries to: Central Information Team
Direct tel: 01603 774775
Direct e-mail: info.services.dcs@norfolk.gov.uk

Organisation type and purpose:
Local government body, public library.

Subject coverage:
History of Norfolk and Norwich; history of 2nd Air Division, 8th US Army Air Force, 1942–1945; USA travel and culture; general subjects.

Museum or gallery collection, archive, or library special collection:
American Memorial Library (US life and history)
Bosworth Harcourt and Buck bequests (theatrical, literary and historical)
Colman and Rye Collections of Local History (seriously affected by the fire of 1994)

continued overleaf

Norwich City Library, 1608 (incunabula, theology and general literature)

Photographic collections by G C Davies, T D Eaton, P H Emerson, Payne Jennings

Publications of the Public Record Office, Historical Manuscripts Commission

Family history resources on microfilm and microfiche include Indexes to Births, Marriages and Deaths (national), Probate Indexes (national) and Census returns and name indexes (local)

Market research, business information, newspapers, etc. online

Database of local organisations (Icon) available in library and via the internet

Non-library collection catalogue:
All or part available online

Library catalogue:
All or part available online

Access to staff:
Contact by letter, by telephone, by fax, by e-mail, in person and via website
Hours: Mon to Fri, 0900 to 2000, Saturday 0900 to 1700

Access for disabled people:
Parking provided, ramped entry, access to all public areas, toilet facilities

Member organisation of:
Anglian Libraries Information Exchange Scheme (ANGLES)

Parent body:
Norfolk Library and Information Service County Hall , Martineau Lane, Norwich; tel: 01603 222049; fax: 01603 222422

NORFOLK & NORWICH NOVI SAD ASSOCIATION

Acronym or abbreviation: NNNSA

Glebelands, Star Lane, Rockland St Mary, Norwich, Norfolk, NR14 7BX

Tel: 01508 480262
Fax: 01508 480262
E-mail: peter@beckleyp.freeserve.co.uk

Enquiries:
Enquiries to: Honorary Secretary

Founded:
1985

Organisation type and purpose:
National organisation, membership association (membership is by subscription).

Subject coverage:
Promoting informal links between people and organisations in the City of Norwich and the County of Norfolk, and those in the municipality of Novi Sad, Serbia; supports the official twinning between the City of Norwich and the City of Novi Sad.

Museum or gallery collection, archive, or library special collection:
Archive material relating to the twinning links between the cities of Norwich and Novi Sad

Printed publications:
Newsletter (3 or 4 times a year)

Access to staff:
Contact by letter, by telephone, by fax and by e-mail
Hours: Mon to Fri, 0900 to 1700

Links with:
City Council Novi Sad
Norfolk County Council
Norwich City Council

NORFOLK AND NORWICH ARCHAEOLOGICAL SOCIETY

Acronym or abbreviation: NNAS

64 The Close, Norwich, NR1 4DH

Tel: 01603 891437

Website:
http://www.nnas.info

Enquiries:
Enquiries to: Librarian

Founded:
1846

Organisation type and purpose:
Learned society (membership is by subscription), present number of members: 400, registered charity (charity number 311116).

Subject coverage:
Archaeology, history, architecture and antiquities of the county of Norfolk.

Museum or gallery collection, archive, or library special collection:
On loan to Norfolk Record Office, County Hall, Norwich:
King Collection of drawings and watercolours of East Anglian specimens of stained and painted glass
Transcripts of Norfolk Parish Registers

Library catalogue:
All or part available online and in-house

Printed publications:
Newsletter (2 times a year)
Norfolk Archaeology (annually)

Access to staff:
Contact by letter, by telephone and via website. Appointment necessary. Access for members only.
Hours: Mon to Fri, 0900 to 1700

Access to building, collection or gallery:
By appointment

NORFOLK ASSOCIATION OF VILLAGE HALLS

Acronym or abbreviation: NAVH

20 Market Place, Hingham, Norwich, Norfolk, NR9 4AF

Tel: 01953 851408
Fax: 01953 850695
E-mail: nrcc@norfolkrcc.org.uk

Enquiries:
Enquiries to: Secretary

Founded:
1984

Organisation type and purpose:
Membership association (membership is by subscription), present number of members: 310, voluntary organisation, registered charity (charity number 1053152).

Subject coverage:
Management of village halls and community centres, training for committee members, sources of funds and charity law.

Access to staff:
Contact by letter, by telephone, by fax and by e-mail. Appointment necessary. Access for members only.
Hours: Mon to Fri, 0900 to 1700

Access to building, collection or gallery:
Prior appointment required

NORFOLK CHURCH TRUST LIMITED

Acronym or abbreviation: NCT

9 The Old Church, St Matthews Road, Norwich, Norfolk, NR1 1SP

Tel: 01603 767576
Fax: 01986 798776
E-mail: secretary@norfolkchurchestrust.co.uk

Website:
http://www.norfolkchurchestrust.co.uk
General information about the Trust.

Enquiries:
Enquiries to: Chief Executive/Company Secretary

Founded:
1976

Organisation type and purpose:
Membership association (membership is by subscription, election or invitation), present number of members: 1,300, voluntary organisation, registered charity (charity number 271176), consultancy.
To ensure Christian Churches remain open as places of worship in Norfolk and the Diocese of Norwich.

Subject coverage:
General state of repair, restoration and maintenance of the churches in Norfolk.

Information services:
Information and guidance on the restoration/conservation/state of the churches in Norfolk.

Printed publications:
Treasure for the Future: A Celebration of the Norfolk Churches Trust 1976–2001 (ed Roberts C)
Sculptured Monuments in Norfolk Churches (Spencer N)
The Brasses of Norfolk Churches (Greenwood R and Norris M)
Order printed publications from: 9 The Old Church, St Matthews Road, Norwich, NR1 1SP

Access to staff:
Contact by letter, by telephone, by fax and by e-mail
Hours: Mon to Sun, 0800 to 2000

NORFOLK COUNTY ASSOCIATION OF PARISH & TOWN COUNCILS

Acronym or abbreviation: NCAPTC

North Wing, County Hall, Norwich, Norfolk, NR1 2UF

Tel: 01603 664869
Fax: 01603 664871
E-mail: enquiries@ncaptc.gov.uk

Enquiries:
Enquiries to: Executive Officer

Founded:
1941

Publications list:
Available in print

Access to staff:
Contact by letter, by telephone, by fax and by e-mail. Access for members only.
Hours: Mon to Fri, 0900 to 1700

Affiliated to:
National Association of Local Councils (NALC)

NORFOLK COUNTY COUNCIL LIBRARY AND INFORMATION SERVICE

County Hall, Martineau Lane, Norwich, Norfolk, NR1 2UA

Tel: 0344 800 8020
Fax: 01603 222422
E-mail: libraries@norfolk.gov.uk

Website:
http://www.norfolk.gov.uk
Key contact details and general information about range of services and locations offered by Norfolk Library and Information Service.

Enquiries:
Enquiries to: Head of Library and Information Service

Founded:
1974

Organisation type and purpose:
Local government body, public library.
Headquarters and administration centre, no library at this address.

Subject coverage:
General.

Museum or gallery collection, archive, or library special collection:
Norwich: Colman and Rye local studies collection
King's Lynn: St Margaret's Parish collection
Thetford: Duleep Singh collection
Thetford: Thomas Paine collection

Non-library collection catalogue:
All or part available online and in-house

Library catalogue:
All or part available online

Access to staff:
Contact by letter, by telephone, by fax and by e-mail. Appointment necessary.
Hours: Mon to Fri, 0900 to 1700

Access to building, collection or gallery:
No prior appointment required

Main libraries:
Great Yarmouth Library
  Tollhouse Street, Great Yarmouth, Norfolk, NR30 2SH; tel: 01943 844551; fax: 01943 857628; e-mail: yarmouth.lib@norfolk.gov.uk
King's Lynn Library
  London Road, King's Lynn, Norfolk, PE30 5EZ; tel: 01553 772568; fax: 01553 769832; e-mail: kings.lynn.lib@norfolk.gov.uk
Norfolk & Norwich Millennium Library
  The Forum, Millennium Plain, Norwich, Norfolk, NR2 1AW; tel: 01603 774774; fax: 01603 774705; e-mail: millennium.lib@norfolk.gov.uk
Thetford Library
  Raymond Street, Thetford, Norfolk, IP24 2EA; tel: 01842 752048; fax: 01842 750125; e-mail: thetford.lib@norfolk.gov.uk

NORFOLK COUNTY PETANQUE ASSOCIATION

Acronym or abbreviation: NCPA

26 Sun Lane, Norwich, NR3 3NF

Tel: 01603 419897

Enquiries:
Enquiries to: Secretary
Direct e-mail: normanguest.petanque@lineone.net

Organisation type and purpose:
Membership association (membership is by subscription), present number of members: 235 (in Norfolk only).
A sporting association.
To promote and foster the game of Pétanque in Norfolk.
To promote and organise Pétanque competitions.

Subject coverage:
The rules of Pétanque and method of play; how to construct, and dimensions of, a playing surface.

Access to staff:
Contact by letter, by telephone and by e-mail
Hours: Mon to Fri, 0900 to 1700

NORFOLK FAMILY HISTORY SOCIETY

Kirby Hall, 70 St Giles Street, Norwich, Norfolk, NR2 1LS

Tel: 01603 763718
E-mail: nfhs@paston.co.uk

Website:
http://www.norfolkfhs.org.uk

Enquiries:
Enquiries to: Company Secretary

Founded:
1968

Organisation type and purpose:
Membership association (membership is by subscription), present number of members: 4000, registered charity (charity number 1055410).

Non-library collection catalogue:
All or part available online

Publications list:
Available online and in print

Access to staff:
Contact by letter and in person
Hours: Tue, Thu, Sun, 1000 to 1300; Wed, 1000 to 1600
Special comments: Donations invited from visiting non-members.

Access to building, collection or gallery:
No prior appointment required

Access for disabled people:
Parking provided, ramped entry, toilet facilities

NORFOLK RECORD OFFICE

The Archive Centre, Martineau Lane, Norwich, Norfolk, NR1 2DQ

Tel: 01603 222599
Fax: 01603 761885
E-mail: norfrec@norfolk.gov.uk

Website:
http://archives.norfolk.gov.uk
Access information, facilities, publications, price list, brief information resources for popular subjects of research, summary guide, online catalogues.

Enquiries:
Enquiries to: County Archivist

Founded:
1963

Organisation type and purpose:
Local government body.
County Record Office.

Subject coverage:
Norfolk Record Office holdings.

Museum or gallery collection, archive, or library special collection:
Archives for the County of Norfolk and Diocese of Norwich, 11th to 21st centuries

Non-library collection catalogue:
All or part available online, in-house and in print

Printed publications:
A Guide to the Records of Norwich Cathedral (F. Meeres, 1998, £6.95 plus p&p)
Norfolk Parish Map: showing the locations of parishes (50p plus p&p)
50 free information leaflets, including guides to sources

Microform publications:
Duplicates of many of the Norfolk Record Office's holdings on film and fiche, including some parish registers, can be purchased

Publications list:
Available online and in print

Access to staff:
Contact by letter, by telephone, by fax, by e-mail, in person and via website. Appointment necessary.

Access to building, collection or gallery:
Hours: Mon, Wed, Thu and Fri, 0900 to 1700; Tue, 0930 to 1700; Sat, 0900 to 1200. Closed bank holidays and Sat before Easter, and spring and summer bank holidays; closed for two weeks in late Nov and early Dec for stocktaking
Special comments: County Archive Research Network reader's ticket required for access to original manuscripts.

NORFOLK YOUTH MUSIC TRUST

Wahnfried, 4 Church Close, Buxton, Norwich, Norfolk, NR10 5ER

Tel: 01603 279742
E-mail: info@norfolk-youth-music-trust.org.uk

Website:
http://norfolk-youth-music-trust.org.uk

Enquiries:
Enquiries to: Chairman / Secretary

Founded:
2001

Formerly called:
Music at Saint George's (year of change 2001)

Organisation type and purpose:
Voluntary organisation, registered charity (charity number 1043945).
To promote, encourage, maintain, develop and improve public education in, and appreciation of, the art and science of music in all its aspects within the county of Norfolk. The trust also aims to help the development of highly-talented Norfolk-based young musicians to pursue careers as professionals by offering annual grants and occasional public performing opportunities. Successful applicants will already be highly skilled in one or more of the six disciplines (brass, keyboard, percussion, strings, voice and woodwind) and will be either undergoing a period of study at a music college or specialist school, or who have made plans to do so.

Subject coverage:
Occasional promotions of young musicians' concerts, plus annual round of grants available to under-30s engaged in studies to become professional musicians.

Museum or gallery collection, archive, or library special collection:
Norfolk 'Icon'

Trade and statistical information:
Database in Local Studies Library, Norwich

Non-library collection catalogue:
All or part available in-house

Library catalogue:
All or part available in-house and in print

Printed publications:
The Music Makers 1977–2001 (132pp, 2001, ISBN 1–903923–00-X, £8.50)
I'll Take You Where the Music's Playing (Hosgood I, 2005, £9.95)
Order printed publications from: Postal address

Electronic and video publications:
WPCD1 and WPCD2 The Last Day 3 Feb 2001 (2 CD Set, £10 per set)
WPCD3 and WPCD4 The Last Day 3 Feb 2001 (2 CD Set, £10 per set)

Access to staff:
Contact by letter, by telephone, by e-mail and via website. Appointment necessary.
Hours: Mon to Fri, 0900 to 1700

Access for disabled people:
Full access for public concerts
Hours: Concert performance times only

NORSKE VERITAS

Acronym or abbreviation: DNV

Palace House, 3 Cathedral Street, London, SE1 9DE

Tel: 020 7357 6080
Fax: 020 7716 6736

Website:
http://www.dnv.com/maritime/publicationlist/index.asp
Publication list.
http://www.dnv.com

Enquiries:
Enquiries to: Information Scientist
Direct tel: 020 7716 6583
Direct fax: 020 7716 6730

Founded:
1864

continued overleaf

Organisation type and purpose:
Service industry, training organisation,
consultancy.
Provides consulting, engineering, verification,
certification and training services.

Subject coverage:
Industrial safety, offshore oil and gas, chemical
industries, risk assessment, safety management,
environmental management, quality management,
marine transport, reliability assessment, loss
prevention, environmental assessment,
environmental risk, safety assessment.

**Museum or gallery collection, archive, or library
special collection:**
Books, reports, documents, periodicals, legislation,
standards, codes, guidelines

Non-library collection catalogue:
All or part available in-house

Library catalogue:
All or part available in-house

Printed publications:
Various publications available for purchase, direct
Rules for Classification
Standards for Certification
Insurance Plans
Offshore Standards
Order printed publications from: For international
orders, Distribution Department
Det Norske Veritas, Norwegian Office, e-mail:
distribution@dnv.com
Information Scientist, Det Norske Veritas
Aberdeen Office

Electronic and video publications:
Some publications available online, free of charge,
and available for purchase, direct

Publications list:
Available online and in print

Access to staff:
Contact by letter, by telephone and by fax
Hours: Mon to Fri, 0900 to 1700

Access to building, collection or gallery:
No access other than to staff

Access for disabled people:
Level entry, access to all public areas

Other offices:
Det Norske Veritas (DNV)
Cromarty House, 67–72 Regent Quay, Aberdeen,
AB11 5AR; tel: 01224 335000; fax: 01244 593311

Parent body:
Det Norske Veritas, Norway (DNV)
Veritasveien 1, 1322 Høvik, Norway; tel: +47 67
57 99 00; fax: +47 67 57 99 11; website: http://
www.dnv.com

NORTH & WESTERN LANCASHIRE CHAMBER OF COMMERCE

Acronym or abbreviation: NWLCC

9–10 Eastway Business Village, Oliver's Place,
Fulwood, Preston, Lancashire, PR2 9WT

Tel: 01772 653000
Fax: 01772 655544
E-mail: info@lancschamber.co.uk

Website:
http://www.lancschamber.co.uk

Enquiries:
Enquiries to: Chief Executive

Founded:
1916

Organisation type and purpose:
Membership association, present number of
members: 1,400.
To promote, protect and develop the local business
community at local, national and international
level.

Subject coverage:
Export, training, market research, business
information, library, databases.

Printed publications:
Chamber Directory/Desk Diary

Publications list:
Available in print

Access to staff:
Contact by letter, by telephone, by fax, by e-mail
and via website. Non-members charged.
Hours: Mon to Fri, 0900 to 1700

Access to building, collection or gallery:
Prior appointment required

Access for disabled people:
Parking provided, ramped entry, toilet facilities

NORTH AYRSHIRE INFORMATION AND CULTURE

Greenwood Centre, Dunlop Crescent, Dreghorn,
KA11 4GZ

Tel: 01294 212716
Fax: 01294 222509
E-mail: libraryhq@north-ayrshire.gov.uk

Website:
http://www.ers.north-ayrshire.gov.uk
Information about the Information and Culture
service as well as the Education Resource Service
support for schools.

Enquiries:
Enquiries to: Manager, Information and Culture
Direct e-mail: asutton@north-ayrshire.gov.uk
Other contacts: Library Operations Manager

Founded:
1996

Organisation type and purpose:
Local government body, public library and
education resource service.

Subject coverage:
Local history and archives relating to
Cunninghame, North Ayrshire, Burghs in that
area, the islands of Arran and Millport.

**Museum or gallery collection, archive, or library
special collection:**
Alexander Wood Memorial Library (local and
Scottish books)

Non-library collection catalogue:
All or part available in-house

Library catalogue:
All or part available online

Printed publications:
The Scottish Co-operative Movement (40p)
Ardrossan Castle
Cunninghame Maps
Town Trails: Ardrossan, Saltcoats and Stevenston
North Ayrshire Street Guides
Other leaflets of local history including:
Ardeer and the Nobel Heritage (£5)
Auchenbarvie Colliery: An early history (£1)
History of the Ancient Society of Archers (25p)
Irvine Carter's Society (£3)
Things that befel in Ayrshire (£4.50)

Publications list:
Available in print

Access to staff:
Contact by letter, by telephone, by fax, by e-mail,
in person and via website. Appointment necessary.
Hours: Mon to Thu, 0900 to 1645; Fri, 0900 to 1630

Access to building, collection or gallery:
No prior appointment required
Hours: Mon to Thu, 0900 to 1645; Fri, 0900 to 1630

Access for disabled people:
Parking provided, ramped entry, toilet facilities

NORTH CORNWALL DISTRICT COUNCIL

Acronym or abbreviation: NCDC

Higher Trenant Road, Wadebridge, Cornwall, PL27
6TW

Tel: 01208 893333
Fax: 01208 893232
E-mail: public.relations@ncdc.gov.uk

Website:
http://www.ncdc.gov.uk

Enquiries:
Enquiries to: Information Officer
Direct tel: 01208 893318

Founded:
1974

Organisation type and purpose:
Local government body.

Access to staff:
Contact by letter, by fax and via website
Hours: Mon to Thu, 0845 to 1700; Fri, 0845 to 1630

Access for disabled people:
Parking provided, ramped entry, toilet facilities

NORTH COUNTRY CHEVIOT SHEEP SOCIETY

Wallacehall West, Waterbeck, Lockerbie, DG11
3HR

Tel: 01461 600646
E-mail: alison.brodie@nc-cheviot.co.uk

Website:
http://www.nc-cheviot.co.uk

Enquiries:
Enquiries to: Secretary

Founded:
1945

Organisation type and purpose:
Membership association (membership is by
subscription), present number of members: 400,
registered charity (charity number SCO 12265).
To promote the North Country Cheviot sheep
breed.

Subject coverage:
Information on the sustainability of North Country
Cheviot sheep in different environments and for
different breeding/crossing programmes.

Printed publications:
Annual Flock Book

Publications list:
Available in print

Access to staff:
Contact by letter, by telephone, by fax, by e-mail,
in person and via website. Appointment necessary.
Hours: Mon to Fri, 0900 to 1700

NORTH DEVON BRITISH MOTORCYCLE OWNERS CLUB

Acronym or abbreviation: NDBMOC

32 Merrythorn Road, Fremington, Barnstaple,
Devon, EX31 3AL

Tel: 01271 379170
E-mail: andylin@andbmocl.freeserve.co.uk

Website:
http://www.ndbmoc.freeserve.co.uk
Details of club, entry forms.

Enquiries:
Enquiries to: Secretary

Founded:
1978

Organisation type and purpose:
Membership association (membership is by
subscription), present number of members: 120,
suitable for ages: 18+.

Subject coverage:
Post-war British motorcycles, mechanical and electrical advice for most popular models: AMC, Ariel, BSA Norton, Triumph, Vincent.

Printed publications:
Magazine (spring and autumn)

Access to staff:
Contact by letter and by telephone
Hours: Any reasonable time after 1800

Access for disabled people:
Ramped entry, access to all public areas, toilet facilities

NORTH DEVON LOCAL STUDIES CENTRE

Library and Record Office, Tuly Street, Barnstaple, Devon, EX31 1EL

Tel: 01271 388607

Enquiries:
Enquiries to: Librarian
Other contacts: (1) Archivist (2) Curator for (1) documents (2) photographs.

Founded:
1988

Organisation type and purpose:
Local government body, public library, suitable for ages: school and adult.

Subject coverage:
Local, house and family history.

Access to staff:
Contact by letter and in person
Hours: Mon, Tue, Thu, Fri, 0930 to 1700; Wed, 0930 to 1300; Sat, 0930 to 1400

Other addresses:
West Country Studies Library
 Castle Street, Exeter; tel: 01392 384216

Parent body:
Devon County Council
 Topsham Road, Exeter

NORTH DEVON RECORD OFFICE

Acronym or abbreviation: NDRO

North Devon Library and Record Office, Tuly Street, Barnstaple, Devon, EX31 1EL

Tel: 01271 388608
Fax: 01271 388608
E-mail: ndevrec@devon.gov.uk

Website:
http://www.devon.gov.uk/record_office.htm
Introduction to holdings, opening times, access requirements, online catalogue.

Enquiries:
Enquiries to: Archivist

Founded:
1988

Organisation type and purpose:
Local government body.

Subject coverage:
Archives for North Devon area.

Museum or gallery collection, archive, or library special collection:
Records of local authorities, Devon County Council; North Devon and Torridge District Councils and their predecessors, the urban and rural district councils; the borough councils of Barnstaple, Bideford, Great Torrington and South Molton; parish councils
Public records, shipping registers, Quarter sessions, Petty Sessional Division records, local hospitals
Poor Law Union and Public Assistance Institution records
Taw and Torridge Fishery Board records
Education records

Ecclesiastical records for the Archdeaconry of Barnstaple, including parish registers and records
Records of nonconformist denominations (including the Bible Christian branch of the Methodist Church founded in North Devon)
Collections of estate records and private papers
Records of local solicitors; businesses; clubs and societies; charities and trusts
Parish registers, electoral registers, wills and land tax assessments (microfilm or microfiche)

Non-library collection catalogue:
All or part available online

Access to staff:
Contact by letter, by telephone, by e-mail and in person. Appointment necessary.

Access for disabled people:
Level entry, access to all public areas, toilet facilities

NORTH EAST CHAMBER OF COMMERCE, TRADE & INDUSTRY

Acronym or abbreviation: NECC

Aykley Heads Business Centre, Aykley Heads, Durham, DH1 5TS

Tel: 0191 386 1133
Fax: 0191 386 1144
E-mail: info@necc.co.uk

Website:
http://www.ne-cc.co.uk
Site includes practical advice and information for business in the North East of England. All Chamber members are included in the Directory section to allow searches for North East companies in particular business sectors.

Enquiries:
Enquiries to: Information Services Manager

Founded:
1995

Organisation type and purpose:
Membership association (membership is by subscription), present number of members: 5,500, service industry, training organisation.
Chamber of commerce.
Business services and representation of members.

Subject coverage:
All aspects of business information with specific reference to commerce and industry in the North East.

Printed publications:
Contact (business magazine, monthly)
North East Regional Business Directory (annually)

Electronic and video publications:
prEview (members only, monthly)

Access to staff:
Contact by letter, by telephone, by fax, by e-mail, in person and via website. Appointment necessary.
Access for members only. Non-members charged.
Hours: Mon to Fri, 0900 to 1700

Member organisation of:
Association of British Chambers of Commerce

Partner in the 5 offices of:
Business Link (North East)

NORTH EAST DERBYSHIRE DISTRICT COUNCIL

Acronym or abbreviation: NEDDC

Council House, Saltergate, Chesterfield, Derbyshire, S40 1LF

Tel: 01246 231111
Fax: 01246 550213
E-mail: connectne@ne-derbyshire.gov.uk

Website:
http://www.ne-derbyshire.gov.uk

Founded:
1974

Organisation type and purpose:
Local government body.

Subject coverage:
Local government services.

Printed publications:
The NEWS (civic newspaper, 3 times a year)

Access to staff:
Contact by letter, by telephone, by fax, by e-mail and via website
Hours: Mon to Fri, 0900 to 1700

NORTH EAST LINCOLNSHIRE ARCHIVES

Town Hall, Town Hall Square, Grimsby, Lincolnshire, DN31 1HX

Tel: 01472 323585
Fax: 01472 323581
E-mail: archives@nelincs.gov.uk

Website:
http://www.nelincs.gov.uk/art-culture-and -leisure/records-and-archives

Enquiries:
Enquiries to: Archivist

Founded:
1951

Formerly called:
Grimsby Borough Archives Office (year of change 1974); South Humberside Area Archives Office (year of change 1996)

Organisation type and purpose:
Local government body.

Subject coverage:
Archives for local authorities in North East Lincolnshire and North Lincolnshire including Grimsby Borough (1201–1996), local boards of health, rural sanitary authorities, urban sanitary authorities, burial boards, school boards, education committees (and over 100 schools), rural district councils, urban district councils (1894–1974), borough councils (1974–1996), parish councils, registers of Grimsby ships (1824–1988), register of Grimsby fishing apprentices (1879–1937) Grimsby fishing vessel crew lists (1864–1914), manorial records, public records.
The office is not a Diocesan Record Office. For original church records, etc. see Lincolnshire Archives, Lincoln.

Museum or gallery collection, archive, or library special collection:
Archives collected by the North Lincolnshire Museum, Scunthorpe
Local and Personal Acts, Private Acts (of Parliament, 1889–1966)
Parish registers of the eleven northern Deaneries of the Diocese of Lincoln (microfiche, appointment required to consult)

Non-library collection catalogue:
All or part available online

Printed publications:
Guidance leaflets

Publications list:
Available in print

Access to staff:
Contact by letter, by telephone, by fax and by e-mail. Appointment necessary.
Hours: Mon to Thu, 0930 to 1230 and 1300 to 1600

Access to building, collection or gallery:
Prior appointment required

Access for disabled people:
Ramped entry, access to all public areas, toilet access

NORTH EAST LINCOLNSHIRE LIBRARY SERVICE

Formal name: North East Lincolnshire Council Public Library Service

Central Library, Town Hall Square, Grimsby, Lincolnshire, DN31 1HG

Tel: 01472 323600
Fax: 01472 323634
E-mail: lib@nelincs.gov.uk

Website:
http://www.nelincs.gov.uk/libraries

Enquiries:
Enquiries to: Head of Cultural Services
Direct tel: 01472 323611
Direct fax: 01472 323618
Direct e-mail: steve.hipkins@nelincs.gov.uk
Other contacts: Principal Librarian (Strategy and Support, tel. 01472 323612)

Founded:
1996

Organisation type and purpose:
Public library.

Subject coverage:
General, local history, family history.

Museum or gallery collection, archive, or library special collection:
Business and company information
Local history collection (Grimsby, Cleethorpes and surrounding area)
Skelton Collection (posters and handbills of local printers), Ruhleben collection WWI

Trade and statistical information:
UK markets.

Non-library collection catalogue:
All or part available online

Library catalogue:
All or part available online and in-house

Access to staff:
Contact by letter, by telephone, by fax, by e-mail, in person and via website
Hours: Mon to Fri, 0830 to 1930; Sat, 0900 to 1600; Sun, 1000 to 1600

Branches:
One central and 10 branch libraries

Parent body:
North East Lincolnshire Council

NORTH EAST OF SCOTLAND DOUBLE BASS SOCIETY

343 Holburn Street, Aberdeen, AB10 7FQ

Tel: 01224 590521

Enquiries:
Enquiries to: Honorary Secretary

Founded:
1996

Organisation type and purpose:
Voluntary organisation.
To promote the enjoyment of, listening to and playing of the double bass repertoire.

Subject coverage:
History of the double bass in North East Scotland.

Access to staff:
Contact by letter
Hours: Mon to Fri, 0900 to 1700

NORTH EAST WORCESTERSHIRE COLLEGE

Acronym or abbreviation: NEW College

Slideslow Drive, Bromsgrove, Worcestershire, B60 1PQ

Tel: 01527 570020
Fax: 01527 572900

Enquiries:
Enquiries to: Assistant Principal, Learner Services
Direct tel: 01527 572517
Direct fax: 01527 572560
Direct e-mail: cduncan@ne-worcs.ac.uk

Founded:
1988

Organisation type and purpose:
Suitable for ages: 16+.
College of further education.

Subject coverage:
Business, management, law, art and design, media studies, music, hospitality and catering, community care, social work, secretarial studies, travel and tourism, IT, automotive, engineering, hair and beauty, childhood studies, sixth form studies, foundation learning, teacher education, public services, sport

Access to staff:
Contact by letter. Appointment necessary. Letter of introduction required.
Hours: Mon to Thu, 0830 to 2000; Fri, 0830 to 1630
Special comments: Access to registered staff and students by arrangement.

Also at:
North East Worcestershire College
Peakman Street, Redditch, B98 8DW; tel: 01527 570020

NORTH EASTERN EDUCATION AND LIBRARY BOARD

Acronym or abbreviation: NEELB/NELS

Library Headquarters, Demesne Avenue, Ballymena, Co Antrim, BT43 7BG

Tel: 028 2566 4100
Fax: 028 2563 2038
E-mail: info.neelb@ni-libraries.net

Website:
http://www.ni-libraries.net

Enquiries:
Enquiries to: Librarian

Organisation type and purpose:
Northern Ireland Government body.
Public and schools library.

Subject coverage:
North Eastern local studies plus all public and schools library subjects.
Community Services Unit.

Non-library collection catalogue:
All or part available online

Library catalogue:
All or part available online

Printed publications:
Library Charter

Access to staff:
Contact by letter, by telephone, by fax, by e-mail, in person and via website
Hours: Mon to Fri, 0900 to 1700
Special comments: Branch libraries have late night and Sat opening.

Access to building, collection or gallery:
No prior appointment required

Access for disabled people:
Ramped entry, access to all public areas, toilet facilities

NORTH HAMPSHIRE CHAMBER OF COMMERCE AND INDUSTRY

Acronym or abbreviation: NHCCI

Winchester Business Centre, 10 Parchment Street, Winchester, Hampshire, SO23 8AT

Tel: 01962 841000
Fax: 01962 870423
E-mail: winchester@nhcci.co.uk

Website:
http://www.nhcci.co.uk/

Enquiries:
Enquiries to: Secretary

Founded:
1918

Subject coverage:
Business information and support.

Printed publications:
Monthly Business Bulletin (free to members)
List of chamber members
List of Winchester businesses

Access to staff:
Contact by letter, by telephone, by fax and in person
Hours: Mon to Fri, 0900 to 1700

Business Helpline:
Hampshire Training and Enterprise Council Limited
25 Thackeray Mall, Fareham, PO16 0PQ; tel: 0800 373833

Member of:
Hampshire Chambers of Commerce

Other addresses:
North
Blackwater Valley Enterprise Trust, Princes Gardens, Aldershot, GU11 1BJ; tel: 0800 132301
South East
South East Hampshire Chamber of Commerce and Industry, 27 Guildhall Walk, Portsmouth, PO1 2RP; tel: 0800 132302
South West
Southampton Chamber of Commerce and Industry, 53 Bugle Street, Southampton, SO14 2LF; tel: 0800 132303

Other local offices at:
Basingstoke Chamber of Commerce (BCC)
Business Support Centre, Deanes Building, London Road, Basingstoke, RG21 7YP; tel: 01256 352275; fax: 01256 479391
North East Hampshire
Civic Offices, Harlington Way, Fleet, GU51 4AE; tel: 01252 811470; fax: 01252 812096
Winchester
Abbey Mill, Colebrook Street, Winchester, SO23 9LH; tel: 01962 841000; fax: 01962 870423

NORTH HERTFORDSHIRE DISTRICT COUNCIL

Acronym or abbreviation: NHDC

Council Offices, Gernon Road, Letchworth, Hertfordshire, SG6 3JF

Tel: 01462 474000
Fax: 01462 474227

Website:
http://www.north-herts.gov.uk

Organisation type and purpose:
Local government body.

Subject coverage:
Housing advice, leisure, community development, planning, building control, environmental health, health and safety, community grants, community safety, economic development, noise and environmental pollution, electoral services, council tax/housing benefits, local government finance.

Museum or gallery collection, archive, or library special collection:
Hitchin and Letchworth museums

Printed publications:
Outlook (residents magazine)
A–Z of Services
Best Value Performance Plan
Comments, Compliments, Complaints (booklet)
Sustainable Community Strategy
Corporate Plan

Access to staff:
Contact by letter, by telephone, by fax, by e-mail and in person

Hours: Mon to Fri, 0900 to 1700

Access to building, collection or gallery:
Hours: Mon to Fri, 0900 to 1700

Access for disabled people:
Fully accessible

Also at:
Finance and Regulatory Services
Town Lodge, Gernon Road, Letchworth,
Hertfordshire, SG6 3HN

NORTH HERTS & DISTRICT CITIZENS ADVICE BUREAU

The Town Hall, Melbourn Street, Royston,
Hertfordshire, SG8 7DA

Tel: 01763 238020
Fax: 01763 238017
E-mail: bureau@roystoncab.cabnet.org.uk

Enquiries:
Enquiries to: Manager
Direct tel: 01763 238017

Organisation type and purpose:
Voluntary organisation, registered charity (charity number 1086489).

Access to staff:
Contact by letter, by fax and by e-mail
Hours: Mon to Fri, 1000 to 1300

NORTH KESTEVEN DISTRICT COUNCIL

Acronym or abbreviation: NKDC

Council Offices, Kesteven Street, Sleaford,
Lincolnshire, NG34 7EF

Tel: 01529 414155
Fax: 01529 413956
E-mail: info@n-kesteven.gov.uk

Website:
http://www.n-kesteven.gov.uk

Enquiries:
Enquiries to: Press and Publications Officer
Direct tel: ext 2467
Direct e-mail: julie_wetton@n.kesteven.gov.uk

Organisation type and purpose:
Local government body, advisory body, statutory body, service industry, training organisation, consultancy, research organisation.

Subject coverage:
Environmental health, planning, council tax, business rates, housing benefits.

Access to staff:
Contact by letter, by telephone, by fax, by e-mail and via website
Hours: Mon to Thu, 0830 to 1700; Fri, 0830 to 1630

Access to building, collection or gallery:
No access other than to staff

Access for disabled people:
Parking provided, ramped entry, toilet facilities

NORTH LANARKSHIRE COUNCIL

PO Box 14, Civic Centre, Windmillhill Street,
Motherwell, North Lanarkshire, ML1 1AB

Tel: 01698 302222
Fax: 01698 275125

Website:
http://www.northlanarkshire.gov.uk

Enquiries:
Enquiries to: Chief Executive

Founded:
1996

Organisation type and purpose:
Local government body.

Subject coverage:
Local government affairs.

NORTH LANARKSHIRE COUNCIL – EDUCATION RESOURCE SERVICE

Acronym or abbreviation: ERS

Department of Education, 8 Kildonan Street,
Coatbridge, Lanarkshire, ML5 3LP

Tel: 01236 434377
Fax: 01236 436224
E-mail: ERSMail@northlan.gov.uk

Website:
http://www.northlan.gov.uk

Enquiries:
Enquiries to: Principal Librarian

Founded:
1996

Organisation type and purpose:
Local government body, suitable for ages: 3 to 18.
School library service.
To provide advice, support and resources to all educational establishments in North Lanarkshire.

Subject coverage:
Educational resources: nursery, primary, special and secondary schools.

Museum or gallery collection, archive, or library special collection:
Artefacts and staff development
Pre 5 years Multimedia collections
5 to 14 years Multimedia collections
Support for Learning

Access to staff:
Contact by letter, by telephone, by fax and by e-mail. Appointment necessary.
Hours: Mon to Thu, 0845 to 1645; Fri, 0845 to 1615
Special comments: Resources available to the general public for reference only.

Affiliated to:
Education Department
Municipal Buildings, Kildonan Street,
Coatbridge, ML5 3BT; tel: 01236 812222; fax: 01236 812247

NORTH LANARKSHIRE COUNCIL – INFORMATION SECTION

Formal name: North Lanarkshire Libraries and Information Service

Motherwell Library, 35 Hamilton Road,
Motherwell, North Lanarkshire, ML1 3BZ

Tel: 01698 332628
Fax: 01698 332625

Website:
http://www.northlan.gov.uk
home page

Enquiries:
Enquiries to: Libraries & Information Manager
Direct tel: 0141 304 1843

Founded:
1904

Organisation type and purpose:
Local government body, public library.

Subject coverage:
General subjects.

Museum or gallery collection, archive, or library special collection:
Chinese collection of books and magazines for children and adults
Gaelic collection of books and magazines for children and adults
Urdu collection of books and magazines for children and adults

Printed publications:
Local history publications
Order printed publications from: North Lanarkshire Libraries and Information Service,
Motherwell Library
tel: 01698 332628

Access to staff:
Contact by letter, by telephone, by fax and via website
Hours: Mon, Tue, Thu, Fri, 0900 to 1930; Wed, 0900 to 1200, lending library, 0900 to 1730 Information library, Sat, 0900 to 1600

Access to building, collection or gallery:
No prior appointment required

Access for disabled people:
Ramped entry, toilet facilities
Special comments: Ramp/lift to ground floor, lift to first floor

Other locations:
24 branches and 6 mobile vans

Parent body:
North Lanarkshire Council

NORTH LANARKSHIRE COUNCIL ARCHIVES

10 Kelvin Road, Lenziemill, Cumbernauld, North Lanarkshire, G67 2BA

Tel: 01236 638980
Fax: 01236 781762
E-mail: museums@northlan.gov.uk

Website:
http://www.northlanarkshire.gov.uk/index
.aspx?articleid=14404

Enquiries:
Enquiries to: Archivist
Direct e-mail: mcgheewi@northlan.gov.uk

Founded:
1996

Organisation type and purpose:
Local government body.
Local authority archive.

Subject coverage:
Holds archives of: landed estates; local firms and individuals; clubs and societies; historical miscellany; prior local authorities (including cemetery and poor law records).

Education services:
Staff available for talks.

Museum or gallery collection, archive, or library special collection:
Archive

Non-library collection catalogue:
All or part available online and in-house

Library catalogue:
All or part available in-house

Access to staff:
Contact by letter, by telephone, by fax, by e-mail and in person. Appointment necessary.
Hours: Mon to Fri, 0930 to 1630

Access to building, collection or gallery:
Prior appointment required

Access for disabled people:
Limited disabled access is available – please enquire for further information

Links with:
North Lanarkshire Museums & Heritage
Museums & Heritage Manager, Lower Ground Floor, Municiple Buildings, Kildonan Street, Coatbridge, ML5 3BT; tel: 0141 812 387

NORTH LINCOLNSHIRE COUNCIL

Pittwood House, Ashby Road, Scunthorpe,
Lincolnshire, DN16 1AB

Tel: 01724 296296\ Minicom no. 01724 296294
Fax: 01724 296079

Website:
http://www.northlincs.gov.uk

Enquiries:
Enquiries to: Library and Information Services Manager

continued overleaf

Direct tel: 01724 297869
Direct fax: 01724 296343
Direct e-mail: customerservice@northlincs.gov.uk

Founded:
1996

Organisation type and purpose:
Local government body.
Created as a unitary council following abolition of
the County of Humberside.
Unitary council responsible for all local
government services, including 82 schools, 25,500
pupils and a gross budget (annual) of £315m.

Subject coverage:
Local government.

Library catalogue:
All or part available online

Access to staff:
Contact by letter, by telephone, by fax, by e-mail
and in person
Hours: Mon to Thu, 0830 to 1700; Fri, 0830 to 1630

Access to building, collection or gallery:
No prior appointment required

Access for disabled people:
Parking provided, ramped entry, access to all
public areas, toilet facilities

NORTH LINCOLNSHIRE LIBRARY AND INFORMATION SERVICES

North Lincolnshire Central Library, Carlton Street,
Scunthorpe, North Lincolnshire, DN15 6TX

Tel: 01724 860161
Fax: 01724 860161
E-mail: library.enquiries@northlincs.gov.uk

Website:
http://www.northlincs.gov.uk/library
Access to library catalogue, online resources,
family and local history information, library events
listings and more.

Enquiries:
Enquiries to: Library and Information Services
Manager

Founded:
1996

Organisation type and purpose:
Local government body, statutory body, service
industry, public library.

Subject coverage:
General, local and family history (North
Lincolnshire), steel industry (Scunthorpe), Wesley
family.

Non-library collection catalogue:
All or part available online and in-house

Library catalogue:
All or part available online

Access to staff:
Contact by letter, by telephone, by fax, by e-mail,
in person and via website
Hours: Mon, Wed, 0900 to 1900; Tue, Thu, Fri, 0900
to 1700; Sat, 0900 to 1630

Access to building, collection or gallery:
See website for opening hours and access

Branches:
14 libraries and two mobile libraries
See website for details

Parent body:
North Lincolnshire Council
website: http://www.northlincs.gov.uk

NORTH NORFOLK DISTRICT COUNCIL

Holt Road, Cromer, Norfolk, NR27 9EL

Tel: 01263 513811
Fax: 01263 515042
E-mail: districtcouncil@north-norfolk.gov.uk

Website:
http://www.north-norfolk.gov.uk

Enquiries:
Enquiries to: Communications Manager
Direct tel: 01263 516344
Direct e-mail: media@north-norfolk.gov.uk

Organisation type and purpose:
Local government body.

Subject coverage:
Local government.

Museum or gallery collection, archive, or library special collection:
Library of photographs of North Norfolk

Printed publications:
Brochures, booklets and leaflets available giving
tourism, business and other district information

Access to building, collection or gallery:
No prior appointment required

NORTH OF ENGLAND INSTITUTE OF MINING AND MECHANICAL ENGINEERS

Neville Hall, Westgate Road, Newcastle upon
Tyne, NE1 1SE

Tel: 0191 232 2201
Fax: 0191 232 2201
E-mail: imm@skynow.net

Enquiries:
Enquiries to: Administrator
Other contacts: Honorary Secretary for qualification
queries.

Founded:
1852

Organisation type and purpose:
Learned society, professional body (membership is
by subscription), present number of members: 480,
registered charity (charity number 220208).

Subject coverage:
Mining and allied subjects: history and technology.

Museum or gallery collection, archive, or library special collection:
A large number of MSS and other collections

Non-library collection catalogue:
All or part available in-house

Library catalogue:
All or part available in-house

Access to staff:
Contact by letter and by telephone. Appointment
necessary. Non-members charged.
Hours: Library: to be arranged.

NORTH OF ENGLAND MULE SHEEP ASSOCIATION

Acronym or abbreviation: NEMSA

Eslaforde, Wear View, Frosterley, Bishop
Auckland, Co Durham, DL13 2RB

Tel: 01388 527411
Fax: 01388 526728

Website:
http://www.nemsa.co.uk

Enquiries:
Enquiries to: Secretary
Direct e-mail: info@nemsa.co.uk

Founded:
1980

Organisation type and purpose:
Membership association (membership is by
subscription), present number of members: 1024,
registered charity.
Breed society, promotional body.

Subject coverage:
The North of England Mule is the top commercial
breeding sheep for prime lamb production.

Printed publications:
Mule News (annually)
Sales booklet (annually)
Order printed publications from: http://
www.nemsa.co.uk

Electronic and video publications:
Mule Views (video)

Publications list:
Available online

Access to staff:
Contact by letter, by telephone, by fax and by e-
mail
Hours: Mon to Fri, 0900 to 1700

NORTH OF ENGLAND ZOOLOGICAL SOCIETY

Formal name: North of England Zoological Society
Acronym or abbreviation: NEZS

Chester Zoo, Caughall Road, Upton by Chester,
Chester, Cheshire, CH2 1LH

Tel: 01244 380280
Fax: 01244 371273
E-mail: marketing@chesterzoo.co.uk

Website:
http://www.chesterzoo.org

Enquiries:
Enquiries to: Director

Founded:
1934

Organisation type and purpose:
International organisation, membership
association (membership is by subscription),
present number of members: 17,000 plus,
registered charity (charity number 306077),
suitable for ages: all.

Subject coverage:
Zoological.

Library catalogue:
All or part available in-house

Printed publications:
Chester Zoo Life (magazine, quarterly for
members)

Electronic and video publications:
Zoo (CD-ROM and videos, also via website or on
site shop)

Access to staff:
Contact by letter and by e-mail
Hours: Mon to Fri, 0900 to 1200

Access to building, collection or gallery:
No prior appointment required
Special comments: Access to library, Mon to Fri, 1200
to 1500

Access for disabled people:
Parking provided, ramped entry, toilet facilities
Special comments: Electric scooters and chairs for
hire, tactile maps.

Member of:
European Association of Zoos and Aquaria
(EAZA)
Federation of Zoological Gardens of Great Britain
and Ireland
World Association of Zoos and Aquariums
(WAZA)

NORTH SOMERSET COUNCIL

Town Hall, Weston-Super-Mare, Somerset, BS23
1UJ

Tel: 01934 888888
Fax: 01934 888822
E-mail: customer.services@n-somerset.gov.uk

Website:
http://www.n-somerset.gov.uk

Enquiries:
Enquiries to: Marketing and Communications
Manager

Direct tel: 01275 888728
Direct e-mail: vanessa.setterington@n-somerset.gov.uk

Founded:
1996

Organisation type and purpose:
Local government body.

Subject coverage:
Local government services.

NORTH STAFFORDSHIRE CHAMBER OF COMMERCE AND INDUSTRY

Commerce House, Festival Park, Stoke-on-Trent, Staffordshire, ST1 5BE

Tel: 01782 202241
Fax: 01782 274394
E-mail: staffordchamber@nscci.co.uk

Website:
http://www.northstaffs.chamber.co.uk
Directory of members, diary of activities.

Enquiries:
Enquiries to: Information Services Manager

Founded:
1949

Organisation type and purpose:
Membership association (membership is by subscription), present number of members: 1054. Chamber of Commerce.

Subject coverage:
Business information and advice; importing and exporting advice and documentation; training; translations; UK and international credit checking; trade missions; UK and overseas marketing and sourcing information.

Trade and statistical information:
Product information on the ceramic industry. Trade in North Staffordshire.

Printed publications:
Business Bulletin (free to members)
Focus (business journal, 6 times a year)
North Staffordshire and South Cheshire Industrial and Commercial Directory (annually)
Overseas Bulletin (free to members)

Publications list:
Available online

Access to staff:
Contact by letter, by telephone and by fax. Non-members charged.
Hours: Mon to Fri, 0900 to 1700

Member of:
Association of British Chambers of Commerce

Partner in:
Business Link Staffordshire

NORTH TRAFFORD COLLEGE LIBRARY

Talbot Road, Stretford, Manchester, M32 0XH

Tel: 0161 886 7012
Fax: 0161 872 7921

Enquiries:
Enquiries to: Senior Librarian
Direct e-mail: jim.temple@ntc.ac.uk

Organisation type and purpose:
College of further education.

Subject coverage:
Gas engineering; chemical process engineering; automotive engineering; mechanical, electrical, electronic engineering; computing; business studies; childcare; building services; CAD; health care; music; science; community studies; social care; basic skills; ESOL; business studies; accounting; teacher training; information technology.

Library catalogue:
All or part available in-house

Access to staff:
Access for members only.
Hours: Mon, Thu, 0845 to 1900; Tues, Wed, Fri, 0845 to 1700

NORTH TYNESIDE LIBRARIES

Central Library, Northumberland Square, North Shields, Tyne and Wear, NE30 1QU

Tel: 0191 200 5424
Fax: 0191 200 6118
E-mail: central@ntlib.demon.co.uk

Website:
http://www.northtyneside.gov.uk/libraries

Enquiries:
Enquiries to: Libraries and Information Manager

Founded:
1870

Organisation type and purpose:
Local government body, public library.

Subject coverage:
General and local studies.

Museum or gallery collection, archive, or library special collection:
Edington collection of prints and engravings (7000 items, Northumberland and Tyne and Wear)
British Standards in microform

Printed publications:
And Then We Moved to Royal Quays
Blyth & Tyne Handbook
Cuddling, Ripyard – Shipyard Muddling (The poems of Jack Davitt)
Full Steam Ahead for Tynemouth Station (published in conjunction with Friends of Tynemouth Station)
How Long Did the Ponies Live?
Lambert's Handbook to Tynemouth and the Blyth and Tyne Railway (facsimile of c. 1865 ed)
Last of the Hunters
North Shields (Hollerton E, local studies librarian)
North Shields: second selection
Richardson History of Wallsend (fascimile ed, published in conjunction with Newcastle City Libraries)
Shipyard muddling
Swans of the Tyne (Swan Hunter ships)
Tynemouth in Old Picture Postcards (Hollerton E, local studies librarian)
Wallsend Pit Disaster
Where the Wall Ends
Whitley Bay Historic Trails 1 & 2
Order printed publications from: Publications Department, Wallsend Library
Ferndale Avenue, Wallsend, NE26 7NB, tel: 0191 200 6968, fax: 0191 200 6967

Access to staff:
Contact by letter, by telephone, by fax, by e-mail and in person
Hours: Central Library: Mon and Fri, 0930 to 1730; Tue and Thu, 0930 to 1900; Sat, 0930 to 1700, Wed, 0930 to 1230.
Times vary for other libraries

Other addresses:
Battle Hill Library
Berwick Drive, Battle Hill, Wallsend, Tyne & Wear, NE28 9EF; tel: 0191 200 6976
Coast Road Library
25 Coast Road, North Shields, NE29 7PG; tel: 0191 200 5857
Cullercoats Library
St George's Road, Cullercoats, North Shields, NE30 3JY; tel: 0191 200 8537
Fordley Library
Fern Drive, Dudley, Northumberland, NE23 7AG; tel: 0191 200 8014
Forest Hall Library
Whitfield Road, Forest Hall, Newcastle, NE12 0LJ; tel: 0191 200 7839

Howdon Library
Churchill Street, Howdon, Wallsend, Tyne & Wear, NE28 7TG; tel: 0191 200 6979
Killingworth Library
White Swan Centre, Citadel East, Killingworth, Newcastle, NE12 6SS; tel: 0191 200 8266
Longbenton Library
Black Friars Way, Longbenton, Newcastle, NE12 8SY; tel: 0191 200 7865
Monkseaton Library
Woodleigh Avenue, Monkseaton, Whitley Bay, NE25 8ET; tel: 0191 200 8538
Shiremoor Library
Stanton Road, Shiremoor, Newcastle upon Tyne, NE27 0PW; tel: 0191 200 8539
Tynemouth Library
Front Street, Tynemouth, North Shields, NE30 4DZ; tel: 0191 200 5856
Wallsend Library
Ferndale Avenue, Wallsend, Tyne & Wear, NE28 7NB; tel: 0191 200 6968; fax: 0191 200 6967
Whitley Bay Library
Park Road, Whitley Bay, NE26 1EJ; tel: 0191 200 8500; fax: 0191 200 8536
Wideopen Library
Canterbury Way, Wideopen, Newcastle, NE13 6JJ; tel: 0191 200 7900

Parent body:
North Tyneside Council

NORTH WALES TOURISM

Acronym or abbreviation: NWT

77 Conway Road, Colwyn Bay, Conwy, LL29 7LN

Tel: 01492 531731
Fax: 01492 530059
E-mail: croeso@nwt.co.uk

Website:
http://www.nwt.co.uk
Descriptive information on North Wales, where to visit, where to stay, where to eat and events.

Enquiries:
Enquiries to: Manager
Other contacts: Visitor Services Manager for management and operation of tourist information centre.

Founded:
1991

Organisation type and purpose:
Advisory body, membership association (membership is by subscription), service industry. Private company. Affiliated local government body. Part statutory body.
To promote North Wales as a holiday destination and provide aftercare services through Tourist Information Centres.

Subject coverage:
North Wales tourist attractions, mountains, Snowdonia National Park, stately homes, castles, Isle of Anglesey, sailing, golf, pony trekking, cycling and walking. All areas of North Wales and its activities.

Printed publications:
Brochures on marketing areas of North Wales, accommodation and attractions information

Publications list:
Available in print

Access to staff:
Contact by letter, by telephone, by fax, by e-mail and via website
Hours: Mon to Fri, 0900 to 1700

Parent body:
Wales Tourist Board
Brunel House, 2 Fitzallan Road, Cardiff, C72 1UY; tel: 029 2049 9909; fax: 029 2048 5031

Tourist Information Centres:
Bangor
Town Hall, Ffordd Deiniol, Bangor, LL57 7RE; tel: 01248 352786; fax: 01248 362701; e-mail: bangor.tic@gwynedd.gov.uk

continued overleaf

Betws-y-Coed
  tel: 01690 710426
Caernarfon
  Oriel Pendeitsh, Castle Street, Caernarfon, LL55
  1SE; tel: 01286 672232; fax: 01285 678209; e-mail:
  caernarfon.tic@gwynedd.gov.uk
Colwyn Bay
  Imperial Building, Princes Drive, Colwyn Bay,
  LL29 8LF; tel: 01492 530478; fax: 01492 534789;
  e-mail: colwynbay.tic@virgin.net
Conwy
  Conwy Castle Visitor Centre, Conwy, LL32 8LD;
  tel: 01492 592248; fax: 01492 573545; e-mail:
  conwy.tic@virgin.net
Holyhead
  Stena Line, Terminal 1, Holyhead, LL65 1DQ; tel:
  01407 762622; fax: 01407 761462; e-mail:
  holyhead.tic@virgin.net
Llanberis
  41a High Street, Llanberis, LL55 4EH; tel: 01286
  870765; fax: 01286 871924; e-mail: llanberis.tic@
  gwynedd.gov.uk
Llandudno
  1–2 Chapel Street, Llandudno, LL30 2YU; tel:
  01492 876413; fax: 01492 872722; e-mail:
  llandudno.tic@virgin.net
Llanfairpwllgwyngyll
  Station Site, Llanfairpwllgwyngyll, LL61 5UJ; tel:
  01248 713177; fax: 01248 715711; e-mail:
  llanfairpwll.tic@virgin.net
Llangollen
  Town Hall, Castle Street, Llangollen, LL20 5PD;
  tel: 01978 860828; fax: 01978 861563; e-mail:
  llangollen.tic@virgin.net
Mold
  Library, Museum and Gallery, Earl Road, Mold,
  CH7 1AP; tel: 01352 759331; fax: 01352 759331;
  e-mail: mold.tic@virgin.net
Porthmadog
  Y Ganolfan, High Street, Porthmadog, LL49 9LP;
  tel: 01766 512981; fax: 01766 515312; e-mail:
  porthmadog.tic@gwynedd.gov.uk
Prestatyn
  Offa's Dyke Centre, Central Beach, Prestatyn,
  LL19 7EY; tel: 01745 889092
Pwllheli
  Min-y-Don, Station Square, Pwllheli, Gwynedd,
  LL53 6HE; fax: 01758 701651; e-mail: pwllheli
  .tic@gwynedd.gov.uk
Rhyl
  Children's Village, The Promenade, Rhyl,
  Denbighshire, LL18 1HZ; tel: 01745 355068; fax:
  01745 342255; e-mail: rhyl.tic@denbighshire.gov
  .uk
Ruthin
  Ruthin Craft Centre, Park Road, Ruthin; tel:
  01824 703992; fax: 01824 703992
Wrexham
  tel: 01978 292015

NORTH WARWICKSHIRE BOROUGH COUNCIL

The Council House, South Street, Atherstone,
Warwickshire, CV9 1BD

Tel: 01827 715341
Fax: 01827 719130
E-mail: customerservices@northwarks.gov.uk

Website:
http://www.northwarks.gov.uk
Information on North Warwickshire and Borough
Council services.

Enquiries:
Enquiries to: Chief Executive

Founded:
1974

Organisation type and purpose:
Local government body.

Printed publications:
Best Value Performance Plan
Guide to North Warwickshire
North Talk (residents newsletter, 2 times a year)
North Warwickshire Commercial Property Guide
Tourism leaflet and Accommodation list

Access to staff:
Contact by letter, by telephone, by fax, by e-mail,
in person and via website. Appointment necessary.
Access for members only.
Hours: Mon to Fri, 0850 to 1715

NORTH WEST EMPLOYERS

Formal name: North Western Local Authorities'
Employers' Organisation
Acronym or abbreviation: NWEO

6th Floor, Delphian House, Riverside, New Bailey
Street, Manchester, M3 5AP

Tel: 0161 834 9362
Fax: 0161 831 7268
E-mail: mail@nweo.org.uk

Website:
http://www.nweo.org.uk

Enquiries:
Enquiries to: Human Resources Adviser
Other contacts: Learning and Development;
Member Development; Human Resources; Local
Government

Founded:
1920

Organisation type and purpose:
Local government body, advisory body, training
organisation, consultancy.

Subject coverage:
Training, conditions of service, industrial relations,
personnel, management.

Printed publications:
see website: http://www.nweo.org.uk

Access to staff:
Contact by letter, by telephone and by e-mail.
Appointment necessary.
Hours: Mon to Fri, 0845 to 1645

NORTH WEST FILM ARCHIVE

Acronym or abbreviation: NWFA

Manchester Metropolitan University, Minshull
House, 47–49 Chorlton Street, Manchester, M1
3EU

Tel: 0161 247 3097
Fax: 0161 247 3098
E-mail: n.w.filmarchive@mmu.ac.uk

Website:
http://www.nwfa.mmu.ac.uk
General information on the Archive's collection,
access services, what's new, etc. Online searchable
film and video database.

Enquiries:
Enquiries to: Collection Assistant

Founded:
1977

Organisation type and purpose:
University department / institute.
Public film archive.
Rescuing and ensuring the survival of moving
images about the North West of England for the
education and enjoyment of the region's people,
both today and in the future.

Subject coverage:
North West of England (Greater Manchester,
Lancashire, Cheshire, Merseyside, Cumbria): mid-
1890s to the present; working life and leisure,
traditions, industry, two World Wars, healthcare,
housing, transport, professional and amateur
material on all gauges.

**Museum or gallery collection, archive, or library
special collection:**
Collection of over 31,500 items dating from pioneer
days of film in mid-1890s to contemporary video
productions, all relating to life in the North West
of England. It includes cinema newsreels,
documentaries, advertising and promotional

material, educational and travel films, home
movies, corporate videos and regional television
programmes
Complementary collections of photographs, taped
interviews and original documentation relating
to North West's film and cinema industries

Non-library collection catalogue:
All or part available online and in-house

Printed publications:
General leaflet on NWFA (free)
The Picture House: a photographic album of North
West film and cinema (1988, £6.95)

Electronic and video publications:
A North West Journey: buses, trams and
trolleybuses 1927–1935 (video, £19.50)
Manchester Ship Canal Centenary Video (£12.99)
Moving Memories, series of video cassette
compilations from 1990 (£14.99)
Primary and Secondary school National
Curriculum video resource packs (prices vary)

Publications list:
Available online

Access to staff:
Contact by letter, by telephone, by fax, by e-mail
and in person. Appointment necessary.
Hours: Mon to Fri, 0900 to 1700

Access for disabled people:
Parking provided, ramped entry, access to all
public areas, toilet facilities

Parent body:
Manchester Metropolitan University Library
Service

NORTH WEST KENT FAMILY HISTORY SOCIETY

Acronym or abbreviation: NWKFHS

51 Newbury Avenue, Maidstone, ME16 0RG

E-mail: secretary@nwkfhs.org.uk

Website:
http://www.nwkfhs.org.uk
Details of all aspects of the society, free indexes,
details and colour photographs of parishes covered
and their churches.

Founded:
1978

Organisation type and purpose:
International organisation, membership
association (membership is by subscription),
present number of members: 2,000, registered
charity (charity number 282627R).
To further education and research in genealogy
and family history.

Subject coverage:
Family history in North West Kent and the South
East area of London once part of the ancient
county of Kent, including Dartford, Sevenoaks,
Bromley, Bexley.

Information services:
Society Library and Resource Centre,
Summerhouse Drive, Joydens Wood Estate, Bexley,
DA5 2EE.

**Museum or gallery collection, archive, or library
special collection:**
Library of indexes and other references for North
West Kent and South East London area, held on
CD, Microfiche or printed form

Non-library collection catalogue:
All or part available in-house

Library catalogue:
All or part available online and in-house

Printed publications:
Journal (quarterly, members)
All publications available from the Society are
listed with current price and p&p in the journal
and on website, these include:

Copies of original parish register, transcriptions, monumental inscriptions, indexes to records in Bromley Journal & West Kent Herald, census indexes
Order printed publications from: NWKFHS, 141 Princes Road, Dartford, DA1 3HJ

Microform publications:
Microfiche publications for sale

Electronic and video publications:
Details advertised on the website of CD-ROMs available; also listed on Parish Chest.
Order electronic and video publications from: 141 Princes Road, Dartford, DA1 3HJ

Publications list:
Available online and in print

Access to staff:
Contact by letter, by e-mail and via website
Hours: None

Branches:
Bromley, Dartford, Sevenoaks, Society Library and Resource Centre, Summerhouse Drive, Joydens Wood Estate, Bexley, DA5 2EE

Member organisation of:
Federation of Family History Societies (FFHS)

Membership Secretary:
North West Kent Family History Society 46 Pollards Oak Crescent. RH8 0JQ; e-mail: membership@nwkfhs.org.uk

NORTH WEST LEICESTERSHIRE DISTRICT COUNCIL

Acronym or abbreviation: NWLDC

Council Offices, Coalville, Leicester, LE67 3FJ

Tel: 01530 454545
Fax: 01530 454546
E-mail: info@nwleicestershire.gov.uk

Website:
http://www.nwleics.gov.uk
Community information, tourist information, economic development/inward investment, the National Forest.

Enquiries:
Enquiries to: Chief Executive

Founded:
1973

Organisation type and purpose:
Local government body.

Subject coverage:
Local government services.

Printed publications:
Free publications include:
Business Information
District Guide
Street Maps
Tourist Information

Access to staff:
Contact by letter, by telephone, by fax, by e-mail and in person
Hours: Mon to Fri, 0900 to 1700

Access for disabled people:
Parking provided, level entry, toilet facilities

NORTH WEST LONDON HOSPITALS NHS TRUST

John Squire Library, Watford Road, Harrow, Middlesex, HA1 3UJ

Tel: 020 8869 3322 (enquiries)
Fax: 020 8869 3332
E-mail: jslib@clara.net

Website:
http://www.jslib.clara.net

Enquiries:
Enquiries to: Head Librarian

Organisation type and purpose:
Hospital.

Subject coverage:
Clinical, medical and complementary basic sciences, nursing and health service management.

Library catalogue:
All or part available online

Printed publications:
Handlist of current journals (annually)
Library Bulletin (monthly)

Access to staff:
Contact in person
Hours: Mon to Fri, 0900 to 1800

Access to building, collection or gallery:
No prior appointment required
Hours: Mon to Fri, 0900 to 1800
Special comments: Must have bona fide need to access library resources.

Funded by:
Central and North West London NHS Foundation Trust
London Deanery
North West London Hospitals NHS Trust

NORTH WEST SOUND ARCHIVE

North West Sound Archive, Clitheroe Museum, Clitheroe Castle, Clitheroe, Lancashire, BB7 1AZ

Tel: 01200 427897
Fax: 01200 427897
E-mail: nwsa@ed.lancscc.gov.uk

Founded:
1979

Organisation type and purpose:
Collects, records and preserves sound recordings relevant to the northwest of England.

Subject coverage:
Sound recordings relating to all aspects of life in the northwest of England.

Education services:
Education packs for schools.

Museum or gallery collection, archive, or library special collection:
Collection includes c. 140,000 recordings on all aspects of northwest life

Library catalogue:
All or part available in-house

Publications list:
Available in print

Access to staff:
Contact by letter, by telephone, by fax, by e-mail and in person. Appointment necessary.
Hours: Mon to Fri, 0845 to 1700

Access to building, collection or gallery:
Hours: Mon to Fri, 0845 to 1700

NORTH WILTSHIRE DISTRICT COUNCIL

Acronym or abbreviation: NWDC

Monkton Park, Chippenham, Wiltshire, SN15 1ER

Tel: 01249 706111
Fax: 01249 443158

Website:
http://www.northwilts.gov.uk

Enquiries:
Enquiries to: Public Relations Manager
Direct tel: 01249 706618
Direct fax: 01249 654999
Direct e-mail: plangcaster@northwilts.gov.uk
Other contacts: Chief Executive

Founded:
1974

Organisation type and purpose:
Local government body.

Subject coverage:
Services and amenities of the District Council.

Printed publications:
Annual reviews
District and town guides
Economic development plans
Forward strategy

Access to staff:
Contact by letter, by telephone and by fax
Hours: Mon to Thu, 0900 to 1700; Fri, 0900 to 1630

NORTH YORK MOORS NATIONAL PARK AUTHORITY

The Old Vicarage, Bondgate, Helmsley, North Yorkshire, YO62 5BP

Tel: 01439 770657
Fax: 01439 770691
E-mail: info@northyorkmoors-npa.gov.uk

Website:
http://www.northyorkmoors.org.uk
Tourist information, education, events, plans and policies, press releases, publications, detailed information and work of the Authority.

Enquiries:
Enquiries to: Information Officer

Founded:
1952

Organisation type and purpose:
Local government body.
National Park administration.
To conserve and enhance the natural beauty, wildlife and cultural heritage of the area, and to promote opportunities for the understanding and enjoyment of the special qualities of the area by the public.

Subject coverage:
North York Moors: history, geography, archaeology, agriculture, ecology, planning, tourism, travel.

Printed publications:
Annual Report
Local history books
Plans and reports
The North York Moors Landscape Heritage
Walks and trail guides
Wild Plants and their Habitats in the North York Moors

Publications list:
Available online and in print

Access to staff:
Contact by letter, by telephone, by fax and by e-mail. Appointment necessary.
Hours: Mon to Thu, 0830 to 1700; Fri, 0830 to 1630

Access for disabled people:
Parking provided, level entry, toilet facilities

Member organisation of:
Association of National Park Authorities

NORTH YORKSHIRE COUNTY COUNCIL, LIBRARY AND INFORMATION CENTRE

Victoria Avenue, Harrogate, North Yorkshire, HG1 1EG

Tel: 0845 0349520
Fax: 01423 523158
E-mail: harrogate.library@northyorks.gov.uk

Website:
http://www.northyorks.gov.uk/libraries
General information about North Yorkshire County Library, service details, library opening times and locations.

Enquiries:
Enquiries to: Community and Information Officer

Founded:
1887

continued overleaf

Organisation type and purpose:
Local government body, public library.

Subject coverage:
General, family history.

Museum or gallery collection, archive, or library special collection:
Illustrated 19th- and 20th-century English books
Mineral waters: books and pamphlets from 1626, with particular reference to Harrogate from 1626

Parent body:
North Yorkshire County Council, Library and Information Centre
21 Grammar School Lane, Northallerton, DL6 1DF; tel: 01609 767800; fax: 01609 780793

NORTH YORKSHIRE COUNTY COUNCIL, LIBRARY AND INFORMATION SERVICES

21 Grammar School Lane, Northallerton, North Yorkshire, DL6 1DF

Tel: 01609 533800
Fax: 01609 780793
E-mail: libraries@northyorks.gov.uk

Website:
http://www.northyorks.gov.uk/libraries

Enquiries:
Enquiries to: Assistant Director (Business and Community Services)

Founded:
1974

Organisation type and purpose:
Local government body, public library.

Subject coverage:
General.

Museum or gallery collection, archive, or library special collection:
Bertram Unne Photograph Collection of Yorkshire landscape, people and buildings 1945–1975
Editions of some 210 titles from private presses (at Stokesley)
Illustrated 19th- and 20th-century English books (at Harrogate)
Mineral waters: books and pamphlets from 1572 with particular reference to Harrogate from 1626 (at Harrogate)
North Yorkshire Census Returns: 1841, 1851, 1861, 1871, 1881 held at local core libraries
Petyt Collection of material on 17th-century history and theology (at Skipton)

Non-library collection catalogue:
All or part available in-house

Library catalogue:
All or part available in-house

Department of the:
North Yorkshire County Council

Has:
42 libraries and 11 mobile libraries in the region

NORTH YORKSHIRE COUNTY RECORD OFFICE

Acronym or abbreviation: NYCRO

Malpas Road, Northallerton, North Yorkshire, DL7 8TB

Tel: 01609 777585
E-mail: archives@northyorks.gov.uk

Enquiries:
Enquiries to: Archives Development Manager

Organisation type and purpose:
Local government body.
Record office.

Subject coverage:
Manuscript sources relating to North Yorkshire, including historical and geographical subjects.

Printed publications:
Guide no. 1: calendars, transcripts and microfilms in the record office (1992 ed.)
Guide no. 2: parish registers, census returns, land tax assessments, tithe apportionments, enclosure awards in the record office
Guide no. 3: maps and plans – list of North Yorkshire and North Riding maps and plans in the record office
Guide no. 4: enclosure awards in the record office (a detailed list)
Guide no. 5: North Yorkshire parish registers – including dates and whereabouts of parish registers, transcripts, microfilm
Guide no. 6: North Yorkshire gazetteer of townships and parishes
Guide no. 7: list of non-conformist and chapel registers, and of monumental inscriptions in the record office
Guide no. 8: North Yorkshire and North Riding railway plans
Guide no. 9: mining plans
Guide no. 10: list of architectural plans in the North Yorkshire County Record Office
Histories of places, people, families and organisations within North Yorkshire, as books, reports, surveys and journals; lists of holdings of parish registers, maps, plans, etc.

Access for disabled people:
Parking provided, level entry, toilet facilities

Parent body:
North Yorkshire County Council

NORTH-EAST CLUB FOR PRE-WAR AUSTINS

Acronym or abbreviation: NECPWA

6 College View, Monkwray, Whitehaven, Cumbria

Tel: 01946 67640
E-mail: john@johnandcarolyn.freeserve.co.uk

Website:
http://www.necpwa.demon.co.uk

Enquiries:
Enquiries to: Honorary Secretary

Founded:
1966

Organisation type and purpose:
Membership association.
Restoration and regular use of historic motor vehicles.

Subject coverage:
The restoration and usage of historic motor vehicles. Members own many different makes of vehicles both pre- and post-war.

Museum or gallery collection, archive, or library special collection:
Club library of obsolete magazines, handbooks, manuals etc

Printed publications:
Newsletter (monthly, members only)

Access to staff:
Contact by letter
Hours: Mon to Fri, 0900 to 1700

NORTHAMPTON BOROUGH COUNCIL

The Guildhall, St Giles Square, Northampton, NN1 1DE

Tel: 01604 838383; minicom: 01604 838970
Fax: 01604 838729
E-mail: enquiries@northampton.gov.uk

Website:
http://www.northampton.gov.uk
The website of Northampton Borough Council.

Organisation type and purpose:
Local government body.

Subject coverage:
Normal range of council subjects, housing, environmental health, planning, council tax, cleansing.

Museum or gallery collection, archive, or library special collection:
Home of the National Boot and Shoe collection

Printed publications:
Bibliographies
Promotional literature on Northampton and its expansion

Access to staff:
Contact by letter, by telephone, by fax, by e-mail, in person and via website. Appointment necessary.
Hours: Mon to Fri, 0900 to 1700

Access for disabled people:
Access to all public areas

Neighbourhood Environmental Services Directorate:
Northampton Borough Council
Westbridge Depot, St James Mill Road, Northampton, NN5 5JW; tel: 01604 838281

Planning and Regeneration Directorate:
Northampton Borough Council
Cliftonville House, Bedford Road, Northampton, NN4 7NR

NORTHAMPTONSHIRE INSPECTION AND ADVISORY SERVICE

Acronym or abbreviation: NIAS

PO Box 216, John Dryden House, 8–10 The Lakes, Northampton, NN4 7DD

Tel: 01604 236242
Fax: 01604 236240
E-mail: nias@northamptonshire.gov.uk

Enquiries:
Enquiries to: Chief Education Adviser
Direct e-mail: cpdnias@northamptonshire.gov.uk

Founded:
1995

Organisation type and purpose:
Local government body, suitable for ages: nursery and 4 to 18, training organisation, consultancy, publishing house.
To provide educational consultancy and training, school inspection and curriculum resources.

Subject coverage:
Specialising in educational consultancy, training, school inspection, curriculum resources.

Printed publications:
NIAS includes in its services the production of a wide range of curriculum products including:
Activity Booklets for KS1 and KS2
Book Study Guides
Picture Packs for KS1 and KS2
Schemes of Work
Science Activities Boxes
Order printed publications from: NIAS Products, Training and Sales
Spencer Centre, Lewis Road, Northampton, NN5 7BJ, tel: 01604 587441, fax: 01604 757799

Electronic and video publications:
Picture Packs for KS2 on CD-ROM (£10)

Publications list:
Available in print

Access to staff:
Contact by letter, by telephone, by fax and by e-mail. Appointment necessary.
Hours: Mon to Fri, 0900 to 1700

Access for disabled people:
Parking provided, level entry, toilet facilities

Administrative Centres:
NIAS Computer/Audio Visual Centre
Covington Street, Northampton, NN15JU; tel: 01604 24190

NIAS Inspection Services
  Cliftonville Middle School, Cliftonville Road, Northampton, NN1 5BW; tel: 01604 259876; e-mail: niasclif@easymail.rmplc.co.uk
NIAS TPS
  Spencer Centre, Lewis Road, Northampton, NN5 7BJ; tel: 01604 758758; e-mail: spencer@rtcnias.rmplc.co.uk

Professional development centres:
Corby PDC
  Firdale, Cottingham Road, Corby, Northamptonshire, NN17 1TD; tel: 01536 266833; e-mail: corby.north@easymail.rmplc.co.uk
Northampton PDC
  Barry Road, Northampton, NN1 5JS; tel: 01604 30815; e-mail: northampton.north@easymail.rmplc.co.uk
Wellingborough PDC
  86 Stanley Road, Wellingborough, Northamptonshire, NN8 1DY; tel: 01933 225104; e-mail: welling.north@easymail.rmplc.co.uk

NORTHAMPTONSHIRE LIBRARIES AND INFORMATION SERVICE

Acronym or abbreviation: NLIS

PO Box 216, John Dryden House, 8–10 The Lakes, Northampton, NN4 7DD

Tel: 01604 236236
Fax: 01604 237937
E-mail: nlis@northamptonshire.gov.uk

Website:
http://www.northamptonshire.gov.uk
Public information service including Northamptonshire, local democracy, people and places, local facilities, community organisations and groups.

Organisation type and purpose:
Local government body, public library.

Museum or gallery collection, archive, or library special collection:
Beeby Thompson Collection (geology)
Charles Bradlaugh Collection (local MP, 19th century)
H. E. Bates Collection
John Clare Collection (poems, MSS, etc. of local poet)
Leather and Footwear Collection
Philip Doddridge Collection (collection of a local minister, 18th century; nonconformist church history)
Sir Henry Dryden Collection (architectural drawings)

Non-library collection catalogue:
All or part available online

Library catalogue:
All or part available online

Printed publications:
Range of greetings cards showing local scenes
Catalogues of some of the special collections
Local history publishing programme of maps, prints, books
Waterways of Northamptonshire (D. Blagrove)
Steaming into Northamptonshire (R. Coleman and J. Rajczonek, eds)
Philip Doddridge of Northampton (M. Deacon)
The Life and Times of H. E. Bates (P. Eads)
The Life and Times of John Clare (D. Powell)
The Life and Times of J. L. Carr (B. Rogers)

Publications list:
Available online and in print

Access to staff:
Contact by letter, by telephone, by fax, by e-mail and via website
Hours: Please contact Enquiries

Branches:
in Northampton, Weston Favell, Corby, Kettering, Wellingborough, Rushden, Daventry, Towcester, and 28 others

Parent body:
Northamptonshire County Council

NORTHAMPTONSHIRE LIBRARIES AND INFORMATION SERVICE – DAVENTRY LIBRARY

Acronym or abbreviation: NLIS

North Street, Daventry, Northamptonshire, NN11 4GH

Tel: 01327 703130
Fax: 01327 300501
E-mail: davlib@northamptonshire.gov.uk

Enquiries:
Enquiries to: Librarian

Organisation type and purpose:
Local government body, public library.

Subject coverage:
General; local information and local history.

Non-library collection catalogue:
All or part available online, in-house and in print

Library catalogue:
All or part available online

Publications list:
Available in print

Access to staff:
Contact by letter, by telephone, by fax, by e-mail and in person. Appointment necessary.
Hours: Mon, Thu, Fri, 0900 to 1800; Tue, 0900 to 1900; Wed, 0900 to 1230; Sat, 0930 to 1600

Access for disabled people:
Parking provided, ramped entry, level entry, access to all public areas, toilet facilities

Parent body:
Northamptonshire Libraries & Information Service (NLIS)
  tel: 01604 236236; fax: 01604 237937; e-mail: nlis@northamptonshire.gov.uk

NORTHAMPTONSHIRE RECORD OFFICE

Acronym or abbreviation: NRO

Wootton Hall Park, Northampton, NN4 8BQ

Tel: 01604 762129
Fax: 01604 767562
E-mail: archivist@northamptonshire.gov.uk

Website:
http://www.northamptonshire.gov.uk
Information leaflet.
Redevelopment in progress.
http://www.a2a.pr.gov.uk
Catalogue for part of the collections.

Enquiries:
Enquiries to: County Archivist

Founded:
1920

Organisation type and purpose:
Local government body.
Record office and archives repository.

Subject coverage:
A great variety of records in different formats are preserved: charters, court rolls, deeds, parish and non-conformist registers, maps, letters, diaries, accounts, minute books, wills, photographs and films. They include the official, judicial and administrative records of the county and other local government authorities, records of the diocese of Peterborough covering Northamptonshire, the Soke of Peterborough and Rutland, probate records for the same area as well as records of local families and estates, business and professional firms and societies.

Education services:
Contact Heritage Education Officer.

Museum or gallery collection, archive, or library special collection:
Houses the Library of the Northamptonshire Antiquarian Society and other donated specialist libraries
Includes records of the former Soke of Peterborough

Non-library collection catalogue:
All or part available online

Printed publications:
Information Leaflet for House Historians
General Information Leaflet
Information Leaflet for Genealogists

Microform publications:
Parish Registers for the Diocese of Peterborough (microfiche)

Access to staff:
Contact by letter, by telephone, by fax, by e-mail and in person
Hours: Tue to Wed, 0900 to 1645; Thu, 0900 to 1945; Fri, 0900 to 1615; 2 Sats each month, 0900 to 12.15

Access to building, collection or gallery:
No prior appointment required

Access for disabled people:
Parking provided, level entry, toilet facilities

Parent body:
Northamptonshire County Council (NCC)

NORTHAMPTONSHIRE RECORD SOCIETY

Wootton Hall Park, Northampton, NN4 8BQ

Tel: 01604 762297

Website:
http://www.northamptonshirerecordsociety.org.uk/

Enquiries:
Enquiries to: Secretary

Founded:
1920

Organisation type and purpose:
Learned society (membership is by subscription), registered charity (charity number 204597).
Historical research of all aspects of the ancient County of Northamptonshire.

Subject coverage:
Local history of Northamptonshire in all its forms.

Museum or gallery collection, archive, or library special collection:
Extensive library, members only, others on request, but not for removal from the premises

Library catalogue:
All or part available in-house

Printed publications:
Annual Report
Northamptonshire Past and Present (journal, annual, prices vary)
Northamptonshire history series (letters, papers, documents etc, but not transcripts of parish registers, every 2 years)
Hardbacked volumes (about every 2 years)
Order printed publications from: Secretary

Publications list:
Available in print

Access to staff:
Contact by letter, by telephone and in person. Access for members only.
Hours: Wed and Thu only, 1000 to 1200 and 1330 to 1630
Special comments: Access to the library normally Wed and Thu, 1030 to 1630, non-members by prior appointment.

Access to building, collection or gallery:
No prior appointment required
Hours: Wed and Thu only, 1000 to 1200 and 1330 to 1630

NORTHBROOK COLLEGE, SUSSEX

Littlehampton Road, Worthing, West Sussex, BN12 6NU

Tel: 01903 606060
Fax: 01903 606007

Enquiries:
Enquiries to: Head of Library Services

Organisation type and purpose:
College of further and higher education.

Subject coverage:
Broad range of curriculum topics in further and higher education.

Access to staff:
Contact by letter
Hours: Mon to Fri, 0900 to 1700

Liaison with:
LASER
West Sussex County Library

Member of:
Circle of Sussex College Librarians (COSCOL)
Surrey and Sussex Libraries in Cooperation (SASLIC)

NORTHERN ARC LIMITED

Acronym or abbreviation: NA

Great Western Business Centre, Emlyn Square, Swindon, Wiltshire, SN1 5BP

Tel: 0845 600 9966
E-mail: info@northernarcltd.co.uk

Website:
http://www.businesslinksw.co.uk

Enquiries:
Enquiries to: Information Officer
Direct e-mail: sarah.harris@businesslinksw.co.uk

Founded:
1995

Formerly called:
Business Link Berkshire and Wiltshire (year of change 2007)

Organisation type and purpose:
Training organisation, consultancy.
Single point of contact for local businesses to access advice, information, training and finance.

Subject coverage:
Business advice, business start-up advice, training for business, property information, innovation advice, information on exporting, market intelligence, economic and demographic information for Wiltshire and Berkshire; local business information including company information, market intelligence and funding searches.

Publications list:
Available in print

Access to staff:
Contact by letter, by telephone, by fax, by e-mail, in person and via website
Hours: Mon to Fri, 0900 to 1700
Special comments: Charges made for most services.

Access to building, collection or gallery:
Prior appointment required

Access for disabled people:
Parking provided, ramped entry

Parent body:
GWEBusiness West Ltd
  Great Western Business Centre, Emlyn Square, Swindon, SN1 5BP; tel: 01793 428320; fax: 01793 428345; e-mail: tony.horn@gwebusinesswest.co.uk; website: http://www.gwebusinesswest.co.uk

NORTHERN HAMSTER CLUB

Acronym or abbreviation: NHC

Club Secretary, 1 Richard Avenue, Smithies, Barnsley. S71 1UZ

Tel: 01226 218439
E-mail: enquiries@northernhamsterclub.co.uk

Website:
http://www.northernhamsterclub.com/

Enquiries:
Enquiries to: Membership Secretary

Founded:
1947

Organisation type and purpose:
Membership association (membership is by subscription), present number of members: 90, voluntary organisation, suitable for ages: all.
Promote the keeping, exhibition and breeding of all species of hamster.

Subject coverage:
Keeping, breeding and exhibition of all species of hamster.

Printed publications:
Journal (monthly, free to members, membership fee £10 a year includes £1.50 registration fee, annual renewal £8.50 a year, printed by the National Hamster Council)
Information sheets (free on request, sae required)

Access to staff:
Contact by letter, by telephone, by e-mail and via website
Hours: Mon to Sun, 0900 to 2100

Affiliated to:
National Hamster Council
  PO Box 154, Rotherham, S66 0FL

NORTHERN IRELAND AGRICULTURAL PRODUCERS' ASSOCIATION

15 Molesworth Street, Cookstown, Co Tyrone, BT80 8NX

Tel: 028 8676 5700
Fax: 028 8675 8598
E-mail: niapa@hotmail.com

Enquiries:
Enquiries to: Information Officer

Founded:
1974

Organisation type and purpose:
Advisory body, membership association (membership is by subscription).
To assist farmers. Farmers representative group, provide farm insurance.

Access to staff:
Contact by letter, by telephone, by fax, by e-mail and in person
Hours: Mon to Fri, 0900 to 1700

NORTHERN IRELAND ARCHERY SOCIETY

Acronym or abbreviation: NIAS

43 Greenwell Street, Newtownards, Co. Down, BT23 7LP

Tel: 028 9181 9529

Website:
http://www.ni-archery.co.uk
Types of archery, how to find a local club, news, events, contacts.

Enquiries:
Enquiries to: President

Founded:
1953

Formerly called:
Ulster Archery Association (year of change late 1970s)

Organisation type and purpose:
One of the smallest Regional Societies within Archery GB, which is the governing body of archery within Great Britain.

Currently has 24 active clubs with a total membership of over 300.

Subject coverage:
All types of archery: indoor target, outdoor target, field and clout, as well as all styles: barebow, recurve, compound and longbow.

Access to staff:
Contact by letter and by telephone

Member organisation of:
Archery GB

NORTHERN IRELAND ASSEMBLY LIBRARY

Parliament Buildings, Stormont, Belfast, BT4 3XX

Tel: 028 9052 1250
Fax: 028 9052 1922
E-mail: issuedesk.library@niassembly.gov.uk

Enquiries:
Enquiries to: Librarian (Resource Team)
Direct e-mail: george.woodman@niassembly.gov.uk

Founded:
1921

Organisation type and purpose:
National government body.
Government library.
To serve staff and members of Northern Ireland Assembly; to act as reference library for Northern Ireland Government Departments.

Subject coverage:
Northern Ireland Parliamentary and Assembly papers, debates and legislation, since 1921; Westminster Parliament Sessional and House of Lords papers and debates; Northern Ireland Departmental papers; Northern Ireland history, politics and government; Irish history; statute law and constitutional law.

Museum or gallery collection, archive, or library special collection:
18th- and 19th-century travel books relating to Ireland
Back runs of Belfast newspapers, Irish Times and Times extending back to at least 1921
Complete set of Hansard dating back to the 1830s
Complete sets of Northern Ireland legislation and very large collection of official publications
Statutes, journals and votes of pre-1800 Irish Parliament

Non-library collection catalogue:
All or part available in-house

Library catalogue:
All or part available in-house

Access to staff:
Contact by letter, by telephone, by fax and by e-mail
Hours: Mon to Fri, 0900 to 1700
Special comments: Access normally limited to members and staff of the NI Assembly and staff of the NI Government Departments.

Access to building, collection or gallery:
Prior appointment required
Hours: Mon to Fri, 0900 to 1700 and when Northern Ireland Assembly is sitting (closes 30 minutes after House rises)

Access for disabled people:
Parking provided, ramped entry, toilet facilities

NORTHERN IRELAND ASSOCIATION OF CITIZENS ADVICE BUREAUX

Acronym or abbreviation: NIACAB

11 Upper Crescent, Belfast, BT7 1NT

Tel: 028 9023 1120
Fax: 028 9023 6522

Website:
http://www.niacab.org

Information on the regional services provided by CAB, job opportunities, publications, news about CAB and developments within the organisation, FAQs, press releases, weekly employment rights columns and bureaux locations, opening times.

Enquiries:
Enquiries to: Senior Information Officer

Founded:
1974

Organisation type and purpose:
Voluntary organisation, registered charity (charity number 85136).
To develop networks with other agencies to ensure that individuals do not suffer through ignorance of either their rights or of the services available to them, or through an inability to explain their needs effectively.

Subject coverage:
General information for CAB workers in Northern Ireland; social policy background information based on evidence from CABx.

Museum or gallery collection, archive, or library special collection:
Northern Ireland statutes and statutory rules

Printed publications:
Annual Report
A Debt Handbook for Advisors in Northern Ireland (£6 inc. p&p)
Basic Questions About Divorce (£2.50 inc. p&p)
CAB Appeals Guide (£19.50 inc. p&p)
Self Help Guides to Claiming Disability Living Allowance and AA
The World of Work Redefined (£4 inc. p&p)
Women and Citizenship by Ruth Lister (£2.50 inc. p&p)

Access to staff:
Contact by letter and by telephone
Hours: Mon to Fri, 0900 to 1700

Subsidiary bureaux throughout:
Northern Ireland

NORTHERN IRELAND ATHLETIC FEDERATION

Acronym or abbreviation: NIAF

Athletics House, Old Coach Road, Belfast, BT9 5PR

Tel: 028 9060 2707
Fax: 028 9030 9939
E-mail: info@niathletics.org

Enquiries:
Enquiries to: Administrator

Founded:
1989

Organisation type and purpose:
Governing body of athletics in Northern Ireland.

Subject coverage:
Amateur athletics.

Access to staff:
Contact by letter and by e-mail
Hours: Mon to Fri, 0900 to 1700

Affiliated to:
UK Athletics

NORTHERN IRELAND CHILDMINDING ASSOCIATION

Acronym or abbreviation: NICMA

16–18 Mill Street, Newtownards, Co Down, BT23 4LU

Tel: 028 9181 1015
Fax: 028 9182 0921
E-mail: bridget.nodder@nicma.org

Website:
http://www.nicma.org

Enquiries:
Enquiries to: Director

Founded:
1984

Organisation type and purpose:
Membership association (membership is by subscription, election or invitation), present number of members: 2500, voluntary organisation, registered charity (charity number XO 549), training organisation.
Child care organisation.
To promote the development of children by providing quality home-based care within registered settings.

Subject coverage:
All aspects of child care provision.

Printed publications:
Annual Report
Publications include:
Accident and Medication Record Book (to enable childminders to fulfil the legal requirements of record keeping)
Children Come First
Child Protection – Policy and Procedures (a good practice guide for registered childminders)
Negotiating with Parents (a guide for childminders and parents when setting fees and drawing up contracts)

Publications list:
Available online and in print

Access to staff:
Contact by letter, by telephone, by fax, by e-mail, in person and via website. Appointment necessary.
Hours: Mon to Fri, 0900 to 1700

Access for disabled people:
Level entry, toilet facilities

NORTHERN IRELAND COMMUNITY RELATIONS COUNCIL

Acronym or abbreviation: CRC

6 Murray Street, Belfast, BT1 6DN

Tel: 028 9022 7500
Fax: 028 9022 7551
E-mail: info@nicrc.org.uk

Website:
http://www.nicrc.org.uk

Enquiries:
Enquiries to: Information Officer

Founded:
1990

Organisation type and purpose:
Advisory body, voluntary organisation, registered charity (charity number XR 16701), consultancy, publishing house.

Subject coverage:
Northern Ireland, peace, conflict resolution, community relations and cultural diversity.

Museum or gallery collection, archive, or library special collection:
Reference library

Library catalogue:
All or part available in-house

Printed publications:
Annual Report, Shared Space (research journal) and others, see website
Order printed publications from: Resource Centre Manager, Community Relations Council, 6 Murray Street, Belfast, BT1 6DN, e-mail: as above

Publications list:
Available online

Access to staff:
Contact by letter, by telephone, by fax, by e-mail, in person and via website. Appointment necessary.
Hours: Information Centre: Mon to Thu, 0900 to 1700; Fri, 0900 to 1630

Access to building, collection or gallery:
No prior appointment required

Access for disabled people:
Ramped entry, toilet facilities
Special comments: Elevator to 1st floor. Toilet facilities on ground floor.

NORTHERN IRELAND COUNCIL FOR VOLUNTARY ACTION

Acronym or abbreviation: NICVA

61 Duncairn Gardens, Belfast, BT15 2GB

Tel: 028 9087 7777; minicom no. 028 9087 7776
Fax: 028 9087 7799
E-mail: info@nicva.org

Website:
http://www.nicva.org
http://www.communityni.org
http://www.grant-tracker.org

Enquiries:
Enquiries to: Information Officer

Founded:
1938

Organisation type and purpose:
Membership association (membership is by subscription), present number of members: over 1,000, voluntary organisation, registered charity (charity number XN47024), training organisation, research organisation.
Umbrella body for voluntary and community groups.

Subject coverage:
Social policy, social action, voluntary action, community development, funding information, research, charity advice.

Museum or gallery collection, archive, or library special collection:
Library (books, grey literature) of more than 2,000 items
Journals and periodicals

Trade and statistical information:
Data on the economic contribution and structure of the voluntary and community sector in Northern Ireland.

Non-library collection catalogue:
All or part available online

Library catalogue:
All or part available in-house

Printed publications:
State of the Sector V – Northern Ireland Voluntary Sector Almanac 2009
NICVA News
eNew
Regular research reports, briefings, advice notes on charity administration and governance
Order printed publications from: Information Officer

Electronic and video publications:
Grant Tracker
Order electronic and video publications from: Online subscription at http://www.grant-tracker.org

Publications list:
Available online and in print

Access to staff:
Contact by letter, by telephone, by fax, by e-mail, in person and via website. Appointment necessary.
Hours: Mon to Thu, 0900 to 1700; Fri, 0900 to 1630
Special comments: Some charges made, e.g. photocopying, consultancy services.

Access to building, collection or gallery:
Prior appointment required for the library
Special comments: Prior appointment required for the library.

Access for disabled people:
Parking provided, ramped entry, level entry, access to all public areas, toilet facilities

NORTHERN IRELAND ENVIRONMENT AGENCY

Acronym or abbreviation: NIEA

continued overleaf

Klondyke Building, Cromac Avenue, Lower
Ormeau Road, Belfast, BT7 2JA

Tel: 028 9056 9230
Fax: 028 9056 9264
E-mail: nieainfo@doeni.gov.uk

Website:
http://www.ni-environment.gov.uk

Enquiries:
Other contacts: Director of Water Quality, Director
of Natural Heritage, Director of Built Heritage (for
specific research)

Formerly called:
Environment and Heritage Service (year of change
2008)

Organisation type and purpose:
National government body.

Subject coverage:
Built Heritage, Natural Heritage, Environmental
Protection.

Printed publications:
Downloadable online
Order printed publications from: at the same address

Access to staff:
Contact by letter, by telephone, by fax and by e-
mail. Appointment necessary.

Access to building, collection or gallery:
Hours: Mon to Fri, 0900 to 1700

Also at:
Northern Ireland Environment Agency
   Water Management Unit, 7 Antrim Road,
   Lisburn; tel: 028 9262 3100; e-mail: waterinfo@
   doeni.gov.uk
Northern Ireland Environment Agency
   Built Heritage, Waterman House, 5–33 Hill
   Street, Belfast, BT1 2LA; tel: 028 9023 5000; fax:
   028 9054 3111; e-mail: bh@doeni.gov.uk

NORTHERN IRELAND ENVIRONMENT AGENCY – MONUMENTS AND BUILDINGS RECORD

Acronym or abbreviation: NIEA–MBR

5–33 Hill Street, Belfast, BT1 2LA

Tel: 028 9054 3159
Fax: 028 9054 3111
E-mail: hmenquiries@doeni.gov.uk

Website:
http://www.ni-environment.gov.uk

Enquiries:
Enquiries to: Secretary

Founded:
1992

Formerly called:
Environment and Heritage Service; Archaeological
Survey

Organisation type and purpose:
National government body.

Subject coverage:
Archaeological sites, listed buildings listings,
photographic and drawings archive library,
historic monuments and buildings, historic
gardens, industrial archaeology, maritime
archaeology.

Education services:
Groups catered for by prior arrangement.

**Museum or gallery collection, archive, or library
special collection:**
Clokey collection (stained glass)
J S Curl photographic collection (of historic
   buildings)
McCutcheon archive (industrial archaeology)
McKinstry and McGeagh architectural archives
Northern Ireland sites and monuments record

Non-library collection catalogue:
All or part available online

Library catalogue:
All or part available online

Printed publications:
Various
Order printed publications from: Postal address for
NIEA, above

Publications list:
Available in print

Access to staff:
Contact by letter, by telephone, by fax, by e-mail
and in person
Hours: 0930 to 1300 and 1400 to 1630

Access to building, collection or gallery:
Hours: As for staff contact

Access for disabled people:
Ramped entry, toilet facilities
Hours: As for staff contact

Parent body:
Department of the Environment
   Clarence Court, Belfast, BT2 8GB; tel: 028 9054
   0540

NORTHERN IRELAND ENVIRONMENT LINK

Acronym or abbreviation: NIEL

89 Loopland Drive, Belfast, BT6 9DW

Tel: 028 9045 5770
Fax: 028 9094 2151
E-mail: info@nienvironmentlink.org

Website:
http://www.nienvironmentlink.org

Enquiries:
Enquiries to: Director
Other contacts: Communications and Membership
Officer

Founded:
1990

Organisation type and purpose:
Membership association (membership is by
subscription), present number of members: 109,
voluntary organisation, registered charity (charity
number XR 19598).
Umbrella and networking body for voluntary
environmental groups.

Subject coverage:
Environmental issues, conservation, pollution and
countryside management, sustainable
development, waste management, biodiversity,
environmental education. Policy and policy
development.

**Museum or gallery collection, archive, or library
special collection:**
Library of recent government and NGO
   publications

Library catalogue:
All or part available in-house

Printed publications:
Case Studies of Environmental Projects
Directory of Environmental Organisations in
   Northern Ireland
Environmental Briefing Notes
Environmental Factsheets (3 a year)
Environmental Strategy (out of print)
Lines from the Environmental Educational Forum
   (6 times a year)
NIEL News (monthly newsletter)
Policy Priorities for Northern Ireland's
   Environment – The Way Ahead

Publications list:
Available online

Access to staff:
Contact by letter, by telephone, by fax, by e-mail,
in person and via website. Appointment necessary.
Hours: Mon to Fri, 0900 to 1700

NORTHERN IRELAND FEDERATION OF CLUBS

1 Sultan Square, Belfast, BT12 4SU

Tel: 028 9029 5134
Fax: 028 9023 3286
E-mail: info@nifederationofclubs.com

Website:
http://www.nifederationofclubs.com/

Enquiries:
Enquiries to: Executive Secretary
Direct e-mail: info@nifederationofclubs.com

Founded:
1983

Organisation type and purpose:
Advisory body, trade union (membership is by
subscription), present number of members: 301,
service industry, voluntary organisation,
consultancy, research organisation.

Subject coverage:
Information on the N Ireland Registration of Clubs
Order and Accounts Regulations 1996. Private
member clubs, management, contracts of
employment for persons employed in registered
clubs, and general advice.

Printed publications:
Club Review (magazine, 10 times a year, free to
   members)
Order printed publications from: Media Marketing
B1.01 Portview Trade Centre, Belfast, BT4 1RX, tel:
028 9045 9864, fax: 028 9045 9034

Access to staff:
Contact by letter, by telephone, by fax, by e-mail
and via website. Appointment necessary.
Hours: Mon to Fri, 0900 to 1700

Access to building, collection or gallery:
Prior appointment required

Access for disabled people:
Access to all public areas, toilet facilities

NORTHERN IRELAND HEALTH AND SOCIAL SERVICES LIBRARY

Queen's University Medical Library, Mulhouse
Building, Mulhouse Road, Belfast, BT12 6DP

Tel: 028 9063 2504
Fax: 028 9063 5038
E-mail: med.office@qub.ac.uk

Enquiries:
Enquiries to: Information Officer

Founded:
1954

Organisation type and purpose:
University department or institute.
University medical and regional health service
library.

Subject coverage:
Medicine, dentistry, nursing, paramedical subjects,
health organisation and social services.

**Museum or gallery collection, archive, or library
special collection:**
Samuel Simms Collection on the history of
   medicine and other historical works
Works by Northern Ireland doctors

Non-library collection catalogue:
All or part available online

Library catalogue:
All or part available online

Access to building, collection or gallery:
No access other than to staff

NORTHERN IRELAND LOCAL GOVERNMENT ASSOCIATION

Acronym or abbreviation: NILGA

Unit 5B, Castlereagh Business Park, 478
Castlereagh Road, Belfast, BT5 6BQ

Tel: 028 9079 8972
Fax: 028 9079 1248

Website:
http://www.nilga.org

Enquiries:
Enquiries to: Chief Executive

Founded:
2001

Organisation type and purpose:
Local government body.
An organisation representing the interests of local government in Northern Ireland.

Subject coverage:
The functions and responsibilities of District Councils in Northern Ireland.

Printed publications:
The Councillors' Handbook (Revised ed. 1994, £10)

Access to staff:
Contact by letter and by fax
Hours: Mon to Fri, 0900 to 1700

Member of:
Local Government International Bureau
  tel: 020 7664 3100

Representing the British section of:
CEMR
IULA

NORTHERN IRELAND MASTER PLUMBERS' ASSOCIATION

Acronym or abbreviation: NIMPA

38 Hill Street, Belfast, BT1 2LB

Tel: 028 9032 1731
Fax: 028 9024 7521
E-mail: info@crawfordsedgwick.co.uk

Enquiries:
Enquiries to: Secretary

Founded:
1931

Organisation type and purpose:
Trade association.

Subject coverage:
Plumbing and mechanical services.

Access to staff:
Contact by letter, by telephone, by fax and by e-mail
Hours: Mon to Fri, 0900 to 1700

Member organisation of:
Scottish & Northern Ireland Plumbing Employers' Federation
  2 Walker Street, Edinburgh, EH3 7LB; tel: 0131 225 2255; fax: 0131 226 7638; e-mail: info@snipef.org; website: http://www.snipef.org

NORTHERN IRELAND OMBUDSMAN

Formal name: Assembly Ombudsman for Northern Ireland/Northern Ireland Commissioner for Complaints

Progressive House, 33 Wellington Place, Belfast, BT1 6HN

Tel: 028 9023 3821; 0800 343424 freephone
Fax: 028 9023 4912
E-mail: ombudsman@ni-ombudsman.org.uk

Website:
http://www.ni-ombudsman.org.uk
General information about the role of the Ombudsman.

Enquiries:
Enquiries to: Office Manager

Founded:
1969

Organisation type and purpose:
Statutory body.

Ombudsman.

Subject coverage:
Complaints from people who claim to have suffered injustice because of maladministration by government departments and public bodies in Northern Ireland.

Printed publications:
Explanatory leaflets available free on request
Annual Report available from website

Publications list:
Available online

Access to staff:
Contact by letter, by telephone, by fax, by e-mail, in person and via website. Appointment necessary.
Hours: Personal callers: Mon to Fri, 0930 to 1600

Access for disabled people:
Level entry, access to all public areas, toilet facilities

NORTHERN IRELAND OPTOMETRIC SOCIETY.

Acronym or abbreviation: NIOS

PO Box 28, Dromore, County Down, BT25 1YH, Northern Ireland

Tel: 028 8224 2137
Fax: 028 8224 9330
E-mail: lizgillespie.nios@btopenworld.com

Website:
http://www.nios.org

Enquiries:
Enquiries to: Secretary

Founded:
1952

Organisation type and purpose:
Professional body (membership is by subscription).

Subject coverage:
The NIOS represents the profession of optometry in Northern Ireland. The core activity of the society is to promote high standards of primary eye care, and to enhance further education and learning.

Trade and statistical information:
Data on number of optometrists resident or practising in Northern Ireland.

Access to staff:
Contact by letter
Hours: Mon to Fri, 0900 to 1700

NORTHERN IRELAND POSTAL CHESS ASSOCIATION

27 Cherry Valley Gardens, Belfast, BT5 6PQ

Tel: 028 9059 1142
E-mail: david.blair4@ntlworld.com

Website:
http://www.chessmail.com

Enquiries:
Enquiries to: Honorary Secretary & Treasurer

Founded:
1985

Organisation type and purpose:
Membership association (membership is by subscription).
To organise and play correspondence chess nationally and internationally.

Subject coverage:
Correspondence chess.

Library catalogue:
All or part available online

Electronic and video publications:
Chessmail (CD-ROM, available)
Order electronic and video publications from: Editor, Chessmail
e-mail: editor@chessmail.com

Publications list:
Available online and in print

Access to staff:
Contact by letter and by e-mail
Hours: Mon to Fri, 1700 to 1900; Sat, Sun, 0900 to 1700
Special comments: No phone Mon to Fri, 0900 to 1700.

Affiliated to:
British Postal Chess Federation

NORTHERN IRELAND TEXTILES & APPAREL ASSOCIATION

c/o Riverside Factory, Victoria Street, Lurgan, Craigavon, County Armagh BT67 9DU

Tel: 028 3831 1399
Fax: 028 3832 1816
E-mail: info@nita.co.uk

Enquiries:
Enquiries to: Director

Organisation type and purpose:
Trade association (membership is by subscription), present number of members: 50.

Subject coverage:
Textiles and apparel.

Access to staff:
Contact by letter, by telephone, by fax, by e-mail and in person. Appointment necessary.
Hours: Mon to Fri, 0900 to 1700

Access for disabled people:
Parking provided, level entry, toilet facilities
Special comments: Access to ground floor only.

Member of:
British Apparel and Textile Confederation (BATC)
  5 Portland Place, London, W1B 1PW; tel: 020 7636 7788; fax: 020 7636 7515; e-mail: batc@dial.pipex.com

NORTHERN IRELAND TOURIST BOARD

Acronym or abbreviation: NITB

St Anne's Court, 59 North Street, Belfast, BT1 1NB

Tel: 028 9023 1221
Fax: 028 9024 0960
E-mail: info@nitb.com

Website:
http://www.ni-tourism.com
http://www.nitb.com

Enquiries:
Enquiries to: Information Officer
Direct e-mail: lking@nitb.com
Other contacts: (1) Research and Information Librarian (2) Photographic Librarian for (1) reports etc (2) film and transparencies.

Founded:
1948

Organisation type and purpose:
Local government body, statutory body.
National tourist board.

Subject coverage:
Northern Ireland tourism facts and figures, accommodation, transport and sightseeing information, activities and events.

Museum or gallery collection, archive, or library special collection:
Photographic library, 30,000 transparencies for loan and hire, plus videos and slides
Research library (5000 titles) NI and UK tourism statistics, market research, planning, environment, annual reports etc
TIC – booklets, brochures, maps – leaflets on particular places or subjects, some free

Printed publications:
Annual Report (£5)
Booklets, brochures and maps (24 titles, most free)

continued overleaf

Illustrated leaflets on particular places (16 titles, free)
Information bulletins on particular subjects (20 titles, free)
Research reports
The Best of Northern Ireland

Access to staff:
Contact by letter, by telephone, by fax, by e-mail, in person and via website. Appointment necessary.
Hours: Mon to Fri, 0900 to 1700
Research Library: Tue, Thu, 0900 to 1700; Wed, 0900 to 1500

NORTHERN IRELAND TRANSPLANT ASSOCIATION

Acronym or abbreviation: NITA

51 Circular Road, Belfast, BT4 2GA

Tel: 028 9076 1394
E-mail: nitransplants@email.com

Website:
http://www.nita.org.uk
Overall view, many personal stories of transplants.

Enquiries:
Enquiries to: Information Officer
Other contacts: Chairman

Founded:
October 1991

Organisation type and purpose:
Membership association (membership is by election or invitation), present number of members: 160, registered charity (charity number XO 19630).
To advise and support those involved with organ transplants, including donor families, and to supply relevant information. To encourage registration of donors and the carrying of organ donor cards.

Subject coverage:
Organ transplantation and donors.

Printed publications:
General leaflets explaining the transplant and donor card programme
Leaflets on personal stories of people who have had transplants
Specialised leaflets on each type of transplant (heart, liver, lung etc)

Electronic and video publications:
Video on various aspects of organ transplantation, lent free to individuals

Access to staff:
Contact by letter, by telephone, by e-mail and via website
Hours: 24-hour telephone answering

NORTHERN IRELAND, WESTERN EDUCATION AND LIBRARY BOARD

Library Headquarters, 1 Spillars Place, Omagh, Co Tyrone, BT78 1HG

Tel: 028 8224 4821
Fax: 028 8224 6716

Website:
http://www.ni-libraries.net

Enquiries:
Enquiries to: Librarian

Organisation type and purpose:
Local government body, statutory body (membership is by election or invitation), present number of members: 21, public library.
Public Library Service; District Libraries at Londonderry, Omagh, Co Tyrone and Enniskillen/County Fermanagh, Limavady and Strabane.
Some material for consultation only.

Subject coverage:
Humanities, history, local history, education, business, fine arts and bibliographical.

Museum or gallery collection, archive, or library special collection:
William Carleton Collection
Nawn Collection (local and Irish history)
Local and Irish history
Material on Ireland; Art; Bibliophily
Irish Joint Fiction Reserve (authors A, F and I)

Trade and statistical information:
Regulatory, economic, financial, technical and marketing material.

Non-library collection catalogue:
All or part available online and in-house

Library catalogue:
All or part available online and in print

Printed publications:
Public Service Current Awareness Bulletins

Access to staff:
Contact by letter, by telephone, by fax, by e-mail, in person and via website. Appointment necessary.
Hours: Library HQ and Divisional HQs, Mon to Fri, 0900 to 1715
Branch libraries vary, all are open Tue pm, Fri, and Sat 1000 to 1300; telephone for more precise details

North West Divisional Library:
Northern Ireland, Western Education and Library Board
35 Foyle Street, Londonderry, BT48 6AL; tel: 028 7127 2300; fax: 028 7126 9084

Other libraries:
Castlederg Library
1a Hospital Road, Castlederg, BT81 7BU; tel: 028 8167 1419; fax: 028 8167 9048; e-mail: castlederg.library@ni-libraries.net
Central Library
35 Foyle Street, Londonderry, BT48 6AL; tel: 028 7126 6888; fax: 028 7126 9084
Creggan Library
59 Central Drive, Creggan Estate, Londonderry, BT48 9QH; tel: 028 7126 6168; fax: 028 7130 8939; e-mail: creggan.library@ni-libraries.net
Dungiven Library
74 Main Street, Dungiven, Co Londonderry, BT47 4LD; tel: 028 7174 1475; e-mail: dungiven.library@ni-libraries.net
Enniskillen Library
Halls Lane, Enniskillen, BT74 7DR; tel: 028 6632 2886; fax: 028 8632 4685; e-mail: enniskillen.library@ni-libraries.net
Fintona Library
112–114 Main Street, Fintona, BT78 2BY; tel: 028 8284 1774; fax: 028 8284 1774; e-mail: fintona.library@ni-libraries.net
Irvinestown Library
Main Street, Irvinestown, Co Fermanagh, BT94 1GT; tel: 028 6862 1383; fax: 028 6862 1383; e-mail: irvinestown.library@ni-libraries.net
Limavady Library
5 Connell Street, Limavady, Co Londonderry, BT49 0EA; tel: 028 7776 2540; fax: 028 7772 2006; e-mail: limavady.library@ni-libraries.net
Lisnaskea Library
Drumhaw, Lisnaskea, Co Fermanagh, BT92 0FC; tel: 028 6772 1222; fax: 028 6772 1222; e-mail: lisnaskea.library@ni-libraries.net
Newtownstewart Library
Main Street, Newtownstewart, BT87 4AA; tel: 028 8266 1245; fax: 028 8266 1245; e-mail: newtonstewart.library@ni-libraries.net
Omagh Library
1 Spillars Place, Omagh, BT78 1HL; tel: 028 8224 4821; fax: 028 8224 6722; e-mail: omagh.library@ni-libraries.net
Shantallow Library
92 Racecourse Road, Shantallow, Co Londonderry, BT4 8DA; tel: 028 7135 4185; fax: 028 7135 4122; e-mail: shantallow.library@ni-libraries.net
Sion Mills Library
Church Square, Sion Mills, BT78 9HA; tel: 028 8265 8513; fax: 028 8265 8513; e-mail: sionmills.library@ni-libraries.net
Strabane Library
1 Railway Road, Strabane, BT82 8AN; tel: 028 7188 3686; fax: 028 7138 2745; e-mail: strabane.library@ni-libraries.net

Strathfoyle Library
Claragh Crescent, Strathfoyle, Co Londonderry, BT47 7HQ; tel: 028 7186 0385; fax: 028 7186 0385; e-mail: strathfoyle.library@ni-libraries.net
Waterside Library
23 Glendermott Road, Waterside, Londonderry, BT47 1BG; tel: 028 7134 2963; fax: 028 7131 8283; e-mail: waterside.library@ni-libraries.net

South West Divisional Library:
Northern Ireland, Western Education and Library Board
Halls Lane, Enniskillen, BT74 7DR; tel: 028 6632 2886; fax: 028 6632 4685; e-mail: enniskillen.library@ni-libraries.net

NORTHERN MINE RESEARCH SOCIETY

Acronym or abbreviation: NMRS

Winshaw Barn, Chapel-le-Dale, Ingleton, Yorkshire, LA6 3AT

Tel: 01524 241851
E-mail: sbassham@nildram.co.uk

Website:
http://www.nmrs.org.uk

Enquiries:
Enquiries to: Publication Sales
Direct tel: 01282 614615
Direct e-mail: mansemins@btopenworld.com
Other contacts: Editor (for publishing enquiries); Recorder (for historical requests)

Founded:
1960

Organisation type and purpose:
Learned society (membership is by subscription), present number of members: 400, registered charity (charity number 326704), suitable for ages: 18+, research organisation, publishing house.
Researching all aspects of the history of Britain's extractive (mining and quarrying) industries.

Subject coverage:
British mining history, mining technology, past and present mining of minerals in UK, some aspects of University field work.

Museum or gallery collection, archive, or library special collection:
Documents, maps and plans relating to British mines
Indexes of mining sites
Mining history books

Trade and statistical information:
Historical data on the production of materials in Britain.

Non-library collection catalogue:
All or part available online and in-house

Library catalogue:
All or part available in-house

Printed publications:
Four Newsletters for members
Individual Survey Series 1966–1974
Memoirs, 1964–2006
Transactions, 1960–1964
British Mining, 1976 to date (see website)

Publications list:
Available online and in print

Access to staff:
Contact by letter and by e-mail
Hours: Recorder only, by appointment.

Access to building, collection or gallery:
Recorder only, by appointment

Access for disabled people:
Recorder only

Member organisation of:
Association for Industrial Archaeology
Council for British Archaeology Group 4
National Association of Mining History Organisations

NORTHERN REGION FILM AND TELEVISION ARCHIVE

Acronym or abbreviation: NRFTA

School of Arts and Media, Teesside University, Middlesborough, Tees Valley, TS1 3BA

Tel: 01642 384022
Fax: 01642 384099
E-mail: enquiries@nrfta.org.uk

Website:
http://www.nrfta.org.uk

Founded:
1998

Organisation type and purpose:
Public-sector moving image archive serving County Durham, Northumberland, Tees Valley and Tyne and Wear.

Subject coverage:
Film and television in County Durham, Northumberland, Tees Valley, and Tyne and Wear.

Museum or gallery collection, archive, or library special collection:
Important collections include:
BBC Look North collection
Tyne Tees Television collection
Border Television collection
Turners' Film Unit collection
Tyne and Wear Archives Service (TWAS) collection

Access to staff:
Contact by letter, by telephone, by e-mail and via website. Appointment necessary.
Hours: Mon to Thu, 0900 to 1700; Fri, 0900 to 1630

NORTHMOOR TRUST

Northmoor Trust, Hill Farm, Little Wittenham, Abingdon, Oxon

Tel: 01865 407792
Fax: 01865 407131
E-mail: admin@northmoortrust.co.uk

Website:
http://www.northmoortrust.co.uk
Work of the trust, activities and events, contact details, visitor centre.

Enquiries:
Enquiries to: Chief Executive

Founded:
1967

Organisation type and purpose:
A conservation charity (registered charity number 1095057) finding working solutions to the challenges faced by farming, conservation and forestry.
To educate and engage people in their local landscape and inspire them to take action to protect it; to demonstrate sustainability in a way that integrates production from the land, wildlife-rich habitats and natural systems.

Subject coverage:
Manages an estate of 300 hectares, including Little Wittenham Nature Reserve and Wittenham Clumps, a conservation farm, a woodland dedicated to forestry research and Project Timescape, the Trust's visitor centre.

Special visitor services:
Varied programme of events, including green birthday parties.

Education services:
Events for primary and secondary schools; farm visits arranged.

Access to staff:
Contact by letter, by telephone, by fax and by e-mail

NORTHUMBERLAND ARCHIVES

Woodhorn Museum and Northumberland Archives

Tel: 01670 528080
Fax: 01670 528083
E-mail: collections@woodhorn.org.uk

Website:
http://www.nationalarchives.gov.uk/a2a
Many catalogue lists available online.
http://www.experiencewoodhorn.com
Many catalogue lists available online, as well as office information and services.

Enquiries:
Enquiries to: Head of Collections

Incorporates the former:
Northumberland Record Office

Organisation type and purpose:
Local government body (charitable trust).
Archive service.

Subject coverage:
Historic records relating to the County of Northumberland.

Museum or gallery collection, archive, or library special collection:
Main map collection for the county including enclosure awards, deposited plans, estate maps, tithe awards, ordnance survey maps
Main photographic collection for the county
Family and estate papers
Manorial
Business
Records of the Society of Antiquaries of Newcastle upon Tyne
Private small collections

Non-library collection catalogue:
All or part available online

Library catalogue:
All or part available online

Printed publications:
Many guidance leaflets including:
Anglican Parish Registers
Civil Cemetery Records
Enclosure Awards in the Northumberland Record Office
Family History Resources for North Northumberland
Historic Census Returns for Northumberland 1841–1891
Historic Maps and Plans
Methodist Registers
Presbyterian and Congregational Registers
Roman Catholic Parish Registers
Trade Directories

Microform publications:
A large number of microfiche copies and transcriptions of censuses, registers, monumental inscriptions, names in wills, school records, directories

Publications list:
Available in print

Access to staff:
Contact by letter, by telephone, by fax, by e-mail, in person and via website
Hours: Wed to Sun, 1000 to 1600; Mon, Tue, closed

Access to building, collection or gallery:
No prior appointment required

Access for disabled people:
Parking provided – charge of £2.50 daily

Branch of:
Berwick Record Office
Council Offices, Wallace Green, Berwick upon Tweed, Northumberland, TD15 1ED; tel: 01289 301865; e-mail: lbankier@woodhorn.org.uk

NORTHUMBERLAND COLLECTIONS SERVICE

Woodhorn Experience, Northumberland Museums and Archives, Queen Elizabeth II Country Park, Ashington, Northumberland, NE63 9YF

Tel: 01670 528080
Fax: 01670 514815

E-mail: ask@northumberland.gov.uk

Website:
www.northumberland.gov.uk/collections/

Enquiries:
Enquiries to: Senior Archivist

Organisation type and purpose:
Local government body.
Archive service.

Subject coverage:
Historic records relating to the county of Northumberland.
Incorporates Northumberland County Archive Service (formerly Northumberland Record Office), Northumberland County Council's Local Studies Collection, and Northumberland County Council's Modern Records Service

Non-library collection catalogue:
All or part available in-house

Printed publications:
Leaflets
Introduction to Record Offices

Publications list:
Available in print

Access to staff:
Contact by letter, by telephone, by fax, by e-mail and in person

Constituent bodies:
Berwick Record Office
Council Offices, Wallace Green, Berwick upon Tweed, Northumberland, TD15 1ED; tel: 01259 330044 ext 230

NORTHUMBERLAND COLLEGE

College Road, Ashington, Northumberland, NE63 9RG

Tel: 01670 814200 extn 240
Fax: 01670 841201
E-mail: lrc@northland.ac.uk

Website:
http://www.northland.ac.uk
Description of college; services and courses provided.

Enquiries:
Enquiries to: Librarian

Organisation type and purpose:
Suitable for ages: 16+.
College of further education.

Subject coverage:
General; particular strengths: sociology and social welfare, tourism, electrical and electronic engineering, business and management studies, European Community. Land-based industries: horticulture, aboriculture, conservation, agriculture, animal husbandry, equine studies, small animals.

Library catalogue:
All or part available online

Printed publications:
Leaflets including services to staff, services to students, information bookmarks, database information

Access to staff:
Contact by letter, by telephone, by fax and by e-mail. Appointment necessary.
Hours: Term time: Mon, Tue, Thu, 0900 to 2000; Fri, 0900 to 1630; Wed, 0900 to 1900
Vacations: Mon to Thu, 0900 to 1630; Fri, 0900 to 1600

Access for disabled people:
Parking provided, ramped entry, access to all public areas, toilet facilities

Also at:
Northumberland College At Kirkley Hall
Kirkley Hall, Ponteland, NE20 0AQ; tel: 01670 814200 extn 519; e-mail: lrc@northland.ac.uk

NORTHUMBERLAND COUNTY LIBRARY – HEXHAM

Queen's Hall, Beaumont Street, Hexham, Northumberland, NE46 3LS

Tel: 01434 652488
Fax: 01434 652490
E-mail: hexhamlibrary@northumberland.gov.uk

Enquiries:
Enquiries to: Librarian

Organisation type and purpose:
Public library.

Museum or gallery collection, archive, or library special collection:
Census returns, parish registers, newspapers all on microfilm
International Genealogical Index (on microfilm)
The Brough Collection: Local History Sources

Non-library collection catalogue:
All or part available in print

Library catalogue:
All or part available online

Printed publications:
Local Studies: resources for family and local historians in the Brough Local Studies Collection, 4th edn

Access to staff:
Contact by letter, by telephone, by fax, by e-mail and in person
Hours: Mon to Wed, 0930 to 1700; Fri, 0930 to 1930; Sat, 0930 to 1230

Access for disabled people:
Level entry

NORTHUMBERLAND COUNTY LIBRARY SERVICE

County Hall, Morpeth, Northumberland, NE61 2EF

Tel: 01670 533000
E-mail: libraries@northumberland.gov.uk

Website:
http://www.northumberlandlibraries.com

Enquiries:
Direct tel: 01670 500391
Direct e-mail: infohelp@northumberland.gov.uk

Founded:
1926

Organisation type and purpose:
Public library.

Subject coverage:
General, modern poetry, cinema, Northumberland.

Museum or gallery collection, archive, or library special collection:
Film and cinema
Modern poetry
Northern Poetry Library
Northumberland

Library catalogue:
All or part available online

Access to staff:
Contact by letter, by telephone, by e-mail, in person and via website
Hours: Mon to Fri, 0900 to 1930; Sat, 0930 to 1230

Parent body:
Northumberland County Council
County Hall, Morpeth, Northumberland, NE61 2EF; tel: 01670 533000; website: http://www.northumberland.gov.uk

NORTHUMBRIA UNIVERSITY – EUROPEAN DOCUMENTATION CENTRE

City Campus Library, Ellison Place, Newcastle upon Tyne, NE1 8ST

Tel: 0191 243 7704

Fax: 0191 227 4563
E-mail: maimie.balfour@northumbria.ac.uk

Website:
http://www.northumbria.ac.uk/edc

Enquiries:
Enquiries to: Information Specialist
Direct e-mail: ask4help@northumbria.ac.uk

Founded:
1974

Organisation type and purpose:
University library.
To provide a service of EU information in the northern region of the United Kingdom to all staff and students internally and in Higher or Further Education institutions, and external clients.

Subject coverage:
EU legislation, EU policy, EU statistics, official publications, etc., including information officially published by all the EC institutions.

Museum or gallery collection, archive, or library special collection:
EU information deposited by the Commission of the EC

Non-library collection catalogue:
All or part available online

Access to staff:
Contact by letter, by telephone, by fax and by e-mail. Appointment necessary.
Hours: http://www.northumbria.ac.uk/edc

NORTHUMBRIA UNIVERSITY – UNIVERSITY LIBRARY

Ellison Place, Newcastle upon Tyne, NE1 8ST

Tel: 0191 227 4125
Fax: 0191 227 4563
E-mail: ask4help@northumbria.ac.uk

Website:
http://www.northumbria.ac.uk/sd/central/library
http://librarycat.northumbria.ac.uk/TalisPrism Web OPAC.

Enquiries:
Enquiries to: Director of Library and Learning Services
Direct tel: 0191 227 4126
Direct e-mail: jane.core@northumbria.ac.uk

Formerly called:
Newcastle Polytechnic (year of change 1992)

Organisation type and purpose:
University Library.

Subject coverage:
Art and design, economics, education, English literature, geography, government, history, law, librarianship and information science, modern languages, nursing, midwifery and allied health, philosophy, politics, psychology, religion, social welfare, sociology, accountancy, building, business, chemistry, civil engineering, electrical and electronic engineering, industrial design, management, marketing, materials science, mathematics, mechanical engineering, statistics, surveying, computing, physics.

Museum or gallery collection, archive, or library special collection:
Thompson Newspaper Archive
Visual Art UK Archives

Library catalogue:
All or part available online

Printed publications:
Guides to the literature of particular subjects
Research reports
University prospectuses, handbooks, etc.

Access to staff:
Contact by letter, by telephone, by e-mail, in person and via website
Hours: Term time: Mon to Thu, 0900 to 2100; Fri, 0900 to 1900; Sat, 0930 to 1700; Sun, 1100 to 1700

Access to building, collection or gallery:
Visitors welcome; Northumbria members and subscribers, smartcard to enter University
Hours: Term time: 24-hour opening, daily; vacations: daily, 0800 to 2400
Special comments: Visitors require proof of identity, incl. photo. No entry without a smartcard outside staff-supervised hours.

Access for disabled people:
Ramped entry, access to all public areas, toilet facilities

NORTHUMBRIAN PIPERS' SOCIETY

Acronym or abbreviation: NPS

Park House, Lynemouth, Morpeth, Northumberland, NE61 5XQ

Tel: 01670 860215
E-mail: secretary@northumbrianpipers.org.uk

Website:
http://www.northumbrianpipers.org.uk
History of society, book catalogue, contacts list.

Enquiries:
Enquiries to: Honorary Secretary

Founded:
1928

Organisation type and purpose:
Unincorporated Association, voluntary society.
To support the playing, making and music of the Northumbrian pipes.

Subject coverage:
Making of the Northumbrian smallpipes and related technical matters; pipe makers, pipe players and availability of music and recordings, materials, etc.; meetings of pipers within and outside Northumberland.

Museum or gallery collection, archive, or library special collection:
W. A. Cocks Collection of Pipes and Manuscripts, held in the Morpeth Chantry Bagpipe Museum

Printed publications:
Magazine (annually)
Members' handbook
Newsletter (quarterly, for members)
Books as listed online
Order printed publications from: e-mail: booksales@northumbrianpipers.org.uk

Publications list:
Available in print

Access to staff:
Contact by letter, by telephone, by e-mail, in person and via website
Hours: By e-mail or phone, any reasonable time; in person by appointment

Also at:
Morpeth Chantry Bagpipe Museum
tel: 01670 500717; e-mail: annemoore02@northumberland.gov.uk

NORTHWEST DEVELOPMENT AGENCY

Acronym or abbreviation: NWDA

PO Box 37, Renaissance House, Centre Park, Warrington, Cheshire, WA1 1XB

Tel: 01925 400100
Fax: 01925 400400
E-mail: information@nwda.co.uk

Website:
http://www.nwda.co.uk
Activities, addresses and reports.

Enquiries:
Enquiries to: Director of Marketing

Founded:
1999

Organisation type and purpose:
Local government body, advisory body, membership association, consultancy.
Regional Development Agency for North West England with remit of economic and social development of the region through business support, inward investment and regeneration.

Subject coverage:
Inward investment into North West England, economic development of North West England, regeneration of North West England, and business support to North West England.

Printed publications:
Annual Report
Brochures on North West England

Electronic and video publications:
Press Releases
Regional Strategy for North West England

Publications list:
Available online

Access to staff:
Contact by letter, by telephone, by fax, by e-mail and via website. Appointment necessary. Non-members charged.
Hours: Mon to Fri, 0830 to 1730

Access to building, collection or gallery:
Prior appointment required

Access for disabled people:
Parking provided, level entry, toilet facilities

Links with:
English Partnerships (EP)
   New Town House, Buttermarket Street, Warrington, WA1 2LF; tel: 01925 644744
Invest in Britain Bureau (IBB)
   1 Victoria Street, London; tel: 020 7215 5000
North West Regional Assembly
   4th Floor, Loops Business Centre, 11 Dorning Street, Wigan, WN1 1HE; tel: 01942 737915

NORTON OWNERS CLUB

Acronym or abbreviation: NOC

Clifton House, 4a Goldington Road, Bedford, MK40 3NF

Tel: 01234 352672
E-mail: secretary@nortonownersclub.org

Website:
http://www.noc.co.uk

Enquiries:
Enquiries to: Secretary

Founded:
1959

Organisation type and purpose:
International organisation, membership association (membership is by subscription), present number of members: 5,000, voluntary organisation.
To promote an interest in Norton Motorcycles.

Subject coverage:
Technical, historical, model, type information on Norton Motorcycles.

Non-library collection catalogue:
All or part available in-house

Library catalogue:
All or part available in-house

Printed publications:
Roadholder (magazine, 6 times a year, to members)

Electronic and video publications:
Engine and Gearbox Strip (videos / DVD)

Publications list:
Available online and in print

Access to staff:
Contact by letter, by telephone and by e-mail

Hours: Mon to Fri, 0900 to 1700

Access to building, collection or gallery:
No access

NORWEGIAN TRADE COUNCIL

Formal name: Royal Norwegian Embassy, Trade and Technology Office

Charles House, 5–11 Regent Street, London, SW1Y 4LR

Tel: 020 7389 8800
Fax: 020 7973 0189
E-mail: london@ntc.no

Website:
http://www.ntclondon.com

Enquiries:
Enquiries to: Information Officer

Organisation type and purpose:
National government body.

Subject coverage:
Companies in Norway, export products, Norwegian companies in UK and Ireland.

Museum or gallery collection, archive, or library special collection:
Norway export brochures

Non-library collection catalogue:
All or part available in-house

Library catalogue:
All or part available in-house

Printed publications:
Publications are free of charge
Norway Export Brochures on:
Aerospace, automotive, building products and services, space, environmental technology, fishing gear, furniture, road and traffic technology, health care, software and multimedia products, oil and gas technology, defence products, pleasure boats, power generation, ships gear, underground facilities, production technology, giftware, seafood, rock engineering, concrete and road technology, Norwegian brands, Norwegian design, aquaculture technology and equipment

Access to staff:
Contact by letter, by telephone, by fax, by e-mail and via website
Hours: Mon to Fri, 0900 to 1700

Access to building, collection or gallery:
No access other than to staff

Access for disabled people:
Level entry

NORWICH CITY COLLEGE OF FURTHER EDUCATION

Library, Ipswich Road, Norwich, Norfolk, NR2 2LJ

Tel: 01603 773224
Fax: 01603 760326
E-mail: tis@ccn.ac.uk

Website:
http://heritage.ccn.ac.uk
Norwich City College catalogue.

Enquiries:
Enquiries to: Learning Resources Manager
Direct tel: 01603 773045

Organisation type and purpose:
FE and HE College library.

Subject coverage:
Business management, hospitality industry, science, construction, electrical and mechanical engineering, hair, beauty, sport and leisure, health, social care and early years education.

Non-library collection catalogue:
All or part available in-house

Library catalogue:
All or part available online

Printed publications:
Information sheets
Library Guide (annually)

Access for disabled people:
Parking provided, access to all public areas, toilet facilities

NORWICH CITY COUNCIL

City Hall, Norwich, Norfolk, NR2 1NH

Tel: 01603 622233\ Minicom no. 01603 212059
Fax: 01603 213000

Website:
http://www.norwich.gov.uk

Enquiries:
Enquiries to: Public Relations Manager

Organisation type and purpose:
Local government body.

Access to staff:
Contact by letter, by telephone, by fax and in person. Appointment necessary.
Hours: Mon to Fri, 0900 to 1700

NORWICH PUPPET THEATRE

Formal name: Norwich Puppet Theatre Trust Ltd
Acronym or abbreviation: NPT

St James's, Whitefriars, Norwich, Norfolk, NR3 1TN

Tel: 01603 615564
Fax: 01603 617578
E-mail: info@puppettheatre.co.uk

Website:
http://www.puppettheatre.co.uk
Information about current events in the Puppet Theatre programme, plus background information on the Theatre's history, place in the puppetry community, and outreach activities.

Enquiries:
Enquiries to: Manager
Other contacts: Marketing Co-ordinator

Founded:
1978

Organisation type and purpose:
Registered charity (charity number 271041).
Theatre.
Puppet theatre with 20-year archive of own puppets, access to some written references.

Subject coverage:
Puppetry and puppet theatre.

Museum or gallery collection, archive, or library special collection:
Puppets from the last 20 years

Access to staff:
Contact by letter, by telephone, by fax, by e-mail and in person. Appointment necessary.
Hours: Mon to Fri, 0930 to 1630

Access to building, collection or gallery:
Mon to Fri; performance Sat
Hours: Mon to Fri, 0930 to 1630; other times by appointment

Access for disabled people:
Level entry, access to all public areas, toilet facilities

NOTTINGHAM BUSINESS CENTRES

Lenton Boulevard, Nottingham, NG7 2BY

Tel: 0115 955 2107/0115 915 9245
Fax: 0115 955 2108
E-mail: info@nottinghambusinesscentres.co.uk

Website:
http://www.nbtg.co.uk

continued overleaf

Information about accommodation available at each business centre, services provided on site and full list of companies currently licensing offices and or workshops.

Enquiries:
Enquiries to: Service Manager

Organisation type and purpose:
Local government body, service industry.
Commercial property provider and business support.
Provide managed workspace (offices and workshops) for start-up and expanding small businesses in Nottingham City area.

Subject coverage:
Commercial property, licensed business accommodation, managed workspace, business centres, support for start-up businesses, support for expanding small businesses, availability of business premises in Nottingham.

Trade and statistical information:
Data on the cost of business premises.
Data on support available for small businesses in Nottingham.

Printed publications:
Brochure (available free, by contacting main switchboard)

Access to staff:
Contact by letter, by telephone and by fax.
Appointment necessary.
Hours: Mon to Fri, 0830 to 1700

Links with:
Nottingham City Council
Design & Property Services, Severns House, Middle Pavement, Nottingham, NG1 7BW; tel: 0115 915 5555; fax: 0115 915 8307

Satellite Offices:
Ashforth Business Centre
Ashforth Street, St Ann's, Nottingham, NG3 4BG; tel: 0115 955 2017/0115 915 9245; fax: 0115 955 2108
Bulwell Business Centre
Sellers Wood Drive, Bulwell, Nottingham, NG6 8GN; tel: 0115 955 2107 (main switchboard); fax: 0115 955 2108
Helston Drive Business Centre

NOTTINGHAM CITY COUNCIL

Loxley House, Station Street, Nottingham, NG2 3NG

Tel: 0115 915 5555

Website:
http://www.nottinghamcity.gov.uk

Enquiries:
Direct fax: 0115 915 4434

Founded:
1996

Organisation type and purpose:
Local government body.

Printed publications:
The Arrow (Civic newspaper)

Publications list:
Available in print

Access to staff:
Contact by letter, by telephone, by fax, in person and via website
Hours: Mon to Fri, 0900 to 1700

Access for disabled people:
Parking provided, ramped entry, level entry, toilet facilities

NOTTINGHAM CITY LIBRARY

Angel Row, Nottingham, NG1 6HP

Tel: 0115 915 2828; minicom no. 0115 915 2847
Fax: 0115 915 2840
E-mail: enquiryline@nottinghamcity.gov.uk

Website:
http://www.mynottingham.gov.uk/libraries

Enquiries:
Enquiries to: Librarian
Direct tel: 0115 915 2842

Founded:
1868

Organisation type and purpose:
Local government body, public library.

Subject coverage:
Information service offered by four subject libraries: arts and music, business, leisure, local studies.

Museum or gallery collection, archive, or library special collection:
British Standards (CD-ROM)
Byron Collection
D. H. Lawrence Collection
Local Printing Collection
Robin Hood Collection
UK street maps

Library catalogue:
All or part available online

Access to staff:
Contact by letter, by telephone, by fax, by e-mail, in person and via website
Hours: Mon to Thurs, 0900 to 1900; Sat, 0900 to 1600

Access for disabled people:
Ramped entry, access to all public areas, toilet facilities

Links with:
Nottinghamshire County Library
Trent Bridge House, Fox Road, West Bridgford, Nottingham, NG2 6BJ; tel: 0115 982 3823; fax: 0115 977 2428

NOTTINGHAM TRENT UNIVERSITY

Libraries and Learning Resources, Boots Library, Goldsmith Street, Nottingham, NG1 5LS

Tel: 0115 848 6434
Fax: 0115 848 4485
E-mail: libweb@ntu.ac.uk

Website:
http://www.ntu.ac.uk/llr
http://opac.ntu.ac.uk
Library online catalogue

Enquiries:
Enquiries to: Administrative Services Manager
Direct tel: 0115 8482775
Direct e-mail: helen.bran@ntu.ac.uk

Organisation type and purpose:
University library.

Subject coverage:
Art and design, humanities, business, law, education, science and technology, social sciences, animal, rural and environmental sciences, architecture, design and the built environment.

Museum or gallery collection, archive, or library special collection:
Lace collection

Trade and statistical information:
Statistics collection (United Kingdom and EC).

Printed publications:
RAM Bulletin (robotics and advanced manufacturing)

Electronic and video publications:
RAM-PC (robotics and advanced manufacturing)

Access to staff:
Contact by letter, by telephone, by fax, by e-mail and in person. Non-members charged.

Access to building, collection or gallery:
Hours: Term time: Mon to Fri, 0830 to 2100; Sat, 0900 to 1700; Sun, 1400 to 1900. Vacations: Mon to Fri, 0830 to 1700; Sat, 1000 to 1400 (closed Sat during August). IT resources rooms open 24 hours.

Also at:
Brackenhurst Campus Library
Nottingham Trent University, Nottingham Road, Southwell, NG25 0QF; tel: 01636 8175249
Clifton Campus Library
Nottingham Trent University, Clifton Lane, Nottingham, NG11 8NS; tel: 0115 848 6612; fax: 0115 848 6304

NOTTINGHAMSHIRE ARCHIVES

County House, Castle Meadow Road, Nottingham, NG2 1AG

Tel: 0115 958 1634; 0115 950 4524
Fax: 0115 941 3997
E-mail: archives@nottscc.gov.uk

Website:
http://www.nottinghamshire.gov.uk/archives
General introduction to services.

Enquiries:
Enquiries to: Archivist

Founded:
1949

Organisation type and purpose:
Local government body.

Subject coverage:
Archives of Nottinghamshire County and Nottingham City, also the Southwell and Nottingham Diocesan Record Office.

Museum or gallery collection, archive, or library special collection:
Local authority records, including county, district and parish councils
Public records, including courts and hospitals
Ecclesiastical records, including parish and non-conformist
Family and estate
Business
Societies and organisations

Non-library collection catalogue:
All or part available online and in-house

Library catalogue:
All or part available in-house

Microform publications:
Nottinghamshire Parish Registers up to 1950
Probate records
Electoral registers
Burial registers
Census returns
GRO index, 1837–1965

Publications list:
Available online and in print

Access to staff:
Contact by letter, by telephone, by fax, by e-mail, in person and via website
Hours: Mon, Wed to Fri, 0900 to 1645; Tue, 0900 to 1915; Sat, 0900 to 1245
Special comments: CARN Readers Ticket required to consult original archives (but not books or microfiche).

Access for disabled people:
Parking provided, level entry, toilet facilities
Special comments: Please ring to book parking space.

NOTTINGHAMSHIRE FAMILY HISTORY SOCIETY

Acronym or abbreviation: NFHS

The Secretary, 8 Westmaner Court, Hall Drive, Chilwell, Nottingham, NG9 5DQ

Tel: 0115 967 7075

Website:
http://www.nottsfhs.org.uk
Surname lists, membership details, publications, computer searches, Society information.

Enquiries:
Enquiries to: Secretary

Founded:
1971

Organisation type and purpose:
Membership association (membership is by subscription), present number of members: 1,800, registered charity (charity number 515898), research organisation.

Subject coverage:
Family history in Nottinghamshire.

Printed publications:
Journal (includes a quarterly update of the publications)
The Records Series (books on a variety of topics such as: rate books, banns registers, alehouse recognisances, Methodist ministers and lay officers, etc.)
Yesterday's Nottingham (a series of books with old postcards of the various areas with a short piece of information about the picture. The cards are mainly from the turn of the 19th/20th centuries.)
Order printed publications from: Notts FHS, 10 Sherwin Walk, St Anns, Nottingham, NG3 1AH

Microform publications:
1841 Census Nottinghamshire – the complete census transcript has been put onto computer; the index is available on microfiche
Census Surname Indexes (pre-1841, 1841, 1851, 1861, 1871, 1881, 1891, microfiche)
Marriages Index (parishes in Phillimore, microfiche)
Marriages Index (parishes not in Phillimore, microfiche)
Members' Interests (annually, April 1998, 2 fiches, £1 plus 45p p&p)
Nottinghamshire 1813–1837 Marriage Index (microfiche)
Monumental Inscriptions (a large number of churches, chapels, cemeteries and burial grounds, microfiche)
Nottinghamshire Marriages Indexes from beginning of registers up to 1900 (over 30 parishes, male and female surname indexes both in alphabetical and chronological order (microfiche)
Surname Indexes to Nottinghamshire Baptisms (microfiche)

Electronic and video publications:
CD-ROM versions of some microform products

Publications list:
Available online and in print

Access to staff:
Contact by letter, by e-mail and via website
Hours: Mon to Fri, 0900 to 2100

NOTTINGHAMSHIRE LIBRARIES, ARCHIVES & INFORMATION

Nottinghamshire County Council, Culture & Community, 4th Floor, County Hall, West Bridgford, Nottingham, NG2 7QP

Tel: 0115 977 4401
Fax: 0115 977 2806
E-mail: cslibraries@nottscc.gov.uk

Website:
http://www.nottscc.gov.uk/libraries
County Library services and sites, Education Library service, Archives service, links to other sites.

Enquiries:
Enquiries to: Librarian
Direct e-mail: contact.libraries@nottscc.gov.uk
Other contacts: Head of Libraries (Libraries, Archives & Information)

Founded:
1998

Organisation type and purpose:
Local government body, public library.

Subject coverage:
General, local archives.

Non-library collection catalogue:
All or part available online

Library catalogue:
All or part available online and in-house

Printed publications:
Amongst many are:
Lost Houses of Nottinghamshire (£5.99)
Timber-Frame Buildings of Nottinghamshire (£3.99)
Victorian Lady's Diary 1838–1842 (£5.95)
Viewing the Lifeless Body, A Coroner and his inquests held In Nottinghamshire Public Houses during the Nineteenth Century 1828–1866 (£7.95)
Discovering Civil War in Nottinghamshire (£2.95)
Muniment Evidences & Writing, The History of Archives in Notts (£1)
Newark Civil War & Seigeworks (£3.99)
Newark the Bounty of Beer (£3.99)
Nottinghamshire Country Houses: Past and Present (£3.95)
In Grandmother Gell's Kitchen (cookery book, £5.95)
Robin Hood Country: The County Guide to Nottinghamshire (£2.95)
A Basketful of Willow – Willow growing (£8.50)
As poor as a stockinger (£3.95)
Great Ancester Hunt (£2.99)
Southwell Inns & Alehouses (£6.95)
These Uncertaine Tymes (£6.95)
Turning back the pages – Raleigh (£3.50)
Turning back the pages – Ravenshead (£3.95)
Turning back the pages – Old Broad Marsh & Narrow Marsh (£3.50)
Turning back the pages in Old Carlton (£3.99)
Turning back the pages in Old Hucknall (£3.99)
Turning back the pages in Old Mansfield Woodhouse (£4.99)
Turning back the pages in Old West Bridgford (£5.95)
Castles of Nottinghamshire (£5.95)
Diaries of Godfrey Tallents of Newark (£7.50)
John Speed Map 1610 (£4.99)
Jones & Smith Map (£5.99)
Moules Map of Nottinghamshire (£2.50)
Order printed publications from: e-mail: carole.tailby@nottscc.gov.uk or contactlibraries@nottscc.gov.uk; 4th Floor County Hall, NG2 7QP

Publications list:
Available online and in print

Access to staff:
Contact by letter, by telephone, by fax, by e-mail and in person
Hours: Public Libraries (core times): Mon to Fri, 0930 to 1700; Sat, 0900 to 1300
Special comments: County Library Headquarters Sections at 4th Floor, County Hall, West Bridgford, Nottingham, NG2 7QP: Mon to Fri, 0830 to 1630; not available Sat.

Branch libraries:
Arnold Library
Front Street, Arnold, Nottingham, NG5 7EE; tel: 0115 920 2247; fax: 0115 967 3378; e-mail: Arnold .library@nottscc.gov.uk
Beeston Library
Foster Avenue, Beeston, Nottingham, NG9 1AE; tel: 0115 925 5168; fax: 0115 922 0841; e-mail: beeston.library@nottscc.gov.uk
Mansfield Library
Four Seasons Centre, Westgate, Mansfield, Nottinghamshire, NG18 1NH; tel: 01623 627591; fax: 01623 629276; e-mail: mansfield.library@ nottscc.gov.uk
Newark Library
Beaumond Gardens, Baldertongate, Newark on Trent, Nottinghamshire, NG24 1UW; tel: 01636 703966; fax: 01636 610045; e-mail: newark .library@nottscc.gov.uk

Nottinghamshire Archives
County House, Castle Meadow Road, Nottingham, NG2 1AG; tel: 0115 950 4524; fax: 0115 941 3997; e-mail: archives@nottscc.gov.uk
Retford Library
Churchgate, Retford, Nottinghamshire, DN22 6PE; tel: 01777 708724; fax: 01777 710020; e-mail: retford.library@nottscc.gov.uk

County Library Headquarters – Education Library Service:
Nottinghamshire County Council
Glaisdale Parkway, Nottingham, NG8 4GP; tel: 0115 985 4200; fax: 0115 928 6400; e-mail: valerie .sawyer@nottscc.gov.uk

NOTTINGHAMSHIRE LOCAL HISTORY ASSOCIATION

Acronym or abbreviation: NLHA

6 Cornwall Road, Retford, DN22 6SH

Tel: 01777 702475

Website:
http://www.nlha.org.uk
News, diary of events, local society contacts and programmes.

Enquiries:
Enquiries to: Chairman
Direct tel: 01623 870515
Other contacts: Membership Secretary (for membership)

Founded:
1960

Organisation type and purpose:
Membership association (membership is by subscription), present number of members: 250, voluntary organisation.
Support to history societies, educational institutes, individuals.

Subject coverage:
Local history of Nottinghamshire.

Printed publications:
Nottinghamshire Historian (2 times a year)
Occasional works on Nottinghamshire local history
Order printed publications from: The Editor, NLHA The Notts Historian, 30 Repton Road, West Bridgford, Nottinghamshire, NG2 7EJ; tel: 0115 923 3901

Access to staff:
Contact by letter and by telephone
Hours: Mon to Fri, 0900 to 1700

NSPCC

Formal name: National Society for the Prevention of Cruelty to Children

Weston House, 42 Curtain Road, London, EC2A 3NH

Tel: 020 7825 2500 (24-hour child protection helpline: 0808 800 5000)
Fax: 020 7825 2525
E-mail: info@nspcc.org.uk

Website:
http://www.nspcc.org.uk/inform
Free, online, specialised child protection resource for practitioners, researchers, trainers, policy-makers and other professionals working to protect children.
http://www.nspcc.org.uk
NSPCC homepage

Enquiries:
Enquiries to: NSPCC and ChildLine Public Enquiry Point
Direct tel: 020 7825 2775
Direct fax: 020 7825 2763
Direct e-mail: info@nspcc.org.uk
Other contacts: Records Manager

Founded:
1884

continued overleaf

Organisation type and purpose:
Voluntary organisation, registered charity (charity number 216401).
Child protection agency.

Subject coverage:
Child protection; child abuse; neglect; domestic violence; child welfare; family therapy; social work; prevention; statistics; child development; positive parenting.

Museum or gallery collection, archive, or library special collection:
Archives and historical material on the NSPCC dating back to 1884

Library catalogue:
All or part available online

Printed publications:
Annual Report
Full publications list available from Publications Sales, tel: 020 7825 7422, or see website.
Order printed publications from: NSPCC Publications tel: 020 7825 7422

Publications list:
Available online and in print

Access to staff:
Contact by letter, by telephone, by e-mail and via website. Appointment necessary.
Hours: Mon to Fri, 0900 to 1700
Special comments: Library suitable for child protection practitioners and researchers by appointment only. Restricted access to some of the archives.

Access for disabled people:
Parking provided, level entry, toilet facilities

NSU OWNERS CLUB

Acronym or abbreviation: NSUOC

Nutleigh, Rabies Heath Road, Bletchingley, Surrey, RH1 4LX

Tel: 01883 744431
Fax: 01883 742437
E-mail: nsuoc@btinternet.com

Website:
http://www.nsuoc.co.uk

Enquiries:
Enquiries to: General Secretary

Founded:
1961

Organisation type and purpose:
International organisation, membership association (membership is by subscription), present number of members: 170.

Subject coverage:
Technical advice on NSU cars, contact address in UK and overseas, sources of new and used parts.

Museum or gallery collection, archive, or library special collection:
Collection of cards, posters, sales brochures, videos, photographs
Repair books, parts books for most models

Trade and statistical information:
Product market values.

Printed publications:
Magazine (quarterly)

Access to staff:
Contact by letter, by telephone and by fax.
Appointment necessary.
Hours: Up to 2130

Affiliated to:
NSU Gmbh
Postfach 1144, 7107 Neckarsulm, Germany

NSU RO80 CLUB GB

Round Barn, Entwistle, Bolton, Lancashire

Tel: 01204 852425

Enquiries:
Enquiries to: Membership Secretary

Founded:
1980

Organisation type and purpose:
Membership association (membership is by subscription), present number of members: 100.
Club association.

Subject coverage:
NSU, Wankel engine motor car.

Printed publications:
Newsletter (4 times a year, £20)

Publications list:
Available in print

Access to staff:
Contact by letter and by telephone
Hours: Mon to Fri, 0800 to 2130

Access to building, collection or gallery:
No access other than to staff

NUCLEAR INDUSTRY ASSOCIATION

Acronym or abbreviation: NIA

First Floor, Whitehall House, 41 Whitehall, London, SW1A 2BY

Tel: 020 7766 6640
Fax: 020 7839 4695
E-mail: info@niauk.org

Website:
http://www.niauk.org

Enquiries:
Enquiries to: Chief Executive
Direct e-mail: john.mcnamara@niauk.org
Other contacts: Information Officer for information requests on nuclear power.

Organisation type and purpose:
NIA was established in the early 1960s; it is the trade association and information and representative body for the British civil nuclear industry; it represents over 80 companies including the operators of the nuclear power stations, those engaged in decommissioning, waste management, nuclear liabilities management and all aspects of the nuclear fuel cycle, nuclear equipment suppliers, engineering and construction firms; nuclear research organisations; and legal, financial and consultancy companies.

Subject coverage:
Nuclear power and its connection with: the environment, UK business, energy costs, pollution and waste, energy strategies, nuclear reactors, DTI and parliament, safety.

Printed publications:
Industry Link (single copies, free)
Nuclear Business Directory (£25)

Access to staff:
Contact by letter, by telephone, by fax, by e-mail and via website. Appointment necessary.
Hours: Mon to Fri, 0900 to 1700

NUFFIELD COLLEGE LIBRARY

New Road, Oxford, OX1 1NF

Tel: 01865 278550
Fax: 01865 278621
E-mail: library-enquiries@nuffield.ox.ac.uk

Website:
http://www.nuffield.ox.ac.uk/library

Enquiries:
Enquiries to: Librarian
Direct e-mail: librarian@nuffield.ox.ac.uk

Founded:
1937

Organisation type and purpose:
Library of a college of the University of Oxford.

Subject coverage:
Social sciences (economics, politics, sociology).

Museum or gallery collection, archive, or library special collection:
G. D. H. Cole Collection
Modern manuscripts (political, social, economic)
William Cobbett Collection
Lord Cherwell Archives

Non-library collection catalogue:
All or part available online

Library catalogue:
All or part available online

Access to staff:
Contact by letter, by telephone, by fax, by e-mail, in person and via website. Appointment necessary.
Hours: Mon to Fri, 0930 to 1730
Special comments: No information service outside the University, except for Archives.

NUFFIELD COUNCIL ON BIOETHICS

Acronym or abbreviation: NCOB

28 Bedford Square, London, WC1B 3JS

Tel: 020 7681 9619
Fax: 020 7637 1712
E-mail: bioethics@nuffieldfoundation.org

Website:
http://www.nuffieldfoundation.org/bioethics

Enquiries:
Enquiries to: Director

Founded:
1991

Organisation type and purpose:
Voluntary organisation.
Voluntary council.

Subject coverage:
Ethical questions raised by recent advances in biological and medical research, home and abroad.

Museum or gallery collection, archive, or library special collection:
Material on bioethics abroad
Press cuttings on bioethics in the UK

Printed publications:
The following publications are available for purchase, direct:
Animal-to-human transplants: the ethics of xenotransplantation
Discussion paper on the ethics of clinical research in developing countries (free)
Genetically Modified Crops: the ethical and social issues
Genetic Screening: Ethical Issues (out of print)
Human Tissue: Ethical and Legal Issues
Mental Disorders and Genetics: the ethical context
Stem Cell Therapy: the ethical issues (discussion paper, free)

Publications list:
Available online

Access to staff:
Contact by letter, by fax and by e-mail
Hours: Mon to Fri, 0900 to 1700

Appointed by the:
Trustees of the Nuffield Foundation

NURSING AND MIDWIFERY COUNCIL

Acronym or abbreviation: NMC

23 Portland Place, London, W1B 1PZ

Tel: 020 7637 7181
Fax: 020 7436 2924
E-mail: communications@nmc-uk.org

Website:
http://www.nmc-uk.org

Enquiries:
Enquiries to: Communications Manager

Direct e-mail: nina.rossi@nmc-uk.org

Founded:
2002

Organisation type and purpose:
Registered charity in England (charity number 1091434) and Scotland (charity number SC038362). Statutory regulatory body.
To safeguard the health and wellbeing of the public by continually regulating, reviewing and promoting nursing and midwifery standards.
Aims to uphold the reputation of the professions in the eyes of the public, government, other healthcare organisations, and nurses and midwives themselves.

Subject coverage:
Issues relating to the Council's statutory responsibilities regarding registration, pre-registration and post-registration education; professional conduct of all nurses and midwives on the Council's register in the United Kingdom.

Printed publications:
An NMC guide for students of nursing and midwifery
Complaints about unfitness to practise: A guide for members of the public (also in Welsh)
Good health and good character: Guidance for students and registrants
Guidance for Continuing Professional Development for Nurse and Midwife Prescribers
Guidelines for records and record keeping (currently under review)
Modern supervision in action: a practical guide for midwives
How to complain about a nurse or midwife (in Arabic, Bengali, Chinese, Greek, Gujarati, Hindi, Punjabi, Somali, Turkish, Urdu, Vietnamese translations)
How to complain about a nurse or midwife in England
How to complain about a nurse or midwife in Northern Ireland
How to complain about a nurse or midwife in Scotland
How to complain about a nurse or midwife in Wales
Midwives rules and standards
NMC Fitness to practise annual reports
Registering as a nurse or midwife in the United Kingdom
Reporting lack of competence: A guide for employers and managers (also in Welsh)
Reporting unfitness to practise: A guide for employers and managers (also in Welsh)
Standards for medicines management
Standards for the preparation and practice of supervisors of midwives
Standards for the supervised practice of midwives
Standards of proficiency for nurse and midwife prescribers
Standards of proficiency for pre-registration midwifery education (also in Welsh)
Standards of proficiency for pre-registration nursing education (also in Welsh)
Standards of proficiency for pre-registration specialist community public health nursing education (in Welsh)
Standards of proficiency for specialist community public health nurses
Standards to support learning and assessment in practice
The Code: Standards of conduct, performance and ethics for nurses and midwives (also in Welsh)
The PREP handbook
What to expect from a nurse or midwife who can prescribe drugs
Order printed publications from: http://nmc-uk.linney.com/orderpage1.aspx

Publications list:
Available online and in print

Access to staff:
Contact by letter, by telephone, by fax, by e-mail, in person and via website
Hours: Mon to Fri, 0800 to 1700

Access to building, collection or gallery:
Prior appointment usually required

Access for disabled people:
Ramped entry, toilet facilities

NUTRICIA LIMITED

New Market Avenue, Whitehorse Business Park, Trowbridge, Wiltshire, BA14 0XQ

Tel: 01225 711677
Fax: 01225 711972

Enquiries:
Enquiries to: Librarian
Direct tel: ext 1731
Direct e-mail: bwilliams@nutricia.co.uk

Organisation type and purpose:
Manufacturing industry.

Subject coverage:
Infant nutrition, general nutrition, food technology and milk technology.

Museum or gallery collection, archive, or library special collection:
Infant feeding bottles dating back to the early 18th century

Library catalogue:
All or part available in-house

Printed publications:
Medical information sheets
Product data cards
Teaching aids and films on infant nutrition

Publications list:
Available in print

Access to staff:
Contact by letter and by e-mail
Hours: Tue to Thu, 0900 to 1600

Access to building, collection or gallery:
No access other than to staff

Access for disabled people:
Parking provided, toilet facilities

Subsidiary of:
Nutricia Limited

NUTRITION SOCIETY

Acronym or abbreviation: Nut Soc

Unit 10, Cambridge Court, 210 Shepherds Bush Road, London, W6 7NJ

Tel: 020 7602 0228
Fax: 020 7602 1756
E-mail: info_officer@nutsoc.org.uk

Website:
http://www.nutritionsociety.org

Enquiries:
Enquiries to: Chief Executive
Direct e-mail: office@nutsoc.org.uk

Founded:
1941

Organisation type and purpose:
Learned society, registered charity (charity number 272071).

Subject coverage:
Nutrition.

Printed publications:
British Journal of Nutrition
Nutrition Research Reviews
Proceedings of the Nutrition Society
Public Health Nutrition

Publications list:
Available online and in print

Access to staff:
Contact by letter, by telephone, by fax, by e-mail and via website
Hours: Mon to Fri, 0900 to 1700

Headquarters address:
Nutrition Society
10 Cambridge Court, 210 Shepherds Bush Road, London, W6 7NJ; tel: 020 7602 0228; fax: 020 7602 1756

OAKLANDS COLLEGE

Smallford Campus, Hatfield Road, St Albans, Hertfordshire, AL4 0JA

Tel: 01727 737700
Fax: 01727 737752
E-mail: gill.hall@oaklands.ac.uk

Website:
http://colleges.herts.ac.uk
Library catalogue
http://www.oaklands.ac.uk

Enquiries:
Enquiries to: Learning Resources Supervisor
Direct tel: 01727 737716/7

Founded:
1921

Organisation type and purpose:
College learning resources centre.

Subject coverage:
Science and husbandry of British agriculture, horticulture, floristry, equine studies and small animal care.

Non-library collection catalogue:
All or part available online

Library catalogue:
All or part available online

Access to staff:
Contact by letter, by telephone, by fax and by e-mail
Hours: Term time: Mon to Thu, 0900 to 2000; Fri, 0900 to 1600
Vacations: Mon to Thu, 0900 to 1700; Fri, 0900 to 1630

Other sites at:
Oakland College
St Albans City Campus; tel: 01727 737000; fax: 01727 737010
Oakland College
Borehamwood Campus; tel: 01727 737400; fax: 01727 737440
Oakland College
Welwyn Garden City Campus, Welwyn Garden City; tel: 01707 737500; fax: 01707 737544

OCCUPATIONAL AND ENVIRONMENTAL DISEASES ASSOCIATION

Acronym or abbreviation: OEDA

PO Box 26, Enfield, Middlesex, EN1 2NT

Tel: 020 8360 6413

Website:
http://www.oeda.demon.co.uk

Enquiries:
Enquiries to: Director
Direct fax: 020 8360 6413

Founded:
1978

Organisation type and purpose:
Voluntary organisation, registered charity (charity number 1031036), consultancy, asbestos research organisation and information resource.
Advice on prevention and information to help those affected by asbestos.

Subject coverage:
Asbestos-related illnesses including asbestosis, mesothelioma, pneumoconiosis, pleural plaques, and asbestos-related lung cancer

Museum or gallery collection, archive, or library special collection:
Early papers on asbestos

continued overleaf

Printed publications:
Information Notes
Newsletters
Asbestos Facts
Asbestos Fibres in Lung Tissue (£10)
Asbestos: To Challenge Fibre Counts (£10)
Report to IIAC (£10)

Publications list:
Available in print

Access to staff:
Contact by letter. Appointment necessary.
Hours: Mon to Fri, 0930 to 1700

Access to building, collection or gallery:
Prior appointment required

Access for disabled people:
Special comments: All communications by letter or phone

OCKENDEN INTERNATIONAL

PO Box 1275, Woking, Surrey GU22 2FT

Tel: 01483 772012
Fax: 01483 750774
E-mail: oi@ockenden.org.uk

Website:
http://www.ockenden.org.uk
General programme.

Enquiries:
Enquiries to: Head of Policy
Direct e-mail: graham.wood@ockenden.org .uk

Founded:
1951

Organisation type and purpose:
International organisation, registered charity
(charity number 1053720).
Assistance to refugees.

Subject coverage:
Support to refugees and displaced people,
primarily overseas but also through reception
services and residential care in the United
Kingdom.

**Museum or gallery collection, archive, or library
special collection:**
Annual Reports of Ockenden Venture's work from
the early 1960s

Printed publications:
Annual Report and Quarterly Newsletter

Electronic and video publications:
Introduction to Ockendon (video)

Access to staff:
Contact by letter, by fax and by e-mail
Hours: Mon to Fri, 0900 to 1730

Access for disabled people:
Parking provided, level entry, toilet facilities

Member agency of the:
British Aid to Afghanistan Group
British Refugee Council
International Consortium for Refugees in Iran

OFCOM

Riverside House, 2a Southwark Bridge Road,
London, SE1 9HA

Tel: 020 7981 3000
Fax: 020 7981 3333

Website:
http://www.ofcom.org.uk
http://www.ofcom.org.uk/consumer_guides/
Comprehensive consumer guides on all aspects of
radio, television, telecommunications and wireless
services.

Enquiries:
Enquiries to: Ofcom Contact Centre
Direct tel: 0845 456 3000\ Textphone: 0845 456 6006
Direct fax: 0845 456 3333
Direct e-mail: contact@ofcom.org.uk

Founded:
2003

Combined from:
Broadcasting Standards Commission, Independent
Television Commission, Oftel, Radio Authority,
Radiocommunications Agency

Organisation type and purpose:
Communications regulator
Responsible for: complaints handling (including
telecommunications, broadcasting content and TV
/ radio interference); general enquiries or queries
regarding licensing spectrum (including fees),
broadcasting or telecommunications; business
radio licensing authorisations; publication requests

Printed publications:
Publications that were created by the original five
regulators will continue to be issued, in some
cases even after the end of 2003. These
publications should be deemed to be Ofcom
approved until such time as they are either
withdrawn or superseded by new Ofcom
publications.

Publications list:
Available online

Access to staff:
Contact by telephone, by fax and by e-mail

OFFA'S DYKE ASSOCIATION

Acronym or abbreviation: ODA

West Street, Knighton, Powys, LD7 1EN

Tel: 01547 528753
E-mail: oda@offasdyke.demon.co.uk

Website:
http://www.offasdyke.demon.co.uk

Enquiries:
Enquiries to: Centre Manager

Founded:
1969

Organisation type and purpose:
Membership association, registered charity
(charity number 503821).
Official tourist information centre.

Subject coverage:
Offa's Dyke as walking route (facilities and
accommodation for walkers), history of Offa and
the Dyke, history of Knighton as tourist centre,
Welsh Border environmental and planning issues.

**Museum or gallery collection, archive, or library
special collection:**
Frank Noble library of books etc on Offa's Dyke
and Welsh Border History

Printed publications:
Newsletter (3 times a year, free to members)
Publications list of numerous titles as well as
charts, maps etc
Strip maps of the Offa's Dyke Path
The ODA Book of Offa's Dyke Path
Where to Stay and Public Transport Guide to Offa's
Dyke Path (revised annually)
Wye Valley Walk
Circular Walks from the Offa's Dyke Path
OD Path South (2007)
OD Path North (2008)
Severn Way

Electronic and video publications:
Tape concerning general information relating to
Association, Dyke and Path can be made
available for sale

Publications list:
Available online and in print

Access to staff:
Contact by letter, by telephone, by fax, by e-mail,
in person and via website
Hours: Easter to end October: daily, 1000 to 1700
End of October to Easter: Mon, Wed, Fri, Sat, 1000
to 1600; Tue, Thu, 1000 to 1700

Access for disabled people:
Parking provided, level entry, access to all public
areas, toilet facilities

Connections with:
Countryside Commission
Countryside Council for Wales
Powys County Council
Wales Tourist Board
Youth Hostels Association

OFFENDER'S TAG ASSOCIATION

Acronym or abbreviation: OTA

128 Kensington Church Street, London, W8 4BH

Tel: 020 7221 7166
Fax: 020 7792 9288
E-mail: ota@stacey-international.co.uk

Website:
http://www.offenderstag.co.uk

Enquiries:
Enquiries to: Director

Founded:
1982

Organisation type and purpose:
Independent organisation.
To promote use of electronic tagging to reduce
offending.

Subject coverage:
Penal affairs, electronic monitoring of offenders.

Printed publications:
Publications list available online

Publications list:
Available online and in print

Access to staff:
Contact by letter, by fax and by e-mail
Hours: Mon to Fri, 0900 to 1700

Access to building, collection or gallery:
No prior appointment required

OFFICE FOR NATIONAL STATISTICS

Acronym or abbreviation: ONS

Government Buildings, Cardiff Road, Newport,
NP10 8XG

Tel: 0845 6013034; minicom no. 01633 812399
Fax: 01633 652747
E-mail: info@statistics.gov.uk

Website:
http://www.ons.gov.uk

Founded:
1996

Organisation type and purpose:
Government department and agency for the
collection and publication of UK industrial and
economic and social statistics, reports to United
Kingdom Statistics Authority.

Subject coverage:
Statistics on national income, finance, balance of
payments, household expenditure; social statistics;
regional statistics; employment/unemployment
data; census; economy.

Trade and statistical information:
Statistics on: manufacturing of specific products,
selected service industries, invisible trade, gross
national product, balance of payments, price
indices, social and regional trends, census and
demographic data, social surveys and social
historical data.

Library catalogue:
All or part available online

Printed publications:
Annual Abstract of Statistics
Britain: An official handbook
Economic and Labour Market Review
Family Spending

Monthly Digest (with annual supplement)
National Income and Expenditure 'Blue Book'
(annual)
Population Trends (quarterly)
Regional Trends (annual)
Social Trends (annual)
UK Balance of Payments 'Pink Book' (annual)
UK National Accounts
Health Statistics Quarterly
Health in England 1998: Investigating the links
between social inequalities and health costs
Order printed publications from: Palgrave Macmillan
for all ONS Publications

Electronic and video publications:
25 years of Social Trends
Health of Adult Britain
Index to British Place Names
Mortality 1900 to date
PACSTAT

Publications list:
Available online and in print

Access to staff:
Contact by letter, by telephone, by fax, by e-mail
and in person. Appointment necessary.
Hours: Mon to Fri, 0900 to 1700

Access for disabled people:
Ramped entry; toilet facilities

Also at:
Office for National Statistics
Segensworth Road, Titchfield, Fareham,
Hampshire, PO15 5RR; tel: 0845 601 3034; e-
mail: info@ons.gov.uk

OFFICE FOR NATIONAL STATISTICS LIBRARY (LONDON)

Acronym or abbreviation: ONS

1 Drummond Gate, London, SW1V 2QQ

Tel: 0845 6013034\ Minicom no. 01633 812399
Fax: 01633 652747
E-mail: info@statistics.gov.uk

Website:
http://www.statistics.gov.uk
General website address for ONS, descriptions of
ONS publications.

Enquiries:
Enquiries to: Librarian

Founded:
1996

Organisation type and purpose:
National government body.

Subject coverage:
Demography, epidemiology, vital registration e.g.
births, deaths and marriages, survey methodology,
census, economic and financial data, business data,
data from the government's statistical service.

**Museum or gallery collection, archive, or library
special collection:**
All published census data from 1801 onwards
Demographic and health statistics 1837 onwards
Government social survey reports 1941 onwards
International statistics, e.g. UN, WHO

Publications list:
Available online

Access to staff:
Contact by letter, by telephone, by fax, by e-mail
and in person
Hours: Mon to Fri, 0900 to 1700

Access to building, collection or gallery:
No prior appointment required
Hours: Mon to Fri, 0900 to 1700

Access for disabled people:
Ramped entry, toilet facilities

Branch library:
Segensworth Road
Titchfield, Fareham, Hampshire, PO15 5RR

Other addresses:
Office for National Statistics Library (Newport)
Government Buildings, Cardiff Road, Newport,
Gwent, NP9 1XG; tel: 0845 6013034

OFFICE OF COMMUNICATIONS

Acronym or abbreviation: OFCOM

Riverside House, 2a Southwark Bridge Road,
London SE1 9HA

Tel: 020 7981 3000
Fax: 020 7981 3333

Website:
http://www.ofcom.org.uk

Enquiries:
Enquiries to: Information Officer
Direct e-mail: ofcomnews@ofcom.org.uk

Founded:
1984

Formerly called:
Office of Telecommunications (OFTEL)

Organisation type and purpose:
National government body.
Non-ministerial government department.

Subject coverage:
Telecommunications, information technology,
consumer affairs and competition policy.

**Museum or gallery collection, archive, or library
special collection:**
Public register of licences, approved apparatus and
approved maintainers of the apparatus (visitors
by prior appointment)

Library catalogue:
All or part available in-house

Printed publications:
Annual Reports (available from The Stationery
Office only)
Consumer Guides including:
Choosing a telephone company, 2001
Economic Working Papers
How to complain about your telephone service,
2001
Your rights as a telephone user, 2001
What is Oftel? 2001
OFTEL Information Notes and Statements
OFTEL News (quarterly)
Statistical Notes
Technical Publications
Variety of publications including those on:
Telecommunication for Disabled and Elderly
People
Statements & Consultative documents
Determinations
Numbering, including: Access Codes for Directory
Enquiries Services (2002)
Licensing

Publications list:
Available online and in print

Access to staff:
Contact by letter, by telephone, by fax, by e-mail
and via website. Appointment necessary.
Hours: Mon to Fri, 0930 to 1200 and 1400 to 1600
Special comments: Access only allowed by prior
appointment.

Parent body:
Department of Trade and Industry – for Library
Service

OFFICE OF FAIR TRADING

Acronym or abbreviation: OFT

Fleetbank House, 2–6 Salisbury Square, London,
EC4Y 8JX

Tel: 020 7211 8000
Fax: 020 7211 8800
E-mail: enquiries@oft.gov.uk

Website:
http://www.oft.gov.uk

Summaries of recent reports, consumer
information, publications list.

Enquiries:
Enquiries to: Publicity Officer
Direct e-mail: laura.osborne@ oft.gsi.gov.uk

Founded:
1973

Organisation type and purpose:
National government body.

Subject coverage:
Consumer affairs, consumer credit (including
trader guidance), competition policy, monopolies,
mergers, restrictive trade practices, anti-
competitive practices, estate agency.

**Museum or gallery collection, archive, or library
special collection:**
Consumer Credit Licences public register
Estate Agents Act public register
Restrictive Trading Agreements public register

Non-library collection catalogue:
All or part available online

Printed publications:
Annual Report
Wide range of leaflets, booklets, posters; videos
covering consumer topics, competition policy,
trader guidance on consumer credit (available
free of charge)

Publications list:
Available online and in print

Access to staff:
Contact by letter, by telephone, by fax, by e-mail
and via website
Hours: Mon to Fri, 0900 to 1700

Access to building, collection or gallery:
Prior appointment required
Special comments: Access only to public registers by
appointment.

Common service ties exist with the:
Department of Trade and Industry

Parliamentary responsibility lies with the:
Secretary of State for Trade and Industry

OFFICE OF GAS AND ELECTRICITY MARKETS

Acronym or abbreviation: Ofgem

9 Millbank, London, SW1P 3GE

Tel: 020 7901 7000
Fax: 020 7901 7066
E-mail: library@ofgem.gov.uk

Website:
http://www.ofgem.gov.uk

Enquiries:
Enquiries to: Librarian
Direct tel: 020 7901 7003
Direct e-mail: keith.smith@ofgem.gov.uk

Founded:
1999

Created by the merger of:
OFFER and OFGAS (year of change 1999)

Organisation type and purpose:
National government body, advisory body,
statutory body, regulatory body.
Independent government watchdog for the gas
and electricity industry.

Subject coverage:
Regulation of the gas and electricity industry.

**Museum or gallery collection, archive, or library
special collection:**
Various journals on the gas, electricity and utility
industry

Library catalogue:
All or part available in-house

Printed publications:
Publications include:
Consultation documents and general reports (free)

continued overleaf

Publications list:
Available online and in print

Access to staff:
Contact by telephone and by e-mail
Hours: Mon to Fri, 800 to 1730

Access to building, collection or gallery:
Prior appointment required

Access for disabled people:
Access to all public areas, toilet facilities

OFFICE OF GOVERNMENT COMMERCE

Acronym or abbreviation: OGC

Rosebery Court, St Andrews Business Park, Norwich, Norfolk, NR7 0HS

Tel: 0845 000 4999
Fax: 01603 704817

OFFICE OF HEALTH ECONOMICS

Acronym or abbreviation: OHE

12 Whitehall, London, SW1A 2DY

Tel: 020 7930 9203
Fax: 020 7747 1419

Website:
http://www.ohe.org
Mostly publications information.

Enquiries:
Enquiries to: Business Manager
Direct tel: 020 7930 9203 ext 1464
Direct e-mail: myork@ohe.org
Other contacts: (1) Associate Director (2) Secretary for (1) work of the OHE (2) OHE publications.

Founded:
1962

Organisation type and purpose:
Consultancy, research organisation, publishing house.

Subject coverage:
Economics of the pharmaceutical industry, healthcare, health technology, assessment, biotechnology industry and related public policy issues.

Trade and statistical information:
Compendium of Health Statistics, providing statistical data on health and healthcare in the UK and comparative data with economically developed nations.
Health Economics Evaluation Database (HEED) containing approximately 23,500 economic evaluations, carefully selected for use by health economists.

Printed publications:
Compendium of Health Statistics
OHE information sheets and briefings
Monographs and briefings on subject areas listed

Electronic and video publications:
HEED – Health Economics Evaluation Database – available from OHE/IFPMA Database Limited, phone and fax as for OHE. Monthly CD-ROM
Compendium of Health Statistics (CD-ROM)
Internet version due to be launched 2002

Publications list:
Available online and in print

Access to staff:
Contact by letter, by telephone, by fax, by e-mail and via website
Hours: Mon to Fri, 0900 to 1700

Access to building, collection or gallery:
Prior appointment required

Access for disabled people:
Ramped entry

Funded by:
Association of the British Pharmaceutical Industry 12 Whitehall, London, SW1A 2DY; tel: 020 7930 3477; fax: 020 7747 1411; e-mail: abpi@abpi.org.uk

OFFICE OF MANPOWER ECONOMICS

Acronym or abbreviation: OME

6th Floor, Kingsgate House, 66–74 Victoria Street, London, SW1E 6SW

Tel: 020 7215 8252
Fax: 020 7215 4445

Website:
http://www.ome.uk.com
Information on the Independent Pay Review Bodies including the Police Negotiating and Advisory Boards.

Enquiries:
Enquiries to: Information Officer

Founded:
1971

Organisation type and purpose:
Secretariat to the Independent Pay Review Bodies and Police Boards

Access to staff:
Contact by letter and by telephone
Hours: Mon to Fri, 0900 to 1700

Access for disabled people:
Toilet facilities

OFFICE OF THE CHIEF RABBI

Formal name: Office of the Chief Rabbi of the United Hebrew Congregations of the Commonwealth

Adler House, 735 High Road, London, N12 0US

Tel: 020 8343 6301
Fax: 020 8343 6310
E-mail: info@chiefrabbi.org

Website:
http://www.chiefrabbi.org

Enquiries:
Enquiries to: Chief Executive
Other contacts: Director of Communications for media.

Founded:
1700

Organisation type and purpose:
Religious institution.

Subject coverage:
Judaism.

Museum or gallery collection, archive, or library special collection:
Anglo-Jewish historical archives

Printed publications:
Radical Then, Radical Now – Letter in the Scroll (American ed., 2001, Harper Collins London)
Celebrating Life (2000, Harper Collins London)
New Revised Edition: Politics of Hope (Vintage, 2000)
Morals and Markets – Institute of Economic Affairs London 1999 (pamphlet, issued by Institute of Economic Affairs)
The Politics of Hope (1997, Jonathan Cape, London)
Christian-Jewish Dialogue (Fry H, Sacks J, 1996, University of Exeter Press)

Publications list:
Available online and in print

Access to staff:
Contact by letter, by telephone, by fax, by e-mail and via website. Appointment necessary.
Hours: Mon to Fri, 0900 to 1700

Access to building, collection or gallery:
Prior appointment required

Houses the:
Chief Rabbinate of the British Commonwealth

Other addresses:
Court of The Chief Rabbi

OFFICE OF THE PARLIAMENTARY AND HEALTH SERVICE OMBUDSMAN

Acronym or abbreviation: PHSO

Millbank Tower, Millbank, London, SW1P 4QP

Tel: 0845 015 4033
Fax: 0300 061 4000
E-mail: phso.enquiries@ombudsman.org.uk

Website:
http://www.ombudsman.org.uk

Enquiries:
Enquiries to: Information Manager
Direct tel: 0300 061 3997
Direct fax: 0300 061 1565
Direct e-mail: lrc@ombudsman.gsi.gov.uk

Founded:
1967

Organisation type and purpose:
Statutory body.
Investigation of complaints by members of the public who have suffered injustice through maladministration by government departments or certain public bodies, or the National Health Service.

Subject coverage:
Ombudsman schemes.

Printed publications:
See list online, or leaflet available

Access to staff:
Contact by letter, by telephone, by fax, by e-mail and via website
Hours: Mon to Fri, 0900 to 1700

Access to building, collection or gallery:
No prior appointment required

OFFICE OF THE REPRESENTATIVE OF NOVI SAD

Acronym or abbreviation: ORNS

Glebelands, Star Lane, Rockland St Mary, Norwich, Norfolk, NR14 7BX

Tel: 01508 480262
Fax: 01508 480262
E-mail: orns@lineone.net

Enquiries:
Enquiries to: Appointed Representative

Founded:
1999

Organisation type and purpose:
To represent the city of Novi Sad in Great Britain and elsewhere.

Subject coverage:
Information on Novi Sad and its environs, information for businesses, assistance in making commercial contacts.

Access to staff:
Contact by letter, by telephone, by fax and by e-mail
Hours: Mon to Fri, 0900 to 1700

Links with:
British Embassy
Belgrade
Serbian Embassy
London

OFFICE OF TIBET

Tibet House, 1 Culworth Street, London, NW8 7AF

Tel: 020 7722 5378
Fax: 020 7722 0362

E-mail: info@tibet.com

Website:
http://www.tibet.com
Information on Tibet including on the Central
Tibetan Administration of His Holiness the Dalai
Lama.

Enquiries:
Enquiries to: Secretary / Press & Information Officer

Founded:
1981

Organisation type and purpose:
To represent the Central Tibetan Administration of
His Holiness the Dalai Lama based in Dharamsala,
India. The Office of Tibet based in London is the
official agency of His Holiness the Dalai Lama for
the UK, Northern Europe, the Baltic States and
Poland.

Subject coverage:
Information on Tibet and Tibetan affairs, including
the Central Tibetan Administration of His Holiness
the Dalai Lama.

**Museum or gallery collection, archive, or library
special collection:**
Small information library on Tibet and Tibetan
affairs

Publications list:
Available in print

Access to staff:
Contact by letter, by telephone, by fax, by e-mail
and via website. Appointment necessary.
Hours: Mon to Fri, 0900 to 1700

Parent body:
Central Tibetan Administration of H H the Dalai
Lama
Dharamsala, India; tel: +91 1892 222457; fax: +91
1892 224957; e-mail: diir@gov.tibet.net; website:
http://www.tibet.net

OFFICE OF WATER SERVICES

Acronym or abbreviation: OFWAT

Centre City Tower, 7 Hill Street, Birmingham, B5
4UA

Tel: 0121 625 1300\ Minicom no. 0121 625 1422
Fax: 0121 625 1400
E-mail: enquiries@ofwat.gsi.gov.uk

Website:
http://www.ofwat.gov.uk

Enquiries:
Enquiries to: Librarian & Information Services
Manager
Direct tel: 0121 625 1361
Direct fax: 0121 625 1362

Founded:
1989

Organisation type and purpose:
National government body.
Central government department.
Economic regulator for the water industry.

Subject coverage:
Water industry; economic regulation, privatisation,
consumer protection.

**Museum or gallery collection, archive, or library
special collection:**
Director General's register

Printed publications:
Annual Report
Customer issues (some free)
Documents on charging for water and water
metering (some free)
Reports, guidelines, consultation, occasional and
research papers, reviews
Variety of information notes and leaflets (free)

Electronic and video publications:
July Return 1996 (CD-ROM)
July Return 1997 (CD-ROM)
July Return 1998 (CD-ROM)
July Return 1999 (CD-ROM)

July Return 2000 (CD-ROM)
Special agreements register (disc)

Publications list:
Available online and in print

Access to staff:
Contact by letter, by telephone, by fax, by e-mail
and via website. Appointment necessary.
Hours: Mon to Fri, 0930 to 1630

Access to building, collection or gallery:
Prior appointment required
Hours: Mon to Fri, 0930 to 1630

Has:
10 Customer Service Committees and Regulates 24
companies

OFFICE OF WATER SERVICES – COMPANIES REGULATED BY OFWAT

**Water and Sewerage Companies Regulated by
OFWAT:**
Anglian Water Services Limited
Henderson House, Lancaster Way, Huntingdon,
Cambridgeshire, PE29 6XQ; tel: 01480 323000;
fax: 01480 323115; website: www.anglianwater
.co.uk
Dwr Cymru Cyfyngedig (Welsh Water)
Pentwyn Road, Nelson, Treharris, Mid
Glamorgan, CF46 6LY; tel: 01443 452300; fax:
01443 452323; website: http://www.dwrcymru.co
.uk
Northumbrian Water Limited
Abbey Road, Pity Me, Durham, DH1 5FJ; tel:
0191 383 2222; fax: 0191 384 1920; website: http://
www.nwl.co.uk/
Severn Trent Water Limited
2297 Coventry Road, Sheldon, Birmingham, B26
3PU; tel: 0121 722 4000; fax: 0121 722 4800;
website: http://www.stwater.co.uk
South West Water Limited
Peninsular House, Rydon Lane, Exeter, EX2 7HR;
tel: 01392 446688; fax: 01392 434966; website:
http://www.south-west-water.co.uk
Southern Water Services Limited
Southern House, Yeoman Road, Worthing,
Sussex, BN13 3NX; tel: 01903 264444; fax: 01903
262185; website: http://www.southernwater.co
.uk
Thames Water Utilities Limited
Clearwater Court, Vastern Road, Reading,
Berkshire, RG1 8DB; tel: 0118 373 8000; fax: 0118
373 8500; website: http://www.thames-water
.com
United Utilities Water plc
Dawson House, Great Sankey, Warrington, WA5
3LW; tel: 01925 234000; fax: 01925 233360;
website: http://www.unitedutilities.com/
Wessex Water Services Limited
Claverton Down Road, Claverton, Bath, BA2
7WW; tel: 01225 526000; fax: 01225 526000;
website: http://www.wessexwater.co.uk
Yorkshire Water Services Limited
Western House, Western Way, Bradford, BD6
2LZ; tel: 01274 691111; fax: 01274 604764;
website: http://www.yorkshirewater.com/

Water only Companies Regulated by OFWAT:
Albion Water (Shotton) Limited
Ground floor Riverview House, Beavor Lane,
Hammersmith, London, W6 9AR; tel: 020 8748
9991; fax: 020 8741 6060; website: http://www
.enviro-logic.com/
Bournemouth and West Hampshire Water plc
George Jessel House, Francis Avenue,
Bournemouth, BH11 8NB; tel: 01202 591111; fax:
01202 597022; website: http://www.bwhwater.co
.uk
Bristol Water plc
PO Box 218, Bridgwater Road, Bristol, BS99 7AU;
tel: 0117 966 5881; fax: 0117 963 4576
Cambridge Water Company pls
41 Rustat Road, Cambridge, CB1 3QS; tel: 01223
403000; fax: 01223 214052; website: http://www
.cambridge-water.co.uk/

Cholderton and District Water Company Limited
Estate House, Cholderton, Salisbury, Wiltshire,
SP4 0DR; tel: 01980 629203; fax: 01980 629307
Dee Valley Water plc
Packsaddle, Wrexham Road, Rhostyllen,
Wrexham, Clwyd, LL14 7EH; tel: 01978 846946;
fax: 01978 846888
Essex and Sufflok Water (Now part of
Northumbrian Water Limited)
Hall Street, Chelmsford, Essex, CM2 0HH; tel:
01245 491234; fax: 01245 212345; website: http://
www.eswater.co.uk
Folkestone and Dover Water Services Limited
Cherry Garden Lane, Folkestone, Kent, CT19
4QB; tel: 01303 298800; fax: 01303 276712;
website: http://www.fdws.co.uk
Hartlepool Water plc
3 Lancaster Road, Hartlepool, TS24 8LW; tel:
01429 868555; fax: 01429 858000
Mid Kent Water plc
PO Box45, High Street, Snodland, Kent, ME6
5AH; tel: 01634 240313; fax: 01634 242764;
website: http://www.midkent.co.uk
Portsmouth Water plc
PO Box 8, West Street, Havant, Hampshire, PO9
1LG; tel: 023 9249 9888; fax: 023 9245 3632;
website: http://www.portsmouthwater.co.uk
South East Water plc
3 Church Road, Haywards Heath, West Sussex,
RH16 3NY; tel: 01444 448200; fax: 01444 413200;
website: http://www.southeastwater.co.uk/
South Staffordshire Water plc
Green Lane, Walsall, West Midlands, WS2 7PD;
tel: 01922 638282; fax: 01922 723631; website:
http://www.south-staffs-water.co.uk/
Sutton and East Surrey Water plc
London Road, Redhill, Surrey, RH1 1LJ; tel:
01737 772000; fax: 01737 766807; website: http://
www.waterplc.com
Tendring Hundred Water Services
Mill Hill, Manningtree, Essex, CO11 2AZ; tel:
01206 399200; fax: 01206 399210; website: http://
www.thws.co.uk
Three Valleys Water plc
PO Box 48, Bishop's Rise, Hatfield, Hertfordshire,
AL10 9HL; tel: 01707 268111; fax: 01707 277333;
website: http://www.3valleys.co.uk

OFFICERS' ASSOCIATION

1st Floor, Mountbarrow House, 6–20 Elizabeth
Street, London, SW1W 9RB

Tel: 020 7808 4160
Fax: 020 7808 4161
E-mail: info@officersassociation.org.uk

Website:
http://www.officersassociation.org.uk

Founded:
1920

Organisation type and purpose:
The Officers' Association, which was founded 90
years ago, is the only charity dedicated exclusively
to supporting officers and ex-officers from all three
services and their dependants.

Subject coverage:
Providing employment services for service leavers
and ex-serving officers at all stages of their
working lives, and benevolence services in the
form of financial and welfare support.

Access to staff:
Contact by letter, by telephone, by fax and by e-
mail
Hours: Mon to Fri, 0900 to 1700

Member organisation of:
COBSEO

OFFSHORE ENGINEERING INFORMATION SERVICE

Heriot-Watt University Library, Edinburgh, EH14
4AS

Tel: 0131 451 3579
Fax: 0131 451 3164

continued overleaf

E-mail: oeis@hw.ac.uk

Website:
http://www.techextra.ac.uk/offshore
Search services, alerting services and the Petroleum and Offshore Engineering Bulletin containing bibliographic information.

Founded:
1974

Organisation type and purpose:
Registered charity, university department or institute, consultancy, research organisation.

Subject coverage:
Petroleum and offshore engineering, marine technology, petroleum and marine environmental protection, offshore health and safety.

Printed publications:
Information Bulletin (monthly)
Marine Technology Microthesaurus

Electronic and video publications:
Information Bulletin (monthly, by email)

Access to staff:
Contact by letter and by e-mail. Appointment necessary. All charged.
Hours: Mon to Fri, 0900 to 1700

Parent body:
Heriot-Watt University Library

OFFSHORE SUPPORT VESSEL ISSUES COMMITTEE

Chamber of Shipping, Carthusian Court, 12 Carthusian Street, London, EC1M 6EZ

Tel: 020 7417 2819
Fax: 020 7600 1534
E-mail: robert.ashdown@british.shipping.org

Website:
http://www.british-shipping.org/

Enquiries:
Enquiries to: Secretary

Organisation type and purpose:
Trade association.
Represents the owners and operators of UK-based Offshore Support Vessels (OSV's).

Subject coverage:
Offshore support vessels serving oil and gas installations.

Access to staff:
Contact by letter and by e-mail
Hours: Mon to Fri, 0900 to 1700

One of the Committees of the:
Chamber of Shipping

OIL AND COLOUR CHEMISTS ASSOCIATION

Acronym or abbreviation: OCCA

Priory House, 967 Harrow Road, Wembley, Middlesex, HA0 2SF

Tel: 020 8908 1086
Fax: 020 8908 1219
E-mail: gensec@occa.org.uk

Website:
http://www.surfex2010.net
http://surfacecoatingsonline.net

Enquiries:
Enquiries to: General Secretary
Direct e-mail: enquiries@occa.org.uk
Other contacts: Assistant General Secretary

Founded:
1917

Organisation type and purpose:
Learned society, professional body (membership is by qualification), registered charity, training organisation.

Subject coverage:
Raw materials, plant, equipment and services for the paint, ink, resins, varnishes, drying oils, lacquers, adhesives, and treated fabrics industries; organic surface coatings in general.

Library catalogue:
All or part available online and in print

Printed publications:
Colour Photography: Past Present and Future
Physical Chemical Aspects of Pigment Application
Pigments: structures and synthetic properties
Student Monograph Series (8 titles to date)
Surface Coatings International (6 issues a year)
Journal of Coatings Technology and Research (4 issues a year)
UK Surface Coatings Handbook (annually)

Electronic and video publications:
UK Surface Coatings Handbook

Publications list:
Available online and in print

Access to staff:
Contact by letter, by telephone, by fax, by e-mail and via website
Hours: Mon to Fri, 0900 to 1700

Access to building, collection or gallery:
No access other than to staff

OLDHAM COLLEGE

Rochdale Road, Oldham, Lancashire, OL9 6AA

Tel: 0161 624 5214
Fax: 0161 785 4234
E-mail: info@oldham.ac.uk

Website:
http://www.oldham.ac.uk/
Prospectus, general college information, employment opportunities.

Enquiries:
Enquiries to: Librarian

Organisation type and purpose:
Suitable for ages: 16+.

Subject coverage:
Mechanical, electrical, electronic and production engineering; building; business studies; mathematics; computing; catering; performing arts.

Access to staff:
Contact by telephone, by fax, by e-mail and via website
Hours: Mon to Fri, 0900 to 1700

Access to building, collection or gallery:
No prior appointment required

Access for disabled people:
Level entry

OLDHAM LIBRARIES

Union Street, Oldham, Lancashire, OL1 1DN

Tel: 0161 911 4634/4645 general; 4643 Reference Library
Fax: 0161 911 4630
E-mail: oldham.library@oldham.gov.uk

Website:
http://www.oldham.gov.uk
Oldham Council web page.

Enquiries:
Enquiries to: Principal Libraries Officer
Direct tel: 0161 911 4632

Organisation type and purpose:
Local government body, public library.

Subject coverage:
General.

Museum or gallery collection, archive, or library special collection:
British Standards on microfiche
Cobbett Collection (books by and about William Cobbett, 1762–1835)

Publications list:
Available in print

Access to staff:
Contact by letter, by telephone, by fax, by e-mail, in person and via website
Hours: Mon, Wed, Thu, 0930 to 1900; Tue, Fri, 9300 to 1700; Sat, 0930 to 1600

Access for disabled people:
Ramped entry, access to all public areas, toilet facilities

OLDHAM LOCAL STUDIES AND ARCHIVES

84 Union Street, Oldham, Lancashire, OL1 1DN

Tel: 0161 770 4654
E-mail: archives@oldham.gov.uk

Website:
http://www.oldham.gov.uk/local_studies
Handouts.

Enquiries:
Enquiries to: Local Studies Officer
Other contacts: Archives Officer (for use of archives)

Founded:
1885

Organisation type and purpose:
Local government body, public library.

Subject coverage:
History of Oldham, records of predecessor authorities, Oldham County Borough, Urban Districts of Chadderton, Crompton, Failsworth, Lees, Royton, Saddleworth, Springhead and Uppermill.

Museum or gallery collection, archive, or library special collection:
Butterworth MSS including press reports 1829 to 1843, notes for Baines History of Lancashire (1836)
Census returns (microfilm)
Extensive record of local Co-operative Society and textile trade unions
Higson antiquarian collection
Newspapers including the Oldham Chronicle 1854 to date, Oldham Standard 1859–1946 (microfilm)
Oldham Walton Archive (collection of material about Sir William Walton)
Oral history
Parish Registers (microfilm)
Personal papers of Dame Sarah and Marjory Lees of Werneth Park including suffragette material
Rowbottom Diaries: daily events in Oldham 1787–1829
Books, pamphlets, maps, press cuttings
20,000 photographs of Oldham's past

Non-library collection catalogue:
All or part available in-house

Printed publications:
Illustrated books on local history including:
Oldham Brave Oldham: An illustrated history of Oldham
Cotton Mills of Oldham
Looking Back At series (Lees, Crompton, Royton)
The Wild Flowers of Oldham

Microform publications:
Butterworth Manuscripts

Publications list:
Available online and in print

Access to staff:
Contact by letter, by telephone, by e-mail and in person
Hours: Mon, Thu, 1000 to 1900; Tue, 1000 to 1400; Wed, Fri, 1000 to 1700; Sat, 1000 to 1600

Access for disabled people:
Ramped entry, toilet facilities

OMNIBUS SOCIETY

Acronym or abbreviation: OS

100 Sandwell Street, Walsall, WS1 3EB

Website:
http://www.omnibussoc.org

Enquiries:
Enquiries to: Secretary

Founded:
1929

Organisation type and purpose:
Voluntary organisation, registered charity (charity number 1048887).
Independent society.
To study every aspect of the history and development of road passenger transport.

Subject coverage:
Public road passenger transport, mainly UK but to a lesser extent abroad, traffic, engineering and methods of operation of buses, coaches, trams and trolleybuses, current and historical.

Museum or gallery collection, archive, or library special collection:
The society has a large collection of timetables, fare tables, directories, tickets and other items, many dating back 60 to 70 years

Printed publications:
Area Bulletins
Historical Bulletins
Omnibus Magazine (6 times a year)

Access to staff:
Contact by letter and via website. Appointment necessary. Non-members charged.
Hours: Mon to Fri, 0900 to 1700

Access for disabled people:
Access available at library

ONE NORTH EAST

Stella House, Goldcrest Way, Newburn Riverside, Newcastle Upon Tyne, NE15 8NY

Tel: 0191 229 6200
Fax: 0191 229 6201
E-mail: enquiries@onenortheast.co.uk

Website:
http://www.onenortheast.co.uk
One North East is the Regional Development Agency set up in April 1999 to help the people of the North East create and sustain jobs, prosperity and a higher quality of life. The Agency is responsible to the people of the North East and to the Government.

Enquiries:
Enquiries to: Corporate Marketing Manager

Founded:
1999

Organisation type and purpose:
Regional development agency.

Subject coverage:
Economic, business and industrial information on the North of England, environment, investment, technologies, statistical data.

Non-library collection catalogue:
All or part available online and in print

Library catalogue:
All or part available online

Printed publications:
Annual Report, Regional Economic Strategy

Publications list:
Available online

Access to staff:
Contact by letter, by telephone, by fax, by e-mail and via website. Appointment necessary.
Hours: Mon to Fri, 0900 to 1700

Access for disabled people:
Ramped entry, access to all public areas, toilet facilities

ONE PARENT FAMILIES SCOTLAND

Acronym or abbreviation: OPFS

13 Gayfield Square, Edinburgh, EH1 3NX

Tel: 0131 556 3899/4563; 0808 801 0323 (Helpline)
Fax: 0131 557 7899
E-mail: info@opfs.org.uk

Website:
http://www.opfs.org.uk

Enquiries:
Enquiries to: Information Officer

Founded:
1945

Organisation type and purpose:
Membership organisation (membership is free), present number of members: 400, a charitable company limited by guarantee (company registered at Edinburgh 94860, charity number SCO 06403).
Informing, supporting and inspiring lone parents and services for lone parents and other families.
Advice and support to lone parents in Scotland

Subject coverage:
One-parent families, all organisations working for one-parent families, children, divorce and separation, conciliation, health, housing, holidays, childcare, poverty, maintenance, social security/tax, rights issues, statistics, women's issues.

Information services:
29 fact sheets for lone parents, a quarterly e-bulletin and a web site.

Special visitor services:
Visits can be arranged for agencies from other countries.

Education services:
Training programme for lone parents and agencies working with lone parents.

Services for disabled people:
Fact sheets for lone-parent families with disabilities.

Museum or gallery collection, archive, or library special collection:
Library of books, leaflets and press cuttings

Printed publications:
29 Fact sheets – free to lone parents
Young Parents Survival Guide
Order printed publications from: e-mail: info@opfs.org.uk

Electronic and video publications:
see website: http://www.opfs.org.uk

Publications list:
Available online and in print

Access to staff:
Contact by letter, by telephone, by fax, by e-mail and via website. Appointment necessary.
Hours: Mon to Fri, 0930 to 1630

Access to building, collection or gallery:
Headquarters office in first floor flat
Hours: Mon to Fri, 0930 to 1630

Access for disabled people:
Limited access

Works in association with:
Parenting Across Scotland
1 Boroughloch Square, Edinburgh, EH8 9NJ; tel: 0131 319 8071; e-mail: pas@children1st.org.uk; website: http://www.parentingacrossscotland.org.

ONE PLUS ONE

Formal name: One Plus One Marriage and Partnership Research

1 Benjamin Street, London, EC1M 5QG

Tel: 020 7553 9530
Fax: 020 7553 9550
E-mail: info@oneplusone.org.uk

Website:
http://www.oneplusone.org.uk

Enquiries:
Enquiries to: Information Officer
Other contacts: Communications Co-ordinator for press enquiries.

Founded:
1971

Organisation type and purpose:
Registered charity (charity number 1087994), research organisation.
To conduct research into all aspects of marriage and partnership, and to put research findings into use in initiatives such as training programmes.

Subject coverage:
All aspects of marriage, divorce and relationships, including both statistics, research reports, international and historical trends.

Information services:
Online resources for academics, students, researchers and practitioners involved in the field of family and relationships.

Museum or gallery collection, archive, or library special collection:
Marriage manuals of historic interest.
Information on One plus One research and projects

Library catalogue:
All or part available in-house

Printed publications:
Growing together of drifting apart? Children with disabilities and their parents' relationship (F. Glenn, available online)
Informing unmarried parents about their legal rights at birth registration (R. Panades, R. Corney, C. Ayles, J. Reynolds, F. Hovsepian, available online)
Fragile Families and Child Wellbeing (One Plus One, available online)
How helping works: Towards a shared model of process (One Plus One, Parentline Plus and The Centre for Parent and Child Support, available online)
Marital Breakdown and the Health of the Nation (F. McAllister, ed., £5)
Not in Front of the Children? (J. Reynolds, ed., £9.99)
One plus One Information Sheets (available free online)
The Relationship Revolution (D. Dormer, £9)

Publications list:
Available online

Access to staff:
Contact by e-mail and via website. Appointment necessary. Non-members charged.
Hours: Mon to Fri, 1000 to 1600

Access to building, collection or gallery:
Prior appointment required.
Hours: Library; Mon to Fri, 1000 to 1600.
Special comments: Library available by appointment only.

Access for disabled people:
Access to all public areas.

ONLINE DATA SERVICES

Acronym or abbreviation: ODS

74 Chancery Lane, London, WC2A 1AA

Tel: 020 7404 2100
Fax: 020 7404 8600
E-mail: theapexgroup@netscapeonline.co.uk

Enquiries:
Enquiries to: Managing Director

Founded:
1998

Organisation type and purpose:
Consultancy, research organisation.
Business and Information Publisher.

continued overleaf

Subject coverage:
Market intelligence reports on business, retailing, leisure, consumer and retail markets. Bespoke market and business analysis.

Trade and statistical information:
Market intelligence on wide variety of UK markets. Special projects on Europe/World by request.

Printed publications:
List of all publications free of charge, by fax, post or email

Publications list:
Available in print

Access to staff:
Contact by letter, by telephone and by fax
Hours: Mon to Fri, 0900 to 1700

Access to building, collection or gallery:
No access other than to staff

Parent body:
The Apex Group
  at the same address

OPEN AND DISTANCE LEARNING QUALITY COUNCIL

Acronym or abbreviation: ODLQC

44 Bedford Row, London, WC1R 4LL

Tel: 020 7447 2543
E-mail: info@odlqc.org.uk

Website:
http://www.odlqc.org.uk

Enquiries:
Enquiries to: Chief Executive

Founded:
1969

Organisation type and purpose:
Registered charity (charity number 325125).
Independent body, formed with the co-operation of the Secretary of State for Education and Science. Accrediting body and advisory service for Open and Distance Learning.

Subject coverage:
Education, training and tuition, open and distance learning methods and activities, standards and improvement, new techniques, assessment, quality control and accreditation.

Printed publications:
Buyer's Guide to Distance Learning and information booklet listing accredited organisations and courses offered (single copies free, possible postal charge for multiple copies)

Access to staff:
Contact by letter, by telephone, by fax, by e-mail and via website
Hours: Mon to Fri, 0900 to 1700

OPEN COLLEGE NETWORK LONDON REGION

Acronym or abbreviation: OCNLR

Unit 15, Angel Gate, 326 City Road, London, EC1V 2SF

Tel: 020 7278 5511
Fax: 020 7833 8289
E-mail: enquiries@ocnlr.org.uk

Website:
http://www.ocnlr.org.uk

Enquiries:
Enquiries to: Chief Executive

Organisation type and purpose:
Awarding body.

Access to staff:
Contact by letter, by telephone, by fax and by e-mail
Hours: Mon to Fri, 0900 to 1700

OPEN COLLEGE OF THE ARTS

Acronym or abbreviation: OCA

Unit 1B, Redbrook Business Park, Wilthorpe Road, Barnsley, South Yorkshire, S75 1JN

Tel: 0800 731 2116
Fax: 01226 730838
E-mail: enquiries@oca-uk.com

Website:
http://www.oca-uk.com
Comprehensive guide to all courses, including BA hons Degrees in creative arts, painting and photography.
http://www.weareoca.com
Open College of the Arts blog.
http://oca-elements.com
This site has been developed to provide fundamental learning 'nuggets' across all the areas in which the Open College of the Arts provides courses. The Elements may be videos, audio or text, and are freely available to all OCA students as well as the general public. The content on this site complements OCA course material, but is not integral to it. It is designed to help students refresh, revise and get up to speed so that they are ready to embark on OCA courses.

Enquiries:
Enquiries to: Academic Services
Direct tel: 01226 730495

Founded:
1987

Organisation type and purpose:
Registered charity (charity number 327446), suitable for ages: 16+.
Distance learning.

Subject coverage:
Art and design, painting, drawing, textiles, sculpture, garden design, interior design, music, calligraphy, creative writing, water colour, printmaking, art history, photography.

Printed publications:
Guide to Courses
Showcase newsletter
Order printed publications from: OCA

Access to staff:
Contact by letter, by telephone, by fax, by e-mail and via website
Hours: Office: Mon to Thu, 0900 to 1700; Fri, 0900 to 1600

Links with:
Buckinghamshire New University

OPEN SPACES SOCIETY

Formal name: Commons, Open Spaces and Footpaths Preservation Society
Acronym or abbreviation: OSS

25A Bell Street, Henley-on-Thames, Oxfordshire, RG9 2BA

Tel: 01491 573535
Fax: 01491 573051
E-mail: hq@oss.org.uk

Website:
http://www.oss.org.uk

Enquiries:
Enquiries to: General Secretary

Founded:
1865

Organisation type and purpose:
Learned society, professional body (membership is by subscription), present number of members: 2,600, voluntary organisation, registered charity (charity number 214753).

Subject coverage:
Public rights of way, protection of common land, village greens, open spaces, public paths, public access to the countryside.

Museum or gallery collection, archive, or library special collection:
Reports of the Society's work since 1868

Printed publications:
Information sheets
Open Space (magazine, 3 times a year)
Our Common Land: law and history of commons and village greens
Getting Greens Registered: a guide to law and procedure for town or village greens

Publications list:
Available online and in print

Access to staff:
Contact by letter, by telephone, by fax and by e-mail. Access for members only.
Hours: Mon to Fri, 0930 to 1730

OPEN UNIVERSITY

Acronym or abbreviation: OUCEM

Centre for Education in Medicine, Walton Hall, Crowther 208, Milton Keynes, Buckinghamshire, MK7 6AA

Tel: 01908 653776
Fax: 01908 659374
E-mail: oucem@open.ac.uk

Website:
http://iet.open.ac.uk/oucem/

Enquiries:
Enquiries to: Personal Assistant

Organisation type and purpose:
University department or institute. Training organisation, consultancy, research organisation, publishing house.
Postgraduate medical education.

Subject coverage:
Postgraduate and continuing medical education.

Printed publications:
An Evaluation Kit for Education in General Practice (£17 plus p&p)
The Place of Research in Medical Training (£15.80 plus p&p)
Career Choice, Development and Change in Medicine (£12.50 plus p&p)
Good Assessment Guide (£19.95)
Making Medical Audit Effective (£12.50 plus p&p)
Approaches to Experimental Learning, Course Delivery and Validation in Medicine (£6 plus p&p)
The Effectiveness in Continuing Professional Development (£8 plus p&p)
PEAKit: Postgraduate Educational Audit Kit (£22 plus p&p)
Pre-Registration House Officer Placements in General Practice (£15 plus p&p)
Evaluation of the Reforms to Higher Specialist Training (£25 plus p&p)
Good CPD Guide – A Practical guide to Managed CPD (£19.95 plus p&p)

Electronic and video publications:
Evaluation of the Reforms to Higher Specialist Training 1996–1999 (CD-ROM, £25 plus p&p)

Publications list:
Available online and in print

Access to staff:
Contact by letter, by telephone, by fax, by e-mail and via website. Appointment necessary.
Hours: Mon to Fri, 0830 to 1700

Access for disabled people:
Parking provided, ramped entry, access to all public areas, toilet facilities

Link with:
Open University (IET)
  Institute of Educational Technology, Milton Keynes, MK7 6AA; tel: 01908 274066; fax: 01908 654173; e-mail: iet-queries@open.ac.uk

OPEN UNIVERSITY LIBRARY AND LEARNING RESOURCES CENTRE

Acronym or abbreviation: OU

Walton Hall, Milton Keynes, Buckinghamshire, MK7 6AA

Tel: 01908 653138
Fax: 01908 653571
E-mail: lib-help@open.ac.uk

Website:
http://library.open.ac.uk
Information about the library, contacts, services to students and staff; online resources; access to OPAC; library news.

Enquiries:
Enquiries to: Director of Library Services
Direct tel: 01908 653254
Direct e-mail: n.whitsed@open.ac.uk

Founded:
1969

Organisation type and purpose:
University library.

Subject coverage:
Modern languages, arts, mathematics, computing, science, social sciences, technology, education, environmental sciences, educational research, management, vocational qualifications, health and social welfare, law.

Museum or gallery collection, archive, or library special collection:
Open University distance teaching materials, including television and radio programmes, illustrations and photographs relating to OU work; Fauvel history of mathematics collection held for the British Association for the History of Mathematics; Jennie Lee papers (archive); Betty Boothroyd papers (archive); Walter Perry (first OU vice-chancellor) papers (archive)

Non-library collection catalogue:
All or part available online

Library catalogue:
All or part available online

Access to staff:
Contact by letter, by telephone, by fax, by e-mail, in person and via website
Hours: Mon, Wed, 0830 to 1930; Tue, Thu, 0830 to 2100; Fri, 0830 to 1700; Sat 0900 to 1700

Access for disabled people:
Parking provided, access to all public areas, toilet facilities

OPEN UNIVERSITY PRESS

Acronym or abbreviation: Open UP

McGraw-Hill House, Shoppenhangers Road, Maidenhead, Berkshire, SL6 2QL

Tel: 01628 502500
Fax: 01628 770224
E-mail: enquiries@openup.co.uk

Website:
http://www.openup.co.uk
Details of books published.

Enquiries:
Enquiries to: Marketing Manager

Organisation type and purpose:
Publishing house.

Subject coverage:
Education, higher education, health and social welfare, sociology, politics, psychology, counselling, management, criminology, and media, film and cultural studies.

Printed publications:
New Books March – August
New Books September – February
Subject Catalogues
Order printed publications from: Open University Press, McGraw-Hill House, Shoppenhangers Road, Maidenhead, SL6 2QL

Publications list:
Available in print

Access to staff:
Contact by letter, by telephone, by fax, by e-mail and via website. Appointment necessary.
Hours: Mon to Fri, 0900 to 1700

OPTICAL CONSUMER COMPLAINTS SERVICE

Acronym or abbreviation: OCCS

PO Box 219, Petersfield, GU32 9BY

Tel: 0844 800 5071
Fax: 01730 265058
E-mail: postbox@opticalcomplaints.co.uk

Website:
http://www.opticalcomplaints.co.uk

Enquiries:
Enquiries to: Administrator

Founded:
1993

Organisation type and purpose:
Advisory body.
Provides mediation in disputes between patients and registered opticians relating to goods or services supplied by opticians.

Subject coverage:
Availability of professional advisers, optical matters, such as eye examination results, prescriptions, dispensing, spectacles, frames, lenses and contact lenses; resolution of complaints by negotiation; communication between practitioners and customers.

Printed publications:
Advice Leaflet
Annual Report

Access to staff:
Contact by letter, by telephone, by fax, by e-mail and via website
Hours: Mon to Fri, 0900 to 1700

Access to building, collection or gallery:
Not open to visitors

OR SOCIETY

Formal name: Operational Research Society
Acronym or abbreviation: ORS

Seymour House, 12 Edward Street, Birmingham, B1 2RX

Tel: 0121 233 9300
Fax: 0121 233 0321
E-mail: email@theorsociety.com

Website:
http://www.theorsociety.com

Enquiries:
Enquiries to: General Secretary

Founded:
1954

Organisation type and purpose:
Learned society, professional body (membership is by subscription), present number of members: 3,000 (charity number 313713), training organisation, research organisation, publishing house.
Conference organisation. Careers information provider.

Subject coverage:
Operational research, management science.

Museum or gallery collection, archive, or library special collection:
The Society has a library based at Brunel University Library, Uxbridge

Trade and statistical information:
Salaries in operational research.

Printed publications:
European Journal of Information Systems (6 times a year, members £8)
Journal of the Operational Research Society (monthly, £8 to members, non-members £880)
Monograph Series
OR Insight (quarterly, members free)
Inside OR (monthly, members only)
Knowledge Management Research and Practice (4 times a year, non-members £212, members £8)
Journal of Simulation

Access to staff:
Contact by letter, by telephone, by fax, by e-mail and via website. Appointment necessary.
Hours: Mon to Fri, 0830 to 1630

Member organisation of:
International Federation of Operational Research Societies (IFORS)

ORAL HISTORY SOCIETY

c/o Department of History, University of Essex, Wivenhoe Park, Colchester, Essex, CO4 3SQ

Tel: 020 7412 7404
Fax: 020 7412 7441
E-mail: rob.perks@bl.uk

Website:
http://www.ohs.org.uk

Enquiries:
Enquiries to: Secretary
Direct tel: 020 7412 7405
Other contacts: Editor

Founded:
1969

Organisation type and purpose:
International organisation, national organisation, advisory body, learned society (membership is by subscription), present number of members: c.1,000, voluntary organisation, registered charity (charity number 288805), training organisation, publishing house.
Regular exchange of information with US oral history organisations and other major fields of oral history activity worldwide.

Subject coverage:
Oral history, life-story research, reminiscence therapy, local history, sound recording and archiving, interviewing skills, women's history, ethnic community history, sociology and social studies.

Museum or gallery collection, archive, or library special collection:
Central oral history database at the British Library Sound Archive
Informed access to oral history collections throughout Great Britain

Printed publications:
Oral History (journal, twice a year)
Various free publicity leaflets

Publications list:
Available in print

Access to staff:
Contact by letter, by telephone, by fax and by e-mail
Hours: Mon to Fri, 1000 to 1800

Administers:
Oral History Society Regional Network
local membership through local representatives

Links with:
British Library Sound Archive
History Workshop Movement

ORCHESTRA OF ST JOHN'S

Acronym or abbreviation: OSJ

The White House, Eltham College, Grove Park Road, London, SE9 4QF

Tel: 020 8857 8579
Fax: 020 8857 9340

continued overleaf

E-mail: info@osj.org.uk

Enquiries:
Enquiries to: Assistant to the Chief Executive
Other contacts: (1) Marketing Manager; (2) Concerts
Director for (1) Promotional/Marketing; (2)
Concerts, Engagements.

Founded:
1967

Organisation type and purpose:
Service industry, registered charity (charity
number 289106), suitable for ages: all.
Orchestra (performing arts).
Education, concerts, activities.

Subject coverage:
Orchestral music.

Printed publications:
Quarterly Magazine, available direct

Electronic and video publications:
CD-ROMs for purchase available direct

Access to staff:
Contact by telephone and by e-mail
Hours: Mon to Fri, 0930 to 1730

Connections with:
Choir of the Orchestra of St John's (COSJ)

ORCHID SOCIETY OF GREAT BRITAIN

Acronym or abbreviation: OSGB

c/o 16 The Rise, Amersham, Buckinghamshire,
HP7 9AG

Tel: 01494 434730
E-mail: annerutter@dsl.pipex.com

Website:
http://www.orchid-society-gb.org.uk

Enquiries:
Enquiries to: Honorary Secretary

Founded:
1951

Organisation type and purpose:
Membership association (membership is by
subscription), present number of members: 1100,
voluntary organisation, registered charity (charity
number 261273).

Subject coverage:
Growing, conservation and identification of
orchids.

**Museum or gallery collection, archive, or library
special collection:**
Books, many out of print
Library of 35mm slides of orchids

Printed publications:
Quarterly journal (members only)

Access to staff:
Contact by letter, by telephone and by e-mail
Hours: Mon to Sun, 0900 to 1700
Special comments: Stamped addressed envelope
required for reply.

Affiliated to:
American Orchid Society
Royal Horticultural Society

ORDERS AND MEDALS RESEARCH SOCIETY

Acronym or abbreviation: OMRS

PO Box 1904, Southam, Warwickshire, CV47 2ZX

Tel: 01295 690009
E-mail: generalsecretary@omrs.org.uk

Website:
http://www.omrs.org.uk
Basic information on the Society.

Enquiries:
Enquiries to: General Secretary
Direct e-mail: membershipsecretary@omrs.org.uk

Founded:
1942

Organisation type and purpose:
Learned society (membership is by subscription,
election or invitation), present number of
members: 2750.

Subject coverage:
British Orders, decorations and medals, foreign
Orders etc, to a lesser extent, history, provenance
and description.

Printed publications:
Journal (quarterly)
Miscellany of Honour (occasional)

Access to staff:
Contact by letter
Hours: Mon to Fri, 0900 to 1700

Also at:
Orders and Medals Research Society
   PO Box 248, Snettisham, Kings Lynn, PE31 7TA

ORDNANCE SURVEY

Acronym or abbreviation: OS

Romsey Road, Maybush, Southampton, SO16 4GU

Tel: 023 8079 5000
Fax: 023 8079 2615
E-mail: customerservice@ordnancesurvey.co.uk

Website:
http://www.ordnancesurvey.co.uk
Catalogues, information papers, location of UK
towns.
http://www.ordsvy.gov.uk/products/Landranger/
lrmsearch.cfm

Enquiries:
Enquiries to: Customer Service Advisor
Direct tel: 08456 050505; 023 8079 2334 (Librarian)
Other contacts: Librarian (for bibliographic
enquiries)

Founded:
1791

Organisation type and purpose:
National government body.
Government agency; national mapping
organisation.

Subject coverage:
Survey and mapping of Great Britain, geodesy,
surveying, photogrammetry, remote sensing,
cartography, GIS.

**Museum or gallery collection, archive, or library
special collection:**
Archive collection of OS maps
Aerial photographs
Books and other published material on relevant
   subjects
Collection of overseas maps and survey data
   (former directorate of overseas surveys library)

Library catalogue:
All or part available in-house

Printed publications:
Administrative maps
Archaeological and historical maps
Educational materials
Map catalogues
Services leaflets
Small and large scale maps
Order printed publications from: Sales are through
agents, a list is available

Electronic and video publications:
Digital map data

Publications list:
Available online and in print

Access to staff:
Contact by letter, by telephone, by fax, by e-mail
and via website
Hours: Mon to Fri, 0830 to 1730
Special comments: Charges made for some services.

Access to building, collection or gallery:
No prior appointment required

Hours: Library: 0930 to 1530
Map Library: 0800 to 1600
Exhibition Centre: 0900 to 1700
Special comments: A charge is made for access to the
Map Library.

ORDNANCE SURVEY OF NORTHERN IRELAND

Acronym or abbreviation: OSNI

Colby House, Stranmillis Court, Belfast, BT9 5BJ

Tel: 028 9025 5755
Fax: 028 9025 5700
E-mail: osni@osni.gov.uk

Website:
http://www.osni.gov.uk

Founded:
1791

Organisation type and purpose:
National government body.
To supply mapping and geographical information
for Northern Ireland.

**Museum or gallery collection, archive, or library
special collection:**
Archive of aerial photographs
Archive of large scale and small scale maps, street
   maps and atlases
Digital topographical archive

Printed publications:
Administrative Maps
Atlases and Guides
Discoverer Series: cover Northern Ireland Scale
   1:50,000
Holiday Map Sheet 1 – Northern Ireland Scale
   1:250,000
Large scale maps of Northern Ireland
Outdoor pursuit Maps

Electronic and video publications:
Colour Raster Data for 1:50,000 and 1:250,000
   mapping
Vector and raster data from the topographical
   archive

Publications list:
Available online and in print

Access to staff:
Contact by letter, by telephone, by fax, by e-mail,
in person and via website
Hours: Mon to Fri, 0900 to 1700

Access for disabled people:
Parking provided, ramped entry, toilet facilities

ORFF SOCIETY UK

7 Rothesay Avenue, Richmond-upon-Thames,
Surrey, TW10 5EB

Tel: 020 8876 1944
Fax: 020 8876 1944
E-mail: orffsocuk@btconnect.com

Website:
http://www.orff.org.uk
Aims of the Orff approach, information about
current teachers' workshops, enquiry form for
joining the Society.

Enquiries:
Enquiries to: Honorary Secretary

Founded:
1964

Organisation type and purpose:
Professional body (membership is by subscription),
present number of members: 127, suitable for all
ages, training organisation.
To promote the experience and understanding of
Carl Orff's approach to music education; a creative
way of teaching music to groups using voices in
speech/singing, movement/dance and percussion
instruments.

Subject coverage:
Information, both specific and related to the Orff approach to music education, as applied to all types of schooling including special education.

Museum or gallery collection, archive, or library special collection:
A wide range of books and articles (some in German) on the subject of Orff-Schulwerk (the international name of the Orff approach to music education) by British and American authors

Printed publications:
Orff Times (magazine for members, Feb, Jun)

Access to staff:
Contact by letter, by telephone, by fax, by e-mail and via website
Hours: Mon to Sun, 0900 to 1900

Access to building, collection or gallery:
Prior appointment required
Hours: By arrangement

ORGANIC FOOD FEDERATION

Acronym or abbreviation: OFF

31 Turbine Way, EcoTech Business Park, Swaffham, Norfolk, PE37 7XD

Tel: 01760 720444
Fax: 01760 720790
E-mail: info@orgfoodfed.com

Enquiries:
Enquiries to: Executive Secretary

Founded:
1986

Organisation type and purpose:
International organisation, membership association (membership is by qualification), present number of members: 350.
Certification body.
To provide certification to producers, processors, importers and retailers of organic food.

Subject coverage:
The Federation provides inspection, certification and registration of organic foods. Represents members' interests in communicating with government and European institutions.

Access to staff:
Contact by letter, by telephone, by fax and by e-mail
Hours: Mon to Fri, 0900 to 1700

Connections with:
Defra
    Nobel House, 17 Smith Square, London, SW1P 3JR; tel: 020 7238 5605

ORGANISATION FOR PROFESSIONALS IN REGULATORY AFFAIRS

Acronym or abbreviation: TOPRA

Bellerive House, 3 Muirfield Crescent, London, E14 9SZ

Tel: 020 7510 2560
Fax: 020 7537 2003
E-mail: info@topra.org

Website:
http://www.topra.org
TOPRA, events, volunteering, special interest networks, careers, services directory, detailed contacts list.
http://www.topra.org/intouch
Interactive website of the In Touch publication.

Enquiries:
Enquiries to: Executive Director

Organisation type and purpose:
A non-profit organisation, the global organisation for regulatory affairs professionals and for those who have an interest in regulatory affairs in the healthcare sector. The current membership is drawn from over 40 countries and members are in

industry, the regulatory agencies and the consultancy community, and work in all sectors including medical technologies, biotech, borderline products and pharmaceuticals.

Subject coverage:
Regulatory affairs in the healthcare sector.

Education services:
Offers an MSc in Regulatory Affairs validated by the University of Wales and an MSc in Medical Technology Regulatory Affairs through collaboration with Cranfield Health Partnership.

Printed publications:
In Touch (monthly)

Electronic and video publications:
Regulatory Rapporteur (journal)
TARIUS news (a global regulatory and compliance regulations database, available to members only)
Updates from The State Institute for Drug Control in the Czech Republic (available to members only)

Publications list:
Available online

Access to staff:
Contact by letter, by telephone, by fax and by e-mail

Links with:
TOPRA North America

ORGANISATION OF BLIND AFRICAN CARIBBEANS

Acronym or abbreviation: OBAC

Gloucester House, 8 Camberwell New Road, London, SE5 0TA

Tel: 020 7735 3400
Fax: 020 7582 8334
E-mail: orgblindafricarib@ukonline.co.uk

Website:
http://www.obac.org.uk
OBAC service provisions, annual reports, newsletter and membership form.

Enquiries:
Enquiries to: Director

Founded:
1988

Organisation type and purpose:
Voluntary organisation, registered charity (charity number 1042756), training organisation.
OBAC provides information, advice and support on a range of issues such as: welfare rights, housing, immigration, training, education, employment issues, counselling, aids and adaptation for visually impaired people.

Subject coverage:
Welfare rights, housing, immigration, training, education, employment issues, counselling, aids and adaptation for visually impaired people.

Printed publications:
OBAC (newsletter, bi-monthly)
The Voice Newspaper (weekly)
The New African Magazine (monthly)

Electronic and video publications:
Tapes and disks are available (free, direct)

Access to staff:
Contact by letter, by telephone, by fax, by e-mail and in person
Hours: Mon to Fri, 0930 to 1730
Special comments: Full disabled access.

Access for disabled people:
Ramped entry, toilet facilities
Special comments: Chairlift.

ORGANON LABORATORIES LIMITED

Cambridge Science Park, Milton Road, Cambridge, CB4 0FL

Tel: 01223 432700
Fax: 01223 424368

Website:
http://www.organon.com

Enquiries:
Enquiries to: Medical Information Officer
Direct tel: 01223 432756

Founded:
1935

Organisation type and purpose:
Manufacturing industry.
Pharmaceutical manufacturing company.

Subject coverage:
Clinical pharmacology; contraception; hormone replacement therapy (HRT), (CNS) depression.

Access to staff:
Contact by letter, by telephone and by fax
Hours: Mon to Fri, 0900 to 1700

Access to building, collection or gallery:
No access other than to staff

Access for disabled people:
Parking provided

Parent body:
AKZO

ORIEL COLLEGE LIBRARY

Oxford, OX1 4EW

Tel: 01865 276558
E-mail: library@oriel.ox.ac.uk

Enquiries:
Enquiries to: Librarian

Founded:
1326

Organisation type and purpose:
University department or institute.
Library of a college of University of Oxford.

Subject coverage:
General, matters relating to old members of the college, Oxford Movement.

Museum or gallery collection, archive, or library special collection:
Orielensia – books by or about old members
Tractarian and Oxford Movement Collection

Access to staff:
Appointment necessary.
Hours: Mon to Fri, 0930 to 1700

Access to building, collection or gallery:
Appointment must be made before entry is allowed

ORKNEY LIBRARY AND ARCHIVE

44 Junction Road, Kirkwall, Orkney, KW15 1AG

Tel: 01856 873166
Fax: 01856 875260
E-mail: general.enquiries@orkneylibrary.org.uk

Website:
http://www.orkneylibrary.org.uk

Enquiries:
Enquiries to: Librarian
Other contacts: Archivist

Founded:
1683

Organisation type and purpose:
Local government body, public library.

Subject coverage:
Orkney.

Museum or gallery collection, archive, or library special collection:
Archives, church records, records of local authority of Orkney, Customs and Excise, Sheriff Court, Earldom Estate, private papers, business archive
Orkney Room collection – books, pamphlets
Photographic archive (40,000 negatives)

continued overleaf

Sound archive (2,000 tapes)

Library catalogue:
All or part available online

Access to staff:
Contact by letter, by telephone, by fax, by e-mail and in person
Hours: Library: Mon to Thu, 0915 to 1900; Fri and Sat, 0915 to 1700
Archive: Mon to Wed and Fri to Sat, 0915 to 1700; Thu, 0915 to 1900

Access to building, collection or gallery:
Main entrance on Junction Road
Hours: As opening hours above

Access for disabled people:
Ramped entry, toilet facilities, lift

ORKNEY TOURIST BOARD

6 Broad Street, Kirkwall, Orkney, KW15 1NX

Tel: 01856 872856/872001
Fax: 01856 875056
E-mail: e. info@visitorkney.com

Website:
http://www.orkney.com
Community, tourism and product information.

Enquiries:
Enquiries to: Chief Executive

Organisation type and purpose:
Statutory body (membership is by subscription), present number of members: 320.
Local area Tourist Board.

Subject coverage:
Tourism in Orkney.

Trade and statistical information:
Tourism in Orkney.

Printed publications:
Annual brochure

Electronic and video publications:
Tourism promotional video

Access to staff:
Contact by letter, by fax and via website.
Appointment necessary.
Hours: Mon to Fri, 0900 to 1700

ORTON TRUST

7 Drake Close, Rothwell, Northamptonshire, NN14 6DJ

Tel: 01536 711600 (Courses Director home telephone)
E-mail: info@ortontrust.org.uk

Website:
http://www.ortontrust.org.uk

Enquiries:
Enquiries to: Courses Director

Founded:
1968

Organisation type and purpose:
Registered charity (charity number 304232), training organisation.

Subject coverage:
Traditional stonemasonry skills, restoration and conservation of historic buildings, stone sculpture and lettering.

Access to staff:
Contact by letter, by telephone, by e-mail and via website
Hours: Mon to Fri, 0900 to 1700

OSCAR WILDE SOCIETY

Secretary, 22 Edric Road, London, SE14 5EL

Tel: 07980 221632
E-mail: michael.seeney@btinternet.com

Website:
http://www.oscarwildesociety.co.uk

Founded:
1990

Organisation type and purpose:
Membership association (membership is by subscription), literary society.
Devoted to the appreciation of Oscar Wilde, promoting knowledge and study of his life, personality and works.

Subject coverage:
Oscar Wilde.

Printed publications:
Oscar Wilde 'Women of Homer'
Thomas Wright 'Death in Genoa'
Order printed publications from: Donald Mead, 63 Lambton Road, London, SW20 0LW; e-mail: donmead@wildean.demon.co.uk

Access to staff:
Contact by letter, by telephone, by e-mail and via website
Hours: No set hours

OUTDOOR INDUSTRIES ASSOCIATION

Acronym or abbreviation: COLA

Morritt House, 58 Station Approach, South Ruislip, Middlesex, HA4 6SA

Tel: 020 8842 1111
Fax: 020 8842 0090
E-mail: info@outdoorindustriesassociation.co.uk

Website:
http://www.outdoorindustriesassociation.co.uk

Enquiries:
Enquiries to: Administration Officer
Direct e-mail: info@outdoorindustriesassociation.co.uk
Other contacts: Director, Financial Controller; Marketing Director

Founded:
1961

Organisation type and purpose:
Trade association.
The Outdoor Industries Association is the UK's leading trade body for manufacturers, suppliers and retailers of outdoor clothing and equipment.

Subject coverage:
Clothing, equipment and accessories for camping, outdoor leisure, climbing, mountaineering, walking, hiking and canoeing, manufacturers' trade names and retailers.

Printed publications:
Go Outdoors Bulletin
Consumer Care Guides
Membership Directory

Access to staff:
Contact by letter, by telephone, by fax and by e-mail
Hours: Mon to Fri, 0900 to 1700

OUTSELL, INC

25 Floral Street, London, WC2E 9DS

Tel: 020 8090 6590
E-mail: info@outsellinc.com

Website:
http://www.outsellinc.com

Enquiries:
Enquiries to: Research and Consultancy Director

Founded:
1985

Incorporates the former:
Electronic Publishing Services (year of change 2008)

Organisation type and purpose:
Consultancy, market research, publishing house.

Subject coverage:
All aspects of the publishing industry and electronic publishing, including online.

Museum or gallery collection, archive, or library special collection:
Library of documents and publications on electronic information products and services

Trade and statistical information:
Data on electronic information services, especially statistics on UK, EU and North American services.

Electronic and video publications:
Data available via website (some available free, most only available to subscribers)

Publications list:
Available online

Access to staff:
Contact by letter, by telephone and by e-mail.
Appointment necessary. All charged.
Hours: Mon to Fri, 0930 to 1730

Access to building, collection or gallery:
Prior appointment required

OUTSIDERS

Formal name: The Outsiders Trust

4S Leroy House, 436 Essex Road, London, N1 3QP

Tel: 020 7354 8291
E-mail: office@outsiders.org.uk

Website:
http://www.outsiders.org.uk

Enquiries:
Enquiries to: Co-ordinator
Direct e-mail: trust@outsiders.org.uk

Founded:
1972

Incorporates the former:
Sexual Health and Disability Alliance; Association to Aid the Personal and Sexual Relationships of People with a Disability (SPOD) helpline (year of change 2002)

Organisation type and purpose:
Registered charity (charity number 290482).
To assist the sexual and personal relationships of people with disabilities.

Information services:
Sex and disability helpline.

Services for disabled people:
Peer support network for people with physical and social disabilities. Local lunches held around the UK.

Printed publications:
Advisory leaflets and resource lists
Membership list
Magazine

Publications list:
Available online and in print

Access to staff:
Contact by letter, by telephone and by e-mail

Access to building, collection or gallery:
No public access

Access for disabled people:
At public lunches

OUTWARD BOUND TRUST

Hackthorpe Hall, Hackthorpe, Penrith, Cumbria, CA10 2HX

Tel: 01931 740000
Fax: 01931 740001
E-mail: enquiries@outwoodbound.org.uk

Website:
http://www.theoutwardboundtrust.org.uk
Centre and course information.

Enquiries:
Enquiries to: Administrator

Founded:
1941

Organisation type and purpose:
Registered charity (charity number 1128090), training organisation.
Educational charity.

Subject coverage:
Outdoor learning, adventure, development training, safety in the outdoors, professional development, personal development.

Printed publications:
Course brochure (annually, free)
Order printed publications from: Marketing, The Outward Bound Trust, Hackthorpe Hall, Hackthorpe, Penrith, Cumbria, CA10 2HX; tel: 01931 740000

Electronic and video publications:
DVD

Access to staff:
Contact by letter, by telephone, by fax, by e-mail and via website
Hours: Mon to Fri, 0900 to 1730

Also at:
The Outward Bound Trust – Aberdovey
    Aberdovey, Gwynedd, LL35 0RA; tel: 01654 767464
The Outward Bound Trust – Eskdale
    Eskdale Green, Holmrook, Cumbria, CA19 1TE; tel: 01946 723281
The Outward Bound Trust – Loch Eil
    Loch Eil, Fort William, Inverness-shire, PH33 7NN; tel: 01397 772866
The Outward Bound Trust – Ullswater
    Penrith, Cumbria, CA11 0JL; tel: 08705 134227

OVERSEAS ADOPTION HELPLINE

64–66 High Street, Barnet, Hertfordshire, EN5 5SJ

Tel: 0870 516 8742 Helpline
Fax: 0208 440 5675
E-mail: info@oah.org.uk

Website:
http://www.oah.org.uk

Enquiries:
Enquiries to: Director
Direct tel: 020 8449 2562

Founded:
1997

Organisation type and purpose:
Registered charity (charity number 1067313).
Provides information and advice to inter-country adopters, inter-country adopted people and their families and also for professionals involved in inter-country adoption.

Subject coverage:
Inter-country adoption.

Printed publications:
General Introductory Pack
Regional Summaries
16 Country Information Booklets

Publications list:
Available online and in print

Access to staff:
Contact by telephone and by e-mail
Hours: Mon to Fri, 0900 to 1300 and 1400 to 1700

OVERSEAS DEVELOPMENT INSTITUTE

Acronym or abbreviation: ODI

111 Westminster Bridge Road, London, SE1 7JD

Tel: 020 7922 0300
Fax: 020 7922 0399
E-mail: odi@odi.org.uk

Website:
http://www.odi.org.uk
Institutional descriptions, full text of free publications, research in progress, publications list, annual report.

Enquiries:
Enquiries to: Publications Officer

Founded:
1960

Organisation type and purpose:
Registered charity (charity number 228248), research organisation.
ODI is Britain's leading independent think-tank on international development and humanitarian issues.
ODI's mission is to inspire and inform policy and practice which lead to the reduction of poverty, the alleviation of suffering and the achievement of sustainable livelihood in developing countries.

Subject coverage:
Overseas development, aid, development policy, trade adjustment, finance, food aid, food security, disasters, environment, agriculture, extension, pastoralism, irrigation, water resources, rural forestry.

Museum or gallery collection, archive, or library special collection:
Grey literature collection of the Rural Resources Management Group

Non-library collection catalogue:
All or part available online and in-house

Library catalogue:
All or part available in-house

Printed publications:
Annual Report
Briefing Papers
Development policy review (quarterly)
Disasters, Journal of Disaster Studies and Management (quarterly)
Economic Crisis in Developing Countries
Index to development literature (6 times a year)
Monetary Policy in Developing Countries
ODI working papers

Publications list:
Available in print

Access to staff:
Contact by letter, by telephone, by fax, by e-mail and in person
Hours: Mon to Fri, 0930 to 1700
Special comments: In person, Mon to Thu, 1000 to 1700 only.

Access to building, collection or gallery:
No prior appointment required

Affiliated to:
European Association of Development Institutes (EADI)
Information for Development Coordinating Committee (IDCC)

Houses the:
Agricultural Administration Unit

Subsidiary body:
Agricultural Research and Extension Network
Humanitarian Policy Group
Humanitarian Practice Network
Pastoral Development Network
Rural Development Forestry Network
Water Resources Group

OVERSEAS SERVICE PENSIONERS' ASSOCIATION

Acronym or abbreviation: OSPA

138 High Street, Tonbridge, Kent, TN9 1AX

Tel: 01732 363836
Fax: 01732 365070
E-mail: mail@ospa.org.uk

Website:
http://www.ospa.org.uk

Enquiries:
Enquiries to: Secretary

Founded:
1960

Organisation type and purpose:
Membership association (membership is by qualification), present number of members: c. 4,200.
To represent, safeguard and promote the interests of members in all matters relating to or affecting Overseas Service pensions, and to promote understanding of all aspects of the former Colonial Service/HMOCS in British colonial rule and development.

Subject coverage:
Matters relating directly or indirectly to Service pensions of former members of the Colonial Service and HM Overseas Civil Service; general interest in past British administration and development in former and present colonial territories.

Printed publications:
The Overseas Pensioner (biannual official membership journal)
Order printed publications from: The Secretary, OSPA, 138 High Street, Tonbridge, Kent TN9 1AX

Access to staff:
Contact by letter, by telephone, by fax and by e-mail. Appointment necessary.
Hours: Mon to Thu, 0900 to 1630

OXFORD BROOKES UNIVERSITY – HARCOURT HILL LIBRARY

Harcourt Hill Campus, Oxford, OX2 9AT

Tel: 01865 488222; 488319 (Wesley Centre)
Fax: 01865 488224
E-mail: library@brookes.ac.uk

Website:
http://www.brookes.ac.uk/library
http://catalogue.brookes.ac.uk
Library catalogue.

Enquiries:
Enquiries to: Head of Learning Resources

Organisation type and purpose:
University library.

Subject coverage:
Education, theology, human development, communication, sport and performing arts.

Museum or gallery collection, archive, or library special collection:
Wesley Historical Society library and archives
Westminster College archives
Art collections such as the Methodist Collection of Modern Christian Art and works by James Smetham
Archives of Bletchley Park College and Lady Spencer Churchill College

Library catalogue:
All or part available online

Access to staff:
Contact by letter, by telephone, by fax, by e-mail and via website
Hours: Term time: Mon to Thu, 0830 to 2100; Fri, 0830 to 1800; Sat, Sun, 1200 to 1800
Vacations: Mon to Fri, 0830 to 1700

OXFORD BROOKES UNIVERSITY – HEADINGTON LIBRARY

Headington Campus, Gipsy Lane, Headington, Oxford, OX3 0BP

Tel: 01865 483156
Fax: 01865 483998
E-mail: library@brookes.ac.uk

Website:
http://www.brookes.ac.uk/library
http://catalogue.brookes.ac.uk
Library catalogue.

continued overleaf

Enquiries:
Enquiries to: Director of Learning Resources and University Librarian

Organisation type and purpose:
University library.

Subject coverage:
Architectural planning and estate management, social sciences, education, management and business studies, humanities, arts, languages, construction, sciences, catering and tourism, publishing, nursing, theology.

Museum or gallery collection, archive, or library special collection:
Andre Deutsch Collection (the published output of Andre Deutsch Ltd and Allan Wingate as well as titles from Deutsch's own personal library)
Dorset House Archive (the history of the first School of Occupational Therapy in the United Kingdom, the Casson family and the wider history of Occupational Therapy education in Britain from 1930 to 1980)
Fuller Collection (books, pamphlets, journals and cuttings on catering, cookery and gastronomy)
Harold Fullard Collection of Atlases
Jane Grigson Collection (books and pamphlets on cookery and gastronomy)
Ken Hom Library (books on cookery and gastronomy)
Medical Sciences Video Archive (biographical interviews with leading medical scientists)
National Brewing Library (a unique English-language collection relating to brewing, other alcoholic beverages and dependent trades)
Oxfordshire Society of Architects Collection (books and journals about architecture and construction, on permanent loan from the local branch of the Royal Institute of British Architects)
Publishing in Africa Collection (materials relating to publishing and the book trade in Africa)

Library catalogue:
All or part available online

Printed publications:
Library guides
Subject journal lists
Wide range of specialist handouts on library services

Access to staff:
Contact by letter, by telephone, by fax, by e-mail and via website
Hours: Term time: Mon to Thu, 0900 to 2200; Fri, 0900 to 2000; Sat and Sun, 1000 to 1600. Vacations: Mon to Fri, 0900 to 1700

OXFORD BROOKES UNIVERSITY – WHEATLEY LIBRARY

Wheatley Campus, Oxford, OX33 1HX

Tel: 01865 485869
Fax: 01865 485750
E-mail: library@brookes.ac.uk

Website:
http://www.brookes.ac.uk/library
http://catalogue.brookes.ac.uk
Library catalogue.

Enquiries:
Enquiries to: Head of Learning Resources

Founded:
1948

Organisation type and purpose:
University library.

Subject coverage:
Business, management, economics, computing, mathematics and engineering

Library catalogue:
All or part available online

Access to staff:
Contact by letter, by telephone, by fax, by e-mail

and via website
Hours: Term time: Mon to Thu, 0900 to 2100; Fri, 0900 to 1800; Sat and Sun, 1000 to 1600. Vacations: Mon to Fri, 0900 to 1700

OXFORD BUSINESS COLLEGE

Acronym or abbreviation: OBC

65 George St, Oxford, OX1 2BQ

Tel: 01865 791908
Fax: 01865 245059
E-mail: enquiries@oxfordbusinesscollege.co.uk

Website:
http://www.oxfordbusinesscollege.co.uk

Enquiries:
Enquiries to: Principal

Founded:
1985

Organisation type and purpose:
Suitable for ages: 17+, training organisation.

Subject coverage:
Marketing, business, management and law; English language, secretarial studies, computing, cookery.

Printed publications:
Prospectus

Access to staff:
Contact by letter, by telephone and by fax
Hours: Mon to Fri, 0900 to 1730

OXFORD CENTRE FOR HEBREW AND JEWISH STUDIES

Yarnton Manor, Church Lane, Yarnton, Oxford, OX5 1PY

Tel: 01865 377946
Fax: 01865 375079
E-mail: enquiries@uchjs.ac.uk

Website:
http://associnst.ox.ac.uk/ochjs

Enquiries:
Enquiries to: President
Other contacts: Librarian for library information, email: muller.library@ochjs.ac.uk

Founded:
1972

Organisation type and purpose:
Registered charity (charity number 309720), university department or institute, suitable for ages: post-graduate.

Subject coverage:
Hebrew and Jewish studies.

Museum or gallery collection, archive, or library special collection:
The Centre's Leopold Muller Memorial Library holds a wide range of collections, for more information contact the Librarian

Non-library collection catalogue:
All or part available in-house

Library catalogue:
All or part available in-house

Printed publications:
Herbert S Frankel: An Economist's Testimony (autobiography, 1992, £25)
Journal of Jewish Studies (2 issues a year, £48 institution subscription, £32 institutions subscription, £18 student subscription, £18 single issue)
Occasional Papers (most are from lectures at the centre)
Publications of The Yarnton Trust (£2.50)
Israel Studies (2 issues a year, copies available from Indiana University Press)
Annual Report (free)
A Bibliography of Publications 1972–1986, 1987 (free)
Newsletter from the Centre (free)

The Kressel Collection (1981, free)
Order printed publications from: For Israel Studies, Journals Division
Indiana University Press, 601 N Morton Street, Bloomington, IN 47404, USA
Other titles, Oxford Centre for Hebrew and Jewish Studies

Publications list:
Available in print

Access to staff:
Contact by letter, by telephone, by fax and by e-mail. Appointment necessary.
Hours: Mon to Fri, 0900 to 1700

Access to building, collection or gallery:
No prior appointment required

OXFORD CENTRE FOR ISLAMIC STUDIES

George Street, Oxford, OX1 2AR

Tel: 01865 278730
Fax: 01865 248942
E-mail: islamic.studies@oxcis.ac.uk

Website:
http://www.oxcis.ac.uk

Enquiries:
Enquiries to: Enquiry Line

Subject coverage:
Islam.

Access to staff:
Contact by letter, by telephone, by fax, by e-mail and via website
Hours: Mon to Fri, 0900 to 1700

OXFORD CITY COUNCIL

St Aldate's Chambers, St Aldate's, Oxford, OX1 1DS

Tel: 01865 249811
Fax: 01865 252338

Website:
http://www.oxford.gov.uk
Web edition of 'The City' newspaper, information from Oxford City Council.

Enquiries:
Enquiries to: Chief Executive

Organisation type and purpose:
Local government body.

Printed publications:
The City (newspaper, 3 times a year, available free on request)
Various corporate publications, leaflets etc

Access to staff:
Contact by letter, by telephone, by fax and in person
Hours: Mon to Fri, 0900 to 1700

OXFORD DOWN SHEEP BREEDERS ASSOCIATION

Hillfields Lodge, Lighthorne, Warwickshire

Tel: 01926 650098
E-mail: cqlfroehlich@hotmail.com

Enquiries:
Enquiries to: Secretary

Founded:
1889

Organisation type and purpose:
Sheep breed society.

Subject coverage:
Oxford Down sheep.

Access to staff:
Contact by letter, by telephone and by e-mail
Hours: Mon to Fri, 0900 to 1700

OXFORD EDUCATIONAL RESOURCES LIMITED

Acronym or abbreviation: OER

PO Box 106, The Barn, Kidlington, Oxfordshire, OX5 1HY

Tel: 01865 842552
Fax: 01865 842551
E-mail: sales@oer.co.uk

Website:
http://www.oer.co.uk

Enquiries:
Enquiries to: Managing Director

Founded:
1978

Organisation type and purpose:
Training organisation.
Publishing and distribution of non-book material.

Subject coverage:
Training material for medicine, health and biology.

Publications list:
Available in print

Access to staff:
Contact by fax and by e-mail
Hours: Mon to Fri, 0900 to 1700

OXFORD INFORMATION CENTRE

Acronym or abbreviation: Oxford TIC

15–16 Broad Street, Oxford, OX1 3AS

Tel: 01865 252200
Fax: 01865 240261
E-mail: tic@oxford.gov.uk

Website:
http://www.visitoxford.org

Enquiries:
Enquiries to: Tourist Information Centre Manager
Direct tel: 01865 252300
Direct e-mail: jbassett@oxford.gov.uk
Other contacts: TIC Team Leader

Founded:
1939

Organisation type and purpose:
Local government body.
Tourist Information Centre.
To assist local people and visitors to make the most of the time they spend in Oxford and the surrounding area.

Subject coverage:
Tourist information including: guided walking tours, maps, guides and accommodation, reservations (B&B), local information, tickets for attractions.

Services for disabled people:
Disabled access, hearing loop

Trade and statistical information:
see website: http://www.visitoxford.org

Non-library collection catalogue:
All or part available online

Printed publications:
What to See and Do in Oxford (60p)
Where to Stay in Oxford

Electronic and video publications:
Various videos
Order electronic and video publications from: Downloadable free

Publications list:
Available online and in print

Access to staff:
Contact by letter, by telephone, by fax, by e-mail, in person and via website
Hours: Mon to Sat, 0930 to 1700; Sun and Public Holidays, 1000 to 1600

Access to building, collection or gallery:
As above

Access for disabled people:
Level entry
Hours: As above

Parent body:
Oxford City Council

OXFORD INSTITUTE OF RETAIL MANAGEMENT

Acronym or abbreviation: OXIRM

Said Business School, University of Oxford, Park End Street, Oxford, OX1 1HP

Tel: 01865 288800
Fax: 01865 288801
E-mail: oxirmenquiries@sbs.ox.ac.uk

Website:
http://www.sbs.ox.ac.uk/oxirm

Enquiries:
Enquiries to: Research Director
Other contacts: Academic Director

Founded:
1985

Organisation type and purpose:
University department or institute, research organisation.

Subject coverage:
Retail management.

Information services:
The Institute is not generally able to assist with ad hoc information requests.

Special visitor services:
Visiting academics and research students can be hosted through established University schemes.

Education services:
Provides executive education for retail and related businesses, conducts research commissioned by private and public sector organizations, and contributes retail education to degree programmes in management studies.

Museum or gallery collection, archive, or library special collection:
Research papers, reports, directories, etc.

Printed publications:
The Retail Digest (quarterly)
E-Business: A Management Perspective (OUP)
Innovation in Retailing
Factors Affecting the Structure and Pattern of Retailing in London
Assessing the Productivity of the UK Retail Sector
Retail Strategy: The View from the Bridge
Internationalisation in Retailing: The Global Performance Perspective
Customer Loyalty Schemes in Retailing Across Europe
Home Shopping
Own Brands in Food Retailing Across Europe
Retailing in the Nordic Countries
Information from Retailers – Individual Customer Information
Order printed publications from: e-mail: oxirmenquiries@sbs.ox.ac.uk

Electronic and video publications:
website: http://oxford-institute.sbsblogs.co.uk

Publications list:
Available online and in print

Access to staff:
Contact by letter, by telephone, by fax and by e-mail. Appointment necessary. Letter of introduction required.
Hours: Mon to Fri, 0900 to 1700

Access to building, collection or gallery:
By invitation only.
Special comments: Academic status generally required.

OXFORD MISSION

General Secretary, PO Box 86, Romsey, Hampshire, SO51 8YD

Tel: 01794 515004
Fax: 01794 515004

Website:
http://www.oxford-mission.org/home/index.html
The Mission, its history and its present work, how to donate, how to volunteer, publications.

Founded:
1879

Organisation type and purpose:
Registered charity, mission.
Runs a boys' orphanage, St. Joseph's Primary School, an English-medium primary school, hostels, training schemes for less academic boys, and an ENT/Eye clinic at Behala, India; boarding schools, Christian students' hostels, St Anne's Medical Centre, an orphanage, a primary school and a Bangladeshi Brotherhood of St. Paul at Barisal, Bangladesh; and a Bangladeshi Sisterhood in Jobarpar to supervise boys' and girls' hostels and a play-centre for small children, help in St Gabriel's School and supervise St. Mary's Home in Barisal.

Subject coverage:
Children's welfare and education.

Printed publications:
Down to the Sea (Bill Down, £17.50 plus £2.50 p&p)
He Leadeth Me (Sister Rosamund S.E., £3.50 incl. p&p)
Bishop James Blair's Diary (ed. Isaac Baroi, £5 incl. p currently out of print)
A Well Watered Garden (compiled and ed. Mabyn Pickering, £5 incl. p&p)
Theodore: Letters from the Oxford Mission, 1946–1993 (ed. Gill Wilson, £5 incl. p&p)
Whether we be many or few (C.E. Millington, £7 incl. p&p)
Newsletter (2 a year)
Order printed publications from: The UK office, except:
Down to the Sea, from The Memoir Club, Stanhope Old Hall, Stanhope, Co. Durham, DL13 2PF
Whether we be many or few, from Christians Aware, Leicester, tel: 0116 254 0770

Electronic and video publications:
Newsletter (2 a year)
Order electronic and video publications from: The UK office

Access to staff:
Contact by letter, by telephone, by fax, by e-mail and via website
Hours: Mon, Tue, Thu, Fri, 0930 to 1530
Special comments: Not Wed.

Also at:
Editor, Oxford Mission News
6 Lodge Vale, East Wellow, Romsey, Hants, SO51 6AU; tel: 01794 323387
Mother Winifred, All Hallows Convent
Ditchingham, Bungay, Suffolk, NR35 2DT
Oxford Mission
Bogra Road, PO Box 21, Barisal, 8200 Bangladesh
Oxford Mission
Barisha, Kolkata 700 008, India
Oxford Mission, Christa Sevika Sangha
PO Box Jobarpar 8240, Barisal Division, Uz. Agailjhara, Bangladesh

OXFORD PRESERVATION TRUST

Acronym or abbreviation: OPT

10 Turn Again Lane, St Ebbes, Oxford, OX1 1QL

Tel: 01865 242918
Fax: 01865 246706
E-mail: info@oxfordpreservation.org.uk

Website:
http://www.oxfordpreservation.org.uk

Enquiries:
Enquiries to: Director

continued overleaf

Founded:
1927

Organisation type and purpose:
Membership association (membership is by subscription), present number of members: 1,000, registered charity (charity number 203043). Area of concern, Oxford and its Green Belt setting.

Subject coverage:
Conservation in Oxford and its Green Belt.

Museum or gallery collection, archive, or library special collection:
Archives accessed through Trust Office

Printed publications:
Annual Report
Newsletter (2 times a year)
Occasional Studies (available in the Local Studies Library and the Bodleian Library)

Access to staff:
Contact by letter, by telephone, by fax and by e-mail. Appointment necessary.
Hours: Mon to Fri, 0900 to 1600

Links with:
Civic Trust
  Europa Nostra
Europa Nostra

OXFORDSHIRE COUNTY COUNCIL

Acronym or abbreviation: OCC

Community Services, Central Library, Westgate, Oxford, OX1 1DJ

Tel: 01865 815549
Fax: 01865 721694
E-mail: oxfordcentral.library@oxfordshire.gov.uk

Website:
http://www.oxfordshire.gov.uk
http://www.libcat.oxfordshire.gov.uk
Oxfordshire County Council Library Catalogue

Enquiries:
Enquiries to: Head of Community Services
Direct tel: 01865 810191
Direct fax: 01865 810187
Other contacts: Principal Librarian Information Services

Organisation type and purpose:
Local government body, public library.

Subject coverage:
Logic, New Testament, international relations, women, costumes, gypsies, customs and folklore, inland waterways, nuclear physics, hydraulic engineering, woodworking, India, Indian religions (Buddhism, etc.), indoor games and amusements, genealogy, heraldry and family history, local studies in Oxfordshire, internal-combustion engines, motor vehicle engineering, cleaning and dyeing, accountancy, rubber technology, business information.

Non-library collection catalogue:
All or part available online

Library catalogue:
All or part available online

Access to staff:
Contact by letter, by telephone, by e-mail and in person
Hours: Contact for details

OXFORDSHIRE FAMILY HISTORY SOCIETY

Acronym or abbreviation: OFHS

19 Mavor Close, Woodstock, Oxford, OX20 1YL

Website:
http://www.ofhs.org.uk
Family history information.

Enquiries:
Enquiries to: Honorary Secretary
Direct tel: 01993 812258

Other contacts: Membership Secretary
Founded:
1976

Organisation type and purpose:
Membership association (membership is by subscription), present number of members: 1300, registered charity (charity number 275891).

Subject coverage:
Family history.

Museum or gallery collection, archive, or library special collection:
Library

Printed publications:
Several family history publications
Order printed publications from: Oxfordshire Family History Society
Windmill Place, Windmill Road, Minchinhampton, Stroud, Gloucestershire, GL6 9EE, tel: 01453 881446, e-mail: HKearsey@aol.com

Microform publications:
Parish registers, marriage index, census index

Publications list:
Available in print

Access to staff:
Contact by letter
Hours: Mon to Fri, 0900 to 1700
Special comments: No office.

OXFORDSHIRE RECORD OFFICE

Acronym or abbreviation: ORO

St Luke's Church, Temple Road, Cowley, Oxford, OX4 2HT

Tel: 01865 398200
Fax: 01865 398201
E-mail: archives@oxfordshire.gov.uk

Website:
http://www.oxfordshire.uk/oro

Enquiries:
Enquiries to: Archives Manager

Founded:
1935

Organisation type and purpose:
Local government body, professional body. Record office.

Subject coverage:
Records of Oxfordshire.

Museum or gallery collection, archive, or library special collection:
Quarter Sessions, local government, diocesan and parish, and private records

Non-library collection catalogue:
All or part available online and in-house

Publications list:
Available in print

Access to staff:
Contact by letter, by telephone, by fax, by e-mail and in person
Hours: Wed to Sat, 0900 to 1700

Access for disabled people:
Parking provided, ramped entry, access to all public areas, toilet facilities

OXFORDSHIRE RECORD SOCIETY

Bodleian Library, Oxford, OX1 3BG

Tel: 01865 277164
E-mail: srt@bodley.ox.ac.uk

Enquiries:
Enquiries to: Secretary

Founded:
1919

Organisation type and purpose:
Learned society.

Exists to publish editions of Oxfordshire local history texts.

Subject coverage:
Oxfordshire local history.

Access to staff:
Contact by letter and by e-mail
Hours: Mon to Fri, 0900 to 1700

OXFORDSHIRE RURAL COMMUNITY COUNCIL

Acronym or abbreviation: ORCC

Jericho Farm, Worton, Near Cassington, Witney, Oxfordshire, OX29 4SZ

Tel: 01865 883488
Fax: 01865 883191
E-mail: oxonrcc@ruralnet.org.uk

Enquiries:
Enquiries to: Chief Executive

Founded:
1920

Organisation type and purpose:
Voluntary organisation, registered charity (charity number 900560).

Subject coverage:
Oxfordshire Rural Community Council (ORCC) supports, promotes and develops local voluntary action and rural services (including shops and rural transport). Offers information on a wide range of local voluntary organisations, community and self-help groups. Provides information and advises village hall management committees and advises on sources of grants for community projects. Also provides parish councils with advice and guidance in partnership with the Oxfordshire Association of Local Councils and the Oxfordshire Playing Fields Association. (All three organisations based at Jericho Farm).

Printed publications:
The following are available free or for purchase upon request
Advice leaflets for community hall committees
Annual Reports
Community Transport in Oxfordshire (Directories)
ORCC News (newsletter, quarterly, for members)
Various publications available for parish councils and community shops

Access to staff:
Contact by letter, by telephone, by fax and by e-mail. Appointment necessary.
Hours: Mon to Fri, 0900 to 1700

Access to building, collection or gallery:
Prior appointment required

Houses the:
Oxfordshire Association of Local Councils
  tel: 01865 883488; fax: 01865 883191; e-mail: oalc@ruralnet.org.uk
Oxfordshire Playing Fields Association
  tel: 01865 883488; fax: 01865 883191; e-mail: oxonrcc@ruralnet.org.uk

OXFORDSHIRE STUDIES

Central Library, Westgate, Oxford, OX1 1DJ

Tel: 01865 815749
Fax: 01865 810187
E-mail: oxfordshire.studies@oxfordshire.gov.uk

Website:
http://www.oxfordshire.gov.uk/oxfordshirestudies
Information about the service and collections, access to online catalogues and images, order forms.
http://www.oxfordshire.gov.uk/heritagesearch
Online catalogue

Enquiries:
Enquiries to: Local Studies Manager

Founded:
1991

Organisation type and purpose:
Local government body, museum, public library.
Local studies and family history resource centre for
Oxfordshire.

Subject coverage:
Oxfordshire local studies, local history and
archaeology, family history, maps, photographs
and oral history.

**Museum or gallery collection, archive, or library
special collection:**
Indexes and databases
Oxfordshire printed materials, microforms, digital
    resources
Photographs and audiotapes
Catalogues

Non-library collection catalogue:
All or part available online and in-house

Library catalogue:
All or part available online and in-house

Access to staff:
Contact by letter, by telephone, by fax, by e-mail
and in person. Appointment necessary.
Special comments: Booking advisable for access to
microfilms and computers, appointments may be
necessary for specialist advice.

Access to building, collection or gallery:
Hours: Tue, Thu, Fri, Sat, 0900 to 1700; Mon, Wed,
Sun closed.

Access for disabled people:
Access to all public areas

Parent body:
Oxfordshire County Council

P & O GROUP

Formal name: The Peninsular and Oriental Steam
Navigation Company

16 Palace Street, London, SW1E 5JQ

Tel: 020 7901 4000
Fax: 020 7901 4015
E-mail: communications@pogroup.com

Website:
http://www.pogroup.com

Founded:
1837

Organisation type and purpose:
Service industry.

Subject coverage:
Shipping, present day and historical (since c. 1830),
other transport and logistics (present day),
constituent companies, history and current
operations of P & O constituent companies.

Access to staff:
Contact by letter, by telephone, by fax, by e-mail,
in person and via website. Appointment necessary.
Hours: Mon to Fri, 0900 to 1700

Access to building, collection or gallery:
Prior appointment required

Access for disabled people:
Ramped entry, access to all public areas, toilet
facilities

PACKAGING AND INDUSTRIAL
FILMS ASSOCIATION

Acronym or abbreviation: PIFA

3rd Floor, Gothic House, Barker Gate, Nottingham,
NG7 7GR

Tel: 0115 959 8389
Fax: 0115 959 9326
E-mail: pifa@pifa.co.uk

Website:
http://www.pifa.co.uk
General information and publications

Enquiries:
Enquiries to: Chief Executive

Other contacts: PR Principal for exhibitions, press
releases, presentations and essential media
contacts.

Founded:
1957

Organisation type and purpose:
National organisation, trade association
(membership is by subscription).
To communicate with Government, Government
Agencies, Ministers and MPs on all issues affecting
the competitiveness, environmental performance
and operation of the industry. To provide factual
and scientific information to universities, schools,
local authorities and other social groups.

Subject coverage:
Production and conversion of plastics films used in
healthcare, agriculture, packaging, building
construction, commerce and industry. Issues
include competitiveness, the environment, safety,
trade matters, processes, products and
applications, education and public awareness.

Trade and statistical information:
Detailed production/consumption, import/export
    and related statistics maintained.

Non-library collection catalogue:
All or part available online and in print

Printed publications:
Environmental statements
PIFA product standards – numbers 1 to 11 (for
    sale)
Technical Reports, Briefings and application
    leaflets including:
A Responsible Approach to the Environmental
    Challenge
A Statement of Environmental Policy
Meeting the Environmental Challenge

Publications list:
Available online and in print

Access to staff:
Contact by letter, by telephone, by fax, by e-mail
and via website. Appointment necessary.
Hours: Mon to Fri, 0900 to 1700

Access to building, collection or gallery:
No prior appointment required

Access for disabled people:
Parking provided, toilet facilities

Affiliated to:
British Plastics Federation

Member of:
C of C
CBI
Plasteurofilm
Polymer NTO

PADDLE STEAMER
PRESERVATION SOCIETY

Acronym or abbreviation: PSPS

17 Stockfield Close, Hazlemere, High Wycombe,
Buckinghamshire, HP15 7LA

Tel: 01494 812979

Enquiries:
Enquiries to: Secretary

Founded:
1959

Organisation type and purpose:
Membership association (membership is by
subscription), present number of members: 4000,
voluntary organisation.
Education of the public in the appreciation of
paddle steamers and their preservation.

Subject coverage:
Paddle steamers of Britain and Europe.

**Museum or gallery collection, archive, or library
special collection:**
Library of Paddle Steamer photographs and books

Printed publications:
Paddle Wheels (quarterly)

Access to staff:
Contact by letter
Hours: Mon to Fri, 0900 to 1700

Affiliated to:
Transport Trust

PAGAN FEDERATION

Acronym or abbreviation: PF

BM Box 7097, London, WC1N 3XX

Tel: 07986 034387
E-mail: secretary@paganfed.org

Website:
http://www.paganfed.org
Information pack, Paganism information, articles
from Pagan Dawn, Pagan events and conferences.
Introduction to Paganism, regional contact details.

Enquiries:
Enquiries to: Secretary
Direct e-mail: secretary@paganfed.org

Founded:
1971

Organisation type and purpose:
To inform the public about Paganism and to
support Pagans in the practice of their religion.

Subject coverage:
Nature, spirituality, goddess worship, Wicca (the
old religion of witchcraft), Druidism, Shamanism,
Pagan folklore and belief, contemporary Pagan
ritual practices, religious and legal rights,
defamation of Pagans, concerns about ritual child
abuse, Pagan ethics, inter-faith dialogue, worship
of traditional European deities.

**Museum or gallery collection, archive, or library
special collection:**
Cuttings collection – stories on Pagan-related
    subjects
Extensive collection of Pagan and esoteric
    magazines, back issues and current issues

Library catalogue:
All or part available in-house

Printed publications:
Pagan Federation Information Pack (£3.25)
Pagan Dawn (magazine, quarterly, £12 a year, £15
    overseas)
Witchcraft Information (£3.25)
Northern Tradition Information Pack (£3.25)
Druidry Information Pack (1998, £3.25)

Publications list:
Available in print

Access to staff:
Contact by letter and by e-mail
Hours: Mon to Fri, 0900 to 1700

Access to building, collection or gallery:
No access other than to staff

PAIN RELIEF FOUNDATION

Acronym or abbreviation: PRF

Clinical Sciences Centre for Research and
Education, University Hospital Aintree, Lower
Lane, Liverpool, L9 7AL

Tel: 0151 529 5820
Fax: 0151 529 5821
E-mail: secretary@painrelieffoundation.org.uk

Website:
http://www.painrelieffoundation.org.uk

Enquiries:
Enquiries to: Information and Education Services
Direct tel: 0151 529 5838
Direct e-mail: mm27@liv.ac.uk

Founded:
1979

continued overleaf

Organisation type and purpose:
Registered charity; research & education.

Subject coverage:
All chronic pain conditions, causes, treatment.

Information services:
Patient/public information leaflets about chronic pain.

Education services:
Postgraduate education courses for health professionals.

Printed publications:
Leaflets about chronic pain conditions
News Bulletins
Order printed publications from: Pain Relief Foundation

Publications list:
Available online

Access to staff:
Contact by letter, by telephone, by fax and by e-mail
Hours: Mon to Fri, 0900 to 1700

Access to building, collection or gallery:
No access other than to staff

Links with:
Pain Research Institute

PAIN SOCIETY

9 Bedford Square, London, WC1B 3RE

Tel: 020 7631 8870
Fax: 020 7323 2015
E-mail: info@painsociety.org

Website:
http://www.painsociety.org

Enquiries:
Enquiries to: Honorary Secretary

Founded:
1967

Organisation type and purpose:
Professional body.

Subject coverage:
Pain research and management, education, organisation of pain clinics.

Printed publications:
Desirable Criteria for Pain Management Programmes (£4)
Information for Patients (free)
Lists of pain clinics in any county (free)

Access to staff:
Contact by letter, by telephone, by fax, by e-mail and via website
Hours: Mon to Fri, 0930 to 1730
Special comments: Letters preferred, no personal callers.

Access to building, collection or gallery:
No access other than to staff

British Chapter of the:
International Association for the Study of Pain

PAINT RESEARCH ASSOCIATION

Acronym or abbreviation: PRA

PRA Coatings Technology Centre, 14 Castle Mews, High Street, Hampton, Middlesex, TW12 2NP

Tel: 020 8487 0800
Fax: 020 8487 0801
E-mail: library@pra-world.com

Website:
http://www.pra-world.com
Details of the organisation, including research projects, information about training courses, conferences, technical & business services and contact details of staff.

Enquiries:
Enquiries to: Librarian
Direct e-mail: n.morgan@pra-world.com

Founded:
1926

Organisation type and purpose:
Research organisation.

Subject coverage:
Paint science and technology; corrosion; deterioration and biodeterioration of materials; pigments; oils; resins; polymers; paint application; health hazards and toxicology; industrial hazards and anti-pollution legislation; organic and inorganic chemistry; analytical chemistry; anti-fouling technology; spectroscopy; rheology; colour science and colourimetry; paint testing; powder coatings; radiation curing; microbiology; building materials; standards, specifications, reports and patents.

Information services:
Literature and patent searches.

Trade and statistical information:
Available in Coatings COMET.

Non-library collection catalogue:
All or part available online

Library catalogue:
All or part available in-house

Printed publications:
Coatings COMET (Companies Markets Economic Trends)
Dispersion Polymers: Technology and Applications (current literature and patent alerting review)
Paint Titles (200 titles; weekly, current awareness service)
Polymer Curing Technologies (current literature and patent alerting review)
RADnews
SHE Alert (Safety, Health and the Environment)
Waterborne and High-solids Coatings (bulletin, monthly)
World Surface Coatings Abstracts (WSCA) (monthly, with SDI Service)

Electronic and video publications:
All publications are available in electronic formats (pdfs)
SHE Alert Online and COMET Search are online searchable databases of Health, Safety and Environment, and Business Information respectively

Publications list:
Available online and in print

Access to staff:
Contact by letter, by telephone, by fax, by e-mail and via website. Non-members charged.
Hours: Mon to Fri, 0900 to 1700

Access to building, collection or gallery:
Prior appointment required

Access for disabled people:
Parking provided, level entry, toilet facilities

Parent body:
PERA
Nottingham Road, Melton Mowbray, Leicestershire LE13 0PB, UK; tel: 01664 501501; fax: 01664 501554; e-mail: innovation@pera.com; website: http://www.pera.com

PAINTING AND DECORATING ASSOCIATION

Acronym or abbreviation: PDA

32 Coton Road, Nuneaton, Warwickshire, CV11 5TW

Tel: 024 7635 3776
Fax: 024 7635 4513
E-mail: info@paintingdecoratingassociation.co.uk

Website:
http://www.paintingdecoratingassociation.co.uk
Complete profile of association.

Enquiries:
Enquiries to: Chief Executive

Founded:
2002

Created by the merger of:
British Decorators Association and Painting and Decorating Federation (year of change 2002)

Organisation type and purpose:
Trade association.

Subject coverage:
All matters relating to the decorating industry, arbitration, insurance, training and education, employment legislation.

Printed publications:
British Decorator (6 times a year, free to members)
Reference Handbook (annually)

Access to staff:
Contact by letter, by telephone, by fax, by e-mail and via website. Appointment necessary. Non-members charged.
Hours: Mon to Fri, 0900 to 1700

Access to building, collection or gallery:
Prior appointment required

Access for disabled people:
Parking provided, level entry, access to all public areas

Member of:
National Specialist Contractors Council (NSCC)
tel: 0870 429 6351

PAINTING AND DECORATING FEDERATION

Acronym or abbreviation: PDF

32 Coton Road, Nuneaton, Warwickshire CV11 5TW

Tel: 02476 353776
Fax: 02476 354513
E-mail: info@paintingdecoratingassociation.co.uk

Website:
http://www.paintingdecoratingassociation.co.uk/

Enquiries:
Enquiries to: Executive Administrator

Founded:
1942

Organisation type and purpose:
Trade association.

Subject coverage:
Painting and decorating.

Printed publications:
Specifiers Guide – incorporating a directory of members
Health and Safety in Painting
Order printed publications from: The Health & Safety in Painting publication is available from, CIP on tel: 0121 722 8200

Access to staff:
Contact by letter, by telephone, by fax, by e-mail and via website
Hours: Mon to Fri, 0930 to 1715

Member of:
National Specialist Contractors Council (NSCC)
tel: 020 7608 5090; fax: 020 7608 5081

PALAEOECOLOGY CENTRE

Queen's University of Belfast, Belfast, BT7 1NN

Tel: 028 9033 5141
Fax: 028 9031 5779
E-mail: g.johnson@qub.ac.uk

Website:
http://www.qub.ac.uk/arcpal
About the School of Archaeology and Palaeoecology at Queen's University, Belfast.

Enquiries:
Enquiries to: Secretary

Founded:
1970

Organisation type and purpose:
University department or institute.

Subject coverage:
Palaeoecology.

Access to staff:
Contact by letter, by telephone and by e-mail
Hours: Mon to Fri, 0915 to 1315

PALAEONTOGRAPHICAL SOCIETY

Department of Palaeontology, Natural History Museum, Cromwell Road, London, SW7 5BD

Tel: 020 7942 5712
E-mail: s.long@nhm.ac.uk

Website:
http://www.palaeosoc.org
General information on the Society, its governing council, membership and publications. Online shop for purchase of Society publications.

Enquiries:
Enquiries to: Secretary

Founded:
1847

Organisation type and purpose:
Learned society.
To figure and describe British fossils by publishing monographs restricted geographically, stratigraphically and palaeontologically.

Subject coverage:
British fossils; study of geology in relation to fossils, particularly by publications upon them.

Non-library collection catalogue:
All or part available online

Printed publications:
Monographs of British fossils
An annual volume published, consisting of a number of complete or part monographs, each enclosed in its own cover
Order printed publications from: Dr Martin Munt, Marketing Manager, Palaeontographical Society, Natural History Museum, Cromwell Road, London SW7 5BD

Publications list:
Available online

Access to staff:
Contact by letter, by e-mail and via website
Hours: Mon to Fri, 1000 to 1600

PALAEONTOLOGICAL ASSOCIATION

Department of Earth Sciences, University of Durham, South Road, Durham, DH1 3LE

Tel: 0191 334 2320
Fax: 0191 334 2301
E-mail: secretary@palass.org

Website:
http://www.palass.org
Newsletter, list of publications, lists of meetings, general information.

Enquiries:
Enquiries to: Secretary
Other contacts: Executive Officer for membership enquiries; publication orders.

Founded:
1957

Organisation type and purpose:
Learned society.

Subject coverage:
Palaeontology.

Printed publications:
Field Guides to Fossils (series)
Palaeontology (6 times a year)
Special Papers on Palaeontology (1 or 2 times a year, over 40 available)
Order printed publications from: Executive Officer

Publications list:
Available online and in print

Access to staff:
Contact by letter, by telephone, by fax and by e-mail. Appointment necessary.
Hours: Mon to Fri, 0900 to 1700

Other address:
Palaeontological Association
Executive Officer, Institute of Geography and Earth Sciences, University of Wales Aberystwyth, Aberystwyth, Ceredigion, SY23 3BD; tel: 01970 627107; fax: 01970 627107; e-mail: palass@palass.org

PANAMANIAN EMBASSY

40 Hertford Street, London, W1J 7SH

Tel: 020 7493 4646
Fax: 020 7493 4333
E-mail: emb.pan@lineone.net

Website:
http://www.panamainfo.com
Tourism.
http://www.presidencia.gob.pa/gobierno.html
Political.
http://www.panamatours.com
Tourism.

Enquiries:
Enquiries to: Counsellor

Organisation type and purpose:
International organisation.

Subject coverage:
Education; economy; culture; politics; historical and geographical information about Panama, tourism etc.

Printed publications:
Press Release

Access to staff:
Contact by letter, by fax and by e-mail
Hours: Mon to Fri, 1030 to 1630

PANHARD ET LEVASSOR CLUB GB

La Dyna, 11 Arterial Avenue, Rainham, Essex, RM13 9PD

Tel: 01708 524425
E-mail: denise.polley@yahoo.co.uk

Website:
http://www.panhardclub.co.uk

Enquiries:
Enquiries to: Vice President/Membership Secretary

Organisation type and purpose:
Membership association (membership is by subscription), present number of members: 55.

Subject coverage:
Deals mainly with the 1950s and 1960s cars, but information can be obtained about any Panhard Levassor cars.

Access to staff:
Contact by letter, by telephone and by e-mail
Hours: Mon to Fri, 0900 to 2100

PANOS LONDON

Formal name: Panos Institute London

9 White Lion Street, London, N1 9PD

Tel: 020 7278 1111
Fax: 020 7278 0345
E-mail: info@panos.org.uk

Website:
http://www.panos.org.uk
Development and environment information, feature articles and briefings.

Enquiries:
Enquiries to: External Relations Assistant
Direct tel: 020 7239 7609

Founded:
1986

Organisation type and purpose:
Panos works to provide the world's poorest people with access to information on issues that affect them, and to make their voices heard on decisions that relate to their lives.

Subject coverage:
Environment, HIV/AIDS, communication for development, technology issues, oral testimony, globalisation and trade, research communication.

Library catalogue:
All or part available online

Printed publications:
Reports
Books
Media Briefings (£5 each or from website)
Photograph Library – commercial notes
Voices from the Mountain – oral testimony series (8 to date)

Publications list:
Available online

Access to staff:
Contact by letter, by telephone, by fax, by e-mail and via website. Appointment necessary. All charged.
Hours: Mon to Fri, 0930 to 1730

Parent body to:
Panos Picture Library
1 Chappel Court, Borough High Street, London, SE1 1HH; tel: 020 7234 0010

Sister organisations:
Worldwide including Asia, Africa, America and the Caribbean

PANOS PICTURE LIBRARY

1 Honduras Street, London, EC1Y OTH

Tel: 020 7253 1424
Fax: 020 7253 2752
E-mail: pics@panos.co.uk

Website:
http://www.panos.co.uk

Enquiries:
Enquiries to: Archive Manager
Direct e-mail: david@panos.co.uk

Subject coverage:
Third world issues.

Parent body:
Panos Institute
9 White Lion Street, London, N1 9PD; tel: 020 7278 1111

PANTHER ENTHUSIASTS CLUB UK

91 Fleet Road, Farnborough, Hampshire, GU14 9RE

Tel: 01252 540217
Fax: 01252 540217
E-mail: george@pantherclub.co.uk

Website:
http://www.pantherclub.co.uk

Enquiries:
Enquiries to: Secretary

Founded:
1998

Organisation type and purpose:
Membership association (membership is by subscription), present number of members: 450.

Subject coverage:
Panther cars.

Access to staff:
Contact by letter, by telephone and by fax
Hours: Mon to Fri, 0900 to 1700

PAPER AGENTS ASSOCIATION

48, Courtmoor Avenue, Fleet, Hampshire, GU52 7UE

Tel: 01252 680449
Fax: 07092 386132
E-mail: info@paa.org.uk

Website:
http://www.paa.org.uk
Aims, directory of members, officers, diary.

Enquiries:
Enquiries to: Director

Organisation type and purpose:
Trade association for the paper and board industry. To promote a better and closer understanding among accredited agents and mill-owned sales offices in the United Kingdom and Eire representing overseas paper and board makers, and to represent their legitimate overall best interests in the local market. There are 42 members of the Association, ranging from small independently owned businesses to the UK sales subsidiaries of multinational paper-making companies. Between them they account for some 40% of all the paper and board consumed in the UK.

Subject coverage:
Members of the Association are divided into four sections representing the various grades of paper and board imported: Publication and Fine Papers; Corrugated Case Materials; Packaging, Industrial and Other Papers; Cartonboards, Industrial and Other Boards.

Electronic and video publications:
PAA News
Order electronic and video publications from:
Download from website

Access to staff:
Contact by letter, by telephone, by fax and by e-mail

Affiliates:
Paper Agents Golfing Society (PAGS)

Associate member of:
Confederation of Paper Industries

Represented on the board of:
Paperpak Limited (the 'paper specific' compliance scheme for members with obligations under the Packaging Waste Regulations)
PEFC UK Limited (Programme for the Endorsement of Forest Certification)

PAPER INDUSTRY TECHNICAL ASSOCIATION

Acronym or abbreviation: PITA

5 Frecheville Court, Bury, Lancashire, BL9 0UF

Tel: 0161 764 5858
Fax: 0161 764 5353
E-mail: info@pita.co.uk

Website:
http://www.pita.co.uk
General information and news of forthcoming events.

Enquiries:
Enquiries to: Chief Executive
Other contacts: Operations Executive for membership enquiries.

Founded:
1920

Organisation type and purpose:
Professional body (membership is by subscription), present number of members: 1700.

Subject coverage:
Papermaking technology, coating technology, finishing, environmental issues.

Museum or gallery collection, archive, or library special collection:
Complete set of Paper Technology formerly Paper Technology and Industry

Conference proceedings for all association events and many others

Non-library collection catalogue:
All or part available online, in-house and in print

Printed publications:
Conference Reports
Numerous reports and Seminar publications
Paper and Board Manufacture
Paper Science & Paper Manufacture (Peel Dr J)
Paper Technology (10 times a year, £100 a year plus p&p)
The Essential Guide to Aqueous Coating of Paper and Board

Electronic and video publications:
How Paper is Made (TAPPI, 3 CD-ROMs)

Publications list:
Available online and in print

Access to staff:
Contact by letter, by telephone, by fax and by e-mail. Appointment necessary.
Hours: Mon to Fri, 0900 to 1730

Access for disabled people:
Parking provided

PAPER MAKERS ALLIED TRADES ASSOCIATION

Acronym or abbreviation: PMATA

24 Beatrice Road, Worsley, Manchester, M28 2TN

Tel: 0161 794 5734
Fax: 0161 793 0827

Enquiries:
Enquiries to: Honorary Secretary

Founded:
1931

Organisation type and purpose:
Trade association (membership is by subscription), manufacturing industry.
Fostering good relations between the paper industry and its suppliers.

Subject coverage:
Paper industry, chemicals and supplies.

PAPERS PAST

Chapel Row, Truro, Cornwall TR1 2EA

Tel: 01872 261220
Fax: 01872 261220

Website:
http://www.paperspast.co.uk/
Service and product description and order form.

Enquiries:
Enquiries to: Archivist

Founded:
1981

Organisation type and purpose:
Mail order birthday/anniversary newspaper supplier.

Subject coverage:
Archive newspapers. Early 19th century to early 21st century.

Museum or gallery collection, archive, or library special collection:
Newspapers

Printed publications:
Original issues of 19th and 20th century newspapers

Access to staff:
Contact by letter, by telephone and by fax
Hours: Mon to Sun, 0900 to 1900

Access to building, collection or gallery:
No access other than to staff

PAPYRUS

Formal name: PAPYRUS prevention of young suicide

Lodge House, Thompson Park, Ormerod Road, Burnley, Lancashire, BB11 2RU

Tel: Helpline – HOPELineUK: 0800 068 4141;
Admin: 01282 432555
Fax: 01282 432777
E-mail: admin@papyrus-uk.org

Website:
http://www.papyrus-uk.org
The organisation and its aims.

Founded:
1997

Organisation type and purpose:
Registered charity (charity number 1070896).
A voluntary organisation committed to the prevention of young suicide and the promotion of mental health and emotional wellbeing.
To promote an understanding of the unique contribution that parents, families and carers can make to suicide prevention and to promote public awareness of the importance of emotional well-being and sound mental health.

Subject coverage:
UK resources and support for those dealing with suicide, depression or emotional distress – particularly teenagers and young adults. Providing assistance to parents and others in a caring or professional role, supporting vulnerable young people, being represented in policy-making decisions at all levels and monitoring their implementation, encouraging, initiating and taking part in the development of learning opportunities for all, encouraging, taking part and/or initiating research into suicide prevention, campaigning for adequate mental health services for young people, and an easily accessible route to such help on an informal basis, promoting awareness of the risk of mental or emotional distress during adolescence and throughout life, and helping to remove the stigma of such occurrences, encouraging the promotion of emotional well-being and sound mental health, in all levels of education, co-operating with professional, statutory and voluntary bodies working in the suicide prevention field, encouraging and disseminating examples of good practice in suicide prevention.

Printed publications:
Not Just a Cry for Help (booklet, single copies free)
Thinking of Ending it All? (booklet, single copies free)
Don't Die of Embarrassment (resource pack for secondary schools, incl. video/DVD, teachers' notes and worksheets)
Making Use of Hindsight (report)
Coping with Exams (leaflet)
Students Mental Health Needs (eds Nicky Stanley and Jill Manthorpe)
Concern and Confidentiality (2004 study)
Are you Worried? (when to call HOPElineUK)
Feelin' Bad, Feelin' Sad (leaflet for young people)
ACTion for Safety on the Internet (leaflet)

Electronic and video publications:
All printed publications available to download from website

Publications list:
Available online

Access to staff:
Contact by letter, by telephone, by fax, by e-mail and via website
Hours: Helpline: Mon to Fri, 1000 to 1700 and 1900 to 2200; Sat, Sun, 1400 to 1700
Admin tel: Mon to Fri, 0900 to 1700

PARENTLINE PLUS

Acronym or abbreviation: PLP

520 Highgate Studios, 53–79 Highgate Road, Kentish Town, London, NW5 1TL

Tel: 0808 800 2222\ Minicom no. 0800 783 6783

Fax: 020 7284 5501
E-mail: parentsupport@parentlineplus.org.uk

Website:
http://www.parentlineplus.org.uk

Enquiries:
Enquiries to: Chief Executive

Founded:
1983

Organisation type and purpose:
Voluntary organisation, registered charity (charity number 1077722).
Provision of advice, support and information, research and training, represents issues to government, encourages informed media coverage.

Subject coverage:
Any parenting issue; stepfamilies, stepparents, stepmothering, stepchildren, shared parenting, post-divorce, remarriage, re-partnering, teenagers and bullying.

Printed publications:
Publications on a variety of family issues including:
Books for children and young people
Divorce, Separation and New Families (12 publications)
Finance
Guides for parents
Helping Children Learn Series (5 leaflets)
Parenting
Resources for Professionals
Stepfamilies
Sexual Health

Electronic and video publications:
Videos for parents and teenagers

Publications list:
Available in print

Access to staff:
Contact by letter, by telephone, by fax, by e-mail and via website
Hours: Mon to Fri, 0900 to 1700

Branches:
Parentline Plus
  Gloucestershire; tel: 01453 768160
Parentline Plus
  Nottingham; tel: 0115 841 0432
Parentline Plus
  Wirral; tel: 0151 201 7876
Parentline Plus
  Croydon; tel: 020 8689 2252
Parentline Plus
  Hadleigh, Essex; tel: 01702 554782
Parentline Plus
  East Midlands; tel: 01780 480893
Parentline Plus
  Hampshire; tel: 0238 061 9826
Parentline Plus
  Hertfordshire; tel: 01707 270696
Parentline Plus
  North East; tel: 01780 480893

PARENTS FOR INCLUSION

Acronym or abbreviation: Pi

Unit 1, Winchester House, Kennington Park Business Centre, Cranmer Road, London, SW9 6EJ

Tel: 020 7735 7735
Fax: 020 7735 3828
E-mail: info@parentsforinclusion.org

Website:
http://www.parentsforinclusion.org

Enquiries:
Enquiries to: Managing Director

Founded:
1984

Organisation type and purpose:
Membership association (membership is by subscription), present number of members: 200, voluntary organisation, registered charity.

To promote inclusive education of special needs children. Parents helping parents so that their disabled children can learn, make friends and have a voice in ordinary school and throughout life. Aims to help parents whose children are said to have special educational needs to get the support their children need in mainstream schools.

Subject coverage:
Disability, inclusive education and training for parents and young people.

Printed publications:
Action for Inclusion (£7 inc. p&p)
Breaking of Relationships (£2.50 inc. p&p)
Disability Equality in the Classroom: A Human Rights Issue (£15)
Parents and Partnership (£2.50 inc. p&p)
The Inclusion Papers: Strategies To Make Inclusion Work (£8.50)

Electronic and video publications:
Altogether Better (video, £7.50 inc p&p)
Audiotapes
Including All Children (video, £10 plus £1 p&p, £5 to parents)

Publications list:
Available in print

Access to staff:
Contact by letter, by telephone, by fax and by e-mail. Appointment necessary.
Hours: Mon to Fri, 0900 to 1700
Special comments: Advice line: Tue, Wed, Thu, 1000 to 1200 and 1300 to 1500.

Access for disabled people:
Parking provided, ramped entry, access to all public areas, toilet facilities

PARKES LIBRARY

The Hartley Library, University of Southampton, Highfield, Southampton, SO17 1BJ

Tel: 023 8059 2721 or 8059 3335
Fax: 023 8059 5451
E-mail: library@soton.ac.uk; archives@soton.ac.uk

Website:
http://www.soton.ac.uk/library/resources/collections/parkes/index.html
http://www-lib.soton.ac.uk
University library catalogue, including the Parkes Library.
http://www.southampton.ac.uk/archives/cataloguedatabases/guideintro.html
Guide to archive collections.

Enquiries:
Enquiries to: Librarian

Organisation type and purpose:
University library.
Library collection within the Southampton University Library; devoted to relations between Jewish and non-Jewish communities.

Subject coverage:
History of Jewish communities; Zionism and Palestine; Middle Eastern history and Israel; Jewish society, religion and ethics; Jewish-Christian relations; anti-Semitism.

Museum or gallery collection, archive, or library special collection:
Manuscript collections covering all aspects of Anglo-Jewry and its origins, relating to national and international organisations and to individuals within the Jewish community

Library catalogue:
All or part available online

Printed publications:
Guide to the Archive and Manuscript Collections of the Hartley Library, University of Southampton
Parkes Library Lectures
Parkes Library Pamphlets (series)
Sources for Research (Special Collections Division, Hartley Library, University of Southampton)
USL Archive lists, catalogues and guides series

Access to staff:
Contact by letter, by telephone, by fax, by e-mail and in person
Hours: Mon to Fri, 0930 to 1700

PARKINSON'S UK

215 Vauxhall Bridge Road, London, SW1V 1EJ

Tel: Helpline: 0808 800 0303
Fax: 020 7233 9908
E-mail: hello@parkinsons.org.uk

Website:
http://www.parkinsons.org.uk

Enquiries:
Enquiries to: Advisory Services Senior Coordinator

Founded:
1969

Organisation type and purpose:
We bring people with Parkinson's, their carers and families together via our network of local groups, our website and free confidential helpline. Specialist nurses, our supporters, staff and publications provide information and training on every aspect of Parkinson's. We also fund major research projects and campaign for better services.

Subject coverage:
We look at why Parkinson's occurs, the wide variety of symptoms the condition may cause and the range of treatments and support available.

Information services:
Information sheets and booklets available to download on all issues relating to Parkinson's.

Printed publications:
Magazine (4 times a year)
Various information materials available.

Electronic and video publications:
Various DVD resources

Publications list:
Available in print

Access to staff:
Contact by letter, by telephone, by fax, by e-mail and via website. Appointment necessary.
Hours: Helpline: Mon to Fri, 0900 to 2000; Sat 1000 to 1400

Access to building, collection or gallery:
Prior appointment required

Branches:
Scotland
  Forsythe House, Lommond Court, Castle Business Park, Stirling, FK9 4TU; tel: 01786 433811; fax: 01786 431811; e-mail: pds.scotland@parkinsons.org.uk; website: http://www.parkinsons.org.uk

Member organisation of:
European Parkinson's Disease Association

Member organisations:
over 300 branches throughout the UK.

PARLIAMENTARY ADVISORY COUNCIL FOR TRANSPORT SAFETY

Acronym or abbreviation: PACTS

St Thomas' Hospital, Governors Hall, Block 5 South Wing, Lambeth Palace Road, London, SE1 7EH

Tel: 020 7922 8112
Fax: 020 7401 8740
E-mail: admin@pacts.org.uk

Website:
http://www.pacts.org.uk
Publications list

Enquiries:
Enquiries to: Administrator

Founded:
1982

continued overleaf

Organisation type and purpose:
Membership association (membership is by subscription), present number of members: 250, voluntary organisation, registered charity (charity number 1068607), research organisation. Parliamentary advisory body (transport safety).

Subject coverage:
Road, rail and air transport safety. PACTS advises parliamentarians on issues of transport safety based on research solutions.

Printed publications:
PACTS' Publications (£10 to £20)

Publications list:
Available online

Access to staff:
Contact by telephone and by e-mail
Hours: Mon to Fri, 0900 to 1700

Founder member of:
European Transport Safety Council (ETSC)
  Rue du Cornet 34, Brussels, B-1040, Belgium

PARLIAMENTARY AND HEALTH SERVICE OMBUDSMAN

Formal name: Office of the Parliamentary Commissioner for Administration and the Health Service Commissioners

Millbank Tower, Millbank, London, SW1P 4QP

Tel: 0300 061 4104
Fax: 0300 061 1565
E-mail: lrc@ombudsman.org.uk

Website:
http://www.ombudsman.org.uk

Enquiries:
Enquiries to: Information Officer

Founded:
1967

Organisation type and purpose:
National organisation.

Subject coverage:
Ombudsman issues.

Printed publications:
Order printed publications from: Stationery Office (for purchase)

Access to staff:
Contact by letter, by telephone, by fax and by e-mail
Hours: Mon to Fri, 0900 to 1700

PARLIAMENTARY AND SCIENTIFIC COMMITTEE

48 Westminster Palace Gardens, Artillery Row, London, SW1P 1RR

Tel: 020 7222 7085
Fax: 020 7222 5355

Enquiries:
Enquiries to: Secretary

Founded:
1939

Organisation type and purpose:
Membership association (membership is by subscription).

Subject coverage:
Parliament and science.

Printed publications:
Science in Parliament (the journal of the Parliamentary and Scientific Committee)

Access to staff:
Contact by letter, by telephone and by fax
Hours: Mon to Fri, 1000 to 1800

PARLIAMENTARY ARCHIVES

Parliamentary Archives, Houses of Parliament, London, SW1A 0PW

Tel: 020 7219 3074
Fax: 020 7219 2570
E-mail: archives@parliament.uk

Website:
http://www.parliament.uk/archives
Index-A-Archives for general information including records held, details of location and access, list of publications in print, on-line exhibitions.
http://www.portcullis.parliament.uk
Catalogue of collections.

Enquiries:
Enquiries to: Clerk of The Records

Founded:
1946

Organisation type and purpose:
One of the Offices of Parliament.
To preserve and make available the archives of Parliament.

Subject coverage:
History of both Houses of Parliament, history of the Palace of Westminster; the Private Bill Records contain a great deal of information about local history, e.g. local government, railways, roads, canals, electricity, gas and water works; political history from the special collections; legal and contemporary issues. Sources for genealogists include certain legislation, Private Bill evidence, Protestation Returns of 1642 and other Lords papers.

Museum or gallery collection, archive, or library special collection:
Records of the House of Lords from 1497 and of the House of Commons from 1547, papers of 1st Viscount Samuel, Lord Beaverbrook, Lloyd George, Bonar Law and others

Trade and statistical information:
Published Parliamentary reports.
Evidence given to select committees.

Non-library collection catalogue:
All or part available online and in-house

Library catalogue:
All or part available online and in-house

Printed publications:
Calendar of the Manuscripts of the House of Lords, volumes I–XII (new series) 1693–1718 (HMSO)
Guide to the Records of Parliament (Bond M F, 1971, pub HMSO)
Annual Review (TSO)
House of Lords Record Office Memoranda including:
Witnesses Before Parliament (1997)
House of Lords Record Office Occasional Publications including:
A Handlist of the Braye Manuscripts in the House of Lords Record Office (HMSO, 1993)
Catalogue of the Beaverbrook Papers in the House of Lords Record Office: Canadian and Business Papers (TSO, 1997)

Microform publications:
Parliamentary Papers (pub Proquest)
Main papers (Harvester)
Minutes, Committee Books, etc. (pub Adam Matthew Publications)

Publications list:
Available online and in print

Access to staff:
Contact by letter, by telephone, by fax, by e-mail and via website. Appointment necessary.
Hours: Mon, Wed to Fri, 0930 to 1700; Tue, 0930 to 2000, booking one week in advance only when Parliament is in session

Access for disabled people:
Toilet facilities
Special comments: Parking by special arrangement, access by lift.

PARLIAMENTARY MONITORING SERVICES

Acronym or abbreviation: PMS

19 Douglas Street, London, SW1P 4PA

Tel: 020 7233 8283
Fax: 020 7821 9352
E-mail: lionel.zetter@parliamentary-monitoring.co.uk

Website:
http://www.politicalwizard.co.uk

Enquiries:
Enquiries to: Managing Director

Founded:
1978

Organisation type and purpose:
Research organisation, publishing house.
We are an independent commercial political research, news and publishing company.

Subject coverage:
Politics: local, national and European Union, legislation, issues and personalities.

Printed publications:
European Public Affairs Directory 1998 (annually, £69)
Legitimate Lobbying (£9)
PMS Guide to Pressure Groups (3rd ed., £17.50)
PMS Parliament Companion (quarterly, £11 per issue, £33 annual subscription)
PMS Update Bulletin (approximately 40 issues a year, £75 annual subscription)
Parliamentary Bulletin for Local Government Executives (weekly, £75 annual subscription)

Electronic and video publications:
Online databases with biographical details on MPs, peers, MEPs and civil servants
PMS Biographical Guide to the Civil Service
PMS Biographical Guide to the House of Commons
PMS Biographical Guide to the House of Lords
PMS Biographical Guides (the three online £900 annual subscription)

Publications list:
Available in print

Access to staff:
Contact by letter, by telephone, by fax and by e-mail. Appointment necessary.
Hours: Mon to Fri, 0900 to 1730

Access to building, collection or gallery:
No prior appointment required

Subsidiary body:
PMS Publications Limited

PARTIALLY SIGHTED SOCIETY

Acronym or abbreviation: PSS

PO Box 322, Doncaster, South Yorkshire, DN1 2XA

Tel: 01302 323132
Fax: 01302 368998
E-mail: info@partsight.org.uk

Enquiries:
Enquiries to: Information Officer

Founded:
1973

Organisation type and purpose:
Membership association, voluntary organisation, registered charity (charity number 254052). Helping the visually impaired make best use of their remaining sight.

Subject coverage:
Education, employment, mobility, daily living, leisure, aids and adaptations in relation to living with partial sight.

Printed publications:
Crossword Books
Good News for the Partially Sighted
Large print crossword book
Light for Low Vision

Mail Order Brochure for daily living aids
Oculus (large print magazine, 4 times a year)

Publications list:
Available in print

Access to staff:
Contact by letter, by telephone, by fax, by e-mail
and via website. Appointment necessary.
Hours: Mon to Fri, 0900 to 1700

PARTNERSHIP FOR THEOLOGICAL EDUCATION

Formal name: Luther King House Library
Acronym or abbreviation: PTE

Luther King House, Brighton Grove, Rusholme,
Manchester, M14 5JP

Tel: 0161 249 2514
Fax: 0161 248 9201
E-mail: library@lkh.co.uk

Website:
http://www.lutherkinghouse.org.uk
http://www.lkhlibrarycatalogue.org.uk
Online catalogue

Enquiries:
Enquiries to: Learning Resources Tutor
Other contacts: Learning Resources Assistant

Founded:
1988

Formerly called:
Manchester Christian Institute (year of change
1992); Northern Federation for Training in
Ministry (year of change 2000)

Organisation type and purpose:
Registered charity, university department or
institute.
Theological college.

Subject coverage:
Theology; Free Church and general ecclesiastical
history; ministry; Bible commentaries; worship;
social sciences; biography; history; philosophy;
ethics; missiology; spirituality; pastoral theology;
ecumenism; comparative religion; community
studies.

**Museum or gallery collection, archive, or library
special collection:**
Collections housed in the John Rylands Library,
    Manchester
Hobill Collection and Primitive Methodist Material
Northern (Congregational College) Collection
Rawdon Collection of historical Baptist material,
    mostly from 18th and 19th centuries (Northern
    Baptist College Deposit)
Unitarian College Collection (McLachlan Library)
    Unitarian and Nonconformist history,
    Socinianism

Non-library collection catalogue:
All or part available online

Library catalogue:
All or part available online

Access to staff:
Contact by letter, by telephone, by fax, by e-mail,
in person and via website. Appointment necessary.
Non-members charged.
Hours: Mon to Fri, 0900 to 1700

Access for disabled people:
Parking provided, ramped entry, toilet facilities

Constituent bodies:
Hartley Victoria College
Luther King House Open College
Northern Baptist College
Northern College (United Reformed and
Congregational)
Unitarian College

Links with:
William Temple Foundation
    at the same address

Recognised by the:
Department of Religions and Theology of the
University of Manchester
Department of Theology and Religious Studies of
the University of Chester

PASSAGE

Formal name: The Passage

St Vincent's Centre, Carlisle Place, London SW1P
1N

E-mail: info@passage.org.uk

Website:
http://www.passage.org.uk
London's homeless and how The Passage helps.

Founded:
1980

Organisation type and purpose:
A Christian charitable organisation.
Runs London's largest voluntary sector day centre
for homeless and vulnerable people: each day it
helps more than 200 men and women.
To provide resources that encourage, inspire, and
challenge homeless people to transform their lives.

Subject coverage:
Day Centre services offering: basic care, individual
assessment and advice, health, housing, pastoral
and spiritual care, education, training and
employment. Outreach services to contact rough
sleepers. Hostel accommodation moving towards
re-settlement and further steps to independence.
Supported semi-independent accommodation
moving towards independence and reintegration.
Welcomes and treats clients with respect and
dignity, finding out what they need and want.
Offers professional and appropriate advice and
help according to client needs and aspirations.
Tries to agree an action plan with clients that is
time-limited, with the aim of supporting clients out
of homelessness.

Electronic and video publications:
Quarterly magazine produced by clients with
    support of staff
Order electronic and video publications from: website:
http://www.writesofpassage.org.uk

Access to staff:
Contact by letter, by telephone and by e-mail

A constitutional partnership between:
Daughters of Charity of St Vincent de Paul and
Westminster Cathedral

PASSENGER SHIPPING ASSOCIATION

Acronym or abbreviation: PSA

1st Floor, 41–42 Eastcastle Street, London, W1W
8DW

Tel: 020 7436 2449
Fax: 020 7636 9206
E-mail: h.tapping@psa-psara.org

Website:
http://www.ferryinformationservice.co.uk
http://www.cruiseinformationservice.co.uk

Enquiries:
Enquiries to: Director
Other contacts: Administrator

Organisation type and purpose:
Membership association (membership is by
subscription).

Subject coverage:
Passenger shipping.

Access to staff:
Contact by e-mail
Hours: Mon to Fri, 0900 to 1700

Access to building, collection or gallery:
No access other than to staff, prior appointment
required

PASSIVE FIRE PROTECTION FEDERATION

Acronym or abbreviation: PFPF

Tournai Hall, Evelyn Woods Road, Aldershot
Hampshire GU11 2LL

Tel: 01252 357841
Fax: 01252 357831
E-mail: admin@pfpf.org

Website:
http://pfpf.org/

Enquiries:
Enquiries to: Secretary
Direct e-mail: membership@pfpf.org

Organisation type and purpose:
Trade association, present number of members: 16.
Federation of trade associations, test houses,
certification and government bodies involved in
passive fire protection.

Subject coverage:
Trade associations, test houses, certification and
government bodies involved in passive fire
protection.

Access to staff:
Contact by letter, by telephone, by fax, by e-mail
and via website
Hours: Mon to Fri, 0900 to 1700

PASTEL SOCIETY

Acronym or abbreviation: PS

17 Carlton House Terrace, London, SW1Y 5BD

Tel: 020 7930 6844
Fax: 020 7839 7830
E-mail: press@mallgalleries.com

Website:
http://www.thepastelsociety.org.uk
http://www.mallgalleries.org.uk
FBA and Mall Galleries information.

Enquiries:
Enquiries to: Secretary
Other contacts: Marketing and Communications
Officer

Founded:
1898

Organisation type and purpose:
Membership association (membership is by
election or invitation), present number of
members: 68, voluntary organisation, registered
charity (charity number 200048).
To foster and promote the art of pastel painting.

Subject coverage:
Pastel art.

**Museum or gallery collection, archive, or library
special collection:**
Examples of pastel artists' work on slides, photos
    and some original pastel paintings

Printed publications:
Annual Exhibition Catalogue
Books on Pastel Painting on sale during annual
    exhibition

Access to staff:
Contact by letter, by telephone, by fax, by e-mail
and via website. Appointment necessary.
Hours: Mon to Fri, 0930 to 1700

Access to building, collection or gallery:
No access other than to staff, prior appointment
required
Hours: Mon to Fri, 0930 to 1700

Access for disabled people:
Stairlift; toilet facilities
Special comments: Stairlift.

Links with:
Federation of British Artists (FBA)
    at the same address

PATENT OFFICE

Cardiff Road, Newport, South Wales, NP10 8QQ

Tel: 01633 814000, Operator; 0845 9500505, Central
Enquiry Unit (local rate)\ Minicom no. 0645 222
250 (local rate)
Fax: 01633 814444
E-mail: enquiries@patent.gov.uk

Website:
http://www.patent.gov.uk
Advice and information regarding patents,
designs, trade and service marks and copyright,
including a search engine for Patents.

Enquiries:
Enquiries to: Information Officer
Direct fax: 01633 813600

Founded:
1852

Organisation type and purpose:
National government body.
Executive agency of the Department of Trade and
Industry.

Subject coverage:
All areas of Intellectual Property incorporating:
Patents, Designs, Trade marks and Copyright.

Printed publications:
An Introduction to the Services of the Patent Office
    and Trade Marks and Design Registries
Design Registration
How to prepare a UK Patent application
Managing Intellectual Property
Official Journal (Patents)
Patent Abstracts
Patent Protection
Registering a Trademark
Trade Mark Journal
What is Intellectual Property
Your Software and How to Protect it

Electronic and video publications:
Managing Intellectual Property
UK Patent applications on CD-ROM available for
    sale

Access to staff:
Contact by letter, by telephone, by fax, by e-mail,
in person and via website
Hours: Mon to Fri, 0900 to 1700

Access to building, collection or gallery:
No prior appointment required
Special comments: Trade Mark Searches in Newport
require an appointment.

Other addresses:
The Patent Office
    Harmsworth House, 13–15 Bouverie Street,
    London, EC4Y 8DP; tel: 020 7596 6518; e-mail:
    enquiries@patent.gov.uk

PATHOLOGICAL SOCIETY OF GREAT BRITAIN AND IRELAND

2 Carlton House Terrace, London, SW1Y 5AF

Tel: 020 7976 1260
Fax: 020 7930 2981
E-mail: admin@pathsoc.org

Website:
http://www.pathsoc.org

Enquiries:
Enquiries to: Administrator

Founded:
1906

Organisation type and purpose:
Learned society (membership is by election or
invitation), present number of members: 1,500
(charity number 214702).
Research communication for the continuing
education of pathologists.

Subject coverage:
Pathology.

Printed publications:
Journal of Pathology (monthly)

Access to staff:
Contact by letter, by telephone, by fax and by e-
mail
Hours: Mon to Fri, 0900 to 1730

PATTERN, MODEL AND MOULDMAKERS ASSOCIATION

Acronym or abbreviation: PMMMA

c/o Eur. Ing. Andrew Turner, National
Metalforming Centre, 47 Birmingham Road, West
Bromwich, West Midlands, B70 6PY

Tel: 0121 601 6976
Fax: 01544 340332
E-mail: andrew@pmmma.co.uk

Website:
http://www.pmmma.co.uk

Organisation type and purpose:
Trade association.

Subject coverage:
Pattern-making, industrial patterns and moulds.

Access to staff:
Contact by letter, by telephone and by fax

PCET PUBLISHING

27 Kirchen Road, London, W13 0UD

Tel: 020 8567 9206 or 5343
Fax: 020 8566 5120
E-mail: info@pcet.co.uk

Website:
http://www.pcet.co.uk
Sample of charts from subject leaflets and
information about teaching, guides, money savers,
photocopiable activity books, catalogue requests.

Enquiries:
Enquiries to: Managing Director
Direct e-mail: Director@pcet.co.uk

Founded:
1964

Organisation type and purpose:
Publishing house.
Non-profit making publisher of educational visual
aids.

Subject coverage:
Educational visual aids in all areas of the National
Curriculum, except modern languages.

Printed publications:
Mail order catalogue (annually, with additional
    supplements)
Titles cover a wide range of subjects including:
Art
Geography
History
Religion
The 20th Century
Mathematics
Music
Sciences
English

Publications list:
Available in print

Access to staff:
Contact by letter, by telephone, by fax, by e-mail
and via website. Appointment necessary.
Hours: Mon to Fri, 0900 to 1700

PDSA

Whitechapel Way, Priorslee, Telford, Shropshire,
TF2 9PQ

Tel: 01952 290999
Fax: 01952 291035
E-mail: pr@pdsa.org.uk

Website:
http://www.pdsa.org.uk

PDSA veterinary services, pet care advice, PDSA
news and fundraising opportunities.

Enquiries:
Enquiries to: Public Relations Manager

Founded:
1917

Organisation type and purpose:
Registered charity (charity number 208217).
The PDSA provides free veterinary treatment to
sick and injured pets whose owners qualify for
help, by receiving either Housing Benefit or
Council Tax Benefit, and live within an area served
by a PDSA PetAid hospital or PetAid practice.

Subject coverage:
Veterinary and associated social and educational
subjects (eg pet care).

Printed publications:
General information leaflets
Pet Care Leaflets

Publications list:
Available in print

Access to staff:
Contact by letter, by telephone, by fax, by e-mail
and via website
Hours: Mon to Fri, 0900 to 1700

PEAK DISTRICT NATIONAL PARK AUTHORITY

Acronym or abbreviation: PDNPA

National Park Office, Aldern House, Baslow Road,
Bakewell, Derbyshire, DE45 1AE

Tel: 01629 816200
Fax: 01629 816310
E-mail: customer.service@peakdistrict.gov.uk

Website:
http://www.peakdistrict.gov.uk

Enquiries:
Enquiries to: Head of Communications (for media
enquiries)
Direct tel: 01629 816356
Direct e-mail: john.fern@peakdistrict.gov.uk

Founded:
1951

Organisation type and purpose:
Local government body, advisory body, statutory
body, training organisation, publishing house.

Subject coverage:
The Peak District National Park, conservation of
the National Park environment, integrated rural
development, moorland erosion, recreation, and
restoration; general information on the history,
geology, agriculture, wildlife, and recreation
opportunities, rural public transport,
environmental education and training.

Printed publications:
Annual Report
National Park Management Plan
Planning publications and official reports
Parklife (2 times a year)
Peak District National Park Cycle Routes

Publications list:
Available in print

Access to staff:
Contact by letter, by telephone, by e-mail and via
website. Appointment necessary.
Hours: Mon to Fri, 0845 to 1700

Access to building, collection or gallery:
Prior appointment required

Access for disabled people:
Parking provided, ramped entry, toilet facilities

PEEBLES AREA LIBRARY

Chambers Institution, High Street, Peebles,
Borders, EH45 8AG

Tel: 01721 720123

Fax: 01721 724424
E-mail: libpeebles@scotborders.gov.uk

Enquiries:
Enquiries to: Area Librarian
Direct e-mail: ptaylor@scotborders.gov.uk

Founded:
1859

Organisation type and purpose:
Local government body, public library.

Subject coverage:
General, Peeblesshire local history, John Buchan
material.

Library catalogue:
All or part available in-house

Access to staff:
Contact by letter, by telephone, by fax, by e-mail
and in person
Hours: Mon, Wed and Fri, 0930 to 1700; Tue and
Thu, 0930 to 1900; Sat, 0900 to 1230

Access for disabled people:
Lift to Library area on first floor only

Parent body:
Scottish Borders Library Service
 St Marys Hill, Selkirk, TD7 5EW; tel: 01750
 20842; fax: 01750 22875

PEMBROKE COLLEGE

McGowin Library, Oxford, OX1 1DW

Tel: 01865 276409
Fax: 01865 276418

Website:
http://www.pmb.ox.ac.uk

Enquiries:
Enquiries to: Librarian/Archivist
Direct e-mail: library@pmb.ox.ac.uk

Founded:
1624

Organisation type and purpose:
College library.

Subject coverage:
Aristotle, Samuel Johnson, College history.

**Museum or gallery collection, archive, or library
special collection:**
Archive of Pembroke College
Aristotle (Chandler Collection)
Samuel Johnson

Access to staff:
Contact by letter, by telephone, by fax and by e-
mail. Appointment necessary. Letter of
introduction required.
Hours: Mon to Fri, 0900 to 1700

PEMBROKESHIRE COAST NATIONAL PARK AUTHORITY

Acronym or abbreviation: PCNPA

Llanion Park, Pembroke Dock, Pembrokeshire,
SA72 6DY

Tel: 0845 345 7275
Fax: 01646 689076
E-mail: info@pembrokeshirecoast.org.uk

Website:
http://www.pcnpa.org.uk

Enquiries:
Enquiries to: Switchboard

Founded:
1952

Organisation type and purpose:
Local government body, advisory body, statutory
body, present number of members: 18
National Park Authority and Local Planning
Authority.

Conservation of landscape, wildlife and culture of
the National Park; promotion of the enjoyment and
understanding of the park's special qualities;
fostering the social and economic well-being of the
local community.

Subject coverage:
Conservation, National Parks, recreation,
countryside access, interpretation, education, local
information, communities, cultural heritage,
wildlife, planning.

**Museum or gallery collection, archive, or library
special collection:**
Local maps and aerial photographs
Planning Records
Teachers' Resources

Trade and statistical information:
Statistics on the National Park (as available).

Printed publications:
Children's Leaflets
Guides to walks in the National Park
Guides for the Coast Path Walker
Subject guides, including wild flowers and beaches
Safety information
Access information (including disabled, etc.)
Easy Access Routes
Order printed publications from: Tenby Information
Centre Manager, Pembrokeshire Coast National
Park Authority, Ruabon House, South Parade,
Tenby, SA70 7DL

Electronic and video publications:
Pembrokeshire Coast Long Distance Path video
Carew Castle Education Pack (includes video)

Publications list:
Available online and in print

Access to staff:
Contact by letter, by telephone, by fax, by e-mail,
in person and via website
Hours: Headquarters: Mon to Thu, 0900 to 1700;
Fri, 0900 to 1630

Access for disabled people:
Parking provided, ramped entry, wheelchair lifts
and toilet facilities

Branches:
Carew Castle and Tidal Mill
 Carew, Pembrokeshire, SA70 8SL; tel: 01646
 651782; fax: 01646 651782; e-mail: enquiries@
 carewcastle.com
Castell Henllys Iron Age Fort
 Meline, Crymych, Pembrokeshire, SA41 3UT; tel:
 01239 891319; fax: 01239 891319; e-mail:
 enquiries@castellhenllys.com
Cilrhedyn Woodland Centre
 Llanychaer, Fishguard, Pembrokeshire, SA65
 9TN; tel: 01348 881441; fax: 01348 881713
National Park Information Centre (all year)
 Ruabon House, South Parade, Tenby, SA70 7DL;
 tel: 01834 845040; fax: 01834 840871; e-mail:
 contact.centre@pembrokeshire.gov.uk
National Park Information Centre (seasonal)
 Bank Cottages, Long Street, Newport, SA42 0TN;
 tel: 01239 820912; fax: 01239 820912
Oriel Y Parc Landscape Gallery and National Park
Information Centre
 The Grove, St Davids, Pembrokeshire, SA62
 6NW; tel: 01437 725087; fax: 01437 720099; e-
 mail: enquiries@stdavids.pembrokeshirecoast
 .org.uk

Links with:
Parc Naturel Regional d'Armorique
 15 place aux Foires, BP 27, 29590 Le Faou,
 France; tel: +33 2 98 81 90 08; fax: +33 2 98 81 90
 09

PEMBROKESHIRE COUNTY COUNCIL

County Hall, Haverfordwest, Pembrokeshire, SA61
1TP

Tel: 01437 764551
Fax: 01437 775303
E-mail: enquiries@pembrokeshire.gov.uk

Website:
http://www.pembrokeshire.gov.uk
Tourism and Inward Investment. General
information re Pembrokeshire and Pembrokeshire
County Council.

Enquiries:
Enquiries to: Head of Marketing Communications
Direct tel: 01437 775850
Direct e-mail: david.thomas@pembrokeshire.gov.uk

Founded:
April 1996

Organisation type and purpose:
Local government body.

Subject coverage:
All local government services.

**Museum or gallery collection, archive, or library
special collection:**
County archives department, county libraries and
county museums

Printed publications:
Community Newspaper (2 times a year, free)
Holiday Brochure for Pembrokeshire (free)
Various other publications and leaflets on services
 provided and policy documents

Access to staff:
Contact by letter, by telephone, by fax, by e-mail,
in person and via website. Appointment necessary.
Hours: Mon to Fri, 0900 to 1700

Access for disabled people:
Parking provided, level entry, toilet facilities

PEMBROKESHIRE RECORD OFFICE

The Castle, Haverfordwest, Pembrokeshire, SA61
2EF

Tel: 01437 763707
Fax: 01437 768539
E-mail: record.office@pembrokeshire.gov.uk

Website:
http://www.pembrokeshire.gov.uk/archives
Brief description of service, with opening hours.

Enquiries:
Enquiries to: Archivist

Founded:
1963

Organisation type and purpose:
Local government body.
Local authority record office.

Subject coverage:
The history of Pembrokeshire.

**Museum or gallery collection, archive, or library
special collection:**
Pembrokeshire historical material, mainly
 manuscript collections

Non-library collection catalogue:
All or part available in-house

Library catalogue:
All or part available in-house

Publications list:
Available in print

Access to staff:
Contact by letter, by telephone, by fax, by e-mail,
in person and via website
Hours: Mon to Thu, 0900 to 1645; Fri, 0900 to 1615

Access to building, collection or gallery:
No access other than to staff and areas available to
the public, i.e. search rooms and toilets
Hours: Mon to Thu, 0900 to 1645; Fri, 0900 to 1615
Special comments: 1st Mon in the month, 1000 to
1645. 1st Sat in the month, except bank holiday
weekends, 0930 to 1230.

Access for disabled people:
Parking provided, ramped entry, access to all
public areas, toilet facilities

PENGUIN COLLECTORS' SOCIETY

Acronym or abbreviation: PCS

c/o 31 Myddelton Square, London, EC1R 1YB

Tel: 020 7278 8064
E-mail: treasurer@penguincollectorssociety.org

Website:
http://www.penguincollectorssociety.com
Details of society, membership application form,
illustrations and descriptions of publications.

Enquiries:
Enquiries to: Secretary / Treasurer

Founded:
1974

Organisation type and purpose:
Charity (membership is by subscription), present
number of members: c. 400.
Study, research, and publishing on 20th-century
books, especially those published by Penguin
Books Limited.

Subject coverage:
Penguin Books, their history and publications.

Printed publications:
Journal and monographs

Publications list:
Available in print

Access to staff:
Contact by e-mail and via website
Hours: PCS has no staff – volunteers only

Access to building, collection or gallery:
PCS has no premises.

PENNINE WAY ASSOCIATION

Acronym or abbreviation: PWA

29 Springfield Park Avenue, Chelmsford, Essex,
CM2 6EL

Tel: 01245 256772
E-mail: penninewayassociation@hotmail.com

Website:
http://www.penninewayassociation.co.uk

Enquiries:
Enquiries to: Chairman
Direct e-mail: penninewayassociation@hotmail.com

Founded:
1971

Formerly called:
Pennine Way Council (year of change 1992)

Organisation type and purpose:
Membership association (membership is by
subscription), present number of members: 360,
voluntary organisation, registered charity (charity
number 511519).

Subject coverage:
To secure the protection of the Pennine Way, to
provide information about the Way to the public,
to educate users of the Way and its environs in a
proper respect for the countryside, and to provide
a forum in which different interests connected with
the Way and its use can discuss problems of
mutual concern.

Printed publications:
Pennine Way woven badge
PW Memento (£3.00 incl. postage)
Pennine Way Accommodation and Camping
  Guide (2008/09 downloadable from the PWA
  website)
Walkers' factsheet (send sae)

Access to staff:
Contact by letter, by telephone, by e-mail and via
website
Hours: Answerphone

PENSIONS ADVISORY SERVICE LTD

Acronym or abbreviation: TPAS

11 Belgrave Road, London, SW1V 1RB

Tel: 0845 6012923
Fax: 020 7233 8016
E-mail: enquiries@pensionsadvisoryservice.org.uk

Website:
http://www.pensionsadvisoryservice.org.uk
Casework reports, leaflets.

Enquiries:
Direct fax: 020 7592 7000

Founded:
1983

Organisation type and purpose:
Advisory body, voluntary organisation.
To provide help and advice on various pension
problems, helps to resolve any difficulties
encountered with the trustees or administrators of
pension schemes.

Subject coverage:
Occupational and personal pensions and state
pensions.

Printed publications:
Getting Information About Your Pension (free)
Ill-Health Retirement (free)
Information (free)
Pension Dispute Procedures (free)
Personal Pension Problems (free)
Transferring a Pension to another Scheme (free)
Where Is My Pension? (free)
Winding Up a Pension Scheme (free)
Women and Pensions (free)

Publications list:
Available online and in print

Access to staff:
Contact by letter, by telephone, by fax and by e-
mail
Hours: Mon to Fri, 0900 to 1700

Access to building, collection or gallery:
No access other than to staff

PENSIONS MANAGEMENT INSTITUTE

Acronym or abbreviation: PMI

PMI House, 4–10 Artillery Lane, London, E1 7LS

Tel: 020 7247 1452
Fax: 020 7365 0603
E-mail: enquiries@pensions-pmi.org.uk

Website:
http://www.pensions-pmi.org.uk

Enquiries:
Enquiries to: Head of Qualifications and Student
Services

Founded:
1976

Organisation type and purpose:
Professional body (membership is by subscription),
present number of members: 4,500.
PMI sets and promotes standards of excellence and
lifelong learning for pensions professionals,
trustees and those working in the employee
benefits field, through its qualifications,
membership and ongoing support services.

Subject coverage:
Pension schemes, administration and
management; pensioners.

Printed publications:
Annual Handbook
Annual Yearbook
Pensions Terminology (Glossary of Pension Terms)
Newsletter (monthly)
Research Papers
Technical News (quarterly)
Study material

Access to staff:
Contact by letter, by telephone, by fax, by e-mail
and via website
Hours: Mon to Fri, 0900 to 1700

PENSIONS OMBUDSMAN

6th Floor, 11 Belgrave Road, London, SW1V 1RB

Tel: 020 7834 9144
Fax: 020 7821 0065

Enquiries:
Enquiries to: Administrator
Direct e-mail: michael.lydon@pensions
-ombudsman.org.uk
Other contacts: Press Officer for press enquiries.

Founded:
1990

Organisation type and purpose:
Independent statutory body.

Subject coverage:
In cases where a complaint or dispute cannot be
resolved, normally after the intervention of OPAS,
an application can be made to the Pensions
Ombudsman for an adjudication. The
Ombudsman can investigate and determine any
complaint or dispute of fact or law involving the
management of occupational and personal pension
schemes. The services of the Ombudsman are
available to scheme members, and prospective
members of schemes, as well as (in some
circumstances) employers, trustees or managers.

Printed publications:
The Pensions Ombudsman – What he can do
  (available free, direct)
The Pensions Ombudsman – Annual Report
  (Stationery Office, charged)

Access to staff:
Contact by letter, by telephone, by fax and by e-
mail
Hours: Mon to Fri, 0900 to 1700
Special comments: No personal callers.

PENSIONS REGULATOR

Napier House, Trafalgar Place, Brighton, East
Sussex, BN1 4DW

Tel: 0870 606 3636
Fax: 0870 241 1144
E-mail: customersupport@thepensionsregulator
.gov.uk

Website:
http://www.thepensionsregulator.gov.uk
http://www.trusteetoolkit.co.uk

Enquiries:
Enquiries to: Customer Support

Founded:
2005

Organisation type and purpose:
Statutory body.
UK regulator of work-based pensions schemes.

Subject coverage:
Work-based pensions industry.

Publications list:
Available online and in print

Access to staff:
Contact by letter, by telephone, by fax, by e-mail
and via website
Hours: Mon to Fri, 0900 to 1730

PENWITH DISTRICT COUNCIL

Council Offices, St Clare, Penzance, Cornwall,
TR18 3QW

Tel: 01736 362341
Fax: 01736 336595

Website:
http://www.penwith.gov.uk

Organisation type and purpose:
Local government body.

PEOPLE & PLANET

51 Union Street, Oxford, OX4 1JP

Tel: 01865 245678
Fax: 01865 791927
E-mail: people@peopleandplanet.org

Website:
http://peopleandplanet.org
People & Planet UK students taking action on
world poverty, human rights and the environment.

Enquiries:
Enquiries to: Administrator

Founded:
1969

Organisation type and purpose:
Student action on world poverty, human rights
and the environment.

Subject coverage:
Global poverty, human rights and the
environment, campaigning and education with UK
students.

Printed publications:
Variety of leaflets, posters, information packs etc

Access to staff:
Hours: Mon to Fri, 1000 to 1600

PEPYS LIBRARY

Magdalene College, Cambridge, CB3 0AG

Tel: 01223 332125
E-mail: pepyslibrary@magd.cam.ac.uk

Website:
http://www.magd.cam.ac.uk/pepys/index.html

Enquiries:
Enquiries to: Pepys Librarian
Direct e-mail: pepyslibrary@magd.cam.ac.uk

Founded:
1703

Organisation type and purpose:
Private library with restricted public access.

Subject coverage:
Pre-1703 printed books and manuscripts (nautical,
musical, literary, ballads, prints and drawings,
calligraphy, medieval manuscripts).

**Museum or gallery collection, archive, or library
special collection:**
Personal library of the diarist and Secretary of the
Admiralty, Samuel Pepys (1633–1703), preserved
in its original presses, closed on his death, and
bequeathed by him to his old college

Library catalogue:
All or part available in print

Printed publications:
Catalogue (Latham R C ed., 16 vols, 1980–1994,
pub. Boydell & Brewer, Woodbridge)
The Pepys Library (booklet, for sale in library)

Access to staff:
Contact by letter and by e-mail. Appointment
necessary. Letter of introduction required.
Special comments: Researchers should make
requests for appointments in writing, giving
details of the nature of research and material
required.
General visitors may visit without appointment.
Groups must not exceed 10 people.

Access to building, collection or gallery:
Hours: Michaelmas and Lent terms: 1430 to 1530
Easter term to end of August: 1130 to 1230 and
1430 to 1530
Exact dates on website
Special comments: Access is via a flight of about 20
stairs; there is no lift

Access for disabled people:
Not accessible by wheelchair.

PERFECT INFORMATION

Acronym or abbreviation: PI

35 Chiswell Street, London, EC1Y 4SE

Tel: 020 7892 4200
Fax: 020 7892 4201
E-mail: research@perfectinfo.com

Website:
http://www.perfectinfo.com

Enquiries:
Enquiries to: Director

Founded:
1990

Organisation type and purpose:
Service industry.

Subject coverage:
All compliance documentation released by UK
listed companies including: directors
shareholdings, board changes, changes in
substantial shareholdings, results, bids,
acquisitions, report and accounts, circulars to
shareholders, all available online in original form
with an archive back to 1982.

**Museum or gallery collection, archive, or library
special collection:**
All UK Company Reports and accounts
EDGAR SEC filings and International Bonds
Entire London Stock Exchange microfiche
collection back to 1982
European and Asian Company Annual Reports
RNS Announcements
UK Company Circulars

Electronic and video publications:
Occasional bureau-based facility can be provided,
call for details
Online service can be accessed via ISDN link, fax
or dedicated Kilostream link

Access to staff:
Contact by letter, by telephone, by fax, by e-mail
and via website. All charged.
Hours: Mon to Fri, 0900 to 1730

Connections with:
Centaur Communications
50 Poland Street, London, W1F 7AX

Other address:
Perfect Information Inc (PI)
245 Park Avenue, 39th Floor, New York, NY
10167, USA; tel: 1 212 792 4350; fax: 1 212 792
4307

PERFORMING RIGHT SOCIETY LIMITED

Acronym or abbreviation: PRS

29–33 Berners Street, London, W1T 3AB

Tel: 020 7580 5544
Fax: 020 7306 4550
E-mail: press@mcps-prs-alliance.co.uk

Website:
http://www.prs.co.uk

Enquiries:
Enquiries to: Chief Executive

Founded:
1914

Organisation type and purpose:
Membership association (membership is by
subscription).
To license the public performance, broadcast and
cable transmission of its composer and publisher
members' copyright.

Subject coverage:
Music copyright and royalties; public performance;
broadcasting; collection and distribution of
performance royalties.

Printed publications:
M (magazine)
PRS Handbook
PRS Yearbook

Access to staff:
Contact by letter, by telephone, by fax, by e-mail
and via website. Appointment necessary.
Hours: Mon to Fri, 0900 to 1700

Access for disabled people:
Ramped entry

Affiliated to:
similar performing right organisations, throughout
the world

Links with:
British Music Rights
Mechanical Copyright Protection Society Limited

PERIODICAL PUBLISHERS ASSOCIATION

Acronym or abbreviation: PPA

Queens House, 28 Kingsway, Holborn, London,
WC2B 6JR

Tel: 020 7404 4166
Fax: 020 7404 4167
E-mail: via website

Website:
http://www.ppa.co.uk
PPA and membership, all about magazines, sector
research, legal and public affairs matters, events.

Enquiries:
Other contacts: Research Manager, tel: 020 7400
7571

Founded:
1913

Formerly called:
Society of Weekly Newspaper and Periodical
Proprietors

Organisation type and purpose:
A trade association, one of the leading magazine
trade bodies world-wide, an issuer of press cards
to journalists.
To promote the interests of the UK magazine and
business media industry.

Subject coverage:
Works at the heart of a network of national and
international alliances across the creative
industries, protecting members from damaging
restrictions on press freedom and on the freedom
to advertise; safeguarding members' intellectual
property; fighting for a cost-effective postal
distribution system; defending members against
unnecessary regulation; and promoting the
editorial and financial health of the industry. Has a
strong interest in training and development, and,
in addition to its own training and qualifications,
credits 12 university courses in the UK.

Printed publications:
Exclusive to members

Electronic and video publications:
Exclusive to members

Access to staff:
Contact by letter, by telephone, by fax and via
website

Also at:
PPA Scotland
22 Rhodes Park, Tantallon Road, North Berwick,
EH39 5NA; tel: 01620 890800; e-mail: kathy
.crawford@ppascotland.co.uk; website: http://
www.ppa.co.uk/ppa-scotland

Constituent bodies:
AOP (Association of Online Publishers)
APA (Association of Publishing Agencies)

Links with:
DPA (Data Publishers Association)
at the same address

Member organisation of:
FAEP (European Federation of Magazine
Publishers)
FIPP (International Federation of the Periodical
Press)

continued overleaf

the funding body for Advertising Standards Authority
the funding body for Press Complaints Commission

PERMANENT WAY INSTITUTION

Acronym or abbreviation: PWI

4 Coombe Road, Folkestone, CT19 4EG

Tel: 01303 275835
E-mail: secretary@permanentwayinstitution.com

Website:
http://www.permanentwayinstitution.com

Enquiries:
Enquiries to: Secretary

Founded:
1884

Organisation type and purpose:
Learned society (membership is by subscription), present number of members: 3,500 British Isles, 1,500 rest of world.

Subject coverage:
Railway permanent way engineering (concerning railway track infrastructure): design, construction and maintenance.

Non-library collection catalogue:
All or part available online

Library catalogue:
All or part available online and in-house

Printed publications:
British Railway Track – Design Construction and Maintenance (7th edn in 12 separate vols; vol. 1, part 3, vols 4, 5 and 9 available) (6th edn, 1993, £30.00)
History of the PWI – the first 100 Years, 1884–1984 (£10 incl. p&p)
Light Rail Supplement, Tracks to the Cities (£10 incl. p&p)
The Evolution of Permanent Way (£5.00 incl. p&p)
Order printed publications from: Secretary, Permanent Way Institution

Publications list:
Available online and in print

Access to staff:
Contact by letter, by telephone and by e-mail
Hours: Mon to Fri, 0900 to 1630

Has:
19 sections in UK, 1 for all Ireland, 5 overseas

Links with:
Union of European Railway Engineer Associations
Verband Deutscher Eisenbahn Ingenieure (VDEI) Germany

Member organisation of:
Union of European Railway Engineer Associations (UEEIV)

PERSONAL FINANCE SOCIETY

Acronym or abbreviation: PFS

42–48 High Road, South Woodford, London, E18 2JP

Tel: 020 8530 0852
Fax: 020 8530 3052
E-mail: customer.serv@thepfs.org

Website:
http://www.thepfs.org/

Enquiries:
Enquiries to: Press and PR Co-ordinator
Direct e-mail: alex.thompson@cii.co.uk

Founded:
2004

Created by the merger of:
The Society of Financial Advisers and the Life Insurance Association (1972)

Organisation type and purpose:
Professional body (membership is by subscription), present number of members: 25,000.

Subject coverage:
Life assurance; pensions; unit-linked products; financial services;
professional education, ethics and standards.

Printed publications:
Prospect (magazine, monthly, for members, £3.50 to non-members or by subscription on application)

Access to staff:
Contact by letter, by telephone, by fax, by e-mail and via website. Appointment necessary.
Hours: Mon to Fri, 0900 to 1700

Associated with:
Chartered Insurance Institute (London)
LIA Ireland
   Dublin
National Association of Life Underwriters
   Washington, DC, USA

Network of:
35 regions in UK and Ireland

PERSONAL SAFETY MANUFACTURERS ASSOCIATION

Acronym or abbreviation: PSMA

Tamesis House, 35 St Philip's Avenue, Worcester Park, Surrey, KT4 8JS

Tel: 020 8330 6446
Fax: 020 8330 7447
E-mail: psma@tamgroup.co.uk

Enquiries:
Enquiries to: General Secretary

Founded:
1998

Organisation type and purpose:
Trade association.

Subject coverage:
Production and marketing of industrial protective and safety equipment within the PSE Directive of the EC.

Printed publications:
C/E Market Product Directory (free on written application enclosing an A5 sae with first class stamp)

Access to staff:
Contact by e-mail
Hours: Mon to Fri, 0900 to 1700

Access to building, collection or gallery:
Prior appointment required

Affiliated to:
British Safety Industry Federation (BSIF)
   St Asaph Business Park, St Asaph, Denbighshire, LL17 0LJ; tel: 01745 585600; fax: 01745 585800; e-mail: info@bsif.co.uk; website: www.bsif.co.uk

PERTH AND KINROSS COUNCIL

2 High Street, Perth, Tayside, PH1 5PH

Tel: 01738 475000
Fax: 01738 475710
E-mail: enquiries@pkc.gov.uk

Website:
http://www.pkc.gov.uk

Enquiries:
Enquiries to: Research and Consultation Assistant
Direct tel: 01738 475084
Direct fax: 01738 475010
Direct e-mail: tbrunton@pkc.gov.uk

Founded:
1996

Organisation type and purpose:
Local government body.

Subject coverage:
Information on the council, tourism, socio-economic property, education, roads, planning, leisure and cultural services, social work, law and administration, environmental health, Europe social policy, finance, human resources, housing.

Access to staff:
Contact by letter
Hours: Mon to Fri, 0900 to 1700

Access for disabled people:
Ramped entry, toilet facilities

PERTH AND KINROSS LIBRARIES

A K Bell Library, York Place, Perth, Perthshire, PH2 8EP

Tel: 01738 444949\ Minicom no. 01738 620114 (textphone)
Fax: 01738 477010
E-mail: library@pkc.gov.uk

Website:
http://www.pkc.gov.uk/library

Enquiries:
Enquiries to: Head of Libraries and Archives
Direct e-mail: mmoir@pkc.gov.uk

Founded:
1996

Organisation type and purpose:
Local government body, public library.

Subject coverage:
General, local history, local archives, Scots language.

Museum or gallery collection, archive, or library special collection:
Atholl Collection (17th and 18th century Scottish folk and dance music)
District archives
Local history
McIntosh Collection (17th century ecclesiastical and general works)
William Soutar Collection (poetry and Scottish literature)

Non-library collection catalogue:
All or part available in print

Printed publications:
A selection of books of particular local interest, including:
A Vision of Perth (Muro D, 2001)
Alert: the War Years in Perth (1989)
Along the A6, The Great North Road (MacDonald A, 2001)
Heritage of Perth (Findlay Dr W H, 1996)
Life in the Atholl Glens (Kerr J, 1993, £9.95)
The Easy Trip (Knaggs B, 2001)
The Story of Errol Station (Beech J, 1993, £2.95)

Publications list:
Available online and in print

Access to staff:
Contact by letter, by telephone, by fax, by e-mail, in person and via website. Appointment necessary.
Hours: Mon, Wed, 0930 to 1700; Tue, Thu, 0930 to 2000; Fri, 0900 to 1700; Sat, 0930 to 1600

Access for disabled people:
Parking provided, level entry, access to all public areas, toilet facilities

Part of:
Perth and Kinross Council
   2 High Street, Perth; tel: 01738 475000; fax: 01738 475710; website: pkc.gov.uk

PERTHES ASSOCIATION

PO Box 773, Guildford, GU1 1XN

Tel: 01483 306637 (helpline); 534431 (admin)
E-mail: info@perthes.org.uk

Website:
http://www.perthes.org.uk

Enquiries:
Enquiries to: Secretary

Founded:
1976

Organisation type and purpose:
National organisation, membership association (membership is by subscription), present number of members: 803 full, 2,000 part members, voluntary organisation, registered charity (charity number 326161), suitable for all ages.

Subject coverage:
Help, advice and support to sufferers of Perthes Disease of the hip, all forms of osteochondritis and MED (multiple epiphyseal dysplasia), in both children and adults; medical information, financial advice (benefits), housing, education, special equipment and clothing, counselling.

Printed publications:
Factsheet (free)
Newsletter (quarterly, members)
Layman's Guide to Osteochondritis, Association Handbook, Your Child in an Immobilising Hip Spica Plaster
Perthes Association Handbook
How to care for your Child in an Immobilising Hip Spica Plaster
Order printed publications from: Secretary, at the same address

Access to staff:
Contact by letter, by telephone, by e-mail and via website. Non-members charged.
Hours: Mon to Fri, 0900 to 1700, tel and e-mail
Special comments: 0900 to 1300 tel.

Links with:
Contact a Family
Long Term Medical Conditions Alliance
NCVO
RADAR

PERTHSHIRE TOURIST BOARD

Acronym or abbreviation: PTB

Administrative Headquarters, Lower City Mills, West Mill Street, Perth, Tayside, PH1 5QP

Tel: 01738 627958/9
Fax: 01738 630416
E-mail: info@perthshire.co.uk

Website:
http://www.perthshire.co.uk/
General information on Perthshire: attractions, events, activities and accommodation.
Visit the 'contact us' section for a list of publications.

Enquiries:
Enquiries to: Chief Executive
Other contacts: Head of Marketing; Head of Visitor Services

Organisation type and purpose:
Statutory body, membership association (membership is by subscription), present number of members: 1300.
Non-governmental public body, area tourist board.
To position Perthshire as a world-class destination, where visitor expectations are exceeded through product quality, delivery of service and unique destination characteristics, in such a manner that Perthshire's maximum potential for long-term economic and social prosperity is realised through a sustainable tourism industry.

Subject coverage:
Information on all matters pertaining to tourism in Perthshire, 2000 square miles in Central Scotland, accommodation, visitor attractions, sporting and recreational facilities, events and entertainments.

Trade and statistical information:
Data on the volume and value of tourism in Perthshire. Research and statistical information.
Marketing advice to Tourist Board members.

Printed publications:
Activity Days Brochure (free)
Angling in Tayside (£5)

An invitation to . . . brief introduction to the eight areas of Perthshire (8 leaflets, free)
Explore Perthshire (free)
A range of factsheets and publications on local walks
Cycling and Mountain Biking in Perthshire (free)
Factsheet for Visitors with Disabilities (free)
Perthshire Conference Brochure (free)
Perthshire: The Essential Guide (£1.50, inc. p&p)
Perthshire Where to Stay Guide (free)
Perthshire Map (£4.30)
Perthshire, Angus and Fife Walks (£10.95)
Perthshire Big Tree Country (free)
Selected Cycle Routes (£1.80)
Snowsports and Winter Activities (free)

Electronic and video publications:
CD-ROM of Perthshire images for use by the press and members of Perthshire Tourist Board

Publications list:
Available online and in print

Access to staff:
Contact by letter, by telephone, by fax, by e-mail, in person and via website
Hours: Mon to Fri, 0900 to 1700
Special comments: Administrative Headquarters is open office hours; tourist information centres open longer, particularly during tourist season.

Tourist Information Centres:
Aberfeldy (open all year)
The Square, Aberfeldy, Perthshire, PH15 2DD; tel: 01887 820276; fax: 01887 829495; e-mail: aberfeldytic@perthshire.co.uk
Auchterarder (open all year)
90 High Street, Auchterarder, Perthshire, PH3 1BJ; tel: 01764 663450; fax: 01764 664235; e-mail: auchterardertic@perthshire.co.uk
Blairgowrie (open all year)
26 Wellmeadow, Blairgowrie, Perthshire, PH10 6AS, Ski-line 875800; tel: 01250 872960; fax: 01250 873701; e-mail: blairgowrietic@perthshire.co.uk
Crieff (open all year)
High Street, Crieff, Perthshire, PH7 3HU; tel: 01764 652578; fax: 01764 655422; e-mail: criefftic@perthshire.co.uk
Dunkeld (open all year)
The Cross, Dunkeld, Perthshire, PH8 0AN; tel: 01350 727688; fax: 01350 727688; e-mail: dunkeldtic@perthshire.co.uk
Kinross (open all year)
Heart of Scotland Visitor Centre, adjacent to service area, Junction 6, M90, Kinross, Perthshire, KY13 7NQ; tel: 01577 863680; Activity line: 01577 861186; fax: 01577 863370; e-mail: kinrosstic@perthshire.co.uk
Perth (open all year)
Lower City Mills, West Mill Street, Perth, PH1 5QP; tel: 01738 450600; fax: 01738 444863; e-mail: perthtic@perthshire.co.uk
Pitlochry (open all year)
22 Atholl Road, Pitlochry, Perthshire, PH16 5BX; tel: 01796 472215 or 472751; fax: 01796 474046; e-mail: pitlochrytic@perthshire.co.uk

PET CARE TRUST

Acronym or abbreviation: PCT

Bedford Business Centre, 170 Mile Road, Bedford, MK42 9TW

Tel: 01234 273933
Fax: 01234 273550
E-mail: info@petcare.org.uk

Website:
http://www.petcare.org.uk
Material about the Trust, its member services and training opportunities.

Enquiries:
Enquiries to: Operations Manager
Direct e-mail: rosie.loft@petcare.org.uk

Founded:
1986

Organisation type and purpose:
National organisation, professional body, trade association (membership is by subscription), present number of members: 1506, service industry, voluntary organisation, registered charity (charity number 1052488), suitable for ages: all, training organisation.
To promote high standards of training in the industry; to promote responsible pet ownership.

Subject coverage:
Training information and information on pet care and related legislation.

Trade and statistical information:
Data on pet care industry, market and population.

Printed publications:
Training manuals and video material
Pet Care Trust – Review (newsletter, once every other month)
UK Pet Trade Year book and Buyers Guide (updated annually)

Access to staff:
Contact by letter, by telephone, by fax and by e-mail. Appointment necessary.
Hours: Mon to Fri, 0830 to 1700

Access to building, collection or gallery:
Prior appointment required

Access for disabled people:
Parking provided, level entry, toilet facilities

Subsidiary body:
British Dog Groomers Association
tel: 01234 273933; fax: 01234 273550; e-mail: pat@petcare.org.uk

PET FOOD MANUFACTURERS' ASSOCIATION LIMITED

Acronym or abbreviation: PFMA

20 Bedford Street, Covent Garden, London, WC2E 9HP

Tel: 020 7379 9009
Fax: 020 7379 8008
E-mail: info@pfma.org.uk

Website:
http://www.pfma.com
Information on the prepared pet food industry in the UK. Also general background on keeping and feeding of pets, information on related charities and organisations.

Enquiries:
Enquiries to: Administration Secretary

Founded:
1971

Organisation type and purpose:
Trade association.

Subject coverage:
General information relating to the UK prepared pet food industry, pet related issues and interests.

Trade and statistical information:
Data on UK prepared pet food market.
Data on UK dog and cat populations.

Access to staff:
Contact by letter, by telephone, by fax and by e-mail
Hours: Mon to Fri, 0900 to 1700

Access to building, collection or gallery:
No access other than to staff

Member of:
FEDIAF
Avenue Louise 89, Brussels, B-1050, Belgium

PETA FOUNDATION

Formal name: People for the Ethical Treatment of Animals Foundation

PO Box 36678, London, SE1 1YE

Tel: 020 7357 9229
Fax: 020 7357 0901

continued overleaf

E-mail: info@peta.org.uk

Website:
http://www.petaf.org.uk
PETA education.

Organisation type and purpose:
Registered charity in England & Wales (charity number 1056453) dedicated to establishing and protecting the rights of all animals. Works mainly in the UK, but also responds to requests for information and resources from overseas.

Subject coverage:
PETA and its affiliates around the world educate policymakers and the public about cruelty to animals and promote an understanding of the right of all animals to be treated with respect.

PETA works through public education, research, legislation, special events, celebrity involvement and protest campaigns.

Education services:
Education Department: events and free education materials.

Electronic and video publications:
e-mail updates
Order electronic and video publications from: via website

Access to staff:
Contact by letter, by telephone, by fax and by e-mail

Links with:
PETA charities in USA, France, Germany, Netherlands, India, Asia-Pacific and Spain

PETERBOROUGH CENTRAL LIBRARY AND THEATRE

Broadway, Peterborough, Cambridgeshire, PE1 1RX

Tel: 01733 864270
Fax: 01733 555277
E-mail: centrallibrary@vivacity-peterborough.com

Website:
http://www.peterborough.gov.uk/leisure_and_culture/libraries.aspx

Organisation type and purpose:
Local government body, public library. Central reference library for the Greater Peterborough area.

Subject coverage:
General, history and study of Peterborough and its area, business information, environmental information, open learning and training materials and information (the Learning Centre), European Union information (European Public Information Centre).

Museum or gallery collection, archive, or library special collection:
John Clare Collection
Local history collection

Non-library collection catalogue:
All or part available online and in-house

Access to staff:
Contact by letter, by telephone, by fax, by e-mail and in person
Hours: Tue, Wed, Fri, 0900 to 1700; Mon, Thu, 0900 to 1900; Sat 0900 to 1600

Access to building, collection or gallery:
No prior appointment required

Access for disabled people:
Parking provided, level entry, access to all public areas, toilet facilities

Parent body:
Peterborough Culture and Leisure Trust

PETERBOROUGH REGIONAL COLLEGE LIBRARY+

Park Crescent, Peterborough, Cambridgeshire, PE1 4DZ

Tel: 01733 762137
Fax: 01733 767986

Website:
http://www.peterborough.ac.uk
College website.

Enquiries:
Enquiries to: Library+ Manager

Organisation type and purpose:
College of further and higher education.

Subject coverage:
Accounting; electrical engineering; mechanical engineering; building construction; chemistry; physics; mathematics; biology; psychology; sociology; economics; geography; geology; English literature; management; catering; media; history; sport; computing; hairdressing; beauty therapy; child care; health & social care; motor vehicles; plumbing; ESOL, foreign languages.

Library catalogue:
All or part available in-house

Access to staff:
Appointment necessary.
Hours: Term time: Mon to Thu, 0830 to 1945; Fri, 0830 to 1700

Access for disabled people:
Parking provided, level entry, toilet facilities

PETERBOROUGH ROYAL FOXHOUND SHOW SOCIETY

East of England Showground, Peterborough, Cambridgeshire, PE2 6XE

Tel: 01733 234451
Fax: 01733 370038
E-mail: andrew@eastofengland.org.uk

Enquiries:
Enquiries to: Secretary

Founded:
1878

Organisation type and purpose:
Foxhound show society.

Subject coverage:
Foxhounds; breeding and showing.

Museum or gallery collection, archive, or library special collection:
Handwritten record books listing winners in each of the above classes, over the years

PETROC

Old Sticklepath Hill, Barnstaple, Devon, EX31 2BQ

Tel: 01271 338170 (main library line)
Fax: 01271 388121
E-mail: library@petroc.ac.uk

Website:
http://www.petroc.ac.uk
Main college website.

Enquiries:
Enquiries to: Learning Centres & e-Resources Manager
Other contacts: Learning Resources Team Leader; Learning Resources Co-ordinators

Created by the merger of:
East Devon College and North Devon College (year of change 2008)

Organisation type and purpose:
Suitable for ages: mainly 16 to 19.
College of further education.

Subject coverage:
Academic subjects and some local material.

Non-library collection catalogue:
All or part available online

Library catalogue:
All or part available online

Access to staff:
Contact by letter, by telephone, by fax and by e-mail
Hours: Term time: Mon to Wed, 0830 to 1900; Thu, Fri, 0830 to 1630
Vacations: Mon to Fri, 0900 to 1300

Access for disabled people:
Parking provided, access to all public areas, toilet facilities

PETROL RETAILERS ASSOCIATION

Acronym or abbreviation: PRA

201 Great Portland Street, London, W1W 5AB

Tel: 020 7307 3593
Fax: 020 7307 3592
E-mail: pra@rmif.co.uk

Website:
http://www.rmif.co.uk

Enquiries:
Enquiries to: Secretary

Founded:
1913

Subject coverage:
Petrol retailing.

Member of the:
Retail Motor Industry Federation

Other addresses:
Petrol Retailers Association
  107a Shore Road, Belfast, BT15 3BB; tel: 028 9037 0137; fax: 028 9037 0706

PETROLEUM OPEN LEARNING

Acronym or abbreviation: OPITO

Minerva House, Bruntland Road, Portlethan, Aberdeen, AB12 4QL

Tel: 01224 787800
Fax: 01224 787830
E-mail: richard.bain@opito.net

Website:
http://www.petroleumopenlearning.com

Enquiries:
Enquiries to: Technical Sales Manager
Direct tel: 01224 787813

Founded:
1988

Organisation type and purpose:
OPITO – The Oil and Gas Academy is the industry's focal point for skills, training and workforce development. The Academy is a self-sustaining, employer- and trade union-led organisation committed to developing and sustaining a safe, skilled and effective workforce now and in the future. This is achieved by working in collaboration with: industry employers, learning and training providers, education and academia and partnership organisations.

Subject coverage:
Oil and gas well technology, petroleum processing technology, health and safety.

Printed publications:
Books and modules for Open learning, include:
Oil and Gas Well Technology Series (3 Modules)
Petroleum Processing Technology Series (10 Modules)
Oil & Gas Electrical Engineering Systems (5 Modules)

Publications list:
Available online and in print

Access to staff:
Contact by letter, by telephone, by fax, by e-mail, in person and via website. Appointment necessary.
Hours: Mon to Fri, 0900 to 1700

Access for disabled people:
Parking provided, ramped entry, level entry, access to all public areas, toilet facilities

Parent body:
OPITO – The Oil and Gas Academy
  Minerva House, Bruntland Road, Portlethen, Aberdeen, AB12 4QL; tel: 01224 787800; fax: 01224 787830; website: http://www.opito.com

PEWTER SOCIETY

37 Hurst Lane, Bollington, Cheshire, SK10 5LT

E-mail: secretary@pewtersociety.org

Website:
http://www.pewtersociety.org

Enquiries:
Enquiries to: Secretary

Founded:
1918

Organisation type and purpose:
Learned society, present number of members: 250, voluntary organisation.

Subject coverage:
Antique pewter – its history, manufacture and social context; identification, conservation and information about specific pewterers.

Museum or gallery collection, archive, or library special collection:
The library holds all British and many foreign books published on pewter and many papers on pewter and pewter-related topics

Library catalogue:
All or part available online and in-house

Printed publications:
Journal of Pewter Society (twice a year, members only but available in some libraries)
Newsletter (twice a year, members only)
Occasional special publications, which are available to non-members, such as:
Irish Pewter (1995)
The Richard Neate Touch Plate (1996)
Books on European Pewter Marks (1999)
Five Centuries of Base Metal Spoons (reprinted 1999)
Pewterers of London 1600–1900 (2001)
English Candlesticks of the Second Half of the 17th Century (2004)
The Records of the York Company of Pewterers (2004)

Electronic and video publications:
Database of British Pewterers and their Marks (online, members only)

Publications list:
Available online

Access to staff:
Contact by letter, by e-mail and via website
Special comments: No access

Access to building, collection or gallery:
No access

PHARMACEUTICAL SOCIETY OF NORTHERN IRELAND

Acronym or abbreviation: PSNI

73 University Street, Belfast, BT7 1HL

Tel: 028 9023 1163
Fax: 028 9043 9919

Enquiries:
Enquiries to: Chief Executive Secretary & Registrar
Direct e-mail: mark.neale@psni.org.uk
Other contacts: Secretary

Founded:
1925

Organisation type and purpose:
Statutory body, professional body (membership is by qualification), present number of members: 1700, service industry.
Registration authority for pharmacists and pharmacies in Northern Ireland.

Subject coverage:
Pharmaceutical matters.

Access to staff:
Contact by letter, by telephone, by fax and by e-mail
Hours: Mon to Fri, 0900 to 1700

PHILADELPHIA ASSOCIATION

Acronym or abbreviation: PA

4 Marty's Yard, 17 Hampstead High Street, London, NW3 1QW

Tel: 020 7794 2652
Fax: 020 7794 2652
E-mail: paoffice@globalnet.co.uk

Enquiries:
Enquiries to: Administrator

Founded:
1965

Organisation type and purpose:
Registered charity.
Charity in the field of mental health.

Subject coverage:
Training in phenomenology and psychoanalytic psychotherapy, residential therapeutic communities, psychotherapy referrals.

Library catalogue:
All or part available in-house

Printed publications:
Information on training and psychotherapy
Thresholds between Philosophy and Psychoanalysis (book)

Access to staff:
Contact by letter, by telephone and by fax. Appointment necessary.
Hours: Mon, 1330 to 1730; Tue, Thu, Fri, 1630 to 2030

Access to building, collection or gallery:
No access other than to staff

PHILATELIC TRADERS SOCIETY LIMITED

Acronym or abbreviation: PTS

PO Box 371, Fleet, Hampshire, GU52 6ZX

Tel: 01252 628006
Fax: 01252 684674
E-mail: info@philatelic-traders-society.co.uk

Website:
http://www.philatelic-traders-society.co.uk
Information on the Society; list of dealers; information on Stampex Exhibitions.

Enquiries:
Enquiries to: General Secretary

Founded:
1949

Organisation type and purpose:
Trade association.

Subject coverage:
Philatelic trade; support for stamp collecting as a hobby; organisers of the two national stamp exhibitions, Spring Stampex and Autumn Stampex.

Printed publications:
Membership Directory (available for purchase)
PTS News (6 times a year, members only)

Access to staff:
Contact by letter, by telephone, by fax, by e-mail and in person. Appointment necessary.
Hours: Mon to Thu, 1000 to 1700; Fri, 1000 to 1300

Constituent bodies:
Stampex Ltd
  tel: 01252 628006; fax: 01252 684674

PHILIPPINE EMBASSY

9a Palace Green, London, W8 4QE

Tel: 020 7937 1600
Fax: 020 7937 2925
E-mail: embassy@philemb.demon.co.uk

Website:
http://www.microtron.net/philemb/index.shtml
Information on Philippines. Philippine Embassy Services, news, visa, passport application forms (downloadable).

Enquiries:
Enquiries to: H E The Ambassador
Direct e-mail: embassy@philemb.co.uk
Other contacts: Information Officer

Organisation type and purpose:
International organisation.

Subject coverage:
The Philippines: Consular matters.

Printed publications:
Information bulletin (limited list of recipients)

Access to staff:
Contact by letter, by telephone, by fax, by e-mail, in person and via website. Appointment necessary.
Hours: Mon to Fri, 0900 to 1700
Special comments: Closed during Philippine holidays.

Access to building, collection or gallery:
No prior appointment required
Hours: Mon to Fri, 0900 to 1700

Other addresses:
Office of the Tourism Attaché
  146 Cromwell Road, London, SW7 4EF; tel: 020 7835 1100; fax: 020 7835 1926; e-mail: Tourism@pdot.co.uk
Philippine Department of Trade
  1A Cumberland House, Kensington Court, London, W8; tel: 020 7937 7998 1898; fax: 020 7937 2747; e-mail: dtilondon@aol.com

PHILOLOGICAL SOCIETY

School of Oriental and African Studies, University of London, Thornhaugh Street, Russell Square, London, WC1H 0XG

Tel: 020 7898 4376
E-mail: secretary@philsoc.org.uk

Website:
http://www.philsoc.org.uk

Enquiries:
Enquiries to: Honorary Secretary

Founded:
1841

Organisation type and purpose:
Learned society, present number of members: 860, registered charity (charity number 1014370).
To investigate and promote the study and knowledge of the structure, affinities, and history of language.

Subject coverage:
Linguistics; philology.

Printed publications:
Transactions of the Philological Society (3 issues per year)
Occasional special publications, for example:
Metaphor and Metonymy: A Diachronic Approach (K. Allan, 2009)
Focus in Hausa (M. Green, 2007)
Universals of Sound Change in Nasalization (J. Hajek, 1997)
The Linguistic Relationship between Armenian and Greek (J. Clackson, 1995)
Order printed publications from: http://www.wiley.com/bw/journal.asp?ref=0079–1636

continued overleaf

Access to staff:
Contact by letter and by e-mail
Hours: Mon to Fri, 0900 to 1700

PHONOGRAPHIC PERFORMANCE LIMITED

Acronym or abbreviation: PPL

1 Upper James Street, London, W1F 9DE

Tel: 020 7534 1000
Fax: 020 7534 1111

Enquiries:
Enquiries to: Public Relations Manager

Founded:
1934

Organisation type and purpose:
Membership association.
Established by the UK record companies as a non-profit company to license the broadcast and public performance of their sound recordings.
Copyright licensing body.

Subject coverage:
Copyright relating to public performance and broadcasting of commercial sound recordings, including records, tapes and re-recordings, in the United Kingdom, on behalf of the British record industry.

Printed publications:
Copyright Protection (information sheet, 1996, free)
Annual Report
Newsletter (quarterly, free)

Publications list:
Available in print

Access to staff:
Contact by letter, by telephone and by fax
Hours: Mon to Fri, 0930 to 1730

Links with:
BPI
IFPI

PHOTO MARKETING ASSOCIATION INTERNATIONAL (UK) LIMITED

Acronym or abbreviation: PMA

Wisteria House, 28 Fulling Mill Lane, Welwyn, Hertfordshire, AL6 9NS

Tel: 0870 240 4542
Fax: 01438 716572
E-mail: pmauk@pmai.org

Website:
http://www.pmai.org

Enquiries:
Enquiries to: Director of UK operations
Other contacts: Administration Manager

Founded:
1923

Organisation type and purpose:
International organisation, trade association (membership is by subscription), consultancy.
To expand the photographic industry and to make its members more profitable.

Subject coverage:
Photographic industry trends – worldwide, consumer research, the photo, video and digital industries, retailers, minilabs, wholesale photo finishers, camera repairers, school photographs.

Trade and statistical information:
Industry trends report – annual statistics on the photo industry.

Printed publications:
Business resources catalogue
Mini Lab Information Package
Promote Your Image and Build Your Business
Who's Who in Photographic Management: A membership, product and service directory

Microform publications:
Photographic Colour Prints

Electronic and video publications:
Mini Lab Training Series (video)
Photofinishing Training Series (video)

Access to staff:
Contact by letter, by telephone, by fax, by e-mail and via website. Appointment necessary. Non-members charged.
Hours: Mon to Fri, 0930 to 1730

Affiliated to:
Photo Marketing Association International
3000 Picture Place, Jackson, Michigan, 49201, USA

Subsidiary body:
APL Services Limited

PHOTOGRAPHIC WASTE MANAGEMENT ASSOCIATION

Acronym or abbreviation: PWMA

Ambassador House, Brigstock Road, Thornton Heath, Surrey, CR7 7JG

Tel: 020 8665 5395
Fax: 020 8665 6447
E-mail: pwma@admin.co.uk

Enquiries:
Enquiries to: Secretary

Founded:
1993

Organisation type and purpose:
Trade association.

Subject coverage:
Photographic waste management.

Printed publications:
Services Guide and List of Members

Access to staff:
Contact by letter
Hours: Mon to Fri, 0900 to 1700

Member of:
British Imaging and Photographic Association

PHYSICAL PROPERTIES DATA SERVICE

Acronym or abbreviation: PPDS

TUV NEL Ltd, Scottish Enterprise Technology Park, East Kilbride, South Lanarkshire, G75 0QU

Tel: 01355 272527
Fax: 01355 272265
E-mail: ppds@tuvnel.com

Website:
http://www.ppds.co.uk
http://www.nelfood.com
Database of physical properties of foods.

Enquiries:
Enquiries to: Manager
Direct tel: 01355 593775
Direct e-mail: ajohns@tuvnel.com

Organisation type and purpose:
Service industry, training organisation, consultancy, research organisation.

Subject coverage:
Constant, thermodynamic and transport properties for over 1,500 organic compounds; vapour liquid equilibrium package containing seven different methods and nine different calculations; data for petroleum fractions and steam; liquid properties for 22 aqueous solutions and 97 commercial heat transfer fluids.

Printed publications:
Newsletter (also available online, free)
Product factsheets

Electronic and video publications:
PPDS Software Package (for calculation of physical properties of pure fluids and their mixtures including equilibria)
http://www.netfood.com (database of properties of foods)

Access to staff:
Contact by letter, by telephone, by fax, by e-mail and via website
Hours: Mon to Fri, 0900 to 1700

Access to building, collection or gallery:
No access other than to staff

PHYSIO FIRST

Minerva House, Tithe Barn Way, Swan Valley, Northampton, NN4 9BA

Tel: 01604 684960
E-mail: minerva@physiofirst.org.uk

Website:
http://www.physiofirst.org.uk

Enquiries:
Enquiries to: General Secretary

Founded:
1951

Formerly called:
Organisation of Chartered Physiotherapists in Private Practice (year of change 2006)

Organisation type and purpose:
Professional body (membership is by subscription, qualification), present number of members: 3,800.
Represents private practitioners, provides members with education, information and legal advice, to ensure patients of high professional standards.

Subject coverage:
Back care, neck care; sports injury treatments, arthritic conditions, neurological stress, chest complaints.

Printed publications:
In Touch (quarterly)

Publications list:
Available in print

Access to staff:
Contact by letter, by telephone, by fax and by e-mail. Appointment necessary.
Hours: Mon to Fri, 0900 to 1700

Access to building, collection or gallery:
Hours: Mon to Fri, 0900 to 1700

Occupational Group of:
Chartered Society of Physiotherapy

PHYSIOLOGICAL SOCIETY, THE

PO Box 11319, London, WC1X 8WP

Tel: 020 7269 5710
Fax: 020 7269 5720
E-mail: admin@physoc.org

Website:
http://www.physoc.org
Publications, meetings, news, special interest groups, grants, membership, vacancies, contacts.

Enquiries:
Enquiries to: Chief Executive

Founded:
1876

Organisation type and purpose:
Learned society (membership is by election or invitation), registered charity (charity number 211585).

Subject coverage:
Physiological and cognate biomedical sciences; special interest groups on autonomic function, blood-brain barrier, cardiovascular control, comparative and invertebrate neuroscience, cellular neurophysiology, comparative physiology, developmental physiology, epithelia and

membrane transport, gastrointestinal tract, heart and cardiac muscle, history of physiology, human physiology, higher sensory functions, ionic channels, microvascular and endothelial physiology, muscle contraction, neuroendocrinology, placental and perinatal physiology, renal physiology, respiratory physiology, sensorimotor control, smooth muscle, somatosensory physiology; physiology as a career.

Museum or gallery collection, archive, or library special collection:
Archives (held at Wellcome Institute for the History of Medicine)
Video and film collection

Printed publications:
Genes and Function, in conjunction with the Genetical Society
Undergraduate booklet on the use of animals in medical experiments (free)
Physiology News (in-house magazine)
Journal of Experimental Physiology (6 times a year)
Journal of Physiology (24 issues a year plus 6 proceedings volumes and index)
Monographs, guides, careers information
Physiology: education and career (careers booklet, free)

Access to staff:
Contact by letter, by telephone, by fax, by e-mail and via website. Appointment necessary.
Hours: Mon to Fri, 0900 to 1700

Access to building, collection or gallery:
Prior appointment required

Accredited society of the:
Foundation for Science and Technology

Affiliated to:
Biosciences Foundation
Institute of Biology

Supports the:
International Union of Physiological Sciences (Munich)

PIANOFORTE TUNERS ASSOCIATION

Acronym or abbreviation: PTA

10 Reculver Road, Herne Bay, Kent, CT6 6LD

Tel: 01227 368808
Fax: 01227 368808
E-mail: secretary@pianotuner.org.uk

Website:
http://www.pianotuner.org.uk

Enquiries:
Enquiries to: Secretary

Founded:
1913

Organisation type and purpose:
Professional body, advisory body.

Subject coverage:
Pianoforte tuning, training facilities, entry into the industry.

Printed publications:
Information leaflet
Sound Advice – Your Piano Your Questions Answered
Sound Advice – Buying a Piano

Access to staff:
Contact by letter, by telephone and by fax
Hours: Including evenings

PILKINGTON GROUP LTD

Pilkington Technology Centre, Hall Lane, Lathom, Ormskirk, Lancashire, L40 5UF

Tel: 01695 50000
Fax: 01695 54366
E-mail: kevin.green@pilkington.com

Enquiries:
Enquiries to: Information Manager
Direct tel: 01695 54231

Founded:
1826

Organisation type and purpose:
Manufacturing industry.

Subject coverage:
Fundamental research in flat glass, applied research leading to improvements in the manufacturing of glass and related materials, development of new processes and products in flat glass, pressed and moulded glass, optical, ophthalmic and other special glasses, surface-treated glass.

Museum or gallery collection, archive, or library special collection:
Comprehensive collection of books on glass

Library catalogue:
All or part available in-house

Access to staff:
Contact by letter, by telephone, by fax and by e-mail. Appointment necessary.
Hours: Mon to Fri, 0900 to 1700
Special comments: By appointment only.

Access to building, collection or gallery:
By appointment only.

PIPER SPORTS AND RACING CAR CLUB

Acronym or abbreviation: The Piper Club

PO Box 55, Bourne, Lincolnshire, PE10 9FX

E-mail: contact@thepiperclub.org.uk

Website:
http://www.thepiperclub.org.uk

Enquiries:
Enquiries to: Secretary

Founded:
1977

Organisation type and purpose:
Membership association, present number of members: 45.

Subject coverage:
Piper cars.

Printed publications:
Newsletter

Access to staff:
Contact by letter and by e-mail

PIRA INTERNATIONAL

Cleeve Road, Leatherhead, Surrey, KT22 7RU

Tel: 01372 802050
Fax: 01372 802239
E-mail: infocentre@pira-international.com

Website:
http://www.pira-international.com

Enquiries:
Enquiries to: Information Services Manager

Organisation type and purpose:
Consultancy.

Subject coverage:
Pulping and pulp evaluation, paper and board making, water and effluent treatment, printing, imaging, inks, packaging, paper and board testing, printing machinery, package development and testing, management, marketing, publishing, nonwovens, statistical and technical information.

Library catalogue:
All or part available in-house

Printed publications:
Packaging Month
Press

Electronic and video publications:
Pira database available online

Publications list:
Available online and in print

Access to staff:
Contact by letter, by e-mail and via website. Appointment necessary. Access for members only. Non-members charged.
Hours: Mon to Fri, 0900 to 1700

Access to building, collection or gallery:
Prior appointment required
Special comments: Members only.

PLACE ARTIST DEVELOPMENT, THE

Acronym or abbreviation: TPAD

17 Dukes Road, London, WC1H 9PY

Tel: 020 7121 1040
Fax: 020 7121 1141
E-mail: artistdevelopment@theplace.org.uk

Website:
http://www.theplace.org.uk
Information on The Place and all its functions including Artist Development, London Contemporary Dance School, The Place: Robin Howard Dance Theatre and Richard Alston Dance Company.

Enquiries:
Enquiries to: Assistant
Direct tel: 020 7121 1040

Founded:
1990

Organisation type and purpose:
Membership association (membership is by subscription), present number of members: 1400. Information and advice service for the independent dance profession.

Subject coverage:
Contemporary dance, venues, promoters, dance artists in the UK and Europe, rehearsal spaces for dance in Greater London, information for new dance companies. Contacts for choreographers, dancers and dance managers in the United Kingdom and the rest of the world.

Museum or gallery collection, archive, or library special collection:
Publicity, annual reports etc from Regional Arts Boards, Venues and Festivals, Funding guides and directories, key reports, periodicals

Printed publications:
Information sheets on useful contacts for those in the Independent Dance Sector (eg: platform events, trusts and funds)
Juice (monthly listings magazine)
New York City Pack

Publications list:
Available in print

Access to staff:
Contact by letter, by telephone, by fax, by e-mail, in person and via website. Appointment necessary.
Hours: Tue to Fri, 1000 to 1800

Access to building, collection or gallery:
No prior appointment required

Access for disabled people:
Parking provided, level entry, access to all public areas, toilet facilities

Parent body:
Contemporary Dance Trust Ltd
The Place, 17 Dukes Road, London, WC1H 9PY; tel: 020 7121 1000; fax: 020 7121 1142

PLAID CYMRU – THE PARTY OF WALES

Tŷ Gwynfor, Marine Chambers, Cwrt Anson Court, Glanfa'r Iwerydd, Caerdydd/Cardiff, CF10 4AL.

continued overleaf

Tel: 029 20472272
Fax: 029 20491 453
E-mail: post@plaidcymru.org

Website:
http://plaidcymru.org
History, aims and goals, press releases.

Enquiries:
Enquiries to: Communications Officer
Other contacts: Press Officer (for press enquiries)

Founded:
1925

Organisation type and purpose:
Membership association (membership is by
subscription), present number of members: 10,800.
Political party.
To achieve full national status for Wales by
electoral means.

Subject coverage:
Politics in Wales.

**Museum or gallery collection, archive, or library
special collection:**
Collections are held on the party's behalf in the
National Library of Wales, including the whole
party archive extending back to 1925

Printed publications:
Ddraig Goch/ Welsh Nation (bilingual – Welsh/
English, quarterly)

Microform publications:
Microfilms available from World Microfilms, 2–6
Foscote Mews, London W9 2HH

Electronic and video publications:
CD-ROM available directly

Publications list:
Available in print

Access to staff:
Contact by letter, by telephone, by fax and by e-
mail. Appointment necessary.
Hours: Mon to Fri, 0830 to 1700

Access to building, collection or gallery:
No prior appointment required
Special comments: Party Archive kept at the
National Library of Wales.

PLAIN LANGUAGE COMMISSION

Formal name: Clearest.co.uk ltd

The Castle, 29 Stoneheads, Whaley Bridge, High
Peak, Derbyshire, SK23 7BB

Tel: 01663 733177
Fax: 01663 735135
E-mail: cutts@clearest.co.uk

Website:
http://www.clearest.co.uk
Publications and details of professional services.

Enquiries:
Enquiries to: Director

Founded:
2006

Organisation type and purpose:
Consultancy.

Subject coverage:
Editorial expertise and training courses on the use
of plain language in business, government
departments, local authorities and the law.

Printed publications:
Lucid Law (Cutts M, £10 direct)
The Oxford Guide to Plain English (Cutts M, £7.99
from bookshops)
Clarifying Eurolaw (Cutts M, £8 direct)
Clarifying EC Regulations (Cutts M & Wagner E,
£8 direct)
Order printed publications from: Web address or
postal address above

Publications list:
Available online

Access to staff:
Contact by letter, by telephone, by fax and by e-
mail. Appointment necessary.
Hours: Mon to Fri, 0900 to 1700

Access to building, collection or gallery:
No access other than to staff

PLANET RETAIL

Greater London House, Hampstead Road, London
NW1 7EJ

Tel: 020 7728 5600
Fax: 020 7728 4999
E-mail: info@planetretail.net

Website:
http://www.planetretail.net

Enquiries:
Enquiries to: Press
Direct e-mail: michael.berggren@planetretail.net

Founded:
1989

Formerly called:
M+M Planet Retail

Organisation type and purpose:
Market research.
On-line database on international retailers.

Subject coverage:
Retail marketing.

Non-library collection catalogue:
All or part available online

Library catalogue:
All or part available online

Printed publications:
Growth Retail Markets Worldwide, Jan 2001 (£200)
Evolution of Retail Structures Worldwide, Jan 2001
(£275)
National Retail Profiles, Dec 2001 including
countries of:
Retailing in Western Europe
Retailing in Central and Eastern Europe
Retailing in Latin America
Retailing in Middle East and Africa
C-Store Retailing: Global Trends and Lessons from
Japan, Dec 2001 (£580)
Global Foodservice Concentration, Jan 2001 (£230)
Foodservice Opportunities in Western Europe, Sep
2001

Electronic and video publications:
Online database, market reports, slides and
newsletter available at www.planetretail.net

Publications list:
Available online

Access to staff:
Contact by e-mail
Hours: Mon to Fri, 0900 to 1700

Holding Company:
M & M Planet Retail SA
Avenue Louise 113, 1050 Brussels, Belgium

Other addresses:
M & M Planet Retail
Dreieichstrasse 59, Frankfurt am Main, D-60594,
Germany; tel: + 49 69 96 21 75 0; fax: + 49 69 96
21 75 40

PLANNED ENVIRONMENT
THERAPY TRUST ARCHIVE AND
STUDY CENTRE

Church Lane, Toddington, Cheltenham,
Gloucestershire, GL54 5DQ

Tel: 01242 620125
E-mail: craig@pettarchiv.org.uk

Website:
http://pettarchiv.org.uk

Founded:
1989

Subject coverage:
Archive, library and other materials related to
planned environment therapy, therapeutic
community, milieu therapy, and progressive,
alternative and democratic education more
generally.

Access to building, collection or gallery:
Hours: Mon to Thu, 0900 to 1500 by appointment;
at other times by special arrangement

PLANT HERITAGE

Formal name: National Council for the
Conservation of Plants and Gardens
Acronym or abbreviation: NCCPG

12 Home Farm, Loseley Park, Guildford, Surrey,
GU3 1HS

Tel: 01483 447540
Fax: 01483 458933
E-mail: info@plantheritage.org.uk

Website:
http://www.plantheritage.com

Enquiries:
Enquiries to: Plant Conservation Officer
Other contacts: Executive Officer

Founded:
1978

Organisation type and purpose:
National organisation overseeing the conservation
of plants in cultivation
through the National Plant Collections scheme;
supported by members and area groups;
registered charity (charity number 1004009).

Subject coverage:
Matters relating to organisation of Plant Heritage/
NCCPG, the National Collection Scheme,
conservation of plants in cultivation and general
conservation information.

**Museum or gallery collection, archive, or library
special collection:**
Plant Heritage co-ordinates the 650 collections
registered under its National Collections Scheme
(50,000 plants held in the collections)

Non-library collection catalogue:
All or part available online

Printed publications:
National Plant Collections Directory 2010 (£6.50
incl. p&p)
Plant Heritage (journal for members)
Booklets are available on:
Cistus, Dianthus, Kalmia, Lathyrus, Lonicera,
Origanum, Polemonium, Russell Lupins, Vireya
Rhododendrons, Viburnum, Yuccas, Garden
Plants of Leicestershire and Rutland, Thyme
Handbook, Echinopsis Hybrids of Abbey Boork
Cactus Nursery

Publications list:
Available online and in print

Access to staff:
Contact by letter, by telephone, by fax, by e-mail
and via website. Appointment necessary.
Hours: Mon to Fri, 0900 to 1700

Access to building, collection or gallery:
Ground floor

Access for disabled people:
Fully accessible

Links with:
all the major horticultural bodies in Great Britain
over 40 county-based groups throughout Great
Britain

PLANTLIFE – THE WILD PLANT
CONSERVATION CHARITY

21 Elizabeth Street, London, SW1W 9RP

Tel: 020 7808 0100
Fax: 020 7730 8377
E-mail: enquiries@plantlife.org.uk

Website:
http://www.plantlife.org.uk

Enquiries:
Enquiries to: Public Relations Manager

Founded:
1989

Organisation type and purpose:
International organisation, membership association (membership is by subscription), present number of members: 11,500 individuals, voluntary organisation, registered charity (charity number 1059559).
Wild plant conservation charity.

Subject coverage:
Conservation of wild plants and their habitats in the British Isles, including lichens, bryophytes, algae, fungi.

Printed publications:
Britain's Rare Flowers (Marren P, £24.95)
Commission of Enquiry into Peat and Peatlands (1992, £10)
Death Knell for Bluebells? (£2.50)
Genes, Crops and Superweeds (report, £3)
Guidelines for Rare Plant Wardening (Church J M, £5.50)
Plantlife Magazine
Plantlife Magazine (back numbers when available £1 each)
Plants and the Proposed EC Habitats Directives Report (1990, £2.50)
Protecting Plants and their Habitats under the EC Habitat Directive (Oldfield S, £5.50)
Red Data Books of Britain and Ireland: Stoneworts (Stewart N F and Church J M, £15)
Seeds of Destruction? (£2.50)
The Acid Test for Plants (£2.50)
The Wild Flower Key (Rose F, £9.99)

Access to staff:
Contact by letter
Hours: Mon to Fri, 0900 to 1700

Members:
Botanical Society of Edinburgh
Botanical Society of The British Isles
British Bryophyte Society
British Ecology Society
British Lichen Society
British Phycological Society
British Pteridological Society
Butterfly Conservation Society
Fauna and Flora International
Friends of the Earth
Royal Society for the Protection of Birds
South London Botanical Institute
Wildflower Society

Other address:
Plantlife
Strome House, North Strome, Lochcarron, Ross-shire, IV54 8YJ; tel: 01520 722588; fax: 01520 722660

PLASTICS & BOARD INDUSTRIES FEDERATION

Acronym or abbreviation: PBIF

Rock House, Maddacombe Road, Kingskerswell, Newton Abbot, Devon, TQ12 5LF

Tel: 01803 403303
Fax: 01803 873167
E-mail: pbifoffice@aol.com

Website:
http://www.pbif.co.uk
Index of members; index of products and services; news; customer enquiries.

Enquiries:
Enquiries to: Chief Executive

Founded:
1987

Organisation type and purpose:
International organisation, trade association (membership is by subscription), present number of members: 150.

Subject coverage:
High frequency welding of thermoplastics; heat sealing and creasing of polypropylene, converting of board.

Library catalogue:
All or part available in-house

Printed publications:
High Frequency Welding Handbook (£40, available direct)

Access to staff:
Contact by letter, by telephone, by fax, by e-mail, in person and via website. Appointment necessary.
Hours: Mon to Fri, 0900 to 1700

PLASTICS HISTORICAL SOCIETY

Acronym or abbreviation: PHS

31A Maylands Drive, Sidcup, Kent, DA14 4SB

Tel: 020 8302 0684
E-mail: r_chambers@lineone.net

Enquiries:
Enquiries to: Honorary Secretary

Founded:
1986

Organisation type and purpose:
International organisation, learned society, membership association (membership is by subscription), present number of members: 250.
Recording the history of plastics and rubber.

Subject coverage:
History of plastics and rubber, conservation and preservation of plastics and rubbers.

Museum or gallery collection, archive, or library special collection:
Collection of plastics artefacts and historical records

Printed publications:
Newsletter (6 times a year, free to members)
Plastiquarian (2 times a year, free to members)

Access to staff:
Contact by letter
Hours: Mon to Fri, 0900 to 1700

Parent body:
Institute of Materials
1 Carlton House Terrace, London, SW1Y 5DB; tel: 020 7451 7300; fax: 020 7839 1702

PLAY WALES

Formal name: Play Wales / Chwarae Cymru

Baltic House, Mount Stuart Street, Cardiff, CF10 5FH

Tel: 029 2048 6050
Fax: 029 2048 9359
E-mail: mail@playwales.org.uk

Website:
http://www.playwales.org.uk
http://www.chwaraecymru.org.uk

Enquiries:
Enquiries to: Information Officer

Organisation type and purpose:
Advisory body, membership association, voluntary organisation, registered charity, consultancy.

Subject coverage:
Children's play; to provide or assist in the provision of children's play facilities and services, to offer advice and training.

Museum or gallery collection, archive, or library special collection:
Specialist Library containing books on children's play (theory and practical books), child development, social and political issues related to children

Library catalogue:
All or part available in-house

Printed publications:
The First Claim . . . a framework for playwork quality assessment
Order printed publications from: Office Manager

Publications list:
Available in print

Access to staff:
Contact by letter, by telephone, by fax and by e-mail. Appointment necessary.
Hours: Tue to Thu, 1000 to 1400
Special comments: At other times by prior appointment.

Access to building, collection or gallery:
Prior appointment required
Hours: Mon to Fri, 0900 to 1700

Access for disabled people:
Parking provided, ramped entry, toilet facilities

Also at:
Play Wales Chwarae Cymru
Station House, Bastion Road, Prestatyn
Play Wales Chwarae Cymru
Units 8/9 Tai Tywyn Business Centre, Sandy Lane, LL19 7SF

PLAYBACK

Formal name: Playback Recording Service for the Blind

Playback Recording Service, Centre for Sensory Impaired, 17 Gullane Street, Glasgow, G11 6AH

Tel: 0141 334 2983
Fax: 0141 334 2983

Website:
http://www.play-back.com

Enquiries:
Enquiries to: Producer
Direct e-mail: peter.fraser@play-back.org.uk
Other contacts: Librarian (for tape library)

Founded:
1987

Organisation type and purpose:
Registered charity (charity number SCO 01189), voluntary organisation.
Provides professional-quality recorded material to all over the UK, as well as parts of the USA, Australia, New Zealand and Canada. Set up to provide a free service to blind and visually impaired people, Playback is also available for individual and commercial recording needs at a small charge or donation. It has never refused to record any material requested, the philosophy being that, if it's available in print, it should be available on tape for all audiences to access.

Subject coverage:
Tape library and reading service, newspapers, magazines.
Playback Magazine continues to be the flagship recording of the service, providing news, information and entertainment to thousands of people, mainly in the West of Scotland, but also throughout the United Kingdom, USA, Canada, Australia and New Zealand.

Museum or gallery collection, archive, or library special collection:
The tape library contains over 1,000 titles spanning a wide range of subjects. Some of the titles, particularly a number of Scottish books, have been recorded by volunteer readers
Audio-described videos

Library catalogue:
All or part available online

Electronic and video publications:
Recordings of:
Playback magazine (monthly, available on cassette, Daisy CD and online as either a series of MP3 files, a podcast or as a Daisy download)
ABC Audio News magazine (6 a year, available on conventional CD and online as a podcast)
Sunday Mail – news and sport (weekly)
Daily Record (weekly)

continued overleaf

Scottish Memories Magazine (monthly, available
on cassette and Daisy CD)
Which Magazine (monthly)
Box & Fiddle – news of accordian & fiddle clubs
(monthly)
Jewish Telegraph – local Jewish news (fortnightly)
The Piping Band Magazine – the official
publication of the Royal Scottish Pipe Band
Association (quarterly)
Glasgow – city council magazine
Tape Library Catalogue – on tape, disc, in print, or
on website
Many newsletters, including those of:
National Federation of the Blind, Glasgow Branch
SAGDO, Scottish Association of Guide Dog
Owners
Retinitis Pigmentosa
International Glaucoma Association
British Diabetic Association Information
News for:
Glasgow Kings Theatre
Citizens Theatre
Tron Theatre
Glasgow Royal Concert Hall
Perth Theatre
Pitlochry Festival Theatre
Scottish Opera
Scottish Ballet

Publications list:
Available online

Access to staff:
Contact by letter, by telephone, by fax and by e-
mail

PLAYBOARD NI

7 Crescent Gardens, Belfast, BT7 1NS

Tel: 028 9080 3380
Fax: 028 9080 3381
E-mail: information@playboard.co.uk

Website:
http://www.playboard.org
General playboard information.

Enquiries:
Enquiries to: Director of Corporate Services &
Finance
Other contacts: Communication / Membership
Officer (for general information requests)

Founded:
1985

Organisation type and purpose:
Advisory body, membership association
(membership is by subscription), present number
of members: 170, voluntary organisation,
registered charity (charity number XO139/90),
training organisation, consultancy, research
organisation.
PlayBoard NI is the lead agency for children's play
in Northern Ireland. It works to promote the child's
right to play by providing quality play
opportunities for all children, supported by
development, policy, information, training and
consultancy services.

Subject coverage:
Information relating to children's play and general
issues impinging on children's lives, particularly in
Northern Ireland.

**Museum or gallery collection, archive, or library
special collection:**
Reference library on issues relating to children's
play and children's lives

Library catalogue:
All or part available in-house

Printed publications:
Action for Play
Games Not Names
Gender Matters
Play, Playtime and Playgrounds
Briefing Papers on relationship between play and
care; education; the environment; social inclusion
(free)
Strategic Plan (free)

Annual Reports (free)
Order printed publications from: Communication /
Membership Officer

Publications list:
Available online and in print

Access to staff:
Contact by letter, by telephone, by fax, by e-mail
and via website. Appointment necessary.
Hours: Mon to Thu, 0930 to 1630; Fri, 0930 to 1530

Access for disabled people:
Level entry, toilet facilities, lift provided

PLAYER PIANO GROUP

Acronym or abbreviation: PPG

'Strets', Church Rd, Lingfield RH7 6AH

Tel: 01342 833 921
E-mail: secretary@playerpianogroup.org.uk

Website:
http://www.playerpianogroup.org.uk

Enquiries:
Enquiries to: Honorary Secretary

Founded:
1959

Organisation type and purpose:
Voluntary organisation.

Subject coverage:
Mechanical music, player pianos, pianolas,
reproducing pianos, piano rolls, performers,
catalogues, sales and exchanges, history of the
instrument, its mechanisms, repair and restoration.

Printed publications:
Bulletin (quarterly, available to members only, free)

Links with:
sister societies in the UK, Germany, Netherlands,
USA, Australia

PLIMSOLL PUBLISHING LIMITED

Scotswood House, Teesdale South, Stockton-on-
Tees, Cleveland, TS17 6SB

Tel: 01642 626400
Fax: 01642 626410
E-mail: enquiries@plimsoll.co.uk

Website:
http://www.plimsoll.co.uk

Enquiries:
Enquiries to: Marketing Officer

Founded:
1986

Organisation type and purpose:
Publishers of financial analysis.

Subject coverage:
Financial analysis of various sectors of UK
industry by the analysis of individual players.

Printed publications:
Analysis of a group of companies, covering all
sectors, in report form: a one-page analysis of
each company in that sector (approximately 700
different industries, available on disc or
hardcopy)

Electronic and video publications:
Electronic versions of all analyses are available

Publications list:
Available online and in print

Access to staff:
Contact by letter, by telephone, by fax, by e-mail
and via website. Appointment necessary.
Hours: Mon to Fri, 0830 to 1700

Access to building, collection or gallery:
Prior appointment required

Access for disabled people:
Access to all public areas

PLUMPTON COLLEGE

Ditchling Road, Plumpton, Lewes, East Sussex,
BN7 3AE

Tel: 01273 890454
Fax: 01273 890071
E-mail: enquiries@plumpton.ac.uk

Website:
http://www.plumpton.ac.uk

Enquiries:
Enquiries to: Librarian
Direct tel: 01273 892041
Direct e-mail: anne.boryer@plumpton.ac.uk

Organisation type and purpose:
College providing land-based courses in
partnership with schools, for those in further
education and for those in higher education.

Subject coverage:
Agriculture, livestock, equestrian, horticulture,
floristry, conservation, wine studies, agricultural
mechanics, animal care, forestry.

Library catalogue:
All or part available online and in-house

Printed publications:
College prospectus & course leaflets

Access to staff:
Contact by telephone, by fax, by e-mail, in person
and via website. Appointment necessary.
Hours: Mon to Fri, 0900 to 2200

Also at:
Ivyland Farm
Netherfield, Battle, East Sussex; tel: 01424 838620

Associate college of:
University of Brighton

PLUNKETT FOUNDATION

The Quadrangle, Woodstock, Oxfordshire, OX20
1LH

Tel: 01993 810730
Fax: 01993 810849
E-mail: info@plunkett.co.uk

Website:
http://www.plunkett.co.uk
Services and information.

Enquiries:
Enquiries to: Information Officer
Direct e-mail: k.targett@plunkett.co.uk
Other contacts: Financial Administrator for book
purchase.

Founded:
1919

Organisation type and purpose:
International organisation, advisory body,
membership association (membership is by
subscription), present number of members: 150,
registered charity (charity number 313743), public
library, training organisation, consultancy, research
organisation.
Information centre.
To provide information, advice and consultancy
about co-operative enterprise and other member-
controlled business models.

Subject coverage:
Co-operative enterprise (all sectors, especially
agriculture), farmer-controlled business,
international project management, rural enterprise
development, co-operative business training and
education, co-operative legislation.

**Museum or gallery collection, archive, or library
special collection:**
Co-operative Congress Reports (1869–1931)
Irish Homestead (vol. I to vol. XXX)
Journals
Library of 30,000 books and documents covering
all aspects of co-operative enterprise
Research reports
Sir Horace Plunkett's Diaries (1881–1932) and
Letters

Yearbook of Co-operative Enterprise 1927–1994
(now retitled World of Co-operative Enterprise
1995–2000)

Trade and statistical information:
Detailed data on the trading activity of farmer-
controlled businesses (including co-operatives)
in the UK, covering farm supplies and the
marketing of farm produce.

Non-library collection catalogue:
All or part available in-house

Library catalogue:
All or part available online

Printed publications:
Directory of Agricultural, Co-operatives and Other
Farmer-Controlled Businesses in the UK
Statistics of UK Agricultural Co-operatives and
Farmer-Controlled Businesses

Access to staff:
Contact by letter, by telephone, by fax, by e-mail
and via website. Appointment necessary.
Hours: Mon to Fri, 0900 to 1700

Access to building, collection or gallery:
Prior appointment required

Access for disabled people:
Parking provided, level entry, toilet facilities

PLYMOUTH AND WEST DEVON RECORD OFFICE

Acronym or abbreviation: PWDRO

Unit 3, Clare Place, Coxside, Plymouth, Devon,
PL4 0JW

Tel: 01752 305940
Fax: 01752 222196
E-mail: pwdro@plymouth.gov.uk

Website:
http://www.plymouth.gov.uk/homepage/
leisureandtourism/archives.htm
Main record office website with information on
services and opening times.
http://www.plymouth.gov.uk/homepage/
leisureandtourism/archives/archivecatalogue.htm
Online record office catalogue for information on
holdings.

Enquiries:
Enquiries to: Archivist

Founded:
1952

Organisation type and purpose:
Local government body. Archive.

Subject coverage:
The records of Plymouth and the West Devon area.

**Museum or gallery collection, archive, or library
special collection:**
Archive

Non-library collection catalogue:
All or part available online and in-house

Access to staff:
Contact by letter, by telephone, by e-mail, in
person and via website. Appointment necessary.
Hours: Tue to Thu, 0930 to 1700; Fri, 0930 to 1600
Special comments: Identification required for visits.

Access to building, collection or gallery:
Hours: Tue to Thu, 0930 to 1700; Fri, 0930 to 1600

Access for disabled people:
By appointment
Hours: Tue to Thu, 0930 to 1700; Fri, 0930 to 1600
Special comments: Disabled access is at the rear.
Please call in advance.

PLYMOUTH ATHENAEUM

Derrys Cross, Plymouth, Devon, PL1 2SW

Tel: 01752 266079
E-mail: bussec@plymouthathenaeum.co.uk

Website:
http://www.plymouthathenaeum.co.uk

Founded:
1812

Organisation type and purpose:
Cultural society and membership organisation
(membership by subscription).

Subject coverage:
Arts, literature, science and technology.

Access to staff:
Contact by letter, by telephone, by fax, by e-mail
and via website
Hours: Mon to Fri, 1000 to 1700

PLYMOUTH CITY COUNCIL

Civic Centre, Armada Way, Plymouth, Devon, PL1
2EW

Tel: 01752 668000
Fax: 01752 264819
E-mail: pccmail@plymouth.gov.uk

Website:
http://www.plymouth.gov.uk

Enquiries:
Direct e-mail: communications@plymouth.gov.uk

Organisation type and purpose:
Local government body.

Access to staff:
Contact by letter, by telephone, by fax, by e-mail
and in person
Hours: Mon to Fri, 0900 to 1700

PLYMOUTH COLLEGE OF ART AND DESIGN LEARNING RESOURCE CENTRE

Acronym or abbreviation: PCAD

Tavistock Place, Plymouth, Devon, PL4 8AT

Tel: 01752 203412
Fax: 01752 203444
E-mail: enquiries@plymouthart.ac.uk

Enquiries:
Enquiries to: Librarian

Organisation type and purpose:
Suitable for ages: 16+.
College of further education and higher education.

Subject coverage:
Architecture; colour; communications; design
crafts; fashion; film and television; fine art; graphic
design; industrial design; painting and decorating;
photography; printing; textiles.

Library catalogue:
All or part available online

Printed publications:
Student Study Guide, for art and design students
(£3)

Access to staff:
Contact by telephone and by e-mail. Appointment
necessary.
Hours: Term time: Mon to Thu, 0845 to 1930; Fri,
0845 to 1730
Vacation time: Mon to Fri, 1000 to 1600

Access to building, collection or gallery:
Hours: Mon to Thu, 0845 to 1900; Fri, 0845 to 1700

Affiliated to:
Open University
University of Plymouth

PLYMOUTH LIBRARY SERVICES

Formal name: City of Plymouth Library and
Information Services

Central Library, Drake Circus, Plymouth, Devon,
PL4 8AL

Tel: 01752 305923

Fax: 01752 305905
E-mail: library@plymouth.gov.uk

Website:
http://www.plymouth.gov.uk/libraries
Extensive information about the public library
service in Plymouth.
http://www.libcat.info
Online catalogue, reservations and renewals.

Founded:
1876

Organisation type and purpose:
Local government body, public library.

Subject coverage:
General, technical, naval history, local studies,
music theory, scores and sets of parts, drama,
patents.

**Museum or gallery collection, archive, or library
special collection:**
Baring-Gould collection (folksongs, folklore,
novels, travel writing)
Eden Phillpotts collection (novels)
Moxon Collection of Ornithology and Travel
(mainly 19th century)
Music collection (orchestral parts and scores)
Local, naval and family History
Patent Abridgements from 1855
Special indexes: Broderick – History of Devonport;
Honeywill – Submarines; Larn – Shipwrecks of
Devon; Akerman – Dictionary of British Fighting
Ships

Library catalogue:
All or part available online

Printed publications:
Various maps, prints, greeting cards

Publications list:
Available online

Access to staff:
Contact by letter, by telephone, by fax, by e-mail,
in person and via website
Hours: Mon to Fri, 0900 to 1900; Sat, 0900 to 1700
Special comments: Patent enquiries, Mon to Fri, 0900
to 1700 only.

Access for disabled people:
Parking provided, level entry, access to all public
areas
Special comments: Lift to 1st floor.

PLYMOUTH LOCAL AND NAVAL STUDIES LIBRARY

Plymouth Central Library, Drake Circus,
Plymouth, PL4 8AL

Tel: 01752 305909
E-mail: library@plymouth.gov.uk

Website:
http://www.plymouth.gov.uk/libraries

Enquiries:
Enquiries to: Librarian

Organisation type and purpose:
Local government body, public library.

Subject coverage:
History of Plymouth, West Devon and South East
Cornwall; family history; naval history.

**Museum or gallery collection, archive, or library
special collection:**
Books and pamphlets, maps, newspapers,
illustrations, family history resources

Library catalogue:
All or part available online

Printed publications:
Selection of books, factsheets, greetings cards and
maps
Order printed publications from: Library or library
website

Publications list:
Available online

continued overleaf

Access to staff:
Contact by letter, by telephone, by e-mail, in person and via website
Hours: Mon to Fri, 0900 to 1900; Sat, 0900 to 1700

Access to building, collection or gallery:
No prior appointment required
Hours: Mon to Fri, 0900 to 1900; Sat 0900 to 1700

Access for disabled people:
Lift to first floor

Member organisation of:
Naval and Maritime Libraries and Archives Group (NMLAG)

PLYMOUTH PROPRIETARY LIBRARY

Alton Terrace, 111 North Hill, Plymouth, Devon, PL4 8JY

Tel: 01752 660515

Enquiries:
Enquiries to: Librarian

Founded:
1810

Organisation type and purpose:
Membership association (membership is by subscription), present number of members: 110, registered charity (charity number 1015700). Private subscription library.

Subject coverage:
General recreational library, nineteenth and twentieth century novels, general non-fiction.

Museum or gallery collection, archive, or library special collection:
Devon and Cornwall local studies section

Library catalogue:
All or part available in-house

Access to staff:
Contact by letter and by telephone. Appointment necessary.
Hours: Mon, Tue, Thu, Fri, 0930 to 1700; Wed, 0930 to 1400; Sat, 0930 to 1230

PMS PUBLICATIONS LIMITED

Formal name: Parliamentary Monitoring Services
Acronym or abbreviation: PMS

19 Douglas Street, Westminster, London, SW1P 4PA

Tel: 020 7233 8283
Fax: 020 7821 9352

Enquiries:
Enquiries to: Managing Director

Founded:
1935

Organisation type and purpose:
Research organisation, publishing house.
News agency for politics and government.
To inform clients of what is happening in government and throughout the UK and the EU.

Subject coverage:
Political, parliamentary, local government, European Union.

Museum or gallery collection, archive, or library special collection:
Databases of biographical information on MPs, peers, top civil servants and local authorities

Printed publications:
European Public Affairs Directory
Parliament and Assemblies of the UK
PMS Guide to Interest Groups
PMS Local Government Companion
PMS Parliamentary Companion
Update Bulletin (weekly)
Parliamentary Bulletin for Local Government Executives (weekly)

Electronic and video publications:
Members of All Parliaments and Assemblies in the UK and European Parliament (CD-ROM)

Publications list:
Available in print

Access to staff:
Contact by letter, by fax and by e-mail. Access for members only.
Hours: Mon to Fri, 0900 to 1700

Also at the same address:
Parliamentary Monitoring Services

POETRY BOOK SOCIETY

Acronym or abbreviation: PBS

Dutch House, 307–308 High Holborn, London, WC1V 7LL

Tel: 020 7831 7468
Fax: 020 7831 6967
E-mail: info@poetrybooks.co.uk

Website:
http://www.poetrybooks.co.uk
Buy books online; history of PBS.

Enquiries:
Enquiries to: Director

Founded:
1953

Organisation type and purpose:
International organisation, membership association (membership is by subscription), present number of members: c. 2,200, registered charity (charity number 313753), suitable for ages: 7+.
A publicly-funded membership book club promoting contemporary poetry.

Subject coverage:
Contemporary poetry published in the UK and Eire since 1953; educational resources for 7 to 18 year olds.

Printed publications:
Bulletin (magazine, quarterly, distributed to members)

Electronic and video publications:
CDs

Access to staff:
Contact by letter, by telephone, by fax, by e-mail and via website
Hours: Mon to Fri, 0930 to 1730

POETRY LIBRARY

Formal name: Saison Poetry Library

Royal Festival Hall, Southbank Centre, London, SE1 8XX

Tel: 020 7921 0943; 020 7921 0664
Fax: 020 7921 0939
E-mail: info@poetrylibrary.org.uk

Website:
http://www.poetrylibrary.org.uk
Outline of library services, 'lost quotations' noticeboard (discussion group), information lists.

Enquiries:
Enquiries to: Poetry Librarian
Direct tel: 020 7921 0940

Founded:
1953

Organisation type and purpose:
National organisation, membership association, present number of members: 21,200, public library, research organisation.
Special arts library.

Subject coverage:
Modern poetry from all English-speaking countries of the world; modern poetry translated from other languages; pre-20th-century poetry translated by

contemporary English language poets; poetry for children, poetry on tape, video, record, CD and CD-ROM.

Museum or gallery collection, archive, or library special collection:
Alec Craig Bequest
Howard Sargent collection of press cuttings
Images of Poets
Large collection of poetry magazines
Rare modern first editions
SIGNAL collection of children's poetry
Sylvia Townsend Warner Bequest
Tapes, records, videos, CD-ROMs

Non-library collection catalogue:
All or part available in-house

Library catalogue:
All or part available in-house

Printed publications:
Current awareness lists
Lists of UK poetry magazines, bookshops, groups and workshops
Short-title catalogue of Books in the Collection (constitutes a bibliography of poetry published 1912–1980)

Publications list:
Available in print

Access to staff:
Contact by letter, by telephone, by fax, by e-mail, in person and via website
Hours: Tue to Sun, 1100 to 2000

Access for disabled people:
Level entry

Parent body:
Arts Council England
South Bank Board

POETRY SOCIETY

22 Betterton Street, London, WC2H 9BX

Tel: 020 7420 9880
Fax: 020 7240 4818
E-mail: info@poetrysociety.org.uk

Website:
http://www.poetrysociety.org.uk

Founded:
1909

Organisation type and purpose:
Membership association, registered charity.
Arts centre for poetry; registered charity supported by the Arts Council.
To promote the study, use and enjoyment of poetry.

Subject coverage:
Poetry and poets, information on writing or publishing poetry, contemporary poetry events, competitions, festivals, teachers' poetry resource.

Services for disabled people:
Audio tapes of Poetry Review and Poetry News for blind and partially-sighted members.

Printed publications:
Teachers' resources
Poetry News (quarterly)
Poetry Review (quarterly)
Information Pack
Jumpstart Poetry in the Secondary School
Poetry Book for Primary Schools
Foyle Young Poets of the Year anthologies

Access to staff:
Contact by letter, by telephone, by fax, by e-mail and via website
Hours: Mon to Fri, 1000 to 1800

Access to building, collection or gallery:
Prior appointment required

Access for disabled people:
Lift to basement performance space; toilet facilities; induction loop

POLAR DATA CENTRE

Acronym or abbreviation: PDC BAS

British Antarctic Survey, High Cross, Madingley Road, Cambridge, CB3 0ET

Tel: 01223 221400
Fax: 01223 362616
E-mail: pdc@bas.ac.uk

Website:
http://www.antarctica.ac.uk/pdc
Information on facilities and projects/support provided by the PDC. Access to the PDC's Metadata System for information on NERC's Antarctic data sets.

Formerly called:
Antarctic Environmental Data Centre (year of change 2009)

Organisation type and purpose:
Research organisation.
A virtual data centre proving a gateway to the distributed data holdings of the British Antarctic Survey. One of the Designated Centres of the UK Natural Environment Research Council (NERC). The UK National Data Centre within the Antarctic Data Management System (ADMS).
Responsible for ensuring the secure, long-term management of BAS data holdings.

Subject coverage:
Information on data sets collected by BAS and other NERC-sponsored organisations in the Antarctic covering: the physical, biological and geological sciences.

Trade and statistical information:
Under Article III(1)(c) of the Antarctic Treaty, data are to be freely exchanged between Treaty parties. Therefore, within the Antarctic scientific community data are made freely available.

Non-library collection catalogue:
All or part available online

Electronic and video publications:
Information on access to data sets from PDC web pages

Access to staff:
Contact by e-mail and via website
Hours: Mon to Fri, 0900 to 1700
Special comments: E-mail is preferred form of contact.

Member organisation of:
One of the Designated Data Centres of the UK Natural Environment Research Council (NERC)
The UK National Antarctic Data Centre within the Antarctic Data Management System

Parent body:
British Antarctic Survey
at the same address

POLICE HISTORY SOCIETY

64 Nore Marsh Road, Wootton Bassett, Wiltshire

Website:
http://www.policehistorysociety.co.uk

Enquiries:
Enquiries to: Honorary Secretary
Other contacts: Membership Secretary (for membership enquiries)

Founded:
1985

Organisation type and purpose:
Membership association (membership is by subscription), present number of members: 400, registered charity, voluntary organisation (charity number 295540).
To bring together those interested in the history of the police and policing. NB: The PHS is not primarily concerned with family historical research and holds no police personnel records.

Subject coverage:
History of policing; history of crime.

Printed publications:
Annual Journal (free to members, otherwise £5 per annum)
Newsletter (free to members 3 or 4 times a year)
Other occasional publications

Access to staff:
Contact by letter and by e-mail
Hours: Mon to Fri, 0900 to 1700
Special comments: SAE for reply essential.

Also at:
Membership Secretary, Police History Society Foxtrot Oscar, 37 South Lawne, Bletchley, Milton Keynes, MK3 6BU; tel: 0161 962 3764

POLICE SUPERINTENDENTS' ASSOCIATION OF ENGLAND AND WALES

67A Reading Road, Pangbourne, Berkshire, RG8 7JD

Tel: 0118 984 4005
Fax: 0118 984 5642
E-mail: enquiries@policesupers.com

Website:
http://www.policesupers.com
The association, news, FAQs.

Founded:
1952

Organisation type and purpose:
The professional association that represents the senior police officers in the 43 Home Office Police Forces, British Transport Police, Civil Nuclear Constabulary and Isle of Man Police in the rank of Superintendent and Chief Superintendent.
To lead and develop the police service to improve the standard of policing; to provide support and advice to members regarding conditions of service, health & welfare; to contribute and influence policing policy and practice at the national strategic level.

Subject coverage:
Policing and senior police officers.

Printed publications:
The Superintendent (quarterly journal)
Order printed publications from: tel: 0118 984 4005

Electronic and video publications:
Annual Report
Press releases
The Superintendent (quarterly journal)
Order electronic and video publications from:
Download from website

Access to staff:
Contact by letter, by telephone, by fax and by e-mail

POLICY PRESS

University of Bristol, Fourth Floor, Beacon House, Queen's Road, Clifton, Bristol, BS8 1QU

Tel: 0117 331 4054
Fax: 0117 331 4093
E-mail: tpp-info@bristol.ac.uk

Website:
http://www.policypress.org.uk

Enquiries:
Enquiries to: Marketing Executive
Direct tel: 0117 331 4096
Other contacts: Director

Founded:
1995

Organisation type and purpose:
Publishing house, publishing policy research.

Subject coverage:
Community care, environment, family policy and child welfare, criminal justice, ageing, education, governance, health, housing, labour markets, urban policy, gender, voluntary sector, welfare and poverty.

Printed publications:
Books, Research and Policy Reports, Practice Guides and Journals, including:
Policy and Politics
Benefits (new)
Order printed publications from: Customer Services, Marston Book Services, PO Box 269, Abingdon, Oxfordshire, OX14 4YN; tel. 01235 465500; fax 01235 465556; e-mail direct.orders@marston.co.uk

Electronic and video publications:
Policy and Politics (online)

Publications list:
Available online and in print

Access to staff:
Contact by letter, by telephone, by fax, by e-mail and via website
Hours: Mon to Fri, 0900 to 1700

Links with:
University of Bristol

POLISH CULTURAL INSTITUTE

Acronym or abbreviation: PCI

34 Portland Place, London, W1B 1HQ

Tel: 0870 774 2300/2
Fax: 020 7637 2190
E-mail: pci@polishculture.org.uk

Website:
http://www.polishculture.org.uk
Details of Institute's events around the country, past events, events in Poland, Polish language courses, the library, general information on Polish culture.

Enquiries:
Enquiries to: Director
Direct tel: 0870 774 2300/2

Organisation type and purpose:
National government body.
Promotion of Polish culture in the UK.

Subject coverage:
Poland and Polish music, film, theatre, literature and art, Polish history, geography.

Museum or gallery collection, archive, or library special collection:
Library of reference books, video, slides and music recordings, newspapers both Polish and English

Trade and statistical information:
Some economic information on Poland.

Non-library collection catalogue:
All or part available online

Library catalogue:
All or part available in-house

Publications list:
Available in print

Access to staff:
Contact by letter, by telephone, by fax, by e-mail and via website
Hours: Mon to Fri,1000 to 1600

Access to building, collection or gallery:
No prior appointment required
Hours: Mon, Tue, Wed, Fri, 1200 to 1600; Thu, 1600 to 2000

Part of:
Polish Embassy in London

POLISH EMBASSY

Formal name: Embassy of the Republic of Poland

47 Portland Place, London, W1B 1JH

Tel: 0870 7742 700
Fax: 020 7323 4018
E-mail: polishembassy@polishembassy.org.uk

Website:
http://www.polishembassy.org.uk

continued overleaf

Website of the Embassy of Poland in London, comprehensive information about the Embassy, Poland and Polish-British relations.
http://www.paiz.gov.pl
Polish Agency of Foreign Investment
http://www.bmb.pl
The promotion of Polish local government with particular emphasis placed upon the investment possibilities of districts
http://www.poland.pl
Poland in brief; Polish Archives; Poland on the web: state and politics, society, geography and tourism, business and economy, computers and telecommunications, art and culture, media and information, science and education, sport and recreation, lifestyle; views from all round Poland, maps; Polish Roots: Poland Genealogy Forum, Dynastic Genealogy, Geneaology & Poland

Enquiries:
Enquiries to: Counsellor (Press & Information)

Organisation type and purpose:
National government body.
Embassy.

Subject coverage:
General enquiries relating to Poland, current political and economic situation, culture and tourism, visas etc.

Trade and statistical information:
Trade information from the Commercial Office.

Printed publications:
Press releases on important issues (not on a regular basis)

Access to staff:
Contact by letter, by fax, by e-mail and via website
Hours: Mon to Fri, 0830 to 1630
Special comments: Visa enquiries should be made to the Consulate General
Tourism enquiries to the Polish National Tourist Office.

Other addresses:
Commercial Counsellors Office to the Embassy of the Republic of Poland
15 Devonshire Street, London, W1N 2AR; tel: 020 7580 5481; fax: 020 7323 0195
Consulate General of the Republic of Poland
73 New Cavendish Street, London, W1N 4HQ; tel: 0870 7742 800; fax: 020 7323 2320; e-mail: consulate@polishconsulate.co.uk; website: www.polishconsulate.co.uk
Consulate General of the Republic of Poland
2 Kinnear Road, Edinburgh, EH3 5PE; tel: 0131 552 0301; fax: 0131 552 1086; e-mail: edinburgh@polishconsulate.org; website: www.polishconsulate.org
Polish Cultural Institute
34 Portland Place, London, W1N 4HQ; tel: 0870 7742 900; fax: 020 7637 2190; e-mail: pci@polishculture.org.uk; website: www.polishculture.org

POLISH LIBRARY

238–246 King Street, London, W6 0RF

Tel: 020 8741 0474
Fax: 020 8741 7724
E-mail: polish.library@posk.org

Enquiries:
Enquiries to: Librarian

Founded:
1942

Organisation type and purpose:
Membership association (membership is by subscription), present number of members: 2000+, voluntary organisation, registered charity (charity number 236745), research organisation, publishing house.
Specialised library. Public library circulating service.
Collecting and the dissemination of information, worldwide, on the subject of Polish emigrés in the UK.

Subject coverage:
Polish culture, history, literature, language, geography, economics, politics, sociology, folklore, arts, philosophy, religious life, militaria.

Museum or gallery collection, archive, or library special collection:
Anglo-Polish relations
Archives of some Polish organisations
Joseph Retinger private papers
Polish emigré publications
Polish underground opposition and Solidarity publications
Works by and about Joseph Conrad

Non-library collection catalogue:
All or part available in-house

Library catalogue:
All or part available in-house

Printed publications:
Annual Report
Bibliographies of books in Polish, or works by Polish scholars, and of books and pamphlets on Katyn
Catalogues of collections and exhibitions
Full list of the publications available from the Library
Joseph Conrad Collection
Polish Library 1942–1979 and 1942–1992
Order printed publications from: e-mail: Polish.library@mailbox.ac.uk

Access to staff:
Contact by letter, by telephone, by fax, by e-mail, in person and via website. Letter of introduction required.
Hours: Mon and Wed, 1000 to 2000; Fri, 1000 to 1700, Sat, 1000 to 1300

Access for disabled people:
Ramped entry, access to all public areas, toilet facilities

Houses the:
Joseph Conrad Society
tel: As for the library

Parent body:
Polish Social and Cultural Association Limited (POSK)
tel: 020 8741 1940; fax: 020 8746 3796; e-mail: admin@posk.org; website: http://www.posk.org

POLITICAL STUDIES ASSOCIATION

Acronym or abbreviation: PSA

National Office, Department of Politics, University of Newcastle, Newcastle-upon-Tyne, NE1 7RU

Tel: 0191 222 8021
Fax: 0191 222 3499
E-mail: psa@ncl.ac.uk

Website:
http://www.psa.ac.uk
PSA, publications, conferences, politics portal, members, specialist groups, politics departments.

Founded:
1950

Organisation type and purpose:
A membership association open to everyone interested in the study of politics, current number of members: over 1,700. Membership spans academics in political science and current affairs, theorists and practitioners, policy-makers, journalists, researchers, politics teachers and students in higher education.
To develop and promote the study of politics.

Subject coverage:
Politics and political science.

Printed publications:
Political Studies (journal, 4 a year, free to members)
Political Insight Magazine (3 a year, free to members)
Political Studies Review (3 a year, free to members)
Politics (3 a year, free to members)

The British Journal of Politics and International Relations (4 a year, free to members)
PSA News (newsletter, 4 a year, free to members)
Annual Directory

Publications list:
Available online

Access to staff:
Contact by letter, by telephone, by fax and by e-mail

PONTEFRACT REGISTER OFFICE

Old Town Hall, Bridge Street, Pontefract, West Yorkshire, WF8 1PG

Tel: 01977 722670
Fax: 01977 722676

Enquiries:
Enquiries to: Superintendent Registrar

Founded:
1837

Organisation type and purpose:
Local government body, statutory body.

Access to staff:
Contact by letter, by telephone, by fax and in person. Appointment necessary.
Hours: Mon to Fri, 0900 to 1630
Special comments: Sat by prior appointment.

Access to building, collection or gallery:
No prior appointment required

Access for disabled people:
Parking provided, ramped entry

PONTELAND LOCAL HISTORY SOCIETY

127 Middle Drive, Darras Hall, Newcastle-upon-Tyne, NE20 9DS

E-mail: jmichaeltaylor@btinternet.com

Website:
http://www.ponthistsoc.freeuk.com

Enquiries:
Enquiries to: Secretary
Direct tel: 01661 823880

Founded:
1968

Organisation type and purpose:
Membership association (membership by subscription).
To promote interest in local history.

Printed publications:
Newsletter (monthly)
Ponte Island News (annually)
Books:
Images of England: Ponteland
Ponteland through the Twentieth Century
Ponteland: One Thousand Years of History
Ponteland: the Garden City

Access to staff:
Contact by letter, by e-mail and via website

Affiliated to:
Association of Northumberland Local History Societies

PONY CLUB OF GREAT BRITAIN

Formal name: The Pony Club

Stoneleigh Park, Kenilworth, Warwickshire, CV8 2RW

Tel: 024 7669 8300
Fax: 024 7669 6836
E-mail: enquiries@pcuk.org

Website:
http://www.pcuk.org

Enquiries:
Enquiries to: Chief Executive

Other contacts: PA to the Chief Executive

Founded:
1929

Organisation type and purpose:
Membership association (membership is by subscription), registered charity (charity number 1050146), suitable for ages: under 25.
To encourage young people to ride and to learn to enjoy horses and riding: to provide instruction in riding, horsemanship and the proper care of their animals: to promote the highest ideals of sportsmanship, citizenship and loyalty.

Subject coverage:
Running an equestrian-orientated youth organisation; information on all matters relating to equestrianism and horse care for young people.

Printed publications:
A variety of publications including:
Gymkhanas and Rally Games
Instructors Handbook
Keeping a Pony at Grass
Manual of Horsemanship
Training Young Horses
A Young Persons Guide to Showjumping

Publications list:
Available in print

Access to staff:
Contact by letter, by telephone, by fax, by e-mail and via website
Hours: Mon to Fri, 0900 to 1700

Has:
2200 affiliated branches overseas in 17 countries
347 branches and over 400 centres in the UK

POOLE CENTRAL LIBRARY

Dolphin Centre, Poole, Dorset, BH15 1QE

Tel: 01202 262424
Fax: 01202 262442
E-mail: libraries@poole.gov.uk

Website:
http://www.boroughofpoole.com/libraries
General description of services, plus access to library catalogue and subscribed online resources.

Enquiries:
Enquiries to: Information Services Librarian
Direct tel: 01202 262421
Other contacts: Central Library Manager

Founded:
1885

Organisation type and purpose:
Local government body, public library.

Subject coverage:
General information.

Non-library collection catalogue:
All or part available in-house

Library catalogue:
All or part available in-house

Access to staff:
Contact by letter, by telephone, by fax, by e-mail, in person and via website
Hours: Mon to Fri, 0900 to 1800; Sat, 0900 to 1700

Access for disabled people:
Access to all public areas, toilet facilities (radar key)
Hours: As above

Parent body:
Borough of Poole, Culture and Community Learning Services
Central Library, Dolphin Centre, Poole, Dorset, BH15 1QE, UK; tel: 01202 262421; fax: 01202 262442; e-mail: libraries@poole.gov.uk; website: http://www.boroughofpoole.com/libraries

POPULATION CONCERN

Studio 325, Highgate Studios, 53–79 Highgate Road, London, NW5 1TL

Tel: 020 7241 8500
Fax: 020 7267 6788
E-mail: info@populationconcern.org.uk

Website:
http://www.populationconcern.org.uk

Enquiries:
Enquiries to: Education Officer

Founded:
1974

Organisation type and purpose:
Registered charity (charity number 1001698). Originally set up as the international division of the UK FPA; an independent charitable organisation since April 1991.

Subject coverage:
Reproductive and sexual health, gender, poverty alleviation, young people, population and related issues.

Trade and statistical information:
Data on world population, youth around the world, young people's sexual and reproductive health, and reproductive risk.

Library catalogue:
All or part available in-house

Printed publications:
Annual Report (free)
Newsletter (annually, free)
Introduction (free)
Meeting the Sexual Health Needs of Young People (free)
2001 World Population Data Sheet (£4 each)
Order printed publications from: Education Officer, Population Concern
e-mail: education@populationconcern.org.uk

Electronic and video publications:
Population Dots (video on issues of population)
Population and Development Database (CD-ROM)

Access to staff:
Contact by letter, by telephone, by fax, by e-mail and via website
Hours: Mon to Fri, 0900 to 1700

Collaborates with:
International Planned Parenthood Federation (IPPF)
Marie Stopes International (MSI)

Recognised by the:
United Nations Population Fund (UNFPA)

POPULATION INVESTIGATION COMMITTEE

Acronym or abbreviation: PIC

London School of Economics and Political Science, Houghton Street, London, WC2A 2AE

Tel: 020 7955 7666
Fax: 020 7955 6831
E-mail: pic@lse.ac.uk

Website:
http://www.lse.ac.uk/depts/pic

Enquiries:
Enquiries to: General Secretary

Founded:
1936

Organisation type and purpose:
Professional body, membership association (membership is by election or invitation), present number of members: 11, registered charity (charity number 263783), research organisation.

Subject coverage:
Demography and population studies.

Printed publications:
A Record of Research and Publications 1936–78 (free, but 75p p&p)
Birth Control Practice and Marital Fertility in Great Britain (C. M. Langford, £2 plus £1.75 p&p)
Demographic Estimation for Developing Societies (N. Carrier and J. Hobcraft, £10.00 plus £1.75 p&p)

Population Research in Britain (M. Murphy and J. Hobcraft, £15 incl. p&p)
Population Studies (journal, 1 vol., 3 parts a year, available online at www.popstudies.net)
Supplements to the Journal
The Demography of the British Peerage (T. H. Hollingsworth, 50p plus £1.50 p&p)
The Population Investigation Committee: A Concise History To Mark Its Fiftieth Anniversary (C. M. Langford, £3 incl. p&p)
Towards a Population Policy for the United Kingdom (50p plus £1.50 p&p)
Order printed publications from: Population Investigation Committee, Room PS201, Houghton Street, London, WC2A 2AE, tel: 020 7955 7666, fax: 020 7955 6831, e-mail: pic@lse.ac.uk

Electronic and video publications:
Order electronic and video publications from: http://www.popstudies.net

Publications list:
Available online

Access to staff:
Contact by letter, by telephone, by fax, by e-mail and via website. Appointment necessary.
Hours: Mon to Fri, 1000 to 1600

PORSCHE CLUB GREAT BRITAIN

Acronym or abbreviation: PCGB

Cornbury House, Cotswold Business Village, London Road, Moreton-in-Marsh, Gloucestershire, GL56 0JQ

Tel: 01608 652911
Fax: 01608 652944
E-mail: cluboffice@porscheclubgb.com

Website:
http://www.porscheclubgb.com

Enquiries:
Enquiries to: Club Manager
Other contacts: Publications Manager

Founded:
1961

Organisation type and purpose:
Membership association (membership is by subscription), present number of members: c.16,000.

Subject coverage:
All information covering Porsche models manufactured from 1948 to the present day; provision of display cars; technical information; Porsche motorsport.

Museum or gallery collection, archive, or library special collection:
Archive of information, photographs, objects and memorabilia relating to Porsche

Printed publications:
Porsche Post (magazine, monthly)
The Real 928

Access to staff:
Contact by letter, by telephone, by fax, by e-mail and via website. Appointment necessary.
Hours: Mon to Fri, 0900 to 1700

Access to building, collection or gallery:
Access for members only
Hours: Mon to Fri, 0900 to 1700

Access for disabled people:
Ramped entry, toilet facilities

PORTIA CAMPAIGN

Acronym or abbreviation: PORTIA

The Croft, West Common, Bowness-on-Solway, Cumbria, CA7 5AG

Tel: 016973 51820
E-mail: ken_portia@ontel.net.uk

Website:
http://www.portia.org

continued overleaf

Enquiries:
Enquiries to: Chairman

Founded:
1971

Organisation type and purpose:
Membership association (membership is by subscription), present number of members: 470, voluntary organisation.
Counselling.

Subject coverage:
Shoplifting allegations, cot-death allegations, risk of baby-snatching, false imprisonment.

Printed publications:
Advice Notes (leaflets, free)
Order printed publications from: Infinity Junction PO Box 64, Neston DO, CH64 0WB, e-mail: http//:www.infinityjunction.com

Electronic and video publications:
The Lynch Mob Syndrome (Internet)

Access to staff:
Contact by letter, by telephone, by fax, by e-mail, in person and via website
Hours: 24 hours

PORTICO LIBRARY AND GALLERY

57 Mosley Street, Manchester, M2 3HY

Tel: 0161 236 6785
Fax: 0161 236 6803
E-mail: librarian@theportico.org.uk

Website:
http://www.theportico.org.uk

Enquiries:
Enquiries to: Librarian
Direct e-mail: librarian@theportico.org.uk
Other contacts: Assistant Librarian

Founded:
1806

Organisation type and purpose:
Independent members' library (membership is by subscription).

Subject coverage:
Travel, biography, topography, novels, poetry, drama, natural philosophy.

Special visitor services:
Group visits by arrangement.

Museum or gallery collection, archive, or library special collection:
Mainly 19th-century collection, archives of the Insitution since 1806. Houses publications of the Lancashire and Cheshire Antiquarian Society

Library catalogue:
All or part available in-house

Printed publications:
In-house monographs on topics mainly related to Manchester, the region and the Library's collection, Portico Library histories, exhibition catalogues
Order printed publications from: Librarian

Publications list:
Available online

Access to staff:
Contact by letter, by telephone, by fax, by e-mail, in person and via website
Hours: 0930 to 1630

Access to building, collection or gallery:
Via entryphone at Charlotte Street entrance
Hours: Mon to Fri, 0930 to 1630 (or as advertised)
Special comments: Subscription only, open to researchers.

Access for disabled people:
No wheelchair access
Special comments: Located upstairs.

Member organisation of:
Association of Independent Libraries
   website: http://www.independentlibraries.co.uk

PORTLAND COLLEGE

Nottingham Road, Mansfield, Nottinghamshire, NG18 4TJ

Tel: 01623 499111
Fax: 01623 499133
E-mail: college@portland.ac.uk

Website:
http://www.portland.ac.uk/

Enquiries:
Enquiries to: Admissions Officer
Direct fax: 01623 499134
Direct e-mail: marketing@portland.ac.uk

Founded:
1950

Organisation type and purpose:
Voluntary organisation, registered charity (charity number 214339).

Subject coverage:
Residential courses for all categories of physically disabled persons, except the totally blind, from 16 years of age upwards; vocational courses in business, technical studies and horticulture; foundation and further education; adult basic education; alternative and augmentative communication skills, unit for head injured (SPAN).

Printed publications:
Prospectus and Annual Report

Access to staff:
Contact by letter, by telephone and by fax.
Appointment necessary.
Hours: Mon to Fri, 0900 to 1700

Recognised by the:
British Accreditation Council

PORTSMOUTH & SOUTH EAST HAMPSHIRE CHAMBER OF COMMERCE AND INDUSTRY

Formal name: Hampshire Chamber of Commerce

Regional Business Centre, Harts Farm Way, Havant, Hampshire, PO9 1HR

Tel: 023 9244 9449
Fax: 023 9244 9444
E-mail: portsmouth@hampshirechamber.co.uk

Website:
http://www.hampshirechamber.co.uk
Directory of members, events, news, business opportunities, training workshops, international trade advice and discussion forum.

Enquiries:
Enquiries to: Membership Services Manager
Direct e-mail: nicholas.hoath@hampshirechamber.co.uk

Founded:
1883

Organisation type and purpose:
Membership association.
Chamber of Commerce.

Subject coverage:
Business information, helpline, export and import advice, documentation, trade missions, training, lobbying and representation.

Information services:
Provision of credit checks and database lists.

Trade and statistical information:
Economic survey of members for ABCC quarterly survey.

Printed publications:
Business News (magazine, monthly)

Access to staff:
Contact by telephone and by e-mail
Hours: Mon to Fri, 0900 to 1700

Access to building, collection or gallery:
No prior appointment required

Hours: Mon to Fri, 0900 to 1700

Access for disabled people:
Parking provided, level entry, access to all public areas, toilet facilities

PORTSMOUTH CITY COUNCIL

Acronym or abbreviation: PCC

Civic Offices, Guildhall Square, Portsmouth, Hampshire, PO1 2BG

Tel: 023 9282 2251
E-mail: general@portsmouthcc.gov.uk

Website:
http://www.portsmouthcc.gov.uk

Enquiries:
Enquiries to: Chief Executive
Direct tel: 023 9283 4009

Organisation type and purpose:
Local government body.

Subject coverage:
Services and amenities of the city council.

PORTSMOUTH CITY COUNCIL LIBRARY SERVICE

Portsmouth Central Library, Guildhall Square, Portsmouth, Hampshire, PO1 2DX

Tel: 023 9281 9311
Fax: 023 9283 9855
E-mail: reference.library@portsmouthcc.gov.uk

Enquiries:
Enquiries to: Library Service Manager
Direct e-mail: chris.goddard@plymouth.gov.uk

Organisation type and purpose:
Local government body, public library.

Subject coverage:
General reference library, particularly strong in areas of law, patent information, business information, art, local history (Hampshire), naval history, genealogy. European Public Information Centre.

Museum or gallery collection, archive, or library special collection:
Art Monographs
British Government Publications
British Standards
Charles Dickens Collection
Conan Doyle Collection
Genealogical Collection
HMSO Collection (selected subjects, 1972-)
Law Library
Local History Collection
Maps Collection
Naval Collection (12,000 vols)
Patent Abridgements, 1607 to 1992
State Papers (Calendars and Rolls)
Statistics Collection
UK Patent bibliographic data and full text 1993 to date on CD-ROM

Trade and statistical information:
Extensive collection of UK and foreign trade directories.
UK and European statistical information.
Some market research material.

Library catalogue:
All or part available online and in-house

Access to staff:
Contact by letter, by telephone, by fax, by e-mail and in person
Hours: Mon to Fri, 0900 to 1900; Sat, 0930 to 1600
Special comments: Access to historical collections requires proof of name and address.

Member of:
HATRICS Centre
Patent Information Network

PORTSMOUTH MUSEUMS AND RECORDS SERVICE

City Museum and Records Office, Museum Road, Portsmouth, Hampshire, PO1 2LJ

Tel: 02392 827261\ Minicom no. 02392 876550
Fax: 02392 875276
E-mail: searchroom@portsmouthcc.gov.uk

Website:
http://www.portsmouthrecordsoffice.co.uk/
http://www.portsmouthmuseums.co.uk

Enquiries:
Enquiries to: Manager
Other contacts: (1) Commercial Manager; (2) Visitor Services Officer for (1) marketing; (2) group bookings.

Founded:
1972

Organisation type and purpose:
Local government body, museum, art gallery.

Subject coverage:
The Story of Portsmouth; Living in Portsmouth; Fine and Decorative Art Gallery; and The Records Office.

Information services:
Special visitor services: Guided tours. Education services: Group education facilities, resources for Key Stages 1 and 2 and 3. Services for disabled people: For the hearing impaired.

Museum or gallery collection, archive, or library special collection:
17th century furniture
Art Deco Furniture
Frank Dobson Sculptures (terracotta and bronze)
Ceri Richards relief work 'Le Piano'.
Ronal Ossory Dunlop painting 'Still Life with Black Bottle'.
JMW Turner RA watercolour 'Gosport, the Entrance to Portsmouth Harbour' c. 1829
Local History:
Sir Alec Rose (Round the World Yachtsman – artefacts)
Verrecchia ice cream parlour and artefacts
Records Office contains the official records of the City of Portsmouth from the 14th century, church registers and records, some of which begin in the reign of Henry VIII, and large collections of deposited records of private, commercial, families and other organisations

Access to staff:
Contact by letter, by telephone, by fax and by e-mail

Access to building, collection or gallery:
No prior appointment required
Hours: Museum: daily, 1000 to 1700 except 24 to 26 Dec
Records Office: Mon to Fri, 1000 to 1700, closed on Public Holidays and 24 to 26 Dec

Access for disabled people:
Parking provided, ramped entry, level entry, access to all public areas, toilet facilities
Special comments: Induction loops.

PORTSMOUTH NHS LIBRARY SERVICE

Library, The Quad, Queen Alexandra Hospital, Portsmouth, Hampshire, PO6 3LY

Tel: 023 9228 6039
Fax: 023 9228 6880
E-mail: library.qah@porthosp.nhs.uk

Website:
http://www.porthosp.nhs/library-services.html

Enquiries:
Enquiries to: Library Services Manager

Organisation type and purpose:
National Health Service library.

Subject coverage:
Multi-disciplinary health care.

Access to staff:
Contact by letter, by telephone, by fax, by e-mail and via website. Appointment necessary.
Hours: Mon to Fri, 0830 to 1630

Branch libraries:
Education Centre
St Mary's Hospital, Portsmouth, Hampshire, PO6 3AD; tel: 023 9228 6000 extn 4855

Parent body:
Portsmouth Hospitals NHS Trust

POST ABORTION COUNSELLING SERVICE

Acronym or abbreviation: PACS

340 Westbourne Park Road, London, W11 1EQ

Tel: 020 7221 9631
E-mail: abortion@pacs.org.uk

Enquiries:
Enquiries to: Counsellor

Founded:
1986

Organisation type and purpose:
Advisory body, professional body, registered charity (charity number 802225), training organisation.
Counselling service.
To offer pre-abortion counselling and training for other professionals in the field.

Subject coverage:
The need for counselling as a result of an abortion.

Printed publications:
It's OK to Talk About Abortion (free)

Access to staff:
Contact by letter and by telephone. Appointment necessary. All charged.
Hours: Mon to Fri, 0900 to 2000
Special comments: 24 hour answerphone, counselling all hours by appointment.

Member of:
British Association of Counselling

POST OFFICE VEHICLE CLUB

Acronym or abbreviation: POVC

32 Russell Way, Leighton Buzzard, Bedfordshire, LU7 3NG

Tel: 01525 382129
E-mail: povehclub@aol.com

Website:
http://www.povehclub.org.uk

Enquiries:
Enquiries to: Honorary Secretary
Direct e-mail: povcmembership@btinternet.com

Founded:
1962

Organisation type and purpose:
Membership association.

Subject coverage:
Preservation of Royal Mail and British Telecom vehicles; DVLA appointed for GPO and Post Office vehicles for V765 registration restoration.

Museum or gallery collection, archive, or library special collection:
Books
Photographs
Vehicle data and manuals
Vehicle records

Non-library collection catalogue:
All or part available in-house and in print

Printed publications:
Post Horn (magazine, monthly)
Order printed publications from: 124 Shenstone Avenue, Norton, Stourbridge, West Midlands, DY8 3EJ

Publications list:
Available in print

Access to staff:
Contact by letter, by telephone, by fax, by e-mail and via website. Appointment necessary. Access for members only.
Hours: Mon to Fri, 1900 to 2100; Sat, Sun, 0900 to 1800

POST VINTAGE HUMBER CAR CLUB

Formal name: PVHCC Ltd

1 Hilberry Rise, Berrydale, Northampton, NN3 5ER

Tel: 01604 404363
E-mail: pvhumber.carclub@talk21.com

Website:
http://www.humber.org.uk

Enquiries:
Enquiries to: Director
Other contacts: Secretary

Founded:
1974

Organisation type and purpose:
Membership association (membership is by subscription), present number of members: 700+. Preservation and enjoyment derived from the ownership and enthusiasm for Humber cars.

Subject coverage:
Humber cars from 1932 to 1976.

Non-library collection catalogue:
All or part available online

Printed publications:
Various publications available (please enquire or see website)

Access to staff:
Contact by letter, by telephone, by e-mail and via website. Appointment necessary.
Hours: Mon to Fri, 0800 to 2200; Sat, Sun, 1000 to 2000

Member organisation of:
Federation of British Historic Vehicle Clubs (FBHVC)

Member organisations:
in more than 20 countries

Parent body:
PVHCC Ltd
1 Hilberry Rise, Northampton, NN3 5ER; tel: 01604 404363

POST-WAR THOROUGHBRED CAR CLUB

Church Villas, 22 Burhill Road, Hersham, Walton on Thames, Surrey, KT12 4JF

Tel: 01932 29101
Fax: 01932 29101

Enquiries:
Enquiries to: Membership Secretary

Founded:
1978

Organisation type and purpose:
Membership association (membership is by subscription), present number of members: 100. Historic car club.

Subject coverage:
British motor vehicles registered between the years 1945–1974.

Access to staff:
Contact by letter
Hours: Mon to Fri, 0900 to 1700

POSTAL HISTORY SOCIETY

Acronym or abbreviation: PHS

continued overleaf

60 Tachbrook Street, London, SW1V 2NA

Tel: 020 7545 7773
Fax: 020 7976 6040
E-mail: home@claireangier.co.uk

Enquiries:
Enquiries to: Membership Secretary

Founded:
1936

Organisation type and purpose:
Learned society (membership is by subscription), present number of members: 416.

Subject coverage:
History of communications by post or telegraph.

Library catalogue:
All or part available in-house

Printed publications:
Postal History (quarterly)
Australian Mails via Suez, 1852–1926 (Kirk)
British Postal Rates 1635–1839 (Sanford & Salt)
British Postal Rates to Europe 1836–76
Devon & Cornwall: a Postal Survey 1500–1791 (Cornelius)
Norwich Post Office 1568–1980 (Sussex)
Official Franking 1800–1840 (Scott)
Royal Mail Steam Packet Co 1842–1879 (Howatt)
Ship Letters (Hendy)
The Bermuda Packet Mails, 1806–1886 (Arnell & Ludington)
Order printed publications from: Publications Officer, Postal History Society
St Andrews Mews, Station Road, Stanley, Ilkeston, Derbyshire, DE7 6FB, tel: 01332 250970, e-mail: nicklynn@standrews85.freeserve.co.uk

Publications list:
Available in print

Access to staff:
Contact by letter, by telephone, by fax and by e-mail
Hours: Mon to Fri, 0900 to 1700

Affiliated to:
Association of British Philatelic Societies Limited
tel: 020 7490 3112

POTATO COUNCIL

4300 Nash Court, John Smith Drive, Oxford Business Park South, Oxford, OX4 2RT

Tel: 01865 714455
Fax: 01865 782200
E-mail: sgerrish@potato.org.uk

Website:
http://www.potato.org.uk

Enquiries:
Enquiries to: Information Resources Manager
Direct tel: 01865 782270
Direct fax: 01865 782283

Founded:
1997

Formerly called:
British Potato Council (year of change 2008)

Organisation type and purpose:
Non-departmental Public Body. Levy funded by the British Potato Industry, providing sponsorship of research and development, knowledge transfer, promotion of British ware and seed potatoes, collection and dissemination of market information and statistics – all activities contributing towards increasing the competitiveness of the British potato industry, and increasing the usage of British potatoes.

Subject coverage:
Potato storage; varieties; pests; diseases; production; marketing; cookery; all aspects, though mainly of UK interest.

Museum or gallery collection, archive, or library special collection:
Some grey literature, collection of published articles going back to 1950s and 1960s on computerised retrieval system

Trade and statistical information:
Data on the production of potatoes in Great Britain and volume of trade throughout the world.
Producer, wholesale and retail prices.
Crop progress reports.

Non-library collection catalogue:
All or part available in-house

Printed publications:
Potato Council Update (newsletter, c.10 a year, sent to all levy payers)
Research and Development Project Reports
Publications for the potato industry, consumers (varieties, cooking), caterers
Order printed publications from: Publications, at the same address, tel: 01865 782222, fax: 01865 782283, e-mail: publications@potato.org.uk

Electronic and video publications:
Many project reports are available on the website

Access to staff:
Contact by letter, by fax and by e-mail.
Appointment necessary.
Hours: Mon to Fri, 0900 to 1700
Special comments: Photocopies cannot be supplied.

Parent body:
Agriculture and Horticulture Development Board (AHDB)
Area 2B, Nobel House, 17 Smith Square, London, SW1P 3JR; tel: 020 7238 3079; e-mail: info@ahdb.org.uk; website: http://www.ahdb.org.uk

POTATO PROCESSORS ASSOCIATION

Acronym or abbreviation: PPA

4a Torphichen Street, Edinburgh, EH3 8JQ

Tel: 0131 229 9415
Fax: 0131 229 9407
E-mail: neil.cuthbert@sfdf.org.uk

Enquiries:
Enquiries to: Secretary

Organisation type and purpose:
Trade association (membership is by subscription).

Subject coverage:
Potato processing.

Access to staff:
Contact by letter, by telephone, by fax and by e-mail. Appointment necessary.
Hours: Mon to Fri, 0900 to 1700

Member of:
EUITP

POWER GENERATION CONTRACTORS ASSOCIATION

Acronym or abbreviation: PGCA

Westminster Tower, 3 Albert Embankment, London, SE1 7SL

Tel: 020 7793 3040
Fax: 020 7793 1576

Enquiries:
Enquiries to: Director

Organisation type and purpose:
Trade association.

Subject coverage:
Project management and engineering services for utility and industrial power stations, water tube and shell boilers; steam, gas, water and wind turbine generators, condensing and feed heating plant, high integrity pipework, auxiliary and ancillary plant, nuclear engineering, environmental systems, retrofit, refurbishment, repair, maintenance and construction services.

Access to staff:
Contact by fax
Hours: Mon to Fri, 0900 to 1700

Federated in:
BEAMA

POWERFUL INFORMATION

City Discovery Centre, Bradwell Abbey, Milton Keynes, Buckinghamshire, MK13 9AP

Tel: 01908 320033
Fax: 01908 320033
E-mail: info@powerfulinformation.org

Website:
http://www.powerfulinformation.org

Enquiries:
Enquiries to: Manager
Direct e-mail: lynne@powerfulinformation.org

Founded:
1990

Organisation type and purpose:
Registered charity, suitable for ages: all, training organisation.

Subject coverage:
Powerful Information is a British charity working to empower communities in low-income countries to tackle the root causes of poverty and injustice and reduce the impact of environmental degradation. It works with and through local partners to provide education and training, and supports practical grassroots initiatives that build social capital, promote social justice and raise public awareness of important social and environmental issues.

Access to staff:
Contact by letter, by telephone and by e-mail.
Appointment necessary.
Hours: Mon to Fri, 0900 to 1700

Access for disabled people:
Parking provided, level entry, access to all public areas, toilet facilities

POWERGEN UK PLC

Power Technology, Ratcliffe on Soar, Nottingham, NG11 0EE

Tel: 0115 936 2000
Fax: 0115 936 2711
E-mail: liz.day@powertech.co.uk

Website:
http://www.powertech.co.uk

Enquiries:
Enquiries to: Information Officer
Direct tel: 0115 936 2360
Direct fax: 0115 362 647

Founded:
1989

Organisation type and purpose:
Service industry.
Electricity and gas utility.

Subject coverage:
Environment; wind power; NDT; metallurgy; combustion and fossil fuel; all subjects relating to electricity production, organisation and maintenance; does not include nuclear generation or electricity transmission.

Museum or gallery collection, archive, or library special collection:
CEGB and Powergen reports

Non-library collection catalogue:
All or part available in-house

Library catalogue:
All or part available in-house

Printed publications:
Public information pamphlets on power stations, Powergen departments and types of power production

Ashes to Assets (booklet)

Access to staff:
Contact by letter, by telephone, by fax, by e-mail and via website. Appointment necessary.
Hours: Mon to Fri, 0900 to 1700

Access for disabled people:
Parking provided, level entry, toilet facilities

Head Office:
Powergen plc
Westwood Way, Westwood Business Park, Coventry, CV4 8LG; tel: 01203 424000; fax: 01203 425432

POWYS COUNTY ARCHIVES OFFICE

County Hall, Llandrindod Wells, Powys, LD1 5LG

Tel: 01597 826088
Fax: 01597 826087
E-mail: archives@powys.gov.uk

Website:
http://archives.powys.gov.uk
http://www.powys.gov.uk
Office guide.

Enquiries:
Enquiries to: Manager
Other contacts: Assistant Archivist

Founded:
1991

Organisation type and purpose:
Local government body.
Archives office.

Subject coverage:
Local history of former counties of Breconshire, Montgomeryshire and Radnorshire, 15th century to 20th century.

Museum or gallery collection, archive, or library special collection:
Public Records, incl. Quarter Sessions records
Official Records
Estate and Solicitors' collections
Records of local historical interest, incl. manuscripts and photographs
Census returns (microfiche)
Parish registers (microfilm)
A growing collection of local history books on Powys

Non-library collection catalogue:
All or part available in-house

Library catalogue:
All or part available online and in-house

Printed publications:
Annual Report (£4 inc. p&p)
Guide to the Powys County Archives Office

Access to staff:
Contact by letter, by telephone, by fax and by e-mail. Appointment necessary.
Hours: Tue to Thu, 1000 to 1230 and 1330 to 1700; Fri, 1000 to 1230 and 1330 to 1600; closed at all other times

Part of:
Powys County Council
Recreation, Culture and Countryside

POWYS COUNTY COUNCIL

County Hall, Llandrindod Wells, Powys, LD1 5LG

Tel: 01597 826000
Fax: 01597 826230
E-mail: customer@powys.gov.uk

Website:
http://www.powys.gov.uk
Council services and information on county.

Enquiries:
Enquiries to: Relevant department

Founded:
1996

Organisation type and purpose:
Local government body.

Subject coverage:
Community services, children, families and lifelong learning, economy and community regeneration, technical and local services.

Access to staff:
Contact by letter, by telephone, by fax, by e-mail and in person
Hours: Mon to Thu, 0900 to 1700; Fri 0900 to 1630

POWYS LIBRARY SERVICE

Library HQ, Cefnllys Lane, Llandrindod Wells, Powys, LD1 5LD

Tel: 01597 826860
Fax: 01597 826872

Website:
http://www.powys.gov.uk/libraries

Enquiries:
Enquiries to: County Librarian

Organisation type and purpose:
Local government body, public library.

Subject coverage:
General.

Museum or gallery collection, archive, or library special collection:
Gregynog Press Collection (at Newtown Area Library)
Local history collections (relating to Powys and to the former counties of Breconshire, Montgomeryshire and Radnorshire)

Library catalogue:
All or part available online and in-house

Access to staff:
Contact by letter, by telephone, by fax, by e-mail, in person and via website
Hours: HQ: Mon to Fri, 0900 to 1700; for branches, see website

Branches:
within the Recreation and Culture directorate of Powys County Council

POWYS SOCIETY

Flat D, 87 Ledbury Road, London, W11 2AG

Tel: 020 7238 4456 (office); 020 7243 0168 (evening)
E-mail: postmaster@powys-society.org

Website:
http://www.powys-society.org

Enquiries:
Enquiries to: Honorary Secretary
Direct e-mail: chris.thd.thomas@hotmail.co.uk

Founded:
1967

Organisation type and purpose:
Learned society (membership is by subscription), present number of members: 298, registered charity (charity number 801332).
Literary society. Aims to publicise the literary and artistic contribution of all members of the Powys Family, in particular John Cowper (1872–1963), Theodore Francis Powys (1875–1953) and Llewelyn Powys (1884–1939), and their wide circle of friends.

Subject coverage:
Lives and works of the three writers: John Cowper Powys, Theodore Francis Powys and Llewelyn Powys, other members of the Powys family and their circle of friends.

Museum or gallery collection, archive, or library special collection:
Major collections of books, manuscripts and letters, etc. relating to the Powys family, held at the Dorset County Museum, Dorchester, Dorset

Non-library collection catalogue:
All or part available in-house

Library catalogue:
All or part available in-house

Printed publications:
The Powys Journal (annual)
The Powys Society Newsletter (3 times a year)
Other occasional publications
Order printed publications from: Publications Manager, The Powys Society, 23 Cleveland Walk, Bath, BA2 6JW, tel: 01225 469004, e-mail: sm@gotadsl.co.uk

Publications list:
Available in print

Access to staff:
Contact by letter, by telephone, by e-mail and via website
Hours: Mon to Fri, 0900 to 1700

Access to building, collection or gallery:
By arrangement only

PRACTICAL ACTION PUBLISHING

The Schumacher Centre for Technology and Development, Bourton-on-Dunsmore, Rugby, CV23 9QZ

Tel: 01926 634501
Fax: 01926 634502
E-mail: publishinginfo@practicalaction.org.uk

Website:
http://www.itdgpublishing.org.uk
Information on publishing company.
http://www.developmentbookshop.com
Thousands of development titles from many publishers. Comprehensive site.

Formerly called:
ITDG Publishing

Organisation type and purpose:
Publishing house.

Subject coverage:
Development technology for developing world, water and sanitation, development and disaster relief, food security.

Library catalogue:
All or part available in-house

Publications list:
Available in print

Access to staff:
Contact by letter and by fax
Hours: Mon to Fri, 0830 to 1730

Access to building, collection or gallery:
Prior appointment required

PRADER-WILLI SYNDROME ASSOCIATION (UK)

Acronym or abbreviation: PWSA (UK)

125A London Road, Derby, DE1 2QQ

Tel: 01332 365676
Fax: 01332 360401
E-mail: admin@pwsa.co.uk

Website:
http://www.pwsa.co.uk
Details of syndrome.

Enquiries:
Enquiries to: Administrator
Other contacts: Welfare Services and Regional Groups Coordinator (for welfare queries, new diagnosis)

Founded:
1981

Organisation type and purpose:
Voluntary organisation, registered charity (charity number 284583).
Voluntary support group.

Subject coverage:
The Prader-Willi Syndrome, support and information for sufferers and carers.

continued overleaf

Library catalogue:
All or part available in-house

Printed publications:
Free information leaflets include:
What is Prader-Willi Syndrome?
So your child has Prader-Willi Syndrome – What
Happens Now?
Diagnostic Criteria for PWS
Prader-Willi Syndrome: A handbook for parents
and carers of babies and children with PWS
(Waters J)
Books for purchase include:
Healthy Eating (free to members, £5 to non-
members)
Handbook for parents and carers of adults with
PWS (£3 members, £4.50 non members)
Prader-Willi Syndrome: A Practical Guide –
Resource materials for teachers (£15)
Our Babies (£3)
Management of PWS (£27.50)
Order printed publications from: above address

Electronic and video publications:
Videos (various for loan)
Prader-Willi Syndrome – Keeping a Balance
(video, £8 members, £12 non members)

Publications list:
Available in print

Access to staff:
Contact by letter, by telephone, by fax, by e-mail,
in person and via website
Hours: Mon to Fri, 0930 to 1530
Special comments: Answerphone available.

Access to building, collection or gallery:
Prior appointment required

Access for disabled people:
Access to first floor offices only

PRE-SCHOOL LEARNING ALLIANCE

National Centre, The Fitzpatrick Building, 188
York Way, London, N7 9AD

Tel: 020 7697 2500
Fax: 020 7700 0319
E-mail: info@pre-school.org.uk

Website:
http://www.pre-school.org.uk

Enquiries:
Enquiries to: Information Services
Direct tel: 020 7697 2595

Founded:
1961

Formerly called:
Pre-school Playgroups Association (year of change
1995)

Organisation type and purpose:
An educational charity specialising in the early
years, and a membership association providing
practical support to over 15,000 early years settings
and contributing to the care and education of over
800,000 young children and their families each
year.

Subject coverage:
Products and services include specialist
publications, childcare services, quality assurance,
campaigning, research, training and family
programmes; offers a range of independent
professional information, advice, support and
guidance tailored especially to meet the needs of
young children and their families, students, early
years practitioners and professionals.

Printed publications:
Extensive publications list covers all aspects of
running an early years setting.
Order printed publications from: www.pre-
school.org.uk/shop

Publications list:
Available online and in print

Access to staff:
Contact by letter, by telephone, by fax and by e-
mail
Hours: Mon to Fri, 0900 to 1700

Constituent bodies:
4 divisional offices, 400 county and branch sub-
committees

PRECAST FLOORING FEDERATION

Acronym or abbreviation: PFF

60 Charles Street, Leicester, LE1 1FB

Tel: 0116 253 6161
Fax: 0116 251 4568
E-mail: info@precastfloors.info

Website:
http://www.precastfloors.info

Enquiries:
Enquiries to: Secretary

Organisation type and purpose:
Trade association.

Subject coverage:
Precast concrete flooring units of all types.

Printed publications:
Code of Practice for the Safe Erection of Precast
Concrete Flooring
Folder and Data Sheets
Members Product Range

Access to staff:
Contact by letter, by telephone, by fax and by e-
mail
Hours: Mon to Fri, 0900 to 1700

Product association of the:
British Precast Concrete Federation

PREHISTORIC SOCIETY

Institute of Archaeology, University College
London, 31–34 Gordon Square, London, WC1H
0PY

Website:
http://www.ucl.ac.uk/prehistoric

Enquiries:
Enquiries to: Administrative Assistant
Direct e-mail: prehistoric@ucl.ac.uk

Founded:
1935

Organisation type and purpose:
Learned society.

Subject coverage:
Prehistory.

Printed publications:
Past (newsletter, 3 times a year)
Proceedings of the Prehistory Society (annually)

Access to staff:
Contact by letter
Hours: Mon to Fri, 0900 to 1700

PREMIER CHRISTIAN RADIO

Formal name: Premier – Christian Radio for London

PO Box 13000, London, SW1E 5PP

Tel: 020 7233 6705
Fax: 020 7233 6706
E-mail: premier@premier.org.uk

Website:
http://www.premier.org.uk
Christian Radio.
http://www.radioondemand.net
Archive Christian programming.
http://www.christianityandrenewal.com
Christian magazine.

Enquiries:
Enquiries to: Administrator
Direct e-mail: crystal.callow@premier.org.uk

Access to staff:
Contact by letter, by telephone, by fax and by e-
mail
Hours: Mon to Fri, 0900 to 1700

Constituent bodies:
4 divisional offices, 400 county and branch sub-
committees

Founded:
1995

Organisation type and purpose:
Registered charity (charity number 287610).
Radio station.

Subject coverage:
Christian broadcasting and publishing, telephone
helpline, internet services via website, Christian
resources.

Printed publications:
Newsletter
Programme schedule
Christianity & Renewal (magazine)
Youthwork magazine

Access to staff:
Contact by letter, by telephone, by fax, by e-mail
and via website
Hours: Mon to Fri, 0900 to 1700

Access to building, collection or gallery:
No access other than to staff

Publishing subsidiary:
Monarch CCP
PO Box 17911, London, SW1E 5ZR; tel: 020 7316
1450; fax: 020 7316 1453; e-mail: monarchccp@
premier.org.uk

Telephone Helpline:
Lifeline
At the same address; tel: 020 7316 0808; e-mail:
lifeline@premier.org.uk

PRESBYTERIAN CHURCH OF WALES

Acronym or abbreviation: PCW

Tabernacle Chapel, 81 Merthyr Road, Whitchurch,
Cardiff, CF14 1DD

Tel: 029 2062 7465
Fax: 029 2061 6188
E-mail: swyddfa.office@ebcpcw.org.uk

Website:
http://www.ebcpcw.org.uk

Enquiries:
Enquiries to: Manager

Organisation type and purpose:
Registered charity.
Christian church, excepted charity.
To propagate the Gospel of Jesus Christ.

Subject coverage:
The history, organisation and current position of
the Presbyterian Church of Wales.

**Museum or gallery collection, archive, or library
special collection:**
The Presbyterian Church of Wales Archive is
housed in the National Library, Aberystwyth

Printed publications:
Books
Treasury (English monthly newspaper)
Y Goleuad (Welsh weekly newspaper)
Yearbook and Diary
Order printed publications from: The Manager, Y
Bwthyn Press, Lôn Ddewi, Caernarfon, Gwynedd,
LL55 1ER, tel: 01286 672018, fax: 01286 677823

Access to staff:
Contact by letter, by telephone, by fax, by e-mail
and via website. Appointment necessary.
Hours: Mon to Fri, 0900 to 1700

PRESBYTERIAN HISTORICAL SOCIETY OF IRELAND

26 College Green, Belfast, BT71LN

Tel: 028 9032 2284 extn 258
Fax: 028 9041 7307
E-mail: phsilibrarian@pcinet.org

Website:
http://www.presbyterianhistoryireland.com

Summary of holdings; list of publications; members have access to 'History of Presbyterian Congregations in Ireland' publication.

Enquiries:
Enquiries to: Librarian/Assistant Secretary

Founded:
1907

Organisation type and purpose:
Learned society (membership is by subscription), present number of members: 350, registered charity.
Historical society for the Presbyterian Church in Ireland; the Non-Subscribing Presbyterian Church of Ireland and the Reformed Presbyterian Church of Ireland.

Subject coverage:
History of Presbyterianism and the Presbyterian Churches in Ireland, with congregational, genealogical and biographical information.

Special visitor services:
Microfilm reader

Museum or gallery collection, archive, or library special collection:
Books and pamphlets (c. 550 to pre-1851)
periodicals
congregational histories
biographies of ministers
photographs of ministers and churches
collection of Irish Presbyterian communion tokens
Presbyterian artefacts including McCahan bequest collection (historical books and manuscripts)
microfilms of church records
some original church records

Library catalogue:
All or part available in-house

Printed publications:
A History of Congregations of the Presbyterian Church in Ireland, 1610–1982 (Supplement published 1996 of additions and amendments)
Helen Waddell, Presbyterian Medievalist (booklet)
Booklets on a number of Presbyterian ministers, including Andrew Weir of Manchuria and Robert Blair of Bangor
Bulletin (annually)
Fasti of the General Assembly of the Presbyterian Church in Ireland, (1840–1910)
Our Presbyterian Heritage (history, for purchase)

Publications list:
Available online

Access to staff:
Contact by letter, by telephone, by e-mail and in person
Hours: Tue, Wed, 0930 to 1630; Thu, 0930 to 1300

Access for disabled people:
Lift available in Church House; at College Green, library faciltiies are on ground floor with disabled toilet facilities

PRESCRIPTION PRICING AUTHORITY

Acronym or abbreviation: PPA

Bridge House, 152 Pilgrim Street, Newcastle upon Tyne, NE1 6SN

Tel: 0191 232 5270
Fax: 0191 232 5250

Website:
http://www.ppa.org.uk

Enquiries:
Enquiries to: Director of Information Technology
Direct fax: 0191 203 5270
Direct e-mail: douglas.ball@ppa.nhs.uk

Founded:
1911

Organisation type and purpose:
Statutory body.
Information on drugs dispensed and prescribed in England. Details on prescribers and dispensers.
Drug coding and descriptive information.

Authorise and make payment to dispensing contractors in England with regard to NHS prescriptions. Provide prescribing information and systems to NHS bodies and prescribers. Detection and prevention of fraud. Management of Low Income Scheme.

Subject coverage:
Drug prescribing in England, volume of drugs in the UK, updates on drug prices, standard drug flle/drug coding systems and information for research groups. Details on prescribing and dispensing contractors.

Printed publications:
Drug file for NHS drugs

Electronic and video publications:
EPACT – Electronic prescribing information access systems
TOOLKIT – Performance indicators

Access to staff:
Contact by letter and by e-mail. Appointment necessary.
Hours: Mon to Fri, 0900 to 1700
Special comments: Access only by appointment.

PRESS ASSOCIATION

Acronym or abbreviation: PA

PA News Library, PA News Centre, Central Park, New Lane, Leeds, West Yorkshire, LS11 5DZ

Tel: 0870 830 6824
Fax: 0870 830 6825
E-mail: newslibrary@pa.press.net

Website:
http://www.palibrary.press.net
Information about the library.

Enquiries:
Enquiries to: News Librarian
Other contacts: Picture Librarian for photo library.

Founded:
1926 (library)

Organisation type and purpose:
National organisation, service industry.
News agency.
Cuttings from all national papers.

Subject coverage:
Archive news material from 1926 to date covering a very wide range of subjects in 15 million press cuttings from all British national newspapers, some back to 1928; domestic news photographs from 1910 to present day.

Museum or gallery collection, archive, or library special collection:
News library
Photo library

Access to staff:
Contact by telephone, by fax, by e-mail and in person. Appointment necessary. All charged.
Hours: Daily, 0700 to 2300

PRESS COMPLAINTS COMMISSION

Acronym or abbreviation: PCC

Halton House, 20–23 Holborn, London, EC1N 2JD

Tel: 020 7831 0022
Fax: 020 7831 0025
E-mail: complaints@pcc.org.uk

Website:
http://www.pcc.org.uk

Enquiries:
Enquiries to: Information and Events Manager
Direct e-mail: pcc@pcc.org.uk

Founded:
1991

Organisation type and purpose:
The PCC is an independent self-regulatory body that deals with complaints about the editorial content of newspapers and magazines (and their websites). It has 17 members drawn from the lay public and the press who form the Commission.

Subject coverage:
The PCC investigates complaints raised with it under the Editors' Code by individuals, companies and organisations. It keeps industry standards high by training journalists and editors, and works pro-actively behind the scenes to prevent harassment and media intrusion. It can also provide pre-publication advice to journalists and the public.

Education services:
Talks/seminars provided for groups of journalism and media studies students by prior appointment.

Printed publications:
Code of Practice
Complaints Reports
How to Complain
How the PCC Can Help You – wallet-sized leaflets

Access to staff:
Contact by letter, by telephone, by fax, by e-mail and via website
Hours: 0900 to 1730
Special comments: 24-hour Advice Line for use in emergencies only: 07659 152656

Access to building, collection or gallery:
Prior appointment required
Hours: 0930 to 1730

PRESSURE GAUGE AND DIAL THERMOMETER ASSOCIATION

Acronym or abbreviation: PGDT

136 Hagley Road, Edgbaston, Birmingham, B16 9PN

Tel: 0121 454 4141
Fax: 0121 454 4949
E-mail: info@pgdt.org

Website:
http://www.pgdt.org

Enquiries:
Enquiries to: Secretary

Organisation type and purpose:
Trade association.

Subject coverage:
Pressure gauges and pressure measurement, temperature gauges and measurement.

Printed publications:
Buyer's Guide

Access to staff:
Contact by e-mail and via website
Hours: Mon to Fri, 0900 to 1700

PRESTON BOROUGH COUNCIL

PO Box 10, Town Hall, Preston, Lancashire, PR1 2RL

Tel: 01772 906000
Fax: 01772 906195
E-mail: yourcouncil@pbcpr.demon.co.uk

Website:
http://www.preston.gov.uk

Enquiries:
Enquiries to: Public Relations Manager
Direct tel: 01772 906464
Direct e-mail: al.mazzafiore@pbcpr.demon.co.uk

Organisation type and purpose:
Local government body.

Subject coverage:
Local government services.

Printed publications:
Annual Report
Prestonian (Citizens' Newsletter, quarterly)

continued overleaf

Access to staff:
Contact by letter and by e-mail
Hours: Mon to Fri, 0900 to 1700

PRESTRESSED CONCRETE ASSOCIATION

Acronym or abbreviation: PCA

4th Floor, 60 Charles Street, Leicester, LE1 1FB

Tel: 0116 253 6161
Fax: 0116 251 4568

Enquiries:
Enquiries to: Secretary

Organisation type and purpose:
Trade association.

Subject coverage:
Precast pretensioned concrete bridge beams, double tee beams and other precast prestressed units.

Printed publications:
Integral Abutments for Prestressed Beam Bridges (£40)
Prestressed Beam Integral Bridges (1991, £10)
Serviceability limit state aspects of continuous bridges using precast concrete beams (£20)
Simple bridge design using Prestressed Beams (£50)

Access to staff:
Contact by letter, by telephone, by fax and by e-mail
Hours: Mon to Fri, 0900 to 1700

Product association of the:
British Precast Concrete Federation

PRIMARY IMMUNODEFICIENCY ASSOCIATION

Acronym or abbreviation: PiA

Alliance House, 12 Caxton Street, London, SW1H 0QS

Tel: 020 7976 7640
Fax: 020 7976 7641
E-mail: info@pia.org.uk

Website:
http://pia.org.uk

Enquiries:
Enquiries to: Chief Executive
Direct e-mail: chris@pia.org.uk

Founded:
1989

Organisation type and purpose:
Membership association, present number of members: 2,000, voluntary organisation, registered charity (charity number 1107233).

Subject coverage:
All primary immunodeficiencies and how they affect individuals.

Publications list:
Available online and in print

Access to staff:
Contact by letter, by telephone, by fax, by e-mail and via website. Appointment necessary.
Hours: Mon to Fri, 0900 to 1700

Member of:
European Patients Primary Immunodeficiency Collaboration (EPPIC)
International Patient of Primary Immunodeficiencies (IPOPI)

PRINCE'S FOUNDATION

Formal name: The Prince's Foundation for the Built Environment
Acronym or abbreviation: PFBE

19–22 Charlotte Road, London, EC2A 3SG

Tel: 020 7613 8500

Fax: 020 7613 8599
E-mail: enquiries@princes-foundation.org

Website:
http://www.princes-foundation.org
Public programme, news, alumni network, project case studies, publications.

Enquiries:
Enquiries to: Librarian
Direct tel: 020 7613 8507
Direct e-mail: library@princes-foundation.org

Founded:
1998

Formerly called:
The Prince of Wales's Institute of Architecture (year of change 2000)

Organisation type and purpose:
Educational charity and architecture and urban design consultancy.

Subject coverage:
Traditional and sustainable architecture and urbanism, community planning, traditional art, building crafts, Islamic arts, environmental building techniques, urban design and regeneration.

Information services:
Members-only Library.

Special visitor services:
By previous arrangement with the librarian.

Museum or gallery collection, archive, or library special collection:
Library includes the collections of the late John Julius Stanton and others, and books on Islamic art and architecture, some donated by Issam El Said
Special Collections: His Royal Highness Collection, books on indefinite loan from the private collection of HRH The Prince of Wales

Non-library collection catalogue:
All or part available in-house

Library catalogue:
All or part available in-house

Printed publications:
Annual Review (free)
Senior Fellows Series: 1, The Architectural Tuning of Settlements, by Leon Krier, PFBE, 2008
Senior Fellows Series: 2, The Place of Dwelling (Ray Gindroz, PFBE, 2008)
Senior Fellows Series: 3, The Roots of Sustainability (David Cadman, PFBE, 2009)
HRH The Prince of Wales's Affordable Rural Housing Initiative. Creating a Sense of Place: A Design Guide
HRH The Prince of Wales's Affordable Rural Housing Initiative. Moving Forward: Further guidance for landowners, businesses and communities
Sustainable Urban Extensions: Planned through design
Taylor & Green Architects 1938–1943: The Spirit of Place in Modern Housing
John Campbell – Rediscovery of an Arts & Crafts Architect (Alam Powers et al.)
Order printed publications from: Tradition & Sustainability available in bookshops from September 2010
Senior Fellows Series can be purchased on-line from the INTBAU website: http://www.intbau.org
Limited availability of back catalogue, enquiries e-mail: library@princes-foundation.org

Electronic and video publications:
DVD: Inside Poundbury: A short film about The Prince of Wales's exemplar development in Dorset, UK, narrated by Dan Cruickshank
Beyond Poundbury DVD Series: DVD 1: Structuring Settlements; DVD 2: Removing the roadblocks; DVD 3: Transit-oriented development; DVD 4: Low Carbon Communities; DVD 5: Mixed Use; DVD 6: Getting the details right

Publications list:
Available in print

Access to staff:
Contact by letter, by telephone, by fax and by e-mail. Appointment necessary.
Hours: Mon to Fri, 1000 to 1730

Access to building, collection or gallery:
Prior appointment required
Hours: Mon to Fri, 0900 to 1700

Access for disabled people:
Ramped entry, access to all public areas, accessible doors to all areas, lift servicing all floors, accessible toilets (fully DDA-compliant)
Hours: Mon to Fri, 0900 to 1700

Links with:
INTBAU, International network for traditonal building, architecture & urbanism
The Prince's Charities
The Prince's Drawing School
The Prince's School of Traditional Art

PRINCE'S TRUST, THE

Head Office, 18 Park Square East, London, NW1 4LH

Tel: 020 7543 1234\ Minicom no. 020 7543 1374
Fax: 020 7543 1200
E-mail: info@princes-trust.org.uk

Website:
http://www.princes-trust.org.uk
Information on all programmes and activities.

Enquiries:
Enquiries to: Press Office
Direct tel: 020 7543 1382
Other contacts: Information Officer for research enquiries.

Founded:
1973

Organisation type and purpose:
Registered charity (charity number 1053579). The Prince's Trust is the UK's leading youth charity, offering 14–30 year olds the training, funding or support they need to gain confidence, improve life skills or get into work.

Subject coverage:
Young people; youth disadvantage; youth unemployment; young people and New Deal; young people and volunteering.

Printed publications:
Various publications including
Annual Review
Yes You Can (booklet)
Abuse and Survival (1998, PAID)
Mapping Disadvantage (PAID)
It's Like That – Young people's hopes and aspirations
The Way It Is
Various factsheets
Order printed publications from: Literature Distribution Service
tel: 020 8957 5190

Electronic and video publications:
Only a Kiss? – helps young people recognise and cope with abusive relationships (video, PAID)
Yes You Can – about the Prince's Trust (video)
Yes You Can (audio tape, booklet)
Yes You Can, Work for Yourself (audio tape)

Publications list:
Available in print

Access to staff:
Contact by letter, by telephone and via website
Hours: Mon to Fri, 0900 to 1700

Access to building, collection or gallery:
No prior appointment required
Special comments: Research/information needs in writing to the Information Officer.

Other addresses:
Various offices across the UK
tel: Freephone 0800 842 842

PRINCIPAL REGISTRY OF THE FAMILY DIVISION (PROBATE DEPARTMENT)

First Avenue House, 42–49 High Holborn, London, WC1V 6NP

Tel: 020 7947 7000
Fax: 020 7947 6946

Website:
http://www.courtservice.gov.uk
Click on forms and leaflets, and probate is towards the end of the list.

Enquiries:
Enquiries to: Manager Probate Department

Organisation type and purpose:
National government body.

Subject coverage:
Wills and grants of probate and administration.

Museum or gallery collection, archive, or library special collection:
All wills in England and Wales since 1858

Printed publications:
How to obtain probate – Form PA2

Access to staff:
Contact by telephone and in person
Hours: Mon to Fri, 1000 to 1630
Special comments: General enquiries only by telephone.

Access for disabled people:
Access to all public areas, toilet facilities

All requests for copies of wills/grants by post:
York Probate Sub-Registry (provide full name of deceased, data of death, locality, where resided, cheque for £5 payable H.M.P.G.)
   Duncombe Place, York, YO1 7EA

PRISON ADVICE AND CARE TRUST

Acronym or abbreviation: PACT

Family Support Services, 254 Caledonian Road, Islington, London, N1 0NG

Tel: 020 7278 3981
Fax: 020 7278 8765
E-mail: familysupport@pact.uk.net

Website:
http://www.imprisonment.org.uk

Enquiries:
Enquiries to: Family Services Manager

Founded:
1974

Organisation type and purpose:
Voluntary organisation, registered charity (charity number 219278).
Gives support advice and help to prisoners' wives, children and any family member or friend who has someone in prison.

Subject coverage:
Welfare benefits, penal systems, 'families and friends' finance, visiting prisons, prison regulations, assisted visits, accommodation.
Overnight accommodation for families visiting London prisons/attending trials/appeals.

Museum or gallery collection, archive, or library special collection:
Leaflets, booklets, books and publications relating to penal establishments, rules etc

Printed publications:
PACT information leaflet

Access to staff:
Contact by letter, by telephone, by fax, by e-mail and via website. Appointment necessary.
Hours: Mon to Fri, 0930 to 1700

Liaison with other groups involved in similar work eg:
Federation of Prisoners' Families Support Groups
NACRO

Prison Reform Trust
Various statutory bodies

Other addresses:
All Day Children's Visits
   HMP Holloway, Parkhurst Road, London, N7 0NU
Holloway Visitors' Centre
   HMP Holloway, Parkhurst Road, London, N7 0NU; tel: 020 7700 1567
Pentonville Visitors' Centre
   HMP Pentonville, Caledonian Road, London, N7 8TT; tel: 020 7609 3860

Registered Office and Administration:
PACT
   Lincoln House, 1–3 Brixton Road, London, SW9 6DE

PRISON OFFICERS' ASSOCIATION

Acronym or abbreviation: POA

Cronin House, 245 Church Street, Edmonton, London, N9 9HW

Tel: 020 8803 0255
Fax: 020 8803 1761

Enquiries:
Enquiries to: General Secretary

Organisation type and purpose:
Trade union, present number of members: 34,000.

Subject coverage:
Trade union view of issues relating to the working and operational conditions of HM Prisons Service.

Access to staff:
Contact by letter. Appointment necessary. Letter of introduction required.
Hours: Mon to Fri, 0900 to 1700

Affiliated to:
EUROFEDOP
TUC

PRISON REFORM TRUST

Acronym or abbreviation: PRT

15 Northburgh Street, London, EC1V 0JR

Tel: 020 7251 5070
Fax: 020 7251 5076
E-mail: prt@prisonreformtrust.org.uk

Website:
http://www.prisonreformtrust.org.uk

Founded:
1981

Organisation type and purpose:
National organisation, voluntary organisation, registered charity (charity number 1035525), research organisation.
The work of the Prison Reform Trust is aimed at creating a just, humane and effective penal system.

Subject coverage:
Prison regimes, alternatives to custody and sentencing policy.

Museum or gallery collection, archive, or library special collection:
News cuttings
Official reports
Prison statistics
Wide variety of UK and international reports and papers

Printed publications:
Monthly newsletter, Bromley Prison Briefing Fact File
Plus many other publications

Publications list:
Available online and in print

Access to staff:
Contact by letter, by telephone, by e-mail and via website
Hours: Mon to Fri, 0930 to 1730

PRISON SERVICE COLLEGE LIBRARY

Prison Service College, Newbold Revel, Rugby, Warwickshire, CV23 0TH

Tel: 01788 804119
Fax: 01788 804114
E-mail: catherine.fell@noms.gsi.gov.uk

Enquiries:
Enquiries to: Librarian

Founded:
1960

Organisation type and purpose:
National government body, training organisation.
Central government training establishment.

Subject coverage:
Penology and criminology; history of the prison service in England and Wales; comparative material on penal establishments in other countries; management and training; forensic psychology and psychiatry.

Museum or gallery collection, archive, or library special collection:
Miscellaneous 19th-century reports on prison-related matters
Reports of Directors of Convict Prisons
Reports of HM Inspectors of Prisons from 1835
Reports of the Prison Commission/Prison Department from 1878

Library catalogue:
All or part available in-house

Printed publications:
Accessions List (6 a year)
Journals Bulletin (monthly)
Miscellaneous reading lists – produced on request

Access to staff:
Contact by letter, by telephone, by fax and by e-mail. Appointment necessary.
Hours: Mon, 1000 to 2030; Tue to Thu, 0830 to 2030; Fri 0830 to 1400

Parent body:
HM Prison Service
   website: http://www.hmprisonservice.gov.uk

PRISONERS ABROAD

Acronym or abbreviation: PA

89–93 Fonthill Road, Finsbury Park, London, N4 3JH

Tel: 020 7561 6820
Fax: 020 7561 6821
E-mail: info@prisonersabroad.org.uk

Website:
http://www.prisonersabroad.org.uk

Founded:
1978

Formerly called:
National Council for the Welfare of Prisoners Abroad (year of change 2003)

Organisation type and purpose:
International organisation, registered charity (charity number 1093710).
Providing information, advice and support to British citizens held in prison abroad, to their families, and when they return to the United Kingdom.

Subject coverage:
Judicial procedures; prisoners' rights; information services; prisoner transfer treaties; extradition; prison conditions; welfare services; resettlement; family support.

Printed publications:
Annual Report
Newsletter (3 times a year)

Publications list:
Available online

continued overleaf

Access to staff:
Contact by letter, by telephone, by fax, by e-mail, in person and via website. Appointment necessary.
Hours: Mon to Fri, 1000 to 1600

Access to building, collection or gallery:
Hours: Mon to Fri, 1000 to 1600

Access for disabled people:
Hours: Mon to Fri, 1000 to 1600

PRIVATE LIBRARIES ASSOCIATION

Acronym or abbreviation: PLA

Ravelston, South View Road, Pinner, Middlesex, HA5 3YD

E-mail: dchambers@aol.com

Website:
http://www.the-old-school.demon.co.uk/pla.htm

Enquiries:
Enquiries to: Chairman

Founded:
1956

Organisation type and purpose:
Learned society.
Society of book collectors.

Subject coverage:
Book collecting.

Trade and statistical information:
Data on privately printed books worldwide in English.

Printed publications:
Books and monographs, including:
Books on book collecting (irregular)
Miniature Libraries for the Young (Alderson B, 1983, £5)
Printing for Pleasure (Ryder J, £10)
The Private Library (journal, quarterly)
Private Press Books (bibliography, annually)
Apart from the Text (Rota A, £24, an account of the externals of the book: its production and sale over the past two centuries)
Early Lithographed Books (Twyman M, £68.50, a study of the design and production of improper books in the age of the hand press, with a catalogue)
Order printed publications from: Publications Secretary, Claude Cox Books
3 Silent Street, Ipswich, IP1 1TF

Publications list:
Available online and in print

Access to staff:
Contact by letter and by e-mail

In liaison with the:
Library Association

Links with:
Society of Private Printers

PROBATE OFFICES

Local offices:
1st Floor, Crown Building, Rivergate, Peterborough, PE1 1EJ, tel: 01733 562802
Bangor Probate Sub-Registry
  Council Offices, Ffordd Gwynedd, Bangor, Gwynedd, LL57 1DT; tel: 01248 362410
Birmingham District Probate Registry
  The Priory Courts, 33 Bull Street, Birmingham, B4 6DU; tel: 0121 681 3400
Bodmin Probate Sub-Registry
  Market Street, Bodmin, Cornwall, PL31 2JW; tel: 01208 72279
Brighton District Probate Registry
  William Street, Brighton, Sussex, BN2 2LG; tel: 01273 684071
Bristol District Probate Registry
  Ground Floor, The Crescent Centre, Temple Back, Bristol, BS1 6EP; tel: 0117 9273915

Carlisle Probate Sub-Registry
  Courts of Justice, Earl Street, Carlisle, Cumbria, CA1 1DJ; tel: 01228 521751
Carmarthen Probate Sub-Registry
  14 King Street, Carmarthen, SA31 1BL; tel: 01267 236238
Chester Probate Sub-Registry
  5th Floor, Hamilton House, Hamilton Place, Chester, CH1 2DA; tel: 01244 345082
Exeter Probate Sub-Registry
  Finance House, Barnfield Road, Exeter, Devon, EX1 1QR; tel: 01392 274515
Gloucester Probate Sub-Registry
  2nd Floor, Combined Court Building, Kimbrose Way, Gloucester, GL1 2DG; tel: 01452 522585
Ipswich District Probate Registry
  Haven House, 17 Lower Brook Street, Ipswich, Suffolk, IP4 1DN; tel: 01473 253724
Lancaster Probate Sub-Registry
  Mitre House, Church Street, Lancaster, LA1 1HE; tel: 01524 36625
Leeds District Probate Registry
  3rd Floor, Coronet House, Queen Street, Leeds, LS1 2BA; tel: 0113 243 1505
Leicester Probate Sub-Registry
  5th Floor, Leicester House, Lee Circle, Leicester, LE1 3RE; tel: 0116 2538558
Lincoln Probate Sub-Registry
  360 High Street, Lincoln, LN5 7PS; tel: 01522 523648
Liverpool District Probate Registry
  Queen Elizabeth II Law Courts, Derby Square, Liverpool, L2 1XA; tel: 0151 236 8264
Maidstone Probate Sub-Registry
  The Law Courts, Barker Road, Maidstone, ME18 8EW; tel: 01622 202048
Manchester District Probate Registry
  9th Floor, Astley House, 23 Quay Street, Manchester, M2 4AT; tel: 0161 834 4319
Middlesbrough Probate Sub-Registry
  Teesside Combined Court Centre, Russell Street, Middlesbrough, Cleveland, TS1 2AE; tel: 01642 340001
Newcastle District Probate Registry
  2nd Floor, Plummer House, Croft Street, Newcastle upon Tyne, NE1 6NP; tel: 0191 261 8383
Norwich Probate Sub-Registry
  Combined Court Building, Bishopsgate, Norwich, NR3 1UR; tel: 01603 728267
Nottingham Probate Sub-Registry
  Butt Dyke House, Park Row, Nottingham, NG1 6GR; tel: 0115 941 4288
Oxford District Probate Registry
  Oxford Combined Court Building, St Aldates, Oxford, OX1 1LY; tel: 01865 793 055
Peterborough Probate Sub-Registry
  1st Floor
Principal Registry of the Family Division
  Probate Department, First Avenue House, 42–49 High Holborn, London, WC1V 6NP; tel: 020 7947 6983
Probate Registry of Wales
  PO Box 474, 2 Park Street, Cardiff, CF10 1TB; tel: 029 2037 6479
Sheffield Probate Sub-Registry
  PO Box 832, The Law Courts, 50 West Bar, Sheffield, S3 3YR; tel: 0114 281 2596
Stoke on Trent Probate Sub-Registry
  Combined Court Centre, Bethesda Street, Hanley, ST1 3BP; tel: 01782 854065
Winchester District Probate Registry
  4th Floor, Cromwell House, Andover Road, Winchester, Hampshire, SO23 7EW; tel: 01962 863771
York Probate Office
  1st Floor, Castle Chambers, Clifford Street, York, YO1 9RG; tel: 01904 666777

PROCESSORS AND GROWERS RESEARCH ORGANISATION

Acronym or abbreviation: PGRO

The Research Station, Great North Road, Thornhaugh, Peterborough, Cambridgeshire, PE8 6HJ

Tel: 01780 782585
Fax: 01780 783993
E-mail: info@pgro.co.uk

Website:
http://www.pgro.co.uk

Enquiries:
Enquiries to: Director

Founded:
1944

Organisation type and purpose:
Research organisation.

Subject coverage:
Production and harvesting of vegetables, primarily for processing for human consumption; seeds and seed health, general agronomy, evaluation of crop protection materials and techniques, evaluation of new varieties.

Printed publications:
Annual Report
Newsletters, papers & advisory leaflets
Pea Growing Handbook
Pea and Bean Progress (4 times per annum, for members)
Vining Peas in England
Field Bran Handbook

PROCTER & GAMBLE TECHNICAL CENTRES LIMITED

Acronym or abbreviation: P&G

Newcastle Technical Centre, PO Box Forest Hall No 2, Newcastle upon Tyne, NE12 9TS

Tel: 0191 228 1000
Fax: 0191 228 1021

Website:
http://www.uk.pg.com
Publications list

Enquiries:
Enquiries to: Business Information Services Manager
Direct tel: 0191 228 1728

Founded:
1837

Organisation type and purpose:
Manufacturing industry, research organisation.
Company technical centre; formerly known as Procter & Gamble Research and Development Laboratories.

Subject coverage:
Soaps and detergents, cleaning products, oils and fats, fatty acids and derivatives, related chemistry and technology.

Non-library collection catalogue:
All or part available in-house

Library catalogue:
All or part available in-house

Publications list:
Available online

Access to staff:
Contact by letter and by fax
Hours: Mon to Fri, 0830 to 1630

Access to building, collection or gallery:
No prior appointment required

PRODUCERS ALLIANCE FOR CINEMA AND TELEVISION

Acronym or abbreviation: PACT

Procter House, 1 Procter Street, Holborn, London, WC1V 6DW

Tel: 020 7067 4367
Fax: 020 7067 4377

Website:
http://www.pact.co.uk

Enquiries:
Enquiries to: Information Manager

Direct e-mail: anish@pact.co.uk

Founded:
1991

Organisation type and purpose:
Trade association.
Represents United Kingdom independent production companies of feature films and broadcast television.

Subject coverage:
Industrial relations within the independent broadcast, television and feature film production industry, copyright, commissioning, financing.

Printed publications:
Art of the Deal
PACT (magazine, monthly, free to members, for sale to non-members)
Members' Directory (annually, £25 to members, £50 to non-members)
Rights Clearance

Publications list:
Available in print

Access to staff:
Contact by telephone. Access for members only.
Hours: Mon to Fri, 0930 to 1800

PRODUCTION MANAGERS ASSOCIATION

Ealing Studios, Ealing Green, Ealing, London, W5 5EP

Tel: 020 8758 8699
E-mail: pma@pma.org.uk

Website:
http://www.pma.org.uk
Member areas, calendar, forum, directory of co-ordinators, directory of accountants, notice board, jobs, business support, training.

Founded:
1991

Organisation type and purpose:
A professional body of film, television, corporate and multi-media production managers. All 200 members have a minimum of 3 years' experience as a Production Manager and at least six broadcast credits (or equivalent).
Within the film and television industry the Association provides a unique network for both freelance and permanently employed Production Managers.

Subject coverage:
Film and television producing.

Information services:
Members can phone for free professional advice on tax, VAT, PAYE, payroll, employment and personnel, health and safety, commercial and legal issues.

Electronic and video publications:
The Bottom Line Newsletter (quarterly)
Order electronic and video publications from:
Download from website

Access to staff:
Contact by letter, by telephone and by e-mail

PROFESSIONAL ASSOCIATION OF NURSERY NURSES

Formal name: VOICE the Union
Acronym or abbreviation: VOICE

2 St James' Court, Friar Gate, Derby, DE1 1BT

Tel: 01332 372337
Fax: 01332 290310
E-mail: triciapritchard@voicetheunion.org.,uk

Website:
http://www.voicetheunion.org.uk

Enquiries:
Enquiries to: Senior Professional Officer

Direct e-mail: richardfraser@voicetheunion.org.uk
(Communications Officer)
Other contacts: Communications Officer

Founded:
1982

Formerly called:
Professional Association of Nursery Nurses (year of change 2008)

Organisation type and purpose:
Professional body, trade union (membership is by subscription), for qualified education professionals, including teachers, support staff, nursery nurses, nannies and other childcarers.

Subject coverage:
Terms and conditions of employment within education and childcare, nannies at home and abroad, contracts, etc., the role of the nursery nurse.

Printed publications:
All you Need to Know About Working as a Nanny
Code of Practice
Role of The Nursery Nurse
Starting a Day Nursery
Variety of booklets and leaflets
Working Together in Powerful Partnership: Nursery Nurses and Teachers
Order printed publications from: e-mail:
publications@voicetheunion.org.uk

Publications list:
Available online and in print

Access to staff:
Contact by letter, by telephone, by fax, by e-mail and via website. Appointment necessary. Access for members only.
Hours: Mon to Fri, 0900 to 1700

Access to building, collection or gallery:
Prior appointment required
Hours: Mon to Fri, 0900 to 1700

Access for disabled people:
Parking provided, level entry

Headquarters address:
Voice
at the same address; tel: 01332 372337; fax: 01332 290310; e-mail: hq@voicetheunion.org.uk; website: http://www.voicetheunion.org.uk

PROFESSIONAL BUSINESS AND TECHNICAL MANAGEMENT

Acronym or abbreviation: PBTM

Warwick Corner, 42 Warwick Road, Kenilworth, Warwickshire, CV8 1HE

Tel: 01926 866623
E-mail: info@group-ims.com

Website:
http://www.group-ims.com

Enquiries:
Enquiries to: Administrative Director

Founded:
1983

Organisation type and purpose:
International organisation, professional body (membership is by subscription, qualification), manufacturing industry, training organisation, professional diploma courses available.

Subject coverage:
Industrial, computing, technological and associated management, education and training.

Printed publications:
Professional Business and Technical Management (3 times a year)

Access to staff:
Contact by letter, by telephone, by e-mail and via website

Links with:
Academy of Executives and Administrators at the same address

Academy of Multi-Skills
at the same address
Institute of Management Specialists
at the same address
Institute of Manufacturing
at the same address

PROFESSIONAL CLASSES AID COUNCIL

Acronym or abbreviation: PCAC

10 St Christopher's Place, London, W1U 1HZ

Tel: 020 7935 0641

Enquiries:
Enquiries to: Secretary
Other contacts: Deputy Secretary

Founded:
1921

Organisation type and purpose:
National organisation, voluntary organisation, registered charity (charity number 207292).

Subject coverage:
Sources of charitable help to those with a professional background.

Printed publications:
Annual Report

Access to staff:
Contact by letter and by telephone
Hours: Mon to Fri, 0930 to 1700

Access to building, collection or gallery:
No access other than to staff

Administers the:
Guild of Aid for Gentlepeople
at the same address

PROFESSIONAL GOLFERS ASSOCIATION

Acronym or abbreviation: PGA

Centenary House, The Belfry, Sutton Coldfield, West Midlands, B76 9PT

Tel: 01675 470333
Fax: 01675 477888
E-mail: media@pga.org.uk

Enquiries:
Enquiries to: Media Department

Founded:
1901

Organisation type and purpose:
Membership association.

Subject coverage:
The game of golf.

Printed publications:
The PGA Professional (magazine, monthly)

Access to staff:
Contact by letter
Hours: Mon to Fri, 0900 to 1700

PROFESSIONAL PHOTOGRAPHIC LABORATORIES ASSOCIATION

Acronym or abbreviation: PPLA

Wisteria House, 28 Fulling Mill Lane, Welwyn, Herts AL6 9NS

Tel: 01438 840367
Fax: 01438 716572
E-mail: pmauk@pmai.org

Website:
http://www.pmai.org

Enquiries:
Enquiries to: Secretary
Other contacts: Administration Manager for office contact.

Founded:
1984

continued overleaf

Organisation type and purpose:
Trade association.
To promote and foster excellence in all areas of
professional photographic laboratory work.

Subject coverage:
Professional photographic processing (silver
halide), digital imaging, inkjet and all normal fields
of output.

Printed publications:
Lablink
Laboratory News Report
PPLA (free to members)

Electronic and video publications:
Fact file covering full membership details, terms of
business, articles of Association and supplier
members (CD-ROM free to members)

Access to staff:
Contact by letter, by telephone, by fax, by e-mail,
in person and via website
Hours: Mon to Fri, 0900 to 1700

A section of:
Photo Marketing Association International

Connections with:
British Photographic Association

PROFESSIONAL SPEAKERS ASSOCIATION

Acronym or abbreviation: PSA

12 Russell Close, Uttoxeter, Staffordshire, ST14
8HZ

Tel: 0845 3700 504
Fax: 0845 3700 503
E-mail: via website

Website:
http://www.professionalspeakersassociation.co.uk
The site is designed to help find a speaker for
meetings, to encourage speakers to join their
professional association and to enable members to
keep in touch with one another and share best
practices in order to raise the standards of
presentation and professionalism.

Enquiries:
Enquiries to: Administration Manager

Founded:
1999

Organisation type and purpose:
Professional association.
Represents 'experts who speak' who are based in
the UK.

Subject coverage:
Public speaking.

Printed publications:
Speakeasy (6 a year)

Access to staff:
Contact by letter, by telephone, by fax and via
website

Member organisation of:
International Federation for Professional Speakers
(IFFPS)

PROPERTY CONSULTANTS SOCIETY LIMITED

Acronym or abbreviation: PCS

Basement Office, Surrey Court, Surrey Street,
Arundel, West Sussex, BN18 9DT

Tel: 01903 889590
Fax: 01903 883787
E-mail: info@propertyconsultantssociety.org

Website:
http://www.propertyconsultantssociety.org

Enquiries:
Enquiries to: Secretary
Direct e-mail: may-david@btconnect.com

Founded:
1954

Organisation type and purpose:
Professional body (membership is by qualification,
election or invitation), present number of
members: 600, service industry.

Subject coverage:
Property consultancy.

Printed publications:
Annual Report
Newsletters (occasional, free to members)

Access to staff:
Contact by letter, by telephone, by fax, by e-mail
and via website
Hours: Mon to Fri
Special comments: Part-time staff only.

PROPERTY OMBUDSMAN

Acronym or abbreviation: TPO

Beckett House, 4 Bridge Street, Salisbury, Wiltshire,
SP1 2LX

Tel: 01722 333306
Fax: 01722 332296
E-mail: admin@tpos.co.uk

Website:
http://www.tpos.co.uk

Enquiries:
Enquiries to: Ombudsman (for initial enquiries)

Founded:
1998

Formerly called:
Ombudsman for Estate Agents (year of change
2009)

Organisation type and purpose:
Membership association (membership is by
subscription, qualification), present number of
members: 583, service industry.

Subject coverage:
Disputes between member agencies and actual or
potential buyers or sellers, tenants or landlords of
property in the UK.

Printed publications:
Annual Report
Code of Practice (available in member agency
  offices)
Consumer Guide (available in member agency
  offices)
Information Package

Electronic and video publications:
Printed products available on website

Access to staff:
Contact by letter, by telephone, by fax, by e-mail
and via website. All charged.
Hours: Mon to Fri, 0900 to 1645

PROPERTY PEOPLE PUBLICATIONS LIMITED

232 Great Guildford Business Square, 30 Great
Guildford Street, London, SE1 0HS

Tel: 020 7401 2075
Fax: 020 7928 4887
E-mail: edit@ppmagazine.co.uk

Website:
http://www.hera-group.co.uk
Editorial information, recruitment advertising.

Enquiries:
Enquiries to: Managing Director
Other contacts: Editor for editorial enquiries.

Founded:
1997

Organisation type and purpose:
Publishing house.

Subject coverage:
People working in housing, students on full-time
housing courses.

Printed publications:
Property People (magazine)

Access to staff:
Contact by letter, by telephone, by fax, by e-mail
and via website
Hours: Mon to Fri, 0900 to 1700

PROQUEST INFORMATION AND LEARNING

The Quorum, Barnwell Road, Cambridge, CB5
8SW

Tel: 01223 215512
Fax: 01223 215513
E-mail: marketing@proquest.co.uk

Website:
http://www.proquest.co.uk/
Catalogue, monthly exhibitions list, contacts.

Enquiries:
Enquiries to: Marketing Manager
Direct e-mail: chesterfield@proquest.co.uk

Founded:
1973

Organisation type and purpose:
Publishing house.

Subject coverage:
Bibliographies, library catalogues, reference works
to archives, official publications, literature, literary
history, newspapers on CD-ROM and the World
Wide Web, performing arts, visual arts and
architecture, history, economics and statistics,
cartography and climate, natural sciences, medical,
education, science and technology reference.

Microform publications:
A wide range of microfiche products

Electronic and video publications:
CD-ROMs and online sites of literature,
  bibliographies, official publications, music and
  performing arts, and history

Publications list:
Available online and in print

Access to staff:
Contact by e-mail
Hours: Mon to Fri, 0900 to 1700

PROSPECT

Prospect House, 75–79 York Road, London, SE1
7AQ

Tel: 020 7902 6600
Fax: 020 7902 6667
E-mail: enquiries@prospect.org.uk

Website:
http://www.prospect.org.uk
Services to members, aims of union, benefits of
membership etc, publications.

Enquiries:
Enquiries to: Assistant General Secretary
Other contacts: Deputy General Secretary

Founded:
1913

Organisation type and purpose:
Trade union (membership is by subscription),
present number of members: c. 100,000.
Statutory body responsible to the Secretary of State
for Industry.

Subject coverage:
Pay and conditions, market testing, trade unions,
public sector pay, privatisation, GCHQ trade union
ban, research, health and safety, equal
opportunities, air traffic control, PFI.

Printed publications:
Annual Report

Network (journal, monthly, on subscription, members)

Electronic and video publications:
Video

Publications list:
Available in print

Access to staff:
Contact by letter, by telephone, by fax and by e-mail. Appointment necessary.
Hours: Mon to Fri, 0900 to 1700

Access for disabled people:
Ramped entry, access to all public areas, toilet facilities
Special comments: Help with parking can be arranged prior to attendance.

Associated with:
Council of Civil Service Unions (CCSU)
IFATSEA
PSI
TUC

Office at:
Prospect Midlands
Unit 4, Midland Court, Central Park, Leicester Road, Lutterworth, LE17 4PN; tel: 01455 555200; fax: 01455 558711
Prospect North West / North Wales
Unit 1F, Ground Floor, Columbus Quay, Riverside Drive, Liverpool, L3 4DB; tel: 0151 728 9028; fax: 0151 728 9072
Prospect Scotland
Suite 4, 1st Floor, Glenarchy House, 20 Union Street, Edinburgh, EH1 3LR; tel: 0131 558 2660; fax: 0131 558 5280
Prospect South East
Flaxman House, Logmore Lane, Chertsey, Surrey, KT16 9JS; tel: 01932 577007; fax: 01932 567707
Prospect South West / Wales
Newminster House, 27–29 Baldwin Street, Bristol, BS1 1LT; tel: 0117 929 4441; fax: 0117 927 6111

PROSTATE CANCER CHARITY

Acronym or abbreviation: PCC

1st Floor Cambridge House, 100 Cambridge House, Hammersmith, London W6 0LE

Tel: 020 8222 7622
Fax: 020 8222 7639
E-mail: info@prostate-cancer.org.uk

Website:
http://www.prostate-cancer.org.uk
Information on prostate cancer and its treatment.

Enquiries:
Enquiries to: Communications Manager
Direct e-mail: carla.blatt@prostate-cancer.org.uk

Founded:
1996

Organisation type and purpose:
National organisation, voluntary organisation, registered charity, research organisation.
Support and information organisation.
Research, support and information.

Subject coverage:
Prostate cancer support and information; information on treatments and their side-effects; general support from counsellors and other sufferers; help for both patients and their families; research into prostate cancer and its treatment.

Printed publications:
Wide range of literature covering all aspects of prostate cancer including:
Factsheets covering issues related to prostate cancer
Prostate Cancer: Everything you need to know (free)
Prostate Cancer – The Facts (free)

Publications list:
Available in print

Access to staff:
Contact by letter, by telephone, by fax, by e-mail, in person and via website
Hours: Mon to Fri, 0900 to 1700
Helpline: Mon to Fri, 1000 to 1600

PROSTATE HELP ASSOCIATION

PHA, Langworth, Lincoln, LN3 5DF

E-mail: philip@bph.org.uk

Website:
http://www.prostatehelp.me.uk

Enquiries:
Enquiries to: Secretary

Founded:
1993

Organisation type and purpose:
Help and information for prostate problems.

Subject coverage:
Prostatitis, BPH and prostatic cancer.

Printed publications:
Books (direct)

Publications list:
Available in print

Access to staff:
Contact by letter, by e-mail and via website
Hours: Mon to Fri, 0900 to 1700

PRS FOR MUSIC

Copyright House, 29–33 Berners Street, London, W1T 3AB

Tel: 020 7580 5544
Fax: 020 7306 4455
E-mail: info@mcps.co.uk

Website:
http://www.prsformusic.com

Enquiries:
Enquiries to: Corporate Communications

Founded:
1997

Created by the merger of:
Mechanical-Copyright Protection Society Limited (MCPS, founded 1924) and PRS

Formerly called:
MCPS–PRS Alliance (year of change 2009)

Organisation type and purpose:
Membership association (membership is by subscription).
Licenses the recording of its composer and publisher members copyright musical works in many different formats.

Subject coverage:
Music copyright and royalties; licensing of music recorded into any format; collection and distribution of mechanical royalties.

Printed publications:
Annual Report
For The Record
On the Right Track

Access to staff:
Contact by letter, by telephone, by fax, by e-mail and via website. Appointment necessary.
Hours: Mon to Fri, 0900 to 1700

Access for disabled people:
Ramped entry

PSORIASIS ASSOCIATION

Dick Coles House, 2 Queensbridge, Northampton, NN4 7BF

Tel: 08456 760076
Fax: 01604 251621
E-mail: mail@psoriasis-association.org.uk

Website:
http://www.psoriasis-association.org.uk

Enquiries:
Enquiries to: Chief Executive
Other contacts: Information Officer

Founded:
1968

Organisation type and purpose:
Membership organisation providing information and support to people affected by psoriasis; aiming to support people who have psoriasis; to raise awareness of psoriasis; to fund research into causes, treatments and care of psoriasis.

Subject coverage:
Psoriasis, psoriatic arthropathy and all aspects relating to them.

Printed publications:
About the Association
What is psoriasis
Scalp psoriasis
Psoriasis in sensitive areas
Psoriasis in children
UV therapy
Psoriatic Arthritis
PsoTeen – Information for teenagers
Psoriasis – a parents' guide
Quarterly Journal
Order printed publications from: Psoriasis Association, Dick Coles House, 2 Queensbridge, Northampton, NN4 7BF

Electronic and video publications:
PsoKids (CD-ROM for children with psoriasis)
Order electronic and video publications from: Psoriasis Association, Dick Coles House, 2 Queensbridge, Northampton, NN4 7BF

Publications list:
Available in print

Access to staff:
Contact by letter, by telephone, by fax and by e-mail. Appointment necessary.
Hours: Mon to Fri, 0915 to 1645

Links with:
AMRC
APPGS
LTCA
Skin Care Campaign

PSYCHIATRIC REHABILITATION ASSOCIATION

Acronym or abbreviation: PRA SERVICES

Bayford Mews, Bayford Street, Hackney, London, E8 3SF

Tel: 020 8985 3570
Fax: 020 8986 1334
E-mail: admin@praservices.org.uk

Website:
http://www.praservices.org.uk
http://www.c4bh.org.uk

Enquiries:
Enquiries to: Director
Other contacts: Association Secretary

Founded:
1959

Organisation type and purpose:
Membership association (membership is by election or invitation), present number of members: 800, voluntary organisation, registered charity (charity number 227891), training organisation, consultancy.
PRA aims to stimulate the individual recovering from mental health problems towards greater initiative and social awareness. It prepares and encourages the individual to play an active part in the community.

Subject coverage:
PRA is a partnership of patients, relatives, friends and professional workers, and has developed a wide range of community care facilities for people

continued overleaf

suffering from mental health problems, study of social problems associated with mental illness, geographical incidence of mental illness, lifestyle analysis, training of professional and voluntary workers, group work.

Information services:
E-mail: info@praservices.org.uk

Non-library collection catalogue:
All or part available online and in-house

Printed publications:
Newsletter (quarterly)
Research publications
HUN newsletter (quarterly)

Microform publications:
Tape and slide teaching aids

Electronic and video publications:
Give Us A Chance (video, £13.50)
Forward with Courage (DVD, £15.00)

Access to staff:
Contact by letter, by telephone, by fax, by e-mail and via website. Appointment necessary.
Hours: Mon to Fri, 0900 to 1700

Administers:
Centre for Better Health (C4BH)
  Bayford Mews, Bayford Street, London, E8 3SF; tel: 020 8985 3570; fax: 020 8986 1334; e-mail: admin@praservices.org.uk; website: http://www.praservices.org.uk
Et Cetera Gallery (Hackney)
  1A Darnley Road, London, E9 6QH; tel: 020 8985 7758; website: http://www.praservices.org.uk
Et Cetera Workshop (Haringey)
  Unit 26G3, N17 Studios, 785/788 High Road, London, N17 0DA; tel: 020 8808 5970; fax: 020 8808 5945; e-mail: etceteraworkshop@praservices.org.uk; website: http://www.praservices.org.uk
Hackney Day Centre
  1A Darnley Road, London, E9 6QH; tel: 020 8985 4617; e-mail: darnleyroad@praservices.org.uk
Mitchley Industrial Education Unit and Day Centre (Haringey)
  Unit 18G, N17 Studios, 784/788 High Road, London, N17 0DA; tel: 020 8808 2833; fax: 020 8880 9075; website: http://www.praservices.org.uk
Southwood Smith Centre (Islington)
  Southwood Smith Street, London, N1 0XN; tel: 020 7226 2244; e-mail: swsmithcentre@praservices.org.uk; website: http://www.praservices.org.uk
Stean Street Industrial Education Unit (Hackney)
  13 Stean Street, London, N8 4ED; tel: 020 7254 9103; fax: 020 7254 2691; e-mail: pramembers@yahoo.co.uk; website: http://www.praservices.org.uk

Member organisations:
Haringey User Network (HUN) (Haringey)
  Unit 26G3, N17 Studios, 784/788 High Road, London, N17 0DA; tel: 020 8885 1258; e-mail: info@haringeyusernetwork.org.uk; website: http://www.haringeyusernetwork.org.uk

PSYCHIATRY RESEARCH TRUST

Box 87, De Crespigny Park, Denmark Hill, London, SE5 8AF

Tel: 020 7703 6217
Fax: 020 7848 5115
E-mail: l.pease@iop.kcl.ac.uk

Website:
http://www.iop.kcl.ac.uk
The trust and the research it funds, information on individual mental illnesses and the research progress being made.

Enquiries:
Enquiries to: Administrator

Founded:
1982

Organisation type and purpose:
Registered charity (number 284286).

Founded with the sole aim of raising funds for research into mental illness and brain disease in support of the vital research work of the Institute of Psychiatry, King's College, University of London.

Subject coverage:
Funds research projects covering a wide spectrum of mental health conditions and brain disease, lectures in aspects of mental health, bursaries to enable students to study and also to carry out research projects, prizes to encourage excellence in research by trainee psychiatrists and basic scientists, the purchase of essential research equipment.

Printed publications:
Information booklets (free on receipt of large sae with 2 1st class stamps affixed):
1. Alzheimer's Disease
2. Schizophrenia
3. Parkinson's Disease / Motor Neurone Disease
4. Epilepsy
5. Antidepressants, Anxiety, Phobias, Obsessive Compulsive Disorder, Chronic Fatigue Syndrome, Post Traumatic Stress Disorder, Seasonal Affective Disorder, Depression
6. Anorexia/Bulimia Nervosa
7. Making a Will
8. Bipolar Disorder (Manic Depression)
9. Introductory Guide to Mental Health Treatments
10. Autism, Asperger's Syndrome, Child Depression, Hyperkinetic Disorder
11. Puerperal Psychosis/Postnatal Depression
12. Hypochondriasis
13. Common sexual disorders
14. Alcoholism
Order printed publications from: Postal address

Access to staff:
Contact by letter, by telephone, by fax and by e-mail

Constituent part of:
The Institute of Psychiatry, King's College, University of London

PSYCHOTHERAPY CENTRE

67 Upper Berkeley Street, London, W1H 7QX

Tel: 020 7723 6173
E-mail: psychotherapy@the-wordsmith.co.uk

Website:
http://www.the-psychotherapy-centre.org.uk

Enquiries:
Enquiries to: Principal

Founded:
1960

Organisation type and purpose:
International organisation, consultancy, research organisation, publishing house.
Treatment and referral centre.
Training college.

Subject coverage:
Psychotherapy, emotional problems, neuroses, compulsions, addictions, relationship problems, psycho-sexual and marital difficulties, phobias, anxiety, alcoholism, insomnia, migraine; parenthood etc.

Printed publications:
Emotional Problems: Different Ways of Dealing with Them
Enjoy Sex
Enjoy Childbirth
Enjoy Parenthood
Selecting a Psychotherapist
Training in Psychotherapy
The Laius Complex
King Lear – Rejection, Abandonment Projection and Paranoia
Nervous Symptoms and Problems
Why be Psycho-Analysed before becoming a Psychotherapist, Hypnotherapist or Counsellor?
How to Assess Therapy Organisations
Two Therapies and After

Experiences of Establishment and Medical Psychotherapy & Psycho-Analysis
The Psychonaut's Handbook
Financing Your Education, Training or Therapy
The Cycle of Deprivation
Group Therapy: We Tried It
Psychotherapy: Is it Helpful or Harmful?
The Psychocate: A Revolution?
Selected Films, Novels and Poems: A List

Publications list:
Available in print

Access to staff:
Contact by letter and by telephone. Appointment necessary.
Hours: Mon to Fri, 0900 to 1700

Access to building, collection or gallery:
Prior appointment required

PUBLIC AND COMMERCIAL SERVICES UNION

Acronym or abbreviation: PCS

160 Falcon Road, London, SW11 2LN

Tel: 020 7924 2727
Fax: 020 7924 1847

Website:
http://www.pcs.org.uk
Latest library acquisitions and press cuttings service.

Enquiries:
Enquiries to: Information Officer
Direct tel: 020 7801 2650
Direct e-mail: info@pcs.org.uk
Other contacts: General Secretary

Founded:
1998

Organisation type and purpose:
Trade union.
Trade Union with its own library.

Subject coverage:
Employment law, health and safety, industrial relations, civil service, childcare/work life balance, Civil Service, conditions of service, economic issues, employment issues, equal opportunities, Europe, government, health and safety, international affairs (ie non-Europe), legislation, maternity/paternity, organisations, parliament, partnership, pay, PCS, pensions, professional management, politics, privatisation – primarily civil service, private sector, public sector, social welfare, trade unions, unemployment.

Library catalogue:
All or part available in-house

Printed publications:
PCS View (Union journal, monthly to members)

Access to staff:
Contact by letter, by telephone, by fax and by e-mail. Access for members only.
Hours: Mon to Fri, 0830 to 1700

Affiliated to:
Council of Civil Service Unions
International Confederation of Free Trade Unions
Public Services International

Member of:
Trades Union Congress
  Congress House, Great Russell Street, London, WC1B 3LS

PUBLIC HEALTH LABORATORY SERVICE – COMMUNICABLE DISEASE SURVEILLANCE CENTRE

Acronym or abbreviation: CDSC

61 Colindale Avenue, London, NW9 5EQ

Tel: 020 8200 6868
Fax: 020 8200 7868

Website:
http://www.phls.co.uk

Enquiries:
Enquiries to: Information Officer
Direct tel: 020 8200 6868 ext 4473
Direct e-mail: eyusuf@phls.org.uk

Organisation type and purpose:
Professional body.
Unit of the Public Health Laboratory Service.
Prevention and control of human communicable
disease through surveillance, epidemiological
investigation, research, teaching and training.

Subject coverage:
Human infectious diseases: prevalence in England
and Wales, and abroad when it is relevant to
England and Wales; control and surveillance of
such disease.

Printed publications:
Communicable Disease Report (weekly)
Communicable Disease and Public Health
(quarterly)

Access to staff:
Contact by letter
Hours: Mon to Fri, 0900 to 1700

Part of:
National Health Service

PUBLIC MONUMENTS AND SCULPTURE ASSOCIATION

Acronym or abbreviation: PMSA

70 Cowcross Street, London, EC1M 6EJ

Tel: 020 7490 5001
E-mail: pmsa@btconnect.com

Website:
http://www.pmsa.org.uk

Enquiries:
Enquiries to: Office Administrator

Founded:
1991

Organisation type and purpose:
Membership association (membership is by
subscription), present number of members: 250,
voluntary organisation, registered charity, suitable
for ages: 18+, consultancy, research organisation.
The promotion, protection and public appreciation
of historic and contemporary public sculpture and
monuments. Preserving Britain's sculptures and
public art for future generations. Save Our
Sculpture project monitors works at risk.
Campaigns for improved conservation and
maintenance. The Association's National
Recording Project, a survey of public works in
Britain, is partially complete: it is a central
information resource for scholars, conservators and
custodians.

Subject coverage:
Art history (sculpture); sculpture conservation;
topographical spread of public works in Britain,
their description, history and condition; British
sculptors; the local and social significance of public
monuments; owners and custodians of same; the
groups involved with public art or similar, either
voluntary or commercial (i.e. commissioning
agencies); regional arts bodies; amenity societies,
e.g. Fountain Society/Twentieth Century Society;
listing and planning regulations.

Information services:
Via e-mail

**Museum or gallery collection, archive, or library
special collection:**
Black and white photographs or colour slides of
public sculptures and monuments

Non-library collection catalogue:
All or part available online and in print

Printed publications:
Public Sculpture in Britain Series (ongoing):
Public Sculpture of Birmingham
Public Sculpture of the City of London
Public Sculpture of Glasgow
Public Sculpture of Greater Manchester
Public Sculpture of Leicestershire and Rutland

Public Sculpture of Liverpool
Public Sculpture of North-East England
Public Sculpture of Staffordshire
Public Sculpture of Warwickshire and the Black
Country
Public Sculpture of South London (Wandsworth,
Lambeth, Southwark, Lewisham)
Sculpture Journal (twice a year)
Order printed publications from: Liverpool
University Press

Electronic and video publications:
PMSA website with NRP database

Publications list:
Available online and in print

Access to staff:
Contact by letter, by telephone, by e-mail, in
person and via website. Appointment necessary.
Hours: Mon to Fri, 1000 to 1700
Special comments: Notice via e-mail required.

Access to building, collection or gallery:
Hours: Mon to Fri, 1100 to 1700

PUBLIC RECORD OFFICE OF NORTHERN IRELAND

Acronym or abbreviation: PRONI

Use website: http://www.proni.gov.uk

E-mail: proni@dcalni.gov.uk

Website:
http://www.proni.gov.uk
Guide to the Public Record Office of Northern
Ireland.
http://www.proni.gov.uk/index/
research_and_records_held.htm
Publications list.
http://www.proni.gov.uk /index/
search_the_archives/ecatalogue.htm
Electronic catalogue: a list of almost all the records
held by PRONI.

Enquiries:
Enquiries to: Head of Public Services

Founded:
1923

Organisation type and purpose:
National government body.
Record office.
To identify, preserve and provide access to
Northern Ireland's archival heritage.

Subject coverage:
Information relating to the political, economic and
social history of Northern Ireland as found in both
official and private records. Genealogy; local
history; government records; non-departmental
public bodies records; academic research.

**Museum or gallery collection, archive, or library
special collection:**
Archives of the Northern Ireland Departments of
government, public bodies and courts of law
Papers of private individuals, estate, school, and
business records, wills, and church records

Non-library collection catalogue:
All or part available online and in-house

Printed publications:
Annual Statutory Reports 1991 to 1996/97 (annual),
1997/98 (statutory)
Annual Reports 1999–present
Reports of the Deputy Keeper of the Records 1960–
1989
PRONI Guides Series including:
Guide to Cabinet Committees (at Stormont, 1921–
1958)
Guide to Education Records
Guide to County Sources: Armagh
Guide to County Sources: Fermanagh
Guide to County Sources: Monaghan
Guide to Tithe Records
Guide to Probate Records

Publications list:
Available online and in print

Access to staff:
Contact by letter, by telephone, by fax, by e-mail,
in person and via website
Hours: Mon, Tue, Wed, Fri, 0915 to 1645; Thu, 0915
to 2045
Special comments: To facilitate staff training, the
office opens at 1000 on first Thu of each month.
Closed for stocktaking, last week of Nov and first
week of Dec each year.

Access to building, collection or gallery:
PRONI will be closed to the public from 3
September 2010 until Spring of 2011 when it will
reopen in new premises in the Titanic Quarter in
Belfast.

Access for disabled people:
Parking provided, ramped entry, access to all
areas; Induction loop for hearing impaired; mono
mouse/computer for enlarging text
Special comments: Staff assistance, if required.
Please ask in advance if possible.

Parent body:
Department of Culture, Arts and Leisure

PUBLIC RELATIONS CONSULTANTS ASSOCIATION LIMITED

Acronym or abbreviation: PRCA

Willow House, Willow Place, London, SW1P 1JH

Tel: 020 7233 6026
Fax: 020 7828 4797
E-mail: katie.goodrum@prca.org.uk

Website:
http://www.prca.org.uk

Enquiries:
Enquiries to: Office Manager

Founded:
1969

Organisation type and purpose:
Trade association (membership is by qualification),
present number of members: 150.

Subject coverage:
Public relations industry, statistics, membership.

**Museum or gallery collection, archive, or library
special collection:**
Archive library

Trade and statistical information:
Case histories
Benchmarking study in PR consultancy industry.

Printed publications:
9 Briefing Papers
25 Educational Guidance Papers
The Public Relations Consultants Year Book
An Insider's Guide to PR
Survival Guides
Order printed publications from: Public Relations
Consultants Association Limited
e-mail: info@prca.org.uk

Publications list:
Available online and in print

Access to staff:
Contact by letter, by telephone, by fax, by e-mail,
in person and via website. Appointment necessary.
Hours: Mon to Fri, 0900 to 1800

Access to building, collection or gallery:
No prior appointment required

PUBLISHERS ASSOCIATION

Acronym or abbreviation: PA

29b Montague Street, London, WC1B 5BW

Tel: 020 7691 9191
Fax: 020 7691 9199
E-mail: mail@publishers.org.uk

Website:
http://www.publishers.org.uk

continued overleaf

Enquiries:
Direct tel: 020 7691 9191
Direct e-mail: mail@publishers.org.uk

Founded:
1896

Organisation type and purpose:
Trade association (membership is by subscription).
Organised into core activity and divisions:
International Division, Educational Publishers
Council, Academic and Professional Division,
Electronic Publishers Forum.

Subject coverage:
Matters relating to publishing; not contracts with
authors or the placing of manuscripts.

**Museum or gallery collection, archive, or library
special collection:**
Books about publishing; list available

Trade and statistical information:
Statistical information on publishing.

Printed publications:
Books, pamphlets, electronic information on
publishing, free or for purchase

Electronic and video publications:
See under printed products

Publications list:
Available online and in print

Access to staff:
Contact by letter, by telephone, by fax, by e-mail
and via website. Access for members only. Non-
members charged.
Hours: Mon to Fri, 0930 to 1730

Access to building, collection or gallery:
Prior appointment required

Affiliated to:
Federation of European Publishers
International Publishers Association

PUBLISHERS LICENSING SOCIETY LIMITED

Acronym or abbreviation: PLS

5 Dryden Street, London, WC2E 9NB

Tel: 020 7829 8486
Fax: 020 7829 8488
E-mail: pls@pls.org.uk

Enquiries:
Enquiries to: Manager

Founded:
1981

Organisation type and purpose:
Trade association, present number of members:
1600.

Subject coverage:
Photocopying and digital licensing. Copyright
information relevant to the publishing industry.

Printed publications:
Annual Report
PLS Newsletter

Publications list:
Available in print

Access to staff:
Contact by letter, by telephone, by fax, by e-mail
and via website
Hours: Mon to Fri, 0900 to 1700

Links with:
Association of Learned and Professional Society
Publishers (ALPSP)
    South House, The Street, Clapham, Worthing,
    Sussex, BN13 3UU; tel: 01903 871686; fax: 01903
    871457; e-mail: sec-gen@alsp.org
Copyright Licensing Agency
    90 Tottenham Court Road, London, W1T 0LP;
    tel: 020 7631 5500; fax: 020 7631 5555; e-mail:
    cla@cla.co.uk

Periodical Publishers Association (PPA)
    Queens House, 28 Kingsway, London, WC2B
    6JR; tel: 020 7404 4166; fax: 020 7404 4167; e-
    mail: info1@ppa.co.uk
Publishers Association (PA)
    29B Montague Street, London, WC1B 5BH; tel:
    020 7691 9191; fax: 020 7691 9199; e-mail: mail@
    publishers.org.uk

PUBLISHING SCOTLAND

Acronym or abbreviation: PS

Scottish Book Centre, 137 Dundee Street,
Edinburgh, EH11 1BG

Tel: 0131 228 6866
Fax: 0131 228 3220
E-mail: enquiries@publishingscotland.org

Website:
http://www.publishingscotland.org
http://www.booksfromscotland.com

Enquiries:
Enquiries to: Training and Information Manager
Direct e-mail: joan@publishingscotland.org

Founded:
1974

Formerly called:
Scottish Publishers Association (year of change
2007)

Organisation type and purpose:
Network and development body, incorporating
trade association (membership is by subscription).

Subject coverage:
Publishing, contracts and copyright, training, trade
fairs, publicity and marketing, information
provision.

Printed publications:
Publishing Scotland Yearbook (annual publication)
Order printed publications from: Publishing Scotland
office

Access to staff:
Contact by letter, by telephone, by fax, by e-mail
and via website. Appointment necessary.
Hours: Mon to Fri, 0900 to 1700

Access to building, collection or gallery:
Prior appointment required
Hours: Mon to Fri, 0900 to 1700

Access for disabled people:
Ramped entry and lift

Constituent bodies:
Booksource
    50 Cambuslang Road, Cambuslang Investment
    Park, Glasgow, G32 8NB; tel: 0845 370 0063; fax:
    0845 370 0064; e-mail: info@booksource.net;
    website: http://www.booksource.net

PUPPET CENTRE TRUST

Acronym or abbreviation: PCT

Battersea Arts Centre, Lavender Hill, London,
SW11 5TN

Tel: 020 7228 5335
E-mail: pct@puppetcentre.org.uk

Website:
http://www.puppetcentre.org.uk
General

Enquiries:
Enquiries to: Administrator

Founded:
1974

Organisation type and purpose:
A national development agency for the art form of
puppetry.

Subject coverage:
The overall mission for the Puppet Centre Trust is
to develop and promote the art form of puppetry
within the context of contemporary performance
practice.

**Museum or gallery collection, archive, or library
special collection:**
Puppetry Archives and Historical Puppet
    Collection now housed in Bridgenorth
Puppet Centre Library housed at Central School of
    Speech and Drama
Both available by appointment

Printed publications:
Animations in Print Volume 1: Animated
    Encounters
Animations in Print Volume 2: Animated
    Advances
Animations in Print Volume 3: Animated Bodies
Order printed publications from: Administrator

Access to staff:
Contact by letter, by telephone and by e-mail.
Appointment necessary.

PURBECK DISTRICT COUNCIL

Acronym or abbreviation: PDC

Westport House, Worgret Road, Wareham, Dorset,
BH20 4PP

Tel: 01929 556561
Fax: 01929 552688
E-mail: performanceunit@purbeck-dc.gov.uk

Website:
http://www.purbeck.gov.uk

Organisation type and purpose:
Local government body.

Subject coverage:
Services and functions of the district council.

Access to staff:
Contact by letter, by telephone, by fax, by e-mail,
in person and via website
Hours: Offices: 0845 to 1645; telephone access: 0830
to 1700

PUSEY HOUSE LIBRARY

Formal name: Dr Pusey's Library

Pusey House, 61 St Giles, Oxford, OX1 3LZ

Tel: 01865 278415
E-mail: chapter@puseyhouse.org.uk

Website:
http:www.puseyhouse.org.uk

Enquiries:
Enquiries to: Custodian
Direct tel: 01865 288024
Other contacts: The Archivist for all enquiries
relating to archive holdings

Founded:
1884

Organisation type and purpose:
Theological resource centre and chaplaincy.

Subject coverage:
Patristics, liturgy, church history (especially Oxford
Movement).

**Museum or gallery collection, archive, or library
special collection:**
19th century pamphlets

Non-library collection catalogue:
All or part available in-house

Library catalogue:
All or part available in-house

Microform publications:
Available from World Microfilms, 70 reels, £2,750:
The Halifax and Church Sub-Collections
Tractarian Pamphlets at Pusey House

Access to staff:
Contact by letter, by telephone, by e-mail, in
person and via website. Appointment necessary.
Access for members only. Letter of introduction
required. All charged.
Hours: Term time: Mon to Fri, 0900 to 1230 and
1400 to 1630; Sat, by appointment only
Vacation opening: by appointment only

QUALIFICATIONS AND CURRICULUM AUTHORITY

Acronym or abbreviation: QCA

83 Piccadilly, London, W1J 8QA

Tel: 020 7509 5555
Fax: 020 7509 6666
E-mail: info@qca.org.uk

Website:
http://www.qca.org.uk
Recent press releases, list of current publications, information newsletter.
http://orderline.qca.org.uk/
Publications catalogue.

Founded:
1997

Organisation type and purpose:
National government body, advisory body.
Set up under the 1997 Education Act.
To promote coherence in education and training, its span of responsibility extends from education for the under fives to occupational standards and lifelong learning. QCA's prime duty is to advise the Secretary of State for Education and Skills.

Subject coverage:
All matters affecting the school curriculum, pupil assessment and all qualifications available in publicly-funded education and training (except for higher education); this includes NVQs, GNVQs, A Levels, GCSEs and the many other qualifications available in schools, colleges and publicly funded training programmes which contribute to the national occupational standards programme currently run by the Department for Education and Skills. Working with the National Training Organisations, awarding bodies and further and higher education, and developing a new regulatory regime which lays down a clear structure of quality assurance.

Printed publications:
The Monitor (journal)
The QCA has an extensive range of titles covering national curriculum, schools, NVQ/GNVQs, Key Stages, statutory tasks, assessment etc

Publications list:
Available online

Access to staff:
Contact by letter, by telephone, by fax, by e-mail and via website
Hours: Mon to Fri, 0900 to 1700

Parent body:
Department for Education and Skills (DfES) Sanctuary Buildings, Great Smith Street, London, SW1P 3BT; tel: 020 7925 5000

QUALITY ASSURANCE AGENCY FOR HIGHER EDUCATION

Acronym or abbreviation: QAA

Southgate House, Southgate Street, Gloucester, GL1 1UB

Tel: 01452 557000
Fax: 01452 557070
E-mail: comms@qaa.ac.uk

Website:
http://www.qaa.ac.uk

Founded:
1997

Formerly called:
Higher Education Quality Council (year of change 1997)

Organisation type and purpose:
An independent public body, a company limited by guarantee, a registered charity (charity numbers 1062746 and SC037786), governed by a Board, which has overall responsibility for the conduct and strategic direction of its business.
Principal role is to safeguard and help to improve the academic standards and quality of higher education.

Subject coverage:
QAA works with universities and colleges to define standards for higher education, through a framework known as the Academic Infrastructure, which includes the qualifications frameworks for the UK. QAA also carries out reviews of higher education institutions against these standards and publishes their outcomes. It advises governments on applications for the grant of degree-awarding powers, university title, or designation as a higher education institution.

Printed publications:
Review reports
The Code of practice for the assurance of academic quality and standards in higher education (10 sections)
Higher quality
Directors reports
Annual reviews
Review method handbooks.
Order printed publications from: Linney Direct, Adams Way, Mansfield, Nottinghamshire, NG18 4FN; tel: 01623 450788; fax: 01623 450481; e-mail: qaa@linneydirect.com

Publications list:
Available online and in print

Access to staff:
Contact by letter, by telephone, by fax, by e-mail and via website. Appointment necessary.
Hours: Mon to Fri, 0900 to 1700

Funded by:
subscriptions from universities and colleges of higher education, and through contracts with the main higher education funding bodies

QUALITY BRITISH CELERY ASSOCIATION

Acronym or abbreviation: QBCA

133 Eastgate, Louth, Lincolnshire, LN11 9QG

Tel: 01507 602427
Fax: 01507 607165
E-mail: crop.association@pvga.co.uk

Enquiries:
Enquiries to: Membership Secretary

Founded:
1980s

Organisation type and purpose:
National organisation, trade association.

Subject coverage:
Celery production.

Access to staff:
Contact by letter, by telephone, by fax and by e-mail
Hours: 0900 to 1700

QUALITY GUILD

Westwinds, Lambley Bank, Scotby, Carlisle, Cumbria, CA4 8BX

Tel: 01228 631681
E-mail: info@qgbiz.co.uk

Website:
http://www.qualityguild.co.uk

QUALITY IMPROVEMENT AGENCY FOR LIFELONG LEARNING

Acronym or abbreviation: QIA

Friars House, Manor House Drive, Coventry, CV1 2TE

Tel: 0870 162 0632
Fax: 0870 162 0633

Website:
http://www.qia.org.uk/
http://www.lsrc.org.uk

Enquiries:
Enquiries to: Communications Officer
Direct tel: 0870 211 3434
Direct e-mail: gillian.dyer@qia.org.uk

Founded:
2006

Formerly a part of:
the Learning and Skills Development Agency

Organisation type and purpose:
Research organisation.
Quango.

Subject coverage:
Further education, research, teaching and learning.

Museum or gallery collection, archive, or library special collection:
Library catalogue

Non-library collection catalogue:
All or part available in-house

Library catalogue:
All or part available in-house

Printed publications:
Books and Reports
Order printed publications from: Learning and Skills Development Agency
Citadel Place, Tinworth Street, London, SE11 5EF, tel: 020 7840 5400, fax: 020 7840 5401, e-mail: p.fielding@lsda.org.uk

Electronic and video publications:
Books, Journals and Reports

Publications list:
Available in print

QUARRY PRODUCTS ASSOCIATION

Acronym or abbreviation: QPA

156 Buckingham Palace Road, London, SW1W 9TR

Tel: 020 7730 8194
Fax: 020 7730 4355
E-mail: info@qpa.org

Website:
http://www.qpa.org

Enquiries:
Enquiries to: Press and Information Officer
Direct e-mail: clements@qpa.org

Founded:
1997

Organisation type and purpose:
Trade association.

Subject coverage:
Construction aggregates, (ie crushed rock, sand, gravel and slag), asphalt and coated macadam for roads and other surfacing uses, (but not asphalts used in roofing, building and waterproofing), lime for building and industrial uses, agricultural lime (information from ALPC).
Ready mixed concrete technology, production, origins, use, specifications and testing, quality assurance.
Sand and gravel industry, planning, technical, environmental, waste management.

Museum or gallery collection, archive, or library special collection:
Overseas periodicals on bitumen, asphalt, concrete and quarrying from 1930s

Trade and statistical information:
Data on UK and European production of ready mix concrete.

Printed publications:
QPA Statistical Yearbook
General information on quarrying
Technical publications

Access to staff:
Contact by letter, by telephone, by fax and by e-mail
Hours: Mon to Fri, 0900 to 1700

continued overleaf

Access to building, collection or gallery:
No access other than to staff

Affiliated to:
European Aggregates Association (UEPG)
European Asphalt Pavement Association
European Ready Mixed Concrete Association

QUEEN ELIZABETH'S FOUNDATION FOR DISABLED PEOPLE

Acronym or abbreviation: QEF

Leatherhead Court, Woodlands Road,
Leatherhead, Surrey, KT22 0BN

Tel: 01372 841100
Fax: 01372 844072
E-mail: info@qef.org.uk

Website:
http://www.qef.org.uk

Enquiries:
Enquiries to: Chief Executive

Founded:
1934

Organisation type and purpose:
Registered charity (charity number 251051).
To provide services for disabled people.

Subject coverage:
Brain injury rehabilitation at Banstead; mobility information advice and assessment at Carshalton; residential vocational training at Leatherhead; development of independent living skills at Leatherhead.

Non-library collection catalogue:
All or part available online and in print

Printed publications:
Annual Report
Leaflets on the various units

Access to staff:
Contact by letter, by telephone and by fax.
Appointment necessary.
Hours: Mon to Fri, 0900 to 1700

Also at:
Banstead, Carshalton, Leatherhead

QUEEN MARGARET UNIVERSITY

Formal name: Queen Margaret University, Edinburgh
Acronym or abbreviation: QMU

Queen Margaret University Drive, Musselburgh, East Lothian, EH21 6UU

Tel: 0131 474 0000
Fax: 0131 474 0001
E-mail: lrchelp@qmu.ac.uk

Website:
http://www.qmu.ac.uk/lb

Founded:
1875

Formerly called:
Queen Margaret University College (year of change 2007)

Organisation type and purpose:
University library.

Subject coverage:
Arts therapies; business and management; dietetics and nutrition; events management; nursing; physiotherapy; occupational therapy; radiography; speech therapy; communication studies; podiatry; retailing; drama; hospitality studies; tourism.

Information services:
Access to books, journals and archive for all users.
Network resources subject to user status.

Special visitor services:
Member of Sconul Access; member of ELISA scheme.

Education services:
Information literacy sessions and workshops; sessions for local schools; regular book swap and reading groups

Services for disabled people:
Assistive technology room available.

Museum or gallery collection, archive, or library special collection:
University archive, especially relating to domestic science

Non-library collection catalogue:
All or part available in-house

Library catalogue:
All or part available online

Access to staff:
Contact by letter, by telephone, by fax, by e-mail, in person and via website. Appointment necessary.
Hours: Term time: Mon to Fri, 0900 to 2100; Sat and Sun, 0900 to 1700
Vacation: Mon to Fri, 0900 to 1700

Access to building, collection or gallery:
Via main reception
Hours: The LRC is open 24/7; however non-University members cannot enter after 2100
Special comments: Visitor card mandatory.

Access for disabled people:
Access to all public areas
Hours: The LRC is open 24/7; however non-University members cannot enter after 2100
Special comments: Visitor card mandatory.

QUEEN MARY, UNIVERSITY OF LONDON

Acronym or abbreviation: QMW

Mile End Road, London, E1 4NS

Tel: 020 7882 3027
Fax: 020 7882 7525
E-mail: j.e.clarke@qmul.ac.uk

Website:
http://www.qmul.ac.uk

Enquiries:
Enquiries to: Public Relations Manager
Direct tel: 020 7882 5314
Direct fax: 020 7882 5556
Direct e-mail: n.relph@qmul.ac.uk

Founded:
1887

Organisation type and purpose:
International organisation, university department or institute.
Constituent college of the University of London.
University college providing higher education and offering research opportunities in medicine, science, engineering, arts and law.

Subject coverage:
Medicine, dentistry; science – physics, chemistry, biochemistry, mathematics, astronomy, computer; engineering – electronic, mechanical, civil, materials, aeronautical; arts – English, German, French, Russian, Hispanic studies, history; law; social sciences – economics, geography, politics.

Non-library collection catalogue:
All or part available online

Access to staff:
Contact by letter, by telephone, by fax, by e-mail and via website
Hours: Mon to Fri, 0900 to 1700

QUEEN MARY, UNIVERSITY OF LONDON – MAIN LIBRARY

Acronym or abbreviation: QMUL

Mile End Road, London, E1 4NS

Tel: 020 7882 3300
Fax: 020 8981 0028
E-mail: library-enquiries@qmul.ac.uk

Website:
http://www.mds.qmw.ac.uk/
General home page for School of Medicine and Dentistry (including libraries).
http://www.qmw.ac.uk
Library services and resources.

Enquiries:
Enquiries to: Director of Academic Information Services
Other contacts: Reference Librarian for telephone enquiries.

Organisation type and purpose:
University library, research organisation.
European Documentation Centre.

Subject coverage:
Arts: language and literature – English, Classical, French, German, Italian, Romanian, Russian, Spanish; history, history of art, drama and theatre; engineering: electrical, electronic, aeronautical, civil, mechanical, geomaterials, materials; informatics and mathematical sciences: computer science, mathematical sciences, information technology, astronomy; physical, biological and basic medical sciences: aquatic biology, microbiology, genetics, ecology, botany, zoology, biochemistry, plant physiology, animal physiology, environmental biology, molecular biology, chemistry (organic, inorganic, physical, structural), physics (astrophysics, mathematical, nuclear, polymer, theoretical, experimental); laws: English law, international law, comparative law, credit and commercial law, legal theory, socio-legal studies, intellectual property law, banking law, international arbitration, international business taxation; social studies: economics, applied econometrics, geography, social analysis, health care, information and planning, political studies, public policy, statistics, operational research, business studies, East London studies.

Museum or gallery collection, archive, or library special collection:
Alumni Collections (St Bartholomew's Hospital, Smithfield)
Alumni Collections (The Royal London Hospital, Whitechapel)
Archives of Westfield College
Camps and Cameron Collection on legal and forensic medicine (written application essential for access)
Constance Maynard Archive
Lyttleton Family Letters and Papers
Manuscripts on the History of Art
People's Palace Archive
Rare book collection (17th and 18th century English and European literature)

Access to staff:
Contact by letter, by telephone, by fax, by e-mail and via website
Hours: Access other than to University members normally restricted to term time: Mon to Fri, 1700 to 2100; Sat, 1000 to 1600 Vacations: Mon to Fri, 0900 to 1700

A college of the:
University of London

Medical Library:
Queen Mary, University of London
Royal London Hospital Medical College, Whitechapel, London, E1 2AD; tel: 020 7882 7112
Queen Mary, University of London
Charterhouse Square, London, EC1M 6BG; tel: 020 7882 6019
Queen Mary, University of London
Medical College of St Bartholomew's Hospital, West Smithfield, London, EC1A 7BE; tel: 020 7601 7853

QUEEN MARY, UNIVERSITY OF LONDON – SCHOOL OF ELECTRONIC ENGINEERING AND COMPUTER SCIENCE

Acronym or abbreviation: QMUL

Mile End Road, London, E1 4NS

Tel: 020 7882 5217
Fax: 020 7882 7064
E-mail: sue.white@eecs.qmul.ac.uk

Website:
http://www.eecs.qmul.ac.uk
Courses, research and publications.

Enquiries:
Enquiries to: Research Co-ordinator

Formerly called:
Queen Mary, University of London – Department
of Computer Science (year of change 2008)

Organisation type and purpose:
University department or institute.

Subject coverage:
Computer science, electronic engineering.

Publications list:
Available online

Access to building, collection or gallery:
Prior appointment required

QUEEN VICTORIA HOSPITAL NHS FOUNDATION TRUST

Acronym or abbreviation: QVH

Library, Holtye Road, East Grinstead, West Sussex,
RH19 3DZ

Tel: 01342 414266
Fax: 01342 414005
E-mail: library@qvh.nhs.uk

Website:
http://ksslks.co.uk/sussex/kqv.asp
Catalogue of items held by Queen Victoria
Hospital Library.

Enquiries:
Enquiries to: Library Services Manager
Other contacts: Library Supervisor

Organisation type and purpose:
Staff library.

Subject coverage:
Burns, plastic and reconstructive surgery, hand
surgery, oral and maxillofacial surgery, ophthalmic
and corneoplastic surgery and nursing.

Library catalogue:
All or part available online

Access to staff:
Contact by letter, by telephone, by fax and by e-
mail. Appointment necessary.
Hours: Mon to Fri, 0930 to 1230

Access to building, collection or gallery:
Prior appointment required; no access to physical
library
Hours: Daily, 24-hour access only for registered
members
Special comments: Library is behind several security
doors.

Access for disabled people:
No access to physical library for disabled people;
however, library staff will provide information on
request
Special comments: Library is on second floor with no
lift.

Constituent part of:
Kent, Surrey and Sussex Library and Knowledge
Services Health Libraries Network
    Calverley House, Tunbridge Wells, Kent, TN1
    2TU; tel: 01892 704240; website: http://www
    .ksslibraries.nhs.uk

QUEEN'S COLLEGE LIBRARY

Oxford, OX1 4AW

Tel: 01865 279130
Fax: 01865 710819
E-mail: library@queens.ox.ac.uk

Website:
http://www.queens.ox.ac.uk

Enquiries:
Enquiries to: Librarian
Direct tel: 01865 279213
Direct e-mail: amanda.saville@queens.ox.ac.uk

Founded:
1341

Organisation type and purpose:
College library.

Subject coverage:
Subject coverage which is likely to be of interest to
others lies in those traditional areas, such as
theology, philosophy etc., where the library has
substantial holdings of older works; theology;
philosophy; classics; history, ancient and modern;
geography (mainly topography); politics; law;
economics; English, French, German, Spanish and
Russian languages and literature.

**Museum or gallery collection, archive, or library
special collection:**
Incunabula (280 items)
Manuscripts (560 items, 10th to 20th centuries)
Oakes Collection (American history)
Peet Memorial Library (Egyptology)
Short Title Catalogue Books

Non-library collection catalogue:
All or part available online and in print

Library catalogue:
All or part available online and in-house

Access to staff:
Contact by letter, by telephone, by fax, by e-mail
and via website. Appointment necessary. Access
for members only.
Hours: Mon to Fri, 0900 to 1700

Access to building, collection or gallery:
Prior appointment required

Access for disabled people:
To ground floor only
Hours: During staffed hours

QUEEN'S NURSING INSTITUTE

Acronym or abbreviation: QNI

3 Albemarle Way, Clerkenwell, London, EC1V
4RQ

Tel: 020 7549 1400
Fax: 020 7490 1269
E-mail: mail@qni.org.uk

Website:
http://www.qni.org.uk

Enquiries:
Enquiries to: Director

Founded:
1887

Formerly called:
Queen's Institute of District Nursing (year of
change 1973)

Organisation type and purpose:
National organisation, professional body,
registered charity (charity number 213128).

Subject coverage:
Community nursing from its foundation in 1887 to
the present day.

**Museum or gallery collection, archive, or library
special collection:**
Archival material in connection with district
    (community) nursing

Printed publications:
Annual Report
Final Reports (by Innovation Award winners)
Newsletter (6 times a year)
QNI leaflet

Microform publications:
Queen's Nurses training records

Electronic and video publications:
Audio tapes, video, disc and CD-ROM

Publications list:
Available online and in print

Access to staff:
Contact by letter, by telephone, by fax, by e-mail
and via website. Appointment necessary.
Hours: Mon to Fri, 0900 to 1730

QUEEN'S UNIVERSITY BELFAST

Acronym or abbreviation: QUB

McClay Library, 10 College Park, Belfast BT7 1LP

Tel: 028 9097 6135
E-mail: library@qub.ac.uk

Website:
http://www.qub.ac.uk/lib
Online catalogue and library services.

Enquiries:
Enquiries to: Library Manager
Direct tel: 028 9097 6144

Organisation type and purpose:
University library.
The McClay Library covers arts, social sciences,
science & engineering; there is also a Medical and
Biomedical Library.

**Museum or gallery collection, archive, or library
special collection:**
Special Collections of early printed and manuscript
    materials

Library catalogue:
All or part available online

Printed publications:
Various documentation relating to electronic
    information sources and aspects of Library
    services

Access to staff:
Contact by letter, by telephone, by e-mail, in
person and via website. Non-members charged.
Hours: See website for details

QUEEN'S UNIVERSITY BELFAST – MCCLAY LIBRARY

Information Services, The McClay Library, 10
College Park, Belfast, BT7 1LP

Tel: 028 9097 6344 (Information Desk)
E-mail: library@qub.ac.uk

Website:
http://www.qub.ac.uk/directorates/
InformationServices/TheLibrary

Organisation type and purpose:
University library, with computing and media
services.

Library catalogue:
All or part available online

QUEKETT MICROSCOPICAL CLUB

Acronym or abbreviation: QMC

The Natural History Museum, Cromwell Road,
London, SW7 5BD

Tel: 020 7938 8921

Website:
http://www.quekett.org.uk/index.html
Current activities and information.

Enquiries:
Enquiries to: Honorary Secretary
Direct e-mail: secretary@quekett.org

Founded:
1865

Organisation type and purpose:
Learned society.

Subject coverage:
Microscopy.

continued overleaf

Museum or gallery collection, archive, or library special collection:
Microscope slides; microscopes

Printed publications:
Bulletin (twice a year)
The Quekett Journal of Microscopy (twice a year)
Order printed publications from: See Quekett website at http://www.quekett.org.uk/files/publications/publications.html

Access to staff:
Contact by letter, by telephone, by e-mail and via website
Hours: Mon to Fri, 0900 to 1700

QUILTERS' GUILD OF THE BRITISH ISLES

Acronym or abbreviation: QGBI

St Anthony's Hall, Peasholme Green, York, YO1 7PW

Tel: 01904 613242
Fax: 01904 632394
E-mail: info@quiltersguild.org.uk

Website:
http://www.quiltersguild.org.uk

Enquiries:
Enquiries to: Guild Administrator

Founded:
1979

Organisation type and purpose:
International organisation, national organisation, membership association (membership is by subscription), present number of members: 7,000, voluntary organisation, registered charity (charity number 1067361), museum, suitable for all ages, research organisation.
To promote and maintain the crafts of quilting, patchwork and appliqué from an educational base and historical perspective.

Subject coverage:
History of quilting, how to quilt, contemporary quilting, patchwork and appliqué.

Museum or gallery collection, archive, or library special collection:
Book library, slide library, study packs, videos
Heritage Quilt Collection
Quilt collection, historical and contemporary

Library catalogue:
All or part available in-house

Printed publications:
Quilt Studies (£10)
Quilt Treasures (2009)
Nineties Catalogue (£10)
The Quilter (quarterly magazine, free to members, £7 to non-members)

Access to staff:
Contact by letter, by telephone, by fax, by e-mail, in person and via website. Appointment necessary. Non-members charged.
Hours: Mon to Thu, 0900 to 1700; Fri, 0900 to 1700

Access to building, collection or gallery:
Hours: Please contact for current opening hours

Access for disabled people:
Access to all public areas, toilet facilities

R J TALBOTT

Springfields, 10 Sandy Lane, Scalford, Leicestershire, LE14 4DS

Tel: 01664 444668
Fax: 01664 444420
E-mail: rjtalbott@rjtalbott.plus.com

Enquiries:
Enquiries to: Director

Founded:
1986

Organisation type and purpose:
Consultancy.
Specialising in videofilm evidence for courts showing disability related to compensation.

Subject coverage:
Medical videofilm maker.

Printed publications:
Leaflets on services available

Access to staff:
Contact by letter and by fax. Appointment necessary.
Hours: Mon to Fri, 0900 to 1700 (but clients are usually visited)

Access to building, collection or gallery:
No access other than to staff

Access for disabled people:
Parking provided

Associated with:
International Paraplegic Claims Service

RAC LIVE – 1740 LIVE TRAFFIC AND WEATHER INFORMATION

RAC Motoring Services, Great Park Road, Bradley Stoke, Bristol, BS32 4QN

Tel: 1740 from any mobile (calls cost up to 59p per minute) also on 0906 470 1740 land-line (calls charged at 60p per minute)

Website:
http://www.rac.co.uk/travelservices/traffic by phone
Information on the 1740 service.
http://www.rac.co.uk
To check the latest traffic information.

Organisation type and purpose:
Membership association (membership is by subscription).
RAC Live is the brand name operated by RAC Trafficmaster Telematics Limited.

Subject coverage:
Live traffic information on your mobile available 24 hours a day:
up to the minute traffic information on over 8,000 miles of motorways and major A roads, latest national and local weather forecasts.
After listening to traffic information, talk to an RAC advisor to find an alternative route, plan routes across UK and Europe, provide general UK and European driving information and traffic regulations.

Access to staff:
Contact by telephone
Hours: Mon to Fri, 0700 to 2000; Sat, 0900 to 1700; Sun 0900 to 1700

RAC LIVE – RAC ROUTE MINDER

RAC Motoring Services, Great Park Road, Bradley Stoke, Bristol, BS32 4QN

Tel: 0800 096 1740

Website:
http://www.rac.co.uk/travelservices/route_minder/
To sign up for a free month's trial.

Organisation type and purpose:
Membership association (membership is by subscription).
RAC Live is the brand name operated by RAC Trafficmaster Telematics Limited.

Subject coverage:
Web-based personalised and proactive traffic information service: delivers relevant traffic information alerts via email and text messages, provides unlimited access to colour map that displays live traffic information.

Access to staff:
Contact by telephone
Hours: Mon to Fri, 0800 to 2000; Sat, 0900 to 1700; Sun, 0900 to 1900

RAC TRAVEL INFORMATION

RAC Live, RAC Motoring Services, Great Park Road, Bradley Stoke, Bristol, BS32 4QN

Tel: 0906 470 1740 (calls charged at 60p per minute)

Website:
http://www.racbusiness.co.uk
http://www.bsm.co.uk
http://www.rac.co.uk
The pages can be used to join the RAC online. Hotel bookings and plans for journeys can be made that take into account traffic conditions and delays. A motorsport section provides members with a virtual tour of British tracks and a diary of events.

Enquiries:
Enquiries to: RAC Travel Information Department

Organisation type and purpose:
Membership association (membership is by subscription).

Subject coverage:
Dynamic traffic updates on the UK motorway and trunk road network: UK and European route information (a charge is made for posted or faxed routes); various UK and European travel-related enquiries.

Access to staff:
Contact by telephone
Hours: Advisors available: Mon to Fri, 0700 to 2000; Sat, 0900 to 1700; Sun, 0900 to 2100
Recorded UK road traffic information is 24 hours

RACE WALKING ASSOCIATION

Acronym or abbreviation: RWA

Hufflers, Heard's Lane, Shenfield, Brentwood, Essex, CM15 0SF

Tel: 01277 220687
Fax: 01277 212380
E-mail: racewalkingassociation@btinternet.com

Website:
http://www.racewalkingassociation.btinternet.co.uk
For other pages add: /AboutTheRWA.html; /archivesandrecords.html; /books.html; /clubcontacts.html; /fixtures.html; /moreinfo.html; /news.html; /outsidecontacts.html; /racewalkingrecord.html; /usefullinks.html; and other more technical pages.

Enquiries:
Enquiries to: Honorary General Secretary

Founded:
1907

Formerly called:
Southern Counties Road Walking Association (year of change 1910); Road Walking Association (year of change 1954)

Organisation type and purpose:
Voluntary organisation, governing body of race walking.
The development, promotion and control of race walking in England, the Isle of Man and the Channel Islands.

Subject coverage:
Policy; organisation and rules; clubs and athletes; coaches, officials and judging; events; history; relations with other sporting organisations.

Information services:
Monthly magazine, archive material, general advice.

Museum or gallery collection, archive, or library special collection:
List of clubs and officials
Lists of events
Historical material
Minutes

Non-library collection catalogue:
All or part available online

Printed publications:
Race Walking Record (monthly)
Fixture List
Handbook
Race Walking (technique and training)
This Is Race Walking (introduction to race walking)
Order printed publications from: Honorary General
Secretary

Electronic and video publications:
Fixture List disc
Handbook disc
Order electronic and video publications from:
Honorary General Secretary

Access to staff:
Contact by letter, by telephone, by fax, by e-mail
and via website
Hours: Mon to Fri, 0800 to 2000

Access to building, collection or gallery:
No access.

Access for disabled people:
No access.

Branches:
Midlands Area RWA
   49, Debdale Avenue, Lyppard Woodgreen,
   Worcester, WR4 0RP; tel: 01905 616718; e-mail:
   perry.sevenacres@worcester.gov.uk
Northern Area RWA
   14, Watery Lane, Dunholme, Lincoln, LN2 3QW;
   tel: 01673 861208; e-mail: rjackson43@hotmail.co
   .uk
Southern Area RWA
   Glenthorne, 65, Liverpool Road, Walmer, Deal,
   CT14 7NN; tel: 01304 368324; e-mail:
   bettychrisf@hotmail.com

RADCLIFFE SCIENCE LIBRARY

Parks Road, Oxford, OX1 3QP

Tel: 01865 272800
Fax: 01865 272821
E-mail: rsl.enquiries@bodleian.ox.ac.uk

Website:
http://www.bodleian.ox.ac.uk
Bodleian Library home page.
http://www.bodleian.ox.ac.uk/science
Guide to the Science Libraries.

Enquiries:
Enquiries to: Keeper of Scientific Books
Direct tel: 01865 272820
Direct fax: 01865 272832
Direct e-mail: rsl.enquiries@bodleian.ox.ac.uk
Other contacts: (1)Subject consultants (2)
Administrator (for bibliographical enquiries or
admin)

Founded:
1749

Organisation type and purpose:
University library, legal deposit library, the main
science lending and reference library of University
of Oxford, part of Bodleian Libraries Services.

Subject coverage:
All pure sciences, mathematics, engineering and
medicine.

**Museum or gallery collection, archive, or library
special collection:**
Acland (medical pamphlets and offprints)
Child (pamphlets and offprints on coconuts)
Hardy (mathematical pamphlets and offprints)
Le Gros Clark (anatomical pamphlets and
   offprints)
Seckerson (pamphlets, offprints and portraits
   related to eponymous syndromes and diseases)
Tylor (anthropological pamphlets and offprints)
Van Heyningen (pamphlets and offprints in
   pathology)

Library catalogue:
All or part available online

Access to staff:
Contact by letter, by telephone, by e-mail, in
person and via website

Hours: Term time: 0830 to 2150
Vacation: 0830 to 1850

Access for disabled people:
Level entry, toilet facilities, accessible lift, disabled
parking bay by appointment

RADIO MANX LIMITED

PO Box 1368, Broadcasting House, Douglas Head,
Douglas, Isle of Man, IM99 1SW, Isle of Man

Tel: 01624 682600
Fax: 01624 682604

Website:
http://www.radiott.com
Information about RadioTT, a concept station
oriented to the Isle of Man TT Races.
http://www.manxradio.com
Programme details, research details, personality
details and general information about Manx Radio.

Enquiries:
Enquiries to: Managing Director
Direct e-mail: stewartwatterson@manxradio.com
Other contacts: (1) News Editor (2) Sales Director
for (1) news releases (2) advertising services.

Founded:
1964

Organisation type and purpose:
Service industry, publishing house.
News and current affairs source – Isle of Man.
Public service broadcaster. Provision of radio
advertising services.

Subject coverage:
News and current affairs; information and views –
Isle of Man.
Isle of Man advertising market.

Trade and statistical information:
Average listenership base – 80% adult population
   of Isle of Man. In consequence, very effective,
   and wide-ranging across all demographics,
   advertising service.

Printed publications:
Advertising and Research Data
Media Pack

Access to staff:
Contact by letter, by fax, by e-mail and via
website
Hours: Mon to Fri, 0900 to 1700

RADIO, ELECTRICAL AND TELEVISION RETAILERS' ASSOCIATION

Acronym or abbreviation: RETRA

Retra House, St John's Terrace, 1 Ampthill Street,
Bedford, MK42 9EY

Tel: 01234 269110
Fax: 01234 269609
E-mail: retra@retra.co.uk

Website:
http://www.retra.co.uk
Member benefits, news, find a retailer, code of
practice, consumer information, consumer rights.

Founded:
1942

Organisation type and purpose:
Trade association for independent electrical
retailers and servicing organisations.
To foster amongst the membership a culture of fair
dealing with consumers; to encourage the
achievement of high standards of retailing and
related service activities within the trade; to
provide members with a range of benefits,
industry information and legal advice; to represent
their interests at a national level – maintaining a
dialogue with manufacturers, government and
other key organisations.

Subject coverage:
Represents more than 1,400 members, operating
from over 2,300 outlets in

the UK; members include electrical retailers,
service engineers, custom installers, computer
stores and electronic music shops.

Access to staff:
Contact by letter, by telephone, by fax and by e-
mail

RADISH GROWERS' ASSOCIATION

133 Eastgate, Louth, Lincolnshire, LN11 9QG

Tel: 01507 602427
Fax: 01507 607165
E-mail: crop.association@pvga.co.uk

Enquiries:
Enquiries to: Membership Secretary

Founded:
c.1980

Organisation type and purpose:
National organisation, trade association.

Subject coverage:
Radishes.

Access to staff:
Contact by letter, by telephone, by fax and by e-
mail

RADNORSHIRE SOCIETY

Pool House, Discoed, Presteigne, Powys, LD8
2NW

Tel: 01547 560318
E-mail: sadiecole@mypostoffice.co.uk

Website:
http://www.radnorshiresociety.org

Enquiries:
Enquiries to: Hon. Secretary

Founded:
1930

Organisation type and purpose:
Learned society (membership is by subscription),
present number of members: 450.

Subject coverage:
History, natural history, archaeology of the old
county of Radnor.

Printed publications:
The Transactions (annually)

Access to staff:
Contact by letter, by telephone and by e-mail.
Appointment necessary. Access for members only.
Hours: Mon to Fri, 0900 to 1700

Access to building, collection or gallery:
No prior appointment required

RADZINOWICZ LIBRARY

Formal name: University of Cambridge, Institute of
Criminology, Radzinowicz Library

Sidgwick Avenue, Cambridge, CB3 9DA

Tel: 01223 335386
Fax: 01223 335356
E-mail: crimlib@hermes.cam.ac.uk

Website:
http://www.crim.cam.ac.uk/library

Enquiries:
Enquiries to: Librarian

Founded:
1960

Organisation type and purpose:
University department or institute. Departmental
library. Research library.

Subject coverage:
Criminology, penology, forensic psychiatry,
forensic psychology, deviance, policing, criminal
justice (foreign and historical materials are
included), criminal law.

continued overleaf

Library catalogue:
All or part available online

Electronic and video publications:
Quarterly accessions list
Order electronic and video publications from: website:
http://www.crim.cam.ac.uk/library/pubs.html

Access to staff:
Contact by letter, by telephone, by fax and by e-mail. Appointment necessary. Letter of introduction required.
Hours: Mon to Fri, 0900 to 1600

RAF CENTRE OF AVIATION MEDICINE

Acronym or abbreviation: RAF CAM

RAF Henlow, Henlow, Bedfordshire, SG16 6DN

Tel: 01462 851515; extn 8045
Fax: 01462 857681
E-mail: rafcamlibrarian@yahoo.co.uk

Website:
http://rafcam.heritage4.com
Online catalogue only.

Enquiries:
Enquiries to: Librarian
Direct tel: extn 8048
Direct e-mail: wilkinsonn807@henlow.raf.mod.uk
Other contacts: Officer Commanding Centre of Aviation Medicine (for non-service personnel who wish to visit the collection)

Founded:
2000

Created by the merger of:
Institute of Aviation Medicine, Farnborough and RAF Institute of Health, RAF Halton

Organisation type and purpose:
National government body, training organisation, research organisation.

Subject coverage:
Medicine, especially those areas most relevant to aviation; physiology; neurology; psychology; occupational health.

Museum or gallery collection, archive, or library special collection:
Technical reports of British and overseas government agencies relevant to aviation and aviation medicine

Non-library collection catalogue:
All or part available in-house

Library catalogue:
All or part available in-house

Access to staff:
Contact by letter, by telephone, by fax and by e-mail. Appointment necessary.
Hours: Mon to Thu, 0900 to 1630; Fri, 0900 to 1600
Special comments: All non-service personnel must first seek the permission of the Officer Commanding by letter.

Access for disabled people:
Level entry, toilet facilities

RAIL PASSENGERS COUNCIL

Acronym or abbreviation: RPC

Freepost WA 1521, Warrington, WA4 6GP

Tel: 08453 022 022
Fax: 0845 850 1392

Website:
http://www.rail-reg.gov.uk

Enquiries:
Enquiries to: External Relations and Policy Manager

Founded:
1994

Organisation type and purpose:
National government body.

Statutory consumer body of 14 members appointed by the Secretary of State, representing the interests of users of rail services and facilities. The Rail Passengers Committees and the LTUC represent passenger interests locally, the RPC on a national scale.

Subject coverage:
Rail users' consumer matters, monitoring and investigating policies and performance of train and station operators.
For passenger complaints, assessing hardship when stations or lines proposed for closure, see RUCCs and LRPC, which represent passengers' interests locally.

Printed publications:
Annual Report
News Releases
Reports and occasional papers
Series of papers on franchising

Access to staff:
Contact by letter, by telephone, by fax and by e-mail. Appointment necessary.
Hours: Mon to Fri, 0900 to 1700

Affiliated to:
London Transport Users Committee (LTUC)
Rail Passengers Committees (RPC)

Branches at:
East RPC Eastern England
  3rd Floor, Stuart House, City Road, Peterborough, Cambridgeshire, PE1 1QF; tel: 01733 312188; fax: 01733 891286
London area See the London Transport Users Committee
Midlands RPC Midlands
  6th Floor, The McLaren Building, 35 Dale End, Birmingham, B4 7LN; tel: 0121 212 2133; fax: 0121 236 6945
North East Also has responsibility for Tyne & Wear Metro services
  Hilary House, St Saviour's Place, York, YO1 7PJ; tel: 01904 625615; fax: 01904 643026
North West Also has responsibility for Greater Manchester Metrolink services
  Third Floor, 82 King Street, Manchester, M2 4WQ; tel: 0161 228 6247; fax: 0161 236 1476
Scotland RPC ScotlandAlso has responsibility for shipping services operated by Caledonian MacBrayne
  Room 514, Corunna House, 29 Cadogan Street, Glasgow, G2 7AB; tel: 0141 221 7760; fax: 0141 221 3393
South RPC Southern England
  3rd Floor, Centric House, 390–391 Strand, London, WC2R 0LY; tel: 020 7240 5308; fax: 020 7240 8923
Wales RPC Wales – Cymru
  St David's House, Wood Street, Cardiff, CF10 1ES; tel: 029 2022 7247; fax: 029 2022 3992
West RPC Western England
  10th Floor, Tower House, Fairfax Street, Bristol, BS1 3BN; tel: 0117 926 5703; fax: 0117 929 4140

Resourced by:
Office of the Rail Regulator

RAILWAY CORRESPONDENCE AND TRAVEL SOCIETY

Acronym or abbreviation: RCTS

Littlecote, 365 Old Bath Road, Cheltenham, Gloucestershire, GL53 9AH

Tel: 01242 523917
E-mail: peter@littlecote.freeserve.co.uk

Website:
http://www.rcts.org.uk
About the society.

Enquiries:
Enquiries to: Book Publications Sales Manager

Founded:
1928

Organisation type and purpose:
Membership association (membership is by subscription), voluntary organisation.

Museum or gallery collection, archive, or library special collection:
Historic working time-tables collection (for members only)
Photographic portfolio (for members only)

Printed publications:
Definitive histories of the locomotives owned by the four British pre-nationalisation companies and their pre-grouping constituents
Other books of general railway interest
Railway Observer (magazine, monthly, members only)

Publications list:
Available online and in print

Access to staff:
Contact by letter, by e-mail and via website
Hours: Mon to Fri, 0900 to 1700

Affiliated to:
a number of similar organisations in the UK and overseas

Has:
26 branches within the UK

RAILWAY HERITAGE TRUST

40 Melton Street, London, NW1 2EE

Tel: 020 7557 8090
Fax: 020 7557 9700
E-mail: rht@networkrail.co.uk

Enquiries:
Enquiries to: Executive Director

Founded:
1985

Organisation type and purpose:
Advisory body.
Independent company, sponsored by Network Rail and BRB (Residuary) Ltd, which offers grant aid for the conservation of listed buildings and structures owned by those sponsors.
Heritage funding agency.

Subject coverage:
Repair, restoration and conservation of listed and historic railway buildings and structures owned by Network Rail and BRB (Residuary) Ltd, grant aid for this purpose.

Printed publications:
Annual Report

Access to staff:
Contact by letter, by telephone, by fax and by e-mail. Appointment necessary.
Hours: Mon to Fri, 0900 to 1700

RAILWAY INDUSTRY ASSOCIATION

Acronym or abbreviation: RIA

22 Headfort Place, London, SW1X 7RY

Tel: 020 7201 0777
Fax: 020 7235 5777
E-mail: ria@riagb.org.uk

Website:
http://www.riagb.org.uk

Enquiries:
Enquiries to: Director

Founded:
1875

Organisation type and purpose:
Trade association.

Subject coverage:
Railway equipment, railway infrastructure, standards and specifications.

Printed publications:
BRB/RIA Technical Specifications (13)
Members and Products (directory)

Publications list:
Available in print

Access to staff:
Contact by letter, by telephone, by fax and by e-mail
Hours: Mon to Fri, 0900 to 1700

RAILWAY PRESERVATION SOCIETY OF IRELAND

Acronym or abbreviation: RPSI

Whitehead Excursion Station, Castleview Road, Whitehead, Carrickfergus, Co Antrim, BT38 9NA

Tel: 028 2826 0803
Fax: 028 2826 0803
E-mail: rpsitrains@hotmail.com

Website:
http://www.steamtrainsireland.com

Enquiries:
Enquiries to: Honorary Secretary
Other contacts: Chairman

Founded:
1964

Organisation type and purpose:
Membership association (membership is by subscription), present number of members: 1,100, voluntary organisation, registered charity. Aims to restore, maintain and operate preserved steam locomotives and historic carriages on the main line railways of Ireland.

Subject coverage:
Irish railway preservation, steam locomotives, vintage rolling stock.

Museum or gallery collection, archive, or library special collection:
Irish steam engines and rolling stock

Non-library collection catalogue:
All or part available online

Printed publications:
Journal (to members)
Newsletters (to members)

Access to staff:
Contact by letter, by e-mail and via website.
Appointment necessary.
Hours: Mon to Fri, 0900 to 1300

Access to building, collection or gallery:
On advertised open days, otherwise by prior appointment.

Access for disabled people:
Parking provided, ramped entry

Member organisation of:
Heritage Railway Association (HRA)

RAJAR

Formal name: Radio Joint Audience Research Limited

2nd floor, 5 Golden Sq., London, W1F 9BS

Tel: 020 7292 9040
Fax: 020 7292 9041
E-mail: info@rajar.co.uk

Website:
http://www.rajar.co.uk
Quarterly summary of radio listening.

Enquiries:
Enquiries to: Chief Executive

Founded:
1992

Organisation type and purpose:
Research organisation.
Joint industry research organisation.
Management of UK's agreed system of radio audience measurement.

Subject coverage:
National and local estimates of radio listening analysis by time period and with demographic breakdowns.

Electronic and video publications:
Electronic access to detailed results available through commercial bureaux

Access to staff:
Contact by letter, by e-mail and via website.
Appointment necessary.
Hours: Mon to Fri, 0930 to 1730

RALEIGH SAFETY SEVEN AND EARLY RELIANT OWNERS CLUB

Acronym or abbreviation: Raleigh/Reliant OC

17 Courtland Avenue, Chingford, London, E4 6DU

Enquiries:
Enquiries to: Secretary

Founded:
1967

Organisation type and purpose:
Membership association (membership is by subscription), present number of members: 180–200.

Subject coverage:
Technical information and spares for all Raleigh motorised vehicles and Reliant vehicles up to the Regal models.

Museum or gallery collection, archive, or library special collection:
Library of Raleigh and Reliant vehicle literature

Printed publications:
Newsletter (quarterly, free to members)

Access to staff:
Contact by letter
Hours: Mon to Fri, 0900 to 1700
Special comments: Stamped addressed envelope with enquiries; Library is open to members only.

RAMBLERS' ASSOCIATION

Acronym or abbreviation: RA

2nd Floor, Camelford House, 89 Albert Embankment, London, SE1 7TW

Tel: 020 7339 8500
Fax: 020 7339 8501
E-mail: ramblers@ramblers.org.uk

Website:
http://www.ramblers.org.uk
Comprehensive source of information on walking in Britain; Ramblers' campaigns, membership and local groups, links to related organisations in Britain and abroad.

Enquiries:
Enquiries to: Information Officer
Direct e-mail: ruths@ramblers.org.uk

Founded:
1935

Organisation type and purpose:
National organisation, membership association (membership is by subscription), present number of members: 140,000, voluntary organisation, registered charity (charity number 306089). Encouraging walking, protecting footpaths, campaigning for responsible freedom to roam, defending the beauty of the countryside.

Subject coverage:
Walking; rights of way and footpath law; care of the countryside and preservation of natural beauty; protection of footpaths and provision of access to open country; long-distance footpath information; all matters connected with walking.

Printed publications:
Fact Sheets and Regional Guides
Footpath Worker (quarterly bulletin)
Path Guides and Accommodation Lists
Policy Statements
Walk (quarterly, members)
Rights of Way publications
The Rambler's Yearbook and Accommodation Guide

Research Reports

Publications list:
Available online and in print

Access to staff:
Contact by letter, by telephone, by fax, by e-mail, in person and via website
Hours: Mon to Fri, 1000 to 1700

Access to building, collection or gallery:
No prior appointment required

Access for disabled people:
Parking provided, ramped entry, access to all public areas, toilet facilities

Other addresses:
Ramblers' Association, Scotland (RA Scotland)
Kingfisher House, Auld Mart Business Park, Milnathort, Kinross, KY13 9DA; tel: 01577 861222; fax: 01577 861333; e-mail: enquiries@scotland.ramblers.org.uk
Ramblers' Association, Wales
Ty'r Cerddwyr, High Street, Gresford, Wrexham, LL12 8PT; tel: 01978 855148; fax: 01978 854445; e-mail: cerddwyr@wales.ramblers.org.uk

RAMSGATE LIBRARY

Guildford Lawn, Ramsgate, Kent, CT11 9AJ

Tel: 01843 593532
Fax: 01843 852692

Enquiries:
Enquiries to: Librarian
Other contacts: Heritage Officer

Founded:
1904

Organisation type and purpose:
Local government body, public library.

Subject coverage:
Parish records, census returns, photographs, newscuttings, maps and ephemera relating to the history of Ramsgate.

Museum or gallery collection, archive, or library special collection:
Ramsgate Archive Collections have been moved to the East Kent Archives Centre, Dover
Collections of books, photographs, maps and postcards relating to the history of Ramsgate

Library catalogue:
All or part available in-house

Access to staff:
Contact by letter, by telephone and by fax
Hours: Mon to Thu, 0930 to 1800; Fri, 0930 to 1900; Sat, 0930 to 1700
Special comments: Heritage staff are available to assist on Thursdays.

Access to building, collection or gallery:
No access other than to staff

Parent body:
Kent County Council
Sessions House, County Hall, Maidstone, Kent

RAPE AND SEXUAL ABUSE SUPPORT CENTRE

Acronym or abbreviation: RASASC

PO Box 383, Croydon, Surrey, CR9 2AW

Tel: 020 8683 3311 (Counselling and Office); minicom no. 020 82391124; 08451 221 331 (Helpline)
Fax: 020 8683 3366
E-mail: info@rasasc.org.uk

Website:
http://www.rasasc.org.uk

Enquiries:
Enquiries to: CEO

Founded:
1984

continued overleaf

Organisation type and purpose:
Voluntary organisation, registered charity (charity number 1085104), training organisation, consultancy.

Subject coverage:
Support to anyone aged 14 and above who has been raped or sexually abused, however long ago. Support and advice to friends / family / partners, and other agencies working with rape or sexual abuse survivors. External training to other organisations. Database of other statutory and otherwise relevant organisations for referral. Helpline support for male survivors.

Printed publications:
Leaflets on the service and other related topics (free of charge)

Access to staff:
Contact by letter, by telephone, by fax, by e-mail and via website. Appointment necessary.
Hours: Mon to Fri, 1000 to 1600
Special comments: Helpline: Mon to Fri, 1200 to 1430 and 1900 to 2130; Sat, Sun and bank holidays, 1430 to 1700
Counselling: Mon to Fri, 1000 to 1600

Access to building, collection or gallery:
No access other than to staff

Access for disabled people:
Parking provided, level entry, toilet facilities
Special comments: Staff only, at present.
(December 2001)

RAPIER REGISTER

The Smithy, Tregynon, Newtown, Powys, SY16 3EH

Tel: 01686 650396

Enquiries:
Enquiries to: Membership Secretary

Founded:
1953

Organisation type and purpose:
International organisation, membership association (membership is by subscription), present number of members: 150, voluntary organisation.
Motor club catering for the needs of persons owning and driving Lagonda Rapiers and Rapier cars built between 1934 and 1938.

Subject coverage:
General and technical information on Lagonda Rapiers and Rapier cars manufactured between 1934 and 1938. Location of available spare parts for same.

Printed publications:
Newsletter (monthly, free to members)
List of Spares (available to members)

Access to staff:
Contact by letter and by telephone
Hours: Mon to Fri, 0900 to 2200

RAPTOR FOUNDATION

Formal name: Bird of Prey Rescue Centre

The Heath, St Ives Road, Woodhurst, Cambridgeshire, PE28 3BT

Tel: 01487 741140
Fax: 01487 841140
E-mail: heleowl@aol.com

Website:
http://www.homepages.tesco.net/~raptor
.foundation
Information about the centre.

Enquiries:
Enquiries to: Director
Other contacts: Founder

Founded:
1989

Organisation type and purpose:
Membership association (membership is by subscription), present number of members: 210, registered charity (charity number 1042085), research organisation.
Care and rehabilitation of raptors.

Trade and statistical information:
Over 350 rescued raptors.

Access to staff:
Contact in person
Hours: 24 hours a day for rescue
daily, 1030 to 1700 for visitors

Access for disabled people:
Parking provided, ramped entry, access to all public areas, toilet facilities

RARE BREEDS SURVIVAL TRUST

Acronym or abbreviation: RBST

National Agricultural Centre, Stoneleigh Park, Kenilworth, Warwickshire, CV8 2LG

Tel: 024 7669 6551
Fax: 024 7669 6706
E-mail: enquiries@rbst.org.uk

Website:
http://www.rbst.org.uk

Enquiries:
Enquiries to: Administrator

Founded:
1973

Organisation type and purpose:
Membership association (membership is by subscription), present number of members: c. 8000, registered charity (charity number 269442).
The conservation of rare breeds of farm livestock.

Subject coverage:
Rare breeds of farm livestock.

Non-library collection catalogue:
All or part available in-house

Access to staff:
Contact by letter, by telephone, by fax, by e-mail and via website. Appointment necessary.
Hours: Mon to Fri, 0900 to 1700

Access to building, collection or gallery:
No prior appointment required

RATHBONE

4th Floor, Churchgate House, 56 Oxford Street, Manchester, M1 6EU

Tel: 0161 236 5358
Fax: 0161 238 6356

Website:
http://www.rathbonetraining.co.uk
Information on services.

Enquiries:
Enquiries to: Helpline Co-ordinator
Direct e-mail: advice@rathbonetraining.co.uk
Other contacts: Marketing and External Affairs Manager for overall responsibility for marketing, public relations and information.

Founded:
1969

Formerly called:
Rathbone Training

Organisation type and purpose:
Advisory body, voluntary organisation, registered charity (charity number 287120), training organisation.
Charity is a training provider. Special education advice line to parents and children with special needs.

Subject coverage:
Advice for parents and children with special needs on all aspects of education, statementing, exclusion etc.

Museum or gallery collection, archive, or library special collection:
Elfrida Rathbone archives

Printed publications:
A4 Poster (free)
Advice Line Business cards (free)
Choosing a School (first copy free, 50p each thereafter)
Finding Funding (first copy free, 25p each thereafter)
General Advice Line Leaflet (free)
How to Complain (first copy free, 25p each thereafter)
Making a Statement: The Parent's Guide to the statementing procedure for a child with special educational needs (£5 for professionals and charities, free to parents although they are asked for a £5 donation if they can afford it)
Making a Statement (summary leaflet) (free)
Organisations which can help (first copy free, 50p each thereafter)
Postcard (free)
Proposed Statements (first copy free, 50p each thereafter)
School Admissions (first copy free, 50p each thereafter)
School Exclusions (first copy free, 50p each thereafter)
School Based Stages (first copy free, 50p each thereafter)
SEAL Newsletter (free)

Publications list:
Available in print

Access to staff:
Contact by letter, by telephone, by fax and by e-mail
Hours: Mon to Fri, 1000 to 1600

Development Officer (London & South):
Rathbone Training
260–268 Poplar High Street, London, E14 0BB; tel: 020 7538 2041; fax: 020 7537 9399

Development Officer (Midlands & Wales):
Rathbone Training
1st Floor, Wrekin House, Market Street, Wellington, Telford, Shropshire, TF1 1DT; tel: 01952 245000; fax: 01952 261771

Development Officer (North):
Rathbone Training
165 Cardigan Road, Leeds, LS6 1QL; tel: 0113 278 9333; fax: 0113 278 9870

Director for Scotland:
Rathbone Training
C.I. Building, Scott Street, Motherwell, ML1 1PN; tel: 01698 252326; fax: 01698 251400

RAVENSBOURNE COLLEGE OF DESIGN AND COMMUNICATION LRC

Walden Road, Chislehurst, Kent, BR7 5SN

Tel: 020 8289 4900
Fax: 020 8325 8320
E-mail: lrc@rave.ac.uk

Website:
http://intranet.rave.ac.uk/lrc

Enquiries:
Enquiries to: Director of Information Services
Direct tel: 020 8289 4919
Direct e-mail: s.bowman@rave.ac.uk

Organisation type and purpose:
College of higher education.

Subject coverage:
Broadcasting, fashion design, furniture design, graphic design, moving image, product design, television.

Library catalogue:
All or part available online

Access to staff:
Contact by letter, by telephone, by fax and by e-mail. Appointment necessary.
Hours: Mon to Fri, 0900 to 1700

Funded by:
HEFCE

RAY SOCIETY

Department of Zoology, The Natural History Museum, Cromwell Road, South Kensington, London, SW7 5BD

Tel: 020 7942 5276
Fax: 020 7942 5433
E-mail: t.ferrero@nhm.ac.uk

Website:
http://www.scionpublishing.com
Listing of available publications.

Enquiries:
Enquiries to: Honorary Secretary

Founded:
1844

Organisation type and purpose:
Learned society (membership is by subscription), present number of members: 357, registered charity (charity number 208082).

Subject coverage:
Natural history; botany; zoology mainly of Britain and NW Europe but also of wider interest.

Printed publications:
Annual Report (yearly)
Ray Society Volumes (irregular, 172 vols to date)
Order printed publications from: Scion Publishing Ltd, The Old Hayloft, Vantage Buisness Park, Bloxham Road, Banbury, OX16 9UX; e-mail: info@scionpublishing.com; tel: 01295 258577; fax: 01295 275624
Concessionary sales to members are available through the Honorary Secretary

Microform publications:
Order microform publications from: Microform Academic Publishers, Microform (Wakefield) Limited, Main Street, East Andsley, Wakefield, WF3 2AT
For purchase of any Ray Society 'I' publications, see addresses for printed publications

Electronic and video publications:
Out of print works available as CD-ROMs
Order electronic and video publications from: Pisces Conservation Ltd, IRC House, The Square, Pennington, Lymington, SO41 8GN; e-mail: pisces@irchouse.demon.co.uk; tel: 01590 676622; fax: 01590 675599

Publications list:
Available online and in print

Access to staff:
Contact by letter, by telephone, by fax, by e-mail and via website. Appointment necessary.
Hours: Mon to Fri, 0900 to 1700
Special comments: Visitor regulations for the Natural History Museum apply.

Access for disabled people:
Parking provided, ramped entry, access to all public areas, toilet facilities

RAYNAUD'S & SCLERODERMA ASSOCIATION

112 Crewe Road, Alsager, Cheshire, ST7 2JA

Tel: 01270 872776
Fax: 01270 883556
E-mail: info@reynauds.org.uk

Website:
http://www.raynauds.org.uk

Enquiries:
Enquiries to: Chief Executive

Founded:
1982

Organisation type and purpose:
Membership association (membership is by subscription), voluntary organisation, registered charity (charity number 326306), research organisation.

Subject coverage:
Raynaud's, Scleroderma, Vibration White Finger, Sjögren's Syndrome, chilblains, Systemic Lupus Erythematosus, Teenage Raynaud's, Erythromelalgia, advances in research, funding for research.

Printed publications:
Leaflets available on the following:
Chilblains
Erythromelalgia
Raynaud's Phenomenon
Scleroderma
Skin Care
Sjörgren's Syndrome
Systemic Lupus Erythematosus
Teenage Raynaud's
Vibration White Finger
CREST (Limited cutaneous systemic sclerosis)
Localised scleroderma in children
Health Professional booklets on the following:
Oral and Dental Aspects of Scleroderma
Raynaud's and Scleroderma, A Reminder for GPs
The Role of the Nurse in Raynaud's and Scleroderma
The Role of a Podiatrist in Raynaud's and Scleroderma
The Role of the Physiotherapist in Raynaud's and Scleroderma
The Role of the Occupational Therapist in Raynaud's and Scleroderma
Available for purchase are the following books:
Scleroderma Patients Booklet
There Are More Questions Than Answers

Electronic and video publications:
DVDs available for purchase

Publications list:
Available in print

Access to staff:
Contact by letter, by telephone, by fax, by e-mail, in person and via website
Hours: Mon to Fri, 0900 to 1700
Special comments: Answering machine available.

Access for disabled people:
Parking provided, level entry, toilet facilities

RE-SOLV – THE SOCIETY FOR THE PREVENTION OF SOLVENT AND VOLATILE SUBSTANCE ABUSE

Acronym or abbreviation: Re-Solv

30a High Street, Stone, Staffordshire, ST15 8AW

Tel: 01785 817885
Fax: 01785 813205
E-mail: information@re-solv.org

Website:
http://www.re-solv.org
Comprehensive information about volatile substance abuse in the United Kingdom.

Enquiries:
Enquiries to: Information Officer

Founded:
1984

Organisation type and purpose:
National organisation, membership association (membership is by subscription), registered charity (charity number 326732).
Aims to prevent death, suffering and crime that may result as a consequence of solvent and volatile substance abuse. Provides information and support to anyone concerned about or interested in solvent and volatile substance misuse issues.

Subject coverage:
Prevention of solvent and volatile substance abuse.

Trade and statistical information:
Solvent and volatile substance abuse statistics, i.e. mortality statistics.

Printed publications:
Training Pack for Social Services Professionals (£20.00)
Toxic Agents Primary School Pack (£35)
Youth Workers Activities Pack (£20)
Greatest Danger leaflet (£4.50 for 50 copies)
Cupboard leaflet (£15 for 50 copies)
Order printed publications from: Website

Electronic and video publications:
A Loaded Gun (DVD with workbook, £20)
The Silent Killer (DVD with booklet, £10)
Order electronic and video publications from: Website

Publications list:
Available online and in print

Access to staff:
Contact by letter, by telephone, by fax, by e-mail and via website
Hours: Mon to Fri, 0900 to 1700; closed public holidays
Special comments: Answerphone services are in operation outside office hours and provide referral details.

Access to building, collection or gallery:
No access other than to staff

Branches:
Re-Solv North East
7 Burrow Street, South Shileds, Tyne and Wear, NE33 1PP; tel: 0191 497 5522; e-mail: northeast@re-solv.org
Re-Solv Scotland
Suite 6, 53–58 South Avenue, Blantyre Industrial Estate, Blantyre, Lanarkshire, G72 0XB; tel: 07505 000024; e-mail: scotland@re-solv.org
Re-Solv Wales
First Floor, 21A Berriew Street, Welshpool, Powys, SY21 7SQ; tel: 01938 556790; e-mail: wales@re-solv.org

READING BOROUGH COUNCIL

Civic Offices, PO Box 17, The Civic Centre, Reading, Berkshire, RG1 7TD

Tel: 0118 939 0900\ Minicom no. 0118 939 0700
Fax: 0118 958 9770

Website:
http://www.reading.gov.uk
A-Z numbers to contact and much more.

Enquiries:
Enquiries to: Public Relations Manager
Direct tel: 0118 939 0333
Direct fax: 0118 939 0282
Direct e-mail: carl.welham@reading.gov.uk

Founded:
1998

Organisation type and purpose:
Local government body.

Subject coverage:
All aspects of local government.

Printed publications:
A guide to getting around the town – buses
A guide to getting around the town – cyclists
Agenda21
Annual report to tenants
Equalities Annual report
Cllr Posters
Equalities statement
Moving Reading Forward (traffic problems and proposals)
On your Bike
Safer Reading Campaign

Electronic and video publications:
Reading (CD-ROM)

Publications list:
Available in print

continued overleaf

Access to staff:
Contact by letter, by telephone, by fax, by e-mail, in person and via website
Hours: Mon to Fri, 0900 to 1700

Access for disabled people:
Parking provided, ramped entry, access to all public areas, toilet facilities

READING CENTRAL LIBRARY

Abbey Square, Reading, Berkshire, RG1 3BQ

Tel: 0118 901 5950
Fax: 0118 901 5954
E-mail: info@readinglibraries.org.uk

Website:
http://www.readinglibraries.org.uk

Enquiries:
Enquiries to: Librarian

Founded:
1883

Organisation type and purpose:
Local government body, public library.

Subject coverage:
General; business information; information on Reading and Berkshire.

Information services:
Internet access provided free of charge at all libraries.

Museum or gallery collection, archive, or library special collection:
Local Studies Library
Mary Russell Mitford collection
Vocal sets collection

Library catalogue:
All or part available online and in-house

Publications list:
Available in print

Access to staff:
Contact by letter, by telephone, by fax, by e-mail, in person and via website
Hours: Mon, Fri, 0900 to 1730; Tue, Thu, 0900 to 1900; Wed, 0900 to 1700; Sat, 0930 to 1700

Access to building, collection or gallery:
No access other than to staff
Hours: Mon, Fri, 0900 to 1730; Tue, Thu, 0900 to 1900; Wed, 0900 to 1700; Sat, 0930 to 1700

Access for disabled people:
Level entry, access to all public areas, toilet facilities

Branch libraries:
Battle Library
    tel: 0118 901 5100; fax: 0118 901 5101
Caversham Library
    tel: 0118 901 5103; fax: 0118 901 5104
Palmer Park Library
    tel: 0118 901 5106; fax: 0118 901 5107
Southcote Library
    tel: 0118 901 5109; fax: 0118 901 5110
Tilehurst Library
    tel: 0118 901 5112; fax: 0118 901 5113
Whitley Library
    tel: 0118 901 5115; fax: 0118 901 5116

Parent body:
Reading Borough Council
    Civic Offices, Reading, Berkshire, RG1 7TD; tel: 0118 939 0900

RECORD OFFICE FOR LEICESTERSHIRE, LEICESTER AND RUTLAND

Long Street, Wigston Magna, Leicester, LE18 2AH

Tel: 0116 257 1080
Fax: 0116 257 1120
E-mail: recordoffice@leics.gov.uk

Enquiries:
Enquiries to: Chief Archivist

Organisation type and purpose:
Local government body.
Record Office.

Subject coverage:
Local archives and local studies including manuscripts, books, maps, photographs and all other archive material relating to Leicestershire, Leicester and Rutland.

Museum or gallery collection, archive, or library special collection:
Collections include:
Books, magazines and pamphlets on Leicestershire and Rutland
Census returns for Leicestershire and Rutland 1841–1901 on microfilm
Directories and electoral registers
Files of local newspapers
Illustrations of people and places
Oral history tapes and sound recordings
Ordnance Survey maps
Photographs and archive films
Archives of:
Leicestershire and Rutland County Councils
Borough of Leicester (from 1103)
Courts of Quarter Sessions and Petty Sessions
Poor Law Unions
Probate Registry (wills from 1858)
Anglican and nonconformist churches
Archdeaconry of Leicester (including wills and inventories from 1496)
Landed estates and families
Solicitors, commercial firms and manufacturers
Clubs, societies and other organisations
Military, Leicestershire Regiment

Non-library collection catalogue:
All or part available online and in-house

Library catalogue:
All or part available online and in-house

Printed publications:
Service leaflet (free)
Various pamphlets on aspects of the service and the stock

Access to staff:
Contact by letter, by telephone, by fax, by e-mail and in person
Hours: Mon, Tue, Thu, 0915 to 1700; Wed, 0915 to 1930; Fri, 0915 to 1645; Sat, 0915 to 1215
Special comments: Readers ticket required (proof of name and address is necessary).

Access for disabled people:
Parking provided, ramped entry, access to all public areas, toilet facilities

Constituent part of:
Leicestershire County Council's Community Services

Part funded by:
Leicester City Council and Rutland County Council

RECORD SOCIETY OF LANCASHIRE AND CHESHIRE

John Rylands University of Manchester Library, Oxford Road, Manchester, M13 9PP

E-mail: rslc@lineone.net

Enquiries:
Enquiries to: Council Secretary

Founded:
1878

Organisation type and purpose:
Membership association, registered charity (charity number 500434).
To transcribe and publish original documents relating to the two palatine counties.

Non-library collection catalogue:
All or part available online

Printed publications:
Over 140 volumes including (from vol 110):

A Lancashire weaver's journal, 1856–64, 1872–75 John O'Neil, Low Moor, Clitheroe (ed Brigg M, Vol 122, £7.50)
Index to wills and administrations formerly preserved in the probate registry, Chester, 1826–30 (ed Dickinson R, vol 113, £9)
Odyssey of an Edwardian Liberal: the political diary of Richard Durning Holt, MP (ed Dutton D J, Vol 129, £18)
Stockport probate records, 1578–1619 (eds Philips C B and Smith J H, Vol 124, £15)
The great diurnal of Nicholas Blundell of Little Crosby, 1702–28 (eds Tyrer F and Bagley J J, Vols 110,112,114, set £30)

Microform publications:
Volumes 1 to 109
Order microform publications from: Chadwyck-Healey Limited, The Quorum, Barnwell Road, Cambridge, CB5 8SW, tel: 01223 215512

Publications list:
Available online and in print

Access to staff:
Contact by letter and by e-mail
Hours: Mon to Fri, 0900 to 1700

RECRUITMENT AND EMPLOYMENT CONFEDERATION

Acronym or abbreviation: REC

3rd Floor, Steward House, 16a Commercial Way, Woking, Surrey, GU21 1ET

Tel: 020 7462 3260
Fax: 01483 714979
E-mail: info@rec.uk.com

Website:
http://www.rec.uk.com

Enquiries:
Enquiries to: Chief Executive

Founded:
1930

Organisation type and purpose:
Professional body (membership is by qualification), present number of members: 6000 Corporate, 7000 Individual, service industry, registered charity (charity number 803141), university department or institute, suitable for ages: 18+, training organisation.

Subject coverage:
Employment consultancy and agency practice; employment legislation relevant to employment agencies; professional qualifications in recruitment and employment agency practice.

Printed publications:
Distance learning materials
Recruitment Matters (magazine, for members)

Access to staff:
Contact by letter, by telephone, by fax, by e-mail and via website
Hours: Mon to Fri, 0830 to 1730

Other office:
REC
    36–38 Mortimer Street, London, W1W 7RG; tel: 020 7462 3260; fax: 020 7255 2878

REDBRIDGE PUBLIC LIBRARIES

Central Library, Clements Road, Ilford, Essex, IG1 1EA

Tel: 020 8708 2414
Fax: 020 8708 2571
E-mail: central.library@redbridge.gov.uk

Website:
http://www.redbridge.gov.uk

Enquiries:
Enquiries to: Chief Librarian
Other contacts: Local Studies Librarian

Organisation type and purpose:
Public library.

Subject coverage:
General; social problems and services, local history of Redbridge, insurance, youth organisations, public health, family history.

Museum or gallery collection, archive, or library special collection:
Local History including part of the Brand Collection (Ilford and Essex history)

Non-library collection catalogue:
All or part available online and in-house

Library catalogue:
All or part available online

Access to staff:
Contact by letter, by telephone, by e-mail and in person
Hours: Mon to Fri, 0930 to 2000; Sat, 0930 to 1600

REDCAR AND CLEVELAND COUNCIL

Town Hall, Fabian Road, South Bank, Middlesbrough, Cleveland, TS6 9AR

Tel: 01642 444000
Fax: 01642 444584

Enquiries:
Enquiries to: Chief Executive

Organisation type and purpose:
Local government body.
Unitary authority.

Access to staff:
Contact by letter, by telephone and by fax.
Appointment necessary.
Hours: Mon to Fri, 0900 to 1700

REDCAR CENTRAL LIBRARY

Reference Library, Coatham Road, Redcar, Cleveland, TS10 1RP

Tel: 01642 489292
Fax: 01642 492253
E-mail: reference_library@redcar-cleveland.gov.uk

Website:
http://www.redcar-cleveland.gov.uk/libraries/index2.htm
Borough library services, including opening hours.

Enquiries:
Enquiries to: Librarian

Organisation type and purpose:
Local government body.
Public library.

Subject coverage:
General reference collection; local history collection, relating largely to North Yorkshire and East Cleveland area; family history resources.

Museum or gallery collection, archive, or library special collection:
Family History Resources: largely in microform, for East Cleveland area, some national coverage
Local history collection: mainly covering the old North Riding of Yorkshire, East Cleveland and the present borough

Non-library collection catalogue:
All or part available online and in-house

Library catalogue:
All or part available online

Access to staff:
Contact by letter, by telephone, by e-mail, in person and via website
Hours: Mon, Tue, Wed, Fri, 0930 to 1900; Thu, 0930 to 1700; Sat, 0930 to 1230
Special comments: Upstairs, lift available.

Access for disabled people:
Level entry, access to all public areas, toilet facilities

Connections with:
Redcar and Cleveland Borough Council
Chief Executive's Department, Redcar and Cleveland House, Kirkleatham Street, Redcar, TS10 1XX
Teesside Archives
Exchange House, 6 Marton Road, Middlesbrough, TS1 1DB; tel: 01642 248321; fax: 01642 248391; e-mail: teesside_archives@middlesbrough.gov.uk

REDDITCH LIBRARY

15 Market Place, Redditch, Worcestershire, B98 8AR

Tel: 01527 63291
Fax: 01527 68571
E-mail: redditchlib@worcestershire.gov.uk

Enquiries:
Enquiries to: Librarian

Organisation type and purpose:
Local government body, public library.

Subject coverage:
Local history of the Redditch area, including Bordesley Abbey, the needle industry, and Redditch New Town.

Museum or gallery collection, archive, or library special collection:
Needle District Almanacs (annual directories 1873–1936)
Redditch census schedules (1841–91)
Redditch Indicator (from 1859)

Non-library collection catalogue:
All or part available online

Library catalogue:
All or part available online

Access to staff:
Contact by letter
Hours: Mon, Thu, Fri, 0930 to 2000; Tue, Wed, 0930 to 1730; Sat, 0930 to 1730
Special comments: Proof of name and address required.

Parent body:
Worcestershire County Council

REFEREES' ASSOCIATION

Unit 12, Ensign Business Centre, Westwood Way, Westwood Business Park, Coventry, CV4 8JA

Tel: 024 7642 0360
Fax: 024 7767 7234
E-mail: ra@footballreferee.org

Website:
http://www.footballreferee.org

Enquiries:
Enquiries to: General Secretary
Direct e-mail: arthur@footballreferee.org

Founded:
1908

Organisation type and purpose:
Membership association (membership is by subscription), training organisation.

Subject coverage:
Implementation of the laws of association football. Recruitment and training of referees.

Printed publications:
Refereeing (a joint publication with the Football Association, quarterly)

Access to staff:
Contact by letter, by telephone, by fax and by e-mail. Appointment necessary.
Hours: Mon to Fri, 0830 to 1630

REFINED SUGAR ASSOCIATION

Acronym or abbreviation: RSA

154 Bishopsgate, London, EC2M 4LN

Tel: 020 7377 2113
Fax: 020 7247 2481
E-mail: durhamn@sugar-assoc.co.uk

Enquiries:
Enquiries to: Secretary

Founded:
1891

Organisation type and purpose:
International organisation, trade association (membership is by election or invitation), present number of members: 115.

Subject coverage:
Sugar.

REFRACTORY USERS FEDERATION

Acronym or abbreviation: RUF

5th Floor, Broadway House, Tothill Street, London, SW1H 9NQ

Tel: 020 7799 2020
Fax: 020 7233 1930

Enquiries:
Enquiries to: Executive Secretary

Founded:
1945

Organisation type and purpose:
Trade association (membership is by subscription), present number of members: 10.

Subject coverage:
Matters relating to refractory contracting, industrial relations, terms and conditions of employment for refractory bricklayers and labourers, and training.

Printed publications:
Blue Booklet Agreement (for refractory bricklayers)
Red Booklet Agreement (for bricklayers labourers)

Access to staff:
Contact by letter, by telephone and by fax
Hours: Mon to Fri, 0900 to 1700

REFUGEE ACTION

The Old Fire Station, 150 Waterloo Road, London, SE1 8SB

Tel: 020 7654 7700
Fax: 020 7654 0696
E-mail: info@refugee-action.org.uk

Website:
http://www.refugee-action.org.uk
Activities, campaigns, news, information, publications, details of local offices.
http://www.refugee-action.org.uk/RAP/default.aspx
Refugee Awareness Project microsite, challenging myths and misinformation about refugees.

Founded:
1981

Organisation type and purpose:
Registered charity (number 283660), an independent national charity that works with refugees to build new lives in the UK.
Provides advice and support to asylum seekers and refugees in the North West, the Midlands, London, South West and South Central. Exists to enable refugees to build new lives, through advice and information, community development, enhancing opportunity, and campaigning for refugee rights.

Subject coverage:
Refugee Action's Asylum Advice teams provide a reception service for newly arrived asylum seekers, as well as advice and advocacy. The Choices service provides independent advice to asylum seekers considering returning voluntarily to their country of origin. Refugee Action's community development workers promote the development of

continued overleaf

refugee communities. It also runs innovative projects to enhance opportunities for refugees and asylum seekers.

Printed publications:
A wide range of publications and videos on the following topics: general, arts, education, training and employment, health, women, young people, housing, handbooks and directories, voluntary return (most are £5, incl. p&p; maternity video £20 incl. p&p)
Order printed publications from: Communications office, tel: 020 7654 7705; e-mail: publications@ refugee-action.org.uk

Electronic and video publications:
Annual report
Asylum advice leaflets and information in a range of languages
Order electronic and video publications from: Download from website

Publications list:
Available online

Access to staff:
Contact by letter, by telephone, by fax and by e-mail
Special comments: Contact local regional offices for asylum advice, community development or volunteering enquiries.

Branches:
Offices across 10 regions of England

REFUGEE COUNCIL

Acronym or abbreviation: BRC

240–250 Ferndale Road, Brixton, London, SW9 8BB

Tel: 020 7346 6700
Fax: 020 7346 6701

Website:
http://www.refugeecouncil.org.uk

Enquiries:
Enquiries to: Media Officer
Direct tel: 020 7346 1214
Direct e-mail: philippa.mcintyre@refugeecouncil .org.uk

Organisation type and purpose:
Voluntary organisation, registered charity (charity number 1014576).

Subject coverage:
Asylum and refugee issues in the UK.

Non-library collection catalogue:
All or part available in-house

Library catalogue:
All or part available in-house

Printed publications:
Order printed publications from: e-shop: http:// www.refugeecouncil.org.uk

Publications list:
Available online

Access to staff:
Contact by letter, by telephone, by fax, by e-mail and in person. Appointment necessary.
Hours: Mon to Fri, 1000 to 1700

Access to building, collection or gallery:
No prior appointment required

Member organisation of:
European Council on Refugees and Exiles (ECRE)
Human Rights Documentation Systems
International Refugee Documentation Network (IRDN)

REGENT'S COLLEGE LIBRARY

Library, Inner Circle, Regent's Park, London, NW1 4NS

Tel: 020 7487 7448

Website:
http://www.regents.ac.uk/library.htm
Library home page.

Enquiries:
Enquiries to: Head Librarian
Direct e-mail: collinsm@regents.ac.uk

Founded:
1985

Organisation type and purpose:
College of higher education.

Subject coverage:
Business, management, psychotherapy and counselling.

Non-library collection catalogue:
All or part available online

Library catalogue:
All or part available online

Access to staff:
Contact by letter, by telephone and by e-mail. Appointment necessary. Access for members only.
Hours: Mon to Fri, 0900 to 1700

REGENT'S PARK COLLEGE

Formal name: Regent's Park College, University of Oxford
Acronym or abbreviation: RPC

Pusey Street, Oxford, OX1 2LB

Tel: 01865 288120
Fax: 01865 288121
E-mail: library@regents.ox.ac.uk

Website:
http://www.rpc.ox.ac.uk
Information on Regent's Park College and various links.
http://www.lib.ox.ac.uk/libraries/guides/REG.html
Brief details about libraries.
http://solo.bodleian.ox.ac.uk
The University catalogue, of which the Regent's Park College holdings are a part.

Enquiries:
Enquiries to: College Librarian
Direct e-mail: emma.walsh@regents.ox.ac.uk
Other contacts: Assistant Librarian (Main Library); Archivist and Library Assistant (Angus Library)

Founded:
1810

Organisation type and purpose:
Registered charity (charity number 309710). Permanent Private Hall of the University of Oxford.
The Angus library also houses the library of the Baptist Union of Great Britain and the archives of the Baptist Missionary Society.

Subject coverage:
Baptist history.

Museum or gallery collection, archive, or library special collection:
Baptist Historical Society, library
Baptist Missionary Society Archives
Baptist Union of Great Britain: minute books, some records, library
David Nicholls Collection: separate location from both libraries
4,000 books on theology, church and state, politics, philosophy, Caribbean studies (especially Haiti)

Non-library collection catalogue:
All or part available online and in-house

Library catalogue:
All or part available online and in-house

Printed publications:
Angus Library, conditions of use
Sources for the study of Baptist History (offprint from the Baptist Quarterly, xxxiv, 6 April 1992, £2)

Microform publications:
200 35mm reels

Electronic and video publications:
Photographs, glass slides, audiotapes, videos

Publications list:
Available online

Access to staff:
Contact by letter, by telephone, by fax and by e-mail. Appointment necessary. Letter of introduction required.
Hours: Mon to Fri, 0930 to 1600
Special comments: College Library: members only. Angus Library: by appointment, with references.

Access to building, collection or gallery:
Hours: Mon to Fri, 0900 to 1700

REGIMENTAL OFFICE ROYAL IRISH REGIMENT

5 Waring Street, Belfast, BT1 2EW

Tel: 028 9023 2086
Fax: 028 9023 2086
E-mail: nirmuseum@yahoo.co.uk

Website:
http://rurmuseum.tripod.com/

Enquiries:
Enquiries to: Curator

Organisation type and purpose:
Professional body.

Subject coverage:
History of the Royal Irish Regiment and the Royal Ulster Rifles.

REGISTER OF APPAREL AND TEXTILE DESIGNERS

Acronym or abbreviation: RATD

5 Portland Place, London, W1B 1PW

Tel: 020 7636 5577
Fax: 020 7636 7848
E-mail: laurian.daries@ukfe.5portlandplace.org.uk

Enquiries:
Enquiries to: Manager

Founded:
1986

Organisation type and purpose:
Trade association (membership is by subscription), present number of members: over 400, consultancy.

Subject coverage:
Design; clothing; textiles; printed textiles; woven textiles; sourcing freelance designers for manufacturers and retailers in the UK and overseas; help and advice to freelance designers who are members of the Register.

Museum or gallery collection, archive, or library special collection:
Library of information relevant to freelance designers

Printed publications:
Specialist Services Directory
Newsletter

Publications list:
Available in print

Access to staff:
Contact by letter, by telephone, by fax and by e-mail. Appointment necessary. Access for members only.
Hours: Mon to Fri, 0900 to 1700
Special comments: Access only available to members of the Register of Apparel and Textile Designers.

Access to building, collection or gallery:
No prior appointment required

Parent bodies:
British Clothing Industry Association
tel: 020 7636 7515
UK Fashion Exports
tel: 020 7636 5577

REGISTER OF UNUSUAL MICRO-CARS

Acronym or abbreviation: RUM Cars

School House Farm, Boarden Lane, Hawkenbury, Staplehurst, Kent, TN12 0EB

Tel: 01580 891377
E-mail: jeanrumcars@cs.com

Enquiries:
Enquiries to: Secretary
Other contacts: Editor tel: 01908 321737 for magazine input.

Founded:
1980

Organisation type and purpose:
National organisation, membership association (membership is by subscription).

Subject coverage:
Three and four wheeled post-war (1947 onwards) road going vehicles with engines of 700cc or less, manufactured in small numbers, small electric vehicles and invalid carriages.

Museum or gallery collection, archive, or library special collection:
Sales brochure, contemporary road tests etc, originals and photostats of magazine articles on all kinds of micro-cars

Printed publications:
RUM Car News (magazine, quarterly)

Access to staff:
Contact by letter, by telephone and by e-mail. Appointment necessary.
Hours: any day, before 2030

Access to building, collection or gallery:
Prior appointment required

REGISTERED NURSING HOME ASSOCIATION

Acronym or abbreviation: RNHA

John Hewitt House, Tunnel Lane, Kings Norton, Birmingham, B30 3JN

Tel: 0121 451 1088
Fax: 0121 486 3175
E-mail: info@rnha.co.uk

Website:
http://www.rnha.co.uk

Enquiries:
Enquiries to: Chief Executive

Founded:
1968

Organisation type and purpose:
Advisory body, trade association (membership is by subscription), present number of members: 1400, service industry.
Independent nursing homes, clinics and hospitals registered under the Care Standards Act 2000.

Subject coverage:
Advice and support, including legal advice, to members; assistance to members of the public in looking for a place in a nursing home; lobbying government and other official bodies.

Library catalogue:
All or part available in-house

Printed publications:
Courier-Bulletin (members only)
Nursing Home News (newspaper, members only, 6 times a year)
Operating Manual (guidelines and standard forms, members only)
Reference Book (£50 to non-members)
Special studies

Publications list:
Available in print

Access to staff:
Contact by letter, by telephone, by fax and by e-mail. Appointment necessary.

Hours: Mon to Thur, 0830 to 1630; Fri, 0830 to 1600

Access for disabled people:
Parking provided

Founder member of:
Independent Care Organisations Network (ICON)
Joint Care Council (JCC)

REGISTRAR OF PUBLIC LENDING RIGHT

Acronym or abbreviation: PLR

Richard House, Sorbonne Close, Stockton-on-Tees, TS17 6DA

Tel: 01642 604699
Fax: 01642 615641
E-mail: theregistrar@plr.uk.com

Website:
http://www.plr.uk.com
The registration service; library information; all about PLR; media centre.

Enquiries:
Enquiries to: Registrar's Personal Assistant

Founded:
1979

Organisation type and purpose:
National government body.
Makes payments to authors for loans of their books from public libraries.

Subject coverage:
Public library book issues and associated statistics.

Printed publications:
Writers Talk
Annual Press Release
Annual Report and Accounts
Information for Authors leaflet
Whose Loan is it Anyway, Essays in Celebration of PLR's 20th Anniversary

Publications list:
Available in print

Access to staff:
Contact by letter, by telephone, by fax, by e-mail and via website. Appointment necessary.
Hours: Mon to Thu, 0900 to 1700; Fri, 0900 to 1630

Funded by:
Department for Culture, Media and Sport
tel: 020 7211 6000; fax: 020 7211 6210

REGISTRY TRUST LIMITED

Acronym or abbreviation: RTL

153–157 Cleveland Street, London, W1T 6QW

Tel: 020 7380 0133
Fax: 020 7388 0672
E-mail: info@registry-trust.org.uk

Website:
http://www.registry-trust.org.uk

Founded:
1986

Organisation type and purpose:
Register of Judgments, Orders and Fines (England and Wales).
Register of Decrees (Scotland).
Registers of Judgments (Northern Ireland, Republic of Ireland, Jersey and Isle of Man).

Subject coverage:
Court money judgments.

Access to staff:
Contact by letter, by telephone, by e-mail and via website. All charged.
Hours: Mon to Fri, 0900 to 1700
Special comments: The staff of Registry Trust Limited do not accept unsolicited sales calls.

Access to building, collection or gallery:
There is no public access to the building or to Registry Trust Limited

RELATE

Herbert Gray College, Little Church Street, Rugby, Warwickshire, CV21 3AP

Tel: 01788 573241
Fax: 01788 535007
E-mail: enquiries@relate.org.uk

Website:
http://www.relate.org.uk
Relate centre addresses. Relate bookshop information. Training.

Enquiries:
Enquiries to: Information Officer
Direct e-mail: kim.atkins@relate.org.uk
Other contacts: Communications Assistant

Founded:
1938

Organisation type and purpose:
Registered charity, training organisation.
Co-ordinates the activities of local marriage guidance centres.

Subject coverage:
Relationship counselling, marriage, family life and personal relationships and educational programmes related to those relationships, sexual problems, divorce, stress and depression.

Printed publications:
Large range of books available through bookshop, Rugby

Access to staff:
Contact by letter, by telephone, by fax and by e-mail. Appointment necessary.
Hours: Mon to Fri, 0900 to 1700

Access to building, collection or gallery:
No access other than to staff

Other addresses:
Local centres in England, Wales and Northern Ireland (see Yellow Pages)

RELATIVES AND RESIDENTS ASSOCIATION

Acronym or abbreviation: RRA

5 Tavistock Place, London, WC1H 9SN

Tel: 020 7692 4302 (admin)
Fax: 020 7916 6093
E-mail: relres@totalise.co.uk

Enquiries:
Enquiries to: Administrator
Other contacts: Advice Line Worker/Co-ordinator for advice offered to callers on the advice line.

Founded:
1992

Organisation type and purpose:
National organisation, membership association (membership is by subscription), voluntary organisation, registered charity (charity number 1020194).

Subject coverage:
Issues relating to long-term care for older people in, or considering admission to, residential or nursing homes. Offers mutual support and advice, facilitates the setting up of groups of relatives in homes. Has a Black and minority ethnic involvement and guides for good practice.

Printed publications:
Involving Relatives and Friends (book, 2001, £10)
As Others See Us (research study including keynote messages, report training pack £26 for members, £29 for non-members, report alone, £10 and £11 respectively, keynote messages £4 for both members and non-members)
Setting Up Relatives' Groups in Homes (1996, £2.50 members, £3 non-members)
Starting up a Local Group (£3 members, £3.50 non-members)
I Have Come to Visit my Wife (Koschland B, 1996, £2 members, £2.50 non-members)

continued overleaf

African Caribbean Elders Directory of Sheltered, Very Sheltered Housing, Residential Care Homes & One Nursing Care Unit (£2.50 members, £3 non-members)
Introductory leaflets (free to individuals, bulk copies available to other organisations: 25 for £3, 50 for £6 and 100 for £12)
Changes and Challenges in Later Life (£10 inc. p&p)

Publications list:
Available in print

Access to staff:
Contact by letter, by telephone and by e-mail
Hours: Advice Line: Mon to Fri, 1000 to 1230 and 1330 to 1700
Admin: Mon to Fri, 0900 to 1700

Access to building, collection or gallery:
No access other than to staff

RELIEF FUND FOR ROMANIA

Acronym or abbreviation: RFFR

54–62 Regent Street, London, W1B 5RE

Tel: 020 7733 7018
Fax: 020 7737 4960
E-mail: mail@relieffundforromania.co.uk

Website:
http://www.relieffundforromania.co.uk

Enquiries:
Enquiries to: Executive Director
Other contacts: Project Director for grant applications.

Founded:
1989

Organisation type and purpose:
International organisation, registered charity (charity number 1046737).

Subject coverage:
Aid and development for children and adults in Romania's institutions, focus on medical improvements, mental health, disabled issues and groups, funding emerging Romanian NGO sector.

Museum or gallery collection, archive, or library special collection:
Photo library and videos of Romanian institutions 1989 to present day
Press cuttings of socio-political and charity subjects from 1989 to present

Access to staff:
Contact by letter, by telephone and by fax
Hours: Mon to Fri, 0930 to 1830

RELIGIOUS EDUCATION

University of Birmingham, Selly Oak Campus, Weoley Park Road, Birmingham, B29 6LL

Tel: 0121 415 8290
Fax: 0121 414 5619
E-mail: g.m.teece@bham.ac.uk

Enquiries:
Enquiries to: Head of Centre
Direct e-mail: c.b.oconnor@bham.ac.uk

Founded:
1974

Formerly called:
Regional Religious Education Centre (Midlands) (year of change 1994)

Organisation type and purpose:
University department or institute.
To promote good practice in religious education.

Subject coverage:
Multi-faith religious education, moral education, personal and social development in education, research and curriculum development.

Museum or gallery collection, archive, or library special collection:
Artefacts

Audio cassettes
Posters
Slides
Videos

Printed publications:
How do I teach RE? (teacher's manual, £10)
How to Write Your School Policy for RE (£10)
Primary Resource packs on Islam and Hinduism
Teacher's manuals on Christianity, Islam and Judaism (£11.50 each)
Westhill Project: RE 5–16 Teachers and pupils books and photopacks (major religious and life themes)

Access to staff:
Contact by letter, by telephone, by fax, by e-mail and in person. Appointment necessary.
Hours: Mon to Fri, 0900 to 1700

Connections with:
National Association of SACREs (NASACRE)

RELIGIOUS SOCIETY OF FRIENDS (QUAKERS) – BRITAIN YEARLY MEETING

Friends House, 173–177 Euston Road, London, NW1 2BJ

Tel: 020 7663 1135
Fax: 020 7663 1001
E-mail: library@quaker.org.uk

Website:
http://www.quaker.org.uk/library
Library information, link to catalogue and subject guides, as part of British Quaker website.

Enquiries:
Enquiries to: Librarian

Founded:
c.1650

Organisation type and purpose:
Religious body, present number of members: c.16,500, voluntary organisation, registered charity (charity number 1127633).
Library for the storage and dissemination of information about Quakers and repository of the central archives of the Religious Society of Friends in Britain and the local archives of London Quaker meetings; point of contact for the Friends Historical Society.

Subject coverage:
Quakers, especially Quaker thought, history and Quakerism, peace, anti-slavery, conscription.

Museum or gallery collection, archive, or library special collection:
Central archives of the Society in Britain
Digest registers of births, marriages and burials on microfilm (search fee payable)
Local Quaker archives for London and Middlesex area
Manuscripts, tracts and pictures
Printed material on Quakers since the mid-17th century
Records of other bodies with Quaker associations

Non-library collection catalogue:
All or part available online and in-house

Library catalogue:
All or part available online and in-house

Printed publications:
The following leaflets are also on the Library website:
Library Rules
Genealogical Sources
Picture Collection
Photocopying and microfilm printouts
The Quaker Calendar – dating of Quaker documents
Quaker Schools in Great Britain and Ireland
Conscientious Objectors and the Peace Movement in Britain 1914–1945
Sources: Abolition of the Slave Trade
Friends Ambulance Unit 1939–1959
Quaker Businesses in Britain : a historical list
Friends Service in the First World War

Elizabeth Fry

Microform publications:
Quaker collections on sale by World Microfilms, London and Academic Microforms, Wick, Scotland
Early English Books (University Microfilms International)
Film copies of some central archives
The Quaker Manuscript Collection (World Microfilms, London)
Quaker Official Correspondence (Academic Microforms, Wick)
Some MSS collections and other materials available direct
Order microform publications from: World Microfilms, London, W9 2HH; website: http:// www.microworld.uk.com
Academic Microforms Ltd, Wick, Scotland, KW1 4DD; website: http:// www.academicmicroforms.com

Access to staff:
Contact by letter, by telephone, by fax, by e-mail, in person and via website
Hours: Tue to Fri, 1000 to 1700
Mon to Fri, 0930 to 1700 for telephone queries
Special comments: Registration, with proof of ID and address, required for admission to the Library. Archives and manuscripts under 50 years old are not normally open. Charge for use of Digest registers of births, marriages & burials microfilms (appointment recommended).

Access to building, collection or gallery:
Wheel chair accessible

Access for disabled people:
Level entry, wheelchair accessible, toilet facilities
Special comments: Access to library reading room; access to basement restaurant by lift only, but level entry to cafe in ground floor Quaker Centre.

Parent body:
Britain Yearly Meeting of the Religious Society of Friends (Quakers)
Friends House, Euston Road, London NW1 2BJ; tel: 020 7663 1000; website: http://www.quaker .org.uk

REMAP

Formal name: Technical Help for Disabled People

D9, Chaucer Business Park, Kemsing, Sevenoaks, Kent, TN15 6YU

Tel: 0845 130 0456
Fax: 0845 130 0789
E-mail: data@remap.org.uk

Website:
http://www.remap.org.uk
Basic information and area contacts throughout the UK.

Founded:
1964

Organisation type and purpose:
Registered charity (charity number 1000456). Has 107 branches (panels) across UK.

Subject coverage:
Design, manufacture and supply or adaptation of equipment to meet the individual needs of a disabled person when there is no suitable equipment on the market; no general information.

Printed publications:
Yearbook and leaflets

Publications list:
Available in print

Access to staff:
Contact by letter, by telephone, by fax and by e-mail
Hours: Mon to Thu, 0930 to 1600; 24-hour answerphone

REMOTE SENSING AND PHOTOGRAMMETRY SOCIETY

Acronym or abbreviation: RSPSoc

School of Geography, University of Nottingham, University Park, Nottingham, NG7 2RD

Tel: 0115 951 5435
Fax: 0115 951 5249
E-mail: rspsoc@nottingham.ac.uk

Website:
http://www.rspsoc.org
Home page.

Enquiries:
Enquiries to: Executive Secretary
Direct tel: 0115 951 5435
Direct fax: 0115 951 5249
Direct e-mail: rspsoc@rspsoc.org

Founded:
2001

Organisation type and purpose:
Learned society (membership is by subscription), present number of members: 1,000, registered charity (charity number 292647).

Subject coverage:
Remote sensing; sensors; platforms; image processing; interpretation equipment; resource surveys; applications of remote sensing in land use, soil mapping, geology, geomorphology, hydrology, meteorology, oceanography; monitoring of pollution and natural hazards; organisations world-wide, photogrammetry.

Printed publications:
Newsletter (quarterly; includes list of publications)
The International Journal of Remote Sensing
The Photogrammetric Record (4 times a year)

Access to staff:
Contact by letter, by telephone, by fax and by e-mail
Hours: Mon to Fri, 0900 to 1700

Associate member of:
International Society for Photogrammetry and Remote Sensing
Joint Branch of International Remote Sensing Activities (JOBRESA)

RENAL ASSOCIATION, THE

Acronym or abbreviation: RA

Secretariat, Durford Mill, Petersfield, Hampshire, GU31 5AZ

Tel: 0870 458 4155
Fax: 0870 442 9940
E-mail: renal@mci-group.com

Website:
http://www.renal.org

Enquiries:
Enquiries to: General Secretary

Founded:
1950

Organisation type and purpose:
Learned society, registered charity (charity number 800733).

Subject coverage:
Research into renal disease, treatment of renal disease.

Printed publications:
Proceedings of the Association's Scientific
   Meetings are published in Kidney International
Provision of Services for Patients with Renal
   Failure (£6)
Treatment of Adult Patients with Renal Failure (£6)

Access to staff:
Contact by letter, by telephone, by fax and by e-mail
Hours: Mon to Fri, 0900 to 1700

Affiliated to:
European Renal Association
International Society of Nephrology

RENAULT CLASSIC CAR CLUB

Acronym or abbreviation: RCCC

5 Evesham Walk, Sandhurst, Berkshire, GU47 0YU

Website:
http://www.renaultclassiccarclub.com
Contact information, pictures and descriptions of models covered, links to other sites.

Enquiries:
Enquiries to: Membership Secretary

Founded:
2001

Organisation type and purpose:
International organisation, membership association (membership is by subscription), present number of members: 70.
Restoration and use of rear-engine Renaults, parts supply and advice, general purchase advice, workshop manuals – printed or on CD-ROM.

Subject coverage:
Restoration and use of classic rear-engine Renaults, parts availability, technical information, buying and selling of parts and cars. Anything that will assist members keeping rear-engine Renault cars on the road.

Museum or gallery collection, archive, or library special collection:
Various technical and workshop manuals

Printed publications:
Club Magazine
Workshop Manuals (enquire for prices)

Electronic and video publications:
Workshop Manuals (CD-ROM, enquire for prices)

Access to staff:
Contact by letter, by e-mail and via website
Hours: Mon to Fri, 0900 to 1700

RENEWABLEUK

Greencoat House, Francis Street, London, SW1P 1DH

Tel: 020 7901 3000
Fax: 020 7901 3001
E-mail: info@renewable-uk.com

Website:
http://www.bwea.com
Onshore and offshore wind, wave & tidal, small wind systems, aviation, Cymru, wind farms in the UK, health & safety, events, publications, news, jobs & courses, membership, company directory, members area; (new website is proposed following name change).

Founded:
1978

Formerly called:
British Wind Energy Association (BWEA) (year of change 2010)

Organisation type and purpose:
The trade and professional body for the UK wind and marine renewables industries, membership organisation (current number of members: 643 corporate members).
Primary purpose is to promote the use of wind, wave and tidal power in and around the UK; acts as a central point for information for members and a lobbying group to promote wind energy and marine renewables to government, industry, the media and the public; researches and finds solutions to current issues and generally acts as the forum for the UK wind, wave and tidal industry.

Subject coverage:
Renewable energy in the UK.

Electronic and video publications:
Real Power (quarterly newsletter)
Briefing Sheets on core wind energy topics
Annual Review
RePLAN (quarterly newsletter for councillors and planning officers in England and Wales)

Install (quarterly news bulletin for manufacturers and installers)
Responses to government consultations
Reports and studies
Order electronic and video publications from: website

Publications list:
Available online

Access to staff:
Contact by letter, by telephone, by fax and by e-mail

Also at:
RenewableUK – Cymru
Temple Court, 13A Cathedral Road, Caerdydd / Cardiff, CF11 9HA; tel: 029 2022 0700; e-mail: cymru@renewable-uk.com

RENFREWSHIRE COUNCIL

Council Headquarters, North Building, Cotton Street, Paisley, Renfrewshire, PA1 1WB

Tel: 0141 842 5000
Fax: 0141 840 3335
E-mail: chiefexex@renfrewshire.gov.uk

Website:
http://www.renfrewshire.gov.uk
Main headings: Welcome to Renfrewshire; The Council; Renfrewshire Magazine; What's On; Contact Us; The Millennium.

Enquiries:
Enquiries to: Chief Executive
Direct tel: 0141 840 3213
Direct fax: 0141 840 3349

Founded:
April 1996

Organisation type and purpose:
Local government body.

Access to staff:
Contact by letter, by telephone, by fax and in person
Hours: Mon to Thu, 0845 to 1645; Fri, 0845 to 1555

RENFREWSHIRE LIBRARY SERVICE

Paisley Museum, High Street, Paisley, PA1 2BA

Tel: 0141 840 6187
Fax: 0141 889 9240
E-mail: libraries.els@renfrewshire.gov.uk

Website:
http://www.renfrewshire.gov.uk
Council website, information on services.

Enquiries:
Enquiries to: Libraries Manager

Organisation type and purpose:
Local government body, public library.

Subject coverage:
General reference; local history; local government; community services; welfare; information for the elderly; library automation.

Museum or gallery collection, archive, or library special collection:
Bannatyne Club collection
Gardner collection (books printed in Paisley)
Local newspapers on microfiche
Maitland Club collection
Rowat collection

Library catalogue:
All or part available online and in-house

Access to staff:
Contact by letter, by telephone, by fax, by e-mail, in person and via website
Hours: Mon to Thu, 0900 to 1700; Fri, 0900 to 1600

Parent body:
Renfrewshire Council
   Education and Leisure Services

RENOLD PLC

Renold House, Styal Road, Wythenshawe, Manchester, M22 5WL

Tel: 0161 498 4500
Fax: 0161 437 7782
E-mail: enquiry@renold.com

Website:
http://www.renold.com

Enquiries:
Enquiries to: Marketing Manager
Direct tel: 0161 498 4531

Organisation type and purpose:
International organisation, manufacturing industry.

Subject coverage:
All aspects of mechanical power transmission, including: roller chains, wheels and pinions; conveying and elevating chains and wheels; gears; worm gear speed reducers; worm gear sets; spur, helical and spiral bevel gearboxes; shaft mounted gear units; geared motors; variable speed drives, couplings, clutches and brakes; sprag clutches for over-running, indexing and backstopping; vibratory shaker drives; power transmission accessories; machine tools; helical rotors for air compressors.

Museum or gallery collection, archive, or library special collection:
Fully classified catalogue collection of archival material relating to the establishment of the power transmission industry in the UK in the late 19th century

Publications list:
Available in print

Access to staff:
Contact by letter, by telephone, by e-mail and via website
Hours: Mon to Thu, 0900 to 1700; Fri, 0900 to 1600

REPETITIVE STRAIN INJURY AWARENESS

Acronym or abbreviation: RSI Awareness

Keytools Ltd, Abacus House, 1 Spring Crescent, Southampton, SO17 2FZ

Tel: 023 8029 4500
Fax: 023 8029 4501
E-mail: rsia@keytools.co.uk

Website:
http://rsi.org.uk

Enquiries:
Enquiries to: Director

Founded:
1989

Formerly called:
Repetitive Strain Injury Association

Organisation type and purpose:
To provide advice, information and support from those concerned about repetitive strain injury.

Subject coverage:
Repetitive strain injuries.

Information services:
Information website, events, advice, workshops, support groups.

Non-library collection catalogue:
All or part available online

Printed publications:
Factsheets (free)
Order printed publications from: Website (factsheets available for download)

Publications list:
Available online and in print

Access to staff:
Contact by letter, by telephone, by fax, by e-mail and via website
Hours: Mon to Fri, 0900 to 1700

Access to building, collection or gallery:
Prior appointment required

Access for disabled people:
Disabled access available
Special comments: By appointment.

RESCUE – THE BRITISH ARCHAEOLOGICAL TRUST

Acronym or abbreviation: RESCUE

15A Bull Plain, Hertford, SG14 1DX

Tel: 01992 553377
E-mail: rescue@rescue-archaeology.freeserve.co.uk

Website:
http://www.rescue-archaeology.org.uk
Basic information.

Enquiries:
Enquiries to: Membership Secretary

Founded:
1972

Organisation type and purpose:
National organisation, membership association (membership is by subscription), registered charity (charity number 1064836).
Independent charitable trust.
To promote and foster the discovery, excavation, preservation, recording and study of archaeology in Great Britain for the public benefit.

Subject coverage:
Organisation and funding of archaeology legislation and archaeology, current archaeological projects and news, recording methods, artefact excavation and storage methods.

Printed publications:
Competitive Tendering in Archaeology (£2.45 members, £2.95 non-members)
Conference Proceedings
First Aid for Finds (Watkinson. David & Neal, Virginia, £18 members, £21 non-members)
Recording Standing Buildings (Hutton B, £1.90 members, £2.90 non-members)
Rescuing the Historic Environment (ed. Hedley Swain, £6.50)
A Manual of Archaeological Field Drawing (Hawker J M, £18 members, £21 non-members)
The Rescue Questionnaire 1990–1991 (Spoerry P, £2.95 members, £3.45 non-members)
The Southern Feeder: The Archaeology of a Gas Pipeline (£4)

Publications list:
Available online and in print

Access to staff:
Contact by letter
Hours: Mon, Fri, 0900 to 1700; Wed, morning only; answerphone when office closed

RESEARCH AND DEVELOPMENT SOCIETY

Acronym or abbreviation: R&D Society

6–9 Carlton House Terrace, London, SW1Y 5AG

Tel: 020 7451 2513
E-mail: rdsociety@royalsociety.org

Website:
http://www.rdsoc.org

Enquiries:
Enquiries to: Administrative Secretary

Founded:
1962

Formerly called:
London Group for the Study of the Administration of Research and Development (LGARD) (year of change 1964)

Organisation type and purpose:
Learned society, membership association (membership is by application), present number of members: 360.

Subject coverage:
Research and development, largely industrial; R&D management; science policy.

Museum or gallery collection, archive, or library special collection:
Symposium Proceedings (9 vols, 1976–87)

Printed publications:
Occasional newsletter and reports

Publications list:
Available online

Access to staff:
Contact by letter, by telephone and by e-mail
Hours: Mon to Fri, 0900 to 1700

Access to building, collection or gallery:
No access other than to staff

RESEARCH DEFENCE SOCIETY

Acronym or abbreviation: RDS

25 Shaftesbury Avenue, London, W1D 7EG

Tel: 020 7287 2818
Fax: 020 7287 2627

Website:
http://www.rds-online.org.uk/

Enquiries:
Enquiries to: Executive Director

Founded:
1908

Organisation type and purpose:
Membership association, present number of members: 9800.

Subject coverage:
Experimental research involving the use of animals; regulations and conditions under which such work is conducted in the UK; importance of such experiments to the welfare of mankind and animals; welfare of laboratory animals; proposed legislative changes; development of alternative methods.

Access to staff:
Contact by letter, by telephone, by fax, by e-mail and via website
Hours: Mon to Fri, 0900 to 1700

RESEARCH INSTITUTE FOR INDUSTRY

Acronym or abbreviation: RIfI

School of Engineering Sciences, University of Southampton, Southampton, SO17 1BJ

Tel: 023 8059 7052
Fax: 023 8059 7051
E-mail: rifi@soton.ac.uk

Website:
http://www.rifi.soton.ac.uk

Founded:
2002

Organisation type and purpose:
University department or institute, consultancy.
To offer to industry the facilities and expertise of the School of Engineering Sciences at the University of Southampton on an applied research or consultancy basis.

Subject coverage:
Composite fabrication and testing, computational fluid dynamics, cryogenics, refrigeration and engineering for low temperatures, electrochemical engineering, electromechanical systems, energy systems, erosion and corrosion, fuel cells and batteries, engineering design and analysis, engineering materials, experimental mechanics, failure analysis and mechanical property determination, finite element analysis, marine technology and industrial aerodynamics, micro electro-mechanical systems (MEMS), nano-indentation, surface engineering and tribology, software engineering, materials testing,

metallographic examination and analysis, fatigue, creep fracture, fracture mechanics, corrosion, wear, surface treatments, heat treatment, welding, significance of defects, plastics, composites, electron microscopy, electron microprobe analysis, failure analysis, machinability and surfacing.

Access to staff:
Contact by letter, by telephone, by fax and by e-mail. Appointment necessary.
Hours: Mon to Fri, 0900 to 1700

RESEARCH INTO AGEING

Acronym or abbreviation: RiA

207–221 Pentonville Road, London, N1 9UZ

Tel: 020 7239 1895
E-mail: helen.rippon@ageing.org

Website:
http://www.ageing.org/
http://research.helptheaged.org.uk/

Enquiries:
Enquiries to: Head of Research
Direct tel: 020 7239 1896
Direct e-mail: james.goodwin@helptheaged.org.uk
Other contacts: Information and Projects Manager

Founded:
1976

Organisation type and purpose:
Voluntary organisation, registered charity (charity number 277468), suitable for ages: 45+, research organisation.
Raises funds to support medical research to investigate the common diseases and disabilities of later life.

Subject coverage:
Research into age-related disease and disability. Makes grants for medical research into diseases of the older generations; osteoporosis, bone disease and loss, visual problems in old age, reaction to drugs, hypothermia, incontinence, loss of smell and taste, exercise and mobility, dementia (including Alzheimer's Disease), nutrition, cellular ageing, urinary incontinence, leg ulcers, breathlessness, nutrition, pressure sores and the ageing process itself.

Trade and statistical information:
Ageing epidemiology/demography, health/diseases in later life.

Printed publications:
Research into Ageing News (newsletter, quarterly)
Annual Report
Exercise for Healthy Ageing (booklet, £5 inc. p&p)
General purpose leaflet (free)
12 Healthy ageing leaflets (free, with a large sae)
Life is for living, and then? (legacy pack, free)
List of sponsored research projects

Electronic and video publications:
More Active More Often: video on chair-based activity (suggested donation of £10 inc. p&p)

Publications list:
Available in print

Access to staff:
Contact by letter, by telephone, by fax and by e-mail. Appointment necessary.
Hours: Mon to Fri, 0930 to 1730

Funded by:
Help the Aged
As above

RESTAURANT ASSOCIATION

Acronym or abbreviation: RA

c/o BHA, Queens House, 55–56 Lincoln's Inn Fields, London, WC2A 3BH

Tel: 0207 404 7744
Fax: 0207 404 7799
E-mail: bha@bha.org.uk

Website:
http://www.ragb.co.uk

Enquiries:
Enquiries to: Commercial Manager
Direct e-mail: pauline.jackson@bha.org.uk
Other contacts: Communications and IT Manager for publications and website.

Founded:
1967

Rejoined the British Hospitality Association (broke away to form the Restaurant Association of Great Britain in 1967):
(year of change 2003)

Organisation type and purpose:
National organisation, advisory body, trade association (membership is by subscription), present number of members: 3000, service industry, research organisation, publishing house.

Subject coverage:
Restaurant industry in Britain.

Trade and statistical information:
Size, diversity, performance and trends of restaurant industry in Britain.

Printed publications:
Dine Out (magazine, quarterly, £2.50)
Digest (newsletter, monthly)
Gold Standard Restaurant Industry Report (annually, £95)
Guidance Notes on recent regulation/legislation (time to time)

Access to staff:
Contact by letter, by telephone, by fax and by e-mail
Hours: Mon to Fri, 0900 to 1730

Trading division of:
British Hospitality Association

RESTORMEL BOROUGH COUNCIL

Borough Offices, Penwinnick Road, St Austell, Cornwall, PL25 5DR

Tel: 01726 223300
Fax: 01726 223301
E-mail: rbc@restormel.gov.uk

Website:
http://www.restormel.gov.uk

Enquiries:
Enquiries to: Chief Executive

Founded:
1974

Organisation type and purpose:
Local government body.

Subject coverage:
All local government issues.

Printed publications:
Corporate Plan
Best Value Performance Plan
Housing Srategy
LA21 Strategy
Taking Stock
Order printed publications from: Corporate Policy Officer, Restormel Borough Council Penwinnick Road, St Austell, Cornwall, PL25 5DR, tel: 01726 223514, fax: 01726 223526, e-mail: fbowler@restormel.gov.uk

Access to staff:
Contact by letter, by telephone, by fax, by e-mail, in person and via website. Appointment necessary.
Hours: Mon to Fri, 0900 to 1700

Access for disabled people:
Parking provided, ramped entry, access to all public areas, toilet facilities

Also at:
Tourism & Publicity Offices
Marcus Hill, Newquay, Cornwall, TR7 1AF; tel: 01637 854000; fax: 01637 854044; e-mail: holidaytime@newquay.org.uk

RETAIL INTELLIGENCE WORLDWIDE

Acronym or abbreviation: RIW Research

Richmond Bridge House, 419 Richmond Road, Twickenham, TW1 2EX

Tel: 020 3005 9862
E-mail: monica.woods@riwresearch.com

Website:
http://www.riwresearch.com

Founded:
1975

Organisation type and purpose:
Information broker.
Specialist retail consulting firm.

Subject coverage:
European retailing and consumer goods research service; information available on companies, distribution, food and drink, leisure, DIY, mail order, clothing, convenience stores, CTNs, newsagents, department stores, electrical stores, footwear, furniture, health and beauty, jewellery, opticians, variety stores, off-licences.

Information services:
Specialist desk research service on retail and consumer markets around the world.

Museum or gallery collection, archive, or library special collection:
Photographic collection of retailers around the world, over 300,000 images

Trade and statistical information:
Information available for all sectors listed.

Library catalogue:
All or part available in-house

Printed publications:
Shopping Index available on the United Kingdom, France, Germany, Italy, Spain and Ireland

Access to staff:
Contact by telephone and by e-mail
Hours: Mon to Fri, 0900 to 1730

RETAIL MOTOR INDUSTRY FEDERATION

Acronym or abbreviation: RMIF

201 Great Portland Street, London, W1W 5AB

Tel: 020 7580 9122
Fax: 020 7580 6376
E-mail: firstnamelastname@rmif.co.uk

Website:
http://www.rmif.co.uk

Founded:
1913

Organisation type and purpose:
Trade association.

Subject coverage:
UK retail motor industry – sales, service and maintenance of new and used cars, trucks and motorcycles, and associated activities.

Trade and statistical information:
Data on sales and service in the UK motor industry.

Printed publications:
Auto Technician (6 times a year, for members)
Forecourt (monthly, for members)
RM Eye (monthly, for members)

Access to staff:
Contact by letter, by telephone, by fax and by e-mail
Hours: Mon to Fri, 0900 to 1700

Members:
Bodyshop Services Division (BSD)
Cherished Numbers Dealers Association (CNDA)
Independent Garage Division (IGD)
Motorcycle Retailers Association (MRA)
Motorcycle Rider Training Association (MRTA)
National Franchised Dealers Association (NFDA)

continued overleaf

Petrol Retailers Association (PRA)
Society of Motor Auctions (SMA)

RETHINK

Formal name: National Schizophrenia Fellowship

15th Floor, 89 Albert Embankment, London, SE1
7TP

Tel: 0845 456 0455
E-mail: welcome. info@rethink.org

Website:
http://www.rethink.org

Founded:
1972

Organisation type and purpose:
Membership association (membership is by
subscription), present number of members: 7,500,
voluntary organisation, registered charity (charity
number 271028). Organisation for people with a
severe mental illness, their families and carers;
membership £15 pa/£6 unwaged.
To help everyone affected by severe mental illness,
including schizophrenia, to recover a better quality
of life.

Subject coverage:
Schizophrenia and severe mental illness, the effect
it has on people with the condition, on relatives
and on friends of sufferers; professional workers
caring for service users or clients (not aspects
involving clinical or medical judgement);
community care.

Printed publications:
Publications on Carers, Complementary Therapy,
   Creative Writing, Mental Illness, Rights,
   Treatments, Services and Advice Guides
Order printed publications from: website: http://
www.mentalhealthshop.rethink.org

Publications list:
Available online and in print

Access to staff:
Contact by letter, by telephone, by fax, by e-mail
and via website. Appointment necessary.
Hours: Mon to Fri, 0900 to 1700

Branches:
120 relative/sufferer local support groups and 380
projects (day care, employment or care homes)
NSF Wales
   Suite C2, Bratt Britannic House, Llandovey,
   Neath, West Glamorgan, SA10 6EL; tel: 01792
   816600; fax: 01792 813056; e-mail: info@wales.nsf
   .org.uk
Operations London and East
   89 Albert Embankment, London, SE1 7TP; tel:
   0845 456 0455; fax: 020 7820 1149; e-mail: info@
   london.rethink.org
Operations North and Midlands
   25A Outram Street, Sutton in Ashfield,
   Nottinghamshire, NG17 4BA; tel: 01623 551338;
   fax: 01623 550547
Operations South and South West
   Fairways House, Mountpleasant Industrial
   Estate, Mountpleasant Road, Southampton, SO4
   0QB; tel: 023 8021 0270; fax: 023 8021 0285; e-
   mail: info@membership.rethink.org
Rethink Information and Advice Service
   89 Albert Embankment, London; tel: 0845 456
   0455; fax: 020 7820 1149; e-mail: info@nsf.org.uk

Member organisation of:
Disability Alliance
EUFAMI
National Council for Voluntary Organisations
Rethink Northern Ireland
   Wyndhurst, Knockbracken Healthcare Park,
   Saintfield Road, Belfast, BT8 8BH; tel: 028 9040
   2323; fax: 028 9040 1616; e-mail: info@nireland
   .nsf.org.uk

RETIRED GREYHOUND TRUST

Acronym or abbreviation: RGT

Park House, Park Terrace, Worcester Park, Surrey,
KT4 7JZ

Tel: 0844 826 8424
Fax: 0844 826 8425

Website:
http://www.retiredgreyhounds.co.uk
Adopting or sponsoring a greyhound, news and
events, how to help, useful contacts, greyhound
care information and other information,
volunteers, online shop.

Organisation type and purpose:
Registered charity (charity number 269668).

Subject coverage:
Welfare of retired greyhounds.

Access to staff:
Contact by letter, by telephone, by fax and via
website

Branches:
Throughout England, Scotland and Wales

RETRAINING OF RACEHORSES

Acronym or abbreviation: RoR

75 High Holborn, London, WC1V 6LS

Tel: 01780 740773
E-mail: info@ror.org.uk

Website:
http://www.ror.org.uk
Information on caring for and retraining an ex-
racehorse.

Enquiries:
Other contacts: Director of Operations (for
applications to enter the RoR Series)

Founded:
2000

Organisation type and purpose:
Registered charity (number 1084787).
British Horseracing's official charity for the welfare
of horses who have retired from racing.

Subject coverage:
Retraining retired racehorses.

Information services:
Horse Helpline, by phone (as above) or e-mail:
asktheexperts@ror.org.uk.

Access to staff:
Contact by letter, by telephone and by e-mail

Also at:
Director of Operations, Retraining of Racehorses
   Ash Cottage, Back Street, East Garston,
   Hungerford, Berkshire, RG17 7EX; tel: 01488
   648998; 07836 293191; e-mail: darbuthnot@ror
   .org.uk

RETREAD MANUFACTURERS
ASSOCIATION

Acronym or abbreviation: RMA

PO Box 320, Crewe, Cheshire, CW2 6WY

Tel: 01270 561014
Fax: 01270 668801
E-mail: rma@greentyres.com

Website:
http://www.retreaders.co.uk
Members directory.
http://www.retreaders.org.uk
Information on retreading.

Enquiries:
Enquiries to: Director
Other contacts: (1) Secretary; (2) Technical
Consultant for (1) In Director's absence; (2)
Technical enquiries only, tel 01782 659674.

Founded:
1946

Organisation type and purpose:
National organisation, trade association
(membership is by subscription), present number
of members: 85.

Subject coverage:
Tyre retreading; standards and tyre disposal, tyre
recycling.

Printed publications:
European Regulations for Retreading

Access to staff:
Contact by letter, by telephone, by fax and by e-
mail. Appointment necessary.
Hours: Mon to Fri, 0930 to 1600

Access for disabled people:
Parking provided, access to all public areas, toilet
facilities

Founder member of:
British Tyre Industry Federation
International Organization of Tyre Retreaders
(BIPAVER)
   Retreading Division; tel: 01782 417777; fax:
   01782 417766; e-mail: retreads@ukonline.co.uk
Tyre Industry Council

RETREAT ASSOCIATION

Acronym or abbreviation: RA

Kerridge House, 42 Woodside Close, Amersham,
Bucks

Tel: 0149 443 3004
Fax: 0871 715 1917
E-mail: info@retreats.org.uk

Website:
http://www.retreats.org.uk

Enquiries:
Enquiries to: Director

Founded:
1989

Organisation type and purpose:
Voluntary organisation, registered charity (charity
number 328746). A federation of 5 member groups.
Has 230 retreats and retreat houses in Britain and
Ireland. Provides information to the public, and
support and networking for organisers.

Subject coverage:
Christian spirituality, spiritual direction.

Information services:
Information and resources in connection with
Christian retreats and spiritual direction.

**Museum or gallery collection, archive, or library
special collection:**
Small specialised library on Christian spirituality

Printed publications:
Books
Free leaflets (19) on retreats and their organisation
List of Training Courses in Spirituality and
   Spiritual Direction
RA Mission Statement
Retreats (journal, annually, £6.00 plus p&p)
Order printed publications from: Order direct or
online

Publications list:
Available online and in print

Access to staff:
Contact by letter, by telephone, by fax, by e-mail
and via website. Appointment necessary.
Hours: 0930 to 1730

Access for disabled people:
There is no access for disabled: the offices are at the
top of a 3-storey buildling with no lift

Member organisation of:
Affiliates of the Retreat Association (non-
denominational) (AFF)
Association for Promoting Retreats (APR)
Baptist Union Retreat Group (BURG)
Catholic Network for Retreats & Spirituality
(CNRS)

Methodist Retreat & Spirituality Network (MRSN)
United Reformed Church Retreats Group (URCG)

RETT SYNDROME ASSOCIATION UK

Acronym or abbreviation: RSAUK

Langham House West, Mill Street, Luton,
Bedfordshire LU1 2NA

Tel: 01582 798910
Fax: 01582 724129
E-mail: info@rettsyndrome.org.uk

Website:
http://www.rettsyndrome.org.uk

Enquiries:
Enquiries to: Office Administrator
Other contacts: Family Support Service Manager

Founded:
1985

Organisation type and purpose:
Membership association (membership is by
subscription), voluntary organisation, registered
charity (charity number 327309).

Subject coverage:
Rett syndrome, treatment and care, research, social
support.

**Museum or gallery collection, archive, or library
special collection:**
Pamphlets, books and videos on Rett Syndrome

Printed publications:
Various publications, free of charge, covering all
aspects of Rett Syndrome including:
Information Packs
Leaflets, which cover varying topics for both
professionals and carers
Magazine (quarterly)
Rett Syndrome: Adolescence & Adulthood
What is Rett Syndrome? (booklet)
What is RS? (leaflet)

Electronic and video publications:
The Lost Girls (video, £9.99 plus £1 p&p UK)
Silent Angels (video, £12 plus £1 p&p UK)

Publications list:
Available online and in print

Access to staff:
Contact by letter, by telephone, by fax, by e-mail
and in person
Hours: Mon to Fri, 0900 to 1700

RETURNED VOLUNTEER ACTION

Acronym or abbreviation: RVA

76 Wentworth Street, London, E1 7SA

Tel: 020 7247 6406
E-mail: retvolact@lineone.net

Enquiries:
Enquiries to: Membership Officer

Founded:
1963

Organisation type and purpose:
Membership association.

Subject coverage:
Advice and help for prospective and returned
overseas volunteers, understanding of the causes
of poverty and inequality, relationship between
north and south.

**Museum or gallery collection, archive, or library
special collection:**
Newsletters, annual reports, catalogues and other
information from development-related UK
groups and campaign organisations, as well as
NGOs

Printed publications:
Books and booklets including:
For Whose Benefit: Racism and Overseas
Development Work (£2.50)

Missing Links: Training for Awareness, Analysis
and Action (£10)
The Only Resource (£2.50)
Thinking about Volunteering Overseas (£2.50)
Handbook for Development Workers Overseas
(£2.50)
Volunteering Overseas: Personal Perceptions (£3)

Publications list:
Available in print

Access to staff:
Contact by letter and by e-mail. Appointment
necessary.
Hours: By appointment
Special comments: Please phone first.

Links with:
Action Village India
76 Wentworth Street, London, E1 7SA; tel: 020
7247 6406; e-mail: info@actionvillageindia.org
.uk; website: http://www.actionvillageindia.org
.uk

REUTERS GROUP PLC

85 Fleet Street, London, EC4P 4AJ

Tel: 020 7250 1122
Fax: 020 7542 4064

Website:
http://www.reuters.com
Information on Reuters, news, financial markets,
stock quotes.

Enquiries:
Enquiries to: Director Corporate Communications
Direct tel: 020 7542 4890
Other contacts: Group Archivist for information on
Reuters history.

Founded:
1851

Organisation type and purpose:
International organisation, service industry.

Subject coverage:
Worldwide news coverage of general, political,
cultural, sports, economic, financial and scientific
matters and events; information and quotes on and
from world's money, fixed-income, equity,
commodity and energy markets.

Printed publications:
Annual Report
The Reuters Magazine (publication for Reuters
clients)

Access to staff:
Contact by letter, by telephone, by fax and by e-
mail
Hours: Mon to Fri, 0900 to 1700

Access to building, collection or gallery:
No access other than to staff

RFCA GREATER LONDON

Formal name: Reserve Forces & Cadets Association
for Greater London

Fulham House, 87 Fulham High Street, London,
SW6 3JS

Tel: 0845 130 7888
E-mail: reception@gl.rfca.mod.uk

Website:
http://www.reserve-forces-london.org.uk

Enquiries:
Enquiries to: Secretary

Founded:
1908

Organisation type and purpose:
National organisation, membership association
(membership is by election or invitation),
voluntary organisation.
Voluntary association, financed by central
government through the Ministry of Defence.
To look after the interests of the Reserve Forces.

Subject coverage:
Recruiting and housing of the Reserves Forces and
Cadets in Greater London.

Access to staff:
Contact by letter, by telephone and via website.
Appointment necessary.
Hours: Mon to Thu, 0900 to 1300, 1400 to 1700; Fri,
0900 to 1300, 1400 to 1600

RHM TECHNOLOGY

Formal name: RHM Technology – a trading name of
RHM Group Ltd

The Lord Rank Centre, Lincoln Road, High
Wycombe, Buckinghamshire, HP12 3QR

Tel: 01494 526191
Fax: 01494 428080

Website:
http://www.rhmtech.co.uk
Information on services offered by RHM
Technology.

Enquiries:
Enquiries to: Commercial Manager
Direct tel: 01494 428153
Direct e-mail: david.scott@rhm.com

Founded:
1963

Organisation type and purpose:
Service industry, consultancy.
Science, engineering and information services for
the food industry.

Subject coverage:
Food science and technology; cereal chemistry;
baking; bread; flour milling, cake, fruit preserves;
electron microscopy; microbial biochemistry; food
analysis and microbiology; mycotoxin analysis;
protein chemistry; process engineering; GM testing
and analysis (quantitative).

Library catalogue:
All or part available in-house

Access to staff:
Appointment necessary.
Hours: Mon to Fri, 0900 to 1700

Research and engineering company within:
Rank Hovis McDougall

RHODODENDRON, CAMELLIA AND MAGNOLIA GROUP OF THE RHS

Acronym or abbreviation: The Rhododendron Group

Botallick, Lanreath, Looe, PL13 2PF

Tel: 01503 220215
E-mail: patbucknell@btinternet.com

Website:
http://www.rhodogroup.rhs.org

Enquiries:
Enquiries to: Honorary Secretary

Organisation type and purpose:
International organisation, membership
association (membership is by subscription),
present number of members: 800.

Subject coverage:
The propagation, preservation and cultivation of
rhododendrons, camellias and magnolias. Group
branch garden visits and lectures. Holidays and
tours for Group members.

Non-library collection catalogue:
All or part available online

Printed publications:
Rhododendrons with Camellias and Magnolias
(yearbook, £11.95, free to members)
Bulletin (3 times a year)

Access to staff:
Contact by letter, by telephone and by e-mail
Hours: Mon to Fri, 0900 to 1700

continued overleaf

Parent body:
Royal Horticultural Society
80 Vincent Square, London, SW1P 2PE; tel: 020
7834 4333

RHONDDA CYNON TAFF COUNTY BOROUGH LIBRARIES

Acronym or abbreviation: RCT CBC

Tel: 01443 773204
Fax: 01443 777047

Website:
http://www.rhondda-cynon-taff.gov.uk/libraries
General information.
http://www.rhondda-cynon-taff.gov.uk/photos
Photographic Archive.

Enquiries:
Enquiries to: Principal Librarian
Direct tel: 01685 880060
Direct fax: 01685 881181
Direct e-mail: norma.d.jones@rhondda-cynon-taff
.gov.uk

Organisation type and purpose:
Local government body, public library.

Subject coverage:
Local history of Rhondda-Cynon-Taff, music,
general.

Library catalogue:
All or part available online

Printed publications:
Cynon Valley Calendar – local events (6 times a
year)
Cynon Valley Community Directory (on OPAC
1996, Taff-Ely in preparation)
Older and Bolder, Rhondda Community Directory
for the over-50s (on OPAC 1996)

Access to staff:
Contact by letter, by telephone, by fax and by e-
mail
Hours: Mon to Fri, 0900 to 1700

Admin Dept.:
Penygraig Library
Tylacelyn Road, Penygraig, Rhondda

Other addresses:
Aberdare Library (Principal Librarian)
Green Street, Aberdare, CF44 7AG; tel: 01685
880050; fax: 01685 881181
Pontypridd Library (Area Librarian-South)
Library Road, Pontypridd; tel: 01443 486850; fax:
01443 493258
The Education Centre (County Borough Librarian)
Grawen Street, Porth, Rhondda; tel: 01443
687666; fax: 01443 680286
Treorchy Library
tel: 01443 773204

Parent body:
Rhondda Cynon Taff County Borough Council
tel: 01443 687666; fax: 01443 680286

RHONDDA CYNON TAFF COUNTY BOROUGH LIBRARIES – ABERDARE

Central Library, Green Street, Aberdare, Mid
Glamorgan, CF44 7AG

Tel: 01685 880050
Fax: 01685 881181
E-mail: aberdare.library@rhondda-cynon-taff.gov
.uk

Website:
http://www.rhondda-cynon-taff.gov.uk/libraries/
index.htm

Enquiries:
Enquiries to: County Borough Librarian

Organisation type and purpose:
Local government body, public library.

Subject coverage:
General, local history of the Cynon Valley.

Museum or gallery collection, archive, or library special collection:
W W Price Collection (local history)

Non-library collection catalogue:
All or part available in-house

Library catalogue:
All or part available online

Printed publications:
Cynon Valley Community Directory

Access to staff:
Contact by letter, by telephone, by fax, by e-mail,
in person and via website
Hours: Mon to Fri, 0900 to 1800; Sat, 0900 to 1300

Access for disabled people:
Ramped entry; lift to Reference Department.

RHONDDA HERITAGE PARK

Lewis Merthyr Colliery, Coed Cae Road, Trehafod,
Pontypridd, Rhondda Cynon Taff, CF37 2NP

Tel: 01443 682036
Fax: 01443 687420
E-mail: reception@rhonddaheritagepark.com

Website:
http://www.rhonddaheritagepark.com
General information about the attraction.

Enquiries:
Enquiries to: County Borough Museums Officer,
Rhondda Cynon Taff
Other contacts: Marketing Officer for promotion/
public relations.

Founded:
1989

Organisation type and purpose:
Local government body, museum, art gallery,
historic building, house or site, suitable for ages:
all. Children's play park, shop, restaurant.
Conference facilities available.
Tourist attraction.

Subject coverage:
Heritage, mining. Black Gold includes 3
audiovisual shows telling the history of the
Rhondda Valleys and mining. A guided tour with
an ex-miner includes a visit to the Grade II listed
pit head buildings and a trip to 'pit bottom' to
experience life as a miner in the 1950s. A
reconstructed village street and art gallery at the
visitor centre.

Special visitor services:
Guided tours, materials and/or activities for
children.

Education services:
Group education facilities, resources for Key
Stages 1 and 2, 3 and 4.

Services for disabled people:
For hearing impaired.

Museum or gallery collection, archive, or library special collection:
Books, photographs, domestic artefacts, shop
artefacts
Variety of mining machinery including:
Hand tools, colliers' tools, 1850–1950
Mine rescue, breathing apparatus, smoke helmets
Mining instruments, methonometers, hygrometers,
dust sampling equipment, etc.
Large colliery machinery and engines, Lewis
Merthyr winding engine, ventilation fans
preserved in situ, 1880/1890

Non-library collection catalogue:
All or part available in-house

Electronic and video publications:
Promotional video available for intending group
visitors

Access to staff:
Contact by letter and by e-mail. Appointment
necessary.
Hours: Mon to Fri, 0900 to 1700

Access to building, collection or gallery:
No prior appointment required
Hours: Daily 1000 to 1800. Closed Dec 25 to 1 Jan
inclusive, and Mondays Oct to Easter

Access for disabled people:
Parking provided, ramped entry, level entry, toilet
facilities, lift. Access to most areas.

Parent body:
Rhondda Cynon Taff County Borough Council
The Pavilions, Clydach Vale, CF40 2XX; tel:
01443 424000

RHS GARDEN HARLOW CARR

Formal name: The Royal Horticultural Society's
Garden Harlow Carr
Acronym or abbreviation: RHS

Crag Lane, Harrogate, North Yorkshire, HG3 1QB

Tel: 01423 565418
Fax: 01423 530663
E-mail: admin-harlowcarr@rhs.org.uk

Enquiries:
Other contacts: Curatorial department for written
enquiries on horticulture.

Founded:
1950

Organisation type and purpose:
Membership association (membership is by
subscription), present number of members:
365,000, registered charity (charity number
222879), museum.
Educational charity.
Selects shrubs, trees and plants to discover their
suitability for northern conditions.

Subject coverage:
Gardening and horticulture, particularly relating to
the conditions in the north of England.

Museum or gallery collection, archive, or library special collection:
Four important national plant collections – rheum
(rhubarb), fuchsia sect. Quelusia (provisional
collection), dryopteris and polypodium (ferns)

Printed publications:
The Garden (monthly)
Harlow Carr Garden (leaflet)

Access to staff:
Contact by letter. Access for members only.
Hours: Mon to Fri, 0900 to 1700

Access for disabled people:
Parking provided, level entry, toilet facilities

RHS LINDLEY LIBRARY

Formal name: Royal Horticultural Society
Acronym or abbreviation: RHS

80 Vincent Square, Westminster, London, SW1P
2PE

Tel: 020 7821 3000
Fax: 020 7630 6060

Website:
http://www.rhs.org.uk/libraries
http://www.rhs.org.uk

Enquiries:
Enquiries to: Head of Library and Archives
Direct tel: 020 7821 3050
Direct fax: 020 7828 3022
Direct e-mail: library.london@rhs.org.uk

Founded:
1804

Organisation type and purpose:
Learned society, professional body, registered
charity, research organisation.

Subject coverage:
Non-commercial horticulture and silviculture, all
plants, trees and shrubs, both ornamental and
culinary, plant pests and diseases, garden design,

history of gardening, floras, botanical art, flower arranging, to a lesser extent books on systematic botany, agriculture and forestry.

Museum or gallery collection, archive, or library special collection:
Bunyard Collection of books on fruit (part of the Lindley Library)
Lindley Library (horticultural and botanical books from the 16th century to the present)
Art Collections – 25,000 original botanical drawings
Horticultural Taxonomy Collection (held at Lindley Library, Wisley)

Library catalogue:
All or part available in-house

Printed publications:
Over 700 publications related to all aspects of horticulture, list available from RHS Enterprises Limited, RHS Garden, Wisley, Woking, Surrey GU23 6QB; tel: 01483 211320; fax: 01483 211003; Mon to Fri, 0900 to 1730
The Garden (monthly)
The Plantsman (quarterly)
Wisley Handbooks and RHS Associated Series including:
Advanced and Technical Books
Art, Floral Craft, Indoor Plants and Herbs
Cacti, Succulents and Orchids
Design and History
Flora and Wild Flowers
General Interest
RHS International Register
Specific Plants and Groupings
Trees and Shrubs
Order printed publications from: RHS Enterprises Ltd, RHS Garden, Wisley, nr Woking, Surrey, GU23 6QB; e-mail: mailorder@rhs.org.uk

Publications list:
Available online

Access to staff:
Contact by letter, by telephone, by fax, by e-mail and in person. Appointment necessary.
Hours: Mon to Fri, 1000 to 1700 excluding Bank hols

Access to building, collection or gallery:
No prior appointment required

Access for disabled people:
Ramped entry

Administers:
Harlow Carr Garden Library
   RHS Garden Harlow Carr, Harrogate, Yorkshire
Hyde Hall Garden Library
   RHS Garden Hyde Hall, Rettendon, Essex
Rosemoor Garden Library
   RHS Garden Rosemoor, Great Torrington, Devon, EX38 8PH

Also at:
RHS Lindley Library, RHS Garden Wisley Woking, Surrey, GU23 6QB; tel: 01483 212428; e-mail: library.wisley@rhs.org.uk; website: http://www.rhs.org.uk/libraries

RICABILITY

Formal name: Research Institute for Consumer Affairs
Acronym or abbreviation: RICA

Unit G03, The Wenlock Business Centre, 50–52 Wharf Road, London, N1 7EU

Tel: 020 7427 2460; textphone no. 020 7427 2469
Fax: 020 7427 2468
E-mail: mail@ricability.org.uk

Website:
http://www.ricability.org.uk
Consumer guides for older and disabled people, covering technology at home, communication, motoring and car information, and childcare products for disabled parents; a who-can-help guide signposting people to useful sources of information.
http://www.ricability-digitaltv.org.uk

Independent consumer test reports on digital TV products to help people choose easy-to-use products for the national digital switchover.
http://www.product-reviews.org.uk
Website where disabled people can register their own opinions about good and bad products or services they use.

Enquiries:
Enquiries to: Administrator

Founded:
1991

Organisation type and purpose:
Voluntary organisation, registered charity (charity number 1007726), research organisation.
Independent charity set up by the Consumers' Association. Ricability is the trading name of the Research Institute for Consumer Affairs.
To carry out research and publish unbiased information on products and services used by consumers who are older or disabled.

Subject coverage:
Consumer information, disabled people, older people, carers, disability equipment, disability services, research, information, product testing and assessment, digital television, digital switchover, product reviews, online product reviews, assistive technology, car adaptations.

Printed publications:
Consumer guides and reports on:
digital TV products (online only), some household products, online car measurement database to search for a car that is easy to get in or out of, car adaptations to help drivers with certain disabilities (amputation, arthritis, cerebral palsy, MS, restricted growth, stroke), wheeled walking frames, pill dispensers, riser recliner chairs

Electronic and video publications:
Audio cassette, audio cd, braille and large-print materials available
Online electric wheelchair/scooter database to help people choose a suitable product to meet particular needs

Publications list:
Available online and in print

Access to staff:
Contact by letter, by telephone, by fax, by e-mail and via website
Hours: Mon to Fri, 0900 to 1700

Access for disabled people:
Access to all public areas, fully adapted toilet
Special comments: Fully accessible and accessible information: tape, braille and large print.

RICARDO UK

Shoreham Technical Centre, Shoreham-by-Sea, West Sussex, BN43 5FG

Tel: 01273 455611
Fax: 01273 464124
E-mail: infoservices@ricardo.com

Website:
http://www.ricardo.com

Enquiries:
Enquiries to: Information Manager
Direct tel: 01273 794230
Direct fax: 01273 794555

Founded:
1915

Organisation type and purpose:
Consultancy.

Subject coverage:
Internal-combustion engineering research, diesel engines, petrol engines, automotive engineering, noise reduction, combustion, exhaust emissions, fuel technology, lubrication, transmissions, finite element stress analysis, computational fluid dynamics, design, vehicle systems, control and electronics.

Library catalogue:
All or part available online

Printed publications:
Components News (details of new powertrain components plans by manufacturers, monthly)
New Engine News (bulletin of new engines and plans by manufacturers, monthly)
Transmissions News (details of new transmissions and plans by manufacturers, monthly)
Alternative Powertrain News, Vehicle Engineering News, Gas Engine News, Control & Electronics News, Fuel Consumption News.

Electronic and video publications:
Ricardo Powerlink Database (250,000 references to the literature of the powertrain and vehicle systems, online)
EMLEG Updating service, covering exhaust emissions legislation (online)

Publications list:
Available online and in print

Access to staff:
Contact by letter, by telephone, by fax, by e-mail and via website. All charged.
Hours: Mon to Fri, 0900 to 1700

Access to building, collection or gallery:
No access other than to staff

Parent body:
Ricardo Group plc
   Shoreham Technical Centre, Shoreham-by-Sea, West Sussex, BN43 5FG; tel: 01273 455611; fax: 01273 464124

RICHARD III SOCIETY

4 Oakley Street, Chelsea, London, SW3 5NN

Tel: 01689 823569
E-mail: information@richardiii.net

Website:
http://www.richardiii.net
Home page re Society, research, publication programmes etc.
http://www.r3.org
US Branch site, materials for students, texts, etc.

Enquiries:
Enquiries to: Secretary
Other contacts: Research Officer for research-related queries.

Founded:
1924

Organisation type and purpose:
Learned society.

Subject coverage:
Life and times of King Richard III and the social and political history of late 15th-century England.

Museum or gallery collection, archive, or library special collection:
Richard III Society Library

Library catalogue:
All or part available in-house

Printed publications:
Catalogues of the Library
The Bulletin (journal, quarterly)
The Ricardian (journal, annual)
Order printed publications from: Membership Dept (also Sales Dept), Time Travellers Limited
Sales Liaison Officer, 42 Pewsey Vale, Forest Park, Bracknell, RG12 9YA

Publications list:
Available online and in print

Access to staff:
Contact by letter, by telephone and by e-mail
Hours: Mon to Fri, 0900 to 1700

RICHARD JEFFERIES SOCIETY

Pear Tree Cottage, Longcot, Oxfordshire, SN7 7SS

Tel: 01793 783040
E-mail: info@richardjefferiessociety.co.uk

continued overleaf

Website:
http://richardjefferiessociety.co.uk
Brief biography of Richard Jefferies plus extracts from his works, Society details, access to publications, events and news.

Enquiries:
Enquiries to: Honorary Secretary

Founded:
1950

Organisation type and purpose:
Learned society (membership is by subscription), present number of members: 300, registered charity (charity number 1042838).
Literary society. Manages the Richard Jefferies Museum at Coate, near Swindon.

Subject coverage:
Life, writings and associations of Richard Jefferies (1848–1887), whose principal subjects are: nature, the Victorian rural scene, agriculture, late Victorian London, gamekeeping and poaching, spiritual philosophy.

Museum or gallery collection, archive, or library special collection:
Library of first and early editions of Jefferies' works, studies and biographies, unpublished essays and letters issued posthumously, photographs, paintings, family memorabilia

Non-library collection catalogue:
All or part available online and in-house

Library catalogue:
All or part available in-house

Printed publications:
Annual Report and Newsletters
Books by and about Richard Jefferies
List of Talks and Articles
Leaflets, cards and postcards
Journal (ISSN 0968–4247, one a year)
Order printed publications from: website: http://richardjefferiessociety.co.uk

Publications list:
Available online

Access to staff:
Contact by letter, by telephone, by e-mail and via website
Hours: Mon to Sun, 0900 to 1600

Access to building, collection or gallery:
No prior appointment required
Hours: Richard Jefferies Museum at Coate, Swindon: Wed, 2nd of month, 1000 to 1600; Sun, May to Sep, 1st, 3rd & 4th of month, 1400 to 1700
Special comments: Other times by appointment.

Access for disabled people:
Museum on 3 floors – no access to 1st and 2nd floors for wheelchairs

Affiliated to:
Alliance of Literary Societies
website: http://www.allianceofliterarysocieties.org.uk

RICHMOND UPON THAMES COLLEGE

Acronym or abbreviation: RuTC

The Library, Egerton Road, Twickenham, Middlesex, TW2 7SJ

Tel: 020 8607 8356
Fax: 020 8607 8360

Website:
http://www.richmond-utcoll.ac.uk

Enquiries:
Enquiries to: Learning Resources Manager

Founded:
1977

Subject coverage:
Humanities, social sciences, literature, science, technology, education, business studies, art and design.

Non-library collection catalogue:
All or part available online

Access to staff:
Contact by letter, by telephone and via website.
Appointment necessary.
Hours: Mon to Fri, 0900 to 1700

Access to building, collection or gallery:
Prior appointment required

Access for disabled people:
Level entry, toilet facilities

RICHMOND UPON THAMES LIBRARIES AND INFORMATION SERVICES

Education and Childen's Services, Regal House, London Road, Twickenham, Middlesex, TW1 3QB

Tel: 020 8831 6136
Fax: 020 8891 7904
E-mail: libraries@richmond.gov.uk

Website:
http://www.richmond.gov.uk

Enquiries:
Enquiries to: Head of Libraries and Culture
Other contacts: Assistant Head of Library and Information Services

Organisation type and purpose:
Local government body, public library.

Subject coverage:
General.

Museum or gallery collection, archive, or library special collection:
Alexander Pope Collection within the Twickenham local collection (Twickenham District Library)
Douglas Sladen Collection of correspondence and printed ephemera relating to his life and interests
George Vancouver Collection
Hansard, House of Commons and House of Lords debates
Other debates and historic journals
Official Journal of the EC
Richmond upon Thames and Barnes local collections
Sir Richard Burton Collection of books and other items
Telephone Directories (microfiche)
Times (microfilm)
Various statistical sources including many OPCS monitors, Annual abstract of Stats, Monthly digest of Stats, Regional Trends, Social Trends, EUROSTAT, United Nations Statistical Year-Book, OECD reports on countries, Europa World Year Book, EC publications, please note most of these would be held at Central Reference Library only

Library catalogue:
All or part available online

Printed publications:
Richmond upon Thames Official Borough Guide (every 2 years, £2.50)
The Official Richmond upon Thames Business Directory (annually, £7.50)
Other publications include irregular local history items

Electronic and video publications:
DVDs available

Access to staff:
Contact by letter, by telephone, by fax, by e-mail, in person and via website
Hours: Mon to Fri, 0900 to 1700

District libraries at:
East Sheen
Richmond
Teddington
Twickenham

Member of:
SHARE

Other addresses:
Reference and Information Services
Old Town Hall, Whittaker Avenue, Richmond-upon-Thames, Surrey, TW9 1TP; tel: 020 8940 5529; fax: 020 8940 6899; e-mail: reference.services@richmond.gov.uk

RICHMOND: THE AMERICAN INTERNATIONAL UNIVERSITY IN LONDON

Queen's Road, Richmond-upon-Thames, Surrey, TW10 6JP

Tel: 020 8332 8210
Fax: 020 8332 3050
E-mail: library@richmond.ac.uk

Website:
http://www.richmond.ac.uk
General information about the university.

Enquiries:
Enquiries to: University librarian
Direct tel: 020 8332 8279
Direct e-mail: trewf@richmond.ac.uk

Founded:
1972

Organisation type and purpose:
University library.
Independent American international university, for liberal arts and professional studies.

Subject coverage:
Business administration, economics, anthropology and sociology, international business, political science, international relations, psychology, women's studies, art history, studio art, theatre arts, British studies, English literature, history, French, computer science, mathematical sciences, communications, environmental studies, modern languages, philosophy and religion, systems engineering and management.

Museum or gallery collection, archive, or library special collection:
N J Cann Bequest (history of art)
Harvard Core Collection (gift of Sir Cyril Taylor and Roger O Walther)
Asa Briggs Collection (gift of Lord Asa Briggs)

Non-library collection catalogue:
All or part available online

Library catalogue:
All or part available online

Access to staff:
Appointment necessary.
Hours: Mon to Fri, 0900 to 1700

Access for disabled people:
Hours: Mon to Thu, 0900 to 2100; Fri, 0900 to 1700; Sat, closed; Sun, 1300 to 2300

Other addresses:
Richmond: the American International University in London
1 Saint Alban's Grove, Kensington, London, W8 5PN; tel: 020 7368 8510

RIDER HAGGARD SOCIETY

Acronym or abbreviation: RHS

27 Deneholm, Whitley Bay, Tyne and Wear, NE25 9AU

Tel: 0191 252 4516
E-mail: rb27allen@blueyonder.co.uk

Website:
http://www.riderhaggardsociety.org.uk
Information and offers to do with Rider Haggard.

Enquiries:
Enquiries to: Honorary Secretary

Founded:
1984

Organisation type and purpose:
International organisation, learned society (membership is by subscription), present number of members: 106.

Subject coverage:
Works by the author Rider Haggard and about him, his family and any relevant ephemera.

Information services:
On request.

Special visitor services:
On request.

Education services:
Research help.

Non-library collection catalogue:
All or part available online and in print

Printed publications:
Books by Haggard
Books about Haggard
RHS Journals
Guides to Haggard fiction and non-fiction
Order printed publications from: Postal address

Publications list:
Available online and in print

Access to staff:
Contact by letter, by telephone, by e-mail, in person and via website. Appointment necessary.
Hours: Any time

Links with:
Alliance of Literary Societies (ALS)

RILEY MOTOR CLUB LIMITED

Treelands, 127 Penn Road, Wolverhampton, West Midlands, WV3 0DU

Tel: 01902 773197

Enquiries:
Enquiries to: Honorary Secretary

Founded:
1925

Organisation type and purpose:
Membership association.

Subject coverage:
History of Riley cars, technical information, source of spares, restoration and maintenance.

Access to staff:
Contact by letter and by telephone
Hours: Mon to Fri, 0900 to 1700

RILEY REGISTER

56 Cheltenham Road, Bishops Cleeve, Cheltenham, Gloucestershire, GL52 8LY

Tel: 01242 673598

Website:
http://www.rileyregister.com

Enquiries:
Enquiries to: Membership Secretary

Founded:
1954

Organisation type and purpose:
Membership association (membership is by subscription).

Subject coverage:
One make car club for Rileys up to 1940; sources of spares.

Printed publications:
Bulletin (quarterly)
Newsletter (every 6 weeks)

Access to staff:
Contact by letter and by telephone
Hours: Mon to Fri, 0900 to 1700

RILEY RM CLUB

509 Preston New Road, Blackburn, Lancashire, BB2 7AN

Tel: 01254 265789
E-mail: gensec@rileyrmclub.org.uk

Website:
http://www.rileyrmclub.org.uk

Enquiries:
Enquiries to: General Secretary

Founded:
1969

Organisation type and purpose:
International organisation, membership association (membership is by subscription).

Subject coverage:
Preservation of RM Rileys, spares, technical information and social activities.

Museum or gallery collection, archive, or library special collection:
Archives covering the majority of cars still in existence
Magazines and technical literature
Spare parts for members' cars

Printed publications:
RMemoranda (club magazine)

Access to staff:
Contact by letter, by telephone and by e-mail
Hours: 0900 to 2100

RIPON CATHEDRAL LIBRARY

Ripon Cathedral, Ripon, North Yorkshire, HG4 1QR

Tel: 01765 603462

Enquiries:
Enquiries to: Canon Librarian

Subject coverage:
Church history; New Testament; personalities and leaders within the church (mainly 20th century); prayer and spirituality.

Museum or gallery collection, archive, or library special collection:
Higgins Library
Library of Canon A Stephenson
Most of the Cathedral's special collections are housed in the Brotherton Library, Leeds University

Access to staff:
Appointment necessary.
Hours: Mon to Fri, 0900 to 1700

RIPON HISTORICAL SOCIETY

Stone Cottage, Wath-in-Nidderdale, Pateley Bridge, North Yorkshire, HG3 5PL

E-mail: gdl@globalnet.co.uk

Website:
http://www.yorksgen.org.uk

Enquiries:
Enquiries to: Honorary Secretary

Founded:
1986

Organisation type and purpose:
Membership association (membership is by subscription), present number of members: 343+, voluntary organisation.

Subject coverage:
The history of the City of Ripon and the surrounding districts, its heritage and the preservation and protection of items of historic or public interest, family history of the area.

Museum or gallery collection, archive, or library special collection:
Microfilms of many of the records of Ripon (held in six Record Offices) are available in the new Ripon County Library

Printed publications:
The Ripon Historian (quarterly, members)
A Guide to Historical Sources for Ripon and District (ed Hebden J R, £3 plus 40p p&p)
Census Index 1851
Kith and Kin: Nidderdale families 1500–1750 (£7.50 plus 85p p&p)
Thirlway Journal: A record of Life in Early Victorian Ripon (£7.50 plus 85p p&p)
Yorkshire Hearth Tax Lists 1672 and 1673 for the North, East and most of the West Ridings and for York
Indexes to 1822/3 Baines Directory for Yorkshire organised by Wapentakes, NRY in 5 parts, WRY 3 parts to date (£2 each)
Order printed publications from: Publications Officer, Ripon Historical Society
Aldergarth, Galphay, Ripon, North Yorkshire, HG4 3NJ, tel: 01765 658602, e-mail: hebden1name@btopenworld.com

Microform publications:
Monumental Inscriptions:
Farnham; Scotton; Staveley; Arkendale (1 fiche)
Killinghall; Burnt Yates; Padside; Ramsgill (1 fiche)
Methodist Chapels: Harrogate circuit; Gracious Street; Knaresborough; Beamsley; West Tanfield (1 fiche)
High Harrogate: Christ Church; St John (Bilton); St Peter; St Wilfred (2 fiche)
Dacre: Providence chapel; Dacre Banks: Holy Trinity (1 fiche)
Census Index 1851:
Harrogate Area
Knaresborough/Wetherby area
Parish Registers: Ripon, Kirkby Malzeard, Dallowgill, Mickley, Winksley, Sawley, Bishop Thornton, Aldfield, Bishop Monkton, Markington, Skelton-on-Ure, Sharow, North Stainley, Holy Trinity Ripon, Ripon Workhouse

Publications list:
Available in print

Access to staff:
Contact by letter and by e-mail
Hours: Mon to Fri, 0900 to 1700

Family history group:
Ripon, Harrogate & District Family History Group
18 Aspin Drive, Knaresborough, North Yorkshire, HG5 8HH

Membership Secretary:
Ripon Historical Society
Downe, Baldersby, Thirsk, North Yorkshire, YO7 4PP; e-mail: dolonic@cs.com

RNIB NATIONAL LIBRARY SERVICE

Far Cromwell Road, Bredbury, Stockport, Cheshire, SK6 2SG

Tel: 0303 123 9999
Fax: 0161 355 2098
E-mail: library@rnib.org.uk

Website:
http://www.rnib.org.uk/library
Provides access to electronic books via OPAC and accessible e-reference materials plus information about library services including reader development tools.

Enquiries:
Enquiries to: Marketing Communications Officer
Direct tel: 0161 355 2080
Direct e-mail: megan.gilks@nlbuk.org

Founded:
1882

Created by the merger of:
National Library for the Blind and RNIB (year of change 2007)

Formerly called:
National Library for the Blind

continued overleaf

Organisation type and purpose:
National organisation (membership is by subscription), voluntary organisation, registered charity (charity number 226227), consultancy. A gateway to free comprehensive library services for those who cannot read print and their intermediaries. Its aim is to enable all visually impaired people to have the same access to library services as sighted people.

Subject coverage:
Library service to blind and partially sighted readers, including a range of electronic library services via the internet.

Museum or gallery collection, archive, or library special collection:
Collection of 40,000 titles in Braille including fiction and non-fiction, books for younger readers (aged eight or over) and Braille sheet music.
Giant Print Library (books in 24pt type) for children, young people and adults.
Small collection of large print books covering classics and standard titles.
Over 17,000 titles in the Talking Book service.

Non-library collection catalogue:
All or part available online

Library catalogue:
All or part available online and in print

Printed publications:
Annual Review (free)
New Books (for members, 6 times per annum, in print, Braille, on disk or by e-mail, free)
Read On (for members, 4 times per annum, in print, Braille, on disk or by e-mail, free)
Order printed publications from: Helpline: 0303 123 9999

Electronic and video publications:
Catalogues and lists available on disk (free)

Publications list:
Available online

Access to staff:
Contact by letter, by telephone, by fax, by e-mail and via website. Appointment necessary.
Hours: Mon to Fri, 0845 to 1800; Sat, 0900 to 1600

Access to building, collection or gallery:
Prior appointment required

Access for disabled people:
Parking provided, ramped entry, access to all public areas

Links with:
IFLA

RNID

19–23 Featherstone Street, London, EC1Y 8SL

Tel: 0808 808 0123 (Textphone 0808 808 9000)
Fax: 020 7296 8199
E-mail: informationline@mid.org.uk

Website:
http://www.rnid.org.uk

Enquiries:
Enquiries to: Information Line
Direct tel: 0808 808 0123
Direct e-mail: informationline@rnid.org.uk

Founded:
1911

Organisation type and purpose:
Registered charity (charity number 207720), working to change the world for the UK's 9 million deaf and hard of hearing people. Does this with the help of members, by campaigning and lobbying, raising awareness of deafness and hearing loss, providing services and through social, medical and technical research.

Subject coverage:
Deafness, hearing loss, hearing, tinnitus, communication support, BSL, sign language, lip-reading, campaigns, information, services, and research into deafness and hearing loss.

Museum or gallery collection, archive, or library special collection:
One of Europe's largest library collections of materials on all aspects of deafness and hearing research
Rare pre-1800 book collection on deafness

Library catalogue:
All or part available in-house

Printed publications:
One in Seven (membership magazine)
RNID provides a range of leaflets, factsheets and priced publications on various aspects of deafness, hearing loss and tinnitus

Publications list:
Available online and in print

Access to staff:
Contact by letter, by telephone, by fax, by e-mail and via website. Appointment necessary.
Hours: Mon to Fri, 0900 to 1700

Access to building, collection or gallery:
Unable to provide a drop-in service – please contact the Information Line before visiting
Hours: 0900 to 1700

Access for disabled people:
Toilet facilities, lifts and BSL interpreters
Special comments: Lift from pavement level

Other addresses:
RNID Products
   1 Haddonbrook Business Centre, Fallodan Road, Orton Southgate, Peterborough, PE2 6YX; tel: 01733 232607 (textphone 01733 238020); fax: 01733 361161; website: www.rnid.org.uk/shop
RNID Typetalk
   PO Box 284, Liverpool, L69 3UZ; tel: 18001 0800 500 888 (textphone users), 0800 7311 888 (hearing people); fax: 0151 709 8119; website: http://www.rnid-typetalk.org.uk

RNID SCOTLAND

Formal name: Royal National Institute for Deaf and Hard of Hearing People (Scotland)

Empire House, 131 West Nile Street, Glasgow, G1 2RX

Tel: 0141 341 5330\ Minicom no. 0141 341 5347
Fax: 0141 354 0176
E-mail: RNIDScotland@rnid.org.uk

Website:
http://www.rnid.org.uk

Enquiries:
Enquiries to: Regional Communications Officer

Founded:
1966

Organisation type and purpose:
Membership association (membership is by subscription), registered charity (charity number 207720).

Subject coverage:
Information, training, specialist telephone services, assistive devices, communication services unit, employment training and skills service.

Non-library collection catalogue:
All or part available online

Printed publications:
One in Seven (magazine, members)
RNID titles cover a wide range of topics dealing with:
Communications
Hearing Aids
Special equipment
Employment
Education
Benefits
Medical
Tinnitus

Publications list:
Available online and in print

Access to staff:
Contact by letter, by telephone, by fax, by e-mail, in person and via website. Appointment necessary.
Hours: Mon to Fri, 0900 to 1700

Access for disabled people:
Toilet facilities, lift

Head Office:
Royal National Institute for Deaf and Hard of Hearing People
   19–23 Featherstone Street, London, EC1Y 8SL; tel: 020 7296 8000; textphone 0808 808 0123 and 0808 808 9000; fax: 020 7296 8199; e-mail: helpline@rnid.org.uk

ROAD OPERATORS SAFETY COUNCIL

Acronym or abbreviation: ROSCO

Cowley House, Watlington Road, Oxford, OX4 6GA

Tel: 01865 775552
Fax: 01865 775552
E-mail: admin@rosco-uk.org

Website:
http://www.rosco.org.uk

Enquiries:
Enquiries to: Executive Secretary

Founded:
1955

Subject coverage:
Road safety in the bus and coach industry, accidents and safe driving.

Printed publications:
Safety First (newsletter)

Access to staff:
Contact by letter, by telephone and by fax
Hours: Mon to Fri, 0900 to 1700

ROADPEACE

Shakespeare Business Centre, 245A Coldharbour Lane, London, SW9 8RR

Tel: 020 7733 1603 (office); 0845 4500 355 (helpline)
E-mail: info@roadpeace.org

Website:
http://www.roadpeace.org

Enquiries:
Enquiries to: Charity Coordinator

Founded:
1992

Organisation type and purpose:
Membership association (charity number 1087192).

Subject coverage:
People bereaved or injured by road crash.

Information services:
Emotional and practical support for those bereaved or injured in a road crash.

Access to staff:
Contact by letter, by telephone, by e-mail and via website
Hours: Mon to Fri, 0900 to 1700

ROBENS CENTRE FOR OCCUPATIONAL HEALTH & SAFETY

University of Surrey, 3–4 Huxley Road, Surrey Research Park, Guildford, Surrey, GU2 7RE

Tel: 01483 686690
Fax: 01483 686691
E-mail: cohs@surrey.ac.uk

Website:
http://www.surrey.ac.uk/Robens/rbhome.html

Enquiries:
Enquiries to: Administrator

Founded:
1978

Organisation type and purpose:
University department or institute, consultancy, research organisation.

Subject coverage:
Toxicology, occupational health and hygiene, environmental health, microbiology, analytical chemistry, psychology, ergonomics, human physiology, epidemiology and overseas development.

Printed publications:
Large selection of published journal articles, conference proceedings and reports available

Publications list:
Available in print

Access to staff:
Contact by letter, by fax and by e-mail
Hours: Mon to Fri, 0900 to 1700

Access for disabled people:
Parking provided

ROBERT GORDON UNIVERSITY – GEORGINA SCOTT SUTHERLAND LIBRARY

Garthdee Road, Garthdee, Aberdeen, AB10 7QE

Tel: 01224 263450
Fax: 01224 263460
E-mail: library@rgu.ac.uk

Website:
http://www.rgu.ac.uk/library
http://www.rgu.ac.uk/library/service/special.htm
Details of staff and assistance available to disabled users.

Enquiries:
Enquiries to: Director of Knowledge and Information Services
Direct tel: 01224 263452
Direct fax: 01224 263455

Organisation type and purpose:
University library.

Subject coverage:
Applied science, architecture, art, business management, computer science, engineering (mechanical, electrical, offshore), food and nutrition, health, librarianship, information studies, mathematics, nursing, pharmacy, public administration, social studies, surveying, law, physiotherapy, occupational therapy, radiography, European information, tourism.

Museum or gallery collection, archive, or library special collection:
Art and architecture antiquarian collection

Library catalogue:
All or part available online

Access to staff:
Contact by letter, by telephone, by fax, by e-mail, in person and via website
Hours: Details of opening hours during term time and vacations (for the Georgina Scott Sutherland Library and the St Andrew Street Library) are available online

Access for disabled people:
Parking provided, ramped entry, level entry, toilet facilities
Special comments: Details of staff contacts and assistance available can be found online.

ROBERT GORDON UNIVERSITY – SCHOOL OF INFORMATION AND MEDIA

Faculty of Management Building, Garthdee Road, Aberdeen, AB10 7QE

Tel: 01224 263900
Fax: 01224 263553
E-mail: sim@rgu.ac.uk

Website:
http://www.rgu.com
Virtual campus, online courses.
http://www.rgu.ac.uk
Courses available; recent research; staff information; links to relevant resources.

Enquiries:
Enquiries to: Head of School
Direct tel: 01224 263901

Founded:
1751

Organisation type and purpose:
University department or institute, training organisation, consultancy, research organisation. The School undertakes teaching and research, consultancy and training in the fields of library and information sciences, publishing, corporate and technical communications, and modern languages.

Printed publications:
From Oct 1999, an increasing range of online course modules at postgraduate level, which can be taken singly or as parts of Masters degree programmes

Electronic and video publications:
Occasional research reports available for downloading free of charge
For details, access the School's Web Pages

Access to staff:
Contact by letter, by telephone, by fax and by e-mail. Appointment necessary. All charged.
Hours: Mon to Fri, 0900 to 1700

Access to building, collection or gallery:
No access other than to staff
Special comments: See separate entry for the University's Library.

ROBINSON COLLEGE LIBRARY

Grange Road, Cambridge, CB3 9AN

Tel: 01223 339100

Enquiries:
Enquiries to: Librarian
Direct tel: 01223 339124

Organisation type and purpose:
University department or institute.
College Library of the University of Cambridge.

Subject coverage:
General, for undergraduate teaching.

Access to staff:
Access for members only.
Hours: Mon to Fri, 0900 to 1700

ROCHDALE LIBRARIES

Wheatsheaf Library, Baillie Street, Rochdale, Lancashire, OL16 1JZ

Tel: 01706 924900
Fax: 01706 924992
E-mail: library.service@rochdale.gov.uk

Website:
http://www.rochdale.gov.uk/
List of addresses, phone numbers, hours of opening, services for visually-impaired people, services for under-5s. Open for learning, British sign language, reminiscence packs, lending. Local studies, reference library, children's services

Enquiries:
Enquiries to: Reference and Information Development Librarian
Direct fax: 01706 924934

Organisation type and purpose:
Local government body, public library.

Subject coverage:
General, local history, international collection on co-operation.

Museum or gallery collection, archive, or library special collection:
Collection of books on the co-operative movement and co-operation (700 items)
Tim Bobbin (John Collier) collection

Non-library collection catalogue:
All or part available online and in-house

Library catalogue:
All or part available online and in-house

Printed publications:
List of periodicals and newspapers held

Access to staff:
Contact by letter, by telephone, by fax, by e-mail and in person
Hours: Mon, 0930 to 1930; Tue to Fri, 0930 to 1730; Sat, 0930 to 1700

Parent body:
Rochdale Metropolitan Borough Council

ROCHFORD DISTRICT COUNCIL

Council Offices, South Street, Rochford, Essex, SS4 1BW

Tel: 01702 546366
Fax: 01702 545737
E-mail: information@rochford.gov.uk

Enquiries:
Enquiries to: Civic and Public Relations Officer
Direct tel: 01702 318144
Direct fax: 01702 318161
Direct e-mail: helen-collins@rochford.gov.uk

Founded:
1974

Organisation type and purpose:
Local government body.

Printed publications:
Official Guide (free, updated every two years)
The Old House (for purchase)
Tourism Guide (free)

Access to staff:
Contact by letter, by telephone, by fax, by e-mail and in person
Hours: Mon to Thu, 0830 to 1700; Fri, 0830 to 1630

ROCKEFELLER MEDICAL LIBRARY

UCL Institute of Neurology, The National Hospital, 23 Queen Square, London, WC1N 3BG

Tel: 020 7829 8709
E-mail: library@ion.ucl.ac.uk

Website:
http://www.ion.ucl.ac.uk/library

Enquiries:
Enquiries to: Librarian

Founded:
1950

Organisation type and purpose:
University department or institute.
Postgraduate medical institute.

Subject coverage:
Clinical neurology and allied fields, historical neurology, neurosurgery and neuroscience.

Museum or gallery collection, archive, or library special collection:
Historical neurology
Queen Square Collection (of staff publications)
Current Neurology, Neurosurgery and Neuroscience books, journals and multimedia

Non-library collection catalogue:
All or part available online

Library catalogue:
All or part available online

Access to staff:
Contact by letter, by telephone, by e-mail, in person and via website. Appointment necessary.
Hours: Mon to Fri, 0900 to 1700

continued overleaf

Access to building, collection or gallery:
Prior appointment required

Links with:
National Hospital for Neurology and
Neurosurgery
University of London

Parent body:
University College London

RODBASTON COLLEGE

Rodbaston, Penkridge, Stafford, ST19 5PH

Tel: 01785 712209
Fax: 01785 715701
E-mail: enquiries@southstaffs.ac.uk

Enquiries:
Enquiries to: Reception

Organisation type and purpose:
Suitable for ages: 16+.
College for training and education in the land-based industries.

Subject coverage:
Courses available in areas of study for the land-based industries.

Access to staff:
Contact by letter
Hours: Mon to Fri, 0900 to 1700

ROEHAMPTON UNIVERSITY

Learning Resources Centre, Roehampton Lane,
London, SW15 5SZ

Tel: 020 8392 3770
Fax: 020 8392 3259

Website:
http://www.roehampton.ac.uk

Enquiries:
Enquiries to: University Librarian and Director of
Learning Services
Direct tel: 020 8392 3051
Direct fax: 020 8392 3026
Direct e-mail: s.clegg@roehampton.ac.uk

Founded:
2000

Organisation type and purpose:
University library.

Subject coverage:
English language and literature, modern
languages, art, drama, dance studies, theology and
religious studies, history, mathematics education,
music, film and TV studies, children's literature,
arts, therapies, arts management, education,
sociology, social policy and administration,
business studies, applied computing, applied
consumer studies, retail and product management,
anthropology, biological sciences, health studies,
human and social biology, natural resource studies,
psychology, counselling, sport studies.

**Museum or gallery collection, archive, or library
special collection:**
Children's Literature Collection
Early Childhood Archive
Froebel Archive

Library catalogue:
All or part available online

Access to staff:
Contact by letter, by telephone, by fax, by e-mail
and via website
Hours: Term time: Mon to Fri, 0800 to 2100; Sat,
1100 to 1800; Sun, 1100 to 1800
Vacations: usually Mon to Fri, 0900 to 1700, but
phone to confirm

Affiliated to:
M25 Consortium of HE Libraries
SCONUL
UK Libraries Plus

Also at:
Roehampton University
    Froebel College
Roehampton University
    Southlands College
Roehampton University
    Whitelands College
Roehampton University
    Digby Stuart College

ROFFEY PARK INSTITUTE

Forest Road, Horsham, West Sussex, RH12 4TD

Tel: 01293 851644
Fax: 01293 851565
E-mail: info@roffeypark.com

Website:
http://www.roffeypark.com

Enquiries:
Enquiries to: Manager, Learning Resource Centre
Direct tel: 01293 854052
Direct e-mail: lrc@roffeypark.com

Founded:
1946

Organisation type and purpose:
Registered charity (charity number 254591),
training organisation, consultancy.
Independent management education institute.

Subject coverage:
Manager development, interpersonal relationships,
developing the developers, personal effectiveness,
assessment centres, self-managed learning,
teamwork, organisational and leadership
development, human resources.

Library catalogue:
All or part available online and in print

Printed publications:
Newsletter
Brochure
Order printed publications from: Marketing
Department

Electronic and video publications:
Research reports (online)

Publications list:
Available online

Access to staff:
Contact by letter, by telephone, by e-mail, in
person and via website. Appointment necessary.
Access for members only. Non-members charged.

Access to building, collection or gallery:
Hours: Mon to Fri, 0900 to 1700
Special comments: Roffey Park course participants
only

ROLLS-ROYCE ENTHUSIASTS' CLUB

Acronym or abbreviation: RREC Limited

The Hunt House, High Street, Paulerspury,
Towcester, Northamptonshire, NN12 7NA

Tel: 01327 811788
Fax: 01327 811797
E-mail: admin@rrec.org.uk

Website:
http://www.rrec.org.uk

Enquiries:
Enquiries to: General Secretary

Founded:
1957

Organisation type and purpose:
International organisation, membership
association (membership is by subscription),
present number of members: 9,800.

Subject coverage:
Rolls-Royce and Bentley archives containing car
build records from 1904 onwards.

Printed publications:
Rolls-Royce Enthusiasts Club Advertiser & the
    Bulletin
R-R EC Bulletin

Access to staff:
Contact by letter, by telephone, by fax and by e-mail. Appointment necessary.
Hours: Mon to Fri, 0900 to 1700

ROLLS-ROYCE PLC

Library Services, Rolls-Royce plc, PO Box 31,
Victory Road, Derby, DE24 8BJ

Tel: 01332 242424
Fax: 01332 247886

Enquiries:
Enquiries to: Technical Librarian
Direct tel: 01332 248277

Organisation type and purpose:
Manufacturing industry.

Subject coverage:
Gas turbines, aerospace, aerodynamics,
mechanical engineering, materials, fluid
mechanics, jet propulsion, aero engines.

Printed publications:
R R Heritage Trust Publications historical series,
    technical series (tel: 01332 248181)
The Jet Engine book (Garry Crook, tel: 01332
    246504)

Access to staff:
Contact by letter, by telephone and by fax
Hours: Mon to Fri, 0800 to 1600

ROMANIAN CULTURAL CENTRE

8th Floor, 54–62 Regent Street, London, W1B 5RE

Tel: 020 7439 4052
Fax: 020 7437 5908
E-mail: mail@romanianculturalcentre.org.uk

Website:
http://www.romanianculturalcentre.org.uk

Organisation type and purpose:
An independent association which promotes
Romanian cultural programmes and acts as a focus
for the Romanian community in Britain.

Subject coverage:
Romanian culture.

ROMANY AND TRAVELLER FAMILY HISTORY SOCIETY

Acronym or abbreviation: RTFHS

c/o Ms. Margaret Montgomery (Secretary), 7 Park
Rise, Northchurch, Berkhamsted, Hertfordshire,
HP4 3RT

Website:
http://www.rtfhs.org.uk

Organisation type and purpose:
A non-political non-profit self-help group, with
membership by subscription.

Subject coverage:
Romany and traveller family history.

Printed publications:
Romany Routes (quarterly journal)

ROOM, THE NATIONAL COUNCIL FOR HOUSING AND PLANNING

RTPI, 41 Botolph Lane, London, EC3R 8DL

Tel: 020 7929 9494
Fax: 020 7929 9490
E-mail: room@rtpi.org.uk

Website:
http://www.room.org.uk

Enquiries:
Enquiries to: External Relations Manager

Other contacts: Assistant Director, Editor of Axis (Journal of Housing, Planning & Regeneration)

Founded:
1900

Organisation type and purpose:
Advisory body, membership association, registered charity.
Campaigning for better housing, planning and regeneration.

Subject coverage:
Housing and planning policy issues, house building and renovation, housing finance, student housing, sheltered housing, community alarms, planning control and policy guidance, regeneration, urban renewal, carbon monoxide/fire control.

Museum or gallery collection, archive, or library special collection:
Historical documents relating to NHPTC

Printed publications:
A Buyers Guide to Retirement Housing (Feb 1995, £4.95)
Axis, the Journal of Housing, Planning and Regeneration (6 times a year)
Best Value for Partnership Housing (Dec 1999, £8.50)
Community Regeneration (June 2001, £5)
Defining Positive Planning (Dec 2000, £5)
Deregulation of the Domestic Energy Market (Aug 1997, £7)
Energy Efficient Design (June 1995, £6)
Financing Partnership Housing (August 1994, £6)
Household Growth – Accommodating Change (Apr 1997, £6)
No Losers-New Users: New Homes from Empty Properties (Sep 1994, £8.50)
Planning Out the Empties (Nov 1998, £5)
Potential Death Traps (Feb 1995, £6)
Regenerating Communities and Neighbourhoods (Apr 1998, £6)
Still Rising High (Feb 1997, £8.50)
Sustaining High Density Living (Dec 1999, £8.50)
Sustainable Living (Jul 2000, £8.50)
Tackling Problem Estates (June 1996, £7)

Publications list:
Available in print

Access to staff:
Contact by letter, by telephone, by fax, by e-mail and via website. Appointment necessary.
Hours: Mon to Fri, 0900 to 1700

Member of:
International Federation of Housing and Planning
The Hague, Netherlands

ROSE BRUFORD COLLEGE

Lamorbey Park, Sidcup, Kent, DA15 9DF

Tel: 020 8308 2600
Fax: 020 8308 0542
E-mail: enquiries@bruford.ac.uk

Website:
http://www.bruford.ac.uk

Enquiries:
Enquiries to: Librarian
Direct tel: 020 8308 2626

Founded:
1950

Organisation type and purpose:
A university sector institution.

Subject coverage:
Theatre, literature, drama, music.

Library catalogue:
All or part available in-house

Printed publications:
Library guide
Library information sheets

Access to staff:
Contact by letter, by telephone, by fax, by e-mail and in person. Appointment necessary.

Hours: Mon to Fri, 0900 to 1700

Access to building, collection or gallery:
By appointment
Hours: Mon to Fri, 0900 to 1700

Access for disabled people:
By appointment
Hours: Mon to Fri, 0900 to 1700

ROSKILL INFORMATION SERVICES LIMITED

27a Leopold Road, London, SW19 7BB

Tel: 020 8944 0066
Fax: 020 8947 9568
E-mail: info@roskill.co.uk

Website:
http://www.roskill.com

Enquiries:
Enquiries to: Information Officer
Other contacts: Managing Director

Founded:
1930

Organisation type and purpose:
Consultancy, publishing house.

Subject coverage:
Publishes reports on the markets for metals and minerals, covering production, consumption, prices of, and trade in, the materials covered; end-use materials covered include plastics, paints and pigments, paper and pulp.

Trade and statistical information:
Production and consumption information on metals and minerals, e.g. base minerals, precious metals, industrial minerals and ferroalloys.
Statistical information on plastics, paper and pulp, paints and pigments, filler materials, etc.

Library catalogue:
All or part available in-house

Printed publications:
Lithium Digest
Roskill's Letter from Japan (monthly)
Roskill's Reports on Metals and Minerals (about 80 on the economics of individual metals and minerals)
Roskill Yearbooks 1996–2000

Publications list:
Available online and in print

Access to staff:
Contact by letter, by telephone, by fax, by e-mail and via website. Appointment necessary.
Hours: Mon to Fri, 0800 to 1700

Access to building, collection or gallery:
No prior appointment required

Affiliated to:
Roskill Consulting Group

Parent body:
Roskill Information Services Limited

ROSPA ADVANCED DRIVERS AND RIDERS

Acronym or abbreviation: RoADAR

Edgbaston Park, 353 Bristol Road, Edgbaston, Birmingham, B5 7ST

Tel: 0121 248 2000
Fax: 0121 248 2001
E-mail: mrae@rospa.com

Website:
http://www.roadar.org

Enquiries:
Enquiries to: Administrator
Direct tel: 0121 248 2099

Organisation type and purpose:
Membership association (membership is by subscription, qualification), registered charity (charity number 207823).

Subject coverage:
Advanced driving; advanced motorcycling; tests and courses; road safety.

Library catalogue:
All or part available in-house

Printed publications:
Care on the Road (newsletter)
Greener Motoring Guide
Essential Minibus Driving
Order printed publications from: Customer Support

Electronic and video publications:
Driver Profiler
Driving for Work film
Driver E-learning
Hazard Perception Challenge
MORR Complete Compliance Tool
Order electronic and video publications from:
jbartlett@rospa.com

Publications list:
Available online and in print

Access to staff:
Contact by letter, by telephone, by fax and by e-mail
Hours: Mon to Fri, 0900 to 1700

Access to building, collection or gallery:
Prior appointment required
Hours: Mon to Fri, 0900 to 1700

Access for disabled people:
Toilet facilities

Constituent part of:
Royal Society for the Prevention of Accidents
tel: 0121 248 2000; fax: 0121 248 2001; e-mail: help@rospa.co.uk; website: http://www.rospa.com

ROSPA DRIVER AND FLEET SOLUTIONS

Formal name: Royal Society for the Prevention of Accidents
Acronym or abbreviation: RoSPA

Edgbaston Park, 353 Bristol Road, Edgbaston, Birmingham, B5 7ST

Tel: 0121 248 2233
Fax: 0121 248 2050
E-mail: sales@rospa.co.uk

Enquiries:
Enquiries to: Manager
Direct tel: 0121 248 2037
Direct e-mail: halcock@rospa.co.uk

Organisation type and purpose:
National organisation, professional body, registered charity (charity number 207823), training organisation, consultancy, research organisation, publishing house. Providing workplace safety and Driver and Fleet Solutions. RoSPA's purpose is to enhance the quality of life by exercising a powerful influence for accident prevention.

Subject coverage:
Training operation in all aspects of defensive driving for companies.

Museum or gallery collection, archive, or library special collection:
General Road Safety/Driving – books, documents and workplace safety.

Non-library collection catalogue:
All or part available in-house

Library catalogue:
All or part available in-house

Publications list:
Available in print

Access to staff:
Contact by letter, by telephone, by fax, by e-mail, in person and via website. Appointment necessary. All charged.
Hours: Mon to Fri, 0900 to 1700

continued overleaf

Access to building, collection or gallery:
No prior appointment required
Hours: Mon to Fri, 0900 to 1700
Special comments: Library available for reference for members only.

Also at:
RoSPA Northern Ireland
Nella House, 4 Dargan Crescent, Belfast, BT3 9JP; tel: 028 9050 1160 / 0870 777 2176; fax: 028 9050 1164 / 0870 777 2186
RoSPA Scotland
Livingstone House, 43 Discovery Terrace, Heriot-Watt University Research Park, Edinburgh, EH14 4AP; tel: 0131 449 9378; fax: 0131 449 9379
RoSPA Wales
7 Cleeve House, Lambourne Crescent, Cardiff, CF14 5GP; tel: 029 2025 0600 / 0870 777 2180; fax: 029 2025 0601 / 0870 777 2181

ROSPA NATIONAL SAFE DRIVING AWARDS

Acronym or abbreviation: NSDA

Edgbaston Park, 353 Bristol Road, Edgbaston, Birmingham, B5 7ST

Tel: 0121 248 2000
Fax: 0121 248 2001

Enquiries:
Enquiries to: Administrator
Direct tel: 0121 248 2106
Direct e-mail: dgrady@rospa.com

Organisation type and purpose:
Voluntary organisation.

Subject coverage:
Safe driving.

Printed publications:
Care on the Road (newsletter)

Access to staff:
Contact by letter, by telephone and by fax
Hours: Mon to Fri, 0900 to 1700

Constituent part of:
Driver and Fleet Solutions – RoSPA

ROTARY INTERNATIONAL IN GREAT BRITAIN AND IRELAND

Acronym or abbreviation: RIBI

Kinwarton Road, Alcester, Warwickshire, B49 6BP

Tel: 01789 765411
Fax: 01789 765570
E-mail: secretary@ribi.org

Website:
http://www.rotary-ribi.org

Enquiries:
Enquiries to: Secretary; CEO
Other contacts: The President

Founded:
1914

Organisation type and purpose:
Membership association.
For charitable, benevolent and philanthropic purposes.

Subject coverage:
Service to the local, national and international communities through projects, ideas and physical assistance, leading to greater international understanding; scholarships and youth exchanges in other countries; ethics in business and professions; the ideal of service.

Printed publications:
Rotary (6 times a year, £1)

Electronic and video publications:
Rotary in Vision (£5 plus p&p)

Access to staff:
Contact by letter, by fax, by e-mail and via website
Hours: Mon to Fri, 0900 to 1700

Access for disabled people:
Parking provided, ramped entry, toilet facilities

Parent body:
Rotary International
One Rotary Center, 1560 Sherman Avenue, Evanston, Illinois, 60201, USA; tel: 00 1 847 866 3000; fax: 00 1 847 328 8554

ROTARY OWNERS' CLUB

Acronym or abbreviation: ROC

Dunbar, Ingatestone Road, Highwood, Chelmsford, Essex, CM1 3QU

E-mail: rotaryoc@aol.com

Website:
www.rotaryownersclub.co.uk
Forum; club shop; gallery.

Enquiries:
Enquiries to: Secretary

Founded:
1982

Organisation type and purpose:
Membership association (membership is by subscription).

Subject coverage:
To encourage the ownership, use of and knowledge relating to the Wankel rotary engine, in particular its application in powered two-wheelers. Information is pooled on the maintenance of such motorcycles; a register is being compiled of all existing machines.

Museum or gallery collection, archive, or library special collection:
Copies of owners' manuals, handbook and parts lists available to members.
Discounted spares (oil, spark plugs, batteries, etc.) available to members.

Printed publications:
The Epitrochoid (club magazine, quarterly, free to members)

Access to staff:
Contact by letter and by e-mail
Hours: Mon to Fri, 0900 to 1700

ROTHAMSTED RESEARCH

Harpenden, Hertfordshire, AL5 2JQ

Tel: 01582 763133
Fax: 01582 760981

Website:
http://www.rothamsted.ac.uk

Enquiries:
Enquiries to: Librarian
Direct e-mail: res.library@bbsrc.ac.uk

Founded:
1843

Organisation type and purpose:
Research organisation.

Subject coverage:
Agricultural research (excluding animal husbandry, diseases, etc., plant breeding and agricultural economics); pure research on many botanical and biochemical aspects of agriculture; entomology; farms; insecticides and fungicides; nematology; pedology; plant pathology; soil microbiology; agricultural computer work; statistics.

Museum or gallery collection, archive, or library special collection:
Agricultural books, 1471–1840
British Farm Livestock, prints and paintings, 1780–1910

Library catalogue:
All or part available online

Printed publications:
Annual Report

Access to staff:
Appointment necessary.
Hours: Mon to Fri, 0900 to 1700

Funded by:
Biotechnology and Biological Sciences Research Council

Links with:
Broom's Barn Experimental Station
Higham, Suffolk, IP28 6NP
North Wyke Research
Okehampton, Devon, EX20 2SB

ROTHER DISTRICT COUNCIL

Town Hall, Bexhill-on-Sea, East Sussex, TN39 3JX

Tel: 01424 787878
Fax: 01424 787879
E-mail: chiefexec@rother.gov.uk

Website:
http://www.rother.gov.uk

Enquiries:
Enquiries to: Chief Executive

Founded:
1974

Organisation type and purpose:
Local government body.

Subject coverage:
Council issues.

Access to staff:
Contact by letter, by telephone, by fax, by e-mail, in person and via website. Appointment necessary.
Hours: Mon to Thu, 0830 to 1700; Fri, 0830 to 1630

Access for disabled people:
Ramped entry

Other addresses:
Community Help Point (Battle)
6 Market Street, Battle, East Sussex, TN33 0XB; tel: 01424 787478; fax: 01424 787479; e-mail: customerservices@rither.gov.uk
Community Help Point (Bexhill)
Amherst Road, Bexhill-on-Sea, East Sussex; tel: 01424 787999; fax: 01424 787766; e-mail: customerservices@rither.gov.uk
Community Help Point (Rye)
25 Cinque Ports Street, Rye, East Sussex, TN31 7AD; tel: 01797 222293; fax: 01797 227576; e-mail: customerservices@rither.gov.uk

ROTHERHAM ARCHIVES AND LOCAL STUDIES SERVICE

Formal name: Rotherham Metropolitan Borough Council: Archives and Local Studies Service

Central Library, Walker Place, Rotherham, South Yorkshire, S65 1JH

Tel: 01709 823616
Fax: 01709 823650
E-mail: archives@rotherham.gov.uk

Website:
http://www.rotherham.gov.uk/info/448/records_and_archives-information_and_advice

Founded:
1986

Organisation type and purpose:
Local government body, public library and archive repository.

Subject coverage:
The local history of the area of Rotherham MBC.

Museum or gallery collection, archive, or library special collection:
Archival holdings include records of Rotherham MBC and predecessor local authorities; quarter sessions and magistrates' courts; hospitals; nonconformist archives; businesses (including iron and steel, glass, coal mining, brass founding, pottery); family and estate records; solicitors

Local studies holdings include books and pamphlets; directories; census returns; newspapers; journals; digital and paper maps

Non-library collection catalogue:
All or part available online and in-house

Library catalogue:
All or part available online and in-house

Printed publications:
Rotherham's Woodland Heritage (M. Jones, Rotherwood Press, 1995, ISBN 0 903666 86 3, £6.95)
A History of Rotherham's Roads and Transport (H. Smith, Rotherham Libraries, 1992, ISBN 0 903666 67 7, £5.95)
A Walk Round Rotherham – the town centre (1994, Rotherham Libraries, ISBN 0 903666 74 X, £2)
Boyhood Memories of Wath (£3.75)
Rotherham and District Transport, vol. 1 (to 1914) (C. C. Hall, Rotherwood Press, 1997, ISBN 0 903666 89 8, £18.95)
Rotherham and District Transport, vol. 2 (1914–39) (C. C. Hall, Rotherwood Press, 1997, ISBN 0 903666 92 8, £16.50)
Rotherham and District Transport, vol. 3 (1940–74; in progress)
Rotherham Town Public Houses (P. Satterthwaite, Rotherham Libraries, 1992, ISBN 0 903666 79 0, £4.50)
The Saltway Trail (£1.50)

Publications list:
Available online and in print

Access to staff:
Contact by letter, by telephone, by fax, by e-mail and in person
Hours: Tue, Wed, Fri, 1000 to 1700; Thu, 1300 to 1700; Sat, 0900 to 1300 and 1400 to 1600

ROTHERHAM CENTRAL LIBRARY AND ARTS CENTRE

Walker Place, Rotherham, South Yorkshire, S65 1JH

Tel: 01709 823611
Fax: 01709 823650
E-mail: central.library@rotherham.gov.uk

Website:
http://www.rotherham.gov.uk
Information on RMBC services, community information, business information.

Enquiries:
Enquiries to: Librarian

Organisation type and purpose:
Local government body, public library.

Subject coverage:
General; local history and study of the Rotherham Metropolitan Borough area; South Yorkshire potteries.

Museum or gallery collection, archive, or library special collection:
Mansell (Rotherham) Parish Library
British Standards (CD-ROM)

Library catalogue:
All or part available online and in-house

Printed publications:
Directory of community information

Access to staff:
Contact by letter, by telephone, by fax, by e-mail, in person and via website
Hours: Mon and Thu, 0830 to 2000; Tue, Wed and Fri, 0830 to 1730; Sat, 0900 to 1600

ROUGH FELL SHEEP BREEDERS ASSOCIATION

High Newstead Farm, Jervaulx, Masham, Ripon, North Yorkshire, HG4 4PJ

Tel: 07746 466794
E-mail: roughfell@fsmail.net

Website:
http://www.roughfellsheep.co.uk

Enquiries:
Enquiries to: Secretary

Subject coverage:
Rough Fell sheep.

Publications list:
Available in print

ROUNDERS ENGLAND

Acronym or abbreviation: RE

PO Box 4458, Sheffield, S20 9DP

Tel: 01142 480357
E-mail: enquiries@roundersengland.co.uk

Website:
http://www.roundersengland.co.uk/rounders/index.cfm
Website of the sport's governing body in England. Provides information about the game, coaching and umpiring courses, tournaments, resources for sale and promotion of the sport at all levels.

Enquiries:
Other contacts: For further contacts, please use the Rounders England website

Founded:
1943

Formerly called:
National Rounders Association (year of change 2009)

Organisation type and purpose:
Rounders England is the sport's governing body in England.

Subject coverage:
Provides a structure for the sport from the board, county associations and clubs, through to individual members and volunteers. It is responsible for the management and training of the England squads and works alongside the other home national governing bodies to provide competition opportunities. Rounders England also co-ordinates a development network that provides a pathway for aspiring players to progress from schools and clubs to the national squad. It provides information about the game, runs coaching and umpiring courses, holds tournaments, sells resources and promotes the sport at all levels.

Museum or gallery collection, archive, or library special collection:
Past publications

Printed publications:
1st Post, 2nd Post, 3rd Post (news sheet)
4th Post (magazine, includes Annual Report)
A range of resources are available for purchase via the Rounders England website: http://www.roundersengland.co.uk/rounders/index.cfm/shop/resources

Publications list:
Available online and in print

Access to staff:
Contact by letter, by telephone, by e-mail and via website
Hours: Mon to Thu, 0900 to 1700; Fri, 0900 to 1600
Special comments: Telephone answering service available at other times.

Access to building, collection or gallery:
No access other than to staff

Links with:
Central Council for Physical Recreation (CCPR)
Sport England
Sportscoach UK
Women's Sports Foundation
Youth Sport Trust

ROUTLEDGE REFERENCE – DIRECTORIES

Albert House, 4th Floor, 1–4 Singer Street, London, EC2A 4BQ

Tel: 020 7017 6000
Fax: 020 7017 6720
E-mail: reference@routledge.co.uk

Website:
http://www.worldwhoswho.com
http://www.routledge.com/reference
http://www.worldoflearning.com
http://www.europaworld.com
http://www.routledgeonline.com

Enquiries:
Enquiries to: Marketing Manager
Direct tel: 020 7017 6566

Organisation type and purpose:
Publishing house.

Subject coverage:
Geographic, economic and political information on every country in the world; current politics; government; political organisations; diplomatic representation; judicial system; religion; the press; publishers; radio and television; finance; trade and industry; transport; tourism; higher education; the environment; biographies; international organisations.

Printed publications:
Directory titles include:
Africa South of the Sahara (annually)
Aslib Directory of Information Sources in the United Kingdom (every two years)
Central & South-Eastern Europe (annually)
Directory of Human Rights
Directory of University Libraries in Europe
Directory of EU Information Sources (annually)
Directory of Trade and Professional Associations in the European Union
Eastern Europe, Russia & Central Asia (annually)
Eastern Europe and the Commonwealth of Independent States (every two years)
Environment Encyclopedia and Directory (irregular)
Europa World Year Book (annually)
European Union Encyclopedia and Directory (annually)
Far East and Australasia (annually)
Guide to EU Information Sources on the Internet
International Directory of Business Information Sources and Services (irregular)
International Directory of Government (annually)
International Foundation Directory (annually)
International Relations Research Directory
International Who's Who (annually)
International Who's Who in Poetry (every two years)
International Who's Who of Authors and Writers (annually)
International Who's Who of Classical Music (annually)
International Who's Who of Popular Music
International Who's Who of Women (every two years)
Middle East and North Africa (annually)
Political & Economic Dictionary of Eastern Europe
South America, Central America and the Caribbean (annually)
South Asia (annually)
Territories of the Russian Federation
USA and Canada (annually)
Western Europe (annually)
Who's Who in International Affairs (every two years)
World of Learning (annually)

Electronic and video publications:
Europa World Plus (online: http://www.europaworld.com)
World Who's Who (online: http://www.worldwhoswho.com)
The Europa World of Learning Online (http://www.worldoflearning.com)
Routledge Online (http://www.routledgeonline.com)

continued overleaf

Publications list:
Available online and in print

Access to staff:
Contact by e-mail
Hours: Mon to Fri, 0900 to 1700

Other office:
Taylor & Francis Books (UK)
2 Park Square, Milton Park, Abingdon,
Oxfordshire, OX14 4RN; tel: 020 7017 6000;
website: http://www.taylorandfrancisgroup.com

Parent body:
Informa plc
4th Floor, 27 Mortimer Street, London, W1; tel:
020 7017 5000; website: http://www.informa.com

ROVER P4 DRIVERS GUILD

32 Arundel Road, Luton, Bedfordshire, LU4 8DY

Tel: 01582 572499
E-mail: colinb@rptdg.freeserve.co.uk

Enquiries:
Enquiries to: Secretary

Founded:
1977

Organisation type and purpose:
International organisation, membership
association, voluntary organisation.

Subject coverage:
Historical, technical, spares sourcing and insurance
information, advertisements, events related to P4
Rover cars built between 1950 and 1964.

Printed publications:
Overdrive (magazine, 6 times a year)
Yearbook

Access to staff:
Contact by letter and by telephone
Hours: Mon to Fri, 0900 to 1700

ROVER P5 CLUB

13 Glen Avenue, Ashford, Middlesex, TW15 2JE

Tel: 01784 258166
Fax: 01784 258166
E-mail: membership@roverp5club.org.uk

Website:
http://www.roverp5club.org.uk
Sample of magazine content, services supplied,
events calendar, etc.

Enquiries:
Enquiries to: Membership Secretary
Other contacts: Cars for sale register (for purchase
or sale of Rover P5 car)

Founded:
1985

Organisation type and purpose:
Membership association (membership is by
subscription), present number of members: 700,
voluntary organisation.
To enable members to keep their examples of the
Rover P5 marque running and in good order so
that they can derive the maximum pleasure from
owning and driving them.

Subject coverage:
All aspects of Rover P5 cars, buying and selling,
technical data, parts supply, maintenance, club
regalia.

**Museum or gallery collection, archive, or library
special collection:**
Technical manuals (available to members only)

Printed publications:
Magazine (6 times a year, free to members)

Access to staff:
Contact by letter, by telephone, by fax and by e-
mail
Hours: Mon to Sun, 0900 to 2100

ROWETT RESEARCH INSTITUTE

Acronym or abbreviation: RRI

Greenburn Road, Bucksburn, Aberdeen, AB21 9SB

Tel: 01224 712751
Fax: 01224 715349
E-mail: enquiries@rowett.ac.uk

Website:
http://www.rowett.ac.uk
General background details.

Enquiries:
Enquiries to: Public Relations Manager
Direct tel: 01224 716668
Direct e-mail: s.bird@rowett.ac.uk

Founded:
1913

Organisation type and purpose:
Registered charity, training organisation,
consultancy, research organisation.
State-aided animal and human nutrition research
centre.

Subject coverage:
Nutrient absorption, nutrient utilisation, trace
elements, growth of skeletal and connective tissue,
growth and metabolism of skeletal muscle,
ruminant science, fermentation biochemistry, lipid
metabolism, appetite control, diet related to health
and disease states.

**Museum or gallery collection, archive, or library
special collection:**
Agriculture in the 18th and 19th centuries

Non-library collection catalogue:
All or part available in-house

Library catalogue:
All or part available in-house

Printed publications:
Corporate brochure

Publications list:
Available online

Access to staff:
Contact by letter, by telephone, by fax and by e-
mail. Appointment necessary.
Hours: Mon to Fri, 0900 to 1700

Access to building, collection or gallery:
Prior appointment required

Access for disabled people:
Parking provided

Links with:
BBSRC
SEERAD

Subsidiary body:
Rowett Research Services

ROWLANDS LIBRARY

Charles Hastings Education Centre, Worcestershire
Royal Hospital, Charles Hastings Way, Worcester,
WR5 1DD

Tel: 01905 760601
Fax: 01905 760866
E-mail: rowlands.enquiries@worcsacute.wmids.nhs
.uk

Website:
http://www.wkp.nhs.uk

Enquiries:
Enquiries to: Librarian

Founded:
1976

Organisation type and purpose:
National government body.
NHS Hospital Trust.

Subject coverage:
Medicine, nursing, midwifery, mental health, social
care, therapies, pathology, public health, health
service management.

**Museum or gallery collection, archive, or library
special collection:**
History of Medicine, Royal College of Nursing
Resource Centre

Non-library collection catalogue:
All or part available online

Access to staff:
Contact by letter, by telephone, by fax, by e-mail
and via website
Hours: Mon to Fri, 0830 to 1700

Access for disabled people:
Parking provided, ramped entry, toilet facilities

ROY CASTLE LUNG CANCER FOUNDATION

The Roy Castle Centre, 4–6 Enterprise Way,
Wavertree Tech Park, Liverpool, Merseyside, L13
1FB

Tel: 0151 254 7200
E-mail: foundation@roycastle.org

Website:
http://www.roycastle.org
Lung cancer and its prevention, research, events
and campaigns, strategic plan, stopping smoking,
sections for health professionals and young people,
details of local support groups, online shop.

Founded:
1990

Formerly called:
Lung Cancer Fund

Organisation type and purpose:
A registered charity (number 1046854 in England
& Wales and SCO37596 in Scotland).
To defeat lung cancer.

Subject coverage:
Lung cancer.

Information services:
Helpline: 0800 358 7200 (UK only); local
information and support groups.

Electronic and video publications:
DVDs and online videos
Information booklets
Fact sheets
Order electronic and video publications from:
Download from website

Publications list:
Available online

Access to staff:
Contact by letter, by telephone, by e-mail and via
website
Hours: Helpline: Mon to Fri, 0900 to 1700

ROYAL ACADEMY OF ARTS

Acronym or abbreviation: RA

Library, Burlington House, Piccadilly, London, W1J
0BD

Tel: 020 7300 5737
Fax: 020 7300 5765
E-mail: library@royalacademy.org.uk

Website:
http://www.racollection.org.uk
General information on the RA, its history,
collections and members, current and forthcoming
exhibitions and events.

Enquiries:
Enquiries to: Librarian

Founded:
1768

Organisation type and purpose:
Learned society.

Subject coverage:
Fine arts, British art since 1750, The Royal
Academy.

Non-library collection catalogue:
All or part available online and in-house

Library catalogue:
All or part available online and in-house

Access to staff:
Contact by letter, by telephone, by fax, by e-mail and via website. Appointment necessary.
Hours: Tue to Fri, 1000 to 1300 and 1400 to 1700

Access to building, collection or gallery:
Hours: Tue to Fri, 1000 to 1300 and 1400 to 1700

Access for disabled people:
Parking provided, ramped entry, toilet facilities

ROYAL ACADEMY OF DANCE

Acronym or abbreviation: RAD

36 Battersea Square, London, SW11 3RA

Tel: 020 7326 8000
Fax: 020 7924 3129
E-mail: info@rad.org.uk

Website:
http://www.rad.org.uk
Royal Academy of Dance promotes knowledge, understanding and practice of dance internationally. It seeks to accomplish its mission through promoting dance, educating and training students and teachers and providing examinations to reward achievement.
http://www.radenterprises.co.uk
RAD Shop – dance wear, footwear, dance-related books and publications, RAD uniforms, RAD syllabi-related music books, DVDs and CDs.
http://www.radacadabra.org
RAD children's website.

Enquiries:
Enquiries to: Acting Communications Manager
Direct tel: 020 7326 8002
Direct e-mail: fcerrone@rad.org.uk
Other contacts: Press and Marketing Manager

Founded:
1920

Organisation type and purpose:
The RAD is a training, membership and examination organisation that promotes knowledge, understanding and practice of dance internationally. It is an international teaching and examining body in classical ballet, and a dance teacher-training body through its Faculty of Education; it holds a specialised reference library and archives and is the home of the Benesh Institute; it is a global organisation involving approximately 13,000 members and present in 79 countries; it is a registered charity England and Wales (number 312826).

Subject coverage:
Dance and related subjects.

Museum or gallery collection, archive, or library special collection:
Benesh Movement Notation Scores
Books, journals, photographs, pictures, programmes, videos and CD-ROMs
Phillip Richardson Library

Library catalogue:
All or part available online, in-house and in print

Printed publications:
dance gazette (3 times a year)
Annual Report and Review (available on request)
Faculty of Education Prospectus (available on request)
Focus on Members (3 times a year)
Examination publication (3 times a year)
Order printed publications from: Royal Academy of Dance Enterprises Ltd; tel. 020 7326 8080; fax 020 7228 6261; e-mail sales@rad.org.uk

Publications list:
Available online

Access to staff:
Contact by letter, by telephone, by fax, by e-mail and via website. Appointment necessary.
Hours: Mon to Thu, 1000 to 1800; Fri, 1000 to 1730

Access to building, collection or gallery:
Prior appointment required

Access for disabled people:
Ramped entry, level entry, toilet facilities

Links with:
University of Surrey
tel: 01483 300800; fax: 01483 300803; website: http://www.surrey.ac.uk

ROYAL ACADEMY OF DRAMATIC ART

Acronym or abbreviation: RADA

18 Chenies Street, London, WC1E 7PA

Tel: 020 7636 7076
Fax: 020 7323 3865

Website:
http://www.rada.org
Information on current courses, forthcoming productions with online booking, history of RADA, and graduate database.

Enquiries:
Enquiries to: Library Manager
Direct tel: 020 7908 4878
Direct e-mail: library@rada.ac.uk

Founded:
1904

Organisation type and purpose:
Registered charity (charity number 312819), suitable for ages: 18 to mid-30s, training organisation.
Academy for professional theatre training, acting and stage management, has 172 full-time students. Provides courses as above and specialist courses in props, electrics, scene painting and wardrobe.

Subject coverage:
Plays, acting, voice and speech, poetry, theatre criticism, theory of drama, theatre history, technical theatre arts, stage management, biography, costume, social history, film.

Museum or gallery collection, archive, or library special collection:
Ivo Currall Bequest (450 books and 46 albums of press cuttings by and about George Bernard Shaw)

Library catalogue:
All or part available in-house

Access to staff:
Contact by letter, by telephone and by e-mail. Appointment necessary. Non-members charged.
Hours: Mon to Wed, 0915 to 1945; Thu, Fri, 1000 to 1830

ROYAL ACADEMY OF ENGINEERING

Acronym or abbreviation: RAEng

29 Great Peter Street, London, SW1P 3LW

Tel: 020 7222 2688
Fax: 020 7233 0054

Website:
http://www.raeng.org.uk

Enquiries:
Enquiries to: Public Relations Manager
Direct tel: 020 7227 0536
Direct fax: 020 7227 7631
Direct e-mail: iffat.memon@raeng.org.uk

Founded:
1976

Organisation type and purpose:
Membership association (membership is by election or invitation), present number of members: 1170, registered charity (charity number 293074).

The pursuit, encouragement and maintenance of excellence in the whole field of engineering in order to promote the advancement of the science, art and practice of engineering for the benefit of the public.

Subject coverage:
Engineering.

Library catalogue:
All or part available in-house

Publications list:
Available online

Access to staff:
Contact by letter, by telephone, by fax, by e-mail and via website
Hours: Mon to Fri, 0900 to 1700

ROYAL ACADEMY OF MUSIC

Acronym or abbreviation: RAM

Marylebone Road, London, NW1 5HT

Tel: 020 7873 7323
Fax: 020 7873 7322
E-mail: library@ram.ac.uk

Website:
http://www.ram.ac.uk

Enquiries:
Enquiries to: Librarian

Founded:
1822

Organisation type and purpose:
Registered charity, suitable for ages: 18+.

Subject coverage:
Music; especially performance, orchestras, choirs, opera, conducting, history of music.

Museum or gallery collection, archive, or library special collection:
Angelina Goetz Library (full scores)
Robert Spencer Collection (lutenist, 1932–1997, early printed music and manuscripts)
Arthur Sullivan archive (research material, books, scores and serials)
David Munrow Library
G. D. Cunningham Collection (organ music)
Mosco Carner Collection (mss, press cuttings, letters, photographs)
Otto Klemperer Collection (scores and books)
R. J. S. Stevens Savage Collection (early printed music and manuscripts)
Sheet music
Sir Henry Wood Library of orchestral material
Foyle Menuhin Archive

Non-library collection catalogue:
All or part available online

Library catalogue:
All or part available online and in-house

Printed publications:
Annual Prospectus
Library guide
Newsletter
Academy of Music, 1988 Research Publications: The Music Collection of the Royal Academy of Music 1988

Access to staff:
Contact by letter, by e-mail and via website
Hours: 0900 to 1800

Access to building, collection or gallery:
Prior appointment required

ROYAL AFRICAN SOCIETY

SOAS, Thornhaugh Street, London, WC1H 0XG

Tel: 020 7898 4390
Fax: 020 7898 4389
E-mail: ras@soas.ac.uk

Enquiries:
Enquiries to: Secretary

continued overleaf

Founded:
1901

Organisation type and purpose:
Voluntary organisation, registered charity (charity number 1062764).

Subject coverage:
African affairs.

Printed publications:
African Affairs (quarterly, membership includes subscription)
African Studies Association Newsletter (quarterly with African Affairs)
Occasional Papers

Access to staff:
Contact by telephone
Hours: Mon to Fri, 0900 to 1700

Affiliated with joint members to the:
African Studies Association of the UK
at the same address

ROYAL AGRICULTURAL COLLEGE

Acronym or abbreviation: RAC

Library, Stroud Road, Cirencester, Gloucestershire, GL7 6JS

Tel: 01285 652531
Fax: 01285 889844
E-mail: library@rac.ac.uk

Website:
http://www.rac.ac.uk

Enquiries:
Enquiries to: Librarian
Direct tel: 01285 652531 extn 2274

Founded:
1845

Organisation type and purpose:
University library, suitable for ages: 18+.
University sector library.
Undergraduate and postgraduate degrees, research and consultancy in land-based industries and development, and related sectors.

Subject coverage:
Agriculture, forestry, horticulture, land use and management including land law, valuation, building construction, taxation, economics, ecology and conservation, farm woodlands, rural planning, business and management, environment, tourism, property agency, wine and viticulture, equine studies, agribusiness, international rural development.

Museum or gallery collection, archive, or library special collection:
British Deer Society collection
Historical collection of books on agriculture and land management

Trade and statistical information:
Agricultural statistics on trade and production, mainly DEFRA, Food and Agriculture Organisation and Eurostat.

Library catalogue:
All or part available online

Access to staff:
Contact by letter, by telephone, by fax, by e-mail and via website. Appointment necessary.
Hours: Term time: Mon to Thu, 0900 to 2000; Fri, 0900 to 1700; Sat, 1200 to 1700; Sun, 1300 to 1700
Vacations: Mon to Fri, 0900 to 1700
Special comments: External membership by subscription.

Access for disabled people:
Parking provided, level entry, access to all public areas, toilet facilities, automatic entrance doors

ROYAL AGRICULTURAL SOCIETY OF ENGLAND

Acronym or abbreviation: RASE

National Agricultural Centre, Stoneleigh Park, Kenilworth, Warwickshire, CV8 2LZ

Tel: 024 7669 6969
Fax: 024 7669 6900
E-mail: jaynesp@rase.org.uk

Website:
http://www.rase.org.uk

Enquiries:
Enquiries to: Press Officer
Other contacts: Marketing Manager

Founded:
1840

Organisation type and purpose:
Learned society, voluntary organisation, registered charity.
Transfer of technology and information related to agriculture and the rural economy.

Subject coverage:
Agriculture in general, horticulture, crop husbandry, machinery, livestock husbandry, entomology.

Museum or gallery collection, archive, or library special collection:
Reference library available by appointment

Printed publications:
Annual Journal
Members Newsletter
Surveys

Access to staff:
Contact by letter, by telephone, by fax, by e-mail and via website. Appointment necessary.
Hours: Mon to Fri, 0900 to 1700

Affiliated with French equivalent:
SAF

Affiliated with German equivalent:
DLG

ROYAL AGRICULTURAL SOCIETY OF THE COMMONWEALTH

Acronym or abbreviation: RASC

2 Grosvenor Gardens, London, SW1W 0DH

Tel: 020 7259 9678
Fax: 020 7259 9675
E-mail: rasc@commagshow.org

Website:
http://www.commagshow.org

Enquiries:
Enquiries to: Honorary Secretary

Founded:
1957

Organisation type and purpose:
International organisation, learned society, voluntary organisation, registered charity (charity number 211322).
Promotes agricultural co-operation between the developed and developing Commonwealth countries etc.

Subject coverage:
Practice and science of agriculture, improvement of methods of crop production and breeding of livestock, improvement of efficiency of agricultural implements and machinery.

Printed publications:
Newsletters (4 times a year)
Reports on Biennial Conferences

Access to staff:
Contact by letter, by telephone, by fax and by e-mail. Appointment necessary.
Hours: Mon to Fri, 0930 to 1700

Comprises the:
42 National Agricultural Show Societies in 21 Commonwealth countries

Links with:
Commonwealth Foundation
Commonwealth Secretariat

International Association of Fairs and Expositions (IAFE)
Royal Commonwealth Society (RCS)

ROYAL AIR FORCE COLLEGE CRANWELL

Acronym or abbreviation: RAFC Cranwell

College Library, Cranwell, Sleaford, Lincolnshire, NG34 8HB

Tel: 01400 261201 extn 6329
Fax: 01400 261201 extn 6266

Website:
http://www.cranwell.raf.mod.uk
General introduction to RAF Cranwell and RAF College Cranwell.

Enquiries:
Enquiries to: Librarian
Direct tel: 01400 266219

Founded:
1920

Organisation type and purpose:
Central government establishment.

Subject coverage:
Aeronautics, military science and history (especially air power), RAF history, defence studies, current affairs, air warfare, management sciences, computer sciences, engineering (mechanical, electrical, electronic, materials, aeronautical, aerospace), mathematics, logistics, warfare, weapons.

Information services:
General enquiry service.

Museum or gallery collection, archive, or library special collection:
College Archives
Part of the library of the late Lord Trenchard
T E Lawrence Collection

Non-library collection catalogue:
All or part available in-house

Library catalogue:
All or part available in-house

Access to staff:
Contact by letter, by telephone and by e-mail. Appointment necessary.
Hours: Mon, Tue, Thu, 0815 to 1700; Wed, Fri, 0815 to 1600

Access to building, collection or gallery:
Access by prior appointment only

Parent body:
Ministry of Defence – Royal Air Force

ROYAL AIR FORCES ASSOCIATION

Acronym or abbreviation: RAFA

CHQ, 117½ Loughborough Road, Leicester, LE4 5ND

Tel: 0116 266 5224
Fax: 0116 266 5012

Website:
http://www.rafa.org.uk/

Enquiries:
Enquiries to: Secretary General

Organisation type and purpose:
Voluntary organisation, registered charity (charity number 226686).
Incorporated by Royal Charter.

Subject coverage:
Advice and assistance to those who are eligible on all aspects of welfare, pensions, disability awards, civilian employment.

Printed publications:
Air Mail (4 times a year, for members)

Access to staff:
Contact by letter and by telephone. Appointment necessary.
Hours: Mon to Fri, 0900 to 1700

Has:
9 area headquarters within the British Isles

ROYAL ALFRED SEAFARERS' SOCIETY

Acronym or abbreviation: RASS

SBC House, Restmor Way, Wallington, Surrey, SM6 7AH

Tel: 020 8401 2889
Fax: 020 8401 2592
E-mail: royalalfred@btopenworld.com

Enquiries:
Enquiries to: General Secretary

Founded:
1867

Organisation type and purpose:
National organisation, registered charity (charity number 209776).
Providing nursing and residential home care, and sheltered housing for retired seafarers, their dependants and persons who have worked in trades or professions allied to the maritime industry.

Subject coverage:
Information on the subject of long-term care facilities for retired seafarers.

Printed publications:
Annual Report

Access to staff:
Contact by letter, by telephone, by fax and by e-mail
Hours: Mon to Fri, 0900 to 1700

Access to building, collection or gallery:
Prior appointment required
Hours: Mon to Fri, 0900 to 1700

Access for disabled people:
Parking provided, level entry, access to all public areas, toilet facilities

Other addresses:
Royal Alfred Seafarers' Society
  Belvedere House, Weston Acres, Woodmansterne Lane, Banstead, Surrey, SM7 3HA; tel: 01737 360106; fax: 01737 353436; e-mail: home.bns@mha.org.uk
Royal Alfred Seafarers' Society
  Royal Alfred House, 5–11 Hartington Place, Eastbourne, BN21 3BS; tel: 01323 721828; fax: 01323 431029; e-mail: home.eas@mha.org.uk

ROYAL AND ANCIENT GOLF CLUB OF ST ANDREWS, THE

Acronym or abbreviation: R&A

St Andrews, Fife, KY16 9JD

Tel: 01334 460000
Fax: 01334 460001
E-mail: webmaster@randa.org

Website:
http://www.randa.org
http://www.opengolf.com

Enquiries:
Enquiries to: Secretary

Founded:
1754

Organisation type and purpose:
International organisation (membership is by election or invitation), present number of members: 1800.
Governing Body for the Rules of Golf and Rules of Amateur Status throughout the world (except USA and Canada).

Subject coverage:
Golf, British championships and international matches, rules of golf, rules of amateur status, golf clubs and balls.

Access to staff:
Contact by letter, by telephone, by fax and by e-mail. Appointment necessary.
Hours: Mon to Fri, 0900 to 1700

ROYAL ANTHROPOLOGICAL INSTITUTE OF GREAT BRITAIN AND IRELAND

Acronym or abbreviation: RAI

50 Fitzroy Street, London, W1T 5BT

Tel: 020 7387 0455
Fax: 020 7388 8817
E-mail: admin@therai.org.uk

Website:
http://www.therai.org.uk
Anthropological Index, information on RAI.

Enquiries:
Enquiries to: Director

Founded:
1843

Organisation type and purpose:
International organisation, national organisation, learned society (membership is by election or invitation), present number of members: 1,600, voluntary organisation (charity number 246269), suitable for ages: 16+, publishing house.

Subject coverage:
Anthropology.

Museum or gallery collection, archive, or library special collection:
Photograph collection at the Institute
The Library, gifted to the British Museum and held at the Centre for Anthropology in London – access to Fellows

Non-library collection catalogue:
All or part available in-house

Library catalogue:
All or part available in-house

Printed publications:
Anthropological Index to Current Periodicals (available free of charge on the internet)
Anthropology Today
Journal of the Royal Anthropological Institute (incorporating 'Man')
Order printed publications from: Wiley-Blackwell, Journals Dept, 9600 Garsington Road, Oxford, OX4 2DQ; tel: 01865 791100; fax: 01865 791347

Electronic and video publications:
Over 200 videos and films; some for sale and some for hire.
Order electronic and video publications from: Articles from backnumbers of JRAI and Anthropology Today available electronically (for a fee) from JSTOR and Ingenta respectively

Publications list:
Available in print

Access to staff:
Contact by letter, by telephone, by fax and by e-mail. Appointment necessary. Non-members charged.
Hours: Mon to Fri, 0930 to 1730

ROYAL ARCHAEOLOGICAL INSTITUTE

Acronym or abbreviation: RAI

Society of Antiquaries, Burlington House, Piccadilly, London, W1J 0BE

E-mail: admin@royalarchaeolinst.org

Enquiries:
Enquiries to: Administrator

Founded:
1844

Organisation type and purpose:
Learned society (membership is by subscription), present number of members: 1,500, registered charity (charity number 226222 ACL), suitable for ages: 18+.

Subject coverage:
Archaeology, art history, architecture.

Library catalogue:
All or part available online and in print

Printed publications:
Archaeological Journal (annually, £80 non-members, £65 members)
Monographs
Newsletters (free to members)

Publications list:
Available in print

Access to staff:
Contact by letter and by e-mail
Special comments: Library (Society of Antiquaries).

ROYAL ARMOURIES LIBRARY – LEEDS

Armouries Drive, Leeds, West Yorkshire, LS10 1LT

Tel: 0113 220 1832
Fax: 0113 220 1934
E-mail: enquiries@armouries.org.uk

Website:
http://www.armouries.org.uk

Enquiries:
Enquiries to: Librarian

Organisation type and purpose:
National government body, museum.
Operates under a Board of Trustees appointed by the Secretary of State for Culture, Media and Sport.

Subject coverage:
The Royal Armouries and its collections, the history and development of European and Oriental arms and armour, including firearms, from the middle ages to the present day; the history of the Tower of London and its institutions.

Museum or gallery collection, archive, or library special collection:
A small number of important manuscripts including the earliest known (13th-century) fencing manual, which shows the use of sword and buckler; a 15th-century firework book, which illustrates the manufacture and use of gunpowder; and an account of the jousts between Jehan Chalons of England and Loys de Beul of France at Tours in 1446
Early books on fencing and the art of warfare
Handbooks and manuals on military small arms and artillery
Catalogues of arms and armour sales
Minute books of the Board of Ordnance (microfilm)
Photographs of objects in the Royal Armouries' own collection, of objects in other collections, and of illustrations of arms and armour in art
40,000 books, pamphlets and journals
150,000 black and white photographs
2,000 colour transparencies

Access to staff:
Contact by letter, by telephone, by fax and by e-mail
Hours: Library: Mon to Fri, 1030 to 1630; closed bank holidays

Access to building, collection or gallery:
No access other than to staff

Also at:
Royal Armouries
  HM Tower of London, London, EC3N 4AB; tel: 020 7480 6358; fax: 020 7481 2922
Royal Armouries
  Fort Nelson, Down End Road, Fareham, Hampshire, PO17 6AN; tel: 01329 233734; fax: 01329 822092

ROYAL ARMOURIES LIBRARY – LONDON

HM Tower of London, London, EC3N 4AB

Tel: 020 3166 6668
Fax: 020 3166 6678
E-mail: enquiries@armouries.org.uk

Website:
http://www.armouries.org.uk

Enquiries:
Enquiries to: Librarian
Other contacts: Keeper of Collections (South)

Organisation type and purpose:
National government body, museum.
Operates under a Board of Trustees appointed by
the Secretary of State for the Environment.

Subject coverage:
History of the Tower of London and its
institutions, including the Board of Ordnance, the
Record office, the Menagerie, the Royal Mint at the
Tower, history of fortification.

**Museum or gallery collection, archive, or library
special collection:**
A small reference collection of books and
pamphlets on arms and armour
Collection of Tower-related prints and manuscripts
Photographic reference archive for Tower-related
material

Non-library collection catalogue:
All or part available in-house and in print

Library catalogue:
All or part available in-house

Printed publications:
Order printed publications from: Royal Armouries
Museum, Armouries Drive, Leeds, LS10 1LT

Publications list:
Available online

Access to staff:
Contact by letter, by telephone, by fax and by e-
mail. Appointment necessary.
Hours: Library: Mon to Fri, 1000 to 1600 by
appointment only

Access to building, collection or gallery:
Hours: Library: Mon to Fri, 1000 to 1600 by
appointment only

Access for disabled people:
Lift

Also at:
Royal Armouries Library
Armouries Drive, Leeds, LS10 1LT; tel: 0113 220
1832

Main Library at:
Royal Armouries Museum, Leeds

Outstation at:
Fort Nelson

ROYAL ARTILLERY HISTORICAL TRUST

Acronym or abbreviation: RAHT

Firepower Royal Artillery Museum, Royal Arsenal
(West), Warren Lane, Woolwich, London, SE18 6ST

Tel: 020 8855 7755
Fax: 020 8855 7100
E-mail: info@firepower.org.uk

Website:
http://www.firepower.org.uk

Enquiries:
Enquiries to: Honorary Secretary
Direct tel: 0208 312 7120

Formerly a part of:
the collections of the Royal Artillery Institution

Organisation type and purpose:
Advisory body.

Subject coverage:
Administration and control of the museum, library,
artefacts and archives.

Non-library collection catalogue:
All or part available in-house

Library catalogue:
All or part available in-house

Access to staff:
Contact by letter, by telephone, by fax, by e-mail,
in person and via website. Appointment necessary.
Hours: Mon to Fri, 1000 to 1600

Administers:
Firepower
James Clavell Library
Firepower, Royal Arsenal (West), Warren Lane,
Woolwich, London, SE18 6ST; tel: 020 8855 7755;
e-mail: research@firepower.org.uk; website:
http://www.firepower.org.uk
Royal Artillery Library and Archives
The Royal Artillery Museum
Royal Arsenal (West), Warren Lane, Woolwich,
London, SE18 6ST; tel: 020 8855 7755; fax: 020
8855 7100; e-mail: research@firepower.org.uk;
website: http://www.firepower.org.uk

ROYAL ARTILLERY INSTITUTION

Acronym or abbreviation: RAI

Artillery House, Royal Artillery Barracks, Larkhill,
Salisbury, Wiltshire, SP4 8QT

Tel: 01980 845528
Fax: 01980 845210
E-mail: ac-rhqra-regtsec@mod.uk

Enquiries:
Enquiries to: Regimental Secretary

Founded:
1839

Organisation type and purpose:
Professional body.
Regimental institution.

Subject coverage:
History of the Royal Regiment of Artillery 1716 to
date; artillery, development, c.1650 onwards;
history of army ordnance, especially post-1715,
military and campaign history; British Army.

**Museum or gallery collection, archive, or library
special collection:**
Kaye collection of military history
The manuscripts of General Sir Alexander Dickson
Wide range of published and manuscript works on
ordnance from 16th century onwards
RA Journals and Minutes of Proceedings of the
RAI

Library catalogue:
All or part available in-house

Printed publications:
History of the Royal Regiment of Artillery (6 vols,
1914–55)
Royal Artillery Historical Society Proceedings
(annually)
Royal Artillery Journal (2 times a year)
Gunner Magazine (monthly)
Order printed publications from: Property Clerk,
Royal Artillery Institution

Access to staff:
Contact by letter, by fax and by e-mail.
Appointment necessary.
Hours: Mon to Fri, 0900 to 1700

Access to building, collection or gallery:
No prior appointment required

Links with:
Firepower, Royal Artillery Museum
Royal Arsenal, Woolwich, London, SE18 6ST; tel:
020 8855 7755; fax: 020 8855 7100; e-mail: info@
firepower.org.uk; website: http://www
.firepower.org.uk
James Clavell Library
Firepower, The Royal Artillery Museum, Old
Laboratory Office, Royal Arsenal (West), Warren
Lane, Woolwich, London, SE18 6ST

Royal Artillery Historical Society
Royal Artillery Barracks, Larkhill, Salisbury,
Wiltshire, SP4 8QT; tel: 01980 845367; e-mail:
rahs@hqdra.army.mod.ac.uk
Royal Artillery Historical Trust
Old Laboratory Office, Royal Arsenal (West),
Warren Lane, Woolwich, London, SE18 6ST; tel:
020 8312 7120; fax: 020 8855 7100; e-mail:
marks@firepower.org.uk

ROYAL ARTILLERY LIBRARY

Formal name: James Clavell Library, Royal Artillery
Museum

James Clavell Library, Royal Arsenal (West),
Warren Lane, Woolwich, London, SE18 6ST

Tel: 020 8312 7125
E-mail: research@firepower.org.uk

Website:
http://www.firepower.org.uk

Enquiries:
Enquiries to: Librarian
Direct tel: 0208 312 7120 (Curator)
Other contacts: Curator :

Organisation type and purpose:
Independently owned, registered charity.
Part of the Firepower Museum Complex.
To record and promote research into the history of
the Royal Artillery and related subjects.

Subject coverage:
Materials on Royal Artillery Regimental History;
artillery equipment, armed forces, warfare, tactics,
training, fortification, military history, military
geography and biography.

**Museum or gallery collection, archive, or library
special collection:**
Books, journals, pamphlets, manuscripts, diaries,
maps, plans, drawings, photographs, film and
microfiche

Non-library collection catalogue:
All or part available in-house

Library catalogue:
All or part available in-house

Printed publications:
History of the Royal Regiment of Artillery (Vols I–
VI available, VII in production)

Access to staff:
Contact by letter, by telephone, by fax, by e-mail,
in person and via website. Appointment necessary.
Hours: Mon to Fri, 0900 to 1600

Access to building, collection or gallery:
Prior appointment required
Hours: David Evans Reading Room, open for
readers Mon to Fri, 1000 to 1600

Links with:
Firepower! Royal Artillery Museum
Royal Regiment of Artillery

Parent body:
Royal Artillery Historical Trust
Royal Artillery Museum, Royal Arsenal (West),
Warren Lane, Woolwich, London, SE18 6ST; tel:
020 8312 7120

ROYAL ASIATIC SOCIETY OF GREAT BRITAIN AND IRELAND

14 Stephenson Way, London, NW1 2HD

Tel: 020 7388 4539
E-mail: cl@royalasiaticsociety.org

Website:
http://www.royalasiaticsociety.org

Enquiries:
Enquiries to: Executive Officer
Direct e-mail: cl@royalasiaticsociety.org

Founded:
1823

Organisation type and purpose:
Membership organisation (membership by election).
To provide a forum for those who are interested in the history, languages, cultures and religions of Asia to meet and exchange ideas through lectures, seminars, research and publishing.
Registered charity (charity number 209629)

Subject coverage:
History, languages, cultures and religions of Asia.

Museum or gallery collection, archive, or library special collection:
Library of 80,000 items, including:
Tod Collection (Indian manuscripts and paintings)
Hodgson Collection (Buddhist and Sanskrit manuscripts)
Ram Raz Collection (architectural drawings)
Raffles and Maxwell Collections (Malay manuscripts)
Howell Collection (early photographs of China and Japan)

Non-library collection catalogue:
All or part available in-house

Library catalogue:
All or part available in-house

Printed publications:
Journal of the Royal Asiatic Society (3 times a year)
Order printed publications from: Books published by the Royal Asiatic Society should be ordered from the Society's publishing partner, RoutledgeCurzon, Taylor and Francis Ltd, 2 Park Square, Milton Park, Abingdon, Oxon., OX14 4RN; tel: 020 7017 6000; fax: 020 7017 6699; internet: www.routledgecurzon.com

Publications list:
Available online

Access to staff:
Contact by letter, by telephone, by e-mail and via website. Appointment necessary.

ROYAL ASSOCIATION FOR DEAF PEOPLE

Acronym or abbreviation: RAD

Centre for Deaf People, Walsingham Road, Colchester, Essex, CO2 7BP

Tel: 01206 509509\ Minicom no. 01206 577090
Fax: 01206 769755
E-mail: info@royaldeaf.org.uk

Website:
http://www.royaldeaf.org.uk
Information and advice about the UK Deaf Community.

Enquiries:
Enquiries to: Administrator

Founded:
1841

Organisation type and purpose:
Registered charity (charity number 1081949).
To promote the spiritual, social and general welfare of deaf people.

Subject coverage:
Profound hearing impairment, blindness and deafness, problems of deaf people in psychiatric and sub-normal hospitals, social casework and welfare service, the Church's ministry to and the spiritual and pastoral care of deaf/blind and deaf people.

Publications list:
Available online and in print

Access to staff:
Contact by letter, by telephone, by fax, by e-mail, in person and via website. Appointment necessary.
Hours: Mon to Fri, 0900 to 1700
Special comments: Access also by minicom.

ROYAL ASSOCIATION FOR DISABILITY AND REHABILITATION

Formal name: Royal Association for Disability Rights
Acronym or abbreviation: RADAR

12 City Forum, 250 City Road, London, EC1V 8AF

Tel: 020 7250 3222; minicom no. 020 7250 4119 (for the hearing impaired only)
Fax: 020 7250 0212
E-mail: radar@radar.org.uk

Website:
http://www.radar.org.uk

Founded:
1977

Organisation type and purpose:
Voluntary organisation, registered charity (charity number 273150).
A major national cross-disability organisation run by and working for disabled people.
Working to end discrimination and to promote the independence of disabled people. Campaigning and lobbying on: independent living; civil rights; employment; education; housing; mobility; leisure; social security; and access.

Subject coverage:
All aspects of physical disability, except the strictly medical (benefits, employment, education, holidays, housing, legislation, civil rights, mobility, social security, social services).

Printed publications:
Bulletin (bi-monthly)
Books and other publications including:
National Key Scheme Guide – Accessible toilets for disabled people (£12.50)
If Only – A guide for newly disabled people, their families and friends (£17.49)
Children First – Guide for parents, carers and families on services for disabled children (£4.75)
Open Britian – Guide for disabled people planning holidays and stress-free travel throughout the UK (£12.49)
Get Mobile – Guide to purchasing a mobility scooter or powered wheelchair (£1)
Get Caravanning – Produced with the support of the Caravan Club – Explore caravanning from a disabled person's perspective (free)
Get Motoring – A guide for disabled motorists – finding, financing and maintaining a car (£1)
Order printed publications from: RADAR, 12 City Forum, 250 City Road, London, EC1V 8AF, or website: http://www.radar-shop.org.uk

Publications list:
Available online and in print

Access to staff:
Contact by letter, by telephone, by fax, by e-mail and via website
Hours: Information Dept: Mon to Thu, 1000 to 1600
Other depts: 0900 to 1700

Access to building, collection or gallery:
Hours: 0930 to 1700

Access for disabled people:
Parking provided, ramped entry, level entry, access to all public areas, toilet facilities

Organisation of:
600 local and national bodies

ROYAL ASSOCIATION OF BRITISH DAIRY FARMERS

Acronym or abbreviation: RABDF

Dairy House, Unit 31, Stoneleigh Deer Park, Stareton, Kenilworth, Warwickshire, CV8 2LY

Tel: 0845 458 2711
Fax: 0845 458 2755
E-mail: office@rabdf.co.uk

Website:
http://www.rabdf.co.uk/

Enquiries:
Enquiries to: Press Officer
Direct tel: 01743 344986
Direct e-mail: lizsnaith@btopenworld.com

Founded:
1876

Organisation type and purpose:
Membership association (membership is by subscription), present number of members: 2000, registered charity (charity number 213782).
The RABDF organises The European Dairy Farming Event – the United Kingdom's largest specialist event for dairy farmers and the dairy farming industry. The Association also organises conferences, publishes regular newsletters, liaises with Government and is involved in training.

Subject coverage:
Dairy farming and other matters related to dairy cattle.

Printed publications:
Dairy Farming Event Catalogue
RABDF News (quarterly magazine, free to members)

Access to staff:
Contact by letter, by telephone and by fax
Hours: Mon to Fri, 0900 to 1700

Organisers of the:
Dairy Event

ROYAL AUTOMOBILE CLUB LIBRARY

89 Pall Mall, London, SW1Y 5HS

Tel: 020 7747 3398
Fax: 0870 4606285
E-mail: library@royalautomobileclub.co.uk

Website:
http://www.royalautomobileclub.co.uk

Enquiries:
Enquiries to: Librarian
Other contacts: Library Assistant

Founded:
1897

Formerly called:
Automobile Club of Great Britain (and later Ireland) (year of change 1907)

Organisation type and purpose:
Private members club (membership by election), present membership approximately 15,000.

Subject coverage:
History of the Royal Autombile Club, history of motoring and motor sport.

Museum or gallery collection, archive, or library special collection:
Long runs of motoring periodicals including: Autocar, The Motor, Autosport; motoring books including: racing and production marques and models, biographies, motor sport, technical and legal material; RAC archives including: club handbooks and journals, personal correspondence, membership records, pamphlets, photographs, exhibition programmes, route guides

Non-library collection catalogue:
All or part available online and in-house

Library catalogue:
All or part available in-house

Printed publications:
The Motoring Century: the story of the Royal Automobile Club (available direct, £15 plus p&p)
Badges of the Royal Automobile Club (available direct, £7.95 plus p&p)

Access to staff:
Contact by letter, by telephone, by fax and by e-mail. Appointment necessary. Access for members only. Letter of introduction required.
Hours: Mon to Fri, 0900 to 1700

continued overleaf

Access to building, collection or gallery:
Special comments: Researchers only

Member organisation of:
international motoring bodies: FIA, FISA, AIT, MSA

ROYAL BIRMINGHAM SOCIETY OF ARTISTS

Acronym or abbreviation: RBSA Gallery

4 Brook Street, St Paul's, Birmingham, B3 1SA

Tel: 0121 236 4353
Fax: 0121 236 4555
E-mail: secretary@rbsa.org.uk

Website:
http://www.rbsa.org.uk
Information about the gallery, current exhibitions and workshops, joining the RBSA and artist opportunities

Enquiries:
Enquiries to: Honorary Secretary
Other contacts: Honorary Curator for gallery hire.

Founded:
1814

Organisation type and purpose:
Independently owned, professional body (membership is by subscription, election or invitation), present number of members: 460 friends, 83 associates, 105 members, registered charity (charity number 528894), museum, art gallery, workshop facilities, suitable for all ages. To actively encourage the learning, practice and appreciation of fine arts and allied crafts. Fulfilment of a vital community purpose by supporting and showcasing the work of local and national professional artists and crafts people and providing opportunities for amateur artists.

Subject coverage:
Practical fine art and allied crafts. History of the Royal Birmingham Society of Artists. All media are represented, from contemporary to traditional. Biennial exhibition of RBSA Permanent Collection.

Museum or gallery collection, archive, or library special collection:
Bound Exhibition Catalogues continuous from the early years of the Society
Paintings, prints, sculptures etc donated by artists when elected as full members
Documentation, membership register, diploma works and more from the early years onwards

Printed publications:
Exhibition Catalogues
The History of the RBSA to 1928 (Hill J and Midgeley W, pub Society and Cornish Brothers Ltd, via Kynoch Press, Birmingham)
Pre-Raphaelite Birmingham (Hartnell R, pub Studley Brewin Books, 1996)
RBSA Members and Friends Newsletter (3 times a year)

Access to staff:
Contact by letter, by telephone, by fax, by e-mail and in person. Non-members charged.
Hours: Mon to Fri, 1030 to 1730

Access to building, collection or gallery:
No prior appointment required
Hours: Mon to Fri, 1030 to 1730; Sat, 1030 to 1700; Sun, 1300 to 1700
Special comments: Archive that houses the RBSA Collection: by prior appointment.
For exhibitions see website, or phone gallery.

Access for disabled people:
Level entry, access to all public areas, toilet facilities

ROYAL BOTANIC GARDEN EDINBURGH

Acronym or abbreviation: RBGE

Library, 20A Inverleith Row, Edinburgh, EH3 5LR

Tel: 0131 552 7171
Fax: 0131 248 2901
E-mail: library@rbge.org.uk

Website:
http://www.rbge.org.uk

Enquiries:
Enquiries to: Librarian
Direct tel: 0131 248 2853

Founded:
1670

Organisation type and purpose:
Research organisation.
Administered by a Board of Trustees.

Subject coverage:
Plant taxonomy; amenity horticulture; history and current practice of gardening; landscaping; conservation; botanical illustration; botanical travels and explorations; plant collecting; floras of the world.

Museum or gallery collection, archive, or library special collection:
Archival material, manuscript and printed, relating to the history of plant sciences and particularly to the Garden (from 1670), and to the Botanical Society of Edinburgh (from 1836)
Correspondence, biographies and portraits of early botanists, horticulturists
Early printed works dating from 1486 on botany, medicine, agriculture, horticulture
Minute Books of the Royal Caledonian Horticulture Society from 1810
Pre-Linnaean botanical literature

Non-library collection catalogue:
All or part available online

Library catalogue:
All or part available online and in-house

Printed publications:
The Botanics (The Royal Botanic Garden Edinburgh quarterly magazine)
Edinburgh Journal of Botany (3 times a year, Cambridge University Press)
British Fungus Flora (irregular, Cambridge University Press)
Sibbaldia (annual)
Catalogue of Plants 2006 (at the Royal Botanic Garden Edinburgh)
Scottish Wild Plants: their history, ecology and conservation (P. Lusby and J. Wright, with photographs by S. Clarke, 1996)
The Scottish Garden: a photographic record (B. Burbridge, with text by F. Young, 1989)
Guidebooks for Inverleith, Benmore Botanic Garden, Logan Botanic Garden, Dawyck Botanic Garden
Order printed publications from: Publications Department

Publications list:
Available online and in print

Access to staff:
Contact by letter, by telephone, by fax, by e-mail, in person and via website
Hours: Mon to Thu, 0930 to 1630; Fri, 0930 to 1600

Access for disabled people:
Parking provided, access to all public areas, toilet facilities

Constituent bodies:
Botanical Society for Edinburgh (1872) Botanical Library
Cleghorn Memorial (1941) Botanical Library
Plinian Society of Edinburgh (1841) Botanical Library
Wernerian Society (1856) Botanical Library

Funded by:
Scottish Executive Environment and Rural Affairs Department

ROYAL BOTANIC GARDENS, KEW

Acronym or abbreviation: RBGK

Library, Art and Archives, Royal Botanic Gardens, Kew, Richmond, Surrey, TW9 3AE

Tel: 020 8332 5414
Fax: 020 8332 5430
E-mail: library@kew.org

Website:
http://www.kew.org
An overview of the programme areas of the Royal Botanic Gardens, Kew, visitor information, science publications catalogue, specialist newsletters and more.

Enquiries:
Enquiries to: Archivist (for Archives enquiries)
Direct tel: 020 8332 5476
Direct e-mail: archives@kew.org; illus@kew.org
Other contacts: Illustrations (for illustrations enquiries)

Founded:
1852 (Library)

Organisation type and purpose:
Registered charity, research organisation.
RBG Kew has charitable status and is an exempt charity under the Charities Act 1960.

Subject coverage:
Botany (plants and fungi of the world), taxonomy, geography, anatomy, biochemistry, cytology, molecular biology, economic botany, horticulture, plant seed physiology, nomenclature, conservation, RBGK reference collections of living and preserved plants.

Museum or gallery collection, archive, or library special collection:
160,000 monographs, 3,800 serials (1,300 current), 150,000 pamphlets, 200,000 prints and drawings, 4,600 archival collections
Adams Collection (diatom books)
Botanists Portraits Collection
Darlington Reprint Collection (genetics)
Kewensia and archives (RBG Kew's public records)
Linnaean Collection
Plant Illustrations, including the Church, Roxburgh and Tankerville Drawings
RGB Kew also has extensive plant and fungi collections: 7m. plant herbarium specimens, 750,000 fungi specimens, 80,000 economic botany specimens, 40,000 living taxa

Non-library collection catalogue:
All or part available online and in-house

Library catalogue:
All or part available online

Printed publications:
Annual Report (includes list of staff publications)
Authors of Plant Names
Curtis's Botanical Magazine
Kew Bulletin
Papers published in periodicals are listed in RBG Kew's Annual Report
Vascular Plant Families and Genera
Volumes on the flora of tropical and other countries, on particular families and genera of plants and fungi, and on topics such as conservation and other general botanical books
Order printed publications from: Orders from booksellers: Publications Sales, RBG Kew, Richmond, Surrey, TW9 3AE; tel: 020 8332 5776; fax: 020 8332 5646; e-mail: kewscbooks@rbgkew.org.uk
UK Retail Sales: KewBooks, Summerfield House, High Street, Brough, Cumbria, CA17 4AX; tel: 01768 341899; fax: 01768 800707; e-mail: kewbooks.com@btinternet.com; website: http://www.kewbooks.com

Electronic and video publications:
Index Kewensis online as part of IPNI – the International Plant Names Index
Electronic Plant Information Centre (ePIC) online – Kew's in-house databases

Publications list:
Available online and in print

Access to staff:
Contact by letter, by fax, by e-mail and via website. Appointment necessary.

Hours: Mon to Fri, 0900 to 1700

Access to building, collection or gallery:
Prior appointment required
Special comments: Only bona-fide researchers.

Access for disabled people:
Parking provided, ramped entry, toilet facilities

Sponsored by:
Department for Environment, Food and Rural Affairs

ROYAL BRITISH LEGION SCOTLAND

Acronym or abbreviation: RBLS

New Haig House, Logie Green Road, Edinburgh, EH7 4HR

Tel: 0131 557 2782
Fax: 0131 557 5819
E-mail: rblshq@care4free.com

Website:
http://www.rblscotland.org.uk

Enquiries:
Enquiries to: Press Officer
Direct e-mail: ehfs.pub@btconnect.com

Founded:
1921

Organisation type and purpose:
Membership association (membership is by subscription), present number of members: 62,000, voluntary organisation, registered charity (charity number SCO 03323).

Subject coverage:
Assistance to ex-service men and women in Scotland, war disability pensions claims, aid during temporary and chronic illness and unemployment, assistance in the provision of surgical appliances, overseas war graves visits for next-of-kin, provision of sheltered accommodation, sports competitions, piping competitions, opportunity to join social club.

Printed publications:
Annual Report
The Scottish Legion News (5 times a year)

Access to staff:
Contact by letter, by telephone, by fax, by e-mail and in person
Hours: Mon to Fri, 0915 to 1630

Access to building, collection or gallery:
No access other than to staff

Access for disabled people:
Parking provided, level entry, toilet facilities

Includes the:
Earl Haig Fund Scotland
Officers Association Scotland

Member of:
British Commonwealth Ex-services League

ROYAL BRITISH LEGION, THE

48 Pall Mall, London, SW1Y 5JY

Tel: 0345 725725
Fax: 020 7973 7399
E-mail: info@britishlegion.org.uk

Website:
http://www.britishlegion.org.uk
Covers all aspects of the organisation and its activities.

Enquiries:
Enquiries to: Secretary General
Direct e-mail: scottam@britishlegion.org.uk
Other contacts: Legionline Coordinator for general enquiries.

Founded:
1921

Organisation type and purpose:
Membership association (membership is by qualification), present number of members: 620,000, registered charity (charity number 219279).
To care for, and raise funds for, the disabled and needy in the ex-service community.

Subject coverage:
War disability pensions and general welfare benefits applicable to ex-servicemen and women and their dependants; overseas war graves visits; the ex-service community generally.

Printed publications:
Annual Report
Legion (journal, 6 times a year)

Access to staff:
Contact by letter, by telephone, by fax, by e-mail and via website
Hours: Mon to Fri, 0900 to 1700

Access for disabled people:
Level entry, access to all public areas, toilet facilities

Member of:
British Commonwealth Ex-Services League
Council of British Services and Ex-Services Organisations
World Veterans Federation

Supports the:
Attendants Company
Disabled Men's Industries Limited
Officers' Association
Royal British Legion Poppy Appeal and Factory
Royal British Legion Women's Section

ROYAL BRITISH SOCIETY OF SCULPTORS

Acronym or abbreviation: RBS

108 Old Brompton Road, London, SW7 3RA

Tel: 020 7373 5554
Fax: 020 7370 3721
E-mail: info@rbs.org.uk

Website:
http://www.rbs.org.uk

Enquiries:
Enquiries to: Administrator

Founded:
1904

Organisation type and purpose:
Advisory body, membership association (membership is by election or invitation), present number of members: over 400, registered charity (charity number 2817292), art gallery.

Subject coverage:
Sculpture.

Access to staff:
Contact by letter, by telephone, by fax and by e-mail. Appointment necessary.
Hours: Mon to Fri, 0930 to 1730

Access to building, collection or gallery:
No prior appointment required
Hours: Mon to Fri, 0930 to 1730

ROYAL CALEDONIAN CURLING CLUB

Acronym or abbreviation: RCCC

Cairnie House, Ingliston Showground, Newbridge, Midlothian, EH28 8NB

Tel: 0131 333 3003
Fax: 0131 333 3323
E-mail: office@royalcaledoniancurling.org

Website:
http://www.rccc.org.uk

Enquiries:
Enquiries to: Manager, Finance and Administration

Other contacts: Director of Development for development of the sport.

Founded:
1838

Organisation type and purpose:
Membership association (membership is by subscription), present number of members: 15,000, training organisation.
Governing body for sport of curling in Scotland.

Subject coverage:
The sport and game of curling.

Museum or gallery collection, archive, or library special collection:
Archive films of grand matches
Royal club annuals from 1839 and many rare books on curling
Various curling artefacts and pictures including trophies and old curling stones

Printed publications:
Royal Club Annual (yearly, £9)
Royal Club Constitution and Rule Book (yearly, £1)
Scottish Curler (monthly, September to April)

Access to staff:
Contact by letter, by telephone, by fax and by e-mail. Appointment necessary.
Hours: Mon to Fri, 0900 to 1700

ROYAL CAMBRIAN ACADEMY OF ART

Acronym or abbreviation: RCA

Crown Lane, Conwy, LL32 8AN

Tel: 01492 593413
Fax: 01492 593413
E-mail: rca@rcaconwy.org

Website:
http://www.rcaconwy.org

Enquiries:
Enquiries to: Curator

Founded:
1882

Organisation type and purpose:
Membership association (membership is by election or invitation), present number of members: 115, registered charity (charity number 219648), art gallery.

Subject coverage:
Past and present members of the Academy since 1882, artists working in Wales.

Museum or gallery collection, archive, or library special collection:
Catalogues of every RCA exhibition since 1882

Printed publications:
Centenary Year (1982) Reference Catalogue (giving history of the Academy)
Exhibition catalogues
Pembrokeshire (Knapp-Fisher J)
Portraits (Williams K)
The Land and the Sea (Williams K)

Access to staff:
Contact by letter, by telephone, by fax, by e-mail and via website
Hours: Tue to Sat, 1100 to 1700; Sun, 1300 to 1630
Special comments: No lift to upstairs gallery.

ROYAL CHORAL SOCIETY

Acronym or abbreviation: RCS

Studio 9, 92 Lots Road, London, SW10 0QD

Tel: 020 7376 3718
Fax: 020 7376 3719

Website:
http://www.royalchoralsociety.co.uk
All information about the choir, concerts, membership, sponsorship

Enquiries:
Enquiries to: Administrator

continued overleaf

Direct e-mail: helenbody@royalchoralsociety.co.uk

Founded:
1871

Organisation type and purpose:
Membership association (membership is by subscription), registered charity.
Choir.

Subject coverage:
Choirs and choral music.

Museum or gallery collection, archive, or library special collection:
Archive material (loaned to the Greater London Public Record Office)

Printed publications:
Annual brochure

Access to staff:
Contact by letter, by telephone, by fax, by e-mail and via website
Hours: Mon to Fri, 0900 to 1700

Links with:
NFMS

Subsidiary body:
Friends of the Royal Choral Society

ROYAL COLLEGE OF ANAESTHETISTS

Churchill House, 35 Red Lion Square, London, WC1R 4SG

Tel: 020 7092 1500
Fax: 020 7092 1730
E-mail: info@rcoa.ac.uk

Website:
http://www.rcoa.ac.uk
About the college, professional standards, information for patients, meetings and events, publications, news.

Organisation type and purpose:
The professional body responsible for the specialty of anaesthesia throughout the UK. Ensures the quality of patient care through the maintenance of standards in anaesthesia, critical care and pain medicine.

Subject coverage:
Anaesthesia is the largest single hospital specialty in the NHS.

Printed publications:
The British Journal of Anaesthesia (members may also access on line)
Continuing Education in Anaesthesia, Critical Care and Pain (members may also access on line)

The British Journal of Anaesthesia

Electronic and video publications:
College Bulletin
Order electronic and video publications from:
Download from website

Publications list:
Available online

Access to staff:
Contact by letter, by telephone, by fax and by e-mail

ROYAL COLLEGE OF ART LIBRARY

Acronym or abbreviation: RCA

Kensington Gore, London, SW7 2EU

Tel: 020 7590 4224
Fax: 020 7590 4500
E-mail: library@rca.ac.uk

Website:
http://www.rca.ac.uk/library

Enquiries:
Enquiries to: Library Manager
Direct tel: 020 7590 4225

Direct e-mail: darlene.maxwell@rca.ac.uk
Other contacts: Head of Information & Learning Services

Organisation type and purpose:
Postgraduate college of art, Institution of University Library status.

Subject coverage:
Art (particularly 20th century), design (industrial, graphic, fashion, textiles, architecture, interior, illustration, vehicle), applied arts (ceramics, metalwork, jewellery), moving image (films, television, animation), photography, humanities.

Museum or gallery collection, archive, or library special collection:
College Archive
Colour Reference Collection covering many aspects of colour, including theory, psychology, symbolism and colour music
Theses Collection

Library catalogue:
All or part available online

Access to staff:
Appointment necessary.
Hours: Term time: Mon to Fri, 0900 to 2100; Sat, 1200 to 1700
Vacations: Mon to Fri, 1000 to 1700

ROYAL COLLEGE OF DEFENCE STUDIES

Acronym or abbreviation: RCDS

37 Belgrave Square, London, SW1X 8NS

Tel: 020 7915 4813
Fax: 020 7915 4800

Website:
http://www.mod.uk.rcds/index.html

Enquiries:
Enquiries to: Librarian

Founded:
1970

Organisation type and purpose:
National government body, learned society (membership is by election or invitation), present number of members: 85 current (on site), historic building, house or site.
Government department.
The house originally known as Sefton House was built in 1842 by the Marquess of Westminster. It may be visited on an Open Day.

Subject coverage:
Defence, international relations, politics, economics, history.

Library catalogue:
All or part available in-house

Printed publications:
Reading Lists
Journal Holdings
New Books Lists
Seaford House Papers (restricted distribution)

Publications list:
Available in print

Access to staff:
Access for members only.
Hours: Mon to Fri, 0900 to 1700
Special comments: Members and OGDs.

Access to building, collection or gallery:
No access other than to staff

Connections with:
Ministry of Defence, London (MOD)

ROYAL COLLEGE OF GENERAL PRACTITIONERS

Acronym or abbreviation: RCGP

14 Princes Gate, Hyde Park, London, SW7 1PU

Tel: 020 7581 3232
Fax: 020 7584 1992

E-mail: library@rcgp.org.uk

Website:
http://www.rcgp.org.uk
General information about the college, its services and products.

Enquiries:
Enquiries to: Information Manager

Founded:
1952

Organisation type and purpose:
Learned society (membership is by qualification), present number of members: 19,000, registered charity (charity number 223106), research organisation.
Encouraging, fostering, and maintaining the highest possible standards in general medical practice.

Subject coverage:
General practice, primary health care, practice management, family practice.

Museum or gallery collection, archive, or library special collection:
General practice theses
College publications
Primary care journals

Library catalogue:
All or part available online and in-house

Printed publications:
Information Sheets (free)
New Books Listings
Journal Holdings

Electronic and video publications:
See Catalogue

Publications list:
Available online and in print

Access to staff:
Contact by letter, by telephone, by fax, by e-mail, in person and via website. Appointment necessary. All charged.
Hours: Mon to Fri, 0900 to 1700
Special comments: Book loans to members only.

ROYAL COLLEGE OF GENERAL PRACTITIONERS (SCOTLAND)

Acronym or abbreviation: RCGP SCOTLAND

25 Queen Street, Edinburgh, EH2 1JX

Tel: 0131 260 6800
Fax: 0131 260 6836
E-mail: scottishc@rcgp.org.uk

Enquiries:
Enquiries to: Deputy Chair (Policy)

Organisation type and purpose:
Professional body, membership association (membership is by qualification), present number of members: 3,018 (Scotland), registered charity (charity number 223106), research organisation.

Subject coverage:
Academic/quality in General Practice.

Access to staff:
Contact by letter and by e-mail
Hours: Mon to Fri, 0900 to 1700

Also at:
Royal College of General Practitioners
14 Princes Gate, Hyde Park, London, SW7 1PU;
tel: 020 7581 3232

ROYAL COLLEGE OF MIDWIVES – EDINBURGH

Acronym or abbreviation: RCM

37 Frederick Street, Edinburgh, EH2 1EP

Tel: 0131 225 1633

Enquiries:
Enquiries to: Director

Organisation type and purpose:
Professional organisation.

Subject coverage:
Midwifery.

Access to staff:
Contact by letter
Hours: Mon to Fri, 0900 to 1700

ROYAL COLLEGE OF MIDWIVES – LONDON

Acronym or abbreviation: RCM

15 Mansfield Street, London, W1G 9NH

Tel: 020 7312 3535
Fax: 020 7312 3536
E-mail: info@rcm.org.uk

Website:
http://www.rcm.org.uk

Enquiries:
Enquiries to: Information Officer

Founded:
1881

Organisation type and purpose:
Professional body, trade union (membership is by subscription, qualification), present number of members: 37,000, registered charity (charity number 275261), suitable for ages: 21+.
To further the art and science of midwifery.

Subject coverage:
Midwifery: education, profession, training and history; obstetrics; neonatal care; ante-natal care; paediatrics; family planning; role of the midwife in the NHS; sociological and psychological aspects of midwifery; further and higher education.

Museum or gallery collection, archive, or library special collection:
(The library and archive collections were placed in storage in 2008 pending the development of plans for the future of the library service.)
Archives
Marion Rabl Collection
Theses and dissertations in midwifery

Non-library collection catalogue:
All or part available in-house

Library catalogue:
All or part available in-house

Printed publications:
Order printed publications from: The Royal College of Midwives Welsh Board
4 Cathedral Road, Cardiff, CF1 9LJ, tel: 029 2022 8111, e-mail: publications@rcmwelshb.org.uk

Publications list:
Available online and in print

Access to staff:
Contact by letter, by telephone, by fax, by e-mail and via website. Appointment necessary. All charged.
Hours: Mon to Fri, 0900 to 1645
Special comments: Non-members when space permits.

Access to building, collection or gallery:
Prior appointment required

Access for disabled people:
Access to all public areas, toilet facilities

ROYAL COLLEGE OF MUSIC

Acronym or abbreviation: RCM

Library, Prince Consort Road, London, SW7 2BS

Tel: 020 7591 4325
Fax: 020 7589 7740
E-mail: pthompson@rcm.ac.uk

Website:
http://www.rcm.ac.uk
Includes Library web pages and access to that part of the catalogue now online.

Enquiries:
Enquiries to: Librarian
Direct tel: 020 7591 4323

Founded:
1883

Organisation type and purpose:
Academic institution and music conservatoire.

Subject coverage:
Music: books, autograph manuscripts, scores, sheet music, orchestral parts, choral sets, audio-visual materials.

Museum or gallery collection, archive, or library special collection:
Collection of manuscripts of British composers
Heron-Allen Collection of books on the violin
Library of the Concerts of Ancient Music
Library of the Sacred Harmonic Society
Maurice Frost collection
Nicanor Zabaleta archive of harp music
Further listings at www.cecilia-uk.org

Non-library collection catalogue:
All or part available online, in-house and in print

Library catalogue:
All or part available in-house

Printed publications:
Catalogue of the Manuscripts of Herbert Howells in the Royal College of Music Library
Catalogues of the Royal College of Music Library (out of print)
Doane: A Musical Directory for the year 1794 (reprint of original edition)
Hummel: Art of Piano Playing, Part 3 (reprint of original edition)
Royal College of Music Library: guide to services
Where to buy and borrow music

Microform publications:
The Music Collection of the Royal College of Music London (Harvester)
Microfilms of individual works available direct

Access to staff:
Contact by letter, by telephone, by fax, by e-mail and in person
Hours: Term time: Mon to Thu, 0900 to 1900; Fri, 0900 to 1730
Vacations: hours may vary
Special comments: Loans to members only.

Access to building, collection or gallery:
No prior appointment required

ROYAL COLLEGE OF MUSIC FRANK BRIDGE BEQUEST

Royal College of Music, Prince Consort Road, London, SW7 2BS

Tel: 020 8749 2268
E-mail: pbanks@rcm.ac.uk

Website:
http://www.cph.rcm.ac.uk/CPHBridge/Pages/Index.htm
Description of the Bequest's activity, details of grants, and a list of publications and recordings sponsored by the Bequest.

Enquiries:
Enquiries to: Chairman

Founded:
1965

Organisation type and purpose:
Promotion of the performance of music by Frank Bridge.

Subject coverage:
Life and music of Frank Bridge (1879–1941).

Museum or gallery collection, archive, or library special collection:
Bridge manuscripts (held in the Library of the Royal College of Music, for access see the entry for the RCM Library)

Publications list:
Available online

Access to staff:
Contact by letter, by telephone, by e-mail and via website
Hours: Mon to Fri, 0900 to 1700

ROYAL COLLEGE OF NURSING OF THE UNITED KINGDOM

Acronym or abbreviation: RCN

20 Cavendish Square, London, W1G 0RN

Tel: 020 7409 3333
Fax: 020 7647 3420
E-mail: rcn.library@rcn.org.uk

Website:
http://www.rcn.org.uk

Enquiries:
Enquiries to: Librarian
Direct tel: 020 7647 3610

Organisation type and purpose:
Professional body, trade union.

Subject coverage:
Professional aspects of nursing; nursing practice, management and education; labour relations and legal matters; social services; health services; hospital management.

Museum or gallery collection, archive, or library special collection:
Seymer Collection (historical books on nursing)
Steinberg Collection of Nursing Research Theses

Library catalogue:
All or part available online

Printed publications:
British Nursing Index
Catalogue of the Steinberg Collection
RCN Library Thesaurus of Nursing Terms

Electronic and video publications:
British Nursing Index

Access to staff:
Contact by letter, by telephone, by fax and by e-mail. Non-members charged.
Hours: Mon, Tue, Thu, Fri, 0900 to 1900; Wed, 1000 to 1900; Sat, 0900 to 1700

Access for disabled people:
Ramped entry, toilet facilities

Also at:
Royal College of Nursing of the United Kingdom Ty Maeth, King George V Drive East, Cardiff, CF4 4XZ; tel: 029 2075 1373
Royal College of Nursing of the United Kingdom 42 Scottish Board, South Oswald Road, Edinburgh, EH9 2HH; tel: 0131 662 1010
Royal College of Nursing of the United Kingdom 17 Windsor Avenue, Belfast, BT9 6EE; tel: 01232 668236

ROYAL COLLEGE OF OBSTETRICIANS AND GYNAECOLOGISTS

Acronym or abbreviation: RCOG

27 Sussex Place, Regent's Park, London, NW1 4RG

Tel: 020 7772 6200

Website:
http://www.rcog.org.uk
http://www.rcog.org.uk/what-we-do/information-services
http://www.rcog.org.uk/our-profession/research-services

Enquiries:
Enquiries to: Librarian
Direct tel: 020 7772 6309
Direct fax: 020 7262 8331
Direct e-mail: library@rcog.org.uk

Founded:
1929

continued overleaf

Organisation type and purpose:
Professional body (membership is by qualification).

Subject coverage:
Obstetrics, gynaecology and closely related subjects (e.g. urogynaecology).

Museum or gallery collection, archive, or library special collection:
Large historical collection in subjects as above
Rare books
College archive
Collection of historical instruments including the Chamberlen forceps

Non-library collection catalogue:
All or part available in-house

Library catalogue:
All or part available online and in-house

Printed publications:
Short-title catalogue of books printed before 1851 in the Library of the RCOG (2nd edn)

Publications list:
Available online

Access to staff:
Contact by letter, by telephone, by fax, by e-mail, in person and via website. Appointment necessary.
Hours: Mon to Fri, 0900 to 1800

Constituent bodies:
National Collaborating Centre for Women's and Children's Health

Houses the:
Faculty of Sexual and Reproductive Health Care
Wellbeing of Women (formerly Birthright)

ROYAL COLLEGE OF OPHTHALMOLOGISTS

17 Cornwall Terrace, London, NW1 4QW

Tel: 020 7935 0702
Fax: 020 7935 9838
E-mail: kathy.evans@rcophth.ac.uk

Website:
http://www.rcophth.ac.uk

Enquiries:
Enquiries to: Chief Executive

Founded:
1988

Organisation type and purpose:
Professional body (membership is by subscription, qualification), present number of members: 4,000, registered charity (charity number 299872).

Subject coverage:
Ophthalmology.

Printed publications:
EYE (journal)

Publications list:
Available in print

Access to staff:
Contact by letter, by telephone, by fax and by e-mail
Hours: Mon to Fri, 0900 to 1700

Access to building, collection or gallery:
Prior appointment required

ROYAL COLLEGE OF ORGANISTS

Acronym or abbreviation: RCO

PO Box 56357, London, SE16 7XL

Tel: 05600 767208
E-mail: admin@rco.org.uk

Website:
http://www.rco.org.uk

Enquiries:
Enquiries to: General Manager
Other contacts: Director of Academic Development

Founded:
1864

Organisation type and purpose:
International organisation, advisory body, learned society, professional body, registered charity (charity number 312847).
Academic institution, especially examining body.

Subject coverage:
The organ and music for the organ.

Museum or gallery collection, archive, or library special collection:
Houses the library of books, music (mainly organ), manuscripts, records, cassettes and CDs
C. H. Trevor Collection
Cruden Collection
Dalton Bequest
Gordon Phillips Collection
John Ella Bequest
Sowerbutts Collection
T. Lea Southgate Bequest
Tickner Collection

Non-library collection catalogue:
All or part available online

Library catalogue:
All or part available online

Printed publications:
Syllabus of examinations plus other items
RCO Journal (annual collection of learned articles)
RCO Newsletter (3 times a year)

Publications list:
Available in print

Access to staff:
Contact by letter, by telephone, by e-mail and in person. Appointment necessary. Non-members charged.
Hours: Mon to Fri, 1000 to 1700

ROYAL COLLEGE OF PAEDIATRICS AND CHILD HEALTH

Acronym or abbreviation: RCPCH

50 Hallam Street, London, W1W 6DE

Tel: 020 7307 5600
Fax: 020 7307 5601
E-mail: enquiries@rcpch.ac.uk

Website:
http://www.rcpch.ac.uk
General information about the College and College activities.

Enquiries:
Enquiries to: Secretary

Founded:
1928

Organisation type and purpose:
Professional body (membership is by qualification, election or invitation), present number of members: 6500, voluntary organisation, registered charity (charity number 1057744).
Members are paediatricians and other professionals active in the field of child health. The RCPCH forms joint standing committees and working parties with several other professional bodies, for example: the Royal College of Physicians, British Association of Paediatric Surgeons, Association of British Paediatric Nurses, National Association for the Welfare of Children in Hospital, Health Visitors Association, Royal College of Midwives, Royal College of Nursing and Royal College of Obstetricians and Gynaecologists. The RCPCH also engages in consultations with a wide range of organisations including voluntary organisations, for example: Foundation for the Study of Infant Deaths.
To advance the art and science of paediatrics; to raise the standard of medical care for children; to educate and examine those concerned with the health of children; to advance the education of the public in child health.

Subject coverage:
Paediatrics, child health, medical training and research.

Non-library collection catalogue:
All or part available in-house

Printed publications:
Archives of Disease in Childhood (monthly, published jointly with the BMA; on subscription)
Fabricated or Induced Illness by Carers (2002)
Guidelines for the Ethical Conduct of Medical Research Involving Children (1992, free on request)
Manual of Childhood Infections
Medicines for Children
Pocket Medicines for Children (2001, £12.99)
Syllabus and Training Records for GPT and HST (£10 each)
Withholding or Withdrawing Life Saving Treatment in Children (1997, £25)
Order printed publications from: RCPCH Bookclub, Direct Books
FREEPOST (BH1879), Ringwood, Hampshire, BH24 3BR, tel: 01425 471719, e-mail: directbooks@bmbc.com

Electronic and video publications:
The following are available on the website http://www.rcpch.ac.uk:
Fabricated or Induced Illness by Carers (2001)
Specimen exam papers for MRCPCH Part I, Part II and DCH
Guidelines for Good Practice
Newsletter for members (quarterly, sent to all members in hardcopy)

Publications list:
Available online and in print

Access to staff:
Contact by letter, by telephone, by fax, by e-mail and via website. Appointment necessary.
Hours: Mon to Fri, 0900 to 1700

Strong connections with the:
Confederation of European Specialists in Paediatrics
International Paediatric Association

ROYAL COLLEGE OF PATHOLOGISTS

Acronym or abbreviation: RCPath

2 Carlton House Terrace, St James's, London, SW1Y 5AF

Tel: 020 7451 6700
Fax: 020 7451 6701
E-mail: info@rcpath.org

Website:
http://www.rcpath.org

Enquiries:
Enquiries to: Chief Executive

Founded:
1962

Organisation type and purpose:
Professional body (membership is by subscription, qualification), present number of members: 7500, registered charity (charity number 261035).

Subject coverage:
History of pathology, pathology as a science, histopathology, cytology, medical microbiology, clinical biochemistry, virology, immunology, genetics, forensic pathology, haematology.

Library catalogue:
All or part available in-house

Printed publications:
Journal (quarterly, members)
Various publications
Order printed publications from: Managing Editor, Publications
tel: 020 7451 6730, fax: 020 7451 6701, e-mail: publications@rcpath.org

Publications list:
Available online

Access to staff:
Contact by letter, by telephone, by fax, by e-mail and via website
Hours: Mon to Fri, 0900 to 1700

Access for disabled people:
Ramped entry, toilet facilities

ROYAL COLLEGE OF PHYSICIANS

Acronym or abbreviation: RCP

Information Centre and Heritage Centre, 11 St Andrews Place, Regent's Park, London, NW1 4LE

Tel: 020 3075 1539
Fax: 020 7486 3729
E-mail: infocentre@rcplondon.ac.uk

Website:
http://www.rcplondon.ac.uk

Founded:
1518

Organisation type and purpose:
International organisation, professional body (membership is by qualification), registered charity (charity number 210508), suitable for ages: postgraduate, training organisation, research organisation, publishing house. To promote the highest standards of medical practice in order to improve health and healthcare.

Subject coverage:
The Information Centre Library covers the College's work, UK health policy and public health. The Heritage Centre covers the history of medicine, medical biography and the history of the College.

Museum or gallery collection, archive, or library special collection:
Archives of the College
Manuscripts (mainly personal papers of physicians)
Portraits and photographs (mainly of Fellows of the College)
H. M. Barlow Collection of Bookplates
Dorchester Library (2,101 titles left to the College by the Marquis of Dorchester), includes the Wilton Psalter dating from 1250
Evan Bedford Library of Cardiology
Heberden Library of Rheumatology
Willan Library of the British Association of Dermatology

Non-library collection catalogue:
All or part available online and in-house

Library catalogue:
All or part available online and in-house

Printed publications:
Catalogue of Engraved Portraits
Evan Bedford Library of Cardiology Catalogue
Order printed publications from: Publications Department, Royal College of Physicians; tel: 020 7935 1174 ext 358; fax: 020 7486 5425; e-mail: publications@rcplondon.ac.uk

Microform publications:
Annals of the Royal College of Physicians, 1518–1915 (pub. Adam Matthew Publications, Calcot, Reading, 1991)

Publications list:
Available online and in print

Access to staff:
Contact by letter, by telephone, by fax, by e-mail, in person and via website. Appointment necessary. Non-members charged.
Hours: Mon to Fri, 0900 to 1700

Access to building, collection or gallery:
Some areas open to public. Prior appointment required to access historical collections

Access for disabled people:
Parking provided, level entry, access to all public areas, toilet facilities

ROYAL COLLEGE OF PHYSICIANS AND SURGEONS OF GLASGOW

Acronym or abbreviation: RCPSG

Library, 232–242 St Vincent Street, Glasgow, G2 5RJ

Tel: 0141 221 6072
Fax: 0141 221 1804
E-mail: library@rcpsg.ac.uk

Website:
http://www.rcpsg.ac.uk
Information on activities, committees, courses run, examinations, library scope and journal holdings.

Enquiries:
Enquiries to: Librarian

Founded:
1698

Organisation type and purpose:
Learned society, professional body (membership is by qualification, election or invitation), present number of members: 8,500.

Subject coverage:
Clinical medicine and surgery, history of medicine, history of Glasgow and West of Scotland.

Museum or gallery collection, archive, or library special collection:
Macewen Collection (papers of Sir William Macewen, surgery, late 19th century)
Mackenzie Collection (papers of Dr William MacKenzie, ophthalmology)
Ross Collection (50% of the papers of Sir Ronald Ross, tropical medicine, 19th century)
Glasgow Collection (history of Glasgow and South West Scotland)

Non-library collection catalogue:
All or part available online and in print

Library catalogue:
All or part available online and in-house

Access to staff:
Contact by letter, by telephone, by fax, by e-mail, in person and via website. Appointment necessary.
Hours: Mon to Fri, 0900 to 1700

Access for disabled people:
Access to all public areas, toilet facilities

ROYAL COLLEGE OF PHYSICIANS OF EDINBURGH

Acronym or abbreviation: RCPE

Library, 9 Queen Street, Edinburgh, EH2 1JQ

Tel: 0131 225 7324
Fax: 0131 220 3939
E-mail: library@rcpe.ac.uk

Website:
http://www.rcpe.ac.uk/library/library.html
History of library, library services, manuscript catalogue.

Enquiries:
Enquiries to: Librarian
Other contacts: Information Librarian for literature searches.

Founded:
1681

Organisation type and purpose:
Advisory body, learned society, professional body (membership is by qualification, election or invitation), present number of members: 7000, registered charity (charity number SCO 09465), research organisation.

Subject coverage:
Medicine, particularly clinical medicine (excluding since 1900, surgery and allied sciences); history of medicine, particularly Scottish medicine.

Museum or gallery collection, archive, or library special collection:
J W Ballantyne Pamphlet Collection on foetal pathology

Manuscripts Collection relating to W Cullen and early Edinburgh Medical School
Sir J Y Simpson Collection on gynaecology and obstetrics

Non-library collection catalogue:
All or part available online and in-house

Library catalogue:
All or part available online and in-house

Printed publications:
Catalogue of sixteenth century medical books in Edinburgh libraries (1982)

Publications list:
Available online and in print

Access to staff:
Contact by letter, by telephone, by fax, by e-mail, in person and via website
Hours: Mon to Fri, 0900 to 1700

ROYAL COLLEGE OF PSYCHIATRISTS

Acronym or abbreviation: RCPsych

17 Belgrave Square, London, SW1X 8PG

Tel: 020 7235 2351
Fax: 020 7245 1231
E-mail: infoservices@rcpsych.ac.uk

Website:
http://www.rcpsych.ac.uk

Enquiries:
Enquiries to: Library and Information Services Manager
Direct tel: 020 7235 2351 ext 6138
Direct fax: 020 7259 6303
Direct e-mail: infoservices@rcpsych.ac.uk

Organisation type and purpose:
Professional body (membership is by qualification).

Subject coverage:
Psychiatry; mental illness and health, history of psychiatry.

Museum or gallery collection, archive, or library special collection:
Antiquarian books on psychiatry

Non-library collection catalogue:
All or part available online and in-house

Library catalogue:
All or part available in-house

Printed publications:
Advances in Psychiatric Treatment (6 times a year)
Books Beyond Words (picture stories, without words, for those with learning difficulties)
Index to Statements, Guidelines and Policy Documents of the College 1971–89 with annual supplements
Mental Health books and leaflets for the general public
British Journal of Psychiatry (monthly)
The Psychiatrist (monthly)
Books for Trainees
Child Psychiatry titles
Clinical Psychiatry titles
College Seminar Series
Public Education Initiatives titles
Service Provision titles
Psychiatric Bulletin (monthly)

Electronic and video publications:
Audio tapes for the general public

Publications list:
Available online and in print

Access to staff:
Contact by letter, by telephone, by fax, by e-mail, in person and via website. Appointment necessary. Access for members only. Letter of introduction required. Non-members charged.
Hours: Mon to Fri, 0930 to 1630

ROYAL COLLEGE OF RADIOLOGISTS

Acronym or abbreviation: RCR

38 Portland Place, London, W1B 1JQ

Tel: 020 7636 4432
Fax: 020 7323 3100
E-mail: enquiries@rcr.ac.uk

Website:
http://www.rcr.ac.uk
Details of all College activities, including online publications and password-protected members' area.

Enquiries:
Enquiries to: Chief Executive

Founded:
1975

Organisation type and purpose:
Professional body (membership is by qualification), present number of members: 8,000, registered charity (charity number 211540).

Subject coverage:
Science and practice of clinical radiology, clinical oncology.

Printed publications:
Clinical Oncology (8 times a year)
Clinical Radiology (monthly)
Faculty Reports and Guidelines: Clinical Radiology and Clinical Oncology (publication free, except where price stated)
Large selection of College Reports and Guidelines (publication free, except where price stated)

Publications list:
Available in print

Access to staff:
Contact by letter, by telephone, by fax and by e-mail. Appointment necessary.
Hours: Mon to Fri, 0900 to 1700

ROYAL COLLEGE OF SPEECH AND LANGUAGE THERAPISTS

Acronym or abbreviation: RCSLT

2–3 White Hart Yard, London, SE1 1NX

Tel: 020 7378 1200
Fax: 020 7403 7254

Website:
http://www.rcslt.org
Information about speech and language therapy as a career, etc.

Enquiries:
Enquiries to: Professional Director
Other contacts: Information Officer for general enquiries re: speech and language therapy profession.

Organisation type and purpose:
National organisation, professional body, registered charity (charity number 273724). Examining and registering body.

Subject coverage:
Disorders of human communication.

Printed publications:
Bulletin (monthly, for Members and Associate Members)
International Journal of Language and Communication Disorders

Access to staff:
Contact by letter and by e-mail
Hours: Mon to Fri, 0900 to 1700

Access to building, collection or gallery:
Prior appointment required

Access for disabled people:
Level entry, toilet facilities

Affiliated to:
International Association of Logopaedics and Phoniatrics
Permanent Liaison Committee of Speech Therapists and Logopaedists (EEC)

ROYAL COLLEGE OF SURGEONS OF EDINBURGH

Acronym or abbreviation: RCSEd

The Library, Nicolson Street, Edinburgh, EH8 9DW

Tel: 0131 527 1630
Fax: 0131 557 6406
E-mail: library@rcsed.ac.uk

Website:
http://www.library.rcsed.ac.uk

Enquiries:
Enquiries to: Librarian

Founded:
1505

Organisation type and purpose:
Membership association (membership is by qualification), registered charity, training organisation, research organisation.

Subject coverage:
Surgery, history of medicine.

Museum or gallery collection, archive, or library special collection:
Records of the institution from 1505; collected papers of notable figures in medicine and surgery, e.g. Joseph Lister, James Young Simpson; large museum; large portrait collection; images collection

Non-library collection catalogue:
All or part available online, in-house and in print

Library catalogue:
All or part available online, in-house and in print

Printed publications:
Current journals list (free, from library)
The Surgeon: Journal of the Royal Colleges of Surgeons of Edinburgh and Ireland
surgeonsnews: the magazine for surgeons everywhere

Publications list:
Available online

Access to staff:
Contact by letter, by telephone, by fax, by e-mail, in person and via website
Hours: Mon to Fri, 0900 to 1700
Special comments: Appointment preferred for non-members, but not essential.

Access for disabled people:
Ramped entry, toilet facilities

ROYAL COLLEGE OF SURGEONS OF ENGLAND

Acronym or abbreviation: RCSEng

35–43 Lincoln's Inn Fields, London, WC2A 3PE

Tel: 020 7869 6555/6556
Fax: 020 7405 4438 (library)
E-mail: library@rcseng.ac.uk; ; museums@rcseng.ac.uk archives@rcseng.ac.uk

Website:
http://www.rcseng.ac.uk/library; www.rcseng.ac.uk/museums
Location; opening hours; catalogues; visitor information; exhibitions; collections and services; contact details; lives of the Fellows of The Royal College of Surgeons of England.

Founded:
1800

Organisation type and purpose:
Medical Royal College, professional body (charity number 212808).

Subject coverage:
Surgery: dental and oral surgery, maxillo-facial surgery, orthopaedics and trauma, cardiovascular surgery, neurosurgery, general surgery, urological surgery, otorhinolaryngology, paediatric surgery, plastic and reconstructive surgery; anatomy; pathology; physiology; history of medicine with special emphasis on surgery.

Museum or gallery collection, archive, or library special collection:
The library, archive and museum collections of The Royal College of Surgeons of England were first assembled in the 18th and early 19th centuries and are unique in their focus and depth in documenting the evolution of surgical knowledge and practice. They are particularly important to understanding not only British but also international surgical history, helping academic researchers, modern practitioners and public alike to understand surgery's development. These collections are joined together by shared creators and owners, shedding light on each other.

The Museums and Archives Department includes the Hunterian Museum, the Wellcome Museum of Anatomy and Pathology and the College Archive collections. The museums and archive collections cover the history of surgery and anatomy from the 17th century to the present. The Hunterian Museum contains one of Britain's greatest medical collections, including over 3,000 anatomical and pathological preparations collected by the surgeon John Hunter (1728–1793). The Wellcome Museum of Anatomy and Pathology contains the College's modern teaching collections. It contains over 2,000 anatomical and pathological specimens as well as other resources. It is open to all individuals with a surgical, medical or relevant profession. The College's archive collections include institutional records documenting the College's activities throughout its history, and a diverse range of deposited manuscript and archive collections relating to medicine and surgery.

The library possesses one of the finest historical medical collections, including many rare and unique items. The collections are particularly strong in anatomy and surgery, though comparative anatomy and natural history are also well represented. Material for the library was initially purchased to support staff working with the Hunterian Collection now housed in the Hunterian Museum. The tracts and pamphlets collection (c. 30,000 items) is one of the largest of its kind in the UK.

Non-library collection catalogue:
All or part available online

Library catalogue:
All or part available online

Printed publications:
Annals of The Royal College of Surgeons of England [also available online]
Bulletin of The Royal College of Surgeons of England [also available online]

Electronic and video publications:
See main College website: http://www.rcseng.ac.uk/publications

Publications list:
Available online

Access to staff:
Contact by letter, by telephone, by fax, by e-mail, in person and via website. Appointment necessary.
Hours: Please check website for opening hours and variations
Special comments: Charges may apply to non-members; please see website.

Access to building, collection or gallery:
Please see website

Access for disabled people:
Please see website

ROYAL COLLEGE OF VETERINARY SURGEONS TRUST

Acronym or abbreviation: RCVS

Library and Information Service, Belgravia House, 62–64 Horseferry Road, London, SW1P 2AF

Tel: 020 7202 0752
Fax: 020 7202 0751
E-mail: library@rcvstrust.org.uk

Website:
http://www.rcvs.org.uk
http://www.rcvslibrary.org.uk

Enquiries:
Enquiries to: Librarian

Founded:
1844

Organisation type and purpose:
Professional body.
Registration and disciplinary body.

Subject coverage:
Veterinary science and surgery, comparative medicine, animal breeding and management.

Museum or gallery collection, archive, or library special collection:
College Archives
Henry Gray Collection (ornithology, late 19th and early 20th centuries)
Historical Collection (books 1514–1850)
J. P. Megnin Collection of drawings, mainly of birds and parasites, and correspondence
Miss Povey Collection of watercolours by Edward Mayhew

Non-library collection catalogue:
All or part available online

Library catalogue:
All or part available online

Publications list:
Available online

Access to staff:
Contact by letter, by telephone, by fax, by e-mail and via website. Appointment necessary. All charged.
Hours: Mon to Fri, 0915 to 1700

Access to building, collection or gallery:
Prior appointment required

ROYAL COMMISSION ON ENVIRONMENTAL POLLUTION

Acronym or abbreviation: RCEP

3rd Floor, 5–8 The Sanctuary, Westminster, London, SW1P 3JS

Tel: 020 7799 8970
Fax: 020 7799 8971
E-mail: enquiries@rcep.org.uk

Enquiries:
Enquiries to: Office Manager
Direct tel: 020 7799 8972

Founded:
1970

Organisation type and purpose:
National government body, advisory body.

Subject coverage:
National and international matters concerning pollution of the environment, further possibilities of danger to the environment, research in this field, transport and the environment, and waste management.

Printed publications:
A Guide to the Commission and its Work
23 reports covering various environmental topics including:
The 'First Report' – A review of the state of the physical environment in Britain at the beginning of the 1970s

Industrial pollution, Air pollution, Nuclear power and the Environment, Agriculture and Pollution, Oil pollution of the Sea, Lead in the Environment, The Release of Genetically Engineered Organisms to the Environment

Publications list:
Available in print

Access to staff:
Contact by letter, by fax, by e-mail and via website
Hours: Mon to Fri, 0900 to 1700

ROYAL COMMISSION ON THE ANCIENT AND HISTORICAL MONUMENTS OF SCOTLAND

Acronym or abbreviation: RCAHMS

John Sinclair House, 16 Bernard Terrace, Edinburgh, EH8 9NX

Tel: 0131 662 1456
Fax: 0131 662 1477
E-mail: info@rcahms.gov.uk

Website:
http://www.rcahms.gov.uk
Information on current work of RCAHMS, new collections and publications, and access to the Canmore database.
http://canmore.rcahms.gov.uk
Canmore is at the heart of the RCAHMS archive, providing searchable, map-based information on over 280,000 buildings and archaeological sites throughout Scotland, as well as a catalogue of the collection items held. Over 130,000 digital images are available to browse and purchase online. Images and information can be shared by registering online with MyCanmore.
http://aerial.rcahms.gov.uk
The National Collection of Aerial Photography is an internationally important collection comprising over 1.6m. images of Scotland, and tens of millions of military intelligence photographs of locations across the globe. Users can browse for digitised imagery, buy images online, request a paid search, or make an appointment to carry out their own searches.
http://www.scran.ac.uk
Scran is an online image archive, which offers subscribers fully searchable access to over 360,000 copyright-cleared resources for educational use, including a fascinating collection of images and information on local and social history.
http://www.scotlandsplaces.gov.uk
Scotlands Places brings authentic information and images together to help to discover places in Scotland. Users can search by place name and county, or browse an online map to discover which buildings and sites are in that area and what information and images are available at RCAHMS and the National Archives of Scotland.
http://www.pastmap.org.uk
PASTMAP brings together information from RCAHMS, Historic Scotland and Local Authority Sites and Monuments Records into one searchable system. An online map may be used to search for information on a specific area, including details of listed buildings, gardens and designed landscapes, and scheduled ancient monuments.
http://hla.rcahms.gov.uk
HLAmap provides map-based analysis of past and present-day land use throughout Scotland. Results can be filtered by land-use type, period and category.

Enquiries:
Enquiries to: Chief Executive
Direct e-mail: diana.murray@rcahms.gov.uk

Founded:
1908

Organisation type and purpose:
National government body, national organisation, advisory body, statutory body, registered charity, public library.
Information relating to the built heritage of Scotland from the earliest times to the present day.

RCAHMS creates and maintains the above record and makes it available to the public online, in the Search Room and through exhibitions and publications.

Subject coverage:
Archaeology, architectural history, landscape history, built heritage, ancient monuments, planning, development and urban history, topography, history, industrial archaeology, aerial photography, and the history of Scotland.

Information services:
RCAHMS searchable online resources; telephone, email, letter and fax enquiry service; free public Search Room; RCAHMS publications; online ordering and licensing of images.

Special visitor services:
Ability to consult Collection items in the Search Room with staff to assist; digital finding aids to research and consult aerial photography; self-service photocopying and lasercopying; four PCs for online research.

Education services:
Group visits; induction and training; lectures; online resources; exhibitions and publications.

Services for disabled people:
Building fully accessible; lifts and toilets.

Museum or gallery collection, archive, or library special collection:
Historic and modern photographs including aerial photographs
Architectural drawings
Books on archaeology, architecture, topography and local history
Manuscripts
National collection of archaeological excavation archives
Papers of many notable Scottish architects
Plans from archaeological excavations and field surveys
The Aerial Reconnaissance Archives (TARA) of international aerial photography

Non-library collection catalogue:
All or part available online, in-house and in print

Library catalogue:
All or part available online and in-house

Printed publications:
A wide range of RCAHMS publications deliver illustrated and researched titles to anyone with an interest in Scotland's history and built heritage
Order printed publications from: BookSource, tel: 0845 370 0067; e-mail: orders@booksource.net

Publications list:
Available online and in print

Access to staff:
Contact by letter, by telephone, by fax, by e-mail, in person and via website
Hours: Monday to Friday, 0930 to 1700

Access to building, collection or gallery:
No prior appointment required
Hours: Mon, Tue, Wed, Fri, 0930 to 1700; Thu, 0930 to 1800
Special comments: Closed on public and local holidays.

Access for disabled people:
Parking provided, ramped entry, access to all public areas, lifts, toilet facilities

Parent body:
The Scottish Government
website: http://www.scotland.gov.uk

ROYAL COMMONWEALTH SOCIETY

Acronym or abbreviation: RCS

18 Northumberland Avenue, London, WC2N 5AP

Tel: 020 7930 6733
Fax: 020 7930 9705
E-mail: info@rcsint.org

continued overleaf

Website:
http://www.rcsint.org

Enquiries:
Enquiries to: Head of Public Affairs
Direct tel: 020 7766 9205
Direct e-mail: miles.giljam@rcsint.org

Founded:
1868

Organisation type and purpose:
International organisation, learned society, membership association (membership is by subscription, election or invitation), present number of members: 6500 affiliated to headquarters and 10,000 worldwide, voluntary organisation, registered charity (charity number 226748), art gallery, university library. International organisation, with 69 self-governing branches and commonwealth societies, operates a private members club, non-governmental organisation.
The RCS promotes, in the UK and internationally, an understanding of the nature and working of the Commonwealth and of the factors that shape the lives of its people and the policies of its governments. Underlying the work of the RCS is the belief that an understanding of the Commonwealth is key to creating successful multicultural societies across the world.

Subject coverage:
The Commonwealth and its members, past and present (virtually all subjects relevant to those countries except scientific and technical); some material on non-Commonwealth countries and on the colonial history of other European countries.

Museum or gallery collection, archive, or library special collection:
Royal Commonwealth Society Collection housed in the Cambridge University Library, West Road, Cambridge, CB3 9DR; includes:
Cobham Collection (on Cyprus)
Photograph Collection

Printed publications:
Annual Report
Meetings & Events Programme (3 times a year)
Newsletter (3 times a year)
Annual Report of the Essay Competition
Occasional reports of seminars and conferences
Various promotional literature
The following are housed in the library at Cambridge:
Biography Catalogue of the Royal Commonwealth Society (1961)
Manuscript Catalogue of the Royal Commonwealth Society (1975)
RCS London Photograph Collection: a unique source of visual documents on Colonial and Commonwealth history (mid-1850s – mid-1980s) on microfiche (Inter Documentation AG, 1987)
Subject Catalogue of the Library of the Royal Empire Society (4 vols, 1930–37)
Subject Catalogue of the Royal Commonwealth Society (7 vols, 1971; supplement, 2 vols, 1977)

Access to staff:
Contact by letter, by telephone, by fax, by e-mail and via website. Appointment necessary.
Hours: Mon to Fri, 0915 to 1715

Access for disabled people:
Ramped entry, toilet facilities

Library housed at:
Cambridge University Library
West Road, Cambridge, CB3 9DR; tel: 01223 333000; fax: 01223 333160

ROYAL CORNWALL AGRICULTURAL ASSOCIATION

Acronym or abbreviation: RCAA

Royal Cornwall Showground, Wadebridge, Cornwall, PL27 7JE

Tel: 01208 812183
Fax: 01208 812713
E-mail: info@royalcornwall.co.uk

Website:
http://www.royalcornwall.co.uk

Enquiries:
Enquiries to: Secretary

Founded:
1793

Organisation type and purpose:
Membership association, registered charity (charity number 250312).
Promotion of agriculture, etc.

Subject coverage:
History of the RCAA, general agricultural history of Cornwall.

Museum or gallery collection, archive, or library special collection:
Archives of the Royal Cornwall Agricultural Association

Printed publications:
History of the Royal Cornwall Show (£5 plus p&p)
Show Catalogue (annually £4 plus p&p)
Souvenir Programme (£3 plus p&p)

Access to staff:
Contact by letter, by telephone, by fax, by e-mail, in person and via website
Hours: Mon to Fri, 0900 to 1700

ROYAL ECONOMIC SOCIETY

Acronym or abbreviation: RES

Secretary-General's Office, School of Economics and Finance, University of St Andrews, St Andrews, Fife, KY16 9AL

Tel: 01334 462479
Fax: 01334 462444
E-mail: royaleconsoc@st-andrews.ac.uk

Website:
http://www.res.org.uk

Enquiries:
Enquiries to: RES Administrator
Other contacts: Administrator (for general enquiries); Secretary-General; Media Consultant

Founded:
1902

Organisation type and purpose:
Learned society (membership is by subscription).
The promotion, encouragement and application of the study of economic science.

Subject coverage:
Economics.

Museum or gallery collection, archive, or library special collection:
Archive of RES within the British Library of Political & Economic Science, London

Printed publications:
Books, including new editions of economics classics (from Blackwell Publishers, Macmillan and CUP)
Economic Journal (8 times a year)
RES Newsletter (quarterly)
Order printed publications from: RES Administrator or Membership Services, Wiley-Blackwell, e-mail: ecove@wiley.com

Electronic and video publications:
Econometrics Journal (online)

Publications list:
Available online

Access to staff:
Contact by letter, by telephone, by fax, by e-mail and via website. Appointment necessary.
Hours: Mon to Fri, 1000 to 1600

ROYAL ENFIELD OWNERS CLUB

Acronym or abbreviation: REOC

30–32 Causeway, Burgh-Le-Marsh, Skegness, Lincolnshire, PE24 5LT

Tel: 01754 810119
E-mail: mickseager@mcmail.com

Website:
http://www.royalenfield.org.uk

Enquiries:
Enquiries to: Membership Secretary

Founded:
1978

Organisation type and purpose:
Membership association (membership is by subscription), present number of members: 3,028

Subject coverage:
Royal Enfield motor cycles.

Printed publications:
The Gun Magazine

Access to staff:
Contact by letter, by telephone, by e-mail and via website
Hours: Mon to Fri, 0900 to 1700

ROYAL ENGINEERS MUSEUM, LIBRARY AND ARCHIVES

Acronym or abbreviation: REMLA

Brompton Barracks, Chatham, Kent, ME4 4UX

Tel: 01634 822221
Fax: 01634 822063
E-mail: mail@re-museum.co.uk

Enquiries:
Enquiries to: Head Curator
Other contacts: Documentation Officer, Deputy Curator

Founded:
1813

Formerly called:
Royal Engineers Library; merged with Royal Engineers Museum (year of change 1993)

Organisation type and purpose:
Military library.

Subject coverage:
All aspects of military engineering world-wide with specific reference to the Royal Engineers; many non-military fields of early technology e.g. photography.

Museum or gallery collection, archive, or library special collection:
2nd copies of RE Units' War Diaries, mainly from the First World War, but some also from other conflicts
Correspondence Books from RE stations, 18th–19th century
Collections of papers of significant Sappers – General Gordon, Kitchener and Burgoyne
Some photographs and maps produced by Engineers, diaries and correspondence relating to members of the Corps from the 18th century to the present day, as well as historical notes by researchers, principally John Connolly, into the early origins of the Corps

Non-library collection catalogue:
All or part available in-house

Library catalogue:
All or part available in-house

Access to staff:
Contact by letter, by telephone and by e-mail.
Appointment necessary.
Hours: Mon to Fri, 0900 to 1700
Special comments: Copying charges apply.

Access to building, collection or gallery:
Hours: Museum open: Tue to Fri, 0900 to 1700; Sat, Sun, 1130 to 1700 (last entry each day at 1600)
Library open: Tue and Wed, 1000 to 1300 and 1400 to 1630
Special comments: Access to the Library is by appointment only. As it is in an active barracks, visitors must be escorted at all times.

Access for disabled people:
Unfortunately the present Library is not accessible for wheelchair users. Please contact staff to make alternative arrangements

Affiliated to:
Royal Engineers Institution
at the same address

ROYAL ENTOMOLOGICAL SOCIETY

Acronym or abbreviation: RES

The Mansion House, Chiswell Green Lane, St Albans, AL2 3NS

Tel: 01727 899387
Fax: 01727 894797
E-mail: val@royensoc.co.uk

Website:
http://www.royensoc.co.uk

Enquiries:
Enquiries to: Librarian

Founded:
1833

Organisation type and purpose:
International organisation, learned society (membership is by election or invitation), registered charity (charity number 213620), suitable for ages: postgraduate +, research organisation, publishing house.
The improvement and diffusion of entomological science.

Subject coverage:
Entomology: all aspects but in particular taxonomy with reference to the western palaeoarctic region.

Museum or gallery collection, archive, or library special collection:
c.750 journal titles
c.11,000 books
c.30,000 reprints, including the Rothschild
collection of siphonaptera reprints (flea)
Archival material
Innumerable monographs
Superb collection of 18th-, 19th- and 20th-century works on insects

Library catalogue:
All or part available in-house

Printed publications:
Agriculture and Forest Entomology (quarterly)
Antenna (house journal of the Society)
Ecological Entomology (quarterly)
Insect Conservation and Diversity
Insect Molecular Biology (quarterly)
Medical and Veterinary Entomology (quarterly)
Physiological Entomology (quarterly)
Systematic Entomology
RES Handbooks for the Identification of British
Insects (11 vols, each vol. in several parts)
Symposia proceedings
A Guide to the Archives of the Royal
Entomological Society

Publications list:
Available online and in print

Access to staff:
Contact by letter, by telephone, by fax and by e-mail. Appointment necessary. Non-members charged.
Hours: Mon to Thu, 0900 to 1600; Fri, 0900 to 1530

Access to building, collection or gallery:
Prior appointment required
Special comments: Access limited to Fellows and Members, except by appointment.

ROYAL ENVIRONMENTAL HEALTH INSTITUTE OF SCOTLAND

Acronym or abbreviation: REHISí

19 Torphichen Street, Edinburgh EH3 8HX

Tel: 0131 229 2968
Fax: 0131 228 2926
E-mail: contact@rehis.com

Website:
http://www.rehis.com
Outline of activities; history of REHIS; REHIS, Our People; REHIS news; the environmental health profession in Scotland; related organisations; contact details for approved training centres; details of qualifications available through the approved centres.

Enquiries:
Enquiries to: Chief Executive

Founded:
1983

Organisation type and purpose:
Membership association (membership is by qualification), present number of members: 1,100, voluntary organisation, registered Scottish charity (charity number SC0 09406). Awarding body for the environmental health profession in Scotland and a UK Competent Authority for the profession. Awarding body for qualifications in food safety, health and safety, food and health, and infection control.

Subject coverage:
Environmental health in Scotland, education and training in environmental health subjects.

Library catalogue:
All or part available online and in-house

Printed publications:
Annual Report
Journal
Occasional publications
e-Newsletter
Order printed publications from: Office

Access to staff:
Contact by letter, by telephone, by e-mail and via website. Appointment necessary.
Hours: Mon to Fri, 0900 to 1700

Access to building, collection or gallery:
Prior appointment required

ROYAL FORESTRY SOCIETY

Acronym or abbreviation: RFS

102 High Street, Tring, Hertfordshire, HP23 4AF

Tel: 01442 822028
Fax: 01442 890395
E-mail: rfshq@rfs.org.uk

Website:
http://www.rfs.org.uk

Enquiries:
Enquiries to: Chief Executive

Founded:
1882

Organisation type and purpose:
Learned society (membership is by subscription).

Subject coverage:
Forestry; arboriculture; careers advice in these fields.

Museum or gallery collection, archive, or library special collection:
Rare forestry books

Printed publications:
Journal of Forestry (quarterly)

Access to staff:
Contact by letter
Hours: Mon to Fri, 0900 to 1700

Access to building, collection or gallery:
No prior appointment required

ROYAL FREE AND UNIVERSITY COLLEGE MEDICAL SCHOOL

Medical Library, Royal Free Hospital, Rowland Hill Street, London, NW3 2PF

Tel: 020 7794 0500
Fax: 020 7794 3534
E-mail: library@rfc.ucl.ac.uk

Website:
http://library.ucl.ac.uk

Enquiries:
Enquiries to: Librarian
Direct tel: 020 7794 0500 ext 3203

Organisation type and purpose:
University library.

Subject coverage:
Medicine, psychiatry and psychology.

Library catalogue:
All or part available online

Access to staff:
Contact by letter. Appointment necessary. Letter of introduction required.
Hours: Mon to Fri, 0900 to 1900;
Sat, 0900 to 1300 (excluding Aug)
Special comments: Members primarily.

Access for disabled people:
Level entry

Parent body:
University College London
(University of London)

ROYAL GEOGRAPHICAL SOCIETY WITH THE INSTITUTE OF BRITISH GEOGRAPHERS

Acronym or abbreviation: RGS-IBG

1 Kensington Gore, London, SW7 2AR

Tel: 020 7591 3000
Fax: 020 7591 3001
E-mail: enquiries@rgs.org

Website:
http://www.rgs.org

Enquiries:
Enquiries to: Principal Librarian
Direct tel: 020 7591 3041
Direct e-mail: e.rae@rgs.org
Other contacts: Deputy Librarian

Founded:
1830

Organisation type and purpose:
Learned society, professional body (membership is by qualification, election or invitation), present number of members: 14,000, registered charity. Study groups in the subjects listed below.
Access to the Society's information resources is available in the Foyle Reading Room.

Subject coverage:
Geography, including exploration and travel; cartography, geography of rural and urban areas, medical, transport and population geography, geomorphology, historical geography, quantitative methods, women and geography, planning and geography, industrial activity and area development, biogeography, geography in higher education, social and political geography, transport geography, careers guidance for all geographers, field science training, major research projects overseas.

Non-library collection catalogue:
All or part available online and in-house

Library catalogue:
All or part available online and in-house

Printed publications:
Area (quarterly)
Geographical Journal (quarterly)
Special publications and book series
Transactions of the Institute of British Geographers
(quarterly)
Order printed publications from: RGS-IBG Book Series

Publications list:
Available in print

continued overleaf

Access to staff:
Contact by letter, by telephone, by fax, by e-mail, in person and via website. Non-members charged.

Access to building, collection or gallery:
Apart from Foyle Reading Room, Members only
Hours: Mon to Fri, 0930 to 1730 (Foyle Reading Room, 1000 to 1700)

Access for disabled people:
Fully accessible

ROYAL GLASGOW INSTITUTE OF THE FINE ARTS, THE

Acronym or abbreviation: RGI

5 Oswald Street, Glasgow, G1 4QR

Tel: 0141 248 7411
Fax: 0141 221 0417
E-mail: rgi@robbferguson.co.uk

Enquiries:
Enquiries to: Secretary

Founded:
1861

Organisation type and purpose:
Membership association (membership is by subscription), present number of members: 1400, registered charity.

Subject coverage:
Promotion of art by means of an open annual exhibition, the third largest in the United Kingdom. The RGI also owns a small gallery for hire for solo or group exhibitions.

Access to staff:
Contact by letter, by telephone and by fax
Hours: Mon to Thu, 0900 to 1600

ROYAL HISTORICAL SOCIETY

Acronym or abbreviation: RHistS

University College London, Gower Street, London, WC1E 6BT

Tel: 020 7387 7532
Fax: 020 7387 7532
E-mail: royalhistsoc@ucl.ac.uk

Website:
http://www.royalhistoricalsociety.org

Enquiries:
Enquiries to: Executive Secretary
Direct e-mail: s.carr@ucl.ac.uk
Other contacts: Administrative Secretary

Founded:
1868

Organisation type and purpose:
Learned society, registered charity.

Subject coverage:
History.

Information services:
see website.

Museum or gallery collection, archive, or library special collection:
A private collection of about 1,000 books dating from 1650 to the present day, some of which are part of the bequest of Sir George Prothero (d. 1922), whose papers are also held in the Society's archives
Collection of publications from national and regional records and historical societies housed within UCL History library
Papers of the Camden Society

Non-library collection catalogue:
All or part available in-house

Library catalogue:
All or part available online

Printed publications:
Studies in History
Camden Series
Guides and Handbooks

Transactions of the Royal Historical Society
Order printed publications from: Camden University Press
Boydell and Brewer

Publications list:
Available online

Access to staff:
Contact by letter, by telephone, by e-mail, in person and via website. Appointment necessary.
Hours: Mon to Fri, 0900 to 1700
Special comments: by appointment

Access to building, collection or gallery:
by appointment

Headquarters address:
University College London
Gower Street, London WC1E 6BT

ROYAL HOLLOWAY INSTITUTE FOR ENVIRONMENTAL RESEARCH

Acronym or abbreviation: RHIER

Huntersdale, Callow Hill, Virginia Water, Surrey, GU25 4LN

Tel: 01784 477404
Fax: 01784 477427
E-mail: rhier@rhbnc.ac.uk

Enquiries:
Enquiries to: Project Development Officer
Direct e-mail: s.kandiah-evans@rhul.ac.uk
Other contacts: Director; e.maltby@rhul.ac.uk

Founded:
1994

Organisation type and purpose:
University department or institute.

Subject coverage:
Wetland management, wetland conservation, wetland ecosystem functioning, hydroacoustic methods for fish survey.
Global Biological Diversity Conservation Policy.

Printed publications:
Ecosystem Management: Questions for Science and Society (£15 inc. p&p)
Technical reports and research papers

Access to staff:
Contact by letter and by e-mail
Hours: Mon to Fri, 0900 to 1700

Access to building, collection or gallery:
Prior appointment required

Access for disabled people:
Parking provided

Connections with:
IUCN Commission on Ecosystem Management
Wetland Ecosystems Research Group
Fish Hydroacoustics Unit; tel: 01784 477404; fax: 01784 477427

Parent body:
Royal Holloway University of London
tel: 01784 434455

ROYAL HOLLOWAY UNIVERSITY OF LONDON – LIBRARY

Formal name: Royal Holloway and Bedford New College University of London
Acronym or abbreviation: RHUL

Egham, Surrey, TW20 0EX

Tel: 01784 443823
Fax: 01784 477670
E-mail: library@rhul.ac.uk

Website:
http://www.rhul.ac.uk/information-services/library
Library catalogue, subject guides, recent acquisitions lists, special collections information

Enquiries:
Enquiries to: Director of Library Services

Other contacts: Information Consultants' Team Co-ordinator

Founded:
1886

Incorporates the former:
Bedford College London (year of change 1986)

Organisation type and purpose:
University library.
College library of the University of London.

Subject coverage:
Arts, classics, drama, theatre studies and film, economics, English and American literature, French, German, Italian language and literature, history, linguistics, management, medical sociology, music, sociology, social administration, social anthropology, Hispanic studies, media arts, history of women.
Sciences: biochemistry, biology, botany, chemistry, geography, geology, mathematics, physics, physiology, psychology and zoology.

Museum or gallery collection, archive, or library special collection:
A. V. Coton collection on dance
Collection on theatre
College Archives
Dawson collection of New Zealand poetry and prose published since 1900
Dom Anselm Hughes collection on medieval religious music (includes his personal letters and papers)
Early printed books from 16th century onwards in classics; English and French literature; history; some science, especially botany
Robert Simpson Society Archives comprising books, scores, records, MS sketches and miscellanea relating to the composer
Sir Alfred Sherman Papers
Small but significant collection of works by or about T. E. Lawrence
South East Asia Geology Library

Non-library collection catalogue:
All or part available online

Library catalogue:
All or part available online

Printed publications:
Guide to the Library (free)

Access to staff:
Contact by letter, by telephone, by fax, by e-mail, in person and via website. Non-members charged.
Special comments: Appointments necessary if specific specialist help required

Access to building, collection or gallery:
No prior appointment required
Hours: Term time: Mon to Thu, 0900 to 2300; Fri, 0900 to 1900; Sat, 1100 to 1700; Sun, 1300 to 2100.
Vacation: Mon to Fri, 0900 to 1700

Access for disabled people:
Good access to Bedford Library; access to Founder's and Music Libraries by arrangement

ROYAL HUMANE SOCIETY

Acronym or abbreviation: RHS

50/51 Temple Chambers, 3–7 Temple Avenue, London, EC4Y 0HP

Tel: 020 7936 2942
Fax: 020 7936 2942
E-mail: info@royalhumanesociety.org.uk

Website:
http://www.royalhumanesociety.org.uk

Enquiries:
Enquiries to: Secretary
Direct e-mail: secretary@royalhumanesociety.org.uk

Founded:
1774

Organisation type and purpose:
Charity
Society incorporated by Royal Charter.

Encourages the saving of human life by the giving of award.

Subject coverage:
Grants non-pecuniary awards for bravery in saving human life and for the restoration of life by resuscitation.

Museum or gallery collection, archive, or library special collection:
Annual reports and casebooks from 1774 to present held by London Metropolitan Archives from autumn 2008

Printed publications:
Medals of the Royal Humane Society
Annual Report
Short History of the Royal Humane Society
Saved from a Watery Grave

Access to staff:
Contact by letter, by telephone, by fax and by e-mail. Appointment necessary. All charged.
Hours: Mon to Thu, 1030 to 1630

ROYAL INCORPORATION OF ARCHITECTS IN SCOTLAND

Acronym or abbreviation: RIAS

15 Rutland Square, Edinburgh, EH1 2BE

Tel: 0131 229 7545
Fax: 0131 228 2188
E-mail: info@rias.org.uk

Website:
http://www.rias.org.uk

Enquiries:
Enquiries to: Secretary

Founded:
1916

Organisation type and purpose:
Professional body, membership association, consultancy.

Subject coverage:
Architecture, architects and services, history of architecture.

Printed publications:
Architectural Guides to Scotland
Members' Newsletter (quarterly)

Access to staff:
Contact by letter, by telephone, by fax, by e-mail and via website. Appointment necessary.
Hours: Mon to Fri, 0900 to 1700

Access to building, collection or gallery:
Hours: Mon to Fri, 0900 to 1700

Branches:
Aberdeen, Dundee, Edinburgh, Glasgow, Inverness and Stirling

Links with:
Royal Institute of British Architects

ROYAL INSTITUTE OF BRITISH ARCHITECTS

Acronym or abbreviation: RIBA

West Midlands, Birmingham and Midland Institute, 9 Margaret Street, Birmingham, B3 3SP

Tel: 0121 233 2321
Fax: 0121 233 4946
E-mail: riba.westmidlands@inst.riba.org

Enquiries:
Enquiries to: Administrator

Organisation type and purpose:
Professional body (membership is by subscription, qualification), present number of members: 1300 in West Midlands, registered charity.

Non-library collection catalogue:
All or part available in-house

Library catalogue:
All or part available in-house

Access to staff:
Contact by letter, by telephone and by fax. Appointment necessary. Non-members charged.
Hours: Mon to Fri, 0900 to 1700
Special comments: Charges to non-members may be appropriate.

Access to building, collection or gallery:
No prior appointment required
Special comments: Library only open on set days, telephone for details.

ROYAL INSTITUTE OF BRITISH ARCHITECTS (NORTH WEST REGION)

Acronym or abbreviation: RIBA NW

Unit 101, The Tea Factory, 82 Wood Street, Liverpool, L1 4DQ

Tel: 0151 703 0107
Fax: 0151 703 0108
E-mail: riba.northwest@inst.riba.org

Website:
http://www.architecture.com
General information.

Enquiries:
Enquiries to: Regional Director

Organisation type and purpose:
Professional body (membership is by subscription).

Subject coverage:
Architecture.

Printed publications:
JCT Contracts and Practice Documents list is available on request
Order printed publications from: RIBA Publications, Construction House, 56–64 Leonard Street, London, EC2A 4LT; tel: 020 7251 0791; fax: 020 7608 2375

Publications list:
Available online and in print

Access to staff:
Contact by letter, by telephone, by fax, by e-mail and in person
Hours: Mon to Fri, 0900 to 1700

Access to building, collection or gallery:
Hours: Mon to Fri, 0900 to 1700

Parent body:
Royal Institute of British Architects (RIBA)
66 Portland Place, London, W1N 4AD

ROYAL INSTITUTE OF INTERNATIONAL AFFAIRS LIBRARY

Acronym or abbreviation: RIIA, Chatham House

Chatham House, 10 St James's Square, London, SW1Y 4LE

Tel: 020 7957 5723
Fax: 020 7957 5710
E-mail: libenquire@chathamhouse.org.uk

Website:
http://www.chathamhouse.org.uk

Founded:
1920

Organisation type and purpose:
International organisation, learned society (membership is by subscription), registered charity, research organisation.
The Royal Institute of International Affairs at Chatham House, London, is one of the world's leading institutes for the analysis of international issues. The Institute is independent of government.

Subject coverage:
International affairs and relations between all states (diplomatic, political, legal, military, economic and financial) since 1918, with special focus on the most recent 30–35 years; international problems and organisations; foreign and defence policies and (on a limited scale) domestic affairs of all countries.

Museum or gallery collection, archive, or library special collection:
British and other government documents relating to foreign policy, 1918 to date
Collection of press cuttings from a wide range of the world's press published in West European languages, closely classified and cross-referenced; the files covering the periods from 1924–August 1939 and 1972–July 1997 (ceased) are at the RIIA (those for September 1939–December 1971 are in the British Library Newspaper Library)
Royal Institute of International Affairs archives by prior application

Library catalogue:
All or part available online

Printed publications:
Chatham House Papers
Classified catalogue of the Library of the RIIA: an introduction (1981)
Briefing Papers
Index to Periodical Articles 1950–78 in the Library of the RIIA (two vols and two supplements)
International Affairs (6 a year)
RIIA Library Thesaurus (1991)
World Today (monthly)

Microform publications:
Classified catalogue of the Library of the RIIA (microfiche)
Index to Periodical Articles 1979–89 in the Library of the RIIA (microfiche edn)

Electronic and video publications:
Briefing papers
Chatham House reports

Publications list:
Available online

Access to staff:
Contact by letter, by e-mail and via website. Appointment necessary. Letter of introduction required. Non-members charged.
Hours: Mon to Fri, 1000 to 1730
Special comments: Primarily for members.

ROYAL INSTITUTE OF NAVIGATION

Acronym or abbreviation: RIN

1 Kensington Gore, London, SW7 2AT

Tel: 020 7591 3130
Fax: 020 7591 3131
E-mail: info@rin.org.uk

Website:
http://www.rin.org.uk
Navigation information, activities, membership details, library and journal search facilities.

Enquiries:
Enquiries to: Director

Founded:
1947

Organisation type and purpose:
International organisation, advisory body, learned society (membership is by subscription), present number of members: 3500, registered charity (charity number 251512), public library, publishing house.
To unite in one body those interested in navigation and to advance its science and practice, and to promote knowledge in navigation.

Subject coverage:
All aspects of air, sea, vehicle and space navigation; navigation technology, satellite navigation, small craft navigation, general and civil aviation navigation, land navigation, traffic routing, animal navigation, personal navigation, history of navigation, astronomy, bridge design, collision avoidance, weather.

continued overleaf

Museum or gallery collection, archive, or library special collection:
Library covering all aspects of navigation

Printed publications:
Journal of Navigation (3 times a year)
Navigation News (6 times a year)

Access to staff:
Contact by letter, by telephone, by fax, by e-mail, in person and via website
Hours: Mon to Fri, 0930 to 1630

Access to building, collection or gallery:
No access other than to staff

Member of:
European Group of Institutes of Navigation (EUGIN)
    tel: + 31 23 540 2485; fax: + 31 23 540 2486; e-mail: navicons@xs4all.nl
International Association of Institutes of Navigation (IAIN)
    tel: 01444 232405; fax: 01444 232405; e-mail: prentpage@aol.com

ROYAL INSTITUTE OF OIL PAINTERS

Acronym or abbreviation: ROI

17 Carlton House Terrace, London, SW1Y 5BD

Tel: 020 7930 6844
Fax: 020 7839 7830
E-mail: press@mallgalleries.com

Website:
http://www.mallgalleries.org.uk

Enquiries:
Enquiries to: Secretary
Other contacts: Marketing and Communications Officer

Founded:
1882

Organisation type and purpose:
Membership association (membership is by election or invitation), present number of members: 68, registered charity (charity number 327615).
To foster and promote the art of oil painting.

Subject coverage:
Oil paintings and painters, annual open exhibition.

Printed publications:
ROI Catalogues available at annual exhibition

Access to staff:
Contact by letter, by telephone, by fax, by e-mail and via website. Appointment necessary.
Hours: Mon to Fri, 0930 to 1700

Access to building, collection or gallery:
No access other than to staff
Hours: Mon to Fri, 0930 to 1700

Access for disabled people:
Stairlift, toilet facilities
Special comments: Stairlift.

Links with:
Federation of British Artists (FBA)
    at the same address

ROYAL INSTITUTE OF PAINTERS IN WATERCOLOURS

Acronym or abbreviation: RI

17 Carlton House Terrace, London, SW1Y 5BD

Tel: 020 7930 6844
Fax: 020 7839 7830
E-mail: press@mallgalleries.com

Website:
http://www.mallgalleries.org.uk

Enquiries:
Enquiries to: Secretary
Other contacts: Marketing and Communications Officer

Founded:
1831

Organisation type and purpose:
Membership association (membership is by election or invitation), present number of members: 78, voluntary organisation, registered charity (charity number 291405).
To foster and promote the art of watercolour painting.

Subject coverage:
Watercolour painting, annual open exhibition.

Printed publications:
RI catalogues available during annual exhibition

Access to staff:
Contact by letter, by telephone, by fax, by e-mail and via website. Appointment necessary.
Hours: Mon to Fri, 0930 to 1700

Access to building, collection or gallery:
No access other than to staff
Hours: Mon to Fri, 0930 to 1700

Access for disabled people:
Stairlift, toilet facilities
Special comments: Stairlift.

Links with:
Federation of British Artists
    at the same address

ROYAL INSTITUTE OF PHILOSOPHY

14 Gordon Square, London, WC1H 0AR

Tel: 020 7387 4130
Fax: 020 7383 4061
E-mail: secretary@royalinstitutephilosophy.org

Website:
http://www.royalinstitutephilosophy.org

Enquiries:
Enquiries to: Secretary

Organisation type and purpose:
Learned society.
To promote the study and discussion of philosophy, arrange and sponsor lectures and conferences.

Subject coverage:
Philosophy: logic, metaphysics, epistemology, ethics, aesthetics, social and political philosophy; the philosophies of science, religion, history, education, mind and language.

Museum or gallery collection, archive, or library special collection:
Bosanquet Collection

Printed publications:
Conference Proceedings (biennial)
Lectures given at the Institute (annual)
Philosophy (quarterly)

Access to staff:
Contact by letter and by e-mail
Hours: Mon to Fri, 0900 to 1700

ROYAL INSTITUTE OF PUBLIC HEALTH

Acronym or abbreviation: RIPH

28 Portland Place, London, W1B 1DE

Tel: 020 7580 2731
Fax: 020 7580 6157
E-mail: info@riph.org.uk

Website:
http://www.riph.org.uk

Enquiries:
Enquiries to: Marketing Communications Officer
Direct tel: 020 7291 8358
Direct e-mail: azilnyk@rsph.org.uk

Founded:
1886

Organisation type and purpose:
Learned society, membership association (membership is by qualification, election or invitation), present number of members: 3000, registered charity (charity number 227746), suitable for ages: 16+, training organisation.

Subject coverage:
Food safety, nutrition, salon hygiene, community care education, health and hygiene, postgraduate training in occupational health.

Printed publications:
Health and Hygiene (journal, quarterly)
Public Health (journal, 6 times a year)
A Handbook of Mortuary Practice & Safety
First Certificate in Food Safety – Student Handbook (1997)
First Certificate in Food Safety – Tutor's Guide (1995)
A Supervisor's Handbook of Food Hygiene and Safety (1998)
HACCP Principles and their Application in Food Safety Training Standards (1995)
Register of Certificated Products
Register of Certificated Training Materials
Symposium Proceedings

Publications list:
Available in print

Access to staff:
Contact by letter, by telephone, by fax and by e-mail
Hours: Mon to Fri, 0900 to 1700

ROYAL INSTITUTION OF CHARTERED SURVEYORS

Acronym or abbreviation: RICS

12 Great George Street, Parliament Square, London, SW1P 3AD

Tel: 0870 333 1600
Fax: 020 7334 3811
E-mail: contactrics@rics.org

Website:
http://www.rics.org
Description of organisation and activities and contact points, press releases, policy submissions listing, Chartered Surveyor Monthly – full text of articles from March 1997, CPD Providers database, RICS Directory of Chartered Surveyors practices database. Details of RICS conferences, research findings, papers and reports. Training and career information.

Enquiries:
Enquiries to: Librarian
Direct fax: 020 7334 3784
Direct e-mail: library@rics.org

Founded:
1868

Organisation type and purpose:
Professional body (membership is by qualification), present number of members: 120,000.

Subject coverage:
Commercial property, leisure property, chartered surveying, property, land, construction, valuation, surveying, town and country planning, construction economics, construction law, housing, agricultural holdings, estate agency, property management, land surveying, hydrographic surveying, landlord and tenant, property tax, quantity surveying, rating, estate management, marine resources.

Museum or gallery collection, archive, or library special collection:
Board of Agriculture Reports, 19th century
Historical Collection (pre-1875) on land, measurement and building economics and topography
Royal Commission Reports, 19th century
Topographical collections

Trade and statistical information:
Construction workload, housing market trend indicator, commercial property market survey, rural market survey and residential lettings.

Library catalogue:
All or part available online

Printed publications:
Knowledge Alert (fortnightly)
RICS Business (monthly)
Chartered Surveyors Directory
New members handbook
Publicity leaflets
RICS Yearbook
Geomatics World
Market Surveys on Residential Property, Commercial Property, Construction, Rural, Residential Lettings
UK Economic Brief
Order printed publications from: Mail Order Department, RICS Books, Surveyor Court, Westwood Way Business Park, Coventry, West Midlands, CV4 8JE, tel: 0870 333 1600, fax: 020 7334 3851, e-mail: mailorder@rics.org, website: ricsbooks.com

Electronic and video publications:
Appraisal and Valuation Manual (CD-ROM and online), isurv Building Surveying, Commercial Property, Construction, Disputes, Environment, Planning, Valuation (all online www.isurv.co.uk)

Publications list:
Available online and in print

Access to staff:
Contact by letter, by telephone, by fax, by e-mail, in person and via website. Non-members charged.
Hours: Mon to Fri, 0930 to 1730
Special comments: Charges made for access to the Library for non-members.

Access for disabled people:
Ramped entry, toilet facilities

Other addresses:
Royal Institution of Chartered Surveyors
Surveyor Court, Westwood Way Business Park, Coventry, CV4 8JE; tel: 0870 333 1600; fax: 020 7334 3811
Royal Institution of Chartered Surveyors
9 Manor Place, Edinburgh, EH3 7DN; tel: 0131 225 7078; fax: 0131 240 0830/31

ROYAL INSTITUTION OF CHARTERED SURVEYORS IN SCOTLAND

Acronym or abbreviation: RICS

9 Manor Place, Edinburgh, EH3 7DN

Tel: 0131 225 7078
Fax: 0131 240 0830
E-mail: edlib@rics.org

Website:
http://www.rics.org/library

Enquiries:
Enquiries to: Library Manager

Founded:
1897

Organisation type and purpose:
International organisation, professional body (membership is by qualification).

Subject coverage:
Surveying, building construction, property, rural practice.

Library catalogue:
All or part available online

Publications list:
Available online

Access to staff:
Contact by letter, by telephone, by fax, by e-mail, in person and via website. Appointment necessary. Non-members charged.
Hours: Mon to Fri, 0900 to 1700

Also at:
The Librarian, Royal Institution of Chartered Surveyors
12 Great George Street, Parliament Square, London, SW1P 3AD; tel: 020 7334 3714; fax: 020 7334 3784; e-mail: library@rics.org

ROYAL INSTITUTION OF CORNWALL

Acronym or abbreviation: RIC

Courtney Library & Cornish History Research Centre, River Street, Truro, Cornwall, TR1 2SJ

Tel: 01872 272205
Fax: 01872 240514
E-mail: RIC@royalcornwallmuseum.org.uk

Enquiries:
Enquiries to: Librarian

Founded:
1818

Organisation type and purpose:
Learned society, registered charity (charity number 221958).
Private members library with public access to study area. The oldest established Cornish history research centre in the county.

Subject coverage:
Cornwall; all aspects of research into Cornish history.

Museum or gallery collection, archive, or library special collection:
19th- and 20th-century photographs of Cornwall (50,000 items)
Doble Collection (hagiography)
Henderson Collection (manuscripts on history, antiquities, topography, Cornwall)
Manuscripts 13th-19th centuries (c. 30,000 items, Cornish estates and people)
Directories and Newspapers 1798–1951 and 1965–1973 (original files, Cornwall)
Parish registers (microfilms and transcripts)
Shaw Collection (Methodist church history, Cornwall)
Staal Collection (ceramics, glass, clocks)

Non-library collection catalogue:
All or part available in-house

Printed publications:
Journal of The Royal Institution of Cornwall (annually since 1864)
Newsletter of The RIC (2 times a year)
Facsimiles of 19th-century posters from RIC Collection
List of Cornish Parish Registers held by RIC as transcripts, 1992
List of Non-Anglican Registers ... Cornwall, 1999
Sources for Maritime Research
Sources for Newspaper Research ... Cornwall, 2000

Microform publications:
List of Cornish Parish Registers held by RIC on microfilm, 1992

Access to staff:
Contact by letter, by telephone, by fax, by e-mail and in person
Hours: Mon to Sat, 1000 to 1300 and 1400 to 1700 Closed Bank Holidays
Special comments: Non-members may be admitted for the purposes of research.

Access for disabled people:
Lift, ramped entry, access to all public areas, toilet facilities

Links with:
Royal Cornwall Museum and Art Gallery

ROYAL INSTITUTION OF GREAT BRITAIN

Acronym or abbreviation: RI

21 Albemarle Street, London, W1S 4BS

Tel: 020 7409 2992

Fax: 020 7629 3569
E-mail: ri@ri.ac.uk

Website:
http://www.rigb.org/

Enquiries:
Enquiries to: Head of Collections and Heritage
Direct tel: 020 7670 2924
Direct e-mail: fjames@ri.ac.uk

Founded:
1799

Organisation type and purpose:
Learned society (membership is by election or invitation), present number of members: c. 3000. Scientific body.

Subject coverage:
Science for the layman, history and philosophy of science, scientific biography, the social relations of science, solid state and surface chemistry and physics, catalysis, computer molecular modelling.

Museum or gallery collection, archive, or library special collection:
Historic apparatus
Manuscripts of famous scientists connected with The Royal Institution eg H Davy, M Faraday, J Tyndall, J Dewar, W H and W L Bragg, G Porter
Pre-1900 scientific books and periodicals
The Royal Institution Administrative Archives

Non-library collection catalogue:
All or part available in-house

Library catalogue:
All or part available in-house

Printed publications:
Annual report

Microform publications:
J Dewar, 1842–1923, catalogue of papers (1991, pub Chadwyck-Healey)
Journals of T A Hirst (Brock W H et al eds, pub Mansell, 1980)
J Tyndall, 1820–1893 (catalogue of papers, Friday J R ed., pub Mansell, 1974)

Electronic and video publications:
RI Christmas Lectures videotapes (via BBC)

Publications list:
Available in print

Access to staff:
Appointment necessary.
Hours: Mon to Fri, 0900 to 1700

Access for disabled people:
Level entry, toilet facilities

Includes the:
Davy-Faraday Research Laboratory
Library and Archives
Michael Faraday Museum
Royal Institution Centre for the History of Science and Technology

ROYAL INSTITUTION OF NAVAL ARCHITECTS

Acronym or abbreviation: RINA

10 Upper Belgrave Street, London, SW1X 8BQ

Tel: 020 7235 4622
Fax: 020 7245 6959
E-mail: hq@rina.org.uk

Website:
http://www.rina.org.uk
Information on all the Institution's activities, publications.

Enquiries:
Enquiries to: Executive Officer
Direct fax: 020 7259 5912

Founded:
1860

continued overleaf

Organisation type and purpose:
International organisation, learned society, professional body (membership is by qualification, election or invitation), registered charity (charity number 211161).

Subject coverage:
Naval architecture, shipbuilding, marine engineering and related subjects.

Non-library collection catalogue:
All or part available online and in print

Library catalogue:
All or part available in-house

Printed publications:
The Naval Architect journal
Occasional publications
Ship and Boat International journal,
Ship Repair and Conversion Technology journal
Warship Technology journal
Offshore Marine Technology journal
International Journal of Maritime Engineering
International Journal on Small Craft Technology
Conference proceedings
Order printed publications from: e-mail: publications@rina.org.uk

Electronic and video publications:
The Naval Architect journal
Occasional publications
Ship and Boat International journal
Ship Repair and Conversion Technology journal
Warship Technology journal
Offshore Marine Technology journal
International Journal of Maritime Engineering
International Journal on Small Craft Technology
Order electronic and video publications from: e-mail: publications@rina.org.uk

Publications list:
Available online and in print

Access to staff:
Contact by letter, by telephone, by fax, by e-mail and via website. Appointment necessary. Non-members charged.
Hours: Mon to Fri, 0930 to 1700

ROYAL INSTITUTION OF SOUTH WALES

Acronym or abbreviation: RISW

c/o Swansea Museum, Victoria Road, Maritime Quarter, Swansea, West Glamorgan, SA1 1SN

Tel: 01792 653763
Fax: 01792 652585
E-mail: swansea.museum@swansea.gov.uk

Website:
http://www.risw.org.uk

Enquiries:
Enquiries to: Honorary Secretary
Direct tel: 01792 874143
Other contacts: Curator for museum/local history

Founded:
1835

Organisation type and purpose:
Learned society (membership is by subscription), voluntary organisation, registered charity. Friends of Swansea Museum.

Subject coverage:
Local history and studies of Swansea and surrounding area, including natural history, biography, culture, early photography, archaeology, ceramics (Swansea and District) and local topography.

Printed publications:
Available for purchase directly
Minerva: The Journal of Swansea History (annually, back numbers available)
History of Swansea Vol 2 (Jones W H)
John Humphrey, God's Own Architect (Farmer D)
Welsh Ceramics in Context, Vols 1–2 (ed Gray J)

Publications list:
Available in print

Access to staff:
Contact by letter, by telephone and by e-mail. Appointment necessary.
Hours: Mon to Fri, 0900 to 1700

Access to building, collection or gallery:
Prior appointment required

Access for disabled people:
Parking provided

ROYAL LANCASHIRE AGRICULTURAL SOCIETY

Acronym or abbreviation: RLAS

PO Box 202, Thornton Cleveleys, FY5 9AW

E-mail: info@rlas.co.uk

Website:
http://www.rlas.co.uk

Enquiries:
Enquiries to: Secretary

Founded:
1767

Organisation type and purpose:
Membership association (membership is by subscription), present number of members: 750, registered charity (charity number 1008403). Promotion of agriculture. Organisation of three-day agricultural show.

Subject coverage:
Royal Lancashire Show.

Museum or gallery collection, archive, or library special collection:
History of Society held in County Records Office
Show Journals over many years

Printed publications:
Annual Report (members only)
Annual Schedules/Prize lists (free)
Newsletter (2 times a year, members only)

Access to staff:
Contact by letter, by telephone, by fax, by e-mail, in person and via website
Hours: Mon to Fri, 0900 to 1700

Access for disabled people:
Access to all public areas

Links with:
Various breed societies

ROYAL LIFE SAVING SOCIETY (UK)

River House, High Street, Broom, Alcester, Warwickshire, B50 4HN

Tel: 01789 773994
Fax: 01789 773995
E-mail: lifesavers@rlss.org.uk

Website:
http://www.lifesavers.org.uk
The society, its branches and clubs, courses, awards.

Founded:
1891

Organisation type and purpose:
A registered charity with a vision to safeguard lives in, on and near water.
The society has more than 11,000 members in 50 branches and 3,000 active lifesaving and lifeguarding clubs and approved training centres throughout the UK and Ireland.

Subject coverage:
Lifesavers and lifesaving.

Electronic and video publications:
Press releases
Order electronic and video publications from: website

Publications list:
Available online

Access to staff:
Contact by letter, by telephone, by fax and by e-mail

ROYAL LONDON HOSPITAL ARCHIVES AND MUSEUM

The Royal London Hospital, Whitechapel, London, E1 1BB

Tel: 020 7377 7608
Fax: 020 7377 7401
E-mail: jonathan.evans@bartsandthelondon.nhs.uk

Website:
http://www.bartsandthelondon.nhs.uk
History of the hospital; general guide to archives and museum.
http://www.a2a.org.uk
Detailed guide to archival holdings.
http://www.aim25.ac.uk
Detailed guide to archival holdings.

Enquiries:
Enquiries to: Archivist

Organisation type and purpose:
National government body, museum, university department or institute,
suitable for ages: 12+.
Archive.

Subject coverage:
Hospitals, medical and nursing history, dentistry, orthodontics, forensic medicine, health records.

Museum or gallery collection, archive, or library special collection:
Archives of the Royal London Hospital
Archives of the London Chest Hospital
Archives of the Queen Elizabeth Hospital for Children
Archives of the London Hospital Medical College
Archives of other hospitals in Tower Hamlets and Newham
Collections of the British Orthodontic Society
Edith Cavell Collection: Nursing history, artefacts and archives 1800s-1915
Eva Luckes Collection
London Hospital Surgical Instruments 18th-20th century
Medical and surgical films
Princess Alexandra School of Nursing: Nursing history, uniforms, equipment etc.1880–1993

Printed publications:
The Royal London Hospital: A Brief History (Collins S M, 1995)
London Pride: The Story of a Voluntary Hospital (Clark-Kennedy A E, 1979)
Emblems, Tokens and Tickets of The London Hospital and the London Hospital Medical College (Gibbs D, 1985)
L.H.M.C. 1785–1985 The Story of England's first Medical School (Ellis J)
The Dental School of The London Hospital Medical College 1911–1991 (Fish S F, 1991)
Learning to care: A history of nursing and midwifery education at the Royal London Hospital, 1740–1983 (Parker E R and Collins S M, 1998)
A History of Radiotherapy at The London Hospital 1896–1996 (Hope-Stone H F, 1999)
Patients are People – Memories of Nursing at 'The London' 1939–1958 (Broadley M E, 1995)
Patients Come First. Nursing at 'The London' between the two World Wars (Broadley M E, 1980)
Edith Cavell: Her Life And Her Art – Sa Vie Et Son Art (Daunton C H G, 1990)
Treves and the Elephant Man (Evans R J, 2003)
Edith Cavell (Evans R J, 2008)

Publications list:
Available online and in print

Access to staff:
Contact by letter, by telephone, by fax, by e-mail, in person and via website. Appointment necessary.
Hours: Mon to Fri, 1000 to 1630

Access to building, collection or gallery:
Open to the public
Hours: Mon to Fri, 1000 to 1630

Access for disabled people:
Disabled access available
Hours: Mon to Fri, 1000 to 1630

Affiliated to:
Queen Mary University of London

Parent body:
Barts and The London Hospital NHS Trust
   Royal London Hospital, London, E1 1BB

ROYAL LONDON SOCIETY FOR THE BLIND

Acronym or abbreviation: RLSB

Dorton House, Seal, Sevenoaks, Kent, TN15 0ED

Tel: 01732 592500
Fax: 01732 592506
E-mail: nicky.josling@rlsb.org.uk

Website:
http://www.rlsb.org.uk

Enquiries:
Enquiries to: Marketing and Communications
Director
Direct e-mail: enquiries@rlsb.org.uk

Founded:
1838

Organisation type and purpose:
Registered charity (charity number 307892).
A national provider of education, training and
employment for people who are visually impaired.

Subject coverage:
Education of blind or partially-sighted children
aged 3 to 16, further education from 16 upwards,
including mature students, training and
rehabilitation, employment in RLSB industrial
Services, SES scheme, homeworkers.

**Museum or gallery collection, archive, or library
special collection:**
Minutes and official reports on the Society dating
   back to its inception in 1838

Printed publications:
Annual Report
Prospectus on school and college
Life Chances (2 times a year)

Electronic and video publications:
Making a will booklet (on tape and Braille)

Access to staff:
Contact by letter, by telephone, by fax and by e-
mail. Appointment necessary.
Hours: Mon to Fri, 0900 to 1700

Member organisation of:
Blindcare
Greater London Fund for the Blind
Opsis

ROYAL MAIL GROUP EDUCATION SERVICE

PO Box 145, Sittingbourne, Kent, ME10 1NH

Tel: 01795 426465
Fax: 01795 437988
E-mail: royalmail@edist.co.uk

Website:
http://www.teacherspost.co.uk

Enquiries:
Enquiries to: Director

Formerly called:
Post Office Film and Video Library, and Education
Service (year of change 2001)

Organisation type and purpose:
Royal Mail education initiatives and resources.

Subject coverage:
Full range of educational resources – primary,
secondary, higher, supported by video
programmes and other material on all aspects of
Royal Mail, Post Office, Counters and Parcelforce.
Library for GPO classic programmes, e.g. 'Night
Mail' on video and many other 1930s subjects. In
addition more recent releases, including videos on
stamps, the Millennium and other subjects.

**Museum or gallery collection, archive, or library
special collection:**
Current Post Office video releases
Archive posters
Classic collection of archive subjects from GPO
   film unit (1930s) (on DVD)
Classic video collection

Library catalogue:
All or part available in print

Printed publications:
Teacher's Post

Publications list:
Available in print

Access to staff:
Contact by letter, by telephone, by fax, by e-mail
and in person
Hours: Mon to Fri, 0900 to 1700

Access to building, collection or gallery:
Prior appointment required

ROYAL MARINES ASSOCIATION

Acronym or abbreviation: RMA

Central Office, Building 32, Whale Island,
Portsmouth, Hants, PO2 8ER

Tel: 023 9265 1519
Fax: 023 9254 7207
E-mail: chiefexec@rma.org.uk

Enquiries:
Enquiries to: Chief Executive

Founded:
1946

Organisation type and purpose:
National organisation, membership association
(membership is by subscription, qualification),
present number of members: 10,000, registered
charity (charity number 206003).
Service charity.

Access to staff:
Contact by letter, by telephone, by fax and by e-
mail
Hours: Mon to Fri, 0900 to 1700

ROYAL MEDICAL SOCIETY

Acronym or abbreviation: RMS

Student Centre, 5/5 Bristo Square, Edinburgh, EH8
9AL

Tel: 0131 650 2672
E-mail: enquiries@royalmedical.co.uk

Website:
http://www.royalmedical.co.uk

Enquiries:
Enquiries to: Secretary

Founded:
1736

Organisation type and purpose:
Learned society.
Historical, medical students' organisation and
library.

Subject coverage:
Edinburgh medical history.

**Museum or gallery collection, archive, or library
special collection:**
Collection of dissertations over last 258 years
Current medical library
Historical medical library
Pathological museum

Printed publications:
RES Medica

Access to staff:
Contact by letter and by e-mail. Appointment
necessary.
Hours: Mon to Fri, 1200 to 1700

ROYAL MICROSCOPICAL SOCIETY

Acronym or abbreviation: RMS

37–38 St Clements, Oxford, OX4 1AJ

Tel: 01865 248768
Fax: 01865 791237
E-mail: info@rms.org.uk

Website:
http://www.rms.org.uk
Information on the Society and its programme of
meetings and courses.

Enquiries:
Enquiries to: Administrator

Founded:
1839

Organisation type and purpose:
Learned society, present number of members:
1,500, registered charity (charity number 241990).
To promote the advancement of microscopical
science by discussion and publication of research
into improvements in the construction and mode
of application of microscopes and into those
branches of science where microscopy is
important.

Subject coverage:
Microscopy.

**Museum or gallery collection, archive, or library
special collection:**
Collection of 18th- and 19th-century microscopes –
housed at the Museum of the History of Science,
Broad Street, Oxford

Non-library collection catalogue:
All or part available in print

Printed publications:
Catalogue of the collection
Journal of Microscopy (monthly, £660 a year)
Proceedings of the Royal Microscopical Society
   (quarterly, £176 a year)
RMS Handbooks Series (1–2 titles a year)

Access to staff:
Contact by letter, by telephone, by fax and by e-
mail
Hours: Mon to Fri, 0900 to 1700

Affiliated to:
International Federation of Societies for
Histochemistry and Cytochemistry (IFSHC)
International Federation of Societies of Electron
Microscopy (IFSEM)

ROYAL MILITARY ACADEMY SANDHURST

Acronym or abbreviation: RMAS

Central Library, Camberley, Surrey, GU15 4PQ

Tel: 01276 412367
Fax: 01276 412359
E-mail: aaorgill@aol.com

Enquiries:
Enquiries to: Librarian

Organisation type and purpose:
Training organisation. Central government
military academy.

Subject coverage:
War studies and military history; international
affairs; political and social studies; Commonwealth
of Independent States and the former republics of
the Soviet Union.

continued overleaf

Museum or gallery collection, archive, or library special collection:
Le Marchant Collection of manuscripts relating to the foundation of Sandhurst
Letter Books, RMA Woolwich, 1787–1895
Register of Gentlemen Cadets, RMA Woolwich, 1790–1793 and 1799–1939
Registers of Gentlemen Cadets, RMC Sandhurst, 1806–1945
Sandhurst Papers, 1857–1939

Non-library collection catalogue:
All or part available in-house

Library catalogue:
All or part available in-house

Printed publications:
Accessions lists

Access to staff:
Contact by letter, by telephone and by e-mail
Hours: Mon to Thu, 0830 to 1800; Fri, 0830 to 1630
Special comments: Visitors strictly by appointment only.

Part of:
Ministry of Defence

ROYAL NATIONAL COLLEGE FOR THE BLIND

Acronym or abbreviation: RNC

College Road, Hereford, HR1 1EB

Tel: 01432 265725
Fax: 01432 376628
E-mail: info@rncb.ac.uk

Website:
http://www.rncb.ac.uk
Prospectus plus additional information.

Enquiries:
Enquiries to: Marketing Manager
Other contacts: Central Admissions for advice/guidance on enrolment procedures.

Founded:
1872

Organisation type and purpose:
Registered charity (charity number 1000388), training organisation.
Further education and training for people who are blind or partially-sighted.

Subject coverage:
Education of the blind and partially sighted, especially education in music technology, piano tuning and repairing, business studies, remedial therapy, computing, performing arts, tele-tutoring, sport and recreation.

Museum or gallery collection, archive, or library special collection:
Annual Reports dating from foundation of College in 1872
Braille Library

Library catalogue:
All or part available online

Printed publications:
Annual Report
Prospectus (braille, large print and standard print)
Individual course leaflets

Electronic and video publications:
Prospectus on disk, tape and CD
Videos/DVD

Access to staff:
Contact by letter, by telephone, by fax, by e-mail and via website. Appointment necessary.
Hours: Mon to Fri, 0900 to 1700

Access for disabled people:
Parking provided, ramped entry, level entry, toilet facilities

Member of:
Natspec
Opsis

ROYAL NATIONAL INSTITUTE OF THE BLIND

Acronym or abbreviation: RNIB

105 Judd Street, London, WC1H 9NE

Tel: 020 7388 1266
Fax: 020 7388 2034
E-mail: helpline@rnib.org.uk

Website:
http://www.rnib.org.uk

Enquiries:
Enquiries to: Communications Systems Officer
Direct tel: 020 7391 2396
Direct fax: 020 7391 2221
Direct e-mail: julie-crispin@rnib.org.uk

Organisation type and purpose:
Registered charity.

Subject coverage:
Advice, support and information for blind and partially-sighted people. Benefit rights, advice on wills and legacies; production of Braille books, periodicals and music; Talking Books; equipment and games for blind and partially sighted people and for deaf-blind people; social and employment rehabilitation and training; education including schools and colleges, advisory and training services; residential services; hotels; research into the prevention of blindness; advice on sport, leisure and the arts; health information service, low-vision expertise, consultancy to health authorities on ophthalmic services.

Information services:
Helpline for advice, support and information.

Museum or gallery collection, archive, or library special collection:
Early embossed literature (some 100 items, Alston, Frere, Lucas, Moon, Braille)

Printed publications:
Catalogue of Braille Books
Catalogue of Braille Music
Catalogue of Print Publications
Catalogue of Talking Books
Directory of Agencies for the Blind in the British Isles and Overseas
New Beacon (RNIB Journal)
Product guides (equipment, games etc)

Publications list:
Available online and in print

Access to staff:
Contact by letter, by telephone, by fax, by e-mail and via website
Hours: Mon to Fri, 0900 to 1700

Access for disabled people:
Ramped entry, access to all public areas, toilet facilities

ROYAL NATIONAL INSTITUTE OF THE BLIND – TALKING BOOK SERVICE

UK Customer Service Centre, PO Box 173, Peterborough, PE2 6WS

Tel: 01733 375000
Fax: 01733 375001
E-mail: cservices@rnib.org.uk

Website:
http://www.rnib.org.uk

Enquiries:
Enquiries to: General Customer Services

Founded:
1935

Organisation type and purpose:
Subscription library, registered charity.
Postal library for blind and partially sighted people, of any age, offering a wide range of professionally recorded books (CD) on special easy to use playback equipment.

Subject coverage:
Talking books.

Publications list:
Available online and in print

Access to staff:
Contact by letter, by e-mail and via website
Hours: Library: Mon to Fri, 0845 to 1800; Sat, 0900 to 1600

Access to building, collection or gallery:
No access other than to staff, prior appointment required

Access for disabled people:
Parking provided, level entry, access to all public areas, toilet facilities

ROYAL NATIONAL LIFEBOAT INSTITUTION

Acronym or abbreviation: RNLI

West Quay Road, Poole, Dorset, BH15 1HZ

Tel: 0845 122 6999
Fax: 01202 663366
E-mail: info@rnli.org.uk

Website:
http://www.rnli.org.uk
General information about the service.

Enquiries:
Enquiries to: Media Relations Manager

Founded:
1824

Organisation type and purpose:
Registered charity.

Subject coverage:
Search and rescue at sea, its organisation and statistics; design and construction of lifeboats and their electronic and other equipment; medical and survival techniques and equipment, lifeboat history (since 1824).

Special visitor services:
Library / archive available by appointment.

Museum or gallery collection, archive, or library special collection:
Lifeboat models
Photographic library (lifeboats since c. 1860)
Royal National Lifeboat Collection
Fine art collection
5 museum sites

Printed publications:
Annual Accounts
Educational Resources
Leaflets and posters
RNLI At Work (Annual review)
Storm Force News (quarterly, for children)
The Lifeboat (quarterly)
Order printed publications from: The Publications Dept, at the above address

Electronic and video publications:
Sea Safety Guidelines and DVDs
DVDs for adults and children
Order electronic and video publications from: Film and Image Unit, at the above address

Access to staff:
Contact by letter, by telephone, by fax, by e-mail and via website
Hours: Mon to Fri, 0900 to 1700

Access to building, collection or gallery:
By appointment
Hours: Mon to Fri, 0900 to 1700

Access for disabled people:
Lifts; access to display area and library
Hours: Mon to Fri, 0900 to 1700

Administers:
Chatham Historic Lifeboat Collection
Grace Darling Museum
Henry Blogg Museum
RNLI Whitby Museum
RNLI Zetland Museum

Provides the secretariat for the:
International Lifeboat Federation

ROYAL NATIONAL MISSION TO DEEP SEA FISHERMEN

Shore Street, Fraserburgh, Aberdeenshire, AB43 9BP

Tel: 01346 518388
Fax: 01346 517664

Enquiries:
Enquiries to: The Superintendent

Founded:
1881

Organisation type and purpose:
Registered charity (charity number 24477).

Subject coverage:
Christian missionary and welfare work for fishing communities.

Access to staff:
Contact by letter
Hours: Mon to Fri, 0900 to 1700

ROYAL NATIONAL MISSION TO DEEP SEA FISHERMEN, SCOTLAND

Acronym or abbreviation: Fishermen's Mission

The Fishermen's Mission, Haypark Business Centre, Marchmont Avenue, Polmont, Falkirk, FK2 0NZ

Tel: 01324 716857
Fax: 01324 716423
E-mail: ian.rnmdsf@talk21.com

Enquiries:
Enquiries to: Director Scotland

Founded:
1881

Organisation type and purpose:
Voluntary organisation, registered charity (charity number 232812).

Subject coverage:
The fishing industry; care of fishermen and their families.

Museum or gallery collection, archive, or library special collection:
Records of magazine (Toilers of the Deep) from 1881 onwards

Printed publications:
Fish and Ships (Stanley Pritchard); the story of 100 years of the fishing industry
They Happened to Me (Stanley Pritchard): the world of Charities in the 1950s-70s, plus comments of characters and social life from the 1920s to the late 1970s
Network (2 times a year)

Access to staff:
Contact by telephone
Hours: Mon to Fri, 0900 to 1700

ROYAL NATIONAL ROSE SOCIETY

Acronym or abbreviation: RNRS

Chiswell Green Lane, St Albans, Hertfordshire, AL2 3NR

Tel: 01727 850461
Fax: 01727 850360
E-mail: mail@rnrs.org.uk

Website:
http://www.rnrs.org.uk

Enquiries:
Enquiries to: Chief Executive

Founded:
1876

Organisation type and purpose:
Membership association (membership is by subscription), present number of members: 3,000, registered charity (charity number 1035848).

Subject coverage:
Roses, cultivation and history, etc; trials and exhibitions.

Museum or gallery collection, archive, or library special collection:
Society library including the Courtney Page Library

Printed publications:
How to grow roses (handbook)
The Rose (quarterly, for members only)

Access to staff:
Contact by letter, by telephone, by fax, by e-mail and via website
Hours: Mon to Fri, 0900 to 1700

Affiliated to:
World Federation of Rose Societies

ROYAL NAVAL ASSOCIATION

Acronym or abbreviation: RNA

Room 210, Semaphore Tower, PP70, HM Naval Base Portsmouth, PO1 3LT

Tel: 023 9272 3747
E-mail: nigel@royalnavalassoc.com

Website:
http://www.royal-naval-association.co.uk

Enquiries:
Enquiries to: General Secretary

Founded:
1954

Incorporates the former:
Royal Naval Old Comrades Assocns (year of change 1953)

Organisation type and purpose:
Registered charity (charity number 266982).

Subject coverage:
Support to ex- and serving Naval Service personnel.

Services for disabled people:
Shared financial support through SSAFA, RNBT.

Access to staff:
Contact by letter and by fax. Access for members only.
Hours: Mon to Fri, 0900 to 1700

Access for disabled people:
Lift available

Branches:
361 in UK; 30 overseas; see website for details

ROYAL NAVAL VOLUNTEER RESERVE OFFICERS ASSOCIATION

Formal name: Royal Naval Volunteer Reserve Officers' Association and Naval Club

38 Hill Street, London, W1J 5NS

Tel: 020 7493 7672
Fax: 020 7629 7995
E-mail: cdr@navalclub.co.uk

Website:
http://www.navalclub.co.uk
Full details of the Club.

Enquiries:
Enquiries to: Chief Executive

Founded:
1946

Organisation type and purpose:
Private members' club (membership is by election or invitation), offering full range of London Club facilities in the heart of Mayfair.

Subject coverage:
RN, RNR and RNVR officers and those connected with the sea and maritime affairs. Corporate membership available.

Access to staff:
Contact by letter, by telephone, by fax, by e-mail and via website. Appointment necessary. Access for members only.
Hours: Mon to Fri, 0900 to 1700

Access to building, collection or gallery:
Hours: 24-hour access

Access for disabled people:
Hours: 24-hour access

ROYAL NORFOLK AGRICULTURAL ASSOCIATION

Acronym or abbreviation: RNAA

The Showground, Dereham Road, New Costessey, Norwich, Norfolk, NR5 0TT

Tel: 01603 748931
Fax: 01603 748729
E-mail: jpurling@norfolkshowground.com

Enquiries:
Enquiries to: Chief Executive
Other contacts: Show Manager

Founded:
1847

Organisation type and purpose:
Membership association (membership is by subscription), present number of members: 3500, registered charity (charity number 289581). County show organiser. Promotes improvement in breeding of livestock and plants, invention and improvement of agricultural machines and implements, and skills in agriculture, horticulture and allied systems of husbandry.

Subject coverage:
Agricultural shows.

Printed publications:
Annual Report
Royal Norfolk Show Catalogue (annually, £4)
Royal Norfolk Show Programme (annually, £2.50)

Access to staff:
Contact by letter, by telephone, by fax and by e-mail. Appointment necessary.
Hours: Mon to Fri, 0900 to 1700

Access for disabled people:
Parking provided, ramped entry

Affiliated to:
Norfolk Showground Ltd

ROYAL NORTHERN AND UNIVERSITY CLUB

Acronym or abbreviation: RNUC

9 Albyn Place, Aberdeen, AB10 1YE

Tel: 01224 583292
Fax: 01224 571082
E-mail: secretary@rnuc.org.uk

Website:
http://www.rnuc.org.uk

Enquiries:
Enquiries to: Secretary

Founded:
1854

Organisation type and purpose:
Membership association (membership is by election or invitation).

Access to staff:
Contact by letter, by fax and by e-mail
Hours: Mon to Fri, 0900 to 1700

Access for disabled people:
Parking provided, ramped entry

ROYAL NORTHERN COLLEGE OF MUSIC

Acronym or abbreviation: RNCM

124 Oxford Road, Manchester, M13 9RD

Tel: 0161 907 5200
Fax: 0161 273 7611
E-mail: library@rncm.ac.uk

Website:
http://www.rncm.ac.uk
http://www.rncm.ac.uk/content/view/27/29
RNCM Library home page.

Enquiries:
Enquiries to: Librarian
Direct tel: 0161 907 5241; 0161 907 5245
Direct e-mail: anna.wright@rncm.ac.uk; geoff
.thomason@rncm.ac.uk
Other contacts: Deputy Librarian

Founded:
1973

Organisation type and purpose:
Music college.

Subject coverage:
Music; recordings; musicology.

Museum or gallery collection, archive, or library special collection:
Adolph Brodsky Collection
Arthur Butterworth manuscripts
Dame Eva Turner Collection of songs
Carl Fuchs Collection
Gordon Green Collection
Halifax Collection
Hansen Collection
Horenstein Collection
Ida Carroll Archive
John Golland manuscripts
Philip Newman Collection
John Ogdon manuscripts
Philip Jones Brass Ensemble Archive
Rawsthorne manuscripts
Richard Hall Collection
RNCM Collection of Historic Musical Instruments, includes Henry Watson Instrument Collection
Rothwell Collection of wind music
Sir Charles Grove Library
Thomas Pitfield Archive

Non-library collection catalogue:
All or part available online

Library catalogue:
All or part available online

Printed publications:
Library Guides
RNCM News
Programme of Events
Prospectus
Annual Report
Catalogue of the RNCM Collection of Historic Musical Instruments

Access to staff:
Contact by letter, by telephone, by fax, by e-mail and via website. Appointment necessary.
Hours: Term time: Mon to Thu, 0900 to 1900; Fri, 0930 to 1700; Sat 0900 to 1300
Vacations: Mon to Fri, 1000 to 1630

Access for disabled people:
The RNCM Library is fully accessible to wheelchair users
Hours: As above

Affiliated to:
IAML
website: http://www.iaml.info

ROYAL NORWEGIAN EMBASSY

25 Belgrave Square, London, SW1X 8QD

Tel: 020 7591 5500
Fax: 020 7245 6993
E-mail: emb.london@mfa.no

Enquiries:
Enquiries to: Press and Information Office

Other contacts: Consular Section (tel: 020 7591 5500 for passports, visas, etc.)

Organisation type and purpose:
Embassy.

Subject coverage:
Norway.

Printed publications:
Various fact sheets and brochures

Access to staff:
Contact by letter, by telephone, by fax, by e-mail and in person
Hours: Mon to Fri, 0900 to 1600
Special comments: Consular matters: Mon to Fri, tel. enquiries, 1000 to 1100 only; Mon, Tue, Thu, Fri, personal visits (passports), 1330 to 1500. Appointment necessary for visa applicants.

Parent body:
Royal Ministry of Foreign Affairs
Oslo

ROYAL NUMISMATIC SOCIETY

Acronym or abbreviation: RNS

Department of Coins & Medals, The British Museum, London, WC1B 3DG

Tel: 020 7323 8228
Fax: 020 7323 8171
E-mail: info@numismatics.org.uk

Website:
http://www.numismatics.org.uk
Information on RNS, catalogue of Numismatic Chronicle, society's calendar of meetings, grants/ funding opportunities, application form.

Enquiries:
Enquiries to: Honorary Secretary

Founded:
1836

Organisation type and purpose:
Learned society.

Subject coverage:
Numismatics.

Museum or gallery collection, archive, or library special collection:
Joint library with British Numismatic Society

Printed publications:
Coin Hoards (occasional)
Numismatic Chronicle (annually)
Special publications (occasional)

Access to staff:
Contact by letter, by telephone, by fax, by e-mail and via website
Hours: Mon to Fri, 0900 to 1700

Affiliated to:
International Numismatic Commission

ROYAL OBSERVATORY GREENWICH

Acronym or abbreviation: ROG

Park Row, London, SE10 9NF

Tel: 020 8858 4422 or 020 8312 6632
Fax: 020 8312 6734
E-mail: comments@nmm.ac.uk

Website:
http://www.nmm.ac.uk/places/royal-observatory

Founded:
1675

Organisation type and purpose:
National government body, museum, suitable for ages: 7 to adult.
Astronomy information.

Subject coverage:
Modern astronomy.

Information services:
Recorded information, tel: 020 8312 6565.

Services for disabled people:
Planetarium shows can be booked in advance for deaf groups and schools using their own sign-interpreter, and Museum runs a programme of signed events. Contact bookings unit, fax: 020 8312 6522; e-mail: bookings@nmm.ac.uk.

Non-library collection catalogue:
All or part available online and in-house

Library catalogue:
All or part available online and in-house

Printed publications:
Astronomy information leaflets (free) and publications
Order printed publications from: Website or direct

Publications list:
Available online and in print

Access to staff:
Contact by letter, by telephone, by fax, by e-mail and via website. Appointment necessary.
Hours: Mon to Fri, 0900 to 1700

Access to building, collection or gallery:
Hours: Mon to Fri, 1000 to 1645; last admission 1630
Special comments: Prior appointment required for reserve collections.

Access for disabled people:
Level access to courtyard, Meridian Line, display of transit instruments and gift shop, complete wheelchair access to new planetarium and education centre, limited wheelchair access to historical buildings of Royal Observatory, level ground floor access and a lift to basement gallery in Flamsteed House, all assistance dogs welcome in museum.
Special comments: No wheelchair access to Octagon Room, 28' telescope and Time & Society gallery.

Also at:
Royal Observatory Greenwich (ROG) (site location)
Greenwich Park, London, SE10 8XJ

ROYAL OCEAN RACING CLUB

Acronym or abbreviation: RORC

20 St James's Place, London, SW1A 1NN

Tel: 020 7493 2248 (4 lines)
Fax: 020 7493 5252
E-mail: info@rorc.org.uk

Enquiries:
Enquiries to: Chief Executive
Direct e-mail: ewo@rorc.org.uk
Other contacts: Accountant Reception (for mailings and computers)

Organisation type and purpose:
International organisation, membership association.

Subject coverage:
Ocean racing in general and British ocean racing in particular, long-distance yacht racing, design, building, navigation and sailing of sailing vessels, navigation and seamanship.

Museum or gallery collection, archive, or library special collection:
British ocean racing records since 1925

Printed publications:
Programme of races and current year's rules and regulations (annually)
Results of RORC races (annually)
Seahorse (on offshore racing, 12 times a year)

Access to staff:
Contact by letter, by fax and by e-mail. Letter of introduction required.
Hours: Mon to Fri, 0900 to 1700

Access to building, collection or gallery:
Prior appointment required

Affiliated to:
Offshore Racing Council
Royal Yachting Association

ROYAL OPERA HOUSE

Acronym or abbreviation: ROH

Covent Garden, London, WC2E 9DD

Tel: 020 7304 4000
Fax: 020 7212 9460

Website:
http://www.royaloperahouse.org
http://www.royalopera.org
Repertoire and booking information, background
information.
http://www.royalballet.org
Repertoire and booking information, background
information.
http://www.artsworld.com

Enquiries:
Enquiries to: Director of Press and Communications
Direct tel: 020 7212 9540
Direct fax: 020 7212 9525
Other contacts: (1) Archivist (2) Mailing List Officer
for (1) historical information (2) performance
details.

Founded:
1858

Organisation type and purpose:
Registered charity (charity number 211775).
The mission of the Royal Opera House is to attract,
excite, uplift and inspire the widest possible
audiences by performing opera and ballet to the
highest international standards at affordable
prices, to develop the art forms and to promote
their appreciation by people of all ages and
backgrounds.

Subject coverage:
The Royal Opera House, The Royal Opera, The
Royal Ballet, historical and current; opera and
ballet generally.

**Museum or gallery collection, archive, or library
special collection:**
Archive of material relating to The Royal Opera
House and its performing companies including:
Administration papers, scores and photos
Costumes and set models

Trade and statistical information:
Statistical details relating specifically to the Royal
Opera House and its performing companies.

Printed publications:
Annual Report
Educational materials (some free, some charged)
Season Guide
Programmes and Libretti (prices vary)
Booking brochures

Electronic and video publications:
CD/Tape: BMG Conifer, Bedford House, 69–79
Fulham High School, London SW6 3JW, tel: 0171
384 7500, fax; 0171 384 7922
Video/Laser disc: Covent Garden Pioneer, Pioneer
House, Hollybush Hill, Stoke Poges, Slough, SL2
4QP, tel: 01753 789661, fax; 01753 789646
Educational CD-ROM in preparation

Access to staff:
Contact by letter, by telephone, by fax and by e-
mail
Hours: Mon to Fri, 1000 to 1530
Special comments: No access for personal callers, or
to Archive, without appointment.

Access for disabled people:
Ramped entry, level entry, access to all public
areas, toilet facilities

Subsidiary body:
The Royal Ballet
at the same address
The Royal Opera
at the same address

ROYAL PAVILION

4–5 Pavilion Buildings, Brighton, East Sussex, BN1
1EE

Tel: 01273 290900

Fax: 01273 292871
E-mail: visitor.services@brighton-hove.gov.uk

Website:
http://www.royalpavilion.org.uk
General information on the Pavilion, prices, etc.

Enquiries:
Enquiries to: Marketing Manager

Founded:
1851

Organisation type and purpose:
Local government body, museum, historic
building, house or site.

Subject coverage:
History and conservation of the Royal Pavilion,
including interior decorations and Regency
gardens.

**Museum or gallery collection, archive, or library
special collection:**
Photographic material
Typescript of the accounts of the Crace Firm of
decorators during their time spent in the
Pavilion, 1802–1804, 1815–1819, 1820–23
Inventory of the Royal Pavilion, 1828
Abstract of accounts of the various firms working
in the Royal Pavilion
Letters
Quantities of letters from or about George, Prince
of Wales, Mrs Fitzherbert, or concerning
Brighton and the Royal Pavilion, but also
including letters by Byron
Also 'Esher' letters, volume containing 56 letters to
or concerning the Prince of Wales and Mrs
Fitzherbert
Plan Registry – Approximately 800 plans of the
Pavilion and the Pavilion Estate
Proceedings of the Pavilion Committee, 1850–1923
Proceedings of the Pavilion and Library
Committee, 1924–1974
Proceedings of the Fine Art Sub-Committee, 1901–
1941

Non-library collection catalogue:
All or part available in-house

Library catalogue:
All or part available in-house

Printed publications:
Guide Book (£4.99)
Order printed publications from: Commercial
Services, Royal Pavilion
at the same address

Access to staff:
Contact by letter, by telephone, by fax, by e-mail
and via website. Appointment necessary.
Hours: Mon to Fri, 0900 to 1730. Closed Christmas
and Boxing Day
Special comments: No office staff at weekends

Access to building, collection or gallery:
No prior appointment required
Hours: Oct to Mar: Daily, 1000 to 1715 (last
admission 1630)
Apr to Sep: Daily, 0930 to 1745 (last admission
1700)
Special comments: Prior appointment required for
guided tours etc.

Access for disabled people:
Level entry, toilet facilities ground floor only
Special comments: Wheelchair access to ground
floor only. 1st floor is NOT wheelchair accessible.

Parent body:
Brighton & Hove City Council

ROYAL PHARMACEUTICAL SOCIETY OF GREAT BRITAIN

Acronym or abbreviation: RPSGB

1 Lambeth High Street, London, SE1 7JN

Tel: 020 7735 9141
Fax: 020 7735 7629
E-mail: enquiries@rpsgb.org.uk

Website:
http://www.pharmpress.com

Pharmaceutical press site for info and online
ordering.
http://www.pharmj.com
The Pharmaceutical Journal online (full text) site.
http://www.rpsgb.org.uk
The Society's official website.

Enquiries:
Enquiries to: Information Librarian
Direct tel: 020 7572 2300
Direct fax: 020 7572 2499
Direct e-mail: library@rpsgb.org.uk

Founded:
1841

Organisation type and purpose:
Professional body (membership is by
qualification), present number of members: 47,000.

Subject coverage:
Pharmacy practice; pharmaceutical science;
pharmacology; therapeutics; medicine; toxicology;
chemistry and botany.

**Museum or gallery collection, archive, or library
special collection:**
Collection on English and foreign proprietary
medicines
Hanbury Library of rare, illustrated, botanical
works
Historical collection (including many herbals) from
1485
London, Edinburgh and Dublin Pharmacopoeias
from 1618
Records relating to pharmacists from 1841
(comprehensive from 1868 when pharmacists
were required to register)

Library catalogue:
All or part available online and in-house

Printed publications:
Publications include:
British National Formulary
BNF for Children
Clarke's Analysis of Drugs and Poisons
Drugs in Use
English Delftware Drug jars
Handbook of Pharmaceutical Excipients
Herbal Medicines
International Journal of Pharmacy Practice (4 a
year)
Journal of Pharmacy and Pharmacology (monthly)
Making Medicines: A Brief History of Pharmacy
and Pharmaceuticals
Martindale: The Complete Drug Reference
Medicines, Ethics and Practice
Patient Care in Community Practice
Pharmaceutical Journal (weekly)
Pharmacy Law and Ethics
Pharmacy Practice
Stockley's Drug Interactions
Order printed publications from: Pharmaceutical
Press, c/o Turpin Distribution, Stratton Business
Park, Pegasus Drive, Biggleswade, Bedfordshire,
SG18 8TQ; tel: 01767 604971; e-mail: custserv@
turpin-distribution.com

Electronic and video publications:
Electronic British National Formulary
Martindale on CD-ROM
Martindale online
MedicinesComplete (online)

Publications list:
Available online and in print

Access to staff:
Contact by letter, by telephone, by fax, by e-mail
and via website. Appointment necessary. Non-
members charged.
Hours: Mon, Tue, Wed, Fri, 0900 to 1700; Thu, 1000
to 1745

Access to building, collection or gallery:
By prior appointment for non-members
Hours: Thu, 1000 to 1745; Mon to Wed and Fri, 0900
to 1700

Access for disabled people:
Level entry, stairlift

ROYAL PHARMACEUTICAL SOCIETY OF GREAT BRITAIN – SCOTTISH DEPARTMENT

36 York Place, Edinburgh, EH1 3HU

Tel: 0131 556 4386
Fax: 0131 558 8850
E-mail: info@rpsis.com

Enquiries:
Enquiries to: Assistant Secretary

Founded:
1852

Organisation type and purpose:
Professional body.

Subject coverage:
Pharmacy.

Museum or gallery collection, archive, or library special collection:
Collection of rare herbals, pharmacopoeias etc

Access to staff:
Appointment necessary.
Hours: Mon to Fri, 0900 to 1300 and 1400 to 1700

ROYAL PHILATELIC SOCIETY

41 Devonshire Place, London, W1G 6JY

Tel: 020 7486 1044
Fax: 020 7486 0803
E-mail: secretary@rpsl.org.uk

Website:
http://www.rpsl.org.uk

Enquiries:
Enquiries to: Honorary Secretary

Founded:
1869

Organisation type and purpose:
Learned society.

Subject coverage:
Philately.

Access to staff:
Contact by letter, by telephone, by fax, by e-mail and via website. Appointment necessary. Access for members only.
Hours: Mon to Fri, 0930 to 1700

ROYAL PHILHARMONIC SOCIETY

Acronym or abbreviation: RPS

10 Stratford Place, London, W1C 1BA

Tel: 020 7491 8110
Fax: 020 7493 7463
E-mail: admin@royalphilharmonicsociety.org.uk

Website:
http://www.royalphilharmonicsociety.org.uk/
lectures.htm
Lectures and debates.
http://www.royalphilharmonicsociety.org.uk/
awards.htm
Awards and opportunities.
http://www.royalphilharmonicsociety.org.uk/
calendar.htm
Calendar of events

Enquiries:
Enquiries to: General Administrator

Founded:
1813

Organisation type and purpose:
National organisation, membership association, registered charity (charity number 213693). Administrators of bequests and trusts, and of awards and competitions.

Subject coverage:
History and activities of the Royal Philharmonic Society since its founding in 1813.

Museum or gallery collection, archive, or library special collection:
Society's Archives (correspondence, scores, manuscripts, programmes etc) held at the British Library, London

Printed publications:
Fanfare from The Royal Philharmonic Society (journal, 2 times a year)
RPS Annual Lecture (1 a year)

Access to staff:
Contact by letter, by fax and by e-mail.
Appointment necessary.
Hours: Mon to Fri, 1000 to 1700
Special comments: Prior appointment only.

ROYAL PHOTOGRAPHIC SOCIETY OF GREAT BRITAIN, THE

Acronym or abbreviation: RPS

The Octagon, Milsom Street, Bath, BA1 1DN

Tel: 01225 462841
Fax: 01225 448688
E-mail: rps@rps.org

Website:
http://www.rps.org
Exhibitions, photographic workshops, 'friends'.
Membership information and distinction information.

Enquiries:
Enquiries to: President
Direct tel: 01225 325720
Direct e-mail: liz@rps.org

Founded:
1853

Organisation type and purpose:
International organisation, learned society (membership is by subscription, election or invitation), present number of members: 10,000, registered charity (charity number 212684).
To promote the art and science of photography.

Subject coverage:
History and science of photography, specialises in the 19th century.

Museum or gallery collection, archive, or library special collection:
Biographic files on photographers
Dumont Collection (19th century books illustrated with photographs)
Notable collection of rare books and periodicals
Photographic collection (strong in 19th century British photographs and the Photo-Secessionists internationally)

Printed publications:
Bulletins of the specialist groups
Imaging Science Journal (4 times a year)
Photographic Journal (10 times a year)
Regional newsletters

Access to staff:
Contact by letter, by telephone, by fax, by e-mail and via website. Appointment necessary. Non-members charged.
Hours: Mon to Fri; 0930 to 1730, closed 24 Dec to 2 Jan

Access to building, collection or gallery:
No access other than to staff

Has:
16 Regions, and 15 Groups and Chapters abroad

ROYAL PIGEON RACING ASSOCIATION

Acronym or abbreviation: RPRA

The Reddings, Cheltenham, Gloucestershire, GL51 6RN

Tel: 01452 713529
Fax: 01452 857119
E-mail: gm@rpra.org

Website:
http://www.rpra.org

Enquiries:
Enquiries to: General Manager
Direct e-mail: dorothyhadley@rpra.org

Founded:
1897

Organisation type and purpose:
Membership association.
Control and administration organisation for the sport of long-distance pigeon racing.

Subject coverage:
Racing and showing of racing pigeons, racing pigeons in general, control and supply of rings, seals, apparatus and appliances.

Museum or gallery collection, archive, or library special collection:
Pigeons in War, Bletchley Park

Printed publications:
British Homing World (weekly)
Yearbook
Order printed publications from: Severn Farm Industrial Estate, Severn Road, Welshpool, Powys, SY21 7DF

Access to staff:
Contact by letter, by telephone, by fax and by e-mail. Appointment necessary.
Hours: Mon to Fri, 0900 to 1700

Affiliated to:
Fédération Colombophile Internationale Brussels

ROYAL PIONEER CORPS ASSOCIATION

c/o 23 Pioneer Regiment Royal Logistic Corps, St David's Barracks, Graven Hill, Bicester, Oxfordshire, OX26 6HF

Tel: 01869 360694
Fax: 01869 360695
E-mail: royalpioneercorps@gmail.com

Website:
http://www.royalpioneercorps.co.uk

Enquiries:
Enquiries to: Controller
Direct e-mail: normanbrown@myself.com

Founded:
1942

Organisation type and purpose:
Membership association (membership is by qualification), present number of members: 3000, registered charity (charity number 801733), suitable for ages: 18+.
To relieve needs, stress and hardship of ex-Pioneers, their wives, widows and dependants.
To foster esprit de corps.

Subject coverage:
Royal Pioneer Corps history.

Printed publications:
Newsletter (2 times a year)

Access to staff:
Contact by letter and by telephone
Hours: Mon to Fri, 0900 to 1700

ROYAL REGIMENT OF FUSILIERS ASSOCIATION LONDON AREA

Acronym or abbreviation: RRF Museum (London)

H M Tower of London, London, EC3N 4AB

Tel: 020 7488 5611
Fax: 020 7481 1093

Enquiries:
Enquiries to: Curator
Direct e-mail: royalfusiliers@fsmail.net
Other contacts: Archivist for research enquiries.

Founded:
1685

Organisation type and purpose:
Membership association (membership is by subscription, qualification), present number of members: 1000, registered charity (charity number 255042), museum.
Regimental Museum.

Subject coverage:
Military and social history.

Museum or gallery collection, archive, or library special collection:
Regimental Archives 1685 to 1968

Non-library collection catalogue:
All or part available in-house

Library catalogue:
All or part available in-house

Printed publications:
Museum Guide (£1.50)
Royal Fusiliers in the Great War (£35)
Royal Fusiliers Victoria Crosses (£2.50)

Access to staff:
Contact by letter. Appointment necessary.
Hours: Archivist only: 0900 to 1500
Special comments: Subject to HM Tower of London.

ROYAL SCHOOL FOR DEAF CHILDREN, MARGATE AND WESTGATE COLLEGE FOR DEAF PEOPLE

Formal name: The John Townsend Trust Ltd
Acronym or abbreviation: RSDC, Margate

Victoria Road, Margate, Kent, CT9 1NB

Tel: 01843 227561; minicom no. 01843 227531
Fax: 01843 227637
E-mail: enquiries@royalschoolfordeaf.kent.sch.uk

Website:
http://www.townsendtrust.org
School.
The school and college.
http://www.johntownsendtrust.org
The charity.

Enquiries:
Enquiries to: Chief Executive
Other contacts: Finance and Resources Director / Principal

Founded:
1792

Incorporates the former:
Royal School for Deaf Children (year of change 2008)

Organisation type and purpose:
National organisation, registered charity (charity number 1127209), suitable for ages: School: 4 to 16, College: 16+, consultancy. Non-maintained special school and specialist college (DfES number 8667017).
Education and training of pupils and students who are deaf.

Subject coverage:
Education of severely to profoundly deaf children and students. All learners have a hearing impairment or associated communication difficulty and many have additional educational, emotional behaviour or medical problems.
Provides 38 weeks of full-time education for learners on either a day or residential basis. Also offers 52-week placements in College and short break facilities during holiday periods for College and School.
A large dedicated team of experienced and qualified staff are able to meet the complex and diverse needs of the young people. They offer a high level of pastoral care and independence skills in addition to the National Curriculum, the 14–19 Vocational Curriculum and a wide range of accredited courses.

Museum or gallery collection, archive, or library special collection:
Minute books and other records from 1792 (not available to the public)

Printed publications:
Prospectus, Royal School for Deaf Children and Westgate College (annually)

Access to staff:
Contact by letter, by telephone, by fax, by e-mail, in person and via website. Appointment necessary.
Hours: Mon to Fri, 0900 to 1700

Access for disabled people:
Parking provided, ramped entry, toilet facilities, electronic doors

Also at:
Westgate College for Deaf People (further education college)
    Victoria Road, Margate, Kent CT9 1NB; tel: 01843 233550; fax: 01843 233551; e-mail: enquiries@westgate-college.org.uk

Member organisation of:
British Association of Teachers of the Deaf (BATOD)
NASEN
National Association of Specialist Colleges (FE) (Charities) (NATSPEC)
National Association of Voluntary Independent and Non-Maintained Schools (Charities) (NASS)

ROYAL SCHOOL OF CHURCH MUSIC

Acronym or abbreviation: RSCM

19 The Close, Salisbury, Wiltshire, SP1 2EB

Tel: 01722 424848
Fax: 01722 424849
E-mail: enquiries@rscm.com

Website:
http://www.rscm.com

Enquiries:
Enquiries to: Administrator
Direct tel: 01722 424855 (Publications Dept); 0845 021 7726 (music sales)

Founded:
1927

Formerly called:
School of English Church Music (year of change 1945)

Organisation type and purpose:
International educational charity, membership association, registered charity, training organisation, publishing house.
Study and promotion of church music.

Subject coverage:
Church music, liturgy, hymnody.

Museum or gallery collection, archive, or library special collection:
Maurice Frost Collection of hymnology (on permanent loan to the Royal College of Music)
Archives of Basil Harwood, G.R.Woodward, Sydney Nicholson and Henry Walford Davies

Library catalogue:
All or part available in-house

Printed publications:
Church Music Quarterly (membership magazine)
Sunday by Sunday (liturgy planner)
New music and scholarly editions of old music
A large range of hymns, anthems, services and other church choral music
Order printed publications from: RSCM Music Direct; tel: 0845 021 7726; fax: 0845 021 8826; e-mail: musicdirect@rscm.com

Publications list:
Available online and in print

Access to staff:
Contact by letter, by telephone, by fax, by e-mail, in person and via website
Hours: Mon to Fri, 0900 to 1700
Special comments: Access to Library by appointment only.

Access to building, collection or gallery:
Prior appointment required (library only)

Hours: Mon to Fri, 0900 to 1700

Access for disabled people:
Parking provided, level entry, toilet facilities

ROYAL SCHOOL OF NEEDLEWORK

Acronym or abbreviation: RSN

Apartment 12a, Hampton Court Palace, Surrey, KT8 9AU

Tel: 020 3166 6932
Fax: 020 8943 4910
E-mail: enquiries@royal-needlework.org.uk

Website:
http://www.royal-needlework.org.uk
Details of the RSN courses, services, events and products.

Enquiries:
Enquiries to: PA & Office Manager
Direct tel: 020 3166 6936

Founded:
1872

Organisation type and purpose:
Registered charity (charity number 312774).
To teach, practise and promote hand embroidery to the widest audience – leisure and professional classes; new embroidery commissions undertaken; restoration and conservation of antique textiles to keep the art of hand embroidery alive.

Subject coverage:
Teaching traditional hand embroidery techniques with technical excellence.

Museum or gallery collection, archive, or library special collection:
Design archive and books on embroidery
Textile collection

Non-library collection catalogue:
All or part available in-house

Printed publications:
Annual Course brochure, promotional leaflets
RSN Friends Newsletter (free with membership)
Royal School of Needlework Embroidery Techniques Book
1880 Handbook of Embroidery – published 2010
Order printed publications from: e-mail: sales@royal -needlework.org.uk

Electronic and video publications:
CD-ROM

Access to staff:
Contact by letter, by telephone, by fax, by e-mail and via website. Appointment necessary.
Hours: Mon to Fri, 0900 to 1700 – by appointment

Access to building, collection or gallery:
Prior appointment required

Access for disabled people:
Parking provided

ROYAL SCOTTISH ACADEMY

Formal name: Royal Scottish Academy of Art and Architecture
Acronym or abbreviation: RSA

The Mound, Edinburgh, EH2 2EL

Tel: 0131 225 6671
Fax: 0131 220 6016

Website:
http://www.royalscottishacademy.org
The RSA maintains a unique position in Scotland as an independently funded institution led by eminent artists and architects whose purpose is to promote and support the creation, understanding and enjoyment of the visual arts through varied exhibitions and related educational events. The RSA also administers scholarships, awards and residencies for artists in Scotland and has an historic collection of Scottish artworks and archive available for consultation by appointment.

continued overleaf

Enquiries:
Enquiries to: Programme Director
Direct e-mail: colingreenslade@
royalscottishacademy.org

Founded:
1826

Organisation type and purpose:
Learned society, professional body (membership is by election or invitation), present number of members: 113, registered charity (charity number SC 004198), art gallery.
Society of elected and nominated Scottish painters, sculptors, architects and printmakers.
The promotion and furtherance of the visual arts in Scotland.

Subject coverage:
Promotion and support of contemporary Scottish art and architecture.

Museum or gallery collection, archive, or library special collection:
RSA Permanent Collection of paintings, drawings, scultpure and other related materials. RSA's own archives (minute books, letter collection, photograph collection, etc.) from 1825 onwards
W G Gillies, RSA Bequest (estate of this artist including letters, pictures, catalogues, etc.)

Non-library collection catalogue:
All or part available in-house

Library catalogue:
All or part available in-house

Printed publications:
The Making of The Royal Scottish Academy
  (Gordon E, £4.95)
Beth Fisher RSA: Grisaille Legacy (£12)
William Littlejohn (£12)
Highland Art –A Window to the West (£10)
Basil's Bairns – Architects from Basil Spence's
  Scottish Studios (£4)
Order + Chaos – Works from the RSA Collection
  (£4)
Survey – Contemporary Sculpture from ESW (£4)
Victoria Crowe – Plant Memory (£4)
Ian McCulloch – Recycled Lives (£4)
RSA John Kinross Scholarships 2006 (£5)
As Others See Us (£4)
The Curious Eye (£4)
FOUND Collective – Stop Look Listen book &
  double CD (£7.50)
Eddie Summerton & Derrick Guild 'Guilding the
  Summer Town' (£10)
Laura Ford – Armour Boys (£4)
RSA New Contemporaries 2010 (£5)
RSA New Contemporaries 2009 (£3)
RSA Annual Exhibition 2009 catalogue (£1)
RSA Annual Exhibition 2008 catalogue (New
  Scots) (£1)
RSA Annual Exhibition 2007 catalogue (Highland)
  (£1)
RSA Annual Exhibition 2006 catalogue (£1)
RSA Annual Exhibition 2005 catalogue (£1)
RSA Student Exhibition 2008 (£1)

Access to staff:
Contact by letter, by telephone, by fax, by e-mail and via website. Appointment necessary.
Hours: Mon to Fri, 1000 to 1700

RSA Permanent Collections located at:
Royal Scottish Academy
  The Dean Gallery, 73 Bedford Road, Edinburgh,
  EH4 3DS; tel: 0131 624 6277

ROYAL SCOTTISH ACADEMY OF MUSIC AND DRAMA

Acronym or abbreviation: RSAMD

100 Renfrew Street, Glasgow, G2 3DB

Tel: 0141 270 8268
Fax: 0141 270 8353
E-mail: library@rsamd.ac.uk

Website:
http://www.rsamd.ac.uk
Library catalogue available online.

Enquiries:
Enquiries to: Head of Information Services
Direct e-mail: c.cochrane@rsamd.ac.uk

Founded:
1847

Organisation type and purpose:
HE Academy.

Subject coverage:
Music and drama.

Library catalogue:
All or part available online

Access to staff:
Contact by letter, by telephone, by fax, by e-mail, in person and via website
Hours: Mon to Fri, 0900 to 1700

Access to building, collection or gallery:
No prior appointment required

Access for disabled people:
Access to all public areas

ROYAL SCOTTISH AUTOMOBILE CLUB (MOTOR SPORT) LTD

Acronym or abbreviation: RSAC

St James Business Centre, Linwood Road, Paisley, PA3 3AT

Tel: 0141 887 9905
Fax: 0141 887 9906

Website:
http://www.motorsport.co.uk
Motor sport information.
http://www.rsac.co.uk
General club information.

Enquiries:
Enquiries to: Secretary
Direct e-mail: mail@rsacmotorsport.co.uk

Founded:
1899

Organisation type and purpose:
Membership association.
Club, for the encouragement of motoring and allied industries and of motor sport.

Subject coverage:
Motoring and motor sport.

Museum or gallery collection, archive, or library special collection:
Hotel Guides
Motoring magazines and other publications from the late 19th century to the present day

Access to staff:
Contact by letter, by telephone, by fax, by e-mail and in person. Appointment necessary. Non-members charged.
Hours: Mon to Fri, 0900 to 1700

Also at the same address:
Royal Scottish Automobile Club (Motor Sport) Limited
  tel: 0141 204 4999; fax: 0141 204 4949; e-mail:
  rsac_motorsport@compuserve.com

Member of:
Alliance Internationale de Tourisme
Standing Joint Committee (AA/RAC/RSAC)

ROYAL SCOTTISH CORPORATION

Formal name: The Scottish Hospital of the Foundation of Charles II
Acronym or abbreviation: ScotsCare

37 King Street, Covent Garden, London, WC2E 8JS

Tel: 020 7240 3718
Fax: 020 7497 0184
E-mail: info@scotscare.com

Website:
http://www.royalscottishcorporation.org.uk
Homepage of Corporation detailing help available.

Enquiries:
Enquiries to: Chief Executive
Other contacts: Welfare Manager for welfare matters.

Founded:
1611

Organisation type and purpose:
Voluntary organisation, registered charity (charity number 207326).

Subject coverage:
Welfare benefits, disability rights, debt advice.

Access to staff:
Contact by letter, by telephone, by fax, by e-mail and via website. Appointment necessary.
Hours: Mon to Fri, 0900 to 1700
Special comments: Callers by strict appointment.

ROYAL SCOTTISH COUNTRY DANCE SOCIETY

Acronym or abbreviation: RSCDS

12 Coates Crescent, Edinburgh, EH3 7AF

Tel: 0131 225 3854
Fax: 0131 225 7783
E-mail: info@rscds.org

Website:
http://www.rscds.org

Enquiries:
Enquiries to: Office Administrator

Founded:
1923

Organisation type and purpose:
International organisation, membership association (membership is by subscription), present number of members: 14,000, registered charity (charity number SC016085), suitable for ages: all.
To promote and develop Scottish country dancing worldwide for the benefit of present and future generations. To publish instructional dance and music books.

Subject coverage:
Scottish country dances, music, practice, teaching, development and preservation (not Highland dancing).

Museum or gallery collection, archive, or library special collection:
Library of old music for Scottish country dancing
  and other related archive material

Printed publications:
Bulletin
Newsbrief
Scottish Country Dances: selection of books with
  printed music

Electronic and video publications:
Music on CD to accompany RSCDS books
Videos to accompany RSCDS books

Publications list:
Available online and in print

Access to staff:
Contact by letter, by telephone, by fax, by e-mail, in person and via website
Hours: Mon to Fri, 1000 to 1600

Access to building, collection or gallery:
Prior appointment may be required
Hours: Mon to Fri, 1000 to 1600

Has:
Local associations known as Branches throughout the world

ROYAL SCOTTISH FORESTRY SOCIETY

Acronym or abbreviation: RSFS

Hagg-on-Esk, Canonbie, Dumfries & Galloway, DG14 0XE

Tel: 013873 71518
Fax: 013873 71418
E-mail: administrator@rsfs.org.uk

Website:
http://www.rsfs.org
History, membership, events diary, news, additional to journal articles.

Enquiries:
Enquiries to: Administrative Director
Other contacts: Editor, Scottish Forestry: editor@rsfs.lumison.co.uk

Founded:
1854

Organisation type and purpose:
National organisation, learned society (membership is by subscription), present number of members: 950, voluntary organisation, registered charity (charity number SCO 02058), suitable for ages: all, publishing house. Independent representative organisation. The advancement of forestry in all its numerous branches.

Subject coverage:
Forestry, woodlands, timber, arboriculture, silviculture, trees, agro forestry, coppicing, community forestry, investment forestry, forestry research, nurseries, forest access, urban forests and trees, social forestry.

Museum or gallery collection, archive, or library special collection:
Books and Journals
Library housed in the University of Edinburgh, Department of Forestry.

Trade and statistical information:
Data on UK forestry.

Printed publications:
Scottish Forestry (quarterly, UK price £13 per issue, overseas £17 per issue)

Electronic and video publications:
Forests For All, Forever (video, 22 mins, with teacher support notes for Scottish schools curriculum 5–14, £7.50)
Scottish Forestry – The Archive 1947–2000 (CD-ROM, single user £100, multi-user £300)
Scottish Forestry – The Archive (CD-ROM, 3 disk set with search engine; single user licence £100, multi-user licence £300)

Access to staff:
Contact by letter, by telephone, by fax, by e-mail and via website. Appointment necessary.
Hours: Mon to Fri, 0900 to 1700

Links with:
CASHEL – A Forest for a Thousand Years
Loch Lomond; tel: Forest Manager 01360 870450; fax: 01668 213555; e-mail: info@cashel.org.uk; website: www.CASHEL.org.uk
RSFS Forest Trust Company

ROYAL SCOTTISH GEOGRAPHICAL SOCIETY

Acronym or abbreviation: RSGS

15–19 North Port, Perth, PH1 5LU

Tel: 01738 455050
E-mail: enquiries@rsgs.org

Website:
http://www.geo.ed.ac.uk/rsgs

Enquiries:
Enquiries to: Chief Executive

Founded:
1884

Organisation type and purpose:
Learned society (charity number SCO15599). To further the science of geography.

Subject coverage:
Geography, topography and travel in Scotland.

Museum or gallery collection, archive, or library special collection:
Early maps of Scotland
Geographical journals

Non-library collection catalogue:
All or part available in-house

Library catalogue:
All or part available online

Printed publications:
Early maps of Scotland (2 volume set)
Newsletter (free, 3 times a year)
Scottish Geographical Journal (4 times a year)
Symposium Volumes (annually)

Publications list:
Available online

Access to staff:
Contact by letter, by telephone, by fax, by e-mail and via website. Appointment necessary.
Hours: Mon to Fri, 0900 to 1700

ROYAL SCOTTISH NATIONAL ORCHESTRA

Acronym or abbreviation: RSNO

73 Claremont Street, Glasgow, G3 7JB

Tel: 0141 226 3868
Fax: 0141 221 4317
E-mail: admin@rsno.org.uk

Website:
http://www.rsno.org.uk

Enquiries:
Enquiries to: Information Officer
Direct tel: 0141 225 3571
Direct e-mail: daniel.pollitt@rsno.org.uk

Founded:
1891

Organisation type and purpose:
Registered charity (charity number SCO10702). To perform symphony concerts throughout Scotland.

Subject coverage:
Orchestral music.

Publications list:
Available online and in print

Access to staff:
Contact by letter, by telephone, by fax, by e-mail and via website
Hours: Mon to Fri, 0900 to 1730

ROYAL SOCIETY

6–9 Carlton House Terrace, London, SW1Y 5AG

Tel: 020 7451 2500
E-mail: via website

Website:
http://royalsociety.org
The Society, fellowship, policy, funding, education, history of science, catalogues, events, library facilities.
http://royalsocietypublishing.org
Royal Society Publishing is the publishing division of the Royal Society.
http://royalsociety.org/Catalogues
Catalogues for the whole library and archives, containing listed papers documenting the history of the Society, portraits, busts and photographs, books and journals dating back to 1660, the details of every past Fellow of the Royal Society and their published works.

Founded:
1660

Organisation type and purpose:
A registered charity (no. 207043), a learned society, a fellowship of the world's most eminent scientists and the oldest scientific academy in continuous existence, the UK's independent national academy of science promoting the natural and applied sciences, and a funding agency.

To expand the frontiers of knowledge by championing the development and use of science, mathematics, engineering and medicine for the benefit of humanity and the good of the planet. Funding schemes are designed to enhance the UK science base and foster collaboration between UK-based and overseas scientists.

Subject coverage:
Natural and applied sciences.

Museum or gallery collection, archive, or library special collection:
Library and Archive contain over 70,000 books, paintings, manuscripts, busts and artefacts; the main strength of the collections is in the 17th and 18th centuries – from the 1680s to the mid-19th century the policy of the Library was to acquire every important scientific publication; collections are of international importance in the history of science; resources include manuscripts, printed books and paintings amassed to provide a record of scientific achievements over almost 350 years; Image Library houses a multitude of beautiful treasures including over 6,000 photographs, engravings and paintings of past and present Fellows and a large collection of images taken from manuscripts and printed works; Raymond and Beverly Sackler Archive Resource is a database of biographical information on past Fellows of the Royal Society from 1660 onwards

Non-library collection catalogue:
All or part available online

Library catalogue:
All or part available online

Printed publications:
See Royal Society Publishing website: http://royalsocietypublishing.org for full list of publications

Microform publications:
Newsletters (e-mail)
Order microform publications from: Website

Publications list:
Available online

Access to staff:
Contact by letter, by telephone and via website
Special comments: Researchers in the scholarly use of the Royal Society's collections are welcomed.

Also at:
Kavli Royal Society International Centre
Chicheley Hall, Buckinghamshire

ROYAL SOCIETY – ICSU INFORMATION SERVICE

Formal name: The Royal Society for Improving Natural Knowledge

6 Carlton House Terrace, London, SW1Y 5AG

Tel: 020 7451 2500
Fax: 020 7451 2692
E-mail: info@royalsoc.ac.uk

Website:
http://www.codata.org/codata
The CODATA Home Page.
http://www.icsu.org
The ICSU Home Page
http://www.royalsoc.ac.uk

Enquiries:
Enquiries to: ICSU Information Officer
Direct tel: extn 2587
Direct e-mail: ruth.cooper@royalsoc.ac.uk

Founded:
1660

Organisation type and purpose:
Learned society (membership is by election or invitation), present number of members: 1,250. The UK National Academy of Science.

Subject coverage:
Information available on all ICSU activities and related journals and publications. Details of union assemblies, conferences and congresses. Advice on

continued overleaf

travel to ICSU conferences and grants available.
Information concerning ICSU projects also
available.

**Museum or gallery collection, archive, or library
special collection:**
Archival centre for ICSU-related publications such
as newsletters, bulletins and journals

Printed publications:
ICSU Focus (newsletter, several times a year, free)

Publications list:
Available online and in print

Access to staff:
Contact by letter, by telephone and via website.
Appointment necessary.
Hours: Mon to Fri, 0900 to 1700

Access for disabled people:
Parking provided, level entry, access to all public
areas, toilet facilities

ROYAL SOCIETY – LIBRARY

6–9 Carlton House Terrace, London, SW1Y 5AG

Tel: 020 7451 2500
Fax: 020 7930 2170
E-mail: library@royalsociety.org

Website:
http://royalsociety.org

Enquiries:
Enquiries to: Librarian
Direct tel: 020 7451 2606

Founded:
1660

Organisation type and purpose:
Learned society, registered charity (charity number
207043).
The Royal Society is an independent academy
promoting the natural and applied sciences.
Founded in 1660, the Society has three roles: as the
UK academy of science, as a learned society, and as
a funding agency. It responds to individual
demand with selection by merit not by field.
Working across the whole range of science,
technology and engineering, the Society aims to:
strengthen UK science by providing support to
excellent individuals; fund excellent research to
push back the frontiers of knowledge; attract and
retain the best scientists; ensure the UK engages
with the best science around the world; support
science communication and education, and
communicate and encourage dialogue with the
public; provide the best independent advice
nationally and internationally; promote
scholarship and encourage research into the
history of science.

Subject coverage:
All sciences, mathematics, statistics, operational
research, physics, space research, crystallography,
chemistry, engineering, metallurgy,
instrumentation, earth sciences, botany,
agriculture, zoology, marine biology, physical
anthropology, biochemistry, biophysics,
physiology, pharmacology, psychology, medicine
(non-clinical), molecular biology, genetics, history
of science and technology, science education,
international scientific relations, science policy.

**Museum or gallery collection, archive, or library
special collection:**
Archives relating to all aspects of the Society and
its Fellows
Books and papers by or about Fellows of the
Society
Books, manuscripts and items relating to Sir Isaac
Newton and other early Fellows
Material on the history of science
Science policy publications

Non-library collection catalogue:
All or part available online, in-house and in print

Library catalogue:
All or part available online

Printed publications:
Review of the Year
Philosophical Transactions of the Royal Society
(Series A – Physical, Mathematical, and Series B
– Biological)
Proceedings of the Royal Society (Series A and B)
Biology Letters
Journal of the Royal Society Interface
Notes and Records of the Royal Society
Biographical Memoirs of Fellows of the Royal
Society
Many occasional publications relating to science
policy and science education
Inside Science
Year Book of the Royal Society
List of Fellows of the Royal Society
Obituaries and Biographical Memoirs of Fellows of
the Royal Society

Publications list:
Available online

Access to staff:
Contact by letter, by telephone, by fax, by e-mail,
in person and via website
Hours: Mon to Fri, 1000 to 1700

Access for disabled people:
Parking provided, disabled lift entry, access to all
public areas, toilet facilities

ROYAL SOCIETY FOR ASIAN AFFAIRS

Acronym or abbreviation: RSAA

2 Belgrave Square, London, SW1X 8PJ

Tel: 020 7235 5122
Fax: 020 7259 6771
E-mail: info@rsaa.org.uk

Website:
http://www.rsaa.org.uk

Enquiries:
Enquiries to: Secretary
Direct e-mail: sec@rsaa.org.uk; editor@rsaa.org.uk
Other contacts: Editor (for Asian affairs)

Founded:
1901

Organisation type and purpose:
Learned society (membership is by qualification,
election or invitation), present number of
members: 1,136 individuals, 13 corporate,
registered charity (charity number 212152).
To promote greater knowledge and understanding
of Asia from the Near and Middle East to Japan.

Subject coverage:
All aspects of Asian affairs.

**Museum or gallery collection, archive, or library
special collection:**
Library of approximately 5,100 books, soon to be
available electronically

Non-library collection catalogue:
All or part available online

Library catalogue:
All or part available online

Printed publications:
Asian Affairs (3 times a year, subscription £40 a
year for individuals, £80 a year for institutions)

Access to staff:
Contact by letter, by telephone, by fax, by e-mail
and via website. Appointment necessary. Access
for members only.
Hours: Mon to Fri, 0930 to 1700
Special comments: One visit to the library is
permitted, after which membership is required.

Access to building, collection or gallery:
No prior appointment required
Hours: Mon to Thu, 1000 to 1300 and 1400 to 1600;
Fri, 1000 to 1300
Special comments: Prior appointment required for
non-members.

ROYAL SOCIETY FOR MENTALLY HANDICAPPED CHILDREN AND ADULTS

Acronym or abbreviation: MENCAP

4 Swan Courtyard, Coventry Road, Birmingham,
B26 1BU

Tel: 0121 707 7877
Fax: 0121 707 3019
E-mail: info@mencap.org.uk

Enquiries:
Enquiries to: Head of Advice and Information
Service

Founded:
1946

Organisation type and purpose:
National organisation, membership association
(membership is by subscription), voluntary
organisation, registered charity (charity number
222377).
Mencap is the leading charity working with
children and adults with learning disabilities in
England, Wales and Northern Ireland. It
campaigns to ensure that people with a learning
disability have the best possible opportunities to
live as full citizens. It aims to influence new
legislation and raise the profile of learning
disability issues. It undertakes research into issues
affecting people with a learning disability.

Subject coverage:
All aspects of learning disabilities, residential,
leisure, holiday, welfare, education and training,
employment services.

Printed publications:
Range of information leaflets (available from
Public Liaison Unit, National Centre)
Viewpoint: The Newspaper of Mencap & Gateway
Order printed publications from: Helpline and
Information Unit, MENCAP
123 Golden Lane, London, EC1Y 0RT, tel: 020 7696
6900/6979

Electronic and video publications:
Use the Tube (video)

Publications list:
Available in print

Access to staff:
Contact by letter, by telephone, by fax, by e-mail
and via website
Hours: Mon to Fri, 0900 to 1700

Access for disabled people:
Level entry, toilet facilities

ROYAL SOCIETY FOR THE ENCOURAGEMENT OF ARTS, MANUFACTURES AND COMMERCE

Acronym or abbreviation: RSA

8 John Adam Street, London, WC2N 6EZ

Tel: 020 7930 5115
Fax: 020 7839 5805
E-mail: library@rsa.org.uk

Website:
http://www.rsa.org.uk
Main RSA website.
http://www.rsa.org.uk/fellowship/facilities.html
Information on library and archive.

Enquiries:
Enquiries to: Librarian
Direct tel: 020 7451 6874
Direct e-mail: library@rsa.org.uk

Founded:
1754

Organisation type and purpose:
International organisation, membership
association (membership is by election or
invitation), present number of members: 23,000,
registered charity (charity number 212424),
research organisation.

Runs conferences and lectures, produces reports relating to education, environment, design, the arts, manufacturing, management.

Subject coverage:
A modern library providing background on the RSA's core concerns: arts, manufacturers and commerce, education, design, environment and management. Also 250 years of archives plus a small library to support access to, and interpretation of, the Society's Archive.

Museum or gallery collection, archive, or library special collection:
Archives of the Society (from 1754 to present). Accessible via AIM25 gateway
Early works (most listed in British Library 18th century catalogue)

Non-library collection catalogue:
All or part available online

Library catalogue:
All or part available online

Printed publications:
RSA Journal (6 issues a year)
Occasional reports relating to RSA project

Publications list:
Available online

Access to staff:
Contact by letter, by telephone, by fax, by e-mail and via website. Appointment necessary.
Hours: Mon to Fri, 0900 to 1700

Access to building, collection or gallery:
Prior appointment required

Access for disabled people:
Ramped entry, access to all public areas, toilet facilities
Special comments: Access has been made by modifications to an 18th-century building, so some routes are circuitous.

ROYAL SOCIETY FOR THE PREVENTION OF ACCIDENTS

Acronym or abbreviation: RoSPA

Edgbaston Park, 353 Bristol Road, Birmingham, B5 7ST

Tel: 0121 248 2000
Fax: 0121 248 2001
E-mail: help@rospa.com

Website:
http://www.rospa.com
General information about all aspects of safety; contact details for publications, products, services of ROSPA.

Enquiries:
Enquiries to: Information Services Manager
Direct tel: 0121 248 2063/66
Direct e-mail: infocentre@rospa.com

Founded:
1917

Organisation type and purpose:
Membership association (membership is by subscription), registered charity, training organisation, consultancy, publishing house. To save lives and reduce injuries.

Subject coverage:
Occupational health and safety, leisure, road, home, play (ground) and water safety, safety education.

Education services:
Training courses.

Museum or gallery collection, archive, or library special collection:
20,000 books and documents
250 journals
British Standards
CD-ROM, Croner, Lawtel
Legislation where relevant to health and safety

Trade and statistical information:
Statistics available, primarily for members (charges).
Technical and advisory service – members only.

Library catalogue:
All or part available in-house

Printed publications:
Care on the Road (6 times a year)
RoSPA Occupational Safety & Health Journal (monthly)
OS&H Bulletin (monthly)
Safety Education (termly)
Safety Express (6 times a year)
Staying Alive (3 times a year)

Electronic and video publications:
Range of videos (for purchase)

Publications list:
Available online and in print

Access to staff:
Contact by letter, by telephone and by e-mail. Appointment necessary.
Hours: Mon to Fri, 0900 to 1600

Access to building, collection or gallery:
Prior appointment required

Access for disabled people:
Parking provided, level entry, access to all public areas, toilet facilities

Administers the:
RoSPA Advanced Drivers and Riders

Links with:
RoSPA Training Centre
Unit 75, Gravelly Industrial Park, Erdington, Birmingham, B24 8TL

Offices in:
Wales, Scotland and N Ireland

ROYAL SOCIETY FOR THE PREVENTION OF CRUELTY TO ANIMALS

Acronym or abbreviation: RSPCA

Wilberforce Way, Horsham, West Sussex, RH13 9RS

Tel: 0300 123 4555
Fax: 0303 123 0100

Website:
http://www.rspca.org.uk
General information on the work and activities of the RSPCA.

Enquiries:
Enquiries to: Information and Records Manager
Direct tel: 0300 123 0188
Direct fax: 0303 123 0188
Direct e-mail: creed@rspca.org.uk

Founded:
1824

Organisation type and purpose:
Registered charity (charity number 219099).

Subject coverage:
Welfare of animals of all types, all aspects, history of animal welfare in the 19th and 20th centuries, suppression of cruelty to animals, animal hospitals, clinics and homes, philosophy and ethics of animal welfare and animal rights.

Museum or gallery collection, archive, or library special collection:
Complete sets of the Society's publications from 1869: Animal Ways, Animal World and Annual Reports
Minute Books of the Society

Non-library collection catalogue:
All or part available in-house

Library catalogue:
All or part available in-house

Printed publications:
Animal Life (quarterly)

Animal Action (children's magazine, 6 times a year)
Booklets, leaflets
Pet care guides
Posters, wall-charts, etc.
Scientific reports
Teaching material

Publications list:
Available online

Access to staff:
Contact by letter, by telephone, by fax and by e-mail. Appointment necessary.
Hours: Mon to Fri, 0930 to 1700

Access for disabled people:
Parking provided, level entry

ROYAL SOCIETY FOR THE PROMOTION OF HEALTH

38a St Georges Drive, London, SW1V 4BH

Tel: 020 7630 0121
Fax: 020 7976 6847

Website:
http://www.rsph.org.uk

Enquiries:
Enquiries to: Chief Executive
Direct fax: 020 7828 8913
Direct e-mail: jtatman@rsph.org.uk
Other contacts: Managing Editor for journal-related enquiries.

Founded:
1876

Organisation type and purpose:
International organisation, learned society, registered charity (charity number 215520). To promote the exchange of knowledge and experience between health-related professions, to influence health-related legislation and planning, to advance the study of health-related subjects.

Subject coverage:
All fields related to medicine, nutrition, hygiene, pharmaceuticals, planning, architecture, housing, environment.

Museum or gallery collection, archive, or library special collection:
Essential Food Hygiene

Printed publications:
Essential Food Hygiene (£2.25)
Journal (6 times a year, £55 per annum, free to members)

Access to staff:
Contact by letter, by telephone, by fax, by e-mail and in person. Appointment necessary.
Hours: Mon to Fri, 0900 to 1700

Affiliated to:
American Public Health Association
World Federation of Public Health Associations

ROYAL SOCIETY FOR THE PROTECTION OF BIRDS

Acronym or abbreviation: RSPB

The Lodge, Potton Road, Sandy, Bedfordshire, SG19 2DL

Tel: 01767 680551
Fax: 01767 692365

Website:
http://www.rspb.org.uk

Enquiries:
Enquiries to: Librarian
Direct e-mail: ian.dawson@rspb.org.uk

Founded:
1889

Organisation type and purpose:
Membership association (membership is by subscription), registered charity (charity number 207076).

continued overleaf

Subject coverage:
Birds and birdwatching (but not aviculture);
especially protection and conservation in Britain.

Museum or gallery collection, archive, or library special collection:
W H Hudson Archive

Library catalogue:
All or part available in-house

Printed publications:
Bird Life (6 times a year)
Birds (quarterly)
Wingbeat (6 times a year)
Wild Times (quarterly)
Miscellaneous reports and publications (see
    website: www.rspb.org.uk)
Information leaflets and educational material on
    birds and wildlife conservation

Publications list:
Available in print

Access to staff:
Appointment necessary.
Hours: Mon to Fri, 0900 to 1700

Member of the global partnership:
BirdLife International

Owns or administers:
over 150 nature reserves in Great Britain and
Northern Ireland

ROYAL SOCIETY FOR THE RELIEF OF INDIGENT GENTLEWOMEN OF SCOTLAND

14 Rutland Square, Edinburgh, EH1 2BD

Tel: 0131 229 2308
Fax: 0131 228 3700

Enquiries:
Enquiries to: Information Officer
Other contacts: General Secretary

Founded:
1847

Organisation type and purpose:
Voluntary organisation, registered charity (charity
number SCO 16095).
To assist ladies of Scottish birth or education with
professional or business backgrounds who exist on
low incomes and have limited savings.
Applications from spinsters, widows and
divorcees of 50 years or over.

Museum or gallery collection, archive, or library special collection:
Records maintained of ladies who made
    applications to the Fund over many years

Access to staff:
Contact by letter, by telephone, by fax and by e-mail
Hours: Mon to Thu, 0900 to 1700; Fri, 0900 to 1600

ROYAL SOCIETY OF BRITISH ARTISTS

Acronym or abbreviation: RBA

17 Carlton House Terrace, London, SW1Y 5BD

Tel: 020 7930 6844
Fax: 020 7839 7830
E-mail: press@mallgalleries.com

Website:
http://www.mallgalleries.org.uk
http://www.the-rba.org.uk

Enquiries:
Enquiries to: Secretary
Other contacts: Marketing and Communications
Officer

Founded:
1824

Organisation type and purpose:
Membership association (membership is by
election or invitation), present number of
members: 115, registered charity (charity number
294590).

Subject coverage:
British art and artists; annual open exhibition of
pictures and sculpture.

Printed publications:
RBA catalogues available during exhibition

Access to staff:
Contact by letter, by telephone, by fax, by e-mail
and via website. Appointment necessary.
Hours: Mon to Fri, 0930 to 1700

Access to building, collection or gallery:
No access other than to staff
Hours: Mon to Fri, 0930 to 1700

Access for disabled people:
Stairlift, toilet facilities
Special comments: Stairlift.

Links with:
Federation of British Artists (FBA)
    at the same address

ROYAL SOCIETY OF CHEMISTRY – LIBRARY AND INFORMATION CENTRE

Acronym or abbreviation: RSC

Burlington House, Piccadilly, London, W1J 0BA

Tel: 020 7440 8656
Fax: 020 7287 9798
E-mail: library@rsc.org

Website:
http://www.rsc.org

Enquiries:
Enquiries to: Librarian

Founded:
1841

Organisation type and purpose:
Learned society.

Subject coverage:
Alchemy, analytical chemistry, biochemistry,
biography, chemical engineering, chemical
industry, chemistry, environment, food science and
technology, hazards, health and safety at work,
inorganic chemistry, organic chemistry,
spectrometry and toxicology.

Museum or gallery collection, archive, or library special collection:
Alchemy and chemistry to 1850 (3,000 vols)
Prints and photographs of distinguished chemists
    (8,000)

Trade and statistical information:
Chemical business statistics on a wide variety of
    chemicals.

Non-library collection catalogue:
All or part available online and in-house

Library catalogue:
All or part available online and in-house

Printed publications:
Chemistry information resources on the Internet
History of Chemistry sources of information
Periodicals list of the LIC

Publications list:
Available online and in print

Access to staff:
Contact by letter, by telephone, by fax, by e-mail
and via website. Appointment necessary. Non-
members charged.
Hours: Mon to Fri, 0930 to 1730

Access for disabled people:
Ramped entry

Constituent bodies:
Analytical, Faraday, Dalton, Perkin, Education and
Industrial Affairs

ROYAL SOCIETY OF CHEMISTRY – SALES AND CUSTOMER CARE DEPARTMENT

Acronym or abbreviation: RSC

Thomas Graham House, Science Park, Milton
Road, Cambridge, CB4 4WF

Tel: 01223 420066
Fax: 01223 426017
E-mail: sales@rsc.org

Website:
http://www.rsc.org
Full publications catalogue plus information of all
RSC services, membership, conferences, journals,
etc.

Enquiries:
Enquiries to: Sales and Customer Care Department
Direct tel: 01223 432360

Founded:
1980

Organisation type and purpose:
Learned society, professional body (membership is
by qualification), present number of members:
47,000, registered charity (charity number 207890),
publishing house.

Subject coverage:
Chemistry (all areas, general, organic, analytical);
mass spectrometry; biology; biotechnology;
biochemistry; food science; nutrition; pesticides;
chemical engineering; toxicology; hazards; health
and safety; agrochemicals; business information.

Museum or gallery collection, archive, or library special collection:
Library located at Burlington House, Piccadilly,
    London

Library catalogue:
All or part available online

Printed publications:
A very large number of journals, books and other
    publications including:
Analytical Abstracts
Chemical Communications (flagship journal)
Chemistry World (monthly)
Dictionary of substances and their effects (DOSE) –
    all chemicals described
Lab on a Chip
Green Chemistry
JAAS
Physical Chemistry Chemical Physics
Soft Matter
RSC Journals Super Archive
A large number of books under the headings:
Analytical and Spectroscopy
Agrochemical Science
Educational and Management
Environmental Chemistry
Food Science and Nutrition
Inorganic and Bio-inorganic Chemistry
Organic and Bio-organic Chemistry
Physical, Industrial and Historical Chemistry
Polymers and Materials

Electronic and video publications:
Electronic journals
Videos and CD-ROMs
Software

Publications list:
Available online and in print

Access to staff:
Contact by letter, by telephone, by fax, by e-mail
and via website
Hours: Mon to Fri, 0900 to 1700

Member of:
Association of Learned and Professional Society
Publishers (ALPSP)

Other address:
Royal Society of Chemistry (RSC)
    Burlington House, Piccadilly, London, W1J 0BA;
    tel: 020 7437 8656; fax: 020 7287 9798

ROYAL SOCIETY OF EDINBURGH

Acronym or abbreviation: RSE

22–26 George Street, Edinburgh, EH2 2PQ

Tel: 0131 240 5000
Fax: 0131 240 5024
E-mail: rse@royalsoced.org.uk

Website:
http://www.royalsoced.org.uk
Details of current activities (meetings, publications, awards) and of offices and staff.

Enquiries:
Enquiries to: Chief Executive
Direct e-mail: bmuldoon@royalsoced.org.uk
Other contacts: Journals & Archive Officer for publications and archive information.

Founded:
1783

Organisation type and purpose:
Learned society.

Subject coverage:
Science and literature; arts and humanities; public administration and business.

Museum or gallery collection, archive, or library special collection:
Charles Piazzi Smyth Archive (now housed at the Royal Observatory Edinburgh, Blackford Hill, Edinburgh)
David Hume manuscripts (now housed at the National Library of Scotland, George IV Bridge, Edinburgh)
RSE Archive, including Minute Books, Correspondence etc, held at National Library of Scotland, George IV Bridge, Edinburgh

Non-library collection catalogue:
All or part available in-house

Library catalogue:
All or part available in-house

Printed publications:
Annual Report (available direct)
Proceedings A – Mathematics (6 times a year)
ReSourcE News – Newsletter (3–4 times a year, available direct)
Transactions – Earth Sciences (quarterly)
Directory & Sessional Review (formerly Year Book)
Annual Review
Order printed publications from: Customer Services, CABI Publishing
Wallingford, Oxfordshire, OX10 8DE, tel: 01491 832111, fax: 01491 829292, e-mail: orders@cabi.org

Access to staff:
Contact by letter, by telephone, by fax, by e-mail and via website. Appointment necessary.
Hours: Mon to Fri, 0900 to 1700

Access for disabled people:
Ramped access, lift access to most rooms, disabled toilet facilities, induction loop

ROYAL SOCIETY OF LITERATURE

Acronym or abbreviation: RSL

Somerset House, Strand, London, WC2R 1LA

Tel: 020 7845 4676
Fax: 020 7845 4679
E-mail: info@rslit.org

Website:
http://www.rslit.org
Pages about the Society's activities, details of how to join.

Enquiries:
Enquiries to: Secretary

Founded:
1820

Organisation type and purpose:
Learned society (membership is by subscription), registered charity.

Subject coverage:
The appreciation of literature in English.

Education services:
Monthly lectures.

Printed publications:
Newsletter

Access to staff:
Contact by letter, by telephone, by fax, by e-mail and via website. Appointment necessary.
Hours: Mon to Thu, 0930 to 1730

Access to building, collection or gallery:
Prior appointment required

Access for disabled people:
Toilet facilities
Special comments: Wheelchair lift available.

ROYAL SOCIETY OF MARINE ARTISTS

Acronym or abbreviation: RSMA

17 Carlton House Terrace, London, SW1Y 5BD

Tel: 020 7930 6844
Fax: 020 7839 7830
E-mail: press@mallgalleries.com

Website:
http://www.mallgalleries.org.uk

Enquiries:
Enquiries to: Secretary
Other contacts: Marketing and Communications Officer

Founded:
1945

Organisation type and purpose:
Membership association (membership is by election or invitation), present number of members: 41, registered charity (charity number 289944).

Subject coverage:
Marine art, annual open exhibition.

Printed publications:
Annual Exhibition Catalogue
Books on marine painting during annual exhibition

Access to staff:
Contact by letter, by telephone, by fax and by e-mail. Appointment necessary.
Hours: Mon to Fri, 0930 to 1700

Access to building, collection or gallery:
Prior appointment required
Hours: Mon to Fri, 0930 to 1700

Access for disabled people:
Stairlift; toilet facilities

Links with:
Federation of British Artists (FBA) at the same address

ROYAL SOCIETY OF MEDICINE

Acronym or abbreviation: RSM

1 Wimpole Street, London, W1G 0AE

Tel: 020 7290 2940/1/2
Fax: 020 7290 2939

Website:
http://www.rsm.ac.uk

Enquiries:
Enquiries to: Director of Information Services
Direct tel: 020 7290 2931
Direct fax: 020 7290 2976
Direct e-mail: ian.snowley@rsm.ac.uk

Founded:
1805

Organisation type and purpose:
Learned society (membership is by subscription, qualification, election or invitation), present number of members: 18,000, registered charity (charity number 206219), publishing house.

Subject coverage:
Medicine in general, biomedical sciences, postgraduate biomedical sciences, archives.

Museum or gallery collection, archive, or library special collection:
Chalmers Collection of early medicine
Comfort Collection on gerontology
Historical Medical Collection from 1474
Major periodicals of Europe and America, 19th and 20th centuries

Non-library collection catalogue:
All or part available online

Library catalogue:
All or part available online

Printed publications:
Regular publishing programme of new medical books
Many journals and other publications
Order printed publications from: Book & Sales Enquiries, RSM Press
1 Wimpole Street, London, W1G 0AE

Publications list:
Available in print

Access to staff:
Contact by letter, by telephone, by fax, by e-mail, in person and via website. Access for members only. Non-members charged.
Hours: Mon to Thur, 0900 to 2030; Fri 0900 to 17.30

Access for disabled people:
Level entry, access to all public areas, toilet facilities

ROYAL SOCIETY OF MINIATURE PAINTERS, SCULPTORS AND GRAVERS

Acronym or abbreviation: RMS

3 Briar Walk, London, SW15 6UD

Tel: 020 8785 2338
E-mail: tremrod@aol.com

Website:
http://www.royal-miniature-society.org.uk
Website archived at the British Library.

Enquiries:
Enquiries to: Executive Secretary

Founded:
1896

Organisation type and purpose:
International organisation, professional body (membership is by election or invitation), present number of members: 160, registered charity (charity number 291389).
Publicising and educating the public about miniature painting.

Subject coverage:
All forms of miniature art: painting in all media, etching, silver-point, sculpture, ceramics, glass engraving, enamelling, gold and silver work, jewellery.

Museum or gallery collection, archive, or library special collection:
Diploma collection

Printed publications:
Annual Catalogue and History of the Society
Centenary Book (1995, containing about 220 lifesize colour reproductions of contemporary members' work)
Order printed publications from: Royal Miniature Society, at the main address

Access to staff:
Contact by letter, by telephone and by e-mail. Appointment necessary.
Hours: Mon to Fri, 0900 to 1700

Access to building, collection or gallery:
No access other than to staff

continued overleaf

Hours: Only during the exhibition.

Access for disabled people:
Ramped entry, access to all public areas, toilet facilities

ROYAL SOCIETY OF MUSICIANS OF GREAT BRITAIN

10 Stratford Place, London, W1C 1BA

Tel: 020 7629 6137
Fax: 020 7629 6137

Enquiries:
Enquiries to: Secretary

Founded:
1738

Organisation type and purpose:
Membership association (membership is by election or invitation), present number of members: 1367, registered charity (charity number 208879).
The world's oldest charity for musicians.
The Society, founded by Handel and over 200 other musicians to support colleagues and their families in distress because of illness, accident or old age, continues to support professional musicians and their dependants.

Subject coverage:
History of music and musicians, from the 18th century, from the records of the Society; personal files of Members; minute books, accounts etc; much material unavailable elsewhere.

Museum or gallery collection, archive, or library special collection:
Manuscript scores (including marches composed for the Society by Haydn, Weber, Cipriani Potter, Bishop and von Winter)

Printed publications:
A History of The Royal Society of Musicians 1738–1988
Handel in London
List of Members 1738–1984
Arthur Sullivan and the Royal Society of Musicians of Great Britain, ed Mackie, D

Access to staff:
Contact by letter, by telephone and by fax
Hours: Mon to Fri, 0900 to 1700

Access to building, collection or gallery:
No prior appointment required

ROYAL SOCIETY OF PORTRAIT PAINTERS

Acronym or abbreviation: RP

17 Carlton House Terrace, London, SW1Y 5BD

Tel: 020 7930 6844
Fax: 020 7839 7830
E-mail: press@mallgalleries.com

Website:
http://www.mallgalleries.org.uk
http://www.therp.co.uk

Enquiries:
Enquiries to: Secretary
Other contacts: Marketing and Communications Officer

Founded:
1891

Organisation type and purpose:
Professional body (membership is by election or invitation), present number of members: 53, registered charity (charity number 327460).
To foster and promote the art of portrait painting.

Subject coverage:
Portrait painting and painters, annual open exhibition.

Museum or gallery collection, archive, or library special collection:
Examples of portrait painters' work on slides, photographs and some original portrait paintings

Printed publications:
Annual Exhibition Catalogue (May)
Book containing details and photographs of the work of some society members

Access to staff:
Contact by letter, by telephone, by fax, by e-mail and via website. Appointment necessary.
Hours: Mon to Fri, 0930 to 1730

Access to building, collection or gallery:
No access other than to staff
Hours: Mon to Fri, 0930 to 1730

Access for disabled people:
Stairlift, toilet facilities
Special comments: Stairlift.

Links with:
Federation of British Artists (FBA)
at the same address

ROYAL SOCIETY OF ST GEORGE

Administration Office, 127 Sandgate Road, Folkestone, Kent, CT20 2BH

Tel: 01303 241795
Fax: 01303 211710
E-mail: info@royalsocietyofstgeorge.com

Website:
http://www.royalsocietyofstgeorge.com
Complete description of the Society, its history, current activities, addresses of branches, extracts from the journal 'England's Standard', forthcoming events and more.

Enquiries:
Enquiries to: Chairman

Founded:
1894

Organisation type and purpose:
Statutory body (membership is by subscription, election or invitation), voluntary organisation, registered charity (charity number 263076).

Subject coverage:
Love of England.

Printed publications:
England's Standard

Access to staff:
Contact by letter, by telephone, by fax, by e-mail and via website
Hours: Mon to Thu, 0900 to 1600

Access to building, collection or gallery:
Hours: Mon to Thu, 0900 to 1600

Has:
some 100 branches, half of which are overseas

ROYAL SOCIETY OF TROPICAL MEDICINE AND HYGIENE

Acronym or abbreviation: RSTMH

50 Bedford Square, London, WC1B 3DP

Tel: 020 7580 2127
Fax: 020 7436 1389
E-mail: mail@rstmh.org

Website:
http://www.rstmh.org
Introduction, structure, history, the journal, fellowship, awards and calendar of meetings.

Enquiries:
Enquiries to: Administrator

Founded:
1907

Organisation type and purpose:
Learned society, registered charity (charity number 208204).

To promote and advance the study, control and prevention of disease in man and other animals in warm climates, to facilitate discussion and the exchange of information among those who are interested in tropical diseases.

Subject coverage:
International health, tropical medicine and hygiene, tropical veterinary science.

Printed publications:
Transactions of the Royal Society of Tropical Medicine and Hygiene (12 times a year)
Order printed publications from: Elsevier, Customer Service Department, PO Box 211, 1000 AE Amsterdam, The Netherlands; tel. +31 20 485 3757; fax. +31 20 485 3432; e-mail: journalscustomerserviceemea@elsevier.com

Publications list:
Available online and in print

Access to staff:
Contact by letter and by e-mail
Hours: Mon to Fri, 0900 to 1700

ROYAL SOCIETY OF ULSTER ARCHITECTS

Acronym or abbreviation: RSUA

2 Mount Charles, Belfast, BT7 1NZ

Tel: 028 9032 3760
Fax: 028 9023 7313
E-mail: info@rsua.org.uk

Enquiries:
Enquiries to: Director

Founded:
1901

Organisation type and purpose:
Professional body (membership is by subscription), registered charity (charity number NI 00069).

Subject coverage:
Advice on selecting an architect. Advice on running architectural competitions.

Access to staff:
Contact by letter, by telephone and by fax. Appointment necessary.
Hours: Mon to Fri, 0900 to 1700

Access for disabled people:
Ramped entry, toilet facilities

ROYAL TOWN PLANNING INSTITUTE

Acronym or abbreviation: RTPI

41 Botolph Lane, London, EC3R 8DL

Tel: 020 7929 9494 (switchboard), 020 7929 9452 (library)
Fax: 020 7929 9490
E-mail: library@rtpi.org.uk

Website:
http://www.rtpi.org.uk
In-house information.
http://www.rtpiconsultants.co.uk
Online directory of planning consultants.
http://www.planningsummerschool.com
Planning Summer School.
http://www.planning.haynet.com
Information from current issues of Planning magazine.
http://www.planningaid.rtpi.org.uk
Planning Aid.

Enquiries:
Enquiries to: Library and Information Manager
Direct tel: 020 7929 9452

Founded:
1914

Organisation type and purpose:
Professional body, present number of members: 17,500.

Subject coverage:
Urban, regional and rural planning, housing, transport, conservation, leisure, spatial planning, recreation, employment, local government.

Non-library collection catalogue:
All or part available online

Library catalogue:
All or part available online

Publications list:
Available online and in print

Access to staff:
Contact by letter, by telephone, by fax, by e-mail and via website. Appointment necessary.

Access to building, collection or gallery:
Prior appointment required

Access for disabled people:
Access to all public areas (including library), toilet facilities

Founder member of:
Commonwealth Association of Planners
now about 20 members, secretariat in Canada

Other office:
RTPI in Scotland
57 Melville Street, Edinburgh, EH3 7HL; tel: 0131 226 1959; fax: 0131 226 1909; e-mail: scotland@rtpi.org.uk

ROYAL TOWN PLANNING INSTITUTE IN SCOTLAND

Acronym or abbreviation: RTPI

57 Melville Street, Edinburgh, EH3 7HL

Tel: 0131 226 1959
Fax: 0131 226 1909
E-mail: scotland@rtpi.org.uk

Website:
http://www.rtpi.org.uk
Policy papers; current news items; member services.

Enquiries:
Enquiries to: National Director

Founded:
1914

Organisation type and purpose:
Professional body (membership is by election or invitation), present number of members: 1,800 in Scotland, 18,000 in UK, registered charity (charity number 262865).
To act as the chartered professional body for town planners and to advance the art and science of town planning at national, regional and local levels.

Subject coverage:
Town planning: services to professional planners; education for planning; policy on national planning systems and practice; assistance to the public through Planning Aid Scotland (the Institute itself cannot provide advice to the public on individual planning cases).

Library catalogue:
All or part available in-house

Printed publications:
Planning (incorporating Planning Week, £65)
Scottish Planner (6 times a year, £15)
Order printed publications from: Royal Town Planning Institute
41 Botolph Lane, London, EC3R 8DL, tel: 020 7929 9494, fax: 020 7929 9490, e-mail: online@rtpi.org.uk

Publications list:
Available in print

Access to staff:
Contact by letter, by telephone, by fax, by e-mail and via website. Appointment necessary.
Hours: Mon to Fri, 0900 to 1700

Access to building, collection or gallery:
Prior appointment required

Parent body:
RTPI
41 Botolph Lane, London, EC3R 8DL; tel: 020 7929 9494; fax: 020 7929 9490; e-mail: online@rtpi.org.uk

ROYAL UNITED SERVICES INSTITUTE FOR DEFENCE AND SECURITY STUDIES

Acronym or abbreviation: RUSI

61, Whitehall, London, SW1A 2ET

Tel: 020 7747 2600
E-mail: defence@rusi.org

Website:
http://www.rusi.org

Enquiries:
Enquiries to: Membership Secretary
Other contacts: Librarian; PA to Director

Founded:
1831

Organisation type and purpose:
Membership association, registered charity (charity number 210639), consultancy, research organisation.

Subject coverage:
Defence and international security.

Museum or gallery collection, archive, or library special collection:
RUSI Library of Military History

Printed publications:
Journal (6 times a year)
Newsbrief (bimonthly)
Whitehall Papers (2 times a year)
RUSI Defence Systems (3 times a year)
Order printed publications from: e-mail: publications@rusi.org

Publications list:
Available online

Access to staff:
Contact by letter, by telephone, by e-mail and via website. Appointment necessary. Access for members only.
Hours: Mon to Fri, 0900 to 1700

Access for disabled people:
Toilet facilities

ROYAL VETERINARY COLLEGE ANIMAL CARE TRUST

Acronym or abbreviation: RVC ACT

The Royal Veterinary College, Hawkshead Lane, Hatfield, Hertfordshire, AL9 7TA

Tel: 01707 666237
Fax: 01707 666382
E-mail: act@rvc.ac.uk

Website:
http://www.rvc.ac.uk/act

Enquiries:
Enquiries to: Director of Fund Raising

Founded:
1982

Organisation type and purpose:
Registered charity (charity number 281571).
To support the work of the Royal Veterinary College.

Subject coverage:
Education of veterinary students and the treatment of animals, veterinary science, veterinary surgery, animal welfare.

Printed publications:
Christmas Gifts Catalogue (annually)
RVC ACT Annual Report
Newsletter (2 times a year)

Access to staff:
Contact by letter, by telephone, by fax, by e-mail and via website. Appointment necessary.
Hours: Mon to Fri, 0900 to 1700

Parent body:
Royal Veterinary College
University of London, Royal College Street, London, NW1 0TU; tel: 020 7468 5000; fax: 020 7388 2342

ROYAL VETERINARY COLLEGE LIBRARY

Acronym or abbreviation: RVC

Royal College Street, Camden, London, NW1 0TU

Tel: 020 7468 5162
Fax: 020 7468 5162
E-mail: sjackson@rvc.ac.uk

Website:
http://www.rvc.ac.uk/aboutus/Services/Libraries/Index.cfm

Enquiries:
Enquiries to: Librarian
Direct tel: 01707 666214
Direct fax: 01707 666214
Other contacts: Deputy Librarian

Founded:
1791

Organisation type and purpose:
University department or institute.

Subject coverage:
Veterinary science and medicine; pre-clinical and historical material at Royal College Street; current veterinary material at Hawkshead.

Museum or gallery collection, archive, or library special collection:
Frank Townend Barton Gift
Granville Penn Gift
Historical collection
James Beart Simonds Collection (veterinary advisor to the Privy Council during the curing of the cattle disease Rhind Pest in the 19th century) scrap-books and extensive notes and photographs
Sir Frederick Smith's Napoleonic manuscripts

Library catalogue:
All or part available online

Printed publications:
College Annual Report
The Historical collections (free)
Library Guide (free)
Prospectus
Services and Price Guide (free)

Microform publications:
James Beart Simonds Collection of scrap-books (microfilm)

Access to staff:
Appointment necessary.
Hours: Mon to Fri, 0900 to 1700

Also at:
Royal Veterinary College Library
Hawkshead House, Hawkshead Lane, North Mymms, Hatfield, Hertfordshire, AL9 7TA; tel: 01707 666 384; e-mail: sjackson@rvc.ac.uk

Parent body:
University of London

ROYAL WATERCOLOUR SOCIETY

Acronym or abbreviation: RWS

Bankside Gallery, 48 Hopton Street, London, SE1 9JH

Tel: 020 7928 7521
Fax: 020 7928 2820
E-mail: rws@banksidegallery.com

Website:
http://www.banksidegallery.com

continued overleaf

Enquiries:
Enquiries to: Gallery Director

Founded:
1804

Organisation type and purpose:
Learned society (membership is by election or invitation), present number of members: 90, registered charity (charity number 258348), art gallery.

Subject coverage:
Watercolour painting and its history, contemporary work by members of the Society, gallery activities.

Museum or gallery collection, archive, or library special collection:
The RWS Diploma collection (1 work from each member of the society, RWS Archive since its inception 200 years ago)

Library catalogue:
All or part available in print

Printed publications:
Bankside Bulletin (journal of the Royal Watercolour Society and the Royal Society of Painter-Printmakers, quarterly, free to members and friends, £2 to the public)

Access to staff:
Contact by letter, by telephone, by fax, by e-mail and via website
Hours: Mon to Fri, 1100 to 1800

Access to building, collection or gallery:
No prior appointment required

Connected with:
Bankside Gallery, home of the RWS

ROYAL WELSH AGRICULTURAL SOCIETY LIMITED

Acronym or abbreviation: RWAS Ltd

Llanelwedd, Builth Wells, Powys, LD2 3SY

Tel: 01982 553683
Fax: 01982 553563
E-mail: requests@rwas.co.uk

Website:
http://www.rwas.co.uk
Information on the Royal Welsh Show, the Royal Welsh Agricultural Winter Fair, and the Royal Welsh Smallholder and Garden Festival.

Enquiries:
Enquiries to: Secretary

Founded:
1904

Formerly called:
Welsh National Agricultural Society (year of change 1922)

Organisation type and purpose:
International organisation, membership association (membership is by subscription), present number of members: 14,000, voluntary organisation, registered charity (charity number 251232), suitable for ages: all.
To promote agriculture, horticulture, forestry and conservation in Wales.

Subject coverage:
Any matters relating to the Royal Welsh Show, the Royal Welsh Agricultural Winter Fair, and the Royal Welsh Smallholder and Garden Festival.

Printed publications:
Official Show Catalogue
Official Show Programme
Promotional Leaflets
RWAS Journal
Section Schedules

Publications list:
Available online and in print

Access to staff:
Contact by letter, by telephone, by fax, by e-mail and via website. Appointment necessary.
Hours: Mon to Fri, 0845 to 1230 and 1330 to 1700

Special comments: Closed on statutory holidays.

Access for disabled people:
Ramped entry, toilet facilities

ROYAL WELSH COLLEGE OF MUSIC & DRAMA LIBRARY

Acronym or abbreviation: RWCMD

Castle Grounds, Cathays Park, Cardiff, CF10 3ER

Tel: 029 2034 2854
Fax: 029 2039 1304
E-mail: library@rwcmd.ac.uk

Website:
http://www.rwcmd.ac.uk

Enquiries:
Enquiries to: Librarian
Direct tel: 029 2039 1330

Founded:
1947

Formerly called:
Welsh College of Music & Drama (year of change 2002)

Merged with:
University of Glamorgan (year of change 2007)

Organisation type and purpose:
Independent higher education college for training in performing arts.

Subject coverage:
Music, theatre, stage design, stage management, creative music technology and recording, technical stage management, music therapy, art management, acting.

Library catalogue:
All or part available online

Access to staff:
Contact by telephone. Appointment necessary.
Hours: Term time: Mon to Thu, 0830 to 2000; Fri, 0830 to 1800; Sat, 1000 to 1400
Vacation: Mon to Thu, 0900 to 1700; Fri, 0900 to 1630; Sat, closed

Links with:
Cardiff Arts Marketing – Organisation of Arts Organisations in Wales
Incorporated Society of Musicians

ROYAL YACHTING ASSOCIATION

Acronym or abbreviation: RYA

RYA House, Romsey Road, Eastleigh, Hampshire, SO50 9YA

Tel: 023 8062 7400
Fax: 023 8062 9924
E-mail: admin@rya.org.uk

Website:
http://www.rya.org.uk

Enquiries:
Enquiries to: Secretary General
Direct tel: 023 8062 7420
Direct e-mail: rod.carr@ry.org.uk
Other contacts: Chief Executive

Founded:
1875

Formerly called:
Yacht Racing Association (YRA)

Organisation type and purpose:
National government body, membership association (membership is by subscription), present number of members: 88,000.
National governing body for recreational boating in the UK.
Represents recreational boating in the UK.

Subject coverage:
Boating matters relating to sail cruising, sail racing, windsurfing, motor cruising, powerboating, personal watercraft.

Museum or gallery collection, archive, or library special collection:
Minute books of the YRA and RYA meetings 1875-present

Library catalogue:
All or part available in-house

Printed publications:
Range of training booklets, foreign cruising notes, legal information etc
RYA Magazine (4 times per annum)

Electronic and video publications:
A range of videos and CDs covering navigation, boat handling, first aid etc

Publications list:
Available in print

Access to staff:
Contact by letter, by fax and by e-mail.
Appointment necessary.
Hours: Mon to Fri, 0900 to 1700

Access to building, collection or gallery:
Prior appointment required

Access for disabled people:
Ramped entry, access to all public areas

Has:
1,500 affiliated clubs and classes, 1,500 RYA recognised schools

Houses the:
RYA Sailability
tel: 02380 647431; fax: 02380 629924; e-mail: info@rya.sailability.org

Links with:
European Boating Association (EBA)
European Sailing Federation (EUROSAF)
International Sailing Federation (ISAF)
Union Internationale Motonautique (UIM)

ROYAL YACHTING ASSOCIATION SCOTLAND

Acronym or abbreviation: RYA Scotland

Caledonia House, 1 Redheughs Rigg, South Gyle, Edinburgh, EH12 9DQ

Tel: 0131 317 7388
Fax: 0131 317 8566
E-mail: admin@ryascotland.org.uk

Organisation type and purpose:
Training organisation.
National governing body for the sports of sailing, windsurfing, powerboating and personal watercrafting in Scotland.

Printed publications:
An extensive publication list of titles on racing, dinghies, power boats, cruising, course notes, club guides, navigation, seamanship, training, etc.
Order printed publications from: Royal Yachting Association, RYA House, Ensign Way, Hamble, Southampton, SO31 4YA; tel: 023 8060 4100; fax: 023 8060 4299

Electronic and video publications:
A range of videos and CDs covering sailing skills, navigation, first aid, etc.

Publications list:
Available online and in print

Access to staff:
Contact by letter, by telephone, by fax, by e-mail and in person
Hours: Mon to Fri, 0900 to 1230 and 1315 to 1645

ROYAL ZOOLOGICAL SOCIETY OF SCOTLAND

Acronym or abbreviation: RZSS

Edinburgh Zoo, 134 Corstorphine Road, Corstorphine, Edinburgh, EH12 6TS

Tel: 0131 334 9171/2/3
Fax: 0131 316 4050

Website:
http://www.edinburghzoo.org

Enquiries:
Enquiries to: Visitor Services Manager
Direct e-mail: marketing@rzss.org.uk

Founded:
1909

Organisation type and purpose:
Learned society (membership is by subscription), present number of members: 13,000, registered charity (charity number SCO040604).
To promote, through the preservation of the Society's living collections, the conservation of animal species and wild places through captive breeding, environmental education and scientific research.

Subject coverage:
Zoo management, animals in captivity, Scottish wildlife, aviculture, conservation education.

Museum or gallery collection, archive, or library special collection:
Animal collection held on the International Species Inventory System (ISIS)

Printed publications:
Annual Report
ARKFILE (newsletter, quarterly)
Guide Book to the Zoo
Guidebook for the Highland Wildlife Park

Access to staff:
Appointment necessary.
Hours: Mon to Fri, 0900 to 1700
Special comments: Seasonal opening hours.

Links with:
European Association of Zoos and Aquaria
International Union for Conservation of Nature and Natural Resources
National Federation of Zoological Gardens of Great Britain and Ireland
World Zoo Organisation (IUDZG)

Manages:
Highland Wildlife Park
    Kincraig; tel: 01540 651270
Scottish National Zoological Park
    Edinburgh

RSABI

Rural Centre, West Mains of Ingliston, Newbridge, EH28 8LT

Tel: 0131 472 4166
Fax: 0131 472 4156
E-mail: rsabi@rsabi.co.uk

Website:
http://www.rsabi.org.uk

Enquiries:
Enquiries to: Chief Executive
Other contacts: Welfare Manager for all beneficiary contact.

Founded:
1897

Formerly called:
Royal Scottish Agricultural Benevolent Institution (year of change 2005)

Organisation type and purpose:
Voluntary organisation, registered charity (charity number SC 009828), suitable for all ages.
To assist those in distress who are or have been in farming, forestry, aquaculture, horticulture and rural estate work in Scotland and their dependants, with modest financial grants and in kind, and welfare assistance tailored to circumstance.

Subject coverage:
Relief of hardship among individuals who have depended on the land in Scotland.

Museum or gallery collection, archive, or library special collection:
Records of all meetings of subscribers since 1897

Printed publications:
Newsletter (2 times a year)

Annual Report
Pamphlets:
Cook Book
Order printed publications from: from the RSABI

Electronic and video publications:
A Farm for All Seasons (DVD)
A Grain of Truth (DVD)

Publications list:
Available online

Access to staff:
Contact by letter, by telephone, by fax, by e-mail, in person and via website. Appointment necessary.
Hours: Mon to Fri, 0900 to 1700

RSS CENTRE FOR STATISTICAL EDUCATION

Formal name: Royal Statistical Society
Acronym or abbreviation: RSS

Nottingham Trent University, Burton Street, Nottingham, NG1 4BU

Tel: 0115 848 4476
Fax: 0115 848 2998
E-mail: rsscse@ntu.ac.uk

Website:
http://science.ntu.ac.uk/rsscse/
Database of available resources. Database of publications available for purchase.

Enquiries:
Enquiries to: Director
Direct tel: 0115 848 2118
Direct e-mail: Neville.Davies@ntu.ac.uk

Founded:
1995

Organisation type and purpose:
Suitable for ages: all, consultancy, research organisation.

Subject coverage:
Teaching statistics at all levels and in all contexts.

Library catalogue:
All or part available online

Printed publications:
Teaching Statistics (journal, 3 times a year)

Publications list:
Available online and in print

Access to staff:
Contact by letter, by telephone, by fax and by e-mail
Hours: Mon to Fri, 0900 to 1700

RUBBER CONSULTANTS

Tun Abdul Razak Research Centre, Brickendonbury, Hertford, SG13 8NL

Tel: 01992 554657
Fax: 01992 504248
E-mail: rubbercon@tarrc.co.uk

Website:
http://www.rubberconsultants.com

Enquiries:
Enquiries to: Manager

Founded:
1984

Organisation type and purpose:
Consultancy, research organisation.

Subject coverage:
All aspects of the science and technology of natural and synthetic rubbers and the use of elastomers in manufactured products, tyre testing, rubber analysis, earthquake protection using structural bearings, information on the rubber industry.

Museum or gallery collection, archive, or library special collection:
MORPHS main database

Trade and statistical information:
Statistical information on the rubber trade and the international trade in rubber products.

Non-library collection catalogue:
All or part available in-house

Library catalogue:
All or part available in-house

Printed publications:
Journal of Rubber Research
Malaysian Rubber Review
Engineering Design with Natural Rubber
NR Engineering Data Sheets
NR Technical Information Sheets
The natural rubber formulary and property index

Electronic and video publications:
Engineering with Rubber
Natural Rubber Bearings for Earthquake Protection (video)

Publications list:
Available online and in print

Access to staff:
Contact by telephone, by fax, by e-mail and via website. Appointment necessary. All charged.
Hours: Mon to Fri, 0900 to 1700

Access to building, collection or gallery:
Special comments: Appointment required

Constituent part of:
Tun Abdul Razak Research Centre

RUBBER STAMP MANUFACTURERS GUILD

Acronym or abbreviation: RSMG

2nd floor, Farringdon Point, 29–35 Farringdon Road, London, EC1M 3JF

Tel: 0845 450 1565
Fax: 0207 405 7784
E-mail: info@rsmg.org.uk

Website:
http://www.rsmg.org.uk
Industry news and information.

Organisation type and purpose:
The trade association for the rubber stamp and associated marking devices industry. Promotes the industry and provides a forum for the exchange of ideas, information and education.

Subject coverage:
Offers members the opportunity to keep up to date with emerging technologies and the development of new and exciting products that help to make their customers more efficient and more profitable; workshops, seminars and social gatherings offer an excellent opportunity for networking within the industry.

Access to staff:
Contact by letter, by telephone, by fax and by e-mail

Links with:
ISEE (International Stamp and Engraving Exhibition)

Member organisation of:
AEGRAFLEX

RUGBY BOROUGH COUNCIL

Town Hall, Evereux Way, Rugby, Warwickshire, CV21 2LB

Tel: 01788 533533
Fax: 01788 533577

Website:
http://www.warwickshire.gov.uk

Enquiries:
Enquiries to: Public Relations Manager

Organisation type and purpose:
Local government body.

continued overleaf

Subject coverage:
Council services and amenities; corporate services, environmental services, finance, housing, legal services, personnel services, planning development, tourism, economic development, technical services, highways, leisure services, council tax and other payments.

RUGBY FIVES ASSOCIATION

Acronym or abbreviation: RFA

66 Brayburne Avenue, Clapham, London, SW4 6AA

Tel: 020 7627 8303
E-mail: andy.pringle@mac.com

Website:
http://www.rfa.org.uk

Enquiries:
Enquiries to: General Secretary
Direct tel: 07760 172904

Founded:
1927

Organisation type and purpose:
Governing body of the sport.
Promotion of the game and organisation of regional and national championships.

Subject coverage:
Rules of the game, championship dates and venues, championship records and past winners, clubs and playing facilities, manufacturers and suppliers of gloves and balls.

Printed publications:
Annual Review (annual, free to members)
Annual Newsletter (annual, free to members)
Members' Pocket Book (annual, free to members)

Publications list:
Available in print

Access to staff:
Contact by letter, by telephone, by e-mail and via website
Hours: No fixed times

RUGBY FOOTBALL UNION

Acronym or abbreviation: RFU

Rugby Road, Twickenham, Middlesex, TW1 1DZ

Tel: 020 8892 2000

Enquiries:
Enquiries to: Sales and Marketing Manager
Direct tel: 020 8831 6737
Direct fax: 020 8891 3254
Direct e-mail: tomhill@rfu.com

Founded:
1871

Formerly called:
England Rugby

Organisation type and purpose:
National organisation, voluntary organisation.
33 constituent unions.
The promotion of rugby union football.

Subject coverage:
Rugby union football; rugby records.

Printed publications:
England Rugby Magazine
Annual Report

Publications list:
Available online

Access to staff:
Access for members only.
Hours: Mon to Fri, 0900 to 1700

Access to building, collection or gallery:
Prior appointment required

Access for disabled people:
Access to all public areas

Affiliated to:
Committee of Home Unions
Committee of Six Nations (England, Scotland, Ireland, Wales, France and Italy)
International Rugby Football Board

RUNNYMEDE BOROUGH COUNCIL

Civic Offices, Station Road, Addlestone, Surrey, KT15 2AH

Tel: 01932 838383
Fax: 01932 855135

Website:
http://www.runnymede.gov.uk

Enquiries:
Enquiries to: Chief Executive
Direct tel: 01932 425500
Direct e-mail: communications@runnymede.gov.uk

Founded:
1974

Organisation type and purpose:
Local government body.

Printed publications:
Annual Report (free)
Borough Guide (free)
Information Directory (£3)
Street Plan (£1)

Access to staff:
Contact by letter, by telephone, by fax and in person
Hours: Mon to Thu, 0830 to 1700; Fri, 0830 to 1630

Access for disabled people:
Parking provided, level entry, toilet facilities

Parent body:
Surrey County Council

RUNNYMEDE TRUST

7 Plough Yard, Shoreditch, London, EC2A 3LP

Tel: 020 7377 9222
Fax: 020 7377 6622
E-mail: info@runnymedetrust.org

Website:
http://www.runnymedetrust.org

Founded:
1968

Formerly called:
Runnymede Educational Trust, Runnymede Housing Trust

Organisation type and purpose:
Voluntary organisation, registered charity (charity number 1063609), research organisation, publishing house.
Educational charity, research body and social policy think-tank.
To promote the development of a successful, equal and culturally diverse society.

Subject coverage:
Social policy issues re multi-ethnicity, race etc. in the UK and how EU legislation affects UK policies.

Museum or gallery collection, archive, or library special collection:
Runnymede Trust Library has been donated to the Middlesex University, Centre for Racial Equality Studies

Printed publications:
The Runnymede Bulletin (quarterly)
A Tale of Two Englands: 'race' and violent crime in the press
A Very Light Sleeper: the persistence & dangers of antisemitism
Black and Ethnic Minority Young People and Educational Disadvantage
Civil Renewal, Diversity and Social Capital in a Multi-Ethnic Britain
Cohesion, Community and Citizenship
Developing Community Cohesion

Equal Respect: ASBOs and race equality
Financial Inclusion and Ethnicity: an agenda for research and policy action
Guardians of Race Equality
Improving Educational Practice
Islamophobia: a challenge for us all
Perpetrators of Racist Violence and Harassment
Preventing Racist Violence
Re(thinking) 'Gangs'
School Choice and Ethnic Segregation
This is Where I Live: stories and pressures in Brixton 1996
Why Preferential Policies Can be Fair
Young People in the UK: attitudes and opinions on Europe, Europeans and the European Union

Publications list:
Available online and in print

Access to staff:
Contact by letter and by e-mail
Hours: Mon to Fri, 0900 to 1700
Special comments: Closed to the public.

Access to building, collection or gallery:
Mon to Fri, 0930 to 1730

Access for disabled people:
Access to all public areas
Special comments: No public access to office except for scheduled appointments.

Links with:
Commission for the Future of Multi-Ethnic Britain

RUPERT BROOKE MUSEUM & SOCIETY

The Orchard, 45–47 Millway, Grantchester, Cambridge, CB3 9ND

Tel: 01223 551118
E-mail: info@rupertbrookemuseum.org.uk

Website:
http://www.rupertbrookemuseum.org.uk
http://www.rupertbrookemuseum.org.uk/rupert-brooke-society

Enquiries:
Enquiries to: Curator
Other contacts: Secretary (for RB Society information)

Founded:
1999

Organisation type and purpose:
International organisation, membership association (membership is by subscription), museum, historic building, house or site.
The Museum covers the life history of Rupert Brooke.
Aims to: foster an interest in the work of Rupert Brooke, increase knowledge and appreciation of Rupert Brooke and of the village of Grantchester, help to preserve places associated with Rupert Brooke.

Subject coverage:
The life and works of Rupert Brooke.

Museum or gallery collection, archive, or library special collection:
Small collection of books

Printed publications:
A selection of books including:
Old Grantchester, A Sketch book (Willmer E N)

Publications list:
Available in print

Access to staff:
Contact by letter, by telephone, by fax, by e-mail and via website
Hours: Mon to Sun, 1100 to 1600

Access to building, collection or gallery:
No prior appointment required
Hours: Jul and Aug: Mon to Sun, 1100 to 1700
Rest of year: Mon to Sun, 1100 to 1600

Access for disabled people:
Parking provided
Special comments: Ramped entry to tea pavilion, steps into museum.

RURAL & INDUSTRIAL DESIGN & BUILDING ASSOCIATION

Acronym or abbreviation: RIDBA

ATSS House, Station Road East, Stowmarket, Suffolk, IP14 1RQ

Tel: 01449 676049
Fax: 01449 770028
E-mail: secretary@ridba.org.uk

Website:
http://www.ridba.org.uk

Enquiries:
Enquiries to: National Secretary

Founded:
1956

Organisation type and purpose:
National organisation, advisory body, trade association (membership is by subscription), present number of members: 320.

Subject coverage:
Members have expertise in all aspects of rural & industrial buildings and cover: planning, design, new construction (steel, timber, concrete and traditional), conversion, fitting out, health and safety, pollution control, education, animal welfare etc. Regular conferences are organised on subjects of interest, plus regular visits to interesting and up-to-date rural & industrial enterprises and an annual study tour usually in Europe.

Museum or gallery collection, archive, or library special collection:
A full set of past journals and newsletters is held and members have access to the old Farm Buildings Centre library at Silsoe College

Trade and statistical information:
Members hold data on all aspects of rural buildings.

Printed publications:
Countryside Building (4 times a year, annual subscription £20, free to members)
Order printed publications from: Editor, Ghyll House Publishing Ltd, ATSS House, Station Road East, Stowmarket, IP14 1RQ, tel: 01449 676049, fax: 01449 770028, e-mail: tony@ghyllhouse.co.uk

Access to staff:
Contact by letter, by telephone, by fax and by e-mail. Appointment necessary.
Hours: Mon to Fri, 0900 to 1700

Access to building, collection or gallery:
No access other than to staff

RURAL CRAFTS ASSOCIATION

Heights Cottage, Brook Road, Wormley, Godalming, Surrey, GU8 5UA

Tel: 01428 682292
Fax: 01428 685969
E-mail: info@ruralcraftsassociation.co.uk

Website:
http://www.ruralcraftsassociation.co.uk

Enquiries:
Enquiries to: Director

Founded:
1970

Organisation type and purpose:
Membership association (membership is by subscription), present number of members: 600. To encourage men and women to make and sell their work and skills, to uphold the quality of work in whatever price range the craft falls, to provide a vigorous forum for the sale of members' work, at a cost they can afford.

Subject coverage:
British craftworkers; contact for members of the association and for those wishing to exhibit and presently exhibiting in Rural Crafts Association pavilions at agricultural and equestrian shows, and game fairs nationwide.

Printed publications:
Year Planner (aims and objectives, activities, shows during the year; members and interested parties)
Newsletter (members)

Access to staff:
Contact by letter, by telephone, by fax and by e-mail
Hours: Mon to Fri, 0900 to 1700

Access for disabled people:
Good access at all events
Hours: At all opening times

RUSHCLIFFE BOROUGH COUNCIL

Civic Centre, Pavilion Road, West Bridgford, Nottinghamshire, NG2 5FE

Tel: 0115 981 9911
Fax: 0115 945 5882
E-mail: customerservices@rushcliffe.gov.uk

Website:
http://www.rushcliffe.gov.uk

Enquiries:
Enquiries to: Public Relations Manager
Direct tel: 0115 9148555
Direct e-mail: media@rushcliffe.gov.uk
Other contacts: Customer Services Centre for all enquiries.

Founded:
1974

Organisation type and purpose:
Local government body.

Subject coverage:
Council services and amenities; corporate services, environmental services, finance, housing, legal services, personnel services, planning development and tourism, property and technical services, roads and transportation, council tax and other payments.

Publications list:
Available online and in print

Access to staff:
Contact by letter, by telephone, by fax, by e-mail, in person and via website
Hours: Mon to Fri, 0730 to 1700

Access to building, collection or gallery:
No prior appointment required
Hours: Mon to Fri, 0830 to 1700

Access for disabled people:
Parking provided, level entry, access to all public areas, toilet facilities

RUSKIN COLLEGE LIBRARY

Walton Street, Oxford, OX1 2HE

Tel: 01865 554331
Fax: 01865 554372
E-mail: library@ruskin.ac.uk

Enquiries:
Enquiries to: Librarian

Founded:
1899

Organisation type and purpose:
Residential college for adult education.

Subject coverage:
Social sciences, labour studies, social work, community and youth work, women's studies, history, literature.

Museum or gallery collection, archive, or library special collection:
Ewan MacColl and Peggy Seeger Archive
Raphael Samuel papers

Access to staff:
Appointment necessary.
Hours: Mon to Fri, 0900 to 1700

RUSKIN LIBRARY

Lancaster University, Lancaster, LA1 4YH

Tel: 01524 593587
Fax: 01524 593580
E-mail: ruskin.library@lancaster.ac.uk

Website:
http://www.lancs.ac.uk/users/ruskinlib
Information for visitors, catalogue of collections.

Enquiries:
Enquiries to: Director
Other contacts: Deputy Curator; Assistant Curator

Founded:
1998

Organisation type and purpose:
Art gallery, university library.

Subject coverage:
Art and architecture, history and literature.

Museum or gallery collection, archive, or library special collection:
Whitehouse Collection of manuscripts, books, photographs and pictures relating to John Ruskin (1819–1900) and his associates

Non-library collection catalogue:
All or part available online

Library catalogue:
All or part available online

Publications list:
Available online

Access to staff:
Contact by letter, by telephone, by fax, by e-mail, in person and via website. Appointment necessary.
Hours: Reading Room: Mon to Fri, 1000 to 1630

Access to building, collection or gallery:
No access other than to staff
Hours: Public Gallery: Mon to Sat, 1100 to 1600; Sun, 1300 to 1600

Access for disabled people:
Ramped entry, access to all public areas, toilet facilities

RUSKIN SOCIETY

1 The Crescent , Witney, Oxfordshire, OX28 2EL

Tel: 01993 201478
E-mail: theruskinsociety@hotmail.co.uk

Website:
http://www.theruskinsociety.com

Founded:
1932

Organisation type and purpose:
The society was founded to promote interest in all aspects of John Ruskin's life and work. These include art, architecture, politics, economics, and social criticism. Membership is by subscription.

Subject coverage:
The life and works of John Ruskin.

Access to staff:
Contact by letter, by telephone and by e-mail

Member organisation of:
Alliance of Literary Societies

RUSSIAN ORTHODOX CHURCH IN GREAT BRITAIN AND IRELAND, DIOCESE OF SOUROZH

Formal name: Russian Orthodox Patriarchal Church in Great Britain and Ireland, Diocese of Sourozh

Cathedral of the Dormition and All Saints, 67 Ennismore Gardens, London, SW7 1NH

Tel: 020 7584 0096

continued overleaf

Fax: 020 7584 9864
E-mail: office@sourozh.org

Website:
http://www.sourozh.org

Enquiries:
Enquiries to: Diocesan Administration

Founded:
1962

Organisation type and purpose:
To administer the Russian Orthodox community in Great Britain and Ireland. Diocese within the Russian Orthodox Patriarchate of Moscow. Registered charity (charity number 254025).

Subject coverage:
Russian Orthodoxy in Great Britain and Ireland.

Access to staff:
Contact by letter and by e-mail

Parent body:
Russian Orthodox Patriarchate of Moscow
website: http://www.mospat.ru

RUSSO-BRITISH CHAMBER OF COMMERCE

Acronym or abbreviation: RBCC

42 Southwark Street, London, SE1 1UN

Tel: 020 7403 1706
Fax: 020 7403 1245
E-mail: office.manager@rbcc.co.uk

Website:
http://www.rbcc.co.uk

Enquiries:
Enquiries to: Office Manager
Direct e-mail: office.manager@rbcc.co.uk

Founded:
1916

Organisation type and purpose:
To facilitate trade between Britain and Russia, through publications, in-depth regional and company profiles, exhibitions, conferences and business advice.

Printed publications:
Newsletter (monthly)

Access to staff:
Contact by letter, by telephone, by fax, by e-mail and via website

RUTHERFORD APPLETON LABORATORY (STFC)

Harwell Science and Innovation Campus, Didcot, Oxfordshire, OX11 0QX

Tel: 01235 445384
Fax: 01235 446403
E-mail: library@stfc.ac.uk

Website:
http://www.e-science.stfc.ac.uk/services/library

Organisation type and purpose:
National government body, research organisation. Formed by Royal Charter in 2007, the Science and Technology Facilities Council is one of Europe's largest multidisciplinary research organisations supporting scientists and engineers worldwide.

Subject coverage:
Elementary particles; computers; lasers; neutron studies; astrophysics; space research; advanced engineering; data collection and transmission; satellites; radio communications; information technology.

Museum or gallery collection, archive, or library special collection:
ESA reports (UK national repository)

Non-library collection catalogue:
All or part available online

Library catalogue:
All or part available online

Access to staff:
Contact by e-mail. Appointment necessary.
Hours: Mon to Fri, 1000 to 1600

Constituent part of:
Science and Technology Facilities Council (STFC)
website: http://www.scitech.ac.uk/Home.aspx

RUTLAND COUNTY LIBRARY

Catmos Street, Oakham, Rutland, LE15 6HW

Tel: 01572 722918
Fax: 01572 724906
E-mail: libraries@rutland.gov.uk

Website:
http://www.rutland.gov.uk/libraries

Enquiries:
Enquiries to: Librarian

Organisation type and purpose:
Public library.

Subject coverage:
General.

Non-library collection catalogue:
All or part available online

Library catalogue:
All or part available online

Access to staff:
Contact by letter, by telephone, by fax, by e-mail, in person and via website. Appointment necessary.
Hours: Mon, Wed, Fri, 0900 to 1900; Tue, 0900 to 1700; Thu, 0900 to 1700; Sat, 0900 to 1600

RUTLAND LOCAL HISTORY & RECORD SOCIETY

Acronym or abbreviation: RLHRS

Rutland County Museum, Catmose Street, Oakham, Rutland, LE15 6HW

Tel: 01572 758440
Fax: 01572 758445
E-mail: enquiries@rutlandhistory.org

Website:
http://www.rutlandhistory.org
Basic details, membership information, activities, research in progress, news, publications list.

Enquiries:
Enquiries to: Honorary Secretary
Direct e-mail: secretary@rutlandhistory.org

Founded:
1979

Incorporates the former:
Rutland Local History Society, Rutland Record Society (year of change 1991); Rutland Field Research Group for Archaeology & History (year of change 1993)

Organisation type and purpose:
Membership association (membership is by subscription), registered charity (charity number 700273).
All aspects of the history of the County of Rutland and the immediate area.

Subject coverage:
History and archaeology of Rutland.

Printed publications:
Rutland Record 1–29, Index of nos 1–10
The Oakham Survey 1305 (ed Chinnery A, 1988)
The Rutland Hearth Tax 1665 (ed Bourn J and Goode A, 1991)
The History of Gilson's Hospital, Morcott (Parkin D, 1995)
The History of the Hospital of St John the Evangelist & St Anne in Oakham (Parkin D, 2000)
The 1712 Land Tax Assessments and the 1710 Poll Book for Rutland (ed Clough, T H McK, 2005)
Common Right and Private Interest: Rutland's Common Fields and their Enclosure (Ryder I E, 2006)

Who Owned Rutland in 1873? Rutland Entries in Return of Owners of land 1873 (Clough, T H McK, 2010)
Tudor Rutland: The County Community under Henry VIII (ed Cornwall J, 1980)
The Weather Journals of a Rutland Squire – Thomas Barker's 18th-century weather, farming and countryside records (ed Kington J, 1988)
Stained Glass in Rutland Churches (Sharpling P, 1997)
Time in Rutland: a history and gazetteer of the bells, scratch dials, sundials and clocks of Rutland (Ovens R & Sleath S, 2002)
The Heritage of Rutland Water (Ovens R & Sleath S, 2nd edn 2008)
Order printed publications from: website: www.rutlandhistory.org or www.genfair.co.uk; or by post from RLHRS

Publications list:
Available online and in print

Access to staff:
Contact by letter, by telephone, by e-mail and via website. Appointment necessary.

Access to building, collection or gallery:
Library access by arrangement: resources combined with those of Rutland County Museum
Hours: Tue to Fri, 1000 to 1700; Sat, 1000 to 1600
Special comments: Closed Sun and Mon.

Access for disabled people:
Accessible

Links with:
Rutland County Museum
at the same address; e-mail: museum@rutland.gov.uk

RWE NPOWER PLC

Windmill Hill Business Park, Whitehill Way, Swindon, Wiltshire, SN5 6PB

Tel: 01793 892565
Fax: 01793 892994

Website:
http://www.rwenpower.com
Company information and news, financial results, direct sales information.

Enquiries:
Enquiries to: Administrator
Direct e-mail: suzanne.botter@rwenpower.com

Founded:
1990

Organisation type and purpose:
Manufacturing industry, research organisation. Electricity generation.

Subject coverage:
Power generation (thermal), electrical engineering, energy, environment, management, fuels.

Museum or gallery collection, archive, or library special collection:
Historical publications on the history of electricity supply in UK
Reports of former CERL, MEL and BNL (microform)

Non-library collection catalogue:
All or part available in-house

Library catalogue:
All or part available in-house

Printed publications:
Research Reports

Access to staff:
Contact by letter, by telephone, by fax and by e-mail. Appointment necessary.
Hours: Tue and Thu, 0900 to 1630
Special comments: Access is discretionary, depending on nature of enquiry and other commitments.

RYEDALE DISTRICT COUNCIL

Acronym or abbreviation: RDC

Ryedale House, Malton, North Yorkshire, YO17 7HH

Tel: 01653 600666
Fax: 01653 696801
E-mail: info@ryedale.gov.uk

Website:
http://www.ryedale.gov.uk

Founded:
1974

Organisation type and purpose:
Local government body.

Subject coverage:
Local government services.

Publications list:
Available online

Access to staff:
Contact by letter, by telephone, by fax, by e-mail, in person and via website. Appointment necessary.
Hours: Mon to Thu, 0830 to 1700; Fri, 0830 to 1630

Access to building, collection or gallery:
Hours: Mon to Thu, 0830 to 1700; Fri, 0830 to 1630

Access for disabled people:
Level, with hearing loop in reception
Hours: Mon to Thu, 0830 to 1700; Fri, 0830 to 1630

SACKLER LIBRARY

1 St John Street, Oxford, OX1 2LG

Tel: 01865 278088 (enquiries and administration)
Fax: 01865 278098
E-mail: james.legg@saclib.ox.ac.uk

Website:
http://www.saclib.ox.ac.uk
Opening hours, subject coverage, catalogues, special collections.

Enquiries:
Enquiries to: Administrator
Direct e-mail: helen.edwards@ouls.ox.ac.uk
Other contacts: Librarian

Founded:
2001

Formerly called:
Ashmolean Museum Library; Ashmolean Library (year of change 1901–2001)

Organisation type and purpose:
University department or institute.

Subject coverage:
Egyptology; Assyriological and Hittite studies; Altertumswissenschaft; papyrology; numismatics; dies and medals; Western art and architecture; Near Eastern classical and European archaeology; Greek and Latin literature; Byzantine studies; patristics.

Library catalogue:
All or part available online

Access to staff:
Contact by letter, by fax and by e-mail. Letter of introduction required.
Hours: Mon to Fri, 0900 to 2200; Sat, 1000 to 1700

Access for disabled people:
Level entry, toilet facilities, lift

Includes the:
Griffith Institute Library of Egyptology
  tel: 01865 288198 or 278089; e-mail: diane
  .bergman@saclib.ox.co.uk
Heberden Coin Room Library
  tel: as main library; e-mail: diane.bergman@
  saclib.ox.ac.uk
Main Library
  tel: 01865 278092; e-mail: jane.bruder@saclib.ox
  .co.uk
Western Art Library
  tel: 01865 278093/4

SACRO

Formal name: Safeguarding Communities – Reducing Offending

1 Broughton Street, Edinburgh, EH3 6NU

Tel: 0131 624 7270
Fax: 0131 624 7269
E-mail: info@national.sacro.org.uk

Website:
http://www.sacro.org.uk

Founded:
1971

Formerly called:
Scottish Association for the Care and Resettlement of Offenders (SACRO) (year of change 1992); SACRO (year of change 1998)

Organisation type and purpose:
Membership association, present number of members: 50+ full members, 2,204 associate members, voluntary organisation (charity number SCO 16293).
To provide advice, assistance and support to people in conflict, and particularly those in trouble with the law, those at risk of becoming so, and their families, by direct services provided at local level.

Subject coverage:
Criminal justice in Scotland, offenders, mediation, supported accommodation for offenders, alcohol education for probationers, intensive probation programmes, families of offenders, volunteer support, dispute resolution, community mediation, restorative justice.

Printed publications:
See website for list of available publications.
Order printed publications from: Communications Officer

Publications list:
Available online and in print

Access to staff:
Contact by letter, by telephone, by fax, by e-mail and via website. Appointment necessary.
Hours: Mon to Fri, 0900 to 1700

Access to building, collection or gallery:
No prior appointment required
Special comments: Non-catalogued, varied filing types; reference only

SADS UK

Formal name: The Ashley Jolly SAD Trust

Suite 6, Churchill House, Horndon Ind. Park, Station Road, West Horndon, CM13 3XD

Tel: 01277 811215
E-mail: sadsuk@btconnect.com

Website:
http://www.sadsuk.org
Events, medical information, contact information, publications.

Founded:
c. 2000

Organisation type and purpose:
Registered charity (charity number 1113681).
SADS UK raises awareness about heart conditions that can cause a sudden arrhythmic death (SAD). It works with government departments to introduce new guidelines to safeguard those who may be at risk from a fatal cardiac arrhythmia. It raises awareness about conditions that may cause SADS and symptoms that need further investigation. It highlights the fact that conditions can be hereditary.

Subject coverage:
SADS UK supports research into the causes of cardiac arrhythmias. This research is essential in order to improve methods of detection and provide even more effective treatments in the future.

Special visitor services:
Events and conferences; monthly bereavement support meetings.

Printed publications:
Newsletter
Leaflets:
Heart disease does not just affect those in the later years of life (booklet)
Supporting families affected by cardiac arrhythmias
The Long QT Syndrome (LQT)
Fainting and the Long QT Syndrome
The Brugada Syndrome
Wolff-Parkinson-White Syndrome (WPW)
Catecholaminergic Polymorphic Ventricular Tachycardia (CPVT)
Cardiac Arrhythmic, Fainting & Syncope
Genetic cardiac conditions and procedure following a sudden death
Order printed publications from: SADS UK, by tel. or e-mail; subscribe to newsletter via website

Publications list:
Available online

Access to staff:
Contact by letter, by telephone and by e-mail

International affiliate of:
SADS Foundation
  Salt Lake City, Utah

Works with:
SADS USA, Canada, Australia and Europe

SAFETY AND RELIABILITY SOCIETY

Acronym or abbreviation: SaRS

Clayton House, 59 Piccadilly, Manchester, M1 2AQ

Tel: 0161 228 7824
Fax: 0161 236 6977
E-mail: secretary@sars.u-net.com

Website:
http://www.sars.org.uk
Membership, aims, branches, publications, news, Body of Knowledge for professionals, jobs.

Founded:
1980

Organisation type and purpose:
Professional institution for all industries.
To represent engineers and scientists working in the important fields of safety and reliability; to enhance the professionalism and reputation of all those involved in safety and reliability technology. Has members in the UK, mainland Europe, the Middle East, USA and the Asia Pacific region; has an affiliate membership scheme for academic institutions, industrial companies, and other organisations with interests in safety and reliability and engineering risk management.

Subject coverage:
Encourages the development and use of safety and reliability technology; provides an international forum for the exchange of information on safety and reliability matters; establishes professional and educational standards for safety and reliability engineers; establishes standard techniques and encourages consistency in their application; encourages organisations and government departments to apply safety and reliability techniques.

Printed publications:
Yearbook
Quarterly Journal
Newsletter

Publications list:
Available online

Access to staff:
Contact by letter, by telephone, by fax and by e-mail

Branches:
6 in England, 1 in Scotland and 1 in Asia

SAFETY ASSESSMENT FEDERATION

Acronym or abbreviation: SAFed

Unit 4, First Floor, 70 South Lambeth Road, Vauxhall, London, SW8 1RL

Tel: 020 7582 3208
Fax: 020 7735 0286
E-mail: diane.mckay@safed.co.uk

Website:
http://www.safed.co.uk

Enquiries:
Enquiries to: Technical Director
Other contacts: Technical Manager for detailed technical information.

Founded:
1995

Formerly called:
Council of Independent Inspecting Authorities (CIIA), Independent Engineering Insurance Committee (IEIC); Associated Offices Technical Committee (AOTC) (year of change 1995)

Organisation type and purpose:
Trade association, present number of members: 8 full, 9 associate.
To represent companies engaged in independent safety inspection, testing and certification of engineering plant and equipment of all types.

Subject coverage:
Engineering inspection and design assessment for plant such as boilers, pressure vessels, lifts, cranes, electrical equipment etc, including welding; NDT techniques; export of engineering plant.

Printed publications:
Fact Sheet: Potential Hazards Created by Water Hammer in Steam Systems (set of ten, £3)
Guidelines for the Periodic Testing and Examination of Fixed Low Voltage Electrical Installations at Quarries (£25)
Lifts Guidelines on the Thorough Examination and Testing of Lifts (£100)
Shell Boilers – Guidelines for the Examination of Longitudinal Seams of Shell Boilers (£30)
Shell Boilers – Guidelines for the Examination of Shell-to-Endplate and Furnace-to-Endplate Welded Joints (£30)
The Use of Accredited Inspection Bodies (£5)
Welding Procedures and Welding Guidelines on Approval Testing (£20)

Publications list:
Available in print

Access to staff:
Contact by letter, by telephone, by fax and by e-mail
Hours: Mon to Fri, 0900 to 1700

UK member of:
Confédération Européenne d'Organismes de Prévention et de Contrôle (CEOC)

SAI GLOBAL

Acronym or abbreviation: SAI

Index House, Ascot, Berkshire, SL5 7EU

Tel: 01344 636400
Fax: 01344 291194
E-mail: standards@saiglobal.com

Website:
http://www.ili.co.uk; http://www.saiglobal.com
World standards catalogue and online ordering facility, plus full product description and access to Standards Infobase, Metals Infobase, Materials Infobase and Eurolaw.

Enquiries:
Enquiries to: Publishing Director
Direct e-mail: richard.boden@saiglobal.com

Founded:
1949

Incorporates the former:
ILI Ltd

Organisation type and purpose:
Service industry, publishing house.
Publishing and distributing technical, legal and regulatory databases.

Subject coverage:
Technical standards and specifications from world-wide sources with special knowledge of US industrial and military standards, agents and distributors for BSI, IEEE, API, ASME, NFPA, DoD, MoD, ASTM and numerous other standards authorities, European law, metals and materials databases.

Museum or gallery collection, archive, or library special collection:
Over 1m. technical specifications and standards, including all British Standards, US Military Standards, MOD Defence Standards, American Standards and others

Non-library collection catalogue:
All or part available online

Electronic and video publications:
Eurolaw CD-ROM and web – full-text European Union Law
Standards Infobase CD-ROM, web and intranet – information on 700,000 national, international and military standards
Metals Infobase CD-ROM and web – information on 74,000 world metal grades
Materials Infobase CD-ROM and web – information on 100,000 non-metallic materials and their suppliers
EU Infobase CD-ROM and web – official bibliographic database of the European Community

Publications list:
Available online

Access to staff:
Contact by letter, by telephone, by fax, by e-mail and via website. Appointment necessary.
Hours: Mon to Fri, 0830 to 1730

Also at:
SAI Global
610 Winters Avenue, Paramus, New Jersey, 07652, USA; tel: +1 201 986 1131; fax: +1 201 986 7886; e-mail: uspubsales@saiglobal.com; website: http://www.saiglobal.com

SAIL TRAINING INTERNATIONAL

Acronym or abbreviation: STI

5 Mumby Road, Gosport, Hampshire, PO12 1AA

Tel: 023 9258 6367
Fax: 023 9258 4661
E-mail: office@sailtraininginternational.org

Website:
http://www.tallshipsraces.com
http://www.sailtraininginternational.com
http://www.ista.co.uk

Enquiries:
Enquiries to: Media Publications Manager
Direct e-mail: corinne.hitching@ sailtraininginternational.org
Other contacts: Business Director

Founded:
1956

Organisation type and purpose:
International organisation.
Operating as a subsidiary of a registered charity, for the development and education of young people through sail training.
Organisers of the Tall Ships Races.

Subject coverage:
Ocean sailing, sail training, race planning, race organisation, event management, adventure activities.

Printed publications:
Tall Ships

Access to staff:
Contact by letter, by telephone, by fax and by e-mail

Hours: Mon to Fri, 0900 to 1700

Parent body:
Sail Training Association
2A The Hard, Portsmouth, Hampshire, PO1 3PT; tel: 023 9283 2055

SAILORS' FAMILIES' SOCIETY

Newland, Cottingham Road, Hull, HU6 7RJ

Tel: 01482 342331
Fax: 01482 447868
E-mail: info@sailors-families.org.uk

Enquiries:
Enquiries to: Chief Executive

Founded:
1821

Organisation type and purpose:
Voluntary organisation.

Subject coverage:
Welfare and care of seafarers and their families. Respite care for disadvantaged children.

SAILORS' SOCIETY

Sailors' Society, 350 Shirley Road, Southampton, Hampshire, SO15 3HY

Tel: 023 8051 5950
Fax: 023 8051 5951
E-mail: admin@sailors-society.org

Website:
http://www.biss.org.uk

Enquiries:
Enquiries to: PR/Fundraising Manager
Direct tel: 023 8063 0789
Direct fax: 023 8063 1789

Founded:
1818

Organisation type and purpose:
Registered charity (charity number 237778).
International Christian charity working amongst seafarers, particularly merchant seamen.

Subject coverage:
Welfare of seafarers.

Museum or gallery collection, archive, or library special collection:
Bound copies of past magazines of Society going back to early 19th century when the Society was founded

Printed publications:
Annual Review (free)
Chart & Compass (annually, free)
Quayways; Magazine of Chaplain's Department (annually, free)

Access to staff:
Contact by letter, by telephone, by fax, by e-mail and in person. Appointment necessary.
Hours: Mon to Fri, 0900 to 1700

Links with:
Sister societies in Canada, New Zealand, South Africa, Ghana and Belgium

Member organisation of:
International Christian Maritime Association
Merchant Navy Welfare Board

SAINT-GOBAIN GYPROC

Information Centre, Gypsum Technical Building, East Leake, Loughborough, Leicestershire, LE12 6JS

Tel: 0115 945 1652
Fax: 0115 945 1678
E-mail: liz.redfern@saint-gobain.com

Enquiries:
Enquiries to: Head of Information Services

Organisation type and purpose:
Manufacturing industry.

Subject coverage:
Gypsum and plaster technology.

Non-library collection catalogue:
All or part available in-house

Library catalogue:
All or part available in-house

Parent body:
Compagnie de Saint-Gobain
  Les Miroirs, 18 avenue d'Alsace, 92096 La
  Defense, Paris, France

SAINT-GOBAIN QUARTZ LTD

PO Box 6, Neptune Road, Wallsend, Tyne and
Wear, NE28 6DG

Tel: 0191 262 5311
Fax: 0191 263 8040
E-mail: quartz.sales@saint-gobain.com

Website:
http://www.quartz.saint-gobain.com

Enquiries:
Enquiries to: Sales Manager
Direct tel: 0191 259 8315

Founded:
1906

Formerly called:
TSL Group PLC; TSL Thermal Syndicate PLC;
Thermal Syndicate Ltd.

Organisation type and purpose:
Manufacturing industry.

Subject coverage:
Transparent and opaque fused quartz, synthetic
transparent, translucent fused silica, ingot, plate,
rod tube and machined components for fibre
optics, semiconductors, heating and lighting,
optical aerospace, foundry, chemical, laboratory
and refractory industries.

Non-library collection catalogue:
All or part available online

Printed publications:
Catalogues, brochures, datasheets

Publications list:
Available online

Access to staff:
Contact by letter, by telephone, by fax, by e-mail
and via website. Appointment necessary.
Hours: Mon to Thu, 0800 to 1615; Fri, 0800 to 1400

Access to building, collection or gallery:
No access other than to staff

SALFORD CITY LIBRARIES

Minerva House, Pendlebury Road, Swinton,
Manchester, M27 4EQ

Tel: 0161 778 0123
Fax: 0161 728 6145
E-mail: robin.culpin@salford.gov.uk

Enquiries:
Enquiries to: Librarian

Founded:
1974

Organisation type and purpose:
Local government body, public library.

Subject coverage:
General, local history, working class movement,
labour movement, James Nasmyth (the engineer).

**Museum or gallery collection, archive, or library
special collection:**
Boothstown Horticultural and Botanical Collection
  (18th century material)
Cowan Collection (theology, 17th century)
Davies Collection (theology, history and literature
  and political pamphlets of 17th-19th centuries)
Photography Collection
Trinity Collection (theology, 17th-19th centuries)

Working Class Movement Library, banners,
  pottery and medallions
Workshops Manuals Collection

Printed publications:
Information leaflets on local topics with
  bibliographies
Various local history publications at various prices

Access to staff:
Contact by letter, by telephone, by fax, by e-mail,
in person and via website. Appointment necessary.
Hours: Mon to Fri, 0900 to 1700

Comprises the:
17 libraries of the City of Salford, Eccles, Irlam,
Swinton and Worsley

SALFORD LOCAL HISTORY LIBRARY

Peel Park Avenue, Salford, Greater Manchester, M5
4WU

Tel: 0161 736 2649
Fax: 0161 745 9490
E-mail: salford.museum@salford.gov.uk

Website:
http://www.lifetimes.org.uk
Information on social and local history library

Enquiries:
Enquiries to: Librarian

Organisation type and purpose:
Local government body, public library, suitable for
ages: 12+.

Subject coverage:
Local history including census returns, parish
registers, documents, maps, and photographs
chronicling the history of Salford City.

Access to staff:
Contact by letter, by telephone, by fax, by e-mail
and in person
Hours: Mon to Fri, 0900 to 1700

Access to building, collection or gallery:
No prior appointment required
Hours: Mon to Fri, 1000 to 1700

Parent body:
Salford Museums Heritage Service
  at same address

SALFORD TOURIST INFORMATION CENTRE

Acronym or abbreviation: Salford TIC

1 The Quays, Salford, Greater Manchester, M50
3SQ

Tel: 0161 848 8601
Fax: 0161 872 3848
E-mail: tic@salford.gov.uk

Website:
http://www.visitsalford.info

Enquiries:
Enquiries to: Manager

Founded:
2000

Organisation type and purpose:
Local government body.

Subject coverage:
Tourist information. Local information, leaflets,
Greater Manchester, arts, theatre, small souvenir
shop, local history books, maps, postcards, videos,
souvenirs, accommodation bookings, boat trips.

Special visitor services:
Free access to tourism websites.

Services for disabled people:
Hearing loop at desk, easy access for wheelchair
users, front desk and internet desk correct height
for wheelchair users.

Printed publications:
Many books and videos on local history including:

Manchester, This Good Old Town (£6)
Mersey Ferry Guide (£1.99)
My Kind of People (Wadlon M, £2)
My Salford (Armstrong A, £4.95)
Recollections of Salford (£5.95)
free self-guided walks leaflets

Electronic and video publications:
Bygone Manchester (video)
Bygone Salford (video)
Manchester Ship Canal Vols 1 and 2 (video)

Publications list:
Available in print

Access to staff:
Contact by letter, by telephone, by fax, by e-mail,
in person and via website
Hours: Tue to Fri 1000 to 1715; Sat 1000 to 1600; Sun
and Bank Holidays 1100 to 1700; closed Mon

Access for disabled people:
Parking provided, level entry, access to all public
areas
Special comments: No disabled toilet facilities inside
TIC but available in The Lowry

Administered by:
Salford City Council

SALISBURY & DISTRICT COUNCIL FOR VOLUNTARY SERVICE

Acronym or abbreviation: Salisbury CVS

42 Salt Lane, Salisbury, Wiltshire, SP1 1EG

Tel: 01722 421747
Fax: 01722 415544
E-mail: salisbury.cvs@ruralnet.org.uk

Enquiries:
Enquiries to: Chief Executive

Founded:
1973

Organisation type and purpose:
Registered charity (charity number 1019716).
Local development agency for community and
voluntary activity.

Access to staff:
Contact by e-mail
Hours: Mon to Fri, 0930 to 1630

Access to building, collection or gallery:
Prior appointment required

Access for disabled people:
Ramped entry, toilet facilities

Connected with:
National Association of Councils for Voluntary
Service (NACVS)

SALMON & TROUT ASSOCIATION

Acronym or abbreviation: S&TA

Fishmongers' Hall, London Bridge, London, EC4R
9EL

Tel: 020 7283 5838
Fax: 020 7626 5137
E-mail: hq@salmon-trout.org

Website:
http://www.salmon-trout.org
The association, its work and membership,
branches, information on fishing, online booking
service.

Founded:
1903

Organisation type and purpose:
Registered charity (number 1123285), membership
association with a UK-wide membership (100,000
individual and club members) of game anglers,
fishery owners/managers, affiliated trades and
members of the public with an interest in
conserving the aquatic environment and its
dependent species.

continued overleaf

Subject coverage:
Addresses all issues relevant to fisheries legislation and regulation, together with environmental and species management and conservation. Has close working relationships with government departments and agencies, advising them over fisheries and angling matters and influencing their decision-making processes on behalf of all those with an interest in the aquatic environment.

Electronic and video publications:
Briefing papers
Order electronic and video publications from:
Download from website

Access to staff:
Contact by letter, by telephone, by fax and by e-mail

Administers:
Salmon & Trout Association's honorary Scientific Advisory Panel

Branches:
in Scotland and Wales and 12 affiliated branches in England

SALMONS TICKFORD REGISTER

Formal name: The Register of Motor Vehicles with Salmons TicKford Bodywork – 1898–1954
Acronym or abbreviation: STR

24 Woodland Rise West, Sheringham, Norfolk, NR26 8PF

Tel: 01263 824045
E-mail: mynard.revarg@tiscali.co.uk

Enquiries:
Enquiries to: Secretary and Registrar
Direct e-mail: mynard@telinco.co.uk

Founded:
1998

Organisation type and purpose:
Membership association (no charge for membership).
To provide information on Salmons and Tickford-bodied motor cars.

Subject coverage:
Salmons and Tickford-bodied cars.

Museum or gallery collection, archive, or library special collection:
Collection of photographs of Salmons/Tickford cars, printed brochures, original manuscripts, etc

Non-library collection catalogue:
All or part available in-house and in print

Printed publications:
Register of surviving cars
Salmons and Sons the Tickford Coachbuilders
Order printed publications from: e-mail: mynard .revarg@tiscali.co.uk

Publications list:
Available in print

Access to staff:
Contact by letter, by telephone, by e-mail and in person. Appointment necessary. Letter of introduction required.
Hours: Sun to Sat, 0900 to 2100

SALT ASSOCIATION

Tel: 015395 68005
E-mail: info@saltinfo.com

Website:
http://www.saltsense.co.uk
Member organisations, salt, its history and uses, health issues, research.

Organisation type and purpose:
Trade association representing UK manufacturers of salt for domestic, catering, water-softening, industrial and de-icing uses.

Subject coverage:
The association supports its members by: representing the technical, social and political views and objectives of the salt industry to relevant government and international organisations; providing a forum where members can exchange knowledge and scientific information on research, legislation, diet and nutrition, technical training, and health and safety issues; promoting balanced exposure for scientific research on salt and human health.

Electronic and video publications:
Press releases
Order electronic and video publications from:
Download from website

Access to staff:
Contact by telephone and by e-mail

Member organisation of:
European Salt Producers' Association (EuSalt)

SALTERS' CHEMISTRY CLUB, THE

Salters' Hall, 4 Fore Street, London, EC2Y 5DE

Tel: 020 7628 5962
Fax: 020 7638 3679
E-mail: club@salters.co.uk

Website:
http://www.salters.co.uk

Enquiries:
Enquiries to: Administrator

Founded:
1991

Organisation type and purpose:
Voluntary organisation, registered charity.

Subject coverage:
Promotion of chemistry in schools by establishing school-based chemistry clubs.

Printed publications:
Newsletter

Access to staff:
Contact by letter, by telephone, by fax and by e-mail
Hours: Mon to Fri, 0900 to 1700

Parent body:
The Salters' Institute
tel: 020 7628 5962; fax: 020 7638 3679; e-mail: institute@salters.co.uk

SALTERS' COMPANY

Formal name: The Worshipful Company of Salters

Salters' Hall, 4 Fore Street, London, EC2Y 5DE

Tel: 020 7588 5216
Fax: 020 7638 3679
E-mail: clerk@salters.co.uk

Website:
http://www.salters.co.uk

Enquiries:
Enquiries to: Clerk

Founded:
1394

Organisation type and purpose:
Membership association, present number of members: 195. A livery company of the City of London with charitable interests.

Subject coverage:
Promoting careers in chemistry and the chemical industries through its flagship charity The Salters' Institute.

Access to staff:
Contact by letter, by telephone, by fax and by e-mail. Appointment necessary. Access for members only.
Hours: Mon to Fri, 0900 to 1700

Access for disabled people:
Toilet facilities

Also at the same address:
Salters' Chemistry Camps
Salters' Chemistry Club
Salters' Institute
The Charities of Nicholas & Beamond
The James' Smiths' Alms House Charity
The Salters' Charities
The Salters' Charity for the Relief of Need

An investment subsidiary at the same address:
The Salters' Management Company Limited

SALTERS' INSTITUTE

Salters' Hall, 4 Fore Street, London, EC2Y 5DE

Tel: 020 7628 5962
Fax: 020 7638 3679
E-mail: institute@salters.co.uk

Website:
http://www.salters.co.uk

Enquiries:
Enquiries to: Institute Manager

Founded:
1918

Formerly called:
Salters' Institute of Industrial Chemistry

Organisation type and purpose:
Membership association, registered charity.

Subject coverage:
Award of Salters' Prizes to final year undergraduates in chemistry or chemical engineering; to Salters' A level chemistry candidates; limited information on research subjects undertaken by Salters Fellows and Scholars; grants for school chemistry libraries and chemistry equipment; no other help given at undergraduate level.

Access to staff:
Contact by letter, by telephone, by fax and by e-mail
Hours: Mon to Fri, 0900 to 1700

Parent body:
The Salters' Company
tel: 020 7588 5216; fax: 020 7638 3679

SALVATION ARMY

United Kingdom Territory, Territorial Headquarters, 101 Newington Causeway, London, SE1 6BN

Tel: 020 7367 4500
Fax: 020 7367 4728
E-mail: thq@salvationarmy.org.uk

Website:
http://www.salvationarmy.org.uk

Enquiries:
Enquiries to: Press Officer
Direct e-mail: sarah.miller@salvationarmy.org.uk
Other contacts: Media contacts, Media and Press Officer tel no: 020 7367 4700

Founded:
1865

Organisation type and purpose:
Voluntary organisation.
Part of the worldwide Christian church, providing social welfare in 108 countries.

Subject coverage:
Evangelism; health; social welfare; housing; education; prison welfare; agriculture; emergency aid; refugees; child care; handicapped ministries; leprosaria; care of the aged; community aid; agricultural development; family tracing; feeding programmes; educational programmes.

Museum or gallery collection, archive, or library special collection:
Historical information and archive material at The Heritage Centre, tel: 0171 387 1656

Printed publications:
146 publications worldwide; in the UK:

The Salvationist
The War Cry
Kids Alive Children's newspaper

Electronic and video publications:
Videos re work of Army from audio-visual
    department, HQ

Access to staff:
Contact by letter, by telephone and by fax.
Appointment necessary.
Hours: Mon to Fri, 0815 to 1630
Special comments: No personal callers without prior
appointment.

SALVATION ARMY FAMILY TRACING SERVICE

101 Newington Causeway, London, SE1 6BN

Tel: 020 7367 4747
E-mail: family.tracing@salvationarmy.org.uk

Website:
http://www.salvationarmy.org.uk/familytracing

Enquiries:
Enquiries to: Director

Founded:
1885

Formerly called:
Salvation Army Investigation Department (year of
change 1990)

Organisation type and purpose:
International organisation, registered charity,
voluntary organisation.
A service for endeavouring to trace members of
family with whom contact has been lost for some
reason, whether recently or in the distant past, for
reconciliation purposes only.
Adoption searches are not accepted.

Subject coverage:
Tracing missing relatives for the purposes of
reconciliation only; counselling for this need
(enquiries for friends, adoption, estate, divorce,
family tree or business reasons are NOT accepted).

Printed publications:
Annual Review and Statistics
Information leaflets and brochures

Access to staff:
Contact by letter and by telephone. All charged.
Hours: Mon to Fri, 0830 to 1545
Special comments: Enclose an sae for a reply.

Parent body:
Salvation Army THQ
    101 Newington Causeway, London, SE1 6BN

SAMARITANS

The Upper Mill, Kingston Road, Ewell, Surrey,
KT17 2AF

Tel: 020 8394 8300
Fax: 020 8394 8301
E-mail: admin@samaritans.org

Website:
http://www.samaritans.org.uk

Founded:
1953

Organisation type and purpose:
Voluntary organisation, registered charity (charity
number 219432). Samaritans is available 24 hours a
day to provide confidential emotional support for
people who are experiencing feelings of distress or
despair, including those which may lead to suicide

Subject coverage:
Suicide and emotional support

**Museum or gallery collection, archive, or library
special collection:**
Books and leaflets on related subjects
Small collection of books on suicide, parasuicide
    (epidemiology, prevention, intervention)

Trade and statistical information:
Suicide statistics – national and international.

Printed publications:
Annual Report
General Information leaflet (free)
Suicide figures (annually, free)

Access to staff:
Contact by letter, by telephone, by e-mail, in
person and via website
Hours: Mon to Fri, 0900 to 1700 (admin only). 24-
hour access to volunteers
Special comments: Confidential emotional support
by phone: 08457 908090; by e-mail:
jo@samaritans.org; by letter: Chris, PO Box 90 90,
Stirling, FK8 2SA

Access to building, collection or gallery:
For individual branches, see website

Access for disabled people:
Please see website

SAMB

Formal name: Scottish Association of Master Bakers

4 Torpichen Street, Edinburgh, EH3 8JQ

Tel: 0131 229 1401
Fax: 0131 229 8239
E-mail: master.bakers@samb.co.uk

Enquiries:
Enquiries to: Chief Executive

Founded:
1891

Organisation type and purpose:
Trade association (membership is by subscription).

Subject coverage:
The baking industry.

Printed publications:
Year Book (£128)

Access to staff:
Contact by letter
Hours: Mon to Fri, 0900 to 1700

SANDWELL AND WEST BIRMINGHAM HOSPITALS NHS TRUST

Acronym or abbreviation: SWBH

Clinical Library, Sandwell General Hospital,
Lyndon, West Bromwich, West Midlands, B71 4HJ

Tel: 0121 507 3587 ext. 3587
Fax: 0121 507 3586
E-mail: clinical.library@swbh.nhs.uk

Enquiries:
Enquiries to: Librarian

Formerly called:
Sandwell General Hospital

Organisation type and purpose:
Hospital.

Subject coverage:
Medicine.

Library catalogue:
All or part available in-house

Access to staff:
Contact by letter, by telephone, by fax and by e-
mail
Hours: Mon to Fri, 0830 to 1700

Also at:
Sandwell and West Birmingham Hospitals NHS
Trust
    Bevan Library, City Hospital, Dudley Road,
    Winson Green, Birmingham B18 4HQ; tel: 0121
    507 5245; e-mail: bevan.library@swbh.nhs.uk

SANDWELL COLLEGE

Learning Centre, Wednesbury Campus, Woden
Road South, Wednesbury, West Midlands, WS10
0PE

Tel: 0121 556 6000, from 0800 to 2000; 505 6000, any
other time
Fax: 0121 253 6069

Website:
http://www.sandwell.ac.uk
College web page.

Enquiries:
Enquiries to: Learning Centre Manager (for each
campus)
Direct tel: ext 6615

Founded:
1986

Formerly called:
Warley College, West Bromwich College

Includes the former:
Warley College

Organisation type and purpose:
College of further and higher education.
Headquarters for the 3 sites of the college:
Wednesbury, West Bromwich and Smethwick.

Subject coverage:
Foundry technology; metallurgy; welding;
marketing; business economics; management;
motor vehicle technology; production and
mechanical engineering; photography (the College
lists over 130 subjects, but excludes agriculture).

**Museum or gallery collection, archive, or library
special collection:**
Diecasting Society Library
Library of the National Foundry College

Non-library collection catalogue:
All or part available in-house

Access to staff:
Contact by letter, by telephone and in person
Hours: Mon to Thu, 0830 to 2000; Fri, 1000 to 1500
Special comments: Reference only, no loans.

Access for disabled people:
Ramped entry, access to all public areas, toilet
facilities

Also at:
Smethwick Campus
    Crochelts Lane, Smethwick, West Midlands
West Bromwich Campus
    High Street, West Bromwich, West Midlands

SANDWELL COMMUNITY HISTORY AND ARCHIVES SERVICE

Acronym or abbreviation: CHAS

Smethwick Library, High Street, Smethwick, West
Midlands, B66 1AA

Tel: 0121 558 2561
Fax: 0121 555 6064
E-mail: archives_service@sandwell.gov.uk

Website:
http://www.archives.sandwell.gov.uk

Founded:
1988

Organisation type and purpose:
Local government body, record office.

Subject coverage:
Local history of area now covered by Metropolitan
Borough of Sandwell.

**Museum or gallery collection, archive, or library
special collection:**
Records of churches, schools, organisations,
    businesses, families and individuals within
    Sandwell Metropolitan Borough. Notable
    collections include:
Public records, e.g. magistrates' court, quarter
    sessions court, coroner's court, hospitals and
    health authority

continued overleaf

Business records, including Patent Shaft
  Steelworks of Wednesbury, T. W. Camm, Stained
  Glass Manufacturer of Smethwick, Chance Bros
  Ltd of Smethwick
Records of the Deanery of Warley and its churches
Records of the Boroughs of Oldbury, Rowley
  Regis, Smethwick, Tipton, Warley, Wednesbury
  and West Bromwich

Non-library collection catalogue:
All or part available online and in-house

Library catalogue:
All or part available online

Access to staff:
Contact by letter, by telephone, by fax, by e-mail,
in person and via website. Appointment necessary.
Hours: Mon, Wed, Fri, 1000 to 1800; Tue, 1030 to
1800; Thu, closed; Sat, 0930 to 1600

Access for disabled people:
Level entry, access to all public areas

Parent body:
Sandwell Metropolitan Borough Council
  Council House, Oldbury, Warley

SANDWELL METROPOLITAN BOROUGH COUNCIL

Sandwell Information Service, Sandwell Central
Library, High Street, West Bromwich, West
Midlands, B70 8DZ

Tel: 0121 569 4911
Fax: 0121 525 9465
E-mail: information_service@sandwell.gov.uk

Website:
http://www.libraries.sandwell.gov.uk

Enquiries:
Enquiries to: Information Librarian

Organisation type and purpose:
Local government body, public library.

Subject coverage:
General; local history, business, Europe, local
council and community.

Non-library collection catalogue:
All or part available in-house

Library catalogue:
All or part available online and in-house

Access to staff:
Contact by letter, by telephone, by fax, by e-mail,
in person and via website
Hours: Mon, Fri, 0930 to 1900; Tue, Thu, 0930 to
1800; Wed, 1030 to 1800; Sat, 0900 to 1600

Access for disabled people:
Level entry

Administers:
Community History and Archive Service
  Smethwick Library, 100 High Street, Smethwick,
  B66 1AA; tel: 0121 558 2561; fax: 0121 555 6064;
  e-mail: archives_service@sandwell.gov.uk;
  website: http://www.libraries.sandwell.gov.uk/
  archives

SANE

Formal name: Schizophrenia – A National
Emergency

1st Floor, Cityside House, 40 Adler Street, London,
E1 1EE

Tel: 020 7375 1002
Fax: 020 7375 2162
E-mail: info@sane.org.uk

Website:
http://www.sane.org.uk
What is SANE? (background information on the
charity and its aims), what is SANELINE?
Research carried out by SANE, supporting SANE
and how to make donations.

Enquiries:
Enquiries to: Communications Officer

Direct tel: 020 7422 5557
Direct e-mail: info@saneline.org
Other contacts: Press Officer

Founded:
1986

Organisation type and purpose:
National organisation, voluntary organisation,
registered charity (charity number 296572),
training organisation, research organisation.
SANE campaigns to combat the prejudice and
intolerance surrounding mental illness, and
improve attitudes and services for individuals
coping with mental health problems and their
families.
SANELINE is a national mental health helpline
providing information and support for people with
mental health problems and those who support
them.

Subject coverage:
Greater public awareness of all mental health
problems.

Printed publications:
Alcohol, Drugs and Mental Illness
Anxiety Phobia and Depression
Community Care and Schizophrenia: The Need for
  Social Research
Depression and Manic Depression
Medical Methods of Treatment
Psychological Methods of Treatment
Schizophrenia: The Forgotten Illness
Schizophrenia92: Catch 22 (Wallace M)
The Forgotten Illness I, II & III
Understanding Clozapine Treatment

Publications list:
Available online and in print

Access to staff:
Contact by letter, by telephone, by fax and by e-
mail. Appointment necessary.
Hours: Mon to Fri, 0900 to 1700
Special comments: SANELINE (helpline), 1300 to
2300 every day.

Access to building, collection or gallery:
Prior appointment required

Access for disabled people:
Parking provided

Has one satellite:
Prince of Wales Research Centre (POWIC), Oxford

SANGAT ADVICE CENTRE

Sancroft Road, Harrow, HA3 7NS

Tel: 020 8427 0659
Fax: 020 8863 2196
E-mail: info@sangat.org.uk

Website:
http://www.asiansinharrow.org

Founded:
1997

Organisation type and purpose:
A not-for-profit company limited by guarantee,
providing the local Asian community with advice
and advocacy in such matters as legal rights,
housing, debt, welfare benefits, immigration and
discrimination.

Access to building, collection or gallery:
Hours: Mon to Fri, 0900 to 1700

Access for disabled people:
Accessible for people with mobility problems

SARUM COLLEGE LIBRARY

19 The Close, Salisbury, Wiltshire, SP1 2EE

Tel: 01722 424803
Fax: 01722 338508
E-mail: library@sarum.ac.uk

Website:
http://www.sarum.ac.uk/library
Includes library catalogue.

Enquiries:
Enquiries to: Librarian
Direct tel: 01722 326899 (Bookshop Manager)
Other contacts: Bookshop Manager

Founded:
1860

Formerly called:
Salisbury and Wells Theological College Library
(year of change 1995)

Organisation type and purpose:
Registered charity (charity number 309501).
Ecumenical centre for theological education,
subscription library.

Subject coverage:
Theology, church history, spirituality, biblical
studies.

Information services:
Online catalogue, enquiry service.

Services for disabled people:
Lift

**Museum or gallery collection, archive, or library
special collection:**
Bishop Hamilton's Library
19th-century theology, including the Markham
  Bequest of 276 bound vols of pamphlets
Sowter Clerical Library, some 12,000 vols including
  local history
Some 6,000 books of historical theology (17th–19th
  centuries)
Christian Socialist Archive supported by the
  Christian Socialist Movement
Jubilee Trust Archive
Michael Vasey papers
Br Tristam's papers
Tom Baker papers (former Principal)

Library catalogue:
All or part available online

Printed publications:
Guide to Library Services

Access to staff:
Contact by letter, by telephone, by fax, by e-mail,
in person and via website. Appointment necessary.
All charged.
Hours: Mon to Fri, 0900 to 1300 and 1400 to 1700
Special comments: Library unstaffed daily, 1300 to
1400.

Access to building, collection or gallery:
Hours: Mon to Fri, 0900 to 1700
Special comments: Library unstaffed between 1 and
2 pm each day

Access for disabled people:
Lift available
Special comments: If wheelchair users phone ahead,
staff will open both doors to library.

Member organisation of:
ABTAPL (Association of British Theological and
Philosophical Libraries)
  website: http://www.le.ac.uk/abtapl

SAVE BRITAIN'S HERITAGE

Acronym or abbreviation: SAVE

70 Cowcross Street, London, EC1M 6EJ

Tel: 020 7253 3500
Fax: 020 7253 3400
E-mail: office@savebritainsheritage.org

Website:
http://www.savebritainsheritage.org
Information on the organisation, publications,
news, database of buildings at risk.

Founded:
1975

Organisation type and purpose:
National organisation, membership association,
present number of members: 1,500, voluntary
organisation, registered charity (charity number
269129), research organisation, publishing house.
Charitable trust supported by Friends.

Campaign group for historic buildings threatened by neglect or demolition.

Subject coverage:
Demolished, threatened or neglected historic buildings; new uses for old buildings and conversions.

Printed publications:
40 publications
Order printed publications from: website: http://www.savebritainsheritage.org/publications/publications_in_print.php

Publications list:
Available online and in print

Access to staff:
Contact by letter, by telephone, by fax and by e-mail
Hours: 0930 to 1730

SBA THE SOLICITORS CHARITY

Formal name: Solicitors Benevolent Association
Acronym or abbreviation: SBA

1 Jaggard Way, London, SW12 8SG

Tel: 020 8675 6440
Fax: 020 8675 6441
E-mail: sec@sba.org.uk

Website:
http://www.sba.org.uk

Enquiries:
Enquiries to: Secretary

Founded:
1858

Organisation type and purpose:
Professional body (membership is by election or invitation), present number of members: 17,000, registered charity (charity number 208878).

Access to staff:
Contact by letter, by telephone, by fax, by e-mail and via website
Hours: Mon to Fri, 0930 to 1730

SCARBOROUGH BOROUGH COUNCIL

Town Hall, St Nicholas Street, Scarborough, North Yorkshire, YO11 2HG

Tel: 01723 232323
Fax: 01723 354979
E-mail: customerfirst@scarborough.gov.uk

Website:
http://www.scarborough.gov.uk
General, contact, members, economic development.

Enquiries:
Enquiries to: Office Manager
Direct tel: 01723 232570
Direct e-mail: janet.deacon@scarborough.gov.uk

Founded:
1974

Organisation type and purpose:
Local government body.

Subject coverage:
All local government services.

Access to staff:
Contact by letter, by telephone, by fax, by e-mail, in person and via website
Hours: Mon to Fri, 0830 to 1700

SCARBOROUGH LIBRARY

Formal name: Scarborough Library and Information Centre

Vernon Road, Scarborough, North Yorkshire, YO11 2NN

Tel: 0845 034 9516
Fax: 01723 353893

E-mail: scarborough.library@northyorks.gov.uk

Website:
htttp://www.northyorks.gov.uk

Enquiries:
Enquiries to: Community Information Officer
Direct tel: 0845 034 9517

Founded:
1930

Organisation type and purpose:
Local government body, public library.

Subject coverage:
General, local studies relating to Scarborough, the Yorkshire coast, North York Moors, Vale of Pickering and Yorkshire Wolds.

Museum or gallery collection, archive, or library special collection:
Censuses 1841–1901
Local newspapers 1839–
GRO indexes 1837–1997

Non-library collection catalogue:
All or part available online

Library catalogue:
All or part available online

Access to staff:
Contact by letter, by telephone, by fax, by e-mail and in person
Hours: Mon, Tue, Fri, 0900 to 1800; Wed, 1000 to 1800; Thu, 0900 to 1900; Sat, 0900 to 1600; Sun, 1100 to 1500
Special comments: Closed public holidays.

Access for disabled people:
Ramped entry

Parent body:
North Yorkshire County Library
Grammar School Lane, Northallerton, North Yorkshire, DL6 1DF; tel: 01609 767829; fax: 01609 780793; website: http://www.northyorks.gov.uk

SCHERING HEALTH CARE LIMITED

The Brow, Burgess Hill, West Sussex, RH15 9NE

Tel: 01444 232323
Fax: 01444 246613

Website:
http://www.schering.co.uk

Enquiries:
Enquiries to: Medical Information Department
Direct e-mail: bsp-communications@bayerhealthcare.com

Organisation type and purpose:
Pharmaceuticals manufacturer.

Subject coverage:
Medicine, especially endocrinology, diagnostic radiology, cardiovascular medicine and surgery, dermatology, neurophysiology and pharmacology, urology, obstetrics and gynaecology.

Printed publications:
Annotated Bibliographies
Patient information leaflets on acne, oral contraceptives, menopause, colposcopy, CT, MRI

Access to staff:
Contact by letter and by telephone
Hours: Mon to Fri, 0900 to 1700
Special comments: Schering Health Care Limited operates under the association of British Pharmaceutical Industry's code of practice and is unable to enter into correspondence with individual patients concerning their treatment.

SCHOOL LIBRARY ASSOCIATION

Acronym or abbreviation: SLA

Unit 2, Lotmead Business Village, Wanborough, Swindon, Wiltshire, SN4 0UY

Tel: 01793 791787
Fax: 01793 791786

E-mail: info@sla.org.uk

Website:
http://www.sla.org.uk

Enquiries:
Enquiries to: Chief Executive

Founded:
1937

Organisation type and purpose:
International organisation, advisory body, professional body (membership is by subscription), registered charity (charity number 313660 & SC039453), suitable for ages: 5 to 19, training organisation, publishing house, branches throughout the United Kingdom.
To support the development of school libraries, through advocacy, advice, training and publications.

Subject coverage:
School librarianship and information literacy, children's literature and literacy.

Printed publications:
The School Librarian (quarterly, free to members)
info@SLA (newsletter, quarterly, free to members)
Annotated booklists and practical guidelines to help those running a school library
Order printed publications from: website: http://www.sla.org.uk

Publications list:
Available online and in print

Access to staff:
Contact by letter, by telephone, by fax and by e-mail. Appointment necessary.
Hours: Mon to Fri, 0900 to 1700

Links with:
Cilip
IFLA

Member organisation of:
IASL

SCHOOL OF MEDITATION

158 Holland Park Avenue, London, W11 4UH

Tel: 020 7603 6116
E-mail: info@schoolofmeditation.org

Website:
http://www.schoolofmeditation.org

Enquiries:
Enquiries to: Administrator

Founded:
1961

Organisation type and purpose:
Membership association (membership is by subscription), present number of members: 700, registered charity (charity number 292171), suitable for ages: 18 to 80.

Subject coverage:
Technique of meditation as passed down through the Vedantic tradition; philosophical background.

Access to staff:
Contact by letter, by telephone and by e-mail. Appointment necessary.
Hours: Mon to Fri, 0930 to 1600

Parent body:
Society for Spiritual Development

SCHOOL OF ORAL & DENTAL SCIENCES

Formal name: University of Bristol School of Oral & Dental Sciences

University of Bristol School of Oral & Dental Sciences & Hospital, Lower Maudlin Street, Bristol, BS1 2LY

Tel: 0117 3424309
E-mail: ann.e.jones@bristol.ac.uk

continued overleaf

Website:
http://www.bris.ac.uk/dental

Enquiries:
Enquiries to: Administrator

Formerly called:
Department of Oral & Dental Science & Dental School (year of change 2010)

Organisation type and purpose:
University School, multiple Research groups, operating within the University of Bristol School of Oral & Dental Sciences with support from Wellcome Trust and Cancer Research Campaign, suitable for ages: 18+.

Subject coverage:
Dental research including the structure, composition and histopathology of teeth; dental caries; periodontal disease; salivary gland disease; oral cancer; viruses and oral disease; lifecourse epidemiology and population oral health, biomaterials.

Access to staff:
Contact by letter, by telephone and by e-mail
Hours: Mon to Fri, 0900 to 1630

Access for disabled people:
Parking provided, ramped entry, toilet facilities

SCHOOL SCIENCE SERVICE

41 Orchard Bank, Edinburgh, EH4 2DS

Tel: 0131 332 9886
Fax: 0131 332 7447
E-mail: anne@sciencesleuth.co.uk

Website:
http://www.sciencesleuth.co.uk

Enquiries:
Enquiries to: Managing Director
Other contacts: Secretary for Bookings Manager.

Founded:
1989

Formerly called:
The Science Sleuth Shop, Science Sleuth

Organisation type and purpose:
Service industry, consultancy.
Practical science workshops for schools, museums and festivals.

Subject coverage:
Educational equipment and resources packaged together for use in Primary School Science. The Science Sleuth visits schools, museums and science festivals with story-based science investigations, science toys.

Trade and statistical information:
World data on science sleuth investigations for primary schools.

Printed publications:
The Science Sleuth – Sense Investigations for Primary 1 to 3
The Science Sleuth – Chemistry and biology experiments for Primary 4 to 7
School Science Resources on a variety of subjects including electricity, magnetism and materials

Publications list:
Available in print

Access to staff:
Contact by letter, by telephone, by fax, by e-mail and via website
Hours: Mon to Fri, 0900 to 1700

Access to building, collection or gallery:
No access other than to staff

Close links with:
Science Sleuth: Colour Chemistry: DC Electricity: Magnetism: Senses Investigations for science festivals or school visits
    tel: 0131 332 7447; fax: 0131 332 7447; e-mail: anne@sciencesleuth.co.uk
The Association for Science Education (ASE) College Lane, Hatfield, AL10 9AA

Other address:
The Science Sleuth Shop (Science Sleuth)
    41 Orchard Bank, Edinburgh, EH4 1HN; tel: 0131 332 7447; fax: 0131 332 7447; e-mail: anne@sciencesleuth.co.uk

SCHUBERT SOCIETY OF BRITAIN

The German YMCA, 35 Craven Terrace, London, W2 3EL

Tel: 020 7723 5684
Fax: 020 7706 2870
E-mail: y-services@german-ymca.org.uk

Website:
http://www.german-ymca.org.uk/schubert.htm
Recital dates and programme offered.

Enquiries:
Enquiries to: Programme Secretary
Direct e-mail: u.bauer@german-ymca.org.uk

Founded:
1957

Organisation type and purpose:
Music Society.
To help young musicians on threshold of a professional career. Recitals given 3pm, third Sunday of month, from Oct to May (except Dec) at Lancaster Hall, Lancaster Hall Hotel, Craven Terrace, London W2, to include at least one work by Franz Schubert.

Subject coverage:
Chamber Music Recitals.

Printed publications:
Recital Programmes via mailing list

Electronic and video publications:
http://www.german-ymca.org.uk/schubert.htm

Publications list:
Available online and in print

Access to staff:
Contact by letter, by telephone, by fax, by e-mail and via website
Hours: Mon to Fri, 0900 to 1700

Access for disabled people:
Level entry
Special comments: Toilets accessible but not adapted for extra support, etc.

SCI

Formal name: Society of Chemical Industry
Acronym or abbreviation: SCI

International Headquarters, 14–15 Belgrave Square, London, SW1X 8PS

Tel: 020 7598 1500
Fax: 020 7598 1545
E-mail: secretariat@soci.org

Website:
http://www.soci.org
The Society of Chemical Industry (SCI) is an international forum where science meets business on independent, impartial ground.
http://www.soci.org/Chemistry-and-Industry
Chemistry & Industry Magazine, a leading source of news and opinion in the arena of chemical technology.
http://www.soci.org/Chemistry-and-Industry/Supply-Line/Company-Listing
Electronic version of Supply Line magazine.
http://www.biofpr.com
Innovation for a sustainable economy. Biofuels, Bioproducts & Biorefining (Biofpr) is a definitive source of information on sustainable products, fuels and energy. Provides an exciting blend of news, patent intelligence and features, and a peer-reviewed journal, with all the latest advances.

Enquiries:
Enquiries to: Web Team
Direct tel: 020 7598 1576
Direct e-mail: web@soci.org

Founded:
1881

Organisation type and purpose:
International organisation, learned society (membership is by subscription), present number of members: 5,000, registered charity (charity number 206883).

Subject coverage:
The science research, investment and industrial interface. Chemical technology and biotechnology, pest management, materials, agriculture, food, fine and heavy chemicals manufacture, environmental protection, corporate management, whole company direction, discovery, marketing and distribution, natural and economic sciences, engineering, law and medicine.

Museum or gallery collection, archive, or library special collection:
The Society's publications (starting 1881)

Non-library collection catalogue:
All or part available online, in-house and in print

Library catalogue:
All or part available online, in-house and in print

Printed publications:
Chemistry & Industry (24 times a year)
SCI Members' News (24 times a year)
The Supply Line (monthly)
Horticulture Newsletter (monthly)
Publisher (with Wiley) of:
Journal of Chemical Technology and Biotechnology
Journal of the Science of Food and Agriculture
Pest Management Science
Polymer International
Biofuels, Bioproducts and Biorefining

Publications list:
Available online and in print

Access to staff:
Contact by letter, by telephone, by fax, by e-mail, in person and via website. Appointment necessary.
Hours: Mon to Fri, 0900 to 1700

Access to building, collection or gallery:
Hours: Mon to Fri, 0900 to 1700

Access for disabled people:
Hours: Mon to Fri, 0900 to 1700

SCIENCE & SOCIETY PICTURE LIBRARY

North Entrance, Science Museum, Exhibition Road, South Kensington, London, SW7 2DD

Tel: 020 7942 4400
Fax: 020 7942 4401
E-mail: piclib@nmsi.ac.uk

Website:
http://www.scienceandsociety.co.uk

Organisation type and purpose:
Represents the collections of the Science Museum, the National Railway Museum and the National Museum of Photography, Film and Television, and other related collections.

Subject coverage:
Science and people's applications of science.

Museum or gallery collection, archive, or library special collection:
More than 150 image collections from within and outside the museums' own core collections, including 70,000 online records and 40,000 digital images. Themes: entertainment and media; medicine and health; natural world; personalities; places; science and technology; society and wars; trade and industry; transport

SCIENCE & TECHNOLOGY FACILITIES COUNCIL

Acronym or abbreviation: STFC

Polaris House, North Star Avenue, Swindon, Wiltshire, SN2 1SZ

Tel: 01793 442000
Fax: 01793 442002
E-mail: stfc@stfc.co.uk

Website:
http://www.stfc.ac.uk
News in particle physics and astronomy, directory of contacts, details of STFC awards.

Enquiries:
Enquiries to: Librarian
Other contacts: Press Officer

Founded:
2007

Created by the merger of:
Particle Physics and Astronomy Research Council (PPARC) and Council for the Central Laboratory of the Research Councils (CCLRC) (year of change 2007)

Organisation type and purpose:
Research organisation.
State-aided organisation.
One of the seven research councils. STFC directs and co-ordinates the funding of United Kingdom research into the physics of the Universe.

Subject coverage:
Astronomy, planetary science, particle physics, science policy.

Printed publications:
Leaflets for schools and the general public about particle physics and astronomy
Order printed publications from: Strategic Planning & Communications, Science & Technology Facilities Council, at the same address

Access to staff:
Contact by letter, by telephone, by fax, by e-mail and via website
Hours: Mon to Fri, 0900 to 1700

Laboratories:
Daresbury Laboratory
Royal Observatory (Edinburgh)
Rutherford Appleton Laboratory

SCIENCE AND ADVICE FOR SCOTTISH AGRICULTURE

Formal name: Science and Advice for Scottish Agriculture (Rural Payments and Inspections Directorate)
Acronym or abbreviation: SASA

Roddinglaw Road, Edinburgh, EH12 9FJ

Tel: 0131 244 8873
Fax: 0131 244 8940
E-mail: library@sasa.gsi.gov.uk

Website:
http://www.sasa.gov.uk

Enquiries:
Enquiries to: Librarian
Direct tel: 0131 244 8826

Founded:
1992

Organisation type and purpose:
National government body, research organisation.
Provides scientific research and advice to the Scottish Government, Environment and Rural Affairs Department.

Subject coverage:
Seed testing, seed potato classification, plant health, nematology, crop entomology, control of pests, pesticide usage, analytical chemistry, plant varieties, diagnostics and molecular biology.

Trade and statistical information:
Pesticide usage surveys for Scotland; pesticide poisoning of animals in Scotland.

Library catalogue:
All or part available in-house

Printed publications:
SASA Scientific Review 1997–2003

SASA Annual Report 1991–2008

Publications list:
Available online

Access to staff:
Contact by letter, by telephone, by fax, by e-mail and via website. Appointment necessary.
Hours: Mon to Fri, 0900 to 1700

Access to building, collection or gallery:
Prior appointment required

Access for disabled people:
Parking provided, level entry, toilet facilities

Parent body:
Scottish Government, Rural Payments and Inspections Directorate
   Broomhouse Drive, Edinburgh, EH11 3XD;
   website: http://www.scotland.gov.uk

SCIENCE COUNCIL

32–36 Loman Street, London, SE1 0EH

Tel: 020 7922 7888
Fax: 020 7922 7879

Website:
http://www.sciencecouncil.org

Enquiries:
Enquiries to: Chief Executive / Registrar
Direct e-mail: d.garnham@sciencecouncil.org

Founded:
2003

Organisation type and purpose:
A membership organisation (current number of member organisations: 30) for learned and professional bodies across science and its applications; works with them to represent this sector to government and others.
Promotes the profession of scientist through the Chartered Scientist designation and the development of codes of practice; promotes awareness of the contribution of professional scientists to science and society and advances science education and increased understanding of the benefits of science; provides a forum for discussion and exchange of views and works to foster collaboration between member organisations and the wider science, technology, engineering, mathematics and medical communities to enable inter-disciplinary contributions to science policy and the application of science.

Subject coverage:
Science and its applications.

Electronic and video publications:
Policy statements
Press releases
Order electronic and video publications from:
Download from website

Access to staff:
Contact by letter, by telephone, by fax and by e-mail

SCIENCE FICTION FOUNDATION COLLECTION

Acronym or abbreviation: SFF

Sydney Jones Library, University of Liverpool, PO Box 123, Liverpool, L69 3DA

Tel: 0151 794 2696
Fax: 0151 794 2681
E-mail: asawyer@liverpool.ac.uk

Website:
http://www.SFHsfhub.ac.uk

Enquiries:
Enquiries to: Librarian
Direct tel: 0151 794 3142

Founded:
1970

Organisation type and purpose:
Learned society, university library, research organisation. Aims to support and encourage research into science fiction.

Subject coverage:
Science fiction and related literary genres, their history and criticism.

Library catalogue:
All or part available online

Printed publications:
Foundation: the review of science fiction (3 times a year)

Access to staff:
Contact by letter, by telephone, by e-mail and via website. Appointment necessary.
Hours: Mon to Fri, 0915 to 1645

Funded by:
Science Fiction Foundation
   website: http://www.sf-foundation.org

Links with:
British Science Fiction Association
   website: http://www.bsfa.co.uk/bsfa

SCIENCE OXFORD

1–5 London Place, St Clements, Oxford, OX4 1BD

Tel: 01865 728953
E-mail: info@scienceoxford.com

Website:
http://www.scienceoxford.com

Organisation type and purpose:
Administered by the Oxford Trust. A registered charity (no. 292664) and a company limited by guarantee (no. 1898691). Science Oxford offers exhibitions, a hands-on science gallery and conference facilities.

Subject coverage:
Science.

Information services:
Information Centre.

Access to building, collection or gallery:
Hours: exhibitions open Mon to Fri, 1000 to 1600; science gallery open Sat in term-time and Mon to Sat during local school holidays

SCIENCE PHOTO LIBRARY

Acronym or abbreviation: SPL

327–329 Harrow Road, London, W9 3RB

Tel: 020 7432 1100
Fax: 020 7286 8668
E-mail: info@sciencephoto.com

Website:
http://www.sciencephoto.com
More than 350,000 images and 15,000 video clips are available to search online and download.

Enquiries:
Enquiries to: Sales Manager
Direct e-mail: mark@sciencephoto.com

Founded:
1979

Organisation type and purpose:
Service industry.
Specialist image and footage library.

Subject coverage:
Images and video clips covering healthcare, science & technology, space, history, environment, animals, plants and flowers.

Education services:
Offers a schools subscription for educational establishments to make use of in their teaching.

Non-library collection catalogue:
All or part available online

continued overleaf

Access to staff:
Contact by letter, by telephone, by fax, by e-mail and via website. Appointment necessary. All charged.
Hours: Mon to Fri, 0930 to 1800

Member organisation of:
British Association of Picture Libraries and Agencies (BAPLA)

SCIENTIFIC AND MEDICAL NETWORK

Acronym or abbreviation: SMN

1 Manchester Court, Moreton-in-Marsh, Gloucestershire GL56 0BY

Tel: 01608 652000
Fax: 01608 652001
E-mail: charla@scimednet.org

Website:
http://www.scimednet.org

Enquiries:
Enquiries to: Network Manager
Other contacts: Secretary

Founded:
1973

Organisation type and purpose:
International organisation, membership association (membership is by subscription, election or invitation), present number of members: 1,500, registered charity (charity number 1101171).

Subject coverage:
Science, medicine and spirituality, consciousness studies.

Printed publications:
Network (3 times a year, subscription £40)
Membership Directory (for private use) available online

Electronic and video publications:
Large selection of audio videos of talks and conferences (available to members only)
Members' Directory (for private use and available to members only)

Publications list:
Available online

Access to staff:
Contact by letter, by telephone, by fax, by e-mail and via website
Hours: Mon to Fri, 0900 to 1700

SCIENTIFIC APPARATUS RECYCLING SCHEME

Acronym or abbreviation: SARS

Department of Biochemistry and Molecular Biology, University College London, London, WC1E 6BT

Tel: 020 7679 2169
Fax: 020 7679 7193
E-mail: p.campbell@biochemsitry.ucl.ac.uk

Organisation type and purpose:
International organisation, voluntary organisation. The purpose of SARS is to collect and despatch scientific equipment, books and journals surplus to the requirements of Western European countries to biochemists in need in Central and Eastern Europe.

Parent body:
Federation of European Biochemical Societies (FEBS)

SCIENTIFIC COMMITTEE ON ANTARCTIC RESEARCH

Acronym or abbreviation: SCAR

SCAR Secretariat, Scott Polar Research Institute, Lensfield Road, Cambridge, CB2 1ER

Tel: 01223 336550
Fax: 01223 336549
E-mail: info@scar.org

Website:
http://www.scar.org

Enquiries:
Enquiries to: Executive Director

Founded:
1958

Organisation type and purpose:
International organisation (membership is by election or invitation), present number of members: 31 full members, 4 associates, 9 international scientific unions. Members are National Academic Societies, e.g. The Royal Society (UK).
To initiate, promote and co-ordinate scientific research in Antarctica and to provide scientific advice to the Antarctic Treaty System.

Subject coverage:
Antarctic biology, geodesy and geographic information, glaciology, human biology and medicine, physics and chemistry of the atmosphere, solar-terrestrial and astrophysical research, geosciences, environment and conservation, global change, astronomy, oceanography.

Publications list:
Available online and in print

Access to staff:
Contact by e-mail
Hours: Mon to Fri, 0900 to 1700

Member organisations:
National Scientific Academies of Argentina, Australia, Belgium, Brazil, Bulgaria, Canada, Chile, People's Republic of China, Denmark (associate mem.), Ecuador, Finland, France, Germany, India, Italy, Japan, Republic of Korea, Malaysia, Netherlands, New Zealand, Norway, Pakistan (associate mem.), Peru, Poland, Portugal (associate mem.), Romania (associate mem.), Russia, South Africa, Spain, Sweden, Switzerland, Ukraine, United Kingdom, Uruguay, USA

Parent body:
International Council of Scientific Unions (ICSU)
ICSU Secretariat, 5 rue Auguste Vacquerie, 75016 Paris, France; tel: +33 1 45 25 03 29; fax: +33 1 42 88 94 31; e-mail: secretariat@icsu.org; website: http://www.icsu.org

SCOLIOSIS ASSOCIATION UK

Acronym or abbreviation: SAUK

4 Ivebury Court, 323–327 Latimer Road, London, W10 6RA

Tel: 020 8964 5343/1166
Fax: 020 8964 5343
E-mail: sauk@sauk.org.uk

Website:
http://www.sauk.org.uk

Enquiries:
Enquiries to: Information Officer

Founded:
1981

Organisation type and purpose:
Membership association, present number of members: 3500, voluntary organisation, registered charity (charity number 285290).
Offers sufferers a chance to share experience of the physical, emotional and social aspects of scoliosis.

Subject coverage:
Scoliosis (ie lateral spinal curvature); information about all aspects of scoliosis, but not individual medical advice.

Printed publications:
Legacy Leaflet (free)
A Twist of Fate (£3)
Clothes to Suit (£3)
Newsletter (twice a year, to members)

Newsletter Index (covers 11 years, with list of reprints available, 20p to 50p)
Schools Fact Sheet (free)
Scoliosis (handbook, £5.50)

Electronic and video publications:
Videos available for purchase or loan

Publications list:
Available in print

Access to staff:
Contact by letter, by telephone, by fax, by e-mail and via website
Hours: Mon to Fri, 1000 to 1730

Links with:
International Federation of Scoliosis Associations

SCOOTACAR REGISTER

18 Holman Close, Aylsham, Norwich, Norfolk, NR11 6DD

Tel: 01263 733861
E-mail: scootacar@btinternet.com

Website:
http://www.scootacar.org.uk
General useful data.

Enquiries:
Enquiries to: Secretary

Founded:
1980

Organisation type and purpose:
Membership association.
To locate and register all Scootacars.

Subject coverage:
Micro cars, bubble cars, location and registration of Scootacars.

Museum or gallery collection, archive, or library special collection:
Photographs
Register of all known cars
Service bulletins
Spares and component numbers
Workshop manuals

Trade and statistical information:
Production figures.
Chassis numbers.
Engine numbers.
Number of cars located.

Printed publications:
Scootabout (newsletter, 2 times a year, £5 annual subscription)

Access to staff:
Contact by letter, by telephone, by e-mail and via website
Hours: Mon to Sun, 0900 to 2100

SCOPE

6 Market Road, London, N7 9PW

Tel: 020 7619 7100
Fax: 020 7619 7360

Website:
http://www.scope.org.uk
Information on cerebral palsy, therapies, education etc.
Information on SCOPE campaigns etc.
Publications list.

Enquiries:
Enquiries to: Library & Information Officer
Direct tel: 020 7619 7340
Direct e-mail: information@scope.org.uk

Founded:
1952

Formerly called:
Spastics Society

Organisation type and purpose:
Voluntary organisation, registered charity (charity number 208231).

To ensure that all people with cerebral palsy and related disabilities, their families and carers have access to properly resourced services that meet their needs and full rights to control their own lives.

Subject coverage:
Cerebral palsy; attitudes to disability; discrimination against disabled people; education and employment of disabled people. Equipment, legislation related to disability; statistics on disability.

Museum or gallery collection, archive, or library special collection:
Complete run of Developmental Medicine & Child Neurology
Full set of Classics in Developmental Medicine
Full set of Clinics in Developmental Medicine

Trade and statistical information:
Disability related statistics eg numbers of disabled people and their income/expenditure, equipment needs etc.

Non-library collection catalogue:
All or part available in-house

Library catalogue:
All or part available in-house

Printed publications:
Disability Now (newspaper, monthly, £1.80)
Other publications (education, conductive education and therapies, parent information leaflets, campaigns and research) include:
A lot to say (Morris J, 2002)
Advocating for Equality
Right From The Start
Focusing on Cerebral Palsy (2001)
Polls Apart
Ready, willing and disabled (2003)
Speak for Yourself (Ford J, 2000)
Stop Press (Cooke C, Daone L, and Morris G, 2000)
That Kind of Life (Morris J, 2002)
Order printed publications from: Library and Information Unit, SCOPE
at the same address, tel: 020 7619 7342, fax: 020 7619 7360, e-mail: information@scope.org.uk

Electronic and video publications:
Disability awareness videos (available for free loan or purchase £15)
All titles can be made available on tape
Order electronic and video publications from:
Education Distribution Service (AV material), SCOPE
Unit 2, Drywall Estate, Castle Road, Marston, Sittingbourne, Kent, ME10 3RL, tel: 01795 427614, fax: 01795 474871

Publications list:
Available online and in print

Access to staff:
Contact by letter, by telephone, by fax, by e-mail, in person and via website
Hours: Helpline (0808 8003333): Mon to Fri, 0900 to 2100; Sat to Sun, 1400 to 1800

Access to building, collection or gallery:
Prior appointment required
Hours: Mon to Fri, 0900 to 1700
Special comments: Prior appointment required for access to library.

Access for disabled people:
Access to all public areas

Has:
a network of local offices around England and Wales providing support
over 200 local groups around England and Wales

Helpline:
Cerebral Palsy Helpline
PO Box 833, Milton Keynes, Buckinghamshire, MK12 5NY; tel: 0808 800 3333; fax: 01908 321051; e-mail: cphelpline@scope.org.uk

SCOPE – RESPONSE

PO Box 833, Milton Keynes, Buckinghamshire, MK12 5NY

Tel: 0808 800 3333; text SCOPE plus message to 80039
Fax: 01908 321051
E-mail: response@scope.org.uk

Website:
http://www.scope.org.uk
Information about cerebral palsy and Scope, sevices and publications.

Formerly called:
The Spastics Society

Organisation type and purpose:
National disability organisation in respect of cerebral palsy, registered charity (charity number 208231).
For disabled people achieving equality; helpline provides free and confidential information, advice and support about cerebral palsy, disability issues and Scope services.

Subject coverage:
Cerebral palsy and associated disabilities.

Printed publications:
A range of publications including:
Cerebral Palsy Helpline (leaflet)
Series of factsheets around cp, therapies and disability issues
Multilingual leaflet
SCOPE for You (leaflet)
Parent Information Leaflets
Factsheets available in large print or Braille on request
Order printed publications from: Scope, CP Helpline, PO Box 833, Milton Keynes, MK12 5NY; tel: 01908 321049 (Publications Line)

Electronic and video publications:
Information in other languages (CD)
Scope videos available

Publications list:
Available online and in print

Access to staff:
Contact by letter, by telephone, by fax, by e-mail and via website
Hours: Mon to Fri, 0900 to 1700; closed weekends and bank holidays

SCOTCH WHISKY ASSOCIATION

Acronym or abbreviation: SWA

20 Atholl Crescent, Edinburgh, EH3 8HF

Tel: 0131 222 9200
Fax: 0131 222 9237
E-mail: contact@swa.org.uk

Website:
http://www.scotch-whisky.org.uk
General information and statistics on Scotch Whisky.

Enquiries:
Enquiries to: Director of Government and Consumer Affairs
Other contacts: Press & Media Relations Manager for press enquiries

Founded:
1943

Organisation type and purpose:
Trade association.
Promotion and protection of Scotch Whisky.

Subject coverage:
Scotch whisky trade worldwide; statistical and industry information.

Printed publications:
Publicity materials
Questions and answers (handbook, for sale)
Statistical report (annually, for sale)

Access to staff:
Contact by letter, by telephone, by fax, by e-mail and via website

Also at:
Scotch Whisky Association
14 Cork Street, London, W1S 3NS; tel: 020 7629 4384; fax: 020 7493 1398

SCOTLAND IS

Suite 41, Geddes House, Kirkton North, Livingston, EH54 6GU

Tel: 01506 472200
Fax: 01506 460615
E-mail: info@scotlandis.com

Website:
http://www.scotlandis.com

Enquiries:
Enquiries to: Membership Liaison Manager
Direct e-mail: karen.meechan@scotlandis.com
Other contacts: General Manager

Founded:
2000

Formerly called:
IMAS, Internet Society (ISOC), Scottish Software Federation (SSF) (year of change 2000)

Organisation type and purpose:
Trade association (membership is by subscription), present number of members: 300 companies.
Representative trade organisation for the ICT industry in Scotland. Members encompass a wide cross-section of companies covering the users, academia, developers, applications providers and service providers.
To make the software industry in Scotland collectively successful.

Subject coverage:
Computer software.

Printed publications:
Switched On (newsletter, available through info@scotlandis.com)
Directory of Member Companies 2002 (£35 plus VAT)

Electronic and video publications:
Members Directory (CD-ROM, available with hard copy £35 plus VAT)

Publications list:
Available online and in print

Access to staff:
Contact by letter, by telephone, by fax, by e-mail and via website
Hours: Mon to Fri, 0900 to 1700

Access to building, collection or gallery:
Prior appointment required

Access for disabled people:
Parking provided, ramped entry

Grampian Office:
Scotland IS
The Software Centre, Aberdeen Science and Technology Park, Campus 2, Balgowie Drive, Bridge of Don, Aberdeen, AB22 8GU; tel: 01224 332182; fax: 01224 332082; e-mail: info@scotlandis.com

SCOTLAND'S GARDENS SCHEME

Acronym or abbreviation: SGS

42A Castle Street, Edinburgh, EH2 3BN

Tel: 0131 226 3714
E-mail: info@sgsgardens.co.uk

Website:
http://www.gardensofscotland.org
Information on gardens open to the public through Scotland's Gardens Scheme.

Enquiries:
Enquiries to: Director

Founded:
1931

Organisation type and purpose:
Registered charity (charity number SCO 11337).
Opening gardens to the public for a range of charities.

Subject coverage:
Opening dates for gardens that open under the scheme in Scotland each year.

continued overleaf

Printed publications:
Gardens of Scotland (annual, for purchase)

Access to staff:
Contact by letter, by telephone and by e-mail
Hours: Mon to Fri, 0900 to 1700

Access to building, collection or gallery:
No access other than to staff

SCOTT BADER COMPANY LIMITED

Wollaston, Wellingborough, Northamptonshire, NN29 7RL

Tel: 01933 663100
Fax: 01933 666608
E-mail: enquiries@scottbader.com

Enquiries:
Enquiries to: Information Officer

Founded:
1920

Organisation type and purpose:
Manufacturing industry.

Subject coverage:
Plastics, synthetic resins, their manufacture and technical applications (specifically unsaturated polyester resins, emulsion and solution polymers), polyesters, reinforced plastics, surface coatings for paper, textiles and other materials, adhesives and thickeners.

Museum or gallery collection, archive, or library special collection:
Ernest Bader's Archives, founder of the company and pioneer in common ownership of companies

Printed publications:
Technical trade literature on polymers, polyesters and their applications in end-use markets

Access to staff:
Appointment necessary.
Hours: Mon to Fri, 0830 to 1700

SCOTT OWNERS' CLUB

Acronym or abbreviation: SOC

Walnut Cottage, Abbey Lane, Aslockton, Nottinghamshire, NG13 9AE

Tel: 01949 851027
Fax: 01949 851027

Website:
http://www.scottownersclub.org
Marque history, membership application details, technical information.

Enquiries:
Enquiries to: Public Relations Officer
Other contacts: (1) Membership Secretary; (2) Machine Registrar; (3) Archivist

Founded:
1958

Organisation type and purpose:
Membership association (membership is by subscription), present number of members: 650. To promote interest in Scott and Silk motorcycles and to provide a spares scheme, library, photographic archives, technical information, a machine register, badges, transfers (decals), and mutual support to members.

Subject coverage:
Scott motorcycles made 1908–1951, Birmingham Scott 1957–1972, Silk Scott 1970s–1980s and the Silk motorcycle which followed.

Museum or gallery collection, archive, or library special collection:
Collections of period photographs, some factory records, engineering drawings, technical information and machine register

Printed publications:
Yowl (club magazine, 6 times a year, for members)

Electronic and video publications:
CD-ROMs – under development

Access to staff:
Contact by letter, by telephone and by fax
Hours: Mon to Fri, 0900 to 1700
Special comments: Enclose SAE if written reply is required.
No access to facilities without membership.

SCOTT POLAR RESEARCH INSTITUTE

Acronym or abbreviation: SPRI

Lensfield Road, Cambridge, CB2 1ER

Tel: 01223 336552
Fax: 01223 336549
E-mail: enquiries@spri.cam.ac.uk

Website:
http://www.spri.cam.ac.uk

Enquiries:
Enquiries to: Librarian and Keeper
Direct e-mail: library@spri.cam.ac.uk
Other contacts: Information Assistant (for general library enquiries)

Founded:
1920

Organisation type and purpose:
Museum, university department or institute.

Subject coverage:
Polar regions; Arctic regions; Antarctic regions including the Falkland Islands; Russian North; snow and ice studies; glaciology; cold regions in general; whaling; sealing; exploration.

Education services:
Polar Museum Education and Outreach Service.

Services for disabled people:
Induction loop.

Museum or gallery collection, archive, or library special collection:
Polar Archives

Non-library collection catalogue:
All or part available online, in-house and in print

Library catalogue:
All or part available online

Printed publications:
Catalogue of the Scott Polar Research Institute Library
Polar Record (quarterly)
Polar and Glaciological Abstracts (3 times a year)
Universal Decimal Classification for use in Polar Libraries

Publications list:
Available in print

Access to staff:
Contact by letter, by telephone, by fax, by e-mail, in person and via website. Appointment necessary.
Hours: Mon to Fri, 0900 to 1300 and 1400 to 1730

Access to building, collection or gallery:
Hours: Mon to Fri, 0900 to 1700; Sat, 1000 to 1600

Access for disabled people:
Lifts to main entrances; internal lifts to all floors

Constituent part of:
University of Cambridge

Houses the:
International Glaciological Society
tel: 01223 355974; e-mail: igsoc@igsoc.org
Scientific Committee on Antarctic Research (SCAR)
tel: 01223 336550; fax: 01223 336549; e-mail: info@scar.org
World Data Centre for Glaciology, Cambridge
tel: 01223 336565; fax: 01223 336549; website: http://wdcgc.spri.cam.ac.uk

SCOTTISH ACCIDENT PREVENTION COUNCIL

Acronym or abbreviation: SAPC

Arcadia Business Centre, Miller Lane, Clydebank, Scotland, G81 1UJ

Tel: 0141 280 0122
Fax: 0141 941 0887
E-mail: secretary@sapc.org.uk

Website:
http://www.sapc.org.uk
The Scottish Accident Prevention Council is the body in Scotland in which organisations involved in accident prevention participate in order to have a stronger voice.
Co-ordinates and stimulates accident prevention in all facets of daily life. Membership and partners are drawn from a wide range of organisations and bodies throughout Scotland who have an involvement in matters affecting accident prevention and safety in the public, private and voluntary sector; also works in partnership with the Scottish Government.

Enquiries:
Enquiries to: Secretary

Founded:
1930

Organisation type and purpose:
Membership association, voluntary organisation, Scottish registered charity.

Subject coverage:
Home, road, water and leisure safety.

Access to staff:
Contact by letter, by telephone, by fax, by e-mail and via website. Appointment necessary.
Hours: Mon to Fri, 0900 to 1700

Administered by:
West Dunbartonshire Community & Volunteering Services
Arcadia Business Centre, Miller Lane, Clydebank, Scotland, G81 1UJ; tel: 0141 941 0886; fax: 0141 941 0887; e-mail: info@wdcvs.com; website: http://www.wdcvs.com

Links with:
local authorities, devolved government, national bodies, other voluntary and charitable organisations

SCOTTISH AGRICULTURAL COLLEGE – EDINBURGH

Acronym or abbreviation: SAC

West Mains Road, Edinburgh, EH9 3JG

Tel: 0131 535 4000
Fax: 0131 535 4246

Website:
http://www.sac.ac.uk/
SAC home page with library details.

Enquiries:
Enquiries to: Librarian
Direct tel: 0131 535 4116
Direct e-mail: m.mullay@ed.sac.ac.uk

Founded:
1990

Formed from:
East of Scotland College of Agriculture, Scottish Agricultural Colleges

Formerly called:
Edinburgh School of Agriculture

Organisation type and purpose:
consultancy, research organisation.

Subject coverage:
All aspects of agriculture excluding fisheries; agricultural economics, farming and engineering; animal nutrition and production; applied plant science; crop production and protection; pests; microbiology; organic and soil science; veterinary medicine; environment; rural affairs.

Museum or gallery collection, archive, or library special collection:
Early agricultural texts

Library catalogue:
All or part available online

Printed publications:
Library Guide

Electronic and video publications:
AGDEX – in-house bibliographic database indexing the popular farming press

Publications list:
Available in print

Access to staff:
Contact by letter and by e-mail. Appointment necessary.
Hours: Term time: Mon to Thu, 0845 to 2100; Fri, 0845 to 1700; Sat, Sun, 1000 to 1700
Vacations: Mon to Fri, 0845 to 1700

Combines the:
Institute of Ecology and Resource Management, University of Edinburgh
Scottish Agricultural College

Other addresses:
Scottish Agricultural College
   Craibstone Estate, Auchincruive, Ayrshire

SCOTTISH AGRICULTURAL COLLEGE, AUCHINCRUIVE

Acronym or abbreviation: SAC

Auchincruive, Ayr, KA6 5HW

Tel: 01292 525209
Fax: 01292 525211
E-mail: libraryau@sac.ac.uk

Website:
http://www.sac.ac.uk/library

Enquiries:
Enquiries to: Librarian
Direct tel: 01292 525209

Founded:
1896

Formerly called:
West of Scotland College of Agriculture (year of change 1990)

Organisation type and purpose:
Research organisation, consultancy, independent body funded by the Scottish Office.
Higher education.

Subject coverage:
Science and economics of agriculture, horticulture, biotechnology, dairying, milk and milk products, poultry husbandry, agricultural engineering, food sciences, water pollution, conservation, environmental science, countryside recreation, tourism and leisure.

Museum or gallery collection, archive, or library special collection:
Historical collection on agriculture and horticulture

Non-library collection catalogue:
All or part available online

Library catalogue:
All or part available online

Printed publications:
Advisory leaflets, etc.
Annual Report
Order printed publications from: Publications Unit, SAC, Kings Buildings, West Mains Road, Edinburgh, EH9 3JG; tel: 0131 535 4000

Publications list:
Available in print

Access to staff:
Contact by letter, by telephone, by fax and by e-mail. Appointment necessary.
Hours: Term time: Mon to Fri, 0845 to 2045; Sat, Sun, 1100 to 1700

Vacations: Mon to Thu, 0845 to 1715; Fri, 0845 to 1645

Access to building, collection or gallery:
No prior appointment required
Hours: Mon to Fri, 0900 to 1630 only

Access for disabled people:
Stairlift available for remote room but library itself inaccessible to wheelchairs
Hours: Mon to Fri, 0900 to 1630 only

Links with:
University of Glasgow

SCOTTISH AMATEUR MUSIC ASSOCIATION

Acronym or abbreviation: SAMA

18 Craigton Crescent, Alva, Clackmannanshire, FK12 5DS

Tel: 01259 760249
E-mail: secretary@sama.org.uk

Website:
http://www.sama.org.uk

Enquiries:
Enquiries to: Honorary Secretary

Founded:
1956

Organisation type and purpose:
Membership association (membership is by election or invitation), registered charity (charity number SCO 14503).

Subject coverage:
The encouragement and stimulation of amateur music-making in Scotland, mainly through summer courses.

Printed publications:
The Gentle Jacobite (a play with music for young people)

Publications list:
Available in print

Access to staff:
Contact by letter, by telephone and by e-mail
Hours: Not always available

SCOTTISH AMATEUR SWIMMING ASSOCIATION

Acronym or abbreviation: SASA

National Swimming Academy, University of Stirling, Stirling, FK9 4LA

Tel: 01786 466520
Fax: 01786 466521
E-mail: info@scottishswimming.com

Website:
http://www.scottishswimming.com

Enquiries:
Enquiries to: Director of Administration
Direct e-mail: e.mackenzie@scottishswimming.com

Founded:
1888

Organisation type and purpose:
Membership association (membership is by subscription), voluntary organisation.
National governing body of the sport.

Subject coverage:
Speed swimming, masters' swimming, synchronised swimming, long distance swimming, water polo.

Printed publications:
Swimming 2000 (magazine, 6 times a year, £7.50)
Scottish Learn to Swim Syllabus (£29.99)
Adult and Child Syllabus (£35)

Access to staff:
Contact by letter, by telephone and by e-mail
Hours: Mon to Thu, 0830 to 1700; Fri, 0830 to 1600

Access to building, collection or gallery:
No prior appointment required

Access for disabled people:
Parking provided, level entry, access to all public areas, toilet facilities

Links with:
Fédération Internationale de Natation Amateur (FINA)
   Avenue de Beaumont 9, Lausanne, CH-1012, Switzerland

SCOTTISH AND NORTHERN IRELAND PLUMBING EMPLOYERS' FEDERATION

Acronym or abbreviation: SNIPEF

2 Walker Street, Edinburgh, EH3 7LB

Tel: 0131 225 2255
Fax: 0131 226 7638
E-mail: info@snipef.org

Website:
http://www.snipef.org
Benefits of using SNIPEF member firms, displays a list of member firms in Scotland and Northern Ireland, membership details available to potential new member firms, history of the Federation.

Enquiries:
Enquiries to: Information Officer

Founded:
1923

Organisation type and purpose:
Trade association (membership is by subscription, qualification), present number of members: 950, service industry.
The national association for all types of firms involved in the plumbing and domestic heating industry in Scotland and Northern Ireland.

Subject coverage:
Customers using SNIPEF members can contact the Federation for advice relating to any plumbing and heating work undertaken by a member firm. In the event that a dispute arises, the customer can contact the Federation, who will advise them on the operation of their complaints procedure through their Code of Fair Trading, which is recognised by the Office of Fair Trading.

Printed publications:
Plumb Heat (trade journal, 4 issues a year, free to members, non-members £20, overseas surface mail £30)
SNIPEF Year book (free to member firms and non-commercial organisations, otherwise £25)

Access to staff:
Contact by letter, by telephone, by fax, by e-mail, in person and via website
Hours: Mon to Thu, 0900 to 1700; Fri, 0900 to 1630

SCOTTISH ANGLERS NATIONAL ASSOCIATION LTD

Acronym or abbreviation: SANA

The National Game Angling Centre, The Pier, Loch Leven, Kinross, Scotland, KY13 8UF

Tel: 01577 861116
Fax: 01577 864769
E-mail: admin@sana.org.uk

Website:
http://www.sana.org.uk

Enquiries:
Enquiries to: Administrator
Other contacts: Secretary

Founded:
1880

Organisation type and purpose:
National organisation, advisory body, membership association (membership is by subscription), service industry, voluntary organisation.

continued overleaf

Governing body for the sport of game fishing in Scotland.

Subject coverage:
Game fishing, especially in Scotland.

Education services:
Angling coaching and instruction

Services for disabled people:
via Disabled Committee

Printed publications:
Annual report
Annual newsletter

Access to staff:
Contact by letter, by telephone, by fax, by e-mail and via website
Hours: 0930 to 1300 and 1400 to 1630
Special comments: Answering machine available.

Access for disabled people:
Good disabled access

SCOTTISH ARCHERY ASSOCIATION

Acronym or abbreviation: SAA

E-mail: via website

Website:
http://www.scottisharchery.org.uk
Archery in Scotland, links to Scottish clubs, events.

Enquiries:
Enquiries to: President
Other contacts: Regional Administrator

Founded:
1949

Organisation type and purpose:
Voluntary association, national body for the development of archery in Scotland, affiliated to the national governing body, ArcheryGB.

Subject coverage:
There are about 70 senior clubs and 36 junior clubs throughout the whole of Scotland, serving the most densely populated areas.

Access to staff:
Contact via website

Affiliated to:
ArcheryGB

Links with:
Scottish Sports Association
SportScotland

SCOTTISH ASIAN ACTION COMMITTEE

Acronym or abbreviation: SAAC

39 Napiershall Street, Glasgow, G20 6EZ

Tel: 0141 341 0025
Fax: 0141 341 0020
E-mail: secretary@saac.freeserve.co.uk

Enquiries:
Enquiries to: Secretary
Other contacts: Development Officer

Founded:
1981

Organisation type and purpose:
Voluntary organisation.
To provide information and advice to black and ethnic minority communities in Scotland. To combat racism and discrimination through campaigning.

Subject coverage:
Black and Asian communities in Scotland, racism, work and equal opportunities, community groups, racial equality standards.

Printed publications:
Newsletter (quarterly)
Annual Report

Access to staff:
Contact by telephone, by fax, by e-mail and in person
Hours: Mon to Fri, 1000 to 1600

SCOTTISH ASSOCIATION FOR MARINE SCIENCE

Acronym or abbreviation: SAMS

Dunstaffnage Marine Laboratory, Dunbeg, Oban, Argyll, PA37 1QA

Tel: 01631 559000
Fax: 01631 559001
E-mail: innfo@sams.ac.uk

Website:
http://www.sams.ac.uk

Enquiries:
Enquiries to: Librarian
Direct tel: 01631 559217
Direct e-mail: olga.kimmins@sams.ac.uk
Other contacts: Director

Founded:
1896

Formerly called:
Scottish Marine Biological Association (SMBA) (year of change 1990)

Organisation type and purpose:
Learned society (membership is by subscription), registered charity (charity number SCO 09206), research organisation.

Subject coverage:
Marine biology, marine ecology, marine chemistry and oceanography.

Library catalogue:
All or part available in-house

Printed publications:
Annual Report

Access to staff:
Contact by letter, by fax and by e-mail
Hours: Mon to Fri, 0900 to 1700
Special comments: SAMS members only. Other bona fide scientists by prior appointment.

Access to building, collection or gallery:
Prior appointment required

Connections with:
Natural Environment Research Council

SCOTTISH ASSOCIATION FOR MARINE SCIENCE

Acronym or abbreviation: SAMS

Scottish Marine Institute, Oban, Argyll, PA37 1QA

Tel: 01631 559000
Fax: 01631 559001
E-mail: info@sams.ac.uk

Website:
http://www.sams.ac.uk

Enquiries:
Enquiries to: Communications officer
Direct e-mail: laila.sadler@sams.ac.uk
Other contacts: Head of Communications

Founded:
1884

Carries out the functions of the former:
Dunstaffnage Marine Laboratory (year of change 2000)

Formerly called:
Scottish Marine Biological Association (year of change 1992)

Organisation type and purpose:
Research and higher education provision in marine science for sustainable seas; learned society; own research vessels, research aquaria, laboratories and advanced sampling and analytical equipment.

Subject coverage:
Marine science; Arctic research; marine renewable energy; marine processes and climate; industrial impacts on oceans; prosperity from marine ecosystems; aquaculture; marine spatial planning; marine biotechnology; fisheries; marine technology; scientific diving;

Museum or gallery collection, archive, or library special collection:
Research library with historic collection; culture collection of algae and protozoa; Scottish Ocean Explorer Centre (under development)

Non-library collection catalogue:
All or part available online and in-house

Library catalogue:
All or part available in-house

Printed publications:
Technical reports on project research work undertaken
Annual reports
Ocean Explorer newsletter

Electronic and video publications:
Some videos

Publications list:
Available online and in print

Access to staff:
Contact by letter, by telephone, by fax, by e-mail and via website. Appointment necessary.
Hours: Mon to Fri, 0900 to 1700

Access to building, collection or gallery:
Prior appointment required

Access for disabled people:
Ramped entry, toilet facilities; lift to upper floors

Links with:
Natural Environment Research Council
Polaris House, North Star Avenue, Swindon, SN2 1EU; tel: 01793 411500; fax: 01793 411501; website: http://www.nerc.ac.uk

Member organisation of:
UHI Millennium Institute
Executive Office, Ness Walk, Inverness, IV3 5SQ; tel: 01463 279000; website: http://www.uhi.ac.uk

SCOTTISH ASSOCIATION FOR PUBLIC TRANSPORT

Acronym or abbreviation: SAPT

11 Queen's Crescent, Glasgow, G4 9BL

Tel: 07760 381729
E-mail: sapt@btinternet.com

Website:
http://www.sapt.org.uk

Enquiries:
Enquiries to: Secretary

Founded:
1962

Formerly called:
Scottish Railway Development Association (SRDA) (year of change 1972)

Organisation type and purpose:
National organisation, membership association (membership is by subscription), present number of members: 150, voluntary organisation.
National organisation (Scotland).
Supporting public transport and environmental improvement.

Subject coverage:
All modes of public transport in Scotland; policy and finance; transport-related environmental issues.

Printed publications:
Annual Report, Scottish Transport Matters (quarterly)
Newsletter (quarterly)
Study papers

Access to staff:
Contact by letter, by telephone and by e-mail

Hours: Mon to Fri, 0900 to 1700

Member organisation of:
Campaign for Better Transport
Environmental Transport Association
TRANSform Scotland
  tel: 0131 467 7714; fax: 0131 554 8656; e-mail:
  campaigns@transformscotland.org.uk

SCOTTISH ATHLETICS LIMITED

Caledonia House, Redheughs Rigg, South Gyle,
Edinburgh, EH12 9DQ

Tel: 0131 317 7320
Fax: 0131 317 7321
E-mail: admin@scottishathletics.org.uk

Website:
http://www.scottishathletics.org.uk

Enquiries:
Enquiries to: General Manager
Other contacts: Press Officer for media relations

Founded:
1992

Formerly called:
Scottish Athletics Federation (SAF) (year of change
2000)

Incorporates the former:
Scottish Amateur Athletics Federation (SAAF),
Scottish Womens Amateur Athletics Federation
(SWAAF)

Organisation type and purpose:
Membership association (membership is by
subscription), present number of members: 6,500,
voluntary organisation, national sports governing
body.
Management, promotion and development of
athletics in Scotland.

Subject coverage:
Track and field athletics, hill, road and cross-
country running, Scottish heavy events, athletics
development packages and support from 5 years
upwards, coaching courses and examinations.

**Museum or gallery collection, archive, or library
special collection:**
Athletics memorabilia

Printed publications:
Awards booklets
Information leaflet and packs
Membership information
Newsletter (4 times a year, members only)

Access to staff:
Contact by letter, by telephone, by fax, by e-mail
and via website. Appointment necessary.
Hours: Mon to Fri, 0900 to 1700

Affiliated to:
Commonwealth Games Council for Scotland
  tel: 0131 336 1924
UK Athletics
  tel: 0121 456 5098; fax: 0121 456 4998

SCOTTISH BIBLE SOCIETY

7 Hampton Terrace, Edinburgh, EH12 5XU

Tel: 0131 337 9701
Fax: 0131 337 0641
E-mail: colin.hay@scottishbiblesociety.org

Website:
http://www.scottishbiblesociety.org

Enquiries:
Enquiries to: Chief Executive
Direct e-mail: elaine.duncan@scottishbiblesociety
.org

Founded:
1809

Formerly called:
National Bible Society of Scotland (year of change
2000)

Organisation type and purpose:
Registered charity (charity number SCO10767)

Non-library collection catalogue:
All or part available online and in print

Printed publications:
Catalogue
Word at Work (magazine)
Read and Pray around the World

Publications list:
Available in print

Access to staff:
Contact by letter, by telephone, by fax and by e-
mail
Hours: Mon to Fri, 0900 to 1700

SCOTTISH BORDERS COUNCIL

Acronym or abbreviation: SBC

Council Headquarters, Newtown St Boswells,
Melrose, Roxburghshire, TD6 0SA

Tel: 01835 824000
Fax: 01835 825001
E-mail: enquiries@scotborders.gov.uk

Website:
http://www.scotborders.org.uk.
Information on all aspects of the Scottish Borders
http://www.scotborders.gov.uk
Information about Scottish Borders Council

Enquiries:
Enquiries to: Head of Communications
Direct tel: 01835 825008
Direct fax: 01825 825059

Founded:
1996

Formed from reorganisation of:
Berwickshire District Council, Borders Regional
Council, Ettrick and Lauderdale District Council,
Roxburgh District Council, Tweeddale District
Council (year of change 1996)

Organisation type and purpose:
Local government body.

Subject coverage:
Services and amenities; corporate services,
education, environmental services, finance,
housing, legal services, personnel services,
planning development and tourism, property and
technical services, roads and transportation, social
services, council tax and other payments,
registration of births, death and marriages, leisure
and recreation, cleansing, environmental health
and trading standards.

Access to staff:
Contact by letter, by telephone, by fax, by e-mail,
in person and via website
Hours: Mon to Thu, 0845 to 1700; Fri, 0845 to 1545

Access for disabled people:
Parking provided, ramped entry, access to all
public areas

SCOTTISH BOWLING ASSOCIATION

Acronym or abbreviation: SBA

National Centre for Bowling, Northfield, Hunters
Avenue, Ayr, KA8 9BL

Tel: 01292 294623
Fax: 01292 294623

Enquiries:
Enquiries to: Secretary

Founded:
1892

Organisation type and purpose:
Membership association.
National Association controlling the level green
game of lawn bowls.

Subject coverage:
All matters relative to level green lawn bowls.

Printed publications:
Bowls for Beginners
Laws of the Game
Newsletter (annually, for clubs)
Year Book (annually)

Access to staff:
Contact by letter, by telephone, by fax and in
person
Hours: Mon to Fri, 0900 to 1630

Associated to:
British Isles Bowls Council (BIBC)
World Bowls Board (WBB)

SCOTTISH BRAILLE PRESS

Craigmillar Park, Edinburgh, EH16 5NB

Tel: 0131 662 4445
Fax: 0131 662 1968
E-mail: info.sbp@royalblind.org

Website:
http://www.royalblind.org

Enquiries:
Enquiries to: Customer Service

Founded:
1881

Organisation type and purpose:
Voluntary organisation, registered charity (charity
number SC 017167), publishing house.
Printers and publishers of Braille, and suppliers of
audio, large-print material, tactile diagrams and
material on disk.

Subject coverage:
Publishing literature and educational textbooks in
Braille, audio and large print.

Non-library collection catalogue:
All or part available online and in print

Printed publications:
A number of weekly and monthly magazines
Publications list is also available in braille
Large selection of books available for purchase,
  direct, including:
Adult fiction
Catalogue of Braille books
Catalogue of Braille magazines
Children's fiction
Educational texts
Homecraft
Music and musical literature
Religion

Electronic and video publications:
CD-ROM

Publications list:
Available online and in print

Access to staff:
Contact by letter, by telephone, by fax, by e-mail,
in person and via website
Hours: Mon to Thu, 0830 to 1630; Fri, 0830 to 1300

Access to building, collection or gallery:
No prior appointment required

Access for disabled people:
Parking provided, ramped entry, access to all
public areas, toilet facilities

Associated with:
Royal Blind Asylum and School

SCOTTISH BREAST CANCER CAMPAIGN

Acronym or abbreviation: SBCC

PO Box 26191, Dunfermline, Fife, KY11 3YG

Tel: 0131 623 0037
Fax: 0131 623 0037
E-mail: enquiries@scottishbreastcancercampaign
.org

Website:
http://www.scottishbreastcancercampaign.org

continued overleaf

Includes information on activities, latest newsletter, merchandise for fundraising.

Enquiries:
Enquiries to: Convener
Direct tel: 07955 170284
Direct e-mail: info@scottishbreastcancercampaign.org
Other contacts: Board member (for general enquiries)

Founded:
1993

Organisation type and purpose:
Membership association (membership is by subscription), present number of members: 100.
Pressure group and support group.

Subject coverage:
Breast cancer services in Scotland.
Campaign for increased state resources for treatment and care for patients and their families and partners, research into the causes (including environmental factors), development and treatment, counselling, and the promotion of local self-help groups.

Printed publications:
Annual Report
News-sheet (4 times a year)
Occasional leaflets

Access to staff:
Contact by letter, by fax, by e-mail and via website
Hours: No office, contact should be made as indicated

SCOTTISH BUILDING

Acronym or abbreviation: SBEF

Crichton House, 4 Crichton's Close, Holyrood, Edinburgh, EH8 8DT

Tel: 0131 556 8866
Fax: 0131 558 5247
E-mail: info@scottish-building.co.uk

Website:
http://www.scottish-building.co.uk

Enquiries:
Enquiries to: Communications and Marketing Manager
Direct e-mail: lynsey@scottish-building.co.uk

Formerly called:
Scottish Building Employers' Federation (SBEF) (year of change 2000)

Organisation type and purpose:
Trade association.

Subject coverage:
Building construction industry, legislation and contracts, education and training, single market, health and safety, industrial relations, technical, environmental.

Printed publications:
Bulletin (fortnightly, members and subscribers)
Building Matters (quarterly)
Directory of Members
Memoranda on specific subjects

Publications list:
Available online and in print

Access to staff:
Contact by letter, by telephone, by fax and by e-mail
Hours: Mon to Thu, 0900 to 1700; Fri, 0900 to 1630

Access to building, collection or gallery:
Prior appointment required

Access for disabled people:
Parking provided, ramped entry, toilet facilities

Affiliated to:
Building Employers' Confederation
Building Guarantee Scheme (Scottish Administration)

SCOTTISH BUSINESS INFORMATION SERVICE

Acronym or abbreviation: SCOTBIS

National Library of Scotland, George IV Bridge, Edinburgh, EH1 1EW

Tel: 0131 623 3818
Fax: 0131 623 3809
E-mail: enquiries@scotbis.com

Website:
http://www.scotbis.com
Provides a guide to the resources and services available from the Scottish Business Information Service.

Enquiries:
Enquiries to: Senior Assistant Librarian, Business Information

Founded:
1989

Organisation type and purpose:
National organisation.
National business information service.

Subject coverage:
Business information, company information, market research, statistics, news information, business journals, remote access to business databases for Scottish residents.

Trade and statistical information:
Extensive industry and trade data held.

Non-library collection catalogue:
All or part available online and in-house

Library catalogue:
All or part available online and in-house

Access to staff:
Contact by letter, by telephone, by fax, by e-mail, in person and via website
Hours: Mon, Tue, Thu, Fri, 0930 to 1700; Wed, 1000 to 1700.
Special comments: Access to business resources in person available via the General Reading Room of the National Library of Scotland.

Also at:
National Library of Scotland
George IV Bridge, Edinburgh, EH1 1EW

SCOTTISH CANOE ASSOCIATION

Acronym or abbreviation: SCA

Caledonia House, South Gyle, Edinburgh, EH12 9DQ

Tel: 0131 317 7314
Fax: 0131 317 7319
E-mail: general.office@canoescotland.com

Website:
http://www.scot-canoe.org
General on sport.

Enquiries:
Enquiries to: Administrator

Founded:
1939

Organisation type and purpose:
Membership association (membership is by subscription), voluntary organisation.
Governing body of the sport.

Subject coverage:
Canoeing.

Non-library collection catalogue:
All or part available online

Printed publications:
Scottish Whitewater (£15.95)
Scottish Canoe Touring (£14.95)

Access to staff:
Contact by letter, by fax, by e-mail and via website
Hours: Mon to Fri, 0830 to 1330

Federal agreement with:
British Canoe Union
tel: 0115 982 1100
Canoe Association for Northern Ireland
Welsh Canoeing Association

SCOTTISH CENTRE FOR CHILDREN WITH MOTOR IMPAIRMENTS

Acronym or abbreviation: SCCMI

Craighalbert Centre, 1 Craighalbert Way, Cumbernauld, Strathclyde, G68 0LS

Tel: 01236 456100
Fax: 01236 736889
E-mail: sccmi@craighalbert.org.uk

Website:
http://www.craighalbert.org.uk

Enquiries:
Enquiries to: Director
Other contacts: Administrative Officer

Founded:
1991

Organisation type and purpose:
Registered charity (charity number SC 008428), suitable for ages: 0–8.
Special needs school.

Subject coverage:
Children with motor impairments.

Access to staff:
Contact by letter, by telephone, by fax and by e-mail. Appointment necessary.
Hours: Mon to Thu, 0830 to 1700; Fri, 0830 to 1600

Access for disabled people:
Fully accessible

SCOTTISH CHAMBER ORCHESTRA LIMITED

Acronym or abbreviation: SCO

4 Royal Terrace, Edinburgh, EH7 5AB

Tel: 0131 557 6800
Fax: 0131 557 6933
E-mail: info@sco.org.uk

Website:
http://www.sco.org.uk

Enquiries:
Enquiries to: Finance Director
Direct tel: 0131 478 8345
Direct e-mail: les@sco.org.uk

Founded:
1974

Created by the merger of:
Scottish Baroque Ensemble, Scottish Philharmonia Society (year of change 1981)

Organisation type and purpose:
Professional body (membership is by election or invitation), registered charity (charity number SCO 15039), company limited by guarantee.
To promote interest in and appreciation of classical music throughout Scotland.

Subject coverage:
Orchestral music.

Printed publications:
Brochure
Concerts in Scotland
Recordings catalogue

Electronic and video publications:
Discography

Publications list:
Available online

Access to staff:
Contact by letter, by e-mail and via website
Hours: Mon to Fri, 0930 to 1730

SCOTTISH CHILD LAW CENTRE

Acronym or abbreviation: SCLC

54 East Cross Causeway, Edinburgh, EH8 9HD

Tel: 0131 667 6333
Fax: 0131 662 1713
E-mail: enquiries@sclc.org.uk

Enquiries:
Enquiries to: Administrator
Other contacts: Director

Founded:
1988

Organisation type and purpose:
National organisation, membership association
(membership is by subscription), present number
of members: 350, registered charity, training
organisation. Advice service, provides training and
publications.

Subject coverage:
All aspects of law relating to children and young
people in Scotland up to age 18; family, childcare,
abduction and education law, divorce, residence,
contact, children's rights, youth offenders and
access to files.

Printed publications:
Various leaflets
Fact Sheet Pack
SCLC's Guide to the Children (Scotland) Act 1995
  (£10)
At What Age Can I Go To See The Doctor? (50p)
Your Views in Court (50p)
Young People and Alcohol (50p)
ASBOs (50p)
Police Power (50p)
What Happens if I am Taken to the Police Station
  (50p)

Publications list:
Available in print

Access to staff:
Contact by letter, by telephone, by fax and by e-
mail
Hours: Mon to Fri, 0930 to 1600

Access to building, collection or gallery:
No access other than to staff

SCOTTISH CHRISTIAN ALLIANCE LTD

3 Nethercairn Place, Newton Mearns, Glasgow,
G77 5SZ

Tel: 0141 571 3804
E-mail: the.director@scottishchristianalliance.org

Enquiries:
Enquiries to: Director

Founded:
1993

Formerly called:
Christian Alliance (Scotland) Ltd

Incorporates the former:
YWCA of Scotland; Keychange Scotland Ltd (year
of change 1997)

Organisation type and purpose:
Voluntary organisation, Scottish charity registered
with OSCR and relevant local projects, registered
with Care Commission.

Subject coverage:
Provision of housing support services.

Printed publications:
Annual Report
Newsletters
Publicity material

Access to staff:
Contact by letter, by telephone and by e-mail
Hours: Mon to Fri, 0900 to 1700

SCOTTISH CHURCH HISTORY SOCIETY

Acronym or abbreviation: SCHS

16 Murrayburn Park, Edingburgh, EH14 2PX

Tel: 0131 442 3772
E-mail: virginia.russell@uas.gov.uk

Enquiries:
Enquiries to: Honorary Secretary

Founded:
1922

Organisation type and purpose:
Learned society.

Subject coverage:
History of the Church in Scotland.

Printed publications:
Records (annually)
Select Critical Bibliographies

Access to staff:
Contact by letter and by e-mail
Hours: Mon to Fri, 0900 to 1700

SCOTTISH COMMUNITY DRAMA ASSOCIATION

Acronym or abbreviation: SCDA

5 York Place, Edinburgh, EH1 3EB

Tel: 0131 557 5552
Fax: 0131 557 5552
E-mail: headquarters@scda.org.uk

Website:
http://www.scda.org.uk
History of the association. Services available.
What's on around Scotland.

Enquiries:
Enquiries to: Administrative Assistant
Other contacts: Chairman for information on
website.

Founded:
1926

Organisation type and purpose:
Membership association, registered charity
(charity number SC021397), training organisation.
Promotes all aspects of amateur/community
theatre in Scotland. Open to all amateur clubs and
interested individuals.

Subject coverage:
Information on all theatre arts, related subjects,
details of theatre libraries for hire of scripts, theatre
arts for the amateur in Scotland. Professional
assistance with amateur productions, workshops
etc.

**Museum or gallery collection, archive, or library
special collection:**
Five libraries of play scripts situated in major cities
  in Scotland

Non-library collection catalogue:
All or part available in-house

Printed publications:
Scene (house magazine, quarterly, free to members,
  non-members £1)

Access to staff:
Contact by letter, by telephone, by fax, by e-mail,
in person and via website
Hours: Mon, 0900 to 1700; Tue, Fri, 1300 to 1700;
Wed, 1000 to 1200 and 1300 to 1700; Thu, 1000 to
1200

Affiliated to:
Central Council for Amateur Theatre
International Amateur Theatre Association

SCOTTISH CONSERVATION BUREAU

Room G20, Longmore House, Salisbury Place,
Edinburgh, EH9 1SH

Tel: 0131 668 8668
Fax: 0131 668 8669
E-mail: hs.conservation.bureau@scotland.gov.uk

Enquiries:
Enquiries to: Bureau Manager

Founded:
1980

Organisation type and purpose:
National government body.
To provide information, advice and support to
those concerned with the conservation of historic
artefacts and cultural property in Scotland.

Subject coverage:
Conservation of historic objects and buildings in
Scotland, careers in conservation, technical
information on conservation.

**Museum or gallery collection, archive, or library
special collection:**
Database of careers information
Database of restorers and conservators working in
  Scotland
Database of suppliers of conservation materials
Library of conservation books, videos,
  photographic material, samples

Library catalogue:
All or part available in-house

Printed publications:
Architects in Conservation (together with RIAS)
Books on stonecleaning
Conservation publications on:
Repair of Historic Buildings in Scotland (£9)
Scottish Conservation Bureau leaflet (free)
Scottish Conservation Handbook (£2.50)
Technical Advice Notes (13 titles, various prices)
Working in Conservation/Training in Conservation
  (£5)

Publications list:
Available in print

Access to staff:
Contact by letter, by telephone, by fax and by e-
mail. Appointment necessary.
Hours: Mon to Fri, 0900 to 1700

Part of:
Historic Scotland

SCOTTISH CONSERVATIVE PARTY

Acronym or abbreviation: SCUP

83 Princes Street, Edinburgh, EH2 2ER

Tel: 0131 247 6890
Fax: 0131 247 6891
E-mail: info@scottishconservatives.com

Enquiries:
Enquiries to: Chairman

Organisation type and purpose:
Advisory body, membership association
(membership is by subscription).
Political organisation.

Subject coverage:
Scottish Conservative Party: history, organisation,
membership, statements, policies.

Access to staff:
Contact by letter, by telephone, by fax and by e-
mail. Appointment necessary.
Hours: Mon to Fri, 0900 to 1700

SCOTTISH COT DEATH TRUST

Acronym or abbreviation: SCDT

Royal Hospital for Sick Children, Yorkhill,
Glasgow, G3 8SJ

Tel: 0141 357 3946
Fax: 0141 334 1376
E-mail: contact@sidscotland.org.uk

Website:
http://www.sidscotland.org.uk

continued overleaf

Enquiries:
Enquiries to: Executive Director

Founded:
1985

Organisation type and purpose:
Registered charity (charity number SCO 03458).

Subject coverage:
Bereavement after cot death, advice on reducing the risks of cot death, information on cot death research.

Education services:
Training for health professionals

Printed publications:
Newsletter (2 times a year)
Information leaflets are available for parents, funeral directors, police officers, health visitors, doctors and the public (free)
Facts about Cot Death

Access to staff:
Contact by letter, by telephone, by fax and by e-mail
Hours: Mon to Thu, 0900 to 1700; Fri, 0900 to 1600

Access for disabled people:
Parking provided, ramped entry

Links with:
SIDS International

SCOTTISH COUNCIL FOR SINGLE HOMELESS

Acronym or abbreviation: SCSH

Wellgate House, 200 Cowgate, Edinburgh, EH1 1NQ

Tel: 0131 226 4382
Fax: 0131 225 4382
E-mail: admin@scsh.org.uk

Website:
http://www.scsh.co.uk
General.

Enquiries:
Enquiries to: Director
Direct e-mail: robert@scsh.org.uk

Founded:
1974

Organisation type and purpose:
Voluntary organisation.
To highlight needs of homeless people, including young people, and offer practical ideas and information to tackle homelessness.

Subject coverage:
Homelessness, benefits, community care, housing, education.

Printed publications:
Streets Ahead (guide for young people)
My Space My Place (young person's guide)
My Space My Place (workers toolkit)
Moving towards independence (the carer's guide)
I'd like to go to college (access to further education)
But what about me? (stock transfer and homelessness)

Publications list:
Available online and in print

Access to staff:
Contact by letter, by telephone, by fax, by e-mail and via website. Appointment necessary.
Hours: Mon to Fri, 0900 to 1700
Special comments: Top floor office, lift available.

SCOTTISH COUNCIL FOR VOLUNTARY ORGANISATIONS

Acronym or abbreviation: SCVO

Mansfield Traquair Centre, 15 Mansfield Place, Edinburgh, EH3 6BB

Tel: 0131 556 3882
Fax: 0131 556 0279
E-mail: enquiries@scvo.org.uk

Website:
http://www.scvo.org.uk

Enquiries:
Enquiries to: Information Service
Direct tel: 0800 169 0022

Founded:
1943

Organisation type and purpose:
Voluntary organisation, recognised Scottish charity (charity number SC003558).

Subject coverage:
Weekly news and current affairs, research, policy and lobbying, conferences and seminars, training courses, information and publications, computer software, office supplies, payroll bureau, pensions, insurance for the sector, project development, Charity Giving Scotland and Give As You Earn, and direct links with Councils for Voluntary Service and national networks.

Printed publications:
Directories, reports, statistics, handbooks, policy papers, workpacks, consultative documents, etc.
Third Force News (weekly)

Publications list:
Available online and in print

Access to staff:
Contact by letter, by telephone, by fax, by e-mail, in person and via website. Appointment necessary.
Hours: Mon to Fri, 1000 to 1600

Access for disabled people:
Fully accessible

SCOTTISH COUNCIL OF INDEPENDENT SCHOOLS

Acronym or abbreviation: SCIS

21 Melville Street, Edinburgh, EH3 7PE

Tel: 0131 220 2106
Fax: 0131 225 8594
E-mail: information@scis.org.uk

Website:
http://www.scis.org.uk
Information for parents, public and press on independent, fee-paying schools in Scotland, including profiles of all member schools.

Enquiries:
Enquiries to: Director

Founded:
1990

Organisation type and purpose:
Advisory body, membership association (membership is by qualification), present number of members: 80 schools, registered charity (charity number SC 018033), suitable for ages: 2 to 18, consultancy.
Key aims are to: provide information, advice and guidance to parents; advance education via curriculum development and the training of teachers; advise member schools and their governing bodies about educational developments and legislation affecting independent schools (e.g. education, taxation, welfare, health and safety); and to communicate and negotiate with the Scottish Parliament, the Government, public and private bodies on behalf of the independent sector.

Trade and statistical information:
Information and data on independent schools in Scotland.

Library catalogue:
All or part available in-house

Printed publications:
Directory of Independent Schools in Scotland (annual, free)
Scottish Independent Schools' Exam Results (free)
What is SCIS? (leaflet, free)
Questions to Consider When Visiting a School (free)
A Guide to the Admissions Process (free)
Boarding Schools in Scotland (free)

Meeting the Cost of School Fees (free)

Publications list:
Available online and in print

Access to staff:
Contact by letter, by telephone, by fax, by e-mail, in person and via website. Appointment necessary.
Hours: Mon to Fri, 0900 to 1700

SCOTTISH COUNCIL ON DEAFNESS

Acronym or abbreviation: SCoD

Suite 62, 1st Floor, Central Chambers, 93 Hope Street, Glasgow, G2 6LD

Tel: 0141 248 2474; textphone: 0141 248 2477
Fax: 0141 248 2479
E-mail: admin@scod.org.uk

Website:
http://www.scod.org.uk

Enquiries:
Enquiries to: Information Officer

Founded:
1927

Organisation type and purpose:
Registered charity (charity number SC016957), organisation for deaf issues in Scotland, represents 90 organisations working with and on behalf of deaf sign language users, deafened, deafblind and hard of hearing people. The membership provides an effective working partnership between the voluntary sector, social work and education departments, NHS Trusts, health boards and the Government.

Subject coverage:
All aspects of deafness, e.g. deaf sign language users, hard of hearing, deafened, deafblind, agencies for deaf people, employment, voluntary help, advice and information.

Printed publications:
Annual Report
History
Range of leaflets
Scottish Directory of Relevant Service Providers

Publications list:
Available online and in print

Access to staff:
Contact by letter, by telephone, by fax, by e-mail, in person and via website. Appointment necessary.
Hours: Mon to Fri, 0900 to 1600

Links with:
organisations working with deaf, hard of hearing and deafblind people.

SCOTTISH CRICKET UNION

Acronym or abbreviation: SCU

National Cricket Academy, MES Sports Centre, Ravelston, Edinburgh, EH4 3NT

Tel: 0131 313 7420
Fax: 0131 313 7430
E-mail: admin.scu@btinternet.com

Website:
http://www.scu.org.uk
General information and results service on Scottish cricket.
http://www.btinternet.com/~sncl
Scottish National Cricket League: results and league tables.

Enquiries:
Enquiries to: Chief Executive

Founded:
1909

Organisation type and purpose:
National government body, advisory body (membership is by subscription), present number of members: 800 members, 168 clubs, training organisation, consultancy.

Governing body of cricket in Scotland.

Subject coverage:
Scottish cricket at domestic and international level.

Printed publications:
Newsletter (annually, free)
SCU coaching cards (£10)
The guide to Scottish cricket (annually, £6)

Access to staff:
Contact by letter, by telephone, by fax, by e-mail
and in person
Hours: Mon to Fri, 0900 to 1700

Affiliated to:
International Cricket Council

SCOTTISH CROP RESEARCH INSTITUTE

Acronym or abbreviation: SCRI

Mylnefield, Invergowrie, Dundee, DD2 5DA

Tel: 01382 562731
Fax: 01382 562426
E-mail: library@scri.ac.uk

Website:
http://www.scri.ac.uk

Enquiries:
Enquiries to: Librarian

Founded:
1922

Organisation type and purpose:
Learned society, registered charity (charity number
SCO 11854), research organisation.

Subject coverage:
All facets of crop research in the northern
hemisphere, plant genetics and breeding, plant
biotechnology and molecular biology, plant
physiology and agronomy, plant pathology and
crop protection, biochemistry and plant analyses,
biomathematics, potatoes, barley and soft fruit,
biodiversity and sustainability in managed arable
ecosystems.

**Museum or gallery collection, archive, or library
special collection:**
Pethybridge Collection on potato pathology, 1870–
1930
Special collections of research literature on
raspberries and potatoes now closed

Library catalogue:
All or part available in-house

Printed publications:
Annual Report

Access to staff:
Appointment necessary.
Hours: Mon to Fri, 0900 to 1700

Constituent part of:
Scottish Research Institutes

Funded by:
Scottish Government

SCOTTISH CULTURAL PRESS & SCOTTISH CHILDREN'S PRESS

Acronym or abbreviation: SCP

Unit 6, Newbattle Abbey Business Park, Newbattle
Road, Dalkeith, Midlothian, EH22 3LJ

Tel: 0131 660 6366
Fax: 0870 285 4846
E-mail: info@scottishbooks.com

Website:
http://www.scottishbooks.com
Publication list.

Enquiries:
Direct tel: 0131 660 4666

Founded:
1992

Organisation type and purpose:
Publisher.

Subject coverage:
Children's Scottish fiction and non-fiction
including history, literature, poetry, environmental
history, biography, Scottish language and folk
tradition.

Printed publications:
Ally Frazer Stories, a selection of historical
adventures (Cameron I, £3.99)
Columba: Iona & the Spread of Christianity
(MacLaverty B, £2.99)
Discover Scotland's History: guide to Scottish
history for children (Cameron A D, £12.99)
Selection of fiction, poetry and children's writing
Selection of Scots language books
Teach the Bairns to Cook: Traditional Scottish
Recipes (Ashworth L, £5.95)
Touching the Past Archaeology 5–14 (Curtis N & E
ed, £4.95)
Order printed publications from: tel: 0131 660 4666;
fax: 0870 285 4846

Publications list:
Available online

Access to staff:
Contact by letter, by telephone, by fax, by e-mail
and via website. Appointment necessary.
Hours: No fixed hours – by appointment only

Access to building, collection or gallery:
No access other than to staff

SCOTTISH CYCLING

Acronym or abbreviation: SC

The Velodrome, London Road, Edinburgh, EH7
6AD

Tel: 0131 652 0187
E-mail: info@scottishcycling.com

Website:
http://www.scottishcycling.com

Enquiries:
Enquiries to: Administrator
Direct e-mail: jackie.davidson@scottishcycling.com

Founded:
1889

Organisation type and purpose:
Membership association (membership is by
subscription), present number of members: 2000.
Governing body for cycle sport in Scotland.

Subject coverage:
Cycle sport, road racing, mountain biking, track
racing, time trialing, cyclo cross, coaching.

Printed publications:
Handbook (annually, £7.50)

Publications list:
Available in print

Access to staff:
Contact by letter, by telephone, by e-mail, in
person and via website. Appointment necessary.
Hours: Mon to Fri, 0900 to 1700

Member of:
British Cycling (BC)
National Cycling Centre, Stuart Street,
Manchester, M11 4DQ; tel: 0870 871 2000; e-mail:
info@britishcycling.org

SCOTTISH DANCE TEACHERS' ALLIANCE

Acronym or abbreviation: SDTA

101 Park Road, Glasgow, G4 9JE

Tel: 0141 339 8944
Fax: 0141 357 4994
E-mail: sdta@btconnect.com

Enquiries:
Enquiries to: Executive Secretary

Founded:
1934

Organisation type and purpose:
International organisation, professional body
(membership is by qualification).

Subject coverage:
Highland, ballet, theatre, ballroom, Latin
American Baton, rock 'n roll, disco dancing, line
dancing and cheer dance.

Printed publications:
SOBHD Text Book
Syllabi and textbooks for all branches of dancing

Electronic and video publications:
Tape/disc/video for purchase directly

Access to staff:
Contact by letter, by telephone, by fax and by e-
mail
Hours: Mon to Fri, 0900 to 1700

Access to building, collection or gallery:
No access other than to staff, no prior appointment
required

Access for disabled people:
Parking provided, ramped entry, level entry, toilet
facilities

Links with:
SOBHD and BCD/WD&DSC

SCOTTISH DECORATORS FEDERATION

Acronym or abbreviation: SDF

Castlecraig Business Park, Players Road, Stirling,
FK7 7SH

Tel: 01786 448838
Fax: 01786 450541
E-mail: info@scottishdecorators.co.uk

Website:
http://www.scottishdecorators.co.uk

Enquiries:
Enquiries to: Chief Executive

Founded:
1878

Organisation type and purpose:
Trade association (membership is by qualification),
service industry.

Subject coverage:
Painting and decorating.

**Museum or gallery collection, archive, or library
special collection:**
Historical collection

Printed publications:
Newsletters
Year Book

Access to staff:
Contact by letter, by telephone and by fax
Hours: Mon to Fri, 0900 to 1700

Member of:
National Specialist Contractors Council (NSCC)

SCOTTISH DEVELOPMENT INTERNATIONAL

Acronym or abbreviation: SDI

150 Broomielaw, Glasgow, G2 8LU

Tel: 0141 228 2828
E-mail: michelle.cowan@scotent.co.uk

Website:
http://www.sdi.co.uk
Range of services.

Enquiries:
Enquiries to: Enquiry Fulfillment and Research
Service
Direct e-mail: investment@scotent.co.uk

Founded:
2001

continued overleaf

Formerly called:
Locate in Scotland (LIS), Scottish Trade
International (STI) (year of change 2001)

Organisation type and purpose:
International organisation.

Subject coverage:
SDI offers help and advice to companies looking
for the ideal investment location for their business
and provides a range of services for businesses
thinking about entering the overseas market.

Access to staff:
Contact by letter, by telephone, by e-mail and via
website
Hours: Mon to Fri, 0900 to 1700

International Offices:
Offices in Brussels, Düsseldorf, Italy, Paris, USA,
Tokyo, Seoul, Taipei, Singapore, China, India,
Russia, & UAE
SDI
  Dover House, Whitehall, London, SW1A 2AU;
  tel: 020 7839 2117; fax: 020 7839 2975

SCOTTISH DISABILITY SPORT

Acronym or abbreviation: SDS

Fife Sports Institute, Viewfield Road, Glenrothes,
Fife, KY6 2RB

Tel: 01592 415700
Fax: 01592 415710
E-mail: ssadsds@aol.com

Website:
http://www.scottishdisabilitysport.com

Enquiries:
Enquiries to: Administrator

Founded:
1962

Formerly called:
Scottish Sports Association for Disabled People
(SSAD)

Organisation type and purpose:
Voluntary organisation.

Subject coverage:
Sport and recreation for people with disabilities.

Transitional office:
Scottish Disability Sport
  Caledonian House, South Gyle, Edinburgh,
  EH12 9DQ; tel: 0131 317 1130; fax: 0131 317 1075;
  e-mail: ssadsds2@aol.com

SCOTTISH DRUGS FORUM

Acronym or abbreviation: SDF

91 Mitchell Street, Glasgow, G1 3LN

Tel: 0141 221 1175
Fax: 0141 248 6414
E-mail: enquiries@sdf.org.uk

Website:
http://www.sdf.org.uk

Enquiries:
Enquiries to: Information Officer
Other contacts: Regional Manager (for specific
drugs issues)

Founded:
1986

Organisation type and purpose:
Membership association (membership is by
subscription), voluntary organisation, registered
charity (charity number 106295).
National policy and information agency working
in partnership with others to co-ordinate effective
responses to drug use in Scotland.

Subject coverage:
Information on drugs issues, information about all
(national) drugs projects and groups in Scotland,
leaflets and brochures for anyone interested in
drugs issues.

Information services:
Library of material relevant to drug use in
Scotland.

Special visitor services:
Visits by appointment.

Printed publications:
SDF Bulletin (10 times a year, free to members,
  subscription rate for non-members)
Policy Statements (single copies free, charges for
  multiples)
Methadone at Work – guidance for employers
Methadone Leaflet
Order printed publications from: website publications
order form

Electronic and video publications:
Where to get help for a drug problem (online) at
  http://www.scottishdrugservices.com

Publications list:
Available online and in print

Access to staff:
Contact by letter, by telephone, by fax, by e-mail,
in person and via website. Appointment necessary.

Access to building, collection or gallery:
Hours: Mon to Fri, 0900 to 1700

Access for disabled people:
Lift is wheelchair accessible
Special comments: No disabled toilet.

Also at:
Scottish Drugs Forum
  139 Morrison Street, Edinburgh, EH3 8AJ; tel:
  0131 221 9300; fax: 0131 221 1556

SCOTTISH ENGINEERING

105 West George Street, Glasgow, G2 1QL

Tel: 0141 221 3181
Fax: 0141 204 1202
E-mail: consult@ScottishEngineering.org.uk

Website:
http://www.ScottishEngineering.org.uk

Enquiries:
Enquiries to: Secretary

Founded:
1865

Formerly called:
Scottish Engineering Employers' Association

Organisation type and purpose:
Advisory body, professional body (membership is
by subscription), present number of members: 400,
manufacturing industry, consultancy.

Subject coverage:
Employee relations; terms and conditions of
employment; employment law and industrial
tribunals; health and safety; training and
development.

Trade and statistical information:
Wage and salary surveys.

Printed publications:
Members Briefings
Quarterly Review

Access to staff:
Contact by letter, by telephone and by fax.
Appointment necessary. Non-members charged.
Hours: Mon to Fri, 0900 to 1700

Links with:
Engineering Employers' Federation

SCOTTISH ENTERPRISE

Acronym or abbreviation: SE

Atrium Court, 50 Waterloo St, Glasgow G2 6HQ

Tel: 0141 248 2700
Fax: 0141 221 3217
E-mail: network.helpline@scotent.co.uk

Website:
http://www.scottish-enterprise.com

Enquiries:
Enquiries to: Manager, Economic Research
Direct tel: 0141 228 2268
Direct e-mail: gail.rogers@scotent.co.uk

Founded:
1991

Formerly called:
Scottish Development Agency (SDA) (year of
change 1991)

Incorporates the former:
Scottish Development Agency, Training Agency

Organisation type and purpose:
National government body.
Economic development of Scotland.

Subject coverage:
Company data, market data, sectoral data,
economic data, county data, government
publications, in-house reports, strategic research,
economic research.

**Museum or gallery collection, archive, or library
special collection:**
Internally generated research

Library catalogue:
All or part available in-house

Access to staff:
Hours: Mon to Fri, 0900 to 1700

Access to building, collection or gallery:
No access other than to staff

SCOTTISH ENVIRONMENT LINK

Acronym or abbreviation: LINK

2 Grosvenor House, Shore Road, Perth, PH2 8BD

Tel: 01738 630804
Fax: 01738 643290
E-mail: enquiries@scotlink.org

Website:
http://www.scotlink.org
Home page.
http://www.scotlink.org/public/publications/
reports.php
Publications list.

Enquiries:
Enquiries to: Information Officer

Founded:
1987

Formerly called:
Scottish Wildlife and Countryside Link (SWCL)

Still known as:
Scottish LINK

Organisation type and purpose:
Membership association, Scottish company limited
by guarantee and without a share capital, and a
Scottish charity (number SC000296).
Voluntary organisations working together to care
for and improve Scotland's environment for people
and nature. Liaison body for 30 of the main
voluntary environmental organisations in
Scotland.

Subject coverage:
Environmental sustainability in Scotland.

Non-library collection catalogue:
All or part available online

Printed publications:
Publications on a variety of environmental issues,
  conference proceedings, reports, audits,
  campaign briefings

Publications list:
Available online and in print

Access to staff:
Contact by letter, by telephone, by fax, by e-mail
and via website
Hours: Mon to Fri, 0900 to 1600

SCOTTISH ENVIRONMENT PROTECTION AGENCY

Acronym or abbreviation: SEPA

Erskine Court, The Castle Business Park, Stirling, FK9 4TR

Tel: 01786 457700
Fax: 01786 446885
E-mail: enquiries@sepa.org.uk

Website:
http://www.sepa.org.uk

Enquiries:
Enquiries to: Information Scientist
Direct e-mail: alison.mackinnon@sepa.org
Other contacts: Press Officer for press enquiries.

Founded:
1996

Formed from:
Her Majesty's Industrial Pollution Inspectorate (HMIPI), The River Protection Boards (RPB) for Forth, Highland, North East, Solway, Tay, Tweed

Formerly called:
Clyde River Purification Board (RPB) (year of change 1996)

Organisation type and purpose:
Statutory body.

Subject coverage:
Environmental regulation, air quality, radioactive substances, water quality, pollution, sustainable development, compliance with EU environmental directives.

Museum or gallery collection, archive, or library special collection:
Environment
Scotland & Northern Ireland Forum on Environmental Research – library of publications: guidance document, statistics, air quality, water quality, radioactive substances
Organisation/Government reports
Legal information – environment

Trade and statistical information:
Statistics: bathing waters; water quality.

Non-library collection catalogue:
All or part available in-house

Library catalogue:
All or part available in-house

Printed publications:
Corporate & Environmental Reports
Information leaflets
Technical papers
Order printed publications from: Publications Officer

Publications list:
Available online

Access to staff:
Contact by telephone, by e-mail and via website. Appointment necessary.
Hours: Mon to Fri, 0900 to 1700

Access to building, collection or gallery:
Prior appointment required

Access for disabled people:
Level entry

Other offices:
SEPA North Region HQ
Graesser House, Fodderty Way, Dingwall, IV15 9XB; tel: 01349 862021
SEPA South East Region HQ
Clearwater House, Heriot Watt Research Park, Avenue North, Riccarton, Edinburgh, EH14 4AP; tel: 0131 449 7296
SEPA South West Region HQ
5 Redwood Crescent, Peel Park, East Kilbride, G74 5PP; tel: 01355 574200

SCOTTISH EXECUTIVE

Information Management Unit, Y Spur, Saughton House, Edinburgh, EH11 3XD

Tel: 0131 244 4556

Fax: 0131 244 4545
E-mail: selibrary@scotland.gsi.gov.uk

Website:
http://www.scotland.gov.uk

Enquiries:
Enquiries to: Information Officer
Direct e-mail: selibrary@scotland.gsi.gov.uk

Formerly called:
Scottish Office (year of change 1999)

Organisation type and purpose:
National government body.
Library and information service, serving the Scottish Executive.

Subject coverage:
Scottish administration, education, health, crime, police, prisons, social work, transport.

Non-library collection catalogue:
All or part available in-house

Library catalogue:
All or part available in-house

Printed publications:
The Scottish Executive Publications List
Order printed publications from: Astron or Blackwells Bookshop, Edinburgh

Publications list:
Available online and in print

Access to staff:
Appointment necessary.
Hours: Mon to Fri, 0900 to 1700

Access for disabled people:
Access to all public areas

SCOTTISH FEDERATION OF HOUSING ASSOCIATIONS LIMITED

Acronym or abbreviation: SFHA

38 York Place, Edinburgh, EH1 3HU

Tel: 0131 556 5777
Fax: 0131 557 6028
E-mail: sfha@sfha.co.uk

Website:
http://www.sfha.co.uk
Current news service, job-search service, information on membership, details of conferences, training, publications, links to related websites.

Enquiries:
Enquiries to: Administrator
Direct tel: 0131 473 6224
Direct e-mail: smorton@sfha.co.uk

Founded:
1976

Organisation type and purpose:
Trade association (membership is by subscription).
Representative body for Registered Social Landlords in Scotland.

Subject coverage:
Information on Scottish Registered Social Landlords, housing policy and practice.

Printed publications:
Briefing Papers on topics such as homelessness, community care, regenerating communities, legislation
Codes of Conduct
Housing Focus (journal, 10 times a year, annual subscription, free to members, £95 non-members)
Guidance Booklets on topics such as contracts for care, stock transfers guidance manual (also with computerised spreadsheet model), internal management plans, planned maintenance and repairs
Raising Standards series of best practice guidance
Model Agreements on tenancy, occupancy, leasing
SCORE (periodic reports, and annual digest)

Access to staff:
Contact by letter, by telephone, by fax, by e-mail and via website. Appointment necessary.
Hours: Mon to Fri, 0900 to 1700

Access to building, collection or gallery:
No access other than to staff

Access for disabled people:
Ramped entry
Special comments: Wheelchair lift (external).

Other addresses:
Scottish Federation of Housing Associations
24 Mauchline Place West, Dundee, DD4 8HS; tel: 01382 510656; fax: 01382 510990
Scottish Federation of Housing Associations
4th Floor, Pegasus House, 375 West George Street, Glasgow, G2 4LW; tel: 0141 332 8113; fax: 0141 332 9684

SCOTTISH FEDERATION OF SEA ANGLERS

Acronym or abbreviation: SFSA

Unit 6, Evans Business Centre, Mitchelston Drive, Mitchelston Industrial Estate, Kirkaldy, Fife, KY1 3NB

Tel: 01592 657520
Fax: 01592 657520

Website:
http://www.sfsa.freeserve.co.uk

Founded:
1961

Organisation type and purpose:
Membership association (membership is by subscription).
Recognised by Sportscotland as the governing body for the sport of sea fishing in Scotland.

Subject coverage:
Sea fishing.

Printed publications:
2006 Handbook (for purchase)

Access to staff:
Contact by letter, by telephone, by fax and in person. Appointment necessary.
Hours: Mon, Tue, Thu, Fri, 0930 to 1300

Links with:
Sea Angling Liaison Committee of Great Britain and Ireland (SALC)
tel: 0626 331 330

SCOTTISH FOOD AND DRINK FEDERATION

Acronym or abbreviation: SFDF

4A Torphichen Street, Edinburgh, EH3 8JQ

Tel: 0131 229 9415
Fax: 0131 229 9407
E-mail: flora.mclean@sfdf.org.uk

Website:
http://www.sfdf.org.uk

Enquiries:
Enquiries to: Director

Founded:
1999

Organisation type and purpose:
Trade association (membership is by subscription).

Subject coverage:
Primarily policy and regulation relating to food and drink manufacturing industry.

Printed publications:
website: http://www.sfdf.org.uk/sfdf/publications.aspx

Electronic and video publications:
website: http://www.sfdf.org.uk/sfdf/home.aspx

Access to staff:
Contact by letter, by telephone, by fax, by e-mail and via website. Appointment necessary.

continued overleaf

Hours: Mon to Fri, 0900 to 1700

Constituent part of:
Food and Drink Federation
Federation House, 6 Catherine Street, London
WC2B 5JJ; tel: 0207 836 2460; fax: 0207 836 0580;
website: http://www.fdf.org.uk

SCOTTISH FOOTBALL ASSOCIATION LIMITED

Acronym or abbreviation: SFA

Hampden Park, Glasgow, G42 9AY

Tel: 0141 616 6000
Fax: 0141 616 6001
E-mail: info@scottishfa.co.uk

Website:
http://www.scottishfa.co.uk

Enquiries:
Enquiries to: Chief Executive

Founded:
1873

Organisation type and purpose:
Governing body for football in Scotland.

Subject coverage:
Player registrations, the laws of the game,
coaching, refereeing, general and specific football
matters of public interest.

**Museum or gallery collection, archive, or library
special collection:**
Old documents, minute books, etc. are now
housed in the Scottish Football Museum at
Hampden Park
Various football trophies and mementos

Printed publications:
SFA Annual Report (free)
SFA Handbook (annually, £12 inc. p&p)

Electronic and video publications:
Various coaching videos (available via football
development department)

Access to staff:
Contact by letter, by telephone, by fax and by e-
mail
Hours: Mon to Fri, 0900 to 1700

Member organisation of:
Fédération Internationale de Football Association
(FIFA)
Union Des Associations Européennes de Football
(UEFA)

SCOTTISH FOOTBALL LEAGUE, THE

Acronym or abbreviation: SFL

Hampden Park, Glasgow, G42 9EB

Tel: 0141 620 4160
Fax: 0141 620 4161
E-mail: info@scottishfootballleague.com

Enquiries:
Enquiries to: Secretary

Founded:
1890

Subject coverage:
Administration, marketing, promotion, fostering
and development of association football, especially
via the SFL championship, league cup, and league
challenge cup competitions.

**Museum or gallery collection, archive, or library
special collection:**
Minute Books 1890–2006
Registration Books 1898–2006
SFL results, appearances, attendances, etc
Various historical documents pertaining to
association football

Printed publications:
Scottish Football League Fixture Booklet (annually)
Scottish Football League Handbook (annually)
The Scottish Football League Review (annually)

Access to staff:
Contact by letter, by telephone and by fax
Hours: Mon to Fri, 0900 to 1700; Sat, 0930 to 1200

SCOTTISH FUNDING COUNCIL

Formal name: Scottish Further and Higher
Education Funding Council
Acronym or abbreviation: SFC

Donaldson House, 97 Haymarket Terrace,
Edinburgh, EH12 5HD

Tel: 0131 313 6500
Fax: 0131 313 6501
E-mail: info@sfc.ac.uk

Website:
http://www.sfc.ac.uk
Circulars, council and committee papers, news
releases, statistics, guidance, etc.

Enquiries:
Enquiries to: Head of Communications
Direct tel: 0131 313 6612
Direct e-mail: communications@sfc.ac.uk

Founded:
2005

Replaced:
Scottish Further Education Funding Council and
Scottish Higher Education Funding Council (year
of change 2005)

Organisation type and purpose:
National government body, advisory body,
funding body supporting universities and colleges
in the provison of high quality learning and
internationally competitive research.

Subject coverage:
Funding policies, guidance on the provision of
learning and teaching, further and higher
education in Scotland.

Trade and statistical information:
Data on numbers of students and staff at further
and higher education institutions in Scotland;
data on income and expenditure of further and
higher education institutions in Scotland.

Printed publications:
Corporate Plan

Publications list:
Available online

Access to staff:
Contact by letter, by telephone, by e-mail and via
website
Hours: Mon to Fri, 0900 to 1700

SCOTTISH GAELIC TEXTS SOCIETY

Acronym or abbreviation: SGTS

c/o McLeish Carswell, 29 St Vincent Place,
Glasgow, G1 2DT

Tel: 0141 248 4134
Fax: 0141 226 3118

Enquiries:
Enquiries to: Honorary Secretary

Founded:
1934

Organisation type and purpose:
Learned society (membership is by subscription),
registered charity.

Subject coverage:
Scottish Gaelic literature generally, but especially
learned texts hitherto unpublished or requiring
revision.

Printed publications:
Texts as they become available (list from the
Society)

Publications list:
Available in print

Access to staff:
Contact by letter
Hours: Mon to Fri, 0900 to 1700

Grant-aided by:
three universities

SCOTTISH GAMES ASSOCIATION

Acronym or abbreviation: SGA

24 Florence Place, Perth, Tayside, PH1 5BH

Tel: 01738 627782
Fax: 01738 639622
E-mail: andrew@highlandgames.org.uk

Website:
http://www.highlandgames-sga.com

Enquiries:
Enquiries to: Honorary Secretary

Founded:
1946

Organisation type and purpose:
Professional body.
National Governing body.

Subject coverage:
Professional activities and participation in most
games and sports in Scotland.

Printed publications:
Annual year book – normally available in February
Order printed publications from: The Secretary,
Scottish Games Association

SCOTTISH GENEALOGY SOCIETY

15 Victoria Terrace, Edinburgh, EH1 2JL

Tel: 0131 220 3677
Fax: 0131 220 3677
E-mail: enquiries@scotsgenealogy.com

Website:
http://www.scotsgenealogy.com
Information on society, membership and sales.

Enquiries:
Enquiries to: Librarian

Founded:
1953

Organisation type and purpose:
Learned society.
Genealogy and Family History Library.

Subject coverage:
Scottish family history and genealogy.

**Museum or gallery collection, archive, or library
special collection:**
Card indexes relating to several families including
Stirling and Mackay
Largest Scottish collection of unpublished lists of
monumental (graveyard) inscriptions

Library catalogue:
All or part available in-house

Printed publications:
A large range of publications on genealogy, local
and family history under the headings Armed
Forces, Burgh Records, Castles of Scotland,
Census 1841, 1851, 1861, Directories, Emigrants
& Immigrants, Jacobites, Mariners and Ships,
People & Poll Tax Lists of 1696, Sources and
Guides, Trades and Professions, Vital Records,
Wills and Testaments,
Monumental Inscriptions (32 volumes)
The Scottish Genealogist (journal, quarterly, free to
members)
Order printed publications from: Above address, or
via website

Microform publications:
Edinburgh Directories (microfiche)
Some Census indexes
Members' Interests

Electronic and video publications:
Inquisitionum Retornatum ad Capellam Domini
Regis Quae in Publicis Archives Scotiae (ed
Thomson T, CD-ROM)
Decennial Indexes to the Services of Heirs in
Scotland, 1700–1859 (CD-ROM)
The Scots Peerage (ed Paul J B, CD-ROM)

Publications list:
Available online and in print

Access to staff:
Contact by letter, by fax, by e-mail, in person and
via website
Hours: Mon, Tue, Thu, 1030 to 1730; Wed, 1030 to
1930; Sat, 1000 to 1700

Member of:
Scottish Association of Family History Societies

SCOTTISH GLADIOLUS SOCIETY

Acronym or abbreviation: SGS

Ardshiel, Bruce Terrace, Kinghorn, Burntisland,
Fife, KY3 9TH

Tel: 01592 892559

Enquiries:
Enquiries to: Secretary

Founded:
1972

Organisation type and purpose:
National organisation, membership association
(membership is by subscription), present number
of members: 40, voluntary organisation, research
organisation.

Subject coverage:
To promote the cultivation, exhibition, research
and hybridisation of gladioli. To contribute
towards gladioli interest in both Britain and
overseas and generally support Scottish flower
shows and Scottish horticulture with exhibits,
expert show judges and lecturers.

Other address:
British Gladiolus Society (BGS)
Honorary Correspondence Secretary, 197 Aston
Clinton Road, Aylesbury, Buckinghamshire,
HP22 5AD

SCOTTISH GROCERS' FEDERATION

222–224 Queensferry Road, Edinburgh, EH4 2BN

Tel: 0131 343 3300
Fax: 0131 343 6147

Enquiries:
Enquiries to: Chief Executive

Founded:
1918

Organisation type and purpose:
Trade association (membership is by subscription).

Printed publications:
Retail News (to members, monthly)

Access to staff:
Contact by letter, by telephone, by fax and in
person. Access for members only.
Hours: Mon to Fri, 0900 to 1700

SCOTTISH GROCERY TRADE EMPLOYERS' ASSOCIATION

222–224 Queensferry Road, Edinburgh, EH4 2BN

Tel: 0131 343 3300
Fax: 0131 343 6147

Enquiries:
Enquiries to: Chief Executive

Organisation type and purpose:
Membership association (membership is by
subscription), present number of members: c. 700.

Access to staff:
Contact by letter, by telephone and by fax.
Appointment necessary. Access for members only.
Hours: Mon to Fri, 0900 to 1700

Parent body:
Scottish Grocers' Federation

SCOTTISH HISTORIC BUILDINGS TRUST

Acronym or abbreviation: SHBT

42 North Castle Street, Edinburgh, EH2 3BN

Tel: 0131 220 5990
Fax: 0131 220 5991
E-mail: info@shbt.org.uk

Website:
http://www.shbt.org.uk

Enquiries:
Enquiries to: Director

Founded:
2003

Created by the merger of:
Scottish Historic Buildings Trust and Cockburn
Conservation Trust (year of change 2010)

Formerly called:
Alba Conservation Trust (year of change 2010)

Organisation type and purpose:
Registered charity.
Building preservation trust.
Acquisition, repair and reuse of buildings of
architectural or historic importance throughout
Scotland.

Subject coverage:
Management and techniques of building
conservation.

**Museum or gallery collection, archive, or library
special collection:**
Books, journals, reports, slides, etc. on building
conservation

Printed publications:
Annual Report and Accounts (£2)
Building Archaeology Reports (individually
priced)
Conservation Plans/Statements

Access to staff:
Contact by letter, by telephone and by e-mail.
Appointment necessary.
Hours: Mon to Fri, 0900 to 1700
Special comments: Information only available to
registered charities and other non-profit making
organisations.

Member organisation of:
UK Association of Preservation Trusts
Alhambra House, 27–31 Charing Cross Road,
London, WC24 0AU; tel: 0207 925 0199

SCOTTISH HISTORY SOCIETY

Acronym or abbreviation: SHS

Dr Katie Stevenson, School of History, University
of St Andrews, St Katharine's Lodge, The Scores, St
Andrews, KY16 9AL

Tel: 01337 831996
E-mail: kcs7@st-andrews.ac.uk

Website:
http://www.scottishhistorysociety.org

Enquiries:
Enquiries to: Honorary Secretary

Organisation type and purpose:
Learned society. Publication of documents relevant
to Scottish history.

Subject coverage:
Scottish history.

Publications list:
Available online and in print

SCOTTISH HOCKEY

589 Lanark Road, Edinburgh, EH14 5DA

Tel: 0131 453 9070
Fax: 0131 453 9079
E-mail: via website

Website:
http://www.scottish-hockey.org.uk
Mission and objectives, national teams, domestic
competition, clubs, coaching, membership, news
and events.

Organisation type and purpose:
The recognised governing body for the sport of
hockey in Scotland, providing for the
development, management and promotion of the
sport across all ages and abilities.

Subject coverage:
Scottish hockey at all levels.

Electronic and video publications:
Ethics Manual 2010–2011
Scottish Hockey Facility Strategy
Order electronic and video publications from:
Download from website

Publications list:
Available online

Access to staff:
Contact by letter, by telephone, by fax and via
website

SCOTTISH HUNTINGTON'S ASSOCIATION

Thistle House, 61 Main Road, Elderslie, Johnstone,
Renfrewshire, PA5 9BA

Tel: 01505 322245
Fax: 01505 382980
E-mail: sha-admin@hdscotland.org

Enquiries:
Enquiries to: Administrator

Founded:
1989

Organisation type and purpose:
Voluntary organisation, registered charity.

Subject coverage:
Huntington's Disease.

Publications list:
Available in print

Access to staff:
Contact by telephone
Hours: Mon to Fri, 0900 to 1700

SCOTTISH JEWISH ARCHIVES CENTRE

Garnethill Synagogue, 129 Hill Street, Glasgow, G3
6UB

Tel: 0141 332 4911
Fax: 0131 332 4911
E-mail: info@sjac.org.uk

Website:
http://www.sjac.org.uk

Enquiries:
Enquiries to: Director
Direct e-mail: rvlkaplan@googlemail.com

Founded:
1987

Organisation type and purpose:
Registered charity, museum, research organisation.

Subject coverage:
History of Jews in Scotland.

Non-library collection catalogue:
All or part available in-house

Library catalogue:
All or part available in-house

continued overleaf

Publications list:
Available online

Access to staff:
Contact by letter, by e-mail and in person.
Appointment necessary.
Hours: Monthly Sun, 1400 to 1600; Fri morning, by
appointment

SCOTTISH JU-JITSU ASSOCIATION

Acronym or abbreviation: SJJA

House of Samurai, 93 Douglas Street, Dundee,
DD1 5AZ

Tel: 01382 201601
Fax: 01382 201601
E-mail: scottishjujitsu@aol.com

Website:
http://www.sjja.eu

Enquiries:
Enquiries to: Executive Administrator
Other contacts: Technical Director; Events Director;
Communications Director; Operations Director;
Projects Director; Director of Junior Training

Founded:
1979

Organisation type and purpose:
National organisation, membership association
(membership is by subscription), governing body
of sport.
To regulate, control and educate in the sport and
art of ju-jitsu.

Subject coverage:
Information on ju-jitsu clubs throughout Scotland,
international ju-jitsu organisations and ko ryu
(traditional systems) organisations.

**Museum or gallery collection, archive, or library
special collection:**
Coaching videos (only available to members), 'The
Essentials' (Robert G. Ross)

Non-library collection catalogue:
All or part available in-house

Library catalogue:
All or part available in-house

Printed publications:
Newsletter (6 times a year, free to members)

Electronic and video publications:
EMBU – paired competition format compulsory
moves (video)
The Syllabus – Series of five videos depicting
association curriculum

Access to staff:
Contact by letter, by telephone, by fax, by e-mail
and via website. Appointment necessary. Access
for members only.
Hours: Mon, Wed and Fri, 1100 to 2200; Tue and
Thu, 1100 to 1500; Sat, 1100 to 1300

Access to building, collection or gallery:
No prior appointment required
Hours: Mon to Fri, 1830 to 2200
Special comments: Main entrance security
controlled.

Member organisation of:
British Association of Sport and Exercise Sciences
tel: 0113 8126162; fax: 0113 8126163; website:
http://www.bases.org.uk
Scottish Schools Sports Association
tel: 0141 353 3215; fax: 0141 353 3815

SCOTTISH LANGUAGE DICTIONARIES LIMITED

Acronym or abbreviation: SLD

25 Buccleuch Place, Edinburgh, EH8 9LN

Tel: 0131 650 4149
E-mail: mail@scotsdictionaries.org.uk

Website:
http://www.scotsdictionaries.org.uk
General information on SLD, information for
schools.

Enquiries:
Enquiries to: Director

Founded:
2002

Formerly called:
Scottish National Dictionary Association Ltd, A
Dictionary of the Older Scottish Tongue (year of
change 2002)

Organisation type and purpose:
Membership association, present number of
members: 150, registered charity (charity number
SC 032910), research organisation, lexicography.

Subject coverage:
The multi-volume dictionaries of Scots language,
which include historical and regional principles,
12th century to 2005; study of Scottish language;
information on Scots language to the present day;
smaller, related publications.

Education services:
Outreach, teaching packs, schools website: http://
www.scuilwab.org.uk

**Museum or gallery collection, archive, or library
special collection:**
Word collection in electronic database, in addition
to published dictionaries

Printed publications:
Concise Scots Dictionary
Dictionary of Scottish Building
Grammar Broonie
Newsletter (2 times a year, members)
Pocket Scots Dictionary
Scots School Dictionary
The Concise English-Scots Dictionary
The Scottish National Dictionary
The Scots Thesaurus
The Scottish National Dictionary (10 volumes)
The Compact SND (2 volumes)
A Dictionary of the Older Scottish Tongue
Say it in Scots Series
Order printed publications from: Amazon via
website: http://www.scotsdictionaries.org.uk

Electronic and video publications:
Cannie Spell (Scots spellchecker on disk)
Electronic Scots School Dictionary (CD-ROM)

Publications list:
Available in print

Access to staff:
Contact by letter, by telephone, by e-mail, in
person and via website. Appointment necessary.
Hours: Mon to Fri, 0900 to 1700
Special comments: Visits by prior appointment only.
Mornings fully covered. Hours in the office are
variable in the afternoon. Please leave message on
answerphone.

SCOTTISH LAW COMMISSION

Acronym or abbreviation: SLC

140 Causewayside, Edinburgh, EH9 1PR

Tel: 0131 668 2131
Fax: 0131 662 4900
E-mail: info@scotlawcom.gov.uk

Website:
http://www.scotlawcom.gov.uk

Enquiries:
Enquiries to: Librarian

Founded:
1965

Organisation type and purpose:
National government body, statutory body.
Law Reform Agency. A statutory body set up
under the Law Commissions Act 1965.

Subject coverage:
Responsible for keeping under review the law of
Scotland and making recommendations for reform.

**Museum or gallery collection, archive, or library
special collection:**
Law reform publications from throughout the
world

Non-library collection catalogue:
All or part available in-house

Library catalogue:
All or part available in-house

Printed publications:
Discussion papers
Reports
Order printed publications from: Stationery Office

Publications list:
Available online

Access to staff:
Contact by letter, by telephone and by e-mail.
Appointment necessary.
Hours: Mon to Fri, 0900 to 1700

Access to building, collection or gallery:
prior appointment required

SCOTTISH LEGAL ACTION GROUP

Acronym or abbreviation: SCOLAG

52 Crossgate, Cupar, Fife, KY15 5JX

Tel: 01334 655150
Fax: 01334 654911
E-mail: company.secretary@scolag.org

Website:
http://www.scolag.org
Details of events, membership and subscriptions to
the monthly legal journal.

Enquiries:
Enquiries to: Administrator
Direct tel: 05600 727138
Direct fax: 05600 727138; 0131 476 5698 (SCOLAG
Legal Journal editor)
Direct e-mail: admin@scolag.org; editor@scolag.org
Other contacts: Editor, SCOLAG Legal Journal

Founded:
1975

Organisation type and purpose:
Membership association (membership is by
subscription).

Subject coverage:
Scots law and socio-legal justice in Scotland.

Non-library collection catalogue:
All or part available online

Library catalogue:
All or part available in print

Printed publications:
SCOLAG Legal Journal (monthly by subscription)
Order printed publications from: Administrator

Access to staff:
Contact by letter, by telephone, by fax, by e-mail
and via website
Hours: Mon to Fri, 0900 to 1700

SCOTTISH LEGAL AID BOARD

44 Drumsheugh Gardens, Edinburgh, EH3 7SW

Tel: 0131 226 7061 \ Helpline 0845 122 8686
Fax: 0131 220 4878
E-mail: general@slab.org.uk

Website:
http://www.slab.org.uk
Information on legal aid in Scotland.

Enquiries:
Enquiries to: Senior Communications Officer

Founded:
1986

Formerly called:
Legal Aid Assessment Office of the Scottish Home and Health Department, The Legal Aid Central Committee of the Law Society of Scotland (year of change 1987)

Organisation type and purpose:
Public body that manages legal aid in Scotland.

Subject coverage:
Expenditure on legal aid in Scotland; volumes of legal aid applications and grants in Scotland.

Non-library collection catalogue:
All or part available online and in print

Printed publications:
Leaflets for the public
Annual Report
Annual Review
Corporate Plan
Various publications for the legal profession

Publications list:
Available online

Access to staff:
Contact by letter, by telephone, by fax, by e-mail and via website. Appointment necessary.
Hours: Mon to Fri, 0900 to 1700

Sponsor body:
Scottish Executive Justice Department
  St Andrews House, Regents Road, Edinburgh; tel: 0131 244 2200

SCOTTISH LIBERAL DEMOCRATS

Acronym or abbreviation: SLD

4 Clifton Terrace, Edinburgh, EH12 5DR

Tel: 0131 337 2314
Fax: 0131 337 3566
E-mail: scotlibdem@cix.co.uk

Website:
http://www.scotlibdems.org.uk

Enquiries:
Enquiries to: Administrator

Founded:
1989

Formerly called:
Scottish Liberal Party, Scottish Social and Liberal Democrats, SDP (Scotland)

Organisation type and purpose:
Membership association (membership is by subscription).
Party political organisation.

Subject coverage:
Local government elections, national elections, Scottish Liberal Democrat policies.

Museum or gallery collection, archive, or library special collection:
Gladstone's Midlothian speeches
Liberal Democrat policy papers

Trade and statistical information:
Election statistics.

Affiliated to:
Liberal Democrats

SCOTTISH LIBRARY AND INFORMATION COUNCIL

Acronym or abbreviation: SLIC

1st Floor, Building C, Brandon Gate, Leechlee Road, Hamilton, ML3 6AU

Tel: 01698 458888
Fax: 01698 283170
E-mail: slic@slainte.org.uk

Website:
http://www.slainte.org.uk/slic
Information about the council and its activities, plus access to information about Scottish libraries.

Enquiries:
Enquiries to: Director

Founded:
1991

Organisation type and purpose:
Advisory body, registered charity.

Subject coverage:
All library and information service issues; networking, internet, social inclusion, open learning, further education, college libraries, higher education, school libraries, public libraries, special libraries, performance indicators.

Printed publications:
SLIC Subscription Newsletter (online, free)
SLIC Annual Review Resources (online, free / hardcopy, free plus p&p)
Range of reports and evaluations (most available online or free to members)

Publications list:
Available online

Access to staff:
Contact by letter, by telephone, by fax and by e-mail. Appointment necessary.
Hours: Mon to Fri, 0900 to 1700

SCOTTISH MASK AND PUPPET CENTRE

Formal name: Scottish Mask and Puppet Centre (The Garret Mask & Puppet Centre Trust Ltd)
Acronym or abbreviation: SMPC

8–10 Balcarres Avenue, Glasgow, G12 0QF

Tel: 0141 339 6185
Fax: 0141 339 8021
E-mail: info@scottishmaskandpuppetcentre.co.uk

Website:
http://www.scottishmaskandpuppetcentre.co.uk
History, aims and objects, HDN Course – professional training, news and events, membership, festival agenda, publications, education and workshops, puppeteers across Scotland, Film and FX Gallery, behind the mask, exhibitions, master classes, contacts.
http://www.maskandpuppetbooks.co.uk
Online mail order book service.

Enquiries:
Enquiries to: Administrator
Other contacts: Exhibitions Curator: malcolm .knight@scottishmaskandpuppetcentre.co.uk

Founded:
1981

Organisation type and purpose:
International organisation, advisory body, professional body, membership association (membership is by subscription), voluntary organisation, registered charity (charity number SCO 14379), training organisation, consultancy, research organisation.
To promote, maintain and develop the ancient art of puppets, masks and performing objects; to seek recognition for the medium as an art form in its own right; to dignify the profession; to network internationally.

Subject coverage:
Masks, puppets, performing objects, exhibitions, workshops, performances, networking, commissions, (no loan or hire), collections, publications.

Museum or gallery collection, archive, or library special collection:
Malcolm Knight Collection of Puppets and Masks
James Arnott Library
Claude Schumacher Library
The Miles Lee Collection of Puppets
The Caricature Theatre Collection
Harry Vernon Punch and Judy Set
Wayang Golek ASEP Collection

Non-library collection catalogue:
All or part available in-house

Library catalogue:
All or part available in-house

Printed publications:
IFCPA Festival Agenda (for purchase)
Masks and Puppets (newsletter, free)
Material suppliers list (free)
Puppeteers across Scotland (free)
Starting a puppet company (free)

Electronic and video publications:
Order electronic and video publications from: website: http://www.maskandpuppetbooks.co.uk

Publications list:
Available online and in print

Access to staff:
Contact by letter, by telephone, by fax, by e-mail and via website. Appointment necessary.
Hours: Mon to Fri, 1000 to 1600; Sat, 1300 to 1700

Access to building, collection or gallery:
Prior appointment required
Hours: Mon to Wed, 1300 to 1600; Sat, 1330 to 1600

Access for disabled people:
Parking provided, ramped entry, toilet facilities
Special comments: Induction loop provided for theatre.

SCOTTISH MASSAGE THERAPISTS ORGANISATION LIMITED

Acronym or abbreviation: SMTO

24 Ellon Road, Bridge of Don, Aberdeen, AB23 8BX

Tel: 01224 822956
Fax: 01224 822960
E-mail: smto@scotmass.co.uk

Enquiries:
Enquiries to: Chairman
Other contacts: General Secretary

Founded:
1992

Organisation type and purpose:
Professional body.

Subject coverage:
Massage, clinical aromatherapy, remedial and sports massage, manipulative therapy, reflexology, on-site seated massage, advanced remedial massage therapy.

Printed publications:
Free brochure on all courses
On The Massage Scene (journal, 3 times a year for members or for £2.50)

Access to staff:
Contact by letter, by telephone, by fax, by e-mail, in person and via website. Appointment necessary.
Hours: Mon to Fri, 0900 to 1700

SCOTTISH MOTOR MUSEUM TRUST

Motoring Heritage Centre, Loch Lomond Outlets, Main Street, Alexandria, Dumbartonshire, G83 0UG

Tel: 01389 607 862
Fax: 01389 607 862
E-mail: info@motoringheritage.co.uk

Website:
http://www.motoringheritage.co.uk
http://www.visitlochlomond.org

Enquiries:
Enquiries to: Honorary Secretary

Founded:
1995

Formerly called:
Argyll Motor Museum

Organisation type and purpose:
Voluntary organisation, registered charity (charity number SCO 28515), museum, historic building, house or site, suitable for ages: 5+.

Subject coverage:
Scottish motoring industry.

Information services:
Library available for reference.

Special visitor services:
Guided tours, materials and/or activities for children.

Museum or gallery collection, archive, or library special collection:
Collection of cine-film on Scottish motoring
Film archive of Scottish motoring
Motor cars of Scottish origin
Photographic archive of Scottish transport 1890 to present day

Non-library collection catalogue:
All or part available in print

Library catalogue:
All or part available in print

Electronic and video publications:
Video tapes

Access to staff:
Contact by letter, by telephone, by fax, by e-mail, in person and via website
Hours: Mon to Fri, 0930 to 1730

Access to building, collection or gallery:
No prior appointment required
Hours: Daily, 0930 to 1730

Access for disabled people:
Parking provided, ramped entry, access to all public areas, toilet facilities

Museum:
Motoring Heritage Centre
at same address

SCOTTISH MOTOR TRADE ASSOCIATION LIMITED

Acronym or abbreviation: SMTA

Palmerston House, 10 The Loan, South Queensfield, EH30 9NS

Tel: 0131 331 5510
Fax: 0131 331 4296
E-mail: info@smta.co.uk

Website:
http://www.smta.co.uk
Services available, news bulletins, membership details, links to related sites.

Enquiries:
Enquiries to: Membership Secretary
Direct e-mail: bill.dunn@smta.co.uk

Founded:
1903

Organisation type and purpose:
Advisory body, trade association (membership is by subscription), present number of members: 1000, training organisation, research organisation.

Subject coverage:
Employment and personnel issues, health and safety, taxation and VAT, legal information, technical information, Scotsure Insurance Co., SMTA (Trading Partners) Ltd.

Museum or gallery collection, archive, or library special collection:
Scottish Motor Show Brochures (1905 to date)
Members Bulletin (monthly)

Trade and statistical information:
New vehicle sales – Scotland.

Access to staff:
Contact by letter, by telephone, by fax, by e-mail, in person and via website. Appointment necessary. Access for members only.
Hours: Mon to Fri, 0900 to 1700

Access to building, collection or gallery:
No access other than to staff
Hours: Mon to Fri, 0900 to 1700

SCOTTISH NATIONAL FEDERATION FOR THE WELFARE OF THE BLIND

Acronym or abbreviation: SNFWB

Richard Mazur, Acting Secretary, c/o Perth Society for the Blind, 14 New Row, Perth, PH1 5QA

Tel: 01738 626969
E-mail: richard.mazur@virgin.net

Website:
http://www.snfwb.org.uk

Enquiries:
Enquiries to: Honorary Secretary

Founded:
1917

Organisation type and purpose:
Voluntary organisation, registered charity (charity number SC 002185).
Parent body for numerous organisations, including local authorities in Scotland, concerned with the welfare of blind and partially sighted people.

Subject coverage:
Social work, education and employment services for the blind and partially sighted.

Printed publications:
Annual Report

Access to staff:
Contact by letter, by telephone, by fax and by e-mail
Hours: Mon to Fri, 0900 to 1700

SCOTTISH NATIONAL INSTITUTION FOR THE WAR BLINDED

Acronym or abbreviation: SNIWB, LINBURN

PO Box 500, Gillespie Crescent, Edinburgh, EH10 4HZ

Tel: 0131 229 1456
Fax: 0131 229 4060
E-mail: enquiries@rbas.org.uk

Enquiries:
Enquiries to: Secretary and Treasurer

Founded:
1915

Organisation type and purpose:
Voluntary organisation, registered charity (charity number SC002652).
Training, employment and aftercare for Scottish ex-services visually impaired.

Subject coverage:
Care and welfare of blind and visually impaired ex-servicemen and women, setting up of specialised workshops, grants.

Printed publications:
Annual Report

Publications list:
Available in print

Access to staff:
Contact by letter, by telephone, by fax and by e-mail. Appointment necessary.
Hours: Mon to Fri, 0900 to 1300 and 1400 to 1700

Access to building, collection or gallery:
No access other than to staff

Access for disabled people:
Parking provided, level entry

Links with:
Royal Blind Asylum and School
at the same address

SCOTTISH NATIONAL PARTY

Acronym or abbreviation: SNP

107 McDonald Road, Edinburgh, EH7 4NW

Tel: 0131 525 8900

Fax: 0131 525 8901
E-mail: snp.hq@snp.org.uk

Website:
http://www.snp.org
About, information, policy, people, join and donations, online shop

Enquiries:
Enquiries to: Policy and information officer
Direct tel: 0131 525 8908

Founded:
1934

Organisation type and purpose:
Membership association (membership is by subscription). Political party.

Subject coverage:
Party policy and information on Scottish independence in Europe.

Printed publications:
Ad hoc publications

Access to staff:
Contact by letter, by telephone, by fax, by e-mail, in person and via website. Appointment necessary.
Hours: Mon to Fri, 0900 to 1700

SCOTTISH NATIONAL SPORTS CENTRE CUMBRAE

Isle of Cumbrae, Millport, Ayrshire, KA28 0HQ

Tel: 01475 530757
Fax: 01475 530013
E-mail: cumbraecentre@sportscotland.org.uk

Website:
http://www.nationalcentrecumbrae.org.uk

Enquiries:
Enquiries to: Principal

Founded:
1974

Organisation type and purpose:
National government body, advisory body, registered charity, training organisation.
To train instructors in watersports, to train the national sailing squads, to offer high level instruction in watersports to all. Scotland's premier watersports training facility.

Subject coverage:
All aspects of watersport; yacht cruising, dinghy sailing and racing, catamaran sailing, windsurfing, sailing, canoeing, powerboating and powerboat racing, sub aqua.

Printed publications:
Brochure (available by phone)

Publications list:
Available in print

Access to staff:
Contact by letter, by telephone, by fax, by e-mail, in person and via website
Hours: Mon to Fri, 0900 to 1700

Access for disabled people:
Parking provided, ramped entry, toilet facilities
Hours: Mon to Fri, 0900 to 1700

Constituent part of:
Scottish Sports Council Trust Company
Caledonian House, South Gyle, Edinburgh; tel: 0131 317 7200; fax: 0131 317 7202; website: http://www.sportscotland.org.uk

SCOTTISH NATIONAL SWEET PEA, ROSE & CARNATION SOCIETY

Acronym or abbreviation: SNSPRCS

Mr Iain Silver, Inglewood, Bogsbank Road West Linton, EH46 7EN

E-mail: society@snsprcs.org.uk

Website:
http://www.snsprcs.org.uk

Sweet pea trial results, international rose trial results, tips and information.

Enquiries:
Enquiries to: General Secretary

Founded:
1919

Organisation type and purpose:
National organisation (membership is by subscription), present number of members: 110, voluntary organisation, registered charity (charity number SC009709).

Subject coverage:
Information on cultivating and exhibiting sweet peas, roses and carnations.

Access to staff:
Contact by letter and by e-mail
Hours: Mon to Fri, 0900 to 1700

SCOTTISH NATURAL HERITAGE, INVERNESS

Great Glen House, Leachkin Road, Inverness, IV3 8NW

Tel: 01463 725290
E-mail: library@snh.gov.uk

Website:
http://www.snh.gov.uk
A variety of information on Scottish National Heritage.

Enquiries:
Enquiries to: Librarian

Founded:
1992

Formerly called:
Countryside Commission for Scotland, Nature Conservancy Council

Organisation type and purpose:
National government body.
Library.

Subject coverage:
All aspects of nature and landscape conservation, land use and recreation especially in relation to Scotland's natural heritage.

Library catalogue:
All or part available in-house

Printed publications:
Several hundred Scottish Natural Heritage publications covering many different aspects of Scotland's Nature: comprehensive online library on website
The Nature of Scotland (magazine, 4 times a year, free)
Order printed publications from: Publications Unit, Scottish National Heritage, Battleby, Redgorton, Perth, PH1 3EW; tel: 01738 458530; e-mail: pubs@snh.gov.uk
or via website publications search: http://www.snh.gov.uk

Publications list:
Available online

Access to staff:
Contact by letter, by telephone and by e-mail
Hours: Mon to Thu, 0900 to 1700; Fri, 0900 to 1630. If travelling from outside the area, please phone in advance to ensure that staff are available.

Access for disabled people:
Library area has wide aisles suitable for wheel chairs.

SCOTTISH NATURAL HISTORY LIBRARY

Acronym or abbreviation: SNHL

Foremount House, Kilbarchan, Renfrewshire, PA10 2EZ

Tel: 01505 702419

Enquiries:
Enquiries to: Chairman
Other contacts: Honorary Librarian

Founded:
1972

Organisation type and purpose:
Learned society, registered charity (charity number SCO 42142), research organisation.
Specialist library.

Subject coverage:
All aspects of Scottish natural history.

Museum or gallery collection, archive, or library special collection:
The largest separate collection of Scottish natural history books and journals anywhere in the world; some 150,000 items, including some 400 periodicals; several specialised Scottish collections which have been presented to the library

Non-library collection catalogue:
All or part available in-house

Library catalogue:
All or part available in-house

Printed publications:
The Scottish Naturalist (founded 1871) (3 times a year, annual subscription £35)

Access to staff:
Contact by letter and by telephone
Hours: Mon to Fri, 0900 to 1700

Access to building, collection or gallery:
Prior appointment required

Works in co-operation with the:
British Library
National Library of Scotland
Natural History Museum
Royal Museum of Scotland
Society for the History of Natural History

SCOTTISH OFFICIAL BOARD OF HIGHLAND DANCING

Acronym or abbreviation: SOBHD

Heritage House, 32 Grange Loan, Edinburgh, EH9 2NR

Tel: 0131 668 3965
Fax: 0131 662 0404
E-mail: admin@sobhd.net

Website:
http://www.sobhd.net

Enquiries:
Enquiries to: Director of Administration

Founded:
1950

Organisation type and purpose:
International organisation, professional body (membership is by election or invitation).
Governing body.

Subject coverage:
Highland dancing world governing body.

Museum or gallery collection, archive, or library special collection:
Collection of books on the subject

Non-library collection catalogue:
All or part available in-house

Printed publications:
Constitution and Rule Book (£4)
Text Book Highland Dancing (£15)
Irish Jig Book (£5)
Sailor's Hornpipe (£5)
Examining body items include:
BATD National Book (£7)
SDTA National Book (£6)
UKA National Book (£5)

Publications list:
Available in print

Access to staff:
Contact by letter, by telephone, by fax, by e-mail, in person and via website
Hours: Mon to Fri, 0900 to 1700

SCOTTISH OPERA

39 Elmbank Crescent, Glasgow, G2 4PT

Tel: 0141 248 4567
Fax: 0141 221 8812

Website:
http://www.scottishopera.org.uk
Preview new season's performances, find out about special ticket offers and forthcoming events.

Enquiries:
Direct tel: 0141 248 4567

Founded:
1962

Organisation type and purpose:
National organisation, registered charity (charity number 37531).

Access to staff:
Contact by letter, by telephone, by fax, by e-mail and in person. Appointment necessary.
Hours: Mon to Fri, 0930 to 1730

Access to building, collection or gallery:
No access other than to staff

SCOTTISH ORNITHOLOGISTS' CLUB

Acronym or abbreviation: SOC

Waterston House, Aberlady, East Lothian, EH32 0PY

Tel: 01875 871330
Fax: 01875 871035
E-mail: mail@the-soc.org.uk

Website:
http://www.the-soc.org.uk

Enquiries:
Enquiries to: Office Manager
Other contacts: Administrative Assistant

Founded:
1936

Organisation type and purpose:
Membership association (membership is by subscription), present number of members: 2500, voluntary organisation, registered charity (charity number KSC009859), publishing house.
To encourage ornithology in Scotland.

Subject coverage:
Conservation and research into birds in Scotland, ornithology in general.

Museum or gallery collection, archive, or library special collection:
Extensive ornithological reference library (The George Waterston Library)
Wildlife art gallery

Library catalogue:
All or part available in-house

Printed publications:
Scottish Raptor Monitoring Scheme Report (annually, free to members)
Scottish Birds (quarterly, free to members or on subscription)

Access to staff:
Contact by letter, by telephone and by e-mail. Appointment necessary.
Hours: Mon to Fri, 0900 to 1700
Special comments: Please phone beforehand.

Access to building, collection or gallery:
Hours: Mon to Fri, 1000 to 1600; Sat and Sun, 1200 to 1800

Access for disabled people:
Wheelchair friendly

continued overleaf

Has:
14 branches throughout Scotland

SCOTTISH PARACHUTE CLUB

Strathallan Airfield, Auchterarder, Perthshire, PH3
1LA

Tel: 01764 662 572
E-mail: andy@afrew.fsnet.co.uk

Website:
http://www.skydivestrathallan.co.uk
Parachuting courses.

Enquiries:
Enquiries to: General Secretary

Founded:
1960

Organisation type and purpose:
National organisation, membership association
(membership is by subscription), present number
of members: 70, voluntary organisation, training
organisation.

Subject coverage:
Parachute training courses for beginners to
experienced jumpers.

Access to staff:
Contact by letter, by telephone, by e-mail, in
person and via website. All charged.
Hours: Fri, 1700 to 2100; Sat, Sun, 0900 to 2100

Access to building, collection or gallery:
No prior appointment required

Access for disabled people:
Parking provided, level entry

Connections with:
British Parachute Association (BPA)
Wharf Way, Glenparva, Leicester, LE2 9TF; tel:
0116 278 5271; fax: 0116 247 7662
Scottish Sport Parachute Association (SSPA)
Strathallan Airfield, Auchterarder, Perthshire,
PH3 1BE; tel: 01698 812 443

SCOTTISH PARENT TEACHER COUNCIL

Acronym or abbreviation: SPTC

53 George Street, Edinburgh, EH2 2HT

Tel: 0131 226 4378/1917
Fax: 08707 065814
E-mail: sptc@sptc.info

Website:
http://www.sptc.info
Current newsletter; insurance information,
responses to consultations.

Enquiries:
Enquiries to: Information Officer
Other contacts: Administrator, Convenor

Founded:
1948

Organisation type and purpose:
Membership association, registered charity.
Educational organisation, open to PAs/PTAs and
others with an interest in education in Scotland.

Subject coverage:
Information about PTAs/PAs in Scotland, Parent/
teacher relationships and general information
about Scottish education.

Printed publications:
Backchat Newsletter (approx 7 times a year, free to
members)
Leaflets on constitutions, devolved school
management, charitable status and setting up
PTAs

Access to staff:
Contact by letter, by telephone, by fax, by e-mail
and via website
Hours: Mon, Tue and Thu, 0900 to 1500; Wed and
Fri, 0900 to 1230

SCOTTISH PARTNERSHIP FOR PALLIATIVE CARE

Acronym or abbreviation: SPPC

1a Cambridge Street, Edinburgh, EH1 2DY

Tel: 0131 229 0538
Fax: 0131 228 2967
E-mail: office@palliativecarescotland.org.uk

Website:
http://www.palliativecarescotland.org.uk

Enquiries:
Enquiries to: Director

Founded:
1991

Formerly called:
Scottish Partnership Agency for Palliative and
Cancer Care (SPAPCC) (year of change 2001)

Organisation type and purpose:
Registered charity (charity number SC017979).

Subject coverage:
Palliative care, specialist palliative care, hospices.

Printed publications:
See website http://
www.palliativecarescotland.org.uk

Access to staff:
Contact by letter, by telephone, by fax and by e-
mail
Hours: Mon to Fri, 0900 to 1700

Access to building, collection or gallery:
No public access to building

Member organisations:
more than 50 voluntary and statutory bodies

SCOTTISH PHARMACEUTICAL FEDERATION

Acronym or abbreviation: SPF

135 Wellington Street, Glasgow, G2 2XD

Tel: 0141 221 1235
Fax: 0141 248 5892
E-mail: spf@npanet.co.uk

Website:
http://www.npa.co.uk

Enquiries:
Enquiries to: Secretary

Founded:
1919

Organisation type and purpose:
Trade association (membership is by subscription),
present number of members: 1040.
Trade association for owners of community
pharmacies in Scotland.

Access to staff:
Contact by letter, by telephone, by fax and by e-
mail
Hours: Mon to Fri, 0900 to 1700

Affiliated to:
The National Pharmaceutical Association
Mallinson House, 38–42 St Peters Street, St
Albans, Hertfordshire, AL1 3NP; tel: 01727
832161; fax: 01727 840858; e-mail: npa@npa.co
.uk

SCOTTISH POETRY LIBRARY

Acronym or abbreviation: SPL

5 Crichton's Close, Edinburgh, EH8 8DT

Tel: 0131 557 2876
Fax: 0131 557 8393
E-mail: reception@spl.org.uk

Website:
http://www.spl.org.uk
General information on the Scottish Poetry Library
and its activities, including events, outreach and
education. Links, online catalogue, Scottish Poetry
Index and enquiry service. Digital essay Poets'

Pub, poets' biographies and European Poetry
Information Centre information including
translation workshops. Canadian and New
Zealand poetry exchanges, poets' A-Z, poet of the
month, poetry news, poetry reading room with
online discussions and reading group resources.

Enquiries:
Enquiries to: Librarian
Direct e-mail: julie.johnstone@spl.org.uk

Founded:
1984

Organisation type and purpose:
Friends association, present number of members:
750, registered charity (charity number SCO
23311), public library.
Borrowing is free to the general public.

Subject coverage:
20th-century Scottish poetry written in English,
Scots and Gaelic; older Scottish poetry; substantial
international collection of poetry from Britain,
Europe and the rest of the world.

**Museum or gallery collection, archive, or library
special collection:**
Edwin Morgan Archive

Non-library collection catalogue:
All or part available online

Library catalogue:
All or part available online

Printed publications:
Free publicity brochure
Lists and bibliographies
Scottish Poetry Index Series, indexing Scottish
poetry periodicals, 1952–1992
SPL Poetry Reader (2 a year)
Handsel: Scottish Poems for Welcoming and
Naming Babies
Lament: Scottish Poems for Funerals and
Consolations
Handfast: Scottish Poems for Weddings and
Affirmations
Intimate Expanses : XXV Scottish Poems 1978–2002
100 Favourite Scottish Poems
The Weaver's Task: a Gaelic Sampler
The Thing that Mattered Most: Scottish poems for
children
Poems United: A Commonwealth Anthology

Electronic and video publications:
The Jewel Box: Contemporary Scottish Poems (CD)

Access to staff:
Contact by letter, by telephone, by fax, by e-mail,
in person and via website
Hours: Tue, Wed, Fri, 1000 to 1700; Thu, 1000 to
2000; Sat, 1000 to 1600

Access to building, collection or gallery:
Hours: Tue, Wed, Fri, 1000 to 1700; Thu, 1000 to
2000; Sat, 1000 to 1600

Access for disabled people:
Level entry, access to all public areas, toilet
facilities

Supported by:
Creative Scotland and others

SCOTTISH PRE-SCHOOL PLAY ASSOCIATION

Acronym or abbreviation: SPPA

21– 23 Granville Street, Glasgow, G3 7EE

Tel: 0141 221 4148
Fax: 0141 221 6043
E-mail: info@sppa.org.uk

Website:
http://www.sppa.org.uk

Enquiries:
Enquiries to: Information Officer

Founded:
1966

Formerly called:
Scottish Pre-School Playgroups Association

Organisation type and purpose:
Membership association (membership is by subscription), present number of members: 1,100, voluntary organisation, registered charity (charity number SC003725).
SPPA supports community-based early years education and childcare services for children and families.

Subject coverage:
The Scottish Pre-school Play Association (SPPA) delivers essential support and guidance to providers of pre-school education and childcare services, including all-day care groups, playgroups, toddler groups and under-fives groups. As a member of SPPA, groups can access a variety of services including an insurance package, a range of early years publications, an information helpline and a quarterly magazine, First Five. SPPA also organises a National Conference which is located in Our Dynamic Earth in Edinburgh in 2010.

Trade and statistical information:
Annual facts and figures relating to the Association and to member groups.

Non-library collection catalogue:
All or part available online

Printed publications:
Early Years Publications
Information packs
First Five (magazine)
Publications and sales list available
Order printed publications from: website: http://www.sppa.org.uk

Electronic and video publications:
Video library

Publications list:
Available online and in print

Access to staff:
Contact by letter, by telephone, by fax, by e-mail and in person
Hours: Mon to Fri, 0900 to 1630

Links with:
Association of Shetland Playgroups
CALA (Highland)
Irish PPA
Northern Ireland PPA
Orkney Pre-School Play Association
PLA (England)
Wales PPA

SCOTTISH PUBLIC SERVICES OMBUDSMAN

Acronym or abbreviation: SPSO

4 Melville Street, Edinburgh, EH3 7NS

Tel: 0800 377 7330
Fax: 0800 377 7331
E-mail: ask@spso.org.uk

Website:
http://www.spso.org.uk

Enquiries:
Enquiries to: Ombudsman
Direct e-mail: gbyrne@spso.org.uk

Founded:
2002

Organisation type and purpose:
Statutory body.
Appointed by the Crown on the recommendation of the Scottish Parliament.
To investigate complaints from members of the public about local government, registered social landlords, NHS and Scottish administration.

Access to staff:
Contact by letter, by telephone, by fax, by e-mail and in person. Appointment necessary.
Hours: Mon, Wed to Fri, 0900 to 1700; Tue, 1000 to 1700

SCOTTISH QUALIFICATIONS AUTHORITY

Acronym or abbreviation: SQA

The Optima Building, 58 Robertson Street, Glasgow, G2 8DQ

Tel: 0845 279 1000
Fax: 0845 213 5000
E-mail: customer@sqa.org.uk

Website:
http://www.sqa.org.uk
Information on Scottish Qualifications Authority and its functions.

Enquiries:
Enquiries to: Customer Contact Centre
Direct tel: 0141 242 2291
Direct fax: 0141 242 2219
Direct e-mail: mike.haggerty@sqa.org.uk

Founded:
1 April 1997

Formed from:
Scottish Examination Board (SEB), Scottish Vocational Educational Council (SCOTVEC)

Organisation type and purpose:
Suitable for ages: all.

Subject coverage:
Education qualifications in Scotland.

Publications list:
Available online and in print

Access to staff:
Contact by letter, by telephone, by fax, by e-mail and via website
Hours: Mon to Fri, 0900 to 1700

Other addresses:
Scottish Qualifications Authority
 Ironmills Road, Dalkeith, Midlothian, EH22 1LE; tel: 0131 663 6601

SCOTTISH RAILWAY PRESERVATION SOCIETY

Acronym or abbreviation: SRPS

The Station, Union Street, Bo'ness, West Lothian, EH51 9AQ

Tel: 01506 825855
Fax: 01506 828766
E-mail: enquiries@srps.org.uk

Website:
http://www.srps.org.uk
Activities of the organisation.

Enquiries:
Enquiries to: SRPS Administrator
Direct e-mail: office@srps.org.uk

Founded:
1961

Organisation type and purpose:
Membership association (membership is by subscription), present number of members: 1300, voluntary organisation, registered charity (charity number SCO02375), museum.
Railway preservation and operation.

Subject coverage:
Railway preservation, restoration of steam locomotives and rolling stock, and their operation; Scottish railways and their historical development; Bo'ness and Kinneil Railway; locations for filming of steam-hauled trains of appropriate vintage; the preservation and display, in work if appropriate, of artefacts pertaining to Scottish railways.

Museum or gallery collection, archive, or library special collection:
Builders' plates for study
Railway artefacts ranging from railway buildings to locomotives (etc)
Small collection of books on practical aspects of railways and rolling stock, also photographs

Printed publications:
Blastpipe (magazine, quarterly, free to members or on subscription)
Bo'ness & Kinneil Railway Guide
Other publications as needed

Access to staff:
Contact by letter, by telephone, by fax and by e-mail. Appointment necessary.
Hours: Mon to Fri, 1000 to 1600

Access for disabled people:
Parking provided, ramped entry, toilet facilities

Links with:
Heritage Railway Association (HRA)
 tel: 01707 643568; fax: 01707 643568

SCOTTISH REFUGEE COUNCIL

Acronym or abbreviation: SRC

Wellgate House, 200 Cowgate, Edinburgh, EH1 1NQ

Tel: 0131 225 9994
Fax: 0131 225 9997
E-mail: info@scottishrefugeecouncil.org.uk

Website:
http://www.scottishrefugeecouncil.org.uk

Enquiries:
Enquiries to: Information Officer
Direct e-mail: media@scottishrefugeecouncil.org.uk
Other contacts: Manager/Policy Development Officer for local services referrals.

Founded:
1985

Organisation type and purpose:
Advisory body, voluntary sector organisation, registered charity (charity number SC008639). To assist and advise local authorities and other agencies on all refugee and related issues by providing training, seminars and briefings and assisting with policy development.
To provide advice, information and assistance to asylum seekers and refugees in Scotland. To promote a strategic response to refugee needs. To campaign to ensure Scotland plays a role in meeting the UK's legal and humanitarian obligations under the 1951 UN Convention on Refugees.

Subject coverage:
Provides advice, information and legal representation to asylum seekers and refugees in Scotland including information on asylum law and procedures, employment, housing, education, health and welfare.

Printed publications:
Finding Asylum (newsletter, quarterly, for members)
Annual Report (printed in December)
Briefings (regular updates)
Information Pack for agencies (printed or online)

Publications list:
Available in print

Access to staff:
Contact by letter, by telephone, by fax, by e-mail and via website. Appointment necessary.
Hours: Mon to Fri, 0900 to 1700

Access for disabled people:
Ramped entry, access to all public areas, toilet facilities

Head Office:
Scottish Refugee Council
 94 Hope Street, Glasgow, G2 6QA; tel: 0141 248 9799; fax: 0141 243 2499

SCOTTISH RIGHTS OF WAY AND ACCESS SOCIETY

Acronym or abbreviation: ScotWays

24 Annandale Street, Edinburgh, EH7 4AN

Tel: 0131 558 1222

continued overleaf

Fax: 0131 558 1222
E-mail: info@scotways.com

Website:
http://www.scotways.com

Enquiries:
Enquiries to: Access Enquiries Officer
Other contacts: National Secretary; Treasurer;
Access Enquiries Assistant; Heritage Paths Project
Officer

Founded:
1845

Formerly called:
Scottish Rights of Way Society (year of change
1999)

Organisation type and purpose:
National, voluntary organisation.
Registered charity (SC015460)
Membership organisation.
The preservation, defence, restoration and
acquisition for the public benefit of rights of access
over land in Scotland, including public rights of
way and their amenity.

Subject coverage:
Public access to the outdoors in Scotland, National
Catalogue of Rights of Way, signposting routes,
advice on access rights under the Land Reform
(Scotland) Act 2003 and public rights of way,
publication of maps and guides, Heritage Paths
Project.

**Museum or gallery collection, archive, or library
special collection:**
Maps and other records of rights of way in
Scotland held in 37 volumes and on 122 special
1:50,000 scale maps; copies available, ask for a
quotation of individual routes/maps

Trade and statistical information:
Data on access routes, especially rights of way, for
every local authority area in Scotland.

Printed publications:
Most publications at a discount to members
Annual Report and Newsletters (annually)
Access Rights and Rights of Way: A Guide to the
Law in Scotland (£10)
Rights of Way: The Authority of Case Law (£5)
Scottish Hill Tracks (revised 4th ed, 2004, £16)
Scottish Hill Tracks Map (free)
Various leaflets (free)

Publications list:
Available online and in print

Access to staff:
Contact by letter, by telephone, by fax, by e-mail
and via website. Appointment necessary. Non-
members charged.
Hours: Mon to Fri, 0900 to 1300

Access for disabled people:
Level entry, access to all public areas
Special comments: No disabled toilet facilities.

SCOTTISH RUGBY UNION

Acronym or abbreviation: SRU

Murrayfield, Edinburgh, EH12 5PJ

Tel: 0131 346 5000
Fax: 0131 346 5001
E-mail: feedback@sru.org.uk

Website:
http://www.sru.org.uk
News, results, facts and figures, games and
competitions.

Enquiries:
Enquiries to: Chief Executive

Founded:
1924

Organisation type and purpose:
International organisation, advisory body,
statutory body, membership association.
Governing body of rugby in Scotland.

Subject coverage:
Promotion and development of rugby union
football in Scotland.

**Museum or gallery collection, archive, or library
special collection:**
Library and museum (closed due to
redevelopment of stadium)

Printed publications:
Calendar (annually)
Coaching brochures (series)
Coaching handbook (annually)
Handbook (annually)
Lawbook (annually)

Access to staff:
Contact by letter, by telephone, by fax, by e-mail
and via website
Hours: Mon to Fri, 0900 to 1700

Member of:
International Rugby Board

SCOTTISH RURAL PROPERTY AND BUSINESS ASSOCIATION

Acronym or abbreviation: SRPBA

Stuart House, Eskmills Business Park,
Musselburgh, Midlothian, EH21 7PB

Tel: 0131 653 5400
Fax: 0131 653 5401
E-mail: info@srpba.com

Website:
http://www.srpba.com

Enquiries:
Enquiries to: Chief Executive

Founded:
1906

Formerly called:
Scottish Landowners' Federation (year of change
2004)

Organisation type and purpose:
Membership association (membership is by
subscription), present number of members: 3500.

Subject coverage:
Land use advice, legal advice on land management
to members only.

Printed publications:
Landbusiness Scotland (journal, six times a year,
free to members)

Access to staff:
Contact by letter, by telephone, by fax, by e-mail
and via website
Hours: Mon to Thu, 0800 to 1700; Fri, 0800 to 1630

SCOTTISH SALMON PRODUCERS ORGANISATION

Acronym or abbreviation: SSPO

Durn, Isla Road, Perth, Tayside, PH2 7HG

Tel: 01738 587000
Fax: 01738 621454
E-mail: enquiries@scottishsalmon.co.uk

Website:
http://www.scottishsalmon.co.uk

Enquiries:
Enquiries to: Chief Executive
Direct e-mail: spatten@scottishsalmon.co.uk
Other contacts: Communications Director for all PR
and marketing issues.

Founded:
2006

Organisation type and purpose:
Trade association (membership is by qualification),
present number of members: 50 companies.
To promote production of farmed Scottish salmon.

Subject coverage:
Farming and production of Scottish salmon.

Trade and statistical information:
Salmon production data, import and export data.

Printed publications:
Corporate brochure
Variety of consumer information

Publications list:
Available in print

Access to staff:
Contact by letter
Hours: Mon to Fri, 0900 to 1700

SCOTTISH SCHOOL OF REFLEXOLOGY, THE

Acronym or abbreviation: SSR

11 Stonefield Park, Ayr, KA7 4HS

Tel: 01292 440730
Fax: 01292 440750

Website:
http://www.reflexscott.co.uk
School training prospectus and reservation form.

Enquiries:
Enquiries to: Principal

Founded:
1985

Organisation type and purpose:
Suitable for ages: 18+, training organisation.
To provide training in knowledge and physical
skills to professional level.

Subject coverage:
Reflexology and anatomy, physiology, pathology.
Magnets and their therapeutic uses, nutritional
herbology.

Printed publications:
Arthritis Relief of Pain Naturally (Bell W D)
Introduction to Nutrition (Bell W D)
Reflexology and the Christian (Bell W D)
Reflexology Foot Charts

Electronic and video publications:
Reflexology Methods (Video, available to purchase
for Graduates only)

Publications list:
Available in print

Access to staff:
Contact by letter, by telephone and by fax
Hours: Mon to Thu, 0930 to 1300 and 1415 to 1700;
Fri, 0930 to 1300; Sat and Sun, closed

SCOTTISH SCHOOLS EQUIPMENT RESEARCH CENTRE LIMITED

Acronym or abbreviation: SSERC

2 Pitreavie Court, South Pitreavie Business Park,
Dunfermline. KY11 8UB

Tel: 01383 626070
Fax: 01383 842793
E-mail: sts@sserc.org.uk

Website:
http://www.sserc.org.uk
Summary of services, publications price list,
sample pages, graphics, etc.

Enquiries:
Enquiries to: Chief Executive Officer
Direct e-mail: fred.young@sserc.org.uk

Founded:
1965

Organisation type and purpose:
Local government body, advisory body,
membership association (membership is by
subscription), present number of members: 32
corporate, 100+ individual, registered charity
(charity number SCO 17884), training organisation,
consultancy, research organisation.
Educational organisation, health and safety
consultancy.

Testing house and laboratory, advisory, consultancy and training services.

Subject coverage:
Technical aspect of science and technology equipment for education, relevant British standards, health and safety literature relevant to science and technology in particular and to education in general; advice, information, training and consultancy on purchase, testing and use (including safety, maintenance and repair) of educational equipment.

Museum or gallery collection, archive, or library special collection:
Selected British and EN standards
Specialised science and technology education journals

Printed publications:
Bulletin, Science and Technology Equipment (journal, quarterly)
Science and Technology Equipment News (quarterly)
Specialised one-offs on IT applications, health and safety in education, etc.
Various leaflets and booklets

Electronic and video publications:
Graphics relevant to science and technology CD-ROM, Acorn Archimedes platform, Apple Mac, PC (metafiles); Science Graphics on application
Hazardous Chemicals: An interactive manual for science education (CD-ROM version, 2nd ed.)

Publications list:
Available online

Access to staff:
Contact by e-mail and via website. Appointment necessary. Non-members charged.
Hours: Mon to Fri, 0900 to 1700
Special comments: Usually only available to members.

Also trading as:
SSERCSOFT
STS (Science, Technology and Safety) Support Services

SCOTTISH SCREEN ARCHIVE

Acronym or abbreviation: SSA

39–41 Montrose Avenue, Hillington Park, Glasgow, G52 4LA

Tel: 0845 366 4600
Fax: 0845 366 4601
E-mail: archive@scottishscreen.com

Website:
http://www.scottishscreen.com
Home page.
http://www.pads.ahds.ac.uk:81/SFTACatalogue .html
Selected catalogue.

Enquiries:
Enquiries to: Librarian
Direct tel: 0141 337 7407
Direct e-mail: ann.beaton@scottishscreen.com
Other contacts: (1) Access and Admin. Assistant; (2) Production Library Administrator; (3) Curator for (1) Enquiries Broadcasters/general; (2) Public/academic research; (3) Educational.

Founded:
1976

Formed from:
Scottish Screen; Scottish Film and Television Archive (SFTA) (year of change 2001)

Formerly called:
Scottish Film Archive (year of change 1997)

Organisation type and purpose:
National government body.
Archive.
To locate and preserve moving images made in or about Scotland.

Subject coverage:
Non-fiction film material relating to Scotland including documentaries, newsreels, educational, advertising and promotional, industrial, broadcasts and amateur film.

Museum or gallery collection, archive, or library special collection:
Film and documentation on the films of Scotland Committee 1938 to 1982
Upper Clyde Shipbuilders 1926 to 1971

Non-library collection catalogue:
All or part available online, in-house and in print

Library catalogue:
All or part available in-house

Printed publications:
Scottish Film Archive Catalogue (1st ed., free plus p&p)
To Speak Its Pride – the work of the Films of Scotland Committee 1938 to 1982, A Scottish Film Monograph (£5 plus p&p)
With an Eye to the Future – A Scottish Film Monograph (Alexander D and Cooper B, Documentary Film Makers, £5 plus p&p)

Electronic and video publications:
Seawards the Great Ships (video, £12.99)
Young At Heart (video, £12.99)
The Rugged Island and Eriskay (video, £12.99)
The Face of Scotland and Wealth of a Nation (video, £12.99)
Various other videos by mail order

Access to staff:
Contact by letter, by telephone, by fax and by e-mail. Appointment necessary.
Hours: Mon to Fri, 0900 to 1700

Parent body:
Scottish Screen
249 West George Street, Glasgow, G2 4QE; tel: 0141 302 1700; fax: 0141 302 1711; e-mail: info@scottishscreen.com

SCOTTISH SECONDARY TEACHERS' ASSOCIATION

Acronym or abbreviation: SSTA

14 West End Place, Edinburgh, EH11 2ED

Tel: 0131 313 7300
Fax: 0131 346 8057
E-mail: info@ssta.org.uk

Enquiries:
Enquiries to: General Secretary

Founded:
1945

Organisation type and purpose:
Trade union (membership is by qualification), present number of members: 8000.

Subject coverage:
Education in secondary schools in Scotland; general education in Scotland.

Access to staff:
Contact by letter, by telephone, by fax and by e-mail. Appointment necessary.
Hours: Mon to Thu, 0900 to 1645; Fri, 0900 to 1615

SCOTTISH SENSORY CENTRE

Acronym or abbreviation: SSC

Moray House School of Education, Holyrood Road, Edinburgh, EH8 8AQ

Tel: 0131 651 6501; minicom no. 0131 651 6067
Fax: 0131 651 6502
E-mail: sscmail@ed.ac.uk

Website:
http://www.ssc.education.ed.ac.uk
http://www.ssc.education.ed.ac.uk/library/list .html
Catalogue.

Enquiries:
Enquiries to: Resource Library Manager

Direct tel: 0131 651 6069
Other contacts: Administrator

Founded:
1991

Created by the merger of:
Scottish Centre for Education of the Deaf (SCED), Visual Impairment Centre (VIC) (year of change 1991)

Organisation type and purpose:
Advisory body, public library, training organisation, educational organisation.
To promote and disseminate effective practices and innovation in the education of children and young people with sensory impairments.

Subject coverage:
All aspects of sensory impairment including visual impairment, deaf education, dual sensory impairment and special educational needs.

Information services:
Postal Lending Library for members; information enquiries from the public; primary documents available online.

Museum or gallery collection, archive, or library special collection:
Resource library contains over 3,000 books, video material, audio cassettes and teaching packs (available for loan to library members)

Library catalogue:
All or part available online, in-house and in print

Printed publications:
Booklet (listing courses, seminars, workshops and open days available free of charge from the Centre)
Centre Newsletter (2 times a year)
Sensory Series (conference proceedings, etc.)
Autism and Visual Impairment Conference (£5 plus £1.50 p&p)
Cerebral Palsy and Visual Impairment in Children: Experience of Collaborative Practice in Scotland (£10 incl. p&p)
Empowerment '97 International conference on Deaf Education (£3.50 incl. p&p)
Empowering Young Deaf and VI People (free)
Managing Change in Visual Impairment Education (£3.50 incl. p&p)
Mobility Education: a Gateway to Learning, Putting Skills in Context (£1.50 incl. p&p)
Moving Through: Stages of the educational journey for deaf children and young people in North Ayrshire – A Parent/Carer Guide (free)
Promoting Social Inclusion of Pupils with Visual Impairment in Mainstream Schools in Scotland (£4.50 incl. p&p)
Self Evaluation by Peripatetic Sensory Services: Quality Assurance in Education Authority Peripatetic Sensory Services (£5 plus £1 p&p)
Video for Visually Impaired Learners (printed version, £10 incl. p&p)
Visual Impairment: Partnership, Networking and Support, Proceedings of the Conference, Sept. 1993 (£3 plus £1.50 p&p)
Order printed publications from: Resource Library Manager, Scottish Sensory Centre; tel. 0131 651 6069; e-mail sscmail@ed.ac.uk

Electronic and video publications:
The Crowded Cottage (in British Sign Language, CD-ROM, free)
IT the VI Way (video)
Let the Fingers do the Reading (video)
Let Me See (video)
Movement, Gesture and Sign (video)
Show Me How to Do It (video)
Video for Visually Impaired Learners (CD-ROM, free)
Vision for Doing (online only)

Publications list:
Available online and in print

Access to staff:
Contact by letter, by telephone, by fax, by e-mail and in person. Appointment necessary.
Hours: Mon to Fri, 0930 to 1300 and 1400 to 1630

continued overleaf

Access for disabled people:
Parking provided, ramped entry and lifts, toilet facilities

Links with:
Moray House School of Education
University of Edinburgh; website: http://www.education.ed.ac.uk

SCOTTISH SNOOKER LIMITED

Acronym or abbreviation: SSL

c/o Baillie, 59 Locher Avenue, Houston, Renfrewshire, PA6 7NX

Tel: 07814 150064
E-mail: scottishsnooker147@yahoo.co.uk

Website:
http://www.scottishsnooker.co.uk
Website of Scottish Snooker – The National Governing Body for Snooker in Scotland.

Enquiries:
Enquiries to: Administrator

Founded:
2001

Created by the merger of:
Scottish Billiards & Snooker Association (SBSA), and Scottish Snooker Association (SSA) (year of change 2001)

Organisation type and purpose:
National government body, national organisation, advisory body, statutory body, membership association (membership is by subscription), present number of members: 200, voluntary organisation, training organisation, consultancy.

Subject coverage:
Snooker.

Access to staff:
Contact by letter, by telephone and by e-mail
Hours: Mon to Fri, 0900 to 1700

SCOTTISH SOCIETY FOR AUTISM

Acronym or abbreviation: SSA

Hilton House, Alloa Business Park, Whins Road, Alloa, Clackmannanshire, FK10 3SA

Tel: 01259 720044
Fax: 01259 720051
E-mail: autism@autism-in-scotland.org.uk

Website:
http://www.autism-in-scotland.org.uk
Information on autism, training and conference services available.

Enquiries:
Enquiries to: HR Director

Founded:
1968

Formerly called:
Scottish Society for Autistic Children (SSAC) (year of change 1999)

Organisation type and purpose:
Voluntary organisation, registered charity (charity number SC009068).
To ensure the provision of the best possible education, care, support and opportunities for those of all ages with autism, to support families, improve understanding, and develop best practice amongst carers, professionals and society at large.

Subject coverage:
Autism and Aspergers Syndrome.

Information services:
Training, advice and support for families and carers of those living with ASD.

Education services:
Day and residential school for pupils with ASD.

Printed publications:
Magazine (members)
Various books related to autism
Newsletters

Information on services for adults, children, respite and training

Publications list:
Available in print

Access to staff:
Contact by letter, by telephone, by fax, by e-mail and via website. Appointment necessary.
Hours: Mon to Thu, 0900 to 1700; Fri, 0900 to 1630

Access for disabled people:
Level entry, access to all public areas, toilet facilities

SCOTTISH SOCIETY FOR CONSERVATION AND RESTORATION

Acronym or abbreviation: SSCR

Chantstown, Tartraven, Bathgate Hills, West Lothian, EH48 4NP

Tel: 01506 811777
Fax: 01506 811777
E-mail: admin@sscr.demon.co.uk

Website:
http://www.sscr.demon.co.uk
Information regarding SSCR, its activities and events.

Enquiries:
Enquiries to: Administrator

Founded:
1977

Organisation type and purpose:
International organisation, learned society, professional body (membership is by subscription), present number of members: 400, voluntary organisation, registered charity (charity number SC017185), suitable for ages: 18+, publishing house.
The purpose of the Society is to improve public knowledge, methods and working standards needed to protect, preserve and to maintain the condition of any work of art or structure of important historic interest and value.

Subject coverage:
All aspects of object conservation and restoration.

Printed publications:
SSCR Journal (3 times a year, members only)
Papers from conferences on: resins ancient and modern, paper and textiles, conservation of furnishing textiles, environmental control and monitoring, decorative wood, conservation and restoration of materials

Publications list:
Available online and in print

Access to staff:
Contact by letter, by telephone, by fax, by e-mail and via website. Appointment necessary.
Hours: Mon to Thu, 1300 to 1700

Member of:
European Confederation for Conservator-Restorers' Organizations (ECCO)
International Institute for Conservation (IIC)
United Kingdom Institute for the Conservation of Historic and Artistic Works (UKIC)

SCOTTISH SOCIETY FOR PSYCHICAL RESEARCH

Acronym or abbreviation: SSPR

5 Church Wynd, Kingskettle, By Cupar, Fife, KY15 7PS

Tel: 01337 830387
Fax: 01337 830387
E-mail: archie.lawrie@ukgateway.net

Enquiries:
Enquiries to: Honorary Secretary

Founded:
1987

Organisation type and purpose:
Learned society, registered charity (charity number SCO 20421), research organisation.

Subject coverage:
All types of phenomena known as paranormal or parapsychological, ghosts, poltergeists.

Museum or gallery collection, archive, or library special collection:
CD and tape library (members only)

Printed publications:
PSI report (newsletter, 9 times a year, £10 a year; as at Jan 2007)

Electronic and video publications:
Tapes of lectures (£3.50)

Access to staff:
Contact by letter, by telephone, by fax and by e-mail
Hours: 0900 to 2100, later in an emergency

SCOTTISH SOCIETY FOR THE PREVENTION OF CRUELTY TO ANIMALS

Acronym or abbreviation: Scottish SPCA

Braehead Mains, 603 Queensferry Road, Edinburgh, EH4 6EA

Tel: 0131 339 0222
Fax: 0131 339 4777
E-mail: enquiries@scottishspca.org

Website:
http://www.scottishspca.org
Locations of animal welfare centres; emergency telephone numbers for reporting an animal in distress; inspectorate; education; membership and volunteering.

Enquiries:
Enquiries to: Public Relations Director
Other contacts: Press Officer

Founded:
1839

Formerly called:
Aberdeen APCA, Glasgow Dog and Cat Home

Organisation type and purpose:
National organisation, advisory body, membership association (membership is by subscription), voluntary organisation, registered charity (charity number SC 006467), suitable for ages: Nursery to Adult.
Main aim is to prevent animal cruelty and to encourage kindness and humanity in their treatment.

Subject coverage:
Prevention of cruelty to animals, animal care, the law regarding animals, education in kind and humane treatment.

Printed publications:
Animal Express (Junior members magazine, quarterly)
Annual Report
Information sheets and leaflets
SSPCA News (members magazine, 6 times a year)

Access to staff:
Contact by letter, by telephone, by fax and by e-mail. Appointment necessary.
Hours: Mon to Fri, 0900 to 1700

Member of:
Eurogroup and World Society for the Protection of Animals (WSPA)

SCOTTISH SOCIETY OF THE HISTORY OF MEDICINE

Acronym or abbreviation: SSHM

c/o Dr Nigel Malcolm-Smith, 13 Craiglea Drive, Edinburgh, EH10 5PB

Tel: 0131 447 2572
E-mail: nigel@malcolm-smith43.wanadoo.co.uk

Website:
http://www.st-andrews.ac.uk/~sshm

Enquiries:
Enquiries to: Honorary Secretary

Founded:
1948

Organisation type and purpose:
Learned society (membership is by subscription), present number of members: 200.

Subject coverage:
History of medicine.

Museum or gallery collection, archive, or library special collection:
Dr Haldane P Tait's book collection is held in the Royal College of Physicians Library, Queen Street, Edinburgh. (subject Paediatrics and Public Health)

Printed publications:
Report of Proceedings

Access to staff:
Contact by letter, by telephone and by e-mail
Hours: Mon to Fri, 0900 to 1700

Affiliated to:
British Society for the History of Medicine

SCOTTISH SPINA BIFIDA ASSOCIATION

Acronym or abbreviation: SSBA

The Dan Young Building, 6 Craighalbert Way, Cumbernauld, G68 0LS

Tel: 01236 794500
Fax: 01236 736435
E-mail: mail@ssba.org.uk

Website:
http://ourworld.compuserve.com/homepages/ssbahq
http://www.ssba.org.uk

Enquiries:
Enquiries to: Family Support Service
Direct tel: 01236 794516
Direct e-mail: familysupport@ssba.org.uk

Founded:
1965

Organisation type and purpose:
Membership association, present number of members: 3,500, registered charity (charity number SCO13328).
To increase public awareness and understanding of spina bifida and/or hydrocephalus. Aims to secure provision for the needs of those with spina bifida and/or hydrocephalus and those of their families.

Subject coverage:
Spina bifida, hydrocephalus and allied disorders.

Printed publications:
Leaflets and booklets including:
Hydrocephalus
Hydrocephalus and You
Incontinence
Medical Aspects
Orthopaedic Aspects
Points for Parents
Pregnancy, Folic Acid and You
Scoliosis
Spina Bifida Occulta
Spina Bifida and Pregnancy
The Learner Driver with Spina Bifida and/or Hydrocephalus
Standard Information Pack

Publications list:
Available online and in print

Access to staff:
Contact by letter, by telephone, by fax, by e-mail, in person and via website
Hours: Mon to Fri, 0900 to 1700

Also at:
Fundraising Office, Scottish Spina Bifida Association
The Dan Young Building, 6 Craighalbert Way, Cumbernauld, G68 0LS; tel: 01236 794500; fax: 01236 736435; e-mail: fundraising@ssba.org.uk; website: http://www.ssba.org.uk
Scottish Spina Bifida Association – Family Support Department
The Dan Young Building, 6 Craighalbert Way, Cumbernauld, G68 0LS; tel: 0645 11 11 12 (lo-call routes); fax: 01236 736435; e-mail: familysupport@ssba.org.uk; website: http://www.ssba.org.uk

SCOTTISH SPORTS ASSOCIATION

Acronym or abbreviation: SSA

Caledonia House, South Gyle, Edinburgh, EH12 9DQ

Tel: 0131 339 8785
Fax: 0131 339 5168
E-mail: david@info-ssa.org.uk

Enquiries:
Enquiries to: Executive Administrator
Other contacts: Chairman

Founded:
1992

Formerly called:
Confederation of National Governing Bodies of Scottish Sport (year of change 1992)

Organisation type and purpose:
Membership association (membership is by election or invitation), present number of members: 78.
To represent the interests of Scottish Sports Governing Bodies.

Subject coverage:
Governing Bodies of sport in Scotland.

Printed publications:
Annual Report
Operational Plan
Running Sport Scotland literature
Saltire (seasonal members information brochure)
Who We Are, What We Do

Access to staff:
Contact by letter, by telephone, by fax and by e-mail
Hours: Mon to Thu, 0900 to 1700

Access for disabled people:
Parking provided, level entry, access to all public areas, toilet facilities

SCOTTISH SQUASH LIMITED

Caledonia House, 1 Redheughs Rigg, South Gyle, Edinburgh, EH12 9DQ

Tel: 0131 317 7343
Fax: 0131 317 7734
E-mail: scottishsquash@aol.com

Enquiries:
Enquiries to: Administration Manager

Formerly called:
Scottish Squash Rackets Association (SSRA)

Organisation type and purpose:
Membership association.

Subject coverage:
Player rankings, events, sources of finance, advice on construction and maintenance, equipment, rules, coaching, training courses, refereeing, history of squash, playing records, fitness.

Electronic and video publications:
Videos on coaching and events

Affiliated to:
European Squash Rackets Federation (ESRF)
World Squash Federation (WSF)

SCOTTISH SUB-AQUA CLUB

Acronym or abbreviation: ScotSAC

Caledonia House, 1 Redheughs Rigg, South Gyle, Edinburgh, EH12 9DQ

Tel: 0131 625 4404
Fax: 0131 317 7202
E-mail: hqssac@ssac.demon.co.uk

Website:
http://www.scotsac.com
Details of ScotSAC and its services.

Enquiries:
Enquiries to: Administrator

Founded:
1953

Organisation type and purpose:
Membership association (membership is by subscription), present number of members: 1,900.
National governing body of the sport.

Subject coverage:
Information on history of diving, dive training methods, diving equipment, salvage methods, underwater medicine, dive sites, construction of ships, underwater life, marine archaeology, video on diving, underwater sport.

Museum or gallery collection, archive, or library special collection:
Library of 760 books on diving, etc.

Printed publications:
Advanced dive training manual
Dive logbook
Dive Training Schedule
Introductory Dive Training Manual
Scottish Diver Magazine

Publications list:
Available in print

Access to staff:
Contact by letter, by telephone, by fax, by e-mail and via website
Hours: Mon to Thu, 0900 to 1700; Fri, 0900 to 1630

Access for disabled people:
Level entry, toilet facilities

SCOTTISH TEXT SOCIETY

Acronym or abbreviation: STS

27 George Square, Edinburgh, EH8 9LD

Tel: 0115 951 5922
Fax: 0115 951 5924
E-mail: editorialsecretary@scottishtextsociety.org

Website:
http://www.scottishtextsociety.org

Enquiries:
Enquiries to: Editorial Secretary

Founded:
1882

Organisation type and purpose:
Learned society, publishing house.
To further the study and teaching of Scottish literature, its language and history, in particular by publishing editions of original texts.

Subject coverage:
Scottish literature especially, although not exclusively, of the medieval and early modern period.

Non-library collection catalogue:
All or part available online

Library catalogue:
All or part available in-house

Printed publications:
List of all the publications (over 120) since 1883, some of which are now out of print, of Scottish poetry and histories, etc.
Recent annual vols include:
The Song Repertoire of Amelia and Jane Harris (ed. E. Lyle, K. McAlpine, A. McLucas)
Older Scots Vowels (A. J. Aitken and C. MacAfee)

continued overleaf

The Poems of Walter Kennedy (ed. N. Meier)
The Shorter Poems of Gavin Douglas (ed. P. Bawcutt)
David Hume of Godscroft, The History of the House of Angus (ed. D. Reid)
Order printed publications from: Boydell and Brewer Ltd, PO Box 9, Woodbridge, Suffolk, IP12 3DF; tel. 01394 610600; fax 01394 610316; e-mail trading@boydell.co.uk

Publications list:
Available online and in print

Access to staff:
Contact by letter, by e-mail and via website. Appointment necessary.
Hours: Mon to Fri, 0900 to 1700

Also at:
Scottish Text Society
c/o Editorial Secretary, 27 George Square, Edinburgh, EH8 9LD

SCOTTISH TOURIST GUIDES ASSOCIATION

Acronym or abbreviation: STGA

Norrie's House, 18b Broad Street, Stirling, FK8 1EF

Tel: 01786 447784
Fax: 01786 447784
E-mail: info@stga.co.uk

Website:
http://www.stga.co.uk

Enquiries:
Enquiries to: Administrator
Other contacts: Booking Secretary for booking guides.

Founded:
1959

Organisation type and purpose:
Professional body (membership is by subscription, qualification), present number of members: 320, service industry, suitable for ages: 25 to 75.

Subject coverage:
Specialised knowledge of Scotland past and present.
Guides are available to conduct tours throughout Scotland.

Printed publications:
List of members: a list of qualified guides, services, Gaelic and other language guides, driver guides
Guide List 2001

Publications list:
Available in print

Access to staff:
Contact by letter, by telephone, by fax, by e-mail and via website. Appointment necessary.
Hours: Mon to Fri, 0900 to 1700
Special comments: Please provide sae for reply.

Centralised booking service:
STGA booking service
tel: 01786 451953; fax: 01786 451953; e-mail: bookings@stga.co.uk

SCOTTISH TRAMWAY AND TRANSPORT SOCIETY

Acronym or abbreviation: STTS

PO Box 78, Glasgow, G3 6ER

Enquiries:
Enquiries to: General Secretary
Direct tel: 0141 445 3883
Direct e-mail: stts.glasgow@virgin.net

Founded:
1951

Organisation type and purpose:
Voluntary organisation.

Subject coverage:
Scottish tramways, trolleybuses and omnibuses. Glasgow Underground Railway, Strathclyde and Lothian Electric Trains.

Museum or gallery collection, archive, or library special collection:
R B Parr photographic collection
Scottish Road Public Transport photographic collection

Printed publications:
Green Cars to Hurlford
Scottish Transport Magazine (annually)
The Glasgow Tramcar (Stewart I G, 1994 ed., £16.95)
The Glasgow Horse Tramways 1872–1902 (Robertson S J T)

Electronic and video publications:
Aberdeen Trams (video, 1994, £19)
Dundee Trams (video, 1996, £16)
Glasgow Trams Part One (video, 1992, £22)
Glasgow Trams Part Two (video, 1993, £22)
Look Back at Glasgow's Trams and Trolleybuses

Publications list:
Available in print

Access to staff:
Contact by letter, by telephone and by e-mail
Hours: Mon to Fri, 0900 to 1700

Affiliated to:
AMTUIR (France)
Tramway Museum Society
Transport Trust

SCOTTISH TRANSPORT STUDIES GROUP

Acronym or abbreviation: STSG

26 Palmerston Place, Edinburgh, EH12 5AL

Tel: 0870 350 4202
E-mail: admin@stsg.org

Website:
http://www.stsg.org
Background information on STSG. Updated list of contacts.

Enquiries:
Enquiries to: Chairman
Direct e-mail: mail@s-b-solutions.co.uk
Other contacts: Organiser

Founded:
1984

Organisation type and purpose:
Membership association (membership is by subscription), present number of members: 100, registered charity.
To stimulate interest in, and awareness of, the transport function and its importance for the Scottish economy; to encourage contacts between operators, public bodies, users, academia and other organisations and individuals with interests in transport in a Scottish context; to issue publications and organise conferences and seminars related to transport policy and research.

Subject coverage:
Transport policy in Scotland.

Non-library collection catalogue:
All or part available online and in print

Library catalogue:
All or part available online and in print

Printed publications:
Scottish Transport Review (quarterly, free to members)
Annual Report and Research Review (free to members)
Occasional Papers (free to members)

Publications list:
Available online

Access to staff:
Contact by letter, by telephone, by fax, by e-mail and via website
Hours: Mon to Fri, 0900 to 1700

SCOTTISH UNIVERSITIES ENVIRONMENTAL RESEARCH CENTRE

Acronym or abbreviation: SUERC

Scottish Enterprise Technology Park, Rankine Avenue, East Kilbride, South Lanarkshire, G75 0QF

Tel: 01355 270139; 01355 270102
Fax: 01355 229898
E-mail: director@suerc.gla.ac.uk

Website:
http://www.gla.ac.uk/suerc

Enquiries:
Enquiries to: Director
Direct tel: 01355 223332

Founded:
2002

Formerly called:
Scottish Universities Research and Reactor Centre (year of change 2002)

Organisation type and purpose:
A collaborative facility operated jointly under a consortium agreement between the University of Glasgow and University of Edinburgh. It hosts five Natural Environment Research Council (NERC) Facilities that are available to UK scientists through competitive application to the relevant Steering Committees. The SUERC Accelerator Mass Spectrometer Laboratory is recognised by NERC as a suitable facility to undertake NERC-funded science.

Subject coverage:
Environmental research.

Access to staff:
Contact by letter, by telephone, by fax, by e-mail, in person and via website

SCOTTISH URBAN ARCHAEOLOGICAL TRUST

Acronym or abbreviation: SUAT

55 South Methven Street, Perth, Tayside, PH1 5NX

Tel: 01738 622393
Fax: 01738 631626

Website:
http://www.suat.demon.co.uk

Enquiries:
Enquiries to: Director

Founded:
1982

Organisation type and purpose:
Registered charity, research organisation, consultancy.
Archaeological research.

Subject coverage:
Urban archaeology in Scotland, general archaeology in Scotland.

Access to staff:
Contact by letter, by telephone and by fax.
Appointment necessary.
Hours: Mon to Fri, 0830 to 1630

Member of:
Council for British Archaeology
Council for Scottish Archaeology
Tayside and Fife Archaeological Committee

SCOTTISH WATER

Castle House, 6 Castle Drive, Carnegie Campus, Dunfermline, Fife, KY11 8GG

Tel: 0845 601 8855

E-mail: customer.service@scottishwater.co.uk

Website:
http://www.scottishwater.co.uk

Enquiries:
Enquiries to: Customer Services

Formed from:
East of Scotland Water (ESW), North of Scotland Water (NoSWA), West of Scotland Water (W'SWA), date of change, 1 April 2002

Subject coverage:
Land analysis, environment management, risk analysis, engineering consultancy, water and waste water analysis, waste management, pipeline installation, water charges, recreation, site surveys and site investigation, education.

Library catalogue:
All or part available in-house

Printed publications:
Information leaflets available on request
Household charges
Code of Practice
Annual Report

Access to staff:
Contact by letter, by telephone, by e-mail and via website
Hours: Mon to Fri, 0900 to 1700

Access to building, collection or gallery:
No access other than to staff

Access for disabled people:
Parking provided, level entry, toilet facilities

SCOTTISH WATER – EDINBURGH

Acronym or abbreviation: SW

55 Buckstone Terrace, Fairmilehead, Edinburgh, EH10 6XH

Tel: 0845 601 8855
Fax: 0131 445 5040
E-mail: customer.services@scottishwater.co.uk

Website:
http://www.scottishwater.co.uk
General information about Scottish Water and its services. Major sections include business and domestic services.

Enquiries:
Enquiries to: Customer Service Adviser
Direct tel: 0845 601 8855
Direct e-mail: customer.services@scottishwater.co.uk
Other contacts: Corporate Communications for press enquiries.

Founded:
2002

Organisation type and purpose:
Statutory body.

Subject coverage:
Supply of water and waste water services to the whole of Scotland

Museum or gallery collection, archive, or library special collection:
Small library of books and reports relating to water and waste water services and the water industry. For internal use only.

Library catalogue:
All or part available in-house

Printed publications:
Annual Report and Accounts
Conditions of Contract – Purchase of Goods and Services Various leaflets
(All the above available electronically)

Publications list:
Available online

Access to staff:
Contact by letter, by telephone, by fax, by e-mail, in person and via website. Appointment necessary.
Hours: Mon to Fri, 0900 to 1700

Access for disabled people:
Hours: Mon to Fri, 0900 to 1700

Area Offices:
Inverness Area Office and Stores
31 Henderson Drive, Longman North, Inverness, IV1 1TR; tel: 0845 601 8855; e-mail: customer.services@scottishwater.co.uk
Scottish Water
Bullion House, Invergowrie, Dundee, DD2 5BB; tel: 0845 601 8855; e-mail: customer.services@scottishwater.co.uk
Scottish Water
Kingshill House, Arnhall Business Park, Westhill, Aberdeen, AB32 6UF; tel: 0845 601 8855; e-mail: customer.services@scottishwater.co.uk
Scottish Water
419 Balmore Road, Glasgow, G22 6NU; tel: 0845 601 8855; e-mail: customer.services@scottishwater.co.uk

Head Office:
Scottish Water
Castle House, 6 Castle Drive, Carnegie Campus, Dunfermline, KY11 8GG; tel: 0845 601 8855; e-mail: customer.services@scottishwater.co.uk

Subsidiary body:
Scottish Water Scientific
Heriot-Watt Research Park, Avenue North, Edinburgh, EH14 4AP; tel: 0845 601 8855; e-mail: customer.services@scottishwater.co.uk

SCOTTISH WATER SKI ASSOCIATION

Acronym or abbreviation: SWSA

Townhill Country Park, Townhill, Dunfermline, Fife, KY12 0HT

Tel: 01383 620123
Fax: 01383 620122
E-mail: info@swsc.fsbusiness.co.uk

Website:
http://www.waterskiscotland.co.uk

Enquiries:
Enquiries to: Administrator
Other contacts: National Co-ordinator for first point of contact.

Founded:
1960

Formerly called:
(SWSA) (year of change 1998)

Organisation type and purpose:
Membership association (membership is by subscription), present number of members: 250, voluntary organisation.
To teach and instruct water skiing and wakeboarding including good driving practice.

Subject coverage:
All aspects relating to the sports of water skiing and waterboarding.

Non-library collection catalogue:
All or part available online

Library catalogue:
All or part available online

Access to staff:
Contact by letter, by fax and by e-mail
Hours: Tue to Fri, 1300 till Dusk; Sat, Sun, 1000 till Dusk
Special comments: Closed Monday.

Access to building, collection or gallery:
No prior appointment required

Access for disabled people:
Parking provided, ramped entry, level entry, access to all public areas, toilet facilities

SCOTTISH WIDER ACCESS PROGRAMME

Acronym or abbreviation: SWAPWest

300 Cathedral Street, Glasgow, G1 2TG

Tel: 0141 553 2471
Fax: 0141 552 6090
E-mail: swapwest@btconnect.com

Website:
http://www.swap2highereducation.com

Enquiries:
Enquiries to: Director

Founded:
1987

Organisation type and purpose:
Membership association (membership is by subscription), present number of members: 30, registered charity (charity number SCO 25833), suitable for adults.

Subject coverage:
All aspects of education for adults with few or no formal qualifications.

Access to staff:
Contact by letter, by telephone, by fax, by e-mail and via website
Hours: Mon to Fri, 0900 to 1700

SCOTTISH WILDLIFE TRUST

Acronym or abbreviation: SWT

Cramond House, 3 Kirk Cramond, off Cramond Glebe Road, Edinburgh, EH4 6HZ

Tel: 0131 312 7765
Fax: 0131 312 8705
E-mail: enquiries@swt.org.uk

Website:
http://www.swt.org.uk

Enquiries:
Enquiries to: Receptionist
Other contacts: Communications Manager (for press and media)

Founded:
1964

Organisation type and purpose:
Advisory body, membership association (membership is by subscription), present number of members: 31,000, voluntary organisation, registered charity (charity number SC005792), training organisation, consultancy, publishing house.
Campaigning environment body, land managers. The protection of all forms of Scottish wildlife and the Scottish environment.

Subject coverage:
Conservation of all forms of wildlife in Scotland, land use for wildlife interest, biological surveying, environmental education, reserves management, practical land management.

Non-library collection catalogue:
All or part available in-house

Library catalogue:
All or part available in-house

Printed publications:
Annual Review (free)
Information leaflets
Scottish Wildlife (magazine, 3 times a year, free to members)
Biodiversity Facts and Figures report

Access to staff:
Contact by letter, by telephone, by fax, by e-mail and via website. Appointment necessary.
Hours: Mon to Fri, 0900 to 1700

Administers:
123 reserves, including three visitor centres

Links with:
People's Postcode Lottery
Scottish Environment Link
Scottish National Heritage
The Scottish Executive
Wildlife Trusts Partnership

SCOTTISH WOMEN'S AID

2nd Floor, 132 Rose Street, Edinburgh, EH2 3JD

Tel: 0131 226 6606
Fax: 0131 226 2996
E-mail: contact@scottishwomensaid.org.uk

Website:
http://www.scottishwomensaid.org.uk

Organisation type and purpose:
Membership association, voluntary organisation,
registered charity (charity number SC001099),
training organisation.

Subject coverage:
Information, support and refuge for women,
children and young people who have been affected
by domestic abuse.

Printed publications:
Children, Young People and Domestic Abuse (30p)
Hello (welcome magazine for young children,
    statutory organisations £2, voluntary
    organisations £1)
Posters for children and young people (Rights, £1;
    Hello, £2; I am important, £2)
Respect (30p)
Welcome (magazine for young people, £2,
    statutory organisations; £1, voluntary
    organisations)
Young People Say (£5, voluntary organisations £4)
Your Rights (leaflet pack, £6 plus 50p p&p or
    singularly at 60p)

Publications list:
Available online and in print

Access to staff:
Contact by letter, by telephone, by fax, by e-mail
and via website. Appointment necessary.
Hours: Mon to Fri, 1000 to 1600; except Tue, 1300 to
1600

Access for disabled people:
Parking provided, ramped entry, level entry, access
to all public areas, toilet facilities

Has:
network of 39 local groups throughout Scotland

SCOTTISH WOMEN'S FOOTBALL

Acronym or abbreviation: SWF

Hampden Park, Glasgow, G42 9DF

Tel: 0141 620 4580
Fax: 0141 620 4581
E-mail: swf@scottish-football.com

Website:
http://www.scottishwomensfootball.com

Enquiries:
Enquiries to: Executive Administrator

Founded:
1972

Formerly called:
Scottish Women's Football Association

Organisation type and purpose:
Membership association (membership is by
subscription), present number of members: 3,000.

Subject coverage:
Women's & girls' football.

Access to staff:
Contact by letter, by telephone, by fax and by e-
mail. Appointment necessary.
Hours: Mon to Fri, 0900 to 1700

SCOTTISH WOMEN'S RURAL INSTITUTES

Acronym or abbreviation: SWRI

42 Heriot Row, Edinburgh, EH3 6ES

Tel: 0131 225 1724
Fax: 0131 225 8129
E-mail: swri@swri.demon.co.uk

Website:
http://www.swri.org.uk

Enquiries:
Enquiries to: General Secretary

Founded:
1917

Organisation type and purpose:
Membership association (membership is by
subscription), present number of members: 26,000,
voluntary organisation, registered charity (charity
number SCO 11901), suitable for ages: 12+, training
organisation, consultancy.

Subject coverage:
Cookery, crafts, village history.

**Museum or gallery collection, archive, or library
special collection:**
Village Histories Collection (histories of many
    villages in Scotland)

Printed publications:
Scottish Home and Country (monthly)

Access to staff:
Contact by letter, by telephone, by fax, by e-mail
and in person
Hours: Mon to Thu, 0900 to 1700; Fri, 0900 to 1530

Access to building, collection or gallery:
No access other than to staff, prior appointment
required

Member organisation of:
Associated Country Women of the World

SCOTTISH YOUTH HOSTELS ASSOCIATION

Acronym or abbreviation: SYHA

7 Glebe Crescent, Stirling, FK8 2JA

Tel: 01786 891400
Fax: 01786 891333
E-mail: syha@syha.org.uk

Website:
http://www.syha.org.uk
Information on all youth hostels in Scotland, travel
details, activity holidays, etc.

Enquiries:
Enquiries to: Public Relations Manager
Direct e-mail: marketing@syha.org.uk

Founded:
1931

Organisation type and purpose:
Voluntary organisation, registered charity (charity
number SCO 13138).

Subject coverage:
Low cost holiday accommodation for all ages;
recreational and activity holidays for young
people; holiday itineraries using youth hostels.

Printed publications:
Annual Report
General information leaflets
Scottish Hosteller (magazine, 2 times a year)
Hostel Guide (annual, free)

Access to staff:
Contact by letter, by telephone, by fax, by e-mail,
in person and via website
Hours: Mon to Fri, 0900 to 1700

Access to building, collection or gallery:
No prior appointment required

Affiliated to:
International Youth Hostels Federation

SCOTTISH YOUTH THEATRE

Acronym or abbreviation: SYT

105 Brunswick Street, Glasgow, G1 1TF

Tel: 0141 552 3988
Fax: 0141 552 7615
E-mail: info@scottishyouththeatre.org

Website:
http://www.scottishyouththeatre.org
Scotland's National Youth Theatre 'for & by' young
people.

Enquiries:
Enquiries to: Marketing Officer
Direct e-mail: emma@scottishyouththeatre.org

Founded:
1976

Organisation type and purpose:
Registered charity (charity number SCO 14283),
suitable for ages: 3 to 25.
National arts organisation.
Giving children and young people in Scotland the
opportunity to reach their creative potential
through a quality theatre arts experience.

Subject coverage:
Theatre, arts, drama, theatrical training, directing,
acting, movement, choreography, technical theatre/
stage management, musical theatre.

Education services:
Contact: karenm@scottishyouththeatre.org

Electronic and video publications:
See website: http://www.scottishyouththeatre.org/
    downloads/publications

Access to staff:
Contact by letter, by telephone, by e-mail, in
person and via website
Hours: Mon to Fri, 1000 to 1730

Funded by:
Glasgow City Council (GCC)
Scottish Arts Council (SAC)

Member organisation of:
Federation of Scottish Theatres (FST)
Independent Theatre Council (ITC)

SCOUT ASSOCIATION

Gilwell Park, Bury Road, Chingford, London, E4
7QW

Tel: 0845 300 1818
Fax: 020 8433 7103
E-mail: scoutbase@scoutbase.org.uk

Website:
http://www.scoutbase.org.uk
Information available on all aspects of scouting,
both home and abroad.

Enquiries:
Enquiries to: Public Relations Officer

Founded:
1907

Organisation type and purpose:
International organisation, membership
association, present number of members: 554,440
members in the UK, registered charity.

Subject coverage:
Scout training; outdoor pursuits, skills training and
service to the community; needs of the physically
handicapped and slow learners; youth education.

**Museum or gallery collection, archive, or library
special collection:**
Archives of 90 years of scouting

Printed publications:
Fact sheets on history or activities
Handbooks and manuals on outdoor pursuits
Publications on scout training and leader training
Scouting (magazine, monthly)

Electronic and video publications:
Rules and fact sheets (CD-ROM)

Publications list:
Available online

Access to staff:
Contact by letter, by telephone, by fax, by e-mail
and via website. Appointment necessary.
Hours: Mon to Fri, 0800 to 2000; Sat 0900 to 1200

Close association with the:
Guides Association

Member of:
National Council for Voluntary Youth Services
World Scout Bureau in Geneva

SCOUTS SCOTLAND

Formal name: The Scottish Council The Scout Association

Fordell Firs, Hillend, near Dunfermline, Fife, KY11 7HQ

Tel: 01383 419073
Fax: 01383 414892
E-mail: shq@scouts-scotland.org.uk

Enquiries:
Enquiries to: Chief Executive

Organisation type and purpose:
Membership association (membership is by subscription), present number of members: 43,828, registered charity (Scottish Charity No. SC017511), training organisation.
The physical, intellectual, social and spiritual development of young people.

Subject coverage:
Development programmes and outdoor activities for young people; training of voluntary adult leaders.

Printed publications:
Scottish Scout News (newsletter 5 times a year)

Access to staff:
Contact by letter, by telephone, by fax, by e-mail and via website
Hours: Mon to Fri, 0900 to 1700
Special comments: Prior appointment recommended.

Affiliated to:
Scout Association UK
Gilwell Park, Chingford, London, E4 7QW; tel: 020 8433 7100; fax: 020 8433 7103; e-mail: scout.association@scout.org.uk

SCREENWRITERS' WORKSHOP

Acronym or abbreviation: SW

Euroscript Ltd, 64 Hemingford Road, London, N1 1DB

Tel: 07958 244 656
E-mail: ask@euroscript.co.uk

Website:
http://www.lsw.org.uk/
Details of upcoming seminars, workshops and industry events with members-only online magazine on screenwriting.

Enquiries:
Enquiries to: Administrator
Direct e-mail: screenoffice@tiscali.co.uk

Founded:
1983

Formerly called:
London Screenwriters Workshop (LSW) (year of change 1998)

Organisation type and purpose:
National organisation, membership association (membership is by subscription), present number of members: 800 approx, training organisation.
To train writers of cinema and TV scripts and offer industry information and networking opportunities.

Subject coverage:
Screenwriting for cinema and TV.
Information on writing and marketing scripts.

Access to staff:
Contact by letter, by telephone, by e-mail and via website. Appointment necessary.
Hours: Mon to Fri, 0900 to 1700
Special comments: By arrangement or at times of advertised meetings, workshops and seminars.

SCRIPTURE UNION

Acronym or abbreviation: SU

207–209 Queensway, Bletchley, Milton Keynes, Buckinghamshire, MK2 2EB

Tel: 01908 856000
Fax: 01908 856111
E-mail: info@scriptureunion.org.uk

Website:
http://www.scriptureunion.org.uk
News from Scripture Union's various ministries across England and Wales.

Enquiries:
Enquiries to: Chief Executive

Founded:
1867

Organisation type and purpose:
International organisation, voluntary organisation, registered charity (charity number 213422), training organisation.
Christian missionary society, member of the Evangelical Alliance.
Evangelising and discipling children, young people and families through school work, missions, holidays, bible ministries, training and resources.

Subject coverage:
Christian outreach to children, young people and families through schools, churches, holidays and missions. Development for church members through training, publications and other resources.

Printed publications:
The Life (magazine, 4 times a year)
A wide range of titles covering many subjects and age ranges:
Up to six years old
Six to eleven year olds
Eleven years plus
School books and resources
Working with children
Bible readings for groups/adults
The Christian Life
Order printed publications from: Scripture Union Mail Order, PO Box 5148, MLO, Milton Keynes, MK2 2YX; tel: 01980 856006; fax: 01980 856020; e-mail: subs@scriptureunion.org.uk

Publications list:
Available in print

Access to staff:
Contact by letter, by telephone, by fax, by e-mail and via website
Hours: Mon to Fri, 0900 to 1700

Access to building, collection or gallery:
No prior appointment required

SEA FISH INDUSTRY AUTHORITY

Acronym or abbreviation: SEAFISH

18 Logie Mill, Logie Green Road, Edinburgh, EH7 4HS

Tel: 0131 558 3331
Fax: 0131 558 1442
E-mail: seafish@seafish.co.uk

Website:
http://www.seafish.co.uk
The work of each department; quality award schemes; publications list with prices; recipes.
http://www.seafish.co.uk/education
Information on fish industry and fish as food, for schools.

Founded:
1981

Formed from:
Herring Industry Board (HIB) and White Fish Authority (WFA)

Organisation type and purpose:
Advisory body, statutory body, training organisation, consultancy, research organisation.

Statutory body; accountable to the Department for Environment, Food and Rural Affairs for broad activities, but funded largely by the fish industry. The Authority works with the fish industry to meet the demands of consumers, to raise standards throughout the industry, to improve the efficiency and unity of the industry, and to secure a prosperous future for all fish industry sectors. The Authority is the Industry Designated Body for training within all sectors of the fish industry, and provides a forum for discussion between sectors.

Subject coverage:
Fishery economics; fish industry statistics (trade, landings, consumption, employment etc), infrastructure economics; fishery management; fish stocks and their assessment; marketing of fish within the UK and abroad; quality assurance throughout the fish industry; technology of fish processing; safety and legal compliance surveys of fishing vessels; grants and loans to the fish industry; EU legislation, and perspective on the UK fish industry; training of workers in all industry sectors; studies of fishing gear behaviour; mariculture.

Museum or gallery collection, archive, or library special collection:
Collection of fisheries statistical publications from Europe, North America, and also international in scope

Trade and statistical information:
Data on UK imports and exports of fish and fish products, data on fish landings into the UK, data on household consumption of fish and fish products in the UK, data on fish landings and trade of European and North American countries (variable information in this case)

Non-library collection catalogue:
All or part available in-house

Library catalogue:
All or part available in-house

Printed publications:
Variety of papers concerning aspects of Seafish Marketing
Annual Reports and accounts
Variety of industry sector newsletters
European Supplies Bulletin (quarterly, plus one data issue annually, UK £85 a year)
Household Fish Consumption in Great Britain (quarterly, UK £75 a year)
Key Indicators (quarterly, UK £35 a year)
UK Trade Bulletin (monthly, UK £35 a year)
Leaflets on the fishing industry, species of fish and fish recipes (free)
Marine Survey: Rules of Construction Series
Variety of economics research papers and seafish technology reports

Electronic and video publications:
Publications Guide (also available by e-mail)

Publications list:
Available online and in print

Access to staff:
Contact by letter, by telephone, by fax, by e-mail and via website. Appointment necessary.
Hours: Mon to Fri, 0900 to 1700

Access to building, collection or gallery:
No prior appointment required

Access for disabled people:
Ramped entry, toilet facilities

Branches at:
Sea Fish Industry Authority
Humber Seafood Institute, Origin Way, Europarc, Grimsby, DN37 9TU; tel: 01472 252300; fax: 01472 268792; e-mail: seafish@seafish.co.uk

SEAFACS INFORMATION AND RESEARCH

Acronym or abbreviation: SIR

PO Box 317, Welwyn Garden City, Hertfordshire, AL8 6DP

continued overleaf

Tel: 01707 334192
E-mail: seafacs@sir.co.uk

Website:
http://www.sir.co.uk

Enquiries:
Enquiries to: Manager

Founded:
1985

Organisation type and purpose:
Information Broker, consultancy.

Subject coverage:
Shipping, marine insurance, commodities.

Electronic and video publications:
P&I ezine Watch
ShipLaw ezine Watch
Commodity ezine Watch

Access to staff:
Contact by letter, by telephone, by e-mail and via
website. All charged.
Hours: Mon to Fri, 0930 to 1730

Access to building, collection or gallery:
No access other than to staff

SEASHELL TRUST

Stanley Road, Cheadle Hulme, Cheshire, SK8 6RQ

Tel: 0161 610 0100
Fax: 0161 610 0101
E-mail: info@seashelltrust.org.uk

Website:
http://www.seashelltrust.org.uk
General information, aims, contact details,
prospectuses.

Enquiries:
Enquiries to: School/College Secretary
Other contacts: Principal & Chief Executive

Founded:
1825

Formerly called:
Royal School for the Deaf

Organisation type and purpose:
Registered charity (charity number 1092655),
school, college and care home provider.
To provide a happy and secure environment for
pupils and students in school, college and
residence and for the service users at Griffin
Lodge; to provide alternative and augmentative
communication systems to ensure learners and
service users are able to access a communication
system appropriate to their needs; to provide an
extended curriculum and activities that meet the
functional and developmental needs of individuals
and promote their independence; to encourage
their participation in the local and wider
community; to realise individual potential by
providing challenges and experiences to develop
self-esteem and confidence.

Subject coverage:
Operates Royal School Manchester, a day and
residential, co-educational, non-maintained special
school; Royal College Manchester, an independent
specialist college on the same campus that caters
for learners of over 19 years; and Griffin Lodge, a
residential care home in the community for 12
young adults with complex learning and social
communication needs, most of whom are also
deaf.

Electronic and video publications:
Prospectuses
Inspection reports
Newsletter
Press releases
Order electronic and video publications from:
Downloadable from website

Publications list:
Available online

Access to staff:
Contact by letter, by telephone, by fax, by e-mail
and via website

SEASONAL AFFECTIVE DISORDER ASSOCIATION

Acronym or abbreviation: SADA

PO Box 989, Steyning, West Sussex, BN44 3HG

Tel: 01903 814942 (recorded message)
Fax: 01903 879939

Website:
http://www.sada.org.uk
Information about SAD and the Association.

Enquiries:
Enquiries to: Administrator

Founded:
1987

Organisation type and purpose:
Membership association (membership is by
subscription), present number of members: c. 1800,
voluntary organisation, registered charity (charity
number 800917).

Subject coverage:
Depression related to lack of sunlight.

Printed publications:
Information leaflet (free with sae)
Information Pack (£5)
Turning the Spotlight on SAD – The Patient
  Perspective (£2)

Publications list:
Available in print

Access to staff:
Contact by letter and by fax
Hours: Mon to Fri, 0900 to 1700

SEDGEMOOR DISTRICT COUNCIL

Bridgwater House, King Square, Bridgwater,
Somerset, TA6 3AR

Tel: 01278 435435
Fax: 01278 446412

Enquiries:
Enquiries to: Media Relations Officer

Organisation type and purpose:
Local government.

SEFTON LIBRARY AND INFORMATION SERVICES

Pavilion Buildings, 99–105 Lord Street, Southport,
Merseyside, PR8 1RJ

Tel: 01704 533133
Fax: 0151 934 2370
E-mail: library.service@leisure.sefton.gov.uk

Website:
http://www.sefton.gov.uk

Enquiries:
Enquiries to: Head of Library and Information
Services

Founded:
1974

Organisation type and purpose:
Local government body, public library.

Library catalogue:
All or part available online

Access to staff:
Contact by letter, by telephone, by fax, by e-mail,
in person and via website. Appointment necessary.

Access for disabled people:
Ramped entry

Parent body:
Sefton Metropolitan Borough Council

SELDEN SOCIETY

School of Law, Queen Mary University of London,
Mile End Road, London, E1 4NS

Tel: 020 7882 3968
Fax: 020 7882 7042
E-mail: selden-society@qmul.ac.uk

Website:
http://www.selden-society.qmul.ac.uk

Enquiries:
Enquiries to: Secretary

Founded:
1887

Organisation type and purpose:
Learned society (membership is by subscription),
present number of members: 1,700, registered
charity (charity number 211536), research
organisation, publishing house.
Promotion of research into history of English law,
and of legal profession, institutions, etc.

Subject coverage:
History of English law and legal institutions, legal
literature and records, palaeography, bibliography,
history of the legal profession, legal biography;
translation, transcription and evaluation of legal
manuscripts.

**Museum or gallery collection, archive, or library
special collection:**
Own publications 1887–2010

Printed publications:
Annual Report
Annual Series and Supplementary Series (over 150
  volumes of early law reports, courts' records,
  legal treatises, etc.)
Centenary Guide to Publications (1987) with
  history of the Society, etc.
Published lectures
Publications, List of Members and Rules
  (handbook)

Publications list:
Available online and in print

Access to staff:
Contact by letter, by telephone, by fax, by e-mail
and via website. Appointment necessary.
Hours: Mon, Tue, Thu, 0900 to 1700

SELECT

Formal name: The Electrical Contractors'
Association of Scotland
Acronym or abbreviation: ECAofS

The Walled Garden, Bush Estate, Midlothian, EH26
0SB

Tel: 0131 445 5577
Fax: 0131 445 5548
E-mail: admin@select.org.uk

Website:
http://www.select.org.uk

Enquiries:
Enquiries to: Head of External Affairs

Founded:
1900

Organisation type and purpose:
Trade association (membership is by qualification).
To represent the electrical, electronic and
communications systems industry. To advance and
promote members interests. To respond to the key
strategic issues facing the industry and the
Association.

Subject coverage:
Electrical installation, safety and security systems,
information technology, telecommunications,
electronics, industrial relations and employment
law matters; commercial and contractual matters;
education, training and health and safety matters;
management; marketing, technical advice and on-
site inspections.

Printed publications:
Annual Report

Cabletalk (magazine, 6 times a year)
Contract Manual
Members' Directory (annually)

Publications list:
Available in print

Access to staff:
Contact by letter, by telephone, by fax, by e-mail and in person
Hours: Mon to Fri, 0900 to 1700
Special comments: Charges to non-members under certain circumstances.

Access for disabled people:
Parking provided, level entry, access to all public areas, toilet facilities

Member of:
International Association of Electrical Contractors (AIE)
Specialist Engineering Contractors Group

Subsidiary body:
Scottish Electrical Contractors Insurance Company

SELEX GALILEO LTD

300 Capability Green, Luton, LU1 3PG

Tel: 01582 886135
Fax: 01582 795861
E-mail: dawn.couzens@selexgalileo.com

Website:
http://www.selexgalileo.com
Corporate website.

Enquiries:
Other contacts: Information Resources Officers (for departmental staff)

Formerly called:
SELEX Sensors and Airborne Systems Ltd; BAE Systems Avionics Ltd; GEC Marconi Ltd (year of change 1998); Marconi Electronic Systems (year of change 1999)

Organisation type and purpose:
International organisation, manufacturing industry.

Subject coverage:
Defence electronics, aerospace engineering and technology.

Non-library collection catalogue:
All or part available in-house

Library catalogue:
All or part available in-house

Access to staff:
Contact by letter, by telephone, by fax and by e-mail
Hours: Mon to Thu, 0845 to 1715; Fri, 0845 to 1645
Special comments: No personal visitors. Most information restricted to employees only.

Part of:
Finmeccanica

SENSE

101 Pentonville Road, London, N1 9LG

Tel: 0845 127 0060; textphone: 0845 127 0062
Fax: 0845 127 0061
E-mail: info@sense.org.uk

Website:
http://www.sense.org.uk

Enquiries:
Enquiries to: Information and Advice Service

Founded:
1955

Organisation type and purpose:
National organisation, membership organisation, voluntary organisation, registered charity (charity number 289868).
Leading national charity that supports and campaigns for children and adults who are deafblind.

Subject coverage:
Provides expert advice and information as well as specialist services to deafblind people, their families, carers and the professionals who work with them; supports people who have sensory impairments with additional disabilities.

Printed publications:
Fact sheets, leaflets, booklets.

Talking Sense (members magazine, 3 times a year)
Order printed publications from: website: http://www.sense.org.uk

Access to staff:
Contact by letter, by telephone, by fax, by e-mail and via website
Hours: Mon to Thu, 0900 to 1730; Fri, 0900 to 1700

Access to building, collection or gallery:
Hours: Mon to Fri, 0900 to 1700

Access for disabled people:
Wheelchair access, entry ramp, lift to 1st floor

SEQUAL TRUST

3 Ploughman's Corner, Wharf Road, Ellesmere, Shropshire, SY12 0EJ

Tel: 01691 624222
Fax: 01691 624222
E-mail: info@thesequaltrust.org.uk

Website:
http://www.thesequaltrust.org.uk

Enquiries:
Enquiries to: Charity Manager
Direct e-mail: liz@thesequaltrust.org.uk

Founded:
1969

Organisation type and purpose:
Membership association (membership is by subscription), registered charity (charity number 260119).
To raise funds to provide communication aids to disabled children and adults on a permanent free loan basis.

Subject coverage:
Communication aids for those with speech, movement or learning difficulties.

Services for disabled people:
Provision of communication aids for those with speech, movement or learning disabilities.

Printed publications:
The Sequal Newsletter (annual)

Publications list:
Available in print

Access to staff:
Contact by letter, by telephone, by fax and by e-mail
Hours: Mon to Fri, 0900 to 1630

Access to building, collection or gallery:
No visits necessary

SERA

Formal name: Socialist Environment and Resources Association

1 London Bridge, Downstream Building, London SE1 9BG

Tel: 020 7022 1985
E-mail: enquiries@sera.org.uk

Website:
http://www.serauk.org.uk

Enquiries:
Enquiries to: National Co-ordinator

Founded:
1973

Organisation type and purpose:
National organisation, membership association (membership is by subscription), present number of members: 1500, voluntary organisation.

Subject coverage:
Environmental issues, politics (Labour party), pollution, green economics, trade union issues.

Printed publications:
New Ground (magazine journal of Green Socialism, two times a year)

Access to staff:
Contact by letter, by telephone and by e-mail
Hours: Mon to Fri, 1000 to 1800

Affiliated to:
Labour Party

SERIES 2 CLUB LTD

PO Box 61, Aberdare, CF44 4AJ

E-mail: info@series2club.co.uk

Website:
http://www.series2club.co.uk
Historical, pictorial, contacts.

Enquiries:
Enquiries to: Membership Secretary

Founded:
1985

Organisation type and purpose:
Membership association (membership is by subscription), present number of members: 800.

Subject coverage:
Land Rover Series II 1958–1971, restoration, operation, history, registration enquiries (DVLA Registered Club).

Museum or gallery collection, archive, or library special collection:
Technical manuals

Printed publications:
Magazine (quarterly)

Access to staff:
Contact by letter. Non-members charged.
Hours: Mon to Fri, 1700 to 2000

Member of:
Association of Rover Clubs
Federation of British Historic Vehicle Clubs

SERVICES CENTRAL LIBRARY

Acronym or abbreviation: SCL

The ACC Memorial Hall, Thornhill Road, Aldershot, Hampshire, GU11 2BG

Tel: 01252 349839
Fax: 01252 349836
E-mail: ets.scl@gtnet.gov.uk

Enquiries:
Enquiries to: Librarian
Direct e-mail: ets.scl@gtnet.gov.uk

Organisation type and purpose:
National government body.

Subject coverage:
General, particularly computing, law and management, no military stock.

Library catalogue:
All or part available in-house

Printed publications:
Subject bibliographies of stock holding

Access to staff:
Contact by letter. Appointment necessary. Access for members only.
Hours: Mon to Fri, 0900 to 1630

Links with:
Army Library Service
Upavon, Pewsey, Wiltshire

SESAME INSTITUTE UK

Acronym or abbreviation: Sesame

Christchurch, 27 Blackfriars Road, London, SE1
8NY

Tel: 020 7633 9690
E-mail: sesameinstituteuk@btinternet.com

Enquiries:
Enquiries to: Director

Founded:
1964

Organisation type and purpose:
Advisory body, professional body (membership is
by subscription), registered charity (charity
number 263155), suitable for ages: 22+, training
organisation.
Recognised by the National Health Service,
Department for Education and the British
Association for Drama Therapists.
Promotes drama and movement in therapy.

Subject coverage:
Drama and movement as therapy in work with the
mentally and physically sick and the physically
handicapped, training in such special skills, direct
patient services.

Printed publications:
Newsletter (quarterly)
Bring White Beads When You Call on the Healer
(Lindkvist M)
Discovering the Self Through Drama and
Movement Therapy – The Sesame Approach
(Pearson J)
Report of Project at Smith Hospital (autistic
children) and at Goodmayes Hospital
(schizophrenic patients)

Microform publications:
Films and videos of Sesame Projects showing the
use of drama with schizophrenic, severely
subnormal and autistic children and adults

Publications list:
Available in print

Access to staff:
Contact by letter, by telephone and by e-mail.
Appointment necessary.
Hours: Tue, 1000 to 1700; Thu, Fri, 1000 to 1700
Special comments: No disabled access.

Affiliated to:
MENCAP
MIND

Member of:
European Consortium for Arts Therapies
Education

SEVENOAKS DISTRICT COUNCIL

Council Offices, Argyle Road, Sevenoaks, Kent,
TN13 1HG

Tel: 01732 227000
Fax: 01732 740693
E-mail: information@sevenoaks.gov.uk

Website:
http://www.sevenoaks.gov.uk
Basic information on authority, expanding into site
containing varied information on Sevenoaks area.

Organisation type and purpose:
Local government body.

Subject coverage:
Planning and building control, car parking, council
tax collection, environmental health, housing
benefits, recycling, refuse collection, community
and environmental services.

Publications list:
Available in print

Access to staff:
Contact by letter, by telephone, by fax, by e-mail,
in person and via website
Hours: Mon to Thu, 0845 to 1700; Fri, 0845 to 1645

Access for disabled people:
Parking provided, level entry, toilet facilities

Local Sub-offices at:
Edenbridge Local Office and Tourist Information
Centre
Stangrove Park, Edenbridge, Kent; tel: 01732
868110; fax: 01732 868114; e-mail:
edenbridgetic@sevenoaks.gov.uk
Swanley Library and Contact Centre
London Road, Swanley, Kent; tel: 01322 614660;
fax: 01322 665082; e-mail: information@
sevenoaks.gov.uk

SEWELLS INFORMATION & RESEARCH

Media House, Lynchwood, Peterborough Business
Park, Peterborough, Cambridgeshire, PE2 6EA

Tel: 01733 468000
Fax: 01733 468349
E-mail: sewells@emap.com

Website:
http://www.sewells.co.uk

Enquiries:
Enquiries to: Information Manager
Direct tel: 01733 468290
Direct fax: 01773 468349
Direct e-mail: eric.carnell@emap.com
Other contacts: Production Manager for
subscriptions and publishing enquiries.

Founded:
1962

Organisation type and purpose:
Advisory body, membership association
(membership is by subscription), service industry,
training organisation, research organisation,
publishing house.
Automotive research information and
publications.

Subject coverage:
Motor trade management, motor industry in the
UK and overseas, statistics, vehicle retailing
companies and manufacturers.

Trade and statistical information:
UK and European motor industry information and
Best Practice publications.

Printed publications:
Aftersales Management (monthly)
Automotive Marketing Review (bi-monthly)
Automotive Digest (weekly)
Automotive Finance (monthly)
Dealer Principal (monthly)
Digital Dealer (monthly)
Fleet Dealer (monthly)
Sales Management (monthly)
Used Car Dealer (monthly)
Management Guides
New Vehicle Registrations
Statistical Reports on Franchise Networks
Weekly Digests of Abstracts

Publications list:
Available online and in print

Access to staff:
Contact by letter, by telephone, by fax and by e-
mail. Non-members charged.
Hours: Mon to Fri, 0900 to 1730

SEWING MACHINE TRADE ASSOCIATION

Acronym or abbreviation: SMTA

Claremont House, 70–72 Alma Road, Windsor,
Berkshire, SL4 3EZ

Tel: 0870 330 8610
Fax: 0870 330 8611
E-mail: info@smta.org.uk

Website:
http://www.sewingmachine.org.uk
STMA and how to join, list of members.

Founded:
1930s

Organisation type and purpose:
A broad-based organisation representing the
interest of high street retailers of household sewing
machines and haberdashery, suppliers of
machinery to the clothing manufacturing industry
and trade distributors. Recognised by local and
national government organisations, educational
institutions and other trade associations as
authoritative voice of the industry.
To offer a courteous and helpful service to the
public and to co-operate nationally with each other
to assist clients who may have made purchases
from other members of the Association.

Subject coverage:
Sewing machines.

Access to staff:
Contact by letter, by telephone, by fax and by e-
mail

SEXUAL HEALTH AND REPRODUCTIVE CARE

Acronym or abbreviation: SHARC

25 Warwick Road, Coventry, CV1 2EZ

Tel: 024 7696 1300
Fax: 024 7696 1339

Enquiries:
Enquiries to: Information Officer
Other contacts: Manager, Clinical Medical Officer,
Senior Nurse

Founded:
1990

Formerly called:
Well Woman Clinic, Well Women's Services,
Women's Health and Information Centre

Organisation type and purpose:
Local government body.
Medical services, information service, support
groups.

Subject coverage:
Women's health, contraception, family planning,
health information, pregnancy.
Specialist genetic, sickle cell and thalassaemia
services, chlamydia screening for ages 16–24.

Access to staff:
Contact by letter, by telephone, by fax and in
person. Appointment necessary.
Hours: Mon to Thu, 0830 to 1900; Fri, 0830 to 1630;
Sat 1300 to 1630
Special comments: Appointments for clinical
services.

Access for disabled people:
Parking provided, ramped entry, access to all
public areas, toilet facilities
Special comments: Hearing loop, magnifier.

Parent body:
Coventry Primary Care Trust
Parkside House, Quinton Road, Coventry, West
Midlands, CV1 2NJ; tel: 024 7655 3344

SHAFTESBURY & DISTRICT HISTORICAL SOCIETY

Gold Hill Museum, Shaftesbury, Dorset, SP7 8JW

Tel: 01747 852157
E-mail: enquiries@goldhillmuseum.org.uk

Website:
http://www.shaftesburyheritage.org.uk

Enquiries:
Enquiries to: Honorary Secretary

Founded:
1946

Organisation type and purpose:
Membership association, voluntary organisation, registered charity (charity number 229883). Local history society and museum.

Subject coverage:
Local history of Shaftesbury and district.

Museum or gallery collection, archive, or library special collection:
With the support of a Heritage Lottery Grant, Gold Hill Musuem will re-open in 2011 with a new exhibition on the social history of the town and 24 villages that surround the town.
Significant objects from the museum collection include:
Dorset buttons
Maps
Shaftesbury Byzant
Lace-making
Victorian social history
World Wars I and II personal mementoes
Photographs and postcards (incl. 700 slides)
John Rutter's scrap album (19th-century)
Medieval alabaster panel, a 1744 fire engine, 2 church bells (16th- & 17th-century), a church font, 1919 Sale of Shaftesbury catalogue
The new Learning Centre will house the Library of local reference books and archival material

Non-library collection catalogue:
All or part available in-house

Library catalogue:
All or part available in-house

Printed publications:
History of The Dorset Button Industry – Gold Hill Museum leaflet
Shaftesbury, a town of slopes and views

Access to staff:
Contact by letter, by telephone, by e-mail, in person and via website. Appointment necessary.

Access to building, collection or gallery:
In 2011 Gold Hill Museum will re-open in Jul and close in Oct; the usal season runs from Apr to Oct; library by appointment only
Hours: 1030 to 1630 during the season
Special comments: By appointment only.

Access for disabled people:
Good disabled access; with the refurbishemnt of the museum, access is currently being improved
Hours: 1030 to 1630 during the season
Special comments: By appointment only.

Links with:
Shaftesbury Abbey Museum & Garden

Member organisation of:
Dorset Museums Association

SHAKESPEARE CENTRE LIBRARY & ARCHIVE

Henley Street, Stratford-upon-Avon, Warwickshire, CV37 6QW

Tel: 01789 208016
Fax: 01789 296083
E-mail: scla@shakespeare.org.uk

Website:
http://www.shakespeare.org.uk/main/3/339
Includes information on library & archive, catalogues, local collections databases, Royal Shakespeare Company Performance Database of productions and production personnel from 1879.

Enquiries:
Enquiries to: Head of Library & Archive

Founded:
1847

Organisation type and purpose:
Registered charity (charity number 209302).

Subject coverage:
Contains combined resources of the Shakespeare Birthplace Trust's Shakespeare Collections, Local Collections and the RSC Archive. Shakespeare Collections cover all aspects of Shakespeare's life, work and time; editions from the 17th century to

present; commentary on the works, translations; theatrical history of the Shakespeare canon; pictorial material including theatrical portraits and illustrations of plays; CDs, films and sound recordings. RSC Archive covers production and administrative archive of the Royal Shakespeare Company and its predecessors from 1879 held on deposit: prompt books; reviews, programmes, photos, and archive video recordings made since 1982. Charges are made for video viewing facilities. Local Collections cover history of Stratford and surrounding area; includes thousands of documents, photos, maps and books, and important documents relating to Shakespeare.

Museum or gallery collection, archive, or library special collection:
Archives of the Shakespeare Memorial Theatre 1879–1960 and of the Royal Shakespeare Company 1961 to date
Joe Cocks Studio Collection (photographs of RSC productions 1969–1991)
Bram Stoker Collection (material relating to Henry Irving at the Lyceum Theatre)
Holte Photographic Collections (photographs of RSC productions 1950s–1981)
Reg Wilson Collection (photographs of RSC productions 1961–1997)
Records of the Stratford-upon-Avon Corporation
Records of leading Warwickshire families
Parish and nonconformist registers for Stratford-upon-Avon
Local newspapers

Non-library collection catalogue:
All or part available online and in-house

Library catalogue:
All or part available online and in-house

Microform publications:
Shakespeare prompt books (microfilm, Harvest Microfilm, 1988, now marketed by Primary Source Media)
Bram Stoker collection on Henry Irving (Harvest Microfilm, 1988, now marketed by Primary Source Media)
Shakespeare at Stratford-upon-Avon (microfiche)

Access to staff:
Contact by letter, by telephone, by fax, by e-mail, in person and via website
Hours: Wed to Fri, 1000 to 1700; Sat, 0930 to 1230; Closed Mon, Tue, all Bank Holidays and the preceding Saturdays
Special comments: ID with address for general use. Letter of introduction required for access to special collections not available in surrogate form.

Access to building, collection or gallery:
No prior appointment required, except for video viewing, but advisable.
Special comments: Letter of introduction required for the use of some materials.

Access for disabled people:
Access to all public areas, toilet facilities
Special comments: Advance notice for wheelchair users advisable. Parking 50 metres.

Constituent bodies:
Royal Shakespeare Company Archive and Library

SHAKESPEARE INSTITUTE LIBRARY

Library Services, University of Birmingham, Mason Croft, Church Street, Stratford-upon-Avon, Warwickshire, CV37 6HP

Tel: 0121 414 9525
Fax: 01789 292021
E-mail: silib@bham.ac.uk

Website:
http://www.library.bham.ac.uk/using/libraries/shakespeare.shtml

Enquiries:
Enquiries to: Librarian
Other contacts: Information Assistant

Founded:
1951

Organisation type and purpose:
University library, university department or institute, postgraduate research institute.

Subject coverage:
Shakespeare; English literature 1475–1640; theatre history.

Museum or gallery collection, archive, or library special collection:
Archive of New Shakespeare Theatre Company
Archive of the Renaissance Theatre Company
E.K. Chambers Papers
Trevor Howard-Hill Archive
Brian Vickers Archive
Unpublished Shakespeare Film Script collection
Shakespeare newscuttings collection 1902–
Early English books 1475–1640 (microform)
Three centuries of English and American plays (microform)

Library catalogue:
All or part available online

Access to staff:
Contact by letter, by telephone, by fax, by e-mail and in person. Appointment necessary.
Hours: Mon to Thu, 0900 to 2000; Fri and Sat, 0900 to 1700; Sun, 1000 to 1700
Special comments: Only members and visitors with valid library cards may be admitted after 1700 and on Sat and Sun. Non-members of the University must bring along at least 2 different forms of ID in order to obtain a library pass.

Parent body:
Library Services (Academic Services)
The University of Birmingham, Edgbaston, Birmingham, B15 2TT; tel: 0121 414 5828; e-mail: library@bham.ac.uk; website: http://www.library.bham.ac.uk

SHAP WORKING PARTY ON WORLD RELIGIONS IN EDUCATION

Acronym or abbreviation: SHAP

National Society's RE Centre, Church House, Great Smith Street, London, SW1P 3NZ

Tel: 020 7898 1495
Fax: 020 7898 1493
E-mail: mike.berry@natsoc.org.uk

Website:
http://dspace.dial.pipex.com/nsrec

Enquiries:
Enquiries to: Secretary

Founded:
1969

Organisation type and purpose:
Advisory body, professional body (membership is by election or invitation), training organisation, consultancy.
Concerned with providing accurate information about world religions for schools and institutions of higher education, police, hospitals, prisons, etc.

Subject coverage:
Religious education and teaching, the world's major religions.

Printed publications:
Calendar of Festivals (annually)
Journal (annually)
Festivals in World Religions
Handbook of World Religions

Publications list:
Available in print

Access to building, collection or gallery:
Prior appointment required
Hours: Mon to Fri, 0900 to 1630

Access for disabled people:
Ramped entry, access to all public areas, toilet facilities

continued overleaf

Associated with:
European Association of World Religions in
Education (EAWRE)

SHAPE

Deane House Studios, 27 Greenwood Place,
London, NW5 1LB

Tel: 0845 521 3457\ Minicom no. 020 7424 7368
Fax: 0845 521 3458
E-mail: info@shape-uk.co.uk

Website:
http://www.shapearts.org.uk

Enquiries:
Enquiries to: Chief Executive
Direct e-mail: mhairi@shapearts.org.uk

Founded:
1976

Organisation type and purpose:
Advisory body, membership association, voluntary
organisation, registered charity (charity number
279184), training organisation.
Ticket Scheme: reduced price tickets and volunteer
escorts/drivers for London arts and entertainment
events for disabled people or those over 70 years of
age. Shape in Education: training for deaf and
disabled artists to work in education settings.
Shape Training: accredited training courses and
placement in all aspects of arts management and
practice. Training Support Network for young
disabled and deaf people wishing to enter arts
industries. Advice and information on training and
employment. Local Arts Development: workshops,
projects and events for disabled people, people
with learning difficulties, mental health system
survivors and older people. Deaf Arts Programme:
national programme of projects and events
promoting deaf arts and equal access to the arts for
deaf and hard of hearing people. Advice,
Information and Consultancy on all aspects of arts
and disability.
Shape opens up access to the arts, enabling greater
participation by disabled and older people.

Subject coverage:
Disability arts, deaf arts, training courses, ticket
scheme with reduced price tickets and volunteer
drivers, training placements and accredited
courses in arts management.

**Museum or gallery collection, archive, or library
special collection:**
Arts related archives specific to Shape, disability
arts

Printed publications:
Disability Arts and Culture Papers

Access to staff:
Contact by letter, by telephone, by fax and by e-
mail
Hours: Mon to Fri, 1000 to 1800

Affiliated to:
Shape network, a federation of independent
disability arts organisations

Other addresses:
Shape in Hammersmith and Fulham
    Polish Arts and Cultural Centre, 238–246 Kings
    Street, Hammersmith, London, W6 0RF; tel: 020
    8741 7548 (answer machine) 020 8563 2894
    (minicom); fax: 020 8741 6375
Shape in Islington
    Room G15, c/o LBI, Arts and Heritage
    Department, Islington Town Hall, Upper Street,
    London, N1 1UD; tel: 020 7527 3850; fax: 020
    7477 3856
Shape in Wandsworth
    BAC, Lavender Hill, London, SW11 5TS; tel: 020
    7924 5287; fax: 020 7978 2507

SHARK ANGLING CLUB OF GREAT BRITAIN

Acronym or abbreviation: SACGB

The Quay, Looe, Cornwall, PL13 1DX

Tel: 01503 262642
Fax: 01503 262642
E-mail: enquiries@sharkanglingclubofgreatbritain
.org.uk

Enquiries:
Enquiries to: Secretary

Organisation type and purpose:
National organisation, membership association
(membership is by subscription), present number
of members: 400.

Subject coverage:
Shark fishing.

Access to staff:
Contact by letter, by telephone, by fax, by e-mail
and in person
Hours: 7 days a week.

Access to building, collection or gallery:
No prior appointment required

SHAW SOCIETY

C/o Alan Knight, 10 Compston Road, London, N1
2PA

Tel: 020 7226 4266

Website:
http://www.shawsociety.org.uk

Enquiries:
Enquiries to: Honorary Secretary
Direct e-mail: anthnyellis@aol.com

Founded:
1941

Organisation type and purpose:
Membership association (membership is by
subscription), present number of members: c. 300,
voluntary organisation.

Subject coverage:
Life and works of Bernard Shaw.

Other addresses:
Membership Secretary
    1 Buckland Court, 37 Belsize Park, London, NW3
    4EB; tel: 020 7794 7014; fax: 020 7431 0816; e-
    mail: shawsociety@blueyonder.co.uk
Newsletter Editor
    C/o Philip Riley, 11 Founders House, Aylesford
    Street, London, SW1V 3QE; tel: 020 7630 1675; e-
    mail: commonroom04@yahoo.com

SHEFFIELD AND DISTRICT FAMILY HISTORY SOCIETY

5 Old Houses, Piccadilly Road, Chesterfield,
Derbyshire, S41 0EH

E-mail: secretary@sheffieldfhs.org.uk

Website:
http://www.sheffieldfhs.org.uk
Aims of the society, area covered, membership
information, officers, meetings and activities,
publications, members e-mail addresses, related
links, maps back to 1600.

Enquiries:
Enquiries to: Honorary Secretary

Founded:
1977

Organisation type and purpose:
Membership association (membership is by
subscription), present number of members: 1050,
voluntary organisation, suitable for ages: all.
To promote, for the benefit and education of the
public, the study of genealogy, family history and
local history in the County of South Yorkshire.

Subject coverage:
Family history, local (Sheffield and District) history,
census records, parish records.

Library catalogue:
All or part available in print

Printed publications:
The Flowing Stream (journal, quarterly, free to
members)
The Small Guide to Parishes in the Sheffield Area
The Small Guide to Nonconformists in Sheffield
Researching Your Family History in Sheffield
Sheffield Ancestors
Sheffield's Volunteer Armies
Changes in Sheffield Street Names 1871
Order printed publications from: Sheffield and
District Family History Society
17 Firshill Road, Sheffield, S4 7BB

Microform publications:
Bradfield Poor Law Documents (microfiche)
Hill Top Chapel and Christ Church Attercliffe,
    indexed transcript of the Baptism Registers
    1719–1840, Marriage Registers 1734–1753 and
    Bishops Transcripts 1693–4 (microfiche)
Militia Men of the Barnsley District 1806 (details of
    3,322 men in 40 townships that comprised the
    Staincross Wapentake, lying to the north and
    west of Sheffield) (microfiche)
St Mary's Ecclesfield, indexed transcript of
    Marriage Registers 1622–1840 and Banns 1653–
    1655, 1754–1775 (Marriages missing 14
    miscellaneous years between 1665 and 1692)
    (microfiche)
St Nicholas Bradfield Marriages 1723–1840
    (microfiche)
St Peter's Church Tankersley, indexed transcript of
    Baptisms, Marriages and Burials 1598–1840,
    Intent of Marriage 1653–1657 and Banns 1754–
    1810 (Registers 1650/1–1661 are missing. 1662 -
    1677 have been compiled from Bishops
    Transcripts) (microfiche)
Hearth Tax Returns for South Yorks, 1672
    (microfiche)
Militia Men of the Barnsley District (microfiche)
Burngreave Cemetery Consecrated Section
    Monumental Inscriptions (microfiche)
Burngreave Cemetery General Section
    Monumental Inscriptions (microfiche)
St Thomas Church Brightside Monumental
    Inscriptions (microfiche)
St Phillip's Churchyard and Wardsend Cemetery
    Monumental Inscriptions (microfiche)
Christ Church Dore Churchyard Monumental
    Inscriptions

Electronic and video publications:
Burial Transcript and Index All Saints, Ecclesall,
    1789–1903 (CD)
Burial Transcript and Index All Saints Rotherham
    1813–1854 (CD)
Burial Transcript and Index St Mary Greasbrough
    1813–1858 (CD)
Burial Transcript and Index Attercliffe Cemetery
    1859–1960 (CD)
Burial Transcript and Index Darnall Cemetery
    1859–1901 (CD)
Burial Transcript and Index Revel Lane Cemetery,
    Woodhouse 1875–1949 (CD)
Burial Transcript and Index Beauchief Abbey
    1813–1988 (CD)
Burial Transcript and Index Christ Church
    Fulwood 1839–1908 (CD)
Burial Transcript and Index St James Norton 1813–
    1947 (CD)
Burial Transcript and Index Christ Church
    Attercliffe 1813–1902 (CD)
Burial Transcript and Index Christ Church
    Stannington 1830–1932 (CD)
Burial Transcript and Index St Mary Bolsterstone
    1813–1856 (CD)
Burial Transcript and Index St Nicholas Bradfield
    1813–1899 (CD)
Burial Transcript and Index Church of the
    Ascension Oughtibridge 1843–1942 (CD)
Burial Transcript and Index St Mary Walkley 1880–
    1901 (CD)
Burial Transcript and Index Holy Trinity Darnall
    1846–1866 (CD)
Burial Transcript and Index Christ Church
    Pitsmoor 1850–1931(CD)
Burial Transcript and Index, St Lawrence Tinsley
    1813–1901(CD)
Burial Transcript and Index Holy Trinity Wicker
    1859 only Burials (CD)

Burial Transcript and Index St George's Portobello 1830–1899 (CD)
Burial Transcript and Index St John Chapeltown 1860–1971 (CD)
Burial Transcript and Index Christ Church Dore 1829–1967 (CD)
Burial Transcript and Index Cholera Burial Ground 1832 (CD)
Burial Transcript and Index St Mary Ecclesfield 1813–1909 (CD)
Burial Transcript and Index St Paul's Church 1813–61 (city centre) (CD)
Burial Transcript and Index St Thomas Brightside 1854–1901 (CD)
Burial Transcript and Index Christ Church Gleadless 1839–1953
Burial Transcript and Index Christ Church Heeley 1848–1906
Burial Transcript and Index St James 1813–55 (city centre)
Burial Transcript and Index St John Park 1830–1908
Burial Transcript and Index St Mary's (Bramall Lane) 1830–1908 (CD)
Burial Transcript and Index St Peter & St Paul (Cathedral) 1813–55 (CD)
Burial Transcript and Index St Philip's 1829–1918 (including Wardsend Cemetery 1857–1905) (CD)
Burial Transcript and Index St Thomas Crookes 1859–1973 (CD)
Burial Transcript and Index Wadsley 1835–1903 (7/5/1891–11/1/1895 records missing) (CD)
Burial Transcript and Index Tinsley Park Cemetery 1882–1973 (CD)
1831 Census Transcript and Index Nether Hallam
1891 Census Transcript and Index Sheffield North, Sheffield West, Sheffield Park, Sheffield South, Ecclesall Bierlow, Nether Hallam, Norton, Upper Hallam, Attercliffe cum Darnall, Brightside Bierlow (CD)
1861 Census Index for Sheffield, Rotherham and Bradfield (CD)
Bradfield Parish Church of St Nicholas Monumental Inscriptions (CD)
Christ Church Heeley Index of Baptisms 1848–1895 (disk)
St James Norton, indexed transcript of Marriages 1559–1837 (disk)
St Mary the Virgin Beighton, indexed transcript of Marriages 1645–1837 (disk)

Publications list:
Available online and in print

Access to staff:
Contact by letter, by e-mail and via website
Hours: Library: Mon to Thu, 0930 to 1730; Fri, closed; Sat, 0900 to 1300 and 1400 to 1630

Library facility held at:
Sheffield Archives
52 Shoreham Street, Sheffield, S1 4SP; tel: 0114 203 9395

Member of:
Federation of Family History Societies (FFHS)

SHEFFIELD ARCHIVES

52 Shoreham Street, Sheffield, South Yorkshire, S1 4SP

Tel: 0114 203 9395
Fax: 0114 203 9398
E-mail: archives@sheffield.gov.uk

Website:
http://www.sheffield.gov.uk/archives

Enquiries:
Enquiries to: Duty Archivist

Organisation type and purpose:
Local government body.

Subject coverage:
Family and estate records, church records (Church of England, Roman Catholic and Nonconformist), business archives, local authority and public records, trade union archives, antiquarian collections, political party records, societies and institutional records.

Museum or gallery collection, archive, or library special collection:
Collections include:
Arundel Castle Manuscripts (Sheffield, Derbyshire, and Nottinghamshire estates of the Dukes of Norfolk)
Business records of industrial history of the area, coal mining, iron and steel, cutlery, silver plate, professional firms, institutions and clubs
Correspondence and papers of Edward Carpenter (1844–1929)
Diocesan records for the Archdeaconry of Sheffield
Papers of the Earls of Wharncliffe
Papers of the Spencer Stanhope and Vernon Wentworth families and estates
Records of the Roman Catholic Diocese of Hallam
Wentworth Woodhouse Muniments (includes the papers of Thomas Wentworth, Earl of Strafford, 2nd Marquis of Rockingham and Edmund Burke)

Non-library collection catalogue:
All or part available online and in print

Printed publications:
A History of Sheffield Castle and Markets (£3.99)
Catalogue of the Arundel Castle Manuscripts in the Sheffield City Libraries (£15)
Diamonds in Brown Paper (£3.95)
Guide to the Fairbank Collection (£1)
Guide to the Manuscript Collections Supplement 1950–1976 (£7)
Essays in the Economic and Social History of South Yorkshire (£2.50)
Local Colour (£1)
Lyceum (£2)
Manuscript Collections in the Sheffield City Libraries (£2.50)
On the Knife Edge (£6.95)
Sheffield Walkabout (£4.95)
Sheffield Official Guide (£1.95)
Sir Francis Chantrey (£1)
The Sword of Sheffield (£1.50)
Family History Guides – listings of the sources available in the Archives (all seven £5 plus £1 p&p UK):
Census Returns, 1841, 1851, 1861, 1871 and 1881 listed alphabetically by place, covers the whole of South Yorkshire. 1981 – Sheffield, Ecclesall, Bierlow, Rotherham and Wortley registration districts
Monumental Inscriptions listed alphabetically by place, both Anglican and Nonconformist records included
Bishop's Transcripts, listed alphabetically by place, covers the whole of South Yorkshire
Parish Registers, Anglican registers from parishes in the Archdeaconry of Sheffield, listed alphabetically by place: Part 1 those in the Archives, Part 2 those churches which keep their own; both with dates
Copies of Parish Registers Held by Other Record Offices, listed alphabetically by place, covers parts of South Yorkshire and Derbyshire
Nonconformist Registers
Registers of Burials in Churchyards, Chapel Yards and Cemeteries, covers the whole of South Yorkshire and includes Anglican churchyards, Nonconformist chapelyards and local authority cemeteries

Publications list:
Available online

Access to staff:
Contact by letter, by telephone, by fax, by e-mail and in person
Hours: Mon, 1000 to 1730; Tue to Thu, 0930 to 1730; Fri, closed; Sat, 0900 to 1300 and 1400 to 1700
Special comments: Users of the searchroom must obtain a reader's ticket, two official proofs of identity required on first visit. Access is suitable for disabled persons and wheelchairs.

Access for disabled people:
Level entry, access to all public areas, toilet facilities

SHEFFIELD ASSAY OFFICE

Acronym or abbreviation: SAO

Guardians Hall, Beulah Road, Hillsborough, Sheffield, South Yorkshire, S6 2AN

Tel: 0114 231 2121
Fax: 0114 233 9079
E-mail: paragreene@assayoffice.co.uk

Website:
http://www.assayoffice.co.uk/resource.htm
Information about library and archives
http://www.assayoffice.co.uk
Services provided, history, contact details, etc.
http://www.assayoffice.co.uk/info.htm
List of publications and ordering details

Enquiries:
Enquiries to: Librarian and Curator
Other contacts: Laboratory Manager

Founded:
1773

Organisation type and purpose:
Statutory, non-profit making body, UKAS accredited laboratory.

Subject coverage:
Jewellery design, silverware design, principally European but worldwide coverage; precious metal assaying including historical material; some information on non-ferrous mining and metallurgy; hallmarking records for Sheffield.

Museum or gallery collection, archive, or library special collection:
Catalogues and records from various silversmithing firms no longer in existence (mainly local)
Daybooks from 1773 to 1830 and 1932 to the present
Office records from 1773 (some stored at Sheffield Archives)

Trade and statistical information:
Hallmarking figures for UK, produced by British Hallmarking Council.

Non-library collection catalogue:
All or part available in-house

Library catalogue:
All or part available in-house

Printed publications:
Bradbury's Book of Hallmarks
Old Silver Platers and their Marks (£25 plus p&p)
Sheffield Assay Office Register 1773/1909 (£9.95 plus p&p)

Access to staff:
Contact by letter, by telephone, by fax, by e-mail and via website. Appointment necessary. Non-members charged.
Hours: Library and collection: Thu and Fri, 0900 to 1600
Archives at Sheffield Archives: Mon to Sat

Access to building, collection or gallery:
No prior appointment required
Hours: Mon to Fri, 0900 to 1600

Access for disabled people:
Parking provided, ramped entry, access to all public areas

SHEFFIELD CITY COUNCIL

Formal name: City of Sheffield Metropolitan District Council
Acronym or abbreviation: SCC

Howden House, 1 Union Street, Sheffield, S1 2HH

Tel: 0114 272 6444
Fax: 0114 273 5003
E-mail: firstpoint@sheffield.gov.uk

Website:
http://www.sheffield.gov.uk/

Enquiries:
Enquiries to: Media Relations Manager
Direct tel: 0114 273 6604
Direct fax: 0114 273 4652

continued overleaf

Direct e-mail: Steph.Cunningham@sheffield.gov.uk

Founded:
1897

Organisation type and purpose:
Local government body.

Subject coverage:
Information about Sheffield, trade, tourism, entertainment, sport, education, social services, housing, parks, environmental health, highways, markets, planning, transport and all other local government services in Sheffield.

Printed publications:
Official Guide to Sheffield (£2)
Official Street Guide to Sheffield (£2)

Access to staff:
Contact by letter, by telephone, by fax, by e-mail and in person
Hours: Mon to Fri, 0900 to 1700

SHEFFIELD GALLERIES & MUSEUMS TRUST

Leader House, Surrey Street, Sheffield, South Yorkshire, S1 2LH

Tel: 0114 278 2600
Fax: 0114 278 2604
E-mail: info@sheffieldgalleries.org.uk

Website:
http://www.sheffieldgalleries.org.uk

Founded:
1998

Organisation type and purpose:
Local government body, registered charity (charity number 1068850).
Administrative body.

Subject coverage:
Galleries and Museums Trust has management responsibility for five musems and galleries in Sheffield, including responsibility for policies, forward planning and performance.

Access to staff:
Contact by letter, by telephone, by fax, by e-mail and via website. Appointment necessary.
Hours: Mon to Fri, 0900 to 1730

Access for disabled people:
Toilet facilities
Special comments: Parking in Surrey Street, one step at door, phone prior to visit if assistance required.

Jointly funded by:
Sheffield City Council and the Arts Council of England

Trust sites:
Bishops' House
   Meersbrook Park, Norton Lees Lane, Sheffield, South Yorkshire, S8 9BE; tel: 0114 278 2600; fax: 0114 278 2604
Graves Art Gallery
   Surrey Street, Sheffield, South Yorkshire, S1 1XZ; tel: 0114 273 5158; fax: 0114 273 4705
Mappin Art Gallery
   Weston Park, Sheffield, South Yorkshire, S10 2TP; tel: 0114 278 2600; fax: 0114 275 0957
Millennium Galleries
   Arundel Gate, Sheffield, South Yorkshire, S1 2PP; tel: 0114 278 2600; fax: 0114 278 2604
Sheffield City Museum
   Weston Park, Sheffield, South Yorkshire, S10 2TP; tel: 0114 278 2600; fax: 0114 275 0957

SHEFFIELD HALLAM UNIVERSITY

Acronym or abbreviation: SHU

City Campus, Pond Street, Sheffield, South Yorkshire, S1 1WB

Tel: 0114 225 3581
Fax: 0114 225 4985

Website:
http://www.shu.ac.uk

Enquiries:
Direct e-mail: pressoffice@shu.ac.uk

Founded:
1843

Organisation type and purpose:
University department or institute.

Printed publications:
Prospectuses (undergraduate and postgraduate)
Course leaflets
Visitors' Guide
Sports Club Guide
Happening at Hallam
Annual Report

Electronic and video publications:
Undergraduate Prospectus (CD-ROM)
Student Life at the University (video)

Publications list:
Available online and in print

Access to staff:
Contact by letter
Hours: Mon to Fri, 0900 to 1700

Access for disabled people:
Access to all public areas

SHEFFIELD HALLAM UNIVERSITY – LEARNING CENTRES, LIBRARY RESOURCES AND IT

Acronym or abbreviation: SHU

Howard Street, Sheffield, South Yorkshire, S1 1WB

Tel: 0114 225 3333
Fax: 0114 225 3859
E-mail: learning.centre@shu.ac.uk

Website:
http://www.shu.ac.uk/services/sls/learning/index.html

Organisation type and purpose:
University library.

Subject coverage:
Adsetts Centre, City Campus: computing, sciences, engineering, built environment, business, management, tourism, hospitality, food, social sciences, history, English, languages, TESOL (Teaching English to Speakers of Other Languages), education, performing arts, communication studies, art, design, fashion, photography, film and media studies, metalwork and jewellery.
Collegiate Learning Centre: health, nursing, midwifery, occupational and physical therapies, paramedicine, radiotherapy and oncology, radiography, operating department practice, sports studies, psychology, social work, social sciences, law and criminology.

Museum or gallery collection, archive, or library special collection:
Adsetts Centre:
Corvey collection (18th- and 19th-century books in English)
18th- and 19th-century books on art and design
Archives of Sheffield School of Art 1843–1969
David Morgan Rees collection (photographs of Yorkshire crafts)
Festival of Britain collection
George Fullard drawings
Photographs of the Miners' strike 1984–85
Public art research archive
Collegiate Learning Centre:
European Documentation Centre

Library catalogue:
All or part available online

Access to staff:
Contact by letter, by telephone, by fax, by e-mail, in person and via website. Appointment necessary.

Access to building, collection or gallery:
Hours: Term time: Mon to Thu, 0845 to 2100; Fri, 0845 to 1800; Sat, Sun, 1000 to 1700

Special comments: 24-hour opening for Sheffield Hallam University students operates during term time.

Access for disabled people:
Ramped entry, access to all public areas, toilet facilities

Also at:
Collegiate Learning Centre
   Sheffield, S10 2BP; tel: 0114 225 3333; fax: 0114 225 2476

SHEFFIELD LIBRARIES, ARCHIVES AND INFORMATION – REFERENCE & INFORMATION

Central Library, Surrey Street, Sheffield, South Yorkshire, S1 1XZ

Tel: 0114 273 4736/7
Fax: 0114 273 5009
E-mail: information.library@sheffield.gov.uk

Website:
http://www.sheffield.gov.uk/informationlibrary
Information on all the services provided by Reference and Information.
http://library.sheffield.gov.uk
Online library catalogue.
http://www.sheffield.gov.uk/libraries
Information about the 28 community libraries, Central Library, archives, mobiles, housebound service, schools' library service, hospitals, special projects and much more.

Enquiries:
Enquiries to: Information Library Officer

Founded:
1934

Organisation type and purpose:
Local government body, public library.

Subject coverage:
Business and commercial information on companies, products, suppliers, importers, exporters, trade names. Company information (general and financial information on local, UK and foreign companies); UK telephone directories. All aspects of science and technology, pure and applied, industry related matters, innovation, trade and technical journals and reports. Official publications, official and non-official national, European and international statistics. Historic and current collection of patents. Current and historic collection of British and world-wide standards and specifications. Metallic materials identification service provided via the World Metal Index (WMI), part of a collection of standards and specifications; trade literature and technical journals on both ferrous and non-ferrous metal. Over 200,000 individual grades are included, both current and historical. MI-21 (Metals Information for the 21st century), a collaboration between the WMI and the Welding Institute (TWI), providing an information resource on metallic materials and welding consumables.

Information services:
24-hour access to search the currently available 20,000 MI-21 World Metal Index datasheets online, by subscription at: http://www.mi-21.com.

Museum or gallery collection, archive, or library special collection:
British directories
FAME company database
Company annual reports
Kompass Worldwide (online)
British Standards (online and paper collection of withdrawn and superseded British Standards)
Foreign and international standards
Company financial data, patents, standards, trademarks (online)
Local company and local economic data
Motor vehicle workshop manuals
Market research databases (online)
Radio and TV servicing data
UK patents 1617 to present
Intellectual property information

Library catalogue:
All or part available in-house

Access to staff:
Contact by letter, by telephone, by fax, by e-mail and in person

Access to building, collection or gallery:
Hours: Mon, 1000 to 2000; Tue, Thu, Fri, Sat, 0930 to 1730; Wed, 0930 to 2000
Special comments: Charges may apply for certain services, e.g. photocopying and printing.

Includes the:
World Metal Index

Member organisation of:
BSI
European Public Information Centre
PatLib UK

Parent body:
Sheffield City Council

SHEFFIELD LIBRARIES, ARCHIVES AND INFORMATION SERVICES – ARTS AND SOCIAL SCIENCES AND SPORTS SECTION

Central Library, Surrey Street, Sheffield, South Yorkshire, S1 1XZ

Tel: 0114 273 4747
Fax: 0114 273 5009
E-mail: artsandsport.library@sheffield.gov.uk

Website:
http://www.sheffield.gov.uk/in-your-area/libraries

Enquiries:
Enquiries to: Librarian

Organisation type and purpose:
Local government body, public library.

Subject coverage:
Social sciences including sociology, politics, education and careers, parliamentary and local government information, social welfare, charities and voluntary sector; the arts, leisure including travel and maps, sport and mountaineering, history, language and literature, census, statistics, government publications, abstracts and indexes.

Museum or gallery collection, archive, or library special collection:
Physical Education Association's sport collection
Climbing and Mountaineering
Funder Finder: charitable trusts database
International Genealogy Index Great Britain and Ireland
Sheffield Philatelic Society Library (on deposit)

Non-library collection catalogue:
All or part available online and in-house

Library catalogue:
All or part available online and in-house

Microform publications:
British Trades Union Histories (Harvester Press)
Tom Harrison Mass Observation Archive

Access to staff:
Contact by letter, by telephone, by fax, by e-mail and in person
Hours: Mon, 1000 to 2000; Tue, Thu, Fri, 0930 to 1730; Wed, 0930 to 2000; Sat, 0930 to 1730

Parent body:
Sheffield City Council

SHEFFIELD LIBRARIES, ARCHIVES AND INFORMATION SERVICES – CENTRAL MUSIC AND FILM LIBRARY

Central Library, Surrey Street, Sheffield, South Yorkshire, S1 1XZ

Tel: 0114 273 4733
Fax: 0114 273 5009
E-mail: musicandav.library@sheffield.gov.uk

Website:
http://www.sheffield.gov.uk/musicandfilm

Organisation type and purpose:
Local government body, public library.

Subject coverage:
Music (books, scores, sets of orchestral parts and vocal scores, sound recordings), music reference services; DVD and Blu-ray lending collection.

Museum or gallery collection, archive, or library special collection:
Bayreuth Collection (Wagner)
Whitworth Collection (organs and organ building)
Both collections now incorporated into the total stock

Library catalogue:
All or part available online and in-house

Printed publications:
Catalogue of Orchestral Sets
Catalogue of Vocal Sets

Access to staff:
Contact by letter, by telephone, by fax, by e-mail and in person
Hours: Mon, 1000 to 2000; Tue, Thu, Fri, Sat, 0930 to 1730; Wed, 0930 to 2000

Access to building, collection or gallery:
Hours: Mon, 1000 to 2000; Tue, Thu, Fri, Sat, 0930 to 1730; Wed, 0930 to 2000

Links with:
Yorkshire and Humberside Joint Library Services

SHEFFIELD LIBRARIES, ARCHIVES AND INFORMATION SERVICES – LOCAL STUDIES LIBRARY

Central Library, Surrey Street, Sheffield, South Yorkshire, S1 1XZ

Tel: 0114 273 4753
Fax: 0114 273 5009
E-mail: local.studies@sheffield.gov.uk

Website:
http://www.picturesheffield.com
Historical image library of Sheffield photographs.
http://www.sheffield.gov.uk/archives

Enquiries:
Enquiries to: Local Studies Officer
Direct e-mail: local.studies.library@sheffield.gov.uk

Organisation type and purpose:
Public library.

Subject coverage:
History, geography, etc. of Sheffield Metropolitan District and surrounding area, articles of local interest in newspapers and periodicals, 19th-century ED returns, 1971/81/91 Small Area Statistics (local census data), trade directories, newspapers, electoral registers.

Museum or gallery collection, archive, or library special collection:
Census records 1841, 51, 61, 71, 81 for Sheffield and parts of South Yorkshire and North Derbyshire on microfilm; 1891 and 1901 on microfiche (name indexes for Sheffield 1841–81)
Ephemera such as playbills, notices, leaflets
Film and video of scenes of life in Sheffield (some access restrictions for preservation reasons)
Map collection (historic and modern)
Newspapers (files of local papers on microfilm)
Oral history recordings
Photographic collection of 60,000 local images
Sheffield street and trade directories from 1774 to 1974

Library catalogue:
All or part available online and in-house

Electronic and video publications:
Online newsletter
Order electronic and video publications from: see website: http://www.sheffield.gov.uk/archives

Publications list:
Available online and in print

Access to staff:
Contact by letter, by telephone, by fax, by e-mail and in person
Hours: Mon, 1000 to 2000; Tue, Thu, Fri, Sat, 0930 to 1730; Wed, 0930 to 2000

SHELL GLOBAL SOLUTIONS (UK), INFORMATION SERVICES

Shell Technology Centre Thornton, Poole Lane, Ince, Cheshire, CH2 4NU

Tel: 0151 373 5900
Fax: 0151 373 5230
E-mail: cip.library@shell.com

Website:
http://www.shell.com/home/content/globalsolutions

Enquiries:
Enquiries to: Information Specialist
Direct tel: 0151 373 5476
Direct e-mail: eddie.carter@shell.com
Other contacts: Librarian; Archivist (for reference and archive enquiries)

Founded:
1940

Formerly called:
Shell Research Limited

Organisation type and purpose:
Shell Global Solutions is part of the Projects & Technology portfolio of Royal Dutch Shell PLC and provides business and operational consultancy to the energy industry and petrochemicals industry worldwide; these services are available both to Shell and non-Shell companies. The Information Centre in the UK is part of a global Information Services team which provides a full range of library, information and archive services to Shell Projects & Technology Staff.

Subject coverage:
Applicational research and development of fuels, lubricants and other petroleum products; combustion; lubrication; environment; analysis and measurement.

Non-library collection catalogue:
All or part available in-house

Library catalogue:
All or part available in-house

Access to staff:
Contact by letter, by telephone, by fax, by e-mail, in person and via website
Hours: Mon to Fri, 0800 to 1700

Access to building, collection or gallery:
Staff only except by prior appointment
Hours: Mon to Fri, 0900 to 1600
Special comments: Access to Library and Information Services is restricted to Shell Staff.

Access for disabled people:
Hours: Mon to Fri, 0900 to 1700

SHELL SERVICES INTERNATIONAL

Business Information Centre, Shell Centre, London, SE1 7NA

Tel: 020 7934 1234
Fax: 020 7934 7679

Enquiries:
Enquiries to: Archivist
Direct tel: 020 7934 2328
Other contacts: Head of Business Information Centre

Organisation type and purpose:
Industrial company.

Subject coverage:
Business aspects of the energy and petrochemical industries worldwide.

Trade and statistical information:
Extensive statistical collection.

Website header section (top of third column)

Access to staff:
Contact by letter, by telephone, by fax, by e-mail and in person
Hours: Mon, 1000 to 2000; Tue, Thu, Fri, Sat, 0930 to 1730; Wed, 0930 to 2000

SHELL UK LTD

1 Altens Farm Road, Nigg, Aberdeen, AB12 3FY

Tel: 01224 882000
E-mail: tullosic-enquiries@shell.com

Enquiries:
Enquiries to: Information Adviser
Direct tel: 01224 882032

Organisation type and purpose:
International organisation.
Oil and gas company.

Subject coverage:
Oil, gas, exploration, production and operation
procedures, offshore safety, offshore engineering.

Access to staff:
Contact by telephone and by e-mail
Hours: Mon to Fri, 0830 to 1630

Access to building, collection or gallery:
Not open to the public.

SHELLFISH ASSOCIATION OF GREAT BRITAIN

Acronym or abbreviation: SAGB

Fishmongers' Hall, London Bridge, London, EC4R
9EL

Tel: 020 7283 8305
Fax: 020 7929 1389
E-mail: SAGB@shellfish.org.uk

Website:
http://www.shellfish.org.uk

Enquiries:
Enquiries to: Secretary
Other contacts: Director

Founded:
1903

Organisation type and purpose:
Trade association.
Represents the UK Shellfish industry.

Subject coverage:
Shellfish stocks, biology, markets, storage,
handling and quality.

Printed publications:
Papers of the Annual Conference

Access to staff:
Contact by letter, by telephone, by fax, by e-mail
and via website. Non-members charged.
Hours: Mon to Fri, 0900 to 1700

Links with:
Association of Scottish Shellfish Growers

SHELTER

88 Old Street, London, EC1V 9HU

Tel: 0844 515 2000
E-mail: info@shelter.org.uk.

Website:
http://england.shelter.org.uk/get_advice
Online housing advice.
http://england.shelter.org.uk
All about Shelter and its services.

Founded:
1966

Organisation type and purpose:
A registered charity (number 263710 in England &
Wales and SC002327 in Scotland).
Works to alleviate the distress caused by
homelessness and bad housing.
To make sure that people in housing need can
access and keep a home; to drive up the supply of
affordable homes in places where people can
thrive.

Subject coverage:
Gives advice, information and advocacy to people
in housing need, and campaigns for lasting
political change to end the housing crisis for good.

Information services:
Free housing advice helpline: 0808 800 4444;
supporter helpdesk (no housing advice): 0300 330
1234; online housing advice (see website);
Children's Service gives children's sector
professionals who are working with families and
young people affected by housing problems direct
access to Shelter's specialist advice and advocacy
services.

Education services:
Online teachers' centre (see website); more than
130 housing and personal development courses to
suit all levels (see website).

**Museum or gallery collection, archive, or library
special collection:**
Online policy library (see website)

Printed publications:
Guide to Housing Benefit and Council Tax Benefit
2010–2011 (2010, £26)
Housing rights guide (£17.50)
Student housing and the law (£20)
A variety of research, policy and good practice
reports, discussion papers and consultations on
housing and homelessness
Order printed publications from: Shelter

Publications list:
Available online and in print

Access to staff:
Contact by letter, by telephone, by fax and by e-
mail
Hours: Reception: Mon to Fri, 0900 to 1730
Supporter Helpdesk: Mon to Fri, 0900 to 2000; Sat,
0900 to 1300

Also at:
Shelter Scotland
4th floor, Scotiabank House, 6 South Charlotte
Street, Edinburgh, EH2 4AW; website: http://
scotland.shelter.org.uk

SHERLOCK HOLMES SOCIETY OF LONDON

15 Copperfield Court, 146 Worple Road,
Wimbledon, London, SW20 8QA

Tel: 020 8879 0332
E-mail: c.cooke@dsl.pipex.com

Website:
http://www.sherlock-holmes.org.uk

Enquiries:
Enquiries to: Secretary

Founded:
1951

Organisation type and purpose:
Membership association.

Subject coverage:
Study of the life, work and times of Sherlock
Holmes and Dr Watson, with more than a passing
interest in the same of Sir Arthur Conan Doyle.

Printed publications:
Occasional other publications on the Society's
expeditions
Sherlock Holmes Journal (twice a year, for
members only)

Access to staff:
Contact by letter, by telephone and by e-mail
Hours: Mon to Fri, 0900 to 1700

SHETLAND ARCHIVES

Formal name: Shetland Museum and Archives

Hay's Dock, Lerwick, Shetland, ZE1 0WP

Tel: 01595 695057 and 01595 741554
Fax: 01595 696729
E-mail: info@shetlandmuseumandarchives.org.uk

Enquiries:
Enquiries to: Archivist

Founded:
1976

Organisation type and purpose:
Trust administering Museum and Archives for
local authority Archives office.

Subject coverage:
Shetland.

**Museum or gallery collection, archive, or library
special collection:**
Archival and some printed historical matter all
concerning Shetland; microfilm copies of
demographic records concerning Shetland, and
of virtually all newspapers with Shetland news,
1830s onwards

Non-library collection catalogue:
All or part available in-house

Printed publications:
Shetland Documents 1195–1579 (Lerwick, 1999)
Shetland Documents 1580–1611 (Lerwick, 1994)
Order printed publications from: Shetland Museum
and Archives

Access to staff:
Contact by letter, by telephone, by fax, by e-mail
and in person
Hours: Mon to Fri, 1000 to 1630; Sat, 1000 to 1300

Access for disabled people:
Parking provided, ramped entry, access to all
public areas, toilet facilities

Administered by:
Shetland Amenity Trust
Garthspool, Lerwick, Shetland; tel: 01595 694688

SHETLAND FAMILY HISTORY SOCIETY

Acronym or abbreviation: SFHS

6 Hillhead, Lerwick, Shetland, ZE1 0EJ

E-mail: secretary@shetland-fhs.org.uk

Website:
http://www.shetland-fhs.org.uk
Society information and contacts.

Enquiries:
Enquiries to: General Secretary
Other contacts: Membership Secretary (for joining
information and application)

Founded:
1991

Organisation type and purpose:
Membership association (membership is by
subscription), present number of members: 900,
registered charity (charity number SCO 20018).
A focus to share, collate and disseminate
genealogical data of Shetland Island families.

Subject coverage:
Genealogy of Shetland families, emigration
worldwide, family trees, monumental inscriptions,
research sources available locally.

Non-library collection catalogue:
All or part available in-house

Library catalogue:
All or part available in-house

Printed publications:
Shetland Surnames, Beattie A M (£7 plus p&p)
Coontin Kin (journal, quarterly £3 plus p&p)
Monumental Inscription Booklets (£3 each, £4 inc.
p&p)
Shetland Pre-1855 Parish Sources for Family
Historians (Beattie A M, £4.50 plus p&p)

Electronic and video publications:
Shetland Censuses 1785/1841, 1851/61, 1871/81,
1891/1901 (CD-ROM, members: £9 plus p&p,
non-members: £12 plus p&p)

Publications list:
Available online and in print

Access to staff:
Contact by letter, by e-mail, in person and via
website. Appointment necessary.
Hours: Mon to Sat, 1400 to 1600; Mon and Thu,
1900 to 2100

Access for disabled people:
Level entry

Links with:
Scottish Association of Family History Societies

SHETLAND ISLANDS COUNCIL

Acronym or abbreviation: SIC

Town Hall, Hillhead, Lerwick, Shetland, ZE1 0HB

Tel: 01595 693535
Fax: 01595 744509
E-mail: sic@sic.shetland.gov.uk

Website:
http://www.shetland.gov.uk

Enquiries:
Enquiries to: Chief Executive

Founded:
1974

Organisation type and purpose:
Local government body.

Subject coverage:
Local government services.

Access to staff:
Contact by letter, by telephone, by fax, by e-mail and in person
Hours: Mon to Fri, 0900 to 1700

SHETLAND LIBRARY

Lower Hillhead, Lerwick, Shetland, ZE1 0EL

Tel: 01595 743868
Fax: 01595 694430
E-mail: shetlandlibrary@sic.shetland.gov.uk

Website:
http://www.shetland-library.gov.uk
Library catalogue, current events and features.

Founded:
1950

Organisation type and purpose:
Local government body, public library.

Subject coverage:
All aspects of Shetland, including its geography, agriculture and local history.

Museum or gallery collection, archive, or library special collection:
Local newspapers (on microfilm)

Non-library collection catalogue:
All or part available online

Library catalogue:
All or part available online

Printed publications:
Court Book of Shetland 1615–1629 (Donaldson G, £8.50)
Da Vaam O, Da Skynbow – Stories of Shetland Music (Morton, T, £5.99)
MacDiarmid in Shetland (Graham L and Smith B, £7.95)
Voes & Sounds (De Luca C, £6.50)
Wast wi da Valkyries (De Luca C, £8.99)
The Placenames of Shetland (Jacobsen J, out-of-print)

Access to staff:
Contact by letter, by telephone, by fax, by e-mail and via website. Appointment necessary.
Hours: Mon, Thu, 0930 to 2000; Tue, Wed, Fri, Sat, 0930 to 1700

Access for disabled people:
Ramped entry, access to all public areas, toilet facilities

SHETLAND PONY STUD-BOOK SOCIETY

Acronym or abbreviation: SPSBS

22 York Place, Perth, Tayside, PH2 8EH

Tel: 01738 623471
Fax: 01738 442274
E-mail: elaineward@shetlandponystudbooksociety.co.uk

Website:
http://www.shetlandponystudbooksociety.co.uk

Enquiries:
Enquiries to: Breed Secretary

Founded:
1891

Organisation type and purpose:
Membership association (membership is by subscription), present number of members: 2000, registered charity (charity number 38044). Breed society. Maintains records and gives advice on registered Shetland Ponies.

Subject coverage:
All subjects concerning Shetland ponies including registrations, pedigrees, performance, exports, welfare, society sales, showing, publications.

Museum or gallery collection, archive, or library special collection:
The Shetland Pony Stud-Book (101 volumes)

Printed publications:
Magazine (annually)
Studbook (annually)

Publications list:
Available online and in print

Access to staff:
Contact by letter, by telephone, by fax and by e-mail. Appointment necessary.
Hours: Mon to Fri, 0900 to 1700
Special comments: Telephone answered 1100 to 1500 daily.

SHINGLES SUPPORT SOCIETY

Acronym or abbreviation: SSS

41 North Road, London, N7 9DP

Tel: 020 7607 9661
E-mail: info@herpes.org.uk

Website:
http://www.shinglessupport.org
Self-help ideas and full details of drug therapies.

Enquiries:
Enquiries to: Director

Founded:
1985

Organisation type and purpose:
Patient support group.

Subject coverage:
Information on drug treatments that a GP can prescribe and self-help therapies.

Printed publications:
Information pack

Publications list:
Available online and in print

Access to staff:
Contact by letter, by telephone and by e-mail. Appointment necessary.
Hours: Mon to Fri, 1000 to 1800

Access to building, collection or gallery:
Prior appointment required

Access for disabled people:
Level entry by circuitous route
Special comments: Disabled access can be arranged if requested in advance.

Parent body:
Herpes Viruses Association (HVA)
same address

SHIPPING GUIDES LIMITED

75 Bell Street, Reigate, Surrey, RH2 7AN

Tel: 01737 242255

Fax: 01737 222449
E-mail: info@portinfo.co.uk

Website:
http://www.portinfo.co.uk

Enquiries:
Enquiries to: Managing Director
Direct e-mail: info@portinfo.co.uk
Other contacts: Director Information Services

Founded:
1970

Organisation type and purpose:
Advisory body, publishing house.
Nautical Advisers.

Subject coverage:
Marine publishers, port information, marine manuals, nautical information, nautical advisers, atlases, maps, books and CDs.

Printed publications:
Guide to Port Entry (2001/2002, £255 UK, £275 overseas)
Guide to Tanker Ports (updated every 8 weeks)
The Shipping World's Map (£20 UK, £25 overseas)
The Ships Atlas (9th ed., 2002, £70 UK, £75 overseas)

Electronic and video publications:
The Guide on CD

Publications list:
Available in print

Access to staff:
Contact by letter, by telephone, by fax, by e-mail and in person
Hours: Mon to Fri, 0900 to 1700

SHOOTERS' RIGHTS ASSOCIATION

Acronym or abbreviation: SRA

PO Box 3, Cardigan, Ceredigion, SA43 1BN

Tel: 01239 698607
Fax: 01239 698614
E-mail: richard.law@btinternet.com

Enquiries:
Enquiries to: Secretary

Founded:
1984

Organisation type and purpose:
International organisation, membership association (membership is by subscription), present number of members: 4500, voluntary organisation, training organisation.
For persons who hold firearm or shotgun certificates, are registered dealers, or who are interested in taking up shooting as a pastime.

Subject coverage:
Firearms licensing; legal problems arising from the possession and use of firearms.

Museum or gallery collection, archive, or library special collection:
Reports about firearms legislation in the UK, including the unpublished Blackwell & McKay Reports

Printed publications:
Newsletter (free to members, for sale to others)
Special Reports (irregular)

Access to staff:
Contact by letter, by telephone, by fax and by e-mail. Appointment necessary.
Hours: Mon to Fri, 0900 to 1700

Access to building, collection or gallery:
Prior appointment required

SHOP AND DISPLAY EQUIPMENT ASSOCIATION

Acronym or abbreviation: sdea

24 Croydon Road, Caterham, Surrey, CR3 6YR

continued overleaf

Tel: 01883 348911
Fax: 01883 343435
E-mail: enquiries@sdea.co.uk

Website:
http://www.shopdisplay.org

Enquiries:
Enquiries to: Administration Manager

Founded:
1947

Organisation type and purpose:
Trade association.

Subject coverage:
Sourcing manufacturers and suppliers of shopfittings and retail display equipment.

Information services:
Information regarding suppliers of shopfittings and retail display equipment

Printed publications:
sdea Directory of Shopfittings and Display (annually, £10)

Access to staff:
Contact by letter, by telephone, by fax, by e-mail and via website
Hours: Mon to Fri, 0900 to 1700

Access to building, collection or gallery:
No access other than to staff

SHORTHORN CATTLE SOCIETY

National Agricultural Centre, Stoneleigh Park, Kenilworth, Warwickshire, CV8 2LG

Tel: 024 7669 6549
Fax: 024 7669 6729
E-mail: shorthorn@shorthorn.co.uk

Website:
http://www.shorthorn.co.uk

Enquiries:
Enquiries to: General Secretary
Other contacts: Secretary

Founded:
1822

Organisation type and purpose:
Membership association (membership is by subscription), present number of members: 1,100, registered charity (charity number 213216).
To keep up a herd book and breed standard, to provide and promote information and advice, genetics and general support for members and supporters of the breed.

Subject coverage:
Shorthorn cattle including membership, registration, classification, semen, breed publicity and general information.

Museum or gallery collection, archive, or library special collection:
Coates' Herd Books
Year Book and Journals
Photographs

Trade and statistical information:
Wordwide Trade for livestock, semen and embryos.

Printed publications:
Dairy Shorthorns (video available for clubs and associations)
Information leaflets and brochures
Genetic Sales list
Journal (2 times a year)

Electronic and video publications:
Northern Beef Shorthorns (video, to purchase)

Access to staff:
Contact by letter, by telephone, by fax, by e-mail and in person
Hours: Mon to Fri, 0900 to 1600

Access for disabled people:
Parking provided

SHREWSBURY COLLEGE OF ARTS & TECHNOLOGY

Learning Resource Centre, London Road, Shrewsbury, Shropshire, SY2 6PR

Tel: 01743 342342
Fax: 01743 342343
E-mail: carolinet@shrewsbury.ac.uk

Website:
http://www.shrewsbury.ac.uk

Enquiries:
Enquiries to: Team Leader – Learning Resources
Direct tel: 01743 342354
Direct e-mail: lrlrc@shrewsbury.ac.uk

Organisation type and purpose:
Suitable for ages: 16+.
College of further education with some HE provision.

Subject coverage:
All areas of further education including accounting, administration, art and design, beauty and holistic therapies, business, care, childcare, computing and IT, construction, engineering, fashion, hairdressing, hospitality and catering, law, media, motor vehicle, music and performing arts, public services, sports and recreation, travel and tourism.

Museum or gallery collection, archive, or library special collection:
Technical indexes

Non-library collection catalogue:
All or part available in-house

Library catalogue:
All or part available in-house

Access to staff:
Contact by letter, by telephone, by fax, by e-mail, in person and via website. Appointment necessary. Non-members charged.
Hours: Mon to Fri, 0900 to 1700

Access for disabled people:
Parking provided, ramped entry, access to all public areas, toilet facilities

Constituent bodies:
Radbrook College Campus
Radbrook Road, Shrewsbury, Shropshire, SY3 9BL; tel: 01743 342642; e-mail: rblrc@shrewsbury.ac.uk

SHREWSBURY SCHOOL LIBRARY

The Schools, Shrewsbury, Shropshire, SY3 7BA

Tel: 01743 280595
Fax: 01743 243107
E-mail: archivist@shrewsbury.org.uk

Website:
http://www.shrewsbury.org.uk
See archives. Brief history of library, images of manuscripts, books and bindings.

Enquiries:
Enquiries to: Taylor Librarian and Archivist

Founded:
1606

Organisation type and purpose:
Independent school library.

Subject coverage:
General, for a school library.

Museum or gallery collection, archive, or library special collection:
Collection of bookbindings, 12th to 20th centuries, and private press books
Collection on early science, natural history and medicine, documented from 1607
Grammar School Library dating from 1606, 7500 vols including medieval manuscripts, incunabula, and books of the 16th and 17th centuries
Letters of Charles Darwin
Manuscripts and watercolours relating to Samuel (Erewhon) Butler

Moser collection of 19th century watercolours
Photographic archive c. 1860 to the present
School and Governing Body Archives, 1552 to the present

Library catalogue:
All or part available in-house

Access to staff:
Contact by letter, by fax and by e-mail. Appointment necessary. Letter of introduction required.
Hours: Mon to Fri, 0900 to 1700

SHROPSHIRE LIBRARIES – REFERENCE LIBRARY

1A Castle Gates, Shrewsbury, Shropshire, SY1 2AQ

Tel: 01743 255380
Fax: 01743 255383
E-mail: ris.enquiries@shropshire.gov.uk

Website:
http://www.shropshire.gov.uk/library.nsf

Enquiries:
Enquiries to: Librarian

Organisation type and purpose:
Local government body, public library.

Subject coverage:
Business information, law, community information, project information for local schools and colleges, European information.

Library catalogue:
All or part available online

Printed publications:
General leaflet
Online Reference Library leaflet

Publications list:
Available online

Access to staff:
Contact by letter, by telephone, by fax, by e-mail, in person and via website
Hours: Mon, Wed, Fri, 0930 to 1700; Tue and Thu, 0930 to 2000; Sat, 0900 to 1700; Sun, 1300 to 1600

Access for disabled people:
Parking provided, toilet facilities

Member organisation of:
European Information Relay

Parent body:
Shropshire Council, Community Services

SHROPSHIRE ARCHAEOLOGICAL AND HISTORICAL SOCIETY

Acronym or abbreviation: SAHS

Glebe House, Vicarage Road, Meole Brace, Shrewsbury, SY3 9EZ

Tel: 01743 236914
E-mail: s.baugh@virgin.net

Website:
http://www.shropshirearchaeology.org.uk

Enquiries:
Enquiries to: Honorary Secretary
Other contacts: Hon. Editor of 'Transactions'; Hon. Membership Secretary

Founded:
1877

Organisation type and purpose:
Learned society (membership is by subscription), present number of members: 329 individual and 40 institutional members.

Subject coverage:
Local history and archaeology of Shropshire, parish registers.

Education services:
Summer field trips; winter lecture series; occasional day schools.

Museum or gallery collection, archive, or library special collection:
J H Smith watercolours of Shropshire churches c. 1840

Non-library collection catalogue:
All or part available in-house

Library catalogue:
All or part available in-house

Printed publications:
Newsletter (2 times a year)
Monographs (irregular)
Parish Register Transcripts (over 80, from the present or former Diocese of St Asaph, Hereford and Lichfield, some indexes only)
Transactions (annually)
New Series (1931 onwards)
From Volume 60 onwards the volumes are not divided into parts
Volume 59 part 2 (£2), part 3 (£3)
Volumes 60 to 75 (various prices)
Shropshire Field Names (Foxall H D G, £5)
The Wealth of Shrewsbury in the Early 14th Century – 6 Local Subsidy Rolls 1297–1322: Text and Commentary (ed Cromarty D & R, £10)
The Cartulary of Lilleshall Abbey (ed Rees U, £10)
Shrewsbury Abbey (ed Baker N, £10)
Order printed publications from: Hon. Publications Secretary

Electronic and video publications:
See http://www.britarch.ac.uk/publications/archlib

Access to staff:
Contact by letter, by telephone, by e-mail, in person and via website

Access to building, collection or gallery:
No prior appointment required

Access for disabled people:
Parking provided, level entry, access to all public areas, toilet facilities

Incorporating the:
Shropshire Parish Register Society

Member of:
Council for British Archaeology

The Society's Library is housed at the:
Shropshire Archives
Castle Gates, Shrewsbury, SY1 2AQ; tel: 01743 255350; fax: 01743 255355; e-mail: archives@shropshire.gov.uk

SHROPSHIRE ARCHIVES

Castle Gates, Shrewsbury, Shropshire, SY1 2AQ

Tel: 01743 255350
Fax: 01743 255355
E-mail: archives@shropshire.gov.uk

Website:
http://www.shropshirearchives.org.uk

Founded:
1885

Organisation type and purpose:
Local government body, public library. Record office.

Subject coverage:
Records and printed works relating to the County of Shropshire; local history, archaeology, genealogy, etc.

Museum or gallery collection, archive, or library special collection:
Archives of Anglican Parishes, Nonconformist Churches, Poor Law Unions, Schools, Quarter Sessions, etc.
Estate Records
J. H. Smith watercolours of Shropshire churches c.1840
Lily F. Chitty Collection (archaeology)
Local Authority Records
Photographic Archive (from 1842)
Prints, drawings and watercolours
Shrewsbury newspapers from 1772
Shropshire censuses 1841–91
Solicitors' Archives

Non-library collection catalogue:
All or part available in-house

Library catalogue:
All or part available in-house

Printed publications:
List of Other Nonconformist and Roman Catholic Registers
List of Original Parish Registers
Family History Guide: An A to Z guide to sources at Shropshire Archives
House History
Guide to the Old Poor Law
Parishes and Townships of Shropshire
Conflict and Memory
Order printed publications from: Shropshire Archives

Microform publications:
Shropshire Directories 1822–1941
Order microform publications from: Shropshire Archives

Publications list:
Available online

Access to staff:
Contact by letter, by telephone, by fax, by e-mail, in person and via website
Hours: Wed, 1000 to 1700; Thu, 1000 to 2000; Sat, 1000 to 1600
Special comments: Shropshire Archives Reader's Ticket needed for access to originals and some printed material.

Access for disabled people:
Parking provided – please book

Houses the library of the:
Shropshire Archaeological and Historical Society

Parent body:
Shropshire Council

SHROPSHIRE CHAMBER OF COMMERCE & ENTERPRISE LTD

Acronym or abbreviation: SCCE

Trevithick House, Stafford Park 4, Telford, Shropshire, TF3 3BA

Tel: 01952 208200
Fax: 01952 208208
E-mail: enquiries@shropshire-chamber.co.uk

Website:
http://www.shropshire-chamber.co.uk

Enquiries:
Enquiries to: Membership / Policy Executive

Organisation type and purpose:
Membership association, training organisation. To offer complete business solutions, to members and non-members.

Subject coverage:
Business services, advice, information.

Library catalogue:
All or part available in-house

Printed publications:
Business Directory
Labour Market Report
Monthly Bulletin
Solutions (magazine)

Access to staff:
Contact by letter, by telephone, by fax, by e-mail, in person and via website. Appointment necessary.
Hours: Mon to Fri, 0900 to 1700
Special comments: Shropshire businesses and members only.

Access to building, collection or gallery:
No access other than to staff, prior appointment required

Access for disabled people:
Parking provided, ramped entry, toilet facilities

Links with:
British Chambers of Commerce

Confederation of West Midlands' Chambers of Commerce
Small Business Service

SHROPSHIRE FAMILY HISTORY SOCIETY

Acronym or abbreviation: SFHS

16 Glentworth Avenue, Oswestry, Shropshire, SY10 9PZ

E-mail: secretary@sfhs.org.uk

Website:
http://www.sfhs.org

Enquiries:
Enquiries to: Honorary Secretary
Other contacts: Membership Secretary (for membership applications)

Founded:
1979

Organisation type and purpose:
Membership association (membership is by subscription), present number of members: 2,000, voluntary organisation, registered charity (charity number 514014).

Subject coverage:
Family history, research, transcription and indexing of historical records such as parish registers, census returns and monumental inscriptions in the county of Shropshire.

Education services:
Talks/courses on family history topics. Voluntary presence in Shropshire Archives to assist the public.

Museum or gallery collection, archive, or library special collection:
1881 Census transcript and index for England and Wales (microfiche)
British Section of the IGI (microfiche)
Early trade directories (microfiche)
Members' Interests (database)
Original Parish Registers Shropshire (microfiche)
Parish Registers of Shropshire (almost complete set of the printed vols)
Quarter Sessions (database)
Shrewsbury Wills from 1858 (database)
Shropshire Monumental Inscriptions (database)
Shropshire Strays (online)

Printed publications:
Census Indexes for 1821, 1831, 1841 (few), 1851 (nearly 200), 1861, 1871, 1881, 1891 (few)
Directory of Members' Interests
Journal (quarterly, members)
Transcripts of Monumental Inscriptions (about 250 sites, some available in microfiche)
Transcripts of registers (particularly nonconformist, for Church of England see Shropshire Archaeological and Historical Society)
Order printed publications from: Shropshire Family History Society, 68 Oakley Street, Belle Vue, Shrewsbury, Shropshire, SY3 7JZ

Electronic and video publications:
Shropshire Burials Index (CD-ROM, edn 4)
Shropshire Marriage Index (CD-ROM, edn 1)
Shropshire Quarter Sessions Index (CD-ROM)
Wrockwardine Poor Law Papers (CD-ROM)
Order electronic and video publications from: Shropshire Family History Society, 19 Upper Bar, Newport, Shropshire, TF10 7EH

Publications list:
Available online and in print

Access to staff:
Contact by letter, by e-mail and via website
Hours: Mon to Fri, 0900 to 1700
Special comments: Please enclose an sae for reply to letters.

Access to building, collection or gallery:
Library access for members only

continued overleaf

Also at:
Membership Secretary
Shropshire Family History Society, 18 Gorse
Lane, Bayston Hill, Shrewsbury, SY3 0JL; e-mail:
monica@emery18g.1com43.net

SHROPSHIRE LIBRARIES

Shirehall, Abbey Foregate, Shrewsbury,
Shropshire, SY2 6ND

Tel: 01743 255000
Fax: 01743 255050
E-mail: libraries@shropshire.gov.uk

Website:
http://www.shropshire.gov.uk/library.nsf
http://www.literaryheritage.org.uk
http://www.shropshireroots.org.uk

Enquiries:
Enquiries to: Librarian

Organisation type and purpose:
Local government body, public library.

Subject coverage:
Music, recorded sound and drama collections,
(Library, Castle Gates, Shrewsbury); local
government and government publications
(Reference Library, Castle Gates, Shrewsbury);
European (EC) Information (Reference Library,
Castle Gates, Shrewsbury); Shropshire local
studies, extensive coverage of Shropshire and the
Welsh Marches (Shropshire Archives, Castle Gates,
Shrewsbury).

**Museum or gallery collection, archive, or library
special collection:**
Shropshire Parochial Libraries (10,000 early
printed and rare volumes; Shropshire Archives)
West Midlands creative literature collection
(Shrewsbury Library)

Library catalogue:
All or part available online

Printed publications:
Disaster Plans
Guide to School Services
Stock Policy

Publications list:
Available in print

Access to staff:
Contact by letter, by telephone, by fax and by e-
mail. Appointment necessary.
Hours: Mon to Thu, 0900 to 1700; Fri, 0900 to 1600

Area libraries at:
Bridgnorth, Oswestry, Shrewsbury

Constituent part of:
Shropshire Council, Community Services
Directorate

SIBTHORP LIBRARY

Bishop Grosseteste University College, Lincoln,
LN1 3DY

Tel: 01522 583790
Fax: 01522 530243
E-mail: library-enquiries@bishopg.ac.uk

Website:
http://www.bishopg.ac.uk/library
General library information.

Enquiries:
Enquiries to: Director of Library and Knowledge
Services
Direct tel: 01522 583744

Founded:
1862

Organisation type and purpose:
Membership association (membership is by
qualification), present number of members: 1,526.
Library of the Church of England college of higher
education, principally training teachers, with 3
humanities first degrees, and several foundation
degrees.

Subject coverage:
Teaching studies; education: history, geography,
English literature, drama, theology, music, art,
children's literature, early education, heritage.

**Museum or gallery collection, archive, or library
special collection:**
Tom Baker Collection – local historical interest
John Tomlinson Collection

Non-library collection catalogue:
All or part available online and in-house

Library catalogue:
All or part available online and in print

Access to staff:
Contact by letter, by telephone, by fax, by e-mail
and in person
Hours: Term time: Mon to Thu, 0830 to 2030; Fri,
0830 to 1900; Sat, 1000 to 1600; Sun, 1330 to 1700

Access for disabled people:
Ramped entry

Constituent school of the:
University of Leicester

Member of:
UK Libraries Plus

SICKLE CELL AND
THALASSAEMIA FOUNDATION

Acronym or abbreviation: SSCATF

A. C. E. Business Centre, 110–120 Wicker,
Sheffield, South Yorkshire, S3 8JD

Tel: 0114 275 3209
Fax: 0114 279 6870
E-mail: sscatf1@btconnect.com

Website:
http://www.sscatf-8m.com

Enquiries:
Enquiries to: Chairman
Other contacts: Health Officer for health issues
specific to the services offered.

Founded:
1997

Subject coverage:
Information and advice about Sickle Cell and
Thalassaemia. Where to get treatment, to be
screened, symptoms of the disorder, applying for
financial or other support, respite care, genetic
counselling, etc.

Printed publications:
A wide range of leaflets about the services and
about the disorders – Sickle Cell and
Thalassaemia in Urdu, Somali, Bangladeshi,
Arabic, Mandarin Chinese and English
A wide range of text books and booklets

Access to staff:
Contact by letter, by telephone, by fax, by e-mail,
in person and via website. Appointment necessary.
Hours: Mon to Fri, 0900 to 1700

Access to building, collection or gallery:
No prior appointment required
Hours: Mon to Fri, 0700 to 1700; Sat, 0900 to 1700

Access for disabled people:
Parking provided, level entry, access to all public
areas, toilet facilities

SICKLE CELL SOCIETY

54 Station Road, London, NW10 4UA

Tel: 020 8961 7795
Fax: 020 8961 8346
E-mail: sicklecellsoc@btinternet.com

Website:
http://www.sicklecellsociety.org

Enquiries:
Enquiries to: Director
Direct e-mail: sickleinfo.line@btinternet.com
Other contacts: Finance Manager; Fundraising
Manager

Founded:
1979

Organisation type and purpose:
Voluntary organisation, registered charity (charity
number 1046631), suitable for ages: all.

Subject coverage:
Information on sickle cell disorders, financial
assistance, educational grants, holiday and
recreational opportunities.

Printed publications:
Not Another Lazy Child (1 copy free)
Nursing Children with Sickle Cell Disorders (1
copy free)
A guide for parents, guardians and families (1
copy free)
Sickle Cell do you Know? (£2)
Living with Sickle Pain (£2)

Publications list:
Available online and in print

Access to staff:
Contact by letter, by telephone, by fax, by e-mail,
in person and via website
Hours: Mon to Fri, 0900 to 1700

Access to building, collection or gallery:
No prior appointment required
Hours: Mon to Fri, 0900 to 1700

Other address:
Brent Sickle Link
25 High Street, Harlesden, NW10; tel: 020 8961
6090

SIGHT SAVERS INTERNATIONAL

Acronym or abbreviation: SSI

Grosvenor Hall, Bolnore Road, Haywards Heath,
West Sussex, RH16 4BX

Tel: 01444 446600
Fax: 01444 446688
E-mail: generalinformation@sightsavers.org

Website:
http://www.sightsavers.org
About sight savers, about blindness and the
blinding diseases, about where SSI works.

Enquiries:
Enquiries to: Internal Communications Manager
Direct tel: 01444 446661
Direct e-mail: kbirrell@sightsaversint.org

Founded:
1950

Organisation type and purpose:
International organisation, registered charity
(charity number 207544).
To prevent and cure blindness in the developing
world, to provide training for incurably blind
children and adults, and to train local staff.

Subject coverage:
Ophthalmology, community ophthalmology
education, prevention and cure of blindness in
developing countries, training of ophthalmic
personnel, training of personnel working with
visually handicapped people, education of blind
children and rehabilitation for blind adults.

**Museum or gallery collection, archive, or library
special collection:**
Small resource centre of books, articles, journals,
slides and photos primarily for internal use but
available for reference by the public by
appointment

Non-library collection catalogue:
All or part available in-house

Printed publications:
Annual accounts
Annual review
Sight Savers News (newsletter, for supporters, 3
times a year)
Try to See it my Way Pack (£8 plus p&p)

Electronic and video publications:
Videos (for loan or free)

Publications list:
Available in print

Access to staff:
Contact by letter, by telephone, by fax, by e-mail and via website. Appointment necessary.
Hours: Mon to Fri, 0900 to 1700

Access to building, collection or gallery:
Prior appointment required
Hours: Mon to Fri, 0900 to 1630

Has consultative status with the:
United Nations

In collaboration with the:
World Health Organisation

Links with:
International Agency for the Prevention of Blindness
International Council for the Education of the Visually Handicapped
World Blind Union

SIGNATURE

Mersey House, Mandale Business Park, Belmont, Durham, DH1 1TH

Tel: 0191 383 1155; minicom no. 0191 383 7915
Fax: 0191 383 7914
E-mail: durham@signature.org.uk

Website:
http://www.signature.org.uk
Publications, factsheets, NVQ information, qualifications, links, NRCPD, awards.

Enquiries:
Enquiries to: Communications Team Support
Direct tel: 0191 383 7922
Direct e-mail: clare.towns@signature.org.uk

Founded:
1982

Organisation type and purpose:
Registered charity. A UK awarding body accredited by Ofqual offering a wide range of high quality qualifications in British Sign Language and other forms of communication used by deaf and deafblind people. Also conducts the selection, training and monitoring of assessors. Promotes the importance of professional standards and working practices amongst those offering linguistic access services. Administers the National Registers for Communication Professionals working with Deaf and Deafblind people.
To provide knowledge and recognise skills in the languages and communication methods used by deaf people.

Subject coverage:
Communicating with deaf and deafblind people, British Sign Language, Lipspeaking, communicating and guiding skills with deafblind people, BSL/English Interpreting, deaf awareness, deafblind awareness.

Education services:
Awarding Body for British Sign Language (BSL) and other Deaf-related qualifications.

Publications list:
Available online and in print

Access to staff:
Contact by letter, by telephone, by fax, by e-mail and via website
Hours: Mon to Thu, 0900 to 1700; Fri, 0900 to 1630
Special comments: All enquiries to Durham office.

Also at:
Signature – Northern Ireland Office
Wilton House, 5 College Square North, Belfast, BT1 6AR; tel: 028 9043 8161 (voice and text); fax: 028 9043 8161; website: http://www.signature.org.uk
Signature – Scotland Office
Touchbase Community Suite, 43 Middlesex Street, Glasgow, G41 1EE; tel: 0141 4187191; fax: 0141 4187192; website: http://www.signature.org.uk

SIGNET LIBRARY

Society of Writers to HM Signet, Parliament Square, Edinburgh, EH1 1RF

Tel: 0131 225 4923
Fax: 0131 220 4016
E-mail: library@wssociety.co.uk

Website:
http://www.signetlibrary.co.uk
Details of history, contacts and developments.

Enquiries:
Enquiries to: Librarian

Founded:
1594

Organisation type and purpose:
Professional body (membership is by qualification), present number of members: 1,000.

Subject coverage:
Law, particularly Scots law; Scottish history and genealogy.

Museum or gallery collection, archive, or library special collection:
Court of Session Papers (2,500 vols)
Roughead Collection of trials (500 vols)

Non-library collection catalogue:
All or part available online and in-house

Library catalogue:
All or part available in-house

Access to staff:
Contact by letter. Appointment necessary. Access for members only. Non-members charged.
Hours: Mon to Fri, 0930 to 1630

Access for disabled people:
Level entry

SIKH EDUCATIONAL ADVISORY SERVICES

Guru Guru House, 42 Park Avenue, Leeds, West Yorkshire, LS15 8EW

Tel: 0113 260 2484

Enquiries:
Enquiries to: Director General
Direct tel: 07973 286585

Founded:
1984

Organisation type and purpose:
Advisory body, professional body, suitable for ages: all, training organisation, consultancy. Spiritual counselling.

Subject coverage:
Religion, culture, Sikh education, stories, drama, dance, music, language, exhibitions, training.

Electronic and video publications:
Stories from Sikh traditions. Price list available

Publications list:
Available in print

Access to staff:
Contact by letter and by telephone
Hours: Sun to Sat, 0700 to 2100

Access to building, collection or gallery:
Prior appointment required

Access for disabled people:
Parking provided, level entry, toilet facilities

SILK ASSOCIATION OF GREAT BRITAIN

Acronym or abbreviation: SAGB

5 Portland Place, London, W1B 1PW

Tel: 020 7636 7788
Fax: 020 7636 7515
E-mail: sagb@dial.pipex.com

Website:
http://www.silk.org.uk

Enquiries:
Enquiries to: Secretary

Organisation type and purpose:
Trade association.

Subject coverage:
All aspects of silk, silk trade and promotion.

Museum or gallery collection, archive, or library special collection:
Samples and literature about silk for teachers, graduates and school children

Trade and statistical information:
Silk in UK.

Printed publications:
Serica (newsletter, quarterly)

Electronic and video publications:
The History of Silk (video)

Access to staff:
Contact by letter, by fax and by e-mail
Hours: Mon to Fri, 0900 to 1700

Incorporated when the:
Silk and Man-made Fibre Users Association was liquidated

Member of:
British Apparel & Textile Confederation
International Silk Association

SILVER SOCIETY

Box 246, 2 Lansdowne Row, London, W1J 6HL

E-mail: secretary@thesilversociety.org

Website:
http://www.thesilversociety.org

Enquiries:
Enquiries to: Secretary
Direct e-mail: editor@thesilversociety.org
Other contacts: Editor

Founded:
1958

Organisation type and purpose:
Learned society (membership is by election or invitation), present number of members: 415, registered charity (charity number 279352).
To encourage an interest in the craft of the goldsmith and silversmith, past and present.

Subject coverage:
Silver; silversmiths; silver workers; gold; goldsmiths; goldworking; plate; plate working/workers; plated wares (Sheffield plate and electroplate); design and designers; social history (as regards the use of gold, silver and plated wares); biographical information on the above.

Library catalogue:
All or part available online

Printed publications:
The Silver Society Journal (annually, £15)
Order printed publications from: website: http://www.thesilversociety.org

Publications list:
Available online

Access to staff:
Contact by letter, by fax, by e-mail and via website

SIMPLIFIED SPELLING SOCIETY

Acronym or abbreviation: SSS

23 Albion Street, New Brighton, Wirral, Merseyside, CH45 9LE

Tel: 0151 327 5837
E-mail: bjhughes71@hotmail.com

Website:
http://www.spellingsociety.org
Aims, texts of leaflets including membership application form, digest of publications.

continued overleaf

Enquiries:
Enquiries to: Secretary

Founded:
1908

Organisation type and purpose:
Learned society (membership is by subscription), voluntary organisation, research organisation. Working for planned change in English spelling for the benefit of learners and users everywhere.

Subject coverage:
Modernisation and simplification of English spelling, English spelling systems, literacy, English language teaching, linguistics, psychology of writing systems, lexicography, typography.

Museum or gallery collection, archive, or library special collection:
Historical collection of Society material (Mont Follick Collection) in Library of Manchester University, Department of General Linguistics

Printed publications:
Bibliography of English language and spelling reform
Cut Spelling Handbook (1992, £10)
Journal (occasional)
New Spelling 90 (1991, £5)
Newsletter (quarterly)
Regularity and Irregularity in English Spelling (1997, £2)
Spelling Reform in Context (1991, £2)

Access to staff:
Contact by letter, by telephone, by e-mail and via website. Appointment necessary.
Hours: Any day, 0900 to 2200

Links with:
British Dyslexia Association
Initial Teaching Alphabet Federation
UK Reading Association

SINGAPORE HIGH COMMISSION

9 Wilton Crescent, London, SW1X 8SP

Tel: 020 7235 8315
Fax: 020 7245 6583
E-mail: singhc_lon@sgmfa.gov.sg

Website:
http://www.singstat.gov.sg
Statistics on Singapore.
http://www.sgnews.info
News on Singapore.
http://www.gov.sg
Singapore Government website.
http://www.mfa.gov.sg/london
Singapore High Commission.

Enquiries:
Enquiries to: Information Officer
Other contacts: Second Secretary (Information)

Organisation type and purpose:
National government body.

Subject coverage:
Singapore in general.

Printed publications:
Singapore
Singapore Facts and Pictures

Electronic and video publications:
Visit website

Access to staff:
Contact by letter, by telephone and by e-mail
Hours: Mon to Fri, 0900 to 1700

Links with:
Contact Singapore
5 Regent Street, Lower Ground Floor, London, SW1 4LR; tel: 020 7321 5600; website: http://www.contactsingapore.org.sg
Trade Development Board
53 Monument Street, London, EC3R 8BU; tel: 020 7626 1717; fax: 020 7626 1711

SINGER OWNERS CLUB

Acronym or abbreviation: SOC

11 Ermine Rise, Great Casterton, Stamford, Lincolnshire, PE9 4AJ

Tel: 01780 762740
E-mail: martyn@singeroc.idps.co.uk

Website:
http://www.singerownersclub.co.uk
Guide to the Singer Owners Club and Singer vehicles from 1880–1970.

Enquiries:
Enquiries to: Secretary

Founded:
1951

Organisation type and purpose:
Membership association (membership is by subscription), present number of members: 800.

Subject coverage:
Singer motor cars and motor cycles 1876–1970, history of George Singer and the Singer motor companies and Rootes group.

Museum or gallery collection, archive, or library special collection:
Photographs and documentation on all Singer models

Printed publications:
The Singer Owner (six times a year, free to members)

Access to staff:
Contact by letter, by telephone, by e-mail and via website
Hours: Mon to Fri, 1900 to 2200

SINO-HIMALAYAN PLANT ASSOCIATION

81 Parlaunt Road, Slough, Berkshire, SL3 8BE

Tel: 01753 542823
Fax: 01753 543823

Enquiries:
Enquiries to: Secretary

Founded:
1991

Organisation type and purpose:
Membership association (membership is by subscription).

Subject coverage:
Sino-Himalayan, i.e. Himalayan and Chinese, mountain plants.

Museum or gallery collection, archive, or library special collection:
P N Kohli Memorial Herbarium of Himalayan plant pressed specimens and Memorial Himalayan Garden

Printed publications:
Newsletter

Access to staff:
Contact by letter

SINTO – THE INFORMATION PARTNERSHIP

Formal name: SINTO – the information partnership for South Yorkshire and North Derbyshire

c/o Learning Centre, Sheffield Hallam University, Collegiate Crescent, Sheffield, South Yorkshire, S10 2BP

Tel: 0114 225 5739; 0114 225 5740
Fax: 0114 225 2476
E-mail: sintoenquiry@shu.ac.uk

Website:
http://www.sinto.org.uk

Enquiries:
Enquiries to: Director
Direct e-mail: c.j.clayton@shu.ac.uk

Founded:
1933

Created by the merger of:
Board for Library and Information Services in Sheffield and SINTO (year of change 1991)

Formerly called:
Scheme for the Interchange of Technical Publications; Sheffield Interchange Organisation; Sheffield Information Organisation

Organisation type and purpose:
Membership association (membership is by subscription).
To promote and develop library and information services through co-operation, planning and partnership. Provides training and CPD events. SINTO is the Library and Information Plan (LIP) for South Yorkshire and North Derbyshire.

Subject coverage:
Access to resources of member libraries with emphasis on business, science and technology.

Printed publications:
Directory of SINTO Members
Learners' Guide to Libraries in South Yorkshire
Subject Guides to Libraries (details on request)

Electronic and video publications:
Fines and Charges in Public Libraries in England and Wales (CD-ROM, annually)

Access to staff:
Contact by letter, by telephone, by fax, by e-mail and via website. Appointment necessary.
Hours: Mon to Fri, 0900 to 1700

SIR ARTHUR SULLIVAN SOCIETY

Acronym or abbreviation: SASS

Captain's Rest , The Old Rectory, Talland Hill, Polperro, Looe, PL13 2RY

Tel: 01503 272874
E-mail: shturnbull@aol.com

Enquiries:
Enquiries to: Secretary
Other contacts: Membership Secretary

Founded:
1977

Organisation type and purpose:
International organisation, learned society, membership association (membership is by subscription), present number of members: 450, voluntary organisation, registered charity (charity number 274022), suitable for ages: all, research organisation, publishing house.
Promotion of the music of Arthur Sullivan.

Subject coverage:
All aspects of the life, career and work of Sir Arthur Sullivan (1842–1900), performances and recordings of his music, musical criticism.

Museum or gallery collection, archive, or library special collection:
Library of performing material for music by Sullivan, including the only extant orchestral parts for a number of major orchestral works (notably Victoria and Merrie England; L'Ile Enchantée; Thespis; The Merry Wives of Windsor); full choral and orchestral material for Kenilworth (Masque); On Shore and Sea (Cantata); also vocal, choral scores for operas Haddon Hall and The Chieftain

Printed publications:
78 rpm record discography (for sale)
CD discography (free to members only, occasional)
Illustrated booklets (commemorating the centenaries of operas and other works by Sullivan, for sale)
Magazine (free to members, for sale to non-members, 3 times a year)
Newsletter (free to members only, one or more per annum)
Newsletter (free, members only, 2 times a year)
Opera Libretti (for sale)
Yearbook (free, members only, annual)

Order printed publications from: The Sales Officer, Sir Arthur Sullivan Society, Fuchsia Cottage, Main Road, Colwich, ST17 0XE; e-mail: elaineatsass@aol .com

Electronic and video publications:
CD recordings (for sale)

Publications list:
Available online and in print

Access to staff:
Contact by letter, by telephone, by e-mail and via website. Appointment necessary.
Hours: Preferred hours for telephone calls: Mon to Fri, 1000 to 2000; any time at weekends

Access to building, collection or gallery:
By appointment

Also at:
Membership Secretary
71 The Heights, Foxgrove Road, Beckenham, BR3 5BZ

SIR ERNEST CASSEL EDUCATIONAL TRUST

5 Grimston Park Mews, Grimston Park, Tadcaster, North Yorkshire, LS24 9DB

Tel: 01937 834730
E-mail: casseltrust@btinternet.com

Enquiries:
Enquiries to: Secretary

Founded:
1919

Organisation type and purpose:
Registered charity.
Educational grant-awarding body.

Subject coverage:
Overseas research grants in the humanities (administered by the British Academy) for more junior teaching members of faculties; Mountbatten Memorial grants to Commonwealth students taking higher education courses in the UK who run into unforeseen financial difficulties in their final year; grants to organisations in the field of adult and higher education.

Access to staff:
Contact by letter, by telephone and by e-mail
Hours: Mon to Fri, 0900 to 1700

SIR NORMAN CHESTER CENTRE FOR FOOTBALL RESEARCH

Acronym or abbreviation: SNCCFR

Department of Sociology, University of Leicester, Leicester, LE1 7RH

Tel: 0116 252 2741
Fax: 0116 252 2746
E-mail: footballresearch@le.ac.uk

Enquiries:
Enquiries to: Administrator

Founded:
1987

Organisation type and purpose:
University department or institute, research organisation.

Subject coverage:
Football.

Publications list:
Available in print

Access to staff:
Contact by letter and by e-mail. Appointment necessary.
Hours: Mon to Fri, 0900 to 1700

Access to building, collection or gallery:
No prior appointment required
Hours: Mon to Fri, 0930 to 1700

SIRSIDYNIX

Formal name: Sirsi Limited

The Chequers, St Mary's Way, Chesham, Buckinghamshire, HP5 1LL

Tel: 01494 777666
Fax: 01494 777555
E-mail: sales-uk@sirsidynix.co.uk

Website:
http://www.sirsidynix.com
Contact, product, and service details.

Enquiries:
Enquiries to: Sales Director
Direct e-mail: david.green@sirsidynix.co.uk

Founded:
1990

Organisation type and purpose:
Consultancy.
European sales and support office for the Symphony/Unicorn/Horizon/Dynix integrated library management systems.

Subject coverage:
Software for libraries and information handlers.

Access to staff:
Contact by letter, by telephone, by fax, by e-mail and via website
Hours: Mon to Fri, 0830 to 1730

SKI CLUB OF GREAT BRITAIN

The White House, 57–63 Church Road, Wimbledon, London, SW19 5SB

Tel: 020 8410 2000
Fax: 020 8410 2001
E-mail: skiers@skiclub.co.uk

Website:
http://www.skiclub.co.uk

Enquiries:
Enquiries to: Information Officer

Founded:
1903

Organisation type and purpose:
Membership association.
Promoting skiing and snowboarding.

Subject coverage:
Recreational skiing, ski mountaineering, ski touring, resorts and holidays, snow conditions, history of skiing, statistics.

Printed publications:
Range of skiing factsheets available
List of dry ski slopes
Ski and Board (club magazine, 5 issues during the skiing season, free to members, for sale to others)

Access to staff:
Contact by letter, by telephone, by fax, by e-mail, in person and via website. Appointment necessary.
Access for members only.
Hours: Mon to Fri, 0900 to 1730 (summer); 0900 to 1800 (winter)

Access to building, collection or gallery:
Prior appointment required
Hours: Mon to Fri, 0900 to 1730
Special comments: Other events held in the library.

Access for disabled people:
Ramped entry, level entry, access to all public areas, toilet facilities

SKILL: NATIONAL BUREAU FOR STUDENTS WITH DISABILITIES

Acronym or abbreviation: Skill

Unit 3, Floor 3, Radisson Court, 219 Long Lane, London, SE1 4PR

Tel: 020 7450 0620; 0800 328 5050 (information); 0800 068 2422 (textphone)
Fax: 020 7450 0650
E-mail: info@skill.org.uk

Website:
http://www.skill.org.uk

Enquiries:
Enquiries to: Information and Services Manager

Founded:
1974

Organisation type and purpose:
Advisory body, membership association (membership is by subscription), present number of members: 1,000, voluntary organisation, registered charity (charity number 801971, also registered in Scotland, number SC039212), suitable for ages: 16+.
Aims to promote opportunities for people with any kind of impairment in 16+ education, training, transition to employment and volunteering.

Subject coverage:
Information and advice for people with disabilities or learning difficulties, their families, friends and people working with them, regarding post-16 education and training.

Printed publications:
Notes and Quotes: Skill's student newsletter
The Skill Journal: articles concerning current developments and projects
The Skill Newsletter: news and information for people working in post-16 education and training
A variety of information booklets and publications including:
Into Teaching
Guides for Disabled Students
Guides to National Policy
Into Higher Education 2009
Order printed publications from: http:// www.skill.org.uk/shop/shop.asp

Electronic and video publications:
Information sheets and publications are available in audio and disk format, and online
Order electronic and video publications from: e-mail: info@skill.org.uk

Publications list:
Available online and in print

Access to staff:
Contact by letter, by telephone, by fax, by e-mail and via website
Hours: Information Service helpline: Tue, 1130 to 1330; Thu, 1330 to 1530

Access to building, collection or gallery:
No access other than to staff

Access for disabled people:
Parking provided, ramped entry, level entry, access to all public areas, toilet facilities

Branches:
Skill Northern Ireland
Unit 2, Jennymount Court, North Derby Street, Belfast, BT15 3HN; tel: 028 9028 7000; fax: 028 9028 7002; e-mail: info@skillni.org.uk; website: http://www.skillni.org.uk
Skill Scotland
Norton Park, 57 Albion Road, Edinburgh, EH7 5QY; tel: 0131 475 2348; fax: 0131 475 2397; e-mail: admin@skillscotland.org.uk; website: http://www.skill.org.uk/scotland
Skill Wales
Skill Wales, Suite 14, 2nd Floor, The Executive Centre, Temple Court, Cathedral Road, Cardiff, CF11 9HA; tel: 029 2078 6506; e-mail: admin@ skillwales.org.uk; website: http://www.skill.org .uk/wales

SKILLS FUNDING AGENCY

26 Kings Hill Avenue, Kings Hill, West Malling, Kent, ME19 4AE

Tel: 0845 377 5000
Fax: 01732 876917
E-mail: info@skillsfundingagency.bis.gov.uk

Website:
http://www.skillsfundingagency.bis.gov.uk

continued overleaf

Enquiries:
Enquiries to: Information Officer

Founded:
2010

Carries out the functions of the former:
Learning & Skills Council (year of change 2010)

Organisation type and purpose:
Service industry, training organisation.
Learning and Business Link.

Subject coverage:
Education and training funding, private training companies, FE colleges, adult and community education initiatives, workforce development, investors in people, business and education partnerships.

Printed publications:
Annual Report
Strategic Plan
Training Provider Directory

Electronic and video publications:
Employer (CD-ROM)

Access to staff:
Contact by letter, by telephone, by fax, by e-mail and via website
Hours: Mon to Fri, 0830 to 1730

Access for disabled people:
Parking provided, level entry, access to all public areas, toilet facilities

SKIN, HIDE AND LEATHER TRADERS ASSOCIATION

Acronym or abbreviation: SHALTA

Douglas House, Douglas Road, Melrose, Roxburghshire, TD6 9QT

Tel: 01896 822233
Fax: 01896 823344
E-mail: offices@andaco.com

Enquiries:
Enquiries to: Secretary General

Founded:
1916

Organisation type and purpose:
Trade association.

Subject coverage:
Trade in hides, skins and leather both nationally and internationally, contractual information, overseas trade missions.

Access to staff:
Contact by letter, by telephone and by fax
Hours: Mon to Fri, 0900 to 1700

Member of:
International Council of Hides, Skins and Leather Traders Associations
Union Européenne des Négociants en Cuir et Peaux Brutes

SKIPTON LIBRARY

High Street, Skipton, North Yorkshire, BD23 1JX

Tel: 01756 792926
Fax: 01756 798056
E-mail: skipton.library@northyorks.gov.uk

Enquiries:
Enquiries to: Librarian
Other contacts: Information Librarian for reference, local and family history.

Founded:
1909

Organisation type and purpose:
Public library.

Subject coverage:
General reference and information sources, including business information and local history material for the Craven area.

Museum or gallery collection, archive, or library special collection:
Petyt Collection of material on 17th century history and theology

Non-library collection catalogue:
All or part available in-house

Library catalogue:
All or part available in-house

Access to staff:
Contact by letter, by telephone, by fax, by e-mail and in person
Hours: Mon, Wed and Thu, 0930 to 1900; Fri, 0930 to 1700; Sat, 0930 to 1600; Tue, closed

Parent body:
North Yorkshire County Library
21 Grammar School Lane, Northallerton, North Yorkshire, DL6 1DF; tel: 01609 780780; fax: 01609 780793

SLOUGH BOROUGH COUNCIL

Acronym or abbreviation: SBC

Town Hall, Bath Road, Slough, Berkshire, SL1 3UQ

Tel: 01753 552288\ Minicom no. 01753 875030
Fax: 01753 692499

Website:
http://www.slough.gov.uk
What the council offers, services.

Enquiries:
Enquiries to: Chief Executive

Organisation type and purpose:
Local government body.

Access to staff:
Contact by telephone
Hours: Mon to Fri, 0900 to 1645

Other addresses:
Wellington House

SLOUGH LIBRARIES

85 High Street, Slough, SL1 1EA

Tel: 01753 535166
Fax: 01753 825050
E-mail: library@slough.gov.uk

Website:
http://www.slough.gov.uk/libraries

Enquiries:
Enquiries to: Information Services Librarian
Direct tel: 01753 787511

Organisation type and purpose:
Local government body, public library.

Subject coverage:
Slough local studies collection; general information; business information; EU information; careers and education.

Library catalogue:
All or part available online and in-house

Access to staff:
Contact by letter, by telephone, by fax, by e-mail, in person and via website
Hours: Mon, Thu, 0900 to 1700; Tue, Fri, 0900 to 1900; Wed, 0930 to 1900; Sat, 0900 to 1600

Access for disabled people:
Ramped entry

SMALL BUSINESS BUREAU LIMITED

Acronym or abbreviation: SBB

Curzon House, Church Road, Windlesham, Surrey, GU20 6BH

Tel: 01276 452010
Fax: 01276 451602
E-mail: info@sbb.org.uk

Website:
http://www.smallbusinessbureau.org.uk

Enquiries:
Enquiries to: Managing Director

Founded:
1976

Organisation type and purpose:
Membership association (membership is by subscription).
Lobbying organisation.

Subject coverage:
Small and medium-sized businesses.

Printed publications:
Small Business News (4 times a year)

Access to staff:
Contact by letter, by telephone, by fax and by e-mail
Hours: Mon to Fri, 0900 to 1700

SMALL ENTERPRISE RESEARCH TEAM

Acronym or abbreviation: SERTeam

Open University Business School, Open University, Walton Hall, Milton Keynes, Buckinghamshire, MK7 6AA

Tel: 01908 655831 / 020 8560 3004
Fax: 01908 655898 / 020 8560 3004
E-mail: oubs-sbrt@open.ac.uk

Website:
http://www.serteam.co.uk
Publications and links to other small business organisations.

Enquiries:
Enquiries to: Secretary

Founded:
1984

Organisation type and purpose:
Registered charity (charity number 1100928), university department or institute, research organisation.
Educational research charity.

Subject coverage:
Management issues, exporting, regional differences, business services, BS5750, small business policy, small business economy. Further education and colleges report, computers in rural small firms across Europe.

Non-library collection catalogue:
All or part available in print

Library catalogue:
All or part available in print

Printed publications:
Some 30 books, reports and research monographs including:
Behind the Veneer of Success: Propensities for UK Franchisor Failure
Enterprise in Britain (out of print)
Ethnic Minorities in Business (1998, £30)
Lloyds Bank/SBRT Quarterly Small Business Management Report (vol. 4, 1996 through to current Volume 10)
NatWest/SBRT Quarterly Survey of Small Business in Britain (vol.16, 2000)
NatWest/SBRT Survey of Exporters (back issues only, discontinued 2000)
Register of Small Business Researchers (hard copy plus disk with the register in Microsoft Access v4, £50)
Risk Capital for Small Firms (guidebook, 1988)
SME Database
The Making of Entrepreneurs
The role of the small firm in the UK economy: Hot Stereotypes and Cool Assessments
Work Status and Self-Employment in the British Construction Industry

Publications list:
Available online and in print

Access to staff:
Contact by telephone, by fax and by e-mail
Hours: Mon to Fri, 0900 to 1700

Access to building, collection or gallery:
No prior appointment required

Other addresses:
Small Enterprise Research Team
45 Clydesdale Close, Isleworth, London, TW7
6ST; tel: 020 8568 3004; fax: 020 8568 3004; e-
mail: b.porter-blake@open.ac.uk

SMALLPEICE ENTERPRISES LIMITED

27 Newbold Terrace East, Leamington Spa,
Warwickshire, CV32 4ES

Tel: 01926 336423
Fax: 01926 450679
E-mail: train@smallpeice.co.uk

Website:
http://www.smallpeice.co.uk
Course descriptions, dates, prices.

Enquiries:
Enquiries to: Marketing Assistant

Founded:
1966

Organisation type and purpose:
Professional body, registered charity, training
organisation, consultancy.
Training Centre.
Smallpeice combines over 30 years' training
experience and specialist industry focus to provide
a total training service for engineering and
manufacturing companies nationwide.

Subject coverage:
Design engineering, Six Sigma; Lean
Manufacturing; Autocad; project management;
management skills; public courses nationwide; in-
company bespoke training; corporate development
partnership; strategic conferences; facilitation and
consultancy; one-to-one training; ICT-based
training partnerships.

Non-library collection catalogue:
All or part available online

Publications list:
Available in print

Access to staff:
Contact by letter, by telephone, by fax, by e-mail
and via website
Hours: Mon to Fri, 0830 to 1730

Parent body:
The Smallpeice Trust
tel: 01926 333200; fax: 01926 333202

SNACK, NUT AND CRISP MANUFACTURERS ASSOCIATION LIMITED

Acronym or abbreviation: SNACMA

37–41 Bedford Row, London, WC1R 4JH

Tel: 020 7611 4660
Fax: 020 7611 4661
E-mail: esa@esa.org.uk

Website:
http://www.esa.org.uk

Enquiries:
Enquiries to: Director General

Founded:
1983

Organisation type and purpose:
Trade association.

Subject coverage:
Snack industry and products; nutritional data;
statistics.

Printed publications:
Periodic distribution of material of educational
nature to schools

Access to staff:
Contact by letter, by telephone, by fax, by e-mail
and via website. Appointment necessary.
Hours: Mon to Fri, 0900 to 1700

Member of:
Food and Drink Federation
tel: 020 7836 2460
Potato Processors Association

SNOWDONIA SOCIETY

Formal name: Cymdeithas Eryri – Snowdonia
Society
Acronym or abbreviation: CESS

Ty Hyll, Capel Curig, Betws-y-Coed, Conwy, LL24
0DS

Tel: 01690 720287
Fax: 01690 720247
E-mail: info@snowdonia-society.org.uk

Website:
http://www.snowdonia-society.org.uk
A broad range of information about the Society
and the Snowdonia National Park; updated
regularly.

Enquiries:
Enquiries to: Assistant to the Director

Founded:
1967

Organisation type and purpose:
Membership association (membership is by
subscription), with approximately 2,000 members,
voluntary organisation, registered charity (charity
number 253231).
Conservation charity for Snowdonia, aiming to
protect the landscape and heritage of Snowdonia.

Subject coverage:
Planning, administration and conservation of the
Snowdonia National Park and district, transport,
wildlife, flora.

Information services:
Information about Snowdonia and planning and
access issues in the Park.

Special visitor services:
The Snowdonia Society's headquarters at Ty Hyll
(the Ugly House) are surrounded by a wildlife
garden and woodland managed for biodiversity
and to preserve native species and encourage
natural regeneration.

Education services:
Works with school and college groups organising
conservation workdays, and several schools are
affiliate members of the Society.

**Museum or gallery collection, archive, or library
special collection:**
Files on past issues within Snowdonia

Printed publications:
The Old Cottages of Snowdonia (out of print)
Annual Report (members, free; non-members, £1)
Snowdonia Society/Cymdeithas Eryri (2 times a
year, members, free; non-members, £1)
The Old Churches of Snowdonia (out of print)
Back issues of Society magazine
Park Under Pressure

Access to staff:
Contact by letter, by telephone, by fax, by e-mail,
in person and via website. Appointment necessary.
Hours: Mon to Fri, 0900 to 1700

Access to building, collection or gallery:
No prior appointment required
Hours: Mon to Fri, 0900 to 1700

Affiliated to:
Campaign for National Parks
6–7 Barnard Mews, London, SW11 1QU; tel: 020
792 44077; website: http://www.cnp.org.uk

SNOWSPORT ENGLAND

Acronym or abbreviation: SSE

Area Library Building, Queensway Mall, The
Cornbow, Halesowen, West Midlands, B63 4AJ

Tel: 0121 501 2314
Fax: 0121 585 6448
E-mail: info@snowsportengland.org.uk

Website:
http://www.snowsportengland.org.uk

Enquiries:
Enquiries to: Chief Executive

Founded:
1978

Formerly called:
English Ski Council (year of change 2004)

Organisation type and purpose:
Governing body for skiing in England.

Subject coverage:
English skiers and skiing, membership scheme,
coaching awards scheme, promotion of events,
design and development of ski slopes.

Printed publications:
Dry Ski Slopes List
National Coaching Scheme Information booklet
SAE required for booklet and list

Publications list:
Available in print

Access to staff:
Contact by letter and by e-mail
Hours: Mon to Fri, 0900 to 1700

Access to building, collection or gallery:
Prior appointment required

Access for disabled people:
Parking provided, ramped entry, access to all
public areas

Grant-aided by:
Sport England

SOAS

Formal name: School of Oriental and African
Studies

Thornhaugh Street, Russell Square, London,
WC1H 0XG

Tel: 020 7637 2388
Fax: 020 7898 4159
E-mail: libenquiry@soas.ac.uk

Website:
http://www.soas.ac.uk/library
Online resources, opening hours, subject guide,
other library guides and access to the rest of SOAS
website.
http://www.soas.ac.uk/archives/home.html
Information on archives.
http://lib.soas.ac.uk
Library online catalogue.

Enquiries:
Enquiries to: Librarian
Direct tel: 020 7898 4150
Other contacts: Archivist

Founded:
1916

Organisation type and purpose:
University library.

Subject coverage:
Asian and African studies in the humanities and
social sciences, with special emphasis on
anthropology, ethnography, history, language,
literature, economics, law, politics, sociology,
philosophy, religion and art (particularly Chinese);
covers the following areas and regions: Africa,
Near and Middle East and Israel, Central Asia,
South Asia, South East Asia, East Asia, Oceania.

**Museum or gallery collection, archive, or library
special collection:**
Major collections of missionary and business
archives relating to Asia and Africa

continued overleaf

Library catalogue:
All or part available online, in-house and in print

Printed publications:
International African Bibliography (quarterly, pub Mansell)
Guide to archives and manuscript collections in the Library, compiled by Rosemary Seton, July 1994
Library Catalogue, 1963, 28 vols Supplement, 1968, 16 vols Supplement, 1973, 16 vols Supplement, 1979, 19 vols (pub G K Hall)
Library Guide and various specialist guides

Microform publications:
Library catalogue supplement, 1978–1989, microfiche (pub IDC)

Publications list:
Available in print

Access to staff:
Contact by fax, by e-mail, in person and via website
Hours: Term time and Christmas and Easter vacations:
Mon to Thu, 0900 to 2330 (issue desk closes at 2000, membership at 1855); Fri, 0900 to 2330 (issue desk and membership close at 1855);
Sat, 1030 to 1800 (staffed: issue and membership desks close at 1745);
Sun, 1030 to 1800 (*unstaffed: self-service only)
Summer vacation:
Mon to Fri, 0900 to 2100 (*unstaffed after 1700);
Sat, 1030 to 1800 (staffed)
Sun, 1030 to 1800 (*unstaffed)
Special comments: Occasional visits allowed for consultation. Non-members of the school may apply for library membership, but a charge may be made and a letter of introduction is required.

Parent body:
University of London

SOCIAL CARE ASSOCIATION

Acronym or abbreviation: SCA

350 West Barnes Lane, Motspur Park, New Malden, KT3 6NB

Tel: 020 8949 5837
Fax: 020 8949 4384
E-mail: via website

Website:
http://www.socialcareassociation.co.uk
The association, aims and membership, services, news, events, publications, jobs.

Founded:
1949

Formerly called:
Residential Child Care Association (RCCA) (year of change 1972); Residential Care Association (RCA) (year of change 1985)

Organisation type and purpose:
A professional membership association for anyone who works in social care at any level, in any role and in any area; a UK-wide organisation that believes in and promotes good practice.

Subject coverage:
Social care practice.

Printed publications:
Adult Social Care Practice Handbook and CD Rom (£50 members, £75 non-members)
Social Care Practice Guides (free to members, at cost to non-members)
Social Caring (quarterly journal, free to members, £10 a year non-members)

Electronic and video publications:
Social Care Practice Guides (free to members)
Social Caring (quarterly journal)
Order electronic and video publications from:
Download from members' section of website

Publications list:
Available online

Access to staff:
Contact by letter, by telephone, by fax and via website

Also at:
Scotland Office
6 School Wynd, Paisley, Renfrewshire, PA1 2DB; tel: 0141 889 6667; fax: 0141 889 4035

Links with:
SCA (Education), a registered charity

SOCIAL CARE INSTITUTE FOR EXCELLENCE

Acronym or abbreviation: SCIE

1st Floor, Goldings House, Hay's Lane, London, SE1 2HB

Tel: 020 7089 6840
Fax: 020 7089 6841
E-mail: info@scie.org.uk

Website:
http://www.scie.org.uk
http://www.scie-socialcareonline.org.uk
Social Care Online
http://www.researchweb.org.uk
ResearchWeb: Scottish social care research
http://www.scie-peoplemanagement.org.uk
People Management
http://www.researchregister.org.uk
Research Register for Social Care

Enquiries:
Enquiries to: Director of Knowledge Management

Founded:
2001

Formerly called:
National Institute for Social Work (year of change 2001)

Organisation type and purpose:
Voluntary organisation; research commissioning body

Subject coverage:
Social welfare policy; personal social services; social care.

Non-library collection catalogue:
All or part available online

Printed publications:
Wide variety of publications available
Order printed publications from: http://www.scie.org.uk/publications/ordering/index.asp

Electronic and video publications:
Social Care Online
ResearchWeb
Research Register for Social Care

Publications list:
Available online and in print

Access to staff:
Contact by e-mail and via website
Hours: Mon to Fri, 1000 to 1700

Access to building, collection or gallery:
No prior appointment required
Hours: Mon to Fri, 1000 to 1700

Access for disabled people:
Parking provided, access to all public areas, toilet facilities

SOCIAL HISTORY SOCIETY

Acronym or abbreviation: SHS

Furness College, Bailrigg, Lancaster, LA1 4YG

Tel: 01524 592547
Fax: 01524 846102
E-mail: l.persson@lancaster.ac.uk

Website:
http://socialhistory.org.uk
Society information, conference information, links.

Enquiries:
Enquiries to: Administrative Secretary

Founded:
1976

Organisation type and purpose:
Learned society.

Subject coverage:
The history of society in all times and places.

Printed publications:
Culture and Social History Journal (4 times a year)

Access to staff:
Contact by letter, by telephone, by fax, by e-mail and via website. Appointment necessary.
Hours: Tue, 0930 to 1630; Wed, 1330 to 1630; Fri, 0930 to 1700

Access for disabled people:
Parking provided, level entry, access to all public areas, toilet facilities

Affiliated to:
Association of Learned Societies in the Social Sciences

SOCIAL RESEARCH ASSOCIATION

Acronym or abbreviation: SRA

PO Box 33660, London, N16 6WE

Tel: 020 8880 5684
Fax: 020 8880 5684
E-mail: admin@the-sra.org.uk

Website:
http://www.the-sra.org.uk
Membership, careers, job adverts, training days, annual conference details and seminars.

Enquiries:
Enquiries to: Administrator

Founded:
1978

Organisation type and purpose:
Membership association.

Subject coverage:
Application and development of social research, methodology, funding, training and policy.

Printed publications:
Directory of members
Newsletter (quarterly)
Commissioning Social Research: a Practical Guide
Ethical Guidelines

Access to staff:
Contact by letter, by telephone, by fax, by e-mail and via website. Appointment necessary.
Hours: Mon to Fri, 0900 to 1700

Affiliated to:
ALSISS
ARCISS
SCASS

SOCIAL, EMOTIONAL AND BEHAVIOURAL DIFFICULTIES ASSOCIATION

Acronym or abbreviation: SEBDA

Room 211, The Triangle, Exchange Square, Manchester, M4 3TR

Tel: 0161 240 2418
Fax: 0161 838 5601
E-mail: admin@sebda.org

Website:
http://www.sebda.org

Enquiries:
Enquiries to: Office Services Manager

Formerly called:
Association of Workers for Children with Emotional and Behavioural Difficulties (AWCEBD); Association of Workers for Maladjusted Children

Organisation type and purpose:
Membership association (membership is by subscription), registered charity (charity number 258730), training organisation, consultancy.

Subject coverage:
Educational and therapeutic care of disturbed children, staff training and support, emotional and behavioural difficulties, policy development.

Printed publications:
Journal
Newsletter
Prospectus

Electronic and video publications:
EBD schools database

Publications list:
Available in print

Access to staff:
Contact by letter, by telephone, by fax, by e-mail and via website
Hours: Response to telephone enquiries 1000 to 1600

Access to building, collection or gallery:
Prior appointment required

Access for disabled people:
Parking provided, level entry, toilet facilities

Member of:
National Children's Bureau
Special Educational Needs National Advisory Council
Young Minds (successor to Child Guidance Trust)

SOCIALIST HEALTH ASSOCIATION

Acronym or abbreviation: SHA

22 Blair Road, Manchester, M16 8NS

Tel: 01612861926
E-mail: admin@sochealth.co.uk

Website:
http://www.sochealth.co.uk
Information about health and health policy in the UK, related organisations, campaigns, current topics, glossary of acronyms, historical and legal materials.

Enquiries:
Enquiries to: Director

Founded:
1930

Formerly called:
Socialist Medical Association (year of change 1980)

Organisation type and purpose:
Membership association (membership is by subscription), present number of members: 720, voluntary organisation.
Political campaigning.

Subject coverage:
Structure and accountability of the National Health Service, community care, local authority health responsibilities, health promotion, politics of health, mental health services, primary health care, health inequalities, public health, inequality.

Museum or gallery collection, archive, or library special collection:
Archives (held at Hull History Centre)

Printed publications:
Annual Report
Discussion papers
Socialism and Health (3 times a year)

Publications list:
Available in print

Access to staff:
Contact by letter, by telephone, by e-mail and via website
Hours: Any reasonable hour

Access to building, collection or gallery:
Prior appointment required

Access for disabled people:
Ramped entry

Affiliated to:
Labour Party

SOCIALIST INTERNATIONAL WOMEN

Acronym or abbreviation: SIW

Maritime House, Old Town, Clapham, London, SW4 0JW

Tel: 020 7627 4449
Fax: 020 7720 4448
E-mail: socintwomen@gn.apc.org

Website:
http://www.socintwomen.org

Enquiries:
Enquiries to: General Secretary
Direct fax: 020 7498 1293

Founded:
1907

Organisation type and purpose:
International organisation.

Subject coverage:
Women; human rights; development; disarmament.

Printed publications:
Women and Politics (magazine, quarterly)

Has:
131 member organisations in different countries
7 fraternal and associated organisations worldwide

SOCIÉTÉ JERSIAISE

7 Pier Road, St Helier, Jersey, JE2 4XW, Channel Islands

Tel: 01534 758314 (office); 730538 (library); 633398 (photo archive)
Fax: 01534 888262
E-mail: library@societe-jersiaise.org

Website:
http://www.societe-jersiaise.org

Enquiries:
Enquiries to: Librarian
Other contacts: Photographic Administrator (for photographic archive)

Founded:
1873

Organisation type and purpose:
Learned society.

Subject coverage:
Local history, natural history with sections on zoology, ornithology, botany, garden history, entomology, marine biology, archaeology, geology, numismatics, bibliography, mycology, environment, the ancient language.

Museum or gallery collection, archive, or library special collection:
Manuscripts, archival documents, correspondence, family papers, ephemera, newspapers, photographs, periodicals and rare books related to Jersey

Non-library collection catalogue:
All or part available online and in-house

Library catalogue:
All or part available online and in-house

Printed publications:
Annual Bulletin (since 1875)
Channel Island Family History Journal
Many publications on historical topics and people, old maps, memoirs and natural history
1851 Census of Jersey
1871 Census of Jersey
A range of publications for children

Publications list:
Available online and in print

Access to staff:
Contact by letter, by telephone, by fax, by e-mail, in person and via website
Hours: Mon to Fri, 0900 to 1700

Links with:
Jersey Archives Service
  tel: 01534 633303; fax: 01534 633301
Jersey Museums Service
  The Weighbridge, St Helier, Jersey, JE2 3NF; tel: 01534 633330; fax: 01534 633301

SOCIETY AND COLLEGE OF RADIOGRAPHERS

Acronym or abbreviation: SCOR

Quartz House, 207 Providence Square, London, SE1 2EW

Tel: 020 7740 7200
Fax: 020 7740 7204
E-mail: info@sor.org

Website:
http://www.sor.org
A range of professional and industrial relations information, members' section.

Enquiries:
Enquiries to: Admin Assistants
Other contacts: Director of Professional Development for professional matters

Organisation type and purpose:
Trade union, present number of members: 18,000.

Subject coverage:
Radiography and related careers.

Education services:
Education for radiographers and related careers.

Printed publications:
Available free or for purchase direct

Publications list:
Available online and in print

Access to staff:
Contact by letter, by telephone, by fax, by e-mail, in person and via website. Appointment necessary.
Hours: Mon to Fri, 0900 to 1700

Access for disabled people:
Parking provided, access to all public areas, toilet facilities

SOCIETY FOR ADVANCED LEGAL STUDIES

Acronym or abbreviation: SALS

17 Russell Square, London, WC1B 5DR

Tel: 020 7862 5865
Fax: 020 7862 5855
E-mail: sals@sas.ac.uk

Website:
http://www.iats.sas.ac.uk/SALS/society.htm

Enquiries:
Enquiries to: Secretary

Founded:
1997

Organisation type and purpose:
Learned society (membership is by subscription, qualification).

Access to staff:
Contact by e-mail
Hours: Mon to Fri, 0900 to 1700

SOCIETY FOR ANGLO-CHINESE UNDERSTANDING

Acronym or abbreviation: SACU

2 Lawnswood Avenue, Poulton-le-Fylde, Lancashire, FY6 7ED

continued overleaf

Tel: 01253 894582

Website:
http://www.sacu.org

Enquiries:
Enquiries to: Information Officer

Founded:
1965

Organisation type and purpose:
Membership association, registered charity.
To promote Anglo-Chinese understanding and
friendship.

Subject coverage:
China and Chinese culture; current events;
calligraphy and brush painting (not specialised
business or academic information).

Printed publications:
China Now
Newsletter

Access to staff:
Contact by letter and by telephone
Hours: Mon to Fri, 0900 to 1700

SOCIETY FOR APPLIED MICROBIOLOGY

Acronym or abbreviation: sfam

Bedford Heights, Brickhill Drive, Bedford, MK41
7PH

Tel: 01234 326661
Fax: 01234 326678
E-mail: info@sfam.org.uk

Website:
http://www.sfam.org.uk
Information on membership, meetings,
publications.

Enquiries:
Enquiries to: Office Manager
Direct e-mail: lucy@sfam.org.uk

Founded:
1931

Organisation type and purpose:
International organisation, learned society
(membership is by subscription), registered charity
(charity number 326509).

Subject coverage:
All aspects of applied bacteriology and
microbiology.

Printed publications:
Environmental Microbiology (bi-monthly, pub
  Blackwell Science)
Journal of Applied Microbiology (monthly, pub
  Blackwell Science)
Letters in Applied Microbiology (monthly, pub
  Blackwell Science)
Order printed publications from: Blackwell Science
Osney Mead, Oxford, OX2 0EL, tel: 01865 206206

Electronic and video publications:
Journals (available online via Blackwell Science)

Publications list:
Available online and in print

Access to staff:
Contact by letter, by telephone, by fax, by e-mail
and via website
Hours: Mon to Fri, 0900 to 1700

Member of:
Federation of European Microbiological Societies
Institute of Biology
International Union of Microbiological Societies

SOCIETY FOR ARMY HISTORICAL RESEARCH

Acronym or abbreviation: SAHR

c/o National Army Museum, Royal Hospital Road,
London, SW3 4HT

Enquiries:
Enquiries to: Honorary Treasurer
Direct tel: 020 3227 0156
Direct fax: 020 3227 0156
Direct e-mail: guysayle@hotmail.com

Founded:
1921

Organisation type and purpose:
Learned society (membership is by subscription),
present number of members: 1,000.
Military historical research.

Subject coverage:
History of British and Commonwealth armies and
their ancillary formations. Members' articles/
research published in quarterly journal.

Printed publications:
Index to the Journal (vols 1–68)
Journal of the Society (commenced publication in
  1921, quarterly)
Special Numbers

Access to staff:
Contact by letter and by telephone. Access for
members only.
Hours: Mon to Fri, 0900 to 1700

SOCIETY FOR CARDIOTHORACIC SURGERY IN GREAT BRITAIN AND IRELAND

Acronym or abbreviation: SCTS

35–43 Lincoln's Inn Fields, London, WC2A 3PE

Tel: 020 7869 6893
Fax: 020 7869 6890
E-mail: sctsadmin@scts.org

Website:
http://www.scts.org
Details of members, events and general
information about the Society.

Enquiries:
Enquiries to: Society Administrator

Organisation type and purpose:
Professional body.

Subject coverage:
Thoracic and cardiac surgery.

Access to staff:
Contact by e-mail
Hours: Mon to Wed, 0800 to 1400; Thur, 0930 to
1430

SOCIETY FOR CO-OPERATION IN RUSSIAN AND SOVIET STUDIES

Acronym or abbreviation: SCRSS

320 Brixton Road, London, SW9 6AB

Tel: 020 7274 2282
Fax: 020 7274 3230
E-mail: ruslibrary@scrss.co.uk

Website:
http://www.scrss.org.uk
Information on lectures and film shows; Russian
courses in Russia; society information; photo
library; SCRSS Information Digest (3 times a year).

Enquiries:
Enquiries to: Librarian

Founded:
1924

Formerly called:
Society for Cultural Relations with the USSR (year
of change 1992)

Organisation type and purpose:
Membership association (membership is by
subscription), present number of members: 500
and 25 affiliated universities/organisations,
voluntary organisation, research organisation.
To facilitate contacts and understanding between
the peoples of the UK and the former Soviet Union
through language courses, information, library etc.

Subject coverage:
Russian history including pre-revolutionary and
Soviet history, geography, literature, art, theatre,
film, ballet, music, education, sport, social sciences
(including ethnography), economics, law.

**Museum or gallery collection, archive, or library
special collection:**
Andrew Rothstein Collection (early Soviet
  documents and pamphlets)
Archive material of the SCR (founded 1924)
Huntly Carter Bequest (early Soviet theatre and
  architecture photographs)
Children's library
Newspaper cuttings files on all subjects plus many
  others maintained, mainly Russian press in
  translation

Trade and statistical information:
Statistics, in cuttings files.
Texts in Russian and English of some laws.
Statistical, economic and political data available in
  variety of subjects.

Non-library collection catalogue:
All or part available in-house

Library catalogue:
All or part available in-house

Printed publications:
SCRSS Information Digest (3 times a year)

Access to staff:
Contact by letter, by telephone, by fax, by e-mail
and in person. Appointment necessary. Non-
members charged.
Hours: Mon to Fri, 1000 to 1300 and 1400 to 1800

Access to building, collection or gallery:
Hours: Mon to Fri, 1000 to 1800
Special comments: Access is by appointment only.

Access for disabled people:
Parking provided, level entry, toilet facilities
Special comments: Prior notice required for parking.

SOCIETY FOR COMPANION ANIMAL STUDIES

Acronym or abbreviation: SCAS

10B Leny Road, Callander, Perthshire, FK17 8BA

Tel: 01877 330996
Fax: 01877 330996

Website:
http://www.scas.org.uk
Details of membership and main aims of SCAS.

Enquiries:
Enquiries to: Executive Director

Founded:
1979

Organisation type and purpose:
Membership association (membership is by
subscription), present number of members: 400,
voluntary organisation, registered charity (charity
number 1070938), suitable for ages: 18+.

Subject coverage:
Relationship between people and their companion
animals; potential therapeutic value in treating
psychological problems, mental illness, impaired
health, promotion of responsible pet ownership to
ensure quality of life of a pet and owner. Training
in providing support for bereaved pet owners.

**Museum or gallery collection, archive, or library
special collection:**
Library for reference in research at general and
  academic level
Requests by phone and letter only

Non-library collection catalogue:
All or part available in print

Library catalogue:
All or part available in-house

Printed publications:
Death of an Animal Friend (1990, £2.50, also on
  audio cassette)

Enriching our Lives (A celebration of the first 20 years of SCAS, £5.50 inc. p&p)
Guidelines for Development and Delivery of Animal Assisted Activity and Therapy Projects (£5 inc. p&p)
Guidelines for the Introduction of Pets into Nursing Homes and other Institutions (1990, £2.50)
Pet Loss and Support for Bereaved Pet Owners (£1.50 inc. p&p)
SCAS Journal (quarterly, £1)

Electronic and video publications:
A Kind Goodbye (video, £10 inc. p&p)

Publications list:
Available online and in print

Access to staff:
Contact by letter, by telephone, by fax and by e-mail. Non-members charged.
Hours: Mon to Fri, 0900 to 1700

Founder member in 1992 of:
International Association of Human/Animal Interaction Organisations (IAHAIO)

Informal links with:
AFIRAC
France
and other members of IAHAIO
DELTA Society
USA
Organisations having similar interests and concerns in the UK and abroad
Pet Fostering Service
Scotland; tel: 01877 331496
The Blue Cross
(Pet Bereavement Support Service 0800 096 6606); tel: 01993 822651; fax: 01993 823083

SOCIETY FOR COMPUTERS AND LAW

Acronym or abbreviation: SCL

10 Hurle Crescent, Clifton, Bristol, BS8 2TA

Tel: 0117 923 7393
Fax: 0117 923 9305
E-mail: ruth.baker@scl.org

Website:
http://www.scl.org
Articles, news, forthcoming events and CPD-accredited courses.

Enquiries:
Enquiries to: General Manager

Founded:
1973

Organisation type and purpose:
National organisation, professional body, membership association (membership is by subscription), present number of members: 2,500, registered charity (charity number 266331).

Subject coverage:
Information technology law, information technology for lawyers.

Information services:
News and articles on IT Law

Education services:
CPD Courses

Printed publications:
Computers & Law (6 times a year, by subscription)
Magazine

Access to staff:
Contact by letter, by telephone, by fax, by e-mail and via website. Appointment necessary.
Hours: Mon to Fri, 0900 to 1700
Special comments: Prior appointment only.

Access to building, collection or gallery:
Prior appointment required
Hours: Mon to Fri, 0900 to 1700

Access for disabled people:
Level entry

Links with:
British and Irish Legal Information Institute (BAILII)
Institute of Advanced Legal Studies, Charles Clore House

Member organisation of:
International Federation of Computer Law Associations
website: http://www.ifcla.com

SOCIETY FOR DANCE RESEARCH

Laban Centre London, Laurie Grove, New Cross, London, SE14 6NH

Tel: 020 8692 4070 ext 120
Fax: 020 8694 8749 or 8691 3792
E-mail: sdr1@tinyworld.co.uk

Enquiries:
Enquiries to: Administrative Secretary
Direct tel: 01903 742019

Founded:
1982

Organisation type and purpose:
Learned society (membership is by subscription), present number of members: 170, voluntary organisation, registered charity, research organisation.
British-based organisation, which promotes and fosters the quality and scope of scholarship and research in all forms of dance.

Subject coverage:
Dance.

Printed publications:
Dance Research (2 times a year)
Newsletter (2 times a year)
Society sponsored reports (occasional)

Access to staff:
Contact by letter, by telephone and by e-mail
Hours: Mon to Fri, 0900 to 1700
Special comments: Please contact by telephone or fax and leave message.

SOCIETY FOR EARTHQUAKE AND CIVIL ENGINEERING DYNAMICS

Acronym or abbreviation: SECED

Institution of Civil Engineers, One Great George Street, London, SW1P 3AA

Tel: 020 7222 7722
Fax: 020 7222 7500

Enquiries:
Enquiries to: Secretary
Direct tel: 020 7655 2238
Direct fax: 020 7799 1325
Direct e-mail: caroline.howe@ice.org.uk

Organisation type and purpose:
Learned society.

Subject coverage:
Earthquakes and engineering; seismology; blast, vibration and impact; soil dynamics and foundation engineering.

Printed publications:
Conference proceedings
Directory of UK practitioners (free)
Earthquake Engineering and Structural Dynamics – Journal of the International Association for Earthquake Engineering (published Wiley)
Earthquake reports

National section of the:
International Association for Earthquake Engineering

SOCIETY FOR EDITORS AND PROOFREADERS

Acronym or abbreviation: SfEP

Erico House, 93–99 Upper Richmond Road, London, SW15 2TG

Tel: 020 8785 5617
Fax: 020 8785 5618
E-mail: administration@sfep.org.uk

Website:
http://www.sfep.org.uk

Enquiries:
Enquiries to: Administrator
Direct e-mail: executive@sfep.org.uk

Founded:
1988

Organisation type and purpose:
Professional body (membership is by subscription), present number of members: c.1,400, training organisation.
Upholding editorial excellence.

Subject coverage:
Copy-editing and proofreading, editorial project management, editorial training, editorial standards. The profession is involved in a wide range of subject areas including: modern languages, business, finance and economics, medicine, music, reference, technical writing, science and computing.

Printed publications:
Newsletter (6 times a year, by subscription, members only)
Directory of Members' Services (annually, free to members, cover price £15 but up to two copies free to bona fide users of freelance editorial services)

Electronic and video publications:
Directory of Members' Services (available online)

Access to staff:
Contact by letter, by telephone, by fax, by e-mail and via website
Hours: 0930 to 1600
Special comments: Personal attendance not encouraged.

SOCIETY FOR ENDOCRINOLOGY

22 Apex Court, Woodlands, Bradley Stoke, Bristol, BS32 4JT

Tel: 01454 642200
Fax: 01454 642222
E-mail: info@endocrinology.org

Website:
http://www.endocrinology.org
Society home pages, ordering information, journal abstracts and contents, full text for institutional subscribers.

Enquiries:
Enquiries to: Society Services Manager

Founded:
1946

Organisation type and purpose:
Learned society, registered charity (charity number 266813), publishing house.
To promote the advancement of public education in endocrinology.

Subject coverage:
Endocrinology; hormones.

Printed publications:
Endocrine-Related Cancer (quarterly)
Journal of Endocrinology (monthly)
Journal of Molecular Endocrinology (6 times a year)
The Endocrinologist (newsletter, quarterly)
Order printed publications from: Portland Press Ltd, Commerce Way, Colchester, Essex, CO2 8HP; tel: 01206 796351; fax: 01206 799331; e-mail: sales@portlandpress.co.uk

Electronic and video publications:
Online versions of journals

Publications list:
Available online

Access to staff:
Contact by letter

continued overleaf

Hours: Mon to Fri, 0900 to 1700

Subsidiary body:
BioScientifica Ltd
22 Apex Court, Woodlands, Bradley Stoke, Bristol, BS32 4JT; tel: 01454 642200; fax: 01454 642222; e-mail: info@endocrinology.org

SOCIETY FOR FOLK LIFE STUDIES

Snibston Discovery Park, Ashby Discovery Park, Ashby Road, Coalville, Leicestershire, LE67 2LN

Tel: 01530 278468
Fax: 01530 813301

Website:
http://www.folklife.org.uk
General description of society, lists of articles in Folklife Journal

Enquiries:
Enquiries to: Secretary
Direct e-mail: seblittlewood@beamish.org.uk

Founded:
1961

Organisation type and purpose:
Learned society (membership is by subscription), present number of members: c. 500, voluntary organisation.

Subject coverage:
Traditional ways of life in Great Britain and Ireland, folk life, popular culture, ethnology.

Printed publications:
Journal of Folk Life Studies (annually)
Newsletter (annually)
Order printed publications from: Society for Folk Life Studies, Welsh Folk Museum
St Fagan's, Cardiff, CF5 6XB, tel: 029 2056 9441, fax: 029 2057 8413

Access to staff:
Contact by letter, by telephone, by fax, by e-mail and via website
Hours: Mon to Fri, 0900 to 1700

SOCIETY FOR GENERAL MICROBIOLOGY

Acronym or abbreviation: SGM

Marlborough House, Basingstoke Road, Spencers Wood, Reading, Berkshire, RG7 1AG

Tel: 0118 988 1800
Fax: 0118 988 5656
E-mail: admin@sgm.ac.uk

Website:
http://www.sgm.ac.uk
Society, membership, subscriptions, forthcoming scientific meetings, publications, availability of publications electronically, external relations and grants, careers, training, microbiology for schools.
http://www.sgmjournals.org
Online journals.

Enquiries:
Enquiries to: Chief Executive
Direct tel: 0118 988 1812
Direct e-mail: r.fraser@sgm.ac.uk

Founded:
1945

Organisation type and purpose:
International organization, learned society (membership is by subscription), present number of members: 5,500, registered charity (charity number 264017), publishing house.
Represents the interests of microbiologists world-wide, particularly in the United Kingdom.

Subject coverage:
Microbiology, virology, biotechnology in response to requests from the general public, academia, industry, government and all levels of education.
Careers and training in microbiology.

Printed publications:
Careers in microbiology (free)

International Journal of Systematic and Evolutionary Microbiology (monthly)
Journal of General Virology (monthly)
Microbiology (monthly)
Microbiology Today (quarterly)
Journal of Medical Microbiology (monthly)
Order printed publications from: website: http://www.sgmjournals.org/subscriptions/pricing

Electronic and video publications:
Online journals
Order electronic and video publications from: website: http://www.sgmjournals.org/subscriptions/pricing

Publications list:
Available online and in print

Access to staff:
Contact by letter, by telephone, by fax, by e-mail and via website. Appointment necessary.
Hours: Mon to Fri, 0900 to 1700

Links with:
Federation of European Microbiology Societies
International Union of Microbiology Societies

SOCIETY FOR INDIVIDUAL FREEDOM

Acronym or abbreviation: SIF

PO Box 744, Bromley, Kent, BR1 4WG

Tel: 01424 713737
Fax: 01424 713737
E-mail: chairman@individualist.org.uk

Website:
http://www.individualist.org.uk
Details on SIF. Tell It.

Enquiries:
Enquiries to: Chairman
Other contacts: President

Founded:
1940

Organisation type and purpose:
Membership association, voluntary organisation.
Lobbying group.
Campaigning for personal freedom.

Subject coverage:
Personal freedom, reducing state control and taxation, fostering free enterprise.

Printed publications:
The Power to Destroy: a study of the British Taxation System (D Myddelton)
The Individual (newsletter)

Publications list:
Available in print

Access to staff:
Contact by letter, by telephone, by e-mail and via website
Hours: Also evenings

SOCIETY FOR INTERNATIONAL FOLK DANCING

Acronym or abbreviation: SIFD

5 South Rise, Carshalton, SM5 4PD

Tel: 020 8395 1400
E-mail: mail@sifd.org

Website:
http://www.sifd.org

Enquiries:
Enquiries to: Publicity Officer

Founded:
1946

Organisation type and purpose:
Membership association (membership is by subscription), present number of members: 400, voluntary organisation, registered charity (charity number 284509), suitable for all ages.
Voluntary society.
Support and co-ordination of work of local bodies.

Subject coverage:
Traditional folk dances of many countries, especially European; costume and music of those countries.

Printed publications:
Newsletter (monthly, members only)
Instruction books
History of Society for International Folk Dancing
Order printed publications from: Publications Secretary, Society for International Folk Dancing, 5 South Rise, Carshalton, Surrey, SM5 4PD, tel: 020 8395 1400

Electronic and video publications:
Music tapes, CDs and a video

Publications list:
Available online

Access to staff:
Contact by letter, by telephone, by e-mail and via website
Hours: Variable

Also at:
63 affiliated and associated UK groups
Society for International Folk Dancing
6 Leveson Crescent, Balsall Common, Coventry, CV7 7DR; tel: 01676 534112
West Midlands Branch

Links with:
Central Council for Physical Recreation (CCPR)
Francis House, Francis Street, London, SW1P 1DE; tel: 020 8828 3163; fax: 020 8630 8820

SOCIETY FOR ITALIC HANDWRITING

Acronym or abbreviation: SIH

205 Dyas Avenue, Great Barr, Birmingham, B42 1HN

Tel: 0121 358 0032
Fax: 0121 358 0032
E-mail: nickthenibs@netscapeonline.co.uk

Enquiries:
Enquiries to: Secretary

Founded:
1952

Organisation type and purpose:
Learned society (membership is by subscription), present number of members: 500, registered charity (charity number 287889R).
To sustain the interest in italic handwriting and to secure the advancement of education in relation to handwriting.

Subject coverage:
Italic handwriting and Renaissance calligraphy.

Printed publications:
A Simple Guide to Italic Handwriting (Winters N, £6 plus £1 p&p)
Writing Matters (formerly the Journal and the Newsletter, 3 times a year to members)

Electronic and video publications:
Good Handwriting Initiative: School's Pack (CD-ROM and copy sheets, £14.50 inc. p&p)

Access to staff:
Contact by letter and by e-mail
Hours: Mon to Fri, 0900 to 1700

Connections with:
Society of Scribes and Illuminators

SOCIETY FOR LIBYAN STUDIES

Institute of Archaeology, 31–34 Gordon Square, London, WC1H 0PY

E-mail: shinleystrong@btconnect.com

Website:
http://www.britac.ac.uk/institutes/libya
Information about the Society, lists of publications, lecture programme, subscription rate, etc.

Enquiries:
Enquiries to: General Secretary

Founded:
1969

Organisation type and purpose:
Learned society.

Subject coverage:
Libyan life and culture, particularly archaeology, history, Islamic law, geography and geomorphology.

Museum or gallery collection, archive, or library special collection:
Specialist works on Libya, including the Goodchild Library

Printed publications:
Annual Journal, Report and Monographs
Publications include:
Excavations at Sidi Khrebish, Bengazi
Farming the Desert: The UNESCO Libyan Valleys Archaeological Survey
Christian Monuments of Cyrenaica
The Severan Buildings of Lepcis Magna
The Archaeology of Fazzan
The Libyan Desert: Natural Resources and Cultural Heritage
Silphium Press publications include:
Travellers in Libya
Libya Archaeological Guides: Tripolitania
The Emergence of Libya
Full publications list on website
Order printed publications from: Website

Publications list:
Available online and in print

Access to staff:
Contact by letter and by e-mail
Hours: Mon to Fri, 0900 to 1700

SOCIETY FOR LINCOLNSHIRE HISTORY AND ARCHAEOLOGY

Acronym or abbreviation: SLHA

Jews' Court, 2 & 3 Steep Hill, Lincoln, LN2 1LS

Tel: 01522 521337
Fax: 01522 521337
E-mail: slha@lincolnshirepast.org.uk

Website:
http://www.lincolnshirepast.org.uk

Enquiries:
Enquiries to: Administrator

Founded:
1974

Organisation type and purpose:
Learned society, membership association (membership is by subscription), present number of members: 600, voluntary organisation, registered charity (charity number 504766), suitable for ages: all.
To promote interest in and the study of all aspects of Lincolnshire history.

Subject coverage:
Lincolnshire history, archaeology, industrial archaeology, topography, architecture, dialect, etc.

Museum or gallery collection, archive, or library special collection:
Library for members (at Jews' Court)
Periodicals and valuable material on deposit at the Lincolnshire Archives Office

Library catalogue:
All or part available in-house

Printed publications:
Bulletin (quarterly)
Diary Dates (quarterly)
Lincolnshire History and Archaeology (annually)
Lincolnshire Past and Present (quarterly)

Publications list:
Available in print

Access to staff:
Contact by letter, by telephone, by fax, by e-mail and in person. Appointment necessary. Access for members only.
Hours: Mon to Thu, 1000 to 1300
Special comments: Library open to members only.

Trading company is:
Lincolnshire Heritage Limited
at the main address; tel: 01522 532280; fax: 01522 521337

SOCIETY FOR LOW TEMPERATURE BIOLOGY

Acronym or abbreviation: SLTB

The General Secretary, c/o Jon Green, Genómica Funcional, CIC-Biogune, Parque Tecnológico de Vizcaya, Edificio 801A, 1pl., 48160-Derio, Spain

Tel: +34 944 061 326
Fax: +34 944 061 301
E-mail: jgreen@cicbiogune.es

Website:
http://www.sltb.info
Information about the society, list of committee members.

Enquiries:
Enquiries to: Treasurer
Direct e-mail: mcurry@lincoln.ac.uk

Founded:
1964

Organisation type and purpose:
International organisation, learned society.

Subject coverage:
Biological effects of low temperature; preservation of cells, tissues, organs, in both plant and animal kingdoms; preservation of genetic stock (plants); adaptation to cold; cryosurgery.

Printed publications:
Newsletter (3 times a year, free to members)

Access to staff:
Contact by letter, by fax, by e-mail and via website
Hours: Mon to Fri, 0900 to 1700

SOCIETY FOR MUCOPOLYSACCHARIDE DISEASES

Acronym or abbreviation: MPS

MPS House, Repton Place, White Lion Road, Amersham, Buckinghamshire, HP7 9LP

Tel: 0845 389 9901
Fax: 0845 389 9902
E-mail: mps@mpssociety.co.uk

Website:
http://www.mpssociety.co.uk

Enquiries:
Enquiries to: Chief Executive

Founded:
1982

Organisation type and purpose:
International organisation, membership association (membership is by qualification), present number of members: 1500, voluntary organisation, registered charity (charity number 287034).
Members who qualify are: those having MPS, parent or carer.
Provides support and advocacy to individuals and their families affected by MPS diseases, brings about public awareness and raises funds for furthering research.

Subject coverage:
Mucopolysaccharide and related diseases; clinical management, gene research, education, home adaptations, welfare benefits, specialist clinics, social events.

Printed publications:
Series of booklets produced by parents and doctors to provide guidance for families and professionals caring for individuals suffering from MPS (£2 each)
Order printed publications from: http://www.mpssociety.co.uk

Publications list:
Available online and in print

Access to staff:
Contact by letter, by telephone, by fax, by e-mail and via website. Appointment necessary.
Hours: Mon to Fri, 0900 to 1700
Out-of-hours helpline: Mon to Fri, 1700 to 2200; Sat, Sun, 0700 to 2200

Access to building, collection or gallery:
Prior appointment preferred.
Hours: Mon to Fri, 0900 to 1700
Special comments: Subject to adequate staffing.

Access for disabled people:
Level entry
Special comments: Limited access to ground floor only.

SOCIETY FOR POPULAR ASTRONOMY

Acronym or abbreviation: SPA

Dept DIS, 36 Fairway, Keyworth, Nottingham, NG12 5DU

E-mail: info@popastro.com

Website:
http://www.popastro.com

Enquiries:
Enquiries to: Honorary Secretary
Other contacts: Editor Popular Astronomy Magazine (for material for review)

Founded:
1953

Organisation type and purpose:
Membership association (membership is by subscription), present number of members: 3,000.
To encourage the study and understanding of astronomy, particularly for beginners of all ages and those who prefer a less technical approach.

Subject coverage:
Astronomy.

Printed publications:
News circulars (6 times a year)
Popular Astronomy (quarterly)

Electronic and video publications:
Electronic News Bulletins (via e-mail, may be requested through website)

Access to staff:
Contact by letter and by e-mail
Hours: Mon to Fri, 0900 to 1700
Special comments: Please send sae with postal enquiries.

Also at:
Editor, Popular Astronomy Magazine
7 Parc-An-Bre Drive, St Dennis, St Austell, PL26 8AS

SOCIETY FOR POST-MEDIEVAL ARCHAEOLOGY, THE

Acronym or abbreviation: SPMA

Department of Medieval and Later Antiquities, British Museum, London, WC1B 3DG

Tel: 0191 482 1037
E-mail: cranstone@btinternet.com

Website:
http://www.spma.org.uk/

Enquiries:
Enquiries to: Honorary Secretary
Direct fax: 0191 487 2343

continued overleaf

Founded:
1966

Organisation type and purpose:
Learned society, registered charity (charity number 281651).

Subject coverage:
Archaeology in the period of European and Colonial history ranging from the close of the Middle Ages up to the twentieth century.

Printed publications:
Newsletter
Post-Medieval Archaeology (annually)
Monograph series

Access to staff:
Contact by letter, by fax and by e-mail
Hours: Mon to Fri, 0900 to 1700

Links with:
Society for Historical Archaeology
USA

Other address:
Secretary
267 Kells Lane, Low Fell, Gateshead, NG9 5HU

SOCIETY FOR PROMOTING CHRISTIAN KNOWLEDGE

Acronym or abbreviation: SPCK

36 Causton Street, London, SW1P 4ST

Tel: 020 7592 3900
Fax: 020 7592 3939
E-mail: spck@spck.org.uk

Website:
http://www.spck.org.uk
Details of all SPCK's activities and services.

Enquiries:
Enquiries to: General Secretary
Direct e-mail: publicity@spck.org.uk

Founded:
1698

Organisation type and purpose:
Membership association (membership is by election or invitation), present number of members: 300, registered charity (charity number 231144), publishing house.
To promote Christian knowledge.

Museum or gallery collection, archive, or library special collection:
Archives of SPCK publications from 1698 (held at Cambridge University Library)

Printed publications:
Annual Report
A wide variety of books on church mission and ministry, prayer and meditation, personal growth and relationships, biblical studies and education, etc.
Order printed publications from: Trade: Marston Book Services, PO Box 269, Abingdon, OX14 4YN; tel: 01235 465521; e-mail: tradeorder@marston.co.uk
Individuals: tel@ 01235 465500; e-mail: directorder@marston.co.uk

Publications list:
Available in print

Access to staff:
Contact by letter, by telephone and by e-mail
Hours: Mon to Fri, 0900 to 1700

Subsidiary bodies:
Azure Books
at the same address
Sheldon Press
at the same address
Triangle Books
at the same address

SOCIETY FOR PSYCHICAL RESEARCH

Acronym or abbreviation: SPR

49 Marloes Road, Kensington, London, W8 6LA

Tel: 020 7937 8984
Fax: 020 7937 8984

Website:
http://www.spr.ac.uk

Enquiries:
Enquiries to: Secretary

Founded:
1882

Organisation type and purpose:
International organisation, learned society (membership is by election or invitation), present number of members: 1,000, voluntary organisation, registered charity (charity number 207325), suitable for ages: 16+, research organisation. To advance the understanding of events and abilities commonly described as psychic or paranormal, without prejudice and in a scientific manner. Houses one of the largest libraries in Europe of psychic material.

Subject coverage:
Inquiry into the reality and nature of paranormal cognition by means of experiments, and by collecting and analysing accounts of spontaneously occurring incidents that appear to be of this nature. The Society operates without prejudice and can offer no corporate view or opinion.

Museum or gallery collection, archive, or library special collection:
Archival material and rare books

Non-library collection catalogue:
All or part available in-house

Library catalogue:
All or part available in-house

Printed publications:
Journal and Newsletter (quarterly)
Objects and Activities (leaflet)
Proceedings (irregular)

Publications list:
Available online and in print

Access to staff:
Contact by letter, by telephone, by fax and in person. Access for members only. Non-members charged.
Hours: Tue, Wed, Thu, 1300 to 1700 for personal callers

Access to building, collection or gallery:
No prior appointment required
Hours: Library: Tue, Wed, Thu, 1300 to 1700
Special comments: Free to members, no appointment required for access to library.

SOCIETY FOR RENAISSANCE STUDIES

Dr Gabriele Neher, Department of Art History, Lakeside Arts Centre, The University of Nottingham, NG7 2RD

Tel: 01159 513184
E-mail: gabriele.neher@nottingham.ac.uk

Website:
http://www.rensoc.org.uk

Enquiries:
Enquiries to: Honorary Secretary

Founded:
1967

Organisation type and purpose:
International organisation, learned society (membership is by subscription), present number of members: 400, registered charity (charity number 1025890).
Promotion of Renaissance studies.

Subject coverage:
Art, history, literature and philosophy of the Renaissance.

Printed publications:
Biennial Bulletin (free to members)

Journal (Wiley-Blackwell, subscription at discount to members)
List of Research Interests of Members
Occasional papers
Renaissance Studies (journal)
Order printed publications from: Journals Marketing, Wiley-Blackwell Publishing, 9600 Garsington Road, Oxford, OX4 2DQ

Access to staff:
Contact by letter, by telephone, by e-mail and via website
Hours: Mon to Fri, 0900 to 1700

Affiliated to:
Institutes for the Study of the Renaissance
International Federation of Societies

SOCIETY FOR REPRODUCTION & FERTILITY

Acronym or abbreviation: SSF

SRF Business Office, Procon Conferences Ltd, Tattersall House, East Parade, Harrogate, North Yorkshire, HG1 5LT

Tel: 01423 564488
Fax: 01423 701433

Website:
http://www.srf-reproduction.org/

Enquiries:
Enquiries to: Secretary
Direct e-mail: SRF@portland-services.com

Founded:
1950

Organisation type and purpose:
Learned society.

Subject coverage:
Reproductive biology, fertility and infertility in animals and man.

Printed publications:
Newsletter (members only)
Reproduction (journal)

Access to staff:
Contact by letter, by e-mail and via website
Hours: Mon to Fri, 0900 to 1700

SOCIETY FOR RESEARCH IN THE PSYCHOLOGY OF MUSIC AND MUSIC EDUCATION

Acronym or abbreviation: SEMPRE

Institute of Education, 20 Bedford Way, London, WC1H 0AL

Tel: 020 7612 6740
Fax: 020 7612 6741
E-mail: membership@sempre.org.uk

Website:
http://www.srpmme.u-net.com/subs.html

Enquiries:
Enquiries to: Membership Secretary

Founded:
1973

Organisation type and purpose:
Learned society.

Subject coverage:
Psychology of music; music education; music education research; music psychology research; music perception psychology; child development (music); music therapy; social psychology of music.

Printed publications:
Psychology of Music (journal, twice a year)

Access to staff:
Contact by letter
Hours: Mon to Fri, 0900 to 1700

Affiliated to:
International Society for Music Education
UK Council for Music Education and Training

SOCIETY FOR THE HISTORY OF ALCHEMY AND CHEMISTRY

Acronym or abbreviation: SHAC

Applied Sciences, Anglia Ruskin University, East Road, Cambridge, CB1 1PT

Tel: 01223 363271 ext 2380
Fax: 01223 417711
E-mail: jhudson@bridge.anglia.ac.uk

Website:
http://www.open.ac.uk/Arts/HST/SHAC/index.html
How to join the society, Ambix – contents of current issue, forthcoming meetings, members of society's council.

Enquiries:
Enquiries to: Honorary Secretary

Founded:
1937

Organisation type and purpose:
Learned society.

Subject coverage:
History of alchemy and chemistry.

Printed publications:
Ambix (journal, 3 times a year, on subscription)

Access to staff:
Contact by letter, by telephone and by e-mail
Hours: Mon to Fri, 0900 to 1700

SOCIETY FOR THE HISTORY OF NATURAL HISTORY

Acronym or abbreviation: SHNH

c/o Natural History Museum, Cromwell Road, London, SW7 5BD

Tel: 020 7887 5261
Fax: 020 7887 5391
E-mail: secretary@shnh.org.uk

Website:
http://www.shnh.org.uk
Objectives, how to join, publications, council members list, forthcoming meetings, news and updates.

Enquiries:
Enquiries to: Honorary Secretary
Other contacts: Treasurer (for sale of publications)

Founded:
1936

Organisation type and purpose:
Learned society, professional body (membership is by subscription), present number of members: 650, registered charity (charity number 210355). Promotes the study of all branches of the history of natural history including biographical and bibliographical studies.

Subject coverage:
History of botany, geology, zoology and other subjects included in the broad term 'natural history'.

Printed publications:
Archives of Natural History (3 times a year)
Essai sur la Géographie des Plantes (1807) (Alexander von Humboldt, 1959, £5)
Newsletter (3 times a year)
A guide to the official archives of The Natural History Museum, London 1998 (Thackray J, £25)
Order printed publications from: Society for the History of Natural History, c/o Natural History Museum, Cromwell Road, London, SW7 5BD

Publications list:
Available online

Access to staff:
Contact by letter, by e-mail and via website. Non-members charged.
Hours: Mon to Fri, 0900 to 1600

Close links with:
The Natural History Museum

SOCIETY FOR THE PROMOTION OF HELLENIC STUDIES

Acronym or abbreviation: SPHS

Senate House, Malet Street, London, WC1E 7HU

Tel: 020 7862 8730
Fax: 020 7862 8731
E-mail: office@hellenicsociety.org.uk

Website:
http://www.hellenicsociety.org.uk

Enquiries:
Enquiries to: Executive Secretary

Founded:
1879

Organisation type and purpose:
Learned society.

Subject coverage:
Greek art, archaeology, architecture, history, literature, law, politics, religion, philosophy, language, and science of the Minoan, Mycenaean and Hellenic world and the Byzantine Empire, and modern periods.

Museum or gallery collection, archive, or library special collection:
Library which (together with the Institute of Classical Studies library) contains some 78,867 monographs and pamphlets and some 15,592 bound vols of periodicals. 526 current periodicals taken
Slides collection of some 6,500 images
Wood donation of the Diaries of Robert Wood and his companions with the sketch books of G. B. Borra

Printed publications:
Archaeological Reports (annually)
Journal of Hellenic Studies (annually)
Occasional publications

Publications list:
Available online and in print

Access to staff:
Contact by letter, by telephone and by e-mail. Access for members only.
Hours: Mon to Fri, 0900 to 1700

Constituent part of:
Hellenic and Roman Societies

Links with:
Institute of Classical Studies Library

SOCIETY FOR THE PROMOTION OF ROMAN STUDIES

Acronym or abbreviation: SPRS

Senate House, Malet Street, London, WC1E 7HU

Tel: 020 7862 8727
Fax: 020 7862 8728
E-mail: office@romansociety.org

Website:
http://icls.sas.ac.uk/library/home.htm
Library information.
http://www.romansociety.org
Activities of the Roman Society, including lectures, grants and publications.

Enquiries:
Enquiries to: Secretary

Founded:
1910

Organisation type and purpose:
Learned society (membership is by subscription), present number of members: 2,600, registered charity (charity number 210644).

Subject coverage:
Archaeology, architecture, art, history, language, religion, philosophy, law, politics, science and literature of Rome and the Roman Empire to about AD 700; Roman Britain.

Museum or gallery collection, archive, or library special collection:
Library, which (together with the Institute of Classical Studies Library) contains some 85,000 monographs and pamphlets and some 16,000 bound vols of periodicals
560 current periodicals taken
Slides collection of some 6,700
Wood donation of the diaries of Robert Wood and his companions with the sketch-books of G. B. Borra

Library catalogue:
All or part available online

Printed publications:
Journal of Roman Studies and Britannia
Monograph Series

Electronic and video publications:
Journal of Roman Studies and Britannia (CD-ROM, 2002–06, available for purchase by members only)

Publications list:
Available online and in print

Access to staff:
Contact by letter, by telephone, by fax, by e-mail and in person. Access for members only.
Hours: Mon to Fri, 0930 to 1730

Links with:
Co-ordinating Committee for Classics
Fédération Internationale des Études Classiques

SOCIETY FOR THE PROTECTION OF ANCIENT BUILDINGS

Acronym or abbreviation: SPAB

37 Spital Square, London, E1 6DY

Tel: 020 7377 1644
Fax: 020 7247 5296
E-mail: info@spab.org.uk

Website:
http://www.spab.org.uk

Enquiries:
Enquiries to: Archivist
Other contacts: Promotions Officer for media enquiries

Founded:
1877

Organisation type and purpose:
Advisory body, learned society, membership association (membership is by subscription), charitable company (company number 5743962, charity number 111 3753, Scottish charity number SC 039244), suitable for ages: adults, training organisation, publishing house.

Subject coverage:
Repair and protection of historic buildings, building conservation in general.

Museum or gallery collection, archive, or library special collection:
Manuscript archive of society's work since 1877, about 15,000 files available to researchers by appointment, mills cases held by Mills Archive Trust, Reading

Library catalogue:
All or part available in-house

Printed publications:
Quarterly magazine (members only)
SPAB technical pamphlets
SPAB information sheets
A range of publications on building conservation and preservation are available from the Society

Publications list:
Available online and in print

Access to staff:
Contact by letter, by telephone, by e-mail and via website. Appointment necessary.
Hours: Technical Helpline: Mon to Fri, 0930 to 1230
Special comments: Archivist is part-time.

continued overleaf

Access to building, collection or gallery:
No prior appointment required
Hours: 0930 to 1730

SOCIETY FOR THE PROTECTION OF ANIMALS ABROAD

Acronym or abbreviation: SPANA

14 John Street, London, WC1N 2EB

Tel: 020 7831 3999
Fax: 020 7831 5999
E-mail: enquiries@spana.org

Website:
http://www.spana.org

Enquiries:
Enquiries to: Chief Executive

Founded:
1923

Organisation type and purpose:
International organisation, advisory body, professional body (membership is by election or invitation), present number of members: 192, voluntary organisation, registered charity (charity number 209015). Aims to improve standards of animal care wherever the need arises.

Access to staff:
Contact by letter, by telephone, by fax, by e-mail and via website
Hours: Mon to Fri, 0900 to 1700

Member organisation of:
IUCN

SOCIETY FOR THE PROTECTION OF UNBORN CHILDREN

Acronym or abbreviation: SPUC

3 Whitacre Mews, Stannary Street, London, SE11 4AB

Tel: 020 7091 7091
Fax: 020 7820 3131
E-mail: information@spuc.org.uk

Website:
http://www.spuc.org.uk
Information on abortion, euthanasia, foetal development, pro-life campaigns, embryo research, etc.

Enquiries:
Enquiries to: General Secretary
Direct e-mail: paultully@spuc.org.uk
Other contacts: Regional development officers (for provision of educational services to schools, voluntary groups, etc.)

Founded:
1966

Organisation type and purpose:
National organisation, membership association (membership is by subscription), present number of members: 46,000, voluntary organisation, suitable for ages: 12+, research organisation. Parliamentary lobby group.
To affirm, defend and promote the existence and value of human life from the moment of conception, and to defend and protect human life especially in the areas of abortion, handicap, euthanasia, embryo experiments and population control. To examine existing or proposed laws, legislation or regulations relating to abortion and to support or oppose such as appropriate.

Subject coverage:
Abortion, human pre-natal development, abortion side-effects, social effects of abortion legislation, handicap, eugenics, euthanasia, infertility treatment and research, human embryo experimentation and population control, cloning, abortifacients (morning-after pill, RU486, 'emergency contraception'), mental incapacity legislation, post-abortion syndrome.

Information services:
e-mail: information@spuc.org.uk

Museum or gallery collection, archive, or library special collection:
Press cuttings and parliamentary debates, questions, speeches, etc. relating to abortion, euthanasia, embryo research

Printed publications:
Pro-Life Times (journal, every other month, 25p)
SPUC – Our Aims, Ethics and Activities (50p)

Electronic and video publications:
Video and audio tapes relating to the various subjects listed

Publications list:
Available in print

Access to staff:
Contact by letter, by telephone, by fax, by e-mail and via website. Appointment necessary.
Hours: Mon to Fri, 0900 to 1730

Access to building, collection or gallery:
Prior appointment required

Access for disabled people:
Level entry, access to all public areas, toilet facilities

Affiliated to:
International Right to Life Federation
Via Niccolò V 44, 00165 Rome, Italy

Links with:
SPUC Educational Research Trust
address as the SPUC

Subsidiary body:
ARCH – Abortion Recovery Care and Helpline
75 Bothwell Street, Glasgow, G2 6TS; tel: 0141 226 5407; 0845 603 8501 (helpline); website: http://www.archtrust.org.uk

SOCIETY FOR THE PROTECTION OF UNBORN CHILDREN – SCOTLAND

Acronym or abbreviation: SPUC Scotland

75 Bothwell Street, Glasgow, G2 6TS

Tel: 0141 221 2094
Fax: 0141 225 3696
E-mail: info@spucscotland.org

Website:
http://spucscotland.org/

Enquiries:
Enquiries to: Director
Other contacts: Development Officer for matters to do with branches.

Organisation type and purpose:
Membership association (membership is by subscription), present number of members: 4500, voluntary organisation.
The protection of all human life from conception to natural death.

Subject coverage:
Abortion, cloning, euthanasia.

Printed publications:
Pro-Life Times (4 page magazine, once every other month)
Various information leaflets

Electronic and video publications:
Videos and Tapes on Abortion, Cloning, Euthanasia, Population

Access to staff:
Contact by letter, by telephone, by fax, by e-mail and in person. Appointment necessary.
Hours: Mon to Fri, 0900 to 1700

Access to building, collection or gallery:
No prior appointment required

SOCIETY FOR THE SOCIAL HISTORY OF MEDICINE

Acronym or abbreviation: SSHM

Department of History, University of Aberdeen, Aberdeen, AB24 3FX

Tel: 01224 272456
Fax: 01224 272203
E-mail: o.walsh@abdn.ac.uk

Website:
http://www.sshm.org

Enquiries:
Enquiries to: Honorary Secretary
Direct tel: 01224 273884

Founded:
1970

Organisation type and purpose:
Learned society (membership is by subscription), registered charity (charity number 278414).

Subject coverage:
Social history of medicine; history of health care and policy.

Printed publications:
Guide to Members' Research and Interests (1995, new edition in preparation)
Social History of Medicine (journal, 3 times a year, Oxford Journals)
Studies in the Social History of Medicine (Book Series, pub Routledge, variable number of publications a year)

Access to staff:
Contact by letter, by telephone, by fax, by e-mail and via website
Hours: Mon to Fri, 0900 to 1700

SOCIETY FOR THEATRE RESEARCH

Acronym or abbreviation: STR

The Theatre Museum, 1E Tavistock Street, London, WC2E 7PR

E-mail: e.cottis@btinternet.com

Website:
http://www.str.org.uk
Prospectus information, list of current lectures, list of members' research interests, online research award form.

Enquiries:
Enquiries to: Honorary Secretary
Direct e-mail: e.cottis@btinternet.com

Founded:
1948

Organisation type and purpose:
Learned society (membership is by subscription), present number of members: 750, registered charity (charity number 266186), publishing house.

Subject coverage:
History and technique of the British theatre, and allied entertainments.

Museum or gallery collection, archive, or library special collection:
The Society's library was amalgamated with that of the Theatre Museum in 1987

Printed publications:
Theatre Notebook (journal, 3 issues per annual volume)
Publications include Journals and Memoirs, Biographies, books on Stage Conditions, on Theatres, Reference Books and others.

Publications list:
Available online and in print

Access to staff:
Contact by letter, by e-mail and via website
Hours: Not applicable

Also at:
Society for Theatre Research
PO Box 3214, Brighton, BN2 1LU

Institutional Friends member of:
Theatres Advisory Council (TAC)
Theatres Trust

SOCIETY FOR UNDERWATER TECHNOLOGY

Acronym or abbreviation: SUT

80 Coleman Street, London, EC2R 5BJ

Tel: 020 7382 2601
Fax: 020 7382 2684
E-mail: info@sut.org

Website:
http://www.sut.org.uk
General information about SUT.

Enquiries:
Enquiries to: Executive Secretary
Other contacts: Press and Publications Officer for media or publications enquiries.

Founded:
1966

Organisation type and purpose:
International organisation, learned society (membership is by subscription), present number of members: 1,600, registered charity (charity number 256659).
Multidisciplinary learned society bringing together individuals and organisations from industry, government and academia with a common interest in underwater technology, marine science and engineering.

Subject coverage:
Marine science and technology applied to: submersible robotic design and operation, diving technology and physiology, scientific diving, underwater acoustics, subsea engineering systems and operations, naval architecture and offshore structures, environmental forces, offshore site investigation, ocean resources, marine pollution and environment, marine biology and archaeology, oceanography, instrumentation, education and training.

Museum or gallery collection, archive, or library special collection:
SUT reference material lodged in the IMarE Marine Information centre

Printed publications:
Advances in Underwater Technology, Ocean Science and Offshore Engineering (conference proceedings series, 34 volumes)
Oceans of Opportunity (careers information pack)
Other collected papers and conference proceedings
SUT News (newsletter, 8 times a year)
Underwater Technology (journal, quarterly)

Electronic and video publications:
Oceans of Opportunities (careers video, £6 including p&p)

Access to staff:
Contact by letter, by fax, by e-mail and via website
Hours: Mon to Fri, 0900 to 1700

Other addresses:
Aberdeen Office
  Innovation Centre, Exploration Drive, Offshore Technology Park, Bridge of Don, Aberdeen, AB23 8GX; tel: 01224 823637; fax: 01224 820236
Southampton branch
  Southampton Oceanography Centre, Empress Dock, Southampton

Parent body for:
Underwater Science Group

SOCIETY OF ACADEMIC & RESEARCH SURGERY

Acronym or abbreviation: SARS

The Royal College of Surgeons of England, 35–43 Lincoln's Inn Fields, London, WC2A 3PE

Tel: 020 7869 6640
Fax: 020 7869 6644
E-mail: sking@rcseng.ac.uk

Website:
http://surgicalresearch.org.uk
SARS, membership, awards, events, publications.

Founded:
c. 1960

Organisation type and purpose:
Professional association for surgeons.
Fosters and enhances research in various disciplines of surgery under its auspices; provides a platform to aspiring surgical trainees to present their laboratory as well as clinical research.

Subject coverage:
Surgery; medical research.

Electronic and video publications:
Yearbook
The Place Of Research and Other Educational Experience in UK Surgical Training – Guidance for Surgical Trainees, April 2010
Surgery in the Undergraduate Curriculum
Order electronic and video publications from:
Download from website

Publications list:
Available online

Access to staff:
Contact by letter, by telephone, by fax and by e-mail

Links with:
other important surgical research forums in USA, Europe and South Africa

SOCIETY OF AFGHAN RESIDENTS IN THE UK

Acronym or abbreviation: SAR

West Acton Community Centre, Churchill Gardens, Acton, London, W3 0JN

Tel: 020 8993 2129
Fax: 020 8993 8168
E-mail: saruk@btconnect.com

Enquiries:
Enquiries to: Chairman
Direct tel: 07947 777705

Founded:
1982

Organisation type and purpose:
National organisation, advisory body, membership association (membership is by subscription, qualification, election or invitation), present number of members: 700, voluntary organisation, registered charity (charity number 800460), public library.
Refugee community organisation.

Subject coverage:
Housing, health, law, welfare benefits, immigration, education, employment.

Museum or gallery collection, archive, or library special collection:
Press cuttings relevant to Afghanistan

Printed publications:
Annual Report
Introductory leaflet
Magazine in Pashto/Dari languages (monthly, 60pp)

Access to staff:
Contact by letter, by telephone, by fax, by e-mail and in person
Hours: Mon to Fri, 0900 to 1600

Access to building, collection or gallery:
Hours: Mon to Fri, 0900 to 1600

Access for disabled people:
Hours: Mon to Fri, 0900 to 1600

Also at:
Offices in Birmingham, Harrow and Northampton

SOCIETY OF ANTIQUARIES OF LONDON

Burlington House, Piccadilly, London, W1J 0BE

Tel: 020 7734 0193
Fax: 020 7287 6967

E-mail: library@sal.org.uk

Website:
http://www.sal.org.uk
Brief details of organisation. Link to on-line catalogue of printed books acquired since 1988.

Enquiries:
Enquiries to: Librarian
Direct tel: 020 7479 7084

Founded:
1707

Organisation type and purpose:
Learned society.

Subject coverage:
Archaeology; architectural history; British topography; art history mostly of decorative arts; heraldry; history (mainly British).

Museum or gallery collection, archive, or library special collection:
Broadsides, proclamations, Civil War tracts
Incunabula
Jackson Collection (Wiltshire)
Manuscripts, photographs and portraits
Prattinton Collection (Worcestershire)
Prints and drawings (18th and 19th centuries)
Rubbings of all the pre-1700 monumental brasses in Britain
Willson Collection (Lincolnshire)

Library catalogue:
All or part available online

Printed publications:
Antiquaries Journal
Archaeologia
Occasional Papers
Reports of the Research Committee

Microform publications:
Medieval and Renaissance Manuscripts from the Society of Antiquaries of London (research publications)

Access to staff:
Contact by letter, by telephone, by fax and by e-mail. Appointment necessary.
Hours: Mon to Fri, 1000 to 1700
Special comments: Closed August.

SOCIETY OF ANTIQUARIES OF NEWCASTLE UPON TYNE

Great North Museum, Hancock, Barras Bridge, Newcastle upon Tyne, NE2 4PT

Tel: 0191 230 2700
E-mail: admin@newcastle-antiquaries.org.uk

Website:
http://www.newcastle-antiquaries.org.uk

Enquiries:
Enquiries to: Membership Secretary
Other contacts: Honorary Secretary

Founded:
1813

Organisation type and purpose:
Learned society (membership is by subscription), present number of members: 750, registered charity (charity number 230888).

Subject coverage:
History and archaeology of Durham, Northumberland and Newcastle upon Tyne.

Museum or gallery collection, archive, or library special collection:
Library of 30,000 volumes

Non-library collection catalogue:
All or part available in-house

Library catalogue:
All or part available in-house

Printed publications:
Archaeologia Aeliana (the Society's journal, annually)
Newsletter (twice a year)
Guidebooks

continued overleaf

Monograph series
Excavations at South Shields Roman Fort Vol 1
(Bidwell P and Speak S, 1994, £35)
Aspects of the Anglo-Norman Design of Durham
Cathedral (Curry I, 1986, £2.95)
The Northumberland Lay Subsidy Roll of 1296 (ed
Fraser CM, 1968, £6)
Newcastle Chamberlains' Accounts 1508–1511 (ed
Fraser C M, 1986 £5)
Bessie Surtees House: Two merchant houses in
Sandhill, Newcastle upon Tyne (Heslop D,
McCombie G and Thompson C, 1995, £2.95)
Chillingham Church – the South Chapel and the
Grey Tomb (Heslop D and Harbottle B, 1999, £3)
Alderman Fenwick's House (Heslop D, Jobling B
and McCombie G, 2001, £4)
Whisky Smuggling on the Border (Philipson J,
1991, £1.50)
The Two Towers of Hexham (Ryder P, 1995, £2.95)

Publications list:
Available online and in print

Access to staff:
Contact by letter, by telephone and by e-mail.
Appointment necessary.
Hours: Library: term-time, 1000 to 1600; vacation
hours, to be announced

Links with:
The Literary and Philosophical Society of
Newcastle upon Tyne
23 Westgate Road, Newcastle upon Tyne, NE1
1SE; tel: 0191 232 0192

SOCIETY OF ANTIQUARIES OF SCOTLAND

Royal Museum, Chambers Street, Edinburgh, EH1
1JF

Tel: 0131 247 4115
Fax: 0131 247 4163
E-mail: f.ashmore@nms.ac.uk

Website:
http://www.socantscot.org
Introduction to the Society, grant information,
publications and Fellow information.

Enquiries:
Enquiries to: Director
Other contacts: Publications Assistant for
monograph sales and publicity.

Founded:
1780

Organisation type and purpose:
Learned society (membership is by election or
invitation), present number of members: 3,500,
registered charity (charity number SC010240).

Subject coverage:
History and archaeology of Scotland.

**Museum or gallery collection, archive, or library
special collection:**
Archaeologia Scotica (irregularly from the Society's
foundation until 1851)

Library catalogue:
All or part available in-house

Printed publications:
Monograph series (irregularly from 1982 to date)
Proceedings of the Society of Antiquaries of
Scotland (annually from 1855 to date)
Order printed publications from: Publications
Administrator, Society of Antiquaries of Scotland
at the same address, tel: 0131 247 4145, e-mail: r
.lancaster@nms.ac.uk

Publications list:
Available online and in print

Access to staff:
Contact by letter and by telephone. Appointment
necessary.
Hours: Mon to Fri, 0900 to 1700
Special comments: Staff work part time – office may
be unsupervised at certain times.

SOCIETY OF ARCHER-ANTIQUARIES

Acronym or abbreviation: SAA

29 Batley Court, Oldland, South Gloucestershire,
BS30 8YZ

Tel: 0117 932 3276
Fax: 0117 932 3276
E-mail: bogaman@btinternet.com

Website:
http://www.societyofarcher-antiquaries.org
Aspects of traditional archery, worldwide.

Enquiries:
Enquiries to: Honorary Secretary

Founded:
1956

Organisation type and purpose:
International organisation, learned society
(membership is by subscription), present number
of members: 250, registered charity, consultancy,
research organisation.

Subject coverage:
General and specialised information on the history
of archery, Asiatic archery, English archery,
crossbows, Middle Eastern archery, ethnographical
archery, literature and constructional information,
bowery, fletchery, legends and practices.

Information services:
Information provided to members upon
application

**Museum or gallery collection, archive, or library
special collection:**
Library and display room

Non-library collection catalogue:
All or part available in-house

Library catalogue:
All or part available in-house

Printed publications:
A Guide to the Crossbow
Journal of the Society of Archer-Antiquaries
Periodic Newsletters
Arrowhead (newsletter booklet)

Access to staff:
Contact by letter, by telephone, by e-mail and via
website. Appointment necessary. Access for
members only.
Hours: Mon to Fri, 1800 to 2000; Sat, Sun, 1000 to
1800

Access to building, collection or gallery:
Prior appointment required. Members only or
visitor with Member
Hours: Two Suns a year

Access for disabled people:
Special comments: Limited disabled access.

Associated with:
Royal Toxophilite Society
Simon Foundation at Manchester University

SOCIETY OF AUTHORS

Acronym or abbreviation: SOA

84 Drayton Gardens, London, SW10 9SB

Tel: 020 7373 6642
Fax: 020 7373 5768
E-mail: info@societyofauthors.org

Website:
http://www.societyofauthors.org
Information about membership benefits,
information for interest groups within the Society.

Enquiries:
Enquiries to: General Secretary

Founded:
1884

Organisation type and purpose:
Trade union.

Subject coverage:
Specialist groups within the Society serve the
needs of broadcasters, literary translators,
educational writers, medical writers, children's
writers, information also on literary agents,
publishers, royalties, contracts, authors' rights,
public lending right.

Printed publications:
Quick Guides (on topics such as copyright and
libel)
The Author (quarterly, £35 a year; free to members)

Publications list:
Available online and in print

Access to staff:
Contact by e-mail and via website. Appointment
necessary. Access for members only. Letter of
introduction required.
Hours: Mon to Thu, 0930 to 1730; Fri, 0930 to 1700

Member of:
British Copyright Council
European Writers Congress
International Confederation of Societies of Authors
and Composers
National Book Committee

SOCIETY OF BIOLOGY

9 Red Lion Court, London, EC4A 3EF

Tel: 020 7936 5900
Fax: 020 7936 5901
E-mail: info@societyofbiology.org

Website:
http://www.societyofbiology.org

Founded:
2009

Created by the merger of:
Institute of Biology and Biosciences Federation
(year of change 2009)

Organisation type and purpose:
Professional body

Subject coverage:
A single unified voice for biology: advising
Government and influencing policy; advancing
education and professional development;
supporting members, and engaging and
encouraging public interest in the life sciences.

Printed publications:
Biologist (quarterly)
Journal of Biological Education (quarterly)

Publications list:
Available online and in print

Access to staff:
Contact by letter, by telephone, by fax, by e-mail
and via website
Hours: Mon to Fri, 0900 to 1700

SOCIETY OF BOOKBINDERS

Acronym or abbreviation: SOB

6 Hillside Road, West Kirby, Wirral, CH48 8BB

Tel: 0151 625 2413
E-mail: nat.secretary@societyofbookbinders.com

Website:
http://www.societyofbookbinders.com
All information appertaining to the Society of
Bookbinders re: national and regional organisation
and events, education and training information,
exhibitions of members' work.

Enquiries:
Enquiries to: Honorary Secretary
Other contacts: Membership Secretary (for
membership enquiries)

Founded:
1974

Organisation type and purpose:
Professional body, trade association, membership association (membership is by subscription), present number of members: 650, registered charity (charity number 1032108), training organisation.

Subject coverage:
All information appertaining to bookbinding.

Printed publications:
Bookbinder (journal, annually)
Educational Leaflets
National Newsletters
Order printed publications from: Society of Bookbinders, Little Broxham, Four Elms Road, Four Elms, Kent, TN8 6LR; e-mail: publications@societyofbookbinders.com

Publications list:
Available online

Access to staff:
Contact by letter, by telephone, by e-mail and via website
Hours: Mon to Fri, 1000 to 1600

Access to building, collection or gallery:
No access other than to staff

Membership Secretary:
Society of Bookbinders
102 Hetherington Road, Shepperton, Middlesex, TW17 0SW; tel: 01746 763896; e-mail: membership@societyofbookbinders.com

SOCIETY OF BORDER LEICESTER SHEEP BREEDERS

Greenend, St Boswells, Melrose, Roxburghshire, TD6 9ES

Tel: 01835 824207
Fax: 01835 824207
E-mail: info@borderleicesters.co.uk

Website:
http://www.borderleicesters.co.uk
Facts and history of Border Leicester Sheep.

Enquiries:
Enquiries to: Membership Secretary

Founded:
1900

Organisation type and purpose:
Membership association (membership is by subscription), present number of members: 250, registered charity (charity number SCO 00011). Pedigree sheep breeding.

Subject coverage:
Border Leicester Sheep Society, pedigree information and records.

Printed publications:
For members only

Publications list:
Available in print

Access to staff:
Contact by letter, by telephone, by fax and in person
Hours: Mon to Fri, 0800 to 2100

Access to building, collection or gallery:
No access other than to staff

SOCIETY OF BOTANICAL ARTISTS

Acronym or abbreviation: SBA

1 Knapp Cottages, Wyke, Gillingham, Dorset, SP8 4NQ

Tel: 01747 825718
Fax: 01747 826835

Website:
http://www.society-botanical-artists.org

Enquiries:
Enquiries to: Executive Secretary
Direct tel: 01747 852718
Direct e-mail: pam@soc-botanical-artists.org

Founded:
1985

Organisation type and purpose:
International organisation, professional body (membership is by election or invitation), present number of members: 190, registered charity (charity number 1047162).
Publicising and educating the public about botanical painting.

Subject coverage:
Botanical painting.

Printed publications:
Annual exhibition catalogue
The Art of Botanical Painting
The Botanical Palette

Access to staff:
Contact by letter, by telephone, by fax and by e-mail. Appointment necessary.
Hours: Mon to Fri, 0900 to 1700

Access for disabled people:
Ramped entry, access to all public areas, toilet facilities

SOCIETY OF BRITISH GAS INDUSTRIES

Acronym or abbreviation: SBGI

36 Holly Walk, Leamington Spa, Warwickshire, CV32 4LY

Tel: 01926 334357
Fax: 01926 450459
E-mail: mail@sbgi.org.uk

Website:
http://www.gasjobs.org.uk
An online job search facility for the gas industry.
http://www.sbgi.org.uk
Comprehensive list of products and services supplied by members. Information on forthcoming events in the United Kingdom and overseas. Useful contact details and relevant industry news.

Enquiries:
Enquiries to: Director
Direct e-mail: claire@sbgi.org.uk

Founded:
1905

Organisation type and purpose:
Trade association (membership is by subscription), present number of members: 170 companies.

Subject coverage:
Gas industry, products and services providers, manufacturers and contractors, gas suppliers/shippers and transporters.

Printed publications:
Directory of Products and Services (annual, free)
Gas Business (journal, quarterly, free)
Review of Activities (annual, free)

Access to staff:
Contact by letter, by telephone, by fax, by e-mail and via website
Hours: Mon to Fri, 0900 to 1700

SOCIETY OF BRITISH WATER & WASTEWATER INDUSTRIES

Acronym or abbreviation: SBWWI

38 Holly Walk, Leamington Spa, Warwickshire, CV32 4HY

Tel: 01926 831530
Fax: 01926 831931
E-mail: hq@sbwwi.co.uk

Website:
http://www.sbwwi.co.uk

Enquiries:
Enquiries to: Executive Director

Founded:
1986

Organisation type and purpose:
Trade association (membership is by subscription, election or invitation), present number of members: 100 companies.
A forum for UK manufacturers and contractors who supply the water industry.
Water industry specific, disseminates information, liaises with water companies and other bodies to help members serve the industry better.

Subject coverage:
Product standards and approval, regulations, training, product suppliers, contractor services providers.

Museum or gallery collection, archive, or library special collection:
OFWAT Reports
Water industry standards

Access to staff:
Contact by letter, by telephone, by fax, by e-mail and via website
Hours: Mon to Fri, 0900 to 1700

SOCIETY OF CABLE TELECOMMUNICATION ENGINEERS

Acronym or abbreviation: SCTE

Fulton House Business Centre, Fulton Road, Wembley Park, Middlesex, HA9 0TF

Tel: 020 8902 8998
Fax: 020 8903 8719
E-mail: office@scte.org.uk

Website:
http://www.scte.org.uk

Enquiries:
Enquiries to: Secretary
Direct e-mail: sara.waddington@scte.org.uk

Founded:
1945

Organisation type and purpose:
Learned society.

Subject coverage:
Cable telecommunications.

Printed publications:
Cable Telecommunication Engineering
Broadband
Members Handbook

Access to staff:
Appointment necessary.
Hours: Mon to Fri, 0900 to 1700

SOCIETY OF COLLEGE, NATIONAL AND UNIVERSITY LIBRARIES

Acronym or abbreviation: SCONUL

102 Euston Street, London, NW1 2HA

Tel: 020 7387 0317
Fax: 020 7383 3197
E-mail: info@sconul.ac.uk

Website:
http://www.sconul.ac.uk

Enquiries:
Enquiries to: Secretary

Founded:
1950

Organisation type and purpose:
International organisation, professional body.

Subject coverage:
British academic libraries; advisory committees on: buildings, copyright, health services, information systems and services, performance indicators, publications, scholarly communication, staffing.

Trade and statistical information:
Data on funding and activities of university libraries.

continued overleaf

Printed publications:
Annual Library Statistics
Performance indicators for university libraries: a
practical guide
The management of integrated Learning Resources
SCONUL Annual Review
Working papers on a range of topics including:
Architects' briefs
Development plans
Management issues: finance, general concerns, in-
house research, staff
Staff development and appraisal, training

Publications list:
Available online and in print

Access to staff:
Contact by letter, by telephone, by fax, by e-mail
and via website. Appointment necessary.
Hours: Mon to Fri, 0900 to 1700

SOCIETY OF CONSTRUCTION LAW

The Cottage, Bullfurlong Lane, Burbage, Hinckley,
LE10 2HQ

Tel: 01455 233253
Fax: 01455 233253
E-mail: via website

Website:
http://www.scl.org.uk
Membership, events, papers, resources, news.

Founded:
1983

Organisation type and purpose:
A membership association, (membership is by
subscription), present number of members: 2,149.
Members come from all sectors of the construction
industry, for example, architects, engineers,
surveyors, contractors, developers, solicitors,
barristers, arbitrators and experts.
Holds meetings, lectures and social events;
publishes papers given to the Society; supports
educational bodies, in particular by funding the
purchase of books; sponsors an annual prize paper;
generally promotes interest in construction law.

Subject coverage:
Construction law.

**Museum or gallery collection, archive, or library
special collection:**
Construction Law library that used to be housed at
the Old Watch House at King's College, London
has now been merged with the Maughan library
in Chancery Lane; any SCL member who wishes
to use the Maughan library should complete the
online application form

Printed publications:
Papers (free to members)

Electronic and video publications:
Papers (free to members)
Newsletter (monthly)
Order electronic and video publications from:
Download from website

Publications list:
Available online

Access to staff:
Contact by letter, by telephone, by fax and via
website

SOCIETY OF CONSULTING MARINE ENGINEERS AND SHIP SURVEYORS

Acronym or abbreviation: SCMS

202 Lambeth Road, London, SE1 7JW

Tel: 020 7261 0869
Fax: 020 7261 0871
E-mail: sec@scmshq.org

Website:
http://www.scmshq.org

Enquiries:
Enquiries to: Secretary

Founded:
1920

Organisation type and purpose:
Learned society.
An MCA appointed certifying authority.

Subject coverage:
The interests of consulting engineers, naval
architects and ship surveyors; shipbuilding,
maritime authorities' activities.

Printed publications:
List of Members (annually)

Access to staff:
Contact by letter, by telephone, by fax and by e-
mail
Hours: Mon to Fri, 0900 to 1700

Access to building, collection or gallery:
Prior appointment required

SOCIETY OF COSMETIC SCIENTISTS

Acronym or abbreviation: SCS

GT House, 24–26 Rothesay Road, Luton,
Bedfordshire, LU1 1QX

Tel: 01582 726661
Fax: 01582 405217
E-mail: ifscc.scs@btconnect.com

Website:
http://www.scs.org.uk

Enquiries:
Enquiries to: Secretary-General

Founded:
1948

Organisation type and purpose:
Learned society.

Subject coverage:
Cosmetic science.

Printed publications:
International Journal of Cosmetic Science (6 times a
year)

Access to staff:
Contact by letter, by telephone, by fax and by e-
mail
Hours: Mon to Fri, 0900 to 1700

**Affiliated to, and providing the secretariat for,
the:**
International Federation of Societies of Cosmetic
Chemists
tel: 01582 726661; fax: 01582 405217; e-mail: ifscc
.scs@btconnect.com

SOCIETY OF DAIRY TECHNOLOGY

Acronym or abbreviation: SDT

PO Box 12, Appleby in Westmorland, CA16 6HH

Tel: 01768 354034
Fax: 01768 352546
E-mail: execdirector@sdt.org

Website:
http://www.sdt.org

Enquiries:
Enquiries to: Executive Director

Founded:
1943

Organisation type and purpose:
Learned society (membership is by election or
invitation), present number of members: 400,
registered charity (charity number 1081615).
Education, training and information transfer in
dairy sciences and technology.

Subject coverage:
Dairy science, dairy technology and dairy research,
including husbandry, engineering and education.

Printed publications:
International Journal of Dairy Technology
(quarterly)
Technical publications
Order printed publications from: Wiley Blackwell

Publications list:
Available online and in print

Access to staff:
Contact by letter, by telephone, by fax, by e-mail
and via website
Hours: Mon to Fri, 0900 to 1700

Access to building, collection or gallery:
No access other than to staff

SOCIETY OF DESIGNER CRAFTSMEN

Acronym or abbreviation: SDC

24 Rivington Street, London, EC2A 3DU

Tel: 020 7739 3663
Fax: 020 7739 3663
E-mail: info@societyofdesignercraftsmen.org.uk

Website:
http://www.societyofdesignercraftsmen.org.uk

Enquiries:
Enquiries to: Hon. Secretary
Other contacts: Chairman

Founded:
1888

Organisation type and purpose:
National organisation, advisory body, membership
association (membership is by election or
invitation), present number of members: 750,
registered charity (charity number 328202),
training organisation, consultancy. Founded by
William Morris and Walter Crane.

Subject coverage:
Information on contemporary practitioners in the
following crafts: basketry, calligraphy, ceramics,
furniture-making, glass-engraving, jewellery,
lettering, metalwork, printmaking, sculpture,
silversmithing, stained glass making, textiles,
toymaking, woodworking.

**Museum or gallery collection, archive, or library
special collection:**
Archives of the Arts and Crafts Exhibition Society
and the Society of Designer Craftsmen, housed at
the Victoria and Albert Museum

Printed publications:
Exhibition Catalogues
Newsletters (5 times a year, for members)

Electronic and video publications:
e-bulletin for Members of the Society

Access to staff:
Contact by letter, by telephone and by e-mail.
Appointment necessary. Access for members only.
Hours: Mon, Wed, Fri, 1400 to 1700

Access to building, collection or gallery:
Prior appointment required

Access for disabled people:
Level entry

SOCIETY OF DYERS AND COLOURISTS

Acronym or abbreviation: SDC

Perkin House, 82 Grattan Road, Bradford, West
Yorkshire, BD1 2LU

Tel: 01274 725138
Fax: 01274 392888
E-mail: info@sdc.org.uk

Website:
http://www.sdc.org.uk

SDC, publications, colour guides, technical information, full list of staff contacts, training, education, news, events, regions.

Founded:
1884

Grant of Royal Charter:
(year of change 1963)

Organisation type and purpose:
A registered charity, a trade association for the dyeing and colouring industry representing members' interests at national and international level, the only international professional society specialising in colour in all its manifestations. To advance the science of colour by disseminating information through the coloration industry and beyond. Has over 2,000 members in almost 50 countries world-wide, from textile artists to designers and colour technologists to educators. Performs standardisation work in relation to colour fastness and colour measurement of textiles.

Subject coverage:
The science of colour.

Special visitor services:
Events and special interest groups for members.

Education services:
Light and Colour Experience for schools, a science-based workshop, allows the delivery of the whole of the Key Stage 2 unit on Light in one entertaining session (tel: 01274 725138; e-mail colour-experience@sdc.org.uk); access to qualifications, training and continuing professional development for members.

Museum or gallery collection, archive, or library special collection:
Online archive of over 2,500 technical articles from SDC's extensive library on colour and coloration

Printed publications:
The Colourist (members' quarterly magazine)
Textile Dyer (members' supplement)
Coloration Technology (flagship journal with peer-reviewed research and review papers, members' discounted price £74)
Large selection of SDC books (available via website)

Electronic and video publications:
e-newsletter (monthly)
Online archive
Large selection of SDC books
Order electronic and video publications from: Website

Publications list:
Available online

Access to staff:
Contact by letter, by telephone, by fax, by e-mail and via website

Has reciprocal affiliate status with:
Hong Kong (SDC) Ltd
SADFA (South Africa)
SDCANZ (Australia and New Zealand)

Regional officers across the UK and in China, India, Pakistan, Bangladesh and Sri Lanka:

SOCIETY OF EDITORS

University Centre, Granta Place, Mill Lane, Cambridge, CB2 1RU

Tel: 01223 304080
Fax: 01223 304090
E-mail: info@societyofeditors.org

Website:
http://www.societyofeditors.org

Enquiries:
Enquiries to: Executive Director
Other contacts: Administrator for administrative matters

Founded:
1946

Organisation type and purpose:
Professional body, over 400 members.

The Society has members in local, regional and national newspapers, magazines, broadcasting, new media, journalism education and media law. The Society provides collective consultation and representation.

Subject coverage:
Collective consultation and representation on all matters of editorial concern including editorial freedom, independence, standards and training, legislation concerning the media. Provision of contacts for media consultancy.

Access to staff:
Contact by letter, by telephone, by fax, by e-mail and via website
Hours: Office hours and 24-hour contact

Access to building, collection or gallery:
No access other than to staff

SOCIETY OF ENGINEERS (INCORPORATED)

Acronym or abbreviation: SOE

Guinea Wiggs, Nayland, Colchester, Essex, CO6 4NF

Tel: 01206 263332
Fax: 01206 262624
E-mail: postmaster@theiet.org

Website:
http://www.society-of-engineers.org.uk
Details of membership, awards, exams, etc.

Enquiries:
Enquiries to: Chief Executive

Founded:
1854

Organisation type and purpose:
International organisation, professional body (membership is by qualification and experience). To promote the interests of multi-disciplinary engineers worldwide and to provide a forum for discussion; to examine engineers in art and science to ensure that they can apply their theoretical knowledge to practical situations.

Subject coverage:
All branches of civil, electrical and mechanical engineering.

Printed publications:
Engineering World (journal, quarterly)
Membership and exam information
Publications list available

Access to staff:
Contact by letter, by telephone, by fax and by e-mail
Hours: Mon to Thurs, 0900 to 1730

SOCIETY OF ENVIRONMENTAL ENGINEERS

Acronym or abbreviation: SEE

The Manor House, High Street, Buntingford, Hertfordshire, SG9 9AB

Tel: 01763 271209
Fax: 01763 273255
E-mail: office@environmental.org.uk

Website:
http://www.environmental.org.uk

Enquiries:
Enquiries to: Chief Executive

Founded:
1959

Organisation type and purpose:
Learned society.
Licensed Member of the Engineering Council (UK) and the Society for the Environment.

Subject coverage:
Climatic contamination control, packaging, vibration shock and noise product assurance and reliability, electromagnetic compatibility.

Printed publications:
Environmental Engineering (quarterly)
Proceedings of Symposia
Test House Directory

Access to staff:
Contact by e-mail
Hours: Mon to Fri, 0900 to 1700

Access to building, collection or gallery:
No access other than to staff

Access for disabled people:
Ramped entry, toilet facilities

SOCIETY OF EVENT ORGANISERS

Acronym or abbreviation: SEO

29A Market Square, Biggleswade, Bedfordshire, SG18 8AQ

Tel: 01767 316255
Fax: 01767 316255
E-mail: peter.cotterell@eou.org.uk

Website:
http://www.seoevent.co.uk

Enquiries:
Enquiries to: Manager

Founded:
1996

Organisation type and purpose:
Trade association.

Subject coverage:
The running of events.

Printed publications:
Newsletters (email, free)

SOCIETY OF FLORISTRY LIMITED

Acronym or abbreviation: SOF

Meadowside, Hall Road, West Bergholt, Colchester, Essex, CO6 3DU

Tel: 0870 241 0432
Fax: 0870 241 0432
E-mail: info@britishfloristassociation.org

Enquiries:
Enquiries to: Secretary
Direct e-mail: secretariat@britishfloristassociation.org

Founded:
1951

Organisation type and purpose:
Professional body (membership is by subscription, qualification), present number of members: 1,164. A non-profit making organisation, founded with the sole purpose of raising the standards of floristry worldwide.

Subject coverage:
Professional floristry, careers information.

Printed publications:
Please enquire for publication details

Publications list:
Available in print

Access to staff:
Contact by letter, by telephone and by fax
Hours: Mon to Fri, 0900 to 1300

SOCIETY OF FOOD HYGIENE TECHNOLOGY, THE

Acronym or abbreviation: SOFHT

The Granary, Middleton House Farm, Tamworth Road, Middleton, Staffs, B78 2BD

Tel: 01827 872500
Fax: 01827 875800
E-mail: admin@sofht.co.uk

Website:
http://www.sofht.co.uk

continued overleaf

Full details of the Society, its activities, publications and membership.

Enquiries:
Enquiries to: Administrator
Direct e-mail: claudetteschlitter@sofht.co.uk

Founded:
1979

Organisation type and purpose:
Learned society (membership is by subscription), present number of members: 750.
Dedicated to improving food hygiene and safety within the food industry.

Subject coverage:
Food hygiene, hygiene technology, hygiene training, food technology, food science, food safety.

Printed publications:
Hygiene in Focus Technical Manual (free to members, £52.50 non members)
Magazine (3 times a year)

Publications list:
Available online and in print

Access to staff:
Contact by letter, by telephone, by fax, by e-mail and via website
Hours: Mon to Fri, 0900 to 1700

Access to building, collection or gallery:
No access other than to staff

SOCIETY OF GARDEN DESIGNERS

Acronym or abbreviation: SGD

Katepwa House, Ashfield Park Avenue, Ross-on-Wye, Herefordshire, HR9 5AX

Tel: 01989 566695
Fax: 01989 567676
E-mail: info@sgd.org.uk

Website:
http://www.sgd.org.uk

Enquiries:
Enquiries to: Administrator

Founded:
1981

Organisation type and purpose:
Professional body.
Promotion of professional standards in garden design.

Subject coverage:
Garden design, accreditation of garden designers, information about journal, visits, events organised by society (some open to public).

Printed publications:
Garden Design Journal (10 a year, £6 per copy)
Register of Designers and their Profiles (free)

Publications list:
Available online

Access to staff:
Contact by letter, by telephone, by fax, by e-mail and via website

Access to building, collection or gallery:
Prior appointment required
Hours: Mon to Fri, 0900 to 1700 (closed bank holidays)

Links with:
Royal Horticultural Society

SOCIETY OF GENEALOGISTS

Acronym or abbreviation: SoG

14 Charterhouse Buildings, Goswell Road, London, EC1M 7BA

Tel: 020 7251 8799
Fax: 020 7250 1800
E-mail: info@sog.org.uk

Website:
http://www.sog.org.uk
http://www.britishorigins.net
Indexes and genealogical data.
http://www.findmypast.com/home.jsp
Indexes and genealogical data.

Enquiries:
Enquiries to: Librarian
Direct tel: 020 7702 5485
Direct e-mail: library@sog.org.uk
Other contacts: Genealogist Officer

Founded:
1911

Organisation type and purpose:
Learned society, present number of members: c.13,000, registered charity (charity number 233701), training organisation, publishing house. Educational Charity.
To promote and encourage the study of genealogy and heraldry.

Subject coverage:
Genealogy, biography, family history, heraldry, history and topography world-wide, but with emphasis on Great Britain, Ireland, former British Colonies, America and Europe.

Education services:
Advice sessions in person or by telephone; lectures, courses and visits; publications.

Services for disabled people:
Portable hearing loop.

Museum or gallery collection, archive, or library special collection:
Australasian Civil Registration indexes to c.1900
Bank of England Wills 1717–1845
Bernau index to pre-1800 Chancery records, etc. (microfilm)
Boyd's Inhabitants of London 16th–18th centuries primarily
Boyd's London Burials (adult males, 1538–1853)
Boyd's Marriage Index (c.12% of pre-1837 English marriages)
Civil Service Irreplaceable Evidences of Age c.1855–c.1939
Estate Duty will indexes 1796–1857 (microfilm)
Family Histories c.15,000
General Register Office, Birth, Marriage and Death Indexes (England and Wales 1837–1925, Scotland 1855–1920) (microfiche and microfilm)
Great Western Railway Probate (Stock Transfer) Registers 1835–1932
Indexes to Scottish Baptisms and Marriages 1558–1854 (microfiche)
International Genealogical Index (c.400m. world-wide entries, CD-ROM and online)
Monumental inscriptions (c.7,000)
Pallot Marriage Index 1780–1837 (online)
Parish Register transcripts (c.10,000)
Teachers' Registration Council Registers 1902–48
Times births, marriages and deaths announcements 1816–1920 and indexes 1785–1920 (microfilm)
Palmer's index to The Times 1790–1905 (CD-ROM)
Trinity House Petitions 1780–1890 (microfilm)
Vital Records Indexes for British Isles, Western Europe, Scandinavia, North America, Middle America covering millions of baptisms and marriages between 1538 and 1905 (CD-ROM)
Principal Probate Registry will indexes 1858–1930 (microfilm)
Vicar General Marriage Allegations 1660–1851 (microfilm)
Faculty Office Marriage Allegations 1715–1851 (microfilm)
Marriage licence and will indexes
1841–1901 census indexes for England, Wales and Scotland and some overseas

Non-library collection catalogue:
All or part available online, in-house and in print

Library catalogue:
All or part available online and in-house

Printed publications:
Full Publications List available from the Society (some 50 titles listed)

Genealogists' Magazine (quarterly)
Order printed publications from: Bookshop Manager, Society of Genealogists Enterprises; tel. 020 7702 5480; e-mail sales@sog.org.uk

Microform publications:
Many on microfiche

Publications list:
Available online and in print

Access to staff:
Contact by letter, by telephone, by fax, by e-mail, in person and via website. Non-members charged.
Hours: Tue, Wed, Sat, 1000 to 1800; Thu, 1000 to 2000
Special comments: Individual staff work a shift system and may not be available during all opening hours.

Access to building, collection or gallery:
Hours: Tue, Wed, Sat, 1000 to 1800; Thu, 1000 to 2000
Special comments: No pens, bags, coats, mobile phones or pagers allowed in the library.

Access for disabled people:
Level entry, access to all public areas, toilet facilities
Special comments: Lift will not take larger wheelchairs.

Member organisation of:
British Genealogical Record Users Committee

SOCIETY OF GLASS TECHNOLOGY

Acronym or abbreviation: SGT

Unit 9, Twelve O'clock Court, 21 Attercliffe Road, Sheffield, S4 7WW

Tel: 0114 263 4455
Fax: 0114 263 4411
E-mail: david@glass.demon.co.uk

Website:
http://www.sgt.org
Links, information services, consultants, journal contents pages.

Enquiries:
Enquiries to: Librarian
Direct tel: 0114 222 7307
Direct e-mail: lisa@glass.demon.co.uk
Other contacts: Managing Editor (for information)

Founded:
1916

Organisation type and purpose:
International organisation, learned society, membership association (membership is by subscription), present number of members: 900, registered charity (charity number 237438), publishing house.
Education charity promoting the use of glass of any and every kind by holding conferences, promoting exchange, publishing books and journals.
Supports student exchanges around the world.

Subject coverage:
Glass science and manufacture, history, art, design and use of glass.

Non-library collection catalogue:
All or part available online

Library catalogue:
All or part available online

Printed publications:
Glass Technology (6 a year)
Physics and Chemistry of Glasses (journal, 6 a year)
Coloured Glasses (W. A. Weyl)
Conference Proceedings
Glass Furnaces; design, construction and operations (translation from German by W. Trier)
Stones and Cord in Glass (C. Clark-Monks and J. M. Parker)
Basic Optical Stress Measurement in Glasses (R. J. Hand and H. W. McKenzie)

Raw Materials for Glass Melting (B.
  Simmingsköld)
The Art of Glass (A. Neri)
Bosc D'Antic on Glass-Making (M. Cable)
Early Nineteenth Century Glass Technology in
  Austria and Germany (M. Cable)
Apsley Pellatt on Glass Making (M. Cable)
Bontemps on Glass Making (M. Cable)
Old English Glass Houses (F. Buckley)
The Window Glass Makers of Saint Helens (R.
  Parkin)
Glass Blowing (C. Bray)
Ceramics and Glass: A Basic Technology (C. Bray)
Practising Stained Glass Safely (M. Stanton Harris)
Glass to Metal Seals (I. Donald)
Refractories in the Glass Industry
Fundamentals of Inorganic Glasses (A. Varshneya)

Electronic and video publications:
ICG 2001 International Congress on Glass –
  collection of invited papers and extended
  abstracts from the meeting (CD-ROM)
Looking Through Glass (DVD)

Publications list:
Available online and in print

Access to staff:
Contact by letter, by telephone, by fax, by e-mail
and via website. Appointment necessary. Access
for members only. Letter of introduction required.
Hours: Mon, 0900 to 1700

Links with:
University of Sheffield
  St George's Library, Mappin Street, Sheffield

Member organisation of:
International Commission on Glass
  website: http://www.icglass.org

SOCIETY OF HOMEOPATHS

11 Brookfield, Duncan Close, Moulton Park,
Northampton, NN3 6WL

Tel: 0845 450 6611
Fax: 0845 450 6622
E-mail: info@homeopathy-soh.org

Website:
http://www.homeopathy-soh.org

Founded:
1978

Organisation type and purpose:
Professional body.

Subject coverage:
Homeopathy.

Printed publications:
Information leaflets
Newsletter (quarterly)
The Homeopath (quarterly)

Publications list:
Available online

Access to staff:
Contact by letter, by telephone, by fax, by e-mail
and via website
Hours: Mon to Fri, 0800 to 1630

Member organisation of:
European Council for Classical Homoeopathy
(ECCH)
International Council for Classical Homoeopathy
(ICCH)

SOCIETY OF INDEXERS

Acronym or abbreviation: SI

Woodbourn Business Centre, 10 Jessell Street,
Sheffield, S9 3HY

Tel: 0114 2449561
E-mail: admin@indexers.org.uk

Website:
http://www.indexers.org.uk

Enquiries:
Enquiries to: Administrator

Founded:
1957

Organisation type and purpose:
Professional body (membership is by subscription).

Subject coverage:
Guidance and support on professional and
technical indexing matters for members, publishers
and authors; indexing of books, periodicals and
other publications; information storage and
retrieval, manual, computer-assisted or fully
automated; the foregoing techniques in virtually all
fields of academic subject specialisation;
improvement of standards; training course for
indexing.

Printed publications:
Occasional papers in indexing
Newsletter (quarterly)
The Indexer (quarterly)
Training in Indexing: Units A–D

Publications list:
Available online and in print

Access to staff:
Contact by letter, by telephone, by e-mail and via
website
Hours: Mon to Fri, 0930 to 1600

Affiliated bodies:
American Society of Indexers
Association of Southern African Bibliographers
and Indexers
Australian & New Zealand Society of Indexers
China Society of Indexers
Indexing & Abstracting Society of Canada

SOCIETY OF JEWELLERY HISTORIANS

Acronym or abbreviation: SJH

Scientific Research, The British Museum, London,
WC1B 3DG

Fax: 01588 620558
E-mail: jewelleryhistorians@yahoo.co.uk

Website:
http://www.societyofjewelleryhistorians.ac.uk

Enquiries:
Enquiries to: Membership Secretary
Direct e-mail: info@societyofjewelleryhistorians.ac
.uk

Founded:
1977

Organisation type and purpose:
Learned society (membership is by subscription),
present number of members: 500, registered
charity (charity number 282160), suitable for ages:
all.

Subject coverage:
History and development of the craft and
craftspeople connected with the manufacture,
design and processes concerning jewellery.

Printed publications:
Jewellery History Today (magazine, free to
  members, available for purchase)
Jewellery Studies (journal, free to members,
  available for purchase)

Publications list:
Available online and in print

Access to staff:
Contact by letter, by fax, by e-mail and via
website

SOCIETY OF LEATHER TECHNOLOGISTS AND CHEMISTS LIMITED

Acronym or abbreviation: SLTC

49 North Park Street, Dewsbury, West Yorkshire,
WF13 4LZ

Tel: 01924460864

Fax: 01924 460864

Website:
http://www.iultcs.org

Enquiries:
Enquiries to: Membership Secretary
Direct e-mail: office@sltc.org

Founded:
1897

Organisation type and purpose:
Learned society.

Subject coverage:
Leather manufacture, science, technology and
testing.

Printed publications:
Journal (6 times a year)
Leather Technologists Pocket Book
Official Methods Analysis
Society handbook

Access to staff:
Contact by e-mail

Founder member of:
International Union of Leather Technologists &
Chemists Societies (IULTCS)

SOCIETY OF LEY HUNTERS

Acronym or abbreviation: SOL

7 Mildmay Road, Romford, Havering, Essex, RM7
7DA

Tel: 01708 732362
E-mail: leyhunter@googlemail.com

Website:
http://www.leyhunter.com
Information on ley lines and research references.

Enquiries:
Enquiries to: Secretary
Direct tel: 01425 273517 (Chairman)
Other contacts: Chairman (for media)

Founded:
2000

Organisation type and purpose:
International organisation, membership
association (membership is by subscription),
voluntary organisation, research organisation.

Subject coverage:
Ley lines, Neolithic archaeology, alignments,
landscape, folklore, pre-Christian religious sites,
pre-literacy farming calendars and energy line
nodes.

**Museum or gallery collection, archive, or library
special collection:**
Archive of researched alignments

Printed publications:
Society of Keyhunters Newsletter
Order printed publications from: Mr G. Frawley, 17
Victoria Street, Cheltenham, Gloucestershire, GL50
4HU

Access to staff:
Contact by letter and by telephone
Hours: Mon to Fri, 0900 to 1700
Special comments: Letter preferred, voluntary staff
availability varies.

Access to building, collection or gallery:
No access other than to staff

Member of:
Stone Circle Webring

SOCIETY OF LICENSED CONVEYANCERS, THE

Chancery House, 110 High Street, Croydon,
Surrey, CR9 1PF

Tel: 020 8681 1001
Fax: 020 8681 6001

Enquiries:
Enquiries to: Chief Executive

continued overleaf

Founded:
1988

Organisation type and purpose:
Professional body (membership is by
qualification), present number of members: 350,
service industry.

Subject coverage:
Licensed conveyancing, residential conveyancing
and related matters.

Trade and statistical information:
Licensed conveyancers' fees and market share in
England and Wales.

Printed publications:
The Licensed Conveyancer (journal, 4 times a year,
£20)

Access to staff:
Contact by letter, by telephone and by fax
Hours: Mon to Fri, 1000 to 1800

Access to building, collection or gallery:
No access other than to staff

Subsidiary:
SLC Lawyer's Services (Provision of seminars,
stationery, books etc to non-members)
   At the same address; tel: 020 8603 5560; fax: 020
   8681 6001; e-mail: slccroydon@netscapeonline.co
   .uk

SOCIETY OF LOCAL COUNCIL CLERKS

No.8 The Crescent, Taunton, Somerset, TA1 4EA

Tel: 01823 253646
Fax: 01823 253681
E-mail: admin@slcc.co.uk

Website:
http://www.slcc.co.uk/

Enquiries:
Enquiries to: External Affairs Officer
Direct tel: 01603 871153
Direct fax: 01603 871153
Direct e-mail: alanfairchild@cawston-pc.gov.uk

Organisation type and purpose:
Local government body.

Access to staff:
Contact by letter, by telephone, by fax and by e-
mail
Hours: Mon to Fri, 0900 to 1700

SOCIETY OF LONDON ART DEALERS

Acronym or abbreviation: SLAD

Ormond House, 3 Duke of York Street, London,
SW1Y 6JP

Tel: 020 7930 6137
Fax: 020 7321 0685
E-mail: sladoffice@aol.com

Website:
http://www.slad.org
List of members. Individual virtual galleries.

Enquiries:
Enquiries to: Director General

Founded:
1932

Organisation type and purpose:
Trade association.
To promote and protect the good name and the
interests of the art trade.

Subject coverage:
Advice on areas of specialisation of London's art
dealers.

Printed publications:
Directory of members (annual)

Access to staff:
Contact by letter, by telephone, by fax and by e-
mail

Hours: Mon to Thu, 1000 to 1730

Members:
British Art Market Federation

SOCIETY OF LONDON THEATRE

Acronym or abbreviation: SOLT

32 Rose Street, London, WC2E 9ET

Tel: 020 7557 6700
Fax: 020 7557 6799
E-mail: enquiries@solttma.co.uk

Website:
http://www.OfficialLondonTheatre.co.uk
London Theatre Guide news, information and
tickets online.

Enquiries:
Enquiries to: Development Manager (Press/
Statistics)
Other contacts: Head of Publications for show
information.

Founded:
1908

Organisation type and purpose:
Trade association.
Representing theatre managers, owners and
producers in the major West End London Theatres.

Subject coverage:
Industrial relations and legal advice, publications,
audience research, promotions, theatre tokens, the
Laurence Olivier Awards and the Leicester Square
half-price ticket booth.

**Museum or gallery collection, archive, or library
special collection:**
London Theatre guides since 1921
Audience data since 1981
Production information

Trade and statistical information:
Trade news for the media and travel trade (by
subscription).
Annual box office data report, audience research.

Printed publications:
Disabled Access Guide to London's West End
Theatres (free)
London Theatre Guide (free)
Theatre list (fortnightly, £30 a year UK)

Access to staff:
Contact by letter, by telephone, by fax, by e-mail
and via website. Appointment necessary.
Hours: Mon to Fri, 1000 to 1800

Access to building, collection or gallery:
No access other than to staff

SOCIETY OF LONDON TOASTMASTERS

Acronym or abbreviation: SOLT

148 Park Crescent, Erith, Kent, DA8 3DY

Tel: 01322 341465
Fax: 01322 402619
E-mail: toastmasters@topfunctions.com

Website:
http://www.societyoflondontoastmasters.co.uk

Enquiries:
Enquiries to: Honorary Secretary

Founded:
1953

Organisation type and purpose:
Membership association (membership is by
qualification, election or invitation), present
number of members: 25, service industry, training
organisation.
To provide toastmasters, announcers for formal
functions, conferences, exhibitions, etc.

Subject coverage:
Art of the professional toastmaster, and master of
ceremonies, the organisation and running of
banquets, conferences, receptions, wedding
receptions, etc.

**Museum or gallery collection, archive, or library
special collection:**
Large collection of banquet invitations,
photographs and menus; books and manuscripts
on banqueting protocol held by individual
members

Access to staff:
Contact by letter, by telephone, by fax, by e-mail,
in person and via website
Hours: Any reasonable time

Access to building, collection or gallery:
No access other than to staff

SOCIETY OF MARITIME INDUSTRIES LIMITED

Acronym or abbreviation: SMI

28–29 Threadneedle Street, London EC2R 8AY

Tel: 020 7628 2555
E-mail: info@maritimeindustries.org

Website:
http://www.maritimeindustries.org

Enquiries:
Enquiries to: Chief Executive
Direct e-mail: ce@maritimeindustries.org

Founded:
1966

Organisation type and purpose:
Trade association.

Subject coverage:
Marine equipment for both merchant and naval
ships ranging from main engines, auxiliaries,
bridge, radar, galley and deck fittings. Also covers
the offshore industry and pollution control
equipment. Facilitation of overseas port
development investment opportunities. Marine
science and technology. Oceanology.

Printed publications:
Guide to Suppliers
Market Information
Members Directory

Access to staff:
Contact by letter, by telephone and by e-mail
Hours: Mon to Fri, 0900 to 1700

Subsidiaries:
Association of British Offshore Industries
   e-mail: aboi@maritimeindustries.org
Association of Marine Scientific Industries
   e-mail: amsi@maritimeindustries.org
British Marine Equipment Association
   e-mail: bmea@maritimeindustries.org
British Naval Equipment Association
   e-mail: bnea@maritimeindustries.org
British Oil Spill Control Association
   e-mail: bosca@maritimeindustries.org
Ports and Terminals Group
   e-mail: ptga@maritimeindustries.org

SOCIETY OF MARTIAL ARTS

Acronym or abbreviation: SMA

PO Box 34, Manchester, M9 8DN

Tel: 0161 702 1660
Fax: 0161 702 1660
E-mail: registrar@societyofmartialarts.org

Website:
http://www.societyofmartialarts.co.uk

Enquiries:
Enquiries to: Registrar
Other contacts: President for founder of the society.

Founded:
1994

Organisation type and purpose:
International organisation, professional body
(membership is by qualification), present number
of members: 50, research organisation.

Subject coverage:
Martial arts education.

Printed publications:
Conference Abstracts
International Journal of Martial Art Research

Access to staff:
Contact by letter, by telephone, by fax and by e-
mail
Hours: Mon to Fri, 0900 to 1700

Access to building, collection or gallery:
No access other than to staff, prior appointment
required

Connections with:
College of Higher Education of Martial Arts
(CHEMA)
    e-mail: principal@chema.co.uk

SOCIETY OF MASTER SADDLERS

Acronym or abbreviation: SMS

Green Lane Farm, Stonham, Stowmarket, Suffolk,
IP14 5DS

Tel: 01449 711642
Fax: 01449 711642
E-mail: enquiries@mastersaddlers.co.uk; master
.saddlers@talk21.com

Website:
http://www.mastersaddlers.co.uk
Aims, categories of membership, news and events,
information on saddle fitting and saddle safety,
training, how to find a member, members' area.

Founded:
1966

Organisation type and purpose:
Formed to serve as a trade association for the craft
retail saddler, but has since embraced all aspects of
the trade.
To safeguard the quality of work, services, training
and qualifications of all those who work in the
saddlery trade, from manufacturers and retailers
through individual craftspeople and saddle fitters.

Subject coverage:
Saddlery.

Access to staff:
Contact by letter, by telephone, by fax and by e-
mail

SOCIETY OF MASTER SHOE REPAIRERS LIMITED

Acronym or abbreviation: SOMSR

St Crispin's House, 21 Station Road, Desborough,
Kettering, Northamptonshire, NN14 2SA

Tel: 01536 760374
Fax: 01536 762348
E-mail: info@msauk.biz

Website:
http://www.somsr.com
List of members (searchable database)

Enquiries:
Enquiries to: General Secretary

Founded:
1963

Organisation type and purpose:
Trade association.

Subject coverage:
Shoe repair, shoe care, independent shoe repairers
in the UK, training.

Printed publications:
Shoe Service (journal, monthly, £12 pa, free to
    members)
Guide to the Code of Practice for Shoe Repairs
    (free)

Access to staff:
Contact by letter, by telephone and by fax.
Appointment necessary.
Hours: Mon to Fri, 0900 to 1700

SOCIETY OF METAPHYSICIANS LIMITED

Acronym or abbreviation: SofM

Archers Court, Stonestile Lane, The Ridge,
Hastings, East Sussex, TN35 4PG

Tel: 01424 751577
Fax: 01424 751577
E-mail: newmeta@btinternet.com

Website:
http://www.metaphysicians.org.uk
e-mail enquiry form and society application form.
Statement of policy, history.
http://www.btinternet.com/~newmeta/index/home
.html
Second-hand book sales list, etc.

Enquiries:
Enquiries to: Managing Director
Other contacts: Founder President

Founded:
1944

Organisation type and purpose:
International organisation, advisory body,
professional body (membership is by qualification,
election or invitation), present number of
members: 298, voluntary organisation, suitable for
ages: all, training organisation, consultancy,
research organisation, publishing house.

Subject coverage:
Neometaphysics (study and application of
fundamental laws), includes all physical and non-
physical sciences, parapsychology, paraphysics,
esoterics, psychic science, biofeedback systems,
bioenergics, psycho-kinetics, neopsychological
studies, healing, energy and mind-based, human
aura, development of infinitely based
administrative systems, alternative medicine.

**Museum or gallery collection, archive, or library
special collection:**
Full research data, photographs, etc. on Aura
    Viewing, including complementary colour
    method, electro-deposition and corona discharge
Bibliography and equipment
Paraphysics, Psychic Science

Trade and statistical information:
World manufactures of aura imaging and
    radiesthetic equipment.

Non-library collection catalogue:
All or part available online

Library catalogue:
All or part available online, in-house and in print

Printed publications:
Abstracts
Bibliographies
Catalogues of current works, rare reprints and
    special issues
Journals
Neo-Metaphysical Digest (journal)
Newsletters
Research Projects
Reprints

Publications list:
Available in print

Access to staff:
Contact by letter, by telephone, by fax, by e-mail
and via website. Appointment necessary.
Hours: Mon to Fri, 1000 to 1400

Access for disabled people:
Parking provided, access to all public areas, toilet
facilities

Also at:
Istituto Italiano di Ricerche Metafisiche
    via Ritmeyer 6-I34/32, Trieste, Italy; fax: 0039 40
    224206; e-mail: istmeta@tin.it

Links with:
Metaphysical Research Group
    tel: 01424 751577; fax: 01424 751577; e-mail:
    newmeta@btinternet.com

SOCIETY OF MODEL SHIPWRIGHTS

Acronym or abbreviation: SMS

5 Lodge Crescent, Orpington, Kent, BR6 0QE

Tel: 01689 827213

Enquiries:
Enquiries to: Honorary Secretary

Founded:
1974

Organisation type and purpose:
Membership association (membership is by
election or invitation), present number of
members: 85, suitable for ages: all.
The society is devoted to the research into and the
construction of accurate scale models of vessels.

Subject coverage:
All matters relating to the construction of scale
models of sailing and powered vessels of any
period.

Access to staff:
Contact by letter and by telephone
Hours: Sun to Sat, 0900 to 2200

SOCIETY OF NURSERY NURSING PRACTITIONERS

Acronym or abbreviation: SNNP

40 Archdale Road, East Dulwich, London, SE22
9HJ

Tel: 0845 643 6832
Fax: 0845 643 6834
E-mail: info@snn.org.uk

Website:
http://www.snnp.org.uk

Enquiries:
Enquiries to: Chief Executive

Founded:
1991

Organisation type and purpose:
Professional body (membership is by subscription,
qualification, election or invitation), suitable for
ages: 18+.

Subject coverage:
Child care education and training.

Printed publications:
Code of Ethics
Prospectus and Syllabus

Access to staff:
Contact by letter, by telephone, by fax, by e-mail
and in person. Appointment necessary.
Hours: Mon to Fri, 0900 to 1700

SOCIETY OF OCCUPATIONAL MEDICINE

Acronym or abbreviation: SOM

6 St Andrews Place, Regents Park, London NW1
4LB

Tel: 020 7486 2641
Fax: 020 7486 0028
E-mail: admin@som.org.uk

Website:
https://www.som.org.uk
SOM, members, meetings, news, OH doctors'
directory.

Founded:
1935

continued overleaf

Formerly called:
Association of Industrial Medical Officers (year of change 1965)

Organisation type and purpose:
A registered charity (number 268555), a learned body for registered medical practitioners with an involvement or interest in the practice of occupational medicine.

Subject coverage:
Protection of the health of people at work, including environmental issues associated with work products and processes. Although the Society does not provide a clinical occupational health service, it seeks to prevent the occurrence of occupational disease and injury across the whole of industry. It also stimulates research and education in occupational medicine and maintains a close relationship with government departments and other agencies in the health and safety field.

Electronic and video publications:
eNews
Order electronic and video publications from: Website

Access to staff:
Contact by letter, by telephone, by fax, by e-mail and via website

Links with:
British Medical Association
Health & Safety Executive

Regional groups in Central Southern England, London, South Wales and the West of England, West Midlands, East Midlands, Yorkshire, North West, North East, Scotland and Northern Ireland:

SOCIETY OF OPERATIONS ENGINEERS

Acronym or abbreviation: SOE

22 Greencoat Place, London, SW1P 1PR

Tel: 020 7630 1111
Fax: 020 7630 6677
E-mail: soe@soe.org.uk

Website:
http://www.iplante.org.uk
http://www.irte.org.uk
http://www.soe.org.uk

Enquiries:
Enquiries to: Chief Executive

Founded:
2000

Organisation type and purpose:
International organisation, learned society, professional body (membership is by election or invitation), present number of members: 18,500, registered charity (charity number 1081753).

Subject coverage:
Plant engineering, maintenance, engineering surveying, and inspection, road transport engineering.

Printed publications:
Guides
Transport Engineer (12 times a year, free to members, non-members by subscription)
The Plant Engineer (6 times a year, free to members, non-members by subscription)
Operations Engineer (10 times a year, free to members)

Publications list:
Available online

Access to staff:
Contact by letter and by e-mail. Appointment necessary. Access for members only.
Hours: Mon to Fri, 0900 to 1700

SOCIETY OF ORTHOPAEDIC MEDICINE

Acronym or abbreviation: SOM

4th Floor, Stanley House, 151 Dale Street, Liverpool, L2 2AH.

Tel: 0151 2373970
Fax: 0151 2373971
E-mail: admin@somed.org

Website:
http://www.somed.org
About the Society, courses, conferences, research grants, journal abstracts.

Founded:
1979

Organisation type and purpose:
International organisation, learned society (membership is by qualification), present number of members: 1,400, registered charity, training organisation.

Subject coverage:
Orthopaedic medicine, musculoskeletal medicine.

Printed publications:
Journal: International Musculoskeletal Medicine (free to members, for sale to non-members)

Access to staff:
Contact by letter, by telephone, by fax, by e-mail and via website
Hours: Mon to Fri, 0900 to 1700

Access to building, collection or gallery:
No access other than to staff

Links with:
British Institute of Musculoskeletal Medicine
Chartered Society of Physiotherapy
Middlesex University
Society of Apothecaries

SOCIETY OF PENSION CONSULTANTS

Acronym or abbreviation: SPC

St Bartholomew House, 92 Fleet Street, London, EC4Y 1DG

Tel: 020 7353 1688
Fax: 020 7353 9296
E-mail: john.mortimer@spc.uk.com

Website:
http://www.spc.uk.com

Enquiries:
Enquiries to: Secretary

Founded:
1958

Organisation type and purpose:
Membership association (membership is by subscription, qualification and election), present number of members: 103 organisations.
Representative body for the providers of the advice and services needed to provide pensions (occupational and personal) and other benefits. Members include pension and actuarial consultants, legal and accounting firms, insurance companies, investment houses and third-party administrators.

Subject coverage:
Occupational pension schemes, personal pension schemes and other employee benefit schemes, interests of organisations involved in providing advice and/or services in connection with the setting up or running of pension schemes.

Information services:
Only available to members.

Museum or gallery collection, archive, or library special collection:
Some records are available through the Pensions Archive Trust

Printed publications:
Newsletter (for members only)
Annual report

Access to staff:
Contact by letter, by e-mail and via website.
Appointment necessary.
Hours: Mon to Fri, 0900 to 1700

Member organisation of:
Occupational Pension Schemes Joint Working Group

SOCIETY OF PLOUGHMEN LIMITED

Quarry Farm, Loversall, Doncaster, South Yorkshire, DN11 9DH

Tel: 01302 852469
Fax: 01302 859880
E-mail: info@ploughmen.co.uk

Website:
http://www.ploughmen.co.uk

Enquiries:
Enquiries to: Secretary

Founded:
1972

Organisation type and purpose:
Membership association (membership is by subscription), registered charity (charity number 1062780).
To promote and encourage the art, skill and science of ploughing the land.

Subject coverage:
Ploughing.

Printed publications:
Handbook for Championships (September/October)
Newsletter (twice a year, members)

Access to staff:
Contact by letter, by telephone, by fax, by e-mail and via website
Hours: Mon to Fri, 0930 to 1630

Links with:
World Ploughing Organisation

SOCIETY OF PROFESSIONAL ENGINEERS

Acronym or abbreviation: SPE

St Mary House, 15 St Mary Street, Chippenham, Wiltshire, SN15 3WD

Tel: 01249 655398
Fax: 01249 443602
E-mail: soc.prof.eng@asi.org.uk

Enquiries:
Enquiries to: Office Co-ordinator

Founded:
1969

Organisation type and purpose:
Professional body.

Subject coverage:
Maintains a register of well qualified professional engineers of whatever discipline. Protects, enhances and promotes the status of the professional engineer and promotes the concept of this title throughout the world. Acts as the secretariat and provider of licences and registration cards to suitably qualified professional engineers on behalf of the UIDIP for the English-speaking countries of the world.
UIDIP is currently on hold until further notice.

Printed publications:
The Professional Engineer (quarterly bulletin, free to members, £2 per issue to non-members)

Access to staff:
Contact by letter, by telephone, by fax and by e-mail
Hours: Mon to Fri, 0900 to 1700

Member of:
Union Internationale des Ingenieurs Professionnels – Currently on hold until further notice (UIDIP) 66 rue de la Rochefoucauld, Paris, F-75009, France

Twinned with the:
Bundesverband der Berufsingenieure
Deutschlands (BDI)
 Germany; tel: 01249 655398
Société Nationale des Ingénieurs Professionnels
France (IPF)
 tel: 01249 655398
South African Society for Professional Engineers
(SASPE)

SOCIETY OF RECORDER PLAYERS

Acronym or abbreviation: SRP

Linkside, 21 Bereweeke Avenue, Winchester, SO22
6BH

E-mail: secretary@srp.org.uk

Website:
http://www.srp.org.uk

Enquiries:
Enquiries to: Secretary

Founded:
1937

Organisation type and purpose:
Membership association (membership is by
subscription), present number of members: 1,500,
voluntary organisation, registered charity (charity
number 282751/SC038422), suitable for all ages.

Subject coverage:
Recorder playing.

Printed publications:
The Recorder Magazine (quarterly)
Teachers' Guide to the Recorder

Access to staff:
Contact by letter, by e-mail, in person and via
website
Hours: Mon to Fri, 0900 to 1700

Also at:
50 regional branches

SOCIETY OF SALES AND MARKETING

Acronym or abbreviation: SSM

40 Archdale Road, East Dulwich, London, SE22
9HJ

Tel: 0845 643 6832
Fax: 0845 643 6834
E-mail: info@ssm.org.uk

Website:
http://www.ssm.org.uk

Enquiries:
Enquiries to: Chief Executive

Founded:
1980

Organisation type and purpose:
International organisation, advisory body,
professional body (membership is by subscription,
qualification, election or invitation).

Subject coverage:
Professional body for those interested in selling
and sales management, marketing, retailing and
international trade.

Printed publications:
Code of Ethics
Journal
Prospectus and syllabus

Access to staff:
Contact by letter, by telephone, by fax, by e-mail
and in person. Appointment necessary.
Hours: Mon to Fri, 0900 to 1700

SOCIETY OF SCRIBES AND ILLUMINATORS

Acronym or abbreviation: SSI

The Art Workers Guild, 6 Queen's Square, London,
WC1N 3AT

Tel: 015242 51534
Fax: 015242 51534
E-mail: scribe@calligraphyonline.org

Website:
http://www.calligraphyonline.org

Enquiries:
Enquiries to: Honorary Secretary

Founded:
1921

Organisation type and purpose:
International organisation, professional body
(Fellowship by election, Lay Membership by
subscription); present number of members: 550,
suitable for ages: 16+.
To perpetuate a tradition of craftsmanship in the
production of manuscript books and documents;
to encourage and influence calligraphy and fine
lettering.

Subject coverage:
Crafts of writing and lettering, production of
manuscript books and documents, fine lettering
and calligraphy, lists of calligraphy courses,
exhibitions, materials and availability, advice on all
aspects of calligraphy and lettering.

**Museum or gallery collection, archive, or library
special collection:**
Rare calligraphy books
Reference library
Small permanent exhibition, with historical and
 modern pieces

Printed publications:
Journal (for members only, twice a year)
Newsletter (3 a year)
Order printed publications from: via website

Access to staff:
Contact by letter, by telephone, by fax, by e-mail
and via website
Hours: Mon to Fri, 0900 to 1700

Access to building, collection or gallery:
No access to building

SOCIETY OF SOLICITORS IN THE SUPREME COURTS OF SCOTLAND

Acronym or abbreviation: SSC Society

SSC Library, Parliament House, 11 Parliament
Square, Edinburgh, EH1 1RF

Tel: 0131 225 6268
Fax: 0131 225 2270
E-mail: enquiries@ssclibrary.co.uk

Website:
http://www.ssclibrary.co.uk

Enquiries:
Enquiries to: Librarian

Founded:
1784

Organisation type and purpose:
Learned society (membership is by subscription),
present number of members: 300.

Subject coverage:
Scottish legal material, statutes, law reports, SIs,
textbooks (comprehensive); English legal material,
statutes, law reports, SIs, limited selection of
textbooks; Scots law in all its branches; UK law
where it is common to Scotland and England.

**Museum or gallery collection, archive, or library
special collection:**
Court of Session and High Court of Justiciary
 Opinions from 1982 to date (open, unreported
 and indexed on database from 1991)
Session papers 1750–1954

Library catalogue:
All or part available in-house

Access to staff:
Contact by letter, by telephone and by e-mail.
Appointment necessary. Access for members only.
Non-members charged.
Hours: Mon to Fri, 0930 to 1600

SOCIETY OF SPORTS THERAPISTS

Acronym or abbreviation: SST

16 Royal Terrace, Glasgow G3 7NY

Tel: 0845 6002613
Fax: 0141 3325335
E-mail: admin@society-of-sports-therapists.org

Website:
http://www.society-of-sports-therapists.org

Enquiries:
Enquiries to: Chairman
Direct e-mail: webmaster@society-of-sports
-therapists.org
Other contacts: Secretary

Founded:
1989

Organisation type and purpose:
National government body, advisory body,
professional body (membership is by subscription,
qualification), present number of members: 1500+,
training organisation, consultancy.
To provide a professional and educational identity
for sports therapists.

Subject coverage:
Sports injury management, treatment and
rehabilitation.

**Museum or gallery collection, archive, or library
special collection:**
Fact sheets, newsletters, book lists and course and
 conference details

Access to staff:
Contact by letter, by telephone, by fax, by e-mail
and via website. Appointment necessary.
Hours: Mon to Fri, 1000 to 1500

Subsidiary body:
Sports Rehab & Education
 tel: 0141 221 1494; fax: 0141 221 1525

SOCIETY OF ST GREGORY

Acronym or abbreviation: SSG

76 Great Bushey Drive, London, N20 8QL

Tel: 020 8445 5724
E-mail: chairman@ssg.org.uk

Website:
http://www.ssg.org.uk

Enquiries:
Enquiries to: Chairman

Founded:
1929

Organisation type and purpose:
Membership association (membership is by
subscription), voluntary organisation, training
organisation.

Subject coverage:
Roman Catholic worship and church music.

**Museum or gallery collection, archive, or library
special collection:**
Church Music
Church Music Association Music Library, 1955–
 1972
Complete sets, 1929 to date:
Life and Worship
Liturgy
Music and Liturgy

Printed publications:
Music and Liturgy (4 times a year)

Access to staff:
Contact by letter, by telephone, by e-mail and via
website
Hours: Any reasonable time

SOCIETY OF TELEVISION LIGHTING AND DESIGN

Acronym or abbreviation: STLD

E-mail: via website

Website:
http://www.stld.org.uk
Technical section, news and events.

Incorporates the former:
Society of Television Lighting Directors (year of change 2009)

Organisation type and purpose:
A membership association (membership is by subscription) for the television lighting profession.

Subject coverage:
Provides a forum that stimulates a free exchange of ideas in all aspects of the television lighting profession.

Printed publications:
Television Lighting (magazine, free to members)
Lighting Director's Planning Diary (magazine, free to members)

Access to staff:
Contact via website

SOCIETY OF TRUST AND ESTATE PRACTITIONERS

Acronym or abbreviation: STEP

Artillery House (South), 11–19 Artillery Row, London, SW1P 1RT

Tel: 020 7340 0500
E-mail: step@step.org

Website:
http://www.step.org
STEP, professional development, communities, branches, resources, publications, STEP TV.

Founded:
1991

Organisation type and purpose:
A professional body providing members with a local, national and international learning and business network focusing on the responsible stewardship of assets today and across the generations. Full members of STEP are the most experienced and senior practitioners in the field of trusts and estates; has over 14,000 members spread throughout the world's major trust and estate jurisdictions. Members advise clients on the broad business of the management of personal finance. Provides education, training, representation and networking for its members.

Subject coverage:
STEP members help families plan their long term financial future, facilitating good stewardship and financial planning across future generations. STEP members also help families comply with the often complex tax rules surrounding trusts, estates and inheritance.

Special visitor services:
STEP TV

Printed publications:
A variety of publications, including:
STEP Guide to Trusts and Investments (members £55.00 plus p&p, non-members £95.00 plus p&p)
STEP Accounting Guidelines (members £8.00 plus p&p, non-members £8.00 plus p&p)
A Practical Guide to Transfer of Trusteeships (members £45.00 plus p&p, non-members £60.00 plus p&p)
The Regulation of Trust and Company Service Providers (members £54.00 plus p&p, non-members £75.00 plus p&p)
Order printed publications from: e-mail: orders@step.org

Electronic and video publications:
STEP Journal
Information leaflets
Wealth Directory
Policy and technical documents

Order electronic and video publications from: Website

Publications list:
Available online

Access to staff:
Contact by letter, by telephone and by e-mail
Hours: Mon to Fri, 0900 to 1730 except bank hols

Branches:
Throughout the world

SOCIETY OF VOLUNTARY ASSOCIATES

Acronym or abbreviation: SOVA

1st Floor, Chichester House, 37 Brixton Road, London, SW9 6DZ

Tel: 020 7793 0404
Fax: 020 7735 4410
E-mail: london@sova.org.uk

Website:
http://www.sova.org.uk/

Enquiries:
Enquiries to: Manager
Direct tel: 0114 282 3187
Direct fax: 0114 282 3292
Direct e-mail: mail@sova.org.uk

Founded:
1975

Organisation type and purpose:
National organisation, voluntary organisation, registered charity (charity number 1073877), training organisation, consultancy.
To involve local communities in community safety, crime reduction and offenders' rehabilitation.

Subject coverage:
Volunteers within the criminal justice system, partnerships between statutory and voluntary agencies, community action, community safety and community support for ex-offenders.

Museum or gallery collection, archive, or library special collection:
Reports on SOVA projects

Printed publications:
Annual Report
Selection of free leaflets
Volunteer Newsletter

Access to staff:
Contact by telephone and by e-mail
Hours: Mon to Fri, 0900 to 1700

Affiliated to:
National Council for Voluntary Organizations

SOCIETY OF WEDDING AND PORTRAIT PHOTOGRAPHERS LIMITED

Acronym or abbreviation: SWPP

Colomendy House, Ivale Road, Denbigh, Clwyd, LL16 3DF

Tel: 01745 815030
E-mail: info@swpp.co.uk

Enquiries:
Enquiries to: Chief Executive
Direct e-mail: info@swpp.co.uk

Founded:
1988

Organisation type and purpose:
Trade association.

Subject coverage:
Training and support in wedding portrait photography and videoing.

Printed publications:
Professional portrait photography (T Hansen, £25)
The A-Z of Wedding photography (T Hansen, £25)
Variety of manuals and videos covering all aspects of wedding photography and videoing

Electronic and video publications:
Barrie Thomas CD-ROMs:
Master Class (£39)
Digital Printing and Presentation (£39)

Publications list:
Available in print

Access to staff:
Contact by letter, by telephone and by fax.
Appointment necessary.
Hours: Mon to Fri, 0900 to 1700

SOCIETY OF WILDLIFE ARTISTS

Acronym or abbreviation: SWLA

17 Carlton House Terrace, London, SW1Y 5BD

Tel: 020 7930 6844
Fax: 020 7839 7830
E-mail: press@mallgalleries.com

Website:
http://www.mallgalleries.org.uk

Enquiries:
Enquiries to: Secretary
Other contacts: Marketing and Communications Officer

Founded:
1964

Organisation type and purpose:
Membership association (membership is by election or invitation), registered charity (charity number 328717).

Subject coverage:
Wildlife art as painting, drawings and sculpture, its exhibition and promotion.

Printed publications:
Catalogue of the annual exhibition

Access to staff:
Contact by letter, by telephone, by fax, by e-mail and via website. Appointment necessary.
Hours: Mon to Fri, 0930 to 1700

Access to building, collection or gallery:
No access other than to staff
Hours: Mon to Fri, 0930 to 1700

Access for disabled people:
Stairlift, toilet facilities
Special comments: Stairlift.

Links with:
Federation of British Artists
at the same address

SOCIETY OF WOMEN ARTISTS, THE

Acronym or abbreviation: SWA

1 Knapp Cottages, Wyke, Gillingham, Dorset, SP8 4NQ

Tel: 01747 825718
Fax: 01747 826835
E-mail: pamhenderson@dial.pipex.com

Website:
http://www.society-women-artists.org.uk

Enquiries:
Enquiries to: Executive Secretary

Founded:
1855

Organisation type and purpose:
International organisation, membership association (membership is by election or invitation), present number of members: 150, registered charity (charity number 298241).

Subject coverage:
Art and women artists; annual exhibition of paintings, drawings, prints and sculpture.

Museum or gallery collection, archive, or library special collection:
Archive of Art and Design, Victoria and Albert Museum, Blythe House, 23 Blythe Road, London W14 0QF

Access to staff:
Contact by letter, by telephone, by fax and by e-mail
Hours: Mon to Fri, 0900 to 1700

Access to building, collection or gallery:
No prior appointment required
Special comments: Archives are kept by the Victoria and Albert Museum's Archive of Art and Design.

SOCIETY OF WOOD ENGRAVERS

Acronym or abbreviation: SWE

The Old Governor's House, Norman Cross, Peterborough, PE7 3TB

Tel: 01733 242833
Fax: 01733 242833
E-mail: swesec@geriwaddington.com

Website:
http://www.woodengravers.co.uk

Enquiries:
Enquiries to: General Secretary

Founded:
1920

Organisation type and purpose:
International organisation, membership association.
Artists' exhibiting society and international contact organisation.

Subject coverage:
Printmaking, relief printmaking, wood engraving, its practice, current practitioners and its history.

Museum or gallery collection, archive, or library special collection:
Society archives

Printed publications:
Journal (4 times a year)
Newsletter (12 times a year)
Occasional fine print books on wood engraving

Access to staff:
Contact by letter, by telephone, by fax, by e-mail and via website
Hours: Mon to Fri, 1000 to 1700

SOG LIMITED

PO Box 13, The Heath, Runcorn, Cheshire, WA7 4QF

Tel: 01928 511888
Fax: 01928 567979
E-mail: heath_library@sog.ltd.uk

Website:
http://www.sog.ltd.uk

Enquiries:
Enquiries to: Librarian
Direct tel: 01928 513438
Direct fax: 01928 513334

Organisation type and purpose:
Service industry.
Facilities management & specialist services.

Subject coverage:
Chlor-alkali; chlorine and inorganic derivatives; caustic soda; electrochemistry and electrochemical technology, water, sewage and effluent treatment chemicals. Processes; chlorinated hydrocarbons and derivatives; cleaning and degreasing solvents; refrigerants; CFC alternatives, fluorinated hydrocarbons and derivatives, chlorine containing monomers and polymers; PVC; fluorine containing monomers and polymers; PTFE.

Non-library collection catalogue:
All or part available in-house

Library catalogue:
All or part available in-house

Publications list:
Available in print

Access to staff:
Contact by letter, by telephone, by fax, by e-mail and via website. Appointment necessary. Access for members only. All charged.
Hours: Mon to Fri, 0830 to 1200 and 1230 to 1630

Access to building, collection or gallery:
Prior appointment required

SOIL ASSOCIATION, THE

Acronym or abbreviation: SA

Bristol House, 40–56 Victoria Street, Bristol, BS1 6BY

Tel: 0117 929 0661
Fax: 0117 314 5000

Website:
http://www.soilassociation.org

Enquiries:
Enquiries to: Information Officer
Direct tel: 0117 914 2444

Founded:
1946

Organisation type and purpose:
Membership association (membership is by subscription), registered charity.

Subject coverage:
Organic food and farming, responsible forestry, agriculture.

Printed publications:
Living Earth (membership magazine, 3 times a year, £18)
Organic Farming (journal, quarterly, £15)

Publications list:
Available online and in print

Access to staff:
Contact by letter, by telephone, by fax and in person. Appointment necessary.
Hours: Mon to Fri, 0900 to 1730

Wholly owned subsidiary of:
Soil Association Certification Limited
at the same address; tel: 0117 914 2405; fax: 0117 925 2504; e-mail: cert@soilassociation.org

SOIL MECHANICS

Acronym or abbreviation: SML

Glossop House, Hogwood Lane, Finchampstead, Wokingham, Berkshire, RG40 4QW

Tel: 0118 932 8888
Fax: 0118 932 8383
E-mail: library@esg.co.uk

Website:
http://www.esg.co.uk

Enquiries:
Enquiries to: Librarian
Direct tel: 0118 932 4459
Direct e-mail: peter.eldred@esg.co.uk

Founded:
1943

Organisation type and purpose:
Service industry, consultancy.

Subject coverage:
Soil mechanics, rock mechanics, geology, geotechnical engineering, site investigation, vibration and dynamics, earthquake engineering, seismicity.

Museum or gallery collection, archive, or library special collection:
Results of site investigations throughout the United Kingdom and some overseas localities (microform and scans)

Non-library collection catalogue:
All or part available in-house

Library catalogue:
All or part available in-house

Access to staff:
Contact by telephone, by fax, by e-mail and in person. Appointment necessary. Non-members charged.
Hours: Mon to Fri, 0900 to 1700

Access to building, collection or gallery:
Prior appointment required
Hours: Mon to Fri, 0900 to 1700

Access for disabled people:
Parking provided, level entry, access to all public areas, toilet facilities

Constituent bodies:
CL Voelcker (CLV)
at the same address
Exploration Associates (EA)
at the same address
TES Bretby
at the same address

Parent body:
Environmental Scientifics Group Limited (ESGL)
at the same address

SOLAR ENERGY SOCIETY

Acronym or abbreviation: UK-ISES

School of Technology, Oxford Brookes University, Headington Campus, Gipsy Lane, Oxford, OX3 0BP

Tel: 01865 484367
Fax: 01865 484263
E-mail: ukises@brookes.ac.uk

Website:
http://www.thesolarline.com

Enquiries:
Enquiries to: Administrator

Founded:
1974

Organisation type and purpose:
Learned society.

Subject coverage:
Solar energy.

Printed publications:
Conference Proceedings (list available)
Solar News (4 times a year)
Refocus (6 times a year)
Heating Water by the Sun: a layman's guide to the use of flat-plate solar collectors for domestic water heating and for heating swimming pools (3rd ed 2000)
Solar Electricity: a layman's guide to the generation of electricity by the direct conversion of solar energy (1999)
Solar Energy Today (1981)
Set of 6 factsheets by the Society for the Solar Trust

Publications list:
Available online and in print

Access to staff:
Contact by e-mail
Hours: Mon to Fri, 0900 to 1700

Access to building, collection or gallery:
No prior appointment required

Section of:
International Solar Energy Society
Freiburg, Germany; tel: + 49 761 4590652; fax: + 49 761 4590699; e-mail: info@ises.org

SOLAR TRADE ASSOCIATION

Acronym or abbreviation: STA

National Energy Centre, Davy Avenue, Knowlhill, Milton Keynes, Buckinghamshire, MK5 8NG

Tel: 01908 442290
Fax: 01908 665577

continued overleaf

E-mail: enquiries@solar-trade.org.uk

Website:
http://www.solar-trade.org.uk

Enquiries:
Enquiries to: Chief Executive

Founded:
1974

Organisation type and purpose:
Trade association (membership is by election or invitation), present number of members: 170, manufacturing industry, service industry, training organisation, consultancy.
National enquiry centre.

Subject coverage:
Solar industry and solar energy utilisation from the commercial point of view, commercial and domestic water heating, swimming pool heating, passive solar design, solar controllers.

Trade and statistical information:
National sales of solar systems.
International sales of solar systems.

Printed publications:
Booklet outlining fundamentals of solar heating and lighting (free)
Membership list (free)

Access to staff:
Contact by letter, by telephone, by fax and by e-mail
Hours: Mon to Fri, 0900 to 1700

Member of:
European Solar Thermal Industries Federation (ESTIF)
The Micropower Council

SOLDIER MAGAZINE

Parsons House, Ordnance Road, Aldershot, Hampshire, GU11 2DU

Tel: 01252 347353
Fax: 01252 347358
E-mail: mail@soldiermagazine.co.uk

Website:
http://www.soldiermagazine.co.uk

Enquiries:
Enquiries to: Archive/Information manager
Direct tel: 01252 355056
Direct e-mail: rkusionowicz@soldiermagazine.co.uk

Founded:
1945

Organisation type and purpose:
National government body, publishing house.

Subject coverage:
The British Army, especially post-1945.

Museum or gallery collection, archive, or library special collection:
Magazine archive of every issue printed since 19th March 1945
Photo archive of photographs used in issues of British Army subjects, in colour, and black and white
Crown copyright of photographs taken by Soldier Magazine staff

Library catalogue:
All or part available in-house

Printed publications:
Soldier Magazine (monthly, £2.50)

Access to staff:
Contact by letter, by telephone, by fax, by e-mail and in person. Appointment necessary.
Hours: Mon to Fri, 0900 to 1600

Access to building, collection or gallery:
Prior appointment required

Access for disabled people:
Parking provided

SOLDIERS, SAILORS, AIRMEN AND FAMILIES ASSOCIATION – FORCES HELP

Acronym or abbreviation: SSAFA Forceshelp

19 Queen Elizabeth Street, London, SE1 2LP

Tel: 020 7403 8783
Fax: 020 7403 8815
E-mail: management@ssafa.org.uk

Website:
http://www.ssafa.org.uk
Connections to Army, Navy, Air Force welfare and ex-service charities.

Enquiries:
Enquiries to: Welfare Advisors
Other contacts: Director of Welfare & Housing

Founded:
1885

Organisation type and purpose:
Voluntary organisation, registered charity (charity number 210760).
Armed Forces National Charity.
Support for serving and ex-service men, women and their families in need.

Subject coverage:
Welfare of Armed Service and ex-Service families and dependants.

Museum or gallery collection, archive, or library special collection:
Small resource library containing up-to-date benefit, housing and welfare advice leaflets and literature

Non-library collection catalogue:
All or part available in-house

Library catalogue:
All or part available in-house

Printed publications:
OnTarget (2 times a year, available for interested persons)
SSAFA News & Views (2 times a year, available to all branches, volunteers and interested persons)
SSAFA Scope (4 times a year, in-house, newsletter for professional and volunteer staff)
In Touch (4 times a year, in-house, update for professional and volunteer staff)

Access to staff:
Contact by letter, by telephone, by fax, by e-mail and via website. Appointment necessary.
Hours: Mon to Fri, 0915 to 1700

Has:
102 Branches throughout the UK and Ireland. Can also be contacted through Citizens Advice Bureaux

SOLICITORS FAMILY LAW ASSOCIATION

Acronym or abbreviation: SFLA

PO Box 302, Orpington, Kent, BR6 8QX

Tel: 01689 850227
Fax: 01689 855833
E-mail: sfla@btinternet.co.uk

Website:
http://www.sfla.co.uk
Seminars, guidance on family law.
http://www.sfla.org.uk
Seminars, guidance on family law.

Enquiries:
Enquiries to: Administrative Director

Founded:
1982

Organisation type and purpose:
Membership association (membership is by subscription, qualification, election or invitation), present number of members: 5,000, voluntary organisation.

Subject coverage:
All solicitor members deal with family law in a constructive rather than aggressive approach to resolving problems flowing from relationship breakdown. The public can contact the Association to receive a list of local members.

Printed publications:
The SFLA Guide to Good Practice for Solicitors Acting for Children (5th ed., 1997, £5)
Precedents for Consent Orders (book 5th ed., 1998, £40 members, £50 non-members)
Precedents – Separation and Pre-Marital Agreements 2001 (book, 1998, £45 members, £60 non-members)
Fairness for Families (free to members)
International Aspects of Family Law – The SFLA Guide to Good Practice and Procedure (£35 members, £45 non-members)

Electronic and video publications:
Please state which WP system when ordering disks:
Precedents for Consent Orders (disk 5th ed., 1998, £20 members, £26 non-members, footnotes not included)
Precedents – Separation and Pre-Marital Agreements 2001 (disk, £25 members, £30 non-members)

Publications list:
Available in print

Access to staff:
Contact by letter, by telephone, by fax and by e-mail
Hours: Mon to Fri, 0900 to 1700

SOLID FUEL ASSOCIATION

Acronym or abbreviation: SFA

7 Swanwick Court, Alfreton, Derbyshire, DE55 7AS

Tel: 01773 835400
Fax: 01773 834351
E-mail: sfa@solidfuel.co.uk

Website:
http://www.solidfuel.co.uk

Enquiries:
Enquiries to: General Secretary

Founded:
1994

Organisation type and purpose:
National organisation, advisory body, trade association (membership is by subscription), present number of members: 38.

Subject coverage:
Utilisation of natural and manufactured solid fuels in domestic heating. Installation and maintenance of solid fuel domestic heating appliances.

Publications list:
Available online

Access to staff:
Contact by letter, by telephone, by fax, by e-mail and via website
Hours: Mon to Fri, 0900 to 1700

Access to building, collection or gallery:
No access other than to staff

SOLIHULL CENTRAL LIBRARY

Homer Road, Solihull, West Midlands, B91 3RG

Tel: 0121 704 6965
Fax: 0121 704 6991
E-mail: libraryarts@solihull.gov.uk

Website:
http://www.solihull.gov.uk/libraries

Enquiries:
Enquiries to: Head of Libraries
Direct tel: 0121 704 6945
Direct e-mail: tcox@solihull.gov.uk

Other contacts: Head of Information & Local Studies Manager; email: dgill@solihull.gov.uk; tel: 0121 704 6808

Organisation type and purpose:
Public library.

Non-library collection catalogue:
All or part available online and in-house

Library catalogue:
All or part available online and in-house

Access to staff:
Contact by letter, by telephone, by fax and by e-mail
Hours: Mon, Thu, 0900 to 2000; Tue, Fri, 0900 to 1800; Wed, 1000 to 1800; Sat, 0900 to 1700

Access to building, collection or gallery:
No prior appointment required

Access for disabled people:
Level entry, access to all public areas, toilet facilities

Branch libraries:
Balsall Common
   283 Kenilworth Road, Balsall Common, CV7 7EL; tel: 01676 532590; fax: 01676 530119
Castle Bromwich
   Hurst Lane North, Castle Bromwich, B36 0EY; tel: 0121 747 3708; fax: 0121 748 5919
Chelmsley Wood
   10 West Mall, Chelmsley Wood Shopping Centre, Chelmsley Wood, Birmingham B37 5TN; tel: 0121 788 4380; fax: 0121 788 4391
Hampton in Arden
   39 Fentham Road, Hampton in Arden, B92 0AY; tel: 01675 442629; fax: 01675 443608
Hobs Moat
   Ulleries Road, Solihull, West Midlands, B92 8EE; tel: 0121 743 4592; fax: 0121 743 2473
Kingshurst
   Marston Drive, Kingshurst, B37 6BD; tel: 0121 770 3451; fax: 0121 770 9388
Knowle
   Chester House, High Street, Knowle, B93 0LL; tel: 01564 775840; fax: 01564 770953
Marston Green
   Land Lane, Marston Green, B37 7DQ; tel: 0121 779 2131; fax: 0121 770 1565
Meriden
   The Green, Meriden, CV7 7LN; tel: 01676 522717; fax: 01676 521146
Olton
   169a Warwick Road, Olton, B92 7AW; tel: 0121 706 3038; fax: 0121 708 0549
Shirley
   Church Road, Shirley, B90 2AY; tel: 0121 744 1076; fax: 0121 744 5047

SOLIHULL CHAMBER OF INDUSTRY AND COMMERCE

142 Lode Lane, Solihull, West Midlands, B91 2HP

Tel: 0121 704 6406
Fax: 0121 704 8259
E-mail: solihull@birminghamchamber.org.uk

Enquiries:
Enquiries to: Information Officer

Organisation type and purpose:
Membership association (membership is by subscription).

Subject coverage:
Business services.

Access to staff:
Contact by letter, by telephone and by fax. Appointment necessary.
Hours: Mon to Fri, 0900 to 1700

Associate of:
Birmingham Chamber of Commerce (BCI)
   75 Harborne Road, Birmingham, B15 3DH; tel: 0121 454 6171

SOLIHULL COLLEGE

Blossomfield Road, Solihull, West Midlands, B91 1SB

Tel: 0121 678 7000
Fax: 0121 678 7200
E-mail: library@solihull.ac.uk

Website:
http://www.solihull.ac.uk
On-line catalogue, useful internet sites.

Enquiries:
Enquiries to: Library and Learning Centre Manager
Direct tel: 0121 678 7205

Organisation type and purpose:
College of further and higher education.

Subject coverage:
Education; business studies; art and design; leisure; travel and tourism; hotel and catering studies; teacher training (further education); counselling; humanities; social sciences.

Library catalogue:
All or part available online

Access to staff:
Contact by letter, by telephone and by e-mail. Appointment necessary.
Hours: Term time: Mon to Thu, 0830 to 2030; Fri, 0830 to 1630; Sat, 0930 to 1300
Vacations: Mon to Fri, 0900 to 1700

SOLIHULL LIBRARY SERVICE

Central Library, Homer Road, Solihull, West Midlands, B91 3RG

Tel: 0121 704 6977
Fax: 0121 704 6212
E-mail: libraryarts@solihull.gov.uk

Website:
http://www.solihull.gov.uk/libraries
Information about all library services.

Enquiries:
Enquiries to: Information and Heritage Services Manager
Direct tel: 0121 704 6808
Direct e-mail: dgill@solihull.gov.uk

Organisation type and purpose:
Local government body, public library.

Subject coverage:
General library, information and reference service; local and family history resources relating to the area covered by the present Metropolitan Borough of Solihull.

Information services:
Business information service, heritage and local studies service.

Education services:
Skills for Life Service (courses via Learndirect); Connexions and NextSteps services hosted.

Museum or gallery collection, archive, or library special collection:
Records relating to Solihull MBC and its predecessor authorities
Birmingham Small Arms (BSA) company archive collection (motorcycles and small arms)
Photographic archive of Cliff Joiner (Solihull press photographer)
Solihull Bowling Club
Archive of Doris Hamilton Smith (artist and pupil of Edith Holden)

Library catalogue:
All or part available online

Access to staff:
Contact by letter, by telephone, by fax, by e-mail, in person and via website
Hours: Mon, Thu, 0900 to 2000; Tue, Fri, 0900 to 1800; Wed, 1000 to 1800; Sat; 0900 to 1700

Access to building, collection or gallery:
Via Library Square, through Touchwood Shopping Centre
Hours: During opening hours

Access for disabled people:
Level entry, access to all public areas, public lift, toilet facilities
Hours: During opening hours
Special comments: Disabled parking in Church Hill car park, special needs parking bays in adjacent Touchwood underground car park, with lifts to Library level.

Parent body:
Solihull Metropolitan Borough Council
   website: http://www.solihull.gov.uk

SOMERSET AND WESSEX EATING DISORDERS ASSOCIATION

Acronym or abbreviation: SWEDA

Strode House, 10 Leigh Road, Street, Somerset, BA16 0HA

Tel: 01458 448611
E-mail: admin@swedauk.org

Website:
http://www.swedauk.org

Enquiries:
Enquiries to: Manager
Direct e-mail: paula@swedauk.org
Other contacts: Administrator

Founded:
1997

Organisation type and purpose:
Membership association, voluntary organisation, registered charity (charity number 1056441), training organisation.
A charity based on the ethos of being user-led and encouraging self-help and improvement, SWEDA aims to reach out to all affected by eating disorders, sufferers, carers and professionals.

Subject coverage:
Eating disorders, helpline and website for sufferers and carers, training and consultation on eating disorders, awareness raising.

Access to staff:
Contact by letter, by telephone, by e-mail, in person and via website. Appointment necessary.
Hours: Administrator: Mon to Fri, 0900 to 1300
Special comments: Answerphone at all other times.

Access to building, collection or gallery:
Prior appointment required
Hours: Wed, 1000 to 1300

SOMERSET ARCHAEOLOGICAL AND NATURAL HISTORY SOCIETY

Acronym or abbreviation: SANHS

Somerset Heritage Centre, Brunel Way, Norton Fitzwarren, Taunton, Somerset TA2 6SF

Tel: 01823 272429
Fax: 01823 272429
E-mail: office@sanhs.org

Website:
http://www.sanhs.org

Enquiries:
Enquiries to: Office Manager
Other contacts: somstud@somerset.gov.uk

Founded:
1849

Organisation type and purpose:
Learned society, registered charity (charity number 201929).

Subject coverage:
History, archaeology and natural history of the pre-1974 county of Somerset.

Museum or gallery collection, archive, or library special collection:
Pigott and Braikenridge Collections (Somerset drawings)
Tite Collection (Somerset books)

continued overleaf

Non-library collection catalogue:
All or part available online, in-house and in print

Library catalogue:
All or part available in-house

Printed publications:
Beetles of Somerset
Flora of Somerset
Decorated medieval floor tiles of Somerset
Maritime History of Somerset
The Taunton Dissenting Academy
Somerset Archaeology and Natural History
(annual vol. from 1849)

Access to staff:
Contact by letter, by telephone, by fax, by e-mail
and in person
Hours: Tue, Wed, Thu, 0900 to 1700

SOMERSET COLLEGE

Wellington Road, Taunton, Somerset, TA1 5AX

Tel: 01823 366331
Fax: 01823 366418
E-mail: enquiries@somerset.ac.uk

Website:
http://www.somerset.ac.uk
General college information and course search.

Enquiries:
Enquiries to: Information Officer

Founded:
1974

Organisation type and purpose:
Suitable for ages: further and higher education.

Subject coverage:
Art and design, performing arts, business and
management studies, information technology,
catering and hospitality, hairdressing and beauty
therapy, community and caring services,
construction, automotive engineering, engineering
technology, humanities, science, access studies, A
levels, health studies, leisure and tourism, sports-
related courses, courses for students with learning
difficulties/disabilities, adult education classes,
commercial courses.

Library catalogue:
All or part available in-house

Printed publications:
The following prospectuses are available free on
request:
Adult & Professional Development Guide
Further Education Prospectus
Higher Education Prospectus

Publications list:
Available online and in print

Access to staff:
Contact by letter, by telephone, by fax, by e-mail,
in person and via website
Hours: Mon to Fri, 0900 to 1700

Access for disabled people:
Parking provided, toilet facilities

SOMERSET COUNSELLING CENTRE

Acronym or abbreviation: SCC

38 Belvedere Road, Taunton, Somerset, TA1 1HD

Tel: 01823 337049
E-mail: info@scctaunton.org.uk

Website:
http://www.wpf.org.uk
http://www.scctaunton.org.uk

Enquiries:
Enquiries to: Centre Manager
Other contacts: Counselling Service Manager for
referral for counselling.

Founded:
1990

Organisation type and purpose:
Voluntary organisation, registered charity (charity
number 1038975), training organisation.
Counselling service and training courses.

Subject coverage:
Counselling Service. Assessment and weekly open-
ended therapeutic counselling, sliding scale of fees.
Training Workshops

Printed publications:
Information pamphlets (free)

Access to staff:
Contact by letter, by telephone, by e-mail and via
website
Hours: Mon, Wed, Fri, Receptionist usually
available 1000 to 1500
Special comments: 24 hours answerphone, calls
returned within one working day.

Access for disabled people:
Toilet facilities

Affiliated to:
Westminster Pastoral Foundation (WPF)
23 Kensington Square, London, W8 5HN; tel: 020
7361 4864; fax: 020 7361 4860; e-mail:
counselling@wpf.org.uk

SOMERSET COUNTY FEDERATION OF WOMEN'S INSTITUTES

11 Trull Road, Taunton, Somerset, TA1 4PT

Tel: 01823 284261
Fax: 01823 322545
E-mail: wiltonlodge@somersetwi.fsbusiness.co.uk

Website:
http://www.somersetwi.fsbusiness.co.uk
Events, etc.

Enquiries:
Enquiries to: County Secretary

Founded:
1918

Organisation type and purpose:
National organisation, membership association
(membership is by subscription), present number
of members: 5,500, voluntary organisation,
registered charity (charity number 1022578),
training organisation.

Access to staff:
Contact by letter, by telephone, by fax and by e-
mail
Hours: Mon, Tue, Wed, 0930 to 1245 and 1315 to
1530

Access for disabled people:
Parking provided, level entry

SOMERSET ENVIRONMENTAL RECORDS CENTRE

Acronym or abbreviation: SERC

Tonedale Mill, Wellington, Somerset, TA20 0AW

Tel: 01823 664450
Fax: 01823 652411
E-mail: info@somerc.com

Website:
http://www.somerc.com
Example Biodiversity data, publications list, IHS,
biological recording.

Founded:
1989

Organisation type and purpose:
Advisory body, training organisation, consultancy.

Subject coverage:
Environmental topics specific to Somerset; wildlife,
biodiversity, flora, fauna, geological, protected
species, habitats, wildlife sites.

Museum or gallery collection, archive, or library special collection:
Site specific and location records of more than
4,000 sites

Printed publications:
Publications – see website

Electronic and video publications:
IHS Integrated Habitat System (CD-ROM)

Access to staff:
Contact by telephone and by e-mail
Hours: Mon to Fri, 0900 to 1700
Special comments: Charges made for some services.

Affiliated to:
National Federation of Biological Recording

Parent body:
Somerset Wildlife Trust

SOMERSET FEDERATION OF YOUNG FARMERS CLUB

Acronym or abbreviation: Somerset YFC

The Old School, School Road, Weston Zoyland,
Bridgwater, Somerset, TA7 0LN

Tel: 01278 681711
Fax: 01278 691912
E-mail: admin@somersetyfc.org.uk

Website:
http://www.somersetyfc.org.uk

Enquiries:
Enquiries to: Federation Co-ordinator

Founded:
1934

Organisation type and purpose:
Membership association (membership is by
subscription), present number of members: 800,
registered charity (charity number 273051).

Subject coverage:
Agriculture, rural youth work, social education.

Publications list:
Available in print

Access to staff:
Contact by letter, by telephone, by fax, by e-mail,
in person and via website. Non-members charged.
Hours: Mon to Fri, 0900 to 1700

Access for disabled people:
Parking provided, level entry, access to all public
areas, toilet facilities

Affiliated to:
National Federation of Young Farmers Clubs
(NFYFC)
Stoneleigh Park, Stoneleigh, Warwickshire, CV8
2LG; tel: 024 7685 7200; fax: 024 7685 7229; e-
mail: post@nfyfc.org.uk; website: www.nfyfc.org
.uk

SOMERSET LIBRARIES

Enquiry Centre, Paul Street, Taunton, Somerset,
TA1 3XZ

Tel: 01823 336370
Fax: 01823 272178
E-mail: enquiry@somerset.gov.uk

Website:
http://www.librarieswest.org.uk
Library catalogue.

Enquiries:
Enquiries to: Senior Librarian: Information

Organisation type and purpose:
Public library.

Library catalogue:
All or part available online

Access to staff:
Contact by letter, by telephone, by fax, by e-mail
and via website
Hours: Mon, Tue, Thu, 0830 to 1800; Wed, Fri, 0830
to 1900; Sat, 0830 to 1630

Parent body:
Library Administration Centre
   Mount Street, Bridgwater, Somerset, TA6 3ES;
tel: 01278 451201; fax: 01278 452787; website:
http://www.somerset.gov.uk

SOMERSET RECORD OFFICE

Formal name: Somerset Heritage and Libraries
Service

Brunel Way, Norton Fitzwarren, Taunton, TA2 6SF

Tel: 01823 278805
Fax: 01823 325402
E-mail: archives@somerset.gov.uk

Website:
http://www.somerset.gov.uk
Guide to holdings, details of services.

Enquiries:
Enquiries to: Archivist

Founded:
1929

Organisation type and purpose:
Local government body.
Archive service.

Subject coverage:
Historic records of the county of Somerset,
churches, societies, businesses and individuals.

Non-library collection catalogue:
All or part available online

Library catalogue:
All or part available online

Printed publications:
Your Somerset Family (£2)
Your Somerset House (£2)

Microform publications:
Images of original records held, especially parish
   records

Electronic and video publications:
Guide to Holdings (CD-ROM)

Publications list:
Available online

Access to staff:
Contact by letter, by telephone, by fax and by e-
mail. Appointment necessary.
Hours: Mon, 1400 to 1650; Tue to Thu, 0900 to 1650;
Fri, 0900 to 1620; Sat, 0915 to 1215
Special comments: Not open every Saturday.

Access to building, collection or gallery:
Prior appointment required

Access for disabled people:
Ramped entry, access to all public areas, toilet
facilities

Parent body:
Somerset County Council

SOMERSET STUDIES LIBRARY

Somerset Heritage Centre, Brunel Way, Norton
Fitzwarren, Taunton, Somerset, TA2 6SF

Tel: 01823 278805
Fax: 01823 347459
E-mail: somstud@somerset.gov.uk

Website:
http://www.librarieswest.org.uk
Library catalogue (combined with the rest of the
public libraries in Somerset and four neighbouring
authorities).

Enquiries:
Enquiries to: Librarian

Founded:
1973

Organisation type and purpose:
County council archives and local studies service.

Subject coverage:
History, archaeology, genealogy and natural
history of historic county of Somerset.

Library catalogue:
All or part available online

Access to staff:
Contact by letter, by telephone, by fax, by e-mail
and in person
Hours: Mon, 1300 to 1700; Tue to Fri, 0900 to 1700
Special comments: Contact for Saturday openings.

Access to building, collection or gallery:
Hours: Mon, 1300 to 1700; Tue to Fri, 0900 to 1700;
contact for Saturday openings
Special comments: Closed until 27th September
2010.

SOMERVILLE COLLEGE LIBRARY

Oxford, OX2 6HD

Tel: 01865 270694
Fax: 01865 270620
E-mail: library@some.ox.ac.uk

Enquiries:
Enquiries to: Librarian

Founded:
1879

Organisation type and purpose:
University department or institute.
College of University of Oxford.

Subject coverage:
Main subjects read in the university.

**Museum or gallery collection, archive, or library
special collection:**
Amelia B Edwards Library and Manuscript
   Collection
John Stuart Mill Library
Margaret Kennedy correspondence
Percy Withers Library and family correspondence
Vernon Lee (Violet Paget) correspondence

Non-library collection catalogue:
All or part available in-house

Library catalogue:
All or part available online

Access to staff:
Contact by letter, by telephone, by fax and by e-
mail. Appointment necessary. Letter of
introduction required.
Hours: Mon to Fri, 0900 to 1700

SONS OF DIVINE PROVIDENCE

Acronym or abbreviation: SDP

13 Lower Teddington Road, Hampton Wick,
Kingston Upon Thames, Surrey, KT1 4EU

Tel: 020 8977 5130
Fax: 020 8977 0105

Website:
http://www.sonsofdivineprovidence.org/literature

Enquiries:
Enquiries to: Senior Administrator

Founded:
1952

Organisation type and purpose:
Registered charity (charity number 1088675).

Subject coverage:
Charitable company running two care homes for
the elderly, three residential care homes for people
with learning disabilities, a horticultural training
centre and units of independent accommodation.

Publications list:
Available online

Access to staff:
Contact by letter, by telephone and via website.
Appointment necessary.
Hours: Mon to Fri, 0900 to 1700

SORIS

PO Box 502, Welwyn Garden City, Hertfordshire,
AL7 9HG

Tel: 01707 321680
Fax: 0870 7059037
E-mail: cdrew@soris.org

Website:
http://www.soris.org

Enquiries:
Enquiries to: Principal Consultant

Founded:
1980

Formerly a part of:
Chemical Industries' Association (year of change
2001); Chemical Industry Regional Centre of
Excellence (CIRCE Ltd) (year of change 2005)

Formerly called:
SORIS Ltd (year of change 1992)

Organisation type and purpose:
International organisation, trade association
(membership is by subscription), service industry,
research organisation.
Provides chemical market intelligence, soft
information and tailored introductions.

Subject coverage:
Chemical intelligence and information broking for
chemistry-using industries.

**Museum or gallery collection, archive, or library
special collection:**
Special Chemical Return to 1993

Access to staff:
Contact by letter, by telephone, by fax, by e-mail
and via website. Appointment necessary. Non-
members charged.
Hours: Mon to Fri, 0900 to 1700

Links with:
Chemical Business Network Group
Chemical Industries Association
Chemical Industry Consultants Association
Chemical Innovation Knowledge Transfer
   Network
Chemicals North West
Royal Society of Chemistry
Society of Chemical Industry
Yorkshire Chemical Focus

SOS CHILDREN

Formal name: SOS Children's Villages

Terrington House, 13–15 Hills Road, Cambridge,
CB2 1NL

Tel: 01223 365589
E-mail: info@soschildrensvillages.org.uk

Website:
http://www.soschildrensvillages.org.uk
The charity and its work, news, child sponsorship,
facts and figures, AIDS in Africa.

Enquiries:
Enquiries to: Chief Executive
Direct e-mail: andrew@soschildrensvillages.org.uk

Founded:
1950s

Organisation type and purpose:
Registered charity (charity number 1069204).
The world's largest orphan and abandoned
children's charity.

Subject coverage:
Provides a new family and home for more than
78,000 children in 500 unique Children's Villages in
124 countries. Also helps a million children and
their families through SOS community outreach
programmes, playing an important role in
supporting the development and sustainability of
their local communities, e.g. building and running
231 SOS nurseries and 185 schools, which are open
to children in its care and to those from the wider
community, and 61 vocational training centres,
which equip more than 174,000 children, teenagers

continued overleaf

and young adults with the practical skills they need to earn a living and lead independent lives. In areas where medical support is scarce or non-existent, it builds SOS medical centres, which provide communities with immediate medical treatment and preventative and palliative care. It also offers skills, training, education, counselling, micro-loans and improved nutrition to vulnerable families, so they are able to provide for their children and stay together through difficult times. In times of conflict, famine or disaster, it provides emergency assistance.

Access to staff:
Contact by letter, by telephone and by e-mail

SOUND AND MUSIC

3rd Floor, South Wing, Somerset House, London, WC2R 1LA

Tel: 020 7759 1800
E-mail: info@soundandmusic.org

Website:
http://www.soundandmusic.org

Founded:
2010

Created by the merger of:
British Music Information Centre, Contemporary Music Network, Society for the Promotion of New Music, and Sonic Arts Network. (year of change 2010)

Organisation type and purpose:
Contemporary arts organisation. A Regularly Funded Organisation of Arts Council England. Registered charity (charity number 1124609).

Subject coverage:
Music and sound.

SOUND RESEARCH LABORATORIES LIMITED

Acronym or abbreviation: SRL

Head Office & Laboratory, Holbrook Hall, Little Waldingfield, Sudbury, Suffolk, CO10 0TH

Tel: 01787 247595
Fax: 01787 248420
E-mail: srl@soundresearch.co.uk

Website:
http://www.soundresearch.co.uk

Enquiries:
Enquiries to: Managing Director

Founded:
1967

Organisation type and purpose:
Consultancy.

Subject coverage:
Acoustics, noise and vibration control, traffic noise, vehicle noise, auditoria acoustics, industrial noise control, laboratory testing, product development.

Printed publications:
Airflow and Acoustic Measurements (lecture manual)
Basic Vibration Control (lecture manual)
Industrial Noise Control (lecture manual)
Mechanical Services Noise Control (lecture manual)
Noise Control in Industry (book)
Noise Control in Mechanical Services (book)
Practical Building Acoustics (lecture manual)
Technical reports

Access to staff:
Contact by letter, by telephone, by fax and by e-mail
Hours: Mon to Fri, 0900 to 1700

Access to building, collection or gallery:
No access other than to staff

Access for disabled people:
Parking provided, level entry, toilet facilities

SOUTH AFRICA HOUSE LIBRARY

South African High Commission, Trafalgar Square, London, WC2N 5DP

Tel: 020 7451 7299
Fax: 020 7451 7289
E-mail: london.general@foreign.gov.za

Website:
http://www.gov.za
South African government portal.
http://www.safrica.info
Official gateway for tourists, immigrants, investors, citizens, South Africans abroad and a wide range of general information.
http://www.artslink.co.za
Arts and cultural events in South Africa.
http://www.southafricahouse.com
General items of relevance to people in Britain on government activity in South Africa. Information includes topical issues, business and economic information, and matters relating to South African passports, visas and residence permits. Also has websites relevant to links between Britain and South Africa.

Enquiries:
Enquiries to: Librarian

Organisation type and purpose:
Government (South Africa).

Subject coverage:
South Africa.

Printed publications:
South Africa Yearbook (to organisations, schools etc only)

Electronic and video publications:
South Africa Yearbook (past Yearbooks in pdf format only)
Order electronic and video publications from: http://www.info.gov.za/aboutsa/index.htm as text version or http://www.gcis.gov.za/docs/publications/yearbook/index.html for pdf format

Access to staff:
Contact by letter and by fax
Hours: Mon to Fri, 0900 to 1300 and 1345 to 1700
Special comments: Fax should be marked Attention Reference Library.

Access to building, collection or gallery:
No access other than to staff
Special comments: Library not on open access, written enquiries only.

SOUTH AFRICAN TOURISM

5–6 Alt Grove, Wimbledon, London, SW19 4DZ

Tel: 020 8971 9351
Fax: 020 8944 6705
E-mail: info@south-african-tourism.org

Website:
http://www.south-african-tourism.org
Order publications
http://www.southafrica.net

Enquiries:
Enquiries to: Information Officer

Organisation type and purpose:
National government body.

Subject coverage:
South African tourism, business travel, special interest tours, conferences and exhibitions, incentives.

Museum or gallery collection, archive, or library special collection:
Film and photographs (colour and black-and-white) libraries

Trade and statistical information:
Tourist data on South Africa.

Printed publications:
South African Tourism Factfiler 2002
Highlights Map 2002

Electronic and video publications:
Photographs available from photo library on website

Access to staff:
Contact by letter, by telephone, by fax, by e-mail, in person and via website
Hours: Mon to Fri, 0900 to 1700
Special comments: Appointments by prior arrangement.

Access for disabled people:
Level entry, toilet facilities

SOUTH AYRSHIRE LIBRARIES

Formal name: South Ayrshire Library and Information Service

Carnegie Library, 12 Main Street, Ayr, KA8 8ED

Tel: 01292 286385
Fax: 01292 611593
E-mail: carnegie.library@south-ayrshire.gov.uk

Website:
http://www.south-ayrshire.gov.uk/libraries
General information about the library service.

Enquiries:
Enquiries to: Libraries Manager
Direct tel: 01292 288820
Direct fax: 01292 619019
Direct e-mail: jean.inness@south-ayrshire.gov.uk

Organisation type and purpose:
Local government body, public library.

Subject coverage:
General, local history of Kyle and Carrick, and South Ayrshire, Robert Burns.

Museum or gallery collection, archive, or library special collection:
Ayrshire (Kyle and Carrick from 1975)
Robert Burns Collection

Non-library collection catalogue:
All or part available in-house

Library catalogue:
All or part available online

Printed publications:
Local history pamphlets and illustrations
Ayr Memories (£4.95)
Girvan Memories (£4.95)
Troon Memories (£4.95)
History of Prestwick (£18)
History of Ayr (£14.95)
Prestwick in the 40s (£5)
Old Parish Records Ayr 1766–1820 (£6.50)
Tarbolton Churchyard Monumental Inscriptions (£4.95)
Smuggling & The Ayrshire Economic Boom (£4)
Order printed publications from: South Ayrshire Book Shop, South Ayrshire Council Library HQ, 26 Green Street, Ayr, KA8 8ED; tel: 01292 288820; fax: 01292 619019; e-mail: jean.inness@south-ayrshire.gov.uk

Publications list:
Available in print

Access to staff:
Contact by letter, by telephone, by fax, by e-mail and in person. Appointment necessary.
Hours: Mon, Tue, Thu, Fri, 0900 to 1930; Wed, Sat, 0900 to 1700

Access for disabled people:
Ramped entry, access to all public areas, toilet facilities

SOUTH BEDFORDSHIRE DISTRICT COUNCIL

The District Offices, High Street North, Dunstable, Bedfordshire, LU6 1LF

Tel: 01582 472222
Fax: 01782 474009 or 01582 474058

Website:
http://www.southbeds.gov.uk

Information for residents, visitors to and businesses in South Bedfordshire, about District Council services and local information.

Enquiries:
Enquiries to: Chief Executive
Direct tel: 01582 474047
Direct e-mail: communications@centralbedfordshire.gov.uk

Organisation type and purpose:
Local government body.

Subject coverage:
Local government services: administrative, technical, financial, planning and estates, environmental health and housing.

Printed publications:
Council Plan (full and summary, annual)
Information (residents magazine)
Housing matters (tenants magazine)

Access to staff:
Contact by letter, by telephone, by fax, by e-mail and in person
Hours: Mon to Thu, 0900 to 1700; Fri, 0900 to 1645

Access to building, collection or gallery:
Mon to Thu, 0900 to 1700; Fri, 0900 to 1645

Access for disabled people:
Hours: Mon to Thu, 0900 to 1700; Fri, 0900 to 1645

SOUTH BUCKS DISTRICT COUNCIL

Council Offices, Windsor Road, Slough, Berkshire, SL1 2HN

Tel: 01753 533333\ Minicom no. 01753 676251
Fax: 01753 731803
E-mail: sbdc@southbucks.gov.uk

Website:
http://www.southbucks.gov.uk

Enquiries:
Enquiries to: Chief Executive

Organisation type and purpose:
Local government body.

Subject coverage:
All usual local government subjects.

Access to staff:
Contact by letter, by telephone, by fax, by e-mail and in person
Hours: Mon to Wed, 0900 to 1730; Thu to Fri, 0900 to 1700

SOUTH DERBYSHIRE DISTRICT COUNCIL

Acronym or abbreviation: SDDC

Civic Offices, Civic Way, Swadlincote, Derbyshire, DE11 0AH

Tel: 01283 221000\ Minicom no. 01283 595849
Fax: 01283 595964
E-mail: civic.offices@south-derbys.gov.uk

Website:
http://www.south-derbys.gov.uk

Enquiries:
Enquiries to: Customer Services
Direct fax: 01283 595854
Direct e-mail: customer.services@south-derbys.gov.uk

Organisation type and purpose:
Local government body.

Subject coverage:
All aspects of local government.

Access to staff:
Contact by letter, by telephone, by fax, by e-mail and via website
Hours: Mon to Fri, 0900 to 1700

Access for disabled people:
Parking provided, ramped entry, level entry, access to all public areas, toilet facilities

SOUTH EAST AREA LIBRARIES INFORMATION CO-OPERATIVE

Acronym or abbreviation: SEAL

Peckham Library, 122 Peckham Hill Street, London, SE15 5JR

Tel: 020 7525 0230
E-mail: wendy.siemaszko@southwark.gov.uk

Enquiries:
Enquiries to: Secretary

Founded:
1969

Organisation type and purpose:
Local information co-operative.

Subject coverage:
The organisation promotes co-operation between all types of libraries located in the London Boroughs of Bexley, Bromley, Greenwich, Lewisham and Southwark, the Medway Council area and the County of Kent. It is not a direct information provider.

Printed publications:
Annual Report and Directory of Members (circulated to member organisations)

Access to staff:
Contact by letter, by telephone and by e-mail. Appointment necessary.

SOUTH EAST ENGLAND TOURIST BOARD

Acronym or abbreviation: SEETB

40 Chamberlayne Road, Eastleigh, Hampshire, SO50 5JH

Tel: 023 8062 5400
E-mail: customerservices@tourismse.com

Website:
http://www.southeastengland.uk.com
Tourist information (accommodation, events, attractions etc)
http://www.tourismsoutheast.com
Tourism statistics, business advice.
http://www.southeastwalks.com
Walking holidays/activities.
http://www.southeastgardens.co.uk
Gardens open to the public.

Enquiries:
Enquiries to: Company Secretary

Founded:
1973

Organisation type and purpose:
Advisory body, membership association (membership is by subscription), service industry.

Subject coverage:
Tourist information on accommodation, visitor attractions, events of special interest and conference venues in South East England i.e. Kent, Surrey, East and West Sussex.

Trade and statistical information:
Tourism volumes and values, hotel occupancies and tourism investments in the area.

Printed publications:
Annual Report
Bed and Breakfast Touring Map (annual, free)
Group Organisers' Guide (annual, free)
Regional Tourism Strategy
Various publications and brochures produced (mainly free of charge)

Access to staff:
Contact by letter, by telephone, by fax and by e-mail
Hours: Mon to Fri, 0900 to 1700

SOUTH EAST LONDON ARMY CADET FORCE

Formal name: Army Cadet Force
Acronym or abbreviation: ACF

Hollyhedge House, Wat Tyler Road, Blackheath, London, SE3 0QZ

Tel: 020 8692 4066
Fax: 020 8694 0566
E-mail: ceoseacf@reserve-forces-london.mod.uk

Enquiries:
Enquiries to: Executive Officer

Organisation type and purpose:
National organisation, voluntary organisation, suitable for ages: 12 to 18.
The Army Cadet Force is a National Voluntary Youth Organisation. It is sponsored by the Army and provides challenging military, adventurous, and community activities. Its aim is to inspire young people to achieve success in life with a spirit of service to the Queen, their country and their local community, and to develop in them the qualities of a good citizen.

Subject coverage:
Adventurous and challenging activities, leadership, character training, work for the community, understanding of the Army and its place in national life.

Printed publications:
Army Cadet National (quarterly, via ACFA, Duke of York's HQ)
Order printed publications from: ACFA, Holderners House, 51–61 Clifton Street, London, EC2A 4DW
South East London ACF
Hollyhedge House, Wat Tyler Road, Blackheath, SE3 0QZ

Publications list:
Available online

Access to staff:
Contact by letter, by telephone, by fax and by e-mail
Hours: Mon to Fri, 0900 to 1700

Links with:
Department for Education and Employment
National Council for Voluntary Youth Services
Territorial Army Volunteer Reserve

Supports the:
Cadet Force which is sponsored by the Army

SOUTH GLOUCESTERSHIRE COUNCIL

Acronym or abbreviation: SGC

Council Offices, Castle Street, Thornbury, Gloucestershire, BS35 1HF

Tel: 01454 868009; minicom no. 01454 868010
Fax: 01454 863886
E-mail: mailbox@southglos.gov.uk

Website:
http://www.southglos.gov.uk

Founded:
1996

Organisation type and purpose:
Local government body.

Subject coverage:
Local government services.

Printed publications:
All available on the website

Publications list:
Available online

Access to staff:
Contact by letter, by telephone, by fax, by e-mail and via website
Hours: Mon to Thu, 0845 to 1700; Fri 0845 to 1630

Access to building, collection or gallery:
No prior appointment required
Hours: Mon to Thu, 0845 to 1700; Fri 0845 to 1630

Access for disabled people:
Parking provided, ramped entry, level entry, access to all public areas, toilet facilities

SOUTH KENT COLLEGE

Shorncliffe Road, Folkestone, Kent, CT20 2TZ

Tel: 01303 858340
Fax: 01303 858400
E-mail: webmaster@southkent.ac.uk

Website:
http://www.southkent.ac.uk

Enquiries:
Enquiries to: Head of Learning Centre
Direct e-mail: pennie.newman@southkent.ac.uk

Organisation type and purpose:
College of further education.

Subject coverage:
Business studies, management, mechanical
engineering, electrical and electronic engineering,
building, education, social sciences, humanities,
sciences, information technology, media studies,
catering, health and social care, hairdressing and
beauty.

Library catalogue:
All or part available online

Access to staff:
Contact in person
Hours: Mon, Wed, 0845 to 1700; Tue, Thu, 0845 to
1930; Fri, 0845 to 1615
Special comments: May be closed during vacations,
so enquire first.

Access for disabled people:
Parking provided, level entry, toilet facilities

Also at:
South Kent College
  Jemmett Road, Ashford, Kent, TN23 4RJ; tel:
  01233 655573; fax: 01233 655501
South Kent College
  Maison Dieu Road, Dover, CT16 1DH; tel: 01304
  244344; fax: 01304 244301

SOUTH KESTEVEN DISTRICT COUNCIL

Acronym or abbreviation: SKDC

Council Offices, St Peters Hill, Grantham,
Lincolnshire, NG31 6PZ

Tel: 01476 406080
Fax: 01476 406000
E-mail: d.nicholls@skdc.com

Website:
http://www.skdc.com

Enquiries:
Enquiries to: Public Relations Manager
Direct tel: 01476 406128
Direct e-mail: pr@southkesteven.gov.uk
Other contacts: Customer Services Manager

Founded:
1974

Organisation type and purpose:
Local government body.

Subject coverage:
All aspects of local government.

Printed publications:
District Line (council newsletter)
Best Value Performance Plan
L A 21 document
Welland Partnership Strategy

Publications list:
Available in print

Access to staff:
Contact by letter, by telephone, by fax, by e-mail
and via website. Appointment necessary.
Hours: Mon to Thu, 0845 to 1715; Fri, 0845 to 1645

Access for disabled people:
Ramped entry, toilet facilities

Connections with:
East Midlands Regional Local Government
Association (EMRLGA)
  The Belvoir Suite, Council Offices, Nottingham
  Road, Melton Mowbray, Leicestershire, LE13
  0UL

Member of:
East Midlands Regional Assembly
Federation of Economic Development Authorities
  FEDA Administrator, 36 Sheep Street, Shipston-
  on-Stour, Warwickshire, CU36 4AE
Lincolnshire Development Partnership
  The Chief Executive, Central Support Team,
  Lincolnshire County Council, Lincoln
Lincolnshire Local Government Association
  The Chief Executive, Lincolnshire County
  Council, Lincoln
Local Government Association
  Local Government House, Smith Square,
  London, SW1P 3HZ

Other addresses:
Bourne Area Office
  Town Hall, North Street, Bourne, PE10 9EA; tel:
  01476 406071
Market Deeping Area Office
  89 High Street, Market Deeping, PE6 8ED; tel:
  01476 406070
Stamford Area Office
  1 Maiden Lane, Stamford, PE9 2AZ; tel: 01476
  406072

SOUTH LANARKSHIRE COUNCIL

Council Building, Almada Street, Hamilton, South
Lanarkshire, ML3 0AA

Tel: 01698 454444
Fax: 01698 454275

Enquiries:
Enquiries to: Chief Executive
Other contacts: Public Relations Manager

Founded:
1996

Organisation type and purpose:
Local government body.
Councillors by election 67. Staff 15,000 by
appointment.
Unitary Council.

Subject coverage:
Local government.

Trade and statistical information:
South Lanarkshire statistical information; South
Lanarkshire statistical profile contains
information on area's characteristics: physical,
population, housing, economy and education.

Access to staff:
Contact by letter, by telephone and by fax.
Appointment necessary.
Hours: Mon to Thu, 0845 to 1645; Fri, 0845 to 1615

Member of:
Convention of Scottish Local Authorities (COSLA)
  Edinburgh

Principal Offices:
Atholl House
  Churchill Avenue, East Kilbride, G74 1LU; tel:
  01355 806000
Civic Centre
  Andrew Street, East Kilbride, G74 1AB; tel:
  01355 806000
Royal Burgh House
  380 King Street, Rutherglen, G73 1DB; tel: 0141
  613 5000
South Vennel
  Lanark, ML11 7JT; tel: 01555 673000

SOUTH LANARKSHIRE COUNCIL ARCHIVES AND INFORMATION MANAGEMENT SERVICE

30 Hawbank Road, College Milton, East Kilbride,
South Lanarkshire, G74 5EX

Tel: 01355 239193

Fax: 01355 242365
E-mail: archives@southlanarkshire.gov.uk

Website:
http://www.southlanarkshire.gov.uk/gateway
Summary of records held
http://www.scan.org.uk
Collection catalogue

Enquiries:
Enquiries to: Archivist

Founded:
1997

Organisation type and purpose:
Local government archive.

Subject coverage:
Local, family, social, economic and administrative
history of South Lanarkshire.

**Museum or gallery collection, archive, or library
special collection:**
Archives of South Lanarkshire Council and
  predecessor local authorities and public
  corporations
Deposited archives of business, voluntary
  organisations and associations in South
  Lanarkshire

Non-library collection catalogue:
All or part available online

Access to staff:
Contact by letter, by telephone, by fax and by e-
mail. Appointment necessary.
Hours: Mon to Fri, 0930 to 1630; other times by
arrangement
Special comments: All visits by appointment only.

SOUTH LANARKSHIRE LIBRARY SERVICE

Education Resources, Council Offices, Almada
Street, Hamilton, South Lanarkshire, ML3 0AE

Tel: 01698 454545
Fax: 01698 454465
E-mail: diana.barr@southlanarkshire.gov.uk

Website:
http://www.southlanarkshire.gov.uk
http://www.slc-learningcentres.org.uk
http://www.library.southlanarkshire.gov.uk
Library catalogue.

Enquiries:
Enquiries to: Manager
Direct tel: 01698 454412; 01698 452220
Other contacts: Information Services Co-ordinator

Founded:
1996

Organisation type and purpose:
Local government body, public library.

Subject coverage:
General, history and topography of South
Lanarkshire, health and safety, government
statistics and other publications.

**Museum or gallery collection, archive, or library
special collection:**
Audio archives, jazz, classical, contemporary
Barbour health and safety microfile
Genealogical index
Statutory government publications
Vehicle technical information
Collection on Robert Owen and New Lanark
  (Lanark Library)
William Smellie Collection (obstetrics, midwifery)
Collection on the estates of the Dukes of Hamilton
  (Hamilton Library)
Lace making (Hamilton Library)

Non-library collection catalogue:
All or part available online and in-house

Library catalogue:
All or part available online

Printed publications:
Book lists of local history

Access to staff:
Contact by letter, by telephone, by fax and by e-mail
Hours: Mon to Fri, 0900 to 1700

Parent body:
South Lanarkshire Council

SOUTH LONDON BOTANICAL INSTITUTE

Acronym or abbreviation: SLBI

323 Norwood Road, London, SE24 9AQ

Tel: 020 8674 5787
Fax: 020 8674 5787
E-mail: info@slbi.org.uk

Website:
http://www.slbi.org.uk

Enquiries:
Enquiries to: Chairman

Founded:
1910

Organisation type and purpose:
Learned society (membership is by subscription),
present number of members: 169, registered
charity (charity number 214251).
Education in botany. Small botanic garden, library
and herbarium.

Subject coverage:
General botany, seed plants, pteridophytes,
bryophytes, lichens.

Education services:
Adult education classes and school groups (pre-book with Education Officer).

**Museum or gallery collection, archive, or library
special collection:**
Extensive herbarium, British and European,
  including the Beeby and Palmer Collection from
  the Orkneys and Shetlands, seed collection,
  pteridophytes, bryophytes, lichen and marine
  algae
Historic floras; 35mm slide collection
Taxonomic library: British and European floras,
  British county floras, world floras

Non-library collection catalogue:
All or part available online

Library catalogue:
All or part available in-house

Printed publications:
Gazette (2 to 3 times a year, free)
Order printed publications from: Administrator

Access to staff:
Contact by letter, by telephone, by fax, by e-mail
and via website. Appointment necessary.
Hours: Thu, 1000 to 1600, or by appointment

Access to building, collection or gallery:
Prior appointment required, except on Thu 1000 to
1600

Access for disabled people:
Garden accessible for wheelchairs

SOUTH NORFOLK DISTRICT COUNCIL

South Norfolk House, Swan Lane, Long Stratton,
Norwich, Norfolk, NR15 2XE

Tel: 01508 533633
Fax: 01508 533695

Website:
http://www.south-norfolk.gov.uk
Tourism, economic development/business, local
services and news.

Organisation type and purpose:
Local government body.

Subject coverage:
District Council Services.

Printed publications:
The Link (community magazine, half yearly)

Access to staff:
Contact by letter, by telephone, by fax, by e-mail,
in person and via website
Hours: Mon to Thu, 0845 to 1700; Fri, 0845 to 1615

Access for disabled people:
Parking provided, level entry, access to all public
areas, toilet facilities

SOUTH NORTHAMPTONSHIRE DISTRICT COUNCIL

Acronym or abbreviation: SNC

Council Offices, Springfields, Towcester,
Northamptonshire, NN12 6AE

Tel: 01327 350211
Fax: 01327 359219

Website:
http://www.southnorthants.gov.uk

Enquiries:
Enquiries to: Head of Community and Leisure
Development
Direct tel: 01327 322340
Direct fax: 01327 322332
Other contacts: Chief Executive

Founded:
1974

Organisation type and purpose:
Local government body.

Subject coverage:
Council services and amenities; corporate services,
education, environmental services, finance,
housing, legal services, personnel services,
planning development, property and technical
services, roads and transportation, social work,
council tax and other payments, leisure and
tourism.

Printed publications:
Council Guide book
Year book

Access to staff:
Contact by letter, by telephone, by fax and in
person
Hours: Mon to Fri, 0900 to 1700

SOUTH NOTTINGHAM COLLEGE

Greythorn Drive, West Bridgford, Nottingham,
NG2 5GA

Tel: 0115 914 6400
Fax: 0115 914 6444
E-mail: enquiries@snc.ac.uk

Enquiries:
Enquiries to: Curriculum Support Manager
Direct tel: 0115 914 6418

Founded:
1971

Organisation type and purpose:
Suitable for ages: 16+.
College of further education.

Subject coverage:
Printing.

Non-library collection catalogue:
All or part available online and in-house

Library catalogue:
All or part available online and in-house

Access to staff:
Contact by letter, by telephone, by fax and by e-mail. Appointment necessary.
Hours: Mon to Thu, 0830 to 1930; Fri, 0830 to 1600
Special comments: Academic term time only.

Access for disabled people:
Parking provided, ramped entry, access to all
public areas, toilet facilities

Associate college of:
Nottingham Trent University

Other addresses:
Charnwood site
  tel: 0115 914 6300; fax: 0115 914 6333

SOUTH OXFORDSHIRE DISTRICT COUNCIL

Acronym or abbreviation: SODC

Benson Lane, Crowmarsh Gifford, Wallingford,
Oxfordshire, OX10 8HQ

Tel: 01491 823000
Fax: 01491 823104

Website:
http://www.southoxon.gov.uk

Enquiries:
Enquiries to: Public Relations Officer
Direct tel: 01491 823748
Direct fax: 01491 823420

Founded:
1974

Organisation type and purpose:
Local government body.

Subject coverage:
Information relating to council issues can be
obtained from the multitude of sources available.

**Museum or gallery collection, archive, or library
special collection:**
Documentation, in general, may be viewed but not
  taken

Printed publications:
Outlook (magazine for all residents of the district)

Access to staff:
Contact by letter, by telephone, by fax, by e-mail
and in person. Appointment necessary.
Hours: Mon to Thu, 0830 to 1700; Fri, 0830 to 1630

Access for disabled people:
Parking provided, level entry, toilet facilities

SOUTH RIBBLE BOROUGH COUNCIL

Civic Centre, West Paddock, Leyland, Lancashire,
PR25 1DH

Tel: 01772 421491
Fax: 01772 622287
E-mail: info@southribble.gov.uk

Website:
http://www.south-ribblebc.gov.uk

Enquiries:
Enquiries to: Public Relations Officer
Direct tel: 01772 625312
Direct e-mail: communications@southribble.gov.uk

Founded:
1974

Organisation type and purpose:
Local government body.

Subject coverage:
Council services and amenities; corporate services,
environmental services, finance, housing, legal
services, personnel services, planning development
and tourism, property and technical services, roads
and transportation, council tax and other
payments.

Printed publications:
Forward (newspaper, quarterly, free to residents)

Access to staff:
Contact by letter, by telephone, by fax and by e-mail
Hours: Mon to Thu, 0830 to 1715; Fri, 0830 to 1645

Access for disabled people:
Parking provided, level entry, access to all public
areas, toilet facilities

SOUTH SHROPSHIRE DISTRICT COUNCIL

Acronym or abbreviation: SSDC

Stone House, Corve Street, Ludlow, Shropshire, SY8 1DG

Tel: 01584 813000
Fax: 01584 813127
E-mail: reception@southshropshire.gov.uk

Website:
http://www.southshropshire.gov.uk/

Enquiries:
Enquiries to: Chief Executive
Direct tel: 01584 813201
Direct fax: 01584 813120
Direct e-mail: gcbiggs_ssdc@btconnect.com

Founded:
1974

Organisation type and purpose:
Local government body.

Access to staff:
Contact by letter, by telephone, by fax, by e-mail, in person and via website
Hours: Mon to Thu, 0840 to 1715; Fri, 0840 to 1630

Access for disabled people:
Parking provided, toilet facilities

SOUTH SOMERSET DISTRICT COUNCIL

Council Offices, Brympton Way, Yeovil, Somerset, BA20 2HT

Tel: 01935 462462
Fax: 01935 462503
E-mail: info@southsomerset.gov.uk

Website:
http://www.southsomerset.gov.uk
500 pages of information about the district, the council and local services and facilities, designed for the local community, businesses and visitors.

Enquiries:
Enquiries to: Communications Manager
Direct tel: 01935 462122

Founded:
1974

Organisation type and purpose:
Local government body.

Subject coverage:
Long distance walking routes in South Somerset, circular walks, cycle routes, horse trails in South Somerset, business premises and opportunities available in South Somerset.

Trade and statistical information:
Statistical information about South Somerset.

Printed publications:
News and Views
Taxing Times
Contact Points

Access to staff:
Contact by letter, by telephone, by fax, by e-mail and in person. Appointment necessary.
Hours: Mon to Fri, 0900 to 1700

SOUTH TYNESIDE COLLEGE – HEBBURN

Acronym or abbreviation: STC

Mill Lane, Hebburn, Tyne and Wear, NE31 2ER

Tel: 0191 427 3614
Fax: 0191 427 3555

Website:
http://www.stc.ac.uk
College website.

Enquiries:
Enquiries to: Assistant Librarian

Founded:
1984

Subject coverage:
Mechanical engineering, health studies, performing arts, welding, automobile engineering, social work, child care, health and safety, management, sports, leisure and tourism.

Museum or gallery collection, archive, or library special collection:
British Standards on CD-ROM
Bound Copies of Hansard 1988–1999

Library catalogue:
All or part available in-house

Access to staff:
Contact by letter, by telephone and by fax
Hours: Mon, Wed, 0900 to 2000; Tue, Thu, 0900 to 1700; Fri, 0900 to 1630

Access for disabled people:
Parking provided, ramped entry

Other Campus at:
South Tyneside College
St Georges Avenue, South Shields, Tyne & Wear, NE34 6ET; tel: 0191 427 3606; fax: 0191 427 3643

SOUTH TYNESIDE COLLEGE – SOUTH SHIELDS

St Georges Avenue, South Shields, Tyne and Wear, NE34 6ET

Tel: 0191 427 3500
Fax: 0191 427 3535
E-mail: margaret.haram@stc.ac.uk

Enquiries:
Enquiries to: Librarian
Direct tel: 0191 427 3605

Organisation type and purpose:
Post-compulsory education, 14–16 provision
College of further and higher education.

Subject coverage:
Sixth form, teacher education, business and professional studies, hairdressing and beauty therapies, health care and early years, nautical studies, marine engineering, general engineering

Library catalogue:
All or part available in-house

Access to staff:
Contact by letter, by telephone and by e-mail
Hours: Term time: Mon to Fri, 0830 to 2000
Vacations: Mon to Fri, 0900 to 1700

Access for disabled people:
Parking provided, ramped entry, level entry, access to all public areas, toilet facilities

SOUTH TYNESIDE LIBRARY

Central Library, Prince George Square, South Shields, Tyne and Wear, NE33 2PE

Tel: 0191 427 1818
Fax: 0191 427 8085
E-mail: reference.library@southtyneside.gov.uk

Website:
http://www.southtyneside.info/
learningandleisure/libraries.asp

Enquiries:
Enquiries to: Libraries Manager
Direct tel: 0191 424 7880
Direct e-mail: mark.freeman@southtyneside.gov.uk

Created by the merger of:
Jarrow, Hebburn, Whitburn, South Shields and Boldon Libraries

Organisation type and purpose:
Local government body, public library.

Subject coverage:
General public library information service, local history of South Tyneside, the Jarrow March, slum clearance, sailing ships, shipbuilding.

Museum or gallery collection, archive, or library special collection:
Jarrow March Collection
Kelly Collection; posters from a South Shields jobbing printer c.1790 to c.1880
Manuscripts and local history: Fox, Wallis and Flagg collections
Photograph collections of South Shields: Willetts, Flagg, Parry, Grimes, Cleet, Peterson and Shields Gazette

Library catalogue:
All or part available online

Printed publications:
Various publications including:
A Victorian Village School: Mr Grundy at Whitburn (S. Reeder, £2.95)
History of Hebburn 1894–1994 (£2.25)
Notes on the History of Shipbuilding in South Shields 1746–1946 (A. C. Flagg, £5.50)
Preservation of Life from Shipwreck: Trilogy on the history of the lifeboat (B. Whitaker, 3 vols, £5.50 each)
South Shields Then and Now (£3.50)
The Borough of South Shields (G. Hodgson, £27 incl. p&p, out of print)
Order printed publications from: Information and Education Co-ordinator, at the same address; tel. 0191 424 7865; fax 0191 455 8085; e-mail hildred .whale@s-tyneside-mbc.gov.uk

Publications list:
Available in print

Access to staff:
Contact by letter, by telephone, by fax, by e-mail, in person and via website
Hours: Mon to Thu, 0900 to 1900; Fri, 0900 to 1700; Sat, 0900 to 1600

Member organisation of:
MLA (NE)

SOUTH WARWICKSHIRE EDUCATION CENTRE

Education Centre Library, John Turner Building, Warwick Hospital, Lakin Road, Warwick, CV34 5BW

Tel: 01926 495321 ext 4287
Fax: 01926 400895
E-mail: veronica.mitchell@swarkhosp-tr.wmids.nhs .uk

Website:
http://www.swec.org.uk

Enquiries:
Enquiries to: Medical Librarian

Organisation type and purpose:
Hospital.

Subject coverage:
Medicine and related disciplines.

Library catalogue:
All or part available in-house

Access to staff:
Contact by letter, by telephone, by fax, by e-mail and via website. Appointment necessary.
Hours: Mon, Wed, 0900 to 1700; Tue, Thu, 0900 to 2000; Fri, 0900 to 1630

Access to building, collection or gallery:
Prior appointment required

Access for disabled people:
Parking provided, level entry, access to all public areas, toilet facilities

SOUTH WEST COAST PATH ASSOCIATION

Acronym or abbreviation: SWCPA

Bowker House, Lee Mill Bridge, Ivybridge, Devon, PL21 9EF

Tel: 01752 896237
Fax: 01752 893654
E-mail: info@swcp.org.uk

Website:
http://www.swcp.org.uk
Photo tour of South West Coast Path, Association history, Association literature, latest news of the Coast Path.

Enquiries:
Enquiries to: Honorary Secretary

Founded:
1973

Organisation type and purpose:
Advisory body, membership association (membership is by subscription), present number of members: 5,000, voluntary organisation, registered charity (charity number 266754). To promote interest in, and the use of, the coast path. To improve standards of waymaking and maintenance.

Subject coverage:
The 630 miles of the South West Coast Path, from Minehead to Poole Harbour via Land's End.

Museum or gallery collection, archive, or library special collection:
8,000 Colour slides of coastal scenery along 630 miles of coast path
Digital archive of 4,000 images of the South West Coast Path

Printed publications:
Annual Guide (£8.00 plus £2 p&p to a UK address, free to members; £3.50 p&p to non-UK)
55 Path Description leaflets of short sections (£1 each inc. p&p)

Publications list:
Available online and in print

Access to staff:
Contact by letter, by telephone, by fax, by e-mail, in person and via website. Appointment necessary.
Hours: Any reasonable time

Access to building, collection or gallery:
No prior appointment required
Hours: Mon to Fri, 0900 to 1300

Access for disabled people:
Yes

SOUTH WESTERN REGIONAL LIBRARY SERVICE

Acronym or abbreviation: SWRLS

c/o Library Headquarters, Ridgewood Centre, 244 Station Road, Yate, South Gloucestershire, BS37 4AF

Tel: 01454 865782
Fax: 01454 863309
E-mail: martin.burton@southglos.gov.uk

Website:
http://www.swrls.org.uk

Enquiries:
Enquiries to: Director
Direct tel: 07504 047625
Direct e-mail: desk2@csndesk.eclipse.co.uk

Founded:
1937

Organisation type and purpose:
Charity aimed at developing library co-operation across the South West of England
Regional library system.

Subject coverage:
General; co-operative library service providing access to material held by members.

Printed publications:
Annual Report

Access to staff:
Contact by e-mail

SOUTHAMPTON AND FAREHAM CHAMBER OF COMMERCE AND INDUSTRY

Bugle House, 53 Bugle Street, Southampton, SO14 2LF

Tel: 023 8022 3541
Fax: 023 8022 7426
E-mail: info@soton-chamber.co.uk

Website:
http://www.soton-chamber.co.uk

Enquiries:
Enquiries to: Information Officer

Founded:
1851

Organisation type and purpose:
Membership association (membership is by subscription), present number of members: 1,500. Chamber of Commerce.

Subject coverage:
Business enquiries, business training, events and seminars, export documentation and advice, French desk, China desk, lobbying/representation.

Museum or gallery collection, archive, or library special collection:
Business directories
Reference books

Printed publications:
Membership directory (yearly)
Gateway (journal, monthly)
Business South Magazine (incorporating Chamber of Commerce News Pages (publ Echo Newspaper))

Access to staff:
Contact by letter, by telephone, by fax, by e-mail, in person and via website. Appointment necessary. Access for members only. Non-members charged.
Hours: Mon to Fri, 0900 to 1700

Access to building, collection or gallery:
No prior appointment required

SOUTHAMPTON CITY ARCHIVES OFFICE

Civic Centre, Southampton, SO14 7LY

Tel: 023 8083 2251
Fax: 023 8083 2156
E-mail: city.archives@southampton.gov.uk

Enquiries:
Enquiries to: Archivist

Founded:
1953

Organisation type and purpose:
Local government body.

Subject coverage:
Southampton records date from 1199, family and local history.

Museum or gallery collection, archive, or library special collection:
Maritime records: crew lists, 1863–1913; Central Index of Merchant Seamen, 1918–1941
Business records: many local firms' records are held
Family records: Southampton Parish Records, 1552 to date
Local government – the Council and its predecessors including the harbour and records of justice

Non-library collection catalogue:
All or part available in-house

Printed publications:
Many guides, histories and maps including:
Information leaflet
Southampton Papers Nos 1–10
Southampton Records 1: A Guide to the Records of Southampton Corporation and Absorbed Authorities (1964, £1)

Sources for Family History in Southampton Archives Office with map showing parish boundaries (£3)
Town Directory – Southampton in 1620 and the Mayflower
Southampton Crew Lists 1863–1913 (printed on request)
Archives Teaching Pack Southampton in the Second World War (£15, to schools £12)
Set of maps of different dates showing the historical development of the city 1611 to 1802 (£3)

Publications list:
Available in print

Access to staff:
Contact by letter, by telephone, by fax, by e-mail, in person and via website
Hours: Tue to Fri, 0930 to 1630
Special comments: One late evening each month, by prior appointment, contact office staff for details. Member of CARN system.

Access for disabled people:
Parking provided, level entry, toilet facilities

SOUTHAMPTON CITY COUNCIL

Civic Centre, Southampton, SO14 7LY

Tel: 023 8022 3855\ Minicom no. 023 8083 2798
Fax: 023 8023 4537
E-mail: webmaster@southampton.gov.uk

Website:
http://www.southampton.gov.uk
Website for Southampton, covering all aspects of the city.

Enquiries:
Direct fax: 023 8023 4527
Other contacts: Head of Marketing and Information Division for head of information services.

Organisation type and purpose:
Local government body.

Subject coverage:
All information about Southampton, its services and amenities, history, heritage, highways, leisure, events, local housing, social services, education, libraries etc.

Museum or gallery collection, archive, or library special collection:
Art gallery
Large variety of accessible information (on request)
Library service including reference

Trade and statistical information:
Electoral register, grant schemes in the local area, local business, tourism and historic information, general city information.

Printed publications:
Annual Report (free)
Southampton City News (6 times a year, free)
Southampton Commercial and Industrial Property Register (6 times a year, free)
Wide variety of leaflets and brochures

Electronic and video publications:
Electoral register (on disk, available for purchase)

Access to staff:
Contact by letter, by telephone, by fax, by e-mail and via website
Hours: Mon to Fri, 0900 to 1700
Special comments: 24-hour emergency hotline 01703 233344.

Also:
Education Services
4th Floor, Frobisher House, Commercial Road, Southampton; tel: 023 8083 2771
Valuation and Estates Services
Marlands House, Civic Centre Road, Southampton, SO14 7PR; tel: 023 8083 2879

SOUTHAMPTON CITY COUNCIL – CULTURAL SERVICES

Civic Centre, Southampton, SO14 7LP

Tel: 023 8022 3855
Fax: 023 8033 7593
E-mail: s.dawtry@southampton.gov.uk

Website:
http://www.southampton.gov.uk/leisure
http://www.southampton.gov.uk
Services provided by the council, leisure services in the city, etc.

Enquiries:
Enquiries to: Manager
Direct tel: 023 8083 2768
Direct e-mail: s.harrington@southampton.gov.uk

Founded:
1912

Organisation type and purpose:
Local government body.

Subject coverage:
Archaeology, particularly British and North European; fine art, particularly 20th century; maritime history; Southampton local history.

Museum or gallery collection, archive, or library special collection:
Buchanan Collection (needlework tools and accessories)
Chipperfield Bequest
Hull-Grundy Gift (jewellery)
Jeffress Bequest
Sandell Collection (miscellaneous)
Smith Bequest
Various local history collections

Non-library collection catalogue:
All or part available in-house

Printed publications:
Various publications on: aspects of the Art Gallery, archaeology, social history (oral and maritime)

Publications list:
Available in print

Access to staff:
Contact by letter, by telephone, by fax, by e-mail and via website. Appointment necessary.
Hours: Mon to Fri, 0900 to 1700

SOUTHAMPTON CITY COUNCIL – HERITAGE ARTS AND ENTERTAINMENT MANAGEMENT

Civic Centre, Southampton, SO14 7LP

Museums and Galleries:
God's House Tower Archaeology Museum
Hawthorns Urban Wildlife Centre
John Hamsard Gallery
 The University, Southampton, SO9 5NH
Southampton City Art Gallery
Southampton Hall of Aviation
Southampton Maritime Museum
Tudor House Museum

SOUTHAMPTON CITY COUNCIL – LIBRARIES

Southampton Central Library, Civic Centre, Southampton, SO14 7LW

Tel: 023 8083 2462
Fax: 023 8033 6305
E-mail: reference.library@southampton.gov.uk

Website:
http://www.southampton.gov.uk/libraries

Enquiries:
Enquiries to: Libraries Manager
Direct tel: 023 8083 2219
Other contacts: Local Studies and Maritime Librarian, Business Librarian

Founded:
1889

Organisation type and purpose:
Local government body, public library.

Subject coverage:
General public library with a reference stock of over 100,000 items; specialisations are: UK and international commerce, shipping (especially ocean liners) and marine transport, nautical almanacs and chronology, standards and specifications, genealogy, Hampshire studies, business and commercial information, British and foreign trade directories, statistics, British Government publications, art monographs, European Union, information, law reports, English history, careers and education, community information.

Museum or gallery collection, archive, or library special collection:
Bowen collection (maritime)
British Government publications
British Standards
European Union (European Public Information Centre)
Hampshire Collection (particularly Southampton)
Maritime Collection (including a collection on the Titanic disaster and ocean-going liners)
Pitt collection (17th- and 18th-century scientific books: restricted access)

Library catalogue:
All or part available online

Printed publications:
Catalogue of the Pitt Collection
Genealogical Sources (1989)
Saints: the glory games (2005)
Shirley: Nuisances and Services (2002)
Southampton Ships (1978)
Titanic Victims and Survivors (2002)
Titanic Voices (2007)
Various leaflets describing collections

Electronic and video publications:
Plimsoll: photographs of Southampton's history (for purchase online)
Southampton Area Census 1871 (CD-ROM, 2003)

Publications list:
Available in print

Access to staff:
Contact by letter, by telephone, by fax, by e-mail, in person and via website
Hours: Mon to Fri, 0930 to 1900; Sat, 0930 to 1600

Constituent bodies:
Level 1 European Public Information Centre
 tel: 023 8083 2958
Southern Area European Information Centre
 tel: 023 8083 2866

Parent body:
Southampton City Council

SOUTHAMPTON SOLENT UNIVERSITY

Acronym or abbreviation: SSU

East Park Terrace, Southampton, SO14 0RJ

Tel: 023 8031 9000
Fax: 023 8022 2259

Website:
http://www.solent.ac.uk/library
Southampton Solent University home page.
http://www.solent.ac.uk
Information on the university, library and sources of information.

Enquiries:
Enquiries to: Deputy University Librarian
Direct tel: 023 8031 9248
Direct e-mail: enquiries@solent.ac.uk

Founded:
1964

Formerly called:
Southampton Institute

Organisation type and purpose:
University department.

Subject coverage:
Accountancy, business studies, e-commerce, law, management, computing, information systems, CAD/CAM, naval architecture, yacht and boat design, condition monitoring, electronics, construction, graphic design, fashion, maritime studies, leisure management, fine art, media communications, film studies.

Museum or gallery collection, archive, or library special collection:
Multimedia collection (video cassettes/DVDs, audio tapes)
Godden collection (antiques and fine art periodicals and sale catalogues)
Ken Russell Collection (film)
Maritime History collection, including Captain Cooper's Letters and Reports, 1922–56
Slide collection (Art & Design)

Library catalogue:
All or part available online

Printed publications:
Yacht and Boat Design: select list of references (irregular)

Access to staff:
Contact by letter, by telephone, by fax, by e-mail, in person and via website
Hours: Term time: Mon to Thu, 0830 to 2100; Fri, 0830 to 1900; Sat, Sun, 1000 to 1700

Access to building, collection or gallery:
Mountbatten Library, East Park Terrace
Hours: Term time: Mon to Thu, 0830 to 2345; Fri, 0830 to 1900; Sat, Sun, 1000 to 1700

Access for disabled people:
Level entry, access to all public areas, toilet facilities

Branch libraries:
Warsash Library
 Newtown Road, Warsash, Southampton, SO31 9ZL; tel: 01489 576161; fax: 01489 573988

Member organisation of:
Hatrics Southern Information Network
 81 North Walls, Winchester, SO23 8BY; tel: 01962 826650; fax: 01962 826615; e-mail: hatricshq@hants.gov.uk; website: www.hants.gov.uk?hatrics/index.html

SOUTHBROOK COMMUNITY MENTAL HEALTH TEAM

Acronym or abbreviation: SCMHT

1 Southbrook Road, London, SE12 8LH

Tel: 020 8318 1330
Fax: 020 8297 1448

Enquiries:
Enquiries to: Manager

Founded:
1978

Organisation type and purpose:
Community Mental Health Team.
Provides support and advice for clients with mental health problems who live within the catchment area of Central and East Lewisham.

Subject coverage:
Mental health.

Access to staff:
Contact by letter, by telephone and in person
Hours: Mon to Fri, 0900 to 1700
Special comments: Residents of Central and East Lewisham only.

Access for disabled people:
Ramped entry, level entry, toilet facilities

Parent body:
Lewisham Social Care and Health
South London and Maudsley NHS/MH Trust

SOUTHEND-ON-SEA BOROUGH LIBRARIES

Southend Library, Victoria Avenue, Southend-on-Sea, Essex, SS2 6EX

Tel: 01702 215011
Fax: 01702 469241
E-mail: library@southend.gov.uk

Website:
http://www.southend.gov.uk/libraries

Enquiries:
Enquiries to: Libraries Services Manager

Organisation type and purpose:
Local government body, public library.

Subject coverage:
Large general library.

Services for disabled people:
Induction loops, magnifying aids, home library service & RNIB talking books.

Museum or gallery collection, archive, or library special collection:
Focal point photographic gallery
Specialist collections for local history

Library catalogue:
All or part available online

Access for disabled people:
Parking provided, level entry, access to all public areas, toilet facilities

Links with:
Essex County Libraries
Thurrock Borough Council library services

SOUTHERN AFRICA BUSINESS ASSOCIATION

Acronym or abbreviation: SABA

Queensland House, 393 Strand, London, WC2R 0JQ

Tel: 020 7836 9980
Fax: 020 7836 6001
E-mail: info@waba.co.uk

Website:
http://www.saba.co.uk
Information about SABA, links to some members' websites.

Enquiries:
Enquiries to: Membership Secretary

Founded:
1995

Organisation type and purpose:
Trade association (membership is by subscription), present number of members: over 130.
To promote investment into the Southern African region and trade within the region.

Subject coverage:
Information on investment effectiveness in the countries of the region: South Africa, Zimbabwe, Mozambique, Zambia, Botswana, Namibia, Malawi, Swaziland, Angola, Lesotho.
General information about the political and economic situation and prospects in each country, investment required, trade agreements.

Printed publications:
Confidential Bulletin (monthly, for members only)
Country Profiles (twice a year)

Publications list:
Available in print

Access to staff:
Contact by letter, by telephone, by fax, by e-mail and via website. Appointment necessary. Non-members charged.
Hours: Mon to Fri, 1000 to 1600

Access to building, collection or gallery:
Prior appointment required

Access for disabled people:
Level entry

SOUTHERN AND SOUTH EAST ENGLAND TOURIST BOARD

Acronym or abbreviation: STB

40 Chamberlayne Road, Eastleigh, Hampshire, SO50 5JH

Tel: 023 8062 5400
Fax: 023 8062 0010
E-mail: info@tourismse.com

Website:
http://www.tourismsoutheast.com

Enquiries:
Enquiries to: Managing Director

Founded:
1977

Organisation type and purpose:
Membership association (membership is by subscription), present number of members: 1,600, service industry.
Promotion and development of tourism.

Subject coverage:
Tourism.

Printed publications:
A wide variety of publications aimed at providing information and advice on tourism in the South East of England

Access to staff:
Contact by letter, by telephone, by fax and by e-mail
Hours: Mon to Thu, 0830 to 1700; Fri, 0830 to 1630

SOUTHERN AREA HOSPICE SERVICES

St John's House, Courtenay Hill, Newry, Co. Down, BT34 2EB

Tel: 028 3026 7711
Fax: 028 3026 8492
E-mail: info@southernareahospiceservices.org

Website:
http://www.southernareahospiceservices.org
The hospice and its services.

Founded:
1989

Organisation type and purpose:
Registered charity (charity number XN47329/2). Provides specialist care for patients affected by cancer, multiple sclerosis, motor neurone disease and other terminal illnesses. Care is provided, without cost, to patients and their families from across the Southern Health Board Area (Northern Ireland). The Hospice provides a holistic approach to care, responding to the physical, psychological and spiritual needs of patients, their relatives and carers. Care is provided by a team of highly trained medics and professionals both at the Hospice and in the community through a wide range of services.

Subject coverage:
Services include: 12-bedded in-patient unit; out-patients clinics; home-care visits; day-hospice unit providing respite for families and carers as well as providing complementary therapies and important social interaction for patients; complementary therapies including physiotherapy, reflexology, hand massage and relaxation techniques for both inpatients and day-care patients; emotional and practical support from social workers for the patient and families, providing advice on benefit entitlements, securing care packages for patients after discharge, and offering patient and family counselling; bereavement counselling to families and carers; chaplaincy service providing spiritual support and counselling to the patient and families; patient helpline; (Donaldson Centre) advice and support to patients and their families at early stages of diagnosis of a terminal illness.

Information services:
Patient helpline, tel: 028 3026 7711 – a patient or relative can phone the Hospice at any time to speak with the nurse in charge, regarding any queries they may have.

Electronic and video publications:
Leaflets:
Your Hospice, Patient Information
Your Hospice, Out-Patient Clinics
Your Hospice, Day Hospice
Your Hospice, Southern Area Hospice Services
Your Hospice, Community Liaison Sister
Your Hospice, Social Work Services
Your Hospice, Bereavement Counselling Services
Your Hospice, Chaplaincy Support Services
Order electronic and video publications from:
Download from website

Access to staff:
Contact by letter, by telephone and by e-mail
Hours: Helpline: any time
Social Work Dept: Mon to Fri, 0830 to 1630
Donaldson Centre: appointments, Mon to Fri, 1000 to1500; drop-ins, Tue, 2000 to 2100; Wed, 1100 to 1200; Thu, 1500 to 1600

SOUTHERN BRICK FEDERATION LIMITED

Brick Development Association, 26 Store Street, London, WC1E 7BT

Tel: 020 7323 7030
Fax: 020 7580 3795
E-mail: brick@brick.org.uk

Enquiries:
Enquiries to: Secretary

Founded:
1970

Organisation type and purpose:
Trade association.

Subject coverage:
Clay brickmakers in the South of England.

Access to staff:
Contact by letter, by telephone, by fax and by e-mail
Hours: Mon to Fri, 0900 to 1700

Links with:
Brick Development Association
   tel: 020 7323 7030; fax: 020 7580 3795; e-mail: brick@brick.org.uk
British Ceramic Confederation
   tel: 01782 744631; fax: 01782 744102; e-mail: bcc@ceramfed.co.uk
British Ceramic Research Limited
   tel: 01782 746476; fax: 01782 412331; e-mail: info@ceram.co.uk

SOUTHERN EDUCATION AND LIBRARY BOARD

Acronym or abbreviation: SELB

Library Headquarters, 1 Markethill Road, Armagh, BT60 1NR

Tel: 028 3752 5353
Fax: 028 3752 6879

Website:
http://www.selb.org
Address and opening hours of branch libraries, staff listing.

Enquiries:
Enquiries to: Chief Librarian
Direct tel: 028 3752 0702

Founded:
1974

Organisation type and purpose:
Local government body, public library.
Schools library service.

Subject coverage:
General, local history, Irish studies.

continued overleaf

Museum or gallery collection, archive, or library special collection:
Crosslé Collection of manuscripts of local Newry families
Irish and local studies collection
Irish folk music record collection

Printed publications:
Annual Report
Bibliographies of Resources available for Northern Ireland Curriculum for Primary Schools
Catalogue of 16mm films (irregular)
Catalogue of video cassettes for education and general interest (yearly)
Public Service Information Bulletin (in collaboration with the other 4 Education and Library Boards) (monthly)
Selected list of recent publications for post-primary schools

Access to staff:
Contact by letter, by telephone, by fax and in person
Hours: Mon to Fri, 0900 to 1700

Access for disabled people:
Parking provided, level entry, access to all public areas, toilet facilities

SOUTHERN WATER

Southern House, Yeoman Road, Worthing, West Sussex, BN13 3NX

Tel: 01903 264444
Fax: 01903 691435

Website:
http://www.southernwater.co.uk
News desk, making water work, providing a quality service, caring for the environment, becoming WaterWise, Water Wise gardening, Bewl Water reservoir.

Enquiries:
Enquiries to: Head of Communications

Organisation type and purpose:
Service industry.

Subject coverage:
Water supply, sewerage services.

Access to staff:
Contact by letter and by fax
Hours: Mon to Fri, 0900 to 1700

Has links with:
Scottish Power

SOUTHGATE COLLEGE

Library and Learning Resources Service, High Street, Southgate, London, N14 6BS

Tel: 020 8982 5123
Fax: 020 8982 5118

Website:
http://www.southgate.ac.uk
Information about the college and its services.

Enquiries:
Enquiries to: Library & Learning Resources Manager
Other contacts: Learning Resources Co-ordinators

Founded:
1963

Organisation type and purpose:
Suitable for ages: 16+.
General further education.

Subject coverage:
General and vocational, including: business, catering, clothing, design, engineering, health and social care, leisure.

Library catalogue:
All or part available in-house

Access to staff:
Contact by letter, by telephone and by e-mail
Hours: Term time only, Mon to Thu, 0900 to 2000; Fri, 0900 to 1630

Special comments: Reference use, for print materials only.

Access to building, collection or gallery:
Prior appointment required

Access for disabled people:
Parking provided, level entry

SOUTHWARK LIBRARY AND INFORMATION SERVICES

15 Spa Road, Bermondsey, London, SE16 3QW

Tel: 020 7525 3920 or 3716/7
Fax: 020 7525 1505
E-mail: adrian.olsen@southwark.gov.uk

Enquiries:
Enquiries to: Librarian
Direct tel: 020 7525 1577
Other contacts: Libraries Development Manager

Founded:
1800s

Organisation type and purpose:
Local government body, public library.

Subject coverage:
General, modern fiction in Swedish, Norwegian and Finnish; local studies; computers and data processing.

Museum or gallery collection, archive, or library special collection:
Greater London Audio Specialisation Scheme (mainly black disc): composers, Berlioz and Messaien; jazz artists, JOO-LED; music minus 1; folk music of SE Asia (at Spa Road)
Joint fiction reserves (English, including play sets by authors whose surnames come within the ranges BAJ-BEL (BOS-CAP and RDA-SHV up to and including 1987 only)) (at Spa Road)
Local history and archives collection relating to the London Borough of Southwark (including civil but not parish records)
Local Studies Library (at John Harvard Library, Borough High Street)
London Special Collection Dewey Nos. 000–009 (at Newington Library)
Mother tongue collection – Bengali, Hindi, Punjabi, Gujerati, Urdu, Chinese, Turkish, Greek, Vietnamese (based at various libraries)
Swedish, Norwegian and Finnish fiction (at Rotherhithe Library)

Library catalogue:
All or part available online and in-house

Printed publications:
Histories of particular areas or aspects of the Borough (irregular)
Occasional specialist booklists (irregular)
Reprinted Ordnance Survey maps of Southwark
Order printed publications from: Local Studies Librarian, London Borough of Southwark
Local Studies Library, 211 Borough High Street, London, SE1 1JA, tel: 020 7403 3507, fax: 020 7403 8633

Access to staff:
Contact by letter, by telephone, by fax and by e-mail. Appointment necessary.
Hours: Mon to Fri, 0900 to 1700

Parent body:
Southwark Environment and Leisure Department Chatelaine House, 186 Walworth Road, London SE17 1JJ; tel: 020 7525 5000

SOUTHWARK LOCAL HISTORY LIBRARY

211 Borough High Street, London, SE1 1JA

Tel: 020 7525 0232
E-mail: local.history.library@southwark.gov.uk

Website:
http://www.southwark.gov.uk/info/200161/local_history_library

Organisation type and purpose:
Local government body, public library.
Local history library and archive for London Borough of Southwark area.

Subject coverage:
Local history and current affairs of London Borough of Southwark area. Includes extensive sources of interest to family historians with ancestors from the area and the archives of local authorities previous to the present London Borough of Southwark and of other organisations, institutions and individuals.

Museum or gallery collection, archive, or library special collection:
The Library Collection includes: printed published books, periodicals, illustrations, maps, cuttings and ephemera, sound recordings, videos
The Archives comprise: the official records of the London Borough of Southwark and its predecessors, the metropolitan boroughs and vestries, and unofficial deposited records of local organisations, institutions, businesses and individuals

Library catalogue:
All or part available online and in print

Printed publications:
Guide to the Archives in Southwark Local Studies Library (Humphrey S)
London Borough of Southwark's Neighbourhood Histories (illustrated pocket histories of the communities within the London Borough of Southwark):
The story of Bermondsey (covers the parishes of St Olaves, St John Horselydown and St Mary, Bermondsey) (Boast M)
The story of Camberwell (Boast M)
The story of Dulwich (Boast M)
The story of Peckham and Nunhead (Beasley J)
The story of Rotherhithe (Humphrey S)
The story of Walworth (covers the parish of St Mary, Newington, the Elephant & Castle and the Old Kent Road) (Boast M)
The story of the Borough (covers the parish of St George the Martyr, Trinity Newington and Borough High Street) (Boast M)
The story of Bankside (covers the parish of St Saviour, Christ Church and part of St George Martyr) (Reilly L and Marshall G)
Southwark; an illustrated history (an overview of Southwark's history, lavishly illustrated with over 100 views) (Reilly L)
Family history in Southwark (a concise introduction to tracing Southwark ancestors) (Reilly L)
Below Southwark (46-page booklet, showing the story of Southwark revealed by excavations over the last 30 years) (Cowan C)
Several others, please apply for prices and postage

Publications list:
Available online and in print

Access to staff:
Contact by letter, by telephone, by e-mail and in person
Hours: Mon and Thu, 10:00 to 19:00; Tue and Fri, 10:00 to 17:00; Sat, 10:00 to 15:00; Wed and Sun, closed

Access to building, collection or gallery:
No prior appointment required

Access for disabled people:
Level entry, access to all public areas, toilet facilities

SOUTHWELL MINSTER LIBRARY

Formal name: Southwell Minster Historic Chapter Library and Theological Library

The Minster Office, Church Street, Southwell, Nottinghamshire, NG25 0HD

Tel: 01636 812649
E-mail: library@southwellminster.org.uk; user274598@aol.com

Enquiries:
Enquiries to: Honorary Librarians (Historic or Theological Library)

Organisation type and purpose:
Cathedral libraries.

Subject coverage:
Genealogy, Bishop's transcripts and marriage licences for Nottinghamshire, theology, history, music, Southwell Minster, its history and archives, biblical studies.

Non-library collection catalogue:
All or part available online

Library catalogue:
All or part available online

Access to staff:
Contact by letter, by telephone and by e-mail.
Appointment necessary.
Hours: Mon to Fri, 0900 to 1700

Access to building, collection or gallery:
Hours: Variable

SPA BUSINESS ASSOCIATION

Acronym or abbreviation: SpaBA

c/o Pennyhill Park Hotel, London Road, Bagshot, Surrey, GU19 5EU

Tel: 01276 478647
Fax: 01276 478635
E-mail: info@spabusinessassociation.co.uk

Website:
http://www.spabusinessassociation.co.uk
UK and Irish Spas and spa-related businesses, links to individual members' sites.

Enquiries:
Enquiries to: General Secretary
Other contacts: Chair, Medical Advisory Committee

Founded:
2004

Organisation type and purpose:
Advisory body, trade association (membership is by subscription), present number of members: 120, training organisation, consultancy, research organisation.
Promotion of businesses in the spa sector, and of the benefits of using spas for health and wellbeing.

Subject coverage:
Spas in the UK and Ireland. Spa Heritage and Tourism. Networking meetings for members and non-members. Quality Standards in spas and promotional campaigns for members.

Printed publications:
Full range of advisory services on Spa regeneration
Glossary of European Spa Terminology
Newsletter
e-newsletter (monthly)

Access to staff:
Contact by letter, by telephone, by fax, by e-mail and via website
Hours: Mon to Fri, 0900 to 1700

Affiliated to:
European Spas Association
1, Avenue de la Renaissance, 1000 Bruxelles, Belgium; tel: +32 2733 2661

SPANISH EMBASSY COMMERCIAL OFFICE

66 Chiltern Street, London, W1M 1PR

Tel: 020 7467 2330
Fax: 020 7487 5586
E-mail: buzon.oficial@londres.ofcomes.mcx.es

Website:
http://www.mcx.es/londres

Enquiries:
Enquiries to: Information Officer

Organisation type and purpose:
National government body.

Embassy department.

Subject coverage:
General information on Spain: commercial or investment, specific department promoting export into Spain, foods and wines from Spain, consumer goods, industrial products and services.

Trade and statistical information:
General statistical information on trade and investment to and from Spain.

Printed publications:
Information material (booklets, brochures, list of companies etc, available by letter, fax or email to the Information Officer)

Access to staff:
Contact by letter, by telephone, by fax, by e-mail and via website
Hours: Mon to Thu, 0900 to 1700; Fri, 0900 to 1500
Special comments: Requests in writing.

Access to building, collection or gallery:
No access other than to staff

Access for disabled people:
Access to all public areas

Connections with:
ICEX
PO Castellana 14–16, 28046 Madrid; tel: 00 34 91 349 3500; fax: 00 34 91 431 6128; website: http://www.icex.es

Parent body:
Spanish Embassy
39 Chesham Place, London, SW1X 8SB; tel: 020 7235 5555; fax: 020 7259 5392; e-mail: embespuk@mail.mae.es

SPANISH TOURIST OFFICE

Acronym or abbreviation: OET

22–23 Manchester Square, London, W1U 3PX

Tel: 020 7486 8077
Fax: 020 7486 8034
E-mail: info.londres@tourspain.es

Website:
http://www.colarioja.es
Regional website for La Rioja.
http://www.comadrid.es
Regional website for Madrid.
http://www.murcia-turismo.es
Regional website for Murcia.
http://www.Tourspain.co.uk
Spanish Tourist Office website.
http://www.andalucia.org
Regional website for Andalucia.
http://www.turismo.cantabria.es
Regional website for Cantabria.
http://www.jccm.es
Regional website for Castilla – La Mancha.
http://www.jcyl.es
Regional website for Castilla Y León.
http://www.gencat.es
Regional website for Cataluña.
http://www.staragon.com
Regional website for Aragon.
http://www.srt.es
Regional website for Asturias.
http://www.caib.es
Regional website for Baleares.
http://www.gobcan.es
Regional website for Canarias.
http://www.juntaex.es
Regional website for Extremadura.
http://www.estancias.es
Accommodation at Spanish historic establishments.
http://www.Tourspain.es
Up-to-date information on Turespaña.
http://www.mcu.es
Cultural events.
http://www.cybermundi.es/vanatur
Rural tourism accommodation.
http://www.ciudad-ceuta.com
Regional website for Ceuta.
http://www.melilla500.com
Regional website for Melilla.

http://www.tourgalicia.es
Regional website for Galicia.
http://www.cfnavarra.es
Regional website for Navarra.
http://www.euskadi.net
Regional website for País Vasco.
http://www.gua.es
Regional website for Comunidad Valenciana.

Enquiries:
Enquiries to: Information Officer

Organisation type and purpose:
National government body.
Tourist information office.

Subject coverage:
Tourist information about Spain.

Museum or gallery collection, archive, or library special collection:
Photographs and slides

Printed publications:
Tourist leaflets on Spanish regions

Electronic and video publications:
Videos on tourist resorts and tourist-related matters

Access to staff:
Contact by letter, by telephone, by fax, by e-mail, in person and via website
Hours: Mon to Fri, 0915 to 1615

Parent body:
Turespaña
José Lazaro Galdiano 6, 28036 Madrid, Spain; tel: 00 34 91 343 3500

SPARTAN OWNERS' CLUB

Acronym or abbreviation: SOC

28 Ashford Drive, Ravenshead, Nottingham, NG15 9DE

Tel: 01623 409351
Fax: 01623 409352

Website:
http://www.spartan-oc.demon.co.uk

Enquiries:
Enquiries to: Secretary

Founded:
1978

Organisation type and purpose:
Membership association (membership is by subscription), present number of members: 350–400, suitable for ages: 17+.
To bring together owners, builders and enthusiasts of the Spartan car.

Subject coverage:
All aspects of the Spartan kit car.

Printed publications:
Spartacus (journal, quarterly, members)

Access to staff:
Contact by letter, by telephone, by fax and via website
Special comments: Telephone between 1800 and 2000 only.

SPEAKABILITY

Formal name: Action for Dysphasic Adults

1 Royal Street, London, SE1 7LL

Tel: 020 7261 9572 (Administration)
Fax: 020 7928 9542
E-mail: speakability@speakability.org.uk

Website:
http://www.speakability.org.uk

Enquiries:
Enquiries to: Chief Executive

Founded:
1979

continued overleaf

Organisation type and purpose:
National organisation, voluntary organisation, registered charity (charity number 295094). Supporting people with aphasia/dysphasia and their carers and friends, through its information service and national network of groups; influencing individuals and organisations in order to improve services for people with aphasia.

Subject coverage:
Dysphasia/Aphasia, speech and language problems after stroke, head injury or neurological condition.

Museum or gallery collection, archive, or library special collection:
Database of information for people with Aphasia, carers and professionals

Printed publications:
Books, posters, leaflets, factsheets, charter for people with Aphasia
Lost for Words – an introductory booklet
Speaking Up – twice yearly newsletter
Workbook for Carers (Dr Marshall J, Carlson E, Moir D)

Electronic and video publications:
Tapes, teaching pack (including DVD and slides) for medical professionals (written by professionals)
Speaking Up About Aphasia (DVD, presented by Andrew Marr, the BBC's Chief Political Editor)

Publications list:
Available in print

Access to staff:
Contact by letter, by telephone, by fax, by e-mail and via website
Hours: Free Helpline: 080 8808 9572 Mon to Fri, 1000 to 1600
24-hour answerphone

Has:
national network of support groups

Links with:
Association of Speech & Language Therapists
British Aphasiology Society (BAS)

SPECIAL EDUCATION CONSORTIUM

8 Wakely Street, London, EC1V 7QE

Tel: 020 7843 6334; 020 7843 6060
Fax: 020 7843 6313
E-mail: cdc@ncb.org.uk

Enquiries:
Enquiries to: SEC Co-ordinator

Organisation type and purpose:
Advisory body, voluntary organisation, registered charity (charity number 258825).
To protect and promote the interests of disabled children and children with special educational needs during the passage of legislation that may affect them.

Subject coverage:
Special educational needs and disability – policy, practice and legislation in this field.

Access to staff:
Contact by letter, by telephone, by fax and by e-mail
Hours: Mon to Fri, 0900 to 1700

Access to building, collection or gallery:
Prior appointment required

Access for disabled people:
Ramped entry, level entry, toilet facilities

Registered under the auspices of:
The Council for Disabled Children
at The National Children's Bureau

SPECIAL EDUCATIONAL NEEDS TRIBUNAL

Acronym or abbreviation: SENT

50 Victoria Street, London, SW1H 0NW

Tel: 020 7925 6902
Fax: 020 7926 6926
E-mail: tribunalqueries@sent.gsi.gov.uk

Website:
http://www.sentribunal.gov.uk
How to appeal and other guidance for parties.

Enquiries:
Enquiries to: Secretary

Founded:
1994

Organisation type and purpose:
Statutory body.

Subject coverage:
Appeals by parents against local decisions about children's special educational needs.

Trade and statistical information:
Volume of SEN appeals by type, nature of SEN and local authority area.

Printed publications:
How to Appeal (booklet)
Annual Reports
Order printed publications from: DfES Publications Centre, Special Educational Needs Tribunal PO Box 5050, Sherwood Park, Annersley, Nottingham, NG15 0DJ, tel: 0845 602 2260, fax: 0845 603 3360, e-mail: dfes@prolog.uk.com

Electronic and video publications:
Right to be Heard (video)
Order electronic and video publications from: SENT As main address

Access to staff:
Contact by letter, by telephone, by fax, by e-mail and via website
Hours: Mon to Fri, 0900 to 1700

Access to building, collection or gallery:
Prior appointment required

SPECIAL OLYMPICS GREAT BRITAIN

Acronym or abbreviation: SOGB

6–8 Great Eastern Street, London, EC2A 3NT

Tel: 020 7247 8891
Fax: 020 7247 2393
E-mail: karen.wallin@sogb.org.uk

Website:
http://www.sogb.org.uk

Enquiries:
Enquiries to: Administrator
Direct e-mail: peju.oriunuta@sogb.org.uk
Other contacts: Chief Executive Officer

Founded:
1978

Organisation type and purpose:
International organisation, national government body, membership association, present number of members: 30,000, registered charity (charity number 800329), suitable for all ages, training organisation.
To provide year-round training and competition in Olympic sports for all with a mental handicap.

Subject coverage:
Sport for people with learning disabilities.

Printed publications:
General information packs
Information leaflets
Special Olympics Summer Sports Rules
Special Olympics Winter Sports Rules
Skill Guides to 23 different sports
Starter packs for new groups

Electronic and video publications:
New Gymnastics Artistic (video and audio cassette)
New Gymnastics Rhythmic (video and audio cassette)
Floor Hockey

Publications list:
Available in print

Access to staff:
Contact by letter, by telephone, by fax, by e-mail and in person. Appointment necessary. Letter of introduction required.
Hours: Mon to Fri, 0900 to 1700

Access to building, collection or gallery:
Prior appointment required

Parent body:
Special Olympics International
1133 19th Street NW, Washington, DC 20036–3604, USA

SPECIALIST CHEESEMAKERS ASSOCIATION

Acronym or abbreviation: SCA

17 Clerkenwell Green, London, EC1R 0DP

Tel: 020 7253 2114
Fax: 020 7608 1645
E-mail: info@specialistcheesemakers.co.uk

Website:
http://www.specialistcheesemakers.co.uk

Enquiries:
Enquiries to: Secretary

Founded:
1989

Organisation type and purpose:
Membership association (membership is by subscription), present number of members: 260.

Subject coverage:
Representation of the interests of specialist cheesemakers, providing a link between cheesemakers, retailers and wholesalers, providing promotional opportunities and own hygiene scheme.

Printed publications:
Specialist Cheesemakers Code of Best Practice

Publications list:
Available online

Access to staff:
Contact by letter, by telephone, by fax, by e-mail and via website
Hours: Mon to Fri, 0900 to 1700

Access to building, collection or gallery:
No access other than to staff

SPELTHORNE BOROUGH COUNCIL

Council Offices, Knowle Green, Staines, TW18 1XB

Tel: 01784 451499
E-mail: customer.services@spelthorne.gov.uk

Website:
http://www.spelthorne.gov.uk
General page.

Enquiries:
Enquiries to: Communications Manager
Direct tel: 01784 446297
Direct e-mail: news@spelthorne.gov.uk
Other contacts: PR and Communications Officer

Organisation type and purpose:
Local government body.

Subject coverage:
Local government services.

Printed publications:
Bulletin (community magazine, four times a year)
Order printed publications from: Louise King, tel: 01784 444260

Publications list:
Available online and in print

Access to staff:
Contact by letter, by telephone, by e-mail, in person and via website
Hours: Mon to Fri, 0900 to 1700

Access for disabled people:
Parking provided, ramped entry, toilet facilities

Parent body:
Surrey County Council

SPINAL INJURIES ASSOCIATION

Acronym or abbreviation: SIA

SIA House, 2 Trueman Place, Oldbrook, Milton Keynes, MK6 2HH

Tel: 0845 678 6633
Fax: 0845 070 6911
E-mail: sia@spinal.co.uk

Website:
http://www.spinal.co.uk

Founded:
1974

Organisation type and purpose:
National organisation, advisory body, membership association (membership is by subscription), present number of members: 5,500, voluntary organisation, registered charity (charity number 1054097), consultancy, publishing house. Self-help group.

Subject coverage:
Paraplegia, tetraplegia, the spinal-cord injured, wheelchair living, self-help aids, personal care, mobility, employment, integration, welfare benefits, sexuality, continence, parenthood, aids and equipment, pain, and an online message board and chat room.

Information services:
Advice line and website with chatroom and message board, as well as access to a range of publications about spinal cord injury.

Library catalogue:
All or part available online and in print

Printed publications:
A variety of factsheets
Books for younger children and teenagers
Forward Magazine
Moving Forward: The Guide to Living with Spinal
  Cord Injury
Directory of Personal Injury Solicitors
Books for medical and healthcare professionals

Electronic and video publications:
Wheelchair Skills (DVD)
Fitness (DVD)
Physiotherapy (DVD)

Publications list:
Available online and in print

Access to staff:
Contact by letter, by telephone, by fax, by e-mail and via website. Appointment necessary.
Hours: Mon to Fri, 0930 to 1630

Access to building, collection or gallery:
Hours: Mon to Fri, 0900 to 1700

Access for disabled people:
Parking provided, level entry, access to all public areas, toilet facilities

Links with:
Scottish Spinal Cord Injuries Association
some 136 other bodies

SPINAL INJURIES SCOTLAND

Acronym or abbreviation: SIS

Festival Business Centre, 150 Brand Street, Glasgow, G51 1DH

Tel: 0141 314 0056
Fax: 0141 427 9258
E-mail: info@sisonline.org

Enquiries:
Enquiries to: Chief Executive

Founded:
1960

Organisation type and purpose:
National organisation, membership association (membership is by subscription), present number of members: c. 700, voluntary organisation, registered charity (charity number SC 015405). Specifically for spinally injured people, their families, friends and carers.

Subject coverage:
Access, accessible holiday information, manufacturers and suppliers of equipment etc.

Printed publications:
Newsline (quarterly, free to members)

Access to staff:
Contact by letter, by telephone, by fax and in person
Hours: Mon to Thu, 0930 to 1700; Fri, 0930 to 1700

Access to building, collection or gallery:
No prior appointment required

Access for disabled people:
Parking provided, level entry, access to all public areas, toilet facilities

Acts in association with the:
Spinal Injuries Association

SPINAL RESEARCH

Formal name: International Spinal Research Trust

Unit 8A, Bramley Business Centre, Station Road, Bramley, Guildford, Surrey, GU5 0AZ

Tel: 01483 898786
Fax: 01483 898763
E-mail: info@spinal-research.org

Website:
http://www.spinal-research.org
General details about spinal research.

Enquiries:
Enquiries to: Chief Executive
Other contacts: Head of Fundraising

Founded:
1981

Organisation type and purpose:
International organisation, registered charity (charity number 281325), research organisation. Spinal Research exists to fund research with the sole aim of finding a treatment for paralysis caused by spinal cord injury.

Subject coverage:
Research into ending the permanence of paralysis caused by spinal cord injury.

Printed publications:
Annual Report (free)
Annual Review (free)
Annual Research Review (free)
Newsletter (twice a year, free)
Research digest (twice a year, free)

Electronic and video publications:
Connections (video)

Access to staff:
Contact by letter, by telephone, by fax, by e-mail, in person and via website
Hours: Mon to Fri, 0900 to 1730

Access to building, collection or gallery:
No prior appointment required

Access for disabled people:
Parking provided, level entry, access to all public areas, toilet facilities

SPLIT SCREEN VAN CLUB

Acronym or abbreviation: SSVC

Old Mills Cottage, Old Mills Road, Elgin, Moray, IV30 1YH

Tel: 01343 550639
E-mail: cjtasker@hotmail.com

Website:
http://www.ssvc.org.uk

Full information, links, forum, contacts for Committee.

Enquiries:
Enquiries to: Information Officer
Other contacts: President/Membership Secretary;
email: president@ssvc.org.uk for membership.

Founded:
1983

Organisation type and purpose:
National organisation, membership association (membership is by subscription), present number of members: 1100.
To preserve and celebrate these unique vintage Volkswagen vans and also the expertise needed to maintain and restore them.

Subject coverage:
Split screen Volkswagen vans, their history, restoration and maintenance.

Museum or gallery collection, archive, or library special collection:
Details of over 500 vans and their histories are collated on the van register.

Printed publications:
Split Screen Scene – packed with photographs, technical articles and advice, restoration hints, van profiles, members anecdotes, letters and classifieds (magazine, 6 times a year)
Order printed publications from: Membership Secretary or via website
e-mail: membership@ssvc.org.uk

Access to staff:
Contact by letter, by telephone, by e-mail and via website
Hours: Mon to Fri, 0900 to 1700

SPORT ENGLAND

3rd Floor Victoria House, Bloomsbury Square, London, WC1B 4SE

Tel: 020 7273 1551
Fax: 020 7383 5740

Website:
http://www.sportengland.org

Enquiries:
Enquiries to: Information Centre
Direct e-mail: jordan.russell@sportengland.org

Founded:
1997

Organisation type and purpose:
National government body. Receives an annual grant-in-aid from the Department for Culture, Media and Sport and in turn distributes grants; 9 regional offices and 5 national sports centres.

Subject coverage:
Sport and physical recreation: administration; grants; design, planning and provision of facilities; technical and architectural factors; development of sport in general; sport for specific groups e.g. unemployed, children etc; governing bodies; sports science and medicine, sports sociology, legislation, sports psychology; individual sports, sporting events.

Museum or gallery collection, archive, or library special collection:
700 Journals
30,000 books and journal articles
Small video collection

Library catalogue:
All or part available in-house

Printed publications:
Best of British Sport (1992, £10)
Injuries in Sport and Exercise (1993, £25)
Planning obligations for sport and recreation – a guide for negotiation and action (£10)
Recreation management (information sheet, free)
Research and technical papers
Select bibliographies on many aspects of sport and its facilities

continued overleaf

The development of sporting talent 1997: how do performers make it to the top (research report 1997, £5)
Order printed publications from: Sport England PO Box 255, Wetherby, West Yorkshire, LS23 7LZ, tel: 0870 521 0255, fax: 0870 521 0266

Publications list:
Available online and in print

Access to staff:
Contact by letter, by telephone, by e-mail, in person and via website. Appointment necessary.
Hours: Mon to Fri, 1330 to 1600
Special comments: Postgraduate students only.

Access for disabled people:
Toilet facilities

Regional Sports Councils are:
East Midlands Region
  Grove House, Bridgford Road, West Bridgford, Nottinghamshire, NG2 6AP; tel: 0115 982 1887; fax: 0115 945 5236
East Region
  Crescent House, 19 The Crescent, Bedford, MK40 2QP; tel: 01234 345222; fax: 01234 359046
London Region
  PO Box 480, Crystal Palace National Sports Centre, Ledrington Road, London, SE19 2BQ; tel: 020 8778 8600; fax: 020 8676 9812
North East Region
  Aykley Heads, Durham, DH1 5UU; tel: 0191 384 9595; fax: 0191 384 5807
North West Region
  Astley House, Quay Street, Manchester, M3 4AE; tel: 0161 834 0388; fax: 0161 835 3678
South East Region
  51A Church Street, Caversham, Reading, Berkshire, RG4 8AX; tel: 0118 948 3311; fax: 0118 947 5935
South West Region
  Ashlands House, Ashlands, Crewkerne, Somerset, TA18 7LQ; tel: 01460 73491; fax: 01460 77263
West Midlands Region
  1 Hagley Road, Five Ways, Edgbaston, Birmingham, B16 8TT; tel: 0121 456 3444; fax: 0121 456 1583
Yorkshire Region
  4th Floor, Minerva House, East Parade, Leeds, LS1 5PS; tel: 0113 243 6443; fax: 0113 242 2189

SPORT HORSE BREEDING OF GREAT BRITAIN

Acronym or abbreviation: SHB(GB)

96 High Street, Edenbridge, Kent, TN8 5AR

Tel: 01732 866277
Fax: 01732 867464
E-mail: office@sporthorsegb.co.uk

Website:
http://www.sporthorsegb.co.uk

Enquiries:
Enquiries to: General Secretary

Founded:
1884

Organisation type and purpose:
Advisory body, membership association (membership is by subscription), present number of members: c. 4000, registered charity.
To develop and improve the breeding of the British sport horse.

Subject coverage:
Horse breeding, registration and shows.

Museum or gallery collection, archive, or library special collection:
Stud Books

Library catalogue:
All or part available in-house

Access to staff:
Contact by letter, by telephone, by fax and by e-mail
Hours: Mon to Fri, 0900 to 1700

SPORTING FIATS CLUB

Acronym or abbreviation: SFC

Elms Farm, Long Clawson, Melton Mowbray, Leicestershire, LE14 4NG

Tel: 01664 822395
E-mail: webmaster@sportingfiatsclub.com

Website:
http://www.sportingfiatsclub.com
Meetings, events, activities and links.

Enquiries:
Enquiries to: Membership Secretary
Other contacts: Chairman for organisational, alliance or regulatory enquiries.

Founded:
1978

Organisation type and purpose:
Membership association (membership is by subscription), present number of members: 500.
To further interest in and enjoyment of Fiat motor cars, worldwide, centred in the UK.

Subject coverage:
Fiat cars.

Printed publications:
Magazine (biannual, glossy)
Newsletter
Books (available through merchandising officer)

Electronic and video publications:
Videos
Photographs (usually in JPEG format)

Access to staff:
Contact by letter, by telephone, by e-mail and via website
Hours: Mon to Fri, 1000 to 2200

Affiliated to:
Group B Car Club
Motor Sport Association
XI/9 Owners Club

SPORTS INDUSTRIES FEDERATION, THE

Acronym or abbreviation: TSIF

Federation House, National Agricultural Centre, Stoneleigh Park, Kenilworth, Warwickshire, CV8 2RF

Tel: 024 7641 4999
Fax: 024 7641 4990
E-mail: admin@sportslife.org.uk

Website:
http://www.sports-life.com

Enquiries:
Enquiries to: Head of Membership & Development
Other contacts: Chief Executive

Founded:
1920

Organisation type and purpose:
Trade association, membership association (membership is by subscription).

Subject coverage:
Lists of suppliers of sports equipment and capital goods equipment. Playground safety guidelines, information on British and European standards relevant to sports industry.

Trade and statistical information:
Data on imports and exports of sports equipment between the United Kingdom and the European Union and non-European Union Countries.
Quarterly United Kingdom sports trends and surveys.
Statistics relating to tennis court construction, sports surfaces, angling trade and play equipment.

Publications list:
Available online

Access to staff:
Contact by letter, by telephone, by fax, by e-mail and via website
Hours: Mon to Fri, 0900 to 1700

Access to building, collection or gallery:
Prior appointment required

Access for disabled people:
Parking provided, toilet facilities

Houses the:
Angling Trade Association
Golf Ball Manufacturers Conference

SPORTS TURF RESEARCH INSTITUTE, THE

Acronym or abbreviation: STRI

St Ives Estate, Bingley, West Yorkshire, BD16 1AU

Tel: 01274 565131
Fax: 01274 561891
E-mail: info@stri.co.uk

Website:
http://www.stri.co.uk
Details of our organisation and the full range of services we offer including details of the book catalogue and publications with order forms for publishing.

Enquiries:
Enquiries to: External Affairs Manager
Other contacts: Chief Executive

Founded:
1929

Organisation type and purpose:
International organisation, advisory body, professional body (membership is by subscription), training organisation, consultancy, research organisation, publishing house.
The STRI is the leading independent organisation in turf grass research and agronomy. Our aims are to carry out research and promote innovation; provide advisory and consultancy services; educate and inform through training and publications.

Subject coverage:
Drainage of sports fields and golf courses, design and construction of golf courses and sports fields, specifications for drainage and construction, irrigation, advisory work including maintenance and management programmes on any sports surface, artificial surfaces, research into turf problems, training courses, publications and books.

Museum or gallery collection, archive, or library special collection:
Library on turf-related publications including rare publications and journals

Library catalogue:
All or part available in-house

Printed publications:
Annual Review (STRI)
Journal of Turfgrass Science (annually)
International Turfgrass Bulletin (4 times a year)
Turfax (US publication, 6 times a year)
Turfgrass Seed (Information booklet, annually)
Miscellaneous books and publications on turf management including:
Cricket Grounds: The Evolution, Maintenance & Construction of Natural Turf Cricket Tables and Outfields (Evans R D C)
International Turf Management Handbook (Aldous D, 1999)
The Care of the Golf Course (Perris J and Evans R D C, 2nd ed., 1996)
The Turfgrass Disease Handbook (Couch H B, 2000)
Winter Games Pitches: The Construction & Maintenance of Natural Turf Pitches for Team Games (Evans R D C, 1994)

Electronic and video publications:
Golf Course Ecology (Video)

Golf Greenkeepers Training Course – Theory
 Notes (CD-ROM, £85 plus VAT plus p&p)
The Bowling Green Maintenance Video (Evans R D
 C)
Turfgrass Diseases – Diagnosis and Management
 (CD-ROM)

Publications list:
Available online and in print

Access to staff:
Contact by letter, by telephone, by fax, by e-mail
and via website. Appointment necessary.
Hours: Mon to Fri, 0900 to 1700

Access to building, collection or gallery:
Prior appointment required

Access for disabled people:
Parking provided, level entry

Links with:
All Sports Governing Bodies including:
Association of Independent Research &
Technology Organisations (AIRTO)
Football Association
Royal & Ancient Golf Club of St Andrews
Sport England
Sports Council

SPORTSCOTLAND

Caledonia House, South Gyle, Edinburgh, EH12
9DQ

Tel: 0131 317 7200
Fax: 0131 317 7202
E-mail: library@sportscotland.org.uk

Website:
http://www.sportscotland.org.uk

Enquiries:
Enquiries to: Information Officer

Founded:
1972

Organisation type and purpose:
Non-departmental public body.
The national agency for sport in Scotland.

Subject coverage:
Sport in Scotland, physical recreation, facilities,
coaching, sports and associated organisations
contacts, participation statistics, sports
sponsorship, drugs in sport.

**Museum or gallery collection, archive, or library
special collection:**
10,000 books and 120 current journals

Trade and statistical information:
Data on sports facilities located in Scotland, data
 on countryside recreation sites located in
 Scotland, National Lottery-funded projects for
 sport in Scotland.

Library catalogue:
All or part available online and in-house

Printed publications:
Advisory information and research in a wide range
 of sports aspects, over 150 titles

Publications list:
Available online

Access to staff:
Contact by letter, by telephone, by fax, by e-mail
and via website. Appointment necessary.
Hours: Mon to Fri, 0900 to 1700

Access to building, collection or gallery:
Prior appointment required
Hours: Mon to Fri, 0900 to 1700

Access for disabled people:
Parking provided, level entry

Funded by:
Central Government under Royal Charter

SPORTSCOTLAND NATIONAL CENTRE INVERCLYDE

Burnside Road, Largs, Ayrshire, KA30 8RW

Tel: 01475 674666
Fax: 01475 674720
E-mail: john.kent@sportscotland.org.uk

Website:
http://www.sportscotland.org.uk

Enquiries:
Enquiries to: Manager
Other contacts: Office Manager for bookings.

Founded:
1970

Organisation type and purpose:
National government body, registered charity.
Residential Sports Centre.
Provision of sport facilities for National Teams,
clubs, society of coaches, education groups,
schools, colleges, sportspeople, conference and
commercial seminars.

Subject coverage:
Sports coaching and awards, educational field
work, fitness testing, sports science and medicine,
residential sports coaching. Corporate team
building, sports days and events.

Trade and statistical information:
United Kingdom market for residential sports
 training for elite athletes, clubs, sports groups
 and corporate activities.

Printed publications:
Brochure on the centre, its services and attractions

Electronic and video publications:
Video available of the Centre, showing all the
 facilities

Publications list:
Available online and in print

Access to staff:
Contact by letter, by telephone, by fax, by e-mail
and via website. Appointment necessary. All
charged.
Hours: Mon to Sun, 0800 to 2300

Access to building, collection or gallery:
Prior appointment required

Access for disabled people:
Parking provided, ramped entry

Parent body:
SportScotland
 tel: 0131 317 7200; fax: 0131 317 7202

SPRAYED CONCRETE ASSOCIATION

Acronym or abbreviation: SCA

Tournai Hall, Evelyn Woods Road, Aldershot,
Hampshire GU11 2LL

Tel: 01252 357842
Fax: 01252 357831
E-mail: admin@sca.org.uk

Website:
http://www.sca.org.uk

Enquiries:
Enquiries to: Secretary
Direct e-mail: admin@sca.org.uk

Founded:
1976

Organisation type and purpose:
Trade association, present number of members: 41.
Contractors, manufacturers and others involved in
sprayed concrete. Operates, through CITB, a
certificate scheme for operatives.

Subject coverage:
Sprayed concrete, gunite, shotcrete.

Printed publications:
Introduction to Sprayed Concrete
Directory of Members
EFNARC specification for sprayed concrete

Publications list:
Available online and in print

Access to staff:
Contact by letter, by telephone, by fax, by e-mail
and via website
Hours: Mon to Fri, 0900 to 1700

SPRU (SCIENCE AND TECHNOLOGY POLICY RESEARCH)

The Freeman Centre, University of Sussex, Falmer,
Brighton, East Sussex, BN1 9QE

Tel: 01273 686758
Fax: 01273 685865
E-mail: b.a.merchant@sussex.ac.uk

Website:
http://www.sussex.ac.uk/spru/library
Information about library and information
services.
http://www.sussex.ac.uk/spru
Research, teaching, library, information,
publications and activities of SPRU.
http://sprulib.central.sussex.ac.uk
SPRU library catalogue.

Enquiries:
Enquiries to: Information Officer
Direct tel: 01273 678178
Direct e-mail: m.e.winder@sussex.ac.uk
Other contacts: Information Services Manager

Founded:
1966

Organisation type and purpose:
University department or institute, research
organisation.

Subject coverage:
Economics of technical change, technology and
innovation management, science and technology
indicators, research evaluation, technology
transfer, technology in developing countries,
energy policy, national science and technology
policies, environmental and social implications of
technical change, chemical, biological and nuclear
arms control. Sectors studied include: energy,
electronics, information and communications
technologies, weapons, building, automobiles,
mining, food, chemicals, pharmaceuticals,
biotechnology, complex systems.

**Museum or gallery collection, archive, or library
special collection:**
Specialist science and technology policy collection,
 including a large holding of grey literature, and a
 core science and technology policy journals
 collection

Trade and statistical information:
Statistics, particularly on R & D expenditure and
 funding, and science and technology.

Printed publications:
Various brochures describing research or teaching
 programmes
Order printed publications from: e-mail:
spru_library@sussex.ac.uk

Access to staff:
Hours: Mon to Fri, 0900 to 1300 and 1400 to 1700
Special comments: Charges to non-academic non-
members.

Houses the former:
Armaments and Disarmaments Information Unit

SSCCI LTD

Ridings House, Ridings Park, Eastern Way,
Cannock, Staffordshire, WS11 2FJ

Tel: 01543 460050
Fax: 01543 462822

Enquiries:
Enquiries to: Chief Executive

Founded:
1994

continued overleaf

Formerly called:
East Mercia Chamber of Commerce and Industry
(EMCCI)

Organisation type and purpose:
Service industry, training organisation,
consultancy.

Subject coverage:
Business information, international trade and
documentation, training, health and safety
consultancy, quality consultancy, environmental
consultancy, late payment of debt and financial
business reports.

**Museum or gallery collection, archive, or library
special collection:**
Comprehensive library of UK and international
business directories

Access to staff:
Contact by letter
Hours: Mon to Fri, 0830 to 1730

ST ALBANS CITY AND DISTRICT COUNCIL

District Council Offices, Civic Centre, St Peter's
Street, St Albans, Hertfordshire, AL1 3JE

Tel: 01727 8662100
Fax: 01727 8662100

Website:
http://www.stalbans.gov.uk
Local information including record offices,
repositories, local researchers.

Enquiries:
Enquiries to: Public Relations Officer

Organisation type and purpose:
Local government body.

Subject coverage:
Local government services.

ST ANDREWS COMMUNITY LIBRARY

Church Square, St Andrews, Fife, KY16 9NN

Tel: 01334 412685
Fax: 01334 413029
E-mail: standrews.library@fife.gov.uk

Enquiries:
Enquiries to: Library Supervisor

Formerly called:
Hay Fleming Library

Organisation type and purpose:
Local government body, public library.

Non-library collection catalogue:
All or part available online and in-house

Library catalogue:
All or part available online and in-house

Access to staff:
Contact by letter, by telephone, by fax and by e-
mail
Hours: Mon, Fri, Sat, 0930 to 1700; Tue, Wed, Thu,
0930 to 1900

Access for disabled people:
Ramped entry, lift to first floor

Branch library of:
Fife Council Library

ST ANNE'S COLLEGE

Library, Woodstock Road, Oxford, OX2 6HS

Tel: 01865 274810
Fax: 01865 274899
E-mail: library@st-annes.ox.ac.uk

Website:
http://www.lib.ox.ac.uk/libraries/guides/ann.html

Enquiries:
Enquiries to: Librarian

Direct e-mail: library@st-annes.ox.ac.uk

Founded:
1879

Organisation type and purpose:
University department or institute.
College library.

Subject coverage:
Most undergraduate subjects in arts, social sciences
and sciences, education and anthropology.

**Museum or gallery collection, archive, or library
special collection:**
Handover Bequest (typography and history of
printing)

Library catalogue:
All or part available online

Access to staff:
Contact by letter. Appointment necessary.
Hours: Mon to Fri, 0900 to 1700

Access to building, collection or gallery:
Only by appointment after prior application to
Librarian

Parent body:
University of Oxford

ST BRIDE LIBRARY

Bride Lane, Fleet Street, London, EC4Y 8EE

Tel: 020 7353 4660
Fax: 020 7583 7073
E-mail: library@stbridefoundation.org

Enquiries:
Enquiries to: Librarian

Founded:
1891

Organisation type and purpose:
Public reference library.

Subject coverage:
Printing (history and technology) and related
subjects (paper, binding, graphic design,
typography, typefaces, calligraphy, illustration,
printmaking, publishing, bookselling, social and
economic aspects of printing and book trades). The
collection comprises books, printing types, antique
presses, photographs, etc.

**Museum or gallery collection, archive, or library
special collection:**
Historical collection dealing with printing,
publishing, graphic design and related subjects,
early technical manuals, trade literature,
manufacturers' prospectuses, type specimens,
trade serials, directories, prints, drawings and
artefacts
Archives and Collections
Broadside Collection (18th century songsheets,
19th century broadsides, chapbooks)
Eric Gill Collection (drawings for printing types
and stone cut inscriptions)
Leaflets, broadsides, union reports on printing
trade relations from 1785
Manuals and periodicals on shorthand (about
3,000 items)
Printing tools and equipment
Prints, drawings and manuscripts

Trade and statistical information:
Data on the printing trade, and also on paper and
publishing.

Library catalogue:
All or part available online and in-house

Access to staff:
Contact by letter, by telephone, by fax, by e-mail
and in person
Hours: Tue, 1200 to 1730; Wed, 1200 to 1900; Thu,
1200 to 1730
Special comments: Reference library.

Parent body:
St Bride Foundation
St Bride Library, Bride Lane, Fleet Street,
London, EC4Y 8EE; tel: 020 7353 4660; fax: 020
7583 7073; e-mail: library@stbrideinstitute.org;
website: www.stbride.org

ST CHRISTOPHER'S FELLOWSHIP

1 Putney High Street, London, SW15 1SZ

Tel: 020 8780 7800
Fax: 020 8780 7801
E-mail: info@stchris.org.uk

Website:
http://www.stchris.org.uk
The charity and its work with children, young
people and vulnerable adults.

Organisation type and purpose:
Registered charity (number 207782), the only
children's charity that is also a housing association.
A leading voluntary provider of services for
children, young people and vulnerable adults,
providing care, accommodation, advice, education
and continuing support, helping to really make a
difference, whether this may be a safe, comfortable
and caring place to stay, help with homework, or
support and advice about education, health,
housing and jobs. Provides a continuum of care to
service users, offering them as much help as they
need to adapt to independent life. Increasingly
reaches out to children who are at risk of being
placed in care or returning there. Also provides
supported housing services, including hostels, flats
and shared houses, and a full range of support in
areas such as further education, training,
employment, and legal issues for young people
who need help to make that vital step towards
fully independent living.

Subject coverage:
Current focus is on adapting therapeutic models of
working to meet the needs of all the people who
require support. By using established academic
theories, the work can be more informed and staff
better able to meet the complex needs of service
users.

Access to staff:
Contact by letter, by telephone, by fax and by e-
mail

ST CHRISTOPHER'S HOSPICE

Halley Stewart Library, 51–59 Lawrie Park Road,
Sydenham, London, SE26 6DZ

Tel: 020 8768 4660
Fax: 020 8776 9345

Website:
http://www.stchristophers.org.uk

Enquiries:
Enquiries to: Librarian
Direct e-mail: n.rattray@stchristophers.org.uk

Founded:
1980 (Library)

Organisation type and purpose:
Voluntary organisation, registered charity (charity
number 210667).
Hospice library (includes information and
education facilities).
Hospice for people with advanced disease.

Subject coverage:
All aspects of hospice and palliative care; death
and dying, ethical issues, bereavement, children's
books on these topics.

**Museum or gallery collection, archive, or library
special collection:**
In-house database on the subject (c.10,000 items –
mainly books, articles and grey literature)

Library catalogue:
All or part available in-house

Printed publications:
Mail order bookshop

Wide range of books available on:
Bereavement, death and dying, ethics and
euthanasia, hospice care, motor neurone disease,
pastoral care, psychosocial aspects, symptom
control, terminal care
Some St Christopher's publications available on
bereaved children

Publications list:
Available in print

Access to staff:
Contact by letter, by telephone, by fax and by e-
mail. Appointment necessary.
Hours: Mon to Fri, 0900 to 1700

Access for disabled people:
Parking provided, ramped entry, toilet facilities

Links with:
Hospice Information

ST DEINIOL'S RESIDENTIAL LIBRARY

Hawarden, Flintshire, CH5 3DF

Tel: 01244 532350
Fax: 01244 520643
E-mail: librarian@st-deiniols.org

Website:
http://www.st-deiniols.org

Enquiries:
Enquiries to: Librarian

Founded:
1896

Organisation type and purpose:
Residential research library founded by the Rt
Hon. W. E. Gladstone.

Subject coverage:
Victorian studies; history; theology; philosophy;
literature; church history; Franciscan studies.

**Museum or gallery collection, archive, or library
special collection:**
Benson Collection (books on Judaism)
Gladstoniana (W. E. Gladstone)
Glynne-Gladstone Collection (over 250,000
manuscripts, family letters, estate, household
and business papers)
Moorman Franciscan Collection (Bishop John R. H.
Moorman)
Pamphlet Collection (over 40,000 from the late 17th
century onwards)
Pre-1800 Collection (biblical studies, philosophy,
church history, European history)

Library catalogue:
All or part available online and in-house

Printed publications:
Bibliographies of special collections, etc.

Access to staff:
Contact by letter, by telephone, by fax, by e-mail,
in person and via website. Letter of introduction
required. All charged.
Hours: External readers: Mon to Sat, 0900 to 1830:
resident readers: daily, 0900 to 2200
Special comments: All users must provide a
testimonial; non-resident readers must purchase an
annual ticket; reference only

ST DUNSTAN'S – AN INDEPENDENT FUTURE FOR BLIND EX-SERVICE MEN & WOMEN

12–14 Harcourt Street, London, W1H 4HD

Tel: 020 7723 5021
Fax: 020 7262 6199
E-mail: pressoffice@st.dunstans.org.uk

Enquiries:
Enquiries to: Head of Public Relations

Founded:
1915

Formerly called:
St Dunstan's Blind ex-Service Men and Women; St
Dunstan's Caring for Men and Women Blinded in
the Service of their Country

Organisation type and purpose:
Registered charity (charity number 216227).
To provide an independent future through
rehabilitation and training for blind ex-service men
and women.

Printed publications:
Annual Brochure
Annual Report
Bi-annual Newsletter

Access to staff:
Contact by letter and by telephone
Hours: Mon to Fri, 0900 to 1700

ST EDMUNDSBURY BOROUGH COUNCIL

Borough Offices, Angel Hill, Bury St Edmunds,
Suffolk, IP33 1XB

Tel: 01284 763233\ Minicom no. 01284 757023
Fax: 01284 757124
E-mail: stedmundsbury@stedsbc.gov.uk

Website:
http://www.stedmundsbury.gov.uk
The heart of East Anglia – a fine place to live, work
and visit.
Council services, press releases, accommodation,
events etc.
http://www.stedmundsbury.gov.uk/moyses.htm
Museums Service

Enquiries:
Enquiries to: Chief Executive

Founded:
1974

Organisation type and purpose:
Local government body.

Subject coverage:
Local government within St Edmundsbury
Borough. Council services, tourist information,
economic development.

Printed publications:
Best Value Performance Plan
Community Spirit

Access to staff:
Contact by letter, by telephone, by fax, by e-mail
and via website
Hours: Mon to Thu, 0900 to 1700; Fri, 0900 to 1600

Access for disabled people:
Parking provided, ramped entry, level entry, toilet
facilities

Other offices:
St Edmundsbury Borough Council
St Edmundsbury House, Western Way, Bury St
Edmunds, Suffolk, IP33 3YS; tel: 01284 763233;
fax: 01284 757378
St Edmundsbury Borough Council
Council Offices, Lower Downs Slade, Haverhill,
Suffolk, CB9 9EE; tel: 01440 702271; fax: 01440
702397

ST FRANCIS LEPROSY GUILD

Acronym or abbreviation: SFLG

73 St Charles Square, London, W10 6EJ

Tel: 020 8969 1345
Fax: 020 8969 3272
E-mail: enquiries@stfrancisleprosy.org

Enquiries:
Enquiries to: General Secretary

Founded:
1895

Organisation type and purpose:
Membership association (membership is by
subscription), registered charity (charity number
208741), voluntary organisation.

Raising funds for the assistance of Catholic priests,
brothers and sisters working among leprosy
sufferers whatever their nationality or creed.

Subject coverage:
Care for leprosy patients; assistance in the
provision of food, drugs, wheelchairs, artificial
limbs, hospital equipment and surgical
instruments, etc.; information on the leprosy
projects and centres assisted.

Printed publications:
Annual Review (free)

Access to staff:
Contact by letter and by e-mail
Hours: Mon to Fri, 1000 to 1700

ST HELENS COLLEGE LIBRARY

Water Street, St Helens, Merseyside, WA10 1PP

Tel: 01744 733766
E-mail: library@sthelens.ac.uk

Website:
http://www.sthelens.ac.uk

Enquiries:
Enquiries to: Head of Information and Library
Services
Direct tel: 01744 623256

Formerly called:
St Helens Community College

Organisation type and purpose:
College of further education.

Subject coverage:
Business studies; office technology; management;
computer-aided design and manufacture; art and
design, health and social care.

Non-library collection catalogue:
All or part available online

Library catalogue:
All or part available online

Printed publications:
College Prospectus
Order printed publications from: Student Services, St
Helens College, at the same address

Access to staff:
Contact by letter, by telephone, by e-mail and in
person. Appointment necessary.
Hours: Term time: Mon to Thu, 0845 to 2000; Fri,
0845 to 1600; Vacations: Mon to Thu, 0900 to 1700;
Fri, 0900 to 1600

Access for disabled people:
Access to all public areas

The College houses the:
St Helens School of Management Studies, a
constituent of the North West Regional
Management Centre

ST HELENS LIBRARIES

Central Library, Gamble Institute, Victoria Square,
St Helens, Merseyside, WA10 1DY

Tel: 01744 456989
Fax: 01744 20836
E-mail: criu@sthelens.gov.uk

Enquiries:
Enquiries to: Librarian

Organisation type and purpose:
Local government body, public library.

Subject coverage:
Local history, glass.

**Museum or gallery collection, archive, or library
special collection:**
Sir Thomas Beecham Archive Collection, not the
original library of the conductor

Access to staff:
Contact by telephone

continued overleaf

Hours: Mon, Wed, 0900 to 2000; Tues, Thurs, Fri, 0900 to 1700; Sat, 0900 to 1600

Access for disabled people:
Access to all public areas

ST HILDA'S COLLEGE LIBRARY

Cowley Place, Oxford, OX4 1DY

Tel: 01865 276884
Fax: 01865 276816

Website:
http://www.sthildas.ox.ac.uk/information/history/archive.htm
http://www.sthildas.ox.ac.uk/information/library/index.htm

Enquiries:
Enquiries to: Librarian
Direct tel: 01865 276848
Direct e-mail: maria.croghan@st-hildas.ox.ac.uk
Other contacts: Archivist for access to the archives and related queries.

Founded:
1893

Organisation type and purpose:
University department or institute.
College library.

Subject coverage:
General undergraduate collection, languages, literature, history, philosophy, theology, geography, politics, economics, biology, physiology, medicine, physics, chemistry, engineering, fine art, music.

Museum or gallery collection, archive, or library special collection:
College archive
History of Women's University Education
Maconchy manuscripts, original music manuscripts of Dame Elizabeth Maconchy (20th century composer)

Non-library collection catalogue:
All or part available in-house

Library catalogue:
All or part available online

Access to staff:
Appointment necessary.
Hours: Mon to Fri, 0900 to 1700

Access for disabled people:
Hours: Mon to Fri, 0900 to 1700

Parent body:
University of Oxford

ST JAMES'S UNIVERSITY HOSPITAL

Medical Library, Level 3, Clinical Sciences Building, Beckett Street, Leeds, West Yorkshire, LS9 7TF

Tel: 0113 2065638
Fax: 0113 2064682

Website:
http://www.leeds.ac.uk/library
Information on all resources available at Leeds University Libraries, including catalogue, databases and other electronic resources.

Enquiries:
Enquiries to: Librarian

Formerly called:
St James's and Seacroft University Hospital

Organisation type and purpose:
University library.

Subject coverage:
Medicine; health care management.

Non-library collection catalogue:
All or part available online

Library catalogue:
All or part available online

Access to staff:
Contact by letter, by telephone and in person.
Access for members only.
Hours: Mon to Thu, 0830 to 1800; Fri, 1000 to 1700

Parent body:
University of Leeds

ST JOHN – THE PRIORY OF SCOTLAND

The Chancery of the Priory of Scotland, St John's House, 21 St John Street, Edinburgh, EH8 8DG

Tel: 0131 556 8711
Fax: 0131 558 3250
E-mail: info@stjohnscotland.org.uk

Website:
http://www.stjohnscotland.org.uk
Aims and projects.
http://www.orderofstjohn.org
Order website.

Founded:
1947

Organisation type and purpose:
Registered Scottish charity (number SC000262).
To improve the safety, health and quality of life of people in need.

Subject coverage:
National rescue support: mountain rescue bases and vehicles, St John rescue boat, Loch Lomond; area initiatives: financial support to a wide range of local schemes, including Maggie's Highland Cancer Caring Centre, Disability Sport Fife and Shopmobility; patient care: St John Patient Transport, Dumfries and Galloway, St John Palliative Care Project, Stranraer; accommodation: Strathtyre Holiday Home, Stirlingshire, Archibald Russell Court, Retirement Complex, Polmont; support for other charities: St John transport for charities, St John Crusader canal cruises, St John's Court, Glasgow; overseas projects: St John Eye Hospital, Jerusalem, St John Malawi Primary Healthcare Project.

Printed publications:
Year Book
Order printed publications from: The Chancery of the Priory of Scotland in Edinburgh

Access to staff:
Contact by letter, by telephone, by fax and by e-mail
Hours: Charity Book Shop open: Tue to Sun

Also at:
St John Book Shop
20 Deanhaugh Street, Stockbridge, Edinburgh

ST JOHN'S COLLEGE LIBRARY

3 South Bailey, Durham, DH1 3RJ

Tel: 0191 334 3500
E-mail: johns.library@durham.ac.uk

Website:
http://www.dur.ac.uk/st-johns.college

Enquiries:
Enquiries to: Librarian
Direct tel: 0191 334 3891
Direct e-mail: richard.briggs@durham.ac.uk
Other contacts: Assistant Librarian

Founded:
1909

Organisation type and purpose:
College library.

Subject coverage:
Mostly theology, some other subject areas.

Library catalogue:
All or part available online

Access to staff:
Contact by letter and by e-mail. Appointment necessary. Non-members charged.
Hours: Mon to Fri, 0900 to 1400

Special comments: Telephone calls morning only.

Access to building, collection or gallery:
Prior appointment required

Parent body:
University of Durham

ST JOHN'S INSTITUTE OF DERMATOLOGY

Education Centre, St Thomas' Hospital, Lambeth Palace Road, London, SE1 7EH

Tel: 020 7188 6255
Fax: 020 7928 1428
E-mail: derm-courses@kcl.ac.uk

Founded:
1947

Formerly called:
Institute of Dermatology

Organisation type and purpose:
University department or institute.
Postgraduate medical school library.

Subject coverage:
Dermatology, dermatopathology, some pathology.

Museum or gallery collection, archive, or library special collection:
As well as the latest books and journals, there is a small collection of historic books over 100 years old on skin and its diseases, including atlases. There is also a collection of moulages on display

Library catalogue:
All or part available in-house

Access to staff:
Contact by e-mail. Appointment necessary.
Hours: Mon to Fri, 0930 to 1730

Parent body:
Guy's, King's and St Thomas' Schools of Medicine, Dentistry and Biomedical Sciences

ST KITTS TOURISM AUTHORITY

10 Kensington Court, London, W8 5DL

Tel: 020 7376 0881
Fax: 020 7937 6742

Website:
http://www.stkitts-tourism.com

Enquiries:
Enquiries to: Manager
Other contacts: Sales Representative

Founded:
1989

Formerly called:
St Kitts and Nevis Department of Tourism

Organisation type and purpose:
National government body.
Tourism promotion.

Subject coverage:
Travel and tourism information for St Kitts and Nevis, also basic investment information.

Trade and statistical information:
Statistical information on tourism arrivals to St Kitts and Nevis.
Relevant cost of a holiday (accommodation, meals and activities).

Printed publications:
Maps and Posters
Promotional Literature
The Secret Caribbean
The Traveller Tourist Guide (free annually)

Publications list:
Available in print

Access to staff:
Contact by telephone
Hours: Mon to Fri, 0930 to 1730

Access to building, collection or gallery:
No prior appointment required

Parent body:
St Kitts and Nevis Department of Tourism
PO Box 132, Basseterre, St Kitts, West Indies

ST LOYE'S FOUNDATION

Brittany House, New North Road, Exeter, Devon, EX4 4EP

Tel: 01392 255428
Fax: 01392 420889
E-mail: info@stloyes.ac.uk

Website:
http://www.stloyesfoundation.org.uk

Founded:
1937

Organisation type and purpose:
Registered charity (number 235434).
Training men and women with disabilities for employment and an independent future with hope and dignity.
To be the preferred choice for people seeking help to realise their potential for financial independence through work.

Subject coverage:
Individually tailored training and personal development programmes to meet clients' needs and support for the whole person on their journey to sustainable, independent working and social inclusion. Includes a range of training programmes, personal development, support services, employability programmes, work experience, work placement, sustainable employment through 'in work' support.

Electronic and video publications:
Newsletter
Order electronic and video publications from: via website

Access to staff:
Contact by letter, by telephone, by fax and by e-mail

Also at:
Sefydliad St Loyes (Cardiff Office)
9 Coopers Yard, Curran Road, Cardiff, CF10 5NB; tel: 02920 003777
St Loye's Enterprises
Unit 64 Basepoint, Yeoford Way, Marsh Barton, Trading Estate, Exeter, EX2 8LB; tel: 01392 826120
St Loye's Foundation (Horticulture Dept)
Westhill Garden Centre, Exmouth Road, Westhill, Ottery St Mary, EX11 1JS; tel: 01404 823684
St Loye's Foundation (Residential Accomodation)
Hope Court, Prince of Wales Road, Exeter, EX4 4PN; tel: 01392 439769
St Loye's Foundation Personal Development Centre
No. 3 The Court Yard, New North Road, Exeter, EX4 4EP; tel: 01392 214955 / 274684

ST LUCIA TOURIST BOARD

Lower Ground Floor, 1 Collingham Gardens, London, SW5 OHW

Tel: 0870 900 7697
Fax: 0207 341 7001

Website:
http://www.bandweb.co.uk/dolphin
Dolphin divers, St Lucia.
http://www.stlucia.org
Tourist board official site.
http://www.interknowledge.com/st-lucia
Tourist information.
http://www.stluciajazz.com
St Lucia jazz festival.
http://www.ansechastanet.com
Anse Chastanet Hotel/diving St Lucia.

Enquiries:
Enquiries to: Information Officer
Direct tel: 020 7431 3675
Direct e-mail: sonia.joseph@axissm.com

Other contacts: Sales Executive
Founded:
1986

Organisation type and purpose:
National Tourist Office.

Subject coverage:
General information on the island, hotels, dining out and places to visit. Incentive groups welcome.

Museum or gallery collection, archive, or library special collection:
Slide library, brochures, posters

Access to staff:
Contact by letter, by telephone, by fax, by e-mail, in person and via website
Hours: Mon to Fri, 0930 to 1730

ST MARY'S UNIVERSITY COLLEGE

Acronym or abbreviation: SMUC

Learning Resources Centre, Waldegrave Road, Strawberry Hill, Twickenham, Middlesex, TW1 4SX

Tel: 020 8240 4097
Fax: 020 8240 4270

Enquiries:
Enquiries to: Public Services Manager
Direct e-mail: enquiry@smuc.ac.uk

Founded:
1850

Organisation type and purpose:
University library, university department or institute.

Subject coverage:
Drama, education, English language and literature, film and television, geography, history, Irish studies, management and business studies, media arts, physical theatre, sociology, sport sciences and theology.

Library catalogue:
All or part available online

Access to staff:
Contact by letter, by telephone, by fax, by e-mail, in person and via website. Appointment necessary.
Hours: 0900 to 2100, term time only

Funded by:
HEFC

ST MARY'S UNIVERSITY COLLEGE LIBRARY (BELFAST)

191 Falls Road, Belfast, BT12 6FE

Tel: 028 9026 8237
Fax: 028 9033 3719
E-mail: library@smucb.ac.uk

Website:
http://www.stmarys-belfast.ac.uk
General information, academic information, services, partnerships, student information, what's new.

Enquiries:
Enquiries to: Librarian
Direct e-mail: f.jones@smucb.ac.uk

Founded:
1900

Formerly called:
St Mary's College Library (Belfast)

Incorporates the former:
St Joseph's College of Education

Organisation type and purpose:
University library, university department or institute.
University College of The Queen's University Belfast.

Education of teachers for the Catholic education system in Northern Ireland, postgraduate diploma for teachers for Irish medium education, masters degree in education, BA degree in liberal arts.

Subject coverage:
Education; religious education; art; physical education; English; drama; history; geography; Celtic; music; mathematics; ICT; science; business studies; European studies, Irish medium, technology and design.

Library catalogue:
All or part available online

Access to staff:
Contact by letter, by telephone, by e-mail, in person and via website
Hours: Mon to Thu, 0830 to 2100; Fri, 0830 to 1700 (term time)
Special comments: Students from other universities may use the library for study purposes if there is sufficient space. They must show a current students union card and sign the visitors book.

Access to building, collection or gallery:
Through front entrance on the Falls Road, or the back entrance on Beechmount Avenue
Hours: Open 0830 to 2100 term time only

Access for disabled people:
Lifts at front and rear of building

Constituent bodies:
Queen's University
Queen's University Belfast, University Road, Belfast, BT7 1NN; tel: 028 9097 3760; e-mail: advisory@qub.ac.uk; website: http://www.qub.ac.uk

ST MUNGO'S COMMUNITY HOUSING ASSOCIATION

Formal name: St Mungo Community Housing Association Limited
Acronym or abbreviation: St Mungo's

Griffin House, 2nd Floor, 161 Hammersmith Road, London, W6 8BS

Tel: 020 8762 5500
Fax: 020 8762 5501
E-mail: info@mungos.org

Website:
http://www.mungos.org

Founded:
1969

Organisation type and purpose:
Housing association (number LH0279), industrial and provident society (number 20598R).
Providing hostels and care homes; offering long-term and intensive support for the single homeless.

Subject coverage:
Rough sleeping, sub-groups of single homeless people (mental health problems, substance misuse, the elderly, women, multiple/complex needs), employment and training for single homeless people, services and facilities for homeless people in London.

Non-library collection catalogue:
All or part available in-house

Printed publications:
Leaflets about St Mungo's services (various, free, available direct)
Annual Report (free, available direct)
Order printed publications from: Marketing and Communications Department

Access to staff:
Contact by letter, by telephone, by fax and by e-mail
Hours: Mon to Fri, 0900 to 1700

Access to building, collection or gallery:
No access other than to staff

ST PAUL'S CATHEDRAL LIBRARY

The Chapter House, St Paul's Churchyard, London, EC4M 8AE

Tel: 020 7246 8342
E-mail: library@stpaulscathedral.org.uk

Website:
http://www.stpauls.co.uk

Enquiries:
Enquiries to: Librarian

Organisation type and purpose:
Private Cathedral library.

Subject coverage:
17th-century theology.

Museum or gallery collection, archive, or library special collection:
Bishop Sumner Collection of 19th-century tracts and pamphlets (6,348 items)
Sacheverell Controversy (233 items)

Access to staff:
Contact by letter, by telephone and by e-mail.
Appointment necessary.
Hours: Mon, Tue, 0900 to 1700; Fri, 1330 to 1700

The archive of Dean and Chapter is currently deposited at:
Guildhall Library
Aldermanbury, London, EC2V 7HH; tel: 020 7332 1868; 020 7332 1870; e-mail: ask.lma@ cityoflondon.gov.uk

ST PAUL'S SCHOOL

Formal name: Walker Library

Lonsdale Road, Barnes, London, SW13 9JT

Tel: 020 8746 5413
Fax: 020 8746 5353
E-mail: ama@stpaulsschool.org.uk

Enquiries:
Enquiries to: Librarian
Direct tel: 020 8746 5433

Founded:
1509

Organisation type and purpose:
School library.

Subject coverage:
General subjects, particularly history and history of the school and Old Paulines.

Museum or gallery collection, archive, or library special collection:
Rare Books Collection (in particular material on John Colet, William Lily, John Milton, G K Chesterton, Laurence Binyon and Edward Thomas)

Library catalogue:
All or part available in-house

Printed publications:
Wecome to the Walker Library
Guides to Subject Areas of the Library
The History of St Paul's Library

Access to staff:
Contact by letter, by telephone, by fax and by e-mail. Appointment necessary. Letter of introduction required.
Hours: Mon to Fri, 0800 to 1600
Special comments: Limited access during school holidays.

ST VINCENT AND THE GRENADINES TOURIST OFFICE

Acronym or abbreviation: SVGTO

10 Kensington Court, London, W8 5DL

Tel: 020 7937 6570
Fax: 020 7937 3611
E-mail: svgtourismeurope@aol.com

Website:
http://www.svgtourism.com

Enquiries:
Enquiries to: Manager

Organisation type and purpose:
National Tourist Office.

Subject coverage:
General information on St. Vincent and the Grenadines, including various types of accommodation, places to go, things to see, sports activities available, climate and all the relevant information required when travelling to the islands.

Printed publications:
Ins and Outs (magazine)
Holiday Bequia (brochure)
Accommodation Guide
Life in St Vincent and the Grenadines

Access to staff:
Contact by letter, by telephone, by fax, by e-mail and in person. Appointment necessary.
Hours: Mon to Fri, 0930 to 1700

Access to building, collection or gallery:
No prior appointment required
Hours: Mon to Fri, 0900 to 1630

STAFF AND EDUCATIONAL DEVELOPMENT ASSOCIATION

Acronym or abbreviation: SEDA

Woburn House, 20–24 Tavistock Square, London, WC1H 9HF

Tel: 020 7380 6767
Fax: 020 7387 2655
E-mail: office@seda.ac.uk

Website:
http://www.seda.ac.uk

Enquiries:
Enquiries to: Administrator

Founded:
1993

Organisation type and purpose:
Professional body (membership is by subscription).

Subject coverage:
Staff and educational development.

Printed publications:
Innovations in Education and Training International (IETI, journal, quarterly)
Educational Developments Magazine (quarterly)
Variety of SEDA papers and specials

Publications list:
Available online and in print

Access to staff:
Contact by letter, by telephone, by fax, by e-mail and via website
Hours: Mon to Fri, 0900 to 1700

Access to building, collection or gallery:
Prior appointment required

STAFFORD BOROUGH COUNCIL

Acronym or abbreviation: SBC

Civic Centre, Riverside, Stafford, ST16 3AQ

Tel: 01785 619000
Fax: 01785 619119

Website:
http://www.staffordbc.gov.uk

Enquiries:
Enquiries to: Chief Executive
Direct e-mail: chiefexecutive@staffordbc.gov.uk

Founded:
1974

Organisation type and purpose:
Local government body.

Subject coverage:
Local government services.

Access to staff:
Contact by letter, by fax and by e-mail.
Appointment necessary.
Hours: Mon to Fri, 0900 to 1700

Access to building, collection or gallery:
No prior appointment required

STAFFORDSHIRE ARCHAEOLOGICAL AND HISTORICAL SOCIETY

Acronym or abbreviation: SAHS

6 Lawson Close, Aldridge, Walsall, West Midlands, WS9 0RX

Tel: 01922 452230
E-mail: sahs@sahs.uk.net

Website:
http://www.sahs.uk.net
General aims of the Society, list of meetings for current season, membership secretary's name and address.

Enquiries:
Enquiries to: Membership Secretary
Direct e-mail: bettysemail@taltalk.net

Founded:
1959

Formerly called:
Lichfield Archaeological and Historical Society (year of change 1961); Lichfield and South Staffordshire Archaeological and Historical Society (year of change 1995)

Organisation type and purpose:
Learned society (membership is by subscription), present number of members: 203, registered charity (charity number 500586), suitable for ages: 16+, publishing house.
Published landscape survey of Shenstone Parish.

Subject coverage:
Local history of Staffordshire, in particular South Staffordshire, archaeology of Staffordshire, concentrating on Lichfield and Tamworth areas.

Museum or gallery collection, archive, or library special collection:
Transactions of 17 similar societies in UK and abroad held at Lichfield Joint Record Office

Library catalogue:
All or part available online, in-house and in print

Printed publications:
Contents of Transactions Volumes I–XLIII
Index to Transactions Volumes I–XXXIV and XXXV–XXXIX
Newsletter (3 or 4 times a year)
Transactions (once a year, free to members, back numbers at various prices)
Order printed publications from: Membership Secretary

Electronic and video publications:
Transactions I–XLII on disc (£50)
Index can be supplied on a disc, but only in its published form, not as a database
Order electronic and video publications from: Membership Secretary

Publications list:
Available online and in print

Access to staff:
Contact by letter, by telephone, by e-mail and via website
Hours: Any time up to 2200

Links with:
Birmingham and District Local History Association
Council for British Archaeology
Friends of Staffordshire and Stoke-on-Trent Archives (FoSSA)

STAFFORDSHIRE LIBRARY AND INFORMATION SERVICES DEPARTMENT

Information Services, Shire Hall Library, Market Street, Stafford, ST16 2LG

Tel: 01785 278350\ Minicom no. 01785 278347
Fax: 01785 278599
E-mail: information.service@staffordshire.gov.uk

Website:
http://www.talisweb.staffordshire.gov.uk
http://www.staffordshire.gov.uk
15,000 pages approximately, county council information, education and training in county, what's on, vacancies, links to other information databases, online electronic tourism brochure.

Enquiries:
Enquiries to: Service Adviser: Knowledge Management, IT & Funding
Direct tel: 01785 278352
Direct fax: 01785 278319
Direct e-mail: lynne.stanley@staffordshire.gov.uk

Organisation type and purpose:
Local government body, public library.

Subject coverage:
Staffordshire, music, coal mining, brewing, industry, playsets.

Museum or gallery collection, archive, or library special collection:
British Standards
Government publications
National Joint Fiction Reserve KB-KEL, KIN-KZ, LAR-LED, LIA-LOD, MAM-MARN, MAY-MAZ

Library catalogue:
All or part available online

Printed publications:
Local studies, publications and reprints

Access to staff:
Contact by letter, by telephone, by fax, by e-mail and via website
Hours: Mon to Fri, 0900 to 1700

Member of:
European Information Association
Midlands On-line User Group
The Library Partnership West Midlands (TLPWM)

Parent body:
Staffordshire County Council

STAFFORDSHIRE MOORLANDS DISTRICT COUNCIL

Acronym or abbreviation: SMDC

Moorlands House, Stockwell Street, Leek, Staffordshire, ST13 6HQ

Tel: 01538 483483
Fax: 01538 483474

Website:
http://www.staffsmoorlands.gov.uk

Enquiries:
Enquiries to: Chief Executive
Direct tel: 01538 483400
Direct fax: 01538 483423
Direct e-mail: simon.baker@staffsmoorlands.gov.uk
Other contacts: PR & Media Communications Officer for press contact.

Founded:
1974

Organisation type and purpose:
Local government body.

Subject coverage:
Local government services: council tax, national non-domestic rates, benefits, housing strategy, tourism, regeneration, industrial and commercial property management, markets, waste collection, street cleaning and public conveniences, waste minimisation and recycling, environmental health, local agenda 21, development control, building

conservation, building control, engineering services, car parks, CCTV, leisure services, countryside management.

Museum or gallery collection, archive, or library special collection:
Permanent collection of artistic and historical artefacts from across Staffordshire Moorlands

Non-library collection catalogue:
All or part available online and in print

Library catalogue:
All or part available in print

Printed publications:
Various publications about local government services
The Moorlands Messenger (newspaper, quarterly, distributed free to every household)
Order printed publications from: Public Relations & Media Communications Officer
tel: 01538 483538, fax: 01538 483423, e-mail: charles .malkin@staffsmoorlands.gov.uk

Electronic and video publications:
The Moorlands Messenger – Council's quarterly newspaper (audio tape, distributed free to around 200 visually impaired subscribers)

Publications list:
Available in print

Access to staff:
Contact by letter, by telephone, by fax, by e-mail, in person and via website. Appointment necessary.
Hours: Mon to Thu, 0900 to 1715; Fri, 0900 to 1645

Access for disabled people:
Parking provided, level entry, toilet facilities

Other addresses:
Biddulph Councils Connect
Biddulph Town Hall, Biddulph, Stoke-on-Trent, Staffordshire, ST8 6AR; tel: 01782 297837; fax: 01782 297846; e-mail: biddulph.connect@ staffsmoorlands.gov.uk
Cheadle Councils Connect
15–17A High Street, Cheadle, Stoke-on-Trent, Staffordshire, ST10 1AA; tel: 01538 483860; fax: 01538 757495; e-mail: cheadle.connect@ staffsmoorlands.gov.uk

STAFFORDSHIRE PARISH REGISTERS SOCIETY

Acronym or abbreviation: SPRS

82 Hilport Avenue, Newcastle under Lyme, Staffordshire, ST5 8QT

Tel: 01782 859078
E-mail: secretary@sprs.org.uk

Website:
http://www.staffs.prs.freeserve.co.uk

Enquiries:
Enquiries to: Honorary Secretary

Founded:
16 January 1900

Organisation type and purpose:
Learned society (membership is by subscription), present number of members: over 150, registered charity (charity number 517646), suitable for ages: all, publishing house.

Subject coverage:
The Society was formed to preserve the contents of the parochial registers in Staffordshire by transcribing and printing them. The long-term aim is to publish all the registers down to 1837 for the county of Staffordshire.

Printed publications:
Nearly 120 volumes of registers have been published and usually two volumes are published each year
Order printed publications from: Honorary Secretary

Microform publications:
All out-of-print registers are on microfiche
Order microform publications from: Birmingham & Midland Society for Genealogy & Heraldry

121 Rowood Drive, Damson Wood, Solihull, West Midlands, B92 9LJ, e-mail: mhbmsgh@aol.com

Publications list:
Available online and in print

Access to staff:
Contact by letter and by e-mail

STAFFORDSHIRE RECORD OFFICE

Eastgate Street, Stafford, ST16 2LZ

Tel: 01785 278379; minicom no. 01785 278376
Fax: 01785 278384
E-mail: staffordshire.record.office@staffordshire .gov.uk

Website:
http://www.staffordshire.gov.uk/archives
Access arrangements and general description of holdings; reprographic and research order forms.

Enquiries:
Enquiries to: Head of Archive Services

Founded:
1947

Organisation type and purpose:
Local government body.
To locate, collect and preserve archive collections relating to past life and activity in the county of Staffordshire and to make these collections available to the public.

Subject coverage:
Archives, local history.

Museum or gallery collection, archive, or library special collection:
Major archive collections relating to the History of Staffordshire

Non-library collection catalogue:
All or part available online

Printed publications:
Family History Pack for Beginners (£7.00 plus P&P)
Advanced Family History Pack (£9.00 plus P&P)
Guide to Parish Registers and Bishop's Transcripts (download free from website)
Nonconformist registers (download free from website)
Maps: parish, county and Ordnance Survey

Microform publications:
Staffordshire Parish Registers (fiche)

Publications list:
Available online and in print

Access to staff:
Contact by letter, by telephone, by fax, by e-mail and in person
Hours: Mon, Tue, Thu, 0900 to 1700; Wed, 0900 to 2000; Fri, 0930 to 1630; Sat, 0900 to 1300

Access to building, collection or gallery:
Prior appointment required
Special comments: Reader's ticket required.

Access for disabled people:
Parking provided, ramped entry, access to all public areas, toilet facilities

Also at:
Lichfield Record Office
The Friary, Lichfield, WS13 6QG; tel: 01543 510720; e-mail: lichfield.record.office@ staffordshire.gov.uk
Stoke on Trent City Archives
City Central Library, Bethesda Street, Hanley, Stoke-on-Trent, Staffordshire; tel: 01782 238420; e-mail: stoke.archives@stoke.gov.uk

STAFFORDSHIRE RECORD SOCIETY

William Salt Library, Eastgate Street, Stafford, ST16 2LZ

E-mail: matthew.blake@btinternet.com

continued overleaf

Enquiries:
Enquiries to: Honorary Secretary

Founded:
1879

Organisation type and purpose:
Learned society (membership is by subscription), present number of members: 300, registered charity.
Publication of historical records relating to the county of Staffordshire.

Subject coverage:
Archives, records and history of Staffordshire.

Printed publications:
Collections for a history of Staffordshire (for members, on sale to the public)

Microform publications:
Microfiche of the collections
Order microform publications from: Chadwyck-Healey, The Quorum, Barnwell Road, Cambridge, CB5 8SW

Access to staff:
Contact by letter and by e-mail

STAFFORDSHIRE UNIVERSITY – THOMPSON LIBRARY

Information Services, Thompson Library, College Road, Stoke-on-Trent, Staffordshire, ST4 2XS

Tel: 01782 294443
Fax: 01782 295799

Website:
http://www.staffs.ac.uk

Enquiries:
Enquiries to: Head of Resources Management
Direct tel: 01782 294961
Direct e-mail: d.j.parkes@staffs.ac.uk

Organisation type and purpose:
University library, university department or institute.

Subject coverage:
Art, law, sciences, social sciences, business, humanities, design, ceramics, engineering, electrical engineering, computing.

Museum or gallery collection, archive, or library special collection:
Arts Archive
Badminton Collection (Badminton Library of Sports and Pastimes)
Centre for the History of Psychology (CHOP) Collection (1600-)
Dorothy Thompson Collection (Chartism 1800-)
Eysenck Collection (H J Eysenck)
Iris Strange Collection (Campaign for pensions for British war widows, mainly WWII)
Mining Archive (worldwide)
Riley Collection
ROAPE (Review of African Studies) Collection
Solon Collection (literature on ceramics)
Staffordshire Film Archive (history of the county and key events)

Library catalogue:
All or part available online

Access to staff:
Contact by letter, by telephone, by e-mail, in person and via website. Non-members charged.
Hours: Mon to Fri, 0900 to 1700

Access to building, collection or gallery:
Hours: (term-time only) Mon to Fri, 0900 to 2000; Sat and Sun, 1300 to 1800

STAG OWNERS CLUB

Acronym or abbreviation: SOC

c/o The Membership Secretary, The Old Rectory, Aslacton, Norfolk, NR15 2JN

Tel: 01379 677735
Fax: 01379 677363
E-mail: membership@stag.org.uk

Website:
http://www.stag.org.uk
Overview of club and activities.

Enquiries:
Enquiries to: Membership Secretary

Founded:
1979

Organisation type and purpose:
Membership association (membership is by subscription), present number of members: 5,000, voluntary organisation.
To further interest in the Triumph Stag motor car.

Subject coverage:
The Triumph Stag.

Printed publications:
Magazine (monthly, members only)

Access to staff:
Contact by letter, by telephone, by e-mail and via website
Hours: Mon to Fri, 0900 to 1700

STAGE MANAGEMENT ASSOCIATION

Acronym or abbreviation: SMA

89 Borough High Street, London, SE1 1NL

Tel: 020 7403 7999
E-mail: admin@stagemanagementassociation.co.uk

Website:
http://www.stagemanagementassociation.co.uk
Information about SMA, training, publications, events, message board.

Enquiries:
Enquiries to: Administrator

Founded:
1954

Organisation type and purpose:
National organisation, professional body (membership is by application), present number of members: 740, representative trade association.
Theatre and television stage management.

Subject coverage:
Supporting, representing and promoting stage management in the UK.

Information services:
Bi-monthly magazine for members, publications, website members' area resources.

Education services:
Short training courses open to members and non-members.

Printed publications:
Company Manager's Notes (£4.50, £7 non-members, inc. p&p)
List of members free for engagements (monthly, free)
Stage Management Notes (£4.50, £7 non-members, inc. p&p)
Stage Management: a career guide
SMA Guide to Props and Propping (£4.50, £7 non-members, inc. p&p)
Paper Props CD 1 (£9.99, inc. p&p)
Order printed publications from: website: http://www.stagemanagementassociation.co.uk

Publications list:
Available online and in print

Access to staff:
Contact by letter, by telephone, by e-mail and via website. Appointment necessary.
Hours: Mon to Fri, 1000 to 1600

Access to building, collection or gallery:
No access other than to staff

In constant correspondence with the:
Stage Managers' Association
USA
Theatrical Management Association (TMA)

Links with:
Association of British Theatre Technicians (ABTT)

British Actors Equity Association
Most theatre organisations
Theatres Trust

Member organisation of:
Independent Theatre Council (ITC)

STAINED GLASS GUILD LTD

4 Grosvenor Gardens, Kingston-Upon-Thames, KT2 5BE

Tel: 020 8274 1562
E-mail: info@stainedglassguild.co.uk

Website:
http://www.stainedglassguild.co.uk
Basic facts and jargon, choosing a style, religious work, galleries.

Founded:
1977

Organisation type and purpose:
The role of the 'guild' is advisory; no charge is made for information on all technical or artistic problems relating to domestic glass from the Victorian/Edwardian period right through to the thirties and Art Deco.

Subject coverage:
Stained glass work for private householders, architects, builders, London boroughs and the church.

Access to staff:
Contact by letter, by telephone, by e-mail and in person. Appointment necessary.
Special comments: Visitors by appointment only.

Links with:
Stained Glass House (working studio)
at the same address; e-mail: stainedglass@mail.com

STANDARD VANGUARD OWNERS CLUB

7 Priory Close, Wilton, Salisbury, Wiltshire, SP2 0LD

Tel: 01722 503101

Enquiries:
Enquiries to: Secretary

Founded:
1989

Organisation type and purpose:
Membership association (membership is by subscription).

Subject coverage:
Standard Vanguard cars, preservation and restoration.

Access to staff:
Contact by letter and by telephone. Appointment necessary.
Hours: 1000 to 2200, any day

STANDING COMMITTEE ON OFFICIAL PUBLICATIONS

Acronym or abbreviation: SCOOP

ISG, SCOOP, c/o CILIP, 7 Ridgmount Street, London, WC1E 7AE

Tel: 020 7255 0500
Fax: 020 7255 0501
E-mail: scoop@nurcombe.com

Website:
http://www.cilip.org.uk/isg

Enquiries:
Enquiries to: Secretary

Founded:
1971

Organisation type and purpose:
Professional body.
To improve access to UK official information.

Subject coverage:
Official publications and information in the UK.

Printed publications:
Directory of Specialists in Official Publications (£7)
Proceedings of seminars and conferences (for sale)
Publicity leaflet (free of charge)
Refer: The Journal of the ISG (£20 subscription)
Order printed publications from: Publications Secretary, SCOOP, 42 Moors Lane, Darnhall, Winsford, Cheshire, CW7 1JX, tel: 01606 558242, e-mail: scoop@nurcombe.com

Publications list:
Available in print

Access to staff:
Contact by letter, by telephone and by e-mail
Hours: Mon to Fri, 0900 to 1700

Sub-group of the:
Library Association's Information Service Group

STANDING CONFERENCE ON LIBRARY MATERIALS ON AFRICA

Acronym or abbreviation: SCOLMA

c/o Commonwealth Secretariat, Marlborough House, Pall Mall, London, SW1Y 5HX

Tel: 020 7747 6253
Fax: 020 7747 6168
E-mail: scolma@hotmail.com

Website:
http://www.lse.ac.uk/library/scolma
Details of SCOLMA and its publications, details on membership, including subscriptions, for full membership and for the SCOLMA journal.

Enquiries:
Enquiries to: Chairman

Founded:
1962

Organisation type and purpose:
Learned society, registered charity (charity number 325086).
African studies.

Subject coverage:
Location of materials relating to African studies, for the following countries and areas: Algeria, Angola, Ascension Island, Benin, Botswana, Burundi, Cameroon, Canary Islands, Cape Verde Islands, Central Africa, Chad, Congo (Brazzaville), Democratic Republic of Congo, Djibouti, Ethiopia, Gabon, Gambia, Ghana, Guinea, Guinea-Bissau, Ivory Coast, Kenya, Lesotho, Liberia, Libya, Madagascar, Madeira, Malawi, Mali, Mauritania, Mauritius, Morocco, Mozambique, Namibia, Niger, Nigeria, Principe, Rwanda, St Helena, St Tomé, Senegal, Seychelles, Sierra Leone, Somalia, South Africa, Sudan, Swaziland, Tanzania, Togo, Tristan da Cunha, Tunisia, Uganda, Upper Volta, Western Sahara, Zimbabwe.

Publications list:
Available online and in print

Access to staff:
Contact by letter, by telephone, by e-mail and in person
Hours: Mon to Fri, 0900 to 1700

STAR PUBLISHERS DISTRIBUTORS

112 Whitfield Street, London, W1T 5EE

Tel: 020 7380 0622
Fax: 020 7419 9169
E-mail: indbooks@aol.com

Organisation type and purpose:
Bookshop.

Subject coverage:
A bookshop exclusively devoted to Indian books. Latest Indian publications (in English, Hindi, Urdu and Punjabi) on art, architecture, fine arts (music, dance, films etc), travel, history, politics, social

sciences, business and economics, women's studies, religion and philosophy, reference and encyclopaedias, language and literature, general subjects, and books for children.

Printed publications:
Bulletin (quarterly)
Catalogue (annually)

Parent body:
Star Publications
  New Delhi, India

STAR, STARLING, STUART & BRITON REGISTER

New Wood Lodge, 2A Hyperion Road, Stourton, Stourbridge, West Midlands, DY7 6SB

Tel: 01384 374329

Website:
http://www.localhistory.scit.wlv.ac.uk/Museum/Transport/Cars/staregister/starreg01.htm

Enquiries:
Enquiries to: Registrar

Founded:
1964

Organisation type and purpose:
Membership association (membership is by election or invitation), present number of members: 200.
To promote the restoration and preservation of vehicles manufactured by the Star and Briton Companies of Wolverhampton, England.

Subject coverage:
Historical and technical information service on Star, Starling, Stuart and Briton cars and commercial vehicles of Wolverhampton.

Museum or gallery collection, archive, or library special collection:
Catalogues, drawings, instructional handbooks and original order specifications on vehicles
Magazine and book references to companies and products, 1869 to 1932

Trade and statistical information:
Order books and statistical data on production between 1927 and 1932.
Data prior to 1927 being compiled.

Printed publications:
List of existing vehicles and current owners (free to members)

Access to staff:
Contact by letter, by telephone and in person
Hours: Mon to Fri, 0900 to 1700

STATE OF SOUTH AUSTRALIA

The Australia Centre, Strand, London, WC2B 4LG

Tel: 020 7836 3455
Fax: 020 7887 5332
E-mail: info@south-aus.org

Enquiries:
Enquiries to: Agent General
Direct tel: 020 7887 5124

Founded:
1858

Organisation type and purpose:
Government trade and investment office.

Publications list:
Available in print

Access to staff:
Contact by letter, by telephone, by fax and by e-mail
Hours: Mon to Fri, 0900 to 1700

Access for disabled people:
Level entry, toilet facilities

STATIONERS' AND NEWSPAPER MAKERS' COMPANY

Stationers' Hall, Ave Maria Lane, London, EC4M 7DD

Tel: 020 7248 2934
Fax: 020 7489 1975
E-mail: admin@stationers.org

Website:
http://www.stationers.org

Enquiries:
Enquiries to: The Clerk

Founded:
1403

Organisation type and purpose:
Membership association (membership is by election or invitation).
City of London Livery Company.

Museum or gallery collection, archive, or library special collection:
Company Archives (1554 to present)

Access to staff:
Contact by letter, by telephone, by fax and by e-mail

STATIONERY OFFICE, THE

Acronym or abbreviation: TSO

St Crispins, Duke Street, Norwich, NR3 1PD

Tel: 01603 622211
E-mail: customer.services@tso.co.uk

Website:
http://www.clicktso.com
http://www.thestationeryoffice.com

Enquiries:
Enquiries to: Press Officer
Direct tel: 01603 622211
Other contacts: Deputy Manager

Founded:
privatised 1996

Organisation type and purpose:
National organisation, publishing house.
Retail bookshops, information provider.

Subject coverage:
Official and regulatory information.

Museum or gallery collection, archive, or library special collection:
The Stationery Office publications
Ordnance Survey
HSE publications
British Standards Distributor including Print on Demand Service

Printed publications:
Various publications available via www.clicktso.com, mail order, from shop

Publications list:
Available online

Access to staff:
Contact by letter, by telephone, by fax, by e-mail, in person and via website
Hours: Mon, Wed, Thu, Fri, 0900 to 1730; Tue, 0930 to 1730; Sat, 1000 to 1500

Access to building, collection or gallery:
No prior appointment required

Access for disabled people:
Level entry

Other addresses:
TSO Bookshop
  9–21 Princess Street, Manchester, M60 8AS; tel: 0161 834 7201
TSO Bookshop
  18–19 High Street, Cardiff, CF10 1PT; tel: 029 2039 5548

Other offices:
TSO Birmingham
  68–69 Bull Street, Birmingham, B4 6AD; tel: 0121 236 9696

continued overleaf

TSO Head Office
  St Crispins, Duke Street, Norwich; tel: 0870 600 5522
TSO Head Office
  51 Nine Elms Lane, London, SW8 5DR; tel: 0870 600 5522
TSO Northern Ireland
  16 Arthur Street, Belfast, BT1 4GD; tel: 028 9023 8451
TSO Scotland
  71 Lothian Road, Edinburgh, EH3 9AZ; tel: 0870 606 5566

STATISTICAL SERVICES CENTRE

Acronym or abbreviation: SSC

University of Reading, Harry Pitt Building, PO Box 240, Reading, Berkshire, RG6 6FN

Tel: 0118 378 8025
Fax: 0118 975 3169
E-mail: l.e.turner@reading.ac.uk

Website:
http://www.reading.ac.uk/ssc/

Enquiries:
Enquiries to: Executive Assistant

Founded:
1982

Organisation type and purpose:
Training organisation, consultancy.

Subject coverage:
Statistical consultancy, statistical training/courses, statistical computing, database management systems.

Electronic and video publications:
Statistical software package INSTAT (a teaching package, free)

Publications list:
Available online

Access to staff:
Contact by letter, by telephone, by fax, by e-mail and via website. Appointment necessary. All charged.
Hours: Mon to Fri, 0900 to 1700

Access for disabled people:
Access to all public areas, toilet facilities
Special comments: Lift

Parent body:
University of Reading

STATUTE LAW SOCIETY

Acronym or abbreviation: SLS

21 Goodwyns Vale, London, N10 2HA

Tel: 020 8883 1700
Fax: 020 8883 7976
E-mail: statutelaw@aol.com

Website:
http://www.statutelawsociety.org

Enquiries:
Enquiries to: Administrator

Founded:
1968

Organisation type and purpose:
Learned society, registered charity (charity number 261226).

Subject coverage:
Statute law and legislation.

Printed publications:
Statute Law Review (pub. OUP)

Access to staff:
Contact by letter, by telephone, by e-mail and via website
Hours: Mon to Fri, 0900 to 1700

STAUNTON SOCIETY, THE

98 Cole Park, Twickenham, Middlesex, TW1 1JA

Tel: 020 8744 2868
Fax: 020 8742 2311

Enquiries:
Enquiries to: General Secretary

Founded:
1993

Organisation type and purpose:
Learned society, membership association (membership is by election or invitation), present number of members: 80.
To further the importance of chess as an educational sport; to provide support and illumination to young players; to make public the achievements of past national figures such as Howard Staunton.

Subject coverage:
The life and works of Howard Staunton (1810–1874), chess player, editor of Shakespeare. Editor of The Great Schools of England, education in the endowed schools. Chess play, historical and contemporary. British chess players 19th and 20th century and foreign nationals who have played here over time.

Museum or gallery collection, archive, or library special collection:
Limited number of Staunton books. Memorabilia

Printed publications:
Staunton Society Newsletter

Access to staff:
Contact by letter, by telephone and by fax
Hours: Sat & Sun inclusive

STEAM BOAT ASSOCIATION OF GREAT BRITAIN

Acronym or abbreviation: SBA

Avoca Cottage, School Lane, Niton, Isle of Wight, PO38 2BP

Tel: 01983 730664

Website:
http://www.steamboat.org.uk

Enquiries:
Enquiries to: Honorary Secretary

Founded:
1972

Organisation type and purpose:
Membership association (membership is by subscription), present number of members: over 1,000.
A society to foster and encourage steamboating and building, development, preservation and restoration of steam boats and steam machinery.

Subject coverage:
Small steam boats and steam launches; other steam machinery.

Museum or gallery collection, archive, or library special collection:
Archive collection

Printed publications:
Journal (quarterly)

Access to staff:
Contact by letter, by telephone and by e-mail
Hours: Any reasonable time.
Special comments: Staff are volunteers, so not always available.

STEEL CONSTRUCTION INSTITUTE

Acronym or abbreviation: SCI

Silwood Park, Buckhurst Road, Ascot, Berkshire, SL5 7QN

Tel: 01344 636525
Fax: 01344 636570

E-mail: library@steel-sci.com

Website:
http://www.steel-sci.org
Information relating to the work of the Steel Construction Institute and services provided to the construction industry.

Enquiries:
Enquiries to: Librarian

Founded:
1986

Organisation type and purpose:
Research organisation.

Subject coverage:
Use of steel in construction onshore and offshore; steel properties, related standards and codes of practice (UK, European and American); steel buildings, bridges, tunnels, offshore platforms.

Printed publications:
A large number of books on topics including: Stainless Steel, Steel and the Environment, Steel Below Ground, Steel Bridges, Offshore Engineering, Light Gauge Steel
Handbooks and Commentaries to BS Codes
New Steel Construction (10 times a year)

Publications list:
Available in print

Access to staff:
Contact by letter, by telephone, by fax, by e-mail and via website. Appointment necessary. Access for members only. Non-members charged.
Hours: Mon to Fri, 0900 to 1700

STEEL WINDOW ASSOCIATION

Acronym or abbreviation: SWA

The Building Centre, 26 Store Street, London, WC1E 7BT

Tel: 020 7637 3571
Fax: 020 7637 3572
E-mail: info@steel-window-association.co.uk

Website:
http://www.steel-window-association.co.uk
List of member companies; specifier's guide to steel windows.

Enquiries:
Enquiries to: Director
Direct e-mail: dns@windows.fsworld.co.uk

Founded:
1967

Organisation type and purpose:
Trade association (membership is by subscription), present number of members: 25.

Subject coverage:
Steel window manufacture, supply and installation, technical advice and information.

Printed publications:
Fact Sheets
List of member companies
Specifier's Guide to Steel Windows (6th ed.)

Access to staff:
Contact by letter, by telephone, by fax, by e-mail, in person and via website. Appointment necessary.
Hours: Mon to Fri, 0900 to 1700

STEPHENSON COLLEGE, COALVILLE

Thornborough Road, Coalville, Leicestershire, LE67 3TN

Tel: 01530 836136
Fax: 01530 814253
E-mail: deniser@stephensoncoll.ac.uk

Website:
http://www.stephensoncoll.ac.uk

Enquiries:
Enquiries to: Library and Learning Resources Manager

Direct tel: 01530 836136 ext. 181

Formerly called:
Coalville Technical College (year of change 1997)

Organisation type and purpose:
Suitable for ages: 16+, training organisation.
Further education establishment.

Subject coverage:
Business and management; motor vehicle
technology; engineering; access to higher
education; construction, information technology,
health and social care; hair and beauty; early years;
uniform services; travel and tourism; teacher
training.

Non-library collection catalogue:
All or part available in-house

Library catalogue:
All or part available in-house

Printed publications:
New Book Lists (occasional)

Access to staff:
Contact by letter, by telephone, by fax, by e-mail
and via website. Appointment necessary. Access
for members only. Letter of introduction required.
Hours: Mon to Thu, 0830 to 2100; Fri, 0830 to 1630

Access for disabled people:
Parking provided, access to all public areas

STERILISED SUTURE MANUFACTURERS ASSOCIATION

Acronym or abbreviation: SSMA

Ethicon Limited, PO Box 408, Bankhead Avenue,
Edinburgh, EH11 4HE

Tel: 0131 453 5555
Fax: 0131 453 6011

Enquiries:
Enquiries to: Honorary Secretary
Other contacts: Chairman of the Technical
Committee for matters of a technical nature or if
the Hon Secretary is unavailable.

Organisation type and purpose:
Trade association (membership is by qualification,
election or invitation), present number of
members: 3, voluntary organisation.

Subject coverage:
Production and supply of surgical sutures.

Access to staff:
Contact by letter, by telephone and by fax
Hours: Mon to Fri, 0900 to 1700

Affiliated to:
European Association of the Surgical Suture
Industry (EASSI)
  tel: 49 69 2556 1338; fax: 49 69 2556 1471

STEVENAGE BOROUGH COUNCIL

Acronym or abbreviation: SBC

Daneshill House, Danestrete, Stevenage,
Hertfordshire, SG1 1HN

Tel: 01438 242242
Fax: 01438 242566

Website:
http://www.stevenage.gov.uk

Enquiries:
Enquiries to: Public Relations Manager

Organisation type and purpose:
Local government body.

Subject coverage:
Local government services.

STEVENAGE BUSINESS INITIATIVE

Acronym or abbreviation: SBI

Business & Technology Centre, Bessemer Drive,
Stevenage, Hertfordshire, SG1 2DX

Tel: 0845 078 0600
Fax: 01438 310001
E-mail: enquiries@sbi-herts.co.uk

Website:
http://www.sbi-herts.co.uk

Enquiries:
Enquiries to: Information Officer

Founded:
1983

Organisation type and purpose:
Service industry.
Enterprise agency, free start-up business advice
service.

Subject coverage:
Business advice.

Access to staff:
Contact by letter, by telephone, by fax, by e-mail,
in person and via website. Appointment necessary.
Hours: Mon to Thu, 0830 to 1730; Fri, 0830 to 1700

STEWART SOCIETY

53 George Street, Edinburgh, EH2 2HT

Tel: 0131 220 4512
Fax: 0131 220 4512
E-mail: info@stewartsociety.org

Website:
http://www.stewartsociety.org

Enquiries:
Enquiries to: Secretary

Founded:
1899

Organisation type and purpose:
International organisation, learned society
(membership is by subscription), present number
of members: 614, voluntary organisation,
registered charity (charity number SC 000692),
museum, research organisation.

Subject coverage:
Stewart and general Scottish history, Stewart
genealogy.

**Museum or gallery collection, archive, or library
special collection:**
Family papers, old books and family trees
  pertaining to the Stewarts and Stuarts, members'
  library

Non-library collection catalogue:
All or part available in-house

Library catalogue:
All or part available in-house

Printed publications:
The Stewarts (magazine, annually)
Stewart News (newsletter)

Publications list:
Available in print

Access to staff:
Contact by letter, by telephone, by fax, by e-mail,
in person and via website. Appointment necessary.
Hours: Mon to Fri, 1000 to 1230

STFC DARESBURY LABORATORY

Formal name: Science and Technology Facilities
Council
Acronym or abbreviation: STFC

Daresbury Science and Innovation Campus,
Keckwick Lane, Daresbury, Warrington, Cheshire,
WA4 4AD

Tel: 01925 603189
Fax: 01925 603779
E-mail: library@dl.ac.uk

Website:
http://www.e-science.stfc.ac.uk/services/library
-services/library.html

Enquiries:
Enquiries to: Library Services Development
Manager

Organisation type and purpose:
UK Research Council

Subject coverage:
Atomic, molecular and condensed matter physics,
synchrotron radiation, nuclear structure,
accelerator physics, computing and computational
science, biological sciences, materials science,
engineering.

Library catalogue:
All or part available online

Printed publications:
Annual Report

Access to staff:
Contact by letter, by telephone, by fax, by e-mail
and in person. Appointment necessary.
Hours: Mon to Fri, 1000 to 1600

Access to building, collection or gallery:
By appointment only

STILLBIRTH AND NEONATAL DEATH CHARITY

Acronym or abbreviation: SANDS

28 Portland Place, London, W1B 1LY

Tel: 020 7436 7940
Fax: 020 7436 3715

Website:
http://www.uk-sands.org
Description of services; how to contact SANDS;
publications list; stillbirth; neonatal death and
baby loss.

Enquiries:
Enquiries to: Administrator
Direct e-mail: katie.duff@)uk-sands.org

Founded:
1981

Organisation type and purpose:
Membership association (membership is by
subscription), present number of members: 970,
voluntary organisation, registered charity (charity
number 299679).
To support parents when their baby dies at or soon
after birth. Training for professionals.

Subject coverage:
Death of a baby at or soon after birth (stillbirth,
neonatal death), pregnancy losses. Incidence of
stillbirth and neonatal death in the UK. Causes of
stillbirth and neonatal death. Support and care of
families affected, funerals for infants.

**Museum or gallery collection, archive, or library
special collection:**
Wide collection on stillbirth, neonatal loss and
  pregnancy losses

Trade and statistical information:
UK stillbirth and neonatal mortality statistics.

Printed publications:
Pregnancy Loss and the Death of a Baby:
  Guidelines for professionals
SANDS Newsletter (3 times a year)
Information leaflets (7 titles, 10p each)
When a baby dies
What has to be done
Saying Goodbye to your baby
Books and leaflets for families and health
  professionals

Publications list:
Available online and in print

Access to staff:
Contact by letter, by telephone, by fax, by e-mail
and via website
Hours: Mon to Fri, 0930 to 1700
Special comments: No disabled access.

Access to building, collection or gallery:
Prior appointment required

STILTON CHEESE MAKERS' ASSOCIATION

Acronym or abbreviation: SCMA

PO Box 384A, Surbiton, Surrey, KT5 9YL

Tel: 020 8255 1334
Fax: 020 8255 1335
E-mail: stilton@stiltoncheese.com

Website:
http://www.stiltoncheese.com

Enquiries:
Enquiries to: Stilton Information Bureau
Direct tel: 0161 923 4994
Direct fax: 0161 923 4760
Direct e-mail: enquiries@stiltoncheese.com

Founded:
1936

Organisation type and purpose:
Trade association (membership is by qualification), present number of members: 5, manufacturing industry.
Promotion of Stilton cheese, protection of Stilton certification trade marks.

Subject coverage:
Stilton cheese: all matters including trade mark, manufacture, methods of storing and serving, sources of supply.

Printed publications:
Recipe leaflets and cards
Order printed publications from: Stilton Information Bureau, c/o BRAZEN, Brazen House, Great Ancoats Street, Manchester, M4 5AJ

Access to staff:
Contact by letter, by telephone and by e-mail
Hours: Mon to Fri, 0900 to 1700

Links with:
Dairy UK
93 Baker Street, London, W1U 6RL; tel: 020 7486 7244; fax: 020 7487 4734

STIRLING CENTRE FOR INTERNATIONAL PUBLISHING AND COMMUNICATION

University of Stirling, Stirling, FK9 4LA

Tel: 01786 467510
Fax: 01786 466210
E-mail: english@stir.ac.uk

Website:
http://www.publishing.stir.ac.uk
Centre information, staff, course content.
http://www.stir.ac.uk
University home page and links.
http://www.english.stir.ac.uk
Department home page, information.

Enquiries:
Enquiries to: Director and Professor in Publishing Studies
Other contacts: Postgraduate secretary (for general course enquiries)

Founded:
1982

Formerly called:
Centre for Publishing Studies

Organisation type and purpose:
University department or institute, training organisation, consultancy, research organisation, publishing house.
Research and teaching in publishing studies (mainly contemporary) on an international basis.

Subject coverage:
Publishing industry, book trade, Scottish publishing industry, textual and scholarly editing, Sir Walter Scott, James Hogg, public support for literature, authorship and the book trade, publishing in Africa, China, Malaysia, developmental issues.

Library catalogue:
All or part available online

Printed publications:
Publishing Studies course leaflet (free)
University Postgraduate Prospectus (annually, free)

Access to staff:
Contact by letter, by telephone, by fax, by e-mail and via website
Hours: Mon to Fri, 0900 to 1700

Cooperative links with similar bodies in:
North America, Far East, Australia, Europe

Member organisation of:
International Association for Publishing Education
UK Association of Publishing Educators

STIRLING COUNCIL ARCHIVE SERVICE

Acronym or abbreviation: SCAS

5 Borrowmeadow Road, Springkerse Industrial Estate, Stirling, FK7 7UW

Tel: 01786 450745
E-mail: archive@stirling.gov.uk

Website:
http://www.stirling.gov.uk/index/access-info/archives.htm

Enquiries:
Enquiries to: Archivist

Founded:
1996

Organisation type and purpose:
Local government body.
Archive.

Subject coverage:
Primary sources relating to the area administered by Stirling Council.

Non-library collection catalogue:
All or part available in-house and in print

Access to staff:
Contact by letter, by telephone, by fax, by e-mail, in person and via website
Hours: Mon to Wed, 0930 to 1630

Access for disabled people:
Level entry

STIRLING COUNCIL LIBRARIES

Administrative Headquarters, Borrowmeadow Road, Springkerse Industrial Estate, Stirling, FK7 7TN

Tel: 01786 432383
Fax: 01786 432395
E-mail: libraryheadquarters@stirling.gov.uk

Website:
http://www.stirling.gov.uk

Enquiries:
Enquiries to: Libraries and Archives Manager
Direct tel: 01786 443398

Founded:
1975

Organisation type and purpose:
Local government body, public library.

Subject coverage:
Local history of the Stirling District (Stirling County to 1975); general.

Museum or gallery collection, archive, or library special collection:
Local and Scottish History Collections
Stirling Journal and Advertiser, local newspaper from 1820–1970
Stirling Observer local newspaper from June 1970
Thomson Collection (theology)

Library catalogue:
All or part available online and in-house

Publications list:
Available online and in print

Access to staff:
Contact by letter, by telephone and by e-mail
Hours: Mon to Fri, 0900 to 1700

Access to building, collection or gallery:
No prior appointment required

Access for disabled people:
Parking provided, ramped entry, access to all public areas

STOCKPORT ARCHIVE SERVICE

Central Library, Wellington Road, Stockport, Cheshire, SK1 3RS

Tel: 0161 474 4530\ Minicom no. 0161 474 4541
Fax: 0161 474 7750
E-mail: localheritagelibrary@stockport.gov.uk

Enquiries:
Enquiries to: Archivist

Organisation type and purpose:
Local government body, public library.

Subject coverage:
Stockport archives, family history, local history.

Museum or gallery collection, archive, or library special collection:
Christy & Co (hat manufacturers) records
Stockport Sunday School records

Non-library collection catalogue:
All or part available in-house

Access to staff:
Contact by letter, by telephone, by fax, by e-mail and in person. Appointment necessary.
Hours: Mon, Tue, 1000 to 2000; Wed, Thu, 0900 to 1700; Fri, 0900 to 2000; Sat, 0900 to 1600
Special comments: Records held in outstore require advance notice.

Access for disabled people:
Lift

STOCKPORT COLLEGE

Wellington Road South, Stockport, Cheshire, SK1 3UQ

Tel: 0161 958 3471
Fax: 0161 958 3469
E-mail: TheLearningCentre@stockport.ac.auk

Website:
http://www.stockport.ac.uk
Information on college facilities and courses offered.

Enquiries:
Enquiries to: Learning Centre Circulation and Operations Manager

Organisation type and purpose:
College of further and higher education. Takes students aged 14–16 and 16+.

Subject coverage:
Art and design; applied social sciences; building and civil engineering; electrical, mechanical and production engineering; general education; management and business studies; science; computing; nursing; travel and tourism; catering.

Museum or gallery collection, archive, or library special collection:
College archives
Video recordings (2500) and DVDs

Non-library collection catalogue:
All or part available online

Library catalogue:
All or part available online

Access to staff:
Contact in person
Hours: Term time: Mon to Thu, 0830 to 2000; Fri, 0830 to 1700
Vacations: Mon to Fri, 0900 to 1700
Special comments: Reference only for non-members (printed materials only).

Access to building, collection or gallery:
Special comments: Please report to main reception as a visitor

Access for disabled people:
Access to all public areas

STOCKSCOTLAND

The Croft Studio, Croft Roy, Crammon Brae, Tain, Ross-shire, IV19 1JG

Tel: 01862 892298
Fax: 01862 892298
E-mail: info@stockscotland.com

Website:
http://www.stockscotland.com
10,000 image catalogue.

Enquiries:
Enquiries to: Proprietor

Founded:
1992

Organisation type and purpose:
Photographic Library.

Subject coverage:
Contemporary images of the highlands and islands of Scotland. Photographs available for landscape, tourism, industry, agriculture, transport, fisheries etc.

Library catalogue:
All or part available online

Printed publications:
Catalogue (free)
Showcard brochure (free)

Electronic and video publications:
CD-ROM catalogue (normally free)

Access to staff:
Contact by letter, by telephone, by fax, by e-mail and via website. Appointment necessary. All charged.
Hours: Mon to Fri, 0900 to 1700

STOCKTON-ON-TEES BOROUGH COUNCIL

PO Box 11, Municipal Buildings, Church Road, Stockton-on-Tees, Cleveland, TS18 1LD

Tel: 01642 393939
Fax: 01642 393092

Website:
http://www.stockton.gov.uk
Service details, councillors details, events, facts and figures.

Enquiries:
Enquiries to: Personnel and Communications Officer

Organisation type and purpose:
Local government body.

Subject coverage:
Stockton-on-Tees borough services and amenities.

Access to staff:
Contact by letter, by telephone, by fax, by e-mail and in person
Hours: Mon to Fri, 0900 to 1700

STOKE-ON-TRENT CLASSIC CAR CLUB

19 Nashe Drive, Blurton, Stoke-on-Trent, Staffordshire, ST3 2HD

Tel: 01782 323167
E-mail: malcolm@classiccarclub.freeserve.co.uk

Enquiries:
Enquiries to: Secretary
Other contacts: Chairman

Founded:
2000

Access to staff:
Contact by letter and by telephone
Hours: Mon to Fri, 0900 to 1700

STOKE-ON-TRENT COLLEGE

Cauldon Campus, Stoke Road, Shelton, Stoke-on-Trent, Staffordshire, ST4 2DG

Tel: 01782 208208
Fax: 01782 603504

Website:
http://www.stokecoll.ac.uk

Enquiries:
Enquiries to: Learning Resources Manager
Other contacts: Cataloguer

Founded:
1947

Organisation type and purpose:
Suitable for ages: 16+.
College of further and higher education.

Subject coverage:
Building construction, management, office skills, social sciences, science, catering, hairdressing, beauty, computer-aided engineering.

Museum or gallery collection, archive, or library special collection:
Construction and Property.Information Centre

Library catalogue:
All or part available online

Printed publications:
Welcome to the LRC

Access to staff:
Contact by letter, by telephone, by fax, by e-mail and in person
Hours: Term time: Mon to Thu, 0830 to 2100; Fri, 0830 to 1800; Sat, 0900 to 1300

Access to building, collection or gallery:
No access other than to staff

Access for disabled people:
Parking provided, ramped entry, level entry, access to all public areas, toilet facilities

Associated with:
Forum for Information Resources in Staffordshire (FIRST)

Includes the:
Construction and Property Information Centre

STOKE-ON-TRENT LIBRARIES, INFORMATION AND ARCHIVES

City Central Library, Bethesda Street, Hanley, Stoke-on-Trent, Staffordshire, ST1 3RS

Tel: 01782 238431
Fax: 01782 238434
E-mail: central.library@stoke.gov.uk

Website:
http://www.stoke.gov.uk/libraries

Enquiries:
Enquiries to: Librarian

Organisation type and purpose:
Public library.

Subject coverage:
General information; ceramics; local history and archives, especially Stoke-on-Trent and Staffordshire.

Museum or gallery collection, archive, or library special collection:
Ceramics
Local history collection and archives

Non-library collection catalogue:
All or part available online

Library catalogue:
All or part available online

Access to staff:
Contact by letter, by telephone, by fax, by e-mail and in person
Hours: Mon, Wed, 0930 to 1900; Tue, Thu, Fri, 0930 to 1700; Sat 09:30 to 1600

Parent body:
Stoke-on-Trent Libraries, Information and Archives
City Central Library, Bethesda Street, Hanley, Stoke-on-Trent, ST1 3RS; tel: 01782 238455; fax: 01782 238499; e-mail: central.library@.stoke.gov.uk

STOKE-ON-TRENT TOURISM GROUP

Trentham Business Centre, Bellringer Road, Trentham Lakes South, Trentham, Stoke-on-Trent, Staffordshire, ST4 8HH

Tel: 01782 232786
Fax: 01782 232910
E-mail: tourism@stoke.gov.uk

Website:
http://www.stoke.gov.uk/tourism

Enquiries:
Enquiries to: Manager

Organisation type and purpose:
Local government body.

Subject coverage:
Tourism in the Stoke-on-Trent area and The Potteries.

Access to staff:
Contact by letter
Hours: Mon to Fri, 0900 to 1700

STORAGE AND HANDLING EQUIPMENT DISTRIBUTORS' ASSOCIATION

Acronym or abbreviation: SHEDA

Heathcote House, 136 Hagley Road, Edgbaston, Birmingham, B16 9PN

Tel: 0121 454 4141
Fax: 0121 454 4949
E-mail: info@sheda.org.uk

Website:
http://sheda.org.uk

Enquiries:
Enquiries to: General Secretary

Founded:
1978

Organisation type and purpose:
National organisation, trade association (membership is by qualification), present number of members: 60.

Subject coverage:
Sources of supply of storage equipment and distributors.

Printed publications:
Newsletters and publications

Access to staff:
Contact by letter, by telephone, by fax, by e-mail and via website
Hours: Mon to Fri, 0900 to 1700

Links with:
Storage Equipment Manufacturers Association (SEMA)

STORAGE EQUIPMENT MANUFACTURERS ASSOCIATION

Acronym or abbreviation: SEMA

The National Metalforming Centre, 47 Birmingham Road, West Bromwich B70 6PY

Tel: 0121 601 6350
Fax: 0121 601 6387

continued overleaf

E-mail: enquiry@sema.org.uk

Website:
http://www.sema.org.uk

Enquiries:
Enquiries to: Information Officer

Founded:
1970

Organisation type and purpose:
Trade association.

Subject coverage:
Storage equipment, racking, shelving etc.

Printed publications:
Code of Practice for the Design of Low Rise Static
  Steel Shelving
Code of Practice for the Design of Static Racking
Code of Practice for the Use of Static Racking
Guide to the Conduct of Palley Racking Surveys
Guideline No. 2 Guide to Erection Tolerances for
  Static Racking
SEMA Guide to the Building Regulations
  Guideline No. 5 Guide to the Design and
  Installation of Mobile Shelving
Terms and Descriptions of Storage Equipment
  (terminology)

Electronic and video publications:
CDM Regulations – Storage Industry
  Interpretation (2000, CD-ROM)
Guidelines for Specifier's of Static Steel Racking
  and Shelving (2000, CD-ROM)

Access to staff:
Contact by letter, by telephone, by fax and by e-
mail
Hours: Mon to Fri, 0900 to 1700

Member of:
British Materials Handling Federation
  tel: 0121 200 2100; fax: 0121 200 1306; e-mail:
  enquiry@bmhf.org.uk

STOURBRIDGE LIBRARY

Crown Centre, Stourbridge, West Midlands, DY8
1YE

Tel: 01384 812945
Fax: 01384 812946
E-mail: stourbridge.library@dudley.gov.uk

Website:
http://www.dudley.gov.uk/libraries
Online catalogue, news, book reviews.

Enquiries:
Enquiries to: Locality Manager
Direct tel: 01384 812951

Organisation type and purpose:
Local government body, public library.

Subject coverage:
Local history of Stourbridge and the surrounding
area, tourist information.

**Museum or gallery collection, archive, or library
special collection:**
County Express (local newspaper) 1856 to present,
  almost all on rollfilm
Stourbridge Census Returns 1841–1901
Stourbridge local history: books, maps,
  photographs, pamphlets, manuscripts, posters,
  newspapers

Library catalogue:
All or part available online

Access to staff:
Contact by letter, by telephone, by fax, by e-mail,
in person and via website

Access to building, collection or gallery:
Hours: Mon, 0930 to 1900; Tue to Fri, 0900 to 1900;
Sat, 0900 to 1700; Sun 1000 to 1400

Access for disabled people:
Level entry

Parent body:
Dudley Libraries
  St James's Road, Dudley

STOURPORT LIBRARY

County Buildings, Worcester Street, Stourport-on-
Severn, Worcestershire, DY13 8EH

Tel: 01905 822722
Fax: 01299 827464
E-mail: stourportlib@worcestershire.gov.uk

Website:
http://www.worcestershire.gov.uk

Enquiries:
Enquiries to: Library Manager

Founded:
1969

Organisation type and purpose:
Public library.

Subject coverage:
General public stock, local history of Stourport,
small canal collection.

**Museum or gallery collection, archive, or library
special collection:**
Local information about Stourport

Library catalogue:
All or part available online

Access to staff:
Contact by letter, by telephone, by e-mail and in
person
Hours: Mon, Tue, Thu, 0900 to 1730; Fri, 0900 to
2000; Sat, 0900 to 1600; Wed, closed

Access to building, collection or gallery:
No prior appointment required

Access for disabled people:
Parking provided, ramped entry, level entry, access
to all public areas

STRATEGIC PLANNING SOCIETY

Acronym or abbreviation: SPS

17 Portland Place, London, W1N 3AF

Tel: 020 7636 7737
Fax: 020 7323 1692
E-mail: enquiries@sps.org.uk

Website:
http://www.sps.org.uk
Dissemination and sharing of strategic
management information, news, tools and society
events.

Enquiries:
Enquiries to: Administration Manager
Direct fax: 020 7636 7737
Direct e-mail: a.claase@sps.org.uk
Other contacts: Marketing Manager email: h
.stones@sps.org.uk

Founded:
1967

Organisation type and purpose:
Learned society, professional body (membership is
by subscription), present number of members:
4,000, registered charity (charity number 253879),
training organisation.
The Society aims to foster and promote research
and best practice in strategic thought and action
for the success of individual members and
organisations.

Subject coverage:
Strategic management and planning knowledge,
applications, techniques and a specialist
membership advisory network; conferences and
workshops; specialist discussion groups.

Trade and statistical information:
Index of published material relating to strategic
  management.

Printed publications:
Long Range Planning (journal, 6 times a year)
Strategy (journal, 6 times a year)

Access to staff:
Contact by letter, by telephone, by fax, by e-mail
and via website. Appointment necessary.
Hours: Mon to Fri, 0900 to 1700

STRATFORD LIBRARY

12 Henley Street, Stratford-upon-Avon,
Warwickshire, CV37 6PZ

Tel: 01789 292209
Fax: 01926 476763
E-mail: stratfordlibrary@warwickshire.gov.uk

Website:
http://www.warwickshire.gov.uk/libraries

Enquiries:
Enquiries to: Information Officer

Organisation type and purpose:
Local government body, public library.

Subject coverage:
General collection ranging from material for young
children to studies at undergraduate level; no
special subject areas.

**Museum or gallery collection, archive, or library
special collection:**
South Warwickshire census returns 1841–1891 held
  on microfilm
Stratford Herald on microfilm

Library catalogue:
All or part available online

Access to staff:
Contact by letter, by telephone, by fax, by e-mail,
in person and via website
Hours: Mon, Wed, Thu, Fri, 0900 to 1730; Tue, 1000
to 1730; Sat, 0930 to 1700; Sun, 1200 to 1600

Parent body:
Warwickshire County Council

STREETBIKE DRAG CLUB

17 Southampton Road, London, NW5 4JS

Tel: 020 7485 0473
Fax: 020 7813 0198

Enquiries:
Enquiries to: Chairman

Founded:
1989

Organisation type and purpose:
Membership association (membership is by
subscription).
To promote street bike drag races.

STRODE COLLEGE & THEATRE

Church Road, Street, Somerset, BA16 0AB

Tel: 01458 844410
Fax: 01458 844415

Website:
http://www.strode-college.ac.uk

Enquiries:
Enquiries to: Head of Learning Resources
Direct tel: 01458 844400 ext 303
Direct e-mail: cbull@strode-college.ac.uk
Other contacts: Learning Centre Manager for
catalogue enquiries, membership.

Founded:
1973

Organisation type and purpose:
Suitable for ages: 16+.
Further education college.

Subject coverage:
Business studies, engineering, secretarial and office
studies, health and beauty, hairdressing, drama,
languages, leisure and tourism, media studies;
degree studies in politics, psychology, sociology,
philosophy, art and design, sport, social care,
childhood studies, information technology,
performing arts, complementary therapies.

Library catalogue:
All or part available online and in-house

Access to staff:
Contact by letter, by telephone and by fax.
Appointment necessary. Access for members only.

Hours: Mon to Thu, 0830 to 2045; Fri, 0830 to 1700; Sat, 0900 to 1245

Access for disabled people:
Parking provided, level entry, access to all public areas, toilet facilities

STROKE ASSOCIATION

Acronym or abbreviation: TSA

Stroke House, 240 City Road, London, EC1V 2PR

Tel: 020 7566 0300; helpline: 0845 303 3100 & 0303 30 33 100
Fax: 020 7490 2686
E-mail: info@stroke.org.uk

Website:
http://www.stroke.org.uk

Enquiries:
Enquiries to: Stroke Information Services

Founded:
1899

Organisation type and purpose:
Registered charity (charity number 211015). Concerned with combating stroke in people of all ages; funds research into prevention, treatment and better methods of rehabilitation; helps stroke patients and their families directly through its Rehabilitation and Support Services, including communication support, family and carer support, information services and welfare grants; campaigns, educates and informs to increase knowledge of stroke.

Subject coverage:
Stroke research, conditions and welfare of sufferers.

Printed publications:
Stroke News (3 times a year)
Six leaflets
40 factsheets
Order printed publications from: The Stroke Association, Publications Department, 1 Sterling Business Park, Salthouse Road, Northampton, NN4 7EX; tel: 01604 687724

Electronic and video publications:
Comprehensive range of information booklets, factsheets and resource sheets (all free online)
Order electronic and video publications from: website: http://www.stroke.org.uk/information/our_publications/index.html

Publications list:
Available online and in print

Access to staff:
Contact by letter, by telephone, by e-mail and via website
Hours: Telephone helpline: Mon to Fri, 0900 to 1700

STROUD DISTRICT COUNCIL

Ebley Mill, Stroud, Gloucestershire, GL5 4UB

Tel: 01453 766321; minicom no. 01453 754949
Fax: 01453 750932
E-mail: customer.services@stroud.gov.uk

Website:
http://www.stroud.gov.uk

Enquiries:
Enquiries to: Principal Marketing Officer
Direct tel: 01453 754385
Direct fax: 01453 754942
Direct e-mail: press@stroud.gov.uk

Founded:
1974

Organisation type and purpose:
Local government body.

Subject coverage:
Stroud district, services and amenities.

Access to staff:
Contact by letter, by telephone, by fax, by e-mail, in person and via website. Appointment necessary.

Hours: Mon to Thu, 0845 to 1700; Fri, 0845 to 1630

Access for disabled people:
Parking provided, level entry, access to all public areas, toilet facilities

STRUCTURAL PRECAST ASSOCIATION

Acronym or abbreviation: SPA

60 Charles Street, Leicester, LE1 1FB

Tel: 0116 253 6161
Fax: 0116 251 4568
E-mail: spa@britishprecast.org

Website:
http://www.structural-precast-association.org.uk

Enquiries:
Enquiries to: Secretary

Founded:
1995

Organisation type and purpose:
Trade association.

Subject coverage:
Precast concrete structural components for building.

Printed publications:
SPANews (newsletter)
Members Products data folder
Code of Practice for the Safe Erection of Precast Concrete Frameworks

Access to staff:
Contact by letter, by telephone, by fax, by e-mail and via website
Hours: Mon to Fri, 0900 to 1700

Parent body:
British Precast Concrete Federation

STUDENT CHRISTIAN MOVEMENT OF GREAT BRITAIN

Acronym or abbreviation: SCM

Unit 308F, The Big Peg, 120 Vyse Street, The Jewellery Quarter, Birmingham, B18 6NF

Tel: 0121 200 3355
E-mail: scm@movement.org.uk

Website:
http://www.movement.org.uk

Enquiries:
Enquiries to: Administrator
Other contacts: Links Worker (for information on events and setting up groups)

Founded:
1889

Organisation type and purpose:
National organisation, membership association, registered charity (charity number 241896), suitable for ages: 16 to 30 (approx).
SCM endeavours to present students in further and higher education with an understanding of the Christian Faith that is enquiring, ecumenical and related to all aspects of life. SCM currently supports a network of around 65 groups across Britain.

Subject coverage:
Introductions to theology, liberation theology, prophecy, feminist theology, Bible studies, sexuality, spirituality, ecumenism, social action, responsibility, politics.

Non-library collection catalogue:
All or part available online

Printed publications:
Common People (Community)
F Word
Fleshing out Faith
God Made Simple
Just Love: sexuality
Movement (termly)
No More Mr Nice Guy

Raging In The Streets
SCM Publications and Resources Guide (free)
Significant Others
The Dying Game (Death)

Publications list:
Available online and in print

Access to staff:
Contact by letter, by telephone, by fax, by e-mail and via website. Appointment necessary.
Hours: Mon to Fri, 0900 to 1630

Access to building, collection or gallery:
No prior appointment required

Access for disabled people:
Level entry

Affiliated to:
Church Together in Britain and Ireland
tel: 020 7523 2139
Churches Together in England
tel: 020 7332 8230
World Student Christian Federation
tel: + 31 20 6754921; e-mail: europe@wscf.xs4all.nl

Has:
Local groups

STUDENTS PARTNERSHIP WORLDWIDE

Acronym or abbreviation: SPW

Faith House, 2nd Floor, 7 Tufton Street, London, SW1P 3QB

Tel: 020 7222 0138
Fax: 020 7233 0008
E-mail: info@spw.org

Website:
http://www.spw.org
Information regarding volunteering in Africa and Asia; country-specific information, SPW's approach, application, support; information about SPW's partners.

Enquiries:
Enquiries to: Operations Manager

Founded:
1985

Subject coverage:
Volunteering; development; education; environment; health; youth development in rural Africa and Asia; community development; non-governmental organisation, focus on HIV/AIDS awareness, nutrition, sanitation; method is youth-to-youth approach through informal activities.

Non-library collection catalogue:
All or part available online and in-house

Library catalogue:
All or part available online and in-house

Printed publications:
Newsletter (free)
Information Pack (free)
Brochure (free)
Annual Report (free)
Information leaflets (free)
Posters (free)

Electronic and video publications:
SPW video of volunteering programmes in Africa

Access to staff:
Contact by letter, by telephone, by fax, by e-mail and via website. Appointment necessary.
Hours: Mon to Fri, 0900 to 1800

Access to building, collection or gallery:
No access other than to staff

Links with:
Duke of Edinburgh
HELP
SAFE

SUBTERRANEA BRITANNICA

Acronym or abbreviation: SB

continued overleaf

c/o CNHSS Ltd, 96A Brighton Road, South Croydon, Surrey, CR2 6AD

Tel: 020 8688 3593

Website:
http://www.subbrit.org.uk

Enquiries:
Enquiries to: Membership Secretary

Founded:
1974

Organisation type and purpose:
Learned society (membership is by subscription), voluntary organisation.
Researches concerning the archaeology and history of man-made and man-used underground space. Mainly (but not exclusively) United Kingdom and Europe.

Subject coverage:
Man-made and man-used underground space of all kinds and all periods – especially miscellaneous (non coal/non metal) mines, tunnels, ice houses, souterrains, deneholes, rockcut cellars, shelters, underground military structures, etc.

Museum or gallery collection, archive, or library special collection:
Correspondence concerning underground sites of all kinds and periods
County files including notes, surveys, newscuttings, offprints, pamphlets
Printed books relating to this subject

Library catalogue:
All or part available in-house

Printed publications:
Subterranea Britannica Guides 1 to 6, include:
The Geological Literature as a Source for Industrial History
Underground Industrial Archaeology in Kent
Wells in Kent
Deneholes and Chalkwells
The Germans' World War II V-weapons sites in France
Why Go Underground for Mineral Sources?
Newsletter (3 times per annum)
Bulletin Subterranea Britannica (irregularly, for sale)

Publications list:
Available in print

Access to staff:
Contact by letter, by telephone and by e-mail.
Appointment necessary.
Hours: Sun to Sat, at any reasonable hour
Special comments: Specific research enquiries only.

Access to building, collection or gallery:
Special comments: The past chairman's personal files/library can be accessed by prior arrangement only.

Links with:
Association for Industrial Archaeology
Council for British Archaeology
National Association of Mining History Organisations

Secretary/Enquiries:
Subterranea Britannica
  14 Maple Close, Sandford, Wareham, Dorset, BH20 7QD; tel: 01929 553872; e-mail: rogerstarling593@btinternet.com

Secretary/Membership:
Subterranea Britannica
  13 Highcroft Cottages, London Road, Swanley, Kent, BR8 8DB; tel: 01322 408081; e-mail: nick@catford.fsbusiness.co.uk

SUE RYDER CARE

114–118 Southampton Row, London, WC1B 5AA

Tel: 0845 050 1953
E-mail: info@suerydercare.org

Website:
http://www.suerydercare.org
About the charity, its research and its work, events.

Organisation type and purpose:
A charity registered in England and Wales (number 1052076) and in Scotland (number SC039578).
A leading provider of palliative and end-of-life care research and education. Through its research the centre seeks to make a valuable contribution to policy and practice in previously under-researched areas of palliative and end-of-life care.

Subject coverage:
Provides health and social care services in local communities; is one of the largest providers of specialist palliative care in the UK; provides indivualised, compassionate care services to people with end-of-life and long-term needs; supports families, friends and carers. Works through innovation and research to improve standards in long-term and end-of-life care; a research partnership with the University of Nottingham is extending skills and knowledge across the sector; has piloted leading hospice-at-home services and holistic care-management programmes for people with complex physical and psychological needs. Its work goes beyond the UK; with fifty projects across 12 countries in Europe and southern Africa, it is positioned at the centre of an international health and social care partnership.

Electronic and video publications:
Filling the void
Order electronic and video publications from:
Download from website

Publications list:
Available online

Access to staff:
Contact by letter, by telephone and by e-mail

Also at:
Doncaster Office
  2 Carr Square, Sidings Court, Doncaster, DN4 5NU; tel: 01302 380080; fax: 01302 380075
Sudbury Office
  First Floor, Kings House, King Street, Sudbury, CO10 2ED; tel: 01787 314200; fax: 01787 319516

Works collaboratively with:
Sue Ryder Care Centre for Palliative and End of Life Studies
  University of Nottingham

SUFFOLK ACRE

Formal name: Suffolk ACRE (Action with Communities in Rural England)
Acronym or abbreviation: ACRE

Brightspace, 160 Hadleigh Road, Ipswich, Suffolk IP2 0HH

Tel: 01473 345300
Fax: 01473 345330
E-mail: info@suffolkacre.org.uk

Website:
http://www.suffolkacre.org.uk
http://www.suffolkonline.net
http://www.brightspace.org
http://www.suffolkcarshare.com

Enquiries:
Enquiries to: Chief Executive

Founded:
1937

Organisation type and purpose:
Membership association, present number of members: 2,000, voluntary organisation, registered charity (charity number 1062038).
Representative and advisory body for the voluntary social services sector in Suffolk; with a membership of a very large number of voluntary and statutory bodies and individuals.
Community development in rural areas of Suffolk.

Subject coverage:
Welfare and quality of life in Suffolk; local communities; village hall regulations; playing fields; job creation programmes; crafts; horticulture; charities; social enterprise; IT; village hall and parish council insurance; transport;

Printed publications:
A–Z Fundraising Ideas
Conducting a Village Appraisal
Information Circulars and Newsletters and Packs (list available)

Publications list:
Available in print

Access to staff:
Contact by letter, by telephone, by fax and by e-mail
Hours: Mon to Fri, 0900 to 1700

Access for disabled people:
Parking provided, ramped entry, access to all public areas, toilet facilities

Affiliated to:
ACRE

SUFFOLK CHAMBER OF COMMERCE, INDUSTRY AND SHIPPING INCORPORATED

Felaw Maltings, South Kiln, 42 Felaw Street, Ipswich, Suffolk, IP2 8SQ

Tel: 01473 680600
Fax: 01473 603888
E-mail: info@suffolkchamber.co.uk

Website:
http://www.suffolkchamber.co.uk

Enquiries:
Enquiries to: Business Information Co-ordinator
Direct tel: 01473 694800
Direct e-mail: wendy@suffolkchamber.co.uk

Founded:
1884

Organisation type and purpose:
Membership association (membership is by subscription), present number of members: 1,400, service industry.
Chamber of commerce.

Subject coverage:
International trade, exporting, business information, business credit checking, personnel assistance.

Museum or gallery collection, archive, or library special collection:
Extensive business library

Printed publications:
SI Trader (newsletter, monthly, members of Suffolk International Trade Association)
Suffolk Business (magazine, monthly, free to members)

Access to staff:
Contact by letter, by telephone, by fax, by e-mail, in person and via website
Hours: Mon to Fri, 0900 to 1700

Affiliated to:
Association of British Chambers of Commerce

SUFFOLK COASTAL DISTRICT COUNCIL

Melton Hill, Woodbridge, Suffolk, IP12 1AU

Tel: 01394 383789; 01394 444211 (minicom)
Fax: 01394 385100
E-mail: scdc@suffolkcoastal.gov.uk

Website:
http://www.suffolkcoastal.gov.uk

Enquiries:
Enquiries to: Communications Manager
Direct tel: 01394 444361
Direct fax: 01394 444690
Direct e-mail: viv.hotten@suffolkcoastal.gov.uk

Founded:
1974

Organisation type and purpose:
Local government body.

Subject coverage:
Local government services, including local planning, environmental protection, housing, recreation and leisure, recycling and waste management, food safety and tourism.

Special visitor services:
Tourist Information Centres at Felixstowe, Woodbridge and Aldeburgh

Printed publications:
CoastLine (magazine)

Publications list:
Available online and in print

Access to staff:
Contact by letter, by telephone, by fax, by e-mail, in person and via website
Hours: Mon to Thu, 0845 to 1715; Fri, 0845 to 1645

Access to building, collection or gallery:
Hours: Mon to Thu, 0845 to 1715; Fri, 0845 to 1645

Access for disabled people:
Parking provided, level entry, toilet facilities

Also at:
Suffolk Coastal District Council (local area office) 91 Undercliffe Road, Felixstowe; tel: 01394 276766

SUFFOLK COLLEGE

Formal name: Suffolk New College

Learning Curve, Rope Walk, Ipswich, Suffolk, IP4 1LT

Tel: 01473 382836
Fax: 01473 230054

Website:
http://www.suffolk.ac.uk
Details of courses available.

Enquiries:
Enquiries to: Learning Curve Co-Ordinator

Founded:
1961

Organisation type and purpose:
College of higher and further education.

Subject coverage:
Computing; engineering; management; construction; social work; nursing; sociology; catering; graphic design; biology; education; midwifery; chemistry; CAD/CAM; personnel management; psychology; business studies; art.

Non-library collection catalogue:
All or part available online

Library catalogue:
All or part available online

Printed publications:
Library Guide

Access to staff:
Contact by letter. Appointment necessary.
Hours: Mon to Fri, 0900 to 1700

Associate college of:
University Campus Suffolk
Waterfront Building, Neptune Quay, Ipswich, IP4 1QJ; tel: 01473 83700; website: http://www .ucs.ac.uk

SUFFOLK HORSE SOCIETY

The Market Hill, Woodbridge, Suffolk, IP12 4LP

Tel: 01394 380643
E-mail: sec@suffolkhorsesociety.org.uk

Website:
http://www.suffolkhorsesociety.org.uk

Enquiries:
Enquiries to: Administrator

Founded:
1877

Organisation type and purpose:
Registered charity (charity number 220756).

Subject coverage:
Breed society for the Suffolk Punch heavy horse.

Museum or gallery collection, archive, or library special collection:
Collections held in the Suffolk Horse Museum

Printed publications:
Stud Book (annually)

Access to staff:
Contact by letter, by telephone and by e-mail. Appointment necessary.
Hours: Mon to Fri, 0930 to 1730

Access for disabled people:
Steps; not suitable for wheelchair access

SUFFOLK LIBRARIES

Formal name: Adult and Community Services Libraries Archives and Information
Acronym or abbreviation: ACS LAI

Endeavour House, 8 Russell Road, Ipswich, Suffolk, IP1 2BX

Tel: 01473 265086
Fax: 01473 216843
E-mail: help@suffolklibraries.co.uk

Website:
http://www.suffolk.gov.uk/LeisureAndCulture/ Libraries/SuffolkLibrariesDirect
Fully searchable library catalogue.
http://www.suffolk.gov.uk/leisureandculture/ libraries
Information about library and record office services in Suffolk; includes a web version of the library catalogue and community information (Suffolk InfoLink).

Enquiries:
Enquiries to: Information Librarian
Direct tel: 01473 583727
Direct e-mail: roger.mcmaster@suffolk.gov.uk
Other contacts: Head of Service

Founded:
1974

Organisation type and purpose:
Local government body, public library.

Subject coverage:
General; local studies; local government; business information.

Museum or gallery collection, archive, or library special collection:
Benjamin Britten Collection (all published works up to 1973); at Lowestoft Central Library
Cullum Collection (family library of a 19th century gentleman, George Milner-Gibson-Cullum) at Bury St Edmunds Record Office
Fitzgerald Collection at Woodbridge Library
Horse Racing Collection (mainly flat racing; sporting reminiscences; history and anatomy of the horse; steeplechasing; includes the Racing Calendar from 1774 and the Bloodstock Breeders Review from 1912) at Newmarket Branch Library, 1A, The Rookery, Newmarket
Ipswich Old Town Library, including incunabula and manuscripts and rare works from the 16th and 17th centuries at Ipswich School by appointment only
Local Studies Collections at: Suffolk Record Office, 77 Raingate Street, Bury St Edmunds; Central Library, Lowestoft; Woodbridge Branch, New Street, Woodbridge (collection on Sutton Hoo); Suffolk Record Office, Gatacre Road, Ipswich
Seckford Collection (local history of East Anglia, with emphasis on a Woodbridge locality; includes the manuscript of a multi-volume work, Suffolk Moated Houses) at Woodbridge Branch Library

Non-library collection catalogue:
All or part available online

Library catalogue:
All or part available online

Access to staff:
Contact by letter, by telephone, by fax, by e-mail, in person and via website
Hours: Mon to Fri, 0900 to 1700

SUFFOLK LOCAL HISTORY COUNCIL

c/o The Honorary Secretary, 5 Cotswold Avenue, Ipswich, Suffolk, IP1 4LL

Tel: 01473 254291
E-mail: admin@slhc.org.uk

Website:
http://www.slhc.org.uk

Enquiries:
Enquiries to: Honorary Secretary

Founded:
1953

Organisation type and purpose:
A registered charity (number is 294270) and voluntary organisation, financed by members and governed by an elected executive committee, all of whom are trustees as well as volunteers; membership is by subscription.
To encourage and support the study of local history and to act as an umbrella organisation for groups and individuals with similar interests in the county of Suffolk.

Subject coverage:
As well as running various events for the membership, organises the Recorders' Scheme to ensure that changes taking place at local level are adequately recorded for future historians.

Non-library collection catalogue:
All or part available online

Printed publications:
Suffolk Review (2 times a year)
Suffolk Local History Council Newsletter (2 times a year)
SLHC Calendar of Events (2 times a year)
Recorders' Booklet (in pack form)

Publications list:
Available online

Access to staff:
Contact by letter, by telephone, by e-mail and via website
Special comments: Variable, not daily.

SUFFOLK RECORD OFFICE

77 Raingate Street, Bury St Edmunds, Suffolk, IP33 2AR

Tel: 01284 352352
E-mail: bury.ro@libher.suffolkcc.gov.uk

Website:
http://www.suffolk.gov.uk/sro

Enquiries:
Enquiries to: Public Service Manager
Direct tel: 01284 352355

Founded:
1974

Organisation type and purpose:
Local government body.

Subject coverage:
Local history, local studies, family history.

Museum or gallery collection, archive, or library special collection:
Records of local authorities, ecclesiastical bodies, families, societies, organisations, businesses and estates relating primarily to Suffolk, 12th to 20th centuries

Non-library collection catalogue:
All or part available online and in-house

Library catalogue:
All or part available online

continued overleaf

Printed publications:
Notes for Searchers: free leaflets on source material for popular areas of research and on major collections (also online)
Guide to Genealogical Sources: parts 1–9 (1998–2000)
Order printed publications from: Suffolk Record Office, Gatacre Road, Ipswich, Suffolk, IP1 2LQ, tel: 01473 584542, fax: 01473 584533, e-mail: ipswich.ro@libher.suffolkcc.gov.uk

Microform publications:
Parish Registers (fiche)
Order microform publications from: Suffolk Record Office, Gatacre Road, Ipswich, Suffolk, IP1 2LQ, tel: 01473 584542, fax: 01473 584533, e-mail: ipswich.ro@libher.suffolkcc.gov.uk

Access to staff:
Contact by letter, by telephone, by fax, by e-mail and in person
Hours: Bury St Edmunds and Ipswich: Mon to Sat, 0900 to 1700
Lowestoft: Mon, Wed, Thu, Fri, 0915 to 1730; Tue, 0900 to 1900; Sat, 0900 to 1700; Sun 1000 to 1600 (no original documents produced on Sunday)
Special comments: CARN ticket required for access to original material.

Also at:
Suffolk Record Office
Gatacre Road, Ipswich, Suffolk, IP1 2LQ; tel: 01473 584541; fax: 01473 584533; e-mail: ipswich .ro@libher.suffolkcc.gov.uk
Suffolk Record Office
Central Library, Clapham Road, Lowestoft, Suffolk, NR32 1DR; tel: 01502 405357; fax: 01502 405350; e-mail: lowestoft.ro@libher.suffolkcc.gov .uk

Parent body:
Suffolk County Council
Endeavour House, Russell Road, Ipswich, IP1 2BX; tel: 01473 583000

SUGAR ASSOCIATION OF LONDON

Acronym or abbreviation: SAL

154 Bishopsgate, London, EC2M 4LN

Tel: 020 7377 2113
Fax: 020 7247 2481
E-mail: durhamn@sugar-assoc.co.uk

Enquiries:
Enquiries to: Secretary

Founded:
1882

Organisation type and purpose:
International organisation, trade association (membership is by election or invitation), present number of members: 130.

Printed publications:
Information Brochure (free)
Book of Rules and Regulations (£60)

Access to staff:
Contact by letter, by telephone and by fax. All charged.
Hours: Mon to Fri, 0900 to 1700

SUGAR BUREAU, THE

6 Catherine Street, London, WC2B 5JS

Tel: 020 7379 6830
Fax: 020 7836 4113
E-mail: info@sugar-bureau.co.uk

Website:
http://www.sugar-bureau.co.uk
Latest research into diet and health for health professionals; publications ordering.

Enquiries:
Enquiries to: Information Manager

Founded:
1964

Organisation type and purpose:
Trade association.

Subject coverage:
Information on sugar (the generic product), diet and health, consumers and the media.

Printed publications:
Nutrition in Practice (for dietitians, health professionals, GP practice nurses, twice a year)
Order printed publications from: See website (resources now mainly online)

Publications list:
Available online

Access to staff:
Contact by letter, by telephone and by e-mail. Appointment necessary.
Hours: Mon to Fri, 0900 to 1700

Access to building, collection or gallery:
No access

Member of:
European Sugar Manufacturers Committee (CEFS)
Food and Drink Federation
World Sugar Research Organisation

SUGAR TRADERS ASSOCIATION OF THE UNITED KINGDOM

Acronym or abbreviation: STAUK

Czarnikow Group Limited, 24 Chiswell Street, London, EC1Y 4SG

Tel: 020 7972 6631
Fax: 020 7972 6699
E-mail: dclark@czarnikow.com

Website:
http://www.sugartraders.co.uk

Enquiries:
Enquiries to: Honorary Secretary

Founded:
1952

Organisation type and purpose:
Trade association (membership is by subscription, election or invitation), present number of members: 12.
To promote, develop and protect the international trade in sugar.

Subject coverage:
Raw cane sugar; beet white sugar.

Access to staff:
Contact by telephone and by e-mail. Access for members only.
Hours: Mon to Fri, 0900 to 1700

Member organisation of:
ASSUC aisbl, European Association of Sugar Traders
Boite 24, Square Ambiorix 32, 1000 Brussels, Belgium; tel: +32 2 7366873; fax: +32 2 7326766; e-mail: assuc@assuc.eu

SUN CHEMICAL LIMITED

Cray Avenue, St Mary Cray, Orpington, Kent, BR5 3PP

Tel: 01689 894000

Website:
http://www.sunchemical.com

Enquiries:
Enquiries to: Manager, Information Department
Direct tel: 01689 894208
Direct fax: 01689 894128
Direct e-mail: barry.hermiston@sunchemical.com

Founded:
1877

Formerly called:
Coates Brothers plc (year of change 2000)

Organisation type and purpose:
Manufacturing industry.

Subject coverage:
Printing inks and printing processes.

Access to staff:
Appointment necessary.
Hours: Mon to Fri, 0900 to 1700

SUNBEAM RAPIER OWNERS CLUB

Acronym or abbreviation: SROC

7 Barnfield, Tattenhall, Chester, CH3 9HE

Tel: 01829 770762
E-mail: sroc.membership@btinternet.com

Website:
http://www.sunbeamrapier.com
All relevant information about the club.

Enquiries:
Enquiries to: Membership Secretary
Other contacts: The Editor, e-mail: sunbeams92@tiscali.co.uk (for magazine advertising)

Founded:
1979

Organisation type and purpose:
Membership association (membership is by subscription), present number of members: 300–350.

Subject coverage:
Sunbeam Rapier cars, details of spare parts availability, technical advice, details and dates of club events, details of cars for sale, objectives of the club.

Museum or gallery collection, archive, or library special collection:
Rootes Archive Centre, Cherwell Business Village, Southam Road, Banbury, Oxon, OX16 2SP

Printed publications:
Cut & Thrust magazine (quarterly)
Order printed publications from: Short Cuts newsletter (occasional issues)

Access to staff:
Contact by letter, by telephone, by e-mail and via website
Hours: Mon to Fri, 1800 to 2200; Sat and Sun, 0900 to 1700

Member organisation of:
Association of Rootes Car Clubs (ARCC)
tel: 01993 878471

SUNBEAM TIGER OWNERS CLUB

8 Villa Real Estate, Consett, Co Durham, DH8 6BJ

Tel: 01207 508296
Fax: 01207 582297

Enquiries:
Enquiries to: Membership Secretary

Founded:
1976

Organisation type and purpose:
International organisation, membership association (membership is by subscription).

Subject coverage:
Sunbeam Tiger cars.

Access to staff:
Contact by letter and by telephone
Hours: Mon to Fri, 0900 to 1700

SUNBEAM VENEZIA TOURING MILANO

Briarstone House, 51 Cheadle Road, Uttoxeter, Staffordshire, ST14 7BX

Tel: 01889 568346
Fax: 01889 568346

Enquiries:
Enquiries to: General Secretary
Direct tel: 00 1 603 675 6622

Direct e-mail: jaars@emailmv.comt

Founded:
1969

Organisation type and purpose:
Membership association (membership is by subscription), present number of members: 10, voluntary organisation, training organisation, consultancy, research organisation.

Subject coverage:
Full and general information club for Rootes, full history of car manufacturers Touring Milano; special mark Sunbeam Venezia, diesel powered cars and transport; technical advice and spares manufacturing.

Museum or gallery collection, archive, or library special collection:
Lord Rootes collection, some paperwork, touring, liquidator, body-builders 1963–5
Photographs, handbooks, spares

Printed publications:
Instruction Books
Parts List
Technical Information
Work Shop Manual

Access to staff:
Contact by letter and by e-mail. Appointment necessary. Non-members charged.
Hours: Mon to Fri, 0900 to 1700

Archives and technical details:
Sunbeam Venezia Touring Milano
    362 Dingleton Hill Road, RR 3 Box 33, Cornish, New Hampshire, NH 03745, USA; tel: +1 603 675 6622; e-mail: jaars@emailmv.com

SUNBED ASSOCIATION

Acronym or abbreviation: TSA

Chess House, 105 High Street, Chesham, Buckinghamshire, HP5 1DE

Tel: 01494 785941
Fax: 01494 786791
E-mail: info@sunbedassociation.org.uk

Website:
http://www.sunbedassociation.org.uk

Enquiries:
Enquiries to: Chief Executive

Founded:
1995

Organisation type and purpose:
Trade association (membership is by subscription), present number of members: 25 manufacturing industry and 1,500 service industry.

Subject coverage:
Manufacture and use of sunbeds.

Museum or gallery collection, archive, or library special collection:
Standards for the manufacture and use of sunbeds

Trade and statistical information:
Comprehensive industry statistics, training programme.

Printed publications:
Industry Statistics
List of Members
Training programme

Access to staff:
Contact by letter, by telephone, by fax and by e-mail
Hours: Mon to Fri, 0900 to 1700

SUNDERLAND CITY COUNCIL, CITY SERVICES DIRECTORATE

City Library and Arts Centre, Fawcett Street, Sunderland, Tyne and Wear, SR1 1RE

Tel: 0191 561 1235
Fax: 0191 565 0506
E-mail: libraries@sunderland.gov.uk

Website:
http://www.sunderland.gov.uk/libraries

Organisation type and purpose:
Local government body, art gallery, public library.

Subject coverage:
General, local studies, commercial and technical fields, and art.

Museum or gallery collection, archive, or library special collection:
Bob Mason Collection (Maritime history)
Local collection on Sunderland and County Durham (8,000 volumes, 12,000 illustrations, 2,000 maps)

Non-library collection catalogue:
All or part available online, in-house and in print

Library catalogue:
All or part available online

Publications list:
Available in print

Access to staff:
Contact by letter, by telephone, by fax and by e-mail
Hours: Mon to Fri, 0900 to 1700

Access for disabled people:
Access to all public areas

Constituent part of:
NETWORK

SUNDERLAND VOLUNTEER LIFE BRIGADE

Acronym or abbreviation: SVLB

The Watch House, Pier View, Roker, Sunderland, Tyne and Wear, SR6 0PR

Tel: 0191 5672579
E-mail: sunderland.vlb@aol.com

Website:
http://www.communigate.co.uk/ne/svlb/index.phtml
The history of the brigade, other information and publications.

Enquiries:
Enquiries to: Secretary
Direct tel: 07847 004983
Direct e-mail: rroberts61@btinternet.com

Founded:
1877

Organisation type and purpose:
Professional body, present number of members: 65 active members, voluntary organisation, registered charity (number 1105980) and company limited by guarantee (number 4978640).
Coastal search, cliff rescue, coastwatch and museum; headquartered at The Watch House, a historic building.

Subject coverage:
Volunteer life brigade, search, rescue, coastwatch and museum; SVLB history – 130 years of life saving on the coast of Sunderland. Volunteers are needed for all teams. Members must be over 18. Duke of Edinburgh Award training is available to 14 to 18 year olds.

Museum or gallery collection, archive, or library special collection:
Model ships, historical photographs and life-saving equipment.

Printed publications:
Include leaflets and postcards
Order printed publications from: Sunderland Volunteer Life Brigade by Kathleen Gill (£12.99)

Publications list:
Available online and in print

Access to staff:
Contact by letter, by telephone, by e-mail and in person
Hours: Sun and bank hols, 1300 to 1630, or by appointment

Access to building, collection or gallery:
Hours: Sun, bank hols and special events, 1300 to 1630

Links with:
RNLI Coastguard

SUPPLY CHAIN KNOWLEDGE CENTRE

Acronym or abbreviation: SCKC

Cranfield Centre for Logistics & Supply Chain, Cranfield School of Management, Cranfield, Bedfordshire, MK43 0AL

Tel: 01234 754931
Fax: 01234 754930
E-mail: sckc@cranfield.ac.uk

Website:
http://www.sckc.info
http://www.logisticsweb.co.uk
Automated database of logistics information searchable by keyword and freetext.
http://www.ila.co.uk
International Logistics Abstracts.

Enquiries:
Enquiries to: Knowledge Manager

Founded:
1970

Organisation type and purpose:
University department or institute.
Information centre (logistics).

Subject coverage:
Logistics, supply chain management, materials handling, warehouse design including cold stores, physical distribution, pallet testing, freight transport, ergonomics.

Museum or gallery collection, archive, or library special collection:
Extensive collection of 35mm slides of materials handling equipment

Printed publications:
Supply Chain Practice (quarterly)
International Logistics Abstracts (6 times a year)

Electronic and video publications:
Automated database of logistics information searchable by keyword and freetext

Publications list:
Available online and in print

Access to staff:
Contact by e-mail and via website. Appointment necessary. Access for members only. Non-members charged.
Hours: Mon to Fri, 0900 to 1730

Division of:
Cranfield Centre for Logistics & Supply Chain

SUPREME COURT LIBRARY

Queen's Building, Royal Courts of Justice, Strand, London, WC2A 2LL

Tel: 020 7947 6587
Fax: 020 7947 6661

Enquiries:
Enquiries to: Librarian
Direct tel: 020 7947 7198

Founded:
1972

Organisation type and purpose:
National government body.
Department for Constitutional Affairs Library and Information Services.
Primarily for the use of the Judiciary and Officials of the Royal Courts of Justice.

Subject coverage:
English law; some coverage of the Commonwealth and EC law.

continued overleaf

Museum or gallery collection, archive, or library special collection:
Old editions of legal textbooks
Transcripts of the Determinations of the Immigration Appeal Tribunal
Transcripts of the judgements of the Court of Appeal (Civil Division, 1951 to date)

Library catalogue:
All or part available in-house

Access to staff:
Contact by letter and by fax. Appointment necessary.
Hours: Mon to Fri, 1000 to 1630; during legal vacations 0930 to 1630

Access for disabled people:
Special comments: Access provided throughout the library and court buildings

SURF LIFE SAVING GB

Formal name: Surf Life Saving Great Britain
Acronym or abbreviation: SLSGB

19 Southernhay West, Exeter, EX1 1PJ

Tel: 01392 218007
Fax: 01392 217808
E-mail: mail@slsgb.org.uk

Website:
http://www.slsgb.org.uk

Enquiries:
Enquiries to: Executive Officer

Founded:
1955

Organisation type and purpose:
Membership association, voluntary organisation, registered charity (charity number 1015668), training organisation.

Subject coverage:
Life-saving on beaches with surf, training, awards, youth development.

Printed publications:
Advanced Resuscitation Guidelines
Competition Manual
Examinations and Awards Manual
IRB Coaching Manual
Professional Surf-Lifeguard Teaching Module
SLSGB Manual

Access to staff:
Contact by letter, by telephone and by fax.
Appointment necessary.
Hours: Mon to Fri, 0900 to 1700

SURFACE ENGINEERING ASSOCIATION

Acronym or abbreviation: SEA

Federation House, 10 Vyse Street, Birmingham, B18 6LT

Tel: 0121 237 1123
Fax: 0121 237 1124
E-mail: info@sea.org.uk

Website:
http://www.sea.org.uk
Surface Engineering Association home page.
http://www.bstsa.org.uk
British Surface Treatment Suppliers Association home page.

Enquiries:
Enquiries to: Chief Executive
Other contacts: Member Services Manager

Founded:
1887

Organisation type and purpose:
Trade association (membership is by subscription), present number of members: 500, manufacturing industry, consultancy.
To promote the interests of the UK surface engineering activity.

Subject coverage:
Metal finishing, coating metal, putting metal coatings on other products, supply of materials or services to companies, sub-contractors for finishing, surface engineering, surface coating materials, economics, health and safety, environmental issues.

Museum or gallery collection, archive, or library special collection:
Standards for surface engineering

Trade and statistical information:
Some data on value of the surface engineering industry.

Printed publications:
Newsletter (quarterly, free of charge to members)
Buyers Guide to Surface Finishing (free of charge to members)

Publications list:
Available online

Access to staff:
Contact by letter, by telephone, by fax, by e-mail and via website. Appointment necessary.
Hours: Mon to Fri, 0900 to 1700
Special comments: Some services are for members only.

Access for disabled people:
Level entry, access to all public areas, toilet facilities

Affiliated to:
CBI
CETS

Member of:
The British Jewellery and Giftware Federation (BJGF)

SURREY ARCHAEOLOGICAL SOCIETY

Castle Arch, Guildford, Surrey, GU1 3SX

Tel: 01483 532454
Fax: 01483 532454
E-mail: info@surreyarchaeology.org.uk

Website:
http://www.surreyarchaeology.org.uk

Enquiries:
Enquiries to: Honorary Secretary

Founded:
1854

Organisation type and purpose:
Learned society.
To promote the study of archaeology and antiquities within the historic county of Surrey.

Subject coverage:
Archaeological, antiquarian or historical material relating to historic county of Surrey including building records, records and manuscripts, cartographic and pictorial material, ceramics, ecclesiastical history and industrial history.

Museum or gallery collection, archive, or library special collection:
The Society's collections, research material and library are housed at Castle Arch

Non-library collection catalogue:
All or part available online and in-house

Library catalogue:
All or part available online and in-house

Printed publications:
Purchased directly from Society

Publications list:
Available online and in print

Access to staff:
Contact by letter, by telephone, by fax, by e-mail, in person and via website. Appointment necessary.
Non-members charged.
Hours: Mon to Fri, 1030 to 1630

Special comments: Non-members, first visit free, subsequent visits £8.00 each

Access to building, collection or gallery:
Prior appointment required

SURREY COMMUNITY ACTION

Acronym or abbreviation: SCA

Astolat, Coniers Way, New Inn Lane, Burpham, Guildford, Surrey, GU4 7HL

Tel: 01483 566072
Fax: 01483 440508 or 0870 0566147
E-mail: info@surreyca.org.uk

Website:
http://www.surreyca.org.uk
Full details of Surrey Community Action and all its projects; directory search facility.

Enquiries:
Enquiries to: Information Officer

Founded:
1950

Organisation type and purpose:
Membership association (membership is by subscription), present number of members: 600, voluntary organisation, registered charity (charity number 1056527).
Independent registered charity working with communities to strengthen voluntary action.
To enhance the quality of life for people in Surrey by promoting, supporting and strengthening voluntary action.

Subject coverage:
Local charities and voluntary groups, including village halls and good neighbour car schemes; volunteering and voluntary transport schemes; local training; rural communities in Surrey; local grant schemes and funding sources.

Printed publications:
Directories (all online via website):
Surrey Health and Social Care
Community Transport
Village & Community Halls
Guidelines: Volunteering, Care groups, Committee procedures

Access to staff:
Contact by letter, by telephone, by fax, by e-mail, in person and via website. Appointment necessary.
Hours: Mon to Fri, 0900 to 1700

Access for disabled people:
Parking provided, level entry, access to all public areas, toilet facilities

SURREY COUNTY ARCHAEOLOGICAL UNIT

Acronym or abbreviation: SCAU

Surrey History Centre, Goldsworth Road, Woking, Surrey, GU21 6ND

Tel: 01483 518777
Fax: 01483 518780
E-mail: archaeology.scau@surreycc.gov.uk

Website:
http://www.surreycc.gov.uk/archaeology

Enquiries:
Enquiries to: Unit Manager
Direct tel: 01483 594630
Other contacts: Archaeological Project Officer

Founded:
1991

Organisation type and purpose:
Local government body, professional body.

Subject coverage:
Archaeological information for Surrey.

Museum or gallery collection, archive, or library special collection:
Archive of archaeological material from a number of sites in Surrey

Printed publications:
Publications on application, for purchase direct or through Surrey Archaeological Society

Access to staff:
Contact by letter, by telephone and by e-mail.
Appointment necessary.
Hours: Mon to Fri, 0800 to 1600

Access to building, collection or gallery:
Prior appointment required

Access for disabled people:
Parking provided, level entry, access to all public areas, toilet facilities

Parent body:
Surrey County Council
County Hall, Kingston upon Thames; tel: 020 8541 8800; fax: 020 8541 9004

SURREY COUNTY COUNCIL LIBRARIES

Surrey County Council, Room 356, County Hall, Kingston upon Thames, Surrey, KT1 2DY

Tel: 01483 543599
Fax: 01483 543597
E-mail: libraries@surreycc.gov.uk

Website:
http://www.surreycc.gov.uk/libraries

Organisation type and purpose:
County council libraries service.

Subject coverage:
Council's 54 libraries.

Library catalogue:
All or part available online

Access to staff:
Contact by letter, by telephone, by fax, by e-mail, in person and via website

SURREY GUILD OF CRAFTSMEN

Acronym or abbreviation: SGC

Surrey Guild Craft Gallery, 1 Moushill Lane, Milford, Godalming, Surrey, GU8 5BH

Tel: 01483 424769
E-mail: enquiries@surreyguild.co.uk

Enquiries:
Enquiries to: Administrator

Organisation type and purpose:
Membership association.

Subject coverage:
Craftworkers in the county; craft activities and techniques; professional craftsmen in Surrey.

Printed publications:
Directory of members and associates (annually)
Newsletter (approximately quarterly)

Access to staff:
Contact by e-mail. Appointment necessary. Access for members only. Letter of introduction required.

Access to building, collection or gallery:
Hours: Mon to Sun, 1030 to 1700

Access for disabled people:
Special comments: Assistance provided, please telephone before visiting

Member of:
South East Arts Association

SURREY HEATH ARCHAEOLOGICAL & HERITAGE TRUST

Acronym or abbreviation: SHAHT

Archaeology Centre, 4–10 London Road, Bagshot, Surrey, GU19 5HN

Tel: 01276 451181

Founded:
1988

Organisation type and purpose:
Learned society (membership is by subscription), present number of members: 200, voluntary organisation, registered charity (charity number 299409), museum, suitable for ages: 9 to 75, training organisation, research organisation.

Subject coverage:
Archaeology of Borough of Surrey Heath; mesolithic to post-industrial revolution.

Non-library collection catalogue:
All or part available in-house

Library catalogue:
All or part available in-house

Access to staff:
Contact by letter and by telephone
Hours: By appointment

Access to building, collection or gallery:
No prior appointment required

SURREY HEATH BOROUGH COUNCIL

Acronym or abbreviation: SHBC

Surrey Heath House, Knoll Road, Camberley, Surrey, GU15 3HD

Tel: 01276 707100
Fax: 01276 707177
E-mail: enquiries@surreyheath.gov.uk

Website:
http://www.surreyheath.gov.uk

Enquiries:
Enquiries to: Chief Executive

Founded:
1974

Organisation type and purpose:
Local government body.

Subject coverage:
Local authority, housing, planning, environmental health, recreation, council tax, benefits.

Printed publications:
Borough Guide (£3)
Directory of Local Organisations (£15)

Access to staff:
Contact by letter, by telephone, by fax, by e-mail, in person and via website
Hours: Mon to Thu, 0830 to 1730; Fri, 0900 to 1700

Access for disabled people:
Parking provided, ramped entry, level entry, toilet facilities

Link with:
Surrey County Council

SURREY HERITAGE

Surrey History Centre, 130 Goldsworth Road, Woking, Surrey, GU21 6ND

Tel: 01483 518737
Fax: 01483 518738
E-mail: shs@surreycc.gov.uk

Website:
http://www.surreycc.gov.uk/surreyhistoryservice
Details of services and events, searchable catalogues of holdings, research guides.

Enquiries:
Enquiries to: Surrey History Centre Helpdesk
Other contacts: Head of Heritage (for matters of overall policy and complaints)

Founded:
1998

Created by the merger of:
Surrey Record Office, Surrey Local Studies Library, Guildford Muniment Room (year of change 1998)

Organisation type and purpose:
Local government body.
County archives and local studies library.

Subject coverage:
Surrey records and history, including material on churches, houses, schools, businesses, charitable institutions (reformatories, asylums, etc.), local government and local legal institutions (i.e. quarter sessions and petty sessions), urban growth and housing development, railways and other public undertakings, family and estate papers; not matters dealt with by central government or heavy industries.

Museum or gallery collection, archive, or library special collection:
John Broadwood and Sons Ltd, piano manufacturers: records
Barclay collection of watercolours by John Hassell (1767–1825)
Dennis Specialist Vehicles Ltd, makers of fire engines, buses and other specialist vehicles: records
Photographs of Surrey by Francis Frith
Papers relating to C. L. Dodgson (Lewis Carroll) and of Dodgson family
Goulburn family of Betchworth: papers, including Henry Goulburn (1784–1856), politician
Gertrude Jekyll (1843–1932), garden designer of Munstead: papers including garden designs
More and More-Molyneux family of Loseley House: papers, particularly relating to Tudor and Stuart Surrey
Queen's Royal Surrey Regiment and predecessors, including Queen's Royal Regiment (West Surrey) and East Surrey Regiment: records
IGI complete

Non-library collection catalogue:
All or part available online and in-house

Library catalogue:
All or part available online

Printed publications:
Guide to parish register holdings
Information sheets (mostly for family history and house history)
Surrey History Service (descriptive leaflet)

Microform publications:
Some fiche and films copies available through bureaux at request of Surrey Heritage; no filming service at present

Publications list:
Available online

Access to staff:
Contact by letter, by telephone, by fax, by e-mail and via website. Appointment necessary.

Access to building, collection or gallery:
Hours: Tue, Wed, Fri, 0930 to 1700; Thu, 0930 to 1930; Sat, 0930 to 1600
Special comments: CARN tickets, Surrey Library cards or ID required

Access for disabled people:
Parking provided, ramped entry, access to all public areas, toilet facilities

SURREY PERFORMING ARTS LIBRARY

Denbies Wine Estate, London Road, Dorking, Surrey, RH5 6AA

Tel: 01306 887509
Fax: 01306 875074
E-mail: performing.arts@surreycc.gov.uk

Website:
http://www.surreycc.gov.uk/libraries

Enquiries:
Enquiries to: Senior Librarian
Direct tel: 01306 875453

Founded:
1981

Organisation type and purpose:
Local government body, public library.

continued overleaf

Subject coverage:
Performing arts, including music, drama, theatre, arts, dance and cinema.

Museum or gallery collection, archive, or library special collection:
CD and DVD collections within the subject areas
Performance materials; sets of plays, vocal scores, orchestral parts, chamber music parts

Non-library collection catalogue:
All or part available online

Library catalogue:
All or part available online

Access to staff:
Contact by letter, by telephone, by fax, by e-mail and in person
Hours: Tue and Fri, 1000 to 1700; Thu, 1000 to 2000; Sat, 0930 to 1300; Mon and Wed, closed

Access to building, collection or gallery:
Hours: Tues and Fri, 1000 to 1700; Thu, 1000 to 2000; Sat, 0930 to 1300; Mon and Wed, closed

Access for disabled people:
Level entry, access to all public areas
Hours: As above

Parent body:
Surrey County Council

SURREY RECORD SOCIETY

c/o Surrey History Centre, 130 Goldsworth Road, Woking, Surrey, GU21 6ND

Tel: 01483 518754
Fax: 01483 518738

Enquiries:
Enquiries to: Honorary Secretary

Founded:
1913

Organisation type and purpose:
Learned society (membership is by subscription). The Society exists to publish records relating to the historic county of Surrey, which includes the parishes of South London as far east as Rotherhithe.

Subject coverage:
Surrey history and genealogy. No research undertaken.

Printed publications:
Transcripts, translations and abstracts of texts ranging in date from the twelfth to the nineteenth century, and in subject from central, county and municipal government to ecclesiastical, manorial, industrial and military history. Manuscript sources held in repositories in and outside the county are thus made accessible
35 volumes to date, not all in print, but including:
Vol VII The Pipe Roll for 1295, Surrey membrane (ed Mills M H, paperback reprint 1968)
Vol XV Surrey Manorial Accounts (ed Briggs H M, paperback reprint, 1968)
Vol XXVIII Kingston upon Thames Register of Apprentices 1563–1703 (ed Daly A, 1974)
Vol XXXIII Minutes of the Board of Directors of the Reading, Guildford and Reigate Railway Company (ed Course E, 1988, members £12.50, non-members £15, overseas £17.50)
Vol XXXIV Parson and Parish in Eighteenth-Century Surrey: Replies to Bishops' Visitations (ed Ward W R, £15 UK)
Vol XXXV The 1851 Religious Census: Surrey (transcribed by Webb C and Robinson D, £25 UK)
Vol XXXVI Gunpowder Mills: Documents of the 17th and 18th centuries (ed Crocker, Crocker, Fairclough and Wilks, 2000, £15 plus £2 p&p UK)
For full list, visit website http://www.surreycc.gov.uk/surreyhistorycentre

Access to staff:
Contact by letter
Hours: Mon to Fri, 0900 to 1700

SURVEY FORCE LIMITED

Algarve House, 140 Borden Lane, Sittingbourne, Kent, ME9 8HW

Tel: 01795 423778
Fax: 01795 423778
E-mail: surveyforce@yahoo.com

Enquiries:
Enquiries to: Director
Other contacts: Sales Managers

Founded:
1974

Organisation type and purpose:
International organisation, service industry, consultancy, research organisation.

Subject coverage:
Market research in chemical, pharmaceutical, health care, electronics, computer, IT, optical, elastomers, rubbers, plastics, food and drink, diagnostics (instrumentation and reagents).

Museum or gallery collection, archive, or library special collection:
Market research studies (over 500) covering world, EU, USA, Japan etc, regularly updated

Trade and statistical information:
Computers – World.
Health care – World and USA.
Pharmaceutical USA, Japan, World.
Electronics – EC, UK, USA, Japan.
Optical – Italy, France, UK, USA.
Elastomers – Europe; USA.
Chemical – World.
IT – World.

Non-library collection catalogue:
All or part available in print

Printed publications:
Over 500 market research studies regularly updated

Electronic and video publications:
Some reports available on CD-ROM
Most databases available on disk or by e-mail

Publications list:
Available in print

Access to staff:
Contact by letter, by telephone, by fax and by e-mail. Appointment necessary.
Hours: Mon to Fri, 0900 to 1700

Access to building, collection or gallery:
Prior appointment required

SUSSEX COUNTY CRICKET CLUB

Eaton Road, Hove, East Sussex, BN3 3AN

Tel: 01273 827100
Fax: 01273 771549

Website:
http://www.sussexcricket.co.uk

Enquiries:
Enquiries to: Business Manager
Direct tel: 01273 827102
Direct e-mail: Russell@sussexcricket.co.uk

Founded:
1839

Organisation type and purpose:
Membership association (membership is by subscription), present number of members: c. 5,000.
Sporting organisation.

Subject coverage:
History of the clubs and its players.

Access to staff:
Contact by letter, by telephone, by fax and via website
Hours: Mon to Fri, 0900 to 1700

SUSSEX INDUSTRIAL ARCHAEOLOGY SOCIETY

Acronym or abbreviation: SIAS

42 Falmer Avenue, Saltdean, Brighton, East Sussex, BN2 8FG

Tel: 01273 271330
E-mail: ronald@martin42.fsnet.co.uk

Website:
http://www.sussexias.co.uk

Enquiries:
Enquiries to: General Secretary
Other contacts: Treasurer for financial matters.

Founded:
1968

Organisation type and purpose:
Membership association (membership is by subscription), present number of members: 350, voluntary organisation, registered charity (charity number 267159), research organisation.

Subject coverage:
Sussex industrial archaeology, mills, brickmaking, railways, ice houses, breweries.

Museum or gallery collection, archive, or library special collection:
Records of industrial archaeology sites in Sussex

Printed publications:
Newsletter (quarterly, 50p)
Sussex Industrial History (annually, £4.25, p&p 75p, back numbers available)

Publications list:
Available in print

Access to staff:
Contact by letter, by telephone and by e-mail
Hours: 0800 to 2300

SUSSEX PAST

Formal name: Sussex Archaeological Society

Bull House, 92 High Street, Lewes, East Sussex, BN7 1XH

Tel: 01273 486260
Fax: 01273 486990
E-mail: admin@sussexpast.co.uk

Website:
http://www.sussexpast.co.uk
Properties open to the public, research, details of organisation and membership.

Enquiries:
Enquiries to: Public Relations Manager
Direct tel: 01273 487188
Direct e-mail: pro@sussexpast.co.uk

Founded:
1846

Organisation type and purpose:
Learned society, registered charity, museum.

Subject coverage:
Sussex archaeology, local history and historic properties.

Special visitor services:
Guided tours.

Education services:
Group education facilities.

Museum or gallery collection, archive, or library special collection:
Artefacts relating to archaeology and history
Collection of prints, pictures, books related to Sussex
Manuscripts

Printed publications:
Sussex Past & Present (magazine, 3 times a year)
Sussex Archaeological Collections (annually, to members or on subscription)

Access to building, collection or gallery:
Prior appointment required
Hours: Mon to Sat, 1000 to 1700; Sun, 1100 to 1700

Special comments: Library: 01273 405738
Museum: 01273 405739

Affiliated to:
Council for British Archaeology

Sussex Past sites:
Anne of Cleves House Museum
52 Southover High Street, Lewes, East Sussex,
BN7 1JA; tel: 01273 474610
Fishbourne Roman Palace and Museum
Salthill Road, Fishbourne, Chichester, West
Sussex, PO19 3QR; tel: 01243 785859; fax: 01243
539266; e-mail: adminfish@sussexpast.co.uk
Lewes Castle & Museums
169 High Street, Lewes, East Sussex, BN7 1YE;
tel: 01273 486290; e-mail: castle@sussexpast.co
.uk
Marlipins Museum
High Street, Shoreham-by-Sea, West Sussex,
BN43 5NN; tel: 01273 462994
Michelham Priory
Upper Dicker, Hailsham, East Sussex, BN27 3QS;
tel: 01323 844224
The Priest House
North Lane, West Hoathly, East Grinstead, West
Sussex, RH19 4PP; tel: 01342 810479; e-mail:
priest@sussexpast.co.uk

SUSSEX RECORD SOCIETY

Barbican House, High Street, Lewes, East Sussex,
BN7 1YE

Website:
http://www.sussexrecordsociety.org.uk

Enquiries:
Enquiries to: Hon. Secretary
Direct e-mail: richard.martin2083@ntlworld.com

Founded:
1901

Organisation type and purpose:
Learned society.

Subject coverage:
Publication of texts relating to the history and
topography of Sussex.

Printed publications:
Annual Report
Annual volumes
Newsletter (annually, for members)

Microform publications:
Volumes 1–61
Order microform publications from: available on
microfiche from Chadwyck-Healey

Electronic and video publications:
Some volumes at website: http://
www.sussexrecordsociety.org.uk/listbooks.asp#

Publications list:
Available in print

Access to staff:
Contact by letter, by e-mail and via website

SUSTAIN: THE ALLIANCE FOR BETTER FOOD FARMING

Acronym or abbreviation: Sustain

94 White Lion Street, London, N1 9PF

Tel: 020 7837 1228
E-mail: sustain@sustainweb.org

Website:
http://www.sustainweb.org
Sustainable food and farming, including
environment, nutrition, animal welfare, local food,
climate change, urban food growing, real bread,
children's food, public sector food.

Enquiries:
Enquiries to: Co-ordinator

Founded:
1985

Created by the merger of:
National Food Alliance, and Sustainable
Agriculture Food and Environment Alliance (year
of change 1999)

Organisation type and purpose:
Membership association (membership is by
application or invitation), present number of
members: c. 100, voluntary organisation, registered
charity (charity number 1018643).
Umbrella group.

Subject coverage:
All aspects of food along the length of the food
chain, including environment, nutrition, farming,
fair trade, animal welfare.

Printed publications:
A wide range of publications, including one-off
reports and regular newsletters, are available
online. Some are freely available, others to
members only – see website for details.
Order printed publications from: via website: http://
www.sustainweb.org/publications

Publications list:
Available online

Access to staff:
Contact by letter, by telephone, by e-mail and via
website. Appointment necessary.
Hours: Mon to Fri, 0900 to 1800

Access to building, collection or gallery:
Prior appointment required

Access for disabled people:
The building is wheelchair accessible

Member organisations:
around 100 member organisations

SUSTRANS

Formal name: Sustainable Transport

2 Cathedral Square, College Green, Bristol, BS1
5DD

Tel: 0117 926 8893
Fax: 0117 929 4173
E-mail: info@sustrans.org.uk

Website:
http://www.sustrans.org.uk
Information about the National Cycle Network,
safe routes to schools and Sustrans. Includes list of
publications.

Enquiries:
Enquiries to: Information Officer
Direct e-mail: press@sustrans.org.uk

Founded:
1978

Organisation type and purpose:
Registered charity (charity number 326550).
Campaigns for and builds cycle and pedestrian
routes.

Subject coverage:
The designing and building of traffic-free routes
for cyclists, pedestrians and wheelchair users, the
National Cycle Network, the need for a new
sustainable transport policy which lessens
dependence on the motor car.

Museum or gallery collection, archive, or library special collection:
About 400 design and policy studies on walking
and particularly cycling facilities

Printed publications:
Recent publications include:
Annual Report
Information Sheets (free)
Making Ways for the bicycle; A Guide to Traffic-
Free Path Construction (1994, £10)
National Cycle Network Route Maps
Safe Routes to Schools: various
The National Cycle Network: Guidelines and
Practical Details; Issue 2 (1997, £29.50 plus p&p)
Order printed publications from: Sustrans
Information Service

PO Box 21, Bristol, BS99 2HA, e-mail: info@
sustrans.org.uk

Publications list:
Available online and in print

Access to staff:
Contact by letter, by telephone, by fax, by e-mail
and via website. Appointment necessary.
Hours: Mon to Fri, 0900 to 1700

Head Office:
Head Office
35 King Street, Bristol, BS1 4DZ; tel: 0117 926
8893; fax: 0117 929 4173

Regions:
North East
Rockwood House, Barn Hill, Stanley, Co
Durham, DH9 8AN; tel: 01207 281259; fax: 01207
28113
Northern Ireland
McAvoy House, 17A Ormeau Avenue, Belfast,
BT2 8HD; tel: 028 9043 4569; fax: 028 9043 4556
Scotland
162 Fountainbridge, Edinburgh, EH3 9RX; tel:
0131 624 7660; fax: 0131 624 7764

SUTTON AND EAST SURREY WATER PLC

Acronym or abbreviation: SESW

London Road, Redhill, Surrey, RH1 1IJ

Tel: 01737 772000
Fax: 01737 766807
E-mail: customer_services@waterplc.com

Website:
http://www.waterplc.com

Enquiries:
Enquiries to: Press Officer
Direct tel: 01372 460111
Direct fax: 01372 470955
Direct e-mail: stuart.hyslop@surreyhouseuk.com

Founded:
1860

Organisation type and purpose:
Utility. Water supply company.

Subject coverage:
Supplies water only to East Surrey and parts of
South London, Sussex and West Kent.

Printed publications:
Your Water (customer magazine, produced once a
year and sent to all customers)
The Wonderful World of Water: H2O. Wide
selection of information leaflets

Electronic and video publications:
Company video material available on request

Publications list:
Available online and in print

Access to staff:
Contact by letter, by telephone, by fax, by e-mail,
in person and via website
Hours: Mon to Fri, 0830 to 1700

Access to building, collection or gallery:
Hours: Mon to Fri, 0830 to 1700

Access for disabled people:
Level entry

SUTTON COLDFIELD LIBRARY

45 Lower Parade, Sutton Coldfield, West Midlands,
B72 1XX

Tel: 0121 464 2274
Fax: 0121 464 0173
E-mail: sutton.coldfield.lending.library@
birmingham.gov.uk

Enquiries:
Enquiries to: Librarian
Direct tel: 0121 464 0164

continued overleaf

Organisation type and purpose:
Public library.

Subject coverage:
Separate reference library, children's library and music library and a substantial local history section.

Non-library collection catalogue:
All or part available online

Library catalogue:
All or part available online

Printed publications:
Societies and Organisations in Sutton Coldfield
Sutton Coldfield (Baxter M)
Sutton Coldfield: the Second Selection (Baxter M)

Access to staff:
Contact by letter, by telephone, by fax, by e-mail, in person and via website
Hours: Mon, Wed, Fri, 0900 to 1800; Tue, Thu, 0900 to 2000; Sat, 0900 to 1700

Access for disabled people:
Toilet facilities

SUTTON LIBRARY AND HERITAGE SERVICES

Central Library, St Nicholas Way, Sutton, Surrey, SM1 1EA

Tel: 020 8770 4700\ Minicom no. 020 8770 4779
Fax: 020 8770 4777
E-mail: sutton.information@sutton.gov.uk

Website:
http://www.sutton-libraries.gov.uk/uhtbin/webcat
List of libraries, services, 'search the catalogue' facility.

Enquiries:
Enquiries to: Librarian

Organisation type and purpose:
Local government body, public library.

Subject coverage:
General, including genealogy and heraldry, local studies.

Museum or gallery collection, archive, or library special collection:
Croydon Airport Collection
River Wandle Collection

Library catalogue:
All or part available online

Printed publications:
Range of local history publications including:
All our Yesterdays: A pictorial record of the London Borough of Sutton over the last century (2nd ed, Bradley I et al)
Courts of the Manors of Bandon and Beddington 1498–1552 (Gowans H ed)
Croydon Airport and the Battle of Britain, 1939–1940 (Bogle J, Cluett D and Learmouth B)
Croydon Airport: The Australian Connection: Flights and other links between Croydon Airport and Australia (Cluett D)
Discovering Sutton's Heritage: The story of five parishes (Cluett D)
Nonsuch: Pearl of the Realm: Henry VIII's fantastic palace (Lister L)
The Story of Little Woodcote and Woodcote Hall (Cunningham M)

Publications list:
Available in print

Access to staff:
Contact by letter, by telephone, by fax, by e-mail and in person
Hours: Mon, closed; Tue to Fri, 0900 to 2000; Sat, 0900 to 1700; Sun, 1400 to 1700

Access for disabled people:
Ramped entry, access to all public areas, toilet facilities

SUZY LAMPLUGH TRUST

National Centre for Personal Safety, Hampton House, 20 Albert Embankment, London, SE1 7TJ

Tel: 020 7091 0014
Fax: 020 7091 0015
E-mail: info@suzylamplugh.org

Website:
http://www.suzylamplugh.org
Complete personal safety information and resources.

Enquiries:
Direct e-mail: press@suzylamplugh.org

Founded:
1986

Organisation type and purpose:
Advisory body, voluntary organisation, registered charity (charity number 802567), suitable for ages: all, training organisation, consultancy, research organisation.
The leading authority on personal safety.
To reduce violence and aggression in society and help everyone – men, women and children – to gain the knowledge and confidence they need to live safer lives.

Subject coverage:
Personal safety, indoors, outdoors, and in the workplace.

Non-library collection catalogue:
All or part available online

Library catalogue:
All or part available in-house

Printed publications:
Living Safely – Personal Safety in Your Daily Life (booklet, versions for adults, teenagers and people with disabilities)
Think Safety (booklet for teenagers) Both of these publications will be sent free on receipt of a sae.
Think Safety Green (£2.50 p&p)
Books and videos for schools, children, and young people, personal safety at work
Research Reports

Electronic and video publications:
Personal Safety At Work (video)
Home Safe (video and pack)
Well Safe (video and pack)
World Wise (video and pack)

Publications list:
Available online and in print

Access to staff:
Contact by letter, by telephone and by fax.
Appointment necessary.
Hours: Mon to Fri, 0900 to 1700

SWALE BOROUGH COUNCIL

Acronym or abbreviation: SBC

Swale House, East Street, Sittingbourne, Kent, ME10 3HT

Tel: 01795 424341
Fax: 01795 417217

Website:
http://www.swale.gov.uk

Enquiries:
Enquiries to: Public Relations Manager
Direct tel: 01795 417400
Direct fax: 01795 417382
Direct e-mail: kimevans@swale.gov.uk

Founded:
1974

Organisation type and purpose:
Local government body.

Subject coverage:
Local government.

Access to staff:
Contact by letter, by telephone, by fax and by e-mail
Hours: Mon to Fri, 0900 to 1700

SWALEDALE SHEEP BREEDERS ASSOCIATION

The Shooting Lodge, High Shipley, Eggleston, Barnard Castle, Co Durham, DL12 0DP

Tel: 01833 650516
Fax: 01833 650516
E-mail: jstephenson@swaledale-sheep.com

Subject coverage:
Breeders and breeding of Swaledale Sheep.

SWANSEA CITY AND COUNTY COUNCIL

County Hall, Swansea, West Glamorgan, SA1 3SN

Tel: 01792 636000
Fax: 01792 637206
E-mail: bob.cuthill@swansea.gov.uk

Website:
http://www.swansea.gov.uk

Enquiries:
Enquiries to: Information Officer
Direct tel: 01792 636737

Founded:
1996

Organisation type and purpose:
Local government body.

Subject coverage:
Policy issues, demography including census of the population, local statistics and modernising local government agenda.

Access to staff:
Contact by letter, by telephone, by fax, by e-mail and via website. Appointment necessary.
Hours: Mon to Fri, 0830 to 1700

Access for disabled people:
Parking provided, ramped entry, level entry, toilet facilities

SWANSEA INSTITUTE OF HIGHER EDUCATION

Acronym or abbreviation: SIHE

Townhill Road, Swansea, West Glamorgan, SA2 0UT

Tel: 01792 481000
Fax: 01792 208683
E-mail: enquiry@sihe.ac.uk

Website:
http://www.sihe.ac.uk

Enquiries:
Enquiries to: Head of Library and Learning Support Services
Direct tel: 01792 481240
Direct fax: 01792 298017
Direct e-mail: t.lamb@sihe.ac.uk

Organisation type and purpose:
Library.

Subject coverage:
Art, stained glass, education – primary teacher training, humanities, construction, business, management, law, tourism, leisure, health care, transport, engineering, manufacturing design, optoelectronics computing, safety in leisure pursuits, motor sport, applied design.

Access to staff:
Non-members charged.
Hours: Mon to Thu, 0845 to 2100; Fri, 0845 to 1630; Sat, 1000 to 1600

Associated college of:
University of Wales

Other addresses:
Swansea Institute of Higher Education
Mount Pleasant, Swansea, SA1 6ED; tel: 01792 481000

SWANSEA TRIBOLOGY SERVICES LIMITED

Acronym or abbreviation: STS Ltd

5 Penrice Court, Fenrod Business Park, Enterprise Park, Swansea, West Glamorgan, SA6 8QW

Tel: 01792 799036
Fax: 01792 799034
E-mail: oiltest@trib.co.uk

Website:
http://www.trib.co.uk

Enquiries:
Enquiries to: Laboratory Director

Founded:
1996

Organisation type and purpose:
International organisation, manufacturing industry, service industry, training organisation, consultancy, research organisation, laboratory.

Subject coverage:
Tribology, condition monitoring, wear debris monitors, oil analysis, maintenance.

Publications list:
Available in print

Access to staff:
Contact by letter, by telephone, by fax, by e-mail, in person and via website. Appointment necessary.
Hours: Mon to Fri, 0900 to 1630

SWANSEA UNIVERSITY – LIBRARY & INFORMATION SERVICES

Singleton Park, Swansea, SA2 8PP

Tel: 01792 295175
Fax: 01792 295851
E-mail: library@swansea.ac.uk

Website:
http://www.swan.ac.uk/lis
Description of Library & Information Services: gateway to other information sources; on-line exhibitions.

Enquiries:
Enquiries to: Director of Library and Information Services

Founded:
1920

Organisation type and purpose:
University library.

Subject coverage:
Humanities, economic and social sciences, physical, natural and engineering sciences, education, business studies, law, history of South Wales coalfield.

Museum or gallery collection, archive, or library special collection:
Archives of the South Wales coalfield and other local archives
British Standards
Strong collections in history, mathematics, Celtic studies, Welsh writers in English

Non-library collection catalogue:
All or part available online and in-house

Library catalogue:
All or part available online

Printed publications:
Guides and leaflets for library users

Microform publications:
University of Wales Swansea Theses can be supplied at a charge.

Access to staff:
Contact by letter, by telephone, by fax, by e-mail and in person
Hours: Term time: Sun to Thu, 0800 to 0200; Fri, Sat, 0800 to 2000
Vacations: Mon to Thu 0800 to 2000; Fri, Sat, 0800 to 1700; Sun, closed

Special comments: Different hours apply in branch libraries.

Access to building, collection or gallery:
No prior appointment required

Access for disabled people:
Ramped entry, access to all public areas, toilet facilities
Special comments: Special facilities for users with visual impairment.

SWEDENBORG SOCIETY

Swedenborg House, 20–21 Bloomsbury Way, London, WC1A 2TH

Tel: 020 7405 7986
E-mail: james@swedenborg.org.uk

Website:
http://www.swedenborg.org.uk
Introduction to the function of the Swedenborg Society, the life, work and influence of Emanuel Swedenborg. Online bookshop. News and events. Library catalogue (partial).

Enquiries:
Enquiries to: Librarian
Other contacts: Secretary

Founded:
1810

Organisation type and purpose:
Learned society (membership is by subscription, election or invitation), present number of members: 850, registered charity (charity number 209172), publishing house.
The Swedenborg Society was established for the purpose of printing and publishing the works of Emanuel Swedenborg.

Subject coverage:
Life and works of Emanuel Swedenborg and related material.

Museum or gallery collection, archive, or library special collection:
Complete works of Swedenborg; all languages and all editions; original archival items re society, Swedenborg, the New Church; collateral works
Completely catalogued reference library
Separate lending library

Non-library collection catalogue:
All or part available online

Library catalogue:
All or part available online and in-house

Printed publications:
Annual Report
Journal
Catalogue: a wide range of books available – theological, Latin editions, facsimile reproductions of first editions, miscellaneous books and booklets
Order printed publications from: http://www.swedenborg.org.uk

Publications list:
Available online and in print

Access to staff:
Contact by letter, by telephone, by e-mail and via website. Appointment necessary.
Hours: Mon to Fri, 0930 to 1700

Access to building, collection or gallery:
Prior appointment required for use of library; please bring ID and proof of address

Links with:
similar bodies world-wide
The Library and Archives of The General Conference of the New Church at the same address

SWEDISH CHAMBER OF COMMERCE FOR THE UNITED KINGDOM

Sweden House, 5 Upper Montagu Street, London, W1H 2AG

Tel: 020 7224 8001
Fax: 020 7224 8884
E-mail: info@scc.org.uk

Website:
http://www.scc.org.uk

Enquiries:
Enquiries to: Managing Director

Founded:
1906

Organisation type and purpose:
Membership association (membership is by subscription), present number of members: 400.

Subject coverage:
General information dealing with Anglo-Swedish trade.

Trade and statistical information:
Data on Anglo-Swedish trade.

Printed publications:
Link Magazine (monthly, free)
Swedish Chamber of Commerce Trade Directory (annually, £79 incl. p&p)

Access to staff:
Contact by letter, by fax, by e-mail, in person and via website. Non-members charged.
Hours: Mon to Fri, 0900 to 1730

SWIFT CLUB

The Croft, Ash Green, Surrey, GU12 6HD

Tel: 01252 344402
Fax: 01252 311187

Enquiries:
Enquiries to: Honorary Secretary

Founded:
1985

Organisation type and purpose:
Membership association (membership is by subscription), present number of members: 67, voluntary organisation.

Subject coverage:
Technical advice on Swift cars produced by the Swift Motor Co. of Coventry between 1901 and 1931.

Printed publications:
Magazine and Newsletter (members only)

Access to staff:
Contact by letter, by telephone, by fax and by e-mail. Appointment necessary.
Hours: Mon to Sun, 0900 to 2200

SWIM WALES

Wales National Pool, Sketty Lane, Swansea, SA2 8QG

Tel: 01792 513636
Fax: 01792 513637
E-mail: secretary@welshasa.co.uk

Website:
http://www.welshasa.co.uk

Enquiries:
Enquiries to: Head of Administration

Founded:
1897

Formerly called:
Welsh Amateur Swimming Association (WASA)

Organisation type and purpose:
Membership association (membership is by subscription), present number of members: 9,500, voluntary organisation.
Recognised as the governing body for swimming in Wales; promotes the sport throughout Wales and develops members' potential to represent Wales and Great Britain at European and World levels in swimming, diving and water polo.

Subject coverage:
Amateur swimming, diving and water polo.

continued overleaf

Access to staff:
Contact by letter, by telephone, by fax and by e-mail
Hours: Mon to Fri, 0900 to 1600

SWIMMING POOL AND ALLIED TRADES ASSOCIATION

Acronym or abbreviation: SPATA

4 Eastgate House, East Street, Andover, Hampshire, SP10 1EP

Tel: 01264 356210
E-mail: admin@spata.co.uk

Website:
http://www.spata.co.uk
SPATA, swimming pools, design awards, members' area, publications.

Organisation type and purpose:
A membership association for the swimming pools and allied trades.
Sets standards governing the construction and operation of pools, spas, saunas and steam rooms, which members have to follow. Inspects pool contractor members' work before they can join, and periodically reinspects afterwards.
Membership includes approx. 200 swimming pool companies in the UK, Ireland and overseas, including contractors, designers, service engineers, trade suppliers, and retailers of pool equipment and ancillaries.

Subject coverage:
Swimming pools, spas, saunas, steam rooms.

Printed publications:
SPATA Standards 2010 for domestic and commercial swimming pools (£395 excl. p&p)
Information Pack, incl. Contract Check List and the SPATA Swimming Pool Guide (free)
Member Factsheets (free)
Order printed publications from: Website

Publications list:
Available online

Access to staff:
Contact by letter, by telephone and by e-mail

Member organisation of:
British Swimming Pool Federation
European Union of Swimming Pool and Spa Associations (EUSA)

SWINDON BOROUGH COUNCIL

Civic Offices, Euclid Street, Swindon, Wiltshire, SN1 2JH

Tel: 01793 463000; minicom no. 01793 436659
Fax: 01793 463930

Website:
http://www.swindon.gov.uk

Enquiries:
Enquiries to: Chief Executive
Direct tel: 01793 463010
Direct e-mail: gjones@swindon.gov.uk

Organisation type and purpose:
Local government body.

Subject coverage:
Local government.

Access to staff:
Contact by letter, by telephone and by fax
Hours: Mon to Fri, 0900 to 1630

SWINDON BOROUGH COUNCIL LIBRARIES

Central Library, Regent Circus, Swindon, SN1 1QG

Tel: 01793 466035
Fax: 01793 529572
E-mail: ajordan@swindon.gov.uk

Website:
http://www.swindon.gov.uk/libraries

Full list of library services and facilities.

Enquiries:
Enquiries to: Library Services Manager

Organisation type and purpose:
Local government body, public library.

Subject coverage:
General, railways.

Museum or gallery collection, archive, or library special collection:
Great Western Railway collection
Richard Jefferies manuscript collection
Swindon and Wiltshire local studies

Non-library collection catalogue:
All or part available online

Library catalogue:
All or part available online

Access to staff:
Contact by letter, by telephone, by fax, by e-mail and in person. Appointment necessary. Access for members only.
Hours: Mon to Fri, 0900 to 1700; Sat, 0930 to 1600

Access to building, collection or gallery:
No prior appointment required

Access for disabled people:
Ramped entry, level entry

Parent body:
Swindon Borough Council
Civic, Offices, Euclid Street, Swindon, SN1 2JH; tel: 01793 445000; e-mail: customerservices@swindon.gov.uk; website: http://www.swindon.gov.uk

Sponsor for:
WILCO
Central Library, Regent Circus, Swindon, SN1 1QG; tel: 01793 463797; fax: 01793 529572; e-mail: rtrayhurn@swindon.gov.uk; website: http://www.wilco.org.uk

SWISS COTTAGE CENTRAL LIBRARY

88 Avenue Road, London, NW3 3HA

Tel: 020 7974 4001
Fax: 020 7974 6532
E-mail: swisscottagelibrary@camden.gov.uk

Website:
http://www.camden.gov.uk/ccm/navigation/leisure/libraries-and-online-learning-centres/swiss-cottage-library/

Enquiries:
Enquiries to: Customer Services Manager
Direct tel: 020 7974 6531 (not a public number)
Other contacts: Service Delivery Manager

Founded:
1964

Organisation type and purpose:
Local government body, public library.

Subject coverage:
General library, reference materials, specialist collection of philosophy and psychology; selected official publications.

Museum or gallery collection, archive, or library special collection:
Maps
Selected official publications of United Kingdom (some EU)
See website: http://www.camden.gov.uk/ccm/content/leisure/libraries-and-online-learning-centres/twocolumn/reference-information.en for current subscription databases

Trade and statistical information:
Selected British official statistics, some EU statistics.

Library catalogue:
All or part available online

Access to staff:
Contact by letter, by telephone, by e-mail and in person
Hours: Mon to Fri, 1000 to 2000; Sat, 1000 to 1700; Sun, 1100 to 1600

Access to building, collection or gallery:
Hours: Mon to Fri, 1000 to 2000; Sat, 1000 to 1700; Sun, 1100 to 1600

Access for disabled people:
Level entry, access to all public areas, toilet facilities

Parent body:
London Borough of Camden, Culture and Environment
Camden Town Hall Extension, Argyle Street, London WC1H 8EQ; tel: 020 7974 5613; website: https://www.camden.gov.uk/ccm/content/contacts/council-contacts/environment/contact-the-environment-department.en

SWISS EMBASSY

Formal name: Embassy of Switzerland

16–18 Montagu Place, London, W1H 2BQ

Tel: 020 7616 6000
Fax: 020 7724 7001
E-mail: swissembassy@lon.rep.admin.ch

Website:
http://www.swissembassy.org.uk

Organisation type and purpose:
National embassy.

Subject coverage:
Switzerland: general, commercial, cultural and educational matters.

SWITZERLAND TOURISM

30 Bedford Street, London, WC2E 9ED

Tel: 020 7420 4900
Fax: 00800 100 200 31
E-mail: info.uk@myswitzerland.com

Website:
http://www.myswitzerland.com
Information, reservations and interaction.

Enquiries:
Enquiries to: Marketing Services

Founded:
1875

Organisation type and purpose:
International organisation.

Access to staff:
Contact by letter, by telephone, by fax and by e-mail
Hours: Mon to Fri, 0900 to 1700

Access to building, collection or gallery:
No access other than to staff, prior appointment required

Access for disabled people:
Ramped entry, toilet facilities

SYBIL CAMPBELL COLLECTION

c/o Mr David Farley, University of Winchester, Winchester, Hampshire, SO22 4NR

Fax: 01962 827479
E-mail: libenquiries@winchester.ac.uk

Website:
http://winchester.ac.uk/library

Enquiries:
Enquiries to: Librarian
Direct tel: 01962 827306

Founded:
1927
Crosby Hall Library

Organisation type and purpose:
Library reference collection reflecting the entrance of women into higher education and into academic and professional life in the late 19th and early 20th century.

Subject coverage:
Women's writing and history in the 19th and 20th centuries, women's education and their personal libraries, (auto)biography, women in wartime (including refugees), early 20th century philosophy, literary criticism, poetry and travel.

Museum or gallery collection, archive, or library special collection:
Library of 8,000 items

Non-library collection catalogue:
All or part available online and in-house

Library catalogue:
All or part available online and in-house

Electronic and video publications:
Order electronic and video publications from: Seminar Monographs (online)

Access to staff:
Contact by letter, by telephone and by e-mail. Appointment necessary.

Administered by:
University of Winchester

Parent body:
University of Winchester

TALIS INFORMATION LIMITED

Knights Court, Solihull Parkway, Birmingham Business Park, B37 7YB

Tel: 0870 400 5000
Fax: 0870 400 5001
E-mail: info@talis.com

Website:
http://www.talis.com
Information, news, web opacs.

Enquiries:
Direct e-mail: sarah.foster@talis.com

Founded:
1969

Organisation type and purpose:
UK's leading provider of library management systems and also provides solutions to manage academic course resources, digitised image collections, and maintain a unique database containing over 19 million bibliographical records.

Subject coverage:
Library automation, library services, unity web, network services, information delivery services, Talislist – guided learning environment, training and consultancy, Invisage – digital content management, OPAC.

Museum or gallery collection, archive, or library special collection:
BLCMP Database of 17 million bibliographic records
Unityweb

Printed publications:
Product Literature for all products

Electronic and video publications:
Talis library automation system
Talis Invisage
Talis List
Talis Message
OPAC
Acquisitions and cataloguing services
Ztarget
Management Information
Circulation & ILL
Talis Inquire
TalisBase database
EDI Gateway services
Unityweb

Access to staff:
Contact by letter, by telephone, by fax, by e-mail and via website. Appointment necessary.
Hours: Mon to Fri, 0900 to 1700

TALKING NEWSPAPER ASSOCIATION OF THE UNITED KINGDOM

Acronym or abbreviation: TNAUK

National Recording Centre, 10 Browning Road, Heathfield, East Sussex, TN21 8DB

Tel: 01435 866102
Fax: 01435 865422
E-mail: info@tnauk.org.uk

Website:
http://www.tnauk.org.uk

Enquiries:
Enquiries to: Director

Founded:
1974

Organisation type and purpose:
Membership association, registered charity (charity number 293656).

Subject coverage:
Recording of over 200 national newspapers and magazines on audio tape, audio CD, Daisy CDs and download with full text versions of many publications on CD-ROM, website download and e-mail for visually impaired and disabled people.

Printed publications:
Catalogue

Electronic and video publications:
Information tape and disk

Publications list:
Available online and in print

Access to staff:
Contact by letter, by telephone, by fax, by e-mail and in person
Hours: Mon to Fri, 0900 to 1700

Links with:
RNIB
tel: 01435 866102; fax: 01435 865422; e-mail: info@tnauk.org.uk

TALL SHIPS YOUTH TRUST

Acronym or abbreviation: STA

2A The Hard, Portsmouth, Hampshire, PO1 3PT

Tel: 023 9283 2055
Fax: 023 9281 5769
E-mail: info@tallships.org

Website:
http://www.tallships.org

Enquiries:
Enquiries to: PR & Events Manager
Other contacts: Reservations Supervisor for voyage enquiry.

Founded:
1956

Formerly called:
STA Schooners (year of change 1995); International STA (year of change 1999); Sail Training Association (year of change 2004)

Organisation type and purpose:
Voluntary organisation, registered charity (charity number 314229), training organisation.
The Tall Ships Youth Trust is dedicated to the personal development of young people, aged 16–25, through the experience of tall ship sailing, aboard one of our Brigs, 'Stavros S Niarchos' and 'Prince William'. Similar opportunities are available on adult voyages (18–75). Voyages are available in the UK, Europe, Caribbean, Mediterranean and transatlantic

Subject coverage:
Tall Ships' Voyages and Cutty Sark Tall Ships' Races, personal development of 16 to 25 year olds.
Adult Voyages for 18–75 year olds.
Day Sails for 18–75 year olds.

Trade and statistical information:
World's largest and leading sail training organisation.

Printed publications:
Aloft (3 times a year, free of charge)

Electronic and video publications:
Tall Ships Youth Trust (Video, DVD, available for purchase)

Access to staff:
Contact by letter, by telephone, by fax, by e-mail, in person and via website
Hours: Mon to Fri, 0900 to 1700

Member of:
Association of Sea Training Organisations
Duke of Edinburgh's Award
tel: 01753 727400; fax: 01753 810666; e-mail: info@theaward.org
Royal Yachting Association
tel: 023 8062 7400; website: www.rya.org

TALYLLYN RAILWAY

Wharf Station, Tywyn, Gwynedd, LL36 9EY

Tel: 01654 710472
Fax: 01654 711755
E-mail: enquiries@talyllyn.co.uk

Website:
http://www.talyllyn.co.uk
Timetables, special events, route, locomotives, history, railway letter service; preservation society, volunteering.

Enquiries:
Enquiries to: Secretary
Direct e-mail: secretary@talyllyn.co.uk
Other contacts: Chief Executive

Founded:
1865

Organisation type and purpose:
Voluntary organisation, museum.
Preservation society. The Talyllyn Railway runs from Tywyn Wharf to Nant Gwernol and was opened in 1866. The Narrow Gauge Railway Museum is at Tywyn.

Subject coverage:
Narrow gauge railways; Welsh slate industry history; narrow gauge railway modelling; maintenance of narrow gauge railways, steam and diesel; volunteering.

Special visitor services:
Opportunities to drive your own steam train; see Driver Experience on website or telephone for details.

Education services:
Narrow Gauge Railway Museum at Tywyn Wharf; facilities for school parties.

Services for disabled people:
All advertised trains except the Victorian Train have accommodation for wheelchairs; accessible lavatories are available at Tywyn Wharf and Abergynolwyn.

Museum or gallery collection, archive, or library special collection:
The Railway operates 6 historic steam locomotives and a number of historic carriages
The Museum houses several locomotives and a large collection of other items from British and Irish narrow gauge lines
Archives are kept in Dolgellau in conjunction with Gwynedd Council

Non-library collection catalogue:
All or part available online

Printed publications:
Timetable, guide, handbook, group travel organisers' guide.

continued overleaf

Quarterly Talyllyn News
Annual Report
Order printed publications from: Talyllyn Railway
Shop, address as above; tel: 01654 711012

Microform publications:
16mm film (for hire)
Order microform publications from: Films Officer,
address as above

Electronic and video publications:
Videos (for purchase)
Order electronic and video publications from: Talyllyn
Railway Shop, address as above; tel: 01654 711012

Publications list:
Available online

Access to staff:
Contact by letter, by telephone, by fax, by e-mail,
in person and via website
Hours: Whenever trains are running; at other times
of year Mon to Fri, 0900 to 1700
See website: http://ngrm.org.uk/ for museum
opening hours
Special comments: Archives only accessible with
introduction; please contact Archives Officer for
details.

Access to building, collection or gallery:
Hours: Stations are open whenever trains are
running, but shops and refreshment rooms may
close earlier. At other times of year at Tywyn
Wharf the shop, refreshment room and museum
are open on certain days; see website or telephone
for details.
See website: http://ngrm.org.uk/ for museum
opening hours.

Access for disabled people:
Tywyn Wharf and Abergynolwyn: all public areas
wheelchair accessible; other stations: please
enquire

TAMBA

Formal name: Twins and Multiple Births
Association

2 The Willows, Gardner Road, Guildford, Surrey,
GU1 4PG

Tel: 01483 304442
Fax: 01483 302483
E-mail: enquiries@tamba.org.uk

Website:
http://www.tamba.org.uk

Enquiries:
Enquiries to: Administrator

Founded:
1978

Formerly called:
Twins Clubs Association

Organisation type and purpose:
Membership association (membership is by
subscription), present number of members: 6000,
registered charity (charity number 1076478).

Subject coverage:
Multiple births (two three, four or more) families;
professional support for parents and carers; ante-
natal and post-natal aspects of management;
network of local twin clubs for parents; fertility
treatment, bereavements; one parent families;
special needs groups; education of twins and
higher multiples. Super Twins (for families of
triplets or more).

**Museum or gallery collection, archive, or library
special collection:**
Educational references
Medical references to twins and higher multiples

Printed publications:
Ante-Natal booklet: Expecting more than one (£5)
Leaflets covering the early years, school and
bereavement
Information for professionals
Personal experience leaflets

Twins & Multiple Births: The Essential Parenting
Guide from Pregnancy to Adulthood

Electronic and video publications:
DVDs, videos

Publications list:
Available in print

Access to staff:
Contact by letter, by telephone and by fax
Hours: Mon to Fri, 0930 to 1600
Special comments: Out of hours answerphone.

TAMESIDE ARCHIVES SERVICE

Formal name: Tameside Local Studies and Archives

Tameside Local Studies and Archives Centre,
Central Library, Old Street, Ashton-under-Lyne,
OL6 7SG

Tel: 0161 342 4242
Fax: 0161 342 4245
E-mail: archives@tameside.gov.uk

Website:
http://www.tameside.gov.uk/history
Brief summary of services offered by Tameside
Local Studies Library.

Enquiries:
Enquiries to: Archivist
Other contacts: Local Studies Librarian

Founded:
1976

Organisation type and purpose:
Local government body.

Subject coverage:
Local public, business, religions, family and
regimental records.

**Museum or gallery collection, archive, or library
special collection:**
Manchester Regiment Archives

Non-library collection catalogue:
All or part available online and in-house

Library catalogue:
All or part available in-house

Printed publications:
Guide to Tameside Archives Service (£12.95, plus
£2.20 p&p)
House History (free)
The Manchester Regiment Archive Collection (free)
Family History (free)
Archives for Family History (free)

Access to staff:
Contact by letter, by telephone, by fax, by e-mail,
in person and via website
Hours: Mon, Tue, Thu, 0900 to 2000; Wed, Fri, 0900
to 1700; Sat, 0900 to 1600

Access for disabled people:
Disabled access available
Hours: As above

Parent body:
Tameside Borough Council
Wellington Road, Ashton-under-Lyne

TAMESIDE LIBRARIES
INFORMATION SERVICE

Tameside Central Library, Old Street, Ashton-
under-Lyne, Lancashire, OL6 7SG

Tel: 0161 342 2031
Fax: 0161 330 4762
E-mail: information.direct@tameside.gov.uk

Website:
http://www.tameside.gov.uk/libraries
Council site with links to library services.

Enquiries:
Enquiries to: Librarian

Organisation type and purpose:
Local government body, public library.

Subject coverage:
General.

**Museum or gallery collection, archive, or library
special collection:**
HMSO publications

Non-library collection catalogue:
All or part available online

Library catalogue:
All or part available online

Access to staff:
Contact by letter, by telephone, by fax, by e-mail,
in person and via website
Hours: Mon, Tue, Thu, 0900 to 2000; Wed, Fri, 0900
to 1700; Sat, 0900 to 1600

Access for disabled people:
Ramp access

Parent body:
Tameside Metropolitan Borough Council,
Community Services

TAMESIDE LOCAL GOVERNMENT
INFORMATION SERVICE AND
MEMBERS SERVICES

Level B, Council Offices, Wellington Road, Ashton-
under-Lyne, Lancashire, OL6 6DL

Tel: 0161 342 8355
Fax: 0161 342 2102
E-mail: tameside-reflib@mcr1.poptel.org.uk

Enquiries:
Enquiries to: Democratic Services Officer
Direct tel: 0161 342 3020

Founded:
1982

Organisation type and purpose:
Local government body.

Subject coverage:
Local government.

Library catalogue:
All or part available in-house

Parent body:
Tameside Metropolitan Borough Council
Borough Solicitor

TAMESIDE LOCAL STUDIES
ARCHIVES CENTRE

Central Library, Old Street, Ashton-under-Lyne,
OL6 7SP

Tel: 0161 342 4242
Fax: 0161 342 4245
E-mail: archives@tameside.gov.uk

Website:
http://www.tameside.gov.uk
Brief summary of services offered.

Enquiries:
Enquiries to: Local Studies Librarian
Other contacts: Archivist

Founded:
1976

Organisation type and purpose:
Local government body, public library.

Subject coverage:
Local history and topography of Tameside area,
and background material on Lancashire and
Cheshire.

**Museum or gallery collection, archive, or library
special collection:**
Manchester Regiment archive collection
Manchester Studies tape collection (oral history
interviews recorded c. 1974–1984)

Non-library collection catalogue:
All or part available in-house

Printed publications:
Ashton and Mossley in Archive Photographs (pub Tempus)
Cotton in Ashton (£1.00)
Denton in Old Photographs (£1.00)
Dukinfield in Old Photographs (£1.00)
Flickering Memories: a history of the cinemas of Ashton (£3)
Folklore of Tameside (£6.99)
General leaflet (2001, free)
Home Front (£3)
Looking Back At Series: books containing a mixture of articles on various aspects of life in the towns including Ashton, Victorian Ashton
Lands and Lordships (volume 6)
The History of Tameside: series of volumes covering the history of the nine towns from earliest times up to World War ll, including:
Tameside Before 1066 (volume 1, £9.95)
Tameside 1066–1700 (volume 2, £9.95)
Tameside in Transition (£9.95)
Tameside 1700–1930 (volume 3, £12.95)
The Buildings of Tameside (volume 5, £13.95)
The People Who Made Tameside (volume 4, £11.95)
Victorian Ashton (£1)
Writings of a Nineteenth Century Working Man (£4.50)
Portland Basin (£7.50)

Publications list:
Available in print

Access to staff:
Contact by letter, by telephone, by fax, by e-mail, in person and via website
Hours: Mon, Tue, Thu, 0900 to 2000; Wed, Fri, 0900 to 1700; Sat 0900 to 1600

Constituent part of:
Sustainable Communities
Community and IT Services, Council Offices, Wellington Road, Ashton-under-Lyne, OL6 6DL

TAMWORTH BOROUGH COUNCIL

Marmion House, Lichfield Street, Tamworth, Staffordshire, B79 7BZ

Tel: 01827 709709
Fax: 01827 709271
E-mail: enquiries@tamworth.gov.uk

Website:
http://www.tamworth.gov.uk

Enquiries:
Enquiries to: Public Relations Officer

Organisation type and purpose:
Local government body.

TANDRIDGE DISTRICT COUNCIL

Station Road East, Oxted, Surrey, RH8 0BT

Tel: 01883 722000
Fax: 01883 722015
E-mail: the.council@tandridge.gov.uk

Website:
http://www.tandridgedc.gov.uk
http://www.tandridge.gov.uk

Enquiries:
Enquiries to: Information Officer

Organisation type and purpose:
Local government body.

Access to staff:
Contact by letter, by telephone, by fax, by e-mail and via website. Appointment necessary.
Hours: Mon to Thu, 0900 to 1700; Fri, 0900 to 1630

Access for disabled people:
Level entry

Parent body:
Surrey County Council

TAUNTON DEANE BOROUGH COUNCIL

The Deane House, Belvedere Road, Taunton, Somerset, TA1 1HE

Tel: 01823 356356\ Minicom no. 01823 356356
Fax: 01823 356329
E-mail: public.relations@tauntondeane.gov.uk

Website:
http://www.tauntondeane.gov.uk/tourism
Tourism, accommodation and local events.

Enquiries:
Enquiries to: Public Relations Manager
Direct tel: 01823 356407

Organisation type and purpose:
Local government body.

Subject coverage:
Local agenda 21 and domestic energy efficiency information for residents of Taunton Deane in addition to normal local authority functions.

Access to staff:
Contact by letter, by telephone, by fax, by e-mail, in person and via website
Hours: Mon to Thu, 0830 to 1730; Fri, 0830 to 1700

Access for disabled people:
Parking provided, level entry, toilet facilities

TAUNTON TOURIST INFORMATION CENTRE

Library, Paul Street, Taunton, Somerset, TA1 3XZ

Tel: 01823 336344
Fax: 01823 340308
E-mail: tauntontic@tauntondeane.gov.uk

Website:
http://www.somerset.gov.uk/libraries

Enquiries:
Enquiries to: Manager

Founded:
1974

Organisation type and purpose:
Local government body.
To provide a wide range of information on the local area and the UK.

Subject coverage:
Tourist information on Taunton and Somerset, holiday information on the whole of the UK, local walks and cycle rides, theatre, gallery and cinema information, local bus and train information. Bookings can be made for National Express coaches, Berrys Coaches, local theatres, local concerts and events, Ticketmaster and YHA membership.

Museum or gallery collection, archive, or library special collection:
Reference books for visitors: hotel and other accommodation, various guides and travel information

Printed publications:
Mini Guide and Heritage Trail (free)
Publications relating to the area – local walks, local cycle trails, maps and books
Taunton Deane Visitor Guide (free)

Electronic and video publications:
Videos of local interest

Access to staff:
Contact by letter, by telephone, by fax, by e-mail, in person and via website
Hours: Mon to Sat, 0930 to 1700; Sun (July and Aug), 1100 to 1500

Access for disabled people:
Access to all public areas

Parent body:
Somerset County Council
Library Headquarters, Mount Street, Bridgewater, Somerset, TA6 3LF; tel: 01278 451201; fax: 01278 452787

TAVISTOCK AND PORTMAN NHS FOUNDATION TRUST LIBRARY

Tavistock Centre, 120 Belsize Lane, London, NW3 5BA

Tel: 020 8938 2520
E-mail: adouglas@tavi-port.org

Website:
http://www.tavistockandportman.ac.uk/library

Enquiries:
Enquiries to: Head of Library and Learning Resources

Founded:
1947

Organisation type and purpose:
Training organisation and outpatient clinic committed to improving mental health and emotional wellbeing. The Trust believes that high quality mental health services should be available for all who need them.

Subject coverage:
Psychoanalysis, psychotherapy, psychology, psychiatry, human relations, social work and social welfare.

Information services:
See website: http://www.tavistockandportman.ac.uk/library/e-library.

Special visitor services:
See website: http://www.tavistockandportman.ac.uk/library/external-members-and-visitors.

Education services:
See website: http://www.tavistockandportman.ac.uk/library/kats-toolbox.

Services for disabled people:
See website: http://www.tavistockandportman.ac.uk/library/in-london/accessibility.

Non-library collection catalogue:
All or part available online

Library catalogue:
All or part available online

Access to staff:
Contact by telephone, by e-mail and via website. Appointment necessary. Non-members charged.
Hours: Mon to Thu, 0930 to 2100; Fri, 1000 to 1800
Special comments: Limited access for non-members in term time.

Access for disabled people:
Parking provided, level entry, access to all public areas, toilet facilities

Parent body:
Tavistock and Portman NHS Foundation Trust
tel: 020 7435 7111; website: http://www.tavistockandportman.ac.uk

TAVISTOCK INSTITUTE OF HUMAN RELATIONS

Acronym or abbreviation: TTI

30 Tabernacle Street, London, EC2A 4UE

Tel: 020 7417 0407
Fax: 020 7417 0566
E-mail: central.admin@tavinstitute.org

Website:
http://www.tavinstitute.org

Enquiries:
Enquiries to: Operations Manager

Founded:
1947

Organisation type and purpose:
Advisory body, registered charity (charity number 209706), training organisation, research organisation.
Independent social science research.

continued overleaf

Subject coverage:
Human relations, community care, community organisations, voluntary action, social welfare, employment, vocational training, telematics, action research, group relations training, organisational change and development, evaluation and review.

Printed publications:
Annual Review
Occasional Papers

Publications list:
Available in print

Access to staff:
Contact by letter. Appointment necessary.
Hours: Mon to Fri, 0930 to 1730

Access to building, collection or gallery:
Prior appointment required

Access for disabled people:
Access to all public areas, toilet facilities

TAVISTOCK SUBSCRIPTION LIBRARY

Court Gate, Guildhall Square, Tavistock, Devon, PL19 0AE

Tel: 01822 612352
E-mail: jackwalkerstar@aol.com

Enquiries:
Enquiries to: Honorary Secretary

Founded:
1799

Organisation type and purpose:
Membership association (membership is by subscription, election or invitation), historic building, house or site.
Independent library.

Subject coverage:
Tavistock (Devon) local books and information.

Museum or gallery collection, archive, or library special collection:
Tavistock and District

Library catalogue:
All or part available in-house and in print

Printed publications:
Various publications available for purchase

Publications list:
Available in print

Access to staff:
Contact by letter, by telephone and by e-mail.
Appointment necessary.
Hours: Mon to Fri, 0900 to 1700

Access to building, collection or gallery:
Prior appointment required

Access for disabled people:
Level entry

Also at:
Honorary Secretary, Tavistock Subscription Library
9 Manor Road, Tavistock, Devon, PL19 0PL; tel: 01822 612352; e-mail: jackwalkerstar@aol.com

Member organisation of:
Independent Library Association

TAXBRIEFS LIMITED

2–5 Benjamin Street, London, EC1M 5QL

Tel: 020 7250 0967
Fax: 020 7251 8867
E-mail: info@taxbriefs.co.uk

Website:
http://www.taxbriefs.co.uk
Details of products, conferences, hot tips and a full listing of publications.

Enquiries:
Enquiries to: Director

Founded:
1975

Organisation type and purpose:
Publishing house.

Subject coverage:
Finance information on pensions, life assurance, taxation.

Library catalogue:
All or part available online and in print

Printed publications:
AFPC Case Studies for G10, G20, G30, G60 and H15
AFPC Manuals for G10, G20, G30, G60, G70 and H25
Financial Timesaver
FP3 Case Study Workbook
Life Assurance and Pensions Handbook
Professional Adviser's Factfile
Report Planner Manual
Stakeholder and Personal Pensions Workbook
The Facts of Life and Health Insurance
The Basic Principles of Tax

Electronic and video publications:
Report Planner (CD-ROM to accompany manual)

Publications list:
Available online and in print

Access to staff:
Contact by letter, by telephone, by fax, by e-mail and via website
Hours: Mon to Fri, 0900 to 1730

Access to building, collection or gallery:
Prior appointment required

TAY VALLEY FAMILY HISTORY SOCIETY

Acronym or abbreviation: TVFHS

Family History Research Centre, 179–181 Princes Street, Dundee, DD4 6DQ

Tel: 01382 461845
Fax: 01382 461845
E-mail: tvfhs@tayvalleyfhs.org.uk

Website:
http://www.tayvalleyfhs.org.uk

Enquiries:
Enquiries to: Honorary Secretary

Organisation type and purpose:
Membership association (membership is by subscription), present number of members: 1,500, registered charity.

Subject coverage:
Family histories, pedigrees, research interests of members, unpublished birth, marriage and death information, census information 1841–91 and collection of monumental inscriptions, all in the counties of Angus, Fife, Kinross and Perth.

Museum or gallery collection, archive, or library special collection:
Extensive collection of family history materials for the counties of Angus, Fife, Kinross and Perth

Library catalogue:
All or part available online

Printed publications:
Books to help family historians in the counties of Angus, Fife, Kinross and Perth
Census Name Indexes 1851 for Angus, Fife, Kinross and Perth
Journal (3 times a year)
Monumental Inscriptions of Local Cemeteries

Microform publications:
Census Indexes: 1841 Dundee and Angus; 1851 Kinross; 1851 parts of Fife (microfiche)

Publications list:
Available in print

Access to staff:
Contact by letter, by telephone, by e-mail, in person and via website. Non-members charged.

Founded:
1975

Access to building, collection or gallery:
Hours: Mon, Tue, Wed, Fri, 1000 to 1600; Sat, 1000 to 1300; Thu, 1000 to 1600 and 1900 to 2100
Special comments: Charge £2 per hour for non-members.

Access for disabled people:
Level entry, toilet facilities

TAYLOR INSTITUTION LIBRARY

Formal name: Taylor Institution Library, One of the Bodleian Libraries of the University of Oxford

St Giles', Oxford, OX1 3NA

Tel: 01865 278158
Fax: 01865 278165
E-mail: tay-enquiries@bodleian.ox.ac.uk

Website:
http://www.bodleian.ox.ac.uk/taylor
Access hours. etc.

Enquiries:
Enquiries to: Reader Services Coordinator
Direct tel: 01865 278155
Direct e-mail: frank.egerton@bodleian.ox.ac.uk

Founded:
1848

Organisation type and purpose:
University department or institute. The Taylor Institution is Oxford University's centre for the study of modern European languages. The building houses two collections: the Taylor Institution (Main) Library, used mainly by postgraduate/academic researchers; and the Modern Languages Faculty Library (MLF), the undergraduate teaching collection. The Taylor Bodleian Slavonic and Modern Greek Library is housed nearby (47 Wellington Square).

Subject coverage:
Medieval and modern continental European (and related) languages and literature, predominantly Spanish and Portuguese, German, French, and Italian; included are those of modern Latin America, the literature of Canada, and North and sub-Saharan Africa; also Linguistics; film studies; women's studies; Celtic; and Dutch, Yiddish, and Afrikaans. Also, at 47 Wellington Square, Russian and other Slavonic (and related) languages, and modern Greek, languages and literature.

Museum or gallery collection, archive, or library special collection:
Butler Clarke Collection (Spanish books)
Dante Collection (Italian)
Dawkins Collection (Byzantine and modern Greek books)
Fiedler Collection of German literary, philological and historical works
Finch Collection of literary and linguistic works printed in the 16th, 17th and 18th centuries (Italian and other)
Martin Collection (Spanish and Portuguese books)
Nevill Forbes and W R Morfill Collections of Slavonic books
Rudler Collection of French books (particularly Benjamin Constant items and early 20th-century French writers)
Besterman Voltaire Bequest: collection of works relating to Voltaire and the French Enlightenment with a world locational index of 18th-century editions of Voltaire
Whitechapel and Schweizer Collections of Yiddish Literature
Collection of European writers' letters and manuscripts
Strachan Collection of French 19th-century 'livres d'artiste'

Non-library collection catalogue:
All or part available online and in print

Library catalogue:
All or part available online

Printed publications:
Catalogues of some of the special collections

Access to staff:
Contact by letter, by fax, by e-mail and via
website. Appointment necessary. Letter of
introduction required.
Hours: See website for details: http://
www.bodleian.ox.ac.uk/taylor

Access to building, collection or gallery:
Visitors are advised to check the library's website
beforehand for times of access

Dependent library:
Taylor Bodleian Slavonic and Modern Greek
Library, University of Oxford
47 Wellington Square, Oxford, OX1 2JF; tel:
01865 270464; fax: 01865 270469; e-mail: tabs
-enquiries@bodleian.ox.ac.uk

Parent body:
University of Oxford

TAYLOR NELSON SOFRES PLC

Westgate, London, W5 1UA

Tel: 020 8967 0007
E-mail: enquiries@tnsofres.com

Website:
http://www.tnsofres.com

Enquiries:
Enquiries to: Director of Social and Political
Research
Direct tel: 020 8332 8551
Direct fax: 020 8332 1090

Organisation type and purpose:
Service industry, research organisation.
Engaged in all forms of social and commercial
survey research.

Subject coverage:
Marketing information – continuous and custom
research in over 80 countries. Specialist expertise in
IT, telecoms, healthcare, automotive, TV, media,
internet, consumer.

Access to staff:
Contact by letter, by telephone, by e-mail and via
website
Hours: Mon to Fri, 0900 to 1730

Access to building, collection or gallery:
No access other than to staff

Member of:
BMRA
Gallup International Association
MRS

Parent body:
SOFRES

TEACHER SCIENTIST NETWORK

Acronym or abbreviation: TSN

John Innes Centre, Norwich Research Park, Colney,
Norwich, Norfolk, NR4 7UH

Tel: 01603 450000
Fax: 01603 450045
E-mail: ts.network@bbsrc.ac.uk

Website:
http://www.tsn.org.uk

Enquiries:
Enquiries to: Co-ordinator

Founded:
1994

Organisation type and purpose:
Membership association (membership is by
qualification and is open to all teachers and
scientists), present number of members: 350.
Collaboration between teachers of science and
professional scientists in the Norfolk area, to
enhance science in schools.

Subject coverage:
Science education (from 5 to 18 years), networking
teachers of science and professional scientists, free
resources available.

Printed publications:
Newsletter (periodic)
Occasional papers

Publications list:
Available online

Access to staff:
Contact by letter, by telephone, by fax, by e-mail
and via website. Appointment necessary.
Hours: Mon to Fri, 0900 to 1700

TEARFUND

100 Church Road, Teddington, Middlesex, TW11
8QE

Tel: 020 8977 9144
Fax: 020 8943 3594
E-mail: enquiry@tearfund.org

Website:
http://www.tearfund.org

Enquiries:
Enquiries to: Supporter Enquiries Team

Founded:
1968

Organisation type and purpose:
International organisation, registered charity
(charity number 265464).
Relief and development charity.

Subject coverage:
Development, overseas aid, evangelical church.

Library catalogue:
All or part available in-house

Printed publications:
Tearfund produce a range of titles under the
following headings:
Books and booklets
Leaflets and magazines
Resource packs
Youth and young people

Electronic and video publications:
Videos, CDs, DVDs and audio cassettes

Publications list:
Available in print

Access to staff:
Contact by letter, by telephone, by e-mail and via
website
Hours: Mon to Fri, 0900 to 1700

Other addresses:
Tearfund Ireland
23 University Street, Belfast, BT7 1FY; tel: 028
9032 4940; fax: 028 9023 6930
Tearfund Scotland
Challenge House, 29 Canal Street, Glasgow, G4
0AD; tel: 0141 332 3621; fax: 0141 400 2980

TECHGNOSIS

PO Box 154, Manchester, M20 3AL

Tel: 0161 445 9757
Fax: 0161 434 2913

Website:
http://www.techgnosis-uk.com
Guides to e-commerce, IT security products and
services; IT market databases

Enquiries:
Enquiries to: Director

Founded:
1988

Organisation type and purpose:
Publishing house, research organisation.
IT information provider.

Subject coverage:
Information technology; computing; computer
security; software development;
telecommunications; office automation, IT end-
user profiles; e-commerce.

Electronic and video publications:
Computer Services Index
Guide to Electronic Commerce Products and
Services
Guide to IT Security Products and Services
The National Computer Index

Publications list:
Available in print

Access to staff:
Contact by letter, by telephone and by fax.
Appointment necessary. All charged.
Hours: Mon to Fri, 0900 to 1700

TECHNICAL HELP TO EXPORTERS

Acronym or abbreviation: THE

British Standards Institution, 389 Chiswick High
Road, London, W4 4AL

Tel: 020 8996 7474
Fax: 020 8996 7048
E-mail: the@bsi-global.com

Website:
http://www.bsi.org.uk

Enquiries:
Enquiries to: Business Development Manager

Organisation type and purpose:
Training organisation, consultancy, research
organisation, publishing house.

Subject coverage:
Overseas technical laws, regulations, standards
and certification requirements; interpretation and
translation of overseas technical requirements;
assistance with technical problems and research
projects; assistance in obtaining test certificates or
approval for products in overseas markets; UK
testing and inspection of goods for export.

**Museum or gallery collection, archive, or library
special collection:**
Library of over 500,000 foreign laws, regulations,
national and non-national standards (BSI library)

Printed publications:
Range of technical publications on engineering
(Europe and International), pressure vessels,
electronic products and general subjects

Electronic and video publications:
BSI Standards Electronic Catalogue (CD-ROM)
PERINORM (database of standards and
regulations, PERINORM Europe and
PERINORM International, CD-ROM)

Access to staff:
Contact by letter, by telephone, by fax and by e-
mail. All charged.
Hours: Mon to Fri 0900 to 1700

TEESSIDE ARCHIVES

Exchange House, 6 Marton Road, Middlesbrough,
Cleveland, TS1 1DB

Tel: 01642 248321
Fax: 01642 248391
E-mail: teesside_archives@middlesbrough.gov.uk

Website:
http://www.middlesbrough.gov.uk/
teessidearchives

Enquiries:
Enquiries to: Archivist

Founded:
1974

Organisation type and purpose:
Local government body.

Subject coverage:
Archives relating to Middlesbrough, Hartlepool,
Stockton on Tees and Redcar and Cleveland
Boroughs (formerly Cleveland County).

Education services:
An outreach service is available for schools and
groups; group visits can be arranged.

continued overleaf

Access to staff:
Contact by letter, by telephone, by fax and by e-mail. Appointment necessary.
Hours: Mon, Wed, Thu, 0900 to 1700; Tue, 0900 to 2100; Fri, 0900 to 1630

Access for disabled people:
Access to all public areas, toilet facilities

TEESWATER SHEEP BREEDERS ASSOCIATION

Wodencroft, Cotherstone, Barnard Castle, Co Durham, DL12 9UQ

Tel: 01833 650032
Fax: 01833 650909
E-mail: wodencroft@freenet.co.uk

Enquiries:
Enquiries to: Secretary

Founded:
1949

Organisation type and purpose:
Membership association (membership is by subscription).

Subject coverage:
Teeswater sheep.

TELECOMMUNICATIONS USERS' ASSOCIATION

Acronym or abbreviation: TUA

Woodgate Studios, 2–8 Games Road, Barnet, Hertfordshire, EN4 9HN

Tel: 020 8449 8844
Fax: 020 8447 4901
E-mail: cma@thecma.com

Website:
http://www.tua.co.uk

Enquiries:
Enquiries to: Chairman

Founded:
1964

Organisation type and purpose:
Independent membership association (membership is by subscription), service industry, training organisation, consultancy, research organisation. Provides information and services to members whilst promoting open competition worldwide.

Subject coverage:
Telecommunications and related industries; open telecommunications environment; to lobby and monitor quality of service; consultancy service to members.

Printed publications:
Factline via FAX broadcast (monthly)
Infocus (newsletter, 4 times a year)
Specialist Research Reports
Telecommunications Users' Association (2 times a year)
TUA Calling Card

Electronic and video publications:
Factline via FAX broadcast (monthly, available as electronic delivery e-factline, PDF format)

Access to staff:
Contact by letter, by telephone, by fax, by e-mail and via website. Access for members only.
Hours: Mon to Fri, 0900 to 1700

TELEPHONE PREFERENCE SERVICE

Acronym or abbreviation: TPS

DMA House, 70 Margaret Street, London, W1W 8SS

Tel: 020 7291 3320
Fax: 020 7323 4226

E-mail: tps@dma.org.uk

Website:
http://www.tpsonline.org.uk
http://www.dma.org.uk

Enquiries:
Enquiries to: Administrator

Founded:
1995

Organisation type and purpose:
Self-regulatory body.
Provide individuals with the opportunity to register not to receive direct marketing telephone calls.

Subject coverage:
Restriction on unsolicited sales and marketing telephone calls to individuals.

Printed publications:
Consumer leaflet and application form
Industry subscriber pack

Electronic and video publications:
TPS file (download from website, diskette or electronic transfer, CD-ROM)

Access to staff:
Contact by letter, by telephone, by fax, by e-mail and via website. Appointment necessary.
Hours: Mon to Fri, 0900 to 1700
Special comments: Charges made to all subscribers (companies making telephone calls).

Affiliated to:
Direct Marketing Association (DMA)
tel: 020 7291 3300; fax: 020 7523 4226; e-mail: dma@dma.org.uk
OFTEL
tel: 020 7434 8700; fax: 020 7434 8893

TELEPHONES FOR THE BLIND FUND

7 Huntersfield Close, Reigate, Surrey, RH2 0DX

Tel: 01737 248032
Fax: 01737 248032

Website:
http://www.tftb.org.uk

Enquiries:
Enquiries to: Hon Secretary

Founded:
1967

Organisation type and purpose:
Voluntary organisation (charity number 255155).

Subject coverage:
Grants towards the provision of telephones for registered blind people. Referrals must be made through Social Services.

Access to staff:
Contact by letter, by telephone and by fax
Hours: Mon to Fri, 1000 to 1600
Special comments: No access to premises allowed.

TELEVISION TRUST FOR THE ENVIRONMENT

Acronym or abbreviation: TVE

21 Elizabeth Street, London, SW1W 9RP

Tel: 020 7901 8855
Fax: 020 7901 8856
E-mail: tve@tve.org.uk

Website:
http://www.tve.org
Information on TVE and publications, list of films available through TVE.

Enquiries:
Enquiries to: Distribution Manager
Direct tel: 020 7901 8834
Direct e-mail: distribution@tve.org.uk

Founded:
1984

Organisation type and purpose:
International organisation, registered charity. Film, video and television producer and distributor.
To inform and educate on environmental, health, human rights and developmental issues.

Subject coverage:
Environment, health, development, human rights, women's issues.

Museum or gallery collection, archive, or library special collection:
Library of over 500 documentaries; substantial archive of environment and development film footage

Non-library collection catalogue:
All or part available online

Electronic and video publications:
Online newsletter distributed regularly to established mailing list
A large number of videos by broadcasters, non-governmental organisations, government organisations, educational institutions, community groups, women's groups, etc. for purchase
Order electronic and video publications from: Distribution manager

Publications list:
Available online

Access to staff:
Contact by letter, by telephone, by fax, by e-mail and via website. Appointment necessary.
Hours: Mon to Fri, 0930 to 1800

Access to building, collection or gallery:
No access other than to staff

Access for disabled people:
No wheelchair access – premises on first floor with narrow stairs.

Affiliated to:
United Nations Environment Programme
WWF UK

Links with:
57 other organisations throughout the world

TELFORD LIBRARY

St Quentin Gate, Telford, Shropshire, TF3 4JG

Tel: 01952 382918
Fax: 01952 382937
E-mail: telford.library@telford.gov.uk

Website:
http://www.telford.gov.uk/libraries

Enquiries:
Enquiries to: Librarian

Organisation type and purpose:
Public library.

Library catalogue:
All or part available online and in-house

Access to staff:
Contact by letter, by telephone, by fax, by e-mail, in person and via website
Hours: Mon, 1000 to 1800; Tue, Wed, Fri, 0930 to 1800; Thu 0930 to 2000; Sat 0930 to 1700

Access for disabled people:
Level entry, access to all public areas, toilet facilities

Parent body:
Telford & Wrekin Council

TEMPLETON COLLEGE

Kennington, Oxford, OX1 5NY

Tel: 01865 422500
Fax: 01865 422501
E-mail: infocent@templeton.ox.ac.uk

Website:
http://www.templeton.ox.ac.uk

Enquiries:
Enquiries to: Information Centre Manager

Founded:
1965

Organisation type and purpose:
Management studies college.

Subject coverage:
Management studies in general; retailing (Oxford Centre of Retail Management); employee relations; information management; food and drink industry; human resource management; industrial relations.

Printed publications:
See website for publications

Publications list:
Available online

Access to staff:
Contact by letter, by telephone and by e-mail
Hours: Mon to Fri, 0830 to 1700

Access to building, collection or gallery:
Prior appointment required
Special comments: Restricted, please ring for information.

Access for disabled people:
Parking provided, ramped entry

Member of:
British Business Schools Librarians Group
European Business Schools Librarians Group

TENANT FARMERS ASSOCIATION

Acronym or abbreviation: TFA

5 Brewery Court, Theale, Reading, Berkshire, RG7 5AJ

Tel: 0118 930 6130
Fax: 0118 930 3424
E-mail: tfa@tfa.org.uk

Website:
http://www.tfa.org.uk

Enquiries:
Enquiries to: Events and Communications Co-ordinator
Other contacts: Membership Co-ordinator

Founded:
1981

Organisation type and purpose:
Trade association (membership is by subscription), present number of members: 4,000.
Provides advice, information and a strong lobby for British tenant farmers.

Subject coverage:
Agricultural tenancies, agricultural policy, tenant farming, landlord/tenant affairs in rural areas.

Trade and statistical information:
Agricultural rent databank (available to tenants only).

Printed publications:
TFA News (6 times a year, members only)
Briefing Notes (weekly, members only)
Guidance Notes (as required, members only)

Access to staff:
Contact by letter, by telephone, by fax, by e-mail and via website. Appointment necessary.
Hours: Mon to Fri, 0900 to 1700
Special comments: Full benefits only available to members.

Access to building, collection or gallery:
No prior appointment required

TENDRING DISTRICT COUNCIL

Town Hall, Station Road, Clacton-on-Sea, Essex, CO15 1SE

Tel: 01255 425501
Fax: 01255 253139
E-mail: Email form on website

Website:
http://www.tendringdc.gov.uk

Enquiries:
Enquiries to: Chief Executive

Organisation type and purpose:
Local government body.

Printed publications:
Civic Newspaper (quarterly)
Annual Report
Citizens Guide

Access to staff:
Contact by letter, by telephone, by fax, by e-mail, in person and via website
Hours: Mon to Fri, 0900 to 1700

Access for disabled people:
Ramped entry, toilet facilities

TENNIS AND RACKETS ASSOCIATION

Acronym or abbreviation: The T&RA

c/o The Queens Club, Palliser Road, West Kensington, London, W14 9EQ

Tel: 020 7386 3447/8
Fax: 020 7385 7424
E-mail: ceo@tennis-rackets.net

Website:
http://www.real-tennis.com

Enquiries:
Enquiries to: Chief Executive

Founded:
1907

Organisation type and purpose:
Membership association (membership is by subscription), present number of members: 2,450, suitable for ages: all.
Governing body of the sports of real tennis and rackets.
To administer and control the games of Tennis (Real Tennis) and Rackets.

Subject coverage:
Real tennis and Rackets (not to be confused with lawn tennis and squash rackets); rules; location of courts; history of the games, championships, sponsorship, development, membership, publicity, fixtures, international liaison.

Printed publications:
Annual and Spring Reports
Historical records back to 18th century

Access to staff:
Contact by letter, by fax and by e-mail.
Appointment necessary.
Hours: Mon to Fri, 0900 to 1700

Member of:
CCPR
Sport England

TENNYSON RESEARCH CENTRE

Formal name: Lincolnshire County Council

Central Library, Free School Lane, Lincoln, LN2 1EZ

Tel: 01522 782040
Fax: 01522 575011
E-mail: grace.timmins@lincolnshire.gov.uk

Website:
http://www.lincolnshire.gov.uk/tennyson

Enquiries:
Enquiries to: Collections Officer
Direct fax: 01522 545011
Direct e-mail: tennyson@lincolnshire.gov.uk

Founded:
1964

Organisation type and purpose:
Research organisation.
Research unit.

Subject coverage:
Alfred, Lord Tennyson: life, works, papers.

Information services:
Please contact the collections officer for information about services.

Museum or gallery collection, archive, or library special collection:
Tennyson Collection includes family libraries, 9,000 letters, manuscripts of the poet's work, family papers, illustrations, proofs, biographical and critical material, including:
Family Libraries: some 350 volumes from the library of Tennyson's father, George Clayton Tennyson, giving an indication of the books Tennyson would have used as a child, when taught by his father. Approximately 2,000 books from Tennyson's own library, reflecting his many interests and often annotated by the poet
Family Papers: family diaries and notebooks including a journal kept by Tennyson's wife, Emily; household books and publishers' accounts
Illustrations: portraits and other illustrative material on Tennyson, his family, contemporaries and places associated with them, including a number of photographs by Julia Margaret Cameron
Letters to and from Tennyson and other members of the family: several thousand letters from eminent Victorians including Browning, Gladstone, Lear and Fitzgerald
Manuscripts: the most complete autograph manuscript of In Memoriam
Plays: Queen Mary, Harold, Becket, The Foresters and an acting copy of The Cup
Proofs: approximately 200 proofs of Tennyson's poetry, a number being significantly corrected in the poet's hand
Biography and Criticism: a comprehensive collection of books and articles, both contemporary and modern, dealing with his life and works
Tennyson's works: an almost complete set of first and other important editions of poetry
'Personalia' includes Tennyson's coat and hat, pipes, spectacles, writing equipment.

Non-library collection catalogue:
All or part available in-house and in print

Library catalogue:
All or part available online, in-house and in print

Printed publications:
Monographs and occasional papers (Tennyson Society)
Tennyson in Lincoln, vols 1 and 2 (Tennyson Society)
Tennyson Research Bulletin (Tennyson Society, annually)
Order printed publications from: The Tennyson Society, c/o Lincoln Central Library, Free School Lane, Lincoln. LN2 1EZ

Access to staff:
Contact by letter, by telephone, by fax, by e-mail and via website. Appointment necessary.
Hours: Mon to Fri, 0930 to 1700

Access for disabled people:
Ramped entry, toilet facilities

Parent body:
Lincolnshire County Council
County Offices, Newland, Lincoln, LN1 1YL; tel: 01522 553207; fax: 01522 552811

TENOVUS, THE CANCER CHARITY

43 The Parade, Cardiff, CF24 3AB

Tel: 029 2048 2000
Fax: 029 2048 4199
E-mail: post@tenovus.com

Website:
http://www.tenovus.com

Enquiries:
Enquiries to: Public Relations Manager
Direct e-mail: natalie.owen@tenovus.org.uk

continued overleaf

Founded:
1943

Organisation type and purpose:
Registered charity (charity number 1054015).

Subject coverage:
Cancer research and patient care.

Museum or gallery collection, archive, or library special collection:
Library holds information on over 200 cancers and support organisations

Trade and statistical information:
Data on cancer in the UK and in Europe.

Printed publications:
Publications free of charge

Publications list:
Available online and in print

Access to staff:
Contact by letter, by telephone, by fax and by e-mail
Hours: Mon to Fri, 0900 to 1700

Access for disabled people:
Parking provided, level entry, toilet facilities

TERRENCE HIGGINS TRUST

Acronym or abbreviation: THT

314–320 Gray's Inn Road, London, WC1X 8DP

Tel: 020 7812 1600; helpline: 0845 122 1200
Fax: 020 7812 1601
E-mail: info@tht.org.uk

Website:
http://www.tht.org.uk

Enquiries:
Enquiries to: Information Officer

Founded:
1982

Organisation type and purpose:
Registered charity, voluntary organisation (charity number 288527).

Subject coverage:
HIV and AIDS, sexual health.

Printed publications:
A range of leaflets on HIV and sexual health, gay and lesbian information
Order printed publications from: Information Department (single copies are free, bulk copies for purchase)

Publications list:
Available online and in print

Access to staff:
Contact by letter, by telephone, by fax, by e-mail, in person and via website
Hours: Mon to Fri, 0930 to 1730

TETRONICS LIMITED

A2 Marston Gate, Stirling Road, South Marston Business Park, Swindon, Wiltshire, SN3 4DE

Tel: 01793 238 500
Fax: 01793 832 533
E-mail: info@tetronics.com

Website:
http://www.tetronics.com

Enquiries:
Enquiries to: Marketing Manager

Founded:
1964

Organisation type and purpose:
Manufacturing industry.
Research and development organisation.

Subject coverage:
Plasma equipment and furnaces, nanopowders, metal melting and heating, new waste treatment processes, melting of incineration ashes, treatment of steel works dusts and hazardous wastes, refractory metal melting.

Access to staff:
Contact by letter, by telephone, by fax and by e-mail
Hours: Mon to Fri, 0900 to 1700

TEXTILE INDUSTRY CHILDREN'S TRUST

Acronym or abbreviation: TICT

Winchester House, 259–269 Old Marylebone Road, London, NW1 5RA

Tel: 020 7170 4117
E-mail: info@tict.org.uk

Website:
http://www.tict.org.uk
The trust and how it can help; case histories.

Founded:
1968

Formerly called:
Purley Children's Trust (year of change 1999)

Organisation type and purpose:
Registered charity (number 257136).
Established to support the education and welfare of children whose parents have worked in fashion, textile retail and manufacturing (UK only). Its mission is to help children achieve their full potential.

Subject coverage:
TICT helps children if they suffer financial hardship as a result of divorce, bereavement or other significant circumstances and, as a result, are unable to make the most of their education. It funds places at specialist schools for children with special educational needs such as dyslexia, autism, ADHD, emotional needs and physical disabilities. It pays for boarding at schools that offer vital pastoral care to children who may have been orphaned or who are living in a desperate home situation. It awards hardship grants to cover the cost of uniforms, specialist equipment such as a home computer or funding towards transport to a school. It helps to nurture the talents of gifted children who would benefit from attendance at a school with a focus on music, sport or artistic performance. It also helps with existing school fees where there has been a dramatic change in family circumstances such as death or debilitating illness.

Access to staff:
Contact by letter, by telephone and by e-mail

TEXTILE INSTITUTE

Formal name: The Textile Institute
Acronym or abbreviation: TI

International Headquarters, 1st Floor, St James's Building, 79 Oxford Street, Manchester, M1 6FQ

Tel: 0161 237 1188
Fax: 0161 236 1991
E-mail: tiihq@textileinst.org.uk

Website:
http://www.textileinstitute.org

Enquiries:
Enquiries to: Professional Affairs Manager
Direct e-mail: escott@textileinst.org.uk
Other contacts: Director of Professional Affairs

Founded:
1910

Organisation type and purpose:
Professional body.

Subject coverage:
Textiles worldwide; textile technology; floorcovering; clothing; industrial textiles; knitting; weaving; design and marketing; finishing, fibre science, footwear.

Non-library collection catalogue:
All or part available in-house

Library catalogue:
All or part available in-house

Printed publications:
International Textile Calendar (12 times a year)
Journal of the Textile Institute (monthly)
Textile Progress (bi-monthly)
Textile Terms and Definitions
Textiles (quarterly)

Publications list:
Available in print

Access to staff:
Contact by letter, by telephone, by fax, by e-mail and via website. Appointment necessary. All charged.
Hours: Mon to Fri, 0900 to 1700

Access to building, collection or gallery:
Prior appointment required

TEXTILE SERVICES ASSOCIATION

Acronym or abbreviation: TSA

Unit 7, Churchill Court, 58 Station Road, North Harrow, Middlesex, HA2 7SA

Tel: 020 8863 7755
Fax: 020 8861 2115
E-mail: tsa@tsa-uk.org

Enquiries:
Enquiries to: Chief Executive

Founded:
1886

Organisation type and purpose:
Trade association (membership is by subscription), present number of members: 600.

Subject coverage:
Developments within the dry-cleaning, laundry and textile rental industry, national and EC legislation affecting the industry e.g. health and safety, workwear etc. NVQs in the textile rental industry.

Printed publications:
A Guide to Workwear Rental (free)
Annual Report and Accounts
Bulletin (monthly, for members)
Career Choices – The Textile Care Industry (careers leaflet, free)
Educational Publications Leaflet for the Laundry and Dry Cleaning Industry (members only)
Fabric and Garment Care
Godly Adjunct (history of the association)
Health, Safety & Environment Management Guidelines
Suede and Leather Care and Cleaning
TSA Code of Practice Booklet
TSA Membership Handbook (members only)
What Your Drycleaner Can Do For You (leaflet for dry cleaning customers, free)

Publications list:
Available in print

Access to staff:
Contact by letter, by telephone, by fax, by e-mail and via website. Non-members charged.
Hours: Mon to Fri, 0900 to 1800

Affiliated to:
International Committee for Textile Care (CINET)

Works closely with:
Guild of Cleaners and Launderers
    Cheshire; tel: 0161 483 4655
SATRA
    Kettering, Northamptonshire; tel: 01536 410000

TFPL LIMITED

2nd Floor, 160 Queen Victoria Street, London, EC4V 4BF

Tel: 020 7332 6000
Fax: 0870 333 7131
E-mail: info@tfpl.com

Website:
http://www.tfpl.com
Information about TFPL, job vacancies, training courses, news, knowledge management, intranets, records management and conferences.

Enquiries:
Enquiries to: Managing Director
Direct e-mail: marketing@tfpl.com

Founded:
1987

Organisation type and purpose:
Service industry, training organisation, consultancy, research organisation, publishing house.
Recruitment and the provision of temporary and contract information staff.
To provide specialist services to the global information market.

Subject coverage:
Employment trends and opportunities for information specialists, training courses and seminars, recruitment, consultancy, European Information World and market research, seminars and conferences.

Printed publications:
Intranet Management: A TFPL Guide to Best Practice
Skills for Knowledge Management
Who's Who in the European Information World (annually)
Who's Who in the UK Information World (annually)

Publications list:
Available in print

Access to staff:
Contact by letter, by telephone, by fax, by e-mail, in person and via website
Hours: Mon to Fri, 0900 to 1800

THAI EMBASSY

Formal name: Royal Thai Embassy

29–30 Queen's Gate, London, SW7 5JB

Tel: 020 7589 2944
Fax: 020 7823 9695
E-mail: thaiduto@btinternet.com

Website:
http://www.thaiembassyuk.org.uk

Enquiries:
Enquiries to: Information Officer
Direct tel: 020 7225 5520
Direct e-mail: thaiembassy.pr@btconnect.com

Organisation type and purpose:
Embassy.

Subject coverage:
Thailand: government, history, culture, society, economy, arts, language, religion, travel.

Museum or gallery collection, archive, or library special collection:
The Embassy's collection is small and mostly in Thai language, though there are a few useful reference books in English

Trade and statistical information:
Contact the Office of Commercial Affairs.

Access to staff:
Contact by letter, by telephone, by fax and by e-mail. Appointment necessary.
Hours: Mon to Fri, 0930 to 1230 and 1400 to 1700
Special comments: Closed on Thai holidays and UK public holidays.

Access to building, collection or gallery:
No prior appointment required

Access for disabled people:
Toilet facilities

Also at:
Office of Commercial Affairs
    11 Hertford Street, Mayfair, London, W1Y 7DX; tel: 020 7493 5749; fax: 020 7493 7416; e-mail: thaicomuk@dial.pipex.com; website: http://www .thaitrade.com
Office of Economics and Financial Affairs
    3rd Floor, 29–30 Queen's Gate, London, SW7 5JB; tel: 020 7589 7266; fax: 020 7589 2624
Office of Educational Affairs
    28 Prince's Gate, London, SW7 1QF; tel: 020 7584 4538; fax: 020 7823 9896; e-mail: info@oealondon .com

THAMES ROWING COUNCIL – LOWER RIVER

Acronym or abbreviation: TRC

45 Sterne Street, London, W12 8AB

Tel: 020 8743 8596

Enquiries:
Enquiries to: Honorary Secretary

Organisation type and purpose:
Membership association (membership is by qualification), voluntary organisation.
Co-ordinating sports body.
To encourage participation in the sport of rowing.

Subject coverage:
Rowing river users, the river Thames.

Access to staff:
Contact by letter
Hours: Mon to Fri, 0900 to 1700

Parent body:
Amateur Rowing Association

THAMES VALLEY CHAMBER OF COMMERCE AND INDUSTRY

Commerce House, 2–6 Bath Road, Slough, Berkshire, SL1 3SB

Tel: 01753 870518
Fax: 01753 524644
E-mail: enquiries@thamesvalleychamber.co.uk

Website:
http://www.thamesvalleychamber.co.uk
General information on products/services, events diary, training course diary.
http://www.euro-info.org.uk
European information centres national site.

Enquiries:
Enquiries to: Information Officer
Direct tel: 01753 870530

Founded:
1927

Organisation type and purpose:
Membership association.
Chamber of Commerce.

Subject coverage:
Business, local and European Information Centre.

Printed publications:
Business Voice (6 times a year)
Europe Matters (6 times a year)

Access to staff:
Contact by letter, by telephone, by fax, by e-mail and via website. Appointment necessary.
Hours: Mon to Thu, 0900 to 1700; Fri, 0900 to 1500
Special comments: Charges for some services.

Hosts:
Thames Valley European Information Centre at the same address

THAMES VALLEY UNIVERSITY

Acronym or abbreviation: TVU

St Mary's Road, London, W5 5RF

Tel: 020 8579 5000

Website:
http://www.tvu.ac.uk
Information about Thames Valley University.

Enquiries:
Enquiries to: Head of Learning and Research Support
Direct tel: 020 8231 2678
Direct fax: 020 8231 2402
Direct e-mail: press@tvu.ac.uk
Other contacts: SMR, LRC Manager for Learning Resource Provision.

Founded:
1993

Organisation type and purpose:
University library, university department or institute.

Subject coverage:
Business, management, accountancy, law, health sciences, humanities, languages, hospitality, music, information studies, technology, art and design, built environment, sports science.

Non-library collection catalogue:
All or part available online

Library catalogue:
All or part available online

Printed publications:
In-house products only

Publications list:
Available online

Access to staff:
Contact by letter, by telephone, by fax and by e-mail. Appointment necessary. Access for members only.
Hours: St Mary's Road; term-time: Mon to Thu, 0830 to 2200; Fri to Sun, 0830 to 1800
Special comments: Reciprocal arrangements with similar institutions. Members only primarily, visitors by prior appointment.

Access to building, collection or gallery:
Prior appointment required
Special comments: 24-hour access to IT facilities during term time – Ealing only

Access for disabled people:
Parking provided, ramped entry, level entry, access to all public areas, toilet facilities

Member of:
M25 Group
SCONUL

Other departments at:
Faculty of Health and Human Sciences
    Westel House, 32 Uxbridge Road, London, W5 2BZ; tel: 020 8280 5043; fax: 020 8280 5045
Paul Hamlyn Learning Resource Centre
    Wellington Street, Slough, Berkshire, SL1 1YG; tel: 01753 697536; fax: 01753 574264
Wolfson School of Health, Sciences Learning Resource Centre
    Royal Berkshire Hospital, Reading, RG1 5AN; tel: 0118 322 7661; fax: 0118 322 8675

THAMES VALLEY UNIVERSITY – LEARNING RESOURCE CENTRE

Acronym or abbreviation: TVU

St Mary's Road, Ealing, London, W5 5RF

Tel: 020 8231 2248
Fax: 020 8231 2631
E-mail: learning.advice@tvu.ac.uk

Website:
http://www.tvu.ac.uk

Enquiries:
Enquiries to: Head of Learning Resources
Direct tel: 020 8231 2678
Direct e-mail: press@tvu.ac.uk
Other contacts: Director of Information Services for all ICT within the University.

continued overleaf

Founded:
1992

Organisation type and purpose:
Learned society, professional body (membership is by qualification), university library, training organisation, research organisation.
Learning Resource Service.

Subject coverage:
Management, including marketing, purchasing, business, accounting, languages, hospitality management, law, music, media, health sciences.

Library catalogue:
All or part available online

Publications list:
Available online

Access to staff:
Contact by letter, by telephone, by fax, by e-mail and via website. Appointment necessary. Access for members only.
Hours: TVU Ealing and PH: Mon to Thu, 0830 to 2200; Fri, Sat, Sun, 0830 to 1800
WIHS Ealing: Mon to Thu, 0830 to 1900; Fri, 1000 to 1700; Sat, 1100 to 1600
Reading: Mon, 1000 to 1930; Tue to Fri, 0830 to 1930; Sat, 0900 to 1300
Special comments: TVU Ealing and PH: Computer access only 2200 to 0600
UK+, SCONUL and M25 Schemes, Shorter hours in vacations, please telephone first.

Access to building, collection or gallery:
Prior appointment required

Access for disabled people:
Parking provided, level entry, access to all public areas, toilet facilities

Location:
Paul Hamlyn Learning Resource Centre
   Wellington Street, Slough, Berkshire, SL1 1YG; tel: 01753 697536; fax: 01753 697538
Wolfson Institute of Health Sciences Learning Resource Centre
   Wexham Park Hospital, Slough, Berkshire, SL2 4HL; tel: 01753 634343; fax: 01753 634344
Wolfson Institute of Health Sciences Learning Resource Centre
   Royal Berkshire Hospital, Reading, RG1 5AN; tel: 0118 987 7661; fax: 0118 986 8675
Wolfson Institute of Health Sciences Learning Resource Centre
   Westel House, 32 Uxbridge Road, Ealing, London, W5 2BS; tel: 020 8280 5043; fax: 020 8280 5045

THE INSTITUTE FOR COMPLEMENTARY AND NATURAL MEDICINE

Acronym or abbreviation: ICNM

Can Mezzanine 32–36 Loman Street, London, SE1 0EH

Tel: 020 7922 7980
Fax: 020 7922 7981
E-mail: info@icnm.org.uk

Website:
http://www.icnm.org.uk

Enquiries:
Enquiries to: General Secretary
Direct e-mail: clive.teal@i-c-m.org.uk

Founded:
1982

Organisation type and purpose:
Professional body (membership is by qualification), registered charity (charity number 326258).

Subject coverage:
Complementary medicine.

Printed publications:
Journal

Access to staff:
Contact by letter, by telephone and by e-mail

Hours: Mon to Fri, 1000 to 1500

Access to building, collection or gallery:
No access other than to staff

Administers:
British Register of Complementary Practitioners (BRCP)

THE UK ASSOCIATION OF PRESERVATION TRUSTS

Acronym or abbreviation: APT

9th Floor, Alhambra House, 27–31 Charing Cross Road, London, WC2H 0AU

Tel: 0207 930 1629
Fax: 0207 930 0295
E-mail: apt@ahfund.org.uk

Website:
http://www.ukapt.org.uk
Information on APT, information about building preservation trusts and completed projects.

Enquiries:
Enquiries to: Administrator
Other contacts: Director

Founded:
1989

Organisation type and purpose:
Advisory body, membership association (membership is by subscription), present number of members: 235, registered charity (charity number 1027919).
Membership open to building preservation trusts. To improve effectiveness of building preservation trusts through advice and information. To represent their views and to provide the public with information about them.

Subject coverage:
Guidance on setting up a preservation trust, information about building preservation trusts and their projects. Advice on rescuing buildings at risk through partnering building preservation trusts.

Trade and statistical information:
Various research data compiled ad hoc. Please ask for further information.

Printed publications:
APT Newsletter
Guidance Notes for Building Preservation Trusts
Order printed publications from: APT

Publications list:
Available in print

Access to staff:
Contact by letter, by telephone, by fax, by e-mail and via website
Hours: Mon to Fri, 0930 to 1730

Has:
9 Area Committees contactable through the London office

THE WORSHIPFUL COMPANY OF INTERNATIONAL BANKERS

12 Austin Friars, London, EC2N 2HE

Tel: 020 7374 0212
Fax: 020 7374 0207
E-mail: tim.woods@internationalbankers.co.uk

Website:
http://www.internationalbankers.co.uk

Enquiries:
Enquiries to: The Clerk

Organisation type and purpose:
Membership association (membership is by election or invitation).
City of London Livery Company.

Access to staff:
Contact by letter, by telephone, by fax, by e-mail and via website

THE-SRDA

Formal name: The Systems Reliability Data Association

Thomson House, Risley, Warrington, Cheshire, WA3 6AT

Tel: 01925 254249
Fax: 01925 254569
E-mail: the-srda@sercoassurance.com

Website:
http://www.the-srda.net
Access to component reliability data online, plus information about data sources, tools and techniques, publications, technical meetings and training courses of interest to safety, reliability and risk professionals.

Enquiries:
Enquiries to: Manager

Founded:
2001

Organisation type and purpose:
Membership association, consultancy.
Providing services to members for annual subscription.

Subject coverage:
Risk assessment, consequence analysis and safety management, reliability analysis and availability management (cross-industry).

Trade and statistical information:
Component reliability data bank online at
   www.the-srda.net (is available to members only).

Printed publications:
SRDA report series

Publications list:
Available online

Part of:
Serco Ltd

THEATRES TRUST

22 Charing Cross Road, London, WC2H 0QL

Tel: 020 7836 8591
Fax: 020 7836 3302
E-mail: info@theatrestrust.org.uk

Website:
http://www.theatrestrust.org.uk
Newsletter articles, advice notes, general information about the work of the trust.

Enquiries:
Enquiries to: Resources Officer
Direct e-mail: info@theatrestrust.org.uk
Other contacts: Planning and Heritage Adviser (for planning/architectural advice)

Founded:
1976

Organisation type and purpose:
Non-departmental public body, statutory body.
To promote the better protection of theatres.

Subject coverage:
History and design of theatre buildings, their planning and architecture.

Museum or gallery collection, archive, or library special collection:
Planning applications relating to theatres in England, Wales and Scotland since 1976, photos

Non-library collection catalogue:
All or part available in-house

Library catalogue:
All or part available in-house

Printed publications:
Advice notes (free)
Annual Report (free)
Theatres Trust Newsletter (subscribers only)
Encore: Strategies for Theatre Renewal
Pilot Study of the Condition of Theatres in England
Theatres: A Guide to Theatre Conservation from English Heritage

Publications list:
Available online and in print

Access to staff:
Contact by letter, by telephone, by fax, by e-mail and via website. Appointment necessary.
Hours: Mon to Fri, 0900 to 1700

Access to building, collection or gallery:
Prior appointment required
Hours: Mon to Fri, 0900 to 1700

Access for disabled people:
No disabled access
Special comments: Steps and narrow lift.

Links with:
Theatres Trust Charitable Fund
  at the same address

THEATRO TECHNIS

26 Crowndale Road, London, NW1 1TT

Tel: 020 7387 6617
Fax: 020 7383 2545
E-mail: info@theatrotechnis.com

Website:
http://www.theatrotechnis.com

Enquiries:
Enquiries to: Co-ordinator

Founded:
1967

Organisation type and purpose:
Advisory body, registered charity (charity number 2808859).
Target/client group: the Greek Cypriot community and other English-speaking communities.

Subject coverage:
Centre for the Cypriot community offering a range of cultural and social activities including multilingual and multicultural theatre. Advice service covering housing, welfare rights, law, language, family life, advocacy, interpreting and translation services.

Access to staff:
Contact by letter, by telephone, by fax and by e-mail. Appointment necessary.
Hours: Mon to Fri, 1000 to 1700

Access to building, collection or gallery:
No access other than to staff

Access for disabled people:
Ramped entry, toilet facilities

THEOSOPHICAL SOCIETY IN ENGLAND

Acronym or abbreviation: TSIE

50 Gloucester Place, London, W1U 8EA

Tel: 020 7935 9261
Fax: 020 7935 9543
E-mail: office@theosoc.org.uk

Enquiries:
Enquiries to: National President

Founded:
1888

Organisation type and purpose:
International organisation, membership association, universal brotherhood.

Subject coverage:
Theosophy, religion, meditation, philosophy, occultism, mysticism.

Museum or gallery collection, archive, or library special collection:
Library of 10,000 vols, bound theosophical magazines.

Printed publications:
Insight (journal, quarterly, free to members, non-members annual fee: UK £9, international £14)

Electronic and video publications:
Cassettes (over 1,000) of past lectures are available

Publications list:
Available in print

Access to staff:
Contact by letter, by telephone, by fax and by e-mail. Appointment necessary.

Access to building, collection or gallery:
No prior appointment required
Hours: Tue to Fri, 1400 to 1830
Special comments: Members and subscribers; some meetings members only

Also at:
sections and lodges in over 60 countries

Parent body:
Theosophical Society
  Adyar, Madras, 600020, India

THERAPY TRAINING COLLEGE

Acronym or abbreviation: LCH

PO Box 10500, Birmingham, B14 4WB

Tel: 0121 430 3336
E-mail: courses@lesserian.co.uk

Website:
http://www.lesserian.co.uk
Information, prospectus, fees and dates of all courses – Introductory, Practical Course, Clinical Supervision, optional workshops, peer supervision, mentoring schemes and other resources for the student and graduate; validated/accredited by all main UK professional bodies.
http://www.lesserian.co.uk/courses.htm
Training courses available to those with no prior experience and to those with training/qualifications in other uses of hypnosis.
http://www.lesserian.co.uk/recommen.htm
Publications about Curative Hypnotherapy and LCH treatment.
http://www.lesserian.co.uk/syllabus.htm
Course syllabus.

Enquiries:
Enquiries to: Director
Direct tel: 0121 430 3336
Direct e-mail: courses@lesserian.co.uk

Founded:
1979

Organisation type and purpose:
Training organisation.
Training in the curative use of hypnosis.

Subject coverage:
The curative use of hypnosis, hypnotherapy and licensed to use 'Lesserian' trademark.

Printed publications:
Details of training courses
Course prospectus
Hypnotherapy Explained (Lesser D, £12.95 inc. p&p)
The Book of Hypnosis (Lesser D, £12.95 inc. p&p)

Electronic and video publications:
Training Course, content, methods explained
  (Video and DVD available, free)

Publications list:
Available online and in print

Access to staff:
Contact by letter, by telephone, by e-mail and via website. Appointment necessary.
Hours: Mon to Thu, 0900 to 1800

THERMAL ENGINEERING INTERNATIONAL LIMITED

Acronym or abbreviation: Tei

PO Box 80, Calder Vale Road, Wakefield, West Yorkshire, WF1 5YS

Tel: 01924 780000
Fax: 01924 201901
E-mail: enquiries@tei.co.uk

Website:
http://www.tei.co.uk

Enquiries:
Enquiries to: Director
Direct e-mail: maddisond@tei.co.uk
Other contacts: Technical Director for Ruislip office.

Founded:
1997

Organisation type and purpose:
International organisation, manufacturing industry, service industry, consultancy.
Design, engineering and commissioning services for utility, industrial and marine boiler plants.

Subject coverage:
Steam boiler plant design and engineering and commissioning for utility, industrial and marine industries.

Museum or gallery collection, archive, or library special collection:
British, European and USA Standards

Printed publications:
Brochures

Access to staff:
Contact by letter, by telephone, by fax and by e-mail. Appointment necessary.
Hours: Mon to Fri, 0730 to 1230 and 1400 to 1700

Head office:
Thermal Engineering International Limited
  Mechanical Services Division, PO Box 80, Calder Vale Road, Wakefield, West Yorkshire, WF1 5PF; tel: 01924 780000; fax: 01924 201901

THERMAL INSULATION CONTRACTORS ASSOCIATION

Acronym or abbreviation: TICA

TICA House, Arlington Way, Yarm Road Business Park, Darlington, Co Durham, DL1 4QB

Tel: 01325 466704
Fax: 01325 487691
E-mail: enquiries@tica-acad.co.uk

Website:
http://www.tica-acad.co.uk

Enquiries:
Enquiries to: Chief Executive

Founded:
1959

Organisation type and purpose:
Trade association, present number of members: 90.
Advisory services for members and representation of their interests.

Subject coverage:
Thermal insulation contracting, hot and cold insulation in power stations, oil refineries, chemical plant and marine projects, including pipework, plant, ductwork, storage tanks, etc., the insulation of heating and ventilation in schools, hospitals, offices and other buildings, asbestos control and removal, firms undertaking such work, technical information, health, safety and training.

Publications list:
Available online and in print

Access to staff:
Contact by letter, by telephone, by fax, by e-mail, in person and via website. Non-members charged.
Hours: Mon to Thu, 0830 to 1700; Fri, 0830 to 1530

Access for disabled people:
Parking provided

Affiliated to:
Fédération Européenne des Syndicats d'Enterprises d'Isolation (FESI)
  TICA House, Allington Way, Darlington, Co. Durham; tel: 0325 466704; fax: 01325 487691; e-mail: ralphbradley@tica-acad.co.uk; website: http://www.fesi.eu
World Insulation and Acoustics Congress Organisation (WIACO)

continued overleaf

Subsidiary bodies:
Asbestos Control and Abatement Division
(ACAD)
  tel: 01325 466704; fax: 01325 487691; e-mail:
  enquiries@tica-acad.co.uk
Insulation and Environmental Training Agency
  tel: 01325 466704; fax: 01325 487691; e-mail: ieta@
  tica-acad.co.uk

THERMAL INSULATION MANUFACTURERS AND SUPPLIERS ASSOCIATION

Acronym or abbreviation: TIMSA

Tournai Hall, Evelyn Woods Road, Aldershot,
Hampshire, GU11 2LL

Tel: 01252 357844
Fax: 01252 357831
E-mail: timsa@associationhouse.org.uk

Website:
http://www.timsa.org.uk

Enquiries:
Enquiries to: Secretary

Founded:
1978

Organisation type and purpose:
Trade association, present number of members: 36.
Represents major manufacturers, specialist
suppliers and distributors and consultants in the
UK thermal insulation industry.

Subject coverage:
Promotes the correct use and application of
thermal insulation and ancillary materials.

Printed publications:
List of Members
Technical Guidance Notes

Publications list:
Available in print

Access to staff:
Contact by letter, by telephone, by fax, by e-mail
and via website
Hours: Mon to Fri, 0900 to 1700

THERMAL SPRAYING AND SURFACE ENGINEERING ASSOCIATION, THE

Acronym or abbreviation: TSSEA

18 Hammeton Way, Wellesbourne, Warwick, CV35
9NT

Tel: 01789 842822
Fax: 01789 842229
E-mail: thermal.sprayers@btinternet.com

Enquiries:
Enquiries to: General Secretary

Founded:
1934

Organisation type and purpose:
International organisation, advisory body, trade
association (membership is by subscription),
service industry, consultancy.

Subject coverage:
Surface coatings on metals or other substrates of
other metals, ceramics and cermets.

Printed publications:
Brochures
Directory of members
Technical information sheets

Access to staff:
Contact by letter, by telephone, by fax and by e-
mail. Appointment necessary.
Hours: Mon to Fri, 0900 to 1700

Affiliated to:
The Institute of Materials (IOM)
  1 Carlton House Terrace, London, SW1Y 5DB

THIRD AGE TRUST

The Old Municipal Buildings, 19 East Street,
Bromley, Kent, BR1 1QE,

Tel: 020 8466 6139
E-mail: via website

Website:
http://www.u3a.org.uk
The trust, U3As and their relationship with the
trust, how to find and join a U3A, how to start a
U3A, list of U3As' websites, online courses.

Organisation type and purpose:
A limited company and a registered charity
(number 288007).
The national representative body for Universities
of the Third Age (U3As) in the UK.
Underpins the work of local U3As by providing
educational and administrative support to their
management committees and to individual
members and assists in the development of new
U3As across the UK.

Subject coverage:
U3As are self-help, self-managed lifelong learning
co-operatives for older people no longer in full-
time work, providing opportunities for their
members to share learning experiences in a wide
range of interest groups and to pursue learning not
for qualifications, but for fun.

Access to staff:
Contact by letter, by telephone and via website
Hours: Tel. lines open: Mon to Thu, 0900 to 1700;
Fri, 0900 to 1300

THISTLE FOUNDATION

Niddrie Mains Road, Edinburgh, EH16 4EA

Tel: 0131 661 3366
Fax: 0131 661 4879
E-mail: via website

Website:
http://www.thistle.org.uk
Services, publications, people's stories.

Founded:
1944

Organisation type and purpose:
A registered Scottish charity (number is SC016816).
Supports people with disabilities and long-term
health conditions.
Aims to give people independence in their own
homes and help bring about a society where
everyone has the right to feel involved and
empowered to live the life they choose, regardless
of their disabilities or health condition.

Subject coverage:
Provides a range of supported living and health
and well-being services for people with disabilities
and health conditions, plus training and
consultancy and conference facilities.

Electronic and video publications:
Focus (newsletter)
Supported living brochure
Course brochures
I don't want to miss a thing (stories of regenerating
  lives from people supported by The Thistle
  Foundation living in Renfrew)
Press releases
Order electronic and video publications from:
Download from website

Publications list:
Available online

Access to staff:
Contact by letter, by telephone, by fax and via
website

Also at:
25 High Mair, Renfrew, PA4 OSD
  tel: 0141 886 3375; fax: 0141 885 1484
Wighton House, East Ct, Edinburgh, EH16 4ED
  tel: 0131 661 1543

THOMAS HARDY SOCIETY

PO Box 1438, Dorchester, Dorset, DT1 1YH

Tel: 01305 251501
Fax: 01305 251501
E-mail: info@hardysociety.org

Website:
http://www.hardysociety.org

Enquiries:
Enquiries to: Honorary Secretary

Founded:
1968

Organisation type and purpose:
Membership association (membership is by
subscription), present number of members: 1,500.
Literary society.

Subject coverage:
Life and work of Thomas Hardy; country
associated with Hardy's writing.

**Museum or gallery collection, archive, or library
special collection:**
Comprehensive collection of books by Hardy and
all literary criticism held at Dorset County
Library, Dorchester
Important Hardy collections at Dorset County
Museum, Dorchester

Printed publications:
Books and pamphlets (18 titles, list available)
The Thomas Hardy Journal (3 times a year)
Tour Guides to the Hardy Country

Publications list:
Available in print

Access to staff:
Contact by letter, by telephone, by fax, by e-mail,
in person and via website. Appointment necessary.
Hours: Mon to Thu, 1400 to 1600

THOMAS LOVELL BEDDOES SOCIETY

9 Amber Court, Belper, Derbyshire, DE56 1HG

Tel: 01773 828066
Fax: 01773 828066
E-mail: john@beddoes.demon.co.uk

Website:
http://www.phantomwooer.org

Enquiries:
Enquiries to: Chair

Founded:
1994

Organisation type and purpose:
International organisation, learned society
(membership is by subscription, election or
invitation), present number of members: 100,
registered charity (charity number 1041402),
research organisation, publishing house.
To research Beddoes' life, times and work and
encourage relevant publications; to further the
reading and appreciation of his works by a wider
public; to liaise with other groups and
organisations; to plan events to further the aims.

Subject coverage:
Life and works of Thomas Lovell Beddoes (1803–
1849).

**Museum or gallery collection, archive, or library
special collection:**
Works of Thomas Lovell Beddoes

Non-library collection catalogue:
All or part available online, in-house and in print

Printed publications:
Newsletter (annually, by membership, or £5 each)
Other publications

Electronic and video publications:
Poems and Songs (audio tape, £5)

Publications list:
Available online and in print

Access to staff:
Contact by letter, by telephone, by fax, by e-mail and in person
Hours: Mon to Fri, 0900 to 1700

Access to building, collection or gallery:
Prior appointment required

Links with:
Alliance of Literary Societies (ALS)
Secretary, 22 Belmont Grove, Havant, Hampshire, PO9 3PU; tel: 01926 337874

THOMAS PAINE SOCIETY

c/o Stuart Hill, 14 Park Drive, Forest Hall, Newcastle, NE12 9JP

E-mail: stuart.hill23@ntlworld.com

Website:
http://www.thomaspainesocietyuk.org.uk

Organisation type and purpose:
Membership association (membership is by subscription). Promotes the recognition of Thomas Paine's contribution to the cause of freedom and seeks to spread a knowledge of his work and activities with a view to encouraging the growth of a similar spirit of constructive criticism in every aspect of public life.

Subject coverage:
The work and activities of Thomas Paine.

Printed publications:
Journal of Radical History

THOMAS PLUME'S LIBRARY

Market Hill, Maldon, Essex, CM9 4PZ

Tel: 01621 854850
Fax: 01621 854850
E-mail: info@thomasplumeslibrary.co.uk

Website:
htpp://www.thomasplumeslibrary.co.uk

Enquiries:
Enquiries to: Librarian

Founded:
1704

Subject coverage:
C17th theology, natural philosophy, chemistry, medicine, physics, mathematics, and astronomy.

Museum or gallery collection, archive, or library special collection:
Thomas Plume Collection of 8,200 vols, post-Plume collection approx. 1,800, Plume's manuscripts and papers.

Library catalogue:
All or part available online and in print

Printed publications:
Catalogue
The Intentions of Thomas Plume
Why do we need so many old books? The value of the Plume Library in the modern world (David Pearson, publication in autumn 2010)
Postcards
Greetings card

Access to staff:
Contact by letter, by telephone, by fax, by e-mail, in person and via website
Hours: Tue to Thu, 1400 to 1600; Sat, 1000 to 1200; Mon, Fri, closed

Access to building, collection or gallery:
Hours: Tue to Thu, 1400 to 1600; Sat, 1000 to 1200; Mon, Fri, closed
Special comments: Spiral staircase to 1st floor.

Access for disabled people:
No disabled access

THOMAS TALLIS SOCIETY

Acronym or abbreviation: TTS

13 Albury Street, London, SE8 3PT

Tel: 020 8691 8337
Fax: 020 8691 8337

Website:
http://www.thomas-tallis-society.org.uk/
http://www.classical-artists.com/tcc

Enquiries:
Enquiries to: Administrator

Founded:
1965

Organisation type and purpose:
Choral society.

Subject coverage:
The music of Thomas Tallis. The choir performs mainly classical music of all periods. Specialising in programmes to suit different venues, themes.

Printed publications:
Brochure (annually)
Newsletter

Access to staff:
Contact by letter, by telephone and by fax
Hours: Mon to Fri, 0900 to 1700

Connections with:
Tallis Chamber Choir (TCC)
13 Albury Street, London, SE8 3PT; tel: 020 8691 8337

THOMPSON HENRY LIMITED

London Road, Sunningdale, Berkshire, SL5 0EP

Tel: 01344 624615
Fax: 01344 626120
E-mail: thl@thompsonhenry.co.uk

Enquiries:
Enquiries to: Managing Director
Direct e-mail: j.dodd@thompsonhenry.co.uk

Founded:
1972

Organisation type and purpose:
Service industry.

Subject coverage:
Publications and services of the academic publishers represented.

Access to staff:
Contact by letter and by e-mail
Hours: Mon to Fri, 0900 to 1700

European agent for:
BIOSIS
CAIRN
H W Wilson Company
NewsBank
RMIT Publishing
STAT!Ref

UK agent for:
LexisNexis Academic & Library Solutions
Readex

THOMSON REUTERS ZOOLOGICAL LTD

Enterprise House, Innovation Way, Heslington, York, YO10 5NY

Tel: 020 7433 4590
Fax: 020 7433 4589

Website:
http://www.thomsonreuters.com
http://www.organismnames.com
Taxonomic name information for life science research.
http://www.biologybrowser.com
Resource index for scientific digital resources in biodiversity, zoology and social sciences.

Enquiries:
Enquiries to: Director, Operations and Development
Direct e-mail: nigel.robinson@thomsonreuters.com

Founded:
1864

Formerly called:
BIOSIS UK

Organisation type and purpose:
Provider of information services and solutions for professionals in life sciences.

Subject coverage:
Life sciences – bibliographic data, zoology.

Printed publications:
Zoological Record (annual bibliography)

Electronic and video publications:
Zoological Record (updated monthly)
Index to Organism Names
Biology Browser
Order electronic and video publications from: Thomson Reuters sales office

Publications list:
Available online

Access to staff:
Contact by letter, by telephone, by fax, by e-mail and via website
Hours: Mon to Fri, 0900 to 1700

Access to building, collection or gallery:
No access other than to staff

Parent body:
Thomson Reuters
77 Hatton Garden, London, EC1N 8JS; website: http://www.thomsonreuters.com

THORESBY SOCIETY

Formal name: The Thoresby Society – The Leeds Historical Society

Claremont, 23 Clarendon Road, Leeds, West Yorkshire, LS2 9NZ

Tel: 0113 247 0704
E-mail: secretary@thoresby.org.uk

Website:
http://www.thoresby.org.uk
The Society's history, programmes of lectures, publications, and articles relating to aspects of the history of the area.

Enquiries:
Enquiries to: Honorary Secretary (for general enquiries)
Direct e-mail: library@thoresby.org.uk
Other contacts: Librarian (for research enquiries)

Founded:
1889

Organisation type and purpose:
Historical society (membership is by subscription), present number of members: c. 350, registered charity (charity number 1126086) and company limited by guarantee (company number 6649783).

Subject coverage:
Local history of Leeds and surrounding areas.

Museum or gallery collection, archive, or library special collection:
Books, pictures, maps and plans, archives

Non-library collection catalogue:
All or part available online and in-house

Library catalogue:
All or part available in-house

Printed publications:
Thoresby Society Publications (annually since 1891). The publications cover a wide variety of subjects on local industrial, social and political history.
The parish registers of Leeds Parish Church have been transcribed and published up to 1776 by the Society, but are currently out of print. They are indexed and contain baptism, marriage and burial entries
Order printed publications from: The Society, by post (address above) or by e-mail: distribution@ thoresby.org.uk

Publications list:
Available online and in print

continued overleaf

Access to staff:
Contact by letter, by telephone, by e-mail and via website. Appointment necessary.
Hours: Tue and Thu, 1000 to 1400; phone messages can be left at other times

Access to building, collection or gallery:
Hours: Tue and Thu, 1000 to 1400

Access for disabled people:
Parking provided; toilet facilities
Special comments: Library is on first floor; there is no lift.

THREE RIVERS DISTRICT COUNCIL

Acronym or abbreviation: TRDC

Three Rivers House, Northway, Rickmansworth, Hertfordshire, WD3 1RL

Tel: 01923 776611
Fax: 01923 896119
E-mail: stuart.marlton@threerivers.gov.uk

Website:
http://www.3rivers.gov.uk

Enquiries:
Enquiries to: Public Relations Manager
Direct tel: 01923 727255
Direct fax: 01923 727258

Founded:
1974

Organisation type and purpose:
Local government body.

Subject coverage:
All local services and amenities covering the Rickmansworth, South Oxhey, Carpenders Park, Chorleywood, Sarratt, Abbots Langley, Moor Park and Maple Cross area, allotments, cemeteries, electoral registration, environmental health, parking, concessionary public transport fares, housing, museums and arts, local planning, building control and development control, council tax and business rates collection, sports and recreation.

Printed publications:
Accommodation Guide (free)
Halls for Hire (free)
How to Contact Your Councillor (free)
Places of Worship (free)
Three Rivers District Guide (free)
Three Rivers Map (free)
Three Rivers Times Magazine (free)

Access to staff:
Contact by letter, by telephone, by fax, by e-mail, in person and via website. Appointment necessary.
Hours: Mon to Thu, 0830 to 1730; Fri, 0830 to 1700

Access for disabled people:
Parking provided, level entry, access to all public areas, toilet facilities

THRIVE

The Geoffrey Udall Centre, Beech Hill, Reading, Berkshire, RG7 2AT

Tel: 0118 988 5688
Fax: 0118 988 5677
E-mail: info@thrive.org.uk

Website:
http://www.thrive.org.uk
http://www.carryongardening.org

Enquiries:
Enquiries to: Information Officer
Direct e-mail: gill.bailey@thrive.org.uk

Founded:
1978

Organisation type and purpose:
Membership association (membership is by subscription), present number of members: 730, voluntary organisation, registered charity (charity number 277570), suitable for all ages; training

organisation, consultancy. To research, educate and promote the use and advantages of gardening for people with a disability.

Subject coverage:
Disability and gardening. Activities focus on promoting the benefits of gardening to individuals and organisations, as well as teaching techniques and practical applications so that anyone with a disability can take part in and benefit from gardening.

Special visitor services:
Two gardens (call office for details)

Museum or gallery collection, archive, or library special collection:
Library containing comprehensive collection on therapeutic horticulture

Printed publications:
Growthpoint (magazine, quarterly)
Children's Gardening
Gardening is for Everyone
Getting on with Gardening (vols 1 & 2)
Getting on with Growing Food
Gardening for Hearts & Minds
Getting on with Growing in Containers
Gardening Year Book
Briefing sheets
Creating Gardening Independence
Cultivating Quality
Horticulture as Therapy
Horticulture in Secure Settings
Evidence & Messages
Health, Wellbeing & Social Inclusion
Growing Together

Publications list:
Available online and in print

Access to staff:
Contact by letter, by telephone, by fax, by e-mail and via website. Appointment necessary.
Hours: Mon to Fri, 0900 to 1700

Links with:
Coventry University
numerous professional and voluntary bodies
Royal Horticultural Society

THROMBOSIS RESEARCH INSTITUTE

Emmanuel Kaye Building, Manresa Road, Chelsea, London, SW3 6LR

Tel: 020 7351 8300
Fax: 020 7351 8317
E-mail: info@tri-london.ac.uk

Website:
http://www.tri-london.ac.uk
The Institute and its research; includes an interactive lecture delivered by the Director of the Institute, focussing on cancer-associated thrombosis.

Founded:
1989

Organisation type and purpose:
Registered charity (charity number 800365). Research institute.
Internationally renowned for pioneering, multi-disciplinary research, the Thrombosis Research Institute was established to conduct research into cardiovascular disease, a major cause of death and disability throughout the world. It comprises two independent charitable foundations based in London, United Kingdom and Bangalore, India (founded 2006). This second facility was set up to study the genetics of heart disease particularly among the South Asian population, who seem to have specific predisposing genetic characteristics, and to develop novel and affordable therapies for disease prevention and treatment.

Subject coverage:
Holds an annual international symposium of clinicians. The two partner institutions contribute to a joint, independent research programme.

Electronic and video publications:
Are you at Risk of DVT? (leaflet)
Are You at risk of DVT in Hospital? (leaflet)

Access to staff:
Contact by letter, by telephone, by fax and by e-mail

Also at:
Thrombosis Research Institute
258A, Bommasandra Industrial Area, Anekal Taluk, Bangalore 560 099, India; tel: +91 80 2783 5303; fax: +91 80 2783 5443

THURROCK AND BASILDON COLLEGE

Woodview Campus, Grays, Essex, RM16 2YR

Tel: 01375 362691
Fax: 01375 373356
E-mail: lbarker@tab.ac.uk

Enquiries:
Enquiries to: Librarian

Founded:
1959

Organisation type and purpose:
College of further education.

Subject coverage:
Management and business studies, office and information technology, hotels and catering, tourism and leisure, language, hair and beauty technology, motor vehicle studies, art and design, caring, pre-school education, vocational.

Library catalogue:
All or part available in-house

Access to staff:
Contact by telephone and in person
Hours: Mon, 0845 to 2130; Tue to Thu, 0845 to 1800; Fri, 0845 to 1645

Access for disabled people:
Parking provided, level entry, toilet facilities

Other address:
Thurrock and Basildon College
Nethermayne Campus, Basildon, Essex, SS16 5NN; tel: 01268 461614

THURROCK UNITARY COUNCIL

Civic Offices, New Road, Grays, Essex, RM17 6SL

Tel: 01375 652652
Fax: 01375 652785
E-mail: general.enquiries@thurrock.gov.uk

Enquiries:
Enquiries to: Head of Corporate Communications
Direct tel: 01375 652016
Direct fax: 01375 652874

Organisation type and purpose:
Local government body.

Subject coverage:
Local government, residential services, regeneration, environmental conservation.

Printed publications:
Thurrock Magazine
corporate literature

Access to staff:
Contact by letter, by telephone and by fax
Hours: Mon to Fri, 0900 to 1700

Access to building, collection or gallery:
Hours: Mon to Fri, 0830 to 1700

Access for disabled people:
Hours: Mon to Fri, 0830 to 1700

TILE ASSOCIATION

Acronym or abbreviation: TTA

Forum Court, 83 Copers Cope Road, Beckenham, Kent, BR3 1NR

Tel: 020 8663 0946
Fax: 020 8663 0949
E-mail: info@tiles.org.uk

Website:
http://www.tiles.org.uk

Enquiries:
Enquiries to: Executive Officer

Founded:
2000

Organisation type and purpose:
Trade association.

Subject coverage:
Generic information on wall and floor tiling.

Printed publications:
Technical literature

Access to staff:
Contact by letter, by telephone, by fax, by e-mail and via website. Appointment necessary.
Hours: Mon to Fri, 0900 to 1700

Member organisation of:
European Ceramic Tile Manufacturers Association (CET)
European Union of Tile Fixers' Associations (EUF)
National Specialist Contractors Council (NSCC)

TILES AND ARCHITECTURAL CERAMICS SOCIETY

Acronym or abbreviation: TACS

'Oakhurst', Cocknage Road, Rough Close, Stoke on Trent, ST3 7NN

Tel: 0151 207 0001
E-mail: kathbertadams@hotmail.com

Website:
http://www.tilesoc.org.uk
Information about the society, information about the tiles, location index and gazetteer project.

Enquiries:
Enquiries to: Secretary

Founded:
1981

Organisation type and purpose:
Advisory body, learned society (membership is by subscription), present number of members: 367, registered charity (charity number 289090), research organisation, publishing house.
The study and protection of tiles and architectural ceramics.

Subject coverage:
All areas of historical and contemporary tile production and functional applications, as well as tile collecting and tile conservation, architectural ceramics.

Printed publications:
Publications list currently being revised
Brightening the Long Days, hospital tile pictures
Fired Earth: 1000 Years of Tiles in Europe:
    Exhibition catalogue
Glazed Expressions (magazine, 3 times a year)
Journal (annual)
Newsletter (quarterly)

Publications list:
Available online and in print

Access to staff:
Contact by letter and by e-mail
Hours: Mon to Fri, 0900 to 1700

TILLENDOVE PICTURE LIBRARY

Bowood, Ewell House Grove, Epsom, Surrey, KT17 1NT

Tel: 07831 598018
Fax: 020 8394 2247
E-mail: tillendove@mailbox.co.uk

Website:
http://www.tillendove.co.uk

Enquiries:
Enquiries to: Partner

Founded:
1993

Organisation type and purpose:
Service industry.
Press photography library.

Subject coverage:
Press photography.

Museum or gallery collection, archive, or library special collection:
Photographs of celebrities, film, TV and music
Photographs of public figures

Non-library collection catalogue:
All or part available online and in-house

Publications list:
Available in print

Access to staff:
Contact by letter, by telephone, by fax and by e-mail. All charged.
Hours: Mon to Fri, 0900 to 1700

Access to building, collection or gallery:
No access other than to staff

TIMBER PACKAGING AND PALLET CONFEDERATION

Acronym or abbreviation: TIMCON

840 Melton Road, Thurmaston, Leicester, LE4 8BN

Tel: 0116 264 0579
Fax: 0116 264 0141
E-mail: timcon@associationhq.org.uk

Website:
http://www.timcon.org

Enquiries:
Enquiries to: Executive Secretary

Organisation type and purpose:
Trade association.

Subject coverage:
Wooden cases and pallets; export packing; technical, legislative, environmental and industrial relations matters in the industry.

Printed publications:
Be Sure with Wood
Code of Practice
Directory of Members
Pallet Buyers Guide

Access to staff:
Contact by letter, by telephone, by fax, by e-mail and via website
Hours: Mon to Fri, 0900 to 1700

Access to building, collection or gallery:
Prior appointment required

Access for disabled people:
Access to all public areas

TIMBER TRADE FEDERATION

Acronym or abbreviation: TTF

The Building Centre, 26 Store Street, London, WC1E 7BT

Tel: 020 3205 0067
E-mail: ttf@ttf.co.uk

Website:
http://www.ttf.co.uk/

Enquiries:
Enquiries to: Director General

Founded:
1892

Organisation type and purpose:
Trade association.

Access to staff:
Contact by letter, by telephone and by e-mail.
Appointment necessary. Non-members charged.

Hours: Mon to Fri, 0900 to 1700

Access to building, collection or gallery:
No prior appointment required

TNS MEDIA INTELLIGENCE LIMITED

Formal name: The Media Monitoring Service

6th Floor, 292 Vauxhall Bridge Road, London, SW1V 1AE

Tel: 0870 202 0100
Fax: 0870 202 0110
E-mail: tnsmi_sales@tnsofres.com

Website:
http://www.tellex.press.net

Enquiries:
Enquiries to: Marketing & Communications Manager
Direct tel: 020 7963 7638
Direct fax: 020 7963 7609

Founded:
1954

Formerly called:
Parker Bishop Limited, TNS Tellex Limited (year of change 2002)

Organisation type and purpose:
Service industry.
Broadcast reporting service monitoring over 350 television and radio stations throughout the UK; a service providing selective broadcast information to the communications industry including: PR agencies, advertising and design agencies, manufacturing and marketing companies, service companies, government organisations, financial PR agencies and companies.

Subject coverage:
Mainly news and current affairs, although any item or station can be monitored with a detailed brief supplied by the client with reasonable notice.

Printed publications:
Blue Book of British Broadcasting (annually in March)
Burgundy Book of European Broadcasting (annually in September)
Order printed publications from: Publications Department
at the same address, tel: 020 7566 3108

Access to staff:
Contact by letter, by telephone, by fax, by e-mail and via website. Appointment necessary.
Hours: Sales office: Mon to Fri, 0700 to 1900

Other addresses:
TNS Media Intelligence
    Manchester; tel: 0161 228 6922
TNS Media Intelligence
    Durham; tel: 0191 386 6767
TNS Media Intelligence
    Leeds; tel: 0113 243 4233
TNS Media Intelligence
    Peterborough, Cambridgeshire; tel: 01733 896776
TNS Media Intelligence
    Cardiff; tel: 029 2039 5313
TNS Media Intelligence
    Worthing, West Sussex; tel: 01903 212731
TNS Media Intelligence
    Edinburgh; tel: 0131 226 2612

Subsidiary of:
Taylor Nelson Sofres plc

TOASTMASTERS FOR ROYAL OCCASIONS

12 Little Bornes, Alleyn Park, Dulwich, London, SE21 8SE

Tel: 020 8670 5585/ 8424
Fax: 020 8670 0055

Enquiries:
Enquiries to: President

continued overleaf

Founded:
1980

Organisation type and purpose:
Professional body, training organisation.

Subject coverage:
Royal visits, state banquets etc, in Britain and overseas; all aspects of the preparation and organisation of these events.

Access to staff:
Contact by letter, by telephone, by fax and by e-mail
Hours: Mon to Fri, 0900 to 1700

Member of:
Guild of International Professional Toastmasters at the same address

TOASTMASTERS OF GREAT BRITAIN

12 Little Bornes, Alleyn Park, Dulwich, London, SE21 8SE

Tel: 020 8670 5585
Fax: 020 8670 0055

Website:
http://www.ivorspencer.com

Enquiries:
Enquiries to: Chief Executive

Founded:
1980

Organisation type and purpose:
Advisory body, professional body.

Subject coverage:
Organisation of royal events, banquets, conferences, and other ceremonies for firms and public bodies.

Access to staff:
Contact by letter, by telephone, by fax and by e-mail. Access for members only.
Hours: Mon to Fri, 0900 to 1700

Member of:
Guild of Professional Toastmasters

TOBACCO MANUFACTURERS' ASSOCIATION

Acronym or abbreviation: TMA

5th Floor, Burwood House, 14/16 Caxton Street, London, SW1H 0ZB

Tel: 020 7544 0100
Fax: 020 7544 0117
E-mail: information@the-tma.org.uk

Website:
http://www.the-tma.org.uk

Enquiries:
Enquiries to: Information and Media Manager
Direct tel: 020 7544 0108

Founded:
1940

Organisation type and purpose:
Trade association.

Subject coverage:
Tobacco industry; smoking issues.

Non-library collection catalogue:
All or part available online, in-house and in print

Access to staff:
Contact by letter, by telephone, by fax and by e-mail
Hours: Mon to Fri, 0900 to 1700

Access to building, collection or gallery:
No access other than to staff

TOC H

3rd Floor, Wing House, Britannia Street, Aylesbury, Buckinghamshire, HP20 1QS

Tel: 01296 331099
Fax: 01296 331135
E-mail: info@toch.org.uk

Website:
http://www.toch.org.uk
Information about the movement. Information on projects and events.

Enquiries:
Enquiries to: Director

Founded:
1915

Organisation type and purpose:
Membership association, present number of members: 3,061, voluntary organisation, registered charity (charity number 211042).
Christian-based, but open to people of all walks of life and faith.
To break down social, racial and cultural barriers by challenging individuals' perceptions of others and the divisions which exist in society.

Subject coverage:
Voluntary work, personal and community service.

Museum or gallery collection, archive, or library special collection:
Archive of Toc H books and photographs

Printed publications:
Royal Charter 1971
Point Three (6 times a year)
Projects and Activities Brochure

Publications list:
Available in print

Access to staff:
Contact by letter, by telephone and by fax
Hours: Mon to Fri, 0900 to 1700

TOGETHER (MACA)

Formal name: Together (The Mental After Care Association)
Acronym or abbreviation: MACA

12 Old Street, London, EC1V 9BE

Tel: 020 7780 7300
Fax: 020 7780 7301
E-mail: contactus@together-uk.org

Website:
http://www.together-uk.org/
General and local services listings.

Enquiries:
Enquiries to: Press and Publications Officer
Direct e-mail: amanda-williamson@together-uk.org

Founded:
1879

Organisation type and purpose:
National organisation, voluntary organisation, registered charity (charity number 211091).
Probably the earliest organisation of its kind, established from 1879.
To provide high quality services for people with mental health needs and their carers and to influence policy and practice in relation to mental health.

Subject coverage:
Services in the community, hospitals and prisons for people with mental health needs and their carers.

Museum or gallery collection, archive, or library special collection:
Archives of the Association dating back to 1879, now held at the Wellcome Trust, London

Library catalogue:
All or part available in-house

Printed publications:
Annual Report
Annual Review
General Information Brochure
Leaflets

Access to staff:
Contact by letter, by telephone, by fax, by e-mail and via website. Appointment necessary.
Hours: Mon to Fri, 0900 to 1730
Special comments: For staff, council members and service users only. No wheelchair access. No public access to library.

Regional Offices:
MACA Development Areas (North, Midlands and Scotland)
   3 Fieldhouse Road, Rochdale, Lancashire, OL12 0AD; tel: 01706 640 027; fax: 01706 640 027; e-mail: maca-midlandsandnorth@maca.org.uk
MACA London and East
   89 Turners Hill, Cheshunt, Hertfordshire, EN8 9BN; tel: 01992 622 000; fax: 01992 622 621; e-mail: maca-londonandeast@maca.org.uk
MACA South
   94b High Street, Epsom, Surrey, KT19 8BJ; tel: 01372 722 970; fax: 01372 722 980; e-mail: maca .south@maca.org.uk

TOLKIEN SOCIETY

8 Queens Lane, Eynsham, Witney, OX2 4HL

E-mail: tolksoc@tolkiensociety.org

Website:
http://www.tolkiensociety.org
Information about the Society, sales catalogue, information request service, articles, seminars

Enquiries:
Enquiries to: Membership Secretary
Direct e-mail: membership@tolkiensociety.org
Other contacts: Archivist –
archives@tolkiensociety.org for access to the Society's archives.

Founded:
1969

Organisation type and purpose:
International organisation, learned society (membership is by subscription), present number of members: 1,245, voluntary organisation, registered charity (charity number 273809).

Subject coverage:
J R R Tolkien, life and works, associated authors, the Inklings etc.

Museum or gallery collection, archive, or library special collection:
Archives of Tolkien-related material including newspaper cuttings, fanzines, merchandise and foreign editions

Non-library collection catalogue:
All or part available in-house

Printed publications:
Amon Hen (bulletin, 6 times a year)
The Best of Amon Hen 1 (£5)
Digging Potatoes, Growing Trees Vol 1, Vol 2 and Vol 3 (£5 each)
First and Second Ages (£5)
Mallorn (journal, annually)
Proceedings of the 1992 Tolkien Centenary Conference (£15pb; £40 hb)
The Ways of Creative Mythologies (£10)
Tolkien, the Sea and Scandinavia (£5)
Travel and Communication in Tolkien's Worlds (£5)
Sindarin Lexicon (£5)
Order printed publications from: Tolkien Society Trading Ltd
8 Chantry Lane, Westbury, Wiltshire, BA13 3BS, tel: 01373 822884, fax: 01373 865001, e-mail: sales@ tolkiensociety.org

Access to staff:
Contact by letter and by e-mail. Appointment necessary.
Hours: Mon to Fri, 0900 to 1700
Special comments: By special appointment and not usually made on weekends.

Access to building, collection or gallery:
Prior appointment required

Affiliated to:
The Alliance of Literary Societies

Has:
23 affiliated local groups (Smials)

TONBRIDGE & MALLING BOROUGH COUNCIL

Acronym or abbreviation: TMBC

Gibson Building, Gibson Drive, Kings Hill, West Malling, Kent, ME19 4LZ

Tel: 01732 844522
Fax: 01732 842170
E-mail: customer.services@tmbc.gov.uk

Website:
http://www.tmbc.gov.uk

Enquiries:
Enquiries to: Media and Communications Manager
Direct tel: 01732 876009
Direct fax: 01732 876004
Direct e-mail: linda.moreau@tmbc.gov.uk

Organisation type and purpose:
Local government body.

Printed publications:
A wide range of literature including:
Tonbridge and Malling – A to Z Guide to Services (free to 47,000 homes)
Leisure guide and other service specific literature (free)
Here and Now (newspaper, free to 47,000 homes)

Access to staff:
Contact by letter, by telephone, by fax, by e-mail and in person
Hours: Mon to Fri, 0830 to 1700

Access for disabled people:
Parking provided, level entry, toilet facilities

TONSIL

Formal name: The Ongoing Singing Liaison Group

35 Old Lynn Road, Wisbech, Cambridgeshire, PE14 7AJ

E-mail: enquiries@tonsil.org.uk

Website:
http://www.tonsil.org.uk/

Enquiries:
Enquiries to: Secretary
Direct e-mail: philliptolley@colcanto.co.uk

Founded:
1988

Organisation type and purpose:
Registered charity. Represents 14 organisations promoting choral singing, supporting over 25,000 member choirs and over 500,000 singers

Subject coverage:
Singing Days, Singing Projects and Animation Schemes, Training for Animateurs and Singing Leaders.

Access to staff:
Contact by letter, by telephone, by fax, by e-mail and via website. Appointment necessary.
Hours: Mon to Fri, 0930 to 1500

Member of:
European Federation of Young Choirs

TOOL AND TRADES HISTORY SOCIETY

Acronym or abbreviation: TATHS

Woodbine Cottage, Budleigh Hill, East Budleigh, Budleigh Salterton, Devon, EX9 7DT

Tel: 01395 443030
E-mail: membership@taths.org.uk

Enquiries:
Enquiries to: Membership Secretary

Founded:
1983

Organisation type and purpose:
International organisation, learned society (membership is by subscription), present number of members: 500, registered charity (charity number 290474).
To advance the education of the general public in the history and development of hand tools and their use, and of the people and trades that used them.

Subject coverage:
Hand tools; traditional trades using hand tools, e.g. blacksmiths, thatchers, coopers, all woodworking trades, furniture-making, clockmaking, jewellery-making, some building trades, medical and scientific instruments.

Library catalogue:
All or part available in print

Printed publications:
Newsletter (quarterly)
The Tool Chest of Benjamin Seaton (1797)
Tools & Trades (journal)
Reprint of Trade Catalogue of James John and Isaac Fussell
Reprint 1787 Directory of Sheffield

Publications list:
Available in print

Access to staff:
Contact by letter, by telephone, by e-mail and via website
Hours: Any evening

Links with:
Early American Industries Association (same field in USA)

TORBAY COUNCIL

Town Hall, Castle Circus, Torquay, Devon, TQ1 3DR

Tel: 01803 201201
Fax: 01803 292677
E-mail: connections @torbay.gov.uk

Website:
http://www.torbay.gov.uk

Founded:
1998

Formerly called:
Torbay Borough Council (year of change 1998)

Organisation type and purpose:
Local government body.

Subject coverage:
Local government services.

Printed publications:
Torbay View

Access to staff:
Contact by letter, by telephone, by fax, by e-mail and via website
Hours: Mon to Thu, 0840 to 1715; Fri, 0840 to 1615

Access to building, collection or gallery:
No access other than to staff

TORBAY LIBRARIES

Torquay Library, Lymington Road, Torquay, Devon, TQ1 3DT

Tel: 01803 208305
Fax: 01803 208307
E-mail: tqreflib@torbay.gov.uk

Website:
http://www.torbay.gov.uk/libraries

Enquiries:
Enquiries to: Head of Library Services

Organisation type and purpose:
Local government body, public library.

Subject coverage:
Devon local studies collection, particularly information on Torbay.

Museum or gallery collection, archive, or library special collection:
Devon local studies collection
Census returns on microfilm (local area only)
Cuttings file
Maps
Newspapers (microfilm)

Non-library collection catalogue:
All or part available online

Library catalogue:
All or part available online

Access to staff:
Contact by letter, by telephone, by fax, by e-mail and in person
Hours: Main Library and Local Studies Library: Mon, Wed, Fri, 0930 to 1900; Tue, 0930 to 1700; Thu, 0930 to 1300; Sat, 0930 to 1600

Access for disabled people:
Ramped entry, lift to first floor.

Parent body:
Torbay Council
e-mail: tqreflib@torbay.gov.uk; website: http://www.torbay.gov.uk/libraries

TORCH TRUST

Formal name: Torch Trust for the Blind

Torch House, Torch Way, Northampton Road, Market Harborough, Leics, LE16 9H

Tel: 01858 438260
Fax: 01858 438275
E-mail: info@torchtrust.org

Website:
http://www.torchtrust.org
Services provided, news and events, details of fellowship groups across the UK, library catalogue, resource catalogue.

Organisation type and purpose:
A registered charity (number 1095094) and voluntary organisation, suitable for children and adults.
Its vision is that blind and partially sighted people should be able to read what they want to read, when they want to read it and in a media that they prefer.

Subject coverage:
Provides a free postal Christian library service for blind and partially sighted people, and a holiday retreat.

Museum or gallery collection, archive, or library special collection:
The Torch Library is the largest collection of Christian books in the English language accessible for those with sight loss – over 2,000 titles covering theological, devotional, missionary, biographical and Christian leisure reading

Library catalogue:
All or part available online

Printed publications:
Magazines produced by Torch Trust are distributed to blind and partially sighted people in over 100 countries

Electronic and video publications:
Publishes six magazines, produces Bibles, hymn books, scripture text calendars, tactile greeting cards, books and booklets, and operates a large free postal library of Christian books in accessible media

Access to staff:
Contact by letter, by telephone, by fax and by e-mail

continued overleaf

Also at:
Torch Holiday and Retreat Centre
4 Hassocks Road, Hurstpierpoint, West Sussex,
BN6 9QN; tel: 01273 832282; e-mail: torchhrc@
torchtrust.org

**Non-denominational Torch Fellowship Groups
meet regularly at 110 locations across the UK:**

TORFAEN COUNTY BOROUGH COUNCIL

Civic Centre, Pontypool, Gwent, NP4 6YB

Tel: 01495 762200
Fax: 01495 755513

Website:
http://www.torfaen.gov.uk

Enquiries:
Enquiries to: Chief Executive
Direct tel: 01495 766069
Direct fax: 01495 766059

Founded:
1 April 1996

Organisation type and purpose:
Local government body.

Printed publications:
Torfaen Guide
Torfaen A-Z of Streets & Services

Access to staff:
Contact by letter
Hours: Mon to Fri, 0900 to 1700

Other office at:
Torfaen County Borough Council
County Hall, Croesyceiliog, Cwmbran

TORFAEN LIBRARY AND INFORMATION SERVICE

Pendragon House, General Rees Square,
Cwmbran, NP44 1AH

Tel: 01633 628941
Fax: 01633 628935
E-mail: Cwmbran.library@torfaen.gov.uk

Website:
http://www.torfaen.gov.uk/en/leisure/property
.php/mid=42

Enquiries:
Enquiries to: Cultural Services Manager
Direct e-mail: Christine.george@torfaen.gov.uk

Founded:
1996

Organisation type and purpose:
Local government body, public library.

Subject coverage:
General, local studies, advice and self help,
bibliotherapy.

Non-library collection catalogue:
All or part available online

Library catalogue:
All or part available online

Publications list:
Available in print

Access to staff:
Contact by letter, by telephone, by fax and by e-
mail
Hours: Mon to Fri, 0900 to 1700

Access for disabled people:
Toilet facilities

Parent body:
Torfaen County Borough Council

TORIT DCE, DONALDSON DUST COLLECTION GROUP

Humberstone Lane, Thurmaston, Leicester, LE4
8HP

Tel: 0116 269 6161
Fax: 0116 269 3028
E-mail: CAP-uk@donaldson.com

Website:
http://www.btrenvironmental.co.uk

Enquiries:
Enquiries to: UK Sales Manger
Other contacts: Marketing Officer for publications.

Founded:
1919

Formerly called:
BTR Environmental Limited; Dust Control
Equipment Limited (DCE) (year of change 1998)

Organisation type and purpose:
Manufacturing industry.

Subject coverage:
Design, manufacture, installation and
commissioning of industrial dust control
equipment; unit collectors; insertable filters;
automatic reverse jet filters; tubular bag filters;
complete plant installations; compact venting
filters; centralised vacuum cleaning systems.

**Museum or gallery collection, archive, or library
special collection:**
Complete Product Literature

Printed publications:
Full literature set available on request (free)

Electronic and video publications:
Product CD-ROM
Product video

Publications list:
Available online

Access to staff:
Contact by letter, by telephone, by fax, by e-mail
and via website. Appointment necessary.
Hours: Mon to Thu, 0830 to 1700; Fri, 0830 to 1545

Access to building, collection or gallery:
Prior appointment required

TORNADO AND STORM RESEARCH ORGANIZATION

Acronym or abbreviation: TORRO

TCO (Thunderstorm) Division, PO Box 84, Oxford,
OX1 4NP

Tel: 01865 483761
Fax: 01865 483937

Website:
http://www.torro.org.uk

Enquiries:
Enquiries to: Director
Direct e-mail: sam.hall@torro.org.uk
Other contacts: Director, Geography Unit, Oxford
Brookes University, Gipsy Lane, Oxford

Founded:
1924

Formerly called:
Thunderstorm Census Organisation (year of
change 1982)

Organisation type and purpose:
Research organisation.
Organisation for data collection, consultancy and
research.

Subject coverage:
Thunderstorm frequency in Great Britain,
geographical distribution in Great Britain, research
into damaging lightning incidents, historical data
collection, thunderstorm climatology, rainfall and
temperature extremes, damaging hailstones,
point rainfalls.

**Museum or gallery collection, archive, or library
special collection:**
Database for tornadoes, damaging hailstorms,
thunderstorms (UK)
Information on temperature and rainfall extremes
Thunderstorm reports and relevant press cuttings
1925 to date

Printed publications:
Monthly summaries of thunderstorm activity
(published in the Journal of Meteorology, UK)
Research papers at periodic intervals (price on
application)

Publications list:
Available in print

Access to staff:
Contact by letter, by e-mail and via website
Hours: Mon to Fri, 0900 to 1700

Parent body:
Tornado and Storm Research Organisation
(TORRO)
Geography Unit, Oxford Brookes University,
Gipsy Lane, Oxford

TORRIDGE DISTRICT COUNCIL

Acronym or abbreviation: TDC

Riverbank House, Bideford, Devon, EX39 2QG

Tel: 01237 428700
Fax: 01237 478849
E-mail: customer.services@torridge.gov.uk

Website:
http://www.torridge.gov.uk

Enquiries:
Enquiries to: Chief Executive
Direct tel: 01237 428705

Founded:
1974

Organisation type and purpose:
Local government body.

TOTAL FINA ELF EXPLORATION UK PLC

Acronym or abbreviation: TFEEUK

Crawpeel Road, Altens Industrial Estate,
Aberdeen, AB12 3FG

Tel: 01224 297000
Fax: 01224 298000

Enquiries:
Enquiries to: Librarian

Formerly called:
Elf Exploration UK plc (EEUK), Total Oil Marine
(TOM) (year of change 2000)

Organisation type and purpose:
Commercial company.

Subject coverage:
Oil, gas, exploration and production.

Library catalogue:
All or part available in-house

TOURETTES ACTION

Formal name: Tourette Syndrome (UK) Association
(Tourettes Action)

Southbank House, Black Prince Road, London, SE1
7SJ

Tel: 0845 458 1252 (helpline)
E-mail: help@tourettes-action.org.uk

Website:
http://www.tourettes-action.org.uk

Enquiries:
Enquiries to: Chief Executive
Direct tel: 020 7793 2355
Direct e-mail: suzanne.dobson@tourettes-action.org
.uk
Other contacts: TS Support Manager

Founded:
1980

Organisation type and purpose:
National organisation, advisory body, membership association (membership is by subscription, qualification, election or invitation), present number of members: 650, voluntary organisation, registered charity (charity number 1003317). The object of the Association is the relief of persons who have the neurological movement disorder Gilles de la Tourette Syndrome.

Subject coverage:
Tourette Syndrome, a neurological disorder causing motor and vocal tics

Information services:
Helpline; information pack available on request.

Printed publications:
General Information Pack
Booklets for teachers
Factsheet on Tourette Syndrome
List of consultants familiar with Tourette
  Syndrome
Order printed publications from: From helpline

Electronic and video publications:
E-mail news bulletins
Newsletter (monthly)

Publications list:
Available online and in print

Access to staff:
Contact by letter, by telephone, by e-mail and via website
Hours: Mon to Fri, 0900 to 1700

Access to building, collection or gallery:
No access other than to staff

TOURISM AUSTRALIA

Acronym or abbreviation: TA

Australia Centre, Australia House, 6th Floor, Melbourne Place/Strand, London, WC2B 4LG

Tel: 020 7438 4601
Fax: 020 7240 6690

Website:
http://www.australia.com
Over 10,000 pages of travel-related information on Australia.
http://www.tourism.australia.com

Enquiries:
Enquiries to: Marketing
Direct e-mail: lcorgan@tourism.australia.com
Other contacts: PR Manager, Advertising Manager

Formerly called:
Australian Tourist Commission (year of change 2004)

Organisation type and purpose:
National government body.
To promote tourism to Australia.

Subject coverage:
Australian travel trade contacts and Australian tourism in general.

Museum or gallery collection, archive, or library special collection:
Image library
Tourism Research
Video footage library

Trade and statistical information:
Statistical details on Australian tourism, arrival statistics.

Printed publications:
Australia Travel Guide (also available in German, French, Italian and Dutch)

Electronic and video publications:
Image Collection on CD-ROM
Video Footage

Access to staff:
Contact by letter, by telephone, by fax, by e-mail and via website
Hours: Mon to Fri, 0900 to 1700

Access to building, collection or gallery:
No prior appointment required

Other addresses:
Main office London, representative offices throughout Europe

TOURISM FOR ALL

c/o Vitalise, Shap Road Industrial Estate, Shap Road, Kendal, Cumbria, LA9 6NZ

Tel: 0845 124 9971
Fax: 01539 735567
E-mail: info@tourismforall.org.uk

Enquiries:
Enquiries to: Manager
Other contacts: Head of Consultancy Services (for consultancy service of the charity)

Founded:
1981

Created by the merger of:
Holiday Care, the Tourism for All Consortium and IndividuALL

Formerly called:
Holiday Care Service (HCS)

Organisation type and purpose:
Voluntary organisation, registered charity (charity number 279169), consultancy, research organisation.

Subject coverage:
The UK's central source of information for disabled people and carers wishing to take a holiday break.

Publications list:
Available in print

Access to staff:
Contact by letter, by telephone, by fax, by e-mail and in person
Hours: Mon to Fri, 0900 to 1700

Access for disabled people:
Access to all public areas, toilet facilities

TOURISM NEW ZEALAND

Acronym or abbreviation: TNZ

New Zealand House, 80 Haymarket, London, SW1Y 4TQ

Tel: 020 7930 1662
Fax: 020 7839 8929

Website:
http://www.newzealand.com

Enquiries:
Enquiries to: Office Manager
Direct e-mail: alisac@tnz.govt.nz

Organisation type and purpose:
National government body.
Government department of New Zealand.

Subject coverage:
Accommodation, transport, sights, vehicle hire, special events, outdoor activities, general tourism information, coach tours re New Zealand.

Printed publications:
New Zealand Motivator Brochure

Access to staff:
Contact by letter, by fax and via website

Member of:
Association of National Tourist Office Representatives
UK Chapter of the Pacific Asia Travel Association

TOURISM SOCIETY

Trinity Court, 34 West Street, Sutton, Surrey, SM1 1SH

Tel: 020 8661 4636
Fax: 020 8661 4637
E-mail: admin@tourismsociety.org

Website:
http://www.tourismsociety.org
Brief history of the society, membership grades, fees, benefits, current events calendar.

Enquiries:
Enquiries to: Executive Director
Other contacts: Conference Co-ordinator for forthcoming events.

Founded:
1977

Organisation type and purpose:
Professional body (membership is by subscription), present number of members: 1,300, service industry, suitable for ages: 15+.
Links tourism sectors, enhances members' professionalism and is the leading tourism network.

Subject coverage:
Education and training in tourism; tourism management, current issues, news.

Printed publications:
Tourism (journal, quarterly)

Publications list:
Available in print

Access to staff:
Contact by letter, by telephone, by fax and by e-mail. Access for members only.
Hours: Mon to Fri, 0900 to 1700

Sub-groups are:
Tourism Management Institute
Tourism Society Consultants Group
Tourism Society Scotland

TOWER HAMLETS LIBRARIES

Bancroft Library, 227 Bancroft Road, London, E1 4DQ

Tel: 020 8980 4366
Fax: 020 8983 4510

Website:
http://www.towerhamlets.gov.uk
Staff and services.

Enquiries:
Enquiries to: Head of Libraries

Organisation type and purpose:
Local government body, public library.

Subject coverage:
General, local history, art, music, languages, general and American literature.

Museum or gallery collection, archive, or library special collection:
Art Library (Whitechapel Library)
Chinese and Vietnamese literature (4,200 volumes Limehouse Library)
Collection of books in Asian languages (Indian, 12,500 volumes Whitechapel Library)
Inner London Special Collection: General and American literature (Limehouse Library)(closed)
Inner London Special Collections: French, German and Portuguese literature (Limehouse Library)
Joint Fiction Reserve: authors OP-PIC (closed), ST-SZ (current, 7000 volumes, Limehouse Library)
Local History Library, including the Bolt Collection on sailing and early steamships (Bancroft Library)
Music and foreign language records (Whitechapel Library)
Play-Reading sets (Whitechapel Library)
Sound recordings (all main libraries, totalling 55,000)

Library catalogue:
All or part available in-house

Printed publications:
Tower Hamlets Libraries Periodical (current)
Union List of Telephone Directories held by central London Reference Libraries (1999)
List of Local History publications – available from the Bancroft Library

continued overleaf

Publications list:
Available in print

Access to staff:
Contact by letter, by telephone, by fax, by e-mail and in person
Hours: Mon, Tue, Thu, 0900 to 2000; Wed, closed; Fri, 0900 to 1800; Sat, 0900 to 1700

Has:
11 branch libraries

Reference & Information Service:
Tower Hamlets Libraries
Bethnal Green Library, Cambridge Heath Road, London, E2 0HL; tel: 020 8980 3902 or 6274; fax: 020 8981 6129; e-mail: 100633.624@compuserve.com

TOWNSWOMEN

Formal name: Townswomen's Guilds
Acronym or abbreviation: TG

Tomlinson House, 1st Floor, 329 Tyburn Road, Erdington, Birmingham, B24 8HJ

Tel: 0121 326 0400
Fax: 0121 326 1976
E-mail: tghq@townswomen.org.uk

Website:
http://www.townswomen.org.uk
Site maintained by head office, giving information on all current Townswomen's Guilds campaigns, activities, structure, aims and objectives.

Enquiries:
Enquiries to: National Secretary
Direct e-mail: joanne@townswomen.org.uk
Other contacts: Public Affairs Officer, Press Officer

Founded:
1928

Formerly called:
National Union of Townswomen's Guilds

Organisation type and purpose:
Membership association (membership is by subscription), registered charity (charity number 306072R).
75,000 members in nearly 1,500 Guilds grouped in 114 Federations campaign on national and regional issues.
Organise national and regional events and conferences, national sport and leisure events and competitions.

Subject coverage:
Education in citizenship for women, current affairs, leadership, sports, environment, consumer affairs, women's health, Europe; current campaigns include the National Lottery, genetically modified food, transport, long-term care, energy conservation, carers, part-time workers.

Museum or gallery collection, archive, or library special collection:
Archives of the Townswomen's Guilds

Printed publications:
Annual Report
Guide to Personal Safety 1996
Townswomen's Guild: Factfile
Townswoman Magazine (4 times a year, for members)
Understanding Genetics 1996
Who Cares in the Long Term? (report on long-term care for the elderly, 1997)

Access to staff:
Contact by letter, by telephone, by fax, by e-mail and via website. Appointment necessary.
Hours: Mon to Fri, 0900 to 1700

Member of:
Associated Countrywomen of the World
Women's National Commission

TOYHORSE SOCIETY

Acronym or abbreviation: THI

Howick Farm, The Haven, Billingshurst, West Sussex, RH14 9BQ

Tel: 01403 822639
Fax: 01403 822014

Enquiries:
Enquiries to: President/Director
Direct e-mail: tikadorian@yahoo.co.uk

Founded:
1992

Formerly called:
British Miniature Horse Society (BMHS)

Organisation type and purpose:
International organisation, membership association (membership is by subscription), present number of members: 100, suitable for ages: 5+, training organisation.
To register the stock of miniature horses; foreign bloodline department formed in 1995. To advise on the welfare of miniature horses and arrange seminars for instruction on training, welfare, showing and exhibiting of miniature horses.

Subject coverage:
Welfare of miniature horses, training for driving etc.

Museum or gallery collection, archive, or library special collection:
AMHA Stud Books
BMHS newsletters, books
BMHS Register
MAFF newsletters
SPSBS Stud Books

Printed publications:
Newsletter (for members)
Information leaflets

Access to staff:
Contact by letter, by telephone and by fax.
Appointment necessary.
Hours: Mon to Fri, 0900 to 1700
Special comments: Charges to non-members for more than basic information.

TOYOTA ENTHUSIASTS' CLUB

Acronym or abbreviation: TEC

11 St Georges Crescent, Gravesend, Kent, DA12 4AR

Tel: 01474 746911

Enquiries:
Enquiries to: Membership Secretary
Other contacts: Newsletter Editor for information.

Founded:
1991

Organisation type and purpose:
Membership association (membership is by subscription).

Subject coverage:
Information on spares and services for all UK import Toyota Models, technical information and vehicle valuation.

Museum or gallery collection, archive, or library special collection:
Comprehensive range of motoring literature on all models of Toyota, both domestic and overseas, road tests, sales brochures and historical references

Printed publications:
Newsletter (quarterly, 40 pages A4)
Tec Topics (free to members, others £2 per copy plus p&p)
Order printed publications from: Newsletter Editor, Toyota Enthusiasts Club
71 Park Road, Chorley, Lancashire, PR7 1QZ, tel: 01257 415795

Access to staff:
Contact by letter and by telephone
Hours: 1900 to 2200, everyday

TR REGISTER

Formal name: TR Owners Club Ltd

1B Hawksworth, Southmead Industrial Park, Didcot, Oxfordshire, OX11 7HR

Tel: 01235 818866
Fax: 01235 818867
E-mail: office@tr-register.co.uk

Website:
http://www.tr-register.co.uk
Club information.

Enquiries:
Enquiries to: General Manager

Founded:
1970

Organisation type and purpose:
Membership association.
Car enthusiast's club.

Subject coverage:
Triumph TR series cars, car register, build records, technical data.

Museum or gallery collection, archive, or library special collection:
Books and archives
Material on TR sports cars

Printed publications:
TR Action (Club magazine, free to members or £2 each to non-members, 8 times a year)

Access to staff:
Contact by letter, by telephone, by fax and by e-mail. Access for members only.
Hours: Mon to Fri, 0900 to 1700

TRADA TECHNOLOGY LIMITED

Acronym or abbreviation: TTL

Stocking Lane, Hughenden Valley, High Wycombe, Buckinghamshire, HP14 4ND

Tel: 01494 569600
Fax: 01494 565487
E-mail: information@trada.co.uk

Website:
http://www.trada.co.uk

Enquiries:
Enquiries to: Manager, TRADA Information Centre
Other contacts: Special technical enquiry line (for enquiries of a technical nature)

Formerly called:
Timber Research and Development Association (TRADA)

Organisation type and purpose:
International organisation (membership is by subscription), training organisation, consultancy, research organisation.
Contracted by TRADA to provide research and information services.

Subject coverage:
Timber research and most aspects of timber utilisation (excluding paper and furniture), with particular reference to timber in construction, fire, finishes, timber engineering, design; testing of structures and components; timber buildings; training; wood-based sheet materials; pallets and packaging; preservation; timber drying. Product conformity services; quality assurance; health and safety; environmental services to a wide-range of industries as well as information services and training courses.

Museum or gallery collection, archive, or library special collection:
Compliance with health and safety and environmental legislation
Construction industry information
Construction products directive-related
European directives
Information on timber and wood-based products
Standards

Printed publications:
Newsletter (members only)

Various books
Order printed publications from: e-mail:
publications@trada.co.uk

Electronic and video publications:
Timberwise CD-ROM
Order electronic and video publications from: e-mail:
publications@trada.co.uk

Publications list:
Available online and in print

Access to staff:
Contact by letter, by telephone, by fax, by e-mail
and in person
Hours: Mon to Fri, 0900 to 1700

Also at:
TRADA Technology Limited
  Stirling; tel: 01786 462122; fax: 01786 474412

Sister company:
BMTRADA Certification Limited
  tel: 01494 569700; fax: 01494 565487
Chiltern International Fire
  tel: 01494 569800; fax: 01494 564895
FIRA International Ltd
  tel: 01438 777700; fax: 01438 777800

TRADES UNION CONGRESS

Acronym or abbreviation: TUC

Congress House, 23–28 Great Russell Street,
London, WC1B 3LS

Tel: 020 7636 4030
Fax: 020 7636 0632
E-mail: info@tuc.org.uk

Website:
http://www.tuc.org.uk

Enquiries:
Enquiries to: Information Manager
Direct fax: 020 7467 1273

Founded:
1868

Organisation type and purpose:
Trade union.

Subject coverage:
Trade unions, TUC policy, international and
overseas trade unions.

Library catalogue:
All or part available in-house

Printed publications:
Annual Report
TUC Budget Submission (annually)
TUC Directory (annually)
TUC General Council Report (annually)
A large number of publications on trade union
  issues, employment and the law, working
  conditions, equal rights for women and black
  workers and other minorities, health and safety,
  personal injury law, disability rights, pensions,
  Europe and international issues, learning and
  skills and TUC history
Order printed publications from: Publications
Department, Trades Union Congress
at the same address, tel: 020 7467 1294, fax: 020
7636 0632, e-mail: smills@tuc.org.uk

Electronic and video publications:
Videos

Publications list:
Available online and in print

Access to staff:
Contact by letter, by telephone, by fax, by e-mail
and via website
Hours: Mon to Fri, 0915 to 1700
Special comments: Not open to the public. TUC
Archive Library at London Metropolitan
University accessible by appointment.

Member of:
European Trade Union Confederation
International Confederation of Free Trade Unions

TUC Library Collection:
London Metropolitan University Learning Centre
  236–250 Holloway Road, London, N7 6PP; tel:
  020 7753 3184; fax: 020 7753 3191; e-mail: c
  .coates@londonmet.ac.uk

TRADES UNION CONGRESS
LIBRARY COLLECTIONS

Acronym or abbreviation: TUC Library Collections

London Metropolitan University, Learning Centre,
236–250 Holloway Road, London, N7 6PP

Tel: 020 7133 3726
Fax: 020 7133 2529
E-mail: tuclib@londonmet.ac.uk

Website:
http://www.londonmet.ac.uk/tuc
http://catalogue.londonmet.ac.uk/search~S7
TUC Library Collections OPAC.
http://www.unionhistory.info
TUC history.
http://www.tuc.org.uk
Trades Union Congress.

Enquiries:
Enquiries to: Librarian
Direct e-mail: c.coates@londonmet.ac.uk

Founded:
1922

Organisation type and purpose:
Trade union, university library.
Research collection.

Subject coverage:
Trade unions, economic, political and social
history, industrial relations, collective bargaining,
international affairs, industrial history, education,
women's history, colonial policy.

**Museum or gallery collection, archive, or library
special collection:**
General Strike Collection
Gertrude Tuckwell Collection (women's trade
  unionism and welfare, 1890–1921)
London Trades Council Records
Marjorie Nicholson Papers (colonial affairs)
Workers' Educational Association Library and
  Archive
Labour Research Department Archive

Non-library collection catalogue:
All or part available online

Library catalogue:
All or part available online and in-house

Printed publications:
Information brochure
Website postcards
Subject source notes

Microform publications:
Microfilm for purchase:
Committee Minutes and Papers 192–253
General Council Minutes 192–146
Gertrude Tuckwell Collection 1890–1920
Parliamentary Committee Minutes 1888–1921
The Mining Crisis and the General Strike 1925–26
TUC Annual Congress Reports 1869–2001
TUC Pamphlets and Leaflets 1887–1972
TUC Periodicals and Serials 1918–1977
TUC publications in Britain and Europe since 1945,
  collection
Women's Trade Union League Papers 1875–1921
Order microform publications from: Contact TUC
Library Collections for distributors' contact details

Access to staff:
Contact by letter, by telephone, by fax, by e-mail
and via website. Appointment necessary.
Hours: Mon to Fri, 0900 to 1700

Access to building, collection or gallery:
Prior appointment required

Access for disabled people:
Toilet facilities, ramped entry to main building,
level entry to collections

Member organisation of:
International Association of Labour History
Institutions (IALHI)

Parent body:
Trades Union Congress
  Congress House, Great Russell Street, London,
  WC1B 3LS; tel: 020 7636 4030

TRADING STANDARDS
INSTITUTE

Acronym or abbreviation: TSI

1 Sylvan Court, Sylvan Way, Southfields Business
Park, Basildon, Essex, SS15 6TH

Tel: 0845 608 9400
Fax: 0845 608 9425
E-mail: institute@tsi.org.uk

Website:
http://www.tradingstandards.gov.uk
General consumer information and information
about courses, events and products available to
trading standards professionals.

Enquiries:
Enquiries to: Chief Executive

Founded:
1881

Formerly called:
Institute of Weights and Measures Administration;
Institute of Trading Standards Administration
(ITSA) (year of change 2000)

Organisation type and purpose:
Professional body (membership is by
qualification).
Society for local government officers in trading
standards departments.

Subject coverage:
Consumer and trade protection legislation,
description of legal requirements, consumer
trends, enforcement interests.

Printed publications:
Directory of Trading Standards Officers in UK (6
  times a year)
The Trading Standards Today (journal, monthly)

Access to staff:
Contact by letter, by telephone, by fax and by e-
mail. Appointment necessary. Access for members
only.
Hours: Mon to Fri, 0900 to 1700

Access for disabled people:
Access to all public areas

TRAFFIC INTERNATIONAL

Acronym or abbreviation: TRAFFIC

219A Huntingdon Road, Cambridge, CB3 0DL

Tel: 01223 277427
Fax: 01223 277237
E-mail: traffic@traffic.org

Website:
http://www.traffic.org

Enquiries:
Enquiries to: Information & Publication Officer
Direct e-mail: susan.vivian@traffic.org

Founded:
1976

Organisation type and purpose:
International non-governmental organisation
(NGO), registered charity (charity number
1076722).

Subject coverage:
The wildlife trade-monitoring network, works to
ensure that trade in wild plants and animals is not
a threat to the conservation of nature.

Trade and statistical information:
Available on request.

continued overleaf

Non-library collection catalogue:
All or part available online

Library catalogue:
All or part available online, in-house and in print

Printed publications:
See Publications section on website: http://www.traffic.org
Order printed publications from: Information & Publication Officer, TRAFFIC International; tel: 01223 277427; e-mail: susan.vivian@traffic.org

Publications list:
Available online and in print

Access to staff:
Contact by letter, by telephone, by fax, by e-mail and via website. Appointment necessary.
Hours: Mon to Fri, 0900 to 1730

Access to building, collection or gallery:
Prior appointment required

Supported by:
IUCN – The World Conservation Union
WWF – World Wide Fund for Nature

TRAFFIC RESEARCH CENTRE

Formal name: Centre for Transport Engineering and Land Use Planning
Acronym or abbreviation: TRC CENTELUP

12 Flamsteed Road, Cambridge, CB1 3QU

Tel: 01223 248444 (answer after 7 rings)

Enquiries:
Enquiries to: Director

Founded:
1982

Formed from:
Arthur Henderson Consultants (year of change 1982)

Formerly called:
Centre for Transport Engineering and Land Use Planning

Organisation type and purpose:
Advisory body, learned society, registered charity (charity number 284449), university library, research organisation.
Charitable research trust.
To research and improve safety standards for pedestrians and all road users, improve the efficiency and convenience of all forms of transport for the movement of passengers and freight with particular reference to rail, air and sea terminals.

Subject coverage:
Traffic engineering, transport planning, highway layout, highway and traffic safety, education, law enforcement, urban junction design, transport systems appraisal, transport economics.

Museum or gallery collection, archive, or library special collection:
Denys Mumby Collection in Transport Economics
London Airport Rapid Transit; Guided Bus concept established 1964

Printed publications:
Design Sheets: loose-leaf system to follow (restricted circulation)

Access to staff:
Contact by letter and by telephone. Appointment necessary.
Hours: Mon to Fri, 0900 to 1700
Special comments: Reference only.

TRAFFORD MBC

Acronym or abbreviation: Trafford Libraries

Waterside House, Sale Waterside, Sale, M33 7ZF

Tel: 0161 912
Fax: 0161 912 2895
E-mail: libraries@trafford.gov.uk

Website:
http://www.trafford.gov.uk

Community information database.

Enquiries:
Enquiries to: Librarian

Founded:
1974

Formerly called:
Trafford MBC Education, Arts and Leisure Department, Recreation and Culture Division

Organisation type and purpose:
Local government body, public library.

Subject coverage:
Local government information, business information and European information at Altrincham library, local studies centre at Sale Library. General public library stock at Altrincham, Urmston, Sale and Stretford libraries. Community and leisure information database and bibliographical services.

Museum or gallery collection, archive, or library special collection:
Photo database (digitised photos)
Cruikshank Collection (some 50 examples of the illustrator's work, housed at Altrincham, access strictly by prior appointment)

Non-library collection catalogue:
All or part available in-house

Printed publications:
Various local history publications
Order printed publications from: Bibliographical Services
As main address

Electronic and video publications:
EnCompass (community information database, online)

Access to staff:
Contact by letter, by telephone, by fax, by e-mail and in person
Hours: Mon to Fri, 0830 to 1630

Access to building, collection or gallery:
Prior appointment required

Access for disabled people:
Parking provided, ramped entry

TRANSLATORS ASSOCIATION

Acronym or abbreviation: TA

84 Drayton Gardens, London, SW10 9SB

Tel: 020 7373 6642
Fax: 020 7373 5768
E-mail: info@societyofauthors.org

Website:
http://www.societyofauthors.org
Criteria for membership, aims and services.

Enquiries:
Enquiries to: Secretary

Founded:
1958

Organisation type and purpose:
Trade association, trade union (membership is by subscription, election or invitation), present number of members: 507.
Specialist section of the Society of Authors, its members are literary translators whose translations of full-length foreign works have already been published in the UK.

Subject coverage:
Interests and problems of translators whose work has been published or produced commercially in the UK, general and legal advice on marketing of work, rates of remuneration, contractual arrangements.

Printed publications:
Guide to Translator/Publisher Agreements (£10 inc. p&p)
In Other Words (journal, twice a year, available to non-members on subscription)
Quick Guide to Literary Translation (£2 inc. p&p)
Specimen Contract (members only)

Access to staff:
Contact by letter, by telephone, by fax and by e-mail. Access for members only.
Hours: Mon to Thu, 0930 to 1730; Fri, 0930 to 1300 and 1400 to 1700

Affiliated to:
Conseil Européen des Associations de Traducteurs Littéraires
Fédération Internationale de Traducteurs

Parent body:
The Society of Authors
at the same address

TRANSPORT & GENERAL WORKERS UNION

Acronym or abbreviation: TGWU (NCTS)

Northern Carpet Trades' Section, 22 Clare Road, Halifax, West Yorkshire, HX1 2HX

Tel: 01422 360492
Fax: 01422 321146

Enquiries:
Enquiries to: Regional Industrial Organiser
Direct e-mail: nhalton@tgwu.org.uk

Founded:
1892

Organisation type and purpose:
Trade union, present number of members: 2,000.

Subject coverage:
Organisation in the carpet industry, staff and shop floor; history; industrial relations.

Museum or gallery collection, archive, or library special collection:
Archives held in Calderdale Central Library (Archives Department)

Printed publications:
Catalogue of historical documents, available in Calderdale Central Library (archives department)
Annual Report
Newsletter (occasional)

Access to staff:
Contact by letter, by telephone, by fax and by e-mail. Appointment necessary. Access for members only.
Hours: Mon to Thur, 0845 to 1645; Fri 0445 to 1545

Access to building, collection or gallery:
No prior appointment required

Affiliated to:
General Federation of Trade Unions (GFTU)
National Affiliation of Carpet Trade Unions (NACTU)
Trades Union Congress

TRANSPORT ASSOCIATION

Peter Acton Associates, 185 Great Tattenhams, Epsom Downs, Surrey, KT18 5RA

Tel: 01737 362232
Fax: 01737 352323
E-mail: secretary@trans-assoc.co.uk

Website:
http://www.trans-assoc.co.uk

Enquiries:
Enquiries to: Secretary

Founded:
1953

Organisation type and purpose:
Trade association (membership is by election or invitation), present number of members: 50+ companies.

Subject coverage:
Road transport.

Access to staff:
Contact by letter, by e-mail and via website
Hours: Mon to Fri, 0900 to 1700

TRANSPORT FOR LONDON

Acronym or abbreviation: TfL

Windsor House, 42–50 Victoria Street, London, SW1H 0TL

Tel: 020 7941 4500
Fax: 020 7941 4572
E-mail: enquiries@tfl.gov.uk

Website:
http://www.transportforlondon.gov.uk
All information on London's Transport and its subsidiaries.

Enquiries:
Enquiries to: Head of Customer Services
Direct tel: 020 7918 4040 Underground; 020 7918 4300 Buses
Direct fax: 020 7918 4093 Underground; 020 7918 3999 Buses
Direct e-mail: Underground: customerservices@email.lul.co.uk;
Other contacts: Buses: customerservices@tfl-buses.co.uk

Founded:
3 July 2000

Formerly (as a holding company):
London Transport (LRT) (LT), date of change, 3 July 2000

Formerly called:
London Underground Limited (LUL), date of change, 3 July 2000

Organisation type and purpose:
Local government body.
TfL is London's integrated transport body. Its role is to implement the Mayor's transport strategy for London and manage the transport services for which the Mayor is responsible.

Subject coverage:
Public transport in London and its operation today.

Museum or gallery collection, archive, or library special collection:
Historic records held by London's Transport Museum

Printed publications:
Annual Report

Publications list:
Available online

Access to staff:
Contact by letter, by telephone, by fax, by e-mail and via website
Hours: Mon to Fri, 0900 to 1700
Special comments: 24 Hours London Travel Information 020 7222 1234.

Access to building, collection or gallery:
No access other than to staff

Historic records:
London's Transport Museum
Covent Garden, London, WC2E 7BB; tel: 020 7379 6344; fax: 020 7836 4118; e-mail: resourcec@ltmuseum.co.uk

Link:
London Underground Limited
55 Broadway, London, SW1H 0BD; tel: 020 7222 5600; fax: 020 7918 3134; e-mail: customerservices@email.lul.co.uk

Responsible to the:
Mayor of London
Romney House, 43 Marsham Street, London, SW1P 3PY; tel: 020 7983 4100; e-mail: enquire@london.gov.uk

Subsidiary bodies:
Docklands Light Railway
Castor Lane, London, E14 0DS; tel: 020 7363 9700
London Buses
172 Buckingham Palace Road, London, SW1W 9TN; tel: 020 7222 5600; fax: 020 7918 3999; e-mail: customerservices@TfL-buses.co.uk
London River Services
Tower Pier, Lower Thames Street, London, EC3N 4DT; tel: 020 7941 2400

Street Management
Windsor House, 42–50 Victoria Street, London, SW1H 0TL; tel: 020 7343 5000; website: www .streetmanagement.org.uk
Victoria Coach Station Limited
164 Buckingham Place, London, SW1W 9TP; tel: 020 7730 3466; website: www .transportforlondon.gov.uk/vcs

TRANSPORT PLANNING SOCIETY

Acronym or abbreviation: TPS

One Great George Street, Westminster, London, SW1P 3AA

Tel: 020 7665 2238
Fax: 020 7799 1325
E-mail: tps@ice.org.uk

Website:
http://www.tps.org.uk
News and events, membership, online document library, regions, careeers and qualifications, jobs.

Founded:
1997

Organisation type and purpose:
Membership association, with over 900 members, a society to facilitate, develop and promote best practice in transport planning and provide a focus for dialogue between all those engaged in it, whatever their background or other professional affiliation.

Subject coverage:
Transport planning.

Electronic and video publications:
Press releases
Online library of transport-related documents
Order electronic and video publications from:
Download from website

Access to staff:
Contact by letter, by telephone, by fax, by e-mail and via website

Links with:
Chartered Institute of Logistics and Transport (UK)
Chartered Institution of Highways and Transportation
Institution of Civil Engineers
Royal Town Planning Institute

TRANSPORT TRUST

202 Lambeth Road, London, SE1 7JW

Tel: 020 7928 6464
Fax: 020 7928 6565
E-mail: hq@thetransporttrust.org.uk

Website:
http://www.thetransporttrust.org.uk

Enquiries:
Enquiries to: Director General
Other contacts: Chairman

Founded:
1965

Organisation type and purpose:
National organisation, membership association (membership is by subscription), present number of members: 1500, voluntary organisation, registered charity (charity number 280943).
To promote and encourage the permanent preservation and where necessary the restoration of transport items of historical or technical interest for the benefit of the nation.

Subject coverage:
Preservation and restoration of all forms of transport: veteran and vintage cars, aircraft, locomotives, all old ships and canal craft plus inland waterway boats etc, cycles, mail and public coaches, buses, trams, trolley buses, military vehicles.

Museum or gallery collection, archive, or library special collection:
An extensive library and archives relating to Britain's transport heritage. Library and archives held at Ironbridge Museum, Shropshire (Tel: 01952 432141)

Library catalogue:
All or part available in-house

Printed publications:
Digest (4 times a year)
List of Transport Museums and Preserved Railways (annually)

Access to staff:
Contact by letter, by telephone, by fax, by e-mail and via website
Hours: Mon to Fri, 0900 to 1700
Special comments: 24-hour answerphone.

Access to building, collection or gallery:
Prior appointment required
Hours: Mon to Fri, 0900 to 1700

Access for disabled people:
Parking provided, ramped entry, access to all public areas, toilet facilities

TRAVEL TRUST ASSOCIATION

Acronym or abbreviation: TTA

Albion House, 3rd Floor, High Street, Woking, Surrey, GU21 6BD

Tel: 01483 545787
Fax: 01483 730746
E-mail: info@traveltrust.co.uk

Website:
http://www.traveltrust.co.uk
Information and advice for people to set up and run their own travel business, information and advice for consumers, online verification of membership, find an agent, member zone, business partner zone.

Enquiries:
Direct tel: 01483 545784 (for membership)
Direct e-mail: enquiries@traveltrust.co.uk
Other contacts: george@traveltrust.co.uk (for membership)

Founded:
c. 1995

Organisation type and purpose:
A travel trade membership association for travel agents, tour operators and travel organisers.
Exists in order to protect the customer, with 100% financial protection.

Subject coverage:
Should a member for any reason financially fail or cease trading, the Travel Trust Association will liaise with the suppliers and tour operators to ensure that the customer's holiday goes ahead unaffected. If for any reason this is not possible, it will administer a claim for a refund of money that the customer has paid to a member for the holiday.

Access to staff:
Contact by letter, by telephone, by fax, by e-mail and via website
Hours: Mon to Fri, 0900 to 1730

Member organisation of:
Travel Partnership Corporation (TTPC)

TREE COUNCIL

51 Catherine Place, London, SW1E 6DY

Tel: 020 7828 9928
Fax: 020 7828 9060
E-mail: info@treecouncil.org.uk

Website:
http://www.treecouncil.org.uk

Enquiries:
Enquiries to: Director General

Founded:
1974

continued overleaf

Organisation type and purpose:
Registered charity.
Company limited by guarantee; promotional, educational and information body; a list of members follows this entry.

Subject coverage:
Trees in the United Kingdom.

Printed publications:
Native Trees and Shrubs for Wildlife (£1)
How to do a Tree Survey (£1)
Select Bibliography on Trees and Woodlands 1984 (free)
Taking Care – Why pay twice for a tree – Tree Planting and Care (free)
Teacher's Handbook – Working with Trees (£6.50, Linden Publications)
Tree Council Forum Notes including: Trees and Property Development; Old trees; Street Trees; Tree Related Subsidence – What are the issues? (£2.50 each title)
Trees of Britain Poster (£2)
Tree News (2 times a year)
The Good Seed Guide (£3.50)
Trees Love Care (leaflet, free)

Electronic and video publications:
Trees of Britain (CD-ROM £19.95, from Main Publishing, City House, 16 City Road, Winchester SO23 8SD tel: 01962 870680)

Access to staff:
Contact by letter, by telephone, by fax, by e-mail and via website
Hours: Mon to Fri, 0900 to 1700

Consultative Members:
Common Ground
Convention of Scottish Local Authorities
Countryside Agency
Countryside Council for Wales
Department for the Environment, Food and Rural Affairs
Department of the Environment for Northern Ireland
Department of Transport, Local Government and the Regions
English Heritage
English Nature
Forestry Commission
Highways Agency
Joint Nature Conservation Committee
Learning Through Landscapes
Ministry of Defence
Scottish Natural Heritage

Full Members:
Ancient Tree Forum
Arboricultural Association
Arid Lands Initiative
British Trust for Conservation Volunteers (BTCV)
Civic Trust
Country Land and Business
Department of Transport, Local Government to the Regions
Forestry & Timber Association
Groundwork Foundation
Horticultural Trades Association
Institute of Chartered Forests
Institute of Horticulture
International Tree Foundation
Landscape Institute
National Association of Tree Officers
National Forest Company
National Memorial Arboretum
National Trust
National Urban Forestry Unit
Royal Agricultural Society of England
Royal Forestry Society of England, Wales & Northern Ireland
Royal Horticultural Society
Royal Institution of Chartered Surveyors
Royal Society for Nature Conservation
Royal Society for the Protection of Birds
Royal Town Planning Institute
Tree Advice Trust
Woodland Trust

TREVITHICK SOCIETY

PO Box 62, Camborne, TR14 7ZN

Tel: 01209 716811
E-mail: k.rickard@trevithick-society.org.uk

Enquiries:
Enquiries to: Honorary Secretary
Direct tel: 01209 711685
Direct e-mail: gbwilson@macace.net

Founded:
1934

Organisation type and purpose:
Membership association (membership is by subscription), present number of members: 450.

Subject coverage:
Industrial archaeology in Cornwall, mines and mining, Cornish engines and engine houses and other restorations, explosives, transport.

Museum or gallery collection, archive, or library special collection:
Collection of artefacts at Geevor Mining Museum, Pendeen, Penzance, and at King Edward Mine, Camborne School of Mines, Cornish mines and engines, Pool, Redruth
Drawings and plans relating to Cornish engines and mines lodged with the County Record Office, Truro

Printed publications:
Journal (annually)
Newsletter (quarterly)

Publications list:
Available in print

Access to staff:
Contact by letter and by e-mail
Hours: Mon to Fri, 0900 to 1700

TRIDENT CAR CLUB

23 Matlock Crescent, Cheam, Sutton, Surrey, SM3 9SS

Tel: 020 8644 9029
E-mail: trident.carclub@virgin.net

Website:
http://www.tridentcarclub.fsnet.co.uk

Enquiries:
Enquiries to: Chairman

Founded:
1980

Organisation type and purpose:
International organisation, membership association (membership is by subscription), present number of members: 36.
Membership open to owners and those interested in Trident cars.

Subject coverage:
Trident cars, technical knowledge, information and experience. Social gatherings.

Printed publications:
Magazine/newsletter (quarterly, members)

Access to staff:
Contact by e-mail and via website

TRIDENT & ROCKET THREE OWNERS CLUB

Acronym or abbreviation: TR3OC

6 Beechnut Drive, Darby Green, Camberley, Surrey, GU17 0DJ

Tel: 01252 861259
E-mail: graham.r@talktalk.net

Website:
http://www.tr3oc.org
Worldwide contact with owners, problems discussed. News, views and sales, also wanted section.

Enquiries:
Enquiries to: Secretary

Founded:
1979

Organisation type and purpose:
International organisation, membership association (membership is by subscription), present number of members: 1,100, voluntary organisation, suitable for ages: all.

Subject coverage:
3-cylinder pushrod-engined machines manufactured by Triumph and BSA between 1968 and 1976 and other machines fitted with these engines; technical information and other areas of interest.

Museum or gallery collection, archive, or library special collection:
Technical data of original machines and developments, including factory records
All published material concerning the 3-cylinder machines

Printed publications:
Triple Echo (6 times a year)
Triple Service Notes (available from Merchandise Secretary)

Access to staff:
Contact by letter, by telephone and by e-mail
Hours: Mon to Fri, 0830 to 2200
Special comments: No visits to Committee Members addresses.

Affiliated to:
BMF

TRINIDAD AND TOBAGO HIGH COMMISSION

Formal name: High Commission for the Republic of Trinidad and Tobago, London, United Kingdom

42 Belgrave Square, London, SW1X 8NT

Tel: 020 7245 9351
Fax: 020 7823 1065
E-mail: tthc@btconnect.com

Website:
http://www.tthighcommission.co.uk
Provides information on consular and immigration services offered to public; opportunities for trade and investment in Trinidad and Tobago; and tourism in Trinidad and Tobago.
http://www.discovertnt.com
http://www.gotrinidadandtobago.com
General information on Trinidad and Tobago.

Enquiries:
Enquiries to: Information Officer

Organisation type and purpose:
Diplomatic Mission.

Subject coverage:
Development of bilateral and multilateral relations with the United Kingdom and other accredited countries and international organisations; and provision of consular and immigration services to nationals and non-nationals/visitors to Trinidad and Tobago.

Printed publications:
London Mission Newsletter

Access to staff:
Contact by letter, by telephone, by fax and by e-mail. Appointment necessary.
Hours: Monday to Friday, 0900 to 1700

TRINITY COLLEGE LIBRARY

Cambridge, CB2 1TQ

Tel: 01223 338488
Fax: 01223 338532
E-mail: trin-lib@lists.cam.ac.uk

Website:
http://www.trin.cam.ac.uk

Enquiries:
Enquiries to: Librarian

Founded:
1546

Organisation type and purpose:
College library in the University of Cambridge.

Subject coverage:
Subjects covered by the special collections.

Museum or gallery collection, archive, or library special collection:
Papers include: R A Butler, J G Frazer, Otto Frisch, Lord Macaulay, R M Milnes, Lord Houghton, D H Robertson, Henry Sidgwick, Piero Sraffa, Alfred, Lord Tennyson, G P Thomson, William Whewell, Ludwig Wittgenstein
Some catalogues available online
Capell Collection of Shakespeareana*
Incunabula (c. 750 items)
Medieval manuscripts (c. 1,500 items)*
Newton Library
Oriental manuscripts*
Rothschild Collection of 18th-century literature*
* indicates that a printed catalogue exists

Access to staff:
Contact by letter, by fax, by e-mail and via website. Appointment necessary. Letter of introduction required.
Hours: Mon to Fri, 0900 to 1700

TRINITY COLLEGE LIBRARY (BRISTOL)

Stoke Hill, Bristol, BS9 1JP

Tel: 0117 968 2803
Fax: 0117 968 7470

Website:
http://www.trinity-bris.ac.uk

Enquiries:
Enquiries to: Librarian

Founded:
1971

Formed by the amalgamation of:
Clifton Theological, Dalton House Colleges; Tyndale Hall (year of change 1971)

Organisation type and purpose:
Theological College.

Subject coverage:
Theology; religion; ecclesiastical history; the Church of England; history; philosophy; ethics; comparative religion.

Library catalogue:
All or part available in-house

Access to staff:
Contact by letter, by telephone, by fax and by e-mail. Non-members charged.
Hours: Mon to Fri, 0900 to 1700
Special comments: Closed Sat and Sun.

Affiliated to:
University of Bristol, which validates the College's degrees

Links with:
Church of England

TRINITY COLLEGE OF MUSIC

Acronym or abbreviation: TCM

Jerwood Library of the Performing Arts, King Charles Court, Old Royal Naval College, Greenwich, London, SE10 9JF

Tel: 020 8305 3950
Fax: 020 8305 9444
E-mail: library@tcm.ac.uk

Website:
http://www.tcm.ac.uk
General information.
http://sirsi3.tcm.ac.uk/uhtbin/webcat
Online catalogue.

Enquiries:
Enquiries to: Head Librarian

Founded:
1872

Organisation type and purpose:
Suitable for ages: 18+.
Specialist college library for students of music and the performing arts.

Subject coverage:
Music.

Museum or gallery collection, archive, or library special collection:
Music Preserved (historic recordings of live performances)
Antonio de Almeida Collection
Barbirolli Collection
Sir Frederick Bridge Library
Centre for Young Musicians Library
Christopher Wood Collection
Frank Cordell Collection
Filmharmonic Archive
Lionel Tertis Collection
Mander & Mitchenson Theatre Collection
Shura Cherkassky Collection
William Lovelock Collection

Non-library collection catalogue:
All or part available in-house

Library catalogue:
All or part available online

Printed publications:
Library guides (available free of charge)

Access to staff:
Contact by letter, by telephone and by e-mail. Appointment necessary.
Hours: Term time: Mon to Thu, 0900 to 1900; Fri, 0900 to 1700
Special comments: Out of term, please telephone.

Access to building, collection or gallery:
Prior appointment required

Access for disabled people:
Parking provided, ramped entry, access to all public areas, toilet facilities

TRIRATNA BUDDHIST ORDER

Acronym or abbreviation: Triratna

London Buddhist Centre, 51 Roman Road, Bethnal Green, London, E2 0HU

Tel: 020 8981 1225; minicom no. 0845 458 4716
E-mail: info@lbc.org.uk

Website:
http://www.lbc.org.uk
Historical, doctrinal and practical introduction, plus listings.

Enquiries:
Enquiries to: Communications Office Director

Founded:
1967

Organisation type and purpose:
International organisation (membership is by election or invitation), present number of members: 3,000, registered charity.
Network of affiliated charities.
Religious, Buddhist, teaching Buddhism and meditation.

Subject coverage:
Buddhism, Buddhist meditation, health and well-being

Non-library collection catalogue:
All or part available online

Library catalogue:
All or part available online

Printed publications:
Urthona magazine: Buddhism and the arts (3 times a year, £3)
Order printed publications from: Numerous titles on Buddhism, Meditation and Triratna from Windhorse Publications Ltd, 169 Mill Road, Cambridge, CB1 3AN UK; tel: (1000 to 1700) 01223 911997; e-mail: info@windhorsepublications.com

Electronic and video publications:
Order electronic and video publications from:
Educational resources from The Clear Vision Trust, 16–20 Turner Street, Manchester, M4 1DZ; tel: 0161 839 9579; e-mail: clearvision@clear-vision.org

Publications list:
Available online and in print

Access to staff:
Contact by letter, by telephone, by e-mail, in person and via website
Hours: Mon to Fri, 1000 to 1700

Access for disabled people:
Access to all public areas

Links with:
30 to 40 other Triratna charities in the United Kingdom and many overseas

Online resource for many audio and transcribed texts important to the Triratna Buddhist Community:
Free Buddhist Audio
website: http://www.freebuddhistaudio.com

TRIUMPH 2000/2500/2.5 REGISTER

10 Gables Close, Chalfont St Peter, Gerrards Cross, Buckinghamshire, SL9 0PR

Tel: 01494 582673
E-mail: t2000register@compuserve.com

Website:
http://www.t2000register.org.uk

Enquiries:
Enquiries to: Secretary

Founded:
1981

Organisation type and purpose:
International organisation, membership association (membership is by subscription), present number of members: 900.

Subject coverage:
Triumph 2000, 2500 and 2.5 cars manufactured between 1963 and 1977.

Printed publications:
Six Appeal

Access to staff:
Contact by letter, by telephone, by fax and by e-mail
Hours: Evenings and weekends

TRIUMPH MAYFLOWER CLUB

19 Broadway North, Walsall, West Midlands, WS1 2QG

Tel: 01922 633042
E-mail: johnchoaker@btinternet.com

Website:
http://www.triumphmayflowerclub.com

Enquiries:
Enquiries to: Membership Secretary

Founded:
1975

Organisation type and purpose:
Membership association (membership is by subscription), present number of members: 152.

Subject coverage:
Workings, both mechanical and non-mechanical, of the Triumph Mayflower; history of Triumph Mayflower; general information and statistics regarding cars still in existence; technical information, sources of spares.

Museum or gallery collection, archive, or library special collection:
Archive of material on the Triumph Mayflower

Printed publications:
Flowerpower (magazine, quarterly)

Publications list:
Available in print

continued overleaf

Access to staff:
Contact by letter and by telephone
Hours: Mon to Fri, 1700 to 1930

TRIUMPH RAZOREDGE OWNERS CLUB

62 Seaward Avenue, Barton-on-Sea, Hampshire, BH25 7HP

Tel: 01425 618074
E-mail: davidwickens@clara.net

Enquiries:
Enquiries to: Secretary General

Founded:
1975

Organisation type and purpose:
Membership association (membership is by subscription), present number of members: 220.

Subject coverage:
Triumph Razoredge saloons manufactured between 1946 and 1954, spare parts, technical information.

Printed publications:
Magazine (6 times a year, free to members)

Access to staff:
Contact by letter, by telephone and by e-mail
Hours: Mon to Fri, 0900 to 1700

Member of:
Historic Vehicle Clubs Committee

TRIUMPH ROADSTER CLUB

Acronym or abbreviation: TRC

15 Lower Hill Road, Epsom, Surrey, KT19 8LS

Tel: 01372 812141
Fax: 01372 812141
E-mail: webmaster@triumphroadster.org.uk

Website:
http://www.triumphroadster.org.uk
Club services and e-mail contact addresses.

Enquiries:
Enquiries to: Secretary

Founded:
1960

Organisation type and purpose:
International organisation, membership association (membership is by subscription), present number of members: 500.
Club for the preservation of Triumph Roadster motor cars (1946–49 18TR and 20TR only).

Subject coverage:
Technical information related to the preservation and restoration of 1946–49 Triumph Roadster models 18TR and 20TR, including sources of replacement components, advice on purchase and registration mark authentication.

Printed publications:
Technical Manual and Restoration Guide
User Manual

Publications list:
Available online

Access to staff:
Contact by letter, by telephone, by fax, by e-mail and via website. Appointment necessary.
Hours: Mon to Fri, 0900 to 1700

Affiliated to:
Federation of British Historic Vehicle Clubs (FBHVC)
Elton House, Church Lane, Tydd St Giles, Wisbech, Cambridgeshire, PE13 5LA; tel: 01945 871295; fax: 01945 870528; e-mail: admin@fbhvc .co.uk; website: www.fbhvc.co.uk

TRIUMPH SPORTS SIX CLUB

Acronym or abbreviation: TSSC LTD

Freepost, Lubenham, Market Harborough, Leicestershire, LE16 9TF

Tel: 01858 434424
Fax: 01858 431936
E-mail: tssc@tssc.org.uk

Website:
http://www.tssc.org.uk

Enquiries:
Enquiries to: Executive Director
Direct e-mail: trudi@tssc.org.uk

Founded:
1977

Organisation type and purpose:
Membership association (membership is by subscription), present number of members: 9,000. Classic car club.

Non-library collection catalogue:
All or part available in-house

Library catalogue:
All or part available in-house

Printed publications:
Accessories Catalogue
The Courier (magazine, monthly, £2.25, free to members)

Publications list:
Available in print

Access to staff:
Contact by letter, by telephone, by fax, by e-mail, in person and via website
Hours: Mon to Fri, 0900 to 1700

Access to building, collection or gallery:
No access other than to staff
Hours: Mon to Fri, 0900 to 1700

Access for disabled people:
Ramped entry, access to all public areas, toilet facilities

TRL LTD

Formal name: Transport Research Laboratory

TRL Library and Information Centre, Crowthorne House, Nine Mile Ride, Wokingham, Berks, RG40 3GA

Tel: 01344 770203
Fax: 01344 770193
E-mail: info@trl.co.uk

Website:
http://www.trl.co.uk

Enquiries:
Enquiries to: Librarian
Other contacts: Document Supply (tel: 01344 770783)

Founded:
1933

Formerly called:
Road Research Laboratory (year of change 1972); Transport and Road Research Laboratory (TRRL) (year of change 1992); Transport Research Laboratory (TRL) (year of change 1992)

Organisation type and purpose:
Consultancy. Provides consultancy on transport, civil engineering, vehicle safety, vehicles and environment both in the UK and overseas.

Subject coverage:
Planning, design, construction and maintenance of roads and highway structures, particularly bridges and tunnels; safe and convenient movement of people and goods, including the layout of roads and traffic networks, control of traffic flow, study of road accidents and methods of reducing their frequency and severity; transport-planning and land-use strategies; existing and projected passenger and freight transport systems; environmental effects; new transport technology, intelligent transport, crash testing, traffic software, vehicle safety.

Non-library collection catalogue:
All or part available in-house

Library catalogue:
All or part available in-house

Printed publications:
Advisory leaflets (free)
Application Guides
Contractor Reports
Current Topics in Transport (bibliographies)
KWIC Indexes to Report Titles
Laboratory Reports
Research Reports
Supplementary Reports
TRL Publications Catalogue (revised annually, free)
TRL Reports (current series)
Order printed publications from: via website, or from IHS; tel: 01344 328039; e-mail: trl@ihs.com

Microform publications:
All TRL's publications to end of 1994

Electronic and video publications:
New Reports (CD-ROM)
Selections from TRL's database

Publications list:
Available online and in print

Access to staff:
Contact by letter, by telephone, by fax, by e-mail and via website. Appointment necessary. All charged.

Access to building, collection or gallery:
Prior appointment required
Hours: Mon to Fri, 0900 to 1700
Special comments: Discounts to academic and non-commercial organisations; one-day visit charge £30.

Access for disabled people:
Access to all public areas, toilet facilities

Links with:
Transport Research Foundation
Crowthorne House, Nine Mile Ride, Wokingham, Berkshire RG40 3GA; tel: 01344 773131; fax: 01344 770356; e-mail: enquiries@trl .co.uk; website: http://www.trl.co.uk

TROON @ AYRSHIRE FAMILY HISTORY SOCIETY

c/o MERC, Troon Public Library, South Beach, Troon, Ayrshire, KA10 6EF

E-mail: info@troonayrshirefhs.org.uk

Website:
http://www.troonayrshirefhs.org.uk
Details of the society, list of publications for sale, membership application form.

Enquiries:
Enquiries to: Secretary

Founded:
1989

Formerly called:
Troon and District Family History Society

Organisation type and purpose:
Membership association, voluntary organisation. Family History research.

Subject coverage:
Family history in the Troon and surrounding area of Ayrshire.

Printed publications:
Death and Burial Records in South Ayrshire
Dundonald Burial Register
Irvine 1820 Census Index (booklet)
Monumental Inscriptions for the Parishes of:
Ayr, Craigie, Coylton, Dailly, Dundonald, Girvan, Kirkoswald, Prestwick & Monkton, St Quivox & Newton on Ayr and Symington Parishes
Sources of Family History in Ayrshire
Galston Census, 1801, 1811, 1821 and 1831
Galston militia 1799 and 1801 with servicemen's letters of 1918
St. Quivox 1821 Census Index

OPR Death & Burial Indexes for Auchinleck, Ballantrae & Girvan, Dalrymple, Irvine, Mauchline, Stair, Symington and Tarbolton
'Airshire News' 1788–1798
'Airshire News' 1800–1810
Order printed publications from: Publications Officer at above address or online (payment by PayPal)

Microform publications:
Irvine Census 1820 – full transcription & Index (set of 2 fiches)
Supplemental Register of births from Kilmarnock 1855 (set of two fiches)

Electronic and video publications:
CDs: Ayrshire OPR Burials; 'Airshire News'; MIs for Crosbie and Dundonald Kirkyards each incorporating additional family notes; Loudoun OPR Burial Transcriptions 1811–1857 as written – 'The Session Clerk's Tale'; Ayrshire War Memorials.

Publications list:
Available online and in print

Access to staff:
Contact by letter and by e-mail

TROPICAL HEALTH AND EDUCATION TRUST

Acronym or abbreviation: THET

5th Floor, 1 Wimpole Street, London, W1G 0AE

Tel: 020 7290 3892
Fax: 020 7290 3890
E-mail: info@thet.org

Website:
http://www.thet.org.uk

Enquiries:
Enquiries to: Project Coordinator

Founded:
1988

Organisation type and purpose:
Registered charity (charity number 800567). To develop capacity for healthcare in Africa through collaboration with training institutions in Africa and the UK.

Subject coverage:
Training for healthcare in Africa.

Non-library collection catalogue:
All or part available online and in-house

Printed publications:
Annual Review
Newsletter

Access to staff:
Contact by letter, by fax and by e-mail. Appointment necessary.
Hours: Mon to Fri, 0900 to 1700

Access to building, collection or gallery:
Prior appointment required

TT SUPPORTERS CLUB

50 Lyndhurst Road, Birmingham, B24 8QS

Tel: 0121 686 3799
Fax: 0121 686 8700

Website:
http://www.ttsupportersclub.com

Enquiries:
Enquiries to: Information Officer

Subject coverage:
The Manx motor cycle TT races.

TUBEROUS SCLEROSIS ASSOCIATION

Acronym or abbreviation: TSA

PO Box 12979, Barnt Green, Birmingham, B45 5AN

Tel: 0121 445 6970

Fax: 0121 445 6970
E-mail: diane.sanson@tuberous-sclerosis.org

Website:
http://www.tuberous-sclerosis.org

Enquiries:
Enquiries to: Support Services Co Ordinator
Other contacts: TS Specialist Advisers; Appeals and Publicity Officer (for advice regarding support and publicity)

Founded:
1977

Organisation type and purpose:
Membership association (membership is by subscription), present number of members: 1,500, voluntary organisation, registered charity (charity number 1039549).

Subject coverage:
Tuberous sclerosis, epilepsy, autism, behaviour generally, renal problems, symptoms, genetic counselling.

Printed publications:
Annual Report
Clinical Guidelines
Factsheets on relevant topics (40 titles)
TSA Scan (newsletter)
What the teacher of a TS Child should know
Your Child with TS – What Happens Next

Electronic and video publications:
CD-ROMs

Publications list:
Available online and in print

Access to staff:
Contact by letter, by telephone, by fax, by e-mail and via website
Hours: Mon to Fri, 0900 to 1700

Links with:
Disability Alliance
  1st Floor, Universal House, 88–94 Wentworth Street, London, E1 7SA; tel: 020 7247 8776
Genetics Interest Group
  Unity 4D, Leroy House, 436 Essex Road, London, N1 3QP; tel: 020 7704 3141; fax: 020 7359 1447
Neurological Alliance
  PO Box 31287, London, NW2 6NL; tel: 020 7831 7522; fax: 020 7831 7522
Tuberous Sclerosis International
  Prins Bernhardlaan 36, 3722 AG Bilthoven, The Netherlands

TUG OF WAR ASSOCIATION

Acronym or abbreviation: ToWA

President

Tel: 01452 532788
E-mail: tonymartin@blueyonder.co.uk

Website:
http://www.tugofwar.co.uk

Enquiries:
Enquiries to: Area Represenatatives (see website for contact details)

Founded:
1958

Organisation type and purpose:
The governing body for tug of war in England. To develop tug of war.

Subject coverage:
Organises men's, women's and youth competitions.

Access to staff:
Contact by telephone and by e-mail

Member organisation of:
Tug of War International Federation (TWIF)

TUN ABDUL RAZAK RESEARCH CENTRE

Acronym or abbreviation: TARRC

Brickendonbury, Hertford, SG13 8NL

Tel: 01992 584966
Fax: 01992 554837
E-mail: general@tarrc.co.uk

Website:
http://www.tarrc.co.uk
Provides an overview of products and services available.

Enquiries:
Enquiries to: Head of Information

Founded:
1938

Formerly called:
Malaysian Rubber Producers' Research Association (MRPRA)

Organisation type and purpose:
Trade association, research organisation.

Subject coverage:
Rubber, especially natural rubber, rubber products.

Museum or gallery collection, archive, or library special collection:
History of Rubber
MORPHS main database 100,000 documents (mainly on microfilm)
Photographs

Trade and statistical information:
SMR Monthly Statistical Bulletin.
Quarterly Statistical Bulletin.

Library catalogue:
All or part available in-house

Printed publications:
Journal of Rubber Research (quarterly)
Malaysian Rubber Review (quarterly)
Malaysian Rubber Board Technology Developments (2 times a year)
Rubber Developments (2 times a year) – ceased in 1997
Books, market research and technical reports, monographs, information packs for schools
MRPRA Publications 1938–1991: author bibliographies
Natural rubber engineering data sheets
Order printed publications from: email: general@tarrc.co.uk

Electronic and video publications:
Natural Rubber Bounces On (video)
Naturally it's Rubber (video)
see also Rubber Consultants

Publications list:
Available in print

Access to staff:
Contact by letter, by telephone, by fax, by e-mail and via website. Appointment necessary.
Hours: Mon to Fri, 0900 to 1700
Special comments: Charges made to some users.

Parent body:
Malaysian Rubber Research and Development Board
  PO Box 10508, Kuala Lumpur, 50716, Malaysia

TUNBRIDGE WELLS FAMILY HISTORY SOCIETY

Yew Tree Byre, Yew Tree Lane, Rotherfield, East Sussex, TN6 3QP

Tel: 01892 852334
E-mail: veronicasiddall@hotmail.co.uk

Website:
http://www.tunwells-fhs.co.uk

Enquiries:
Enquiries to: Secretary

Founded:
1991

Organisation type and purpose:
Membership association (membership is by subscription), present number of members: 250. To promote genealogical studies and family history, particularly in the Tunbridge Wells area.

continued overleaf

Subject coverage:
Family history research in Tunbridge Wells area for members.

Printed publications:
Journal (three times a year, for members)
Other publications include:
Memorials and other Inscriptions St Mark's Church, Broadwater Down, Tunbridge Wells
Tonbridge Area, incl. Tunbridge Wells
Census Index 1851, A–L and M–Z
Speldhurst Church CD Burials 1558–1837 and other records
Frant Church CD of parish records,
Census returns for 1801, 1821, 1831, 1841 and 1851 for some East Sussex Parishes (fiche or hard copy)
Rolls of Honour and War Memorials in some East Sussex and Kent Villages
Local history books including:
Crowborough – Bygone Crowborough (M. Payne and L. Batchelor)
Place Names of Kent (J. Glover)
Groombridge – An Illustrated History of the Village
Royal Tunbridge Wells (R. Farthing)
Southborough and High Brooms (C. McCooey)
Order printed publications from: Tunbridge Wells Family History Society, 16 Hydehurst Close, Crowborough, East Sussex, TN6 1EN

Electronic and video publications:
1891 Census Index for the Tunbridge Wells Area RG12/0676–0683 (£5.50 plus p&p)

Publications list:
Available in print

Access to staff:
Contact by letter, by e-mail and via website
Hours: Mon to Fri, 0900 to 1700
Special comments: Evenings (private residence)

TUNNEL LINING MANUFACTURERS ASSOCIATION

Acronym or abbreviation: TLMA

60 Charles Street, Leicester, LE1 1FB

Tel: 0116 253 6161
Fax: 0116 251 4568
E-mail: info@britishprecast.org

Enquiries:
Enquiries to: Secretary

Organisation type and purpose:
Trade association.

Subject coverage:
Tunnel linings.

Parent body:
British Precast Concrete Federation

TURKISH CYPRIOT CULTURAL ASSOCIATION

14a Graham Road, Hackney, London, E8 1BZ

Tel: 020 7249 7410
Fax: 020 7241 5643

Enquiries:
Enquiries to: Chairman
Other contacts: Co-ordinator

Founded:
1977

Organisation type and purpose:
Membership association (membership is by subscription), present number of members: About 400, voluntary organisation, registered charity (charity number 285799).

Subject coverage:
Social and cultural problems of the Turkish community and the Turkish Cypriot community in particular.

Access to staff:
Contact by letter and by telephone

Hours: Tue to Fri, 1000 to 1700

Access to building, collection or gallery:
No access other than to staff
Hours: Mon to Fri, 1000 to 1700

TURKISH EMBASSY

Education Counsellor's Office, Tigris House, 256 Edgware Road, London, W2 1DS

Tel: 020 7724 1511
Fax: 020 7724 9989

Enquiries:
Enquiries to: Education Counsellor

Organisation type and purpose:
National government body.
Education for Turkish students.

Subject coverage:
Advice and guidance to Turkish students in UK; Turkish education system and scholarships offered by the Turkish government.

Access to staff:
Contact by letter, by telephone and by fax
Hours: Mon to Fri, 0930 to 1630, by telephone; Mon to Fri, 0930 to 1330, in person

Unit of the:
Turkish Ministry of National Education in Turkey

TURKISH TOURIST OFFICE

Acronym or abbreviation: TTO

4th Floor, 29–30 St James's Street, London, SW1A 1HB

Tel: 020 78397778
Fax: 020 7925 1388
E-mail: info@gototurkey.co.uk

Website:
http://www.gototurkey.co.uk
General, regional, practical.

Enquiries:
Enquiries to: Public Relations Officer
Direct e-mail: tourismturkey.mediauk@fd.com

Formerly called:
Turkish Information Office

Organisation type and purpose:
National government body.
Section of the Turkish Embassy.

Subject coverage:
Tourist information on Turkey.

Printed publications:
Brochures, posters, slides, films, and video cassettes
General holiday guide
List of tour operators

Access to staff:
Contact by letter, by telephone, by fax, by e-mail, in person and via website
Hours: Mon to Fri, 0930 to 1730

Affiliated to:
Ministry of Tourism in Turkey
tel: +312 212 8300; fax: +312 212 8391; e-mail: tanitma@turizm.gov.tr

TURNER LIBRARY

Whitefield Schools and Centre, Macdonald Road, Walthamstow, London, E17 4AZ

Tel: 020 8531 8703
Fax: 020 8527 0907
E-mail: lib@whitefield.org.uk

Website:
http://www.whitefield.org.uk

Enquiries:
Enquiries to: Librarian

Organisation type and purpose:
Membership association (membership is by subscription), service industry.

Professional library, with national and international membership, for all who have an interest in special educational needs; based at Whitefield Special School, the largest special school in the United Kingdom.
Current awareness service by post.

Subject coverage:
All aspects of special educational needs: curriculum; management; policy; legislation; syndromes and disorders; integration; support teaching.

Museum or gallery collection, archive, or library special collection:
Large periodical collection of national and international journals relating to special education, early years education and curriculum

Printed publications:
Current awareness bulletin (6 times a year, with back-up photocopying service on subscription)

Access to staff:
Contact by letter, by telephone, by fax, by e-mail and in person. Non-members charged.
Hours: Mon, Thu, 0900 to 1830; Tue, Wed, 0900 to 1700; Fri, 0900 to 1630
Aug, half-terms, Easter: Tue, Wed, Thu, 0900 to 1600
Please check opening hours before visiting during holiday periods
Special comments: Closed all other days and for two weeks at Christmas and New Year.

Access for disabled people:
Wheelchair access, disabled lift, lift to seminar rooms

TURNER REGISTER

21 Ellsworth Road, High Wycombe, Buckinghamshire, HP11 2TU

Tel: 01494 445636

Enquiries:
Enquiries to: Registrar

Founded:
1960

Organisation type and purpose:
Membership association.

Subject coverage:
Information relating to design, manufacture, restoration and maintenance of Turner sports and racing cars manufactured by Mr J H Turner in Wolverhampton 1949–1966.

Museum or gallery collection, archive, or library special collection:
Copies of original works publications
Manufacturing records of vehicles built
Road Tests from motoring journals

Printed publications:
Club Newsletter (11 times a year, members only)

Access to staff:
Contact by letter
Hours: Mon to Fri, 0900 to 1700

Parent body:
Fairthorpe Sports Car Club (Turner Register)
9 Lynhurst Crescent, Hillingdon, Middlesex, UB10 9EF

TURNER SOCIETY

BCM Box Turner, London, WC1N 3XX

Website:
http://www.turnersociety.org.uk

Enquiries:
Enquiries to: Chairman

Founded:
1975

Organisation type and purpose:
Learned society (membership is by subscription), present number of members: c. 400, registered charity (charity number 269832).

To further interest in the life and work of J M W Turner RA.

Subject coverage:
The life, work and influence of J M W Turner, RA.

Printed publications:
Turner Society News (twice a year)

Access to staff:
Contact by letter

TWI LTD

Granta Park, Great Abington, Cambridgeshire, CB21 6AL

Tel: 01223 899000
Fax: 01223 894342
E-mail: library@twi.co.uk

Website:
http://www.twi.co.uk

Enquiries:
Enquiries to: Manager, Information Services
Direct e-mail: linda.dumper@twi.co.uk;
weldasearch@twi.co.uk (Technical Enquiries)

Founded:
1968

Formerly called:
British Welding Research Association, Institute of Welding (year of change 1968); The Welding Institute (year of change 1991)

Organisation type and purpose:
International organisation, professional body, training organisation, consultancy, research organisation.

Subject coverage:
Technology and practice of welding; brazing; soldering; thermal cutting; weld surfacing; metal spraying; inspection and non-destructive testing; QA systems; welding design; welding and joining metallurgy and materials science; performance of welded assemblies (failure, fatigue, brittle fracture, corrosion); fabrication and construction; quality control; joining of plastics and ceramics; adhesives.

Museum or gallery collection, archive, or library special collection:
Materials identification
Trade literature on welding equipment and consumables

Library catalogue:
All or part available online and in-house

Printed publications:
Connect
Welding Abstracts (abstracts journal, monthly)

Electronic and video publications:
Software programmes (c.15)
WELDASEARCH (online file on QUESTEL/ORBIT, Dialog, CINECA (Italy), FIZ-TECHNIK and via CSA web-based search services and through the TWI website at http://www.twi.co.uk)

Publications list:
Available in print

Access to staff:
Contact by letter, by telephone, by fax, by e-mail and via website. Appointment necessary. Access for members only.
Hours: Mon to Thu, 0830 to 1630; Fri, 0830 to 1615

Constituent bodies:
Certification Scheme for Welding and Inspection Personnel (CSWIP)
Institute of Rail Welding (IORW)
School of Applied Non-Destructive Testing (SANDT)
School of Welding Technology (SWT)
Welding and Joining Society (WJS)

TYNDALE HOUSE BIBLICAL STUDIES RESEARCH CENTRE

Tyndale House, 36 Selwyn Gardens, Cambridge, CB3 9BA

Tel: 01223 566601
Fax: 01223 566608
E-mail: librarian@tyndale.cam.ac.uk

Website:
http://www.tyndale.cam.ac.uk
Details of the library, facilities and staff; access to other libraries and centres for biblical research; access to online databases and journals useful to biblical research.

Enquiries:
Enquiries to: Librarian
Direct tel: 01223 566604

Founded:
c.1940

Organisation type and purpose:
Registered charity, university department or institute, research organisation, publishing house.

Subject coverage:
Biblical studies and research; theology.

Information services:
Photocopy and scanning service accessed from web site.

Museum or gallery collection, archive, or library special collection:
Maps of Palestine
The library is said to contain one of the best collections of books and electronic resources on biblical studies in the world

Library catalogue:
All or part available online

Printed publications:
Tyndale Bulletin (twice a year)

Access to staff:
Contact via website. Appointment necessary. Letter of introduction required.
Hours: Mon to Fri, 0900 to 1730

Parent body:
Universities and Colleges Christian Fellowship

TYNE & WEAR ARCHIVES

Formal name: Tyne & Wear Archives & Museums
Acronym or abbreviation: TWAM

Discovery Museum, Blandford Square, Newcastle upon Tyne, NE1 4JA

Tel: 0191 277 2248
Fax: 0191 230 2614
E-mail: archives@twmuseums.org.uk

Website:
http://www.twmuseums.org.uk/archives
General information, online catalogue.

Enquiries:
Enquiries to: Chief Archivist

Founded:
1974

Created by the merger of:
Tyne & Wear Archives Service and Tyne & Wear Museums (year of change 2009)

Formerly called:
Tyne & Wear Archives Service (year of change 2009)

Organisation type and purpose:
Local government body.
Archives service.

Subject coverage:
Tyne and Wear, shipbuilding, family history, other aspects of the North-East.

Museum or gallery collection, archive, or library special collection:
Records of many organisations, industries and individuals relating to Tyne and Wear

Non-library collection catalogue:
All or part available online and in-house

Library catalogue:
All or part available online and in-house

Printed publications:
Newcastle upon Tyne Charters (out of print)
Combination and Confederacy Chartist Pack (£2)
Newcastle Quayside – Heart of a City Pack (£5)
Pressgangs and Privateers (£6.95)
South Shields in the Nineteenth Century Pack (£2)
Sunderland Builds the Ships (£1.95)
Tyne and Wear at Work (£2.95)

Access to staff:
Contact by letter, by telephone, by fax, by e-mail, in person and via website
Hours: Mon, Wed, Thu, Fri, 0900 to 1700; Tue, 0900 to 2030; first Sat every month, 0900 to 1700
Special comments: Appointments are essential for Tue evening.

Access for disabled people:
Parking provided, ramped entry, level entry, access to all areas, toilet facilities

TYNE METROPOLITAN COLLEGE

The Library, Embleton Avenue, Wallsend, Tyne and Wear, NE28 9NJ

Tel: 0191 229 5301
Fax: 0191 229 5243
E-mail: enquiries@tynemet.ac.uk

Website:
http://www.tynemet.ac.uk

Enquiries:
Enquiries to: Head of Library Resources

Organisation type and purpose:
Suitable for ages: 14+
College of further education.

Subject coverage:
All areas covered particularly international baccalaureate, A-levels, art and design, media, engineering, hairdressing

Trade and statistical information:
FEFC documents.

Non-library collection catalogue:
All or part available online

Library catalogue:
All or part available online and in-house

Printed publications:
Library user guide (annually)

Access to staff:
Contact by letter, by telephone, by fax and by e-mail. Appointment necessary. Access for members only.
Hours: Mon to Thu, 0900 to 2000; Fri, 0900 to 1600; Sat, 1000 to 1300
Vacations: 0900 to 1600

TYNEDALE COUNCIL

Hexham House, Hexham, Northumberland, NE46 3NH

Tel: 01434 652200\ Minicom no. 01434 652323
Fax: 01434 652420
E-mail: enquiries@tynedale.gov.uk

Website:
http://www.tynedale.gov.uk
Tourist information, economic development information.

Enquiries:
Enquiries to: Chief Executive
Other contacts: Public Relations and Marketing Officer for sources of information about the council.

Founded:
1974

Organisation type and purpose:
Local government body.
District Council.

Subject coverage:
Public information about the work of the Tynedale Council.

continued overleaf

Printed publications:
Annual Report
A-Z Council Services
Local Performance Plan
Tynedale Community Plan

Access to staff:
Contact by letter, by telephone, by fax, by e-mail,
in person and via website
Hours: Mon to Thu, 0830 to 1700; Fri, 0830 to 1630

TYNWALD LIBRARY

Legislative Buildings, Finch Road, Douglas, Isle of
Man, IM1 3PW

Tel: 01624 685520
Fax: 01624 685522
E-mail: library@tynwald.org.im

Website:
http://www.tynwald.org.im
Information and documentation relating to the
parliament of the Isle of Man and parliamentary
business considered by Tynwald and its branches,
the House of Keys and the Legislative Council.

Enquiries:
Enquiries to: Librarian

Founded:
1975

Core collection dates from 1938:

Formerly called:
Central Reference Library (year of change 1987)

Organisation type and purpose:
National government body.
Parliamentary library.
To provide a comprehensive source of information
and documentation relevant to the work of the
Legislature of the Isle of Man.

Subject coverage:
General reference collection, especially social
sciences, Manx affairs, law, parliament, executive
government, official documents.

Information services:
Public access to library collections. Research
services for Members, Clerks and Officers of
Tynwald only. One-stop shop for official and
parliamentary papers, Manx Statutes and
subordinate legislation.

Special visitor services:
Regular tours of the legislative chambers twice
weekly. Limited gift shop.

Education services:
School tours, Junior Tynwald for Sixth form
students.

Services for disabled people:
Library is disabled-friendly, other disabled
facilities available.

**Museum or gallery collection, archive, or library
special collection:**
Documents produced by the Isle of Man
Government (Civil Service)
Laws of the Isle of Man
Parliamentary and any other papers considered by
the Legislature of the Isle of Man
Report of the Official Proceedings: Isle of Man
(Hansard)

Trade and statistical information:
Isle of Man Digest of Economic and Social Statistics
(annual)
Isle of Man Government Policy Review (annual).
Census reports
(also on www.gov.im)

Non-library collection catalogue:
All or part available in-house

Library catalogue:
All or part available online

Printed publications:
Publications include:
Reports and Bills laid before the Legislature
Acts of Tynwald
Statutory Documents of the Isle of Man

Tynwald Calendar
Tynwald Ceremony (booklet, annual)
Isle of Man Orders in Council (2nd ed, 1996)
Chronological Table of Acts of Parliament
extending to the Isle of Man (2003)
Tynwald Companion 2010
Standing Orders of Tynwald, House of Keys,
Legislative Council
Notes on Petitions for Redress (Tynwald Day)
Official Report of Proceedings (Hansard)
Order Papers, Question Papers, Votes and
Proceedings relating to parliamentary sittings
Order printed publications from: Tynwald Library

Access to staff:
Contact by letter, by telephone, by fax, by e-mail,
in person and via website
Hours: Mon to Fri, 0900 to 1730
Special comments: Research staff unable to
undertake research for members of the public.

Access to building, collection or gallery:
Ground floor public access
Hours: Mon to Fri, 0900 to 1700; evening tours by
arrangement

Access for disabled people:
Parking provided, toilet facilities, lifts
Hours: Mon to Fri, 0900 to 1700
Special comments: Public tours available, prior
notification of attendance of disabled persons
appreciated as alternate route is necessary.

Parent body:
Clerk of Tynwald's Department
at the same address; tel: 01624 685000; fax: 01624
685004; e-mail: enquiries@tynwald.org.in

UACE

Formal name: Universities Association for
Continuing Education

University of Cambridge, Board of Continuing
Education, Madingley Hall, Madingley,
Cambridge, CB3 8AQ

Tel: 01954 280279
Fax: 01954 280200
E-mail: mer1000@cam.ac.uk

Website:
http://www.uace.org.uk
Publications list; membership list.

Enquiries:
Enquiries to: Secretary
Direct e-mail: sm120@cam.ac.uk

Formerly called:
Polytechnic Association for Continuing Education
(PACE), Universities Council for Adult and
Continuing Education

Organisation type and purpose:
Professional body.
Consultative body for universities and university
colleges; information centre for continuing and
adult education; liaison and collaborative body
with, for example, the Department for Education
and Skills.
Co-ordinating policy development for the whole
field of continuing education at university level in
the UK; acting as a source of information and,
where appropriate, pressure on Universities UK,
Department for Education and Skills.

Subject coverage:
Continuing education, continuing vocational
education, part-time student and non-standard
student matters in HE, FE/HE links, access and
other flexible entry routes, flexible study patterns
in higher education, research in continuing
education, European and international links in CE
development and research, CE provision to
counter educational disadvantage (including
targeted work with specific groups such as
minority ethnic communities, disabled people,
unwaged people, socio-economically
disadvantaged groups, universities in their
relations with the community, workers' education).

Trade and statistical information:
Statistical information available on all aspects of
CE provision in the higher education sector in
the UK.

Printed publications:
Annual Report
Membership List
Newsletters
Range of scholarly and good practice
documentation

Publications list:
Available online and in print

Access to staff:
Contact by e-mail
Hours: Mon to Fri, 0900 to 1700

Access to building, collection or gallery:
No access other than to staff

UCL EASTMAN DENTAL INSTITUTE

Formal name: Eastman Dental Institute for Oral
Health Care Sciences

Eastman Dental Hospital, 256 Gray's Inn Road,
London, WC1X 8LD

Tel: 020 7915 1092
Fax: 020 7915 1274
E-mail: academic@eastman.ucl.ac.uk

Website:
http://www.eastman.ucl.ac.uk

Enquiries:
Enquiries to: Admissions Officer

Formerly called:
Institute of Dental Surgery

Organisation type and purpose:
University department or institute, research
organisation.
Postgraduate teaching and research.

Subject coverage:
Dentistry, dental research, dental education.

Publications list:
Available online

Access to staff:
Contact by telephone, by e-mail and via website
Hours: Mon to Fri, 0900 to 1700

Postgraduate institute affiliated to:
University College London

UCL INSTITUTE OF CHILD HEALTH LIBRARY

Acronym or abbreviation: ICH

30 Guilford Street, London, WC1N 1EH

Tel: 020 7242 9789 extn 2424
Fax: 020 7831 0488
E-mail: library@ich.ucl.ac.uk

Website:
http://www.ich.ucl.ac.uk/library

Enquiries:
Enquiries to: Librarian or Deputy Librarian
Other contacts: Assistant Librarian (for SOURCE
collection)

Founded:
1945

Organisation type and purpose:
University department or institute.

Subject coverage:
Paediatrics, diseases of children, SOURCE
collection covers disability, mother and child
health, HIV/AIDS, poverty and health in less
developed countries.

Museum or gallery collection, archive, or library special collection:
SOURCE collection: an international information support centre designed to strengthen the management, use and impact of information in health and disability; jointly owned by ICH, Healthlink Worldwide and Handicap International.

Non-library collection catalogue:
All or part available online

Library catalogue:
All or part available online

Access to staff:
Contact by letter, by telephone, by fax, by e-mail, in person and via website. Appointment necessary.
Hours: Mon to Fri, 0900 to 1800

Access for disabled people:
Ramped entry, access to all public areas, chairlifts, toilet facilities
Special comments: Chairlifts

Constituent part of:
University College London
Gower Street, London; tel: 020 7679 7700; fax: 020 7679 7373; e-mail: library@ucl.ac.uk; website: http://www.ucl.ac.uk

Links with:
Hospital for Sick Children
Great Ormond Street, London; tel: 020 7405 9200; fax: 020 7829 8643; e-mail: info@gosh.nhs.uk

UCL LANGUAGE & SPEECH SCIENCE LIBRARY

Acronym or abbreviation: NICeST: National Information Centre for Speech-Language Therapy

UCL Language & Speech Science Library, Chandler House, 2 Wakefield Street, London, WC1N 1PF

Tel: 020 7679 4207
Fax: 020 7679 4238
E-mail: library@langsci.ucl.ac.uk

Website:
http://www.langsci.ucl.ac.uk/library/index.php
Information about the library, catalogue, links to online resources (UCL members only), links to other speech and language therapy sites, blog.
http://www.ucl.ac.uk/Library/hcslib.shtml
Library information.
http://www.ucl.ac.uk/Library/blog/hcs/
Library blog for news, information and Resource of the Week.

Enquiries:
Enquiries to: Librarian

Founded:
1987

Formerly called:
National Hospital's College of Speech Science (NHCSS) (year of change 1995); UCL Human Communication Science Library (HCS) (year of change 2008)

Organisation type and purpose:
University department or institute.

Subject coverage:
Speech, language, and communication disorders; speech and language therapy; linguistics; phonetics.

Museum or gallery collection, archive, or library special collection:
Tests and assessments used in clinics and placements; historical collection of books and pamphlets (held in offsite storage).

Non-library collection catalogue:
All or part available online

Library catalogue:
All or part available online

Access to staff:
Contact by telephone, by e-mail and via website. Appointment necessary. Access for members only. Non-members charged.

Hours: Mon to Thu, 0915 to 1900; Fri, 1000 to 1900; Sat in UCL term and Easter vacation, 1100 to 1800.
Special comments: Vacations, please telephone.

Access to building, collection or gallery:
Hours: As library opening hours

Access for disabled people:
Ramp, and automatic doors at building entrance; lift, accessible toilets on each floor
Hours: As library opening hours
Special comments: Lift cannot be used for emergency evacuation; library is on 2nd floor.

Branch of:
UCL Library Services
Gower St, London WC1

UCLH CHARITABLE FOUNDATION

3rd Floor East, 250 Euston Road, London, NW1 2PG

Tel: 020 7380 9558

Website:
http://www.uclh.nhs.uk/Charities+at+UCLH/UCL+Hospitals+Charitable+Foundation
Current projects, events, news.

Organisation type and purpose:
A registered charity (number 1077638).
The main fundraising charity for key research, building and equipment projects across all University College London Hospitals.

Subject coverage:
With support from the general public, has helped to fund an ultrasound scanner for the Fetal Medicine Unit, research into the treatment and detection of early lung cancer, and the building of a new Cellular Therapy Unit for cancer patients receiving high dose chemo and radiotherapy.

Access to staff:
Contact by letter and by telephone
Hours: Mon to Fri, 0800 to 1600

Links with:
University College London Hospitals NHS Foundation Trust (UCLH)
250 Euston Road, London, NW1 2PG; tel: 0845 1555 000

UCLH CHARITY

Trustees Department, 250 Euston Road, 5th Floor East, London, NW1 2PG

Tel: 020 7380 9605
Fax: 020 7380 9544
E-mail: trustees@uclh.nhs.uk

Website:
http://www.uclhcharity.org.uk
Support for patients, staff and research.

Organisation type and purpose:
A registered charity (number 229771).
The main charity associated with the 7 general and specialist hospitals of the University College London Hospitals NHS Foundation Trust.

Subject coverage:
Provides support for patients (equipment, services), staff (health and welfare) and research.

Electronic and video publications:
Newsletter
Order electronic and video publications from:
Download from website

Publications list:
Available online

Access to staff:
Contact by letter, by telephone, by fax and by e-mail

Links with:
University College London Hospitals NHS Foundation Trust (UCLH)
250 Euston Road, London, NW1 2PG; tel: 0845 1555 000

UFO MONITORS EAST KENT

Acronym or abbreviation: UFOMEK

23 Brabner Close, Folkestone, Kent, CT19 6LW

Tel: 07968 583435 / 07091 020078
E-mail: astratech@supanet.com

Website:
http://www.homestead.com/kentufowatch/homepage.html
http://www.homestead.com/kentufowatch/ufomek.html

Enquiries:
Enquiries to: Director of Research and Investigations

Founded:
Dec 1995

Formerly called:
National UFO Research Centre

Organisation type and purpose:
National organisation, voluntary organisation, research organisation.
Investigation and research into aerial phenomena.

Subject coverage:
Information on investigations and research into aerial phenomena in the county of Kent, first and foremost, and nationally in the regions of the UK.

Access to staff:
Contact by letter, by telephone, by e-mail and via website
Hours: Sun to Sat, 0900 to 2100

Access to building, collection or gallery:
No access other than to staff

Connections with:
UFO-Trek Information Service
UFO-Trek, c/o 23 Brabner Close, Folkestone, Kent, CT19 6LW; tel: 07091 020078

UK CLEANING PRODUCTS INDUSTRY ASSOCIATION

Acronym or abbreviation: UKCPI

1st Floor, Century House, High Street, Tattenhall, Cheshire, CH3 9RJ

Tel: 01829 770055
Fax: 01829 770101
E-mail: ukcpi@ukcpi.org

Website:
http://www.ukcpi.org

Enquiries:
Enquiries to: Secretary

Founded:
1939

Organisation type and purpose:
Trade association.

Subject coverage:
Effect of detergents on the environment, human health and safety; regulations affecting the cleaning products industry; history of the UK soap industry.

Trade and statistical information:
Basic consumption statistics.

Printed publications:
A–Z of Detergents
Health and Hygiene
Cleaning with Care (Guide for Local Authorities)
Hooray for Handwashing

Access to staff:
Contact by letter, by telephone, by fax and by e-mail
Hours: Mon to Fri, 0900 to 1215

Links with:
Chemical Industries Association

Member organisation of:
Association Internationale de la Savonnerie et de la Détergence (AISE)

UK COLLEGE FOR COMPLEMENTARY HEALTHCARE STUDIES

Acronym or abbreviation: UK College

St Charles Hospital, Exmoor Street, London, W10 6DZ

Tel: 020 8964 1206
Fax: 020 8964 1207
E-mail: info@ukcollege.com

Website:
http://www.ukcollege.com

Enquiries:
Enquiries to: Administrator
Other contacts: Principal or Director for areas of expertise.

Founded:
1985

Formerly called:
UK Training College for Hypnotherapy and Counselling

Organisation type and purpose:
Suitable for ages: Mature students 19+, training organisation.
For complementary healthcare.

Subject coverage:
Accredited courses for complementary therapies; BTEC, City and Guilds and VTCT, massage, hypnotherapy, reflexology, counselling, first aid, and aromatherapy, NLP one- and two-day introductory courses.

Museum or gallery collection, archive, or library special collection:
Register of Practitioners in United Kingdom (telephone only for nearest one in location)

Library catalogue:
All or part available in-house

Printed publications:
Prospectus

Access to staff:
Contact by letter, by telephone, by fax, by e-mail and via website. Appointment necessary.
Hours: Mon to Fri, 0900 to 1700

Access to building, collection or gallery:
Prior appointment required

Access for disabled people:
Parking provided, access to all public areas, toilet facilities

UK DATA ARCHIVE

Acronym or abbreviation: UKDA

University of Essex, Wivenhoe Park, Colchester, Essex, CO4 3SQ

Tel: 01206 872001
Fax: 01206 872003
E-mail: info@data-archive.ac.uk

Website:
http://www.data-archive.ac.uk

Enquiries:
Enquiries to: Helpdesk

Founded:
1967

Formerly called:
ESRC Data Bank, ESRC Survey Archive; ESRC Data Archive (year of change 1996); The Data Archive (year of change 2000)

Organisation type and purpose:
University department or institute.
To preserve, maintain and disseminate research data.

Subject coverage:
The UK Data Archive (UKDA) acquires, preserves, disseminates and promotes data, including digital data in the social sciences and humanities.

The UKDA provides resource discovery and support for secondary use of quantitative and qualitative data in research, teaching and learning as a lead partner of the Economic and Social Data Service (ESDS). The UKDA provides preservation services for other data organisations, facilitates international data exchange, carries out research in digital preservation and provides advice in data management.

Museum or gallery collection, archive, or library special collection:
The UKDA houses over 6,000 datasets of interest to researchers, students and teachers in the HE/FE sectors and from many disciplines; datasets cover the full range of the social sciences and most aspects of social and economic study

Non-library collection catalogue:
All or part available online and in-house

Printed publications:
UK Data Archive News (newsletter, quarterly, free, online or printed copy)

Publications list:
Available online

Access to staff:
Contact by letter, by telephone, by fax, by e-mail, in person and via website. Appointment necessary.
Hours: Mon to Fri, 0900 to 1700

Funded by:
Economic and Social Research Council (ESRC)
Joint Information Systems Committee (JISC)
University of Essex

UK FASHION EXPORTS

Acronym or abbreviation: UKFE

5 Portland Place, London, W1B 1PW

Tel: 020 7636 5577
Fax: 020 7636 7848
E-mail: info@ukfashionexports.com

Website:
http://www.ukfashionexports.com
Full description of aims and activities of UK Fashion Exports and of the services available to members and non-members.

Enquiries:
Enquiries to: Executive Director

Founded:
1940

Formed by the amalgamation of:
British Knitting Export Council (BKEC), Clothing Export Council of Great Britain (CECGB) (year of change 1984)

Formerly called:
British Knitting and Clothing Export Council (BKCEC) (year of change 2000)

Organisation type and purpose:
Trade association (membership is by subscription).
To promote the export from UK of all clothing and fashion-related accessories.

Subject coverage:
Export markets and marketing, export statistics, export procedures and tariffs, information on overseas markets for clothing (members only), general information, to potential buyers of British clothing etc, all relevant details of appropriate UK suppliers.

Museum or gallery collection, archive, or library special collection:
Library of commercial information available to member companies (directories, export regulations, buyer information, trade journals (UK and foreign) etc)

Trade and statistical information:
Via associated organisations in the British Apparel and Textile Confederation, details of production in UK, numbers employed etc.

Library catalogue:
All or part available in-house

Printed publications:
Annual Report and Accounts
The BKCEC Exporter (monthly bulletin, free to members only)
The Fashion Buyer's Guide to Britain (formerly British Apparel Directory; free to overseas buyers or agents)
Various promotional leaflets

Access to staff:
Contact by letter, by telephone, by fax, by e-mail and via website. Appointment necessary.
Hours: Mon to Fri, 0900 to 1800

Affiliated to:
British Apparel and Textile Confederation at the same address
British Clothing Industry Association at the same address

Subsidiary body:
Apparel Marketing Services (Export) Ltd at the same address

UK HYDROGRAPHIC OFFICE

Acronym or abbreviation: UKHO

Admiralty Way, Taunton, Somerset, TA1 2DN

Tel: 01823 337900
Fax: 01823 284077
E-mail: via website www.ukho.gov.uk

Website:
http://www.ukho.gov.uk

Enquiries:
Enquiries to: Archives Research Manager
Direct tel: 01823 337900 ext 3409
Direct e-mail: research@ukho.gov.uk

Founded:
1795

Organisation type and purpose:
National government body, research organisation.
Producer of navigational charts and related publications.
An appointed place of deposit for its own records under the Public Records Act 1958.

Subject coverage:
Navigation; hydrographic surveying; geodesy; photogrammetry; cartography; geophysics; oceanography; meteorology; shipping and ports.

Museum or gallery collection, archive, or library special collection:
Archives of hydrographic surveys, Admiralty Charts, navigational information, books, letters

Non-library collection catalogue:
All or part available in-house

Library catalogue:
All or part available in-house

Printed publications:
Catalogue of Admiralty Charts and other hydrographic publications available via worldwide network of agents
Order printed publications from: List of agents for UKHO publications available on website

Microform publications:
Microform copies of historical material available for purchase directly, subject to copyright restrictions

Electronic and video publications:
Some data may be purchased in electronic format where held subject to copyright restrictions

Access to staff:
Contact by letter, by telephone, by fax and by e-mail. Appointment necessary.
Hours: Mon to Fri, 0930 to 1630

Access to building, collection or gallery:
Prior appointment required

Access for disabled people:
Parking provided, toilet facilities, level access, lift to Research Room

A Trading Fund Agency within the:
Ministry of Defence

UK INDUSTRIAL VISION ASSOCIATION

Acronym or abbreviation: UKIVA

PO Box 25, Royston, Herts, SG8 6TL

Tel: 01763 220981
E-mail: info@ukiva.org

Website:
http://www.ukiva.org
Members, news and events, list of academic members, courses, hints and tips, publications, jobs.

Organisation type and purpose:
To promote the use of vision and imaging technology by industry and science in the UK.

Subject coverage:
Provides information about image processing and machine vision systems.

Electronic and video publications:
A Series of Technology Briefings on Various Subjects: 100% digital image acquisition for vision; Options for Inspection of Moving Products; Using Colour Information in Machine Vision
Guide to Machine Vision
21 Financial Justifications for using Vision
Past Seminars that UKIVA has presented
Order electronic and video publications from: Available to download from free resources section of website by registered visitors

Publications list:
Available online

Access to staff:
Contact by letter, by telephone, by e-mail and via website

UK INNOVATION RELAY CENTRES

Avon:
Bristol
 tel: 0117 221 016

Cambridgeshire:
Cambridge
 tel: 01954 261199

Hampshire:
Farnborough
 tel: 01252 394607

Kent:
Canterbury
 tel: 01227 763414

Merseyside:
St Helens
 tel: 01744 453366

Northern Ireland:
Belfast
 tel: 028 9052 9475
Belfast
 tel: 028 9049 1031

Oxfordshire:
Oxford
 tel: 01865 784888

Scotland:
Aberdeen
 tel: 01224 211500
Glasgow
 tel: 0141 946 0500
Glasgow
 tel: 0141 221 0999
Inverness
 tel: 01463 715400
Sterling
 tel: 01786 448333

South Yorkshire:
Barnsley
 tel: 01226 249590

Tyne & Wear:
Sunderland
 tel: 0191 383 3336

Wales:
Cardiff
 tel: 029 2082 8739

West Midlands:
Coventry
 tel: 024 7683 8140

UK JEEP CLUB

Jeep Books Ltd/Jeep Promotions Ltd, 5 Chestnut Avenue, Wheatley Hills, Doncaster, South Yorkshire, DN2 5SW

Tel: 01302 739000
Fax: 01302 739001
E-mail: info@jeepworld.co.uk

Website:
http://www.jeepworld.co.uk

Enquiries:
Enquiries to: Editor

Founded:
1990

Formerly called:
C J Jeep Club UK, Jeep Club UK

Organisation type and purpose:
Membership association (membership is by subscription), voluntary organisation.

Subject coverage:
Jeeps for sale, jeep parts new and used, suppliers, insurance, technical advice, information, events, everything for real jeeps from 1941 Willys to new CJs, Wranglers and Cherokees.

Museum or gallery collection, archive, or library special collection:
Many books, magazines, manuals for helping club members, but not for loan

Non-library collection catalogue:
All or part available online, in-house and in print

Library catalogue:
All or part available in-house and in print

Printed publications:
Magazine (6 times a year)

Publications list:
Available online

Access to staff:
Contact by letter, by telephone, by e-mail and via website
Hours: Mon to Fri, 0900 to 1700

UK LUBRICANTS ASSOCIATION LTD

Acronym or abbreviation: UKLA

Berkhamsted House, 121 High Street, Berkhamsted, Hertfordshire, HP4 2DJ

Tel: 01442 230589
Fax: 01442 259232
E-mail: enquiries@ukla.org.uk

Website:
http://www.ukla.org.uk

Enquiries:
Enquiries to: Executive Director

Founded:
1921

Organisation type and purpose:
Trade association.

Subject coverage:
Lubrication and additives, all aspects of manufacture, distribution and marketing of lubricants.

Printed publications:
Exposure to Hard Metals in Metalworking Fluids during Machining Operations
Lube (Association magazine)
Membership Handbook
Membership Lists

Access to staff:
Contact by letter, by fax, by e-mail and via website
Hours: Mon to Fri, 0900 to 1700

UK MAJOR PORTS GROUP

Acronym or abbreviation: UKMPG

4th floor, Carthusian Court, 12 Carthusian Street, London, EC1M 6EZ

Tel: 020 7260 1785
Fax: 020 7260 1785
E-mail: richardbird@ukmajorports.org.uk

Website:
http://www.ukmajorports.org.uk

Enquiries:
Enquiries to: Executive Director

Founded:
1993

Formerly called:
British Ports Federation (year of change 1992)

Organisation type and purpose:
Trade association.

Subject coverage:
Policy issues affecting the major ports arising from UK Government, European Commission or other action.

Printed publications:
Brochure (free)

Access to staff:
Contact by letter, by telephone, by fax and by e-mail
Hours: Mon to Fri, 0900 to 1700

UK NATIONAL COMMITTEE FOR THE PREVENTION OF ALCOHOL AND DRUG DEPENDENCY

Acronym or abbreviation: NCPA

BUC Office, Stanborough Park, Watford, Hertfordshire, WD25 9JZ

Tel: 01923 665553
Fax: 01923 893212

Enquiries:
Enquiries to: Executive Director

Organisation type and purpose:
Membership association (membership is by election or invitation), registered charity (charity number 1008129).

Printed publications:
Cannabis and Mental Function (£2 plus pp)

Access to staff:
Contact by letter, by telephone and by fax
Hours: Fri, 0900 to 1200

Affiliated to:
International Commission for the Prevention of Alcoholism and Drug Dependency (an NGO of the WHO and UN)
 12501 Old Columbia Pike, Silver Spring, MD 20904, USA

UK PAYMENTS

Formal name: UK Payments Administration Ltd

2 Thomas More Square, London, E1W 1YN

Tel: 020 3217 8200
Fax: 020 7488 4232
E-mail: enquiries@ukpayments.org.uk

Website:
http://www.ukpayments.org.uk
One-stop shop for information on payments in the UK and a way to access different UK payment industry sites for the Payments Council, The UK Cards Association, Bacs, CHAPS and Cheque & Credit Clearing.

continued overleaf

Enquiries:
Enquiries to: Director of Communications
Direct tel: 020 3217 8234

Founded:
1985

Formerly called:
APACS Administration Ltd (year of change 2009)

Organisation type and purpose:
A service company for the UK payments industry, providing people, facilities and expertise. The payments industry has different players and separate industry groups with UK Payments supplying different services to a wide range of companies with separate external identities.

Subject coverage:
UK payments issues including plastic cards, card fraud, cheques, electronic payments and cash.

Printed publications:
See website

Publications list:
Available online

Access to staff:
Contact by letter and by e-mail
Hours: Mon to Fri, 0900 to 1700

Links with:
Payments Council
2 Thomas More Square, London, E1W 1YN; tel: 020 3217 8200; e-mail: enquiries@ukpayments .org.uk; website: http://www.paymentscouncil .org.uk
The UK Cards Association
2 Thomas More Square, London, E1W 1YN; tel: 020 3217 8200; e-mail: support@ukcards.org.uk; website: http://www.theukcardsassociation.org .uk

UK SOCIETY OF INVESTMENT PROFESSIONALS

Acronym or abbreviation: UKSIP

21 Ironmonger Lane, London, EC2V 8EY

Tel: 020 7796 3000
Fax: 020 7796 3333
E-mail: uksipstaff@uksip.org

Website:
http://www.uksip.org

Enquiries:
Enquiries to: Chief Executive
Other contacts: (1) Director of Finance; (2) Director of Education and IT

Founded:
2000

Formerly called:
Institute of Investment Management and Research (IIMR) (year of change 2000)

Organisation type and purpose:
National organisation, professional body (membership is by qualification), present number of members: 4400.
To set standards in profession of fund management and investment research.

Subject coverage:
Techniques of investment; stocks and shares and other securities; investment analysis; portfolio management. Careers in investment analysis and fund management.

Printed publications:
Headline Earnings (booklet)
Investment Management Certificate Training Manual
Journal (monthly)
Past Examination Papers and Examiners Reports
Career Booklet

Publications list:
Available in print

Access to staff:
Contact by letter, by telephone, by fax, by e-mail and via website

Hours: Mon to Fri, 0930 to 1730

Member society of the:
Association for Investment Management & Research (AIMR)
tel: 00 1 434 951 5489

UK SPRING MANUFACTURERS' ASSOCIATION

Acronym or abbreviation: UKSMA

Tel: 0114 252 7997
E-mail: uksma@uksma.org.uk

Website:
http://www.uksma.org.uk
Find a spring maker, news, events, sales leads, products and services.

Organisation type and purpose:
Trade association providing business support for UK spring makers.

Subject coverage:
Actively promotes the UK spring industry, encourages business development, provides information, networking and support.

Access to staff:
Contact by telephone and by e-mail

Administered by:
Institute of Spring Technology
Henry Street, Sheffield, S3 7EQ; tel: 0114 276 0771; fax: 0114 252 7997; e-mail: ist@ist.org; website: http://www.ist.org.uk

UK STEEL

Broadway House, Tothill Street, London, SW1H 9NQ

Tel: 020 7222 7777
Fax: 020 7222 2782
E-mail: steel@eef.org.uk

Website:
http://www.eef.org.uk/uksteel

Enquiries:
Enquiries to: Director
Direct tel: 020 7654 1519
Direct e-mail: irodgers@eef.org.uk

Founded:
1967

Organisation type and purpose:
Trade association for the UK steel industry, representing the industry to policy and opinion formers, promoting the industry and the importance of steel to the public, and providing information and services to its members.

Subject coverage:
UK steel industry, including its structure, performance (nationally and internationally) and its contribution to the UK economy and everyday life. Specialist knowledge of steel production, processing and steel products; steel standards and steel sourcing; environmental issues relating to the production, processing and recyclability of steel; legislation and representation to government in the United Kingdom, Europe and elsewhere; international trade in steel; other issues affecting steel companies such as transport and haulage, careers in the UK steel industry, and health and safety.

Trade and statistical information:
Key statistics for the United Kingdom steel industry available free; other statistics (United Kingdom, Europe, worldwide) available on request and online.

Printed publications:
Annual Review (free)
Key Statistics (free)
Steel Specifications – contains detailed information about the chemical, mechanical and physical properties of steels specified in British, European and other standards together with details of UK steel industry producers (13th edn, approx. £100)

Electronic and video publications:
SteelSpec (online version of Steel Specifications, subscriptions start at £90 per year)

Publications list:
Available online

Access to staff:
Contact by letter, by telephone, by fax and by e-mail
Hours: Mon to Fri, 0900 to 1700

Also at:
UK Steel
Swinden House, Rotherham, S60 3AR; tel: 01709 362288; fax: 01709 724999; e-mail: rruddlestone@ eef.org.uk

Constituent bodies:
ISSB Limited
1 Carlton House Terrace, London, SW1Y 5DB; tel: 020 7343 3900; fax: 020 7343 3902; e-mail: enquiries@issb.co.uk

Member organisation of:
Energy Intensive Users Group (EIUG)
Broadway House, Tothill Street, London, SW1H 9NQ; tel: 020 7654 1536; fax: 020 7222 2782

Sponsor of:
Challenge of Materials Gallery
Science Museum, Exhibition Road, London, SW7 2DD; tel: 020 7938 8000

UK STEM CELL FOUNDATION

Acronym or abbreviation: UKSCF

20 Park Crescent, London, W1B 1AL

Tel: 020 7670 5370
E-mail: info@ukscf.org

Website:
http://www.ukscf.org/foundation
Aims, stem cell research, current research projects.

Founded:
2005

Organisation type and purpose:
A registered charity (number 1110009).
To support the advance of pioneering stem cell research into medical practice.
Directly funds innovative UK clinical projects with the greatest potential for saving and improving people's lives.

We are determined to fill the critical gap between currently available UK funding and the many promising research projects in need of financial assistance.

Subject coverage:
Leading biomedical scientists the world over believe that stem cell research holds the key to curing society's most intractable diseases including Parkinson's, Alzheimer's, multiple sclerosis and heart attack. The scientific and therapeutic benefits to be gained are potentially enormous.

Electronic and video publications:
Newsletter
Brochure
Order electronic and video publications from:
Download from website

Access to staff:
Contact by letter, by telephone and by e-mail

Also at:
UK Stem Cell Foundation
Abbey House, 83 Princes Street, Edinburgh EH2 2ER; tel: 0131 718 0684; e-mail: info@ukscf.org

UK THALASSAEMIA SOCIETY

Acronym or abbreviation: UKTS

19 The Broadway, Southgate Circus, London, N14 6PH

Tel: 020 882 0011
Fax: 020 8882 8618
E-mail: office@ukts.org

Website:
http://www.ukts.org

Enquiries:
Enquiries to: Honorary Secretary

Founded:
1976

Organisation type and purpose:
Registered charity (number 275107).

Subject coverage:
Information on thalassaemia.

Printed publications:
Books, posters and leaflets including:
What is Thalassaemia
Management protocol for the treatment of
thalassaemia patients
Information for people who have haemoglobin H
disease
Standards for the Clinical Care of Children and
Adults with Thalassaemia in the UK

Access to staff:
Contact by letter, by telephone, by fax, by e-mail,
in person and via website
Hours: Mon to Fri, 0900 to 1700

Access for disabled people:
Level entry

UK TRADE & INVESTMENT

Acronym or abbreviation: UKTI

Kingsgate House, 66–74 Victoria Street, London,
SW1E 6SW

Tel: 020 7215 8000
Fax: 020 7828 1281

Website:
http://www.ukinvest.gov.uk/

Enquiries:
Enquiries to: Information Officer

Founded:
1977

Formerly called:
Invest-UK, Trade Partners UK, Invest in Britain
Bureau (year of change 2003)

Organisation type and purpose:
National government body.
Unit of the Department of Trade and Industry and
Foreign and Commonwealth Office.
The major role of UKTI is to assist and encourage
overseas companies with internationally mobile
manufacturing and service sector projects to locate
their activities in this country. Particularly
interested in securing those projects which bring
long-term jobs or which introduce new
technologies or management techniques and which
improve the UK's competitive manufacturing
position. UKTI works in partnership with national
development agencies in Scotland, Wales and
Northern Ireland and the English regional
development agencies.

Subject coverage:
The Government's main inward investment agency
in the United Kingdom, assisting firms with all
aspects of locating or relocating a business or
expanding existing facilities. UKTI offers a one-
stop advisory service in drawing together
information from government and public agencies,
and can put together a complete package of
locations, financial incentives, employment,
taxation, entry clearance and immigration,
company formation, training, research assistance
and product sector advice. The service is both free
and confidential.

Trade and statistical information:
Comparison statistics for above subjects between
UK and EU countries.

Printed publications:
Operations Review
Flagship Brochure
Briefing in Britain
Sector Brochures

Information Sheets
Order printed publications from: DTI Publications
tel: 0870 150 2500, fax: 0870 150 2333, e-mail:
publications@dti.gsi.gov.uk

Microform publications:
Some material available through the DTI Library,
tel: 020 7215 5000

Publications list:
Available online and in print

Access to staff:
Contact by letter, by telephone, by fax, by e-mail
and via website
Hours: Mon to Fri, 0900 to 1700

Parent body:
Department of Trade and Industry

UK TRADE AND INVESTMENT, HONG KONG AND MACAO DESK

Acronym or abbreviation: UKTI

Bay 960, Kingsgate House, 66–74 Victoria Street,
London, SW1E 6SW

Tel: 020 7215 8095
Fax: 020 7215 4074
E-mail: michael.opoku@ukti.gsi.gov.uk

Website:
http://www.uktradeinvest.gov.uk

Enquiries:
Enquiries to: Country Manager

Formerly a part of:
Department of Trade and Industry (DTI) (year of
change 2007)

Organisation type and purpose:
National government body.
Trade promotion.

Subject coverage:
Exporting to Hong Kong, prospects for investment
and other forms of commercial co-operation.

Publications list:
Available in print

Access to staff:
Contact by letter, by telephone, by fax and by e-
mail
Hours: Mon to Fri, 0900 to 1700

Access for disabled people:
Access to all public areas

Constituent part of:
BERR

UK YOUTH

3rd Floor, Lancaster House, 33 Islington High
Street, London, N1 9LH

Tel: 0845 862 0155
Fax: 0845 862 0155
E-mail: info@ukyouth.org

Website:
http://www.ukyouth.org
Youth work, projects, magazines, publications, etc.

Enquiries:
Enquiries to: Chief Executive
Direct tel: 0845 862 0157
Direct e-mail: jo@ukyouth.org

Founded:
1911

Formerly called:
National Association of Youth Clubs; Youth Clubs
UK (YCUK) (year of change 1999)

Organisation type and purpose:
Voluntary organisation, registered charity (charity
number 306066).

Subject coverage:
Youth, youth work and services.

Non-library collection catalogue:
All or part available online and in print

Library catalogue:
All or part available online and in print

Printed publications:
Videos catalogue
UK Youth (magazine, quarterly)
ninety-five per cent (magazine, quarterly)
Books, booklets, action packs, posters, including:
Actual Reality – a programme for young people
beyond 2000: the report
Foundations – the guide to running a youth group
Making Connections – the role of youth work
Perspectives on Young Carers
The Art of Youth Work
Understanding Anger – a group work programme
Youth Listens – training & support for peer
mentors

Electronic and video publications:
Videos (over 50 titles)

Publications list:
Available online and in print

Access to staff:
Contact by letter, by telephone, by fax, by e-mail
and via website. Appointment necessary.
Hours: Mon to Fri, 0900 to 1700

Access to building, collection or gallery:
Prior appointment required

Access for disabled people:
Level entry

Affiliated to:
European Confederation of Youth Club
Organisations (ECYC)
Ornevej 45, Copenhagen NV, DK-2400,
Denmark; tel: 00 45 38 10 80 38
National Council for Voluntary Organisations
National Council for Voluntary Youth Services

Has:
3 divisions (Scotland, Wales and Northern Ireland)
43 local associations of youth clubs

UK-IDF

c/o Dairy UK, 93 Baker Street, London W1U 6QQ

Tel: 0207 467 2621
Fax: 0207 487 4734
E-mail: iwakeling@dairyuk.org

Website:
http://www.ukidf.org/
Publications.

Enquiries:
Enquiries to: Secretary

Founded:
1950

Formerly called:
United Kingdom Dairy Association

Organisation type and purpose:
Membership association (membership is by
subscription).
UK National Committee of the International Dairy
Federation.

Subject coverage:
Hygiene, dairy technology, economics, analytical
techniques, nutrition and education.

Printed publications:
IDF bulletins and special issues

Access to staff:
Contact by letter, by telephone, by fax and by e-
mail
Hours: Mon to Fri, 0900 to 1700

UKCISA: THE COUNCIL FOR INTERNATIONAL STUDENT AFFAIRS

9–17 St Albans Place, London, N1 0NX

Tel: 020 7107 9922
Fax: 020 7288 4360

continued overleaf

Website:
http://www.ukcisa.org.uk

Enquiries:
Enquiries to: Membership Secretary

Founded:
1968

Formerly called:
UKCOSA: The Council for International Education

Organisation type and purpose:
Advisory body, membership association
(membership is by subscription), voluntary
organisation, registered charity (charity number
1095294), training organisation, consultancy,
research organisation.
To promote the interests of international students.

Subject coverage:
All matters affecting international students in the
UK.

Trade and statistical information:
Comparative statistics on international students.

Printed publications:
Good Practice publications
Guidance Notes for Students (21 titles)
Research reports
Manual
Order printed publications from: Publications Officer,
UKCOSA
e-mail: publications@ukcosa.org.uk

Electronic and video publications:
Onyx: the electronic guide to regulations and
procedures for international students
CD-ROM
Videos

Publications list:
Available online and in print

Access to staff:
Contact by letter, by telephone, by fax, by e-mail
and via website
Hours: Telephone: 020 7354 5210: Mon to Fri, 1300
to 1600

UKERNA

Formal name: United Kingdom Education and
Research Networking Association

Atlas Centre, Chilton, Didcot, Oxfordshire, OX11
0QS

Tel: 01235 822212
Fax: 01235 822397
E-mail: service@ukerna.ac.uk

Website:
http://www.ja.net
Holds information about JANET, the UK's
academic and research network.
http://www.ukerna.ac.uk

Enquiries:
Enquiries to: Customer Service Director

Founded:
1993

Organisation type and purpose:
Statutory body.
UKERNA is responsible for the co-ordination and
management of the networking programme of the
UK education and research community known as
JANET.

Subject coverage:
Internetworking for the UK academic and research
community, multiservice networking, information
superhighway for education, managing the JANET
network.

Printed publications:
Annual Report
Networking Programme Report
UKERNA News (3 times a year)

Access to staff:
Contact by letter, by telephone, by fax and by e-
mail. Appointment necessary.
Hours: Mon to Fri, 0800 to 1800

Affiliated to:
JISC, HEFCE
Northavon House, Coldharbour Lane, Bristol,
BS16 1QD

UKOLN

Library and Learning Centre, University of Bath,
Claverton Down, Bath, BA2 7AY

Tel: 01225 386580
Fax: 01225 386838
E-mail: ukoln@ukoln.ac.uk

Website:
http://www.ukoln.ac.uk

Enquiries:
Enquiries to: Resource Co-ordinator
Direct tel: 01225 386250
Direct e-mail: b.r.robinson@ukoln.ac.uk
Other contacts: Events Manager (for conference
organisation)

Founded:
1977

Organisation type and purpose:
Advisory body, research organization.

Subject coverage:
UKOLN is a research organisation that aims to
inform practice and influence policy in the areas of:
digital libraries, information systems, bibliographic
management, and web technologies. It provides
network information services, including the
Ariadne magazine, and runs workshops and
conferences.

Printed publications:
Reports, briefing papers, etc.

Electronic and video publications:
Ariadne (online)

Access to staff:
Contact by letter, by telephone, by e-mail and via
website
Hours: Mon to Fri, 0900 to 1700

Funded by:
European Union Project Funding
Joint Information Systems Committee of the
Higher and Further Education Funding Councils
Museums, Libraries and Archives Council (MLA)

Supported by:
University of Bath

UKSPACE

Acronym or abbreviation: SBAC

Salamanca Square, 9 Albert Embankment, London,
SE1 7SP

Tel: 020 7091 4500
Fax: 020 7091 4545

Website:
http://www.sbac.co.uk

Enquiries:
Enquiries to: Policy and Communications
Direct e-mail: mark.watson@sbac.co.uk

Founded:
1975

Formerly called:
United Kingdom Industrial Space Committee
(UKISC)

Organisation type and purpose:
National organisation, trade association, present
number of members: 40. Represents the collective
interests of its member companies in increasing
space and space-related business, and their share
of the home and export markets.

Subject coverage:
UK Space Industry – policy and capability. Links to
specialist sources.

Access to staff:
Contact by letter
Hours: Mon to Fri, 0900 to 1700

Access to building, collection or gallery:
No access other than to staff

Connections with:
Federation of the Electronics Industry
Russell Square House, London, WC1B 5EE; tel:
020 7331 2000
Society of British Aerospace Companies (SBAC)
60 Petty France, London, SW1H 9EU; tel: 020
7227 1000

UKSPILL ASSOCIATION

PO Box 21, Over Wallop, Stockbridge, Hampshire,
SO20 8WY

Tel: 0870 4868980
Fax: (0870 4863235
E-mail: info@ukspill.org

Website:
http://www.ukspill.org

Enquiries:
Enquiries to: Director

Founded:
1981

Organisation type and purpose:
Trade association.

Subject coverage:
All aspects of the prevention, control and clean-up
of marine, inland and industrial pollution, both in
the UK and overseas.

Access to staff:
Contact by letter
Hours: Mon to Fri, 0900 to 1700

ULSTER COLLEGE OF MUSIC

13 Windsor Avenue, Belfast, BT9 6EE

Tel: 028 9038 1314

Website:
http://www.ulstercollegeofmusic.com

Enquiries:
Enquiries to: Administrator
Direct e-mail: annestafford@btinternet.com
Other contacts: Chairman

Founded:
1966

Organisation type and purpose:
College of Music.
The training of musicians on all instruments and
voice, or vocal and instrumental tuition.

Subject coverage:
All aspects of the profession of music.

Library catalogue:
All or part available in-house

Access to staff:
Contact by letter, by telephone, by e-mail, in
person and via website
Hours: Mon to Fri, 1400 to 2030; Sat, 0900 to 1700

Access for disabled people:
Toilet facilities
Special comments: Disabled access to ground and
first floor only.

ULSTER HISTORICAL FOUNDATION

Acronym or abbreviation: UHF

49 Malone Road, Belfast, Co. Antrim, BT9 6RY

Tel: 028 9066 1988
Fax: 028 90661977
E-mail: enquiry@uhf.org.uk

Website:
http://www.ancestryireland.com
http://www.booksireland.org.uk

Enquiries:
Enquiries to: Executive Director
Direct e-mail: fintan@uhf.org.uk

Founded:
1956

Organisation type and purpose:
Voluntary organisation, registered charity (charity number XN48460), research organisation, publishing house.
Genealogical research, computerisation of historical records, publications.

Subject coverage:
Genealogical research for all of Ireland, history of Ulster, particularly migration to and from, Irish Genealogical Project (for the computerisation of all pre-1900 church and civil records in Ireland), designated centre for Co. Antrim and Co. Down (including Belfast).

Museum or gallery collection, archive, or library special collection:
Completed searches regarding Ulster families (approx. 13,000)

Printed publications:
Directory of Irish Family History Research (Subscribers' interest list, annually, some back volumes available)
Familia: Ulster Genealogical Review (annually, some back volumes available)
Newsletter (annually)
Gravestone Inscription Series (28 volumes, some in hardcopy, some also as fiche, some only as fiche)
Historical series includes:
Essays in Scotch-Irish History (ed Green E R R)
A Century of Northern Life – The Irish News & 100 Years of Ulster History 1890s–1990s
A Past Apart: Studies in the History of Catholic Belfast (1996)
Buildings of County Antrim
Clergy of Connor
Clergy of Down and Dromore
Down Cathedral: The Church of St Patrick of Down (Rankin J F)
Merchants in Plenty
New Light at the Cape of Good Hope
Nine Ulster Lives
Northern Ireland and the Second World War (1995)
People's Champion
Presbyterians and The Irish Language (Blaney R)
Private Life and Public Fortune: Macartney of Lisanaire (Roebuck P ed.)
Scottish Migration to Ulster in the Reign of James I (rev 1999, Perceval-Maxwell M)
Two Acres of Irish History: A Study Through Time of Friars Bush and Belfast (Phoenix E)
The Famine in Ulster (Kinealy C and Parkhill T)
Ulster Emigration to Colonial America 1718–1775 (Dickson R J, 2nd reprint 1996)
Ulster Libraries, Archives, Museums & Ancestral Heritage Centres: A visitors guide (O'Neill R K)
Penal Era and Golden Age: Essays in Irish history 1690–1800
Scottish Covenanters and Irish Confederates

Microform publications:
Gravestone Inscription Series for Co. Down and Co. Antrim including Belfast (all 27 volumes of the series in microfiche, £6 per individual volume inc. p&p)

Publications list:
Available online and in print

Access to staff:
Contact by letter, by telephone, by fax, by e-mail, in person and via website
Hours: Mon to Fri, 0930 to 1630

Access to building, collection or gallery:
No prior appointment required
Hours: Mon to Fri, 0930 to 1630

Links with:
Federation of Family History Societies
Irish Family History Foundation
Irish Genealogical Project
Ulster Genealogical and Historical Guild

ULSTER UNIONIST PARTY

Acronym or abbreviation: UUP

First Floor, 174 Albertbridge Road, Belfast, BT5 4GS

Tel: 028 9046 3200
Fax: 028 9045 6899
E-mail: uup@uup.org

Website:
http://www.uup.org
General party information; history, policies, objectives, documents, press statements, election results, contact details for elected representatives.

Enquiries:
Enquiries to: Party Admin Manager
Direct tel: 028 9046 3201
Direct e-mail: hazel.legge@uup.org

Founded:
1905

Organisation type and purpose:
Membership association (membership is by subscription).
Political party.

Access to staff:
Contact by letter, by telephone, by fax, by e-mail, in person and via website
Hours: Mon to Fri, 0900 to 1700

Access to building, collection or gallery:
Hours: Mon to Fri, 0900 to 1700

Access for disabled people:
Hours: Mon to Fri, 0900 to 1700

ULSTER WILDLIFE TRUST

Acronym or abbreviation: UWT

Ulster Wildlife Trust, 3 New Line, Crossgar, Downpatrick, Co. Down, BT30 9EP

Tel: 028 4483 0282
Fax: 028 4483 0888
E-mail: info@ulsterwildlifetrust.org

Website:
http://www.ulsterwildlifetrust.org

Enquiries:
Enquiries to: Marketing Manager
Other contacts: Membership Officer (for membership issues)

Founded:
1978

Organisation type and purpose:
Registered charity.

Subject coverage:
Nature conservation, biodiversity, marine, planning, environmental education.

Printed publications:
Irish Hare (membership magazine)
Natural World (membership magazine)
Wildife gardening guides

Publications list:
Available online

Access to staff:
Contact by letter, by telephone and by e-mail.
Appointment necessary.
Hours: Mon to Fri, 0900 to 1700

Member organisation of:
The Wildlife Trust
The Kiln, Waterside, Mather Road, Newark, Nottinghamshire, NG24 1WT; tel: 01636 677711; fax: 01636 670001; e-mail: enquiry@wildlifetrusts.org; website: http://www.wildlifetrusts.org

UNICEF UK

Formal name: United Nations Children's Fund
Acronym or abbreviation: UNICEF

Africa House, 64–78 Kingsway, London, WC2B 6NB

Tel: 020 7405 5592
Fax: 020 7405 2332
E-mail: helpdesk@unicef.org.uk

Website:
http://www.unicef.org.uk
Information on UNICEF and situation of children; video clips; interviews.

Enquiries:
Enquiries to: Information Department

Founded:
1947

Organisation type and purpose:
International organisation, registered charity (charity number 1072612).
Fund raising and advocacy organisation, supporting the work of UNICEF in over 160 countries. Helping to provide basic services for children and promoting children's rights.

Subject coverage:
Health, children's rights, child labour, nutrition, water and sanitation, children in conflict, education, aid and development work for the improvement of conditions for mothers and children in developing countries; children's issues and rights in the industrialised world.

Museum or gallery collection, archive, or library special collection:
Photographs (black and white) and colour transparencies
UNICEF international publications, board papers, speeches

Trade and statistical information:
Statistics on child births, deaths, performance, malnutrition, immunisation, primary education, maternal deaths.

Printed publications:
A large number of publications on child rights, economic policies, local government, urban children in difficult circumstances
Annual Report
Financial Statement
News in Brief (monthly)
Publicity material
Resources for Schools (a series of publications and videos for Key Stage 1 to adult)
The Progress of Nations (annually)
The State of the World's Children (annually)
Order printed publications from: UNICEF
Unit 1, Rignals Lane, Chelmsford, Essex, CM2 8TU, tel: 01245 476315, fax: 01245 477394

Publications list:
Available in print

Access to staff:
Contact by letter, by telephone, by fax, by e-mail and via website
Hours: Mon to Fri, 0930 to 1730

Access to building, collection or gallery:
No access other than to staff

Parent body:
United Nations

UNION OF MUSLIM ORGANISATIONS OF UK AND EIRE

Acronym or abbreviation: UMO

109 Campden Hill Road, London, W8 7TL

Tel: 020 7221 6608 or 7229 0538
Fax: 020 7792 2130 (on request)

Enquiries:
Enquiries to: Secretary-General
Other contacts: Assistant Secretary.

Founded:
1970

Organisation type and purpose:
National organisation, membership association (membership is by subscription), present number of members: 214, voluntary organisation.
Voluntary religious organisation, representative body of the Muslim community in UK and Eire.

continued overleaf

To co-ordinate the activities of Muslim organisations in the UK and Eire, to negotiate with government departments and serve the religious rights of the British Muslim community.

Subject coverage:
Islam; Islamic education; social and cultural aspects of British Muslim activities, including youth activities in the UK; current Mosque projects dealing with any problems faced by Muslim students or workers in the observance of their religions duties.

Printed publications:
Islamic books
Press releases issued after major events

Publications list:
Available in print

Access to staff:
Contact by letter, by telephone and by fax.
Appointment necessary.
Hours: Mon to Fri, 0900 to 1700

Has as members:
Local Muslim organisations in UK and Eire

Houses the:
National Muslim Education Council and the UMO Youth Council of UK and Eire
  tel: 020 7221 6608; fax: 020 7792 2130 (on request)
UMO Board of Ulama, UK
UMO Trust

UNION OF SHOP, DISTRIBUTIVE AND ALLIED WORKERS

Acronym or abbreviation: USDAW

188 Wilmslow Road, Fallowfield, Manchester, M14 6LJ

Tel: 0161 224 2804
Fax: 0161 257 2566
E-mail: enquiries@usdaw.org.uk

Website:
http://www.usdaw.org.uk

Enquiries:
Enquiries to: Head of Media and Communications (applications to use library and archive facilities need to be in writing)

Organisation type and purpose:
Trade union, present number of members: 340,000.
The Supervisory, Administrative and Technical Association (SATA) is the white collar section.

Subject coverage:
Trade union activity and industrial relations matters in retail and wholesale distribution and associated sectors of food and chemical processing and the catering and hairdressing trades; wages councils; shopping hours and Sunday trading; history of USDAW and earlier shopworker unions.

Museum or gallery collection, archive, or library special collection:
Copies of Union journals: New Dawn, The Shop Assistant, Dawn and Usdaw Today, Agenda, Arena, Network
Union's Official Records since the 1880s

Printed publications:
Network (6 times a year)
Arena (4 times a year)

Access to staff:
Contact by letter, by telephone, by fax, by e-mail and via website. Appointment necessary.
Hours: Mon to Fri, 0900 to 1700

UNISON

1 Mabledon Place, London, WC1H 9AJ

Tel: 0845 355 0845

Website:
http://www.unison.org.uk
Information on UNISON.

Founded:
1993

Organisation type and purpose:
Trade union.

Subject coverage:
Trade unions and industrial relations, pay and conditions, public services.

Printed publications:
See website
Order printed publications from: UNISON Communications, tel: 020 7551 1115

Publications list:
Available online and in print

Access to staff:
Contact by letter, by telephone, by fax and by e-mail. Appointment necessary.
Hours: Mon to Fri, 0900 to 1700

Affiliated to:
Labour Party
Public Services International
Trades Union Congress
  website: http://www.tuc.org.uk

UNIT FOR RESEARCH INTO CHANGING INSTITUTIONS

Acronym or abbreviation: URCHIN

115 Poplar High Street, London, E14 0AE

Tel: 020 7987 3600
Fax: 020 7515 8627
E-mail: info@meridian.org.uk

Website:
http://www.meridian.org.uk

Enquiries:
Enquiries to: Executive Director

Founded:
1981

Organisation type and purpose:
Registered charity (charity number 284542), research organisation.
To carry out research into ways to implement and advance the capacity of society and its associated institutions to adapt to change in a functional and realistic manner.

Subject coverage:
Management of change, organisational learning, psychoanalysis, social dynamics, pre- and perinatal psychology, primal integration.

Non-library collection catalogue:
All or part available online

Library catalogue:
All or part available online

Printed publications:
All publications free and online

Publications list:
Available online and in print

Access to staff:
Contact by letter
Hours: Mon to Fri, 0900 to 1700

UNITARIAN GENERAL ASSEMBLY

Formal name: General Assembly of Unitarian and Free Christian Churches
Acronym or abbreviation: GAUFCC

Essex Hall, 1–6 Essex Street, London, WC2R 3HY

Tel: 020 7240 2384
Fax: 020 7240 3089
E-mail: info@unitarian.org.uk

Website:
http://www.unitarian.org.uk
Publicity material, list of congregations with addresses and service times, forthcoming events, affiliated groups and periodicals.

Enquiries:
Enquiries to: Information Officer

Founded:
1928

Organisation type and purpose:
Membership association, registered charity (charity number 250788).
Religious, Unitarianism.
Spreads information about liberal religion and provides support services for member groups.

Subject coverage:
Current British Unitarian beliefs and practices; liberal religious ideas and principles; personalised weddings, baptisms, child namings and funerals; liberal religious movements abroad, blessings of same-sex relationships.

Museum or gallery collection, archive, or library special collection:
Year Books, 1870 to date

Printed publications:
Annual Directory
Other occasional publications

Publications list:
Available in print

Access to staff:
Contact by letter, by telephone, by fax, by e-mail and via website. Appointment necessary. Access for members only.
Hours: Mon to Fri, 0900 to 1700
Special comments: Please telephone first.

UNITARIAN HISTORICAL SOCIETY

Acronym or abbreviation: UHS

223 Upper Lisburn Road, Belfast, BT10 0LL

E-mail: nspresb@hotmail.com

Website:
http://www.unitarianhistory.org.uk

Enquiries:
Enquiries to: Honorary Secretary

Founded:
1916

Organisation type and purpose:
Learned society (membership is by subscription), present number of members: 350.

Subject coverage:
Unitarian history.

Museum or gallery collection, archive, or library special collection:
For library, see Dr Williams's Library

Printed publications:
Transactions of the Unitarian Historical Society (annually)

Access to staff:
Contact by letter and by e-mail
Hours: Mon to Fri, 0900 to 1700

Associated with:
General Assembly of Unitarian and Free Christian Churches

UNITED KINGDOM ACCREDITATION SERVICE

Acronym or abbreviation: UKAS

21–47 High Street, Feltham, Middlesex, TW13 4UN

Tel: 020 8917 8400
Fax: 020 8917 8500
E-mail: info@ukas.com

Website:
http://www.ukas.com
General information about UKAS and its purpose.

Enquiries:
Enquiries to: Head of Corporate Communications
Direct tel: 020 8917 8554
Direct fax: 020 8917 8754
Direct e-mail: ukas@clear-group.co.uk

Founded:
1995

Organisation type and purpose:
Statutory body, service industry.
Accreditation of conformity assessment bodies.

Subject coverage:
Interpretation and clarification of conformity assessment standards; calibration: electrical (dc, lf, rf and microwave), mechanical, fluids, thermal, radiological, thermal conductivity, acoustics, humidity, force, mass, accelerometry, magnetic, pressure, hardness, optical, fibre; testing: acoustical, ballistic, biological, chemical, corrosion, dimensional, electrical, EMC, environmental, fire, geological, health and hygiene, information technology, mechanical, metallurgical, NDDT, performance, physical, safety.

Printed publications:
Directory of Accredited Laboratories

Access to staff:
Contact by letter, by telephone, by fax, by e-mail and via website
Hours: Mon to Fri, 0900 to 1700

UNITED KINGDOM ALLIANCE

Acronym or abbreviation: UKA

176 Blackfriars Road, London, SE1 8ET

Tel: 07985 011029

Enquiries:
Enquiries to: General Secretary

Founded:
1853

Organisation type and purpose:
Membership association (membership is by subscription), present number of members: 500, voluntary organisation, registered charity (charity number 293067).
Education in respect of alcohol and drug abuse.

Subject coverage:
Advising on the dangers of alcohol and drug abuse.

Access to staff:
Contact by letter
Hours: Mon to Fri, 0900 to 1700

Access to building, collection or gallery:
No access other than to staff

UNITED KINGDOM ASSOCIATION OF MANUFACTURERS OF BAKERS' YEAST

Acronym or abbreviation: UKAMBY

6 Catherine Street, London, WC2B 5JJ

Tel: 020 7420 7109
Fax: 020 7836 0580
E-mail: tom.hollis@fdf.org.uk

Enquiries:
Enquiries to: Executive Secretary

Organisation type and purpose:
Trade association (membership is by subscription), manufacturing industry.

Subject coverage:
Bakers' yeast, legislative developments.

Printed publications:
Annual Report

Access to staff:
Contact by letter, by fax and by e-mail
Hours: Mon to Fri, 0900 to 1700

Member of:
Food & Drink Federation

UNITED KINGDOM ASTRONOMY TECHNOLOGY CENTRE

Acronym or abbreviation: UK ATC

The Library, Royal Observatory, Blackford Hill, Edinburgh, EH9 3HJ

Tel: Switchboard 0131 668 8100 \ Library 0131 668 8395
Fax: 0131 668 8264
E-mail: user@roe.ac.uk

Website:
http://www.roe.ac.uk/atc/library
Astronomical literature

Enquiries:
Enquiries to: Librarian
Direct tel: 0131 668 8395
Direct e-mail: library@roe.ac.uk

Founded:
1896

Organisation type and purpose:
Research organisation.

Subject coverage:
National centre for the design and production of state-of-the-art astronomical instrumentation and associated technology, in collaboration with UK organisations and/or overseas partners.

Museum or gallery collection, archive, or library special collection:
Crawford Collection of historical books and manuscripts on astronomy, and related subjects from 13th to late 19th century, c. 15,000 items

Non-library collection catalogue:
All or part available online

Library catalogue:
All or part available online

Printed publications:
Annual Report of the James Clerk Maxwell Telescope
Annual Report of the United Kingdom Infrared Telescope
JCMT Newsletter (irregular)
Research and Facilities/Royal Observatory, Edinburgh (1981-)
Spectrum (quarterly)
Supplement to the Catalogue of the Crawford Library of the Royal Observatory, Edinburgh (1977)

Publications list:
Available in print

Access to staff:
Contact by letter, by telephone, by fax, by e-mail, in person and via website. Appointment necessary.
Hours: Mon to Fri, 0900 to 1730
Special comments: Not open to the public

Funded by:
Science & Technology Facilities Council
Polaris House, North Star Avenue, Swindon, SN2 1SZ; website: http://www.scitech.ac.uk

UNITED KINGDOM ATOMIC ENERGY AUTHORITY

Formal name: United Kingdom Atomic Energy Authority, Culham Centre for Fusion Energy

Fusion Library, Culham Science Centre, Abingdon, Oxfordshire, OX14 3DB

Tel: 01235 466347
Fax: 01235 466507
E-mail: helen.bloxham@ukaea.org.uk

Website:
http://www.ccfe.ac.uk

Enquiries:
Enquiries to: Library Manager

Founded:
1961

Organisation type and purpose:
National government body, research organisation.
Fusion research and development.

Subject coverage:
Nuclear fusion, plasma physics.

Museum or gallery collection, archive, or library special collection:
UKAEA Fusion Reports
JET Reports

Non-library collection catalogue:
All or part available online and in-house

Library catalogue:
All or part available in-house

Electronic and video publications:
Order electronic and video publications from: via website

Publications list:
Available online

Access to staff:
Contact by letter, by telephone, by fax, by e-mail, in person and via website. Appointment necessary. Access for members only. Non-members charged.
Hours: Mon to Fri, 0815 to 1630

Access to building, collection or gallery:
Prior appointment required

UNITED KINGDOM CENTRE FOR ECONOMIC AND ENVIRONMENTAL DEVELOPMENT

Acronym or abbreviation: UK CEED

Suite 1, Priestgate House, 3–7 Priestgate, Peterborough, Cambridgeshire, PE1 1JN

Tel: 01733 311644
Fax: 01733 312782
E-mail: info@ukceed.org

Website:
http://www.ukceed.org
Company description and information on project areas.

Enquiries:
Enquiries to: Information Officer

Founded:
1984

Organisation type and purpose:
National organisation, registered charity (charity number 289469), research organisation.

Subject coverage:
All aspects of environmental economics including energy, coastal, marine, leisure, packaging, sustainable development, land use planning, nuclear, business ethics and corporate environmental reporting, and information and communication technologies; public participation; tourism.

Non-library collection catalogue:
All or part available online and in print

Printed publications:
Conference proceedings
UK CEED Bulletin (4 times a year)
UK CEED Discussion Papers (irregular)
Atmospheric Emissions from Private Motor Vehicles (1995)
Cleaner Technology (1992)
Digital Futures – Living in a Dot-Com World (Feb 2001)
Inland, Coastal and Estuarine Waters Magazine (bi-monthy, by subscription)
Leicestershire Rural Partnership Citizen's Jury on Rural Issues (May 2001)
Monitoring and Retrievability of Radioactive Waste (I) (Dec 2000)
Monitoring and Retrievabililty of Radioactive Waste (II) (Feb 2001)
Signposting the Sustainable Development Strategy (1994)
The Impacts of Recreation on Marine Special Areas of Conservation (mSAC) (Mar 2000)

Access to staff:
Contact by letter, by telephone, by fax, by e-mail and via website
Hours: Mon to Fri, 0900 to 1700

UNITED KINGDOM CERTIFICATION AUTHORITY FOR REINFORCING STEELS

Acronym or abbreviation: UK CARES

Pembroke House, 21 Pembroke Road, Sevenoaks, Kent, TN13 1XR

Tel: 01732 450000
Fax: 01732 455917
E-mail: general@ukcares.com

Website:
http://www.ukcares.com

Enquiries:
Enquiries to: Company Secretary

Founded:
1983

Organisation type and purpose:
Third party certification body.

Subject coverage:
Reinforcing steels.

Printed publications:
List of approved firms

Publications list:
Available online and in print

Access to staff:
Contact by letter, by telephone, by fax and by e-mail
Hours: Mon to Fri, 0900 to 1700

UNITED KINGDOM CLINICAL PHARMACY ASSOCIATION

Acronym or abbreviation: UKCPA

1st Floor, Publicity House, 59 Long Street, Wigston, Leicester, LE18 2AJ

Tel: 0116 277 6999
Fax: 0116 277 6272
E-mail: admin@ukcpa.com

Website:
http://www.ukcpa.org

Enquiries:
Enquiries to: General Manager
Direct e-mail: mmatthews@ukcpa.com

Founded:
1981

Organisation type and purpose:
Advisory body, professional body (membership is by subscription), present number of members: 2,000+, training organisation.
Promotes pharmaceutical care for the benefit of patients.

Subject coverage:
Clinical pharmacy, education and training, safety and quality of medicines, critical care, care of the elderly, surgery, infection management, respiratory, cardiac, diabetes, emergency care, IT, leadership development, pain management, community, gastroenterology/hepatology and haemostasis, anticoagulation and thrombosis.

Information services:
Resource centre, online discussion forums.

Education services:
Study days, symposia.

Printed publications:
Clinical Pharmacy Models of Care
Newsletter (quarterly, free to members)
Symposia abstract booklets (free to members)

Publications list:
Available in print

Access to staff:
Contact by letter, by telephone, by fax, by e-mail and via website
Hours: Mon to Fri, 0900 to 1700

UNITED KINGDOM FLIGHT SAFETY COMMITTEE

Acronym or abbreviation: UKFSC

Graham Suite, Fairoaks Airport, Chobham, Woking, Surrey, GU24 8HX

Tel: 01276 855193
Fax: 01276 855195
E-mail: admin@ukfsc.co.uk

Website:
http://www.ukfsc.co.uk

Enquiries:
Enquiries to: Chief Executive

Founded:
1959

Organisation type and purpose:
Advisory body, professional body (membership is by subscription, election or invitation), present number of members: 85, voluntary organisation.
To improve aviation safety.

Subject coverage:
Aviation safety.

Information services:
Website and magazine

Education services:
Flight Safety Familiarisation Course

Trade and statistical information:
Aviation safety articles and statistics.

Library catalogue:
All or part available in-house

Printed publications:
Focus on Commercial Aviation Safety (FOCUS)

Publications list:
Available online

Access to staff:
Contact by letter, by telephone, by fax and by e-mail
Hours: Mon to Fri, 0900 to 1630

UNITED KINGDOM FORTIFICATIONS CLUB

Acronym or abbreviation: UKFC

4 Mablethorpe Road, Wymering, Portsmouth, Hampshire, PO6 3LJ

Tel: 023 9238 7794

Website:
http://www.mysite.freeserve.com/ukfc

Enquiries:
Enquiries to: Chairman
Direct tel: 023 9238 7794 (24 hours)
Other contacts: Webmaster for Internet enquiries email Peter.Cobb@btopenworld.com.

Founded:
1972

Organisation type and purpose:
International organisation, membership association (membership is by subscription), voluntary organisation, research organisation.

Subject coverage:
All types of fortification within UK and certain other nations overseas from 2,500 BC to the present day; specifically Iron Age hill and promontory forts, Romano-British camps, forts and towers etc; castle construction; Tudor fortifications: Martello towers and 18th and 19th century fortifications; Georgian and Victorian defences and armoured works; coast artillery, anti-aircraft artillery and field fortifications from both World Wars; Northern Ireland defences; airfield layouts and offshore fortified structures (any period); 130 different subject groupings.

Museum or gallery collection, archive, or library special collection:
Cobb Family Archive
Rare books on fortifications, military archaeology and nautical matters

Slide and photographic archives
UKFC Central Archive (over 115 subjects in many volumes)
W E J Parker Archive (Gosport)

Non-library collection catalogue:
All or part available in print

Library catalogue:
All or part available in-house

Printed publications:
Book and reports on general and particular sites include:
ALDIS, newsletter (free to members; at cost plus postage to non-members)
Muster of Archive/Additions to UKFC collections (annually, free to members)
Solent Papers (on sale only)

Publications list:
Available online and in print

Access to staff:
Contact by letter, by telephone, by e-mail and in person. Appointment necessary.
Hours: Mon to Sat, 0800 to 1130 and 2100 to 2230; Sun and bank holidays, 0830 to 2100

Access to building, collection or gallery:
Prior appointment required

Connections with:
Airfield Research Group
CAMP
  USA
CDSG
  USA
Coast Defence Study Group
Kent Defence Research Group
  tel: 01304 205885
Palmerston Forts Society
  tel: 023 9258 6575
Pill Box Study Group
  tel: 01502 710149; e-mail: gkdesignresearch@tiscali.co.uk
Society for Army Historical Research

UNITED KINGDOM HOME CARE ASSOCIATION

Acronym or abbreviation: UKHCA

Group House, 52 Sutton Court Road, Sutton, SM1 4SL

Tel: 020 8288 1551
Fax: 020 8288 1550
E-mail: enquiries@ukhca.co.uk

Website:
http://www.ukhca.co.uk

Enquiries:
Enquiries to: Information Officer

Founded:
1988

Organisation type and purpose:
National professional and representative association for the independent, voluntary, and statutory homecare sector, representing 1,600 organisations.

Subject coverage:
Domiciliary care, community care, social services, health and safety, contracting services and training, welfare of clients and welfare of care workers.

Printed publications:
Choosing Care in Your Home (leaflet, members only)
UKHCA Careworker handbook (£5.99 members, £8.99 non-members)
The Code of Practice (members only)
Costing Mode (online, free to members and non-members)
Who Cares Now?

Publications list:
Available in print

Access to staff:
Contact by letter, by telephone, by fax and by e-mail

Hours: Mon to Fri, 0900 to 1700

Access to building, collection or gallery:
No access other than to staff

Affiliated to:
Care Forum Wales
CCC
NCVO

UNITED KINGDOM ISLAMIC MISSION

Al Furqan School, 27 Arlington Street, Glasgow, G3 6DT

Tel: 0141 331 1119
Fax: 0141 332 2811
E-mail: ukimgla@yahoo.co.uk

Website:
http://www.ukim.org

Enquiries:
Enquiries to: Information Officer
Other contacts: President

Founded:
1920

Organisation type and purpose:
Membership association (membership is by subscription), present number of members: 45, voluntary organisation.
Provides information, training and resources on Islam/Muslims.

Subject coverage:
Islam/Muslim religion and culture.

Printed publications:
Zeal (magazine)
Islamic books (some free, mostly for purchase)

Publications list:
Available in print

Access to staff:
Contact by letter, by telephone, by fax, by e-mail and in person. Appointment necessary.
Hours: 1230 to 1630

Also at:
United Kingdom Islamic Mission
19 Carrington Street, Glasgow, G4 6AJ

UNITED KINGDOM PASSPORT SERVICE

Acronym or abbreviation: UKPS

Globe House, 89 Eccleston Square, London, SW1V 1PX

Tel: 0870 521 0410

Website:
http://www.passport/gov.uk
How to obtain a British passport.

Enquiries:
Enquiries to: Private Office of Headquarters of UKPS
Direct tel: 020 7901 2428

Organisation type and purpose:
National government body.
Executive agency of the Home Office; 7 regional offices.

Subject coverage:
Issue of UK passports to British citizens, British Dependent Territories citizens, British Nationals (Overseas); British Overseas citizens, British Subjects and British Protected Persons.

Museum or gallery collection, archive, or library special collection:
Records of all UK passport issues including those issued at British Consular posts abroad (at Hayes)

Printed publications:
Advice leaflets (free)

Access to staff:
Contact by letter and by telephone. Appointment necessary.
Hours: Mon to Fri, 0830 to 1800; Sat, 0900 to 1500
Special comments: Prior appointment is required – 0870 521 0410.

Regional Offices:
Belfast Passport Office
tel: 0870 521 0410
Durham Passport Office
tel: 0870 521 0410
Glasgow Passport Office
tel: 0870 521 0410
Liverpool Passport Office
tel: 0870 521 0410
London Passport Office
tel: 0870 521 0410
Newport Passport Office
tel: 0870 521 0410
Peterborough Passport Office
tel: 0870 521 0410

UNITED KINGDOM PETROLEUM INDUSTRY ASSOCIATION LIMITED

Acronym or abbreviation: UKPIA

Quality House, Quality Court, Chancery Lane, London, WC2A 1HP

Tel: 020 7269 7600
Fax: 020 7269 7608
E-mail: info@ukpia

Website:
http://www.ukpia.com

Enquiries:
Enquiries to: Director General

Founded:
1978

Organisation type and purpose:
Trade association.

Subject coverage:
The downstream oil industry (supply, refining and distribution of petroleum products in the UK and Northern Ireland).

Publications list:
Available online

Access to staff:
Contact by telephone and via website

Close liaison with:
Europia
Institute of Petroleum
Oil & Gas UK
other organisations serving the petroleum field

UNITED KINGDOM SCIENCE PARK ASSOCIATION, THE

Acronym or abbreviation: UKSPA

Chesterford Research Park, Little Chesterford, Saffron Walden, Essex, CB10 1XL

Tel: 01779 532050
Fax: 01779 532049
E-mail: info@ukspa.org.uk

Website:
http://www.ukspa.org.uk

Enquiries:
Enquiries to: UKSPA Administrator
Other contacts: Business Development Manager

Founded:
1984

Organisation type and purpose:
Membership Association.

Subject coverage:
UK science parks; tenant companies of UK science parks; science parks finance, premises, types of business.

Printed publications:
Annual Report
The Planning, Development and Operation of Science Parks, 2nd edn, 2006 (£50 plus p&p)
Research (economic) main report
Science Park Directory – 14th edition (£50 plus p&p)
Evaluation of the Past and Future Economic Contribution of the UK Science Park Movement (report)

Publications list:
Available online and in print

Access to staff:
Contact by letter, by telephone, by fax and by e-mail. Appointment necessary.
Hours: Mon to Fri, 0900 to 1700

Affiliated to:
AURIL (Association for University Research and Industry Links)
Queens University Belfast, Lanyon North, University Road, Belfast, BT7 1NN; tel: 028 9027 2588; fax: 028 9027 2570; website: www.auril.org.uk
International Association of Science Parks (IASP)

UNITED KINGDOM TRANSPLANT CO-ORDINATORS ASSOCIATION

Acronym or abbreviation: UKTCA

PO Box 6300, Birmingham, B15 2RN

Tel: 07071 223171
Fax: 07071 223171
E-mail: alex@uktca.org.uk

Enquiries:
Enquiries to: The Secretariat

Founded:
1983

Organisation type and purpose:
Professional body (membership is by subscription), registered charity (charity number 1065609).
To increase transplantation and organ donation within the UK and Eire.

Subject coverage:
Transplantation and organ donation.

Access to staff:
Contact by letter, by telephone, by fax and by e-mail
Hours: Mon to Fri, 0900 to 1700

UNITED KINGDOM VINEYARDS ASSOCIATION

Acronym or abbreviation: UKVA

PO Box 985, Bottisham, Cambridge, CB5 9WW

Tel: 01223 813812
E-mail: info@ukva.org.uk

Enquiries:
Enquiries to: General Secretary

Founded:
1996

Organisation type and purpose:
Trade association.
Central body for the affiliated regional associations.

Subject coverage:
The growth of the wine trade and the cultivation of vines and making of wine in the United Kingdom; negotiation with central and local government in matters such as planning, rating and taxation, and EC and its wine regulations; the interchange of technical and other information concerning wine or the vine; Quality wine scheme for English and Welsh Wine; and the annual competition and awards for the English and Welsh Wine of the Year.

Printed publications:
Grape Press (2 times a year, for members)

continued overleaf

Access to staff:
Contact by letter, by telephone, by fax and by e-mail. Appointment necessary.
Hours: Mon to Fri, 0900 to 1700

Affiliated to the:
National Farmers Union
Wine and Spirit Association of Great Britain

UNITED KINGDOM WAREHOUSING ASSOCIATION

Acronym or abbreviation: UKWA

Walter House, 418–422 Strand, London, WC2R 0PT

Tel: 020 7836 5522
Fax: 020 7438 9379
E-mail: dg@ukwa.org.uk

Website:
http://www.ukwa.org.uk

Founded:
1944

Organisation type and purpose:
Trade association.

Subject coverage:
Public warehousing information in the UK, warehousing standards, European legislation.

Printed publications:
BS5750 Quality Manuals
Newsletter (monthly)
Warehousing Manual

Access to staff:
Contact by letter, by telephone, by fax, by e-mail and in person. Appointment necessary.
Hours: Mon to Fri, 0900 to 1700

Member organisation of:
European Warehousing and Logistics Confederation
International Federation of Warehousing Logistics Associations

UNITED LIBRARY

Old Coates House, 32 Manor Place, Edinburgh, EH3 7EB

Tel: 0131 225 4911
E-mail: tisec@scotland.anglican.org

Enquiries:
Enquiries to: Librarian

Founded:
1995

Subject coverage:
Theology, counselling.

Library catalogue:
All or part available in-house

Access to staff:
Contact by letter, by telephone, by e-mail and in person. Non-members charged.
Hours: Tue to Fri, 0900 to 1230
Special comments: Annual subscription for borrowing to non-members.

Combined library from:
Scottish Congregational College
Scottish Episcopal Theological College
St Colm's College (Church of Scotland) Pastoral Foundation

Parent body:
Scottish Episcopal Church
    tel: 0131 225 6357; fax: 0131 346 7247

UNITED LODGE OF THEOSOPHISTS

Acronym or abbreviation: ULT

62 Queens Gardens, London, W2 3AL

Tel: 020 7723 0688
Fax: 020 7262 8639

E-mail: ult@ultlon.freeserve.co.uk

Website:
http://www.ultlon.freeserve.co.uk

Enquiries:
Enquiries to: Information Officer

Founded:
1925

Organisation type and purpose:
International organisation, voluntary organisation.

Subject coverage:
Theosophy and comparative religions, psychic powers in man and philosophies.

Museum or gallery collection, archive, or library special collection:
19th-century magazines on theosophy: Lucifer, Theosophy and other now extinct publications

Non-library collection catalogue:
All or part available online, in-house and in print

Library catalogue:
All or part available in-house and in print

Printed publications:
Theosophy Magazine
Pamphlets, books and magazines

Publications list:
Available online and in print

Access to staff:
Contact by letter, by telephone, by fax, by e-mail, in person and via website. Appointment necessary. Letter of introduction required.
Hours: Mon to Fri, 1000 to 1400; at other times by appointment

Access to building, collection or gallery:
Prior appointment required
Hours: by appointment on Wed and Sun

UNITED NATIONS ASSOCIATION OF GREAT BRITAIN AND NORTHERN IRELAND

Acronym or abbreviation: UNA-UK

3 Whitehall Court, London, SW1A 2EL

Tel: 020 7766 3444
Fax: 020 7930 5893
E-mail: info@una-uk.org

Website:
http://www.una.org.uk

Enquiries:
Enquiries to: Deputy Director
Direct tel: 020 7766 3469
Direct e-mail: southgate@una.org.uk
Other contacts: Head of Advocacy, Executive Director

Founded:
1945

Organisation type and purpose:
Voluntary organisation.
Educational and lobbying body.

Subject coverage:
United Nations activities and international affairs, especially United Nations and conflict, human rights, environment and development.

Museum or gallery collection, archive, or library special collection:
Current UN documents and material relating to 1996

Printed publications:
Briefings (4 times a year, on particular UN interests; 8pp A4 usually)
New World (journal primarily for members and others interested in UN, every 3 months)

Publications list:
Available online and in print

Access to staff:
Contact by letter, by telephone and by e-mail. Appointment necessary.
Hours: Mon to Fri, 1000 to 1600

Links with:
UNA Trust

Member of:
World Federation of UNAs
    Which has consultative status grade 1 with United Nations Economic and Social Council

UNITED NATIONS HIGH COMMISSIONER FOR REFUGEES

Acronym or abbreviation: UNHCR

21st Floor, Millbank Tower, 21–24 Millbank, London, SW1P 4QP

Tel: 020 7828 9191
Fax: 020 7630 5349
E-mail: gbrloea@unhcr.org

Website:
http://www.unhcr.ch
Refugee statistics, section for teachers, country information.
http://www.ukforunhcr.com
Website of national charitable organisation.
Information on UK issues.

Enquiries:
Enquiries to: Information Assistant
Direct e-mail: gbrloea@unhcr.org

Founded:
1951

Organisation type and purpose:
International organisation.
To assist and protect asylum seekers and refugees.

Subject coverage:
Information on refugee situations worldwide, refugee statistics, work of UNHCR and type of assistance provided to refugees.

Museum or gallery collection, archive, or library special collection:
Photographs

Trade and statistical information:
Statistics on refugees.

Printed publications:
REFUGEES Magazine (quarterly)
Variety of books, posters, leaflets, educational resources
The State of the World's Refugees – In search of Solutions (every 2 years)

Electronic and video publications:
Videos available on loan, list available includes:
UNHCR: A Global View
Educational Videos available to schools include:
To Feel At Home

Access to staff:
Contact by letter, by telephone and by fax. Appointment necessary.
Hours: Mon to Thu, 0900 to 1730; Fri, 0900 to 1500

Parent body:
United Nations

UNITED REFORMED CHURCH

Acronym or abbreviation: URC

86 Tavistock Place, London, WC1H 9RT

Tel: 020 7916 2020
Fax: 020 7916 2121
E-mail: urc@urc.org.uk

Website:
http://www.urc.org.uk

Enquiries:
Enquiries to: General Secretary

Founded:
1972

Organisation type and purpose:
Membership association.
Christian Church.

Subject coverage:
United Reformed Church affairs and history.

Museum or gallery collection, archive, or library special collection:
United Reformed Church Historical Society Library (now at Westminster College, Madingley Road, Cambridge CB3 0AA)

Printed publications:
Journal of the URC History Society
Reform (monthly except August)
Year Book

Publications list:
Available in print

Access to staff:
Contact by e-mail. Appointment necessary.
Hours: Mon to Fri, 0900 to 1630

Member of:
Churches Together in Britain and Ireland
Churches Together in England
World Alliance of Reformed Churches
World Council of Churches

Partner in:
Council for World Mission

UNITED REFORMED CHURCH HISTORY SOCIETY

Acronym or abbreviation: URC History Society

Westminster College, Madingley Road, Cambridge, CB3 0AA

Tel: 01223 741300
Fax: 01223 300765
E-mail: mt212@cam.ac.uk

Enquiries:
Enquiries to: Administrator

Founded:
1972

Incorporates the former:
Congregational Historical Society, Presbyterian Historical Society of England and Churches of Christ Historical Society

Organisation type and purpose:
Learned society (membership is by subscription), present number of members: 250.

Subject coverage:
Denominational church history, in particular that of the United Reformed Church in England and Wales, the Congregational Church of England and Wales and the Presbyterian Church of England.

Museum or gallery collection, archive, or library special collection:
Library of Presbyterian Church of England and central/organisational archives of that church
Carruthers Collection of 17th-century dissenting pamphlets

Non-library collection catalogue:
All or part available in-house

Library catalogue:
All or part available online and in-house

Printed publications:
Journal (2 times a year)
Order printed publications from: Address above

Access to staff:
Contact by letter, by telephone, by fax and by e-mail. Appointment necessary. Non-members charged.
Hours: Mon to Wed, 0930 to 1530 (but may change as result of new appointment in 2010)

Access to building, collection or gallery:
Mon to Wed, 0930 to 1530

Access for disabled people:
Hours: Mon to Wed, 0930 to 1530

UNITED SOCIETY FOR CHRISTIAN LITERATURE

Acronym or abbreviation: USCL

Park Place, 12 Lawn Lane, London SW8 1UD

Tel: 020 7582 3535
Fax: 020 7735 7617
E-mail: info@feedtheminds.org

Enquiries:
Enquiries to: Information Officer

Founded:
1799

Organisation type and purpose:
Registered charity (charity number 226512).

Subject coverage:
Christian literature in developing countries, including development of publishing houses through training, etc., training of pastors and ministers.

Museum or gallery collection, archive, or library special collection:
Lutterworth Press archive, held at SOAS, London

Printed publications:
Annual Report
Information Sheet

Access to staff:
Contact by letter, by telephone, by fax and by e-mail. Appointment necessary.
Hours: Mon to Fri, 0900 to 1700

Links with:
Feed the Minds
at the same address

UNITED SYNAGOGUE AGENCY FOR JEWISH EDUCATION

Acronym or abbreviation: AJE

Bet Meir Building, 44b Albert Road, Hendon, London, NW4 2SG

Tel: 020 8457 9700
Fax: 020 8457 9707
E-mail: info@aje.org.uk

Website:
http://www.aje.org.uk
Full Agency for Jewish Education information, publications, catalogue and order facility.

Enquiries:
Enquiries to: Resource Centre Manager
Direct tel: 020 8457 9717
Direct e-mail: resources@aje.org.uk

Founded:
1995

Formed from:
United Synagogue Board of Religious Education; Institute of Jewish Education (year of change 1995)

Formerly called:
Agency for Jewish Education (year of change 2004)

Organisation type and purpose:
Membership association, registered charity, training organisation, publishing house.
Education resource centre.

Subject coverage:
All aspects of Jewish Studies teaching, training and information.

Museum or gallery collection, archive, or library special collection:
Education Library containing books on Jewish Studies and teaching methodology

Printed publications:
The Jewish Educator (journal)
Wide variety of teaching resources including curriculum guidance, posters, maps, charts and resource packs

Publications list:
Available online

Access to staff:
Contact by letter, by telephone, by fax, by e-mail, in person and via website. Appointment necessary. Non-members charged.
Hours: Mon to Thu, 0900 to 1700; Fri, 0900 to 1300

UNITED WORLD COLLEGE OF THE ATLANTIC LIMITED

Acronym or abbreviation: UWC AC

St Donat's Castle, Llantwit Major, Vale of Glamorgan, CF61 1WF

Tel: 01446 799000
Fax: 01446 799013
E-mail: principal@atlanticcollege.org

Website:
http://www.atlanticcollege.org
Prospectus and student views.

Enquiries:
Enquiries to: Principal
Other contacts: Director of College Operations

Founded:
1962

Organisation type and purpose:
International organisation, registered charity.
International residential 6th form college.
International understanding through education and service.

Subject coverage:
International baccalaureate, international education, emergency sea rescue services, community service, environmental monitoring (marine).

Printed publications:
Extramural centre prospectus
Handbook
Prospectus

Access to staff:
Contact by letter, by telephone, by fax, by e-mail and via website. Appointment necessary.
Hours: Mon to Fri, 0830 to 1630

Access to building, collection or gallery:
Only by prior appointment

UNITED WORLD COLLEGES (INTERNATIONAL)

Formal name: The United World Colleges (International) Ltd
Acronym or abbreviation: UWC

Second floor, 17–21 Emerald Street, London, WC1N 3QN

Tel: 020 7269 7800
Fax: 020 7405 4374
E-mail: uwcio@uwc.org

Website:
http://www.uwc.org
Overview of the UWC International Movement.

Enquiries:
Enquiries to: Executive Director
Other contacts: Communications Co-ordinator

Founded:
1962

Organisation type and purpose:
International organisation, membership association (membership is by qualification), present number of members: 33,000, voluntary organisation, registered charity (charity number 313690), suitable for ages: 16 to 19.
The UWC International Office is a co-ordinating office for an international educational movement.
The aims of the movement are international education for responsible citizenship with emphasis on service, peace, justice, international understanding and environmental concern.

Printed publications:
College Prospectuses and Publications
UWC United World Magazine
UWC: An Overview

Electronic and video publications:
UWC Promotional Video – Preparing Tomorrow's International Leaders

continued overleaf

Access to staff:
Contact by letter, by telephone, by fax and by e-mail
Hours: Mon to Fri, 0900 to 1730
Special comments: Closed weekends and holidays.

A member college is:
United World College of the Atlantic
St. Donat's Castle, Llantwit Major, Vale of
Glamorgan, CF61 1WF; tel: 01446 799000; fax:
01446 799013; e-mail: principal@uwcac.uwc.org

Has:
12 Member Colleges
132 National Committees

UNIVERSITIES AND COLLEGES ADMISSIONS SERVICE

Acronym or abbreviation: UCAS

Rosehill, New Barn Lane, Cheltenham,
Gloucestershire, GL52 3LZ

Tel: 01242 544879; minicom no. 01242 544942
Fax: 01242 544954

Website:
http://www.ucas.com
Higher education, getting into university or
college, university/college details, course research,
statistical information, press releases.

Enquiries:
Enquiries to: Director of Outreach Department
Direct tel: 0870 1122211 (for information and advice
on application to higher education)
Direct e-mail: g.jordan@ucas.ac.uk

Founded:
1993

Organisation type and purpose:
Higher education admissions service. Managed by
representatives of universities and schools.

Subject coverage:
Applications for admission to full-time and
sandwich first degree, diploma HND, HNC, and
Certificate of Higher Education courses at United
Kingdom universities (not Open University) and in
most colleges of higher education; also manages
separate systems for diplomas in social work,
nursing and midwifery, and for postgraduate
teacher training; promotion of opportunities
available in higher education.

Trade and statistical information:
Application statistics and related information on
access to higher education.

Printed publications:
GTTR Guide for Applicants
Mature Students Guide to Higher Education
Parents' Guide to Higher Education
UCAS Annual Report
UCAS Directory
Order printed publications from: tel: 01242 544610; e-mail: distribution@ucas.ac.uk

Electronic and video publications:
Online application via website: http://
www.ucas.com
UCAStv

Access to staff:
Contact by letter, by telephone, by fax, by e-mail
and via website
Hours: Mon to Fri, 0900 to 1700

Access for disabled people:
Parking provided, level entry

UNIVERSITIES FEDERATION FOR ANIMAL WELFARE

Acronym or abbreviation: UFAW

The Old School, Brewhouse Hill,
Wheathampstead, Hertfordshire, AL4 8AN

Tel: 01582 831818
Fax: 01582 831414
E-mail: ufaw@ufaw.org.uk

Website:
http://www.ufaw.org.uk

Enquiries:
Enquiries to: Secretary
Other contacts: Scientific Officer (for grants);
Editorial Assistant (for Animal Welfare journal);
Development Officer (for general scientific
information)

Founded:
1926

Organisation type and purpose:
Membership association (membership is by
subscription), present number of members: 900,
registered charity (charity number 207996),
research organisation.
Extensive publications and educational aids on
animal welfare.
Promotion of human behaviour towards wild and
domestic animals in the UK and abroad.

Subject coverage:
Care and management of laboratory, farm, wild,
zoo and companion animals, humane killing, pest
control, welfare of animals in the wild.

Printed publications:
Animal Welfare (journal, quarterly)
Annual Report
Information leaflets
News Sheet (annually)
Proceedings of Symposia
Animal Welfare Books

Electronic and video publications:
Videos

Publications list:
Available in print

Access to staff:
Contact by letter, by telephone, by fax and by e-mail. Appointment necessary.
Hours: Mon to Fri, 0900 to 1600

Access to building, collection or gallery:
Prior appointment required

UNIVERSITY AND COLLEGE UNION (SCOTLAND)

Acronym or abbreviation: UCU (Scotland)

6 Castle Street, Edinburgh, EH2 3AT

Tel: 0131 226 6694
Fax: 0131 226 2066
E-mail: edinburgh@ucu.org.uk

Website:
http://www.ucu.org.uk

Enquiries:
Other contacts: Research Officer
Association of University Teachers (Scotland)

Organisation type and purpose:
Trade union.

Subject coverage:
Professional and trade union interests of academic
and academically-related staff in Scottish
Universities; University teaching, quality assurance
and research in Scotland.

Access to staff:
Contact by letter, by telephone, by fax and by e-mail. Appointment necessary.
Hours: Mon to Fri, 0900 to 1645

Affiliated to:
Scottish Trades Union Congress

UNIVERSITY ASSOCIATION FOR CONTEMPORARY EUROPEAN STUDIES

Acronym or abbreviation: UACES

UACES Secretariat, King's College London, Strand,
London, WC2R 2LS

Tel: 020 7240 0206
Fax: 020 7240 0206

E-mail: admin@uaces.org

Website:
http://www.uaces.org
Information on Association, its activities, register
of courses and publications and links to other
relevant sites.

Enquiries:
Enquiries to: Executive Director

Founded:
1970

Organisation type and purpose:
International organisation, professional body
(membership is by subscription), present number
of members: 800, registered charity (charity
number 274470).

Subject coverage:
Contemporary European studies, European
integration, European Union.

Printed publications:
Contemporary European Studies (series)
Journal of Common Market Studies: The European
Union Annual Review 2000/2001
Negotiating a European Energy Policy: Role Play
Simulation (George S, Haythorne D and Wright
P, 1995, £5)
Register of Courses in European Studies 1998/2000
in UK Universities and University Colleges
(biennial, £6) now on website
Register of Current Research in European
Integration 1999/2001 in the UK (biennial, £10)
Order printed publications from: Contemporary
European Studies Series, Sheffield Academic Press,
c/o Orca Book Services, Stanley House, 3 Fleets
Lane, Poole, Dorset, BH15 3AJ, tel: 01202 665 432,
fax: 01202 666 219
For Journal of Common Market Studies/The EU:
Annual Review, Contemporary European Studies
Series, Blackwell Publishers, PO Box 805, 108
Cowley Road, Oxford, OX4 1FH, tel: 01865 244083,
fax: 01865 381381, e-mail: jnlinfo@
blackwellpublishers.co.uk

Electronic and video publications:
UACES Online Essays

Publications list:
Available online and in print

Access to staff:
Contact by letter, by fax, by e-mail and via
website
Hours: Mon to Fri, 0900 to 1700

UNIVERSITY COLLEGE FALMOUTH LIBRARY

Woodlane, Falmouth, Cornwall, TR11 4RH

Tel: 01326 213815
Fax: 01326 213827
E-mail: library@falmouth.ac.uk

Website:
http://www.falmouth.ac.uk

Enquiries:
Enquiries to: Head of Library and Information
Services
Direct tel: extn 3815
Direct e-mail: dawn.lawrence@falmouth.ac.uk

Formerly called:
Falmouth School of Art and Design

Organisation type and purpose:
University department or institute.

Subject coverage:
Undergraduate and postgraduate courses in art,
design, media and performance. See website for
full details.

**Museum or gallery collection, archive, or library
special collection:**
35,000 books/exhibition catalogues
230 current journal subjects in art, design and
media studies
Journals Collection – extensive range of
contemporary international art and design titles

Broadcasting; journalism, media collection
Illustrated books and graphic novels special
collection
Contemporary artists catalogues
Video library (art, film, general)
Cornwall artists

Printed publications:
Journals listing
Library Guide

Electronic and video publications:
Newsletter

Access to staff:
Contact by letter, by telephone, by e-mail and via
website. Appointment necessary.
Hours: Term time: Mon to Thu, 0900 to 2000; Fri,
0900 to 1700; Sat, 1000 to 1800
Vacations: Mon to Fri, 0900 to 1700

Access for disabled people:
Level entry, access to all public areas, toilet
facilities

UNIVERSITY COLLEGE LONDON – BARTLETT LIBRARY

Formal name: UCL Bartlett Built Environment
Library

5th Floor, Wates House, 22 Gordon Street, London,
WC1H 0QB

Tel: 020 7679 4900
Fax: 020 7679 7373
E-mail: library@ucl.ac.uk

Website:
http://www.ucl.ac.uk/library
Library services, opening hours, catalogue, etc. for
all UCL library sites.

Enquiries:
Enquiries to: Librarian

Organisation type and purpose:
University library.

Subject coverage:
Architecture, town planning, construction
management, development planning.

Library catalogue:
All or part available online

Access to staff:
Contact by e-mail. Appointment necessary.
Hours: Term time: Mon, Thu, 0900 to 2000; Tue,
Wed, Fri, 0030 to 1900; Sat, 0930 to 1630
Vacation: Mon to Fri, 0930 to 1900

Constituent part of:
University College London Library
 tel: 020 7679 2000; fax: 020 7679 7373; e-mail:
 library@ucl.ac.uk

UNIVERSITY COLLEGE LONDON – CRUCIFORM LIBRARY

Acronym or abbreviation: UCL

Cruciform Building, Gower Street, London, WC1E
6BT

Tel: 020 7679 6079
Fax: 020 7679 6981
E-mail: clinscilib@ucl.ac.uk

Website:
http://www.ucl.ac.uk/library/crucilib.shtml

Enquiries:
Enquiries to: Librarian

Founded:
1907

Organisation type and purpose:
University department or institute.

Subject coverage:
Clinical medicine, urology

Library catalogue:
All or part available online

Access to staff:
Contact by letter, by telephone, by e-mail, in
person and via website. Appointment necessary.
Non-members charged.
Hours: Mon to Fri, 0900 to 1700

Access for disabled people:
Ramped entry, toilet facilities
Special comments: Internal lift.

Part of:
Royal Free and University College Medical School
UCL Library Services

UNIVERSITY COLLEGE LONDON – JEWISH STUDIES LIBRARY

Acronym or abbreviation: UCL

Gower Street, London, WC1E 6BT

Tel: 020 7679 7700
Fax: 020 7679 7373
E-mail: library@ucl.ac.uk

Website:
http://www.ucl.ac.uk/library

Enquiries:
Enquiries to: Jewish Studies Librarian
Direct tel: 020 7679 2598
Direct e-mail: v.freedman@ucl.ac.uk

Founded:
1826

Incorporates the former:
Mocatta Library

Organisation type and purpose:
University library.
Library of the Jewish Historical Society of England.

Subject coverage:
Jewish history, Hebrew and Semitic languages,
Bible, Rabbinic literature, mysticism, Jewish
philosophy, Hebrew literature and Yiddish
language and literature.

Services for disabled people:
Alternative-format leaflets, catalogue terminal
with large-format keyboard and screen, book
fetching service, induction loop, visual magnifiers.

**Museum or gallery collection, archive, or library
special collection:**
Abramsky Collection
Albert Hyamson Collection
Altmann Collection
Asher Myers Collection
F. D. Mocatta Collection
Lucien Wolf Genealogical Papers
Moses Gaster Papers
Schachar Collection (of Hassidism)
William Margulies Yiddish Library

Non-library collection catalogue:
All or part available online

Library catalogue:
All or part available online

Printed publications:
The Gaster Papers (1976, occasional publications
no. 2)
Order printed publications from: e-mail: library@ucl
.ac.uk

Access to staff:
Contact by letter, by telephone, by fax, by e-mail
and in person

Access to building, collection or gallery:
Membership required (see website for details);
appointment required for access to special
collections
Hours: Term time: Mon to Thu, 0845 to 2230; Fri,
0845 to 1900; Sat, 1100 to 1745; Sun, 1100 to 2100
Summer vacation: Mon to Fri, 0845 to 1900

Access for disabled people:
Building accessible (entrance, lift); some items
inaccessible, but can be fetched by staff; toilet
facilities

Constituent part of:
University College London

UNIVERSITY COLLEGE LONDON – JOINT LIBRARY OF OPHTHALMOLOGY

Formal name: Joint Library of Ophthalmology,
Moorfields Eye Hospital and UCL Institute of
Ophthalmology

11–43, Bath Street, London, EC1V 9EL

Tel: 020 7608 6814
E-mail: ophthlib@ucl.ac.uk

Website:
http://www.ucl.ac.uk/library/iophth.shtml

Enquiries:
Enquiries to: Librarian
Direct tel: 020 7608 6815
Direct e-mail: d.heatlie@ucl.ac.uk

Founded:
1947

Organisation type and purpose:
University department or institute.
Post-graduate and medical research.

Subject coverage:
Ophthalmology and visual sciences, clinical optics
(postgraduate only).

**Museum or gallery collection, archive, or library
special collection:**
Long runs of journals in European languages
Collection of Historical Works on ophthalmology,
 optics and visual science, including
Sir Edward Nettleship Papers and Ophthalmic
 instruments

Library catalogue:
All or part available online

Access to staff:
Contact by letter, by telephone and by e-mail.
Appointment necessary. Non-members charged.
Hours: Mon to Fri, 0900 to 1700

**The Joint Library of Ophthalmology serves the
employees of:**
Moorfields Eye Hospital NHS Foundation Trust

UNIVERSITY COLLEGE LONDON – LIBRARY OF THE INSTITUTE OF ARCHAEOLOGY

31–34 Gordon Square, London, WC1H 0PY

Tel: 020 7679 7485
Fax: 020 7383 2572
E-mail: library@ucl.ac.uk

Website:
http://library.ucl.ac.uk/

Enquiries:
Enquiries to: Institute Librarian
Direct e-mail: r.kirby@ucl.ac.uk
Other contacts: Library Admission Officer for
requests for use of library, cost and access.

Organisation type and purpose:
University library, university department or
institute.

Subject coverage:
Archaeology, particularly general prehistoric, pre-
Columbian Latin American, Roman Provinces,
Egyptology, pre-Islamic Western Asiatic, Medieval
European; environmental archaeology, scientific
basis of archaeology; technology and conservation
of archaeological material; museology, museum
studies and cultural heritage studies.

**Museum or gallery collection, archive, or library
special collection:**
Tylecote Collection (archaeometallurgy)
The following have been relocated to The Special
 Collection Library services at University College:
The Edwards Collection of Egyptology
Air survey photographs of Near Eastern sites
De Navarro Collection (books and journals dealing
 with La Tène period)
Margaret Wood Collection (English architectural
 history)
Records of Near Eastern excavations

continued overleaf

Library catalogue:
All or part available online

Printed publications:
Archaeology International (annually)
Papers from The Institute of Archaeology

Access to staff:
Contact by letter, by telephone and by e-mail.
Appointment necessary. Non-members charged.
Hours: Mon to Fri, 0900 to 1700

Houses the:
Institute for Archaeometallurgical Studies

Part of:
University College London Library

UNIVERSITY COLLEGE LONDON – LIBRARY OF THE INSTITUTE OF ORTHOPAEDICS

Royal National Orthopaedic Hospital, Brockley Hill, Stanmore, Middlesex, HA7 4LP

Tel: 020 8909 5351
Fax: 020 8909 5390
E-mail: orthlib@ucl.ac.uk

Website:
http://www.ucl.ac.uk/library/iorthlib.shtml

Enquiries:
Enquiries to: Institute Librarian

Founded:
1946

Organisation type and purpose:
University department or institute.
To form a special collection on orthopaedics.

Subject coverage:
Orthopaedics.

Museum or gallery collection, archive, or library special collection:
Historical orthopaedic books

Non-library collection catalogue:
All or part available online

Library catalogue:
All or part available online

Access to staff:
Contact by letter, by telephone, by fax, by e-mail and in person. Appointment necessary.
Hours: Mon, Thu, 0830 to 1830; Tue, Wed, Fri, 0830 to 1700

Access to building, collection or gallery:
Mon, Thu, 0830 to 1830; Tue, Wed, Fri, 0830 to 1700

Constituent part of:
University College London Library
University College London Medical School

UNIVERSITY COLLEGE LONDON – LIBRARY SERVICES

Gower Street, London, WC1E 6BT

Tel: 020 7387 7700
Fax: 020 7380 7373
E-mail: library@ucl.ac.uk

Website:
http://www.ucl.ac.uk/library

Enquiries:
Enquiries to: Director of Library Services
Direct tel: 020 7380 7834
Direct e-mail: p.ayris@ucl.ac.uk

Founded:
1826

Organisation type and purpose:
University library.

Subject coverage:
American history, anthropology, archaeology, architecture, art (fine art and history of art), biological sciences, Celtic, classical studies, clinical sciences, comparative philology, computer science, Dutch, economics, Egyptology, earth sciences, engineering, English, film studies, geography,

German, Hebrew, history, human rights, Jewish studies, Latin American studies, law, library, archive and information studies, life sciences, linguistics, London history, mathematical sciences, medical sciences, management, philosophy, phonetics, physical sciences, planning, politics, psychology, public policy, Romance languages, Scandinavian studies, science and technology studies, Slavonic and East European studies.

Museum or gallery collection, archive, or library special collection:
Libraries of learned societies housed in the College Library (some in Special Collections – see later entry):
British Society of Franciscan Studies
Folklore Society
Gaelic Society
Geologists Association
Hertfordshire Natural History and Field Club
Huguenot Society
Jeremy Bentham Society
Jewish Historical Society of England
London Mathematical Society (now incorporated into the maths collections)
Malacological Society
Mocatta Library of Anglo-Judaica
Philological Society
Royal Historical Society
Royal Statistical Society
Viking Society for Northern Research (now incorporated into the Scandinavian collections)

Non-library collection catalogue:
All or part available in-house

Library catalogue:
All or part available online

Access to staff:
Contact by letter, by telephone, by fax, by e-mail and in person
Hours: Various: see website

Constituent part of:
University of London

Houses the:
RNID Library for deaf and hard-of-hearing people

UNIVERSITY COLLEGE LONDON – SPECIAL COLLECTIONS

Acronym or abbreviation: UCL

Library Services, Gower Sreet, London, WC1E 6BT

Tel: 020 7679 5197
Fax: 020 7679 5157
E-mail: spec.coll@ucl.ac.uk

Website:
http://www.ucl.ac.uk/Library/special-coll/index.shtml
General information, site information, directory of special collections and library catalogue.

Enquiries:
Enquiries to: Archivist

Organisation type and purpose:
University library.

Subject coverage:
Special collections from the medieval to the present day covering a wide range of subjects. Highlights include the C K Ogden and Graves Libraries of rare books, incunabula and medieval manuscripts, rich in the fields of science, language and literature; 19th-century collections, notably Jeremy Bentham's manuscripts and the papers of Lord Brougham, renowned in the field of social, political, legal and educational reform, as well as particular strengths in medical and scientific innovation; and 20th-century professorial manuscripts, literary collections and papers, notably the Orwell Archive and the Little Magazines collection.

Museum or gallery collection, archive, or library special collection:
Some of the more important special collections are:
G C Allen Papers
Bagehot Notebooks
Bank of London and South America archives

Arnold Bennett Papers
Bentham Collection and Manuscripts (Jeremy Bentham 1748–1832)
Joseph Black lecture notes (chemistry)
John Bright letters (1811–1889)
Brougham Papers (Lord Brougham, 1778–1868)
Carswell Drawings
Chadwick
Dante Collection
De Morgan Papers (mathematics)
Early Renaissance Manuscripts
Flaxman Collection (drawings)
Folklore Society Collection and Archives
Sir Ambrose Fleming Papers
Gaelic Society Collection
Hugh Gaitskell Papers
Graves Library
Haldane Papers
Hertfordshire Natural History Society
Laurence Housman Collection (1865–1959)
Hume Tracts
Incunabula
Jewish Studies
Johnston Lavis Collection
Josephus Collection
James Joyce Collection
Learned Society Libraries
London History Collection
London Mathematical Society Archive
Kathleen Lonsdale Papers
Malacological Society
Medieval Manuscripts
Moses Montefiore Collection and family papers
Charles Kay Ogden Library and Papers (including Basic English)
George Orwell Archive
Mervyn Peake Manuscripts
L. S. Penrose Papers
Piranesi Collection (Books)
William Ramsey Papers
Rossetti Letters
Routledge & Kegan Paul Archives
John Russell Papers
Lord Odo Russell Collection
Julia Strachey Papers
Thane Papers
Underground Presses
David M S Watson Papers (palaeontology, zoology, geology)
Sir Arthur Smith Woodward Papers (palaeontology)
J Z Young Papers
Zola Letters

Non-library collection catalogue:
All or part available online, in-house and in print

Library catalogue:
All or part available online and in-house

Access to staff:
Contact by letter, by telephone, by fax, by e-mail, in person and via website. Appointment necessary.
Hours: Mon to Thu, 0930 to 1700; Fri, 0930 to 1645
Closed Sat and Sun

Access to building, collection or gallery:
Prior appointment required
Hours: Mon to Thu, 0930 to 1700, Fri 0930 to 1645
Closed Sat and Sun
Special comments: Admission is by UCL ID and/or by completing a reader application form for consultation for manuscripts and archives.

UNIVERSITY COLLEGE PLYMOUTH ST MARK AND ST JOHN

Acronym or abbreviation: UCP Marjon Library

Derriford Road, Plymouth, Devon, PL6 8BH

Tel: 01752 636700
Fax: 01752 636820
E-mail: wevans@marjon.ac.uk

Website:
http://www.marjon.ac.uk
General information about the institution and the prospectus.
http://www.marjon.ac.uk/facilities/library

Enquiries:
Enquiries to: Head of Library
Direct tel: 01752 636700 ext.n 4206
Direct e-mail: libraryenquiries@marjon.ac.uk
Other contacts: Senior Assistant Librarian; Assistant Librarian

Founded:
1840

Organisation type and purpose:
Registered charity (charity number 312929). Higher education.

Subject coverage:
Education and teacher training, children, youth and community, English language, literature and writing, speech and language therapy, sport, health, coaching and physical education, drama, live music, media, outdoor adventure, English language teaching

Museum or gallery collection, archive, or library special collection:
College archive material 1840 to the present

Library catalogue:
All or part available online

Access to staff:
Contact by letter, by telephone, by fax, by e-mail and via website. Appointment necessary. Non-members charged.
Hours: Term time: Mon to Fri, 0830 to 2000; Sat and Sun, 1000 to 1645
Summer holidays: Mon to Fri, 0900 to 1700

Access for disabled people:
Parking provided, ramped entry, toilet facilities, lifts

UNIVERSITY HOSPITAL LEWISHAM

The Robin Stott Library, Education Centre, Lewisham High Street, London, SE13 6LH

Tel: 020 8333 3030 ext 6454
Fax: 020 8333 3247
E-mail: library@uhl.nhs.uk

Enquiries:
Enquiries to: Library Manager
Direct tel: 020 8333 3439
Direct e-mail: jane.coyte@uhl.nhs.uk

Founded:
1969

Organisation type and purpose:
Trust hospital, multidisciplinary library.
To provide all Trust staff with the evidence base of health care.

Subject coverage:
Medicine and subjects allied to medicine, the National Health Service and health services in general.

Library catalogue:
All or part available in-house

Electronic and video publications:
CINAHL database
Medline database
The Cochrane Library database

Access to staff:
Contact by letter, by telephone, by fax, by e-mail and in person. Appointment necessary.
Hours: Term time: Mon to Thu, 0900 to 1900; Fri, 0900 to 1700
Vacations: Mon to Fri, 0900 to 1700

UNIVERSITY HOSPITALS BRISTOL NHS FOUNDATION TRUST

Acronym or abbreviation: UHBristol

University Hospitals, Bristol Learning Resource Centre, Education Centre, Upper Maudlin Street, Bristol, BS2 8AE

Tel: 0117 342 0105
Fax: 0117 917 0161

E-mail: elizabeth.jordan@uhbristol.nhs.uk

Website:
http://www.uhbristol.nhs.uk/library

Enquiries:
Enquiries to: Learning Resource Services Manager
Direct tel: 0117 342 0102
Direct e-mail: learningresources@uhbristol.nhs.uk

Founded:
1957

Organisation type and purpose:
Libraries of a teaching hospital.

Subject coverage:
All health-related information.

Museum or gallery collection, archive, or library special collection:
Richard Smith Bibliographical Collection of Manuscripts (medicine in Bristol in the 18th and 19th centuries; housed in the Bristol City Archives)

Non-library collection catalogue:
All or part available online

Library catalogue:
All or part available online

Printed publications:
Learning Resource Services User's Guide

Access to staff:
Appointment necessary.
Hours: Mon to Fri, 0900 to 1700

Access to building, collection or gallery:
Prior appointment required

Access for disabled people:
Access to all public areas

Also at:
Bristol Eye Hospital
Bristol General Hospital
Bristol Haematology and Oncology Centre
St Michael's Hospital

UNIVERSITY OF ABERDEEN – DIRECTORATE OF INFORMATION SYSTEMS AND SERVICES: HISTORIC COLLECTIONS, SPECIAL LIBRARIES AND ARCHIVES

King's College, Aberdeen, AB24 3SW

Tel: 01224 272598
Fax: 01224 273891
E-mail: speclib@abdn.ac.uk

Website:
http://www.abdn.ac.uk/historic
Introductory, searchable database of descriptive lists of manuscripts, library catalogue, digitised resources.

Enquiries:
Enquiries to: Reading Room Manager

Founded:
1495

Formerly called:
Aberdeen University Library, Department of Special Collections and Archives (year of change 1997)

Organisation type and purpose:
University library.

Subject coverage:
Humanism, renaissance science and medicine, maps, Jacobitism, travel and transport, North-East Scotland.

Museum or gallery collection, archive, or library special collection:
Gregory Collection (early science and medicine)
Local Collection (NE Scotland)
Local estate papers
Macbean Jacobite Collection
O'Dell Railway Collection
Taylor Psalmody Collection

Theological Library
Bernard C. Lloyd Walter Scott Collection

Non-library collection catalogue:
All or part available online and in print

Library catalogue:
All or part available online

Access to staff:
Contact by letter, by telephone, by fax, by e-mail, in person and via website
Hours: Mon to Fri, 0930 to 1630

Access for disabled people:
Ramped entry

UNIVERSITY OF ABERDEEN – QUEEN MOTHER LIBRARY

Meston Walk, Aberdeen, AB24 3UE

Tel: 01224 273600
Fax: 01224 273956
E-mail: library@abdn.ac.uk

Website:
http://www.abdn.ac.uk
Information about the University, departments, courses and research, information for prospective students, graduates, visitors and businesses.

Enquiries:
Enquiries to: Head of Administration & Planning
Direct tel: 01224 273321

Founded:
1495

Incorporates the former:
Northern College of Education, Aberdeen Campus Library (year of change 2001); MacRobert Library (year of change 2001); Reid Library, Rowett Research Institute (year of change 2007)

Organisation type and purpose:
University library.

Subject coverage:
All subjects covered by the Colleges of Arts and Social Sciences (divinity, history and philosophy; education; language and literature; law; social sciences; business school),
Life Sciences and Medicine (biological sciences, medical sciences, medicine, psychology),
Physical Sciences (engineering and physical sciences, geosciences)

Museum or gallery collection, archive, or library special collection:
Aberdeen Harbour Board
Archives and Local Collection (history of the University and of the North East of Scotland)
Biesenthal Collection (Hebraica)
Celtic literature
European Documentation Centre
George Washington Wilson (Victorian and Edwardian Photographic Archive)
Gregory Collection (history of science and medicine)
Macbean Collection (Jacobites)
Melvin Collection (classics)
Music Scores
O'Dell Collection (railways)
Taylor Collection (psalmody)
Victorian Literature Collection

Non-library collection catalogue:
All or part available online

Library catalogue:
All or part available online

Access to staff:
Contact by letter, by telephone, by fax, by e-mail and in person. Appointment necessary.
Hours: Term time: Mon to Thur, 0900 to 2200; Fri 0900 to 2000; Sat 0900 to 2200; Sun 1100 to 2200
Vacations: Mon to Fri, 0900 to 1700

Constituent bodies:
Medical Library, Foresterhill
tel: 01224 552488; fax: 01224 685157
Queen Mother Library
tel: 01224 273600; fax: 01224 273956; e-mail: library@abdn.ac.uk

continued overleaf

Special Libraries and Archives, Historic Collections at King's College
   tel: 01224 272598; fax: 01224 273891
Taylor Library
   tel: 01224 272601; fax: 01224 273893

UNIVERSITY OF ABERTAY DUNDEE

Acronym or abbreviation: UAD

Kydd Building, 40 Bell Street, Dundee, DD1 1HG

Tel: 01382 308000
Fax: 01382 308877
E-mail: infodesk@abertay.ac.uk

Website:
http://www.abertay.ac.uk
Library: details on academic schools: Steps theatre information.

Enquiries:
Enquiries to: Information Officer
Direct tel: 01382 308080
Direct fax: 01382 308081
Direct e-mail: iro@abertay.ac.uk

Founded:
1888

Organisation type and purpose:
International organisation, advisory body, membership association, university library, university department or institute, suitable for ages: all, training organisation, consultancy, research organisation, publishing house. To provide a high quality learning and scholarly environment for students and staff and to contribute to the development of local companies and the regional economy.

Subject coverage:
Accountancy, behavioural science, biology and biotechnology, building sciences, business studies; civil, mechanical, electronic, electrical engineering; chemistry, sciences, social science, mathematics, computing sciences, economics, law, environmental technology, forest product technology, information management, law and European business law, nursing, physics, psychology, quantity surveying, travel and tourism, sport, golf tourism, sports coaching, Japanese, construction management, chemistry, French, German, Spanish, computer games technology, computer arts, management, forensic psychobiology, sport science, internet communications, mechatronics, software engineering, sociology, financial services, taxation, commercialisation, urban water technology, tourism, hospitality management, marketing, forensic sciences, food and consumer services, animation, health and exercise, web design, communication, counselling.

Non-library collection catalogue:
All or part available online

Library catalogue:
All or part available online

Printed publications:
A.D. Alumni (magazine, annual)
Abertay Beacon newsletter (quarterly, free)
Abertay Sociology Papers
Conference proceedings
Guide to Finance (free)
Guide for International Students (free)
Guide to sport and recreation (free)
School proceedings
Undergraduate and postgraduate leaflets (free)
Undergraduate and postgraduate prospectus (free)

Electronic and video publications:
CD-ROM
Video

Publications list:
Available online and in print

Access to staff:
Contact by letter, by telephone, by fax, by e-mail and via website. Appointment necessary.
Hours: Mon to Fri, 0845 to 1700

Access to building, collection or gallery:
No access other than to staff
Hours: Term time: Mon to Thu, 0830 to 2200; Fri, 0830 to 2100; Sat, 1000 to 1700; Sun, 1200 to 1700.
Vacations: Mon to Fri, 0845 to 1700
Special comments: External membership required for non-members

Access for disabled people:
Parking provided, ramped entry, level entry, toilet facilities

UNIVERSITY OF BATH

The Library, Claverton Down, Bath, BA2 7AY

Tel: 01225 385000
Fax: 01225 386229
E-mail: library@bath.ac.uk

Website:
http://www.bath.ac.uk/library

Enquiries:
Enquiries to: Office of the University Librarian
Direct tel: 01225 826084

Founded:
1966

Organisation type and purpose:
University library.

Subject coverage:
Architecture; biological sciences; chemical engineering; chemistry; economics; education; electrical and electronic engineering; management; materials science; mathematics; mechanical engineering; French, German, Italian, Russian and Spanish, modern European studies; modern languages; pharmacy and pharmacology; physics; psychology; social and policy studies; statistics; sports science; medical sciences; computer science.

Museum or gallery collection, archive, or library special collection:
The Holburne Museum of Art Library
Pitman Collection (shorthand and phonographic systems, initial teaching alphabet)
Royal Bath & West & Southern Counties Society Library
Watkins/Hudson Industrial Archaeology Collection

Trade and statistical information:
European Documentation Centre and other statistical compilations.

Non-library collection catalogue:
All or part available online

Library catalogue:
All or part available online

Access to staff:
Contact by letter, by telephone, by fax, by e-mail and via website. Appointment necessary.
Hours: Term time: Mon to Fri, 0900 to 1900
Special comments: See website: http://www.bath.ac.uk/library

Access for disabled people:
Level entry, access to all public areas, toilet facilities

UNIVERSITY OF BEDFORDSHIRE

Park Square, Luton, Bedfordshire, LU1 3JU

Tel: 01582 734111
Fax: 01582 489325

Website:
http://www.beds.ac.uk
Prospectus information.
http://www.lrweb.beds.ac.uk
Learning resources information and gateway to resources

Enquiries:
Enquiries to: Librarian
Direct tel: 01582 489312
Direct e-mail: tim.stone@luton.ac.uk

Founded:
2006

Organisation type and purpose:
University library.

Subject coverage:
Business; health care and social studies; management; media studies, nursing, psychology, biology and geology.

Non-library collection catalogue:
All or part available online

Library catalogue:
All or part available online

Access to staff:
Contact by letter
Hours: Mon to Thu, 0830 to 2200

Access to building, collection or gallery:
Prior appointment required

Access for disabled people:
Level entry, access to all public areas, toilet facilities

UNIVERSITY OF BIRMINGHAM – EDUCATION LIBRARY

Edgbaston, Birmingham, B15 2TT

Tel: 0121 414 4869
Fax: 0121 471 4691
E-mail: library@bham.ac.uk

Website:
http://www.is.bham.ac.uk/education/
Location and opening hours; enquiries; staff; admissions and borrowing arrangements of the library; services for users with disabilities; subject resources; services to distance learners.

Enquiries:
Enquiries to: Librarian

Organisation type and purpose:
University library.

Subject coverage:
Education, special education, education management, educational psychology, curriculum subjects particularly: religious education, English, maths, geography, history, modern languages, science, physical education.

Museum or gallery collection, archive, or library special collection:
Archives of the British Association of Teachers of the Deaf (BATOD)

Access to staff:
Contact by letter, by telephone, by fax and by e-mail. Appointment necessary.
Hours: Mon to Fri, 0900 to 1700

UNIVERSITY OF BIRMINGHAM – INFORMATION SERVICES

Edgbaston, Birmingham, B15 2TT

Tel: 0121 414 5817
Fax: 0121 471 4691
E-mail: library@bham.ac.uk

Website:
http://www.is.bham.ac.uk/publications/index.htm
Index page for all publications produced by Information Services.
http://www.is.bham.ac.uk/
Home page for Information Services, leading to Information Services website and full details of all facilities and services offered.

Enquiries:
Enquiries to: Director of Information Services
Direct tel: 0121 414 5828
Other contacts: Head of Special Collections

Founded:
1880

Formerly called:
University of Birmingham Library

Organisation type and purpose:
University library.

Subject coverage:
All subjects taught and researched at the University of Birmingham. Arts: American studies; ancient history and archaeology; Canadian studies; classical studies (Latin, classical and modern Greek, Byzantine and Ottoman studies); drama and theatre arts; Dutch; English; film studies; fine art; French studies; German studies; history; Italian; linguistics; Middle and Near Eastern ancient history; music; philosophy; Romanian; Russian and other Slavonic languages (e.g. Czech, Polish, Serbo-Croat); Scandinavian (Danish, Icelandic, Norwegian, Swedish); Spanish and Portuguese (including Latin America); theology; cultural studies; West African studies; commerce and social sciences: accounting and finance; business; development administration; economic and social history; economics; education; international studies; local government studies; management; political science; Russian and East European studies; social administration; social policy; social work; sociology; urban and regional studies; law (all in the Harding Law Library); medicine (all in the Barnes Medical Library): anaesthetics; anatomy; cancer studies; general practice; geriatric medicine; haematology; immunology; intensive care; medical microbiology; medicine; neurology; neurosurgery; nursing studies; obstetrics and gynaecology; occupational health; paediatrics and child health; pathology; pharmacology; physiology; psychiatry; rheumatology; public health and epidemiology; social medicine; surgery; dentistry (all in the Ronald Cohen Dental Library, in the Birmingham Dental Hospital); physical education and recreation; sports science; science and engineering as follows: biochemistry; computer science; earth sciences; mathematics and statistics; physics; space research; chemistry; biological sciences (including botany, environmental health, genetics, microbiology, zoology and comparative physiology); psychology; geography; manufacturing and mechanical engineering; civil engineering; electronic and electrical engineering; chemical engineering; metallurgy and materials; minerals engineering.

Museum or gallery collection, archive, or library special collection:
Main Library (Heslop Room)
Alma Tadema Collection
Birmingham and West Midlands general local history (including Canal Collection, Cannock Chase Colliery Collection, Priestley Collection, Seward Letters, Slade-Baker Correspondence, West Midland Group on Post-War Planning and Reconstruction Papers)
British business and economic history of the eighteenth to twentieth centuries (including British Cotton Growing Association Papers, Cadbury Papers, Canal Collection, Cannock Chase Colliery Collection, Nineteenth century Industry Collection)
British Nonconformist history (including Catholic Apostolic Church Collection, Dale Papers, Martineau Collection, Weatherhead Archive)
British Recusant history (including Jerningham Letters, Little Malvern Court Collection)
Church of England history in the nineteenth and twentieth centuries (including Dr Ernest William Barnes, Bishop of Birmingham 1924–1953 Papers, Church Missionary Society Papers, Church Pastoral Aid Society Papers, Stafford Letters)
English literature and drama (including Edgeworth Letters, Marsh Letters, Harriet Martineau Collection, Mill Collection, Modern Poetry Collection, Nicoll Collection, Reed Collection, Seward Letters, Theatre Collection, Wedgwood Collection (philology), Francis Brett Young Collection, David Lodge papers, Noel Coward collection)
English political and related archives of the nineteenth and twentieth centuries (including Lord Avon Papers, Chamberlain Papers (Arthur

Neville, Joseph and Sir Joseph Austen), Dale Papers, Dawson Papers, Dixon Letters, Masterman Papers)
General theology and Church history (including Bengeworth Library, Hetherington Collection, St Mary's Warwick Parish Library, Thomas Wigan Library of 17th and 18th century literature and theology)
History of The University of Birmingham
History of science (including Priestley Collection)
Printing history (including Baskerville Collection, Birmingham School of Printing Collection, Bodoni Collection of Early Italian Books, English Special Period 1660–69, Foulis Collection, Kelmscott Press Collection, Mandeville Press Collection, Sceptre Press Collection, Shakespeare Head Press Collection)
Russian history of the late nineteenth and early twentieth centuries (including Dolgorukov Papers, Pashkov Papers, Shishkin Papers)
West Africana (including Bradbury Papers, British Cotton Growing Association Papers, Cadbury Papers (mainly photographs of archaeological interest), Church Missionary Society Papers, Matacong Island Papers)
Archives of special educational associations (National Special Schools Union, National Association of Teachers of the Deaf)
Other English general local and family history (including Jerningham Letters, Mingana collection of Middle Eastern historical manuscripts, Mytton Papers, Shaw Letters, Stafford Letters)
Barber Fine Art Library
Art and architecture topography
Items related to specific works of art in the Barber Collection
Sale catalogues and the history of collecting
Barber Music Library
Barber Opera Archive
Early 20th century classical recordings
English and European instrumental music (including Feeney Collection, Shaw-Hellier Collection)
English and European musical treatises and libretti of the seventeenth and eighteenth centuries
English and European vocal music of the seventeenth and eighteenth centuries (including Shaw-Hellier Collection)
Granville Bantock Collection
Barnes Library
History of medicine (including Birmingham Medical Institute Historical Collection, William Withering Collection)
Baykov Library (European Resource Centre)
History and social sciences of pre- and, especially, post-Revolutionary Russia and of Ukraine, Poland, Hungary and most of the republics of the former Soviet Union (including Pares Collection)
Sports history (especially Olympic Games and athletics, including Abrahams Collection)
Sports science
The Ronald Cohen Dental Library
History of dentistry
Education Library
Children's books, c. 1790–1970
History of education
Mathematics textbooks
Harding Law Library
History of English law
Shakespeare Institute Library
Corelli Collection
18th to 20th century editions of Shakespeare
English Renaissance literature
History of drama and the theatre (including Press Cuttings Collection)
Sources and analogues for Shakespeare's plays

Non-library collection catalogue:
All or part available online and in print

Library catalogue:
All or part available online

Printed publications:
Information Services Bulletin (3 times a year)
Large number of User Guides to specific subjects and/or services (print and web versions)
Heslopian (once a year)
Vision (once a year)

Publications list:
Available online

Access to staff:
Contact by letter, by telephone, by fax, by e-mail, in person and via website. Appointment necessary. All charged.
Hours: Mon to Fri, 0900 to 1700

Access to building, collection or gallery:
Special comments: ID required for non-members; limited number of visits per year

Access for disabled people:
Parking provided, level entry, access to all public areas, toilet facilities

UNIVERSITY OF BIRMINGHAM – ORCHARD LEARNING RESOURCES CENTRE

Hamilton Drive, Weoley Park Road, Selly Oak, Birmingham, B29 6QW

Tel: 0121 415 2255
Fax: 0121 415 2273
E-mail: olrc@bham.ac.uk

Website:
http://www.olrc.bham.ac.uk
Catalogue of books and serials. Summary of subjects covered. List of relevant CD-ROMs and websites.

Enquiries:
Enquiries to: Manager
Direct tel: 0121 414 8598
Direct e-mail: d.n.vuong@bham.ac.uk

Founded:
1997

Formerly called:
Selly Oak Colleges Central Library, Westhill College of Higher Education

Organisation type and purpose:
University department or institute.

Subject coverage:
Art in general, community care and service, dance and movement, design, disability, educational studies, English language, English literature, history, Islamics, leisure, physical education, religious education, Christian ministry, missiology, theology, youth studies, youth work and services, counselling.
Christian theology; Bible; Islam and Christian-Muslim relations; Judaism; world religions; community welfare; social work; overseas development studies; church overseas; church history; mission studies; English as a foreign language; peace studies; Syriac studies; education; Quaker studies (in Woodbrooke College).

Museum or gallery collection, archive, or library special collection:
Harold W Turner Collection of New Religious Movements
Mingana Collection of Islamic and Syriac Manuscripts
Rare books 1475–1830
Rendel Harris Collection of Greek papyri

Printed publications:
Catalogues of the special collections
Alphonse Mingana 1878–1937 (Samir Samir Khali, Selly Oak Colleges, 1990)
The Mingana and Related Collections (Hunt L, Selly Oak Colleges, 1997)

Microform publications:
Mingana Collection of Oriental Manuscripts (for purchase)
Harold Turner Collection of New Religious Movements (for purchase)

Access to staff:
Contact by letter, by fax, by e-mail and via website. Appointment necessary.
Hours: Mon to Fri, 0900 to 1700

Access to building, collection or gallery:
Prior appointment required
Hours: Mon to Fri, 0900 to 1700

continued overleaf

Access for disabled people:
Parking provided, toilet facilities

Parent body:
University of Birmingham
Information Services, Main Library, Edgbaston,
Birmingham, B15 2TT; tel: 0121 414 5805; fax:
0121 471 4691; e-mail: library@bham.ac.uk

UNIVERSITY OF BOLTON

Deane Road, Bolton, Lancashire, BL3 5AB

Tel: 01204 903090
Fax: 01204 903166
E-mail: christine.smith@bolton.ac.uk

Website:
http://www.bolton.ac.uk
Links to library information at http://
www.bolton.ac.uk/learning.

Enquiries:
Enquiries to: Collection Development Manager
Direct tel: 01204 903563
Other contacts: Library Administrator

Founded:
1982

Formerly called:
Bolton Art College, Bolton College of Education
(Technical), Bolton Institute of Technology, Bolton
Institute of Higher Education (year of change 2005)

Organisation type and purpose:
Educational institution.

Subject coverage:
Textiles, business studies, psychology, electrical,
mechanical and civil engineering, teacher
education (FE/HE), art and design.

Library catalogue:
All or part available online

Publications list:
Available online

Access to staff:
Contact via website. Non-members charged.
Hours: Mon to Fri, 0845 to 2100; Sat, 0930 to 1230

Access for disabled people:
Access to all public areas, toilet facilities

Member organisation of:
SCONUL NoWAL

UNIVERSITY OF BRADFORD – LEARNING SUPPORT SERVICES

Richmond Road, Bradford, West Yorkshire, BD7
1DP

Tel: 01274 233301\ Minicom no. 01274 233687
Fax: 01274 233398
E-mail: Library@bradford.ac.uk

Website:
http://www.brad.ac.uk/lss/library
News, services, catalogue.

Enquiries:
Enquiries to: Librarian
Direct e-mail: p.m.ketley@bradford.ac.uk

Founded:
1966

Organisation type and purpose:
University Library.

**Museum or gallery collection, archive, or library
special collection:**
Arthur Raistrick Map Collection
Calvin Wells Collection (archaeological sciences)
Commonweal Collection – non-violence and peace
History of Dyeing Collection
History of Pharmacy Collection
Mitrinovic Library
WR Mitchell Collection (the 'Dalesman' archive)
The Joel M Halpern Balkan Collection
The Waddington – Feather Collection (Yorkshire
dialect and poetry)
JB Priestley Collection

Library catalogue:
All or part available online

Access to staff:
Contact by letter
Hours: Mon to Fri, 0845 to 1730

Access for disabled people:
Level entry, access to all public areas, toilet
facilities

Includes the:
Health Studies Library
tel: 01274 236375; fax: 01274 236470
J B Priestley Library
Yvette Jacobson Library (Management Library)
tel: 01274 234401; fax: 01274 234398

UNIVERSITY OF BRIGHTON – EASTBOURNE SITE

The Queenwood Library, Darley Road,
Eastbourne, East Sussex, BN20 7UN

Tel: 01273 643822
Fax: 01273 643825
E-mail: askqueenwood@brighton.ac.uk

Website:
http://library.brighton.ac.uk

Enquiries:
Enquiries to: Information Services Manager
Direct tel: 01273 643820
Other contacts: User Services Librarian (for most
appropriate opening hours, membership queries)

Founded:
1992

Created by the merger of:
Queenwood Library with the Welkin Library and
the Podiatry Library (Leaf Hospital) (year of
change 2000)

Organisation type and purpose:
University library.

Subject coverage:
Queenwood Library: physical education, dance,
sports and exercise science, leisure and sports
studies/management; physiotherapy, occupational
therapy, nursing, podiatry; service management,
tourism, hospitality, culinary arts and event
management; retail marketing; policing studies
Health Sciences Library, Eastbourne District
General Hospital: nursing, midwifery, medicine.

Access to staff:
Contact by letter and by telephone. Appointment
necessary.
Hours: Mon to Fri, 0900 to 1730

Access for disabled people:
Parking provided, ramped entry, access to all
public areas, toilet facilities

Also at:
Eastbourne District General Hospital Health
Sciences Library
King's Drive, Eastbourne, East Sussex, BN21
2UD; tel: 01323 417400 ext n 4048

UNIVERSITY OF BRIGHTON – GRAND PARADE SITE

St Peter's House Library, 16–18 Richmond Place,
Brighton, BN2 9NA

Tel: 01273 643221
Fax: 01273 607532
E-mail: asksph@brighton.ac.uk

Website:
http://library.brighton.ac.uk
Library catalogue.
http://www.brighton.ac.uk
Opening hours, services.

Enquiries:
Enquiries to: Enquiry Desk Team

Founded:
1992

Organisation type and purpose:
University library.

Subject coverage:
Art and design history, fine arts, graphic design,
photography, fashion and textiles, crafts,
performing arts, humanities.

Library catalogue:
All or part available online

Printed publications:
Guides to Library Services (free)

Access to staff:
Contact by letter, by telephone, by fax, by e-mail,
in person and via website

Access to building, collection or gallery:
Hours: Term time: Mon to Thu, 0900 to 2000; Fri,
0900 to 1800; Sat, Sun, 1300 to 1700
Vacations: Mon to Fri, 0900 to 1700

Access for disabled people:
Ground floor only

UNIVERSITY OF BRISTOL – LIBRARY

Tyndall Avenue, Bristol, BS8 1TJ

Tel: 0117 928 8000
Fax: 0117 925 5334
E-mail: library-enquiries@bristol.ac.uk

Website:
http://www.bristol.ac.uk/is/library

Enquiries:
Enquiries to: Librarian
Other contacts: Special Collections Librarian

Founded:
1876

Organisation type and purpose:
University library, with 11 branch libraries.

Subject coverage:
Arts, law, social sciences, science, medicine,
engineering and education.

**Museum or gallery collection, archive, or library
special collection:**
British philosophers
Business histories
Courtesy books
Early English novels
Early mathematics
Early medical works (including some on spas and
mineral waters)
European Documentation Centre
Eyles Collection of early geology
Family papers (Dorset and West Indies, 1650–1948)
General election addresses (acquired with the
purchase of the National Liberal Club Library)
Historical chemistry
I K Brunel's papers
Landscape gardening
Penguin Publishing Archives
Sir Allen Lane Collection of Penguin Books, most
of them signed by their authors
Somerset Miners Association papers
West Indies papers
Wiglesworth Ornithological Library

Non-library collection catalogue:
All or part available online and in-house

Library catalogue:
All or part available online and in-house

Access to staff:
Contact by letter, by telephone, by fax and by e-
mail. Appointment necessary.
Hours: Special Collections: Mon to Wed, 0915 to
1845; Thu, 0945 to 1845; Fri, 0915 to 1645

Constituent part of:
Information Services (includes Library and
Computing Services)

UNIVERSITY OF BUCKINGHAM LIBRARY

Hunter Street, Buckingham, MK18 1EG

Tel: 01280 814080
Fax: 01280 820312
E-mail: library@buckingham.ac.uk

Website:
http://www.buckingham.ac.uk/library

Enquiries:
Enquiries to: Assistant Librarian
Direct tel: 01280 820218

Founded:
1976

Organisation type and purpose:
University library.

Subject coverage:
Law, politics, economics, accounting and finance, management, history, English and modern languages, information systems, psychology.

Museum or gallery collection, archive, or library special collection:
Denning Law Library

Library catalogue:
All or part available online

Printed publications:
Denning Law Journal

Access to staff:
Contact by letter, by telephone, by fax, by e-mail and in person
Hours: Mon to Fri, 0900 to 1700

UNIVERSITY OF CAMBRIDGE – BALFOUR AND NEWTON LIBRARIES OF THE DEPARTMENT OF ZOOLOGY

Downing Street, Cambridge, CB2 3EJ

Tel: 01223 336600
Fax: 01223 336676
E-mail: library@zoo.cam.ac.uk

Website:
http://www.zoo.cam.ac.uk/library/index.html
Admissions, opening times, contacts, exam papers, reprints, theses, print journals, facilities, disabled access, rules.

Enquiries:
Enquiries to: Librarian
Direct tel: 01223 336648
Direct e-mail: library@zoo.cam.ac.uk
Other contacts: Academic Librarian for letter of application to use library.

Organisation type and purpose:
University department or institute.
Departmental library. Balfour Library founded 1883, Newton Library founded 1907.

Subject coverage:
Zoology and ecology.

Museum or gallery collection, archive, or library special collection:
Newton Collection (ornithology and natural history)
Strickland Collection (ornithology)

Non-library collection catalogue:
All or part available online

Library catalogue:
All or part available online and in-house

Access to staff:
Contact by letter, by telephone, by fax, by e-mail and via website. Appointment necessary. Letter of introduction required.
Hours: Mon to Fri, 0830 to 1700
Special comments: Membership is restricted to members of Cambridge University. Application for access by others by letter to the Academic Librarian.

Access to building, collection or gallery:
Please telephone in advance of your visit

Hours: Mon to Fri, 0830 to 1700

Access for disabled people:
Lift, wheelchair accessible, disabled parking, toilet facilities available
Hours: Mon to Fri, 0830 to 1700
Special comments: Please telephone in advance of your visit

UNIVERSITY OF CAMBRIDGE – BETTY AND GORDON MOORE LIBRARY

Wilberforce Road, Cambridge, CB3 0WD

Tel: 01223 765670
Fax: 01223 765678
E-mail: moore-library@lib.cam.ac.uk

Website:
http://www.lib.cam.ac.uk/BGML

Enquiries:
Enquiries to: Librarian

Founded:
2001

Incorporates the former:
Department of Applied Mathematics and Theoretical Physics Library, Department of Pure Mathematics and Mathematical Statistics Library, Wishart Library

Organisation type and purpose:
University library.

Subject coverage:
Mathematics, physics, astronomy, computer science, materials science and engineering.

Museum or gallery collection, archive, or library special collection:
University collections for mathematics, physics, astronomy, computer science, materials science and engineering.

Library catalogue:
All or part available online

Access to staff:
Contact by letter, by telephone, by e-mail, in person and via website. Appointment necessary.
Hours: Mon to Fri, 0900 to 1700; Sat, 0900 to 1300

Parent body:
University of Cambridge Library
West Road, Cambridge, CB3 9DR; tel: 01223 333000; fax: 01223 333160; e-mail: library@lib.cam.ac.uk; website: http://www.lib.cam.ac.uk

UNIVERSITY OF CAMBRIDGE – BOTANIC GARDEN

Cory Lodge, Bateman Street, Cambridge, CB2 1JF

Tel: 01223 336265
Fax: 01223 336278
E-mail: enquiries@botanic.cam.ac.uk

Website:
http://www.botanic.cam.ac.uk

Enquiries:
Enquiries to: Information Officer
Direct tel: 01223 336265
Direct e-mail: enquiries@botanic.cam.ac.uk

Founded:
1762

Organisation type and purpose:
University department or institute.
Sub-department library, of the Department of Plant Sciences.

Subject coverage:
Taxonomy of vascular plants; horticulture; the history of botany and horticulture; information on plants within the Garden.

Museum or gallery collection, archive, or library special collection:
Indexed collection of living plants
Library of books on horticulture and botany
Nurserymen's catalogues

Slide collection of plants

Publications list:
Available in print

Access to staff:
Contact by letter and by telephone. Appointment necessary.
Hours: Mon to Fri, 0900 to 1700

Houses the:
Cory Library

UNIVERSITY OF CAMBRIDGE – CENTRAL SCIENCE LIBRARY

Arts School, Bene't Street, Cambridge, CB2 3PY

Tel: 01223 334742
Fax: 01223 334748

Website:
http://www.lib.cam.ac.uk/CSL/

Enquiries:
Enquiries to: Librarian
Direct tel: 01223 334744
Direct e-mail: mlw1003@cam.ac.uk

Founded:
1820

Organisation type and purpose:
University library.

Subject coverage:
Biological, Chemical, Earth and Environmental Sciences.

Museum or gallery collection, archive, or library special collection:
19th century scientific books
Biffen Collection on plant breeding (reprints)
Buttress Collection (books and journals on agriculture, formerly the library of the Department of Applied Biology)
Marshall Collection on animal reproduction (reprints)

Non-library collection catalogue:
All or part available online

Library catalogue:
All or part available online

Access to staff:
Contact by letter, by e-mail and via website. Appointment necessary.
Hours: Mon to Fri, 0900 to 1700

Originally the library, but still houses the offices, of the:
Cambridge Philosophical Society

Parent body:
Cambridge University Library

UNIVERSITY OF CAMBRIDGE – CENTRE OF ISLAMIC STUDIES

Acronym or abbreviation: CIS

Faculty of Asian and Middle Eastern Studies, Sidgwick Avenue, Cambridge, CB3 9DA

Tel: 01223 335103
Fax: 01223 335110
E-mail: secretary@cis.cam.ac.uk

Website:
http://www.cis.cam.ac.uk
History of the centre, lectures, activities.

Founded:
1960

Formerly called:
Centre of Middle Eastern and Islamic Studies (CMEIS) (year of change 1999)

Organisation type and purpose:
University department or institute, consultancy.
Development of a constructive and critical awareness of the role of Islam in wider society, initially through research programmes about Islam in the United Kingdom and Europe.

continued overleaf

Subject coverage:
Modern history, culture, politics and economics of the Middle East through research and outreach programmes to interact with policy makers and wider society.

Electronic and video publications:
Religious Broadcasting Report
Contextualising Islam in Britain Report
Annual Report 2008–2009
Order electronic and video publications from: PDF files available online: http://www.cis.cam.ac.uk/Reports.htm

Publications list:
Available online

Access to staff:
Contact by letter, by telephone, by fax, by e-mail, in person and via website. Appointment necessary.
Hours: Mon to Fri, 0900 to 1700
Special comments: Questions and queries can usually be answered by mail; of potential use to traders, politicians and academics.

Links with:
Faculty of Asian and Middle Eastern Studies
Sidgwick Avenue, Cambridge CB3 9DA; tel: 01223 335106; fax: 01223 335110; e-mail: enquiries@ames.cam.ac.uk; website: http://www.ames.cam.ac.uk

UNIVERSITY OF CAMBRIDGE – COLMAN LIBRARY OF THE DEPARTMENT OF BIOCHEMISTRY

Tennis Court Road, Cambridge, CB2 1QW

Tel: 01223 333600
Fax: 01223 333345
E-mail: librarian@bioc.cam.ac.uk

Website:
http://www.bio.cam.ac.uk/dept/biochem/ColmanLibrary/index.html

Enquiries:
Enquiries to: Librarian
Direct tel: 01223 333613

Founded:
1924

Organisation type and purpose:
University department or institute.

Subject coverage:
Biochemistry.

Museum or gallery collection, archive, or library special collection:
Departmental papers
Departmental archives

Non-library collection catalogue:
All or part available online

Library catalogue:
All or part available online

Printed publications:
List of Research Projects (Postgraduate Prospectus)

Access to staff:
Contact by telephone, by fax, by e-mail and in person. Appointment necessary. Access for members only.
Hours: Mon to Thu, 0830 to 1700; Fri, 0830 to 1600
Special comments: Non-members by arrangement.

Access to building, collection or gallery:
Card needed
Hours: Mon to Thu, 0830 to 1700; Fri, 0830 to 1600

Access for disabled people:
Hours: Mon to Thu, 0830 to 1700; Fri, 0830 to 1600

UNIVERSITY OF CAMBRIDGE – FACULTY OF EDUCATION LIBRARY AND INFORMATION SERVICE

184 Hills Road, Cambridge, CB2 8PQ

Tel: 01223 767700

E-mail: library@educ.cam.ac.uk

Website:
http://www.educ.cam.ac.uk/library

Enquiries:
Enquiries to: Faculty Librarian

Founded:
2001

Formerly called:
Department of Education, Institute of Education (year of change 1997); School of Education (year of change 2001)

Organisation type and purpose:
University department or institute.

Subject coverage:
Education, including educational research, children with special needs, in-service training of teachers and related subjects, e.g. psychology, philosophy, sociology.

Museum or gallery collection, archive, or library special collection:
Collections of school textbooks and books on teaching method in the fields of English, classics, modern languages, science (general), physics, chemistry, biology, mathematics, history, geography
Source material on history of education now transferred to University of Cambridge Library

Library catalogue:
All or part available online

Printed publications:
Library Guides (annually, free)

Access to staff:
Contact by letter, by telephone, by e-mail, in person and via website
Hours: Mon to Fri, 0930 to 1700

Parent body:
University of Cambridge
website: http://www.cam.ac.uk

UNIVERSITY OF CAMBRIDGE – GEOGRAPHY DEPARTMENT LIBRARY

Department of Geography, Downing Place, Cambridge, CB2 3EN

Tel: 01223 333391
Fax: 01223 333392
E-mail: library@geog.cam.ac.uk

Website:
http://www.lib.cam.ac.uk
University library home page with access to catalogue. The department is part of the Union Catalogue. Periodicals listed in Union list of Serials. Clark Collection and offprints accessed via card catalogue.

Enquiries:
Enquiries to: Librarian
Direct e-mail: rcc23@hermes.cam.ac.uk

Organisation type and purpose:
University department or institute.

Subject coverage:
Geography and its related subjects: ecology, sociology, cultural studies, economics, politics, history and historical geography, cartography, statistics, research techniques, glaciology, some geology, geomorphology, hydrology, climatology, environmental science, environmental policy etc; remote sensing, geographical information systems, urban planning, substantial regional collections covering India, Africa, North and South America, Soviet and post-Soviet Russia.

Museum or gallery collection, archive, or library special collection:
Clark Collection (primarily 18th- and 19th-century books on travel and exploration)

Non-library collection catalogue:
All or part available online and in-house

Library catalogue:
All or part available online

Access to staff:
Contact by letter, by telephone, by e-mail and in person
Hours: Term time: Mon to Fri, 0845 to 1800; Sat, 0845 to 1245
Vacations: Mon to Thu, 0900 to 1300 and 1400 to 1630; Fri, 0900 to 1300 and 1400 to 1530; Sat, closed
Special comments: Visitors by prior appointment during term time. Vacation hours may vary, phone in advance.

UNIVERSITY OF CAMBRIDGE – HADDON LIBRARY OF THE FACULTY OF ARCHAEOLOGY AND ANTHROPOLOGY

Downing Street, Cambridge, CB2 3DZ

Tel: 01223 333505/6
Fax: 01223 333503
E-mail: haddon-library@lists.cam.ac.uk

Website:
http://haddon.archanth.cam.ac.uk
Library guide and Cambridge Union Catalogue.

Enquiries:
Enquiries to: Librarian

Founded:
1920

Organisation type and purpose:
University department or institute.

Subject coverage:
Archaeology; biological anthropology; social anthropology.

Museum or gallery collection, archive, or library special collection:
Burkitt Collection: archaeology (Europe)
Bushnell Collection: archaeology (Americas)
Clarke bequest (archaeology)
De Navarro Collection: archaeology (Europe)
Frazer bequest (anthropology)
McBurney bequest (archaeology)
McBurney Collection: archaeology and anthropology (world-wide)
Offprints
Pitt-Rivers Collection: archaeology and anthropology (19th century)
Rare books collection: c.600 vols, archaeology and anthropology (17th to 19th centuries)

Library catalogue:
All or part available online

Access to staff:
Contact by letter, by telephone, by fax, by e-mail and in person. Appointment necessary. Letter of introduction required.
Hours: Mon to Fri, 0900 to 1700

Constituent bodies:
Cambridge Antiquarian Society Library

UNIVERSITY OF CAMBRIDGE – INSTITUTE OF ASTRONOMY LIBRARY

Acronym or abbreviation: IoA

The Observatories, Madingley Road, Cambridge, CB3 0HA

Tel: 01223 337548
Fax: 01223 337523
E-mail: ioalib@ast.cam.ac.uk

Website:
http://www.ast.cam.ac.uk/library
Online catalogue of holdings; information about the library; resource listings, pictures and photographs from the historical collection.

Enquiries:
Enquiries to: Departmental Librarian
Direct tel: 01223 337537

Founded:
1823

Formerly called:
Institute of Theoretical Astronomy, Library of the Observatories, Cambridge Observatory Library (year of change 1972)

Organisation type and purpose:
University department or institute.
Departmental library.

Subject coverage:
Astronomy and astrophysics.

Museum or gallery collection, archive, or library special collection:
John Couch Adams Collection of astronomy books, mostly pre-1850

Library catalogue:
All or part available online

Access to staff:
Contact by letter, by telephone and by e-mail.
Appointment necessary.
Hours: Mon to Fri, 0900 to 1700

UNIVERSITY OF CAMBRIDGE – JOINT LIBRARY OF THE FACULTY OF CLASSICS AND MUSEUM OF CLASSICAL ARCHAEOLOGY

Sidgwick Avenue, Cambridge, CB3 9DA

Tel: 01223 335154
Fax: 01223 335409
E-mail: library@classics.cam.ac.uk

Website:
http://www.classics.cam.ac.uk/library
Guide to in-house/local resources and other classical resources.

Enquiries:
Enquiries to: Librarian

Founded:
1982

Created by the merger of:
Faculty of Classics Library and Museum of Classical Archaeology Library (year of change 1982)

Organisation type and purpose:
University department or institute.
Teaching and research needs of the Faculty of Classics.

Subject coverage:
Classics, Greek and Latin literature, ancient history, ancient philosophy, classical philology, classical archaeology, classical art, palaeography, epigraphy and modern Greek.

Museum or gallery collection, archive, or library special collection:
J. E. Sandys Collection (classical books)
Owen Collection (ancient philosophy books)
Sir Ellis Minns Collection (palaeography)
Sir Stephen Gaselee Collection (palaeography)
William Martin Leake Collection (classical books and notebooks)

Non-library collection catalogue:
All or part available online

Library catalogue:
All or part available online

Printed publications:
Guide to the Museum of Classical Archaeology (£4)

Access to staff:
Contact by letter, by telephone and by e-mail.
Appointment necessary. Letter of introduction required.
Hours: Mon to Fri, 0900 to 1700; Sat (term time) 0900 to 1300

Access for disabled people:
Level entry, access to all public areas, toilet facilities

UNIVERSITY OF CAMBRIDGE – KANTHACK & NUTTALL LIBRARY OF THE DEPARTMENT OF PATHOLOGY

Tennis Court Road, Cambridge, CB2 1QP

Tel: 01223 333690
Fax: 01223 333346
E-mail: librarian@path.cam.ac.uk

Website:
http://www.path.cam.ac.uk/~library

Enquiries:
Enquiries to: Librarian
Direct tel: 01223 333698
Direct fax: 01223 333698
Other contacts: Library Administrator

Formerly called:
Nuttall Library

Incorporates the former:
Molteno Institute, Parasitology Library

Organisation type and purpose:
University department or institute.

Subject coverage:
Pathology; microbiology; virology; immunology; parasitology; oncology.

Non-library collection catalogue:
All or part available online and in-house

Access to staff:
Contact by letter and by telephone. Appointment necessary. Access for members only.
Hours: Mon to Fri, 0900 to 1600
Special comments: Non-members by prior arrangement.

Access for disabled people:
Ramped entry, toilet facilities

UNIVERSITY OF CAMBRIDGE – LIBRARY OF THE ASIAN AND MIDDLE EASTERN STUDIES

Formal name: University of Cambridge – Faculty of Asian and Middle Eastern Studies Library
Acronym or abbreviation: FAMES

Sidgwick Avenue, Cambridge, CB3 9DA

Tel: 01223 335111/2
Fax: 01223 335110
E-mail: library@ames.cam.ac.uk

Website:
http://www.ames.cam.ac.uk/faclib/index.html
http://www.ames.cam.ac.uk

Enquiries:
Enquiries to: Head of Library

Founded:
1935

Organisation type and purpose:
University department or institute.
Faculty library; the collection of the Middle East Centre.

Subject coverage:
Chinese, Japanese, Sanskrit, modern Indian languages, Persian, Turkish, Arabic, Hebrew; Egyptology, Assyriology, Indian history and archaeology, coverage of the language, literature, history, religion and general culture of all countries of the Middle and Far East Indian sub-continent and Central Asia (but excluding south-east Asia).

Museum or gallery collection, archive, or library special collection:
I. B. Horner Collection (paper and letters, etc.)
Israel Abrahams Collection (Rabbinics)
Lattimore Collection on Central Asia and Mongolia
Marshall Collection of Indian photographs (5,000 items on Indian monuments and antiquities)
Middle East Centre Library (modern Middle East – especially the Arabian peninsula and Yemen)
Queens' College Oriental Collection
W. Lockhart Collection (Persian)

Wheeler Collection (700 photographs of Indian archaeology)

Non-library collection catalogue:
All or part available online

Library catalogue:
All or part available online

Access to staff:
Contact by letter, by telephone, by e-mail, in person and via website. Appointment necessary.
Letter of introduction required.
Hours: Mon to Fri, 0900 to 1730

Access for disabled people:
Special comments: Appointment needed.

UNIVERSITY OF CAMBRIDGE – LIBRARY OF THE DEPARTMENT OF CHEMISTRY

Lensfield Road, Cambridge, CB2 1EW

Tel: 01223 336300
Fax: 01223 336362
E-mail: library@ch.cam.ac.uk

Website:
http://www-library.ch.cam.ac.uk

Enquiries:
Enquiries to: Librarian
Direct tel: 01223 336329
Other contacts: Deputy Librarian

Organisation type and purpose:
University department or institute.

Subject coverage:
Inorganic, organic, physical and theoretical chemistry.

Library catalogue:
All or part available online

Access to staff:
Contact by letter, by telephone, by fax, by e-mail, in person and via website. Appointment necessary.
Letter of introduction required.
Hours: Mon to Fri, 0800 to 1630

Access for disabled people:
By arrangement

UNIVERSITY OF CAMBRIDGE – LIBRARY OF THE DEPARTMENT OF EARTH SCIENCES

Downing Street, Cambridge, CB2 3EQ

Tel: 01223 333429
Fax: 01223 333450
E-mail: libraryhelp@esc.cam.ac.uk

Website:
http://www.esc.cam.ac.uk
List of publications written by department members from the beginning of 1993; database of publications is now being migrated to e-prints and contains abstracts and pdf copies with restricted access; parts of most of the collections are available through this site; links to university on-line journals.

Enquiries:
Enquiries to: Librarian

Founded:
1980

Created by the merger of:
Departments of Geology, Mineralogy & Petrology and Geodesy & Geophysics (year of change 1980)

Organisation type and purpose:
University department or institute.

Subject coverage:
Earth sciences, palaeontology, mineralogy, geophysics, mineral physics, climate change.

Museum or gallery collection, archive, or library special collection:
Black Collection
Collection of geological reprints

continued overleaf

Collection of mineralogical reprints
Godwin Collection
Extensive geological map collection
W A Dear Collection
Bullard Collection
R G West Collection
Sedgwick Collection
Bulman Collection
Harker Collection
N F Hughes Collection
Macfadyen Collection
Tilley Collection
Whittington Collection
Collection of geophysics offprints

Non-library collection catalogue:
All or part available online and in-house

Library catalogue:
All or part available online

Printed publications:
Annual Report, which includes a bibliography of
    work published by members of the department

Publications list:
Available online

Access to staff:
Contact by letter, by telephone, by fax, by e-mail,
in person and via website. Letter of introduction
required.
Hours: Term time: Mon to Fri, 0900 to 1800; Sat,
1000 to 1300
Vacations: Mon to Fri, 0900 to 1700; Sat, closed
Bullard Laboratory Library is staffed for a couple
of hours on Mon, Wed and Fri

Access to building, collection or gallery:
Access to Bullard is only ever by prior
arrangement

Also at:
Bullard Laboratory Library
    Madingley Road, Cambridge; e-mail:
    libraryhelp@esc.cam.ac.uk

UNIVERSITY OF CAMBRIDGE – LIBRARY OF THE DEPARTMENT OF GENETICS

Downing Street, Cambridge, CB2 3EH

Tel: 01223 333973
Fax: 01223 333992
E-mail: library@gen.cam.ac.uk (preferred means of
contact)

Website:
http://www.gen.cam.ac.uk/department/library/
index.html

Enquiries:
Enquiries to: Librarian

Organisation type and purpose:
University department or institute.

Subject coverage:
Genetics; cytology; parts of biochemistry, cell
biology.

**Museum or gallery collection, archive, or library
special collection:**
Offprints of papers by past department members
    and eminent geneticists

Non-library collection catalogue:
All or part available in-house

Library catalogue:
All or part available online

Access to staff:
Contact by letter, by telephone, by fax and by e-
mail. Appointment necessary.
Hours: Mon to Fri, 0900 to 1700

Access to building, collection or gallery:
Must be let in by receptionist
Hours: Mon to Fri, 0900 to 1700, excluding
lunchtimes

Access for disabled people:
Wheelchair lift and push-button for doors
Hours: as above
Special comments: Some parts of library inaccessible.

UNIVERSITY OF CAMBRIDGE – LIBRARY OF THE DEPARTMENT OF PHYSIOLOGY, DEVELOPMENT AND NEUROSCIENCE

Acronym or abbreviation: PDN Library

Downing Street, Cambridge, CB2 3EG

Tel: 01223 333899
Fax: 01223 333840
E-mail: library@pdn.cam.ac.uk

Website:
http://www.pdn.cam.ac.uk/library

Enquiries:
Enquiries to: Librarian
Direct tel: 01223 333821

Created by the merger of:
School of Anatomy Library and Department of
Physiology Library (year of change 2006)

Organisation type and purpose:
University department or institute.

Subject coverage:
Physiology, human and veterinary anatomy,
embryology, developmental biology, neurobiology.

**Museum or gallery collection, archive, or library
special collection:**
Boyd histological collection (slides), embryological
    collection, compiled by Professor J. D. Boyd
History of physiology

Non-library collection catalogue:
All or part available in-house

Library catalogue:
All or part available online, in-house and in print

Access to staff:
Contact by letter, by telephone, by fax and by e-
mail. Appointment necessary. Letter of
introduction required.
Hours: Mon to Fri, 0900 to 1230 and 1400 to 1700
Special comments: Advanced notice required for
consultations.

Access to building, collection or gallery:
Prior appointment required
Hours: Mon to Fri, 0900 to 1230 and 1330 to 1700
Special comments: Prior appointment required for
Library and Collections.

Access for disabled people:
Fully accessible

UNIVERSITY OF CAMBRIDGE – LIBRARY OF THE DEPARTMENT OF PLANT SCIENCES

Downing Street, Cambridge, CB2 3EA

Tel: 01223 333900
Fax: 01223 333953
E-mail: library@plantsci.cam.ac.uk

Enquiries:
Enquiries to: Librarian
Direct tel: 01223 333930

Formerly called:
Botany School, University of Cambridge

Organisation type and purpose:
University department or institute.

Subject coverage:
All aspects of plant sciences: genetics,
biochemistry, physiology, ecology and taxonomy,
excluding agriculture and forestry, but including
quaternary vegetation.

**Museum or gallery collection, archive, or library
special collection:**
Early herbals
Simpson Collection of local floras

Access to staff:
Contact by letter, by telephone, by fax and by e-
mail. Appointment necessary.
Hours: Mon to Fri, 0900 to 1700

UNIVERSITY OF CAMBRIDGE – LIBRARY OF THE DEPARTMENT OF VETERINARY MEDICINE

Madingley Road, Cambridge, CB3 0ES

Tel: 01223 337600
Fax: 01223 337610

Website:
http://www.vet.cam.ac.uk

Enquiries:
Enquiries to: Librarian
Direct tel: 01223 337633
Direct e-mail: lel1000@hermes.cam.ac.uk

Founded:
1955

Organisation type and purpose:
University department or institute.

Subject coverage:
Veterinary medicine.

**Museum or gallery collection, archive, or library
special collection:**
Rare book collection

Library catalogue:
All or part available online

Printed publications:
Library Users Guide (free)
List of new accessions (quarterly, free)

Access to staff:
Contact by letter, by telephone, by fax and by e-
mail. Appointment necessary.
Hours: Mon to Fri, 0900 to 0430

Access to building, collection or gallery:
Special comments: Card access only

UNIVERSITY OF CAMBRIDGE – LIBRARY OF THE EXPERIMENTAL PSYCHOLOGY LABORATORY

Downing Street, Cambridge, CB2 3EB

Tel: 01223 333554
Fax: 01223 333564
E-mail: library@psychol.cam.ac.uk

Enquiries:
Enquiries to: Librarian

Organisation type and purpose:
University department or institute.
Teaching and research unit of the University of
Cambridge.

Subject coverage:
Experimental psychology and psychopathology.

**Museum or gallery collection, archive, or library
special collection:**
McCurdy Psychopathology Library (1900-, about
    1000 books)
Oldfield Collection (material on vision, 1900–1940,
    about 100 books)

Access to staff:
Appointment necessary.
Hours: Mon to Fri, 0930 to 1700 during full term
Special comments: Please telephone for an
appointment outside full term.

UNIVERSITY OF CAMBRIDGE – LIBRARY OF THE FACULTY OF ARCHITECTURE AND HISTORY OF ART

1 Scroope Terrace, Trumpington Street,
Cambridge, CB2 1PX

Tel: 01223 332953
Fax: 01223 332960

E-mail: mb151@cam.ac.uk

Website:
http://www.arct.cam.ac.uk/library.html
Library guide and catalogue

Enquiries:
Enquiries to: Librarian

Organisation type and purpose:
University department or institute.

Subject coverage:
Architecture; history of art; architecture and design.

Museum or gallery collection, archive, or library special collection:
16th–19th-century architectural special collection
19th- and 20th-century architectural periodicals, mainly European

Library catalogue:
All or part available online

Access to staff:
Contact by letter
Hours: Term time: 0915 to 1730
Vacation: opening hours vary, but usually 0930 to 1230 and 1430 to 1730

UNIVERSITY OF CAMBRIDGE – LIBRARY OF THE FACULTY OF DIVINITY

West Road, Cambridge, CB3 9BS

Tel: 01223 763040
Fax: 01223 763003
E-mail: library@divinity.cam.ac.uk

Website:
http://www.divinity.cam.ac.uk/library.html
http://www.lib.cam.ac.uk/newton
Catalogue

Enquiries:
Enquiries to: Librarian

Founded:
1879

Organisation type and purpose:
University department or institute.

Subject coverage:
Theology, ecclesiastical history, biblical studies, Judaism, Islam, Hinduism, Buddhism, ethics, philosophy of religion, psychology of religion, sociology of religion, science and religion, patristics, liturgy.

Museum or gallery collection, archive, or library special collection:
Feltoe Bequest (liturgy)
Lightfoot Bequest (library of Bishop J. B. Lightfoot 1828–89)

Non-library collection catalogue:
All or part available online

Library catalogue:
All or part available online

Access to staff:
Contact by letter and by e-mail. Appointment necessary. Access for members only.
Hours: Term time: Mon to Fri, 0900 to 1700
Vacations: Mon to Fri, 0900 to 1255 and 1400 to 1630

Access to building, collection or gallery:
Prior appointment required

Access for disabled people:
Access to all public areas

UNIVERSITY OF CAMBRIDGE – MILL LANE LIBRARY OF THE DEPARTMENT OF LAND ECONOMY

Acronym or abbreviation: DLE

8 Mill Lane, Cambridge, CB2 1RX

Tel: 01223 337110

Fax: 01223 337130
E-mail: wt10000@cus.cam.ac.uk

Website:
http://www.landecon.cam.ac.uk/library/library.htm
http://www.landecon.cam.ac.uk
http://www.lib.cam.ac.uk/catalogues/opac/union.shtml
Catalogue.

Enquiries:
Enquiries to: Librarian
Direct e-mail: wt10000@cam.ac.uk

Founded:
1950

Organisation type and purpose:
University department or institute.

Subject coverage:
Agriculture economics, architecture, environmental policy and law, forestry, housing, land economics, land law, land tenure, land values, regional economics, rural development, town and country planning.

Non-library collection catalogue:
All or part available online

Library catalogue:
All or part available online

Printed publications:
Handbook of the Department
Research and Publications (annually)

Publications list:
Available in print

Access to staff:
Contact by letter, by telephone, by e-mail, in person and via website
Hours: Mon to Fri, 0900 to 1700
Special comments: No disabled access.

UNIVERSITY OF CAMBRIDGE – MODERN AND MEDIEVAL LANGUAGES LIBRARY

Acronym or abbreviation: MML Library

Sidgwick Avenue, Cambridge, CB3 9DA

Tel: 01223 335041
Fax: 01223 335062
E-mail: mmllib@hermes.cam.ac.uk

Website:
http://www.mml.cam.ac.uk/library

Enquiries:
Enquiries to: Librarian
Direct tel: 01223 335047
Direct e-mail: aec25@cam.ac.uk

Organisation type and purpose:
University department or institute.

Subject coverage:
Most Continental European languages and literatures (no Greek); Germanic, Romance and Slavonic groups; linguistics, cinema, literary theory; DVDs and videos.

Museum or gallery collection, archive, or library special collection:
Beit Library (German research material)

Library catalogue:
All or part available online

Printed publications:
Annual Report
Readers' Guide

Access to staff:
Contact by letter, by telephone, by fax, by e-mail and in person
Hours: Term time: Mon to Fri, 0900 to 1900; Sat, 1000 to 1600
Vacations: Mon to Fri, 0900 to 1700

Access to building, collection or gallery:
Hours: Term time: Mon to Fri, 0900 to 1900; Sat, 1000 to 1600
Vacations: Mon to Fri, 0900 to 1700

UNIVERSITY OF CAMBRIDGE – RAYLEIGH LIBRARY OF THE DEPARTMENT OF PHYSICS

J.J. Thomson Avenue, Cambridge, CB3 0HE

Tel: 01223 337414
E-mail: librarian@phy.cam.ac.uk

Website:
http://www.phy.cam.ac.uk/library

Enquiries:
Enquiries to: Librarian

Organisation type and purpose:
University department or institute.
Departmental library.

Subject coverage:
Physics, meteorology.

Museum or gallery collection, archive, or library special collection:
Maxwell Collection
Napier Shaw Meteorology Library (books and periodicals)
Rayleigh Library (books and periodicals)
History of science

Non-library collection catalogue:
All or part available in-house

Library catalogue:
All or part available online

Access to staff:
Contact by letter, by telephone, by e-mail, in person and via website. Appointment necessary.
Hours: Mon to Fri, 0900 to 1700

Access for disabled people:
Parking provided

UNIVERSITY OF CAMBRIDGE – SQUIRE LAW LIBRARY

10 West Road, Cambridge, CB3 9DZ

Tel: 01223 330077
Fax: 01223 330057
E-mail: dfw1003@cus.cam.ac.uk

Website:
http://www.lib.cam.ac.uk

Enquiries:
Enquiries to: Librarian
Other contacts: Deputy Librarian

Founded:
1904

Organisation type and purpose:
University library.

Subject coverage:
English, Scottish and Irish Law; legal history; Roman law; US law; comparative law; international law; Commonwealth law.

Museum or gallery collection, archive, or library special collection:
Commonwealth Law Reform Commissions
International Law Treaty Series
Nominate Reports, pre-1800 Law Books and Manuscripts

Library catalogue:
All or part available online

Printed publications:
Guides to the Library and its Collections (Commonwealth, European Communities, International, American) are available in the Library

Access to staff:
Contact by letter, by telephone, by e-mail and via website. Letter of introduction required.
Hours: Mon to Fri, 0900 to 1700

Access for disabled people:
Toilet facilities

Part of:
Cambridge University Library

UNIVERSITY OF CAMBRIDGE – THE MARSHALL LIBRARY OF ECONOMICS

Sidgwick Avenue, Cambridge, CB3 9DB

Tel: 01223 335217
Fax: 01223 335475
E-mail: marshlib@econ.cam.ac.uk

Website:
http://www.econ.cam.ac.uk/marshlib

Enquiries:
Enquiries to: Librarian
Direct tel: 01223 335215

Organisation type and purpose:
University department or institute, research organisation.
Research library.

Subject coverage:
Economics, statistics.

Non-library collection catalogue:
All or part available online and in-house

Printed publications:
Monograph Series and Occasional Papers (pub. CUP)
Working papers

Access to staff:
Contact by letter, by telephone, by fax, by e-mail and in person
Hours: Mon to Fri, 0900 to 1700

Access for disabled people:
Access to all public areas, toilet facilities

UNIVERSITY OF CAMBRIDGE – WHIPPLE LIBRARY OF THE DEPARTMENT OF HISTORY AND PHILOSOPHY OF SCIENCE

Free School Lane, Cambridge, CB2 3RH

Tel: 01223 334547
Fax: 01223 334554
E-mail: hpslib@hermes.cam.ac.uk

Website:
http://www.hps.cam.ac.uk/library/Fpage.html

Enquiries:
Enquiries to: Librarian
Direct e-mail: tje25@cam.ac.uk

Founded:
1944

Organisation type and purpose:
University department or institute.
Departmental library attached to the Department of History and Philosophy of Science.

Subject coverage:
History and philosophy of science and of medicine, scientific instruments and instrument makers.

Museum or gallery collection, archive, or library special collection:
Phrenology Collection
Scientific works of 16th–19th centuries
Works of Robert Boyle
Foster Pamphlet Collection (physiology)

Library catalogue:
All or part available online

Access to staff:
Appointment necessary.
Hours: Term time: 0930 to 1730
Vacations: 0930 to 1700

Access for disabled people:
Lift, Library on 1st floor, please telephone or e-mail in advance of visit
Special comments: lift, Library on 1st floor, please telephone or e-mail in advance of your visit

UNIVERSITY OF CENTRAL LANCASHIRE

Acronym or abbreviation: LIS

Learning and Information Services, Preston. Lancashire, PR1 2HE

Tel: 01772 892261
Fax: 01772 892937
E-mail: mahern@uclan.ac.uk

Website:
http://www.uclan.ac.uk/information/services/lis/index.php
Library mission statement, opening hours, services, staff names, subject specialist information, FAQs.

Enquiries:
Enquiries to: Director of Learning and Information Services
Other contacts: Head of Library Services

Organisation type and purpose:
University library, suitable for ages: 18+.

Subject coverage:
Social sciences; nursing and midwifery; education; humanities; accountancy; business; management; astronomy; biology; chemistry; mathematics; physics; computing science; electrical and electronic engineering; mechanical engineering; production engineering; construction and urban studies.

Museum or gallery collection, archive, or library special collection:
Illustrated Books Collection
Joseph Livesey Collection (temperance)
Local history collections
Preston Incorporated Law Society Library

Non-library collection catalogue:
All or part available online

Library catalogue:
All or part available online

Printed publications:
Miscellaneous library subject guides and IT guides

Access to staff:
Contact by letter, by telephone, by fax, by e-mail and via website. Appointment necessary. Non-members charged.
Hours: Term time: Mon to Thu, 0830 to 2300; Fri, 0830 to 2000; Sat, Sun, 1000 to 1800
Vacations: Mon, Wed, Fri, 0845 to 1700; Tue, Thu, 0845 to 2000; Sat, 1200 to 1800

Access to building, collection or gallery:
Prior appointment required
Special comments: Access to non-members by prior arrangement in writing and to Lancashire County Library members via library card.

Access for disabled people:
Ramped entry, access to all public areas

UNIVERSITY OF CHESTER

Parkgate Road, Chester, Cheshire, CH1 4BJ

Tel: 01244 511000 (University); 511234 (Learning and information services)
Fax: 01244 511300 (University); 511325 (Learning and information service
E-mail: lis.helpdesk@chester.ac.uk

Website:
http://www.chester.ac.uk/lr
Details of learning resources, including library services, catalogue access.

Enquiries:
Enquiries to: Customer Services Manager

Founded:
1839

Formerly called:
Chester College of Higher Education (year of change 2003); University College Chester (year of change 2005)

Organisation type and purpose:
University library.

Subject coverage:
Art, education, biological science, business and management, computing, criminology, drama, English literature, history, geography, languages, mathematics, nursing and midwifery, social work, sports science, religious studies, psychology, journalism, media and communications, law, graphic design, nutrition and dietetics.

Information services:
Helpdesk and reference services.

Services for disabled people:
Adjustable tables, specialist software.

Museum or gallery collection, archive, or library special collection:
310,000-vol. academic library

Non-library collection catalogue:
All or part available online

Library catalogue:
All or part available online and in-house

Electronic and video publications:
DVDs, videos

Access to staff:
Contact by letter, by telephone, by e-mail and in person
Hours: Term time: Mon to Thu, 0830 to 2100; Fri, 0830 to 2000; Sat, Sun, 1200 to 1800
Vacations: Mon, Tue, Thu, Fri, 0900 to 1730; Wed, 0900 to 2000

Access for disabled people:
Ramped entry, toilet facilities, lift

UNIVERSITY OF CHICHESTER LIBRARY

Acronym or abbreviation: UoC

Bishop Otter Campus, College Lane, Chichester, West Sussex, PO19 6PE

Tel: 01243 816089
Fax: 01243 816096

Website:
http://www.chi.ac.uk/info/lrc.cfm

Enquiries:
Enquiries to: Head of Library Services
Direct tel: 01243 816090
Direct e-mail: s.robertson@chi.ac.uk

Founded:
1977

Created by the merger of:
Bishop Otter College and Bognor Regis College (year of change 1977)

Formerly called:
West Sussex Institute of Higher Education (year of change 1995); Chichester Institute of Higher Education (year of change 1999); University College Chichester (year of change 2005)

Organisation type and purpose:
University library.

Subject coverage:
History, English, theology, media studies, fine art, music, dance, performing arts, childhood and youth studies, counselling, social work, sport studies, sport science, sport therapy, physical education, adventure education, management, education, business studies, applied language studies.

Museum or gallery collection, archive, or library special collection:
Otter Gallery
Bishop Otter art collection
Chichester Theological Collection
Professor J Dunn collection
Ted Walker Archive
Dance Videos
Children's Resources (Bognor)
Gerard Young Collection (Bognor local history) (Bognor)
Bishop Kemp Collection (Bognor)
John Fines Collection (Bognor)

Trade and statistical information:
Social and health statistics.

Library catalogue:
All or part available online

Access to staff:
Contact by letter, by telephone, by fax, by e-mail, in person and via website. Appointment necessary.
Hours: Term time: Mon to Thu, 0845 to 2145; Fri, 0845 to 1700; Sat, Sun, 1000 to 1700
Vacation: Mon to Fri, 0900 to 1700

Access to building, collection or gallery:
No prior appointment required
Hours: Term time: Mon to Thu, 0845 to 2145; Fri, 0845 to 1700; Sat, Sun, 1000 to 1700
Vacation: Mon to Fri, 0900 to 1700
Special comments: Half-hour only parking, 0800 to 1700

Access for disabled people:
Parking provided, ramped entry, level entry, lift, access to all public areas, toilet facilities

Branch libraries:
Bognor Regis Campus Library
   Upper Bognor Road, Bognor Regis, West Sussex, PO21 1HR; tel: 01243 812099; fax: 01243 812081

UNIVERSITY OF CUMBRIA

Learning and Information Services, Harold Bridges Library, University of Cumbria, Bowerham Road, Lancaster, LA1 3JD

Tel: 01524 384243
Fax: 01524 384588

Website:
http://www.cumbria.ac.uk/services/lis/home.aspx

Enquiries:
Enquiries to: Head of Learning and Information Services
Direct tel: 01524 384238
Other contacts: Site Library Managers for Ambleside, Carlisle Fusehill Street, Lancaster; Campus Library Managers for Carlisle Brampton Road, Newton Rigg Libraries

Founded:
1964

Created by the merger of:
St Martin's College, Cumbria Institute of the Arts, Cumbria campuses of University of Central Lancashire (year of change 2007)

Formerly called:
University College of St Martin, Lancaster (year of change 1998)

Incorporates the former:
Charlotte Mason College, Ambleside (year of change 1996)

Organisation type and purpose:
Multi-site university library.

Subject coverage:
Education, humanities, health studies, management, nursing, radiography, occupational therapy and midwifery, social studies, outdoor studies

Museum or gallery collection, archive, or library special collection:
Large collection of children's books, and teaching and learning materials
Local studies collection (Lancashire, Cumbria and Yorkshire)
Religious and moral studies collection.

Non-library collection catalogue:
All or part available online

Library catalogue:
All or part available online

Access to staff:
Contact by telephone, by fax, by e-mail and in person
Hours: Mon to Fri, 0900 to 1700

Access to building, collection or gallery:
No prior appointment required

Access for disabled people:
Parking provided, ramped entry, access to all public areas, toilet facilities

Also at:
The Library, University of Cumbria
   Fusehill Street, Carlisle, CA1 2HH; tel: 01228 616218; fax: 01228 616263; e-mail: libcarfs@ cumbria.ac.uk
The Library, University of Cumbria
   Rydal Road, Ambleside, Cumbria, LA22 9BB; tel: 015314 30274; fax: 015394 30371; e-mail: libamb@ cumbria.ac.uk
The Library, University of Cumbria
   Newton Rigg, Penrith, Cumbria, CA11 0AH; tel: 01768 893503; fax: 01768 893506; e-mail: libpen@ cumbria.ac.uk
The Library, University of Cumbria
   Brampton Road, Carlisle, Cumbria, CA3 9AY; tel: 01228 400312; fax: 01228 514491; e-mail: libcarbr@cumbria.ac.uk

Associated health-related libraries in:
Westmoreland and Cumbria

Funded by:
Health Authorities
HEFCE
TTA

UNIVERSITY OF DUNDEE – LIBRARY

Small's Wynd, Dundee, DD1 4HN

Tel: 01382 344087
Fax: 01382 229190
E-mail: library@dundee.ac.uk

Website:
http://www.dundee.ac.uk/library/
Library catalogue, library services, library tour, bibliographic and related resources.

Enquiries:
Enquiries to: Librarian
Direct tel: 01382 344082
Direct e-mail: j.m.bagnall@dundee.ac.uk

Organisation type and purpose:
University library.

Subject coverage:
Arts, art and design, social sciences, education, environmental studies, law, medicine, dentistry, nursing, science, engineering and applied science including architecture.

Museum or gallery collection, archive, or library special collection:
Brechin Diocesan Library
Joan Auld Memorial Collection
Kinnear Allan Ramsay Collection
Kinnear Local Collection
Leng Collection (Scottish philosophical writers)
Nicoll Collection (books on the fine arts)
Thoms mineralogical collection
William Lyon Mackenzie Collection (Canadiana)

Printed publications:
Catalogue of Allan Ramsay Collection (1990)
Guides to Library Services
University Education in Dundee, 1881–1981: a pictorial history (1982, £3.50)

Microform publications:
University theses on request subject to copyright restrictions

Access to staff:
Contact by letter, by telephone, by fax and by e-mail
Hours: Mon to Fri, 0900 to 1700

UNIVERSITY OF DUNDEE – NINEWELLS LIBRARY

Ninewells Hospital and Medical School, Dundee, DD1 9SY

Tel: 01382 632519
Fax: 01382 566179
E-mail: ninewells-library@dundee.ac.uk

Website:
http://www.dundee.ac.uk/library
Library pages including access to catalogue.

Organisation type and purpose:
University library.

Subject coverage:
Medicine and nursing.

Library catalogue:
All or part available online

Access to staff:
Contact by letter, by telephone, by e-mail, in person and via website
Hours: Mon to Fri, 0845 to 2200; Sat, 1200 to 1700
Closed over Christmas vacation

Access to building, collection or gallery:
No prior appointment required

UNIVERSITY OF EAST ANGLIA

Formal name: School of International Development
Acronym or abbreviation: DEV

University of East Anglia, Norwich, Norfolk, NR4 7TJ

Tel: 01603 591472
Fax: 01603 451999
E-mail: dev.general@uea.ac.uk

Website:
http://www.uea.ac.uk/dev/co
Details of consultancy activities, research experience and training courses.
http://www.uea.ac.uk/dev/publications
Publications Link – faculty publications since 1996; commercially published books, articles in academic journals, some work is available to download from the website.
http://www.uea.ac.uk/dev
Details of School, faculty information, research, publications, courses available, application forms.

Enquiries:
Enquiries to: Local Office Administrator
Other contacts: PA to Head of School

Founded:
1973

Formerly called:
School of Development Studies (year of change 2009)

Organisation type and purpose:
University department affiliated to the School of International Development, consultancy and research organisation.
Teaching, research and consultancy in international development.

Subject coverage:
Research addresses contemporary challenges in developing and transition economies via disciplinary and multi/interdisciplinary approaches in the following groups: Ageing and development; Behavioural and experimental development economics; Business, accountability, regulation and development; Climate change and development; Educational diversity, literacy & development; Global environmental justice; Health policy and practice; Land resources; Social identities, institutions and justice; Social protection and mobile livelihoods.
Consultancy services in: Gender and social development; Literacy and development; Globalisation and transition; Livelihoods and well-being; Natural resources and environment and climate change; Health and HIV and AIDS.
Training courses include: Climate change and development; Gender and development; Gender and internal organisational change; Management information systems for M&E; Monitoring and evaluation for development activities; Water security for policy makers and practitioners.

Printed publications:
Development (annual newsletter), prospectuses and brochures

continued overleaf

Publications list:
Available online

Access to staff:
Contact by letter, by telephone, by fax, by e-mail and via website. Appointment necessary.
Hours: Mon to Fri, 0900 to 1700

Access to building, collection or gallery:
Hours: Mon to Fri, 0900 to 1700

Access for disabled people:
Ramped entry
Hours: Mon to Fri, 0900 to 1700

Attached consultancy group:
International Development, University of East Anglia
   University of East Anglia, Norwich, Norfolk, NR4 7TJ UK; tel: 0603 592813; fax: 01603 591170; e-mail: devco.gen@uea.ac.uk

UNIVERSITY OF EAST ANGLIA – LIBRARY

Acronym or abbreviation: UEA Library

University of East Anglia, Norwich, Norfolk, NR4 7TJ

Tel: 01603 592993
Fax: 01603 591010
E-mail: lib.helpdesk@uea.ac.uk

Website:
http://www.uea.ac.uk/is/lib

Enquiries:
Enquiries to: Head of User Services
Direct tel: 01603 593440
Direct e-mail: heather.wells@uea.ac.uk

Founded:
1963

Organisation type and purpose:
University library.

Subject coverage:
Social sciences and the humanities; history; law; education; development studies; biological, chemical, environmental, mathematical, physical and computing sciences; accounting; management; information systems; health sciences; film studies; medicine; pharmacy.

Special visitor services:
See: http://www.uea.ac.uk/is/borrowing/externalusers.

Museum or gallery collection, archive, or library special collection:
Abbott Collection (English literature)
Anthony Grey Archive
Archives of Modern Writing and Literary Translation
Doris Lessing Archive
European Documentation Centre (Selective)
Everest Collection
Fisher Theatre, Bungay
G.S. Callendar Archive
H.H. Lamb Archive
Hill Papers
Holloway Collection of Contemporary Culture Records
Illustrated Books
Kenney Papers
Ketton-Cremer Collection (local history)
Lorna Sage Archive
Peterborough Literary Society
Pevsner Art Catalogue Collection
Pritchard Archive
Roger Deakin Archive
Theatre Quarterly Archive
Tinkler and Williams' Theatre Collection
Zuckerman Archive

Non-library collection catalogue:
All or part available online

Library catalogue:
All or part available online

Access to staff:
Contact by letter, by telephone, by fax, by e-mail, in person and via website

Hours: Mon to Fri, 0900 to 1700
Special comments: Reference-only to non-registered borrowers.

Access for disabled people:
Level entry, access to all public areas, toilet facilities

Links with:
Centre for Environment, Fisheries and Agriculture Sciences (CEFAS)
   Lowestoft
East Anglian Film Archive
Institute of Food Research (Norwich)
John Innes Centre
Norfolk and Norwich University Hospital
Norwich University College of the Arts
   Norwich, Norfolk
Otley College
   Ipswich
Suffolk New College
   Ipswich
University Campus Suffolk
West Suffolk College

Member organisation of:
ANGLES (formerly NINES)

UNIVERSITY OF EAST ANGLIA – SCHOOL OF ENVIRONMENTAL SCIENCES

Acronym or abbreviation: ENV, UEA

University Plain, Norwich, Norfolk, NR4 7TJ

Tel: 01603 592994
Fax: 01603 593035
E-mail: j.darch@uea.ac.uk

Website:
http://www.uea.ac.uk/env/

Enquiries:
Enquiries to: Research Administrator

Organisation type and purpose:
University department or institute.

Subject coverage:
Environmental sciences, atmospheric chemistry, climatic change, climatic modelling, wind energy, ecology, geophysics, oceanography, health, planning, risk assessment, cost-benefit analysis, environmental assessment and appraisal, geology, geomorphology, quaternary period, global environmental change, air-sea interactions, GIS, waste management, hydrology and hydrogeology, estuaries, soils and land use planning.

Printed publications:
Annual Report
CERM working papers
Climatic Research Unit Research Publications (occasional)
Centre for Social and Economic Research on the Global Environment (CSERGE) (working papers)

Electronic and video publications:
Climatic Monitor (online)
Various items available online or CD-ROM, for purchase

Publications list:
Available online and in print

Access to staff:
Contact by letter, by fax, by e-mail and via website. Appointment necessary.
Hours: Mon to Fri, 0900 to 1700

Includes the:
Centre for Environmental Risk
   tel: 01603 593129; fax: 01603 507719; e-mail: n.pidgeon@uea.ac.uk
Centre for Social and Economic Research on the Global Environment (CSERGE)
   tel: 01603 592551; fax: 01603 250588; e-mail: n.k.turner@uea.ac.uk
Climatic Research Unit
   tel: 01603 593647; fax: 01603 507784; e-mail: j.palativiof@uea.ac.uk
Tyndall Centre for Climate Change

UNIVERSITY OF EAST LONDON – DOCKLANDS LIBRARY AND LEARNING CENTRE

Acronym or abbreviation: UEL

University Way, London, E16 2RD

Tel: 020 8223 3434
Fax: 020 8223 7497
E-mail: j.a.preece@uel.ac.uk

Website:
http://www.uel.ac.uk

Enquiries:
Enquiries to: Manager

Founded:
1999

Organisation type and purpose:
University library.

Subject coverage:
Art and architecture, social sciences, cultural studies, business studies, computing and engineering.

Museum or gallery collection, archive, or library special collection:
Refugee Archive
British Olympic Archive
Diversity Art Forum

Library catalogue:
All or part available online

Access to staff:
Contact by telephone, by e-mail and via website
Hours: Mon to Fri, 0900 to 1700

Access to building, collection or gallery:
Prior appointment required
Special comments: No prior appointment required for students and staff of UEL and SCONUL Access scheme card holders.
All other visitors must make advance application.

Access for disabled people:
Parking provided, ramped entry, level entry, access to all public areas, toilet facilities

UNIVERSITY OF EAST LONDON – STRATFORD LEARNING RESOURCE CENTRE

Acronym or abbreviation: UEL

Holbrook Annexe, Holbrook Road, Stratford, London, E15 3EA

Tel: 020 8223 3251
Fax: 020 8223 3296

Website:
http://www.uel.ac.uk/library

Enquiries:
Enquiries to: Manager
Direct e-mail: s.p.lyes@uel.ac.uk

Organisation type and purpose:
University library.

Subject coverage:
Architecture, building, planning.

Museum or gallery collection, archive, or library special collection:
Collection of architectural slides
Collection on architecture (RIBA trade literature)

Library catalogue:
All or part available online

Access to staff:
Contact by letter, by telephone, by e-mail and via website. Appointment necessary.
Hours: Mon to Thu, 0900 to 1900; Fri, 0900 to 1700
Vacations have varying opening hours

Access to building, collection or gallery:
Prior appointment required

Access for disabled people:
Level entry

UNIVERSITY OF EDINBURGH – CENTRE FOR EDUCATIONAL SOCIOLOGY

Acronym or abbreviation: CES

St John's Land, Holyrood Road, Edinburgh, EH8 8AQ

Tel: 0131 651 6238
Fax: 0131 651 6239
E-mail: ces@ed.ac.uk

Website:
http://www.ces.ed.ac.uk
Information about the Centre, personnel, projects and publications.

Enquiries:
Enquiries to: Administrator
Direct tel: 0131 651 6238
Direct e-mail: ces@ed.ac.uk

Founded:
1972

Organisation type and purpose:
University department or institute, research organisation.

Subject coverage:
Education, training, youth labour market, transitions to adulthood, information systems.

Library catalogue:
All or part available in-house

Publications list:
Available online and in print

Access to staff:
Contact by letter, by telephone, by fax, by e-mail, in person and via website. Appointment necessary.
Hours: Mon to Fri, 0900 to 1700

Access for disabled people:
Access to all public areas, toilet facilities

UNIVERSITY OF EDINBURGH – UNIVERSITY LIBRARY

Acronym or abbreviation: EUL

Main Library, George Square, Edinburgh, EH8 9LJ

Tel: 0131 650 3409
Fax: 0131 651 5041
E-mail: is.helpdesk@ed.ac.uk

Website:
http://www.ed.ac.uk/is/library-museum-gallery
Library, museum and gallery services: using the library; finding resources; library help; Centre for Research Collections; museums and galleries.
http://www.ed.ac.uk/is
Information services home page: information about library, museums and galleries, computing, learning technology, and research support.

Enquiries:
Enquiries to: Director of Library & Collections
Direct tel: 0131 650 3381 (administration); 0131 650 8379 (Centre for Research Collections – CRC)
Direct fax: 0131 650 4978, administration (0131 650 2922 – CRC)
Other contacts: Director of University Collections, e-mail: john.scally@ed.ac.uk; Director of User Services, e-mail bryan.macgregor@ed.ac.uk

Founded:
1580

Organisation type and purpose:
University library.
The books acquired by the Library between its foundation in 1580 and the publication of its 3-volume printed catalogue in 1918–23, especially during the period 1710–1837 when it was a library of copyright deposit, now represent a significant historical research resource in most branches of the humanities, especially on the history of Scotland and the United Kingdom, European history and literature, and the Commonwealth and British expansion overseas. The Library also has significant collections of early printed books, and mediaeval and modern Western and Oriental manuscripts. It is a European Documentation Centre, and this facility is focused on the Law and Europa Library.

Subject coverage:
The Library serves the needs of the 3 University Colleges and Schools within them: College of Humanities and Social Science; College of Medicine and Veterinary Medicine; College of Science and Engineering. It holds general academic collections in all these fields as well as in-depth collections in many of them.
Astronomy (Royal Observatory), botany (Darwin Library), chemistry (Darwin Library), engineering and geology (Robertson Engineering and Science Library), forestry (Darwin Library), genetics (Darwin Library), mathematics, computer science and physics (James Clerk Maxwell Library), zoology (Darwin Library).
Medicine and medical sciences, dentistry, psychiatry, community medicine (Main Library).
European Union, German public law and political organisation (Law and Europa Library).
Scottish ethnology, folklore, folk tales, oral traditions, customs and belief, literature, dialectology, material culture, ethnomusicology, song, place-names, social history and organisation, urban ethnology, ethnology of religion, emigrant traditions (Scottish Studies Library).
Christianity and Church history, biblical studies, theology, patristics, Church missions, non-Christian religions in relation to Christianity (New College Library), education, psychology, English language teaching, physical education, movement, leisure studies, sports science and recreational management (Moray House Library), veterinary anatomy, biochemistry, medicine, parasitology, pathology, pharmacology, physiology; animal health and reproduction (Royal (Dick) School of Veterinary Studies Library).

Museum or gallery collection, archive, or library special collection:
Size of collections: the Library holds over 3,400,000 printed volumes and pamphlets, as well as many manuscripts and archives of international importance; largest university library in Scotland; its electronic data, including full-text journals and other resources which are now core to its collections, are accessible across the University network and increasingly off-campus
Named special collections, with year of acquisition, include:
Lord Abercromby, 1924 (archaeology, ethnology, linguistics)
Auden, 1982 (W H Auden and associated writers of the 1930s)
John Stuart Blackie, 1895 (Greek)
Blondal, 1950 (Icelandic studies)
Bruce, 1921 (oceanography and Polar studies)
Cameron, 1889 (Celtic studies and theology)
Hugh Cleghorn, 1895 (Indian forestry, land use and botany)
Compton, 1997 (American history)
Corson, 1989 (Sir Walter Scott)
Cumming, 1939 (Italian studies)
William Drummond of Hawthornden, 1620–30 (English, Latin, Italian, French and Spanish literature)
East Asian Studies
Will Foret Archive (Scottish studies)
Geikie, 1915 (geology)
Halliwell-Phillipps, 1866, 1872 (Shakespeare, 17th- and 18th-century English drama)
W B Hodgson, 1880 (economics)
Jameson Collection (mineralogy)
Berriedale Keith, 1944 (Indian literature, history and politics and the constitutional history of the British Commonwealth)
Kennedy-Fraser, c. 1950 (Scottish music, dance, history and literature)
Arthur Koestler, 1985 (literature)
David Laing, 1878 (3,000 Scottish charters, mediaeval and modern manuscripts on Scottish history and literature, early Scottish music texts, and letters of artists)
Kenneth Leighton Manuscripts (music)
John Levy archive (oriental music) (Scottish Studies)
Clement Littill, 1580 (theology)
Lyell Collection (geology)
Mackinnon, 1924 (Celtic studies and theology)
Sir John Murray, 1921 (zoology, geography, geology)
James Nairn, 1678 (theology, philosophy, history and literature)
Penguin Books 1935–1985
Adam Smith, 18th century (literature, classics, political economy, science)
Serjeant, 1996 (Middle East)
Dugald Stewart, 18th–19th centuries (political economy, moral philosophy, mathematics)
James Thin, 1880 (hymnology)
Sir Donald F Tovey, 1940 (music scores and books)
Weiss, 1948 (books on Beethoven)
Watt, 1997 (Arabic)
Un-named special collections:
18th- and 19th-century books on agriculture
Audio-visual Archive (Scottish Studies)
Bundesgesetzblatt
Cases of the European Court of Human Rights
Collection of early printed books on music theory
Debates of the European Parliament
Ecumenical Collection (includes all World Council of Churches and British Council of Churches publications)
European Courts Reports (English, French, German and Dutch language)
Historical collections of Scottish churchmen (books, pamphlets and portraits)
Historical collection of veterinary science, nucleus of which belonged to the school's founder, William Dick
Manuscript collections (mainly Scottish church history, including Thomas Chalmers, 1780–1847, archive of c. 20,000 letters)
Official Journal of the European Union (Communities) (C and L series)
Photographic Archive (Scottish studies)
Sound Archive (10,000 tapes, Scottish studies)
Verhandlungen des Deutschen Bundestages
Libraries of the:
Dumfries Presbytery
Edinburgh Geological Society
Edinburgh Mathematical Society
Lothian Health Services Archives
Royal Physical Society
Royal Scottish Forestry Society
University of Edinburgh Archives
Manuscripts of various scientific societies
Subject specialisations:
African studies
Canadian studies
History of medicine and science
Landscape architecture
New Zealand studies
Scandinavian studies
Modern Scottish and English literature
Scottish studies
South Asian studies
The Church of Scotland
The Scottish Enlightenment
The University of Edinburgh
Poets and writers:
W H Auden
George Mackay Brown
Thomas and Jane Welsh Carlyle
Thomas Chalmers
Helen B Cruikshank
Christopher Murray Grieve ('Hugh MacDairmid')
Norman McCaig
James Leslie Mitchell ('Lewis Grassic Gibbon')
John Middleton Murry
Poets of Scottish Literary Renaissance
Sydney Goodsir Smith
Sir Walter Scott
John Wain

Non-library collection catalogue:
All or part available online

Library catalogue:
All or part available online

Printed publications:
Publications list available on request
Catalogue of manuscripts, printed music and books on music up to 1850 in the Main Library

continued overleaf

Catalogue of the Printed Books in the Library of the University, 3 vols (1918–1923)

Index to [post-mediaeval Western] manuscripts, 2 vols and supplement to 1978

Library Guide 9, Library services for external users (free)

Pre-1985 catalogues: Main Library Guard-Book catalogue 1580–1984 available in situ and on microfiche

Catalogues of older material are still in manual form in most Faculty Libraries

Scottish Studies (annual volume)

Union list of Current Serials received in Edinburgh University Library and some other research libraries in Edinburgh

Small range of publications available on request

Order printed publications from: Publications, Edinburgh University Library, George Square, Edinburgh, EH8 9LJ, tel: 0131 650 3409, fax: 0131 651 5041, e-mail: IS.Helpdesk@ed.ac.uk

Electronic and video publications:
The Library Catalogue (online)

Access to staff:
Contact by letter, by telephone, by fax, by e-mail and via website. Appointment necessary. Letter of introduction required. Non-members charged.
Hours: For opening hours information please check website: http://www.ed.ac.uk/is/library-opening
Semester time: Main Library, Mon to Thu, 0900 to 2200; Fri, 0900 to 1900; Sat, 0900 to 1700; Sun, 1200 to 1900; most other major College and School Libraries, Mon to Thu, 0900 to 2200; Fri, Sat 0900 to 1700; Sun, 1200 to 1700;
Vacations: Main Library, Mon to Thurs, 0900 to 2000; Fri, 0900 to 1700; Sat, 1000 to 1300; other libraries vary
Special comments: Members of the University of Edinburgh have full access as of right. They may borrow free of charge and are charged for photocopying, photography and inter-library loans.
External users may be charged for access (consultation and/or borrowing), photocopying, photography and inter-library loans.
Undergraduate students from other European Union HEIs during EUL vacations may have access for reference purposes free of charge on production of their own current ID cards. They may have borrowing facilities on payment of the current external fee. During term-time they are admitted only by prior arrangement with their own institutions' librarians. Postgraduate students are admitted at all times.
Staff, postgraduate students and undergraduate students from overseas HEIs, including members of Universitas 21, Coimbra, and other groups, will be charged external fees for borrowing unless they are official academic visitors to the University.
Advanced Higher Students, School students and equivalent project-based course students may have access to the Library for consultation purposes free of charge, provided that prior arrangements have been made between each School and the University Library. Other school students are not normally admitted to the Library.
Corporate membership is available on application and by subscription.
Prices, which may be adjusted at any time, are available on request or online: http://www.ed.ac.uk/is/library-museum-gallery.

Access for disabled people:
Parking provided, ramped entry, level entry, access to all public areas, toilet facilities
Special comments: These facilities apply to the Main Library. On other sites the provision will vary.

College of Medicine and Veterinary Medicine:
Easter Bush Veterinary Centre Library
Royal (Dick) School of Veterinary Studies, Easter Bush, Roslin, Midlothian, EH25 9RG; tel: 0131 650 6405; e-mail: ebvc.library@ed.ac.uk
Roslin Institute Library
Roslin Institute, Roslin Biocentre, Roslin, Midlothian, EH25 9RG; tel: 0131 527 4200; fax: 0131 440 0434; e-mail: roslin.library@roslin.ed.ac.uk

Royal (Dick) School of Veterinary Studies Library
Royal (Dick) School of Veterinary Studies, Summerhall, Edinburgh, EH9 1QH; tel: 0131 650 6175; fax: 0131 650 6593; e-mail: dick.vetlib@ed.ac.uk
Royal Infirmary Library
Chancellor's Building, 49 Little France Crescent, Edinburgh, EH16 4SB; tel: 0131 242 6340; fax: 0131 242 6338; e-mail: royal.infirmary.library@ed.ac.uk
Western General Hospital Library
Western General Hospital, Crewe Road South, Edinburgh, EH4 2XU; tel: 0131 537 2299; e-mail: western.general.library@ed.ac.uk

College of Science and Engineering:
Darwin Library
Darwin Building, The King's Buildings, West Mains Road, Edinburgh, EH9 3JU; tel: 0131 650 5784; fax: 0131 650 6702; e-mail: darwin.library@ed.ac.uk
James Clerk Maxwell Library
James Clerk Maxwell Building, The King's Buildings, West Mains Road, Edinburgh, EH9 3JZ; tel: 0131 650 5784
Robertson Engineering and Science Library
James Clerk Maxwell Building, The King's Buildings, West Mains Road, Edinburgh, EH9 3JF; tel: 0131 650 5666; fax: 0131 650 6702; e-mail: robertson.library@ed.ac.uk

Moray House School of Education:
Moray House Library
Dalhousie Land, St John Street, Edinburgh, EH8 8AQ; tel: 0131 651 6193; e-mail: morayhse@staffmail.ed.ac.uk

School of Divinity:
New College Library
School of Divinity, Mound Place, Edinburgh, EH1 2LU; tel: 0131 650 8957; fax: 0131 650 7952; e-mail: new.college.library@ed.ac.uk

School of Law:
Law and Europa Library (European Documentation Centre)
Old College, South Bridge, Edinburgh, EH8 9YL; tel: 0131 650 2044; e-mail: law.europa.library@ed.ac.uk

School of Literatures, Languages and Cultures:
Scottish Studies Library
School of Scottish Studies, 27– 29 George Square, Edinburgh, EH8 9LD; tel: 0131 650 3060; e-mail: scottish.studies@ed.ac.uk

UNIVERSITY OF ESSEX LIBRARY

Formal name: The Albert Sloman Library, University of Essex

Wivenhoe Park, Colchester, Essex, CO4 3SQ

Tel: 01206 873333
Fax: 01206 872289
E-mail: librarian@essex.ac.uk

Website:
http://libwww.essex.ac.uk
Catalogues and library guides.

Enquiries:
Enquiries to: Librarian

Founded:
1963

Organisation type and purpose:
University library.

Subject coverage:
Biology, computing science, electronics, health sciences, mathematics, psychology; art, history, language and linguistics, literature and philosophy; accounting and financial management, business studies, economics, government, law, psychoanalysis, sociology. Special emphasis on Latin America, USA and the former Soviet Union.

Museum or gallery collection, archive, or library special collection:
Archives of Mrs Mary Whitehouse, CBE

Archives of SCOPE-ENUWAR (Scientific Committee on Problems of the Environmental Consequences of Nuclear War)
Archives of the National Viewers' and Listeners' Association
Archives of the Rowhedge Ironworks Company (1904–1964)
Archives of the Social Democratic Party (SDP)
Lord Rogers of Quarrybank (SDP papers)
Baron Newby of Rothwell (SDP papers)
Archives of the Tawney Society (the SDP 'Think Tank')
Bassingbourn Parish Library
Bean Collection on William Blake
Donald Davie Archive
Edgell Rickword Collection
European Documentation, from 1977
S E Finer Papers (UK transport policy)
George Goddeck Archive (psychoanalysis)
Hervey Benham Sound Archive (local history)
Historical Collection of the Royal Statistical Society
David Kerr Papers (UK health policy)
Letters of T E Lawrence
Levene/Sky Television Political interviews Video Archive
Nolan Committee Papers (Committee of Standards of Conduct in Public Life) 1995–1997
Letters, papers and diaries of Henri and Sophie Gaudier Brzeska
Letters, papers and diaries of John Hassall
National Social Policy and Social Change Archive (QUALIDATA)
Library of the Essex Society for Archaeology and History
Papers and printed books of the Colchester and Coggeshall Meetings of the Society of Friends
Papers of Enid Balint (psychoanalysis)
Papers (1992–93) of the Boundary Commission for England
Papers and Diaries of S L Bensusan
Papers of Lord Alport (Rhodesia, House of Lords, Colchester and Essex)
Papers of Lord Brimelow (Yalta Repatriation Agreement)
Papers on the Third London Airport controversy
Paul Sieghart Human Rights Archive
Russell Collection Family Archive
Sigmund Freud Collection (psychoanalysis)
Sir Vincent Evans Collection (European Court of Human Rights)
Watergate Collection
Windscale Inquiry Papers, 1977 (Nuclear reactor fuel reprocessing)
Margery Allingham / Philip Youngman Carter literary archives
Charter88 Archives (civil, political and human rights)
Bernie Hamilton Archive (human rights)
Colchester Medical Society Library (historical books)

Library catalogue:
All or part available online

Printed publications:
English Law 2001
European Documentation 2001
Guide to the Latin American Collection 2001
Human Rights 2001
Guides and bibliographies
Microforms 1998
Library guide 2000/01

Publications list:
Available online and in print

Access to staff:
Contact by letter and by fax. Appointment necessary. Letter of introduction required.
Hours: Term time: Mon to Fri, 0800 to 2200; Sat, 0900 to 1800; Sun, 1400 to 1900
Vacations: Mon to Fri, 0900 to 1730

Access for disabled people:
Level entry, access to all public areas, toilet facilities

UNIVERSITY OF EXETER – CAMBORNE SCHOOL OF MINES

Acronym or abbreviation: CSM

Pool, Redruth, Cornwall, TR15 3SE

Tel: 01209 714866
Fax: 01209 719677
E-mail: libcsm@csm.ex.ac.uk

Enquiries:
Enquiries to: Librarian
Direct e-mail: jfoote@csm.ex.ac.uk

Formerly called:
Camborne School of Mines

Organisation type and purpose:
University department or institute.
Education and research in mining engineering,
extractive metallurgy, industrial geology,
surveying and minerals resource management,
environmental management.

Subject coverage:
Metalliferous mining, mineral processing,
extractive metallurgy, industrial geology,
surveying, minerals resource management,
environmental and waste management, mined
land reclamation.

UNIVERSITY OF EXETER – LAW LIBRARY

Amory Building, Rennes Drive, Exeter, Devon,
EX4 4RJ

Tel: 01392 263356
Fax: 01392 263196

Website:
http://www.library.ex.ac.uk/internet
European studies and law pages on the Exeter
library resources page.

Enquiries:
Enquiries to: Librarian
Direct e-mail: p.c.overy@ex.ac.uk

Founded:
1974

Organisation type and purpose:
University library.

Subject coverage:
English, European and international law.

Museum or gallery collection, archive, or library special collection:
European Documentation Centre: European
   Commission publications

Trade and statistical information:
EU Statistics.

Non-library collection catalogue:
All or part available online

Library catalogue:
All or part available online

Access to staff:
Contact by letter, by telephone and by e-mail.
Appointment necessary.
Hours: Mon to Fri, 0900 to 1700

Member of:
European Information Association

UNIVERSITY OF EXETER – ST LUKE'S CAMPUS LIBRARY

Heavitree Road, Exeter, Devon, EX1 2LU

Tel: 01392 264785
Fax: 01392 264784
E-mail: roy.davies@ex.ac.uk

Website:
http://www.ex.ac.uk/library

Enquiries:
Enquiries to: Librarian
Direct tel: 01392 264782

Founded:
1837

Formerly called:
Institute of Education

Organisation type and purpose:
University library, university department or
institute.
Library of university faculty.

Subject coverage:
Education, social work, exercise and sport science.

Museum or gallery collection, archive, or library special collection:
National curriculum archive

Non-library collection catalogue:
All or part available online

Library catalogue:
All or part available online

Access to staff:
Contact by letter, by telephone, by fax, by e-mail,
in person and via website
Hours: Term time: Mon to Thu, 0900 to 2100; Fri,
0900 to 1715; Sat, 0900 to 1700, Sun 1400 to 1800
Vacations: Mon to Fri, 0900 to 1715, Sat 1300 to
1700, Sun 1400 to 1800

Access for disabled people:
Parking provided, level entry, toilet facilities, lift,
stair-lift

Parent body:
University of Exeter Library

UNIVERSITY OF EXETER – UNIVERSITY LIBRARY

Stocker Road, Exeter, Devon, EX4 4PT

Tel: 01392 263869
Fax: 01392 263871
E-mail: library@exeter.ac.uk

Website:
http://www.as.exeter.ac.uk/library
Details of academic services and staff.

Enquiries:
Enquiries to: Assistant Director, Collections and
Research Support

Founded:
1855

Organisation type and purpose:
University library. Serving the community as well
as the university staff and students.

Subject coverage:
Arts, law, social studies, science and technology.

Museum or gallery collection, archive, or library special collection:
Arabic and Gulf Studies
Audio-visual resources
Books and recordings related to American music,
   especially popular music
Dan Davin book collection of New Zealand
   literature
Imperial Institute collection of photographs
Bill Douglas Centre for Film Studies
Crediton, Ottery St Mary and Totnes Parish
   Libraries
Dodderidge Collection
Ghana Collection (Scolma Area Specialization
   Plan)
MSS Collections (West Country authors)
Syon Abbey Collection

Non-library collection catalogue:
All or part available online

Library catalogue:
All or part available online

Access to staff:
Contact by letter, by telephone, by fax and by e-
mail. Appointment necessary.
Hours: Mon to Fri, 0900 to 1700

Includes the:
Devon and Exeter Institution Library
Exeter University (St Luke's) Library

UNIVERSITY OF GLAMORGAN

Learning Resources Centre, Pontypridd, Rhondda
Cynon Taff, CF37 1DL

Tel: 01443 482625\ Minicom no. 01443 482322
Fax: 01443 482629
E-mail: smorgan1@glam.ac.uk

Website:
http://www.glam.ac.uk/lrc/home.htm
Information; including learning resources centre
guide, news, guide to selected internet resources,
staff directory, connection to the OPAC.

Enquiries:
Enquiries to: Librarian
Direct e-mail: press@glam.ac.uk
Other contacts: Head of Learning Resources Centre

Organisation type and purpose:
University library.

Subject coverage:
Mathematics; computer science; physics;
chemistry; life sciences; geology; chemical, civil,
mechanical, manufacturing, electrical and
electronic engineering; information technology;
building; quantity surveying; estate management;
law; politics; public administration; behavioural
and communication studies; accountancy; business
studies and management; arts and humanities;
statistics; safety; languages; nursing and
midwifery.

Museum or gallery collection, archive, or library special collection:
Centre for the Study of Welsh Writing in English
   Collection

Printed publications:
Learning Resources Centre Guide
Specialised publications, on particular facilities,
   services, databases
Some publications are available via the Learning
   Resource Centre's WWW pages

Access to staff:
Contact by letter, by telephone, by fax and by e-
mail
Hours: Mon to Fri, 0900 to 1700

UNIVERSITY OF GLASGOW – ARCHIVE SERVICES

77–87 Dumbarton Road, Glasgow, G11 6PW

Tel: 0141 330 5515
Fax: 0141 330 4158
E-mail: enquiries@archives.gla.ac.uk

Website:
http://www.gla.ac.uk/archives
Information about collections and services.
http://www.universitystory.gla.ac.uk
The story of the people who have contributed to
the development of the University.

Enquiries:
Enquiries to: Duty Archivist

Formerly called:
Glasgow University Archives & Business Records
Centre; Business Records Centre (year of change
2000)

Organisation type and purpose:
University department or institute.
Archive repository.

Subject coverage:
Higher education archives and history, business
archives, retail, shipbuilding, engineering and
textiles archives, Scottish culture, Scottish history.

Information services:
Research service available.

Services for disabled people:
Wheelchair-accessible, ground-level searchroom
available by appointment.

continued overleaf

Museum or gallery collection, archive, or library special collection:
Glasgow University Archives from 1451
Scottish Business Archives

Non-library collection catalogue:
All or part available online and in-house

Library catalogue:
All or part available in-house

Printed publications:
Source Lists

Access to staff:
Contact by letter, by telephone, by fax, by e-mail, in person and via website. Appointment necessary.
Hours: Mon: 1330 to 1700; Tue, Wed, Fri: 0930 to 1700; Thu: 0930 to 2000

Access for disabled people:
Parking provided, toilet facilities, ground-level searchroom (appointment required)

Also at:
Searchroom, Glasgow University Archive Services
13 Thurso Street, Glasgow, G11 6PE

UNIVERSITY OF GLASGOW – DIVISION OF VIROLOGY

Institute of Virology, Church Street, Glasgow, G11 5JR

Tel: 0141 330 4017 or 4029
Fax: 0141 337 2236

Website:
http://www.vir.gla.ac.uk/staff.shtml
Summaries of current research.

Enquiries:
Enquiries to: Joint Heads of Division
Direct tel: 0141 330 4029

Founded:
1958

Formerly called:
Institute of Virology (year of change 1994)

Organisation type and purpose:
University department or institute.

Subject coverage:
Herpes virus genomic and evolutionary biology, herpes virus gene control and latency, herpes virus genome replication, viral structure and assembly; antivirals, vaccines and immunological reagents; eukaryotic mRNA processing in virus infected cells; genomic and functional analysis of bunyavirus; molecular biology of hepatitis B virus; molecular biology of hepatitis C virus, molecular biology of RSV, molecular biology of picorna viruses.

Printed publications:
Research results are published in the primary scientific journals

Access to staff:
Contact by letter, by telephone, by fax and by e-mail
Hours: Mon to Fri, 0900 to 1700
Special comments: Books and journals not available for outside loan.

Access to building, collection or gallery:
Prior appointment required

Access for disabled people:
Ramped entry

Parent body:
Medical Research Council
University of Glasgow

UNIVERSITY OF GLASGOW – LANGUAGE CENTRE LIBRARY

Acronym or abbreviation: UGLC

Hetherington Building, Bute Gardens, Glasgow, G12 8RS

Tel: 0141 330 4117
Fax: 0141 330 4114

E-mail: lc-librarian@arts.glasgow.ac.uk

Website:
http://www.glasgow.ac.uk/langcent/library

Enquiries:
Enquiries to: Librarian

Founded:
1985

Organisation type and purpose:
University department or institute.

Subject coverage:
Language learning – holdings in Catalan, Czech, French, German, Italian, Polish, Portuguese, Spanish, Russian and 35 other languages.

Non-library collection catalogue:
All or part available online

Library catalogue:
All or part available online

Printed publications:
Library guide

Access to staff:
Contact by letter, by telephone, by fax, by e-mail and in person
Hours: Term time: Mon to Thu, 0930 to 2000; Fri, 0900 to 1645
Vacation: Mon to Fri, 0930 to 1645
Special comments: Please phone as opening times vary.

Access for disabled people:
Ramped entry, toilet facilities, lift

UNIVERSITY OF GLASGOW – UNIVERSITY LIBRARY

Hillhead Street, Glasgow, G12 8QE

Tel: 0141 330 6704/5
Fax: 0141 330 4952
E-mail: library@lib.gla.ac.uk

Website:
http://www.lib.gla.ac.uk/index.html
Library catalogue, news and information; bibliographic, reference and network resources and exhibition information.

Enquiries:
Enquiries to: Head of Enquiry Service
Direct e-mail: enquiries@lib.gla.ac.uk
Other contacts: Keeper of Special Collections

Founded:
1451

Organisation type and purpose:
University library.

Subject coverage:
Social sciences, humanities and medicine; administrative medicine; adult and continuing education; anaesthesia; ancient Near Eastern history; Arabic and Islamic studies; archaeology; architecture; art history; bibliography; cardiac surgery; cartography; Celtic; child and adolescent psychiatry; child health; clinical medicine; clinical physics; clinical surgery; community medicine; constitutional law and history; Czech; dental medicine; dermatology; drama; ecclesiastical history; economic history; economics; education; emblem studies; English language and literature; European Community; financial studies; fine art; forensic medicine; French; general practice (medicine); geography; geriatric medicine; German; Greek; haematology; Hebrew and Semitic languages; Hispanic studies; history; immunology; industrial relations; infectious diseases; international economic studies; Italian; Latin; Latin American studies; law; linguistics and phonetics; logic; media studies; medical genetics; medicine; music; neurology; neuropathology; neurosurgery; nursing studies; obstetrics and gynaecology; oncology; ophthalmology; orthopaedics; otolaryngology; pathology; pharmacology; philosophy; plastic surgery; Polish; politics; psychological medicine; psychology; religious studies; Russian; Scottish history; Scottish literature; social and economic research; social

administration and social work; sociology; Soviet and East European studies; surgery; theology; veterinary medicine; science and technology; aeronautics and fluid mechanics; agriculture; anatomy; animal developmental biology; animal nutrition; astronomy; bacteriology and immunology; biochemistry; biology; botany; cell biology; chemical physics; chemistry; civil engineering; computing science; conveyancing; economics; electronics and electrical engineering; genetics; geology; history of science; management studies; mathematics; mechanical engineering; mercantile law; microbiology; naval architecture; ocean engineering; parasitology; pathology; physics; physiology; statistics; taxation; topographic science; virology; zoology.

Museum or gallery collection, archive, or library special collection:
Blau (200 vols, 16th-century Hebrew books)
Bourgeois (2,000 vols on philology)
Broady and Bisset (2,000 left-wing pamphlets)
Caricatures (3,000 French political caricatures of the Commune and Franco-Prussian war)
Eadie (8,000 vols of biblical studies and early printing)
Euing (15,000 vols including 400 black-letter ballads, 15th- and 16th-century books)
Euing Music (5,300 vols of scores, early printed music, history of music)
Farmer (the library of Henry George Farmer comprising 1,600 printed vols and 600 MSS with special emphasis on oriental and military music)
Ferguson (8,000 vols on alchemy, chemistry, witchcraft, gypsies and secret societies)
Gemmell (90 vols on the Dance of Death)
Geological Society of Glasgow: foreign periodicals
Hamilton (8,000 vols on philosophy)
Hepburn (300 vols mainly of 19th-century English literature)
Hunterian (10,000 vols including 534 incunabula, 649 MSS, especially strong in history of medicine and anatomy)
Institution of Engineers and Shipbuilders in Scotland: Library
Kelvin (papers relating to Lord Kelvin, William Thomson)
MacColl (6,000 letters to and from the art critic and poet, D. S. MacColl)
McGrigor (650 vols and 1,000 pamphlets on Palestine)
Mearns (3,000 vols on hymnology)
Morgan (papers of the poet, Edwin Morgan)
Munro (300 vols of editions of Sir Thomas Browne)
Murray (15,000 vols on bibliography and history of the West of Scotland)
Ogilvie (1,700 vols of 17th-century material and civil war pamphlets)
Robertson (1,000 vols on oriental languages)
Scottish Theatre Archive (playscripts, programmes, press cuttings, financial records, photographs, plans, taped interviews and correspondence)
Simson, Robert, mathematical library (850 vols of early mathematics and astronomy)
Smith (350 vols mostly of rare Glasgow pamphlets)
Spencer (111 vols of books and MSs relating to the Darien Scheme)
Stevenson (900 vols on Semitic languages, literature and archaeology)
Stirling Maxwell (2,000 vols of emblem and fête books)
Tischendorf (2,500 vols on biblical studies, codicology and topography from the library of Konstantin von Tischendorf)
Veitch (600 vols of medieval philosophy)
Walker-Arnott Botanical Collection
Whistler (3,300 vols of letters, MSs and papers of James McNeill Whistler)
Wright (the papers of Harold Wright, mainly concerning late 19th- and early 20th-century British artists and print-makers)
Wylie (1,000 vols on the history and antiquities of Glasgow)

Non-library collection catalogue:
All or part available online

Library catalogue:
All or part available online

Printed publications:
A guide to the major collections in the Department of Special Collections
Cell Biology, Molecular Biology and Genetics
Directory of British Government publications in GUL
Kelvin Papers: Index to the Manuscript Collection of William Thomson, Baron Kelvin
St Mungo's Bairns – some notable Glasgow students down the centuries
Starting Research in... (series)
The Book as a Modern Artefact
Whistler, MacColl, Wright: art history papers, 1850–1950, in GUL

Microform publications:
Guardbook catalogue (fiche)
Presentation of Medical and Scientific Theses According to British Standard 4821:1972 (tape/slide guide)
Serials list (fiche)

Publications list:
Available in print

Access to staff:
Contact by letter, by telephone, by fax, by e-mail, in person and via website. Appointment necessary.
Hours: Mon to Fri, 0900 to 1955; Sat, 1300 to 1655

Access to building, collection or gallery:
Hours: Mon to Sun, 0715 to 2000
Special comments: Special Collections: Mon to Fri, 0900 to 1700; Sat, 0900 to 1230

Access for disabled people:
Level entry, access to all public areas, toilet facilities
Special comments: Emergency egress when lifts not in use by protected stairwells only. Refuge areas available on levels 4 to 11.

UNIVERSITY OF GLOUCESTERSHIRE

Acronym or abbreviation: UoG

The Park Campus, Cheltenham, Gloucestershire, GL50 2RH

Tel: 01242 715442

Website:
http://insight.glos.ac.uk/departments/lis/Pages/default.aspx
Services and locations of Learning Centres.
http://aleph.glos.ac.uk/F?RN=368518371
Online catalogue.

Enquiries:
Enquiries to: LIS Administrator
Direct e-mail: rbashford@glos.ac.uk
Other contacts: Senior Information Adviser (Archives) (for access to archive collections)

Founded:
1834

Incorporates the former:
Cheltenham Mechanical Institute (year of change 1834); Gloucester Mechanical Institute (year of change 1840); Church Training College, Cheltenham (year of change 1847); St Paul's College of Education (year of change 1920); St Mary's College of Education (year of change 1920); Gloucestershire College of Education (year of change 1967); College of St Paul and St Mary (year of change 1979); Higher Education Section, Gloucestershire College of Arts and Technology (year of change 1980); Cheltenham and Gloucester College of Higher Education (year of change 1990)

Organisation type and purpose:
University library.
University, providing foundation degrees, undergraduate and taught postgraduate degrees, research programmes.

Subject coverage:
Advertising; animal biology; animation and interactive media; biology; business and management; creative writing; criminology; digital film; education; English language; English literature; environmental policy and management;

film and media; fine art – painting and drawing; geography; graphic design; health studies; history; illustration; IT and computing; journalism; landscape architecture; law; leisure, tourism, hospitality and events management; photography; playwork; popular music; psychology; public relations; publishing; religion, philosophy, ethics; social work; sociology; sports and exercise science; sports development and coaching; teacher training; television and radio production.

Museum or gallery collection, archive, or library special collection:
Bristol and Gloucestershire Archaeological Society Library
College archive, 1840–
Gloucestershire Poets, Writers and Artists collection: Dymock Poets Archive and Study Centre – L. Abercrombie; E. Thomas; R. Frost; W. Gibson; R. Brooke; J. Drinkwater; James Elroy Flecker; Ivor Gurney; W. H. Davies; U. A. Fanthorpe
Paul Oliver Collection of African-American Music
Local Heritage Initiative Archive
History of physical education
Whittington Press – private press, founded 1972

Non-library collection catalogue:
All or part available online and in-house

Library catalogue:
All or part available online

Access to staff:
Contact by letter, by telephone, by e-mail, in person and via website. Appointment necessary. Non-members charged.
Hours: Mon to Fri, 0900 to 1700

Access to building, collection or gallery:
Hours: Mon to Fri, 0900 to 1700

Access for disabled people:
Parking provided, ramped entry, toilet facilities

UNIVERSITY OF GREENWICH – INFORMATION SERVICES AND LIBRARY, WOOLWICH CAMPUS/ GREENWICH CAMPUS

Queen Mary Court, Old Royal Naval College, Park Row, Greenwich, London, SE10 9LS

Tel: 020 8331 8000 (switchboard)
E-mail: a.e.murphy@gre.ac.uk

Website:
http://www.gre.ac.uk/offices/ils/ls

Enquiries:
Enquiries to: Head of Learning Services
Direct tel: 020 8331 8196
Direct fax: 020 8331 9084

Founded:
1891

Incorporates the former:
Dartford College of Education (year of change 1972); Avery Hill College (year of change 1985); Garnett College (year of change 1989); Thames College of Health Care Studies, Thames Polytechnic (year of change 1993); Natural Resources Institute (year of change 1996)

Organisation type and purpose:
University library.

Subject coverage:
Architecture and landscape architecture, built environment, civil engineering, surveying, construction management, biology, chemistry, pharmaceutical science, pharmacy, business and management, computing, IT, earth sciences, engineering, environmental sciences, natural resources, humanities, law, mathematics, statistics, education, social sciences, health, sport science, maritime studies.

Museum or gallery collection, archive, or library special collection:
Sidney Keyes Archive

Institutional archives of Woolwich Polytechnic, Thames Polytechnic, Dartford College of Education, Avery Hill College of Education, Garnett College

Library catalogue:
All or part available online

Publications list:
Available online

Access to staff:
Contact by fax, by e-mail and via website. Appointment necessary. Non-members charged.

Access to building, collection or gallery:
Hours: Term time: hours vary across campuses, usually: Mon to Thu, 0830 to 2100; Fri, 0900 to 1700; Sat and Sun, 1100 to 1700; vacation: Mon to Fri, 0900 to 1700; (see website for details)

Access for disabled people:
Parking provided, ramped entry, level entry, toilet facilities

Branch libraries:
University of Greenwich
  Drill Hall Library, North Road, Chatham Maritime, Kent, ME4 4TB; tel: 01634 883278; fax: 01634 883567; e-mail: v.g.malone@gre.ac.uk
University of Greenwich
  Dreadnought Library, Maritime Greenwich Campus, 30 Park Row, Greenwich, London, SE10 9LS; tel: 020 8331 7788; fax: 020 8331 7775; e-mail: t.harland@gre.ac.uk
University of Greenwich
  Avery Hill Campus Library, Bexley Road, London, SE9 2PQ; tel: 020 8331 9656; fax: 020 8331 8756; e-mail: r.m.moon@gre.ac.uk

UNIVERSITY OF GREENWICH – LIBRARY

Central Avenue, Chatham Maritime, Chatham, Kent, ME4 4TB

Tel: 020 8331 9617
Fax: 020 8331 9837
E-mail: info@greenwich.ac.uk

Website:
http://www.gre.ac.uk:8080/www-bin/www_talis32
Library catalogue.
http://www.greenwich.ac.uk
General university information.

Enquiries:
Enquiries to: Librarian
Direct tel: 01634 883419
Direct e-mail: mghsslibteam@gre.ac.uk

Founded:
1894

Formerly called:
Centre of Overseas Pest Research, Land Resources Department, Natural Resources Institute Library, Overseas Development Natural Resources Institute, Tropical Products Institute

Formerly owned by:
Department for International Development

Organisation type and purpose:
University library, consultancy, research organisation.
Principal aim is to alleviate poverty and hardship in developing countries by increasing the productivity of their renewable resources.

Subject coverage:
Agriculture including: tropical agriculture, forestry and fisheries, land resource assessment, tropical environment, soil science, pests and pest control, water resources, tropical diseases and vectors of tropical diseases, climatology, use of natural resources in developing countries, geography, geology, environmental sciences, engineering.

Library catalogue:
All or part available online

continued overleaf

Printed publications:
A wide range of titles on crops, fisheries, food storage, forestry, land resources, soils and water, livestock, etc.
Order printed publications from: NRI Catalogue Services, CABI, Wallingford, Oxfordshire, OX10 8DE

Publications list:
Available in print

Access to staff:
Appointment necessary.
Hours: Term time: 0900 to 2100

Headquarters address:
University of Greenwich
Southwood House, Avery Hill Road, Eltham, London, SE9 2UG; tel: 020 8331 8000; fax: 020 8331 8145; e-mail: info@greenwich.ac.uk

UNIVERSITY OF HERTFORDSHIRE

Information Hertfordshire, College Lane, Hatfield, Hertfordshire, AL10 9AB

Tel: 01707 284653
Fax: 01707 284666
E-mail: lihsbuoffice@herts.ac.uk

Website:
http://www.herts.ac.uk/lis
http://www.voyager.herts.ac.uk
Collection catalogue.
http://www.herts.ac.uk/uhpress
Publications list.

Enquiries:
Enquiries to: Dean / CIO

Founded:
1952

Formerly called:
Hatfield Polytechnic

Organisation type and purpose:
University library.

Subject coverage:
Accounting, art, biosciences, careers and employment information, computing, design, economics, education, engineering, film and theatre, health, history, law, linguistics, literature, management, marketing, mathematics, midwifery, music, nursing, paramedic sciences, pharmacy, philosophy, physical sciences, physiotherapy, psychology, radiography, social care, social sciences, sports science, technology, tourism.

Non-library collection catalogue:
All or part available online

Library catalogue:
All or part available online

Printed publications:
Order printed publications from: UH Press, tel: 01707 284681

Publications list:
Available online and in print

Access to building, collection or gallery:
No prior appointment required
Hours: Mon to Fri, 0830 to 2200; Sat, Sun, 1100 to 1800
Special comments: Visual ID required for issue of Visitors Day Pass.

Access for disabled people:
Parking provided, level entry, toilet facilities

UNIVERSITY OF HUDDERSFIELD – LIBRARY AND COMPUTING CENTRE

Queensgate, Huddersfield, West Yorkshire, HD1 3DH

Tel: 01484 422288
Fax: 01484 517897
E-mail: s.a.white@hud.ac.uk

Website:
http://www.hud.ac.uk/cls
Catalogue and e-resources.

Enquiries:
Enquiries to: Head of Library Services
Direct tel: 01484 472784
Other contacts: Director of Computing and Library Services

Founded:
1841

Organisation type and purpose:
University library.

Subject coverage:
Architecture, art and design, drama, English, history, hospitality and logistics, chemistry, computing, education, engineering, law, management, marketing, media, music, paramedical subjects including podiatry, social sciences, social work, teacher training, textiles.

Museum or gallery collection, archive, or library special collection:
Colne Valley Constituency Labour Party archives
G. H. Wood Collection (free trade, women's employment, co-operative movement)
Huddersfield Labour Party archives
Huddersfield Mechanics Institute archives
Rugby League archive
Wesley Historical Society (Yorkshire)
Engineering Industry archives

Non-library collection catalogue:
All or part available online

Library catalogue:
All or part available online

Access to staff:
Contact by letter, by telephone, by fax, by e-mail, in person and via website
Hours: Term time: Mon to Fri, 0800 to 1900 hours; Sat and Sun afternoons

Access to building, collection or gallery:
Access via Student Centre, 4th Floor, Central Services Building
Hours: Term time: Mon to Thu, 0800 to 2400; Fri, 0800 to 2100; Sat, 0930 to 2100; Sun, 1300 to 2100
Vacations: Mon to Thu, 0845 to 2000; Fri, 0845 to 1700
Special comments: Personal reference use only.

Access for disabled people:
Level entry, toilet facilities

UNIVERSITY OF HULL – ACADEMIC SERVICES LIBRARIES

Brynmor Jones Library, Cottingham Road, Hull, East Yorkshire, HU6 7RX

Tel: 01482 466581
Fax: 01482 466205
E-mail: libhelp@hull.ac.uk

Website:
http://www.hull.ac.uk/lib

Enquiries:
Enquiries to: Director of Academic Services and Librarian
Direct tel: 01482 465436
Direct e-mail: r.g.heseltine@hull.ac.uk

Founded:
1927

Organisation type and purpose:
University library.

Subject coverage:
Arts, humanities, social sciences, law, pure sciences, applied physics, electronic engineering, education, health sciences.

Museum or gallery collection, archive, or library special collection:
South-East Asia Collection
Labour history
Contemporary papers of political and social interest
Local archives

Non-library collection catalogue:
All or part available in-house

Library catalogue:
All or part available online

Access to staff:
Contact by letter, by telephone, by fax, by e-mail and via website. Appointment necessary.
Hours: Mon to Fri, 0900 to 1700

Access to building, collection or gallery:
Hours: Mon to Thu, 0830 to 2200; Fri, 0830 to 2100; Sat, 0900 to 2100; Sun, 1300 to 2100 (term-time hours)

Access for disabled people:
Ramped entry, toilet facilities

UNIVERSITY OF KENT – TEMPLEMAN LIBRARY

Canterbury, Kent, CT2 7NU

Tel: 01227 764000
Fax: 01227 823984
E-mail: library-enquiry@ukc.ac.uk

Website:
http://www.library.ukc.ac.uk/library
Library web catalogue.
http://www.library.ukc.ac.uk/librarycollections.htm
Links to special collections, EDC.
http://www.library.ukc.ac.uk/cartoons
Centre for the study of Cartoons and Caricatures (with searchable image database).
http://www.library.ukc.ac.uk/library/bysubject.htm
Library guides by subject.
http://www.library.ukc.ac.uk/special
Weatherill Papers.

Enquiries:
Enquiries to: Director of Information Services and Librarian
Direct tel: 01227 823565
Direct e-mail: m.m.coutts@ukc.ac.uk
Other contacts: Deputy Librarian

Founded:
1963

Organisation type and purpose:
University library.

Subject coverage:
Humanities: drama and theatre studies; English and American literature; history; classical and archaeological studies, comparative literature; Colonial and Post-Colonial studies, Medieval and Tudor studies; American studies; French, German, Italian, Spanish, linguistics and English language; philosophy, theology and religious studies; applied ethics; propaganda; history of science; modern cultural studies; European culture and languages, cartoons and caricature.
Sciences: chemistry; physics; biosciences; biotechnology; space sciences and astrophysics; materials research; medicine and health sciences; psychotherapy; computing; electronics; mathematics and statistics.
Social Sciences: accounting; anthropology; business; economics; law; politics and international relations; psychology; social and public policy; social work; sociology; conservation and ecology; social anthropology and computing; European regional and transport economics; health behaviour; group processes; health services; urban and regional studies; women's studies; geography; European studies.

Museum or gallery collection, archive, or library special collection:
British Chess Federation Library
Cartoons: 20th century cartoons and caricatures
Drama and Theatre:
Frank Pettingell Collection (19th century, texts, mss, playbills)
Melville Collection (1870–1930: typescripts, playbills, theatre records, memorabilia)
Reading-Raynor Collection (texts: biographical, critical, historical)

Richard Fawkes Collection (material on Dion Boucicault)
English Literature:
John Crow Collection
Bonamy Dobree Collection
T S Eliot Collection
Modern Poetry Collection
History of Science:
Maddison Collection of the History of Science
Miscellaneous:
Weatherill Collection (papers of the Speaker of the House of Commons)
C P Davies Wind- and Water-mill Collection
Muggeridge Collection of Windmill Photographs
Lloyd George Collection (signed copies from his library)
European Documentation Centre
Madagascar (formerly SCOLMA SPECIALISATION)
Slide Collection (135,000 slides, chiefly fine arts)
Microfilm Collection:
British Sessional Papers 1801–1969 (microcard)
Landmarks of Science (microcard)
Three Centuries of Drama (microcard)

Non-library collection catalogue:
All or part available online

Library catalogue:
All or part available online

Printed publications:
Centre for the study of Cartoons and Caricatures (see list of publications at website)

Microform publications:
Pettingell (microfilms from Research Publications Inc)

Electronic and video publications:
Cartoons (database at website)
Weatherill Papers (at website)

Publications list:
Available online and in print

Access to staff:
Contact by letter, by telephone, by fax, by e-mail, in person and via website. Appointment necessary. Non-members charged.
Hours: Mon to Fri, 0900 to 1700
Special comments: Limited availability in evenings and at weekends.

Access to building, collection or gallery:
No access other than to staff
Hours: Term time: Mon to Fri, 0845 to 2200; Sat, Sun, 1000 to 2200
Vacations: Mon to Fri, 0900 to 1900; Sat, 1100 to 1900; Sun, closed

Access for disabled people:
Level entry, access to all public areas, toilet facilities

UNIVERSITY OF LEEDS – DEPARTMENT OF ARABIC AND MIDDLE EASTERN STUDIES

Leeds, West Yorkshire, LS2 9JT

Tel: 0113 343 3421
Fax: 0113 343 3517
E-mail: a.spellman@leeds.ac.uk

Enquiries:
Enquiries to: Secretary

Organisation type and purpose:
University department.

Subject coverage:
Arabic language; Islamic religion and culture; Mediterranean studies and culture.

Printed publications:
Middle East Sources (Netton I R, available via publisher Curzon Press)

Access to staff:
Contact by letter, by telephone, by fax and by e-mail
Hours: Mon to Fri, 0900 to 1700

UNIVERSITY OF LEEDS – EDUCATION COLLECTION

University Library, Leeds, West Yorkshire, LS2 9JT

Tel: 0113 233 5517
Fax: 0113 233 5539
E-mail: libjms@library.novell.leeds.ac.uk

Website:
http://www.leeds.ac.uk/library/library.html
Information on all the university's libraries.

Enquiries:
Enquiries to: Assistant Librarian

Organisation type and purpose:
University library.

Subject coverage:
Education, psychology, teaching methods of curricular subjects.

Museum or gallery collection, archive, or library special collection:
W B Thompson Collection of Greek and Latin school textbooks
Historical collection of biology school textbooks
19th century educational sources and texts

Printed publications:
British Education Index, (annually from 1986, contact British Education Index at this address)
British Education Thesaurus (1st ed., 1988, 2nd ed., 1991, contact British Education Index at this address)
Improved Visibility: an international bibliography on the education of women and girls 1978–1989 (LISE Publications 1991 £8)

Electronic and video publications:
International Eric CD-ROM (contact British Education Index at this address)

Access to staff:
Contact by letter and by e-mail. Appointment necessary.
Hours: Mon to Fri, 0900 to 1700

UNIVERSITY OF LEEDS – UNIVERSITY LIBRARY

Leeds, West Yorkshire, LS2 9JT

Tel: 0113 343 5501
Fax: 0113 343 3556
E-mail: library@library.novell.leeds.ac.uk

Website:
http://www.leeds.ac.uk/library/spcoll/
Information on special collections.
http://www.leeds.ac.uk/library/library.html
Information on library services, contacts, holdings.

Enquiries:
Enquiries to: Librarian
Direct tel: 0113 343 5663

Founded:
1874

Organisation type and purpose:
University library.

Subject coverage:
Agriculture; Arabic; architecture; astronomy; bibliography; biology; biophysics; botany; ceramics; chemical engineering and technology; chemistry; China and Chinese studies; civil engineering; classical studies; dentistry; dyes and dyeing; economics; education; electrical engineering; engineering in general; English; food science and technology; French; fuels and fuel technology; geography and topography; geology; German; history; Italian; law; leather and leatherwork; linguistics; mathematics; mechanical engineering; medicine; metallurgy; meteorology; mines and mining; music; numismatics; palaeontology; philosophy; physics; politics; Portuguese; psychology; Russian; science; seismology; Semitics; Slavonic studies; social sciences; Spanish; technology in general; textiles; theology; translations; transport; Yorkshire; zoology.

Law Library: English, European, Commonwealth and American Law, criminology, police studies.

Museum or gallery collection, archive, or library special collection:
All Souls' College and Chaston Chapman Collections of early science
Anglo-French Collection (French books reflecting the influence of Great Britain on France to 1850)
Blanche Leigh, J F Preston and Camden Collections (historical books on cookery and domestic management)
Brotherton Collection (rare books and MSS, especially on English literature of the 17th, 18th and 19th centuries and on Romany literature)
Business archives of the West Yorkshire wool textile industry (18th to 20th centuries)
European Documentation Centre
Icelandic Collection
Leeds and West Riding Medico-Chirurgical Society Collection
Leeds Philosophical and Literary Society Library
Leeds Russian Archive (literary and historical MSS)
Liddle Collection of First World War archive materials
Medical classics, originally of the library of the old Infirmary
19th and 20th century educational sources, texts and archives
Quaker literature
Ripon Cathedral Library, and archives of the Dean and Chapter
Roth Collection of Judaica
W B Thompson Collection of Greek and Latin school textbooks
Wentworth-Woolley Hall estate papers (16th to 20th centuries)
Whitaker Collection of Atlases (mainly of the British Isles)
Yorkshire Geological Society Library
Yorkshire Quaker Archives (17th to 20th centuries)

Non-library collection catalogue:
All or part available online and in print

Library catalogue:
All or part available online

Printed publications:
The Brotherton Collection, University of Leeds; its contents described with illustrations of fifty books and manuscripts (£20)
Current periodicals in the University Libraries
Duplicated handlists of many of the Special Collections
German literature printed in the 17th and 18th centuries
Icelandic Collection
Printed catalogues of some of the collections

Electronic and video publications:
British Education Index

Publications list:
Available in print

Access to staff:
Contact by letter. Non-members charged.
Hours: Mon to Fri, 0900 to 1700

Access for disabled people:
Access to all public areas

UNIVERSITY OF LEICESTER – CLINICAL SCIENCES LIBRARY

Robert Kilpatrick Clinical Sciences Building, PO Box 65, Leicester Royal Infirmary, Leicester, LE2 7LX

Tel: 0116 252 3104
Fax: 0116 252 3107
E-mail: clinlib@leicester.ac.uk

Website:
http://www.le.ac.uk/library/clinical/clinlib.htm

Founded:
1978

Organisation type and purpose:
University library.

continued overleaf

Hospital library of the Medical School of the University of Leicester.

Subject coverage:
Medicine, health, nursing, midwifery and professions allied to medicine and social care.

Non-library collection catalogue:
All or part available online

Library catalogue:
All or part available online

Access to staff:
Contact by letter, by telephone, by fax, by e-mail, in person and via website. Appointment necessary. *Hours:* Mon to Fri, 0900 to 2100; Sat, 0900 to 1800; Sun, 1400 to 1800

Access to building, collection or gallery:
No prior appointment required
Hours: 24-hour access
Special comments: Outside staffed hours, access for University of Leicester staff and students, and NHS staff only.

Access for disabled people:
Level entry, access to all public areas, toilet facilities

Links with:
Other hospital libraries in the region

UNIVERSITY OF LEICESTER – DAVID WILSON LIBRARY

Box 248, University Road, Leicester, LE1 9QD

Tel: 0116 252 2043
Fax: 0116 252 2066
E-mail: libdesk@le.ac.uk

Website:
http://www.le.ac.uk/library

Enquiries:
Enquiries to: Enquiry service

Organisation type and purpose:
University library.

Subject coverage:
Archaeology; art history; astronomy; biological sciences; chemistry; computing; economic and social history; economics; engineering; English; French; genetics; geography; geology; German; history; Italian; law; local history; management; mass communications; mathematics; microbiology; museum studies; physics; politics; pre-clinical medicine; psychology; social work; sociology; zoology.

Museum or gallery collection, archive, or library special collection:
Burrows Collection (20th-century music)
English local history
European documentation
Fairclough Collection (17th century)
Leicester Medical Society
Mathematical Association Library
Orton Papers
Sue Townsend collection

Non-library collection catalogue:
All or part available online

Library catalogue:
All or part available online

Access to staff:
Contact by letter, by telephone, by fax, by e-mail, in person and via website. Appointment necessary. Letter of introduction required. Non-members charged.
Hours: Sep to Jun: Mon to Fri, 0900 to 2100; Sat, 0900 to 1700; Sun, 1200 to 1800
Jul and Aug: Mon to Sat, 0900 to 1700

Access to building, collection or gallery:
Hours: Sep to Jun: Mon to Fri, 0800 to 0000; Sat, Sun, 0900 to 0000
Jul and Aug: Mon to Fri, 0900 to 1730; Sat 0900 to 1800

Branch libraries:
Clinical Sciences Library

UNIVERSITY OF LINCOLN – UNIVERSITY LIBRARY

Brayford Pool, Lincoln, LN6 7TS

Tel: 01522 886664
Fax: 01522 886311
E-mail: acquisitions@lincoln.ac.uk

Website:
http://www.lincoln.ac.uk

Enquiries:
Enquiries to: University Librarian
Direct tel: 01522 886310
Direct e-mail: isnowley@lincoln.ac.uk

Formerly called:
University of Lincolnshire and Humberside

Organisation type and purpose:
University library.

Subject coverage:
Accountancy, architecture, art and design, building, business, communications, criminology, design, economics, English, environment, film, finance, food management, history, housing, humanities, languages, law, literature, management, marketing, media studies, photography, politics, printing, printmaking, psychology, radio, social policy, social science, social work, sociology, statistics and tourism.

Access to staff:
Contact via website

UNIVERSITY OF LIVERPOOL – UNIVERSITY LIBRARY

PO Box 123, Liverpool, L69 3DA

Tel: 0151 794 2674
Fax: 0151 794 2681

Website:
http://www.liv.ac.uk/library

Enquiries:
Enquiries to: Librarian
Direct tel: 0151 794 2673
Other contacts: Head of Special Collections and Archives

Organisation type and purpose:
University library.

Subject coverage:
The main holdings in humanities, social sciences and special collections are housed in the Sydney Jones Library; those in science, medicine, engineering, veterinary and dental science and archives are in the Harold Cohen Library; there are departmental libraries in education, law, archaeology, chemistry, civic design, continuing education, geology, music, oceanography, physics, marine biology (Port Erin, Isle of Man), veterinary science (Leahurst, Wirral).

Museum or gallery collection, archive, or library special collection:
Blake Collection (items by and about William Blake)
Brunner Papers (letter-books, accounts, diaries, etc. of Sir John Brunner, 1842–1919, including material on chemical industry)
Campbell Brown Collection (414 books of the 16th-19th centuries, on alchemy and chemistry)
Comte Collection (Positivism)
Fraser Collection (includes about 900 items on tobacco art, English literature, Scottish books, positivism, phrenology, some manuscript material)
Grace Collection (158 books on mathematics, printed 17th-19th centuries)
Manuscript collections of Joseph Blanco White, Charles Booth, John and Katharine Bruce Glasier, Josephine Butler
Noble Collection (fine printed and limited editions of English books of the late 19th and early 20th centuries and many examples of the private presses)
Peers Collection (Spanish Civil War)

Rathbone Papers (family and business papers of the Rathbones, Greenbank, Liverpool, 18th-20th centuries)
Rendall Collection (a. Marcus Aurelius; b. Shakespeare controversy)
Robert Graves Collection
Salisbury Collection (340 scientific books of the 19th century, mostly English)
Science Fiction Foundation Collection (books and magazines of science fiction and fantasy, including critical works and journals. Much foreign-language material, including the Myers Collection of Russian SF; manuscript and archive material of a number of SF writers; pseudo-science material including the Flat Earth Society Papers. c. 25,000 items)
Scott-MacFie Collection (works on Romany and Gypsy lore, books, manuscripts, broadsides, prints, photographs, sheet music, records and tape)
Simey Collection (women in society)
Stapledon Collection (philosophy and science fiction)
Merseyside Poets Collection (manuscripts, first drafts)
Thomson Collection (114 bound volumes of c. 1200 English pamphlets, 1689–1789)
Un-named collections on the history of medicine, 19th century documents of the US Congress, Latin American topography, selected modern poets
Whale Collection (309 books and pamphlets of the 19th-20th centuries on finance and banking)

Library catalogue:
All or part available online

Printed publications:
User guides to main libraries

Access to staff:
Contact by letter, by telephone, by e-mail and in person
Hours: Special collections and archives, Mon to Fri, 0930 to 1645
Special comments: Visitors by appointment for special collections and archives.

Access for disabled people:
Ramped entry, access to all public areas, toilet facilities

UNIVERSITY OF LONDON – GERMANIC STUDIES LIBRARY

29 Russell Square, London, WC1B 5DP

Tel: 020 7862 8967
Fax: 020 7862 8970
E-mail: igslib@sas.ac.uk

Enquiries:
Enquiries to: Librarian

Founded:
1950

Organisation type and purpose:
University library.

Subject coverage:
German language and literature of all periods (including Austria and Switzerland).

Museum or gallery collection, archive, or library special collection:
Friedrich Gundolf Archive
Lexicography, dialect dictionaries and grammars
Priebsch-Closs Collection (first and early edns of 18th- and early 19th-century authors)
Reference library of some 100,000 vols and 300 current periodicals

Library catalogue:
All or part available online

Access to staff:
Contact by letter, by telephone, by fax, by e-mail and in person
Hours: Mon to Fri, 0945 to 1730

Access to building, collection or gallery:
Hours: Mon to Fri, 0945 to 1745

Constituent part of:
University of London Research Library Services

UNIVERSITY OF LONDON – INTERNATIONAL SCHOOL EFFECTIVENESS AND IMPROVEMENT CENTRE

Acronym or abbreviation: ISEIC

Institute of Education, 20 Bedford Way, London, WC1H 0AL

Tel: 020 7612 6347/6323/6409
Fax: 020 7612 6344
E-mail: iseic.admin@ioe.ac.uk

Website:
http://www.ioe.ac.uk/iseic

Enquiries:
Enquiries to: Administrator

Founded:
1994

Organisation type and purpose:
Membership association (membership is by subscription), present number of members: 1100, university department or institute, research organisation.
Research and consultancy.

Subject coverage:
ISEIC brings together academics and professionals involved in research and development work in the fields of school effectiveness and improvement. It engages in consultancy work for LEAs and schools, and runs NSIN, the National School Improvement Network.

Printed publications:
Research Matters Series
NSIN Newsletter
Books and articles on school effectiveness and improvement topics

Publications list:
Available online and in print

Access to staff:
Contact by letter, by telephone, by fax and by e-mail. Non-members charged.
Hours: Mon to Fri, 0900 to 1700

Subsidiary body:
National School Improvement Network (NSIN) at the same address

UNIVERSITY OF NORTHAMPTON

Park Campus, Boughton Green Road, Northampton, NN2 7AL

Tel: 01604 735500
Fax: 01604 718819

Website:
http://library.northampton.ac.uk

Enquiries:
Enquiries to: Director of Information Services
Direct tel: 01604 892045
Direct e-mail: Hilary.Johnson@northampton.ac.uk

Organisation type and purpose:
University .

Subject coverage:
Whole range of social sciences and humanities, education, history of Northamptonshire, American studies, health studies, nursing, leather technology, waste management.

Museum or gallery collection, archive, or library special collection:
Collection of the National Leathersellers Centre
Osborne Robinson Collection of posters (1890 onwards) (School of Art and Design)
AEA Technology Wastes Management Collection

Library catalogue:
All or part available online

Access to staff:
Contact by letter, by telephone, by fax and by e-mail. Appointment necessary.
Hours: Term time: Mon to Fri, 0830 to 2200; Sat, 1000 to 1700; Sun, 1300 to 1700

Access for disabled people:
Access to all public areas, toilet facilities

Other address:
Avenue Campus
  St George's Avenue, Northampton, NN2 6JD

UNIVERSITY OF NOTTINGHAM – DJANOGLY LEARNING RESOURCE CENTRE

Acronym or abbreviation: DLRC

Jubilee Campus, Nottingham, NG8 1BB

Website:
http://www.nottingham.ac.uk/is

Organisation type and purpose:
University library.

Subject coverage:
Education and computer science.

Library catalogue:
All or part available online

UNIVERSITY OF NOTTINGHAM – GEORGE GREEN LIBRARY OF SCIENCE AND ENGINEERING

University Park, Nottingham, NG7 2RD

Tel: 0115 951 4570
Fax: 0115 951 4578

Website:
http://www.nottingham.ac.uk/is
List of staff contacts.

Enquiries:
Enquiries to: Librarian
Direct tel: 0115 846 7463

Organisation type and purpose:
Constituent part of the University library.

Subject coverage:
Botany; chemical engineering; chemistry; civil engineering; computer science; electrical and electronic engineering; geology; manufacturing engineering; materials science; mathematics; mechanical engineering; metallurgy; mineral resources engineering; pharmacy; physics; psychology; remote sensing; theoretical mechanics; zoology.

Museum or gallery collection, archive, or library special collection:
British Standards
Porter Collection (on ornithology)

Trade and statistical information:
International metal statistics.

UNIVERSITY OF NOTTINGHAM – GREENFIELD MEDICAL LIBRARY

Queen's Medical Centre, Nottingham, NG7 2UH

Tel: 0115 970 9441
Fax: 0115 970 9449
E-mail: library-medical-enquiries@nottingham.ac.uk

Website:
http://www.nottingham.ac.uk/is/locations/library/greenfield

Enquiries:
Enquiries to: Medical Librarian
Direct e-mail: wendy.stanton@nottingham.ac.uk

Founded:
1968

Organisation type and purpose:
University library.

Subject coverage:
Biochemistry; child health; community health; human anatomy; genetics; medicine; obstetrics and gynaecology; nursing; midwifery; pathology; physiology; pharmacology; psychiatry; surgery; therapeutics; anaesthetics; chemical pathology; chest medicine; dermatology; geriatrics; haematology; histopathology; learning disabilities; neurology; ophthalmology; paediatrics; radiology; rheumatology.

Museum or gallery collection, archive, or library special collection:
F H Jacob History of Medicine Collection

Library catalogue:
All or part available online

Access to staff:
Contact by letter, by telephone, by fax, by e-mail, in person and via website. Non-members charged.
Hours: Mon to Fri, 0800 to 2300

Access for disabled people:
Ramped entry, toilet facilities

Other affiliated libraries:
School of Nursing Library
  Mansfield
School of Nursing Library
  Derby

Serves the:
Nottingham University
  Faculty of Medicine and Health Sciences
University Hospital NHS Trust
  Queens Medical Centre

UNIVERSITY OF NOTTINGHAM – HALLWARD LIBRARY

University Park, Nottingham, NG7 2RD

Tel: 0115 951 4557
Fax: 0115 951 4558

Website:
http://www.nottingham.ac.uk/library

Enquiries:
Enquiries to: Librarian

Organisation type and purpose:
University library.

Subject coverage:
American studies (literature and history), archaeology, architecture, art history, child development, classics, economic, industrial and social history, economics, education, including adult education, educational psychology, English language and literature, film and cinema, French language and literature, geography, German language and literature, Hispanic studies (Spanish, Catalan, Portuguese), history, insurance, local government and administration, management, money and banking, music, philosophy; planning and development, politics, Slavonic studies, including Russian, Yugoslav, Serbian, Croatian and Slovene; social administration, social work, sociology, textile history, theology, trade unions and Viking studies.

Museum or gallery collection, archive, or library special collection:
Archive of newspaper cuttings (approximately 750,000 cuttings) relating to the politics, social, economic and cultural conditions in Germany (especially East Germany) 1946–1981
Holdings from former East German library (Diesdorf, Magdeburg)
Mellish Collection (meteorology)
Waldheim: A Commission of Enquiry – documentary research material collected by Thames Television for a television programme June 1988
Large collection of microforms, mainly in the arts and humanities
Large collection of CD-ROMs

Trade and statistical information:
Large collection of UK government and international statistics.

continued overleaf

Library catalogue:
All or part available online

Printed publications:
Introductory guide and index to archive of newspaper cuttings

Microform publications:
Large numbers mainly in the arts and humanities

Electronic and video publications:
Large collection of CD-ROMs and web-based products

Branch library of:
Nottingham University
  Music Library

UNIVERSITY OF NOTTINGHAM – JAMES CAMERON GIFFORD LIBRARY

Sutton Bonington Campus, Loughborough, Leicestershire, LE12 5RD

Tel: 0115 951 6390
Fax: 0115 951 6389
E-mail: suzanna.rogers@nottingham.ac.uk

Website:
http://www.nottingham.ac.uk/is

Enquiries:
Enquiries to: Librarian
Direct e-mail: library-biosciences-enquiries@nottingham.ac.uk

Organisation type and purpose:
University library.

Subject coverage:
Agriculture, horticulture, farm management, food science and microbiology, animal and plant biochemistry and physiology, environmental biology, soil science, applied biology, animal production, nutrition and dietetics, veterinary medicine and science.

Library catalogue:
All or part available online

Publications list:
Available online

Access to staff:
Contact by letter and by e-mail
Hours: Mon to Fri, 0900 to 1700

Constituent part of:
University of Nottingham Information Services

UNIVERSITY OF NOTTINGHAM – MANUSCRIPTS AND SPECIAL COLLECTIONS

King's Meadow Campus, Lenton Lane, Nottingham, NG7 2NR

Tel: 0115 951 4565
Fax: 0115 846 8651
E-mail: mss-library@nottingham.ac.uk

Website:
http://www.nottingham.ac.uk/mss
Reader services, including opening hours, descriptions of holdings, catalogues, online resources, e-learning and skills resources, exhibitions and digital gallery.

Enquiries:
Enquiries to: Manuscripts and Special Collections

Organisation type and purpose:
University library.

Museum or gallery collection, archive, or library special collection:
Manuscript and Archive Collections:
Includes local ecclesiastical, industrial and trade union collections, substantial collections of local family and estate papers; records of the Severn-Trent Water Authority and its forerunners from the 17th century; records of the General Hospital and other Nottingham hospitals

Manuscript collections in Restoration verse, William of Orange and the 1688 Revolution, the Jacobite Rising of 1745, the American War of Independence, the Peninsular War, the Crimean War, 18th- and 19th-century British and Irish politics and foreign affairs, India of the early 19th century, British colonies of the mid-19th century, history of nonconformity, draining of the Fens, the 17th-century naturalists John Ray and Francis Willoughby
D. H. Lawrence Collection (literary papers, books)
Germany 1946–1981: Archive of Newspaper Cuttings (in German)
Mellish Collection (meteorological papers)
Printed Books Collections:
Benedikz Collection (Icelandic literature, mainly in Icelandic)
Briggs Collection (educational books before 1851)
Cambridge Drama Collection (English plays 1750–1850)
Cambridge Shakespeare Collection (edns of Shakespeare's plays)
East Midlands Collection (Derbyshire, Leicestershire, Lincolnshire, Nottinghamshire, Rutland)
Medical Rare Books Collection
French Revolution Collection
Nottingham Medico-Chirurgical Society Collection
Oakham and Elston Parochial Libraries (17th century)
Coleorton Parish Library Collection
Parker Woodward Collection (on the Bacon-Shakespeare controversy)
Porter Ornithological Collection

Non-library collection catalogue:
All or part available online

Library catalogue:
All or part available online

Printed publications:
Children in War: Reminiscences of the Second World War
World War (1989)
D. H. Lawrence Exhibition Catalogues (1985)
Lawrence in Love: Letters from D. H. Lawrence to Louie Burrows (J. Boulton ed. 1968)
Nottinghamshire Marriage Bonds 1791–1800 (1987)
Campus Collection: A Photographic Record of the University of Nottingham (Ablett and Johnston 1989)
Politics and Society in Germany, Austria and Switzerland (vols 2 to 5)
Mender of disorders: court and community in the Archdeaconry of Nottingham, 1560–1756 (K. Holland, ed., 2004)

Microform publications:
Soviet War Posters, c.1940–1945: the Tass Poster Series from the Hallward Library, University of Nottingham
Guide with fiche/film (1992, Adam Matthew Publications)

Electronic and video publications:
D. H. Lawrence at the University of Nottingham (DVD, video, 2003)

Publications list:
Available online

Access to staff:
Contact by letter, by telephone, by fax, by e-mail and via website. Appointment necessary.
Hours: Mon to Fri, 0900 to 1700
Special comments: ID required for reader ticket.

UNIVERSITY OF OXFORD – BALFOUR LIBRARY (PITT RIVERS MUSEUM)

School of Anthropology and Museum Ethnography, South Parks Road, Oxford, OX1 3PP

Tel: 01865 270928
Fax: 01865 270943
E-mail: librarian@prm.ox.ac.uk

Website:
http://www.lib.ox.ac.uk/olis

OLIS, union catalogue.
http://www.prm.ox.ac.uk

Enquiries:
Enquiries to: Librarian
Direct tel: 01865 270939
Direct e-mail: library@prm.ox.ac.uk
Other contacts: Director of the Museum

Founded:
1884

Organisation type and purpose:
Museum, university library, suitable for ages: 18+.

Subject coverage:
Anthropology, ethnology, prehistoric archaeology, material culture, museum studies, ethnomusicology, visual anthropology (including ethnographic film and photography), ethnographic art.

Museum or gallery collection, archive, or library special collection:
Books owned by Henry Balfour, first curator of the Museum
Collection of over 100,000 anthropological photographs from c.1850 onwards
Collections of papers of Henry Balfour, E. B. Tyler, W. Baldwin Spencer and others who have made important contributions to the history of anthropology and archaeology (separate Manuscript and Photographic Archive, see website)
Ellen Ettlinger Bequest of books on folklore
June Bedford collection of books on ethnographic art

Non-library collection catalogue:
All or part available online

Library catalogue:
All or part available online and in-house

Printed publications:
Annual Report
Catalogue of the Australian Collections
Catalogue of the Native American Collection
Monograph series
Occasional papers on technology, archaeology, miscellaneous publications
The Origin and Development of the Pitt Museum

Publications list:
Available online and in print

Access to staff:
Contact by letter, by telephone, by fax and by e-mail. Appointment necessary.
Hours: Term time: Mon to Fri, 0900 to 1700
Vacations: 0900 to 1230 and 1400 to 1600; closed August
For Christmas and Easter hours, please phone or e-mail
Special comments: Reference only for non-members of the University.

Access for disabled people:
Parking provided

Links with:
Institute of Social and Cultural Anthropology
Tylor Library, University of Oxford

UNIVERSITY OF OXFORD – BODLEIAN EDUCATION LIBRARY

Acronym or abbreviation: EDU

15 Norham Gardens, Oxford, OX2 6PY

Tel: 01865 274028
Fax: 01865 274027
E-mail: education.library@bodleian.ox.ac.uk

Website:
http://www.education.ox.ac.uk/library

Formerly called:
Department of Educational Studies Library (year of change 2007); Education Library (year of change 2010)

Organisation type and purpose:
University department or institute.

Subject coverage:
Education; educational psychology; sociology of education; applied social sciences; methodology of teaching of subjects in the secondary school curriculum.

Services for disabled people:
Equipment available: magnifier, hearing loop, variable height chairs, lift to library level.
Services available: extended loan periods, book fetching.
Please let staff know if there is anything else they can do to improve your library experience.

Museum or gallery collection, archive, or library special collection:
Histories of individual schools and universities
Pre-1918 government publications on education

Library catalogue:
All or part available online

Access to staff:
Contact by letter, by telephone, by fax, by e-mail and in person
Hours: Term time: Mon to Thu, 0830 to 2030; Fri, 0830 to 1900; Sat, 1300 to 1700; Sun, 1200 to 1600
Vacation: Mon to Fri, 0900 to 1730

Access to building, collection or gallery:
Hours: Term time: Mon to Thu, 0830 to 2030; Fri, 0830 to 1900; Sat, 1300 to 1700; Sun, 1200 to 1600
Vacation: Mon to Fri, 0900 to 1730
Special comments: Visitors should have a Bodleian Reader's Card, available from http://www.bodleian.ox.ac.uk/services/admissions.

Access for disabled people:
Parking and lift available
Hours: Office hours (other times by appointment)
Special comments: There is a lift to the library; one reading room is reached by stairs only. Staff will happily fetch any books that are out of reach.

Constituent part of:
Bodleian Libraries
Bodleian Library, Broad Street, Oxford, OX1 3BG; tel: 01865 277162; fax: 01865 277182; e-mail: reader.services@bodleian.ox.ac.uk; website: http://www.bodleian.ox.ac.uk

UNIVERSITY OF OXFORD – BODLEIAN SOCIAL SCIENCE LIBRARY

Manor Road Building, Manor Road, Oxford, OX1 3UL

Tel: 01865 271093
Fax: 01865 271072
E-mail: library@ssl.ox.ac.uk

Website:
http://www.ssl.ox.ac.uk

Founded:
2004

Organisation type and purpose:
University library.

Subject coverage:
Criminology, economics, international development, politics and international relations, refugee studies, Russian and East European studies, social policy and social work, socio-legal studies, sociology.

Museum or gallery collection, archive, or library special collection:
150,000 vols, 1,000 journal and serial subscriptions
Economics and international development working papers from 200 institutions
African and Latin American collections

Trade and statistical information:
Data on all international trade.

Library catalogue:
All or part available online

Access to staff:
Contact by letter, by telephone, by fax, by e-mail and via website. Appointment necessary. Access for members only.

Hours: Mon to Fri, 0900 to 1730

Access to building, collection or gallery:
Term time: Mon to Fri, 0900 to 2200; Sat, 1000 to 1800; Sun, 1200 to 1800
Vacation: Mon to Fri, 0900 to 1900; Sat, 1000 to 1600; Sun, closed

Access for disabled people:
Ramped entry, wide doorway, toilet facilities

UNIVERSITY OF OXFORD – COMPUTING LABORATORY

The Library, Wolfson Building, Parks Road, Oxford, OX1 3QD

Tel: 01865 273838
Fax: 01865 273839
E-mail: library@comlab.ox.ac.uk

Website:
http://www.comlab.ox.ac.uk/
Information about courses, research and personnel with links to other parts and Oxford University.

Enquiries:
Enquiries to: Librarian
Direct tel: 01865 273837
Direct e-mail: Gordon.Riddell@comlab.ox.ac.uk

Organisation type and purpose:
University department or institute, research organisation.

Subject coverage:
Scientific computation including formal methods, numerical analysis and computational fluid dynamics, and general computing science.

Library catalogue:
All or part available online

Printed publications:
PRG Research Reports

Access to staff:
Appointment necessary.
Hours: Mon to Fri, 0900 to 1700

Subsidiary body:
Centre for Requirements and Foundations
Numerical Analysis Group (NAGp)
Programming Research Group (PRG)

UNIVERSITY OF OXFORD – DEPARTMENT OF EARTH SCIENCES

Parks Road, Oxford, OX1 3PR

Tel: 01865 272000
Fax: 01865 272072
E-mail: jennyc@earth.ox.ac.uk

Enquiries:
Enquiries to: Librarian
Direct tel: 01865 272050

Organisation type and purpose:
University department or institute.

Subject coverage:
Earth sciences; geology; geodesy; mineralogy; geochemistry; geophysics; oceanography; stratigraphy; tectonics; crystallography; petrology; sedimentology.

Museum or gallery collection, archive, or library special collection:
Collection of reprints
Wager, Lawrence Rickard (1904–1965) collection

Access to staff:
Contact by letter, by telephone, by fax and by e-mail. Appointment necessary. Letter of introduction required.
Hours: Term time; Mon to Thu, 0900 to 1730; Fri, 0900 to 1630
Vacations; Mon to Thu, 0900 to 1730

Access to building, collection or gallery:
No prior appointment required
Special comments: Bodleian Readers Card required

Access for disabled people:
Toilet facilities
Special comments: One step at entrance

UNIVERSITY OF OXFORD – DEPARTMENT OF PHYSICS

Denys Wilkinson Building, Keble Road, Oxford, OX1 3RH

Tel: 01865 273333
Fax: 01865 273418

Website:
http://www2.physics.ox.ac.uk/library/default.asp

Enquiries:
Enquiries to: Librarian
Direct tel: 01865 273421
Direct e-mail: library@physics.ox.ac.uk

Organisation type and purpose:
University department or institute.

Subject coverage:
Theoretical and observational cosmology, galactic astronomy, stellar and interstellar physics, telescopes and instrumentation, nuclear physics, particle physics.

Museum or gallery collection, archive, or library special collection:
Astronomical library (not open to the public)

Library catalogue:
All or part available in-house

Publications list:
Available in print

Access to staff:
Access for members only.
Hours: Mon to Fri, 1400 to 1700

Access to building, collection or gallery:
No access other than to staff

Access for disabled people:
Level entry, access to all public areas, toilet facilities

UNIVERSITY OF OXFORD – ENGINEERING SCIENCE LIBRARY

Department of Engineering Science, Parks Road, Oxford, OX1 3PJ

Tel: 01865 273193
Fax: 01865 273010
E-mail: library@eng.ox.ac.uk

Website:
http://www.eng.ox.ac.uk/home.html
General information on department and its research.

Enquiries:
Enquiries to: Librarian
Direct e-mail: anne.greig@eng.ox.ac.uk

Organisation type and purpose:
University department or institute.

Subject coverage:
Engineering.

Printed publications:
OUEL Reports (Departmental reports)
Annual summaries of current research projects

Access to staff:
Contact by letter, by telephone and by e-mail.
Appointment necessary.
Hours: Mon to Fri, 0900 to 1700

Parent body:
Oxford University

UNIVERSITY OF OXFORD – ENGLISH FACULTY LIBRARY

St Cross Building, Manor Road, Oxford, OX1 3UQ

Tel: 01865 271050
Fax: 01865 271054

continued overleaf

Website:
http://www.lib.ox.ac.uk
Oxford University libraries home page.
http://users.ox.ac.uk/~enginfo/
Library home page.

Enquiries:
Enquiries to: Librarian
Direct tel: 01865 271051
Direct e-mail: susan.usher@efl.ox.ac.uk

Founded:
1914

Organisation type and purpose:
University library.

Subject coverage:
English language and literature; Old Norse
language and literature.

**Museum or gallery collection, archive, or library
special collection:**
E H W Meyerstein's published books and
manuscripts
Old Norse: working libraries of E O G Turville-
Petre, W P Ker, G Vigfússon, and F York Powell
(the last two on loan from Christ Church)
Wilfred Owen Collection (his library, some
manuscripts and memorabilia)

Access to staff:
Contact by letter, by telephone, by fax and by e-
mail. Appointment necessary.
Hours: Termtime: Mon to Fri, 0930 to 1900, Sat 0930
to 1230
Vacations: Mon to Fri, 0930 to 1700
Special comments: Visitors from other academic
institutions may normally use the library for
reference purposes in the vacations only.

Access for disabled people:
Parking provided, ramped entry, level entry, access
to all public areas, toilet facilities

UNIVERSITY OF OXFORD –
MODERN LANGUAGES FACULTY
LIBRARY

Taylor Institution, St Giles, Oxford, OX1 3NA

Tel: 01865 278152
E-mail: library@modern-languages-library.oxford
.ac.uk

Website:
http://www.ox.ac.uk
Oxford University home page.
http://users.ox.ac.uk/~mlflinfo/index.html
Home page – some details of publications and
information, including classification, layout and
services; it also links to other web pages of interest
to modern linguists.
http://www.lib.ox.ac.uk
Oxford University libraries home page.

Enquiries:
Enquiries to: Librarian
Direct tel: 01865 278155
Direct e-mail: gordon.robson@mlfl.ox.ac.uk
Other contacts: Deputy Librarian for Spanish and
Portuguese.

Founded:
1960

Organisation type and purpose:
University department or institute.

Subject coverage:
Modern European languages and literature;
general linguistics, German, French, Italian,
Spanish, Portuguese, Latin American, Catalan,
Occitan; European cinema.

**Museum or gallery collection, archive, or library
special collection:**
Collection of European Newspapers (in original
form). This collection is to be disposed of owing
to lack of space. Any request from libraries for
any part of it will be welcome.
Recordings on audio and video cassette of
European literary, historical and cultural works,
and cinema

Non-library collection catalogue:
All or part available online

Library catalogue:
All or part available online

Printed publications:
Library Rules and Information

Access to staff:
Contact by letter, by telephone, by e-mail and in
person. Letter of introduction required.
Hours: Term time: Mon to Fri, 0900 to 1800
Vacations: 0900 to 1300 and 1400 to 1730
Summer: 0900 to 1300 and 1400 to 1700

UNIVERSITY OF OXFORD –
MUSIC FACULTY LIBRARY

Formal name: Bodleian Music Faculty Library

St Aldate's, Oxford, OX1 1DB

Tel: 01865 276148
E-mail: music.library@bodleian.ox.ac.uk

Website:
http://www.bodleian.ox.ac.uk/music
Library website.
http://www.solo.bodleian.ox.ac.uk
Library catalogue (partial holdings only).

Enquiries:
Enquiries to: Librarian
Other contacts: Deputy Librarian

Founded:
c.1950

Organisation type and purpose:
University library.

Subject coverage:
Music (western classical tradition).

**Museum or gallery collection, archive, or library
special collection:**
Byzantine music
Howes folk music collection
Music from the Oxford University Music Society
Library

Library catalogue:
All or part available online and in-house

Printed publications:
Library guide (free)

Access to staff:
Contact by telephone, by e-mail and in person
Hours: Term time: Mon to Fri, 0900 to 1800; Sat,
1000 to 1300
Vacations: shorter hours
Special comments: Non-university members have
reference-only access at the discretion of library
staff.

UNIVERSITY OF OXFORD –
PHYSICAL AND THEORETICAL
CHEMISTRY LABORATORY

South Parks Road, Oxford, OX1 3QZ

Tel: 01865 275400
Fax: 01865 275410
E-mail: jacob.klein@chem.ox.ac.uk

Website:
http://physchem.ox.ac.uk
General information on department.

Enquiries:
Enquiries to: Head of Department
Direct tel: 01865 275402

Organisation type and purpose:
University department or institute.

Subject coverage:
Physical, theoretical and computational chemistry.

Access to staff:
Contact by letter, by telephone, by fax, by e-mail
and via website
Hours: Mon to Fri, 0900 to 1700

UNIVERSITY OF OXFORD –
SCHOOL OF GEOGRAPHY AND
THE ENVIRONMENT LIBRARY

Parks Road, Oxford, OX1 3QP

Website:
http://www.bodleian.ox.ac.uk/science

Enquiries:
Enquiries to: Reader Services Librarian Geography
Direct tel: 01865 272800
Direct e-mail: enquiries.rsl@bodleian.ox.ac.uk

Founded:
1887

Housed in the:
Radcliffe Science Library (year of change 2007)

Organisation type and purpose:
University library.

Subject coverage:
Geography, environmental sciences and allied
subjects, mountaineering.

**Museum or gallery collection, archive, or library
special collection:**
Oxford Mountaineering Library
Radcliffe Meteorological Collection held within
School of Geography; access for visitors is via the
Library

Non-library collection catalogue:
All or part available online

Library catalogue:
All or part available online

Access to staff:
Contact by letter, by telephone, by fax, by e-mail
and in person. Appointment necessary.
Hours: Term time: Mon to Fri, 0830 to 2200; Sat,
1000 to 1600; Sun, 1100 to 1700
Vacations: Mon to Fri, 0830 to 1900; Sat, 1000 to
1400

Access for disabled people:
Ramped entry, toilet facilities

UNIVERSITY OF OXFORD –
SHERARDIAN LIBRARY OF PLANT
TAXONOMY

Department of Plant Sciences, South Parks Road,
Oxford, OX1 3RB

Tel: 01865 275025
E-mail: enquiries.plant@bodleian.ox.ac.uk

Website:
http://www.bodleian.ox.ac.uk/science

Enquiries:
Enquiries to: Sherardian Librarian
Direct tel: 01865 275025
Direct e-mail: anne.townsend@bodleian.ox.ac.uk

Founded:
1621

Previously part of:
Plant Sciences Library, which merged with
Radcliffe Science Library (year of change 2010)

Organisation type and purpose:
University library.

Subject coverage:
Plant taxonomy.

**Museum or gallery collection, archive, or library
special collection:**
Sibthorpian and Sherard Collections (historic
botanical works)

Non-library collection catalogue:
All or part available online and in-house

Library catalogue:
All or part available online

Printed publications:
Tropical Forestry Papers

Access to staff:
Contact by letter, by telephone, by fax, by e-mail,
in person and via website. Appointment necessary.

Hours: Mon to Fri, 0900 to 1730

Access for disabled people:
Access to all public areas, toilet facilities

Parent body:
University of Oxford, Bodleian Libraries

UNIVERSITY OF PLYMOUTH

Charles Seale-Hayne Library, Drake Circus,
Plymouth, Devon, PL4 8AA

Tel: 01752 587140
Fax: 01752 587100

Website:
http://www.plymouth.ac.uk/library
Opening hours, access to catalogue, information
for visitors and Associate Membership scheme.

Enquiries:
Enquiries to: Head of Customer Services
Direct tel: 01752 588725
Direct e-mail: libraryservices@plymouth.ac.uk

Organisation type and purpose:
University library.

Subject coverage:
Agriculture, architecture, art and design,
computing, civil engineering, economics,
education, electronic engineering, English
literature, environmental sciences, geography,
geology, health services, history, law, life sciences,
management, marine sciences, mathematics,
mechanical engineering, medicine, petroleum
geology, politics, psychology, shipping, social
work, sociology, transport.

Trade and statistical information:
UK core statistical data.

Library catalogue:
All or part available online

Access to staff:
Contact by letter, by telephone, by e-mail and via
website
Hours: Mon to Fri, 0900 to 1700
Special comments: See website for detailed opening
hours.
Reference only, except for Associate Membership
scheme.
Limited access to electronic information.

UNIVERSITY OF PORTSMOUTH

University Library, Cambridge Road, Portsmouth,
Hampshire, PO1 2ST

Tel: 023 9284 3228
Fax: 023 9284 3233
E-mail: library@port.ac.uk

Website:
http://www.port.ac.uk
General information on the University of
Portsmouth, courses, departments, library
information services.

Enquiries:
Enquiries to: Librarian

Organisation type and purpose:
University library.

Subject coverage:
Business studies; economics; management; law
and criminology; engineering and technology;
computing; environmental studies; social sciences;
physical and life sciences; health studies;
psychology; marine resources; languages and area
studies; literature; history; art and design;
European studies; media studies.

**Museum or gallery collection, archive, or library
special collection:**
Bolton collection (history of architecture)
European Documentation Centre

Library catalogue:
All or part available online

Access to staff:
Contact by letter, by telephone, by fax, by e-mail,
in person and via website. Non-members charged.
Hours: Mon to Fri, 0900 to 2045; Sat, Sun, 1000 to
1600
See website for holiday and vacation hours

Access to building, collection or gallery:
No prior appointment required

Access for disabled people:
Level entry, access to all public areas, toilet
facilities

UNIVERSITY OF READING – BULMERSHE LIBRARY

Woodlands Avenue, Reading, Berkshire, RG6 1HY

Tel: 0118 378 8652
Fax: 0118 378 8651
E-mail: g.connell@reading.ac.uk

Website:
http://www.library.rdg.ac.uk/about/bulmershe/
index.html
http://www.reading.ac.uk/library/using/sites/lib
-bulmershe.asp

Enquiries:
Enquiries to: Faculty Team Manager

Founded:
1964

Organisation type and purpose:
University library.

Subject coverage:
Education and related social sciences, community
health, social work, drama, film, history, children's
literature, and music.

UNIVERSITY OF READING – DEPARTMENT OF FOOD AND NUTRITIONAL SCIENCES

PO Box 226, Whiteknights, Reading, Berkshire,
RG6 6AP

Tel: 0118 378 8722
Fax: 0118 931 0080
E-mail: r.a.wilbey@reading.ac.uk

Website:
http://www.rdg.ac.uk
Historic collection of books relating to food science
and technology.

Enquiries:
Enquiries to: Librarian

Founded:
1892

Formerly called:
Department of Food Biosciences (year of change
2009)

Organisation type and purpose:
University department or institute.

Subject coverage:
Food, science and technology, nutrition,
biotechnology, industrial microbiology and
fermentation technology.

**Museum or gallery collection, archive, or library
special collection:**
McLachlan Library (food science and technology)

Library catalogue:
All or part available in-house

Access to staff:
Contact by e-mail
Hours: Mon to Fri, 0900 to 1700

UNIVERSITY OF READING – EUROPEAN DOCUMENTATION CENTRE

Acronym or abbreviation: EDC

Main Library, Whiteknights, PO Box 223, Reading,
Berkshire, RG6 6AE

Tel: 0118 378 8782
Fax: 0118 378 6636
E-mail: library-edc@reading.ac.uk

Website:
http://www.reading.ac.uk/library

Enquiries:
Enquiries to: EDC Librarian

Founded:
1967

Organisation type and purpose:
University library.

Subject coverage:
European Communities, European Union.

**Museum or gallery collection, archive, or library
special collection:**
Collection of European Communities and
European Union published material, donated for
the use of the University and local community

Library catalogue:
All or part available online

Access to staff:
Contact by letter, by telephone, by fax, by e-mail
and in person. Appointment necessary.
Hours: Mon to Fri, 0900 to 1700; evenings and
weekends during term time

Access to building, collection or gallery:
No prior appointment required

Access for disabled people:
Parking provided, access to all public areas

UNIVERSITY OF READING LIBRARY

Whiteknights, PO Box 223, Reading, Berkshire,
RG6 6AE

Tel: 0118 378 8770
Fax: 0118 378 6636
E-mail: library@reading.ac.uk

Website:
http://www.reading.ac.uk/library
Information about library services and collections.

Enquiries:
Enquiries to: Circulation Services Manager

Founded:
1926

Organisation type and purpose:
University library.

Subject coverage:
Agriculture (including history), archaeology,
classics, community studies, contemporary
European studies, economics, education, English,
fine art, French, physical sciences, earth sciences,
biological sciences, geography, German history,
history of art, Italian, land management, law,
linguistics, medieval studies, music, philosophy,
politics, psychology, sociology, typography and
graphic communication.

**Museum or gallery collection, archive, or library
special collection:**
Agricultural history
Farm Records
Publishers' and Printers' Archives
Children's Collection (and H. M. Brock)
Cole Library (history of zoology, comparative
anatomy and early medicine)
Finzi Collections of English Literature and Music
Henley Parish Library (history, philosophy and
literature)
Isotype Collection (statistical information in
graphic form)
Music (printed by lithography) and Victorian
music covers
Overstone Library (economics, literature, history
and travel)
Papers of Lord and Lady Astor
Printed ephemera

continued overleaf

Printing history (including Robert Gibbings)
Samuel Beckett Archive
Stenton Library (medieval history)
Turner Collection (French Revolution)

Non-library collection catalogue:
All or part available in-house

Library catalogue:
All or part available online

Printed publications:
Beckett at Reading: Catalogue of the Beckett manuscript collection
Catalogue of the collection of children's books, 1617–1939
Cole Library of Early English Medicine and Zoology (catalogue)
Historical Farm Records

Publications list:
Available online

Access to staff:
Contact by letter, by telephone and by e-mail
Hours: See information online

Access to building, collection or gallery:
No prior appointment required at Main and Bulmershe Libraries
Special comments: Prior appointment advisable to visit University archives and special collections at Special Collections Services, Redlands Road.

Access for disabled people:
Parking provided, ramped entry, level entry, access to all public areas, toilet facilities

Branch libraries:
Bulmershe Library (until Summer 2011 when role transfers to Main Library, Whiteknights)
Bulmershe Court, Earley, Reading, Berkshire, RG6 1HY; tel: 0118 378 8652; fax: 0118 378 8651

Links with:
Special Collections Services
University of Reading, Redlands Road, Reading, RG1 5EX; tel: 0118 378 6660; fax: 0118 378 5632; e-mail: specialcollections@reading.ac.uk; website: http://www.reading.ac.uk/special -collections

UNIVERSITY OF SALFORD, THE LIBRARY

Acronym or abbreviation: The Library

The Crescent, Salford, Manchester, M5 4WT

Tel: 0161 295 2444
Fax: 0161 295 6624
E-mail: its-servicedesk@salford.ac.uk

Website:
http://www.library.salford.ac.uk
http://www.salford.ac.uk

Founded:
1967

Formerly called:
Information Services Division (ISD) (year of change 2008); Information & Learning Services (year of change 2010)

Organisation type and purpose:
University library, information and learning services.

Subject coverage:
Art and design; built environment; business; computing, science and engineering; English, sociology, politics and contemporary history; environment and life sciences; health and social care; law; media, music and performance.

Museum or gallery collection, archive, or library special collection:
Arthur Hopcraft Archive
Badnall Papers
Bartington Hall Papers
Bridgewater Estates Archive
British Election Campaign Material
Changing Face of Salford Collection
Dockray Collection
Duke of Bridgewater Archive

English Velvet and Cord Dyers' Association Archive
Lancashire and Yorkshire Railway Drawings
Phil May and Leo Cheney Cartoons
Mather Papers
Oldham and Son Ltd Archive
Revans Collection
Salford Technical and Engineering Association Archive
Stanley Houghton Collection
University of Salford Local Collection
Walter Greenwood Collection
Willink Archive

Trade and statistical information:
General statistics issued by UK government departments.

Non-library collection catalogue:
All or part available online

Library catalogue:
All or part available online

Electronic and video publications:
Guides available, see website: http://www.library.salford.ac.uk

Publications list:
Available online

Access to staff:
Contact by letter, by telephone, by fax, by e-mail and via website. Appointment necessary.

Access to building, collection or gallery:
Hours: Term time, main library: Mon to Fri, 0800 to 0000; Sat, 1200 to 1800; Sun, 1200 to 1800
Visit website for other library opening times

Access for disabled people:
All libraries have ramp access, toilet facilities, lift

UNIVERSITY OF SHEFFIELD

Formal name: Information School, The University of Sheffield
Acronym or abbreviation: iSchool @ Sheffield

Information School, Regent Court, 211 Portobello Street, Sheffield, South Yorkshire, S1 4DP

Tel: 0114 222 2630
Fax: 0114 278 0300
E-mail: is@sheffield.ac.uk

Website:
http://www.shef.ac.uk/is
Information about the iSchool, its staff, its programmes of study and its research.
http://www.shef.ac.uk/is/publications
Provides information about publications produced by the iSchool.

Enquiries:
Enquiries to: Head of School
Direct tel: 0114 222 2638
Direct e-mail: p.levy@sheffield.ac.uk
Other contacts: Teaching and Learning Manager

Founded:
1963

Formerly called:
Department of Information Studies (year of change 2010)

Organisation type and purpose:
University department or institute.

Subject coverage:
The iSchool offers a number of taught degree programmes both at graduate (PGCert, PGDip, MA, MSc, MRes, MPhil, PhD) and undergraduate (BA and BSc) level, in the areas of librarianship, digital library management, information literacy, information management, multilingual information management, information systems, chemoinformatics and health informatics. In addition the iSchool has an international research profile within which two main research groups operate: Computational Informatics; and Library and Information Management. The research areas of study undertaken by these groups include: chemoinformatics; information retrieval;

information systems; information literacy; reader development; social inclusion; library management; knowledge and information management; health informatics; and educational informatics.

Information services:
Consultancy in all aspects of library and information management and information systems.

Education services:
Training in all aspects of library and information management and information systems. Occasional short courses. Bespoke training by arrangement.

Printed publications:
Occasional reports

Electronic and video publications:
Research reports

Publications list:
Available online

Access to staff:
Contact by letter, by telephone, by fax, by e-mail and via website
Hours: Mon to Fri, 0900 to 1700

Access to building, collection or gallery:
Hours: Mon to Fri, 0900 to 1700
Special comments: Access only from Portobello Street entrance.

Access for disabled people:
Ramped entry, toilet facilities
Hours: Mon to Fri, 0900 to 1700

UNIVERSITY OF SHEFFIELD – LIBRARY

Western Bank, Sheffield, South Yorkshire, S10 2TN

Tel: 0114 222 7200
Fax: 0114 222 7290
E-mail: library@sheffield.ac.uk

Website:
http://www.shef.ac.uk/library

Enquiries:
Enquiries to: Director of Library Services

Organisation type and purpose:
University library.

Subject coverage:
Arts; pure and life sciences; applied sciences; social sciences; engineering; medicine and dentistry; law; architectural studies; educational studies.

Museum or gallery collection, archive, or library special collection:
Collection of books on glass
Firth Collection of 19th-century ballads
Firth Collection of Civil War pamphlets
Hans Krebs Archives
Innes Smith collection of medical illustrations
Japanese and Korean Collection
Papers of Samuel Hartlib, W S Hewins and A J Mundella
Royal Infirmary donation of medical books
Sir Thomas Beecham Archive

Library catalogue:
All or part available online

Electronic and video publications:
Hartlib Papers (CD-ROM, pub. UMI)

Access to staff:
Contact by letter, by telephone, by e-mail, in person and via website
Hours: Mon to Thu, 0900 to 1900; Fri 1000 to 1900; Sat and Sun, 1200 to 1800 (WBL)

Access for disabled people:
Parking provided, ramped entry, toilet facilities

Constituent bodies:
Health Sciences Library
tel: 0114 271 2030; fax: 0114 278 0923; e-mail: lib -hsl@sheffield.ac.uk

St George's Library
   tel: 0114 222 7301; fax: 0114 222 7290; e-mail: lib
   -sgl@sheffield.ac.uk
Western Bank Library
   tel: 0114 222 7296; fax: 0114 222 7290; e-mail: lib
   -wbl@sheffield.ac.uk

UNIVERSITY OF SHEFFIELD – METALS ADVISORY CENTRE

Acronym or abbreviation: SUMAC

Department of Engineering Materials, Sir Robert
Hadfield Building, Mappin Street, Sheffield, South
Yorkshire, S1 3JD

Tel: 0114 222 5497
Fax: 0114 222 5493
E-mail: sumac@sheffield.ac.uk

Website:
http://www.sumac.group.shef.ac.uk
Promotional and services information.

Enquiries:
Enquiries to: Senior Consultant

Founded:
1981

Organisation type and purpose:
Advisory body, professional body, university
department or institute, consultancy, research
organisation.

Subject coverage:
Metal component failures, materials selection,
mechanical testing, chemical analysis, electron
microscopy, materials consultancy service.
Machinery, vehicle and structural malfunction.
Engineering Measurements on operating
machinery and plant.

Access to staff:
Contact by letter, by telephone, by fax and by e-
mail. Appointment necessary.
Hours: Mon to Fri, 0900 to 1700

Access to building, collection or gallery:
Prior appointment required

Access for disabled people:
Parking provided, level entry, access to all public
areas, toilet facilities

UNIVERSITY OF SHEFFIELD – THE INSTITUTE FOR LIFELONG LEARNING

Acronym or abbreviation: TILL

196–198 West Street, Sheffield, South Yorkshire, S1
4ET

Tel: 0114 222 7000
Fax: 0114 222 7001
E-mail: till@sheffield.ac.uk

Website:
http://www.shef.ac.uk/till

Enquiries:
Enquiries to: Publicity Officer
Direct tel: 0114 222 7009
Direct e-mail: k.wainwright@sheffield.ac.uk

Organisation type and purpose:
University library, university department or
institute, research organisation.
To make the resources of the university available to
the public, with a focus on continuing, part-time
and flexible education for adults.

Subject coverage:
Archaeology, arts, computing and information
technology, creative writing, earth sciences,
education, film, health, humanities, history,
language (French and Spanish), literature, music,
natural science, religious studies, theatre studies,
social and political studies, botanical illustration,
local studies; also part-time degree and certificate
courses.

Printed publications:
Part-time Degrees and Certificates brochure –
named awards (free)
Courses for Everyone brochure – general
programme (free)
Order printed publications from: via http://
coursesforeverone.co.uk

Access to staff:
Contact by letter, by telephone, by fax, by e-mail
and in person. Appointment necessary.
Hours: Mon to Fri, 0930 to 1640

Access to building, collection or gallery:
Customers via West Street Reception area
Hours: Mon to Fri, 0930 to 1630

UNIVERSITY OF SOUTHAMPTON LIBRARY

University Road, Highfield, Southampton, SO17
1BJ

Tel: 023 8059 2180
Fax: 023 8059 3007
E-mail: libenqs@soton.ac.uk

Website:
http://www.soton.ac.uk/library
Guide to services and information resources.

Enquiries:
Enquiries to: Librarian

Organisation type and purpose:
University library.

Subject coverage:
All subjects covered by the faculties and
departments of the university.

**Museum or gallery collection, archive, or library
special collection:**
Cope Collection on Hampshire and the Isle of
   Wight (Hartley)
European Documentation Centre (Hartley)
Ford Collection of British Official Publications
   (Hartley)
Parkes Library on relations between the Jewish and
   non-Jewish peoples (Hartley)
Perkins Agricultural Library (British and Irish
   writers on agriculture published before 1901;
   Hartley)
Manuscript collections, principally of 19th and
   20th centuries (Hartley) including:
Papers of the first Duke of Wellington
The Palmerston papers
The Mountbatten papers
The Broadlands collections

Non-library collection catalogue:
All or part available online

Library catalogue:
All or part available online

Printed publications:
Archive lists, Catalogues and Guides Series
Isle of Wight Photographers 1840–1940
Users' Guides

Publications list:
Available online

Access to staff:
Contact by letter, by telephone, by fax, by e-mail,
in person and via website
Hours: Mon to Fri, 0900 to 1700
Special comments: Library collections available for
reference only.
Evening and weekend opening at selected sites.
Visitors by prior appointment at the National
Oceanographic Library and the Winchester School
of Art.

Branch libraries:
Avenue Library
   Avenue Campus, University of Southampton,
   Highfield Road, Southampton, SO17 1BF; tel:
   023 8059 5432; e-mail: alengs@soton.ac.uk
Hartley Library
   University of Southampton, Highfield,
   Southampton, SO17 1BJ; tel: 023 8059 2180; fax:
   023 8059 3007; e-mail: libenqs@soton.ac.uk

Health Services Library
   MP883, Level A, South Academic Block,
   Southampton General Hospital, Tremona Road,
   Southampton, SO16 6YD; tel: 023 8079 6547; e-
   mail: hslib@soton.ac.uk
National Oceanographic Library
   National Oceanography Centre,Southampton,
   University of Southampton, Waterfront Campus,
   European Way, Southampton, SO14 3ZH; tel:
   023 8059 6116; fax: 023 8059 6115; e-mail: nol@
   soc.soton.ac.uk
Parkes Library
   Hartley Library, University of Southampton,
   Highfield, Southampton, SO17 1BJ; tel: 023 8059
   3335; fax: 023 8059 3007; e-mail: libenqs@soton
   .ac.uk
Winchester School of Art Library
   Park Avenue, Winchester, Hampshire, SO23
   8DL; tel: 023 8059 6982; e-mail: wsa@soton.ac.uk

UNIVERSITY OF ST ANDREWS LIBRARY

Formal name: University Library, University of St
Andrews

North Street, St Andrews, Fife, KY16 9TR

Tel: 01334 462281
Fax: 01334 462282
E-mail: library@st-andrews.ac.uk

Website:
http://www.st-andrews.ac.uk/library
General information about the library and its
services.

Enquiries:
Enquiries to: Director of Library Services
Direct tel: 01334 462301
Direct e-mail: jcu1@st-andrews.ac.uk

Founded:
1411

Organisation type and purpose:
University library.

Subject coverage:
Subjects of the Faculties of Arts, Divinity, Science
and Medicine.

**Museum or gallery collection, archive, or library
special collection:**
Large collection of United Kingdom and European
   community statistical publications
16th-century books (c. 3,500 items)
Andrew Lang Collection
Beveridge Collection (includes bee culture)
Bible Collection
Buchanan Collection (George Buchanan's works)
Copyright deposit collection, 1710–1837
Donaldson Collection (classics)
Finzi Collection (18th-century music scores)
Forbes Collection (early and rare science works)
Incunabula (150 items)
MacGillivray Collection (Celtic history and
   literature)
Mackay Collection (mathematics)
Manuscripts (over 100,000)
Photographs and prints (c. 300,000)
Runciman Collection
Simson and Wedderburn Collection (early medical
   books)
STC items (over 1,000 titles)
Valentine Collection (photographs and postcards)
von Hugel Collection (theology and philosophy)

Non-library collection catalogue:
All or part available online

Library catalogue:
All or part available online

Printed publications:
Dundee in 1793 and 1833: the First And Second
   Statistical Accounts
Living in St Andrews
Sheriffs of Scotland
St Andrews in 1793 and 1838: the First and Second
   Statistical Accounts
The Carved Stones of St Andrews
The Coins of St Andrews

continued overleaf

The University of St Andrews: a Short History

Publications list:
Available in print

Access to staff:
Contact by letter, by telephone, by fax and by e-mail. Appointment necessary.
Hours: Mon to Fri, 0845 to 0000; Sat, 0900 to 2100; Sun, 1300 to 0000
Vacations: Mon to Fri, 0900 to 2000

Access to building, collection or gallery:
University ID required or sign in at Security Desk

Access for disabled people:
Level entry, access to all public areas, lift, toilet facilities

Member organisation of:
Consortium of European Research Libraries
Scottish Confederation of University and Research Libraries
Tayside and Fife Library Information Network

UNIVERSITY OF STIRLING LIBRARY

Library, Andrew Miller Building, University of Stirling, Stirling, FK9 4LA

Tel: 01786 467235
Fax: 01786 466866
E-mail: library@stir.ac.uk

Website:
http://www.external.stir.ac.uk
http://www.is.stir.ac.uk
Library catalogue and holdings information, opening hours, borrowing information.

Enquiries:
Enquiries to: Director of Information Services
Other contacts: University Librarian

Founded:
1967

Organisation type and purpose:
University library.

Subject coverage:
General academic subjects (no engineering).

Museum or gallery collection, archive, or library special collection:
Lindsay Anderson Archive
Drummond Collection (religious tracts)
Howietoun Fish Farm Archive
John Grierson Archive (papers relating to the documentary film movement)
Leighton Library (personal collection of Archbishop Leighton 1611–84, 4,000 vols, 16th to 19th centuries)
MacLeod Collection (Scottish theatrical history)
Sir Walter Scott and Scottish authors contemporary with Scott
Tait Collection (left-wing political pamphlets)
Watson Collection (labour history)

Trade and statistical information:
General statistical reference section.

Non-library collection catalogue:
All or part available online

Library catalogue:
All or part available online

Printed publications:
John Grierson Archive Occasional Papers
Tait Pamphlet Collection: a checklist (1983)
Checklist of newspapers and periodicals in the Tait and Watson Collections: Stirling University Library (1990)
Two glossaries by Robert Burns: the glossaries to the Edinburgh and Kilmarnock Poems reproduced in facsimile (1987)
Inchnadamph and other poems (Norman MacCaig, 1978)
Rob Stene's dream (David Reid ed., 1989)
Catalogue of manuscripts: Leighton Library (Gordon Willis, 1981)
The Stirling Tract Enterprise and the Drummonds (Mike Cormack, 1984)

J. D. Fergusson at Stirling: an illustrated catalogue with an introduction by Guy Peploe (1991)
Order printed publications from: Library Office, University of Stirling Library, Andrew Miller Building, University of Stirling, Stirling, FK9 4LA

Publications list:
Available online

Access to staff:
Contact by letter, by telephone, by fax, by e-mail, in person and via website. Appointment necessary. Non-members charged.
Hours: Mon to Fri, 0900 to 1700

Access to building, collection or gallery:
A major redevelopment of the Library building is due to be completed in late August 2010. Please contact library@stir.ac.uk for information about access to the building and collections in summer 2010.
Hours: Please check website for current opening hours

Access for disabled people:
Lift access to all floors

Also at:
Highland Health Sciences Library
University of Stirling – Highland Campus, Centre for Health Science, Old Perth Road, Inverness, IV2 3JH; tel: 01463 255600 (extn 7600); fax: 01463 255605; e-mail: hhsl-inverness@stir.ac.uk

UNIVERSITY OF STRATHCLYDE – ANDERSONIAN LIBRARY

Curran Building, 101 St James Road, Glasgow, G4 0NS

Tel: 0141 548 4620
Fax: 0141 552 3304
E-mail: library@strath.ac.uk

Website:
http://www.lib.strath.ac.uk

Enquiries:
Enquiries to: Assistant Director: Information Services Directorate (Library & Information Resources)
Direct tel: 0141 548 4602
Direct e-mail: m.roberts@strath.ac.uk

Founded:
1964

Organisation type and purpose:
University library.

Subject coverage:
All subjects studied in the Faculties of Science, Engineering, Humanities and Social Sciences (including Education) and in the Strathclyde Business School.

Special visitor services:
http://www.lib.strath.ac.uk/visitors.htm

Services for disabled people:
http://www.lib.strath.ac.uk/libdis.htm

Museum or gallery collection, archive, or library special collection:
Aldred Collection (pamphlets on anarchism)
Anderson Collection (founder's library, 1726–1796)
British Standards on microfiche
Jordanhill Archive (Scottish education)
Laing Collection (mathematics, 17th–19th centuries)
Major British company reports
Robertson Collection (West of Scotland)
Royal Scottish Geographical Society Library
Strathclyde collection (publications by University staff or departments)
Young Collection (alchemy, chemistry, pharmacy, 16th–19th centuries)

Non-library collection catalogue:
All or part available online

Library catalogue:
All or part available online

Printed publications:
Annual Report
Guides to Library Services

Access to staff:
Contact by e-mail
Hours: Mon to Fri, 0900 to 1700

Access to building, collection or gallery:
Hours: see website: http://www.lib.strath.ac.uk/hours.htm

Access for disabled people:
Access to all public areas
Special comments: Lift access to all floors of Andersonian Library.

Constituent bodies:
Jordanhill Library
tel: 0141 950 3300; fax: 0141 950 3150; e-mail: jordanhill.library@strath.ac.uk

UNIVERSITY OF STRATHCLYDE – GRADUATE SCHOOL OF ENVIRONMENTAL STUDIES

Acronym or abbreviation: GSES

Graham Hills Building, 50 Richmond Street, Glasgow, G1 1XN

Tel: 0141 548 4078
Fax: 0141 548 3489
E-mail: g.s.e.s@strath.ac.uk

Website:
http://www.strath.ac.uk/Departments/GSES/
Course details, general information on department, staff, etc.

Enquiries:
Enquiries to: Director
Direct e-mail: p.h.booth@strath.ac.uk

Founded:
1992

Organisation type and purpose:
University department or institute.

Subject coverage:
Environmental issues.

Printed publications:
Course Details (free)

Publications list:
Available online and in print

Access to staff:
Contact by letter, by telephone, by fax and by e-mail. Appointment necessary.
Hours: Mon to Fri, 0900 to 1700

UNIVERSITY OF STRATHCLYDE – JORDANHILL LIBRARY

76 Southbrae Drive, Glasgow, G13 1PP

Tel: 0141 950 3300
Fax: 0141 950 3150
E-mail: jordanhill.library@strath.ac.uk

Website:
http://www.strath.ac.uk/jhlibrary

Enquiries:
Enquiries to: Campus Librarian

Founded:
1828

Organisation type and purpose:
University library.

Subject coverage:
Teacher education, social work, community education, sport and leisure, community arts, speech therapy, children's literature, Scottish and Gaelic language and literature, music, counselling.

Library catalogue:
All or part available online

Printed publications:
Library user leaflets (annually)

College History – Teaching the Teachers: The History of Jordanhill College of Education 1828–1993

Access to staff:
Contact by letter, by telephone, by fax, by e-mail, in person and via website. Appointment necessary.
Hours: Term time: Mon to Thu, 0900 to 2100; Fri and Sat, 0900 to 1700; Sun, 1100 to 1700
Vacations: Mon to Fri, 0900 to 1700; Sat, 0900 to 1200; Sun, 1100 to 1700

Access for disabled people:
Parking provided, ramped entry, access to all public areas
Special comments: Toilet facilities outside library.

UNIVERSITY OF SUNDERLAND – ASHBURNE LIBRARY

Ashburne House, Backhouse Park, Ryhope Road, Sunderland, Tyne and Wear, SR2 7EF

Tel: 0191 515 2119
Fax: 0191 515 3166
E-mail: jan.dodshon@sunderland.ac.uk

Website:
http://www.library.sunderland.ac.uk/
Library information and catalogue.

Enquiries:
Enquiries to: Librarian

Organisation type and purpose:
University library.

Subject coverage:
Art history, design history, sculpture, ceramics, illustration, design, glass, painting, printmaking, photography, model making.

Museum or gallery collection, archive, or library special collection:
40,000 books
Slide collection of 60,000 slides

Non-library collection catalogue:
All or part available online

Library catalogue:
All or part available online

Access to staff:
Contact by letter, by telephone and by e-mail. Appointment necessary. Non-members charged.
Hours: Term Time: Mon, Tue, 0900 to 2100; Wed, Thu, 0900 to 2000; Fri, 0900 to 1700, Sat, 1000 to 1300
Vacation: Mon to Fri, 0900 to 1700
Special comments: Charges to non-members for borrowing; open to general public for reference.

Access to building, collection or gallery:
No prior appointment required
Hours: As before

Access for disabled people:
Parking provided
Special comments: Library on 1st floor – no lift.

UNIVERSITY OF SUNDERLAND – MURRAY LIBRARY

Information Services, The Murray Library, Chester Road, Sunderland, Tyne and Wear, SR1 3SD

Tel: 0191 515 2900
Fax: 0191 515 2904
E-mail: andrew.mcdonald@sunderland.ac.uk

Website:
http://www.library.sunderland.ac.uk

Enquiries:
Enquiries to: Director
Direct tel: 0191 515 2905
Direct fax: 0191 515 3914
Other contacts: Assistant Director Information Services

Organisation type and purpose:
University library.

Subject coverage:
Art and design, education, business management, law, humanities, social studies, computing, mathematics, science, engineering, technology, pharmacy, health studies, environmental studies.

Printed publications:
Prospectus

Access to staff:
Contact by letter, by fax and by e-mail
Hours: Term time: Mon to Thu, 0830 to 2200; Fri, 0830 to 2100; Sat 0945 to 1800; Sun 0945 to 1800
Vacations: Mon to Fri, 0900 to 1700

UNIVERSITY OF SURREY – UNIVERSITY LIBRARY

Acronym or abbreviation: UniS

Guildford, Surrey, GU2 7XH

Tel: 01483 683325
Fax: 01483 689500
E-mail: library-enquiries@surrey.ac.uk

Website:
http://talis-prism.lib.surrey.ac.uk/TalisPrism/
Library catalogue.
http://portal.surrey.ac.uk:7778/portal/
page?_pageid=734,1&_dad=portal&_schema=
PORTAL
Library name-page.

Enquiries:
Enquiries to: The Librarian

Organisation type and purpose:
University library.

Subject coverage:
Biomedical sciences, biochemistry, toxicology, nutrition, chemical engineering, environmental strategy, civil engineering, electronic engineering (including satellite research), computing science, mechanical engineering, physics, chemistry, microbiology, economics, sociology, law, dance studies, statistics, politics, psychology, hotel, catering and tourism management, linguistics, music, mathematics, materials science, industrial and environmental health, nursing and midwifery, occupational health and safety, biomedical engineering, translation, sound recording.

Museum or gallery collection, archive, or library special collection:
European Documentation Centre (catalogue online)
National Resource Centre for Dance
E H Shepard Archive, original drawings and manuscripts

Non-library collection catalogue:
All or part available online

Library catalogue:
All or part available online

Access to staff:
Contact by telephone, by e-mail and via website
Hours: During semester: Mon to Fri, 0830 to 2100; Sat, 1400 to 1800; Sun, 1400 to 1800
Special comments: Hours alter during vacations – see library website.

Access for disabled people:
Parking provided, toilet facilities

Connections with:
M25 Consortium of Higher Education Libraries
Surrey and Sussex Libraries in Co-operation (SASLIC)
UK Libraries Plus Scheme

UNIVERSITY OF SUSSEX

The Library, Falmer, Brighton, East Sussex, BN1 9QL

Tel: 01273 678163
Fax: 01273 678441
E-mail: library@sussex.ac.uk

Website:
http://www.sussex.ac.uk/library

Enquiries:
Enquiries to: Librarian
Direct tel: 01273 678158; 01273 678157 (Special Collections)
Direct e-mail: library.specialcoll@sussex.ac.uk (Special Collections)
Other contacts: Head of Special Collections (for access to special collections, MSS and rare books)

Founded:
1962

Incorporates the former:
Education Library

Organisation type and purpose:
University library.

Subject coverage:
All arts and social sciences, applied science and technology, biological sciences, mathematics, physical sciences, molecular science, economics (including commerce).

Museum or gallery collection, archive, or library special collection:
Special Collections: manuscripts, archives and rare books
Allsop Collection (correspondence, notes and drafts of Kenneth Allsop)
Baker Collection of Fine Books (mainly 19th century, some 180 titles)
Caffyn Books (first and other editions of works by Shelley, and some critical and biographical studies, some 28 items, together with copies of 22 letters from Shelley and other non-printed material)
Carrington Collection (papers of C. E. Carrington and others c.1935–79 on Rudyard Kipling)
Charleston Collection (personal correspondence of members of the Bloomsbury Group)
Common Wealth Collection (papers of the British political organisation 1940 onwards)
Crowther Collection (on scientific journalism and politics, 1920–74)
Benn W. Levy Collection (collection of Benn Wolfe Levy on politics and the theatre, c.1930–70)
Eugene Shulkind Commune collection (periodicals, newspapers, monographs, posters and cartoons from and about the Paris Commune, 1871, some 2,500 items)
Gorer Collection (papers, correspondence, photographs, notebooks, c.1930–80, of Geoffrey Gorer, social anthropologist)
Gregory Collection (papers of Sir Richard Gregory, astronomer and editor of 'Nature' on scientific affairs and journalism, c.1880–1952)
Hogarth Press Collection (items from Leonard Woolf's file collection of Hogarth Press books, augmented by purchases and gifts)
James Stevenson Collection (Baron Stevenson of Holmbury, 1873–1926)
John Hilton Bureau Collection (papers, press-cuttings, written evidence for official enquiries, etc., of the John Hilton Bureau, News of the World Ltd, 1945–68)
Kingsley Martin Collection (correspondence, diaries, notes, pamphlets and press cuttings 1910–69)
Kipling Collection (correspondence, literary manuscripts, press cuttings, drawings, photographs, India and England 1870–1940 of Rudyard Kipling and John Lockwood Kipling, on deposit from the National Trust)
Leonard Woolf Collection (papers of Leonard Woolf on literary, political, domestic and personal affairs c.1890–1969)
Leys Collection (papers of Professor C. T. Leys on the politics and administration of Uganda, 1962–66)
Madge Papers (early poetry, notebooks and correspondence of Charles Madge, 1920–96)
Mass-Observation Archive (see separate entry)
Matusow Collection I (correspondence, press cuttings, court reports, diaries, photographs, tape recordings and films particularly on the politics of the McCarthy period 1950–55)
Matusow Collection II (USA underground ephemera, alternative society material, and Harvey Matusow personalia 1960s–80s)

continued overleaf

Monks House Collection (literary papers and correspondence 1900–42 of Virginia Woolf and associated collection of Virginia Woolf books)

Muir/Norden archive (radio comedy scripts and notes 1948–70)

New Statesman Collection (editorial correspondence, drafts, business papers, etc., from the files of The New Statesman 1943–88)

Pledge Collection (papers on the history of science and knowledge, 1919–60, of Humphrey Thomas Pledge, Assistant Keeper and then Keeper of the Science Museum Library)

Reckitt Collection (papers, correspondence and press cuttings of Maurice Benington Reckitt on religion in politics and social questions, and Christian socialism 1915–70)

Rolph Collection (papers of C. H. Rolph including correspondence, news cuttings, etc., relating to Kingsley Martin and The New Statesman)

Rosey Pool Collection (papers, correspondence, photographs, music, etc., on black American literature 1945–70)

Stamp Collection (papers on geographical subjects, especially land use, 1910–65, of Sir Laurence Dudley Stamp, Director of the Land-Use Survey (International Geographical Union))

Travers Collection (mainly 15th- and 16th-century printed books, some 350 titles)

Wartime Social Survey Collection (papers, principally interviews and survey reports, on economic and social conditions in Britain, 1940–41)

World Parliament Association Collection (papers, photographs, minutes, reports, correspondence and programmes, mostly on federalism and world government)

Non-library collection catalogue:
All or part available online

Library catalogue:
All or part available online

Printed publications:
All Special Collections catalogues available online
General helpsheets and information leaflets available in-house to support use of library

Publications list:
Available online

Access to staff:
Contact by letter, by telephone, by fax, by e-mail, in person and via website
Hours: Term time: 24-hour access from Mon, 0845 to Sat, 1930; Sun, 1230 to 1930
Vacations: Mon, Wed, Thu, Fri, 0900 to 1730; Tue, 0900 to 2000; Sat, closed; Sun, 1300 to 1800

UNIVERSITY OF SUSSEX SPECIAL COLLECTIONS

The Library, University of Sussex, Brighton, East Sussex, BN1 9QL

Tel: 01273 678157
Fax: 01273 678441
E-mail: library.specialcoll@sussex.ac.uk

Website:
http://www.sussex.ac.uk/library/speccoll

Enquiries:
Enquiries to: Special Collections Manager

Founded:
1964

Organisation type and purpose:
To provide public access to and care for the archives, manuscripts, rare books and art works of the University of Sussex, including the Mass-Observation Archive which is a registered charity. The Mass-Observation Archive continues to operate as a research unit specialising in the collection of autobiographical accounts of everyday life in Britain.

Subject coverage:
The University of Sussex holds a number of internationally acclaimed archival, manuscript and rare book collections, mostly relating to 20th-century literary, political and social history.

Museum or gallery collection, archive, or library special collection:
Over 80 collections, including:
Several Rare Book collections (Travis and Baker)
Bloomsbury related collections, including the Monks House Papers (Virginia Woolf)
Archive of Rudyard Kipling
Eugene Schulkind Paris Commune Collection
New Statesman Archive
Mass-Observation Archive: 1937 to mid-1950s
Mass-Observation Archive (phase 2) from 1981 to the present
Related collections of diaries, letters, personal collections and photographs

Non-library collection catalogue:
All or part available online

Printed publications:
Mass-Observation Archive publications include:
Occasional Papers Series (12 titles) includes:
Beneath the Mourning Veil: Mass Observation and the Death of Diana (J. Thomas, 2002)
Damned Anecdotes and Dangerous Confabulations: Mass Observation as Life History (D. Sheridan, 1996)
Health, Sickness and the Work Ethic (H. Busby, 2000)
Observing the Other: Mass Observation and Race (T. Kushner, 1995)
Order printed publications from: All original Mass-Observation book publications and selected collections 1937–55 by
theme available from Adam Matthew Publications.

Electronic and video publications:
Mass-Observation File Report Sequence (Primary Media Services)

Publications list:
Available online and in print

Access to staff:
Contact by letter, by telephone, by fax, by e-mail and in person. Appointment necessary.

Access to building, collection or gallery:
ID required (including photograph and address); visits to Special Collections by appointment only
Hours: Mon to Thu, 0915 to 1700
Special comments: Charges made to some non-academic users.

Access for disabled people:
Level entry, toilet facilities. Assistive technology available in reading room.

Links with:
University of Sussex Library
tel: 01273 678163; fax: 01273 678441; website: http://www.sussex.ac.uk/library

UNIVERSITY OF THE ARTS LONDON – CHELSEA COLLEGE OF ART AND DESIGN

Millbank, London, SW1P 4JU

Tel: 020 7514 7773
Fax: 020 7514 7785
E-mail: enquiries@chelsea.arts.ac.uk

Website:
http://www.arts.ac.uk/library
University of the Arts London Library Services webpage, includes online catalogue.

Enquiries:
Enquiries to: Assistant Learning Resources Manager
Other contacts: Reader and Information Services Librarian

Founded:
1890

Formerly called:
Chelsea School of Art

Organisation type and purpose:
University department or institute. Partnered with Camberwell College of Arts, Central Saint Martins College of Art and Design, London College of Communication, London College of Fashion and Wimbledon College of Art.

Subject coverage:
Fine art; modern art history; applied arts; design and design history; women's art.

Museum or gallery collection, archive, or library special collection:
Archives of the College
African-Caribbean, Asian and African Art in Britain Archive
Artists' books
Artists' Multiples
European and American Art and Design History from 1850
Exhibition catalogues
Jean Spencer Archive
Kurt Schwitters Archive
Modern Art Periodicals
Women's International Art Club Archive

Non-library collection catalogue:
All or part available online

Library catalogue:
All or part available online

Microform publications:
Contemporary Art Slide Scheme (subscription service)

Access to staff:
Appointment necessary.
Hours: Mon to Fri, 0900 to 1700

Access to building, collection or gallery:
By appointment only
Hours: Mon to Fri, 0900 to 1700

Access for disabled people:
Lift access available
Hours: Mon to Fri, 0900 to 1700

Part of:
University of the Arts London

UNIVERSITY OF THE WEST OF ENGLAND – FRENCHAY CAMPUS (BOLLAND) LIBRARY

Acronym or abbreviation: UWE

Coldharbour Lane, Bristol, BS16 1QY

Tel: 0117 328 2404
Fax: 0117 328 2407
E-mail: library.admin@uwe.ac.uk

Website:
http://www.uwe.ac.uk/library

Enquiries:
Enquiries to: Head of Library Services
Direct tel: 0117 328 2406
Direct e-mail: catherine.rex@uwe.ac.uk

Formerly called:
Bristol Polytechnic (year of change 1992)

Organisation type and purpose:
University library.

Subject coverage:
Nursing and allied health professions (Glenside, Hartpury).
Architecture, languages, law, management, social sciences, built environment, business, mathematics, computing, education, engineering, applied science, psychology, environmental health, geography, information science (Frenchay Campus (Bolland) Library).
History, literature, cultural studies, drama, music therapy (St Matthias).
Animal and land sciences, sports sciences (Hartpury).
Art, media and design (Bower Ashton).

Library catalogue:
All or part available online

Access to staff:
Contact by letter, by telephone, by fax, by e-mail, in person and via website. Non-members charged.
Hours: Term time: Mon to Thu, 0900 to 2000; Fri, 0900 to 1900; Sat, 1000 to 1600
Vacations: Mon to Thu, 0900 to 1700; Fri, 0900 to 1630; Sat, 0930 to 1300

Special comments: No charges for use of the library for reference.

Branch libraries:
Bower Ashton
  UWE Library Services, Kennel Lodge Road, Bristol, BS3 2JT; tel: 0117 328 4750; fax: 0117 328 4745
Glenside
  UWE Library Services, Blackberry Hill, Stapleton, Bristol, BS16 1DD; tel: 0117 328 8404; fax: 0117 328 8402
St Matthias
  UWE Library Services, Oldbury Court Road, Fishponds, Bristol, BS16 2JP; tel: 0117 328 4472
The Frank Parkinson Learning Resources Centre
  UWE Library Services, Hartpury College, Hartpury House, Gloucester, GL19 3BE; tel: 01452 702160; fax: 01452 702161

UNIVERSITY OF THE WEST OF SCOTLAND

Acronym or abbreviation: UWS

Paisley, Renfrewshire, PA1 2BE

Tel: 0141 848 3758
Fax: 0141 848 3761

Website:
http://www.uws.ac.uk
Access to online catalogues.

Enquiries:
Enquiries to: University Librarian
Direct tel: 0141 848 3750
Direct fax: 0141 887 0812
Direct e-mail: philomena.millar@uws.ac.uk

Founded:
2007

Created by the merger of:
University of Paisley and Bell College Hamilton (year of change 2007)

Organisation type and purpose:
University library, university department or institute.

Subject coverage:
Computing, land economics, business economics, mathematics, physics, chemistry, biology, electronics, electrical engineering, mechanical engineering, industrial engineering, civil engineering, chemical engineering, applied social studies, information technology, management, nursing and health care.

Museum or gallery collection, archive, or library special collection:
Aviation history collection
Norman Buchan parliamentary papers
Collection of material on Scottish railways including maps
Hugh MacDiarmid collection
L. F. Richardson archive
IUP 19th-century government papers
SLGIU Scottish Poll Tax Archive
Hugh McMahon EU Papers
West of Scotland Community Relations Council Archive
Scottish Milk Marketing Board Archive
20th-century American literature archive and collection
Stuart Harvey Papers

Non-library collection catalogue:
All or part available online

Library catalogue:
All or part available online

Printed publications:
Calendar of Scottish Railway Maps
Forward by Degrees: the University of Paisley 1897–1997
L. F. Richardson Calendar
Paisley Poets: A Critical Re-appraisal
Renfrewshire Studies

Access to staff:
Contact by letter, by telephone, by fax and by e-mail. Appointment necessary.

Hours: Term time: 0900 to 2100
Special comments: Enquiries involving the use of special information units, to the Director of the Technology and Business Centre; reference and lending services available to external users without charge; fees charged for bibliographic work, online searches, loans from other libraries and telecommunications services.

Access for disabled people:
Level entry, access to all public areas, toilet facilities
Special comments: Parking available.

Also at:
Ayr Campus
  Beech Grove, Ayr, KA8 0SR; tel: 01292 886345; fax: 01292 886006; e-mail: margo.stewart@paisley.ac.uk
Dumfries Campus
  The Crichton Library, Dumfries and Galloway College Building, Bankend Road, Dumfries, DG1 4FD; tel: 01387 734275; e-mail: avril.goodwin@uws.ac.uk
Hamilton Campus
  Almada Street, Hamilton, ML3 0JB; tel: 01698 283100; e-mail: john.burke@uws.ac.uk

Constituent bodies:
Ayrshire Management Centre
  tel: 01292 886400; fax: 01292 886401; e-mail: amc-info@paisley.ac.uk
Biotechnology Transfer Centre
  e-mail: biology@paisley.ac.uk
Centre for Alcohol and Drug Studies
  tel: 0141 848 3140
Centre for Gerontology and Health Studies
  tel: 0141 848 3771; fax: 0141 848 3891; e-mail: m.gilhooly@paisley.ac.uk
Centre for Particular Characterization and Analysis
  tel: 0141 848 3241; fax: 0141 848 3204
Comhairle: The Scottish Centre for European Public Sector Studies
  tel: 0141 848 3351; fax: 0141 848 3395; e-mail: comhairle@paisley.ac.uk
Electromagnetic Compatibility Centre
  tel: 0141 848 3419; fax: 0141 848 3404; e-mail: emcc@paisley.ac.uk
Land Value Information Unit
  tel: 0141 848 3747; fax: 0141 848 9799; e-mail: lviu@paisley.ac.uk
Materials and Components Development and Testing Association
  tel: 0141 848 3000
Microelectronics in Business Centre
  tel: 0141 848 3419; fax: 0141 848 3404; e-mail: mib-ee@paisley.ac.uk
Scottish Property Network
  tel: 0141 561 7300; fax: 0141 561 7319; e-mail: spn@paisley.ac.uk
Technology and Business Centre
  tel: 0141 848 3302; fax: 0141 848 3542; e-mail: brian.cross@paisley.ac.uk

UNIVERSITY OF THE WEST OF SCOTLAND – AYR CAMPUS

Acronym or abbreviation: UWS Ayr

Beech Grove, Ayr, KA8 0SR

Tel: 01292 886000
Fax: 01292 886006

Website:
http://www.uws.ac.uk/schoolsdepts/library

Enquiries:
Enquiries to: Librarian
Direct tel: 01292 886345
Direct fax: 01292 886288
Direct e-mail: neal.buchanan@uws.ac.uk

Founded:
1965

Created by the merger of:
University of Paisley and Bell College (year of change 2007)

Formerly called:
Craigie College of Education (year of change 1993)

Organisation type and purpose:
University library.

Subject coverage:
Education, educational psychology, children's books, nursing, health care studies, management and business studies, media studies, film studies, commercial music, digital art.

Museum or gallery collection, archive, or library special collection:
Scottish Poetry Library (branch)
West of Scotland Development Education Centre (collection)

Non-library collection catalogue:
All or part available online

Library catalogue:
All or part available online

Access to staff:
Contact by letter, by telephone, by e-mail, in person and via website
Hours: Term time: Mon to Thu, 0900 to 2050; Fri, Sat, 0900 to 1650
Vacations: Mon to Sat, 0900 to 1650

Branch of:
University of the West of Scotland
  Robertson Trust Library and Learning Resources, High Street, Paisley, PA1 2BE; tel: 0141 848 3000; e-mail: library@uws.ac.uk

UNIVERSITY OF ULSTER

Acronym or abbreviation: UU

Information Services Department, Cromore Road, Coleraine, Co Londonderry, BT52 1SA

Tel: 08700 400 700

Website:
http://www.ulster.ac.uk/
University's home page.
http://www.ulster.ac.uk/library/
Library's home page, library online catalogue, staff, services, facilities, news and announcements. Connect to the University of Ulster Library Catalogue and other library catalogues in the UK.

Enquiries:
Enquiries to: Director of Information Services

Founded:
1984

Formed by the merger of:
New University of Ulster, Ulster Polytechnic (year of change 1984)

Organisation type and purpose:
University library.

Subject coverage:
Economics, social administration, social organisation, social anthropology, conflict studies, media studies, education, English, Irish, French, German and, Spanish languages and literature, linguistics, classics, history, business studies, nursing, psychology, geography, environmental studies, communication studies, biological and biomedical sciences and surface science.

Museum or gallery collection, archive, or library special collection:
Denis Johnston Manuscripts
E N Carrothers Collection of Bookplates
English linguistics collection, microfiche
European Documentation Centre
Francis Stewart Archive of literary manuscripts
Headlam-Morley Collection, library of books, pamphlets and manuscripts relating to World War I and the Peace Treaty
Henry Davis gift of incunabula, fine bindings etc
Henry Morris Irish Collection
Irish Travelling People: Resource Collection
John Hewitt Library
Paul Ricard Library relating to World War II
Shiels plays
Stelfox Natural History Collection

Non-library collection catalogue:
All or part available in-house

continued overleaf

Library catalogue:
All or part available online

Printed publications:
Guides to the use of the library and services

Access to staff:
Contact by letter, by telephone, by fax, by e-mail
and via website. Appointment necessary. Letter of
introduction required.
Hours: Term time: Mon to Fri, 0845 to 2200; Sat,
0100 to 1700
Vacations: Mon to Fri, 0900 to 1700; Sat, closed

Access for disabled people:
Parking provided, ramped entry, level entry, toilet
facilities

Other campuses at:
Belfast campus
  York Street, Belfast, BT15 1ED; tel: 08700 400 700
Jordanstown campus
  Shore Road, Newtownabbey, Co Antrim, BT37
  0BQ; tel: 08700 400 700
Magee campus
  Northland Road, Londonderry, BT48 7JL; tel:
  08700 400 700

UNIVERSITY OF WALES CENTRE FOR ADVANCED WELSH AND CELTIC STUDIES

Acronym or abbreviation: CAWCS

National Library of Wales, Aberystwyth,
Ceredigion, SY23 3HH

Tel: 01970 636543
Fax: 01970 639090
E-mail: cawcs@wales.ac.uk

Website:
http://www.wales.ac.uk/cawcs
Details of research undertaken at the centre,
publications, fora, seminars, conferences.

Enquiries:
Enquiries to: Director
Direct e-mail: d.r.johnston@wales.ac.uk
Other contacts: Administrative Officer (for
publications)

Organisation type and purpose:
Research organisation.
Research, Welsh and Celtic study.

Subject coverage:
Language, literature, history and culture of Wales
and the other Celtic countries.

**Museum or gallery collection, archive, or library
special collection:**
Library books and periodicals – mainly Celtic- and
  Welsh-language material

Library catalogue:
All or part available in-house

Printed publications:
See website for full list of publications
Centre Research Papers (29 papers)
Memorial Lectures (T. H. Parry-Williams)
Poets of the Nobility Series (36 vols)
Poets of the Princes Series (8 vols, University of
  Wales Press)
The Effects of Tourism on the Welsh Language in
  North-West Wales (D. Phillips, C. Thomas)
Wales and the Welsh 2000: proceedings of the
  Millennium Conference of the University of
  Wales Centre for Advanced Welsh and Celtic
  Studies (ed. G. Jenkins)

Publications list:
Available online and in print

Access to staff:
Contact by letter, by telephone, by fax and by e-
mail. Appointment necessary.
Hours: Mon to Fri, 0900 to 1700

Access for disabled people:
Level entry, toilet facilities

Constituent part of:
University of Wales

UNIVERSITY OF WALES INSTITUTE, CARDIFF

Acronym or abbreviation: UWIC

Western Avenue, Llandaff, Cardiff, CF5 2YB

Tel: 029 2041 6244
Fax: 029 2041 6908

Website:
http://www.uwic.ac.uk/library/

Enquiries:
Enquiries to: Head of Library Division
Direct tel: 029 2041 6240
Direct e-mail: priley@uwic.ac.uk

Founded:
1976

Organisation type and purpose:
University department or institute.

Subject coverage:
Business; computing; food science and technology;
education; art education; physical education;
human movement and sport studies; art and
design; applied sciences; health and social sciences;
product and engineering design.

Library catalogue:
All or part available online

Printed publications:
Bullying – a positive response (1991)

Access to staff:
Contact by letter, by telephone, by fax, by e-mail
and via website. Letter of introduction required.
Hours: Mon to Fri, 0900 to 2030; Sat, 0900 to 1300

Access to building, collection or gallery:
Prior appointment required

Access for disabled people:
Parking provided, level entry, access to all public
areas, toilet facilities

Other addresses:
Colchester Avenue Library, UWIC
  Colchester Avenue, Cardiff, CF3 7XR; tel: 029
  2041 6241
Cyncoed Library, UWIC
  Cyncoed Road, Cardiff, CF23 6XD; tel: 029 2041
  6242
Howard Gardens Library, UWIC
  Howard Gardens, Cardiff, CF24 1SP; tel: 029
  2041 6243

UNIVERSITY OF WALES, LAMPETER

Lampeter, Ceredigion, SA48 7ED

Tel: 01570 424997
E-mail: library@lamp.ac.uk

Website:
http://www.lamp.ac.uk/founders_library
Home page of Founders' Library (pre-1850
collections) with access and contact information.
http://www.lamp.ac.uk/library/
Library home page with library information and
links to online bibliographic resources and to
information about University of Wales, Lampeter.

Enquiries:
Enquiries to: Library Administrator
Direct e-mail: j.bracher@lamp.ac.uk

Founded:
1822

Formerly called:
St David's University College Library

Organisation type and purpose:
University library.

Subject coverage:
Anthropology, archaeology, classics, film and
media, German, history, informatics, philosophy,
theology and religious studies, Welsh.

**Museum or gallery collection, archive, or library
special collection:**
Early Welsh periodicals

MSS collection includes 15th century Books of
  Hours and other service books
Pre-1850 material (over 20,000 volumes) includes
  Tract Collection (printed catalogue published
  1975), Incunabula (ca. 60 items representing most
  early centres of printing)
Welsh Bibles, prayerbooks etc

Library catalogue:
All or part available online

Printed publications:
Exhibition guides and other occasional items
Notes for readers, revised annually

Access to staff:
Contact by letter, by telephone, by fax, by e-mail,
in person and via website
Hours: Term time: Mon to Thu, 0900 to 2145; Fri,
0900 to 1945; Sat, 1300 to 1645; Sun, 1300 to 1645
Vacations: Mon to Fri, 0900 to 1645

Access for disabled people:
Parking provided, level entry, toilet facilities
Special comments: Ask at counter for access to lift
between floors.

Constituent Institution of the:
University of Wales

UNIVERSITY OF WALES, NEWPORT

Library and Information Services, Caerleon
Campus, PO Box 179, Newport, Gwent, NP18 3YG

Tel: 01633 432101
Fax: 01633 432105
E-mail: lis@newport.ac.uk

Website:
http://www.lis.newport.ac.uk
Provides access to catalogue, location maps, user
guides and useful internet links.

Enquiries:
Enquiries to: Librarian
Direct tel: 01633 432103
Direct fax: 01633 432920
Direct e-mail: lesley.may@newport.ac.uk

Founded:
1974

Formerly called:
Gwent College of Higher Education Library (year
of change 1995); University of Wales College,
Newport (year of change 2004)

Organisation type and purpose:
University library.

Subject coverage:
Art and design, interactive arts, documentary
photography, archaeology, education, humanities,
environmental science, business, accountancy,
human resource management, counselling,
technology, computing, electrical and electronic
engineering, mechatronics, sports studies,
psychology, social sciences.

**Museum or gallery collection, archive, or library
special collection:**
David Hurn collection of documentary
  photography materials
Newport Survey Collection of photographic
  images

Trade and statistical information:
General statistics for Wales.
Education statistics.

Non-library collection catalogue:
All or part available online

Library catalogue:
All or part available online

Printed publications:
How to study successfully
Library and Information Services Annual Report
Making References Using Harvard
Various guides to subjects

Access to staff:
Contact by letter, by telephone, by fax, by e-mail
and via website. Appointment necessary.

Hours: Term time: Mon to Thu, 0830 to 2000; Fri, 0930 to 1700; Sat, Sun, 1300 to 1700
Special comments: Access to electronic databases may be restricted.

Access to building, collection or gallery:
Hours: Term time: Mon to Thu, 0830 to 2000; Fri, 0930 to 1700; Sat, Sun, 1300 to 1700
Special comments: Vacation opening hours available on the website.

Access for disabled people:
Wheelchair access and lift to upper floor, automatic doors

Also at:
Library and Information Services
Allt yr yn Campus, PO Box 180, Newport, NP20 5XR; tel: 01633 432310; fax: 01633 432343; e-mail: dawne.leatherdale@newport.ac.uk

UNIVERSITY OF WARWICK – MAIN LIBRARY

Coventry, Warwickshire, CV4 7AL

Tel: 024 7652 2026
Fax: 024 7652 4211
E-mail: library@warwick.ac.uk

Website:
http://www.warwick.ac.uk/services/library
Library information, including staff contacts.
http://www.warwick.ac.uk/services/library/mrc/mrc.html
Information on the Modern Records Centre.
http://www2.warwick.ac.uk/services/library/researchexchange
Information on the Wolfson Research Exchange.
http://www2.warwick.ac.uk/services/library/teachinggrid
Information on the Teaching Grid.

Founded:
1965

Organisation type and purpose:
University library.

Subject coverage:
Social sciences including law; humanities (Western languages only); trade unions, pressure groups and radical political movements; statistics; biological sciences; chemistry; molecular sciences; computer science; engineering; economics; environmental studies; mathematics; physics; business studies; United Kingdom official publications; European Documentation Centre; statistical series.

Services for disabled people:
Fetch-and-carry service.

Museum or gallery collection, archive, or library special collection:
Economics and Management Working Papers
Employers' Records collections
French Theatre 18th–19th centuries
Modern Records Centre tel no: 024 7652 4219 (collection of British trade union (eg NUR), and employers' records, and records relating to pressure groups and political movements; they include the CBI and TUC archives and the private papers of Sir Victor Gollancz)
Statistics Collection (current and historical)

Non-library collection catalogue:
All or part available online

Printed publications:
Guides to the Modern Records Centre
Modern Records Centre Information Bulletin (quarterly)

Access to staff:
Contact by letter, by telephone, by fax, by e-mail, in person and via website
Hours: Term time: Mon to Sun, 0830 to 2130
Opening times may vary during vacations and the summer term
Special comments: Members of the public may access the Library for reference provided they show photographic proof of ID and proof of address.

Access to building, collection or gallery:
Hours: Term time: Mon to Sun, 0830 to 0000
Opening times may vary during vacations and the summer term
Special comments: Visitor access during staff access hours.

Access for disabled people:
Parking provided, lift, toilet facilities
Hours: As above

UNIVERSITY OF WESTMINSTER

Headquarter Building, 309 Regent Street, London, W1B 2UW

Tel: 020 7911 5000
Fax: 020 7911 5858
E-mail: course-enquiries@westminster.ac.uk

Website:
http://www.westminster.ac.uk
Course information, events/open days, job vacancies.

Founded:
1838

Formerly called:
Royal Polytechnic Institution (year of change 1882); Regent Street Polytechnic (year of change 1970); Polytechnic of Central London (PCL) (year of change 1992)

Organisation type and purpose:
University department or institute, suitable for ages: 18+, teaching and research organisation.

Subject coverage:
Business, management, psychology and social sciences, biosciences, computer sciences, integrated health and complementary therapies, English and linguistics, architecture and the built environment, communications, languages, law, media, arts and design, electronics.

Information services:
See: http://www.westminster.ac.uk/study/library-and-it-services.

Museum or gallery collection, archive, or library special collection:
University of Westminster Archive Services holds mainly the records of the University and its predecessor bodies, going back to the Royal Polytechnic Institution founded in 1838, and including Regent Street Polytechnic and the Polytechnic of Central London; it also holds records of the Polytechnic Sports and Social Clubs; in addition there are a number of collections deposited or donated to support research, notably in the areas of architecture and town planning
For full details of holdings please see website: http://www.westminster.ac.uk/about/archive-services

Library catalogue:
All or part available online and in-house

Printed publications:
Individual course brochures
Prospectuses (undergraduate and postgraduate)
Financial Statements
Order printed publications from: Marketing, Communications and Development Department (for list), Cavendish House, 101 New Cavendish St, London, W1W 6XH

Publications list:
Available online

Access to staff:
Contact by letter, by telephone, by fax, by e-mail and via website
Hours: Mon to Fri, 0900 to 1700
24-hour telephone enquiry service

Access to building, collection or gallery:
Hours differ at each campus; please contact for details

Access for disabled people:
Facilities differ at each site; please contact for details

Special comments: Contact Disabilities Officer for further details: see http://www.westminster.ac.uk/study/disability-services

Also at:

115 New Cavendish Street, London, W1W 6UW

Watford Road, Northwich Park, Harrow, London, HA1 3TP

35 Marylebone Road, London, NW1 5LS

4–12 Little Titchfield Street, London, W1W 7UW

UNIVERSITY OF WESTMINSTER – INFORMATION SYSTEMS & LIBRARY SERVICES

115 New Cavendish Street, London, W1W 6UW

Tel: 020 7911 5095
Fax: 020 7911 5093

Website:
http://www.westminster.ac.uk/library
Information on libraries and their services, plus links to Information Systems and Computing.

Enquiries:
Enquiries to: Director, Information Systems & Library Services
Other contacts: Library Managers for campus-related enquiries.

Founded:
1839

Formed by the merger of:
Holborn College of Law, Languages and Commerce, Regent Street Polytechnic

Formerly called:
Polytechnic of Central London (PCL) (year of change 1992)

Organisation type and purpose:
University library, on 4 campuses.

Subject coverage:
Planning, architecture, construction, tourism, transport, business management and economics, at 35 Marylebone Road, NW1 5LS (tel. no. for this site and the following sites 020 7911 5000 ext 3047)
Women's studies, economics, economic history, law, politics, psychology, sociology, and languages, civil rights, criminology, EC and Commonwealth law, English law, international law, sociology of law at 4 -12 Little Titchfield Street, London, W1P 7FW, ext 2516
Art and design, communications, film, radio and television, journalism, mass media, computing, photography, business management, engineering, at Harrow Learning Resources Centre, ext 5954
Technical and scientific subjects including mathematics, computing, chemistry, biological sciences, electronic engineering, systems engineering at 115 New Cavendish Street, W1M 8JS ext 3628.

Museum or gallery collection, archive, or library special collection:
University Archive: record of predecessor institutions including Royal Polytechnic Institution (1838 – 1881), Regent Street Polytechnic (1881 – 1970), the Polytechnic of Central London (1970 – 1992). Access by appointment

Non-library collection catalogue:
All or part available in-house

Library catalogue:
All or part available online

Access to staff:
Appointment necessary. Access for members only. Non-members charged.
Hours: Term time: Mon to Fri, 0915 to 2100; Sat, Sun, 1100 to 1700
Vacations: Mon to Fri, 0915 to 1700
Special comments: Members only: plus M25, Access schemes members and UK Libraries Plus members.

continued overleaf

Access for disabled people:
Ramped entry
Special comments: Otherwise varies from campus to campus.

UNIVERSITY OF WINCHESTER LIBRARY

Formal name: Martial Rose Library

Sparkford Road, Winchester, Hampshire, SO22 4NR

Tel: 01962 827306
Fax: 01962 827443
E-mail: libenquiries@winchester.ac.uk

Website:
http://www.winchester.ac.uk/library

Enquiries:
Enquiries to: Librarian

Founded:
1840

Formerly called:
King Alfred's College (year of change 2005)

Organisation type and purpose:
University library.

Subject coverage:
Art, biology, design and technology, drama, education, English, environmental studies, geography, history, human movement studies, mathematics, music, religious studies, psychology, television studies, archaeology, learning difficulties, American studies, Japanese studies, business studies, sports studies, leisure management, tourism.

Museum or gallery collection, archive, or library special collection:
Sybil Campbell Collection; Thorold & Lyttelton Collection

Library catalogue:
All or part available online

Printed publications:
Guide to the Library

Access to staff:
Contact by letter, by telephone, by e-mail and via website
Hours: Mon to Fri, 0900 to 1700

Access for disabled people:
Access to all public areas

UNIVERSITY OF WOLVERHAMPTON – LEARNING CENTRE

Telford Campus, Priorslee, Telford, Shropshire, TF2 9NT

Tel: 01902 323983
Fax: 01902 323985

Website:
http://www.wlv.ac.uk/lib
Access to catalogues and access information.

Enquiries:
Enquiries to: Librarian
Direct tel: 01902 312672

Founded:
1992

Formerly called:
Wolverhampton Polytechnic

Organisation type and purpose:
University library.

Subject coverage:
Business and management, social work, engineering design.

Trade and statistical information:
United Kingdom statistics.

Library catalogue:
All or part available online

Access to staff:
Contact in person
Hours: Term time: Mon to Fri, 0900 to 2200; Sat & Sun, 1330 to 1730. Vacations: Mon to Fri, 1000 to 1700
Special comments: No staff or counter access until 1100.
Visitors must check in at Reception for Identity Day Pass.

Access for disabled people:
Parking provided, level entry, access to all public areas, toilet facilities

UNIVERSITY OF WORCESTER

Peirson Building, Henwick Grove, Worcester, WR2 6AJ

Tel: 01905 855341
Fax: 01905 855197
E-mail: a.hannaford@worc.ac.uk

Website:
http://www.worc.ac.uk/ils

Enquiries:
Enquiries to: Director of Information and Learning Services
Other contacts: Customer Services Manager (for use of library)

Subject coverage:
Education, humanities, social sciences, environmental science, health, nursing, midwifery, sport studies, business, IT, digital media.

Library catalogue:
All or part available online

Publications list:
Available online

Access to staff:
Contact by telephone, by e-mail and via website. Appointment necessary.
Hours: Mon to Fri, 0900 to 1700
Special comments: Longer opening hours during semester, check with library.

Access to building, collection or gallery:
No prior appointment required

Access for disabled people:
Level entry, access to all public areas, toilet facilities

UNIVERSITY OF YORK

J B Morrell and Raymond Burton Libraries, Heslington, York, YO10 5DD

Tel: 01904 433873
Fax: 01904 433866
E-mail: lib-enquiry@york.ac.uk

Website:
http://www.york.ac.uk/library
Includes notes on all libraries in University of York, including King's Manor Library, their contents and opening hours. It also leads to the York Subject Tree, linking in turn to home pages for Departments in the University.

Enquiries:
Enquiries to: Director of Information

Founded:
1962

Organisation type and purpose:
University library and archives.

Subject coverage:
Economics; politics; psychology; sociology; social administration; social work; archaeology; education; English and related literature; history; language and linguistics; music; philosophy; biochemistry; biology; chemistry; computer science; electronics; mathematics; physics; architecture; history of art; health sciences; medicine; environment; law; theatre; film; television (J B Morrell and Raymond Burton Libraries). Architecture in general; architectural history and conservation in particular;

conservation of historic parks and gardens; continuing education for architectural and related professions (King's Manor Library).

Museum or gallery collection, archive, or library special collection:
Copland Collection (scores composed by Aaron Copland)
Cooper Abbs Collection (library of an 18th-century clergyman)
Dyson Collection (English literature of the 17th, 18th and early 19th centuries)
Eliot Collection (20th-century English literature first editions)
Halifax Parish Library (17th-century parish library)
Milner-White Collection (English detective stories)
Milnes-Walker Collection (medicine)
Mirfield Collection (theology pre-1800)
Raymond Burton Yorkshire Collection (books on Yorkshire)
Smith Collection (British engraving and painting in 18th and 19th century)
Slaithwaite Collection (18th-century theology)
York Medical Society Library (medicine)

Non-library collection catalogue:
All or part available online

Library catalogue:
All or part available online

Printed publications:
Library Guides (updated as required)

Access to staff:
Contact by letter, by telephone, by fax, by e-mail, in person and via website
Hours: Term time opening: Mon to Fri, 0800 to 0000; Sat and Sun, 1000 to 0000 (includes the weekends immediately before and after term)
Special comments: Vacation opening hours vary: see website.

Subsidiary library:
King's Manor Library (formerly, up to 1996, the library of the Institute of Advanced Architectural Studies)
Exhibition Square, York, YO1 7EP; tel: 01904 433969; fax: 01904 433949

UPKEEP

22–25 Finsbury Square, London, EC2A 1DX

Tel: 020 7256 7646
Fax: 020 7022 1575
E-mail: info@upkeep.org.uk

Website:
http://www.upkeep.org.uk

Enquiries:
Enquiries to: Director

Founded:
1983

Formerly called:
The Building Conservation Trust

Organisation type and purpose:
Registered charity (charity number 277351), educational charity.
Promotes good practice in building care; provides training courses and education relating to the care, maintenance and refurbishment of buildings of all ages; also operates the Charities Facilities Management Group, a national network for people who look after property in the voluntary sector.

Subject coverage:
Building care, repairs, maintenance, facilities management.

Museum or gallery collection, archive, or library special collection:
Upkeep Exhibition

Printed publications:
Guide to the Exhibition, resource packs for schools ranging from Key Stage 1 to College level

Access to staff:
Contact by letter, by telephone, by fax, by e-mail and via website. Appointment necessary.
Hours: Mon to Fri, 0900 to 1700

UPPER NORWOOD JOINT LIBRARY

Acronym or abbreviation: UNJL

Westow Hill, Upper Norwood, London, SE19 1TJ

Tel: 020 8670 2551
Fax: 020 8670 5468
E-mail: jsavage@uppernorwood.akhter.com

Website:
http://www.uppernorwoodlibrary.org

Enquiries:
Enquiries to: Chief Librarian

Founded:
1898

Organisation type and purpose:
Local government body, public library.

Subject coverage:
History of both Crystal Palaces (Hyde Park and Norwood); the Great Exhibition 1851, the history of Norwood (especially Upper Norwood). Gerald Massey, 1828–1907 (Victorian Chartist, poet, Spiritualist and Egyptologist), Chartist Movement.

Museum or gallery collection, archive, or library special collection:
Material relating to Gerald Massey (1828–1907), Victorian Chartist, poet, spiritualist and Egyptologist
Gerald Massey collection
Oral history collection of taped interviews (c. 60) with people who remember Crystal Palace, collected by the Crystal Palace Foundation
The J B Wilson Collection: materials and photographs of the Norwood Area, particularly West Norwood, collected by J B Wilson (d. 1949)

Non-library collection catalogue:
All or part available in-house

Library catalogue:
All or part available in-house

Access to staff:
Contact by letter, by telephone, by fax, by e-mail and in person
Hours: Mon, 1000 to 1900; Tue, Thu, Fri, 0900 to 1900; Sat, 0900 to 1700; Wed and Sun, closed

Access to building, collection or gallery:
Hours: Mon, 1000 to 1900; Tue, Thu, Fri, 0900 to 1900; Sat, 0900 to 1700; Wed and Sun, closed

Access for disabled people:
Disabled access available

Funded by:
London Boroughs of Croydon and Lambeth

URBAN AND ECONOMICAL DEVELOPMENT GROUP

Acronym or abbreviation: URBED

41 Old Birley Street, Manchester, M16 5RF

Tel: 0161 226 5078
Fax: 0161 226 7307
E-mail: urbed@urbed.co.uk

Website:
http://www.urbed.co.uk
General material on activities of the organisation.

Enquiries:
Enquiries to: Director

Founded:
1976

Organisation type and purpose:
National organisation, consultancy, research organisation.
Urban Regeneration Consultants.

Subject coverage:
Town centres, housing, sustainable development and urban regeneration.

Museum or gallery collection, archive, or library special collection:
Library of 4000 journals, books and publications of sustainable urban development

Library catalogue:
All or part available in-house

Printed publications:
Sun Dial (newsletter, quarterly)
Building the 21st Century Home (Architectural Press 1999)
Building to Last (21st Century Homes) Joseph Rowntree Foundation, 1995
But Would You Live There (Urban Task Force 1999)
Tomorrow a Peaceful Path to Urban Returns (Friends of the Earth, 1998)

Publications list:
Available in print

Access to staff:
Contact by letter, by telephone, by fax and by e-mail. Appointment necessary.
Hours: Mon to Fri, 0900 to 1700

Other addresses:
Urban and Economical Development Group
19 Store Street, London, WC1E 7DH; tel: 020 7436 8050; fax: 020 7436 8083; e-mail: n.falk@urbed.co.uk

UROSTOMY ASSOCIATION

Acronym or abbreviation: UA

18 Foxglove Avenue, Uttoxeter, Staffordshire, ST14 8UN

Tel: 0845 241 2159; 01889 563191
E-mail: secretary.ua@classmail.co.uk

Website:
http://www.urostomyassociation.org.uk

Enquiries:
Enquiries to: National Secretary

Founded:
1971

Organisation type and purpose:
Voluntary organisation, registered charity (charity number 1131072).

Subject coverage:
The Urostomy Association aims to assist all who are about to undergo, or have undergone surgery resulting in the diversion or removal of the bladder with such information, help and support as may be necessary to assist them to resume as full a life as possible with every confidence.

Special visitor services:
Trained visitors available.

Printed publications:
Journal (3 times a year)
Membership information (leaflet)
Information request (leaflet)
What is a Urostomy? (leaflet)
Travel advice (leaflet)
Active living (leaflet)
Coping with urinary infections (leaflet)
How you can help the UA with a legacy (leaflet)
Neo-bladder/reconstruction – An alternative to Urostomy (leaflet)
Understanding problems that may occur (leaflet)
Sexual Matters (Male and Female, leaflet)
Travel Hints (leaflet)
Suprapubic catheter (leaflet)
Continent Diversion (leaflet)
Order printed publications from: The National Secretary, Urostomy Association 18 Foxglove Avenue, Uttoxeter, Staffordshire, ST14 8UN; tel. 08452 412159, 01889 563191; e-mail secretary.ua@classmail.co.uk

Electronic and video publications:
Living with Cancer (DVD)
Recorded version of Journal (cassette tape)
Order electronic and video publications from: The National Secretary, 18 Foxglove Avenue, Uttoxeter, Staffordshire, ST14 8UN; tel. 08452 412159, 01889 563191; e-mail secretary.ua@classmail.co.uk

Publications list:
Available online and in print

Access to staff:
Contact by letter, by telephone, by e-mail, in person and via website. Appointment necessary.
Hours: Mon to Fri, 0900 to 1730

Access to building, collection or gallery:
By appointment only

Links with:
International Ostomy Association

US-UK FULBRIGHT COMMISSION

Fulbright House, 62 Doughty Street, London, WC1N 2JZ

Tel: 020 7404 6994
Fax: 020 7404 6874
E-mail: education@fulbright.co.uk

Website:
http://www.fulbright.co.uk

Enquiries:
Enquiries to: Educational Adviser

Founded:
1948

Also:
US-UK Educational Commission

Organisation type and purpose:
Anglo-American scholarship organisation (Fulbright grants). Specialised US education library and resource centre.
To promote educational and cultural exchanges between the United States and the United Kingdom. Advisory service on all aspects of education in the USA.

Subject coverage:
Education in the US at all levels and for most disciplines; exchanges for British students.

Museum or gallery collection, archive, or library special collection:
Application forms for US admissions tests (SAT, GRE, GMAT, TOEFL, USMLE, LSAT, MCAT, ACT) and test preparation books
Reference collection of US education directories

Printed publications:
A Few Things You Should Know Before You Go (1999–2000 ed, £5.50)
Postgraduate Study in the United States (£5)
Undergraduate Study in the United States (£3.50)
Postgraduate Test Review Publications
Undergraduate Test Review Publications

Electronic and video publications:
TOEFL Test Preparation Kit (2nd ed)

Publications list:
Available online and in print

Access to staff:
Contact by letter and via website
Hours: Mon, 1330 to 1900; Wed and Fri, 1330 to 1700

USHAW COLLEGE LIBRARY

Formal name: St Cuthbert's College, Durham

Ushaw College, Durham, DH7 9RH

Tel: 0191 373 8516
E-mail: matthew.watson@ushaw.ac.uk

Website:
http://www.ushaw.ac.uk

Enquiries:
Enquiries to: Librarian

Founded:
1808

Organisation type and purpose:
Library of a Roman Catholic seminary.

Subject coverage:
Recusant history, church councils, medieval church history, English civil law to 1840, liturgy.

continued overleaf

Museum or gallery collection, archive, or library special collection:
18th century lectures from English College, Douai
John Lingard's Correspondence with Newsham and Wiseman
Lisbon Collection (Archives of English College, Lisbon, 1628–1971)
Printed books from Durham Priory
Weld Bank Parish Library

Non-library collection catalogue:
All or part available in-house

Library catalogue:
All or part available in-house

Printed publications:
In Illo Tempore

Access to staff:
Contact by letter, by telephone and by e-mail. Appointment necessary.
Hours: No regular hours – e-mail contact preferred
Special comments: Visits by appointment only.

Access to building, collection or gallery:
Visits by appointment only

Access for disabled people:
Parking provided, toilet facilities
Hours: As above, appointment only

Links with:
University of Durham

USPG: ANGLICANS IN WORLD MISSION

Formal name: United Society for the Propagation of the Gospel
Acronym or abbreviation: USPG

200 Great Dover Street, London, SE1 4YB

Tel: 020 7378 5678 or 0845 273 1701
Fax: 020 7378 5650
E-mail: enquiries@uspg.org.uk

Website:
http://www.uspg.org.uk
http://shop.uspg.org.uk/acatalog
Publications and free resources.

Enquiries:
Enquiries to: Supporter Care Coordinator
Direct e-mail: archive@uspg.org.uk
Other contacts: Archivist (for archival and historical enquiries)

Founded:
1701

Created by the merger of:
Society for the Propagation of the Gospel in Foreign Parts
Universities' Mission to Central Africa
Cambridge Mission to Delhi (joined USPG in 1968) (year of change 1965)

Organisation type and purpose:
Voluntary organisation, registered charity (charity number 234518).
USPG is an Anglican mission agency, which works in direct partnership with Anglican Churches in over 50 countries, helping to support vital church work, including healthcare, education, leadership training and action for social justice.

Subject coverage:
Anglican church life and mission in many areas of the world, predominantly but not exclusively in the Commonwealth.
The Archive contains the records of USPG and its predecessor Societies from 1701 onwards, including information about former missionaries of the Societies.

Museum or gallery collection, archive, or library special collection:
Photograph library (current collection of prints, slides and digital images).
The Society's archives from approximately 1965, plus all files on individual missionaries from the mid-19th century onwards.

Most of the archives to 1965 are at the Rhodes House Library, South Parks Road, Oxford, OX1 3RG and these include:
The historic library collection
Photographs to the 1950s
Records of the Society for the Propagation of the Gospel, 1701–1965
Records of the Universities' Mission to Central Africa, 1858 –1965
Records of the Cambridge Mission to Delhi, 1877–1968.

Non-library collection catalogue:
All or part available in-house

Printed publications:
Born Among Us (resource pack, £18)
The Christ We Share (resource pack, £18)
Three Centuries of Mission: The United Society for the Propagation of the Gospel, 1701–2001 (O'Connor D et al, hb £25, pb £12.50)
From Shore to Shore (£5.99)
Today! The Mission of Jesus in the Gospel of Luke (£5)
Transmission (quarterly)
USPG Prayer Diary (quarterly)
Order printed publications from: USPG

Microform publications:
A number of SPG and UMCA archive series are available on microfilm or online from Microform Academic Publishers
Order microform publications from: Microform Academic Publishers, Main Street, East Ardsley, Wakefield, WF3 2AT; tel: 01924 825700; website: http//www.microform.co.uk

Electronic and video publications:
The Life We Share (resource pack, £10)
Rethinking Mission at website: http:// www.rethinkingmission.org
Order electronic and video publications from: USPG

Publications list:
Available online

Access to staff:
Contact by letter, by telephone, by fax, by e-mail and via website. Appointment necessary.
Hours: Mon to Fri, 0900 to 1700
Special comments: The Archivist's post is part time.

Member organisation of:
Churches Network for Mission
  tel: 020 7901 4090; fax: 020 7901 4894; e-mail: info@ctbi.org.uk
Partnership for World Mission (PWM)
  tel: 020 7898 1328; e-mail: pwm@c-of-e.org.uk

UTTLESFORD DISTRICT COUNCIL

London Road, Saffron Walden, Essex, CB11 4ER

Tel: 01799 510510\ Minicom no. 01799 5104129
Fax: 01799 510510
E-mail: postroom@uttlesford.gov.uk

Enquiries:
Enquiries to: Chief Executive

Founded:
1974

Organisation type and purpose:
Local government body

Subject coverage:
Local government services

Access to staff:
Contact by letter, by telephone, by fax, by e-mail, in person and via website. Appointment necessary.
Hours: Mon to Thur, 0900 to 1700, Fri 0900 to 1630

VALE OF GLAMORGAN COUNCIL

Civic Offices, Holton Road, Barry, Vale of Glamorgan, CF63 4RU

Tel: 01446 700111
Fax: 01446 421479
E-mail: civ@valeofglamorgan.gov.uk

Website:
http://www.valeofglamorgan.gov.uk

Organisation type and purpose:
Local government body.

VALE OF GLAMORGAN RAILWAY COMPANY LIMITED

Acronym or abbreviation: VOGR

Barry Island Station, Romanwell Road, Barry Island, Vale of Glamorgan, CF62 5TH

Tel: 01446 748816
Fax: 01446 749018
E-mail: valeofglamrail@hotmail.com

Website:
http://www.valeglamrail.co.uk
Information on Barry Island Steam Railway and Heritage Centre

Enquiries:
Enquiries to: Librarian and Archivist

Founded:
1994

Organisation type and purpose:
Museum, historic building, house or site, suitable for ages: all.
Steam Heritage Centre for pleasure and educational purposes.

Subject coverage:
General railway history (especially South Wales railways), history and information on the Woodham Locomotive Scrapyard.

Information services:
Library available for reference

Special visitor services:
Guided tours, materials and/or activities for children.

Education services:
Group education facilities, resources for Key Stages 1 and 2.

Services for disabled people:
Displays and/or information at wheelchair height.

Museum or gallery collection, archive, or library special collection:
Reference library
Railwayiana
Victorian Station Building
Steam and diesel locomotives
Coaches, including a Taff Vale Railway one of 1874 being restored
Cranes, steam and hand operated
Woodham collection (photos and scrapbooks)

Library catalogue:
All or part available in-house

Printed publications:
Barry Island Steam Railway and Heritage Centre Handbook (£4.99)
Barry Island Steam Railway and Heritage Centre Colouring Book (99p)
Steam Heritage Centre, Barry Island Station, Timetable and Information 2002/2003 Events (free)

Access to staff:
Contact by letter, by telephone, by fax, by e-mail, in person and via website

Access for disabled people:
Parking provided, level entry, access to all public areas, toilet facilities
Special comments: Ramped entry to coaches

Affiliated to the:
Council for Museums in Wales

VALE OF WHITE HORSE DISTRICT COUNCIL

The Abbey House, Abbey Close, Abingdon, Oxfordshire, OX14 3JE

Tel: 01235 520202

Fax: 01235 554960

Website:
http://www.oxfordshire.gov.ukio.idc-ioid=6.htm/

Organisation type and purpose:
Local government body.
District council.

Subject coverage:
Waste collection and recycling, housing register, homelessness, planning, building control, leisure facilities, housing benefit, council tax collection, non-domestic rates, car parks, electoral registration.

Access to staff:
Contact by letter, by telephone, by fax, by e-mail and in person
Hours: Mon to Fri, 0845 to 1700

Access for disabled people:
Ramped entry, access to all public areas, toilet facilities

VALUES INTO ACTION

Acronym or abbreviation: VIA

Oxford House, Derbyshire Street, London, E2 6HG

Tel: 020 7729 5436
Fax: 020 7729 7797
E-mail: general@viauk.org

Website:
http://www.viauk.org
Membership, publications, current work.

Enquiries:
Enquiries to: Manager
Other contacts: Administrator

Founded:
1971

Formerly called:
Campaign for People with Mental Handicaps (CPMH) (year of change 1989)

Organisation type and purpose:
Membership association (membership is by subscription), voluntary organisation, registered charity (charity number 1057249), training organisation, research organisation.
VIA is committed to achieving laws, services and public attitudes which will allow people with learning difficulties to become valued citizens.

Subject coverage:
Learning difficulties, research training.

Printed publications:
A range of publications including:
The Principle of Normalisation
One Law for All
Setting up a Tenants' Group
The Cost of Opportunity

Electronic and video publications:
It's My House: Your Rights as a Tenant (video)
Make Your Move – video guide to independent living (Holman A, 1998)
Telesafe 2 video resource pack
Good Support (DVD)
Mission Possible – DVD about Mental Capacity Act made by and for people with learning difficulties

Publications list:
Available online and in print

Access to staff:
Contact by letter, by telephone, by fax and by e-mail. Appointment necessary.
Hours: Mon to Fri, 0930 to 1630

VANGUARD 3 OWNERS CLUB

14 Kennet Rise, Axford, Marlborough, Wiltshire, SN8 2EZ

Tel: 01672 520154

Enquiries:
Enquiries to: General Secretary

Founded:
1990

Organisation type and purpose:
Membership association (membership is by subscription).

Subject coverage:
Technical information and sources of spares for Vanguard 3 cars.

Museum or gallery collection, archive, or library special collection:
Factory workshop manuals
Technical Bulletins

Printed publications:
Newsletter (quarterly)

Access to staff:
Contact by letter and by telephone
Hours: Mon to Fri, 0900 to 1700, also evenings and weekends

VARIETY CLUB OF GREAT BRITAIN

93 Bayham Street, London, NW1 0AG

Tel: 020 7428 8100
E-mail: info@varietyclub.org.uk

Website:
http://www.varietyclub.org.uk

Enquiries:
Enquiries to: Chief Executive

Founded:
October 1949

Organisation type and purpose:
Registered charity (charity number 209259).
Has 53 chapters in 14 countries and ten regional offices in the UK.
To give financial help to projects and individual disadvantaged children. Recipients include hospitals, schools, youth groups and individuals. The club helps to provide equipment such as Sunshine Coaches (minibuses), mobility equipment or other specialised equipment for disabled or disadvantaged children.

Subject coverage:
Support for disabled and disadvantaged children.

Parent body:
Variety Clubs International
350 Fifth Avenue, Suite 1119, New York, 10118, USA; tel: 00 1 212 695 3818; fax: 00 1 212 695 3857; e-mail: vci@interport.net

VAUGHAN LIBRARY

Harrow School, High Street, Harrow on the Hill, Middlesex, HA1 3HT

Tel: 020 8872 8278
Fax: 020 8872 8013
E-mail: mek@harrowschool.org.uk

Website:
http://www.harrowschool.org.uk
Whole school information with library link.

Enquiries:
Enquiries to: Librarian
Other contacts: Archivist (for school history)

Founded:
1863

Organisation type and purpose:
Suitable for ages: 13 to 18.
Independent school library.

Subject coverage:
General.

Museum or gallery collection, archive, or library special collection:
Aldine Collection
Byron Collection
Churchill Collection
Harrow School Archive
Sheridan Collection

Non-library collection catalogue:
All or part available online

Library catalogue:
All or part available online

Access to staff:
Contact by letter and by e-mail. Appointment necessary.
Hours: Mon to Fri, 0830 to 1830

VAUXHALL CONVERTIBLE CAR CLUB

Acronym or abbreviation: VCCC

47 Brooklands Close, Luton, Bedfordshire, LU4 9EH

Tel: 01582 573269
E-mail: ronnie.goddard@ntlworld.com

Website:
http://www.vccc.org.uk
Club information.

Enquiries:
Enquiries to: Membership Secretary

Founded:
1990

Formerly called:
Vauxhall Cavalier Convertible Club

Organisation type and purpose:
Membership association, voluntary organisation.
Independent organisation to promote the use of Vauxhall convertible cars.

Subject coverage:
All aspects of Vauxhall convertible cars; conversion of Cavalier, Astra and Nova cars; agreed value insurance.

Printed publications:
Convertible correspondence (magazine)
Newsletter
Order printed publications from: Regalia Officer, Vauxhall Convertible Car Club
28 Deans Meadow, Dagnall, Berkhamsted, Hertfordshire, HP4 1RW, e-mail: tonycoates@btinternet.com

Access to staff:
Contact by letter and by telephone
Hours: Mon to Fri, 0900 to 1700

VAUXHALL DROOP SNOOT GROUP

Acronym or abbreviation: DSG

17 Priors Road, Tadley, Hampshire, RG26 4QJ

Tel: 0118 981 5238

Website:
http://come.to/droop.snoot.group

Enquiries:
Enquiries to: Information Officer
Other contacts: Public Relations Manager

Founded:
1981

Organisation type and purpose:
International organisation, membership association (membership is by subscription), present number of members: 350–400, voluntary organisation. Performance/classic car owners.

Subject coverage:
Vauxhall Firenza, Magnum, HP Firenza, Sportshatch, and HS/HSR Chevette vehicle data and specification; production history; competition history; original vehicle data and authentication data; modification/technical material; spares schedules and information; vehicle insurance validations.

Trade and statistical information:
Vauxhall performance, race and rally cars 1970–1985.

continued overleaf

Non-library collection catalogue:
All or part available in-house

Printed publications:
The Droop Snoot Noos (quarterly)

Microform publications:
Available for viewing only

Publications list:
Available in print

Access to staff:
Contact by letter and by telephone
Hours: Mon to Fri, 1930 to 2230

Links with:
Vauxhall Bedford Opel Association (VBOA)

Publicity Office:
Vauxhall Droop Snoot Group
11 New Road, Sands, High Wycombe, Bucks,
HP12 4LH; tel: 01494 525948

VAUXHALL OWNERS CLUB (1903–1957)

Acronym or abbreviation: VOC

1 Horseshoe Drive, Red Lodge, Bury St Edmunds,
Suffolk, IP28 8ER

Tel: 01638 751275
E-mail: roychilders@onetec.com

Website:
http://www.vauxhallownersclub-1903-1957.co.uk
Membership, magazine, events and contact details.

Enquiries:
Enquiries to: Membership Secretary

Founded:
1976

Organisation type and purpose:
Membership association (membership is by
subscription), present number of members: 400.

Subject coverage:
Details of 1903–1957 Vauxhall cars, advice on
restoration and use, spares scheme.

**Museum or gallery collection, archive, or library
special collection:**
Some sales brochures, technical data and house
magazines

Printed publications:
Newsletter (monthly)
Register

Access to staff:
Contact by letter and by telephone
Hours: Evenings and weekends

VAUXHALL VIVA OWNERS CLUB

The Thatches, Snetterton North End, Snetterton,
Norwich, Norfolk, NR16 2LD

Tel: 01953 498818
E-mail: adrian@vivaclub.freeserve.co.uk

Website:
http://www.vivaclub.freeserve.co.uk

Enquiries:
Enquiries to: Membership Secretary

Founded:
1982

Organisation type and purpose:
Membership association (membership is by
subscription), present number of members: 1000,
voluntary organisation.

Subject coverage:
Vauxhall Viva motorcars.

Printed publications:
Viva Owners Club Newsletter (quarterly)

Access to staff:
Contact by letter, by telephone, by fax and by e-
mail. Appointment necessary. Access for members
only.
Hours: Mon to Fri, 0900 to 1730 only

Member of:
Vauxhall/Bedford/Opel Association (VBOA)

VEGAN SOCIETY

Donald Watson House, 7 Battle Road, St Leonards-
on-Sea, East Sussex, TN37 7AA

Tel: 01424 427393
Fax: 01424 717064
E-mail: info@vegansociety.com

Website:
http://www.vegansociety.com
News, information, catalogue, membership,
contact/links.

Enquiries:
Enquiries to: Information Officer
Direct e-mail: media@vegansociety.com
Other contacts: Fundraising Officer, Email:
fundraising@vegansociety.com for adverts,
trademark licensing, legacies.

Founded:
1944

Organisation type and purpose:
Membership association (membership is by
subscription), present number of members: 4500,
registered charity (charity number 279228).
Provides information on all aspects of veganism –
including nutrition and health – to the public,
schools, media, healthcare professionals, caterers,
food manufacturers etc.

Subject coverage:
Vegan diets, animal welfare, land use, nutrition,
environment, health.

Non-library collection catalogue:
All or part available online

Printed publications:
The Animal-Free Shopper (shopping guide), Plant
Based Nutrition and Health (nutrition guide),
Vegan Passport (travel / language guide), Vegan
Stories (lifestyle book), Why Vegan? (booklet),
The Vegan (quarterly magazine)
Books, cookbooks, leaflets, pamphlets and booklets

Electronic and video publications:
Leaflets, booklets, website

Publications list:
Available online and in print

Access to staff:
Contact by letter, by telephone, by fax, by e-mail
and via website. Appointment necessary.
Hours: Mon to Fri, 0900 to 1700

Access to building, collection or gallery:
Prior appointment required

VEGETARIAN SOCIETY OF THE UNITED KINGDOM

Acronym or abbreviation: VSUK

Parkdale, Dunham Road, Altrincham, Cheshire,
WA14 4QG

Tel: 0161 925 2000
Fax: 0161 926 9182
E-mail: info@vegsoc.org

Website:
http://www.vegsoc.org

Enquiries:
Enquiries to: Information Officer

Founded:
1847

Formed by the amalgamation of:
London Vegetarian Society, Vegetarian Society

Organisation type and purpose:
Membership association (membership is by
subscription), present number of members: 18,000,
registered charity (charity number 259358),
consultancy.

Subject coverage:
Vegetarianism.

**Museum or gallery collection, archive, or library
special collection:**
Collection of books on vegetarianism and Society
Journals dating back to 1848

Printed publications:
Leaflets on the movement
The Vegetarian (magazine, quarterly)

Electronic and video publications:
Food Without Fear (video)
Devour the Earth (video)
Vegetarian Nutrition (GCSE) (video)

Access to staff:
Contact by letter, by telephone, by fax, by e-mail
and via website. Appointment necessary.
Hours: Mon to Fri, 0900 to 1700

Access to building, collection or gallery:
Prior appointment required

Access for disabled people:
Ramped entry, toilet facilities

Affiliated to:
International Vegetarian Union (IVU)

VEHICLE AND OPERATOR SERVICES AGENCY

Acronym or abbreviation: VOSA

Berkeley House, Croydon Street, Bristol, BS5 0DA

Tel: 0117 954 3200
Fax: 0117 954 3212
E-mail: enquiries@vosa.gov.uk

Website:
http://www.vosa.gov.uk/
General information about the work of Vehicle
Inspectorate and the services it provides. Details of
addresses and telephone numbers of regional
offices; publications; complaints procedure;
training courses.

Enquiries:
Enquiries to: Agency Secretariat

Founded:
2003

Created by the merger of:
the Vehicle Inspectorate and the Traffic Area
Network Division of the Department for Transport

Organisation type and purpose:
National government body.

Subject coverage:
Conducting statutory testing of lorries, coaches
and buses; supervising the MOT scheme; carrying
out roadside checks and other spot checks to
ensure vehicles comply with legal standards and
regulations; undertaking specialised vehicle
inspections; investigating accidents and defects,
and overseeing vehicle recall campaigns.

Printed publications:
A wide range of leaflets and general information
are available from local VI offices and in html
and pdf versions on the Internet.
About twenty technical manuals and instruction
for the testing of all vehicles
Order printed publications from: Vehicle Inspectorate
PO Box 12, Swansea, SA1 1BP, tel: 01792 454320

Electronic and video publications:
A series of twenty videos to support its education
and development programme

Publications list:
Available online and in print

Access to staff:
Contact by letter, by telephone, by fax, by e-mail,
in person and via website
Hours: Mon to Fri, 0900 to 1700

VEHICLE BUILDERS AND REPAIRERS ASSOCIATION LIMITED

Acronym or abbreviation: VBRA

Belmont House, Finkle Lane, Gildersome, Leeds, West Yorkshire, LS27 7TW

Tel: 0113 253 8333
Fax: 0113 238 0496
E-mail: vbra@vbra.co.uk

Website:
http://www.vbra.co.uk

Enquiries:
Enquiries to: Director General

Founded:
1914

Organisation type and purpose:
Trade association.
1,300 members engaged in vehicle building and repairing industry. To ensure VBRA membership is recognised as a sign of the professional builder and repairer. To develop membership criteria, profitability and relationships with key industry players. To improve communications within the industry. To provide membership benefits and assistance.

Subject coverage:
Working conditions and wages in the vehicle body building industry, material and data relating to commercial vehicle body building and body repair, car body repair, market research.

Printed publications:
Body (magazine, 10 times a year, free to members, £4.50 per issue for non-members)

Electronic and video publications:
TIPS (online, tips on vehicle repair, updated quarterly, members free, non-members £120)

Access to staff:
Contact by letter, by telephone, by fax, by e-mail and via website. Appointment necessary. Non-members charged.
Hours: Mon to Fri, 0830 to 1630

Access for disabled people:
Ramped entry

Affiliated to:
International Association of Vehicle Body Builders and Repairers (AIRC)

VEHICLE CERTIFICATION AGENCY

Acronym or abbreviation: VCA

1, The Eastgate Office Centre, Eastgate Road, Bristol, BS5 6XX

Tel: 0117 952 4119
Fax: 0117 952 4103

Website:
http://www.vca.gov.uk

Enquiries:
Enquiries to: Librarian

Founded:
1989

Organisation type and purpose:
National government body.

Subject coverage:
National testing and certification service for new models of road and agricultural vehicles and vehicle parts, administers the compulsory national vehicle type approval schemes and the European whole vehicle approval schemes.

Access to staff:
Contact by letter and by e-mail
Hours: Mon to Fri, 0830 to 1700

Access to building, collection or gallery:
No access other than to staff

Executive Agency of:
Department of Transport
e-mail: enquiries@vca.gov.uk

VELOCETTE OWNERS CLUB

12A Hampton Close, Newport, Shropshire, TF10 7RB

Website:
http://www.velocetteowners.com

Enquiries:
Enquiries to: Public Relations Officer

Founded:
1957

Organisation type and purpose:
Membership association (membership is by subscription), present number of members: 1,700.

Subject coverage:
Velocette motorcycles.

Access to staff:
Contact by letter
Hours: Mon to Fri, 0900 to 1700

VERE HARMSWORTH LIBRARY

Acronym or abbreviation: VHL

Rothermere American Institute, 1a South Parks Road, Oxford, OX1 3UB

Tel: 01865 282700
Fax: 01865 282709
E-mail: vhl@bodleian.ox.ac.uk

Website:
http://www.bodleian.ox.ac.uk/vhl

Enquiries:
Enquiries to: Librarian

Founded:
2002

Organisation type and purpose:
University library, university department or institute.

Subject coverage:
History of the USA, political, economic and social.

Library catalogue:
All or part available online

Access to staff:
Contact by letter, by telephone, by fax, by e-mail, in person and via website
Hours: Oct to Jun: Mon to Fri, 0900 to 1900; May to Jun also: Sat, 0900 to 1300
Jul to Sep: Mon to Fri, 0900 to 1700

Access for disabled people:
Level entry, access to all public areas, toilet facilities

Parent body:
Bodleian Libraries, Oxford University

VERIFICATION RESEARCH, TRAINING AND INFORMATION CENTRE

Acronym or abbreviation: VERTIC

Development House, 56–64 Leonard Street, London EC2A 4LT,

Tel: 020 7065 0880
Fax: 020 7065 0890
E-mail: info@vertic.org

Website:
http://www.vertic.org/
Monthly newsletter 'Trust and Verify' and summary of VERTIC and current activities pages, VERTIC briefing papers available free on-line.

Enquiries:
Enquiries to: Information Officer
Direct e-mail: rocio.escauriaza@vertic.org

Founded:
1986

Formerly called:
Verification Technology Information Centre (VERTIC) (year of change 1998)

Organisation type and purpose:
International organisation, registered charity (charity number 1073051), consultancy, research organisation.
Non-Governmental Organisation.

Subject coverage:
Research on verification and confidence-building measures in international treaties and agreements, spanning arms control and disarmament, conflict resolution and the environment; nuclear testing; greenhouse gas emissions, climate change.

Museum or gallery collection, archive, or library special collection:
Library containing books, journals, news clippings, documents, papers and Hansard on all research areas dating from 1985

Printed publications:
Annual Reports 'VERTIC Matters' 1986 to 1995

Microform publications:
Trust and Verify (6 times a year, £20 individuals, £25 organisations)
Verification: The VERTIC Year Book (1997 edition, 2000 edition)
VERTIC Briefing Papers (occasional papers)
VERTIC Research Reports (occasional papers)

Electronic and video publications:
Trust and Verify (available free on website, or by email on request)

Publications list:
Available online and in print

Access to staff:
Contact by letter, by telephone, by fax, by e-mail and via website. Appointment necessary.
Hours: Mon to Fri, 1000 to 1730
Special comments: Charges for photocopies, free access to the library.

Access to building, collection or gallery:
No prior appointment required

VERNACULAR ARCHITECTURE GROUP

Acronym or abbreviation: VAG

Ashley, Willows Green, Chelmsford, Essex, CM3 1QD

Tel: 01245 361408

Website:
http://www.vag.org.uk
Information on group and links to other compatible sites.

Enquiries:
Enquiries to: Honorary Secretary

Founded:
1952

Organisation type and purpose:
Learned society, registered charity (charity number 279839).

Subject coverage:
Vernacular (smaller traditional) architecture, particularly in the UK.

Printed publications:
Bibliography of Vernacular Architecture (irregularly, 4 vols. to date)
Newsletter (2 times a year)
Vernacular Architecture (annually)

VETERAN CAR CLUB OF GREAT BRITAIN

Acronym or abbreviation: VCC

Jessamine Court, 15 High Street, Ashwell, Hertfordshire, SG7 5NL

Tel: 01462 742818
Fax: 01462 742997
E-mail: hq@vccofgb.co.uk

Website:
http://www.vccofgb.co.uk

continued overleaf

Enquiries:
Enquiries to: Secretary

Founded:
1930

Organisation type and purpose:
International organisation, membership association (membership is by subscription, election or invitation), present number of members: 1600.

Subject coverage:
Preservation and use of Veteran and Edwardian cars manufactured before 1919.

Museum or gallery collection, archive, or library special collection:
Early motoring period literature

Library catalogue:
All or part available in-house

Printed publications:
Club magazine (6 times a year)

Access to staff:
Contact by letter and by fax. Appointment necessary. Access for members only. Letter of introduction required.
Hours: Mon to Fri, 0930 to 1700

VETERANS AID

Acronym or abbreviation: VA

40 Buckingham Palace Road, London, SW1W 0RE

Tel: 020 7828 2468
Fax: 020 7630 6780

Website:
info@veterans-aid.net

Enquiries:
Enquiries to: Administrator

Founded:
1932

Formerly called:
Ex-Services Fellowship Centre (year of change 2007)

Organisation type and purpose:
Registered charity (charity number 209667). To relieve distress among ex-service, including merchant service, men and women.

Subject coverage:
Assistance to ex-service persons in need.

Access to staff:
Contact by letter, by telephone, by fax, by e-mail, in person and via website
Hours: Mon to Thurs, 0900 to 1530; Fri 0900 to 1330

Also at:
New Belvedere House (Hostel for the Homeless) Whitehorse Road, London, E1 0ND; tel: 020 7790 1474; fax: 020 7253 4997

VETERINARY LABORATORIES AGENCY

Acronym or abbreviation: VLA

Woodham Lane, New Haw, Addlestone, Surrey, KT15 3NB

Tel: 01932 341111
Fax: 01932 347046
E-mail: enquiries@vla.defra.gsi.gov.uk

Website:
http://www.defra.gov.uk/vla

Enquiries:
Enquiries to: Librarian
Direct tel: 01932 357314
Direct fax: 01932 357608
Direct e-mail: library@defra.vla.gov.uk
Other contacts: Library Services Manager

Founded:
1995

Organisation type and purpose:
National government body, consultancy, research organisation.
To provide consultancy, surveillance, research, laboratory services and products to promote animal health and welfare and to minimise hazards associated with animals that are important to public health and the environment.

Subject coverage:
Investigation and control of diseases of commercial farm animals, animal husbandry, biochemistry, veterinary science and medicine, life sciences as related to animals.

Information services:
Library, Information and Records Management.

Museum or gallery collection, archive, or library special collection:
10,000 books, 40,000 bound periodicals, 300 current subscriptions, 10,000 pamphlets, 300 annual reports, collection of staff papers and posters, 3,000 slides

Trade and statistical information:
Statistics on outbreaks of animal diseases in the United Kingdom.

Library catalogue:
All or part available in-house

Printed publications:
VLA Annual Report
Veterinary Surveillance Report – VIDA
Salmonella in Livestock Production in Great Britain

Electronic and video publications:
Library Current Awareness Bulletin (weekly e-mail for members)

Publications list:
Available in print

Access to staff:
Contact by letter, by telephone, by fax, by e-mail and via website. Appointment necessary. Non-members charged.
Hours: Mon to Fri, 0900 to 1645

Access to building, collection or gallery:
Limited access, appointment necessary

Also at:
Central research facility at Weybridge

Constituent bodies:
Network of 15 regional laboratories across the UK

Constituent part of:
Department for Environment, Food and Rural Affairs (DEFRA)

VICTIM SUPPORT

National Centre, Hallam House, 56–60 Hallam Street, London, W1W 6JL

Tel: 020 7268 0200
Fax: 020 7268 0210
E-mail: contact@victimsupport.org.uk

Website:
http://www.victimsupport.org.uk

Enquiries:
Enquiries to: Information Officer
Direct tel: 020 7268 0281
Direct e-mail: info@victimsupport.org.uk
Other contacts: Library/Information Officer for arrangements to use library resources

Founded:
1974

Organisation type and purpose:
Voluntary organisation, registered charity (charity number 298028).
Provides emotional support, information and practical help to victims and witnesses of crime and their families. Raises awareness of victims' rights and the effects of crime.

Subject coverage:
Services for victims of crime, effects of crime, victims' rights, victims in the criminal justice system, victim policy.

Trade and statistical information:
Statistics of referrals to Victim Support by crime. Statistics on use of the Witness Service and Victim Supportline.

Non-library collection catalogue:
All or part available in-house

Library catalogue:
All or part available in-house

Printed publications:
View (twice yearly)

Access to staff:
Contact by letter, by telephone, by fax, by e-mail and via website. Appointment necessary.
Hours: Mon to Fri, 0900 to 1730
Special comments: Access to the collection for reference by postgraduates and professional users only, and by prior appointment with the Library/Information Officer.

Access to building, collection or gallery:
Prior appointment required

Affiliated to:
European Forum for Victim Services
National Council for Voluntary Organisations
Volunteering England
World Society of Victimology

Victim Support has:
a Witness Service in every Crown Court and magistrate's court in England and Wales about 400 local Victim Support services throughout England, Wales and N Ireland

VICTIM SUPPORT SCOTLAND

Acronym or abbreviation: VSS

15–23 Hardwell Close, Edinburgh, EH8 9RX

Tel: 0131 668 4486
Fax: 0131 662 5400
E-mail: info@victimsupportsco.org.co.uk

Website:
http://www.victimsupport.sco.org.uk

Enquiries:
Enquiries to: Head of Communications and Fundraising
Direct tel: 0131 662 5409
Direct fax: 0131 662 8209
Direct e-mail: david.sinclair@victimsupportsco.org.uk
Other contacts: Communications Officer

Founded:
1985

Organisation type and purpose:
Registered charity (charity number SC002138). Helping the victims and witnesses of crime.

Subject coverage:
Information on help available to victims of crime; practical and emotional support and essential information.

Printed publications:
Voice newsletter

Publications list:
Available online and in print

Access to staff:
Contact by letter, by telephone, by fax, by e-mail and via website. Appointment necessary.
Hours: Mon to Fri, 0900 to 1700
24-hour helpline 08456 039213; 24-hour media line 07803 970320

Also at:
32 local victim support branches and witness service offices
15–23 Hardwell Close, Edinburgh, EH8 9RX; tel: 0131 668 4486; website: http://www.victimsupportsco.org.uk

VICTORIA COLLEGE EXAMINATIONS

Acronym or abbreviation: VCM

52 Bedford Row, London, WC1R 4LR

Tel: 020 7405 6483
E-mail: vcmexams@aol.com

Website:
http://www.vcmexams.com

Enquiries:
Enquiries to: Chief Executive

Founded:
1890

Incorporates the former:
Victoria College of Music, London (year of change 2000); College of Violinists (year of change 2000)

Organisation type and purpose:
Examining body in music, speech and drama.

Subject coverage:
Examinations in performing arts.

Printed publications:
Music for VCM Exams in Clarinet Playing
Music for VCM Exams in Electronic Organ Playing
Music for VCM Exams in Flute Playing
Music for VCM Exams in Guitar Playing
Music for VCM Exams in Keyboard Playing
Music for VCM Exams in Pianoforte Playing
Music for VCM Exams in Pipe Organ Playing
Music for VCM Exams in Recorder Playing
Music for VCM Exams in Singing
Music for VCM Exams in Violin Playing
Music for VCM Exams in Harpischord Playing
Music for VCM Exams in Ukelele Playing
Music for Exams in Ocarina Playing
Past Papers: Theory of Music/Speech Exams
Order printed publications from: website: http://www.whitepublishing.co.uk

Publications list:
Available online and in print

Access to staff:
Contact by letter, by telephone, by e-mail and via website
Hours: All times

Access to building, collection or gallery:
No access other than to staff

Constituent bodies:
College of Violinists
London Music Press (publications department of Victoria College)

Member organisation of:
Association of British Choral Directors (ABCD)
European Piano Teachers Association (EPTA)
European Recorder Teachers Association (ERTA)
European String Teachers Association (ESTA)
Music Education Council (MEC)
Society of Teachers of Recorder Players (STRP)
Society of Teachers of Speech and Drama (STSD)

VICTORIA COUNTY HISTORY

Formal name: Victoria History of the Counties of England

Institute of Historical Research, University of London, Senate House, Malet Street, London, WC1E 7HU

Tel: 020 7862 8770
Fax: 020 7862 8749
E-mail: vchevents@sas.ac.uk

Website:
http://www.victoriacountyhistory.ac.uk

Enquiries:
Enquiries to: Publications Manager
Direct e-mail: jessica.davies@sas.ac.uk

Founded:
1899

Organisation type and purpose:
An encyclopaedic record of England's places and people from earliest times to the present day, written by historians working in counties across England.
To produce an encyclopaedic national history in a series of volumes that cover, county by county, and parish by parish, the general and detailed history of England from earliest times to the present.

Printed publications:
County volumes
Parish volumes
Order printed publications from: Boydell & Brewer

Electronic and video publications:
Order electronic and video publications from: Text of some vols available online at: http://www.british-history.ac.uk

Publications list:
Available online

Access to staff:
Contact by letter, by telephone and by e-mail

VICTORIA INSTITUTE OR PHILOSOPHICAL SOCIETY OF GREAT BRITAIN

Acronym or abbreviation: VI

c/o The Secretary to the Trustees, 41 Marne Avenue, Welling, Kent, DA16 2EY

Tel: 020 8303 0465
Fax: 020 8303 0465

Website:
http://www.faithandthought.org.uk

Enquiries:
Enquiries to: Honorary Treasurer
Direct tel: 01279 422661
Direct e-mail: johnbuxton@tesco.net
Other contacts: Editor for publication and material reviews: 110 Flemming Avenue, Leigh-on-Sea, Essex, SS9 3AX, tel: 01702 475110

Founded:
1865

Operating as:
Faith and Thought

Organisation type and purpose:
Learned society (membership is by subscription), registered charity (charity number 285871).
Faith and thought.

Subject coverage:
The interface between science (increasing knowledge) and the Christian revelation contained in the Holy Bible, investigating apparent contradictions and seeking reconciliation.

Museum or gallery collection, archive, or library special collection:
Back numbers of Faith and Thought, its predecessor the Journal of the Transactions of the Victoria Institute 1867 to 1989 and its successor Science and Christian Belief from 1989

Printed publications:
Brochure
Faith and Thought Bulletin (2 times a year)
Science and Christian Belief (published jointly with Christians in Science, 2 times a year)

Access to staff:
Contact by letter and by telephone
Hours: Mon to Fri, 0900 to 1700
Special comments: The society does not have regular opening times.

Editor (also for book reviews):
Faith & Thought
110 Flemming Avenue, Leigh-on-Sea, Essex, SS9 3AX; tel: 01702 475110; e-mail: reg@luhman.freeserve.co.uk

Editorial Consultant:
Victoria Institute or Philosophical Society of Great Britain
185 Wickham Road, Croydon, Surrey, CR0 8TF; tel: 020 8654 4887

In association with:
Christians in Science
The Secretary, 4 Sackville Close, Sevenoaks, Kent, TN13 3QD; tel: 01732 451907; fax: 01732 464253; e-mail: cberry@centrenet.co.uk

VICTORIAN SOCIETY

1 Priory Gardens, Bedford Park, London, W4 1TT

Tel: 020 8994 1019
Fax: 020 8747 5899
E-mail: library@victoriansociety.org.uk

Website:
http://www.victoriansociety.org.uk

Enquiries:
Enquiries to: Administrator

Founded:
1958

Organisation type and purpose:
Statutory body, learned society, registered charity (charity number 1081435).
Pressure group.
Campaigns for the Victorian and Edwardian historic environment and promotes public understanding of the architecture and decorative arts of the period.

Subject coverage:
19th- and early 20th-century architectural history, conservation legislation and protection of historic buildings, conservation and refurbishment advice, care for Victorian houses.

Museum or gallery collection, archive, or library special collection:
Case files relating to individual buildings that have been the subject of listed building consent applications

Non-library collection catalogue:
All or part available in-house

Library catalogue:
All or part available in-house

Printed publications:
Care of Victorian Houses
Reports, books, conference papers
Journal

Publications list:
Available online and in print

Access to staff:
Contact by letter, by telephone and by e-mail.
Appointment necessary.

Access to building, collection or gallery:
Prior appointment required

VIDEO PERFORMANCE LIMITED

Acronym or abbreviation: VPL

1 Upper James Street, London, W1F 9DE

Tel: 020 7534 1400
Fax: 020 7534 1414

Founded:
1984

Organisation type and purpose:
Trade association, present number of members: 800.
Music video licensing.

Subject coverage:
Music videos.

Access to staff:
Contact by letter, by telephone, by fax and by e-mail
Hours: Mon to Fri, 0900 to 1700

Trading division:
Music Mall
at the same address; tel: 020 7534 1444; fax: 020 7534 1440; e-mail: info@musicmall.co.uk

VIKING SOCIETY FOR NORTHERN RESEARCH

Department of Scandinavian Studies, University College London, Gower Street, London, WC1E 6BT

Tel: 020 7679 7176
Fax: 020 7679 7750
E-mail: vsnr@ucl.ac.uk

Website:
http://www.nolt.ac.uk/~aezjj/homepage.html

Enquiries:
Enquiries to: Honorary Secretary

Founded:
1892

Organisation type and purpose:
Learned society.

Subject coverage:
Old Norse literature; medieval Scandinavian literature, languages and history; the history and culture of The North (the Viking Age, Viking settlements in British Isles, runes etc).

Museum or gallery collection, archive, or library special collection:
Viking Society Library (now housed as part of the University College Collection)

Printed publications:
Dorothea Coke Memorial Lectures (occasional publication, free to members)
Saga Book (free to members)
Text series and books covering history, sagas, and other Viking-related subjects

Publications list:
Available in print

Access to staff:
Contact by letter, by telephone, by fax, by e-mail and in person
Hours: Mon to Fri, 1100 to 1700

Links with:
Scottish Society for Northern Studies

VINTAGE AUSTIN REGISTER LTD

The Briars, Four Lane Ends, Oakerthorpe, Alfreton, Derbyshire, DE55 7LH

Tel: 01773 831646
E-mail: frank.smith7@tesco.net

Enquiries:
Enquiries to: Honorary Secretary

Founded:
1958

Organisation type and purpose:
Membership association, voluntary organisation.

Subject coverage:
Information on all Austin motor cars produced between 1906 and 1930.

Museum or gallery collection, archive, or library special collection:
Handbooks, spares lists, sales brochures for most Austin motor cars 1906–1930

Printed publications:
VAR Newsletter (monthly, free to members)
The Vintage Austin Magazine (quarterly, free to members)

Access to staff:
Contact by letter, by telephone and by e-mail
Hours: Mon to Fri, 0900 to 1700

VINTAGE GLIDER CLUB

Acronym or abbreviation: VGC

Arewa, Shootersway Lane, Berkhamsted, Hertfordshire, HP4 3NP

Tel: 01442 873258
Fax: 01442 873258
E-mail: geoffmoore@madasafish.com

Website:
http://www.vintagegliderclub.org.uk

Enquiries:
Enquiries to: Membership Secretary

Founded:
1972

Organisation type and purpose:
International organisation, membership association (membership is by subscription), present number of members: 800 internationally, museum.
Museum – flying, restoration.

Subject coverage:
History of gliding since the early 1920s, plans of vintage gliders, whereabouts of vintage gliders, gliding museums, dates of rallies and similar events.

Museum or gallery collection, archive, or library special collection:
Collection of photographs
Construction plans of gliders especially Slingsby drawings held at Lasham Airfield and microfilm covering a wider range including Slingsby

Printed publications:
Technical Articles
Vintage (Glider) News (3 times a year)

Access to staff:
Contact by letter, by fax, by e-mail and via website
Hours: 24-hour answerphone and fax

Associated with:
British Gliding Association

VINTAGE MOTOR CYCLE CLUB LIMITED

Acronym or abbreviation: VMCC

Allen House, Wetmore Road, Burton on Trent, Staffordshire, DE14 1TR

Tel: 01283 495102
Fax: 01283 510547
E-mail: library@vmcc.net

Website:
http://www.vmcc.net
Membership details, history, section details.

Enquiries:
Enquiries to: Librarian

Founded:
1946

Organisation type and purpose:
International organisation, membership association (membership is by subscription), present number of members: 15,573, suitable for ages: all, research organisation.

Subject coverage:
Information on motorcycling and motorcycles with related accessories from 1890s to the present. Preservation and use of motorcycles over 25 years old.

Museum or gallery collection, archive, or library special collection:
Complete sets of Motorcycle, Motorcycling etc.; Ariel, BSA, Norton, Royal Enfield (early), Scott, Triumph, Velocette (early) and late Zenith works records; other collections held; handbooks, technical information etc.
Photograph collection

Non-library collection catalogue:
All or part available online and in-house

Library catalogue:
All or part available online and in-house

Printed publications:
Magazine (monthly, members)

Publications list:
Available online and in print

Access to staff:
Contact by letter, by telephone, by fax, by e-mail, in person and via website
Hours: Mon to Thu, 0900 to 1730; Fri 0900 to 1600

Access to building, collection or gallery:
Hours: Mon to Thu, 0900 to 1730; Fri, 0900 to 1600
Special comments: Library and archives situated on first floor, no lift access.

Access for disabled people:
Access to ground floor; no lift access to first floor.

Affiliated Member of:
Auto Cycle Union
tel: 01788 566400; fax: 01788 573585; e-mail: admin@acu.org.uk
Federation of British Historic Vehicle Clubs

Associated Member of:
Royal Automobile Club

VINTAGE SPORTS-CAR CLUB LIMITED

Acronym or abbreviation: VSCC

The Old Post Office, West Street, Chipping Norton, Oxfordshire, OX7 5EL

Tel: 01608 644777
Fax: 01608 644888
E-mail: info@vscc.co.uk

Enquiries:
Enquiries to: Secretary

Founded:
1934

Organisation type and purpose:
Membership association.

Subject coverage:
General and specialised information on pre-war cars and historic racing cars; mechanical data, history and whereabouts of existing cars; specialist firms; racing and competitions up to the last war; addresses of one-make and other clubs specialising in old cars in the UK and abroad; emphasis on vintage cars made 1919–1930.

Museum or gallery collection, archive, or library special collection:
Book library
Film library

Printed publications:
Bulletin (quarterly)
Circular (monthly)

Access to staff:
Contact by letter, by fax and by e-mail
Hours: Mon to Fri, 0900 to 1700

Access to building, collection or gallery:
No prior appointment required
Hours: Mon to Fri, 0900 to 1700
Special comments: Wednesday preferred.

Member of:
Fédération Internationale des Voitures Anciennes
Federation of British Historic Vehicle Clubs

VINTNERS' COMPANY

Vintners' Hall, Upper Thames Street, London, EC4V 3BG

Tel: 020 7236 1863
E-mail: info@vintnershall.co.uk

Website:
http://www.vintnershall.co.uk

Enquiries:
Enquiries to: The Clerk

Founded:
1363

Organisation type and purpose:
Membership association (membership is by election or invitation).
City of London Livery Company.

Access to staff:
Contact by letter, by telephone, by e-mail and via website

VIOLA DA GAMBA SOCIETY

Acronym or abbreviation: VdGS

28 Freelands Road, Oxford, OX4 4BT

Tel: 01865 723778
E-mail: admin@vdgs.org.uk

Website:
http://www.vdgs.org.uk

Enquiries:
Enquiries to: Administrator

Founded:
1948

Organisation type and purpose:
International organisation, learned society (membership is by subscription), present number of members: 530, voluntary organisation, registered charity (charity number 258544), publishing house, research organisation.

Subject coverage:
Printed and manuscript sources of music for viols, particularly English sources; limited information on instruments and on original treatises on playing technique.

Printed publications:
The Viol (quarterly)
Membership List (annually)
Music for Viols
Newsletter (quarterly)
Thematic Index of Music for Viols (6 vols)

Electronic and video publications:
Online Journal

Access to staff:
Contact by letter, by telephone, by fax, by e-mail, in person and via website
Hours: Afternoons and weekends

Links with:
Lute Society
Viola da Gamba Society of America

VIRGINIA WOOLF SOCIETY OF GREAT BRITAIN

Acronym or abbreviation: VWSGB

Fairhaven, Charnleys Lane, Banks, Southport, Merseyside, PR9 8HJ

Tel: 01704 225232
E-mail: stuart.n.clarke@btinternet.com

Website:
http://www.virginiawoolfsociety.org.uk

Enquiries:
Enquiries to: Membership Secretary

Founded:
1998

Organisation type and purpose:
Learned society (membership is by subscription), number of members: 400, literary society.

Subject coverage:
Virginia Woolf and the Bloomsbury Group.

Printed publications:
Annual Virginia Woolf Birthday Lectures
Virginia Woolf Bulletin (3 times a year)
Society Postcards (set of 5 costs £2, £2.50 overseas, inc. p&p)

Publications list:
Available online

Access to staff:
Contact by e-mail
Hours: Mon to Fri, 0900 to 1700

VISIBILITY

2 Queen's Crescent, St George's Cross, Glasgow, G4 9BW

Tel: 0141 332 4632
Fax: 0141 353 2981
E-mail: info@visibility.org.uk

Website:
http://www.visibility.org.uk
Outline of Society services.

Enquiries:
Enquiries to: Operational Director
Direct tel: 0141 572 0744
Direct e-mail: val@visibility.org.uk
Other contacts: Chief Executive Officer for organisational issues, funding, promotion and advertising.

Founded:
1859

Formerly called:
Glasgow & West of Scotland Society for the Blind; Mission To The Outdoor Blind

Organisation type and purpose:
Voluntary organisation, registered charity (charity number SCO 009738).
To support the independence of people with a visual impairment by providing information, welfare rights, home support, social and recreational opportunities, and volunteer support. To raise awareness of the issues of people who are visually impaired. Research.

Subject coverage:
Visual impairment and issues of concern to those working with people with sight impairment. Awareness of visual impairment/access issues for employers/service providers.

Trade and statistical information:
Data on registration in West of Scotland.

Printed publications:
Annual Report (free)
Information newsletter (free)
Project Leaflets (free)

Electronic and video publications:
Other printed information available on audio tape, disc, braille

Access to staff:
Contact by letter, by telephone, by fax and by e-mail. Appointment necessary.
Hours: Mon to Thu, 0900 to 1700; Fri, 0900 to 1630

Access to building, collection or gallery:
No prior appointment required

Access for disabled people:
Ramped entry, access to all public areas, toilet facilities

Members of:
National Association of Local Societies for the Visually Impaired (NALSVI)
tel: 01582 391848
SCVO

VISIT CORNWALL

Formal name: Cornwall Development Company
Acronym or abbreviation: VC

Pydar House, Pydar Street, Truro, Cornwall, TR1 1EA

Tel: 01872 322900
Fax: 01872 322919
E-mail: enquiries@visitcornwall.com

Website:
http://www.visitcornwall.com
The official online guide to holidays in Cornwall.

Enquiries:
Enquiries to: Administrator
Other contacts: Head of Marketing

Formerly called:
Cornwall Tourist Board

Organisation type and purpose:
Tourism.

Subject coverage:
Marketing and promotion of Cornwall as a tourism destination.

Trade and statistical information:
Various surveys giving statistical information on aspects of tourism in Cornwall.

Printed publications:
Cornwall Accommodation Guide
Gardens of Cornwall Map Guide
Cornwall Destination Guide
Dogs on Beaches – guide to dog-friendly beaches in Cornwall
Get Married in Cornwall – guide to wedding venues and services in Cornwall

Access to staff:
Contact by letter, by telephone, by fax, by e-mail and via website. Appointment necessary. Access for members only.
Hours: Answerphone out of office hours

Parent body:
Cornwall Development Company
Pydar House, Pydar Street, Truro, Cornwall, TR1 1EA; tel: 01872 322800; e-mail: mail@ cornwalldevelopmentcompany.co.uk; website: http://www.cornwalldevelopmentcompany.co .uk

VISIT FINLAND

Formal name: Visit Finland, Finland Trade Centre UK

177–179 Hammersmith Road, London, W6 8BS

Tel: 020 8600 7260 (trade and press only)

Website:
http://www.visitfinland.com/uk
Travel information on Finland.

Organisation type and purpose:
National government body, professional body. National tourist board, promoting Finland in the UK and Ireland.
Working closely with local travel trade and press.

Subject coverage:
Travelling to and in Finland; tourism facilities in Finland; addresses and contacts within the travel trade in Finland; timetables; packages available; statistics; tourist attractions.

Museum or gallery collection, archive, or library special collection:
Brochures, posters
Photographic library
Video films available on loan

Trade and statistical information:
Statistics on tourism to and in Finland.

Non-library collection catalogue:
All or part available online

Library catalogue:
All or part available online

Printed publications:
Summer and Winter brochures, lists of tour operators, activities and events
Order printed publications from: Website

Electronic and video publications:
Videos

Access to staff:
Contact via website. Appointment necessary.
Special comments: Not open to public. Visitors by prior appointment only.

Access to building, collection or gallery:
Prior appointment required
Hours: Mon to Fri, 0900 to 1700

Parent body:
Finnish Tourist Board
PO Box 625, Helsinki, 00101, Finland; tel: + 358 9 4176911; fax: + 358 9 41769399; e-mail: mek@mek .fi

VISIT LONDON

5th Floor, 1 Warwick Row, London, SW1E 5ER

Tel: 020 7234 5800
Fax: 020 7234 5751

Website:
http://www.visitlondon.com

Enquiries:
Enquiries to: Information Officer
Direct e-mail: kkelling@visitlondon.com

Organisation type and purpose:
Tourist Board.

Subject coverage:
What to see, and where to go and stay in London.

Printed publications:
London Breaks
London for the Travel Trade
Where to stay and what to do
Where to stay on a Budget

Publications list:
Available online and in print

Access to staff:
Contact by letter, by telephone, by fax, by e-mail
and via website

VISIT SWEDEN

Sweden House, 5 Upper Montagu Street, London,
W1H 2AG

Tel: 020 7108 6168
Fax: 020 7724 5872
E-mail: uk@visitsweden.com

Website:
http://www.visitsweden.com

Enquiries:
Enquiries to: Director
Direct tel: 020 7870 5601
Direct e-mail: semmy.rulf@visitsweden.com

Organisation type and purpose:
National government body.
Tourist office.

Subject coverage:
All aspects of travel to and in Sweden, including
ferry routes, airlines, suggested holiday areas.

Access to staff:
Contact by letter, by telephone, by fax, by e-mail
and via website
Hours: Mon to Fri, 0900 to 1700

VISITDENMARK

55 Sloane Street, London, SW1X 9SY

Fax: 020 7259 5955
E-mail: london@visitdenmark.com

Website:
http://www.visitdenmark.com

Founded:
1948

Organisation type and purpose:
National tourist board.

Subject coverage:
Travel and tourism to and in Denmark.

Museum or gallery collection, archive, or library special collection:
Tourist information, brochures, images, posters

Trade and statistical information:
Information for educational purposes is obtainable
from the Press and Cultural Department of the
Royal Danish Embassy.

Printed publications:
Tourist brochures are free, please contact
VisitDenmark for further information

Access to staff:
Contact by letter, by fax, by e-mail and via
website

Links with:
VisitDenmark
Islands Brygge 43–3, 2300 Copenhagen S,
Denmark

VISITGUERNSEY

PO Box 23, St Peter Port, Guernsey, GY1 3AN,
Channel Islands

Tel: 01481 726611
Fax: 01481 721246
E-mail: enquiries@visitguernsey.com

Website:
http://www.visitguernsey.com

Founded:
1946

Organisation type and purpose:
Local government body.
Tourist office.

Subject coverage:
All aspects of the tourism and conference business
of the Bailiwick of Guernsey.

Trade and statistical information:
Data on the number of visitors to the Island each
year.

Electronic and video publications:
Image Library (CD-ROM)

Access to staff:
Contact by letter, by telephone, by fax, by e-mail
and via website
Hours: Mon to Fri, 0900 to 1700

Access for disabled people:
Ramped entry, toilet facilities

Parent body:
States of Guernsey
Sir Charles Frossard House, La Charroterie, St
Peter Port, GY1 1FH, Guernsey

VISITSCOTLAND

Fairways Business Park, Deer Park Avenue,
Livingston, EH54 8AF

Tel: 01506 832213

Website:
http://www.visitscotland.com

Enquiries:
Enquiries to: Information Services Manager
Direct e-mail: tom.maxwell@visitscotland.com

Formerly called:
Scottish Tourist Board (STB)

Organisation type and purpose:
National government body.

Subject coverage:
Tourism: development, marketing, research,
tourist information.

Printed publications:
Accommodation guides (4 titles)
Information fact sheets
Promotional leaflets
Research publications

Access to staff:
Contact by letter, by telephone, by fax, by e-mail
and via website
Hours: Mon to Fri, 0900 to 1700

VISITSCOTLAND (HIGHLANDS)

Peffery House, Strathpeffer, Ross-shire, IV14 9HA

Tel: 01997 421160
Fax: 01997 421168
E-mail: info@visitscotland.com

Website:
http://www.visithighlands.com

Enquiries:
Enquiries to: Chief Executive

Direct e-mail: lorna.maclennan@visitscotland.com

Founded:
1996

Created by the merger of:
Aviemore and Spey Tourist Board, Caithness
Tourist Board, Fort William and Lochaber Tourist
Board, Inverness, Loch Ness and Nairn Tourist
Board, Isle of Skye Tourist Board, Ross and
Cromarty Tourist Board, Sutherland Tourist Board
(year of change 1996)

Organisation type and purpose:
Statutory body.
Tourism marketing.

Subject coverage:
Tourism in the Highlands of Scotland.

Trade and statistical information:
Data on volume and value of tourism in the
Highlands.

Printed publications:
Freedom of the Highlands (brochure, free)

Electronic and video publications:
Tourism and the Arts in the Highlands of Scotland
(CD-ROM)

Access to staff:
Contact by letter, by telephone, by fax and by e-
mail
Hours: Mon to Fri, 0900 to 1700

Access for disabled people:
Level entry, toilet facilities

VISITSCOTTISHBORDERS

VisitScotland, Ocean Point One, 94 Ocean Drive,
Edinburgh, EH6 6JH

Tel: 01750 20555
Fax: 01750 21886
E-mail: sbtb@scot-borders.co.uk

Website:
www.visitscottishborders.com
Wide range of consumer tourism related material.
http://www.scot-borders.co.uk

Enquiries:
Enquiries to: Chief Executive
Direct tel: 01750 23800
Direct e-mail: rgraham@scot-borders.co.uk
Other contacts: Director of Customer Marketing;
Director of Development

Founded:
1982

Formed from:
Borders Regional Council (Tourism Division),
Borders Tourist Association (year of change 1983)

Formerly called:
Scottish Borders Tourist Board (year of change
2006)

Organisation type and purpose:
Statutory body, membership association
(membership is by subscription), present number
of members: 994.
Area Tourist Board.

Subject coverage:
Tourism in the Scottish Borders, the attractions,
activities, accommodation, business advice,
marketing, statistics and research.

Museum or gallery collection, archive, or library special collection:
Collection includes 10,000 slide transparencies of
the Scottish Borders

Trade and statistical information:
Data on visitor statistics, market research, and
tourism revenue, wide range of local statistical
data on local and national tourism.

Library catalogue:
All or part available in-house

Printed publications:
Annual Report and Statement of Accounts
Variety of general guides and leaflets, including:

Angling Guide
Borders Historic Route Guide
Cycling Guide
Freedom of Fairways (golf)
Gardens Guide
Meeting and Incentives Guide
Scottish Borders Holiday Planner (annually)
Scottish Borders Essential Guide (annually)
Shopping Guide
Walking Guide
Welcome leaflet

Publications list:
Available online and in print

Access to staff:
Contact by letter, by telephone, by fax, by e-mail, in person and via website. Appointment necessary.
Hours: Mon to Thu, 0900 to 1700; Fri, 0900 to 1630
Special comments: Tourist information centre opening times vary according to the time of the year.

Access to building, collection or gallery:
No prior appointment required

Access for disabled people:
Parking provided, ramped entry, access to all public areas

Tourist Information Centres:
Coldstream
  Town Hall, 76 High Street, Coldstream, TD12 4DH; tel: 01890 882607; e-mail: coldstream@scot-borders.co.uk
Eyemouth
  Auld Kirk, Market Square, Eyemouth, TD14 5HE; tel: 01890 750678; e-mail: eyemouth@scot-borders.co.uk
Hawick
  Drumlanrig's Tower, Tower Knowe, Hawick, TD9 9EN; tel: 01450 327457; fax: 01450 373993; e-mail: hawick@scot-borders.co.uk
Jedburgh
  Murrays Green, Jedburgh, TD8 6BE; tel: 01835 863688 or 863435; fax: 01835 864099; e-mail: info@scot-borders.co.uk
Kelso
  Town House, The Square, Kelso, TD5 7HF; tel: 01573 223464; e-mail: kelso@scot-borders.co.uk
Melrose
  Abbey House, Abbey Street, Melrose, Roxburghshire, TD6 LG; tel: 01896 822555; e-mail: melrose@scot-borders.co.uk
Peebles
  High Street, Peebles, EH45 8AG; tel: 01721 720138; fax: 01721 724401; e-mail: peebles@scot-borders.co.uk
Selkirk
  Halliwells House, Selkirk, TD7 4BL; tel: 01750 20054; e-mail: selkirk@scot-borders.co.uk

VITAL INFORMATION LIMITED

Stowe Castle Business Park, Buckingham, MK18 5AB

Tel: 01280 827078
Fax: 01280 827077
E-mail: maggie@vitalinformation.co.uk

Website:
http://www.vitalinformation.co.uk

Enquiries:
Enquiries to: Director

Founded:
1984

Organisation type and purpose:
Information business.

Subject coverage:
Life sciences; biology; medicine; veterinary medicine; agriculture; food science; environmental sciences; biotechnology; pharmaceuticals; toxicology; diagnostics; health care; general news services.

Information services:
Literature searching, abstracting, indexing, desk research, thesaurus/taxonomy construction.

Access to staff:
Contact by letter, by telephone, by fax, by e-mail and via website. Appointment necessary. All charged.
Hours: Mon to Fri, 0900 to 1730

VOCATIONAL AWARDS INTERNATIONAL LIMITED

Acronym or abbreviation: VAI

3rd Floor, Eastleigh House, Market Street, Eastleigh, Hampshire, SO50 9FD

Tel: 01243 842064
Fax: 01243 842489
E-mail: info@vtct.org.uk

Website:
http://www.vtct.org.uk

Enquiries:
Enquiries to: Information Officer
Other contacts: Head of Quality Assurance, telephone: 023 8068 4500 for training centres as opposed to individual enquiries.

Founded:
1986

Formerly a division of:
International Health and Beauty Council (year of change 1986)

Organisation type and purpose:
International organisation.
Promotes qualifications of Vocational Training Charitable Trust (VTCT) internationally.

Subject coverage:
Availability of qualifications for beauty, hairdressing, health and fitness and complementary therapies. Also centres providing training.

Printed publications:
Publications only available to approved training centres
List of approved centres for training is available on website

Access to staff:
Contact by letter
Hours: Mon to Fri, 0900 to 1700

Parent body:
Vocational Training Charitable Trust
  at the same address; tel: 023 8068 4500; fax: 023 8065 1493

VOICE OF THE LISTENER AND VIEWER

Acronym or abbreviation: VLV

PO Box 401, Gravesend, Kent, DA12 9FY

Tel: 01474 338711; 01474 338716
Fax: 01474 425440
E-mail: info@vlv.org.uk

Website:
http://www.vlv.org.uk

Enquiries:
Enquiries to: Chairman

Founded:
1983

Incorporates the former:
Broadcasting Research Unit (Archive) (BRU) (year of change 1990); Voice of the Listener (VOL) (year of change 1991); British Action for Children's Television (Archive) (BACTV) (year of change 1995)

Organisation type and purpose:
Membership association (membership is by subscription), present number of members: 2,000, voluntary organisation, registered charity (charity number 296207), research organisation, publishing house.

To support high quality, independence and diversity in broadcasting; to maintain the principle of public service in broadcasting; and to represent the interests of listeners and viewers, citizens and consumers in broadcasting.

Subject coverage:
Radio and television, broadcasting policy, children's radio and television educational broadcasting, public service broadcasting in the UK, Europe and world-wide.

Museum or gallery collection, archive, or library special collection:
British Action for Children's Television (BACTV) Archive, 1988–1995
Broadcasting Research Unit (BRU) Archive, 1980–1991
Voice of the Listener and Viewer Archive, 1984–

Non-library collection catalogue:
All or part available online and in print

Library catalogue:
All or part available in-house

Printed publications:
Responses to Radio Authority, Independent Television Commission and Broadcasting Standards Commission Consultations
Conference reports
Responses to UK Government, Council of Europe and European Commission Consultations
Information sample pack (free)
Newsletter (quarterly)
Order printed publications from: Publications Secretary

Electronic and video publications:
Newsletter (quarterly, on audio tape, mainly for the blind)
Audio tapes of conference proceedings

Publications list:
Available online and in print

Access to staff:
Contact by letter, by telephone, by fax and by e-mail
Hours: Mon to Thurs, 0900 to 1700

Access to building, collection or gallery:
Prior appointment required

VOICE: THE UNION FOR EDUCATION PROFESSIONALS

2 St James' Court, Friar Gate, Derby, DE1 1BT

Tel: 01332 372337
Fax: 01332 290310
E-mail: enquiries@voicetheunion.org.uk

Website:
http://www.voicetheunion.org.uk
News, booklets, information sheets, information packs, surveys; information or actual copies available online.

Enquiries:
Enquiries to: General Secretary
Direct e-mail: pressoffice@voicetheunion.org.uk (for media)
Other contacts: Communications Officer (for media).

Founded:
1970

Formerly called:
Professional Association of Teachers (PAT) (year of change 2008)

Incorporates the former:
Professional Association of Nursery Nurses (PANN) (year of change 2008)

Organisation type and purpose:
Professional body, trade union (membership is by subscription), present number of members: 38,000. Teachers, lecturers, education support staff and childcarers.

Subject coverage:
Matters of interest to the teaching and child care professions at all levels and in all sectors.

continued overleaf

Printed publications:
Your Voice (4 times a year)
Advice booklets, factsheets and information packs
on pay and conditions, education and childcare
practice
Some publications available free online (some to
members only, some to all)
Order printed publications from: e-mail:
publications@voicetheunion.org.uk

Publications list:
Available online and in print

Access to staff:
Contact by letter, by telephone, by fax, by e-mail
and via website. Appointment necessary. Access
for members only.
Hours: Mon to Fri, 0900 to 1700

Access to building, collection or gallery:
Prior appointment required
Hours: Mon to Fri, 0900 to 1700

Access for disabled people:
Parking provided, level entry

Also at:
Voice (Scotland)
4–6 Oak Lane, Edinburgh, EH12 6XH; tel: 0131
220 8241; fax: 0131 220 8350; e-mail: scotland@
voicetheunion.org.uk

VOLKSWAGEN TYPE 2 OWNERS' CLUB

Acronym or abbreviation: VWT20C

57 Humphrey Avenue, Charford, Bromsgrove,
Worcestershire, B60 3JD

Tel: 01527 872194
Fax: 01527 872194
E-mail: philshawvw@cs.com

Website:
http://www.vwt2oc.org.uk
http://www.vanfest.org

Enquiries:
Enquiries to: Honorary Club Secretary

Founded:
1991

Organisation type and purpose:
International organisation, advisory body,
membership association (membership is by
subscription), present number of members: 2500,
voluntary organisation.

Subject coverage:
Volkswagen Type 2 vehicles, advice and help given
to members with any related problem.

Museum or gallery collection, archive, or library special collection:
Wide range of printed information concerning
Volkswagen Type 2 vehicles

Library catalogue:
All or part available in-house

Printed publications:
Magazine (6 times a year, members)

Access to staff:
Contact by letter, by telephone, by fax, by e-mail,
in person and via website. Appointment necessary.
Hours: 7 days, 1000 to 2200

VOLUNTARY SERVICE OVERSEAS

Acronym or abbreviation: VSO

317 Putney Bridge Road, London, SW15 2PN

Tel: 020 8780 7200\ Minicom no. 020 8780 7440
Fax: 020 8780 7300
E-mail: enquiry@vso.org.uk

Website:
http://www.vso.org.uk
Job information, campaigns and events,
information provision, publishing working papers,
magazine, overseas programmes, fundraising
events.

Enquiries:
Enquiries to: Enquiries Unit
Direct tel: 020 8780 7500
Direct fax: 020 8780 7207
Direct e-mail: press@vso.org.uk

Founded:
1958

Organisation type and purpose:
International organisation, present number of
members: 1939, voluntary organisation, registered
charity (charity number 313757).
Development agency that works through
volunteers to tackle disadvantage in developing
communities worldwide.

Subject coverage:
Advice on volunteering opportunities with VSO.

Publications list:
Available online and in print

Access to staff:
Contact by letter, by telephone, by fax, by e-mail
and via website
Hours: Enquiries unit: Mon to Fri, 0900 to 1700

Access to building, collection or gallery:
No prior appointment required
Hours: Library: Mon to Fri, 0900 to 1700; Sat, 1000
to 1630

Access for disabled people:
Ramped entry, toilet facilities

VOLUNTEER CENTRE

Formal name: Centre for Community Action,
Volunteering & Employment Initiatives
Acronym or abbreviation: VC

4th Floor, 84 Miller Street, Glasgow, G1 1DT

Tel: 0141 226 3431
Fax: 0141 221 0716
E-mail: info@volunteerglasgow.org

Website:
http://www.volunteerglasgow.org
Information on all the services provided.
Soon – online database of volunteering
opportunties.

Enquiries:
Enquiries to: Information Officer

Founded:
1970

Organisation type and purpose:
Membership association (membership is by
election or invitation), present number of
members: 99, registered charity (charity number
SCO 05462).
A catalogue of volunteering opportunities
available in Glasgow. A resource library of
publications relating to volunteering and issues
affecting the voluntary sector.
The Centre aims to improve the quality of life for
the people of Glasgow by offering opportunities to
use and develop their skills in volunteering,
training and personal development. In addition,
the Centre works in neighbourhoods to develop
informal care and support services with vulnerable
families and individuals; and in partnership with
charitable trusts, local authorities and other
organisations to deliver community care services.

Subject coverage:
Volunteering, good practice in working with
volunteers, befriending, carers, employment issues
for voluntary and community organisations,
community care, employment training for
physically disabled people, health and wellbeing.

Museum or gallery collection, archive, or library special collection:
Resource library of books and documents relating
to volunteering, the voluntary sector, health and
social care, community care, disability, health
and safety, employment, education etc
Catalogue of voluntary opportunities for potential
volunteers

Non-library collection catalogue:
All or part available online

Printed publications:
Newsletter for volunteers (2 times a year, free)
Newsletter for organisations that involve
volunteers (2 times a year)
A Guide to Good Practice on Employment and
Management Issues for Voluntary Organisations
(ISBN 1 87175901 3, £19 plus £1.95 p&p)
Good practice factsheets for organisations
involving volunteers (free)

Access to staff:
Contact by letter, by telephone, by fax, by e-mail,
in person and via website
Hours: Mon to Thu, 0900 to 1700; Fri, 0900 to 1600

Access to building, collection or gallery:
No access other than to staff

VOLUNTEER NOW

34 Shaftesbury Square, Belfast, BT2 7DB

Tel: 028 9020 0850
Fax: 028 9020 0860
E-mail: reception@volunteernow.co.uk

Website:
http://www.volunteernow.co.uk

Enquiries:
Enquiries to: Co-ordinator

Founded:
2010

Formerly called:
VSB (year of change 2010)

Organisation type and purpose:
Volunteer Now is a regional to local organisation
that works to promote, develop and support
volunteering across Northern Ireland. The
organisation enhances recognition for the
contribution volunteers make, provides access to
opportunities and encourages people to volunteer.
Volunteer Now also provides training,
information, guidance and support to volunteer-
involving organisations on issues of good practice
and policy regarding volunteering, volunteer
management, child protection and governance.

Subject coverage:
Information on volunteer opportunities
throughout Northern Ireland.

Publications list:
Available online

Access to staff:
Contact by letter, by telephone, by fax, by e-mail,
in person and via website. All charged.
Hours: Mon to Fri, 0900 to 1700

Branches:
Antrim, Armagh, Bangor, Downpatrick,
Dungannon, Enniskillen, Larne, Lisburn, Newry
website: http://www.volunteernow.co.uk

VOLUNTEERING ENGLAND

Acronym or abbreviation: VE

Regents Wharf, 8 All Saints Street, London, N1
9RL

Tel: 0845 305 6979
Fax: 020 7520 8910
E-mail: volunteering@volunteeringengland.org

Website:
http://www.volunteering.org.uk/

Enquiries:
Enquiries to: Head of Information

Founded:
2004

Created by the merger of:
the Consortium on Opportunities for Volunteering,
the National Centre for Volunteering and
Volunteer Development England. Subsequently
merged with Student Volunteering England (in
2007).

Organisation type and purpose:
Voluntary organisation, registered charity (charity number 1102770).
National development agency for volunteering.

Subject coverage:
Information, training and support to organisations who work with volunteers, campaign on public policy.

Museum or gallery collection, archive, or library special collection:
Largest library on volunteering in the UK

Library catalogue:
All or part available in-house

Printed publications:
Volunteering (magazine, 10 times a year, UK £20)
Many leaflets and books including:
Managing Volunteers
The 1997 National Survey of Volunteering in the UK
Volunteering in Europe: Opportunities and challenges for the 90s
Working With Volunteers (4 booklets, personnel issues, recruitment and selection, training, support)
Order printed publications from: MJF Data Management
River House, Riverside Way, Uxbridge, UB8 2YF, tel: 01895 909050, fax: 01895 909060

Publications list:
Available in print

Access to staff:
Contact by letter, by telephone, by fax and by e-mail. Appointment necessary.
Hours: Mon to Fri, 1000 to 1700

Access to building, collection or gallery:
Prior appointment required

Access for disabled people:
Access to all public areas, toilet facilities

VOLVO ENTHUSIASTS CLUB

Acronym or abbreviation: VEC

127 Kidderminster Road, Wribbenhall, Bewdley, Worcestershire, DY12 1JE

Tel: 01872 553740 or 01425 476425
Fax: 01872 553740 (phone first)

Website:
http://www.volvo1800.co.uk
http://www.volvoenthusiastsclub.co.uk

Enquiries:
Enquiries to: Chairman/Founder

Founded:
1989

Organisation type and purpose:
International organisation, membership association (membership is by subscription), present number of members: 1500, voluntary organisation.
To encourage ownership, interest, preservation and correct maintenance of all Volvos over 15 years old or out of production, and to serve as a source of technical information and parts through a friendly family style club.

Subject coverage:
Historic and technical information on all Volvo cars, buses and trucks over 15 years old, spares location and availability, restoration advice, guide to purchase, classic Volvo historical data P1800 (Saint Volvo), 120 (Amazon) etc, international register, historic rally-race preparation-information and data-race/rally register.

Museum or gallery collection, archive, or library special collection:
Complete Volvo production data for P1800 1961–63 – first 6000 vehicles built by Jensen
Sales brochures – P1800, 120 etc
Technical library – Volvo workshop manuals, parts lists etc
Homologation papers 120, 1800-PV-140 etc

Volvo special tuning data B18/B20 engines and vehicles fitted with these units
Volvo special tools

Trade and statistical information:
Production data pre 1990 – rolling over 15 years, all models.
Production data from original records of P1800 1961–1963.
Current vehicle values and trends.

Printed publications:
Buyers Guides for each model covered by the Club
Club Magazine (quarterly, free to members)
List of Cars For Sale or Wanted
Volvo Enthusiasts Club Magazine

Access to staff:
Contact by letter and by telephone. Non-members charged.
Hours: Mon to Fri, 0900 to 1700

VOLVO OWNERS CLUB

18 Macaulay Avenue, Portsmouth, Hampshire, PO6 4NY

Tel: 023 9238 1494
Fax: 023 9238 1494
E-mail: membership@volvoclub.org.uk

Website:
http://www.Volvoclub.org.uk
Information relating to the Club.

Enquiries:
Enquiries to: Membership Secretary

Organisation type and purpose:
Membership association (membership is by subscription), present number of members: 5000.
Club for owners and enthusiasts of Volvo cars.

Subject coverage:
All aspects of the ownership and maintenance of Volvo cars.

Access to staff:
Contact by letter, by telephone, by fax, by e-mail and via website
Hours: Mon to Sun

VTCT

Third Floor, Eastleigh House, Market Street, Eastleigh, Hampshire, SO50 9FD

Tel: 023 8068 4500
Fax: 023 8065 1493
E-mail: info@vtct.org.uk

Website:
http://www.vtct.org.uk

Enquiries:
Enquiries to: Customer Service Department
Direct e-mail: customerservice@vtct.org.uk
Other contacts: Head of Quality Assurance for potential training centres.

Founded:
1986

Formed from:
International Health and Beauty Council (IHBC) (year of change 1986)

Organisation type and purpose:
International organisation, registered charity (charity number 295192). Awarding body (service sector). National and international qualifications in hairdressing, beauty, fitness, sport, holistic and complementary therapies. Supportive qualifications in business organisation, customer service and keyskills.

Subject coverage:
Availability of National and Scottish vocational qualifications (NVQs and S/NVQs) and international qualifications in beauty, hairdressing, holistic and complementary, fitness and sports therapies. Courses are provided across the British Isles, primarily in Colleges of Further Education.

Access to staff:
Contact by letter, by telephone and by e-mail
Hours: Mon to Fri, 0900 to 1700
Special comments: No visitors in person.

VW OWNERS' CLUB GB

Acronym or abbreviation: VWOC (GB)

PO Box 7, Burntwood, Walsall, West Midlands, WS7 2SB

E-mail: info@vwocgb.com

Website:
http://www.vwocgb.com
Technical information, vehicle age verification, online membership, articles, adverts and discounts.

Founded:
1953

Organisation type and purpose:
Membership association (membership is by subscription), present number of members: 1,000, voluntary organisation.
To provide a focal group for all enthusiasts of Volkswagen Group vehicles both old and modern. Also, to obtain from associated trades any financial benefits possible for members.

Subject coverage:
VW cars including all Volkswagen Group Companies.

Printed publications:
Quarterly magazine, Club News

Access to staff:
Contact by letter, by e-mail and via website
Hours: Mon to Fri, 0900 to 1700

WADE SPRING LIMITED

Highfield Street, Long Eaton, Nottingham, NG10 4GY

Tel: 0115 946 3000
Fax: 0115 946 1361
E-mail: sales@wade-spring.co.uk

Website:
http://www.wade-spring.co.uk

Enquiries:
Enquiries to: Technical Director

Founded:
1926

Incorporates the former:
Elson & Robbins Limited

Organisation type and purpose:
Manufacturing industry.

Subject coverage:
Spring cases and assemblies for upholstery and bedding trades.

Access to staff:
Contact by letter, by telephone, by fax and by e-mail
Hours: Mon to Fri, 0900 to 1700

WADHAM COLLEGE

The Library, Oxford, OX1 3PN

Tel: 01865 277900
E-mail: library@wadham.ox.ac.uk

Enquiries:
Enquiries to: Librarian

Founded:
1613

Organisation type and purpose:
University department or institute.
College library.

Subject coverage:
General undergraduate material; Spanish (16th and 17th centuries); Persian.

continued overleaf

Museum or gallery collection, archive, or library special collection:
16th-century theology (2,000 vols)
16th- and 17th-century Spanish books (1,000 vols)
Persian and Arabic manuscripts (800 items)
Persian lithographs (200 items)
Printed books in Persian, Arabic and European languages on Persian classical literature and history, up to the end of the Constitutional Persian Revolution in 1911

Non-library collection catalogue:
All or part available online and in-house

Library catalogue:
All or part available online and in-house

Access to staff:
Contact by letter, by telephone and by e-mail. Appointment necessary.
Hours: Mon to Fri, 0900 to 1700

Parent body:
University of Oxford

WAKEFIELD COLLEGE

Margaret Street, Wakefield, West Yorkshire, WF1 2DH

Tel: 01924 789789\ Minicom no. 01924 789270
Fax: 01924 789340
E-mail: staffmember@wakcoll.ac.uk

Website:
http://www.wakcoll.ac.uk

Enquiries:
Enquiries to: Marketing Manager
Direct tel: 01924 789162
Direct fax: 01924 789362

Formerly called:
Wakefield District College

Organisation type and purpose:
Suitable for ages: 16+.
Further Education College.

Subject coverage:
GCSEs, 'A' levels, GNVQs, HNDs, HNCs, NVQs, computer studies, languages, health, child and social care, hospitality, leisure and tourism, business and secretarial, building, technology, CAD/CAM, art, drama, media, graphics, adult education, engineering, hair and beauty, sport studies, public services, horticulture.

Printed publications:
Corporate Business Courses Literature – Service to Business
Full Time Prospectus (full time courses for young people)
Part Time Prospectus
HE Prospectus

Electronic and video publications:
Full Time and HE Courses (CD-ROM, free)

Publications list:
Available in print

Access to staff:
Contact by letter
Hours: Mon to Fri, 0900 to 1700

Access to building, collection or gallery:
No prior appointment required
Special comments: Report to main reception.

Access for disabled people:
Parking provided, ramped entry, access to all public areas, toilet facilities

Connections with:
Learndirect Learning Centre
tel: 01924 789333; e-mail: c.furbisher@wakcoll.ac.uk

Other Campuses:
Hemsworth SkillsBank
Bank Street, Hemsworth, West Yorkshire, WF9 4JX; tel: 01924 789789 Minicom: 01977 619784; fax: 01977 619480

Thornes Park Campus
Thornes Park, Horbury Road, Wakefield, West Yorkshire, WF2 8QZ; tel: 01924 789789 Minicom: 01924 789800; fax: 01924 789821
Whitwood Campus
Four Lane Ends, Castleford, West Yorkshire, WF10 5NF; tel: 01924 789789 Minicom: 01924 789431; fax: 01924 789478

WAKEFIELD HISTORICAL SOCIETY

19 Pinders Grove, Wakefield, WF1 4AH

E-mail: kate@airtime.co.uk

Website:
http://www.wakefieldhistoricalsoc.org.uk

Enquiries:
Enquiries to: President

Founded:
1924

Organisation type and purpose:
Historical Society.
To bring together those with an interest in local or national history.

Access to staff:
Contact by letter, by e-mail and via website

WAKEFIELD LIBRARIES AND INFORMATION SERVICE

Library Headquarters, Balne Lane, Wakefield, West Yorkshire, WF2 0DQ

Tel: 01924 302210; typetalk no. 01924 302210
Fax: 01924 302245
E-mail: lib.admin@wakefield.gov.uk

Website:
http://www.wakefield.gov.uk/libraries
Description of service, service point addresses and opening hours, access to online library resources.

Enquiries:
Enquiries to: Libraries & Information Services Manager

Founded:
1974

Organisation type and purpose:
Local government body, public library.

Subject coverage:
General, local and family history.

Museum or gallery collection, archive, or library special collection:
British Official Publications, 1974 onwards, all parliamentary and selected non-parliamentary
British Standards
Cryer Collection
J S Fletcher Collection
George Gissing Collection
Henry Moore Collection
Local and Family History (District and Yorkshire) Collection
School Library Service including:
books, posters, audio cassettes, videos
Yorkshire Libraries & Information collections:
Music and drama services (single copies and sets of plays and music)
Provincial Fiction Reserve (N-S section)

Non-library collection catalogue:
All or part available in-house

Library catalogue:
All or part available in-house

Access to staff:
Contact by letter, by telephone, by fax, by e-mail and via website
Hours: Mon to Fri, 0900 to 1700

Access for disabled people:
Parking provided, level entry, toilet facilities

Administers:
Yorkshire Libraries & Information (YLI)
tel: 01924 302214; fax: 01924 302245; e-mail: kholliday@wakefield.gov.uk

WALES COUNCIL FOR VOLUNTARY ACTION

Acronym or abbreviation: WCVA

Cyngor Gweithredu Gwirfoddol Cymru, Baltic House, Mount Stuart Square, Cardiff, CF10 5FH

Tel: 0800 2888 329; minicom no. 0808 1 804080
Fax: 029 2043 1701
E-mail: help@wcva.org.uk

Website:
http://www.wcva.org.uk

Enquiries:
Enquiries to: WCVA Helpdesk

Founded:
1934

Organisation type and purpose:
Trade union (membership is by subscription), present number of members: 3,000 approx, service industry, voluntary organisation, registered charity (charity number 218093).
Promotes and supports voluntary action and community development in Wales.

Subject coverage:
Information relating to the voluntary sector in Wales; legal matters, funding advice, Europe and European funding, training, community care, contracting, volunteering matters, community development, voluntary sector liaison with the National Assembly for Wales.

Museum or gallery collection, archive, or library special collection:
Comprehensive collection of material relating to the voluntary sector, with particular emphasis on Wales

Trade and statistical information:
Database of voluntary organisations in Wales.

Library catalogue:
All or part available in-house

Printed publications:
Best Value and the voluntary sector: A Guide (2001, £5)
Dance with the Dragon – A guide to devolution in Wales for UK voluntary organisations (bilingual, 1999, £5)
Faith and hope don't run charities (trustees do) – a practical guide for voluntary members of management committees (1999, £10)
National Voluntary Organisations in Wales: Directory 2000 (2000, £10)
Wales Funding Handbook 2000 (£17)
Wales voluntary sector almanac 2002 – Key facts and figures
Wales voluntary sector almanac 2002 – Mapping the sector
Briefing and consultation documents
Information sheets
Network Wales (newsletter, fortnightly)
Order printed publications from: WCVA Publications, WCVA, at the same address; tel: 029 2043 1723; fax: 029 2043 1701; e-mail: publications@wcva.org.uk

Electronic and video publications:
Disc version (customised) of Directory of Voluntary Organisations in Wales: National contacts

Publications list:
Available in print

Access to staff:
Contact by letter, by telephone, by fax, by e-mail and via website. Appointment necessary. Non-members charged.
Hours: Mon to Fri, 0900 to 1700

Access for disabled people:
Parking provided, ramped entry, access to all public areas, toilet facilities

Also at:
WCVA – Mid Wales
Unit 2, Science Park, Cefn Llan, Aberystwyth, Ceredigion, SY23 3AH; tel: 0800 2888 329; e-mail: help@wcva.org.uk
WCVA – North Wales Office
Morfa Hall, Bath Street, Rhyl, Denbighshire, LL18 3EB; tel: 0800 2888 329; e-mail: help@wcva.org.uk

WALES TOURIST BOARD

Acronym or abbreviation: WTB

Brunel House, 2 Fitzalan Road, Cardiff, CF24 0UY

Tel: 029 2049 9909
Fax: 029 2048 5031

Website:
http://www.visitwales.com
Product, statistical and grant aid information for Wales, a gateway to information on visiting Wales, Wales as a nation and the work of the Wales Tourist Board.

Enquiries:
Enquiries to: Information Development Officer
Direct tel: 029 2047 5277
Direct e-mail: kathryn.newton@wales.gsi.gov.uk

Organisation type and purpose:
National government body.
Statutory body.

Subject coverage:
Development, marketing and advisory functions relating to tourism in Wales, events, attractions, activities, holidays and accommodation.

Trade and statistical information:
Data on the number of overseas visitors, domestic visitors, visitors to attractions in Wales.

Printed publications:
Events Listings
Maps
Promotional publications
Tourist guides

Electronic and video publications:
Heritage of a Nation (video)
Homecoming 2000 (video)
Rugby World Cup (video)
The Wonder of Wales (video)
Welcome to Wales (CD-ROM)
Voices from Wales (CD)

Publications list:
Available in print

Access to staff:
Contact by letter, by telephone, by fax and by e-mail
Hours: Mon to Fri, 0900 to 1700

Associated with:
British Tourist Authority

WALLCOVERINGS SECTOR COUNCIL

Acronym or abbreviation: WSC

British Coatings Federation, The Stables, Thorncroft Manor, Leatherhead, Surrey, KT22 8JB

Tel: 01372 700848
Fax: 01372 700851
E-mail: alison.brown@bcf.co.uk

Enquiries:
Enquiries to: Administrator

Founded:
2005

Created by the merger of:
Wallcovering Manufacturers' Association of Great Britain Limited (f. 1970) and British Coatings Federation (year of change 2005)

Organisation type and purpose:
Trade association, membership association (membership is by subscription, election or invitation), present number of members: 15.

Subject coverage:
Wallcovering manufacture, product standards, pattern book names.

Trade and statistical information:
Statistics (very selective distribution).

Access to staff:
Contact by letter, by fax and by e-mail
Hours: Mon to Fri, 0900 to 1700

WALLPAPER HISTORY SOCIETY

Acronym or abbreviation: WHS

c/o Victoria and Albert Museum, South Kensington, London, SW7 2RL

Tel: 020 7942 2560

Enquiries:
Enquiries to: Secretary
Direct tel: 020 8977 4978

Founded:
1986

Organisation type and purpose:
Research organisation.

Subject coverage:
History of wallpaper, bibliography, specialist conservation sources, manufacturers specialising in the production of reproduction historic papers, details of museums and archives holding wallpapers.

Museum or gallery collection, archive, or library special collection:
Please note that the Society itself holds no collections, though it has members and contacts in institutions which do have collections of wallpaper

Printed publications:
Wallpaper History Review

Access to staff:
Contact by letter and by telephone
Hours: Mon to Fri, 0900 to 1700

WALMSLEY SOCIETY

April Cottage, 1 Brand Road, Hampden Park, Eastbourne, East Sussex, BN2 9PX

Tel: 01323 506447

Website:
http://www.walmsleysoc.org

Enquiries:
Enquiries to: Honorary Secretary
Other contacts: Membership Secretary (for membership enquiries only)

Founded:
1985

Organisation type and purpose:
International organisation (membership is by subscription). Literary society. To promote and encourage an appreciation of the literary and artistic heritage left by Leo and J Ulric Walmsley.

Subject coverage:
Appreciation of the work of Leo Walmsley (author) and the work of James Ulric Walmsley (artist).

Museum or gallery collection, archive, or library special collection:
Various items and information applicable to the aims of the society

Printed publications:
Society Journal (two a year, members free, £3 non-members)
Various booklets (prices on application)
Reprints by publisher of some of Leo Walmsley's books (price on application)
Order printed publications from: via website

Electronic and video publications:
Turn of The Tide (video, £13.95 incl p&p, J Arthur Rank's first feature film based on Leo Walmsley's book 'Three Fevers')

Publications list:
Available online and in print

Access to staff:
Contact by letter, by telephone and via website
Hours: Anytime within reason

Also at:
Membership Secretary (letter only)
21 The Crescent, Hipperholme, Halifax, Yorkshire, HX3 8NQ

Member organisation of:
The Alliance of Literary Societies

WALSALL HOSPITAL NHS TRUST

Manor Hospital Postgraduate Medical Centre, Medical Library, Moat Road, Walsall, West Midlands, WS2 9PS

Tel: 01922 721172

Enquiries:
Enquiries to: Librarian

WALSALL LOCAL HISTORY CENTRE

Essex Street, Walsall, West Midlands, WS2 7AS

Tel: 01922 721305
Fax: 01922 634954
E-mail: localhistorycentre@walsall.gov.uk

Website:
http://www.walsall.gov.uk/localhistorycentre

Enquiries:
Enquiries to: Archivist/Local Studies Officer

Founded:
1986

Formerly called:
Walsall Archives Service

Organisation type and purpose:
Local government body, public library.
Record office, archive and local studies library.

Subject coverage:
All aspects of the history of Walsall Metropolitan Borough and its constituent towns: Aldridge, Bloxwich, Brownhills, Darlaston, Willenhall and Walsall. Photographic, map, oral history, ephemera, newspapers, printed materials, archives and family history.

Non-library collection catalogue:
All or part available online and in-house

Library catalogue:
All or part available online and in-house

Printed publications:
A large number of publications, many with photographs, on the Black Country, its people, industry and history
Many books on specific areas including:
Aldridge, Bloxwich, Brownhills, Caldmore and Palfrey, Darlaston, Pheasey, Streetly, Walsall, Willenhall

Publications list:
Available online and in print

Access to staff:
Contact by letter, by telephone, by fax, by e-mail, in person and via website
Hours: Mon, closed; Tue and Thu, 0930 to 1730; Wed, 0930 to 1900; Fri, 0930 to 1700; Sat, 0930 to 1300

Access for disabled people:
Ramped entry, access to all public areas, toilet facilities

WALTHAM FOREST ARCHIVES AND LOCAL STUDIES LIBRARY

Waltham Forest Archives and Local Studies Library, Vestry House Museum, Vestry Road, Walthamstow, London, E17 9NH

continued overleaf

Tel: 020 8496 4381
E-mail: vhm.enquiries@walthamforest.gov.uk

Website:
http://www.walthamforest.gov.uk/index/leisure/
museums-galleries/archives-local-studies.htm

Enquiries:
Enquiries to: Archivist
Other contacts: Local Studies Librarian

Founded:
Late 1970s

Organisation type and purpose:
Local government body, public library.

Subject coverage:
History and development of the area covered by
the London Borough of Waltham Forest
(comprising the former boroughs of Chingford,
Leyton and Walthamstow).

**Museum or gallery collection, archive, or library
special collection:**
Records of Waltham Forest Deanery (including
parish records)

Non-library collection catalogue:
All or part available in-house

Library catalogue:
All or part available in-house

Printed publications:
Victoria County History (extracts from the Victoria
History of the Counties of England – A History
of Essex Vol. V and Vol. VI, extracts for
Chingford and Leyton, published by LBWF)
War over Walthamstow (Ross Wyld, LBWF)
Alfred Hitchcock: From Leytonstone to Hollywood
(Nigel Sadler and Victoria Coxon)
Walthamstow Historical Society Publications:
Waltham Forest Revisited, 1910–1940
Some Old Walthamstow Houses
A Brief History of Courtenay Warner and the
Warner Estate
Bullseyes
Chingford Historical Society Publications:
Chingford As It Was
Chingford in History
The Chingflier (extracts from the Chingford Royal
Naval Air Station magazine, WWI)
Waltham Forest Oral History Society Publications:
Walthamstow Village
We Want Winns
Jenny Hammond – the life of a Labour Councillor
One Door Closes, Another Opens
Order printed publications from: Linda Weston at
Vestry House Museum, Vestry Road,
Walthamstow, London, E17 9NH; tel: 020 8496
4391

Publications list:
Available in print

Access to staff:
Contact by letter, by telephone, by e-mail and in
person. Appointment necessary.
Hours: By prior appointment; Thu, Fri and Sat,
1000 to 1300 and 1400 to 1700

Access for disabled people:
Stairs to Searchroom (located in a listed building),
but appointments can take place in an accessible
ground floor room by prior arrangement.

WALTHAM FOREST COLLEGE

Library, Forest Road, Walthamstow, London, E17
4JB

Tel: 020 8501 8501
Fax: 020 8501 8302
E-mail: 2learn@waltham.ac.uk

Website:
http://www.waltham.ac.uk

Enquiries:
Enquiries to: Learning Resources Manager
Direct tel: 020 8501 8026
Direct e-mail: pauline.nash@waltham.ac.uk

Founded:
1938

Organisation type and purpose:
College of higher education.

Subject coverage:
Business studies, management, office technology,
computing, electrical and electronic engineering,
manufacturing, automobile engineering, art and
design, fashion technology, caring, health studies,
counselling, ESOL, EFL, catering, meat technology,
travel and tourism, hotel management, performing
arts, media studies, general education, science,
beauty therapy, hairdressing, built environment.

Library catalogue:
All or part available in-house

Access to staff:
Contact by letter, by telephone, by fax and by e-
mail. Appointment necessary.
Hours: Mon to Thu, 0845 to 1900; Fri, 0845 to 1600

WALTHAM FOREST HEALTHCARE
LIBRARY

Acronym or abbreviation: WXUHT

Whipps Cross Hospital, Leytonstone, London, E11
1NR

Tel: 020 8535 6860
Fax: 020 8535 6973
E-mail: library@whippsx.nhs.uk

Website:
http://www.libnel.nhs.uk

Enquiries:
Enquiries to: Librarian
Direct e-mail: angela.head@whippsx.nhs.uk

Organisation type and purpose:
NHS Trust Library supporting library and
information needs of health and social care staff
based in the local health economy.

Subject coverage:
Clinical medicine and health and social care.

Library catalogue:
All or part available online and in-house

Access to staff:
Contact by letter, by telephone, by fax, by e-mail,
in person and via website. Non-members charged.
Hours: Mon, Tue, Wed, Fri, 0830 to 1700; Thu, 0830
to 1900

Access for disabled people:
Lift access, toilet facilities

WALTHAM FOREST LIBRARIES,
MUSEUM & GALLERY SERVICES

Silver Birch House, Uplands Business Park, Black
Horse Lane, Walthamstow, London E17 5SD

Tel: 020 8496 3652
E-mail: wf.libs@walthamforest.gov.uk

Website:
http://www.walthamforest.gov.uk/libraries
Waltham Forest Council's home page.

Enquiries:
Enquiries to: Head of Libraries, Museum & Gallery
Services
Direct tel: 020 8496 3203; 020 8496 3643 (Libraries
Development Manager)
Direct e-mail: lorna.lee@walthamforest.gov.uk
Other contacts: Libraries Development Manager

Formerly called:
Waltham Forest Libraries & Cultural Services

Organisation type and purpose:
Local government body, public library.

Subject coverage:
General; domestic arts and sciences.

**Museum or gallery collection, archive, or library
special collection:**
Laser subject specialisation, Dewey 640–649, 663–
664, 338.47663–338.47664
William Morris Collection

Access to staff:
Contact by letter, by telephone, by e-mail, in
person and via website
Hours: Mon to Fri, 0900 to 1700

WALTHAMSTOW HISTORICAL
SOCIETY

Vestry House Museum, Vestry Road, London, E17
9NH

Tel: 020 8509 1917
E-mail: ellingham@clara.co.uk

Website:
http://www.walthamstowhistoricalsociety.org

Enquiries:
Enquiries to: Publications Secretary

Founded:
1914

Formerly called:
Walthamstow Antiquarian Society (year of change
1986)

Organisation type and purpose:
Membership association, registered charity
(charity number 277823).
Local history society.

Subject coverage:
Local history of Walthamstow and Waltham
Forest.

Publications list:
Available in print

WANDSWORTH HERITAGE
SERVICE

Battersea Library, 265 Lavender Hill, London,
SW11 1JB

Tel: 020 8871 7753
Fax: 020 7978 4376
E-mail: heritage@wandsworth.gov.uk

Website:
http://www.wandsworth.gov.uk
Summary of holdings and services, opening hours.

Enquiries:
Enquiries to: Heritage Officer
Other contacts: Assistant Heritage Officer

Organisation type and purpose:
Public library.

Subject coverage:
Local history library for Wandsworth area.

**Museum or gallery collection, archive, or library
special collection:**
Photograph collection
Archives of London Borough of Wandsworth and
predecessor authorities, local institutions and
societies including WWII records, electoral
registers
Microfilm resources: Census returns 1841 to 1901
(local area); IGI (1992 edition) for England; local
newspapers c.1853 to 1990s (some gaps); maps of
local area mid-17th century to present day
Cuttings collections of Mayors of Wandsworth
circa 1950s to 1960s
Cuttings collections of Alfred Hurley, proprietor of
Tooting and Balham Gazette 1900 to 1947
Wandsworth Scrapbooks circa 1880 to 1939
Slides of local area (approx. 3,000) loan service
Wandsworth Museum holds original watercolours
and prints; printed ephemera and photograph
collections
Battersea Scrapbooks 1901–1939

Non-library collection catalogue:
All or part available online and in-house

Library catalogue:
All or part available online

Printed publications:
Modern reproductions of postcards and paintings;
maps and prints (prices available on application)

Local history publications produced by local authors, etc. (also on sale)

Access to staff:
Contact by letter, by telephone, by fax, by e-mail, in person and via website
Hours: Mon to Thu, 0930 to 2000; Fri, 0930 to 1800; Sat, 0930 to 1730; Sun, 1300 to 1700
Special comments: Qualified staff only available Thu, Fri and Sat mornings.

Access for disabled people:
Located on the first floor, please call and arrangements will be made to bring material downstairs

WANDSWORTH LIBRARIES

Formal name: Wandsworth Library and Heritage Service

Department of Leisure & Amenity Services, Wandsworth Town Hall, Wandsworth High Street, London, SW18 2PU

Tel: 020 8871 6369
Fax: 020 8871 7630
E-mail: libraries@wandsworth.gov.uk

Website:
http://www.wandsworth.gov.uk/libraries

Enquiries:
Enquiries to: Librarian

Organisation type and purpose:
Local government body, public library.
11 libraries, reference and local archives service.

Museum or gallery collection, archive, or library special collection:
Early children's books (tel: 020 8871 7090)
Edward Thomas Collection
G A Henty Collection
William Blake Collection
World War One and Two

Library catalogue:
All or part available online

Access to staff:
Contact by letter, by telephone, by fax, by e-mail and in person
Hours: Mon to Fri, 0900 to 1700

WAR WIDOWS' ASSOCIATION OF GREAT BRITAIN

c/o 199 Borough High Street, London, SE1 1AA

Tel: 0845 241 2189
E-mail: info@warwidowsassociation.org.uk

Website:
http://www.warwidowsassociation.org.uk

Enquiries:
Enquiries to: Secretary

Founded:
1971

Organisation type and purpose:
Membership association (membership is by subscription), present number of members: 4,000 voluntary organisation, registered charity (charity number 1002656).
The improvement of War Widows' Pensions and the regulations pertaining to them; support for War Widows; not grant-making.

Subject coverage:
War Widows' pensions; associated DSS benefits.

Printed publications:
Courage

Publications list:
Available in print

Access to staff:
Contact by letter, by telephone, by e-mail and via website
Hours: Mon to Fri, 0900 to 1700

WARBURG INSTITUTE

Woburn Square, London, WC1H 0AB

Tel: 020 7862 8949
Fax: 020 7862 8955
E-mail: warburg@sas.ac.uk

Website:
http://www.warburg.sas.ac.uk

Enquiries:
Enquiries to: Secretary

Founded:
1921

Organisation type and purpose:
University department or institute.
Postgraduate research institute.

Subject coverage:
History of the classical tradition: those elements of European thought, literature, art and institutions that derive from the ancient world.

Education services:
Postgraduate degrees.

Museum or gallery collection, archive, or library special collection:
Library (305,000 vols) on the classical tradition
Collection of photographs, primarily designed for the study of iconography
Archive

Non-library collection catalogue:
All or part available online and in-house

Library catalogue:
All or part available online

Printed publications:
Journal of the Warburg and Courtauld Institutes (annually, £110 plus p&p)
Fritz Saxl (1890–1948, a biographical memoir, reprint 1998, £5)
Journals (set of six vols 32–37 plus index, £30 plus p&p)
Studies, texts, colloquia and surveys (lists available at end of each issue of the above Journal)
Legal Documents of the Hellenistic World (eds M. J. Geller and H. Maehler, with A. D. E. Lewis, 1995, £30)
Order printed publications from: e-mail: warburg .books@sas.ac.uk

Publications list:
Available online and in print

Access to staff:
Contact by letter, by telephone, by fax, by e-mail, in person and via website. Letter of introduction required.
Hours: Mon to Fri, 1000 to 1800

Access to building, collection or gallery:
Access to library by library ticket
Hours: Mon to Fri, 1000 to 1800; Sat opening varies

Access for disabled people:
Ramped entry front and rear, access to all public areas, toilet facilities
Special comments: Lift access to floors other than ground floor and basement.

Houses the library of:
British Numismatic Society
   tel: 020 7862 8951 (part time)
Folklore Society
   tel: 020 7862 8564 (part time)
Royal Numismatic Society

Parent body:
University of London, School of Advanced Study
   tel: 020 7862 8659; fax: 020 7862 8657

WARRINGTON BOROUGH COUNCIL

Town Hall, Warrington, Cheshire, WA1 1UH

Tel: 01925 444400
Fax: 01925 442138

Website:
http://www.warrington.gov.uk

Enquiries:
Enquiries to: Head of Communications
Direct tel: 01925 442042
Direct fax: 01925 442024
Direct e-mail: bwilliams@warrington.gov.uk

Organisation type and purpose:
Local government body.

Subject coverage:
Council services and amenities; corporate services, education, environmental services, finance, housing, legal services, personnel services, planning development and tourism, property and technical services, roads and transportation, social work, council tax and other payments.

Printed publications:
Contacting the Council (free)
Warrington News (4 times a year)
Warrington Official Handbook (free)
Warrington Official Street Guide

Access to staff:
Contact by letter, by telephone and by fax.
Appointment necessary.
Hours: Mon to Fri, 0900 to 1700

WARRINGTON CHAMBER OF COMMERCE AND INDUSTRY

International Business Centre, Delta Crescent, Westbrook, Warrington, Cheshire, WA5 7WQ

Tel: 01925 715150
Fax: 01925 715159
E-mail: info@warrington-chamber.co.uk

Website:
http://www.warrington-chamber.co.uk
Details of Chamber activities.

Enquiries:
Enquiries to: Chief Executive

Founded:
1876

Organisation type and purpose:
Trade association. Provides advice and guidance on matters of commercial and industrial concern.

Subject coverage:
Export documentation and advice; seminars and training; language provision; general information in fields of industrial and commercial interest.

Printed publications:
Annual members' handbook
Newspaper (quarterly, free to members)
News-sheets (monthly, free to members)

Access to staff:
Contact by letter, by telephone, by fax, by e-mail and via website. Appointment necessary.
Hours: Mon to Thu, 0900 to 1700; Fri, 0900 to 1630

Member organisation of:
Chambers of Commerce North West
North Cheshire & Wirral Consortium of Chambers of Commerce

WARRINGTON COLLEGIATE

Winwick Road Campus, Winwick Road, Warrington, Cheshire, WA2 8QA

Tel: 01925 494422
Fax: 01925 494422
E-mail: swatkiss@warrington.ac.uk

Website:
http://www.warrington.ac.uk
Information about the college, library catalogue, links to other organisations.

Founded:
1979

Formerly called:
North Cheshire College

Organisation type and purpose:
Further and higher education.

continued overleaf

Subject coverage:
Construction, engineering, business studies, leisure, media, performing arts and sports studies, travel and tourism, creative arts, health and social care, hairdressing, beauty therapy, holistics.

Museum or gallery collection, archive, or library special collection:
Lewis Carroll

Library catalogue:
All or part available online and in-house

Access to staff:
Contact by letter and by telephone
Hours: Mon to Thu, 0845 to 2000; Fri, 0845 to 1630
Winwick Campus: Sat, 0900 to 1300

Access for disabled people:
Parking provided, ramped entry, access to all public areas, toilet facilities

WARRINGTON LIBRARY

Museum Street, Warrington, Cheshire, WA1 1JB

Tel: 01925 442889
Fax: 01925 443257
E-mail: library@warrington.gov.uk

Website:
http://www.warrington.gov.uk/libraries

Enquiries:
Enquiries to: Information Services Manager

Founded:
1848

Organisation type and purpose:
Local government body, public library.

Subject coverage:
Soap industry and manufacture, wire manufacture, welding, general.

Museum or gallery collection, archive, or library special collection:
Substantial body of material held on local area in terms of local and family history including: a large collection of manuscripts and archives; local studies books and pamphlets; photographs and other images; voters' lists; maps; ephemera; microform copies of censuses, newspapers, and parish and other church records

Library catalogue:
All or part available online

Access to staff:
Contact by letter, by telephone, by fax, by e-mail, in person and via website
Hours: Mon to Wed, 0900 to 1800; Thu, 0900 to 1900, Fri, 0900 to 1700; Sat, 0900 to 1600

Access to building, collection or gallery:
No prior appointment required

Access for disabled people:
Disabled access to main entrance, access to all public areas

Parent body:
Warrington Borough Council Culture, Libraries and Heritage Service
website: http://www.warrington.gov.uk

WARWICKSHIRE COLLEGE

Warwick New Road, Leamington Spa, Warwickshire, CV35 5JE

Tel: 01926 318000
Fax: 01926 318111
E-mail: enquiries@warkscol.co.uk

Website:
http://www.warkscol.ac.uk

Enquiries:
Enquiries to: Admission
Direct tel: 0800 783 6767
Other contacts: The Principal

Founded:
1949

Organisation type and purpose:
Training and education. Further and higher education.

Subject coverage:
Art and design, building and construction, business, accounting and management studies, caring, nursing and social welfare, computing and administration, engineering technology, agriculture, horticulture, machinery, equine studies, animal care, business studies, education, training, media, music, performing arts, veterinary nursing, arboriculture, spa management, English as a foreign language, English as a second language, GCE A levels, GCSEs, hairdressing and beauty therapy, hospitality and catering, languages, motor vehicle technology, sports studies, leisure and tourism, return to learn courses, adult basic education and programmes for students with learning difficulties and disabilities.

Printed publications:
Prospectus (free)

Publications list:
Available online and in print

Access to staff:
Contact by letter, by telephone, by fax, by e-mail, in person and via website
Hours: Mon to Fri, 0900 to 1700

WARWICKSHIRE COLLEGE – MORETON MORRELL CENTRE

Formal name: Warwickshire College Royal Leamington Spa and Moreton Morrell

Moreton Morrell, Warwick, CV35 9BL

Tel: 01926 318278
Fax: 01926 318300
E-mail: librarymm@warkscol.ac.uk

Website:
http://www.warkscol.ac.uk
Select student intranet

Enquiries:
Enquiries to: Librarian

Founded:
1949

Formerly called:
Warwickshire College of Agriculture (year of change 1996)

Organisation type and purpose:
Suitable for ages: Further and Higher Education. College for land-based industries.

Subject coverage:
Agriculture; agricultural engineering; amenity and commercial horticulture; business studies; equine studies; horse management and horse business management; small animal care; green-keeping; landscaping; woodland and estate maintenance; animal care; pre-veterinary nursing; arboriculture; countryside and rural affairs; human sports science.

Museum or gallery collection, archive, or library special collection:
LOOI Horticultural Library
British Horse Society Library

Non-library collection catalogue:
All or part available in-house

Library catalogue:
All or part available in-house

Printed publications:
Equine Business Guide 2002 (4th ed.)
Equine distance learning materials (Equi Study)
Order printed publications from: Equi Study at the same address, tel: 01926 318340

Electronic and video publications:
EQUIRY, computerised index of library-held equine periodical articles

Access to staff:
Contact by letter, by telephone, by fax, by e-mail and via website. Appointment necessary. Non-members charged.
Hours: Term time: Mon to Thu, 0830 to 2200; Fri, 0830 to 1700; Sat, 1000 to 1600
Vacations: Mon to Fri, 0915 to 1645
Special comments: One free visit, then have to become members; charges to non-members.

Access for disabled people:
Level entry, access to all public areas, toilet facilities

Other site at:
Warwickshire College
Leamington Centre, Warwick New Road, Leamington Spa, Warwickshire, CV32 5JE; tel: 01926 318000; fax: 01926 318111

WARWICKSHIRE COUNTY RECORD OFFICE

Priory Park, Cape Road, Warwick, CV34 4JS

Tel: 01926 738959
Fax: 01926 738969
E-mail: recordoffice@warwickshire.gov.uk

Website:
http://www.warwickshire.gov.uk/countyrecordoffice
http://www.a2a.org.uk
Catalogue of part of the collection online.

Enquiries:
Enquiries to: Head of Archive Service

Founded:
1933

Organisation type and purpose:
Local government body.
Record office.
To collect, preserve and make accessible the historic records of the County.

Subject coverage:
Warwickshire historical records (largely excluding Birmingham and Coventry).

Museum or gallery collection, archive, or library special collection:
Warwickshire Historical Manuscripts
Warwickshire Local History Library (printed works)
Warwickshire Map Collection
Warwickshire Photograph Collection
Small reference library of books on Warwickshire

Non-library collection catalogue:
All or part available online and in-house

Library catalogue:
All or part available in-house

Printed publications:
Parish Register and Census Holdings (1992, £1.50)

Access to staff:
Contact by letter, by telephone, by fax, by e-mail, in person and via website
Hours: Tue, Wed, Thu, 0900 to 1730; Fri, 0900 to 1700; Sat, 0900 to 1230
Closed to the public for the first full week of each calendar month.
Special comments: Identification required.

Access to building, collection or gallery:
Special comments: Members and public must be in possession of a CARN reader's ticket or bring proof of ID including name, address and signature to obtain a ticket

Access for disabled people:
Limited parking provided (please phone to reserve a space), access to all public areas, readers' tea room, toilet facilities

Parent body:
Warwickshire County Council
Shire Hall, Warwick, CV34 4SA; tel: 01926 410410; e-mail: http://www.warwickshire.gov.uk

WARWICKSHIRE FAMILY HISTORY SOCIETY

7 Mersey Road, Bulkington, Nuneaton, Warwickshire, CV12 9QB

E-mail: chairman@wfhs.org.uk

Website:
http://www.wfhs.org.uk

Enquiries:
Enquiries to: Chairman
Direct e-mail: secretary@wfhs.org.uk

Founded:
1986

Organisation type and purpose:
Membership association (membership is by subscription).

Subject coverage:
Family history and genealogy, in particular of Warwickshire.

Museum or gallery collection, archive, or library special collection:
IGI
Census 1881

Printed publications:
Leaflet detailing the publications of the Society, some of which are on disc
WFHS Pamphlets including Bedworth Inclosure 1861; Shipston upon Stour – short history and 1874 Directory; Warwickshire Poor Law Unions; School Admission Registers.
Blue Coat School, Coventry (£2.50 plus 35p p&p)
Canal Miscellanea (£3.50 plus 60p p&p)
Early Admission registers for Nuneaton Charity Schools (a must for Nuneaton tracers) (£2.50 plus 90p p&p)
General Baptist Registers – Salem Births 1785 – 1837 (Longford, Foleshill) (£2 plus 35p p&p)
I remember Coventry's War – a compilation of memories, facts and archival information. (£2 plus 60p p&p)
It grew by Industry – The story of Bedworth (£3 plus 60p p&p)
Warwickshire Militia Lists 1758–60 (including Birmingham but not Coventry, £2.50 plus 60p p&p)
Order printed publications from: Publications, Warwickshire Family History Society
26 Flude Road, Binley Woods, Coventry, CV7 9AQ

Publications list:
Available online and in print

Access to staff:
Contact by letter and by e-mail
Hours: Mon to Fri, 0900 to 1700

Access for disabled people:
Parking provided

WARWICKSHIRE LIBRARY AND INFORMATION SERVICE

Barrack Street, Warwick, CV34 4TH

Tel: 01926 412164
Fax: 01926 412165
E-mail: librarieslearningandculture@warwickshire.gov.uk

Website:
http://www.warwickshire.gov.uk/libraries

Enquiries:
Enquiries to: Head of Libraries, Learning and Culture

Founded:
1920

Formerly called:
Warwickshire County Library

Organisation type and purpose:
Local government body, public library.

Subject coverage:
General information service, tourist information, local history.

Museum or gallery collection, archive, or library special collection:
George Eliot Collection at Nuneaton Library
Local History collections at Warwick, Leamington, Nuneaton and Rugby Libraries
Michael Drayton Collection at Nuneaton Library
Warwickshire collection at Warwick Library
Music and Drama Collection at Warwick Library

Non-library collection catalogue:
All or part available in-house

Library catalogue:
All or part available online and in-house

Printed publications:
Current periodicals list
Information leaflets

Access to staff:
Contact by letter, by telephone, by fax, by e-mail, in person and via website
Hours: Mon to Fri, 0900 to 1700

Access to building, collection or gallery:
No access other than to staff

Branch libraries:
in 34 locations

Parent body:
Warwickshire County Council

WARWICKSHIRE LOCAL HISTORY SOCIETY

Acronym or abbreviation: WLHS

c/o Jackie Bland, Hon. Secretary, 607 Kenilworth Road, Balsall Common, West Midlands, CV7 7DT

Tel: 01676 532349
E-mail: info@warwickshirehistory.org.uk

Website:
http://www.warwickshirehistory.org.uk

Enquiries:
Enquiries to: Honorary Secretary

Founded:
1965

Organisation type and purpose:
Learned society (membership is by subscription), present number of members: 222, voluntary organisation.

Subject coverage:
Warwickshire history.

Printed publications:
Bulletin (2–3 times a year)
Warwickshire History (2 times a year)
Order printed publications from: Warwickshire Local History Society
28 Lillington Road, Leamington Spa, Warwickshire, CV32 5YY, tel: 01926 422628

Publications list:
Available in print

Access to staff:
Contact by letter
Hours: Mon to Fri, 0900 to 1700

Member of:
British Association for Local History

WASTE WATCH

96 Tooley Street, London, SE1 2TH

Tel: 020 7089 2100
Fax: 020 7403 4802
E-mail: info@wastewatch.org.uk

Website:
http://www.wastewatch.org.uk
http://www.nrf.org.uk
The UK Recycled Products Guide

Enquiries:
Enquiries to: Waste Watch Wasteline
Direct tel: 0870 243 0136
Direct e-mail: sam.jarvis@wastewatch.org.uk

Founded:
1991

Organisation type and purpose:
Voluntary organisation, registered charity (charity number 1005417).
To promote and support action on waste reduction and recycling.

Subject coverage:
Recycling, waste management, waste reduction, recycled products.

Printed publications:
Community Recycling (4th ed, 1999, £4.95)
Educational resources (free for sae)
Information sheets (free set for three 1st class stamps plus A4 sae)
The National Recycling Directory (6th ed., Nov 2001, £37.50)
Work at Waste at School (1997, £5.50)
Work at Waste at Work (£9.95)

Publications list:
Available online and in print

Access to staff:
Contact by letter, by telephone, by fax and via website. Appointment necessary.
Hours: Mon to Fri, 1000 to 1700

Access to building, collection or gallery:
No prior appointment required

Part funded by:
Department of the Environment's Environmental Action Fund

WATER MANAGEMENT SOCIETY

Acronym or abbreviation: WMSoc

6 Sir Robert Peel Mill, Tolson's Enterprise Park, Fazeley, Tamworth, B78 3QD

Tel: 01827 289558
Fax: 01827 250408
E-mail: wmsoc@btconnect.com

Website:
http://www.wmsoc.org.uk
Membership.
Training courses, conferences – both online booking.
Publications – online ordering.

Enquiries:
Enquiries to: Information Officer

Founded:
1975

Organisation type and purpose:
Professional body, membership association (membership is by qualification), present number of members: 565.

Subject coverage:
Specification, selection and operating of equipment and systems applied to the use and re-use of water; cooling systems; cooling towers; air conditioning plants; heat exchangers; de-aeration; boiler and condensate systems; hot water systems; effluents and wastes from water preparation processes; recovery systems; environmental aspects and optimisation of available supplies of water; water audits; risk assessment of water services; in-house treatment for reducing effluent costs; current legislation.

Printed publications:
Conference papers, codes of practice, technical literature
Waterline (journal, quarterly, free to members; available on subscription also)

Publications list:
Available in print

Access to staff:
Contact by letter, by telephone, by fax, by e-mail and via website
Hours: Mon to Fri, 0900 to 1600

Access to building, collection or gallery:
No access other than to staff

WATER UK

1 Queen Anne's Gate, London, SW1H 9BT

Tel: 020 7344 1844
Fax: 020 7344 1866
E-mail: info@water.org.uk

Website:
http://www.water.org.uk

Enquiries:
Enquiries to: Chief Executive

Founded:
1998

Formerly called:
Water Companies Association (WCA), Water
Services Association (WSA) (year of change 1998)

Organisation type and purpose:
Trade association.
Water UK is the industry association that
represents water and waste water service suppliers
at national and European level.

Subject coverage:
Water and wastewater services.

Printed publications:
Publications include:
Water (magazine, fortnightly)

Publications list:
Available online and in print

Access to staff:
Contact by letter, by e-mail and via website
Hours: Mon to Fri, 0900 to 1700

Members of the Association are:
24 water and wastewater companies in England
and Wales
Northern Ireland Water Service
  website: www.water.org.uk
Scottish Water
  website: see water uk website

WAVENEY DISTRICT COUNCIL

Town Hall, High Street, Lowestoft, Suffolk, NR32
1HS

Tel: 01502 562111
Fax: 01502 589327
E-mail: webmaster@waveney.gov.uk

Website:
http://www.waveney.gov.uk

Enquiries:
Enquiries to: Chief Executive
Direct tel: 01502 523210

Organisation type and purpose:
Local government body.

Printed publications:
Each department provides many leaflets on its
  own areas (eg housing, planning)
A-Z of Services
Councillor Information booklet

Access to staff:
Contact by letter, by telephone, by fax, by e-mail,
in person and via website
Hours: Mon to Thu, 0900 to 1700; Fri, 0900 to 1630

Local Offices at:
Beccles District Office
  6 Market Street, Beccles, Suffolk, NR34 9QD; tel:
  01502 713113; fax: 01502 713113
Bungay District Office
  Broad Street, Bungay, Suffolk, NR35 1EE; tel:
  01986 892176
Halesworth District Office
  London Road, Halesworth, Suffolk, IP9 8LW; tel:
  01986 873162; fax: 01986 874516
Tourist Information
  Town Hall, Southwold, Suffolk, IP18 6EF; tel:
  01502 722366

WAVERLEY CARE HIV AND HEPATITIS C INFORMATION SERVICE

Waverley Care, 2–4 Abbeymount, Edinburgh, EH8
8EJ

Tel: 0131 661 0982
Fax: 0131 652 1780
E-mail: info@waverleycare.org

Website:
http://www.waverleycare.org

Enquiries:
Enquiries to: Information Worker
Other contacts: Manager, Waverley Care SOLAS

Founded:
1991

Organisation type and purpose:
Voluntary organisation, registered charity (charity
number SCO 036500).
HIV and Hepatitis C information and support.

Subject coverage:
Supporting the HIV and Hepatitis C community in
Scotland

Electronic and video publications:
Newletter (pdf, online)

Access to staff:
Contact by letter, by telephone, by fax, by e-mail,
in person and via website
Hours: Mon to Fri, 0900 to 1700

Access to building, collection or gallery:
No prior appointment required
Hours: Mon to Fri, 0830 to 1530

Access for disabled people:
Ramped entry
Special comments: Wheelchair access to ground
floor only

Constituent bodies:
Waverley Care Milestone Respite Unit
  113 Oxgangs Road North, Edinburgh, EH14 1EB;
  tel: 0131 441 6989

Parent body:
Waverley Care
  Old Coates House, 32 Manor Place, Edinburgh,
  EH3 7EB; tel: 0131 226 2206; fax: 0131 226 2209

WAX CHANDLERS' COMPANY

Formal name: Worshipful Company of Wax
Chandlers

Wax Chandlers' Hall, Gresham Street, London,
EC2V 7AD

Tel: 020 7606 3591/2
Fax: 020 7600 5462
E-mail: info@waxchandlershall.co.uk

Website:
http://www.waxchandlershall.co.uk
Banqueting, meeting and reception facilities and
history, charities.

Enquiries:
Enquiries to: Clerk
Other contacts: Beadle for bookings for meetings
and banquets.

Founded:
Before 1371

Organisation type and purpose:
Membership association, service industry.
City of London livery company, provider of
banqueting and meeting facilities.

**Museum or gallery collection, archive, or library
special collection:**
The Company's archive is lodged at Guildhall
  Library, London, EC2 and is open for public
  inspection

Printed publications:
A chronology of the history of the Company, and a
  brochure on hall letting facilities (available for
  download via website)

Access to staff:
Contact by letter, by telephone, by fax, by e-mail
and in person
Hours: Mon to Fri, 0900 to 1700

WEALDEN IRON RESEARCH GROUP

2 West Street Farm Cottages, Maynards Green,
Heathfield, Sussex, TN21 0DG

Tel: 01435 812506
E-mail: wirghonsec@hotmail.com

Website:
http://www.wealdeniron.org.uk

Founded:
1968

Organisation type and purpose:
A charity whose objects are to advance the
education of the public in historical and
archaeological study and, in particular, to promote
investigation and collate information concerning
the Wealden iron industry and related activities for
the benefit of the public. In furtherance of this
objective:
(1) to publish such information both in regular
bulletins and by any other means which the
Trustees shall think fit;
(2) to co-operate with and affiliate to other
organizations with allied aims as may seem
desirable.

Subject coverage:
The extinct iron industry of the Weald of Sussex,
Kent and Surrey.

Printed publications:
Wealden Iron
Newsletter
Order printed publications from: The Publications
Officer, 1 Stirling Way, East Grinstead RH19 3HG

Publications list:
Available online

Access to staff:
Contact by letter, by telephone, by e-mail, in
person and via website

WELL DRILLERS ASSOCIATION

Acronym or abbreviation: WDA

PO Box 4595, Nuneaton, Warwicks, CV11 9DX

Tel: 07885 957 9583
E-mail: david.s.duke@gmail.com

Website:
http://www.welldrillers.org.uk

Enquiries:
Enquiries to: Executive Secretary
Other contacts: Chairman and Treasurer

Founded:
pre-1940

Organisation type and purpose:
Trade association.
Association of water well drillers in the United
Kingdom.

Subject coverage:
Water-well drilling, pump installation and
maintenance.

Printed publications:
Guidance Notes for the Construction of Boreholes
  for Water Supply
Membership list

Access to staff:
Contact by letter, by telephone and by e-mail
Hours: Mon to Fri, 0900 to 1800

WELLCHILD

16 Royal Crescent, Cheltenham, Gloucestershire,
GL50 3DA

Tel: 0845 458 8171

Fax: 01242 530008
E-mail: info@wellchild.org.uk

Website:
http://www.wellchild.org.uk

Enquiries:
Enquiries to: Chief Executive

Founded:
1977

Organisation type and purpose:
Registered charity (charity no. 289600).
WellChild is the national charity for sick children.
It helps children and young people who are
seriously ill or have complex conditions and their
families throughout the UK by focusing on three
key areas – care, support and research.

Subject coverage:
Children's health.

Printed publications:
General
Newsletter
Leaflets on events
Annual Review
Helpline leaflet

Access to staff:
Contact by letter, by telephone, by fax, by e-mail
and via website. Appointment necessary.
Hours: Mon to Fri, 0900 to 1700

WELLCOME LIBRARY

183 Euston Road, London, NW1 2BE

Tel: 020 7611 8722
Fax: 020 7611 8369
E-mail: library@wellcome.ac.uk

Website:
http://library.wellcome.ac.uk

Enquiries:
Enquiries to: User Services Manager
Other contacts: Librarian

Founded:
1949

Organisation type and purpose:
Registered charity (charity number 210183),
research organisation.

Subject coverage:
Medicine and its role in society, past and present,
including popular science, biomedical ethics and
the public understanding of science.

**Museum or gallery collection, archive, or library
special collection:**
Over 600,000 books and journals
13,000 original letters and facsimiles of letters by
Florence Nightingale, Lord Lister and Melanie
Klein
Records of numerous organisations and bodies
involved in medical science and health care
Autograph Letters (100,000)
Books from the library of William Morris
(including 67 incunabula)
Ethnology and travel c.1800 to c.1940; thereafter
medically-oriented ethnology and anthropology
Incunabula (over 600 items); early printed books
(over 7,000 pre-1641; over 66,000 1641–1850),
including about 11,000 items from the Library of
the Medical Society of London
Library of the Royal Society of Health
Library of the Society for the Study of Addiction
Microforms (1,600)
Asian collection of 12,000 MSS in 43 eastern
languages including Sanskrit, Arabic, Persian,
Hebrew, Chinese, Japanese, (c.70 microfilm rolls
in oriental languages); 3,000 items printed in
Oriental scripts and topographical and other
works relevant to oriental studies in Western
languages
American Collection including medical imprints
from the Hispanic and Portuguese American
Empires 1557–1833 and from the British Colonies
in America 1720–1820; also material on
Amerindian medicine, manuscripts and much
reference material, especially bibliographies

200,000 prints, drawings; paintings and
photographs, from the Orient to the Americas,
(middle ages to present)
Western Manuscripts (9,000)

Non-library collection catalogue:
All or part available online, in-house and in print

Library catalogue:
All or part available online

Printed publications:
Catalogue of Arabic Manuscripts on Medicine and
Science in the Wellcome Historical Medical
Library
Catalogue of Printed Books in the Wellcome
Historical Medical Library: Vol. I, Books printed
before 1641; Vol. II, Books printed from 1641 to
1850 A–E; Vol. III, Books printed from 1641 to
1850 F–L; Vol. IV, Books printed from 1641 to
1850 M–R; Vol. V, Books printed from 1641 to
1850 S–Z.
Catalogue of Western Manuscripts on Medicine
and Science in the Wellcome Historical Medical
Library: Vol. I, Manuscripts written before 1650;
Vol. II, Manuscripts written after 1650 (2 vols)
Handlist of Sanskrit and Prakrit manuscripts in the
library of the Wellcome Institute for the History
of Medicine, vol. I and 2
Order printed publications from: Mrs Tracy Tillotson,
tel. 020 7611 8486; fax 020 7611 8369; e-mail t
.tillotson@wellcome.ac.uk

Access to staff:
Contact by letter, by telephone, by fax, by e-mail,
in person and via website
Hours: Mon, Tue, Wed, Fri, 1000 to 1800; Thu, 1000
to 2000; Sat, 1000 to 1600

Funded by:
Wellcome Trust

Links with:
University College London

WELLCOME LIBRARY – MOVING IMAGE AND SOUND COLLECTION

183 Euston Road, London, NW1 2BE

Tel: 020 7611 8766
Fax: 020 7611 8577
E-mail: misc@wellcome.ac.uk

Website:
http://library.wellcome.ac.uk

Enquiries:
Enquiries to: Curator

Formerly called:
Wellcome Trust Medical Film and Video Library

Organisation type and purpose:
Research organisation.

Subject coverage:
Moving image and sound materials illustrating the
evolution of medicine and health over the last 100
years. A primary source in the study of the use of
media as a communication tool in medical science
and practice.

**Museum or gallery collection, archive, or library
special collection:**
Approx 3,000 film items, 3,000 video items and
2,000 sound items. Mostly available for reference
only with a limited number of titles for loan and/
or licensing

Non-library collection catalogue:
All or part available online and in-house

Library catalogue:
All or part available online

Electronic and video publications:
60 Wellcome Trust copyright videos (VHS/DVD
PAL or NTSC for purchase)

Publications list:
Available online

Access to staff:
Contact by letter, by telephone, by fax, by e-mail,
in person and via website. Appointment necessary.
Hours: Mon to Fri, 1000 to 1700

Access to building, collection or gallery:
Hours: Mon, Tue, Wed, Fri, 1000 to 1800; Thu, 1000
to 2000; Sat, 1000 to 1600

Access for disabled people:
Fully accessible

WELLCOME TRUST MEDICAL PHOTOGRAPHIC LIBRARY

210 Euston Road, London, NW1 2BE

Tel: 020 7611 8348
Fax: 020 7611 8577
E-mail: photolib@wellcome.ac.uk

Website:
http://www.wellcome.ac.uk/mpl

Enquiries:
Direct e-mail: photolib@wellcome.ac.uk

Formerly called:
Wellcome Library for the History and
Understanding of Medicine

Organisation type and purpose:
Research organisation.

Subject coverage:
Images of medical and social history, photographs
of clinical medicine and biomedical sciences.

**Museum or gallery collection, archive, or library
special collection:**
Over 160,000 images of medical and social history;
17,000 photos of modern clinical medicine and
biomedical sciences

Non-library collection catalogue:
All or part available online and in-house

Library catalogue:
All or part available online

Publications list:
Available online and in print

Access to staff:
Contact by letter, by telephone, by fax, by e-mail
and via website. Appointment necessary.
Hours: Mon to Fri, 0930 to 1730

Access to building, collection or gallery:
Prior appointment required
Hours: Mon to Fri, 0930 to 1730

WELLCOME-BEIT PRIZE FELLOWSHIPS

The Wellcome Trust

Enquiries:
Enquiries to: Secretary

Founded:
1909

Organisation type and purpose:
Registered charity, research organisation.

Subject coverage:
Advancement by research of medicine and of the
allied sciences in their relation to medicine.

WELLINGBOROUGH BOROUGH COUNCIL

Council Offices, Swanspool House,
Wellingborough, Northamptonshire, NN8 1BP

Tel: 01933 229777
Fax: 01933 231629
E-mail: customerservices@wellingborough.gov.uk

Website:
http://www.wellingborough.gov.uk/

Organisation type and purpose:
Local government body.

WELLS AND WALSINGHAM LIGHT RAILWAY

Acronym or abbreviation: WWLR

Wells-Next-the-Sea, Norfolk, NR23 1QB

Tel: 01328 710631

Enquiries:
Enquiries to: Owner
Direct tel: 01328 711630

Founded:
1982

Organisation type and purpose:
Membership association (membership is by subscription), present number of members: 120.

Subject coverage:
Steam railway preservation.

Printed publications:
Guide to Line (obtainable by post or visit)

Access to staff:
Contact by letter, by telephone and in person
Hours: Mon to Fri, 0900 to 1700

WELSH ASSEMBLY GOVERNMENT – CENTRAL REGISTER OF AERIAL PHOTOGRAPHY FOR WALES

Statistical Division, Room G-073a, Crown Offices, Cathays Park, Cardiff, CF10 3NQ

Tel: 029 2082 3819
Fax: 029 2082 3080
E-mail: aerialphotoofficer@wales.gsi.gov.uk

Enquiries:
Enquiries to: Aerial Photographs Officer

Organisation type and purpose:
National government body, central government department.

Subject coverage:
The Central Register aims to index all vertical air survey coverage of Wales flown by the Royal Air Force, Ordnance Survey, commercial air survey companies and other air survey organisations. The Register is a comprehensive source of information about the aerial photography of Wales and advises all interested users. Customers need to supply a map or OS National Grid Reference of their area of interest to perform a cover search.

Museum or gallery collection, archive, or library special collection:
The Aerial Photographs Library holds an extensive collection of photographs covering Wales at various dates and scales. The base of the collection is the national 1:10,000 aerial survey flown 1945–52 by the RAF. To this has been added other RAF photographs including the 1969 and 1981 small-scale national surveys; Ordnance Survey 1958–2002; Medmenham 1940–45; and Meridian 1952–83. The Welsh Assembly has continued to update the collection, which now includes extensive coverage in colour 1983–97. Some oblique and infrared photos are held of the Welsh coastline and also MAFF/ADAS (black and white and colour) from the 1970s–80s.
Full cover of Wales by Getmapping (1999–2000), COWI (2006) is available to view in colour on screen

Printed publications:
Reprints of some of the collection are available for sale

Access to staff:
Contact by letter, by telephone, by fax and by e-mail. Appointment necessary.
Hours: Mon to Fri, 0900 to 1700

Access to building, collection or gallery:
Prior appointment required

Special comments: Hand luggage will be liable to search and x-ray to meet security requirements.

Access for disabled people:
Parking provided, level entry, toilet facilities

WELSH ASSOCIATION OF MOTOR CLUBS

Acronym or abbreviation: WAMC

General Secretary, 63 Maes y Sarn, Pentyrch, Cardiff, CF15 9QR

Tel: 029 2089 1314
E-mail: secretary@wamcweb.com

Website:
http://www.wamcweb.com/

Enquiries:
Enquiries to: Press Officer
Direct e-mail: wamc.pressoffice@wamcweb.com

Founded:
1957

Organisation type and purpose:
National government body, membership association (membership is by qualification), present number of members: 100.

Subject coverage:
Motor sport in Wales.

Printed publications:
Annual Year Book

Access to staff:
Contact by letter, by telephone and by fax
Hours: Mon to Fri, 1800 to 2100; Sat, Sun, 1000 to 1800

Associated with:
MSA
  Motorsport House, Colnbrook, Slough, Berkshire, SL3 0HG

WELSH BLACK CATTLE SOCIETY

13 Bangor Street, Caernarfon, Gwynedd, LL55 1AP

Tel: 01286 672391
Fax: 01286 672022
E-mail: welshblack@btclick.com

Website:
http://www.welshblackcattlesociety.com

Enquiries:
Enquiries to: Chief Executive

Founded:
1904

Organisation type and purpose:
International organisation (membership is by subscription, qualification, election or invitation), present number of members: 960, registered charity (charity number 244415/acl).

Subject coverage:
Breeding of Welsh Black cattle.

Printed publications:
Annual Herdbook (£22)

Access to staff:
Contact by letter, by telephone, by fax, by e-mail and in person
Hours: Mon to Fri, 0900 to 1700

Also at:
Welsh Black Cattle Society
  Royal Welsh Showground, Llanelwedd, Builth Wells, Powys, LD2 3NJ; tel: 01982 551111; fax: 01982 551333

WELSH BOOKS COUNCIL

Formal name: Cyngor Llyfrau Cymru – Welsh Books Council

Castell Brychan, Aberystwyth, Ceredigion, SY23 2JB

Tel: 01970 624151

Fax: 01970 625385
E-mail: castellbrychan@cllc.org.uk

Website:
http://www.gwales.com
Complete online catalogue and ordering facility.
http://www.wbc.org.uk
Welsh Books Council's website (including bestseller lists, pdfs of latest catalogues).

Enquiries:
Enquiries to: Head of Administration
Direct e-mail: moelwen.gwyndaf@cllc.org.uk
Other contacts: Distribution Centre Manager (for visiting the Distribution Centre); Head of Children's Books Department (for visiting the Children's Books Collection)

Founded:
1961

Organisation type and purpose:
National organisation, trade association.

Subject coverage:
Welsh language and English language Welsh-interest books and magazines, books for learning Welsh, books for children (Welsh and Welsh interest).

Education services:
The service of School Officers in Wales to supply information on the latest children's books.

Museum or gallery collection, archive, or library special collection:
Complete collection of Welsh language and Welsh interest Children's books published during previous 10 years and that are still in print

Library catalogue:
All or part available online

Printed publications:
Subject catalogues, brochures, leaflets
Order printed publications from: Head of Sales and Marketing, Welsh Books Council, Uned 16 Parc Menter Glanyrafon, Llanbadarn, Aberystwyth, Ceredigion, SY23 3AQ; tel: 01970 624455

Publications list:
Available online

Access to staff:
Contact by letter, by telephone, by fax, by e-mail and via website. Appointment necessary.
Hours: Mon to Thu, 0900 to 1700; Fri, 0900 to 1630
Special comments: Only account holders at Distribution Centre may purchase titles during visit.

Access to building, collection or gallery:
Prior appointment required

Access for disabled people:
Parking provided, level entry

Also at:
Cyngor Llyfrau Cymru/Welsh Books Council (CLLC)
  Uned 16 Parc Menter Glanyrafon, Llanbadarn, Aberystwyth, Ceredigion, SY23 3AQ; tel: 01970 624455; fax: 01970 625506; e-mail: canolfan.ddosbarthu@cllc.org.uk

WELSH CENTRE FOR INTERNATIONAL AFFAIRS / CANOLFAN MATERION RHYNGWLADOL CYMRU

Acronym or abbreviation: WCIA

Temple of Peace, Cathays Park, Cardiff, CF10 3AP, Cymru/Wales

Tel: 029 2022 8549
Fax: 029 2064 0333
E-mail: centre@wcia.org.uk

Website:
http://www.wcia.org.uk
Events (forthcoming, plus past lecture/conference content), getting actively involved inc. volunteering, membership details, educational materials for schools, United Nations Association Wales information.

Enquiries:
Enquiries to: Administrative Officer
Direct e-mail: suecoles@wcia.org.uk
Other contacts: Programme Co-ordinator

Founded:
1973

Incorporates the former:
Welsh League of Nations Union, Welsh National
Council of the United Nations Association (UNA
Wales), Council for Education in World
Citizenship-Cymru (CEWC-Cymru) (year of
change Various amalgamations)

Organisation type and purpose:
International organisation, membership
association (membership is by subscription),
present number of members: 500. voluntary
organisation, suitable for ages 15+.
To promote public awareness of international
affairs.

Subject coverage:
International political, economic and social affairs;
international affairs generally including the UN
and its agencies, EU and European affairs,
disarmament, development and humanitarian
issues.

Information services:
Public interpretation displays and interactive sites
on the building's history and the work that the
institution does.

Special visitor services:
Viewing of the First World War National Book of
Remembrance for Wales in the building's crypt.

Education services:
Global citizenship, sustainable development,
human rights and international affairs education –
for young people in particular.

Services for disabled people:
The Temple of Peace is a fully accessible building
for disabled people.

**Museum or gallery collection, archive, or library
special collection:**
A library with a good collection on international
politics between the two world wars (1918–1939)

Printed publications:
Newsletter (2 times a year)
Non-Violence Training Handbook for Wales
(Cynefin y Werin, 2008)
Wise and Foolish Dreamers – Wales and the
Spanish Civil War (Cope P, 2007)
Passport to the UN (bilingual, 2006)
Various posters and booklets on the Universal
Declaration of Human Rights and on the
Convention on the Rights of the Child (bilingual,
2005, passim)
The Temple of Peace and Health 1938–1998: Its
Impact on Wales and the World (Davies W R,
1998)
The UN at Fifty: The Welsh Contribution (ed.
Davies W R, 1995)
Order printed publications from: Sue Coles, at the
above address/contact details

Electronic and video publications:
DVD of Wise and Foolish Dreamers – Wales and
the Spanish Civil War
Order electronic and video publications from: Sue
Coles, at the above address/contact details

Publications list:
Available in print

Access to staff:
Contact by letter, by telephone, by fax, by e-mail,
in person and via website
Hours: Mon to Fri, 0900 to 1700

Access to building, collection or gallery:
No prior appointment required
Hours: Mon to Fri, 0900 to 1700

Access for disabled people:
All areas of the building are fully accessible to
disabled people
Hours: as above

WELSH COLLEGE OF HORTICULTURE

Holywell Road, Northop, Mold, Flintshire, CH7
6AA

Tel: 01352 841000
Fax: 01352 841031
E-mail: info@wcoh.ac.uk

Website:
http://www.wcoh.ac.uk

Enquiries:
Enquiries to: Information Centre

Founded:
1953

Organisation type and purpose:
Suitable for ages: 16+, training organisation.
College offering courses in land-based subjects for
students aged 16+.

Subject coverage:
Floristry, landscape design and construction; turf
management, market gardening, biological control,
equine studies, environmental studies, small
animal care, IT, garden centre practices, crop
production, nursery stock production, machinery.

**Museum or gallery collection, archive, or library
special collection:**
Distance learning courses in floristry and
management

Printed publications:
Prospectus (on application)

Access to staff:
Contact by letter, by telephone and by fax.
Appointment necessary.
Hours: Mon to Fri, 0900 to 1700

Access to building, collection or gallery:
Prior appointment required

Access for disabled people:
Parking provided, ramped entry, level entry, access
to all public areas, toilet facilities

WELSH FOLK DANCE SOCIETY

Acronym or abbreviation: WFDS/CDdWC

Cymdeithas Ddawns Werin Cymru, Ffynnonlwyd,
Trelech, Carmarthen, SA33 6QZ

Tel: 01994 484496
E-mail: dafydd.evans@ic24.net

Website:
http://www.welshfolkdance.org.uk

Enquiries:
Enquiries to: Honorary Secretary

Founded:
1949

Organisation type and purpose:
Membership association (membership is by
subscription), present number of members: 264
individuals, 20 groups, voluntary organisation,
registered charity (charity number 1023817).
To promote traditional dance and music.

Subject coverage:
Welsh folk dancing and music.

**Museum or gallery collection, archive, or library
special collection:**
Library at the Welsh Folk Museum, St Fagans,
Cardiff of early dance manuals and notations

Printed publications:
Annual Report
Dance and Music notations and books
Dawns (magazine, annually)
Newsletters
Order printed publications from: Sales Point,
Cymdeithas Ddawns Werin Cymru/Welsh Folk
Dance Society, Palas Print, 10 Stryd y Plas,
Caernarfon, Gwynedd, LL55 1RR; tel. 01286
674631; e-mail siop@palasprint.com

Electronic and video publications:
CD and DVD

Publications list:
Available online and in print

Access to staff:
Contact by letter, by telephone, by e-mail and via
website
Hours: Mon to Fri, 0900 to 1700

Affiliated to:
Welsh Amateur Music Federation
Welsh Arts Council

Librarian:
Welsh Folk Dance Society
8 St Cyre's Road, Penarth, South Glamorgan

WELSH JUDO ASSOCIATION

Acronym or abbreviation: WJA

Welsh Institute of Sport, Sophia Gardens, Cardiff,
CF11 9SW

Tel: 029 2033 4945
E-mail: office@welshjudo.com

Website:
http://www.welshjudo.com
About judo, clubs, coaching, competitions,
membership, national squads, news, calendar.

Organisation type and purpose:
Governing body for the sport of judo in Wales,
with various services devolved to it by the British
governing body, the British Judo Association; has
over 60 member clubs.

Subject coverage:
Judo in Wales at all levels.

Electronic and video publications:
Annual report
Newsletters
Order electronic and video publications from:
Download from website

Publications list:
Available online

Access to staff:
Contact by letter, by telephone and by e-mail
Hours: Office hours: Mon to Fri, 1000 to 1400

WELSH LANGUAGE SOCIETY

Pen Roc, Rhodfa'r Môr, Aberystwyth, Ceredigion,
SY23 2AZ

Tel: 01970 624501
Fax: 01970 627122
E-mail: swyddfa@cymdeithas.com

Website:
http://www.cymdeithas.com
Online version of the quarterly magazine, together
with information on all aspects of the society's
work.

Enquiries:
Enquiries to: Administrative Officer
Direct e-mail: dafydd@cymdeithas.org
Other contacts: Assembly Campaigns Officer

Founded:
1962

Organisation type and purpose:
Voluntary organisation.
Political pressure group.
To campaign for the Welsh language and Welsh
communities.

Subject coverage:
Welsh language: its future and campaigns to
secure its future; socio-linguistic planning and
education; official status of the Welsh language.

Printed publications:
Manifesto (in Welsh and English)
Tafod y Ddraig (quarterly)
Various policy documents, leaflets etc

Access to staff:
Contact by letter, by fax, by e-mail and via
website. Appointment necessary.
Hours: Mon to Fri, 0930 to 1730

WELSH TEACHERS' UNION

Acronym or abbreviation: UCAC

Prif Swyddfa UCAC, Ffordd Penglais,
Aberystwyth, Ceredigion, SY23 2EU

Tel: 01970 639950
Fax: 01970 626765
E-mail: ucac@athrawon.com

Website:
http://www.athrawon.com

Enquiries:
Enquiries to: General Secretary

Founded:
1940

Organisation type and purpose:
Trade union (membership is by subscription),
present number of members: c.4,800.
As well as safeguarding the rights of teachers and
lecturers and ensuring fair salaries, pensions and
conditions of employment, UCAC has always
campaigned for an independent education system
for Wales.

**Museum or gallery collection, archive, or library
special collection:**
Archive, Cardiff University

Publications list:
Available online

Access to staff:
Contact by letter, by telephone, by fax and by e-
mail. Appointment necessary. Non-members
charged.
Hours: Mon to Thu, 0900 to 1700; Fri, 0900 to 1600
Special comments: Office is closed for a fortnight
over Christmas, on St David's Day and during the
first week in August; emergency tel. number on
office answerphone.

Access for disabled people:
yes

WELWYN HATFIELD BOROUGH COUNCIL

Council Offices, Welwyn Garden City,
Hertfordshire, AL8 6AE

Tel: 01707 357000
Fax: 01707 357257
E-mail: contact-whc@welhat.gov.uk

Website:
http://www.welhat.gov.uk
General service information.

Enquiries:
Enquiries to: Customer Services Officer

Founded:
1974

Organisation type and purpose:
Local government body.

Printed publications:
Welwyn Hatfield Life (external, quarterly)

Publications list:
Available online and in print

Access to staff:
Contact by letter, by telephone, by e-mail and via
website. Appointment necessary.
Hours: Mon to Thu, 0845 to 1715; Fri, 0845 to 1645

Access to building, collection or gallery:
Hours: Mon to Thu, 0845 to 1715; Fri, 0845 to 1645

Access for disabled people:
Parking provided, level entry

WENDY WARR & ASSOCIATES

6 Berwick Court, Holmes Chapel, Cheshire, CW4
7HZ

Tel: 01477 533837
Fax: 01477 533837
E-mail: wendy@warr.com

Website:
http://www.warr.com

Enquiries:
Enquiries to: Principal Consultant

Founded:
1992

Organisation type and purpose:
Consultancy.

Subject coverage:
Cheminformatics, chemical information, scientific,
technical and medical information systems,
electronic publishing, computational chemistry,
drug discovery.

Printed publications:
About 70 learned publications including nine
books
Reports as commissioned by clients

Publications list:
Available online and in print

Access to staff:
Contact by letter, by telephone, by fax, by e-mail,
in person and via website
Hours: Mon to Fri, 0900 to 1700

WENSLEYDALE LONGWOOL SHEEP BREEDERS' ASSOCIATION

Acronym or abbreviation: WLSBA

Breed Secretary, Coffin Walk, Sheep Dip Lane,
Princethorpe, Rugby, Warwickshire, CV23 9SP

Tel: 01926 633439

Website:
http://www.wensleydale-sheep.com
Breed characteristics, history, sales and news items.

Enquiries:
Enquiries to: Membership Secretary
Direct tel: 01388 777852

Founded:
1890

Organisation type and purpose:
Membership association (membership is by
subscription), present number of members: 210.
Breeding and promotion of Wensleydale sheep.

Subject coverage:
Breed characteristics and sales of Wensleydale
sheep.

Printed publications:
Breed brochure (free)
Journal (£2.50)

Access to staff:
Contact by letter and by telephone
Hours: Mon to Fri, 0900 to 1700

WESLEY HISTORICAL SOCIETY

Acronym or abbreviation: WHS

7 Haugh Shaw Road, Halifax, HX1 3AH

Tel: 01422 250780
E-mail: johnahargreaves@blueyonder.co.uk

Website:
http://www.wesleyhistoricalsociety.org.uk

Enquiries:
Enquiries to: General Secretary
Direct e-mail: jandclenton@blueyonder.co.uk
Other contacts: Registrar (for membership);
Librarian (for access to collections); Editor (for offer
of articles, advertising rates)

Founded:
1893

Organisation type and purpose:
Learned society (membership is by subscription),
present number of members: 850, registered
charity (charity number 283012).

To promote the study of the history and literature
of all branches of Methodism, to accumulate exact
knowledge, and to provide a medium of
intercourse on all related subjects.

Subject coverage:
Methodist history, literature, Methodism,
Methodist portraits. No genealogical Methodist
records held.

**Museum or gallery collection, archive, or library
special collection:**
Bretherton Collection
Reference library housed at Westminster Institute
of Education. Contact library before visiting

Non-library collection catalogue:
All or part available online and in-house

Library catalogue:
All or part available online and in-house

Printed publications:
Annual Lecture (published separately on occasion,
depending on the subject)
Annual listings of Methodist historical literature
Proceedings (3 times a year, free to members, with
index to each vol., 6 issues per vol.)
Order printed publications from: c/o The Registrar,
Wesley Historical Society, 15 Foxlands Drive,
Lloyd Hill, Penn, Wolverhampton, WV4 5NB

Publications list:
Available in print

Access to staff:
Contact by letter, by telephone and by e-mail.
Appointment necessary. Non-members charged.
Hours: Mon to Fri, 0900 to 1700
Special comments: Check library opening times with
WHS Library; tel: 01865 488319.

Access to building, collection or gallery:
Prior appointment required

Access for disabled people:
Please telephone in advance to make arrangements

Branch libraries:
Wesley Historical Society Library
Westminster Institute of Education, Harcourt
Hill Campus, Oxford Brookes University,
Oxford, OX2 9AT; e-mail: peter@forsaith-oxon
.demon.co.uk; website: http://opac.brookes.ac
.uk:8001/wes

Branches:
Network of 17 Methodist regional historical
societies
c/o Regional Historical Societies Liaison Officer,
Wesley Historical Society, 50 Well Oak Park,
Dryden Road, Exeter, Devon, EX2 5BB; e-mail:
rthorne@fish.co.uk

WEST DUNBARTONSHIRE COUNCIL

Garshake Road, Dumbarton, Strathclyde, G82 3PU

Tel: 01389 737000
Fax: 01389 737070
E-mail: wdcmgr@post.allmac.co.uk

Website:
http://www.west-dunbarton.gov.uk

Enquiries:
Enquiries to: Public Relations Manager
Direct tel: 01389 737296
Direct fax: 01389 737578
Direct e-mail: joe.cox@west-dunbarton.gov.uk

Founded:
April 1996

Organisation type and purpose:
Local government body.

Subject coverage:
All local government services.

Non-library collection catalogue:
All or part available online

Printed publications:
Publications on request

Publications list:
Available in print

Access to staff:
Contact by letter, by telephone, by e-mail and via website
Hours: Mon to Fri, 0900 to 1700

Access for disabled people:
Parking provided, ramped entry, toilet facilities

WEST DUNBARTONSHIRE LIBRARIES

Headquarters, Levenford House, Helenslee Road, Dumbarton, Strathclyde, G82 4AH

Tel: 01389 608041
Fax: 01389 608044

Enquiries:
Enquiries to: Service Manager
Direct e-mail: dumbarton.library@west-dunbarton.gov.uk

Founded:
1996

Organisation type and purpose:
Local government body, public library.

Subject coverage:
General and local history of Dunbartonshire, Clyde shipbuilding, sewing machine manufacture, textile industry

Museum or gallery collection, archive, or library special collection:
West-Dunbartonshire Archives
Singer sewing machines, Dennystown Forge, Dumbarton Burgh Council minutes, 1599–1975
Thompson Collection (local history)
Watchmeal Collection (local history)

Non-library collection catalogue:
All or part available online and in-house

Library catalogue:
All or part available online and in-house

Printed publications:
Local history books and pamphlets including:
Beardmore Built: The Rise and Fall of a Clydeside Shipyard (Ian Johnston, £9.95)
Clydebank in Old Picture Postcards (£4)
History of The Parish of West or Old Kilpatrick (John Bruce, £7.95)
Marchstones in the Kilpatrick Hills (Dr R A Rankine)
Historic Dumbarton, Scottish Burgh Survey (E. Patricia Dennison & Russel Coleman, £14.95)

Electronic and video publications:
Clydebank – Building on the Past (video, £10)
Clydebank Memories (Singer, video, £10)
From Canoes to Cunarders (video, £8)
Music for a Christmas Evening VI (video, £5)

Access to staff:
Contact by letter, by telephone, by fax, by e-mail, in person and via website. Appointment necessary.
Hours: Mon to Fri, 0830 to 1615
Special comments: Telephone switchboard operates from Mon to Fri, 0830 to 1615.

Affiliated to:
Glasgow & West of Scotland Family History Society
Library Association
Scottish Genealogy Society
Scottish History Society
Scottish Library and Information Council
Scottish Local Government Information Unit
Scottish Museum Council
Scottish Poetry Library
Scottish Records Association

WEST GLAMORGAN ARCHIVE SERVICE

Acronym or abbreviation: WGAS

Civic Centre, Oystermouth Road, Swansea, SA1 3SN

Tel: 01792 636589
Fax: 01792 637130
E-mail: westglam.archives@swansea.gov.uk

Website:
http://www.swansea.gov.uk/westglamorganarchives
Catalogue information and description of service including online guide, locations, opening times and facilities.

Enquiries:
Enquiries to: Archivist

Organisation type and purpose:
Local government body.
Archive service.

Subject coverage:
Local and family history in West Glamorgan.

Museum or gallery collection, archive, or library special collection:
Usual local authority holdings

Non-library collection catalogue:
All or part available online, in-house and in print

Printed publications:
Various books and booklets, including:
Annual Reports of the West Glamorgan County Archivist
A Guide to the Collections
Recent publications include:
Historic Swansea
George Orlean Delamotte: A South Wales Sketch Album c1816–1835
Rhossili: The Land, Landscape and People

Publications list:
Available online and in print

Access to staff:
Contact by letter, by telephone, by fax, by e-mail and in person
Hours: Tue, 0900 to 1900; Wed to Fri, 0900 to 1700; Sat, 1000 to 1600 (Family History Centre only)

Access for disabled people:
Parking provided, ramped entry, level entry, access to all public areas, toilet facilities

Also at:
Neath Antiquarian Society Archives
The Mechanics Institute, 4 Church Place, Neath, SA11 3LL; tel: 01639 620139
Port Talbot Family and Local History Centre
Aberafan Library, Port Talbot, SA13 1PB; tel: 01639 763430

WEST HERTS COLLEGE

Cassio Campus Teaching and Learning Resources Service, Langley Road, Watford, Hertfordshire, WD7 4YH

Tel: 01923 812231
Fax: 01923 812232
E-mail: anne.h@westherts.ac.uk

Website:
http://colleges.herts.ac.uk
Voyager.

Enquiries:
Enquiries to: Learning Resources Manager
Direct tel: 01923 812200

Created by the merger of:
Cassio College (year of change 1991)

Organisation type and purpose:
Suitable for ages: 16+.
College of further and higher education.

Subject coverage:
Catering, retail and distribution services, travel and tourism, NVQ business administration, GNVQ business and finance, social and community courses, hairdressing, A levels and GCSEs, languages.

Library catalogue:
All or part available online

Printed publications:
Occasional booklists

Publications list:
Available online

Access to staff:
Contact by letter, by telephone and by fax. Appointment necessary.
Hours: Mon, 0845 to 1700; Tue to Thu, 0845 to 2000; Fri, 0845 to 1630
College holidays: Mon to Thu, 0900 to 1230 and 1330 to 1700; Fri, 0900 to 1230 and 1330 to 1630
Special comments: Phone to make prior appointment, required because of security checks.

Access to building, collection or gallery:
No prior appointment required

Access for disabled people:
Parking provided
Special comments: Library on first floor, no lift – arrangements can be made for access to learning centre (ground floor).

WEST KENT COLLEGE

Acronym or abbreviation: WKC

Brook Street, Tonbridge, Kent, TN9 2PW

Tel: 01732 358101\ Minicom no. 01732 350763
Fax: 01732 771415
E-mail: marketing@wkc.ac.uk

Enquiries:
Enquiries to: Admissions Officer
Direct tel: 01732 358101
Direct fax: 01732 771415

Organisation type and purpose:
Training organisation.

Subject coverage:
Further and higher education, training courses for business and commerce, professional development courses.

Printed publications:
Order printed publications from: Student Services at the same address, tel: 01732 358101, fax: 01732 771415, e-mail: enquiries@wkc.ac.uk

Access to staff:
Contact by letter, by telephone, by fax, by e-mail, in person and via website
Hours: Mon to Fri, 0900 to 1730

In association with:
University of Greenwich

WEST LANCASHIRE DISTRICT COUNCIL

52 Derby Street, Ormskirk, Lancashire, L39 2DF

Tel: 01695 577177
Fax: 01695 585082

Website:
http://www.westlancsdc.gov.uk

Enquiries:
Enquiries to: Public Relations Manager
Direct tel: 01695 585011
Direct fax: 01695 585220
Direct e-mail: public.relations@westlancsdc.gov.uk

Founded:
1974

Organisation type and purpose:
Local government body.

Subject coverage:
Policy issues, public relations, leisure, planning, housing, economic development, finance and council tax, civic administration, building control, contract services, environmental health, refuse collection.

Printed publications:
Citizens Guide and Visitors Guide
Information on council services

Access to staff:
Contact by letter, by telephone, by fax, by e-mail, in person and via website

continued overleaf

Hours: Mon to Fri, 0900 to 1700

Access for disabled people:
Parking provided

WEST LOTHIAN COUNCIL

Libraries Department, Connolly House, Hopefield Road, Blackburn, West Lothian, EH47 7HZ

Tel: 01506 776336
Fax: 01506 776345
E-mail: library.info@westlothian.gov.uk

Website:
http://www.westlothian.gov.uk/libraries
Online catalogue.

Enquiries:
Enquiries to: Library Services Manager

Founded:
1996

Organisation type and purpose:
Local government body, public library.

Subject coverage:
General, local studies, local government.

Museum or gallery collection, archive, or library special collection:
Local history, local government

Non-library collection catalogue:
All or part available online

Library catalogue:
All or part available online

Access to staff:
Contact by letter, by telephone, by fax, by e-mail and in person
Hours: Mon to Thu, 0900 to 1700; Fri, 0900 to 1600

WEST LOTHIAN COUNCIL ARCHIVES AND RECORDS CENTRE

Acronym or abbreviation: WLC ARC

9 Dunlop Square, Deans Industrial Estate, Livingston, EH54 8SB

Tel: 01506 773770
Fax: 01506 773775
E-mail: archive@westlothian.gov.uk

Website:
http://www.westlothian.gov.uk/tourism/libservices/ves

Enquiries:
Enquiries to: Archivist
Other contacts: Local History Librarian (for genealogy enquiries, secondary (published) sources)

Founded:
1995

Formerly called:
Lothian Regional Council (West Lothian Area), West Lothian District Council (year of change 1996); Livingston Development Corporation (year of change 1997)

Organisation type and purpose:
Local government body.
Archive Office.

Subject coverage:
New town development (Livingston) in West Lothian.
Archives of local government, private depository.

Education services:
Education packs and source boxes available for loan to local schools.

Museum or gallery collection, archive, or library special collection:
Livingston Development Corporation Collection (computerised finding aid)

Access to staff:
Contact by letter, by telephone and by fax. Appointment necessary.
Hours: Mon to Thu, 0900 to 1700; Fri, 0900 to 1600

Access to building, collection or gallery:
Prior appointment required

Access for disabled people:
Search room is fully accessible
Hours: As above; please phone first

WEST OF SCOTLAND VW CLUB

Formal name: West of Scotland Volkswagen Club

20 Greenlaw Avenue, Paisley, Renfrewshire, PA1 3RD

Tel: 0141 889 6914

Enquiries:
Enquiries to: Chairman
Other contacts: Membership Secretary for Club information.

Founded:
1963

Organisation type and purpose:
Advisory body, membership association (membership is by subscription), present number of members: 200, consultancy.
Social gatherings, motoring events, helping members with technical and mechanical problems regarding their vehicles.

Subject coverage:
General or technical information regarding Volkswagen vehicles, and other relevant makes of vehicles in the V.A.G. group, e.g. Audi.

Printed publications:
Club newsletter (5 times a year, members only)

Access to staff:
Contact by letter and by telephone
Hours: Mon to Fri, 0900 to 2300
Special comments: All services and information for members only.

Memberships:
Harold Cameron
  8 Allander Drive, Torrance, Glasgow, G64 4LG; tel: 01360 622766

WEST OXFORDSHIRE DISTRICT COUNCIL

Council Offices, Woodgreen, Witney, Oxfordshire, OX28 1NB

Tel: 01993 702941
Fax: 01993 770255
E-mail: enquiries@westoxon.gov.uk

Enquiries:
Enquiries to: Chief Executive
Other contacts: Visitor and Information Centre Manager for publications.

Organisation type and purpose:
Local government body.

Subject coverage:
Information for visitors to the district of West Oxfordshire.

Printed publications:
Leaflets on places of interest, places to visit etc within the District of West Oxfordshire

Access to staff:
Contact by letter, by telephone, by fax, by e-mail, in person and via website
Hours: Mon to Thu, 0830 to 1730; Fri, 0830 to 1700

Access for disabled people:
Parking provided, ramped entry, level entry, toilet facilities

Other offices:
West Oxfordshire District Council
  26 Church Green, Witney, Oxfordshire, OX28 4AU; tel: 01993 702941; fax: 01993 770155

WEST RIDING TRADE PROTECTION ASSOCIATION

Acronym or abbreviation: WRTPA

Protection House, 16–17 East Parade, Leeds, West Yorkshire, LS1 2BS

Tel: 0113 243 2561
Fax: 0113 244 3901
E-mail: wrtpa@cwcom.net

Website:
http://www.wrtpa.com

Enquiries:
Enquiries to: General Manager
Other contacts: Company Secretary

Founded:
1848

Organisation type and purpose:
Membership association (membership is by subscription), present number of members: 4500.
Credit information and debt recovery agency.

Subject coverage:
Debt recovery specialists in both UK and overseas, company monitoring, tracing agents, business and credit information specialists.

Printed publications:
Brochure (available free, on request)

Publications list:
Available in print

Access to staff:
Contact by letter, by telephone, by fax, by e-mail, in person and via website. Appointment necessary.
Access for members only.
Hours: Mon to Fri, 0900 to 1700

WEST SURREY FAMILY HISTORY SOCIETY

Acronym or abbreviation: WSFHS

21 Sheppard Road, Basingstoke, Hampshire, RG21 3HT

Tel: 01256 358454
E-mail: secretary@wsfhs.org

Website:
http://www.surreyweb.org.uk/wsfhs/index.html
All society details, meetings, list of publications, etc.
http://www.wsfhs.org

Enquiries:
Enquiries to: Secretary

Founded:
1974

Organisation type and purpose:
Membership association (membership is by subscription), present number of members: 1,200, voluntary organisation, registered charity (charity number 278091), research organisation.
To collect, index, co-ordinate, publish and make accessible, in the interests of genealogy, any documents or records relating to the ancient County of Surrey; to promote their preservation; to encourage the study of genealogy.

Subject coverage:
Genealogy and family history.

Special visitor services:
Regular meetings are held most months of the year at venues in West Surrey: Camberley, Farnham, Guildford, Walton on Thames, and a computer group meets at Pyrford.

Non-library collection catalogue:
All or part available online, in-house and in print

Printed publications:
Handbook (members only)
Vast range of research aids, records, maps, all of which are detailed on the website at: http://www.wsfhs.org/publications.htm
Order printed publications from: Publications Officer, West Surrey Family History Society, 17 Lane End Drive, Knaphill, Woking, Surrey, GU21 2QQ

Microform publications:
All are detailed on the website at: http://www.wsfhs.org/publications.htm
They include:
Census and hearth tax records, monumental inscriptions, Surrey early wills, including:
1851 Census Index of Western Surrey (£10)
1861 Census Index for 13 areas
Transcriptions and indexes of parishes registers (over 80; £1.20 to £5.20)
Archdeaconry Court of Surrey Early Wills (fiche)

Electronic and video publications:
All are detailed on the website at: http://www.wsfhs.org/publications.htm
They include The Surrey Marriage Index, Surrey Burials Index, Surrey Baptisms not in the IGI and Surrey Poor Law (CD-ROM), plus several more.

Publications list:
Available online and in print

Access to staff:
Contact by letter, by e-mail and via website
Hours: Mon to Fri, 0900 to 1700
Special comments: Some charges to non-members.

Access for disabled people:
Check in advance

WEST SUSSEX COUNTY COUNCIL

County Hall, West Street, Chichester, West Sussex, PO19 1RQ

Tel: 01243 777100
Fax: 01243 777950
E-mail: webmaster@westsussex.gov.uk

Website:
http://www.westsussex.gov.uk
Information about the County Council and the county of West Sussex.

Enquiries:
Enquiries to: News Manager
Direct tel: 01243 777117
Direct fax: 01243 777266
Direct e-mail: nigel.galloway@westsussex.gov.uk

Founded:
1889

Organisation type and purpose:
Local government body.

Access to staff:
Contact by letter, by telephone, by fax, by e-mail, in person and via website
Hours: Mon to Fri, 0900 to 1700

Access for disabled people:
Parking provided, toilet facilities
Special comments: Lift into the building

WEST SUSSEX LIBRARY SERVICE

Worthing Reference Library, Richmond Road, Worthing, BN11 1HD

Tel: 01903 704824
Fax: 01903 821902
E-mail: worthing.reference.library@westsussex.gov.uk

Website:
http://www.westsussex.gov.uk

Enquiries:
Enquiries to: Information Librarian

Organisation type and purpose:
Local government body, public library.

Subject coverage:
Local history; art; folklore; ornithology; zoology; business information sources; law; government publications, European information, Family History.

Non-library collection catalogue:
All or part available online

Library catalogue:
All or part available online

Access to staff:
Contact by letter, by telephone, by fax, by e-mail and in person
Hours: Mon to Fri, 0900 to 1900; Sat, 0900 to 1700

Access for disabled people:
Ramped entry

WEST SUSSEX RECORD OFFICE

Acronym or abbreviation: WSRO

County Hall, Chichester, West Sussex, PO19 1RN

Tel: 01243 753600
Fax: 01243 533959
E-mail: records.office@westsussex.gov.uk

Website:
http://www.westsussex.gov.uk/ccm/navigation/libraries-and-archives/record-office/
General introduction to the office.

Enquiries:
Enquiries to: Archivist

Founded:
1946

Organisation type and purpose:
Local government body, research organisation.

Subject coverage:
1200 years of the County's history, including the Diocese of Chichester, and the county's landed estates (especially Goodwood, Petworth, Cowdray and Wiston), family papers including Richard Cobden, WS Blunt, and the Wilberforce and Maxse families, and the Royal Sussex Regiment.

Museum or gallery collection, archive, or library special collection:
Garland Photographic Collection (70,000 photographs)
South East Film and Video Archive
William Blake (Crookshank Collection)

Non-library collection catalogue:
All or part available online, in-house and in print

Library catalogue:
All or part available in-house

Printed publications:
Some 70 publications including:
A Catalogue of the Records of the Bishop, Archdeacons and Former Exempt Jurisdictions (compiled by Steer F W £15)
Cinema West Sussex: The First Hundred Years (Eyles A et al, £15.95)
Genealogists Guide to the West Sussex Record Office (Wilkinson P M, reprinting 2002)
Petworth House Archives Vol 1 (Steer F W ed, £10)
The Goodwood Estate Archives Vol 1 (Steer F W ed, £15)
The Royal Sussex Regiment: A Catalogue of Records (Readman A E ed, £25)
West Sussex Local History Mini Guides to Sources, 15 titles (£1 each)
West Sussex Census Returns 1841–1901
The Wiston Archives (Booker J M L ed, £15)
General Register Office Indexes

Microform publications:
Copies of West Sussex Parish Registers (microfiche)

Electronic and video publications:
Scanned images of West Sussex photographs, pictures and documents (prints or disk)

Access to staff:
Contact by letter, by telephone, by fax, by e-mail, in person and via website
Hours: Mon to Fri, 0915 to 1645; Sat, 0915 to 1230 and 1330 to 1630
Special comments: A valid County Archives Research Network Ticket is required to use the search room. This is available free of charge on proof of identity on arrival.

Access for disabled people:
Ramped entry, access to all public areas, toilet facilities

Parent body:
West Sussex County Council
County Hall, Chichester, PO19 1RG; tel: 01243 777100; fax: 01243 777952

WEST THAMES COLLEGE

London Road, Isleworth, Middlesex, TW7 4HS

Tel: 020 8326 2308
Fax: 020 8569 7787
E-mail: library.services@west-thames.ac.uk

Website:
http://www.west-thames.ac.uk

Enquiries:
Enquiries to: Library Services Manager
Direct tel: 020 8326 2310
Direct e-mail: karen.kelly@west-thames.ac.uk

Formerly called:
Hounslow Borough College

Organisation type and purpose:
Further education.

Subject coverage:
Psychology; social sciences; education; computing; language; art; literature; history; biography; art history; graphic design; architecture, physics, chemistry, catering, hairdressing and beauty, health and care, ESOL (English for Speakers of Other Languages), business studies, engineering, construction trade skills, biology.

Museum or gallery collection, archive, or library special collection:
Collection relating to Joseph Banks

Library catalogue:
All or part available in-house

Printed publications:
Course Prospectus

Publications list:
Available in print

Access to staff:
Contact by letter, by telephone, by fax and by e-mail
Hours: Mon, Fri, 0845 to 1600; Tue, Wed, Thu, 0845 to 2000

Access to building, collection or gallery:
Prior appointment required

Access for disabled people:
Parking provided, ramped entry, toilet facilities
Special comments: Lifts

WEST YORKSHIRE ARCHAEOLOGY ADVISORY SERVICE

Acronym or abbreviation: WYAAS

Registry of Deeds, Newstead Road, Wakefield, West Yorkshire, WF1 2DE

Tel: 01924 306797
Fax: 01924 306810
E-mail: wysmr@wyjs.org.uk

Website:
http://www.archaeology.wyjs.org.uk

Enquiries:
Enquiries to: Historic Environment Record (HER) Officer (for information on archaeological sites and findspots and some historic buildings)

Organisation type and purpose:
Local government body, advisory body, suitable for ages: all.
Provision of advice to local authorities on archaeological matters.

Subject coverage:
The area served by the Metropolitan Districts of Bradford, Calderdale, Kirklees, Leeds and Wakefield.

continued overleaf

All aspects of the archaeology of the area, for all periods up to and including the 'Cold War'. The HER is interested in all new discoveries of sites, artefacts, cartographic, photographic and documentary sources.
Planning and research enquiries, site management and heritage issues. The service includes a Historic Buildings Officer and an outreach Education Officer. The HER includes a reference library, the principal oblique aerial photographic collection for West Yorkshire, a number of significant archaeological surveys, as well as details of all known sites, find spots and archaeological monuments within the five Metropolitan Districts. The HER is interested in liaising with other local and national groups and with individuals who possess information on archaeological sites and historic buildings within West Yorkshire.

Printed publications:
Available to purchase online
Order printed publications from: Resources, West Yorkshire Archaeology Service, PO Box 30, Nepshaw Lane South, Morley, Leeds, LS27 0UG; tel: 0113 383 6404

Electronic and video publications:
Some archaeological information via e-mail

Publications list:
Available in print

Access to staff:
Contact by letter, by telephone, by fax and by e-mail. Appointment necessary.
Hours: Mon to Fri, 1000 to 1700, by appointment only

WEST YORKSHIRE ARCHIVE SERVICE – BRADFORD

Acronym or abbreviation: WYAS

Bradford Central Library, Prince's Way, Bradford, BD1 1NN,

Tel: 01274 435099
E-mail: bradford@wyjs.org.uk

Website:
http://www.archives.wyjs.org.uk

Enquiries:
Enquiries to: Archivist

Founded:
1982

Organisation type and purpose:
Local government body.
Record office.

Subject coverage:
Primary source material for historical and other purposes.

Museum or gallery collection, archive, or library special collection:
Local authority records, parish and nonconformist records, family and estate records, business records, political and trade union records, etc.

Non-library collection catalogue:
All or part available online, in-house and in print

Printed publications:
Guide to the Bradford District Archives (to purchase)
Information leaflets, i.e. the West Yorkshire Archive Service and Bradford District Archives (free)
Guide for Family Historians (to purchase)

Publications list:
Available online

Access to staff:
Contact by letter, by telephone, by fax, by e-mail and in person. Appointment necessary.
Hours: Mon, Tue, Thu, 0930 to 1700; Wed, closed

Constituent part of:
West Yorkshire Archive Service
West Yorkshire Joint Services
tel: 0113 289 8214; e-mail: info@wyjs.org.uk; website: http://www.wyjs.org.uk

Supported by:
Metropolitan District Councils of Bradford, Calderdale, Kirklees, Leeds and Wakefield

WEST YORKSHIRE ARCHIVE SERVICE – CALDERDALE

Central Library, Northgate, Halifax, West Yorkshire, HX1 1UN

Tel: 01422 392636
E-mail: calderdale@wyjs.org.uk

Website:
http://www.archives.wyjs.org.uk
Leaflets, general information etc, catalogues.

Enquiries:
Enquiries to: Visitor Services Co-ordinator
Direct tel: 01422 392635

Founded:
1964

Formerly called:
Calderdale District Archive Service (year of change 1983)

Organisation type and purpose:
Local government body.
A county-wide archive service.

Subject coverage:
Primary source material for historical and other purposes.

Museum or gallery collection, archive, or library special collection:
Local authority records, nonconformist records, family and estate records, business records, charities and societies records, political and trade union records, etc.

Non-library collection catalogue:
All or part available online, in-house and in print

Printed publications:
Calderdale Archives 1964–1989: an illustrated guide to Calderdale District Archives 1990, supplement 1990–1998
Information leaflets re the West Yorkshire Archive Service and Collections and User Guides (free)
See also entry for Service HQ at Wakefield

Publications list:
Available online and in print

Access to staff:
Contact by letter, by telephone, by e-mail, in person and via website. Appointment necessary.
Hours: Mon, Tue, Thu, Fri, 0930 to 1700; Wed, closed

Access for disabled people:
Parking provided, level entry, access to all public areas

Constituent part of:
West Yorkshire Archive Service

Supported by:
Metropolitan District Councils of Bradford, Calderdale, Kirklees, Leeds and Wakefield

WEST YORKSHIRE ARCHIVE SERVICE – KIRKLEES

Acronym or abbreviation: WYAS, Kirklees

Central Library, Princess Alexandra Walk, Huddersfield, West Yorkshire, HD1 2SU

Tel: 01484 221966
E-mail: kirklees@wyjs.org.uk

Website:
http://www.archives.wyjs.org.uk

Enquiries:
Enquiries to: Archivist

Founded:
1982

Organisation type and purpose:
Local government body.

Subject coverage:
Primary source material for historical and other purposes relating to the Kirklees District.

Museum or gallery collection, archive, or library special collection:
Local authority records, nonconformist records, family and estate records, business records (especially textile industry), society records, etc.

Non-library collection catalogue:
All or part available online, in-house and in print

Printed publications:
Leeds Archives 1938–1988: an illustrated guide to Leeds District Archives
Information leaflets re the West Yorkshire Archive Service and Kirklees District Archives (free)
Kirklees Archives 1959–1989 (guide, supplement 1989–1995)
Sources of information at Kirklees Archives on specific topics
Order printed publications from: Publication Sales Office, West Yorkshire Archive Service HQ Registry of Deeds, Newstead Road, Wakefield, WF1 2DE; tel: 01924 305982; fax: 01924 305983; e-mail: wakefield@wyjs.org.uk

Microform publications:
See WYAS Wakefield Headquarters

Publications list:
Available online and in print

Access to staff:
Contact by letter, by telephone, by e-mail and in person. Appointment necessary.
Hours: Mon, Tues, Thu, 0930 to 1700; Wed and Fri, closed; 3rd Sat of month, 0930 to 1300

Constituent part of:
West Yorkshire Archive Service

Parent body:
West Yorkshire Joint Services
PO Box 5, Nepshaw Lane South, Morley, Leeds, LS27 0QP; tel: 0113 2530241; fax: 0113 2530311; e-mail: info@wyjs.org.uk; website: http://www.wyjs.org.uk

Supported by:
Metropolitan District Councils of Bradford, Calderdale, Kirklees, Leeds and Wakefield

WEST YORKSHIRE ARCHIVE SERVICE – LEEDS

Acronym or abbreviation: WYAS

2 Chapeltown Road, Sheepscar, Leeds, West Yorkshire, LS7 3AP

Tel: 0113 214 5814
E-mail: leeds@wyjs.org.uk

Website:
http://www.archives.wyjs.org.uk
Office leaflet style pages providing brief summary of records held and access details.

Founded:
1938

Organisation type and purpose:
Local government body.
Archive service.

Subject coverage:
Primary source material for historical and other purposes.

Museum or gallery collection, archive, or library special collection:
Local authority records
Parish and nonconformist records; family and estate records; business records; voluntary bodies, charities and societies records, political and trade union records, manorial records, tithe records, solicitors and estate agents papers
Major deposited collections:
Family and estate archives including:
Baines family of Leeds
Gascoigne family of Parlington
Earl of Mexborough
Earl of Harewood

Ingilby family of Ripley Castle
Lane Fox family of Bramham Park
Newby Hall Estate
Nostell Priory
Ramsden family of Byram
Samuel Smiles papers
Studley Royal Estate including Fountains Abbey
Temple Newsam
Business records, including:
T and M Bairstow
British Coal
Burton Group
Joshua Tetley
John Wilson
Yorkshire Patent Steam Waggon Co

Non-library collection catalogue:
All or part available online, in-house and in print

Printed publications:
Around Leeds: archive photographs (Young M and Payne D, 1995, £8.99 plus £1.50 p&p)
Information leaflets re. the West Yorkshire Archive Service and collections and user guides (free)
Leeds Archives 1938–1988 (guide)
Leeds in the News: Britain in Old Photographs (Harrison B, £8.99 plus £1.50 p&p)
Order printed publications from: Sue Pad, WYAS, Wakefield, Newstead Road, Wakefield, WF1 2DE

Microform publications:
Various Parish Registers of West Yorkshire and beyond
Order microform publications from: Sue Pad, WYAS, Wakefield, Newstead Road, Wakefield, WF1 2DE

Publications list:
Available online and in print

Access to staff:
Contact by letter, by telephone, by e-mail, in person and via website. Appointment necessary.
Hours: Mon, Tue, Thur 0900 to 1700; Wed, Fri, closed

Constituent part of:
West Yorkshire Archive Service

Supported by:
Metropolitan District Councils of Bradford, Calderdale, Kirklees, Leeds and Wakefield

WEST YORKSHIRE ARCHIVE SERVICE – WAKEFIELD

Acronym or abbreviation: WYAS

Registry of Deeds Building, Newstead Road, Wakefield, West Yorkshire, WF1 2DE

Tel: 01924 305980
Fax: 01924 305983
E-mail: wakefield@wyjs.org.uk

Website:
http://www.archives.wyjs.org.uk
Introduction to offices, publications, information for family historians, events.

Enquiries:
Enquiries to: Archivist

Organisation type and purpose:
Local government body. Archive service.

Subject coverage:
Primary source material for historical and other purposes, including administration at county, district and parish levels, religion, law and order, education, health, historical geography, transport, property rights, rights of way, industry.

Museum or gallery collection, archive, or library special collection:
Manuscript documentation on the West Riding and on Wakefield District from the Middle Ages to the present day; West Riding Quarter Sessions records; local authority records including former West Riding County Council and West Yorkshire Metropolitan County Council; West Riding Registry of Deeds records; records of public bodies and utilities; county-wide records; Wakefield Diocesan parish records and records of public bodies; nonconformist records; family

and estate records; business records; charities and societies records; courts, coroners, estates, schools, probate registry, hospitals, political and trade union records, etc.

Trade and statistical information:
1971 Census of distribution maps. 1960 Land utilisation maps. 19th- and 20th-century records of businesses.

Non-library collection catalogue:
All or part available online and in print

Library catalogue:
All or part available online and in print

Printed publications:
Guide for Family Historians, a list of parish and nonconformist and other related records held by the West Yorkshire Archive Service (3rd edition, £2.99 + £2.50 p&p)
Information leaflets re the West Yorkshire Archive Service and Wakefield Headquarters (free)
Bradford Archives 1974–1995: an illustrated guide to Bradford District Archives (1996, 220pp, £4 plus £2 p&p)
Calderdale Archives 1964–1989: an illustrated guide to Calderdale District Archives (1990, 120pp, £4 plus £2 p&p)
Calderdale Archives, Supplement 1990–1998 (1999, 87pp, £1 plus 50p p&p)
Kirklees Archives 1959–1989: an illustrated guide to Kirklees District Archives (1989, 80pp, £4 plus £1 p&p)
Leeds Archives 1938–1988: an illustrated guide to Leeds District Archives (1989, 72pp £4 plus £1 p&p)
Order printed publications from: Administration Officer, West Yorkshire Archive Service, at the same address; tel: 01924 305982; e-mail: spad@wyjs.org.ukuk

Microform publications:
Microfiche of parish registers, etc. (for sale)
Order microform publications from: Administration Officer, as above

Publications list:
Available online and in print

Access to staff:
Contact by letter, by telephone, by fax, by e-mail, in person and via website. Appointment necessary.
Hours: Mon, Tue, Thu, 0930 to 1700; 2nd & 4th Mon, 0930 to 2000; 2nd Sat in month, 0930 to 1300; closed Wed, Fri, Sun
Special comments: CARN tickets required. Appointment recommended as the searchrooms can get very busy.

Access for disabled people:
Parking provided
Special comments: Disabled access not available; wheelchair users have to be lifted into building or, if able to walk a little, use handrails by steps.

Constituent part of:
West Yorkshire Joint Service
PO Box 5, Nepshaw Lane South, Morley, Leeds, LS27 0PQ; tel: 0113 289 8214; e-mail: info@wyjs.org.uk; website: http://www.wyjs.org.uk

Supported by:
Metropolitan District Councils of Bradford, Calderdale, Kirklees, Leeds and Wakefield

Works under the guidance of the:
Lord Chancellor's Department with regard to public records
Master of the Rolls with regard to tithe and manorial records

WESTCOUNTRY STUDIES LIBRARY

Acronym or abbreviation: WSL

Exeter Central Library, Castle Street, Exeter, Devon, EX4 3PQ

Tel: 01392 384216
Fax: 01392 384228
E-mail: westcountry.library@devon.gov.uk

Website:
http://www.devon.gov.uk/localstudies

Enquiries:
Enquiries to: Westcountry Studies Librarian

Founded:
1870

Formerly called:
Royal Albert Memorial; Exeter City Library (year of change 1974)

Organisation type and purpose:
Local government body, public library. Main local studies collection for Devon Library and Information Services. Reference library.

Subject coverage:
All aspects of Devon and the adjoining counties, past and present.

Museum or gallery collection, archive, or library special collection:
Brooking Rowe collection (local history, brass rubbings, bookplates)
Burnet Morris index on Devon history
Devon and Cornwall Record Society (collections and unpublished transcripts, available to members; membership can be taken out in the library)
Devon Folk Life Register
Heber Mardon Collection of Napoleonic illustrations
Pike Ward collection (Iceland)
Pocknell collection of shorthand books

Non-library collection catalogue:
All or part available online

Library catalogue:
All or part available in-house

Printed publications:
Publications include:
Abbots Bickington to Zeal Monachorum: a handlist of parish histories compiled on the occasion of the centenary of parish councils 1994
An Index of Brass Rubbings in the Westcountry Studies Library 1991 (Andrew G, also on web)
Devon Bibliography (1985 to date, annually, also on web since 1999)
Devon's Testimony of War (1995)
Devon Topographical Prints 1660–1870: a catalogue and guide
Facsimiles of maps
In Pursuit of Devon's History (Maxted I, Devon Books 1997, partly on web)
Resource Guides: three series of leaflets on genealogy, house history, parish history etc, giving details of resources available for local studies research in Devon (also on web)
The Devon Collection of Children's Books 1692–1849 (Moon M, also on web)
Various handlists and guides to resources (many also on web)

Microform publications:
Microfiche of early trade directories from 1791 onwards and some other historical sources (details available on request)

Electronic and video publications:
Extracts from local studies database in dBase or ASCII format can be provided on request on disc or can be downloaded from the web

Publications list:
Available online

Access to staff:
Contact by letter, by telephone, by e-mail, in person and via website
Hours: Mon and Fri, 0930 to 1800; Tue and Thu, 0930 to 1900; Wed, 1000 to 1700; Sat, 0930 to 1600

Branch library:
North Devon Local Studies Centre
Tuly Street, Barnstaple, Devon, EX32 7EJ; tel: 01271 388607

Parent body:
Devon Library and Information Services
Devon County Council; tel: 01392 384315

WESTERKIRK PARISH LIBRARY

Bentpath, Langholm, Dumfriesshire, DB13 0PB

Enquiries:
Enquiries to: Chairman of the Trustees
Direct tel: 013873 70201
Other contacts: Mrs M. Sanderson, Chairman of the
Trustees: Westerkirk Schoolhouse, Langholm
DG13 0PB, tel: 013873 70201

Founded:
1793

Organisation type and purpose:
Library.
Registered Scottish charity (charity number
SCO20308)

Subject coverage:
Parish records

**Museum or gallery collection, archive, or library
special collection:**
8,000 books (mid-18th century to the present)

Access to staff:
Contact by letter and by telephone. Appointment
necessary.

Access to building, collection or gallery:
Hours: 1st Mon of month, 1900 to 2000 (by
appointment with staff)

WESTERN ISLES LIBRARIES

19 Cromwell Street, Stornoway, Isle of Lewis, HS1
2DA

Tel: 01851 708631
Fax: 01851 708676

Website:
http://www.cne-siar.gov.uk
Details of services provided by the library can be
found from the Council's home page.

Enquiries:
Enquiries to: Chief Librarian
Direct tel: 01851 708641
Other contacts: Senior Librarian Adult Services,
Senior Librarian Youth Services

Organisation type and purpose:
Local government body, public library.

Subject coverage:
General, local history, Gaelic.

**Museum or gallery collection, archive, or library
special collection:**
An Comunn Gaidhealach collection of Gaelic and
  Highland language and history
Donald MacDonald Papers
Gaelic Collection including recorded sound,
  language, learning, books and periodicals
Local history of the Western Isles
Morrison Manuscripts
School Board minute books
School log books
T B Macaulay photographs collection

Library catalogue:
All or part available online

Access to staff:
Contact by letter, by telephone, by fax and in
person
Hours: Mon to Wed, 1000 to 1700; Thu and Fri, 1000
to 1800; Sat, 1000 to 1700

Access for disabled people:
Access to all public areas, toilet facilities

Parent body:
Comhairle Nan Eilean Siar (formerly Western Isles
Islands Council)

WESTERN KURDISTAN
ASSOCIATION

Palingswick House, 241 King Street, London, W6
9LP

Tel: 020 8748 7874
Fax: 020 8741 6436

E-mail: info@westernkurdistan.org.uk
Website:
http://www.westernkurdistan.org.uk

Organisation type and purpose:
Community centre for Kurdish refugees, offering
help in matters such as immigration, welfare,
housing and health, and courses in English
language and other subjects. Administers a
Kurdish museum, library and archive.

Information services:
Nesletter, websites radio and TV broadcasting in
Kurdish, English and other languages.

Special visitor services:
Kurdish Museum, Library and Archive.

Education services:
Courses in English language, computers, internet,
media and film-making.

**Museum or gallery collection, archive, or library
special collection:**
Historical and cultural archive of the Kurdish
  community

Access to building, collection or gallery:
Hours: Mon to Fri, 1000 to 1700
Special comments: Access to archive is by
appointment only.

WESTMINSTER (ROMAN
CATHOLIC) DIOCESAN ARCHIVES

16a Abingdon Road, Kensington, London, W8 6AF

Tel: 020 7938 3580

Enquiries:
Enquiries to: Administrator

Organisation type and purpose:
Diocesan archive.

Subject coverage:
History of England's post-reformation Roman
Catholic community.

Non-library collection catalogue:
All or part available in-house

Library catalogue:
All or part available in-house

Access to staff:
Contact by letter and by telephone. Appointment
necessary.
Hours: Tue, Wed, Thu, 1000 to 1600

Access to building, collection or gallery:
Prior appointment required
Hours: Tue, Wed, Thu, 1000 to 1600
Special comments: The Archive is private. Letter of
introduction required.

WESTMINSTER ABBEY

Library and Muniment Room, London, SW1P 3PA

Tel: 020 7654 4830
Fax: 020 7654 4827
E-mail: library@westminster-abbey.org

Website:
http://www.westminster-abbey.org/library

Enquiries:
Enquiries to: Librarian
Direct tel: 020 7654 4826
Other contacts: Keeper of the Muniments (for
archives)

Founded:
1623

Organisation type and purpose:
Abbey church library and archives collection.

Subject coverage:
History of Westminster Abbey and its precincts,
coronations, St Margaret's Westminster.

**Museum or gallery collection, archive, or library
special collection:**
c. 14,000 early printed books

c. 70,000 documents relating to the Abbey since
  1066
Collection of books on the history of Westminster
  Abbey
Collection of illuminated and other medieval
  manuscripts
Collection of Pamphlets belonging to William
  Camden (1551–1623)
K H Oldaker Collection of English Bookbindings,
  1655–1920
Langley collection of prints and drawings
Large photographic collection
Music Collection (mainly late 16th and 17th
  centuries)

Non-library collection catalogue:
All or part available in print

Library catalogue:
All or part available in-house

Printed publications:
Westminster Abbey Record Series Vol 1 (1997–) –
in progress, 4 volumes published to date

Microform publications:
Early music and manuscript collections available
from World Microfilms, POB 35488, St John's
Wood, London NW8 6WD

Access to staff:
Contact by letter, by telephone, by fax, by e-mail
and via website. Appointment necessary.
Hours: Mon to Fri, 1000 to 1300 and 1400 to 1645

Access for disabled people:
Medieval building with staircases. Please consult
staff about alternative arrangements for access to
library materials

WESTMINSTER COLLEGE
LIBRARY (CAMBRIDGE)

Madingley Road, Cambridge, CB3 0AA

Tel: 01223 741084
Fax: 01223 300765

Website:
http://www.westminster.cam.ac.uk
Brief description of the college and courses.

Enquiries:
Enquiries to: Librarian
Direct tel: 01223 741043
Direct e-mail: cr248@cam.ac.uk

Founded:
1844

Created by the merger of:
Presbyterian theological college and a
Congregational College

Formerly called:
Cheshunt College, Westminster College

Organisation type and purpose:
Suitable for ages: 18+.
Preparation of men and women for the Christian
ministry.

Subject coverage:
Theological and Biblical studies, particularly
Reformed theology and church history, philosophy
of religion, Christian ethics and pastoral studies.

**Museum or gallery collection, archive, or library
special collection:**
Archives of the Countess of Huntingdon's colleges
  and chapels
Archive material of the Ecclesiastical History
  Society of the United Reformed Church
Elias Library of Hymnology
Lewis and Gibson Collection of manuscripts from
  the Cairo Synagogue Genizah (complements the
  University Library's Taylor-Schechter Collection)
Library of the Ecclesiastical History Society of the
  United Reformed Church
Todd Collection of liturgical works

Non-library collection catalogue:
All or part available online and in-house

Library catalogue:
All or part available online

Access to staff:
Contact by letter and by e-mail. Appointment necessary. Letter of introduction required. Non-members charged.
Hours: Mon to Fri, 0900 to 1600
Special comments: Open to members of the Cambridge Theological Federation, ministers of the United Reformed Church and approved external members only.

Parent body:
United Reformed Church

WESTMINSTER LIBRARIES AND ARCHIVES

Charing Cross Library, 4 Charing Cross Road, London, WC2H 0HF

Tel: 020 7641 6573
Fax: 020 7641 6551

Website:
http://www.westminster.gov.uk/index/libraries .cfm

Enquiries:
Enquiries to: Westminster Libraries Manager
Direct e-mail: a.stevens@dial.pipex.com
Other contacts: Archives Centre for full list of current publications tel no: 020 7641 5180.

Formerly called:
Westminster City Archives and Libraries

Organisation type and purpose:
Local government body.
Public library and archive.

Subject coverage:
Local studies and archives at City of Westminster Archives; music at Westminster Music Library; art and design, official publications, EU at Westminster Reference Library.

Museum or gallery collection, archive, or library special collection:
Archive and local history collections (City of Westminster Archives)
Ashbridge Collection (City of Westminster Archives)
Gillow Archives (furniture design history, Victoria Library)
Sherlock Holmes Collection (Marylebone Library)

Non-library collection catalogue:
All or part available online

Library catalogue:
All or part available online

Printed publications:
Contact Archives Centre tel: 020 7641 5180 for full list
Artisans and Avenues: A History of the Queen's Park Estate (E McDonald and D J Smith, 2nd ed., 1990)
Blitz over Westminster: City of Westminster Civil Defence bomb incident photographs 1940–1944 (R Harrison, City of Westminster Libraries, 1990)
Catalogue of Orchestral Sets held at Westminster Music Library
Greetings cards: 18th Century Westminster Views
Old Westminster Parish Maps from John Strype's 1755 edition of John Stow's Survey of London
Pineapples and Pantomimes: A History of Church Street and Lisson Green (E McDonald and D J Smith, 1992)
The Contents of a Lumber Room – A catalogue of the Sherlock Holmes Collection

Publications list:
Available in print

Access to staff:
Contact by letter, by telephone and by e-mail
Hours: Mon to Fri, 0900 to 1700
Special comments: Please telephone individual sites for opening hours and to establish restrictions on access.

Headquarters:
Westminster Libraries and Archives Headquarters
Westminster City Hall, Victoria Street, London, SW1E 6QP; tel: 020 7641 2496

Other addresses:
Charing Cross Library
Charing Cross Road, London, WC2H 0HG; tel: 020 7641 4628
Church Street Library
Church Street, London, NW8 8EU; tel: 020 7641 5479
City of Westminster Archives Centre
10 St Ann's Street, London, SW1T 2XR; tel: 020 7641 5180
Maida Vale Library
Sutherland Avenue, London, W9 2QT; tel: 020 7641 3659
Marylebone Library
Marylebone Road, London, NW1 5PS; tel: 020 7641 1037
Mayfair Library
25 South Audley Street, London, W1Y 5DJ; tel: 020 7641 4903
Paddington Library
Porchester Road, London, W2 5DU; tel: 020 7641 4475
Pimlico Library
Rampayne Street, London, SW1V 2PU; tel: 020 7641 2983
Queen's Park Library
666 Harrow Road, London, W10 4NE; tel: 020 7641 4575
St James's Library
62 Victoria Street, London, SW1E 6QP; tel: 020 7641 2989
St John's Wood Library
20 Circus Road, London, NW8 6PD; tel: 020 7641 5087
Victoria Library
160 Buckingham Palace Road, London, SW1W 9UD; tel: 020 7641 4287
Westminster Music Library
Victoria Library, 160 Buckingham Palace Road, London, SW1W 9UD; tel: 020 7641 4292
Westminster Reference Library
St Martin's Street, London, WC2H 7HP; tel: 020 7641 4636

Parent body:
Westminster City Council

WESTMINSTER REFERENCE LIBRARY

35 St Martins Street, London, WC2H 7HP

Tel: 020 7641 4634/4636/4638
Fax: 020 7641 4606
E-mail: westreflib@dial.pipex.com

Website:
http://www.westminster.gov.uk/libraries/search Catalogue.
http://www.westminster.gov.uk/libraries/libraries/ westref
Information about the library.

Enquiries:
Enquiries to: Manager
Direct tel: 020 7641 5260
Direct e-mail: tarathoon@dial.pipex.com

Formerly called:
Westminster Central Reference Library

Organisation type and purpose:
Local government body, public library.

Subject coverage:
A general public reference library specialising in the following key areas:
Business: market research, business directories and international telephone directories, company information.
Official Publications: HMSO publications since 1947, Parliamentary papers since 1906, Hansard since 1803, EU Official Publications.
Arts: covering art, fine arts, painting, drawing, sculpture, ceramics, glassware, coins, tapestry, carpets, furniture, jewellery, interior design,

costume, goldsmiths' work, silverware, arms and armour, architecture, antiques, collecting, cinema, film, theatre, radio and television and dance.

Museum or gallery collection, archive, or library special collection:
EU Depository Library

Trade and statistical information:
Wide range of UK, EU and International statistics.

Non-library collection catalogue:
All or part available online

Library catalogue:
All or part available online

Access to staff:
Contact by letter, by telephone, by fax, by e-mail, in person and via website
Hours: Mon to Fri, 1000 to 2000; Sat, 1000 to 1700
Special comments: Reference library.

Also at:
Marylebone Information Service (MIS)
109–117 Marylebone Road, London, NW1 5PS; tel: 020 7641 1031; fax: 020 7641 1028; e-mail: m.i .s@dial.pipex.com

Parent body:
Westminster City Council

WESTON COLLEGE

Learning Resources Centre, Knightstone Road, Weston-super-Mare, Somerset, BS23 2AL

Tel: 01934 411411
Fax: 01934 411410
E-mail: college@weston.ac.uk

Website:
http://www.weston.ac.uk
College home page.

Enquiries:
Enquiries to: Librarian
Direct tel: 01934 411409
Direct e-mail: lrc@weston.ac.uk

Formerly called:
Weston-Super-Mare College of Further Education

Organisation type and purpose:
Further Education.

Subject coverage:
General, psychology, sociology, social sciences, catering, hairdressing, electronics, engineering, business, care, art, leisure, drugs information base, computer studies, information technology, music technology, sciences, languages, EFL, humanities, education, sign language.

Museum or gallery collection, archive, or library special collection:
Drugs information base

Printed publications:
General information (opening hours, borrowing rights)
CD guides
Subject guides
Web site guides

Access to staff:
Contact by letter, by telephone, by fax, by e-mail, in person and via website
Hours: Term time: Mon to Thu, 0845 to 2100, Fri, 0845 to 1700
Vacations: Mon to Fri, 0900 to 1700

Access for disabled people:
Parking provided, ramped entry, toilet facilities

Also at:
Weston College 6th Form Library
Loxton Road, Weston-super-Mare, Somerset; tel: 01934 411615

WESTONBIRT, THE NATIONAL ARBORETUM

Forestry Commission England, Tetbury, Gloucestershire, GL8 8QS

continued overleaf

Tel: 01666 880220
Fax: 01666 880559
E-mail: westonbirt@forestry.gov.uk

Website:
http://www.forestry.gov.uk/westonbirt
Official Westonbirt pages.
http://www.fowa.org.uk
Friends of Westonbirt Arboretum pages.

Enquiries:
Enquiries to: Curator
Other contacts: Visitor Services Manager

Founded:
1829

Organisation type and purpose:
Government Department

Subject coverage:
Arboriculture, forestry, trees and shrubs in general.

Services for disabled people:
All main paths and facilities are accessible for less able visitors. Electric scooters and wheelchairs are also available to hire, pre-book on: 01666 881218.

Museum or gallery collection, archive, or library special collection:
600 acres of picturesque, historic landscape, covered by 17 miles of paths; a collection of 16,000 trees, some of the oldest, rarest and largest of their kind in the UK; tree and shrub collection on computer database, over 18,000 records

Non-library collection catalogue:
All or part available in-house

Printed publications:
Westonbirt Tree Forestry

Access to staff:
Contact by letter, by telephone, by fax and by e-mail. Appointment necessary.

Access to building, collection or gallery:
Hours: Grounds and Visitor Centre open every day of the year; please check website for current times and prices

Access for disabled people:
Parking provided, ramped entry, toilet facilities, mobility scooters can be booked

Constituent part of:
Forestry Commission

WEYMOUTH COLLEGE

Library, Cranford Avenue, Weymouth, Dorset, DT4 7LQ

Tel: 01305 208820
Fax: 01305 208912
E-mail: library@weymouth.ac.uk

Website:
http://www.weymouth.ac.uk

Enquiries:
Enquiries to: Librarian

Founded:
1985

Organisation type and purpose:
Further education college with some HE courses.

Subject coverage:
Art, biology, classics, business studies, careers, catering, chemistry, computer studies, conservation, construction, engineering, geography, hairdressing, history, literature, maths, physics, physical education, recreation management, sociology, tourism, education, religion, stone carving, beauty, dance, drama, music, management, public services

Museum or gallery collection, archive, or library special collection:
Fleet Study archive

Library catalogue:
All or part available online and in-house

Printed publications:
Resource lists of library stock

Access to staff:
Contact by letter, by telephone, by fax, by e-mail and in person
Hours: Term time: Mon to Thu, 0830 to 2000; Fri, 0830 to 1700; Sat, Sun, closed
Vacations: daily, 0830 to 1700

Access for disabled people:
Level entry, access to all public areas, toilet facilities

WHALE AND DOLPHIN CONSERVATION SOCIETY

Acronym or abbreviation: WDCS

Brookfield House, 38 St Paul Street, Chippenham, Wiltshire, SN15 1LY

Tel: 01249 449500
Fax: 01249 449501
E-mail: info@wdcs.org

Website:
http://www.bluetravel.co.uk
WDCS travel wing/conservation holidays (out of the blue).
http://www.wdcs.org
WDCS homepage.

Founded:
1987

Organisation type and purpose:
Registered charity (charity number 1014705). The global voice for the protection of whales, dolphins and their environment.

Subject coverage:
Conservation of all species of whale, dolphin and porpoise.

Printed publications:
Journey Under the Sea – Getting to Know Orcas and Other Whales, Dolphins and Porpoises (education pack for Key Stages 1–3, includes video and poster)
Various on captivity, fisheries, oil and gas, UK cetaceans, sightings and strandings, whale watching and whaling available as PDF Files from websites

Access to staff:
Contact by letter, by telephone, by fax, by e-mail and via website
Hours: Mon to Fri, 0900 to 1700

WHEELYBOAT TRUST, THE

North Lodge, Burton Park, Petworth, West Sussex, GU28 0JT

Tel: 01798 342222
Fax: 01798 342222
E-mail: wheelyboats@tiscali.co.uk

Website:
http://www.wheelyboats.org
Work of the Trust, wheelyboat locations list.

Enquiries:
Enquiries to: Director

Founded:
1984

Formerly called:
Handicapped Anglers Trust – Boating for the Disabled

Organisation type and purpose:
Registered charity (charity number 292216). Promoting solutions for access by disabled people to fisheries, waterways and other bodies of water.

Subject coverage:
Access by disabled people to fisheries and other waterways. Disability Discrimination Act 1995 – advice on implications of the act on fisheries and other waterways.

Access to staff:
Contact by letter, by telephone, by fax and by e-mail

Hours: Mon to Fri, 0900 to 1700

Access to building, collection or gallery:
No access other than to staff

WHERNSIDE MANOR

Formal name: Whernside Manor Bunkhouses

Cave and Fell Centre, Dent, Sedburgh, Cumbria, LA10 5RE

Tel: 01539 625213
E-mail: whernsidemanor@aol.com

Website:
http://www.whernsidemanor.com

Enquiries:
Enquiries to: Manager

Founded:
2000
Changed ownership (year of change 2000)

Organisation type and purpose:
Historic building, house or site.

Subject coverage:
Caving, walking.

Printed publications:
Leaflets available on request

Access to staff:
Contact by letter. Appointment necessary.
Hours: Mon to Fri, 0900 to 1700

Access to building, collection or gallery:
Prior appointment required

WHICHINTRO.COM

18 Thayer Street, London, W1U 3JY

Tel: 020 7935 6408
Fax: 020 7486 3817
E-mail: info@whichintro.com

Website:
http://www.whichintro.com
Database providing comprehensive details of every organisation offering introductions; advice and guidance to individuals considering joining an agency.

Enquiries:
Enquiries to: Information Officer

Founded:
1970

Formerly called:
Society of Marriage Bureaux (SMB) (year of change 1999)

Organisation type and purpose:
National organisation (membership is by subscription), service industry, research organisation.
Searchable database on all organisations in UK offering introduction services; plus advice and guidance on selecting and using such agencies.

Subject coverage:
Joining a marriage bureau or introductory agency, things to be aware of and alert to, general information about the industry, objective comment on proposed legislation and news items.
Comprehensive information on fees, methodology, specialisms and location of introduction agencies.

Museum or gallery collection, archive, or library special collection:
Many brochures from introduction agencies
Various books on marriage and finding partners

Trade and statistical information:
Number of active agencies; membership numbers; agencies ceasing to trade; new agencies.

Printed publications:
Happily Ever After, advising 30-something young women on relationships (book, available from website)

Electronic and video publications:
Codes of conduct

Watchdog (leaflet, available online to subscribers)

Access to staff:
Contact by letter, by telephone, by e-mail and via website
Hours: Mon to Fri, 0900 to 1700 by telephone.

WHITAKER

Woolmead House West, Bear Lane, Farnham, Surrey, GU9 7LG

Tel: 01252 742500
Fax: 01252 742501

Enquiries:
Enquiries to: Sales Manager

Organisation type and purpose:
Publishing house.

Subject coverage:
Bibliographic files of English language books published in the UK and over 70 other countries which are or were in print and those which are forthcoming.

Trade and statistical information:
Data on the publication of English language titles published in the UK or with a stock holding distributor in the UK.

Printed publications:
The Bookseller (weekly)
Directory of Publishers (annually)
Whitaker's Almanack (annually)
Whitaker's Books in Print (annually)

Microform publications:
ISBN Listing (fiche)
New and Forthcoming (weekly fiche)
Out-of-Print (fiche)
Whitaker's Books in Print (annual fiche)
Whitaker's Book List (fiche)

Electronic and video publications:
BookBank (CD-ROM)
BookBank OP (CD-ROM)
BookBank with SABIP (CD-ROM)
BookBank with ThorpeROM (includes database of Australasian books) (CD-ROM)
Global BookBank (finder) (CD-ROM)
Global BookBank, Premium (CD-ROM)
Whitaker's Books in Print (magnetic tape)

Access to staff:
Contact by letter, by telephone, by fax and by e-mail
Hours: Mon to Fri, 0900 to 1700

Associated with:
BookTrack Limited
  tel: 01252 542555; e-mail: booktrack.info@ booktrack.co.uk
Teleordering Limited

Connections with:
Standard Book Numbering Agency Limited
  12 Dyott Street, London, WC1A 1DF

WHITWELL LOCAL HISTORY GROUP

10 Jubilee Road, Whitwell, Nottinghamshire, S80 4PL

Tel: 01909 723230
E-mail: wlhg@hopkins-uk.co.uk

Website:
http://www.wlhg.co.uk

Enquiries:
Enquiries to: Secretary

Founded:
1986

Organisation type and purpose:
Local history group.

Subject coverage:
Local and national history, allied topics on a variety of subjects.

Education services:
Contact with local school.

Printed publications:
Whitwell Miscellany (journal, occasional)
Whitwell, A Parish History

Access to staff:
Contact by letter, by telephone, by e-mail and via website

WIENER LIBRARY

Formal name: Wiener Library Institute of Contemporary History

4 Devonshire Street, London, W1W 5BH

Tel: 020 7636 7247/8
Fax: 020 7436 6428
E-mail: info@wienerlibrary.co.uk

Website:
http://www.wienerlibrary.co.uk
The oldest Holocaust Library in the world, collecting material on the Holocaust, its causes and legacies.

Enquiries:
Enquiries to: Librarian
Direct e-mail: library@wienerlibrary.co.uk
Other contacts: Senior Librarian

Founded:
1933

Formerly called:
Institute of Contemporary History and Wiener Library; Jewish Central Information Office

Organisation type and purpose:
Registered charity (number 313015), research library, open to the public.
Extensive archive on the Holocaust and Nazi era, with a collection of over 1m. items.

Subject coverage:
Holocaust, Third Reich, fascism, neo-fascism, German-Jewish history, exile and refugee studies, anti-Semitism.

Museum or gallery collection, archive, or library special collection:
Books and pamphlets (c. 60,000)
Periodicals (c. 3,000 titles and 140 current subscriptions)
Document collections (c. 1,300)
Eyewitness accounts (of survivors of the Holocaust)
Photo Archive (over 10,000)
Press Archive

Non-library collection catalogue:
All or part available online

Library catalogue:
All or part available online

Printed publications:
Newsletter (twice a year)

Electronic and video publications:
E-newsletter

Access to staff:
Contact by letter, by telephone, by fax, by e-mail, in person and via website. Letter of introduction required.
Hours: Mon to Fri, 1000 to 1715

Access to building, collection or gallery:
4 steps from the street
Hours: Mon to Fri, 1000 to 1715

Links with:
Institute of Contemporary History

WIGAN ARCHIVES SERVICE

Town Hall, Leigh, Lancashire, WN7 1DY

Tel: 01942 404430
Fax: 01942 404425
E-mail: heritage@wlct.org

Enquiries:
Enquiries to: Archivist

Founded:
1968

Formerly called:
Wigan Record Office

Organisation type and purpose:
Local government body.

Museum or gallery collection, archive, or library special collection:
Archive

Non-library collection catalogue:
All or part available online, in-house and in print

Printed publications:
Guide to the Archives
Genealogical Services

Access to staff:
Contact by letter, by telephone, by fax, by e-mail and in person. Appointment necessary.
Hours: Tue to Thu, 1000 to 1300 and 1400 to 1630

Access to building, collection or gallery:
Prior appointment required
Hours: To view documents: Tue to Thu, 1000 to 1300 and 1400 to 1630

Access for disabled people:
Access to all public areas

Parent body:
Wigan Leisure and Culture Trust
  Department of Leisure; tel: 01942 244991

WIGAN HERITAGE SERVICE

The History Shop, Library Street, Wigan, Lancashire, WN1 1NU

Tel: 01942 828128
Fax: 01942 827645
E-mail: heritage@wlct.org

Enquiries:
Enquiries to: Visitor Services Manager
Other contacts: Collection Department Manager for collections.

Founded:
1992

Organisation type and purpose:
Local government body, museum, suitable for ages: 12+.

Subject coverage:
Local history – all types, genealogy.

Services for disabled people:
Displays and/or information at wheelchair height.

Museum or gallery collection, archive, or library special collection:
Social and industrial history
Family history, parish records, census material

Access to staff:
Contact by letter, by telephone, by fax, by e-mail and in person

Access to building, collection or gallery:
No prior appointment required
Hours: Mon, 1000 to 1900; Tue to Fri, 1000 to 1700; Sat, 1000 to 1300

Access for disabled people:
Ramped entry, toilet facilities
Special comments: Access to ground floor only.

WIGAN LIBRARY

College Avenue, Wigan, Lancashire, WN1 1DQ

Tel: 01942 827621
Fax: 01942 827640
E-mail: wigan.library@wlct.org

Website:
http://www.wlct.org

Enquiries:
Enquiries to: Information Services Officer
Direct tel: 01942 827619

continued overleaf

Organisation type and purpose:
Public library.

Subject coverage:
General subjects.

Museum or gallery collection, archive, or library special collection:
All the following collections now in the Museum of Wigan Life (Heritage Services) or the Central Reserve Store, Leigh Library
Dootson Collection (Lancashire and local history at Leigh Library)
Eckersley Collection and Leyland Collections (personal, general collections at Hindley Library)
Fine Bindings Collection
Incunabula Collection

Non-library collection catalogue:
All or part available online

Library catalogue:
All or part available online

Access to staff:
Contact by letter, by telephone, by fax, by e-mail, in person and via website
Hours: Mon, 1000 to 1830; Tues, Wed, Thu, 0930 To 1830; Fri, 0930 to 1700; Sat, 1000 to 1600
Special comments: Prior arrangement required to consult the Dootson Collection, Incunabula, etc.

Access for disabled people:
Ramped entry, toilet facilities

Parent body:
Wigan Leisure & Culture Trust
Loire Drive, Robin Park, Wigan, WN5 0UL; tel: 01942 828508; fax: 01942 828540; website: http://www.wlct.org

WILCO

Central Library, Regent Circus, Swindon, Wiltshire, SN1 1QG

Tel: 01793 463796/7
Fax: 01793 541319
E-mail: rtrayhurn@swindon.gov.uk

Website:
http://www.wilco.org.uk

Enquiries:
Enquiries to: Secretary
Other contacts: Treasurer

Founded:
1974

Formerly called:
Wiltshire Libraries in Co-operation

Organisation type and purpose:
Local government body, membership association (membership is by election or invitation), present number of members: 20 Full, 10 Associate.
Library co-operative scheme between public, government, academic, research and industrial libraries.

Subject coverage:
Business, commercial and industrial information, standards, journals, reports, serials, monographs, in a wide range of business topics.

Non-library collection catalogue:
All or part available online

Access to staff:
Contact by telephone, by fax and by e-mail.
Access for members only.
Hours: Mon to Fri, 0930 to 1900; Sat, 0930 to 1600

WILDFOWL & WETLANDS TRUST

Acronym or abbreviation: WWT

Slimbridge, Gloucestershire, GL2 7BT

Tel: 01453 891900
Fax: 01453 890827
E-mail: information@wwt.org.uk

Website:
http://www.wwt.org.uk

Enquiries:
Enquiries to: Managing Director
Direct e-mail: marketing@wwt.org.uk

Founded:
1946

Formerly called:
Wildfowl Trust

Organisation type and purpose:
Registered charity (charity number 1030884).
Trust for conservation, education, and research; 8 visitors centres throughout the UK.

Subject coverage:
Conservation of: wildfowl and their habitat, mainly geese, ducks and swans but also considerable data on other waterfowl; wildfowl populations, behaviour, migration, nutrition and disease; breeding of wildfowl; wetlands; ponds, streams, lakes, rivers, marshes, bogs, wet meadows, ecology, management, conservation, aviculture.

Museum or gallery collection, archive, or library special collection:
Library of books and documents on wildfowl and wetlands

Printed publications:
Wildfowl and Wetlands (4 times a year, free to members)
Wildfowl: an annual collection of scientific papers

Publications list:
Available in print

Access to staff:
Contact by letter, by telephone and by fax
Hours: Mon to Fri, 0900 to 1700

Also at:
London Wetland Centre
Queen Elizabeth's Walk, Barnes, London, SW13 9WT; tel: 020 8409 4400; e-mail: info.london@wwt.org.uk
National Wetlands Centre Wales
Llanelli Centre, Penclawydd, Llwynhendy, Llanelli, SA14 9SH; tel: 01554 741087; fax: 01554 744101; e-mail: info.llanelli@wwt.org.uk
Wildfowl & Wetlands Trust
Castle Espie, Ballydrain Road, Comber, Co Down, BT23 6EA; tel: 028 9187 4146; fax: 028 9187 3857; e-mail: info.castleespie@wwt.org.uk
Wildfowl & Wetlands Trust
Pintail House, Hundred Foot Bank, Welney, Wisbech, Cambridgeshire, PE14 9TN; tel: 01353 860711; fax: 01353 860711; e-mail: info.welney@wwt.org.uk
Wildfowl & Wetlands Trust
Martin Mere, Burscough, Ormskirk, Lancashire, L40 0TA; tel: 01704 895181; fax: 01704 892343; e-mail: info.martinmere@wwt.org.uk
Wildfowl & Wetlands Trust
District 15, Washington, Tyne & Wear, NE38 8LE; tel: 0191 416 5454; fax: 0191 416 5801; e-mail: info.washington@wwt.org.uk
Wildfowl & Wetlands Trust
Mill Road, Arundel, West Sussex, BN18 9PB; tel: 01903 883355; fax: 01903 884834; e-mail: info.arundel@wwt.org.uk
Wildfowl & Wetlands Trust
Eastpark Farm, Caerlaverock, Dumfriesshire, DG1 4RS; tel: 01387 770200; fax: 01387 770539; e-mail: info.caerlaverock@wwt.org.uk

Constituent bodies:
Wildfowl & Wetlands Trust (Consulting) Ltd
Slimbridge, Gloucestershire, GL2 7BT; tel: 01453 891905; fax: 01453 890827; e-mail: consulting@wwt.org.uk; website: http://www.wwtconsulting.co.uk
Wildfowl & Wetlands Trust (Property) Ltd

WILDLIFE TRUSTS

The Kiln, Mather Road, Waterside, Newark, Nottinghamshire, NG24 1WT

Tel: 01636 677711
Fax: 01636 670001
E-mail: info@wildlife-trusts.cix.co.uk

Website:
http://www.wildlifetrust.org

Enquiries:
Enquiries to: Information Officer

Founded:
1912

Formerly called:
Royal Society for Nature Conservation

Organisation type and purpose:
Voluntary organisation, registered charity (charity number 207238).
The protection of local countryside and wildlife inhabitants.

Subject coverage:
Nature conservation, protection and enhancement of species and habitats in the UK; wildlife legislation; history of nature conservation; environmental education; membership and work of Wildlife Trusts.

Printed publications:
Annual Report and Accounts
Annual Review
Natural World (3 times a year, members only)
A variety of leaflets, newsletters (free of charge)
Many books for sale including:
Guide to Nature Reserves in Bedfordshire and Cambridgeshire
The Wildlife Trusts' Nature Reserves Guide

Publications list:
Available in print

Access to staff:
Contact by letter, by e-mail and via website
Hours: Mon to Fri, 0900 to 1700

Member of:
European Environment Bureau
International Union for the Conservation of Nature
Wildlife Link

Regional Offices:
Avon Wildlife Trust
Wildlife Centre, 32 Jacob's Wells Road, Bristol, BS8 1DR; tel: 0117 926 8018; fax: 0117 929 7273; e-mail: avonwt@cix.compulink.co.uk
Berkshire, Buckinghamshire & Oxfordshire Wildlife Trust
The Lodge, 1 Armstrong Road, Littlemore, Oxford, OX4 4XT; tel: 01865 775476; fax: 01865 711301; e-mail: bbowt@cix.co.uk
Brecknock Wildlife Trust
Lion House, Bethel Square, Brecon, Powys, LD3 7AY; tel: 01874 625708; fax: 01874 625708; e-mail: brecknockwt@cix.co.uk
Cheshire Wildlife Trust
Grebe House, Reaseheath, Nantwich, Cheshire, CW5 6DG; tel: 01270 610180; fax: 01270 610430; e-mail: cheshirewt@cix.co.uk
Cornwall Wildlife Trust
Five Acres, Aller, Truro, Cornwall, TR4 9DJ; tel: 01872 273939; fax: 01872 225476; e-mail: cornwt@cix.co.uk
Cumbria Wildlife Trust
Brockhole, Windermere, Cumbria, LA23 1LJ; tel: 015394 48280; fax: 015394 48281; e-mail: cumbriawt@cix.co.uk
Derbyshire Wildlife Trust
East Mill, Bridgefoot, Belper, Derby, DE56 1XH; tel: 01773 881188; fax: 01773 821826; e-mail: derbywt@cix.co.uk
Devon Wildlife Trust
Shirehampton House, 35–37 St David's Hill, Exeter, Devon, EX4 4DA; tel: 01392 279244; fax: 01392 433221; e-mail: devonwt@cix.co.uk
Dorset Wildlife Trust
Brooklands Farm, Forston, Dorchester, DT2 7AA; tel: 01305 264620; fax: 01305 251120; e-mail: dorsetwt@cix.co.uk
Durham Wildlife Trust
Rainton Meadows, Chilton Moor, Houghton-le-Spring, Tyne & Wear, DH4 6PU; tel: 0191 584 3112; fax: 0191 584 3934; e-mail: durhamwt@cix.co.uk

Essex Wildlife Trust
  Abbotts Hall Farm, Great Wigborough,
  Colchester, Essex, CO5 7RZ; tel: 01621 862960;
  fax: 01621 862990; e-mail: admin@essexwt.org.uk
Glamorgan Wildlife Trust
  Nature Centre, Fountain Road, Tondu, Bridgend,
  Mid Glamorgan, CF32 0EH; tel: 01656 724100;
  fax: 01656 729880; e-mail: glamorganwt@cix.co
  .uk
Gloucestershire Wildlife Trust
  Dulverton Building, Robinswood Hill Country
  Park, Reservoir Road, Gloucester, GL4 6SX; tel:
  01452 383333; fax: 01452 383334; e-mail: gmcg@
  cix.co.uk
Gwent Wildlife Trust
  16 White Swan Court, Church Street,
  Monmouth, Gwent, NP25 3NY; tel: 01600
  715501; fax: 01600 715832; e-mail:
  gwentwildlife@cix.co.uk
Hampshire & Isle of Wight Wildlife Trust
  Woodside House, Woodside Road, Eastleigh,
  Hampshire, SO50 4ET; tel: 023 8061 3636; fax:
  023 8068 8900; e-mail: hampswt@cix.co.uk
Herefordshire Nature Trust
  Lower House Farm, Ledbury Road, Tupsley,
  Hereford, HR1 1UT; tel: 01432 356872; fax: 01432
  275489; e-mail: herefordwt@cix.co.uk
Hertfordshire & Middlesex Wildlife Trust
  Grebe House, St Michael's Street, St Albans,
  Hertfordshire, AL3 4SN; tel: 01727 858901; fax:
  01727 854542; e-mail: hertswt@cix.co.uk
Kent Wildlife Trust
  Tyland Barn, Sandling, Maidstone, Kent, ME14
  3BD; tel: 01622 662012; fax: 01622 671390; e-mail:
  kentwildlife@cix.co.uk
Lancashire Wildlife Trust
  Cuerdon Park Wildlife Centre, Shady Lane,
  Bamber Bridge, Preston, PR5 6AU; tel: 01772
  324129; fax: 01772 628849
Leicestershire & Rutland Wildlife Trust
  Longfellow Road, Knighton Fields, Leicester,
  LE2 6BT; tel: 01162 702999; fax: 01162 709555; e-
  mail: leicswt@cix.compulink.co.uk
Lincolnshire Wildlife Trust
  Banovallum House, Manor House Street,
  Horncastle, Lincolnshire, LN9 5HF; tel: 01507
  526667; fax: 01507 525732; e-mail: lincstrust@cix
  .compulink.co.uk
London Wildlife Trust
  Harling House, 47–51 Great Suffolk Street,
  London, SE1 0BS; tel: 020 7261 0447; fax: 020
  7261 0538; e-mail: londonwt@cix.compulink.co
  .uk
Manx Wildlife Trust
  Conservation Centre, The Courtyard, Tynwald
  Mills, St Johns, Isle of Man; tel: 01624 801985;
  fax: 01624 801022; e-mail: manxwt@cix.co.uk
Montgomeryshire Wildlife Trust
  Collott House, 20 Severn Street, Welshpool,
  Powys, SY21 7AD; tel: 01938 555654; fax: 01938
  556161; e-mail: montwt@cix.compulink.co.uk
Norfolk Wildlife Trust
  72 Cathedral Close, Norwich, Norfolk, NR1 4DF;
  tel: 01603 625540; fax: 01603 630593; e-mail:
  nwt@cix.compulink.co.uk
North Wales Wildlife Trust
  376 High Street, Bangor, Gwynedd, LL57 1YE;
  tel: 01248 351541; fax: 01248 353192; e-mail:
  nwwt@cix.compulink.co.uk
Northumberland Wildlife Trust
  The Garden House, St Nicholas Park, Jubilee
  Road, Newcastle upon Tyne, NE3 3XT; tel: 0191
  284 6884; fax: 0191 284 6794; e-mail:
  northwdlife@cix.compulink.co.uk
Nottinghamshire Wildlife Trust
  The Old Ragged School, Brook Street,
  Nottingham, NG1 1EA; tel: 0115 958 8242; fax:
  0115 924 3175; e-mail: nottswt@cix.compulink.co
  .uk
Radnorshire Wildlife Trust
  Warwick House, High Street, Llandrindod Wells,
  Powys, LD1 6AG; tel: 01597 823298; fax: 01597
  823274; e-mail: radnorshirewt@cix.compulink.co
  .uk

Scottish Wildlife Trust
  Crammond House, Kirk Crammond, Crammond
  Glebe Road, Edinburgh, EH4 6NS; tel: 0131 312
  7765; fax: 0131 312 8705; e-mail: scottishwt@cix
  .compulink.co.uk
Sheffield Wildlife Trust
  37 Stafford Road, Sheffield, S2 2FS; tel: 0114 263
  4335; fax: 0114 263 4345; e-mail: sheffieldwt@cix
  .co.uk
Shropshire Wildlife Trust
  193 Abbey Foregate, Shrewsbury, Shropshire; tel:
  01743 284280; fax: 01743 284281; e-mail:
  shropshirewt@cix.co.uk
Somerset Wildlife Trust
  Fyne Court, Broomfield, Bridgwater, Somerset,
  TA5 2EQ; tel: 01823 451587; fax: 01823 451671; e-
  mail: somwt@cix.co.uk
Staffordshire Wildlife Trust
  Coutts House, Sandon, Staffordshire, ST18 0DN;
  tel: 01889 508534; fax: 01889 508422; e-mail:
  staffswt@cix.co.uk
Suffolk Wildlife Trust
  Brooke House, The Green, Ashbocking, Ipswich,
  Suffolk, IP6 9JY; tel: 01473 890089; fax: 01473
  890165; e-mail: suffolkwt@cix.co.uk
Surrey Wildlife Trust
  School Lane, Pirbright, Woking, Surrey, GU24
  0JN; tel: 01483 488055; fax: 01483 486505; e-mail:
  surreywt@cix.co.uk
Sussex Wildlife Trust
  Woods Mill, Shoreham Road, Henfield, West
  Sussex, BN5 9SD; tel: 01273 492630; fax: 01273
  494500; e-mail: sussexwt@cix.co.uk
Tees Valley Wildlife Trust
  Bellamy Pavilion, Kirkleatham Old Hall,
  Kirkleatham, Redcar, Cleveland, TS10 5NW; tel:
  01642 759900; fax: 01642 480401; e-mail:
  clevelandwt@cix.co.uk
Ulster Wildlife Trust
  3 New Line, Crossgar, Co Down, BT30 9EP; tel:
  028 9083 0282; fax: 028 9083 0888; e-mail:
  ulsterwt@cix.co.uk
Warwickshire Wildlife Trust
  Brandon Marsh Nature Centre, Brandon Lane,
  Coventry, CV3 3GW; tel: 01203 302912; fax:
  01203 639556; e-mail: warkswt@cix.co.uk
Wildlife Trust for Bedfordshire, Cambridgeshire,
Northamptonshire and Peterborough
  3B Langford Arch, London Road, Sawston,
  Cambridge, CB2 4EE; tel: 01223 712400; fax:
  01223 712412; e-mail: cambswt@cix.co.uk
Wildlife Trust for Birmingham & Black Country
  Unit 310, Jubilee Trade Centre, 130 Pershore
  Street, Birmingham, B5 6ND; tel: 0121 666 7474;
  fax: 0121 622 4443; e-mail: urbanwt@cix.co.uk
Wildlife Trust: West Wales
  7 Market Street, Haverfordwest, Dyfed, SA61
  1NF; tel: 01437 765462; fax: 01437 767163; e-mail:
  wildlife@wildlife-wales.org.uk
Wiltshire Wildlife Trust
  Elm Tree Court, Long Street, Devizes, Wiltshire,
  SN10 1NH; tel: 01380 725670; fax: 01380 729017;
  e-mail: wiltswt@cix.co.uk
Worcestershire Wildlife Trust
  Lower Smite Farm, Smite Hill, Hindlip,
  Worcester, WR3 8SZ; tel: 01905 754919; fax:
  01905 755868; e-mail: worcswt@cix.co.uk
Yorkshire Wildlife Trust
  10 Toft Green, York, YO1 6JT; tel: 01904 659570;
  fax: 01904 613467; e-mail: yorkshirewt@cix.co.uk

The national association of UK's:
Urban Wildlife Groups
Wildlife Trusts
Wildlife Watch (the junior branch)

WILDLIFE WATCH

The Kiln, Waterside, Mather Road, Newark,
Nottinghamshire, NG24 1WT

Tel: 0870 036 7711
Fax: 0870 036 0101
E-mail: watch@wildlife-trusts.cix.co.uk

Website:
http://www.wildlifetrusts.org/watch

Enquiries:
Enquiries to: Development Officer

Direct e-mail: arawson@wildlife-trusts.cix.co.uk
Other contacts: Membership Officer

Founded:
1971

Formerly called:
Watch Trust for Environmental Education, Wildlife
WATCH

Organisation type and purpose:
Membership association (membership is by
subscription), present number of members: 20,000,
voluntary organisation, registered charity (charity
number 207238), suitable for ages: 7 to 14.
Junior Branch of The Wildlife Trust.
To encourage young people to investigate and help
solve environmental problems.

Subject coverage:
Nature conservation, environmental education,
activities and projects, advice to teachers and
educationalists, site interpretation via local
Wildlife Trusts.

Printed publications:
Wildlife Extra – An A4 children's magazine that
  folds out to a full-colour poster (£1.20)
Wildlife Extra – Compost Café: Composting and
  the life in your compost heap (£1.20)
Wildlife Extra – Butterfly Bonanza: A look at how
  to attract butterflies to your garden (£1.20)
Wildlife Extra – Pondemonium: Taking action for
  amphibians (£1.20)
Wildlife Extra – Water For Life: How to avoid
  wasting water (£1.20)
Wildlife Extra – Twilight Zone: Bat stars of the
  night sky (£1.20)
Wildlife Extra – Snug as Bugs: The winter survival
  challenge of minibeasts (£1.20)
Watchword (magazine, £1.80)
Ready For Action? (leaflet on Wildlife Watch and
  its club for animal fans, etc., children aged 8–14,
  SAE)
Watch Activity Books (£5 each, £22.50 for set of 5)
Young Voices – Turning ideas into action (£7.50)
Rescuing Ratty (1999, free)
Various factsheets (free; 5 or more implies a
  donation of £1 towards postage)

Publications list:
Available in print

Access to staff:
Contact by letter, by telephone, by fax, by e-mail
and via website. Appointment necessary.
Hours: Mon to Fri, 0900 to 1700

WILKIE COLLINS SOCIETY

Acronym or abbreviation: WCS

21 Huson Close, London, NW3 3JW

E-mail: apogee@apgee.co.uk

Website:
http://www.wilkie-collins.info/
wilkie_collins_society.htm

Enquiries:
Enquiries to: Chairman
Other contacts: Membership Secretary
(paul@paullewis.co.uk)

Founded:
1980

Organisation type and purpose:
International organisation, membership
association (membership is by subscription),
present number of members: 145.
To foster interest in the life and works of Wilkie
Collins.

Subject coverage:
Wilkie Collins: biographical, literary works.

Printed publications:
Reprints of out-of-print Collins short pieces (free
  with membership or for separate purchase)
Journal (annually, free with membership or for
  separate purchase)
Newsletters (3 times a year, free with membership
  or for separate purchase)

continued overleaf

Order printed publications from: Membership Secretary, Wilkie Collins Society, 4 Ernest Gardens, London, W4 3QU; e-mail paul@paullewis.co.uk

Publications list:
Available in print

Access to staff:
Contact by letter and by e-mail
Hours: Mon to Fri, 0900 to 1700

Links with:
Alliance of Literary Societies

WILLIAM COBBETT SOCIETY

c/o Charles Stuart, 6 Lynch Road, Farnham, Surrey, GU9 8BZ

Website:
http://www.williamcobbett.org.uk

Enquiries:
Enquiries to: Chairman
Direct tel: 01252 722947
Direct e-mail: charles-stuart3@talktalk.net
Other contacts: Honorary Membership Secretary (for details of membership)

Founded:
1976

Organisation type and purpose:
Learned society.

Subject coverage:
Life, times and writings of William Cobbett, 1763–1835.

Museum or gallery collection, archive, or library special collection:
Complete set of Cobbett's State Trials
Complete set of political registers 1802–31
Large collection of books by and about Cobbett

Printed publications:
The Life of William Cobbett by Himself
Cobbett's New Register
William Cobbett in America (Molly Townsend)
Anne Cobbett's Account of the Family
The Jolly Farmer: William Cobbett in Hampshire 1804–20

Publications list:
Available online and in print

Access to staff:
Contact by letter, by telephone and by e-mail
Hours: Mon to Fri, 0900 to 1700

Also at:
Honorary Membership Secretary
  1 Meadow View, Spring Grove, Burlesdon, SO31 8BB; tel: 023 8045 5848

WILLIAM HARVEY LIBRARY

GETEC, George Eliot Hospital NHS Trust, College Street, Nuneaton, Warwickshire, CV10 7DJ

Tel: 024 7686 5464
E-mail: library@geh.nhs.uk

Enquiries:
Enquiries to: Library Services Manager
Other contacts: Clinical Librarian

Formerly called:
George Eliot Postgraduate Education Centre Library (year of change 2006)

Organisation type and purpose:
National Health Service.

Subject coverage:
Medicine, nursing, allied health, mental health, health management.

Library catalogue:
All or part available online

Access to staff:
Contact by letter, by telephone and by e-mail.
Access for members only. Non-members charged.
Hours: Mon to Thu, 0830 to 1700; Fri, 0830 to 1630

Access to building, collection or gallery:
Hours: Mon to Fri, 0800 to 1700
Special comments: Outside normal opening hours access is by staff swipe card.

Access for disabled people:
Toilet facilities

WILLIAM MORRIS SOCIETY

Kelmscott House, 26 Upper Mall, Hammersmith, London, W6 9TA

Tel: 020 8741 3735
Fax: 020 8748 5207
E-mail: william.morris@care4free.net

Website:
http://www.morrissociety.org
Information on Morris's life and work, including photographs and links to related sites.

Enquiries:
Enquiries to: Curator

Founded:
1956

Formerly called:
Kelmscott Fellowship, William Morris Society

Organisation type and purpose:
Learned society (membership is by subscription), present number of members: 1,500, voluntary organisation, registered charity (charity number 261437), museum.

Subject coverage:
The life and works of William Morris, his associates and successors in art, craft, design, literature and politics.

Museum or gallery collection, archive, or library special collection:
Library of work by and about William Morris, his associates and followers

Non-library collection catalogue:
All or part available in-house

Library catalogue:
All or part available in-house

Printed publications:
Journal (twice a year, members only)
A range of titles on William Morris, his life and works including:
A History of Kelmscott House (Elletson, H, 2009, £5.00)
Red House – A Guide (1993, £3.95)
The Story of Kormak, the Son of Ogmund (Morris, William & Magnusson, Eirikir, £10)
Three William Morris Songs for soprano and piano (1990, £3)
William Morris and the Printed Book (Kelmscott Lecture, 1986, £5)

Publications list:
Available in print

Access to staff:
Contact by letter, by telephone, by fax, by e-mail, in person and via website
Hours: Thu and Sat, 1400 to 1700

Access to building, collection or gallery:
No access other than to staff
Hours: Thu & Sat, 1400 to 1700

Access for disabled people:
Level entry, toilet facilities

WILLIAM REED PUBLISHING LIMITED

Broadfield Park, Crawley, West Sussex, RH11 9RT

Tel: 01293 613400
Fax: 01293 610322

Website:
http://www.products-online.co.uk
http://www.william-reed.co.uk

Enquiries:
Enquiries to: Information Officer

Founded:
1862

Organisation type and purpose:
Publishing house.

Subject coverage:
Food and drink manufacturing, retailing, distribution, food and drink industry, petrol forecourt shops, shopping centres; some European coverage.

Museum or gallery collection, archive, or library special collection:
Complete runs of journals published eg The Grocer 1865 to date, Off Licence News, Convenience Store, Forecourt Trader, Shopping Centre

Trade and statistical information:
Food Marketing Database.

Printed publications:
Directories, Guides and Reports on the food, drink and retail industries, including:
Food & Drink From Britain Buyers Guide
Shopping Centre & Retail Directory
The Grocer Food & Drink Manufacturers & Suppliers
The Grocer Directory of Non Food Manufacturers & Suppliers
The Mardek Guide to the UK Catering Industry
The Mardek Guide to the UK Grocery Retailers
The Grocer (weekly £60 a year)
Order printed publications from: website http://www.products-online.co.uk

Publications list:
Available online and in print

Access to staff:
Contact by telephone and by e-mail. Appointment necessary. All charged.
Hours: Mon to Fri, 1100 to 1600

WILLIAM SALT LIBRARY

19 Eastgate Street, Stafford, ST16 2LZ

Tel: 01785 278372
Fax: 01785 278414
E-mail: william.salt.library@staffordshire.gov.uk

Website:
http://www.staffordshire.gov.uk/salt.htm

Enquiries:
Enquiries to: Librarian

Founded:
1872

Organisation type and purpose:
Registered charity (charity number 528570). The library aims to preserve printed books, manuscripts, pamphlets and illustrative material relating to Staffordshire for future generations.

Subject coverage:
Staffordshire local history.

Museum or gallery collection, archive, or library special collection:
Collections relating to Staffordshire history, including parish and family histories, topographical histories, pictorial collections, pamphlets, newspapers, periodicals, manuscripts and notes

Non-library collection catalogue:
All or part available online and in-house

Library catalogue:
All or part available online and in-house

Access to staff:
Contact by letter, by telephone, by fax, by e-mail, in person and via website

Access to building, collection or gallery:
No prior appointment required
Hours: Tue to Thu, 0900 to 1300 and 1400 to 1700; Fri, 0930 to 1300 and 1400 to 1630; first Sat in each month, 0900 to 1300; closed Mon
Special comments: Reader's ticket is required. No children under age of 11 unless accompanied by an adult. Reader registration system is in operation.

Links with:
Staffordshire Record Office
  Eastgate Street, Stafford, ST16 2LZ; tel: 01785
  278379; fax: 01785 278384

WILLIAM SNYDER PUBLISHING ASSOCIATES

5 Five Mile Drive, Oxford, OX2 8HT

Tel: 01865 513186
Fax: 01865 513186
E-mail: snyderpub@aol.com

Website:
http://www.hoovers-europe.com

Enquiries:
Enquiries to: Managing Director

Founded:
1992

Organisation type and purpose:
Publishing house.

Subject coverage:
Distributer of business, health and general
reference publications

Library catalogue:
All or part available online and in print

Printed publications:
International business directories, mainly from
  America, and some from UK, Europe and the
  world
Titles covering international business
Europe's 15,000 Largest Companies (also on CD-
  ROM)
Asia's 10,000 Largest Companies (also on CD-
  ROM)
UK's 5,000 Largest Companies (also on CD-ROM)
Europe's Largest Banks Corporate Snapshots

Electronic and video publications:
Europe's 15,000 Largest Companies (for use on
  user's own databases, wordprocessing or
  spreadsheets)

Publications list:
Available online and in print

Access to staff:
Contact by letter, by telephone, by fax, by e-mail
and via website

WILTSHIRE & SWINDON USERS NETWORK

Formal name: Wiltshire Community Care User
Involvement Network
Acronym or abbreviation: WCCUIN

The Independent Living Centre, St George's Road,
Semington, BA14 6JQ

Tel: 01380 871800
Fax: 01380 871507
E-mail: adminwsun@btconnect.com

Website:
http://www.wsun.co.uk

Founded:
1993

Organisation type and purpose:
Voluntary organisation.
Service-user controlled organisation.

Subject coverage:
User involvement in all aspects of community care.

Printed publications:
I am in Control – a report of user-controlled
  research into disabled people's views of Wiltshire
  Independent Living Fund (£5)
From Bobble Hats to Red Jackets – A history of the
  first 5 years of Wiltshire and Swindon Users
  Network (Evans, C C)
Tall oaks from little acorns – an account of user
  participation in care management training
  (Evans and Hughes, £3.50)

The Trowbridge Experience – A guide to involving
  older people and their carers in planning of local
  health and social core services

Publications list:
Available in print

Access to staff:
Contact by letter
Hours: Mon to Fri, 0900 to 1700

WILTSHIRE AND SWINDON RECORD OFFICE

Formal name: Wiltshire and Swindon Archives
Acronym or abbreviation: WSA

Wiltshire and Swindon History Centre,
Cocklebury Road, Chippenham SN15 3QN

Tel: 01249 705500
Fax: 01249 705527
E-mail: archives@wiltshire.gov.uk

Website:
http://www.wshc.eu

Enquiries:
Enquiries to: Archivist

Founded:
1947

Organisation type and purpose:
Local authority-funded archive service.

Non-library collection catalogue:
All or part available online and in-house

Access to staff:
Contact by letter, by telephone, by fax, by e-mail
and in person
Hours: Tue to Sat, 0930 to 1730

Access for disabled people:
Good disabled access

WILTSHIRE ARCHAEOLOGICAL AND NATURAL HISTORY SOCIETY

Acronym or abbreviation: WANHS

Wiltshire Heritage Museum, 41 Long Street,
Devizes, Wiltshire, SN10 1NS

Tel: 01380 727369
Fax: 01380 722150
E-mail: wanhs@wiltshireheritage.org.uk

Website:
http://www.wiltshireheritage.org.uk
Website database of collections and information
about exhibitions and events.

Enquiries:
Enquiries to: Director
Direct e-mail: david.dawson@wiltshireheritage.org
.uk

Founded:
1853

Organisation type and purpose:
Learned society (membership is by subscription),
present number of members: c. 1,000, registered
charity (charity number 1080096), museum.

Subject coverage:
Archaeology, natural history and local history of
the county of Wiltshire; prehistoric, Roman and
medieval antiquities; family history, biological
records, etc.

Information services:
Research archive and library, with extensive
collections about the archaeology, history and
natural history of Wiltshire.

Services for disabled people:
The Archive and Library is on the first floor, so it is
not easily accessible to those with mobility
impairments, but there is a dedicated research area
on the ground floor available on request.

**Museum or gallery collection, archive, or library
special collection:**
Designated as being of national significance, with
  important archaeological collections from the
  Stonehenge and Avebury World Heritage Site, as
  well as natural history and art collections.

Non-library collection catalogue:
All or part available online, in-house and in print

Library catalogue:
All or part available in-house

Printed publications:
Wiltshire Archaeological and Natural History
  Magazine (the county's archaeological journal,
  published annually)
Trilithon newsletter and Annual Reports
A range of other monographs about the history
  and archaeology of the County
Order printed publications from: Website and direct
from the Museum

Publications list:
Available online

Access to staff:
Contact by letter, by telephone, by e-mail and via
website
Hours: Mon to Fri, 0900 to 1700

Access to building, collection or gallery:
Hours: Mon to Sat, 1000 to 1700; Sun, 1200 to 1600
Special comments: Library open Tue to Fri, 1000 to
1700; Sat, 1000 to 1700; closed 1st Sat of every
month

WILTSHIRE ASSOCIATION OF LOCAL COUNCILS

Acronym or abbreviation: WALC

Wyndhams, St Josephs Place, Devizes, Wiltshire,
SN10 1DD

Tel: 01380 729549
Fax: 01380 728476
E-mail: office@wiltshire-alc.org.uk

Website:
http://www.wiltshire-alc.org.uk/

Enquiries:
Enquiries to: County Secretary
Direct tel: 01380 729549
Other contacts: Local Councils' Adviser

Organisation type and purpose:
Advisory body, membership association
(membership is by subscription), present number
of members: 220.

Access to staff:
Contact by letter and by e-mail
Hours: Mon to Fri, 0930 to 1530

WILTSHIRE COLLEGE

The Learning Resources Centre, Southampton
Road, Salisbury, Wiltshire, SP1 2LW

Tel: 01722 344325; minicom no. 01722 344307
Fax: 01722 344345
E-mail: lrc_sa@wiltshire.ac.uk

Website:
http://www.wiltshire.ac.uk

Enquiries:
Enquiries to: Senior LRC Team Leader
Direct e-mail: sandy.black@wiltshire.ac.uk
Other contacts: Library Learning Assistants (for
general enquiries regarding bookstock and loans)

Created by the merger of:
Salisbury College and Wiltshire College (year of
change 2008)

Organisation type and purpose:
Suitable for ages: 16+.
College Learning Resources Centre.

Subject coverage:
Computing and administration, management
studies, basic and key skills, built environment,
foundation studies, technology and science,

continued overleaf

information technology, performing arts, humanities, social sciences, fashion, art and design, graphics, film, TV and media, health and social care, food and hospitality, tourism, leisure and recreation, construction crafts, hairdressing, beauty therapy, business studies, teacher education.

Non-library collection catalogue:
All or part available online and in-house

Library catalogue:
All or part available online and in-house

Access to staff:
Contact by letter, by telephone, by fax, by e-mail, in person and via website. Appointment necessary. Non-members charged.
Hours: Mon, 0845 to 1700; Tue and Wed, 0845 to 2000; Thu, 0845 to 1830; Fri, 1000 to 1615

Access for disabled people:
Parking provided, access to all public areas, toilet facilities

WILTSHIRE COLLEGE LACKHAM

Library & Learning Resources, Lacock, Chippenham, Wiltshire, SN15 2NY

Tel: 01249 466800
Fax: 01249 444474
E-mail: lackham@wiltscoll.ac.uk

Website:
http://www.wiltscoll.ac.uk

Enquiries:
Enquiries to: Manager Library and Learning Resources
Direct tel: 01249 466814
Direct e-mail: obrihn@wiltscoll.ac.uk

Founded:
1946

Formed by the merger of:
Lackham College of Agriculture Library; Lackham College Library (year of change 2001)

Organisation type and purpose:
College of further education.

Subject coverage:
Agriculture; agricultural economics, horticulture, small animal care, land-based industries, equine studies.

Non-library collection catalogue:
All or part available online

Library catalogue:
All or part available online

Access to staff:
Contact by telephone and by e-mail
Hours: Mon, to Thu, 0845 to 1700; Fri, 1000 to 1700

Access to building, collection or gallery:
Prior appointment required

Access for disabled people:
Lift, toilet facilities

Other addresses:
Wiltshire College Chippenham
   Cocklebury Road, Chippenham, Wiltshire, SN15 3QD; tel: 01249 464644; e-mail: chippenham@wiltscoll.ac.uk
Wiltshire College Trowbridge
   College Road, Trowbridge, Wiltshire, BA14 0ES; tel: 01225 766241; e-mail: trowbridge@wiltscoll.ac.uk

WILTSHIRE COUNTY COUNCIL LIBRARIES AND HERITAGE

Library Headquarters, Community Services Department, Bythesea Road, Trowbridge, Wiltshire, BA14 8BS

Tel: 01225 713701
Fax: 01225 713993
E-mail: libraryenquiries@wiltshire.gov.uk

Website:
http://www.wiltshire.gov.uk

Library catalogue, CI database.

Enquiries:
Enquiries to: Information Manager

Organisation type and purpose:
Local government body, public library.

Subject coverage:
Archaeology of Wiltshire; Christology; conservation of moveable objects of archaeological and historical significance; museums and museology; Wiltshire local studies; European information.

Museum or gallery collection, archive, or library special collection:
David Long Collection
Early English Children's Books
Tatham Collection of Girls' School Stories
Wiltshire Collection

Library catalogue:
All or part available online

Electronic and video publications:
Community Information Database with over 9,000 contact names and addresses
Sites and Monuments Database
Museum Objects Database

Access to staff:
Contact by letter, by telephone, by fax, by e-mail, in person and via website
Hours: Admin: Mon to Fri, 0900 to 1700

Access to building, collection or gallery:
No prior appointment required

Branch libraries:
Chippenham Public Library
   tel: 01249 650536; fax: 01249 443793
Devizes Public Library
   tel: 01380 726878; fax: 01380 722161
Salisbury Public Library
   tel: 01722 324145; fax: 01722 413214

Parent body:
Wiltshire County Council

WILTSHIRE EDUCATION & LIBRARIES

Salisbury Library and Galleries, Market Place, Salisbury, Wiltshire, SP1 1BL

Tel: 01722 324145
Fax: 01722 413214

Website:
http://www.wiltshire.gov.uk
Full county website.
http://www.wiltshire.gov.uk/library
Online catalogue, renewals, reservations and information.

Enquiries:
Enquiries to: District Librarian
Direct tel: 01722 330606
Direct e-mail: chrisharling@wiltshire.gov.uk
Other contacts: Art Curator, tel: 01722 410614; Reference and Local Studies Library, tel: 01722 411098

Formerly called:
Wiltshire Library and Museum Service

Organisation type and purpose:
Local government body, art gallery, public library.

Subject coverage:
History of Salisbury and Wiltshire; arts; general subjects.

Museum or gallery collection, archive, or library special collection:
Edwin Young Watercolour collection – Victorian watercolours of Salisbury
Creasey Collection of contemporary art
Robin Tonner Collection – 1930s Children's Art
Edgar Barclay Collection – Victorian paintings of Stonehenge
Jerram Collection of Bellringing Books (Guild of Campanologists Collection of books and documents, many hand-annotated, formerly in the Sowter Clerical Library)

John Creasey Literary Museum

Library catalogue:
All or part available online

Printed publications:
Business Key leaflet, and many others
For under 5s: What's On? and Education Fact Sheets (free)

Access to staff:
Contact by letter, by telephone, by fax, in person and via website
Hours: Mon to Fri, 0900 to 1700

Access for disabled people:
Level entry
Special comments: Level entry via side entrance.

Member of:
WILCO

Parent body:
Wiltshire County Council

WILTSHIRE FAMILY HISTORY SOCIETY

10 Castle Lane, Devizes, Wiltshire, SN10 1HJ

E-mail: society@wiltshirefhs.co.uk

Website:
http://www.wiltshire.fhs.co.uk
http://www.genfair.com

Enquiries:
Other contacts: Membership Secretary; Research Co-ordinator

Founded:
1981

Organisation type and purpose:
Membership association (membership is by subscription), present number of members: 2600, voluntary organisation, registered charity (charity number 290284), suitable for ages: adults, research organisation.

Subject coverage:
Family and local history in Wiltshire.

Non-library collection catalogue:
All or part available online and in-house

Library catalogue:
All or part available in-house

Printed publications:
Wiltshire Family History Society Journal
Local Censuses in Wiltshire
Parish Registers

Microform publications:
Bishop's Marriage Licence Bonds
Parish Registers
Wiltshire Apprentices
Early Censuses (various in the period 1695–1887)
1851 Census Surname Index
Wiltshire Strays

Publications list:
Available online and in print

Access to staff:
Contact by letter and by e-mail. Appointment necessary. All charged.
Hours: Variable

Access to building, collection or gallery:
Prior appointment required
Hours: By arrangement

Access for disabled people:
Special comments: By arrangement.

WILTSHIRE LIBRARIES AND HERITAGE

Libraries and Heritage Branch, Corporate & Library Services Department, Bythesea Road, Trowbridge, Wiltshire, BA14 8BS

Tel: 01225 713700
Fax: 01225 713993
E-mail: libraryenquiries@wiltshire.gov.uk

Enquiries:
Enquiries to: Head of Libraries and Heritage Branch

Organisation type and purpose:
Local government body.
Museums Service.

Subject coverage:
Wiltshire County Historic Photograph Collection.

Museum or gallery collection, archive, or library special collection:
Wiltshire County Historic Photograph Collection, 35,000 records
Museum Objects Database, 155,000 records

Non-library collection catalogue:
All or part available in-house

Library catalogue:
All or part available online and in-house

Electronic and video publications:
Museum Objects Database, 155,000 records
Historic Photograph Database, 35,000 records

Access to staff:
Contact by letter, by telephone, by fax and by e-mail
Hours: Mon to Fri, 0900 to 1700

Access to building, collection or gallery:
No prior appointment required
Hours: Mon, Thu, Fri, 0900 to 1900; Tue, 0900 to 1700; Wed, 1000 to 1700; Sat, 0900 to 1600

Access for disabled people:
Parking provided, level entry, access to all public areas, toilet facilities

Parent body:
Wiltshire County Council

WILTSHIRE MUSIC CENTRE

Formal name: Wiltshire Music Centre Trust Limited

Ashley Road, Bradford-on-Avon, Wiltshire, BA15 1DZ

Tel: 01225 860110; Box Office: 01225 860100
Fax: 01225 860111
E-mail: enquiries@wiltsmusiccentre.fsnet.co.uk

Website:
http://www.wiltshiremusic.org.uk

Enquiries:
Enquiries to: Operations Manager
Direct e-mail: info@wiltshiremusic.org.uk

Organisation type and purpose:
Registered charity (charity number 1026160).
Purpose-built concert hall and music centre.
Music education, performance, recording and creation.

Subject coverage:
The Wiltshire Music Centre Trust has three closely related objectives: the advancement of music education for all ages and levels of ability, in and around the county of Wiltshire, placing the work of young musicians at the heart of this programme; the development of a high quality, varied and stimulating programme in terms of the scope of activity, breadth of musical cultures and range of people involved; to work with artists, other arts organisations and arts development agencies to achieve sustainable growth in participation, the development of audiences and of the art form.

Printed publications:
Available, free

Publications list:
Available in print

Access to staff:
Contact by letter, by telephone, by fax, by e-mail and in person
Hours: Mon to Fri, 0900 to 1800

Access for disabled people:
Parking provided, ramped entry, level entry, toilet facilities
Special comments: Infrared sound relay system; access to all areas on ground floor.

WILTSHIRE RECORD SOCIETY

Acronym or abbreviation: WRS

Wiltshire and Swindon History Centre,
Cocklebury Road, Chippenham, SN15 3QN

Tel: 01249 705500
Fax: 01249 705527
E-mail: stevenhobbs@wiltshire.gov.uk

Enquiries:
Enquiries to: Secretary
Direct e-mail: james5.lee@uwe.ac.uk

Founded:
1936

Organisation type and purpose:
Learned society.
Originated as a branch of the Wiltshire Archaeological and Natural History Society but autonomous since 1964.

Subject coverage:
The publication of Wiltshire's historical archives.

Printed publications:
Vol. of edited historical records (63 to date, annually)

Publications list:
Available in print

WIMBLEDON COLLEGE OF ART

Main Building, Merton Hall Road, London, SW19 3QA

Tel: 020 7514 9641
Fax: 020 7514 9642

Website:
http://www.wimbledon.arts.ac.uk
Learning Resources Centre information (Library, Slide Library, IT Centre) and link to Library catalogue.

Enquiries:
Enquiries to: Head of Learning and Information Resources
Direct tel: 020 8408 5039
Direct e-mail: pjennett@wimbledon.ac.uk

Founded:
1963

Formerly called:
Wimbledon School of Art (year of change 2006)

Organisation type and purpose:
Independent art school.

Subject coverage:
Fine art, art history, scenography, costume history, dramatic literature.

Museum or gallery collection, archive, or library special collection:
Books, journals and video tapes, slides, CD-ROM databases

Library catalogue:
All or part available online

Access to staff:
Contact by letter, by telephone, by fax and by e-mail. Appointment necessary.
Hours: Mon to Thu, 1000 to 2030; Fri, 1000 to 1930

Access to building, collection or gallery:
Prior appointment required
Hours: Mon to Thu, 1000 to 2030; Fri, 1000 to 1930

Access for disabled people:
Parking provided

Parent body:
University of the Arts London

WIMBLEDON LIBRARY

Wimbledon Hill Road, London, SW19 7NB

Tel: 020 8274 5758 (central reference library)
Fax: 020 8944 6804
E-mail: wimbledon.library@merton.gov.uk

Website:
http://www.merton.gov.uk/learning/libraries/findalibrary/wimlib.htm

Enquiries:
Enquiries to: Librarian

Organisation type and purpose:
Public library.

Subject coverage:
General.

Museum or gallery collection, archive, or library special collection:
Local studies – materials for the study of Wimbledon, Mitcham, Morden and Merton at Local Studies Centre

Non-library collection catalogue:
All or part available online and in-house

Library catalogue:
All or part available in-house

Printed publications:
Order printed publications from: Local Studies Centre, Morden Library, London Road, Morden, Surrey, SM4 5DX; tel: 020 8545 3239; fax: 020 8545 4037

Access to staff:
Contact by letter, by telephone, by fax, by e-mail and in person
Hours: Mon, Tue, Thu, Fri, 0930 to 1900; Wed, 0930 to 1300; Sat, 0930 to 1700

Access to building, collection or gallery:
No prior appointment required

Access for disabled people:
Level entry, toilet facilities

Central reference library for:
Merton Library Service

Local studies centre at:
Morden Library
Merton Civic Centre, London Road, Morden, Surrey, SM4 5DX; tel: 020 8545 3239; fax: 020 8545 4037

WINCHESTER CITY COUNCIL

City Offices, Colebrook Street, Winchester, Hampshire, SO23 9LJ

Tel: 01962 840222
Fax: 01962 841365
E-mail: info@winchester.gov.uk

Website:
http://www.winchester.gov.uk
Information on council services.

Enquiries:
Enquiries to: Information Officer

Organisation type and purpose:
Local government body.
Provision of local government services to 110,000 residents in the City Council district, which covers 250 sq miles.

Access to staff:
Contact by letter, by telephone, by fax, by e-mail, in person and via website
Hours: Mon to Fri, 0900 to 1700

WINCHESTER MUSEUMS

Winchester City Council, City Offices, Colebrook Street, Winchester SO23 9LJ

Tel: 01962 848269
E-mail: museums@winchester.gov.uk

Website:
http://www.winchester.gov.uk/LeisureAndCulture/MuseumsAndGalleries

Enquiries:
Enquiries to: Head of Museums
Direct tel: 01962 848396
Direct e-mail: gdenford@winchester.gov.uk
Other contacts: Education Officer

continued overleaf

Founded:
1847

Organisation type and purpose:
Local government body, museum, art gallery, historic building, house or site, suitable for ages: all.

Subject coverage:
Winchester Museums is responsible for public galleries at the City Museum, Westgate Museum and City Space. The Historic Environment Centre exists for those visitors and researchers wishing to consult the collections and staff: this is by appointment only.

Special visitor services:
Materials and/or activities for children.

Education services:
Group education facilities, resources for Key Stages 1 and 2 and Further or Higher Education.

Museum or gallery collection, archive, or library special collection:
Archaeology and local history of Winchester and district including topographical prints, photographs and numismatics
Books relating to the history of Winchester and its district

Non-library collection catalogue:
All or part available online and in-house

Library catalogue:
All or part available in-house

Printed publications:
Various booklets and leaflets, maps, prints and posters
Joint English Heritage-funded backlog project: publication of suburban and defensive sites from archaeological excavations undertaken in the 1970s and 1980s

Publications list:
Available online and in print

Access to staff:
Contact by letter, by telephone, by e-mail, in person and via website. Appointment necessary.
Hours: Mon to Fri, 0900 to 1700

Branch museums:
City Museum
   The Square, Winchester
City Space
   Winchester Discovery Centre, Jewry Street, Winchester
Historic Environment Centre
   Guildhall, Winchester
Westgate Museum
   High Street, Winchester

WINE AND SPIRIT TRADE ASSOCIATION

Acronym or abbreviation: WSTA

International Wine and Spirit Centre, 39–45 Bermondsey Street, London SE1 3XF

Tel: 020 7089 3877
Fax: 020 7089 3870
E-mail: info@wsta.co.uk

Website:
http://www.wsta.co.uk
Information on the WSTA.

Enquiries:
Enquiries to: Press Officer
Direct e-mail: gavin@wsta.co.uk

Founded:
1824

Formerly called:
Wine and Spirit Association of Great Britain and Northern Ireland (year of change 1999)

Organisation type and purpose:
Trade association (membership is by subscription). The WSTA is the UK organisation for the wine and spirit industry representing over 310 companies producing, importing, transporting and selling

wines and spirits. It campaigns to promote the industry's interests with governments at home and abroad and works with its members to promote the responsible production, marketing and sale of alcohol.

Subject coverage:
Wine and spirit trade.

Printed publications:
The following available to purchase directly:
Checklists
Freight Forwarders Booklet
WSTA Guide to setting up a Wine and Spirit Business
WSTA Guide to Licensing Act 2003 – Wholesalers
WSTA Guide to Licensing Act 2003 – Retailers
WSTA Guide to Licensing Act 2003 – Wine Producers
WSTA Guide to Licensing Act 2003 – Distance Sellers
Code of practice for the transportation of wines, spirits and concentrated grape must
Order printed publications from: tel: 020 7089 3877

Publications list:
Available online and in print

Access to staff:
Contact by letter, by telephone, by fax, by e-mail and via website. Appointment necessary. Access for members only.
Hours: Mon to Fri, 0915 to 1715

Access to building, collection or gallery:
Prior appointment required

Affiliated to:
Comité Européen de Vins
   Brussels, Belgium; tel: 00 32 2 2309970
European Federation of Wine & Spirit Importers and Distributors, London (EFWSID)
   London; tel: 020 7248 5377; fax: 020 7489 0322; e-mail: efwsid@wsa.org.uk
FIVS
   Paris, France; tel: 00 33 1 42 68 82 48

WINE AUSTRALIA

Australia Centre, Strand, London, WC2B 4LG

Tel: 020 7887 5259
Fax: 020 7240 9429
E-mail: uk@wineaustralia.com

Website:
http://www.wineaustralia.com/uk

Founded:
1987

Organisation type and purpose:
Generic marketing organisation.

Subject coverage:
Australian wine.

Trade and statistical information:
World data on export/import of Australian wines – value and volume.

Printed publications:
Promotional leaflets, posters

Access to staff:
Contact by letter, by telephone, by fax, by e-mail and via website
Hours: Mon to Fri, 0900 to 1700

Access to building, collection or gallery:
Prior appointment required

Parent body:
Australian Wine & Brandy Corporation
   tel: +61 8 8228 2000; fax: +61 8 8228 2022; e-mail: awbc@awbc.com.au

WINSTON CHURCHILL MEMORIAL TRUST

29 Great Smith Street, London, SW1P 3AZ

Tel: 020 7799 1660
Fax: 020 7799 1667
E-mail: office@wcmt.org.uk

Website:
http://www.wcmt.org.uk

Founded:
1965

Organisation type and purpose:
Registered charity (charity number 313952). To provide Travelling Fellowships overseas for British citizens resident in the United Kingdom.

Access to staff:
Contact by letter, by telephone, by fax, by e-mail and via website
Hours: Mon to Thu, 0930 to 1700; Fri, 0930 to 1600

WIRELESS FOR THE BEDRIDDEN

159a High Street, Hornchurch, Essex, RM11 3YD

Tel: 01708 621101 or Freephone: 0800 182137
Fax: 01708 620816
E-mail: info@w4b.org.uk

Enquiries:
Enquiries to: Chief Executive

Founded:
1939

Organisation type and purpose:
Registered charity (charity number 207400). To provide radio and television sets to the housebound, disabled and elderly who cannot afford to buy or rent for themselves.

Subject coverage:
Provision of radio and television facilities for the needy, elderly, disabled, handicapped or housebound.

Access to staff:
Contact by letter, by telephone, by fax and by e-mail
Hours: Mon to Fri, 0830 to 1630

WIRRAL ARCHIVES SERVICE

Wirral Museum, Hamilton Square, Birkenhead, Wirral, CH41 5BR

Tel: 0151 666 3903
E-mail: archives@wirral-libraries.net

Enquiries:
Enquiries to: Archivist
Other contacts: Information Services Librarian

Founded:
1974

Organisation type and purpose:
Public library.

Subject coverage:
Deposit for public records: schools, hospitals, local government and Poor Law. Business and private records. Antiquarian collections.

Museum or gallery collection, archive, or library special collection:
Archives of local hospitals
Cammell Laird Shipbuilders archive
Local government records
Macclesfield Collection
Poor Law Records
School records
Unichema Chemicals Limited (Price's Patent Candle Company)

Non-library collection catalogue:
All or part available in-house

Library catalogue:
All or part available in-house

Access to staff:
Contact by letter, by telephone, by fax, by e-mail and in person
Hours: Thu, Fri, 1000 to 1700; Sat, 1000 to 1300

Access for disabled people:
Ramped entry, access to all public areas

WIRRAL LIBRARIES

Acronym or abbreviation: WIZ

Central Library, Borough Road, Birkenhead, Merseyside, CH41 2XB

Tel: 0151 652 6106/7/8 ext 7
Fax: 0151 653 7320
E-mail: birkenhead.ref@wirral-library.net

Website:
http://www.wirral-libraries.net

Enquiries:
Enquiries to: Librarian
Other contacts: Information Services Librarian.

Founded:
1856

Created by the merger of:
Birkenhead, Bebington, Wallasey and Cheshire County Library Services, Wirral (year of change 1974)

Organisation type and purpose:
Local government body, public library.

Subject coverage:
General public library stock range.

Museum or gallery collection, archive, or library special collection:
Birkenhead Photographic Survey 1900–1920 and 1971–1974
Hopps Paintings of Wallasey 1910–1950
Macclesfield Collection
Price Collection (Price's Patent Candle Company and Model Village records 1840–1960)
Priestley Collection of Photographs 1890–1930
Wirral and Cheshire Photographic Survey 1900–1910
Wirral Borough Council Public Records 1833 to date
Wirral Photographic Survey, 1974-to date

Non-library collection catalogue:
All or part available in-house

Library catalogue:
All or part available online

Access to staff:
Contact by letter, by telephone, by fax, by e-mail and in person. Appointment necessary.
Hours: Mon, Tue, Thu, 0900 to 2000; Fri and Sat, 0900 to 1700; closed Wed and Sun

Access to building, collection or gallery:
Mon, Tue, Thu, 0900 to 2000; Fri and Sat, 0900 to 1700; closed Wed and Sun

Access for disabled people:
Ramped entry only; limited disabled access to Reference Department; no ground floor toilets

WIRRAL METROPOLITAN COLLEGE

Carlett Park, Eastham, Merseyside, CH62 0AY

Tel: 0151 551 7866
Fax: 0151 551 7751

Website:
http://www.wmc.ac.uk

Enquiries:
Enquiries to: Information Officer
Direct tel: 0151 551 7751
Direct e-mail: pat.roberts@wmc.ac.uk

Organisation type and purpose:
Suitable for ages: 16+.
College of further education.

Subject coverage:
Management, engineering, social sciences, sciences.

Access to staff:
Contact by letter, by telephone, by fax, by e-mail, in person and via website
Hours: Mon to Fri, 0900 to 1700

Other sites:
International Business and Management Centre
Europa Boulevard, Conway Park, Birkenhead, L41 4NT; tel: 0151 551 7067
Wirral Metropolitan College
Borough Road, Birkenhead, L42 9QD; tel: 0151 551 7476

WIRRAL METROPOLITAN COLLEGE – TWELVE QUAYS CAMPUS

Acronym or abbreviation: Wirral Met

Shore Road, Birkenhead, Merseyside, CH41 1AG

Tel: 0151 551 7476
Fax: 0151 551 7476
E-mail: steve.cropper@wmc.ac.uk

Website:
http://www.wmc.ac.uk
General description of WMC and its facilities.

Enquiries:
Enquiries to: Senior Librarian

Founded:
2003

Organisation type and purpose:
Further Education College

Subject coverage:
Construction, engineering, caring professions, leisure, tourism and catering, humanities, sciences

Non-library collection catalogue:
All or part available in-house

Library catalogue:
All or part available online, in-house and in print

Access to staff:
Contact by letter, by telephone, by fax and by e-mail. Appointment necessary.
Hours: Mon to Thu, 0845 to 2000; Fri, 0845 to 1600
Special comments: Reference use of collections only.

Access for disabled people:
Electric doors, lifts

Other addresses:
Wirral Metropolitan College Library
Carlett Park Campus, Eastham, Wirral, CH62 0AY; tel: 0151 551 7866

WISE VEHICLE PROGRAMME

Formal name: Women into Science and Engineering
Acronym or abbreviation: WISE

Nottingham Trent University, Burton Street, Nottingham, NG1 4BU

Tel: 0115 848 2101
Fax: 0115 947 2780
E-mail: joyce.bullimore@ntu.ac.uk

Enquiries:
Enquiries to: Operational Manager

Founded:
1992

Organisation type and purpose:
Suitable for ages: 13 to 14 (girls).

Subject coverage:
Women's education.

Access to staff:
Contact by letter, by fax and by e-mail
Hours: Mon to Fri, 0900 to 1600

WJEC

245 Western Avenue, Cardiff, CF5 2YX

Tel: 029 2026 5000
Fax: 029 2057 5894
E-mail: info@wjec.co.uk

Website:
http://www.wjec.co.uk/publicat.html
Publications programme.

Enquiries:
Enquiries to: Chief Executive

Founded:
1948

Organisation type and purpose:
Registered charity (charity number 3150875). Until local government reorganisation in 1996, it was a body established under a statutory order following the 1944 Education Act. Now established as a company limited by guarantee and a charity. The WJEC provides a range of educational services; as an awarding body offering a range of academic and vocational qualifications; support of these qualifications through in-service training for teachers (INSET); support for the Welsh language and culture through the work of the National Language Unit of Wales; and support in relation to the expressive arts, including the administration of the National Youth Orchestra of Wales and the National Youth Theatre of Wales.

Subject coverage:
Examinations at GCE, AEA, GCSE and Entry level, Key Skills, Welsh Baccalaureate, INSET, National Language Unit teaching resources, Welsh for Adults, Welsh Language INSET scheme, Expressive Arts support of National Youth Orchestra of Wales (NYOW), and National Youth Theatre of Wales (NYTW).

Printed publications:
Examinations catalogue of past question papers, marking schemes, specifications and other related materials in print form
Order printed publications from: WJEC Bookshop
tel: 029 2026 5112

Electronic and video publications:
Online catalogue of educational publications and teaching resources (available from the National Language Unit)

Access to staff:
Contact by letter, by telephone, by fax, by e-mail, in person and via website. Appointment necessary.
Hours: Mon to Fri, 0900 to 1700

Access for disabled people:
Parking provided, ramped entry

WM ENTERPRISE

Formal name: West Midlands Enterprise Ltd

Wellington House, 31–34 Waterloo Street, Birmingham, B2 5TJ

Tel: 0121 236 8855
Fax: 0121 233 3942
E-mail: mail@wm-enterprise.co.uk

Enquiries:
Enquiries to: Marketing Manager

Founded:
1981

Formerly called:
West Midlands Enterprise Board (WMEB)

Organisation type and purpose:
Consultancy, socio-economic research organisation.
Venture capital provider.

Subject coverage:
All aspects of the management of local and regional economic development within the UK, Europe and Asia, development of small and medium sized enterprises, business start-up and marketing support.

Access to staff:
Contact by letter, by telephone, by fax and by e-mail
Hours: Mon to Fri, 0900 to 1700

WOKING BOROUGH COUNCIL

Civic Offices, Gloucester Square, Woking, Surrey, GU21 1YL

Tel: 01483 755855

continued overleaf

Fax: 01483 768746

Website:
http://www.woking.gov.uk
Tourism and leisure information, location maps,
council information (e.g., list of services, telephone
numbers). Links to local websites, business
information, vacant commercial property.

Enquiries:
Enquiries to: Public Relations Manager
Direct tel: 01483 743022
Direct fax: 01483 743055
Other contacts: Business Liaison Officer for business
enquiries.

Founded:
1895

Organisation type and purpose:
Local government body.

Subject coverage:
Economic information, population characteristics,
vacant sites and business in the area, and tourist
information.

**Museum or gallery collection, archive, or library
special collection:**
Photographic library of Woking

Printed publications:
Business Contacts in Woking
Commercial and Industrial Property Register
Discovering Ponds – a guide to encourage primary
    and secondary schools to use ponds as an
    educational resource
Economical Development Plan for Woking
Employment Sites Register
The Council Tax 1996–1997 and A-Z of Services for
    Woking Borough
The Woking Magazine
Where to Stay Guide
Where to Eat Guide
Woking – A visitors' guide to the town centre
Woking Business to Business Directory – lists over
    800 local companies

Electronic and video publications:
Information video on the borough of Woking

Publications list:
Available in print

Access to staff:
Contact by letter, by telephone and by fax.
Appointment necessary.
Hours: Mon to Fri, 0900 to 1700 (telephone
enquiries)
Mon to Fri, 0900 to 1645 (personal enquiries)

Twin town with:
Amstelveen
    Amstelveen, The Netherlands
Le Plessis Robinson
    France

WOKINGHAM LIBRARIES AND INFORMATION SERVICE

Shute End, Wokingham, Berkshire, RG40 1WN

Tel: 0118 974 6000
E-mail: libraries@wokingham.gov.uk

Website:
http://www.wokingham.gov.uk/libraries
Library catalogues

Founded:
1998

Formerly a part of:
Berkshire County Council (year of change 1998)

Organisation type and purpose:
Public library.

Subject coverage:
General (public library network).

Library catalogue:
All or part available online

Access to staff:
Contact by letter, by telephone, by fax, by e-mail,
in person and via website

Hours: Library opening hours vary

Branch libraries:
Aborfield Container Library
    Parish Council Car Park, Swallowfield Road,
    Arborfield Cross; tel: 07801 664520
Lower Earley Library
    Chalfont Close, Chalfont Way, Lower Earley; tel:
    0118 931 2150; fax: 0118 975 0162
Maiden Erlegh Library
    Maiden Erlegh Drive, Earley; tel: 0118 966 6630;
    fax: 0118 966 6630
Spencers Wood Library
    Basingstoke Road, Spencers Wood; tel: 0118 988
    4771; fax: 0118 988 4771
Twyford Library
    Polehampton Close, Twyford; tel: 0118 934 0800;
    fax: 0118 934 5399
Wargrave Library
    Woodclyffe Hostel, Church Street, Wargrave; tel:
    0118 940 4656; fax: 0118 940 4656
Winnersh Library
    Robin Hood Lane, Winnersh; tel: 0118 974 7979;
    fax: 0118 974 7989
Woodley Library
    Headley Road, Woodley; tel: 0118 940 0304; fax:
    0118 969 9807

Headquarters address:
Wokingham Library
    Denmark Street, Wokingham; tel: 0118 978 1368;
    fax: 0118 989 1214

WOLFSON CENTRE FOR MAGNETICS TECHNOLOGY

Cardiff School of Engineering, Cardiff University,
PO Box 925, Newport Road, Cardiff, CF24 0YF

Tel: 029 2087 6729
Fax: 029 2087 6729
E-mail: wolfson@cf.ac.uk

Website:
http://www.cf.ac.uk/engin/research/wolfson

Enquiries:
Enquiries to: Director

Founded:
1969

Organisation type and purpose:
University department or institute.
University research centre; formerly Wolfson
Centre for the Technology of Soft Magnetic
Materials.

Subject coverage:
Applications and performance of magnetic
materials.

Printed publications:
List of published papers
List of research projects

Publications list:
Available online and in print

Access to staff:
Contact by letter, by telephone, by fax, by e-mail
and via website. Appointment necessary.
Hours: Mon to Fri, 0900 to 1700

Access to building, collection or gallery:
Prior appointment required

Access for disabled people:
Parking provided, ramped entry, level entry, toilet
facilities

WOLFSON ELECTROSTATICS, UNIVERSITY OF SOUTHAMPTON

Department of Electronics and Computer Science,
University of Southampton, Southampton, SO17
1BJ

Tel: 023 8055 2266
Fax: 023 8059 3015
E-mail: wolfson@soton.ac.uk

Website:
http://www.soton.ac.uk/~wolfson

Enquiries:
Enquiries to: Technical Director

Founded:
1971

Formerly called:
Wolfson Electrical Engineering Consultancy
Service (year of change 1987); Wolfson
Electrostatics Advisory Unit (year of change 1990)

Organisation type and purpose:
University department or institute, consultancy,
research organisation.

Subject coverage:
Electrostatic hazard analysis, explosion prevention
and protection, loss prevention, classification of
flammable materials, safety audits, electrostatic
applications including: liquid and dry powder
coatings, precipitation and electrostatic separation,
high voltage testing.

Access to staff:
Contact by letter, by telephone, by fax and by e-
mail. Appointment necessary.
Hours: Mon to Fri, 0900 to 1700

Access for disabled people:
Level entry, toilet facilities
Special comments: Lifts

WOLFSON FOUNDATION

8 Queen Anne Street, London, W1G 9LD

Tel: 020 7323 5730
Fax: 020 7323 3241

Website:
http://www.wolfson.org.uk

Enquiries:
Enquiries to: Chief Executive

Founded:
1955

Organisation type and purpose:
Registered charity (charity number 206495).

Subject coverage:
Funding of charities or exempt charities such as
universities in areas such as medicine and health
care, research, science, technology and education,
arts and the humanities.

Printed publications:
Annual Report

Access to staff:
Contact by letter
Hours: Mon to Fri, 0900 to 1700

Sister trust:
Wolfson Family Charitable Trust
    tel: 020 7323 5730; fax: 020 7323 3241

WOLFSON HEAT TREATMENT CENTRE

Acronym or abbreviation: WHTC

Federation House, 10 Vyse Street, Birmingham,
B18 6LT

Tel: 0121 237 1122
Fax: 0121 237 1124
E-mail: derek.close@sea.org.uk

Website:
http://www.sea.org.uk/whtc

Enquiries:
Enquiries to: Information Officer
Direct tel: 0121 237 1122

Founded:
1973

Organisation type and purpose:
Subscription service for information, advice centre
on heat treatment of metals, consultancy, courses.

Subject coverage:
Heat treatment of metals, metallurgy, materials
standards and specifications, consultancy, failure
investigations and reports, heat treatment courses,

conferences, safety in heat treatment, heat treatment processes and equipment, location of contract heat treatment facilities for engineering companies.

Museum or gallery collection, archive, or library special collection:
Library of heat treatment books
Trade literature, equipment suppliers

Trade and statistical information:
Data on heat treatment equipment suppliers and suppliers of consumables to the trade.

Printed publications:
Heat Treatment of Metals (journal, quarterly)

Publications list:
Available in print

Access to staff:
Contact by letter, by telephone and by e-mail. Appointment necessary. Access for members only. Non-members charged.
Hours: Mon to Fri, 0800 to 1600
Special comments: Free to subscribers, consultancy fee for non-subscribers

Associated with:
Surface Engineering Association

WOLFSON MICROELECTRONICS LIMITED

Westfield House, 26 Westfield Road, Edinburgh, EH11 2QB

Tel: 0131 272 7000
Fax: 0131 272 7001
E-mail: europe@wolfsonmicro.com

Website:
http://www.wolfsonmicro.com
Full site information, publications

Enquiries:
Enquiries to: Product Marketing Engineer

Founded:
1985

Organisation type and purpose:
Manufacturing industry.
Design and manufacture of semiconductor devices.

Subject coverage:
Integrated circuit design and manufacture for consumer, PC, audio and imaging applications.

Non-library collection catalogue:
All or part available online

Printed publications:
Data sheets

Access to staff:
Contact by letter, by telephone, by fax, by e-mail and via website
Hours: Mon to Fri, 0900 to 1700

Access for disabled people:
Access to all public areas
Special comments: Level entrance at back of building

Associated with:
Edinburgh University

WOLFSON UNIT FOR MARINE TECHNOLOGY AND INDUSTRIAL AERODYNAMICS

Acronym or abbreviation: WUMTIA

University of Southampton, Southampton, SO17 1BJ

Tel: 023 8058 5044
Fax: 023 8059 7594
E-mail: wumtia@soton.ac.uk

Website:
http://www.wolfsonunit.com
Services, products and personnel.

Enquiries:
Enquiries to: Secretary

Founded:
1968

Organisation type and purpose:
Commercial consultancy and research organisation, using skills, knowledge and facilities of university; feedback of commercial problems to academics.

Subject coverage:
Towing tank testing of ship models; wind tunnel testing of sailing vessel rigs, keels, superstructures, buildings, road vehicles; computer program bureau service in hydrostatics and stability, ship motions and propulsion, model testing; trials data acquisition; computer modelling; material testing/failure analysis; feasibility studies; expert witnesses.

Electronic and video publications:
Software for Naval Architects including hydrostatics and stability, ship motions, powering and propulsion, lines fairing (for sale)

Access to staff:
Contact by letter, by telephone, by fax, by e-mail, in person and via website
Hours: Mon to Fri, 0900 to 1700

Parent body:
University of Southampton, Department of Ship Science

WOLSELEY 6/80 & MORRIS OXFORD CLUB

21 Bates Lane, Weston Turville, Aylesbury, Bucks, HP22 5SL

Tel: 01296 614065
E-mail: brianspost1@myway.com

Enquiries:
Enquiries to: Membership Secretary

Founded:
1977

Organisation type and purpose:
Membership association (membership is by subscription).

Subject coverage:
Technical information and sources of spares for Wolseley 6/80 and Morris Oxford cars.

Museum or gallery collection, archive, or library special collection:
A small collection of workshop manuals and technical data

Printed publications:
News sheet (quarterly)

Access to staff:
Contact by letter, by telephone, by e-mail and in person
Hours: Sun to Sat, 0900 to 2200
Special comments: Enclose an sae for reply.

WOLVERHAMPTON ARCHIVES AND LOCAL STUDIES

Acronym or abbreviation: WALS

Molineux Hotel Building, Whitmore Hill, Wolverhampton WV1 1SF

Tel: 01902 552480; minicom no. 01902 552479
Fax: 01902 552481
E-mail: archives@wolverhampton.gov.uk

Website:
http://www.wolverhampton.gov.uk/archives
http://www.wolverhampton.gov.uk/library/archives.htm
Information on holdings and services; opening hours; details of postal search service; leaflets(leaflets available in PDF format); location map.

Enquiries:
Enquiries to: City Archivist

Founded:
1978

Organisation type and purpose:
Local government body, suitable for ages: 8+.
Archive repository.
To ensure the long-term preservation of the City's documentary heritage and to encourage and develop the use of these materials by the general public and within the council itself.

Subject coverage:
Archive and local studies material, local history, genealogy.

Non-library collection catalogue:
All or part available in-house

Library catalogue:
All or part available in-house

Printed publications:
Education Service leaflet
Family History Fact Sheets – brief guides for beginners – records of births, marriages and deaths, census returns and parish registers, etc. (£1)
Family History Forms pack (£1.50)
General information leaflet
Guide to Church of England Parish Registers
Guide to Nonconformist Registers and Roman Catholic Registers
Guide to the Contents of Wolverhampton Archives and Local Studies (£4.99)
Map of Wolverhampton 1750 (surveyed by Taylor I, £2.50)
Mapping the Past – Wolverhampton 1577–1986 (£4.50)
Tracing your Army Ancestors
Tracing your family tree leaflet
Town Centre Timeline – A Guide to Using the Story of Wolverhampton's past as a Source for National Curriculum History (1997, £6)

Electronic and video publications:
Bilston in the 19th Century (CD-ROM, £6.99)

Publications list:
Available online and in print

Access to staff:
Contact by letter, by telephone, by fax, by e-mail, in person and via website
Hours: Sun & Mon closed; Tue, Thu and Fri, 1000 to 1700; Wed, 1000 to 1900; Sat 1000 to 1300

Access for disabled people:
Ramped entry, access to all research facilities, toilet facilities
Hours: Normal opening hours

WOLVERHAMPTON LIBRARIES AND INFORMATION SERVICES

Central Library, Snow Hill, Wolverhampton, West Midlands, WV1 3AX

Tel: 01902 552025; minicom no. 01902 552020
Fax: 01902 552024
E-mail: libraries@wolverhampton.gov.uk

Website:
http://www.wolverhampton.gov.uk/libraries
Locations, opening hours, catalogue, events, readers and writers' groups, links to council information and useful websites.

Enquiries:
Enquiries to: Information Officer (Reference)

Organisation type and purpose:
Local government body, public library.

Subject coverage:
General information in all fields, materials in Asian languages, materials of African-Caribbean interest. On-line resources: business information, newspapers, European information, Wolverhampton local history; popular and classical music on CD; educational and instructional DVDs; music scores.

Special visitor services:
Public internet access at all service points.

continued overleaf

Library catalogue:
All or part available online and in-house

Printed publications:
Directories of local organisations

Access to staff:
Contact by letter, by telephone, by fax, by e-mail, in person and via website
Hours: Mon to Thu, 0900 to 1900; Fri and Sat, 0900 to 1700 at Central Library. Other libraries' opening hours vary – please check for details.

Access to building, collection or gallery:
No prior appointment required

Access for disabled people:
Ramped entry, toilet facilities, adaptive technologies on PCs

Has:
15 service points throughout the City

Links with:
MLA, BCLiP, CIlip and SCL

WOLVERHAMPTON MEDICAL INSTITUTE

Bell Library, New Cross Hospital, Wolverhampton, West Midlands, WV10 0QP

Tel: 01902 695322
Fax: 01902 723037
E-mail: jean.paterson@rwh-tr.nhs.uk

Enquiries:
Enquiries to: Medical Librarian

Founded:
1971

Formerly called:
South Staffordshire Medical Centre Library

Organisation type and purpose:
A group of medical libraries in the NHS including the Eye Infirmary Library, Wolverhampton.

Subject coverage:
Medicine, dentistry, veterinary surgery, pharmacy, ophthalmology, physiotherapy, nursing.

Access to staff:
Contact by letter, by telephone, by fax and by e-mail
Hours: Mon to Wed, 0830 to 1700; Thu, 0830 to 1830; Fri, 0830 to 1630

WOMEN AGAINST RAPE

Acronym or abbreviation: WAR

Crossroads Women's Centre, 230a Kentish Town Road, London, NW5 2AB

Tel: 020 7482 2496\ Minicom no. 020 7482 2496
Fax: 020 7209 4761
E-mail: war@womenagainstrape.net

Website:
http://www.womenagainstrape.net

Enquiries:
Enquiries to: Secretary

Founded:
1976

Organisation type and purpose:
Voluntary organisation.
Pressure group.
To campaign for reform of the law and legal system with respect to violence against women and children.

Subject coverage:
Counselling, legal advice, support for women and girls who have been raped or sexually assaulted, compensation and other resources for recovery and the prevention of violence against women and children. Help with reporting attacks, legal action, testifying in court, health referrals, rehousing, claiming benefits and compensation, including for immigrant wives facing domestic violence and refugees who are rape survivors seeking asylum.

Printed publications:
Ask Any Woman
Rape in the Media
The Power to Refuse
The Rapist Who Pays the Rent

Publications list:
Available in print

Access to staff:
Contact by letter, by telephone, by fax and by e-mail
Hours: Telephone open, Mon to Fri, 1330 to 1600
Centre opening hours, Tue and Wed, 1200 to 1600; Thu, 1700 to 1900
Special comments: Letters should be addressed to PO Box 287, London NW6 5QU.

Other address:
Women Against Rape
PO Box 287, London, NW6 5QU

WOMEN IN FILM AND TELEVISION

Acronym or abbreviation: WFTV

4th Floor, Unit 2 Wedgwood Mews, 12–13 Greek Street, London, W1D 4BB

Tel: 020 7287 1400
Fax: 020 7287 1500
E-mail: info@wftv.org.uk

Website:
http://www.wftv.org.uk

Enquiries:
Enquiries to: Administrator
Direct e-mail: administrator@wftv.org.uk

Founded:
1990

Organisation type and purpose:
Trade association (membership is by qualification), present number of members: 1,000.

Access to staff:
Contact by letter, by telephone and by e-mail
Hours: Mon to Fri, 1000 to 1800

WOMEN'S AID FEDERATION OF ENGLAND

Acronym or abbreviation: Women's Aid

PO Box 391, Bristol, BS99 7WS

Tel: 0117 944 4411
Fax: 0117 924 1703
E-mail: info@womensaid.org.uk

Website:
http://www.womensaid.org.uk

Enquiries:
Enquiries to: Information Officer

Founded:
1974

Organisation type and purpose:
Membership association (membership is by subscription), present number of members: 120 full, 280 associate, voluntary organisation, registered charity (charity number 1054154).
Co-ordinate work of refuges in England, campaigning and lobbying on behalf of women and children. Provides Freephone 24 hour national domestic violence helpline: 0808 2000 247. Run in partnership between Women's Aid and Refuge.

Subject coverage:
Domestic violence in the form of physical violence, sexual abuse and psychological abuse, and related issues: housing, social security, legal rights, women's rights, children.

Library catalogue:
All or part available in-house

Printed publications:
Many books and leaflets including:
Children, Domestic Violence and Refuges: a study of needs and responses (£14.50)

Getting Free from Domestic Violence – language leaflets for women available in eleven different languages
Children Living with Domestic Violence (1994, £17)
It's Just a Domestic (£4.50)
Posters
The Gold Book: The Women's Aid Directory of Domestic Violence Refuge and Helpline Services 2005 (£25)
Strengthening Diversity: Good practice in delivering domestic violence services to Black women and children (£12)
It hurts me too – Children's experiences of domestic violence and refuge life (£7)

Publications list:
Available online and in print

Access to staff:
Contact by letter, by telephone, by fax, by e-mail and via website
Hours: Office: 1000 to 1600 only by telephone
Helpline: 24 hours

Access to building, collection or gallery:
No access other than to staff

Access for disabled people:
Ramped entry

Has:
over 160 member Refuge Groups in England

WOMEN'S DESIGN SERVICE

Acronym or abbreviation: WDS

52–54 Featherstone Street, London, EC1Y 8RT

Tel: 020 7490 5210
Fax: 020 7490 5212
E-mail: info@wds.org.uk

Website:
http://www.wds.org.uk

Enquiries:
Enquiries to: Director

Founded:
1986

Organisation type and purpose:
Advisory body, membership association (membership is by election or invitation), voluntary organisation, registered charity (charity number 801282), public library, consultancy, research organisation.
Information and research on women's needs in the built environment.

Subject coverage:
Women's issues relating to the urban environment, including: architecture, planning, design, safety, transport, work environments, childcare, housing, tenant participation, access, disability, technical aid hazards, regeneration.

Museum or gallery collection, archive, or library special collection:
EX-GLC reports
EX-LPAC reports
Reports of proceedings of London Women and Planning Forum

Printed publications:
Accessible Offices (£5.50)
At Women's Convenience (£6.50)
Designing Housing for Older Women (£6.50)
Disability and Regeneration (£18)
Good Practice Manual on Tenant Participation (£8)
Housing for Independence (£18)
It's Not All Swings and Roundabouts (£6.50)
Making Safer Places (£15)
Removing the Goalposts (£18)
Shoppers' Creches (£6.50)
Thinking Of Small Children – Access, Provision and Play (£3.50)
Women's Safety On Housing Estates (£6.50)
Many broadsheets on related subjects are also available (£2 or £3 each)

Publications list:
Available in print

Access to staff:
Contact by letter, by telephone, by fax, by e-mail, in person and via website
Hours: Mon to Fri, 1000 to 1700

Access to building, collection or gallery:
Prior appointment required

Access for disabled people:
Ramped entry, toilet facilities

WOMEN'S EMPLOYMENT ENTERPRISE & TRAINING UNIT

Acronym or abbreviation: WEETU

2 Redwell Street, Norwich, NR2 4SN

Tel: 01603 230625
Fax: 01603 776426
E-mail: admin@weetu.org

Website:
http://www.weetu.org

Enquiries:
Enquiries to: Chief Executive

Founded:
1988

Organisation type and purpose:
Voluntary organisation, training organisation.
To help women deal with economic change, and to improve access to and experience of employment and training, as well as providing information and advice on these issues.

Subject coverage:
Adult guidance: women (all ages); women returners; women's self employment; existing network for women who run their own businesses.

Access to staff:
Contact by letter, by telephone, by fax and by e-mail
Hours: Mon to Fri, 0900 to 1700

WOMEN'S ENGINEERING SOCIETY

Acronym or abbreviation: WES

2 Queen Anne's Gate Buildings, Dartmouth Street, London, SW1H 9BP

Tel: 020 7233 1974
Fax: 020 7233 1973
E-mail: info@wes.org.uk

Website:
http://www.wes.org.uk
Society news, views, information, publicity, some job vacancies, etc.

Enquiries:
Enquiries to: Secretary
Other contacts: President

Founded:
1920

Organisation type and purpose:
Professional body, registered charity (charity number 1008913).
To promote the study and practice of engineering among women.

Subject coverage:
Engineering, all levels, all fields, particularly relating to women's careers, bursaries, career breaks, equal opportunities, continuing professional development.

Trade and statistical information:
Data on women in engineering.

Printed publications:
Free leaflets publicising the society and its activities
The Woman Engineer (journal, quarterly by subscription £20 pa UK, £25 overseas, or free to members)

Access to staff:
Contact by letter, by telephone, by fax, by e-mail and via website

Hours: Not Friday

Affiliated to:
International Conference of Women Engineers & Scientists (ICWES)
Verena Holmes Lecture Fund

WOMEN'S ENVIRONMENTAL NETWORK

Acronym or abbreviation: WEN

Real Nappy Project, PO Box 30626, London, E1 1TZ

Tel: 020 7481 9004
Fax: 020 7481 9144
E-mail: info@wen.org.uk

Website:
http://www.wen.org.uk
See nappy pages from subjects page 3.

Enquiries:
Enquiries to: Project Worker
Direct e-mail: comms@wen.org.uk
Other contacts: Project Assistant for second-hand nappy exchange.

Founded:
2000

Subject coverage:
Information on the environmental impact and the economic, social and health aspects of disposable nappies. Life cycle analyses and other studies on environmental impacts of real versus disposable nappies.

Trade and statistical information:
Nappy waste statistics in the UK, and other information relating to the environment, health and economics. List of retailers and businesses (including non-profit) who provide washable cotton nappies for home washing or via nappy laundry delivery service.

Library catalogue:
All or part available online

Printed publications:
WEN Nappy Briefing
Real Nappy Project Leaflet
Preventing Nappy Waste (Report 1996)
Health Professionals' Pack
Local Authorities' Information Pack
Parents' Information Pack
Real Nappy Activists' Pack
Information Packs available only by post, on receipt of a large SAE with two 1st or 2nd class stamps
Order printed publications from: Real Nappy Association
PO Box 3704, London, SE26 4RX

Publications list:
Available online and in print

Access to staff:
Contact by letter, by telephone, by fax, by e-mail and via website. Appointment necessary.
Hours: Mon to Fri, 1000 to 1800

Access to building, collection or gallery:
Prior appointment required

Access for disabled people:
Level entry

WOMEN'S FARM AND GARDEN ASSOCIATION

Acronym or abbreviation: WFGA

175 Gloucester Street, Cirencester, Gloucestershire, GL7 2DP

Tel: 01285 658339
E-mail: admin@wfga.org.uk

Website:
http://www.wfga.org
History and background on the charity, membership application, member log-in, Member's Forum, Women Returners to Amenity

Gardening Scheme, detail of workshops, tours and weekend visits, and details of funding scheme The Christine Ladley Fund.

Enquiries:
Enquiries to: Director

Founded:
1899

Organisation type and purpose:
Membership association (membership is by subscription), present number of members: 1,000, registered charity (charity number 212527), training organisation.
Association for professional women in all aspects of agriculture and horticulture. To provide advice and practical training in horticulture through the Women Returners to Amenity Gardening Scheme; to represent women in agriculture and horticulture.

Subject coverage:
Careers advice for women in agriculture and horticulture; national, European and international information on women's affairs; practical horticultural training; funding for projects in horticulture through the Christine Ladley Fund.

Museum or gallery collection, archive, or library special collection:
Archives covering 100 years

Non-library collection catalogue:
All or part available in-house

Printed publications:
Growing Vegetables booklet (£2)
Potted History (£2)
Set of 3 postcards of gardening trainees in the 1920s (£1.50 per set)
Role of Women in British Agriculture (£2)
The Hidden Workforce: a self-help guide to Safeguards and Benefits for Women (£2)
Women Rule the Plot, the story of the 100-year fight to establish Women's place in farm and garden (£12 + £2 p&p)
Order printed publications from: Available from the office in Cirencester

Access to staff:
Contact by letter, by telephone, by e-mail and via website
Hours: Mon to Fri, 0900 to 1700

WOMEN'S FOOD AND FARMING UNION

Acronym or abbreviation: WFU

WFU c/o Cargill plc, Witham St Hughs, Lincoln, LN6 9TN

Tel: 0844 335 0342
Fax: 0844 335 0342
E-mail: secretary@wfu.org.uk

Website:
http://www.wfu.org.uk
WFU news and activities, policies and official responses, CEC information.

Enquiries:
Enquiries to: President
Direct tel: 07800 664701
Direct e-mail: president@wfu.org.uk
Other contacts: Administrator (for policy administration)

Founded:
1979

Formerly called:
Women's Farming Union (year of change 1997)

Organisation type and purpose:
Membership association (membership is by subscription), voluntary organisation, suitable for ages: 18+, training organisation, research organisation.
To link consumer and producer.

continued overleaf

Subject coverage:
All aspects of food production, the concerns of consumers, the co-operation between industries related to food and farming; monitors production methods, scientific developments, retail products and the presentation of food in the market place.

Electronic and video publications:
DVD Beyond the Farm gate
Order electronic and video publications from: free on application to Secretary

Access to staff:
Contact by letter, by telephone, by e-mail and via website
Hours: Mon to Fri, 0900 to 1700
Special comments: Not weekends.

WOMEN'S HEALTH

52 Featherstone Street, London, EC1Y 8RT

Tel: 020 7251 6333\ Minicom no. 020 7490 5489
Fax: 020 7608 0928
E-mail: womenshealth@pop3.poptel.org.uk

Website:
http://www.womenshealthlondon.org.uk

Enquiries:
Enquiries to: Information Officer

Founded:
1982

Formerly called:
Women's Health and Reproductive Rights Information Centre

Organisation type and purpose:
National organisation, membership association (membership is by subscription), voluntary organisation, registered charity (charity number 296002), research organisation.
Health information organisation.
To provide health information that enables women to make informed decisions about their health.

Subject coverage:
Women's health: menstruation, menopause, gynaecology; abortion, hysterectomy, fibroids, polycystic ovaries, pelvic inflammatory disease.

Museum or gallery collection, archive, or library special collection:
Over 5700 books, cuttings, reports on women's
    health issues

Printed publications:
Newsletter (quarterly, by subscription)
Publications list of over 50 titles (send sae)
Leaflets on various aspects of women's health
    describe a problem or situation and give
    practical solutions, plus leaflets for women with
    learning difficulties

Electronic and video publications:
Leaflets are all available on tape

Publications list:
Available online and in print

Access to staff:
Contact by letter, by telephone, by fax and by e-mail. Appointment necessary.
Hours: Office: Mon to Fri, 0900 to 1700
Helpline enquiries: Mon to Fri, 0930 to 1330

Access for disabled people:
Parking provided, ramped entry, toilet facilities

WOMEN'S HEALTH CONCERN

Acronym or abbreviation: WHC

4–6 Eton Place, Marlow, Buckinghamshire, SL7 2QA

Tel: 01628 478473
Fax: 01628 482743
E-mail: advice@womens-health-concern.org

Website:
http://www.womens-health-concern.org

Enquiries:
Enquiries to: Chief Executive
Direct e-mail: info@womens-health-concern.org

Founded:
1979

Organisation type and purpose:
Registered charity (charity number 279651).
Provides advice and counselling about the menopause, and information about, and treatment for, sexual health and gynaecological conditions.

Subject coverage:
Women's sexual and gynaecological problems and other health matters.

Education services:
Professional development seminars (see website)

Electronic and video publications:
Series of factsheets (online)

Publications list:
Available online

Access to staff:
Contact by letter, by telephone, by e-mail and via website
Hours: Mon to Fri, 0900 to 1700

Access to building, collection or gallery:
No access other than to staff

WOMEN'S INTERNATIONAL LEAGUE FOR PEACE AND FREEDOM UK SECTION

Acronym or abbreviation: WILPF

WILPF UK Section, Tindlemanor, 52–54 Featherstone Street, London, EC1Y 8RT

Tel: 020 7250 1968
E-mail: office@ukwilpf.org.uk

Website:
http://www.ukwilpf.org.uk

Founded:
1915

Organisation type and purpose:
The WILPF is an international non-government organisation with national sections in 35 countries.
To lobby the UN and its agencies formally on issues related to peace, disarmament and economic justice.

Subject coverage:
National and international lobbying, campaigning and networking on all issues affecting peace, civil liberties and human rights, status of all women and disarmament.

Museum or gallery collection, archive, or library special collection:
The archives of WILPF and the Women's Peace
    Movement are held in the LSE library, London

Printed publications:
Annual Report
Peace and Freedom News
Various reports of seminars, etc.
Order printed publications from: See contact details above

Publications list:
Available in print

Access to staff:
Contact by letter, by telephone, by e-mail and via website
Hours: Mon to Fri, 1100 to 1600

Access to building, collection or gallery:
By prior arrangement

Access for disabled people:
Fully accessible

Parent body:
WILPF
    1, rue de Varembé, Case Postale 28, 1121 Geneva
    20, Switzerland; tel: +41 22919 7080; fax: +41
    22919 7081; e-mail: inforequest@wilpf.ch;
    website: http://www.wilpfinternational.org

WOMEN'S INTERNATIONAL SQUASH PLAYERS ASSOCIATION

Acronym or abbreviation: WISPA

27 Westminster Palace Gardens, Artillery Row, London, SW1P 1RR

Tel: 020 7222 1667
Fax: 020 7976 8778
E-mail: wispahq@aol.com

Website:
http://www.wispa.net

Enquiries:
Enquiries to: Administrator

Founded:
1983

Organisation type and purpose:
International organisation, professional body (membership is by subscription), present number of members: 300.

Subject coverage:
To promote and administer professional squash for women; to promote squash as a game; to advise and assist squash promoters / media / players / officials on all aspects of the game.

Access to staff:
Contact by letter, by telephone, by fax, by e-mail and via website
Hours: Mon to Fri, 0900 to 1700

WOMEN'S LEAGUE OF HEALTH AND BEAUTY

Acronym or abbreviation: WLHB

6 Station Parade, Sunningdale, Berkshire, SL5 0EP

Tel: 01344 874787
Fax: 01344 873887
E-mail: tfi@thefitnessleague.com

Website:
http://www.thefitnessleague.com

Enquiries:
Enquiries to: Administrator

Founded:
1930

Formerly called:
The Fitness League (year of change 1999)

Trading as:
Health and Beauty Exercise

Organisation type and purpose:
Membership association (membership is by subscription), present number of members: 14,000, registered charity (charity number 226127).
To promote health through exercise.

Printed publications:
Magazine (3 times a year, free to members)
Various leaflets

Electronic and video publications:
MANFIT (exercise video)

Access to staff:
Contact by letter, by telephone, by e-mail and via website
Hours: Mon to Fri, 1000 to 1600

WOMEN'S LIBRARY

London Metropolitan University, Old Castle Street, London, E1 7NT

Tel: 020 7320 2222
Fax: 020 7320 2333
E-mail: moreinfo@thewomenslibrary.ac.uk

Website:
http://www.thewomenslibrary.ac.uk

Enquiries:
Enquiries to: Librarian
Direct tel: 020 7320 3515
Direct e-mail: enquirydesk@thewomenslibrary.ac.uk

Other contacts: Archivist (for non-published material, manuscripts, etc); Curator (for pictorial material)

Founded:
1926

Formerly called:
The Fawcett Society (year of change 2001)

Incorporates the former:
Fawcett Library, London Guildhall University
(year of change 2001)

Organisation type and purpose:
Membership association, university library.

Subject coverage:
Women's studies and women's history, particularly in Britain and the Commonwealth.

Museum or gallery collection, archive, or library special collection:
Archives of many feminist organisations and of some individual women
Cavendish Bentinck Library
Josephine Butler Society Library
Sadd Brown Library

Non-library collection catalogue:
All or part available online

Library catalogue:
All or part available online

Printed publications:
Information leaflet
Newsletter (4 times a year)

Access to staff:
Contact by letter, by telephone, by fax, by e-mail, in person and via website
Hours: Mon, closed; Tue, Wed and Fri, 0930 to 1700; Thu, 0930 to 2000

Access to building, collection or gallery:
No prior appointment required
Hours: Mon, closed; Tue, Wed and Fri, 0930 to 1700; Thu, 0930 to 2000; Sat, 1000 to 1600

Access for disabled people:
Access to all public areas, toilet facilities

WOMEN'S NATIONAL COMMISSION

Acronym or abbreviation: WNC

1st Floor, Cabinet Office, 35 Great Smith Street, London, SW1P 3BQ

Tel: 020 7276 2555
Fax: 020 7276 2563
E-mail: wnc@cabinet-office.x.gsi.gov.uk

Website:
http://www.thewnc.org.uk

Enquiries:
Enquiries to: Director
Direct e-mail: jveitch@cabinet-office.x.gsi.gov.uk

Founded:
1969

Organisation type and purpose:
Advisory body, membership association.
Advisory body funded and staffed, but not controlled, by the government; composed of women's organisations, including national organisations, women's sections of major political parties, trade unions, professional and business bodies, churches.

Subject coverage:
Helsinki fund, women's organisations, public appointments, women returners, older women, women's point of view contributed to the deliberations of Government, in, for example, health and social services, education, prostitution, illegitimacy, family law, income tax. International work on women's equality, particularly on CEDAW and CSW. Advice on women's organisations in the UK and contact between them and Government.

Printed publications:
Future Female
Growing Up Female in the UK
National Agenda for Action
Reports of Working Parties
WNC Business Report 1999/01
Women's Organisations in United Kingdom 1997
Women in Public Life
World Conference Against Racism (WACR)

Publications list:
Available online and in print

Access to staff:
Contact by letter, by fax, by e-mail and via website. Appointment necessary.
Hours: Mon to Fri, 0900 to 1700

WOMEN'S SPORTS FOUNDATION

Acronym or abbreviation: WSF

3rd Floor, Victoria House, Bloomsbury Square, London, WC1B 4SE

Tel: 020 7273 1740
Fax: 020 7273 1981
E-mail: info@wsff.org.uk

Website:
http://www.wsf.org.uk
Role and function of Women's Sports Foundation, current news, student pages, links to other organisations.

Enquiries:
Enquiries to: Head of Communications
Direct tel: 020 7273 1744
Other contacts: Membership & Administrative Officer for routine enquiries, resource orders, membership applications.

Founded:
1984

Organisation type and purpose:
Advisory body, membership association (membership is by subscription), present number of members: 450.
To develop and promote women's sport.

Subject coverage:
Women's sport, participation, careers, coaching, media contacts, funding and sponsorship, resources (posters and photographs). Single sex sport and leisure provision.

Museum or gallery collection, archive, or library special collection:
Range of resources and publications on women's sport

Trade and statistical information:
Data on women's involvement in sport.

Printed publications:
A Booklet on Careers in Sport and Recreation for Women and Girls (1994, £2)
Careers in Sport (1997, £3 plus £1.75 p&p)
Factsheets (1998–1999, £1)
Photographic displays for hire
Poster Set (1999, £10)
Single Sex Sport Provision (1998, free)
Syllabus Guide (2000, £20)
Women and Coaching Information Pack (1994, free with sae for 98p)
Women and Sport Information Pack (Mar 2000, £2)

Electronic and video publications:
Time of Change (video, 1995, £7.50 plus £5 p&p)
Women and Sport (VHS video, 22 mins)

Publications list:
Available online and in print

Access to staff:
Contact by letter, by e-mail and via website
Hours: Mon to Fri, 0900 to 1700

Access to building, collection or gallery:
No prior appointment required

WOOD BUREAU

PO Box 9, Farnborough, Hampshire, GU14 6WE

Tel: 01252 522545
Fax: 01252 522546
E-mail: enquiries@woodbureau.co.uk

Website:
http://www.woodbureau.co.uk

Organisation type and purpose:
Voluntary organisation.
Wood awareness campaign.

Subject coverage:
The promotion of a better understanding of wood, as a basic fibre, common and vital to many and varied industries, to encourage a rational approach to the utilisation of both wood fibre and the forest resource.

WOOD GREEN ANIMAL SHELTERS

Acronym or abbreviation: WGAS

King's Bush Farm, London Road, Godmanchester, Cambridgeshire, PE29 2NH

Tel: 0844 248 8181
Fax: 01480 832815
E-mail: info@woodgreen.org.uk

Website:
http://www.woodgreen.org.uk
Official site for the charity.

Enquiries:
Enquiries to: Fundraising Department
Direct e-mail: rhiannon.swannell@woodgreen.org.uk
Other contacts: Press and PR officer

Founded:
1924

Organisation type and purpose:
Registered charity (charity number 298348).
Animal Welfare organisation.

Subject coverage:
Animal rehoming charity, animal welfare, protection, surgery and veterinary services.

Printed publications:
Annual Review
Animals Matter (3 a year)
WAGS – for junior members (quarterly, free to members, 50p to non-members)

Publications list:
Available online

Access to staff:
Contact by letter, by telephone, by fax, by e-mail, in person and via website
Hours: 24-hour service, 365 days a year; open to visitors, 1000 to 1600

Access for disabled people:
Parking provided, ramped entry, toilet facilities

Affiliated to:
Wood Green Enterprises Ltd
King's Bush Farm, London Road, Godmanchester, Cambridgeshire, PE29 2NH; tel: 08701 904090; e-mail: tina.jeffery@woodgreen.org.uk; website: http://www.woodgreen.org.uk

Also at:
Wood Green Animal Shelter
601 Lordship Lane, Wood Green, London, N22 5LG; tel: 08701 904440; fax: 020 8889 0245; e-mail: info@woodgreen.org.uk; website: http://www.woodgreen.org.uk
Wood Green Animal Shelter
Chishill Road, Heydon, Royston, Hertfordshire, SG8 8PN; tel: 08701 909099; fax: 01763 838824; e-mail: info@woodgreen.org.uk; website: http://www.woodgreen.org.uk

WOOD PANEL INDUSTRIES FEDERATION

Acronym or abbreviation: WPIF

28 Market Place, Grantham, Lincolnshire, NG31 6LR

continued overleaf

Tel: 01476 563707
Fax: 01476 579314
E-mail: enquiries@wpif.org.uk

Website:
http://www.wpif.org.uk

Enquiries:
Enquiries to: Director General

Founded:
1995

Organisation type and purpose:
Trade association (membership is by subscription), present number of members: 25.

Subject coverage:
Industrial, professional or DIY use of particle boards, chipboard, oriented strand board and medium density fibreboard (MDF); fire and building regulations; design and application data; fixing methods; finishing techniques.

Trade and statistical information:
Data on the imports of particle boards and fibreboards into the UK; UK production.

Publications list:
Available in print

Access to staff:
Contact by letter, by telephone, by fax, by e-mail, in person and via website. Appointment necessary.
Hours: Mon to Fri, 0900 to 1700

Member organisation of:
BWF
CEI-BOIS
CPA
EPF
FIRA
TRADA
TTF
WPA

WOODBROOKE QUAKER STUDY CENTRE

1046 Bristol Road, Selly Oak, Birmingham, B29 6LJ

Tel: 0121 472 5171
Fax: 0121 472 5173
E-mail: library@woodbrooke.org.uk

Website:
http://www.woodbrooke.org.uk/woodbrooke
Contains library pages.

Enquiries:
Enquiries to: Librarian
Other contacts: Director

Founded:
1903

Organisation type and purpose:
Registered charity (charity number 313816).
Adult religious educational college for Quakers and others.

Subject coverage:
Quaker studies, theology.

Museum or gallery collection, archive, or library special collection:
Bevan Naish Library of 17th and 18th century Quaker books and pamphlets
Powicke Collection of Richard Baxter books

Non-library collection catalogue:
All or part available in-house

Library catalogue:
All or part available in-house

Printed publications:
The Woodbrooke Journal (occasional)

Access to staff:
Contact by letter, by telephone, by fax and by e-mail. Appointment necessary.
Hours: Variable, please enquire

WOODLAND HERITAGE CENTRE

Brokerswood Country Park, Westbury, Wiltshire, BA13 4EH

Tel: 01373 822238
Fax: 01373 858474

Enquiries:
Enquiries to: Education Officer
Direct e-mail: woodland.park@virgin.net

Founded:
1971

Formerly called:
Phillip's Countryside Museum; Woodland Heritage Museum (year of change 1997)

Organisation type and purpose:
Registered charity (charity number L246167), museum, suitable for ages: all, but primarily 5 to 11.

Subject coverage:
Forestry and forest management, forests for leisure and recreation, public participation in forestry, natural history, botany, flora, fauna, ornithology, ecology and conservation of woodland.

Museum or gallery collection, archive, or library special collection:
Barber Collection of Birds' Eggs of the World (approximately 2000 species)

Printed publications:
Details of educational facilities (on request)

Access to staff:
Contact by letter, by fax and by e-mail
Hours: Mon to Fri, 0900 to 1700
Special comments: Opening dependent on season, please phone in advance.

Access to building, collection or gallery:
Prior appointment required
Hours: Mon to Fri, 1000 to 1600; Sat, Sun, 1100 to 1600
Winter: Mon to Fri, 1000 to 1600; Sat, Sun, 1200 to 1600

WOODLAND TRUST

Autumn Park, Dysart Road, Grantham, Lincolnshire, NG31 6LL

Tel: 01476 581111
Fax: 01476 590808
E-mail: enquiries@woodlandtrust.org.uk

Website:
http://www.woodlandtrust.org.uk
Electronic versions of most Trust publications, including annual reports, press releases, policy information, Woodfinder, etc.

Enquiries:
Enquiries to: Public Enquiries Officer
Direct tel: 01476 581135

Founded:
1972

Organisation type and purpose:
Membership association (membership is by subscription), present number of members: just under 200,000, voluntary organisation, registered charity (charity number 294344).
Woodland conservation and creation.

Subject coverage:
Conservation and planting of native broadleaved woodland.

Museum or gallery collection, archive, or library special collection:
Photographic collection relating to Trust properties

Printed publications:
Broadleaf (members' magazine)
Woodland Trust directory of Trust woods
Misc. other publications
Order printed publications from: website: http://www.woodlandtrust.org.uk/publications

Publications list:
Available online

Access to staff:
Contact by letter, by telephone, by fax, by e-mail and via website
Hours: Mon to Fri, 0830 to 1700

WORCESTER COLLEGE OF TECHNOLOGY

Acronym or abbreviation: WCT

Deansway, Worcester, WR1 2JF

Tel: 01905 725555
Fax: 01905 725600
E-mail: library@wortech.ac.uk

Website:
http://www.wortech.ac.uk
Main college website.
http://www.wortech.ac.uk/campus/studycentres/Pages/default.aspx
Study Centre webpages.

Enquiries:
Enquiries to: Head of Library and Study Centres
Direct tel: 01905 725576
Direct e-mail: wparry@wortech.ac.uk

Organisation type and purpose:
Further education college.

Subject coverage:
General education, construction, business studies, hospitality, engineering, electronics, science, mathematics, caring, art and design, local government, personnel, law, accountancy, travel & tourism, sports, management, IT.

Services for disabled people:
See: http://www.wortech.ac.uk/campus/campusbuildings/Pages/buildingaccessibility.aspx.

Library catalogue:
All or part available online and in-house

Access to staff:
Contact by letter, by telephone, by e-mail, in person and via website. Appointment necessary.
Hours: Term time: Tues to Thur, 0830 to 2100; Mon and Fri, 0830 to 1700;
Vacations: 0900 to 1600

Access for disabled people:
Ramped entry, access to all public areas

WORCESTERSHIRE ARCHAEOLOGICAL SOCIETY

E-mail: secretary@worcestershirearchaeologicalsociety.org.uk

Enquiries:
Enquiries to: Librarian
Direct tel: 01905 361827
Other contacts: Museum Collections Manager (for library and Honorary Librarian)

Organisation type and purpose:
Learned society (membership is by subscription).

Subject coverage:
Archaeology, architecture, history.

Non-library collection catalogue:
All or part available in-house

Library catalogue:
All or part available in-house

Printed publications:
Worcestershire Archaeological Society's Transactions
The Recorder
Order printed publications from: Honorary Editor, Worcestershire Archaeological Society, 14 Scobell Close, Pershore, Worcestershire, WR10 1QJ; tel: 01905 766353

Access to staff:
Contact by letter, by telephone and by e-mail. Appointment necessary.
Hours: Mon, 1000 to 1700; or by arrangement

Access to building, collection or gallery:
Prior appointment required

Access for disabled people:
Parking provided, level entry, toilet facilities

Links with:
Worcester City Museums
  at the same address; tel: 01905 361820

WORCESTERSHIRE HISTORIC ENVIRONMENT AND ARCHAEOLOGY SERVICE

Formal name: Historic Environment and
Archaeology Service, Worcestershire County
Council
Acronym or abbreviation: WHEAS

Woodbury, University of Worcester, Henwick
Grove, Worcester, WR2 9AJ

Tel: 01905 855455
Fax: 01905 855035
E-mail: archaeology@worcestershire.gov.uk

Website:
http://www.worcestershire.gov.uk/archaeology
Information on sites (Historic Environment
Record), guidance on planning applications,
directory of local societies, commercial services,
educational resources and advice, projects, links to
specialist websites, unpublished reports.

Founded:
1974

Formerly a part of:
Hereford and Worcester County Council (year of
change 1998)

Organisation type and purpose:
Local government, public library (non-issue),
commercial project contracts.

Subject coverage:
Archaeology in general and of Worcestershire in
particular, historic buildings, aerial photographs,
industrial archaeology, archaeological projects.

Non-library collection catalogue:
All or part available online and in-house

Library catalogue:
All or part available online

Printed publications:
Archaeology Newsletter (twice a year)
Project Reports (on excavations and fieldwork; c.
  60 p.a.)
Information leaflets (various)

Publications list:
Available online

Access to staff:
Contact by letter, by telephone, by fax, by e-mail,
in person and via website. Appointment necessary.
Hours: Mon to Fri, 1000 to 1630
Special comments: closed bank holidays.

Parent body:
Worcestershire County Council

WORCESTERSHIRE LIBRARIES AND LEARNING SERVICE

Libraries and Learning, County Hall, Spetchley
Road, Worcester, WR5 2NP

Tel: 01905 822819
Fax: 01905 766930
E-mail: librarieshq@worcestershire.gov.uk

Website:
http://www.worcestershire.gov.uk/libraries

Enquiries:
Enquiries to: Strategic Libraries and Learning
Manager
Direct tel: 01905 766946
Other contacts: Personal Assistant/Admin

Founded:
1920

Organisation type and purpose:
Local government body, public library.

21 branch libraries, 4 mobile libraries, 1 Library
Service at Home vehicle

Subject coverage:
General, local history (all libraries), carpet and
textile industry (at Kidderminster), needle industry
(at Redditch), business information (particularly at
Worcester, Kidderminster and Redditch).

**Museum or gallery collection, archive, or library
special collection:**
Carpets and Textile Collection (Kidderminster)
A. E. Housman and L. Housman Collection
  (Bromsgrove)
Needle Industry (Redditch)
Stuart Period Collection (Worcester)
Willis Bund Collection (local studies material,
  Worcester)

Library catalogue:
All or part available online

Access to staff:
Contact by letter, by telephone, by fax, by e-mail,
in person and via website. Appointment necessary.
Hours: Please see opening times at: http://
www.worcestershire.gov.uk/libraries

Access to building, collection or gallery:
Prior appointment required
Hours: Headquarters: office hours
Branch libraries have various opening hours
including some evenings and some Sat; please see:
http://www.worcestershire.gov.uk/libraries

Access for disabled people:
Avaiable at most libraries; please see: http://
www.worcestershire.gov.uk/libraries

Member organisation of:
SCL West Midlands
TLP West Midlands

Parent body:
Worcestershire County Council

WORCESTERSHIRE RECORD OFFICE

County Hall, Spetchley Road, Worcester, WR5 2NP

Tel: 01905 766351; minicom no. 01905 766399
Fax: 01905 766363
E-mail: recordoffice@worcestershire.gov.uk

Website:
http://www.worcestershire.gov.uk/records
General information concerning Worcestershire
County Council, including Record Office and
heritage function.

Enquiries:
Enquiries to: Archivist

Founded:
1947

Organisation type and purpose:
Local government body.

Subject coverage:
Local authority, quarter sessions, petty sessions,
hospital, coroners, schools, parish, diocesan and
privately deposited records relating to
Worcestershire.

**Museum or gallery collection, archive, or library
special collection:**
Worcestershire photographic survey

Non-library collection catalogue:
All or part available in-house

Library catalogue:
All or part available online

Printed publications:
General information (leaflet, free)
House Hunting at the Worcestershire Record
  Office (leaflet, free)
Worcestershire Research Service (leaflet, free)
Local History at Worcestershire Library and
  History Centre (leaflet, free)
Using the Worcestershire Library and History
  Centre for Family History Research (leaflet, free)
The Photographic Survey (leaflet, free)

Publications list:
Available in print

Access to staff:
Contact by letter, by telephone, by fax, by e-mail,
in person and via website
Hours: Mon, Fri, 0930 to 1900; Tue to Thu, 0930 to
1730; Sat 0930 to 1600

Access to building, collection or gallery:
No prior appointment required
Special comments: Reader's ticket required for
consultation of original documents.

Access for disabled people:
Parking provided, ramped entry

Branches:
Worcestershire Library and History Centre
(WLHC)
  Trinity Street, Worcester, WR1 2PW; tel: 01905
  765922; fax: 01905 765925; e-mail: wlhc@
  worcestershire.gov.uk

WORK FOUNDATION, THE

Peter Runge House, 3 Carlton House, London
SW1Y 5DG

Tel: 0870 165 6700
Fax: 0870 165 6701
E-mail: enquiries@theworkfoundation.com

Website:
http://www.theworkfoundation.com

Enquiries:
Enquiries to: Information Officer

Organisation type and purpose:
Membership association, registered charity,
training organisation, consultancy, research
organisation.
Promoting best practice at work.

Subject coverage:
Conditions of employment, health and safety,
training, leadership, equal opportunities,
employment law, communication at work, total
quality.

Printed publications:
A large range of books in all aspects of people
  management and development

Electronic and video publications:
Right First Time (video)
Say the Right Thing (video)
Team Briefing for the 21st Century (video)
Wish You Were Here (video)

Publications list:
Available in print

Access to staff:
Appointment necessary. Non-members charged.
Hours: Mon to Fri, 0900 to 1700

WORKERS' EDUCATIONAL ASSOCIATION

Acronym or abbreviation: WEA

Third Floor, 70 Clifton Street, London, EC2A 4HB

Tel: 020 7426 3450
Fax: 020 7426 3451
E-mail: national@wea.org.uk

Website:
http://www.wea.org.uk

Founded:
1903

Organisation type and purpose:
The WEA is the largest voluntary sector adult
education provider in Britain, reaching over 80,000
people each year. Courses respond to local need,
often in partnership with community groups and
local charities. Registered charity (number 111275).

continued overleaf

Subject coverage:
Adult education, day, evening, weekend courses in a wide range of subjects, in liberal academic studies, workplace learning, partnership work, community adult education. See website: http://www.wea.org.uk for full details.

Education services:
Runs short (typically ten-week) community adult education courses across England and Scotland.

Museum or gallery collection, archive, or library special collection:
The WEA Archive is held at London Metropolitan University, see website: http://www.wea.org.uk/weaarchive/index.htm

Non-library collection catalogue:
All or part available in print

Library catalogue:
All or part available in print

Printed publications:
Course guides, newsletters and a small number of other publications. See website: http://www.wea.org.uk

Publications list:
Available in print

Access to staff:
Contact by letter, by telephone, by e-mail, in person and via website. Appointment necessary.
Hours: Mon to Fri, 0900 to 1700

Also at:
WEA East Midlands
  39 Mapperley Road, Mapperley Park, Nottingham, NG3 5AQ; tel: 0115 962 8400; fax: 0115 962 8401; e-mail: eastmidland@wea.org.uk
WEA Eastern Region
  Cintra House, 12 Hills Road, Cambridge, CB2 1JP; tel: 01223 350978; fax: 01223 300911; e-mail: eastern@wea.org.uk
WEA London Region
  4 Luke Street, London, EC2A 4XW; tel: 020 7426 1950; fax: 020 7729 9821; e-mail: london@wea.org.uk
WEA National Archive
  London Metropolitan University, Learning Centre, 236 Holloway Road, London, N7 6PP; tel: 020 7753 3184; fax: 020 7753 3191; e-mail: c.coates@unl.ac.uk
WEA North East
  21 Portland Terrace, Jesmond, Newcastle upon Tyne, NE2 1QQ; tel: 0191 212 6100; fax: 0191 212 6101; e-mail: northeast@wea.org.uk
WEA North West
  Suite 405, The Cotton Exchange Building, Old Hall Street, Liverpool, L3 9JR; tel: 0151 243 5340; fax: 0151 243 5359; e-mail: northwest@wea.org.uk
WEA Scottish Association
  Riddle's Court, 322 Lawnmarket, Edinburgh, EH1 2PG; tel: 0131 226 3456; fax: 0131 220 0306; e-mail: scotland@wea.org.uk
WEA South West
  Bradninch Court, Castle Street, Exeter, EX4 3PL; tel: 01392 457300; e-mail: southwest@wea.org.uk
WEA Southern Region
  57 Riverside, 2 Sir Thomas Longley Road, Rochester, Kent, ME2 4DP; tel: 01634 298600; fax: 01634 298601; e-mail: southern@wea.org.uk
WEA West Midlands
  Fourth Floor, Lancaster House, 67 Newhall Street, Birmingham, B3 1NQ; tel: 0121 237 8120; fax: 0121 237 8121; e-mail: westmidlands@wea.org.uk
WEA Yorkshire and Humber
  6 Woodhouse Square, Leeds, LS3 1AD; tel: 01132 453304; fax: 01132 450883; website: http://yorkshumberwea.org.uk

Member organisation of:
National Council for Voluntary Organisations
National Institute of Adult Continuing Education

WORKING CLASS MOVEMENT LIBRARY

Acronym or abbreviation: WCML

Jubilee House, 51 The Crescent, Salford, M5 4WX

Tel: 0161 736 3601
Fax: 0161 737 4115
E-mail: enquiries@wcml.org.uk

Website:
http://www.wcml.org.uk
Online catalogue of books, pamphlets and archival material, plus introduction to the Library's varied collections.

Enquiries:
Enquiries to: Library Manager

Founded:
c.1950

Organisation type and purpose:
Registered charity (charity number 1115731), public library, historic building, house or site, suitable for ages: adults/students.
To assist in the study and research of labour history, the working class and political struggles from 1770 to the present day.

Subject coverage:
Trade unions, campaigns for change from Chartism to the present day, poverty and social conditions, politics, economics, working class education, Co-operative Movement.

Museum or gallery collection, archive, or library special collection:
Records from brushmakers, shipwrights, boilermakers and many other unions
Papers from playwright Jim Allen, activists such as Benny Rothman and Angela Tuckett, and the Library's founders Eddie and Ruth Frow
Papers relating to the International Brigade in the Spanish Civil War, with a specific focus on volunteers from the North West of England
Banners, photographs, poetry, songs, posters, badges, cartoons and much more

Non-library collection catalogue:
All or part available online and in-house

Library catalogue:
All or part available online and in-house

Printed publications:
Shelf Life (quarterly bulletin for Friends of the Library)
Publications include:
From Manchester to Spain (£5)
Essays on the Irish in Manchester (£1.50)
Karl Marx in Manchester (£5)
Frederick Engels in Manchester (£1.50)
William Morris in Manchester and Salford (£2.50)
Manchester and Salford Chartists (£4)
Order printed publications from: WCML

Microform publications:
Nelson Gazette, 1928–1962
Order microform publications from: Microform Academic Publishers, Main Street, East Ardsley, Wakefield, WF3 2AP

Publications list:
Available online

Access to staff:
Contact by letter, by telephone, by fax, by e-mail and via website. Appointment necessary.
Hours: Tue to Fri, 1000 to 1700; third Sat of the month, 1000 to 1600

Access to building, collection or gallery:
Prior appointment required
Hours: Tue to Fri, 1000 to 1700; third Sat of the month, 1000 to 1600

Access for disabled people:
Parking provided, ramped entry, toilet facilities

Administered by:
Board of Trustees
  at the same address

WORLD AHLUL BAYT ISLAMIC LEAGUE

Acronym or abbreviation: WABIL

19 Chelmsford Square, London, NW10 3AP

Tel: 020 8459 8475
Fax: 020 8451 7059
E-mail: wabil@wabil.com

Website:
http://www.cealpha1.swan.ac.uk
Information on Islam, Quran, Islamic books, history, lives of Islam's personalities.
http://www.wabil.com

Enquiries:
Enquiries to: Secretary General
Direct tel: 020 8459 6051
Direct e-mail: mmusawi@gmail.com
Other contacts: Public Relations Officer

Founded:
1983

Organisation type and purpose:
International organisation, voluntary organisation, registered charity (charity number 291922).

Subject coverage:
Islam, Shiaism, jurisprudence, scholars' welfare in poor countries, books, charity.

Printed publications:
Ahlul Bayt Journal (available in English, Arabic and French)
Ja'fari Observer

Electronic and video publications:
Islamic & Educational Subjects available (CD-ROM)

Publications list:
Available in print

Access to staff:
Contact by letter, by fax and by e-mail
Hours: Mon to Fri, 0900 to 1700

WORLD ARABIAN HORSE ORGANIZATION

Acronym or abbreviation: WAHO

Newbarn Farmhouse, Forthampton, Gloucestershire, GL19 4QD

Tel: 01684 274455
Fax: 01684 274422
E-mail: waho@compuserve.com

Website:
http://www.waho.org

Enquiries:
Enquiries to: Executive Secretary

Founded:
1972

Organisation type and purpose:
International organisation, membership association, present number of members: 54 member countries, 1000 individual associate members, registered charity.

Subject coverage:
Arabian horses.

Printed publications:
Members Directory

Access to staff:
Contact by letter, by telephone, by fax, by e-mail and via website. Appointment necessary.
Hours: Mon to Fri, 0900 to 1700

WORLD BOWLS LIMITED

SportScotland, Caledonia House, 1 Redheughs Rigg, South Gyle, Edinburgh, EH12 9DQ

Tel: 0131 317 9764
Fax: 0131 317 9765
E-mail: worldbows@btconnect.com

Website:
http://www.worldbowlsltd.co.uk

Enquiries:
Enquiries to: Chief Executive Officer

Founded:
1907

Formed by the amalgamation of:
International Womens Bowling Board (IWBB),
World Bowls Board (year of change 2001)

Formerly called:
International Bowling Board (IBB) (year of change
1992)

Organisation type and purpose:
International organisation, advisory body,
membership association (membership is by
subscription), present number of members: 53
National Authorities.
Governing body of the sport.

Subject coverage:
International competition, laws of game,
manufacture and testing of bowls, standards for
bowling green surfaces.

Printed publications:
Constitution and By-Laws (free)
Joint Laws of the Game (£1.50)
Performance Standard for Artificial Flat Green
  Bowls Surfaces (£10)

Electronic and video publications:
Umpiring and Marking Skills DVD (£10)

Access to staff:
Contact by letter, by telephone, by fax and by e-
mail
Hours: Mon to Fri, 0900 to 1700

Access for disabled people:
Parking provided, level entry, access to all public
areas, toilet facilities

WORLD CANCER RESEARCH FUND (WCRF UK)

Acronym or abbreviation: WCRF UK

22 Bedford Square, London WC1B 3HH

Tel: 020 7343 4200
Fax: 020 7343 4201
E-mail: wcrf@wcrf.org

Website:
http://www.wcrf-uk.org
Practical advice on preventing cancer through diet,
physical activity and weight management.

Enquiries:
Enquiries to: Supporter Services Department
Direct tel: 020 7343 4205

Founded:
1990

Organisation type and purpose:
Registered charity (charity number 1000739),
suitable for ages: all, research organisation.
To raise awareness of cancer as a preventable
disease; to provide advice for healthy living; to
translate scientific research findings into accessible
form; to motivate individuals to change to
healthier diets and lifestyles; to provide supporter
services.

Subject coverage:
Diet, nutrition, physical activity, weight
management and cancer prevention.

Information services:
Education department; tel: 020 7343 4200

Education services:
Education department; tel: 020 7343 4200

Printed publications:
A series of booklets and fact sheets available free
  (although donations to cover postage and
  printing gratefully received) including:
Recommendations for Cancer Prevention
Guidelines for Cancer Prevention
Reducing Your Risk series
A Closer Look at series
Finding the Balance series
Cookbooks
Health Aids, such as BMI Calculators
Order printed publications from: website: http://
www.wcrf-uk.org/publications or telephone 020
7343 4205

Electronic and video publications:
A series of booklets and fact sheets available free,
  including:
Recommendations for Cancer Prevention
Guidelines for Cancer Prevention
Reducing Your Risk series
A Closer Look at series
Finding the Balance series
Cookbooks
Health Aids, such as BMI Calculators
Order electronic and video publications from: website:
http://www.wcrf-uk.org/publications

Publications list:
Available online and in print

Access to staff:
Contact by letter, by telephone, by fax, by e-mail
and via website. Appointment necessary.
Hours: Mon to Fri, 0900 to 1730

Access to building, collection or gallery:
No access other than to staff

Affiliated to:
American Institute for Cancer Research
  website: http://www.aicr.org
World Cancer Research Fund Hong Kong
  website: http://www.wcrf-hk.org
World Cancer Research Fund Netherlands
  Netherlands; website: http://www.wcrf-nl.org

WORLD CONFEDERATION FOR PHYSICAL THERAPY

Acronym or abbreviation: WCPT

Victoria Charity Centre, 11 Belgrave Road,
London, SW1V 1RB

Tel: 020 7931 6465
Fax: 020 7931 6494
E-mail: info@wcpt.org

Website:
http://www.wcpt.org

Enquiries:
Enquiries to: Secretary-General

Founded:
1951

Organisation type and purpose:
International organisation, professional body
(membership is by qualification), present number
of members: 92, registered charity (charity number
234307).
WCPT is a confederation of 92 national
professional associates around the world. It aims to
improve global health care by representing
physical therapists (physiotherapists)
internationally, enabling information exchange and
co-operation among physical therapists across the
world, and encouraging high standards of
research, education and practice in physical
therapy.

Printed publications:
Single copies of most publications are free of
  charge to member organisations
Newsletter (available by subscription, £16 for 2
  years, 8 issues)

Publications list:
Available online and in print

Access to staff:
Contact by letter and by e-mail. Appointment
necessary.
Hours: Mon to Fri, 0900 to 1700

Access to building, collection or gallery:
No prior appointment required

WORLD CURLING FEDERATION

Acronym or abbreviation: WCF

74 Tay Street, Perth, Tayside, PH2 8NP

Tel: 01738 451630
Fax: 01738 451641
E-mail: wcf@dial.pipex.com

Website:
http://www.worldcurling.org

Enquiries:
Enquiries to: Secretary-General
Other contacts: Media Relations Officer

Founded:
1966

Formerly called:
International Curling Federation (ICF) (year of
change 1991)

Organisation type and purpose:
International organisation, membership
association.
Represents 44 member associations and promotes
the sport of curling world-wide.

Subject coverage:
The sport of curling world-wide, details of
participants and performance, venues of World
and World Junior Curling Championships since
1959, organisation of all World and World
Wheelchair Curling Championships.

Printed publications:
Coaching Manuals (various)
WCF Constitution and By-Laws
WCF Rules of Curling and Competition
Curling Ice-Making Manual
Order printed publications from: World Curling
Federation, 74 Tay Street, Perth, PH2 8NP

Publications list:
Available in print

Access to staff:
Contact by letter, by telephone, by fax and by e-
mail. Appointment necessary.
Hours: Mon to Fri, 0900 to 1700

Access for disabled people:
Ramped entry

WORLD EDUCATION DEVELOPMENT GROUP

Acronym or abbreviation: WEDG

98A Broad Street, Canterbury, Kent, CT1 2LU

Tel: 01227 766552
Fax: 01227 766552
E-mail: info@wedg.org.uk

Website:
http://www.wedg.org.uk

Enquiries:
Enquiries to: Projects Leader
Other contacts: Development Education Co-
ordinator

Founded:
1987

Organisation type and purpose:
Development Education Centre

Subject coverage:
TWEDG engages with schools, universities,
community groups and other educators in East
Kent to promote global education and make issues
such as sustainable development, social justice and
human rights accessible to all. Provides training, a
resources centre, workshops, assemblies, support
and advice through projects.

**Museum or gallery collection, archive, or library
special collection:**
A variety of material for educational use in
  geography, RE, English, science, etc.
Reference information on Peace, Human Rights,
  Environment and Development including
  teachers' packs

Non-library collection catalogue:
All or part available online

Printed publications:
Dolls Defying Discrimination
Young Diasporas – Longing and Belonging
Order printed publications from: WEDG

continued overleaf

Electronic and video publications:
Videos and slides

Access to staff:
Contact by letter, by telephone, by fax, by e-mail and via website. Appointment necessary. Non-members charged.
Hours: Wed, 1400 to 1800; first Sat of month, 1100 to 1300; by appointment at other times

Access to building, collection or gallery:
No access other than to staff, no prior appointment required
Hours: Wed, 1400 to 1800; first Sat of month, 1100 to 1300

Access for disabled people:
Ramped entry

Links with:
Kent and the Wider World
   website: http://www.commonwork.org/kww/default.htm
PIDEC
   website: http://www.pestalozzi.org.uk

Member organisation of:
DEA
   CAN Mezzanine, 32–36 Loman Street, London, SE1 0EH; website: http://www.dea.org.uk
Local4Global
   website: http://www.local4global.org.uk

WORLD EMERGENCY RELIEF

Acronym or abbreviation: WER

20 York Buildings, London, WC2N 6JU

Tel: 020 7839 3854
Fax: 020 7839 8202
E-mail: info@wer-uk.org

Website:
http://www.wer-uk.org
Details of charity operation and accounts.

Enquiries:
Enquiries to: Executive Director
Direct e-mail: alex@wer-uk.org

Founded:
1994

Organisation type and purpose:
Registered charity (charity number 1045672).

Access to staff:
Contact by letter and by e-mail
Hours: Mon to Fri, 0900 to 1700

Access for disabled people:
Access to all public areas

WORLD ENERGY COUNCIL

Acronym or abbreviation: WEC

5th Floor, Regency House, 1–4 Warwick Street, London, W1B 5LT

Tel: 020 7734 5996
Fax: 020 7734 5926

Website:
http://www.worldenergy.org
Publication list

Enquiries:
Enquiries to: Information Officer

Founded:
1924

Formerly called:
World Energy Congress

Organisation type and purpose:
International organisation, membership association, registered charity (charity number 1086559).
To promote the sustainable supply and use of energy for the greatest benefit of all.

Subject coverage:
Energy (all forms, fossil, renewables, nuclear), provision and use thereof, energy-related issues including environmental, efficiency and conservation, economic and social development, financing, technology, policy.

Museum or gallery collection, archive, or library special collection:
Small energy library

Trade and statistical information:
Triennial surveys of energy resources and national energy databases
Special publications, e.g. WEC Commission report, renewable energy resources, combined heat and power schemes

Printed publications:
For purchase:
Survey of Energy Resources 2001 £25
Renewable Energy in South Asia: Status and Prospects £15
Drivers of the Energy Scene 2004 (PDF only) £55
Drivers of the Energy Scene 2004 (CD package) £70
Drivers of the Energy Scene 2004 (hardcopy volume) £95
Renewable Energy Projects Handbook (PDF) £20
Comparison of Energy Systems Using Life Cycle Analysis £45
Regulating District Heating and Cogeneration in Central and Eastern Europe (Hard Copy) £40
Regulating District Heating and Cogeneration in Central and Eastern Europe (PDF version) £25
Energy Market Reforms: Lessons Learned and Next Steps (Hard Copy) £100
Energy Market Reforms: Lessons Learned and Next Steps (PDF version) £75
Comparison of Energy Systems Using Life Cycle Analysis (PDF version) £30
Energy Efficiency: A Worldwide Review (Hard Copy) £75
Energy Efficiency: A Worldwide Review (PDF version) £55
Performance of Generating Plant: New Realities, New Needs (Hard Copy) £85
Performance of Generating Plant: New Realities, New Needs (PDF version) £60
Sustainable Global Energy Development: The Case of Coal (Hard Copy) £70
Sustainable Global Energy Development: The Case of Coal (PDF version) £60
Energy End-Use Technologies for the 21st Century (PDF version) £75
Energy End-Use Technologies for the 21st Century (Hard Copy) £100
Comparación de los Sistemas Energéticos Utilizando Evaluación del Ciclo de Vida (PDF) £30
Global Energy Perspectives (1998) £15
Online:
Déclaration 2004 du CME: Réflexions sur la dynamique des marchés du pétrole et du gaz naturel (also in hard copy)
Electricity Market Design and Creation in Asia Pacific Report 2001
Energy & Climate Change Working Paper 2004
Energy Efficiency Policies and Indicators Report 2001
Energy for Tomorrow's World – Acting Now! Report 2000
Energy Markets in Transition: The Latin American and Caribbean Experience Report 2001
Energy Technologies for the 21st Century Report
Living in One World (also in hard copy)
Mensaje del CME para 2003: Cuotas de la Energía
Performance of Generating Plant Report 2001
Performance of Thermal Generating Plant (PTGP) Monographs Report 1998
Potentiel de développement intégré de l'énergie au plan régional en Afrique Report 2003
Pricing Energy in Developing Countries Report 2001
Renewable Energy in South Asia Report 2000 (also in hard copy)
Report on COP-5: A Bonn Outcome or Bad?
Climate Change Report No. 13, 1999
Report on COP-6: Lack of Progress at COP 6
Climate Change Report No. 14, 2000
Restructuring and Privatizing the Coal Industries in Central and Eastern Europe and the CIS Report 2000 (also in hard copy)
Survey of Energy Resources Report 2001 (also on CD)
The Benefits and Deficiencies of Energy Sector Liberalisation Report 1998
The Challenge of Rural Energy Poverty in Developing Countries Report 1999
The Potential for Regionally Integrated Energy Development in Africa Report 2003
Towards Local Energy Systems: Revitalizing District Heating and Co-Generation in Central and Eastern Europe
WEC Statement 2001: Pricing Energy in Developing Countries – Summary Only
WEC Statement 2002: Energy for People, Energy for Peace Only
WEC Statement 2003: Renewable Energy Targets Only
WEC Statement 2004: Reflections on the Dynamics of Oil and Natural Gas Markets (also in hard copy)
Order printed publications from: London Office, WEC
at the same adddress, e-mail: info@worldenergy .org

Electronic and video publications:
All Publications available on the Council's website
Survey of Energy Resources (online 1998, 2001, CD-ROM)
Energy for Tomorrow's World – Acting Now (online 2000)
Living in One World (online 2001)
Renewables in S Asia (online 2001)
The Challenge of Rural Energy Poverty (online 1999)

Publications list:
Available online and in print

Access to staff:
Contact by letter, by telephone, by fax and by e-mail. Appointment necessary.
Hours: Mon to Fri, 1000 to 1600

Has:
96 affiliated national energy associations worldwide

WORLD HERITAGE

Heritage House, 25 High West Street, Dorchester, Dorset, DT1 1UW

Tel: 01305 269741
Fax: 01305 268885
E-mail: info@world-heritage.org.uk

Website:
http://www.thedinosaurmuseum.com
http://www.world-heritage.org.uk
http://www.tutankhamun-exhibition.co.uk
http://www.teddybearmuseum.co.uk
http://www.terracottawarriors.co.uk

Enquiries:
Enquiries to: Manager

Founded:
1989

Organisation type and purpose:
Museum.
A consortium of independent museums and exhibitions; also operates literature distribution and tourism services.

Subject coverage:
Egyptology, dinosaurs, fossils, geology, teddy bears, tourism, museum management, terracotta warriors, photography.

Printed publications:
Wide selection of books produced by other publishers, available by mail order or direct from one of the museum shops
Main themes of books: Egyptology, dinosaurs, teddy bears (price lists available)

Access to staff:
Contact by letter, by telephone, by fax, by e-mail and via website. Appointment necessary.

Hours: Mon to Fri, 0900 to 1700

Access to building, collection or gallery:
All the museums are open daily.
Hours: Times vary for different museums but they are all open through the core times of 1000 to 1630
Special comments: Entrance to the museums is charged for.

Branch museums:
Dinosaur Museum
 Icen Way, Dorchester, DT1 1EW; tel: 01305 269880; fax: 01305 268885; e-mail: info@ thedinosaurmuseum.com; website: http://www .thedinosaurmuseum.com
Teddy Bear Museum
 corner of High East Street and Salisbury Street, Dorchester, DT1 1JU; tel: 01305 266040; fax: 01305 268885; e-mail: info@teddybearmuseum.co .uk; website: http://www.teddybearmuseum.co .uk
Terracotta Warriors Museum
 Salisbury Street, Dorchester, Dorset, DT1 1JU; tel: 01305 266040; fax: 01305 268885; e-mail: info@terracottawarriors.co.uk; website: http:// www.terracottawarriors.co.uk
Tutankhamun Exhibition
 High West Street, Dorchester, DT1 1UW; tel: 01305 269571; fax: 01305 268885; e-mail: info@ tutankhamun-exhibition.co.uk; website: http:// www.tutankhamun-exhibition.co.uk

WORLD HORSE WELFARE

Anne Colvin House, Snetterton, Norfolk, NR16 2LR

Tel: 01953 498682
Fax: 01953 498373
E-mail: info@worldhorsewelfare.org

Website:
http://www.worldhorsewelfare.org

Founded:
1927

Formerly called:
International League for the Protection of Horses

Organisation type and purpose:
International organisation, registered charity (charity number 206658).
Equine welfare organisation.
Working for a world where the horse is used but never abused.

Subject coverage:
Equine care and management; transportation of equines for slaughter – overseas; recovery and rehabilitation of equines – UK; NGO training on saddlery, farriery, horse management and nutrition in developing countries.

Printed publications:
Mail Order catalogue
Newsletter (quarterly)
Individual leaflets on each of the 4 UK Equine recovery and rehabilitation centres
Order printed publications from: Communications Manager

Access to staff:
Contact by letter, by telephone, by fax, by e-mail, in person and via website. Appointment necessary.
Hours: Mon to Fri, 0900 to 1700

Collaboration with other major equine organisations eg:
Animal Health Trust
 Newmarket, Suffolk
International Equestrian Federation, Lausanne, Switzerland (FEI)
Liverpool University
 Department of Veterinary Clinical Science and Animal Husbandry
Royal (Dick) School of Veterinary Studies, University of Edinburgh

WORLD LAND TRUST

Blyth House, Bridge Street, Halesworth, Suffolk, IP19 8AB

Tel: 0845 054 4422 (local rate, UK only); 01986 874422
Fax: 01986 874425
E-mail: info@worldlandtrust.org

Website:
http://www.worldlandtrust.org
About the trust and its work, news, events.
http://www.carbonbalanced.org
Projects that both offset carbon dioxide (CO2) emissions and conserve biodiversity.
http://www.focusonforests.org
Rainforest education for 11–14 year olds.
http://www.wildlifefocus.org
Website for wildlife and nature lovers everywhere.

Enquiries:
Other contacts: Education, Training & Outreach Officer

Founded:
1989

Formerly called:
World Wide Land Conservation Trust

Organisation type and purpose:
An international conservation charity (registered charity number 1001291).
Takes direct action to save rainforest and other wildlife habitats by providing funds for partner organisations, so that they can purchase land and establish permanent wildlife reserves; works to preserve the world's most biologically important and threatened lands, and has helped purchase and protect over 400,000 acres of habitats rich in wildlife, in Asia, Central and South America and the UK.

Subject coverage:
Has a policy of working with local partner organisations, and the Trust does not normally play a direct role in the ownership or the management of the land it conserves.

Education services:
Resource packs for schools; internships; Graduate Diploma in Conservation and Project Administration in conjunction with the University of East Anglia.

Electronic and video publications:
eBulletin (monthly conservation news)
Order electronic and video publications from:
Download from website

Publications list:
Available online

Access to staff:
Contact by letter, by telephone, by fax, by e-mail and via website

Links with:
World Land Trust-US
 2806 P Street NW, Washington, DC 20007, USA; fax: +1 603 284 7134; e-mail: info@worldlandtrust -us.org; website: http://www.worldlandtrust-us .org

WORLD NUCLEAR ASSOCIATION

Acronym or abbreviation: WNA

Carlton House, 22a St James's Square, London, SW1Y 4JH

Tel: 020 7451 1520
Fax: 020 7839 1501
E-mail: wna@world-nuclear.org

Website:
http://www.world-nuclear.org
All aspects of uranium and nuclear energy industries, including forthcoming conferences, statistics, information papers.

Founded:
1975

Organisation type and purpose:
International organisation, trade association (membership is by subscription), present number of members: 120, research organisation.

Subject coverage:
Uranium: supply and demand, geology, mining, processing, laws and regulations, trade, safety, environmental issues; nuclear power: status world-wide, technology.

Trade and statistical information:
Uranium production statistics, international by country; nuclear energy statistics, international by country.

Non-library collection catalogue:
All or part available in-house

Printed publications:
Pocket Guides (free) on:
Nuclear Power Reactor Characteristics
Uranium: From Mine to Mill
Nuclear Power: Energy and the Environment
Market Report (every 2 years, price on application)
Order printed publications from: website

Electronic and video publications:
Information papers (online)
Symposium proceedings (online)

Publications list:
Available online

Access to staff:
Contact by letter, by telephone, by fax, by e-mail and via website. Appointment necessary.
Hours: Mon to Fri, 1000 to 1600

WORLD OWL TRUST

The World Owl Centre, Muncaster Castle, Ravenglass, Cumbria, CA18 1RQ

Tel: 01229 717393
Fax: 01229 717107
E-mail: via website

Website:
http://www.owls.org
Contacts, membership, general and specific owl information, owl first aid, online shop.

Organisation type and purpose:
Registered charity (number 1107529).
Exists to advance wildlife conservation by primarily focusing on all owl species and their ecology. Through the promotion of habitat management and restoration, research, captive breeding programmes, and its own education policy, the Trust intends to bring an awareness of conservation and environmental sustainability to all levels of society. On-site facilities are maintained to provide treatment and rehabilitation for sick and injured owls and other wildlife.

Subject coverage:
Conservation programmes protect populations of endangered owls until their habitat has been restored and birds held at the Owl Centre can be reintroduced back into the wild.

Special visitor services:
Owl Centre, Muncaster Castle; tel: 01229 717614

Electronic and video publications:
Save an Owl for a £1 Information Pack
Newsletter (2 or 3 a year)
Annual report
Order electronic and video publications from:
Download from website

Publications list:
Available online

Access to staff:
Contact by letter, by telephone, by fax, in person and via website

Access to building, collection or gallery:
Free coach and car parking opposite the main gate, with disabled parking
Hours: The Gardens, Owl Centre and MeadowVole Maze open Mon to Sun all year (except Jan), 1030 to 1800 (or dusk if earlier)

Access for disabled people:
The main areas of the Gardens and Owl Centre and MeadowVole Maze allow wheelchair access; the ground floor of the Castle (where the majority

continued overleaf

of the audio tour takes place) is also accessible by wheelchair; accessible toilets are available in the Stable Yard and the Coach Park; dogs are welcome in the Gardens and the Owl Centre if kept on a lead and under control; guide dogs, only, in the Castle, MeadowVole Maze and Café.

Member organisation of:
British and Irish Association of Zoos and Aquariums (BIAZA)
European Association of Zoos and Aquariums (EAZA)

WORLD PARROT TRUST

Acronym or abbreviation: WPT

Glanmor House, Hayle, Cornwall, TR27 4HB

Tel: 01736 751026
Fax: 01736 751028
E-mail: uk@worldparrottrust.org

Website:
http://www.parrots.org

Enquiries:
Enquiries to: Administrator
Other contacts: Chairman

Founded:
1989

Organisation type and purpose:
International organisation, membership association (membership is by subscription), present number of members: 2,116, registered charity (charity number 800944).
Conservation and welfare of parrots.

Subject coverage:
Parrot conservation projects, the welfare of pet parrots and aviculture.

Printed publications:
Parrot Action Plan 2000–2005
Leaflets on pet care welfare – Happy, Healthy Parrot
PsittaScene (quarterly newsletter, free to members or £3 each)

Access to staff:
Contact by letter, by telephone, by fax, by e-mail and via website
Hours: Mon to Fri, 0900 to 1700

Links with:
Paradise Park (wildlife sanctuary)
   tel: 01736 751026; fax: 01736 751028

WORLD PHEASANT ASSOCIATION

Acronym or abbreviation: WPA

Biology Field Station, Newcastle University, Close House Estate, Heddon-on-the-Wall, Newcastle-upon-Tyne, NE15 0HT

Tel: 01661 853397
Fax: 01661 853397
E-mail: office@pheasant.org.uk

Website:
http://www.pheasant.org.uk

Enquiries:
Enquiries to: Administrator
Direct e-mail: Barbara.Ingman@pheasant.org.uk
Other contacts: Director

Founded:
1975

Formerly called:
WPA International (WPA)

Organisation type and purpose:
International organisation, membership association, voluntary organisation, registered charity (charity number 271203).

Subject coverage:
Conservation, breeding and management of galliformes (pheasants, grouse, quail etc) field studies.

Trade and statistical information:
Data on the status and distribution of galliformes worldwide.

Printed publications:
Annual Review
WPA News (2 a year)

Electronic and video publications:
Under development (bibliographic database)

Publications list:
Available online and in print

Access to staff:
Contact by letter, by telephone, by fax and by e-mail. Appointment necessary.
Hours: Mon to Fri, 0900 to 1700

Access for disabled people:
Parking provided, level entry, access to all public areas, toilet facilities

Specialist group for:
Birdlife International

WORLD PLOUGHING ORGANIZATION

Acronym or abbreviation: WPO

26 Gable Avenue, Cockermouth, Cumbria, CA13 9BU

Tel: 01900 825686
Fax: 01900 68736

Website:
http://www.worldploughing.org

Enquiries:
Enquiries to: Treasurer

Founded:
1952

Organisation type and purpose:
Voluntary organisation.

Subject coverage:
Standards of ploughmanship, the rules for ploughing, competition ploughing as an incentive to good husbandry of the soil, soil tillage demonstrations and machinery exhibition.

Printed publications:
WPO Bulletin of News and Information (annually)
WPO Contest Handbook (annually)

Access to staff:
Contact by letter
Hours: Mon to Fri, 0900 to 1700

WORLD PROFESSIONAL BILLIARDS AND SNOOKER ASSOCIATION LIMITED

Acronym or abbreviation: WPBSA

Suite 2/1, Albert House, 111–117 Victoria Street, Bristol, BS1 6AX

Tel: 0117 317 8200
Fax: 0117 317 8300
E-mail: enq@worldsnooker.com

Website:
http://www.worldsnooker.com

Enquiries:
Enquiries to: Company Secretary

Organisation type and purpose:
Membership association.
Governing body of the games.

Subject coverage:
Details of the professional and amateur games of billiards and snooker.

Museum or gallery collection, archive, or library special collection:
Books and records of snooker and billiards from the commencement of the games in 1887 and founding of a formal Snooker and Billiards Association in that year

Access to staff:
Contact by letter
Hours: Mon to Fri, 0900 to 1700

WORLD SIKH FOUNDATION

33 Wargrave Road, South Harrow, Middlesex, HA2 8LL

Tel: 020 8864 9228
E-mail: bablibharara@hotmail.com

Enquiries:
Enquiries to: Secretary
Direct e-mail: worldsikhfoundation@hotmail.com

Founded:
1960

Formerly called:
Sikh Cultural Society of Great Britain (year of change 1993)

Organisation type and purpose:
International organisation, learned society (membership is by subscription), present number of members: 850, voluntary organisation, registered charity (charity number 1054913), publishing house.
Religious society.
To spread message of Sikhism worldwide.

Subject coverage:
The Sikh religion.

Printed publications:
Pamphlets
Sikh Courier International (journal)

Access to staff:
Contact by letter and by telephone
Hours: Mon to Fri, 0900 to 1700

Also at the same address:
Guru Nanak Foundation UK

WORLD SOCIETY FOR THE PROTECTION OF ANIMALS

Acronym or abbreviation: WSPA

89 Albert Embankment, London, SE1 7TP

Tel: 020 7587 5000
Fax: 020 7793 0208
E-mail: wspa@wspa.org.uk

Website:
http://www.wspa.org.uk

Enquiries:
Enquiries to: Supporter Services

Founded:
1980

Formerly called:
ISPA; WFPA (year of change 1980)

Organisation type and purpose:
Membership association, present number of members: 953 member societies in 154 countries, registered charity (charity number 1081849).
Animal welfare charity.

Subject coverage:
Wildlife, companion animals, farm animals, animal welfare legislation, disaster relief, humane education, animal protection.

Printed publications:
Annual Report
Membership Communication Material
Ongoing Animal Reports

Electronic and video publications:
Campaign videos

Publications list:
Available in print

Access to staff:
Contact by letter, by telephone, by fax and by e-mail. Appointment necessary.
Hours: Mon to Fri, 0900 to 1700

Access for disabled people:
Parking provided, ramped entry, toilet facilities

Access to staff:
Contact by letter
Hours: Mon to Fri, 0900 to 1700

Also at:

World Society for the Protection of Animals
90 Eglington Avenue East, Suite 960, Toronto, Ontario, M4P 2Y3, Canada; tel: +1 416 369 0044; fax: +1 416 369 0147; e-mail: wspa@wspa.ca; website: http://www.wspa.ca

World Society for the Protection of Animals
Mall Paseo las Flores Business Center, 5th floor, Apdo Postal 516–3000, Heredia, Costa Rica; tel: +506 2562 1200; fax: +506 2562 1225; e-mail: info@wspala.org; website: http://wspa.or.cr

World Society for the Protection of Animals
PO Box 105476, Dar es Salaam, Tanzania; tel: +255 22 270 1032; fax: +255 22 270 1033; e-mail: enquiries@wspaafrica.org; website: http://www .wspa-international.org

World Society for the Protection of Animals
Lincoln Plaza, Suite 201, 89 South Street, Boston 02111, USA; tel: +1 617 896 9214; fax: +1 617 737 4404; e-mail: wspa@wspausa.org; website: http://www.wspa-usa.org

World Society for the Protection of Animals
19th Floor, Olympia Thai Tower, 444 Ratchadaphisek Road, Huay Kwang, Bangkok 10310, Thailand; tel: +66 2 513 0475; fax: +66 2 513 0477; e-mail: thailand.enquiries@wspa-asia .org; website: http://www.wspa-international .org

World Society for the Protection of Animals
GPO Box 3294, Sydney, NSW 2001, Australia; tel: +61 2 9902 8000; fax: +61 2 9906 1166; e-mail: wspa@wspa.org.au; website: http://www.wspa .org.au

World Society for the Protection of Animals
Av. Princesa Isabel, 323 – 8 andar, Copacabana, 22011–901, Rio de Janeiro, Brazil; tel: +55 21 3820 8200; fax: +55 21 3820 8229; e-mail: wspabrasil@ wspabr.org; website: http://www.wspabrasil.org

World Society for the Protection of Animals
501B, Dong Wai Diplomatic Building, No. 23, Dongzhimen Wai Avenue, Beijing 100600, People's Republic of China; tel: +86 10 85325211 – 8008; fax: +86 10 85324211; e-mail: alyceyu@ wspa-asia.org; website: http://www.wspa -international.org

World Society for the Protection of Animals
Carrera 13 #29–21 Of. 234, Manzana 1, Parque Central Bavaria, Bogotá, Colombia; tel: +571 288 8829; fax: +571 232 1361; e-mail: wspa@wspa.org .co; website: http://www.wspa-international.org

World Society for the Protection of Animals
Kaiserstrasse 22, 53113, Bonn, Germany; tel: +49 228 956 3455; fax: +49 228 956 3454; e-mail: info@ wspa.de; website: http://www.wspa.de

World Society for the Protection of Animals
Benoordenhoutseweg 23, 2596 BA Den Haag, The Netherlands; tel: +31 70 314 2800; fax: +31 70 314 2809; e-mail: info@wspa.nl; website: http:// www.wspa.nl

World Society for the Protection of Animals
Private Bag 93220, Parnell 1151, Auckland, New Zealand; tel: +64 9 309 3901; fax: +64 9 336 1947; e-mail: wspa@wspa.org.nz; website: http://www .wspa.org.nz

World Society for the Protection of Animals
Vesterbrogade 34, 1, 1620 Copenhagen V, Denmark; tel: +45 33 93 7212; fax: +45 33 93 7210; e-mail: info@wspa.dk; website: http://www .wspa.dk

Links with:
United Nations (consultative status)

Member organisation of:
Eurogroup for Animal Welfare

WORLD SQUASH FEDERATION LIMITED

Acronym or abbreviation: WSF

6 Havelock Road, Hastings, East Sussex, TN34 1BP

Tel: 01424 429245
Fax: 01424 429250
E-mail: squash@worldsquash.org

Website:
http://www.squash.org
The Internet Squash Federation.

Enquiries:
Enquiries to: Chief Executive
Other contacts: Executive Assistant

Founded:
1967

Formerly called:
International Squash Rackets Federation (ISRF) (year of change 1992)

Organisation type and purpose:
International organisation.

Subject coverage:
The sport of squash, court, clothing, ball, racket specifications; rules, refereeing, coaching, world championships.

Access to staff:
Contact by letter, by telephone, by fax, by e-mail and via website. Appointment necessary.
Hours: Mon to Fri, 0900 to 1700

WORLD UNION FOR PROGRESSIVE JUDAISM EUROPEAN BOARD

Acronym or abbreviation: WUPJ

Sternberg Centre for Judaism, 80 East End Road, London, N3 2SY

Tel: 020 8349 3779
Fax: 020 8343 5699
E-mail: europeanjudaism@directmail.org

Enquiries:
Enquiries to: Administrator

Founded:
1926

Organisation type and purpose:
International organisation (membership is by election or invitation), registered charity (charity number 253000).
Nurture and develop progressive Jewish communities in Europe.

Printed publications:
European Eye (newsletter, quarterly)

Access to staff:
Contact by letter, by fax and by e-mail
Hours: Mon to Thu, 1030 to 1600

Parent body:
World Union for Progressive Judaism
13 King David Street, Jerusalem 94101, Israel; tel: 00 972 2 6203447; fax: 00 972 2 6203525; e-mail: wupjis@wupj.org.il; website: http://www.wupj .org

WORLD WAR TWO RAILWAY STUDY GROUP

17 Balmoral Crescent, West Molesey, Surrey, KT8 1QA

Tel: 020 8783 1024
E-mail: tcane@ww2rsg.u-net.com

Website:
http://www.2rsg.org

Organisation type and purpose:
Membership association.
Research into the use of railways in World War II.

Subject coverage:
Use of railways in World War Two, mainly UK railways and the overseas use of railways by British forces. Topics include civil engineering, ambulance trains, rail guns etc.

Printed publications:
Newsletter 4–5 times a year

WORLD'S POULTRY SCIENCE ASSOCIATION UK BRANCH

Acronym or abbreviation: WPSA

Woodlands, Bradfield St Clare, Bury St Edmunds, Suffolk, IP30 0EQ

Tel: 01284 386520
Fax: 01284 386520
E-mail: wpsa@hotmail.co.uk

Website:
http://www.wpsa-uk.com
Details of membership, meetings and publications.

Enquiries:
Enquiries to: Honorary Secretary

Founded:
1946

Organisation type and purpose:
Membership association (membership is by subscription), present number of members: 280, voluntary organisation, registered charity (charity number 803616).
To promote the spread and exchange of information on poultry science and the poultry industry.

Subject coverage:
Poultry science and technology, poultry industry.

Printed publications:
Membership Directory
Newsletter (3 times a year)
Poultry Science Symposia (every two years)
World's Poultry Science Journal (4 times a year)

Publications list:
Available online

Access to staff:
Contact by letter, by telephone, by fax, by e-mail and via website. Access for members only.
Hours: variable part time

Access to building, collection or gallery:
No

Parent body:
World's Poultry Science Association (WPSA)
tel: + 31 55 506 6534; fax: + 31 55 506 4858; e-mail: wpsa@xs4all.nl; website: www.wpsa.com

WORLDSCALE ASSOCIATION (LONDON) LIMITED

Acronym or abbreviation: Worldscale

Copenhagen House, 5–10 Bury Street, London, EC3A 5AT

Tel: 020 7456 6600
Fax: 020 7456 6601
E-mail: wscale@worldscale.co.uk

Website:
http://www.worldscale.co.uk
As per published book but extended dataset (approximately 4 times as much).

Enquiries:
Enquiries to: Managing Director

Founded:
1962

Organisation type and purpose:
Consultancy.

Subject coverage:
Standard of reference for nominal freight scale to the oil tanker industry.

Trade and statistical information:
Nominal oil tanker freight rates for worldwide trade.

Printed publications:
Worldscale Schedule (annual, book)

Publications list:
Available in print

Access to staff:
Contact by letter, by telephone, by fax and by e-mail. Appointment necessary.
Hours: Mon to Fri, 0930 to 1730
Special comments: Services offered on an annual subscription basis.

continued overleaf

Joint publishers:
Worldscale Association (NYC) Inc
116 John Street, Suite 620, New York, NY 10038,
USA; tel: + 1 212 422 2786; fax: +1 212 344 4169;
e-mail: worldscale@worldscale-usa.com;
website: http://www.worldscale-usa.com

WORSHIPFUL COMPANY OF ACTUARIES

3rd Floor, Cheapside House, 138 Cheapside,
London, EC2V 6BW

Tel: 020 7776 3880
E-mail: clerk@actuariescompany.co.uk

Website:
http://www.actuariescompany.co.uk

Enquiries:
Enquiries to: The Clerk

Founded:
1979

Organisation type and purpose:
Membership association (membership is by
election or invitation).
City of London Livery Company.
To extend recognition and understanding of the
work of actuaries within the City and beyond
through educational and charitable works.

Access to staff:
Contact by letter, by telephone, by e-mail and via
website

WORSHIPFUL COMPANY OF ARBITRATORS

13 Hall Gardens, Colney Heath, St Albans,
Hertfordshire, AL4 0QF

Tel: 01727 826578
Fax: 01727 822652
E-mail: clerk@arbitratorscompany.org

Website:
http://www.arbitratorscompany.org

Enquiries:
Enquiries to: The Clerk
Direct tel: 01727 826578
Direct e-mail: clerk@arbitratorscompany.org

Founded:
1981

Organisation type and purpose:
Membership association (membership is by
election or invitation).
City of London Livery Company. Promotes
arbitration and interest in arbitration of the City of
London, and supports education in the field of
arbitration through charitable works.

Access to staff:
Contact by letter, by telephone, by fax, by e-mail
and via website. Non-members charged.

WORSHIPFUL COMPANY OF ARMOURERS & BRASIERS

Armourers' Hall, 81 Coleman Street, London,
EC2R 5BJ

Tel: 020 7374 4000
Fax: 020 7606 7481

Enquiries:
Enquiries to: The Clerk

Founded:
1322

Organisation type and purpose:
Livery company.

Access to staff:
Contact by letter
Hours: Mon to Fri, 0900 to 1700

Access to building, collection or gallery:
No access other than to staff

WORSHIPFUL COMPANY OF BAKERS

Bakers' Hall, Harp Lane, London, EC3R 6DP

Tel: 020 7623 2223
Fax: 020 7621 1924
E-mail: clerk@bakers.co.uk

Website:
http://www.bakers.co.uk

Founded:
c. 12th century

Organisation type and purpose:
Membership association (membership is by
election or invitation).
City of London Livery Company.

Access to staff:
Contact by letter, by telephone, by fax, by e-mail
and via website

WORSHIPFUL COMPANY OF BARBERS, THE

Acronym or abbreviation: The Barbers' Company

Barber-Surgeons' Hall, Monkwell Square, Wood
Street, London, EC2Y 5BL

Tel: 020 7606 0741
Fax: 020 7606 3857

Website:
http://www.barberscompany.org

Enquiries:
Enquiries to: The Clerk

Founded:
1308

Organisation type and purpose:
Learned society (membership is by election or
invitation).
City of London Livery Company.

Subject coverage:
Surgery (up to 1745) and barbery.

Printed publications:
Newsletter (issued to members)

Access to staff:
Contact by letter
Hours: Mon to Fri, 0930 to 1700

Access to building, collection or gallery:
No access other than to staff

WORSHIPFUL COMPANY OF BASKETMAKERS

29 Ingram House, Park Road, Hampton Wick,
Kingston upon Thames, Surrey, KT1 4BA

Tel: 020 8943 2343
Fax: 020 8977 6793
E-mail: clerk@basketmakersco.org

Website:
http://www.basketmakersco.org

Enquiries:
Enquiries to: The Clerk
Direct tel: 020 8943 2343
Direct fax: 020 8977 6793
Direct e-mail: clerk@basketmakersco.org

Founded:
1569

Organisation type and purpose:
Membership association (membership is by
election or invitation).
City of London Livery Company.

Access to staff:
Contact by letter, by telephone, by fax, by e-mail
and via website

WORSHIPFUL COMPANY OF BLACKSMITHS

48 Upwood Road, Lee, London, SE12 8AN

Tel: 020 8318 9684
Fax: 020 8318 9687
E-mail: hammerandhand@supanet.com

Website:
http://www.blacksmithscompany.org.uk

Enquiries:
Enquiries to: Clerk

Founded:
1325

Organisation type and purpose:
Membership association.
City of London Livery Company.

Subject coverage:
The blacksmith craft.

Printed publications:
History of the Company – booklet and leaflet
Directory of Blacksmiths in the UK

Access to staff:
Contact by letter
Hours: Mon to Fri, 0900 to 1700

WORSHIPFUL COMPANY OF BOWYERS

Archer House, Vicarage Crescent, London, SW11
3LF

E-mail: clerk@bowyers.com

Website:
http://www.bowyers.com/public

Enquiries:
Enquiries to: The Clerk
Direct e-mail: clerk@bowyers.com

Founded:
1363

Organisation type and purpose:
Membership association (membership is by
election or invitation).
City of London Livery Company.
Registered charity (charity number 270702).

Access to staff:
Contact by letter and by e-mail

WORSHIPFUL COMPANY OF BRODERERS

Ember House, 35–37 Creek Road, East Molesey,
Surrey, KT8 9BE

Tel: 020 8941 3116
Fax: 020 8979 5934
E-mail: clerk@broderers.co.uk

Website:
http://www.broderers.co.uk

Enquiries:
Enquiries to: Clerk
Direct e-mail: office@newbycrouch.co.uk

Founded:
1400

Organisation type and purpose:
City of London Livery Company.

Subject coverage:
The Worshipful Company of Broderers.

Printed publications:
History notes of the Worshipful Company of
Broderers and 'Plain Dealing Fellows' (Squadron
Leader P R Levy MBE, £20)

Access to staff:
Contact by letter, by telephone, by fax, by e-mail
and via website
Hours: Mon to Fri, 0900 to 1730

WORSHIPFUL COMPANY OF BUILDERS' MERCHANTS

4 College Hill, London, EC4R 2RB

Tel: 020 7329 2189

E-mail: wcobm@aol.com

Enquiries:
Enquiries to: The Clerk
Direct e-mail: wcobm@aol.com

Organisation type and purpose:
Membership association (membership is by election or invitation).
City of London Livery Company.

Access to staff:
Contact by letter, by telephone and by e-mail

WORSHIPFUL COMPANY OF BUTCHERS

Acronym or abbreviation: Butchers' Company

Butchers' Hall, 87 Bartholomew Close, London, EC1A 7EB

Tel: 020 7606 4106
Fax: 020 7606 4108

Enquiries:
Enquiries to: Clerk to the Company

Founded:
1198

Organisation type and purpose:
Learned society (membership is by election or invitation), present number of members: 690.

Subject coverage:
City Livery Companies, City of London.

Library catalogue:
All or part available in-house

Printed publications:
Butchers' Company brochure

Access to staff:
Contact by letter, by telephone, by fax and by e-mail. Appointment necessary.
Hours: Mon to Fri, 0900 to 1700

Access to building, collection or gallery:
Prior appointment required
Hours: Mon to Fri, 0900 to 1700

Access for disabled people:
Ramped entry, access to all public areas, toilet facilities

WORSHIPFUL COMPANY OF CARMEN

Five Kings House, 1 Queen Street Place, London EC4R 1QS

Tel: 020 7489 8289
Fax: 020 7236 3313
E-mail: enquiries@thecarmen.co.uk

Website:
http://thecarmen.co.uk

Enquiries:
Enquiries to: Clerk
Direct e-mail: theclerk@thecarmen.co.uk

Founded:
1517

Organisation type and purpose:
Membership association (membership is by election or invitation), present number of members: 550, voluntary organisation.
City of London Livery Company.

Printed publications:
Carr and Carman (Birch C, available for purchase, direct)

Access to staff:
Contact by letter, by telephone, by fax, by e-mail, in person and via website. Appointment necessary. Letter of introduction required. All charged.
Hours: Mon to Fri, 0900 to 1700

WORSHIPFUL COMPANY OF CHARTERED ACCOUNTANTS IN ENGLAND AND WALES

Larksfield, Kent Hatch Road, Crockham Hill, Edenbridge, Kent, TN8 6SX

Tel: 01732 866423
E-mail: clerk@wccaew.org.uk

Website:
http://www.wccaew.org.uk

Enquiries:
Enquiries to: The Clerk

Founded:
1977

Organisation type and purpose:
Membership association (membership is by election or invitation).
City of London Livery Company.
To foster the profession of accountancy and to provide social intercourse and mutual information between members of the Institute of Chartered Accountants in England and Wales.

Access to staff:
Contact by letter, by telephone, by e-mail and via website

WORSHIPFUL COMPANY OF CHARTERED ARCHITECTS

82A Muswell Hill Road, London, N10 3JR

Tel: 020 8292 4893
Fax: 020 8292 4893
E-mail: coleadams@architects-livery-company.org

Website:
http://www.architects-livery-company.org

Enquiries:
Enquiries to: The Clerk
Direct tel: 020 8292 4893
Direct fax: 020 8292 4893
Direct e-mail: coleadams@architects-livery -company.org

Founded:
1988

Organisation type and purpose:
Membership association (membership is by election or invitation). City of London Livery Company. To advance the profession of architecture, to act as an independent forum for fellowship and exchange of ideas between members.

Access to staff:
Contact by letter, by telephone, by fax, by e-mail and via website

WORSHIPFUL COMPANY OF CHARTERED SECRETARIES AND ADMINISTRATORS

Saddlers' House, 3rd Floor, 40 Gutter Lane, London, EC2V 6BR

Tel: 020 7726 2955
E-mail: clerk@wccsa.org.uk

Website:
http://www.wccsa.org.uk

Enquiries:
Enquiries to: Clerk

Organisation type and purpose:
Membership association (membership is by election or invitation).
City of London Livery Company.

Access to staff:
Contact by letter, by telephone and by e-mail

WORSHIPFUL COMPANY OF CLOCKMAKERS

The Salters' Hall, Fore Street, London EC2Y 5DE

Tel: 020 7638 5500
Fax: 020 7638 5522
E-mail: clerk@clockmakers.org

Website:
http://www.clockmakers.org
A City of London Livery Company founded by Royal Charter 1631 – its history and customs, charities, museum, and horology generally.

Enquiries:
Enquiries to: Clerk

Founded:
1631

Organisation type and purpose:
Membership association (membership is by election or invitation), present number of members: 500, registered charity (charity number 275380), museum.

Subject coverage:
Antiquarian horology – in particular clockmaking in London.

Museum or gallery collection, archive, or library special collection:
Horological library (founded 1813) consisting of books and manuscripts, together with a collection of clocks and watches, which were also originally (1817) intended for reference purposes

Non-library collection catalogue:
All or part available in print

Printed publications:
Photographs of the Collection from Bridgeman Art Library
see: http://www.bridgemanart.com

Access to staff:
Contact by letter, by telephone, by fax, by e-mail and via website. Appointment necessary.
Hours: Mon, Wed, Fri, 1000 to 1600

Clockmakers' Museum is at the:
Guildhall Library
Aldermanbury, London, EC2P 2EJ; tel: 020 7332 1865

WORSHIPFUL COMPANY OF COACHMAKERS AND COACH HARNESS MAKERS OF LONDON

48 Alderney Street, London, SW1V 4EX

Tel: 07505 089841
E-mail: clerk@coachmakers.co.uk

Website:
http://www.coachmakers.co.uk

Enquiries:
Enquiries to: The Clerk

Founded:
1677

Organisation type and purpose:
Membership association (membership is by election or invitation).
City of London Livery Company.

Access to staff:
Contact by letter, by telephone, by fax and via website

WORSHIPFUL COMPANY OF CONSTRUCTORS

Ragby House, 157 Sidney Road, Walton on Thames, Surrey, KT12 3SA

Tel: 01932 253212
E-mail: m.kearsley1@ntworld.com

Website:
http://www.constructorscompany.co.uk

Enquiries:
Enquiries to: The Clerk

Founded:
1990

continued overleaf

Organisation type and purpose:
Membership association (membership is by
election or invitation).
City of London Livery Company.
To bring together those professionally qualified
individuals concerned with all aspects of building
design, execution, management, vision and
economic appraisal within the framework of
Guildery and Livery in the City of London.

Access to staff:
Contact by letter, by telephone and by e-mail

WORSHIPFUL COMPANY OF COOKS

Coombe Ridge, Thursley Road, Churt, Farnham,
Surrey, GU10 2LQ

Tel: 01428 606670
E-mail: clerk@cookslivery.org.uk

Website:
http://www.cookslivery.org.uk

Enquiries:
Enquiries to: The Clerk
Direct tel: 01428 606670
Direct e-mail: clerk@cookslivery.org.uk

Founded:
1482

Organisation type and purpose:
Membership association (membership is by
election or invitation).
City of London Livery Company.
To support the City, the modern catering trade and
charitable activities.

Access to staff:
Contact by letter, by telephone and by e-mail

WORSHIPFUL COMPANY OF COOPERS

Coopers' Hall, 13 Devonshire Square, London,
EC2M 4TH

Tel: 020 7247 9577
Fax: 020 7377 8061
E-mail: clerk@coopers-hall.co.uk

Website:
http://www.coopers-hall.co.uk

Enquiries:
Enquiries to: The Clerk
Direct e-mail: clerk@coopers-hall.co.uk

Founded:
1501

Organisation type and purpose:
Membership association (membership is by
election or invitation).
City of London Livery Company.

Access to staff:
Contact by letter, by telephone, by fax, by e-mail
and via website

WORSHIPFUL COMPANY OF CORDWAINERS

Acronym or abbreviation: Cordwainers Company

Clothworkers' Hall, Dunster Court, Mincing Lane,
London, EC3R 7AH

Tel: 020 7929 1121
Fax: 020 7929 1124

Enquiries:
Enquiries to: The Clerk (Chief Executive)
Direct e-mail: office@cordwainers.org

Founded:
1272

Organisation type and purpose:
Membership association (membership is by
election or invitation), present number of
members: 161.
City Livery Company.

**Museum or gallery collection, archive, or library
special collection:**
Archives and records are held in The Guildhall
Library

Access to staff:
Contact by letter
Hours: Mon to Fri, 0900 to 1700

Access to building, collection or gallery:
Prior appointment required

WORSHIPFUL COMPANY OF CURRIERS

Hedgerley, The Leaze, Ashton Keynes, Wiltshire,
SN6 6PE

Tel: 01285 861017
E-mail: clerk@curriers.co.uk

Website:
http://www.curriers.co.uk

Enquiries:
Enquiries to: The Clerk

Founded:
1367

Granted Royal Charter of Incorporation:
(year of change 1605)

Organisation type and purpose:
City of London Livery Company.
Membership association (membership is by
election or invitation).
Historical, charitable, social

Subject coverage:
Original trade – preparers and finishers of heavy
hides for the leather industry.

Access to staff:
Contact by letter, by telephone, by e-mail and via
website

WORSHIPFUL COMPANY OF CUTLERS

Cutlers' Hall, Warwick Lane, London, EC4M 7BR

Tel: 020 7248 1866
E-mail: clerk@cutlerslondon.co.uk

Website:
http://www.cutlerslondon.co.uk

Enquiries:
Enquiries to: The Clerk
Direct tel: 020 7248 1866
Direct e-mail: clerk@cutlerslondon.co.uk

Founded:
1416

Organisation type and purpose:
Membership association (membership is by
election or invitation).
City of London Livery Company.

**Museum or gallery collection, archive, or library
special collection:**
Cutlery
Medals

Access to staff:
Contact by letter, by telephone, by e-mail and via
website

WORSHIPFUL COMPANY OF DISTILLERS

71 Lincoln's Inn Fields, London, WC2A 3JF

Tel: 020 7405 7091
E-mail: chughes@bcmw.co.uk

Enquiries:
Enquiries to: The Clerk

Organisation type and purpose:
Membership association (membership is by
election or invitation).
City of London Livery Company.

Access to staff:
Contact by letter, by telephone and by e-mail

WORSHIPFUL COMPANY OF DYERS

Dyers Hall, 11–13 Dowgate Hill, London, EC4R
2ST

Tel: 020 7236 7197
Fax: 020 7248 0774
E-mail: clerk@dyerscompany.com

Website:
http://www.dyerscompany.co.uk

Organisation type and purpose:
City of London Livery Company.

WORSHIPFUL COMPANY OF ENGINEERS

Wax Chandlers' Hall, 6 Gresham Street, London,
EC2V 7AD

Tel: 020 7726 4830
Fax: 020 7726 4820
E-mail: clerk@engineerscompany.org.uk

Website:
http://www.engineerscompany.org.uk

Enquiries:
Enquiries to: The Clerk

Organisation type and purpose:
Membership association (membership is by
election or invitation).
City of London Livery Company.
To promote the development and advancement of
the science, art and practice of engineering through
a series of lectures, events and visits.

Access to staff:
Contact by letter, by telephone, by fax, by e-mail
and via website

WORSHIPFUL COMPANY OF ENVIRONMENTAL CLEANERS

Acronym or abbreviation: WCEC

121 Hacton Lane, Upminster, RM14 2NL

Tel: 01708 505548
E-mail: neil.morley@environmental-cleaners.com

Website:
http://www.environmental-cleaners.com

Enquiries:
Enquiries to: Clerk of the Company

Founded:
1986

Organisation type and purpose:
Membership association (membership is by
election or invitation).
City of London Livery Company.
To encourage and maintain high standards of
practice and integrity through social and
professional exchange, while supporting and
promoting education, training and research
projects within the industry.

Access to staff:
Contact by letter, by telephone, by e-mail and via
website

WORSHIPFUL COMPANY OF FAN MAKERS

Skinners' Hall, 8 Dowgate Hill, London, EC4R 2SP

Tel: 020 7329 4633
Fax: 020 7329 4633
E-mail: clerk@fanmakers.com

Website:
http://www.fanmakers.com

Enquiries:
Enquiries to: The Clerk

Founded:
1709

Organisation type and purpose:
Membership association (membership is by election or invitation).
City of London Livery Company.

Museum or gallery collection, archive, or library special collection:
Collection of 250 fans

Access to staff:
Contact by letter, by telephone, by fax, by e-mail and via website

WORSHIPFUL COMPANY OF FARMERS

Red Copse End, Red Copse Lane, Boars Hill, Oxford, OX1 5ER

Tel: 01865 321580
E-mail: clerk@farmerslivery.org.uk

Enquiries:
Enquiries to: The Clerk

Founded:
1952

Organisation type and purpose:
Membership association (membership is by election or invitation).
City of London Livery Company.

Access to staff:
Contact by letter, by telephone and by e-mail

WORSHIPFUL COMPANY OF FARRIERS

19 Queen Street, Chipperfield, Kings Langley, Hertfordshire, WD4 9BT

Tel: 01923 260747
Fax: 01923 261677
E-mail: theclerk@wcf.org.uk

Website:
http://www.wcf.org.uk

Enquiries:
Enquiries to: Clerk

Founded:
1356

Organisation type and purpose:
Membership association.
City of London Livery Company.

Subject coverage:
The welfare of the horse through farriery.

Access to staff:
Contact by letter, by telephone, by fax and by e-mail
Hours: Mon to Fri, 0900 to 1700

WORSHIPFUL COMPANY OF FELTMAKERS

Formal name: The Worshipful Company of Feltmakers of London

Clerk to the Trustees, Post Cottage, Greywell, Hook, Hampshire, RG29 1DA

Website:
http://www.feltmakers.co.uk

Enquiries:
Enquiries to: The Clerk

Founded:
1604

Organisation type and purpose:
Membership association (membership is by election or invitation).
City of London Livery Company.

Access to staff:
Contact by letter, by telephone and by e-mail

Administers:
The Feltmakers Charitable Foundation (Charity No. 259906)

WORSHIPFUL COMPANY OF FIREFIGHTERS

20 Aldermanbury, London, EC2V 7GF

Tel: 020 7600 1666
Fax: 020 7600 1666
E-mail: clerk@firefighterscompany.org

Website:
http://www.firefighterscompany.org

Enquiries:
Enquiries to: The Clerk

Founded:
1988

Formerly called:
The Company of Firefighters, The Guild of Firefighters

Organisation type and purpose:
Membership association (membership is by subscription, election or invitation), present number of members: 155, registered charity.
Livery company.

Subject coverage:
Firefighting and associated products, industry and activities.

Trade and statistical information:
Fire fighting and protection.

Access to staff:
Contact by letter
Hours: Mon to Fri, 0900 to 1700

WORSHIPFUL COMPANY OF FISHMONGERS

Acronym or abbreviation: The Fishmongers' Company

Fishmongers' Hall, London Bridge, London, EC4R 9EL

Tel: 020 7626 3531
Fax: 020 7929 1389
E-mail: clerk@fishhall.org.uk

Website:
http://www.fishhall.org.uk

Enquiries:
Enquiries to: The Clerk
Other contacts: Chief Fisheries Inspector (for Billingsgate Market or other trade enquiries)

Founded:
1272

Organisation type and purpose:
Membership association (membership is by election or invitation), present number of members: 800.
Quality control, health and hygiene inspection service at Billingsgate Market.
Promotion of a healthy, prosperous and sustainable fish and fisheries sector for the long-term benefit of the United Kingdom.

Library catalogue:
All or part available in-house

Printed publications:
Fishmongers' Company Cook Book and Simply! Fish
Order printed publications from: Fishmongers' Hall

Publications list:
Available in print

Access to staff:
Contact by letter, by telephone, by fax and by e-mail. Appointment necessary.
Hours: Mon to Fri, 0900 to 1700

Access to building, collection or gallery:
Prior appointment required.

Links with:
Gresham's School
Cromer Road, Holt, Norfolk, NR25 6EA; tel: 01263 714500

WORSHIPFUL COMPANY OF FLETCHERS

Farmers' and Fletchers' Hall, 3 Cloth Street, EC1A 7LD

Tel: 020 7600 2204
Fax: 020 7606 4971
E-mail: ff@chesterboyd.co.uk

Website:
http://www.fletchers.org.uk

Enquiries:
Enquiries to: The Clerk
Direct e-mail: fletchersclerk@aol.com

Founded:
1371

Organisation type and purpose:
Membership association (membership is by election or invitation).
City of London Livery Company.

Access to staff:
Contact by letter, by telephone, by fax and by e-mail

WORSHIPFUL COMPANY OF FOUNDERS

Founders' Hall, Number One, Cloth Fair, London, EC1A 7JQ

E-mail: founderscompany@aol.com

Website:
http://www.foundersco.org.uk

Enquiries:
Enquiries to: The Clerk
Direct tel: 01273 858700
Direct fax: 01273 858900
Direct e-mail: founderscompany@aol.com

Organisation type and purpose:
Membership association (membership is by election or invitation).
City of London Livery Company.
To promote technical education and research in founding.

Access to staff:
Contact by letter, by telephone, by fax and by e-mail

WORSHIPFUL COMPANY OF FRAMEWORK KNITTERS, THE

86 Park Drive, Upminster, Essex, RM14 3AS

Tel: 01708 510439
Fax: 01708 510439
E-mail: clerk@frameworkknitters.co.uk

Website:
http://www.frameworkknitters.co.uk

Enquiries:
Enquiries to: Clerk to the Company

Founded:
1713

Organisation type and purpose:
Membership association (membership is by election or invitation), present number of members: 215.
A City of London livery company.

Printed publications:
A history of the company

Access to staff:
Contact by letter, by telephone, by fax, by e-mail, in person and via website. Appointment necessary.
Hours: Upminster: Mon to Fri, 0900 to 1700
Oadby: Mon to Fri, 0930 to 1330

continued overleaf

Access to building, collection or gallery:
Prior appointment required
Special comments: Archives are deposited at the Guildhall Library.

Subsidiary:
Framework Knitters Homes
Corah House, Framework Knitters Cottages, Stoughton Road, Oadby, Leicestershire, LE2 4FQ; tel: 01162 712171; fax: 01162 713894; e-mail: fwkcottages@oadby.fs.business.co.uk

WORSHIPFUL COMPANY OF FRUITERERS

Chapelstones, 84 High Street, Codford St Mary, Warminster, Wiltshire, BA12 0ND

Tel: 01985 850682
E-mail: clerk@fruiterers.org.uk

Website:
http://www.fruit-baskets.co.uk/asp/default.asp

Enquiries:
Enquiries to: The Clerk
Direct tel: 01985 850682
Direct e-mail: clerk@fruiterers.org.uk

Founded:
1463

Organisation type and purpose:
Membership association (membership is by election or invitation).
City of London Livery Company.
To promote excellence across all sectors of the fruit industry and to support education and research within it.

Access to staff:
Contact by letter, by telephone, by fax and by e-mail

WORSHIPFUL COMPANY OF FUELLERS

26 Merrick Square, London, SE1 4JB

E-mail: clerk@fuellers.co.uk

Website:
http://www.fuellers.co.uk

Enquiries:
Enquiries to: The Clerk
Direct tel: 020 7234 0760
Direct e-mail: clerk@fuellers.co.uk

Organisation type and purpose:
Membership association (membership is by election or invitation).
City of London Livery Company.
To foster the business of persons involved in providing energy for the home, industry, commerce and export.

Access to staff:
Contact by letter, by telephone, by e-mail and via website

WORSHIPFUL COMPANY OF FURNITURE MAKERS

Furniture Makers' Hall, 12 Austin Friars, London, EC2N 2HE

Tel: 020 7256 5558
Fax: 020 7256 5155
E-mail: clerk@furnituremakers.org.uk

Website:
http://www.furnituremakers.org.uk

Enquiries:
Enquiries to: The Clerk

Founded:
1951

Organisation type and purpose:
Membership association (membership is by election or invitation).
City of London Livery Company.

To foster both the craft and the industry of furniture-making, marketing and retailing in the United Kingdom.

Access to staff:
Contact by letter, by fax, by e-mail and via website

WORSHIPFUL COMPANY OF GARDENERS OF LONDON

25 Luke Street, London, EC2A 4AR

Tel: 020 7953 2321
E-mail: clerk@gardenerscompany.org.uk

Website:
http://www.gardenerscompany.org.uk

Enquiries:
Enquiries to: The Clerk
Direct tel: 020 7149 6696

Organisation type and purpose:
Membership association (membership is by election or invitation).
City of London Livery Company.
To promote the art and practice of good gardening throughout the country and especially in the London area, to support charitable activities connected with horticulture or the City of London, and to beautify the City of London by encouraging the display of flowers and foliage.

Access to staff:
Contact by letter, by telephone, by e-mail and via website

WORSHIPFUL COMPANY OF GIRDLERS

Girdlers' Hall, Basinghall Avenue, London, EC2V 5DD

Tel: 020 7638 0488
E-mail: clerk@girdlers.co.uk

Enquiries:
Enquiries to: The Clerk
Direct e-mail: clerk@girdlers.co.uk

Founded:
1327

Organisation type and purpose:
Membership association (membership is by election or invitation).
City of London Livery Company.

Access to staff:
Contact by letter, by telephone, by e-mail and via website

WORSHIPFUL COMPANY OF GLASS SELLERS

57 Witley Court, Coram Street, London, WC1N 1HD

Tel: 020 7837 2231
Fax: 020 7837 2231
E-mail: info@glass-sellers.co.uk

Website:
http://www.glass-sellers.co.uk

Enquiries:
Enquiries to: The Honorary Clerk
Direct tel: 020 7837 2231
Direct e-mail: info@glass-sellers.co.uk

Founded:
1664

Organisation type and purpose:
Membership association (membership is by election or invitation).
City of London Livery Company.
To stimulate interest in glass in all its aspects and to carry out charitable works, with special emphasis on education.

Access to staff:
Contact by letter, by telephone, by fax, by e-mail and via website

WORSHIPFUL COMPANY OF GLAZIERS AND PAINTERS OF GLASS

Acronym or abbreviation: Glaziers Company

Glaziers' Hall, 9 Montague Close, London Bridge, London, SE1 9DD

Tel: 020 7403 6652
Fax: 020 7403 6652
E-mail: info@worshipfulglaziers.com

Website:
http://www.worshipfulglaziers.com

Enquiries:
Enquiries to: Clerk
Direct e-mail: clerk@worshipfulglaziers.com

Founded:
1638

Organisation type and purpose:
City of London Livery Company.
Membership association (membership is by election or invitation), present number of members: 300.

Subject coverage:
Advice on stained glass, particularly on conservation of historic glass.

Museum or gallery collection, archive, or library special collection:
Library on stained glass

Library catalogue:
All or part available in-house

Access to staff:
Contact by letter, by telephone, by fax and by e-mail. Appointment necessary.
Hours: Mon to Fri, 1000 to 1600

Access for disabled people:
Ramped entry, access to all public areas, toilet facilities

WORSHIPFUL COMPANY OF GLOVERS

Cherry Tree Cottage, 73 Clapham Manor Street, London, SW4 6DS

E-mail: clerk@thegloverscompany.org

Website:
http://www.thegloverscompany.org

Enquiries:
Enquiries to: The Clerk
Direct e-mail: clerk@thegloverscompany.org

Founded:
1349

Organisation type and purpose:
Membership association (membership is by election or invitation).
City of London Livery Company.

Access to staff:
Contact by letter, by e-mail and via website

WORSHIPFUL COMPANY OF GOLD AND SILVER WYRE DRAWERS

Bee Cottage, North Heath, Chieveley, Berkshire, RG20 8UA

Tel: 01635 247014
Fax: 01635 247014
E-mail: clerk@gswd.co.uk

Website:
http://www.gswd.co.uk

Enquiries:
Direct tel: 01635 247014

Direct fax: 01635 247014
Direct e-mail: clerk@gswd.co.uk

Founded:
1423

Organisation type and purpose:
Membership association (membership is by election or invitation).
City of London Livery Company.

Access to staff:
Contact by letter, by telephone, by fax, by e-mail and via website

WORSHIPFUL COMPANY OF GOLDSMITHS

Goldsmiths' Hall, Foster Lane, London, EC2V 6BN

Tel: 020 7606 7010
Fax: 020 7606 1511
E-mail: library@thegoldsmiths.co.uk

Website:
http://www.thegoldsmiths.co.uk
Basic information on the Goldsmiths' Company, history and publications.

Enquiries:
Enquiries to: Librarian
Other contacts: Assistant to the Librarian (with special responsibility for A-V material)

Founded:
1327

Organisation type and purpose:
Membership association (membership is by qualification), present number of members: 1,500.
The Goldsmiths' Company is one of the Twelve Great Livery Companies of the City of London with its roots in the trade guilds of the Middle Ages.
It is responsible for: operating the London Assay Office which hallmarks precious metal articles, gold, silver and platinum; promoting excellence in design and craftmanship of silver and jewellery, through exhibitions and other projects; administering charitable trusts to help the disadvantaged; and specific areas of education.

Subject coverage:
Assaying and hallmarking of precious metals, gold plate, silver and jewellery, antique and modern, regalia.

Museum or gallery collection, archive, or library special collection:
Archives of the Company from 1334
Photographic collection
Slide collection
Twining Collection (books on regalia)
Collection of antique and modern silver, modern jewellery and modern art medals

Non-library collection catalogue:
All or part available in-house

Library catalogue:
All or part available in-house

Printed publications:
Unravelling the Mystery: The Story of the Goldsmiths' Company in the C20th (Jenkins P)
Treasures of the C20th (Ransome Wallis R)
Goldsmiths' Review (annually)
Variety of catalogues and booklets

Microform publications:
Film loan collection (list available)

Electronic and video publications:
Video loan collection (list available)

Publications list:
Available online and in print

Access to staff:
Contact by letter, by telephone, by fax and by e-mail. Appointment necessary.
Hours: Mon to Fri, 1000 to 1645

Access to building, collection or gallery:
Prior appointment required

Access for disabled people:
Disabled entrance, bathroom facilities, street parking
Special comments: Parking subject to availability; entry assisted by a device and staff.

Subsidiary body:
Assay Office London

WORSHIPFUL COMPANY OF GROCERS

Grocers' Hall, Princes Street, London, EC2R 8AD

Tel: 020 7606 3113
Fax: 020 7600 3082
E-mail: clerk@grocershall.co.uk

Website:
http://www.grocershall.co.uk

Enquiries:
Enquiries to: The Clerk

Founded:
c. 12th century

Organisation type and purpose:
Membership association (membership is by election or invitation).
City of London Livery Company.

Access to staff:
Contact by letter, by telephone, by fax, by e-mail and via website

WORSHIPFUL COMPANY OF GUNMAKERS

Proof House, 48–50 Commercial Road, London, E1 1LP

Tel: 020 7481 2695
E-mail: clerk@gunmakers.org.uk

Enquiries:
Enquiries to: The Clerk
Direct tel: 020 7481 2695
Direct e-mail: clerk@gunmakers.org.uk

Founded:
1637

Organisation type and purpose:
Membership assocation (membership is by election or invitation).
City of London Livery Company.

Access to staff:
Contact by letter, by telephone, by e-mail and via website

WORSHIPFUL COMPANY OF HACKNEY CARRIAGE DRIVERS

25 The Grove, Parkfield Latimer, Buckinghamshire, HP5 1VE

Website:
http://www.wchcd.com

Enquiries:
Enquiries to: The Clerk

Founded:
2004

Organisation type and purpose:
Membership association (membership is by election or invitation).
City of London Livery Company.
To raise public awareness of the extremely high standards of the London Hackney Carriage trade and industry.

Access to staff:
Contact by letter

WORSHIPFUL COMPANY OF HORNERS

C/o St Stephens House, Hide Place, London, SW1P 4NJ

Tel: 020 7834 1575
E-mail: horners.clerk@btinternet.com

Website:
http://www.horners.org.uk

Enquiries:
Enquiries to: The Clerk

Founded:
Royal Charter 1638

Organisation type and purpose:
Membership association (membership is by election).
City of London Livery Company.

Museum or gallery collection, archive, or library special collection:
Collection of horn artefacts housed in the Museum of Design in Plastics, part of the Arts University College, Bournemouth

Access to staff:
Contact by letter, by telephone and by e-mail

WORSHIPFUL COMPANY OF INFORMATION TECHNOLOGISTS

39A Bartholomew Close, London, EC1A 7JN

Tel: 020 7600 1992
Fax: 020 7600 1991
E-mail: info@wcit.org.uk

Website:
http://www.wcit.org.uk

Enquiries:
Enquiries to: The Clerk
Direct e-mail: michael@wcit.org.uk

Founded:
1992

Organisation type and purpose:
Membership association (membership is by election or invitation).
City of London Livery Company.

Access to staff:
Contact by letter, by telephone, by fax, by e-mail and via website

WORSHIPFUL COMPANY OF INNHOLDERS

Innholders' Hall, 29–30 College Street, London, EC4R 2RH

Tel: 020 7236 6703
Fax: 020 7236 0059
E-mail: mail@innholders.co.uk

Enquiries:
Enquiries to: The Clerk

Founded:
1514

Organisation type and purpose:
Voluntary organisation.

Access to staff:
Contact by letter, by telephone, by fax and by e-mail
Hours: Mon to Fri, 0900 to 1700

Access to building, collection or gallery:
No access other than to staff

Access for disabled people:
Limited – please enquire prior to visit

WORSHIPFUL COMPANY OF INSURERS

The Insurance Hall, 20 Aldermanbury, London, EC2V 7HY

Tel: 020 7600 4006
Fax: 020 7972 0153
E-mail: enquiries@wci.org.uk

Website:
http://www.wci.org.uk

continued overleaf

Enquiries:
Enquiries to: The Clerk

Founded:
1970

Organisation type and purpose:
Membership association (membership is by election or invitation).
City of London Livery Company.
To foster the business of Insurers and to provide social intercourse and mutual information between members of that business

Access to staff:
Contact by letter, by telephone, by fax, by e-mail and via website

WORSHIPFUL COMPANY OF IRONMONGERS, THE

Ironmongers' Hall, Shaftesbury Place, Barbican, London, EC2Y 8AA

Tel: 020 7606 2726
Fax: 020 7600 3519
E-mail: beadle@ironhall.co.uk

Enquiries:
Enquiries to: The Clerk
Other contacts: Hall Manager for conferences and facilities hire.

Founded:
1463

Organisation type and purpose:
Membership association (membership is by election or invitation), voluntary organisation.

Access to staff:
Contact by letter, by telephone and by e-mail
Hours: Mon to Fri, 0900 to 1700

Access to building, collection or gallery:
Prior appointment required

Access for disabled people:
Ramped entry, access to all public areas, toilet facilities

WORSHIPFUL COMPANY OF JOINERS AND CEILERS

75 Meadway Drive, Horsell, Woking, Surrey, GU21 4TF

Fax: 01483 720098
E-mail: info@joinersandceilers.co.uk

Website:
http://www.joinersandceilers.co.uk

Enquiries:
Enquiries to: The Clerk
Direct fax: 01483 720098
Direct e-mail: info@joinersandceilers.co.uk

Organisation type and purpose:
Membership association (membership is by election or invitation).
City of London Livery Company.

Access to staff:
Contact by letter, by telephone, by e-mail and via website

WORSHIPFUL COMPANY OF LAUNDERERS

Launderers' Hall, 9 Montague Close, London, SE1 9DD

Enquiries:
Enquiries to: The Clerk
Direct tel: 020 7378 1430

Organisation type and purpose:
Membership association (membership is by election or invitation).
City of London Livery Company.

Access to staff:
Contact by letter

WORSHIPFUL COMPANY OF LEATHERSELLERS

Acronym or abbreviation: Leathersellers

Leathersellers Hall, St Helen's Place, London, EC3A 6DQ

Tel: 020 7330 1444
Fax: 020 7330 1445
E-mail: enquiries@leathersellers.co.uk

Website:
http://www.leathersellers.co.uk
Background on Company activities.

Enquiries:
Enquiries to: Chief Executive

Founded:
1444

Organisation type and purpose:
National organisation, membership association (membership is by election or invitation), present number of members: 150, voluntary organisation, registered charity (charity number 278072). Investment company and grant giving foundation.

Subject coverage:
History of leather trade, history of livery companies.

Library catalogue:
All or part available in-house

Access to staff:
Contact by letter, by telephone and by e-mail
Hours: Mon to Fri, 0900 to 1700

Access to building, collection or gallery:
Prior appointment required
Hours: Mon to Fri, 1000 to 1600
Special comments: Bona fide researchers only.

WORSHIPFUL COMPANY OF LIGHTMONGERS

Crown Wharf, 11A Coldharbour, Blackwall Reach, London, E14 9NS

Tel: 020 7515 9055
Fax: 020 7538 5466
E-mail: clerk@lightmongers.org.uk

Website:
http://www.lightmongers.org.uk

Enquiries:
Enquiries to: The Clerk
Direct tel: 020 7515 9055
Direct e-mail: clerk@lightmongers.org.uk

Founded:
1967

Organisation type and purpose:
Membership association (membership is by election or invitation).
City of London Livery Company.

Access to staff:
Contact via website

WORSHIPFUL COMPANY OF LORINERS

8 Portland Square, Wapping, London, E1W 2QR

Tel: 020 7709 0222
E-mail: clerk@loriner.co.uk

Website:
http://www.loriner.co.uk

Enquiries:
Enquiries to: The Clerk
Direct e-mail: clerk@loriner.co.uk

Founded:
1261

Organisation type and purpose:
Membership association (membership is by election or invitation).
City of London Livery Company.

To maintain manufacturing standards in the trade and the encouragement of the proper use of bits, spurs, stirrups, buckles, bridles, saddle trees and other metal parts of horse tack, together with support for the Mayoralty of the City of London and good fellowship amongst the Livery.

Access to staff:
Contact by letter, by telephone and by e-mail

WORSHIPFUL COMPANY OF MAKERS OF PLAYING CARDS

Acronym or abbreviation: WCMPC

Flat 5, 15 Greycoat Place, London, SW1P 1SB

Tel: 020 7799 3556
Fax: 020 7799 3557

Enquiries:
Enquiries to: Archivist
Other contacts: Clerk

Founded:
1628

Organisation type and purpose:
Membership association (membership is by election or invitation).
City of London Livery Company, with its own, separate Charitable Trust.

Subject coverage:
Origins of playing cards worldwide, their manufacture, history, use and games, also ancillary items such as card games, tarot cards etc.

Museum or gallery collection, archive, or library special collection:
Famous and large collection of playing cards, kept (on permanent loan) at the Guildhall Library. Prior notice is required for an examination of most exhibits

Printed publications:
Small history booklet available to genuinely interested enquirers

Access to staff:
Contact by letter, by telephone, by fax and by e-mail
Hours: Mon to Fri, 0900 to 1700

WORSHIPFUL COMPANY OF MANAGEMENT CONSULTANTS

Copperfield, The Ridgeway, Cranleigh, Surrey, GU6 7HR

Tel: 01483 271459
E-mail: clerk@wcomc.org

Website:
http://www.comc.org.uk

Enquiries:
Enquiries to: The Clerk
Direct tel: 01483 271459
Direct e-mail: clerk@wcomc.org.uk

Founded:
1993

Organisation type and purpose:
Membership association (membership is by election or invitation).
City of London Livery Company.

Access to staff:
Contact by letter, by telephone and by e-mail

WORSHIPFUL COMPANY OF MARKETORS

13 Hall Gardens, Colney Heath, St Alban's, Hertfordshire, AL4 0QF

Tel: 01727 824446
Fax: 01727 822652
E-mail: clerk@marketors.org

Website:
http://www.marketors.co.uk

Enquiries:
Enquiries to: The Clerk

Founded:
1978

Organisation type and purpose:
Membership association (membership is by election or invitation).
City of London Livery Company.
To promote excellence in marketing practice and education, support for the interests of the City of London as well as fellowship amongst its members.

Access to staff:
Contact by letter, by telephone, by fax, by e-mail and via website

WORSHIPFUL COMPANY OF MASONS

22 Cannon Hill, Southgate, London, N14 6LG

Tel: 020 8882 9520
Fax: 020 8882 9520
E-mail: thecompanyclerk@masonslivery.org

Website:
http://www.masonslivery.org

Enquiries:
Enquiries to: Clerk

Founded:
1472

Organisation type and purpose:
City of London Livery Company.

Subject coverage:
City of London, stonemasonry.

Access to staff:
Contact by letter, by telephone, by fax and by e-mail
Hours: Mon to Fri, 0900 to 1700; leave a message if call not answered

WORSHIPFUL COMPANY OF MERCERS

Acronym or abbreviation: Mercers' Company

Mercers' Hall, Ironmonger Lane, London, EC2V 8HE

Tel: 020 7726 4991
Fax: 020 7600 1158
E-mail: mail@mercers.co.uk

Website:
http://www.mercers.co.uk

Enquiries:
Enquiries to: Archivist and Curator
Direct e-mail: janer@mercers.co.uk

Founded:
1394

Organisation type and purpose:
Membership association (membership is by election or invitation), present number of members: 300+.
City of London Livery Company.
Fraternity, corporate body and charitable foundation.

Subject coverage:
History of the Mercers' Company and its associated trusts and charities.

Museum or gallery collection, archive, or library special collection:
Mercers' Company archives and art collection, 1347 to present

Non-library collection catalogue:
All or part available in-house

Library catalogue:
All or part available in-house

Printed publications:
General information booklets and Company History

Access to staff:
Contact by letter and by e-mail. Appointment necessary.

Access to building, collection or gallery:
By prior appointment only
Special comments: Access to external researchers will be severely limited from 2010 due to reorganisation.

Access for disabled people:
Level entry, toilet facilities

WORSHIPFUL COMPANY OF MUSICIANS

6th Floor, 2 London Wall Buildings, London, EC2M 5PP

Tel: 020 7496 8980
Fax: 020 7588 3633

Website:
http://www.wcom.org.uk
General information on the livery and details of awards and grants.

Enquiries:
Enquiries to: Clerk
Other contacts: Deputy Clerk; email: deputyclerk@wcom.org.uk

Founded:
1500

Organisation type and purpose:
Membership association (membership is by election or invitation), registered charity.

Subject coverage:
Grants.

Museum or gallery collection, archive, or library special collection:
Archives deposited at the Guildhall Library

Access to staff:
Contact by letter and by e-mail
Hours: Mon to Fri, 0900 to 1700

WORSHIPFUL COMPANY OF NEEDLEMAKERS

5 Staple Inn, London, WC1V 7QH

Tel: 020 7242 5031

Enquiries:
Enquiries to: The Clerk
Direct tel: 020 7242 5031
Direct e-mail: michael@hobsonarditti.com

Founded:
1656

Organisation type and purpose:
Membership association (membership is by election or invitation).
City of London Livery Company.

Access to staff:
Contact by letter, by telephone and by e-mail

WORSHIPFUL COMPANY OF PAINTER-STAINERS

Acronym or abbreviation: Painters' Company

Painters' Hall, 9 Little Trinity Lane, London, EC4V 2AD

Tel: 020 7236 6258
Fax: 020 7236 0500
E-mail: beadle@painters-hall.co.uk

Website:
http://www.painters-hall.co.uk
Brief history and details of Painters' Hall. Basic listing and details of the various rooms available for hire at Painters' Hall.

Enquiries:
Enquiries to: Clerk
Direct tel: 020 7236 7070
Direct fax: 020 7236 7074

Direct e-mail: clerk@painters-hall.co.uk

Founded:
1268/1283

Created by the merger of:
Worshipful Company of Painters and Worshipful Company of Stainers (year of change 1502)

Organisation type and purpose:
Membership association (membership is by election or invitation), present number of members: 520, registered charity (charity number 200001), historic building, house or site, suitable for ages: 16+.
City of London Livery Company.

Subject coverage:
Historical details of the Company and its membership.

Museum or gallery collection, archive, or library special collection:
Assorted paintings and silver of varying degrees of interest
Charters and other documents of historical interest

Non-library collection catalogue:
All or part available in-house

Access to staff:
Contact by letter, by telephone, by fax and by e-mail. Appointment necessary.
Hours: Mon to Fri, 0900 to 1700

Access to building, collection or gallery:
Prior appointment required

Access for disabled people:
Access to all public areas, toilet facilities

WORSHIPFUL COMPANY OF PATTENMAKERS

3 The High Street, Sutton Valence, Kent, ME17 3AG

Tel: 01622 842440
E-mail: rwmurfin@btinternet.com

Website:
http://www.pattenmakers.co.uk

Enquiries:
Enquiries to: The Clerk

Founded:
c. 14th century

Organisation type and purpose:
Membership association (membership is by election or invitation).
City of London Livery Company.

Access to staff:
Contact by letter, by telephone, by e-mail and via website

WORSHIPFUL COMPANY OF PAVIORS

3 Ridgemount Gardens, Enfield, Middlesex, EN2 8QL

Tel: 020 8366 1566
E-mail: clerk@paviorscompany.org.uk

Website:
http://www.paviors.org.uk

Enquiries:
Enquiries to: The Clerk
Direct tel: 020 8366 1566
Direct e-mail: clerk@paviorscompany.org.uk

Founded:
1479

Organisation type and purpose:
Membership association (membership is by election or invitation).
City of London Livery Company.

Access to staff:
Contact by letter, by telephone and by e-mail

WORSHIPFUL COMPANY OF PEWTERERS

Acronym or abbreviation: The Pewterers' Company

Pewterers' Hall, Oat Lane, London, EC2V 7DE

Tel: 020 7397 8190
Fax: 020 7600 3896
E-mail: clerk@pewterers.org.uk

Website:
http://www.pewterers.org.uk

Enquiries:
Enquiries to: Clerk (Chief Executive)

Founded:
1474

Organisation type and purpose:
Membership association (membership is by election or invitation), present number of members: 230, voluntary organisation.
City of London Livery Company.
Custodians of the history of pewter and the pewter trade. Promote pewter and the trade, particularly through youth education.

Subject coverage:
All aspects of antique and modern pewter.

Museum or gallery collection, archive, or library special collection:
Collection of antique pewterware
Comprehensive records of pewter and pewterers since the company's first charter in 1474

Printed publications:
Englefields – Two Centuries of Pewtering in London (1996)
History of British Pewter
Short History of the Worshipful Company of Pewterers of London and a Catalogue of Pewterware in its Possession (1968)
Supplementary Catalogue of Pewterware (1979)
Shire Album, Pewter
Techniques of Pewtersmithing (1984)

Access to staff:
Contact by letter, by telephone and by fax.
Appointment necessary.
Hours: Mon to Fri, 0900 to 1700

Headquarters of the:
Association of British Pewter Craftsmen
tel: 0114 266 3084; fax: 0114 267 0910
European Pewter Union
tel: 020 7606 9363; fax: 020 7600 3896; e-mail: epu@pewterers.org.uk

WORSHIPFUL COMPANY OF PLAISTERERS

1 London Wall, London, EC2Y 5JU

Tel: 020 7796 4333
Fax: 020 7796 4334
E-mail: clerk@plaistererslivery.co.uk

Website:
http://www.plaistererslivery.co.uk

Enquiries:
Enquiries to: The Clerk

Founded:
1501

Organisation type and purpose:
Membership association (membership is by election or invitation).
City of London Livery Company.

Access to staff:
Contact by letter, by telephone, by fax and by e-mail

WORSHIPFUL COMPANY OF PLUMBERS

Acronym or abbreviation: WCP

Wax Chandlers' Hall, 6 Gresham Street, London, EC2V 7AD

Tel: 020 7796 2468
Fax: 020 7796 2468
E-mail: clerk@plumberscompany.org.uk

Website:
http://www.plumberscompany.org

Enquiries:
Enquiries to: Clerk

Founded:
1365

Organisation type and purpose:
Membership association.
City of London Livery Company.

Subject coverage:
Plumbing.

Museum or gallery collection, archive, or library special collection:
Records back to 1365 deposited in the Guildhall Museum

Printed publications:
Short History of Company 1365–1988

Access to staff:
Contact by letter
Hours: Mon to Thu, 0900 to 1700

Connections with:
Chartered Institute of Plumbing and Heating Engineering (for registered plumbers)
CORGI (for registered gas fitters)

WORSHIPFUL COMPANY OF SADDLERS

40 Gutter Lane, Cheapside, London, EC2V 6BR

Tel: 020 7726 8661
Fax: 020 7600 0386
E-mail: clerk@saddlersco.co.uk

Enquiries:
Enquiries to: Clerk

Founded:
early 12th century

Organisation type and purpose:
City of London Livery Company.
Support of trade of saddlery, support of education and charity.

Non-library collection catalogue:
All or part available in-house

Library catalogue:
All or part available in-house

Access to staff:
Contact by letter, by telephone, by fax and by e-mail. Appointment necessary.
Hours: Mon to Fri, 0900 to 1700

WORSHIPFUL COMPANY OF SCIENTIFIC INSTRUMENT MAKERS

Glaziers Hall, 9 Montague Close, London, SE1 9DD

Tel: 020 7407 4832
Fax: 020 7407 1565
E-mail: theclerk@wcsim.co.uk

Website:
http://www.wcsim.co.uk

Enquiries:
Enquiries to: The Clerk
Direct tel: 020 7407 4832
Direct e-mail: theclerk@wcsim.co.uk

Founded:
1956

Organisation type and purpose:
Membership association (membership is by election or invitation).
City of London Livery Company.

Access to staff:
Contact by letter, by telephone, by fax, by e-mail and via website

WORSHIPFUL COMPANY OF SCRIVENERS

HQS Wellington, Temple Stairs, Victoria Embankment, London, WC2R 2PN

Tel: 020 7240 0529
Fax: 020 7497 0645
E-mail: clerk@scriveners.org.uk

Website:
http://www.scriveners.org.uk
News, history, membership applications, professional qualification requirements for Scrivener Notaries and forthcoming events.

Enquiries:
Enquiries to: Clerk

Founded:
1373

Formerly called:
Mysterie of the Writers of the Court Letter

Organisation type and purpose:
Membership association (membership is by election or invitation), present number of members: 200, registered charity.
Livery Company of the City of London.
Regulating the standards of Scrivener Notaries

Subject coverage:
The profession of public notary principally within the City of London, its history and regulation.

Museum or gallery collection, archive, or library special collection:
History and former membership of the company, for which all records are deposited in the City of London Guildhall Library, Aldermanbury, London, EC2P 2EJ

Printed publications:
Regulations and Syllabuses (occasional, free to firms of Scriveners' Notaries and to intending apprentices)
Scriveners' Apprentices Examinations (for London notaries) – Rules

Access to staff:
Contact by letter, by telephone and by e-mail
Hours: Mon, Wed and Thu, 1000 to 1700

WORSHIPFUL COMPANY OF SHIPWRIGHTS

Ironmongers' Hall, Shaftesbury Place, London, EC2Y 8AA

Tel: 020 7606 2376
Fax: 020 7600 8117

Website:
http://www.shipwrights.co.uk

Enquiries:
Enquiries to: Clerk
Direct e-mail: clerk@shipwrights.co.uk

Founded:
pre 1199

Organisation type and purpose:
Membership association (membership is by election or invitation), present number of members: 460, registered charity (charity number 262043 313249).
City of London Livery Company.

Subject coverage:
History of the company.

Access to staff:
Contact by letter, by telephone, by fax and by e-mail. Appointment necessary.
Hours: Mon to Fri, 0900 to 1700

WORSHIPFUL COMPANY OF SKINNERS

Skinners' Hall, 8 Dowgate Hill, EC4R 2SP

Tel: 020 7236 5629
E-mail: beadle@skinners.org.uk

Website:
http://www.skinnershall.co.uk

Enquiries:
Enquiries to: The Clerk

Organisation type and purpose:
Membership association (membership is by election or invitation).
City of London Livery Company.
To increase the prosperity of the Company and to support Skinners' schools.

Access to staff:
Contact by letter, by telephone and by e-mail

WORSHIPFUL COMPANY OF SPECTACLE MAKERS

Formal name: Also known as The Spectacle Makers Company
Acronym or abbreviation: SMC

Apothecaries' Hall, Black Friars Lane, London, EC4V 6EL

Tel: 020 7236 2932
Fax: 020 7329 3249
E-mail: clerk@spectaclemakers.com

Website:
http://www.spectaclemakers.com
Training courses, history.

Enquiries:
Enquiries to: Clerk

Founded:
1629

Organisation type and purpose:
Professional body.
City of London Livery Company.

Subject coverage:
Livery company, optical technicians, optics, history of the company.

Museum or gallery collection, archive, or library special collection:
Company Records
Library, city history, histories of livery companies

Printed publications:
Programmed Learning Booklet
The Barrow Lectures (Fay and Bennett)
Worshipful Company of Spectacle Makers (Frank Law)

Access to staff:
Contact by letter
Hours: Mon to Fri, 0900 to 1700

WORSHIPFUL COMPANY OF TALLOW CHANDLERS

4 Dowgate Hill, London, EC4R 2SH

Tel: 020 7248 4726
Fax: 020 7236 0844
E-mail: clerk@tallowchandlers.org

Website:
http://www.tallowchandlers.org

Enquiries:
Enquiries to: Clerk

Founded:
1462

Organisation type and purpose:
Membership association.
City of London Livery Company.

Subject coverage:
Tallow and candles, tallow trade, oils and fats

Museum or gallery collection, archive, or library special collection:
Company documents from 1456

Access to staff:
Contact by letter and by e-mail
Hours: Mon to Fri, 0900 to 1700

WORSHIPFUL COMPANY OF TAX ADVISERS

191 West End Road, Ruislip, HA4 6LD

Tel: 01895 625817
E-mail: clerk@taxadvisers.org.uk

Website:
http://www.taxadvisers.org.uk

Enquiries:
Enquiries to: The Clerk

Founded:
1995

Organisation type and purpose:
Membership association (membership is by election or invitation).
City of London Livery Company.

Access to staff:
Contact by letter, by telephone and by e-mail

WORSHIPFUL COMPANY OF TIN PLATE WORKERS ALIAS WIRE WORKERS

Acronym or abbreviation: Tin Plate Workers' Company

Highbanks, Ferry Road, Surlingham, Norfolk, NR14 7AR

Tel: 08456 439967
E-mail: clerk@tinplateworkers.co.uk

Website:
http://www.tinplateworkers.co.uk

Enquiries:
Enquiries to: The Clerk

Founded:
1670

Organisation type and purpose:
Membership association (membership is by election or invitation).
City of London Livery Company.

Printed publications:
The Lanthorn (newsletter, annually)

Access to staff:
Contact by letter, by telephone, by e-mail and via website

WORSHIPFUL COMPANY OF TOBACCO PIPE MAKERS AND TOBACCO BLENDERS

Hackhurst Farm, Lower Dicker, Hailsham, East Sussex, BN27 4BP

Tel: 01323 844267
Fax: 01323 441199
E-mail: nickhp@prhack.demon.co.uk

Enquiries:
Enquiries to: Clerk

Founded:
1619/1954

Organisation type and purpose:
Membership association (membership is by election or invitation), present number of members: 200.
City of London Livery Company.
Charitable.

Subject coverage:
Tobacco products, pipes.

WORSHIPFUL COMPANY OF TURNERS OF LONDON

Skinners' Hall, 8 Dowgate Hill, London, EC4R 2SP

Tel: 020 7236 3605
E-mail: clerk@turnersco.com

Website:
http://www.turnersco.com

Enquiries:
Enquiries to: The Clerk

Founded:
1604

Organisation type and purpose:
Membership association (membership is by election or invitation).
City of London Livery Company.
To promote the craft of turning, to participate in the life of the City of London and to support related charities.

Access to staff:
Contact by letter, by telephone, by e-mail and via website

WORSHIPFUL COMPANY OF TYLERS AND BRICKLAYERS

30 Shelley Avenue, Tiptree, Essex, CO5 0SF

Tel: 01621 816592
E-mail: tandbclerk@aol.com

Website:
http://www.tylersandbricklayers.co.uk

Enquiries:
Enquiries to: The Clerk

Founded:
1568

Organisation type and purpose:
Membership association (membership is by election or invitation).
City of London Livery Company.

Access to staff:
Contact by letter, by telephone and by e-mail

WORSHIPFUL COMPANY OF UPHOLDERS

C/o K.E.S. Limited, 46 Quail Gardens, Selsdon, South Croydon, Surrey, CR2 8TF

Tel: 020 8651 3303
Fax: 020 8651 3454
E-mail: clerk@codyranch.co.uk

Website:
http://www.upholders.co.uk

Enquiries:
Enquiries to: The Clerk

Founded:
1626

Organisation type and purpose:
Membership association (membership is by election or invitation).
City of London Livery Company.

Access to staff:
Contact by letter, by telephone, by fax and by e-mail

WORSHIPFUL COMPANY OF WATER CONSERVATORS

The Lark, 2 Bell Lane, Worlington, Bury St Edmunds, Suffolk, IP28 8SE

Tel: 01638 510626
Fax: 01638 510626
E-mail: clerk@waterconservators.org

Website:
http://www.waterconservators.org

Enquiries:
Enquiries to: The Clerk
Direct tel: 020 8421 0305

Founded:
1994

Organisation type and purpose:
Membership association (membership is by election or invitation).
City of London Livery Company.

continued overleaf

To promote the development and advancement of the science, art and practice of water and environmental management and the various scientific subjects related thereto.

Access to staff:
Contact by letter, by telephone, by fax and by e-mail

WORSHIPFUL COMPANY OF WAX CHANDLERS

Wax Chandlers Hall, 6 Gresham Street, London, EC2V 7AD

Tel: 020 7726 0710
Fax: 020 7600 5462
E-mail: enquiries@waxchandlershall.co.uk

Website:
http://www.waxchandlershall.co.uk

Enquiries:
Enquiries to: The Clerk

Organisation type and purpose:
Membership association (membership is by election or invitation).
City of London Livery Company.

Museum or gallery collection, archive, or library special collection:
Archive held by Guildhall Library (open access)

Access to staff:
Contact by letter, by telephone, by fax and by e-mail

WORSHIPFUL COMPANY OF WEAVERS

Saddlers' House, Gutter Lane, London, EC2V 6BS

Tel: 020 7606 1155
Fax: 020 7606 1119
E-mail: weavers@weavers.org.uk

Website:
http://www.weavers.org.uk

Enquiries:
Enquiries to: Clerk

Founded:
1130

Organisation type and purpose:
Membership association (membership is by election or invitation), present number of members: 150.
City of London Livery Company.

Subject coverage:
History of the company.

Museum or gallery collection, archive, or library special collection:
The company's historical records and admission records are deposited at Guildhall Library

Printed publications:
The Weavers Company in the City of London (booklet)

Microform publications:
Microfilms of company's records (through World Microfilms)

Publications list:
Available in print

Access to staff:
Contact by letter
Hours: Mon to Fri, 0900 to 1700

WORSHIPFUL COMPANY OF WHEELWRIGHTS

7 Glengall Road, Bexleyheath, Kent, DA7 4AL

Tel: 020 8306 5119
Fax: 020 8979 5934
E-mail: enquiries@wheelwrights.org

Website:
http://www.wheelwrights.org

Enquiries:
Enquiries to: Clerk

Founded:
1670

Organisation type and purpose:
Membership association (membership is by election or invitation), present number of members: 220.

Subject coverage:
The craft of wheelwrighting. List of working wheelwrights in the United Kingdom.

Printed publications:
The Worshipful Company of Wheelwrights of the City of London 1670–1970 (Bennett E, 1970, £3 plus p&p)
Making a Wheel (Wright J and Hurford R, 1997, The Rural Development Commission, £10 plus p&p)

Access to staff:
Contact by letter, by e-mail and via website
Hours: Mon to Fri, 0900 to 1700

WORSHIPFUL COMPANY OF WOOLMEN

Brewers' Hall, Aldermanbury Square, London, EC2V 7HR

Tel: 020 7606 1301
Fax: 020 7796 3557

Website:
http://www.woolmen.com

Enquiries:
Enquiries to: The Clerk
Direct e-mail: clerk@woolmen.com

Founded:
c. 12th century

Organisation type and purpose:
Membership association (membership is by election or invitation).
City of London Livery Company.

Access to staff:
Contact by letter, by telephone, by fax and by e-mail

WORSHIPFUL COMPANY OF WORLD TRADERS

Acronym or abbreviation: World Traders

13 Hall Gardens, Colney Heath, St Albans, Herts, AL4 0QF

Tel: 01727 822181
E-mail: clerk@world-traders.org

Website:
http://www.world-traders.org

Enquiries:
Enquiries to: Clerk

Founded:
2000

Organisation type and purpose:
Membership association (membership is by election or invitation).
City of London Livery Company.

Access to staff:
Contact by telephone and by e-mail

Access to building, collection or gallery:
No access

WORSHIPFUL SOCIETY OF APOTHECARIES OF LONDON

Apothecaries' Hall, Black Friars Lane, London, EC4V 6EJ

Tel: 020 7236 1189

Fax: 020 7329 3177
E-mail: clerk@apothecaries.org

Website:
http://www.apothecaries.org
Information on the Society and the Hall, details of all Society examinations.

Enquiries:
Enquiries to: The Clerk

Founded:
1617

Organisation type and purpose:
Learned society.
City of London Livery Company.

Subject coverage:
History of the Society, membership lists since 1617, medical historical matters, non-university medical examination and licensing matters, the following examinations: Licentiate in Medicine and Surgery of the Society of Apothecaries, Diploma in the History of Medicine, Mastership in Medical Jurisprudence, Diploma in Medical Jurisprudence, Diploma in Genito-Urinary Medicine, Diploma in the Philosophy of Medicine, Diploma in Sports Medicine, Diploma in Musculo-Skeletal Medicine, Diploma in Medical Care of Catastrophes, Diploma in Regulatory Toxicology.

Museum or gallery collection, archive, or library special collection:
Medical examination matters from 1815
Some records from 1617 to date

Access to staff:
Contact by letter, by telephone, by fax and by e-mail. Appointment necessary.
Hours: Mon to Fri, 0900 to 1700

Access to building, collection or gallery:
Prior appointment required

Access for disabled people:
Ramped entry, access to all public areas

Links with:
Faculty of the History and Philosophy of Medicine and Pharmacy

WORTHING BOROUGH COUNCIL

Town Hall, Chapel Road, Worthing, West Sussex, BN11 1HA

Tel: 01903 239999\ Minicom no. 01903 204500
Fax: 01903 236552
E-mail: enquiries@worthing.gov.uk

Website:
http://www.worthing.gov.uk

Enquiries:
Enquiries to: Public Relations Manager

Founded:
1890

Organisation type and purpose:
Local government body.

Subject coverage:
Two tier authority. Provider of public services within Worthing Borough.

Access to staff:
Contact by letter, by telephone, by fax, by e-mail and via website
Hours: Mon to Fri, 0900 to 1700

Access for disabled people:
Parking provided, ramped entry, toilet facilities

WOTTON-UNDER-EDGE HISTORICAL SOCIETY

Wotton-under-Edge Heritage Centre, The Chipping, Wotton-under-Edge, Gloucestershire, GL12 7AD

Tel: 01453 521541
E-mail: info@wottonheritage.com

Website:
http://www.wottonheritage.com

Information provided on opening hours, displays and collections held at the Centre.

Enquiries:
Enquiries to: Honorary Administrator
Other contacts: Society Chairman

Founded:
1945

Organisation type and purpose:
Membership association, present number of members: 70, voluntary organisation, registered charity (charity number 291936), museum, suitable for ages: all.

Subject coverage:
Local history of Wotton-under-Edge and adjoining parishes, local family history, Wotton-under-Edge and adjoining parishes, tourist information point.

Information services:
Tourist Information Point.

Special visitor services:
Facilities for local and family history research.

Education services:
Education packs available for loan to local schools.

Services for disabled people:
Displays and/or information at wheelchair height.

Museum or gallery collection, archive, or library special collection:
Books, documents, manuscripts, pictures, photographs and artefacts, all in computerised database
Parish registers and 1891 census on microfiche and 1881 census on CD-ROM

Non-library collection catalogue:
All or part available in-house

Printed publications:
Annual Journal
Local information booklets
Order printed publications from: Wotton Heritage Centre

Microform publications:
Parish registers and 1891 census (microfiche)

Electronic and video publications:
1881 census (CD-ROM)

Publications list:
Available online

Access to staff:
Contact by letter, by telephone, by e-mail and in person
Hours: As for access to building

Access to building, collection or gallery:
No prior appointment required
Hours: Tue to Fri, 1000 to 1300 and 1400 to 1700 (1600 in winter); Sat, 1000 to 1300; some Sun in summer, 1430 to 1700
Special comments: Charges made for the use of research facilities only.

Access for disabled people:
Parking provided, level entry, access to all public areas, toilet facilities
Hours: As above

WOUND CARE SOCIETY

Acronym or abbreviation: WCS

PO Box 170, Huntingdon, Cambridgeshire, PE29 1PL

Tel: 01480 434401
Fax: 01480 434401
E-mail: wound.care.society@talk21.com

Enquiries:
Enquiries to: Administrator

Founded:
1987

Subject coverage:
WCS is a charitable organisation concerned with all aspects of wound care. It is a registered charity which provides educational material to nursing professionals.

Printed publications:
Educational Booklets (available for purchase, £2.50 per booklet)

Access to staff:
Contact by letter, by telephone, by fax, by e-mail and via website
Hours: 24 hours Answer Machine

Access to building, collection or gallery:
No access other than to staff

WPF COUNSELLING AND PSYCHOTHERAPY

Formal name: Westminster Pastoral Foundation Counselling and Psychotherapy
Acronym or abbreviation: WPF

23 Magdalen Street, London, SE1 2EN

Tel: 020 7378 2000
Fax: 020 7378 2010
E-mail: reception@wpf.org.uk

Website:
http://www.wpf.org.uk
Counselling service, training department.

Enquiries:
Enquiries to: Secretary
Other contacts: Appointments Office tel no: 020 7361 4803

Founded:
1970

Organisation type and purpose:
Registered charity (charity number 273434), training organisation, consultancy.
Counselling service.
To provide affordable counselling and psychotherapy, to train counsellors and psychotherapists.

Subject coverage:
Counselling and psychotherapy.

Access to staff:
Contact by telephone
Hours: Mon to Fri, 0900 to 1700

Access for disabled people:
Parking provided, ramped entry, toilet facilities

Affiliated Counselling Centres:
WPF Counselling and Psychotherapy
23 Kensington Square, London, W8 5HN; tel: 020 7361 4864

WRC PLC

Frankland Road, Blagrove, Swindon, Wiltshire, SN5 8YF

Tel: 01793 865000
Fax: 01793 865001
E-mail: solutions@wrcplc.co.uk

Website:
http://www.wrcplc.co.uk

Enquiries:
Enquiries to: Librarian
Direct tel: 01793 865056
Direct e-mail: martine.gibbons@wrcplc.co.uk

Founded:
1927

Formerly called:
Water Research Centre (WRc)

Organisation type and purpose:
Consultancy, research organisation.

Subject coverage:
Water supply, drinking water analysis, environmental chemistry, microbiology, quality and health matters, legislation; water pollution; solid wastes and sewage sludge disposal;

ecotoxicology; water and waste water treatment; sewage treatment and disposal; sludge treatment; processes automation and control; sewers and sewerage; water mains; marine and freshwater studies including modelling; computing; Water Byelaws Advisory Service.

Printed publications:
Annual Report
Order printed publications from: Publications Department, WRc Information Resources, Frankland Road, Blagrove, Swindon, Wiltshire, SN5 8YF; tel: 01793 865138; fax: 01793 514562; e-mail: sales@webookshop.com; website: http://www.webookshop.com

Access to staff:
Contact by letter, by telephone, by fax, by e-mail and via website
Hours: Mon to Fri, 0930 to 1630

Access to building, collection or gallery:
No access other than to staff

Also at:
WRc-NSF
Unit 30, Fern Close, Pen-y-Fan Industrial Estate, Oakdale, Gwent, NP11 3EH; tel: 01495 236260; fax: 01495 249234; e-mail: info@wrcnsf.com; website: http://www.wrcnsf.com

WREXHAM COUNTY BOROUGH COUNCIL

Acronym or abbreviation: WCBC

Guildhall, Wrexham, Clwyd, LL11 1AY

Tel: 01978 292000
Fax: 01978 292106

Website:
http://www.wrexham.gov.uk

Enquiries:
Enquiries to: Public Relations Manager
Direct tel: 01978 292275
Direct fax: 01978 292252
Direct e-mail: sue.wynjones@wrexham.gov.uk

Founded:
1996

Organisation type and purpose:
Local government body.

Printed publications:
Connect – Local residents magazine (2 times a year)
Order printed publications from: Publicity Officer, tel: 01978 292274; fax: 01978 297448; e-mail: kesah .trowell@wrexham.gov.uk

Electronic and video publications:
See website

Access to staff:
Contact by letter, by telephone, by fax, by e-mail, in person and via website. Appointment necessary.
Hours: Mon to Thu, 0845 to 1715; Fri, 0845 to 1645

Access to building, collection or gallery:
No prior appointment required
Hours: Hours vary

Access for disabled people:
Parking provided

WRITERS GUILD OF GREAT BRITAIN

Acronym or abbreviation: WGGB

430 Edgware Road, London, W2 1EH

Tel: 020 7723 8074
Fax: 020 7706 2413
E-mail: admin@writersguild.org.uk

Website:
http://www.writersguild.org.uk

Enquiries:
Enquiries to: General Secretary

Founded:
1957

continued overleaf

Organisation type and purpose:
Professional body, trade union, present number of members: 2,000.

Subject coverage:
Professional writing in TV, radio, films, theatre, books and multimedia.

Printed publications:
Writers' Newsletter (6 times a year, £25 annual subscription)

Access to staff:
Contact by letter, by telephone, by fax, by e-mail and via website. Appointment necessary.
Hours: Mon to Fri, 0930 to 1730

Incorporates the:
Theatre Writers Union

WRITTLE COLLEGE

Chelmsford, Essex, CM1 3RR

Tel: 01245 424200
Fax: 01245 420456
E-mail: info@writtle.ac.uk

Website:
http://www.writtle.ac.uk

Enquiries:
Enquiries to: Librarian

Founded:
1893

Formerly called:
Writtle Agriculture College (year of change 1993)

Organisation type and purpose:
Local government body, university library. Higher Education College.

Subject coverage:
Agriculture; agricultural engineering; horticulture (amenity and commercial); agricultural diversification; plant and animal science; soil science; farm and horticultural enterprise management, equine science.

Museum or gallery collection, archive, or library special collection:
Collection of 18th- and 19th-century books on agriculture and horticulture

Library catalogue:
All or part available online

WWF-UK

Acronym or abbreviation: WWF

Panda House, Weyside Park, Godalming, Surrey, GU7 1XR

Tel: 01483 426444
Fax: 01483 426409

Website:
http://www.wwf.org.uk
Website updated frequently.
http://www.wwflearning.org.uk

Enquiries:
Enquiries to: Supporter Relations

Founded:
1961

Formerly called:
World Wildlife Fund (WWF) (year of change 1986); Worldwide Fund for Nature (WWF) (year of change 2001)

Organisation type and purpose:
International organisation, registered charity (charity number 201707).
To conserve species of animals and plants and their habitats, and to reconcile the needs of people with the conservation of the natural environment upon which they depend.

Subject coverage:
Climate change, forests, freshwater, marine and coasts, rare species, toxics, agriculture, plants, tourism, economics, trade and investment, international development, oil, gas and mining, UK social change.

Library catalogue:
All or part available in-house

Printed publications:
UK Factsheets: A selection of 30 factsheets on the most often-requested topics
Specialist Reports
WWF Annual Review
Action (magazine, members, quarterly)
Order printed publications from: Education resources only, WWF-UK
Education Distribution, PO Box 963, Slough, SL2 3RS, tel: 01753 643104, fax: 01753 646553

Electronic and video publications:
Computerised data bulletins (educational software): for 7 to 11 years: Exploring Coasts, Exploring Farms, Exploring Rivers, Exploring Towns and Cities
Computerised data bulletins (educational software): for 13 to 16 years
Climate Chaos (for teachers)
Stimulus (video pack 11 to 16 yrs)

Publications list:
Available online and in print

Access to staff:
Contact by letter, by telephone, by fax and by e-mail. Appointment necessary.
Hours: Mon to Fri, 0900 to 1700
Special comments: Library use by appointment.

Access to building, collection or gallery:
Prior appointment required

Access for disabled people:
Parking provided

Affiliated to:
International Union for Conservation of Nature and Natural Resources (IUCN)

Other addresses:
WWF Cymru
Room 313, Baltic House, Mount Stuart Square, Cardiff, CF10 5FH; tel: 029 2045 4970; fax: 029 2045 1306; e-mail: wwf-uk-wales@wwf.org.uk
WWF Northern Ireland
13 West Street, Carrickfergus, Co Antrim, BT38 7AR; tel: 028 9335 5166; fax: 028 9336 4448; e-mail: wwf-uk-ni@wwf.org.uk
WWF Scotland
Little Dunkeld, Dunkeld, Perthshire, PH8 0AD; tel: 01887 820449

Parent body:
WWF International
Avenue du Mont Blanc, Gland, CH-1196, Switzerland

WYRE BOROUGH COUNCIL

Civic Centre, Breck Road, Poulton-le-Fylde, Lancashire, FY6 7PU

Tel: 01253 891000
Fax: 01253 899000
E-mail: mailroom@wyrebc.gov.uk

Website:
http://www.wyrebc.gov.uk

Enquiries:
Enquiries to: Corporate Support Officer
Direct tel: 01253 887503
Direct fax: 01253 887499
Direct e-mail: jporter@wyrebc.gov.uk

Founded:
1974

Organisation type and purpose:
Local government body.

Subject coverage:
Provision of local government services by a district council, council tax, environmental health, health and safety, housing, transport, sport, leisure and recreation, planning, personnel and management services, tourism.

Printed publications:
Index of free leaflets available to the public

Publications list:
Available in print

Access to staff:
Contact by letter, by telephone, by e-mail, in person and via website
Hours: Mon to Fri, 0900 to 1700

Access to building, collection or gallery:
Mon to Fri
Hours: 0830 to 1700

Access for disabled people:
Parking provided, ramped entry, level entry, access to all public areas, toilet facilities

XENOPHON

98 Cambridge Gardens, London, W10 6HS

Tel: 020 8968 1360
E-mail: wolstan-dixie@hotmail.co.uk

Enquiries:
Enquiries to: Information Officer

Founded:
1979

Organisation type and purpose:
Learned society (membership is by election or invitation).

Subject coverage:
Recreational and historical cryptography, i.e. codes, ciphers, cryptanalysis, signs, signals, steganography, secret and hidden artificial languages and their recovery.

Museum or gallery collection, archive, or library special collection:
Books
Pamphlets
Magazines
Grey literature
Press clippings

Non-library collection catalogue:
All or part available in-house

Library catalogue:
All or part available in-house

Printed publications:
Crypt (newsletter, irregular)
Wordpattern Dictionary

Electronic and video publications:
Decrypting programs
IBM PC encrypting
Random text program
Wordsearch programs

Access to staff:
Contact by letter, by telephone and by e-mail.
Non-members charged.
Hours: Mon to Fri, 1000 to 1700

XR OWNERS CLUB

Acronym or abbreviation: XROC

9 Cope Place, Earls Court Road, Kensington, London, W8 6AA

Tel: 020 7937 7595
E-mail: info@xroc.co.uk

Website:
http://www.interford.co.uk
http://www.xrownersclub.co.uk
Membership information.
http://www.xroc.co.uk

Enquiries:
Enquiries to: National Co-ordinator
Direct e-mail: john@xroc.co.uk

Founded:
1983

May be looked for as:
Ford XR Owners Club

Organisation type and purpose:
Car Club.

Subject coverage:
Ford XR2, XR3, XR4, XR6 and XR8 information, supersport register, classic car insurance, technical information and national day track event.

Printed publications:
Xtra (magazine, 5 times a year, members)

Access to staff:
Contact by letter, by telephone, by fax, by e-mail and via website
Hours: Mon to Fri, 1000 to 1900; Sat, 1000 to 1600

Access to building, collection or gallery:
No access other than to staff

YACHT DESIGNERS AND SURVEYORS ASSOCIATION

Acronym or abbreviation: YDSA

The Glass Works, Penns Road, Petersfield, Hampshire, GU32 2EW

Tel: 01730 710425/710490
Fax: 01730 710423
E-mail: info@ybdsa.co.uk

Website:
http://www.ydsa.co.uk

Enquiries:
Enquiries to: Chief Executive
Other contacts: Certifying Authority (for MCA Code vessel work)

Founded:
1912

Organisation type and purpose:
Professional body (membership is by election or invitation), present number of members: 150. Training and maintaining of standards.

Subject coverage:
Surveyors and designers of small craft, marine surveyors, training, tonnage measurement for registration, certification under the MCA Small Commercial Vessel Code.

Museum or gallery collection, archive, or library special collection:
Wide selection of books relating to small craft, dating back to early 20th century

Library catalogue:
All or part available in-house

Printed publications:
Brochures and leaflets

Access to staff:
Contact by letter, by telephone, by fax, by e-mail, in person and via website. Appointment necessary.
Hours: Mon to Fri, 0900 to 1700

Access to building, collection or gallery:
Prior appointment required
Hours: Mon to Fri, 0900 to 1700

Access for disabled people:
Some parking

Links with:
Association of Brokers & Yacht Agents (ABYA)
Professional Charter Association (PCA)
Yacht Brokers Designers & Surveyors Association (YBDSA)

YACHT HARBOUR ASSOCIATION

Marine House, Thorpe Lea Road, Egham, Surrey, TW20 8BF

Tel: 01784 223817
Fax: 01784 475870
E-mail: lgordon@britishmarine.co.uk

Website:
http://www.yachtharbourassociation.com
The association and its services, code of practice, link to Berth Search for boat users.
http://www.berthsearch.com
Displays all the vacant berths at member marinas.

Enquiries:
Enquiries to: Administrator
Other contacts: General Manager; Chairman

Organisation type and purpose:
Marina trade association.
To develop the marine industry by specifically supporting marina members of the British Marine Federation.
Helps boat users find good quality marinas and helps marina businesses improve their services and operate to high, modern standards. Offers advice in a range of issues, marketing and promotional tools, specific training for marina management and the opportunity to work with other businesses to find the best way to address problems.

Subject coverage:
Marina and mooring operators; boatyards; consultants; suppliers of equipment and services to the marina industry, both in the UK and overseas.

Printed publications:
Fore & Aft (quarterly international publication for marina managers and industry businesses)

Access to staff:
Contact by letter, by telephone, by fax, by e-mail and via website

Links with:
British Marine Federation (BMF)

YEHUDI MENUHIN SCHOOL

Stoke d'Abernon, Cobham, Surrey KT11 3QQ

Tel: 01932 864739
E-mail: reception@yehudimenuhinschool.co.uk

Website:
http://www.yehudimenuhinschool.co.uk

Enquiries:
Enquiries to: Headmaster and PA
Direct tel: 01932 584795
Direct fax: 01932 864633
Direct e-mail: nicolaschisholm@yehudimenuhinschool.co.uk
Other contacts: Friends Secretary

Founded:
1963

Organisation type and purpose:
Registered charity. Has special status as a Centre of Excellence for the Performing Arts.
Aims to develop the musical potential of gifted young people regardless of race, creed or financial background, both for their own fulfilment and for the benefit and enrichment of others, within an academic environment that supports and develops their social, emotional, aesthetic and physical needs.

Subject coverage:
Educates more than 60 talented boys and girls between the ages of 8 and 18. The range of instruments is limited to violin, viola, cello, double bass, guitar and piano. All pupils sing in one of two choirs and all string players also play the piano.

Education services:
Partnerships with Surrey County Arts and local maintained schools; works with many Surrey primary and secondary schools to share resources and expertise, supplementing existing music education provision.

Electronic and video publications:
Newsletter (3 a year)
Order electronic and video publications from: Download from website

Access to staff:
Contact by letter, by telephone, by fax and by e-mail

YEMEN EMBASSY

57 Cromwell Road, London, SW7 2ED

Tel: 020 7584 6607
Fax: 020 7584 3759

Enquiries:
Enquiries to: Information Officer

Organisation type and purpose:
National government body.

Subject coverage:
The Yemen.

Access to staff:
Contact by letter, by telephone and by fax
Hours: Mon to Fri, 0900 to 1700

YEOVIL NIGHT SHELTER PROJECT

13 Wyndham Street, Yeovil, Somerset, BA20 1JH

Tel: 01935 412052
E-mail: support@yeovilnightshelter.com

Website:
http://www.yeovilnightshelter.com
Services, manager's report, volunteering.

Enquiries:
Enquiries to: Manager
Direct tel: 07814 235855
Direct e-mail: chris@yeovilnightshelter.com

Organisation type and purpose:
Operation of a night shelter for about 12, where all are welcome, no-one is refused and everyone is fed.

Subject coverage:
Clients pay 50p a night to contribute towards a hot nutritious meal, a bed for the night and toast in the morning. Clients while at the shelter have access to shower and laundry facilities. There is a store of clothing for those in need of renewing clothes, and also items in store for those living on the street so that when clients get settled with accommodation they have belongings to take with them. The shelter offers advice on addiction, puts people in touch with services (hospital, doctors, dentists, etc.) and provides support with everyday issues on housing and work information.

Education services:
In-house training for volunteers; plans to welcome Year 1 social work students to the project as a first placement and to invite police trainees from Portishead training facility, so that new police can have a better understanding of homeless issues.

Access to staff:
Contact by letter, by telephone, by e-mail and via website

Access to building, collection or gallery:
Shelter open: Sun/Mon night to Thu/Fri night, 2030 to 0830

YHA (ENGLAND AND WALES)

Formal name: YHA (England and Wales) Ltd
Acronym or abbreviation: YHA

Trevelyan House, Dimple Road, Matlock, Derbyshire, DE4 3YH

Tel: 01629 592600
Fax: 01629 592702

Website:
http://www.yha.org.uk

Enquiries:
Enquiries to: PR assistant
Direct tel: 01629 592779
Direct e-mail: hannahcurzon@yha.org.uk

Founded:
1930

Formerly called:
Youth Hostels Association (England and Wales)

continued overleaf

Organisation type and purpose:
Registered charity (charity number 301657). To help all, especially young people of limited means, to a greater knowledge, love and care of the countryside, and appreciation of the cultural values of towns and cities, particularly by providing Youth Hostels or other accommodation for them in their travels, and thus to promote their health, recreation and education.

Subject coverage:
Young people, education, travel.

Printed publications:
YHA News 9 (twice a year)
YHA Accommodation Guide (listing all hostels) and YHA map

Access to staff:
Contact by telephone and by e-mail
Hours: Mon to Fri, 0900 to 1700

Access for disabled people:
Parking provided, ramped entry, toilet facilities at National Office

YMCA ENGLAND

Formal name: Young Men's Christian Associations of England
Acronym or abbreviation: YMCA

National Council of YMCAs, 640 Forest Road, London, E17 3DZ

Tel: 020 8520 5599
Fax: 020 8509 3190
E-mail: info@england.ymca.org.uk

Website:
http://www.ymca.org.uk
Information on housing and the other work carried out by the YMCA.

Enquiries:
Enquiries to: Senior Media Officer
Direct tel: 020 7061 3324
Direct fax: 0845 873 6644
Direct e-mail: press@england.ymca.org.uk

Founded:
1844

Organisation type and purpose:
International organisation, membership association, voluntary organisation, registered charity (charity number 212810), training organisation.

Subject coverage:
Youth and community work; mentoring for young people; rehabilitation of young offenders; sport, health, exercise and fitness; education and training for young people; youth homelessness; residential facilities for young people; adult education; outdoor education; drugs education, extended schools.

Museum or gallery collection, archive, or library special collection:
Archive material, photographs and memorabilia relating to the history of the YMCA

Printed publications:
Anniversary Review (12pp history booklet, 1844–1994)
Annual Report
Annual Review
Publications relating to specific projects
Unity (newsletter, 4 times a year)
Y Care International's annual review, booklet on Street Children and educational material. (Y Care International is the international development agency of the English, Scottish, Welsh and Irish national councils of YMCAs)
YMCA in Focus
YMCA World (3 times a year)

Electronic and video publications:
Chasing the Bandwagon (video and teaching pack for drugs education)
Videos about the YMCA's work (for loan)

Publications list:
Available in print

Access to staff:
Contact by letter, by telephone, by fax and by e-mail. Appointment necessary.
Hours: Mon to Fri, 0900 to 1730

Access to building, collection or gallery:
Hours: Mon to Fri, 0900 to 1700

Branch office:
YMCA Metropolitan Region
53 Parker Street, London, WC2B 5PT

Has:
160 local YMCA Associations

Member of:
National Council for Voluntary Youth Services

YORK ARCHAEOLOGICAL TRUST

Formal name: York Archaeological Trust for Excavation and Research Limited
Acronym or abbreviation: YAT

Cromwell House, 13 Ogleforth, York, YO1 7FG

Tel: 01904 663000
Fax: 01904 640024
E-mail: postmaster@yorkarchaeology.co.uk

Website:
http://www.yorkarchaeology.co.uk
http://www.vikingjorvik.com
Information on Jorvik Viking Centre.

Enquiries:
Enquiries to: Director
Direct tel: 01904 663001
Direct fax: 01904 663024
Direct e-mail: pvaddyman@yorkarchaeology.co.uk
Other contacts: Head of Finance and Administration for administrative matters.

Founded:
1972

Organisation type and purpose:
Membership association (membership is by election or invitation), present number of members: c. 100, registered charity (charity number 509060), museum, suitable for ages: all, research organisation, publishing house.

Subject coverage:
Archaeology of York and its region; Roman, Anglo Saxon, Viking and medieval archaeology, Jorvik Viking Centre, Archaeological Resource Centre, Barley Hall Medieval Centre, archaeological techniques, visitors' centre and attraction development and management; collections management, maintenance and archaeological artefact conservation, waterlogged archaeological materials.

Museum or gallery collection, archive, or library special collection:
Air photographic collections for Yorkshire
Archaeological picture library, with worldwide coverage but specialisation in York, Britain and Viking topics
Artefacts and excavation records relating to the archaeology of York 1972 onwards
CD-ROM on Viking and other subjects
Exhibited collections in Jorvik Viking Centre (Viking age) and of replicas in Barley Hall (medieval)

Printed publications:
Annual Report
Yorkshire Archaeology Today Vol 1 ongoing
The Archaeology of York Vols 1–21 ongoing

Microform publications:
Archive materials (copies of certain site records)

Electronic and video publications:
Facing the Past (video)
Roman Britain (CD-ROM)
World of the Vikings (CD-ROM)

Publications list:
Available online and in print

Access to staff:
Contact by letter, by telephone, by fax, by e-mail, in person and via website. Appointment necessary.

Hours: Mon to Fri, 0900 to 1700

Access for disabled people:
Level entry, access to all public areas, toilet facilities
Special comments: Visitor Centres: Disabled access available to most areas.
Other Offices: Conditions vary.

Connections with:
Archaeological Resource Centre (ARC)
St Saviour's Church, St Saviour Gate, York, YO1 8NN; tel: 01904 643211
JORVIK
Coppergate, York, YO1 9WT; tel: 01904 543400; fax: 01904 627097; e-mail: enquiries@vikingjorvik.com

YORK COLLEGE

Acronym or abbreviation: YC

Tadcaster Road, Dringhouses, York, YO24 1UA

Tel: 01904 770400
Fax: 01904 770499

Website:
http://www.yorkcollege.ac.uk

Enquiries:
Enquiries to: Customer Services
Direct e-mail: customer-services@yorkcollege.ac.uk
Other contacts: Marketing Manager, 01904 770543

Founded:
1827

Formed by the merger of:
York College of Further and Higher Education (YCFHE), York Sixth Form College (YSFC) (year of change 1999)

Organisation type and purpose:
Suitable for ages: 16+, training organisation, consultancy.

Subject coverage:
Art and design, business, catering, computing, construction, engineering, hair and beauty, health and social care, sport and leisure, fashion, performing arts and A-Levels, etc.

Non-library collection catalogue:
All or part available in-house

Library catalogue:
All or part available in-house

Printed publications:
Branding Information
Prospectuses: Full Time, Higher Education, Part-time (annually, free)
Annual Report

Access to staff:
Contact by letter, by telephone, by fax, by e-mail and via website. Appointment necessary.
Hours: Mon to Thu, 0830 to 1930; Fri, 0830 to 1800

Access for disabled people:
Parking provided, ramped entry, level entry, toilet facilities

Sixth Form Site:
York College
Sim Balk Lane, York; tel: 01904 704141

YORK COUNCIL FOR VOLUNTARY SERVICE

Acronym or abbreviation: York CVS

Priory Street Centre, 15 Priory Street, York, YO1 6ET

Tel: 01904 621133
Fax: 01904 630361
E-mail: yorkcvs@yorkcvs.org.uk

Website:
http://www.yorkcvs.org.uk
Citizen's Guide entries, Voluntary Voice articles, topical information.

Enquiries:
Enquiries to: Information & Development Manager

Founded:
1939

Organisation type and purpose:
Registered charity (charity number 225087).
York CVS provides information and advice on
issues which are common to all charities and
voluntary groups – fundraising, legal
constitutions, volunteering, accounts, etc.

Subject coverage:
How to set up and run a voluntary group or
charity.

**Museum or gallery collection, archive, or library
special collection:**
Books and pamphlets relating to issues concerning
the voluntary sector

Printed publications:
Citizen's Guide (annually updated directory of
local voluntary groups)
Voluntary Voice (newsletter, 10 times a year)

Access to staff:
Contact by letter, by telephone, by fax, by e-mail
and in person. Appointment necessary.
Hours: Mon to Fri, 0900 to 1630

Access for disabled people:
Parking provided, ramped entry, level entry, access
to all public areas, toilet facilities
Special comments: Hearing loops in meeting rooms

YORK HOSPITAL

Health Library and Information Service, 3rd Floor,
Administration Block, York Hospital, Wigginton
Road, York, YO31 8HE

Tel: 01904 726712
Fax: 01904 675583
E-mail: hslibydh@york.ac.uk

Enquiries:
Enquiries to: Librarian

Founded:
1971

Organisation type and purpose:
Health library.

Subject coverage:
Medicine, nursing, management and all health-
related subjects.

Library catalogue:
All or part available online

Printed publications:
Journal holdings
Library guide

Access to staff:
Contact by letter, by telephone, by fax, by e-mail,
in person and via website. Appointment necessary.
Letter of introduction required. Non-members
charged.
Hours: Mon to Thu, 0830 to 2000; Fri, 0830 to 1700;
Sat, 1000 to 1300

Also at:
Bootham Park Library

At the same address:
Bootham Park Hospital Library

Parent bodies:
York Hospitals NHS Trust

YORK MINSTER LIBRARY AND ARCHIVES

Dean's Park, York, YO1 7JQ

Tel: 01904 625308 (library); 01904 611118 (archives)
Fax: 01904 611119
E-mail: antonioj@yorkminster.org

Website:
http://www.yorkminster.org/learning/library
-archives-conservation

Enquiries:
Enquiries to: Librarian
Direct e-mail: archivist@yorkminsterlibrary.org.uk

Other contacts: Archivist

Founded:
627

Formerly called:
York Minster Library

Organisation type and purpose:
Registered charity.
Cathedral library and archives.

Subject coverage:
Church history, history of York Minster and its
attendant bodies (but not the archdiocese),
medieval manuscripts, illuminated manuscripts,
literature, theology, religious art and architecture,
religious literature (poetry, drama), York and
Yorkshire local history, historical bibliography,
music (religious and secular).

**Museum or gallery collection, archive, or library
special collection:**
Library: General Collection; Old Library
collections, including items from the collections
of Revd Dr Marmaduke Fothergill (d. 1731) and
Canon T. F. Simmons (d. 1884); Yorkshire
collections, including the Hailstone Collection
(printed matter; Edward Hailstone (d. 1890)) and
the Foot-Walker Collection; and Yorkshire Parish
Library collections.
Archives: Minster archives, from c.1148, including
the archives of the Vicars Choral (1252–1936) and
the Minster School; small archives of other
organisations; personal papers; manuscript
collections (MSS XVI and MSS Add.), from late-
10th century; music manuscripts, 16th–20th
centuries; Hailstone Collection (chiefly
documents and manuscript material, 12th–19th
centuries); modern media, including
photographs, and video and sound recordings.

Non-library collection catalogue:
All or part available in-house

Library catalogue:
All or part available online

Printed publications:
A Catalogue of the Printed Music Published before
1850 in York Minster Library (D. Griffiths, 1977)
A Catalogue of Music Manuscripts in York Minster
Library (D. Griffiths, 1982)
A Catalogue of the Printed Books in the Library of
the Dean and Chapter of York (J. Raine, York,
1896)
Probate Inventories of the York Diocese, 1350–1500
(P. M. Stell trans., York Archaeological Trust,
2006)

Access to staff:
Contact by letter, by telephone, by fax, by e-mail
and via website. Appointment necessary. Letter of
introduction required.
Hours: Mon to Fri, 0900 to 1700

Access for disabled people:
One parking space, by appointment; lift to first
floor reading room; ground floor toilet facilities

Administered by:
Dean and Chapter of York
tel: 01904 557200; website: http://yorkminster.org

Links with:
University of York

YORK ST JOHN UNIVERSITY

Acronym or abbreviation: YSJ

Lord Mayors' Walk, York, YO31 7EX

Tel: 01904 876700
Fax: 01904 876342
E-mail: library@yorksj.ac.uk

Website:
http://www.yorksj.ac.uk/library
Library home page; library catalogue and search
tools; information on library services, databases
and collections; guides to resources by subject, etc.

Enquiries:
Enquiries to: Librarian

Founded:
1841

Created by the merger of:
Ripon College and St John's College, York (year of
change 1975)

Formerly called:
College of Ripon and York St John; York St John
College (year of change 2008)

Organisation type and purpose:
University department or institute, suitable for
ages: 18+.

Subject coverage:
Art, design and technology, English literature,
history, business studies, linguistics, psychology,
theology and religious studies, counselling, film,
TV, performance studies, occupational therapy,
physiotherapy, sports and exercise science,
teaching studies.
Postgraduate courses in humanities, teaching
studies, professional and management studies,
health and life sciences, international education.

**Museum or gallery collection, archive, or library
special collection:**
University Archive
Language Resources Centre (language teaching
materials)
Rees-Williams Collection of 19th-century
Children's Literature
York Theatre Royal Contemporary Archive
Religious Education Centre
School library resource collections
Yorkshire Film Archive

Non-library collection catalogue:
All or part available online

Library catalogue:
All or part available online

Printed publications:
Library guides for most subject areas

Publications list:
Available online

Access to staff:
Contact by letter, by telephone, by fax, by e-mail,
in person and via website. Non-members charged.
Hours: Term time: Mon to Thu, 0800 to 2130; Fri,
0800 to 1900; Sat, 0930 to 1700; Sun, 1330 to 1900
Vacations: Mon to Fri, 0900 to 1700

Access for disabled people:
Level entry

Constituent bodies:
David Hope Religious Education Centre
Yorkshire Film Archive

YORKSHIRE ARCHAEOLOGICAL SOCIETY

Acronym or abbreviation: YAS

Claremont, 23 Clarendon Road, Leeds, West
Yorkshire, LS2 9NZ

Tel: 0113 245 7910
Fax: 0113 245 7992
E-mail: yas.library@gmail.com

Website:
http://www.users.globalnet.co.uk/~gdl/yasfhs.htm
Family History Section.

Enquiries:
Enquiries to: Librarian
Other contacts: Assistant Librarian

Founded:
1863

Organisation type and purpose:
Learned society (membership is by subscription),
registered charity (charity number 224083).

Subject coverage:
Historical sciences, including archaeology, local
history, genealogy, with particular emphasis on
Yorkshire, but some material on the North of
England and England in general.

continued overleaf

Museum or gallery collection, archive, or library special collection:
Archival material on Yorkshire, 12th to 20th century, including the Wakefield Court Rolls and parish register transcripts
Large collection of national and international periodicals
Extensive collection of books, maps, photographs, etc. on Yorkshire

Non-library collection catalogue:
All or part available online and in-house

Library catalogue:
All or part available in-house

Printed publications:
Maps and Plans
Wakefield Court Rolls Series
Y.A.S. Parish Register Section
Y.A.S. Record Series
Yorkshire Archaeological Journal (annually)
Yorkshire Archaeological Reports

Microform publications:
Parish registers available on microfiche (details on application)
Indexes of wills available (microfiche)

Publications list:
Available online

Access to staff:
Contact by letter, by telephone, by fax, by e-mail, in person and via website
Hours: Tue and Wed, 1400 to 2030; Thu, 1000 to 1730; Fri 1000 to 1300; Sat, 0930 to 1700
Special comments: Appointment necessary for visit to archives.

Access for disabled people:
Parking provided
Special comments: Limited access for disabled.

Separate subscription sections at the same address:
Family History and Population Studies Section
Industrial History Section
Medieval Section
Parish Register Section
Prehistory Research Section
Roman Antiquities Section

YORKSHIRE DIALECT SOCIETY

Acronym or abbreviation: YDS

19 Prospect Close, Swinefleet, East Yorkshire, DN14 8FB

Website:
http://www.yorkshiredialectsociety.org.uk
General information about the Society's aims, meetings, publications, etc.

Enquiries:
Enquiries to: Hon Publicity & Information Officer

Founded:
1897

Organisation type and purpose:
International organisation, membership association (membership is by subscription), present number of members: 500.
The study, publication, recording and research of dialects, mainly Yorkshire.

Subject coverage:
Yorkshire dialects.

Printed publications:
Summer Bulletin (annually, free to members)
Transactions (annually, free to members)
Many books and anthologies including:
The Yorkshire Dictionary of Dialect, Tradition and Folklore (Kellett A)

Electronic and video publications:
Tapes and CDs

Publications list:
Available in print

Access to staff:
Contact by letter
Hours: Mon to Fri, 0900 to 1700

YORKSHIRE GEOLOGICAL SOCIETY

Acronym or abbreviation: YGS

19 Thorngate, Barnard Castle, Co Durham, DL12 8QB

Tel: 01833 638893
E-mail: tjm4@tutor.open.ac.uk

Website:
http://www.yorkgeolsoc.org.uk
Society news.

Enquiries:
Enquiries to: General Secretary

Founded:
1837

Organisation type and purpose:
Learned society (membership is by subscription), present number of members: 794 all sections, voluntary organisation, registered charity.

Subject coverage:
Geology.

Printed publications:
Circular of the Yorkshire Geological Society
Occasional publications
Proceedings of the Yorkshire Geological Society

Access to staff:
Contact by letter, by telephone, by e-mail and via website
Hours: Mon to Fri, 0900 to 1800

Affiliated to:
Geologists' Association

YORKSHIRE PHILOSOPHICAL SOCIETY

Acronym or abbreviation: YPS

The Lodge, Museum Gardens, York, YO1 7DR

Tel: 01904 656713
Fax: 01904 656713
E-mail: info@yorksphilsoc.org.uk

Website:
http://www.yorksphilsoc.org.uk

Enquiries:
Enquiries to: Honorary Archivist
Other contacts: Clerk to the Society (for general information and membership)

Founded:
1822

Organisation type and purpose:
Learned society (membership is by subscription, election or invitation), present number of members: 500, registered charity (charity number 529709).

Subject coverage:
Natural history, science, archaeology and history of York, Yorkshire and elsewhere.

Museum or gallery collection, archive, or library special collection:
Records and publications of the Society from 1822

Printed publications:
Annual Reports from 1825 to 2009 (£1.50 each)
An Index to the Articles and Obituaries in the Annual Reports 1823–1995 (£2.50, £1.50 to members)
A Brief Index to the Annual Reports 1995–2009 (price on enquiry)
BAAS jubilee poster of 1881 (black and white print, £5)
The Gardens of the Yorkshire Philosophical Society (colour print, £15, £12.50 to members)
Philosophers and Provincials: The Yorkshire Philosophical Society from 1822 to 1844 (A. D. Orange, £2, £1.50 to members)
Sir George Cayley 1773–1857, the inventor or the aeroplane (Leonard S. Rivet, 50p)
St Mary's Abbey and the City of York (Dr Jane Burton, £1.50, £1 to members)

The Mythical Norman Element in the 1822 Bishophill (York) find of Anglo-Saxon Coins (Michael Dolley, 50p)
York Observatory (leaflet, 25p)
Yorkshire People and Places: A Millennium Celebration (eds, Sylvia Hogarth and Veronica Wallace, 2001, £7.50)
Postage extra on all publications

Publications list:
Available in print

Access to staff:
Contact by letter, by telephone, by fax, by e-mail, in person and via website
Hours: Mon and Wed, 1000 to 1600; Fri, 1000 to 1200

YORKSHIRE TOURIST BOARD

Acronym or abbreviation: YTB

312 Tadcaster Road, York, YO24 1GS

Tel: 01904 707961
Fax: 01904 701414
E-mail: info@ytb.org.uk

Website:
http://www.yorkshirevisitor.com
Consumer site for planning a visit to Yorkshire
http://www.yorkshiretouristboard.net
Business to business site
http://www.venueyorkshire.com
Conference and venue site
http://www.grouptravelyorkshire.com
site for group travel

Enquiries:
Enquiries to: Marketing Assistant

Formerly called:
Yorkshire and Humberside Tourist Board

Organisation type and purpose:
Regional tourist board.

Subject coverage:
General tourist information for Yorkshire.

Printed publications:
Yorkshire Visitor Guide
Conference & Venue Guide

Publications list:
Available online

Access to staff:
Contact by letter, by telephone, by fax and by e-mail
Hours: Mon to Fri, 0900 to 1730

Access for disabled people:
Parking provided, ramped entry, level entry, access to all public areas, toilet facilities

YOUNG CONCERT ARTISTS TRUST

Acronym or abbreviation: YCAT

23 Garrick Street, London, WC2E 9BN

Tel: 020 7379 8477
Fax: 020 7379 8467
E-mail: info@ycat.co.uk

Website:
http://www.ycat.co.uk
Directory of artists, list of concerts, booking artists, CDs for sale.

Founded:
1984

Organisation type and purpose:
Registered charity (number 326490).
Nurtures and promotes outstanding young classical soloists and chamber ensembles trained in the UK.

Subject coverage:
As a classical musicians agency, YCAT liaises with event promoters in the UK and abroad providing performance opportunities and engagements for its artists. As a classical event promoter, it presents

concerts to showcase its artists, including concerts in London as part of the YCAT Wigmore Lunchtime Series, Southbank Purcell Room Presentation Concerts and performances in Manchester at the Bridgewater Hall.

Special visitor services:
Annual auditions to identify exciting new talent who could benefit from the charity's work, culminating in a public final at Wigmore Hall.

Electronic and video publications:
Selection of current CDs of young artists performing
Order electronic and video publications from: The Trust, or online stores

Access to staff:
Contact by letter, by telephone, by fax and by e-mail

YOUNG LANCASHIRE

10 Fishergate Hill, Preston, Lancashire, PR1 8JB

Tel: 01772 556127
Fax: 01772 251334
E-mail: mail@younglancashire.org.uk

Website:
http://www.younglancashire.org.uk

Enquiries:
Enquiries to: Director

Founded:
1923

Formerly called:
Lancashire Youth Clubs Association (year of change 2000); Lancashire Youth Association (year of change 2009)

Organisation type and purpose:
Membership association, present number of members: 107 youth groups and clubs, voluntary organisation, registered charity (charity number 518147), suitable for ages: year 12 students, training organisation.
Youth service.

Subject coverage:
Personal and social development of young people including those who have disabilities, support and advice to youth groups/clubs, links with other voluntary youth organisations, links with local government youth and community services.

Printed publications:
Annual Report
Grassroots (newsletter, for members)

Access to staff:
Contact by letter, by telephone, by fax, by e-mail and via website. Appointment necessary.
Hours: Mon to Fri, 0930 to 1630

Affiliated to:
British Confederation of Youth Clubs
European Federation of Youth Clubs
Irish Confederation of Youth Clubs
UK Youth
    11 Bride Street, London, EC4A 4AS

YOUNG WRITER CHARITABLE TRUST

Secretary, The Glebe House, Church Road, Weobley, Herefordshire, HR4 8SD

Tel: 01544 318901
Fax: 01544 318901
E-mail: info@youngwritertrust.org

Website:
http://www.youngwritertrust.org
Trustees, online writing games.

Organisation type and purpose:
Registered charity (number 1095083).
To support young people through their writing.

Education services:
Online games for young writers.

Access to staff:
Contact by letter, by telephone, by fax and by e-mail

YOUNGMINDS

48–50 St John Street, London, EC1M 4DG

Tel: 020 7336 8445
Fax: 020 7336 8446
E-mail: enquiries@youngminds.org.uk

Website:
http://www.youngminds.org.uk

Founded:
1992

Organisation type and purpose:
Voluntary organisation, registered charity (charity number 1016968).
A voice for young people's mental health and well-being.

Subject coverage:
UK charity committed to improving the emotional well-being and mental health of children and young people and empowering their parents or carers.

Trade and statistical information:
See website: http://www.youngminds.org.uk/ym-newsroom

Printed publications:
Booklets for Young People
Leaflets including:
Bullying – Why it Matters
Children and Young People Get Depressed Too
Why do Young Minds Matter?
Worried about a Young Person's Eating Problems?
Resource Sheets
YoungMinds Magazine
YoungMinds Directory of Services
Order printed publications from: website: http://www.youngminds.org.uk

Publications list:
Available online and in print

Access to staff:
Contact by letter, by telephone, by fax, by e-mail and via website
Hours: Mon to Fri, 0930 to 1730

Access to building, collection or gallery:
Prior appointment required

YOUTH CYMRU

Unit 5, Ty Nant Court, Morganstown, Cardiff, CF15 8LW

Tel: 029 2081 4335
E-mail: mailbox@youthcymru.org.uk

Website:
http://www.youthcymru.org.uk

Enquiries:
Enquiries to: Chief Executive

Founded:
1934

Formerly called:
Welsh Association of Youth Clubs (WAYC) (year of change 2003)

Organisation type and purpose:
National organisation, membership association (membership is by subscription, qualification), present number of members: 200+ youth groups, voluntary organisation, registered charity (charity number 524480).

Subject coverage:
All aspects of youth and community work.

Printed publications:
Ad hoc papers and information sheets
Conference Report
Training Programme
Annual Report
Corporate Plan
Newsletters (one a term)

Access to staff:
Contact by letter, by telephone, by fax and by e-mail. Appointment necessary.
Hours: Mon to Fri, 0845 to 1615

Access to building, collection or gallery:
Prior appointment required

Access for disabled people:
Parking provided, ramped entry, level entry, access to all public areas, toilet facilities

YOUTH LINK SCOTLAND

Central Hall, West Tollcross, Edinburgh, EH3 9BP

Tel: 0131 229 0339
Fax: 0131 229 0339
E-mail: info@youthlink.co.uk

Website:
http://www.youthlink.co.uk
Overview of Youthlink Scotland's activities. Links to member organisation websites.

Enquiries:
Enquiries to: Administrator
Direct e-mail: rdambrosio@youthlink.co.uk

Founded:
1942

Formerly called:
Scottish Standing Conference of Voluntary Youth Organisations (SSCVYO) (year of change 1996)

Organisation type and purpose:
Voluntary organisation.
Umbrella/intermediary organisation supporting voluntary youth organisations.

Subject coverage:
Range of youth issues and related topics such as funding, charity law, peer education, youth work and sustainable development, sport and the arts.

Museum or gallery collection, archive, or library special collection:
Catalogue currently being developed

Printed publications:
Wide range of publications, leaflets etc. related to youth work including own publications
Annual Report

Publications list:
Available in print

Access to staff:
Contact by letter, by telephone, by fax, by e-mail and via website. Appointment necessary. Non-members charged.
Hours: Mon to Fri, 0900 to 1700

Members include:
51 youth organisations

ZEPHYR & ZODIAC MKIV OWNERS CLUB

94 Claremont Road, Rugby, Warwickshire, CV21 3LU

Tel: 01788 574884

Enquiries:
Enquiries to: Treasurer

Founded:
1983

Organisation type and purpose:
Membership association (membership is by subscription), present number of members: 110, voluntary organisation.

Subject coverage:
All aspects of Zephyr and Zodiac MkIV cars.

Printed publications:
Quarterly magazine

Publications list:
Available in print

continued overleaf

Access to staff:
Contact by letter and by telephone
Hours: Evenings and weekends
Special comments: Not after 2100.

ZINC INFORMATION CENTRE

Acronym or abbreviation: ZINC

Wrens Court, 56 Victoria Road, Sutton Coldfield,
West Midlands, B72 1SY

Tel: 0121 362 1201
Fax: 0121 355 8727
E-mail: zincinfocentre@hdg.org.uk

Enquiries:
Enquiries to: Director

Founded:
2001

Formerly called:
Zinc Development Association (ceased trading)
(year of change 2000)

Organisation type and purpose:
Trade association.

Subject coverage:
A source of information on zinc and its uses.

Printed publications:
Publications and films on zinc

Access to staff:
Contact by letter, by telephone, by fax and by e-
mail
Hours: Mon to Fri, 0900 to 1700

Operated in conjunction with the:
Galvanizers Association

ZOOLOGICAL SOCIETY OF GLASGOW AND WEST OF SCOTLAND

Secretary: George W.H. Thomson, Morrisbank,
Bathgate, EH48 1JU

Tel: 0845 108 1426
Fax: 0845 108 1426

Website:
http://www.glasgowzoopark.org.uk
Current and historical information on zoos in
Glasgow.

Enquiries:
Enquiries to: Secretary
Direct e-mail: registrar@rzss.org.uk

Founded:
1936

Organisation type and purpose:
Membership association (membership is by
election or invitation), present number of
members: 200, registered charity (charity number
SCO 02651).

Subject coverage:
Zoo biology, biodiversity, environment.

**Museum or gallery collection, archive, or library
special collection:**
Books and photographs

Printed publications:
Annual Report (£10)

Access to staff:
Special comments: Volunteer staff only

Access to building, collection or gallery:
Prior appointment required

ZOOLOGICAL SOCIETY OF LONDON

Acronym or abbreviation: ZSL

Library, Regent's Park, London, NW1 4RY

Tel: 020 7449 6293
Fax: 020 7586 5743
E-mail: library@zsl.org

Website:
http://www.zsl.org

Enquiries:
Enquiries to: Librarian

Founded:
1826

Organisation type and purpose:
Learned society (membership is by subscription),
present number of members: 25,000, registered
charity (charity number 208728), research
organisation.
ZSL aims to achieve and promote the worldwide
conservation of animals and their habitats.

Subject coverage:
Zoology, animal conservation, zoo management.

**Museum or gallery collection, archive, or library
special collection:**
Archives of ZSL
Current journals on all aspects of zoology, animal
conservation and zoos
An extensive photographic collection covering the
diversity of nature with special emphasis on
endangered and extinct animals
Library specialising in historical taxonomy
(200,000 vols)

Collection of works of Gould, Wolf, Tickell,
Reeves, Lear and Elliott

Non-library collection catalogue:
All or part available online and in-house

Library catalogue:
All or part available online and in-house

Printed publications:
Animal Conservation (journal, bimonthly, Wiley)
Conservation Biology Series (Wiley)
International Zoo Yearbook
Journal of Zoology (monthly, Wiley)
Wild About
Nomenclator Zoologicus

Access to staff:
Appointment necessary.
Hours: Mon to Fri, 0930 to 1730

Access to building, collection or gallery:
Photographic ID and proof of address required

Access for disabled people:
Special comments: Reading Room accessed via steps
or small lift. Facilities are available to use the
online catalogue and consult material elsewhere if
the Reading Room cannot be accessed.

Parent body:
Institute of Zoology
ZSL London Zoo
ZSL Whipsnade Wild Animal Park

ZURICH RISK ENGINEERING UK

Zurich Risk Engineering UK, Park House, Bristol
Road South, Rubery, Birmingham, B45 9AH

Tel: 0121 698 5810
E-mail: riskengineering@zurich.co.uk

Enquiries:
Enquiries to: Librarian

Formerly called:
Zurich Risk Services; Eagle Star Insurance
Company

Organisation type and purpose:
Service industry.

Access to staff:
Contact by letter
Hours: Mon to Fri, 0900 to 1700

Access to building, collection or gallery:
No access other than to staff

Index of
Abbreviations and Acronyms

The abbreviations and acronyms listed here are cross-referenced by page number to their respective organisations in the Main Directory.

ANMW	Association of Newspaper and Magazine Wholesalers, *page 79*	ARMA	Association of Residential Managing Agents Ltd, *page 84*
ANSA	Association of Nurses in Substance Abuse, *page 80*	ARMMS	Heriot-Watt University – Archive, Records Management and Museum Service, *page 563*
ANTOR	Association of National Tourist Office Representatives, *page 79*	ARMS	Association of Researchers in Medicine & Science, *page 84*
ANTS	Anglo-Norman Text Society, *page 35*	ARS	Anaesthetic Research Society, *page 31*
AOC	Aromatherapy Council, *page 46*	ARS	Army Records Society, *page 45*
AoC	Association of Colleges, *page 69*	ARTSM	Association for Road Traffic Safety and Management, *page 59*
AOI	Association of Illustrators, *page 75*		
AOP	Association of Optometrists, *page 80*	ARU	Anglia Ruskin University, *page 33*
AOP	Association of Photographers Limited, *page 80*	ARX	Advocacy Resource Exchange, *page 16*
AoR	Association of Reflexologists (UK), *page 83*	AS	Alzheimer's Society, *page 28*
AOT	Association of Tutors, *page 87*	AS IN GB	Anthroposophical Society in Great Britain, *page 37*
APA	Association of Practising Accountants, *page 82*		
APA	Association of Publishing Agencies, *page 83*	ASA	Advertising Standards Authority, *page 15*
APAC	British Library – Asia, Pacific and Africa Collections, *page 191*	ASA	Amateur Swimming Association, *page 28*
		ASA	Amateur Swimming Association, Water Polo Committee, *page 29*
APCE / SNPA	Awdurdod Parc Cenedlaethol Eryri / Snowdonia National Park Authority, *page 96*	ASA	Association of Social Anthropologists of the Commonwealth, *page 85*
APCIMS	Association of Private Client Investment Managers and Stockbrokers, *page 82*	ASAO	Association of Show and Agricultural Organisations, *page 85*
APCMH	Association for Pastoral Care of the Mentally Ill, *page 57*	ASAUK	African Studies Association of the United Kingdom, *page 18*
APCO/CBA	Association of Pleasure Craft Operators / Canal Boatbuilders Association, *page 81*	ASBAH	Association for Spina Bifida and Hydrocephalus, *page 60*
APCP	Association of Paediatric Chartered Physiotherapists, *page 80*	ASBCI	Association of Suppliers to the British Clothing Industry, *page 85*
APEC	Action on Pre-eclampsia, *page 12*	ASC	Asian Studies Centre, *page 52*
APHA	Association of Port Health Authorities, *page 82*	ASCC	Association of Scottish Community Councils, *page 84*
APHC	Association of Plumbing and Heating Contractors, *page 81*	ASCL	Association of School and College Leaders, *page 84*
API	Association of Play Industries, *page 81*	ASCO	Association of Singer Car Owners, *page 85*
APIL	Association of Personal Injury Lawyers, *page 80*	ASDMA	Architectural and Specialist Door Manufacturers Association, *page 41*
APIRA	Avon Park International Racing Association, *page 95*		
APL	Association of Professional Landscapers, *page 82*	ASE	Association for Science Education, *page 59*
APM	Association for Palliative Medicine of Great Britain and Ireland, *page 57*	ASFAD	Association of Stainless Fastener Distributors, *page 85*
APM	Association for Project Management, *page 58*	ASFP	Association for Specialist Fire Protection, *page 59*
APMC	Association of Pioneer Motor Cyclists, *page 81*	ASGBI	Anatomical Society of Great Britain and Ireland, *page 32*
APMI	Association of Printing Machinery Importers, *page 82*	ASGBI	Association of Surgeons of Great Britain and Ireland, *page 86*
APMM	Association of Policy Market Makers, *page 81*		
APMT	Association of Professional Music Therapists, *page 82*	ASH	Action on Smoking and Health, *page 12*
APNI	Association for Post Natal Illness, *page 57*	ASI	Ambulance Service Institute, *page 29*
APNT	Association of Physical & Natural Therapists, *page 81*	ASI	Architecture and Surveying Institute, *page 43*
		ASLS	Association for Scottish Literary Studies, *page 59*
APR	Aslib Professional Recruitment Limited, *page 52*	ASM	Association of Supervisors of Midwives, *page 85*
APRS	Association of Professional Recording Services Limited, *page 83*	ASP	Anglia Support Partnership, *page 33*
APS	Apostrophe Protection Society, *page 39*	ASS	Advisory Service for Squatters, *page 16*
APS	Australasian Plant Society, *page 92*	AST	Atlantic Salmon Trust Limited, *page 90*
APSA	Association for Professionals in Services for Adolescents, *page 58*	ASTO	Association of Sea Training Organisations, *page 85*
APSE	Association for Public Service Excellence, *page 58*	ASUC	ASUCplus, *page 90*
APT	The UK Association of Preservation Trusts, *page 1152*	ASVA	Association of Scottish Visitor Attractions, *page 84*
APTG	Association of Professional Tourist Guides, *page 83*	ASWA	Anglican Society for the Welfare of Animals, *page 33*
APV	Association of Professional Videomakers, *page 83*	ATC	Aromatherapy Trade Council, *page 46*
		ATC	Association of Translation Companies Limited, *page 87*
ARA	Aircraft Research Association Limited, *page 22*	ATCM	Association of Tank and Cistern Manufacturers, *page 86*
ARA	Archives and Records Association, *page 43*		
ARA	Association of Relocation Agents, *page 84*	ATCM	Association of Town Centre Management, *page 87*
ARB	Architects Registration Board, *page 41*	ATLAS	Association of Technical Lighting and Access Specialists, *page 86*
ARC	ARC Antenatal Results & Choices, *page 40*		
ARC Unit	Arthritis Research Campaign Epidemiology Unit, *page 47*	ATM	Association of Teachers of Mathematics, *page 86*
ARCA	Adult Residential Colleges Association, *page 15*	ATMA	Adhesive Tape Manufacturers Association, *page 14*
ARLA	Association of Residential Letting Agents, *page 84*	ATP	American Technical Publishers Limited, *page 30*
ARLIS/UK & Ireland	Art Libraries Society of the UK and Ireland, *page 47*		
ARM	Association of Radical Midwives, *page 83*	ATT	Association of Taxation Technicians, *page 86*

BSA	Boarding Schools' Association, *page 128*
BSA	British Society of Aesthetics, *page 219*
BSA	British Society of Audiology, *page 219*
BSA	British Sociological Association, *page 221*
BSA	British Stammering Association, *page 222*
BSA	British Surfing Association, *page 223*
BSA	Building Societies Association, *page 241*
BSA	Business Services Association, *page 246*
BSA	Business Software Alliance, *page 246*
BSA at NIACE	Basic Skills Agency at NIACE, *page 103*
BSAC	British Sub-Aqua Club, *page 222*
BSACI	British Society for Allergy and Clinical Immunology, *page 216*
BSAFWDC	BSA Front-Wheel Drive Club, *page 236*
BSAS	British Society of Animal Science, *page 219*
BSAT	British Sporting Art Trust, *page 222*
BSAVA	British Small Animal Veterinary Association, *page 215*
BSBI	Botanical Society of the British Isles, *page 132*
BSC	British Safety Council, *page 213*
BSCA	British Schools Cycling Association, *page 213*
BSCAH	British Society of Clinical and Academic Hypnosis, *page 219*
BSCB	British Society for Cell Biology, *page 216*
BSCC	British Society for Clinical Cytology, *page 216*
BSD	British Society of Dowsers, *page 219*
BSDA	British Soft Drinks Association Limited, *page 221*
BSDB	British Society for Developmental Biology, *page 216*
BSDR	British Society for Dental Research, *page 216*
BSES Expeditions	British Schools Exploring Society, *page 214*
BSF	British Sikh Federation, *page 215*
BSF	British Softball Federation, *page 222*
BSFA	British Science Fiction Association Limited, *page 214*
BSG	British Society for Geomorphology, *page 216*
BSG	British Society of Gastroenterology, *page 220*
BSG	British Society of Gerontology, *page 220*
BSGA	British Schools Gymnastic Association, *page 214*
BSGA	British Sign & Graphics Association, *page 215*
BSH	British Society for Haematology, *page 217*
BSH	British Society of Hypnotherapists, *page 220*
BSHAA	British Society of Hearing Aid Audiologists, *page 220*
BSHP	British Society for the History of Pharmacy, *page 218*
BSHS	British Society for the History of Science, *page 218*
BSI	British Society for Immunology, *page 217*
BSI	British Suzuki Institute, *page 223*
BSI	BSI Product Services, *page 237*
BSIA	British Security Industry Association Limited, *page 214*
BSIA	British Starch Industry Association, *page 222*
BSIF	British Safety Industry Federation, *page 213*
BSJA	British Show Jumping Association, *page 215*
BSMDH (MET&S)	British Society for Medical and Dental Hypnosis, *page 217*
BSME	British Society of Magazine Editors, *page 220*
BSMFD	British Society for Mercury Free Dentistry, *page 217*
BSMGP	British Society of Master Glass Painters, *page 220*
BSMT	British Society for Music Therapy, *page 217*
BSNR	British Society of Neuroradiologists, *page 221*
BSO	British School of Osteopathy, *page 213*
BSP	British Society for Parasitology, *page 218*
BSP	British Society of Periodontology, *page 221*
BSPB	British Society of Plant Breeders Limited, *page 221*
BSR	British Society for Rheumatology, *page 218*
BSRD	British Society for Restorative Dentistry, *page 218*
BSS	Botanical Society of Scotland, *page 132*
BSS	British Standards Society, *page 222*
BSS	British Sundial Society, *page 223*
BSS-Do	British School of Shiatsu-Do, *page 213*
BSSAA	British Snoring and Sleep Apnoea Association Limited, *page 216*
BSSC	British Shooting Sports Council, *page 214*
BSSM	British Society for Strain Measurement, *page 218*
BSSPD	British Society for the Study of Prosthetic Dentistry, *page 219*
BSSS	British Society of Soil Science, *page 221*
BSY GROUP	British School of Yoga, *page 213*
BTA	British Tinnitus Association, *page 224*
BTA	British Trout Association, *page 225*
BTBA	British Tenpin Bowling Association, *page 224*
BTCV	BTCV – Wallingford, *page 238*
BTCV Scotland	British Trust for Conservation Volunteers Scotland, *page 225*
BTF	British Thyroid Foundation, *page 224*
BTG	British Toymakers Guild, *page 225*
BTHA	British Toy & Hobby Association Limited, *page 224*
BTMA	British Textile Machinery Association, *page 224*
BTMA	British Turned Parts Manufacturers Association, *page 226*
BTO	British Trust for Ornithology, *page 225*
BTS	British Tarantula Society, *page 223*
BTS	British Trolleybus Society, *page 225*
BTS	British Tunnelling Society, *page 226*
BTS	Business and Trade Statistics Limited, *page 243*
BUAV	British Union for the Abolition of Vivisection, *page 226*
BUC	British Union Conference of Seventh-day Adventists, *page 226*
BUFORA	British Unidentified Flying Object Research Association, *page 226*
BUFVC	British Universities Film & Video Council, *page 227*
BURA	British Urban Regeneration Association, *page 227*
Bury Metro	Metropolitan Borough of Bury, *page 775*
BUSA	British Universities Sports Association, *page 227*
BUSWE	British Union of Social Work Employees, *page 227*
Butchers' Company	Worshipful Company of Butchers, *page 1279*
BVA	British Veterinary Association, *page 228*
BVA	British Video Association, *page 228*
BVA	British Voice Association, *page 229*
BVAMA	British Valve & Actuator Association, *page 228*
BVNA	British Veterinary Nursing Association, *page 228*
BVS	Battery Vehicle Society, *page 105*
BVSS	British Vendeen Sheep Society, *page 228*
BWA	Bitumen Waterproofing Association (UK) Ltd, *page 123*
BWBF	British Wireless for the Blind Fund, *page 230*
BWCMG	British Watch and Clockmakers Guild, *page 229*
BWF	British Woodworking Federation, *page 231*
BWLA	British Weight Lifters Association Limited, *page 229*
BWMA	British Weights and Measures Association, *page 230*
BWPA	British Women Pilots' Association, *page 231*
BWRC	British Wildlife Rescue Centre, *page 230*
BWSF	British Wheelchair Sports Foundation, *page 230*
BYC	British Youth Council, *page 231*
CA	Classical Association, *page 321*
CA	Consumers' Association, *page 347*
CA	Croquet Association, *page 365*
CA	Cruising Association, *page 368*
CAA	Cement Admixtures Association, *page 267*
CAA	Cinema Advertising Association Limited, *page 313*
CAA	Civil Aviation Authority, *page 319*
CAA	Club for Acts and Actors, *page 323*
CAABU	Council for the Advancement of Arab-British Understanding, *page 356*
CAAT	Campaign Against Arms Trade, *page 254*
Cab	Christians Abroad, *page 309*
CAB	Council for Aluminium in Building, *page 354*

GROS	General Register Office for Scotland, *page 513*	HDRA	Home Decoration Retailers Association, *page 576*
GSA	Glasgow School of Art, *page 522*	HEART UK	Hyperlipidaemia Education & Atherosclerosis Research Trust UK, *page 589*
GSEIS	Graduate School of European and International Studies, *page 529*	HECSU	Graduate Prospects Ltd, *page 529*
GSES	University of Strathclyde – Graduate School of Environmental Studies, *page 1216*	HEFCE	Higher Education Funding Council for England, *page 568*
GSG	Good Schools Guide, *page 527*	HEFCW	Higher Education Funding Council for Wales, *page 568*
GSMD	Guildhall School of Music and Drama, *page 539*	Henry George Foundation	Henry George Foundation of Gt Britain Limited, *page 559*
GSP	Global School Partnerships, *page 524*	Herefordshire Council	County of Herefordshire District Council, *page 359*
GT	Gender Trust, *page 511*	HESA	Higher Education Statistics Agency, *page 568*
GTA	Gun Trade Association Limited, *page 540*	HFAN (UK)	Health for All Network (UK) Ltd, *page 554*
GTC Scotland	General Teaching Council for Scotland, *page 513*	HFBG	Historic Farm Buildings Group, *page 571*
GTCW	General Teaching Council for Wales, *page 513*	HFHS	Herefordshire Family History Society, *page 562*
GTMA	Gauge and Tool Makers' Association, *page 510*	HFHS	Highland Family History Society, *page 569*
GTPU	Guys' and St Thomas' Poisons Unit, Guy's and St Thomas' NHS Foundation Trust, *page 541*	HFMA	Health Food Manufacturers' Association, *page 554*
GTT Ltd	Growth Through Training (GTT) Limited, *page 534*	HGWS	H G Wells Society, The, *page 542*
GVA	Gin and Vodka Association, *page 518*	HHA	Historic Houses Association, *page 571*
GWCT	Game and Wildlife Conservation Trust, *page 508*	HHC	Holistic Health College, *page 575*
GWL	Glasgow Women's Library, *page 523*	HIE	Highlands & Islands Enterprise, *page 569*
GWP	Guild of Photographers (United Kingdom), *page 538*	HKTB	Hong Kong Tourism Board, *page 578*
		HLBC	Canning House Library, *page 257*
GWS	Great Western Society Limited, *page 531*	HLF	Heritage Lottery Fund, *page 564*
H&D FHS	Huddersfield and District Family History Society, *page 584*	HLIS	Hampshire Library and Information Service – Farnborough, *page 547*
H4H	Help for Heroes, *page 559*	HLN	Hounslow Library Network, *page 581*
HA	Historical Association, *page 572*	HLR	Historic Lotus Register, *page 571*
HA	Huntingdonshire Archives, *page 587*	HLS	Huntingdon Life Sciences, *page 587*
HABIA	Hair and Beauty Industry Authority (HABIA), *page 543*	HLSI	Highgate Literary and Scientific Institution, *page 569*
HAC	Help Advisory Centre, *page 558*	HMBCE	English Heritage (South West Region), *page 439*
HACSG	Hyperactive Children's Support Group, *page 588*	HMC	Headmasters' and Headmistresses' Conference, *page 552*
HAE	Hire Association Europe, *page 571*	HMD	Home Mission Desk, *page 577*
HALS	Hampshire Archives and Local Studies, *page 545*	HMLR	HM Land Registry, *page 574*
		HMNAO	HM Nautical Almanac Office, *page 575*
HALS	Hertfordshire Archives and Local Studies, *page 565*	HMRS	Historical Model Railway Society, *page 573*
Hants Field Club	Hampshire Field Club and Archaeological Society, *page 546*	HMS	Historical Metallurgical Society Limited, *page 573*
HAPPA	Horses and Ponies Protection Association, *page 579*	HMSTC	Hertfordshire Multiple Sclerosis Therapy Centre, *page 565*
HAT Archive	History of Advertising Trust, *page 573*	HNHS	Hertfordshire Natural History Society, *page 566*
HAT Archive	History of Advertising Trust Archive, *page 573*	HOS	Housing Ombudsman Service, *page 582*
HBC	Havant Borough Council, *page 550*	HOT	Hawk and Owl Trust, *page 551*
HBMC or EH	English Heritage, *page 436*	HP CDS	Hewlett-Packard CDS, *page 566*
HBP	Housebuilder Publications, *page 582*	HPA	Health Protection Agency, *page 555*
HBS	Havergal Brian Society, *page 551*	HPA	Health Protection Agency – Centre for Infections, *page 556*
HC	Hairdressing Council, *page 543*	
HCA	Hall-Carpenter Archives, *page 544*	HPA	Heat Pump Association, *page 558*
HCA	Holiday Centres Association, *page 575*	HPA	Hurlingham Polo Association, The, *page 588*
HCC	Hospital Chaplaincies Council, *page 580*	HPA CRCE	Health Protection Agency – Centre for Radiation, Chemical and Environmental Hazards, *page 556*
HCC	Hungarian Cultural Centre, *page 587*	
HCFHE	Havering College of Further and Higher Education, *page 551*	HPA MRL	Health Protection Agency – Mycology Reference Laboratory, *page 556*
HCGB	Hovercraft Club of Great Britain, *page 582*	HPANI	Health Promotion Agency for Northern Ireland, *page 555*
HCIMA	Hotel and Catering International Management Association, *page 581*	HPC	Health Professions Council, *page 555*
HCIO	House of Commons Information Office, *page 581*	HPLB	Hewlett-Packard Laboratories, *page 566*
		HR	Human Rights, *page 586*
HCIS	British Library – Health Care Information Service, *page 193*	HRA	Heritage Railway Association, *page 564*
HCKC	Hillman Commer & Karrier Club, *page 570*	HRI	Hannah Research Institute, *page 547*
HCMM	Honourable Company of Master Mariners, *page 578*	HRI	Horticulture Research International, *page 580*
		HRO	Herefordshire Record Office, *page 562*
HCPT	HCPT – The Pilgrimage Trust, *page 552*	HRUK	Heart Research UK, *page 557*
HCSA	Hospital Consultants and Specialists Association, *page 581*	HS	Historic Scotland, *page 572*
		HSA	Humane Slaughter Association, *page 587*
HCST	H C Starck Limited, *page 542*	hsbp	Henshaws Society for Blind People, *page 560*
HCT	Herefordshire College of Technology – Hereford Campus, *page 562*	HSCC	Historic Sports Car Club, *page 572*
		HSE	Health and Safety Executive, *page 553*
HCVS	Historic Commercial Vehicle Society, *page 571*	HSE	Health and Safety Executive – Information Services, *page 553*
HDA	Health Development Agency, *page 554*	
HDA	Huntington's Disease Association, *page 588*	HSGBI	Hymn Society of Great Britain and Ireland, *page 588*
HDC	Horticultural Development Company, *page 580*	HSL	Health and Safety Laboratory, *page 553*

ITC Ltd	Individual Travellers Co Ltd, *page 598*	JMC	Jewish Marriage Council, *page 680*
ITDG	Intermediate Technology Development Group Limited, *page 643*	JMF Soc	John Meade Falkner Society, *page 682*
		JMI	Jewish Music Institute, *page 680*
ITEC	International Therapy Examination Council, *page 663*	JMTC	Johnson Matthey Technology Centre, *page 683*
		JNCC	Joint Nature Conservation Committee, *page 684*
ITF	International Transport Workers' Federation, *page 663*	JNTO	Japan National Tourist Organization, *page 676*
ITF	International Tree Foundation, *page 664*	JOAC	Jupiter Owners' Auto Club, *page 687*
ITI	Institute of Translation and Interpreting, *page 636*	John Cabot CTC	John Cabot City Technology College, *page 681*
		JPR	Institute for Jewish Policy Research, *page 605*
ITI	International Theatre Institute Limited, *page 663*	JRF	Joseph Rowntree Foundation, *page 685*
ITL	Imperial Tobacco Limited, *page 594*	JRULM	John Rylands University Library of Manchester, *page 682*
ITMA	Institute of Trade Mark Attorneys, *page 635*	JRULM	Methodist Archives and Research Centre, *page 774*
ITOPF	International Tanker Owners Pollution Federation Limited, *page 662*	JSCSC	Joint Services Command & Staff College Library, *page 685*
ITS	Institute for Transport Studies, *page 607*		
ITS	Irish Texts Society, *page 669*	JTSMA	Jennifer Trust for Spinal Muscular Atrophy, *page 677*
ITT	Institute of Travel and Tourism, *page 636*		
ITTF	International Table Tennis Federation, *page 662*	JVC	JVC Professional Europe Ltd., *page 688*
IUA	International Underwriting Association, *page 664*	JVDC	Justice for all Vaccine-Damaged Children, *page 687*
IVCA	International Visual Communication Association, *page 664*	K&ESR	Kent and East Sussex Railway, *page 690*
		KAS	Kent Archaeological Society, *page 690*
IVE	Institute of Vitreous Enamellers, *page 637*	KC	Kirklees College – Huddersfield Centre, *page 695*
IVehE	Institute of Vehicle Engineers, *page 636*		
IVS	International Voluntary Service (North), *page 664*	KCC Libraries and Archive	Kent County Council Libraries and Archives, *page 690*
IVS GB	International Voluntary Service, *page 664*	KCL	King's College London – St Thomas' House Information Services Centre, *page 693*
IWA	Inland Waterways Association, *page 601*		
IWA	International Water Association, *page 665*	KCL	King's College London – Stamford Street Information Services Centre, *page 693*
IWater	Institute of Water, *page 637*		
IWC	International Whaling Commission, *page 665*	KFAT	National Union of Knitwear, Footwear and Apparel Trades, *page 858*
IWCCTI	Isle of Wight Chamber of Commerce, Tourism and Industry, *page 672*		
		KFHS	Kent Family History Society, *page 690*
IWCT	International Wildlife Coalition Trust, *page 665*	KIAD	Kent Institute of Art and Design at Maidstone, *page 690*
IWFS	International Wine & Food Society, *page 665*		
IWH	Institute of Women's Health, *page 637*	KIB	Kodály Institute of Britain, *page 696*
IWM	Imperial War Museum, *page 594*	KIF	Knitting Industries' Federation, *page 696*
IWPPA	Independent Waste Paper Processors Association, *page 597*	KNTO	Korea National Tourism Organization, *page 696*
		KSGB	Kite Society of Great Britain, *page 695*
IWR	Information World Review, *page 601*	KSL	Kate Sharpley Library, *page 688*
IWSc	IWSc: The Wood Technology Society, *page 675*	L&I	List and Index Society, *page 724*
IYF	International Youth Foundation of Great Britain, *page 666*	L&LR	Leukaemia & Lymphoma Research, *page 717*
		L&SWLFHS	Liverpool & SW Lancashire Family History Society, *page 726*
IZAUK	International Zen Association (United Kingdom), *page 666*		
		LA	Libertarian Alliance, *page 719*
JACT	Joint Association of Classical Teachers, *page 683*	LA	Lighting Association, *page 721*
JAMPRO	Jamaica Trade Commission, *page 675*	LA	Lincolnshire Archives, *page 723*
Jane's	Jane's Information Group, *page 676*	LA	Lymphoma Association, *page 749*
JBD	Jewish Blind and Disabled, *page 679*	LAACTSA	Local Authority Action for Southern Africa, *page 729*
JBS	Josephine Butler Society, *page 686*		
JBSoc	John Buchan Society, *page 681*	LACA	Local Authority Caterers Association, *page 730*
JCCI	Japanese Chamber of Commerce and Industry in the United Kingdom, *page 677*	LACORS	Local Authorities Coordinators of Regulatory Services, *page 729*
JCI	Junior Chamber International London, *page 687*	LACS	League Against Cruel Sports Limited, *page 708*
JCLI	Joint Council for Landscape Industries, *page 683*	LAD	Liverpool Association of Disabled People, *page 726*
JCWI	Joint Council for the Welfare of Immigrants, *page 684*	LADD	London Academy of Dressmaking and Design, *page 731*
JDA	Jewellery Distributors' Association, *page 679*	LAG	Legal Action Group, *page 713*
JDRF	Juvenile Diabetes Research Foundation, *page 687*	LAHS	Leicestershire Archaeological and Historical Society, *page 714*
JEB	Jewish Education Bureau, *page 680*	LAMAS	London and Middlesex Archaeological Society, *page 732*
JEC	Jaguar Enthusiasts' Club, *page 675*		
JEC	Jewel & Esk College, *page 679*	LAPADA	Association of Art & Antiques Dealers, *page 61*
JEECS	Jewish East End Celebration Society, *page 679*	LAPP	London Association of Primal Psychotherapists, *page 732*
JET	Joint Educational Trust, *page 684*		
JETRO	JETRO London, *page 678*	LASA	Laboratory Animal Science Association, *page 697*
JHSE	Jewish Historical Society of England, *page 680*		
JIB	Joint Industry Board for the Electrical Contracting Industry, *page 684*	LBA	London Baptist Association, *page 732*
		LBC	Leo Baeck College Library, *page 715*
JIB	Jordan Information Bureau, *page 685*	LBC	London Buddhist Centre, *page 734*
JIC	John Innes Centre and Sainsbury Laboratory, *page 681*	LBH	London Borough of Hounslow, *page 734*
		LBN	London Bereavement Network, *page 732*
JICC	Japanese Embassy, *page 677*	LBS	London Business School, *page 735*
JIMA	John Innes Manufacturers Association, *page 682*	LCAS	Lancashire and Cheshire Antiquarian Society, *page 700*
JKJ Society	Jerome K Jerome Society, *page 677*	LCC	London College of Communication, *page 736*

NATE	National Association for the Teaching of English, *page 806*	NDCS	National Deaf Children's Society (NDCS), *page 823*
NATLL	National Association of Toy and Leisure Libraries, *page 813*	NDFS	National Deposit Friendly Society Limited, *page 823*
NatSCA	Natural Sciences Collections Association, *page 862*	NDL	National Debtline, *page 823*
NAVCA	National Association for Voluntary and Community Action, *page 806*	NDNA	National Day Nurseries Association, *page 823*
		NDRO	North Devon Record Office, *page 877*
NAVH	Norfolk Association of Village Halls, *page 874*	NEA	National Energy Action, *page 824*
NAW	National Association of Widows, *page 814*	NEA	National Exhibitors Association, *page 825*
NAWC	National Association of Women's Clubs, *page 814*	NEAC	New English Art Club, *page 866*
		NEBOSH	National Examination Board in Occupational Safety and Health, *page 825*
NAWP	National Association of Women Pharmacists, *page 814*	NEC	National Extension College, *page 825*
NAWP	Newham Asian Women's Project, *page 868*	NECC	North East Chamber of Commerce, Trade & Industry, *page 877*
NAWT	National Animal Welfare Trust, *page 801*	NECPWA	North-East Club for Pre-War Austins, *page 884*
NAYO	National Association of Youth Orchestras, *page 814*	NEDDC	North East Derbyshire District Council, *page 877*
NAYT	National Association of Youth Theatres, *page 814*	NEELB/NELS	North Eastern Education and Library Board, *page 878*
NBA	National Beef Association, *page 816*	NEF	National Energy Foundation, *page 825*
NBA	National Blood Authority, *page 816*	NEMA	National Early Music Association, *page 824*
NBF	National Bed Federation, *page 815*	NEMSA	North of England Mule Sheep Association, *page 880*
NBGW	National Botanic Garden of Wales, The, *page 816*	NERC	National Eye Research Centre, *page 826*
NBI	National Benevolent Institution, *page 816*	NERC	Natural Environment Research Council, *page 861*
NCAPTC	Norfolk County Association of Parish & Town Councils, *page 874*	NES	National Eczema Society, *page 824*
NCC	National Caravan Council Limited, *page 817*	NEVAC	National Electronic and Video Archive of the Crafts, *page 824*
NCC	National Computing Centre Limited, *page 820*	NEVL	National Educational Video Library, *page 824*
NCCA	National Carpet Cleaners Association, *page 817*	NEW College	North East Worcestershire College, *page 878*
NCCF	National Consumer Credit Federation, *page 821*	NEZS	North of England Zoological Society, *page 880*
NCCPG	Plant Heritage, *page 930*	NFA	National Federation of Anglers, *page 828*
NCDC	North Cornwall District Council, *page 876*	NFB	National Federation of Builders, *page 828*
NCDS	National Council for the Divorced and Separated, *page 821*	NFB	National Film Board of Canada, *page 830*
		NFBUK	National Federation of the Blind of the United Kingdom, *page 829*
NCDT	National Council for Drama Training, *page 821*	NFCU	Ace Credit Union Services, *page 10*
NCEC	National Chemical Emergency Centre, *page 818*	NFDC LTD	National Federation of Demolition Contractors Limited, *page 828*
NCEM	National Centre for Early Music, *page 817*	NFFF	National Federation of Fish Friers Limited, *page 828*
NCF	National Consumer Federation, *page 821*		
NcfeD	National Centre for Eating Disorders, *page 818*	NFHS	Nottinghamshire Family History Society, *page 894*
NCFS	National Campaign for Firework Safety, *page 816*	NFM	National Family Mediation, *page 826*
NCHA	National Care Association, *page 817*	NFMFT	National Federation of Meat and Food Traders, The, *page 828*
NCHP	National College of Hypnosis and Psychotherapy, *page 820*	NFMS	Making Music, *page 752*
NCNE	National Campaign for Nursery Education, *page 817*	NFPB & CS	New Forest Pony Breeding and Cattle Society, *page 866*
NCOB	Nuffield Council on Bioethics, *page 896*	NFRC	National Federation of Roofing Contractors Limited, *page 828*
NCOPO	National Council of Pakistani Organisations (UK), *page 822*	NFSP	National Federation of SubPostmasters, *page 828*
NCPA	Norfolk County Petanque Association, *page 875*	NFT	National Film Theatre, *page 830*
NCPA	UK National Committee for the Prevention of Alcohol and Drug Dependency, *page 1175*	NFTMMS	National Federation of Terrazzo Marble & Mosaic Specialists, *page 829*
NCS	National Chrysanthemum Society, *page 819*	NFTS	National Film and Television School, *page 829*
NCSS	National Council for School Sport, *page 821*	NFU	National Farmers' Union, *page 827*
NCT	Norfolk Church Trust Limited, *page 874*	NFUS	NFU Scotland, *page 870*
NCTC	National Collection of Type Cultures, *page 820*	NFWI	National Federation of Women's Institutes, *page 829*
NCTEPO	National Centre for Training and Education in Prosthetics and Orthotics, *page 818*	NFWI–Wales	National Federation of Women's Institutes – Wales, *page 829*
NCTJ	National Council for the Training of Journalists, *page 821*	NFWS	National Fox Welfare Society, *page 830*
NCUACS	National Cataloguing Unit for the Archives of Contemporary Scientists, *page 817*	NGA	National Governors' Association, *page 831*
		ngb2b	Newport and Gwent Chamber of Commerce and Industry, *page 868*
NCVCCO	National Council of Voluntary Child Care Organisations, *page 822*	NGC	Gypsy Council, The, *page 542*
NCVO	National Council for Voluntary Organisations, *page 822*	NGS	National Gerbil Society, *page 831*
NCVYS	National Council for Voluntary Youth Services, *page 822*	NGS	NGS: Gardens Open for Charity, *page 870*
NCW	National Council of Women of Great Britain, *page 822*	NHA	National Housewives Association, *page 833*
NCYPE	National Centre for Young People with Epilepsy, *page 818*	NHC	National Hamster Council, *page 832*
		NHC	Northern Hamster Club, *page 886*
NDAF	National Disability Arts Forum, *page 823*	NHCCI	North Hampshire Chamber of Commerce and Industry, *page 878*
NDBMOC	North Devon British Motorcycle Owners Club, *page 876*	NHDC	North Hertfordshire District Council, *page 878*

NSPS	National Sweet Pea Society, *page 848*
NSRA	National Small-bore Rifle Association, *page 846*
NSRA	National Society for Research into Allergy, *page 847*
NSS	National Schools Sevens, *page 845*
NSS	National Secular Society, *page 846*
NSSAW	National Screen and Sound Archive of Wales, *page 845*
NSUOC	NSU Owners Club, *page 896*
NT	National Theatre, *page 849*
NT	National Trust, *page 850*
NT	National Trust (Devon & Cornwall Regional Offices) – Bodmin, *page 850*
NT	National Trust (Devon & Cornwall Regional Offices) – Exeter, *page 850*
NT	National Trust (East Midlands Regional Office), *page 851*
NT	National Trust (East of England Regional Office), *page 851*
NT	National Trust (North West Regional Office), *page 852*
NT	National Trust (South East Regional Office), *page 852*
NT	National Trust (Thames and Solent Regional Office), *page 853*
NT	National Trust (Wessex Regional Office), *page 853*
NT	National Trust (Yorkshire & North East Regional Offices) – Morpeth, *page 854*
NT	National Trust (Yorkshire & North East Regional Offices) – York, *page 854*
NT	National Trust Midlands (West), *page 857*
NT	National Trust Office for Wales, *page 857*
NTA	National Taxi Association, *page 849*
NTA	National Trolleybus Association, *page 849*
NTDA	National Tyre Distributors Association, *page 858*
NTET	National Traction Engine Trust, *page 849*
NTS	National Trust for Scotland, *page 854*
NTS	National Trust for Scotland (North-East Region), *page 855*
NTS	National Trust for Scotland (South Region), *page 855*
NTS	National Trust for Scotland (West Region), *page 856*
NTS	National Trust for Scotland Highlands and Islands Office (North), *page 856*
NTS	National Trust for Scotland Highlands and Islands Office (South), *page 856*
NTTC	Australia's Northern Territory Tourist Commission, *page 93*
NURA	National Union of Residents Associations, *page 858*
NUS	National Union of Students, *page 858*
NUT	National Union of Teachers, *page 858*
Nut Soc	Nutrition Society, *page 897*
NVCAS	Civil Aid, *page 318*
NVTEC	National Vintage Tractor and Engine Club, *page 859*
NWDA	Northwest Development Agency, *page 892*
NWDC	North Wiltshire District Council, *page 883*
NWEO	North West Employers, *page 882*
NWFA	North West Film Archive, *page 882*
NWKFHS	North West Kent Family History Society, *page 882*
NWLCC	North & Western Lancashire Chamber of Commerce, *page 876*
NWLDC	North West Leicestershire District Council, *page 883*
NWLH	National Waiting List Helpline, *page 859*
NWML	National Weights and Measures Laboratory, *page 859*
NWR	National Women's Register, *page 859*
NWT	North Wales Tourism, *page 881*
NYCRO	North Yorkshire County Record Office, *page 884*
NYJO	National Youth Jazz Orchestra of Great Britain, *page 860*
NYOS	National Youth Orchestras of Scotland, *page 860*
NYT	National Youth Theatre of Great Britain, *page 860*
OBAC	Organisation of Blind African Caribbeans, *page 907*
OBC	Oxford Business College, *page 910*
OCA	Open College of the Arts, *page 904*
OCC	Oxfordshire County Council, *page 912*
OCCA	Oil and Colour Chemists Association, *page 902*
OCCS	Optical Consumer Complaints Service, *page 905*
OCNLR	Open College Network London Region, *page 904*
ODA	Offa's Dyke Association, *page 898*
ODI	Overseas Development Institute, *page 909*
ODLQC	Open and Distance Learning Quality Council, *page 904*
ODS	Online Data Services, *page 903*
OEDA	Occupational and Environmental Diseases Association, *page 897*
OER	Oxford Educational Resources Limited, *page 911*
OET	Spanish Tourist Office, *page 1113*
OFCOM	Office of Communications, *page 899*
OFF	Organic Food Federation, *page 907*
Ofgem	Office of Gas and Electricity Markets, *page 899*
OFHS	Oxfordshire Family History Society, *page 912*
OFT	Office of Fair Trading, *page 899*
OFWAT	Office of Water Services, *page 901*
OGC	Office of Government Commerce, *page 900*
OHE	Office of Health Economics, *page 900*
OME	Office of Manpower Economics, *page 900*
OMRS	Orders and Medals Research Society, *page 906*
ONS	Office for National Statistics, *page 898*
ONS	Office for National Statistics Library (London), *page 899*
Open UP	Open University Press, *page 905*
OPFS	One Parent Families Scotland, *page 903*
OPITO	Petroleum Open Learning, *page 926*
OPT	Oxford Preservation Trust, *page 911*
ORCC	Oxfordshire Rural Community Council, *page 912*
ORNS	Office of the Representative of Novi Sad, *page 900*
ORO	Oxfordshire Record Office, *page 912*
ORS	OR Society, *page 905*
OS	Omnibus Society, *page 902*
OS	Ordnance Survey, *page 906*
OSGB	Orchid Society of Great Britain, *page 906*
OSJ	Orchestra of St John's, *page 905*
OSNI	Ordnance Survey of Northern Ireland, *page 906*
OSPA	Overseas Service Pensioners' Association, *page 909*
OSS	Open Spaces Society, *page 904*
OTA	Offender's Tag Association, *page 898*
OU	Open University Library and Learning Resources Centre, *page 905*
OUCEM	Open University, *page 904*
Oxford TIC	Oxford Information Centre, *page 911*
OXIRM	Oxford Institute of Retail Management, *page 911*
P&G	Procter & Gamble Technical Centres Limited, *page 946*
PA	Living Streets, *page 728*
PA	Philadelphia Association, *page 927*
PA	Press Association, *page 943*
PA	Prisoners Abroad, *page 945*
PA	Publishers Association, *page 951*
PACS	Post Abortion Counselling Service, *page 939*
PACT	Prison Advice and Care Trust, *page 945*
PACT	Producers Alliance for Cinema and Television, *page 946*
PACTS	Parliamentary Advisory Council for Transport Safety, *page 917*
Painters' Company	Worshipful Company of Painter-Stainers, *page 1285*
PBIF	Plastics & Board Industries Federation, *page 931*

SFHS	Shetland Family History Society, *page 1068*
SFHS	Shropshire Family History Society, *page 1071*
SFL	Scottish Football League, The, *page 1044*
SFLA	Solicitors Family Law Association, *page 1100*
SFLG	St Francis Leprosy Guild, *page 1119*
SFSA	Scottish Federation of Sea Anglers, *page 1043*
SFTAH	Autism Independent UK, *page 93*
SGA	Scottish Games Association, *page 1044*
SGC	South Gloucestershire Council, *page 1105*
SGC	Surrey Guild of Craftsmen, *page 1137*
SGD	Society of Garden Designers, *page 1092*
SGM	Society for General Microbiology, *page 1082*
SGS	Scotland's Gardens Scheme, *page 1033*
SGS	Scottish Gladiolus Society, *page 1045*
SGT	Society of Glass Technology, *page 1092*
SGTS	Scottish Gaelic Texts Society, *page 1044*
SHA	Socialist Health Association, *page 1079*
SHAC	Society for the History of Alchemy and Chemistry, *page 1085*
SHAHT	Surrey Heath Archaeological & Heritage Trust, *page 1137*
SHALTA	Skin, Hide and Leather Traders Association, *page 1076*
SHAP	Shap Working Party on World Religions in Education, *page 1063*
SHARC	Sexual Health and Reproductive Care, *page 1062*
SHB(GB)	Sport Horse Breeding of Great Britain, *page 1116*
SHBA	Homes for Scotland, *page 577*
SHBC	Surrey Heath Borough Council, *page 1137*
SHBT	Scottish Historic Buildings Trust, *page 1045*
SHEDA	Storage and Handling Equipment Distributors' Association, *page 1129*
SHNH	Society for the History of Natural History, *page 1085*
SHS	Scottish History Society, *page 1045*
SHS	Social History Society, *page 1078*
SHU	Sheffield Hallam University, *page 1066*
SHU	Sheffield Hallam University – Learning Centres, Library Resources and IT, *page 1066*
SI	Society of Indexers, *page 1093*
SIA	Spinal Injuries Association, *page 1115*
SIAS	Sussex Industrial Archaeology Society, *page 1138*
SIC	Shetland Islands Council, *page 1069*
SIF	Society for Individual Freedom, *page 1082*
SIFD	Society for International Folk Dancing, *page 1082*
SIH	Society for Italic Handwriting, *page 1082*
SIHE	Swansea Institute of Higher Education, *page 1140*
SIR	Seafacs Information and Research, *page 1059*
SIS	Spinal Injuries Scotland, *page 1115*
SIW	Socialist International Women, *page 1079*
SJH	Society of Jewellery Historians, *page 1093*
SJJA	Scottish Ju-Jitsu Association, *page 1046*
SKDC	South Kesteven District Council, *page 1106*
Skill	Skill: National Bureau for Students with Disabilities, *page 1075*
SLA	School Library Association, *page 1029*
SLAD	Society of London Art Dealers, *page 1094*
SLBI	South London Botanical Institute, *page 1107*
SLC	Scottish Law Commission, *page 1046*
SLCVS	Council for Voluntary Service – South Lakeland, *page 356*
SLD	Scottish Language Dictionaries Limited, *page 1046*
SLD	Scottish Liberal Democrats, *page 1047*
SLHA	Society for Lincolnshire History and Archaeology, *page 1083*
SLIC	Scottish Library and Information Council, *page 1047*
Slovak Embassy	Embassy of the Slovak Republic, *page 428*
SLS	Statute Law Society, *page 1126*
SLSGB	Surf Life Saving GB, *page 1136*
SLTB	Society for Low Temperature Biology, *page 1083*

SLTC	Society of Leather Technologists and Chemists Limited, *page 1093*
SMA	Society of Martial Arts, *page 1094*
SMA	Stage Management Association, *page 1124*
SMC	Worshipful Company of Spectacle Makers, *page 1287*
SMDC	Staffordshire Moorlands District Council, *page 1123*
SMI	Society of Maritime Industries Limited, *page 1094*
SML	Soil Mechanics, *page 1099*
SMN	Scientific and Medical Network, *page 1032*
SMPC	Scottish Mask and Puppet Centre, *page 1047*
SMS	Society of Master Saddlers, *page 1095*
SMS	Society of Model Shipwrights, *page 1095*
SMTA	Scottish Motor Trade Association Limited, *page 1048*
SMTA	Sewing Machine Trade Association, *page 1062*
SMTO	Scottish Massage Therapists Organisation Limited, *page 1047*
SMUC	St Mary's University College, *page 1121*
SNACMA	Snack, Nut and Crisp Manufacturers Association Limited, *page 1077*
SNC	South Northamptonshire District Council, *page 1107*
SNCCFR	Sir Norman Chester Centre for Football Research, *page 1075*
SNFWB	Scottish National Federation for the Welfare of the Blind, *page 1048*
SNHL	Scottish Natural History Library, *page 1049*
SNIPEF	Scottish and Northern Ireland Plumbing Employers' Federation, *page 1035*
SNIWB, LINBURN	Scottish National Institution for the War Blinded, *page 1048*
SNNP	Society of Nursery Nursing Practitioners, *page 1095*
SNP	Scottish National Party, *page 1048*
SNSPRCS	Scottish National Sweet Pea, Rose & Carnation Society, *page 1048*
SoA	Broadcasting Group of the Society of Authors, *page 233*
SOA	Society of Authors, *page 1088*
SOB	Society of Bookbinders, *page 1088*
SOBHD	Scottish Official Board of Highland Dancing, *page 1049*
SOC	Scott Owners' Club, *page 1034*
SOC	Scottish Ornithologists' Club, *page 1049*
SOC	Singer Owners Club, *page 1074*
SOC	Spartan Owners' Club, *page 1113*
SOC	Stag Owners Club, *page 1124*
SODC	South Oxfordshire District Council, *page 1107*
SOE	Society of Engineers (Incorporated), *page 1091*
SOE	Society of Operations Engineers, *page 1096*
SOF	Society of Floristry Limited, *page 1091*
SOFHT	Society of Food Hygiene Technology, The, *page 1091*
SofM	Society of Metaphysicians Limited, *page 1095*
SoG	Society of Genealogists, *page 1092*
SOGB	Special Olympics Great Britain, *page 1114*
SOL	Society of Ley Hunters, *page 1093*
SOLT	Society of London Theatre, *page 1094*
SOLT	Society of London Toastmasters, *page 1094*
SOM	Society of Occupational Medicine, *page 1095*
SOM	Society of Orthopaedic Medicine, *page 1096*
Somerset YFC	Somerset Federation of Young Farmers Club, *page 1102*
SOMSR	Society of Master Shoe Repairers Limited, *page 1095*
SOVA	Society of Voluntary Associates, *page 1098*
SPA	Society for Popular Astronomy, *page 1083*
SPA	Structural Precast Association, *page 1131*
SPAB	Society for the Protection of Ancient Buildings, *page 1085*
SpaBA	Spa Business Association, *page 1113*
SPANA	Society for the Protection of Animals Abroad, *page 1086*
SPATA	Swimming Pool and Allied Trades Association, *page 1142*
SPC	Society of Pension Consultants, *page 1096*

SPCK	Society for Promoting Christian Knowledge, *page 1084*	
SPE	Society of Professional Engineers, *page 1096*	
SPF	Scottish Pharmaceutical Federation, *page 1050*	
SPHS	Society for the Promotion of Hellenic Studies, *page 1085*	
SPL	Science Photo Library, *page 1031*	
SPL	Scottish Poetry Library, *page 1050*	
SPMA	Society for Post-Medieval Archaeology, The, *page 1083*	
SPPA	Scottish Pre-School Play Association, *page 1050*	
SPPC	Scottish Partnership for Palliative Care, *page 1050*	
SPR	Society for Psychical Research, *page 1084*	
SPRI	Scott Polar Research Institute, *page 1034*	
SPRS	Society for the Promotion of Roman Studies, *page 1085*	
SPRS	Staffordshire Parish Registers Society, *page 1123*	
SPS	Strategic Planning Society, *page 1130*	
SPSBS	Shetland Pony Stud-book Society, *page 1069*	
SPSO	Scottish Public Services Ombudsman, *page 1051*	
SPTC	Scottish Parent Teacher Council, *page 1050*	
SPUC	Society for the Protection of Unborn Children, *page 1086*	
SPUC Scotland	Society for the Protection of Unborn Children – Scotland, *page 1086*	
SPW	Students Partnership Worldwide, *page 1131*	
SQA	Scottish Qualifications Authority, *page 1051*	
SRA	Shooters' Rights Association, *page 1069*	
SRA	Social Research Association, *page 1078*	
SRC	Scottish Refugee Council, *page 1051*	
SRL	Sound Research Laboratories Limited, *page 1104*	
SROC	Sunbeam Rapier Owners Club, *page 1134*	
SRP	Society of Recorder Players, *page 1097*	
SRPBA	Scottish Rural Property and Business Association, *page 1052*	
SRPS	Scottish Railway Preservation Society, *page 1051*	
SRU	Scottish Rugby Union, *page 1052*	
SSA	Scottish Screen Archive, *page 1053*	
SSA	Scottish Society for Autism, *page 1054*	
SSA	Scottish Sports Association, *page 1055*	
SSAFA Forceshelp	Soldiers, Sailors, Airmen and Families Association – Forces Help, *page 1100*	
SSBA	Scottish Spina Bifida Association, *page 1055*	
SSC	Scottish Sensory Centre, *page 1053*	
SSC	Statistical Services Centre, *page 1126*	
SSC Society	Society of Solicitors in the Supreme Courts of Scotland, *page 1097*	
SSCATF	Sickle Cell and Thalassaemia Foundation, *page 1072*	
SSCR	Scottish Society for Conservation and Restoration, *page 1054*	
SSDC	South Shropshire District Council, *page 1108*	
SSE	Snowsport England, *page 1077*	
SSERC	Scottish Schools Equipment Research Centre Limited, *page 1052*	
SSF	Society for Reproduction & Fertility, *page 1084*	
SSG	Society of St Gregory, *page 1097*	
SSHM	Scottish Society of the History of Medicine, *page 1054*	
SSHM	Society for the Social History of Medicine, *page 1086*	
SSI	Sight Savers International, *page 1072*	
SSI	Society of Scribes and Illuminators, *page 1097*	
SSL	Scottish Snooker Limited, *page 1054*	
SSLRC	National Soil Resources Institute, *page 847*	
SSM	Society of Sales and Marketing, *page 1097*	
SSMA	Sterilised Suture Manufacturers Association, *page 1127*	
SSPO	Scottish Salmon Producers Organisation, *page 1052*	
SSPR	Scottish Society for Psychical Research, *page 1054*	
SSR	Scottish School of Reflexology, The, *page 1052*	
SSS	Shingles Support Society, *page 1069*	

SSS	Simplified Spelling Society, *page 1073*	
SST	Society of Sports Therapists, *page 1097*	
SSTA	Scottish Secondary Teachers' Association, *page 1053*	
SSU	Southampton Solent University, *page 1110*	
SSVC	Split Screen Van Club, *page 1115*	
St Mungo's	St Mungo's Community Housing Association, *page 1121*	
STA	Solar Trade Association, *page 1099*	
STA	Tall Ships Youth Trust, *page 1143*	
STAUK	Sugar Traders Association of the United Kingdom, *page 1134*	
STB	Southern and South East England Tourist Board, *page 1111*	
STC	South Tyneside College – Hebburn, *page 1108*	
STEP	Society of Trust and Estate Practitioners, *page 1098*	
STFC	Science & Technology Facilities Council, *page 1030*	
STFC	STFC Daresbury Laboratory, *page 1127*	
STGA	Scottish Tourist Guides Association, *page 1056*	
STI	Sail Training International, *page 1024*	
STLD	Society of Television Lighting and Design, *page 1098*	
STR	Salmons Tickford Register, *page 1026*	
STR	Society for Theatre Research, *page 1086*	
STRI	Sports Turf Research Institute, The, *page 1116*	
STS	Scottish Text Society, *page 1055*	
STS Ltd	Swansea Tribology Services Limited, *page 1141*	
STSG	Scottish Transport Studies Group, *page 1056*	
STTS	Scottish Tramway and Transport Society, *page 1056*	
SU	Scripture Union, *page 1059*	
SUAT	Scottish Urban Archaeological Trust, *page 1056*	
SUERC	Scottish Universities Environmental Research Centre, *page 1056*	
SUMAC	University of Sheffield – Metals Advisory Centre, *page 1215*	
Sustain	Sustain: The Alliance for Better Food Farming, *page 1139*	
SUT	Society for Underwater Technology, *page 1087*	
SVGTO	St Vincent and the Grenadines Tourist Office, *page 1122*	
SVLB	Sunderland Volunteer Life Brigade, *page 1135*	
SW	Scottish Water – Edinburgh, *page 1057*	
SW	Screenwriters' Workshop, *page 1059*	
SWA	Scotch Whisky Association, *page 1033*	
SWA	Society of Women Artists, The, *page 1098*	
SWA	Steel Window Association, *page 1126*	
SWAPWest	Scottish Wider Access Programme, *page 1057*	
SWBH	Sandwell and West Birmingham Hospitals NHS Trust, *page 1027*	
SWCPA	South West Coast Path Association, *page 1108*	
SWE	Society of Wood Engravers, *page 1099*	
SWEDA	Somerset and Wessex Eating Disorders Association, *page 1101*	
SWF	Scottish Women's Football, *page 1058*	
SWLA	Society of Wildlife Artists, *page 1098*	
SWPP	Society of Wedding and Portrait Photographers Limited, *page 1098*	
SWRI	Scottish Women's Rural Institutes, *page 1058*	
SWRLS	South Western Regional Library Service, *page 1109*	
SWSA	Scottish Water Ski Association, *page 1057*	
SWT	Scottish Wildlife Trust, *page 1057*	
SYHA	Scottish Youth Hostels Association, *page 1058*	
SYT	Scottish Youth Theatre, *page 1058*	
TA	Tourism Australia, *page 1161*	
TA	Translators Association, *page 1164*	
TAC	Aeroplane Collection Limited, *page 17*	
TACS	Tiles and Architectural Ceramics Society, *page 1157*	
TACT	Adolescent and Children's Trust, *page 14*	
TAE	Academy of Experts, *page 9*	
TARRC	Tun Abdul Razak Research Centre, *page 1169*	
TATHS	Tool and Trades History Society, *page 1159*	
TAU	Foreign and Commonwealth Office – Travel Advice Unit, *page 496*	
TCCR	Centre for Couple Relationships, *page 273*	

UK CEED	United Kingdom Centre for Economic and Environmental Development, *page* 1181	UWC AC	United World College of the Atlantic Limited, *page* 1185
UK College	UK College for Complementary Healthcare Studies, *page* 1174	UWE	University of the West of England – Frenchay Campus (Bolland) Library, *page* 1218
UK-ISES	Solar Energy Society, *page* 1099	UWE, Bristol	Faculty of Creative Arts Library, University of the West of England, Bristol, *page* 470
UKA	United Kingdom Alliance, *page* 1181		
UKAMBY	United Kingdom Association of Manufacturers of Bakers' Yeast, *page* 1181	UWIC	University of Wales Institute, Cardiff, *page* 1220
		UWS	University of the West of Scotland, *page* 1219
UKAS	United Kingdom Accreditation Service, *page* 1180	UWS Ayr	University of the West of Scotland – Ayr Campus, *page* 1219
UKCPA	United Kingdom Clinical Pharmacy Association, *page* 1182	UWT	Ulster Wildlife Trust, *page* 1179
		VA	Veterans Aid, *page* 1228
UKCPI	UK Cleaning Products Industry Association, *page* 1173	VAG	Vernacular Architecture Group, *page* 1227
UKDA	UK Data Archive, *page* 1174	VAI	Vocational Awards International Limited, *page* 1233
UKFC	United Kingdom Fortifications Club, *page* 1182	VBRA	Vehicle Builders and Repairers Association Limited, *page* 1226
UKFE	UK Fashion Exports, *page* 1174		
UKFSC	United Kingdom Flight Safety Committee, *page* 1182	VC	Visit Cornwall, *page* 1231
		VC	Volunteer Centre, *page* 1234
UKHCA	United Kingdom Home Care Association, *page* 1182	VCA	Vehicle Certification Agency, *page* 1227
		VCC	Veteran Car Club of Great Britain, *page* 1227
UKHO	UK Hydrographic Office, *page* 1174	VCCC	Vauxhall Convertible Car Club, *page* 1225
UKIVA	UK Industrial Vision Association, *page* 1175	VCM	Victoria College Examinations, *page* 1229
UKLA	UK Lubricants Association Ltd, *page* 1175	VdGS	Viola da Gamba Society, *page* 1231
UKMPG	UK Major Ports Group, *page* 1175	VE	Volunteering England, *page* 1234
UKPIA	United Kingdom Petroleum Industry Association Limited, *page* 1183	VEC	Volvo Enthusiasts Club, *page* 1235
		VERTIC	Verification Research, Training and Information Centre, *page* 1227
UKPS	United Kingdom Passport Service, *page* 1183		
UKSCF	UK Stem Cell Foundation, *page* 1176	VGC	Vintage Glider Club, *page* 1230
UKSIP	UK Society of Investment Professionals, *page* 1176	VHL	Vere Harmsworth Library, *page* 1227
		VI	Victoria Institute or Philosophical Society of Great Britain, *page* 1229
UKSMA	UK Spring Manufacturers' Association, *page* 1176		
		VIA	Values into Action, *page* 1225
UKSPA	United Kingdom Science Park Association, The, *page* 1183	VLA	Veterinary Laboratories Agency, *page* 1228
		VLV	Voice of the Listener and Viewer, *page* 1233
UKTCA	United Kingdom Transplant Co-ordinators Association, *page* 1183	VMCC	Vintage Motor Cycle Club Limited, *page* 1230
		VOC	Vauxhall Owners Club (1903–1957), *page* 1226
UKTI	UK Trade & Investment, *page* 1177	VOGR	Vale of Glamorgan Railway Company Limited, *page* 1224
UKTI	UK Trade and Investment, Hong Kong and Macao Desk, *page* 1177		
		VOICE	Professional Association of Nursery Nurses, *page* 947
UKTS	UK Thalassaemia Society, *page* 1176		
UKVA	United Kingdom Vineyards Association, *page* 1183	VOSA	Vehicle and Operator Services Agency, *page* 1226
UKWA	United Kingdom Warehousing Association, *page* 1184	VPL	Video Performance Limited, *page* 1229
		VSCC	Vintage Sports-Car Club Limited, *page* 1230
ULT	United Lodge of Theosophists, *page* 1184	VSO	Voluntary Service Overseas, *page* 1234
UMO	Union of Muslim Organisations of UK and Eire, *page* 1179	VSS	Victim Support Scotland, *page* 1228
		VSUK	Vegetarian Society of the United Kingdom, *page* 1226
UNA-UK	United Nations Association of Great Britain and Northern Ireland, *page* 1184		
		VWOC (GB)	VW Owners' Club GB, *page* 1235
UNHCR	United Nations High Commissioner for Refugees, *page* 1184	VWSGB	Virginia Woolf Society of Great Britain, *page* 1231
UNICEF	UNICEF UK, *page* 1179	VWT20C	Volkswagen Type 2 Owners' Club, *page* 1234
UniS	University of Surrey – University Library, *page* 1217	WABIL	World Ahlul Bayt Islamic League, *page* 1272
		WAHO	World Arabian Horse Organization, *page* 1272
Unite/CPHVA	Community Practitioners and Health Visiting Association, *page* 338	WALC	Wiltshire Association of Local Councils, *page* 1259
UNJL	Upper Norwood Joint Library, *page* 1223	WALS	Wolverhampton Archives and Local Studies, *page* 1265
UoC	University of Chichester Library, *page* 1198		
UoG	University of Gloucestershire, *page* 1205	WAMC	Welsh Association of Motor Clubs, *page* 1244
URBED	Urban and Economical Development Group, *page* 1223	WANHS	Wiltshire Archaeological and Natural History Society, *page* 1259
		WAR	Women Against Rape, *page* 1266
URC	United Reformed Church, *page* 1184	WCBC	Wrexham County Borough Council, *page* 1289
URC History Society	United Reformed Church History Society, *page* 1185	WCCUIN	Wiltshire & Swindon Users Network, *page* 1259
		WCEC	Worshipful Company of Environmental Cleaners, *page* 1280
URCHIN	Unit for Research into Changing Institutions, *page* 1180		
USCL	United Society for Christian Literature, *page* 1185	WCF	World Curling Federation, *page* 1273
		WCIA	Welsh Centre for International Affairs / Canolfan Materion Rhyngwladol Cymru, *page* 1244
USDAW	Union of Shop, Distributive and Allied Workers, *page* 1180		
		WCML	Working Class Movement Library, *page* 1272
USPG	USPG: Anglicans in World Mission, *page* 1224	WCMPC	Worshipful Company of Makers of Playing Cards, *page* 1284
UU	University of Ulster, *page* 1219		
UUP	Ulster Unionist Party, *page* 1179	WCP	Worshipful Company of Plumbers, *page* 1286
UWB	Bangor University – Library and Archive Service, *page* 98	WCPT	World Confederation for Physical Therapy, *page* 1273
UWC	United World Colleges (International), *page* 1185	WCRF UK	World Cancer Research Fund (WCRF UK), *page* 1273

Subject Index

Entries in the Subject Index refer the reader to the page numbers of full entries in the Main Directory.

Subject Index ASLIB DIRECTORY of INFORMATION SOURCES

brazing
European Association for Brazing and Soldering ... 455
TWI Ltd ... 1171
bread
Federation of Bakers ... 475
Flour Advisory Bureau Limited ... 492
National Association of Master Bakers ... 811
RHM Technology ... 971
breakfast
Association of Cereal Food Manufacturers ... 66
breastfeeding
Association of Breastfeeding Mothers ... 62
Association of Radical Midwives ... 83
Health Promotion Agency for Northern Ireland ... 555
La Leche League (Great Britain) ... 696
NCT ... 864
breathing apparatus
Dstl Knowledge Services – Information Centre 400
Brechin Diocesan Library
University of Dundee – Library ... 1199
Brecknock Militia
Howell Harris Museum ... 583
Brecon Beacons
Brecon Beacons National Park Authority ... 138
Brecon Beacons National Park Visitor Centre . 139
Breconshire
Powys Library Service ... 941
Brent
Brent Archives ... 139
Brian, Havergal (1876–1972)
Havergal Brian Society ... 551
bricks, brickmaking and brickwork
British Brick Society ... 161
British Ceramic Plant and Machinery Manufacturers Association ... 164
CERAM Research Ltd ... 287
Dudley College ... 401
Mortar Industry Association ... 790
Refractory Users Federation ... 963
Southern Brick Federation Limited ... 1111
Sussex Industrial Archaeology Society ... 1138
Worshipful Company of Tylers and Bricklayers ... 1287
– special collection
CERAM Research Ltd ... 287
bridge
English Bridge Union Limited ... 434
Bridge, Frank (1879–1941)
Royal College of Music Frank Bridge Bequest 991
Trinity College of Music ... 1167
bridges
Forum for the Built Environment ... 499
Institution of Structural Engineers ... 641
Ironbridge Gorge Museum Trust – Museum Library ... 669
Prestressed Concrete Association ... 944
Royal Institute of Navigation ... 999
Scottish Rights of Way and Access Society ... 1051
Steel Construction Institute ... 1126
TRL Ltd ... 1168
Bridgewater, Francis, *3rd Duke* (1726–1803)
University of Salford, The Library ... 1214
Bridgnorth
Bridgnorth & District Historical Society ... 140
Bridgnorth District Council ... 140
briefcases
British Luggage and Leathergoods Association 197
Bright, John (1811–1889)
University College London – Special Collections ... 1188
Brighton
East Sussex Library and Information Service .. 414
Brinson, Peter
Laban Centre London ... 697
Bristol
Avon Local History and Archaeology ... 95
Bristol and Gloucestershire Archaeological Society ... 141
Bristol Central Library ... 141
Bristol City Council ... 141
Bristol Record Office ... 142
Business West ... 246
English Heritage (South West Region) ... 439
Britain and British way of life
Institute of Historical Research ... 622
Society for Folk Life Studies ... 1082
British army
Air Despatch Association ... 21
British Association of Teachers of the Deaf
University of Birmingham – Education Library ... 1190
British Cave Research Association
Derbyshire County Council ... 384
British Fire Prevention Committee
Building Research Establishment Limited ... 240
British Ports Authority
Museum of London Docklands ... 796
British Theatre Association
Drama Association of Wales ... 398
Britten, *Sir* Benjamin (1913–1976)
Britten-Pears Library ... 232
Britten-Pears Young Artist Programme ... 232
– special collection
Britten-Pears Library ... 232
Suffolk Libraries ... 1133
broadcasting
Association of Broadcasting Doctors ... 65
BBC Information and Archive ... 106
BBC Scotland ... 106
BBC Written Archives Centre ... 106
British Library Sound Archive ... 196
Broadcasting, Entertainment, Cinematograph and Theatre Union ... 233
Celtic Media Festival ... 267
Chartered Institute of Journalists ... 292
Commonwealth Broadcasting Association ... 331
Community Service Volunteers ... 338
Dentists' Media Group ... 380
Department for Culture, Media and Sport ... 380
Dorothy L Sayers Society ... 395
Environmental Communicators' Organization 446
International Institute of Communications ... 655
London College of Communication ... 736
Mediawatch–UK ... 764
Nottingham Trent University ... 894
Ofcom ... 898
Performing Right Society Limited ... 923
Phonographic Performance Limited ... 928
RAJAR ... 959
Ravensbourne College of Design and Communication LRC ... 960
Society of Editors ... 1091
TNS Media Intelligence Limited ... 1157
University College Falmouth Library ... 1186
Voice of the Listener and Viewer ... 1233
broadsides
Chetham's Library ... 302
Lincoln Cathedral Library ... 722
Manchester Room@City Library ... 756
Newcastle University ... 868
Society of Antiquaries of London ... 1087
St Bride Library ... 1118
Broadwood, John (1732–1812)
Surrey Heritage ... 1137
Brodsky, Adolph
Royal Northern College of Music ... 1006
brokers and brokerage
National Association of Commercial Finance Brokers ... 808
Yacht Designers and Surveyors Association .. 1291
Bromham Parish Library
Central Bedfordshire Libraries ... 268
Bromley
Bromley Public Libraries ... 234
Business Link in London ... 244
Bromyard
Bromyard and District Local History Society .. 234
Brontë family
Brontë Society ... 234
Calderdale Libraries ... 250
– special collection
Brontë Society ... 234
Manchester Language and Literature Library . 755
Bronze Age
Wiltshire Archaeological and Natural History Society ... 1259
Brooke, Rupert Chawner (1887–1915)
King's College Library ... 692
Rupert Brooke Museum & Society ... 1020
University of Gloucestershire ... 1205
Brooke-Popham, *ACM Sir* Robert (1878–1953)
Liddell Hart Centre for Military Archives ... 720
Brougham, *Lord* Henry Peter (1778–1868)
University College London – Special Collections ... 1188
Brown, Ann Memorial Library
Alzheimer's Society ... 28
Natural History Museum ... 861
Brown, George Mackay
University of Edinburgh – University Library 1201
Browne, *Sir* Thomas (1605–1682)
University of Glasgow – University Library . 1204
Browning, Robert (1812–1889) and Elizabeth Barrett (1806–1861)
Tennyson Research Centre ... 1149
Broxbourne
Broxbourne Borough Council ... 235
Bruce, Robert (1274–1329)
Glasgow Libraries, Information & Learning ... 521
Brunel, Isambard Kingdom (1769–1849)
Brunel University ... 236
Centre for the History of Technology, Science and Society ... 285
Institution of Civil Engineers ... 638
Institution of Mechanical Engineers ... 640
Bryant, *Sir* Arthur (1899–1985)
Liddell Hart Centre for Military Archives ... 720
Buccleuch *Duke of*
Cumbria Archive Service – Barrow-in-Furness 369
Buchan, John (1875–1940)
John Buchan Society ... 681
Peebles Area Library ... 920
Buchan, Norman
University of the West of Scotland ... 1219
Buchan, Norman and Janey
Glasgow Caledonian University Library in the Saltire Centre ... 520
Buckinghamshire
Berkshire, Buckinghamshire and Oxfordshire Wildlife Trust ... 112
Buckinghamshire Archaeological Society ... 239
Buckinghamshire Family History Society ... 239
Buckinghamshire Library Service ... 239
Buckinghamshire Record Society ... 239
Centre for Buckinghamshire Studies ... 271
Milton Keynes Council ... 780
Milton Keynes Learning City Libraries Network ... 780
South Bucks District Council ... 1105
Buckler's Hard
Beaulieu Archives ... 107
Buckley
Flintshire Record Office ... 492
Buddhism
British Buddhist Association ... 161
Buddhist Society ... 240
Institute of Buddhist Studies ... 611
International Zen Association (United Kingdom) ... 666
London Buddhist Centre ... 734
London Buddhist Vihara ... 735
Oxfordshire County Council ... 912
Triratna Buddhist Order ... 1167
University of Cambridge – Library of the Faculty of Divinity ... 1197
Bugatti, Ettore (1882–1947)
Bugatti Owners' Club Limited ... 240
building construction
Architecture and Surveying Institute ... 43
Association of Building Component Manufacturers Limited ... 66
Association of Building Engineers ... 66
Basingstoke College of Technology ... 103
Bedford College ... 108
Birmingham City University ... 120
Birmingham Libraries ... 121
Bishop Auckland College Library ... 122
Bournemouth and Poole College ... 133
Bovis Lend Lease Limited (Europe) ... 134
British Architectural Library ... 147
British Constructional Steelwork Association Limited ... 166
British Expertise ... 173
British Precast Concrete Federation ... 208
Buckinghamshire Chilterns University College 239
Building Research Establishment Limited ... 240
Burton College Library ... 241
Calderdale College ... 249
Carmarthenshire College (Coleg Sir Gar) ... 262
Central Sussex College ... 270

– special collection

general practice

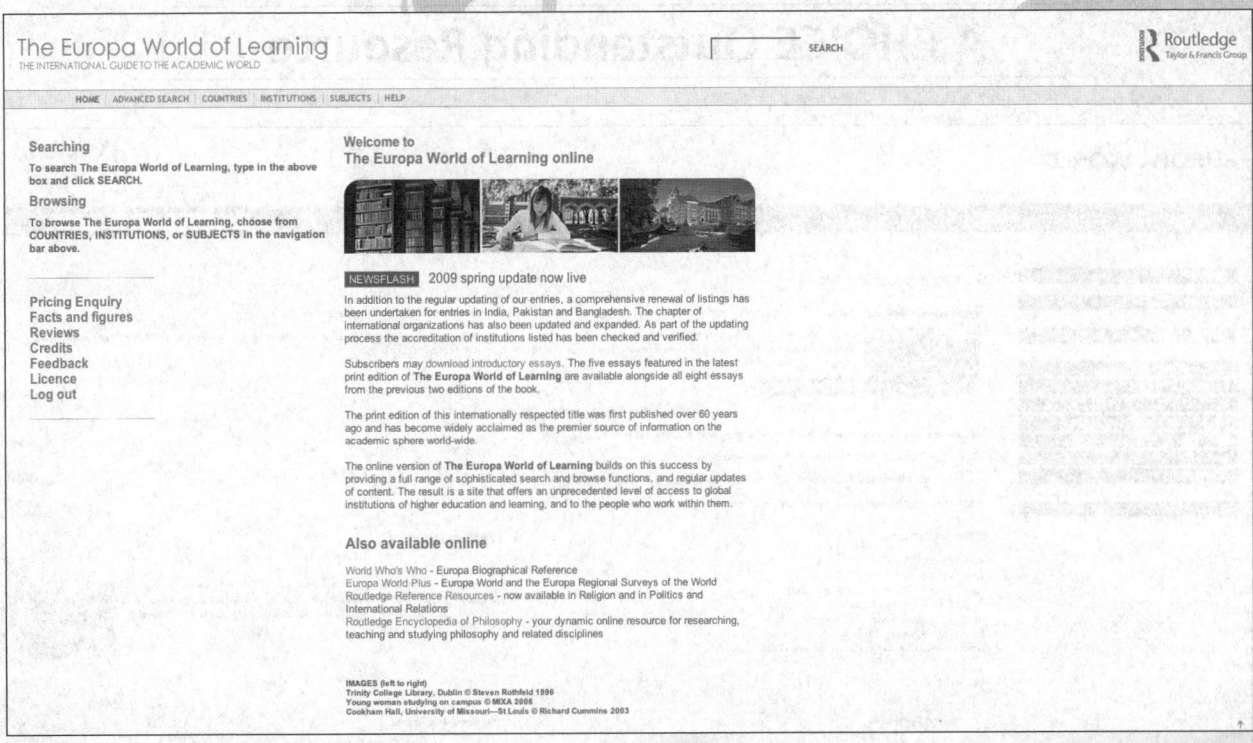

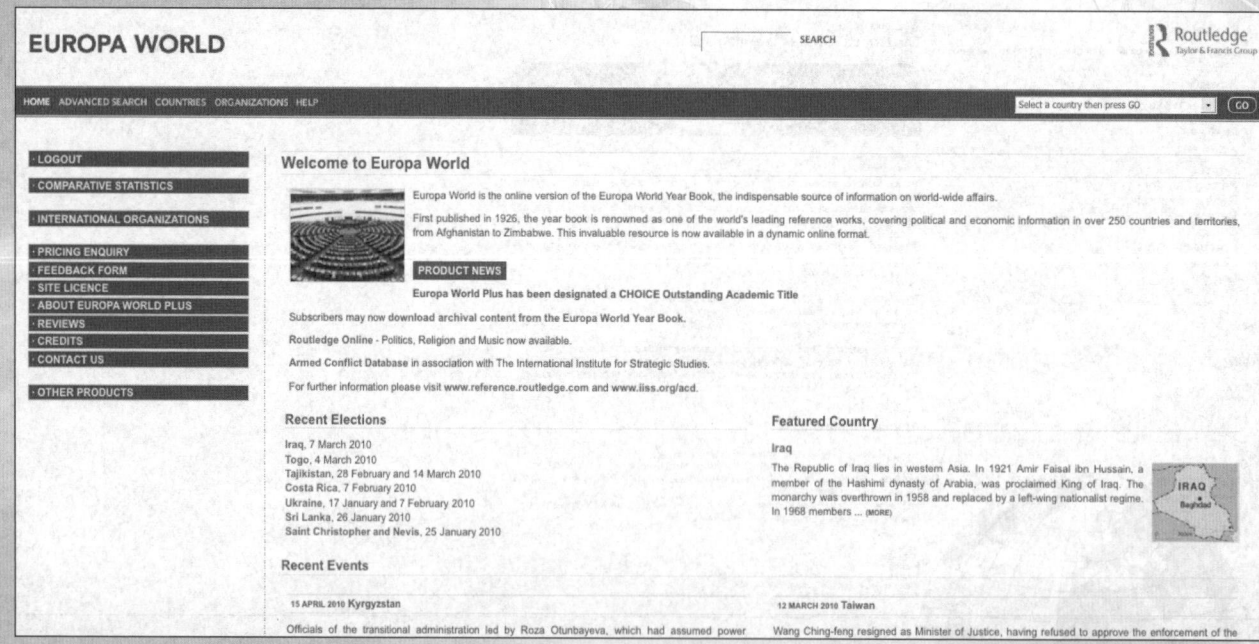

EUROPA REGIONAL SURVEYS OF THE WORLD

This nine-volume set covers each of the major world regions. As well as offering expert review of topics critical to the region as a whole, each volume provides a comprehensive range of background information, statistics, directory listings and analysis for all countries of the region.

Titles include:

- Africa South of the Sahara
- Central and South-Eastern Europe
- Eastern Europe, Russia and Central Asia
- The Far East and Australasia
- The Middle East and North Africa
- South America, Central America and the Caribbean
- South Asia
- The USA and Canada
- Western Europe

  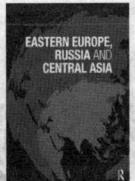   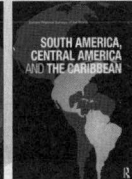   

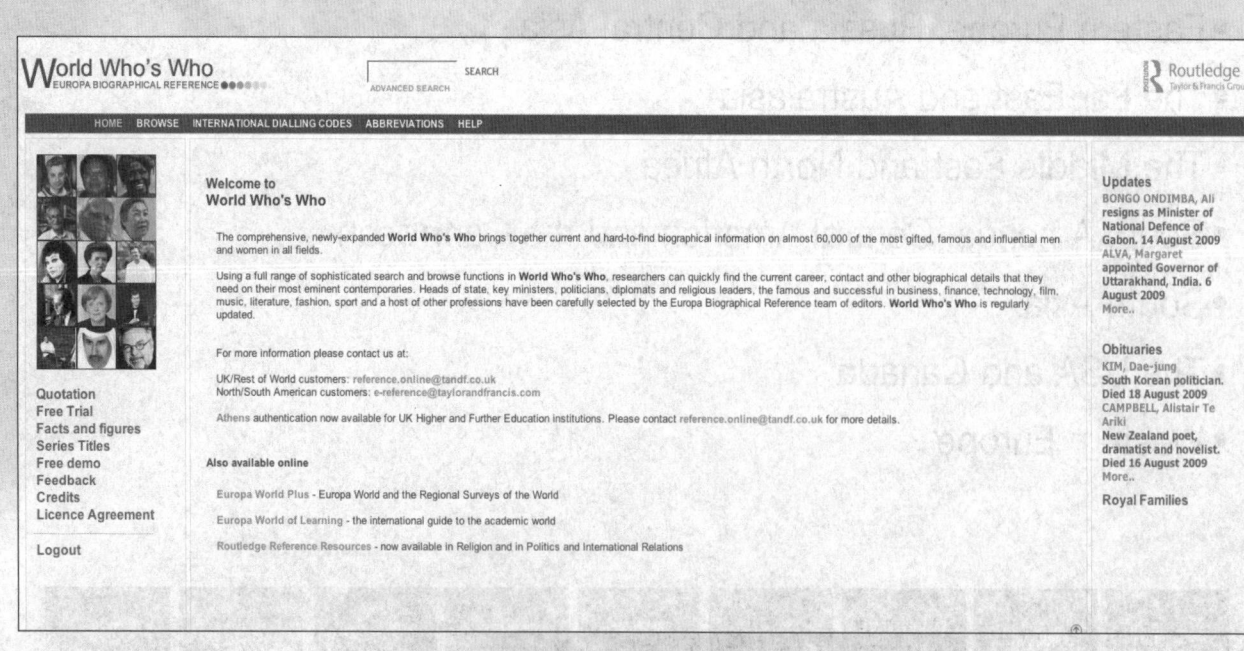